THE CONCISE REFERENCE ENCYCLOPEDIA & DICTIONARY

THE CONCISE REFERENCE ENCYCLOPEDIA & DICTIONARY

Bay Books
in association with Oxford University Press

Credits

Photographs and Illustrations
Popperfoto; Bay Books Pty Ltd; Bay Picture Library; Adelaide Festival Centre Trust; Antarctic Division of D.S.I.R.; Australian Army; Australian Broadcasting Commission; Australian Glass Manufactures Company; Australian Information Service; Australian Inland Mission; Australian Jaycees; Australian News and Information Bureau; The Australian Opera; Australian Tourist Commission; A. Bradley; Broken Hill Prop. Company Ltd; Bullers Book of Birds; J. Cann; Carlton United Breweries; Marshall Cavendish; Cement and Concrete Association of New South Wales; M. C. Cohen and Company; Neville Coleman; Colonial Sugar Refinery; Commonwealth Science and Industrial Research Organization, Australia; Consulate Republic of Cuba; Ben Cropp; B. Cummins; Dairy Industry Authority of New South Wales; Department of Agriculture, Australia; Department of Information and Extension Services, PNG; Department of Main Roads, New South Wales; Department of Mines, New South Wales; Department of Overseas Trade, Victoria; Department of Science, Victoria; Douglass Baglin Photography; Alan Foley; A. M. Fox; Fritz Prenzel Photo Library; Garuda Indonesian Airways; Keith Gillet; Globe Theatre (NZ); John Goode; Robert Goodman; Hong Kong Government Information Service; Robert Horton; Alan Hutchison; Japan National Tourist Organisation; Lan Chile Airways; Lutheran Publishing House; Magic Carpet Tours, Sydney; Malaysian Airline System; Malaysian Government; Metropolitan Water Sewerage and Drainage Board, Sydney; Motor Cycle Weekly; New South Wales Tourist Bureau; New Zealand Lamb Information Bureau; New Zealand Travel Commission; New Zealand Wildlife Service; Northern Territory Tourist Board; Old Tote Theatre Company, Sydney; Overseas Telecommunications Centre, Sydney; P&O Australia; Photographic Library of Australia; Rentokil; Royal Australian Navy; A. J. Salter; Salvation Army; Scoopix, Victoria; Brian Shirley; Sir Colin Mackenzie Sanctuary; Snowy Mountains Hydro-electric Authority, New South Wales; South Australian Government Tourist Bureau; Spasm Australia Pty. Ltd.; State Electricity Commission of Victoria; State Library of Victoria; TAA Australia; Telecom Australia; UTA French Airlines; Victorian Ministry of Tourism; Water Conservation and Irrigation Committee, New South Wales; Western Australian Department of Development and Decentralization; Eric Worrell.

Published by Bay Books
61-69 Anzac Parade, Kensington, NSW 2033

Compiled in association with Oxford University Press
This edition first published 1987, reprinted 1988.

ISBN 1 86256 025 0
Printed in Singapore by Toppan Printing Company.

How to use the Dictionary

A dictionary normally takes the uses of words and phrases as such for its subject-matter and is concerned with giving information about the things for which these words and phrases stand only so far as correct use of the words depends upon knowledge of the things. In an encyclopaedia, on the other hand, the emphasis will be much more on the nature of the things for which the words and phrases stand. That is the distinction between a dictionary and an encyclopaedia made by H. W. Fowler in the preface to the *Concise Oxford Dictionary.*

This new work attempts to combine in a form that can be easily and pleasurably used the essential features of dictionary and encyclopaedia. As well as giving the meanings of words in common or not-so-common currency, the work contains hundreds of entries on famous people and places, animals and plants. Some things are more easily explained by pictures or diagrams than by words and prolific use is made throughout this encyclopaedic dictionary of illustrations as an aid to definition and as visual amplification of the text entries. As well as colour photographs, explanatory cut-away and other diagrams, and maps, the dictionary contains reproductions of many famous paintings and specially commissioned original illustrations.

Vocabulary

The general reader for whom the book is intended may not always have another dictionary or encyclopaedia to hand and so the vocabulary has been chosen with an eye to the needs of one who may require either type of information.

The vocabulary should be more than adequate for the reader who consults the book for ordinary dictionary purposes. But it also contains terms in everyday use which would be excluded from an ordinary dictionary because of their technical and scientific character or which would be very briefly dealt with; familiar words in semi-technical use (e.g. *vertical trust, combine,* etc.); the names of famous people (e.g. statesmen, explorers, inventors, artists, and writers), historical, contemporary, or fictitious; and the names of important places and events.

Special pains have been taken to ensure that scientific and technical terms are up to date and accurate in selection and in definition, and at the same time intelligible to the user, but the present pace of development in science and technology is so swift that no reference book which deals with them in even the most general way can ever be completely up to date: between the time the book is compiled and its publication new words and senses will have come into use and existing words and senses will have acquired fresh shades of meaning or become obsolescent.

In order to keep the work within reasonable compass obsolete words and phrases have been omitted except for a few which some special interest has made it desirable to retain.

Illustrations

The illustrations have been planned to complement the text. Each of them is independent but adjacent to or near the relevant text entry, and is fully captioned. Each is intended to show the meaning of a word or indicate the character of the thing for which the word stands; to bring a diffuse subject into sharp visual focus or explain diagrammatically how a complex piece of machinery or technical process works. To avoid wasteful repetition some subjects have been grouped together, especially where the members of the group help to explain one another: the picture of a machine, for example, may not only illustrate the machine itself but exhibit the nature of its parts, and their relation to one another and to the whole.

Words are often best defined in general terms but a drawing has to be of a particular thing and therefore gives an example of the particular use of the word rather than a generalized statement. Thus the human body may be chosen to show the different bones of the skeleton, although the same terms are used for comparable bones in other vertebrates.

The subjects chosen for illustration are those of general interest, many of them being easier to define by illustration than verbally. Examples with a wide range of reference have usually been chosen; thus the illustrations of animals show at least one example from each major group.

Abbreviations

Abbreviations in current use appear in their alphabetical place in the body of the text to save a separate alphabet. But there is a separate list (see page xiii) of those abbreviations used in the dictionary itself.

Etymology

For the sake of space, derivations have been omitted with a few exceptions. These occur where the etymology is especially interesting or unexpected (e.g. *penicillin, derrick*), or when a thing has been named after its inventor or place of origin (e.g. *Fortin barometer, Borstal*). In these cases the etymology is given in square brackets at the end of the entry.

Cross-references

Where a word is given in small capitals in a definition, this indicates that reference to the word in its alphabetical place will provide further information (e.g. INSULIN in the entry for *pancreas*) or discuss the term which is given in comparison or contradistinction (e.g. NOBLE or PRECIOUS metals as opposed to *base* metals).

Pronunciation

1. **Accent** The accentuation mark ′ is placed after the vowel or vowel sound in the stressed syllable.

2. **Phonetic system** Where the pronunciation of a word or part of a word cannot be shown by the ordinary spelling and markings, a phonetic spelling is given in round brackets immediately after the black-type word. The phonetic scheme is as follows:

CONSONANTS: b; ch (ch*in*); d; dh (dh*e* = the); f; g (go); h; j; k; l; m; n; ng (*sing*); ngg (*finger*); p; r; s (*sip*); sh (sh*ip*); t; th (th*in*); v; w; y; z; zh (*vizhon* = vision).

ṅ indicates French nasalization of preceding vowel.

The symbol χ represents the ch in *Bach*, *loch*, pronounced as a guttural sound or as k.

VOWEL COMBINATIONS:

ā ē ī ō ū o͞o (mate mete mite mote mute moot)
ă ĕ ĭ ŏ ŭ o͝o (rack reck rick rock ruck rook)
ār ēr īr ūr (mare mere mire mure)
ar͡ er͡ or͡ (part pert port)
ah aw oi oor ow (bah bawl boil boor brow)

Vowels and combinations (as *er*) printed in italic within the brackets indicate vague sounds frequently indistinguishable from each other.

Vowels marked ̆̄ may be pronounced either way, e.g. **pă′trĭot** (pā- or pă-).

3. **Pronunciation without respelling.** As far as possible pronunciation is shown without respelling by placing symbols over the words (e.g. **ā, ĕ, ār, ēr, o͝o,** etc.) in the black type. Unmarked vowels in the black-type words indicate vague sounds.

(*a*) The ordinary spelling often coincides with the phonetic system described in paragraph 2.

(*b*) The following additional symbols are used in the black type:

ė=ĭ (nā′kėd, rėlȳ′, cŏ′llėge, prī′vėt)
ir͡, ur͡=**er͡** (bir͡th, bur͡n)
ȳ ў=ī, ĭ (ĭmplȳ′, sŭ′nnў)
ȳr=īr (lȳre)

(*c*) Final *e* when unmarked is mute, i.e. not to be pronounced. Thus **āpe** is to be pronounced āp. Where final *e* is pronounced, it is marked as in **rĕ′cipė.** Where *e* is mute in the headword it is mute also (unless marked) in derivatives placed in the same entry, e.g. **bāre, bār′ely, bār′eness.**

(*d*) A double consonant is pronounced as single **(sĭ′llў, mă′nnish)** unless indicated as in **plai′nnėss** (-n-n-).

(*e*) The following letters and combinations have the usual values in American spelling which are shown alongside them:

Vowel Combinations

ae=ē (aegis)
ai=ā (pain)
air=ār (fair)
au=aw (maul)
ay=ā (say)
ea, ee=ē (mean, meet)
ear, eer=ēr (fear, beer)
ei=ē (ceiling)
eu, ew=ū (feud, few)
ey=ĭ(donkey)
ie=ē (thief)
ier=ēr (pier)
oa=ō (boat)
ou=ow (bound)
our=ow*er* (flour)
oy=oi (boy)

Consonants

c is hard and=k (cob, cry, talc) *but* **c** before **e, i, y,** is soft and=s (ice, icy, city)
ck=k (back)
dg before **e, i, y,**=j (judgement)
g before **e, i, y,** is soft and=j (age, gin, orgy), except when doubled (digger, haggis, baggy)
n before **k,** hard **c, q, x**=ng (zinc, uncle, tank, banquet, minx)
ph=f (photo)
qu=kw (quit)
tch=ch (batch)
wh=w or hw (when)
x=ks (fox)

Thus in **gĕm** the pronunciation of *g* is not marked because it comes under the rule above for soft *g*, but **gĕt** is followed by (g-) to show that here exceptionally **g** before **e** is hard as in *go*.

The following combinations have the values shown:
-age=-ĭj (garbage)
-al, -el preceded by *d, n, t*=-l (Handel, mental)
-en, -ent preceded by *d, t,*=-n, -nt (madden, fatten, student)
-nch when final=-nsh or -nch (trench)
-ous=*-us* (furious)
-sion after consonants=-sh*o*n (passion, tension)
-sion after vowels=-zh*o*n (division)
-sm=-zm (atheism, spasm)
-tion=-sh*o*n (salvation)
-tual, -tue, -ture=-chōō*a*l, -chōō, -ch*er* as well as -tū*a*l, -tū, -tūr, esp. in common words

Swung Dash(~)

The 'swung dash' or 'tilde' is frequently used to save space in the body of the entry. It represents the headword (or a derivative of the headword printed in black type in the same entry) when this is repeated as a different part of speech or when it is used in combination with another word, either hyphenated or detached (but not when it has become part of a complete new word). For example, in the article **pitch**[1] *n.* we have ~ *v.t.* when the headword becomes a new part of speech, and ~ *black* and ~ *-pine* when it is in combination (but *pitchblende* as a whole word). The addition of an initial letter to the swung dash indicates a change from a small letter in the headword to a capital or vice versa (e.g. *F*~ in the article **flood** represents the Flood recorded in Genesis).

Contents

Abbreviations used in the dictionary

A Ab./original
abbrev./iation, -iated
abl./ative
abs./olute(ly)
acc./ording
accus./ative
act./ive
adj(s)., adjective(s)
adv(s)., adverb(s)
aeron./autics
AF, Anglo-French
Afr./ican
alg./ebra
allus./ive(ly)
Amer./ican
anal./ogy
anat./omy
Anglo-Ind./ian
anon./ymous
antiq./uities
anthrop./ology
app./arently
Arab./ic
Aram./aic
arbitr./ary
archaeol./ogy
archit./ecture
arith./metic
assim./ilated
assoc./iated
astrol./ogy
astron./omy
at. wt, atomic weight
attrib./utive(ly)
augment./ative
Austral./ian
av./oirdupois

B b./orn
back form./ation
bibl./ical
bibliog./raphy
biochem./istry
biol./ogy
Boh./emian
bot./any
Br./itish
Braz./ilian
Bulg./arian
Burm./ese
Byz./antine

C c./entury
Camb./ridge
c/*irca*
cap./ital
Celt./ic
cf., compare
Ch./urch
chem./istry
Chin./ese
chronol./ogy
cinemat./ography
cogn./ate
collect./ive(ly)
colloq./uial(ly)
com./mon
comb./ination
commerc./ial
comp., compar./ative
compl./ement
conch./ology
confus./ion
conj., conjunction, conjugation
conn./ected
constr./uction
contempt./uous(ly)
contr./action
cop./ulative
correl./ative
corresp./onding
corrupt./ion
cryst./allography
cu./bic

D d./ied
Dan./ish
dat./ive
demonstr./ative
deriv./ative
derog./atory
dial./ect
dict./ionary
diff./erent
dim./inutive
diplom./acy
dist./inct, -inguished
distrib./utive
Du./tch
dub./ious

E E., east(ern)
eccles./iastical
ecol./ogy
econ./omics
Egyptol./ogy
E. Ind., East Indian
(i.e. of the East Indies)
elect./ricity
ellipt./ical
embryol./ogy
emphat./ic(ally)
eng., engin./eering
Engl., England, English
entom./ology
erron./eous(ly)
esp./ecial(ly)
ethnol./ogy
etym./ology
euphem./ism
Eur./ope(an)
exagg./eration
exc./ept
exch./ange
excl., exclamation, exclusive
expr./essing etc.

F f./rom
facet./ious etc.

fam./iliar etc.
fem./inine etc.
fig./urative etc.
Fl./emish
foll./owing (word)
footb./all
fort./ification
Fr./ench
freq./uent(ly)
frequent./ative(ly)
fut./ure (tense)

G
Gael./ic
gen., general(ly), genitive
geog./raphy
geol./ogy
geom./etry
Ger./man
Gk, Greek
govt., government
gram./mar

H
Heb./rew
her./aldry
Hind./ustani
hist./orical, history
hort./iculture

I
i., intransitive
Icel./andic
ill./ustration
illit./erate
imit./ative
imp., imper./ative
imperf./ect
impers./onal
improp./er(ly)
incl./uding, inclusive
Ind./ian (i.e. of the Indian sub-continent)
ind., indicative, indirect
indecl./inable
indef./inite
inf./initive
infl./uence(d)
instr./umental (case)
int./erjection
interrog./ative(ly)
intrans./itive
Ir./ish
iron./ically
irreg./ular(ly)
It., Ital./ian

J
Jap./anese
Jew/ish
joc./ular(ly)

L
L, Latin
lang./uage
l.c., lower case
LG, Low German
lit./eral(ly)
Lith./uanian
LL, late Latin

M
magn./etism
manuf./acture
masc./uline
math./ematics
MDu., Middle Dutch
ME, Middle English
mech./anics
med./icine
med. L, medieval Latin
metall./urgy
metaph./or(ically)
metaphys./ics
meteor./ology
Mex./ican
MG, Middle German
MHG, Middle High German
mil./itary
min./eralogy
MLG, Middle Low German
mod./ern
morphol./ogy
mus./ic
myth./ology

N
N., north(ern)
n./oun
N. Amer., North America(n)
nat. hist., natural history
naut./ical
nav./al
nec./essary, -essarily
neg./ative(ly)
neut./er
nom./inative
Norm./an
north./ern
Norw./egian
ns., nouns
N.T., New Testament
num./eral

O
obj./ect
obl./ique
obs./olete
obsolesc./ent
occas./ional(ly)
OE, Old English
OF, Old French
OHG, Old High German
OIr., Old Irish
OLG, Old Low German
ON, Old Norse
onomat./opoeic
ophthalm./ology
opp., (as) opposed (to), opposite
ord./inary, -inarily
orig./inal(ly)
ornith./ology
O.T., Old Testament

P
p./age
paint./ing
palaeog./raphy

palaeont./ology
parenth./etic(ally)
parl./iament(ary)
part./iciple, -icipial
pass./ive(ly)
past t./ense
path./ology
pedant./ic(ally)
perf./ect (tense)
perh./aps
Pers./ian
pers./on(al)
Peruv./ian
pharm./acy, -acology
philol./ogy
philos./ophy
phon., phonet./ics
phot., photog./raphy
phr./ase
phrr., phrases
phys./ics
phys. chem., physical chemistry
physiol./ogy
pl./ural
pluperf./ect
poet./ical
Pol./ish
pol./itics etc.
pol. econ., political economy
pop./ular(ly)
Port./uguese
poss./essive
pp., pages
pr./onounced
prec., (the) preceding (word)
pred./icate, -icative
pref./ix
prep./osition(al)
pres./ent (tense)
pret./erite
print./ing
prob./able, -ably
pron., pronoun, pronounced, pronunciation
prop./er(ly)
pros./ody
psych., psychol./ogy
psychoanal./ysis

R railw./ay
R.C./Roman Catholic
ref./erence
refl./exive(ly)
rel./ative
repr./esent
rhet./oric
Rom./an
Russ./ian

S S., south(ern)
S. Afr., South African
Sansk./rit
Sax./on
Sc./ottish
Scand./inavian
sculp./ture
sent./ence
Serb./ian
sing./ular
Slav./onic
sociol./ogy
sp./elling
Span./ish
spec./ial(ly)
specif./ic(ally)
sport./ing
Stock Exch., Stock Exchange
subj., subject, subjunctive
superl./ative
surg./ery
surv./eying
Swed./ish
syn./onym

T tech./nical (ly)
teleg./raphy
term./ination
Teut./onic
theatr./ical
theol./ogy
trans./itive
transf., in transferred sense
transl./ation
trig./onometry
Turk./ish
typ./ography

U U.K., United Kingdom
ult./imate(ly)
unexpl./ained
Univ./ersity
Univv., Universities
U.S., United States
usu./al(ly)

V v./erb
var., variant, various
varr., variants
v. aux., verb auxiliary
vbl, verbal
vbs., verbs
v.i., verb intransitive
voc./ative
v.r., verb reflexive
v.t., verb transitive
vulg./ar(ly)

W W., west(ern)
w./ith
W. Afr., West African
wd, word
wds, words
W. Ind., West Indian (i.e. of the West Indies)

Y yr(s), year(s)

Z zool./ogy

Form of the letter **A, a** has evolved with successive cultures (see examples on right). Originally the letter may have been based on the symbol of an ox head. Left: construction of capital A in 1525 by Albrecht Dürer, the great Renaissance artist. He designed the strokes within a square according to geometrical ratios.

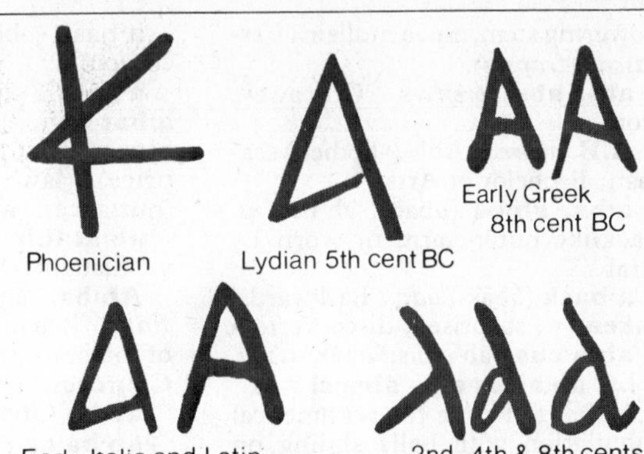

Many abbreviations, especially those consisting of initial letters, may be written with or without points.

A, a (ā) (pl. **A's, a's** or **As, as**). 1. First letter of modern English and ancient Roman alphabet, descended, through Greek and Latin, from first letter, **a·leph** (ah'lĕf) (א), of Hebrew and Phoenician alphabets, in English representing orig. a low–back–wide vowel sound and now a number of vowel sounds. 2. First in series, order, or class, esp. (alg. etc.) first known quantity. 3. Grade or mark indicating highest quality. 4. **A**, (mus.) sixth note of natural scale (C major); scale or key with this note for tonic. 5. **A 1** (ā'wŭn'), applied in Lloyd's Register to ships in first-class condition in regard to both hull (designated by A) and equipment (1); hence, (also **A one**), first class, prime, perfect. 6. **A-frame**, building with main frame or shape forming inverted V; **A–O.K.** (slang), in perfect order.

A *abbrev.* Ampere(s); angstrom(s).

a (*a*; emphat. ā), **an** *indefinite articles.* One; some, any; (in, to, for) each.

a- *prefix.* 1. On, in, at. 2. (also **an-**) Without, not.

A.A. *abbrev.* Anti-aircraft; Alcoholics Anonymous; Associate in Arts.

A.A.A. *abbrev.* American Automobile Association; anti-aircraft artillery.

Aa·chen (ah'ken, -χen). (Fr. *Aix-la-Chapelle*) Ancient city of Germany near Belgian and Dutch borders, scene of coronation of German kings until 16th c.

Aal·borg (awl'boorg). Historic city and port of N. Denmark.

Aal·to (ahl'taw), **Alvar** (1898–1976). Finnish architect, designer, and planner; his works have influenced modern design throughout the world.

Aar (ar̄), **Aa·re** (ar̄'*e*). River in Switzerland flowing from the Bernese Alps NE. to the Rhine.

aard·vark (ar̄k'var̄k) *n.* S. Afr. ant-eating quadruped (*Orycteropus afer*) with long extensile tongue. [Du., = "earth-pig"]

aard·wolf (ar̄d'wo͞olf) *n.* (pl. **-wolves** pr. -wo͞olvz). Carnivorous mammal (*Proteles cristatus*) resembling the hyena.

Aar·on (ar̄'on, ăr'-). Brother of Moses and traditional founder of Jewish priesthood; **~'s rod,** (Numbers 17) plant with tall

The Cape anteater, ***aardvark,*** *reaches its prey first by destroying the nests with its large claws, then by grubbing with its tapering snout. It has a long thread-like tongue.*

The 'earth-wolf' of southern Africa, ***aardwolf*** *resembles the hyena but is smaller. It lives chiefly off termites, eggs and lizards. Glands release a musk smell when it is attacked.*

flowering stem, esp. a mullein (*Verbascum trapsus*).

ab-, abs- *prefixes.* Off, away, from.

A.B. *abbrev.* Able (-bodied) seaman; Bachelor of Arts.

a·ba, ab·ba (*a*bah′, ah′b*a*) *ns.* Sacklike outer garment worn by Arabs.

a·back (*a*băk′) *adv.* Backwards; **taken ~**, surprised, disconcerted.

ab·a·cus (ăb′*a*k*u*s; *a*băk′*u*s) *n.* (pl. **ab·a·cus·es, ab·a·ci** pr. ăb′*a*sī). 1. Frame for arithmetical calculation with balls sliding on wires, used before the adoption of the nine figures and zero, and still used in China etc. and in elementary teaching. 2. (archit.) Upper member, often a square flat slab, of capital, supporting architrave.

A·ba·dan (ahbahdahn′). Port and oil-refining center on the Persian Gulf in SW. Iran.

A·bad·don (*a*băd′*o*n). Hebrew name of APOLLYON.

a·baft (*a*băft′) *adv.* On or toward stern of ship. ~ *prep.* Aft of, behind.

ab·a·lo·ne (ăb*a*lō′nē) *n.* Edible mollusk of genus *Haliotis*, with ear-shaped shell lined with mother-of-pearl.

a·ban·don (*a*băn′d*o*n) *v.t.* Give up, surrender, forsake. ~*n.* Careless freedom. **a·ban′don·ment** *n.* **a·ban·doned** (*a*băn′d*o*nd) *adj.* (esp.) Profligate.

a·base (*a*bās′) *v.t.* (**a·based, a·bas·ing**). Humiliate, lower, make base. **a·base′ment** *n.*

a·bash (*a*băsh′) *v.t.* Embarrass, confound.

a·bate (*a*bāt′) *v.* (**a·bat·ed, a·bat·ing**). Diminish, make or become less; lower; deduct (part of price); (law) quash (action), end (nuisance). **a·bate′ment** *n.*

ab·at·toir (ăb′*a*twa͡r, ăb*a*twa͡r′) *n.* Slaughterhouse.

Ab·ba (ăb′*a*). Used (in "~, *Father*") in invocations to God; title of bishops in Syriac and Coptic Churches. [Aram. = "father"]

ab·ba (*a*bah′, ah′b*a*) = ABA.

ab·ba·cy (ăb′*a*sē) *n.* (pl. **-cies**). Office, jurisdiction, or tenure of abbot or abbess.

Ab·bas (ăb′*a*s, *a*bahs′) (566–652). Uncle of Muhammad.

Ab·bas·id (ăb′*a*sĭd, *a*băs′ĭd) *n.* Member of dynasty of caliphs ruling in Baghdad 750–1258, claiming descent from ABBAS.

ab·ba·tial (*a*bā′sh*a*l) *adj.* Of an abbey, abbot, or abbess.

ab·bé (ăbā′, ăb′ā) *n.* 1. (esp. in France) Abbot. 2. Title of respect for a priest or any ecclesiastical figure.

ab·bess (ăb′*e*s) *n.* Female superior of community of nuns, in those orders in which monks are governed by abbots.

Abbe·vil·li·an (ăbvĭl′ē*a*n) *adj.* & *n.* (Culture) of the earliest paleolithic period in Europe, represented by the remains found at Abbeville, N. France (formerly called CHELLEAN).

ab·bey (ăb′ē) *n.* (pl. **-beys**). Body of monks or nuns governed by an abbot or abbess; monastic buildings; church or house once an abbey or part of it.

Ab·bey (ăb′ē) **Theatre.** Irish national theater, located since 1904 on Abbey St., Dublin.

ab·bot (ăb′*o*t) *n.* Superior of community of monks (now chiefly in Benedictine and Augustinian orders), usu. elected by the monks for life or period of years, and freq. holding certain episcopal rights. [Aram. *abba* father]

abbr., abbrev. *abbrevs.* Abbreviated; abbreviation.

ab·bre·vi·ate (*a*brē′vēāt) *v.t.* (**-at·ed, -at·ing**). Shorten, contract (esp. word, by writing part for the whole). **ab·bre·vi·a·tion** (*a*brēvēā′sh*o*n) *n.*

ABC (ābēsē′) *n.* (pl. **ABC's, ABCs**). Alphabet, rudiments of subject.

ab·di·cate (ăb′dĭkāt) *v.* (**-cat·ed, -cat·ing**). Renounce, relinquish (esp. crown) formally or by default. **ab·di·ca·tion** (ăbdĭkā′sh*o*n) *n.*

ab·do·men (ăb′d*o*m*e*n, ăbdō′-) *n.* 1. (anat.) Part of body between diaphragm and floor of pelvis, containing digestive and other organs. 2. (zool.) Hind part, not bearing walking limbs, of insects, spiders, etc. **ab·dom·i·nal** (ăbdŏm′*i*n*a*l) *adj.*

ab·duct (ăbdŭkt′) *v.t.* Carry off person (esp. by force), kidnap; (of muscle etc.) draw limb from normal position. **ab·duc′tion, ab·duc′tor** *ns.*

a·beam (*a*bēm′) *adv.* On a line

*Above: Earliest calculating device of the ancient world before adoption of the nine figures and zero, the **abacus** is still commonly used in the East for commercial purposes. The word is thought to derive from the Hebrew 'ābāq', which described sand strewn on a surface to be written on.*

*Right: St. Mary's Abbey, York, U.K. Historically an **abbey** housed a religious community governed by an abbot or abbess. Before the Reformation, abbeys were dominant locally.*

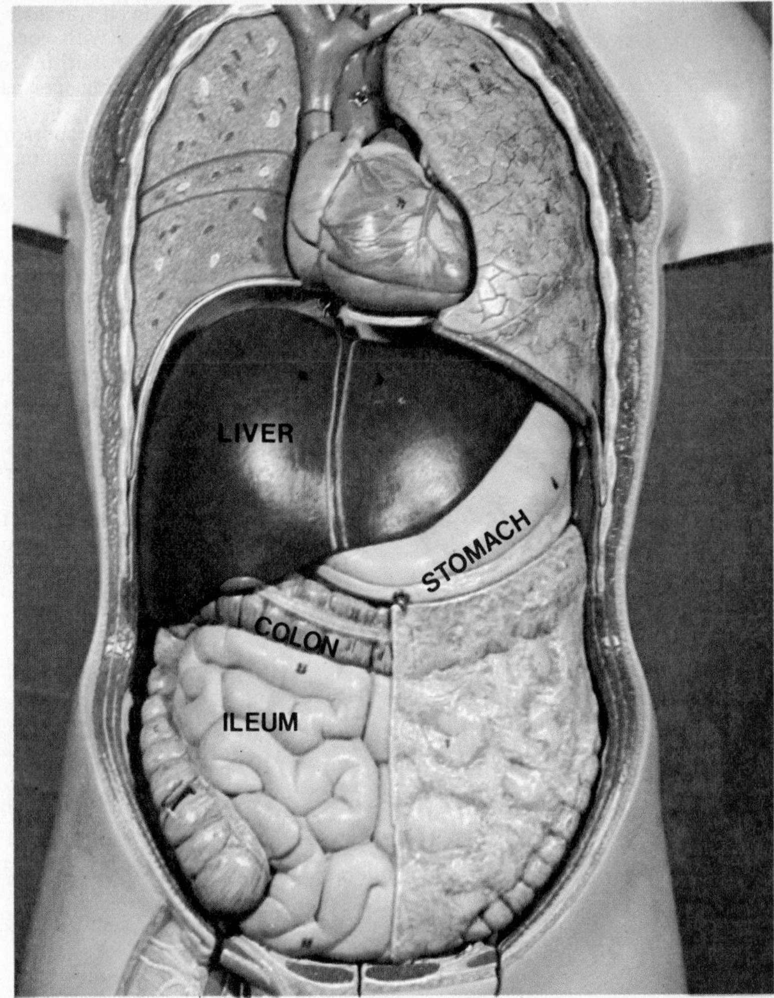

*All the organs of the **abdomen** shown in the illustration are crucial to digestion. When food is eaten, its digestion starts in the stomach and is continued in the ileum and the colon. The liver stores products of digestion and converts them into other substances needed by the body, or to be excreted.*

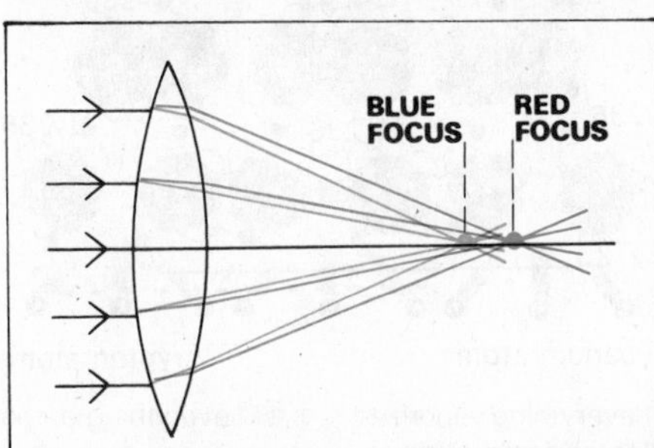

*Left: In chromatic **aberration,** when light passes through a convex lens the rays of various colors in the light are variously bent. Not a single focus but a sequence of foci results.*

*Below: **Aberdeen Angus,** famous breed of beef cattle notable for its quality of flesh. The Angus won world rank after its introduction to the U.S.A. in 1873.*

at right angles to ship's or aircraft's length; opposite the middle of ship's or aircraft's side.

a·be·ce·dar·i·an (ābēsēdār′ēan) *adj.* 1. Arranged alphabetically, as the 119th Psalm. 2. Elementary. ~ *n.* Pupil learning the alphabet; beginner, novice.

à Beck·et (*a* běk′ĭt), **Thomas**: see BECKET.

a·bed (*a*běd′) *adv.* (archaic, poet.) In bed.

A·bed·ne·go (*a*běd′negō). Jewish youth who, with Shadrach and Meshach, came unharmed from a furnace into which they had been thrown by Nebuchadnezzar (Dan. 3).

A·bel (ā′bel). Second son of Adam, killed by his brother Cain (Gen. 4).

Ab·é·lard (ăb′elard; *Fr.* ăbālar′), **Pierre** (1079–1142). French philosopher; advocate of rational theological inquiry and founder of scholastic theology. (See also HÉLOÏSE.)

a·bele (*a*bēl′, ā′bel) *n.* White poplar (*Populus alba*).

Ab·er·deen (ăb*er*dēn′). City on E. coast of N. Scotland; university, 1494; ~ (ăb′*er*dēn) **Angus,** (one of) a breed of polled black beef cattle; **Ab·er·do·ni·an** (ăb*er*dō′nēan) *adj.* & *n.*

ab·er·rant (*a*bĕr′*a*nt) *adj.* 1. Wandering, straying from moral standard. 2. Diverging from normal type. **ab·er′rance** *n.*

ab·er·ra·tion (ăberā′shon) *n.* 1. Mental or moral slip or error; deviation from type. 2. (optics) Nonconvergence of rays to one focus. 3. (astron., also ~ **of light**) Displacement of true position of heavenly body to observer on Earth, due to Earth's motion and noninstantaneous transmission of light; **planetary** ~, aberration due to motion of the planet itself.

a·bet (*a*bĕt′) *v.t.* (**a·bet·ted, a·bet·ting**). Help or encourage, esp. in wrongdoing. **a·bet′ter, a·bet′tor** *ns.*

a·bey·ance (*a*bā′*a*ns) *n.* State of suspension, dormant condition (of rights etc.).

ab·hor (ăbhor′) *v.t.* (**-horred, -hor·ring**). Regard with disgust and hatred. **ab·hor·rent** (ăbhor′-*e*nt, -har′-) *adj.* Inspiring disgust, repugnant, detestable. **ab·hor′rent·ly** *adv.* **ab·hor′rence** *n.*

a·bide (*a*bīd′) *v.* (**a·bode** pr. *a*bōd′, **a·bid·ed, a·bid·ing**). Remain; continue; dwell (archaic); wait for (archaic); (with neg.) tolerate; ~ **by**, remain faithful to. **a·bid′ing** *adj.* Enduring, permanent. **a·bid′ing·ly** *adv.*

Ab·i·djan (ăbĭjahn′). Seaport on the Gulf of Guinea; former capital of the Ivory Coast.

Ab·i·gail (ăb′igāl). 1. Wife of Nabal and subsequently of David (I Sam. 25). 2. In Beaumont and Fletcher's *Scornful Lady*, the waiting gentlewoman (cf. I Sam. 25); hence (**a** ~), lady's maid.

Ab·i·lene (ăb′ilēn). City in Kansas west of Topeka; boyhood home of Dwight D. Eisenhower.

a·bil·i·ty (abĭl′ĭtē) *n.* (pl. **-ties**). Sufficient power, capacity (*to* do); legal competency (to act); cleverness, talent, mental power.

A·bim·e·lech (abĭm′elĕk). 1. Son of Gideon, one of the judges of Israel (Judges 8, 9). 2. King of Gerar, southern Palestine (Gen. 20, 26).

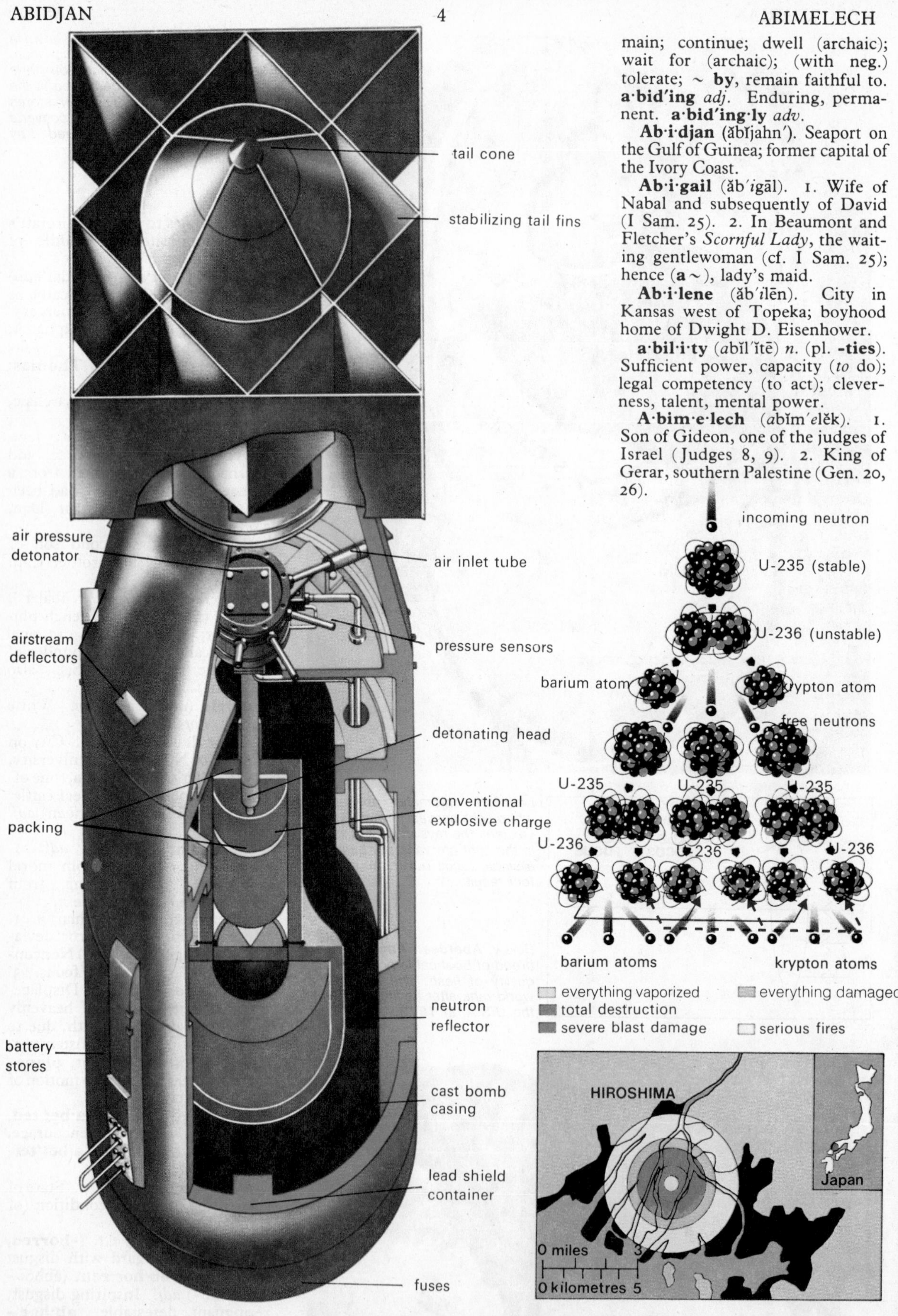

Inside view of uranium bomb 'Little Boy' (U-235), first ***A-bomb*** *which was dropped on and destroyed Hiroshima, August 1945. Shown also: chain reaction that fuelled it. Atomic bombs work by nuclear fission (splitting atoms); hydrogen bombs by fusion. Atomic energy is now harnessed to engineering projects and mining.*

ab in·i·ti·o (ăb ĭnĭsh′ēō). From the beginning (abbrev. *ab init.*). [L.]

a·bi·o·gen·e·sis (ābīōjĕn′ĭsĭs, ăbē-) *n.* T.H. Huxley's term for spontaneous generation (opp. BIOGENESIS).

ab·ject (ăb′jĕkt, ăbjĕkt′) *adj.* Brought low, miserable, craven, degraded. **ab·ject′ly** *adv.*

ab·jure (ăbjoor′) *v.t.* (**-jured, -jur·ing**). Renounce on oath. **ab·ju·ra·tion** (ăbjo͝orā′shon) *n.*

abl. *abbrev.* Ablative.

ab·la·tion (ăblā′shon) *n.* 1. Removal (esp. in surgery, of part of body). 2. (geol.) Waste of a glacier by evaporation and melting. 3. (of a rocket) Burning away of nose material on reentry into Earth's atmosphere.

ab·la·tive (ăb′latĭv) *adj.* (gram.) Of the case (in Latin and other languages) denoting direction from a place, also time and source, agent, or instrument. ~ *n.* (Word in) ablative case; ~ **absolute**, Latin construction of noun and participle (both in ablative case) expressing time, occasion, or circumstances.

ab·laut (ahb′lowt; ăb′-) *n.* (philol.) Systematic vowel permutation (not due to influence of contiguous sounds) in root of word to show changes in tense, meaning, etc., as in s*i*ng, s*a*ng, s*u*ng.

a·blaze (ablāz′) *adv.* Blazing; on fire; gleaming, brilliant.

a·ble (ā′bel) *adj.* (**a·bler, a·blest**). Having the power or ability; talented, clever; ~**-bodied**, physically fit, robust; ~ (**-bodied**) **seaman**, (abbrev. A.B.) certified merchant seaman.

-able *suffix.* Close in meaning to the word *able*; by addition to nouns and verbs used to form many adjectives with sense "that can, may or must be" (*bearable, readable, washable*); "that can be made the subject of" (*objectionable*); "that is in accordance with" (*fashionable, reasonable*).

ab·lu·tion (ăblo͞o′shon, ablo͞o′-) *n.* Ceremonial washing; water or wine used in this; (pl.) process of washing oneself.

ABM *abbrev.* Antiballistic missile.

ab·ne·gate (ăb′negāt) *v.t.* (**-gat·ed, -gat·ing**). Deny oneself (thing), renounce (right, belief). **ab·ne·ga·tion** (ăbnegā′shon) *n.*

ab·nor·mal (ăbnōr′mal) *adj.* Deviating from type, exceptional, irregular. **ab·nor′mal·ly** *adv.* **ab·nor·mal·i·ty** (ăbnōrmăl′ĭtē) *n.* (pl. **-ties**).

ab·nor·mi·ty (ăbnōr′mĭtē) *n.* (pl. **-ties**). Irregularity; monstrosity.

a·board (abōrd′, abōrd′) *adv.* & *prep.* On board (ship, train, etc.).

a·bode (abōd′) *n.* 1. Dwelling place. 2. See ABIDE.

a·bol·ish (abŏl′ĭsh) *v.t.* Put an end to.

ab·o·li·tion (ăbolĭsh′on) *n.* Action or fact of abolishing; in 18th and 19th centuries esp. in U.S. history, movement against slavery, usu. **A~. ab·o·li′tion·ism** *n.* **ab·o·li·tion·ist** *n.* One advocating abolition, esp. of slavery.

ab·o·ma·sum (ăbomā′sum) *n.* (pl. **-sa** pr. -sa). Fourth stomach of ruminant.

Australian ***Aboriginal*** *hunter stands poised to spear fish in a swamp. The Aboriginals have been in Australia for at least 40,000 years. They now number about 160,000.*

A-bomb (ā′bŏm) *n.* Atom(ic) bomb.

a·bom·i·na·ble (abŏm′inabel) *adj.* Morally or physically loathsome, detestable, odious, revolting; **A~ Snowman** = YETI. **a·bom′·i·na·bly** *adv.*

a·bom·i·nate (abŏm′ināt) *v.t.* (**-nat·ed, -nat·ing**). Loathe, dislike strongly.

a·bom·i·na·tion (abŏminā′shon) *n.* Loathing; object or practice deserving of aversion or disgust.

ab·o·rig·i·nal (ăborĭj′inal) *adj.* Indigenous, existing or present at dawn of history or before arrival of colonists or invaders. ~ *n.* Aboriginal inhabitant (esp. of Australia).

ab·o·rig·i·nes (ăborĭj′inēz) *n.pl.* Aboriginal inhabitants, plants, etc. **ab·o·rig′i·ne** *n.* (colloq.) Aboriginal inhabitant.

a·bort (abōrt′) *v.* 1. (Cause to) miscarry; (biol.) become sterile, remain undeveloped. 2. Fail, cease prematurely. 3. (aeronaut.) Terminate (mission, flight) prematurely. ~ *n.* (aeronaut.) Premature termination of mission flight.

a·bor·ti·fa·cient (abōrtifā′shent) *adj.* & *n.* (Drug etc.) causing abortion.

a·bor·tion (abōr′shon) *n.* 1. Termination of pregnancy by expulsion of fetus, esp. before 28th week of pregnancy; (pop.) operation etc. inducing this. 2. Fetus expelled in abortion. 3. Misshapen creature; failed project or action. **a·bor′·tion·ist** *n.* One who performs abortion.

a·bor·tive (abōr′tĭv) *adj.* Premature; fruitless; rudimentary. **a·bor′tive·ly** *adv.* **a·bor′tive·ness** *n.*

A·bou·kir (ahbo͞okēr′) **Bay** = ABUKIR BAY.

a·bou·li·a (abo͞o′lēa) = ABULIA.

a·bound (abownd′) *v.i.* Be plentiful; be rich (*in*), teem or be infested (*with*).

a·bout (abowt′) *adv.* On every side; near; somewhere around; here and there; astir; almost; (naut.) on or to the opposite tack (so **come, put** ~, = TACK[1] *v.* def. 2); **be ~ to** (do), be on the point of doing; **come** ~, happen; ~ **face**, (mil.) turn so as to face in opposite direction. **about** *prep.* 1. On every side of; near; with. 2. Concerning. 3. Occupied with. 4. Here and there in, on, etc.

a·bout·face (abowt′fās′) *n.* Reversal of direction, opinion, policy, or behavior.

a·bove (abŭv′) *adv.* Higher up, overhead; upstream; earlier in a book etc. ~ *prep.* Over, higher than, of higher rank, etc., than; in addition to; ~ **all**, more important than everything else; of higher rank than. **a·bove′board**, without concealment; fair, open, honest.

ab·ra·ca·dab·ra (ăbr*a*k*a*dăb′r*a*) *n.* Cabalistic word formerly used as charm, orig. by Gnostics, and believed to have power of curing agues etc., esp. when written on amulet; (now) spell, mysterious formula, gibberish.

a·brade (*a*brād′) *v.t.* (**a·brad·ed, a·brad·ing**). Scrape off, wear away, injure, by rubbing.

A·bra·ham (ā′br*a*hăm). Hebrew patriarch, from whom all Jews trace their descent (Gen. 11); **~'s bosom**, heavenly abode of the blessed dead (Luke 16); **Plains of ~**, plateau near Quebec, scaled from St. Lawrence River by English army under WOLFE[1] (1759) and scene of subsequent battle with French under MONTCALM, which decided fate of Canada.

a·bra·sion (*a*brā′zh*o*n) *n.* Rubbing or scraping off; rough or sore place on skin caused by this; (geol.) wearing away of Earth's surface by wind-borne particles of rock or sand (cf. EROSION).

a·bra·sive (*a*brā′sĭv, -zĭv) *adj.* Tending to produce abrasion. **~** *n.* Any substance, as emery, Carborundum, etc., used for grinding or polishing.

ab·re·ac·tion (ăbrēăk′sh*o*n) *n.* (psychiatry) Removal, by revival and expression, of the emotion associated with an event that has undergone repression in memory.

a·breast (*a*brĕst′) *adv.* Side by side and facing the same way; **~ of**, keeping up with, not behind (times etc.).

a·bridge (*a*brĭj′) *v.t.* (**a·bridged, a·bridg·ing**). Condense, shorten, curtail. **a·bridg′ment,** Brit. **a·bridge′ment** *ns.* Curtailment; epitome, abstract.

a·broad (*a*brawd′) *adv.* In or to foreign lands; broadly, in different directions; out of doors; (of rumor etc.) current; **from ~**, from foreign countries.

ab·ro·gate (ăb′r*o*gāt) *v.t.* (**-gat·ed, -gat·ing**). Repeal, cancel. **ab·ro·ga·tion** (ăbr*o*gā′sh*o*n) *n.*

ab·rupt (*a*brŭpt′) *adj.* Sudden, hasty; brusque; disconnected; steep; (bot.) truncated. **ab·rupt′ly** *adv.* **ab·rupt′ness** *n.*

A·bruz·zi e Mo·li·se (ahbrōōt′sē ĕ mawlē′zĕ). Region of central Italy between the Apennines and the Adriatic.

abs-: see AB-.

Ab·sa·lom (ăb′s*a*lom). Third and favorite son of DAVID[1], killed while leading rebellion against his father (2 Sam.).

ab·scess (ăb′sĕs) *n.* Local inflammation of body tissues with deep suppuration caused by bacteria that destroy the cells in the center of the area and leave a cavity filled with pus.

ab·scis·sa (ăbsĭs′*a*) *n.* (pl. **-scis·sas, -scis·sae** pr. -sĭs′ē). (geom.) Part of line between fixed point on it and ordinate to it from any other point; coordinate parallel to *x*-axis (horizontal axis) in a system of coordinates.

ab·scis·sion (ăbsĭzh′*o*n) *n.* Cutting off; (bot.) separation.

ab·scond (ăbskŏnd′) *v.i.* Go away secretly, fly from the law.

ab·sence (ăb′s*e*ns) *n.* Being away or absent; nonexistence, lack (*of*); abstracted state.

ab·sent (ăb′s*e*nt) *adj.* Not present; not existing; abstracted in mind; **~-minded**, abstracted, preoccupied; forgetful; **~-mindedly** (*adv.*), **~-mindedness** (*n.*); **absent without leave**, (mil.) absent from military duties without authorization, but without intending to desert, abbrev. AWOL or A.W.O.L. **absent** (ăbsĕnt′) *v.t.* Keep (oneself) away, withdraw (oneself).

ab·sen·tee (ăbs*e*ntē′) *n.* Person not present; person who absents himself or herself from duties etc.; **~ ballot**, ballot cast by mail by a voter away from his or her usual voting place; **~ vote**, absentee ballots collectively. **ab·sen·tee′ism** *n.*

ab·sinthe, ab·sinth (ăb′sĭnth) *ns.* Wormwood, the plant or its essence; strong greenish-gray liqueur flavored with wormwood and anise.

ab·so·lute (ăb′s*o*lōōt) *adj.* Complete, perfect, pure; unrestricted, independent; despotic, ruling arbitrarily; not in (the usual) grammatical relation with other words; real, not relative or comparative; unqualified; self-existent and conceivable without relation to other things; **~ alcohol**, containing at least 99% pure alcohol by weight; **~ magnitude**, magnitude of a star as it would appear at a distance of 10 parsecs; **~ music**, self-dependent instrumental music without literary or other extraneous suggestions (opp. PROGRAM music); **~ pitch**, (mus.) ability to recognize or reproduce pitch of notes; pitch of a note defined scientifically in terms of vibrations per second; **~ temperature**, temperature measured on a Centigrade (Celsius) scale, which has its zero at absolute zero; **~ zero**: see ZERO. **ab·so·lute·ly** (ăb′s*o*lōōtlē, ăbs*o*lōōt′-) *adv.*

'Improvisation', by Kandinsky is an example of ***abstract*** *art, a term which covers the non-figurative painting and sculpture of this century. Abstract art rejects dominance of subject matter.*

Completely, independently; yes, quite so.

ab·so·lu·tion (ăbsoloo′shon) *n.* Formal forgiveness, esp. ecclesiastical declaration of forgiveness of sins; remission of penance.

ab·so·lut·ism (ăb′solootĭzem) *n.* (pol.) Principle of absolute government, despotism. **ab′so·lut·ist** *n.*

ab·solve (ăbzŏlv′, -sŏlv′) *v.t.* (**-solved, -solv·ing**). Set or pronounce free from blame etc.; acquit.

ab·sorb (ăbsorb′, -zorb′) *v.t.* Swallow up, incorporate; engross the attention of; suck in (liquid); take in (heat, light, etc.); assume (an expense). **ab·sorb′a·ble** *adj.* That can be absorbed.

ab·sorb·ent (ăbsor′bent, -zor′-) *adj.* Having a tendency to absorb. ~ *n.* Absorbent substance.

ab·sorp·tion (ăbsorp′shon, -zorp′-) *n.* Action of absorbing, fact of being absorbed.

ab·stain (ăbstān′) *v.i.* Keep oneself from doing something, esp. from drinking alcohol. **ab·stain′er** *n.*

ab·ste·mi·ous (ăbstē′mēus) *adj.* Sparing or moderate in food, drink, etc. **ab·ste′mi·ous·ly** *adv.* **ab·ste′mi·ous·ness** *n.*

ab·sten·tion (ăbstĕn′shon) *n.* Refraining or holding back; not using one's vote.

ab·sti·nence (ăb′stinens) *n.* Abstaining from food, pleasure, alcohol, etc. **ab′sti·nent** *adj.* Practicing abstinence.

ab·stract (ăb′străkt) *adj.* Not concrete; theoretical, not practical; (of art etc.) concerned with pure form and pattern, free from representational qualities; ~ **expressionism**, form of abstract art in which paint is applied by spontaneous or random action of artist. **abstract** *n.* 1. **the** ~, ideal or theoretical way of regarding things. 2. Epitome, summary. 3. Abstraction, abstract term. ~ (ăbstrăkt′) *v.t.* Deduct, remove; steal; disengage (attention etc.); summarize. **ab·stract′ed** *adj.* Withdrawn in thought, not attending.

ab·strac·tion (ăbstrăk′shon) *n.* Withdrawal, removal; abstract idea; absent-mindedness; abstract art.

ab·struse (ăbstroos′) *adj.* Hard to understand, profound. **ab·struse′ly** *adv.* **ab·struse′ness** *n.*

ab·surd (ăbserd′, -zerd′) *adj.* Incongruous, unreasonable, ridiculous.

A·bu Dha·bi (aboo′ dah′bē). City on the Persian Gulf; capital of the United Arab Emirates.

A·bu·kir (ahbooker′) **Bay, Aboukir Bay.** Bay at the mouth of the Nile, N. Egypt; British fleet defeated French fleet here in 1798.

a·bu·li·a (abū′lēa), **a·bou·li·a** (aboo′lēa) *ns.* Loss of willpower (as mental disorder).

a·bun·dance (abŭn′dans) *n.* Plenty, more than enough; affluence; (phys.) amount present.

a·bun′dant *adj.* Plentiful, rich, in abundance. **a·bun′dant·ly** *adv.*

a·buse (abūz′) *v.t.* (**a·bused, a·bus·ing**). Make bad use of, misuse; speak insultingly to or about. ~ (abūs′) *n.* Misuse, perversion; unjust or corrupt practice; insulting speech. **a·bu′sive** *adj.* **a·bu′sive·ly** *adv.* **a·bu′sive·ness** *n.*

A·bu Sim·bel (aboo′ sĭm′bĕl). Village on the Nile S. of Aswan, Egypt; site of ancient Egyptian rock temples built by Rameses II.

a·but (abŭt′) *v.* (**a·but·ted, a·but·ting**). Have common boundary with; border (*on*); end *on*, lean *against*. **a·but′ment** *n.* (archit.) Support from which arch, vault, etc. springs, and which receives the lateral thrust. **a·but′ter** *n.*

a·bysm (abĭz′em) *n.* (poet.) Abyss.

a·bys·mal (abĭz′mal) *adj.* Bottomless (esp. fig.); extremely bad. **a·bys′mal·ly** *adv.*

a·byss (abĭs′) *n.* Primal chaos; bottomless chasm; deep gorge.

a·bys·sal (abĭs′al) *adj.* Of lowest depths of ocean.

Ab·ys·sin·i·a (ăbĭsĭn′ēa). Former name of Ethiopia. **Ab·ys·sin′i·an** *adj.* & *n.*

AC, A.C., ac *abbrevs.* Alternating current.

A/C, a/c *abbrevs.* Account; account current.

a.c. *abbrev.* (in prescriptions) Before meals.

A large genus of trees and shrubs belonging to the pea family, the ***acacia*** *is most commonly found in Africa and Australia. Of some 900 species, about 650 grow only in Australia.*

Trail down the Grand Canyon, Arizona, the immense ***abyss*** *cut by the Colorado River. The winding course of the gorge extends to 217 miles and in width it ranges from some 4 to 18 miles.*

a·ca·cia (*akā'sha*) *n.* 1. Leguminous shrub or tree of genus *A*~ (subfamily Mimoseae), found in warmer regions of Europe and Australia, some species of which yield gum arabic, dyes, etc. 2. N. Amer. locust tree (*Robinia pseudoacacia*, false ~), with sweet-scented pea-like flowers.

ac·a·deme (ăk'*adēm*) *n.* (properly) = ACADEMUS; (used by mistake in poet. style for) the Greek ACADEMY, hence, college, university. [Gk.; mistake perh. caused by Milton's "grove of Academe," (in *Paradise Regained*) i.e. Academus]

ac·a·dem·ic (ăk*adĕm'ĭk*) *adj.* 1. Of an academy or academician; of a university or college. 2. Of the philosophic school of Plato, skeptical. 3. Scholarly; abstract, cold, merely logical; impractical; theoretical, conventional. ~ *n.* Member of university.

ac·a·dem·i·cal (ăk*adĕm'ĭkal*) *adj.* Of a college or university. **ac·a·dem'i·cal·ly** *adv.*

a·cad·e·mi·cian (*akădemĭsh'an*, ăk*ade-*) *n.* Member of art, literary, or scientific academy; teacher.

A·ca·dé·mie Fran·çaise (ăkădāmē frahṅsĕz'). French honorary literary academy, founded by Richelieu (1635); membership, limited to 40, is considered the highest distinction for men of letters.

Ac·a·de·mus (ăk*adē'mus*). (Gk. legend) Hero who revealed hiding place of their sister Helen to the Dioscuri when they invaded Attica.

a·cad·e·my (*akăd'emē*) *n.* (pl. **-mies**). 1. **A**~, pleasure garden near Athens (said to have belonged to ACADEMUS) in which Plato taught; Plato's followers, the philosophical school founded by him. 2. A secondary or high school (esp. private). 3. Place of training in a special art. 4. Society for cultivating literature, art, etc.; **the A**~, (esp.) the Royal Academy of Arts, the *Académie Française*, the U.S.S.R. Academy of Science, etc.

A·ca·di·a (*akā'dēa*). Name given by French to district in what is now known as Nova Scotia, first settled by them at end of 16th c. **A·ca'·di·an** *adj.* & *n.* (Native, inhabitant) of Acadia; (descendant) of Acadians. **Acadia National Park,** scenic recreation area on Mount Desert Island off the S. coast of Maine.

ac·an·thop·ter·yg·i·an (ăk*an*thŏpterĭj'ēan) *adj.* & *n.* (Fish) of group Acanthopterygii, usu. with hard spiny rays in dorsal and anal fins.

a·can·thus (*akăn'thus*) *n.* (pl. **-thus·es, -thi** pr. -thī). 1. Herbaceous plant of genus *A*~ with large, deeply cut, hairy, shining leaves, native to southern Europe, Asia, and Africa. 2. (archit.) Conventionalized leaf of *A. mollis* or *A. spinosus* (with narrower spiny-toothed leaves) used as ornament, esp. on the Corinthian and Composite capitals.

a cap·pel·la (ah k*apĕl'a*). (of choral music) Unaccompanied.

A·ca·pul·co (ăk*apōōl'kō*; *Sp.* ahkahpōōl'kaw). Port and resort city on the Pacific coast of Mexico.

ac·a·rid (ăk'*arĭd*) *n.* Arachnid of family Acaridae, a mite or tick.

acc. *abbrev.* Account; accusative.

Ac·cad (ăk'ăd, ah'kahd), **Ac·ca·di·an** (*akā'dēan*, *akah'*-): see AKKAD.

ac·cede (ăksēd') *v.i.* (**-ced·ed, -ced·ing**). Consent, agree (*to*); (also ~ *to*) enter upon office.

ac·ce·le·ran·do (ahchĕl*erahn'dō*) *adv.*, *adj.*, & *n.* (pl. **-dos**). (mus.) (Passage performed) with gradual increase of speed. [It.]

ac·cel·er·ate (ăksĕl'*erāt*) *v.* (**-at·ed, -at·ing**). Make, become, quicker; cause to happen earlier; **accelerated particle,** (phys.) one subjected to acceleration, esp. by electrical or magnetic means.

ac·cel·er·a·tion (ăksĕl*erā'shon*) *n.* Accelerating; vehicle's power to accelerate; (phys.) rate of increase in velocity of moving body (written, e.g., 10 fps/sec. if body moves 10 feet per second faster in every second).

ac·cel·er·a·tor (ăksĕl'*erāter*) *n.* Thing that increases anything's speed; pedal that operates throttle of internal combustion engine; substance added to mixture to reduce time taken by chemical reaction; electrical or magnetic apparatus (also *atom smasher*) giving high velocities to free electrons or other atomic particles.

ac·cent (ăk'sĕnt) *n.* Prominence given to syllable by stress or pitch; mark used to indicate syllabic pitch, vowel quality, etc. (see ACUTE, CIRCUMFLEX, GRAVE[2], ~); individual, local, or national mode of pronunciation; (pl.) speech; (pros.) rhythmical stress; (mus.) stress recurring at intervals; (fig.) distinctive character; emphasis *on*.

ac·cent (ăk'sĕnt, ăksĕnt') *v.t.* Pronounce with accent or stress, emphasize; mark with (written) accents; intensify, make conspicuous.

ac·cen·tu·al (ăksĕn'chōō*al*) *adj.* Of accent; (esp. of verse) in which meter or rhythm results from alternation of strong and weak (not long and short) syllables. **ac·cen'·tu·al·ly** *adv.*

ac·cen·tu·ate (ăksĕn'chōōāt) *v.t.* (**-at·ed, -at·ing**). Accent (esp. in fig. senses). **ac·cen·tu·a·tion** (ăksĕnchōōā'sh*on*) *n.*

ac·cept (ăksĕpt') *v.t.* Consent to receive; answer (invitation etc.) affirmatively; receive or regard as

*1968: 'Saturn' rocket blasts off with a supreme feat of **acceleration** — the rate of change, with time, in the velocity of a moving object.*

***Acadia National Park** in south-east Maine on the Atlantic coast was established in 1919. An abundance of wildlife inhabits the area and there are several museums and nature centers.*

adequate, satisfactory, or true; tolerate; agree to pay; undertake (office, responsibility). **ac·cept′ance, ac·cep′tor** *ns.*

ac·cept·a·ble (ăksĕp′t*a*b*e*l) *adj.* Worth accepting; adequate; satisfactory. **ac·cept′a·bly** *adv.* **ac·cept·a·bil·i·ty** (ăksĕpt*a*bĭl′ĭtē) *n.*

ac·cept·ed (ăksĕp′tĭd) *adj.* Generally approved, recognized, or believed in.

ac·cess (ăk′sĕs) *n.* 1. Approach; addition; right or means of approach; being approached. 2. Attack or outburst.

ac·ces·si·ble (ăksĕs′ĭb*e*l) *adj.* Able to be reached, entered, or obtained; open to influence (of). **ac·ces′si·bly** *adv.* **ac·ces′si·bil·i·ty** (ăksĕsibĭl′ĭtē) *n.*

ac·ces·sion (ăksĕsh′*o*n) *n.* Acceding or attaining (esp. to throne or manhood); joining, addition; (law) addition to property by natural growth or artificial improvement.

ac·ces·so·ry (ăksĕs′*e*rē) *adj.* Additional, subordinately contributive, adventitious. ~ *n.* (pl. **-ries**). 1. Person who aids or encourages lawbreaker before (~ **before the fact**) or after (~ **after the fact**) the commission of a criminal act. 2. Accompaniment, adjunct; (pl., commerc.) smaller articles of (esp. woman's) dress, as shoes, gloves, etc.; minor fittings for car, camera, etc.

ac·ci·dent (ăk′sĭd*e*nt) *n.* 1. Event without apparent cause, the unexpected; unintentional act, chance misfortune, mishap. 2. Property or quality not essential to our conception of a substance, attribute; mere accessory. **ac·ci·den·tal** (ăksĭdĕn′t*a*l) *adj.* **ac·ci·den′tal·ly** *adv.* **ac·ci·dent′tal** *n.* (mus.) Sharp ♯, flat ♭, or natural ♮ sign occurring not in key signature but before particular note.

ac·ci·die (ăk′sĭdē) *n.* Sloth; laziness or indifference.

ac·claim (*a*klām′) *v.t.* Welcome or applaud loudly, hail. ~ *n.* Shout or applause or welcome.

ac·cla·ma·tion (ăkl*a*mā′sh*o*n) *n.* Loud and eager assent; (pl.) shouting in person's honor.

ac·cli·mate (*a*klī′m*i*t, ăk′l*i*māt) *v.t.* (**-mat·ed, -mat·ing**). Habituate to new climate or surroundings. **ac·cli·ma·tion** (ăkl*i*mā′sh*o*n) *n.*

ac·cli·ma·tize (*a*klī′m*a*tīz) *v.t.* (**-tized, -tiz·ing**) = ACCLIMATE. **ac·cli·ma·ti·za·tion** (*a*klīm*a*tīzā′sh*o*n) *n.* Fact, process, of acclimating, esp. (biol.) in ref. to transference of plants or animals to a new environment.

ac·cliv·i·ty (*a*klĭv′ĭtē) *n.* (pl. **-ties**). Upward slope.

ac·co·lade (ăk′*o*lād, ăk*o*lād′) *n.* 1. Ceremony of conferring knighthood, formerly an embrace, now usu. by stroke on shoulder with flat of sword. 2. Expression of praise or approval.

Arch of Independence enshrining the eternal flame in ***Accra,*** *seaport and capital of Ghana, West Africa. Accra developed from Dutch and English forts established in the 17th century.*

ac·com·mo·date (*a*kŏm′*o*dāt) *v.t.* (**-dat·ed, -dat·ing**). 1. Adapt (*to*); harmonize; reconcile, settle differences between. 2. Equip, supply (*with*); oblige, confer favor on; find lodging for; contain comfortably. **ac·com′mo·dat·ing** *adj.* Obliging.

ac·com·mo·da·tion (*a*kŏm*o*dā′sh*o*n) *n.* 1. Adaptation, adjustment; (of eye) adjustment of shape of lens to bring light rays from various distances to focus upon retina. 2. Settlement, compromise. 3. Serviceable thing, convenience. 4. Lodgings. 5. Loan.

ac·com·pa·ni·ment (*a*kŭm′p*a*nēm*e*nt) *n.* Accompanying thing; appendage; (mus.) subsidiary part, gen. instrumental, supporting a solo instrument or voice, choir, etc.

ac·com·pa·nist (*a*kŭm′p*a*nĭst) *n.* Performer of accompaniment.

ac·com·pa·ny (*a*kŭm′p*a*nē) *v.t.* (**-nied, -ny·ing**). Go with, escort, attend; coexist with; (mus.) support (player, singer, chorus, etc.) by performing subsidiary part.

ac·com·plice (*a*kŏm′plĭs) *n.* Associate, usu. subordinate, in guilt or crime.

ac·com·plish (*a*kŏm′plĭsh) *v.t.* Perform, carry out, succeed in doing. **ac·com′plished** *adj.* Done, existing; skilled, having accomplishments. **ac·com′plish·ment** *n.* Achievement, fulfillment; social attainment.

ac·cord (*a*kōrd′) *v.* 1. Agree, be consistent (*with*). 2. Grant (indulgence, request, etc.). ~ *n.* Consent; mutual agreement; harmonious correspondence in color, tone, etc.; volition (as **of one's own** ~). **ac·cord′ance** *n.* Conformity, agreement. **ac·cord′ant** *adj.*

ac·cord·ing (*a*kōr′dĭng) *adv.* ~ **to,** in a manner consistent with; on the authority of. **ac·cord′ing·ly** *adv.* Correspondingly; in accordance with what might be expected; in due course; therefore.

ac·cor·di·on (*a*kōr′dē*o*n) *n.* Small portable musical instrument with bellows and keyboard admitting wind to metal reeds when keys are depressed; ~ **door,** ~ **file,** having a series of folds like the bellows of an accordion.

ac·cost (*a*kawst, *a*kŏst′) *v.t.* Approach and address (esp. boldly); (of prostitute) solicit.

ac·couche·ment (ăkōōshmahṅ′) *n.* Lying-in, delivery. **ac·cou·cheur** (ăkōōshẽr′) *n.* Male midwife. **ac·cou·cheuse** (ăkōōshöz′) *n.* Midwife. [Fr.]

ac·count (*a*kownt′) *n.* 1. Counting, reckoning. 2. Amount of money deposited with a bank; credit facilities allowed by shop etc. to customer; statement of money received and expended, with balance; statement of discharge of responsibilities generally, answering for conduct; final account at judgment seat of God; **balance, square** ~**s** (*with*), settle account by payment of money due (freq. fig.); **for** ~ **of,** to be sold on behalf of; **give** (*good*) ~ **of oneself,** be successful, give favorable impression; **keep** ~**s,** keep statement of expenditure and receipts; **on** ~, as interim payment; **on** ~ **of,** in consideration of, because of; **on no** ~, not for any reason, certainly not; **on one's own** ~, for one's own purposes and at one's own risk; **on someone's** ~, in a person's interest, for someone's sake. 3. Reckoning in one's favor, profit, advantage. 4. Estimation; **leave out of, take into,** ~, (fail to) take into consideration. 5. Narration, report, description (*of*). 6. ~ **executive,** person in an advertising agency or other service business who is responsible for managing a client's account. **account** *v.* 1. Consider, regard as. 2. ~ **for,** give reckoning for; answer for; explain cause of, serve as explanation of.

ac·count·a·ble (*a*kown′t*a*b*e*l) *adj.* 1. Bound to give account, responsible, liable. 2. Explicable. **ac·count·a·bil·i·ty** (*a*kownt*a*bĭl′ĭtē) *n.*

ac·count·an·cy (*a*kown′t*a*nsē) *n.* Profession or duties of accountant.

ac·count·ant (*a*kown′t*a*nt) *n.* Professional keeper or inspector of accounts, esp. **certified public** ~, one having official certificate as ~.

ac·cou·ter (*a*kōō′t*e*r) *v.t.* Attire, equip. esp. for military duty (chiefly in past part. **accoutered**).

ac·cou·ter·ment (*a*kōō′t*e*rm*e*nt) *n.* (usu. *n.pl.*) Equipment, trappings.

ac·cou·tre (*a*kōō′t*e*r) *v.t.* (**-tred, -tring**). (esp. Brit.) = ACCOUTER. **ac·cou·tre·ment** (*a*kōō′trem*e*nt) *n.*

Ac·cra (ăk′r*a*, *a*krah′). W. Afr. seaport on Gulf of Guinea, capital

*The **acetylene** torch is used in the welding and cutting of practically all industrial metals. This colorless, gaseous hydrocarbon is mixed with oxygen for use in industry.*

of Ghana.

ac·cred·it (*a*krĕd'ĭt) *v.t.* Gain credit for; provide with credentials, as an ambassador; certify as meeting specific requirements; attribute *to*. **ac·cred'it·ed** *adj.* Officially recognized; generally accepted.

ac·crete (*a*krēt') *v.i.* (**-cret·ed, -cret·ing**). Grow together or into one; form around or on (*to*), as around a nucleus. **ac·cre·tion** (*a*krē'sh*o*n) *n.* Growth by organic enlargement; increase by external additions; adhesion of extraneous matter; matter so added, extraneous addition.

ac·crue (*a*kroo') *v.i.* (**-crued, -cru·ing**). Fall (*to* one) as a natural growth, advantage, or result (esp. of interest on invested money).

ac·cu·mu·late (*a*kū'my*u*lāt) *v.* (**-lat·ed, -lat·ing**). Heap up, amass; grow numerous, form increasing mass or heap. **ac·cu·mu·la·tion** (*a*kūmy*u*lā'sh*o*n) *n.* **ac·cu·mu·la·tive** (*a*kū'my*u*lātĭv, -l*a*tĭv) *adj.*

ac·cu·mu·la·tor (*a*kū'my*u*lāt*er*) *n.* 1. One who collects. 2. Equipment for collecting and storing energy. 3. (Brit.) Storage battery.

ac·cu·rate (ăk'y*e*rĭt) *adj.* Precise, exact, correct. **ac'cu·rate·ly** *adv.* **ac'cu·ra·cy** *n.* (pl. **-cies**).

ac·curs·ed (*a*kẽr'sĭd, *a*kẽrst'), **ac·curst** (*a*kẽrst') *adjs.* Lying under a curse; execrable, detestable.

ac·cu·sa·tion (ăky*u*zā'sh*o*n) *n.* Accusing; allegation, indictment.

ac·cu·sa·tive (*a*kū'z*a*tĭv) *adj.* (gram.) Of the case (also *objective* case) chiefly denoting the direct object of a verb or used following certain prepositions. ~ *n.* (Word in) accusative case. **ac·cu'sa·tive·ly** *adv.*

ac·cu·sa·to·ry (*a*kū'z*a*tōrē, -tōrē) *adj.* Conveying or implying accusation.

ac·cuse (*a*kūz') *v.t.* (**-cused, -cus·ing**). Charge with fault, indict; blame, lay fault on; **the accused**, defendant in criminal case.

ac·cus·tom (*a*kŭs't*o*m) *v.t.* Familiarize by habit or custom. **ac·cus'tomed** *adj.* Customary, usual; used.

ace (ās) *n.* 1. Card, die face, etc., with one pip. 2. Fighter pilot who has shot down many enemy planes; person excelling in any sport or skill; (tennis etc.) unreturnable service; point thus scored; (golf) a hole in one; the hole thus made; ~ **in the hole,** ~ **up one's sleeve**, something effective kept in reserve. **ace** *v.t.* (**aced, ac·ing**). 1. (tennis) Score an ace against (one's opponent). 2. (golf) Reach (a hole) from the tee in a single stroke. ~ *adj.* (colloq.) Excellent, of high quality, outstanding.

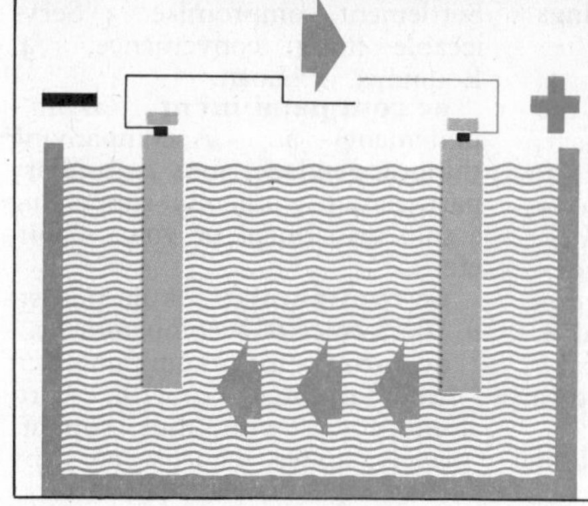

*In a lead–acid **accumulator** (diagram), chemical reactions between lead plate, and lead dioxide plate, both immersed in dilute sulphuric acid, produce electrical energy.*

a·ce·di·a (*a*sē'dē*a*) = ACCIDIE.

a·ceph·a·lous (āsĕf'*a*l*u*s) *adj.* Headless; (zool.) having no part of body specially organized as head; (bot.) with head aborted or cut off; (pros.) lacking the regular first syllable.

a·cer·bi·ty (*a*sẽr'b*i*tē) *n.* Astringent sourness; bitterness of speech, manner, or temper.

ac·e·tal (ăs'*e*tăl) *n.* Colorless pleasant-smelling liquid formed by slow oxidation of alcohol; class of complex ethers, derivatives of aldehyde, of which this is the type.

ac·et·al·de·hyde (ăsĭtăl'd*e*hīd) *n.* Aldehyde.

ac·et·an·i·lide (ăsĭtăn'*i*līd) *n.* White crystalline solid made by action of acetic acid on aniline and used as febrifuge and analgesic.

ac·e·tate (ăs'ĭtāt) *n.* Salt of acetic acid; synthetic material in the manufacture of which acetic acid is used; ~ **fiber**, textile fiber made from cellulose acetate.

a·ce·tic (*a*sē'tĭk, *a*sĕt'ĭk) *adj.* Of, producing, vinegar; ~ **acid**, colorless pungent biting organic acid (CH_3COOH) which gives vinegar its characteristic taste.

a·cet·i·fy (*a*sĕt'*i*fī) *v.* (**-fied, -fy·ing**). Turn into vinegar, make or become sour. **a·cet·i·fi·ca·tion** (*a*sĕt*i*f*i*kā'sh*o*n) *n.*

aceto-, acet- *prefixes.* (chem.) Derived from, connected with, acetic acid or acetyl.

ac·e·tone (ăs´ĭtōn) *n.* Colorless fragrant inflammable liquid ketone (CH_3COCH_3) widely used as an organic solvent and in making chloroform etc.

a·ce·tyl (asē´tĭl, ăs´e-) *n.* Monovalent radical (CH_3CO) of acetic acid. **a·cet·y·la·tion** (asĕtĭlā´shon) *n.* Introduction of acetyl group(s) into a compound by means of a chemical reaction. **a·cet·y·late** (asĕt´ĭlāt) *v.* (**-lat·ed, -lat·ing**).

a·cet·y·lene (asĕt´ĭlēn, -lĭn) *n.* Colorless, nearly odorless (when pure), highly inflammable gaseous hydrocarbon, usu. prepared by adding water to calcium carbide (impurities in which produce the characteristic unpleasant smell), and used for lighting, for welding, and for cutting metals, etc., hence, ~ **torch.**

a·ce·tyl·sal·i·cyl·ic (asē´tĭlsălĭsĭl´ĭk) **acid.** Aspirin.

A·chae·a (akē´a). 1. District of ancient Greece along S. shore of Gulf of Corinth. 2. Roman province comprising all the southern part of Greece. **A·chae´an** *adj.* & *n.* 1. In Homer, apparently = Greek; hence, (one) of the early Greeks; of the early Greek civilization. 2. In classical times, (inhabitant) of Achaea.

A·cha·tes (akā´tēz). (Gk. & Rom. legend) Faithful friend of Aeneas.

ache (āk) *v.i.* (**ached, ach·ing**). 1. Suffer, be a source of continuous dull pain. 2. Yearn, long *for.* ~ *n.* Continuous or prolonged dull pain.

Ach·er·on (ăk´erŏn). (Gk. myth.) One of the rivers of Hades, over which the dead were carried by Charon's ferry.

A·cheu·le·an, A·cheu·li·an (ashōō´lēan) *adjs.* & *ns.* (Of) the paleolithic period succeeding the Abbevillian. [*St. Acheul*, Amiens, France]

a·chieve (achēv´) *v.t.* (**a·chieved, a·chiev·ing**). Accomplish; acquire; reach (an end). **a·chieve´ment** *n.* Completion, accomplishment; thing accomplished.

A·chil·les (akĭl´ēz). (Gk. legend) Hero of the Trojan war, son of Peleus and Thetis; was killed by Paris with a poisoned arrow that pierced his heel where his mother held him in infancy when she plunged him into the Styx to make him invulnerable; hence, **Achilles' heel**, vulnerable part; ~ **tendon**, tendon in heel by which calf muscles extend foot.

ach·ro·mat·ic (ăkromăt´ĭk) *adj.* Colorless; transmitting light without dispersing it into its constituent colors; ~ **lens**, pair of lenses, the dispersion of one correcting the dispersion of the other. **a·chro·ma·tism** (ākrō´matĭzem) *n.* Achromatic quality. **a·chro´ma·tize** *v.t.* (**-tized, -tiz·ing**).

A loudspeaker being tested in the anechoic chamber of E.M.I. laboratories, Middlesex, U.K. A building's ***acoustical*** *quality governs audibility and clarity equally with quality of transmission.*

ac·id (ăs´ĭd) *adj.* 1. Sour, sharp to the taste; (fig.) biting, severe. 2. Having properties of an acid. ~ *n.* 1. Sour substance. 2. (chem.) One of a class of compounds in which hydrogen may be replaced by metals to form salts, neutralizing alkalis, usu. corroding or dissolving metals, and having sour taste. 3. (slang) The drug LSD; **ac´idhead,** user of this. 4. **acid test**, testing for gold by means of aqua fortis; (fig.) crucial test.

a·cid·ic (asĭd´ĭk) *adj.* Acid; acid forming.

a·cid·i·fy (asĭd´ĭfī) *v.* (**-fied, -fy·ing**). Change or make into acid; become or make sour.

a·cid·i·ty (asĭd´ĭtē) *n.* Acid property.

ac·i·do·sis (ăsĭdō´sĭs) *n.* (path.) Acid condition of blood and body tissues.

a·cid·u·lous (asĭj´ulus) *adj.* Somewhat acid; sharp, caustic.

-acious *suffix.* Forming adjs. with sense "inclined to" (*pugnacious*), "abounding in" (*capacious*).

-acity *suffix.* Forming nouns of quality corresponding to adjectives in **-acious.**

ac·knowl·edge (ăknŏl´ĭj) *v.t.* (**-edged, -edg·ing**). Admit the truth of, admit, own; announce receipt of; express appreciation of. **ac·knowl´edg·ment**, Brit. **ac·knowl´edge·ment** *ns.* Acknowledging; thing given or done in return for service etc.

A.C.L.U. *abbrev.* American Civil Liberties Union.

ac·me (ăk´mē) *n.* Highest point or pitch, culmination; (fig.) point of perfection.

ac·ne (ăk´nē) *n.* Skin eruption due to inflammation of sebaceous glands, common in adolescence, and characterized by pimples esp. on face.

ac·o·lyte (ăk´olīt) *n.* Altar attendant, esp. of priests and deacons, lighting and carrying candles etc.; assistant.

ac·o·nite (ăk´onīt) *n.* Plant of poisonous ranunculaceous genus *Aconitum*, with five blue or yellow sepals, of which one is helmet shaped, as *A. lycoctonum*, wolfsbane; dried root of this plant used in treatment of disease and as poison.

a·corn (ā´kōrn) *n.* Fruit of oak, oval nut growing in shallow woody cup; ~ **squash**, acorn-shaped type of squash.

a·cot·y·le·don (ākŏtelē´don) *n.* (bot.) Plant with no distinct cotyledons or seed leaves, as fern, moss, etc. **a·cot·y·le´don·ous** *adj.*

a·cous·tic (akōō´stĭk) *adj.* Of the sense of hearing; of sound, of acoustics; (of building material) sound-absorbent; operated by sound waves. **a·cous´tics** *n.* 1. (usu. considered sing.) Science of sound. 2. (considered pl.) Properties of building, room, etc., in regard to audibility of sounds. **a·cous'ti·cal** *adj.* **a·cous'ti·cal·ly** *adv.*

ac·quaint (*a*kwānt') *v.t.* Make aware or familiar, inform; **be acquainted with**, have personal knowledge of. **ac·quaint'ance** *n.* Personal knowledge; person with whom one is acquainted but not intimate. **ac·quaint'ance·ship** *n.*

ac·qui·esce (ăkwēĕs') *v.t.* (**-esced, -esc·ing**). Agree, esp. tacitly; not object. **ac·qui·es'cence** *n.* **ac·qui·es'cent** *adj.*

ac·quire (*a*kwīr') *v.t.* (**-quired, -quir·ing**). Gain, get, come to have; **acquired characteristic**, characteristic gained through influence of environment, and not inherited from parents. **ac·quire'-ment** *n.* Acquiring.

ac·qui·si·tion (ăkwĭzĭsh'*o*n) *n.* Acquiring; thing acquired, useful or pleasant addition.

ac·quis·i·tive (*a*kwĭz'ĭtĭv) *adj.* Inclined or disposed to acquire things. **ac·quis'i·tive·ly** *adj.* **ac·quis'i·tive·ness** *n.*

ac·quit (*a*kwĭt') *v.t.* (**-quit·ted, -quit·ting**). Pay (debt); declare not guilty, free from blame or obligation; ~ **oneself** (*well, ill,* etc.), perform one's part or duty.

ac·quit·tal (*a*kwĭt'*a*l) *n.* Discharge from debt; performance (of duty); deliverance from a charge by verdict etc.

A·cre (ah'k*e*r, ā'k*e*r). Seaport of Israel; captured by Christians in Third Crusade, 1191. **Bay of** ~, inlet of the Mediterranean in NW. Israel.

a·cre (ā'k*e*r) *n.* Land measure, legally 4,840 sq. yds. (4,047 sq. m); (pl.) lands, fields. **a·cre·age** (ā'k*e*rĭj) *n.* Amount of acres, acres collectively.

ac·rid (ăk'rĭd) *adj.* Bitterly pungent, irritating; of bitter temper or manner. **ac'rid·ly** *adv.* **a·crid·i·ty** (*a*krĭd'ĭtē) *n.*

ac·ri·dine (ăk'r*i*dēn) *n.* Colorless crystalline compound derived from coal tar, source of dyes and drugs.

ac·ri·mo·ni·ous (ăkr*i*mō'nē*u*s) *adj.* Marked by acrimony. **ac·ri·mo'ni·ous·ly** *adv.* **ac·ri·mo'ni·ous·ness** *n.*

ac·ri·mo·ny (ăk'r*i*mōnē) *n.* Bitterness of temper or manner.

ac·ro·bat (ăk'r*o*băt) *n.* Performer of daring and spectacular gymnastic feats. **ac·ro·bat·ic** (ăkr*o*băt'ĭk) *adj.* **ac·ro·bat'i·cal·ly** *adv.* **ac·ro·bat'ics** *n.*

ac·ro·meg·a·ly (ăkr*o*mĕg'*a*lē) *n.* Disease due to overactivity of pituitary gland, resulting in overgrowth of bones esp. of extremities and skull.

ac·ro·nym (ăk'r*o*nĭm) *n.* Word formed from initial letters of words in a phrase, e.g. *NATO* (*N*orth *A*tlantic *T*reaty *O*rganization), *scuba* (*s*elf-*c*ontained *u*nderwater *b*reathing *a*pparatus).

ac·ro·pho·bi·a (ăkr*o*fō'bē*a*) *n.* (psych.) Pathological dread of high places.

a·crop·o·lis (*a*krŏp'*o*lĭs) *n.* Citadel or upper fortified part of ancient Greek city, esp. (**A**~) that of Athens, situated on a hill about 250 ft. high and richly adorned, esp. in 5th c. B.C., with architecture and sculpture

a·cross (*a*kraws', *a*krŏs') *prep.* & *adv.* From side to side (of), to or on the other side (of), forming a cross with, making angles with; ~ **the board**, generally.

a·cros·tic (*a*kraw'stĭk, *a*krŏs'tĭk) *n.* Poem or series of written lines in which first or first and last letters or other letters of lines form word(s), the alphabet, etc.; puzzle so made.

a·cryl·ic (*a*krĭl'ĭk) *adj.* ~ **acid**, monobasic acid (CH_2:CH. COOH); ~ **fiber, resin**, synthetic substance prepared from acrylic acid or its derivatives. **acrylic** *n.* Acrylic fiber, resin, etc.; artist's paint with acrylic resin as a vehicle.

act (ăkt) *n.* 1. Thing done, deed; process of doing something. 2. Decree passed by legislative body, court of justice, etc.; statute. 3. Each of main divisions of dramatic work, in which definite part of whole action is completed. 4. Short performance that is part of variety show, circus, etc. 5. **Acts** (**of the Apostles**), fifth book of New Testament, relating early history of Christian Church and dealing largely with the lives and work of the Apostles Peter and Paul; traditionally ascribed to St. Luke. 6. ~ **of God**, (law) sudden and

General view of the Acropolis, Athens, with the Parthenon crowning the classical hill site. In Greek, ***acropolis*** *means 'city at the top'.*

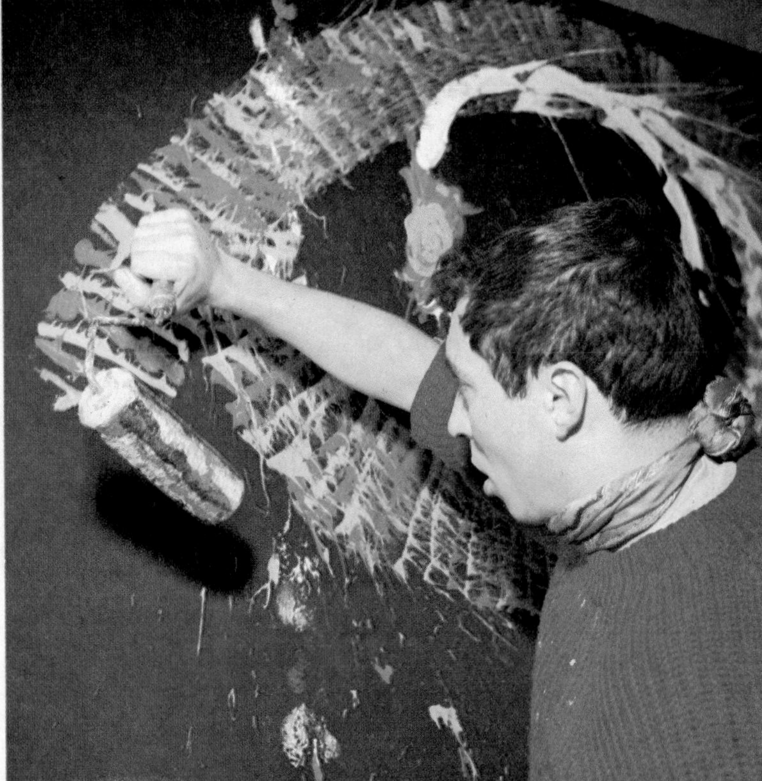

*Composing an **action painting,** a form of abstract art in which the artist works spontaneously, perhaps throwing a can of paint at the composition or impressing the rim of a tyre across it.*

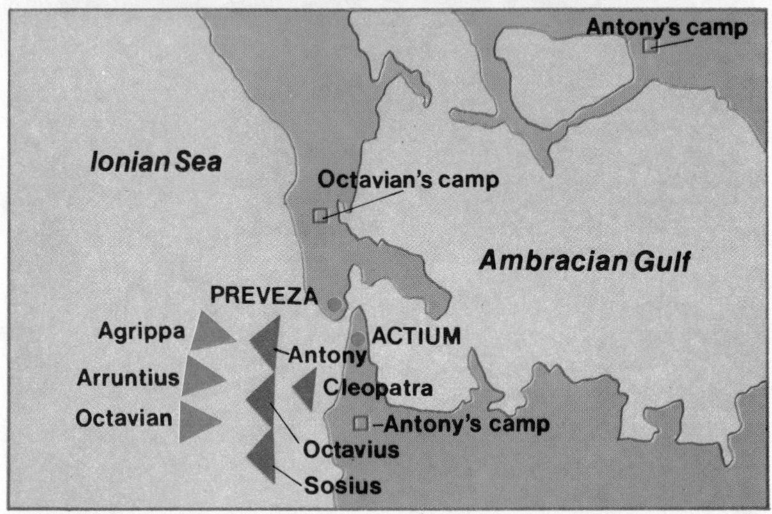

*Deployment of forces at the **Battle of Actium.** Near this Greek promontory in 31 B.C., Octavian (Augustus) defeated Mark Antony and Cleopatra to become master of the Roman world.*

overwhelming natural occurrence (hurricane, earthquake, etc.) that could not reasonably have been expected or prevented. **act** *v.* 1. Represent in mimic action, perform (play); play part of (on stage or fig. in real life); perform on stage. 2. Perform actions, do things; perform special functions; (of things) work, fulfill functions; ~ **as,** serve as; ~ **on,** influence, affect; regulate one's conduct by, put into practice.

Ac·tae·on (ăktē′*o*n). (Gk. myth.) Hunter who, because he accidentally saw Artemis bathing, was changed into a stag and killed by his own hounds.

ACTH *abbrev.* Adrenocorticotropic hormone.

act·ing (ăk′tĭng) *adj.* (esp., prefixed to title) Temporarily doing duties of; doing alone duties nominally shared with others. ~ *n.* Art or profession of performing parts in plays, films, etc.

ac·tin·ic (ăktĭn′ĭk) *adj.* Of actinism; ~ **rays,** rays possessing actinism, as the green, blue, violet, and ultraviolet rays of sunlight, which have a marked photochemical effect.

ac·ti·nide (ăk′t*i*nīd) *n.* Element with atomic number between 89 (actinium) and 103.

ac·ti·nism (ăk′t*i*nĭz*e*m) *n.* That property of radiant energy, found esp. in the shorter wavelengths of the spectrum, by which chemical changes are produced, as in photography.

ac·tin·i·um (ăktĭn′ē*u*m) *n.* (chem.) Radioactive element, found in pitchblende; symbol Ac, at. no. 89, principal isotope at. wt. 227.

ac·ti·nom·e·ter (ăkt*i*nŏm′ĭt*e*r) *n.* Instrument for measuring heat radiation.

ac·ti·no·mor·phic (ăkt*i*nōmōr′fĭk) *adj.* (biol.) Radially symmetrical. **ac·ti·no·mor′phism** *n.*

ac·ti·no·my·cet·es (ăkt*i*nōmīsē′tēz) *n.pl.* Group of minute organisms of the order Actinomycetales, commonly held to be filamentous bacteria.

ac·tion (ăk′sh*o*n) *n.* 1. Process of acting, exertion of energy or influence; **out of** ~, not functioning. 2. Thing done. 3. Series of events represented (in drama). 4. Mode of acting; mechanism of instruments etc. 5. Legal process; **take** ~, institute legal proceedings; take steps in regard to any matter. 6. Battle, engagement between opposing forces. 7. (slang) Activity, usu. of pleasurable or illicit nature. **ac′tion·a·ble** *adj.* Affording ground for action at law.

Ac·ti·um (ăk′tē*u*m). Promontory of W. coast of Greece (opposite modern Preveza on Gulf of Amurakia), near which, in 31 B.C., the fleets of Mark Antony and Cleopatra were decisively defeated by Octavian (Augustus).

ac·ti·vate (ăk′t*i*vāt) *v.t.* (**-vat·ed, -vat·ing**). Make active, esp. (phys.) radioactive; render (molecules) capable of reacting chemically; **activated charcoal,** charcoal treated to increase its adsorptive power. **ac·ti·va·tion** (ăkt*i*vā′sh*o*n) *n.*

ac·tive (ăk′tĭv) *adj.* 1. Working, acting, operative; consisting in or marked by action; energetic, busy, diligent; (of volcano) liable to erupt; ~ **service,** full-time service in one of the armed forces. 2. (gram.) Applied to a voice of the verb comprising all forms of intransitive verbs, and those forms of transitive verbs that attribute the verbal action to the person or thing it precedes; (loosely, of verb) in which the subject acts on or affects something else. ~ *n.* Active voice or form of verb. **ac′tive·ly** *adv.*

ac·tiv·ism (ăk′t*i*vĭz*e*m) *n.* Policy of vigorous action in politics.

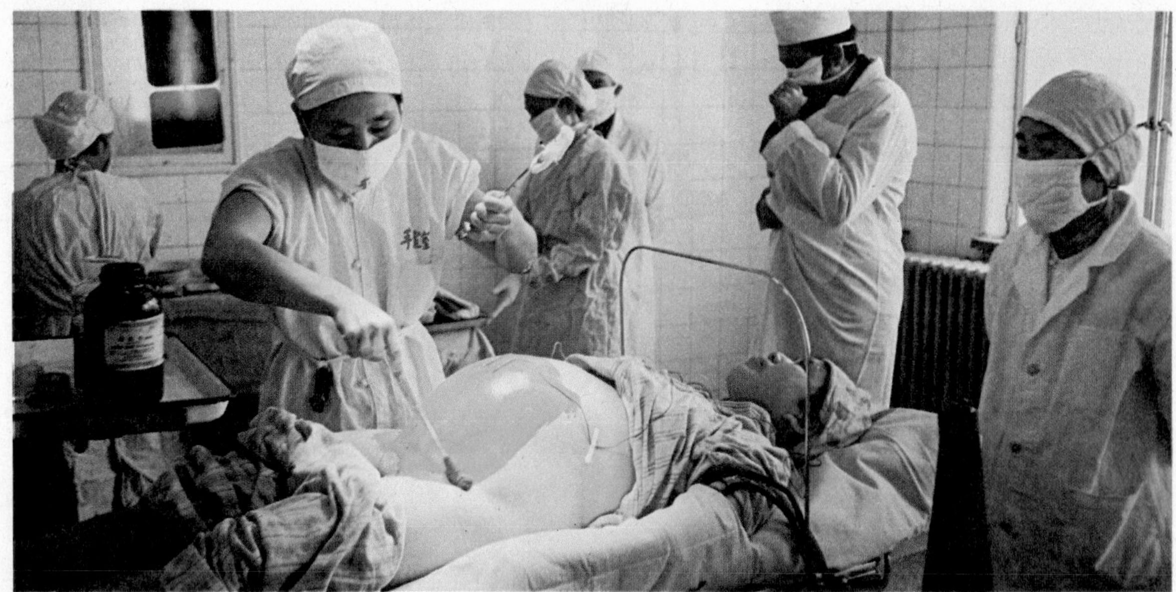

Above: Preparing a patient for Caesarean operation without anesthetic, using the techniques of ***acupuncture,*** *a medical procedure of Chinese origin. Needles of various sizes are inserted into prescribed places on the body. Right: A patient undergoing treatment by acupuncture. In this instance, the needles have been inserted in lines parallel to the spine.*

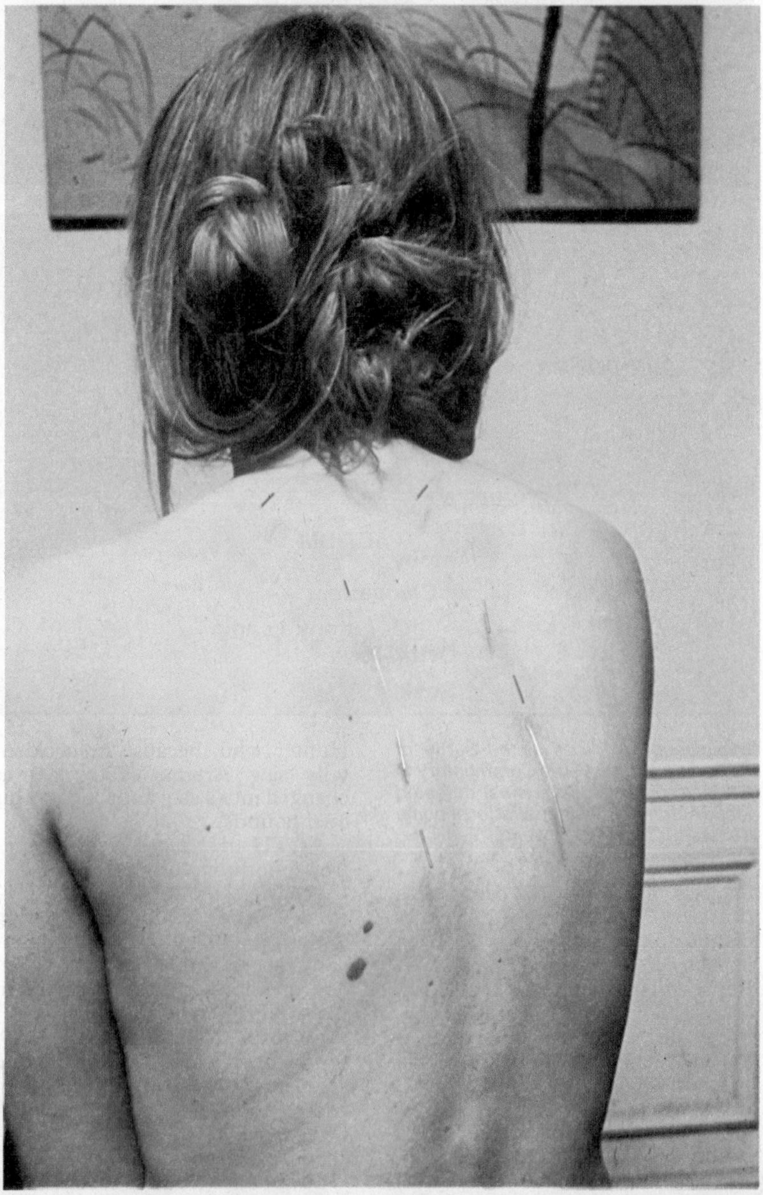

ac′tiv·ist *n.*

ac·tiv·i·ty (ăktĭv′ĭtē) *n.* (pl. **-ties**). Exertion of energy; state or quality of being active, energy, diligence, liveliness; active force or operation; specific deed or action; work or occupation.

Ac·ton (ăk′t*o*n), (**Emerich Edward Dalberg-Acton**) **Lord John,** 1st Baron (1834–1902). English historian; leader of English Roman Catholics.

ac·tor (ăk′t*er*), fem. **ac·tress** (ăk′trĭs) *ns.* Dramatic performer.

ac·tu·al (ăk′chōō*a*l) *adj.* Existing, real, present, current. **ac′tu·al·ly** *adv.* In actual fact, really, even, as a matter of fact.

ac·tu·al·i·ty (ăkchōōăl′ĭtē) *n.* (pl. **-ties**). Reality.

ac·tu·al·ize (ăk′chōō*a*līz) *v.t.* (**-ized, -iz·ing**). Realize in action. **ac·tu·al·i·za·tion** (ăkchōō*a*lĭzā′sh*o*n) *n.*

ac·tu·ar·y (ăk′chōōĕrē) *n.* (pl. **-ar·ies**). Expert on insurance who calculates risks and premiums. **ac·tu·ar·i·al** (ăkchōōâr′ēal) *adj.*

ac·tu·ate (ăk′chōōāt) *v.t.* (**-at·ed, -at·ing**). Serve as motive to; put into action. **ac·tu·a·tion** (ăkchōōā′sh*o*n), **ac′tu·a·tor** *ns.*

a·cu·i·ty (*a*kū′ĭtē) *n.* (pl. **-ties**). Sharpness, acuteness.

a·cu·men (*a*kū′m*e*n, ăk′y*u*-) *n.* Keen discernment, penetration.

ac·u·punc·ture (ăk′yōōpŭngkch*er*) *n.* (med.) Practice of puncturing areas of skin or tissues with needles for therapeutic

John Adams was the first vice-president and second president of the U.S.A. A strong supporter of the revolutionary cause, he was a central figure in negotiating peace with Britain and was appointed the first U.S. minister to the English court.

purposes.

a·cute (akūt′) *adj.* 1. Sharp, keen, penetrating; clever. 2. (of disease) Coming sharply to a crisis, not chronic. 3. (of sound) Sharp, shrill; having acute accent. 4. (fig.) Severe, crucial. 5. ~ **accent**, accent ′, originally indicating a high or rising pitch on the vowel so marked; ~ **angle**: see angle¹. **a·cute′ly** *adv.* **a·cute′ness** *n.*

ad (ăd) *n.* (colloq.) Advertisement.

ad- *prefix.* To, with sense of motion or direction to, reduction or change into, addition, adherence, increase, or intensification.

A.D. *abbrev.* Anno Domini, (of the Christian era). [f. L. *Anno Domini*, "in the year of our Lord"]

ad·age (ăd′ĭj) *n.* Traditional maxim.

a·da·gio (adah′jō, -zhēō) *adv., adj., n.* (pl. **-gios**). (mus.) Leisurely (passage or movement); ~ **dancing**, that involving feats of balance etc. [It.]

Ad·al·bert (ăd′albert), **St.** (*c*955–97). Missionary in N. Germany and Poland, called "apostle of the Prussians," martyred in Bremen, commemorated April 23.

Ad·am¹ (ăd′am). (in Hebrew tradition) The first man (Gen. 2 and 3), who lived with Eve in the Garden of Eden, but was driven from it for eating the fruit (traditionally an apple) of "the tree of the knowledge of good and evil"; ~**'s ale**, water; ~**'s apple**, projection formed by the thyroid cartilage, particularly prominent in males. [Heb., = "man"]

Ad·am² (ăd′am). 1. **Robert** (1728–92). The best known of a family of Scottish architects; introduced into Britain a neoclassical style of decoration, furniture, etc., based on ancient Roman and Italian Renaissance designs. 2. **James** (1730–94), architect, his brother.

ad·a·mant¹ (ăd′amant, -mănt) *n.* Legendary stone of extreme hardness. **ad·a·man·tine** (ădamăn′tĭn, -tēn) *adj.*

ad·a·mant² (ăd′amant, -mănt) *adj.* 1. Of extreme hardness. 2. Unshakable, inflexible. **ad′a·mant·ly** *adv.*

Ad·a·mite (ăd′amīt) *n.* Child of Adam, human being; unclothed man.

Ad·ams¹ (ăd′amz). Name of a family of American politicians, statesmen, and writers, including: 1. **John** (1735–1826) 2nd president of U.S. (1797–1801); member of committee formed to draft Declaration of Independence; 2. his wife, **Abigail Smith** (1744–1818); 3. his son, **John Quincy** (1767–1848) 6th president of U.S. (1825–9); 4. John Quincy's grandson, **Henry Brooks** (1838–1918) historian and philosopher.

Ad·ams² (ăd′amz), **Maude** (1872–1953). American actress; best known for starring role in *Peter Pan.*

Ad·ams³ (ăd′amz), **Mount.** A mountain in the Cascade Range of S. Washington.

Ad·ams⁴ (ăd′amz), **Samuel** (1722–1803). American propagandist, statesman, and leader in the American Revolution.

a·dapt (adăpt′) *v.* Suit, make suitable, fit (*to, for*); alter, modify, so as to make suitable for new surroundings, purpose, etc. **a·dapt·a·bil·i·ty** (ădăptabĭl′ĭtē) *n.* **a·dapt′a·ble** *adj.* **a·dapt′er, a·dap′tor** *ns.* (esp.) Device allowing connection of pieces of equipment not orig. designed to be connected.

ad·ap·ta·tion (ădaptā′shon) *n.* (esp. biol.) Process, characteristic of living matter, by which organism or species becomes adjusted to its environment; that which is so adapted.

A.D.C. *abbrev.* Aide-de-camp.

add (ăd) *v.* Join by way of increase or supplement; perform arithmetical process of addition; say or write further; ~ **up**, add a column of figures; find sum of; make desired total; (colloq.) seem logical or reasonable; **adding machine**, machine that performs arithmetical processes.

Ad·dams (ăd′amz), **Jane** (1860–1935). American social worker and peace advocate; founded Hull House in Chicago, 1889; shared Nobel Peace Prize, 1931.

ad·dax (ăd′ăks) *n.* Large light-colored antelope (*Addax nasomaculatus*) of N. Afr. deserts, with spiral horns.

ad·den·dum (adĕn′dum) *n.* (pl. **-da** pr. -da). Something to be

Festival Theatre, **Adelaide,** Australia, where many international artists have performed. Adelaide, encircled by parkland, is the capital of South Australia.

Aden, near entrance to Red Sea, was of strategic importance in 1939–45 war. Until 1967 a British colony, Aden is capital of People's Democratic Republic of Yemen.

added, addition, appendix.

ad·der (ăd′*er*) *n.* Small venomous snake, viper (*Vipera berus*); **death ~, horned ~, puff ~**, highly poisonous African and Australian species of Viperidae; **adder's-tongue** *n.* fern (*Ophioglossum vulgatum*); white- or yellow-flowered dogtooth violet.

ad·dict (ăd′ĭkt) *n.* One addicted to drugs etc.; devotee of pastime etc. ~ (*a*dĭkt′) *v.t.* Apply habitually or compulsively (*to* a practice). **ad·dict′ed** *adj.* Devoted *to* or physiologically or psychologically dependent on drug, pastime, etc. **ad·dic′tion** *n.* **ad·dic′tive** *adj.* Causing addiction.

Ad·dis Ab·a·ba (ah′dĭs ah′*ba*-bah). Capital of and largest city in Ethiopia.

Ad·di·son[1] (ăd′ĭs*o*n), **Joseph** (1672–1719). English essayist and poet; contributor to *Tatler* and joint author (with STEELE) of *Spectator*.

Ad·di·son[2] (ăd′ĭs*o*n), **Thomas** (1793–1860). English physician; first to recognize **A~'s disease**, disease connected with defective functioning of suprarenal glands and freq. characterized by bronzy pigmentation of skin.

ad·di·tion (*a*dĭsh′*o*n) *n.* Adding; arithmetical process of putting together two or more numbers or amounts to form a total; thing added; **in ~**, as an added thing etc. (*to*). **ad·di′tion·al** *adj.* **ad·di′tion·al·ly** *adv.*

ad·di·tive (ăd′ĭtĭv) *adj.* Of addition; to be added. ~ *n.* Substance added to mixture or alloy in order to impart specific qualities to the resulting product.

ad·dle (ăd′*e*l) *v.* (**-dled, -dling**). Make or become addled. ~ *adj.*

ad′dlebrained, ad′dleheaded, ad′dlepated, *adjs.* Confused in mind. **ad′dled** *adj.* (of egg) Rotten; muddled, crazy.

ad·dress (*a*drĕs′, ăd′rĕs) *n.* 1. (obs.) Readiness, skill, adroitness. 2. Place to which letters etc. are directed; place of residence. 3. Manner, bearing, in conversation; way of addressing person. 4. Discourse delivered to audience. 5. (pl.) Courteous approach, courtship. ~ (*a*drĕs′) *v.t.* 1. Direct in speech or writing; speak to; send as written message (*to*); write address on outside of (letter etc.) 2. Apply *oneself*, direct one's skill or energies (*to*). 3. (golf) ~ **the ball**, take aim, prepare to make a stroke.

ad·dress·ee (ădrĕsē′) *n.* Person to whom letter etc. is addressed.

ad·duce (*a*dōōs′, *a*dūs′) *v.t.* (**-duced, -duc·ing**). Cite as proof or instance.

ad·duct (*a*dŭkt′) *v.t.* Draw to a common center or toward median line or long axis of body. **ad·duc′tion, ad·duc′tor** *ns.*

-ade *suffix.* Forming nouns with following senses: 1. action done (*blockade, tirade*). 2. body or person concerned in action or process (*cavalcade, renegade*). 3. product of material or action (*arcade, lemonade, masquerade*).

Ad·e·laide (ăd′*e*lād). Seaport and capital of South Australia.

A·dé·lie (*a*dā′lē) **Land.** French territory in coastal region of Antarctica, south of Australia.

A·den (ah′d*e*n, ā′d*e*n). Seaport in SW. Arabia near entrance to Red Sea; capital city of the People's Democratic Republic of Yemen.

A·de·nau·er (ăd′*e*now*e*r, ah′-d*e*-), **Konrad** (1876–1967). First chancellor, Federal Republic of Germany.

ad·e·noids (ăd′*e*noidz) *n.pl.* Pathological enlargement of lymphoid tissue between back of nose and throat, occurring usu. in children and often obstructing breathing. **ad·e·noi·dal** (ăd*e*noi′-d*a*l) *adj.*

a·dept (*a*dĕpt′) *adj.* Thoroughly proficient (*in*). **ad·ept** (ăd′ĕpt, *a*dĕpt′) *n.* Adept person.

ad·e·quate (ăd′*e*kwĭt) *adj.* Proportionate to what is necessary; sufficient. **ad′e·quate·ly** *adv.* **ad·e·qua·cy** (ăd′*e*kw*a*sē) *n.*

ad·here (ăd-hēr′) *v.i.* (**-hered, -her·ing**). Stick fast, cleave (*to*); give support *to* (agreement, opinion, party).

ad·her·ent (ăd-hēr′*e*nt, -hĕr′-) *adj.* Sticking; adhering. ~ *n.* Supporter (of party etc.). **ad·her′ence** *n.*

ad·he·sion (ăd-hē′zh*o*n) *n.* Adhering; (chem.) molecular force of attraction between different kinds of molecules (opp. COHESION); (med.) abnormal union of tissue as a result of inflammation.

ad·he·sive (ăd-hē′sĭv, -zĭv) *adj.* & *n.* Adhering, sticky or gummed (substance or material); ~ **tape,** tape coated on one side with a sticky substance. **ad·he'sive·ly** *adv.* **ad·he'sive·ness** *n.*

ad hoc (ăd hŏk'). Arranged for this purpose; special(ly). [L.]

ad·i·a·bat·ic (ădēabăt'ĭk, ādīa-) *adj.* (of physical change) Involving neither loss nor gain of heat.

a·dieu (adōō', adū; *Fr.* ădyö') *int.* & *n.* (pl. **a·dieus, a·dieux** pr. adōōz', adūz'; *Fr.* ădyö') Goodby. [Fr. *à Dieu* to God]

ad in·fi·ni·tum (ăd ĭnfīnī'tum). Without limit, for ever. [L.]

ad·i·os (ădēōs', ahdē-) *int.* Goodby. [Sp.]

ad·i·pose (ăd'ĭpōs) *adj.* Of fat, fatty; ~ **tissue**, connective tissue cells in animal body containing large globules of fat. **ad·i·pos·i·ty** (ădipŏs'ĭtē) *n.*

Ad·i·ron·dack (ădirŏn'dăk) **Mountains.** (also **Adirondacks**) Group of mountains in NE. New York.

ad·it (ăd'ĭt) *n.* Horizontal entrance to, or passage in, mine.

adj. *abbrev.* Adjutant; adjective.

ad·ja·cent (ajā'sent) *adj.* Lying near *to*, contiguous. **ad·ja'cen·cy** *n.*

ad·jec·tive (ăj'ĭktĭv) *n.* (gram.) Name of attribute added to noun to describe it more fully or definitely; modifier of noun. **ad·jec·ti·val** (ăjĭktī'val) *adj.* **ad·jec·ti'val·ly** *adv.*

ad·join (ajoin') *v.* Be contiguous or connected (with).

ad·journ (ajẽrn') *v.* Suspend the meeting or proceedings of (a legislature etc.); move *to* another place (esp. during such a suspension). **ad·journ'ment** *n.*

ad·judge (ajŭj') *v.t.* (**-judged, -judg·ing**). Adjudicate upon; pronounce or award judicially.

ad·ju·di·cate (ajōō'dĭkāt) *v.* (**-cat·ed, -cat·ing**). Decide upon; pronounce; sit in judgment and pronounce sentence. **ad·ju·di·ca·tion** (ajōōdĭkā'shon), **ad·ju'di·ca·tor** *ns.*

ad·junct (ăj'ŭngkt) *n.* Subordinate or incidental thing, accompaniment; (gram.) amplification of the predicate, subject, etc.; (logic) nonessential attribute. **ad·junc·tive** (ajŭngk'tĭv) *adj.* **ad·junc'tive·ly** *adv.*

ad·jure (ajoor') *v.t.* (**-jured, -jur·ing**). Charge under oath or penalty of curse *to* do; request earnestly. **ad·ju·ra·tion** (ăjōōrā'shon) *n.*

ad·just (ajŭst') *v.* Arrange, put in order; harmonize; adapt (*to*); settle; (insurance) determine the amount to be paid to settle (a claim). **ad·just'a·ble** *adj.* **ad·just'ment** *n.*

ad·ju·tant (ăj'utant) *n.* 1. (mil.) Officer assisting commanding officer by communicating orders, conducting correspondence, etc.; ~ **general**, adjutant of a U.S. Army unit having a general staff; **A~ General**, chief administrative officer of the U.S. Army. 2. (also ~ **stork**, ~ **bird**) Large stork of genus *Leptoptilos*, esp. Indian *L. dubius*, walking with stiff-legged gait.

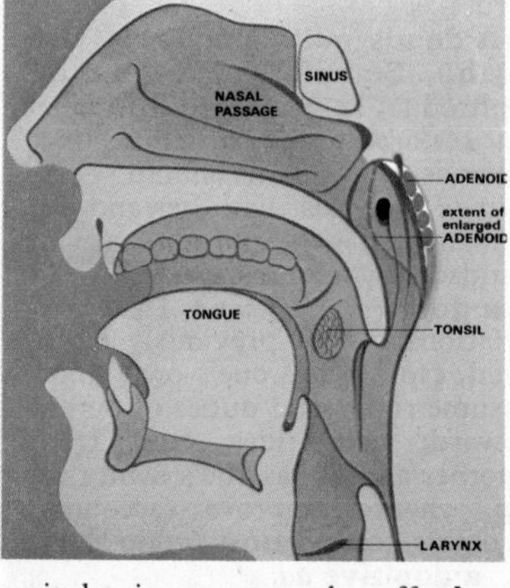

Diagram shows ***adenoids,*** *enlargement of tissue between back of nose and throat. Large adenoids tend to obstruct breathing through the nose. Normally they decrease in size after childhood.*

Ad·ler[1] (ăd'ler), **Alfred** (1870–1937). Austrian psychiatrist; put forward theory of inferiority complex.

Ad·ler[2] (ăd'ler), **Felix** (1851–1933). German-born American educator and reformer; founder of the Society for Ethical Culture.

ad lib (ăd lĭb') *n.* Words, gestures, etc. ad-libbed. ~ *adv.* To any desired extent. **ad-lib** *v.* (**-libbed, -lib·bing**). Speak, act, etc. without preparation; improvise. **ad-lib** *adj.* Extemporaneous; improvised; spontaneous. **ad-lib'ber** *n.*

ad lib·i·tum (ăd lĭb'ĭtum). 1. To the extent etc. desired. 2. (mus.) That can be omitted. [L.]

Adm. *abbrev.* Admiral.

adm., admin. *abbrevs.* Administration; administrative.

Ad·me·tus (ădmē'tus). (Gk. legend) Husband of ALCESTIS.

ad·min·is·ter (ădmĭn'ĭster) *v.* 1. Manage (affairs, estate, etc.); dispense (justice, sacraments, etc.); act as administrator. 2. Formally present (oath to be sworn) *to.* 3. Furnish, give; apply (remedies). 4. Contribute *to* (one's comfort etc.).

ad·min·is·tra·tion (ădmĭnĭstrā'shon) *n.* 1. Administering; management; management of public affairs, government; (law) management of deceased person's estate. 2. Body of administrators; government. **ad·min·is·trate** (ădmĭn'ĭstrāt) *v.* (**-trat·ed, -trat·ing**). Administer. **ad·min·is·tra·tive** (ădmĭn'ĭstrātĭv, -stra-) *adj.* Of administration; executive. **ad·min'is·tra·tor** *n.*

ad·mi·ra·ble (ăd'merabel) *adj.* Worthy of admiration; estimable, excellent. **ad'mi·ra·bly** *adv.*

ad·mi·ral (ăd'meral) *n.* Naval officer commanding fleet or subdivision of fleet; (hist.) commander in chief of navy; **A~ of the Fleet**, highest rank of British naval officers; **Fleet ~**: see FLEET. [Arab. 'amīr commander]

Ad·mi·ral·ty (ăd'meraltē) *n.* (Brit.) Former name of government department superintending the Royal Navy.

Ad·mi·ral·ty (ăd'meraltē) **Island.** Island in the Alexander Archipelago of southeastern Alaska; **Admiralties**, group of small islands of Bismarck Archipelago, under Australian administration; **Admiralty Range**, mountain range in Victoria, Antarctica, NW. of Ross Sea.

ad·mire (admīr') *v.t.* (**-mired, -mir·ing**). Regard with pleased surprise or approval; express admiration of. **ad·mir'er** *n.* One

The ***adjutant bird*** *is a large stork with a stiff-legged gait. There are species in Africa, India and S.E. Asia. The largest adjutant bird, Leptoptilus dubius, is between 6 and 7 ft. tall.*

who admires. **ad·mi·ra·tion** (ădmerā′shon) *n.*

ad·mis·si·ble (ădmĭs′ibel) *adj.* 1. That may be accepted or considered. 2. (law) That may be allowed as evidence in court. **ad·mis·si·bil·i·ty** (ădmĭsibĭl′ĭtē) *n.* **ad·mis′si·bly** *adv.*

ad·mis·sion (ădmĭsh′on) *n.* Admitting, being admitted, fee for this; acknowledgement that something is true.

ad·mit (ădmĭt′) *v.* (**-mit·ted, -mit·ting**). 1. Allow entrance or access (*to*). 2. Allow, permit; accept as valid or true; acknowledge; ~ **of**, be capable of or compatible with; leave room for. **ad·mit′tance** *n.* **ad·mit′ted·ly** *adv.*

ad·mix (ădmĭks′) *v.* Add as an ingredient, mingle *with*. **ad·mix·ture** (ădmĭks′cher) *n.*

ad·mon·ish (ădmŏn′ĭsh) *v.t.* Urge; give advice; warn; remind, inform. **ad·mon′ish·ment** *n.*

ad·mo·ni·tion (ădmonĭsh′on) *n.* Admonishing; warning, reproof. **ad·mon·i·to·ry** (ădmŏn′itorē, -tōrē) *adj.*

ad nau·se·am (ăd naw′zēam, -ăm, -shē-, -zhē-). To a disgusting extent. [L.]

a·do (adōō′) *n.* Fuss; confused activity, bustling.

a·do·be (adō′bē) *n.* Sun-dried clay used for building etc.; house made of such clay bricks. [Span., f. *adobar* daub, plaster]

ad·o·les·cent (ădolĕs′ent) *adj.* & *n.* (Person) between childhood and maturity. **ad·o·les′cence** *n.*

A·do·nai (ahdōnoi′, -nī′). Hebrew title of reverence for God, pronounced as substitute for the tetragrammaton. [Heb., = "my lord(s)"]

A·do·nis (adŏn′ĭs, adō′nĭs). (Gk. myth.) Beautiful youth loved by Aphrodite; he was killed by a boar but restored to life by Persephone; Zeus decreed that he should spend part of each year with her and the rest on earth with Aphrodite; hence, handsome young man.

a·dopt (adŏpt′) *v.t.* Take into relationship not previously occupied, esp. take as one's own child, assume rights and duties of parent toward; take (idea etc.) from another and use as one's own; take up, choose; approve (accounts, report). **a·dop·tion** (adŏp′shon) *n.* **a·dop′tive** *adj.*

a·dore (adōr,′ adōr′) *v.t.* (**a·dored, a·dor·ing**). Regard with very deep respect and affection; worship as a deity; like very much; (R.C. Ch.) offer form of reverence to. **a·dor′a·ble** *adj.* **a·dor′a·bly** *adv.* **ad·o·ra·tion** (ăderā′shon) *n.*

a·dor·er (adōr′er, -dōr′-) *n.* Worshipper; ardent admirer, lover.

a·dorn (adōrn′) *v.t.* Add beauty or luster to, esp. with ornament(s). **a·dorn′ment** *n.*

a·dre·nal (adrē′nal) adj. At or near kidney; of, produced by the adrenal glands; ~ **gland**, suprarenal gland, one of two yellowish-brown ductless glands lying on upper anterior surface of kidneys. ~ *n.* Adrenal gland.

a·dren·a·line (adrĕn′alĭn) *n.* Hormone secreted by adrenal glands and affecting circulation and muscular action; this obtained from these glands in animals or prepared synthetically, used in medicine as a stimulant.

a·dre·no·cor·ti·co·trop·ic (*a*-drē′nōkōrtikōtrŏp′ĭk) **hormone.** Hormone secreted by pituitary gland and stimulating adrenal cortex.

A frenzied reaction to pop groups is one mark of ***adolescence,*** *which has been described as the period when a youngster starts learning to control and properly direct sexual urges. Various hormones are responsible for the physical changes of adolescence both in males and females.*

A·dri·an (ā′drēan). Name of six popes including **Adrian IV** (Nicholas Breakspear), pope 1154–1159, the only English pope.

A·dri·at·ic (ādrēăt′ĭk, ădrē-) *adj.* ~ **Sea**, arm of Mediterranean lying between Italy and Balkan peninsula. **Adriatic** *n.* Adriatic Sea.

a·drift (adrĭft′) *adj.* Drifting; at mercy of wind and tide or of circumstances.

a·droit (adroit′) *adj.* Dextrous, deft. **a·droit′ly** *adv.* **a·droit′ness** *n.*

ad·sorb (ădsōrb′, -zōrb′) *v.t.* Act as adsorbent of. **ad·sor′bent** *adj.* & *n.* (Substance) producing adsorption.

ad·sorp·tion (ădsōrp′shon, -zōrp′-) *n.* Process by which specific gases, vapors, or substances in solution adhere to exposed surfaces of certain, usu. solid, materials. **ad·sorp′tive** *adj.*

ad·u·late (ăj′ulāt) *v.t.* (**-lat·ed, -lat·ing**). Flatter, admire excessively. **ad·u·la·tion** (ăjulā′shon) *n.* **ad·u·la·to·ry** (ăj′ulatōrē, -tōrē) *adj.*

a·dult (adŭlt′, ăd′ŭlt) *adj.* Fully grown, mature; befitting adults; intended for or restricted to adults only. ~ *n.* Adult person, animal,

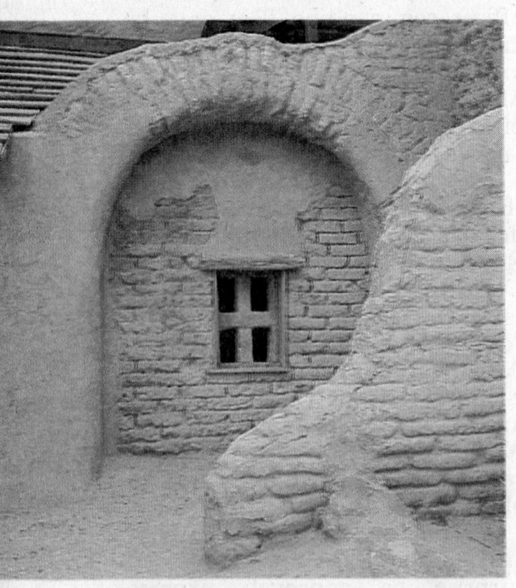

Adobe *bricks have been used for centuries by the American Indians as a convenient, durable building material.*

The ***Adriatic Sea*** *forms a part of the Mediterranean lying between Italy and the Balkan Peninsula. The average width of the Adriatic is 110 miles and it is a rich fishing ground.*

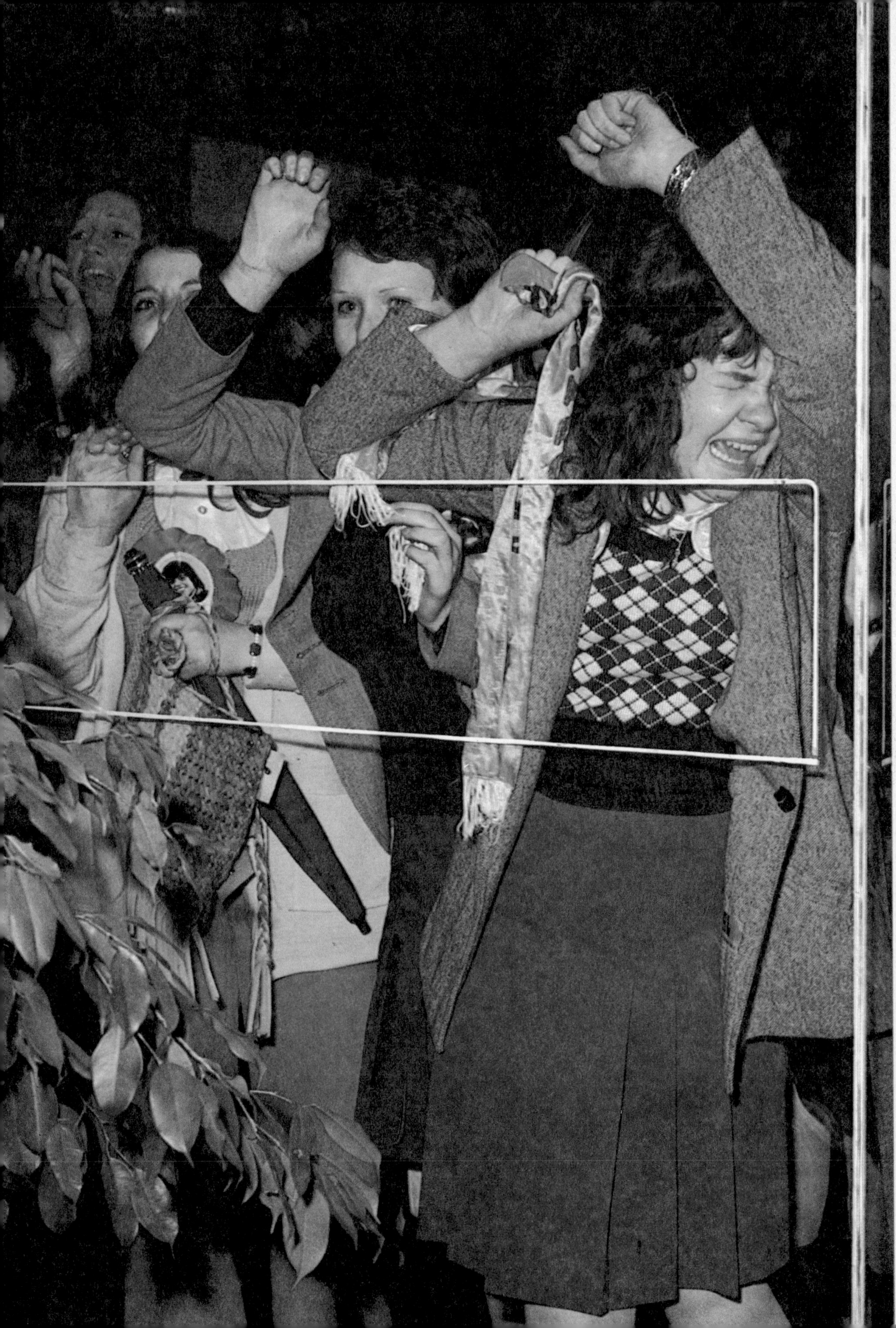

*Mangrove trees with bared **adventitious** roots: Biscayne Bay, Florida. In addition to the main root, adventitious roots are secondary roots which can grow from other parts of the plant.*

plant, etc.; ~ **education**, courses etc. provided for persons over school age.

a·dul·ter·ant (*a*dŭl′t*e*r*a*nt) *adj.* & *n.* (Thing) employed in adulterating.

a·dul·ter·ate (*a*dŭl′t*e*rāt) *v.t.* (**-at·ed, -at·ing**). Falsify, corrupt, debase, esp. by admixture of baser ingredients. **a·dul·ter·a·tion** (*a*dŭlt*e*rā′sh*o*n) *n.*

a·dul·ter·er (*a*dŭl′t*e*r*e*r), fem. **a·dul·ter·ess** (*a*dŭl′t*e*rĭs, -trĭs) *ns.* Person guilty of adultery.

a·dul·ter·y (*a*dŭl′t*e*rē) *n.* (pl. **-ter·ies**). Voluntary sexual intercourse of married person with one who is not his or her spouse. **a·dul′ter·ous** *adj.* **a·dul′ter·ous·ly** *adv.*

ad·um·brate (ăd′*u*mbrāt, ădŭm′-) *v.t.* (**-brat·ed, -brat·ing**). Represent in outline; faintly indicate; typify, foreshadow; overshadow. **ad·um·bra·tion** (ăd*u*mbrā′sh*o*n) *n.*

adv. *abbrev.* Adverb; advertisement.

ad va·lo·rem (ăd valōr′*e*m, -lōr′-). (of taxes or duties) In proportion to (estimated) value of goods. [L.]

ad·vance (ădvăns′ -vahns′) *n.* 1. Going forward, progress; improvement, promotion. 2. Personal approach, overture; (pl.) amorous approaches. 3. Increase, as in a figure, price, etc. 4. Payment beforehand; loan. 5. **in** ~, in front, ahead; beforehand; ~ **copy**, copy of book etc., supplied before publication; ~ **guard**, guard before main body of army. **advance** *v.* (**-vanced, -vanc·ing**). Move or put forward; bring forward (claims etc.); present for consideration; accelerate (events); pay (money) before it is due; lend; help on, promote; make progress; improve, show improvement; raise (price), rise (in price). **ad·vanced′** *adj.* Far on in progress; ahead of times, others, etc. **ad·vance′ment** *n.* (esp.) Promotion, preferment; furtherance, improvement.

ad·van·tage (ădvăn′tĭj) *n.* Better position, precedence, superiority; favorable circumstance; (tennis) next point won after deuce; **mechanical** ~: see MECHANICAL; **take** ~ **of**, use (circumstance) profitably; exploit (person) unfairly. **ad·van·ta·geous** (ădv*a*ntā′j*u*s) *adj.* **ad·van·ta′geous·ly** *adv.*

ad·vent (ăd′vĕnt) *n.* 1. Arrival, esp. important one. 2. Coming into being. 3. **A**~, season before Christmas, beginning on 4th Sunday before it; coming of Christ.

*Neon signs in the heart of the city. The first **advertisements** were by public criers. A 3,000-year-old written advertisement, found in ruins of Thebes, offered a gold coin for return of a runaway slave. Advertising media include newspapers, magazines, posters, T.V., radio and illuminated signs.*

ad·ven·ti·tious (ădv*e*ntĭsh′*u*s) *adj.* 1. Accidental, casual; not essential or intrinsic. 2. (bot.) In an unusual position, sporadic. **ad·ven·ti′tious·ly** *adv.*

ad·ven·ture (ădvĕn′ch*e*r) *n.* Unexpected or exciting experience; daring enterprise, hazardous activity. ~ *v.i.* (**-tured, -tur·ing**). 1. Venture. 2. Venture to say.

ad·ven·tur·er (ădvĕn′ch*e*r*e*r), fem. **ad·ven·tur·ess** (ădvĕn′ch*e*rĭs) *ns.* One who seeks adventure; speculator; one who lives by his or her wits.

ad·ven·tur·ous (ădvĕn′ch*e*r*u*s) *adj.* Venturesome, enterprising. **ad·ven′tur·ous·ly** *adv.*

ad·verb (ăd′vėrb) *n.* (gram.) Word that modifies a verb, adjective, or another adverb, expressing any relation of place, time, circumstance, causality, manner, or degree. **ad·ver·bi·al** (ădvėr′bē*a*l) *adj.* **ad·ver′bi·al·ly** *adv.*

ad·ver·sar·y (ăd′v*e*rsĕrē) *n.* (pl.

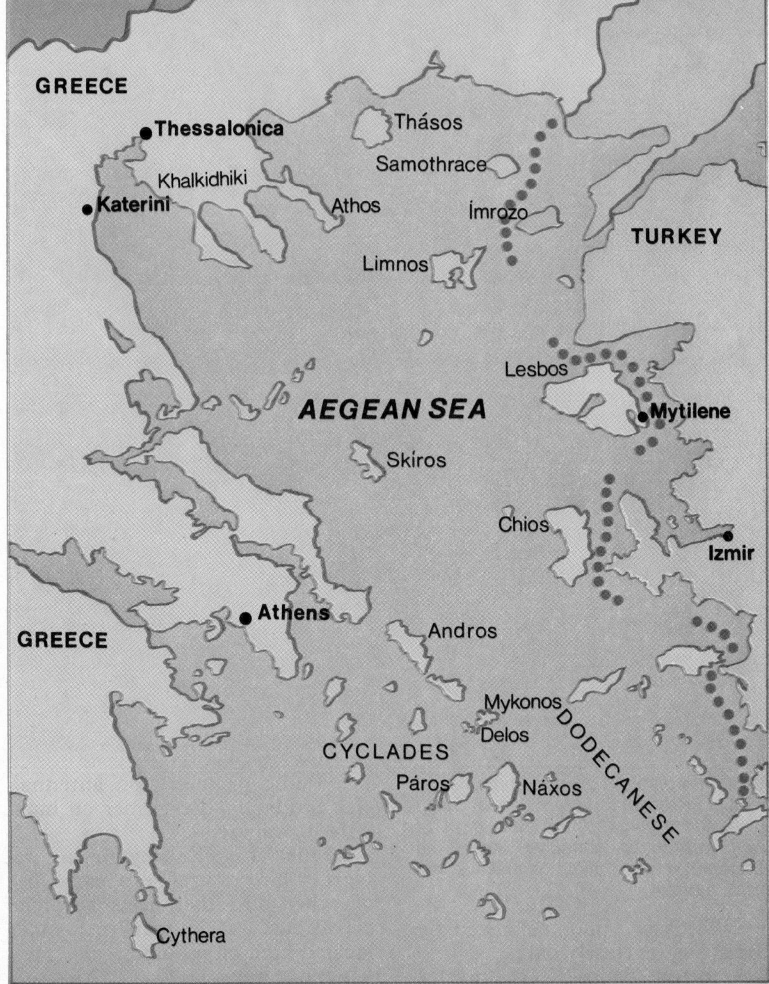

*Top: The northern **Aegean Sea** seen from Khalkidhiki, at the extremity of Thessalonica, Greece.*
Below: The Aegean Sea, between Greece and Asia Minor, was the heart of the ancient Greek world. The Greek people, said Plato, lived along its shores like frogs around a pond.

-sar·ies). Opponent, enemy.

ad·verse (ădvẽrs′, ăd′vẽrs) *adj.* Contrary, hostile *to*; hurtful, injurious. **ad·verse′ly** *adv.*

ad·ver·si·ty (ădvẽr′s*i*tē) *n.* (pl. **-ties**). Condition of adverse fortune; misfortune.

ad·vert (ădvẽrt′) *v.i.* Refer *to.*

ad·ver·tise (ăd′vertīz) *v.* (**-tised, -tis·ing**). Notify, warn, inform; make generally or publicly known; proclaim merits of; esp., try to encourage sales of (product) by public announcement; ~ **for**, ask for by public notice. **ad′ver·tis·er** *n.*

ad·ver·tise·ment (ădv*e*rtīz′m*e*nt, -vẽr′tĭs-) *n.* Advertising; public announcement (in newspapers, by posters, etc.).

ad·vice (ădvīs′) *n.* Opinion given or offered as to action; information given, news.

ad·vis·a·ble (ădvī′z*a*bel) *adj.* To be recommended; expedient. **ad·vis·a·bil·i·ty** (ădvīz*a*bĭl′ĭtē) *n.*

ad·vise (ădvīz′) *v.* (**-vised, -vis·ing**). Offer advice (to); recommend; notify, inform. **ad·vised′** *adj.* Deliberate, considered. **ad·vis·ed·ly** (ădvī′zĭdlē) *adv.*

ad·vis·er, ad·vi·sor (ădvī′z*er*) *ns.* Counselor, esp. person habitually consulted; **legal** ~, lawyer.

ad·vi·so·ry (ădvī′z*e*rē) *adj.* Giving advice; consisting in giving advice. ~ *n.* (pl. **-ries**). An announcement, esp. a warning, such as a radio weather forecast.

ad·vo·ca·cy (ăd′v*o*k*a*sē) *n.* (pl. **-cies**). Function of advocate; pleading in support *of.*

ad·vo·cate (ăd′v*o*kĭt, -kāt) *n.* Professional pleader in court of justice, counsel (technical title in Roman law courts and in countries retaining Roman law, as Scotland, France, etc.); one who pleads for another; one who speaks for cause etc. ~ (ăd′v*o*kāt) *v.t.* (**-cat·ed, -cat·ing**). Plead for, support (policy etc.).

advt. *abbrev.* Advertisement.

ad·y·tum (ăd′ĭt*u*m) *n.* (pl. **-ta** pr. -t*a*) Innermost part of ancient temple. [Gk. *aduton* not to be entered (*duō* enter)]

adz, adze (ădz) *ns.* Carpenter's tool for cutting away surface of wood, like ax with arched blade at right angles to handle.

A. E. Pseudonym of G(eorge) W(illiam) Russell (1867–1935). Irish poet and painter.

ae·dile (ē′dīl) *n.* (Rom. hist.) Magistrate who superintended public buildings, games, shows, etc.

A.E.F. *abbrev.* American Expeditionary Forces.

Ae·ge·an (ĭjē′*a*n) *adj.* ~ **Sea**, arm of Mediterranean between Greece and Asia Minor; ~ **Civilization**, Bronze Age civilization of the coasts and islands of the Aegean Sea, the Minoan and Mycenaean civilizations. **Aegean** *n.* Aegean Sea.

Ae·gir (ā′jĭr). (Scand. myth.) Chief of the sea giants, representing the peaceful ocean.

ae·gis (ē′jĭs) *n.* (Gk. myth.) Shield of Zeus or Athena; **under the** ~ **of**, under the protection or sponsorship of.

Ae·gis·thus (ĭjĭs′th*u*s). (Gk. legend) Nephew of Atreus, whom he murdered, and lover of Clytemnestra, who helped him murder her husband Agamemnon.

Æl·fric (ăl′frĭk) (*c*955–1020). English abbot and writer, chiefly of homilies and lives of saints.

***Aerobatic** displays are a common sight at most airshows today, but never fail to excite the crowds. In the early days of flight, aerobatic displays were an important way for pilots to make some extra money.*

Ae·ne·as (ĭnē′*a*s). (Gk. & Rom. legend) Trojan hero; son of Anchises and Aphrodite; escaped after fall of Troy and after long wandering reached the Tiber; regarded by Romans as founder of Rome.

Ae·ne·id (ĭnē′ĭd). Epic poem by Virgil in twelve books of Latin hexameters relating story of Aeneas after fall of Troy.

Ae·o·li·an (ēō′lē*a*n) *adj.* 1. Of Aeolis. 2. Of Aeolus; caused by, relating to, wind; ~ **harp**, musical instrument consisting of rectangular box on or in which are stretched strings or wires producing musical sounds as the wind passes across them; ~ **Islands**, ancient name of Lipari Islands; ~ **mode**, (mus.) ancient Greek mode; ninth of ecclesiastical modes, with A as final and E as dominant.

Ae·o·lis (ē′*o*lĭs). Coastal district of NW. Asia Minor colonized by Greeks at very early date.

Ae·o·lus (ē′*o*lu̥s). (Gk. myth.) God of the winds.

ae·on, e·on (ē′*o*n, ē′ŏn) *ns.* Immeasurable period; eternity.

aer·ate (ār′āt, ā′*e*rāt) *v.t.* (**-at·ed, -at·ing**). Expose to mechanical or chemical action of air; charge, treat, or supply with air or a gas. **aer·a·tion** (ārā′sh*o*n), **aer′a·tor** *ns.*

aer·i·al (ār′ē*a*l, āēr′ē*a*l) *adj.* Of air, gaseous; ethereal; immaterial, imaginary; atmospheric; existing, moving, happening, in the air; conducted by aircraft. **aerial** (ār′ē*a*l) *n.* Radio or television antenna. **aer′i·al·ist** *n.* Performer on high wire or trapeze.

aer·ie (ār′ē, ēr′ē), **ey·rie** *ns.* 1. Nest of bird of prey, esp. eagle, or of other bird that nests at high elevations. 2. Human residence located high on mountain etc.

aero-, aer- *prefixes.* Air-; of aircraft.

aer·o·bat·ics (ār*o*băt′ĭks) *n.pl.* Spectacular feats of flying performed by airplanes. **aer·o·bat′ic** *adj.*

aer·obe (ār′ōb) *n.* Microorganism capable of living only in the presence of atmospheric oxygen; opp. ANAEROBE. **aer·o·bic** (ārō′bĭk) *adj.* **aerobic exercise**, sustained physical exercise that increases the body's intake of oxygen.

aer·o·drome (ār′*o*drōm) (Brit.) = AIRdrome.

*Radio Australia repeater station at Cox Peninsula, near Darwin. An **aerial** has identical transmitting and receiving properties and may be used simultaneously for both functions.*

aer·o·dy·nam·ics (ārōdīnăm′ĭks) *n.* (usu. considered sing.) Branch of dynamics dealing with the effects produced in air by the motion of solid bodies through it and the effects produced on such bodies by the air through which they pass. **aer·o·dy·nam′ic, aer·o·dy·nam′i·cal** *adjs.* **aer·o·dy·nam′i·cal·ly** *adv.* **aer·o·dy·nam·i·cist** (ārōdīnăm′ĭsĭst) *n.*

aer·o·naut (ār′*o*nawt, -nŏt) *n.* Navigator or pilot of balloon or other lighter-than-air craft. **aer·o·nau·tic** (ār*o*naw′tĭk, -nŏt′ĭk), **aer·o·nau′ti·cal** *adjs.* Of, pertaining to, aeronautics. **aer·o·nau′tics** *n.pl.* (usu. considered sing.) Science or practice of flight.

aer·o·plane (ār′*o*plān) (Brit.) = AIRplane.

aer·o·sol (ār′*o*sōl, -sawl, -sŏl) *n.* System of colloidal particles dispersed in a gas, as mist, fog, etc.; container, also called ~ **bomb**, holding substance packed under pressure with spraying device; this substance.

*Boeing 747 Jumbo Jet is powered by 4 turbo-fan engines. Front-mounted fan blows air through ducts around the jet exhausts, improving quietness and fuel economy. the Jumbo **aeroplane** can take 450 passengers.*

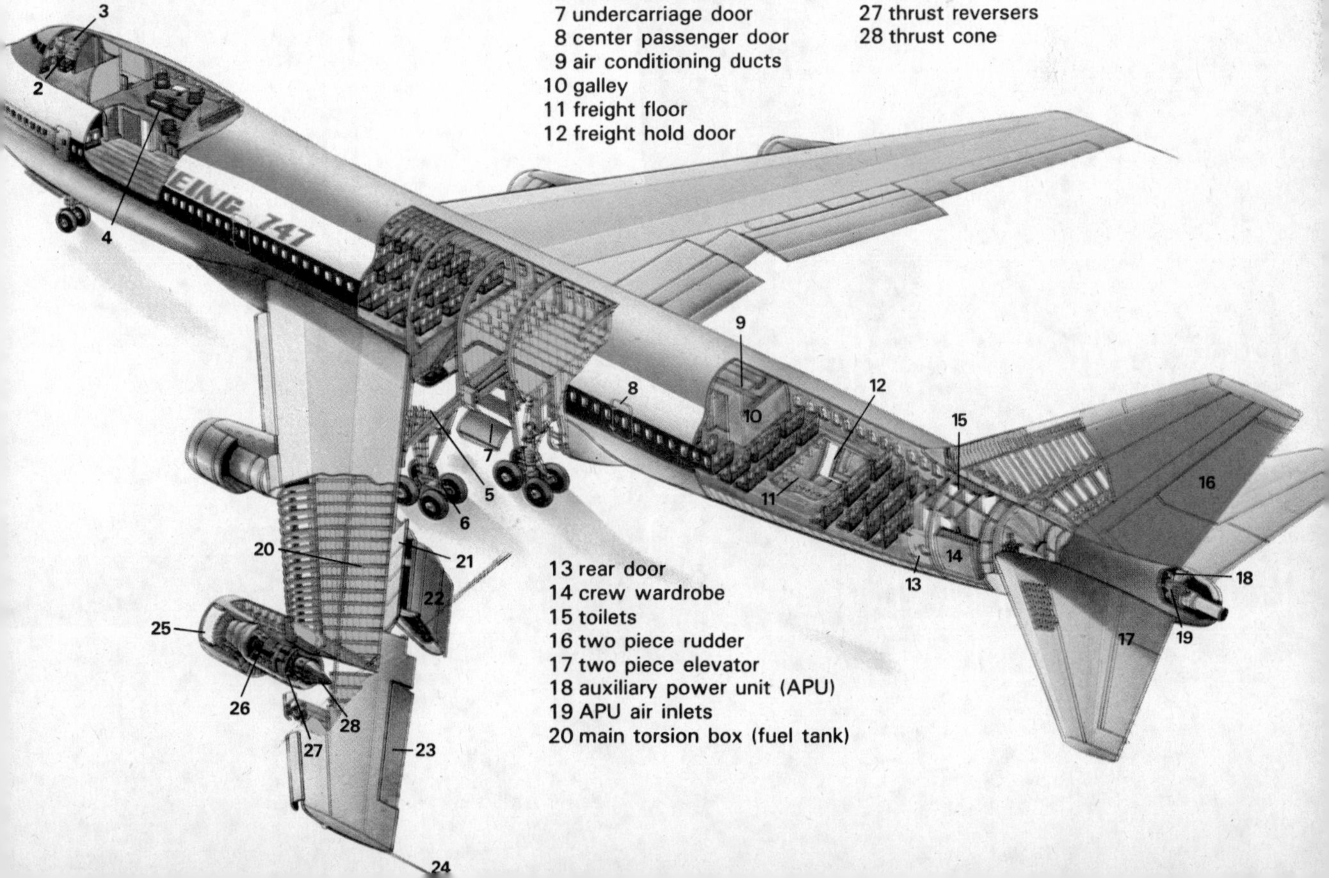

1 glass fiber radar cone
2 flight engineer's seat
3 flt eng electronics panel
4 upper first class lounge
5 retraction jacks
6 brake reaction link
7 undercarriage door
8 center passenger door
9 air conditioning ducts
10 galley
11 freight floor
12 freight hold door
13 rear door
14 crew wardrobe
15 toilets
16 two piece rudder
17 two piece elevator
18 auxiliary power unit (APU)
19 APU air inlets
20 main torsion box (fuel tank)
21 spoilers
22 triple slotted flaps
23 aileron
24 HF aerial
25 fan
26 cooler
27 thrust reversers
28 thrust cone

USAF

The displays in Washington's National Air and Space Museum cover many aspects of the U.S. ***aerospace*** *program. Exhibits include space exploration equipment and moon rock samples.*

aer·o·space (ār′ospās) *n.* Earth's atmosphere and outer space; (attrib.) of (industry concerned with) missiles, satellites, vehicles, etc. for operation in aerospace.

Aes·chy·lus (ĕs′kīlus) (525–456 B.C.). Athenian poet regarded as founder of Greek tragic drama; of his many tragedies only seven are extant: *The Persians*, *Seven Against Thebes*, *Prometheus Bound*, *The Suppliant Maidens*, and the Orestes trilogy: *Agamemnon*, *Choephori*, *Eumenides*.

Aes·cu·la·pi·us (ĕskyulā′pēus). (Rom. myth.) = ASCLEPIUS.

Æ·sir (ā′sĭr). (Scand. myth.) Collective name of the gods.

Ae·sop (ē′sŏp, ē′sop) (6th c. B.C.). Semilegendary Phrygian teller of fables about animals, said to have been a slave in Samos; the fables attributed to him are prob. compiled from various sources.

The Atlas Centaur rocket was originally designed by ***aerospace*** *engineers as a missile but is now used as a booster for spacecraft.*

aes·thete (ĕs′thēt) *n.* Professed lover of beauty.

aes·thet·ic (ĕsthĕt′ĭk) *adj.* Of appreciation of the beautiful; having such appreciation; in accordance with principles of good taste; **A ~ Movement**, movement in late 19th-c. England advocating "art for art's sake." **aes·thet′i·cal·ly** *adv.* **aes·thet′i·cism** *n.* **aes·thet′-ics** *n.* (usu. considered sing.) Philosophy of the beautiful; philosophy of art.

aes·ti·val (ĕs′tival) *adj.* Of summer.

aes·ti·vate (ĕs′tivāt) *v.i.* (**-vat·ed, -vat·ing**). Spend the summer, esp. (zool.) in state of torpor.

aes·ti·va·tion (ĕstivā′shon) *n.* (zool.) Aestivating; (bot.) arrangement of petals in flower bud before expansion.

Æth·el·red (ĕth′elrĕd) = ETHELRED.

AF *abbrev.* Air Force.

A.F. *abbrev.* Air Force; audio frequency.

a·far (afār′) *adv.* At, to, a distance; **from ~**, from a distance.

af·fa·ble (ăf′abel) *adj.* Easy to approach and converse with; courteous, friendly. **af′fa·bly** *adv.* **af·fa·bil·i·ty** (ăfabĭl′ĭtē) *n.*

af·fair (afār′) *n.* Business, concern; love affair; social event; (pl.) ordinary pursuits of life; (pl.) public commercial, or professional business or transactions.

af·fect[1] (afĕkt′) *v.t.* Practice, use, assume (character); pretend to have or feel; pretend (*to* do). **af·fect′ed** *adj.* Artificially assumed or displayed; full of affectation. **af·fect′ed·ly** *adv.*

af·fect[2] (afĕkt′) *v.t.* Attack (as disease); move, touch; produce (material effect on). **af·fect′ing** *adj.* Emotionally moving. **af·fect′-ing·ly** *adv.*

af·fect[3] (ăf′ĕkt) *n.* (psychol.) Emotion, feeling, as antecedent of action.

af·fec·ta·tion (ăfĕktā′shon) *n.* Studied display *of*; artificiality of manner; pretense.

af·fec·tion (afĕk′shon) *n.* 1. Affecting, being affected. 2. Mental state, emotion; kindly feeling, love. 3. Bodily state due to any influence; (esp.) malady, disease. **af·fec·tion·ate** (afĕk′shonĭt) *adj.* Loving, fond; showing love or tenderness. **af·fec′tion·ate·ly** *adv.*

af·fec·tive (afĕk′tĭv) *adj.* Of the affections, emotional.

af·fer·ent (ăf′erent) *adj.* (of blood and lymph vessels, nerves, etc.) Bringing, conducting, inwards or towards.

af·fi·ance (afī′ans) *v.t.* (**-anced, -anc·ing**). Promise solemnly in marriage, betroth.

af·fi·da·vit (ăfĭdā′vĭt) *n.* Written statement, confirmed by oath, to be used as judicial proof. [L., = "has stated on oath"]

af·fil·i·ate (afĭl′ēāt) *v.t.* (**-at·ed, -at·ing**). 1. (of institution) Adopt (persons as members, societies as branches); attach *to*, connect *with* (a society). 2. (law) Fix paternity of (illegitimate child) for purpose of maintenance; father (thing) *upon*, trace *to*. **af·fil·i·ate** (afĭl′ēĭt, -āt) *n.* Person, group, business, etc. that is affiliated. **af·fil·i·a·tion** (afĭlēā′-shon) *n.*

af·fin·i·ty (afĭn′ĭtē) *n.* (pl. **-ties**). Relationship, relations, by marriage or in general; structural resemblance; similarity of character suggesting relationship; liking, attraction; (chem.) tendency of substance to combine with others.

af·firm (afērm′) *v.* Assert strongly; make formal declaration or affirmation; state in the affirmative; ratify (judgment). **af·fir·ma·tion** (ăfermā′shon) *n.* Affirming.

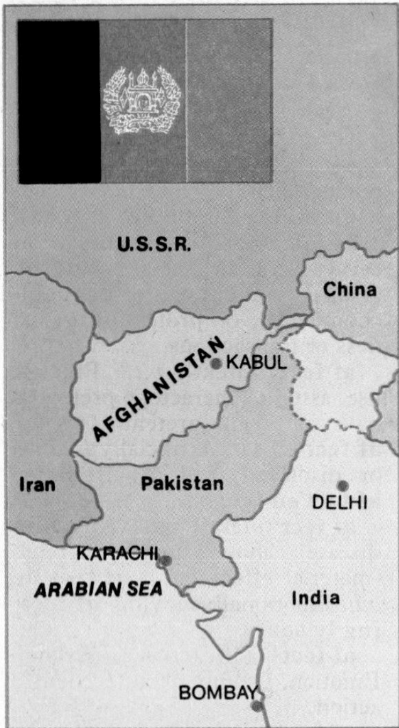

*Map and flag of **Afghanistan** and view of its rugged landscape: Salang Pass crosses Hindu Kush, at a height of 11,000 ft. Since 1979 there has been fighting between government forces backed by the U.S.S.R. and the Muslim tribesmen.*

af·firm·a·tive (*a*fẽr′matĭv) *adj.* Affirming, expressing assent; (logic) expressing agreement of the two terms of a proposition; ~ **action,** (law) process to counteract the effects of previously unfavorable allotment or refusal of jobs to persons because of their race or sex. **affirmative** *n.* Affirmative answer; the side that affirms a proposition in a debate. **af·firm′a·tive·ly** *adv.*

af·fix (*a*fĭks′) *v.t.* Fasten, append, attach. ~ (ăf′ĭks) *n.* Appendage, addition; (gram.) prefix or suffix.

af·fla·tus (*a*flā′*tus*) *n.* Divine or creative inspiration.

af·flict (*a*flĭkt′) *v.t.* Distress with bodily or mental suffering. **af·flic·tion** (*a*flĭk′sh*o*n) *n.* Misery, distress; pain, calamity.

af·flu·ent (ăf′lo͞oent) *adj.* Flowing freely; abounding; wealthy. ~ *n.* Tributary stream. **af′flu·ence** *n.* Wealth, abundance.

af·flux (ăf′lŭks) *n.* Flow toward a point; accession.

af·ford (*a*fōrd′, *a*fo͞rd′) *v.t.* 1. (with *can*) Have the means, be rich enough, manage to spare (time etc.). 2. Supply, provide. 3. Bestow. 4. Yield supply of. 5. Be in a position *to* do.

af·for·est (*a*fŏr′ĭst; *a*fa͞r′-) *v.t.* Convert into a forest; plant with trees. **af·for·est·a·tion** (*a*fŏrĭstā′-sh*o*n, *a*fa͞r-) *n.*

af·fray (*a*frā′) *n.* Breach of peace caused by fighting or rioting in public place.

af·front (*a*frŭnt′) *v.t.* Insult openly; face defiantly. **af·front′ed** *adj.* **affront** *n.* Open insult.

Af·ghan (ăf′găn, -g*a*n) *adj.* Of Afghanistan or its people; (strictly) of a tribe of Pathans who inhabit E. Afghanistan and speak Pashto; of the Pashto language; ~ **hound,** hunting dog of ancient breed with long silky hair and tuft on head. **Afghan** *n.* 1. Afghan person or language. 2. (**a**~) knitted or crocheted woolen coverlet.

Af·ghan·i·stan (ăfgăn′ĭstăn). Inland republic of SW. Asia bounded on W. by Iran, on S. and E. by Pakistan and on N. by U.S.S.R.; founded in 18th c. by tribe of Pathans who broke away from Mogul Empire; later under British protection but declared a sovereign state in 1921; inhabited by various chiefly Muslim peoples, including Afghans and Tajiks, speaking several languages of which the principal are Pashto and Persian (the official language); capital, Kabul.

a·fi·cio·na·do (*a*fĭsēonah′dō, -fĭsh*o*-; *Sp.* ahfēthyawnah′dhaw) *n.* (pl. **-dos**). Devotee of bullfighting (or other sport or pastime). [Sp.]

a·field (*a*fēld′) *adv.* On, in, or to the field; away, at a distance, astray.

a·fire (*a*fīr′) *adv.* & *pred. adj.* On fire.

a·flame (*a*flām′) *adv.* & *pred. adj.* In flames; in a glow of light.

AFL-CIO *abbrev.* American Federation of Labor and Congress of Industrial Organizations.

a·float (*a*flōt′) *adv.* & *pred. adj.* Floating, drifting; at sea, on board ship; full of water.

a·flut·ter (*a*flŭt′*er*) *adj.* In a flutter.

a·foot (*a*fo͝ot′) *adv.* & *pred. adj.* On one's feet; astir; in the process of being done.

a·fore (*a*fōr′, *a*fo͞r′) *adv.* & *prep.* (naut.) In front (of); (archaic, dial.) before, previously. **afore′-mentioned** *adj.* Mentioned previously or earlier. **afore′said** *adj.* Spoken of or named earlier or above. **afore′thought** *adj.* Thought out or planned beforehand, premeditated.

a for·ti·o·ri (ā fōrshēōr′ē, ā fo͞rshēo͞r′ē; *Lat.* ah fo͞rtēo͞r′ē). With stronger reason, all the more. [L.]

a·foul (*a*fowl′) *adj.* & *adv.* In a state of collision, conflict, or entanglement; **run** (or **fall**) ~ **of,** come into conflict with.

Afr. *abbrev.* Africa; African.

a·fraid (*a*frād′) *pred. adj.* Alarmed, frightened; sorry to say or suspect.

a·fresh (*a*frĕsh′) *adv.* Anew, with fresh beginning.

Af·ri·ca (ăf′rĭk*a*). Continent between Atlantic and Indian oceans extending nearly as far southward of equator as northward; its indigenous inhabitants are dark-skinned peoples varying in color from light copper in N. to black in equatorial and southern parts; it was visited by Portuguese from

*Face of an **African** tribesman, member of the pastoral Samburu tribe in northern Kenya. The political face of the African continent has changed rapidly since 1946 with former colonies gaining independence and then rejecting Europeans and their influence.*

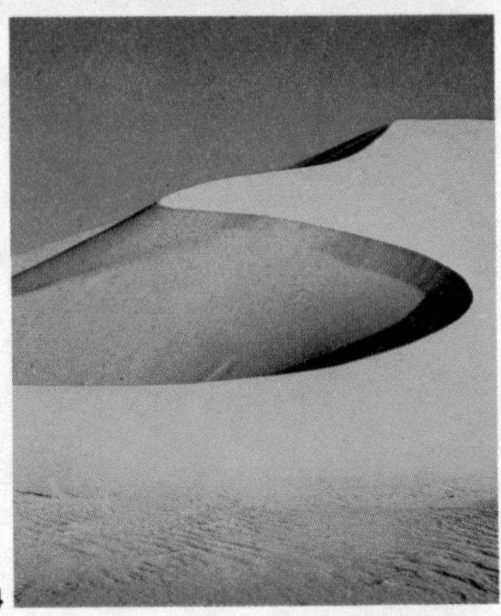

The second largest continent (after Asia). ***Africa*** *stretches about the same distance north and south of the Equator. Although archaeological evidence suggests East Africa was a center of early human evolution, to the outside world Africa remained the unexplored 'Dark Continent' until the mid-19th century. 1. Giraffe in the protected terrain of Amboseli Reserve, Kenya. Wildlife reserves may save many species from extinction. 2. View from the Escom building of Johannesburg, largest city of the Republic of South Africa. 3. Victoria Falls, Zambesi River. The chasm is 355 ft. deep and water falls almost vertically with a deafening roar in a cloud of spray. 4. Looking as though sculpted by human hands: a sand dune at Tassili, near Djanet in Algeria.*

15th c. onwards but remained largely unknown, except for limited colonization by the Dutch and British in the Cape region and by the French in Algeria, until mid-19th c.; in the 1880s the leading European nations competed for colonies, and the continent was divided between them, Liberia and Ethiopia alone remaining independent; after World War II most former colonies secured political independence.

Af·ri·can (ăf′rĭkan) *adj.* Of Africa or its people; ~ **violet**, a widely cultivated house plant (*Saintpaulia ionantha*) having white, pink, or violet flowers. **African** *n.* African person, esp. dark-skinned person as dist. from European or Asiatic settlers or their descendants. **Af′ri·can·ism** *n.* (esp.) African nationalism. **Af′ri·can·ist** *adj.* & *n.* **Af·ri·can·ize** (ăf′rĭkanīz) *v.t.* (**-ized, -iz·ing**). Subject to rule of African blacks. **Af·ri·can·i·za·tion** (ăfrĭkanīzā′shon) *n.*

Af·ri·kaans (ăfrĭkahns′, -kahnz′) *n.* Language, derived from 17th-century Dutch, used in the Republic of South Africa. ~ *adj.* Of Afrikaans or its speakers.

Af·ri·kan·der (ăfrĭkăn′der) *n.* 1. (hist.) Afrikaner. 2. (One of) a breed of hump-backed, large-horned beef cattle developed in South Africa.

Af·ri·ka·ner (ăfrĭkah′ner) *n.* (Esp. Afrikaans-speaking) descendant of Dutch settlers of South Africa.

Af·ro (ăf′rō) *adj.* Of Afro-Americans, black traditions, etc. ~ *n.* Bushy hairstyle.

Afro- *prefix.* African; African and —.

Af·ro-A·mer·i·can (ăfrōamĕr′ĭkan) *adj.* & *n.* (An American, esp. a black) from Africa or descended from Africans.

aft (ăft) *adv.* In, to, or toward stern of ship or tail of aircraft.

af·ter (ăf′ter) *adv.* Behind; later. ~ *prep.* Behind; in pursuit of; following in point of time; in view of; below in importance or rank; according to; in imitation of; ~ **all**, in spite of everything that has happened, been said, done, etc. **after** *conj.* In or at a time subsequent to that when. ~ *adj.* Later, following; nearer stern of ship or tail of aircraft; **af′terbirth**, placenta and membrane enveloping fetus in womb, extruded after the child; **af′terburner**, device for increasing jet-engine thrust by burning extra fuel through use of hot exhaust gases; device for burning undesirable exhaust fumes, as from internal combustion engine or incinerator; **af′tercare**, attention given to person after discharge from hospital, prison, etc.; **af′tereffect**, delayed effect; effect following after an interval; **af′terglow**, glow in west after sunset; pleasant remembrance; **af′terlife**, life after death; later period of person's life; **af′termath**, (fig.) results, consequences; **af′terpains**, pains caused by uterine contraction after childbirth; **af′tertaste**, taste remaining or recurring after eating or drinking (freq. fig.); **af′terthought**, reflection after the act; later expedient or explanation.

af·ter·noon (ăfternōōn′) *n.* Time between noon and evening.

af·ter·ward (ăf′terwerd), **af·ter·wards** (ăf′terwerdz) *advs.* Later, subsequently.

Ag *symbol.* Silver.

A.G. *abbrev.* Adjutant General.

a·ga (ah′ga) *n.* Commander or chief officer in Ottoman Empire; **Aga Khan**, title given to Hasan Ali Shah (1800–81) when he fled from Persia and settled in Bombay under British protection, and subsequently held by his successors; as direct descendant of Muhammad's son-in-law Ali, the Aga Khan is spiritual leader (Imam) of the Ismaili sect of Muslims. [Turk. *aghā* master, *khan* ruler, king]

a·gain (agen′) *adv.* Another time, once more; further, besides; on the other hand; in return, in response; **~ and ~**, repeatedly; **as much ~**, twice as much; **half as much ~**, one-and-a-half times as much.

a·gainst (agĕnst′) *prep.* In opposition to; in contrast to; in anticipation of; into collision with; in contact with; as a protection from; in payment towards; opposite to (usu. **over ~**).

Ag·a·mem·non (ăgamĕm′nŏn, -non). (Gk. legend) King of Argos, brother of Menelaus and commander of the Greeks in the Trojan War; murdered on his return from Troy by his wife Clytemnestra and her lover Aegisthus.

a·gape[1] (agāp′, agăp′) *adv.* & *pred. adj.* Gaping.

a·ga·pe[2] (ahgah′pā, ah′ga-) *n.* 1. Love feast held by early Christians in connection with Lord's Supper. 2. Spiritual love (opp. EROS). [Gk., = "brotherly love"]

a·gar (ah′gar̄, ăg′er), **a′gar-a′gar** *ns.* Gelatinous substance obtained from various seaweeds and used as laxative, as solidifying agent in culture media for bacteria etc., and in East as food. [Malay]

Ag·as·siz (ăg′asē), **(Jean) Louis (Rodolphe)** (1807–73). Swiss-born American naturalist, educator, and writer.

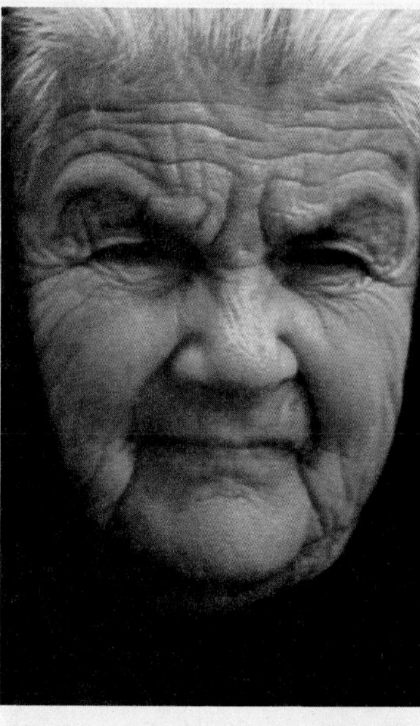

*Portrait of **age**. Average length of the human life has much increased. The average in N.W. Europe and N. America in late 18th century was 35–40 years. By 1970 it exceeded 70 years.*

a·gate (ăg′ĭt) *n.* 1. Any of various semiprecious stones, semi-pellucid and variegated, usu. having a banded appearance and consisting largely of silica. 2. (print.) 5½-point type.

a·ga·ve (agah′vē, agā′-) *n.* Tropical American plant of genus *A~* (family Amaryllidaceae), including century plant, of which some species are ornamental, and some yield rope and other fibers and are sources of beverages.

age (āj) *n.* 1. Length of life or of existence; a generation; (colloq., esp. in pl.) long time. 2. Particular length of life qualifying one for a purpose; **~ of consent**, (law) age at which consent is valid; **come of ~**, (law) attain age of 18 (formerly 21) years, assume rights and responsibilities of adult; **under ~**, not of full age; of less than age required. 3. Latter part of life (also **old ~**). 4. Great period, as **Ice A~**; **~-old**, having existed for a very long time. **age** *v.* (**aged, ag·ing** or **age·ing**). 1. (Cause to) grow old. 2. Become mature. **ag′ing, age′ing** *ns.* (esp.) Change of properties occurring in some metals after heat treatment or cold working. **aged** *adj.* 1. (ājd) Of the age of. 2. (ā′jĭd) Old; **the ~**, old persons. **age′less** *adj.* Never becoming old or outmoded. **age′less·ness** *n.*

*A variety of semi-precious stones, the **agate**, found in eruptive rocks, consists largely of silica. Uses vary from jewelry and paper-knives to laboratory mortars and pestles.*

a·gen·cy (ā′jensē) *n.* (pl. **-cies**). Active operation, action; instrumentality; action personified; office of agent; agent's business establishment; government bureau.

a·gen·da (ajĕn′da) *n.* List of things to be done, items of business to be considered at a meeting.

a·gent (ā′jent) *n.* One who, thing that, exerts power or produces effect; one acting for another in business, law, politics, etc.; spy; natural force acting on matter.

a·gent pro·vo·ca·teur (ăzhahn′ prawvawkătör′). Person employed to detect suspected offenders by tempting them to overt action. [Fr.]

ag·glom·er·ate[1] (aglŏm′erāt) *v.* (**-at·ed, -at·ing**). Collect into a mass. **ag·glom·er·a·tion** (aglŏmerā′shon) *n.* **ag·glom·er·a·tive** (aglŏm′erātĭv, -eratĭv) *adj.*

ag·glom·er·ate[2] (aglŏm′erĭt, -rāt) *adj.* Collected into a mass. **~** *n.* Mass; (geol.) aggregate of angular fragments of rock (of any or of several kinds) that has been shattered by volcanic action and subsequently consolidated into a mass.

ag·glu·ti·nate (aglōō′tinăt) *v.* (**-nat·ed, -nat·ing**). 1. Unite as with glue; combine simple words to express compound ideas without important change of form or loss of meaning. 2. Turn into glue. **ag·glu·ti·na·tion** (aglōōtĭnā′shon) *n.* **ag·glu·ti·na·tive** (aglōō′tĭnātĭv) *adj.* (of languages) Characterized by the joining of simple roots to express compound ideas without material change of form or loss of meaning.

ag·gran·dize (agrăn′dīz, ăg′ran-) *v.t.* (**-dized, -diz·ing**). Increase the power, rank, wealth, etc., of; exaggerate. **ag·gran·dize·ment** (agrăn′dĭzment) *n.*

ag·gra·vate (ăg′ravāt) *v.t.* (**-vat·ed, -vat·ing**). Increase the severity of; make more serious or worse; (colloq.) exasperate; annoy. **ag·gra·va·tion** (ăgravā′shon) *n.*

ag·gre·gate[1] (ăg′regāt) *v.* (**-gat·ed, -gat·ing**). Collect together; unite; amount to. **ag·gre·ga·tion** (ăgregā′shon) *n.*

ag·gre·gate[2] (ăg′regĭt, -gāt) *adj.*

How the opposing forces lined up at the ***Battle of Agincourt*** *(Pas-de-Calais). The St. Crispin's Day battle was won in 1415 by the English under Henry V against the French in a crucial encounter of the Hundred Years War.*

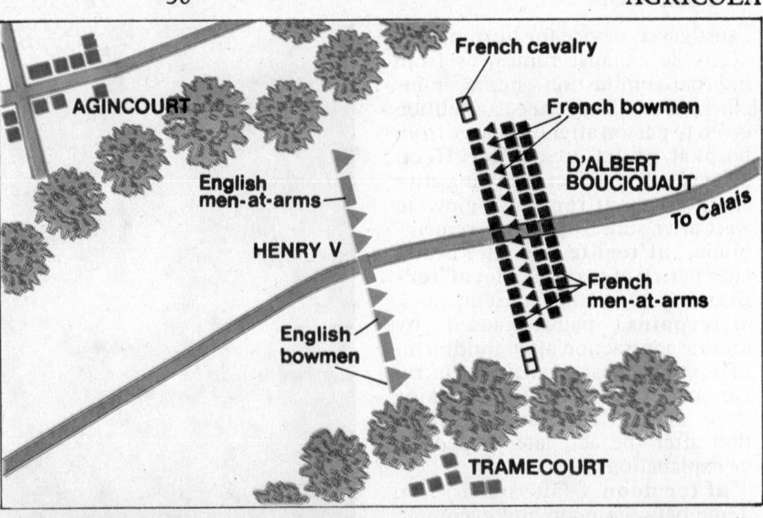

Collected into one body; collective total; (law) composed of associated individuals; (bot., of fruit) formed from carpels of one flower (as raspberry). ~ *n.* Total; assemblage, collection; (phys.) mass formed by union of homogeneous particles; (geol.) mass of minerals formed into one rock; (building) material mixed with lime, cement, bitumen, etc., to make concrete.

ag·gres·sion (agrĕsh′*o*n) *n.* Unprovoked attack; (psych.) Hostile or destructive tendency or behavior. **ag·gres·sor** (agrĕs′*er*) *n.*

ag·gres·sive (agrĕs′ĭv) *adj.* Of attack, offensive; disposed to attack; self-assertive. **ag·gres′sive·ly** *adv.* **ag·gres′sive·ness** *n.*

ag·grieved (agrēvd′) *pred. adj.* Distressed, oppressed; injured, having a grievance.

a·ghast (agăst′) *adj.* Terrified; struck with amazement.

ag·ile (ăj′*i*l) *adj.* Quick-moving; nimble, active. **ag′ile·ly** *adv.* **a·gil·i·ty** (ajĭl′ĭtē) *n.*

Ag·in·court (ăj′ĭnkōrt; *Fr.* ăzhahṅkoor′). Village of NW. France, scene of victory (1415) of Henry V of England over French.

ag·i·tate (ăj′ĭtāt) *v.* (**-tat·ed, -tat·ing**). 1. Shake, move; disturb, excite. 2. Revolve mentally, keep up an agitation (*for*).

ag·i·ta·tion (ăjĭtā′sh*o*n) *n.* 1. Shaking. 2. Commotion, disturbance. 3. Keeping of matter constantly before public; public excitement.

ag·i·ta·to (ăjĭtah′tō) *adv.* (mus.) In an agitated manner. [It.]

ag·i·ta·tor (ăj′ĭtāt*er*) *n.* 1. Person who creates excitement or disturbance, esp. for political ends. 2. Mechanical device for keeping liquid etc. in motion.

A·gla·ia (aglā′*a*). (Gk. myth.) One of the three Graces (see GRACE *n.* def. 3).

a·glit·ter (aglĭt′*er*) *adj.* Glittering; sparkling.

Ag·nes (ăg′nĭs), **St.** (4th c.). Patron saint of virgins, martyred in the persecution of Diocletian and commemorated Jan. 21.

Ag·new (ăg′nōō, -nū), **Spiro Theodore** (1918–). Vice president of the U.S. (1969–1973) under Richard Nixon; resigned Oct. 10, 1973.

Ag·ni (ăg′nē). (Vedic myth.) God of fire.

ag·nos·tic (ăgnos′tĭk) *n.* One who holds that nothing is known, or likely to be known, of the existence of God or gods or of anything beyond material phenomena. ~ *adj.* Pertaining to agnostics or agnosticism. **ag·nos·ti·cism** (ăgnŏs′tĭsĭzem) *n.* [Gk. *agnōstos* (*theos*) unknown (god); taken by T. H. Huxley f. Acts 17]

Taj Mahal, ***Agra,*** *India, erected 1631-45. Thought by some to be the world's most sublime building, it was built by the Mogul emperor Shah Jahan as a mausoleum in memory of his beloved wife.*

Ag·nus De·i (ăg′n*u*s dē′ī, ahn′yōōs dĕ′ē). Part of the Mass beginning with these words; figure of lamb as emblem of Christ bearing cross or banner; small disk of wax stamped with this figure and blessed by pope. [L., = "lamb of God"]

a·go (agō′) *adv.* Past, gone by; since.

a·gog (agŏg′) *adv.* & *pred. adj.* Eager(ly), expectant(ly).

ag·o·nize (ăg′*o*nīz) *v.* (**-nized, -niz·ing**). Torture; suffer agony, writhe in anguish; make desperate efforts for effect.

ag·o·ny (ăg′*o*nē) *n.* (pl. **-nies**). Extreme bodily or mental suffering; the last sufferings of Jesus Christ before the Crucifixion; **death ~**, **last ~**, death pangs.

ag·o·ra·pho·bi·a (ăg*e*rafō′bē*a* *n.* Morbid dread of open spaces.

a·gou·ti (agōō′tē) *n.* (pl. **-tis, -ties**). Rodent (several species in genus *Dasyprocta*) of tropical America, related to guinea pig.

agr. *abbrev.* Agricultural; agriculture.

A·gra (ah′gr*a*). City on river Jumna in Uttar Pradesh, capital of Mogul emperors from early 16th to mid-17th c.; site of the TAJ MAHAL.

a·grar·i·an (agrār′ēan) *adj.* Of landed property or cultivated land. **a·grar′i·an·ism** *n.*

a·gree (agrē′) *v.* (**a·greed, a·gree·ing**). Consent (*to*); be in accord, harmonize in opinion etc. (*with*); (gram.) have same number, gender, case, or person.

a·gree·a·ble (agrē′*a*bel) *adj.* Pleasing (*to*); (colloq.) well disposed (*to, to* do); **a·gree′a·bly** *adv.*

a·gree·ment (agrē′m*e*nt) *n.* Mutual understanding, covenant; (law) contract legally binding on parties; accordance in opinion; (gram.) concord in number, gender, case, person.

A·gric·o·la (agrĭk′*o*la), **Gnaeus**

Contrasts in present day ***agriculture.*** *Left: A cotton harvester in Louisiana collects the cotton bolls for processing. Above: In Cordova, Spain, a peasant plows a furrow with two mules — in much the same way that his ancestors have done over the centuries.*

Julius (40–93 A.D.). Roman general; governor of Britain for several years from 78.

ag·ri·cul·ture (ăg′rĭkŭlcher) *n.* Cultivation of the soil. **ag·ri·cul·tur·al** (ăgrĭkŭl′cheral) *adj.* **ag·ri·cul′tur·ist, ag·ri·cul′tur·al·ist** *ns.*

ag·ri·mo·ny (ăg′rimōnē) *n.* (pl. **-nies**). Perennial plant of the rose family, esp. *Agrimonia eupatoria*, which has yellow flowers and hooked clinging fruit; **hemp ~**, see HEMP.

A·grip·pa (agrĭp′a), **Marcus Vipsanius** (*c*63–12 B.C.). Roman general, son-in-law of the Emperor Augustus.

a·gron·o·my (agrŏn′omē) *n.* Rural economy, husbandry. **ag·ro·nom·ic** (ăgronŏm′ĭk), **ag·ro·nom′i·cal** *adjs.* **a·gron′o·mist** *n.*

a·ground (agrownd′) *adv.* & *pred. adj.* On the bottom of shallow water.

a·gue (ā′gū) *n.* Malarial fever; cold shivering stage of this; shivering fit.

ah (ah) *int.* Exclamation of joy, sorrow, surprise, entreaty, etc.

a·ha (ah-hah′) *int.* Exclamation of surprise, triumph, mockery.

A·hab (ā′hăb). King of Israel (1 Kings 16–22).

A·haz (ā′hăz). King of Judah (2 Kings 16).

a·head (ahĕd′) *adv.* & *pred. adj.* In advance *of*, in or direct line forward, onward; in or toward a more advantageous position or situation.

a·hoy (ahoi′) *int.* (naut.) Call used in hailing.

Ah·ri·man (ah′rĭman). Principle of evil in the Zoroastrian system.

A·hu·ra Maz·da (ah′hoora măz′da) = ORMAZD.

ai (ah′ē) *n.* (pl. **a·is**). Three-toed sloth (*Bradypus tridactylus*) of S. America. [f. its cry]

AID *abbrev.* Agency for International Development.

aid (ād) *v.t.* Help, assist, promote. **~** *n.* Help, assistance; helper; material source of help.

aide (ād) *n.* Aide-de-camp; assistant.

aide-de-camp (ād′dekămp′) *n.* (pl. **aides-de-camp**). Military officer acting as confidential assistant to senior officer. [Fr.]

ai·grette (ā′grĕt, āgrĕt′) *n.* Ornamental tuft of upright plumes, esp. from the long white tail feathers of egret; spray of gems or other ornaments resembling this.

ail (āl) *v.* Trouble, afflict; be ill. **ail′ment** *n.* Illness, esp. slight one.

ai·le·ron (ā′lerŏn) *n.* Hinged flap on trailing edge of aircraft wing, providing variation of lift on either side and used, for example, to execute the movement known as banking. [Fr., = "little wing, fin," dim. of *aile* wing]

ai·lu·ro·pho·bi·a (īloorofō′bēa) *n.* Morbid fear of cats. **ai·lu·ro·phobe** (īloor′ofōb) *n.* One having this fear.

aim (ām) *v.* Direct *at*; point (gun etc.); deliver blow, discharge missile *at*; form designs, try. **~** *n.* Direction of or act of directing a missile or weapon towards an object; design, purpose, object. **aim′less** *adj.* **aim′less·ly** *adv.* **aim′less·ness** *n.*

ain't (ānt) 1. Contraction of *am not*. 2. Also contraction of *is not*, *are not*, *has not*, *have not*. In all senses *ain't* is considered substandard usage in speech or writing.

Ai·nu (ī′nōō) *n.* (pl. **-nus**, collect. **-nu**). (Member of) a Caucasoid people in Japan and U.S.S.R. with hairy bodies; their language.

air (ār) *n.* 1. Invisible, odorless, and tasteless mixture of gases enveloping Earth, consisting chiefly of oxygen and nitrogen, with some carbon dioxide and traces of other gases, and breathed by all land animals; atmosphere; unconfined space; breeze; **on the ~**, broadcast(ing) by radio or television transmission. 2. Appearance; mien; affected manner. 3. (mus.) Melody, tune, aria. 4.

(attrib.) Of aircraft or flying; containing air or inflated by air. 5. ~ **bag**, safety device filling with air to protect automobile passengers in a collision; ~ **base**, center for military aircraft; **air'borne**, transported by air; in air after taking off; **air brake**, brake operated by piston driven by compressed air; also, brake consisting of flaps or other movable surfaces, normally lying parallel to airflow, turned through 90° to retard progress of aircraft or automobile; **air'brush**, fine spray for paint used in commercial art and for retouching photographs; **air cavalry**, airborne troops; **air conditioning**, process of controlling temperature and humidity of air before it enters a room, building, etc.; **air-cooled**, (*adj.*) cooled by exposure to stream of air; **air'craft**, (pl. same) any kind of flying machine, including airplanes, airships, helicopters, etc.; these collectively; **aircraft carrier**, ship designed to carry airplanes with special deck for take-off and landing; **air cushion**, cushion inflated by air; body of air serving to provide support, esp. in **air-cushion vehicle**, hovercraft; **air'drome, air'field**, area of land where aircraft are accommodated and maintained and may take off or land; **air'foil**, any or all of the lift-producing surfaces of an aircraft, as wings, ailerons, fins, etc.; **air force**, branch of armed forces using aircraft in fighting; **air'frame**, body of aircraft as distinct from engine(s); **air freight**, freight carried by aircraft; charge for this service; **air gun**, gun from which missile is discharged by compressed air; **air lane**, regular route of travel for aircraft; **air'lift**, transportation of troops, supplies, etc. by air to or from an area cut off from normal communications; (*v.t.*) transport thus; **air'line**, line of aircraft for public service; **air'liner**, large passenger airplane; **air lock**, stoppage of flow of liquid in pump or pipe by bubble of air; also, see LOCK[2] *n.* def. 2; **air mail**, mail carried by aircraft; **air'man**, member of crew of aircraft; enlisted man or woman in air force; **air mattress**, inflatable pad used as mattress; **air piracy**, hijacking an airplane; **air'plane**, powered winged heavier-than-air flying machine; **air pocket**, local condition of atmosphere, as a down current or sudden change of wind velocity, that causes aircraft to lose altitude suddenly; **air'port**, airdrome for transport of passengers and goods by air; **air power**, power of offensive and defensive action dependent upon a supply of aircraft; **air pressure**, atmospheric pressure, see ATMOSPHERE; pressure exerted by compressed air; **air pump**, pump for exhausting vessel etc. of its air; (also compressor); **air raid**, attack by aircraft; **air rifle**, air gun with rifled barrel; **air shaft**, passage for ventilating mine, tunnel, or building; **air'ship**, self-propelled lighter-than-air craft; dirigible balloon; **air'sickness**, nausea sometimes affecting airplane crew or passengers; **air'space**, space containing air; air lying over a par-

*The ancients believed that the **air** sustained flight; da Vinci and later Galileo established that, on the contrary, it resisted movement of a solid object. That was the spur to the development of aerodynamics. Right: An **aircraft carrier** with support ships. Below: One of the 160-ton hovercraft that ply across the English Channel. Bottom right: Goodyear **airship** 'Europa'. Photographing sports events is one role of airships today.*

ticular territory and considered subject to its jurisdiction; **air′-speed**, speed of aircraft in relation to the air, as dist. from *groundspeed*; **air′strip**, strip of land prepared for the taking off and landing of aircraft, often for temporary use; **air terminal**, airport building equipped for reception of passengers; **air′tight**, impermeable to air; **air traffic control**, regulation of aircraft operating in air lanes; **air′waves**, medium for transmission of radio and television signals; **air′way**, ventilating passage in mine; air lane; **air′worthy**, (of aircraft) in fit condition to be flown. **air** *v.t.* Expose to open air, ventilate; express (one's grievances, opinions, etc.).

Aire·dale (ār′dāl) *n.* One of a breed of large terriers with rough reddish-brown coats. [valley of river Aire, West Yorkshire]

air·less (ār′lĭs) *adj.* Stuffy; breezeless, still. **air′less·ness** *n.*

air·y (ār′ē) *adj.* (**air·i·er, air·i·est**). Breezy; light, thin; immaterial; sprightly, graceful, delicate; superficial, flippant. **air′i·ly** *adv.*

aisle (īl) *n.* Division of church, esp. parallel to nave, choir, or transept, and divided from it by pillars; passage between rows of seats, in church, theater, etc. [L. *ala* wing]

Aix-en-Pro·vence (ĕks-ahn̄-prawvahn̄s′). City in S. France, N. of Marseilles.

Aix-la-Cha·pelle (ĕks-lah-shahpĕl′). French name of AACHEN.

a·jar (*a*jār′) *adv.* (of a door) Slightly open.

A·jax (ā′jăks). (Gk. legend) 1. Greek hero of the Trojan war, son of Telamon king of Salamis. 2. Another Greek, son of Oileus king of Locris, who was killed after a shipwreck on his homeward journey after the fall of Troy.

AK *abbrev.* Alaska.

a.k.a. *abbrev.* Also known as.

Ak·bar (ăk′bār). **Jalaludin Muhammad** (1542–1605), Mogul emperor; enlarged the Mogul Empire in India to its greatest extent.

à Kempis, Thomas: see THOMAS À KEMPIS.

Akh·na·ton (ahknah′t*o*n), **Ikhnaton.** Name (lit. "glory of the sun") taken by Amenhotep IV, king of Egypt of 18th dynasty (14th c. B.C.), husband of NEFERTITI, who tried to replace the worship of Ammon by that of Ra, and built a new capital at Tell el Amarna, away from Thebes where the old priesthood was established.

a·kim·bo (*a*kĭm′bō) *adv.* & *adj.* (of arms) With hands on hips and elbows out.

a·kin (*a*kĭn′) *pred. adj.* Related by blood; (fig.) of similar character.

Ak·kad (ăk′ăd, ah′kahd). Northern part of ancient Babylonia; also, the city (Agade) founded by Sargon *c*2300 B.C. **Ak·ka·di·an** (*a*kā′dē*a*n) *adj.* & *n.* (Native or inhabitant) of Akkad; (of) the language of this people, the oldest known Semitic language.

Ak·ron (ăk′r*o*n). Manufacturing and industrial city in NE. Ohio.

ak·va·vit (ahk′vahvēt) = AQUAVIT.

AL *abbrev.* Alabama.

Al *symbol.* Aluminum.

-al *suffix.* 1. Forming adjectives from L. (*general, central*), Gk. (*tropical*) etc. 2. Forming nouns (*animal, rival*), esp. of verbal action (*arrival, withdrawal*).

à la, a la (ah′lah, ăl′*a*). After the manner of. [Fr.]

Ala. *abbrev.* Alabama.

A.L.A. *abbrev.* American Library Association.

Al·a·bam·a (ăl*a*băm′*a*). State in southeastern U.S., admitted to the Union in 1819; capital, Montgomery.

al·a·bas·ter (ăl′*a*băst*e*r) *n.* Translucent granular gypsum rock of white, pink, or yellowish color, used for statues etc. ~ *adj.* Of alabaster; resembling it in whiteness or smoothness.

à la carte (ăl *a* kārt′, ah l*a*). (of meal) Ordered by separate items from the bill of fare, with a stated price for each item (opp. *table d'hôte*). [Fr.]

a·lac·ri·ty (*a*lăk′rĭtē) *n.* Briskness, cheerful readiness.

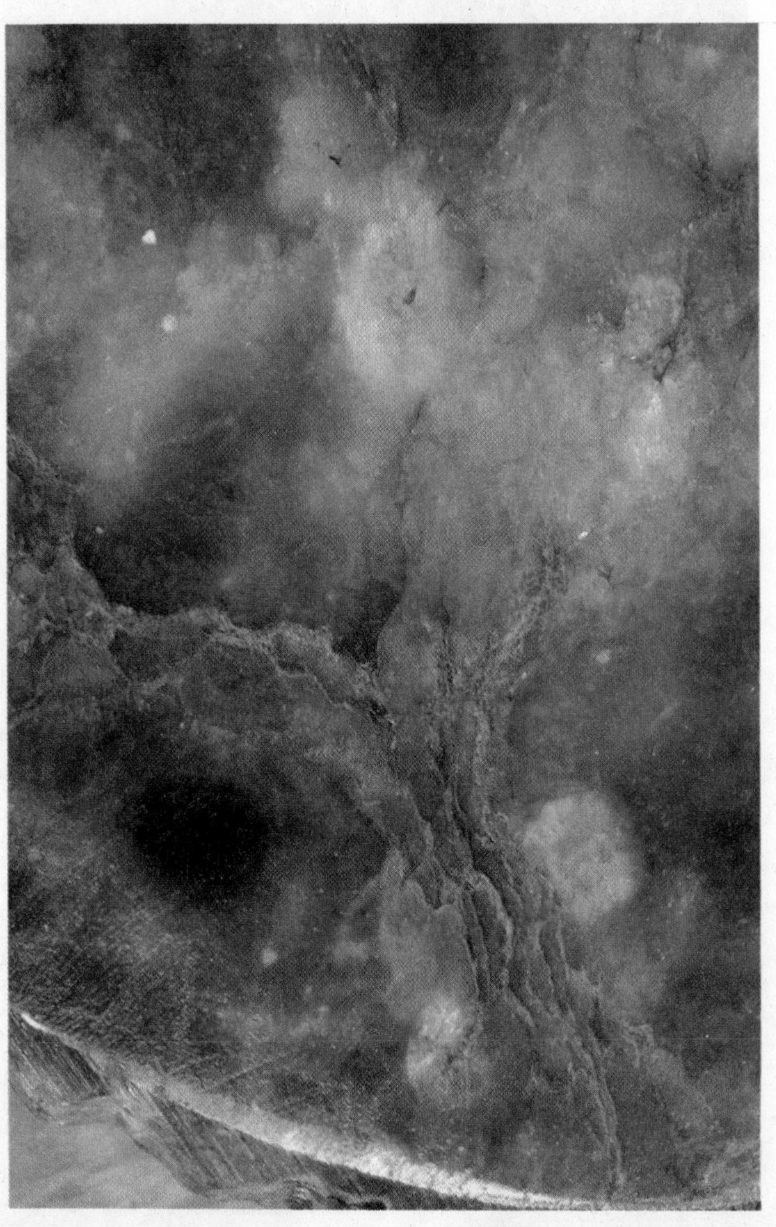

*This **alabaster** rock in Denver, Colorado, is a good example of the translucent gypsum rock that has been used for centuries to make statues, carvings and other ornaments.*

A·lad·din (*a*lăd′*i*n). Hero of a story in *Arabian Nights*, who acquired a lamp the rubbing of which brought a genie to do the will of the owner.

à la king (ah l*a* kĭng′, ăl *a*). (of food) Creamed with green pepper or pimento etc.

Al·a·mo (ăl′*a*mō). Fort and former Franciscan mission in San Antonio, Texas; site of a massacre of Texans by Mexican troops in 1836, from which came the battle-cry "Remember the Alamo!"

à la mode (ăl *a* mōd′, ah l*a*). In the fashion, fashionable; (of pie etc.) served with ice cream on top; (of beef) braised with vegetables in wine and/or with a brown sauce.

Å·land (aw'l*a*nd) **Islands.** Group of islands in the Gulf of Bothnia constituting a department of Finland.

a·lar (ā′l*e*r) *adj.* Pertaining to wings; wing-shaped, winglike; axillary.

Al·a·ric (ăl′*e*rĭk) (*c*370–410). A Visigoth, the first Germanic conqueror of Rome (410 A.D.).

a·larm (*a*lârm′) *n.* Call to arms; warning sound giving notice of danger; warning; frightened anticipation of danger; sudden uneasiness; mechanism that sounds alarm; ~ **clock**, clock with apparatus that can be set to ring at predetermined time; ~**s and excursions**, (joc.) noise and bustle. **alarm** *v.t.* Arouse to sense of danger; disturb, agitate. **a·larm′ing** *adj.* **a·larm′ing·ly** *adv.* [It. *all' arme* to arms]

a·larm·ist (*a*lâr′mĭst) *n.* One who raises alarm on slight grounds; panic monger.

a·lar·um (*a*lăr′*u*m, *a*lâr′-) *n.* (archiac) Alarm.

a·las (*a*lăs′) *int.* Exclamation of grief, pity, concern.

A·las·ka (*a*lăs′k*a*). State of the U.S. in the extreme NW. of N. America, with coasts on Arctic Ocean, Bering Sea, and North Pacific; discovered by Russian explorers (under Vitus Bering) in 1741, and further explored by Cook, Vancouver, and others during the last quarter of 18th c.; the territory was purchased from Russia in 1867 and admitted to the Union in 1959; capital, Juneau. Construction of new capital, at Willow, is planned. **A·las′kan** *adj.* & *n.* **Gulf of Alaska**, inlet of the Pacific Ocean between the Alaska Peninsula and the Alexander Archipelago; **Alaska Highway**, also called "Alcan Highway," highway 1,671 miles (2,689 km) long built by the U.S. and Canada between Dawson Creek, B.C., and Fairbanks, Alaska.

alb (ălb) *n.* Vestment reaching to feet, worn by celebrant at Eucharist over the cassock and by some consecrated kings.

At 20,300 ft. Mt. McKinley, in the south of ***Alaska,*** *is the highest mountain in North America. Alaska, the largest State of U.S.A., was once known as Russian America.*

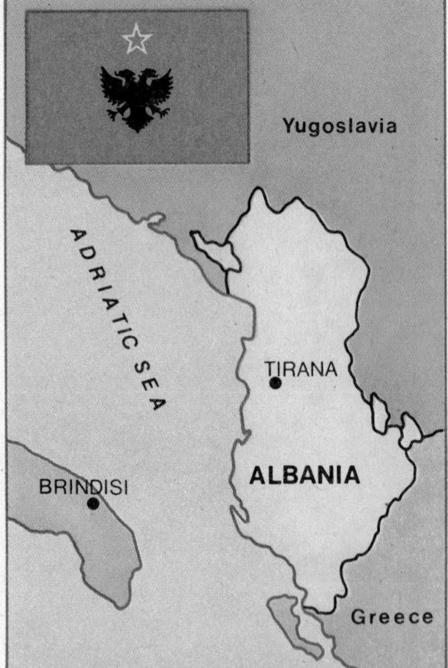

Map of ***Albania*** *with its flag. Proclaimed People's Republic in 1946, it was first a satellite of Yugoslavia, then of U.S.S.R. It is now more closely aligned with communist China.*

al·ba·core (ăl′b*a*kōr, -kôr) *n.* (pl. **-cores**, collect. **-core**). Large species of fish of E. and W. coasts of North America (*Thunnus alalunga*) allied to tuna; other fish of the same genus. [Arab. *al* the, *bakr* young camel]

Al·ba·ni·a (ălbā′nē*a*, awl-). Balkan state between Greece and Yugoslavia; under Turkish rule 16th c. until 1912; a republic from 1925 until 1928 when it was changed into a monarchy; again proclaimed a republic, the People's Republic of Albania, in 1946; capital, Tirana. **Al·ba′ni·an** *adj.* & *n.* (Native, inhabitant, language) of Albania.

Al·ba·ny[1] (awl′b*a*nē). Ancient poetic name, of Gaelic origin, for the N. part of Britain.

Al·ba·ny[2] (awl′b*a*nē). Capital of New York State, on the Hudson River 145 miles (233 km) N. of New York City.

al·ba·tross (ăl′b*a*traws, -trŏs) *n.* Very long-winged oceanic bird (genus *Diomedea*), allied to petrel, found chiefly in the S. hemisphere; **wandering** ~, one of the largest sea-birds (*D. exulans*), white when adult, with dark wings and hooked beak. [f. obs. *alcatras* frigate bird, f. Span. and Port., f. Arab *al-qadus* the bucket (name for the pelican, from its supposed water-carrying habit)]

Al·bee (awl′bē), **Edward** (1928–). American playwright; author of *Who's Afraid of Virginia Woolf?* etc.

al·be·it (awlbē′ĭt) *conj.* Though.

Al·be·marle (ăl′b*e*mârl) **Sound.** Inlet (about 50 miles long) of the Atlantic Ocean in North Carolina.

Al·bé·niz (ahlbā′nĭs; *Sp.* ahlvĕ′-nĕth), **Isaac** (1860–1909). Spanish pianist and composer, famous

The long-winged oceanic ***albatross*** *ranges the high seas for months on end. Inset: Courtship dance of the wandering albatross (Diomedea exulans). The male claps its bill, waves its neck and spreads its wings.*

Calgary Stampede, ***Alberta,*** *annual rodeo that attracts visitors from all over North America. Alberta, prairie province of Canada, is bordered on the west by the Rocky Mountains.*

chiefly for works based on the rhythm of Spanish popular music.

Al·ber·ich (ăl'berĭk). (Scand. myth.) King of the elves, guardian of the treasure of the Nibelungs, stolen from him by Siegfried.

Al·bert (ăl'b*e*rt), **Prince** (1819–1861). Prince of Saxe-Coburg-Gotha; cousin and consort (1840) of Queen Victoria; **Lake ~**, large shallow lake in Uganda, discovered in 1864, renamed *Lake Mobutu Sese Seko*, 1973.

Al·ber·ta (ălbēr't*a*). Western prairie province of Canada, bounded on the south by the U.S., and on the west by the Rocky Mountains; capital, Edmonton.

Al·ber·tus Mag·nus (ălbēr't*u*s măg'n*u*s) (1193 or 1206–1280). Swabian Dominican monk, one of the great scholastic philosophers; known as "Doctor Universalis."

Al·bi·gen·ses (ălbĭjĕn'sēz) *n.pl.* Members of a heretical sect preaching a form of Manichaean dualism in S. France, 11th–13th c. **Al·bi·gen·si·an** (ălbĭjĕn'sē*a*n, -sh*a*n) *adj.* & *n.* [L. f. town of *Albi*]

Snowball, the ***albino*** *gorilla. Albinotic animals and humans lack pigments in skin, hair, eyes. The condition is inherited. 'Albus' is Latin for white.*

al·bi·no (ălbī'nō) *n.* (pl. **-nos**). Animal or human being marked by congenital absence of pigment in skin and hair, which is white, and eyes, which are pink or very pale blue and unduly sensitive to light; plant lacking normal coloring. **al·bi·not·ic** (ălbĭnŏt'ik) *adj.* **al·bi·nism** (ăl'bĭnĭz*e*m) *n.*

Al·bi·on (ăl'bē*o*n). Ancient poetical name for Britain.

al·bum (ăl'b*u*m) *n.* Blank book for insertion of autographs, photographs, etc.; long-playing record or set of records.

al·bu·men (ălbū'm*e*n) *n.* White of egg.

al·bu·me·nize (ălbū'm*e*nīz) *v.t.* (**-nized, -niz·ing**). Coat (paper) with an albuminous solution.

al·bu·min (ălbū'm*i*n) *n.* Any of a class of water-soluble proteins, including the main constituent of white of egg; (bot.) substance found between skin and embryo of many seeds, usu. the edible part. **al·bu·mi·nose** (ălbū'm*i*nōs), **al·bu'mi·nous** *adjs.*

al·bu·mi·noid (ălbū'm*i*noid) *n.* Any of a class of organic compounds forming chief parts of organs and tissues of animals and plants; protein. **al·bu·mi·noid·al** (ălbūm*i*noi'd*a*l) *adj.*

Al·bu·quer·que[1] (ăl'b*u*kērkē), **Alfonso d'** (1453–1515). Portuguese navigator, founder of Portuguese power in India.

Al·bu·quer·que[2] (ăl'b*u*kērkē). City on the Rio Grande in central New Mexico; established as a Spanish settlement in 1706.

al·bur·num (ălbēr'n*u*m) *n.* Recently formed wood in trees, sapwood.

Al·cae·us (ălsē'*u*s) (b. *c*620 B.C.). Greek lyric poet of Mitylene in Lesbos. **al·ca·ic** (ălkāĭk) *adj.* (esp.) Of a meter invented by Alcaeus, a stanza of four lines.

Al·can (ăl´kăn) **Highway** = ALASKA Highway.

Al·ca·traz (ăl´katrăz). Island in San Francisco Bay, California; former site of U.S. federal prison.

Al·ces·tis (ălsĕs´tĭs). (Gk. legend) Wife of Admetus, whose life she saved by giving her own; she was brought back from Hades by Hercules.

al·che·my (ăl´kemē) *n.* Medieval forerunner of chemistry, primarily the attempt to transmute base metals into gold or silver. **al·chem·ic** (ălkĕm´ĭk), **al·chem'i·cal** *adjs.* **al·che·mist** (ăl´kemĭst) *n.* [Arab. *al-kimia*, f. *al* the, Gk. *khēmeia* transmutation of metals]

Al·ci·bi·a·des (ălsibī´adēz) (*c*450–404 B.C.). Athenian general and politician to whose irresponsibility the defeat of Athens in the Peloponnesian War was partly due.

Al·cin·o·üs (ălsĭn´ōus). (Gk. legend) King of Phaeacia and father of Nausicaa; entertained Ulysses during his journey home from Troy.

Alc·me·ne (ălkmē´nē). (Gk. myth.) Wife of Amphitryon and mother of Hercules by Zeus.

al·co·hol (ăl´kohawl, -hŏl) *n.* 1. Colorless volatile inflammable liquid, also called **ethyl** ~ (C_2H_5OH), formed by fermentation of sugars and contained in wine, beer, whiskey, etc., of which it is the intoxicating principle, also used in medicine and industry as a solvent for fats, oils, etc., and as a fuel. 2. Any liquor containing alcohol. 3. (chem.) Any of a class of compounds analogous to alcohol in constitution and derived from hydrocarbons by the replacement of hydrogen atoms by hydroxyl groups. [Arab. *al* the, *koh'l* powder (for staining eyelids)]

al·co·hol·ic (ălkohaw´lĭk, -hŏl´ĭk) *adj.* Pertaining to, containing, alcohol. ~ *n.* Person suffering from alcoholism.

al·co·hol·ism (ăl´kohawlĭzem, -hŏlĭz-) *n.* Diseased condition caused by excessive consumption of alcoholic liquors.

Al·cott (awl´kot), **Louisa May** (1832–88). American writer of popular novels; author of *Little Women, Little Men,* etc.

al·cove (ăl´kōv) *n.* Recess in room wall; recess in garden wall or hedge; summer house or secluded garden enclosure. [Arab. *al-qobbah* the vault]

Al·cy·o·ne (ălsī´onē). (Gk. legend) Wife of Ceyx; threw herself into the sea after finding the body of her shipwrecked husband on the shore; the gods changed both into kingfishers, and the sea is said to be calm while they are nesting; hence the expression "halcyon days."

al·de·hyde (ăl´dehīd) *n.* Any of a class of organic compounds containing the group CHO— in their structures, esp. acetaldehyde, CH_3CHO. [abbrev. of L. *al*cohol *dehyd*rogenatum (deprived of hydrogen)]

*The **alder** tree with its leaf and catkins, male and female. The alder group of trees and shrubs belongs to the birch family and is found throughout the N. hemisphere and in western S. America.*

***Alcatraz** was a U.S. prison from 1868, originally for military purposes. Between 1934–63 it held the most dangerous federal prisoners. Since 1972 it has been a National Recreation Area.*

Al·den (awl´den), **John** (1599?–1687). A signer of the Mayflower Compact and a founder of the Plymouth Colony in Massachusetts, 1620; married Priscilla Mullens.

al·der (awl´der) *n.* Shrub or tree (genus *Alnus*) of birch family, esp. *A. glutinosa*, growing by lakes and streams and in marshy ground.

al·der·man (awl´derman) *n.* (pl. **-men** pr. -men). 1. (hist.) Co-opted member of an English county or borough council, next in dignity to mayor; as an Anglo-Saxon title, a noble or person of high rank. 2. In some U.S. towns and cities, a member of municipal governing body. **al·der·man·ic** (awldermăn´ĭk) *adj.*

Al·drin (awl´drin), **Edwin Eugene, Jr.** (1930–). American astronaut; second man to walk on moon (1969).

ale (āl) *n.* Liquor made from an infusion of malt by fermentation, flavored with hops etc., similar to but stronger and more bitter than beer; **ale'wife** *n.* (pl. **-wives** pr. -wīvz) Fish of N. Amer. Atlantic waters, *Alosa pseudoharengus*, allied to the herring.

A·lec·to (alĕk´tō). (Gk. myth.) One of the Furies (see FURY).

a·lee (alē´) *adv.* & *pred. adj.* On the lee side of a ship, to leeward.

A·len·çon (alĕn´son; *Fr.* ălahṅsawṅ´). Town in NW. France, famous for the manufacture of needlepoint lace orig. copied from Venetian lace.

A·lep·po (alĕp´ō). Ancient city in Syria, twice besieged (though not taken) during the Crusades.

a·lert (alert´) *adj.* Watchful, vigilant; lively, nimble. ~ *n.* Warning call, alarm; warning of air raid etc., period of warning; **on the** ~, on the lookout. **a·lert'ly** *adv.* **a·lert'ness** *n.* **alert** *v.t.* Make alert, warn. [It. *all' erta* to the watchtower]

A·leu·tian (aloo´shan) **Islands** (also **Aleutians**). Group of islands in U.S. possession extending SW. from Alaska. **Aleutian Range,** volcanic mountain range extending along the Alaska Peninsula and into the Aleutian Islands; site of Katmai National Monument.

Al·ex·an·der[1] (ălĭgzăn´der) (356–323 B.C.), "the Great." King of Macedon; son of Philip II of Macedon; educated by Aristotle;

***Alfalfa,** also called lucerne, is a native of Europe but grown widely in the U.S.A. as a fodder crop of great economic value. Crops are pollinated by strategically placing bee colonies in the fields.*

became king 336 B.C.; was nominated by the Greek states to conduct the war against Persia, in which he was victorious; he extended his conquests to Egypt (where he founded Alexandria) and India.

Al·ex·an·der[2] (ălĭgzăn′d*er*). Name of three emperors of Russia: **Alexander I** (1777–1825), emperor 1801–25 during the Napoleonic Wars; sponsor of the Holy Alliance; **Alexander II** (1818–81), emperor 1855–81; emancipated serfs 1861; assassinated in St. Petersburg; **Alexander III** (1845–94), emperor 1881–94.

Al·ex·an·der Nev·ski (ălĭgzăn′d*er* nĕv′skē, nĕf′-) (1220–63). Russian Saint and national hero, called "Nevski" from the river Neva, on the banks of which he defeated the Swedes.

Al·ex·an·dri·a (ălĭgzăn′drē*a*). City and seaport of Egypt, founded by Alexander the Great 332 B.C.; capital of Egypt under the Ptolemies; until the Roman conquest of Egypt it was a center of Greek culture. **Al·ex·an′dri·an** *adj.* Of Alexandria; ~ **period,** period of Hellenistic literature with Alexandria as its chief center from end of the time of Alexander the Great to the Roman conquest of Greece, 300–146 B.C.

al·ex·an·drine (ălĭgzăn′drĭn, -drēn) *adj.* & *n.* (pros.) (Line) of six iambic feet, or 12 syllables, the French heroic verse. [so called because it was used in early poems on the subject of Alexander the Great]

al·fal·fa (ălfăl′f*a*) *n.* Leguminous plant (*Medicago sativa*) with trifoliate leaves and bluish-purple cloverlike flowers, used for fodder.

Al·fon·so (ălfŏn′sō). Name of several kings of Spain, the last of whom, **Alfonso XIII** (1886–1941), was deposed in 1931 when Spain became a republic.

Al·fon·so I (ălfŏn′sō) (1112–85). First king of independent Portugal (1139–85).

Al·fred (ăl′frĭd) (849–899), **the Great.** King of the West Saxons 871; drove the Danes from his territories; built a navy; composed a code of laws; encouraged the revival of letters in the W. of England, himself translating Latin works into English.

al·fres·co (ălfrĕs′kō) *adv.* & *adj.* In the open air, out of doors.

al·gae (ăl′jē) *n.pl.* (sing. **al·ga** pr. ăl′g*a*). Any of the Algae, a division of primitive cryptogamic plants including green, brown, and red seaweeds, pond scums, and many microscopic water plants showing immense diversity of structure.

Al·gar·ve (ahlgar̄′vē). Province on the S. coast of Portugal; originally a Moorish kingdom.

al·ge·bra (ăl′j*e*br*a*) *n.* Branch of mathematics dealing with relations and properties of numbers by means of letters and other general symbols. **al·ge·bra·ic** (ălj*e*brā′ĭk), **al·ge·bra′i·cal** *adjs.* **al·ge·bra′i·cal·ly** *adv.* **al·ge·bra·ist** (ăl′j*e*brāĭst) *n.* [Arab. *al–jebr* the reunion of fragments]

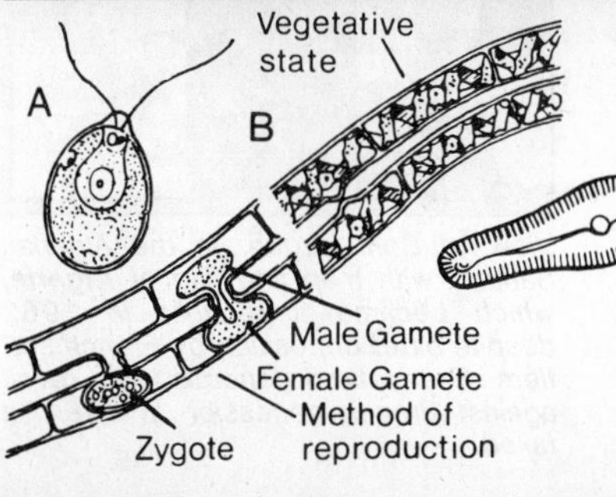

A
B
C
D
Vegetative state
Male Gamete
Female Gamete
Method of reproduction
Zygote

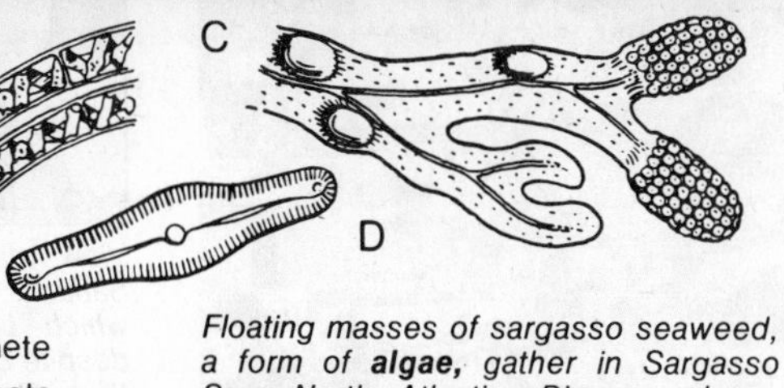

*Floating masses of sargasso seaweed, a form of **algae,** gather in Sargasso Sea, North Atlantic. Diagram shows (left) method of reproduction of algae and (right) vegetative state.*

Key: A = Chlamydomonas; B = Spirogyra; C = Bladderwrack; D = Diatom. Some marine algae are used in food, 'Irish moss' seaweed, for example, in blancmange and other puddings.

Al·ge·ri·a (ăljēr'ēa). Republic in N. Africa; under French rule until 1962; capital, Algiers. **Al·ge'·ri·an** *adj.* & *n.*

Al·giers (ăljērz'). City and port on the Mediterranean; capital of Algeria.

ALGOL (ăl'gŏl) *n.* International algebraic language for use in programming computers. [*algo*rithmic *l*anguage]

Al·gon·qui·an (ălgŏng'kēan, -kwēan) *n.* (pl. **-ans**, collect. **-an**) & *adj.* (One) of a group of languages spoken by N. Amer. Indians from Labrador to the Carolinas and west to the Mississippi; Algonquin.

Al·gon·quin (ălgŏng'kĭn,-kwĭn) *n.* (pl. **-quins**, collect. **-quin**) & *adj.* (Member) of a group of Algonquian-speaking N. Amer. Indian tribes; Algonquian.

al·go·rism (ăl'gerĭzem) *n.* Arabic system of notation. [med. L. *algorismus*, f. Arab. *al-Khowarazmi* the man of Khiva, surname of a 9th-c. Muslim mathematician]

al·go·rithm (ăl'gerĭdhem) *n.* 1. = ALGORISM. 2. Process or rules, usu. expressed algebraically, for (esp. machine) calculation etc. **al·go·rith·mic** (ălgerĭdh'mĭk) *adj.*

Al·ham·bra (ălhăm'bra). Palace of the Moorish kings at Granada, built in 13th c. [Arab. *al* the *hamra'* red: thought to refer to the color of the bricks or the name of the founder]

A·li (ah'lē, ahlē'). Cousin and son-in-law of Muhammad; regarded by some Muslims as the first caliph, his three predecessors being considered interlopers.

a·li·as (ā'lēas) *n.* (pl.**-as·es**). Assumed name, esp. of criminal. ~ *adv.* Otherwise named; called as assumed name.

A·li Ba·ba (ah'lē bah'ba, ăl'ē băb'a). Hero of a story supposed to be from the *Arabian Nights*; discovered the magic formula ("Open Sesame!") which opened the cave in which 40 robbers kept the treasures they had accumulated.

al·i·bi (ăl'ibī) *n.* (pl. **-bis**). Defense by an accused person that when an act allegedly took place he or she was elsewhere; (colloq.) excuse. ~ *v.* (colloq.) Make an excuse.

al·i·dade (ăl'ĭdād) *n.* Movable arm of quadrant etc. carrying the sights and indicating degrees cut off on the arc. [Arab. *al-'idada* the revolving radius (upper arm)]

al·ien (āl'yen, ā'lēen) *adj.* Not one's own; foreign; differing in nature (*from*); repugnant (*to*). ~ *n.* Person born in, citizen of, a country other than the one he or she lives in; foreigner, stranger. **al'ien·a·ble** *adj.* Capable of being sold. **al·ien·a·bil·i·ty** (ālyenabĭl'ĭtē, ālēena-) *n.*

al·ien·ate (āl'yenāt, ā'lēe-) *v.t.* (**-at·ed, -at·ing**). Estrange, (law) transfer ownership of; divert (*from*). **al·ien·a·tion** (ālyenā'shon, ālēe-) *n.* Estrangement; (law) transference of ownership; diversion to different purpose.

A·li·ghie·ri (ălĭgyār'ē): see DANTE.

a·light[1] (alīt') *v.i.* (**a·light·ed, a·lit** pr. alĭt', **a·light·ing**). Dismount, descend (*from*); settle, come to earth (from the air).

a·light[2] (alīt') *pred. adj.* Kindled, on fire, lighted up.

a·lign (alīn') *v.* Place, lay, in a line; bring into line; form a line; ally (oneself) *with* a cause, group, side, etc. **a·lign'ment** *n.* Act of aligning; formation in a straight line.

a·like (alīk') *adj.* Similar, like. ~ *adv.* In like manner.

al·i·ment (ăl'iment) *n.* Food; mental sustenance. **al·i·men·tal** (ălimĕn'tal) *adj.* **al·i·men'tal·ly** *adv.*

al·i·men·ta·ry (ălimĕn'terē, -trē) *adj.* Nourishing; performing functions of nutrition; providing maintenance; ~ **canal**, channel in animal body through which food passes, including whole length from mouth through the intestines to the anus.

al·i·men·ta·tion (ălimĕntā'shon) *n.* Nourishment; maintenance.

al·i·mo·ny (ăl'imōnē) *n.* Maintenance allowance made to divorced person by (former) spouse after legal separation or divorce.

al·i·phat·ic (ălifăt'ĭk) *adj.* (chem.) Fatty; belonging to the group of organic compounds in which the carbon atoms are linked in open chains as opposed to rings.

al·i·quot (ăl'ikwŏt, -kwot) *adj.* & *n.* (math.) (Part) contained by the whole an integral number of times, thus, 6 is an aliquot part of 18.

a·lit (alĭt') *v.i.* past t. and past part. of ALIGHT.[1]

a·live (alīv') *pred. adj.* Living; active, brisk; fully susceptible *to*; swarming *with*.

al·ka·li (ăl'kalī) *n.* (pl. **-lies, -lis**). (chem.) Any of a number of substances having strongly basic properties and including the carbonates and hydroxides of the alkali metals of ammonium and the hydroxides of some other reactive metals; ~ **metal**, any of a group of highly reactive metallic elements including lithium, sodium, and potassium. **al·ka·line** (ăl'kalĭn,

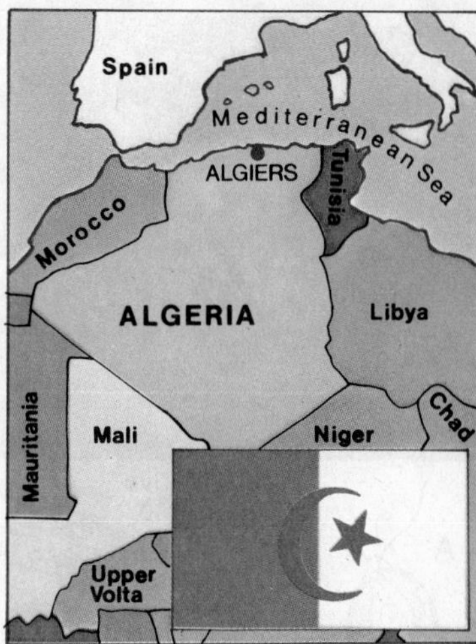

View of Beni Izzgen, in the Algerian Sahara, with map and flag of ***Algeria,*** *which became a republic in 1962 despite bitter opposition by French settlers. Four retired generals led a revolt against French secession in 1961: it failed.*

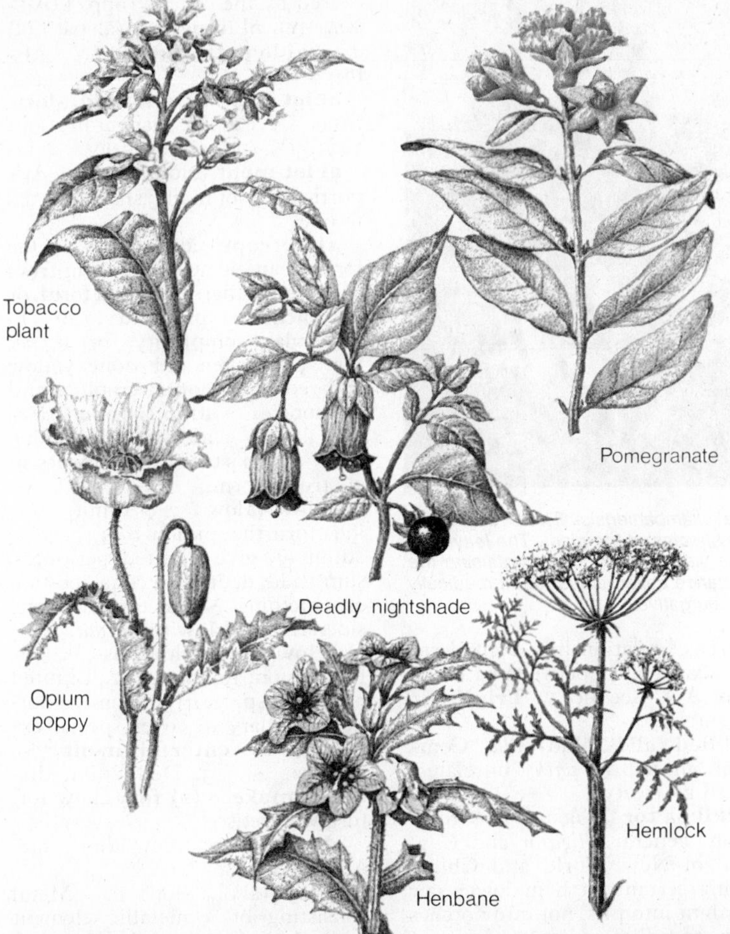

Morphine, quinine, nicotine, cocaine and strychnine are ***alkaloids,*** *complex compounds in plants that may affect men and animals physiologically. Alkaline plants illustrated are: Tobacco plant, pomegranate, deadly nightshade, opium poppy, henbane and hemlock. The number of alkaloids identified is nearly 1,000.*

'Birth of Venus' by Botticelli (Uffizi, Florence), is an example of what may be termed ***allegorical*** *painting. Botticelli (1444–1510) was one of the greatest Renaissance painters.*

-lĭn) *adj.* **al·ka·lin·i·ty** (ălk*a*lĭn′ĭtē) *n.* [Arab. *al* the, *qily* cinders, lye]

al·ka·loid (ăl′k*a*loid) *n.* Any of a large group of nitrogenous organic substances of vegetable origin having basic or alkaline properties, many, as morphine, strychnine, cocaine, etc., being used as drugs.

al·kane (ăl′kān) *n.* Any member of the paraffin series of hydrocarbons.

al·kene (ăl′kēn) *n.* Any member of the ethylene series of hydrocarbons; olefin.

al·kyl (ăl′k*i*l) *adj.* Derived from, or related to, the paraffin series of hydrocarbons; ~ **radical**, any of the series of radicals derived from paraffin hydrocarbons by removal of a hydrogen atom, e.g. methyl (CH_3), ethyl (C_2H_5).

all (awl) *adj.* Entire, every, any; the greatest possible; the entire number of; ~**-American**, *adj.* of Americans only; typically American; chosen as best in any U.S. sport; *n.* all-American player; **all but**, nearly; **all clear**, signal giving information that there is no danger; esp., signal that hostile aircraft have left the neighborhood; **All Fools' Day** = APRIL Fools' Day: **All Hallows**, (archaic) All Saints' Day; **All Saints' Day**, Nov. 1, day on which there is a general celebration of all Christian saints; **All Souls' Day**, Nov. 2, day on which Roman Catholics and some Anglicans offer prayers for the souls of all the faithful deceased; **all-star**, made up of star performers; **all-time**, (colloq.) (of records) hitherto unsurpassed; of all time; **all** *n.* All people; the whole, every one, everything; **at** ~, in any way; in any degree; of any kind; ~ **one**, just the same. **all** *adv.* Wholly, quite; ~ **in**, (colloq.) quite exhausted; ~ **in** ~, taken as a whole; of supreme importance; ~ **out**, using or involving all resources; fully extended; at top speed; **allover**, (colloq.) finished; everywhere; in characteristic behavior; **all right**, safe and sound, in good state; satisfactorily; (as sentence) I consent; all is well; **all-around**, *adj.* having ability and skill of all kinds, esp. in a game; **all there**, (colloq.) having all one's wits about one; **all the same**, in spite of this, notwithstanding.

Al·lah (ăl′*a*, ah′l*a*). Muslim name of God. [Arab., f. *al* the, *ilah* god, cf. Heb. *eloah*]

Al·lah·a·bad (ăl*a*h*a*băd′, ahl*a*h*a*bahd′). Indian city at the confluence of the Jumna with the Ganges; capital of Uttar Pradesh; a place of Hindu pilgrimage.

al·lay (*a*lā′) *v.t.* Put down, repress; alleviate; diminish.

al·le·ga·tion (ălĭgā′sh*o*n) *n.* Alleging; assertion (esp. one not proved).

al·lege (*a*lĕj′) *v.t.* (**-leged, -leg·ing**). Assert; affirm, advance as argument or excuse.

Al·le·ghe·ny (ăl*e*gā′nē) **Mountains** (also **Al·le·ghe′nies**). Ranges of the Appalachian system in eastern U.S. **Allegheny River,** river flowing S. through Pennsylvania; it unites with the Monongahela at Pittsburgh to form the Ohio River.

al·le·giance (*a*lē′j*a*ns) *n.* Loyalty of citizen to government or sovereign; devotion to group or cause.

al·le·go·rize (ăl′egerīz) *v.* (**-rized, -riz·ing**). Treat as an allegory, make allegories.

al·le·go·ry (ăl′egōrē, -gōrē) *n.* (pl. **-ries**). Narrative description of subject under guise of another suggestively similar; figurative story. **al·le·gor·ic** (ălegōr′ĭk, -gār′-), **al·le·gor′i·cal** *adjs.* **al·le·gor′i·cal·ly** *adv.*

al·le·gret·to (ălegrĕt′ō, ahle-) *adv.*, *adj.*, & *n.* (pl. **-tos**). (mus.) (Passage or movement played) somewhat briskly. [It.]

al·le·gro (alĕg′rō, alā′grō) *adj.*, *adv.*, & *n.* (pl. **-gros**). (mus.) Lively, gay (passage or movement), in brisk time. [It.]

al·lele (alēl′), **a·le·lo·morph** (alē′lomōrf, alĕl′e-) *ns.* Gene that occupies the same relative position on homologous chromosomes.

al·le·lu·ia (ălelōō′ya) = HALLELUJAH.

Al·len (ăl′en), **Ethan** (1738–89). American Revolutionary War hero and commander of the Green Mountain Boys of Vermont.

al·ler·gen (ăl′erjĕn) *n.* Substance causing allergic reaction; **al·ler·gen′ic** *adj.*

al·ler·gist (ăl′erjĭst) *n.* Physician who specializes in the treatment of allergies.

al·ler·gy (ăl′erjē) *n.* (pl. **-gies**). Hypersensitivity of body tissues esp. to the action of some particular foreign material, as certain foods, pollens, microorganisms, etc.; (fig.) antipathy; **al·ler·gic** (alēr′jĭk) *adj.* Of, possessing, allergy; susceptible *to* (also fig.).

al·le·vi·ate (alē′vēāt) *v.t.* (**-at·ed, -at·ing**). Make less burdensome or severe. **al·le·vi·a·tion** (alēvēā′shon) *n.* **al·le·vi·a·tive** (alē′vēātĭv, -atĭv), **al·le·vi·a·to·ry** (alē′ēatōrē, -tōrē) *adjs.*

al·ley (ăl′ē) *n.* (pl. **-leys**). Narrow street between or behind buildings; walk, path; also **al′leyway**; ~ **cat**, homeless city cat; **bowling** ~: see BOWLING; **up one's** ~, (slang) fitting one's interests or abilities.

al·li·ance (alī′ans) *n.* Act, state, of allying or being allied; union by

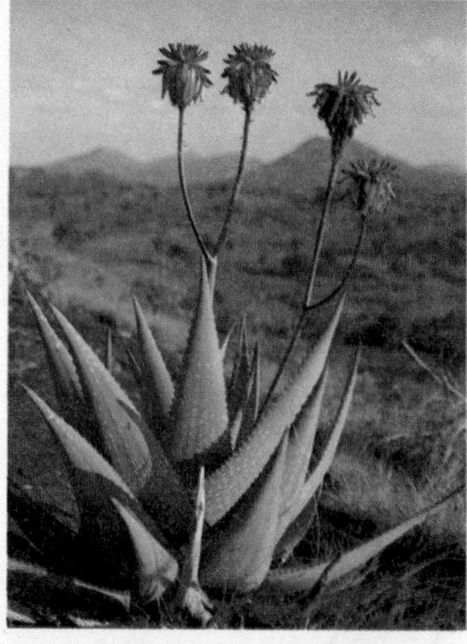

Aloe ukambaniensis. There are about 180 species of the plant. The leaves of some yield a bitter juice containing the substance called aloes, used medically as a purgative.

marriage; relationship; confederation, league (esp. between nations); **Holy A**~: see HOLY; **Triple** ~: see TRIPLE.

al·lied (alīd′, ăl′īd) *adj.* Combined, united (*to, with*), unrelated, linked by treaty.

al·li·ga·tor (ăl′igāter) *n.* Crocodilian (genera *Alligator* and *Cayman*) of New World and China, having certain teeth in lower jaw which fit into pits, not into notches as in crocodiles proper; ~ **pear** = AVOCADO. [Span. *el lagarto*, f. L. *lacerta* lizard]

al·lit·er·a·tion (alĭterā′shon) *n.* Commencement of two or more words in close connection with the same letter or sound, esp. as a device in verse. **al·lit·er·ate** (alĭt′erāt) *v.i.* (**-at·ed, -at·ing**). (Contain words that) begin with the same sound. **al·lit·er·a·tive** (alĭt′erātĭv, -atĭv) *adj.* **al·lit′er·a·tive·ly** *adv.*

al·lo·cate (ăl′okāt) *v.t.* (**-cat·ed, -cat·ing**). Assign (*to*). **al·lo·ca·tion** (ălokā′shon) *n.* Apportionment.

al·lop·a·thy (alŏp′athē) *n.* Traditional medical practice that aims at curing disease by remedies having opposite effect to that caused by the disease (opp. HOMEOPATHY). **al·lo·path·ic** (ălopăth′ĭk) *adj.* **al·lo·path′i·cal·ly** *adv.* **al·lop′a·thist** *n.*

al·lot (alŏt′) *v.t.* (**-lot·ted, -lot·ting**). Give as due share or portion; assign for special purpose.

al·lot·ment (alŏt′ment) *n.* Apportioning; lot in life; share allotted to one.

al·lo·trope (ăl′otrōp) *n.* One form of an element, differing from another or others in crystal form, or in chemical properties, or in molecular complexity, or in all three (as oxygen and ozone; yellow and red phosphorus; graphite and diamond). **al·lo·trop·ic** (ălotrŏp′ĭk) *adj.* **al·lot·ro·py** (alŏt′ropē) *n.* Existence of elements in allotropic form.

al·low (alow′) *v.* Admit; (colloq.) form the opinion (*that*); permit; admit *of*; give (limited periodical sum); add, deduct, in consideration of something; ~ **for**, take into consideration. **al·low′a·ble** *adj.*

al·low·ance (alow′ans) *n.* 1. Permission; tolerance. 2. Limited portion, esp. yearly income; addition to salary to cover special expenses, as **entertainment** ~, overseas ~. 3. Deduction, discount; **make** ~**(s) for**, allow for, forgive, excuse.

al·low·ed·ly (alow′ĭdlē) *adv.* Admittedly.

al·loy (ăl′oi, aloi′) *n.* Metal consisting of a metallic element with admixture of another metal or nonmetals, usu. having more useful properties than its constituents (e.g. brass is an alloy of copper and zinc). ~ (aloi′) *v.t.* 1. Form an alloy (of). 2. Debase.

all·spice (awl′spīs) *n.* Berry of *Pimenta officinalis*, supposed to combine flavor of cinnamon, nutmeg, and cloves.

al·lude (alōōd′) *v.i.* (**-lud·ed, -lud·ing**). Make indirect or passing reference *to*.

al·lure (aloor′) *v.t.* (**-lured, -lur·ing**). Tempt, entice; fasci-

Swamps, rivers and lakes of the tropics and sub-tropics are habitat of the ***alligator.*** *Alligator mississippiensis (U.S.A.) averages 10 ft. in length; the Chinese species averages 5 ft.*

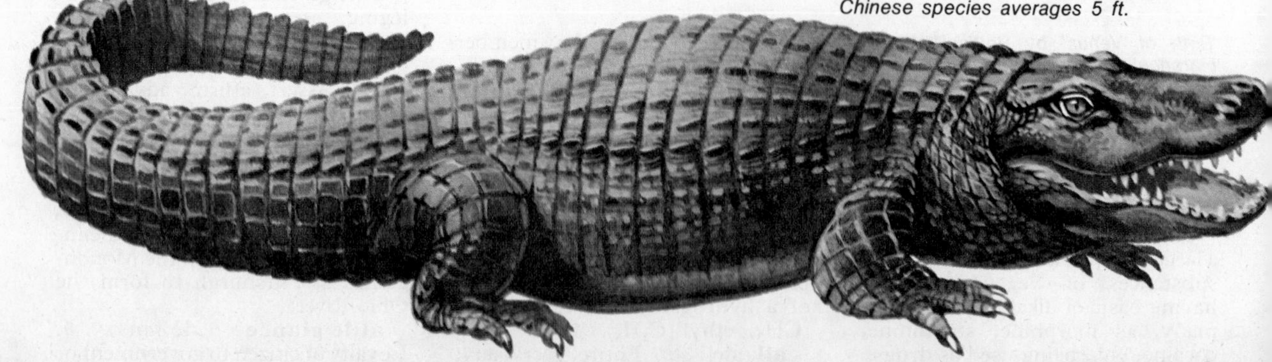

*An **almond** orchard in springtime. There are two types of nut. The sweet variety is edible and used in confectionery or for its oil; the bitter almond is processed for flavoring extracts.*

nate, charm. ~ *n.* Personal charm. **al·lure′ment** *n.*

al·lu·sion (*a*lo͞o′zh*o*n) *n.* Indirect or passing reference.

al·lu·sive (*a*lo͞o′sĭv) *adj.* Containing an allusion, full of allusions. **al·lu′sive·ly** *adv.* **al·lu′sive·ness** *n.*

al·lu·vi·on (*a*lo͞o′vē*o*n) *n.* Wash of sea against shore or of river against banks; flood; (esp.) alluvium; (law) formation of new land by action of water.

al·lu·vi·um (*a*lo͞o′vē*u*m) *n.* (pl. **-vi·ums, -vi·a** pr. -vē*a*). Deposit of earth, sand, etc., left by flood esp. in river valleys and deltas. **al·lu′vi·al** *adj.* ~ **fan, cone**, deposit left by swift stream entering a valley or plain. **al·lu′vi·al·ly** *adv.*

al·ly (*a*lī′) *v.t.* (**-lied, -ly·ing**). Combine, unite, for special object. ~ (ăl′ī, *a*lī′) *n.* (pl. **-lies**). Person, nation, etc., allied with another; **the Allies**, U.S., France, Britain, Russia, etc., united against Central Powers in World War I, and against Axis Powers in World War II.

al·ma ma·ter (ăl′m*a* mah′t*e*r, ahl′-, mā′t*e*r). Title used in reference to one's university, college, or school. [L., = "fostering mother"]

al·ma·nac (awl′m*a*năk) *n.* Annual publication with calendar of months and days, and with astronomical and other data.

Al·me·rí·a (ahlmĕrē′ah). Seaport in SE. Spain on the Mediterranean.

al·might·y (awlmī′tē) *adj.* All-powerful; **the A**~, God.

al·mond (ah′m*o*nd, ăm′-) *n.* Kernel or stone of two varieties of *Prunus amygdalus* (**sweet, bitter** ~), allied to plum and peach; the tree; anything almond-shaped.

al·most (awl′mōst, awlmōst′) *adv.* Very nearly.

alms (ahmz) *n.* (sing. or pl.). Charitable relief of the poor; donation; **alms′house** (chiefly Brit.), institution founded by charity for reception of poor, usu. old, people; **alms′man**, one supported by alms.

al·oe (ăl′ō) *n.* Liliaceous plant of genus *A*~, with erect spikes of flowers, rosettes of fleshy leaves (often spiny), and bitter juice; (pl.) purgative drug procured from juice of aloes. **al·o·et·ic** (ălōĕt′ik) *adj.* (med.) Containing aloes.

a·loft (*a*lawft′, *a*lŏft′) *adv.* & *adj.* High up; upward; in the air; esp. in(to) the upper parts of a ship's rigging.

a·lo·ha (*a*lō′*a*, ahlō′hah) *int.* & *n.* Greetings; farewell; love; friendship. [Hawaiian]

a·lone (*a*lōn′) *pred. adj.* Not with others, solitary. ~ *adv.* Only, exclusively.

a·long (*a*lawng′) *prep.* From end to end of, through any part of the length of; **along′side**, close to the side of (ship, car, etc.); **alongside of**, side by side with. **along** *adv.* In company or conjunction *with*; **all** ~, all the time; **be** ~, (colloq.) arrive.

a·loof (*a*lo͞of′) *adv.* & *adj.* Away, apart; reserved, indifferent.

al·o·pe·ci·a (ălopē′shē*a*, -sh*a*) *n.* (med.) Baldness. [Gk. *alopekia* fox mange f. *alopex* fox]

a·loud (*a*lowd′) *adv.* Audibly, not in a whisper; (archaic) loudly.

alp (ălp) *n.* Mountain peak; a high mountain, esp. in the Alps.

al·pa·ca (ălpăk′*a*) *n.* S. Amer. domesticated camel-like hoofed mammal, bred in Andes for its long woolly hair; its fleece; fabric of alpaca hair mixed with cotton; any of various silk, cotton or rayon fabrics more or less resembling this. [Arab *al* the, Peruvian name *paco*]

al·pen·horn (ăl′p*e*nhōrn) *n.* Long wooden horn used by Swiss herdsmen.

al·pen·stock (ăl′p*e*nstŏk) *n.* Staff with iron point used in mountain climbing.

al·pha (ăl′f*a*) *n.* First letter of Greek alphabet (Α, α), corresponding to *a*, used in enumerations etc.; (astron.) chief or brightest star of constellation; ~ **and omega**, first and last letters of Greek alphabet; hence, beginning and end (Rev. I); ~ **particles, rays**, first of three types of radiation emitted by radioactive substances, consisting of positively charged particles.

al·pha·bet (ăl′f*a*bĕt) *n.* Set of letters (in customary order) used in a language; first rudiments; symbols representing speech sounds (**phonetic** ~); ~ **soup**, broth containing small noodles shaped like

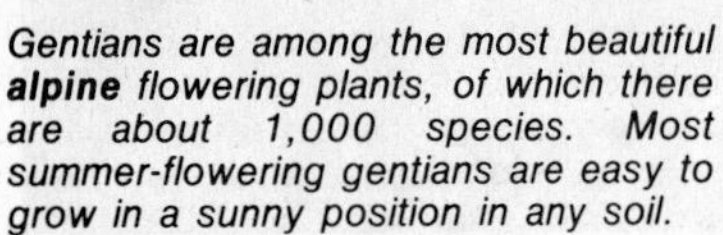

Gentians are among the most beautiful ***alpine*** *flowering plants, of which there are about 1,000 species. Most summer-flowering gentians are easy to grow in a sunny position in any soil.*

Petit France in Strasbourg, made capital of ***Alsace*** *when the French occupied it in 1681. Alsace-Lorraine went to Germany in 1871, to France 1919, Germany 1940, France 1946.*

letters; (*joc.*) profusion of alphabetic and acronymic government agencies; **deaf-and-dumb** ~: see DEAF. **al·pha·bet·i·cal** (ălf*a*bĕt′ĭk*a*l) *adj.* Of the alphabet; esp. in ~ **order. al·pha·bet′i·cal·ly** *adv.* [Gk. *alpha, beta,* first two letters of alphabet]

al·pha·bet·ize (ăl′f*a*betīz) *v.t.* (**-ized, -iz·ing**). Arrange in alphabetical order.

al·pha·nu·mer·ic (ălf*a*nōōmĕr′ĭk, -nū-) *adj.* Consisting of letters, numbers, and other symbols for computer work.

al·pine (ăl′pīn) *adj.* Of the Alps or other lofty mountains; (geol.) of a European episode of mountain formation during the Tertiary era; ~ **plant**, plant native to these regions, or (loosely) to mountain districts, or suited to similar conditions. **al·pin·ist** (ăl′pĭnĭst) *n.* Alpine climber.

Alps (ălps). Mountain range extending from Ligurian Sea and Rhône valley through Switzerland to the western Hungarian plain.

al·ready (awlrĕd′ē) *adv.* Beforehand; by this time, thus early.

Al·sace (ăl′săs, ălsăs′, -săs′). French province W. of the Rhine; annexed with part of Lorraine (the annexed territory was known as Alsace-Lorraine) by Germany after the Franco-Prussian war of 1870; restored to France after the 1914–18 war.

Al·sa·tia (ălsā′sh*a*). Old name of Alsace. **Al·sa′tian** *adj* & *n.* (Native, inhabitant) of Alsace; (Brit.) German shepherd dog.

al·so (awl′sō) *adv.* In addition to; ~**-ran**, horse not among first three in a race; (fig.) person etc. not distinguished in contest.

alt (ălt) *n.* (mus.) High note; **in** ~, in the octave (beginning with G) above the treble stave.

alt. *abbrev.* Altitude.

Al·tai (ăl′tī, ahl′-) **Mountains.** A major mountain system of central Asia, in the Soviet Union, Mongolia and China.

Al·ta·ic (ăltā′ĭk) *adj.* & *n.* (Of) a family of languages comprising Turkish, Mongol, and Tungus.

Al·ta·mi·ra (ălt*a*mēr′*a*). A cave in N. Spain famous for prehistoric paintings.

al·tar (awl′t*e*r) *n.* Flat-topped block for offerings to deity; Communion table; **lead to the** ~, marry (a woman); ~ **boy**, acolyte; ~ **cloth**, linen cloth used at Communion or Mass; silk frontal and super frontal; **al′tarpiece**, painting or sculpture above back of altar.

al·ter (awl′t*e*r) *v.* Change in size, appearance, character, etc.; castrate or spay. **al·ter·a·tion** (awlt*e*rā′sh*o*n) *n.*

al·ter·cate (awl′t*e*rkāt) *v.i.* (**-cat·ed, -cat·ing**). Dispute hotly, wrangle. **al·ter·ca·tion** (awlt*e*rkā′sh*o*n) *n.*

al·ter e·go (awl′t*e*r ē′gō, ĕg′ō). One's other self, intimate friend. [L.]

al·ter·nate (awl′t*e*rnĭt, ăl′-) *adj.* (of things of two kinds) Coming each after one of the other kind; placed on alternate sides (of line, stem, etc.). ~ *n.* Deputy, substitute. **al′ter·nate·ly** *adv.* **al·ter·nate** (awl′t*e*rnāt, ăl′-) *v.* (**-nat·ed, -nat·ing**). Arrange, perform, alternately; interchange (one thing) alternately *with*, by another; succeed each other by turns; consist of alternate things; **al′ternating current**, (abbrev. A.C. or a.c.) electric current reversing its direction at regular intervals. **al·ter·na·tion** (awlt*e*rnā′sh*o*n, ăl-) *n.*

al·ter·na·tive (awltēr′n*a*tĭv, ăl-) *adj.* Available in place of another (thing); (of two things) mutually exclusive. ~ *n.* Permission to choose between two things; either of two possible courses; one of more than two possibilities. **al·ter′na·tive·ly** *adv.*

al·ter·na·tor (awl′t*e*rnāt*e*r, ăl′-) *n.* Generator producing alternating current.

al·tho (awldhō′) = ALTHOUGH.

alt·horn (ălt′hōrn), **alto horn** *ns.* Alto saxhorn, brass wind instrument like the French horn.

al·though (awldhō′) *conj.* Though.

al·tim·e·ter (ăltĭm′ĭt*e*r, ăl′tĭmēt*e*r) *n.* Aneroid barometer indicating altitude reached, as in aviation.

al·ti·tude (ăl′tĭtōōd, -tūd) *n.* 1. Height. 2. (geom.) Length of perpendicular from vertex to base. 3. (geog.) Height above mean sea level. 4. (astron., of heavenly body) Angular distance above horizon. 5. High place, (fig.) eminence.

al·to (ăl′tō) *n.* (pl. **-tos**). Highest adult male voice; female voice of

Grandeur of the ***Alps.*** *The village of Les Praz nestles at the foot of Aiguille Rouge and La Flegere Mountains. The mountain system extends from the Gulf of Genoa in the west to Vienna in the east.*

similar range, contralto; singer with alto voice; musical part for this. ~ *adj.* (of instrument) Tenor.

al·to·cu·mu·lus (ăltōkū′my*ulus*) *n.* (meteor.) Type of cloud, of medium height, in form of thin patches often very close together or almost joined.

al·to·geth·er (awlt*o*gĕdh′*er*, awl′t*o*gĕdh*er*) *adv.* Totally; on the whole. ~ *n.* **in the** ~, completely naked.

al·to·stra·tus (ăltōstrā′t*us*) *n.* (meteor.) Continuous veil of cloud, thin or thick, of medium height.

al·tru·ism (ăl′trooĭz*e*m) *n.* Unselfish concern for others as a principle of action. **al·tru·is′tic** *adj.* **al·tru·is′ti·cal·ly** *adv.*

al·um (ăl′*u*m) *n.* One of series of double sulfates, esp. that of potassium and aluminum, used industrially, esp. in paper-making and leather tanning, and medically, as astringent and styptic.

a·lu·mi·na (*a*loo′m*ina*) *n.* Aluminum oxide (Al_2O_3), which occurs as ruby, sapphire, etc., and as bauxite from which aluminum is obtained. **a·lu·mi·nate** (*a*loo′m*i*nāt) *n.* Compound of alumina with one of the stronger bases.

al·u·min·i·um (ăly*u*mĭn′ē*u*m) (Brit.) = ALUMINUM.

a·lu·mi·nize (*a*loo′m*i*nīz) *v.t.* (**-nized, -niz·ing**). Coat with aluminum.

a·lu·mi·num (*a*loo′m*inu*m) *n.* (chem.) Light silvery white metallic element (symbol Al, at. no. 13, at. wt. 26.9815), not found naturally but widely distributed in the form of compounds, obtained by electrolysis and widely used esp. in alloys for construction of aircraft etc.

a·lum·na (*a*lŭm′n*a*) *n.* (pl. **-nae** pr. -nē). Female former student of a school or college.

a·lum·nus (*a*lŭm′n*us*) *n.* (pl. **-ni** pr. -nī). Male former student of a school or college. [L., = "foster child"]

al·ve·o·lar (ălvē′*oler*) *adj.* Of an alveolus; (of a consonant) pronounced with tongue tip behind upper teeth; ~ *n.* alveolar sound or consonant.

al·ve·o·late (ălvē′*o*lĭt, -lāt) *adj.* Honeycombed, pitted with small cavities.

al·ve·o·lus (ălvē′*olus*) *n.* (pl. **-li** pr. lī). Small cavity, socket of a tooth; terminal air sac of lung in which exchange of gases between lung and blood takes place; cell of honeycomb; conical chamber of belemnite.

al·ways (awl′wāz, -wĭz) *adv.* At all times, on all occasions, in all circumstances; forever, constantly.

am (ăm) *v.* First pers. sing. pres. indicative of BE.

A.M. *abbrev.* Master of Arts; amplitude modulation.

__Altocumulus__ (patchy) cloud over the Aspen Pass, Colorado. There are 10 main cloud groups, classified according to height (up to 45,000 ft.). Sighting aids weather forecasts.

Skyscrapers in Dallas, with __aluminum__ cladding. Aluminum was developed in 1855. Use of decorative aluminum sheeting on external walls became popular from the 1950s.

a.m. *abbrev. Anno mundi* (L., = in the year of the world); *ante meridiem* (L., = before noon).

Am·a·lek·ite (ăm′*a*lĕkīt, *a*măl′-ekīt) *adj.* & *n.* (Member) of a nomadic people descended from Esau (Gen. 36), proverbial for treachery.

a·mal·gam (*a*măl′g*a*m) *n.* Alloy of a metal or metals, with mercury, freq. plastic and used, e.g., in dentistry; (fig.) a mixture, combination.

a·mal·ga·mate (*a*măl′g*a*māt) *v.* (**-mat·ed, -mat·ing**). Combine, unite (esp. of business firms); mix; (of metals) alloy with mercury. **a·mal·ga·ma·tion** (*a*mălg*a*mā′-sh*o*n) *n.*

a·man·u·en·sis (*a*mănūĕn′sĭs) *n.* (pl. **-ses** pr. -sēz). One who writes from dictation, or copies; literary assistant.

am·a·ranth (ăm′*a*rănth) *n.* Imaginary unfading flower; plant of genus *Amaranthus*, as pigweed, tumbleweed, etc.; purple color. **am·a·ran·thine** (ăm*a*răn′thĭn, -thīn) *adj.* (poet.) Unfading; purple.

Am·a·ril·lo (ăm*a*rĭl′ō). Commercial and industrial city in NW. Texas.

am·a·ryl·lis (ăm*a*rĭl′ĭs) *n.*

Autumn-flowering bulbous plant of genus *A*~ comprising only one species, *A. belladonna* from Cape of Good Hope, also called belladonna lily. [Gk. *Amarullis* name of a country girl in Theocritus and Virgil]

a·mass (*a*măs′) *v.t.* Heap together; accumulate.

am·a·teur (ăm′*a*t*er*, -choor, -tūr, -ch*er*) *n.* One who engages in an activity, esp. an art or sport, for pleasure rather than financial benefit; inexperienced, unskillful person (freq. opp. *professional*). **am·a·teur′ish** *adj.* Like an amateur; imperfect in execution, unskillful. **am·a·teur′ish·ly** *adv.* **am·a·teur′ish·ness, am′a·teur·ism** *ns.*

A·ma·ti (ahmah′tē). Name of a family of violin makers of Cremona, flourishing *c*1550–*c*1700: **Nicola** ~ (1596–1684) taught Antonio Stradivari.

am·a·tive (ăm′*a*tĭv) *adj.* Disposed to loving. **am′a·tive·ness** *n.*

am·a·tory (ăm′*a*tōrē, -tōrē) *adj.* Pertaining to a lover, making love, or expressions of sexual love.

a·maze (*a*māz′) *v.t.* (**a·mazed, a·maz·ing**). Overwhelm with wonder. **a·maz′ed·ly, a·maz′ing·ly** *advs.* **a·maze′ment** *n.*

Am·a·zon[1] (ăm′*a*zŏn, -zon). (Gk. myth.) One of a race of female warriors alleged by Herodotus to exist in Scythia; hence, tall, strong, or athletic woman.

Am·a·zon[2] (ăm′*a*zŏn, -zon). Great river of S. America, flowing into the southern Atlantic on N. coast of Brazil; it was named because of a legend that a tribe of female warriors lived somewhere on its banks.

Am·a·zo·ni·an (ăm*a*zō′nē*a*n) *adj.* Of the Amazons; of the Amazon River.

am·bas·sa·dor (ămbăs′*a*d*er*) *n.* Diplomatic official of the highest rank sent by one country to another as its representative. **am·bas·sa·do·ri·al** (ămbăs*a*dōr′ē*a*l -dōr′-) *adj.* **am·bas·sa·dress** (ămbăs′*a*drĭs) *n.* Female ambassador; ambassador's wife.

am·ber (ăm′b*er*) *n.* & *adj.* (Made of, colored like) yellow translucent fossil resin found chiefly on S. shore of Baltic and valued as ornament. **am·ber·jack** (ăm′b*er*jăk) *n.* Any of several large food and game marine fishes of genus *Seriola*. [Fr. *ambre*, f. Arab. *anbar ambergris*, to which the name originally belonged]

am·ber·gris (ăm′b*er*grĭs, -grēs) *n.* Waxlike gray or blackish substance found floating in tropical seas, and in intestines of sperm whale, odoriferous and used in perfumery. [Fr. *ambre gris* gray amber]

am·bi·dex·trous (ămbĭdek′-

*Course of the mighty **Amazon,** largest river in the world. For centuries a challenge to explorers, the river drains 40 per cent of South America, including a vast belt of tropical forest.*

str*u*s) *adj.* Able to use both hands equally well. **am·bi·dex′trous·ly** *adv.* **am·bi·dex′trous·ness** *n.*

am·bi·ent (ăm′bēent) *adj.* Surrounding. **am·bi·ence, am·bi·ance** (ăm′bēens, ahmbēahns′) *n.* Environment, surroundings; atmosphere.

am·big·u·ous (ămbĭg′ū*u*s) *adj.* Obscure; of double meaning; of doubtful classification. **am·big′u·ous·ly** *adv.* **am·big′u·ous·ness** *n.* **am·bi·gu·i·ty** (ămbĭgū′ĭtē) *n.* (pl. **-ties**). Double meaning; expression capable of more than one meaning.

am·bi·tion (ămbĭsh′*o*n) *n.* Ardent desire for distinction; aspiration *to* (be or do); object of such desire.

am·bi·tious (ămbĭsh′*u*s) *adj.* Full of or showing ambition; strongly desirous. **am·bi′tious·ly** *adv.* **am·bi′tious·ness** *n.* [L. *ambitio* canvassing for votes, f. *ambire* go round]

am·biv·a·lence (ămbiv′*a*l*e*ns) *n.* State of having either or both of two contrary values or qualities; coexistence in one person of contradictory emotions (as love and hatred) toward the same person or thing. **am·biv′a·lent** *adj.*

am·ble (ăm′b*e*l) *v.i.* (**-bled, -bling**). (of horse, etc.) Move by lifting two feet on one side together; walk at a leisurely pace. ~ *n.* Pace of an ambling horse; easy pace.

am·bly·o·pi·a (ămblēō′pē*a*) *n.* Dimness of vision without discernible change in the eye. **am·bly·op·ic** (ămblēŏp′ĭk) *adj.*

am·bro·sia (ămbrō′zh*a*) *n.* (myth.) Food of the gods; anything delightful to taste or smell; beebread. **am·bro′sial** *adj.* [L. f. Gk. f. *ambrotos* immortal]

am·bu·lance (ăm′by*u*l*a*ns) *n.* Vehicle for conveyance of sick or injured persons.

am·bu·lant (ăm′by*u*l*a*nt) *adj.* (med.) Walking, not confined to bed.

am·bu·la·to·ry (ăm′by*u*l*a*tōrē, -tōrē) *adj.* Pertaining to, adapted for, or capable of walking, movable; not permanent. ~ *n.* (pl. **-ries**). Place for walking; arcade, cloister; esp., aisle around apse at east end of church.

am·bus·cade (ămb*u*skād′) *n.* & *v.* (**-cad·ed, -cad·ing**). Ambush.

am·bush (ăm′bŏŏsh) *v.* & *n.* (Make) a surprise attack from concealment; (wait in) a concealed position.

a·meer (*a*mēr′) = EMIR.

a·mel·io·rate (*a*mēl′yerāt) *v.* (**-rat·ed, -rat·ing**). (Cause to) become better. **a·mel·io·ra·tion** (*a*mēlyerā′sh*o*n) *n.* **a·mel·io·ra·tive** (*a*mēl′yerātĭv; -*a*tĭv) *adj.*

A·men (ah′m*e*n). Supreme god of the ancient Egyptians in the Theban religion, represented as a man with a ram's head; his worship spread to Greece, where he was identified with Zeus, and to Rome, where he was known as Jupiter Ammon.

a·men (ā′mĕn′, ah′-) *int.* So be it (used at end of prayer etc.). ~ *n.* Utterance of "amen"; expression of assent. [Heb. *āmēn* certainly, truly]

a·me·na·ble (*a*mē′n*a*bel, *a*mĕn′*a*-) *adj.* Responsive, willing to listen or yield; responsible, liable, or subject (*to*). **a·me′na·ble·ness, a·me·na·bil·i·ty** (*a*mēn*a*bĭl′ĭtē) *ns.* **a·me′na·bly** *adv.*

a·mend (*a*mĕnd′) *v.t.* Correct an error in (document), modify (measure before a legislature, proposal, etc.); make better, rectify.

a·mend·ment (*a*mĕnd′m*e*nt) *n.* Improvement; addition to or correction of a document, bill, or law.

a·mends (*a*mĕndz′) *n.* (sing. or pl.) Reparation, restitution, compensation.

A·men·ho·tep (ahm*e*nhō′tĕp, ăm′*e*n-). Name of four pharaohs of the 18th dynasty in Egypt; ~ **IV**: see AKHNATON.

a·men·i·ty (*a*mĕn′ĭtē) *n.* (pl. **-ties**). Quality of being pleasant, agreeable; (characteristic of) situation, climate, disposition, etc., that is agreeable or pleasant (often pl.); (in pl.) pleasant manners or features; agreeableness.

Am·e·no·phis (ăm*e*nō′fĭs) = AMENHOTEP.

a·men·or·rhe·a (āmĕn*o*rē′*a*) *n.* (physiol). Absence of menstruation.

am·ent (ăm′*e*nt, ā′m*e*nt) *n.* Catkin. **am·en·ta·ceous** (ăm*e*ntā′sh*u*s), **am·en·tif·er·ous** (ăm*e*ntĭf′*e*r*u*s) *adjs.*

Amer. *abbrev.* America, American.

A·mer·i·ca (*a*mĕr′ĭk*a*). Continent of the New World or western hemisphere, consisting of great land masses, **North** ~ and **South** ~, joined by the narrow isthmus of **Central** ~; N. America comprises Canada, the U.S., and Mexico; Central and S. America are divided into a number of independent nations. N. America was prob. visited by Norse seamen *c*1000 A.D., but for the modern world the continent was discovered by Christopher Columbus, who reached the W. Indies in 1492 and the S. American mainland in 1498. (See also UNITED STATES OF AMERICA.) [named after *Amerigo* VESPUCCI]

A·mer·i·can (*a*mĕr′ĭk*a*n) *adj.* Of the continents of N. or S. America or their people; of the United States or its people; ~ **Beauty**, a type of rose with purplish-red flowers; ~ **cheese**, a mild cheddar; ~ **eagle** = BALD eagle; ~ **English**, English spoken in the U.S., also called **American**; ~ **Expeditionary Forces**, abbreviated A.E.F., U.S. troops in Europe in World War I; ~ **Falls**, the section of Niagara Falls within the U.S.; ~ **Federation of Labor** (A.F.L.), a federation of U.S. labor unions founded in 1886, merged with the C.I.O. in 1955; ~ **Indian**: see INDIAN; ~ **Legion**, organization of veterans of U.S. armed forces, establ. 1919; ~ **plan**, (rate for) hotel room with inclusion of meals; ~ **Revolution,** ~ **War of Independence**, war (1775–83) between Great Britain and her colonies in N. America in which 13 colonies won independence and subsequently formed the U.S.; ~ **Samoa**, seven islands in the S. Pacific with a combined area of 76 square miles, a U.S. possession since 1951; capital, Pago Pago (see also SAMOA); ~ **Spanish**, Spanish as spoken in the Americas; ~ **Standard Version**, also called ~ **Revised Version**, a U.S. revision of the King James Bible, published in 1901. **American** *n.* 1. Citizen of the Americas. 2. Citizen of the U.S. 3. American English.

The bald eagle, Haliaetus leucocephalus, commonly known as the ***American Eagle,*** *has been the U.S. national emblem since 1782. It is the only eagle native solely to N. America.*

A·mer·i·ca·na (*a*mĕrĭkăn′*a*, -kah′n*a*) *n.* Books, memorabilia, etc., relating to America, esp. to U.S. history.

A·mer·i·can·ism (*a*mĕr′ĭk*a*nĭz*e*m) *n.* 1. Devotion to U.S. and its institutions. 2. Word or idiom characteristic of American English. 3. Something peculiar to U.S.

A·mer·i·can·ize (*a*mĕr′ĭk*a*nīz) *v.* (**-ized, -iz·ing**). Naturalize as an American; make, become American in character. **A·mer·i·can·i·za·tion** (*a*mĕrĭk*a*nĭzā′sh*o*n) *n.*

America's Cup. Yachting trophy orig. won by schooner *America* for race around Isle of Wight (1851); later offered as challenge trophy for international matches.

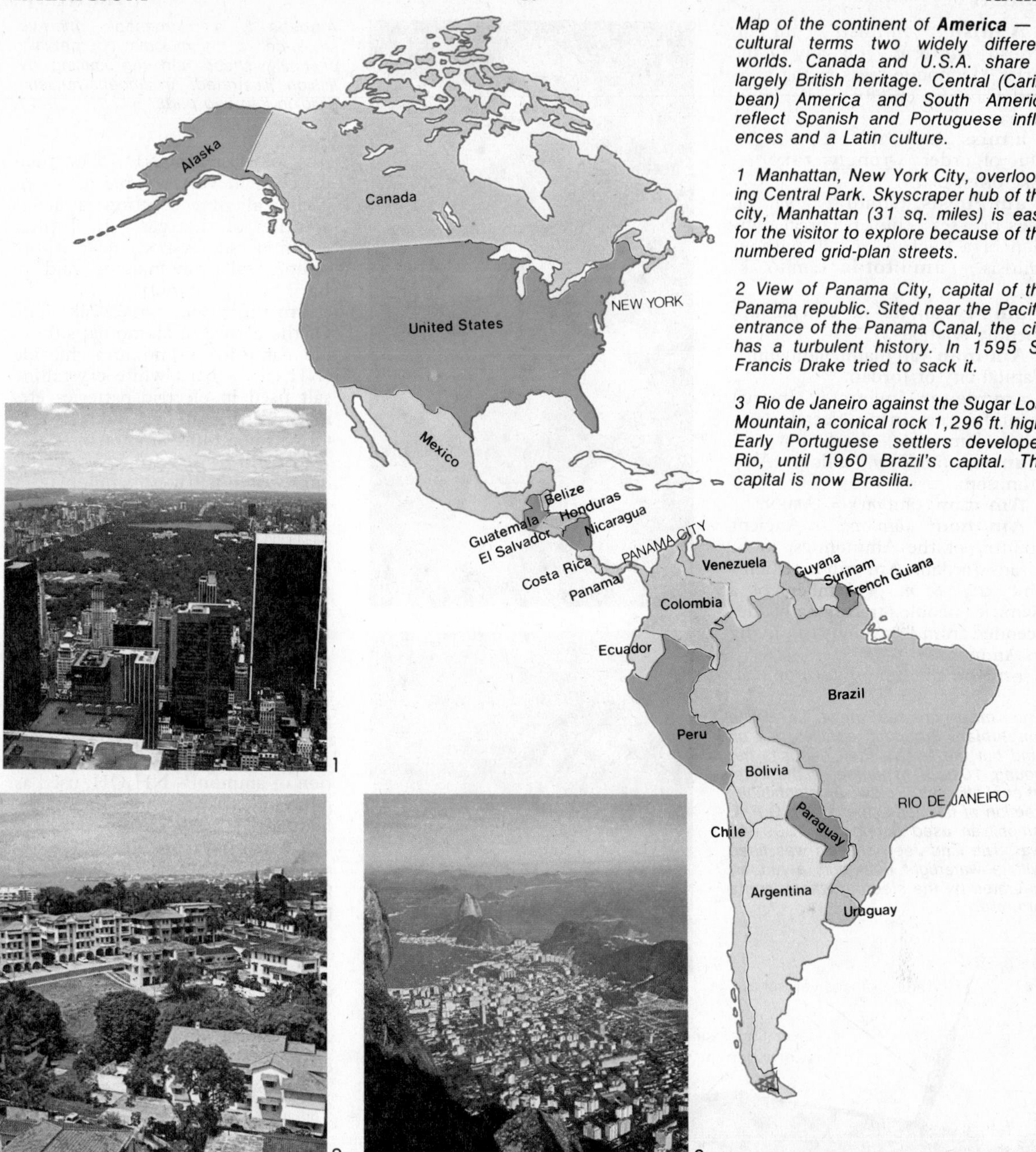

*Map of the continent of **America** — in cultural terms two widely different worlds. Canada and U.S.A. share a largely British heritage. Central (Caribbean) America and South America reflect Spanish and Portuguese influences and a Latin culture.*

1 Manhattan, New York City, overlooking Central Park. Skyscraper hub of the city, Manhattan (31 sq. miles) is easy for the visitor to explore because of the numbered grid-plan streets.

2 View of Panama City, capital of the Panama republic. Sited near the Pacific entrance of the Panama Canal, the city has a turbulent history. In 1595 Sir Francis Drake tried to sack it.

3 Rio de Janeiro against the Sugar Loaf Mountain, a conical rock 1,296 ft. high. Early Portuguese settlers developed Rio, until 1960 Brazil's capital. The capital is now Brasilia.

am·er·i·ci·um (ămerĭsh´ēum) *n.* (chem.) Metallic radioactive element; symbol Am, at. no. 95, principal isotope at. wt. 241. [f. *America* (first made at Berkeley, California)]

Am·er·ind (ăm´erĭnd) *n.*, **Am·er·in·di·an** (ămerĭn´dēan) *adj.* & *n.* See INDIAN.

am·e·thyst (ăm´ĭthĭst) *n.* Purple or violet precious stone, a variety of quartz colored by manganese; purplish color. **am·e·thys·tine** (ămĭthĭs´tĭn, -tīn) *adj.* [Gk. *amethustos* not drunken (*methu* wine), because the stone was supposed to have the power of preventing intoxication]

Am·har·a (ahmhar´*a*). Former province of NW. Ethiopia, the dominant province from the 12th c.–19th c.

Am·har·ic (ămhăr´ĭk, ahmhar´-) *adj.* & *n.* (Of) the official language of Ethiopia, a Semitic language related to ancient Ethiopic.

a·mi·a·ble (ā´mēabel) *adj.* Friendly, good-natured. **a·mi·a·bil·i·ty** (āmēabĭl´ĭtē) *n.* **a´mi·a·bly** *adv.*

am·i·ca·ble (ăm´ĭkabel) *adj.* Friendly. **am·i·ca·bil·i·ty** (ămĭkabĭl´ĭtē) *n.* **am´i·ca·bly** *adv.*

a·mi·cus cu·ri·ae (amī´kus kūr´ēē) (pl. **a·mi·ci cu·ri·ae** pr. amī´kī). Disinterested adviser. [L., = "friend of the court"]

a·mid (amĭd´) *prep.* In the middle of; in the course of.

am·ide (ăm´īd, -ĭd) *n.* Compound formed from ammonia by replacement of one or more hydrogen atoms by a metal or acid radical.

a·mid·ships (amĭd´shĭps) *adv.* In or toward the middle part of a ship or aircraft.

a·midst (amĭdst´) *prep.* (poet.) Amid.

a·mine (amēn´, ăm´ĭn) *n.* (chem.) Compound derived from ammonia by replacing one or more of the hydrogen atoms by certain aliphatic or aromatic radicals.

a·mi·no (amē´nō, ăm´ĭnō) *adj.* (chem.) Pertaining to or containing the group NH_2; **~ acid**, any organic compound containing both an amino group and a carboxyl group; some are the building blocks of proteins.

amino- *prefix.* Containing an amino group.

a·mir (amēr´) = EMIR.

A·mish (ah'mĭsh, ăm'ĭsh, ā'mĭsh) *adj.* & *n.* (Of) any of the strict Mennonite sects in the U.S. and Canada, chiefly in Pennsylvania.

a·miss (*a*mĭs') *adv.* & *pred. adj.* Out of order; wrongly; **take ~**, take offense at.

am·i·to·sis (ămĭtō'sĭs) *n.* (pl. **-ses** pr. -sēz). (biol.) Direct division of a nucleus or cell without mitosis. **am·i·tot·ic** (ămĭtŏt'ĭk) *adj.*

am·i·ty (ăm'ĭtē) *n.* Friendship, friendly relations.

Am·man (ah'mahn, ahmahn'). Capital city of Jordan.

am·me·ter (ăm'ēt*e*r) *n.* Instrument for measuring electric currents. [am-(pere) + meter]

am·mo (ăm'ō) *n.* (colloq.) Ammunition.

Am·mon[1] (ăm'*o*n) = AMEN.

Am·mon[2] (ăm'*o*n). Ancient country of the Ammonites, in S. Trans-Jordan. **Am·mo·nite** (ăm'*o*nīt) *adj.* & *n.* (Member) of a Semitic people traditionally descended from Lot (Gen. 19), living in Ammon.

am·mo·nia (*a*mōn'y*a*, *a*mō'nē*a*) *n.* Colorless gas (NH_3) with pungent smell, very soluble in water, giving alkaline solution; aqueous solution of this gas. [f. Jupiter Ammon (see AMEN), near whose temple sal ammoniac is said to have been prepared]

am·mo·ni·ac (*a*mō'nēăk) *adj.* Of the nature of ammonia; **sal ~**, old name for ammonium chloride (NH_4Cl), a hard white crystalline salt used in electric batteries etc. **am·mo·ni·a·cal** (ăm*o*nī'*a*k*a*l) *adj.* Of or resembling ammonia.

am·mo·ni·at·ed (*a*mō'nēātĭd) *adj.* Combined with ammonia.

Am·mo·nite (ăm'*o*nīt): see AMMON[2].

am·mo·nite (ăm'*o*nīt) *n.* Member of an extinct group of cephalopods with chambered shell coiled in a flat spiral, freq. found fossilized in some Mesozoic rocks. [L. *cornu Ammonis* horn of AMMON[1]]

am·mo·ni·um (*a*mō'nē*u*m) *n.* (chem.) Radical (NH_4), whose compounds resemble those of the alkali metals; **~ chloride** = sal AMMONIAC; **~ hydroxide**, aqueous solution of ammonia, NH_4OH, used as household cleanser and in manufacturing.

am·mu·ni·tion (ămy*u*nĭsh'*o*n) *n.* Military stores (now only of projectiles with their necessary propellants, detonators, fuses, etc.); (fig.) facts, arguments, etc. used in attack or defense.

am·ne·sia (ămnē'zh*a*) *n.* Loss of memory.

am·nes·ty (ăm'nĭstē) *n.* (pl. **-ties**). General pardon, usu. to a group and often before trial, for

Ectoplasm
Endoplasm
Food vacuoles
Nucleus
Contractile vacuole

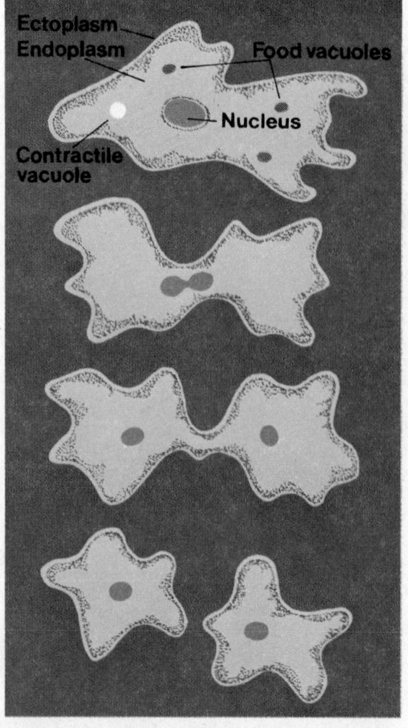

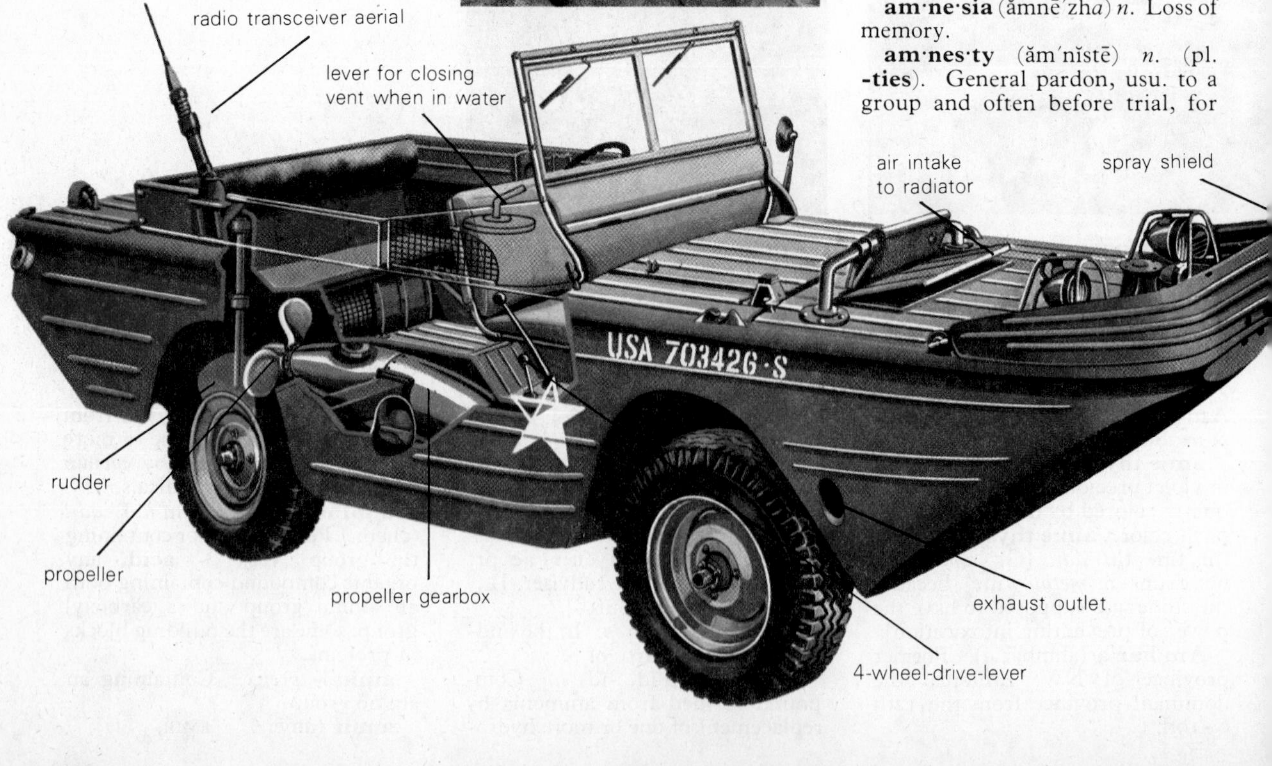

***Amoeba** is a microscopic primitive single-celled animalcule perpetually changing shape and reproducing by fission. Illustrated: An amoeba nucleus dividing into two parts.*

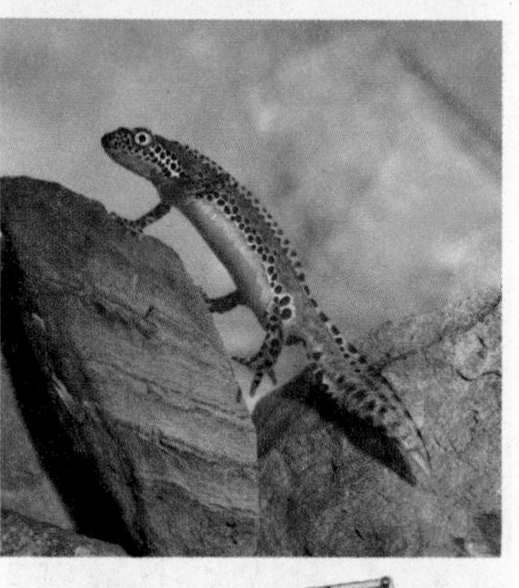

*The male crested newt, a tailed **amphibian.** European species pair on land but the female then deposits her young, 10 to 50 in number, in the water of cool streams. Below: An amphibious version of the Jeep, the ¼-ton G.P.A. Amphibian used during the 1939–45 war. The land Jeep chassis was fitted with a watertight boat hull, a rudder, operated by the steering wheel, and a propeller.*

radio transceiver aerial
lever for closing vent when in water
air intake to radiator
spray shield
USA 703426-S
rudder
propeller
propeller gearbox
exhaust outlet
4-wheel-drive-lever

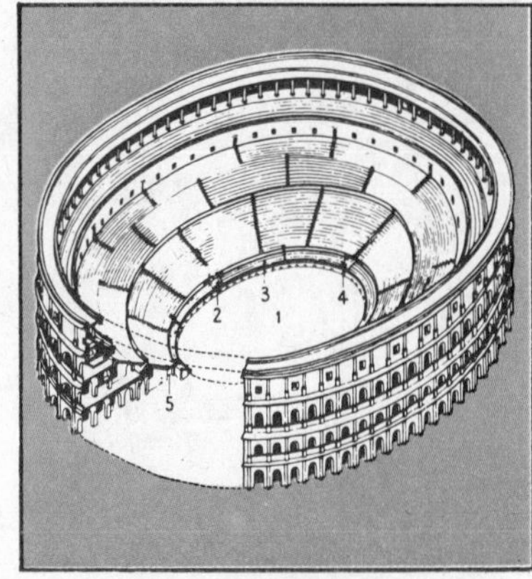

Above: A Roman ***amphitheater.*** *Key: 1. Arena. 2. Emperor's or consul's box. 3. Podium. 4. Animals' entrance. 5. Animals' dens. Left: General view of the Coliseum in Rome, so named because of its size. It was erected by the emperors Vespasian and Titus on the site of Nero's Golden House. The Coliseum could seat up to 50,000 people.*

offenses usu. political. ~ *v.t.* (**-tied, -ty·ing**). Give amnesty to.

am·ni·on (ăm'nēŏn, -*o*n) *n.* (pl. **-ni·ons, -ni·a** pr. -nē*a*). (zool., physiol.) Membrane enclosing embryo or fetus. **am·ni·ot·ic** (ămnēot'ĭk) *adj.* Of the amnion; ~ **fluid**, fluid filling amniotic sac; ~ **sac**, cavity enclosed by amnion.

a·moe·ba (*a*mē'b*a*) *n.* (pl. **-bas, -bae** pr. -bē). Single-celled protozoan, constantly changing shape, occurring in water and soil and as internal parasite. **a·moe'bic, a·moe'boid** *adjs.*

a·mok (*a*mŭk', *a*mŏk) = AMUCK.

a·mong (*a*mŭng'), **a·mongst** (*a*mŭngst') *preps.* In the assemblage or number of; surrounded by, within the limits of; by joint action of; between.

a·mon·til·la·do (*a*mŏnt*i*lah'dō) *n.* One of the principal types of dry sherry, with nutty flavor. [Span., = "made like (the wine of) *Montilla*" (place in Cordova)]

a·mor·al (āmŏr'*a*l, ă-, -măr'-) *adj.* Nonmoral; outside the sphere of morals.

Am·o·rite (ăm'*o*rīt) *adj.* & *n.* (Member) of an ancient Semitic people of the Middle East.

am·o·rous (ăm'*e*r*u*s) *adj.* Inclined to (esp. sexual) love; in love; of or pertaining to love. **am'o·rous·ly** *adv.* **am'o·rous·ness** *n.*

a·mor·phous (*a*mŏr'f*u*s) *adj.* Formless; indeterminate; (chem., min.) not crystalline. **a·mor'phism** *n.* **a·mor'phous·ly** *adv.* **a·mor'phous·ness** *n.*

am·or·tize (ăm'*e*rtīz, *a*mŏr'-) *v.t.* (**-tized, -tiz·ing**). Pay off (debt, mortgage) by periodic payments; gradually write off initial cost of (asset). **am·or·ti·za·tion** (ăm*e*rtĭzā'sh*o*n, *a*mŏr-) *n.*

A·mos (ā'm*o*s) (*c*760 B.C.). Hebrew minor prophet; book of Old Testament containing his prophecies.

a·mount (*a*mownt') *v.t.* Be equivalent *to*; add up *to*. ~ *n.* Total, quantity.

a·mour (*a*moor') *n.* Love affair, esp. an illicit one.

amp (ămp) = AMPERE.

am·pe·lop·sis (ămp*e*lŏp'sĭs) *n.* Climbing plant allied to vine, esp. Virginia creeper. [Gk., = "looking like a vine" (*ampelos* vine, *opsis* appearance)]

am·per·age (ăm'p*e*rĭj, ămpēr'-) *n.* Strength of current of electricity measured in amperes.

Am·père (ahṅpār'), **Andre-Marie** (1775–1836). French physicist and mathematician; established the relation between magnetism and electricity.

am·pere (ăm'pēr, ămpēr') *n.* Unit of electric current; the current produced by one volt acting through resistance of one ohm (abbreviation A). [f. AMPÈRE]

am·per·sand (ăm'p*e*rsănd, ămp*e*rsănd') *n.* The sign "&" (= *and*). [f. phrase "and *per se* (= by itself) and"]

am·phet·a·mine (ămfĕt'*a*mēn, -mĭn) *n.* Powerful synthetic drug that stimulates the heart and respiration, constricts blood vessels, and induces sleeplessness.

amphi-, amph- *prefixes.* Both, of both kinds, on both sides, around.

am·phib·i·an (ămfĭb'ē*a*n) *adj.* & *n.* 1. (Animal) living both on land and in water; (animal) of the Amphibia, a class of vertebrates intermediate between reptiles and fishes and including anurans and caecilians. 2. (*adj.*) Amphibious. [Gk. *amphibios* leading a double life]

am·phib·i·ous (ămfĭb'ē*u*s) *adj.* Living both on land and in water, connected with both; (airplane, car, tank, etc.) able to operate both on land and water; (mil.) involving both land and sea forces.

am·phi·brach (ăm'f*i*brăk) *n.* Metrical foot of three syllables, one long between two short, or one accented between two unaccented (⏑ – ⏑).

am·phip·ro·style (ămfĭp'r*o*stīl, -f*i*prō'-) *adj.* & *n.* (Building) with portico at both ends.

am·phis·bae·na (ămfĭsbē'n*a*) *n.* 1. Fabulous serpent with head at each end. 2. (zool.) Wormlike lizard of genus *A*~. [Gk. *amphis* both ways, *baino* go]

am·phi·the·a·ter, am·phi·the·a·tre (ăm'f*i*thē*a*t*e*r) *ns.* 1. Oval, circular, or semicircular building or arena with seats rising in tiers around a central open space; natural formation resembling this; (fig.) scene of a contest. 2. Room having tiers of seats arranged above a central area for students and others to listen to lectures and observe surgery etc.

Am·phi·tri·te (ămf*i*trī'tē). (Gk. myth.) Sea goddess, the wife of Poseidon.

Am·phit·ry·on (ămfĭt'rē*o*n). (Gk. myth.) Husband of Alcmene, while he was absent Zeus impersonated him and became the father of Hercules by Alcmene.

am·pho·ra (ăm'f*e*r*a*) *n.* (pl. **-rae** pr. -rē, **-ras**). Greek or Roman two-handled vase, esp. used to store wine, oil, etc.

am·ple (ăm´p*e*l) *adj.* (**-pler, -plest**). Spacious, extensive; abundant; quite enough. **am'ply** *adv.*

am·pli·fy (ăm´pl*i*fī) *v.* (**-fied, -fy·ing**). Enlarge; increase strength of (electric current, signal, etc.); add details. **am·pli·fi·ca·tion** (ămpl*i*fĭkā´sh*o*n) *n.* **am'pli·fi·er** *n.* (esp.) Appliance for increasing strength of electrical signals.

am·pli·tude (ăm´plĭtōōd, -tūd) *n.* 1. Breadth; abundance; wide range. 2. (astron.) Distance from due east or west at which celestial body rises or sets. 3. (phys.) Maximum displacement from mean position of vibrating body etc.; ~ **modulation**: see MODULATE.

am·pule, am·pul, am·poule (ăm´pūl) *ns.* (med.) Small sealed glass vessel used for storing sterilized materials prepared for injection.

am·pu·tate (ăm´py*u*tāt) *v.t.* (**-tat·ed, -tat·ing**). Cut off (esp. part of animal body). **am·pu·ta·tion** (ămpy*u*tā´sh*o*n) *n.*

am·pu·tee (ămpy*u*tē´) *n.* One who has lost limb etc. by amputation.

Am·ster·dam (ăm´st*e*rdăm). Capital of the Netherlands.

Am·trak (ăm´trăk) *n.* A U.S. national rail-passenger system.

a·muck (*a*mŭk´) *adv.* **run** ~, run about in murderous frenzy; get out of control. [Malay *amok*, rushing in frenzy]

am·u·let (ăm´y*u*lĭt) *n.* Thing worn as charm against evil.

A · mund · sen (ah´m*u*nds*e*n), **Roald** (1872–1928). Norwegian explorer; explored Northwest Passage 1903–6; reached S. Pole 1911.

A·mund·sen (ah´m*u*nds*e*n) **Sea.** Arm of the South Pacific Ocean, off the Antarctic coast W. of the Ross Sea.

A·mur (ahmoor´). River in NE. Asia rising in Mongolia, flowing to the Sea of Okhotsk, forming part of the Soviet-Chinese border.

a·muse (*a*mūz´) *v.t.* (**a·mused, a·mus·ing**). Cause laughter or smiles; be or find diversion or light occupation for; entertain. **a·mus·ing** *adj.* **a·mus'ing·ly** *adv.* **a·muse'ment** *n.* Pleasant diversion; excitement of laughter or smiles; pastime; ~ **park**, park with refreshments and merry-go-rounds, roller coasters, etc.

AMVETS (ăm´vĕts) *n.* Organization of U.S. veterans of World War II and Korean War.

Capital of the Netherlands, ***Amsterdam*** *'Venice of the North'. Some 50 miles of canals divide the city into 70 islands linked by 500 bridges. Highstep gables characterize old houses.*

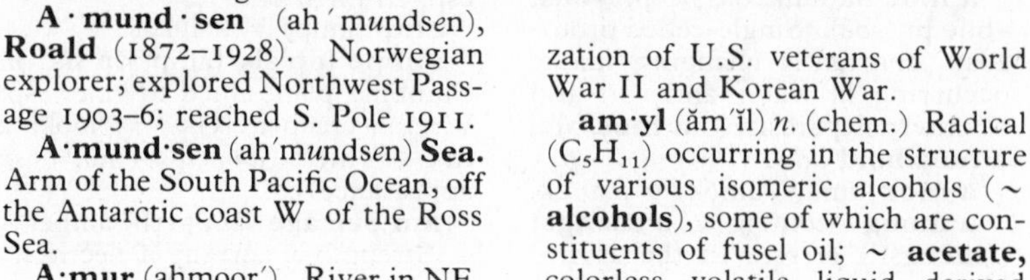

am·yl (ăm´ĭl) *n.* (chem.) Radical (C_5H_{11}) occurring in the structure of various isomeric alcohols (~ **alcohols**), some of which are constituents of fusel oil; ~ **acetate,** colorless volatile liquid derived from amyl alcohol and acetic acid, with odor of pears, used in making artificial fruit essences and as solvent of cellulose acetate. [Gk. *amulon* fine meal]

am·y·la·ceous (ăm*i*lā´sh*u*s) *adj.* Of starch, starchy.

an (*a*n; emphat. ăn) *indef. article*: see A.

an-[1]: see A- def. 2.

-an *suffix.* Forming adjectives or nouns, esp. names of places, systems, zool. classes, and founders (e.g., *Canadian*, *Anglican*, *crusta-*

A boa inhabiting swamps and rivers in South America, the non-venomous ***anaconda*** *up to 30 ft. in length, rivals the reticulated python as world's largest snake. There are 35 boa species.*

cean, Lutheran).

ana-, an-[2] *prefixes*. Up, back, again, anew.

a·na (ā´na, ah´na) *n*. Collection of person's sayings; anecdotes, literary gossip, about a person.

-ana *suffix*. Appended to a name with the meaning: sayings of, anecdotes about, publications bearing on, persons or places.

An·a·bap·tist (ănabăp´tĭst) *n*. & *adj*. (Member) of a sect that arose in Germany in 1521, was heavily persecuted by both Catholics and Protestants, and suppressed (lit., = "one who baptizes over again" because the Anabaptists held that infant baptism was ineffectual, and some of them rebaptized adults); also (opprobriously) = BAPTIST. **An·a·bap'tism** *n*.

a·nab·o·lism (anăb´olĭzem) *n*. Synthesis by living things of complex molecules from simpler ones.

a·nach·ro·nism (anăk´ronĭzem) *n*. Error in computing time; event or thing that would be incongruous in the period in which it is supposed to have happened or existed. **a·nach·ro·nis'tic** *adj*.

an·a·con·da (ănakŏn´da) *n*. Tropical S. Amer. aquatic and arboreal boa (*Eunectes murinus*).

A·nac·re·on (anăk´rēon) (*c*563–478 B.C.). Greek lyric poet, of whose poems very few genuine fragments survive. **A·nac·re·on·tic** (anăkrēŏn´tĭk) *adj*. & *n*. (Poem) in the manner or meter of Anacreon's lyrics; convivial and amatory.

a·nae·mi·a (anē´mēa) = ANEMIA.

an·aer·obe (ăn´erōb, ănār´-) *n*. Microorganism that can live and reproduce in the absence of atmospheric oxygen. **an·aer·o·bic** (ănerō´bĭk, ănĕrō´-) *adj*.

an·aes·the·sia (ănĭsthē´zha) = ANESTHESIA.

an·aes·thet·ic (ănĭsthĕt´ĭk) = ANESTHETIC.

a·naes·the·tist (anĕs´thetĭst) = ANESTHETIST.

a·naes·the·tize (anĕs´thetīz) = ANESTHETIZE.

an·a·gram (ăn´agrăm) *n*. Word or phrase formed by transposing letters of another.

An·a·heim (ăn´ahīm). City in S. California, near Los Angeles; site of Disneyland.

a·nal (ā´nal) *adj*. Of or near the anus; (psych.) of or pertaining to infantile psychosexual development in which attention is centered on the anus.

an·a·lects (ăn´alĕkts), **an·a·lec·ta** (ănalĕk´ta) *ns.pl*. Literary gleanings.

an·al·ge·si·a (ănaljē´zēa, -sēa) *n*. Absence of pain; relief of pain. **an·al·ge·sic** (ănaljē´zĭk, -sĭk) *adj*. & *n*. (Drug) giving analgesia.

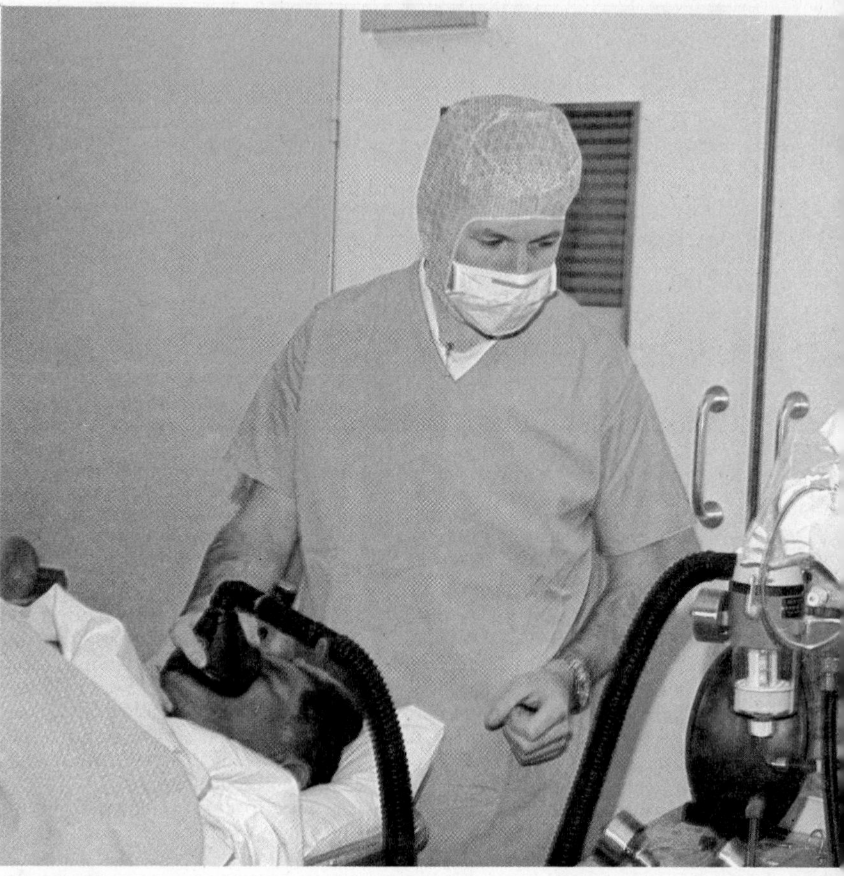

Administering ***anesthetic*** *before a surgical operation. Ether to desensitize pain was first demonstrated in 1846; local anesthesia in 1884, using cocaine for eye surgery.*

a·nal·o·gous (anăl´ogus) *adj*. Similar, parallel (*to*); (biol., of limb or organ) similar in function but not necessarily in structure or position (cf. HOMOLOGOUS). **a·nal'o·gous·ly** *adv*.

an·a·logue, an·a·log (ăn´alawg, -lŏg) *ns*. Analogous word or thing; ~ **computer**: see COMPUTER.

a·nal·o·gy (anăl´ojē) *n*. (pl. **-gies**). Agreement, similarity; analogue; (math.) proportion; (logic) process of reasoning from parallel cases; (gram.) process whereby words and grammatical forms are built up on the model of others.

an·a·lyse (ăn´alīz) (*Brit.*) = ANALYZE.

a·nal·y·sis (anăl´ĭsĭs) *n*. (pl. **-ses** pr. -sēz). Resolution into simple elements; PSYCHOANALYSIS; (math.) branch of mathematics using algebraic and calculus methods; (philos.) clarification of concepts and knowledge; **chemical** ~, determination of composition of substances; **qualitative** ~, identification of elements or compounds present; **quantitative** ~, determination of precise amounts of elements etc. present. **an·a·lyst** (ăn´alĭst) *n*. One skilled in (chemical) analysis; PSYCHOANALYSIS. **an·a·lyt·ic** (ănalĭt´ĭk) *adj*. Pertaining to analysis; **an·a·lyt'i·cal** *adj*. Employing the method of analysis; (of language) using separate words instead of inflections; ~ **psychology**: see PSYCHOLOGY. **an·a·lyt'i·cal·ly** *adv*.

an·a·lyze (ăn´alīz) *vbs*. (**-lyzed, -lyz·ing**). Examine minutely the constitution of; conduct a PSYCHOANALYSIS; (chem.) ascertain the elements present in a compound or the constituents of a mixture, sample of food, etc.; (gram.) resolve into grammatical elements.

An·a·ni·as (ănanī´as). 1. Jewish high priest before whom Paul was brought (Acts 23). 2. Husband of Sapphira, struck dead because he "lied unto God" (Acts 5).

an·a·pest (ăn´apĕst) *n*. Metrical foot of three syllables, the first two short and the last long (⏑⏑–). **an·a·pes'tic** *adj*.

a·naph·o·ra (anăf´era) *n*. 1. (also **A**~) Part of Eucharistic service in the Greek Orthodox Church; (R.C. Ch.) Canon of the Mass. 2. Repetition of words or phrases at beginning of a succession of clauses.

an·ar·chist (ăn´erkĭst) *n*. Advocate of anarchism. **an'ar·chism** *n*. System or theory that conceives of society without government.

an·ar·chy (ăn´erkē) *n*. Absence of government; disorder, political

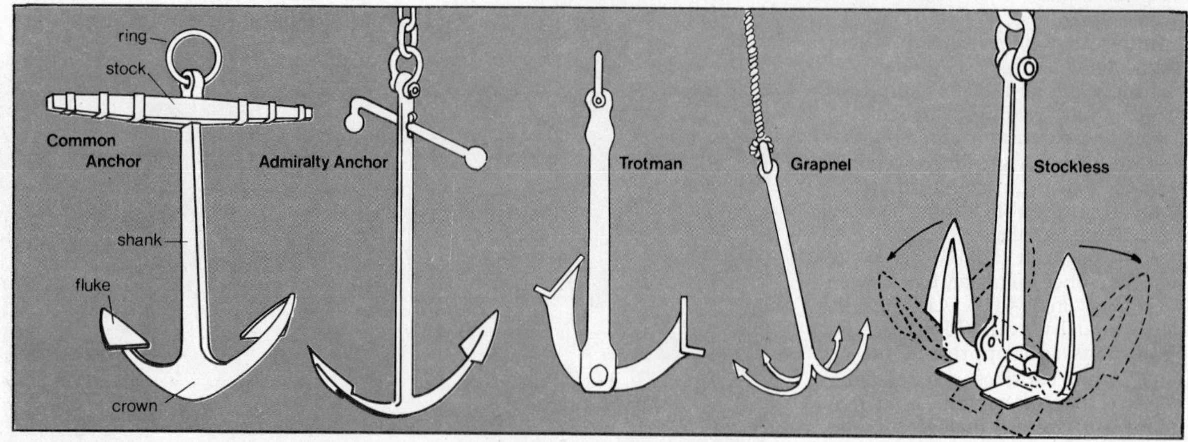

A ship's ***anchor*** *is shaped so that a horizontal pull on the cable secures it to the sea bed and an upward pull dislodges it easily. Shown (left to right): Traditional anchor with flukes (digging ends); admiralty or stowing anchor, held in place by the metal key; Trotman's anchor with flukes on pivoted arms for angled anchorage; the grapnel with arms to grasp sea-bed projections; stockless anchor as used in most large modern ships.*

and social confusion. **an·ar·chic** (ănar´kĭk), **an·ar´chi·cal** *adjs.* Lawless. **an·ar´chi·cal·ly** *adv.*

an·as·tig·mat·ic (ăn*a*stĭgmăt´ĭk, *a*năs-) *adj.* Free from astigmatism (used esp. of photographic lenses in which this error is corrected).

anat. *abbrev.* Anatomy.

a·nath·e·ma (*a*năth´*ema*) *n.* Accursed thing; curse of God; curse of the Church, excommunication; imprecation. **a·nath´e·ma·tize** *v.* (**-tized, -tiz·ing**). Curse. [Gk. *anathema* thing devoted, (later) accursed thing]

An·a·to·li·a (ăn*a*tō´lē*a*). Asiatic part of Turkey; (in ancient usage) Asia Minor. **An·a·tol·ic** (ăn*a*tŏl´ĭk) *adj.* **An·a·to´li·an** *adj.* & *n.*

an·a·tom·i·cal (ăn*a*tŏm´ĭk*a*l) *adj.* Belonging to anatomy; structural. **an·a·tom´i·cal·ly** *adv.*

a·nat·o·mist (*a*năt´*o*mĭst) *n.* Dissecter of bodies; one skilled in anatomy. **a·nat´o·mize** *v.* (**-mized, -miz·ing**). Dissect; (fig.) analyze.

a·nat·o·my (*a*năt´*o*mē) *n.* (pl. **-mies**). (Science of) bodily structure; dissection; analysis.

An·ax·ag·o·ras (ănăksăg´*era*s) (5th c. B.C.). Greek philosopher and scientist; he explained solar eclipses.

-ance *suffix.* Forming nouns of quality (e.g., *arrogance*) or action (e.g., *assistance*).

an·ces·tor (ăn´sĕst*er*) *n.* Any of those from whom one's father or mother is descended, progenitor.

an·ces·tral (ănsĕs´tr*a*l) *adj.* Belonging to, inherited from, ancestors.

an·ces·try (ăn´sĕstrē) *n.* (pl. **-tries**). Ancestral lineage; ancient descent; ancestors.

an·chor (ăng´k*er*) *n.* Heavy implement consisting usu. of long shank and (curved) barbed arms, used for mooring ship to bottom of sea etc.; **at ~**, thus moored; **~ man, ~ woman**, one playing vital or central part in a team game or broadcast. **~ plate**, heavy piece of metal or timber as point of support. **anchor** *v.* Secure (ship) with anchor; (fig.) fix firmly; drop anchor, lie at anchor.

An·chor·age (ăng´k*er*ĭj). Largest city in Alaska, in S. at the head of Cook Inlet.

an·chor·age (ăng´k*er*ĭj) *n.* Anchoring; lying at anchor; anchoring ground.

an·cho·rite (ăng´k*er*īt), fem. **an·cho·ress** (ăng´k*er*ĭs) *ns.* Hermit, recluse. **an·cho·rit·ic** (ăngk*e*rĭt´ĭk) *adj.*

an·cho·vy (ăn´chōvē, ănchō´-) *n.* (pl. **-vies**). Small fish of herring family, esp. the Mediterranean *Engraulis encrasicholus*, used as food fish.

an·cien ré·gime (ahṅsyăṅ´rāzhēm´). System of government in France before the Revolution; (transf.) former regime. [Fr., = "old rule"]

an·cient (ān´sh*e*nt) *adj.* Belonging to times long past; having existed, lived, long; **~ history**: see HISTORY. **ancient** *n.* **the ~s**, civilized people of antiquity. **an´cient·ly** *adv.* **an´cient·ness** *n.*

an·cil·lar·y (ăn´s*i*lĕrē, ănsĭl´*e*rē) *adj.* Subordinate; auxiliary.

-ancy *suffix.* Indicating state or quality but not action (e.g., *infancy*, *constancy*).

and (*a*nd; emphat. ănd) *conj.* Word connecting words, clauses, and sentences.

An·da·man (ăn´d*a*m*a*n) **Islands.** Large group of islands in Bay of Bengal; administered (with

View of Colombian ***Andes.*** *The mountain system ranges the length of western S. America from Tierra del Fuego 4,000 miles north to Caribbean coast. Ten peaks top 22,000 ft.*

Nicobar Islands) by India; chief city, Port Blair.

an·dan·te (ahndahn'tā) *adv.* & *n.* (mus.) (Movement) in moderately slow time.

An·der·sen (ăn'dersen), **Hans Christian** (1805–75). Danish poet and dramatist, best known for his fairy tales.

An·der·son[1] (ăn'derson), **Carl David** (1905–). American physicist; discovered the positron in cosmic rays; shared Nobel Prize for physics, 1936.

An·der·son[2] (ăn'derson), **Marian** (1902–). American concert contralto.

An·der·son[3] (ăn'derson), **Maxwell** (1888–1959). American playwright; author of *Elizabeth the Queen, Winterset, Key Largo*, etc.

An·der·son[4] (ăn'derson), **Sherwood** (1878–1941). American novelist and short story writer; author of *Winesburg, Ohio*; *Dark Laughter*, etc.

An·der·son·ville (ăn'dersonvĭl). Village in SW. Georgia; site of an infamous Confederate prison for Union troops during the Civil War.

An·des (ăn'dēz). Mountain range running from N. to S. along the whole of the Pacific coast of S. America.

An·dhra Pra·desh (ahn'dra pradāsh'). State of SE. India; chief city, Hyderabad.

and·i·ron (ănd'īern, -īrn) *n.* One of a pair of stands for logs in a fireplace; fire dog.

and/or (ănd'ōr') *conj.* Indicating that either of two things named may be applicable, or both.

An·dor·ra (ăndōr'a). Small republic in the Pyrenees, on the border between France and Spain; capital, Andorra la Vella. **An·dor'ran** *adj.* & *n.*

An·dre (ahn'drā), **John** (1751–1780). British army major hanged as a spy during the Revolutionary War for conspiring with Benedict Arnold to betray West Point.

An·dre·a del Sar·to (ahndrā'a dĕl sartō) (1486–1531). Florentine painter.

An·drew (ăn'drōō), **St.** Apostle and patron saint of Scotland, commemorated, Nov. 30; **St. ~'s cross**, cross shaped like the letter ×.

An·dro·cles (ăn'droklēz). Runaway slave in story by Aulus Gellius (2nd c. A.D.) who extracted a thorn from the paw of a lion that later recognized and refrained from attacking him in the arena.

an·dro·gen (ăn'drojen) *n.* Any organic compound that promotes development of masculine characteristics. **an·dro·gen·ic** (ăndrojĕn'ĭk) *adj.*

an·drog·y·nous (ăndrŏj'inus) *adj.* Hermaphroditic; (bot.) with both staminate and pistillate flowers in a cluster. **an·drog'y·ny** *n.*

an·droid (ăn'droid) *n.* Robot with human form.

An·drom·a·che (ăndrŏm'akē). (Gk. legend) Wife of HECTOR, captured by the Greeks at the fall of Troy.

An·drom·e·da (ăndrŏm'ĭda). 1. (Gk. legend) Daughter of Cassiopeia; was rescued by Perseus from a sea monster for whom she was fastened to a rock. 2. (astron.) Constellation, conspicuous for its great spiral nebula. **An·drom·e·des** (ăndrŏm'ĭdēz), **An·drom·e·dids** (ăndrŏm'ĭdĭdz) *ns. pl.* (astron.) System of meteors appearing to radiate from a point in Andromeda and usu. seen in November.

an·ec·dote (ăn'ĭkdōt) *n.* Short narrative of amusing or interesting incident. **an·ec·dot·age** (ăn'ĭkdōtĭj) *n.* Anecdotes; (joc.) garrulous old age. **an'ec·dot·ist** *n.* **an'ec·do·tal, an·ec·dot·ic** (ănĭkdŏt'ĭk), **an·ec·dot'i·cal** *adjs.*

a·ne·mi·a (anē'mēa) *n.* Deficiency of red blood corpuscles or their hemoglobin, often causing paleness; **pernicious ~**: see PERNICIOUS. **a·ne·mic** (anē'mĭk) *adj.* (often fig.).

an·e·mom·e·ter (ănemŏm'ĭter) *n.* Instrument for measuring speed (sometimes also direction) of wind. **an·e·mo·met·ric** (ănemōmĕt'rĭk) *adj.* **an·e·mom'e·try** *n.*

a·nem·o·ne (anĕm'onē) *n.* Plant of the buttercup family of genus *A~* with flowers of various colors. [Gk., = "windflower"]

a·nent (anĕnt') *prep.* (archaic) Concerning.

an·e·roid (ăn'eroid) *adj.* & *n.* (Barometer) that measures air pressure by its action on the flexible lid of a metal box nearly exhausted of air, not by height of fluid column.

an·es·the·sia, an·aes·the·sia (ănĭsthē'zha) *ns.* Loss of sensation; insensibility, esp. to pain, induced by certain drugs; **general ~**, anesthesia of the whole body; **local ~**, anesthesia induced in a limited area of the body. **an·es·the·si·ol·o·gy** (ănĭsthēzēŏl'ojē), **an·es-**

*A small semi-independent State, **Andorra,** some 175 sq. miles, lies in the Pyrenees between France and Spain. It is a haven for smugglers of tobacco and cars especially.*

***Anemones** are a group of mainly herbaceous and rock garden plants grown mostly from corms. The corms are able to survive all but the most severe winters.*

the·si·ol′o·gist *ns.*

an·es·thet·ic, an·aes·thet·ic (ănĭsthĕt′ĭk) *adjs.* & *ns.* (Drug) inducing local or general anesthesia, used esp. in surgical operations.

a·nes·the·tist, a·naes·the·tist (anĕs′thetĭst) *ns.* One who administers anesthetics during surgical operation.

a·nes·the·tize, a·naes·the·tize (anĕs′thetīz) *vbs.* (**-tized, -tiz·ing**). Render insensible; administer anesthetics to.

an·eu·rysm, an·eu·rism (ăn′yerĭzem) *ns.* (path.) Localized dilation of an artery caused by a weakening in its wall.

a·new (anōō′, anū′) *adv.* Again; in a different way.

an·gel (ān′jel) *n.* 1. Divine messenger; a celestial attendant of God; member of one of nine orders to which angels were held to belong in medieval theology, namely: seraphim, cherubim, thrones; dominations, virtues, powers; principalities, archangels, angels. 2. Lovely or innocent being; loving or obliging person. 3. Financial backer, esp. of theatrical production. 4. **an′gelfish,** (esp.) S. Amer. fresh water fish (various species of *Pterophyllum*), laterally flattened, with bars of black and silver; ~ **food cake,** very light sponge cake. [Gk. *aggelos* messenger]

An·gel (ān′jel) **Fall.** Highest uninterrupted waterfall in the world, over 3,000 feet (914 m); in SE. Venezuela.

An·ge·la Me·ri·ci (ăn′jela merē′chē), **St.** (1474?–1540). Italian Roman Catholic nun; founder of the Ursuline Order.

an·gel·ic (ănjĕl′ĭk) *adj.* Like an angel.

an·gel·i·ca (ănjĕl′ĭka) *n.* Aromatic umbelliferous plant used in cooking and medicine; candied stalk of this.

An·ge·li·co (ănjĕl′ĭkō), **Fra.** Fra Giovanni da Fiesole (1387–1455), painter of religious subjects, active in Florence and Rome.

An·ge·lus (ăn′jelus) *n.* (R.C. Ch.) Devotional exercise (also **angelus**) (beginning *Angelus domini*; L., = "the angel of the Lord") commemorating the Incarnation, said morning, noon, and evening, at sound of bell; bell for this.

an·ger (ăng′ger) *n.* Hot displeasure, rage. ~ *v.t.* Make angry, enrage. [ON. *angr* affliction]

An·ge·vin (ăn′jevĭn) *adj.* Of Anjou or its ruling house; ~ **kings,** PLANTAGENET kings of England.

an·gi·na (ănjī′na) *n.* Constrictive sensation or pain, as in quinsy, croup, etc.; ~ **pectoris** (pĕk′terĭs), intense pain in chest, accompanied by sense of suffocation, caused by insufficient blood supply to heart.

an·gi·o·sperm (ăn′jēospẽrm) *n.* Flowering plant, i.e. one that has ovules enclosed in an ovary (opp. GYMNOSPERM).

Ang·kor (ăng′ker, -kōr). Group of ruins in NW. Kampuchea (formerly Cambodia), the most famous of which are the temple Angkor Wat and the ancient Khmer capital, Angkor Thom.

an·gle[1] (ăng′gel) *n.* Space between two meeting lines or planes; inclination of two lines to each other (**acute** ~, angle smaller than 90°; **obtuse** ~, greater than 90°; **right** ~, angle of 90°; **reflex** ~, angle greater than 180°); corner, sharp projection; (colloq.) point of view; aspect of a situation; **angle iron,** metal plate of L-shaped section. **an′gled** *adj.*

an·gle[2] (ăng′gel) *v.i.* (**-gled, -gling**). Fish with hook and bait; (fig.) use artifice, hints, etc., to obtain something. **an′gler** *n.* 1. Fisherman. 2. (zool.) Fish (esp. *Lophius piscatorius*) that preys on smaller fish, attracting them by filaments attached to its head and mouth. **an′gleworm** *n.* Earthworm used as bait in fishing.

An·gles (ăng′gelz) *n.pl.* One of the Germanic tribes that settled in Britain in the 5th c. A.D., where they formed the kingdoms of Northumbria, Mercia, and East Anglia, and finally gave their name to England and the English.

An·gli·can (ăng′glĭkan) *adj.* Of the reformed Church of England or any Church in the Anglican Communion, such as the Protestant Episcopal Church; ~ **Communion,** Churches in communion with, and recognizing the leadership of, the see of Canterbury. **Anglican** *n.* Member of Anglican Church. **An′gli·can·ism** *n.*

An·gli·cize (ăng′glĭsīz) *v.* (**-cized, -ciz·ing**). Make, become, English in form or character. **An′gli·cism** *n.* English idiom, Briticism; a typical English custom or trait.

An·glo (ăng′glō) *n.* (pl. **-glos**). (colloq.) English-speaking white American.

Anglo- *prefix.* English; English and—, as ~-American.

An·glo·phile (ăng′glofīl), **An·glo·phil** (ăng′glofĭl) *ns.* One who loves the English. **An·glo·phil·i·a** (ăngglofĭl′ēa) *n.* **An·glo·phil′i·ac** *adj.*

An·glo·phobe (ăng′glofōb) *n.* One who hates the English. **An·glo·pho·bi·a** (ăngglofō′bēa) *n.* **An·glo·pho·bic** (ăngglofō′bĭk) *adj.*

An·glo-Sax·on (ăng′glō săk′son) *adj.* & *n.* 1. (Member, language) of the Germanic tribes that settled in England in the 5th and 6th c. and remained dominant until 1066. 2. (Person) of English descent. 3. (colloq.) Plain English (language).

An·go·la (ănggō′la). Former Portuguese province of W. Africa, N. of SW. Africa and W. of Zambia; independent Nov. 1975.

An·go·ra (ănggōr′a, -gōr′a). Former name of ANKARA; fabric made from fleece of Angora goat or of sheep's wool mixed with hair of Angora rabbit; ~ **cat, goat, rabbit,** varieties of these animals with long silky hair.

An·gos·tu·ra (ănggostoor′a, -tūr′a). Former name of Ciudad Bolivar, town in Venezuela on Orinoco; **a** ~ (**bark**), aromatic bark formerly used as tonic and febrifuge, obtained from S. Amer. tree of family Rutaceae; ~ **bitters,** (trademark) tonic and flavoring made from this bark.

an·gry (ăng′grē) *adj.* (**-gri·er, -gri·est**). Enraged, resentful; irritable; (of wound etc.) inflamed, painful; ~ **young man,** (Brit.) one of a group of British writers of the 1950's noted for social protest; any similarly rebellious young person. **an′gri·ly** *adv.*

angst (ahngst) *n.* Anxiety; remorse. [Ger.]

Ang·ström (ăng′strom), **Anders Jonas** (1814–74). Swedish physicist and astronomer; **angstrom** (also **angstrom unit**), unit (abbrev. Å) used for measuring electromagnetic wavelengths, one hundred millionth of a centimeter.

An·guil·la (ănggwĭl′a). Island in the West Indies, under British rule.

an·guish (ăng′gwĭsh) *n.* Severe mental or bodily pain.

an·gu·lar (ăng′gyuler) *adj.* Having angles; sharp cornered; placed in, at, an angle; bony, gaunt; awkward. ~ **momentum,** product of moment of inertia of a body moving about its axis and its angular velocity.

An·gus (ăng′gus). Former county of E. Scotland; a breed of hornless beef cattle originally raised there.

an·he·dral (ănhē′dral) *adj.* Of a rock that does not have its characteristic crystalline form.

an·hin·ga (ănhĭng′ga) *n.* Dark bird (*A* ~ *anhinga*) with long, snakelike neck living in tropical swamps; also called darter, water turkey, snakebird.

An·hui (ahn′hwā′) = ANHWEI.

An·hwei (ahn′hwā′). Province of China on the Yangtze Kiang.

an·hy·dride (ănhī′drīd) *n.* Substance formed by removal of water from a compound; substance that combines with water to form an acid or base.

an·hy·drous (ănhī′drus) *adj.* (chem.) Having no water; deprived of water of crystallization.

This picture was taken in Luanda on ***Angola's*** *'Independence Day' following the factional war. The child is a member of the M.P.L.A. pioneer youth wing, the 'lollipop army'.*

an·i·line (ăn′ilĭn, -līn) *n.* Phenylamine ($C_6H_5NH_2$), an oily liquid with characteristic smell, made by reduction of nitrobenzene and used in the manufacture of many chemicals, dyestuffs, drugs, etc. ~ *adj.* Derived from aniline; ~ **dye**, (pop.) any synthetic dyestuff. [formerly obtained from *anil*, the shrub indigo]

an·i·ma (ăn′ima) *n.* 1. The soul. 2. (psych.) Inner personality (opp. PERSONA); feminine part of a man's personality. [L., "breath," "soul"]

an·i·mad·ver·sion (ănimăd-vēr′zhon, -shon) *n.* Criticism, censure. **an·i·mad·vert** (ănimăd-vērt′) *v.i.* Pass criticism or censure *on*.

an·i·mal (ăn′ımal) *n.* Organized being endowed with life, sensation, and voluntary motion; animal other than man; quadruped; brutish man. ~ *adj.* Pertaining to the functions of animals; pertaining to animals as opp. to vegetables; carnal; ~ **crackers**, small cookies baked in shapes of animals; ~ **kingdom**, all animals collectively; ~ **magnetism**, (hist.) mesmerism; magnetic personality, sensuality; ~ **spirits**, natural buoyancy. [L. *anima* breath]

an·i·mal·cule (ănimăl′kūl) *n.* Microscopic animal.

an·i·mal·ism (ăn′imalĭzem) *n.* Animal activity; sensuality; doctrine that men are mere animals.

an·i·mal·ize (ăn′ımalīz) *v.t.* (**-ized, -iz·ing**). 1. (art, religion) Represent as an animal, give animal features to. 2. Make coarse or brutal; sensualize.

an·i·mate (ăn′imĭt) *adj.* Living, lively. ~ (ăn′imāt) *v.t.* (**-mat·ed, -mat·ing**). Give life to; make lively; encourage; **animated cartoon**: see CARTOON. **an·i·ma·tion** (ănimā′shon) *n.* **an′i·mat·ed·ly** *adv.*

an·i·mism (ăn′imĭzem) *n.* Attribution of living soul to inanimate objects and natural phenomena. **an′i·mist** *n.* **an·i·mis·tic** (ănimĭs′-tĭk) *adj.*

an·i·mos·i·ty (ănimŏs′ĭtē) *n.* (pl. **-ties**). Active enmity.

an·i·mus (ăn′imus) *n.* 1. Animating spirit; animosity. 2. (psych.) Masculine part of a woman's personality.

an·i·on (ăn′īon, -ŏn) *n.*: see ION. **an·i·on·ic** (ănīŏn′ĭk) *adj.* Of anions; having an active anion. [Gk. *ana* up, + ION]

an·ise (ăn′ĭs) *n.* Umbelliferous plant (*Pimpinella anisum*) with aromatic fruits and licorice-flavored seeds.

an·i·seed (an′isēd) *n.* Seed of anise, used to flavor liqueurs, desserts, etc.

an·i·sette (ănĭsĕt′, -zĕt′, ăn′ĭsĕt, -zĕt) *n.* Colorless sweet liqueur flavored with aniseed.

An·ka·ra (ăng′kera). Capital city of Turkey since 1923.

ankh (ăngk) *n.* Keylike cross used in ancient Egypt as symbol of life. [Egypt., = "life, soul"]

an·kle (ăng′kel) *n.* Joint connecting foot with leg; slender part between this and calf. **an·klet** (ăng′klĭt) *n.* Fetter or ornamental band around ankle; short sock just covering ankle.

Ann (ăn), **Cape.** Peninsula near Gloucester in N. Massachusetts, projecting into the Atlantic Ocean.

an·nals (ăn′alz) *n.pl.* Narrative of events year by year; historical records. **an·nal·ist** (ăn′alĭst) *n.* Writer of annals.

An·nap·o·lis (anăp′olĭs). Capital of Maryland, site of the U.S. Naval Academy.

An·na·pur·na (ănapoor′na, -pēr′-). Part of the Himalayas in central Nepal; the highest elevation, Annapurna I, 26,502 feet (8,078 m).

Ann (ăn) **Arbor.** City in SE. Michigan.

Anne[1] (ăn) (1665–1714). Queen of Great Britain (1702–14); second daughter of James II; succeeded William, husband of her sister Mary, in 1702; **Queen** ~, (archit.) applied to a style of red brick and stone houses of *c*1660–*c*1720.

Anne[2] (ăn), **St.** Mother of the Virgin Mary; commemorated July 26.

an·neal (anēl′) *v.t.* Toughen (glass or metals) by heating and then cooling; temper.

Anne Boleyn: see BOLEYN.

an·ne·lid (ăn′elĭd) *n.* One of the phylum Annelida, segmented worms (including earthworms, leeches, etc.).

Anne of Cleves (klēvz) (1515–1557). Daughter of John, Duke of Cleves, and fourth wife of Henry VIII of England; the marriage (1540) was annulled after a few months.

an·nex (anĕks′) *v.t.* Add as subordinate (part); append; take possession of (territory). **an·nex·a·tion** (ănĕksā′shon) *n.* **an·nex** (ăn′ĕks) *n.* Addition to document; building added to larger one, esp. to provide extra accommodation.

An·nie Oak·ley (ăn′ē ōk′lē) (1860–1926). Real name, Phoebe Anne Oakley Mozee. Famous American rider and markswoman; starred in Buffalo Bill's Wild West Show; hence a ticket (esp. a free ticket, meal ticket, etc.), so called from the similarity of a punched ticket to a bullet-riddled target.

an·ni·hi·late (anī′ilāt) *v.t.* (**-lat·ed, -lat·ing**). Demolish, destroy utterly. **an·ni·hi·la·tion** (anīilā′shon) *n.* Utter destruction.

an·ni·ver·sa·ry (ănivēr′serē) *n.* (pl. **-ries**). Yearly return of a date, celebration of this.

An·no Dom·i·ni (ă′nō dŏm′inē, -nī). In the year of our Lord, of the Christian era (abbrev. A.D.). [L.]

an·no·tate (ăn′ōtāt) *v.t.* (**-tat·ed, -tat·ing**). Furnish (a text) with notes. **an·no·ta·tion** (ănōtā′shon), **an′no·ta·tor** *ns.*

Ulus Square, ***Ankara.*** *Kemal Ataturk, founder of modern Turkey, chose Ankara as capital in 1923 because its 100-mile distance from the Black Sea made it easy to defend.*

*Giant earthworms mating. Segmented worms, **annelids** include leeches. Anatomically an annelid is a tube (alimentary canal) within a tube (body wall) separated by the coelum.*

*Rockport on **Cape Ann,** north-eastern Massachusetts. Cape Ann, noted for its scenery, resorts, fishing villages and artists' colonies, was named after Queen Anne, wife of James I of Gt. Britain.*

an·nounce (*anowns'*) *v.t.* (**-nounced, -nounc·ing**). Declare, make publicly known; intimate the approach of; serve as an announcement of. **an·nounce'·ment** *n.* **an·nounc'er** *n.* (esp.) Person who announces program, reads news items, etc., over radio or television.

an·noy (*anoi'*) *v.t.* Irritate; molest, harass. **an·noy'ance** *n.* (Thing that causes) molestation; vexation; disgust.

an·nu·al (ăn'ūal) *adj.* Reckoned by the year; recurring yearly; lasting for one year; that lives only for a year; published yearly; ~ **ring,** ring in cross section of tree, fish, etc., from one year's growth. **annual** *n.* Plant that lives for one year; book etc. published yearly. **an'nu·al·ly** *adv.*

an·nu·i·ty (*anoo'ite, anū'-*) *n.* (pl. **-ties**). Sum payable in regard to a particular year; yearly grant; investment of money entitling investors to series of equal annual sums. **an·nu·i·tant** (*anoo'itant, anū'-*) *n.* One who holds an annuity.

an·nul (*anŭl'*) *v.t.* (**-nulled, -nul·ling**). Abolish, cancel; declare invalid, esp. of a marriage that was never consummated or was invalid to begin with. **an·nul'ment** *n.*

an·nu·lar (ăn'*yuler*) *adj.* Ringlike; ~ **eclipse,** partial eclipse of sun, during which a ring of the sun's surface can be seen surrounding the moon's disk.

an·nu·late (ăn'*yulĭt*, -lāt), **an·nu·lat·ed** (ăn'*yulātĭd*) *adjs.* Furnished, marked, with rings; formed of rings.

an·nu·lus (ăn'*yulus*) *n.* (pl. **-li** pr. -lī, **-lus·es**). Ring, ringlike body.

an·nun·ci·ate (*anŭn'sēāt*, -shē-) *v.t.* (**-at·ed, -at·ing**). Announce.

an·nun·ci·a·tion (*anŭnsēā'shon*) *n.* Announcement; **the A~,** the announcement of the Incarnation made by the angel Gabriel to the Virgin Mary (Luke 1); festival commemorating this, March 25.

an·ode (ăn'ōd) *n.* (elect.) 1. Positively charged electrode. 2. Negative terminal of cell or storage battery. **an·od·ic** (ănŏd'ĭk) *adj.* **an·o·dize** (ăn'*odīz*) *v.t.* (**-dized, -diz·ing**). Cover (metal) with a protective film by electrolysis in which the metal acts as the anode. [Gk. *anodos* way up]

an·o·dyne (ăn'*odīn*) *adj.* & *n.* (Medicine, drug) able to assuage pain; (anything) mentally soothing.

a·noint (*anoint'*) *v.t.* Apply ointment, oil, to, esp. as religious ceremony at baptism or on consecration as priest or king.

a·nom·a·lous (*anŏm'alus*) *adj.* Irregular, abnormal. **a·nom'a·lous·ly** *adv.* **a·nom'a·lous·ness** *n.*

a·nom·a·ly (*anŏm'alē*) *n.* (pl. **-lies**). Irregularity; (astron.) angular distance of planet or satellite from its last perihelion or perigee.

a·non (*anŏn'*) *adv.* (archaic) Soon, presently; at another time.

anon. *abbrev.* Anonymous.

an·o·nym (ăn'*onĭm*) *n.* Person whose name is not revealed; pseudonym. **an·o·nym·i·ty** (ăno*nĭm'ĭtē*) *n.*

a·non·y·mous (*anŏn'imus*) *adj.* Not named; not bearing author's, painter's, etc., name; (fig.) lacking individuality. **a·non'y·mous·ly** *adv.*

a·noph·e·les (*anŏf'elēz*) *n.* Mosquito of genus *A~*, comprising numerous species, many of which are carriers of malaria. [Gk., = "hurtful"]

an·o·rex·i·a (ăn*erĕk'sēa*) *n.* (path.) Loss of appetite; ~ **ner·vo·sa** (*nervō'sa*), syndrome in which chronic anorexia is induced by emotional disturbance.

an·oth·er (*anŭdh'er*) *adj.* Additional, different; a similar (one). ~ *pron.* Additional one; someone else, something else.

A·nouilh (ahnwē'), **Jean** (1910–). French dramatist, author of *le Bal des Voleurs, Antigone,* etc.

ans. *abbrev.* Answer.

An·schluss (ahn'shloos) *n.* Annexation, esp. of Austria to Germany. [Ger., = "union"]

an·swer (ăn'*ser*) *v.* Give answer; reply to (charge); be responsible *for*; fulfill (purpose); suffice; correspond *to* (description etc.); act or operate in response (*to*); ~ **back,** reply impertinently. **answer** *n.* Something said or done in response to a question, accusation, etc.; defense; solution; (mus.) repetition of theme by another voice or instrument, esp. in fugue. **an'-swer·a·ble** *adj.* Responsible.

-ant *suffix.* Forms adjectives denoting existence of action (*repentant*) and nouns denoting agent (*applicant*).

ant (ănt) *n.* Small hymenopterous insect of superfamily Formicoidea, with complex instincts and social system, proverbial for industry; **ant'eater**, any of various tropical American mammals of the family Myrmecophagidae, feeding chiefly on ants and termites, esp. *Myrmecophaga tridactyla*, or giant anteater; also such mammals as ECHIDNA and PANGOLIN. **ant hill**, mound over ants' nest; (fig.) crowded dwelling(s) swarming with people.

ant. *abbrev.* Antenna; antonym.

ant- = ANTI-.

ant·ac·id (ăntăs'ĭd) *adj.* & *n.* (Agent) neutralizing acidity, esp. in stomach.

An·tae·us (ăntē'*us*). (Gk. myth.) Libyan giant, son of Poseidon and Ge; when Hercules wrestled with him, Antaeus was only overcome when lifted from the earth, from which he drew new strength whenever he touched it.

an·tag·o·nism (ăntăg'*o*nĭz*e*m) *n.* Active opposition; opposing principle.

an·tag·o·nist (ăntăg'*o*nĭst) *n.* 1. Opponent. 2. (physiol.) Counteracting muscle. **an·tag·o·nis·tic** (ăntăg*o*nĭs'tĭk) *adj.*

an·tag·o·nize (ăntăg'*o*nīz) *v.* (**-nized, -niz·ing**). Evoke hostility in, make into an enemy.

ant·arc·tic (ăntârk'tĭk, -âr'tĭk) *adj.* Of the south polar regions. **A~ Circle**, parallel of 66 33'S., south of which the sun does not rise at midwinter or set at midsummer. **A~ Ocean**, southern extensions of the Atlantic, Pacific, and Indian Oceans which constitute the waters surrounding Antarctica. **Antarctic** *n.* Regions (both land and sea) around the S. Pole. [Gk. *anti* opposite + ARCTIC]

Ant·arc·ti·ca (ăntârk'tĭk*a*, -âr'tĭ-). Continent mainly within the Antarctic Circle, almost entirely covered by ice sheet.

an·te (ăn'tē) *n.* (poker etc.) Stake put up before being dealt one's hand or drawing new cards; (slang) price, cost; one's share of the cost; **penny ~**: see PENNY.

ante- *prefix.* Before.

an·te·bel·lum (ăn'tēbĕl'*u*m) *adj.* Before the war; specif., of the U.S. South before the Civil War. [L.]

an·te·ced·ent (ăntĭsē'd*e*nt) *adj.* Previous; presumptive. ~ *n.* Preceding thing or circumstance; (logic) part of conditional proposition on which other part depends; (gram.) noun, clause, etc., to which a following pronoun refers; (math.) first term of ratio; (pl.) ancestors.

an·te·cham·ber (ăn'tēchāmb*e*r) *n.* Room leading to chief apartment.

an·te·date (ăn'tĭdāt, ăntĭdāt') *v.t.* (**-dat·ed, -dat·ing**). Affix, assign, an earlier than the true date to; precede; anticipate.

an·te·di·lu·vi·an (ăntēdĭlōō'vē*a*n) *adj.* Belonging, referring, appropriate, to the time before the Flood; very old, old-fashioned. ~ *n.* Antediluvian person.

an·te·lope (ăn'tel*ō*p) *n.* (pl. **-lopes**, collect. **-lope**). Any of several cloven-hoofed, horned ruminants of the family Bovidae

Australian green tree ***ants.*** *Ant species exceed 10,000. Most colonies have three castes (male, female, worker). A winged potential queen takes off coupled to a winged male. Workers cannot mate.* ***Anteaters*** *are mammals. Illustrated: The great anteater is more than 5 ft. long including its bushy tail. The scaly anteater. The echidna or spiny anteater is native to Australia and New Guinea and the marsupial banded anteater (numbat).*

The flag flies 24 hours a day at the passenger terminal of Williams Field, the main airfield of ***Antarctica.*** *The base lies on the 150 ft. thick edge of the Ross Ice Shelf in the Ross Sea.*

(related to deer, goats, and cattle) including the chamois, gazelle, and gnu.

an·te me·rid·i·em (ăn′tē merĭd′ēĕm, -*e*m). (abbrev. a.m.) Between midnight and noon. **an·te·me·rid′i·an** *adj.* [L.]

an·ten·na (ăntĕn′*a*) *n.* 1. (pl. **-ten·nae** pr. -tĕn′ē). Sensory organ found in pairs on heads of insects and crustacea, usually long slender projections like horns, sometimes knobbed. 2. (pl. **-ten·nas**). Wire(s) or rod(s) used to transmit or receive radio waves; aerial. [L., = "sail-yard"]

an·te·pe·nult (ăntēpē′nŭlt, -pĭ-nŭlt′), **an·te·pe·nul·ti·mate** (ăntĭ-pĭnŭl′t*i*mĭt) *adjs.* & *ns.* (Syllable) last but two.

an·te·ri·or (ăntēr′ē*e*r) *adj.* In or toward the front; prior *to.*

an·te·room (ăn′tĕro͞om, -ro͞om) *n.* Room leading to another, antechamber; waiting room.

an·them (ăn′th*e*m) *n.* Hymn of praise or patriotism; nonmetrical musical setting of sacred words; religious composition sung antiphonally.

an·ther (ăn′th*e*r) *n.* Terminal part of stamen containing pollen in pollen sacs.

an·thol·o·gy (ănthŏl′*o*jē) *n.* (pl. **-gies**). Collection of small choice literary pieces or extracts; literary collection; collection of songs etc. **an·thol′o·gize** *v.* (**-gized, -giz·-ing**). Make an anthology *from.* [Gk. *anthologia*, f. *anthos* flower, *-logia* collection (*legō* gather)]

An·tho·ny[1] (ăn′th*o*nē), **St.** (*c*251–356). Born in Egypt, the first Christian monk; **St. ~'s cross,** T-shaped cross.

An·tho·ny[2] (ăn′th*o*nē) **of Padua, St.** (1195–1231). Portuguese Franciscan monk, patron saint of Portugal.

An·tho·ny[3] (ăn′th*o*nē), **Susan B(rownell)** (1820–1906). American leader of the women's suffrage movement; organized the National Woman Suffrage Association, 1869.

an·tho·zo·an (ănthozō′*a*n) *adj.* & *n.* (Aquatic animal) of the class Anthozoa, including corals, sea anemones, etc. [Gk. *anthos* flower, *zōon* animal]

an·thra·cite (ăn′thr*a*sīt) *n.* Glossy variety of coal containing much carbon and low percentage of volatile matter, burning with hot smokeless flame and leaving little ash. **an·thra·cit·ic** (ănthr*a*sĭt′ĭk) *adj.*

an·thrax (ăn′thrăks) *n.* Disease of sheep and cattle, transmitted to man by infected wool, bristles, etc., and characterized by inflammatory

Antelopes *include chamois, gazelles and gnus, horned ruminants of the Bovidea family to which deer, sheep goats and cattle also belong. The brindled gnu ranges over central Africa. The eland is the largest antelope; adult bulls standing nearly 5 ft. at the shoulder. Grant's gazelle was named after a Scottish explorer.*

skin lesions, caused by a bacillus (*B. anthracis*).

anthrop. *abbrev.* Anthropology.

an·thro·poid (ăn'thropoid) *adj.* Resembling man; ~ **ape**, one of the primates most nearly related to man, i.e., chimpanzees, gibbons, orangutans, and gorillas. ~ *n.* Anthropoid ape.

an·thro·pol·o·gy (ănthrŏpŏl'ojē) *n.* Science of man, his origins, customs, etc.; study of man as an animal (**physical** ~) and of human, esp. primitive, societies (**social** ~). **an·thro·po·log·i·cal** (ănthropolŏj'ĭkal) *adj.* **an·thro·po·log'i·cal·ly** *adv.* **an·thro·pol'o·gist** *n.*

an·thro·po·mor·phism (ănthropomōr'fĭzem) *n.* Ascription of human form and attributes to a god or to a thing not human. **an·thro·po·mor'phic** *adj.*

an·thro·po·mor·phous (ănthropomōr'fus) *adj.* Having human form. **an·thro·po·mor'phize** *v.* (**-phized, -phiz·ing**). Regard as anthropomorphous.

anti-, ant- *prefixes.* Opposite, against; (in the arts, literature, etc.) unlike the conventional form.

an·ti·air·craft (ăntēār'krăft, -krahft) *adj.* & *n.* (Force) for shooting down, or for defense against, hostile aircraft (abbrev. A.A.).

an·ti·bal·lis·tic (ăntēbalĭs'tĭk) **missile.** Defensive missile designed to intercept and destroy an attacking ballistic missile.

An·tibes (ăntēbz'; *Fr.* ahṅtēb'). Port and popular resort on the Riviera, in SE. France.

an·ti·bi·o·sis (ăntēbīō'sĭs, ăntī-) *n.* Condition of antagonism between organisms, esp. microorganisms (opp. SYMBIOSIS).

an·ti·bi·ot·ic (ăntĭbīŏt'ĭk, ăntī-, ăntē-) *adj.* & *n.* (Substance, drug, as penicillin, streptomycin) obtained from a mold, fungus, or other microorganism, or prepared synthetically, and having the power to inhibit the growth of other microorganisms, e.g. bacteria.

an·ti·bod·y (ăn'tĭbŏdē) *n.* (pl. **-bod·ies**). (physiol.) Protein formed within the body to inactivate compounds (esp. bacterial toxins and viruses) that are foreign to it.

an·tic (ăn'tĭk) *n.* (often pl.) Grotesque posture or gesture; playful prank.

An·ti·christ (ăn'tĭkrīst). Great personal opponent of Christ expected by early Christians to appear before the end of the world; person hostile to Christ and his teaching.

an·ti·chris·tian (ăntĭkrĭs'chan) *adj.* Opposed to Christianity.

an·tic·i·pate (ăntĭs'ipāt) *v.t.* (**-pat·ed, -pat·ing**). Look forward to, expect; perform action before (another person or event), (of event) happen before (another event); satisfy (wish), obey (command), before it is expressed; use in advance. **an·tic·i·pa·tive** (ăntĭs'ipātĭv, -patĭv), **an·tic·i·pa·to·ry** (ăntĭs'ipatōrē, -tōrē) *adjs.* **an·tic·i·pa·tion** (ăntĭsipā'shon) *n.*

an·ti·cler·i·cal (ăntēklĕr'ĭkal, ăntī-) *adj.* & *n.* (Person) opposed to undue influence of clergy or to existence of organized clerical hierarchy. **an·ti·cler'i·cal·ism** *n.*

an·ti·cli·max (ăntĭklī'măks) *n.* Lame end to anything promising a climax.

an·ti·cline (ăn'tĭklīn) *n.* (geol.) Archlike fold in bed(s) of rock (opp. SYNCLINE). **an·ti·cli·nal** (ăntĭklī'nal) *adj.*

an·ti·co·ag·u·lant (ăntēkōăg'yulant) *adj.* & *n.* (Drug) retarding or preventing the clotting of blood.

an·ti·cy·clone (ăntĭsī'klōn) *n.* Atmospheric system in which barometric pressure is high, and from center of which air tends to flow spirally outward (clockwise in N. hemisphere, counterclockwise in S. hemisphere).

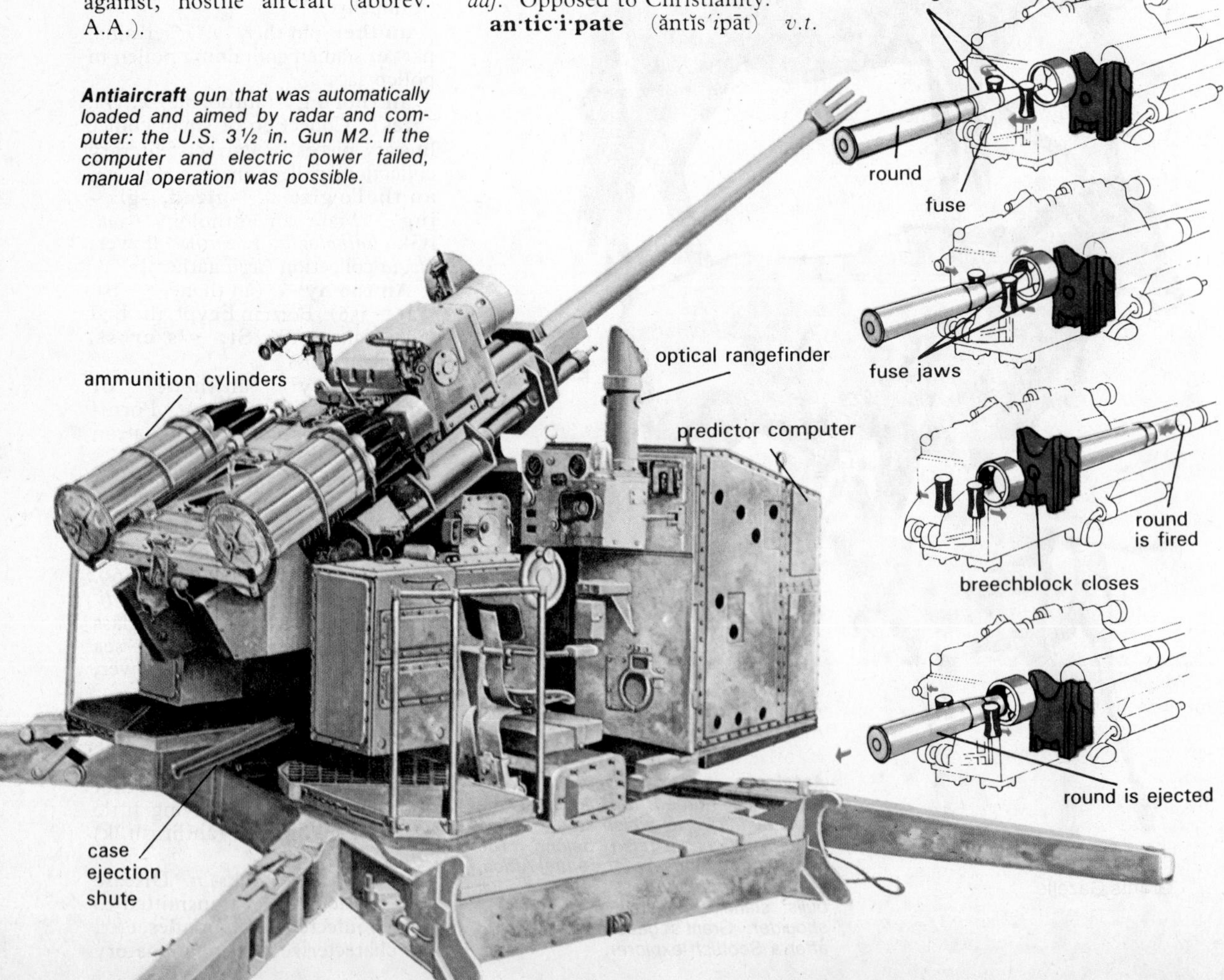

Antiaircraft *gun that was automatically loaded and aimed by radar and computer: the U.S. 3½ in. Gun M2. If the computer and electric power failed, manual operation was possible.*

English Harbor, former naval base at ***Antigua*** *where Nelson met his future wife, Frances Nisbet. A British possession from 1632, Antigua became independent in 1967.*

an·ti·de·pres·sant (ăntēdĭprĕs′-ant) *n.* Drug used in the treatment of mental depression to elevate spirits.

an·ti·dote (ăn′tĭdōt) *n.* Medicine etc. used to counteract disease or poison.

An·tie·tam (ăntē′tam). Creek near the town of Sharpsburg in W. Maryland; site of a major Civil War battle, 1862, in which the Confederates under Gen. Robert E. Lee were defeated by Union armies under Gen. McClellan.

an·ti·freeze (ăn′tĭfrēz) *n.* Chemical agent (usu. ethylene glycol) added to water to lower its freezing point, esp. in a car's radiator in winter.

an·ti·gen (ăn′tĭjen) *n.* Substance that stimulates production of an antibody when introduced into a living organism.

An·tig·o·ne (ăntĭg′onē). (Gk. legend) Daughter of Oedipus and Jocasta; she buried the body of her brother Polynices by night, against the order of her uncle King Creon; he condemned her to death but she took her own life.

an·ti·grav·i·ty (ăntēgrăv′ĭtē, ăntī-) *n.* Hypothetical force opposing gravity.

An·ti·gua (ăntē′gwa, -tĭg′wa). One of the Leeward Islands, in the West Indies, discovered in 1493 by Columbus; independent since 1967; capital, St. John's.

an·ti-he·ro (ăn′tē-hērō, ăntī-) *n.* (pl. **-roes**). Hero of unconventional type in novel etc.

an·ti·his·ta·mine (ăntĭhĭs′ta-mēn, -mĭn) *adj.* & *n.* (Drug) that counteracts the effect of histamine, used esp. in treatment of allergic conditions.

An·til·les (ăntĭl′ēz). Chain of West Indian islands separating the Caribbean Sea from the Atlantic Ocean; **Greater ~**, Cuba, Jamaica, Hispaniola (Haiti and the Dominican Republic), and Puerto Rico; **Lesser ~**, group of smaller islands to the SE.

an·ti·log (ăn′tĭlawg, -lŏg), **an·ti·log·a·rithm** (ăntĭlaw′gerĭ-dhem, -lŏg′e-) *ns.* Number to which a logarithm belongs (100 is the ~ of 2 to the base 10).

an·ti·ma·cas·sar (ăntĭmakăs′er) *n.* Covering on chair back to protect it from hair grease or as ornament. [f. *Macassar oil*, pop. as hair oil in 19th c.]

an·ti·mag·net·ic (ăntēmăgnĕt′-ik, ăntī-) *adj.* Resistant to magnetization, esp. of watch movements.

an·ti·mat·ter (ăn′tēmăter, ăn′-tī-) *n.* (Hypothetical) matter composed solely of antiparticles.

ant·i·mo·ny (ăn′timōnē) *n.* (chem.) Brittle metallic element, bluish-white, of flaky crystalline texture, used in alloys, esp. with lead, and in medicine; symbol Sb, at. no. 51, at. wt. 121.75.

an·ti·no·mi·an (ăntĭnō′mēan) *adj.* & *n.* (Person) holding that the moral law is not binding on Christians on the ground that faith alone is sufficient to salvation. **an·ti·no′mi·an·ism** *n.*

an·tin·o·my (ăntĭn′omē) *n.* (pl. **-mies**). Contradiction in a law, or between laws, principles, etc.

An·ti·och (ăn′tēŏk). Name of several ancient cities of the Near East, esp. (1) the capital of Syria under the Seleucid kings (now Antakya in Turkey near the Syrian border); (2) "Antioch toward Pisidia" in the Roman province of Galatia (near the present Yalvac in SW. Anatolia, Turkey).

an·ti·par·ti·cle (ăn′tēpārtĭkel, ăn′tī-) *n.* (phys.) One of a pair of particles of equal mass but with opposite electrical charge (e.g. electron and positron) or direction of magnetic moment.

an·ti·pas·to (ăntĭpahs′tō, -păs′-) *n.* (pl. **-tos,** *It.* **-ti** pr. -tē). Assorted appetizers such as smoked meats, fish, olives, etc.; hors d'oeuvre.

an·tip·a·thy (ăntĭp′athē) *n.* (pl. **-thies**). Constitutional or settled aversion (*to, against, between*). **an·ti·pa·thet·ic** (ăntĭpathĕt′ĭk) *adj.*

an·ti·per·son·nel (ăntēpērso-nĕl′, ăntī-) *adj.* (of bombs, mines, etc.) Designed to kill or injure persons.

an·ti·per·spi·rant (ăntĭpēr′-sperant) *n.* Substance applied to the

Anzac Day commemoration, Sydney, Australia. Remembrance services are held each year on April 25th to honor the Australian and New Zealand forces who fought in the 1914–18 and 1939–45 wars.

skin to reduce perspiration.

an·tiph·o·nal (ăntĭf′*o*nal) *adj.* Sung alternately.

an·tip·o·des (ăntĭp′*o*dēz) *n.pl.* Places on opposite sides of the earth; **A~**, Australasia as region diametrically opposite to Europe. **an·tip′o·dal** *adj.* **an·tip·o·de·an** (ăntĭp*o*dē′*a*n) *adj.* & *n.* [Gk., = "having the feet opposite"]

an·ti·pope (ăn′tĭpōp) *n.* Pope in opposition to one (held to be) canonically chosen.

an·ti·py·ret·ic (ăntēpīrĕt′ĭk) *adj.* & *n.* (Drug) allaying or preventing fever.

an·ti·quar·y (ăn′tĭkwĕrē) *n.* (pl. **-quar·ies**). Student or collector of antiques or antiquities. **an·ti·quar·i·an** (ăntĭkwār′ē*a*n) *adj.* & *n.* **an·ti·quar′i·an·ism** *n.*

an·ti·quat·ed (ăn′tĭkwātĭd) *adj.* Out of date; antique.

an·tique (ăntēk′) *adj.* Of or existing from old times; old-fashioned; of the ancients. ~ *n.* Relic of ancient art or of old times; piece of old furniture, work of art, etc., regarded as valuable esp. by collectors.

an·tiq·ui·ty (ăntĭk′wĭtē) *n.* (pl. **-ties**). Ancientness; ancient times, esp. (**classical ~**) the period of the ancient Greek and Roman civilizations; (pl.) customs, practices, etc., of ancient times, objects surviving from them.

an·ti·scor·bu·tic (ăntĭskôrbū′tĭk, ăntī-) *adj.* & *n.* (Medicine etc.) preventing or curing scurvy.

an·ti-Sem·ite (ăntēsĕm′īt, ăntī-) *adj.* & *n.* (Person) hostile to Jews. **an·ti-Se·mit·ic** (ăntēs*e*mĭt′ĭk, ăntī-) *adj.* **an·ti-Sem·i·tism** (ăntēsĕm′ĭtĭz*e*m, antī-) *n.*

an·ti·sep·sis (ăntĭsĕp′sĭs) *n.* (med.) Antiseptic treatment or condition.

an·ti·sep·tic (ăntĭsĕp′tĭk) *adj.* & *n.* 1. (Agent) counteracting sepsis; germicide. 2. Clean, sterile. **an·ti·sep′ti·cal·ly** *adv.*

an·ti·so·cial (ăntēsō′sh*a*l, ăntī-) *adj.* Opposed to principles on which society is based; hostile, antagonistic to others. **an·ti·so′cial·ly** *adv.*

an·ti·spas·mod·ic (ăntĭspăzmŏd′ĭk, ăntī-) *adj.* & *n.* (Drug) that relieves spasms.

An·tis·the·nes (ăntĭs′th*e*nēz) (5th c. B.C.). Athenian philosopher, pupil of Socrates and founder of the Cynic school of philosophy.

an·tith·e·sis (ăntĭth′ĭsĭs) *n.* (pl. **-ses** pr. -sēz). Contrast of ideas marked by parallelism of strongly contrasted words; direct opposite.

an·ti·thet·ic (ănt*i*thĕt′ĭk), **an·ti·thet′i·cal** *adjs.*

an·ti·tox·in (ăntĭtŏk′sĭn) *n.* Substance serving to neutralize a toxin. **an·ti·tox′ic** *adj.*

an·ti·trust (ăntētrŭst′, ăntī-) *adj.* (of law) Opposed to or intended to regulate trusts and monopolies.

an·ti·ven·in (ăntēvĕn′ĭn, ăntī-) *n.* Antitoxin, esp. against snake poison.

ant·ler (ănt′l*e*r) *n.* Whole or any branch of either horn of deer.

ant·li·on (ănt′lī*o*n) *n.* Any insect of the family Myrmeleontidae whose larva digs holes in sand to trap ants.

An·to·ni·nus Pi·us (ănt*o*nī′n*u*s pī′*u*s) (A.D. 86–161). Roman emperor 138–161.

an·ton·o·ma·sia (ănt*o*n*o*mā′zh*a*) *n.* Substitution of epithet etc. for proper name; use of proper name to express general idea (e.g. *a Solomon*).

An·to·ny (ăn′t*o*nē), **Mark.** Marcus Antonius (*c*83–30 B.C.), Roman general and consul; member of 2nd triumvirate; became enthralled by Cleopatra; was deprived of his powers (32 B.C.) by the senate and defeated at battle of Actium.

an·to·nym (ăn′t*o*nĭm) *n.* Word of contrary meaning to another.

an·trum (ăn′tr*u*m) *n.* (pl. **-tra** pr. -tr*a*). Cavity in the body, esp. one in the upper jawbone.

Ant·werp (ăn′twĕrp). (Fl. *Antwerpen*, Fr. *Anvers*) Belgian port city.

A·nu·bis (*a*nōō′bĭs, *a*nū′-). (Egyptian myth.) Jackal-headed deity, ruler of the dead, whom he conducts to the shades.

an·u·ran (anoor′*a*n, *a*nūr′-) *adj.* & *n.* (Member) of the Anura, an order of the Amphibia comprising frogs and toads, the adult forms of which have no tails or gills but have strong hind legs for leaping and swimming.

a·nus (ā′n*u*s) *n.* (pl. **a·nus·es**). Opening at end of alimentary canal through which solid matter is excreted.

an·vil (ăn′vĭl) *n.* Block (usu. of steel) on which metal is worked by smith; thing resembling this.

anx·i·e·ty (ăngzī′ĭtē) *n.* (pl. **-ties**). Uneasiness, concern; solicitous desire; neurotic fear. **anx·ious** (ăngk′sh*u*s, ăng′-) *adj.* Troubled, uneasy; earnestly desirous; causing anxiety. **anx′ious·ly** *adv.*

an·y (ĕn′ē) *adj.* & *pron.* One or some but no matter which; whichever is chosen. ~ *adv.* At all, in some degree.

an·y·bod·y (ĕn′ēbŏdē, -bŭdē) *n.* & *pron.* Any person.

an·y·how (ĕn′ēhow) *adv.* Anyway; in any case.

an·y·more (ĕnēmōr′, -môr′) *adv.* (colloq.) Now, henceforth (in neg. and interrog. constructions).

an·y·one (ĕn′ēwŭn) *n.* & *pron.* Anybody.

an·y·place (ĕn′ēplās) *adv.* (colloq.) Anywhere.

an·y·thing (ĕn′ēthĭng) *n.* & *pron.* Whatever thing; a thing, no matter which.

an·y·time (ĕn′ētīm) *adv.* At any time.

an·y·way (ĕn′ēwā) *adv.* In any way whatever; anyhow; (colloq.) carelessly.

an·y·where (ĕn′ēhwâr -wâr) *adv.* & *pron.* (In to) any place; **get ~**, (colloq.) attain success, make progress.

An·zac (ăn′zăk) *adj.* & *n.* (Belonging to, member of) the Australian and New Zealand Army Corps (Anzacs) in World War I; also applied to any Austral. and N.Z. group, characteristic, etc. [initials of name]

*The **Apache** Indians, forced out of their tribal lands by white settlers live mainly on reservations in New Mexico and Arizona where they farm small plots of land.*

*Renaissance town hall in Grote Markt, **Antwerp,** Belgium's chief port on the Scheldt about 55 miles from North Sea, for centuries a center of commerce and the arts. Rubens lived there.*

A-O.K., A-OK, A-O·Kay (ā'ō kā') *adjs.* Perfectly all right, excellent.

a·or·ta (āor'ta) *n.* (pl. **-tas, -tae** pr. -tē). Great artery issuing from left ventricle of heart, carrying blood through its branches to all other parts of body.

a·pace (apās') *adv.* Swiftly.

A·pach·e (apăch'ē) *n.* (pl. **A·pach·es,** collect. **A·pach·e**) & *adj.* (Member) of tribe of southwestern U.S. Indians, fierce and skillful in raiding.

a·pache (apăsh') *n.* Violent street ruffian in Paris; member of Parisian underworld; ~ **dance,** vigorous dance for two.

Ap·a·lach·i·co·la (ăpalăchĭkō'la) **River.** River in NW. Florida flowing from Georgia border 112 miles (180km) S. to the Gulf of Mexico.

a·part (apart') *adv.* Aside, separately; into pieces; to or at a

*The **ape** has manlike basic structure of head, neck, shoulder, girdle and arms. Illustrated: Orang-utan, a long-armed mainly arboreal ape up to 5½ ft. tall; gorilla, the largest anthropoid ape; the chimpanzee, most resembling man and allied to the gorilla; and the gibbon, arboreal and supremely agile.*

distance; ~ **from**, not considering, with the exception of. ~ *adj.* Unique.

a·part·heid (*a*pârt′hāt, -hīt) *n.* Policy of racial segregation in S. Africa; similar policy elsewhere. [Afrikaans]

a·part·ment (*a*pârt′m*e*nt) *n.* Single room or set of rooms for use as a dwelling; ~ **house**, building divided into apartments.

ap·a·thy (ăp′*a*thē) *n.* Insensibility to suffering; indifference; mental indolence. **ap·a·thet·ic** (ăp*a*thĕt′ĭk) *adj.* **ap·a·thet′i·cal·ly** *adv.*

ape (āp) *n.* Anthropoid ape (see ANTHROPOID); (pop.) monkey; big, stupid, clumsy man; **great ~s**, gorilla, chimpanzee, orangutan; **ape-man**, pithecanthrope. **ape** *v.t.* (**aped, ap·ing**). Imitate, mimic.

Ap·en·nines (ăp′*e*nīnz). Mountain range running down the length of Italy.

a·per·i·tif (*a*pĕrĭtēf′) *n.* Alcoholic drink taken before meal to stimulate appetite.

ap·er·ture (ăp′*e*rch*e*r) *n.* Opening, gap; space through which light passes in camera or other optical instrument.

a·pet·al·ous (āpĕt′*a*l*u*s) *adj.* Without petals.

a·pex (ā′pĕks) *n.* (pl. **a·pex·es, a·pi·ces** pr. ā′pĭsēz, ăp′ĭ-). Tip, top; vertex (of cone, triangle).

a·pha·sia (*a*fā′zh*a*) *n.* Loss of speech, partial or total, or loss of power to understand written or spoken language as result of damage to the brain.

a·phe·li·on (*a*fē′lē*o*n) *n.* (pl. **-li·a** pr. -lē*a*). Point of planet's or comet's orbit farthest from sun.

a·phid (ā′fĭd, ăf′ĭd) *n.* Small, soft-bodied insect of family Aphididae, infesting leaves and stems of plants.

a·phis (ā′fĭs, ăf′ĭs) *n.* (pl. **aph·i·des** pr. ăf′ĭdēz) = APHID.

aph·o·rism (ăf′*e*rĭz*e*m) *n.* Short, pithy statement or maxim. **aph·o·ris·tic** (ăf*e*rĭstĭk) *adj.*

aph·ro·dis·i·ac (ăfr*o*dĭz′ēăk) *adj.* & *n.* (Drug, food, etc.) provoking sexual desire. [f. APHRODITE]

Aph·ro·di·te (ăfr*o*dī′tē). (Gk. myth.) Goddess of love (esp. sensual), beauty, and fertility, born of the sea foam; identified by the

*Gran Sasso d'Italia, **Apennines,** mountain backbone of Italy, ranging some 838 miles in length, 25–80 miles in width.*

Romans with Venus; her cult was of eastern origin, and she was identified with Astarte, Ishtar, etc.

A·pi·a (ah′pĭy*a*). Capital of Western Samoa.

a·pi·ar·y (ā′pēĕrē) *n.* (pl. **-ar·ies**). Place where bees are kept.
a·pi·a·rist (ā′pēĕrĭst) *n.* Beekeeper.

ap·i·cal (ăp′ĭk*a*l, ā′pĭ-) *adj.* Belonging to an apex; placed at the tip; (phon., of sound) articulated with tip of tongue.

a·pi·cul·ture (ā′pĭkŭlch*er*) *n.* Beekeeping.

a·piece (*a*pēs′) *adv.* Severally, each.

A·pis (ā′pĭs). (Egyptian myth.) God, the incarnation as a bull of the sun-god Ptah, represented as a bull with the disk of the sun between his horns.

ap·ish (ā′pĭsh) *adj.* Like an ape.

a·plomb (*a*plŏm′, *a*plŭm′) *n.* Self-possession; poise.

A.P.O. *abbrev.* Army Post Office.

A·poc·a·lypse (*a*pŏk′*a*lĭps) *n.* Revelation, esp. that made to St. John in the island of Patmos; book of New Testament ("Revelation of St. John the Divine") recording this; cataclysmic event such as described in this book; end of the world. **a·poc·a·lyp·tic** (*a*pŏk*a*lĭp′tĭk) *adj.* Of or pertaining to this revelation or to such violent events. **a·poc·a·lyp′ti·cal** *adj.* **a·poc·a·lyp′ti·cal·ly** *adv.*

a·poc·o·pe (*a*pŏk′*o*pē) *n.* Cutting off of last sound or syllable of word.

Apocr. *abbrev.* Apocrypha.

a·poc·ry·pha (*a*pŏk′rĭf*a*) *n.pl.* 1. **the A ~**, books of Old Testament included in Septuagint and Vulgate, but not in Hebrew Bible and not in all modern Bibles. 2. Other writings of doubtful authenticity.

a·poc′ry·phal *adj.* 1. Of the Apocrypha; also applied to a number of early Christian writings in similar form to the canonical books of New Testament. 2. Of doubtful authenticity, spurious. [Gk. *apokrupha* hidden or secret (writings), i.e. those reserved for the initiated and often falsely ascribed]

ap·o·dal (ăp′*o*d*a*l) *adj.* & *n.* (zool.) Limbless (creature); (member) of the Apoda, an order of the Amphibia containing tropical legless wormlike animals, some of which have scales; (fish) with no ventral fin.

ap·o·gee (ăp′*o*jē) *n.* Point in orbit of moon, planet, or artificial satellite farthest from Earth; (fig.) highest point. **ap·o·ge·an** (ăp*o*jē′*a*n) *adj.*

a·po·lit·i·cal (āp*o*lĭt′ĭk*a*l) *adj.* Unconcerned with or detached from politics. **a·po·lit′i·cal·ly** *adv.*

A · pol · li · naire (ăp*a*wlēnĕr′), **Guillaume** (1880–1918). Pen name of Wilhelm Apollinaris de Kostrowitzky, Polish-born French poet and man of letters.

A·pol·lo (*a*pŏl′ō). (Gk. and Rom. myth.) God sometimes identified with the sun and called *Phoebus* (*Apollo*); son of Zeus and Leto and brother of Artemis; represented ideal type of manly beauty; associated esp. with music, poetry, and prophecy.

A·pol·lyon (*a*pŏl′y*o*n). "The destroyer," the angel of the bottomless pit (Rev. 9).

*The **Temple of Apollo** at Delphi, the shrine of the most famous Greek oracle. Apollo, a God of prophecy, was consulted if trouble threatened. The reply was often cryptic.*

a·pol·o·get·ic (*a*pŏl*o*jĕt′ĭk) *adj.* Regretfully acknowledging, excusing, fault or failure; of the nature of an apology. **a·pol·o·get′i·cal·ly** *adv.* **a·pol·o·get′ics** *n.pl.* (usu. considered sing.) Reasoned defense, esp. of Christianity. **a·pol·o·gist** (*a*pŏl′*o*jĭst) *n.* One who defends by argument. **a·pol′o·gize** *v.i.* (**-gized, -giz·ing**). Make an apology.

ap·o·lo·gi·a (ăp*o*lō′jē*a*) *n.* Defense or justification of conduct or opinions.

a·pol·ogy (*a*pŏl′*o*jē) *n.* (pl. **-gies**). Regretful acknowledgement of offense; statement of regret; apologia; ~ **for**, poor or scanty specimen of.

ap·o·phthegm (ăp′*o*thĕm) *n.*, **ap·o·phtheg·mat·ic** (ăp*o*thĕg′măt′ĭk) *adj.*: see APOTHEGM.

ap·o·plec·tic (ăp*o*plĕk′tĭk) *adj.* Pertaining to, causing, apoplexy; liable to, suffering from, apoplexy. **ap·o·plec′ti·cal·ly** *adv.*

ap·o·plex·y (ăp′*o*plĕksē) *n.* Seizure caused by blockage or rupture of an artery in the brain.

a·port (*a*pōrt′, *a*pōrt′) *adv.* (naut.) On or toward the port (left) side.

ap·o·si·o·pe·sis (ăp*o*sī*o*pē′sĭs) *n.* (pl. **-ses** pr. -sēz). (rhet.) Breaking off short for effect.

a·pos·ta·sy (*a*pŏs′t*a*sē) *n.* (pl. **-sies**). Renunciation of religious vows, faith, party, etc.

a·pos·tate (*a*pŏs′tāt, -tĭt) *n.* & *adj.* (One) guilty of apostasy. **a·pos·ta·tize** (*a*pŏs′t*a*tīz) *v.i.* (**-tized, -tiz·ing**). Become an apostate.

a pos·te·ri·o·ri (ā pŏstērēōr′ī, -ōr′ī, -ōr′ē, -ōr′ē). (Reasoning) from effects to causes. [L., = "from what comes after"]

a·pos·tle (*a*pŏs′*e*l) *n.* Messenger, esp. (**A ~**) any of the 12 disciples sent forth by Christ to preach Gospel (Matt. 10); first successful Christian missionary in a country; leader of reform; **Apostles' Creed**, simplest and prob. oldest of the Christian creeds, ascribed by tradition to the Apostles and beginning "I believe in God the Father Almighty." **ap·os·tol·ic** (ăp*o*stŏl′ĭk) *adj.* Of the Apostles; of the character of an Apostle; of the pope, esp. as successor of St. Peter.

a·pos·tro·phe (*a*pŏs′tr*o*fē) *n.* The sign (') of omission of letter(s); also used in possessive case of nouns and to indicate plurals of numbers, omission of letters, etc.

a·poth·e·car·y (*a*pŏth′ekĕrē) *n.* (pl. **-car·ies**). (obsolesc.) Pharmacist, druggist; pharmacy, drugstore. **apothecaries' measure, weight**, system of liquid measures, weights, used in pharmacy. [Gk. *apothēkē* storehouse]

ap·o·thegm, ap·o·phthegm (ăp′*o*thĕm) *ns.* Terse or pithy

*The **Appalachian Mountains** extend for about 1,200 miles from Canada to Alabama. The Appalachian Trail offers spectacular hiking through 14 States and 8 national forests.*

saying. **ap·o·theg·mat·ic, ap·o·phtheg·mat·ic** (ăpothĕgmăt´ĭk) *adjs.*

a·poth·e·o·sis (*a*pŏthēō´sĭs, ăp*o*thē´*o*sĭs) *n.* (pl. **-ses** pr. -sēz). Deification; deified ideal. **a·poth·e·o·size** (*a*pŏth´ē*o*sīz, ăp*o*thē´*o*sīz) *v.t.* (**-sized, -siz·ing**).

app. *abbrev.* Appendix; apparent(ly).

Ap·pa·la·chi·a (ăp*a*lā´chē*a*, -ch*a*, -lăch´ē*a*, -lăch´*a*, -lā´kē*a*). Region in SE. U.S., in the area of the S. Appalachian Mountains, noted for scenery, coal mining, and poverty. **Ap·pa·la′chi·an** *adj.* ~ **Mountains**, chief mountain chain of eastern N. America, from Ala. to S. Quebec; highest peak Mt. Mitchell (6,684 feet, 2,037m) in S.C.; ~ **Trail**, system of trails through the ~ **Mountains** extending 2,000 miles from Maine to Georgia.

ap·pall (*a*pawl´) *v.t.* Dismay, terrify. **ap·pall′ing** *adj.* Horrifying; (colloq.) very bad.

Ap·pa·loo·sa (ăp*a*lōō´s*a*) *n.* Horse of western Amer. breed with dark spots on light background.

ap·pa·ra·tus (ăp*a*răt´*u*s, -rā´t*u*s) *n.* (pl. **-tus, -tus·es**). 1. Mechanical requisites, an appliance, for doing something, esp. for scientific experiment; a complex machine. 2. Organs effecting a natural process. 3. A political organization.

ap·par·el (*a*păr´el) *v.t.* (**-eled, -el·ing**; *Brit.* **-elled, -el·ling**). (archaic) Dress, clothe. ~ *n.* Dress, clothing.

ap·par·ent (*a*păr´ent, *a*pār´-) *adj.* Manifest; seeming; **heir** ~, one who cannot be superseded by birth of nearer heir (cf. PRESUMPTIVE). **ap·par′ent·ly** *adv.*

ap·pa·ri·tion (ăp*a*rĭsh´*o*n) *n.* Appearance, esp. of ghostly or startling kind; thing thought to be seen but having no material existence.

ap·peal (*a*pēl´) *v.i.* Application *to* higher court for alteration of decision of lower; call (*to* witness) for corroboration, (*to* person) for assistance etc.; make earnest request; ~ **to**, be, prove, attractive to. ~ *n.* Act or right of appealing; earnest request, entreaty; quality that appeals; **Court of Appeals**, one hearing cases previously tried in a lower court.

ap·pear (*a*pēr´) *v.i.* Become visible; present oneself; seem; be manifest; come before the public; be present; (law) come before a court. **ap·pear·ance** (*a*pēr´*a*ns) *n.* Appearing; look, aspect; (pl.) outward show (of prosperity etc.); apparition.

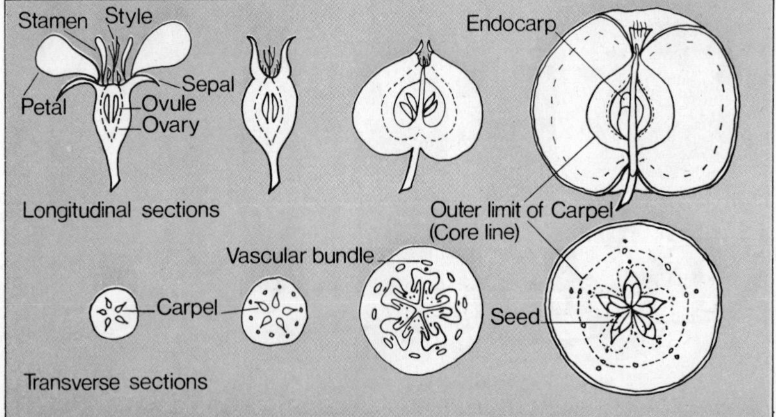

*Cutting away the stamens of **apple** blossom on an apple farm in Kent U.K. In the U.K. alone there are 2,000 varieties of apple; it is the most widely cultivated fruit of temperate climates. It thrives in any good, well-drained soil but is susceptible to frost and a large number of pests. The drawing shows successive stages in the apple from flower to fruit.*

ap·pease (apēz′) *v.t.* (**-peased, -peas·ing**). Pacify, soothe; make concessions to (an aggressor); satisfy. **ap·pease′ment** *n.*

ap·pel·lant (apĕl′ant) *n.* One who appeals to higher court. **ap·pel·late** (apĕl′ĭt) *adj.* Having authority to hear appeals and reverse decisions, as an ~ **court.**

ap·pel·la·tion (ăpelā′shon) *n.* Identifying name, title.

ap·pend (apĕnd′) *v.t.* Attach to as an accessory; add, esp. in writing. **ap·pend·age** (apĕn′dĭj) *n.*

ap·pen·dec·to·my (ăpendĕk′-tomē) *n.* (pl. **-mies**). (surg.) Excision of appendix.

ap·pen·di·ci·tis (apĕndisī′tĭs) *n.* Inflammation of vermiform appendix.

ap·pen·dix (apĕn′dĭks) *n.* (pl. **-dix·es, -di·ces** pr. -dĭsēz). 1. Subsidiary addition (*to* book etc.) 2. Small process developed from organ, esp. vermiform appendix of the intestine.

ap·per·tain (ăpertān′) *v.i.* Belong, be appropriate, relate *to.*

ap·pe·tite (ăp′ĭtīt) *n.* Desire, inclination (*for* food, pleasure, etc.); relish. **ap·pe·tiz·er** (ăp′ĭtīzer) *n.* Anything taken to give appetite for a meal. **ap·pe·tiz·ing** (ăp′etīzĭng) *adj.* Inducing appetite.

Ap·pi·an (ăp′ēan) **Way.** Roman highway running SE. from Rome to Brundisium (Brindisi), begun by the censor Appius Claudius Caecus, 312 B.C.

ap·plaud (aplawd′) *v.* Express approval (of), esp. by handclapping; praise.

ap·plause (aplawz′) *n.* Approval loudly expressed, esp. by handclapping.

ap·ple (ăp′el) *n.* Firm, fleshy, edible fruit of a rosaceous tree of genus *Malus;* ~ **butter**, jam made from apples; **upset person's applecart**, spoil plans; **ap′plejack** (*n.*), spirit distilled from cider; apple brandy; **apple of discord**, (Gk. myth.) golden apple, inscribed "For the fairest," contended for by Hera, Athene, and Aphrodite; see PARIS[2]; hence, cause, subject, of dispute; **apple of one's eye**, pupil, treasured person; **apple pandowd′y**, thick-crusted dessert of apples, sugar, and spices; **apple-pie order**, extreme neatness; **apple-polish** (*v.i.*), (colloq.) curry favor; **apple polisher** *n.*; **ap′plesauce** *n.*, apples sweetened and stewed to a pulp; (slang) nonsense.

Ap·ple·seed (ăp′elsēd), **Johnny** (1774–1845). Nickname of John Chapman, American pioneer and legendary hero; ranged over the Ohio River Valley planting and nurturing apple trees.

ap·pli·ance (aplī′ans) *n.* Any device or machine, esp. electrical or for household use.

ap·pli·ca·ble (ăp′lĭkabel, aplĭk′-) *adj.* Capable of being applied. **ap·pli·ca·bil·i·ty** (ăplĭkabĭl′ĭtē) *n.*

ap·pli·cant (ăp′lĭkant) *n.* One who applies.

ap·pli·ca·tion (ăplĭkā′shon) *n.* Applying; thing applied; request; relevancy; diligence; printed form to make a request on (as for a job).

ap·pli·ca·tor (ap′lĭkāter) *n.* Device for applying a substance.

ap·pli·qué (ăplĭkā′) *n.* & *adj.* (Needlework) consisting of pieces of material cut out and sewn to the surface of other material of different color or texture; material so applied. ~ *v.t.* (**-quéd, -qué·ing**). Sew (material) to another as appliqué.

ap·ply (aplī′) *v.* (**-plied, -ply·ing**). Put in contact; administer (remedy); be relevant or suitable; devote (*to*); address oneself (*for* help etc.) *to*; make application (*for*); make use of; **applied** (*adj.*), put to practical use.

ap·point (apoint′) *v.t.* Fix (time etc.); assign *to* an office or position; **well appointed, badly appointed**, so equipped. **ap·point·ee** (apointē′) *n.* Person appointed.

ap·point·ment (apoint′ment) *n.* Act of appointing; agreement to meet at specific time; office assigned; (pl.) furnishings, equipment.

Ap·po·mat·tox (ăpomăt′oks). Town in central Virginia; site of courthouse where Gen. Robert E. Lee surrendered to Gen. Ulysses S. Grant on April 9, 1865, ending the Civil War.

ap·por·tion (apōr′shon, -pōr′-) *v.t.* Give as due share; portion out. **ap·por′tion·ment** *n.*

ap·po·site (ăp′ozĭt) *adj.* Well put; appropriate. **ap·po·si·tion** (ăpozĭsh′on) *n.* Placing side by side; **in** ~, (gram.) syntactically parallel; in same case etc.

ap·praise (aprāz′) *v.t.* (**-praised, -prais·ing**). Fix or estimate value of; estimate. **ap·prais′al, ap·praise′ment** *ns.*

ap·pre·cia·ble (aprē′shabel) *adj.* Enough to be seen or estimated perceptible. **ap·pre′cia·bly** *adv*

ap·pre·ci·ate (aprē′shēāt) *v.* (**-at·ed, -at·ing**). Estimate rightly; recognize, understand; be thankful for; be sensitive to; esteem highly; raise, rise, in value. **ap·pre·ci·a·tion** (aprēshēā′shon) *n.* **ap·pre·cia·tive** (aprē′shatĭv, -shēā-) *adj.*

ap·pre·hend (ăprĭhĕnd′) *v.t.* Seize, arrest; understand; anticipate with fear.

ap·pre·hen·si·ble (ăprĭhĕn′sibel) *adj.* Perceptible to senses.

ap·pre·hen·sion (ăprĭhĕn′shon) *n.* 1. Arrest; capture. 2. Understanding. 3. Uneasiness.

ap·pre·hen·sive (ăprĭhĕn′sĭv) *adj.* Relating to sensory perception, or intellectual understanding; uneasy in mind. **ap·pre·hen′sive·ly** *adv.* **ap·pre·hen′sive·ness** *n.*

ap·pren·tice (aprĕn′tĭs) *n.* Learner of a craft, formerly bound to serve, and entitled to instruction from, his employer for a specified term; a beginner. ~ *v.t.* (**-ticed, -tic·ing**). Bind or place as apprentice (*to*). **ap·pren′tice·ship** *n.*

ap·prise (aprīz′) *v.t.* (**-prised, -pris·ing**). Give notice *of*, inform.

ap·proach (aprōch′) *v.* Come near or nearer (to); set about (task); make overtures to. ~ *n.* Approaching; access, passage; (golf) shot that is intended to reach green. **ap·proach′a·ble** *adj.* Easy of access; welcoming, friendly to advances.

ap·pro·ba·tion (ăprobā′shon) *n.* Sanction, approval.

ap·pro·pri·ate (aprō′prēĭt) *adj.* Suitable, proper. **ap·pro′pri·ate·ly** *adv.* **ap·pro·pri·ate** (aprō′prēāt) *v.t.* (**-at·ed, -at·ing**). Take possession of; devote to special purposes. **ap·pro·pri·a·tion** (aprōprēā′shon) *n.* Funds set aside for a particular purpose.

ap·prove (aprōōv′) *v.* (**-proved, -prov·ing**). Confirm, sanction, commend; ~ **of**, pronounce or consider good. **ap·prov·al** (aprōō′val) *n.* Approving; **on** ~, (of goods supplied) to be returned if not satisfactory.

approx. *abbrev.* Approximate, approximately.

ap·prox·i·mate (aprŏk′sĭmĭt) *adj.* Very near; fairly correct. **ap·prox′i·mate·ly** *adv.* **ap·prox·i·mate** (aprŏk′sĭmāt) *v.* (**-mat·ed, -mat·ing**). Bring or come near (*to*). **ap·prox·i·ma·tion** (aprŏksimā′shon) *n.*

ap·pur·te·nance (apēr′tenans) *n.* Appendage, accessory; belonging. **ap·pur′te·nant** *adj.* Belonging, appertaining.

Apr. *abbrev.* April.

a·près-ski (ăprāskē′, ah-) *n.* & *adj.* (Of, suitable for) time, period of relaxation, after skiing.

ap·ri·cot (ăp′rĭkŏt, ā′pri-) *n.* Succulent orange-pink fruit, with smooth stone, of the rosaceous tree *Prunus armeniaca*; this tree; color of the fruit.

A·pril (ā′pril). Fourth month of Gregorian (2nd of Julian) calendar, with 30 days; ~ **Fools' Day**, April 1 (the celebration of which is probably a survival of ancient festivities held at spring equinox), when the unsuspecting are made victims of practical jokes or sent on fools' errands.

a pri·o·ri (ā prīōr′ī, -ōr′ī, ā prēōr′ē, -ōr′ē, ah prē-) *adv.* & *adj. phr.* (Reasoning) from cause to effect; deductive(ly); presumptive(ly), without investigation; (of knowledge) obtained by deduction without sensory experience. [L., =

"from what is before"]

a·pron (ā′pron) *n.* 1. Garment worn in front of body to protect clothes; **tied to ~ strings of** (mother, wife, etc.), unduly dependent on. 2. Part of ceremonial dress (of bishops, freemasons, etc.). 3. (theatr.) Advanced strip of stage for playing scenes before proscenium arch. 4. Area near hangars of airfield for accommodation of aircraft maneuvering on ground.

ap·ro·pos (ăpropō′) *adv.* To the purpose; in respect *of.* ~ *adj.* Pertinent.

apse (ăps) *n.* Semicircular or polygonal recess, usu. with vaulted roof, in church or other building.

ap·sis (ăp′sĭs) *n.* (pl. **ap·si·des** pr. ăp′sĭdēz). Aphelion or perihelion of planet; apogee or perigee of moon.

apt (ăpt) *adj.* Suitable, appropriate; quick, ready; inclined (*to*). **apt′ly** *adv.* **apt′ness** *n.*

ap·ter·ous (ăp′terus) *adj.* (zool.) Wingless.

ap·ti·tude (ăp′tĭtōōd, -tūd) *n.* Fitness, natural propensity; ability; (psychol.) capacity to acquire skill in a particular field of bodily or mental performance.

Ap·u·le·ius (ăpyulē′us), **Lucius** (b. *c*123 A.D.). Platonic philosopher, of Madaura in N. Africa; author of the satire known as *The Golden Ass.*

A·pu·lia (apūl′ya). Ancient country and modern region (It. *Puglia*) forming the so-called heel of SE. Italy. **A·pu′lian** *adj.* & *n.*

A·qa·ba (ah′kahbah). Seaport in SW. Jordan; **Gulf of ~**, an extension of the Red Sea between Saudi Arabia and the Sinai Peninsula.

aq·ua (ăk′wa, ah′kwa) *n.* (pl. **aq·uae** pr. ăk′wē, ah′kwē, **aq·uas**). 1. Water. 2. Aquamarine. 3. (pharm.) Liquid; solution, esp. in water.

aq·ua (ăk′wa, ah′kwa) **for·tis** (fŏr′tĭs). (obs.) Nitric acid. [L., = "strong water"]

Aq·ua-Lung (ăk′walŭng, ah′-kwa-) *n.* (trademark) Diver's portable breathing apparatus, consisting of cylinders of compressed air with valve and mouthpiece.

aq·ua·ma·rine (ăkwamarēn′, ahkwa-) *n.* Bluish-green transparent beryl; color of this. [L. *aqua marina* sea water]

aq·ua·naut (ăk′wanawt, -nŏt, ah′kwa-) *n.* Underwater explorer or swimmer, esp. one who lives in underwater installation for an extended time.

aq·ua·plane (ăk′waplān, ah′-kwa-) *n.* Board towed behind speed boat, carrying a rider. ~ *v.i.* (**-planed, -plan·ing**). 1. Ride on aquaplane. 2. (of vehicle traveling on wet surface) Lose contact with surface through build-up of water beneath tires.

aq·ua (ăk′wa, ah′kwa) **re·gia** (rē′ja, rē′jēa). Mixture of concentrated nitric and hydrochloric acids, able to dissolve gold and platinum, which are not attacked by the unmixed acids. [L., = "royal water"]

aq·ua·relle (ăkwarĕl′, ahkwa-) *n.* (Painting in) transparent watercolor.

a·quar·i·um (akwār′ēum) *n.* (pl. **a·quar·i·ums, a·quar·i·a** pr. akwār′ēa). Artificial pond or tank for keeping live aquatic plants, fishes, or animals; park, building, or room, etc. containing such tanks.

A·quar·i·us (akwār′ēus). The Water Carrier, a constellation; 11th sign (♒) of the zodiac, which the sun enters about Jan. 21. **A·quar′-i·an** *adj.* & *n.*

a·quat·ic (akwăt′ĭk, akwŏt′-) *adj.* Living in or frequenting water; (of sports) conducted in or on water. ~ *n.* Aquatic plant or animal; (pl.) aquatic sports.

aq·ua·vit (ah′kwavēt, ăk′wa-) *n.* Colorless or yellowish alcoholic liquor distilled from potatoes or other starch-containing plant; schnapps.

aq·ua (ăk′wa, ah′kwa) **vi·tae** (vī′tē). (obs.) Brandy or other alcoholic spirit; (alchemy) alcohol. [L., = "water of life"]

aq·ue·duct (ăk′wĭdŭkt) *n.* Artificial channel, esp. elevated structure of masonry across valley etc. for conveyance of water.

a·que·ous (ā′kwēus, ăk′wē-) *adj.* Of water, watery; (geol.) produced by the action of water.

aq·ui·cul·ture (ăk′wikŭlcher) *n.* Cultivation of plants or breeding of animals in water; hydroponics.

aq·ui·le·gia (ăkwilē′ja) *n.* Plant of genus *A ~*; columbine.

aq·ui·line (ăk′wilīn, -lĭn) *adj.* Of an eagle; eagle-like; curved like eagle's beak.

A·qui·nas (akwī′nas), **St. Thomas** (*c*1225–74). Italian theologian and philosopher, a Dominican friar, whose writings, notably his *Summa Totius Theologiae*, represent the culmination of scholastic philosophy.

AR *abbrev.* Arkansas.

Ar *symbol.* Argon.

Ar·ab (ăr′ab) *n.* 1. One of an orig. Semitic people inhabiting Saudi Arabia and neighboring countries. 2. = ARABIAN horse. 3. **street a ~**, homeless child. 4. **~ League**, confederation of Arab states established 1945 and augmented later; headquarters in Cairo; members Egypt, Saudi Arabia, Syria, etc. **Arab** *adj.*

ar·a·besque (ărabĕsk′) *adj.* Arabian; Moorish, esp. in design; fantastic. ~ *n.* 1. Decoration of fancifully twisted scrollwork, leaves, etc., orig. devised by Muslim artists owing to ban on images. 2. Musical composition suggestive of this decoration. 3. (ballet) Pose in which dancer stands on one foot with one arm extended in front and the other arm and leg extended behind.

The Romans were the best if not the earliest builders of ***aqueducts.*** *Water from mountain springs was channelled through a duct. Below: The Pont du Gard, which supplied water to Nimes, southern France.*

The ***Aqua-Lung*** *(scuba) has been widely used since the 1939–45 war where it was developed by naval frogmen to facilitate underwater demolition work. Scuba diving has since become a popular sport.*

SR 2000

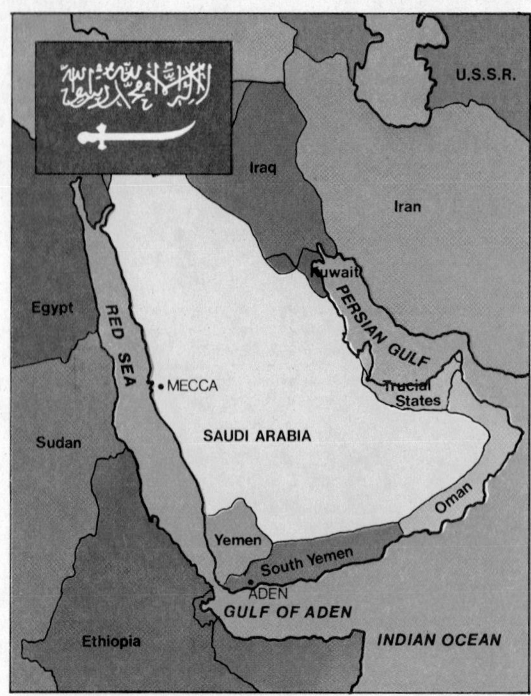

Left: Arabian Hall in Lord Leighton's house, London, U.K.: an example of ***arabesque*** *decoration. A successful 19th-century painter, Leighton toured the East in 1873 to collect objects for his house. Right: Map of* ***Arabia,*** *linked to Africa by the Sinai Peninsula. The length of this vast region, from N.E. to S.W., is 1,800 miles; its maximum width from the Yemen to Oman 1,300 miles. Total area is about 1 million square miles.*

A·ra·bi·a (*a*rā′bē*a*). Peninsula of SW. Asia, largely desert, lying between the Red Sea and the Persian Gulf and bounded on the north by Jordan and Iraq. See SAUDI ~.

A·ra·bi·an (*a*rā′bē*a*n) *adj.* Of Arabia or the Arabs; ~ **camel** = DROMEDARY; ~ **Desert**, Egyptian desert area between the Nile and the Red Sea; ~ **horse**, orig. bred in Arabia, noted for its graceful build and speed; ~ **Nights' (Entertainments)**, also called the *Thousand and One Nights*, a collection of Arabian fairy stories and fantastic romances linked together by a framework of Persian origin; the tales themselves were probably collected in Egypt during the 14th–16th centuries; ~ **Sea**, NW. part of Indian Ocean, between Arabia and India. **Arabian** *n.* Arab.

Ar·a·bic (ăr′*a*bĭk) *adj.* Arabian; **gum a~**, gum exuded from various kinds of acacia and used in the manufacture of adhesives, confectionery, and in textile printing, pharmacy, etc.; ~ **numerals**, those (1, 2, 3, etc.) now in common use in all western countries, most of which were first used in India and were introduced into the west by the Arabs. **Arabic** *n.* Semitic language, orig. that of the Arabs, but now spoken in a large part of N. Africa, Syria, and neighboring countries.

Ar·ab·ist (ăr′*a*bĭst) *n.* Student of Arabic or of Arab civilization etc.

ar·a·ble (ăr′*a*bel) *adj.* & *n.* (Land) suitable for plowing.

Ar·a·by (ăr′*a*bē). (poet.) Arabia.

a·ra·ceous (*a*rā′sh*u*s) *adj.* Of the Araceae or arum family of plants.

A·rach·ne (*a*răk′nē). (Gk. legend) Skillful weaver who challenged Athena to a contest; Athena tore the work up and when Arachne hanged herself changed her into a spider.

a·rach·nid (*a*răk′nĭd) *n.* (zool.) Member of the Arachnida, a class of wingless arthropods including spiders, scorpions, mites, king crabs, and others, and distinguished from insects esp. by having eight or more legs and no antennae.

a·rach·noid (*a*răk′noid) *adj.* 1. Of the arachnids. 2. (anat.) Of the three membranes surrounding the brain and supporting the blood-vessels. ~ *n.* Arachnoid membrane.

Ar·a·gon (ăr′*a*gŏn). Region of Spain, bounded on N. by the Pyrenees and on E. by Catalonia and Valencia.

Ar·al (ăr′*a*l) **Sea.** Inland sea of U.S.S.R., E. of Caspian Sea.

Ar·am (ăr′*a*m, ār′-). Biblical name of Syria. **Ar·a·mae·an** (ăr*a*mē′*a*n) *adj.* & *n.*

Ar·a·ma·ic (ăr*a*mā′ĭk) *adj.* & *n.* (Of) the NW. Semitic language, closely related to Hebrew, spoken in SW. Asia in the later Babylonian Empire and until *c*7th c. A.D.

Ar·an (ăr′*a*n) **Islands.** Group of three islands off W. coast of Ireland, lying across mouth of Galway Bay. **Ar′an** *adj.*

A·rap·a·ho (*a*răp′*a*hō) *n.* (pl. **-hos**, collect. **-ho**). (Member, language) of a tribe of N. Amer. Indians of Algonquian speech group, formerly living in Nebraska and Kansas, now in Wyoming and Oklahoma.

Ar·a·rat (ăr′*a*răt). Either of two peaks of the Armenian plateau, in which region Noah's ark is said (Gen. 8) to have rested after the Flood (**Great** ~, 5,165 m, 16,945 ft.).

ar·bi·ter (ār′bĭt*e*r) *n.* Judge; one appointed to settle dispute; one with entire control *of*.

ar·bi·trage (ār′bĭtrahzh) *n.* Buying of stocks, etc., for immediate sale in other markets at higher prices. **ar′bi·trag·er** *n.*

ar·bi·trar·y (ār′bĭtrĕrē) *adj.* Derived from mere opinion, capricious; despotic; (law) discretionary. **ar·bi·trar·i·ly** (ār′bĭtrĕr*i*lē, ārbĭtrār′-) *adv.*

ar·bi·trate (ār′bĭtrāt) *v.* (**-trat·ed, -trat·ing**). Decide by arbitration. **ar·bi·tra·tion** (ārbĭtrā′sh*o*n) *n.* Settlement of dispute by an arbiter.

ar·bi·tra·tor (ār′bĭtrāt*e*r) *n.* One chosen to settle dispute.

ar·bor (ār′b*e*r) *n.* Shady retreat with sides and roof of trees or climbing plants; bower; **A~ Day**, day annually appointed in many states for public tree-planting.

ar·bo·ra·ceous (ārb*e*rā′sh*u*s) *adj.* Tree-like; wooded.

ar·bo·re·al (ārbōr′ē*a*l, -bōr′-) *adj.* Of, living in, trees.

*Scorpions comprise one of the main orders of **arachnids.** Shown is a large African species that hides in a burrow in the daytime. The poisonous sting in the tail is used to kill prey.*

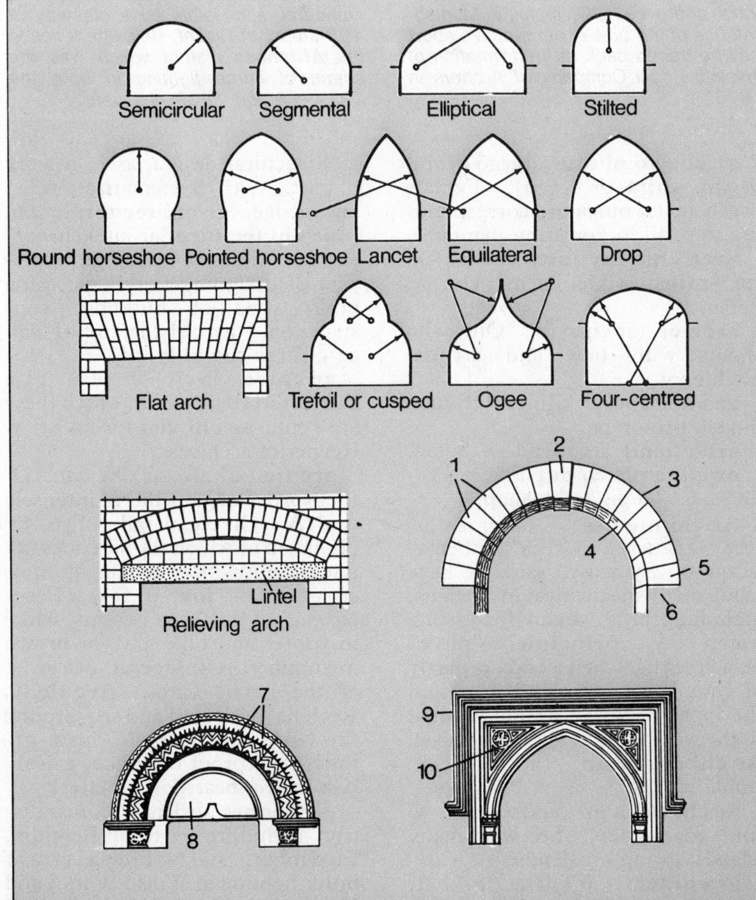

*Diagrams show various types of **arches** and their construction. Key: 1. Voussoirs. 2. Keystone. 3. Extrados. 4. Intrados. 5. Springer. 6. Impost. 7. Orders. 8. Tympanum. 9. Hoodmold, dripstone or label. 10. Spandrel. The keystone is crucial, 'locking' the structure.*

ar·bo·re·ous (ar̄bōr′ēus, -bōr′-) *adj.* Wooded; arboreal; arborescent.

ar·bo·res·cent (ar̄berĕs′ent) *adj.* Treelike; branching. **ar·bo·res′-cence** *n.*

ar·bo·re·tum (ar̄berē′tum) *n.* (pl. **-tums, -ta** pr. -ta). Tree garden.

ar·bor·i·cul·ture (ar̄′berĭkŭlcher) *n.* Cultivation of trees and shrubs. **ar·bor·i·cul·tu·ral** (ar̄berĭkŭl′cheral) *adj.* **ar·bor·i·cul′tur·ist** *n.*

ar·bor·vi·tae (ar̄bervī′tē) *n.* Coniferous evergreen shrub of genus *Thuja*.

ar·bu·tus (ar̄bū′tus) *n.* (pl. **-tus·es**). Evergreen plant of genus *A*~ of the heather family with red berries.

arc (ar̄k) *n.* 1. Part of circumference of circle or other curve. 2. (elect.) Intense electrical discharge in gas or vapor, a luminous bridge of conducting gas formed between two separate electrical poles; ~ **lamp,** ~ **light**, lamp using this; ~ **welding**: see WELD².

ar·cade (ar̄kād′) *n.* 1. Passage arched over; any covered walk, esp. one with shops etc. at side(s). 2. (archit.) Series of arches supported by columns.

Ar·ca·di·a (ar̄kā′dēa). Mountainous district in the Peloponnese, taken as an ideal region of rustic contentment (in this sense also **Ar·ca·dy** pr. ar̄′kadē). **Ar·ca′-di·an** *adj.* & *n.* (Native, inhabitant) of Arcadia; ideal(ly) rustic.

ar·cane (ar̄kān′) *adj.* Mysterious, secret.

ar·ca·num (ar̄kā′num) *n.* (usu. in pl. **-na** pr. -na). Mystery, secret.

arch¹ (ar̄ch) *n.* Structure, usu. curved, consisting of wedge-shaped pieces so arranged as to support one another by mutual pressure, and used to carry weight of roof, wall, etc., or as ornament; any curved structure resembling this in form and function; curve; vault; (anat.) curve on inner side of foot; **arch′-way** *n.*, arched passage or entrance. **arch** *v.* Furnish with, form into, form, an arch; span.

arch² (ar̄ch) *adj.* Making hints or allusions in a jocose affected manner. **arch′ly** *adv.* **arch′ness** *n.*

arch. *abbrev.* Archaic; architect; architecture.

arch- *comb. form.* Chief, superior; leading; extreme; first.

ar·chae·ol·o·gy (ar̄kēŏl′ojē) *n.* Study of ancient peoples and cultures through their material remains. **ar·chae·o·log·i·cal** (ar̄kē-

The U.S. ***archer,*** *John Williams, in action at the 1972 Olympics in Munich. The use of the bow in competitive sport may be traced back to the formation of Britain's Royal Company of Archers in 1676.*

The 11th-century cliff-top citadel and cathedral, accessible by a stairway of 408 steps, at Dinant, Belgium. It lies in the ***Ardennes*** *district which was the scene of fierce fighting in both the 1914–18 and 1939–45 wars.*

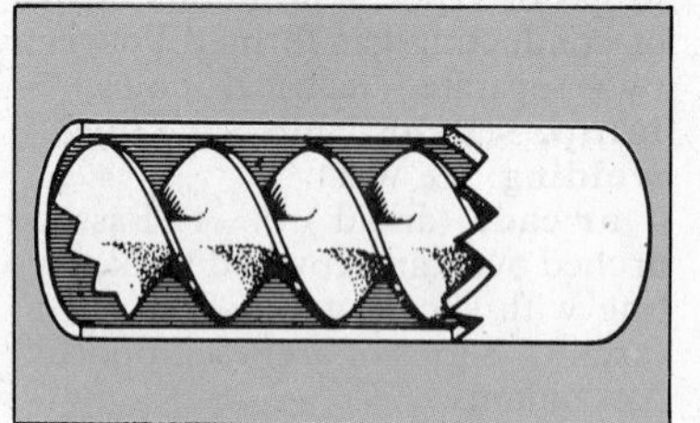

Archimedes *was an early master of mechanics and hydrostatics. He invented the pulley and probably the hydrometer. His Archimedean screw (shown) is a method of raising water by turning a tube with a screw inside it.*

*o*lŏj′ĭk*a*l) *adj.* **ar·chae·o·log′i·cal·ly** *adv.* **ar·chae·ol′o·gist** *n.*

ar·chae·op·ter·yx (ar̄kēŏp′t*e*-rĭks) *n.* Extinct primitive bird of the Jurassic period, transitional between reptile and bird.

ar·cha·ic (ar̄kā′ĭk) *adj.* Primitive, antiquated; no longer in common use. **ar·cha′i·cal·ly** *adv.*

ar·cha·ism (ar̄′kēĭz*e*m, -kā-) *n.* Obsolete word or phrase; retention or imitation of the old or obsolete (esp. in language and art).

arch·an·gel (ar̄k′ānj*e*l) *n.* Angel of highest rank (see ANGEL).

arch·bish·op (ar̄chbĭsh′*o*p) *n.* Chief bishop. **arch·bish′op·ric** *n.*

arch·dea·con (ar̄chdē′k*o*n) *n.* Ecclesiastical dignitary next below bishop.

arch·di·o·cese (ar̄chdī′*o*sĭs, -sēz) *n.* Archbishop's diocese.

arch·duke (ar̄ch′dōōk′, -dūk′) *n.* Prince of former imperial house of Austria. **arch′du′cal** *adj.* **arch·duch·ess** (ar̄ch′dŭch′ĭs) *n.*

ar·che·go·ni·um (ar̄k*e*gō′nē*u*m) *n.* (pl. **-ni·a** pr. -nē*a*). Female organ in cryptogams, corresponding to pistil in flowering plants.

arch·en·e·my (ar̄ch′ĕn′*e*mē) *n.* (pl. **-mies**). Chief enemy; **the ~**, Satan.

arch·er (ar̄′ch*e*r) *n.* One who shoots with bow and arrows. **arch′er·y** *n.*

ar·che·type (ar̄′kĭtīp) *n.* Original model, prototype.

arch·fiend (ar̄ch′fēnd′) *n.* Satan.

ar·chi·e·pis·co·pal (ar̄kēĭpĭs′k*o*-p*a*l) *adj.* Of an archbishop.

Ar·chi·me·des (ar̄k*i*mē′dēz) (*c*287–212 B.C.). Greek mathematician of Syracuse; said to have made many mechanical inventions, including the ~ **screw** for raising water; ~ **principle**, (phys.) principle that when a body is partly or completely immersed in a fluid the apparent loss of weight is equal to the weight of the fluid displaced. **Ar·chi·me·de·an** (ar̄k*i*mē′dē*a*n, -mĭdē′*a*n) *adj.*

ar·chi·pel·a·go (ar̄k*i*pĕl′*a*gō) *n.* (pl. **-gos, -goes**). Sea with many islands; group of islands.

ar·chi·tect (ar̄′kĭtĕkt) *n.* 1. Designer of buildings who prepares plans and superintends execution; **marine** ~, designer of ship. 2. (fig.) Designer.

ar·chi·tec·ton·ics (ar̄kĭtĕktŏn′-ĭks) *n.* 1. Science of architecture. 2. Structural design, as in a work of art. 3. Systematization of knowledge. **ar·chi·tec·ton′ic** *adj.*

ar·chi·tec·ture (ar̄′kĭtĕkch*e*r) *n.* Art or science of building; profession of designing buildings; thing built; style of building; construction. **ar·chi·tec′tur·al** *adj.* **ar·chi·tec′tur·al·ly** *adv.*

ar·chive (ar̄′kīv) *n.* (usu. pl.). Public records; place in which these are kept. **ar·chi·vist** (ar̄′k*i*vĭst) *n.* Keeper of archives.

arc·tic (ar̄k′tĭk, ar̄′tĭk) *adj.* Of the North Pole; northern; intensely cold; **A ~ Circle**, parallel of 66° 32′ N., north of which the sun does not rise at midwinter or set at midsummer; ~ **fox**, a fox (*Alopex lagopus*) of northern regions, white in winter and blue-gray or brown in summer; **A ~ Ocean**, ocean N. of the Arctic Circle. **Arc′tic** *n.* Regions (both land and sea) around the North Pole; **arctic**, (usu. pl.) thick waterproof overshoe; galosh. [Gk. *arktos* bear, Ursa Major]

Ar·dennes (ar̄dĕn′). Forest district including parts of Belgium, Luxemburg, and N. France, area of bitter fighting in World Wars I and II.

ar·dent (ar̄′d*e*nt) *adj.* Eager, zealous, fervent; having strong feelings esp. of desire or devotion. **ar′dent·ly** *adv.*

ar·dor, Brit. **ar·dour** (ar̄′d*e*r) *ns.*

The Manhattan skyline, New York. The distinctive ***architecture*** *of Manhattan reflects its reputation as one of the principal financial, commercial and industrial centers of the world. Its development began in 1626.*

Zeal; ardent feelings.

ar·du·ous (ăr´jo͞ous) *adj.* Hard, laborious; strenuous. **ar´du·ous·ly** *adv.* **ar´du·ous·ness** *n.*

are[1] (ăr, ār) *n.* Unit of square measure, = 100 square meters.

are[2] (ăr) *v.* Second pers. sing. and first, second, third pers. pl., pres. ind. of BE.

ar·e·a (ār´ēa) *n.* Extent of space or surface; region; space intended for specific use, as *dining, parking,* ~; scope, range; field of study or competence; measure of a plane or of the surface of a solid; **~ code**, 3-digit number identifying telephone area in U.S. and Canada, used in long-distance calls; **ar´e·a·way** *n.*, sunk court in front of house basement.

ar·e·ca (ăr´eka, arē´-) *n.* Tropical Asiatic palm of genus *A*~, bearing pungent astringent fruit.

A·re·ci·bo (ārĭsē´bō). Seaport in N. Puerto Rico.

a·re·na (arē´na) *n.* Central part of amphitheater, in which contests etc. took place; central part of stadium; scene of conflict or action.

aren't (ărnt, ăr´ent) *contr.* Are not.

a·re·o·la (arē´ola) *n.* (pl. **-lae** pr. -lē, **-las**). Interstice; small pigmented area, e.g. that surrounding nipple or pupil.

Ar·e·op·a·gus (ărēŏp´agus). Hill at Athens where (in antiquity) highest judicial court met; hence, this court. **Ar·e·op·a·gite** (ărēŏp´ajīt, -gīt) *n.* Member of court of Areopagus. [Gk. *Areios pagus* hill of Ares]

A·re·qui·pa (ārekē´pah). City in S. Peru founded by Pizarro on the site of an Incan town; now a major commercial center.

Ar·es (ār´ēz). (Gk. myth.) God of war, son of Zeus and Hera; identified with the Roman MARS.

Ar·e·thu·sa (ărethōō´za). (Gk. legend) Water nymph who fled from Greece to Ortygia in Sicily, pursued by the river god Alpheus.

ar·gent (ăr´jent) *n.* & *adj.* Silver (color, esp. in heraldry).

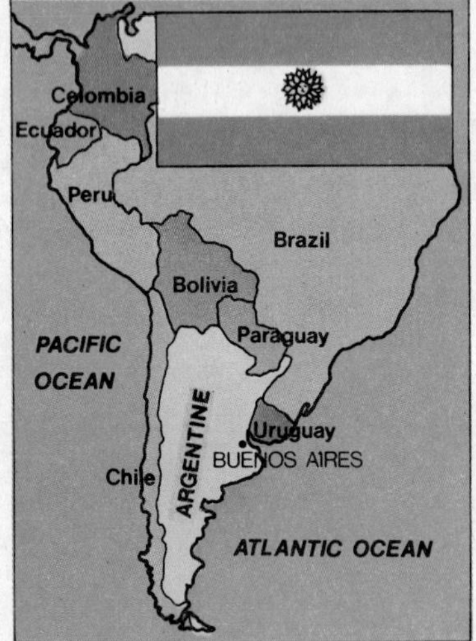

*The **Argentine** is a vast land of great contrasts—from the high Andes in the west to the lowland pampas in the center. Top left: Peon of the Salta Province in northern Argentine. Top right: The Igassu Falls, Miseones Province, which marks the border between Argentine and Brazil. Above left: Map of the Argentine showing its narrow shape, over 2,000 miles long, and the national flag. Above right: These two ice cream vendors in **Argentina** are typical of the young street workers who are forced into employment from a very early age due to family poverty.*

Ar·gen·ti·na (ar̄jentē′n*a*). Republic occupying most of S. part of S. America E. of the Andes; settled by Spaniards (1526 onward); remained a Spanish colony until 1816; capital, Buenos Aires. **Ar·gen·tine** (ar̄′jentēn, -tīn), **Ar·gen·tin·e·an** (ar̄jentĭn′ē*a*n) *adjs.* & *ns.* [L. *argentum* silver, because the Rio de la Plata district exported it]

ar·gen·tine (ar̄′jentīn; -tēn) *adj.* Of silver; silvery.

Ar·go (ar̄′go) *n.*: see ARGONAUTS.

ar·gon (ar̄gŏn) *n.* (chem.) Inert gaseous element, present to extent of about 1% in the air, used in gas-filled electric light bulbs etc.; symbol Ar, at. no. 18, at. wt. 39.948.

Ar·go·nauts (ar̄′gonawts) *n. pl.* (Gk. legend) Heroes who accompanied Jason on board the ship *Argo* on the quest for the Golden Fleece.

Ar·gonne (ar̄′gŏn; *Fr.* ărgawn′) **Forest.** Wooded area in NE. France; site of heavy fighting during World Wars I and II.

Ar·gos (ar̄′gŏs). Ancient Greek town of the E. Peloponnese.

ar·go·sy (ar̄′gosē) *n.* (pl. **-sies**). (hist., poet.) Large vessel (orig. of Ragusa or Venice) carrying rich merchandise. [prob. from It. *Ragusea (nave)* (ship) of Ragusa]

ar·got (ar̄′gō, -g*o*t) *n.* Jargon, slang, of a class or group, esp. of criminals.

ar·gue (ar̄′gū) *v.* (**-gued, -gu·ing**). Maintain by reasoning; reason; prove, indicate; raise objections, dispute. **ar′gu·a·ble** *adj.*

ar·gu·ment (ar̄′gy*u*m*e*nt) *n.* Reason advanced; verbal dispute, debate; summary of subject matter of book etc. **ar·gu·men·ta·tion** (ar̄gy*u*mĕntā′sh*o*n) *n.* Methodical reasoning; debate.

ar·gu·men·ta·tive (ar̄gy*u*mĕn′tatĭv) *adj.* Logical; fond of arguing. **ar·gu·men′ta·tive·ly** *adv.* **ar·gu·men′ta·tive·ness** *n.*

Ar·gus (ar′g*u*s). 1. (Gk. myth.) Fabulous person with 100 eyes, slain by Hermes; after his death Hera transferred his eyes to the tail of the peacock. 2. (Gk. legend) Dog of Ulysses, who recognized his master on his return from Troy after an absence of 20 years.

ar·gyle (ar̄′gīl) *n.* Diamond-shaped varicolored knit pattern, esp. for socks; such a sock.

a·ri·a (ar̄′ēa) *n.* Long accompanied song for one voice in opera and oratorio; songlike movement in instrumental composition. [It.]

Ar·i·ad·ne (ărēăd′nē, ar̄ēahd′nĕ). (Gk. myth.) Daughter of Minos, king of Crete; gave Theseus the thread with which to find his way out of the labyrinth of the Minotaur; then became his wife, but he deserted her, and she

*Portrait of **Aristotle** (left) in 'The School of Athens', a painting by Raphael. The philosopher believed in three types of soul: 'rational' (man), 'sensitive' (animals), 'nutritive' (plants).*

*Cattle around a waterhole in **Arizona's** Painted Desert. The State is on the Mexican border. Its most spectacular feature is the Grand Canyon formed by the Colorado River.*

married Dionysus.

ar·id (ăr′ĭd) *adj.* Dry, parched; (geog., of climate or region) having insufficient water to support vegetation. **a·rid·i·ty** (*a*rĭd′ĭtē) *n.*

Ar·i·el (ār′ēel). In Shakespeare's *The Tempest*, a spirit released by the magician Prospero from imprisonment by a witch, Sycorax.

Ar·ies (ār′ēz). The Ram, a constellation; 1st sign (♈) of the zodiac, which the sun enters at the vernal equinox.

a·right (*a*rīt′) *adv.* Rightly.

Ar·i·ma·the·a (ăr*i*m*a*thē′*a*): see JOSEPH[1], def. 3.

A·ri·on (*a*rī′*o*n) (7th c. B.C.). Greek poet and musician of Lesbos; said to have perfected the dithyramb; acc. to legend, sailors on a ship resolved to murder him, but he begged first to play a tune, did so, and leapt overboard; dolphins were attracted by the music, and one bore him on its back to land.

A·ri·os·to (āreŏs′tō), **Lodovico** (1474–1533). Italian poet, author of the romantic epic *Orlando Furioso*.

a·rise (*a*rīz′) *v.i.* (**a·rose** pr. *a*rōz′, **a·ris·en** pr. *a*rĭz′*e*n, **a·ris·ing**). Appear, spring up, occur, get up, rise.

Ar·is·tar·chus[1] (ărĭstār′k*u*s) **of Samos** (3rd c. B.C.). Astronomer and mathematician; maintained that the Earth revolved around the sun.

Ar·is·tar·chus[2] (ărĭstār′k*u*s) **of Samothrace** (*c*217–*c*145 B.C.). Librarian at Alexandria; edited the Greek classics.

Ar·is·ti·des (ărĭstī′dēz) (d. *c*466 B.C.). Athenian general and statesman, called "the Just"; commanded his tribe at the battle of Marathon.

Ar·is·tip·pus (ărĭstĭp′*u*s). Name of two Greek philosophers; the elder (late 5th c. B.C.), a native of Cyrene and friend of Socrates, is freq. called the founder of the Cyrenaic school, prob. by confusion with the younger, his grandson (fl. *c*400–365), who taught that immediate pleasure is the only end of action.

ar·is·toc·ra·cy (ărĭstŏk′r*a*sē) *n.* (pl. **-cies**). The nobility; government by nobles; best representatives (of intellect etc.); any class deemed superior.

a·ris·to·crat (*a*rĭs′t*o*krăt, ăr′ĭs-) *n.* Member of aristocracy. **a·ris·to·crat·ic** (*a*rĭst*o*krăt′ĭk) *adj.* Belonging to the aristocracy; having distinguished bearing and manners. **a·ris·to·crat′i·cal·ly** *adv.*

Ar·is·toph·a·nes (ărĭstŏf′*a*nēz) (*c*445–*c*385 B.C.). Athenian comic dramatist; author of comedies (the *Birds, Frogs, Wasps*, etc.) caricaturing his contemporaries and their attitude to public affairs.

Ar·is·tot·le (ăr′ĭstŏt*e*l) (384–322 B.C.). Greek philosopher; pupil of Plato at Athens; tutor of Alexander the Great; conducted the PERIPATETIC school; wrote the *Ethics, Politics*, and *Poetics*, and works of zoology, physics, metaphysics, deductive logic, and rhetoric. **Ar·is·to·te·lian** (ărĭst*o*tēl′y*a*n) *adj.* & *n.*

arith. *abbrev.* Arithmetic.

a·rith·me·tic (*a*rĭth′m*e*tĭk) *n.* Science of numbers; computation. ~ (ărĭthmĕt′ĭk), **ar·ith·met·i·cal** (ărĭthmĕt′ĭk*a*l) *adjs.* **arithmetic progression**, (series of numbers showing) increase or decrease by a constant quantity, as 2, 5, 8, 11, etc., or 26, 21, 16, 11, etc. **ar·ith·met′i·cal·ly** *adv.* **a·rith·me·ti·cian** (*a*rĭthm*e*tĭsh′*a*n, ărĭth-) *n.*

Ar·i·us (ār′ē*u*s, *a*rī′*u*s) (*c*250–*c*336). Priest of Alexandria; denied the true Divinity of Christ. **Ar′i·an** *adj.* & *n.* (Supporter) of Arius or his heresy. **Ar′i·an·ism** *n.*

Ariz. *abbrev.* Arizona.

Ar·i·zo·na (ărĭzō′n*a*). State in southwestern U.S., admitted to the Union in 1912; capital, Phoenix.

ark (ārk) *n.* 1. Chest, box; **A~ of the Covenant**, wooden coffer containing tables of Jewish law, the most sacred religious symbol of early Israel (also **~ of the Law**), chest or cupboard in synagogue containing scrolls of the Law. 2. Covered floating vessel in which NOAH was saved at the time of the Flood.

Ark. *abbrev.* Arkansas.

Ar·kan·sas (ār′k*a*nsaw). State in south-central U.S., admitted to the

Arlington National Cemetery. *Monument to the cutter Tampa which sank in 1918. Some of the dead of each war fought by the U.S.A. are buried here at the nation's foremost military cemetery.*

Union in 1836; capital, Little Rock. ~ **River**, river rising in the Rocky Mountains of central Colorado and flowing 1,460 miles (2,350 km) SE. to the Mississippi River.

Ark·wright (ärk'rīt), **Sir Richard** (1732–92). English engineer, inventor of the spinning jenny.

Ar·ling·ton (ar'lĭngton). Suburban area in Virginia on the Potomac River, opposite Washington, D.C.; site of Arlington National Cemetery; ~ **National Cemetery**, U.S. military cemetery; former estate of Gen. Robert E. Lee; site of Tomb of the Unknown Soldier.

arm[1] (arm) *n.* Upper limb of human body; sleeve; branch; armlike thing; support for arm on chair or sofa; (fig.) power, authority; **with open ~s**, cordially; **arm'-chair**, chair with supports for arms; (fig.) applied to persons who theorize without actively participating; **arm'hole**, (in garment) hole through which arm is put; **arm'pit**, hollow under arm at shoulder; **arm'rest**, support for arm on chair, car door, etc. **arm'-ful** *n.* (pl. **-fuls**). **arm'less** *adj.*

arm[2] (arm) *n.* 1. Particular kind of weapon; (pl.) weapons, esp. firearms; branch of the military service; **up in ~s**, actively rebelling (*against*, lit. or fig.; *about*, fig.). 2. (pl.) Heraldic devices; **coat of ~s**: see COAT. **arm** *v.* Furnish with arms; take up arms; provide, furnish *with*; **armed forces, services**, military forces of a nation.

ar·ma·da (armah'da). 1. (also **Spanish ~**) Fleet sent by Philip II of Spain against England in 1588; it was defeated in the English Channel and dispersed by the English fleet under Lord Howard of Effingham and such captains as Drake, Frobisher, and Hawkins. 2. Fleet of warships, planes, etc.

ar·ma·dil·lo (armadĭl'ō) *n.* (pl. **-los**). Burrowing, usu. nocturnal, mammal, protected by bony plates resembling armor. [Span. dim. of *armado* armed creature]

Ar·ma·ged·don (armagĕd'on). (Scene of) supreme or large-scale conflict between nations. (Rev. 16).

ar·ma·ment (ar'mament) *n.* Force equipped for war; military weapons and munitions; process of equipping for war; (pl.) all the forces and weapons of a nation.

ar·ma·ture (ar'macher) *n.* 1. Armor, defensive covering of animals or plants. 2. Piece of soft iron placed in contact with poles of a magnet to preserve the intensity of magnetization or to support a load; core of laminated iron wound with coils of insulated copper wire, that part of a dynamo which rotates in the magnetic field.

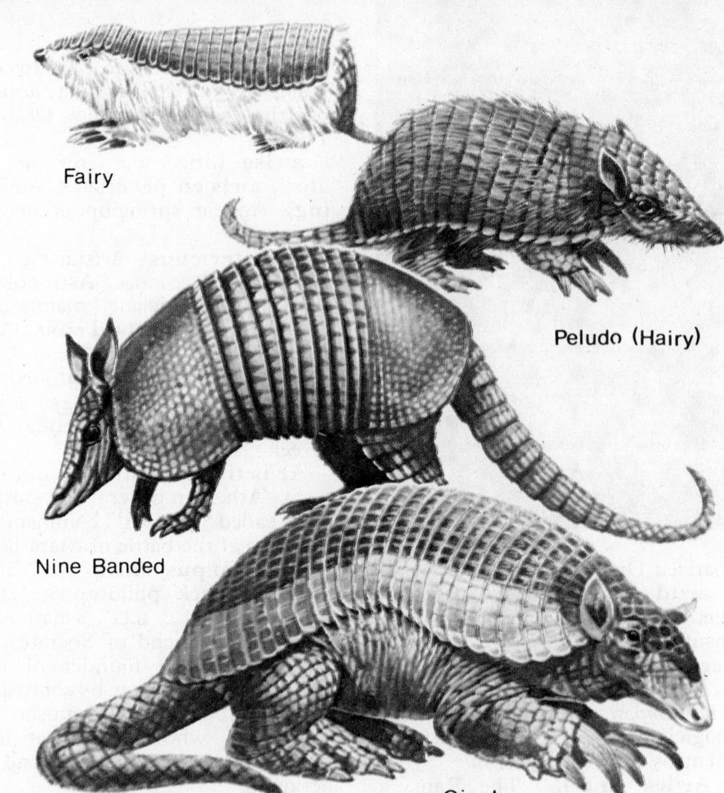

*The plates of the **armadillo** are articulated, allowing it to roll itself into a ball when danger threatens. It feeds on plants and insects, tearing open anthills with its claws and catching the insects with its long, sticky tongue. In Mexico armadillos are hunted for food.*

Ar·me·ni·a (armē'nēa, -mēn'ya). Constituent republic (properly *Armenian Soviet Socialist Republic*) of U.S.S.R., lying S. of the Caucasus, part of the former kingdom of Armenia, most of which was under Turkish rule from the 16th c.; capital, Erivan.

Ar·me·ni·an (armē'nēan, -mēn'yan) *adj.* Of Armenia or its people or language. ~ *n.* Armenian person or language.

ar·mi·stice (ar̄´mĭstĭs) *n.* Cessation of hostilities by agreement between belligerents; short truce; **A~ Day**, Nov 11, anniversary of the armistice that ended hostilities in World War I; since 1954 celebrated as VETERANS' DAY. [L. *arma* arms + *-stitium* stopping]

arm·let (ar̄m´lĭt) *n.* Band worn around arm.

ar·moire (ar̄mwar̄´) *n.* Ornate wardrobe cabinet.

ar·mor (ar̄´m*er*) *n.* 1. (hist.) Defensive covering for body worn in fighting. 2. (also ~ **plate**) Steel plates etc. protecting ship, tank, car, etc., from projectiles etc. (so **~plated**); tanks and other fighting vehicles equipped with such armor. ~ *v.t.* Furnish with such protective covering; **armored car, train**, one supplied with protective armor; **armored column, division**, etc., one equipped with armored cars, tanks, etc.

ar·mor·er (ar̄´m*er*er) *n.* Maker of arms or armor; one in charge of small arms.

ar·mo·ri·al (ar̄mōr´ēal, mōr´-) *adj.* Of heraldic arms.

ar·mor·y (ar̄´m*er*ē) *n.* (pl. **-mor·ies**). Place where arms are kept; arsenal; armorer's workshop.

Arm·strong[1] (ar̄m´strawng), (**Daniel**) **Louis "Satchmo"** (1900–71). American jazz musician and trumpet player.

Arm·strong[2] (ar̄m´strawng), **Edwin Howard** (1890–1954). American electrical engineer; developed FM radio.

Israeli Centurion tanks form up during the six-day Arab–Israeli war, 1967. Mechanized ***armor*** *was introduced in 1898: a four-wheeled motor cycle with armored shield and machine-gun.*

Arm·strong[3] (ar̄m´strawng), **Neil Alden** (1930–). U.S. astronaut; first man to walk on moon, 1969.

ar·my (ar̄´mē) *n.* (pl. **-mies**). Organized force armed for fighting on land; the military profession; large number; organized body for a cause; (U.S. mil.) a military unit consisting of two or more army corps, a headquarters, and auxiliary forces; ~ **ant**, any of the tropical Amer. ants that move in vast numbers.

ar·ni·ca (ar̄´nĭk*a*) *n.* Composite plant of genus *A~*, largely American, having yellow flowers; tincture, prepared from root and flowers of this and used for bruises, sprains, etc.

Ar·no (ar̄´nō). River of N. Italy, flowing through Florence and Pisa.

Ar·nold[1] (ar̄´n*o*ld), **Benedict** (1741–1801). American army officer in the Revolutionary War; while commander of West Point turned traitor and arranged its surrender to British; plot discovered; escaped to England where he later died.

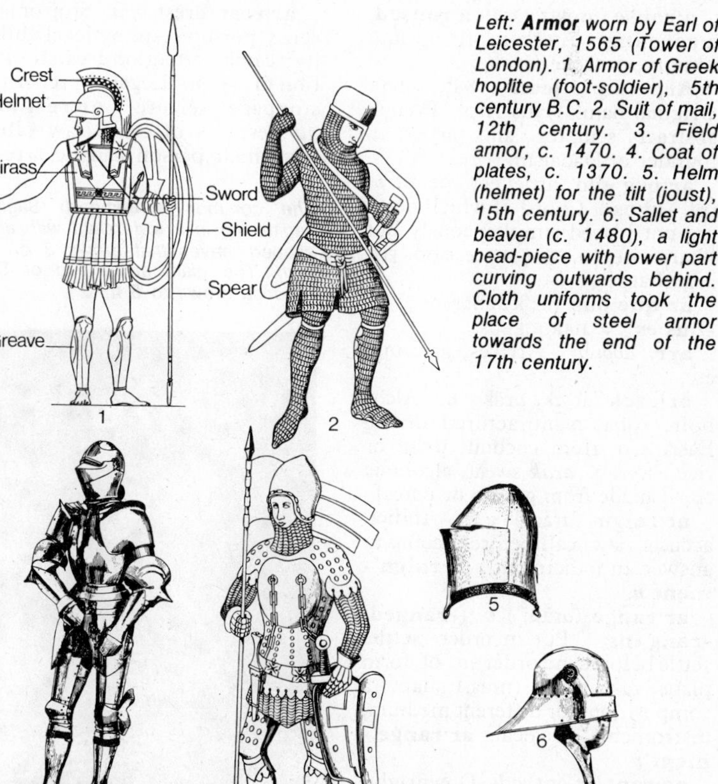

Left: ***Armor*** *worn by Earl of Leicester, 1565 (Tower of London). 1. Armor of Greek hoplite (foot-soldier), 5th century B.C. 2. Suit of mail, 12th century. 3. Field armor, c. 1470. 4. Coat of plates, c. 1370. 5. Helm (helmet) for the tilt (joust), 15th century. 6. Sallet and beaver (c. 1480), a light head-piece with lower part curving outwards behind. Cloth uniforms took the place of steel armor towards the end of the 17th century.*

Aromatic plants (from left): Sage, a hardy evergreen with leaves used as a culinary herb; thyme, the shoots of which give flavoring; peppermint, a herb yielding an oil which flavors confectionery and toothpaste; Mexican orange, which bears capsular fruit; blue-gum eucalyptus; parsley.

Ar·nold[2] (ār′nold), **Henry Hurley "Hap"** (1886–1950). American army general; chief of U.S. air forces during World War II.

Ar·nold[3] (ār′nold), **Matthew** (1822–88). English poet, critic, and educator.

a·ro·ma (*a*rō′m*a*) *n.* Fragrance; subtle pervasive quality.

ar·o·mat·ic (ăr*o*măt′ĭk) *adj.* 1. Fragrant, spicy. 2. (chem.) Of the group of organic compounds in which the carbon atoms are arranged in 6-membered rings (as in benzene).

a·rose (*a*rōz′): see ARISE.

a·round (*a*rownd′) *adv.* On every side; round; nearby; here and there. ~ *prep.* All round; about; enveloping; near; at the edge of; approximately; ~ **the clock** = ROUND-THE-CLOCK (see ROUND[3]).

a·rouse (*a*rowz′) *v.t.* (**a·roused, a·rous·ing**). Awaken; stir up into activity, provoke, excite.

Arp (ārp), **Jean** (1887–1966). Original name Hans Arp. French abstract sculptor and artist; a founder of Dadaism.

ar·peg·gi·o (ārpĕj′ēō, -pĕj′ō) *n.* (pl. **-gi·os**). Chord of which notes are not played simultaneously but "harpwise," i.e. in succession. [It. *arpa* harp]

ar·que·bus (ār′kw*e*b*u*s) *n.* (pl. **-bus·es**) = HARQUEBUS.

arr. *abbrev.* Arrives, arriving, etc.

ar·rack (ăr′*a*k, *a*răk′) *n.* Alcoholic spirit manufactured in the East, esp. from coconut palm or rice. [Arab. *'arak* sweat, alcoholic spirit made from grapes or dates]

ar·raign (*a*rān′) *v.t.* Indict, accuse; (law) call before a court to answer an indictment. **ar·raign′ment** *n.*

ar·range (*a*rānj′) *v.* (**-ranged, -rang·ing**). Put in order; settle; settle beforehand order etc. of; form plans, take steps; (mus.) adapt (a composition) for different medium, instrumental or vocal. **ar·range′ment** *n.*

ar·rant (ăr′*a*nt) *adj.* Downright, notorious.

Ar·ras (*a*rahs′, ăr′*a*s). Town in NE. France famous in 13th–16th centuries for tapestry weaving.

ar·ras (ăr′*a*s) *n.* Rich tapestry; hangings of this around walls of room. [f. ARRAS]

ar·ray (*a*rā′) *v.t.* Dress, esp. with display; marshal (forces). ~ *n.* Dress; imposing series; martial order; orderly arrangement; (radio) assembly of antennas.

ar·rear (*a*rēr′) *n.* (usu. pl.) Outstanding debts; what remains undone; **in ~s**, behindhand, esp. in payment.

ar·rest (*a*rĕst′) *v.t.* Stop or slow; seize (person) esp. by legal authority; catch (attention); catch attention of. ~ *n.* Legal apprehension; stoppage; seizure. **ar·rest′a·ble** *adj.* (esp.) ~ **offense,** (law) offense for which person can be arrested without a warrant.

*The common **arrowhead** (Sagittaria sagittifolia) is a waterplant with arrow-shaped leaves that grows 3 or 4 ft. high. The giant arrowhead of South America grows to 6 ft.*

ar·rive (*a*rīv′) *v.i.* (**-rived, -riv·ing**). Come to destination or end of journey; be brought; come; establish one's reputation or position. **ar·ri′val** *n.*

ar·ri·ve·der·ci (ahrēvēdĕr′chē) *int.* Goodby, till we meet again. [It.]

ar·ro·gant (ăr′*o*g*a*nt) *adj.* Overbearing, presumptuous. **ar′ro·gant·ly** *adv.* **ar′ro·gance** *n.*

ar·ro·gate (ăr′*o*gāt) *v.t.* (**-gat·ed, -gat·ing**). Claim unduly. **ar·ro·ga·tion** (ăr*o*gāsh*o*n) *n.*

ar·row (ăr′ō) *n.* Missile shot from bow, usu. consisting of straight slender shaft with sharp point or head of stone or metal, and feathers fastened to the butt; figure or symbol like an arrow or arrowhead, often used as indication of direction etc.; **ar′rowhead,** pointed tip of an arrow; water plant (*Sagittaria sagittifolia*) with arrow-shaped leaves, growing in ponds and slow streams; **ar′rowroot,** tropical plant *Maranta arundinacea*; starch obtained from its rhizomes, used as food esp. for invalids.

ar·roy·o (*a*roi′ō) *n.* (pl. **-os**). Deep gully cut by a (usu. dry) stream; brook, stream. [Sp.]

ar·se·nal (ār′s*e*n*a*l) *n.* Government establishment where weapons and ammunition are made or stored; supply of weapons. [Arab. *dār aṣ-ṣinā'a* factory, place where fighting ships are equipped]

ar·se·nic (ār′s*e*nĭk, ārs′nĭk) *n.* (chem.) Brittle steel-gray semimetallic element, symbol As, at. no. 33, at. wt. 74.9216; (pop.) white mineral substance (~ **trioxide**), a violent poison used as an insecticide and in the manufacture of paint, glass, etc. **ar·sen·ic** (ārsĕn′ĭk) *adj.* Of arsenic; (chem.) applied to compounds in which arsenic is pentavalent. **ar·sen′i·cal** *adj.* [Gk. *arsenikon,* f. Arab. *az-zirnīḵ,* orpiment, arsenic]

ar·son (ār′s*o*n) *n.* Willful setting on fire of houses or other property. **ar·son·ist** (ār′s*o*nĭst) *n.* One who commits arson.

art[1] (ārt) *n.* Skill, esp. applied to

design, representation, or imaginative creation; human skill as opp. to nature; things embodying this, as paintings, statues, etc.; cunning, stratagem; subject in which skill may be exercised; (pl.) certain courses of study (**liberal ~s**) in school or college, esp. languages, history, philosophy, as distinct from sciences; **bachelor, master of ~s**, degree denoting a standard of attainment in these studies; one who has received such degree; **decorative ~s**, those concerned with the design and decoration of objects in practical use, handicrafts; **fine ~s**, (usu.) paintings, architecture, sculpture, music, and poetry; **A~ Deco** (ar̄′dĕkō; ar̄t′-), decorative art style of 1920's and 1930's; **~ form**, established form of composition (e.g., novel, sonata, sonnet); medium of artistic expression; **A~ Nouveau**: see ART NOUVEAU.

art[2] (ar̄t) *v.* (archaic) Second pers. sing. pres. ind. of verb BE.

Ar·te·mis (ar̄′temĭs). (Gk. myth.) Goddess of chastity and of hunting; daughter of Leto; twin sister of Apollo, identified with Selene and DIANA.

ar·te·ri·al (ar̄tēr′ēal) *adj.* Belonging to, of the nature of, an artery. **~** *n.* Highway around a city, also **~ highway.**

ar·te·ri·ole (ar̄tēr′ēōl) *n.* Small artery.

ar·te·ri·o·scle·ro·sis (ar̄tērēōsklerō′sĭs) *n.* Hardening and thickening of the walls of arteries.

ar·te·ry (ar̄′terē) *n.* (pl. **-ries**). 1. Muscular-walled blood vessel conveying the blood impelled by the heart to the small vessels which supply the tissues. 2. Something serving as channel of supplies, e.g. main road.

ar·te·sian (ar̄tē′zhan) *adj.* **~ well**, perpendicular bore into a curved or slanting water-saturated stratum, penetrating it at a level lower than the source of the water, which rises spontaneously to the surface in a continuous flow. [f. *Artois*, Fr. province]

art·ful (ar̄t′ful) *adj.* Cunning, crafty.

ar·thri·tis (ar̄thrī′tĭs) *n.* Inflammation of joint. **ar·thrit·ic** (ar̄thrĭt′ĭk) *adj.*

ar·thro·pod (ar̄′thropŏd) *n.* One of the Arthropoda, the largest animal phylum, comprising insects, arachnids, myriapods, crustaceans, and trilobites, and characterized by jointed limbs and a hard jointed external skeleton.

Ar·thur[1] (ar̄′ther). King of Britain; historically perh. a 5th- or 6th-c. chieftain or general; acc. to legend he was the son of Uther Pendragon and Igerne; became king of Britain at age 15; married Guinevere; held court at Caerleon-on-Usk and established there a company of knights whose seats were at a round table so that none had precedence; was mortally wounded at Camelford in battle against his usurping nephew Modred; was then borne off in a magic boat to Avalon, from which he will one day return. **Ar·thu·ri·an** (ar̄thoor′ēan) *adj.*

Ar·thur[2] (ar̄′ther), **Chester Alan** (1830–86). American politician and lawyer; 21st president of U.S., 1881–5.

ar·ti·choke (ar̄′tĭchōk) *n.* 1. Plant, *Cynara scolymus* (of which bottom of flower and bases of its scales are edible), allied to thistle. 2. **Jerusalem ~**, species of sunflower with edible tuberous roots. [It. *articiocco*, f. Arab. *alkaršūfa*; Jerusalem, corrupt, of It. *girasole* sunflower]

ar·ti·cle (ar̄′tĭkel) *n.* Separate portion of anything written; separate clause, piece of nonfiction writing forming part of magazine etc.; particular; particular thing, as an **~ of clothing**; (gram.) either of the adjectives "a, an" (**indefinite ~**) and "the" (**definite ~**), or their equivalents in other languages.

ar·tic·u·late (ar̄tĭk′yulĭt) *adj.* Having joints; distinctly jointed, distinguishable; able to express oneself well; (of speech) clearly defined. **~** (ar̄tĭk′yulāt) *v.* (**-lat·ed, -lat·ing**). Connect by joints; divide into words, pronounce distinctly; speak distinctly; express clearly; relate coherently the various parts (of a complex work of art, philosophy, etc.). **ar·tic·u·la·to·ry** (ar̄tĭk′yulatōrē, -tōrē) *adj.*

ar·tic·u·la·tion (ar̄tĭkyulā′shon) *n.* Articulate utterance, speech; jointing.

ar·ti·fact (ar̄′tĭfăkt) *n.* Object, as paleolithic flint, made by human workmanship.

ar·ti·fice (ar̄′tĭfĭs) *n.* Cunning; skill; clever stratagem. **ar·tif·i·cer** (ar̄tĭf′ĭser) *n.* Craftsman; ingenious person.

ar·ti·fi·cial (ar̄tĭfĭsh′al) *adj.* Produced by art; not natural, made in imitation, as **~** *hand*; affected; not real; **~ insemination**, injection of semen into uterus by artifical means; **~ language**, invented language, esp. one designed for international use; **~ respiration**: see RESPIRATION. **ar·ti·fi′cial·ly** *adv.* **ar·ti·fi·ci·al·i·ty** (ar̄tĭfĭsheăl′ĭtē) *n.*

ar·til·ler·y (ar̄tĭl′erē) *n.* Large mounted firearms or missile

*This tropical tree millipede, 4 ins. long, belongs to the **arthropod** phylum, which comprises three-quarters of all known animal species — from mites to the giant land-crab.*

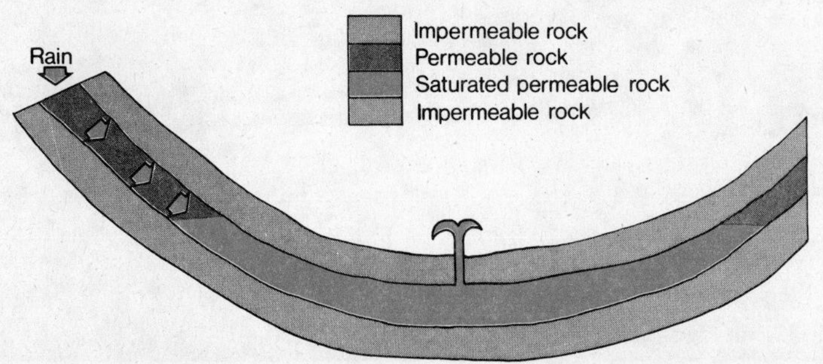

*Curved rock strata with **artesian well** bore penetrating to a level lower than the water source. Water rises to the surface through resultant pressure. Artesian wells have reached depths of several hundred feet. In Europe they date from the 12th century.*

launchers; cannon; branch of army that uses these; **artil′leryman**, one belonging to the artillery, gunner. **ar·til·ler·ist** (ārtĭl′erĭst) *n.* Artilleryman.

ar·ti·san (ār′tĭzan) *n.* Mechanic; handicraftsman.

art·ist (ār′tĭst) *n.* One who practices one of the fine arts, esp. painting; one who makes his craft a fine art; artiste. **ar·tis·tic** (ārtĭs′-tĭk) *adj.* **ar·tis·try** (ār′tĭstrē) *n.*

ar·tiste (ārtēst′) *n.* Professional singer, dancer, etc.

art·less (ārt′lĭs) *adj.* Guileless, simple; lacking art, crude. **art′-less·ly** *adv.* **art′less·ness** *n.*

Art Nou·veau (ār nōōvō′, ārt). Decorative style (*c*1880–*c*1910) using flowing curves and naturalistic motifs. [Fr., = "new art"]

art·y (ār′tē) *adj.* (**art·i·er, art·i·est**). Having artistic pretensions.

A·ru·ba (arōō′ba). Island resort in the Netherlands Antilles, in the Caribbean; site of huge oil refineries.

ar·um (ār′*u*m) *n.* Plant of genus *A*~, having arrow-shaped leaves and an inflorescence on a spadix enclosed within a spathe.

-ary *suffix.* Forming adjectives (*arbitrary, contrary, military*) and nouns (*dictionary, granary*).

Ar·y·an (ăr′ēan, ār′-) *adj.* & *n.* 1. (archaic) Indo-European; (esp.) Indo-Iranian. 2. (loosely) (Member) of a people speaking an Indo-European language; in Nazi Germany esp. contrasted with SEMITE. [Sansk. *ārya* noble (in earlier use a national name comprising worshippers of the gods of the Brahmans); the earlier *Arian* is f. L. *Arianus*, of Aria (f. Gk. *Areia* eastern Persia)]

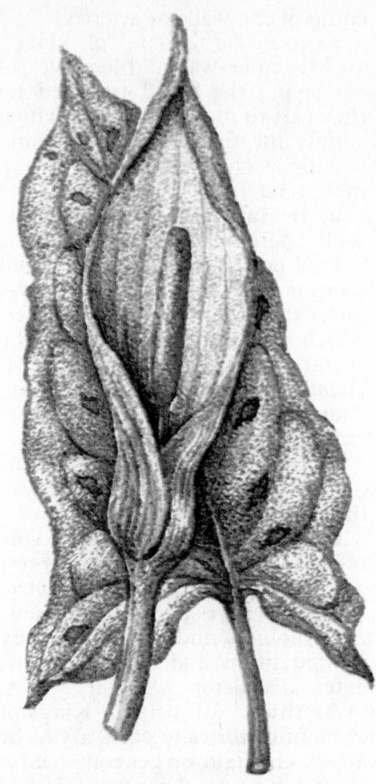

*The decorative **arum** lily belongs to a genus of tuberous-rooted herbs. There are some 20 species in Europe and the Mediterranean region. The water arum is a related plant.*

as (ăz) *adv.* In the same degree; similarly; for example. ~ *conj.* While, when; since, seeing that. ~ *prep.* In the capacity or role of; ~ **for, to**, with reference to; ~ **if, though**, as it would be if; ~ **is**, in the existing state; ~ **of**, as from, as at (date).

A.S. *abbrev.* Anglo-Saxon.

as·a·fet·i·da (ăsafĕt′ĭda) *n.* Concreted resinous gum of various Persian plants of genus *Ferula* with strong smell of garlic and bitter taste, used in medicine. [Pers. *aza* mastic, L. *foetida* stinking]

A·sa·ma (ah′sah′mah′), **Mount.** Continuously active volcano on Honshu Island, Japan.

as·bes·tos (ăsbĕs′tos, ăz-) *n.* White or gray fibrous mineral (consisting largely of calcium and

*Light **artillery** such as this howitzer are used as highly maneuverable support for close combat troops and anti-tank defense.*

Sea squirts or **ascidians,** a primitive group of marine animals found along the sea shore. They are hermaphrodites each producing both sperm and eggs.

magnesium silicates) that can be woven into an incombustible fabric used for fireproof clothing, thermal insulation of pipes, etc., or formed into light sheet material for roofing. [Gk., = "unquenchable"]

as·cend (*a*sĕnd′) *v.* Go or come up; rise, mount, climb; succeed to (a throne, high office, etc.).

as·cend·an·cy, as·cend·en·cy (*a*sĕn′densē) *ns.* Dominant control, powerful influence.

as·cend·ant, as·cend·ent (*a*sĕn′dent) *adjs.* Rising; (astron.) rising toward zenith; (astrol.) just rising above eastern horizon; predominant. ~ *n.* Dominant position, etc., as *in the ascendant*; (astrol.) ascendant point of ecliptic or degree of zodiac.

as·cen·sion (*a*sĕn′sh*o*n) *n.* Ascent; **A** ~, bodily ascent of Christ into heaven on 40th day after resurrection; rising of a celestial body; **A** ~ **Day**, day commemorating Christ's ascension, the 40th day after Easter.

As·cen·sion (*a*sĕn′sh*o*n) **Island.** Small island in S. Atlantic, discovered by Portuguese on Ascension Day 1501.

as·cent (*a*sĕnt′) *n.* Ascending, rising; upward path or slope.

as·cer·tain (ăs*er*tān′) *v.t.* Find out. **as·cer·tain′a·ble** *adj.* **as·cer·tain′ment** *n.*

as·cet·ic (*a*sĕt′ĭk) *adj.* Severely abstinent, austere. ~ *n.* One who practices severe self-discipline, esp. for religious reasons. **as·cet′i·cal·ly** *adv.* **as·cet′i·cism** *n.*

Asch (ăsh), **Sholem** (1880–1957). Polish-born American novelist and playwright; author of *Mottke the Thief*, *Uncle Moses*, *Song of the Valley*, etc.

As·cham (ăs′k*a*m), **Roger** (1515–68). English scholar and prose writer, tutor to Elizabeth I, and author of *The Scholemaster*, a treatise on education.

as·cid·i·an (*a*sĭd′ē*a*n) *n.* Tunicate of the order Ascidiacea. [Gk. *askidion* dim. of *askos* wineskin]

As·cle·pi·us (*a*sklē′pē*u*s). (Gk. myth.) Hero and god of healing, freq. represented bearing staff with serpent coiled around it.

as·co·my·cete (ăskōmī′sēt, -mīsēt′) *n.* Fungus, including the yeasts and mildews, producing spores in a sac-like structure.

a·scor·bic (*a*skor′bĭk) *adj.* ~ **acid**, vitamin C, which occurs in fresh foods, esp. fruits and vegetables, and is necessary to prevent scurvy.

as·cot (ăs′k*o*t) *n.* Broad scarflike tie looped under chin.

as·cribe (*a*skrīb′) *v.t.* (**-cribed, -crib·ing**). Attribute, impute; consider as belonging *to.* **as·crip·tion** (*a*skrĭp′sh*o*n) *n.*

a·sep·sis (āsĕp′sĭs, *a*-) *n.* Absence of putrefactive matter or harmful bacteria.

a·sep·tic (āsĕp′tĭk, *a*-) *adj.* Free from living disease germs.

a·sex·u·al (āsĕk′sho͞o*a*l) *adj.* Not sexual, without sex.

ash[1] (ăsh) *n.* Forest tree of genus *Fraxinus* with silver-gray bark, pinnate leaves, and close-grained wood; wood of this.

Orange picking in California. Citrus fruit is an important source of **ascorbic acid,** or vitamin C, which prevents scurvy.

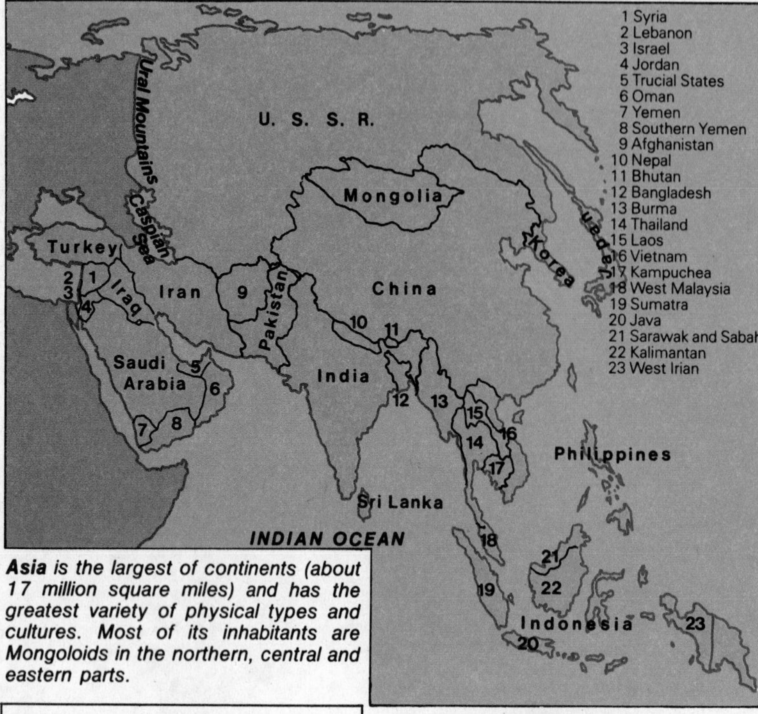

***Asia** is the largest of continents (about 17 million square miles) and has the greatest variety of physical types and cultures. Most of its inhabitants are Mongoloids in the northern, central and eastern parts.*

*The **asp** is a venomous viper. 'Aspis' is the classical name for snake. A bite in the breast by a viper was held to be a quick and merciful death for a condemned prisoner.*

*The **aspen,** a deciduous tree of the poplar genus. The quaking, or golden, aspen is commonly found in the mountains of western U.S.A.*

ash[2] (ăsh) *n.* (freq. pl.) Powdery residue left after combustion of any substance; (pl.) mortal remains after cremation. ~ **blond(e)** *adj.* light blond; *n.* person with ash-blond hair; **A~ Wednesday**, first day of Lent (from custom of placing ashes on penitents' foreheads); **ash'tray**, receptacle for tobacco ash etc.

a·shamed (*a*shāmd') *adj.* Abashed, upset by consciousness of guilt.

ash·en (ăsh'*e*n) *adj.* Pale; of, resembling ashes.

Ash·er (ăsh'*er*). Hebrew patriarch, son of Jacob (Gen. 30); tribe of Israel, traditionally descended from him.

Ash·ke·naz·i (ahshk*e*nah'zē) *n.* (pl. **-naz·im** pr. -nah'zĭm). Central or eastern European Jew, esp. a Yiddish-speaking one. (Cf. SEPHARDI) [Mod. Heb., f. *Ashkenaz*, Gen. 10]

ash·ram (ahsh'r*a*m) *n.* (in India) Place of religious retreat, hermitage.

ash·y (ăsh'ē) *adj.* (**ash·i·er, ash·i·est**). Of ashes; ash-colored, pale.

A·sia (ā'zh*a*, ā'sh*a*). Continent of N. hemisphere, E. part of the great land mass formed by the Old World; separated from Europe by the Ural Mountains and the Caspian Sea; home of the oldest known civilizations; ~ **Minor**, westernmost part of Asia, a peninsula bounded by the Black Sea, the Aegean, and the Mediterranean, and comprising most of Turkey; Anatolia. **A'sian, A·si·at·ic** (āzhēăt'ĭk) *adjs.* & *ns.*

a·side (*a*sīd') *adv.* To or on one side; away, apart. ~ *n.* Words spoken by an actor and supposed not to be heard by other performers. ~ **from**, in addition to, excluding; except for.

as·i·nine (ăs'*i*nīn) *adj.* Of asses; stupid.

ask (ăsk) *v.* Call for an answer to; request information (about), make a request (for); invite; demand, require.

a·skance (*a*skăns') *adv.* Sideways; **look ~ at,** view suspiciously.

a·skew (*a*skū') *adv.* Obliquely, awry.

a·slant (*a*slănt') *adv.* Obliquely.

a·sleep (*a*slēp') *adv.* In a state of sleep. ~ *pred. adj.* (of limbs) Benumbed.

As·ma·ra (ahsmar'ah). Old Abyssinian town; now capital of Eritrea, N. Ethiopia.

A·so (ah'sō'). Volcano on Kyushu Island, Japan; one of the largest craters in the world.

a·so·cial (āsō'sh*a*l) *adj.* Antagonistic to or withdrawn from society.

A·so·ka (*a*sō'k*a*) (d. *c*232 B.C.). Emperor of India from *c*269 B.C.; was converted to Buddhism, did much to propagate it, and is revered by Buddhists.

asp (ăsp) *n.* 1. Small viper of S. Europe (*Vipera aspis*). 2. Viper of N. Africa and Arabia (species of *Cerastes*).

as·par·a·gus (*a*spăr'*a*g*u*s) *n.* Liliaceous plant of genus *A~* with many-branched fine stems, and leaves reduced to scales; species of this (*A. officinalis*) whose vernal shoots are a table delicacy.

A.S.P.C.A. *abbrev.* American Society for the Prevention of Cruelty to Animals.

as·pect (ăs'pěkt) *n.* Way a thing presents itself to eye or mind; side (of building etc.) looking, fronting, in a given direction; appearance; (philol.) form of the verb expressing duration, completion, etc., of an action.

as·pen (ăs'p*e*n) *n.* Any of several varieties of poplar tree, esp. *Populus*

tremuloides, with leaves tremulous on account of their long thin leaf stalks.

as·per·i·ty (aspĕr′ĭtē) *n.* Roughness; severity; harshness.

as·perse (aspẽrs′) *v.t.* (**-persed, -pers·ing**). Attack the reputation of, calumniate. **as·per·sion** (aspẽr′zhon, -shon) *n.* Defamatory statement, slander.

as·phalt (ăs′fawlt) *n.* 1. Solid or plastic pitch derived from petroleum. 2. Mixture of this with sand etc. used for surfacing roads etc. ~ *v.t.* Pave (road) with asphalt.

as·pho·del (ăs′fodĕl) *n.* Any of various hardy liliaceous plants from the Mediterranean and India, including classical *Asphodeline lutea* in Greece; (poet.) immortal flower in Elysium.

as·phyx·i·a (ăsfĭk′sēa) *n.* Lack of oxygen and excess of carbon dioxide in the blood, causing loss of consciousness or death. **as·phyx·i·ate** (ăsfĭk′sēāt) *v.* (**-at·ed, -at·ing**). Kill by asphyxia, suffocate. **as·phyx·i·a·tion** (ăsfĭksēā′shon) *n.* [Gk. *a-* not, *sphuxis* pulse]

*A road construction gang shovels **asphalt** onto the road surface from the hopper preparing it for the roller which will even the surface.*

as·pic (ăs′pĭk) *n.* Gelatin used as a garnish or for making molds of cooked meat, fish, eggs, etc.

A favorite house plant in 19th-century England. The ***aspidistra*** *is easy to grow indoors. It tolerates bad light and fluctuations in temperature. There are eight species.*

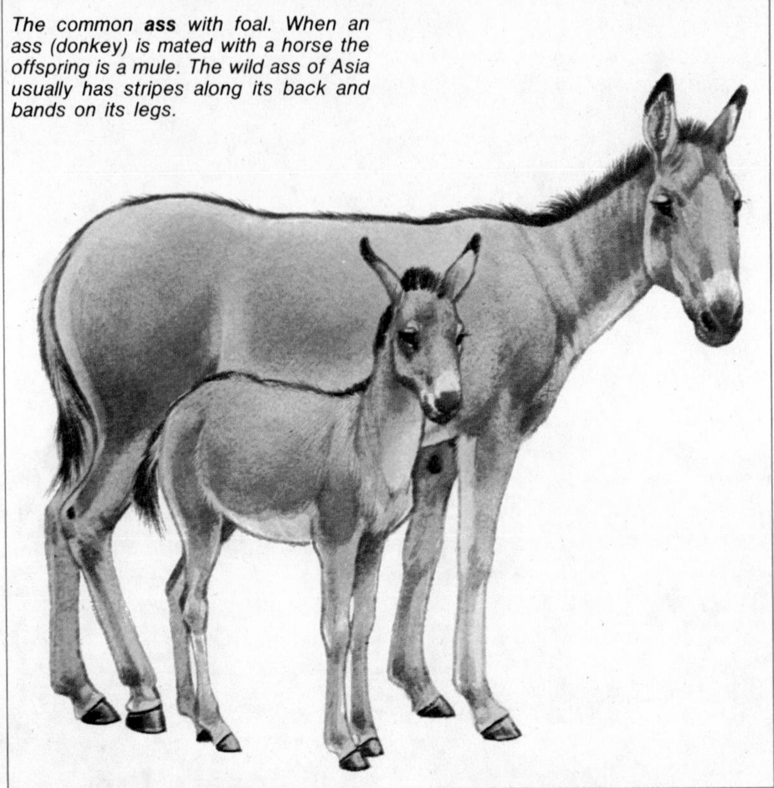

The common ***ass*** *with foal. When an ass (donkey) is mated with a horse the offspring is a mule. The wild ass of Asia usually has stripes along its back and bands on its legs.*

as·pi·dis·tra (ăspĭdĭs′tr*a*) *n.* Plant of the lily family, with broad tapering leaves, freq. grown as a house plant. [Gk. *aspis* shield]

as·pi·rant (ăs′p*e*rant, aspīr′*a*nt) *n.* One who aspires.

as·pi·rate (ăs′perĭt) *adj.* Aspirated; begun with the sound of the letter h. ~ *n.* Aspirated consonant; the sound of *h.* ~ (ăs′perāt) *v.t.* (**-rat·ed, -rat·ing**). 1. Pronounce with a breathing, blended with the sound of *h.* 2. Draw out by suction.

as·pi·ra·tion (ăsp*e*rā′sh*o*n) *n.* Drawing of breath; strong desire; desired goal.

as·pi·ra·tor (ăs′perāt*er*) *n.* Apparatus using suction to remove fluids or gases from a space, esp. one used in medicine to draw fluids from the body.

as·pire (*a*spīr′) *v.i.* (**-pired, -pir·ing**). Feel earnest desire or ambition; (fig.) reach high.

as·pi·rin (ăs′perĭn, -prĭn) *n.* (pl. **-rin, -rins**). Compound of acetylsalicylic acid, used to relieve pain and fever; tablet of this.

ass[1] (ăs) *n.* 1. Quadruped of the genus *Equus*, related to the horse, but smaller; esp. *E. asinus asinus* the domestic donkey descended from the African wild ass *E. asinus*, and *E. hemionus* the wild ass of Asia; donkey. 2. (slang) Ignorant or stupid person.

ass[2] (ăs) *n.* (vulg.) Buttocks, rump; anus.

as·sail (*a*sāl′) *v.t.* Attack, assault. **as·sail′ant** *n.* One who assails.

as·sas·sin (*a*săs′ĭn) *n.* One who undertakes to kill for reasons of fanaticism or financial gain. [Arab. *hashshāshĭn*, oblique pl. of *hashshàsh* hashish addict]

as·sas·si·nate (*a*săs′*i*nāt) *v.t.* (**-nat·ed, -nat·ing**). Kill (person) for political or sectarian reasons. **as·sas·si·na·tion** (*a*săs*i*nā′sh*o*n) *n.*

as·sault (*a*sawlt′) *n.* Hostile attack; rush against walls of fortress etc.; (law) unlawful personal attack or threat of it. ~ **and battery**, (law) threat to make an unlawful personal attack followed by the attack itself. **assault** *v.t.* Make attack upon.

as·say[1] (ăs′ā, *a*sā′) *n.* Testing of an alloy or ore to determine the proportion of a given metal.

as·say[2] (*a*sā′) *v.* 1. Try, attempt; put to a test. 2. (metall.) Analyze (ore etc.) to determine the amount of gold or other valuable components in it. 3. Subject (a drug) to analysis in order to determine its strength. 4. Evaluate after examination or analysis.

as·sem·blage (*a*sĕm′blĭj) *n.* Collection, assembly; (art) (also pr. ahsawṅblahzh′) object made of unrelated things joined together.

as·sem·ble (*a*sĕm′b*e*l) *v.* (**-bled, -bling**). Bring or come together; collect; fit together parts of (machine etc.).

as·sem·bly (*a*sĕm′blē) *n.* (pl. **-blies**). 1. Group of persons gathered together for discussion, worship, recreation, or other particular purpose. 2. Gathering of student body in auditorium for a special program. 3. **A** ~, legislative body, esp. the lower house of the legislature in some states; **assem′blyman, assem′blywoman**, member of a legislative assembly. 4. Act of assembling; state of being assembled. 5. Military call by drum, bugle, etc. for troops to make formation. 6. (eng.) Assembling of those parts of a machine etc. that form a unit; parts so assembled; **assembly line**, sequence of machines and workers for assembly of product.

as·sent (*a*sĕnt′) *v.i.* Agree (*to*), defer (*to*); express agreement; say yes. ~ *n.* Concurrence; sanction.

as·sert (*a*sẽrt′) *v.t.* Maintain a claim to (rights); declare; ~ **oneself**, put oneself forward insistently, act confidently.

as·ser·tion (*a*sẽr′sh*o*n) *n.* Insistence upon a right; affirmation, positive statement.

as·ser·tive (*a*sẽr′tĭv) *adj.* Given to assertion; positive, dogmatic. **as·ser′tive·ly** *adv.* **as·ser′tive·ness** *n.*

as·sess (*a*sĕs′) *v.t.* Fix amount of (taxes, fine); fine, tax; estimate value of (esp. for taxation); evaluate. **as·sess′ment** *n.*

as·ses·sor (*a*sĕs′*er*) *n.* One who assesses taxes or estimates value of property for purpose of taxation; special adviser to judge.

as·set (ăs′ĕt) *n.* 1. (pl.) Total resources of cash, property, etc.; (law) property available for payment of debts. 2. (loosely) Any valuable possession; any useful quality. [med. L. *ad satis* sufficiently]

as·sev·er·ate (*a*sĕv′erāt) *v.t.* (**-at·ed, -at·ing**). Solemnly de-

*Basilica di San Francesco in **Assisi,** where St. Francis (1181?–1226) was born and died. He founded the Franciscans, friars who emphasize tending the sick and the poor.*

*This **assembly** of college students is just one of thousands of graduation ceremonies that take place at the end of each school year all over the U.S.A.*

clare. **as·sev·er·a·tion** (*a*sĕv*e*rā´sh*o*n) *n.*

as·si·du·i·ty (ăsĭdōō´ĭtē, -dū´-) *n.* (pl. **-ties**). Close attention, persistent application.

as·sid·u·ous (*a*sĭj´ōō*u*s) *adj.* Persevering, diligent. **as·sid´u·ous·ly** *adv.* **as·sid´u·ous·ness** *n.*

as·sign (*a*sīn´) *v.t.* Transfer (property, rights, etc.) formally; allot; appoint; ascribe. ~ *n.* One to whom a property, right, etc., is legally transferred.

as·sig·na·tion (ăsĭgnā´sh*o*n) *n.* Assigning; appointment (of time and place), esp. a tryst or rendezvous of lovers.

as·sign·ee (*a*sīnē´, ăsĭnē´) *n.* One appointed to act for another; assign.

as·sign·ment (*a*sīn´m*e*nt) *n.* Allotment; legal transference; task, commission.

as·sim·i·late (*a*sĭm´*i*lāt) *v.* (**-lat·ed, -lat·ing**). Make or become like; absorb, be absorbed into the system. **as·sim·i·la·tion** (*a*sĭm*i*lā´sh*o*n) *n.* **as·sim·i·la·tive** (*a*sĭm´*i*lātĭv, -l*a*tĭv), **as·sim·i·la·to·ry** (*a*sĭm´*i*l*a*tōrē; -tōrē) *adjs.*

As·si·si (*a*sē´zē). Town of Umbria, central Italy; birthplace of St. Francis.

as·sist (*a*sĭst´) *v.* Help; ~ *n.* Act of assisting (esp., as in sports, a play that leads to a teammate's scoring a goal etc.). **as·sis·tance** (*a*sĭs´t*a*ns) *n.*

as·sis·tant (*a*sĭs´t*a*nt) *adj.* Helping; subordinate, holding an auxiliary position, auxiliary. ~ *n.* Helper, subordinate worker; ~ **professor**, faculty member in a college or university ranking above an instructor and below an associate professor.

as·size (*a*sīz´) *n.* (hist.) (usu. pl.) Periodic criminal and civil court sessions held in counties of England and Wales by circuit judges; their time or place.

assoc. *abbrev.* Association; associate.

as·so·ci·ate (*a*sō´sēāt, -shē-) *v.* (**-at·ed, -at·ing**). Join; connect in idea; combine; have frequent dealings (*with*); ~ (*a*sō´sēĭt, -shē-) *adj.* Joined, allied; subordinate. ~ *n.* Partner, colleague; subordinate member of an association; thing connected with another; ~ **professor**, faculty member in a college or university ranking above an assistant professor and below a professor. **as·so´ci·a·tive** *adj.*

as·so·ci·a·tion (*a*sōsēā´sh*o*n; -shē-) *n.* Associating; organized body of persons; connection of ideas; intercourse; **free** ~: see FREE.

as·so·nance (ăs´*o*n*a*ns) *n.* Resemblance of sound between two syllables; rhyming of one word with another in the accented vowel but not in the following consonants (e.g. *sonnet, porridge*). **as´so·nant** *adj.*

as·sort (*a*sōrt´) *v.t.* Arrange or distribute according to kind, class, etc. **as·sort·ed** (*a*sōr´tĭd) *adj.* Of various sorts, mixed.

as·sort·ment (*a*sōrt´m*e*nt) *n.* Assorting; mixed collection.

ASSR *abbrev.* Autonomous Soviet Socialist Republic.

asst. *abbrev.* Assistant.

as·suage (*a*swāj´) *v.t.* (**-suaged, -suag·ing**). Calm, soothe; appease; make milder or less severe. **as·suage´ment** *n.*

as·sume (*a*sōōm´) *v.t.* (**-sumed, -sum·ing**). Take upon oneself; undertake; take to be true or for granted for purpose of argument or action; pretend to be or have. **as·sum´ing** *adj.* Taking much upon oneself, arrogant.

as·sump·tion (*a*sŭmp´sh*o*n) *n.* Assuming; thing assumed; arrogance; **the A**~, the bodily taking up of the Virgin Mary into heaven; feast in honor of this, Aug. 15.

as·sur·ance (*a*shoor´*a*ns) *n.* Positive assertion, pledge; self-confidence, sureness; impudence; (Brit.) (life) insurance.

as·sure (*a*shoor´) *v.t.* (**-sured, -sur·ing**). Tell (person) confi-

*The **aster** is a genus of hardy herbaceous perennials. Its flowers can be obtained in shades of blue, mauve, pink, crimson, white and yellow.*

dently (*of* a thing, *of* its being so, *that* it is so), reassure; make (person) sure (of fact); make certain, ensure the happening etc. of; make safe or secure; (Brit.) insure, as against loss. **as·sur·ed·ly** (*a*shoor′ĭdlē) *adv.*

As·syr·i·a (*a*sĭr′ē*a*). More northerly of the two ancient empires of Mesopotamia; capital, Assur; supremacy ended soon after the death of Assur-bani-pal (7th c. B.C.), who had subdued rebellious Egypt and Elam.

As·syr·i·an (*a*sĭr′ē*a*n) *adj.* & *n.* (Member) of the Assyrian people, a mixed Semitic race; (of) the Assyrian language, a dialect of Akkadian.

As·tar·te (ăstar̄′tē). Goddess of love and fertility; Phoenician equivalent of Aphrodite.

as·ta·tine (ăs′t*a*tēn) *n.* (chem.) Radioactive element of short life (symbol At, at. no. 85, principal isotope at. wt. 211), which does not occur in nature but can be made artificially; the heaviest element of the halogen group. [Gk. *astatos* unstable]

as·ter (ăs′t*er*) *n.* Herbaceous plant of genus *A*~ with showy radiated flowers of various colors. [Gk. *aster* star]

as·ter·isk (ăs′t*e*rĭsk) *n.* Star * used to mark words for reference or distinction, or fill up space in a line where something is omitted. ~ *v.t.* Mark with asterisk.

a·stern (*a*stẽrn′) *adv.* In, at, the stern; behind.

as·ter·oid (ăs′t*e*roid) *n.* 1. (astron.) Any of the thousands of small celestial bodies revolving around the sun mainly between the orbits of Mars and Jupiter. 2. (zool.) One of the class of Asteroidea or starfishes. **as·ter·oi·dal** (ăst*e*roi′d*a*l) *adj.* [Gk. *asteroeidēs* starlike]

asth·ma (ăz′m*a*) *n.* Disorder, usu. of allergic origin, characterized by paroxysms of difficult breathing. **asth·mat·ic** (ăzmăt′ĭk) *adj.* & *n.* (Person) suffering from asthma. **asth·mat′i·cal·ly** *adv.*

As·ti (ah′stē). Town in Piedmont producing wines, including the sweet white sparkling ~ **spumante.**

a·stig·ma·tism (*a*stĭg′m*a*tĭzem) *n.* Structural defect in eye or lens, preventing rays of light from being brought to a common focus, arising from unequal refraction at different points. **as·tig·mat·ic** (ăstĭgmăt′ĭk) *adj.* **as·tig·mat′i·cal·ly** *adv.*

a·stir (*a*stẽr′) *adv.* In motion; out of bed.

as·ton·ish (*a*stŏn′ĭsh) *v.* Amaze, surprise. **as·ton′ish·ment** *n.*

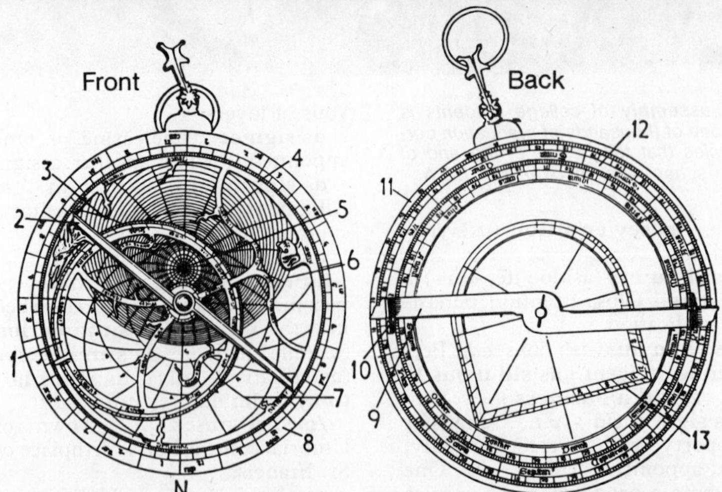

*Front and back views of an **astrolabe,** used by astronomers. 1. Ecliptic ring. 2. Index. 3. Star pointer. 4. Tropic of Capricorn ring. 5. Zenith. 6. Horizon. 7. Unequal hour line. 8. Equal hour scales. 9. Alidade. 10. Sight. 11. Scale of degrees. 12. Zodiac calendar scales. 13. Shadow square.*

*The 150 in. (3.8 m.) Anglo-Australian reflecting telescope at Siding Springs, N.S.W. The larger the diameter (aperture) of an **astronomical** telescope, the greater the distance it can probe into space. The mirrors of the telescope shown are made of ceramic material which unlike glass prevents distortion due to changes in temperature.*

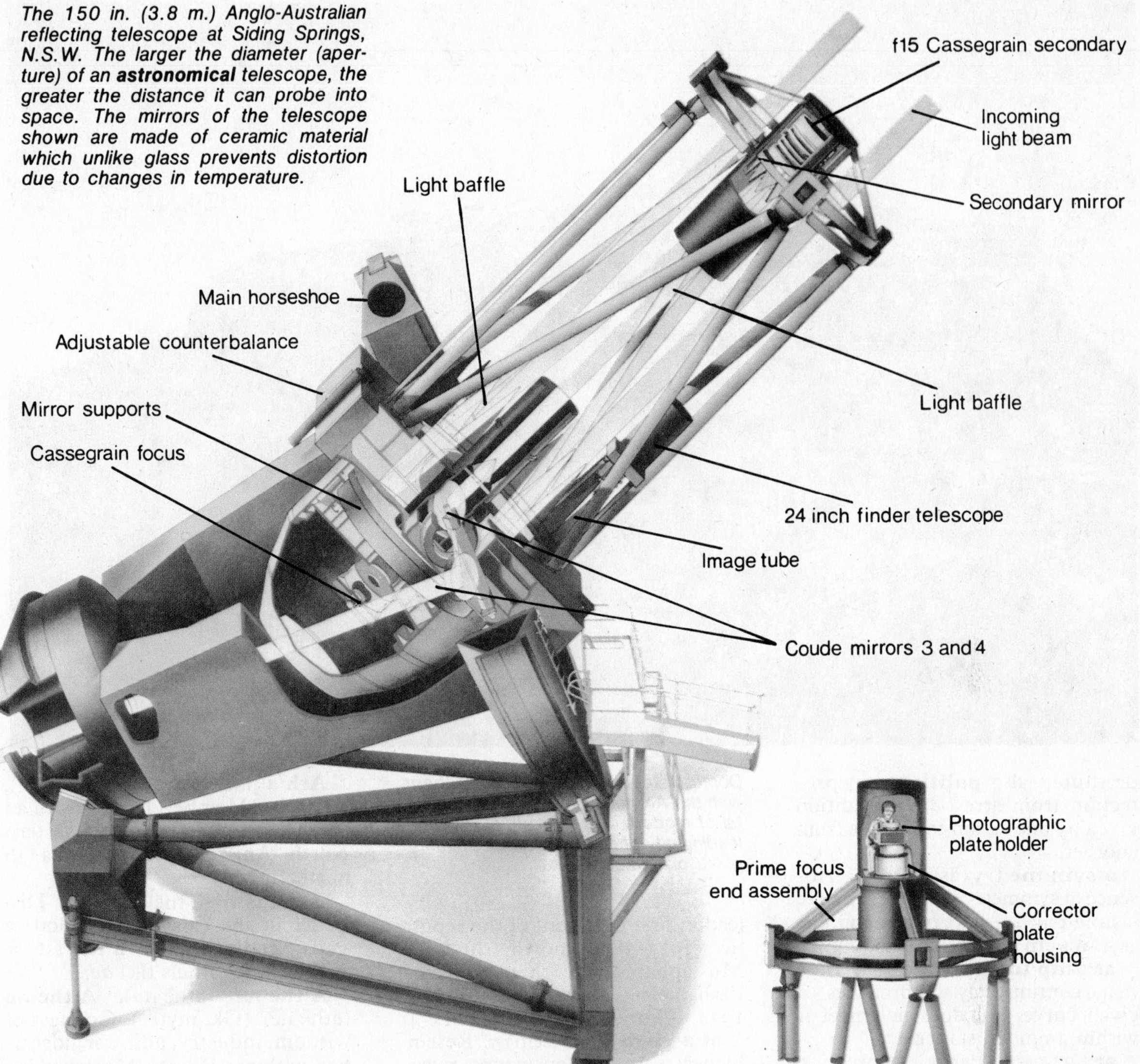

as·tound (*a*stownd′) *v.t.* Shock with alarm or surprise; amaze.

as·tra·khan (ăs′tr*a*k*a*n, -kăn) *n.* 1. Dark curly fleece of young lambs from Astrakhan, U.S.S.R. 2. Cloth imitating this.

as·tral (ăs′tr*a*l) *adj.* Connected with, consisting of, stars; ~ **body,** (theosophy) ethereal counterpart of the human body accompanying it in life, and surviving its death.

a·stray (*a*strā′) *adv.* Out of the right way; (esp., fig.) in or into error or sin.

a·stride (*a*strīd′) *adv.* & *prep.* With a leg on either side (*of*); extending across.

as·trin·gent (*a*strĭn′jent) *adj.* Causing to contract, styptic; severe; austere. ~ *n.* Astringent substance.

astro- *comb. form.* 1. Star, heavenly body, as *astronomy, astrophysics.* 2. Outer space, as *astronaut.*

as·tro·labe (ăs′trolāb) *n.* Instrument formerly used to take altitudes of celestial bodies and solve other problems of practical astronomy.

as·trol·o·gy (*a*strŏl′*o*jē) *n.* Art of understanding the reputed occult influence of the stars on human affairs. **as·trol′o·ger** *n.* **as·tro·log·i·cal** (ăstrolŏj′ĭk*a*l) *adj.* **as·tro·log′i·cal·ly** *adv.*

as·tro·naut (ăs′tr*o*nawt) *n.* Person who travels in interplanetary space as pilot, navigator, etc. of a spacecraft.

as·tro·nau·tics (ăstr*o*naw′tĭks) *n.* (considered sing.) Science and technology of space flight. **as·tro·nau′tic, as·tro·nau′ti·cal** *adjs.*

as·tro·nom·i·cal (ăstr*o*nŏm′ĭk*a*l) *adj.* Relating to, concerned with, astronomy; (of numbers, distances, etc.) very big, immense; ~ **unit,** (abbreviation a.u.) mean distance of the Earth from the sun as unit of measurement, approx. 150 million kilometers (93 million miles). **as·tro·nom′i·cal·ly** *adj.*

as·tron·o·my (*a*strŏn′*o*mē) *n.* Science of the heavenly bodies. **as·tron′o·mer** *n.* One who studies astronomy.

as·tro·phys·ics (ăstrōfĭz′ĭks) *n.* (considered sing.) That branch of physics which deals with the physical or chemical properties of heavenly bodies. **as·tro·phys′i·cal** *adj.* **as·tro·phys·i·cist** (ăstrōfĭz′ĭsĭst) *n.*

as·tute (*a*stōōt′, *a*stūt′) *adj.* Of great discernment or mental penetration; shrewd; crafty. **as·tute′ly** *adv.* **as·tute′ness** *n.*

A·sun·ción (ahs ōōnsēawn′). Capital city of Paraguay.

a·sun·der (*a*sŭn′der) *adv.* Apart; to pieces.

A.S.V. *abbrev.* American Standard Version (of the Bible).

As·wan (ăs′wahn) **Dam.** Dam (1⅓ miles long) built on the Nile at Aswan in SE. Egypt 1902, enlarged 1933; **Aswan High Dam,** larger dam, about 4 miles upstream, completed 1969.

a·sy·lum (*a*sī′l*u*m) *n.* Sanctuary, place of refuge; (formerly) institution for the care of the insane or

Dome of the New Metropolis, ***Athens,*** *with the Acropolis in background. Capital of modern Greece, Athens was the leading city of ancient Greece and birthplace of democracy.*

destitute; (also **political** ~) protection from arrest or extradition given by one nation to refugee from another.

a·sym·me·try (āsĭm´ĭtrē) *n.* Absence of symmetry. **a·sym·met·ric** (ās*i*mĕ´trĭk), **a·sym·met′ri·cal** *adjs.* **a·sym·met′ri·cal·ly** *adv.*

as·ymp·tote (ăs´ĭmtōt) *n.* Line that continuously approaches a given curve, but does not meet it within a finite distance.

at (ăt) *prep.* Particle expressing exact, approximate, or vague position (*at Chicago, at school, at dinner*) or time of day (*at one o'clock*), amount (*at 50 miles an hour*), involvement (*at work*), condition (*at peace*), etc.; ~ **that,** at that estimate, moreover.

At·a·brine (ăt´*a*brĭn, -brēn) *n.* (trademark) Quinacrine hydrochloride.

A·ta·ca·ma (ăt´*a*kăm´*a*) **Desert.** Barren area of N. Chile; contains major nitrate deposits.

At·a·hual·pa (ahtawahl´p*a*) (1500?–33). Last emperor of the Incas; put to death by Pizarro for refusing to become a Christian.

At·a·lan·ta (ăt*a*lăn´t*a*). (Gk. legend) Huntress and athlete; she required all her suitors to run a race with her and killed them if they lost; but Milanion (or Hippomenes) won the race by throwing down three golden apples given to him by Aphrodite, which were so beautiful that Atalanta stopped to pick them up.

At·a·türk (ăt´*a*tĕrk), **Kemal** (*c*1880–1938). Turkish nationalist leader; first president of the republic 1923–38; known first as Mustapha Kemal, then as Kemal Pasha; took surname Atatürk in 1934. [Turk., = "father-Turk"]

at·a·vism (ăt´*a*vĭzem) *n.* Resemblance to remote ancestors, reversion to earlier type. **at·a·vis·tic** (ăt*a*vĭs´tĭk) *adj.* **at·a·vis′ti·cal·ly** *adv.* [L. *atavus* great-grandfather's grandfather]

a·tax·i·a (atăk´sē*a*) *n.* Loss or lack of control of coordinated movement. **a·tax′ic** *adj.*

ate (āt): see EAT.

-ate *suffix.* Forming nouns denoting (1) office, state, function, group, or product (*episcopate, magistrate, electorate, filtrate*); adjectives (*desolate, ornate*); and verbs (*fascinate, hyphenate*); and (2) (chem.) a salt of an acid with corresponding name in *-ic* (*chlorate, nitrate*).

at·el·ier (ătelyā´) *n.* Artist's workshop, studio.

Ath·a·bas·ca (ăth*a*băs´k*a*). Lake in N. Alberta and Saskatchewan Provinces, Canada; over 3,000 square miles in area. **Ath·a·bas·can, Ath·a·pas·can** = ATHAPASKAN.

Ath·a·na·sius (ăth*a*nā´sh*u*s), **St.** (*c*296–373). Bishop of Alexandria. Doctor of the church. **Ath·a·na·sian** (ăth*a*nā´zhan) *adj.*

Ath·a·pas·kan (ăth*a*păs´k*a*n), *adj.* & *n.* (Member, language) of an American Indian people in western North America from Alaska to northern Mexico.

a·the·ism (ā´thēĭzem) *n.* Disbelief in the existence of God or gods; godlessness. **a′the·ist** *n.* **a·the·is·tic** (āthēĭs´tĭk) *adj.*

A·the·na (*a*thē´n*a*), **A·the·ne** (*a*thē´nē). (Gk. myth.) Goddess of wisdom, industry, and war, identified with the Roman Minerva; she sprang fully grown and armed from the brain of her father, Zeus; her emblem was an owl.

ath·e·nae·um, ath·e·ne·um (ăthenē´*u*m) *ns.* 1. Institution for the promotion of learning. 2. Library or reading room. 3. **A**~, college of rhetoric and poetry, founded at Rome *c*133 A.D. by the Emperor Hadrian. [L. f. Gk. *Athēnaion* temple of ATHENA]

Ath·ens (ăth´ĭnz). (Gk. *Athenai*) Leading city of ancient Greece; capital of modern Greece. **A·the·ni·an** (*a*thē´nē*a*n) *adj.* & *n.*

a·thirst (*a*thĕrst´) *pred. adj.* Thirsty; eager (*for*).

ath·lete (ăth´lēt) *n.* One who competes or excels in sports or physical exercises; ~**'s foot,** contagious ringworm of the feet.

ath·let·ic (ăthlĕt´ĭk) *adj.* Pertaining to athletes; physically active or powerful. **ath·let′ics** *n.pl.* Athletic sports (e.g. running, jumping, hurdling, etc.), games, or exercises. **at·let·i·cism** (ăthlĕt´-isĭzem) *n.*

a·thwart (*a*thwŏrt´) *adv.* Across

from side to side (usu. obliquely). ~ *prep.* Across.

A·ti·tlan (ah'tĭtlahn). Crater lake in SW. Guatemala; volcano S. of the lake.

At·lan·ta (ătlăn'ta). Commercial and industrial city in NW. Georgia; the state capital.

At·lan·tic (ătlăn'tĭk) *adj.* Of, adjoining the Atlantic Ocean; ~ **Ocean**, great ocean lying between Europe and Africa on E. and America on W. ~ *n.* Atlantic ocean; **Battle of the ~**, German offensive against Allied Atlantic shipping during World War II. [f. ATLAS]

Atlantic City. Resort and convention city on the SE. coast of New Jersey; famous for its 4-mile-long boardwalk.

At·lan·tis (ătlăn'tĭs). (Gk. legend) Fabled island in the ocean W. of the Pillars of Hercules; it was beautiful and prosperous, the seat of an empire that dominated part of Europe and Africa, but was overwhelmed by the sea because of the impiety of its inhabitants.

At·las (ăt'las). (Gk. legend) One of the Titans, who was punished for revolting against Zeus by being made to support the heavens with his head and hands; acc. to another legend Perseus, with the aid of Medusa's head, turned him into a mountain (the ~ **Mountains** of N. Africa).

at·las (ăt'las) *n.* 1. Collection of maps in a volume, so called from the use of a figure of ATLAS supporting the heavens as a frontispiece. 2. Uppermost vertebra of backbone, supporting the skull.

Atlanta, *Georgia at night. The State's capital was badly damaged during the Civil War but experienced a rapid renaissance in the latter part of the 19th century.*

at·man (aht'man) *n.* (Hinduism) 1. The individual soul. 2. The principle of life. 3. **A~**, the supreme universal soul, source of all individual souls.

at·mos·phere (ăt'mosfēr) *n.* Gaseous envelope surrounding a heavenly body, esp. the envelope of air surrounding the Earth, which consists of gases (nitrogen, oxygen, argon, carbon dioxide, helium, and others) and water vapor, and is rarer as distance from the Earth increases; air (of a place); mental or moral environment or mood. **at·mos·pher·ic** (ătmosfĕr'ĭk) *adj.* ~ **pressure**, pressure of the column of air above a given point, equivalent on the Earth's surface to about 14.7 pounds per square inch, but decreasing with increasing altitude above the Earth. **at·mos·pher'ics** *n.pl.* Atmospheric disturbances of electrical origin causing interference in telecommunications; crackling or other interference so caused.

at. no. *abbrev.* Atomic number.

at·oll (ăt'awl, -ŏl, -ōl, atawl', atŏl', atōl') *n.* Ring-shaped coral

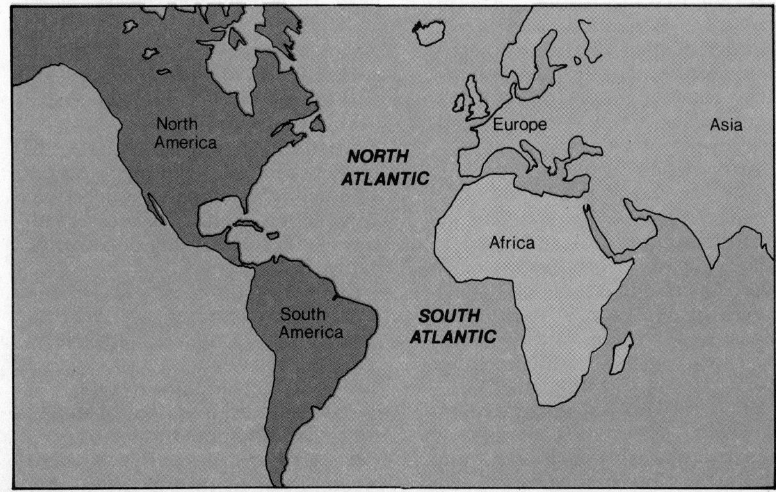

*The **Atlantic Ocean** dividing Europe and Africa from the Americas. In area about 32½ million square miles, it is second only to the Pacific Ocean in size.*

reef enclosing lagoon. [Malay]

at·om (ăt′*o*m) *n.* 1. Body too small to be divided; minute portion, small thing. 2. (chem.) Smallest particle of an element that cannot be further subdivided without destroying its identity, regarded as consisting of a minute central positively charged nucleus in which almost all the mass is concentrated, and a number of negative electrons arranged around the nucleus; ~ **bomb** = ATOMIC bomb; ~ **smasher**: see ACCELERATOR.

a·tom·ic (*a*tŏm′ĭk) *adj.* Of atoms; of, using, concerned with, atomic energy or weapons; ~ **bomb**, bomb deriving its destructive power from ~ **energy**, released by fission of atomic nuclei of certain heavy elements such as uranium 235 or plutonium or by the fusion of light nuclei; ~ **mass**, mass of an atom measured in units based on $\frac{1}{12}$ of the mass of the carbon-12 atom; ~ **number**, (abbreviated at. no.) number of unit positive charges carried by the nucleus of an atom or protons of an element, number determining the position of the element in the periodic table; ~ **pile** or ~ **reactor**: see REACTOR, def. 3; ~ **theory**, theory that elements consist of atoms of definite relative weight and that atoms of different elements unite with one another in fixed proportions; (philos.) atomism; ~ **weight**, (abbreviated at. wt.) = *atomic mass* (see above). **a·tom′i·cal·ly** *adv.*

at·om·ism (ăt′*o*mĭzem) *n.* (philos.) Theory that all matter consists of minute indivisible particles. **at′om·ist** *n.* **at·om·is·tic** (ăt*o*mĭs′tĭk) *adj.*

at·om·ize (ăt′*o*mīz) *v.t.* (**-ized, -iz·ing**). Reduce to atoms; reduce to fine particles or spray. **at′om·iz·er** *n.* Instrument for reducing liquids to a fine spray.

a·ton·al (ātō′n*a*l) *adj.* (mus.) Not conforming to any system of key or mode. **a·to·nal·i·ty** (ātōnăl′ĭtē) *n.*

a·tone (*a*tōn′) *v.i.* (**a·toned, a·ton·ing**). Make amends; ~ **for**, expiate. **a·tone′ment** *n.* **the A**~, expiation of man's sin by Christ; **Day of A**~: see YOM KIPPUR.

a·top (*a*tŏp′) *adj.* & *adv.* At or on the top. ~ *prep.* On the top of.

A·tre·us (ā′trē*u*s, ā′trōōs). (Gk. legend) King of Argos, who set the flesh of his brother Thyestes' children before their father at a banquet in revenge because Thyestes had seduced his wife; he was himself murdered by Aegisthus.

a·tri·um (ā′trē*u*m) *n.* (pl. **a·tri·a** pr. ā′trē*a*, **a·tri·ums**). 1. Central court of Roman house. 2. Either of the two upper cavities (*left* and *right* ~) of the heart into which the veins pour the blood.

Nuclear plant at Oyster Creek, Long Island. A nuclear or ***atomic*** *reactor contains fissionable material arranged to keep up a controlled nuclear chain reaction.*

a·tro·cious (*a*trō′sh*u*s) *adj.* Extremely wicked; very bad. **a·tro′cious·ly** *adv.*

a·troc·i·ty (*a*trŏs′ĭtē) *n.* (pl. **-ties**). Atrocious deed; bad blunder; (colloq.) hideous object.

at·ro·phy (ăt′r*o*fē) *n.* Wasting away through imperfect nourishment or lack of use. ~ *v.* (**-phied, -phy·ing**). Waste away.

at·ro·pine (ăt′r*o*pēn, -pĭn) *n.* White crystal-like alkaloid prepared from *Atropa belladonna* (deadly nightshade) and used to dilate the pupil of the eye or to relieve pain. [f. ATROPOS]

At·ro·pos (ăt′r*o*pŏs). (Gk. myth.) Eldest of the three Fates, who cut the thread of human life with her shears. [Gk., = "inflexible"]

att. *abbrev.* Attached; attention; attorney.

at·tach (*a*tăch′) *v.* Fasten, join; attribute (importance etc. *to*); adhere, be incident *to*; seize by legal authority; bind in friendship, make devoted. **at·tach′ment** *n.*

at·ta·ché (ăt*a*shā′, ătă-) *n.* Diplomatic or military officer attached to an embassy or legation; ~ **case**, rectangular briefcase with rigid sides for carrying documents, papers, etc.

at·tack (*a*tăk′) *v.* Take the initiative in fighting; act destructively on; criticize adversely; (colloq.) set about (a task) vigorously; rape or attempt to rape. ~ *n.* Act of attacking; bout of illness etc.; rape, attempted rape.

at·tain (*a*tān′) *v.* Reach, gain, accomplish. **at·tain′ment** *n.* Attaining; thing attained; (pl.) personal accomplishments.

at·tar (ăt´er) *n.* Fragrant essential oil distilled from flowers, esp. roses. [ult. F, Arab. *'itr* perfume]

at·tempt (atĕmpt´) *v.t.* Try; try to master. ~ *n.* Attempting; endeavor.

at·tend (atĕnd´) *v.* 1. Turn the mind, apply oneself (*to*). 2. Be present (*at*); go regularly to (school, church, etc.). 3. Wait upon; serve; escort; accompany.

at·tend·ance (atĕn´dans) *n.* Attending (ATTEND *v.* defs 2, 3); number of persons present.

at·tend·ant (atĕn´dant) *n.* 1. One who attends or provides service. 2. One who is present. 3. Thing or circumstance that accompanies; concomitant or consequence. ~ *adj.* 1. Being present, accompanying. 2. Consequent, associated, related.

at·ten·tion (atĕn´shon) *n.* Act or faculty of attending (ATTEND *v.* def. 1); consideration, care; (pl.) ceremonious politeness; courtship, addresses; **at** ~, (mil.) formal attitude of troops standing in erect position as dist. from *at* EASE; (as command) order to stand thus.

at·ten·tive (atĕn´tĭv) *adj.* Giving or paying attention. **at·ten´tive·ly** *adv.* **at·ten´tive·ness** *n.*

at·ten·u·ate (atĕn´ūāt) *v.t.* (**-at·ed, -at·ing**). Make slender or thin; reduce in force or value. **at·ten·u·a·tion** (atĕnūā´shon) *n.* **attenuate** (atĕn´ūĭt) *adj.* Slender; rarefied.

at·test (atĕst´) *v.* Testify, certify; put on oath or solemn declaration. **at·tes·ta·tion** (ătestā´shon) *n.*

Att. Gen. *abbrev.* Attorney General.

At·tic (ăt´ĭk) *adj.* Of Attica; ~ **dialect**, Greek spoken by ancient Athenians; ~ **order**, square column of any of the five orders (see ORDER def. 6). **Attic** *n.* Attic dialect.

at·tic (ăt´ĭk) *n.* 1. (archit.) Structure consisting of small order placed above another of greater height. 2. (Room in) highest story of building, usu. immediately under the roof and not having a flat ceiling. [Fr. *attique* upper part of house, so called from Attic order of architecture]

At·ti·ca (ăt´ĭka). District of ancient Greece of which Athens was the capital.

At·ti·la (atĭl´a, ăt´ila) (d. 453 A.D.). King of the Huns, known as the "scourge of God"; ravaged the Eastern Roman Empire (445–50); after making peace with Theodosius invaded the Western Empire and was defeated at Châlons by Aëtius in 451.

at·tire (atīr´) *v.t.* (**-tired, -tir·ing**) & *n.* Dress, array.

At·tis (ă´tĭs). (myth.) Youthful consort of CYBELE; his death was mourned for days in the spring, and his recovery (when his spirit passed into a pine tree and violets sprang up from his blood) then celebrated.

at·ti·tude (ăt´ĭtōōd, -tūd) *n.* 1. Posture of body; settled behavior, as indicating opinion. 2. Manner, feeling toward a person, idea, or thing. 3. Angular relation between aircraft's or spacecraft's axis and the wind, course, etc.

at·ti·tu·di·nize (ătĭtōō´dinīz, -tū´-) *v.i.* (**-nized, -niz·ing**). Practice attitudes; act, speak, etc. affectedly.

at·tor·ney (atêr´nē) *n.* (pl. **-neys**). Lawyer, esp. an attorney-at-law; **power of** ~, a legal document authorizing one person or party to act as attorney or agent for another; ~ **general** (pl. ~**s general** or ~ **generals**), chief law officer and legal counsel of a national or state government; the **A**~ **General** of the United States is head of the Department of Justice and a member of the Cabinet.

at·tract (atrăkt´) *v.t.* Draw to itself or oneself; excite pleasurable emotions of; draw forth and fix on oneself (attention etc.). **at·trac·tion** (atrăk´shon) *n.* Attracting; thing that attracts; attractive qualities. **at·trac·tive** (atrăk´tĭv) *adj.* **at·trac´tive·ly** *adv.* **at·trac´tive·ness** *n.*

at·trib·ute (atrĭb´ūt) *v.t.* (**-ut·ed, -ut·ing**). ~ **to**, consider as caused by, resulting or originating from, made or composed by; consider as belonging or appropriate *to*. **at·tri·bu·tion** (ătribū´shon) *n.* **attribute** (ăt´ribūt) *n.* Quality ascribed to anything; material object regarded as appropriate to person or office; characteristic quality; (gram.) attributive word, adjective.

at·trib·u·tive (atrĭb´yutĭv) *adj.* Assigning an attribute to a subject; (gram.) expressing an attribute, qualifying. ~ *n.* Word denoting an attribute. **at·trib´u·tive·ly** *adv.*

at·tri·tion (atrĭsh´on) *n.* Wearing down by friction; wearing out; gradual reduction of staff through retirement, resignation, etc.; weakening by harassment.

At·tucks (ăt´uks), **Crispus** (1723?–70). American patriot and leader of mob at Boston Massacre in which he was killed; may have been a runaway slave.

at·tune (atōōn´, atūn´) *v.t.* (**at·tuned, at·tun·ing**). Bring into (musical) accord; adapt.

Atty. Gen. *abbrev.* Attorney General.

ATV (ā´tē´vē´) *abbrev.* All-terrain vehicle, one capable of traveling on rough off-the-road terrain and going over water.

a·twit·ter (atwĭt´er) *adj.* Excited; nervous; agitated; twittering.

at. wt. *abbrev.* Atomic weight.

a·typ·i·cal (ātĭp´ĭkal) *adj.* Not typical.

a.u. *abbrev.* Astronomical unit.

au·brie·tia (ōbrē´sha) *n.* Spring-flowering dwarf perennial plant of genus *Aubrieta* of mustard family, with flowers of colors ranging through purple, red, and blue. [after Claude *Aubriet* (d. 1743), French painter of flowers and animals]

au·burn (aw´bern) *n.* & *adj.* Reddish brown (usu. of hair).

Au·bus·son (ōbüsawn´). Town in central France, famous since the 16th c. for the manufacture of tapestries and carpets.

Auck·land (awk´land). Largest city and chief seaport of New Zealand.

au cou·rant (ō kōōrahn´). Acquainted *with* what is going on, well informed; up-to-date. [Fr.]

auc·tion (awk´shon) *n.* 1. Public sale at which articles are sold to person making the highest bid. 2. (Also ~ **bridge**): see BRIDGE². ~ *v.t.* Sell (*off*) by auction.

auc·tion·eer (awkshonēr´) *n.* One who conducts auctions.

au·da·cious (awdā´shus) *adj.* Daring, bold; impudent. **au·da´cious·ly** *adv.* **au·da´cious·ness, au·dac·i·ty** (awdăs´ĭtē) *ns.*

Au·den (aw´den), **Wystan Hugh** (1907–73). English-born poet and dramatist.

*The Temple of Zeus, built in 130 A.D., is in Athens, the chief city of **Attica,** a region of ancient Greece which was controlled and dominated by Athens from the 5th century B.C.*

*A large **audience** gathered for a concert. At outdoor concerts and sporting events, the audience may total more than 100,000 people.*

au·di·ble (aw′d*i*b*e*l) *adj.* That can be heard. **au′di·bly** *adv.* **au·di·bil·i·ty** (awd*i*bĭl′ĭtē) *n.*

au·di·ence (aw′dē*e*ns) *n.* Hearing; formal interview; persons within hearing; group of listeners or spectators.

au·di·o (aw′dēō) *adj.* Of (the reproduction of) sound; ~ **frequency**: see FREQUENCY. ~ *n.* 1. Reproduction of sound. 2. Audio element of television.

au·di·ol·o·gy (awdēŏl′*o*jē) *n.* Science of hearing. **au·di·ol′o·gist** *n.*

au·di·om·e·ter (awdēŏm′ĭt*e*r) *n.* Instrument for measuring the sensitivity of the ear to sounds.

au·di·o·phile (aw′dē*o*fīl) *n.* Devotee of high-fidelity sound reproduction (on radios, record players, etc.).

au·di·o·vis·u·al (awdēōvĭzh′-ōō*a*l) *adj.* Of or pertaining to both hearing and sight, esp. in educational materials such as movies, filmstrips, recordings, etc.

au·dit (aw′dĭt) *n.* Official examination of financial records or accounts. ~ *v.t.* 1. Examine (financial records) officially. 2. Register for and attend (class) without intending to obtain credits.

au·di·tion (awdĭsh′*o*n) *n.* Hearing; trial hearing of actor, singer, etc., seeking employment. ~ *v.* Test, be tested, by an audition.

au·di·tor (aw′dĭt*e*r) *n.* 1. One who audits financial records. 2. College or university student who audits classes.

au·di·to·ri·um (awdĭtōr′ē*u*m, -tōr′-) *n.* 1. Room in a theater, school, or other building where audience sits. 2. Building for public meetings, concerts, theatrical performances, etc.

au·di·to·ry (aw′dĭtōrē, -tōrē) *adj.* Of hearing.

Au·du·bon (aw′d*u*bŏn, -b*o*n), **John James** (1785–1851). Amer. naturalist and painter; author of *Birds of America*, engraved in aquatint (1827–38).

auf Wie·der·seh·en (owf vē′d*e*r-zā*e*n). (Goodby) till we meet again. [Ger.]

Aug. *abbrev.* August.

Au·ge·an (awjē′*a*n) *adj.* Abominably filthy; resembling the stables of Augeas, legendary king of Elis, which went uncleaned for many years until Hercules, as one of his labors, accomplished the cleaning by diverting the river Alpheus through them.

au·ger (aw′g*e*r) *n.* Tool for boring holes in wood, having a long shank with cutting edge and screw point, and handle at right angles.

*Illustration of an oriole, one of 435 plates from 'Birds of America'. The book is the masterpiece of **J. J. Audubon** (1785–1851), the American naturalist painter and author.*

aught[1], **ought** (awt) *ns.* Anything.

aught[2] (awt) = OUGHT[1].

aug·ment (awgmĕnt′) *v.* Increase, enlarge. **aug·ment′ed** *adj.* (esp., mus., of an interval) Widened by a semitone. **aug·men·ta·tion** (awgmĕntā′sh*o*n) *n.* Enlargement; addition; (mus.) repetition of a passage in notes longer than those of the original.

au grat·in (ō grah′t*i*n, ō grăt′*i*n). Cooked with crisp brown crust usu. of bread crumbs or grated cheese.

au·gur (aw′g*e*r) *n.* 1. (Rom. antiq.) Religious official who foretold future events by observing flight or notes of birds etc. 2. Soothsayer. ~ *v.* Forebode, anticipate; ~ **well, ill**, have good (bad) implications or expectations *of, for.* **au·gu·ry** (aw′gy*e*rē) *n.* (pl. **-ries**). Divination; omen.

Au·gust (aw′g*u*st). Eighth month of Gregorian (5th of Julian) calendar, with 31 days. [named after Rom. emperor AUGUSTUS]

au·gust (awgŭst′) *adj.* Majestic, venerable. **au·gust′ly** *adv.* **au·gust′ness** *n.* [L. *augustus* consecrated, venerable]

Au·gus·ta[1] (awgŭs′t*a*). City in E. Georgia; the former state capital.

Au·gus·ta[2] (awgŭs′t*a*). Capital city of Maine, in the SW. on the Kennebec River.

Au·gus·tan (awgŭs′t*a*n) *adj.* Of AUGUSTUS; ~ **Age**, period of literary eminence in the life of a nation, so called because Virgil, Horace, Ovid, etc., all flourished

*The great **auk** (Pinguinus impennis), now extinct. Auks are short-winged sea-divers, ranging from 7 to 30 ins. in length. There are 22 species.*

*'St. Augustine in his Cell' by Botticelli. **St. Augustine** (354–430 A.D.). Bishop of Hippo in N. Africa, was in his day the dominant personality of the Western church.*

during Augustus' reign; in English literary history, the period of Pope and Addison.

Au·gus·tine[1] (aw'gustēn, awgŭs'tĭn), **St.** (354–430). Doctor of the church; son of a pagan father and Christian mother (St. Monica); was for a time attracted by Manicheanism, but baptized as a Christian 387; became bishop of Hippo in N. Africa 391; defended Christianity in numerous writings, of which the best known are the *City of God* (*Civitas Dei*) and the autobiographical *Confessions*; commemorated Aug. 28.

Au·gus·tine[2] (aw'gustēn, awgŭs'tĭn), **St.** (d. 604). First archbishop of Canterbury; led mission to England from Rome and founded a monastery at Canterbury; commemorated in England May 26, elsewhere May 28.

Au·gus·tin·i·an (awgustĭn'ēan) *adj.* Of St. AUGUSTINE[1] of Hippo; ~ **Friars**, mendicant order founded *c*1250 and following Augustinian principles.

Au·gus·tus (awgŭs'tus) (63 B.C.–14 A.D.). Gaius Octavius ("Octavian"), named Gaius Julius Caesar Octavianus after his adoption by Julius Caesar, his great-uncle; member of the 2nd triumvirate and first Roman emperor; the title of Augustus was conferred on him by senate and people in 27 B.C. and was borne by all subsequent Roman emperors.

au jus (ō zhōō', ō jōōs'). (of meat) Served with the natural juices obtained during roasting.

auk (awk) *n.* Any of the Alcidae, a family of seabirds that includes the guillemot, puffin, razorbill, little auk (*Plautus alle*), and the great auk (*Pinguinus impennis*), formerly inhabiting N. Atlantic but extinct since mid-19th c.

auld lang syne (awld' lăng zīn', sīn', ōld'). The days of long ago. [Sc., old long since]

Au·lis (aw'lis). Ancient Greek town on Boeotian coast, where (in legend) the Greek fleet was detained by contrary winds before the Trojan War, and where Iphigenia was offered for sacrifice.

au na·tu·rel (ō nătyürĕl'). (Cooked) in the simplest way; uncooked, in a natural state; nude. [Fr.]

aunt (ănt, ahnt) *n.* Father's or mother's sister; uncle's wife.

aunt·ie, aunt·y (ăn'tē, ahn'tē) *ns.* (pl. **aunt·ies**). (colloq.) Aunt.

au pair (ō pār'). (Person, esp. young girl) performing domestic duties in foreign country in return for room and board or a small salary. ~ *adv. phr.* [Fr.]

au·ra (ōr'a) *n.* Subtle emanation; atmosphere diffused by or attending a person etc. (esp. in mystical use as definite envelope of body or spirit).

au·ral (ōr'al) *adj.* Of, received by, the ear. **au'ral·ly** *adv.*

Au·re·li·an (awrē'lēan, -rēl'yan). Lucius Domitius Aurelianus (*c*212–75 A.D.). Roman emperor, 270–5.

au·re·ole (ōr'ēōl), **au·re·o·la** (awrē'ola) *ns.* Celestial crown or halo worn by martyrs, saints, virgins, etc.; halo, esp. that of the sun seen in eclipses. [L. *aureola* (*corona*) golden crown]

Au·re·o·my·cin (ōrēōmī'sĭn) *n.* (trademark) Chlortetracycline.

au re·voir (ō revwār'). (Goodby) till we meet again. [Fr.]

au·ri·cle (ōr'ĭkel) *n.* 1. External ear of animals; earlike part. 2. Small appendage of the ATRIUM, def. 2.

au·ric·u·la (awrĭk'yula) *n.* Species of alpine primula with ear-shaped leaf. [L. *auris* ear]

au·ric·u·lar (awrĭk'yuler) *adj.* Pertaining to or like the ear; aural; pertaining to auricle of the heart.

au·rif·er·ous (awrĭf'erus) *adj.* Yielding gold.

Au·ri·gna·cian (ōrĭnyā'shan) *adj.* & *n.* (Of) a paleolithic culture believed to have existed in France *c*11,500–10,000 B.C. [f. *Aurignac* in Haute-Garonne, SW. France, where flint implements were found]

Au·ro·ra (awrōr'a, -rōr'a).

University of Texas at **Austin,** the capital of Texas, founded in 1840, originally named Waterloo.

(Rom. myth.) Goddess of the dawn, corresponding to the Greek Eos.

au·ro·ra (awrōr′*a*, -rōr′*a*) *n.* (poet.) Dawn; ~ **aus·tra·lis** (awstrā′lĭs), phenomenon similar to aurora borealis, seen in southern latitudes; ~ **bo·re·al·is** (bōrēăl′ĭs, bōr-), luminous phenomenon, popularly called the *northern lights*, seen in northern latitudes esp. at night, usu. appearing as streamers of many colors ascending from above the northern horizon and supposed to be of electrical origin.

Ausch·witz (owsh′vĭts). City in S. Poland; site of an infamous Nazi concentration camp during World War II.

aus·cul·ta·tion (awsk*u*ltā′sh*o*n) *n.* Act of listening, esp. (med.) to movement of heart, lungs, etc., as with a stethoscope. **aus·cul′ta·to·ry** (awskŭl′t*a*tōrē, -tōrē) *adj.*

Map and flag of **Austria,** a republic in 1918 after break-up of the Austro-Hungarian Empire. It was annexed by Hitler in 1938, freed in 1945 and became a republic again in 1955.

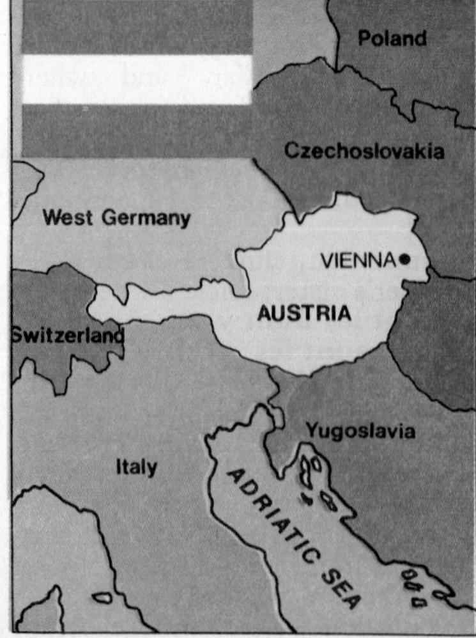

aus·pice (aw′spĭs) *n.* (pl. **aus·pic·es** pr. aw′spĭsĭz, -sēz). Observation of birds for purpose of taking omens; omen, sign; (pl.) patronage; approving support. **aus·pi·cious** (awspĭsh′*u*s) *adj.* Of good omen; favorable; prosperous. **aus·pi′cious·ly** *adv.* **aus·pi′cious·ness** *n.*

Aus·sie (aw′sē) *n.* (slang) Australian, orig. of Australian troops in World War I.

Aus·ten (aw′sten), **Jane** (1775–1817). English author of six novels: *Pride and Prejudice*, *Northanger Abbey*, *Sense and Sensibility*, *Mansfield Park*, *Emma*, and *Persuasion*.

aus·tere (awstēr′) *adj.* Harsh; stern; stringently moral; severely simple; frugal; thrifty. **aus·tere′ly** *adv.* **aus·tere′ness** *n.* **aus·ter·i·ty** (awstĕr′ĭtē) *n.* (pl. **-ties**). Quality of being austere; severity, austere or ascetic practice.

Aus·ter·litz (aw′st*e*rlĭts, ow′-). Town in Moravia, scene in 1805 of Napoleon's defeat of the Austrians and Russians.

Aus·tin[1] (aws′tĭn). Capital city of Texas, in the central part on the Colorado River.

Aus·tin[2] (aws′tĭn), **Stephen Fuller** (1793–1836). American colonizer and political leader of the Texas Republic; worked toward Texas statehood.

aus·tral (aw′str*a*l) *adj.* Southern. [L. *Auster*, the south wind]

Aus·tral·a·sia (awstr*a*lā′zh*a*, -sha). Term used loosely to include Australia and the islands scattered over the SW. Pacific. **Aus·tral·a′sian** *adj.* & *n.*

Aus·tral·ia (awstrāl′y*a*). Continent of S. hemisphere in the SW. Pacific; federal commonwealth, member nation of the British Commonwealth. The existence of a *Terra Australis* ("southern land") was known in Europe in the 16th c.; British colonization began in 1788; in 1901 the six colonies (New South Wales, Victoria, Queensland, South Australia, Western Australia, and Tasmania) federated as sovereign states of the **Commonwealth of** ~, which also administers Northern Territory, Capital Territory (site of the federal capital, Canberra), and certain areas outside the continent.

Aus·tral·ian (awstrāl′y*a*n) *adj.* Of Australia; ~ **ballot,** ballot listing all the candidates, given to the voter at the polls and marked in secret; ~ **crawl,** form of crawl stroke in swimming originating in Australia. **Australian** *n.* Native or inhabitant of Australia.

Aus·tra·loid (aw′str*a*loid), **Aus·tra·li·oid** (awstrā′lēoid) *adjs.* & *ns.* (Of) the ethnological types of Australian Aborigines.

Aus·tri·a (aw′strē*a*). German-speaking country of central Europe,

*The island continent of **Australia** in the S.W. Pacific is rich in fauna and flora, and mineral resources. Its climate is diverse, hot and arid in much of the interior, temperate in the S.E. and S.W. British colonization began in 1788. Top: View across Sydney Harbor, showing the Opera House, originally controversial but now one of the most admired of modern buildings. Center: A view of Ayers Rock, the world's largest monolith rising 1,104 ft. above an open plain in S.W. Northern Territory. Bottom: Harvesting in progress at Humpty Doo, Northern Territory.*

which became a republic in 1918; formerly it was the nucleus of the Austro-Hungarian Empire; it became a duchy in 1156 and later the seat of the Hapsburg emperors; in 1918 the empire was divided between Hungary, Poland, Czechoslovakia, Italy, Rumania, Yugoslavia, and Austria itself; in March 1938 Austria was forcibly annexed to the Third Reich; it was liberated from Nazi rule in 1945; capital, Vienna. **Aus'tri·an** *adj.* & *n.* (Native) of Austria.

Aus·tro·ne·sia (awstrōnē'zh*a*, -sh*a*). Islands of the central and south Pacific Ocean including Indonesia, Micronesia, Melanesia, and Polynesia.

au·tar·chy (aw'tarkē) *n.* (pl. **-chies**). Absolute sovereignty, despotism. [Gk. *autarkhia* (*arkhō* rule)]

auth. *abbrev.* Author; authorized.

au·then·tic (awthĕn'tĭk) *adj.* Reliable, trustworthy; of undisputed origin. **au·then'ti·cal·ly** *adv.* **au·then·tic·i·ty** (awthĕntĭs'ĭtē) *n.*

au·then·ti·cate (awthĕn'tĭkāt) *v.t.* (**-cat·ed, -cat·ing**). Establish the truth or authorship of; make valid.

au·thor (aw'th*er*), fem. **au·thor·ess** (aw'therĭs) *ns.* Originator; writer of book etc. ~ *v.t.* Be the author or. **au'thor·ship** *n.*

au·thor·i·tar·i·an (awthŏrĭtār'ēan, -thăr-) *adj.* Favoring obedience to authority as opp. to individual liberty; of, pertaining to, a dictatorship. ~ *n.* Authoritarian person.

au·thor·i·ta·tive (*a*thŏr'ĭtātĭv, *a*thăr'-) *adj.* Possessing or claiming authority. **au·thor'i·ta·tive·ly** *adv.*

au·thor·i·ty (*a*thŏr'ĭtē, *a*thăr'-) *n.* (pl. **-ties**). Power or right to act, command, or enforce obedience; delegated power; person etc. having authority; personal influence; expert.

au·thor·ize (aw'therīz) *v.t.* (**-ized, -iz·ing**). Sanction; give ground for; give authority to; **Authorized Version,** (of the Bible) the English translation of 1611, the *King James Bible.*

au·tism (aw'tĭzem) *n.* Morbid absorption in fantasy; condition, esp. in children, preventing proper response to environment. **au·tis·tic** (awtĭs'tĭk) *adj.*

au·to (aw'tō) *n.* (pl. **-tos**). Automobile.

auto-, aut- *prefixes.* Self, by one's or its own agency.

au·to·bahn (aw't*o*bahn) *n.* In Germany, an express highway. [Ger.]

au·to·bi·og·ra·phy (awt*o*bīŏg'r*a*fē, -bē-) *n.* (pl. **-phies**). Writing the story of one's own life; the story

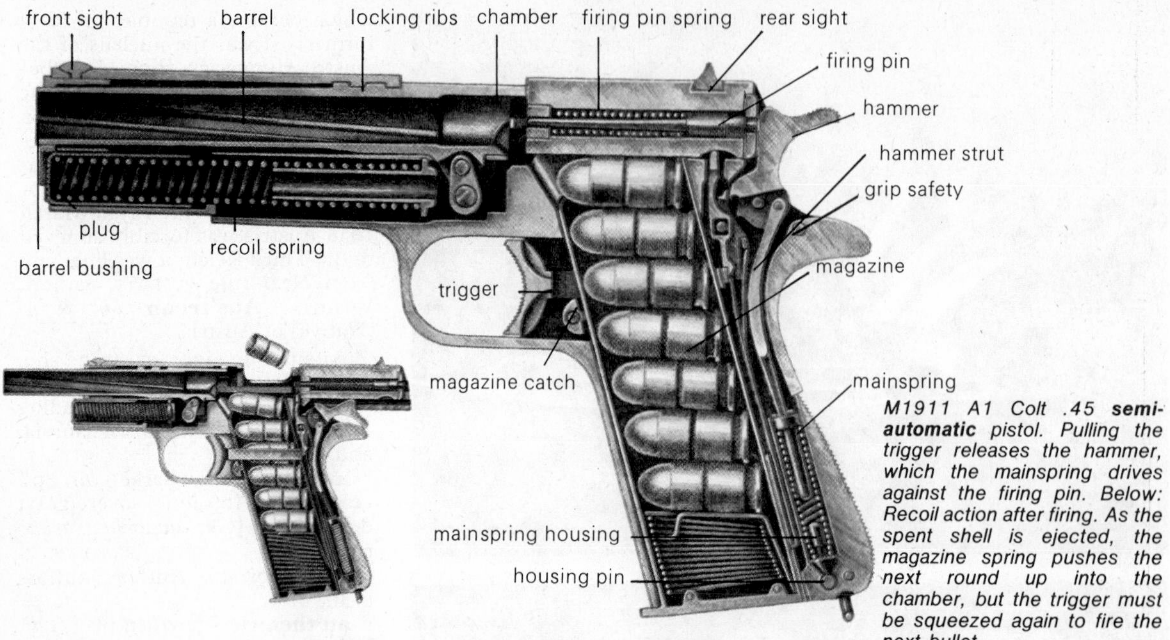

M1911 A1 Colt .45 ***semi-automatic*** *pistol. Pulling the trigger releases the hammer, which the mainspring drives against the firing pin. Below: Recoil action after firing. As the spent shell is ejected, the magazine spring pushes the next round up into the chamber, but the trigger must be squeezed again to fire the next bullet.*

so written. **au·to·bi·o·graph·i·cal** (awtobīogrăf′ĭkal), **au·to·bi·o·graph′ic** *adjs.* **au·to·bi·og′ra·pher** *n.*

au·toch·thon (awtŏk′thon) *n.* (pl. **-thons, -tho·nes** pr. -thonēz). Original inhabitant. **au·toch·tho·nous** (awtŏk′thonus) *adj.*

au·to·clave (aw′toklāv) *n.* Vessel in which chemical reactions take place at high temperatures under pressure; apparatus for sterilizing by steam at high pressure. ~ *v.* (**-claved, -clav·ing**).

au·toc·ra·cy (awtŏk′rasē) *n.* (pl. **-cies**). Absolute government.

au·to·crat (aw′tokrăt) *n.* Absolute ruler; dictatorial overbearing person. **au·to·crat·ic** (awtokrăt′ĭk) *adj.* **au·to·crat′i·cal·ly** *adv.*

au·to-da-fé (awtōdafā′) *n.* (pl. **au·tos-da-fé**). Sentence of the Spanish Inquisition; execution of this, esp. burning of a heretic. [Port., = "act of faith"]

au·to·gi·ro (awtojīr′ō) *n.* (pl. **-ros**). Early form of helicopter with a conventional propeller for forward motion and freely rotating horizontal vanes that provide lift, keep the craft airborne, and permit slow and steep descent.

au·to·graph (aw′togrăf, -grahf) *n.* Person's own handwriting, esp. signature for keeping as a memento; document signed by its author, as dist. from HOLOGRAPH, one wholly written in his hand (freq. attrib., as ~ **letter**). ~ *v.t.* Write one's signature on or in; sign. **au·to·graph·ic** (awtogrăf′ĭk), **au·to·graph′i·cal** *adjs.* **au·to·graph′i·cal·ly** *adv.*

au·to·mat (aw′tomăt) *n.* Cafeteria in which meals etc. are provided from closed compartments into which customers deposit coins.

au·to·mate (aw′tomāt) *v.* (**-mat·ed, -mat·ing**). Apply automation (to).

au·to·mat·ic (awtomăt′ĭk) *adj.* Working of itself, without direct human actuation; mechanical; unconscious; necessary, inevitable; ~ **control**, device enabling machine to maintain a predetermined temperature, pressure, speed, etc., without intervention of operator; ~ **pilot**, similar device in aircraft for maintaining a set course or altitude; ~ **pistol**, **rifle**, firearm which, after each shot is exploded, by gas pressure or force of recoil automatically ejects the empty case, loads another into the chamber, and fires, repeating this movement until the ammunition in the mechanism is exhausted or pressure on the trigger is released; ~ **transmission**, system in motor vehicle in which gears engage automatically according to the speed of the vehicle or by means of a torque converter. **automatic** *n.* Automatic pistol; machine, tool, etc. operated automatically. **au·to·mat′i·cal·ly** *adv.*

au·to·ma·tion (awtomā′shon) *n.* Completely automatic control of a

A 1956 U.S. designed Thunderbird. The first true ***automobile*** *was built in 1769 by Frenchman Nicolas-Joseph Cugnot, whose cumbersome steam-driven tricycle travelled at 2.25 m.p.h.*

manufactured product through a number of successive stages; use of automatic mechanical or electronic devices.

au·tom·a·ton (awtŏm´*a*tŏn, -t*o*n) *n.* (pl. **-tons, -ta** pr. -t*a*). Robot; person whose actions are mechanical, following a customary routine.

au·to·mo·bile (awt*o*mōbēl´, aw´t*o*m*o*bēl, awt*o*mō´bēl, -bĭl) *n.* Motor-driven passenger road vehicle, usu. four-wheeled and propelled by an internal-combustion engine.

au·to·mo·tive (awt*o*mō´tĭv) *adj.* Concerned with motor vehicles.

au·to·nom·ic (awt*o*nŏm´ĭk) *adj.* (physiol.) Of that part of the nervous system (~ or *involuntary nervous system*) which functions more or less independently of the will, comprising the sympathetic and parasympathetic nervous systems.

au·ton·o·mous (awtŏn´*o*m*u*s) *adj.* 1. Self-governing. 2. (physiol., path.) Independent of the usual processes that regulate the growth of an organism. **au·ton´o·mous·ly** *adv.*

au·ton·o·my (awtŏn´*o*mē) *n.* Right of self-government; freedom of the will.

au·to·pis·ta (aw´t*o*pĭst*a*) *n.* In Spain and Spanish-speaking countries, an express highway. [Span.]

au·top·sy (aw´tŏpsē, -t*o*p-) *n.* (pl. **-sies**). Examination of a corpse to determine the cause of death; post-mortem examination.

au·to·route (aw´tōrōōt) *n.* In France, an express highway. [Fr.]

au·to·stra·da (awtōstrah´d*a*) *n.* In Italy, an express highway. [It.]

au·tumn (aw´t*u*m) *n.*: see FALL (*n.* def. 2); (fig.) season of incipient decay. **au·tum·nal** (awtŭm´n*a*l) *adj.* Of autumn.

aux·il·ia·ry (awgzĭl´y*e*rē, -zĭl´-*e*rē) *adj.* Helpful; supplemental; subsidiary; (gram., of verbs) serving to form tenses, moods, voices, of other verbs. ~ *n.* (pl. **-ries**). 1. Auxiliary person, group, theory. 2. (esp. pl.) Foreign troops serving with another country in war; (naval) vessel auxiliary to fighting vessels, as tanker, supply ship, etc.

av. *abbrev.* Average; avoirdupois.

A.V. *abbrev.* Authorized Version (of the Bible).

a·vail (*a*vāl´) *v.* Be of use or assistance (to); help, benefit. ~ *n.* Use, profit.

a·vail·a·ble (*a*vā´l*a*b*e*l) *adj.* At one's disposal, at hand; capable of being used. **a·vail·a·bil·i·ty** (*a*vāl*a*bĭl´ĭtē) *n.*

av·a·lanche (ăv´*a*lănch, -lahnch) *n.* Mass of snow, rock, and ice, sliding suddenly down mountain (also fig.).

Av·a·lon (ăv´*a*lŏn). In the Arthurian legend, the place to which ARTHUR[1] was conveyed after death; (Welsh myth.) kingdom of the dead.

a·vant-garde (ăvahntgard´, *a*-vănt-) *n.* Pioneers or innovators, esp. in any art in a particular period (freq. attrib.). [Fr.]

av·a·rice (ăv´*e*rĭs) *n.* Greed for gain, cupidity. **av·a·ri·cious** (ăv*e*-rĭsh´*u*s) *adj.* **av·a·ri´cious·ly** *adv.*

a·vast (*a*văst´) *int.* (naut.) Stop, cease. [Du. *houd vast* hold fast]

av·a·tar (ăv´*a*tar) *n.* (Hinduism) Descent to earth and incarnation of a deity.

a·vaunt (*a*vawnt´) *int.* (archaic) Begone.

avdp. *abbrev.* Avoirdupois.

ave. *abbrev.* Avenue.

Ave·bur·y (āv´b*e*rē). Village in Wiltshire, England, site of a very large prehistoric stone circle.

A·ve Ma·ri·a (ah´vā m*a*rē´*a*), **A·ve Mar·y** (ah´vē mar´ē, ah´vā). (= Hail, Mary!), the angelic salutation to the Virgin (Luke 1:28), combined with that of Elizabeth (Luke 1:42), used as a devotional recitation, together with a prayer to the Virgin. ~ *n.* Utterance of this recitation and prayer. [L. *ave* hail]

a·venge (*a*vĕnj´) *v.t.* (**a·venged, a·veng·ing**). Inflict retribution on behalf of; exact retribution for.

av·ens (ăv´*e*nz) *n.* Small rose-aceous plant of genus *Jeum.*

Av·en·tine (ăv´*e*ntīn). Most southerly of the seven Hills of Rome.

a·ven·tu·rine (*a*vĕn´ch*e*rĭn) *n.* Brownish glass with copper crystals, first manufactured near Venice; quartz, spangled with mica or hematite, resembling this. [It. *avventura* chance (from its accidental discovery)]

Avant-garde *art challenges current and historical presumptions about the nature of art. Jackson Pollock's 'Alchemy', below, challenged concepts of orderly organization.*

The **avocet,** a wading bird about 18 ins. long which feeds in shallows by sifting water through its up-curved beak. There are four species distributed round the world.

Avocado with segment showing the large seed. In 1519 a Spanish explorer was the first European to discover the tree and fruit near Santa Marta, Colombia.

av·e·nue (ăv′enū, -nōō) *n.* Way of approach; approach to large house, bordered by trees; roadway with trees etc. at regular intervals; wide street, main thoroughfare.

a·ver (avẽr′) *v.t.* (**a·verred, a·ver·ring**). Assert, affirm.

av·er·age (ăv′erĭj, ăv′rĭj) *n.* Arithmetical mean; generally prevailing amount, degree; **on the ~**, usually; typically; generally. **average** *adj.* Estimated by average; typical, ordinary. ~ *v.t.* (**-aged, -ag·ing**). Calculate an average value for; ~ **out**, achieve or end with an average. [Arab. *ʻawārīya* damaged goods]

A·ver·ro·ës (avĕr′ōēz). Abul Walid Muhammad ben Ahmed ibn Rushd (1126–98), Muslim doctor born at Cordova, philosopher, and author of a famous commentary on Aristotle.

a·verse (avẽrs′) *adj.* Opposed, disciplined (*to, from*); unwilling.

a·ver·sion (avẽr′zhon, -shon) *n.* Dislike, unwillingness; object of dislike.

a·vert (avẽrt′) *v.t.* Turn away; ward off.

A·ves·ta (avĕs′ta) *n.* Collection of sacred Zoroastrian writings. **A·ves′tan, A·ves′tic** *adjs.* & *ns.* (Of) the ancient E. Iranian language in which the Avesta is written.

a·vi·an (ā′vēan) *adj.* Of birds.

a·vi·ar·y (ā′vēĕrē) *n.* (pl. **-ar·ies**). Large cage or building for keeping birds.

a·vi·a·tion (āvēā′shon, ăvē-) *n.* 1. Method or practice of flying aircraft; operation of aircraft. 2. Design and manufacture of aircraft.

a·vi·a·tor (ā′vēāter, ăv′ē-) *n.* (fem. **a·vi·a·trix** pr. āvēā′trĭks, ăvē-). Aircraft pilot.

av·id (ăv′ĭd) *adj.* Eager, greedy. **av′id·ly** *adv.* **a·vid·i·ty** (avĭd′ĭtē) *n.*

A·vi·gnon (ăvēnyawn′). City on river Rhône, in S. France, to which Clement V removed the papal seat in 1308; it remained there until 1377, and after the papal schism in 1378 two antipopes, Clement VII and Benedict XIII, resided there; the latter was expelled in 1408, but the city remained in papal possession until 1791.

a·vi·on·ics (āvēŏn′ĭks, ăv′ē-) *n.* Application of electronics in aviation. **a·vi·on′ic** *adj.*

av·o·ca·do (ăvokah′dō, ahvo-) *n.* (pl. **-dos**). Succulent pear-shaped fruit, a drupe with soft-coated seed, borne by the tropical Amer. and W. Indian tree *Persea gratissima.* [Span. *avocado* advocate, corrupt. of Mex. name]

av·o·ca·tion (ăvokā′shon) *n.* Minor occupation; hobby.

av·o·cet (ăv′osĕt) *n.* Wading bird with long upturned beak (*Recurvirostra americana*).

A·vo·ga·dro (ahvogah′drō), **Amadeo** (1776–1856). Italian physicist; **~'s law**, hypothesis that equal volumes of all gases at the same temperature and pressure contain equal numbers of molecules; **~'s number**, number of molecules in the gram-molecular weight of any gas; value, 6.02×10^{23}.

a·void (avoid′) *v.t.* Shun, refrain from; evade, escape. **a·void′a·ble** *adj.* **a·void′a·bly** *adj.* **a·void′ance** *n.*

av·oir·du·pois (ăverdupoiz′) *n.* System of weights and measures based on ounces and pounds, a pound containing 16 ounces or 7,000 grains and equal to 453.59 grams. [corrupt. of Fr. *avoir de pois* goods of weight]

A·von[1] (ā′von, ăv′on). River, flowing through Warwickshire, England, a tributary of the Severn (**Bard of ~**, sobriquet for Shakespeare, who was born at Stratford-upon-Avon).

A·von[2] (ā′von, ăv′on). County of SW. England.

a·vow (avow′) *v.t.* Admit, confess. **a·vow′al** *n.* **a·vow′ed·ly** *adv.*

a·vun·cu·lar (avŭng′kyuler) *adj.* Of, resembling, an uncle.

aw (aw) *int.* Expression of mild remonstrance, commiseration, protest, etc.

a·wait (awāt′) *v.t.* Wait for.

a·wake (awāk′) *v.* (**a·woke** pr. awōk′ or **a·waked, a·wak·ing**). Cease to sleep; rouse from sleep. ~ *pred. adj.* Not asleep; vigilant. **a·wak′en** *v.* Awake. **a·wak′en·ing** *adj.* Rousing, stirring. ~ *n.* 1. Act of awaking from sleep. 2. Arousal of interest or attention. 3. Entering into state of awareness about something. 4. Revival of interest in religion.

a·ward (awõrd′) *v.t.* Give as payment, prize, etc.; grant, assign. ~ *n.* Judicial decision; payment, penalty, assigned by this; prize; grant.

a·ware (awãr′) *pred. adj.* Conscious, not ignorant (*of, that*). **a·ware′ness** *n.*

a·wash (awŏsh′, awawsh′) *pred. adj.* Flush with or washed by the waves.

a·way (awā′) *adv.* To or at a distance; on opponent's ground; far, separate; aside, to a different place; ~ **with**, go away, take away. **away** *adj.* Absent; distant; (of game) played on opponent's ground.

awe (aw) *n.* Reverential fear. ~ *v.t.* (**awed, aw·ing**). Inspire with awe. **awe·some** (aw′som) *adj.* **awe·strick·en** (aw′strĭken), **awe·struck** (aw′strŭk) *adjs.* Struck with awe.

a·weigh (awā′) *adv.* (of anchor) Just raised from bottom in weighing.

aw·ful (aw′ful) *adj.* Inspiring awe, fear, or dread; (colloq.) very bad, ugly, disliked, etc. **aw·ful·ly** (aw′fulē, aw′flē) *adv.* (esp. colloq.) Extremely. **aw′ful·ness** *n.*

a·while (ahwīl′, awīl′) *adv.* For a short time.

awk·ward (awk′werd) *adj.* Ill adapted for use; hard to deal with; clumsy; inconvenient, embarrass-

*The **axolotl**, a salamander found in mountain lakes of Mexico and southwestern U.S.A. The name applies to any neotenic salamander i.e. one that matures sexually in the larval stage.*

*The **aye-aye** is a tree-climbing, nocturnal primate 31 to 41 ins. long, including the tail. It is now rare because most of its forest habitat in Madagascar has been destroyed.*

ing. **awk'ward·ly** *adv.* **awk'-ward·ness** *n.*

awl (awl) *n.* Small pointed tool for piercing holes in leather, wood, etc., esp. that used by shoemakers.

awn·ing (aw'nĭng) *n.* Sheet of canvas etc. stretched on framework as protection from sun etc.

a·woke (*a*wōk') *v.*: see AWAKE.

A.W.O.L. *abbrev.* Absent without leave.

a·wry (*a*rī') *adv.* & *pred. adj.* Crookedly; amiss.

ax, axe (ăks) *ns.* (pl. **ax·es** pr. ăk'sĭz). Metal tool for chopping, cleaving, etc., with wooden handle; **get the ~**, (colloq.) to be dismissed from one's job. **ax, axe** *vbs. t.* (**axed, ax·ing**). Cut down (personnel, expenses, etc.); put an end to (project); **have an ~ to grind**, (colloq.) to have one's own special interest to promote.

ax·i·al (ăk'sē*a*l) *adj.* Forming, belonging to, an axis. **ax'i·al·ly** *adv.*

ax·il (ăk'sĭl) *n.* Upper angle between leaf and stem it springs from, or between branch and trunk.

ax·i·om (ăk'sē*o*m) *n.* Self-evident truth; established principle; maxim; (geom.) self-evident theorem. **ax·i·o·mat·ic** (ăksē*o*măt'ĭk) *adj.* **ax·i·o·mat'i·cal·ly** *adv.*

ax·is (ăk'sĭs) *n.* (pl. **ax·es** pr. ăk'sēz). 1. Line about which a body rotates; straight line from end to end of a body. 2. (math.) Line dividing a regular figure symmetrically; line by revolution about which a plane figure is conceived as generating a solid. 3. (bot.) Main stem or shoot; **floral ~**, that part of a shoot which bears the floral organs, receptacle. 4. (anat.) Second cervical vertebra, on which the head turns. 5. Alliance between two or more countries; **the A~**, alliance between Germany and Italy, and later Japan, during World War II.

ax·le (ăk's*e*l) *n.* Spindle on or with which wheel revolves; end of axletree; axletree; **ax'letree**, bar connecting wheels of carriage etc.

Ax·min·ster (ăks'mĭnst*er*). Small town in Devon, England; **~ carpet**, carpet of cut pile, first made at Axminster, orig. in imitation of hand-knotted oriental carpets.

ax·o·lotl (ăk'sol*ŏ*t*e*l) *n.* Salamander of genus *Ambystoma* of mountain lakes of Mexico and southwestern U.S., usu. retaining larval form throughout life. [Aztec]

ax·on (ăk'sŏn), **ax·one** (ăk'sōn) *ns.* That part of the nerve which is its conducting element or nerve fiber.

a·yah (ah'y*a*) *n.* Hindu nurse. [Port. *aia* fem. of *aio* tutor]

a·ya·tol·lah (ahyahtō'l*a*) *n.* Chief spiritual leader of Shiite Muslims.

aye[1], **ay**[1] (ī) *advs.* (esp. Sc. & dial.) Yes. **~** *n.* (pl. **ayes**). Affirmative answer or vote.

aye[2], **ay**[2] (ā) *adv*s. (literary) Always; **for ~**, for ever.

aye-aye (ī'ī) *n.* Small tree-climbing animal (genus *Daubentonia*) found in Madagascar, a primate related to the lemurs.

Ayr·shire (ār'shēr, -sh*er*). Former county of SW. Scotland; hence, breed of dairy cattle, mostly white with reddish or black markings, orig. raised there; kind of bacon cured in Ayrshire.

AZ *abbrev.* Arizona.

a·zal·ea (*a*zāl'y*a*) *n.* Flowering shrubby plant of the genus *Rhododendron*, chiefly native of N. America and China. [mod. L. f. Gk. *azaleos* parched, because Linnaeus believed them to grow in dry situations]

A·zer·bai·jan, A·zer·bai·dzhan (ahzerbījahn', ăz*er*-). 1. One of the constituent republics (properly *Azerbaijan Soviet Socialist Republic*) of the U.S.S.R., lying between the Black and Caspian Seas; capital Baku. 2. Former province of NW. Iran, now divided into **Eastern ~** and **Western ~**. **A·zer·bai·ja·ni** (ahz*er*bījah'nē, ăz*er*-) *n.* (pl. **-ja·nis**, collect. **-ja·ni**). (Native, inhabitant, language) of Azerbaijan.

az·i·muth (ăz'*i*m*u*th) *n.* Arc of the heavens extending from the zenith to the horizon, which it cuts at right angles; (in full, **true ~** of a heavenly body) arc of horizon intercepted between north (in S. hemisphere, south) point of horizon and the point where the vertical circle passing through the body cuts the horizon. [Arab. *al samt* the way, road, used in astron. for azimuth]

az·o (ăz'ō) *adj.* (chem.) Containing the **azo group**, —N = N—, where both bonds are attached to carbon atoms.

A·zores (*a*zōrz', *a*zōrz', ā'zōrz, ā'zōrz). Group of islands in N. Atlantic, some 800 miles W. of Portugal; in Portuguese possession.

Az·tec (ăz'tĕk) *adj.* & *n.* (Member, language) of an Indian people first known (*c*1100 A.D.) as inhabitants of the valley of Mexico; they built their capital (on the same site as modern Mexico City) in 1324 and extended their conquests in the 15th c., their most successful leader being Montezuma I (reigned 1440–1469); they were conquered by the invading Spaniards under Cortez, early in the 16th c.

A·zu·ma (ah'zōō'mah'). Volcano on Honshu Island, Japan.

az·ure (ăzh'*er*) *adj.* & *n.* Sky blue; blue of unclouded sky; lapis lazuli; (heraldry) blue. [Arab. *al lāzuward* lapis lazuli, cerulean blue, f. Pers. *lazhward*]

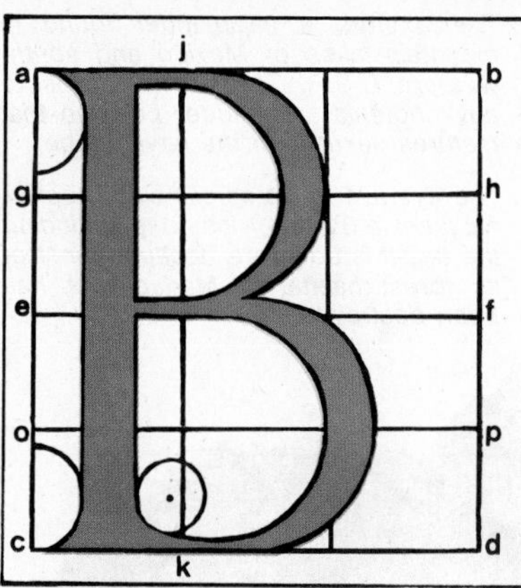

How (right) the written form of the letter ***B, b*** *has evolved through the ages. Left: the classical grid on which the capital letter is constructed. The letter derives from the Greek beta and the Phoenician and Hebrew beth. It has, from the earliest times, been second letter of nearly all European alphabets.*

Phoenician — Early Greek — Early Etruscan

Classical Latin — Anglo-Saxon — Italian (Roman)

B, b (bē) (pl. **B's, b's** or **Bs, bs**). 1. Second letter of modern English and ancient Roman alphabet, representing a voiced bilabial stop, and derived from the Greek *beta* (*β*) and Phoenician and Hebrew *beth* (𐤁, ב). 2. Second in series, order, or class. 3. **B**, (mus.) Seventh note in the natural scale (C major); scale or key with this note for tonic. 4. Grade or mark indicating good but not highest quality.

B. *abbrev.* Beatus (fem. -*a*) (L., = blessed); British; Bible; (music) bass, basso; book.

b. *abbrev.* Born; (baseball) base; brother.

B.A. *abbrev.* Bachelor of Arts.

baa (bă, bah) *n.* & *v.* (**baaed, baa·ing**). (of sheep) Bleat.

Ba·al (bā′*a*l, bāl) (pl. **Ba·al·im** pr. bā′*a*lĭm). God of the ancient Phoenicians and Canaanites; false god. **Ba′al·ism, Ba′al·ist, Ba′al·ite** *ns.* [Heb. *ba'al* lord, master]

Baal·bek (bahl′bĕk, bā′*a*l-, bāl′-). Site in Lebanon of the Roman colony of Heliopolis (1st–3rd centuries A.D.), a center of worship of the sun-god Helios, identified with BAAL.

ba·ba (bah′b*a*) *n.* (also **baba au rhum** pr. bah′b*a* ō rŭm′). Small rich spongecake soaked in rum syrup.

Ba·bar (bah′b*e*r) = BABER.

Bab·bitt (băb′ĭt). Hero of a novel (1922) by Sinclair Lewis; hence a materialistic complacent businessman. **Bab′bitt·ry** *n.*

bab·bitt (băb′ĭt) *n.* (also **Babbitt metal**). Soft alloy of tin, copper, and antimony, used for machine bearings. [I. *Babbitt* (1799–1862), Amer. inventor]

bab·ble (băb′*e*l) *v.* (**-bled, -bling**). Talk half articulately, incoherently, foolishly, or excessively; murmur (of stream etc.). ~ *n.* Foolish or childish talk. **bab′ble·ment** *n.* **bab′bler** *n.* Chatterer; teller of secrets.

babe (bāb) *n.* Baby; (slang) an attractive young girl or woman.

Ba·bel (bā′b*e*l, băb′*e*l). (Heb. myth.) = BABYLON; its people (Gen. 11) tried to build a tower that would reach heaven, but God prevented them by "confounding" their language (so that they could not understand one another) and scattering them abroad.

ba·bel (bā′b*e*l, băb′*e*l) *n.* Scene of confusion and uproar; confused mixture of voices or sounds. [f. BABEL]

Ba·ber, Ba·bar, Bab·ur (bah′b*e*r) (1483–1530). First Mogul emperor, descended from Tamburlaine; he conquered most of India *c*1525.

bab·i·ru·sa, bab·i·rous·sa, bab·i·rus·sa (băb*i*rōō′s*a*, bahb*i*-) *ns.* Wild hog (*Babirusa babyrussa*), male of which has long upper canine teeth which pierce the lip and grow upward like horns; found only in islands of Celebes and Buru. [Malagasy, = "hog deer"]

Ba·bi Yar (bah′bē yar̄′). Ravine outside Kiev, U.S.S.R., where the Jews of the city were slaughtered by German troops in 1941.

ba·boon (bă*b*ōōn′) *n.* Medium-sized monkey (several species in genus *Papio*) of Arabia and Africa S. and E. of Sahara, living in bands in open rocky country, occas. tree-climbing, characterized by doglike snout, cheek prominences, and colored bare patches on the buttocks; (slang) brutish or ungentlemanly person.

Ba·bur (bah′b*e*r) = BABER.

ba·bush·ka (b*a*bōōsh′k*a*) *n.* Kerchief tied under chin. [Russ., = grandmother]

ba·by (bā′bē) *n.* (pl. **-bies**). Infant, very young child; childish person; very young animal; thing small of its kind; (fig.) one's responsibility; one's particular interest; (slang) an attractive young girl or woman; ~ **beef**, beef from a calf 12 to 20 months old; ~ **blue**, pale blue; ~**'s-breath**, plant of the genus *Gypsophila* with branching clusters of small fragrant white flowers; ~ **buggy,** ~ **carriage**, carriage for one or two children, usu. with four wheels, pushed by hand; ~ **face(d)**, (of an adult) having a smooth, plump babylike

The ***babirusa,*** *a wandering wild pig, is a night hunter of the dense forests of Celebes and Buru, Indonesia. A peculiarity of the male is the exaggerated development of its canines.*

Left: The ***baboon*** *lives closely with a band or troop of other baboons under a dominant male leader jealous of his harem. Baboons can prove dangerous adversaries.*

Facing page: The six preserved columns, 62 ft. high, 7½ ft. in diameter, of the Temple of Jupiter at ***Baalbek,*** *Lebanon. The columns are notable for their carved entablature.*

face; ~ **grand (piano),** see PIANO²; ~ **talk,** the early speech of a very young child or an adult's imitation of it; infantile or mincing speech; ~ **tooth,** milk tooth. **ba'by·hood** *n.* **ba'by·ish** *adj.* **ba'by·ish·ly** *adv.* **ba'by·ish·ness** *n.* **ba'by·-like** *adj.* **baby** *v.t.* (**-bied, -by·ing**). Treat like a baby. **ba'by-sit** *v.i.* (**-sat, -sit·ting**). Act as **baby-sitter,** person who looks after child when its parents go out.

Bab·y·lon (băb'*ilon*, -lŏn). Capital city, on the Euphrates, of the ancient Chaldean Empire; the Jews were brought there in captivity by Nebuchadnezzar (597 and 586 B.C.); its **hanging** (i.e. terraced) **gardens** were one of the Seven Wonders of the ancient world; it was sacked by Cyrus of Persia in 538 B.C. **Bab·y·lo·ni·a** (băb*i*-lō'nē*a*). Empire of Babylon. **Bab·y·lo'ni·an** *adj.* & *n.*

bac·ca·lau·re·ate (băk*a*lōr'ēĭt) *n.* 1. Bachelor's degree. 2. Sermon delivered at a commencement.

bac·ca·rat, bac·ca·ra (bahk*a*-rah', băk*a*-, băh'k*a*rah, băk'*a*-) *ns.* Gambling card game, played against banker by players betting that their hands will be closest to totaling nine.

bac·cha·nal (bahk*a*nahl', băk*a*-năl', băk'*a*nal) *adj.* Of Bacchus or his rites. ~ *n.* Drunken revelry, wild party.

Bac·cha·na·lia (băk*a*nāl'y*a*, -nā'lē*a*) *n.pl.* Festival held in honor of Bacchus; drunken revelry, orgy. **bac·cha·na'lian** *adj.*

bac·chic (băk'ĭk) *adj.* Of Bacchus or his worship; riotous, drunken.

Bac·chus (băk'*u*s). (Gk. and Rom. myth.) God of wine: see DIONYSUS.

bac·cif·er·ous (băksĭf'*er*us), **bac·ci·form** (băk's*i*fōrm), **bac·-civ·or·ous** (băksĭv'*er*us) *adjs.* Berry-bearing, -shaped, -eating.

bach (băch) *v.* ~ **it,** live alone as a bachelor. [abbreviation of bachelor]

Bach (bah*χ*), **Johann Sebastian** (1685–1750). German composer of many fugues and works for organ and other keyboard instruments, a great Mass, and much other choral church music.

bach·e·lor (băch'*e*ler, băch'ler) *n.* Unmarried man; bachelor's degree; **B ~ of Arts** (B.A.), **of Science** (B.Sc.), etc., holder of a bachelor's degree, one awarded by a college or university to a person who successfully completes 4-year undergraduate study program; the degree itself; **~'s button,** any of various flowers of round or button-like form such as the cornflower, orig. the double variety of *Ranunculus acris*; ~ **girl,** (archaic) young unmarried woman living independently. **Bach'e·lor·dom, bach'e·lor·hood, bach'e·lor·ship** *ns.*

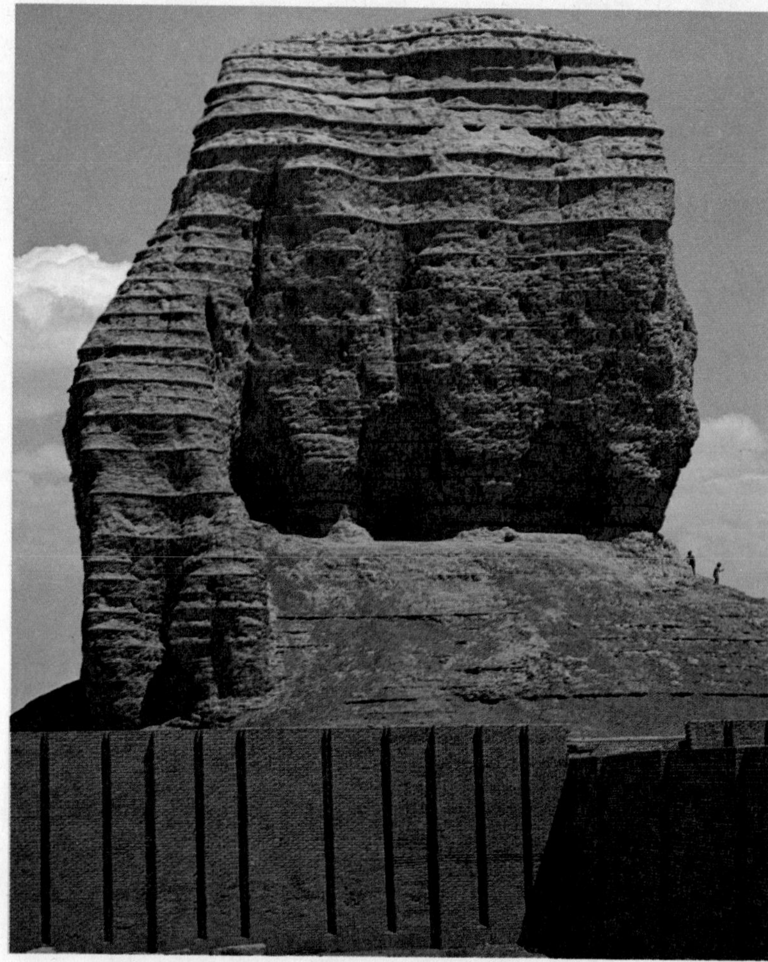

Ziggurat (temple) of Aqar Quf evokes ***Babylon.*** *This famous city of antiquity with its hanging gardens lay just north of the modern town of Hillah in southern Iraq.*

ba·cil·lar (b*a*sĭl'*er*, băs'*i*ler), **bac·il·lar·y** (băs'*i*lĕrē) *adjs.* Consisting of little rods; connected with bacilli.

ba·cil·li·form (b*a*sĭl'*i*fōrm) *adj.* Rod-shaped.

ba·cil·lus (b*a*sĭl'*u*s) *n.* (pl. **-cil·li** pr. -sĭl'ī). Any straight rod-shaped bacterium; (loosely and usu. pl.) disease-producing bacteria. [L. dim. of *baculus* stick]

back (băk) *n.* Rear surface of human body, part of this between shoulders and hips; corresponding part of animal's body; side or part away from or farther from spectator or direction of motion; side of hand opposite palm; part or area forming rear of anything; backbone, spine; (football) player stationed behind scrimmage line; **behind (someone's)** ~, without his knowledge, treacherously; **get (one's)** ~ **up,** make (person) angry or stubborn; **turn (one's)** ~ **on,** forsake. **back** *adj.* Situated behind or at rear; remote; of, pertaining to, the back; in arrears, overdue; ~ **country,** area away from settled districts. **back** *adv.* To or at the rear; in(to) an earlier position; to or in a remote position. ~ *v.* Put, or be, a back, lining, support, or background to; sponsor; support with money, argument, etc. (also ~ **up**); bet on; (cause to) move back; lay (sail) against the wind; (of wind) change counterclockwise (cf. VEER); ~ **down,** abandon claim; ~ **off,** retreat; ~ **out** (*of*), withdraw (from). **back'er** *n.* One who backs or supports. **back'ing** *n.* Support, assistance. **back-** combining form: **back'ache,** pain in the back; **back'bite** (*v.*) (**-bit, -bit** or **-bit·-ten, -bit·ing**), slander; **back'biter** (*n.*); **back'board,** (basketball) board to which basket is attached; **back'bone,** spine, main support, firmness of character; **back'breaking,** arduous; **(on the) back burner,** deemed less important, tabled; **back'court,** (as in tennis) the area between service line and baseline, or (as in basketball) area near basket being defended; **back-date** (*v.*) (**-dat·ed, -dat·ing**), affix earlier date to (document etc.); **back'door** (*adj.*), clandestine; **back'drop,** painted curtain hung at back of stage; setting; **back'field,** (football) the backs, or the area they play in; **back'fire** (*n.*), fire

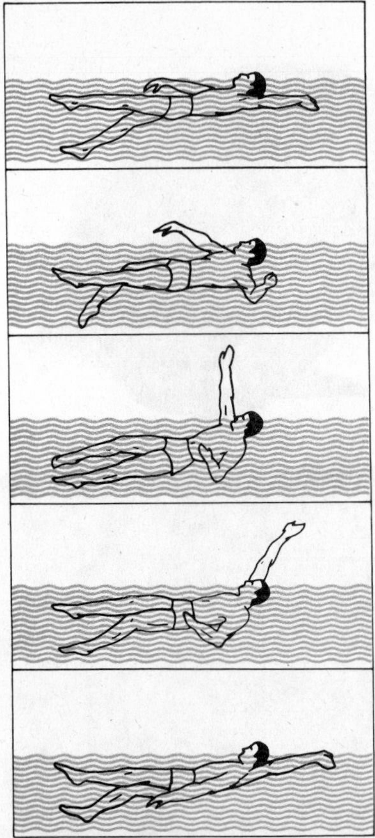

*Action of the S-pull **backstroke,** used by most world-class swimmers. The hand, forming a lengthened 's' shape, catches the water about 6 ins. below the surface (top) as the pull starts. The hand pulls back and the forearm rotates. The pull ends with a final thrust back and down. Normally the legs are kicked six times during every arm cycle.*

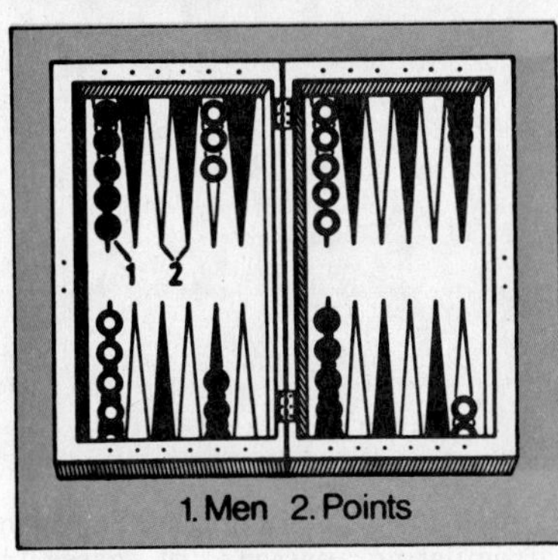

***Backgammon** board. The game is one of the oldest known, possibly dating back to 3,000 B.C. The rules were codified in 1743 by Edmond Hoyle.*

deliberately set to create burned area as protection against oncoming fire; (of internal combustion engine) premature explosion in cylinder or explosion in exhaust pipe; (*v.*) (**-fired, -fir·ing**), to explode thus; (fig. of plan etc.) go wrong, have adverse effect on instigator; **back formation**, the creation of a word by dropping an apparent affix in another word, as *burgle* from *burglar;* word so formed; **back'ground** (*n.*), back part of scene or picture; social surroundings, circumstances, origins, environment; (*adj.*), in, providing, a background; **back'hand**, (tennis etc.) (stroke) with back of hand turned in the direction of movement; **back'handed**, of a similar stroke; (fig.) ambiguous, equivocal; **back'lash**, sudden or violent recoil; (fig.) hostile reaction esp. to real or fancied threat posed by social or racial reforms; **back'log**, large log at back of hearth to keep up fire; accumulation or reserve, of work, business, stock, etc.; **back number**, an out-of-date periodical; (colloq.) anything out of date; **back order** (*n.* & *v.*), (place) an order to be sent or filled at a future time; **back'pack**, knapsack usu. mounted on a light frame; (*v.i.*), hike while carrying a backpack; **back'packer** (*n.*); **back-pedal** (*v.i.*) (**-ped·aled** or **-ped·alled, -ped·al·ing** or **-ped·al·ling**), slow (a bicycle) by pedaling backwards; retreat; **back'rest**, a rest for one's back; **back road**, a relatively unused country road, often unpaved; **back seat**, humble or obscure position; **back-seat driver**, one who gives unwanted advice; **back'side**, buttocks; **back'slapper**, a noisy, overly effusive person; **back'slide** (*v.i.*) (**-slid, -slid** or **-slid·den, -slid·ing**), relapse into sin, error, etc.; **back'space** (*v.i.*) (**-spaced, -spac·ing**), move typewriter carriage backward by striking designated key; (*n.*), such a key; **back'spin,** reverse spin imparted to a ball to slow it or change its direction or bounce; **back'stage**, (part of theater) behind the scenes; also fig.; **back'stairs** (*adj.*), underhand, secret; **back'stitch** (*v.*), sew by inserting needle each time behind the place where it has just been brought out; (*n.*), stitch made thus; **back'stop**, a barrier to stop a ball from going too far out of playing area; (baseball, colloq.) the catcher; (colloq.) a substitute or support in case of need; (*v.i.*) (**-stopped, -stop·ping**), to act as backstop; **back'stroke**, stroke made by swimmer lying on his or her back; **back talk**, impudent repartee; **back'track** (*v.*), take the same route back; retreat; reverse policy; **back'up**, one who supports; a stoppage (as of traffic, plumbing, etc.); substitute mechanism or program ready if original fails; **back'wash**, motion of receding wave; motion of water caused by passage of vessel; **back'water**, stretch of still water parallel with a stream and fed from it at the lower end; (fig.) a stagnant place or condition; **backwoods'**, remote, only partially settled forest land; **backwoods'man** (pl. **-men**), settler in backwoods; **back'yard'**, yard behind a house etc.; (fig.) a familiar or nearby place (esp. one's *own backyard*).

back·gam·mon (băk'găm*o*n, băkgăm'-) *n.* Game for two persons, played by moving pieces according to the throw of dice, on a board of two tables, each marked off into 12 spaces of alternating colors.

back·less (băk'lĭs) *adj.* Having no back; (of dress etc.) cut low at the back.

back·ward (băk'w*e*rd) *adv.* (also **back'wards**). Back foremost; back toward the starting point; the reverse way; toward the rear; ~ **and forward**, to and fro. **backward** *adj.* Directed to rear or starting point; reversed; slow in learning or developing; bashful, hesitant. **back'ward·ly** *adv.* **back'ward·ness** *n.*

ba·con (bā'k*o*n) *n.* Cured meat from back and sides of a hog; **bring home the** ~, (colloq.) succeed.

Ba·con[1] (bā'k*o*n), **Francis, Baron Verulam and Viscount St. Albans** (1561–1626). Lord Chancellor of England (1618–20), philosopher and essayist. **Ba·co·ni·an** (bākō'nē*a*n) *adj.* & *n.* (Advocate) of the theory that Bacon wrote the plays of Shakespeare.

Ba·con[2] (bā'k*o*n), **Roger** (1214?–94). English Franciscan, philosopher and student of experimental science (esp. optics) at Paris and Oxford; credited, then and later, with magical powers.

bac·te·ri·a (băktēr'ē*a*) *n.pl.* (sing. **-te·ri·um** pr. -tēr'ē*u*m). Any of several types of microscopic or ultramicroscopic single-celled organisms occurring in enormous numbers everywhere in nature, not only in land, sea, and air, but also on or in many parts of the tissues of plants and animals, and forming one of the main biologically interdependent groups of organisms by virtue of the chemical changes that many of them bring about, e.g. many forms of decay, certain diseases, and the building up of nitrogen compounds in the soil. **bac·te'ri·al** *adj.* Of or caused by bacteria. **bac·te'ri·al·ly** *adv.* [Gk. dim. of *baktron* stick]

bac·te·ri·cide (băktēr'ĭsīd) *n.* Substance that destroys bacteria. **bac·te·ri·cid·al** (băktērĭsī'd*a*l) *adj.*

bac·te·ri·ol·o·gy (băktērēŏl'*o*jē) *n.* Study of bacteria, esp. as a branch of medicine. **bac·te·ri·o·log·i·cal** (băktērēolŏj'ĭk*a*l) *adj.* ~ **warfare**, use of bacteria to spread disease in the enemy. **bac·te·ri·o·log'i·cal·ly** *adv.* **bac·te·ri·ol'o·gist** *n.*

bac·te·ri·o·phage (băktēr'ēofāj) *n.* Virus capable of destroying bacteria. **bac·te·ri·o·phag·ic**

A nocturnal mammal, the ***badger*** *digs rapidly, far more quickly than a man with a shovel. For long periods it remains underground, where its young are usually born.*

(băktērēofăj′ĭk) *adj.*

Bac·tri·a (băk′trē*a*). Ancient country of central Asia (now *Balkh* in N. Afghanistan).

Bac·tri·an (băk′trē*a*n) *adj.* Of Bactria or its people; ~ **camel**, two-humped camel of central Asia, *Camelus bactrianus*. **Bactrian** *n.* Native or inhabitant of Bactria.

bad (băd) *adj.* (**worse, worst**). 1. Worthless, inferior; defective, inefficient; not valid; unpleasant; (of coinage) counterfeit; rotten, spoiled; **go** ~, decay; **not** ~, (colloq.) rather good; ~ **debt**, one not recoverable; **bad′lands**, arid rocky region seamed with deep vertical gullies by erosion and thus uncultivable; see BAD LANDS; **bad-tempered**, ill-humored, surly. 2. Wicked, vicious; **bad egg, apple**, a dishonest or untrustworthy person; **bad′man** (pl. **-men**), desperado; **bad′mouth** (*v.*), (slang) slander, denigrate. 3. Painful; harmful; **bad blood**, ill feeling. 4. Ill, in pain. **bad** *n.* Ill fortune, ruin; **go to the** ~, go to ruin, degenerate. **bad′ly** *adv.* **bad′ness** *n.*

Ba·den-Ba·den (bah′d*e*n bah′-d*e*n). Health resort, with mineral springs, in Baden-Wurtemberg, the Federal Republic of Germany.

Ba·den-Pow·ell (bā′d*e*n pō′*e*l, băd′*e*n pow′*e*l), **Robert Stephenson Smyth, 1st Baron Baden-Powell of Gilwell** (1857–1941). English soldier; defended Mafeking, 1900; founded the Boy Scout organization, 1908.

badge (băj) *n.* Distinctive emblem or mark as a sign of office, membership, etc.

badg·er (băj′*e*r) *n.* Nocturnal plantigrade quadruped (*Taxidea taxus*) intermediate between weasel and bear, with coarse dark fur and a white blaze on the forehead, which digs a burrow, hibernates, and defends itself fiercely against attack; **badger game**, extortion scheme in which a man is lured into a compromising situation and then surprised and blackmailed. **badger** *v.* Pester as dogs worry a badger; tease, torment.

bad·i·nage (băd*i*nahzh′) *n.* Banter.

Bad Lands. Extensive barren eroded region of SW. South Dakota and NW. Nebraska; ~ **National Monument**, tract of this region in South Dakota set aside to preserve fossils and rock formations.

bad·min·ton (băd′mĭnt*o*n) *n.* Game like tennis played with shuttlecocks and rackets over a high net. [name of the country seat of

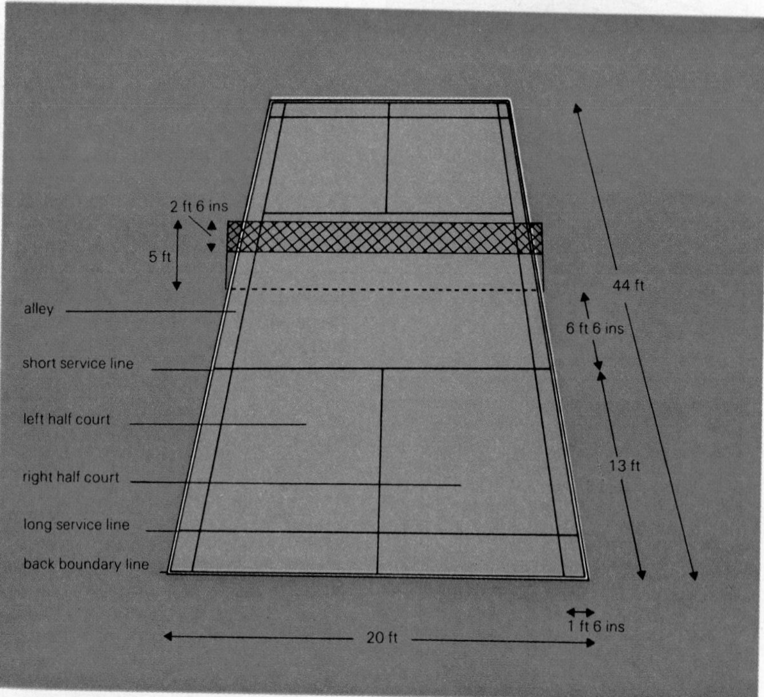

The dimensions and markings of a ***badminton*** *court. This racket game is mostly played indoors either as singles or doubles. It derives from battledore and shuttlecock.*

Duke of Beaufort in Gloucestershire, Eng.]

Bae·de·ker (bā′d*i*k*e*r) *n.* Any of the travel guidebooks issued by **Karl** ~ (1801–59), German publisher, and his successors; hence, any guidebook.

Baf·fin (băf′ĭn), **William** (1584?–1622). English navigator and explorer; discovered ~ **Island**, large island off the NE. coast of Canada and ~ **Bay**, sea between it and Greenland.

baf·fle (băf′*e*l) *v.t.* (**-fled, -fling**). Foil, frustrate, perplex. **baf′fler** *n.* **baf′fling** *adj.* Bewildering. **baffle** *n.* Shielding device or structure; esp. one checking or deflecting sound waves, improving tone of loudspeaker by hindering return of sound waves to back of speaker; one hindering or regulating passage of gases or fluids.

bag (băg) *n.* Receptacle of flexible material with an opening usu. at the top; suitcase, handbag, or purse; amount of game taken in hunting; pouch or pouch-like part; (baseball) a base; (slang) ugly girl or woman; (slang) one's special interest or avocation; (esp. pl.) folds of loose skin beneath the eyes; ~ **and baggage**, with all belongings, completely; **in the** ~, assured of success; **bag′man** (pl. **-men**), (slang) agent who collects or distributes money for illicit purposes. **bag** *v.* (**bagged, bag·ging**). Put in a bag; secure game; bulge, hang loosely, droop, swell.

ba·gasse (b*a*găs′) *n.* Residue of sugar cane after processing.

bag·a·telle (băg*a*tĕl′) *n.* 1. Mere trifle; short unpretentious piece of music. 2. Game played on a table with a semicircular end, the object

*The New Mosque in **Baghdad,** with the monument to an Iraqi unknown warrior in foreground. The city was for centuries a prosperous trading center under the caliphs.*

*The **Bad Lands** National Monument is in harsh, barren country in South Dakota. Opened in 1939, many fossils have been found in the area, such as the saber-toothed tiger and the three-toed horse.*

being to strike balls into numbered holes with a cue.

ba·gel (bā'gel) *n.* Hard ring-shaped bread roll. [Yiddish]

bag·gage (băg'ĭj) *n.* Portable equipment of an army; luggage; (joc.) saucy girl; ~ **master**, person in charge of baggage in rail or bus terminal.

bag·gy (băg'ē) *adj.* (**bag·gi·er, bag·gi·est**). That bags or hangs loosely.

Bagh·dad, Bag·dad (băg'dăd, bahgdahd'). City on the Tigris, now the capital of Iraq.

bagn·io (băn'yō, bahn'-) *n.* (pl. **-ios**). Brothel.

bag·pipe (băg'pīp) *n.* (freq. pl.) Musical instrument consisting of several pipes, including drones and a chanter through which air is forced by pressure on a windbag held under the arm; now associated chiefly with Scotland.

ba·guette, ba·guet (băgĕt') *ns.* Gem cut in long rectangular shape.

Ba·guio (bah'gyō). Summer capital of the Republic of the Philippines on N. Luzon.

bah (bah, bă) *int.* Expression of contempt.

Ba·ha·mas (b*a*hah'm*a*z). (also **Bahama Islands**) Archipelago of British W. Indies, the first land touched by Columbus in 1492; first colonized by Spaniards and later (in 17th c.) by the English; British colony 1783–1973; independent 1973; capital, Nassau. **Ba·ha·mi·an** (b*a*hā'mē*a*n; -hah'-) *adj.* & *n.*

Ba·hi·a (bah-ē'*a*). Atlantic coast state of E. Brazil; capital, Salvador.

Bah·rain, Bah·rein (bahrān', -rīn'). Independent sheikdom consisting of a group of islands, the largest being Bahrain Island, in the Persian Gulf; capital, Manama.

Bai·kal (bīkahl'), **Lake.** Large lake in S. Siberia, U.S.S.R., containing largest volume of fresh water anywhere in the world.

bail[1] (bāl) *n.* 1. Security for a prisoner's appearance for trial; person providing this; release from prison granted in return for bail money; the privilege or right of being so released. ~ *v.t.* Secure the liberation of on bail.

bail[2] (bāl) *n.* Bar separating horses in an open stable.

bail[3] (bāl) *v.* Scoop water out of (boat etc.); ~ **out**, parachute from airplane; relieve or assist person in (esp. financial) crisis; (fig.) escape. **bail'er** *n.* Utensil for bailing.

bail[4] (bāl) *n.* Handle of a bucket etc.

bail·iff (bā'lĭf) *n.* Court attendant entrusted with custody of prisoners under arraignment, protecting jurors, maintaining order in courtroom, etc.

bail·i·wick (bā'l*i*wĭk) *n.* One's area of knowledge, skill, etc.

Bai·ram (bīrahm', bī'rahm) *n.* Each of the two principal festivals of the Muslim year, **Lesser** ~ (lasting three days) following the fast of Ramadan, and **Greater** ~ (lasting four days) 70 days later.

bairn (bārn) *n.* (Sc.) Child.

bait (bāt) *v.* 1. Worry (animal) by setting dogs at it; worry (person) by jeers. 2. Put bait on or in (fishhook, trap, etc.). ~ *n.* Food etc. used to entice prey; allurement.

baize (bāz) *n.* Coarse woolen usu. green fabric used chiefly for coverings, linings, etc.

Ba·ja (bah'hah) **California.** State of Mexico and resort area in the N. part of the Lower California Peninsula; capital, Mexicali.

bake (bāk) *v.* (**baked, bak·ing**). Cook by dry heat, as in an oven; harden by heat; be or become baked; **baked Alaska**, dessert of cake, ice cream, and meringue browned quickly in oven; **baked beans**, beans so cooked (esp. as a canned food, in tomato sauce); **baking powder**, powder consisting of sodium bicarbonate and cream of tartar with a filling of starch or flour, used instead of yeast to make cakes etc. rise; **baking soda**, sodium bicarbonate.

bak·er (bā'k*e*r) *n.* One who bakes and sells bread; ~**'s dozen**, 13 objects of any kind. **bak'er·y** *n.* (pl. **-er·ies**). Bakehouse; trade of baking.

Baker Street. Street in London where the fictional detective Sherlock Holmes resided.

ba·kla·va (bahkl*a*vah', bah'kl*a*vah) *n.* Dessert of flaky pastry, honey, and nuts. [Turkish]

bak·sheesh, bak·shish (băk'-shēsh, băkshēsh') *ns.* Small gift of money. [Pers. *bakhshish* gift, munificence]

Ba·ku (bahkōō'). Capital of Azerbaijan, on the shore of the Caspian Sea; a center of the petroleum industry.

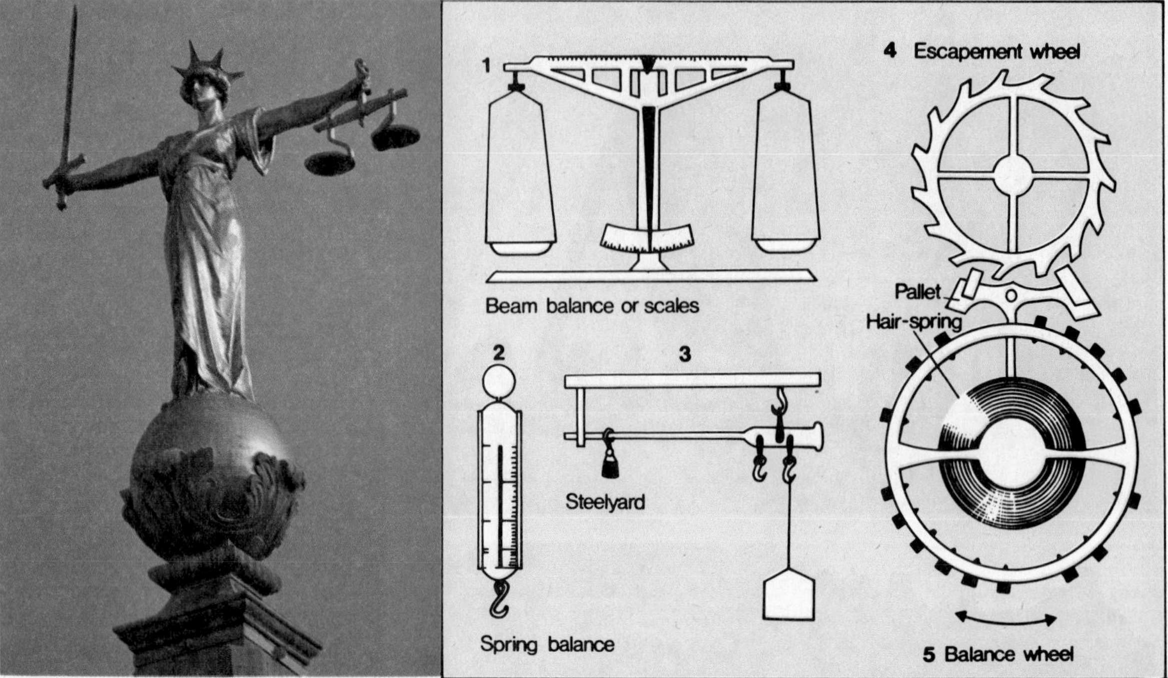

*Above: The Scales of Justice on the roof of the Old Bailey, London, U.K. Above right: 1. Beam **balance.** 2. Spring balance. 3. Steelyard. 4. Escapement wheel. 5. Balance wheel.*

In a watch the pallet allows the escapement wheel to unwind one tooth at a time, rocking to and fro before letting it go. It is the movement that makes a watch tick.

Bal·a·kla·va (băl*a*klah′v*a*, bahl*a*-). Crimean village near Sevastopol, scene of battle (1854) of the Crimean War during which occurred the Charge of the Light Brigade.

bal·a·lai·ka (băl*a*lī′k*a*) *n.* Russian stringed instrument played by plucking, resembling guitar but with triangular body and two, three, or four strings.

bal·ance (băl′*a*ns) *n.* 1. Weighing apparatus consisting of a beam moving freely on a central pivot with a pan at either end; spring or lever substitute for this; scale; ~ **(wheel),** regulating gear of a clock, watch, etc. 2. (State of) even distribution of weight or amount; state of stability, harmony, etc. 3. Preponderating weight or amount. 4. Excess of assets over liabilities or vice versa. 5. Remainder. 6. ~ **beam,** horizontal beam for gymnastic exercises; ~ **of payments,** difference of value between payments into and out of a country; ~ **of power,** equilibrium of military and political power between several nations; ~ **of trade,** difference between the value of total exports and total imports of a country, **favorable** if exports exceed imports; ~ **sheet,** statement of assets and liabilities, esp. of a business. **balance** *v.* (**-anced, -anc·ing**). 1. Weigh. 2. Equalize, match; bring or come into equilibrium. 3. Find the balance of assets and liabilities in (an account book). **bal′anced** *adj.* (esp., of diet) Containing essential nutriments in suitable proportions.

Bal·an·chine (băl′*a*nshēn, băl*a*nshēn′), **George** (1904–). Russian-born American ballet dancer and choreographer.

bal·bo·a (bălbō′*a*) *n.* Principal monetary unit of Panama.

Bal·bo·a (bălbō′*a*), **Vasco Nuñez de** (1475–1517). Spanish explorer, esp. of Central America; first sighted the Pacific Ocean in 1513.

bal·brig·gan (bălbrĭg′*a*n) *n.* Knitted cotton cloth; (esp. pl.) underclothes of this material. [from Balbriggan, Ireland]

bal·co·ny (băl′k*o*nē) *n.* (pl. **-nies**). 1. Balustraded or railed platform on the outside of a building with access from an upper-floor window. 2. In a theater, the seats above the dress or upper circle.

bald (bawld) *adj.* 1. Having the scalp wholly or partly hairless; (of animal, bird) without fur, feathers, etc.; (zool.) having white on head; ~ **eagle,** a N. Amer. eagle (*Haliaeetus leucocephalus*) with white head and tail, also called "American eagle," a symbol of the U.S. 2. Bare; meager; undisguised, obvious. **bald′ly** *adv.* **bald′ness** *n.*

bal·der·dash (bawl′d*e*rdăsh) *n.* Nonsense, rubbish.

bald·ing (bawl′dĭng) *adj.* Becoming bald.

bal·dric (bawl′drĭk) *n.* Belt for supporting a sword, bugle, etc., worn over shoulder and across body to opposite hip.

Bald·win (bawld′wĭn), **Stanley** (1867–1947), **1st Earl Baldwin of Bewdley.** British Conservative statesman; prime minister 1923–4, 1924–9, 1935–7.

bale[1] (bāl) *n.* (archaic) Evil, destruction, woe.

bale[2] (bāl) *n.* Large bundle or package, esp. of merchandise, usu. wrapped and corded or looped. ~ *v.t.* (**baled, bal·ing**). Make up into bales. **bal′er** *n.*

Bal·e·ar·ic (bălēăr′ĭk) **Islands.** Group of islands, including Majorca and Minorca, off E. coast of Spain; a province of Spain.

ba·leen (b*a*lēn′) *n.* Whalebone.

bale·ful (bāl′f*u*l) *adj.* Pernicious, destructive, malignant. **bale′ful·ly** *adv.* **bale′ful·ness** *n.*

Ba·li (bah′lē, băl′ē). Mountainous island, area 2,146 square miles, famous for its beautiful scenery, near the E. end of Java; capital Singaradja. **Ba·li·nese** (bahl*i*nēz′, -nes′) *adj.* & *n.* (pl. **-nese**). (Native, language, people) of the island of Bali.

balk (bawk) *v.* 1. Thwart, hinder, discourage. 2. Shy. 3. (baseball) Commit a balk. ~ *n.* (baseball) Illegal motion made by pitcher while preparing to pitch when there is a runner or runners on base. **balk′er** *n.*

Bal·kan (bawl′k*a*n) *adj.* Of the Balkan Peninsula or States; ~ **Peninsula,** peninsula of Europe south of the Danube and Sava rivers; home of various peoples (Albanians, Vlachs, Greeks, Serbs, Bulgars, and Turks) with differing cultures. From the 3rd to the 7th

*Fishing boats in the bay at Santa Ponsa, Majorca. Together with Minorca, Ibiza, Formentera and Cabrera, Majorca is one of the **Balearic Islands.***

centuries the peninsula was nominally ruled by the Byzantine emperors; in 1356 the Ottoman invasion began; Constantinople fell to the Turks in 1453, and by 1478 most of the peninsula was in their power; the subject nations did not recover independence until the 19th c.; in 1912–13 Turkey was attacked and defeated by other Balkan peoples in alliance; during World War I Turkey and Bulgaria sided with Austria and Germany and the other Balkan States with the Allies; after the war the peninsula was divided among Greece, Bulgaria, Albania, and Yugoslavia, with Turkey retaining only Constantinople and the surrounding land; ~ **States**, countries of the Balkan Peninsula. **Bal′kans** *n.pl.* Balkan States.

Bal·khash (bahl*x*ahsh′). Lake, area 7,100 square miles, in Kazakhstan, central Asia.

ball[1] (bawl) *n.* 1. Solid or hollow sphere, esp. one used in a game; rounded mass (as of snow, string, etc.); game played with a ball, as esp. baseball; (*pl.*, vulg.) testicles; ~ **of foot, thumb**, rounded base of big toe, thumb; **have a** ~, enjoy oneself; **on the** ~, (colloq.) alert; **play** ~, (colloq.) cooperate (with). 2. (baseball) Pitch outside the strike zone not swung at by the batter. 3. Missile for cannon, rifles, etc. 4. ~ **bearing**, bearing in which revolving parts of a machine turn upon a number of hard balls running in grooves, which diminish friction; one of these balls; ~ **of fire**, very energetic, able person; ~ **park**, stadium for ball games; ~ **player**, professional player esp. of baseball; ~**-point (pen)**, writing instrument having for point a small ball bearing moistened from a reservoir of semiliquid ink. **ball** *v.* (of snow etc.) Form lumps; (vulg.) have sexual intercourse (with); ~ **up**, (slang) confuse or bungle.

ball[2] (bawl) *n.* Social assembly for dancing; **ball′room**, large room suitable for this.

bal·lad (băl′*a*d) *n.* 1. Narrative poem (esp. traditional) designed to be sung, with the same melody for each verse. 2. Any poem in similar style; = BALLADE, def. 1. 3. Any light simple song. **bal·lad·eer** (băl*a*dēr′) *n.* **bal′lad·ry** *n.* Ballad poetry. [Provençal *ballada*, dancing song]

bal·lade (b*a*lahd′, bă-) *n.* 1. Poem of one or more triplets of seven or eight lined stanzas, each ending with the same line as refrain, followed by an envoi freq. of 4 lines. 2. Piece of esp. lyrical or romantic

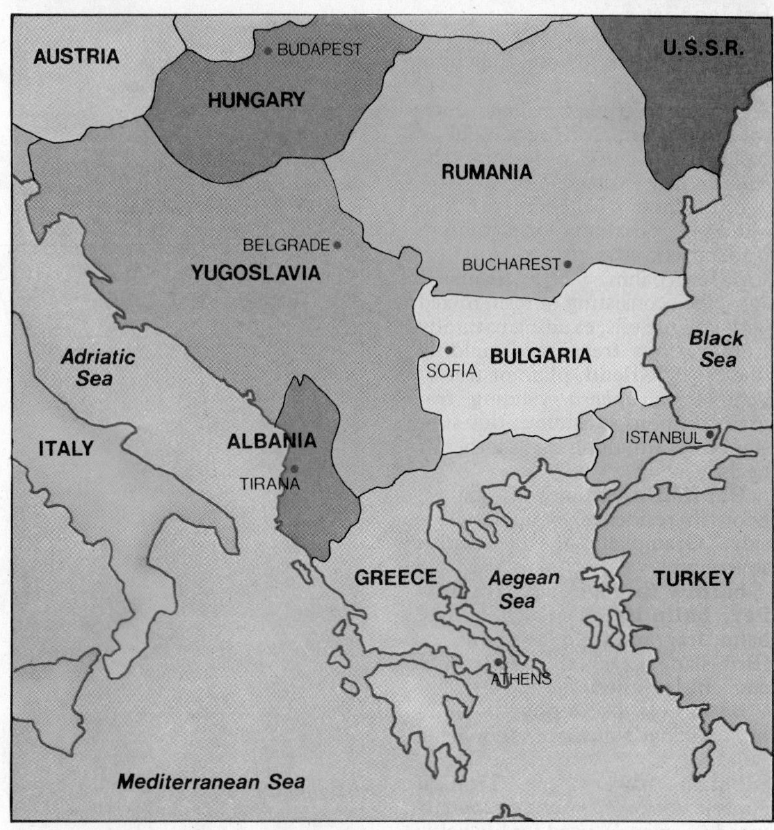

*Map showing the countries within the **Balkan Peninsula.** The name derives from the Turkish word for 'mountain'. From the 15th century until 1912–13, the Turks dominated the region through satrap governments and by setting one country against another.*

instrumental music.

bal·last (băl′*a*st) *n.* 1. Heavy material, as sand or water, placed in a ship's hold or carried in a balloon or airship for stability. 2. Coarse stone, clinker, etc., forming bed of railway. ~ *v.t.* Furnish with ballast.

bal·le·ri·na (băl*e*rē′n*a*) *n.* Female ballet dancer (strictly, dancer who takes one or more of certain classical roles).

bal·let (bălā′, băl′ā) *n.* Classical dance form demanding precision and grace; theatrical performance of dancing and mime to music; company performing this; musical score for this.

bal·lis·ta (b*a*lĭs′t*a*) *n.* (pl. **-tae** pr. -tē). Ancient military machine for hurling stones etc.

bal·lis·tic (b*a*lĭs′tĭk) *adj.* Of projectiles; ~ **missile**, one that is powered and possibly guided during the initial stage of its flight, and then travels unpowered. **bal·lis′tics** *n.* Science of projectiles.

bal·loon (b*a*loo͞n′) *n.* Large air-

*Hot-air **ballooning** near Bristol, U.K. The first manned balloon flights were made in France in 1756 in the Montgolfiers' experimental hot-air balloons.*

tight envelope of silk or other light material inflated with gas lighter than air so as to rise in the air, sometimes provided with a basket or car slung beneath from a net enclosing the envelope, used for making observations and as an antiaircraft defense; small usu. rubber envelope inflated with air as toy; (colloq.) balloon-shaped outline enclosing speech or thought of character in strip cartoon etc. or added matter for printing etc.; ~ **tire**, low-pressure motor tire of large section. **balloon** *v.* Swell out like a balloon; ride in a balloon. **bal·loon′ist** *n.*

bal·lot (băl′ot) *n.* (Usu. secret) voting; the right to vote, franchise; paper used in voting; ~ **box**, receptacle for voters' ballots. **ballot** *v.* (**-lot·ed, -lot·ing**). Vote by ballot (*for*); cause to do this. [It. *ballotta* little ball]

bal·ly·hoo (băl′ēhōō) *n.* (pl. **-hoos**). Sensational or clamorous publicity or advertising.

balm (bahm) *n.* 1. Aromatic substance consisting of resin mixed with volatile oils, exuding naturally from various trees; tree yielding this; ~ **of Gilead**, plant or tree of genus *Commiphora* yielding fragrant resinous substance; this substance. 2. Anything that soothes or heals.

Bal·mor·al (bălmōr′al, -mar′-). Scottish residence in upper Deeside, Grampian, of the British sovereign.

balm·y (bah′mē) *adj.* (**balm·i·er, balm·i·est**). 1. Of or like balm; fragrant, mild, soothing. 2. (Brit. slang) Crazy, silly. **balm′i·ly** *adv.* **balm′i·ness** *n.*

ba·lo·ney, bo·lo·ney (balō′nē) *ns.* 1. (slang) Nonsense. 2. Bologna sausage.

bal·sa (bawl′sa) *n.* Tropical American tree, *Ochroma lagopus*; its wood (~ **wood**), used for life belts, model airplanes, etc., because of its extreme lightness.

bal·sam (bawl′sam) *n.* 1. = BALM 1; balm of Gilead. 2. Aromatic ointment, of various substances dissolved in oil or turpentine. 3. Tree yielding balm. 4. Flowering plant of genus *Impatiens*, with hooded and spurred colored sepals and thick succulent stem; ~ **fir**, N. Amer. evergreen (*Abies balsamea*) widely used as Christmas tree.

Balt (bawlt) *n.* Native or inhabitant of one of the Baltic States of Lithuania, Latvia, and Estonia, esp. a German inhabitant. ~ *adj.*

Bal·tha·zar (bălthā′zer, -thăz′-er, bawl′thazar, băl′-). 1. = BELSHAZZAR. 2. Traditional name of one of the three Magi, represented as king of Chaldea.

Bal·tic (bawl′tĭk) *adj.* Of the Baltic Sea, States, or languages; ~

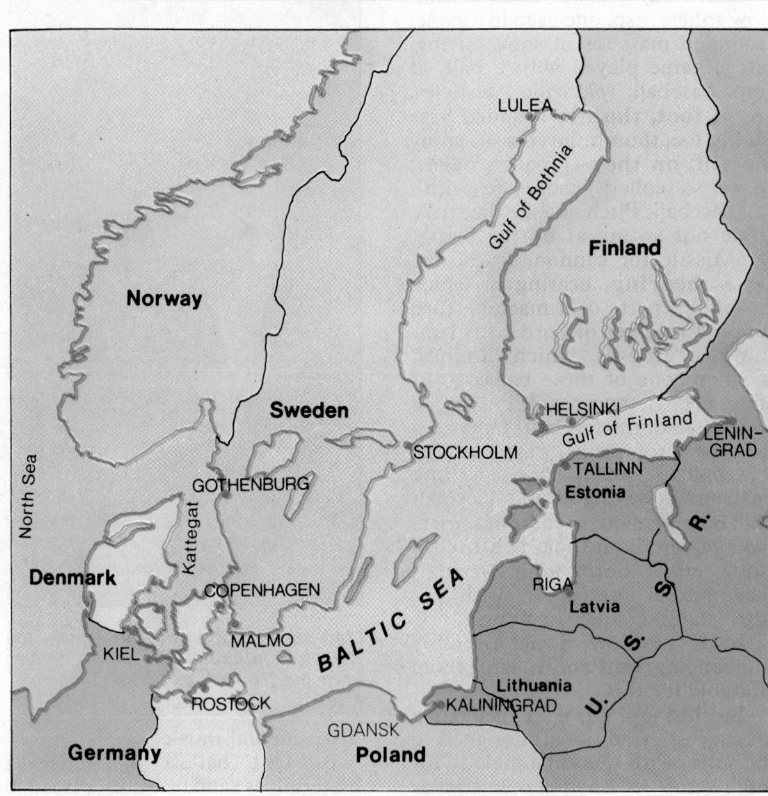

*Map of the almost land-locked **Baltic Sea,** connected to the North Sea by a channel between Denmark and Sweden. Its average width is about 124 miles. Low salinity leads to freezing of the surface in winter, and Baltic ports are frequently closed to ships.*

Facing page:
*Polling booths in the U.S.A. use the **ballot** system established in the 1880s which allows the voting public to register their vote in private without pressure or harassment from party supporters.*

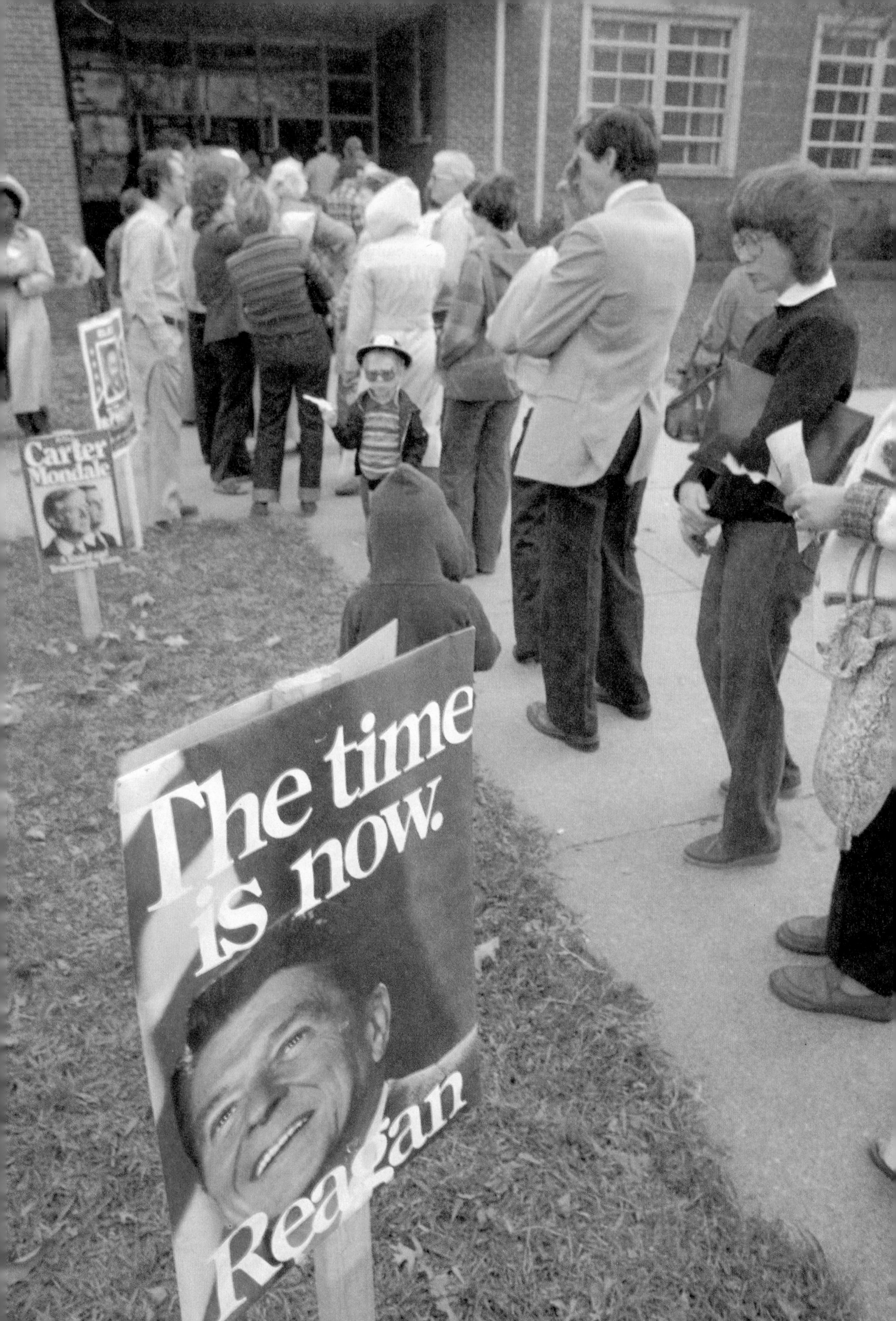
Carter
Mondale
The time is now.
Reagan

language, branch of Indo-European languages containing Lithuanian, Lettish, and Old Prussian; ~ **Sea**, almost landlocked sea in N. Europe, bordered by Sweden, U.S.S.R., Germany, Denmark, etc.; ~ **States**, former independent republics of Estonia, Latvia, and Lithuania. **Baltic** *n.* Baltic Sea.

Bal·ti·more (bawl'tĭmōr, -mōr). Seaport in N. Maryland; ~ **oriole**, N. American bird (*Icterus galbula*), whose colors, black and orange, are like the coat of arms of Lord Baltimore. [Lord *Baltimore* (d. 1632), English proprietor of territory that later became Maryland]

Bal·to-Sla·vic (bawl'tō slah'vĭk, -slăv'ĭk) *adj.* & *n.* (Of) the group of languages including the Baltic and Slavic branches.

Ba·lu·chi (balōō'chē) *n.* (pl. **-chis**, collect. **-chi**). Native or inhabitant of, the Iranian language of, Baluchistan. **Ba·lu·chi·stan** (balōōchĭstahn', -stăn'). Mountainous region in West Pakistan.

bal·us·ter (băl'uster) *n.* Any of the closely spaced posts supporting a railing.

bal·us·trade (băl'ustrād) *n.* Row of balusters with a rail or coping as the parapet of a balcony or along a staircase.

Bal·zac (bawl'zăk, băl'-; *Fr.* bălzăk'), **Honoré de** (1799–1850). French realistic novelist, whose *Comédie Humaine* is a long series of novels intended to depict the whole of contemporary French society.

Ba·ma·ko (băm'akō). Largest city and capital of Mali, on the Niger River.

bam·boo (bămbōō') *n.* (pl. **-boos**). Tropical giant grass of genus *Bambusa*, with hollow jointed stem; stem of this as a stick, as material etc.; ~ **curtain**, ideological and political barrier to passage of persons and information at borders of China.

bam·boo·zle (bămbōō'zel) *v.t.* (**-zled, -zling**). Hoax, mystify. **bam·boo'zle·ment, bam·boo'zler** *ns.*

ban (băn) *v.t.* (**banned, ban·ning**). Prohibit, interdict. ~ *n.* Curse, formal prohibition.

ba·nal (banăl', -nahl', bā'nal) *adj.* Commonplace, trite. **ba·nal·i·ty** (banăl'ĭtē, bā-) *n.* (pl. **-ties**). **ba·nal·ly** (bā'nalē) *adv.*

ba·nan·a (banăn'a) *n.* Tropical treelike plant (*Musa sapientum*); finger-shaped yellow pulpy fruit of this, growing in clusters or bunches; **ba·nan'as**, (slang) crazy, insane; **banana republic**, (esp. derog.) any small Latin American country whose economy depends on export of fruit; **banana split**, large sundae made of bananas, ice cream, etc. [Port. or Span., f. native name in Guinea]

band (bănd) *n.* 1. Thing that binds, bond (archaic). 2. Strip or hoop of material for supporting or holding things together or for decoration etc.; belt, strap; strip forming part of garment, esp. binding the neck or waist; (pl.). pair of white linen strips worn at neck as part of legal, ecclesiastical, or academic dress. 3. Body of musicians playing together, esp. wind instrument performers (**brass, dance, military** ~); organized company or group of persons. 4. (elect.) Range of frequencies or wavelengths falling between two limits (also **wave** ~). 5. (phys.) Group of closely spaced lines in a molecular spectrum. 6. **B~-Aid**, (trademark) a small adhesive bandage for minor wounds; (fig.) superficial or inadequate remedy for a major problem; **band'box**, box for hats (orig. for neckbands); (*adj.*) conspicuously neat and clean; **band'master**, conductor of a band of musicians; **band saw**, endless saw running over wheels; **bands'man** (pl. **-men**), member of a mili-

*A row of balusters with a rail or coping form a **balustrade.** 1. Pier. 2. Baluster. During the Italian Renaissance, designers excelled in producing richly molded balusters.*

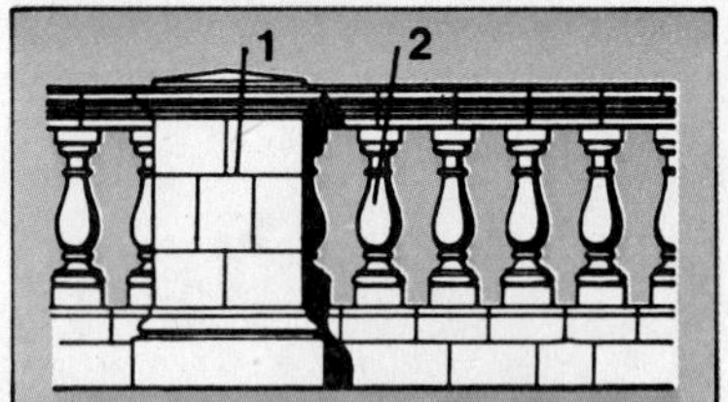

*Snow-covered Kholpur Bolan in **Baluchistan,** the mountainous western province of Pakistan. Following Pakistan autonomy, 50,000 Hindus and Sikhs left for India.*

*Statue of **Honoré de Balzac** by his French compatriot, Auguste Rodin. One of the world's greatest novelists Balzac was attracted by the theme of the individual in conflict with society.*

*A **band** of young musicians and singers at Disneyland attracts the crowds and adds to the holiday atmosphere during an open-air concert.*

tary or brass band; **band'stand**, (covered, open-air) platform for musicians; **band'wagon**, wagon carrying the band at the head of a procession; **climb, jump, on the bandwagon**, join an enterprise that is likely to be successful. **band** *v.* Form into band or league; put a band on; **band'ed**, (bot., zool.) marked with colored bands or bars.

band·age (băn'dĭj) *n.* Strip or band of textile material used to bind a wound, sore, etc., or for blindfolding the eyes. ~ *v.t.* (**-aged, -ag·ing**). Bind up with a bandage.

ban·dan·na, ban·dan·a (băndăn'*a*) *ns.* Large brightly colored handkerchief esp. with yellow or white spots. [prob. from Hind. *bāndhnū*, a method of dyeing in different colors]

ban·deau (băndō') *n.* (pl. **-deaux** pr.-dōz'). Band of ribbon etc. around the head; narrow hair band.

ban·de·ril·la (bănd*e*rē'*a*, -rēl'-y*a*) *n.* Decorated dart thrust into bull's neck or shoulders in bullfight. **ban·de·ril·le·ro** (băndĕrēâr'ō, -rēlyâr'ō) *n.* (pl. **-ros**). Bullfighter or matador's assistant using banderillas.

ban·de·role, ban·de·rol (băn'dĕrōl) *ns.* Long narrow flag with cleft end flying from a ship, lance, etc.; ribbonlike scroll; (archit.) feature resembling this and bearing inscription.

ban·dit (băn'dĭt) *n.* (pl. **ban·dits, ban·dit·ti** pr. băndĭt'ē). Outlaw, brigand; lawless and violent robber, esp. member of an organized gang.

ban·do·leer, ban·do·lier (băndol*ē*r') *ns.* Shoulder belt with loops or pockets for cartridges.

ban·dore (băndōr', -dōr', ban'dōr, -dōr), **ban·do·ra** (băndōr'*a*, -dōr'*a*) *ns.* Wire-stringed musical instrument resembling the cittern. Also **pandora, pandore**.

ban·dy (băn'dē) *v.t.* (**-died, -dy·ing**). Throw or pass to and fro; discuss; exchange. ~ *adj.* (of legs) Curving outward at the knees; so ~ **-leg·ged** (-lĕgĭd, -lĕgd).

bane (bān) *n.* Ruin; poison. **bane'ful** *adj.* Poisonous; pernicious; injurious. **bane'ful·ly** *adv.* **bane'ful·ness** *n.*

bang[1] (băng) *v.* Strike or shut noisily; make sound as of a blow or explosion; thrash. ~ *n.* Sharp blow; loud noise; (slang) a thrill; **bang'tail**, (slang) a race horse. **bang** *adv.* (colloq.) Right, exactly; suddenly and loudly.

bang[2] (băng) = BHANG.

bang[3] (băng) *n.* & *v.t.* (Cut *hair* in) a fringe.

Bang·kok (băng'kŏk). Capital city of Thailand.

Bang·la·desh (băng'gl*a*dĕsh, bănggl*a*dĕsh'). Muslim country in SE. Asia, formerly East Pakistan; member nation of the British Commonwealth, independent since 1971; capital Dacca. [Bengali, = "land of Bengal"]

ban·gle (băng'g*e*l) *n.* Ring bracelet or anklet.

Ban·gor (băng'gōr, -g*er*). Port city on the Penobscot River in E. Maine.

Ban·gui (bahnggē'). Largest city and capital of the Central African Republic, in the SW., on the Ubangi River.

ban·ian (băn'y*a*n) = BANYAN.

ban·ish (băn'ĭsh) *v.t.* Condemn to exile; drive away; dismiss from one's presence or mind. **ban'ish·er, ban'ish·ment** *ns.*

ban·is·ter, ban·nis·ter (băn'ĭst*er*) *ns.* Post supporting handrail of a staircase; posts and handrail together. [corrupt. of BALUSTER]

ban·jo (băn'jō) *n.* (pl. **-jos, -joes**). Musical instrument having four, five, six, or seven strings, head and neck like guitar, and body like tambourine, played with fingers or with plectrum; ~ **clock**, pendulum clock shaped like a banjo. **ban'jo·ist** *n.* [Gk. *pandoura* three-stringed mus. instrument]

Ban·jul (bahnjōōl'). Capital of The Gambia, on the island of St. Mary at the mouth of the Gambia River.

bank[1] (băngk) *n.* 1. Raised shelf of ground; transverse slope of a road or curve, etc. 2. Ground at edge of river. 3. Mass of cloud. ~ *v.* 1. Contain or confine as or with bank(s). 2. Make (road, track) higher at outer edge of a bend to facilitate cornering at high speeds;

(aeronaut.) incline (aircraft) laterally in turning so as to avoid a side-slip; heap up; cover (a fire) with ashes, etc., to make it burn slowly.

bank[2] (băngk) *n.* 1. Establishment for receiving, safeguarding, and lending money; building housing this; **central** ~: see CENTRAL; **savings** ~: see SAVINGS; **bank'-book**, book showing the state of a customer's account at a bank; **bank holiday**, weekday on which banks are legally closed, (Brit.) usu. kept as a general holiday; **bank'note**, authorized bank's promissory note circulating as money; **bank'roll** (*n.*), roll of banknotes, ready money; (*v.*), finance. 2. Money box; **piggy bank**: see PIGGY. 3. Money before keeper of a gaming table. 4. Store or storage place, reserve supply (of blood, organs, etc.). **bank** *v.* Deposit money in a bank; have an account with a bank; act as a bank or banker; handle funds; ~ **on**, count or rely on.

bank[3] (băngk) *n.* Galley rowers' bench; tier (of oars) in galley; row of organ keys; group of similar objects in line or in tiers.

bank·er (băng'k*er*) *n.* 1. Proprietor or director of a BANK[2]; keeper of money. 2. Keeper of money staked at gaming table.

bank·ing (băng'kĭng) *n.* Business of a banker or BANK[2].

bank·rupt (băngk'rŭpt, -r*u*pt) *n.* (law) Insolvent person whose property is administered and distributed for the benefit of all his or her creditors; (pop.) any insolvent person. ~ *adj.* Declared a bankrupt; insolvent; (fig.) bereft (of some quality). **bank'rupt·cy** *n.* (pl. **-cies**).

Banks (băngks) **Island.** Westernmost island of the Arctic Archipelago, about 25,000 square miles.

Ban·nek·er (băn'*e*k*er*), **Benjamin** (1731–1806). American mathematician, astronomer, and black colonial leader; member of the group appointed to survey and lay out the site for Washington, D.C.

ban·ner (băn'*er*) *n.* Rectangular flag of a country, army, king, etc.; strip or piece of fabric bearing emblem or slogan etc.; (also ~ **headline**) newspaper headline in large type, esp. running across whole page. ~ *adj.* Preeminent (as in *banner year*, *crop*). **ban'-nered** *adj.*

ban·nis·ter (băn'ĭst*er*) = BANISTER.

banns (bănz) *n.pl.* Notice of intended marriage, read three times in church, in order that any objec-

Below: Gold nuggets in a Sierra Nevada ***bank.*** *About 60 per cent of all gold mined is held in banks. Below right: The U.S. cent is made of copper with a zinc and tin alloy.*

*Above: The **baptistery** of the cathedral at Pisa. Until the 11th century a baptistery, with its apse and font, was usually built separate from the main church.*

*Above left: Members of a **Bantu** tribe celebrating a festival in South Africa. Bantu-speaking peoples inhabit the equatorial and southern regions of the continent.*

*Barrel-like trunk of a **baobab** tree. Some trees reach 30 ft. in diameter. The edible fruit pulp is called monkey bread and can be used in the preparation of cooling drinks.*

tions may be lodged.

ban·quet (băng′kwĭt) *n.* Sumptuous feast; ceremonious dinner with speeches. ~ *v.* (**-quet·ed, -quet·ing**). Regale with, take part in, banquet. [Fr. f. It. *banchetto*, dim. of *banco* bench]

ban·quette (băngkĕt′) *n.* Firing step in trenches; upholstered seat along a wall.

ban·shee, ban·shie (băn′shē) *ns.* Spirit supposed by Irish and Highland superstition to wail under the windows of a house in which one of the inhabitants is about to die. [Ir., = "fairy woman"]

ban·tam (băn′tam) *n.* 1. Small variety of domestic fowl, of which the cock is a spirited fighter. 2. Small but spirited person. 3. **ban′tamweight**, boxer of weight between 112 and 118 pounds. [f. *Bantam*, seaport in W. Java]

ban·ter (băn′ter) *n.* Humorous ridicule. **ban′ter·er** *n.* **ban′ter·ing·ly** *adv.* **banter** *v.* Make good-humored fun of, rally; jest.

Ban·tu (băn′tōō) *n.* (pl. **-tus**, collect. **-tu**). (Member of) an extensive group of black peoples inhabiting the equatorial and southern region of Africa; language(s) spoken by them.

Ban · tu · stan (băntōōstahn′, -stăn) *n.* Any of several segregated territories for Bantus in S. Africa.

ban·yan, banian (băn′yan) *ns.* (also ~ **tree**) E. Indian fig tree (*Ficus bengalensis*), whose branches root themselves like new trees over a large area.

ban·zai (bahnzī′, bahn′zī) *int.* Japanese patriotic greeting or cheer. ~ *adj.* Suicidal, desperate (of an attack or charge). [Jap., = 10,000 years (of life to you)]

ba·o·bab (bā′ōbăb, bah′-) *n.* African tree (*Adansonia digitata*), naturalized also in Australia, India, and Ceylon, having extremely thick stem and large woody fruit with edible pulp, known as "monkey-bread."

bap·tism (băp′tĭzem) *n.* Religious rite of immersing in or sprinkling with water in sign of moral or spiritual purification or regeneration, and initiation into the (Christian) church; any initiation or initiation ceremony; ~ **of fire**, soldier's first experience of battle. **bap·tis·mal** (băptĭz′mal) *adj.* **bap·tis′mal·ly** *adv.* **baptismal name** = CHRISTIAN[1] name.

bap·tist (băp′tĭst) *n.* One who baptizes; **St. John the B**~: see JOHN[5]; **B**~, member of a Protestant Christian sect, founded early in the 17th c., which holds that baptism should be administered only to believers, not to infants, and by immersion.

bap·tis·ter·y, bap·tist·ry (băp-tĭstrē) *ns.* (pl. **-ries**). Part of church (or in early times separate building) used for baptism.

bap·tize (băp′tīz, băptīz′) *v.t.* (**-tized, -tiz·ing**). Administer baptism to; christen; name. **bap·-**

tiz'er *n.*

BAR *abbrev.* BROWNING[1] automatic rifle.

bar[1] (bār) *n.* 1. Long piece of rigid material; straight strip; **bar'bell**, iron bar with heavy ball at each end for weight lifting; **bar chart, ~ graph**, graph using parallel bars showing numbers, costs, etc. 2. Rectangular piece (of soap, chocolate, etc.). 3. Strip of silver below clasp of medal as additional distinction. 4. (mus.) Vertical line across stave dividing composition into sections of equal time value (also **~ line**); such a section. 5. (her.) Stripe across shield; **~ sinister**, erron. for BEND[1] sinister. 6. Rod or pole used to confine or obstruct; bolt or beam for fastening door etc. 7. Barrier of any shape; obstacle, hindrance; **sand ~**: see SAND. 8. Barrier limiting access etc.; place in court where prisoner stands; **the B~**, the legal profession. 9. Counter in tavern, restaurant, **bar and grill**, etc. across which drinks or food are served directly to customers; room or place containing this; **~ car**, railroad car with a bar at which drinks etc. are served; **bar'fly** (pl. **-flies**), one who frequents bars; **bar'keep(er), bar'maid, bar'man** (pl. **-men**), **bar'tender**, attendant at bar serving alcoholic drinks; **bar'stool**, high stool for sitting at a bar. **bar** *v.t.* (**barred, bar·ring**). 1. Fasten with bars, keep in or out thus; obstruct, prevent. 2. Mark with stripes. **~** *prep.* Except, excluding.

bar[2] (bār) *n.* Unit of barometric pressure, = 10^5 newtons per square centimeter.

Bar·ab·bas (barăb'*a*s). Robber released instead of Jesus Christ (Matt. 27).

barb (bārb) *n.* Secondary backward-projecting point of arrow, fishhook, etc.; sting, wounding remark; beardlike feelers of barbel etc.; lateral filament branching from shaft of feather. **~** *v.t.* Furnish with barb; **barb(ed) wire**, wire used in fencing and as an obstruction in war, with short pointed pieces of wire twisted in at intervals. [L. *barba* beard]

Bar·ba·dos (bārbā'dōs, -dōz). Island in W. Indies settled by the British 1627, member nation of the British Commonwealth 1966; capital, Bridgetown. **Bar·ba·di·an** (bārbā'dē*a*n) *adj.* & *n.*

bar·bar·i·an (bārbār'ē*a*n, -băr'-) *n.* 1. Rough, wild, uncultured or uncivilized person, savage (orig. foreigner, one differing in language and customs). 2. (hist.) Non-Greek; person outside the Roman Empire; person outside the civilization of Christendom. **~** *adj.* Of or like a barbarian. **bar·bar'i·an·ism** *n.*

bar·bar·ic (bārbăr'ĭk) *adj.* Rough, uncultured; of barbarians. **bar·bar'i·cal·ly** *adv.*

bar·ba·rism (bār'b*a*rĭzem) *n.* Savagery; absence of culture; ignorance; (use of) word or expression not in accordance with the established standard of a language.

bar·bar·i·ty (bārbăr'ĭtē) *n.* (pl. **-ties**). Savage or barbarous cruelty.

bar·ba·rize (bār'b*a*rīz) *v.* (**-rized, -riz·ing**). Make, become, barbarous. **bar·ba·ri·za·tion** (bārb*a*rĭzā'sh*o*n) *n.*

Bar·ba·ros·sa (bārb*a*rŏs'*a*): see FREDERICK[1].

bar·ba·rous (bār'b*a*r*u*s) *adj.* Uncivilized, uncultured, savage. **bar'ba·rous·ly** *adv.* **bar'ba·rous·ness** *n.*

*Norwegian **bark** (or barque). Now serving as training ships, barks had their heyday before the 1860s. The 5-masted bark 'France', 418 ft. long, was the largest sailing ship ever built.*

Bar·ba·ry (bār'b*a*rē). Old name for the western part of N. Africa; **~ ape**, large tailless ape of N. Africa and Gibraltar; **~ Coast**, the Mediterranean coastal area of Barbary; a district of San Francisco notorious before 1906 for gambling and prostitution; **~ sheep**, wild N. Afr. sheep with large horns.

bar·be·cue (bār'b*e*kū) *n.* 1. Framework for cooking meat above an open fire. 2. Barbecued meat, fowl, or fish; animal roasted whole; **~ sauce**, highly seasoned sauce of vinegar, spices, etc. 3. (Open-air) social gathering where barbecue is served. **barbecue** *v.t.* (**-cued, -cu·ing**). Cook on barbecue or with barbecue sauce. [Haitian *barbacòa* grate on posts]

bar·bel (bār'b*e*l) *n.* Large European freshwater fish of genus *Barbus* with fleshy filaments hanging from mouth; such a filament.

bar·ber (bār'b*e*r) *n.* One who cuts hair and shaves beards; **bar'-**

bershop (*adj.*) (fig., colloq.) in the style of close-harmony male quartet; **~'s itch**, ringworm of face communicated by (unsterilized) shaving apparatus; **~'s pole**, pole painted spirally with red and white stripes, used as barber's sign.

Bar·ber (bar̄ʹber), **Samuel** (1910–). American composer; winner of two Pulitzer Prizes, for the opera *Vanessa*, 1958, and for *Piano Concerto No. 1*, 1963.

bar·ber·ry (bar̄ʹbĕrē, -berē) *n.* (pl. **-ries**). Shrub, especially *Berberis vulgaris*, with spiny shoots and small yellow flowers; oblong, red, sharply acid berry of this.

bar·bi·tu·rate (bar̄bĭchʹerĭt, -erāt) *n.* (chem.) Salt of barbituric acid; (pharmac.) any of various sedatives and hypnotic substances derived from barbituric acid. **bar·bi·tu·ric** (bar̄bĭtoorʹĭk, -tūrʹ-) *adj.* **~ acid**, white crystalline substance ($C_4H_4O_3N_2$) from which barbiturates are derived.

Bar·bi·zon (bar̄ʹbĭzŏn). Village near Fontainebleau, near Paris, frequented in mid-19th c. by the **~ School**, a colony of painters (T. Rousseau, Millet, Daubigny, and others) who produced naturalistic pictures of landscapes and peasant life.

Bar·bour (bar̄ʹber), **John** (1316–1395). Author of "The Bruce" (*c*1375), a long historical poem; regarded as father of Scottish poetry.

bar·ca·role, bar·ca·rolle (bar̄ʹkarōl) *ns.* Gondolier's song; imitation of this.

Bar·ce·lo·na (bar̄selōʹna). City and province of Catalonia, NE. Spain.

bard (bar̄d) *n.* Celtic minstrel; poet; **~ of Avon**: see AVON[1]. **bardʹic** *adj.*

'The Church at Marisse' by Jean Corot, the 19th-century French landscape painter (Louvre, Paris). Corot influenced the ***Barbizon*** *school of naturalistic landscape painting.*

bare (bar̄) *adj.* (**barʹer, barʹest**). Unclothed, uncovered; exposed; unadorned; scanty; mere; unarmed; unconcealed; undisguised; with less than usual ornaments, furnishings; **bareʹback**, (*adj.* & *adv.*) on unsaddled horse; **bareʹfaced**, shameless, impudent; **bareʹfoot**, (*adj.* & *adv.*) with bare feet; **bareʹhanded**, (*adj.* & *adv.*) without tools or weapons; **bareʹheaded**, with head uncovered. **bareʹly** *adv.* Scarcely, only just. **bareʹness** *n.* **bare** *v.t.* (**bared, bar·ing**). Make bare, strip, expose.

Bar·ents (bărʹents, bar̄ʹ-), **Willem** (d. 1597). Dutch Arctic explorer, after whom is named the **~ Sea**, the extreme NE. part of the Atlantic Ocean.

bar·gain (bar̄ʹgĭn) *n.* Agreement on terms of transaction between two parties, compact; thing acquired by bargaining; something offered for sale cheaper than usual; advantageous purchase; **in(to) the ~**, moreover; **strike a ~**, come to terms. **~** *v.i.* Haggle over terms of transaction; stipulate; **~ for**, be prepared for, expect.

barge (bar̄j) *n.* Flat-bottomed freight boat for canals and rivers; ceremonial vessel used in pageants. **bargeʹman** *n.* (pl. **-men**). **barge** *v.i.* (**barged, barg·ing**). (colloq.) Lurch or rush heavily *into*.

bar·ite (bar̄ʹīt, bărʹ-) *n.* Barium sulfate, ore of barium.

bar·i·tone (bărʹĭtōn) *n.* Male voice between tenor and bass; singer with this voice. **~** *adj.*

bar·i·um (bar̄ʹēum, bărʹ-) *n.* (chem.) White metallic element occurring chiefly as barite; symbol Ba, at. no. 56, at. wt. 137.34; **~ sulfate**, white, very insoluble heavy powder ($BaSO_4$), opaque to X-rays, used in a mixture in radiological examination of the alimentary tract and as a pigment in paints.

bark[1] (bar̄k) *n.* Rind or outer sheath of the trunk and branches of trees; bark used in tanning. **~** *v.* Strip bark from; rub the skin off, as of the shins. **barkʹless** *adj.*

bark[2], **barque** (bar̄k) *ns.* Three-masted vessel with foremasts and mainmasts square-rigged, and mizen fore-and-aft rigged; (poet.) ship, boat.

bark[3] (bar̄k) *v.* (of dogs etc.) Utter sharp explosive cry; make sound like this; speak sharply or petulantly; (slang) cough; **~ up the wrong tree**, (fig.) be on the wrong track. **~** *n.* Sharp explosive cry of dogs, foxes, etc.; sound of gunfire; cough. **barkʹer** *n.*, one who stands at entrance to a show soliciting customers with loud and extravagant shouts.

bar·ken·tine (bar̄ʹkentēn) *n.* Vessel with three or more masts, of which only the foremast is square-rigged.

Bark·ley (bārk'lē), **Alben (William)** (1877–1956). Congressman from Kentucky, 1913–49; Senate majority leader, 1937–47; Vice President of the U.S. under Harry Truman, 1949–53.

bar·ley (bār'lē) *n.* Cereal (*Hordeum distichon* and *H. vulgare*), used as food and in the preparation of malt; grain of this; **bar'leycorn**, grain of barley; **John Bar'leycorn**, personification of whiskey in general; malt liquor.

barm (bārm) *n.* Froth from fermenting malt liquor, used as leaven; yeast.

bar mitz·vah (bār mĭts'va; *Heb.* bār mētsvah'). (Religious initiation ceremony for) Jewish boy aged 13. [Heb., = "son of commandment"]

barn (bārn) *n.* Farm building for storing grain (or hay, straw, etc.) and housing livestock; ~ **door**, large door of this; target too big to be easily missed; ~ **owl**, owl (*Tyto alba*) often found in barns; **barn'storm**, act as **barn'stormer**, itinerant actor; **barn swallow**, fork-tailed swallow (*Hirundo rustica erythrogaster*) often nesting in barns; **barn'yard**, area surrounding a barn.

Bar·na·bas (bār'nabas), **St. Joseph**, surnamed Barnabas, an early leader of the Christian Church and companion of St. Paul on his missionary journeys (Acts 4, 9, 11, etc.).

bar·na·cle (bār'nakel) *n.* 1. Wild goose, *Branta leucopsis*, also called ~ **goose**, of N. Europe and Greenland. 2. Crustacean of the subclass Cirripedia; **goose** ~, one found attached to ships' bottoms etc.; **acorn** or **rock** ~, one found attached to rocks. **bar'na·cled** *adj.*

Bar·nard (bār'nārd), **Christiaan N.** (1923–). South African surgeon; performed first human heart transplant, 1967.

bar·o·gram (băr'ogrăm) *n.* Record of variations in atmospheric pressure.

bar·o·graph (băr'ogrăf) *n.* Barometer with apparatus (usu. paper roll on drum rotated by clockwork) for making a barogram. **bar·o·graph'ic** *adj.*

ba·rom·e·ter (barŏm'ĭter) *n.* Instrument for measuring atmospheric pressure (and hence for predicting changes in the weather) by means of a tube containing a column of mercury (which rises and falls according to the weight of the atmosphere) or of a vacuum box (see ANEROID ~). **bar·o·met·ric** (băromĕt'rĭk), **bar·o·met'ri·cal** *adjs.* **bar·o·met'ri·cal·ly** *adv.* **ba·rom'e·try** *n.*

bar·on (băr'on) *n.* 1. (hist.) Great noble, noble holding directly from the king by military service. 2. Member of lowest order of nobility in British peerage; important financier or merchant (as **beef** ~). 3. ~ **of beef**, cut consisting of two sirloins left uncut at backbone. **bar·on·ess** (băr'onĭs) *n.* Wife, widow, of baron; woman with baronial title in her own right. **ba·ro·ni·al** (barō'nēal) *adj.* **bar'o·ny** *n.* (pl. **-nies**). Domain or rank of baron.

*Gooseneck **barnacles,** stalked marine crustaceans that foul the hulls of ships in the open sea. Some barnacle species cling to almost any surface, e.g. rocks or shells of crabs.*

bar·on·age (băr'onĭj) *n.* Barons collectively.

bar·on·et (băr'onĭt, -nĕt) *n.* Member of the lowest hereditary titled British order, ranking as a commoner.

ba·roque (barōk') *adj.* 1. Irregularly shaped (of jewels, esp. pearls); grotesque, odd. 2. Of the style of art that evolved in Italy *c*1600 out of that of the Renaissance and prevailed in Europe (chiefly in Catholic countries) until *c*1720, being characterized by massive and complex design in which architecture was combined with painting, sculpture, etc., and esp. by vigorous, restless or violent movement; of the music or literature of this period. 3. Applied loosely to any style with similar characteristics. ~ *n.* Baroque style. [Fr. f. Span. *barrueco* rough pearl]

ba·rouche (baroōsh') *n.* Four-wheeled horse-drawn carriage with a seat in front for the driver, and seats inside for two couples facing each other.

barque (bārk) = BARK[2].

bar·quen·tine (bār'kentēn) = BARKENTINE.

bar·racks (băr'aks) *n.pl.* Building(s) for lodging soldiers; large building of severely plain, dull, or dreary appearance.

bar·ra·cu·da (băr*a*koō'd*a*) *n.* (pl. **-das**, collect. **-da**). Voracious fish, including great ~ and Pacific ~, of family Sphyraenidae found in warm seas.

bar·rage (barahzh'; *Brit.* bar'ij for def. 1, băr'ahzh for def. 2) *n.* 1. Artificial obstruction in river or watercourse. 2. (mil.) A barrier of artillery fire from a large number of guns (also fig.); ~ **balloon**, large balloon supporting steel cable in an almost vertical position, esp. as one of a series forming antiaircraft defense. **barrage** *v.* (**-raged, -rag·ing**). Subject to a barrage.

bar·ra·tor, bar·ra·ter (băr'*a*-*ter*) *ns.* One who vexatiously incites to litigation or raises discord.

bar·ra·try (băr'*a*trē) *n.* 1. Purchase or sale of ecclesiastical preferments or offices of state. 2. Vexatious persistence in or incitement to litigation. 3. Fraud or gross and criminal negligence of ship's master or crew at the expense of the owners. **bar'ra·trous** *adj.* **bar'ra·trous·ly** *adv.*

bar·rel (băr'*e*l) *n.* 1. Wooden vessel of curved staves bound by hoops, with flat ends; contents or capacity of such a vessel. 2. Revolving cylinder in capstan, watch, etc. 3. Cylindrical body of object; belly and loins of horse. 4. Metal tube of firearm, through which the missile is projected. 5. ~ **organ**, musical instrument with pin-studded cylinder turned by a handle and operating a mechanism that opens the pipes, the handle also serving to work the bellows; piano organ; ~ **roll**, maneuver by an airplane that makes a complete rotation about its longitudinal axis.

bar·ren (băr'*e*n) *adj.* Not bearing, incapable of bearing (children, fruit, etc.); waste; unprofitable. ~ *n.* (usu. pl.) Barren land; elevated plains on which grow small trees and shrubs, but no timber. **bar'ren·ly** *adv.* **bar'ren·ness** *n.*

Bar·rett (băr'ĭt), **Elizabeth**: see BROWNING[2].

bar·rette (barĕt') *n.* Bar-shaped clip for woman's hair.

bar·ri·cade (băr'ĭkād, bărĭkād') *n.* (Defensive) barrier, esp. one hastily erected across street etc. ~ *v.t.* (**-cad·ed, -cad·ing**). Block or defend with a barricade. **bar'ri·cad·er** *n.* [Span. *barrica* cask]

Bar·rie (băr'ē), **Sir James Matthew** (1860–1937). Scottish writer of comedies and short stories, author of *Peter Pan*, *Quality Street*, etc.

*Facing page: A masterpiece of the **baroque** style: the ceiling of the Banqueting Hall, Whitehall, London, U.K., painted by the great Flemish artist, Rubens, in 1634. His English contemporary, Inigo Jones, was architect of the building.*

bar·ri·er (băr′ēer) *n.* Fence barring advance or preventing access; any obstacle, boundary, or agency that keeps apart, or prevents communication, success, etc.; ~ **reef**, high wall of coral rock separated from land by a broad deep channel and with a precipitous face on the seaward side.

bar·ri·o (bār′ēō, băr′-) *n.* (pl. **-ri·os**). Spanish-speaking quarter of a U.S. city. [Sp., = district of a town]

bar·ris·ter (băr′ĭster) *n.* (Brit.) Attorney who has the privilege of practicing as advocate in the superior courts of law.

bar·row[1] (băr′ō) *n.* Prehistoric grave mound.

bar·row[2] (băr′ō) *n.* Rectangular frame with short shafts for carrying loads; shallow box with two shafts and one wheel; small two-wheeled handcart; wheelbarrow.

bar·row[3] (băr′ō) *n.* A castrated pig.

Bar·row (băr′ō), **Point.** Northernmost point in Alaska, on the Arctic Ocean.

Butch Hobson of the Red Sox ***baseball*** *team. The rules of modern baseball were formulated by the Knickerbocker Baseball Club, established in 1845. The origins of the game are disputed. Some claim it's English, others all-American.*

Bar·ry·more (băr′ĭmōr, -mōr). Family of American actors including: **Maurice** (real name Herbert Blythe) (1847–1905), English-born stage actor; his son, **Lionel** (1878–1954); his daughter, **Ethel** (1879–1959); and his son, **John** (1882–1942), known as "the great profile," and famous for his portrayal of Hamlet in Shakespeare's *Hamlet*.

bar·ter (bār′ter) *v.* Exchange (goods, rights, etc.) *for* things of like kind. ~ *n.* Act or practice of business involving exchange of goods or services rather than payment. **bar′ter·er** *n.*

Barth (bārt), **Karl** (1886–1968). Swiss Protestant theologian.

Bar·thol·di (bārthŏl′dē; *Fr.* bărtawldē′), **Frédéric Auguste** (1834–1904). French sculptor; creator of the Statue of Liberty in New York harbor.

Bar·thol·o·mew (bārthŏl′omū), **St.** One of the 12 Apostles, commemorated on Aug. 24.

Bart·lett (bārt′lĭt) *n.* Large, yellow juicy variety of pear. [f. Enoch *Bartlett* (1779–1860), U.S. merchant]

Bar·tók (bār′tŏk; *Hung.* bŭr′-tawk), **Béla** (1881–1945). Hungarian composer and collector of Hungarian folk music.

Bar·ton (bār′ton), **Clara** (1821–1912). Founder of the American Red Cross, 1881.

bar·y·on (băr′ēŏn) *n.* (phys.) Elementary particle whose mass is equal to or greater than that of a proton.

bar·y·sphere (băr′ĭsfēr) *n.* Core of the earth, consisting of a very heavy substance, prob. nickel iron.

ba·ry·ta (barī′ta) *n.* Barium monoxide, an alkaline earth distinguished by its great density.

bar·y·tone (băr´ĭtōn) = BARITONE.

ba·sal (bā´sal, -zal) *adj.* Of or at the base; ~ **metabolism**, (physiol.) minimum amount of energy needed by an organism at rest. **bas´al·ly** *adv.*

ba·salt (basawlt´, bā´sawlt, băs´-awlt) *n.* 1. Dark fine-grained rock occurring as a lava or as an intrusion, often showing columnar structure. 2. Black porcelain invented by Wedgwood. **ba·sal´tic** *adj.*

bas·cule (băs´kūl) *n.* Lever apparatus often used in a drawbridge balanced by a counterpoise that rises or falls as the bridge is lowered or raised.

base[1] (bās) *adj.* (**bas·er, bas·est**). Morally low, mean, ignoble, debased; menial; **base´born**, of low birth; illegitimate; **base metals**, those that quickly corrode or tarnish (opp. NOBLE or PRECIOUS **metals**). **base´ly** *adv.* **base´ness** *n.*

base[2] (bās) *n.* 1. That on which anything stands or depends; support, foundation, principle, groundwork, starting point, principal element; substance used as first layer (of paint, make-up, etc.). 2. (biol.) End at which an organ is attached to trunk. 3. (geom.) Line or surface on which a plane or solid figure is held to stand. 4. (surv., also ~ **line**) Known line used as geometrical base for trigonometry. 5. (math.) Starting number for system of numeration or logarithms (as 10 in decimal counting). 6. (chem.) Antithesis of ACID, substance (including ALKALI) capable of combining with an acid to form a salt. 7. (archit.) Part of column between shaft or pedestal and pavement; **base´board**, narrow board around wall of room close to floor. 8. (mil.) Town or other area in rear of an army where supplies, hospital, etc., are concentrated; military camp. 9. (gram.) Form of a word to which suffixes are attached. 10. One of the four corners of the baseball diamond, marked by a bag or home plate; ~ **hit**, fair ball allowing batter to reach first base without an error or force play; ~ **line**, (surv.) see sense 4; (tennis) line at end of court; (baseball) line between successive bases; **base´man** (pl. **-men**), fielder assigned to first, second, or third base; **base on balls** (pl. **bases on balls**), advancement to first base of batter after four balls; **base runner**, member of baseball team at bat who is on or running to a base; **off base** (baseball) not touching the base occupied; (fig.) mistaken, unprepared. **base** *v.t.* (**based, bas·ing**). Found or establish *on.*

A small all-purpose hunting dog of African breed, the ***basenji*** *seldom barks. This dog was portrayed in ancient Egyptian murals.*

base·ball (bās´bawl) *n.* Game played between two teams of nine (ten, counting the designated hitter) players on a diamond-shaped field with four bases around which the batter runs in order to score; ball used in this game.

base·less (bās´lĭs) *adj.* Groundless, unfounded.

base·ment (bās´ment) *n.* Lowest part of a structure; inhabited story partly or wholly below ground level.

ba·sen·ji (basĕn´jē) *n.* Small hunting dog of African breed that rarely barks.

bash (băsh) *v.t.* Strike heavily so as to smash *in.* ~ *n.* Heavy blow; (slang) party.

bash·ful (băsh´ful) *adj.* Shy, sheepish. **bash´ful·ly** *adv.* **bash´ful·ness** *n.*

ba·sic (bā´sĭk) *adj.* 1. Of, forming or serving as a base or basis, fundamental. 2. (chem.) Having the chemical properties of a base. 3. (min., of igneous rocks) Having little silica in proportion to the amount of lime, potash, etc. 4. **B~ English**, system of English comprising a select vocabulary of 850 words, devised by C. K. Ogden of Cambridge, England, as a medium of international communication. **ba´si·cal·ly** *adv.*

ba·sic·i·ty (bāsĭs´ĭtē) *n.* (chem.) Number of equivalents of a base with which one molecule of an acid can react.

ba·sid·i·um (basĭd´ēum) *n.* (pl. **-sid·i·a** pr. -sĭd´ēa). Spore-bearing structure in some fungi.

bas·il (băz´il, bā´zil) *n.* Aromatic herb of the genus *Ocimum*, esp. **sweet** ~ (*O. basilicum*) and the dwarf **bush** ~ (*O. minimum*), the leaves of which are used for flavoring soups, salads, etc. [L. *basilisca* the plant (supposed antidote to basilisk's bite)]

Bas·il (băz´il, băs´-), **St.** (*c*330–379). Doctor of the church, founder of a monastic rule that is still the basis of monasticism in the Orthodox Church.

ba·sil·i·ca (basĭl´ĭka, -zĭl´-) *n.* 1. (in ancient Rome) Large oblong building used as exchange or law court, having an apse at one or each end and freq. side aisles; colonnaded hall, resembling this, in Roman house. 2. Church of similar

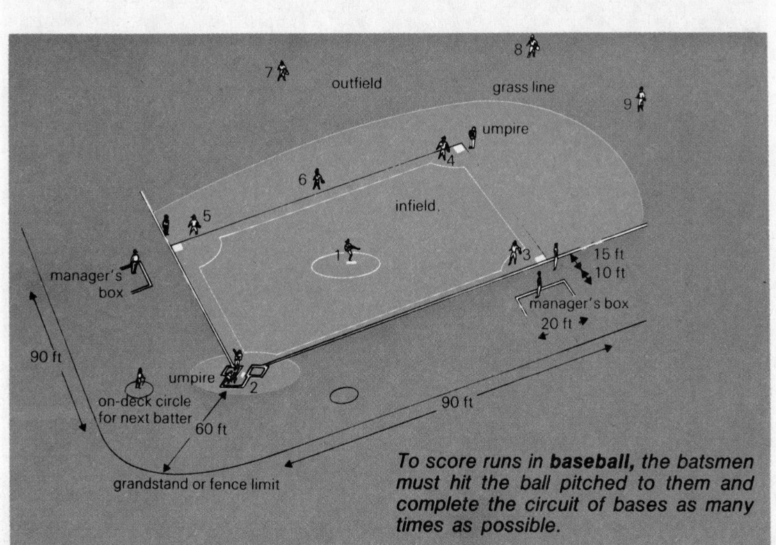

To score runs in ***baseball,*** *the batsmen must hit the ball pitched to them and complete the circuit of bases as many times as possible.*

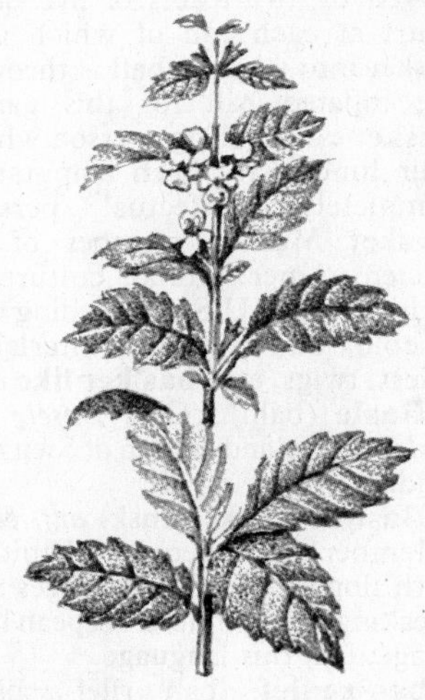

Basil *is a hardy annual grown as a culinary herb. Its leaves have a distinctive flavor and can be used fresh or dried.*

*The object of **basketball** is to score points by throwing the ball into the opposing team's basket. The game is played by 2 teams of 5 players who are allowed to pass, throw, roll, bat, or dribble the ball.*

shape, having a wide nave with aisles, and an apse at one (orig. western) end. **ba·sil'i·can** *adj.* [Gk. *basilika* (*oikia*) royal (house), f. *basileus* king]

bas·i·lisk (băs'ĭlĭsk, băz'-) *n.* 1. Cockatrice, fabulous reptile hatched by a serpent from a cock's egg, said to kill by its breath or glance. 2. Small C. Amer. and S. Amer. lizard of the family Iguanidae, with a hollow crest that can be inflated at will. [L. *basilicus* kind of lizard, f. Gk. *basiliskos* little king]

ba·sin (bā'sĭn) *n.* 1. Circular or oval vessel of greater width than depth and with sloping or curving sides, for holding water etc.; contents of a basin. 2. Hollow depression; circular or oval valley; tract of country drained by river and its tributaries. 3. = DOCK[3] defs. 1, 2; landlocked harbor. **ba'sined, ba'sin·like** *adjs.*

ba·sis (bā'sĭs) *n.* (pl. **-ses** pr. -sēz). Base; foundation, beginning, determining principle; main ingredient; common ground for negotiation etc.

bask (băsk) *v.i.* Revel in warmth and light (*in* the sun, firelight, etc.); **bask'ing shark**, one of the largest species of shark (*Cetorhinus maximus*), found in northern seas, so called from its habit of lying near surface of water.

bas·ket (băs'kĭt) *n.* Receptacle of plaited or interwoven canes, osiers, etc.; contents of this; (basketball) horizontal hoop attached to a raised backboard and suspending an open net through which a basketball is thrown; the score (one or two points) made by such a throw; **bas'ketball**, game played by two teams of five on a court at each end of which is a basket into which a ball is thrown; the inflated ball for this game; **basket case**, (slang) person whose four limbs have been amputated; completely ineffectual person; **Basket Maker**, member of an ancient Amer. Indian culture of southwestern U.S., preceding the Pueblo; **bas'ketwork**, interlaced osiers, twigs, etc. **bas'ket·like** *adj.*

Basle (bahl). (Ger. *Basel*, Fr. *Bâle*) Town and canton of Switzerland.

Basque (băsk, bahsk) *adj.* & *n.* (Member) of a people inhabiting both slopes of the W. Pyrenees and speaking a non-Indo-European language; (of) this language.

bas-re·lief (bah rĭlēf', băs-, bah'rĭlēf, băs'-) *n.* Low relief, carving or modeling in which figures project less than one-half of

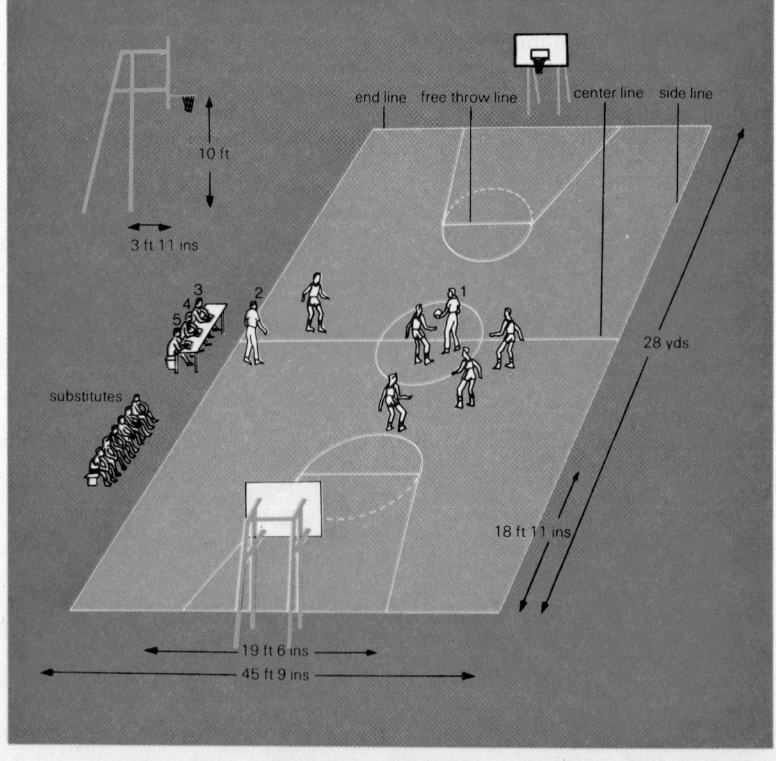

*The **bas-reliefs** of Trajan's Column in Rome illustrate his victories over the Dacians (2nd century A.D.). The scenes wind around the shaft in marble spirals, a supreme example of continuous narration in classical art.*

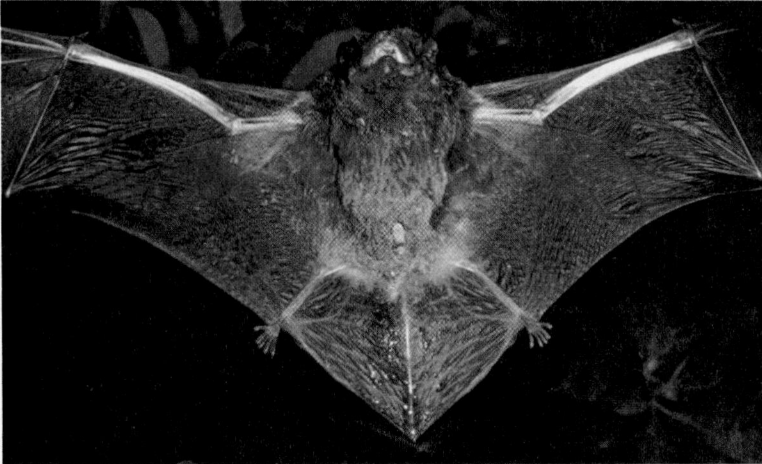

*Grey-headed fruit **bat**, Australia. Of the order Chiroptera (meaning 'hand wings' in Greek), bats are the only winged mammals. Nocturnal creatures, they sleep hanging upside down in the dark. The hind feet, toes and sharply curved claws are modified for clinging without strain.*

their true proportions from the background.

bass[1] (bǎs) *n.* (pl. **bass·es**, collect. **bass**). Any of a large group of fishes in sea or fresh water, including **sea ~** (family Serranidae), **striped ~** (*Roccus saxatilis*) etc.

bass[2] (bās) *adj.* Deep sounding; of, suited to, lowest part in harmonized music; having a voice extending 1 1/2 octaves or more below middle C; **~ clef**: see CLEF; **~ drum**: see DRUM; **~ viol**, double bass, viola da gamba. **~** *n.* Bass part; music for, singer with, bass voice; **bass'ist**, player of the DOUBLE BASS.

bass[3] (bǎs) = BAST.

bas·set (bǎs'ĭt) *n.* (also **~ hound**) Short-legged dog of breed originating in France, used in hunting hares or badgers, followed on foot.

bas·set (bǎs'ĭt) **horn.** Tenor clarinet, of somewhat greater range than the ordinary clarinet.

bas·si·net (bǎsĭnět', bǎs'ĭnět) *n.* Hooded cradle for infants.

bas·so (bǎs'ō, bah'sō; *It.* bahs'saw) *adj.* & *n.* (pl. **-sos**, *It.* **-si** pr. -sē). (mus.) Bass; **~ profundo**, (singer having) deep bass voice.

bas·soon (bǎsōōn', ba-) *n.* Double-reed musical instrument, the bass of the woodwind family, having an 8-ft. pipe turned back so that the whole instrument measures only 4 ft. **bas·soon'ist** *n.*

bast (bǎst) *n.* (also **bass**[3], **bass'-wood**). Inner bark of linden tree (*Tilia americana*) which, cut into strips and coarsely woven, is used for matting etc.; similar fiber obtained from leaf bases or leaf stalks of certain palms and used for ropes, brooms, etc.; any flexible or fibrous bark.

bas·tard (bǎs'terd) *n.* Person born out of wedlock; hybrid, counterfeit thing; (slang) disliked person or thing. **bas'tard·ly** *adj.* **bas'tar·dy** *n.* (pl. **-dies**).

bas·tard·ize (bǎs'terdīz) *v.t.* (**-ized, -iz·ing**). Declare or render bastard; debase, corrupt. **bas·tard·i·za·tion** (bǎsterdīzā'shon) *n.*

baste[1] (bāst) *v.t.* (**bast·ed, bast·ing**). Sew together loosely, sew with long loose stitches, tack.

baste[2] (bāst) *v.t.* (**bast·ed, bast·ing**). 1. Moisten (roasting meat etc.) by pouring melted fat, gravy, etc. over (it). 2. (colloq.) Thrash, cudgel.

bas·tille, bas·tile (bǎstēl'; *Fr.* bǎstē'ye) *ns.* (pl. **bas·tilles** pr. bǎstēlz'; *Fr.* bǎstē'ye). 1. Prison. 2. **B~**, 14th-c. prison fortress in Paris, used for political and other prisoners, stormed and destroyed by the revolutionary mob on July 14, 1789; the anniversary of its fall (**B~ Day**), marking the end of absolute monarchy in France and the beginning of the French Revolution, the national holiday of republican France.

bas·ti·na·do (bǎstinā'dō) *n.* (pl. **-does**) & *v.t.* (**-doed, -do·ing**). (Punish with) caning or cudgeling on the soles of the feet.

bas·tion (bǎs'chon) *n.* Mass of masonry or brick- or stone-faced earthwork projecting from fortification in the form of an irregular pentagon; (fig.) stronghold. **bas'-tioned** *adj.*

Bas·togne (bǎstōn'; *Fr.* bǎs-tawn'ye). Town in SE. Belgium; a key point in the Allied line of defense during the Battle of the Bulge, 1944–5, in World War II.

Ba·su·to (basōō'tō) *n.* (pl. **-tos**, collect. **-to**). (Member of) a S. African people of Bantu stock; **Basutoland**, former name of LESOTHO.

bat[1] (bǎt) *n.* Small nocturnal mammal of the order Chiroptera, resembling a mouse, with leathery wings consisting of a membrane stretched from neck over forearms and elongated fingers, and along sides of body to hind limbs and (usu.) tail; (slang) a mean old woman; **have ~s in the belfry**, (slang) be insane, hence **bats** (slang) insane, crazy.

bat[2] (bǎt) *n.* Stout wooden stick used as cudgel; a blow, as from a bat; long, round stick with handle at one end used in baseball; similar stick used in other games; **at ~**, (baseball, cricket) taking one's turn as batter; **go to ~ for**, (colloq.) support or defend (someone); **right off the ~**, (colloq.) immediately; **bat'ter**, baseball player at bat. **bat** *v.* (**bat·ted, bat·ting**). 1. Hit, strike with a bat. 2. (esp. baseball) Take one's turn at bat.

bat[3] (bǎt) *v.t.* (**bat·ted, bat·**-

ting). (colloq.) Blink; **not to ~ an eye(lid)**, (fig.) be unperturbed.

Ba·taan (b*a*tăn′, -tahn′). Peninsula of W. Luzon, Republic of the Philippines; surrendered and recaptured by American forces during World War II; famous as scene of Gen. MacArthur's promise: "I shall return."

Ba·ta·vi·a (b*a*tā′vē*a*). 1. Former name of DJAKARTA. 2. (hist.) Region between Rhine and Waal, inhabited in Roman times by a Celtic tribe, the Batavi.

batch (băch) *n.* Quantity of loaves etc. baked at one time; quantity, number, or set of people or things associated together, esp. in time.

bate (bāt) *v.t.* (**bat·ed, bat·ing**). Let down; restrain (breath); **with bated breath**, anxiously.

ba·teau (bătō′; *Fr.* bătō′) *n.* (pl. **-teaux** pr. -tōz′; *Fr.* -tō′). Light river boat, esp. the long, tapering, flat-bottomed boat used by French Canadians.

Bath (băth, bahth). City in SW. England noted for its hot springs and mineral baths since its Roman days.

bath (băth, bahth) *n.* (pl. **baths** pr. bădhz, bahdhz, băths, bahths). Immersion or washing, esp. of the body, in water etc; water for this; room for this; bathtub; (usu. pl.) spa; **Order of the B~**, high order of British knighthood, founded 1725 as revival of the "Knights of the Bath," first created 1399 at coronation of Henry IV and so named from the ceremonial bath that preceded installation; **bath′-house**, building with dressing room for bathers; **bath′robe**, dressing gown; **bath′room**, room with bathtub or shower and usu. washbasin and toilet; (euphem.) toilet; **bath′tub**, vessel for bathing in.

bathe (bādh) *v.* (**bathed, bath·ing**). Immerse in liquid (as for cleaning); wet thoroughly; envelop; go swimming; **bathing suit**, garment for bathing or swimming in; **bath′er** *n.*

bath·o·lith (băth′*o*lĭth), **bath·o·lite** (băth′*o*līt) *ns.* Large body of intrusive rock (e.g. granite) such as is found esp. along Pacific coast of America.

ba·thos (bā′thŏs) *n.* Fall from sublime to ridiculous; anticlimax; insincere pathos. **ba·thet·ic** (b*a*thĕt′ĭk) *adj.*

Bath·she·ba (băthshē′b*a*, băth′-sh*e*-). Wife of Uriah the Hittite (2 Sam. 11); she became one of the wives of David and the mother of Solomon.

bath·y·scaphe (băth′ĭskăf, -skăf), **bath·y·scaph** (băth′ĭskăf), **bath·y·scape** (băth′ĭskāp) *ns.* Vessel for deep-sea diving and exploration. [Fr., f. Gk. *bathus* deep + *skaphos* ship; coined by A. Piccard (1884–1962), Swiss physicist]

bath·y·sphere (băth′ĭsfēr) *n.* Spherical diving apparatus for deep-sea observation.

ba·tik (b*a*tēk′, bă-, băt′ĭk) *n.* Javanese method, practiced also in the West, of executing designs on textiles by painting parts of the

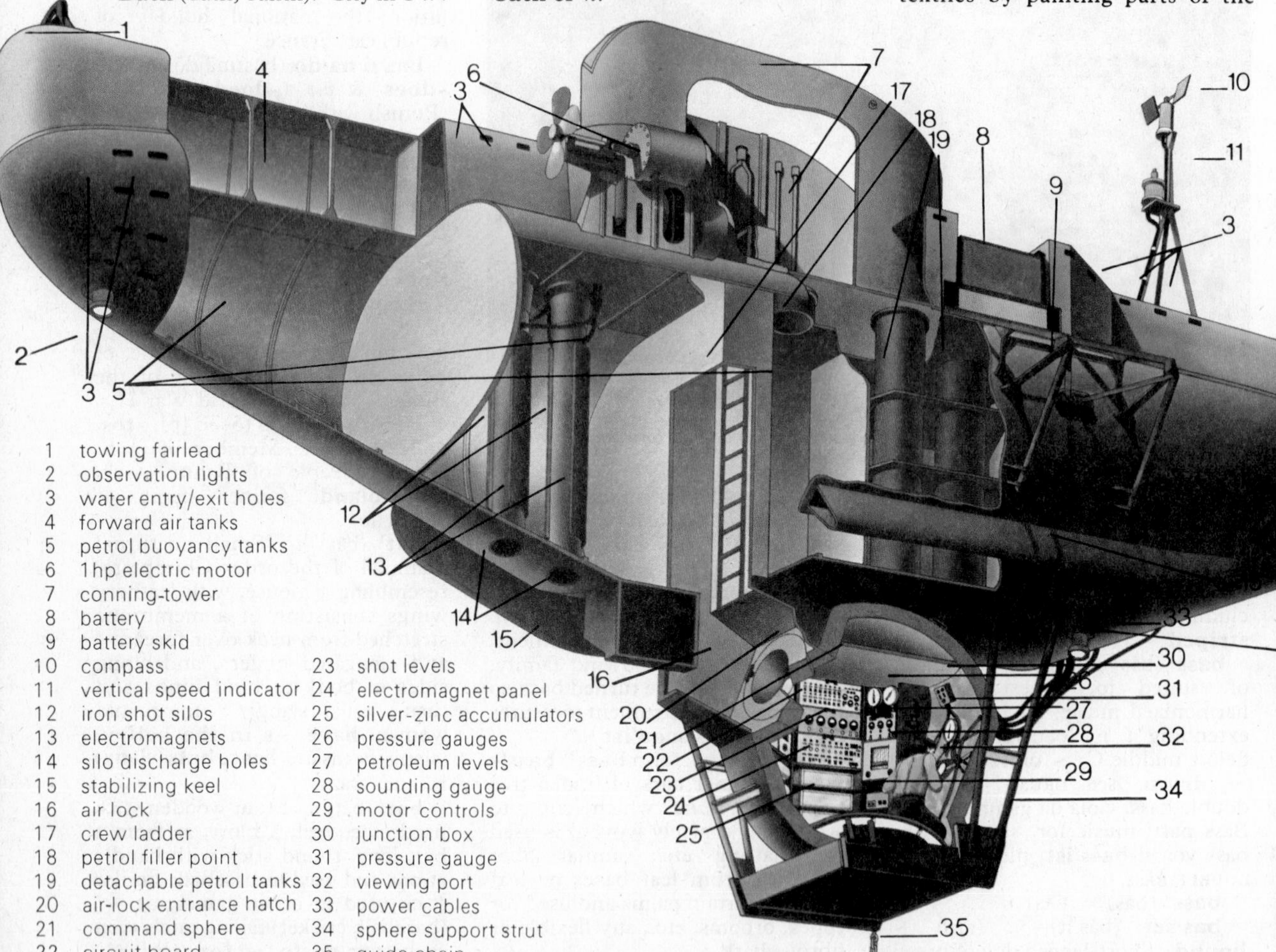

*Cutaway illustration of a **bathyscaphe,** used for deep-sea exploration. Electric motors power the vessel. It is cast in two hemispheres designed so that watertightness increases with external pressure. Some compartments contain buoyant gasoline; others are open to the sea, equalizing pressure in the float with sea pressure. Ballast is provided by iron shot and detachable gasoline tanks, which can be jettisoned electromagnetically.*

*Facing page: The Javanese craft of **batik** has been widely adopted by Western textile designers. Parts of the pattern are painted in wax. The parts which are left exposed are dyed. The wax is then removed.*

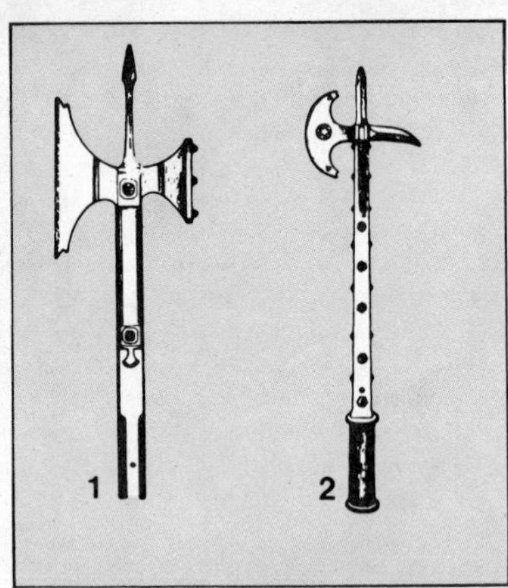

Organized ***battle*** *is as old as civilization. Top: Tableaux of Custer's Last Stand at Little Bighorn in 1876. Left: Battleship U.S.S. Alabama at Mobile. Below: Baton Rouge, capital of Louisiana and location of 3 major battles between 1779 and 1863, is now the site of the U.S.'s biggest oil refinery. Above: Battle-axes. 1. Poleax c. 1470. 2. Horseman's ax c. 1520. Ax remains dating back 30,000 years have been found.*

pattern in wax, dyeing the parts left exposed, and then removing the wax; material dyed thus. [Javanese, = "drawing"]

Ba·tis·ta (bahtēs′tah), **Fulgencio** (1901–73). Cuban dictator, 1933–40, and president 1940–4, 1952–9; ousted by Fidel Castro.

ba·tiste (b*a*tēst′, bă-) *n.* Fine light cotton or other fine, smooth fabric. [Fr., f. *Baptiste* of Cambrai, first maker]

bat·man (băt′m*a*n) *n.* (pl. **-men** pr. -m*e*n) (fem. **-wom·an** pr. -wo͝om*a*n; pl. **-wom·en** pr. -wĭmĭn). Member of British army or air force acting as officer's servant. [orig. man who carried officer's baggage (Fr. *bât* pack-saddle)]

bat mitz·vah (baht mĭts'v*a*; *Heb.* baht mētsvah') (Religious initiation ceremony for) Jewish girl aged 12 to 14. [Heb., = "daughter of commandment"]

ba·ton (bătŏn', b*a*-, băt'*o*n) *n.* 1. Staff of office. 2. (mus.) Conductor's wand for beating time. 3. Short rod passed from one runner to another in a relay race.

Ba·ton Rouge (băt'*o*n ro͞ozh'). Capital and important port of Louisiana, in the S., on the Mississippi River.

ba·tra·chi·an (b*a*trā'kē*a*n) *adj.* Of, concerning, like tailless amphibians, e.g., frogs and toads; ANURAN. ~ *n.* Tailless leaping amphibian.

bat·tal·ion (b*a*tăl'y*o*n) *n.* Unit of infantry (*or* artillery) consisting of three or four companies (*or* batteries).

bat·ten[1] (băt'*e*n) *n.* Long, thin strip of wood used in carpentry. ~ *v.t.* Strengthen, fasten *down*, with battens.

bat·ten[2] (băt'*e*n) *v.i.* (archaic) Feed gluttonously *on*; grow fat, (fig.) thrive at another's expense.

bat·ter (băt'*e*r) *v.* Strike repeatedly so as to bruise or break; beat out of shape; handle severely; **bat'tered child**, young child with injuries inflicted by a parent; **battered wife**, a woman habitually beaten by her husband; **bat'tering ram**, heavy beam used for battering down walls or doors. **batter** *n.* Mixture of flour and eggs beaten up with liquid for cooking.

bat·ter·y (băt'*e*rē) *n.* (pl. **-ter·ies**). 1. (law) Infliction of a blow or blows on another person. 2. (mil.) Set of guns with their men, and vehicles; group of guns on a warship; the basic tactical artillery unit. 3. Set of similar or connected instruments, utensils, etc.; cell or set of cells (**storage battery**) generating electrical current by chemical action. 4. (baseball) Team's pitcher and catcher in a game.

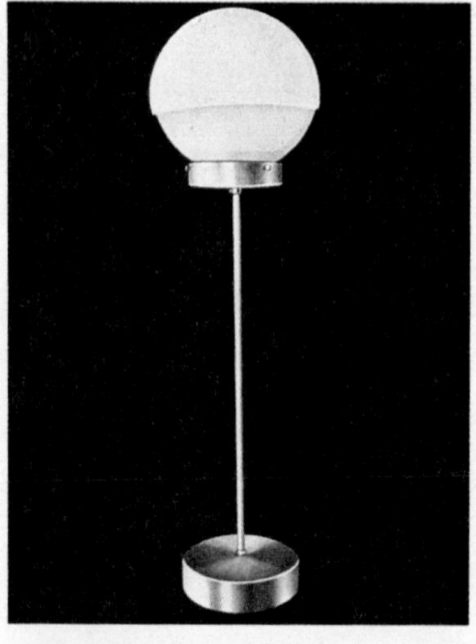

*Globelight, 1927, a product of the **Bauhaus** movement. The aim of the movement was to close the gap between the creative artist and the industrial craftsman.*

Bat·ter·y (băt'*e*rē), **The.** (Park on) the S. tip of Manhattan Island; the site of defensive artillery during the Colonial era.

bat·tle (băt'*e*l) *n.* Combat, esp. between large organized forces; **line of ~**, troops or ships drawn up to fight; **~-ax**, kind of long-handled ax used as a medieval weapon; (fig.) formidable or domineering woman; **~ cry**, war cry, slogan; **~ dress**, (formerly) soldier's etc. fighting uniform; **~ fatigue**, mental disorder due to stress in wartime combat; **bat'tlefield**, scene of battle; **bat'tleship**, warship of the largest and most powerfully armed class; **battle station(s)**, position(s) assigned for battle; **battle wagon**, (slang) battleship. **battle** *v.* (**-tled, -tling**). Struggle *with* or *against* or *for*; fight against; fight (one's way etc.). **bat'tler** *n.*

bat·tle·dore (băt'*e*ldōr) *n.* An early form of badminton (also called **~ and shuttlecock**); the light wooden paddle or racket used in this game. [prob. f. Span. *batallador* champion]

bat·tle·ment (băt'*e*lm*e*nt) *n.* Indented parapet at top of wall etc., orig. for purposes of defense against assailants.

bat·ty (băt'ē) *adj.* (**-ti·er, -ti·est**). (slang) Crazy.

bau·ble (baw'b*e*l) *n.* 1. Showy trinket. 2. Baton surmounted by fantastic head with asses' ears carried by court fool or jester.

Bau·de·laire (bōd*e*lār', bō'd*e*lār), **Charles Pierre** (1821–67). French lyric poet, author of *Les Fleurs du Mal* (1857).

Bau·douin I (bōdwăn') (1930–). King of Belgium since 1951.

Bau·haus (bow'hows). School of design founded by Walter Gropius (1883–1969) in Weimar, Germany in 1919; closed in 1933.

baulk (bawk) = BALK.

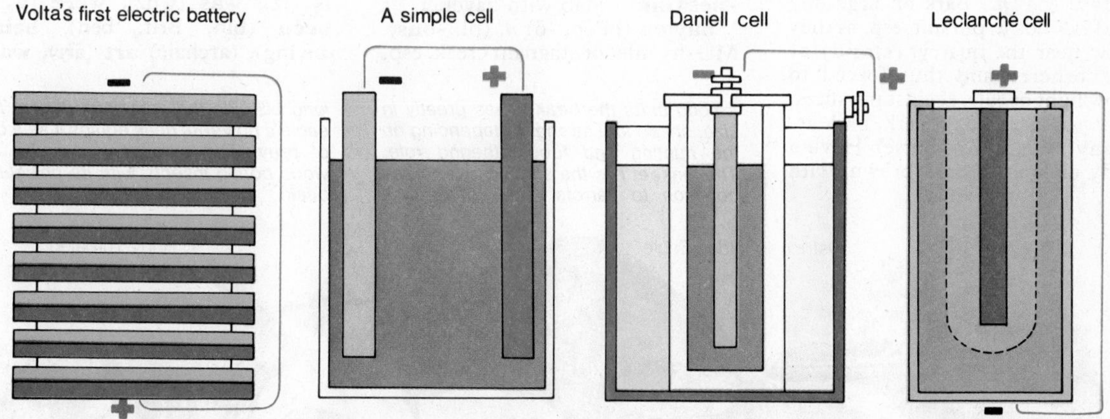

*An Italian, Alessandro Volta, described the first electric **battery** in 1800. He found he could cause a current to pass through a wire by immersing 2 different metals in a salt solution. Englishman John Daniell developed the first cell free of 'polarization' in 1836: a zinc negative electrode dipped in a sulphuric acid electrolyte, and a positive electrode of copper dipped in copper sulfate solution. 'Dry' batteries with a depolarizer derive from the Leclanché cell. In fact the electrolyte is not dry but is made up in the form of a paste or jelly.*

Baum (bahm, bawm), **L(yman) Frank** (1856–1919). American journalist and playwright; author of the children's classic, *Wonderful Wizard of Oz*.

baux·ite (bawk′sīt, bŏk′-) *n.* The principal ore of aluminum, containing aluminum hydroxide, ferric oxide, and silica. [originally found at *Les Baux* near Arles, France]

Ba·var·i·a (b*a*vār′ē*a*). Former state of S. Germany, now a province of The Federal Republic; capital, Munich. **Ba·var′i·an** *adj.* & *n.*

bawd (bawd) *n.* (archaic) Procuress, brothel madam; prostitute.

bawd·y (baw′dē) *adj.* (**bawd·i·er, bawd·i·est**). Humorously vulgar or indecent; **baw′dy-house**, brothel. **bawd′i·ly** *adv.* **bawd′i·ness** *n.*

bawl (bawl) *v.* Shout or weep at the top of one's voice; ~ **out**, (slang) reprimand severely. **bawl′er** *n.*

bay[1] (bā) *n.* 1. Kind of laurel, esp. the sweet bay or bay laurel, (*Laurus nobilis*), with deep-green leaves (~ **leaf**) (used to flavor soups etc.) and many dark purple berries. 2. (also **bay′berry**) West Indian tree (*Pimenta acris*), bearing small green berries; the berry; **bay rum**, aromatic liquid made from its leaves, used as an astringent.

bay[2] (bā) *n.* Part of sea filling wide-mouthed opening of land.

bay[3] (bā) *n.* 1. Division of wall between columns or buttresses. 2. Recess, alcove; compartment; **sick** ~, part of ship's deck used as hospital; part of building similarly used. 3. Space added to room by advancing window from wall line; **B~ State**, Massachusetts; ~ **window**, window in a bay; (slang) a protruding stomach.

bay[4] (bā) *n.* Bark of large dog or of hounds in pursuit, esp. as they draw near the quarry; **(stand) at** ~, cornered and thus forced to show fight or turn against pursuers. ~ *v.* (of large dog) Bark, bark at.

bay[5] (bā) *adj.* (of horse) Having body of light to dark brown, with black mane and tail; reddish brown. ~ *n.* Bay horse.

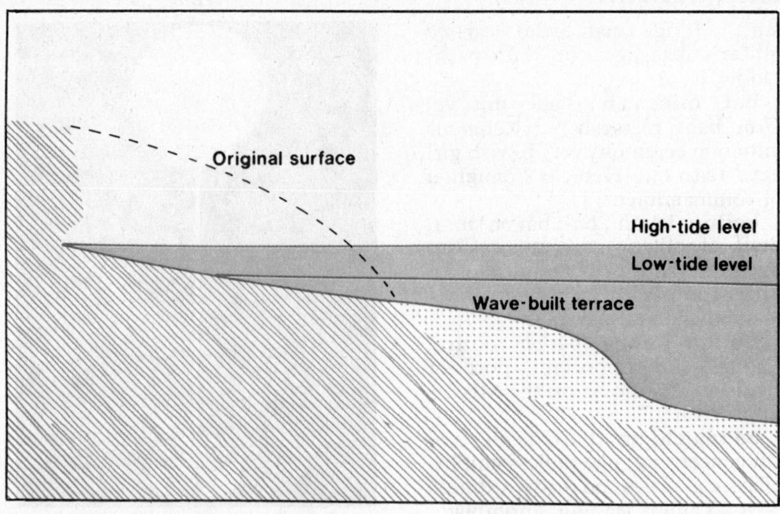

How ebb and flow of the tide acts on the shore to form a ***beach.*** *The line of the shore, the water movement along it and the materials composing the beach influence the form the beach takes.*

Ba·yeux (bāyo͞o′, bah-; *Fr.* bahyö′) **tapestry.** An 11th- or 12th-c. embroidered linen tapestry 231 ft. long by 20 in. wide with scenes depicting the Norman Conquest of England and preserved in the cathedral of Bayeux, France.

Bayle (bāl), **Pierre** (1647–1706). French philosopher and skeptic, author of a *Dictionnaire historique et critique* (1695–7), which had great influence on Voltaire and other 18th-c. French skeptics.

bay·o·net (bā′*o*nĭt, -nĕt, bā*o*nĕt′) *n.* Stabbing blade that can be attached to rifle muzzle. ~ *v.t.* (**-net·ed** or **-net·ted, -net·ing** or **-net·ting**). Stab with bayonet.

bay·ou (bī′o͞o, -ō) *n.* (pl. **-ous**). Marshy inlet or stagnant creek, esp. in southern U.S.

ba·zaar, ba·zar (b*a*zâr′) *ns.* Oriental marketplace or shopping quarters; fancy shop, boutique; sale of goods for charities. [Pers. *bāzār* street of shops]

ba·zoo·ka (b*a*zo͞o′k*a*) *n.* 1. Crude trombone-like musical instrument. 2. Infantry's portable rocket launcher for firing armor-piercing (esp. antitank) rockets.

BB (bē′bē) *n.* A .18-inch diameter pellet shot by firing from an air rifle.

B.B.A. *abbrev.* Bachelor of Business Administration.

BBC *abbrev.* British Broadcasting Corporation.

B.C. *abbrev.* Before Christ; British Columbia.

bd. *abbrev.* Board.

B.D. *abbrev.* Bachelor of Divinity.

bdrm. *abbrev.* Bedroom.

Be *symbol.* Beryllium.

be (bē) *v.i.* [**am** (ăm), **are** (âr), **is** (ĭz), **was** (wŭz), **were** (wẽr), **been** (bĭn, Brit. bēn), **being** (bē′ĭng), (archaic) **art** (ârt), **wast**

Among birds the ***beak*** *varies greatly in size, shape and strength, depending on the hunting and food-gathering role. The lorikeet has the short hooked beak common to parrots. The cormorant's long bill aids the voracious fisher. The eagle's powerful beak equips it as a bird of prey. The woodpecker grubs out wood-boring insects with its chisel-like beak.*

*Zulu girls at a gathering in Natal, South Africa. Many tribal peoples believe **beads** have magical or talismanic properties as well as being decorative. Early explorers used beads of metal or glass to barter with native tribes.*

(wŭst), **wert** (wĕrt)] Exist, occur; occupy a position; remain, continue; have a certain state or quality (specified by following noun, adj., etc.); **~-all and end-all**, absolutely everything, the whole *of*; ~ **off**, go away.

beach (bēch) *n.* Sandy or pebbly shore of the sea (or lake or large river); ~ **ball**, large inflated ball for games on beach; ~ **buggy**, lightweight or framework vehicle with oversized tires for driving on sand beaches; **beach′comber**, long wave rolling onto the beach; person who lives by gathering salable jetsam or refuse from beaches; **beach grass**, grass of the genus *Ammophila* growing on sandy shores and dunes and having long clusters of spikelets. **beach′head**, fortified position of troops landed on a beach; **beach plum**, (edible plum-like fruit of) New England coastal shrub (*Prunus maritima*) bearing white flowers. **beach** *v.t.* Run (ship etc.) ashore, haul up.

Beach-la-Mar (bēch l*a* mar′) = BÊCHE-DE-MER. [Port. *bicho do mar* sea-worm]

bea·con (bē′k*o*n) *n.* 1. Guiding or warning signal light or fire, signal fire on hill. 2. Conspicuous hill or tower suitable for a beacon. 3. Lighthouse; conspicuous object. 4. Radio transmitter sending out signals enabling ship or aircraft to fix position.

bead (bēd) *n.* 1. Small perforated ornamental ball etc. for threading with others on a string or for sewing on to fabric; small bubble or drop of liquid; (pl.) necklace; rosary; **tell (count, say) one's ~s**, say prayers with rosary beads. 2. Small metal knob forming front sight of gun (**draw a bead on**, take aim at). **bead** *v.* Furnish or adorn with beads; form or grow into beads. [OE, = "prayer," from the use of strings of beads for keeping count of the number of prayers said] **bead′ed** *adj.* **bead′ing** *n.*

bea·dle (bē′d*e*l) *n.* 1. (hist.) Inferior parish officer appointed to keep order in church, punish petty offenses, and carry messages, etc. 2. Official who prepares and walks before procession, macebearer [in the Engl. universities usu. spelled *bedel*(*1*)].

bead·y (bē′dē) *adj.* (**bead·i·er, bead·i·est**). (of eyes) Small and bright like beads, esp. as indicating cunning, greed, or meanness.

bea·gle (bē′g*e*l) *n.* Small hound with long ears and short legs, orig. bred for hunting hares.

beak (bēk) *n.* Horny projecting mandibles of bird; bill; extremities, often horny in structure, of mandibles of other animals (as turtles); hooked nose; projection at prow of ancient ships, esp. war galleys. **beaked** (bēkt, bē′kĭd), **beak′less, beak′like** *adjs.*

beak·er (bē′k*e*r) *n.* 1. Large drinking cup. 2. Straight-sided lipped glass for scientific experiments.

beam (bēm) *n.* 1. Long piece of squared timber such as is used in building houses or ships; horizontal support in building. 2. Transverse bar of balance. 3. Transverse horizontal timber of a ship; hence, the greatest breadth of a ship; **broad in the ~**, (colloq.) wide; having wide hips or a wide rear end. 4. Ray or group of nearly parallel rays of light, or of electric radiation, etc.; (also **radio ~**) radio waves sent as a beam (i.e. not dispersed or broadcast); directional radio or radar signal used to guide aircraft or missiles; course indicated by this;

(phys.) directional flow of radiation or particles; **off the ~**, (colloq.) mistaken, on the wrong track; **on the ~**, (colloq.) correct, on the right track. 5. Radiance, bright look, smile. **beam** *v.* Emit (light, affection, etc.); direct, aim (radio signals etc.); shine, smile radiantly. **beamed, beam'ing, beam'less, beam'like** *adjs.* **beam'ing·ly** *adv.*

bean (bēn) *n.* 1. Edible kidney-shaped non-endospermic seed borne in pods of the family Leguminosae; plant producing such seeds; (slang) a person's head; **bean'pole**, tall, slender pole for supporting growing bean plants; (slang) tall, thin person. 2. Similar seed of other plants, as coffee. 3. **full of ~s**, (slang) in high spirits; **spill the ~s**, (slang) disclose a secret. **bean'er·y** *n.* (pl. **-er·ies**), (slang) cheap restaurant. 4. **beanbag**, small cloth bag filled with beans, used as a toy, ornament, etc.; **bean ball**, baseball pitch deliberately thrown at batter's head; **bean curd**, creamy white cake of soybean cheese used in oriental cooking; **bean'stalk**, stem of the bean plant. **bean** *v.t.* (slang) Hit on the head.

bear[1] (bār) *n.* (pl. **bears**, collect. **bear**). 1. Heavily built, thick-furred plantigrade quadruped of family Ursidae. 2. Rough, gruff, or clumsy person. 3. (stock exch.) Person who believes price of stocks will decline; **~ market**, one with falling prices. 4. **Great, Little B~**: see URSA. 5. **~ baiting**, (hist.) setting dogs to attack captive bear; **~ hug**, tight embrace; **bear'-skin**, skin or pelt of a bear; garment, rug, etc., made from this. **bear'ish** *adj.* Rough mannered, surly; (of stock market or prices) tending to fall.

'J'ai baisé ta bouche Iokanaan' by ***Aubrey Beardsley*** *(1872–98), English artist and illustrator of 'Yellow Book' fame whose unconventional drawings many considered decadent.*

bear[2] (bār) *v.* (**bore, borne, bear·ing**). 1. Carry, bring; support; wear; **~ out**, confirm. 2. Endure, tolerate; **~ up**, endure, keep up one's courage; **~ with**, be patient with. 3. (past. part. **born** in passive) Give birth to. 4. Produce, yield. 5. Apply weight; press or push against; tend, incline; move, tend in the direction of; **~ down**, strive harder; **~ down on**, move toward; **~ hard on**, oppress; **~ on**, relate to; **bring to ~**, apply. **bear'er** *n.*

Beard (bērd). Name of two American educators and historians: **Charles Austin** (1874–1948) and his wife, **Mary Ritter** (1876–1958); authors of *The Rise of American Civilization*.

beard (bērd) *n.* Hair on lower part of man's face (now usu. excluding moustache and whiskers); chin tuft of animal. **beard'ed, beard'like** *adjs.* **beard'less** *adj.* Youthful, immature. **beard** *v.t.* Oppose openly, defy.

Beard·sley (bērdz'lē), **Aubrey Vincent** (1872–98). English artist and illustrator, worked in style of art nouveau.

bear·ing (bār'ĭng) *n.* (esp.) 1. Behavior. 2. Act, capability, or period of birth or bringing forth. 3. Relation, reference, aspect; tendency to exert influence *on.* 4. Part of machine that supports and guides a shaft, pivot, etc. 5. Situation or direction of one point, object, etc., with respect to another; determination of this; (pl.) relative position or direction (also fig.).

beast (bēst) *n.* 1. Animal; quadruped as dist. from birds, man, insects, etc.; **~ of burden**, animal used for carrying heavy loads. 2. Cruel, coarse person; brutal, savage man. **beast'like** *adj.*

beast·ly (bēst'lē) *adj.* (**-li·er, -li·est**). Like a beast or its ways; (colloq.) unpleasant. **beast'li·ness** *n.*

Despite its massive body, a ***bear*** *can run at 30 m.p.h. Left to right: Grizzly bear, long-clawed and very fierce; Polar bear, which lives on Arctic ice-floes; Himalayan black bear has V-shaped blaze on its chest; Kodiak bear, a variety of Grizzly, is the largest land carnivore and often over 9 ft. tall.*

beat (bēt) *v.* (**beat, beat·en** or **beat, beat·ing**). 1. Strike repeatedly; (of sun etc.) strike *upon*. 2. Thrash soundly; defeat, overcome, surpass; be too hard for, perplex. 3. (of wings etc.) Move up and down; (of heart etc.) pulsate, throb; ~ **it**, (slang) go away; ~ **time**, mark the time of music by the beat of a wand, tapping with the foot, etc. 4. Shift, drive, alter, deform, or shape by blows; make (a path) by repeated treading; (also ~ **up**) stir vigorously. 5. Strike bushes etc. to rouse game. 6. ~ (person) **up**, (colloq.) attack and injure person by blows and kicks. ~ *n.* 1. Stroke or blow; drum signal; movement of conductor's baton; measured sequence of strokes or sounds; marking of metrical divisions of music; accent or stress in music or poetry; a throb or throbbing. 2. Policeman's appointed course; newspaper reporter's habitual round. 3. (colloq.) = BEATNIK. ~ *adj.* (colloq.) Exhausted, worn out; ~**-up**, (colloq.) dilapidated.

beat·en (bē'ten) *adj.*: see BEAT; (esp.) ~ **gold** etc., gold etc. hammered into foil, shaped by the hammer; ~ **track, way**, well-trodden way (also fig.).

beat·er (bē'ter) *n.* (esp.) Man employed to rouse game; man who beats gold etc.; implement that beats, as **egg'beater** etc.

beat (bēt) **generation.** Young people (esp. after World War II) adopting unconventional dress, manners, habits, etc., as a means of self-expression and social protest and espousing mystical detachment. [Prob. f. *beat* = "exhausted"; perh. infl. by *beat* = "rhythm"; but coined by novelist J. Kerouac (b. 1922), connecting *beat* with *beatitude*]

be·a·tif·ic (bēatĭf'ĭk) *adj.* Bestowing bliss; blissful, saintly. **be·a·tif'·i·cal·ly** *adv.*

be·at·i·fy (bēăt'ĭfī) *v.t.* (**-fied, -fy·ing**). Make supremely happy or blessed; (R.C. Ch.) declare to be in enjoyment of heavenly bliss (as the first step toward canonization). **be·at·i·fi·ca·tion** (bēătĭfĭkā'shon) *n.* **be·at·i·tude** (bēăt'ĭtōōd, -tūd) *n.* Supreme blessedness; declaration of blessedness, esp. (pl.) those pronouced by Jesus Christ in the Sermon on the Mount (Matt. 5).

beat·nik (bēt'nĭk) *n.* Member and adherent of the beat generation.

beau (bō) *n.* Fop, dandy; suitor, lover; **B ~ Brummell**, like George Bryan Brummell (1778–1840). English dandy and fashion leader.

Beau·fort (bō'fert) **scale.** Series of numbers used by meteorologists to indicate force of wind (measured at 10 m above level ground), thus:

Force	*m.p.h.*		*knots*
0	less than 1	calm	less than 1
1	1–3	light air	1–3
2	4–7	light breeze	4–6
3	8–12	gentle breeze	7–10
4	13–18	moderate breeze	11–16
5	19–24	fresh breeze	17–21
6	25–31	strong breeze	22–27
7	32–38	near gale	28–33
8	39–46	gale	34–40
9	47–54	strong gale	41–47
10	55–63	storm	48–55
11	64–72	violent storm	56–63
12	73 or more	hurricane	64 or more

[devised by Admiral Sir F. *Beaufort* (1774–1857)]

beau geste (bō zhĕst') (pl. **beaux gestes** pr. bō zhĕst'). Display of magnanimity. [Fr., = "beautiful (or splendid) gesture"]

Beau·jo·lais (bōzholā') *n.* Red or (less freq.) white Burgundy from the Beaujolais district in the Rhône department of France.

Beau·mar·chais (bōmărshā'), **Pierre Augustin Caron de** (1732–90). French dramatist, author of famous comedies *Le Barbier de Seville* (1775), *Le Mariage de Figaro* (1778).

beau monde (bō mawnd'). Fashionable society. [Fr., = "beautiful world"]

Beau·mont (bō'mŏnt). Industrial city and port on the Gulf of Mexico in E. Texas.

Beau·mont (bō'mŏnt), **Francis** (1584–1616). English playwright, collaborator with John Fletcher from *c*1606 to 1616.

Beau·re·gard (bō'regārd), **Pierre Gustave Toutant de** (1818–93). American Confederate army general; in command of bombardment of Fort Sumter.

beaut (būt) *n.* (slang abbreviation) Something beautiful or excellent.

beau·te·ous (bū'tēus, -tyus) *adj.* (archaic and poet.) Endowed with beauty. **beau'te·ous·ly** *adv.* **beau'te·ous·ness** *n.*

beau·ti·cian (būtĭsh'an) *n.* One skilled in giving beauty treatments, as in a beauty parlor.

beau·ti·ful (bū'tiful) *adj.* Having beauty; excellent; (colloq.) typical; ~ **people**, wealthy trendsetters, fashionable people; **the beautiful**, beauty in the abstract. **beau'ti·ful·ly** *adv.* **beau'ti·ful·ness** *n.*

beau·ti·fy (bū'tifī) *v.t.* (**-fied, -fy·ing**). Make beautiful.

beau·ty (bū'tē) *n.* (pl. **-ties**). Combination of qualities (as form, color, etc.) that delights the eye; combined qualities delighting the other senses, the moral sense, or the mind; beautiful trait or feature; person or thing possessing beauty; something excellent; (colloq.) a typical example; ~ **parlor**, (also ~ **shop**), establishment for hairdressing, manicuring, or other beauty treatment of women; ~ **sleep**, sleep obtained before midnight; (fig.) enough sleep to keep one beautiful; ~ **spot**, small patch placed on woman's face as foil to a beautiful complexion; beautiful place or scene; ~ **treatment**, use of massage, cosmetics, exercise,

*The vineyards that produce **Beaujolais** wine stretch from a little south of Anse to slightly north of Tournis in a narrow fertile strip along the west bank of the River Saône.*

etc., in an attempt to improve personal beauty.

beaux arts (bōzar̄′) *n.pl.* The fine arts. [Fr.]

bea·ver (bē′v*e*r) *n.* (pl. **-vers,** collect. **-ver**). 1. Amphibious rodent of genus *Castor* with broad, oval, horizontally flattened tail, webbed hind feet, soft fur, and hard incisor teeth with which it cuts down trees: remarkable for its industry esp. in constructing dams of wood and mud; **bea′verboard**, a kind of fiberboard; **eager beaver**, (colloq.) zealous person. 2. Soft, short, rather wooly light brown fur of this animal; tall hat for men made from this.

be·bop (bē′bŏp) *n.* A style of jazz music.

be·calm (bĭkahm′) *v.t.* Deprive (a sailing ship) of wind necessary to move it.

became (bĭkām′): see BECOME.

be·cause (bĭkawz′) *adv.* By reason of. ~ *conj.* For the reason that.

bé·cha·mel (bā′sh*a*mĕl; *Fr.* bāshămĕl′) **sauce.** Rich white sauce of butter, flour, cream, and seasoning. [f. its inventor, Marquis de *Béchamel*, steward of Louis XIV]

bêche-de-mer (bĕsh d*e* mar̄′) (also **beach-la-mar**) *n.* (pl. **bêches-de-mer**, collect. **bêche-de-mer** for def. 1). 1. = TREPANG (sea cucumber). 2. Lingua franca of the SW. Pacific combining Malay and English.

Bech·u·an·a (bĕch o͞oah′n*a*, bĕkū-) *n.* (pl. **-nas**, collect. **-na**) = TSWANA.

beck (bĕk) *n.* Beckoning gesture, nod, etc.; **at the ~ and call of**, completely at the service of.

Beck·et (bĕk′ĭt), **St. Thomas à** (1117–70). Archbishop of Canterbury (1162) and Chancellor of England (1158) under Henry II; he successfully opposed Henry's policy in taxation and other matters, and was murdered by Henry's orders, in Canterbury Cathedral; he was canonized in 1173.

Beck·ett (bĕk′ĭt), **Samuel** (1906–). Irish novelist and dramatist, many of whose works are written first in French; author of the play *Waiting for Godot*; winner of the Nobel Prize for literature 1969.

beck·on (bĕk′*o*n) *v.* Summon, call attention of, by gesture; make mute signal *to*.

be·cloud (bĭklowd′) *v.t.* Cover with clouds, obscure.

be·come (bĭkŭm′) *v.* (**be·came** pr. bĭkām′, **be·come, be·com·ing**). 1. Come into being; begin to be; **~ of,** (past t. and fut.) happen to, as in *what has, will, become of him?*. 2. Suit, befit, look well on. **be·com′ing** *adj.* Suitable; (of clothes etc.) giving pleasing appearance. **be·com′ing·ly** *adv.*

bed (bĕd) *n.* 1. Thing to sleep or rest on, esp. framework with mattress and coverings; animal's resting place or bedding; **go to ~ with**, (esp.) have sexual intercourse with. 2. Flat base on which anything rests; foundation of road or railroad; garden plot for plants; bottom of sea, river, etc.; stratum. 3. **~ and board**, sleeping accommodations and meals, as at a rooming house; **bed′board**, thin board placed under mattress to make bed firm; **bed′bug**, flat, evil-smelling, sucking insect (*Cimex lectularius*) infesting beds etc.; **bed′chamber**, (archaic) bedroom; **bed′clothes**, sheets, pillows, blankets, etc., of bed; **bed′fellow**, sharer of bed; (fig.) associate; **bed linen**, sheets and pillowcases; **bed′pan**, shallow TOILET pan for persons confined to bed; **bed′post**, upright support of bedstead; **bed′rid·den**, (*adj.*) confined to bed by infirmity; **bed′rock**, solid rock underlying soil etc., of earth's surface; **bed′roll**, bedding rolled into a bundle; **bed′room**, room for sleeping; **bed′side**, side of bed, esp. in **bedside manner**, of tactful doctor; **bed′sore**, sore developed by long

***Beavers** fell small trees which they roll into the water as building material for their lodges: covered islands of branches and twigs cemented together with mud. Here the beavers raise their young and hibernate in winter, living off small shoots and twigs stored away in the fall.*

periods of lying in bed; **bed'-spread**, outer covering for a bed, coverlet; **bed'stead**, framework of bed; **bed'time**, hour for going to bed. **bed** *v.* (**bed·ded, bed·ding**). 1. Provide with a bed; put or go to bed; provide bedding for horses etc. 2. Plant *out* in a garden bed. 3. Cover up or fix firmly in something; embed. 4. Arrange as, be or form, a layer. **bed'less, bed'like** *adjs.*

be·daub (bĭdawb') *v.t.* Smear or daub with paint, mud, etc.

be·daz·zle (bĭdăz'el) *v.t.* (**-zled, -zling**). Completely dazzle; confuse (person).

bed·ding (bĕd'ĭng) *n.* (esp.) 1. Mattress and bedclothes; litter, straw, etc. for animals to sleep on.

The ***Great Bed of Ware*** *(top) stands 8 ft. 9 ins. high and is 10 ft. 8 ins. square. Made c. 1590 of oak, it is richly carved and inlaid. The novelist Charles Dickens was captivated by its grandeur and purchased it in 1864. The State Bed at Osterley Park, in Middlesex, U.K., was designed by the Scottish architect Robert Adam in 1776 in a style of the greatest elegance.*

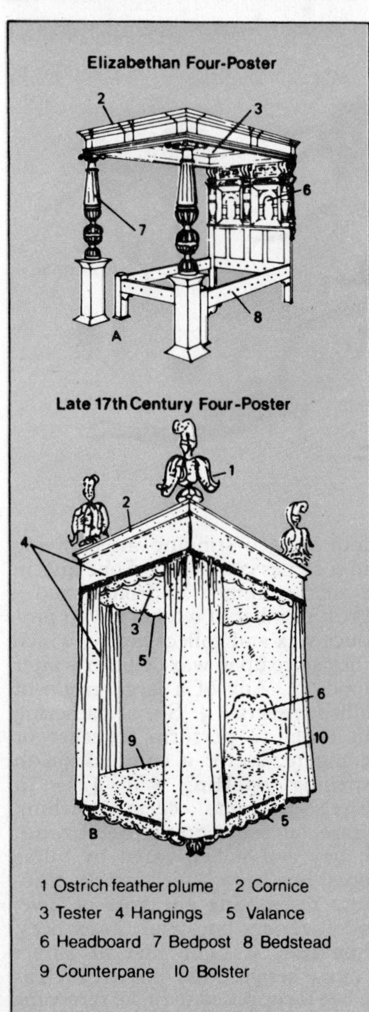

Honey bee

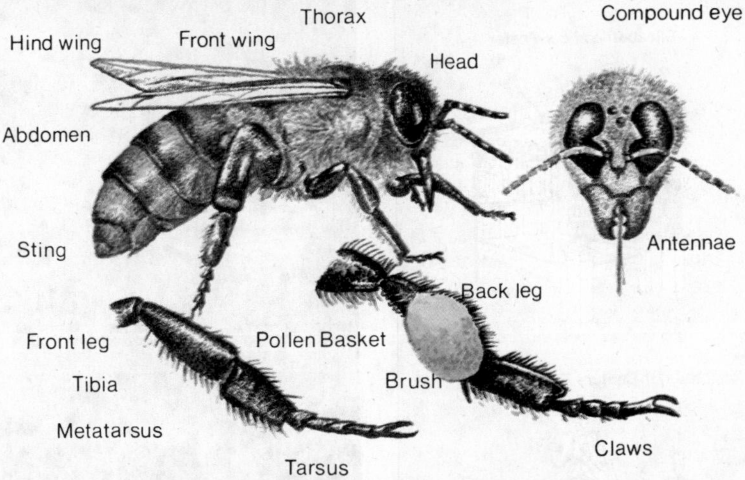

*A honey **bee** (top) collects pollen from a flower. The pollen adheres to hairs on its legs, and the bee brushes most of it to pollen baskets on its hind legs (right). Three types of bees live in a hive: one queen lays thousands of eggs after mating with drones; the worker bees gather pollen and maintain the hive.*

2. (geol.) Layered structure visible in some rocks resulting from their deposition in water in layers or beds.

Bede (bēd), **St.** (*c*673–735). English historian and scholar, a monk of Jarrow; author of a Latin history of the English Church and many other works in Latin; known since 9th c. as "the Venerable Bede."

be·deck (bĭdĕk′) *v.t.* Adorn.

be·dev·il (bĭdĕv′*i*l) *v.t.* (**-iled, -il·ing**; Brit. **-illed, -il·ling**). Torment diabolically, bewitch. **be·dev′il·ment** *n.*

be·dew (bĭdo͞o′, -dū′) *v.t.* Cover with drops of or like dew.

be·diz·en (bĭdī′zen, -dĭz′*e*n) *v.t.* Deck out gaudily.

Bed·lam (bĕd′l*a*m). (hist.) Popular name for the hospital of St. Mary of Bethlehem, former asylum in London for the insane.

bed·lam (bĕd′l*a*m) *n.* 1. (hist.) Lunatic asylum. 2. Scene of uproar and confusion.

Bed·ling·ton (bĕd′lĭngt*o*n) *n.* (also ~ **terrier**) Curly-haired, gray English terrier with narrow head, short body and longish legs. [*Bedlington*, England]

Bed·ou·in (bĕd′o͞oĭn, bĕd′wĭn) *n.* (pl. **-ins**, collect. **-in**). Arab of the desert. [Arab. *badawiyyūn*, oblique case *badawiyyīn* desert dwellers]

be·drag·gle (bĭdrăg′*e*l) *v.t.* (**-gled, -gling**). Wet (dress etc.) by trailing it, or so that it trails or hangs limp. **be·drag′gled** *adj.* **be·drag′gle·ment** *n.*

bee (bē) *n.* 1. Hymenopterous four-winged stinging insect living in societies composed of one queen, a small number of drones, and a great number of workers, who produce wax and collect honey, which they store up in wax cells for winter food. 2. Any of a large group of allied insects. 3. Social gathering in order to perform together or compete, as for a competition in spelling (**spelling** ~). 4. ~ **in one's bonnet**, eccentric whim, craze on some point; **bee′bread**, honey and pollen eaten by nurse bees; **bee′hive**, HIVE; domed structure resembling one type of hive; **bee′keeper**, one who raises bees; **bee′line**, straight line or direct course between two points, such as a bee is supposed to make returning to the hive; **bees′wax**, *n.* & *v.t.*

(polish with) wax secreted by bees (see WAX¹, 1).

beech (bēch) *n.* Tree of the genus *Fagus* (esp. *F. grandifolia* of Eastern North America and *F. sylvatica* of Europe), with thin smooth light-colored bark, glossy oval leaves, and bearing a small, edible three-sided nut (**beech'nut**) in a rough or prickly involucre; its wood.

Bee·cham (bē'cham), **Sir Thomas, 2nd Bt.** (1879–1961). English conductor of opera and symphony orchestras.

Bee·cher (bē'cher), **Henry Ward** (1813–87). American Protestant clergyman, editor, and abolitionist leader; father of Harriet Beecher STOWE.

beef (bēf) *n.* (pl. **beeves** pr. bēvz, **beefs** for slang sense). Flesh of steer, bull, or cow used as food; adult steer, bull, or cow raised for its meat; (slang) complaint, ground for this; **beef'burger**, a hamburger; **beef'eaters**, a yeoman of the English royal guard or a warder of the Tower of London (both wear the same uniform); (slang) an Englishman; **beef'steak**, slice of beef cut from hind-quarters and suitable for broiling, frying, etc.; **beef tea**, broth made from beef extract or boiled beef juice. **beef'y** *adj.* (**beef·i·er, beef·i·est**). Solid, muscular; stolid. **beef** *v.i.* (slang) Complain, grumble; ~ **up**, (colloq.) to strengthen.

*In the forests of central and southern Europe the nuts of the **beech** tree, or mast, are harvested for their oil. They are also used in some countries as food for pigs.*

Be·el·ze·bub (bēĕl'zebŭb). Canaanite god, mentioned in 2 Kings as the "god of Ekron," and in the New Testament as "prince of demons"; the Devil. [Heb. *ba'al-zebûb* fly lord]

been (bĭn; *Brit.* bēn): see BE.

beep (bēp) *n.* Short high-pitched sound of various devices. ~ *v.* Emit beep. **beep'er** *n.* Device to indicate that telephone conversation is being recorded; pocket paging device; beeping alarm.

beer (bēr) *n.* Alcoholic beverage made from fermented malt flavored with hops; (in trade usage) any of the liquors brewed from malt, as ale, stout, porter, lager.

Beer·bohm (bēr'bōm), **Sir Max** (1872–1956). English author and caricaturist.

beer·y (bēr'ē) *adj.* (**beer·i·er, beer·i·est**). Of or like beer; betraying its influence.

beet (bēt) *n.* Any of several widely cultivated plants with edible roots and leaves sometimes eaten as greens (varieties of *Beta vulgaris*), including sugar beet, garden beet, etc.; the bulbous root of this plant, characteristically dark red in color.

Bee·tho·ven (bā'tōven; *Ger.* bāt'hōfen), **Ludwig van** (1770–1827). German composer of Flemish descent; worked mainly in Vienna; wrote nine symphonies, an opera, many piano sonatas, string quartets, and other orchestral and chamber music.

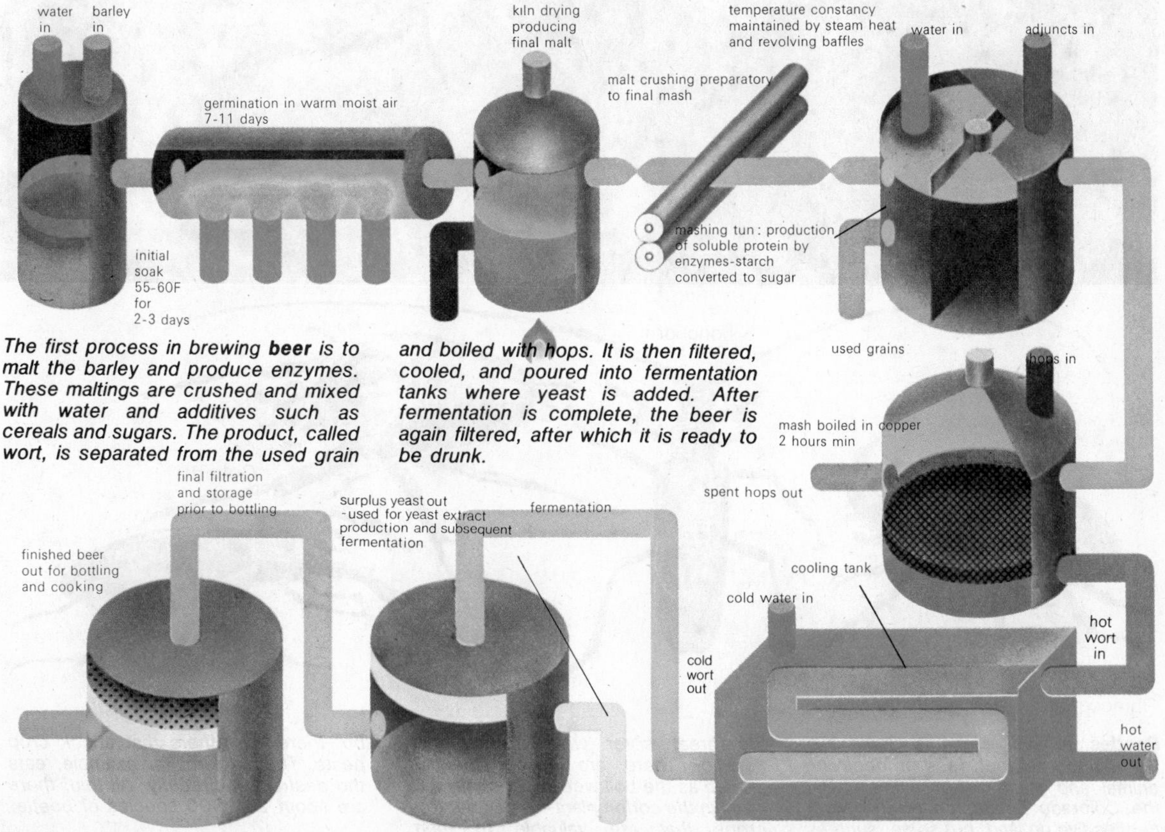

*The first process in brewing **beer** is to malt the barley and produce enzymes. These maltings are crushed and mixed with water and additives such as cereals and sugars. The product, called wort, is separated from the used grain and boiled with hops. It is then filtered, cooled, and poured into fermentation tanks where yeast is added. After fermentation is complete, the beer is again filtered, after which it is ready to be drunk.*

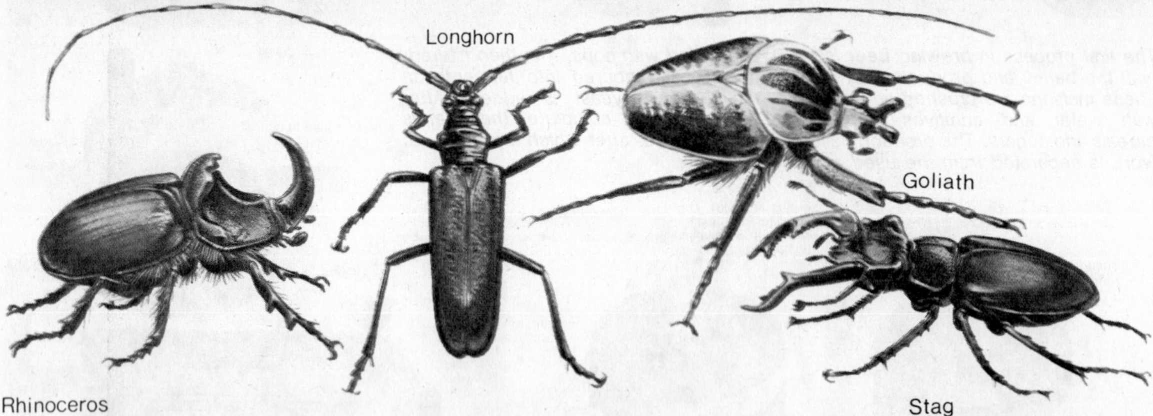

***Beetles** are diverse insects. Some, like the rhinoceros (top), feed on decaying animal and plant matter. Others, like the Colorado beetle, on plants. Most beetles live on land, but some, such as the great silver water beetle, are aquatic. There are several beetles —such as the boll weevil, which lays its eggs in the cotton plant—which destroy crops that are valuable to man, but there are others that attack crop pests. The ladybird, for example, eats the destructive greenfly. All told, there are about 250,000 species of beetle.*

bee·tle[1] (bē'tel) *n.* Tool with handle and heavy head for crushing, ramming, etc., mallet; machine for finishing cloth.

bee·tle[2] (bē'tel) *n.* Any coleopterous insect with front wings converted into hard sheaths or wing cases, which close over the back and protect the lower or true wings; (colloq.) insect resembling these.

bee·tle[3] (bētel) *v.i.* (**-tled, -tling**). Overhang, project. ~ *adj.* (in ~**brows,** ~**-browed**) Projecting, scowling.

B.E.F. *abbrev.* British Expeditionary Force.

be·fall (bĭfawl') *v.* (**-fell, -fall·en, -fall·ing**). Happen, happen to.

be·fit (bĭfĭt') *v.t.* (**-fit·ted, -fit·ting**). Be suited to, become.

be·fog (bĭfŏg', fawg') *v.t.* (**-fogged, -fog·ging**). Envelop in fog; confuse, obscure.

be·fore (bĭfōr', -fōr') *adv.* Ahead; in front; at an earlier time, already. ~ *prep.* In front of, ahead of; in the presence of; earlier than. ~ *conj.* Before the time when; rather than.

be·fore·hand (bĭfōr'hănd, -fōr'-) *adv.* In anticipation; in advance, early.

be·foul (bĭfowl') *v.t.* Make foul or dirty.

be·friend (bĭfrĕnd') *v.t.* Act as a friend to, help.

be·fud·dle (bĭfŭd'el) *v.t.* Make drunk; confuse. **be·fud'dler, be·fud'dle·ment** *ns.*

beg (bĕg) *v.* (**begged, beg·ging**). 1. Ask for (food, money, etc.) as alms or charity; live by alms. 2. Ask earnestly or humbly, entreat. 3. (of dog etc.) Sit up with forepaws raised expectantly. 4. ~ **the question**, take for granted the matter in dispute, assume by implication what one is trying to prove; (pop.) avoid, evade, an issue.

be·gan (bĭgăn'): see BEGIN.

be·get (bĭgĕt') *v.t.* (**be·got** or archaic **be·gat, be·got·ten** or **be·got, be·get·ting**) Procreate, esp. be the father of; give rise to, occasion.

beg·gar (bĕg'er) *n.* One who begs, esp. one who lives by begging; poor person; (colloq.) fellow. ~ *v.t.* Reduce to poverty; exhaust resources of; go beyond, as description. **beg'gar·dom, beg'gar·hood** *ns.*

beg·gar·ly (bĕg'erlē) *adj.* Needy, poverty-stricken; mean, sordid, inadequate. **beg'gar·li·ness** *n.*

beg·gar·y (bĕg'erē) *n.* Extreme poverty.

Beg·hard (bĕg'erd, bĭgărd') *n.* Member of lay brotherhoods which arose in the Low Countries in 13th c.; the name was soon adopted by many who were simply idle mendicants, and the brotherhoods were

*The natural habitat of the **begonia** is in the American tropics, but it is cultivated widely as a bedding plant. Begonias may be grown from seed, or easily propagated from cuttings.*

denounced by popes and councils and persecuted by the Inquisition.

be·gin (bĭgĭn') *v.* (**be·gan, be·gun, be·gin·ning**). Start, perform first part of, set about; be the first; originate; come into being, arise. **be·gin'ner** *n.* (esp.) Tyro, learner. **be·gin'ning** *n.* (esp.) Time at which anything begins; source, origin; first part.

Be·gin (bā'gĭn), **Menachem** 1913–). Prime Minister of Israel, 1977–1985; co-winner of the Nobel Peace Prize, 1978.

be·gird (bĭgērd') *v.t.* (**-girt, -gird·ed, -gird·ing**). Gird, encircle.

be·gone (bĭgawn', -gŏn') *v.imp.* Be off, away with you.

be·gon·ia (bigōn'ya, -gō'nēa) *n.* Tropical plant of genus *B*~, having flowers with brightly colored perianths (but no petals) and often richly colored foliage; often cultivated as an ornamental plant. [Michel *Bégon*, Fr. patron of science (1638–1710)]

be·got·ten (bĭgŏt'en): see BEGET.

be·grime (bĭgrīm') *v.t.* (**-grimed, -grim·ing**). Make grimy.

be·grudge (bĭgrŭj') *v.t.* (**-grudged, -grudg·ing**). Envy the good fortune or pleasure of; be reluctant to give or permit.

be·guile (bĭgīl') *v.t.* (**-guiled, -guil·ing**). Delude; cheat; charm, amuse; divert attention from (passage of time etc.). **be·guil'er** *n.* **be·guil'ing·ly** *adv.* **be·guile'·ment** *n.*

Beg·uine (bĕg'ēn) *n.* Member of certain lay sisterhoods, small communities of which still exist esp. in Belgium, first founded in the Netherlands in the 12th c., who devoted themselves to a religious life but did not bind themselves by strict vows. [f. Lambert *Bègue* (or *le bègue* the stammerer), the founder]

beg·uine (bĭgēn') *n.* A W. Indian native dance; ballroom dance based on this; kind of syncopated bolero dance rhythm.

be·gum (bē'gum) *n.* Indian Muslim woman of high rank. [Turk. *bīgam*, fem. of *beg* lord]

be·gun (bĭgŭn'): see BEGIN.

be·half (bĭhăf', -hahf') *n.* **On** or **in the** ~ **of,** for, as a representative for.

be·have (bĭhāv') *v.i.* & *refl.* (**-haved, -hav·ing**). Act in a particular way (~ **well, badly**, etc.); show good manners.

be·hav·ior, Brit. **be·hav·iour** (bĭhāv'yer) *ns.* Manners, conduct, way of behaving. **be·hav'ior·al** *adj.* ~ **science**, any of various sciences, as sociology or psychology, concerned with human behavior.

be·hav·ior·ism (bĭhāv'yerĭzem) *n.* Psychological doctrine, based on the objective study of behavior, that all human actions admit of analysis into stimulus and response. **be·hav'ior·ist** *n.* & *adj.* **be·hav·ior·is·tic** (bĕhāvyerĭs'tĭk) *adj.*

be·head (bĭhĕd') *v.t.* Cut off the head of.

be·held (bĭhĕld'): see BEHOLD.

be·he·moth (bĭhē'moth, bē'e-) *n.* Enormous creature; in Job 40, prob. the hippopotamus.

be·hest (bĭhĕst') *n.* Command; earnest request, entreaty.

be·hind (bĭhīnd') *adv.* In or to the rear; past, too late; in concealment or unrevealed by; in arrears. ~ *prep.* In or to the rear of; hidden by; supporting. ~ *n.* (colloq.) The buttocks.

be·hind·hand (bĭhīnd'hănd) *adv.* & *pred. adj.* Late; backward, out of date.

Behn (bān), **Mrs. Aphra** (1640–1689). English dramatist and novelist, author of *Oroonoko.*

be·hold (bĭhōld') *v.t.* (**-held, -hold·ing**). (archaic and rhet.) See; take notice, attend. **be·hold'er** *n.*

be·hold·en (bĭhōl'den) *pred. adj.* Under obligation *to.*

be·hoof (bĭhōōf') *n.* (pl. **-hooves** pr. -hōōvz'). (archaic) Benefit, advantage.

be·hoove (bĭhōōv'), **be·hove** (bĭhōv') *vbs.t. impers.* (**-hooved, -hoov·ing**) (**-hoved, -hov·ing**). Be incumbent on; befit.

Behring = BERING.

beige (bāzh) *n.* Yellowish-gray or grayish-brown color of unbleached wool. ~ *adj.* Of color of beige.

Bei·jing (bā'jĭng') = PEKING.

be·ing (bē'ĭng) *n.* (esp.) Existence; constitution, nature, essence, anything that exists; person.

Bei·rut (bārōōt', bā'rōōt). Principal port and the capital of Lebanon, on the E. Mediterranean.

be·jew·el (bĭjōō'el) *v.t.* (**-eled,**

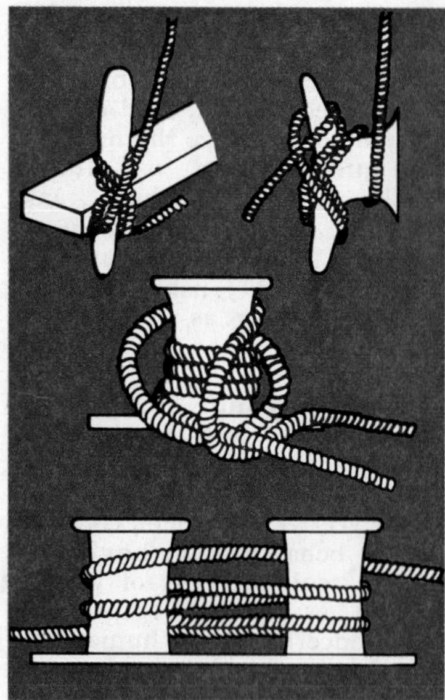

The **belay** (above) is one of the most widely used methods of securing a running rope to a belaying pin, cleat, single bollard or to a twin bollard.

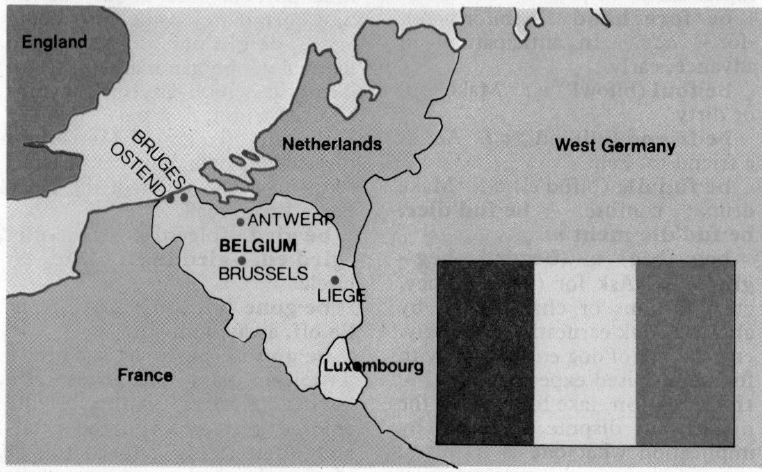

Many of the principal cities of **Belgium**—map and flag (right)— are linked by waterways. Canals like the Speigelrei in Bruges (above right) serve the nation so well that Belgium has become one of the leading countries of Europe in the shipping and transit trade.

-el·ing, Brit. **-elled, -el·ling**). Adorn with jewels.

Bel (bāl, bĕl). (Babylonian and Assyrian myth.) = BAAL.

be·la·bor, Brit. **be·la·bour** (bĭlā´b*er*) *vbs.t.* Thrash, beat repeatedly; discuss at unreasonable length.

be·lat·ed (bĭlā´tĭd) *adj.* Coming late. **be·lat´ed·ly** *adv.* **be·lat´ed·ness** *n.*

be·lay (bĭlā´) *v.t.* (**-layed, -lay·ing**). Coil (running rope) around cleat etc., to secure it; *imp.* (naut.) stop!; **belaying pin**, fixed wooden or iron pin for belaying on.

bel can·to (bĕl´ kăn´tō, kahn´-). Singing in the Italian manner, characterized by full rich tone and accomplished technique. [It.]

belch (bĕlch) *v.* Emit gas noisily from stomach through mouth; utter noisily or drunkenly; (of gun or volcano) emit (fire, smoke, etc.). ~ *n.* Belching.

bel·dam (bĕl´d*a*m), **bel·dame** (bĕl´d*a*m, -dām) *ns.* Old woman, hag; virago.

be·lea·guer (bĭlē´g*er*) *v.t.* Besiege. **be·lea´guered** *adj.* **be·lea´guer·er** *n.*

Be·lém (bĕlĕm´). Port city on the Para River in N. Brazil.

bel·em·nite (bĕl´*e*mnīt) *n.* Common fossil, occurring in Mesozoic rocks, consisting of the hard part of an extinct marine animal similar to the squid, freq. torpedo shaped. [Gk. *belemnon* dart]

Bel·fast (bĕl´făst, -fahst, bĕlfăst´, -fahst´). Seaport in Ulster, capital city of N. Ireland.

bel·fry (bĕl´frē) *n.* (pl **-fries**). Bell tower; room or story in which the bells are hung.

Bel·gian (bĕl´j*a*n) *adj.* & *n.* (Native or inhabitant) of Belgium.

Bel·gium (bĕl´j*u*m). Small kingdom of N.W. Europe, the S. part of the Low Countries (see NETHERLANDS, 2), inhabited by people of French and Flemish stock speaking both languages; established in 1831; capital, Brussels. [L. territory occupied by the *Belgae*]

Bel·grade (bĕlgrād´, bĕl´grād). (Serbo-Croatian *Beograd*) City on the Danube, capital of Yugoslavia.

Bel·gra·vi·a (bĕlgrā´vē*a*). Fashionable residential district of London. [f. *Belgrave* Square, named after Belgrave, England]

Be·li·al (bē´lē*a*l, bēl´y*a*l). 1. (Old Testament) Spirit of evil personified (as **sons of** ~); (2 Cor.) the Devil. 2. (in Milton) Fallen angel representing impurity. [Heb. *b^{e}līyyaʿal* without use, without avail]

be·lie (bĭlī´) *v.t.* (**-lied, -ly·ing**). Show to be false; fail to justify or act up to; give false notion of.

be·lief (bĭlēf´) *n.* Trust, confidence (*in*); acceptance of any received theology; religious tenet; acceptance as true or existing; thing believed.

be·lieve (bĭlēv´) *v.* (**-lieved, -liev·ing**). Have faith (*in*), trust word of; accept as true; suppose, think; be of opinion *that*. **be·liev´a·ble** *adj.* **be·liev´er** *n.* **be·liev´ing·ly** *adv.*

be·lit·tle (bĭlĭt´*e*l) *v.t.* (**-tled, -tling**). Disparage.

Be·lize (bĕlēz´). Formerly

British Honduras; a British Crown Colony in Central America on the Caribbean Sea; capital Belpoman.

bell (bĕl) *n.* 1. Hollow object of cast metal esp. in deep cup shape widening at lip, made to emit clear musical sound when struck by a tongue or clapper suspended inside it or by a hammer impelled by a spring or by electricity etc. 2. Sound of this, esp. as signal; (naut.) **one** to **eight** ~**s**, half-hours of watch, indicated by strokes of bell. 3. Bell-shaped object or part. 4. **bell′bird**, any of several tropical American birds of the family Cotingidae having a bell-like call; **bell-bottomed**, (of trousers) widening from below knee to bottom of leg; **bell′boy**, man employed to carry luggage, run errands, etc., at a hotel; **bell buoy**, buoy with a bell rung by the motion of the sea; **bell glass**, bell jar; **bell′hop**, bellboy; **bell jar**, bell-shaped glass used to protect instruments or contain gases etc. in a laboratory; **bell′-ringing**, ringing a peal of bells in a series of different sequences; **bell′-wether**, leading sheep of flock, with bell on neck (also fig.).

Bell[1] (bĕl), **Alexander Graham** (1847–1922). Scottish-born American inventor of the telephone.

Bell[2] (bĕl), **Currer, Ellis,** and **Acton.** Pen names of Charlotte, Emily, and Anne Brontë.

bel·la·don·na (bĕladŏn′*a*) *n.* Specific name of the deadly nightshade (*Atropa belladonna*), with dark purple flowers and poisonous black berries; dried parts of this, containing atropine and related alkaloids, used as a drug to dilate the pupils; ~ **lily**, amaryllis. [It., = "fair lady"]

Bel·lay (bĕlā′), **Joachim du** (*c*1524–60). French poet and critic.

belle (bĕl) *n.* Handsome woman; reigning beauty.

Bel·leau (bĕl′ō; *Fr.* bĕlō′) **Wood.** Forest near Chateau Thierry, N.E. France; site of 1918 World War I battle during which German drive to Paris was halted by U.S. troops.

Bel·ler·o·phon (belĕr′*o*fŏn). (Gk. legend) Hero who slew the Chimera with the help of Pegasus.

belles-let·tres (bĕl lĕ′tr*e*) *n.pl.* Studies, writings, of a purely literary kind; essays, literary criticism, etc., as a division of literature. **bel·let·rist** (bĕllĕ′trĭst) *n.* **bel·let·ris·tic** (bĕletrĭs′tĭk) *adj.*

bel·li·cose (bĕl′*i*kōs) *adj.* Inclined to war or fighting. **bel′li·cose·ly** *adv.* **bel′li·cose·ness, bel·li·cos·i·ty** (bĕl*i*kŏs′ĭtē) *ns.*

bel·lig·er·ent (belĭj′erent) *adj.* Waging war, bellicose. ~ *n.* Belligerent nation, party, or person. **bel·lig′er·en·cy** *n.* **bel·lig′er·ent·ly** *adv.*

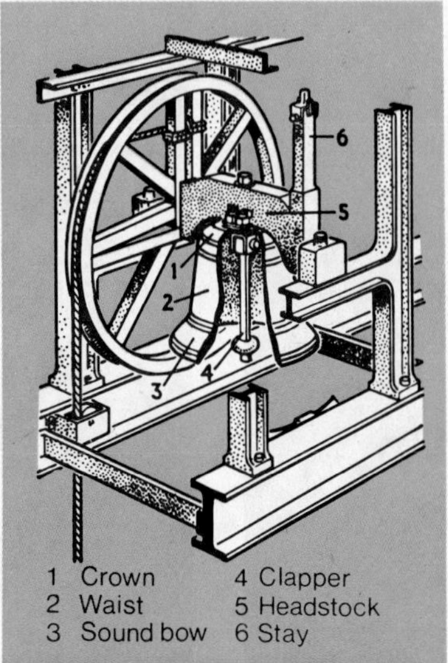

*The **bell** (above) is turned through a full circle and produces a more resonant sound than a bell played by the carillon method, where the clapper strikes the bell while it is held steady.*

Bel·li·ni[1] (b*e*lē′nē; *It.* bĕlē′nē), **Giovanni** (*c*1435–1516). Italian painter of the Venetian School; his father **Jacopo** (*c*1400–70) and brother **Gentile** (1429?–1507) were also painters.

Bel·li·ni[2] (b*e*lē′nē; *It.* bĕlē′nē), **Vincenzo** (1801–35). Italian composer of operas.

Bel·loc (bĕl′*o*k, -ŏk), **Joseph Hilaire Pierre** (1870–1953). English essayist, novelist, and poet, born in France.

Bel·lo·na (b*e*lō′n*a*). (Rom. myth.) Goddess of war.

bel·low (bĕl′ō) *v.* Roar as a bull; shout, roar, bawl with pain; shout loudly and angrily. ~ *n.* Bellowing sound. **bel′low·er** *n.*

Bel·low (bĕl′ō), **Saul** (1915–). American novelist; awarded Nobel Prize for literature, 1976; author of *Adventures of Augie March, Herzog,* etc.

bel·lows (bĕl′ōz) *n.pl.* 1. Instrument or machine for driving strong blast of air into fire, organ, etc., in its simplest form consisting of a pair of boards joined by flexible leather sides, with a valve through which air enters when the boards are moved apart, and a nozzle or tube through which air is forced as they are brought together. 2. Expandable portion of folding camera.

Bel·lows (bĕl′ōz), **George Wesley** (1882–1925). American realistic painter and lithographer; his most famous lithographs depict boxing scenes.

bel·ly (bĕl′ē) *n.* (pl. **-lies**). Abdomen; stomach; underpart of animal; underside, cavity, or bulging part of anything; **bel′lyache,** pain in abdomen or stomach, as from eating foods that disagree with one; (*v.i.*, slang) complain; **bel′ly-button,** (colloq.) navel; **belly dance,** erotic oriental dance involving movements of the abdominal muscles; so **belly dancer; belly flop,** (*n.*, colloq.) dive in which abdomen hits the water (also **belly flopper**); **bel′lyful,** (colloq.) as much as one can tolerate; **belly-landing,** (of aircraft) crash-landing on underside of fuselage; **belly laugh,** (colloq.) deep unrestrained laugh. **belly** *v.* (**-lied, -ly·ing**). Swell out.

Bel·mon·te (bĕlmawn′tē), **Juan** (1893–1962). Spanish bullfighter; known as the father of modern bullfighting.

be·long (bĭlawng′, -lŏng′) *v.i.* Have a rightful or appropriate place or position; fit an environment etc.; ~ **to**, (esp.) be a member or adherent etc. of; be a possession of. **be·long·ings** (bĭlawng′ĭngz, -lŏng′-) *n.pl.* Person's movable property etc.

Be·lo·rus·sia (byĕl*o*rŭsh′*a*, bĕl*o*-) = Byelorussia.

be·lov·ed (bĭlŭv′ĭd, -lŭvd′) *adj.* Dearly loved; ~ *n.* Beloved person.

be·low (bĭlō′) *adv.* At or to a lower level or part; in a lower position or rank; on earth (rather than up in heaven). ~ *prep.* Lower in position, amount, degree, rank, etc., than; unworthy of, beneath.

Bel·shaz·zar (bĕlshăz′*er*). (also **Balthazar**) Acc. to Old Testament (Dan. 5), son of Nebuchadnezzar and last king of Babylon, who was killed in the sack of the city by Cyrus (538 B.C.); but in inscriptions and documents from Ur, Belshazzar was the son of the last king of Babylon, Nabonidos, and did not himself reign.

belt (bĕlt) *n.* 1. Broadish flat strip of leather etc., used to gird or encircle the person, confine some part of the dress, or support various articles; such an article awarded to boxing champion or sash worn as a mark of rank, as by a knight or earl. 2. Strip of color etc., line of trees, around or on anything; zone or district; endless band to connect pulleys in machinery or to transmit motion, convey objects, etc.; flexible strip holding machine gun cartridges and carrying them to firing chamber. 3. (slang) A hard blow, hit; (slang) a drink of liquor; (slang) a thrill. ~ *v.* Put belt around, fasten with belt; (slang) give a hard blow (to); (slang) drink (liquor); (slang) sing (a song) loudly.

be·lu·ga (b*e*lo͞o′g*a*) *n.* White sturgeon, valued as a source of caviar; white whale.

bel·ve·dere (bĕl′v*e*dēr) *n.* Raised turret or lantern, summer house, to view scenery from. [It. =

Monte Cassino, once a pagan shrine, was chosen by **St. Benedict of Nursia** for the site of his abbey. The building was destroyed in the 1939–45 war and subsequently rebuilt.

Above right: The Church's tradition of fine craftsmanship is maintained. The **Benedictine** monks of Prinknash Abbey, Gloucestershire (now Avon), England show vestments to visitors.

"fine view"]

Be·mel·mans (bē'melmanz, bĕm'el-), **Ludwig** (1898–1962). Austrian-born American painter, illustrator, and writer.

be·moan (bĭmōn') *v.t.* Lament.

be·muse (bĭmūz') *v.t.* (**-mused, -mus·ing**). Cause to be preoccupied, esp. to point of confusion; (pop.) amuse. **be·mused'** *adj.*

Be·nar·es (benar̄'ĭs, -ēz) = VARANASI.

bench (bĕnch) *n.* 1. Long seat for several persons. 2. Judge's or official's seat; office of judge, law court (**King's ~, Queen's ~**); **on the ~**, serving as judge; (sports) (team member) not participating in the game. 3. Working table in carpenter's shop, laboratory, etc., workbench; **~ mark**, surveyor's mark put on stone etc. to indicate a point of known elevation; **~ warrant**, one issued by a judge. ~ *v.t.* Exhibit (dog) at show; (sports) remove (player) from a game. **bench'less** *adj.*

Bench·ley (bĕnch'lē), **Robert Charles** (1889–1945). American humorist; wrote for *Vanity Fair*, *Life*, and *New Yorker* magazines.

bend[1] (bĕnd) *n.* 1. (naut.) Knot. 2. (her.) Diagonal band from upper right (dexter) to lower left (sinister) of shield; **~ sinister**, bend in the opposite direction, a mark of bastardy.

bend[2] (bĕnd) *v.* (**bent,** archaic **bend·ed, bend·ing**). 1. Force into, receive, curved or angular shape. 2. Attach (sail etc.) with bend or knot. 3. Turn in a particular direction. 4. Incline from perpendicular; bow, stoop, submit, force to submit. 5. Direct, apply (oneself) *to*. 6. Modify or interpret (law, rule, etc.) for one's own purposes. ~ *n.* 1. Bending, curve; bent part. 2. (pl.) Caisson disease. 3. **round the ~**, (Brit. slang) insane. **bend'a·ble** *adj.*

bend·ed (bĕn'dĭd) *adj.* (of knee) Bent.

bend·er (bĕn'der) *n.* (slang) Drinking spree.

be·neath (bĭnēth') *adv.* & *prep.* Below, under, underneath; ~ **one's contempt**, not even worth despising.

ben·e·dict (bĕn'edĭkt) *n.* Newly married man, esp. one who has long been a bachelor. [*Benedick*, in Shakespeare's *Much Ado About Nothing*]

The full economic union of the **Benelux** countries—map below— was gradually established by a series of treaties. The first was signed in 1922, followed by a customs union in 1947, and a final treaty in 1960.

Ben·e·dict (bĕn'edĭkt), **St.** (c480–543). Italian monk, founder (529) of the first of the monastic orders of the Western Church, for which he built the abbey of Monte Cassino.

Ben·e·dic·tine (bĕnedĭk'tĭn, **-tēn, -tīn** for *adj.* & *n.* 1; bĕnedĭk'tēn for *n.* 2) *adj.* Of the order of St. Benedict; ~ **Rule**, rule written for it by St. Benedict, later adopted by other monastic communities. **Benedictine** *n.* 1. Benedictine monk. 2. Liqueur of brandy flavored with herbs etc., made at Fécamp in Normandy, orig. by the monks of the Benedictine abbey there.

ben·e·dic·tion (bĕnedĭk'shon) *n.* Utterance of blessing, at end of religious service, or at table. **ben·e·dic'tion·al, ben·e·dic'to·ry** *adjs.*

ben·e·fac·tion (bĕnefăk'shon, bĕn'efăk-) *n.* Doing good; charitable gift.

ben·e·fac·tor (bĕn'efăkter, bĕnefăk'-) *n.* Person who has given friendly aid; patron of, or donor to, cause or charity.

ben·e·fice (bĕn'efĭs) *n.* (eccles.) Material livelihood of incumbent of a parish; rectory, vicarage, or perpetual curacy. ~ *v.* (**-ficed, -fic·ing**). Provide with a benefice.

be·nef·i·cent (bĕnĕf'ĭsent) *adj.* Doing good, showing active kindness. **be·nef'i·cence** *n.* **be·nef'i·cent·ly** *adv.*

ben·e·fi·cial (bĕnefĭsh'al) *adj.* 1. Advantageous. 2. (law) Of, having the right to receive proceeds or other advantages, as from property. **ben·e·fi'cial·ly** *adv.*

ben·e·fi·ci·ar·y (bĕnefĭsh'ēērē, -fĭsh'erē) *n.* (pl. **-ar·ies**). Receiver of benefits; recipient of funds etc., under a will, insurance policy, or

The view of ***Ben Nevis,*** *Inverness-shire, (now part of Highland), Scotland, seen from the bank of the Caledonian Canal. It is the highest peak in the British Isles, 4,406 ft.*

trust.

ben·e·fit (bĕn′efĭt) *n.* 1. Advantage. 2. Allowance, pension, etc. to which person is entitled; e.g. during sickness, unemployment, etc. 3. Theater performance, game, etc., of which proceeds go to particular players or charity. ~ *v.* (**-fit·ed, -fit·ing**). Do good to; receive benefit. **ben′e·fit·er** *n.*

Ben·e·lux (bĕn′elŭks). Collective name for *Be*lgium, the *Ne*therlands, and *Lux*emburg, esp. with reference to their economic collaboration.

Be·nét (benā′), **William Rose** (1886–1950). American editor and writer; his brother, **Stephen Vincent** (1898–1943), poet and short story writer; Pulitzer Prize winner, 1929; author of *The Devil and Daniel Webster*, *John Brown's Body*, etc.

be·nev·o·lent (benĕv′olent) *adj.* Desirous of doing good; charitable. **be·nev′o·lent·ly** *adv.* **be·nev′o·lence** *n.*

Ben·gal (bĕngawl′, bĕnggawl′, bĕn′gal, bĕng′-). District of the Ganges delta, formerly a province of British India, divided into **West** ~, a state of India (capital, Calcutta), and Bangladesh; **Bay of** ~, part of Indian Ocean lying between Indian peninsula and Burma; **Bengal tiger**, the tiger proper, so called from its abundance in lower Bengal.

Ben·gal·i (bĕngaw′lē, bĕnggaw′lē) *adj.* & *n.* (Of) the Indo-European language spoken in Bengal; (native) of Bengal.

Ben-Gur·i·on (bĕngoor′ēon), **David** (1886–1973). Polish-born first Prime Minister of Israel, 1948–1953 and 1955–63.

be·nign (bĭnīn′) *adj.* Kind, gracious, gentle; beneficial, favorable; (path., of disease) mild, not malignant; (of tumor) not cancerous, displacing but not destroying surrounding tissue (opp. MALIGNANT).

be·nig·nant (bĭnĭg′nant) *adj.* Kind, kindly, to inferiors; gracious; beneficial. **be·nig′nan·cy** (pl. **-cies**), **be·nig′ni·ty** (pl. **-ties**) *ns.* **be·nig′nant·ly** *adv.*

Be·nin (benēn′). Formerly Dahomey, republic in W. Africa; independent since 1960; capital, Porto Novo.

ben·i·son (bĕn′ĭzon, -son) *n.* (archaic) Blessing.

Ben·ja·min (bĕn′jamĭn). Hebrew patriarch, youngest and favorite son of Jacob (Gen. 35); smallest tribe of Israel, traditionally descended from him.

Ben·nett (bĕn′ĭt), **Enoch Arnold** (1867–1931). English novelist; author of *The Old Wives' Tale* etc.

Ben Ne·vis (bĕn nē′vĭs, nĕv′ĭs). Mountain in the Grampians, Scotland, the highest peak (4,406 ft. 1,343 m) in the British Isles.

Ben·ning·ton (bĕn′ĭngton). Town in S. Vermont, near site of Revolutionary War battle (1777) in which Americans defeated the British.

ben·ny (bĕn′ē) *n.* (pl. **-nies**). (slang) An amphetamine tablet.

bent[1] (bĕnt) *n.* Reedy or rushlike stiff-stemmed grass of various kinds; old stalk, of grasses; heath, unenclosed pasture.

bent[2] (bĕnt) *n.* Inclination, bias.

bent[3] (bĕnt) *adj.*: see BEND[2] *v.* (esp.) curved, crooked; (slang) dishonest, perverted.

Ben·tham (bĕn′tham, -tam), **Jeremy** (1748–1832). English Utilitarian philosopher, reformer, and writer on ethics, jurisprudence, and political economy; he believed that the highest morality is the pursuit of the greatest happiness of the greatest number. **Ben′tham·ism, Ben′tham·ite** *ns.*

Ben·ton (bĕn′ton), **Thomas Hart** (1889–). American painter and muralist; known for realistic paintings of ordinary people and scenes of life in the Midwest and South.

be·numb (bĭnŭm′) *v.t.* Make torpid; paralyze.

Benz (bĕnts), **Karl Friedrich** (1844–1929). German engineer and pioneer in the construction of motor-driven vehicles; built first gasoline-powered automobile, 1885.

Ben·ze·drine (bĕn′zedrēn, -drĭn) *n.* (trademark) Amphetamine.

ben·zene (bĕn′zēn, bĕnzēn′) *n.* (chem.) Aromatic hydrocarbon (C_6H_6), a colorless, volatile, and highly inflammable liquid obtained from coal tar etc., used as a solvent and in the chemical industry; ~ **ring**, ring-like hexagon arrangement of the six carbon atoms in the benzene molecule.

ben·zine (bĕn′zēn, bĕnzēn′) *n.* Mixture of hydrocarbons obtained from petroleum and used as a solvent, for removing grease stains etc.

ben·zo·caine (bĕn′zokān) *n.* White crystalline ester used as a local anesthetic.

ben·zo·in (bĕn′zōĭn, -zoin, bĕnzō′ĭn) *n.* 1. (also **gum** ~) Fragrant aromatic resin obtained from various trees of the genus *Styrax* from Sumatra and Thailand, and used in perfumery, medicine, etc. 2. (chem.) Constituent of gum benzoin. **ben·zo·ic** (bĕnzō′ĭk) *adj.* (chem.) Of or derived from benzoin or benzoic acid; **benzoic acid**, benzene carboxylic acid (C_6H_5COOH). [Fr. *benjoin* f. Arab. *lubān jāwī* Java frankincense]

ben·zol (bĕn′zōl, -zawl, -zŏl) *n.* (obs.) Benzene.

Be·o·wulf (bā′owo͝olf). Legendary Swedish hero celebrated in the Old English epic poem *Beowulf*, anonymous, believed to have been written in northern England between 650 and 750 A.D.

be·queath (bĭkwēdh′, -kwēth′) *v.t.* Leave by will; hand down. **be·queath′a·ble** *adj.*, **be·queath′al, be·queath′ment** *ns.*

be·quest (bĭkwĕst′) *n.* Bequeathing; thing bequeathed, legacy.

be·rate (bĭrāt′) *v.t.* (**-rat·ed, -rat·ing**). Scold.

Ber·ber (bẽr′ber) *adj.* & *n.* (Member) of a fair-skinned aboriginal people of N. Africa.

ber·ceuse (bĕrsöz′) *n.* (pl. **-ceuses** pr. *Fr.* -söz′). Lullaby; composition in style of this.

Berch·tes·ga·den (bĕrx′tesgah′den). Resort town in SE. West Germany, 10 miles S. of Salzburg, Austria: Adolf Hitler maintained a

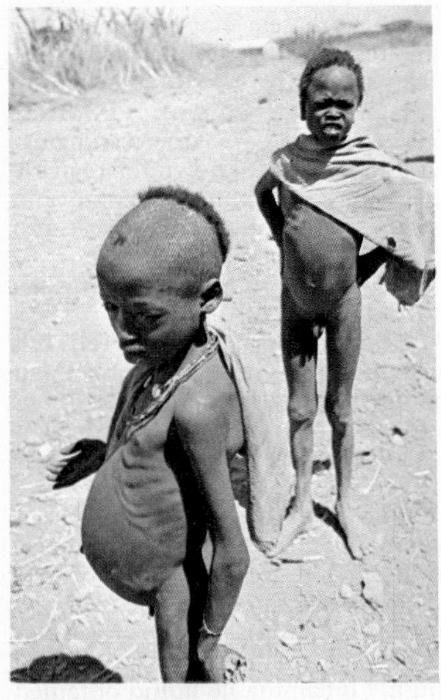

*The Kenyan child (above) has symptoms of **beriberi,** probably caused by a diet of highly refined grain. If left untreated, the condition may cause paralysis and death, but it can be cured with large doses of thiamine.*

*The Brandenburg Gate (above) was one of the few monuments of old **Berlin** to survive the devastation of the 1939–45 war. The Gate stands on the city's East/West boundary, established in 1945.*

retreat here during World War II.

be·reave (bĭrēv′) *v.t.* (**-reaved** or **-reft, -reav·ing**). 1. Deprive *of* ruthlessly or by force. 2. Deprive by death of relation, wife, etc.; leave desolate. **be·reave′ment** *n.*

beret (berā′) *n.* (pl. **berets** pr. berāz′). Round flat visorless cloth cap, worn orig. by Basque farmers.

berg (bẽrg) *n.* Iceberg (see ICE, def. 3).

ber·ga·mot[1] (bẽr′gamŏt) *n.* 1. Small, spiny tree (*Citrus bergamia*) bearing sour pear-shaped fruit; fragrant oil (also called ~ **oil**) extracted from its fruit. 2. Any of various plants of the family Labiatae, esp. *Monarda* species. [f. *Bergamo* in Italy]

ber·ga·mot[2] (bẽr′gamŏt) *n.* Fine kind of pear. [Turk. *beg* prince, *armūdī* pear]

Ber·gen (bĕr′gen). Seaport and the second largest city in Norway, in the SW.

Ber·ge·rac (bẽr′zherăk), **Cyrano de** (1619–55). French soldier and author of comedies; said to have fought over 1,000 duels.

Berg·man (bẽrg′man), **Ingmar** (1918–). Swedish writer of screenplays and director of motion pictures.

berg·schrund (bĕrk′shrŏont) *n.* Crevasse or gap at head of glacier, separating moving ice from stationary ice.

Berg·son (bẽrg′son; *Fr.* bĕrgsawṅ′), **Henri** (1859–1941). French philosopher who regarded reality as change and movement, "becoming" rather than "being." **Berg·so·ni·an** (bẽrgsō′nēan) *adj.* & *n.*

ber·i·ber·i (bĕr′ēbĕr′e) *n.* Disease of the peripheral nervous system caused by deficiency of vitamin B_1 in diet and characterized by emaciation, anemia, and partial paralysis of the extremities. [Sinhalese *beri* weakness]

Ber·ing, Behr·ing (bār′ĭng, bĕr′-, bẽr′-), **Vitus Jonassen** (1680–1741). Danish navigator who explored Arctic seas on behalf of Russia; ~ **Sea**, northernmost part of Pacific between Alaska and Siberia; ~ **Strait**, strait between Asia and America, connecting Bering Sea with Arctic Ocean.

Berke·ley[1] (bẽrk′lē). City in N. California on San Francisco Bay across from San Francisco.

Berke·ley[2] (bẽrk′lē; *Brit.*bärk′lē), **George** (1685–1753). Irish Protestant bishop and idealist philosopher, active in America (1728–31). **Berke·le′ian** *adj.* & *n.*

berke·li·um (bẽrk′lē*u*m, *ber*kē′-) *n.* (chem.) Metallic radioactive synthetic element; symbol Bk, at. no. 97, principal isotope at. wt. 243. [*Berkeley*, Calif., where first made]

Ber·lin (bẽrlĭn′; *Ger.* bĕrlēn′). Chief city of Germany; on river Spree; capital of Germany from 1871; since 1945 divided into **East** ~, capital of East Germany, and **West** ~, an isolated part of West Germany. ~ **wall**, Soviet- and East German-built wall dividing East and West Berlin. **Ber·lin′er** *n.* Native, inhabitant, of Berlin.

ber·lin (bẽrlĭn, bẽr′lĭn) *n.* Four-wheeled covered carriage with hooded seat behind, invented in Berlin in 17th c., popular in France and England in the 18th c.

Ber·li·oz (bĕr′lēōz), **Hector** (1803–69). French composer of operas, symphonic works, etc.

*The first journeys of **Vitus Bering** carried him north to the straits subsequently named after him. On his last voyage he crossed from the Siberian coast to Alaska.*

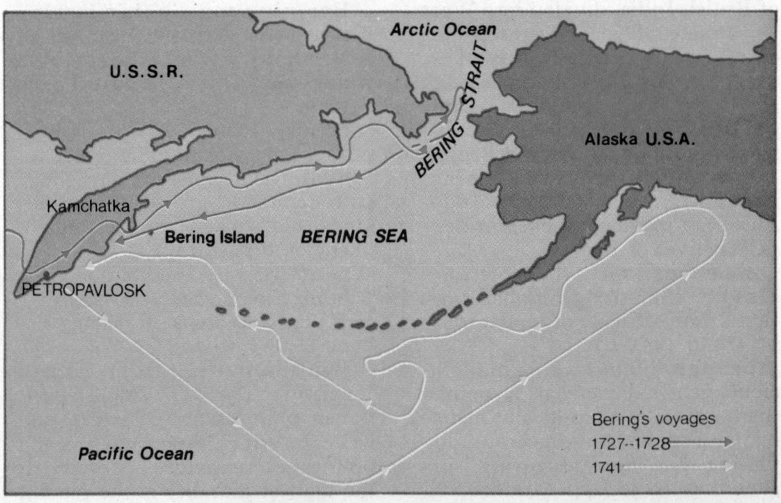

*The 'divine Sarah', as Oscar Wilde called **Sarah Bernhardt,** was the chief romantic and classical actress of the French stage from about 1870 to 1915. Mucha painted posters for her plays.*

berm, berme (bẽrm) *ns.* Narrow space or ledge; (esp., fort.) space between ditch and parapet.

Ber·mu·da (bermū'da). (also ~ **Islands, Bermudas**) Group of over 350 small islands in W. Atlantic about 570 miles (917 km) SE. of North Carolina; a British colony with a total area of about 21 square miles; capital, Hamilton; ~ **grass**, wiry grass (*Cynodon dactylon*) used for lawns and pasturage in warm regions; ~ **onion**, large, mild, yellow-skinned variety of onion; ~ **rig**, fore-and-aft rig carrying a tall triangular mainsail, used on cruising and racing yachts; ~ **shorts**, (also **Bermudas**) knee-length shorts. **Ber·mu'di·an** *adj.* & *n.*

Bern (bẽrn; *Fr.* & *Ger.* běrn). (also **Berne**) Canton and capital city of Switzerland. **Ber·nese** (bẽrnēz', -nēs') *adj.* & *n.*

Ber·na·dette (bẽr'nadět, bernadět'), **St.** (1844–79). Original name, Marie Bérnarde Soubirous; French peasant girl of Lourdes, France, who claimed to have seen the Virgin Mary; a shrine was subsequently established at LOURDES.

***Bernini** was the leading sculptor of the Italian baroque. He worked for most of his life for papal patrons, and like the 'Fountain of the Rivers' shown here almost all his sculpture is to be found in Rome.*

Ber·na·dotte[1] (bẽr'nadŏt), **Count Folke** (1895–1948). Swedish humanitarian; assassinated while acting as United Nations mediator in Palestine.

Ber·na·dotte[2] (bẽr'nadŏt; *Fr.* běrnădawt'), **Jean Baptiste** (1763–1844). French soldier; one of Napoleon's marshals; was adopted by Charles XIII of Sweden in 1810 and himself became king (as Charles XIV) in 1818, thus founding the present royal house.

Ber·nard[1] (bernard'; *Fr.* běrnăr'), **St.** (923–1008). Priest of Menthon; founder of the Alpine hospices of the Great and Little St. Bernard; **St. ~ (dog)**, dog of large and intelligent breed, of the mastiff type, usu. light brown and white, orig. bred by the monks of the St. Bernard hospices and trained to search for travelers lost in the snowdrifts of the Alpine passes.

Ber·nard[2] (bernard'; *Fr.* běrnăr'), **St.** (1090–1153). French churchman, first abbot of Clairvaux; he reformed the Cistercian Order and preached the 2nd Crusade.

Ber·nard[3] (bernard; *Fr.* běrnăr'), **Claude** (1813–78). French physiologist; famous for his research on the pancreas and the glycogenic function of the liver, and his discovery of the vasomotor system.

Berne = BERN.

Bern·hardt (bẽrn'hart, běrn'-), **Sarah.** Name adopted by the French romantic and tragic actress Rosine Bernard (1845–1923).

Ber·ni·ni (bernē'nē; *It.* běrnē'nē), **Giovanni Lorenzo** (1598–1680). Italian baroque architect and sculptor; designer of the colonnade of St. Peter's in Rome.

Ber·noul·li (bernōō'lē). Surname of Swiss family including several eminent mathematicians and scientists, including **Jacob** or **James** (1654–1705) and **Daniel** (1700–82); ~ **effect**, the decrease in pressure of a fluid as its velocity increases; **~'s law**, statement of this relation, (essentially = CONSERVATION OF ENERGY). [from Daniel *Bernoulli*]

Bern·stein (bẽrn'stīn, -stēn), **Leonard** (1918–). American conductor, composer, and pianist.

ber·ry (běr'ē) *n.* (pl. **-ries**). 1. Any small round or oval juicy fruit without a stone; dry seed or kernel (of wheat etc.). 2. (bot.) Fruit of any size with seed(s) enclosed in pulp.

ber·serk (bersẽrk', -zẽrk') *adj.* & *adv.* Destructively or frenetically violent; deranged; **go** ~, behave thus. [Icel., prob. = "bearcoat" as worn by a *berserkr*, a fierce warrier]

berth (bẽrth) *n.* 1. Convenient searoom; room for ship to swing at anchor; ship's place at wharf; **give a wide ~ to**, avoid. 2. Sleeping place in ship, railroad car, etc. 3. Job, appointment. ~ *v.t.* Moor (ship).

ber·yl (běr'el) *n.* Transparent precious stone of pale green color or of light blue, yellow, or white, chemically beryllium aluminum silicate, the chief ore of beryllium.

be·ryl·li·um (berĭl'ēum) *n.* (chem.) Very light metallic element obtained from beryl; symbol Be, at. no. 4, at. wt. 9.01218.

bes·ant = BEZANT.

Bes·ant (běz'ant), **Mrs. Annie** (1847–1933). English writer, socialist and agnostic; became president of the Theosophical Society in 1907; active in the cause of Indian self-government.

be·seech (bĭsēch′) *v.t.* (**-seeched** or **-sought** pr. -sawt′, **-seech·ing**). Ask earnestly for; entreat.

be·set (bĭsĕt′) *v.t.* (**-set, -set·ting**). Hem in, surround; harass constantly.

be·side (bĭsīd′) *prep.* At the side of, close to; compared with; wide of; ~ **oneself**, strongly moved by emotion.

be·sides (bĭsīdz′) *adv.* In addition; otherwise, else. ~ *prep.* In addition to; except.

be·siege (bĭsēj′) *v.t.* (**-sieged, -sieg·ing**). Lay siege to; assail, crowd around. **be·sieg′er** *n.*

be·smear (bĭsmēr′) *v.t.* Smear, bedaub.

be·smirch (bĭsmērch′) *v.t.* Soil; sully. **be·smirch′er, be·smirch′ment** *ns.*

be·som (bē′zom) *n.* Bundle of twigs tied around stick for sweeping.

be·sot·ted (bĭsŏt′ĭd) *adj.* Stupefied (esp. with drink).

be·sought (bĭsawt′): see BESEECH.

be·spat·ter (bĭspăt′*er*) *v.t.* Spatter; slander.

be·speak (bĭspēk′) *v.t.* (**-spoke, -spok·en, -speak·ing**). (Brit.) Engage beforehand; order; speak to (poet.); indicate, be evidence of. **be·spoke′** *v.* & *adj.* Ordered (now only in ~ **tailoring, footwear**, etc., opp. ready-made, or of tradesman making goods to order).

be·sprin·kle (bĭsprĭng′kel) *v.t.* (**-kled, -kling**). Sprinkle.

Bes·sa·ra·bi·a (bĕs*a*rā′bē*a*). Former Rumanian region now part of the Moldavian S.S.R.

Bes·se·mer (bĕs′*e*mer), **Sir Henry** (1813–98). English engineer; inventor of ~ **process**, process for making steel (~ **steel**) in which iron is decarbonized by blowing a blast of air through the molten metal in a large pear-shaped metal container (~ **converter**).

best (bĕst) *adj.* (superl. of *good*). Of the most excellent kind; most advantageous, desirable, or serviceable; ~ **man**, bridegroom's chief attendant at wedding; the ~ **part**, most; ~ **seller**, book with large sale, esp. one that is among those having the largest sales during a given period. **best** *adv.* (superl. of *well*) In the most excellent way etc.; **had** ~, would find it wisest. ~ *n.* That which is best; (collect.) most excellent persons, (colloq.) kindest regards; **at** ~, under the most favorable circumstances; **for the** ~, with good intentions or outcome; **get the** ~ **of**, gain the advantage over, defeat; **make the** ~ **of**, manage as well as one can under adverse circumstances.

bes·tial (bĕs′ch*a*l, bĕst′y*a*l) *adj.* Of, like a beast; brutish, barbarous; depraved, obscene. **bes·ti·al·i·ty** (bĕschēăl′ĭtē, tēăl′) *n.* (pl. **-ties**). (esp. law) Crime of person having sexual intercourse with animal. **bes′tial·ly** *adv.* **bes′tial·ize** *v.t.* (**-ized, -iz·ing**).

bes·ti·ar·y (bĕs′chēērē, -tē-) *n.* (pl. **-ar·ies**). Medieval moralizing treatise on beasts. **bes·ti·a·rist** (bĕs′chēerĭst, -tē-, -che-) *n.*

be·stir (bĭstēr′) *v.refl.* (**-stirred, -stir·ring**). Exert, rouse.

be·stow (bĭstō′) *v.t.* Confer as gift. **be·stow′a·ble** *adj.* **be·stow′al, be·stow′er, be·stow′ment** *ns.*

be·strew (bĭstrōō′) *v.t.* (**-strewed, -strewn, -strew·ing**). Strew.

be·stride (bĭstrīd′) *v.t.* (**-strode** pr. -strōd, **-strid·den** pr. -strĭd′*e*n, **-strid·ing**). Get or sit upon with legs astride; stand astride over.

bet (bĕt) *v.* (**bet, bet·ted, bet·ting**). Risk one's money etc. against another's on result of doubtful event; (loosely) think, reckon (something to be true etc.); ~ *n.* Act of betting; money etc. so risked; thing, event, etc. bet on.

be·ta (bā′t*a*; *Brit.* bē′t*a*) *n.* Second letter of Gk. alphabet (B, β), corresponding to *b*, used of the 2nd star in a constellation; and in other classifications; ~ **particles**, fast-moving electrons emitted by radioactive substances, orig. regarded as rays (~ **rays**) and having greater penetrating power than alpha particles and less than gamma rays.

be·take (bĭtāk′) *v.refl.* (**-took** pr. -tŏŏk, **-tak·en, -tak·ing**). (archaic) Commit (oneself) *to* some cause or means; go.

be·ta·tron (bā′t*a*trŏn) *n.* (phys.) Apparatus for accelerating electrons.

be·tel (bē′t*e*l) *n.* Shrubby East Indian pepper plant (*Piper betle*); leaf of this plant, which is wrapped around parings of areca nut and chewed by people of India etc. for stimulating and narcotic effects; hence ~ **nut**, areca nut. [Malayalam *vettila*]

Be·tel·geuse, Be·tel·geux (bē′t*e*ljōōz, bĕt′*e*ljöz) *ns.* Yellowish-red variable star, the brightest in the

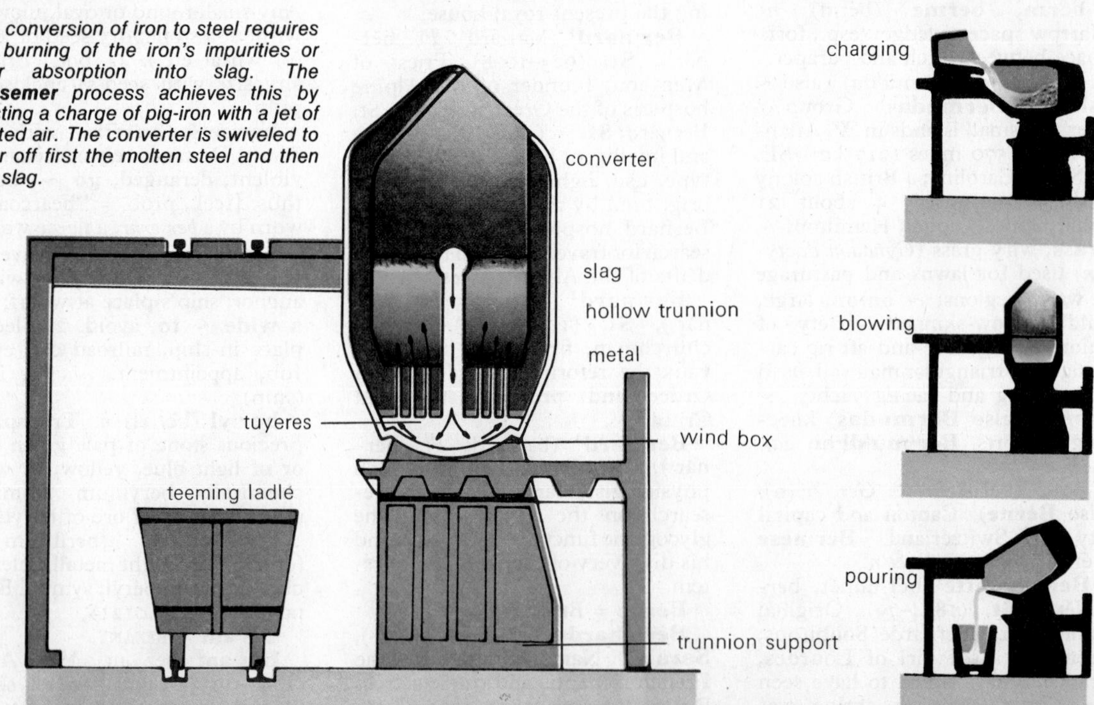

The conversion of iron to steel requires the burning of the iron's impurities or their absorption into slag. The ***Bessemer*** *process achieves this by blasting a charge of pig-iron with a jet of heated air. The converter is swiveled to pour off first the molten steel and then the slag.*

Containing one of the world's great shrines, ***Bethlehem*** *is situated on a slope overlooking the Dead Sea. Many of its inhabitants make a living from pilgrims to the shrine.*

constellation of Orion.

bête noire (bāt nwar̄'; *Fr.* bĕt nwăr') (pl. **bêtes noires** pr. bāt nwar̄z'; *Fr.* bĕt nwăr'). Person or thing one particularly dislikes or dreads. [Fr.]

Beth·a·ny (bĕth'anē). Village near Jerusalem where Lazarus was raised from the dead by Christ (John 11).

Beth·el (bĕth'*el*, bĕthĕl'). Town near Jerusalem, considered a holy place after JACOB's dream there. [Heb., = "house of God"; Gen. 28]

beth·el (bĕth'*el*) *n.* Hallowed spot; seamen's church (ashore or floating).

be·think (bĭthĭngk') *v.refl.* (**-thought** pr. -thawt', **-think·ing**). (archaic) Reflect, stop to think; remind oneself.

Beth·le·hem (bĕth'lĭhĕm, -lēem). Town near Jerusalem; birthplace of Jesus Christ.

Be·thune (bĕthūn'), **Mary McLeod** (1875–1955). American educator; president of Bethune-Cookman College from 1923.

be·tide (bĭtīd') *v.* (**-tid·ed, -tid·ing**). (archaic) Happen, befall.

be·times (bĭtīmz') *adv.* Early; in good time.

Bet·je·man (bĕch'*e*man), **Sir John** (1906–1984). English poet, poet laureate, 1972.

be·to·ken (bĭtō'ken) *v.t.* Be token of; presage; indicate. **be·to'ken·er** *n.*

bet·o·ny (bĕt'*o*nē) *n.* (pl. **-nies**). Labiate plant (*Stachys officinalis*), with spike of reddish-purple flowers.

be·tray (bĭtrā') *v.t.* Give up or reveal treacherously; be disloyal or unfaithful to; lead astray; (archaic) seduce and desert (a woman); reveal involuntarily; be evidence or symptom of. **be·tray'al, be·tray'er** *ns.*

be·troth (bĭtrōdh', -trawth') *v.t.* Bind with a promise to marry. **be·troth'al** *n.* **be·trothed'** *adj.* & *n.*

bet·ter (bĕt'*er*) *adj.* (comp. of *good*). Of a more excellent kind; superior use or value, etc.; larger, greater; ~ **half** (joc.) wife; ~ **part**, greater part. **better** *adv.* (comp. of *well*). In a more excellent way; more; (of person) (partially) recovered from illness; ~ **off**, in better circumstances; **had** ~, would find it wiser; **think** ~ **of**, reconsider, decide more wisely. **better** *n.* Person of higher rank (usu. pl.); that which has greater excellence; **for the** ~, in a way that is an improvement; **get the** ~ **of**, defeat, outwit. **better** *v.* Improve, surpass. **bet'ter·ment** *n.* Improvement.

bet·tor (bĕt'*er*) *n.* Person who bets.

be·tween (bĭtwēn') *prep.* In, into, along, or across, a space or interval bounded by, *lies* ~ *Paris and Rouen; happened* ~ *Monday and Friday*; separating; connecting; intermediately in time, place, degree, quantity or order; shared by, confined to; to and from; reciprocally on the part of; ~ **ourselves,** ~ **you and me**, confidentially. **between** *adv.* Between two points or times.

be·twixt (bĭtwĭkst') *prep.* & *adv.* 1. (archaic) Between. 2. ~ **and between,** in position intermediate between; neither one thing nor the other.

Beu·lah (bū'l*a*). Biblical name for land of Israel (Isaiah 62); the land of peace described by Bunyan in *Pilgrim's Progress*.

bev·el (bĕv'*el*) *n.* 1. Carpenter's and mason's tool, a flat rule with movable tongue or arm stiffly connected to one end, for marking angles. 2. Slope from right angle, or from horizontal or vertical, surface so sloped; ~ **gear**, gear with toothed surface oblique with the axis usu. meshing with another set at right angles. ~ *v.* (**-eled, -el·ing**; *Brit.* **-elled, -el·ling**). Impart bevel to, slant.

bev·er·age (bĕv'*er*ĭj, bĕv'rĭj) *n.* Any liquid for drinking, esp. other than water.

Bev·er·ly (bĕv'*er*lē) **Hills.** City in the Los Angeles area of S. California; known for its wealth and

Stories from the ***Bible*** *inspired many of the early Christian artists. The 12th-century plaque (right) shows St. Paul escaping from Damascus, lowered from the walls in a basket and met below by his friends.*

homes of movie celebrities.

bev·y (bĕv′ē) *n.* (pl. **bev·ies**). Flock (of birds, esp. quail); group (of girls or women).

be·wail (bĭwāl′) *v.t.* Wail over, mourn for. **be·wail′er** *n.*

be·ware (bĭwār′) *v.* (used without inflections). Be cautious (of), take heed (*of, lest, how*).

be·wil·der (bĭwĭl′d*e*r) *v.t.* Confuse, perplex. **be·wil′dered** *adj.* **be·wil′dered·ly** *adv.* **be·wil′der·ing** *adj.* **be·wil′der·ing·ly** *adv.* **be·wil′der·ment** *n.*

be·witch (bĭwĭch′) *v.t.* Affect by witchcraft; charm, enchant. **be·witch′er** *n.* **be·witch′ing** *adj.* **be·witch′ing·ly** *adv.*

bey (bā) *n.* (formerly) Turkish provincial governor; native ruler of former kingdom of Tunis or Tunisia; Turkish title of honor and respect. [Turk., = "lord"]

Beyle (bāl), **Henri**: see STENDHAL.

be·yond (bĭyŏnd′) *adv.* & *prep.* At, to, the farther side (of) past, besides; out of reach, comprehension or range (of). ~ *n.* Future life after death, the unknown.

bez·ant, bes·ant (bĕz′*a*nt, bĭzănt′) *ns.* (hist.) Gold coin issued in Byzantium. [f. *Byzantium* where orig. struck]

bez·el (bĕz′*e*l) *n.* Sloped edge or face of chisel etc.; oblique side or face of cut gem; groove holding gem or watch glass in setting.

be·zique (b*e*zēk′) *n.* Card game similar to pinochle and played by two players using deck of 64 cards; combination of queen of spades and jack of diamonds in this game.

b.f. *abbrev.* Bold face (type); (accounting) brought forward.

B.F.A. *abbrev.* Bachelor of Fine Arts.

bhang, bang (băng) *ns.* Indian hemp plant; leaves of this mixed with resin used as intoxicant and narcotic.

b.h.p. *abbrev.* Brake horsepower.

Bhu·tan (bōōtahn′). Independent kingdom, a protectorate of the Republic of India, lying on the SE. of the Himalayas; capital, Thimphu.

Bi *symbol.* Bismuth.

bi- *prefix.* Twice, doubly, having two.

Bi·a·fra (bēah′fr*a*). Region of E. Nigeria; an attempt to secede and set up the Republic of Biafra failed in 1970.

Bia·ly·stock (byăl′ĭstŏk; *Pol.* byah′wĭstawk). Industrial city and important railroad junction in NE. Poland.

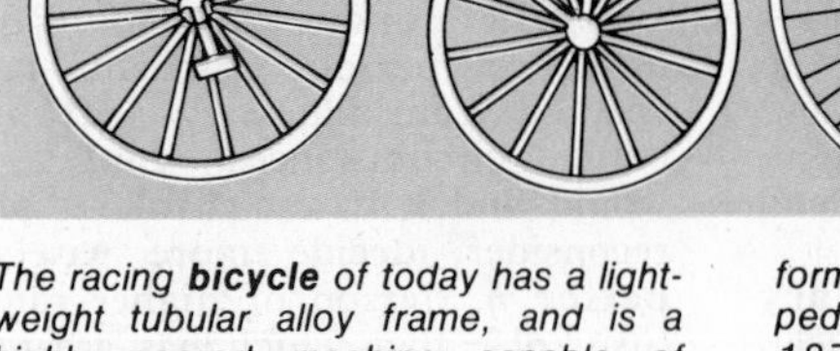

The racing ***bicycle*** *of today has a lightweight tubular alloy frame, and is a highly geared machine capable of speeds in excess of 40 m.p.h. Early forms of bicycle, such as the velocipede of 1865 and the penny-farthing of 1875, had crude springs to support their saddles.*

Bi·ar·ritz (bē′*e*rĭts; *Fr.* byărĕts′). Resort city on the Bay of Biscay in SW. France.

bi·as (bī′*a*s) *n.* 1. Inclination, predisposition, prejudice, influence; (statistics) systematic distortion; (elect.) steady voltage or current applied to electronic device. 2. Diagonal line of direction, esp. across a fabric. ~ *v.t.* (**bi·ased, bi·as·ing**; *Brit.* **bi·assed, bi·as·sing**). Give bias to, influence, prejudice.

bib[1] (bĭb) *v.i.* (**bibbed, bib·bing**). (archaic) Drink much or often, tipple.

bib[2] (bĭb) *n.* Cloth, etc. placed under child's chin to protect its clothing from spilled food; apron top.

bib·cock (bĭb′kŏk) *n.* Faucet with bent down nozzle (dist. from stopcock).

Bi·ble (bī′bel) *n.* Sacred book of Christianity comprising the Old and New Testaments (and sometimes the Apocrypha); sacred writings of Judaism, comprising the Old Testament only; edition or copy of either of these; sacred book, (colloq.) authoritative book, set of rules, etc.; ~ **Belt**, those parts of the Southern and Midwestern U.S. that are strongly fundamentalist.

bib·li·cal (bĭb′lĭkal) *adj.* Of, in, concerning, the Bible; (of language) of the Authorized Version. **bib′li·cal·ly** *adv.*

bib·li·og·ra·phy (bĭblēŏg′rafē) *n.* (pl. **-phies**). History of books, their publication, editions, etc.; list of books of any author, subject, etc. **bib·li·o·graph·ic** (bĭblēograf′ĭk), **bib·li·o·graph′i·cal** *adjs.* **bib·li·o·graph′i·cal·ly** *adv.* **bib·li·og′ra·pher** *n.*

bib·li·o·ma·ni·a (bĭblēomā′nēa, -mān′ya) *n.* Mania for collecting books. **bib·li·o·ma′ni·ac** *n.* & *adj.*

bib·li·o·phile (bĭb′lēofīl) *n.* Book lover; book collector. **bib·li·oph·i·lism** (bĭblēŏf′ilĭzem) *n.*

bib·u·lous (bĭb′yulus) *adj.* Addicted to alcoholic drinking.

bi·cam·er·al (bīkăm′eral) *adj.* With two (legislative) branches.

bi·car·bon·ate (bīkar′bonĭt, -nāt) *n.* 1. Salt of carbonic acid in which only one hydrogen atom is replaced by a metal. 2. (pop., also ~ **of soda**) Sodium bicarbonate ($NaHCO_3$) used in medicine and as constituent of baking powder etc.

bi·cen·te·nar·y (bīsĕn′tenĕrē, -sĕntĕn′erē) *n.* (pl. **-nar·ies**). Bicentennial.

bi·cen·ten·ni·al (bīsĕntĕn′ēal, -yal) *adj.* Occurring every, lasting for, 200 years. ~ *n.* 200th anniversary.

bi·ceps (bī′sĕps) *n.* & *adj.* (pl. **-ceps·es, -ceps**). (Muscle) with two heads or attachments, esp. that on front of upper arm, which bends forearm.

bick·er (bĭk′er) *v.i.* & *n.* Quarrel, wrangle.

bi·cus·pid (bīkŭs′pĭd) *adj.* & *n.* (Tooth) with two cusps.

bi·cy·cle (bī′sĭkel, -sikel) *n.* Vehicle having two wheels one behind the other and a seat on which the rider sits astride, driven by two pedals and having handlebars for steering. ~ *v.i.* (**-cled, -cling**). Ride bicycle. **bi′cy·cler, bi′cy·clist** *ns.*

bid (bĭd) *v.* (**bade** pr. băd, băd, **bad** or **bid, bid·den** or **bid, bid·ding**). Command to; invite; salute with (greeting etc.); (past t. and past part. **bid**) offer (price) for a thing; (at bridge) made a bid. **bid′der** *n.* **bid** *n.* Offer of price, esp. at an auction; (at bridge) announcement of the number of tricks that a player will undertake to win at no trump or with a specified suit as trump; attempt; invitation.

bid·da·ble (bĭd′abel) *adj.* 1. (archaic) Obedient. 2. (Of a suit in a hand at bridge) on which a bid can reasonably be made.

bide (bīd) *v.* (**bid·ed** or **bode**, pr. bōd, **bid·ed** or archaic **bid, bid·ing**). Abide (archaic except in ~ **one's time**, wait for a favorable opportunity).

bi·det (bēdā′, bĭdĕt′) *n.* Bathroom fixture with low bowl-like basin and faucets, used for bathing the crotch.

bi·en·ni·al (bīĕn′ēal) *adj.* Lasting, recurring, or completing the normal term of life every two years. **bi·en′ni·al·ly** *adv.* **biennial** *n.* Plant that springs from seed one year and flowers, fructifies, and dies the next.

bier (bēr) *n.* Movable frame on which corpse or coffin is laid before burial.

Bierce (bērs), **Ambrose** (1842–1914?). American journalist and short story writer; known for caustic wit and cynicism; disappeared in Mexico, 1913.

biff (bĭf) *n.* (slang) Blow, whack. ~ *v.t.* Strike, hit.

bi·fid (bī′fĭd) *adj.* Divided by a deep cleft into two lobes.

bi·fo·cal (bīfō′kal, bī′fō-) *adj.* (of spectacle lenses) Having two segments of different focal lengths, the upper for distant, the lower for near, vision. **bi·fo′cals** *n.pl.* Bifocal spectacles.

bi·fo·li·ate (bīfō′lēĭt, -āt) *adj.* Of two leaves.

bi·fur·cate (bī′ferkāt, bīfer′-) *v.* (**-cat·ed, -cat·ing**). Divide into two branches, fork. ~ *adj.* (bīferkĭt, bīfer′-, -kāt). Forked. **bi·fur·ca·tion** (bīferkā′shon) *n.*

big (bĭg) *adj.* (**big·ger, big·gest**). Large; grown-up; important, successful; boastful; loud; (colloq.) major, outstanding; elder (as in ~ **brother,** ~ **sister**); (colloq.) magnanimous; ~ **with child**, advanced in pregnancy; **B ~ Apple**, (slang) any large city esp. New York City; **big bang theory**, theory that the universe was created from an explosion of compressed elementary particles and is still expanding; opp. STEADY STATE. **B ~ Ben**, great bell in clock tower of Houses of Parliament in London, England, hence the clock itself; **B ~ Bertha**, large cannon used by the Germans in World War I, esp. to bombard Paris in 1918 [Frau Berta Krupp, head of the Krupp steel manufacturing family in Germany]; **B ~ Brother**, head of state in George Orwell's novel *1984*, hence, head of authoritarian organization exercising dictatorial pseudobenevolent power; ~ **business**, commerce on grand scale; **Big′foot**: see SASQUATCH; **big′headed,** (colloq.) conceited; **big game**, large wild animals hunted for sport, as deer, lions, etc.; **big gun**, (fig.) important person; **big-hearted**, kind, generous; **big′horn**, wild sheep (*Ovis canadenis*) of the Rocky Mountains, having massive curving horns; **big-league**, (adj.) of major league baseball, major, important; **big money**, large amount of money; **big′-mouth**, (slang) loud, talkative person, esp. one who lacks discretion; ~ **shot**, (slang) important or influential person; **big three, four**, etc., predominant few; **big toe**, innermost, largest toe; **big top**, main circus tent, circus; **big′wig**, (colloq.) important person. **big** *adv.* **big′ness** *n.*

big·a·my (bĭg′amē) *n.* (pl. **-mies**). Crime of marrying while one has a legal spouse still living. **big′a·mist** *n.* **big′a·mous** *adj.* **big′a·mous·ly** *adv.*

Big Bend National Park. Mountain and desert area in W. Texas on the Mexican border.

Big Horn Mountains. Mountain range in N. Wyoming, part of the Rocky Mountains.

bight (bīt) *n.* Loop of a rope; curve or recess, of coast, river, etc., bay.

big·ot (bĭg′ot) *n.* Person obstinately and unreasonably holding some creed or view and intolerant toward others. **big′ot·ed** *adj.* **big′ot·ed·ly** *adv.* **big′ot·ry** *n.*

bi·jou (bē′zhōō, bēzhōō′) *n.* Small, exquisite trinket. ~ *adj.* Small and elegant.

bike (bīke) *n.* & *v.i.* (**biked, bik·ing**). (colloq.) Bicycle; motorcycle; motorbike; **bike′way**, road, path, or lane especially for bicycle traffic.

Bi·ki·ni (bĭkē′nē). Atoll in the Marshall Islands of the W. Pacific Ocean; site of U.S. atomic bomb test, 1946.

bi·ki·ni (bĭkē′nē) *n.* Scanty two-piece bathing suit for women.

bi·la·bi·al (bīlā′bēal) *adj.* & *n.* (phon.) (Consonant) produced by the junction or apposition of both lips.

bi·lat·er·al (bīlăt′eral) *adj.* Of, on, with, two sides; affecting, between, two parties; ~ **symmetry**, symmetry about a plane, such that one half is a mirror image of the other (as left and right in general outward appearance of human body and in all other vertebrate and many invertebrate animals). **bi·lat′er·al·ism, bi·lat′er·al·ness** *ns.* **bi·lat′er·al·ly** *adv.*

Bil·ba·o (bēlbah′aw). Commercial, manufacturing, and port city in N. Spain on an inlet of the Bay of Biscay.

bil·ber·ry (bĭl′bĕrē) *n.* (pl. **-ries**). Small blue-black edible berry of dwarf hardy shrub

(*Vaccinium myrtillus*) of N. Europe (also *whortleberry*, *blueberry*).

bil·bo (bĭl′bō) *n.* (pl. **-boes**). Iron bar with sliding shackles for prisoner's ankles.

bile (bīl) *n.* Bitter, brownish-yellow fluid secreted by the liver and poured into the duodenum in the process of digestion; (hist.) one of the four humors (see HUMOR, 4); (fig.) anger, peevishness.

bilge (bĭlj) *n.* Nearly horizontal part of ship's bottom; foulness that collects in the bilge; (slang) nonsense, rot; ~ **water**, foul water that collects in ship's bilge.

bil·har·zi·a·sis (bĭlhārzī′asĭs) *n.* Disease produced by trematode worm of genus *Bilharzia*, parasitic in veins of human pelvic region and urinary organs, esp. in Africa. [f. Theodor *Bilharz* (1825–62), German physician]

bil·i·ar·y (bĭl′ēērē) *adj.* Of the bile.

bi·lin·gual (bīlĭng′gwal) *adj.* Having, written in, speaking, etc., two languages. **bi·lin′gual·ism** *n.* **bi·lin′gual·ly** *adv.* **bi·lin′guist** *n.*

bil·ious (bĭl′yus) *adj.* Arising from derangement of the bile; liable to, affected by, this; peevish, irritable. **bil′ious·ly** *adv.* **bil′ious·ness** *n.*

bilk (bĭlk) *v.t.* Evade payment of (creditor or bill); cheat, defraud. **bilk′er** *n.*

bill[1] (bil) *n.* 1. Halberd or similar obsolete weapon with a hooked blade and long handle. 2. (also **bill′hook**) Implement used for pruning etc., having long blade with concave edge, and a wooden handle in line with blade.

bill[2] (bĭl) *n.* Bird's beak, esp. when slender or flattened; horny beak of platypus. ~ *v.i.* Stroke bill with bill (as doves); ~ **and coo**, exchange caresses, whisper endearments.

bill[3] (bĭl) *n.* 1. Draft of statute presented to legislature. 2. (law) Written statement of (plaintiff's) case; proposed indictment submitted to a court. 3. Statement of charges for goods delivered or services rendered. 4. Poster, placard; program of entertainment; **fill the** ~, (colloq.) suffice. 5. (also ~ **of exchange**) Written order to pay sum on given date to drawer or named payee. 6. Bank note. 7. **bill′board**, structure for the display of large advertisements; **bill′fold**, a wallet; **bill of fare**, list of dishes to be served, menu; **bill of health**, certificate regarding infectious disease on ship or in port at time of sailing; **bill of lading**, receipt given by a carrier for goods accepted for transportation; **bill of rights**, statement of rights and liberties of a nation or group of people; (cap. B & R) the first ten amendments to the U.S. Constitution; (cap. B & R) English Statute of 1689; **bill of sale**, document transferring personal property from seller to buyer; **bill** *v.t.* Announce, put in the program; plaster with placards; send a bill to, enter as a charge on a bill. **bill′a·ble** *adj.* **bill′er** *n.*

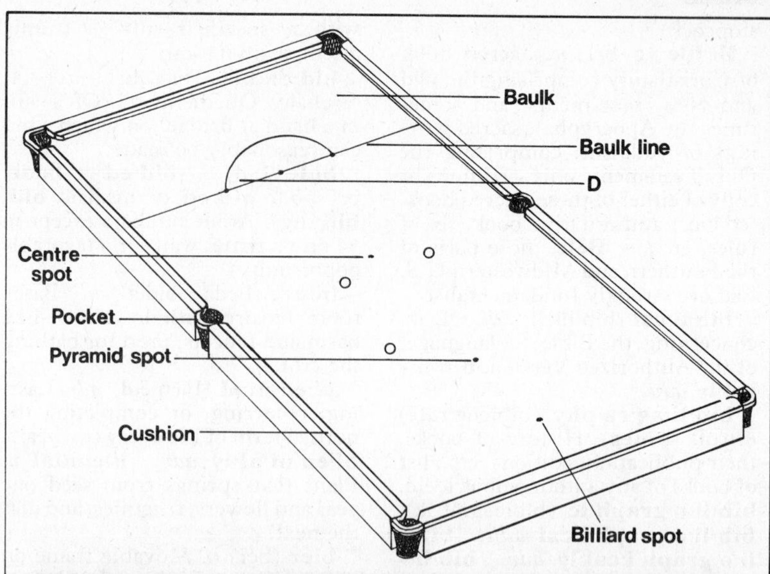

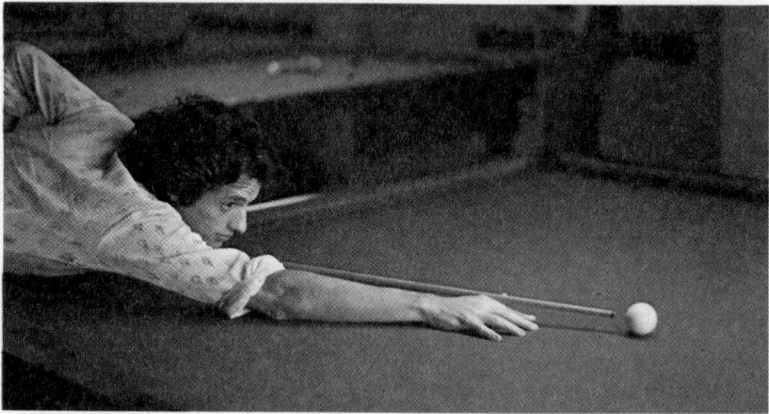

*From the 16th century, the game of **billiards** and its variants has been popular in Europe. The table is generally 6 ft. by 12 ft., with a slate bed, ground perfectly flat, and covered in green baize. Above: the player makes a 'bridge' with his fingers to control the action of the cue.*

bill·a·bong (bĭl′abŏng) *n.* (Austral.) Branch or effluent of river forming backwater or stagnant pool. [Ab. *Billibang*, old name of Bell River, f. *billa* water, *bang* of uncertain meaning]

bil·let (bĭl′ĭt) *n.* Order requiring householder to board and lodge soldier etc. bearing it; place where such a person is lodged; appointment, job. ~ *v.t.* (**-let·ed, -let·ing**). Quarter (soldiers etc.) *on* town, householder, etc., *in*, *at*, place.

bil·let-doux (bĭl′ēdōō′, -ā-; *Fr.* bēyĕdōō′) *n.* (pl. **bil·lets-doux** pr. bĭl′ēdōōz′, -ā-; *Fr.* bēyĕdōō′). Love letter.

bil·liards (bĭl′yerdz) *n.pl.* Game played with three small solid balls, driven about by cues on a horizontal rectangular table covered with smooth green cloth, surrounded by a cushioned ledge; any of several similar games, such as one played on a similar table with pockets at the corners and in the middle of the long sides; **billiard ball, cue, table**, etc., one used in billiards (cf. POOL[2]). **bil′liard·ist** *n.*

Bil·lings·gate (bĭl′ĭngzgāt; *Brit.* bĭl′ĭngzgĭt). Fish market established at one of the old city gates of London; hence (also **b** ~), foul language (for which the market was famous in 17th c.).

bil·lion (bĭl′yon) *n.* (pl. **-lions**, **-lion** following a numeral). (U.S.) One thousand millions; (Brit.) one million millions. **bil·lion·aire** (bĭlyonār′) *n.* One whose wealth is a billion (dollars, pounds, etc.) or more.

bil·lon (bĭl′on) *n.* Alloy of gold

or silver with a predominating amount of some base metal, used for coinage.

bil·low (bĭl′ō) *n.* Great wave; anything that sweeps along, as smoke, sound, etc. ~ *v.i.* Rise, move, in billows. **bil′low·y** *adj.* (**-low·i·er, -low·i·est**).

bil·ly[1] (bĭl′ē) *n.* (pl. **-lies**). (Austral.) Tin can with (lid and) wire handle used as kettle etc. in camping out and as container for foodstuffs; so **bil′lycan**.

bil·ly[2] (bĭl′ē) = BILLY GOAT.

bil·ly·cock (bĭl′ēkŏk), **billycock hat.** (Brit.) Man's round, low-crowned, hard felt hat; bowler.

bil·ly (bĭl′ē) **goat.** Male goat.

Bil·ly (bĭl′ē) **the Kid** (1859–81). Real name, William H. Bonney; notorious and legendary American bandit of the Southwest; killed in ambush.

bi·lobed (bī′lōbd) *adj.* Having, or divided into, two lobes.

Bi·lox·i (bĭlŏk′sē, -lŭk′-). Resort and commercial fishing city on the Gulf of Mexico in S. Mississippi.

bi·me·tal·lic (bīmetăl′ĭk) *adj.* 1. Of two metals. 2. Using both gold and silver at fixed ratio to each other, as a monetary standard. **bi·met·al·lism** (bīmĕt′*a*lĭzem), **bi·met′al·list** *ns.*

Bim·i·ni (bĭm′inē). Two small islands SE. of Florida in the Bahamas.

bi·month·ly (bīmŭnth′lē) *adj.* & *n.* (pl. **-lies**). (Periodical) produced or occurring every two months.

bin (bĭn) *n.* Receptacle or enclosed place for corn, coal, etc. ~ *v.* (**binned, bin·ning**).

bi·na·ry (bī′nerē) *adj.* (pl. **-ries**). Dual, of or involving pairs; ~ **compound,** (chem.) one consisting of two elements; ~ **star,** system of two stars revolving around their common center of mass and often appearing as a single visual object.

bind (bīnd) *v.* (**bound, bind·ing**). Tie, fasten; put in bonds, restrain; fasten, encircle, or hold together; cause to cohere; (of clothing) to restrict or chafe. 2. Be obligatory, impose constraint or duty upon; unite by legal or moral tie; (pass.) be required by duty; subject to legal obligation; indenture as apprentice; ~ **over,** (esp.) put person under bond to appear in court as required. 3. Bandage; edge *with* braid, iron, etc.; fasten (sheets, book) into cover. **bind** *n.* 1. Something that binds. 2. (mus.) = TIE *n.* def. 4. 3. (slang) Predicament.

bind·ing (bīn′dĭng) *adj.* Obligatory (*on*). ~ *n.* (esp.) Book cover; braid etc. for binding raw edges of textiles. **bind′ing·ly** *adv.* **bind′-ing·ness** *n.*

bin·dle (bĭn′d*e*l) **stiff.** (slang) Itinerant worker who carries his own bedroll. [*bindle,* alteration of bundle]

bind·weed (bīnd′wēd) *n.* Convolvulus or other twining plant, related to the morning glory.

bine (bīn) *n.* Flexible shoot; stem of climbing plant, esp. the hop.

Bin·et (bĭnā′), **Alfred** (1857–1911). French psychologist; experimented in the measurement of intelligence and was the first to devise intelligence tests; ~ **(-Simon) scale,** ~ **(-Simon) test,** one for measuring relative mental development, esp. in children, usu. expressed in an intelligence quotient (see INTELLIGENCE).

binge (bĭnj) *n.* (colloq.) Spree of excessive indulgence, as in eating or esp. drinking of alcoholic beverages.

bin·go (bĭng′gō) *n.* Form of lotto in which columns of numbered squares are headed with the letters B,I,N,G, and O. ~ *int.* Used to express pleasurable surprise or unexpected success.

bin·na·cle (bĭn′*a*kel) *n.* Box for compass on a ship.

bin·oc·u·lar (b*i*nŏk′*yu*ler) *adj.* Adapted for both eyes; ~ **vision,** type of vision, peculiar to man and some other primates, in which both eyes cooperate in observing the same object and receive a stereoscopic impression. ~ *n.* (usu. pl.) Binocular instrument, as field or opera glasses.

bi·no·mi·al (bīnō′mēal) *adj.* Consisting of two terms or names; ~ **theorem,** general algebraic formula, discovered by Newton, by which any power of a binomial quantity may be found without performing the progressive multiplications. **binomial** *n.* 1. Algebraic expression consisting of two terms joined by + or −, as $3x + 2y$ and $x^2 - 3y$. 2. (zool. and bot.) A taxonomic name consisting of a generic and a specific term.

bio- *prefix.* (Course of) life of, concerning, organic life; biological.

bi·o·chem·is·try (bīōkĕm′ĭstrē) *n.* Science dealing with the chemical properties of the parts of

*Some species of the **bindweed** family called morning glory are cultivated as ornamental plants. They grow prolifically and their blossoms often open only in the morning. The related moonflower blooms only at night.*

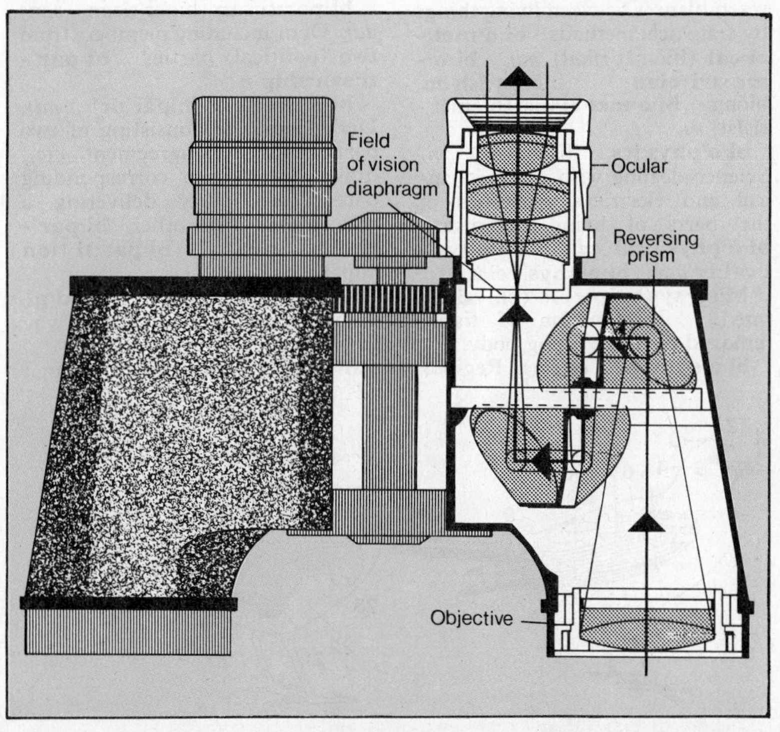

*A viewer sees images of greater depth through **binoculars** than through a telescope. Binoculars are specified by two numbers. The first indicates the magnification, the second the diameter of the object lenses.*

living organisms. **bi·o·chem·i·cal** (bīōkĕm′ĭk*a*l), **bi·o·chem′ic** *adjs.* **bi·o·chem′i·cal·ly** *adv.* **bi·o·chem′ist** *n.*

bi·o·gen·e·sis (bīōjĕn′*e*sĭs) *n.* Postulate that living matter arises only from living matter; synthesis of chemical substances by living matter; hypothetical development of living matter from complex inanimate substances. **bi·o·ge·net·ic** (bīōj*e*nĕt′ĭk), **bi·o·ge·net′i·cal** *adjs.* **bi·o·ge·net′i·cal·ly** *adv.*

bi·o·ge·og·ra·phy (bīōjēŏg′r*a*fē) *n.* Study of the geographical distribution of animals and plants.

bi·og·ra·phy (bīŏg′r*a*fē) *n.* (pl. **-phies**). Written account of another person's life; branch of literature dealing with such writing. **bi·og′ra·pher** *n.* **bi·o·graph·i·cal** (bīogrăf′ik*a*l), **bi·o·graph′ic** *adjs.* **bi·o·graph′i·cal·ly** *adv.*

bi·ol·o·gy (bīŏl′*o*jē) *n.* Science of life, dealing with the morphology, physiology, behavior, origin, and distribution of animals and plants. **bi·ol′o·gist** *n.*

bi·o·log·i·cal (bī*o*lŏj′ĭk*a*l) *adj.* Of biology; ~ **control**, control of pests by the use of other organisms which devour or destroy them; ~ **warfare**, use of bacteria, viruses, etc., against an enemy or his animals or crops. **bi·o·log′i·cal·ly** *adv.*

bi·o·lu·mi·nes·cence (bīōlōō-mĭnĕs′*e*ns) *n.* Emission of light by living organisms. **bi·o·lu·mi·nes′cent** *adj.*

bi·ome (bī′ōm) *n.* (ecol.) Biotic community of plants and animals.

bi·om·e·try (bīŏm′ĭtrē) *n.* Application of mathematics to biology, esp. the study of resemblances between living things by statistical methods. **bi·o·met·ri·cal** (bīōmĕt′rĭk*a*l) *adj.* **bi·o·me·tri·cian** (bīōm*e*trĭsh′*a*n, bīōm*e*-), **bi·o·met·ri·cist** (bīōmĕt′rĭsĭst) *ns.*

bi·o·phys·ics (bīōfĭz′ĭks) *n.* Science dealing with the mechanical and electrical properties of the parts of living organisms. **bi·o·phys′i·cal** *adj.* **bi·o·phys′i·cal·ly** *adv.* **bi·o·phys′i·cist** *n.*

bi·op·sy (bī′ŏpsē) *n.* (pl. **-sies**). (med.) Examination of tissue removed from the living body.

bi·o·sphere (bī′*o*sfēr) *n.* Regions of Earth's crust and atmosphere occupied by living organisms.

*There are many varieties of the **birch** tree. Oil similar to oil of wintergreen is extracted from black birch; the bark of the others is used in tanning.*

bi·ot·ic (bīŏt′ĭk) *adj.* (biol.) Relating to life; peculiar to living organisms.

bi·par·ti·san (bīpar′tĭz*a*n, -*s*an) *adj.* Of or including members from two (political) parties. **bi·par′ti·san·ship** *n.*

bi·par·tite (bīpar′tīt) *adj.* Divided into or consisting of two parts; (law, of agreement etc.) drawn up in two corresponding parts, each party delivering a counterpart to the other. **bi·par′tite·ly** *adv.* **bi·par·ti·tion** (bīpartĭsh′*o*n) *n.*

bi·ped (bī′pĕd), **bi·ped·al** (bī′pĕd*a*l, bĭp′*e*-) *ns.* & *adjs.* Two-footed (animal).

bi·pin·nate (bīpĭn′āt) *adj.* (bot.) Having leaflets arranged in two rows on either side of leafstalk, the leaflets being themselves subdivided.

bi·plane (bī′plān) *n.* Airplane with two sets of wings, one above the other.

bi·quad·rat·ic (bīkwŏdrăt′ĭk) *adj.* Of, raised to, the square of a square (or 4th power) of a number; ~ **equation**, one in which the unknown quantity is biquadratic. **biquadratic** *n.* Biquadratic equation; 4th power of a number.

birch (bẽrch) *n.* 1. Hardy, northern forest tree of genus *Betula* with smooth tough bark and slender graceful branches; wood of this; **birch′bark canoe**, one made of the bark of *B. papyrifera.* 2. Birch rod or bundle of birch twigs used for flogging. **birch** *v.t.* Flog with birch. **birch′en** *adj.* Made of birch.

bird (bẽrd) *n.* 1. Any feathered vertebrate animal, member of a class nearly allied to reptiles but distinguished by warm blood, feathers, and adaptation of the forelimbs as wings. 2. Game bird. 3. (slang) Young woman; (joc.) person; ~**s of a feather**, people with opinions or interests in common; **for the** ~**s**, (slang) contemptible or ridiculous. 4. **get the** ~, (slang, esp. theatr.) be hissed, booed, etc.; so **give the** ~; **bird′bath**, dish of water, often on pedestal, set in garden for birds' use; **bird′brain(ed)**, (person) with small brain, dolt, scatterbrain; **bird cage**, cage for bird(s), object of similar design; **bird call**, note of bird; instrument imitating this; **bird cherry**, species of Eurasian cherry tree (*Prunus padus*) with white flowers and small black fruit; **bird dog**, dog used for hunting birds; (fig.) one who hunts out something for another; **bird′ lime**, sticky substance made from holly bark for catching small birds; **bird of paradise**, bird of family Paradiseidae native to New Guinea and notable for its brilliant colors and elegant plumes; **bird of**

*The only creature in the world to have a covering of feathers, the **bird** is ideally adapted to flight. Facing page: The male and female of the strikingly colored flamingo incubate their eggs in turn.*

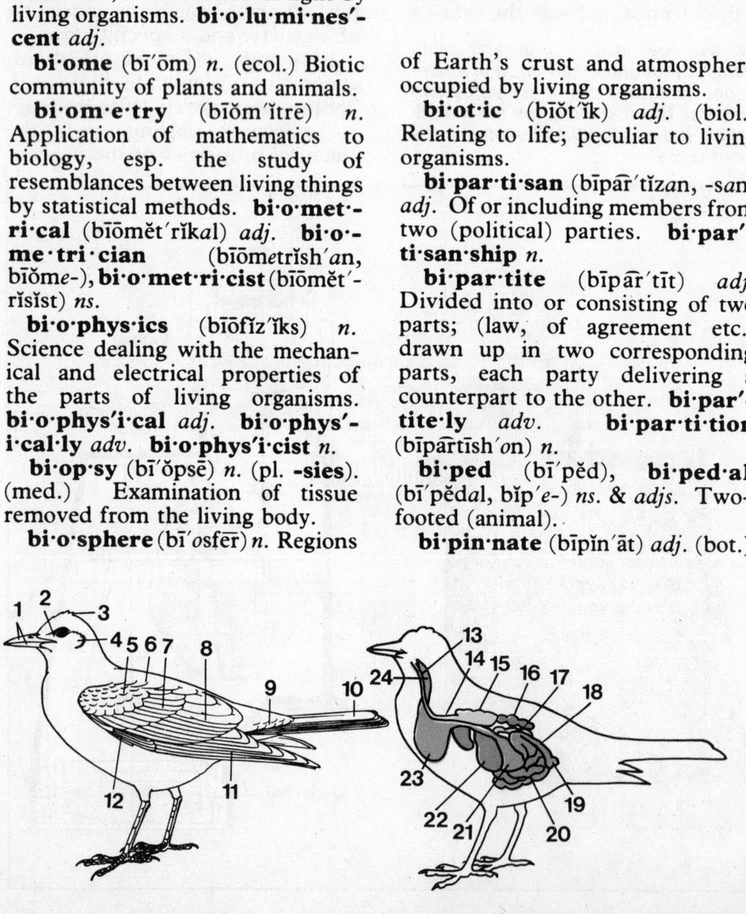

Exterior	Internal
1 culmen	13 trachea
2 lore	14 syrinx
3 crest	15 lung
4 ear feathers	16 kidney
5 lesser wing coverts	17 testes
6 scapulars	18 rectum
7 greater wing coverts	19 cloaca
8 secondaries	20 intestines
9 upper tail coverts	21 gizzard
10 retrices	22 liver
11 primaries	23 lung
12 primary coverts	24 crop
	25 esophagus

*The Iron Chancellor, **Otto von Bismarck,** was the architect of the German Empire. His success in uniting the German States into a nation was matched by that of his diplomacy, as at the Congress of Berlin (left), 1878.*

*The **bison** that roamed the North American prairies in great herds is now much reduced in numbers. The male stands about 5 ft. 10 ins. tall and weighs about 1,800 lb.*

passage, migratory bird (also fig. of sojourner); **bird of prey**, any of various predatory birds such as hawks and owls; **bird sanctuary**, area where birds are protected by law; **bird'seed**, any of various kinds of seed used for feeding birds; **bird's-eye**, any of several plants with small round bright flowers; **bird's-eye maple**, wood of the sugar maple when full of little knots; **bird's-eye view**, view of landscape from above; résumé of a subject; **bird's-nest soup**, Chinese soup made from edible nest of certain swallows found in the China Sea; **bird-watcher**, one who studies birds in their natural surroundings; **bird-watching**, this occupation. **bird'like** *adj.*

Birds·eye (bẽrdz'ī), **Clarence** (1886–1956). American inventor; pioneered first practical method of freezing foods.

bi·reme (bī'rēm) *n.* Ancient galley with two banks of oars.

bi·ret·ta, bir·ret·ta, be·ret·ta, ber·ret·ta (berĕt'*a*) *ns.* Square cap with three projections worn by Roman Catholic and some Anglican clerics.

Bir·ming·ham[1] (bẽr'mĭng-hăm). Industrial center and largest city in N. central Alabama.

Bir·ming·ham[2] (bẽr'mĭng*a*m). Industrial midland city in England; 2nd largest city in England.

birth (bẽrth) *n.* 1. Emergence of child or animal from body of female parent; process of producing young; **give ~ to**, (of female parent) produce (young) from body (also fig.). 2. Origin, beginning. 3. Parentage, descent; noble lineage. 4. **~ certificate**, form showing date and place etc. of birth; **~ control**, regulation of the number of one's children through restriction of ovulation, intercourse, or conception; **birth'day**, (anniversary of) day of one's birth; **birthday suit**, (slang) state of nakedness; **birth'mark**, congenital mark on the body; **birth'place**, place at which one was born; **birth rate**, number of births per 1,000 of population per annum; **birth'-right**, rights, privilege, or position to which one is entitled by birth.

Bis·cay (bĭs'kā, bĭskā'), **Bay of.** Part of N. Atlantic between N. coast of Spain and W. coast of France, notorious for storms.

Bis·cayne (bĭs'kān, bĭskān') **Bay.** Inlet of the Atlantic Ocean along SE. coast of Florida; Miami is on NW. shore and Key Biscayne is on NE.

bis·cuit (bĭs'kĭt) *n.* 1. Small cake of shortened bread raised with baking powder or soda. 2. (Brit.) Cracker or cookie. 3. Pottery after firing but before glazing and painting.

bi·sect (bīsĕkt', bī'sĕkt) *v.t.* Cut or divide into two (usu. equal) parts. **bi·sec'tion** *n.* **bi·sec'tion·al** *adj.* **bi·sec'tion·al·ly** *adv.* **bi·sec'tor** *n.* Bisecting line.

bi·sex·u·al (bīsĕk'sh*oo*al) *adj.* Of both sexes; having both sexes in one individual, hermaphrodite; sexually responsive to both sexes. ~ *n.* Bisexual person. **bi·sex·u·al·i·ty** (bīsĕkshōōăl'ĭtē) *n.*

bish·op (bĭsh'*o*p) *n.* 1. Clergyman consecrated as ecclesiastical governor of a diocese. 2. Miter-shaped chessman moved diagonally. **bish'op·ric** *n.* Diocese or office of a bishop.

Bis·marck[1] (bĭz'mark). Capital of North Dakota, in the SW. part, on the Missouri River.

Bis·marck[2] (bĭz'mark), **Prince Otto Eduard von Leopold** (1815–1898). Prussian and German statesman; first chancellor of the German Empire, 1871–90.

Bis·marck[3] (bĭz'mark) **Archipelago.** Group of small islands in the Pacific, NE. of New Guinea, under Australian administration.

bis·muth (bĭz'm*u*th) *n.* (chem.) Reddish-white brittle metallic element melting at low temperatures; symbol Bi, at. no. 83, at. wt. 208. 9806. **bis'muth·al** *adj.*

bi·son (bī'son, -zon) *n.* (pl. **-son**). 1. Species of wild ox (*Bison europaeus*) of heavy build with humped shoulders, formerly common in Europe and still existing in the Caucasus. 2. N. Amer. wild ox (*B. americanus*) formerly roaming in vast herds over the continent, now almost extinct except in protected areas.

bisque[1] (bĭsk) *n.* Advantage given to inferior player in certain games, esp. a free point or extra turn taken when desired.

bisque[2], **bisk** (bĭsk) *ns.* Thick, rich soup made with shellfish etc.

bis·sex·tile (bīsĕks′tĭl, bĭ-) *adj.* & *n.* (Of or pertaining to) a leap year or its extra day. [L. *bis sextilis* (*annus*) (year) containing the doubled sixth day (because in the Julian calendar the day repeated, Feb. 24, was acc. to the Roman method of reckoning the sixth before the Calends of March)]

bis·tou·ry (bĭs′terē) *n.* (pl. **-ries**). Surgical knife for minor incisions.

bit[1] (bĭt) *n.* 1. Biting or cutting end or part of tool, as boring piece of drill; part of key that engages with levers of lock. 2. Mouthpiece of horse's bridle.

bit[2] (bĭt) *n.* 1. Morsel of food; something to eat. 2. Small piece of anything; small portion or quantity; a single character of computer language; a short time; (slang) an act, performance, or routine; **do one's ~**, play one's part; **~ part, player**, (theatr.) (player of) very small part.

bit[3] (bĭt): see BITE.

bitch (bĭch) *n.* 1. Female of dog, fox, wolf. 2. (colloq.) Malicious, ill-tempered or lewd woman; (slang) difficult or unpleasant thing; (slang) complaint; ~ *v.* (slang) Complain. **bitch'y** *adj.* (**bitch·i·er, bitch·i·est**). **bitch'i·ness** *n.*

bite (bīt) *v.* (**bit** pr. bĭt, **bit·ten** or **bit, bit·ing**). 1. Cut into or off, nip or grip with teeth; (of insects etc.) sting, suck. **~ the bullet**, accept, confront an unpleasant situation; **~ the dust**, be killed, esp. in battle. 2. (of fish) Accept bait; accept, express interest in an offer, esp. one intended to deceive. 3. Cause glowing, smarting pain to. 4. Corrode. 5. (of wheels, screw, etc.) Grip. ~ *n.* Act of, wound made by, piece detached by, biting; a morsel or mouthful of food; small meal, snack; dental occlusion; taking of bait by fish; snack; grip, hold. **bit'er** *n.* **bit'ing·ly** *adv.* **bit'ing·ness** *n.*

Bi·thyn·i·a (bĭthĭn′ēa). Ancient region of NW. Asia Minor. **Bi·thyn'i·an** *adj.* & *n.*

bit·ing (bī′tĭng) *adj.* (esp.) Nipping, keen; pungent, stinging, sarcastic.

bit·ter (bĭt′er) *adj.* Tasting like wormwood, quinine, aloes, etc., obnoxious, irritating, or unfavorably stimulating to the gustatory sense; unpalatable to the mind, full of affliction; resentful, hostile, or cynical; virulent, relentless; biting, harsh; piercingly cold; **~ end**, (nautical) end of rope wound around a deck post (*bitt*) hence (colloq.) final or unpleasant end; **bit'tersweet** *adj.*, both bitter and sweet to the taste; mingling pleasure with pain or regret; **bittersweet** *n.*, any of various climbing plants, such as *Solanum dulcamara*, with bright berries or seeds. **bit'ter·ish** *adj.* **bit'ter·ly** *adv.* **bit'ter·ness** *n.* **bitter** *n.* 1. Bitterness. 2. (Brit.) Bitter beer; (pl.) (usually alcoholic) liquor in which bitter herbs or roots have steeped, used to flavor mixed drinks or as a tonic.

bit·tern (bĭt′ern) *n.* Bird of genus *Botaurus*, allied to herons, but smaller; noted for booming cry; **American ~**, *B. lentiginosus.*

bi·tu·men (bĭto͞o′men, -tū′-, bĭch′o͞o-) *n.* Mineral pitch, asphalt; any of various kinds of native oxygenated hydrocarbon, as naphtha, petroleum. **bi·tu'mi·noid, bi·tu'mi·nous** *adjs.*

bi·va·lent (bīvā′lent, bĭv′*a*-) *adj.* (chem). Having a valence of two.

bi·valve (bī′vălv) *adj.* Having two valves, having two shells hinged together. ~ *n.* Mollusk, as the clam, with shell consisting of two halves hinged together by elastic ligament.

biv·ou·ac (bĭv′o͞oăk, bĭv′wăk) *n.* Temporary encampment made with tents or improvised shelter. ~ *v.i.* (**-acked, -ack·ing**). Remain, esp. during the night, in a bivouac.

bi·zarre (bĭzär′) *adj.* Eccentric, fantastic, grotesque, mixed in style. **bi·zarre'ly** *adv.* **bi·zarre'ness** *n.* [Span. *bizarro* brave, handsome]

Bi·zet (bēzā′), **Georges** (1838–1875). French composer of *Carmen* and other operas.

blab (blăb) *v.* (**blabbed, blab·bing**). Talk or tell foolishly or indiscreetly, reveal, let out; hence, **blab'bermouth**, one who cannot keep a secret. **blab'ber** *n.* **blab** *n.* Blabbing.

black (blăk) *adj.* 1. Opposite of white, colorless from the absence or complete absorption of all light; so near this as to have no distinguishable color; very dark colored; dark; dusky, gloomy; dirty. 2. (sometimes **B ~**) Of, belonging to, a dark-skinned ethnic group of African origin. 3. Deadly, sinister, wicked; dismal; angry, lowering; implying disgrace or condemnation (as **~ mark** etc.); existing, bought, sold, in contravention of economic regulations. 4. **~ -and-blue**, discolored with bruise(s); **B ~ and Tans**, (from their black and khaki uniform), the Royal Irish Constabulary, about 6,000 British soldiers specially recruited and sent to Ireland to suppress the Sinn Fein rebellion in 1919–21; **~ and white**, written etc. in black ink on white paper; (of film etc.) not in color; (fig.) comprising opposite extremes; (**down in**) **~ and white**, recorded in writing or print; **~ art**, divination through alleged communication with the dead; sorcery; **black'ball**, (*v.t.*) exclude from club, society, etc. (orig. by putting black ball into urn or ballot box to express adverse vote); **black bear**, N. Amer. bear (*Ursus americanus*); **black belt**, (belt worn by) person who has attained a certain degree of proficiency in judo or karate; (colloq.) area, section predominantly inhabited by blacks; **black'berry**, bramble (*Rubus fruticosus*) or its fruit; **black'bird**, any of various birds of the family Icteridae, as grackles, redwings, etc.; European songbird (*Turdus merula*); **black'board**, large black or dark-colored board, panel, etc., used in schools and lecture rooms for writing or drawing on in chalk; **black box**, (esp.) device in aircraft recording details of flight or performing other functions electronically; **black coffee**, coffee without milk or cream; **black currant**, shrub *Ribes nigrum*; its small black fruit; **black'damp**, chokedamp of coal mines; **Black Death**, outbreak of plague, mostly in bubonic form, which spread into Europe from Asia in the 14th c., so called from the symptom of internal hemorrhages that blackened the skin of sufferers; **black earth**, dark soil rich in humus; **black eye**, eye with dark iris; discoloration around eye due to bruise; (colloq.) poor

*The superb camouflage of the **bittern** is demonstrated to good effect when the bird assumes an upright pose in keeping with the background of tall reeds.*

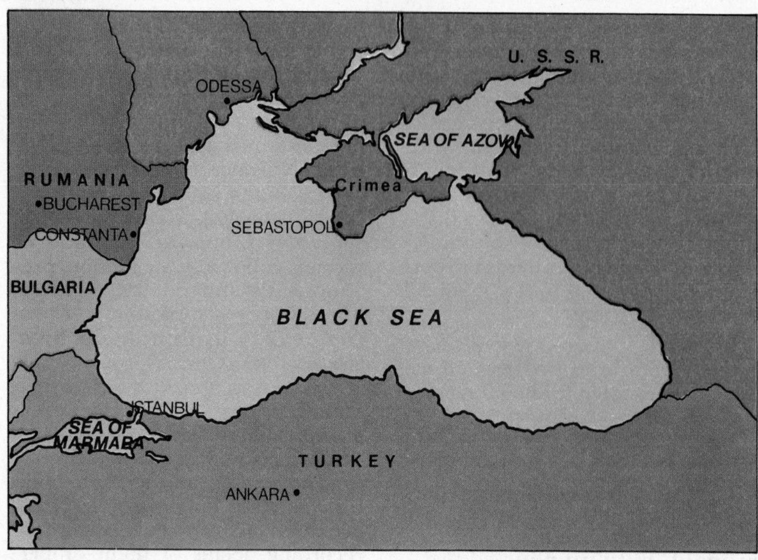

*An inland sea of about 160,000 sq. miles, the **Black Sea** is linked to the Mediterranean by a narrow strait, called the Bosphorus, which is overlooked by the city of Istanbul.*

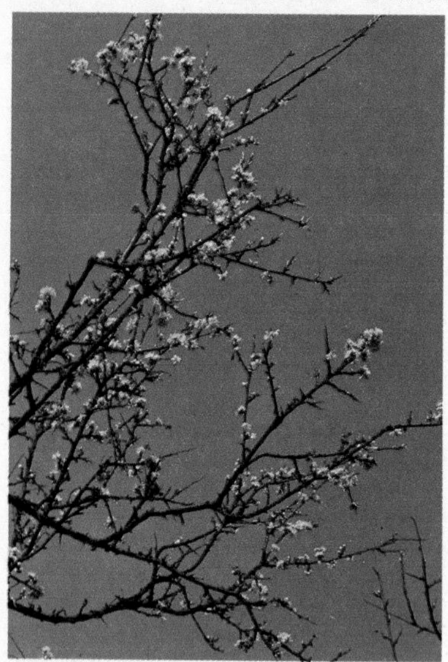

*The white flowers of **blackthorn** are followed by small purple fruits. These may be used to flavor gin and brandy. The blackthorn can be trained to form a strong hedge.*

reputation, dishonor; **black-eyed Susan**, flower with light usu. yellow petals and dark center, esp. *Thunbergia alata* and *Rudbeckia hirta*; **black′face**, make-up for minstrel show; **black′fish**, any of several saltwater and freshwater bass-like edible fish; **black fly**, any of the small, dark, biting gnats of the family Simuliidae; **Black Friar**, Dominican; **blackguard** (blăg′ĕrd) (*adj.* & *n.*) scoundrel(ly); **Black Hand**, (hist.) secret terrorist society, composed largely of Sicilians, in U.S. in early 20th c.; any similar group; **black′head**, black-headed greasy plug in mouth of hair follicle; **black′hearted**, evil; **black hole**, (astron.) region from which no matter or radiation can escape; any dark hole or deep cell, esp. (hist.) punishment cell or guardroom in barracks; **Black Hole of Calcutta**, punishment cell of the barracks in Fort William, Calcutta, in which 146 Europeans were confined for a night (1756) by order of Suraj ud Daula and only 23 survived until the morning; **black′jack**, flexible loaded club; pirates' black flag; **black′leg**, strikebreaker; disease of sheep and cattle; **blacklist**, list of persons, groups, etc. under disfavor, esp. those to whom jobs are not to be given; **black′list** (*v.t.*); **black′mail**, payment extorted by threats or pressure, esp. by threatening to reveal discrediting secret; extortion of such payment; so **black′mail** (*v.t.*); **black′mailer** (*n.*); **Black Maria**, prison van; **black mark**: see sense 3; **black market**, illegitimate traffic in controlled goods, currencies, or commodities; hence **black marketeer**, (*n.* & *v.i.*); **black mass** (often **B~ Mass**), mass for the dead, at which vestments and drapings are black; travesty of this, used in the cult of Satanism; **black monk**, Benedictine (from the color of his habit); **Black Muslim**, member of black organization advocating Islam; **black pepper**: see PEPPER; **Black Power**, U.S. movement of blacks in support of civil rights; the power of black Americans as a group; **Black Prince**, 16th-c. name given, for unknown reasons, to Edward (1330–76), the eldest son of Edward III; **Black Sea**, tideless sea between U.S.S.R. and Turkey; **black sheep**, scoundrel, unsatisfactory or disreputable member *of* (family etc.); **Black Shirt**, Fascist (from black shirt in uniform of Fascist militia); **black′smith**, smith working in iron, esp. one who makes horseshoes and shoes horses; **black′snake**, any of various dark non-venomous snakes of N. Amer., esp. *Coluber constrictor*; **black′strap (molasses)**, dark, very thick molasses used to make alcohol and as cattle feed; **black-tailed deer**, also **Columbian black-tailed deer**, deer of the western slope of the Rocky Mountains (*Odocoileus hemionus columbianus*); **black tea**: see TEA; **black′thorn**, sloe (*Prunus spinosa*), a thorny shrub bearing white flowers before the leaves and small dark purple fruits; **black tie**, tie worn with tuxedo or dinner jacket; the jacket and attire as a whole; **black velvet**, mixture of stout and champagne; **black′water fever**, tropical fever, originating in malarial infection, characterized by brown or blue-black urine; **black widow**, small, jet-black spider (*Latrodectus mactans*), female of which is venomous. **black′ish** *adj.* **black′ly** *adv.* **black′ness** *n.* **black** *n.* 1. Black color, paint, etc.; **in the ~**, (bookkeeping) operating at a profit. 2. Black substance, as soot etc.; fungus, smut, in wheat etc. 3. Black variety of anything; black cloth or clothing. 4. (sometimes Black) Member of dark-skinned people of African descent. 5. (Player using) dark pieces in chess etc. **black** *v.t.* Make black, polish with blacking; obscure (window, street, etc.) so that no light is visible from outside or from the air; extinguish lights during stage performance; become unconscious; **black′out** (*n.*) (1) (period of) obscuration of artificial lights, esp. in wartime; (2) failure or stoppage of electrical power, radio signal, etc.; suspension or suppression of news; (3) temporary loss of vision and consciousness; (4) temporary loss of memory.

black·a·moor (blăk′*a*moor) *n.* (archaic) Black person.

Black·beard (blăk′bērd) (d. 1718). Real name Edward Teach or Thatch. British pirate along the Spanish Main, the Bahamas, and off the coasts of Virginia and Carolina; protected by corrupt governor of N. Carolina; killed in attack by naval ships sent by governor of Virginia.

Black Canyon. Colorado River canyon between Arizona and Nevada; site of Hoover Dam.

black·en (blăk′*e*n) *v.* Make grow, black or dark; speak evil of. **black′en·er** *n.*

Black Forest. Wooded mountainous resort region in S.W. West Germany.

Black Hawk (1767–1838). American Indian leader of the Fox and Sauk during the Black Hawk War, 1832.

Black Hills. Group of mountains rich in mineral deposits in S.W. South Dakota and N.E. Wyoming.

black·ing (blăk′ĭng) *n.* (esp.) Paste or liquid for blacking or polishing boots.

Black·more (blăk′mōr), **Richard Dodridge** (1825–1900). English novelist, author of *Lorna Doone*.

Black·pool (blăk′pōōl). Seaside resort in N.W. England on the Irish sea.

Black·stone (blăk′stōn), **Sir William** (1723–80). English jurist, author of *Commentaries on the Laws of England* (1765–9).

Black · well (blăk′wĕl), **Elizabeth** (1821–1910). American and British physician; resident of the U.S. 1832–69; first woman doctor in modern times; established private dispensary in New York, 1851, which became New York Infirmary and College for Women.

blad·der (blăd′*er*) *n.* 1. Membranous bag in human and other animal bodies, esp. urinary bladder; animal's bladder or part of it prepared for various uses, inflated, etc. 2. Anything inflated and hollow, inflated pericarp or vesicle in plants and seaweeds. **blad′der·like, blad′der·y** *adjs.*

blade (blād) *n.* 1. Flat lanceolate leaf of grass and cereals; (bot.) broad thin expanded part of leaf as opp. to petiole or leafstalk. 2. Broad flattened leaflike part of instrument, as oar, paddle, spade, aircraft propeller, etc.; broad flattened bone, esp. shoulder blade. 3. Thin cutting part of edged tool or weapon; a sword; detachable usu. two-edged cutting part of safety razor; sharp part of ice skate in contact with the ice. 4. Swordsman; a gallant, dashing fellow. **blade′less, blade′like** *adjs.*

blain (blān) *n.* Inflamed swelling or sore on skin.

Blair (blār), **Eric Arthur**: see George ORWELL.

Blake (blāk), **William** (1757–1827). English poet, painter, and mystic; engraved, and sometimes colored by hand, many of his own works, which included the lyrical *Songs of Innocence* (1789) and *Songs of Experience* (1794), and the *Prophetic Books* (1793–1804).

blame (blām) *n.* Censure; responsibility for bad result. ~ *v.t.* (**blamed, blam·ing**). Find fault with; fix responsibility on. **blame′less** *adj.* Innocent. **blame′ful** *adj.* **blame′ful·ly** *adv.* **blame′ful·ness** *n.* **blame′less·ly** *adv.* **blame′less·ness** *n.* **blame′wor·thy** *adj.*

blanch (blănch) *v.* Make white by withdrawing color, peeling (almonds), immersing in boiling water, or depriving of light (plants); make or grow pale with fear, cold, etc.

blanc · mange (bl*a*mahnj′, -mahṅzh′) *n.* Flavored, sweetened milk pudding thickened with cornstarch.

bland (blănd) *adj.* Pleasantly agreeable, gentle; mild; (of food) nonspicy, soothing or nonirritating; unemotional, indifferent. **bland′ly** *adv.* **bland′ness** *n.*

blan·dish (blăn′dĭsh) *v.* Flatter, coax. **blan′dish·er, blan′dish·ment** *ns.*

blank (blăngk) *adj.* 1. Not written or printed on; with spaces left for signature or details. 2. Empty, not filled. 3. Void of interest, incident, result, or expression; unrelieved, sheer. 4. ~ **check**, check signed by drawer, with amount left for payee to fill in; hence, full discretionary power; ~ **verse**, unrhymed, metrical verse esp. of five-foot iambics; ~ **wall**, wall without opening; (fig.) impassable obstacle. **blank′ly** *adv.* **blank′ness** *n.* **blank** *n.* 1. Void; space left to be filled up in document; printed form containing such spaces; dash (—) written in place of omitted letter or word(s). 2. Gun cartridge containing powder but no bullet. 3. Piece of metal ready for stamping as coin, medal, etc. 4. Blank (losing) ticket in drawing; **draw (a)** ~, elicit no response, fail. **blank** *v.t.* 1. To keep (an opponent) from scoring in a game. 2. ~ **out**, cross out, obliterate, delete.

blan·ket (blăng′kĭt) *n.* Rectangular piece of woolen etc. material used for warmth esp. as bed covering; any covering, as a ~ **of snow**; (as *adj.*) covering or including all contingencies etc.; **wet** ~, (fig.) discouraging person. **blanket** *v.t.* Cover with blanket, stifle. **blan′ket·less** *adj.*

blan·ket·ing (blăng′kĭtĭng) *n.*

William Blake *was a visionary poet and artist. His illustrations for other poets' works are imbued with his distinctive image of the world. Here, one of his illustrations for Dante's 'Commedia' shows the poet at hell's gates.*

(esp.) Material for blankets.

blare (blār) *n.* & *v.* (**blared, blar·ing**). (Make) sound of trumpet; utter loudly.

Blar·ney (blār'nē). Village near Cork in S. Ireland; ~ **stone**, inscribed stone, very difficult to reach, in the Castle of Blarney, supposed to confer upon anyone who kisses it a cajoling tongue and the art of flattery or of telling lies with unblushing effrontery.

blar·ney (blār'nē) *n.* & *v.* (**-neyed, -ney·ing**). (Use, assail with) flattering or cajoling talk; nonsense.

bla·sé (blahzā', blah'zā) *adj.* Bored, indifferent from an excess of worldliness.

blas·pheme (blăsfēm', blăs'fēm) *v.* (**-phemed, -phem·ing**). Talk impiously; utter profanity about, revile. **blas·phem'er, blas·phe·my** (blăs'fəmē) *ns.* (pl. **-mies**). **blas'phe·mous** *adj.* **blas'phe·mous·ly** *adv.*

blast (blăst) *n.* Strong gust of wind; violent gust of air caused by explosion of bomb, etc.; explosion; blowing or sound of trumpet or other wind instruments; sudden loud noise; strong current of air used in smelting etc.; quantity of explosion used in blasting; (colloq.) violent reprimand; (slang) a party, esp. a wild one; (**at**) **full** ~, (colloq.) at maximum speed, capacity, etc.; ~ **furnace**, smelting furnace into which a blast of compressed heated air is driven by blower. **blast** *v.t.* 1. Blow up, break, dislodge, with explosives; criticize loudly or vigorously. 2. Wither, shrivel, blight. 3. (of rocket or spacecraft) ~**-off**, take off, be launched into space; use power in flight; **blast'off** (*n.*); **blast** *v.i.* Make a loud, blaring sound. **blast'ed** *adj.* (esp., colloq.) Damnable.

blas·to·derm (blăs'tədērm) *n.* External layer of cells formed as a result of cleavage of a yolked egg, characteristic of eggs of reptiles, birds, and in a different form, insects.

blas·tu·la (blăs'choolə) *n.* (pl. **-las, -lae** pr. -lē). (biol.) Early embryonic stage, usu. a hollow ball of cells, produced by cleavage of an egg. (cf. GASTRULA).

bla·tant (blā'tənt) *adj.* Noisy, vulgarly clamorous; palpably obvious. **bla'tan·cy** *n.* **bla'tant·ly** *adv.*

blath·er (blădh'ər) *n.* & *v.* (Utter) foolish talk; **blath'erskite**, a babbling, foolish person; foolish talk.

Bla·vat·sky (bləvăt'skē), **Helena Petrovna** (1831–91). Russian spiritualist, founder (in New York) of the Theosophical Society.

blaze[1] (blāz) *v.i.* (**blazed, blaz·ing**). Burn with bright flame; be brilliantly lighted; burn with excitement etc.; show bright colors; emit light. ~ *n.* Bright flame or fire; glow of color, bright display; **go to** ~**s**, (slang) go to hell. **blaz'ing·ly** *adv.*

*A **blast furnace** is fueled with ore, coke, and a flux, usually limestone, at the top. Pre-heated air is pumped through the mixture from the base to ignite the coke which reduces the ore to molten iron and slag.*

blaze[2] (blāz) *n.* White mark on face of horse or cow; white mark made on tree by chipping off bark, to indicate path, boundary, etc. ~ *v.t.* (**blazed, blaz·ing**). Mark (tree, path) with blaze; (fig.) ~ **a trail**, show a new way by pioneering activity.

blaze[3] (blāz) *v.t.* (**blazed, blaz·ing**). Proclaim (news) as with trumpet.

blaz·er (blā'zər) *n.* Brightly colored sport jacket, usu. with badge on pocket, and often part of school uniform; solid color sport jacket, esp. one with metal buttons.

bla·zon (blā'zən) *n.* Heraldic shield, coat of arms, bearings, or banner; record, description, esp. of virtues etc. ~ *v.t.* Describe or paint (arms) heraldically; inscribe with arms etc. in colors; give luster to; set forth in fitting words; proclaim. **bla'zon·er, bla'zon·ment** *ns.* **bla'zon·ry** *n.* (Art of describing or painting) heraldic devices, armorial bearings; brightly colored display.

bleach (blēch) *v.* Whiten by exposure to sunlight or chemical process; **bleaching powder**, chemical, such as chloride of lime, used for bleaching. **bleach** *n.* Bleaching process or substance. **bleach'er** *n.* (usually ~**s**), roofless section of (cheapest) seats in baseball park (so called because spectators there are exposed to sun); **bleach'erite**, a spectator who sits in the bleachers, esp. an emotional fan of a team. **bleach'er, bleach'er·y** *ns.*

bleak (blēk) *adj.* Bare of vegetation; exposed, wind-swept; cold, chilly, dreary; offering little hope; (of person) depressed, lifeless. **bleak'ly** *adv.* **bleak'ness** *n.*

blear (blēr) *adj.* Dim, filmy, rheumy; misty, indistinct. ~ *v.t.* Dim (eyes) with tears, rheum, etc.; blur. **blear'y** *adj.* (**blear·i·er, blear·i·est**). **blear'i·ly** *adv.* **blear'i·ness** *n.*

bleat (blēt) *v.* (of sheep, goat, etc.) Utter characteristic tremulous cry; make sound resembling this, speak feebly or foolishly. ~ *n.* Cry of sheep, goat, etc.; any similar sound. **bleat'er** *n.* **bleat'ing·ly** *adv.*

bleed (blēd) *v.* (**bled** pr. blĕd, **bleed·ing**). 1. Emit blood; suffer wounds or violent death; feel pity, sorrow, or anguish; (of plants) emit sap; (of dyes) come out in water. 2. Draw blood surgically from; allow (liquid or gas) to escape from (a container). 3. Part with money, suffer extortion; extort money from. 4. (print.) Let illustration run to edge of page, without margin.

bleed·er (blē'dər) *n.* (esp.) Person suffering from hemophilia.

bleep (blēp) *n.* & *v.i.* (Emit) high-pitched intermittent sound; censor word or words from television or radio program by deleting them electronically.

blem·ish (blĕm'ĭsh) *v.t.* Mar, spoil beauty or perfection of, sully. ~ *n.* Physical or moral defect, stain, flaw. **blem'ish·er** *n.*

blench (blĕnch) *v.i.* (archaic) Start aside, flinch, quail. **blench'er** *n.*

blend (blĕnd) *v.* (**blend·ed** or **blent, blend·ing**). Mix, mingle (esp. sorts of tea, tobacco, whiskey, etc., to produce a certain quality); mingle intimately *with*; mix so as to be inseparable and indistinguishable; pass imperceptibly into each other; fit, relate, or match. ~ *n.* Blending; mixture made by blending. **blend'er** *n.* (esp.) Kitchen appliance for combining cooking ingredients.

blende (blĕnd) *n.* Zinc sulfide. [Ger. *blenden* deceive, because although it often resembled galena, it did not yield lead]

blen·ny (blĕn'ē) *n.* (pl. **-nies**). Small spiny-finned fish of genus *Blennius* of family Blenniidae,

*Facing page, top: Prescribed burning by the United States Forest Service prevents uncontrollable **blazes.** Below: **Bleachers** provide inexpensive outdoor seating for enthusiastic spectators.*

A closed-circuit T.V. with lens attachment magnifies the text of an ordinary book. Technological advancements have made it possible for near ***blind*** *and partially sighted people to lead more fulfilling lives.*

mostly shore fish found in shallow pools. **blen·ni·oid** (blĕn′ēoid) *adj.*

blent (blĕnt): see BLEND.

bleph·a·ri·tis (blĕferī′tĭs) *n.* Inflammation of the eyelids.

bless (blĕs) *v.t.* (**bless·ed** or **blest, bless·ing**). 1. Consecrate (esp. food); sanctify by making sign of cross. 2. Call holy, adore; glorify for benefits received. 3. Pronounce words (held) to confer supernatural favor and well-being upon; make happy or successful; make happy *with* some gift; *bless me! bless you!*, (**God**) **bless my soul!**, etc., exclamations of surprise or indignation.

bless·ed (blĕs′ĭd; sometimes blĕst) *adj.* 1. Consecrated; revered; fortunate; in paradise; beatified. 2. Blissful, bringing happiness. 3. (euphem.) Cursed etc. **bless′ed·ly** *adv.* **bless′ed·ness** *n.*

bless·ing (blĕs′ĭng) *n.* Declaration, invocation, or bestowal, of divine favor; grace before or after food; gift of God, nature, etc., that one is glad of; approval; ~ **in disguise**, misfortune that works for eventual good.

blest (blĕst): see BLESS.

Bligh (blī), **William** (1754–1817). English vice-admiral, explorer, and colonial administrator; as a lieutenant he commanded the BOUNTY.

blight (blīt) *n.* 1. Disease of plants caused by fungoid parasites. 2. Any malignant withering influence. ~ *v.t.* Affect with blight; exert baleful influence on; nip in the bud, mar, frustrate.

blight·er (blī′ter) *n.* (Brit. slang) Contemptible or annoying person or thing; fellow, thing.

bli·mey (blī′mē) *int.* (Brit. slang) Exclamation of surprise or contempt. [f. *Gorblimey* = God blind me!]

blimp (blĭmp) *n.* Small, nonrigid type of airship.

Blimp (blĭmp), **Colonel.** Character invented by the English cartoonist David Low (1891–1963) representing a muddleheaded, obese, elderly gentleman, pop. interpreted as type of diehard or reactionary.

blind (blīnd) *adj.* 1. Without sight; (aeronaut.) without direct observation of objects etc., relying on instruments. 2. Without foresight, discernment, or moral or intellectual light; reckless; not ruled by purpose, reason, or control (as a ~ **chance**). 3. Secret, obscure, concealed (as a ~ **driveway**); without windows or openings; walled up; closed at one end, not leading anywhere (as ~ **alley**). 4. (slang) Very drunk. 5. ~ **date**, social engagement between two persons of opposite sex who have not met before; either of these persons; **blind′man's buff**, game in which blindfolded player tries to catch and identify one of the others; **blind spot**, point in the retina not sensitive to light, where the optic nerve passes through the inner coat of the eyeball, hence (fig.) a subject, area, etc. about which one is ignorant, intolerant, or overly emotional; **blind-stamping** (bookbinding), stamping without the use of ink or gold leaf. **blind** *adv.* **blind′ing** *adj.* **blind′ing·ly, blind′ly** *advs.* **blind′ness** *n.* **blind** *v.t.* Deprive of sight permanently or temporarily; take away power of judgment, deceive. ~ *n.* Obstruction to sight or light; screen for windows etc., esp. on roller; pretext; shelter of canvas, leaves, etc. for concealing hunters, as a **duck** ~.

blind·fold (blīnd′fōld) *adj.* With eyes covered with cloth; without circumspection. ~ *v.t.* Deprive of sight by covering eyes with cloth. ~ *n.* A cloth covering the eyes to prevent seeing.

blink (blĭngk) *v.* 1. Shut one's eyelids momentarily, esp. in-

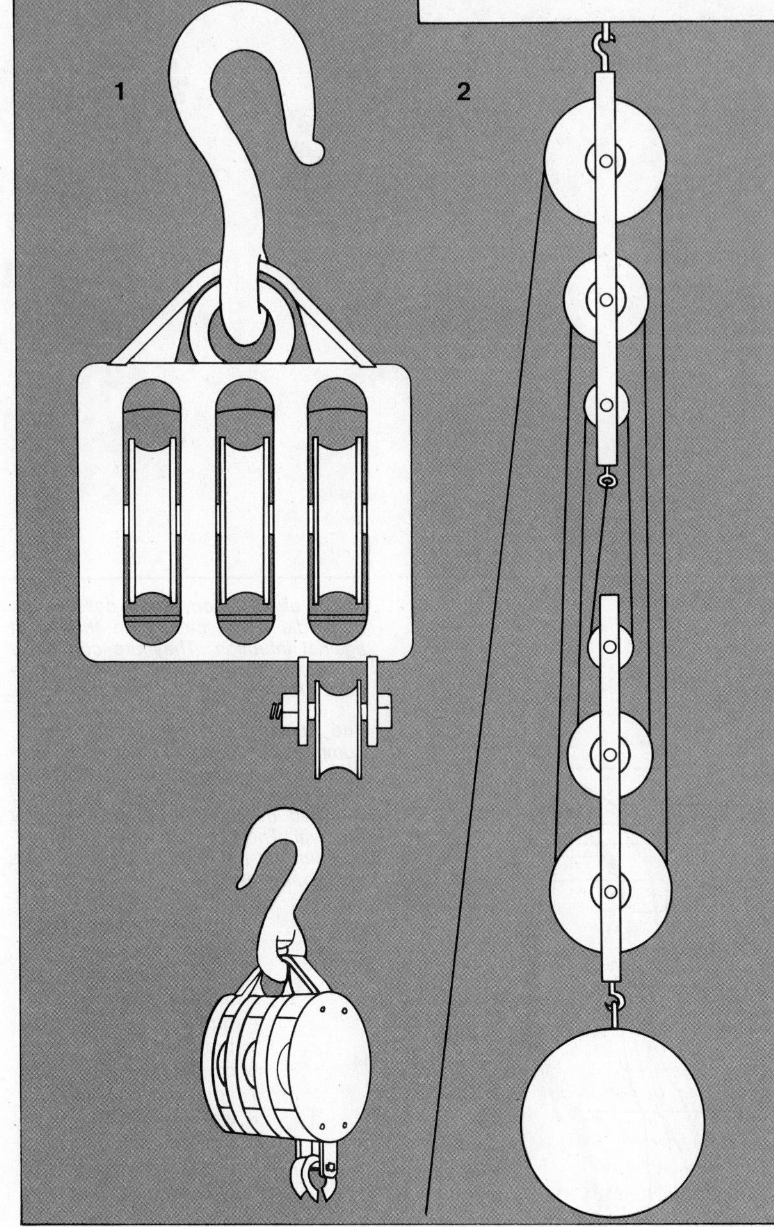

*When a **block** is fitted with pulley wheels and linked by rope or belt to other pulleys it reduces the effort required to lift a weight. 1. A triple block with internal straps and side hook. Parts of the strap go through the block to form a becket. 2. A multiple block and tackle.*

voluntarily; (of eyes) shut thus. 2. (fig.) Shut one's eyes to, evade. 3. Send (tears etc.) away by blinking. 4. Shine suddenly or momentarily. ~ *n.* Blinking; momentary gleam or glimpse.

blink·er (blĭng'k*er*) *n.* 1. Either of two flaps on horse's bridle preventing it from seeing sideways. 2. A device for flashing light signals; a blinking signal light, as for signaling or warning motorists.

blip (blĭp) *n.* (radar) Image of object as projected on screen.

bliss (blĭs) *n.* Gladness, enjoyment; the joy of heaven, perfect happiness, blessedness; being in heaven. **bliss'ful** *adj.* **bliss'ful·ly** *adv.* **bliss'ful·ness** *n.*

blis·ter (blĭs'*ter*) *n.* Thin vesicle on skin filled with serum, caused by friction, a burn, etc.; similar swelling on plant, metal, painted surface, etc.; rounded compartment protruding from body of airplane. ~ *v.* Raise blister on, be or become covered with blisters; (fig.) criticize scathingly. **blis'ter·y** *adj.*

blithe (blīdh) *adj.* (poet.) Gay, joyous. **blithe'ly** *adv.* **blithe'ness** *n.* **blithe'some** *adj.*

B.Litt. *abbrev. Baccalaureus Literarum.* (L., = Bachelor of Letters).

blitz (blĭts) *n.* Quick, violent attack intended to bring speedy victory, intensive air attack. ~ *v.t.* Attack suddenly and violently. [Ger. *Blitzkrieg* lightning war]

bliz·zard (blĭz'*erd*) *n.* Heavy snowstorm with driving winds.

bloat[1] (blōt) *v.t.* Cure (herring) by salting and smoking. **bloat'er** *n.* (esp. Brit.) Herring cured by bloating.

bloat[2] (blōt) *v.* Inflate, swell. **bloat'ed** *adj.* Inflated, swollen; (fig.) swollen with pride, excessive wealth, etc.

blob (blŏb) *n.* Drop of liquid; small roundish mass; spot of color. ~ *v.* (**blobbed, blob·bing**).

bloc (blŏk) *n.* Combination of political parties, or of governments, groups, etc., formed to forward some interest.

block (blŏk) *n.* 1. Log of wood; large piece of wood for chopping or hammering on, mounting horse from, etc., (hist.) on which condemned persons were beheaded. 2. Compact usu. solid piece of any substance; unhewn lump of rock; prepared piece of building stone; mold or form on which something is shaped or displayed; piece of wood or metal engraved for printing; (mech.) pulley, system of pulleys mounted in case; (slang) head. 3. Section, compact set or group; group of buildings surrounded by (usu. four) streets. 4. Obstruction; (psychol.) mental obstruction preventing a particular thought or expression; (path.) obstruction of a nervous or muscular impulse. 5. **block'-buster**, (slang) large high-explosive bomb; overwhelmingly impressive object or idea, such as a novel or film; **block'busting**, inducing people to sell their homes at a low price by warning of change in racial patterns of a neighborhood; **block'head**, stupid person; **block'house**, detached fort (orig. one blocking passage), occas. one of connected chain of posts; one-storied timber building with loopholes; reinforced concrete shelter; **block letters, writing**, (writing with) detached letters, as in printing, usu. capitals; **block printing**, hand printing of fabrics with wooden blocks on which design is carved. **block** *v.t.* Obstruct (passage etc.); put obstacles in way of; restrict use or conversion of currency etc.; shape on block; ~ **in, out**, sketch roughly, plan.

Block (blŏk), **Adriaen.** Seventeenth c. Dutch navigator, discoverer of Block Island; ~ **Island,** island and summer resort off the coast of Rhode Island at the entrance to Long Island Sound.

block·ade (blŏkād') *n.* Surrounding of place, blocking of harbor, etc., by hostile forces to prevent goods etc. from reaching or leaving it; **raise, run the** ~, remove, evade, the blockading force. **blockade** *v.t.* (**-ad·ed, -ad·ing**). Subject to blockade. **block·ad′er** *n.*

block·age (blŏk′ĭj) *n.* Obstruction.

bloke (blōk) *n.* (Brit. slang) Man, fellow.

blond (blŏnd) *adj.* (of hair) Light colored, flaxen; (of complexion) fair. ~ *n.* Person with blond hair. **blonde** *n.* Woman with blond hair. **blond′ness** *n.*

blood (blŭd) *n.* 1. Liquid circulating in the veins and arteries of vertebrates, carrying nourishment and oxygen to all parts of the body and bringing away waste products to be excreted, consisting of a serum or plasma in which corpuscles are suspended and usu. red because of their hemoglobin content; (hist.) one of the four humors (see HUMOR, 4). 2. Analogous liquid in invertebrates performing (some of) the same functions. 3. Taking of life, guilt of bloodshed; passion, temperament, mettle. 4. Race, relationship, kin, descent, parentage. 5. Dandy, man of fashion. 6. ~ **bank**, place where supply of blood for transfusion is stored; ~ **bath**, massacre; ~ **brother**, brother by birth; one bound to another in solemn friendship by ceremonial mingling of blood; ~ **count**, (determination of) number of blood cells in a given volume of blood; ~ **donor**: see DONOR; ~ **group**, one of several types into which human blood may be divided on basis of its compatibility with that of other persons; **blood′hound**, large keen-scented dog used for tracking cattle, criminals, etc.; **blood′letting**, surgical removal of some of patient's blood; **blood′-mobile**, truck equipped for receiving and transporting blood donated for transfusions; **blood money**, that gained ruthlessly through others' suffering; that paid to a hired assassin; (hist.) that paid to next of kin for slaughter of relative; **blood poisoning**, condition caused by presence of pathogenic bacteria in the blood; **blood pressure**, pressure of blood against walls of arteries as it is impelled along them, freq. measured in diagnosis because in certain conditions it may be higher (hypertension) or lower (hypotension) than normal; **blood relation**, one related by virtue of common descent, not by marriage; **blood′shed**, spilling of blood, slaughter; **blood′shot**, (of eye) suffused, tinged, with blood; **blood sport**, sport involving killing of animals, esp. hunting; **blood′-stone**, green chalcedony with spots

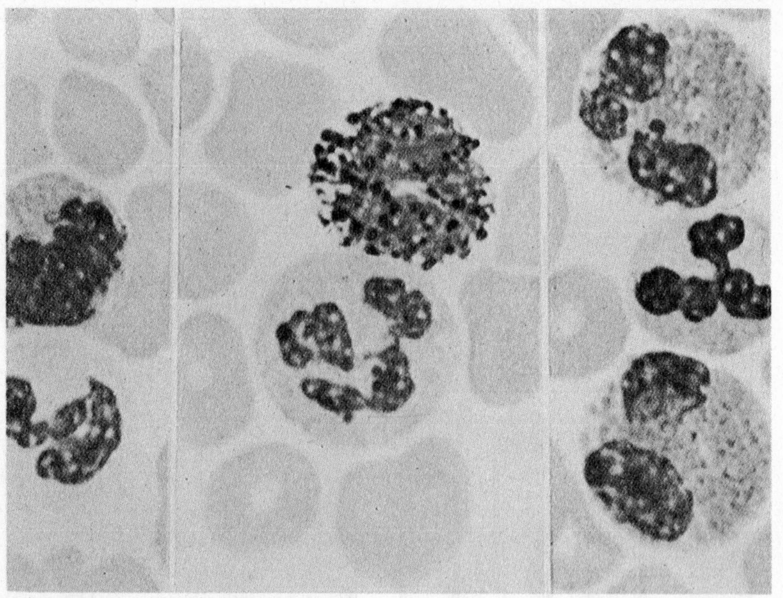

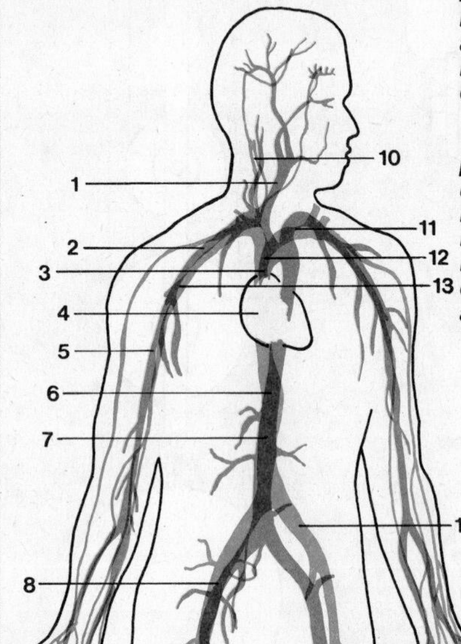

*About eight million **blood** cells in the body die every second in their fight against infection. They are constantly renewed. Above: Here, red and white cells are seen under a microscope.*

The human heart can, under stress, pump up to 12 pints of blood every minute. Oxygen-enriched blood is forced round the arterial system (red) and returned through the veins (blue) for renewal. The blood is supplied to various parts of the body by blood vessels and capillaries.

Arterial System (red)
1 common carotid
2 right subclavian
3 ascending aorta
4 heart
5 brachial
6 coeliac artery
7 abdominal aorta
8 exterior iliac
9 femoral artery
Venous System (blue)
10 external jugular vein
11 innominate vein
12 vena azygos
13 brachial
14 common iliac
15 long saphenous vein
16 femoral vein

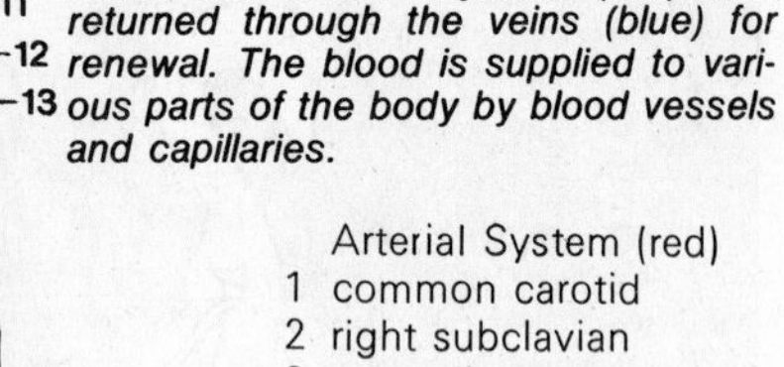

Veins have a series of valves that act as a check on the direction of flow. While the blood flows correctly (A), the valves remain open, but when the blood flows back in the wrong direction (B) it flicks the valve across the vein and closes it.

*Its acute sense of smell and inborn skill in tracking makes the **bloodhound** valuable to hunters. It pursues its quarry but does not kill. A hound stands 25–27 ins. at the shoulder.*

***Bluebottles** or blowflies are flies of metallic hue belonging to the family Calliphoridae. Some are a serious pest of sheep as they lay eggs in damp wool and the larvae cause wounds which become infected.*

or veins of red jasper; heliotrope; **blood'stream**, circulating blood in human or animal system; **blood'sucker**, leech; extortioner; **blood'thirsty**, eager for bloodshed; **blood vessel**, vein, artery, or capillary conveying blood. **blood** *v.t.* Remove surgically some of the blood of; smear face of (novice at hunting) with blood of fox after kill. **blood'less** *adj.* Without blood; unfeeling; pale; without bloodshed. **blood'like** *adj.*

blood·y (blŭd'ē) *adj.* (**blood·i·er, blood·i·est**). 1. Of, like, running or smeared with, blood. 2. Involving, loving, resulting from, bloodshed; cruel. 3. (Brit. slang) Damned. ~ *adv.* (Brit. slang) Confoundedly, very. ~ *v.t.* (**blood·ied, blood·y·ing**). Make bloody; stain with blood. **blood'i·ly** *adv.* **blood'i·ness** *n.*

bloom (bloo͞m) *n.* Flower, esp. of plants grown or admired chiefly for the flower, florescence. 2. Prime, perfection; flush, glow; delicate powdery deposit on grapes, plums, etc.; cloudiness on a shiny surface; freshness. ~ *v.* Bear flowers, be in flower; come into, be in, full beauty; flourish.

Bloom·er (bloo͞'mer), **Mrs. Amelia Jenks** (1818–94). American temperance leader, feminist, and popularizer of "rational dress" for women. **bloom'ers** *n.pl.* Costume with loose knee-length trousers formerly worn by women for gymnastics, cycling, etc.; undergarments of this shape.

Blooms·bur·y (bloo͞mz'berē, -brē). District of London containing British Museum and many buildings of London University, formerly a fashionable and later a literary quarter.

blos·som (blŏs'om) *v.i.* Open into flower (lit. and fig.). ~ *n.* Flower, mass of flowers on fruit tree etc.; early stage of growth, promise. **blos'som·y** *adj.*

blot[1] (blŏt) *n.* Spot or stain of ink etc., dark patch; disfigurement, blemish, defect; disgraceful act or quality in good character. ~ *v.* (**blot·ted, blot·ting**). 1. Spot or stain with ink, etc.; make blots; smudge; sully, detract from; obliterate (writing etc.) with blot, destroy. 2. Dry with **blotting paper**, absorbent paper for soaking up wet ink. **blot'less** *adj.*

blot[2] (blŏt) *n.* Exposed piece in backgammon.

blotch (blŏch) *n.* Discolored or inflamed patch on skin; irregular patch of ink, color, etc. **blotch'y** *adj.* (**blotch·i·er, blotch·i·est**).

blot·ter (blŏt'*er*) *n.* Piece or pad of blotting paper; record book of daily occurrences or transactions; so **police** ~, book listing police arrests, calls answered, etc., each day.

blot·to (blŏt'ō) *adj.* (slang) Very drunk.

blouse (blows, blowz) *n.* 1. Woman's or child's loose garment for upper part of body, usu. worn tucked into skirt or trousers. 2. Upper part of battle dress, fitting closely at waist. ~ *v.* (**bloused, blous·ing**). Arrange (material, bodice), be arranged, in loose light folds like a blouse. **blouse'like** *adj.*

blow[1] (blō) *v.* (**blew** pr. bloo͞, **blown** pr. blōn, **blow·ing**). 1. Move as wind does, act as current of air; send current of air from mouth; pant, puff; (of whales etc.) eject water and air; cause to pant, put out of breath. 2. Drive, be driven, by blowing; sound (wind instrument, or note *on* or *with* this); direct air current at; clear, empty, by air current; break *in* or send flying *off*, *out*, *up*, by explosion; (of instrument) sound; ~ **up** (*v.*), inflate, shatter or be shattered by explosion; (photog., colloq.) enlarge. 3. (of electric fuse or lamp filament) Melt when overloaded. 4. (slang) Curse, confound; squander. 5. **blow'fly**, fly that lays its eggs on carrion etc.; **blow'gun**, pipe through which darts or pellets are blown by the breath; **blow'hard**, braggart; **blow'hole**, each of two holes (containing the nostrils) at top of head in whales etc. through which they blow; hole in ice through which seals etc. can breathe; **blow'out**, bursting (of automobile tire etc.); (slang) large meal, feast; **blow'pipe**, tube for heating flame by blowing air or other gas into it; **blow'torch**, apparatus for directing very hot flame on a selected spot; apparatus for heating or cutting metals; **blow'up** (*n.*), explosion; (colloq.) enlargement; (colloq.) outburst of temper; **blow** *n.* Blowing; blowing of flute, one's nose, etc. **blow'er** *n.*

blow[2] (blō) *n.* Hard stroke with fist, hammer, etc.; disaster, shock; **~-by-~** *adj.*, (of narrative) giving all details in sequence.

blow·er (blō'*er*) *n.* (esp.) 1. Apparatus for increasing draft of fire. 2. (Brit. slang) Telephone.

blown (blōn): see BLOW[1].

blow·y (blō'ē) *adj.* (**blow·i·er,**

Above: The black-crested ***Steller's blue jay*** *is one of up to 35 species of the largely omnivorous jay found in the U.S.A.*

Right: A typical farm building in the ***Blue Ridge Mountains*** *which have a diverse farming community as well as tourist attractions.*

blow·i·est). Windy.

blowz·y (blow'zē) *adj.* (**blowz·i·er, blowz·i·est**). (of woman) Red-faced, coarse looking; slatternly.

blub·ber (blŭb'*er*) *n.* 1. Fatty tissue of aquatic mammals which keeps them warm, esp. **whale ~**, used as source of oil. 2. Weeping. **blubber** *adj.* (of lips) Swollen, protruding. ~ *v.* Utter with sobs, weep noisily. **blub'ber·er** *n.* **blub'ber·ing·ly** *adv.*

blu·cher (bloo͞'k*er*, -ch*er*) *n.* (19th-c.) Strong leather half boot or high shoe. [f. BLÜCHER]

Blü·cher (bloo͞'k*er*, -ch*er*; *Ger.* blü'χ*er*), **Gebhard Leberecht von** (1742–1819). Prussian field marshal, led the Prussian army at the battle of WATERLOO.

bludg·eon (blŭj'*on*) *n.* Short heavy-headed stick. ~ *v.t.* Strike heavily or repeatedly with or as with bludgeon.

blue (bloo͞) *adj.* (**blu·er, blu·est**). 1. Colored like the cloudless sky, or with darker or paler shades of this color; livid, leaden colored. 2. Affected with fear, discomfort, anxiety, low spirits, etc. 3. Dressed in blue; (of talk etc.) indecent, obscene. 4. ~ **baby**, infant suffering from congenital cyanosis; **blue'bell**, any of various plants with blue, bell-shaped flowers, e.g. harebell, (*Scilla monscripta*, of Europe), lungwort (*Mertensia virginica*). **blue'berry**, (blue fruit of) one of several plants of genus *Vaccinium*; **blue'bird**, any of three N. Amer. songbirds of genus *Sialis*, of mostly blue plumage, esp. *S. sialis*, the eastern bluebird; **blue blood**, high birth; **blue'bonnet**, round flat blue woolen cap formerly generally worn in Scotland; (hist.) Scottish soldier wearing this; wildflower with blue blossoms (*Lupinus subcarnosus*) common in SW. U.S.; **blue book**, student's examination booklet in blue paper cover; **blue'bottle**, dipterous insect with blue body of genus *Calliphora* (esp. *C. vomitoria* and *C. erythrocephala*), which deposits eggs on meat, carrion, etc.; **blue cheese**, cheese with veins of blue mold; **blue-chip**, (stock exch.) stock that is a fairly reliable investment, paying good dividends; (also attrib.); **blue-collar worker**, manual or industrial (opp. office) worker; **blue'fish**, voracious game fish (*Pomatomus saltatrix*); **blue'-grass**, species of *Poa* (esp. *P. pratensis*), as found in Kentucky and Virginia; hence, **the Blue'-grass**, region in central Kentucky famous for this grass and the breeding of race horses; **blue'-jacket**, seaman; **blue jay**, common crested jay (*Cyanocitta cristata*) of N. Amer.; **blue jeans**, blue denim trousers with reinforced seams and seat; **blue law**, severely Puritanical law; **blue mold**, fungus of genus *Penicillium* forming on food; **once in a blue moon**, very rarely; **Blue Nile**: see NILE; **blue pencil**, pencil making blue mark, used chiefly in making corrections, obliterations, etc.; **blue-pencil** (*v.t.*) make marks, cuts, or alterations in; censor; **blue'point**, small, tasty oyster from south shore of Long Island [f. name of headland]; **blue'print**, photographic print of white lines on blue ground or blue lines on white ground, used in copying plans, machine drawings, etc.; (fig.) detailed plan, scheme; **blue ribbon**, first prize; greatest honor or distinction in any sphere; **blue-sky laws**, regulations forbidding sales to gullible investors; **blue'-stocking**, woman having or affecting literary tastes and learning [f. *Blue Stocking Society*, name given in 18th c. to meetings for literary conversation etc. at the houses of Mrs. Elizabeth Montagu (1720–1800) and her circle, from the fact that the men attending might wear the blue worsted stockings of ordinary daytime dress instead of the black silk of evening]; **blue water**, deep water, the open sea. **blu'ish** *adj.* **blue'ness** *n.*

blue *n.* 1. Blue color or pigment; blue cloth etc. 2. Sky, sea (**the** ~); **out of the** ~, unexpectedly. 3. (pl.) Melancholy; (type of) melancholy song of U.S. black origin; **the blues**. **blue** *v.t.* (**blued, blu·ing**). Make blue; treat with laundering blue.

Blue·beard (blōō´bẽrd). Hero of a popular tale, who killed several wives in turn because they showed undue curiosity about a locked room.

Blue Ridge Mountains. SE. range of the Appalachian Mountains from S. Pennsylvania to N. Georgia; contains many scenic and resort areas.

bluff[1] (blŭf) *adj.* Having perpendicular broad front; abrupt, blunt, frank, hearty. **bluff'ly** *adv.* **bluff'ness** *n.* **bluff** *n.* Headland with perpendicular broad face.

bluff[2] (blŭf) *v.* Make pretense of strength to gain advantage etc. (orig. in poker); mislead thus. ~ *n.* Bluffing; **call person's** ~, challenge his attempted bluff. **bluff'er** *n.*

Blum (blŭm), **Léon** (1872–1950). French political leader; premier of France, 1936–7 and 1946–7.

blun·der (blŭn´d*e*r) *v.* Move blindly, stumble; make gross mistake. ~ *n.* Stupid or careless mistake. **blun'der·er** *n.* **blun'der·ing·ly** *adv.*

blun·der·buss (blŭn´d*e*rbŭs) *n.* Short flintlock gun with large bore, firing many balls or slugs, used esp. in 17th and 18th centuries. [corrupt. of Du. *donderbus* lit. thunder gun]

blunt (blŭnt) *adj.* Dull, not sensitive; without sharp edge or point; outspoken. **blunt'ly** *adj.* **blunt'ness** *n.* **blunt** *v.t.* Make less sharp or sensitive.

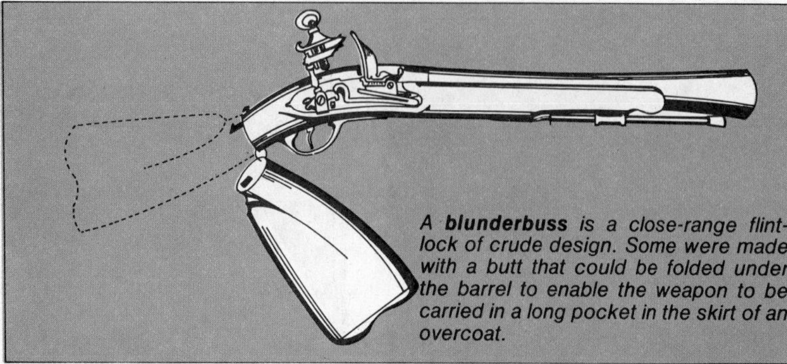

A ***blunderbuss*** *is a close-range flintlock of crude design. Some were made with a butt that could be folded under the barrel to enable the weapon to be carried in a long pocket in the skirt of an overcoat.*

blur (blẽr) *n.* Smear of ink etc.; dimness, confused effect. ~ *v.* (**blurred, blur·ring**). Smear with ink etc.; sully, disfigure; make indistinct; efface; dim.

blurb (blẽrb) *n.* Publisher's description of book printed on jacket etc.; descriptive or commendatory paragraph.

blurt (blẽrt) *v.t.* Burst *out* with, utter abruptly.

blush (blŭsh) *v.i.* Become red with shame or other emotion; be ashamed; be red or pink. ~ *n.* Glance, glimpse; reddening of face in shame etc.; rosy glow, flush of light. **blush'er** *n.* **blush'ful** *adj.* **blush'ing·ly** *adv.*

blus·ter (blŭs´t*e*r) *v.* Storm boisterously; utter overbearingly. **blus'ter·er** *n.* **blus'ter·ing·ly** *adv.* **blus'ter·y, blus'ter·ous** *adjs.* **bluster** *n.* Boisterous blowing, noisy self-assertive talk, threats.

Bly (blī), **Nellie** (1867–1922). Pseudonym of Elizabeth Cochrane Seaman; American journalist, famous for trip made around the world in the record time of 72 days, 6 hours, 11 minutes; had herself committed to New York City insane ward to write *Ten Days in a Madhouse*; also wrote *Around the World in Seventy-Two Days.*

BM *abbrev.* Basal metabolism; (colloq.) bowel movement.

BMR *abbrev.* Basal metabolic rate.

bn. *abbrev.* Battalion.

B'nai B'rith (b*i*nā´ brĭth´). Jewish organization promoting welfare of Jews and social and educational improvement. [Hebrew, = "sons of the covenant"]

B.O. *abbrev.* Body odor; box office.

bo·a (bō´*a*) *n.* (pl. **bo·as**). 1. S. Amer. tropical nonpoisonous snake of family Boidae that kills its prey by constriction or compression (pop. extended to pythons); ~ **constrictor**, large Brazilian species of boa; any great crushing snake. 2. Long round fur or feather wrap formerly worn around throat by women.

Bo·ad·i·ce·a (bōăd*i*sē´*a*). (d. 62 A.D.). British queen, led revolt against the Romans, took poison when finally defeated by Suetonius Paulinus. Also **Boudicca.**

boar (bōr, bŏr) *n.* Uncastrated

The African wild ***boar*** *(below), like those of Asia and Europe, is dangerous when cornered. It feeds on roots and berries and grows to about 3 ft. high at the shoulder.*

A constrictor snake (above) is of the ***boa*** *family which includes the largest snake in the world, the anaconda. South American constrictors rarely exceed 12 ft. but the Central American type may be 15 ft. long.*

Many racing yachts and other small* boats *have hulls built from molded glass-reinforced plastics. The method allows the forming of a strong, well-shaped, and smooth hull that enables the boat to slip unhindered through the water.

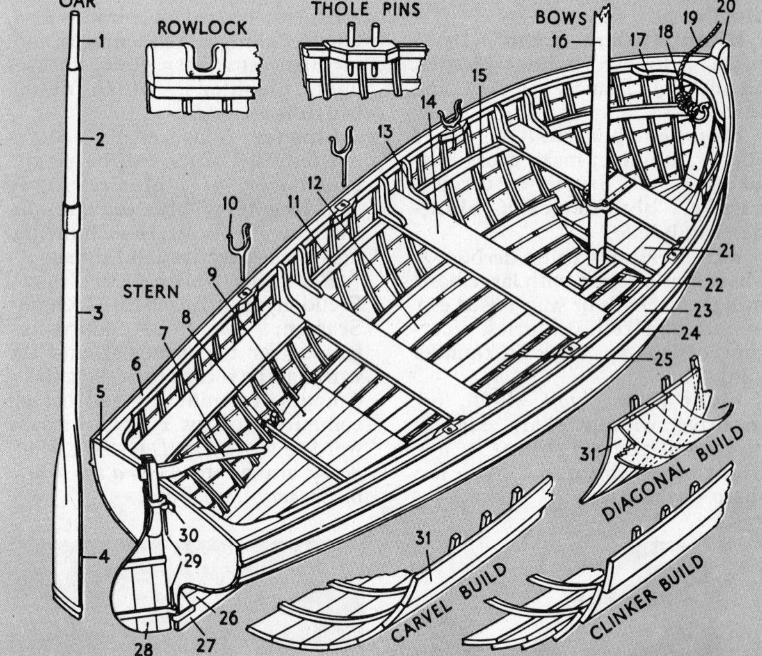

1 grip
2 loom
3 shaft
4 blade
5 transom
6 gunwale
7 tiller
8 stretcher
9 stern sheets
10 rowlock
11 rising
12 bottom boards
13 knee
14 thwart
15 rib
16 mast
17 breast hook
18 apron
19 painter
20 stem
21 foresheets
22 mast step
23 top strake
24 rubbing piece
25 keelson
26 garboard strake
27 keel
28 rudder
29 pintle
30 gudgeon
31 plank

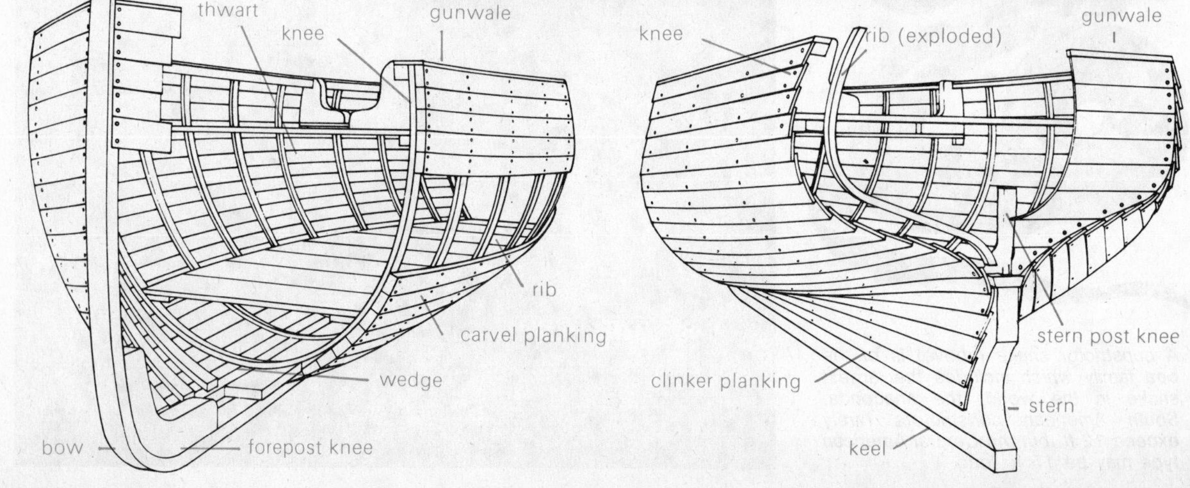

male swine (wild or tame); flesh of this; **wild** ~, European wild swine (*Sus scrofa*), domesticated throughout the U.S.

board (bōrd, bo͞rd) *n.* 1. Thin piece of timber, usu. rectangular, and of greater length than breadth; one or more pieces of this or similar substance, used in games, for posting notices, etc.; (pl.) the stage; thick stiff paper used in bookbinding etc.; **across the** ~, embracing all categories. 2. Table spread for meals; food served, daily meals provided at contract price or in return for services; official group directing organization; ~ **of directors;** ~ **of education**, body elected or appointed to provide and maintain colleges, public schools, etc. (also SCHOOLBOARD) in public school sense; **B** ~ **of Trade**, association of businessmen etc. to promote trade. 3. Ship's side (only in certain phrases); (naut.) tack; **on** ~, aboard, in or into ship, train, etc. 4. **board'walk**, footway of boards or planks. **board** *v.* 1. Cover with boards. 2. Provide with, receive, stated meals at fixed rate. 3. Go on board, enter (ship, train, etc.); (naut.) come alongside and force one's way on board (ship).

board·er (bōr'd*er*, bo͞r'-) *n.* One who boards with someone; boy or girl at boarding school; one who boards a ship to capture it.

board·ing (bōr'dĭng, bo͞r'-) *n.* (esp.) **board'inghouse**, house in which persons are boarded and lodged for payment; ~ **school**, school in which pupils live during term, as dist. from day school.

boast (bōst) *n.* Exceedingly proud statement; cause of pride. ~ *v.* Praise oneself, make boast(s) (*of, about*); possess as thing to be proud of. **boast'er** *n.* **boast'ful** *adj.* **boast'ful·ly** *adv.* **boast'ful·ness** *n.*

boat (bōt) *n.* 1. Small open vessel; fishing vessel, mail packet, small steamer; occas. large seagoing vessel; **in the same** ~, in the same predicament or circumstances. 2. Boat-shaped dish for gravy etc. 3. ~ **hook**, long pole with hook and spike; **boat'house**, shed at water's edge for keeping boat; **boat'man**, hirer, or rower or sailer of boat for hire; **boat·swain** (bō's*u*n), **bo'sun**, (naut.) ship's officer in charge of sails, rigging, etc., and summoning men to duty with whistle; **boat train**, train having connection with a steamer at a port. **boat** *v.i.* Go in boat, esp. for pleasure.

boat·er (bō't*er*) *n.* Straw hat with flat crown and brim.

Bo·az (bō'ăz): see RUTH[1].

bob[1] (bŏb) *n.* 1. Weight on pendulum, plumb line, or kite tail. 2. Knot of hair, tassel-shaped curl; horses's docked tail; bobbed hair. ~ *v.t.* (**bobbed, bob·bing**). Cut (hair) to hang short of the shoulders.

bob[2] (bŏb) *n.* Jerk, bouncing movement; curtsy. ~ *v.i.* (**bobbed, bob·bing**). Move up and down, dance, rebound; curtsy; ~ **for**, try to catch (floating apples, etc.) with the mouth.

bob[3] (bŏb) *n.* (pl. **bob**). (Brit. slang) Shilling.

bob·bin (bŏb'ĭn) *n.* 1. Cylinder on which thread, wire, etc., may be wound; reel, spool; ~ **lace**: see LACE. 2. Rounded piece of wood attached to a string, for raising door latch.

bob·ble (bŏb'*e*l) *v.* (**-bled, -bling**). 1. Bob up and down. 2. Fumble (a ball); blunder. ~ *n.* Fumble, blunder.

bob·by (bŏb'ē) *n.* (pl. **-bies**). (Brit. slang) Policeman. [Nickname for *Robert*, in allusion to Sir Robert Peel, who was British Home Secretary when the Metropolitan Police Act was passed in 1828]

bob·by·socks, bob·by·sox (bŏb'ēsŏks) *ns.pl.* Socks reaching just above the ankle, once worn esp. by teenage girls. **bob'by·sox·er** *n.* (freq. derog.) Girl wearing bobbysocks.

bob·cat (bŏb'kăt) *n.* American wildcat (*Lynx rufus*), with stumpy tail, tufted ears, and spotted reddish-brown fur.

*The **boardwalk** in Atlantic City, New Jersey was the first ever, built in 1870. It extends for 5 miles and is 60 ft. wide with amusement piers built out into the ocean which enhance the festive seaside atmosphere.*

*In the second **Boer War** one of the few clear successes for British forces was achieved when Lord Roberts forced Piet Cronge's surrender at Paardeberg in February, 1900, after the destruction of his laager.*

*The rapid firing capacity of the **Bofors** gun makes it ideal for an anti-aircraft role. It forms part of the armament of most ships in the navies of NATO. It is also effective against small ships.*

bob·o·link (bŏb′əlĭngk) *n.* N. Amer. songbird, also called ricebird (*Dolichonyx oryzivorus*). [orig. *Bob (o') Lincoln*; imit. of its call]

bob·sled (bŏb′slĕd) *n.* 1. Racing sled with two pairs of runners, brake, and steering mechanism. 2. Sled formed by two short sleds operating in tandem. ~ *v.i.* Ride on a bobsled.

bob·stay (bŏb′stā) *n.* (naut.) Rope or chain used to steady a bowsprit.

bob·tail (bŏb′tāl) *n.* (Horse or dog with) docked tail; **tag, rag, and** ~, rabble.

bob·white (bŏb′wīt′) *n.* Small chunky game bird, *Colinus virginianus*, of eastern U.S., named from its call.

Boc·cac·ci·o (bōkah′chēō), **Giovanni** (1313–75). Italian novelist, poet, and humanist, author of the *Decameron*.

Boc·che·ri·ni (bŏkerē′nē), **Luigi** (1740–1805). Italian composer and cellist.

Boche (bŏsh, bawsh) *n.* & *adj.* (derog. slang, esp. in World War I) German.

bock (bŏk) *n.* (also ~ **beer**). Strong dark-colored German beer, usu. brewed for drinking in spring months. [Ger. f. *Einbockbier*, beer from *Einbeck*, in Hanover]

bode (bōd) *v.* (**bod·ed, bod·ing**). Foresee, foretell (evil); portend, foreshow; promise *well, ill.*

bo·de·ga (bōdē′ga; *Span.* bawdhĕ′gah) *n.* (pl. **-gas** pr. -gaz; *Span.* -gahs). Wine warehouse or wineshop; (esp. in Puerto Rican city neighborhoods) grocery store. [Sp., f. L., f. Gk. *apothēkē* store]

bo·dhi·satt·va (bōdĭsăt′wă) *n.* (Buddhism) Person who is entitled by his good deeds to enter Nirvana but who, out of compassion for human suffering, delays doing so in order to save others.

bod·ice (bŏd′ĭs) *n.* Upper part of woman's dress, down to waist; undergarment for same part of body. [orig. (pair of) *bodies*, stays, corset]

bod·i·less (bŏd′ēlĭs) *adj.* Incorporeal, separated from the body.

bod·i·ly (bŏd′ĭlē) *adj.* Of, affecting, the human body or physical nature (opp. *spiritual*). ~ *adv.* With the whole bulk, as a whole.

bod·kin (bŏd′kĭn) *n.* 1. Thick, blunt needle with large eye for threading tape or ribbon through a series of loops or a hem. 2. Small pointed instrument for piercing holes in cloth or leather; long ornamental hairpin.

Bod·lei·an (bŏd′lēan, bŏdlē′-) **Library.** (also **the Bodlei′an**) Library of Oxford University, a major scholarly and British copyright library.

bod·y (bŏd′ē) *n.* (pl. **bod·ies**). 1. Material frame of man or animal; corpse. 2. Trunk apart from head and limbs; main portion of anything; part of vehicle etc. fitted to receive the load; shank of piece of type. 3. Bulk, majority. 4. Person. 5. Aggregate of persons or things; collection; **in a** ~, in a group. 6. Piece of matter (**heavenly** ~); mass of tissue forming a structure; solidity, substance; (of wine) rich full flavor. 7. ~ **English**, twisting of the body by pool player and

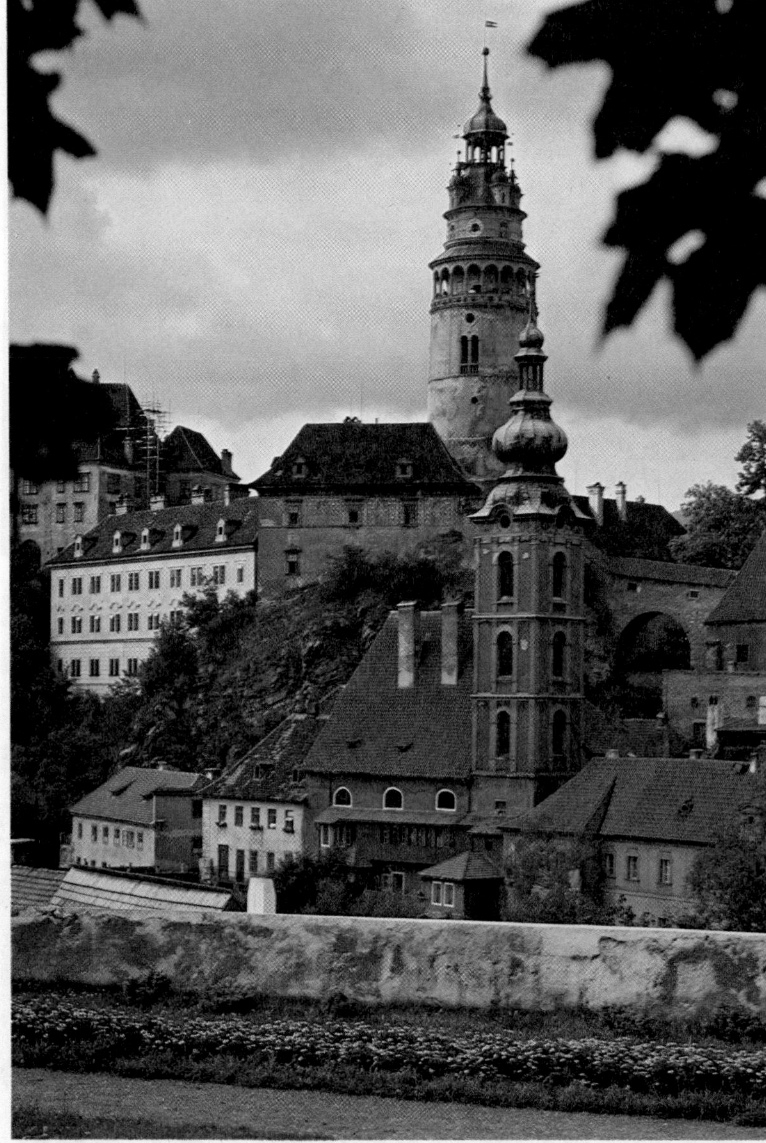

Bohemia encompasses some 20,000 sq. miles of what is now western Czechoslovakia. The spas of the region still attract visitors to towns such as Český Krumlov.

others as if to help a ball travel in the desired path; **bod′yguard**, guard for the person (esp. of dignitary), retinue, escort; **the body politic**, the nation; **body snatcher**, (hist.) one who secretly disinters corpses to sell them for dissection; **body stocking**, woman's undergarment covering trunk and legs.

Boehme (böm), **Jakob** (1575–1624). German mystic; held that will is the original force, that every manifestation involves opposition, and that existence is a process of conflict between pairs of contrasted principles, which are ultimately resolved into a new unity.

Boer (bōr, bōr; *Du.* boor) *n.* S. Afr. farmer of Dutch origin; ~ **War**, each of two wars fought by Great Britain: the first (1880–1) against Transvaal, which, annexed by Britain in 1877, had proclaimed its independence; the 2nd, and most important (1899–1902), against the Transvaal and Orange Free State, resulting in their annexation by Great Britain.

Bo·e·thi·us (bōē′thēus), **Anicius Manlius Severinus** (*c*475–525). Roman Christian philosopher, consul, and translator of Aristotle; he wrote *De Consolatione Philosophiae*, professing Neoplatonic and stoic ideas that had great influence throughout the Middle Ages.

Bo·fors (bō′fōrz, -fōrs) **gun.** Clip-fed, rapid-firing, double-barreled light anti-aircraft gun. [name of a munitions works in Örebro Län, Sweden]

bog (bŏg, bawg) *n.* (Piece of) wet spongy ground, consisting chiefly of decayed or decaying moss or other vegetable matter; **bog′gy** *adj.* **bog′gi·ness** *n.* **bog′gish** *adj.* **bog** *v.t.* (**bogged, bog·ging**). Submerge in bog; ~ **down** (fig.).

bo·gey (bō′gē) *n.* (pl. **-geys**). 1. Bogy. 2. (golf) One stroke over par for a hole. 3. (military slang) Unidentified flying aircraft; enemy aircraft. ~ *v.t.* (**-geyed, -gey·ing**). (golf) Make one stroke over par on a hole. [app. jocular application of *bogy*, "something to be afraid of"]

bog·gle (bŏg′el) *v.i.* (**-gled, -gling**). Start with fright, shy; hesitate, demur, *at*.

bo·gie (bō′gē) *n.* (pl. **-gies**). Undercarriage with two or more pairs of wheels, pivoted below front part of railroad engine or ends of long railroad car, streetcar, etc., to facilitate traveling around curves.

Bo·go·tá (bōgotah′). Capital and largest city of Colombia, South America.

bo·gus (bō′gus) *adj.* Sham, fictitious, spurious.

bo·gy, bo·gey, bo·gie (bō′gē, bŏŏg′ē) *ns.* (pl. **-gies, -geys, -gies**). 1. (esp. **Old B**~) The Devil. 2. Goblin. 3. Bugbear.

Bo·hea (bōhē′) *n.* Black tea of lowest quality, the last crop of the season (in 18th c., the finest kinds of black tea). [Chin. *Wu-i* district]

Bo·he·mi·a (bōhē′mēa, -hēm′ya). Slavonic kingdom of central Europe; came under Austrian rule, 1526; by the treaty of Versailles (1919) became a province of Czechoslovakia; now a region of Czechoslovakia. **Bo·he′mi·an** *adj.* & *n.* 1. (Native, inhabitant) of Bohemia. 2. (Person, esp. artist or writer) of free and easy habits, manners, and sometimes morals (from mistaken belief that gypsies came orig. from Bohemia).

Bohr (bōr, bōr), **Niels Henrik David** (1885–1962). Danish physicist; applied the quantum theory to the problem of atomic structure; won the Nobel Prize for physics in 1922.

boil[1] (boil *n.* Hard, inflamed suppurating tumor.

boil[2] (boil) *v.* (of a liquid) Reach or be at that temperature (**boiling point**) where the vapor pressure is equal to the pressure of the atmosphere above its surface and vapor is consequently evolved in bubbles from all parts of the liquid (also used of containing vessel); be agitated by the evolution, rising, and bursting of such bubbles; bring a liquid by the application of heat to this temperature; subject to heat of boiling water, cook, be cooked thus; (fig.) be agitated with anger etc.; ~ **down**, reduce by boiling; ~ **down to**, (fig.) mean basically; ~ **over**, bubble up so as to run over sides of vessel; said also of the vessel; **boiled shirt**, dress shirt. **boil** *n.* Boiling, boiling point.

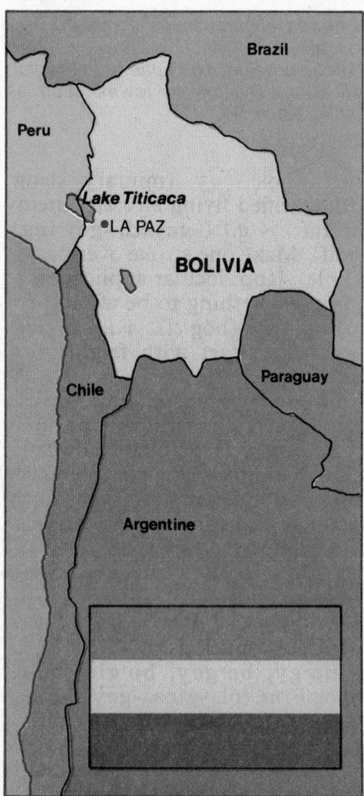

Above: The map and flag of ***Bolivia,*** *a land-locked country of S. America. It is about 424,000 sq. miles in area and has a population of about 5½ millions, more than half being Indians. The photographs are of Lake Titicaca (upper right) and a market scene (right).*

boil·er (boi′l*er*) *n.* Vessel for boiling, esp. for making steam under pressure; tank for heating water for domestic use; metal tub in which laundry is boiled; **boil′er-maker**, one who builds or repairs boilers; (colloq.) whiskey with a beer chaser.

boil·ing (boi′lĭng) *n.* ~ **point**: see BOIL². ~ *adj.* (esp.) ~ **hot,** (colloq.) very hot.

Bois de Bou·logne (bwah d*e* bo͞olawn′y*e*). Park in Paris, France.

Boi·se (boi′zē). Capital and largest city of Idaho, in the SW.

bois·ter·ous (boi′ster*u*s, -str*u*s) *adj.* Violent, rough; noisily cheerful. **bois′ter·ous·ly** *adv.* **bois′-ter·ous·ness** *n.*

bold (bōld) *adj.* Courageous, enterprising, confident; forward, immodest; vigorous, free, well-marked, clear; **bold′face(d),** (type) having a thick face; **bold-faced,** impudent. **bold′ly** *adv.* **bold′ness** *n.*

bole¹ (bōl) *n.* Stem or trunk of tree.

bole² (bōl) *n.* Fine, compact earthy or unctuous clay, usu. reddish brown with iron oxide; reddish brown.

bo·lec·tion (bōlĕk′sh*o*n) *adj.* & *n.* (Molding) placed around a panel, which it holds in a groove.

bo·le·ro (bōlār′ō, b*o*-) *n.* (pl. **-ros**). 1. Lively Spanish dance, music for this. 2. Short jacket coming barely to the waist.

Bol·eyn (bo͝ol′ĭn, bolĭn′), **Anne** (*c*1507–36). Second wife of English King Henry VIII and mother of Elizabeth I; she was beheaded on a charge of unfaithfulness.

bol·i·var (bŏl′*iver*; *Span.* bawlē-vār′) *n.* (pl. **-vars, -va·res** pr. *Span.* -vah′rĕs). Monetary unit of Venezuela.

Bol·i·var (bŏl′*iver*; *Span.* bawlē-vār′), **Simon** (1783–1830). Venezuelan patriot and statesman, called "the Liberator"; founded (1819) the Republic of Colombia, uniting Venezuela, New Granada (Colombia), and Ecuador; became dictator of Peru; formed the Republic of Bolivia.

Bo·liv·i·a (bōlĭv′ē*a*). S. Amer. inland republic, formerly part of the Incan Empire, and subsequently of the Spanish possession of Peru; capital, La Paz. **Bo·liv′i·an** *adj.* & *n.*

boll (bōl) *n.* Rounded seed pod, as in flax or cotton; ~ **weevil,** weevil (*Anthonomus grandis*), destructive to the cotton plant.

Bo·lo·gna (bawlawn′yah). Manufacturing city and railroad center in N. Italy; site of oldest European university, founded 1088.

bo·lo·gna (bolō′nē, -lōn′y*a*) *n.* Large sausage of veal, bacon, pork, etc. [orig. made at BOLOGNA]

bo·lom·e·ter (bōlŏm′*eter*, b*o*-) *n.* Electrical instrument for measuring radiant heat. **bo·lo·met·ric** (bōlomĕt′rĭk) *adj.*

bo·lo·ney (bolō′nē) = BALONEY.

Bol·she·vik, bol·she·vik (bŏl′-shevĭk, bŏl′-; *Russ.* bawlshevēk′) *ns.*

*A replica of the atom **bomb** that destroyed Hiroshima on 6 August 1945 and killed or injured about 75,000 people. Many thousands died later as a result of exposure to radioactivity.*

& *adjs.* (pl. **-viks, -vik·i** pr. -vĭkē, -vēkē; *Russ.* -vĭkē´). 1. (Member) of the Revolutionary party led by Lenin, which seized power in Russia in 1917 in the name of the proletariat and based its rule on the ideas of Karl Marx. 2. (loosely) (Of) a socialist or person suspected of subversive ideas. **Bol´she·vist, bol´she·vist** *ns.* & *adjs.* **Bol·she·vis´tic, bol·she·vis´tic** *adjs.* **Bol´she·vism** *n.* [Russ. *Bol'shevik* majority man (i.e. member of majority group in the Social-Democratic Party) f. *bol'shiv* more]

bol·ster (bōl´st*er*) *n.* Long, stuffed cushion for bed, sofa, etc. ~ *v.t.* (usu. with *up*) Support with bolster, prop; aid and abet, countenance; give fictitious support to (something unable to stand of itself); pad. **bol´ster·er** *n.*

bolt[1] (bōlt) *n.* 1. Short heavy arrow of crossbow. 2. Discharge of lightning; ~ **from the blue**, complete surprise. 3. Door fastening of sliding bar and staple; sliding part of mortise lock. 4. Sliding part of rifle that contains striker and mainspring and that locks the breech. 5. Metal pin with head, for holding things together, usu. secured by riveting or by a nut. 6. Length of fabric woven on a loom in one operation. ~ *adv.* ~ **upright**, stiffly upright.

bolt[2] (bōlt) *v.* 1. Dart off or away; (of horse) break from control, make violent dash. 2. Gulp down (food) hastily or unchewed. 3. Fasten (door etc.) with bolt; fasten together with bolts. ~ *n.* Sudden start; running away.

bolt[3] (bōlt) *v.t.* Sift, pass through a sieve.

bo·lus (bō´l*us*) *n.* (pl. **-lus·es**). Large pill, esp. one administered to an animal; lump of food at moment of swallowing.

bomb (bŏm) *n.* Case filled with explosive, inflammable material, gas, etc., fired from a gun, dropped from aircraft, or thrown or deposited by hand; **the B~**, (esp.) nuclear bomb; ~ **bay**, compartment in aircraft for holding bombs; **bomb´proof**, strong enough to resist explosion of a bomb; **bomb´shell**, artillery bomb; shell; (fig.) cause of great surprise. **bomb** *v.* Assail with bombs, throw bombs.

bom·bard (bŏm´bârd) *n.* Earliest kind of cannon, throwing stone ball or very large shot. ~ (bŏmbârd´) *v.t.* Batter with shot and shell; assail persistently with abuse, argument, etc.; (phys.) subject to a stream of (charged) atoms

*The city of **Bombay** is built on low lying islands near the coast, where it forms the only deep-water harbor of western India. The city is a great commercial center and has a thriving cotton spinning industry.*

or subatomic particles. **bom·bard´er, bom·bard´ment** *ns.*

bom·bar·dier (bŏmb*er*dēr´) *n.* Member of aircraft crew who aims and releases bombs from aircraft.

bom · bar · don (bŏm´b*er*d*on*, bŏmbâr´-) *n.* (mus.) Low-pitched brass instrument; organ stop imitating this.

bom·bast (bŏm´băst) *n.* Pompous language, tall talk. **bom·bas·tic** (bŏmbăs´tĭk) *adj.* **bom·bas´ti·cal·ly** *adv.* [orig. = cotton wool, used in 16th c. as padding for clothes; f. Gk. *bombux* silk, silkworm]

Bom·bay (bŏmbā´). Capital city of Maharashtra, on W. coast of India; ~ **duck**, dried, salted fish used as a relish with curry.

bom · ba · zine (bŏmb*a*zēn´, bŏm´b*a*zēn) *n.* Twilled dress material of worsted formerly used for mourning.

bombe (bŏm, bŏmb; *Fr.* bawnb) *n.* Conical or cup-shaped frozen melon or mold dessert containing layers of ice cream.

bomb·er (bŏm´*er*) *n.* Aircraft designed to carry bombs.

bo·na fide (bō´n*a* fīd, bŏn´*a*, bō´n*a* fīdē). Genuine, authentic, sincere.

bo·nan·za (b*o*năn´z*a*, bō-) *n.* Prosperity, large output (esp. of mines); run of luck, fine weather, good crops, etc. ~ *adj.* Yielding great wealth or a large output. [Sp., = "fair weather"]

Bo·na·parte (bō´n*a*pârt). Name of Corsican family including NAPOLEON I; **Joseph** ~, (1775–1844), brother of Napoleon I; king of Naples 1806; king of Spain 1808.

Bon·a·ven·ture (bŏn'avĕncher, bŏnavĕn'-), **St.** (1221–74). John of Fidanza, Italian Franciscan, scholastic theologian, and mystic; commemorated July 14.

bon·bon (bŏn'bŏn; *Fr.* bawṅ-bawṅ') *n.* Piece of confectionery, sweet.

bond[1] (bŏnd) *n.* 1. (archaic, chiefly pl.) Thing restraining bodily freedom, shackle; restraining or uniting force; connection; adhesion between two surfaces etc.; (chem.) = VALENCE bond. 2. Binding agreement; document by which one binds oneself and one's heirs etc. to pay a sum to others; government's or public company's document undertaking to repay borrowed money, usu. with fixed rate of interest; any of various kinds of investment; **in ~**, (of goods) stored under charge of customs in bonded warehouse until importer pays duty; **bond'holder**, person holding bond(s) of another person or of company or government; **bond paper**, paper of superior quality as used for bonds. 3. Bond paper. **bond** *v.t.* Bind together; connect with a bond; put (goods) into bond; **bonded warehouse**, customs warehouse in which goods in bond are stored.

bond[2] (bŏnd) *adj.* (archaic) In serfdom or slavery; not free; so **bond'maid, bond'man, bond' servant, bond'slave, bonds'-man.**

bond·age (bŏn'dĭj) *n.* Serfdom, slavery; subjection to some influence or obligation.

Bond (bŏnd) **Street.** London street noted for its fashionable shops. [named after Sir Thomas *Bond*, who began its construction *c*1688]

bone (bōn) *n.* One of the parts making up the skeleton of a human being or other vertebrate; substance (mainly calcium phosphate and fibrous protein) of which these consist; article made of this substance; strip of stiff substance in corset etc.; (pl.) skeleton, bodily frame, body, mortal remains; **~ to pick, ~ of contention**, subject of dispute; **make no ~s of** or **about**, make no attempt to hide; admit without hesitation; **~ china**, chinaware made of clay mixed with bonedust or phosphate of lime; **~-dry**, quite dry; **bone'head**, blockhead; **bone meal**, animal food, fertilizer, made from finely crushed bone. **bone** *v.t.* (**boned, bon·ing**). Take out bones from; stiffen with bone. **bone'less, bone'like** *adjs.*

bon·fire (bŏn'fīr) *n.* Large fire in the open air.

bong (bŏng) *n.* Deep, resonant sound as of a large bell. ~ *v.i.* Produce such a sound.

bon·go[1] (bŏng'gō, bawng'-) *n.* (pl. **-gos**, collect. **-go**). Large striped African antelope (*Boocercus eurycerus*), related to bushbuck, living in dense forests.

bon·go[2] (bŏng'gō, bawng'-) *n.* (pl. **-gos, -goes**). (also **~ drum**) One of a pair of small drums played with the fingers.

bon·ho·mie, bon·hom·mie (bŏn'omē) *ns.* Good nature; geniality.

bon·i·face (bŏn'ifās) *n.* Jovial innkeeper. [name of the jovial innkeeper in Farquhar's *Beaux Stratagem* (1707)]

Bon·i·face (bŏn'ifās), **St.** (680–755). Winfrith, English Benedictine, apostle to the Germans under Pope Gregory II; commemorated June 5.

bon mot (bawn' mō'; *Fr.* bawṅ mō') (pl. **bons mots** pr. bawn'mōz; *Fr.* bawṅ mō'). Witty saying [Fr.]

Bonn (bŏn). Capital of the German Federal Republic, in the NW., on the Rhine River; site of famous 13th c. cathedral.

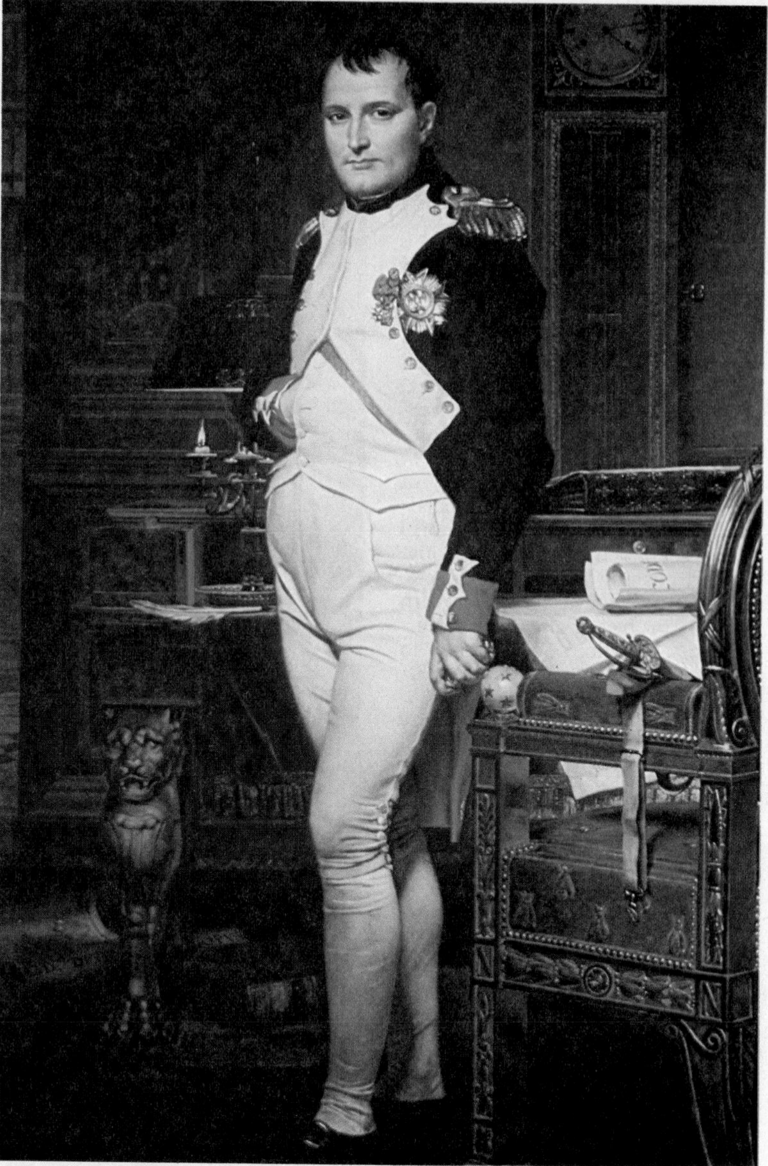

The greatest of the ***Bonaparte*** *family was Napoleon I, whose portrait by Jacques Louis David is shown here. Napoleon established members of his family on various European thrones in the early 1800s.*

Bon·nard (bawnăr'), **Pierre** (1867–1947). French impressionist painter, lithographer, and etcher.

bon·net (bŏn'ĭt) *n.* 1. Woman's outdoor headdress with strings. 2. (Sc.) Man's cap. 3. (Brit.) Automobile hood.

Bon·ne·ville (bŏn'evĭl) **Salt Flats.** Stretch of barren land in NW. Utah; part of the bed of prehistoric Bonneville Lake; site where several world records were made in automobile speed tests.

bon·ny, bon·nie (bŏn'ē) *adjs.* (**-ni·er, -ni·est**). 1. (chiefly Sc.) Comely. 2. Healthy looking. **bon'ni·ly** *adv.* **bon'ni·ness** *n.*

bon·sai (bōn'sī, bŏn'-) *n.* Potted plant or shrub artificially dwarfed

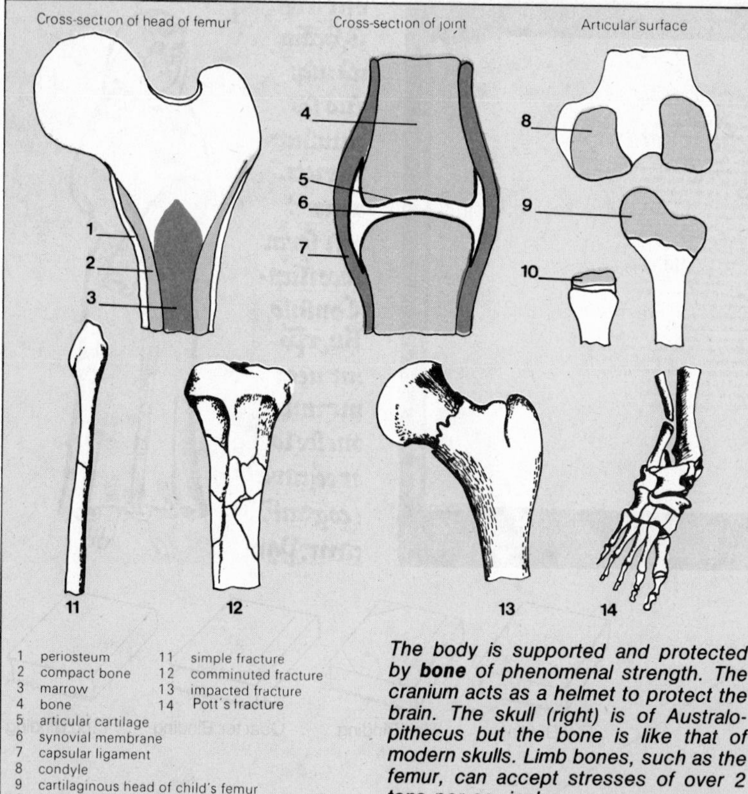

*The body is supported and protected by **bone** of phenomenal strength. The cranium acts as a helmet to protect the brain. The skull (right) is of Australopithecus but the bone is like that of modern skulls. Limb bones, such as the femur, can accept stresses of over 2 tons per sq. inch.*

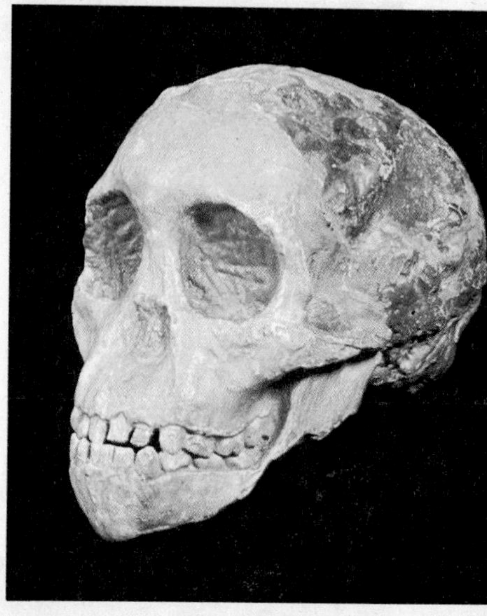

*Below: The 3-foot horns of the **bongo** make it a prized trophy for hunters. Found in equatorial Africa, the bongo is a large antelope, males standing about 4 ft. high at the shoulder.*

as ornament; method of cultivating this. [Jap.]

bo·nus (bō′n*u*s) *n.* Something to the good, into the bargain; (esp.) extra dividend to company's shareholders, distribution of profits to holders of insurance policies, gratuity to employees beyond their wages; ~ **army,** demonstration by war veterans in Washington, D.C., in 1932 demanding bonuses for their military service in World War I.

bon vi·vant (bawṅ vēvahṅ′) (pl. **bons vi·vants** pr. bawṅ vēvahṅ′). Gourmand. [Fr.]

bon voy·age (bŏn voiahzh′; *Fr.* bawṅ vwahyahzh′). Pleasant journey (used as expression of farewell to a traveler). [Fr.]

bon·y (bō′nē) *adj.* (**bon·i·er, bon·i·est**). Of, like, bone; big-boned; with little flesh; ~ **fishes,** those (including most of the common species) that have bones as opp. to cartilage. **bon′i·ness** *n.*

bonze (bŏnz) *n.* (European name for) Japanese or Chinese Buddhist priest.

boo (bo͞o) *int., n.* (pl. **boos**), & *v.* (**booed, boo·ing**). (Make) sound of disapproval or contempt (at); jeer (at); sound made to frighten, as by ghost or person wishing to startle or surprise another.

boo·by (bo͞o′bē) *n.* (pl. **-bies**). Stupid or babyish person; ~ **prize,** prize given in derision or fun to player with worst score; ~ **trap,** (mil.) harmless-looking object concealing an explosive charge, designed to go off when disturbed.

boo·dle (bo͞o′d*e*l) *n.* (slang) Money, esp. for political bribery.

boo·gie-woo·gie (bo͝og′ē wo͝og′ē, bo͞o′gē wo͞o′gē) *n.* (also **boogie**) Style of playing blues or jazz, usu. on the piano, marked by persistent bass rhythm.

book (bo͝ok) *n.* 1. Treatise written or printed on a number of sheets which are folded, fastened together in hinge-wise fashion at the folded edges, and protected by a binding or cover; in antiquity, set of written sheets pasted together to form a roll; literary composition that would fill a book; main division of literary composition or of the Bible; libretto; anything from which one may learn; (colloq.) magazine. 2. Blank sheets of paper for keeping accounts, taking notes, etc., fastened together in the shape of a book; anything bound together in this shape, as checks, stamps, tickets, etc. 3. Betting book, record of bets made; (pl.) merchants' accounts. 4. **book′binder, book′binding,** binder, binding, of books; **book′case,** case containing bookshelves; **book club,** business that sells books through the mails at reduced prices to its members;

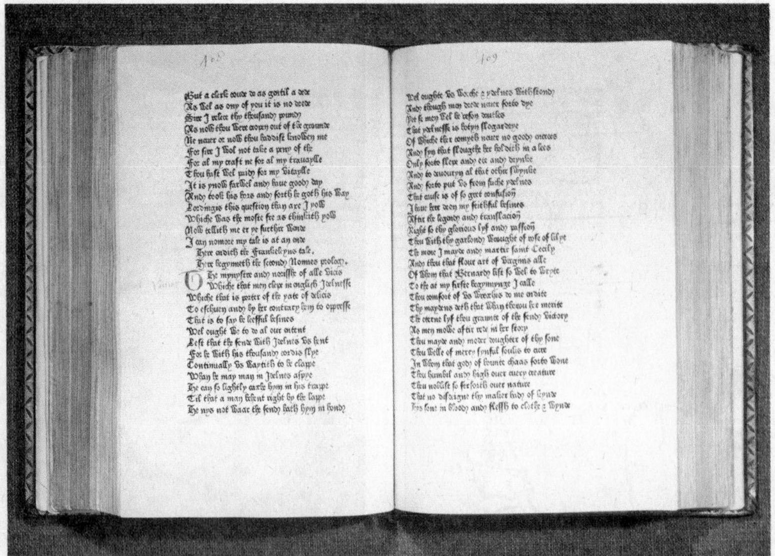

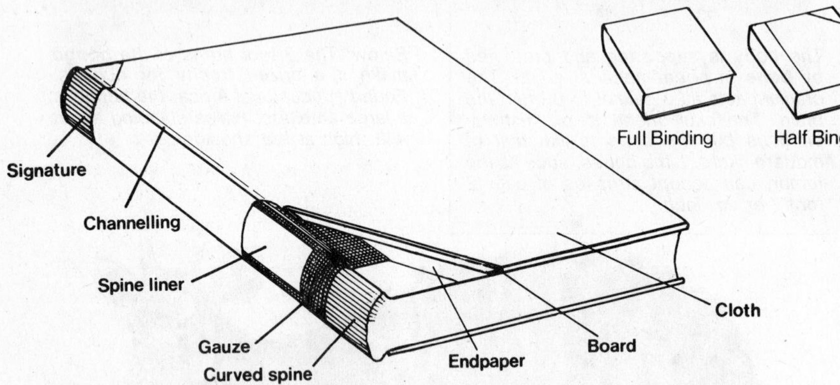

In the 1st century A.D. ***books*** *began to supersede scrolls, and throughout the Middle Ages they were copied and illuminated by monks. Top right: This copy of Matthew Paris's 'Chronica Majora' dates from the 13th century. Top left: The technique of printing was brought to England in 1476.*

book'ends, pair of (ornamental) props used to keep row of books upright; **book'keeper, book'keeping**, one who keeps, art of keeping, accounts of merchant etc.; **book learning**, knowledge gained from books not life; **book'maker**, (esp.) professional gambler who accepts bets on horse racing and other sports; **book'mobile**, mobile library; **book'plate**, label with owner's name for pasting into books; **book'shelf**, shelf for standing books on; **book value**, value of a commodity as entered in a firm's books (opp. *market value*); **book work**, study involving reading, opp. practical experiment etc.; paper work; **book'worm**, larva of various moths or beetles, that burrows into or destroys pages of books; (fig.) person who is always poring over books. **book** *v.* Enter in book or list; (esp. Brit.) secure seat etc. in advance; (Brit.) issue, obtain, ticket for journey etc.; enter (name) in police register etc. for alleged offense.

book·ie (bŏŏk'ē) *n.* (slang) Bookmaker.

book·ish (bŏŏk'ĭsh) *adj.* Literary; addicted to reading books. **book'ish·ly** *adv.* **book'ish·ness** *n.*

book·let (bŏŏk'lĭt) *n.* Small usu. paper-covered book, pamphlet.

Boole (bōōl), **George** (1815–1864). English mathematician and logician; **Bool'ean algebra**, abstract system of postulates and symbols applicable to logical problems.

boom[1] (bōōm) *n.* Long spar used to keep the bottom of a sail extended; floating barrier across mouth of a river, entrance to a harbor etc.; beam of derrick supporting weights; extendable arm carrying microphone or camera.

boom[2] (bōōm) *n.* & *v.i.* (Make, speak, etc., with) deep resonant sound.

boom[3] (bōōm) *v.* & *n.* (Show) sudden increase or development (esp. of prices, commercial ventures, etc.: opp. SLUMP).

boom·er·ang (bōō'merăng) *n.* Australian missile of thin curved wood that can be thrown so as to return to the thrower; (fig.) scheme etc. that backfires on its originator. ~ *v.i.* Backfire on originator.

boon[1] (bōōn) *n.* Benefit, advantage.

boon[2] (bōōn) *adj.* ~ **companion,** congenial companion.

boon·docks (bōōn'dŏks) *n.pl.* (slang) Rough or isolated country. [Tagalog *bundok* = mountain]

boon·dog·gle (bōōn'dŏgel) *n.* & *v.* (**-gled, -gling**). (slang) (Engage in) trivial or unnecessary work.

Boone (bōōn), **Daniel** (1735–1820). American pioneer; explored and opened up Kentucky for settlement.

boor (boor) *n.* Ill-mannered fellow. **boor'ish** *adj.* **boor'ish·ly** *adv.* **boor'ish·ness** *n.*

boost (bōōst) *v.t.* 1. Push from below; advance the progress of; praise. 2. Raise power of electromotive force in (engine, circuit, etc.). ~ *n.* Boosting. **boost'er** *n.* (esp.) Auxiliary rocket giving acceleration; one who praises, esp. an enthusiastic supporter; (med.) dose increasing or renewing effect of earlier one.

boot[1] (bōōt) *n.* Advantage (now only in **to** ~, as well). ~ *v.t.* (archaic; usu. impers. & abs.) Do good (*to*), avail. **boot'less** *adj.* Unavailing.

boot[2] (bōōt) *n.* 1. Outer foot covering of leather etc., reaching above the ankle; **give (person) the** ~, dismiss; **boot'black**, shoeshine, see SHOE def. 3; **boot'jack**, contrivance for pulling off boots;

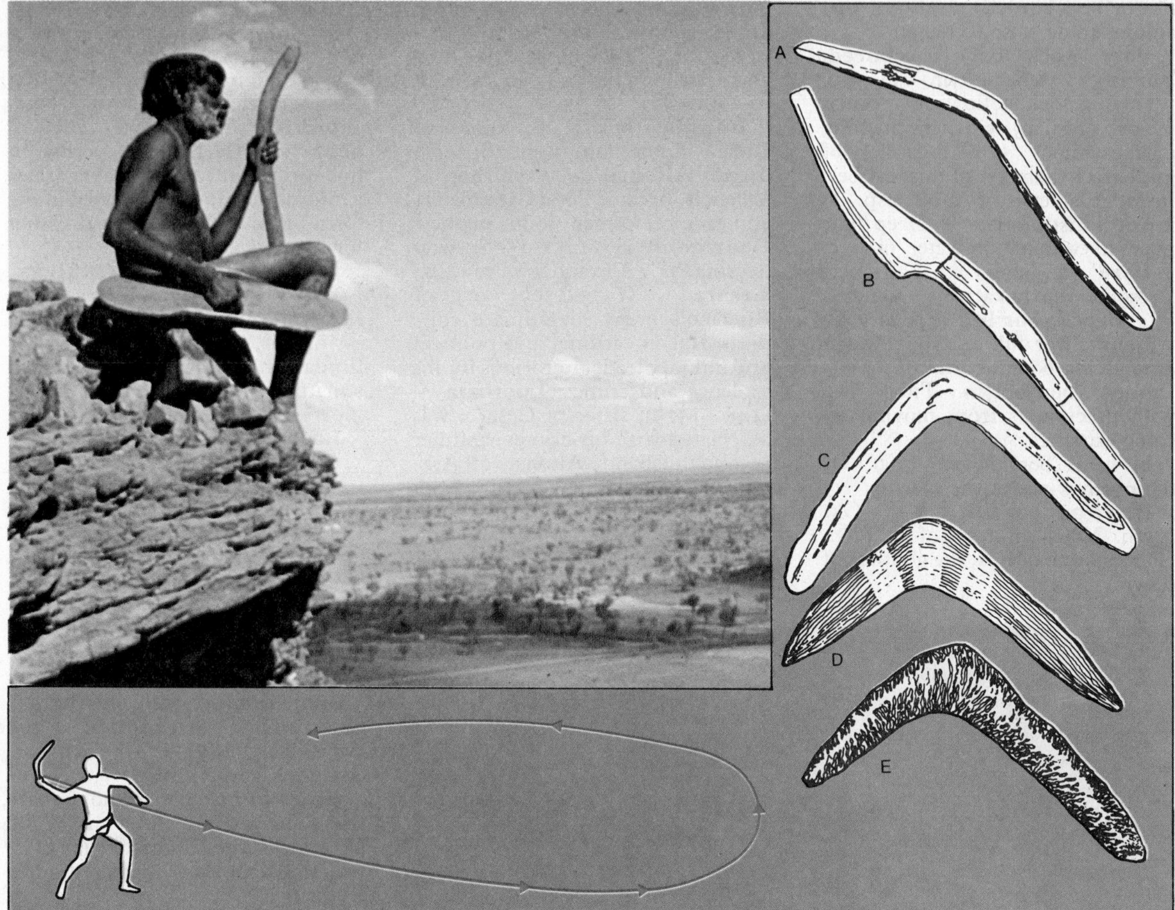

*Top left: Australian Aboriginals can use the **boomerang** skillfully in hunting to stun small animals. There are two main types of this missile: straight fliers (A and B) and returners (C, D and E). The missile's aerodynamic shape, plano-convex in section, enables it to 'fly', giving it a range of about 200 yards in straight flight. Lower left: A simple return flight is useful if the hunter misses his quarry. Right: A and B are neolithic boomerangs found in East Jutland; C, D and E are Australian returning boomerangs.*

boot'lace, lace fastening boots; **boot'leg**, smuggled, sold illicitly; **boot'legger, boot'legging**, smuggler, smuggling, of liquor (esp. during the prohibition period); **boot'licker**, (slang) toady. 2. (hist.) Instrument of torture encasing the foot. 3. (Brit.) Automobile trunk. **boot** *v.t.* Kick; (slang) kick (person) *out* (of the house, of employment, etc.). **boot'ed** *adj.* Wearing boots.

boot·ee (bo͞o'tē) *n.* Infant's knitted or crocheted boot.

booth (bo͞oth, bo͞odh) *n.* (pl. **booths** pr. bo͞odhz, bo͞oths). Temporary shelter of canvas etc., covered stall in market, tent at fair, etc.; compartment, as **telephone** ~, one containing a telephone; **polling** ~, place where one votes at election.

Booth[1] (bo͞oth), **Edwin Thomas** (1833–93). American actor; his brother, **John Wilkes**, (1838–65), also an actor, assassinated President Abraham Lincoln, 1865.

Booth[2] (bo͞oth; *Brit.* bo͞odh), **William** (1829–1912). English revivalist preacher, founder and first general of the Salvation Army.

boo·ty (bo͞o'tē) *n.* (pl. **-ties**). Plunder or profit acquired in common and to be divided; spoil, prize, plunder.

booze (bo͞oz) *n.* (colloq.) Alcoholic drink; a drinking bout. ~ *v.i.* (**boozed, booz·ing**). Drink deeply, go on drinking. **booz'er** *n.* Drinker. **booz'y** *adj.* (**booz·i·er, booz·i·est**).

Bo·phu·that·swa·na (bōfo͞o-thahtswah'nah). Republic in S. central Africa; achieved independence from Republic of South Africa, December 1977; capital Mmabatho.

bor·age (bẽr'ĭj, bŏr'-, băr'-) *n.* Blue-flowered, hairy-leaved plant (*Borago officinalis*).

bo·rate (bōr'āt, bōr'-, -ĭt) *n.* Salt of boric acid. **bo'rat·ed** *adj.*

bo·rax (bōr'ăks, bōr'-) *n.* (pl. **bo·rax·es, bo·ra·ces** pr. bōr'-*a*sēz, bōr'-). Sodium borate ($Na_2B_4O_7.IOH_2O$), a white crystalline substance giving a slightly alkaline solution, used in manufacture of glass and ceramics and as a cleansing agent.

bor·a·zon (bōr'*a*zŏn, bōr'-) *n.* Crystalline compound of boron nitride, extremely hard and resistant to oxidation at high temperatures.

Bor·deaux (bōrdō'). City and port of SW. France; any of the wines of the district about Bordeaux, including Graves, Sauternes, and Medoc.

Bor·den (bōr'd*e*n), **Lizzie Andrew** (1860–1927). Central figure in famous American murder trial in Fall River, Massachusetts, 1892; tried for the ax murder of her father and stepmother, but acquitted.

bor·der (bōr'd*er*) *n.* Side, edge, boundary or part near it; frontier of country; continuous bed around garden or part of it, or along path, etc.; distinct edging for strength or ornament or definition around or along anything; **bor'derland**, land or district on or near a border (also fig.); **bor'derline**, strip of land along border; (*adj.*) near the margin of anything; uncertain or indefinite; marginal, as in ~ **case. border** *v.*

Put or be a border to; (also ~ **on**) adjoin; come close to being.

bore[1] (bōr, bōr) *v.* (**bored, bor·ing**). Make hole in, usu. with revolving tool; hollow out evenly; make by boring, persistent pushing or excavation. ~ *n.* 1. Hollow of gunbarrel; diameter of this, caliber; inside diameter of tube, esp. in musical instrument. 2. Deep hole made in earth to find water, oil, etc.

bore[2] (bōr, bōr) *n.* Nuisance; tiresome, esp. talkative, person. ~ *v.t.* (**bored, bor·ing**). Weary by tedious talk or dullness. **bore'dom** *adj.* Being bored, ennui.

bore[3] (bōr, bōr) *n.* Tidal wave with precipitous front moving up some estuaries.

bo·re·al (bōr'ēal, bōr'-) *adj.* Of the north wind; of the North.

Bo·re·as (bōr'ēas, bōr'-). (Gk. myth.) North wind, son of the Titan Astraeus and of Eos, the goddess of dawn.

Bor·ghe·se (bōrgĕ'zĕ). Name of Italian noble family from Siena; noted for its famous art collection and active in politics from the 16th to 19th c.

Bor·gia (bōr'ja). Name of Italian noble family of Spanish origin: **Alfonso de** ~, bishop of Valencia, became Pope Calixtus III and gave preferment to his nephew **Rodrigo de** ~ (1431–1503), who became Pope Alexander VI in 1492; **Cesare** ~ (1475–1507), one of Rodrigo's many illegitimate children, Italian cardinal and political and military leader notorious for his violence and crimes; **Lucrezia** ~ (1480–1519), sister of Cesare, was associated with his crimes, and her second husband, Alfonso of Aragon, was murdered by his direction; she later married Alfonso d'Este, heir of the Duke of Ferrara, and her court became a center for artists, poets, and scholars.

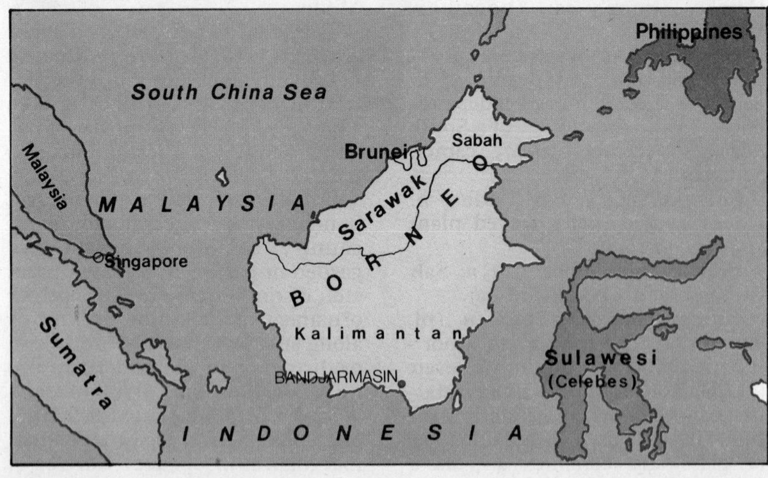

*The world's third largest island, **Borneo**, has about 287,000 sq. miles of dense jungle and rugged mountains that make communications difficult. The rivers are navigable and small boats carry trade to villages of the interior. The photograph shows a Dyak woman, with tattooed hands, and her children.*

Bor·glum (bōr'glum), **Gutzon** (1867–1941). American sculptor and painter best known for sculpting the figures of presidents on Mount Rushmore in South Dakota.

bo·ric (bōr'ĭk, bōr'-) *adj.* ~ **acid,** acid (H_3BO_3) occurring in hot springs in some volcanic areas, a mild antiseptic, widely used in the form of an ointment as a dressing for wounds and sores.

born (bōrn) *adj.*: see BEAR[2]; (esp.) ~ **of**, owing origin to; ~ **fool, idiot**, etc., utter, hopeless, fool, etc. ~ **again**, regenerate, (esp. of a fundamentalist Christian) reborn spiritually; ~ **yesterday**, naive, inexperienced, simple.

borne (bōrn, bōrn): see BEAR[2].

Bor·ne·o (bōr'nēō). Large island of Malay archipelago, comprising (1) Kalimantan, a region of Indonesia; (2) Sabah and Sarawak, formerly British colonies, now parts of Malaysia; (3) Brunei, a British protected State.

Born·holm (bōrn'hōm, -hōlm). Danish island in the Baltic, 227 square miles in area.

Bo·ro·din (bōr'odĭn, -dēn; *Russ.* bawrawdēn'), **Alexander Porfiryevich** (1834–87). Russian composer and chemist.

Bo·ro·di·no (bŏrŏdē'nō). Village some 120 miles (193 km) W. of Moscow; scene of a battle (1812) in which Napoleon defeated the Russians.

bo·ron (bōr'ŏn, bōr'-) *n.* (chem.) Dark-brown or greenish-brown nonmetallic solid element; symbol B, at. no. 5, at. wt. 10.81.

bor·ough (bẽr'ō, bŭr'ō) *n.* Incorporated town or village; **pocket** ~, (Brit. hist.) borough in which election of member of parliament was controlled by one person; **rotten** ~, (Brit. hist.) one that no longer had any real constituency.

bor·row (bar'ō, bōr'ō) *v.t.* Obtain or take temporary use of (something to be returned); adopt, use without being the true or original owner or inventor, import from an alien source; **borrowed time**, unexpected extension of time, esp. of life. **bor'row·er** *n.*

borscht, borsht (bōrsht), **borsch** (bōrsh) *ns.* Beet soup served hot or cold, often with sour cream, made esp. in Russia and Poland.

Bor·stal (bōr'stal) *n.* One of a number of institutions in Great Britain to which young offenders may be sent for reformative train-

Established in 1630 by John Winthrop the elder, ***Boston*** *has grown to be the largest city in New England. It is a busy port and a market for fish and wool. It has industries for food processing and for textile manufacture.*

ing; ~ **boy**, a boy in or from such an institution. [f. *Borstal*, village in Kent where first experimental training was carried out]

bort (bōrt) *n.* Coarse diamonds; diamond fragments made in cutting.

bor·zoi (bōr'zoi) *n.* (pl. **-zois**). Dog of large high-standing breed, called also Russian or Siberian wolfhound, of greyhound type, but with thick silky coat, usu. white with yellow markings. [Russ. *bórziy* swift]

bos·cage (bŏs'kĭj) *n.* Mass of growing trees or shrubs; thicket, grove.

Bosch (bŏsh, bawsh), **Hieronymus** (1450–1516). Original name, van Aken; Dutch painter noted for caricatures and fantasy representations of monstrosities and gruesome subjects.

bosh (bŏsh) *n.* (slang) Contemptible nonsense. [Turk., = "empty," "worthless" (popularized by Morier's novel *Ayesha*, 1834)]

bosk·y (bŏs'kē) *adj.* (**bosk·i·er, bosk·i·est**). Wooded, bushy.

Bos·ni·a (bŏz'nēa). Federal unit of Yugoslavia, formerly a province of the Austro-Hungarian Empire. **Bos'ni·an** *adj.* & *n.*

bos·om (bo͝oz'om, bo͞o'zom) *n.* Breast; enclosure formed by breast and arms; breast of dress, space between dress and breast; surface of sea, ground, etc.; heart, thoughts, desires, etc.; ~ **friend**, especially intimate or beloved friend.

Bos·po·rus (bŏs'perus), **Bos·pho·rus** (bŏs'ferus). Strait connecting the Black Sea and the Sea of Marmara.

boss[1] (baws, bŏs) *n.* Protuberance; round metal knob or stud on center of shield or ornamental work; (archit.) projection, freq. carved, at intersecting point of vault ribs. **boss'y**[1] *adj.* (**boss·i·er, boss·i·est**).

boss[2] (baws, bŏs) *n.* Master, person in authority; employer, manager, supervisor; politician who controls a political organization. ~ *v.t.* Be master or manager of. **boss'y**[2] *adj.* (**boss·i·er, boss·i·est**). Domineering. [orig. U.S., f. Du. *baas* master]

bos·sa no·va (bŏs'a nō'va). Brazilian dance like samba; music for it.

Bos·ton (baws'ton, bŏs'-). Capital city and seaport of Massachusetts, founded *c*1630 and named after Boston, town in Lincolnshire, England; ~ **Tea Party**, throwing of a cargo of tea into Boston harbor by colonists, 1773, as a protest against the British tea tax, a prelude to the Revolutionary War. **Bos·to·ni·an** (bawstō'nēan, bŏs-) *adj.* & *n.*

bo·sun (bō'sun) *n.* (naut.) Boatswain (see BOAT).

Bos·well (bŏz'wĕl, -wel), **James** (1740–94). Scotsman, a lawyer who became a friend of Samuel Johnson and recorded his conversation in a biography published in 1791. **Bos·well·i·an** (bŏzwĕl'ēan) *adj.* **Bos'well·ize** *v.* (**-ized, -iz·ing**).

bot (bŏt) *n.* Parasitic larva of the **bot'fly**, an insect of genus *Oestrus*; **botts**, disease of horses, cattle, etc., caused by this.

bot·a·nize (bŏt'anīz) *v.i.* (**-nized, -niz·ing**). Study plants, esp. by seeking them as they grow.

bot·a·ny (bŏt'anē) *n.* (pl. **-nies**). Science of plants. **bo·tan·ic** (botăn'ĭk), **bo·tan'i·cal** *adjs.* (esp.) ~ **garden**, garden for the display and study of plants. **bo·tan'i·cal·ly** *adv.* **bot·a·nist** (bŏt'anĭst) *n.*

Bot·a·ny (bŏt'anē) **Bay.** Bay on E. coast of New South Wales, Australia, (5 miles, 8 km, S. of modern Sydney) where Capt. Cook first landed in 1770, so named because of the variety of its plant life; site of an 18th-c. English penal settlement.

botch (bŏch) *n.* Bungled work. ~ *v.t.* Spoil by unskillful work, bungle. **botch'er, botch'er·y** *ns.* **botch'y** *adj.* (**botch·i·er, botch·i·est**).

both (bōth) *adj.* & *pron.* The two (and not merely one of them); the pair (of). ~ *adv.* ~ **... and**, not only . . . but also.

both·er (bŏdh'er) *v.* Pester, worry; be troublesome; worry oneself, take trouble. ~ *n.* Minor trouble, worry; fuss; worried state. ~ *int.* Exclamation of impatience.

both·er·a·tion (bŏdherā'shon) *n.* & *int.* Bother.

both·er·some (bŏdh'ersom) *adj.* Annoying, troublesome.

Both·ni·a (bŏth'nēa), **Gulf of.** Northern arm of the Baltic Sea between Sweden and Finland.

Bot·swa·na (bŏtswah'nah). Republic of south central Africa; capital, Gaborone.

bott (bŏt): see BOT.

Bot·ti·cel·li (bŏtĭchĕl'ē), **Sandro** (1447–1510). Alessandro Filipepi, Florentine painter of the Renaissance.

bot·tle (bŏt'el) *n.* Narrow-necked vessel of glass or plastic

*Madame de Pompadour was a pupil of her portrait painter, **Francois Boucher.** His elegant paintings made him the most fashionable artist of his day and brought him theater commissions too.*

(orig. of leather) for storing liquid; amount of liquid in it; feeding bottle; ~**-fed**, (of infant or young animal) fed on milk etc. from a feeding bottle, not from breast; ~ **glass**, coarse dark-green glass; ~ **green**, dark green; **bot'tleneck**, narrow stretch of road, narrow outlet, esp. one causing congestion of traffic (freq. fig.); **bottle-nosed dolphin, whale**, dolphin of genus *Tursiops*, whale of genus *Hyperoödon*, with bottle-shaped snout; **bottle party**, party to which guests contribute drinks; **bottle washer**, factotum, underling. **bottle** *v.t.* (**-tled, -tling**). Store in bottles; ~ **up**, conceal, restrain for a time. **bot'tler** *n.*

bot·tom (bŏt′*o*m) *n.* 1. Lowest part, part on which thing rests; buttocks; seat (of chair). 2. Ground under water of lake etc.; river basin etc., low-lying land. 3. Less honorable end of table, class, etc., person occupying this. 4. Keel, horizontal part near keel, hull; ship, esp. as cargo carrier. 5. Basis, origin; essential character, reality; **at the ~ of**, causing, responsible for. **bottom** *adj.* Lowest; last; ~ **line**, line showing profit or loss in a financial statement; final consideration. **bottom** *v.* Put bottom to; base *on.*

bot·tom·less (bŏt′*o*mlĭs) *adj.* Unfathomable.

bot·u·lism (bŏch′*u*lĭzem) *n.* Poisoning caused by eating food that contains *botulinus* toxin, an exceptionally powerful toxin poisonous to nerve tissue, produced by a bacillus (*Clostridium botulinum*) usu. in preserved foods that have been imperfectly sterilized.

Bou·cher (bo͞oshā′), **François** (1703–70). French rococo painter of elegantly artificial pastorals.

bou·clé (bo͝oklā′) *n.* Yarn of looped or curled ply; fabric of this.

Bou·dic·ca (bo͞odĭk′*a*) = BOADICEA.

bou·doir (bo͞od′wâr, -wôr) *n.* Woman's private sitting room, dressing room, or bedroom. [Fr., = "sulking place" (*bouder* sulk)]

bouf·fant (bo͞ofahṅ′) *adj.* Puffed out.

Bou·gain·ville (bo͞ogăṅvēl′). Largest of the Solomon Islands in the SW. Pacific Ocean, part of the trust territory of New Guinea.

Bou·gain·ville (bo͞ogăṅvēl′), **Louis Antoine de** (1729–1811). French navigator, military leader, and scientist.

bou·gain·vil·le·a, bou·gain·vil·lae·a (bo͞og*i*nvĭl′ē*a*, -vĭl′y*a*) *ns.* Tropical climbing plant of genus ***B***~, with large bright-colored bracts. [named after L. A. de BOUGANVILLE]

bough (bow) *n.* Tree branch.

bought (bawt): see BUY.

bou·gie (bo͞o′jē, -zhē, bo͞ozhē′) *n.* Wax candle; thin, flexible surgical instrument for exploring, dilating, etc., passages of the body. [*Bougie*, Algerian town with wax trade]

bouil·la·baisse (bo͞ol′y*a*bās, bo͞oly*a*bās′; *Fr.* bo͞oyăbĕs′) *n.* Provençal dish of various kinds of Mediterranean fish stewed in water or spiced white wine; fish and shellfish stew.

bouil·lon (bo͞ol′yŏn, -yon; *Fr.* bo͞oyawṅ′) *n.* Broth.

boul·der (bōl′d*e*r) *n.* Large irregular water worn or weather worn stone; (geol.) rounded rock fragment about the size of a basketball or larger.

Boul·der (bōl′d*e*r) **Dam.** Former name of HOOVER DAM on the Colorado River.

boul·e·vard (bo͞ol′*e*vârd, bo͞o′l*e*-) *n.* Wide city street, often lined with trees or landscaped.

Boulle (bo͞ol). Name of a French family of cabinet makers (esp. **André Charles** ~, 1642–1732), noted for ebony furniture inlaid with brass, tortoise shell, etc., and mounted with gilt bronze.

boulle, buhl, boule (bo͞ol) *adjs.* & *ns.* (Furniture, ornament) of the type made by the BOULLE family.

bounce (bowns) *n.* Rebound. ~ *v.* (**bounced, bounc·ing**). Rebound, bound like a ball; throw oneself about; burst *into, out of*, etc.; swagger; (of check) be returned because the account has insufficient funds to cover it. **bounc'ing** *adj.* Big and lively; boisterous; **bouncing Bet**: see SOAPWORT. **bounc'y** *adj.* (**bounc·i·er, bounc·i·est**). That bounces; springy.

bound[1] (bownd) *n.* Limit of territory etc.; (pl.) limitation, restriction, limit beyond which schoolchildren, students, soldiers, etc., may not pass. ~ *v.t.* Set bounds to, limit; be boundary of. **bound'less** *adj.*

bound[2] (bownd) *n.* Springy movement upward or forward; recoil (of ball etc.). ~ *v.i.* (of ball etc.) Recoil from wall or ground, bounce; spring, leap, or advance lightly.

bound[3] (bownd) *adj.* Ready to start, having started (*for*).

bound[4] (bownd): see BIND.

bound·a·ry (bown′d*e*rē, -drē) *n.* (pl. **-ries**). That which serves to indicate bounds or limits of anything; bounds.

bound·en (bown′d*e*n) *adj.* Obliged, beholden, indebted, esp. ~ **duty.**

bound·er (bown′d*e*r) *n.* (slang) Cad.

boun·te·ous (bown′tē*u*s) *adj.* Beneficent, liberal; freely bestowed. **boun'te·ous·ly** *adv.* **boun'te·ous·ness** *n.*

boun·ti·ful (bown′tiful) *adj.* Bounteous; generous. **boun'ti·ful·ly** *adv.* **boun'ti·ful·ness** *n.*

boun·ty (bown′tē) *n.* (pl. **-ties**). Munificence, liberality in giving; gift, gratuity; subsidy; prize money, esp. that offered by a government.

Boun·ty (bown′tē), **Mutiny of**

The flowers of the **bougainvillea** have a flamboyance that attracts gardeners throughout the world. The plant is native to South America.

*Above: Replica of the **Bounty** at St. Petersburgh, Florida. This supply ship was made famous in 1789 by the mutiny of the crew, led by Fletcher Christian, on a voyage from Tahiti.*

*Below: **Boulder Dam** was completed in 1936 and renamed for President Herbert Hoover in 1947. Straddling the Arizona-Nevada border, it services the surrounding area.*

the. Mutiny (April 28, 1789) of the crew of H.M.S. *Bounty*, bound from Tahiti to the Cape of Good Hope, against their captain, Lieut. BLIGH. He and eighteen companions, set adrift in an open boat, succeeded in reaching Timor, nearly 4,000 miles away. Some of the mutineers eventually went on to Pitcairn Island, founding a settlement there which was not discovered until 1808.

bou·quet (bōkā′, bo͞o-) *n.* (pl. **-quets** pr. -kāz′). Bunch of flowers, esp. one presented as a compliment (also fig.); characteristic perfume of wine.

Bour·bon (boor′bon). Surname of branch of royal family of France; they became the ruling monarchs when Henry IV succeeded to the throne in 1589; members of this family also became kings of Spain (1700–1931) and of Naples.

bour·bon (bẽr′bon) *n.* (also ~ **whiskey**). Whiskey distilled from corn and rye, orig. made in Bourbon County, Kentucky.

bour·don (boor′don) *n.* Low-pitched (usu. 16-ft.) stop in organ; drone bass of bagpipe (ill. BAGPIPE). [Fr., = "drone bee, bass stop in organ"]

bour·geois[1] (boorzhwah′, boor′-zhwah) *n.* (pl. **-geois**) & *adj.* 1. (orig.) (Of) a French citizen or freeman of a small city or town. 2.

(Member) of shopkeeping or mercantile middle class; (person) of humdrum middle-class ideas (now freq. a rather vague term of abuse). **bour·geoi·sie** (boorzhwahzē′) *n.* Middle class.

bour·geois[2] (berjois′) *n.* Size of type (approx. 9 point). [Perh. f. a French printer's name]

Bour·geois (boorzhwah′, boor′-zhwah), **Léon Victor Auguste** (1851–1925). French statesman; a founder and first chairman of the League of Nations; awarded the Nobel Peace Prize in 1920.

bour·rée (bo͞orā′; *Fr.* bo͞orā′) *n.* (pl. **-rées** pr. -rāz; *Fr.* -rā′). Lively dance, in duple time, of French or Spanish origin; music suitable for or derived from this, esp. as a movement in a suite.

bourse (boors) *n.* Money market, esp. (**B**~) the Paris stock exchange.

bout (bowt) *n.* 1. Spell or turn of work, illness, exercise, etc.; fit of drinking. 2. Prizefight, contest, trial of strength.

bou·tique (bo͞otēk′) *n.* Small shop or department selling fashionable clothes or accessories.

bo·vine (bō′vīn, -vēn, -vĭn) *adj.* Of, like, a cow; inert, dull.

bow[1] (bō) *n.* 1. Curve. 2. Weapon for shooting arrows, a strip of flexible wood or other material held in bent position, when in use, by a string stretched between its two ends. 3. Appliance for playing instruments of violin class, rod with a number of horsehairs stretched from end to end, for drawing across the strings. 4. Slipknot with double or single loop, ribbon etc. so tied. 5. ~ **compass(es)**, drawing compass with jointed legs; **bowlegged** (bō′lĕgĭd), having legs bowed or curved outward; bandylegged; **bow′man**, archer; **bow tie**, necktie tied in a bow. **bow** *v.* Play with bow (on violin etc.), use bow.

bow[2] (bow) *v.* Submit *to*; bend or kneel in sign of submission or reverence, incline head in greeting or assent; express by bowing, usher *in, out,* by bowing; cause to bend. ~ *n.* Bending of head or body in salutation, respect, content, etc.

bow[3] (bow) *n.* Fore end of boat or ship from where it begins to arch inward (often pl.).

Bow (bō) **bells.** Peal of bells of St. Mary-le-Bow, a church in Cheapside near the center of London; hence, **within the sound of** ~, within the City of London.

Bow·ditch (bow′dĭch), **Nathaniel** (1773–1838). American astronomer, mathematician and navigational expert; prepared the American edition of *The Practical Navigator*, 1802.

Bowd·ler (bowd′ler, bōd′-), **Thomas** (1754–1825). M.D. of Edinburgh, editor of *Family Shakespeare* (1818), an edition "in which those words and expressions are omitted which cannot with propriety be read aloud in a family."

*The **bow** was probably invented in the paleolithic period. Right: A New Guinea tribesman uses a light hunting bow. Below: Archer using a modern recurve bow fully-equipped for competitive archery.*

*The male **bowerbird** is sexually active during a long breeding season and, once it has made its arena or bower, will attract several females to mate. The plainer the species, the more elaborate is its courting bower. MacGregor's bowerbird makes a simple bower of twigs, but the plainer crestless bowerbird builds a roofed stage and garden. The female regent bowerbird is better camouflaged than her mate, a vital survival factor.*

MacGregor's Bower Bird

Crestless Bower Bird

Regent's Bower Bird

bowd'ler·ize *v.t.* (**-ized, -iz·ing**). Expurgate.

bow·el (bow'*el*) *n.* Division of alimentary canal below stomach, intestine; (pl.) entrails, inside of body; pity, tender feeling; inside of anything, esp. in **~s of the earth**. **bowel** (**-eled, -el·ing;** *Brit.* **-elled, -el·ling**). Disembowel.

bow·er[1] (bow'*er*) *n.* 1. (poet.) Dwelling, abode; inner room, boudoir. 2. Place closed in with foliage, arbor, summerhouse; **bow'erbird**, any of several Australian birds (e.g., **satin, regent, spotted ~**) of starling family, remarkable for their habit of building bowers or runs and adorning them with feathers, shells, etc., in courtship. **bow'er·like** *adj.*

bow·er[2] (bow'*er*) *n.* Each of the two highest cards at euchre, the jack of trumps (**right ~**) and the jack of the other suit of the same color (**left ~**). [Ger. *Bauer* peasant]

Bow·er·y (bow'*er*ē, bow'rē), **The.** Street and section in lower part of Manhattan, formerly notorious as a haunt of criminals and, later, of derelicts. [Du. *bouwerij* husbandry, farm]

bow·ie (bō'ē) *n.* (also **~knife**) Large hunting knife with long hollow-ground blade, curved and double-edged near the point and having a hilt and crosspiece. [Popularized by James *Bowie*, probably designed by his brother Retzin P. *Bowie*]

Bow·ie (bō'ē, bo͞o'ē), **James** (1799–1836). Georgia-born Texas colonist and colonel in Texan army; became Mexican citizen, 1830; leader of opposition to Mexican control of Texas; killed at Battle of the Alamo, 1836.

bowl[1] (bōl) *n.* Deep, rounded basin for holding liquid or food; drinking vessel; contents of a bowl; bowl-shaped part of a tobacco pipe, spoon, etc.; bowl-shaped topographical depression; flat region noted for specific item, crop, etc.; bowl-shaped football stadium; **~ game**, championship or important football game played by selected teams in such a bowl after regular season (as **Rose B~, Cotton B~, Super B~**).

bowl[2] (bōl) *n.* 1. Wooden ball made slightly out of spherical shape (formerly spherical and weighted on one side) to make it run in a curved course; (pl.) game played on a bowling green with bowls, the object being to lay the bowls near a spike. **~** *v.* Play bowls; roll (bowl, hoop, etc.); roll like bowl or hoop, move on wheels; play a game of, roll a bowl in, bowling; **~ over**, knock down; disconcert, render helpless.

bowl·er[1] (bō'l*er*) *n.* One who bowls.

bowl·er[2] (bō'l*er*) *n.* (chiefly Brit.) (also **~ hat**) Hard round felt hat; derby.

bow·line (bō'lĭn, -līn) *n.* Rope in ship's rigging from weather side of square sail to bow; (also **bow'knot**) simple but very secure knot used in fastening bowline to sail.

bowl·ing (bō'lĭng) *n.* Playing bowls; playing skittles; game played by rolling a **~ ball** down a wooden

Since the day early in the 19th century when a young woman first bowled over-arm in the game of cricket, the way was open for more complex ***bowling*** *styles. Dennis Lillee, an Australian fast bowler, made great impact in the 1970s. The game of* ***bowls*** *may be played between two single players, pairs or fours, using wooden bowls weighing up to 3½ lb.*

Boxers *are placed in categories according to weight and here fight for the world championship.*

alley to knock down as many as possible of a triangular group of ten pins; ~ **alley**, the wooden alley used in bowling; building housing such alleys; ~ **green**, lawn for playing bowls.

bow·sprit (bow′sprĭt, bō′-) *n.* Spar running out from ship's stem, to which forestays are fastened.

box[1] (bŏks) *n.* (pl. **box·es**). Evergreen shrub or small tree of genus *Buxus* (esp. *B. sempervirens*), with small dark-green leathery leaves, much used in garden borders and hedges; (also **box′wood**), wood of this.

box[2] (bŏks) *n.* (pl. **box·es**). 1. Receptacle (usu. with lid, rectangular or cylindrical, and for solids) of wood, cardboard, etc.; quantity contained in this; receptacle at newspaper office for replies to advertisement; **post-office** ~: see POST[2]. 2. Coachman's seat. 3. Small separate compartment in theater etc., or for horse in stable or railroad car; jury box; witness stand; hut for sentry etc. 4. Protective case for piece of mechanism etc.; (typ.) space enclosed by rules etc. 5. ~ **camera**, box-shaped camera; ~ **kite**, kite with light, rectangular frame at each end; ~ **office**, ticket office at a theater, stadium, etc.; (fig.) quality of entertainment etc. likely to attract audiences; ~ **pleat**: see PLEAT; ~ **spring**, one of a set of pocketed springs in a mattress etc.; hence ~**-spring mattress** or ~ **spring**, mattress containing such springs. **box** *v.t.* Provide with, put into, confine as in, box; partition *off* from other compartments; ~ **in**, block the movement of (a vehicle) so that it cannot maneuver; ~ **the compass**, (naut.) repeat compass points in correct order; (fig.) make complete revolution and end where one began; (Brit.) **Boxing Day**, first weekday after Christmas, observed as a holiday, traditional day for giving of Christmas gift boxes to servants and other service workers. **box′like** *adj.*

box[3] (bŏks) *v.* 1. Slap (person's) ears. 2. Fight with fists, usu. in padded leather gloves. **box′ing** *n.* (esp.) Act or sport of fighting with fists, usu. in padded leather gloves (~ **gloves**); ~ **match**, match between pugilists fighting in boxing gloves; **box** *n.* (pl. **box·es**). Slap with hand *on the ear*.

Table of Boxing Weights

Amateur

Weight	Not more than	
light fly	48 kg	7st 8lb
fly	51 kg	8st
bantam	54 kg	8st 6lb
feather	57 kg	9st
light	60 kg	9st 7lb
light welter	63.5 kg	10st
welter	67 kg	10st 8lb
light middle	71 kg	11st 2lb
middle	75 kg	11st 11lb
light heavy	81 kg	12st 10lb
heavy	81 kg and over	12st 10lb

Professional

Weight	Not more than
fly	8st
bantam	8st 8lb
feather	9st
light	9st 9lb
welter	10st 7lb
middle	11st 6lb
light heavy	12st 7lb
heavy	12st 7lb and over

Box·er (bŏk′ser) *n.* Member of a Chinese secret society that attempted to drive foreigners from China (1900) by violence and by besieging the legations at Peking, and tried to force Chinese Christians to renounce their religion. [transl. of Chinese word meaning "fist of harmony"]

box·er[1] (bŏk′sẽr) *n.* Person who fights in boxing match(es), pugilist.

box·er[2] (bŏk′sẽr) *n.* Dog of smooth-coated brown breed and having a short, square muzzle.

box·y (bŏk′sē) *adj.* (**box·i·er, box·i·est**). Resembling a box (BOX[2]) in shape.

boy (boi) *n.* Male child or youth, son; man retaining boy's character, tastes, etc.; (derog.) male servant or laborer; (derog.) familiarly as term of address; **boy′-friend**, woman's usual or preferred male companion; **Boy Scout**: see SCOUT. **boy** *int.* (colloq.; also **oh ~**) Exclamation of surprise, approval, etc.

boy·cott (boi′kŏt) *v.t.* Combine to punish or coerce by systematic refusal of social or commercial relations; abstain from (goods etc.) with this aim. **~** *n.* Boycotting. [f. Captain *Boycott*, an Irish landlord, victim of this treatment]

boy·hood (boi′ho͝od) *n.* Boyish age; boys.

boy·ish (boi′ĭsh) adj. Of or like boys. **boy′ish·ly** *adv.* **boy′ish·ness** *n.*

Boyle (boil), **Hon. Robert** (1627–91). English natural philosopher and chemist; **~'s law**, law, formulated by him, that the volume of a given quantity of gas varies inversely with the pressure when the temperature is constant.

Boz (bŏz). Pseudonym used by Charles DICKENS.

bp *abbrev.* Bishop.

B.P. *abbrev.* Bills payable; blood pressure.

b.p. *abbrev.* Bills payable; boiling point.

bpl. *abbrev.* Birthplace.

B.P.O.E. *abbrev.* Benevolent and Protective Order of Elks.

bra (brah) *n.* (colloq.) Brassiere.

Bra·bant (brabănt′, brah′bant). Former duchy in W. Europe, now divided into 2 provinces: **~** in Belgium and **N. ~** in the Netherlands.

brace (brās) *v.t.* (**braced, brac·ing**). Strengthen or tighten; make taut; give firmness to, invigorate. **~** *n.* 1. Thing that braces or connects; connecting mark in printing or writing ({); strengthening piece of iron or timber in buildings; (dentistry) wire device for straightening teeth; (naut.) rope attached to yard for trimming sail; (pl., Brit.) suspenders; **~ and bit**, tool for boring in which the bit is made to rotate by turning the brace etc. 2. Couple, pair, esp. of dogs or game.

brace·let (brās′lĭt) *n.* Ornamental band, chain, etc., for wrist or arm; (pl., slang) handcuffs.

brac·er (brā′sẽr) *n.* Stimulating drink; tonic.

bra·chi·al (brā′kēal) *adj.* Of the arm; like an arm.

brach·y·ce·phal·ic (brăkēsefăl′ĭk) *adj.* Short headed; with width of skull at least 4/5 of length. **brach·y·ceph·a·ly** (brăkēsĕf′alē), **brach·y·ceph′a·lism** *ns.*

brack·en (brăk′en) *n.* Kind of large fern (*Pteridium aquilinum*), abundant on heaths etc.; mass of this.

brack·et (brăk′ĭt) *n.* 1. Flat-topped projection from wall serving as support; shelf with slanting underprop for hanging against wall; wooden or metal angular support. 2. (freq. pl.) Pair of marks [ ] used for enclosing words, figures, etc., so as to separate them from the context. 3. (artillery) Specified distance between pair of shots fired beyond target and short of it, in finding range. 4. Group bracketed together as of equal standing or falling between certain limits (as **income ~**). **~** *v.t.* Enclose in brackets; couple with brace, imply connection or equality between; (artillery) fire shots beyond and short of target (see above).

brack·ish (brăk′ĭsh) *adj.* (of water) Rather salty; unpalatable. **brack′ish·ness** *n.*

bract (brăkt) *n.* (bot.) Modified usu. small leaf or scale below flower.

brac·te·ate (brăk′tēĭt, -āt) *adj.* Bearing bracts.

brac·te·ole (brăk′tēōl) *n.* (bot.) Small bract on flower stalk.

brad (brăd) *n.* Thin flattish nail of same thickness throughout.

Brad·dock (brăd′ok), **Edward** (1695–1755). Commander in chief of British troops in America during the French and Indian War; was defeated and died in surprise attack at Fort Duquesne, 1755.

Brad·ford (brăd′fẽrd), **William** (1590–1657). English Puritan colonist in America; signer of the Mayflower Compact; governor of

*The **boxer,** sometimes known as a German bulldog, stands 21–24 ins. at the shoulder and may be brindled or have white markings. Active and strong, it makes a good guard dog.*

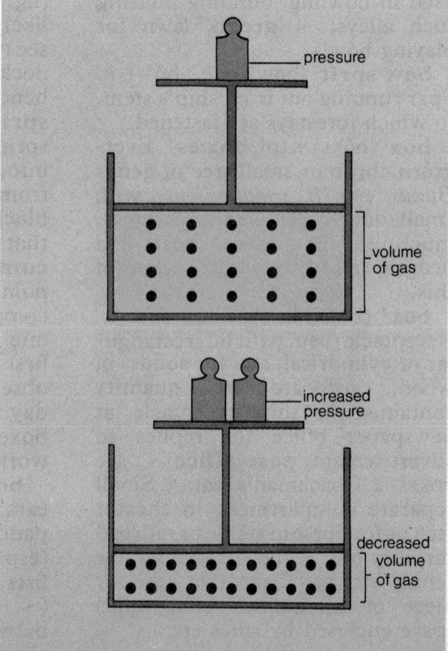

***Boyle's Law** states that the volume of a gas at constant temperature varies in inverse proportion to pressure acting upon it. If the pressure is doubled the volume is halved; trebled the volume is reduced to one third.*

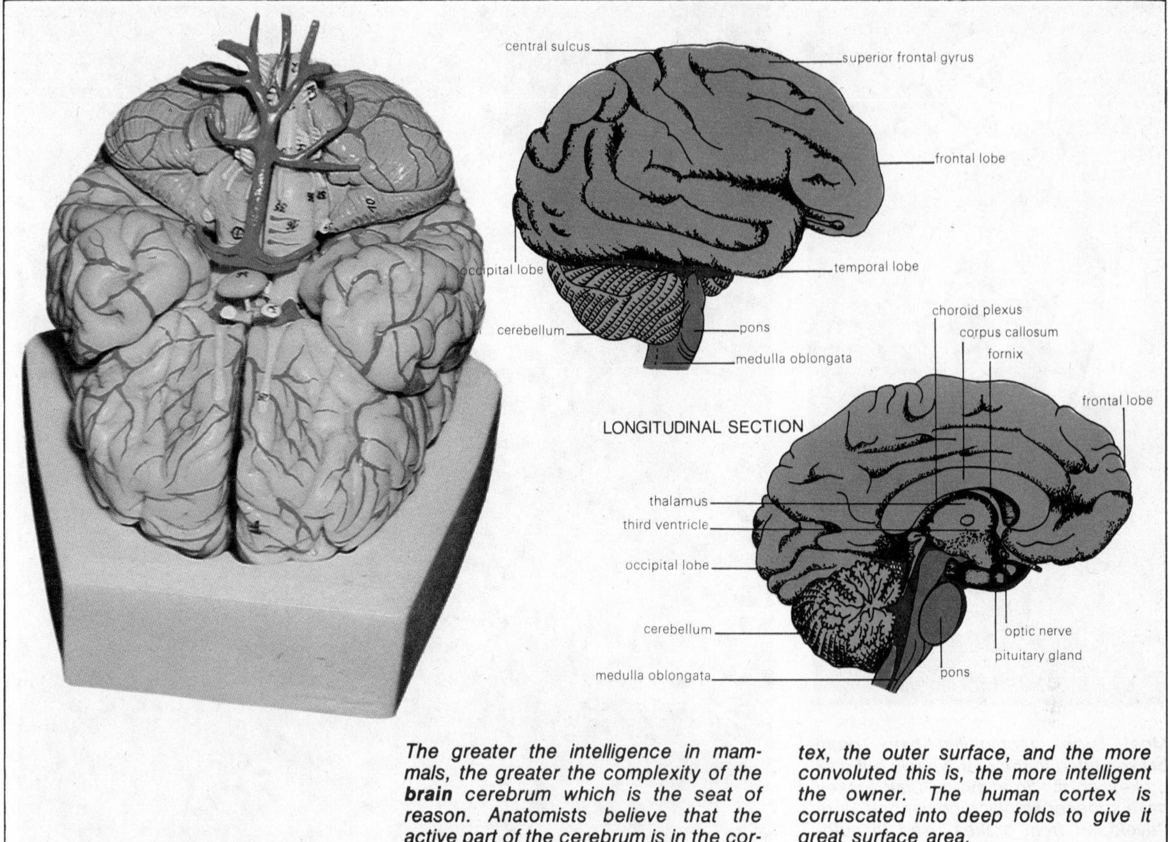

The greater the intelligence in mammals, the greater the complexity of the ***brain*** *cerebrum which is the seat of reason. Anatomists believe that the active part of the cerebrum is in the cortex, the outer surface, and the more convoluted this is, the more intelligent the owner. The human cortex is corruscated into deep folds to give it great surface area.*

Plymouth Colony five times.

Brad·ley (brăd′lē), **Omar Nelson** (1893–). American army general; commander of the 12th Army Group, largest American combat force during World War II European campaign; first chairman, Joint Chiefs of Staff, 1949.

Brad·street (brăd′strēt), **Anne Dudley** (1612–72). Puritan colonist in America, 1630; first colonial American woman poet, author of *The Tenth Muse*.

Bra·dy (brā′dē), **Matthew B.** (1823?–96). American pioneer photographer; best known for photographing the Civil War.

brae (brā) *n.* (Sc.) Steep bank, hillside.

brag (brăg) *v.* (**bragged, brag·ging**). Talk boastfully. ~ *n.* Boastful talk. **brag′ger** *n.*

brag·ga·do·ci·o (brăg*a*dō′shēō) *n.* (pl. **-ci·os**). Empty boasting. [formed by Spenser from *brag* as proper name of personification of vainglory]

brag·gart (brăg′*ert*) *n.* & *adj.* (Person) given to bragging.

Brahe (brah, brah′hē), **Tycho** (1546–1601). Danish astronomer; his observations of the sun prepared the way for the discoveries of Kepler (who worked under him) but he did not accept the Copernican system.

Brah·ma (brah′m*a*). (Hinduism) Supreme God, the divine reality, of which the entire universe is only a manifestation.

Brah·man, Brah·min (brah′m*a*n) *ns.* (pl. **-mans, -mins**). Member of the highest or priestly caste among Hindus; (colloq.) highly cultured or intellectual aloof person. **Brah·man·ic** (brahmăn′ĭk), **Brah·man′i·cal** *adjs.* **Brah′man·ism** *n.*

Brahms (brahmz), **Johannes** (1833–97). German composer of symphonies, chamber music, songs, etc.

braid (brād) *n.* 1. Entwined hair, plait; band, etc., entwined with the hair. 2. Woven fabric of silk, linen, etc., in the form of a band. ~ *v.t.* Plait, interweave, arrange in braids; trim, edge, with braid. **braid′er, braid′ing** *ns.*

Braille, braille (brāl) *ns.* System of printing for the blind consisting of embossed characters recognizable by touch, invented by Louis BRAILLE. ~ *v.t.* (**Brailled, Brail·ling**). Print in Braille.

Braille (brāl), **Louis** (1809–52). French educator and musician; blind from childhood; devised system of printing for the blind.

brain (brān) *n.* 1. Convoluted mass of nervous tissue, contained in the skull, which controls the processes of sensation, learning, and memory in vertebrates and is regarded as the center of thought and intellectual power in man; **fore′brain, mid′brain, hind′brain,** parts that develop from the three main parts of the primitive brain; **great ~**, cerebrum; **lesser ~**, cerebellum; **~ stem**, medulla oblongata. 2. In many invertebrates, the part of the nervous system that corresponds to the vertebrate brain in function and position. 3. (colloq.) Very intelligent person; **the ~s**, cleverest person or major planner (of group, movement, etc.). 4. **brain′child**, invention, scheme; **brain drain**, (colloq.) emigration of highly qualified persons, esp. from England to U.S.; **brain fever**, (archaic) inflammation of the brain; **brain′pan**, part of skull containing the brain, cranium; **brain′storm**, sudden idea; **brain′storming**, spontaneous discussion in search for new ideas; **brain trust**, (hist.) group of advisers called in by President Franklin Roosevelt; group of experts advising a government; **brain′washing**, systematic elimination from person's mind of (esp. political) established ideas, esp. coercive conversion of dissidents in totalitarian state; so **brain′wash** (*v.t.*); **brain wave**,

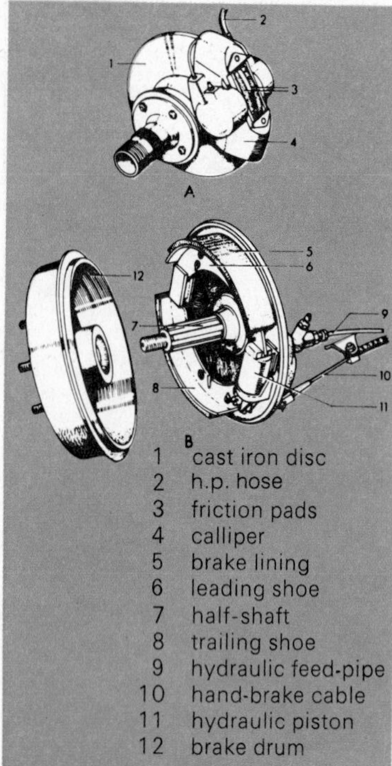

*Most large automobiles have drum **brakes** fitted to the rear wheels but disk brakes on the front ones. Disk brakes have superior stopping power and were developed from brakes used in automobile racing.*

***Brambles** of the genus* Rubus *grow wild throughout North America and are also cultivated for their fruit, the blackberry, which is a source of vitamin C.*

sudden inspiration, bright thought. **brain'less** *adj.* **brain** *v.t.* Dash out brains of.

brain·y (brā'nē) *adj.* (**brain·i·er, brain·i·est**). (colloq.) Intelligent.

braise (brāz) *v.t.* (**braised, brais·ing**). Cook by browning in fat and then simmering in small quantity of liquid in a covered container.

brake[1] (brāk) *n.* Bracken.

brake[2] (brāk) *n.* Thicket, brushwood.

brake[3] (brāk) *n.* Toothed instrument for braking flax and hemp; a heavy harrow. ~ *v.t.* (**braked, brak·ing**). Crush (flax, hemp) by beating.

brake[4] (brāk) *n.* Frictional apparatus for checking motion of vehicle or machine by pressure, usu. applied to circumference of wheel or to special drum or hub on axle; (also ~ **pedal**) pedal operating this; ~ **horsepower,** (abbrev. b.h.p.) horsepower of an engine measured by an absorption dynamometer (orig. by resistance of an applied brake); **brake'man** (also Brit. **brakes'man**), trainman, assistant to conductor. **brake** *v.* (**braked, brak·ing**). Apply brake; check with brake.

bram·ble (brăm'bel) *n.* Rough, prickly rambling shrub, esp. the blackberry. **bram'bly** *adj.* (**-bli·er, -bli·est**).

bran (brăn) *n.* Husks of grain separated from flour after grinding.

branch (brănch) *n.* Limb of tree etc. growing from stem or bough; lateral extension or subdivision of river, road, family, business, etc.; small stream. ~ *v.i.* Put branches *out, forth,* spring *out*; spread *forth,* tend *away, off,* diverge *into.* **branch'ing** *adj.* & *n.* **branch'less** *adj.*

bran·chi·a (brăng'kēa) *n.* (pl. **-chi·ae** pr. -kēē). (zool.) Gill. **bran'chi·al, bran·chi·ate** (brăng'kēĭt, -āt) *adjs.*

Bran·cu·si (brahngkōō'zē), **Constantin** (1876–1957). Rumanian-born French sculptor, associated with modern school of art and symbolism.

brand (brănd) *n.* 1. Burning or charred piece of wood from hearth. 2. Mark made by burning with hot iron; stigma; trademark, goods of particular make or trademark; ~**-new**, perfectly new. 3. Iron instrument for branding. 4. (poet.) Sword. **brand** *v.t.* Burn with hot iron; impress on memory; stigmatize; **branding iron**, instrument for branding. **brand'er** *n.*

Bran·deis (brăn'dīs), **Louis Dembitz** (1856–1941). U.S. lawyer and jurist; counsel in famous cases for limiting hours of the work week and against New England railroad monopoly; Supreme Court associate justice, 1916–39.

bran·dish (brăn'dĭsh) *v.t.* Wave about, flourish, in display or threat.

bran·dy (brăn'dē) *n.* (pl. **-dies**). Strong alcoholic spirit distilled from wine. **bran'died** *adj.* [Du. *brandewijn*, burnt, distilled wine]

Bran·dy·wine (brăn'dēwīn). Creek in SE. Pennsylvania and NW Delaware; site of victory of British over Americans during Revolutionary War, 1777.

brant (brănt) *n.* (pl. **brants,** collect. **brant**). (also Brit. *brent*) Any of several species of wild goose (esp. *Branta bernicla*); breeds in Arctic.

Braque (brahk), **Georges** (1882–1963). French Cubist painter and friend of Picasso.

brash (brăsh) *adj.* Vulgarly

assertive, impudent. **brash'ly** *adv.* **brash'ness** *n.* **brash'y** *adj.* (**brash·i·er, brash·i·est**).

Bra·síl·ia (brahzēl'ya). City of central Brazil, especially constructed as its capital; capital since 1960.

brass (brăs, brahs) *n.* 1. (hist.) Alloy of copper with tin or zinc, bronze; (now) yellow alloy of copper and zinc, usu. with about 1/3 total weight of zinc. 2. Monumental or sepulchral tablet of inscribed brass or similar alloy; musical instruments of brass. 3. Effrontery, shamelessness. 4. (slang; also **top** ~) Brass hats; senior officials. **brass** *adj.* Made of brass; ~ **band,** band of musicians with brass instruments; ~ **hat,** (slang) officer of high rank; ~ **knuckles,** metal device worn to protect knuckles from injury during fist-fighting and to increase effectiveness of punches; ~ **tacks,** (slang) actual details, real business.

bras·sard (brăs'ärd) *n.* Cloth badge worn on arm; piece of armor for protecting the arm.

brass·ie (brăs'ē, brah'sē) *n.* (pl. **brass·ies**). Wooden-headed golf club with brass plate under the head, for hitting long, low shots; number 2 wood.

bras·siere (brazēr') *n.* Woman's undergarment supporting breasts.

brass·y (brăs'ē, brah'sē) *adj.* (**brass·i·er, brass·i·est**). Yellow like brass; sounding like brass; impudent, shameless. **brass'i·ly** *adv.* **brass'i·ness** *n.*

brat (brăt) *n.* (contempt.) Child.

Bra·ti·sla·va (brah'tĭslahvah). Historic port and industrial city on the Danube in S. central Czechoslovakia.

brat·wurst (brăt'werst, -woorst, braht'-; *Ger.* braht'voorsht) *n.* Spiced pork sausage.

Braun[1] (brown), **Eva** (1910–45). German mistress and wife, just before their joint deaths, of Adolf Hitler.

Braun[2] (brown), **Karl Ferdinand** (1850–1918). German physicist and pioneer in telegraphy; invented a cathode ray tube; co-winner of the Nobel Prize in physics, 1909.

Braun·schwei·ger (brown'-shwīger; *Ger.* brown'shvīger) *n.* (also **braunschweiger**) Smoked and spiced liver sausage.

bra·va·do (bravah'dō) *n.* (pl. **-does, -dos**). Show of courage, bold front.

brave (brāv) *adj.* (**brav·er, brav·est**). 1. Ready to confront and steady in enduring danger or pain. 2. Splendid, spectacular. ~ *n.* N. Amer. Indian warrior. **brave'ly** *adv.* **brave'ness** *n.* **brave** *v.t.* (**braved, brav·ing**). Defy, meet with courage.

brav·er·y (brā'verē) *n.* (pl. **-er·ies**). Brave conduct; splendor.

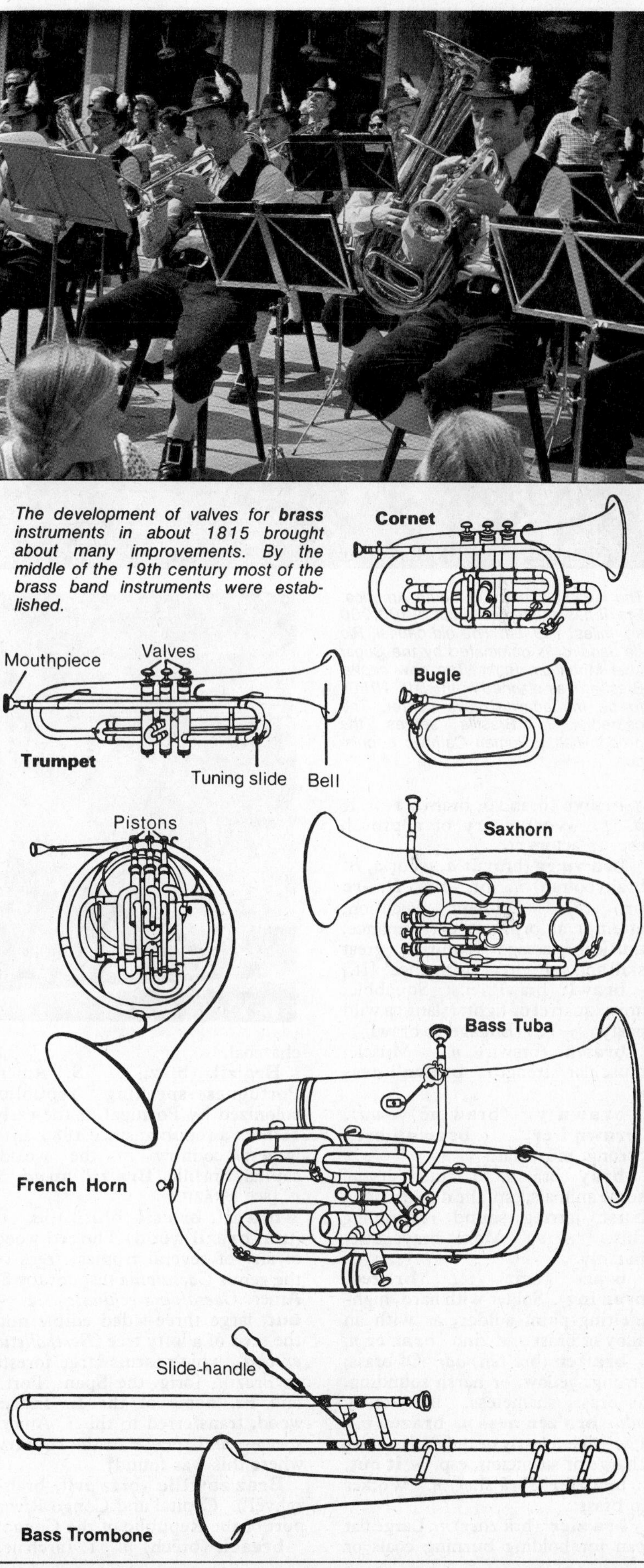

The development of valves for ***brass*** *instruments in about 1815 brought about many improvements. By the middle of the 19th century most of the brass band instruments were established.*

*The largest country in South America, **Brazil** has an area of about 3,300,000 sq. miles. Top left: The old capital, Rio de Janeiro, is dominated by the Sugar Loaf Mountain. Right: The new capital Brasilia, was planned in the late 1950s to be the administrative center. The cathedral in Brasilia serves the predominantly Roman Catholic population.*

bra·vo (brah´vō, brahvō´) *int.* & *n.* (pl. **-vos**). Cry of approval, esp. to actors etc.

bra·vu·ra (br*a*vūr´*a*, -voor´*a*; *It.* brahvōō´rah) *n.* (pl. **-ras**; *It.* **-re** pr. -rĕ). Brilliant execution, attempt at brilliant performance; musical passage requiring great skill and spirit in performance. [It.]

brawl (brawl) *n.* Squabble, noisy quarrel or fight; (slang) a wild party. ~ *v.i.* Engage in brawl.

brawn (brawn) *n.* Muscle; muscular strength. **brawn´i·ness** *n.*

brawn·y (braw´nē) *adj.* (**brawn·i·er, brawn·i·est**). Strong, muscular.

bray (brā) *n.* Peculiar cry of some animals, esp. the donkey; loud harsh jarring sound resembling this. ~ *v.* Make bray; utter harshly.

braze (brāz) *v.t.* (**brazed, braz·ing**). Solder with hard, high-melting-point solder, as with an alloy of brass and zinc. **braz´er** *n.*

bra·zen (brā´zen) *adj.* Of brass; strong, yellow, or harsh sounding, as brass; shameless. **bra´zen·ly** *adv.* **bra´zen·ness** *n.* **brazen** *v.t.* Face shamelessly or defiantly under charge or suspicion, esp. ~ **it out**.

bra·zier[1] (brā´zh*e*r) *n.* Worker in brass.

bra·zier[2] (brā´zh*e*r) *n.* Large flat pan for holding burning coals or charcoal.

Bra·zil (br*a*zĭl´). S. Amer. Portuguese-speaking republic; colonized by Portugal in the early 16th c.; a republic since 1889; fifth largest country in the world; capital, Brasília. **Bra·zil´ian** *adj.* & *n.* [see BRAZIL]

bra·zil, bra·sil (br*a*zĭl´) *ns.* 1. (usu. **brazil´wood**) The red wood of any of several tropical trees of the genus *Caesalpina* (esp. of the S. Amer. *Caesalpina echinata*). 2. ~ **nut**, large three-sided edible nut, the seed of a lofty tree (*Bertholletia excelsa*), which forms large forests in Brazil. [orig. the Span., Port., and Fr. name of the E. Indian wood; transferred to the S. Amer. species, and thence to the country where this was found]

Braz·za·ville (brăz´*a*vĭl, brah-zahvēl´). Capital and Congo River port of the Republic of the Congo.

breach (brēch) *n.* 1. (archaic, also ~ **of the sea**) Breaking of waves. 2. Breaking or neglect (of rule, duty, promise, etc.); breaking of relations, alienation, quarrel; ~ **of the peace**, disturbance of public peace by brawl, riot, etc.; ~ **of promise**, (esp.) breaking of promise to marry. 3. Injury, broken place, gap, esp. in wall or fortification; **breach** *v.t.* Break through, make gap in.

bread (brĕd) *n.* Flour moistened, usu. leavened, kneaded into dough, and baked in loaves; this as staple article of food; livelihood, means of subsistence; ~ **and butter**, livelihood, means of support: **~-and-butter letter**, letter of thanks for hospitality; **bread´-board**, board to knead or cut bread on; **bread´fruit**, starchy fruit, about the size of a melon, and with whitish pulp like new bread, of the **bread´fruit tree** (*Artocarpus incisa*) of the South Sea islands etc.;

bread'winner, person supporting a family or household. **bread** *v.t.* Coat (food) with bread crumbs before cooking.

breadth (brĕdth) *n.* 1. Broadness, measure from side to side; piece (of cloth etc.) of full standard breadth. 2. Wide extent or scope; largeness, liberality, catholicity. **breadth'ways, breadth'wise** *advs.*

break (brāk) *v.* (**broke** or archaic **brake, bro·ken** or archaic **broke, break·ing**). 1. Divide, disperse, split, separate, otherwise than by cutting; tame, subdue, crush; fall to pieces; burst, issue, *forth*; solve (cipher etc.); (of voice) crack, change tone (at puberty); (boxing) come out of clinch; **~down,** (*v.i.*) collapse; lose control, become tearful; **break'down,** (of machine etc.) cease to function; (trans.) itemize, analyze; **break even**, emerge with neither loss nor gain; **break in**, tame, discipline; teach the rudiments; enter by force or stealth, as to rob; hence, **break-in** (*n.*); **break out**, burst from restraint or concealment; **break up**, disband; separate, obtain a legal separation (of a married couple). 2. Ruin financially, make bankrupt. 3. Interrupt, change; put an end to; act contrary to (agreement, law, etc.). 4. Make a way through, with suddenness or violence; disclose; (of news) be disclosed; (of day) dawn; (of a storm) begin violently. 5. (of baseball pitch) Curve. 6. **break'away,** (*adj.*, esp.) seceding; **break'down**, collapse, stoppage; failure of health or (esp. mental) power(s); act of disintegrating or analyzing a substance; analysis of statistical figures etc.; **break'neck**, endangering the neck, headlong; **break'through**, (esp.) significant advance in knowledge, achievement, etc.; **break'up**, disintegration, collapse, dispersal; **break'-water**, barrier built to break force of waves. **break'a·ble** *adj.* **break'age** *n.* **break** *n.* Breaking; breach, gap, broken place; pause in work etc.; escape; curve of baseball after pitching; (billiards) the opening shot, points scored continuously; (slang) stroke of luck.

break·er[1] (brā'ker) *n.* (esp.) Heavy ocean wave breaking on coast or over reefs; (CB radio use) one wishing to transmit a message.

break·er[2] (brā'ker) *n.* (naut.) Small keg, esp. for a lifeboat.

break·fast (brĕk'fast) *n.* First meal of the day. **~** *v.i.* Take breakfast. **break'fast·er** *n.*

bream (brēm) *n.* (collect. **bream**, pl. **breams**). Any of several fresh-water fishes of genus *Abramis* with high-arched back; any of various porgies, such as the sea bream (*Archosargus rhomboidalis*); also various fresh-water sunfishes of genus *Lepomis*.

breast (brĕst) *n.* 1. Each of two soft protuberances on woman's thorax, secreting milk for feeding young; corresponding rudimentary organ of man. 2. Upper front part of human body; corresponding part in animals, this as cut of meat; part of dress, coat, etc., covering this. 3. Heart, emotions, thoughts. 4. **breast'bone**, sternum; **breast-fed**, (of infant) fed at mother's breast; **breast'plate**, piece of embroidered fabric embellished with 12 precious stones, representing the 12 tribes of Israel, worn on breast of Jewish high priest; (hist.) piece of armor covering breast; **breast'stroke**, stroke in swimming in which breast is squarely opposed to the water; **breast'work**, temporary defense or parapet a few feet high. **breast** *v.t.* Oppose breast to, face, contend with.

breath (brĕth) *n.* 1. Exhalation as perceptible to sight or smell; slight movement of air; whiff. 2. Air taken into and expelled from lungs; respiration; power of breathing; whisper, murmur; **take person's ~ away**, dumbfound him or her; so **breath'taking** (*adj.*). 3. (phon.) Voiceless expiration of air, as in the articulation of *s* and *p*.

*The mass production of **bread** begins with a mixture in which all the ingredients except sugar and salt are present. The mixture stands for two or three hours before sugar and salt are added. After standing until it is risen, the dough is divided and molded. The dough's elasticity is replaced by kneading, and a final molding leads to the ovens.*

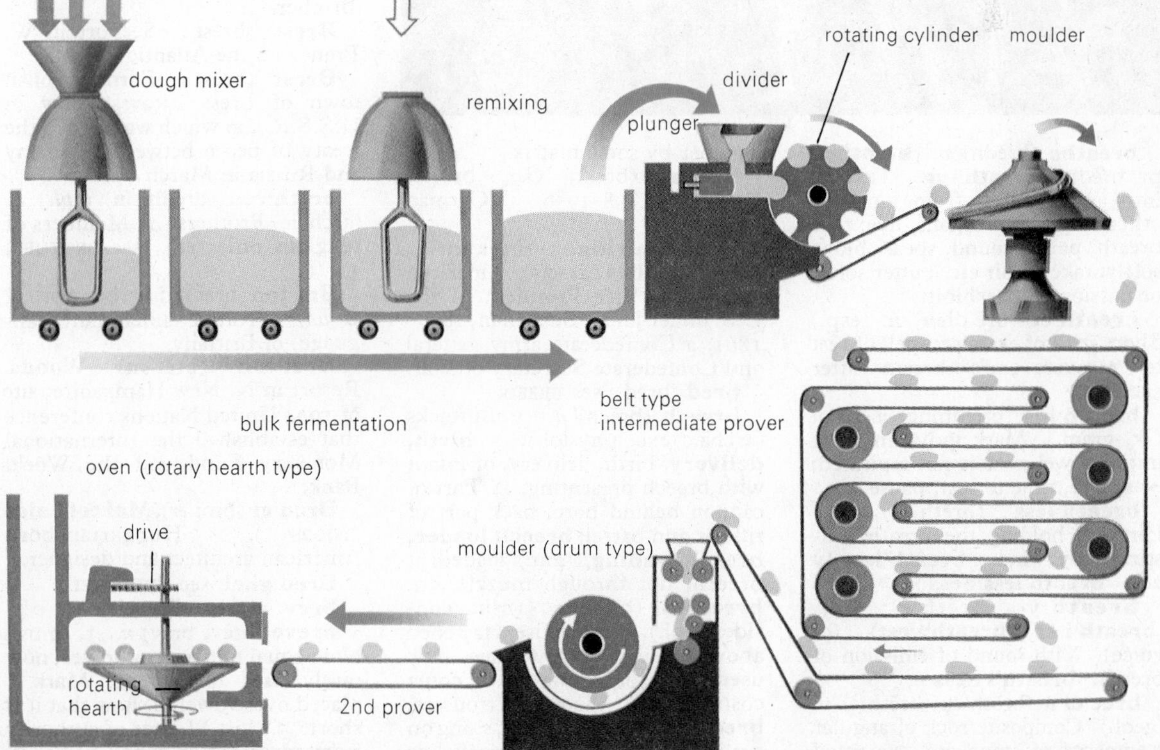

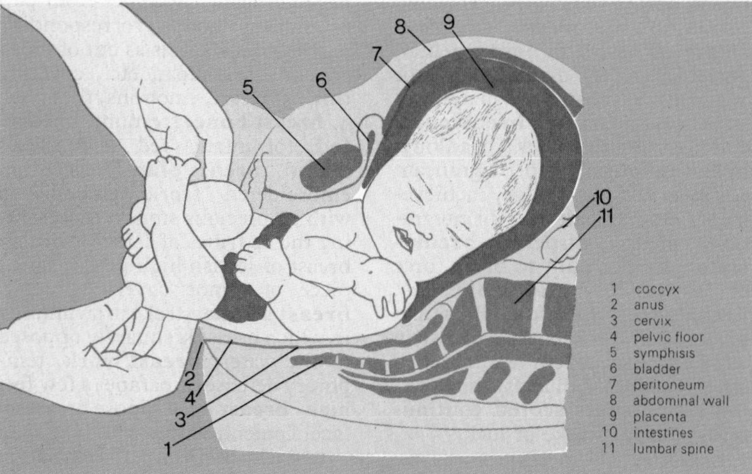

*Above: When a baby does not turn to present its head to the opening of the uterus, it may be born naturally but bottom first—a **breech birth.***

*Below: Collies are trained as herding dogs for their capacity to learn and obey commands. **Breeding** them as show dogs is also popular.*

breathe (brēdh) *v.* (**breathed** pr. brēdhd, **breath·ing**). Take air into and expel it from lungs or other respiratory organs; live; take breath, pause; sound, speak, blow, softly; take in (air etc.); utter softly or passionately, exhibit.

breath·er (brē′dh*er*) *n.* (esp.) Short spell of exercise; spell of rest to recover one's breath after exertion.

breath·ing (brē′dhĭng) *n.* (esp. Gk. gram.) Mark indicating that initial vowel is or is not aspirated; ~ **space**, time to rest, pause.

breath·less (brĕth′lĭs) *adj.* Panting; holding the breath; unstirred by wind. **breath′less·ly** *adv.* **breath′less·ness** *n.*

breath·y (brĕth′ē) *adj.* (**breath·i·er, breath·i·est**). (of voice) With sound of emission of breath. **breath′i·ness** *n.*

brec·ci·a (brĕch′ē*a*, brĕsh′-) *n.* (geol.) Composite rock of angular fragments of stone etc. cemented together by some matrix.

Brecht (brĕkt; *Ger.* brĕχt), **Bertolt** (1898–1956). German playwright.

Breck·in·ridge (brĕk′*i*nrĭj), **John Cabell** (1821–75). American statesman; Vice President of the U.S. under James Buchanan, 1857–1861; a Confederate army general and Confederate Secretary of War.

bred (brĕd): see BREED.

breech (brēch) *n.* 1. Buttocks (archaic exc. physiol.); ~ **birth, delivery**, birth, delivery, of infant with breech presenting. 2. Part of cannon behind bore; back part of rifle or gun barrel; **breech′loader, breech′loading**, (gun) loaded at breech, not through muzzle. 3. **breeches** (brĭch′ĭz), (usu. considered pl.) Short trousers fastened above or (esp.) below knee, now used only for riding or in court costume etc.; (loosely) trousers; **breeches buoy**, life buoy, slung on a pulley, with canvas supports like breeches for the legs.

breed (brēd) *v.* (**bred, breed·ing**). 1. Bear, generate; (make) propagate; yield, produce, result in; arise, spread. 2. Train; fit for being, adapt *to*, bring up. 3. (phys.) Create fissile material from nonfissile by nuclear reaction. ~ *n.* 1. Strain of animals etc. visibly resembling each other, esp. developed under control of man; similar group of plants. 2. Stock, lineage. 3. Sort, kind.

breed·er (brē′d*er*) *n.* One who breeds cattle etc.; animal that breeds; (phys., also ~ **reactor**) reactor that can create more fissile material than it consumes in the chain reaction.

breed·ing (brē′dĭng) *n.* (esp.) Result of training, (good) behavior or manners.

breeze (brēz) *n.* 1. Gentle wind; wind blowing in from sea during day (**sea** ~), or from land to sea during night (**land** ~); (meteor.): see BEAUFORT scale. 2. (colloq.) An easy task, sure thing. ~ *v.i.* (**breezed, breez·ing**). (colloq.) Move *along* briskly; come *in*. **breeze′less** *adj.*

breez·y (brē′zē) *adj.* (**breez·i·er, breez·i·est**). Wind-swept; pleasantly windy; lively, jovial. **breez′i·ly** *adv.* **breez′i·ness** *n.*

Bre·men (brĕm′*e*n; *Ger.* brā′m*e*n). State in W. Germany; its capital, a seaport on river Weser.

Bren·ner (brĕn′*er*) **Pass.** Strategic pass through the Alps between Austria and Italy.

brent (brĕnt) = BRANT.

br'er (brẽr, brâr) *n.* (Southern dial.; as title prefixed to name) Brother.

Brest[1] (brĕst). Seaport in W. France on the Atlantic Ocean.

Brest[2] (brĕst). Former Polish town of Brest Litovsk (now in U.S.S.R.), in which was signed the treaty of peace between Germany and Russia in March 1918.

breth·ren (brĕdh′rĭn) *n.pl.* 1. (archaic) Brothers. 2. Members of religious order etc. (see BROTHER, 3).

Bre·ton (brĕt′*o*n; *Fr.* br*e*tawṅ) *n.* & *adj.* (Native, inhabitant, language) of Brittany.

Bret·ton (brĕt′*o*n) **Woods.** Resort in N. New Hampshire; site of 1944 United Nations conference that established the International Monetary Fund and the World Bank.

Breu·er (broi′*er*), **Marcel Lajos** (1902–). Hungarian-born American architect and designer.

Breu·ghel: see BRUEGHEL.

brev. *abbrev.* Brevet.

breve (brēv, brĕv) *n.* 1. (mus.) Note equal to two semibreves, now rarely used (‖O‖). 2. Mark ˘ placed over vowel to show that it is short. 3. (hist.) Letter of authority from sovereign or pope.

bre·vet (br*e*vĕt′; *Brit.* brĕv′ĭt) *n.* Document, commission, often granted as an honor, promoting military officer in rank without an increase in authority or pay. ~ *v.t.* (**-vet·ted, -vet·ting** or **-vet·ed, -vet·ing**). Confer brevet rank on. **bre·vet′cy** *n.*

bre·vi·ar·y (brē′vēērē, brĕv′ē-) *n.* (pl. **-ar·ies**). Book containing prayers, psalms, etc., for each canonical hour, to be recited by those in (Roman Catholic or Anglican) orders.

brev·i·ty (brĕv′ĭtē) *n.* Shortness, briefness.

brew (broo͞) *v.* 1. Make (beer etc.) by steeping, boiling, and fermentation, or (tea, punch) by steeping or mixture. 2. Concoct, set in motion; fester, gather force. ~ *n.* Brewing; amount brewed; beverage etc. brewed.

brew·er (broo͞′*er*) *n.* (esp.) One who brews beer. **brew′er·y** *n.* (pl. **-er·ies**). Establishment where brewing is carried out.

Brew·ster (broo͞′st*er*), **William** (1567–1644). English Puritan colonist in America; signer of Mayflower Compact; Pilgrim leader of Plymouth Colony.

Brezh·nev (brĕzh′nĕf; *Russ.* brĕzhnyĕf′), **Leonid Ilyich** (1906–1982). Soviet statesman; first secretary of the Communist Party, from 1964.

Bri·an Bo·ru (brī′*a*n bōroo͞′, brēn′) (926–1014). King of Munster; defeated the Danes and in 1002 became high king of Ireland; was killed after a great victory over the Danes at Clontarf.

Bri·and (brēahnd′; *Fr.* brēahn′), **Aristide** (1862–1932). French statesman; 11 times premier of France.

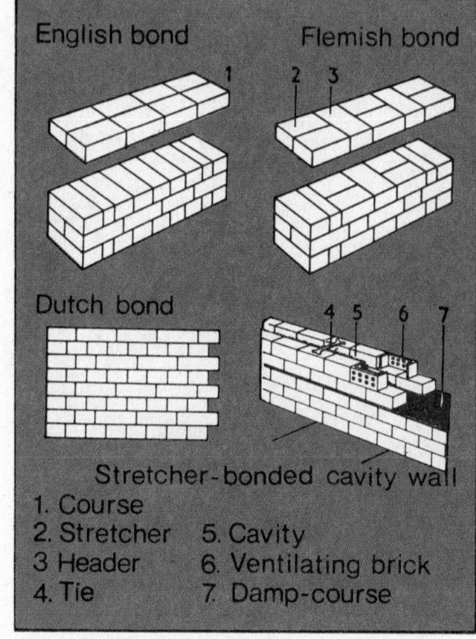

***Bricks** were first used by the ancient Sumerians, and the technique of brick making was carried throughout Europe by the Romans. After a break, building in brick revived at the end of the Middle Ages.*

bri·ar (brī′*er*): see BRIER[2]; ~ **pipe**, smoking pipe made of brier-root. **bri′ar·y** *adj.*

Bri·ar·e·us (brīār′ē*u*s). (Gk. myth.) Giant with 100 hands and 50 heads, confined under Mt. Etna for fighting, with the other giants, against the gods.

bribe (brīb) *n.* Money or other inducement offered to procure (often illegal or dishonest) action in favor of the giver. ~ *v.t.* (**bribed, brib·ing**). Persuade by bribe. **brib′a·ble** *adj.* **brib′er, brib′er·y** (pl. **-er·ies**) *ns.*

bric-a-brac (brĭk′*a*brăk) *n.* (Collection of) miscellaneous old ornaments, furniture, trinkets, etc.

brick (brĭk) *n.* 1. Clay kneaded, molded, and baked by fire or sun, used as a building material; rectangular block of this. 2. Brick-shaped block; child's toy building block. 3. (slang) Generous or loyal person. 4. **brick′bat**, piece of brick, esp. as missile (also fig.); **brick′layer**, workman who lays bricks in building; **brick red**, color of red brick; **brick′work**, brick construction. **brick** *v.t.* Block *up* with brickwork. **brick′like, brick′y** *adjs.*

brid·al (brī′d*a*l) *adj.* Of bride or wedding.

Brid·al·veil (brī′d*a*lvāl). Waterfall in Yosemite National Park, California, 620 feet (189 m) high.

bride (brīd) *n.* Woman on her wedding day and shortly before or after it.

Bride (brīd), **St.**: see BRIDGET.

bride·groom (brīd′groo͞m) *n.* Man on his wedding day and shortly before or after it.

brides·maid (brīdz′mād) *n.* Woman, usu. young and unmarried or girl, as flower girl, attending bride at wedding.

bridge[1] (brĭj) *n.* 1. Structure

*The double-leaf bascule of **Tower Bridge,** London, U.K., allows the road bridge to be raised when a ship passes under it. Built between 1886 and 1894 the bridge has a center opening of 200 ft.*

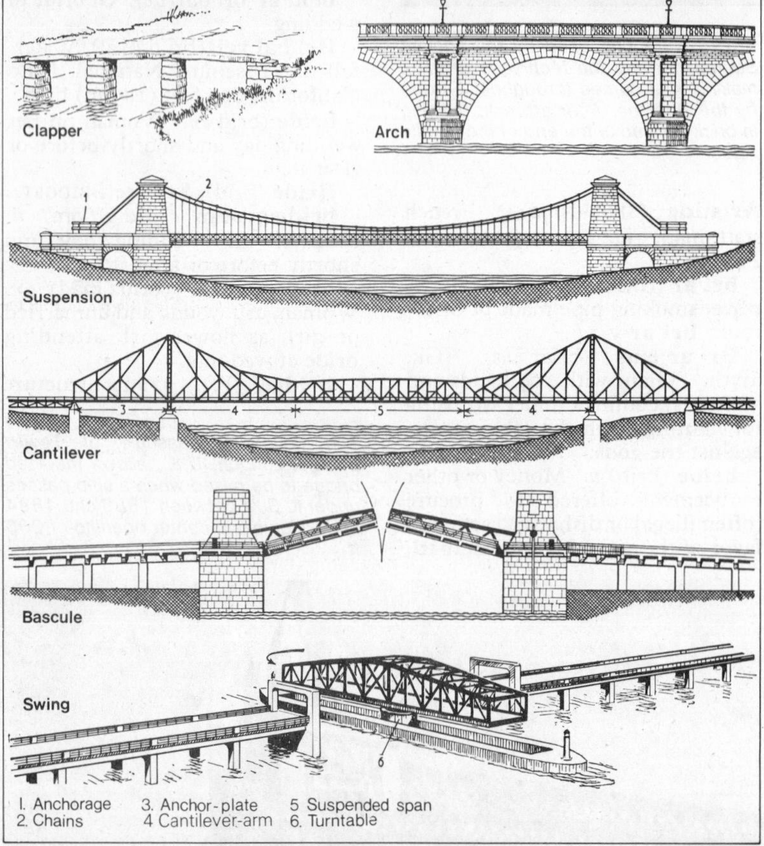

carrying road, path, etc., across stream, ravine, road, etc.; **B~ of Sighs**, 16th-c. bridge in Venice between the Doges' Palace and the prison, crossed by prisoners on way to execution. 2. (naut.) Platform amidships for officer in command. 3. Upper bony part of nose. 4. Movable piece over which strings of violin etc. are stretched. 5. (billiards) Support for cue formed with hand; contrivance consisting of a long stick with device at end to support cue. 6. (dentistry; also **bridge'work**) Partial denture supported by teeth on each side. 7. **bridge'head**, (mil.) Fortification, post, at end of bridge or on side of a river nearest enemy; any position established in face of enemy, e.g. by landing force. **bridge** *v.t.* (**bridged, bridg·ing**). Form bridge; span as if with a bridge.

bridge[2] (brĭj) *n.* (orig.) Card game based on whist (now esp.) contract bridge; **auction ~**, variety of bridge in which the right to name trumps and play with the dummy goes, with each deal, to the player who makes the highest bid; **contract ~**, the most usual form of bridge, in which only the tricks the declarer has undertaken to make count toward the game.

Bridg·et (brĭj'ĭt), **St.** (also **Brigid**, in England **Bride**) Second patron saint of Ireland, traditionally held to have been born in Louth in the time of St. Patrick; commemorated Feb. 1.

Bridge·town (brĭj'town). Port and capital on the SW. coast of Barbados, West Indies.

bri·dle (brī'del) *n.* Headgear of harness, including headstall, bit, and rein; restraint, curb; **~ path**, trail for saddle horses. **~** *v.* (**-dled, -dling**). Put bridle on, curb, control; express resentment, vanity, etc., by throwing up head and drawing in chin. **bri'dler** *n.*

Brie (brē) *n.* White, soft mold-ripened dessert cheese produced in Brie, a district of N. France.

brief[1] (brēf) *n.* 1. Papal letter on matter of discipline (less formal than BULL[1]). 2. (law) Summary of facts and points of law of a case filed by attorney before arguing the case

*The size and type of obstacle to be crossed and the traffic that crosses it determine the type of **bridge** built. Top: The **Verrazano-Narrows Bridge,** New York City, which has the longest central span of any suspension bridge (4,260 ft.). Center: The development of bridging technology has produced a variety of ways of supporting spans. Left: The cantilevered structure of the old Forth Bridge, Scotland, has two 1,710 ft. spans of steel, shown here before the new bridge was built. Right: Bridge builders still use vines, as seen in this suspension bridge in Papua New Guinea.*

in court; abstract or condensation of document or series of documents; short or condensed statement or argument; **brief'case**, rectangular case for carrying documents etc. **brief** *v.t.* Instruct by brief; give instructions, necessary information, etc., to.

brief[2] (brēf) *adj.* Short, concise. **brief'ly** *adv.* **brief'ness** *n.*

briefs (brēfs) *n.pl.* Very short or legless tight-fitting underpants.

bri·er[1], **bri·ar**[1] (brī'*er*) *ns.* Prickly bush, esp. wild rose. **bri'er·y** *adj.*

bri·er[2], **bri·ar**[2] (brī'*er*) *ns.* White heath (*Erica arborea*) native to S. France, Corsica, etc.; smoking pipe made from brierroot.

brig[1] (brĭg) *n.* Two-masted square-rigged vessel having additional lower fore-and-aft sail with a gaff and boom on the mainmast.

brig[2] (brĭg) *n.* Ship's prison; (slang) military prison, guardhouse.

Brig. *abbrev.* Brigadier, brigade.

bri·gade (brĭgād') *n.* Major military unit, usually consisting of several regiments or battalions; organized or uniformed band of workers.

brig·a·dier (brĭgadēr') *n.* (~ **general**) Officer ranking immediately above colonel and below major general in the U.S. Army, Air Force, and Marine Corps.

brig·and (brĭg'*a*nd) *n.* Bandit, robber. **brig'and·ish** *adj.* **brig'and·age, brig'and·ism** *ns.*

brig·an·tine (brĭg'*a*ntēn, -tīn) *n.* Two-masted vessel with square-rigged foremast and fore-and-aft rigged mainmast.

bright (brīt) *adj.* Emitting or reflecting much light, shining; lit up with joy etc.; vivid; illustrious; vivacious; quick-witted. **bright'ly** *adv.* **bright'ness** *n.* **bright'en** *v.t.* & *v.i.* **bright** *adv.* Brightly.

Bright's (brīts) **disease.** Granular degeneration of the kidneys. [Dr. Richard *Bright*, English physician (1789–1858)]

Brig·id (brĭj'ĭd, brē'ĭd): see BRIDGET.

Bril·lat-Sa·va·rin (brēyă'săvărăn'), **Anthelme** (1755–1826). French statesman, writer, and journalist; author of a literary work on gastronomy, *The Physiology of Taste.*

bril·liant (brĭl'yant) *adj.* Bright, sparkling; illustrious; highly talented; showy. **bril'liant·ly** *adv.* **bril'liance, bril'lian·cy** *ns.* **brilliant** *n.* 1. Diamond or other gem of faceted cut; ~**-cut**, faceted; (in diamond) cut designed to give maximum brilliance, usu. consisting of 58 facets. 2. (print.) Very small size of type, approx. 3 1/2 point.

bril·lian·tine (brĭl'yantēn) *n.* Oily preparation for keeping hair smooth and glossy.

*During the 18th and 19th centuries, **brigantines** were found in all the world's oceans as trading vessels and as naval ships. Being small and maneuverable, they were ideal for river trading, scouting and chasing.*

brim (brĭm) *n.* Edge or lip of cup, bowl, or hollow; projecting edge of hat; **brim'ful**, full to the brim. **brim** *v.* (**brimmed, brim·ming**). Fill, be full, to the brim. **brim'less** *adj.*

brim·stone (brĭm'stōn) *n.* (obs.) Sulfur fuel of hellfire.

brin·dled (brĭn'deld) *adj.* Brownish or tawny with streaks of other color; **brin'dle** *adj.* **brindle** *n.* A brindled color or animal.

brine (brīn) *n.* Water saturated, or strongly impregnated, with salt; the sea. ~ *v.t.* (**brined, brin·ing**). Steep or pickle in brine.

bring (brĭng) *v.* (**brought** pr. brawt, **bring·ing**). Cause to come, come with or convey in any fashion; cause, result in; prefer (charge), adduce (argument); cause to become; persuade; ~ **about**, cause to happen; ~ **around**, convince; revive, restore to consciousness; ~ **down**, kill or wound, cause to fall, cause (penalty) to alight *on*, abase, lower, continue (record) *to* a point; ~ **down the house**, (colloq.) receive loud applause; ~ **forth**, bear, produce; cause; ~ **in**, produce, introduce; pronounce (verdict); ~ **off**, conduct with success; ~ **to**, restore to consciousness; ~ **to mind**, cause (oneself) to remember; ~ **to pass**, cause to happen; ~ **up**, rear, educate, come to a stop, call attention (*again*) to.

brink (brĭngk) *n.* Edge of steep place; border of water, esp. when steep; verge (also fig.). **brink·man·ship** (brĭngk′m*a*nshĭp) *n.* Policy of advancing to the very brink of war but not engaging in it.

brin·y (brī′nē) *adj.* (**brin·i·er, brin·i·est**). Very salty. ~ *n.* (slang) The sea.

bri·o (brē′ō) *n.* Vivacity, vigor, dash. [It.]

bri·quette, bri·quet (brĭkĕt′) *ns.* Block of compressed coal dust or charcoal, usu. with addition of binding substance such as pitch.

Bris·bane (brĭz′bān, -bĭn). Capital, chief port, and main industrial center of Queensland, in NE. Australia.

brisk (brĭsk) *adj.* Active, lively; enlivening, keen. **brisk′ly** *adv.* **brisk′ness** *n.*

bris·ket (brĭs′kĭt) *n.* Chest of animals; meat from this part.

bris·ling (brĭs′lĭng) *n.* Young herring or sprat.

bris·tle (brĭs′*e*l) *n.* Stiff hair (esp. of hog's back and sides), used for brushes; anything resembling this. **bris′tly** *adj.* (**-tli·er, -tli·est**).

The ancient port of ***Bristol,*** *in Gloucestershire (now Avon), U.K., received its first charter in 1155. St. Mary Redcliffe shown here is one of several fine buildings in the city. It is one of England's largest parish churches.*

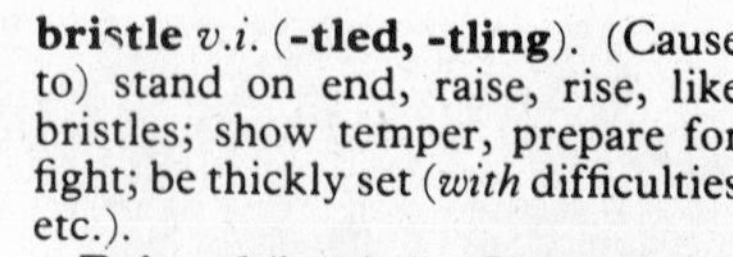

bristle *v.i.* (**-tled, -tling**). (Cause to) stand on end, raise, rise, like bristles; show temper, prepare for fight; be thickly set (*with* difficulties etc.).

Bris·tol (brĭs′tol). City and port on river Avon, in SW. England; ~

Brisbane, *capital and principal port of Queensland, is Australia's 3rd-largest city. Founded in 1824 as a penal colony, it was proclaimed a city in 1902.*

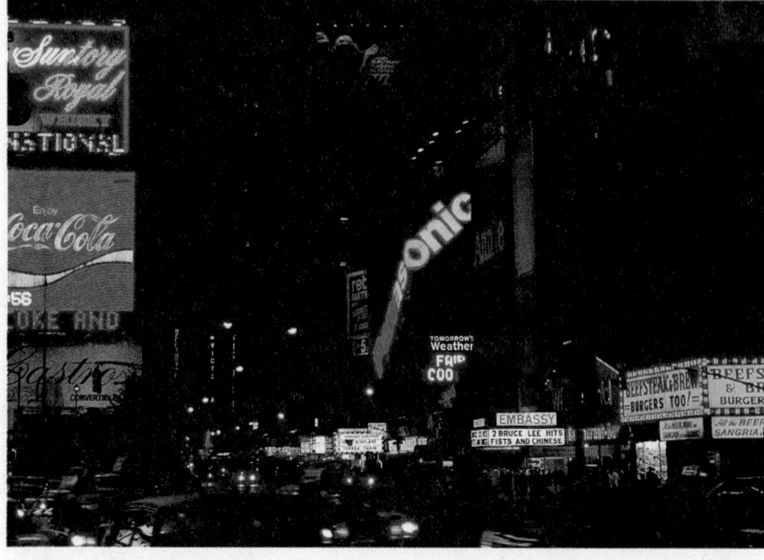

*The peoples who have contributed to the history of **Britain** have left behind them many traces of their cultures. Top: Stonehenge, Wiltshire, is a mysterious ruin raised in various stages from about 2100 to 1400 B.C. Above left: The sculptor of this Anglo-Saxon cross at Irton, Cumbria, belonged to one of the peoples that invaded Britain during the Dark Ages.*

*Above: **Broadway,** the New York City thoroughfare which runs through Manhattan is most famed as the theater district.*

board, fine cardboard for drawing; ~ **Channel**, arm of the Atlantic between Wales and SW. England.

Brit. *abbrev.* Britain; British.

Brit·ain (brĭt′*i*n). (also **Great** ~) Island containing England, Wales, and Scotland, with their dependencies; **Battle of** ~, series of air battles (Aug.–Sept. 1940) over London and SE. England between British and German air forces in which British victory ended the threat of German invasion.

Bri·tan·ni·a (brĭtăn′ē*a*, -tăn′-y*a*). 1. (poet.) Great Britain. 2. Britain personified, usu. represented (e.g. on coins) as a woman with shield, helmet, and trident. 3. ~ **metal**, an alloy of tin with copper, antimony, and sometimes bismuth, used for tableware etc. [L.]

Bri·tan·nic (brĭtăn′ĭk) *adj.* (now chiefly in **His, Her** ~ **Majesty**) Of Britain. **Brit·i·cism** (brĭt′ĭsĭz*e*m) *n.* Word or idiom used in Great Britain but not in U.S. etc. Also **Britishism**.

Brit·ish (brĭt′ĭsh) *adj.* 1. Of Great Britain; (loosely) of the United Kingdom, or the British Empire or Commonwealth; ~ **Broadcasting Corporation**, (abbreviation B.B.C.) public corporation responsible for all radio and noncommercial television broadcasting in the United Kingdom; ~ **Commonwealth of Nations**: see COMMONWEALTH; ~ **Empire**, (formerly) territories under leadership or control of Great Britain; ~ **Library**, national library of Britain, one of the COPYRIGHT libraries; **Order of the** ~ **Empire**, military and civil award (instituted 1917) for services rendered to the British Empire; ~ **Museum**, British national museum of antiquities etc. in Bloomsbury, London; ~ **thermal unit**: see THERMAL. **British** *n.* People of Britain.

Brit·ish (brĭt′ĭsh) **Columbia.** Westernmost province of Canada, bordering on the Pacific Ocean; capital, Victoria.

Brit·ish·er (brĭt′ĭsh*e*r) *n.* Native or inhabitant of Great Britain.

Brit·ish (brit′ish) **Isles.** Britain and Ireland, with the islands near their coasts.

Brit·ish·ism (brĭt′ĭshĭz*e*m) (Brit.) = BRITICISM.

Bri·ton (brĭt′*o*n) *n.* 1. Inhabitant of Great Britain. 2. (also **ancient** ~) Celtic inhabitant of the S. part of ancient Britain at the time of the Roman invasion.

Brit·ta·ny (brĭt′*a*nē). (*Fr.* Bretagne) NW. district of France, an ancient province and duchy, largely inhabited by a Celtic stock related to that of Britain.

Brit·ten (brĭt'en). **Edward Benjamin** (1913–1976). British composer of operas (*Peter Grimes* etc.) and other music.

brit·tle (brĭt'el) *adj.* (**-tler, -tlest**). Apt to break, fragile. ~ *n.* Brittle candy made from melted sugar, usu. containing nuts, as **peanut ~**.

broach[1] (brōch) *n.* 1. Spit for roasting. 2. Tool for shaping and enlarging holes. ~ *v.t.* Pierce (cask) to draw liquor, begin drawing (liquor), open (bale, box, etc.); begin discussion of (subject). **broach'er** *n.*

broach[2] (brōch) *v.* (usu. ~ **to**) Veer, cause (ship) to veer and present side to wind and waves.

broad (brawd) *adj.* 1. Large across, wide, not narrow; in width, as *20 ft.* ~; extensive. 2. Full, clear, main, explicit; general; tolerant; bold in effect or style; (of humor) coarse; (of speech) strongly dialectal. 3. ~ **bean**, (seed of) a variety of edible bean (*Vicia faba*); **broad'cloth**, fine twilled woolen cloth, (also) plainly woven cotton cloth (the name refers rather to quality than width); **broad'loom**, (carpet) woven in width greater than 54 in.; loom weaving this; **broad-minded**, tolerant or liberal in thought or opinion; **broad'side**, ship's side above water between bow and quarter; (discharge of) all guns on one side of ship; (fig.) direct attack; large sheet of paper printed on one side as an advertisement; **broad'sword**, broadbladed cutting sword; **broad'tail**, [transl. Ger. *breitschwanz*] karacul fur. **broad** *n.* Broad part; (slang) a woman. **broad'ish** *adj.* **broad'ly** *adv.* **broad'ness** *n.* **broad** *adv.* Broadly.

broad·cast (brawd'kăst) *adj.* 1. (of seed) Scattered freely, not in drills or rows. 2. (of information, news, music, etc.) Sent or received by broadcasting. ~ *adv.* (Sown, disseminated) in this manner. ~ *n.* Action of broadcasting; broadcast program etc. ~ *v.* (**-cast** or **-cast·ed, -cast·ing**). 1. Sow (seed) broadcast. 2. Disseminate (news, musical performances, etc.) from a radio or television transmitting station; said also of performer etc. **broad'cast·er** *n.* **broad'-cast·ing** *n.* & *adj.*

broad·en (braw'den) *v.* Make, grow, broader.

Broad·way (brawd'wā). Street in New York City extending the entire length of Manhattan and famous for its commerce and theaters; (colloq.) the professional New York City theater.

Brob·ding·nag (brŏb'dĭngnăg). In Swift's *Gulliver's Travels*, a country inhabited by giants. **Brob·ding·nag'i·an** *adj.* & *n.*

bro·cade (brōkād') *n.* 1. Fabric, of any weave or yarn, enriched by a design that is formed by additional weft threads, often of metal, running back and forth across each motif only (not from selvage to selvage). 2. Fabric superficially resembling this, produced by Jacquard loom. ~ *v.t.* (**-cad·ed, -cad·ing**). Enrich (fabric) with design by these means. **bro·cad'ed** *adj.*

broc·co·li (brŏk'olē) *n.* Cultivated plant of genus *Brassica* resembling cauliflower, eaten as vegetable before the green buds open.

bro·chure (brōshoor') *n.* Booklet, pamphlet.

brogue[1] (brōg) *n.* Rough Irish and Scottish Highland shoe of untanned leather; strong outdoor shoe with bands of ornamental perforations.

brogue[2] (brōg) *n.* Dialectal, esp. Irish, accent.

broil[1] (broil) *n.* Quarrel, tumult.

broil[2] (broil) *v.* Cook (meat), be cooked, by exposure to radiant heat; scorch, make or be very hot.

broil·er (broi'ler) *n.* (esp.) 1. Tender young chicken suitable for broiling. 2. Part of stove used for broiling; small electric appliance used for broiling.

broke (brōk) *adj.* (colloq.)

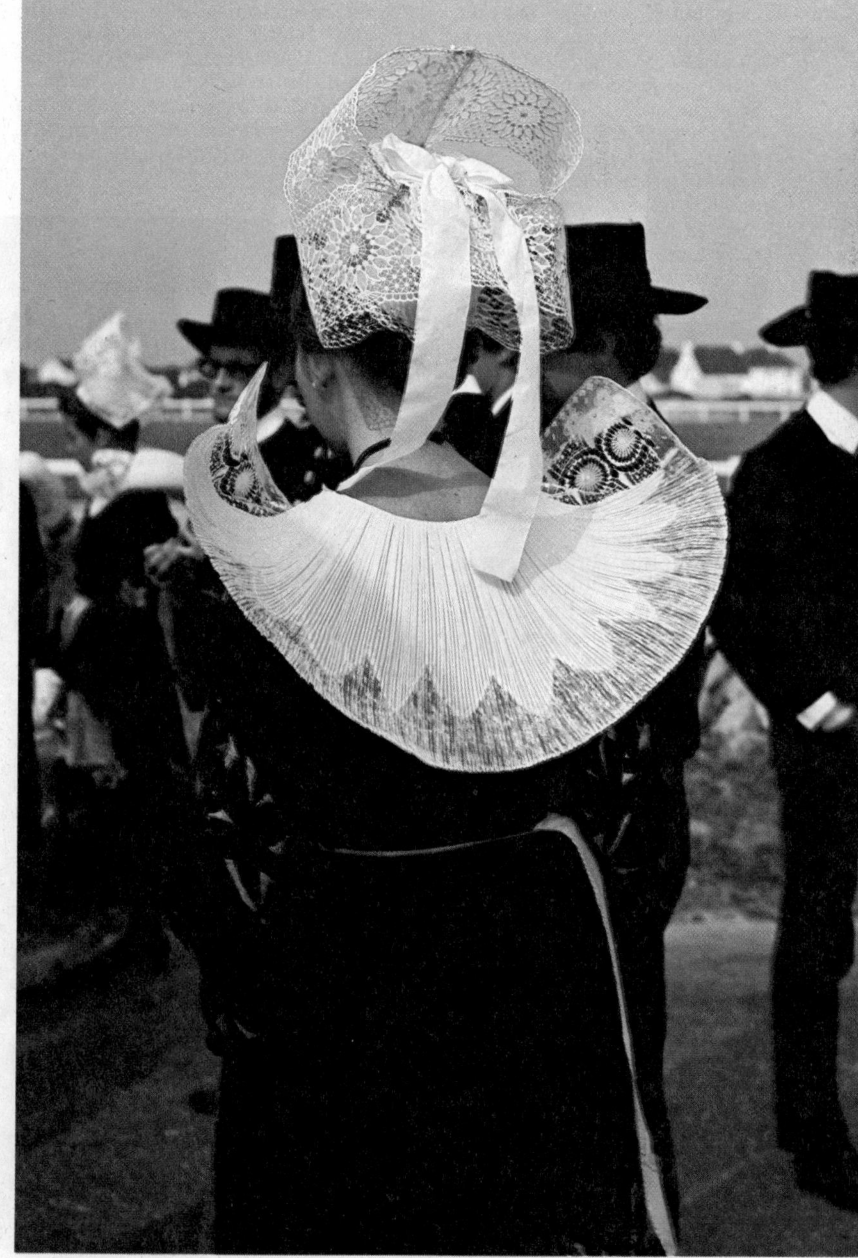

*The people of **Brittany,** in France, maintain many old customs and styles of dress. The coif is worn daily by older women, and the young women wear it for festivals.*

Ruined, penniless.

bro·ken (brō′ken) *adj.*: see BREAK; ~ **English** etc., imperfect English spoken often with a strong foreign accent; ~ **ground**, uneven ground; ~**-hearted**, crushed by grief. **bro′ken·ly** *adv.* Spasmodically, by jerks, with breaks. **bro′ken·ness** *n.*

bro·ker (brō′ker) *n.* Middleman, agent; stockbroker. **bro′ker·age** *n.* Broker's fees or commission, esp. on stock exchange transactions. [OF. *brocheor* "broacher," retailer of wine]

bro·me·li·ad (brōmĕ′lēăd) *n.* Any of various Amer. chiefly epiphytic plants of the family Bromeliaceae, including the pineapple, Spanish moss, and many ornamental species.

bro·mide (brō′mīd) *n.* 1. Compound of bromine with an element of organic radical. 2. Potassium bromide, KBr, taken as a sedative; (fig., colloq.) conventional and commonplace person or remark.

bro·mine (brō′mēn) *n.* (chem.) Non-metallic element, closely resembling chlorine in its properties and compounds; dark reddish-black heavy liquid with a strong irritating smell; symbol Br, at. no. 35, at. wt. 79.904. [Gk. *brōmos* stink]

bron·chi·a (brŏng′kēa) *n.pl.* Ramifications of bronchi in lungs.

bron·chi·al (brŏng′kēal) *adj.* Of the bronchi or bronchia.

bron·chi·tis (brŏngkī′tĭs) *n.* Inflammation of bronchial mucous membrane.

bron·cho·scope (brŏng′koskōp) *n.* Instrument for inspecting interior of bronchi.

bron·chus (brŏng′kus) *n.* (pl. **-chi** pr. -kī). Either of the two main divisions of the windpipe.

bron·co, bron·cho (brŏng′kō) *ns.* (pl. **-cos, -chos**). Wild or half-tamed horse or pony of Western U.S.; **bron′cobuster**, cowboy who breaks in broncos.

Bron·të (brŏn′tē), **Charlotte** (1816–55), **Emily** (1818–48), and **Anne** (1820–49). Novelists, daughters of a Yorkshire clergyman of Irish descent; wrote under pseudonyms of Currer, Ellis, and Acton Bell; Charlotte is famous esp. for *Jane Eyre* (1847), Emily for *Wuthering Heights* (1848).

bron·to·saur (brŏn′tosōr) *n.* Herbivorous dinosaur of genus *Brontosaurus* from the Jurassic and Cretaceous periods, one of the largest terrestrial vertebrates. [Gk. *brontē* thunder, *sauros* lizard]

Bronx (brŏngks), **The.** One of the five boroughs of New York City.

bronze (brŏnz) *n.* Brown alloy chiefly of copper and tin; work of art made of bronze; color of bronze; **B~ Age**, that stage of a people's culture, between the Stone Age and Iron Age, during which its weapons etc. were made of bronze. **bronze** *adj.* Made of, colored, like, bronze. ~ *v.* (**bronzed, bronz·ing**). Give bronze-like surface to; make or become brown, tan. **bronz′y** *adj.* (**bronz·i·er, bronz·i·est**). [L. (*aes*) *Brundisinum* (brass) from Brundisium (Brindisi)]

brooch (brōch, brŏŏch) *n.* Ornamental clasp worn on dress etc., secured by hinged pin and catch.

brood (brŏŏd) *n.* Young birds etc. produced at one hatch; (usu. joc.) human family, children. ~ *adj.* For breeding. ~ *v.i.* 1. (of bird) Sit on eggs to be hatched. 2. Hang close *over, on*; meditate, often sullenly or with resentment (*on, over*, etc.). **brood′ing·ly** *adv.*

brood·y (brŏŏ′dē) *adj.* (**brood·i·er, brood·i·est**). (of hen) Wanting to remain on nest to hatch eggs; (of person) moody, gloomy.

brook[1] (brŏŏk) *n.* Small stream.

brook[2] (brŏŏk) *v.t.* Put up with, tolerate.

Brooke (brŏŏk), **Rupert** (1887–1915). English poet famous for his poems on World War I, in which he died.

Brook (brŏŏk) **Farm.** Utopian socialist community in West Roxbury, Mass., 1841–7; noted for its association with Emerson and other literary figures.

Brook·lyn (brŏŏk′lĭn). One of the five boroughs of New York City.

Brooks (brŏŏks), **Van Wyck** (1886–1963). American essayist, critic, and translator; author of *America's Coming-of-Age, The Flowering of New England*, etc.

broom (brŏŏm) *n.* 1. Yellow-flowered shrub of the genus *Cytisus*, growing on sandy banks, heaths, etc.; shrub of related genus *Genista*; **broom′rape**, brown leafless fleshy-stemmed parasitic plant

A typical tenement in the largely-residential area of the ***Bronx,*** *New York City, also renowned for its zoo, refurbished in the 1960s, and the Yankee Stadium.*

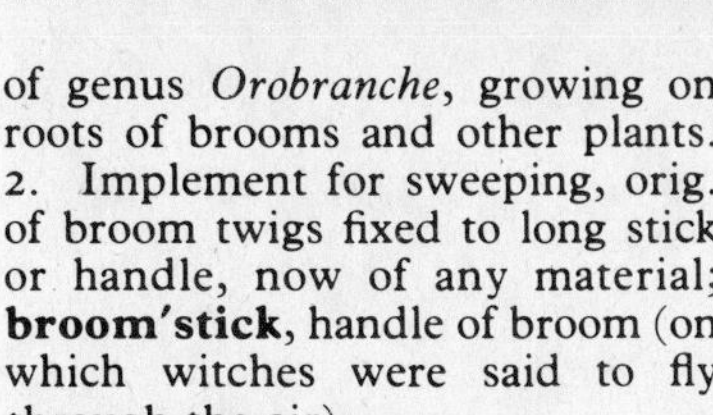

of genus *Orobranche*, growing on roots of brooms and other plants. 2. Implement for sweeping, orig. of broom twigs fixed to long stick or handle, now of any material; **broom'stick**, handle of broom (on which witches were said to fly through the air).

bros. *abbrev.* Brothers.

broth (brawth, brŏth) *n.* Uncleared meat or fish stock used for making soup; thin, clear soup.

broth·el (brŏth'*e*l, brŏdh'-, braw'th*e*l, -dh*e*l) *n.* House where prostitutes are available.

broth·er (brŭdh'*er*) *n.* 1. Male with the same parents as another person. 2. Fellow, companion, equal. 3. (with pl. **breth·ren** pr. brĕdh'r*e*n) Member of religious order, fellow member of church, guild, order, etc. 4. **~-in-law**, brother of one's husband or wife, husband of one's sister. **broth'er·ly** *adj.* Of, like, a brother('s), fraternal. **broth'er·li·ness** *n.*

broth·er·hood (brŭdh'*er*hŏŏd) *n.* Fraternal tie; companionship; (members of) association for mutual help etc.

brougham (brōōm, brōō'*e*m, brōm, brō'*e*m) *n.* One-horse, four-wheeled closed carriage with an open driver's seat in front; closed electrically-driven carriage for four or five passengers; limousine with open seat for driver. [f. Lord *Brougham* (1778–1868), lawyer, politician, and Lord Chancellor of England]

brought (brawt): see BRING.

brow (brow) *n.* Arch of hair over eye (usu. in pl.); forehead; edge, projection, of cliff etc., top of hill in road.

brow·beat (brow'bēt) *v.t.* (**-beat, -beat·en, -beat·ing**). Bully, bear down, with looks and words. **brow'beat·er** *n.*

brown (brown) *adj.* 1. Of the color produced by a mixture of orange and black pigments, or by partial charring of starch or woody fiber, as in toasted bread, etc. 2.

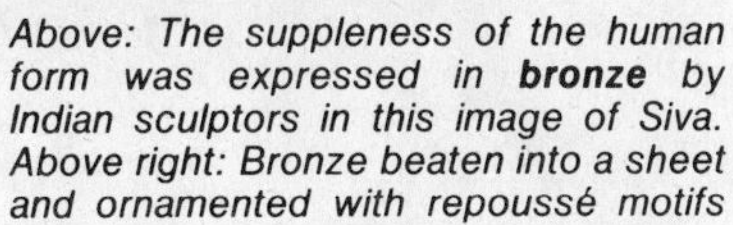

Above: The suppleness of the human form was expressed in ***bronze*** *by Indian sculptors in this image of Siva. Above right: Bronze beaten into a sheet and ornamented with repoussé motifs and enamel bosses shows the skills of Celtic workmanship. Above: African smiths in Benin, now south-west Nigeria, produced beautiful cast figures and heads in bronze.*

Dark, dark skinned; tanned. 3. ~ **bread**, bread of dark flour; ~ **paper**, unbleached paper used for packing, etc.; **brown'shirt**, Nazi storm trooper; **brown'stone**, dark brown sandstone used in building; a building made of this; ~ **study**, reverie; ~ **sugar**, unrefined or partially refined sugar. **brown** *n.* Brown color or pigment; (ellipt.) brown clothes, etc. ~ *v.* Make or become brown by roasting, chemical process, etc.

Brown (brown), **John** (1800–1859). Abolitionist leader who with only 18 men seized the Federal arsenal at Harper's Ferry, Virginia (1859); pursued and caught by army troops under Robert E. Lee; hanged at Charlestown, Virginia; hero of popular songs, poems, etc.

Browne (brown), **Sir Thomas** (1605–82). English physician, author of *Religio Medici* (1642).

Brown·i·an (brow'nēan) **movement.** Irregular oscillatory movement of microscopic particles in fluids, due to molecular bombardment. [discovered by Robert *Brown* (1773–1858), Scottish botanist]

brown·ie (brow'nē) *n.* 1. Benevolent shaggy goblin (a "wee brown man") said to haunt houses and do household work secretly. 2. **B**~, member of junior branch of Girl Scouts at ages seven and eight. 3. A square, moist cake-like chocolate cookie.

Brown·ing[1] (brow'nĭng) *n.* (also ~ **automatic rifle**). A .30 caliber air-cooled automatic and semiautomatic gas-operated magazine rifle used in World Wars I and II; ~ **machine gun**, .30 caliber automatic machine gun; .50 caliber automatic machine gun. [J.M. *Browning* (1885–1926), Amer. firearms designer]

Brown·ing[2] (brow'nĭng), **Elizabeth Barrett** (1806–61). English poet, wife of Robert Browning.

Brown·ing[3] (brow'nĭng), **Robert** (1812–89). English poet, author of numerous philosophical and dramatic lyrics and of several dramas.

browse (browz) *v.* (**browsed, brows·ing**). Feed *on*, crop (leaves, twigs, scanty vegetation); feed thus; (fig.) read desultorily for enjoyment. ~ *n.* Browsing. **brows'er** *n.*

Bruce (bro͞os), **Robert de** (1274–1329). Robert I, king of Scotland (1306–29), which he

The Dome of Florence Cathederal (Il Duomo) seen by night from Piazza Michelangelo. ***Filippo Bruneleschi*** *was responsible for the design of the dome, and the machines that were required to carry out the work, from 1420 until 1446.*

liberated from the English.

bru·cel·lo·sis (brōōselō'sĭs) *n.* Disease caused by bacteria of genus *Brucella*, causing abortion in cattle; (in man) undulant fever.

bru·cine (brōō'sēn, -sĭn) *n.* Highly poisonous vegetable alkaloid found in false Angostura bark and in nux vomica.

Bruck·ner (brŭk'ner; *Ger.* brŏŏk'ner), **Anton** (1824–96). Austrian composer of church music and symphonies.

Brue·ghel, Breu·ghel, Brue·gel (broi'gel, brōō'-; *Flem.* brö'gel). Surname of a large family of Flemish painters, the most famous of whom is **Pieter Bruegel the Elder** (*c*1520–69), painter of lively peasant scenes.

Bru·ges (brōōzh; *Fr.* brüzh). (*Fl.* Brugge) City in Belgium, capital of West Flanders, famous for its bells and canals.

bru·in (brōō'ĭn) *n.* Bear. [Name of bear in fable of Reynard the Fox, f. Du., = BROWN]

bruise (brōōz) *n.* Injury by blow to body, fruit, etc., discoloring skin. ~ *v.* (**bruised, bruis·ing**). Injure by blow that discolors skin without breaking it; batter; pound, grind small; show effects of blow. **bruis'er** *n.* (esp.) Big strong man.

bruit (brōōt) *v.t.* Spread (a rumor) *abroad, about.*

Bru·maire (brōōmār'; *Fr.* brümĕr') *n.* Second month in French Revolutionary calendar, Oct. 22–Nov. 20; **18** ~, Nov. 9, 1799, day on which Napoleon Bonaparte became First Consul. [Fr. *brume* mist]

Bru·nei (brōōnī'). British protected state on NW. coast of Borneo; capital Bandar Seri Begawan.

Bru·nel·les·chi (brōōnelĕs'kē), **Bru·nel·les·co** (brōōnelĕs'kō), **Filippo** (1377–1446). Florentine architect and engineer; designed dome of Cathedral of Florence.

*'Children Playing' by **Pieter Brueghel** the Elder, is typical of the lively and humorous paintings made early in his life. Later, many of his works show a more satirical view of the world.*

*The city of **Bruges,** capital of the West Flanders province of Belgium, retains some of its old street trades. Here a woman is seen making bobbin lace.*

bru·nette (brōōnĕt') *n.* & *adj.* Dark-skinned and brown-haired (woman); **brunet**, such a person.

Brun·hild, Bryn·hild (brōōn'hĭld). In the *Nibelungenlied*, wife of Gunther, who instigated the murder of Siegfried; in Norse versions, a Valkyrie whom Sigurd wins by penetrating the wall of fire behind which she lies in an enchanted sleep.

Bru·no[1] (brōō'nō), **Giordano** (*c*1548–*c*99). Italian philosopher; regarded God as the unity reconciling spirit and matter; was condemned to death by the Inquisition.

Bruno[2] (broōnō), **St.** (*c*1035–1101). Founder of the Carthusian order.

brunt (brŭnt) *n.* Chief stress of shock or attack etc.

brush (brŭsh) *n.* 1. Thicket, brushwood, growing or cut in faggots; land covered with thicket; backwoods; dense forests, undergrowth and thickets of small trees. 2. Implement of bristles, hair, wire, etc., set in wood etc. for sweeping or scrubbing dust and dirt from a surface, usu. named acc. to its use, as **clothes'brush, hair'brush**; bunch of hairs etc. in straight handle for painting etc.; application of brush, brushing; (mus.) one of a pair of devices with wire bristles for striking drums etc. 3. Tail, esp. of fox; brushlike tuft. 4. (elect.) Brushlike discharge of sparks; strip of conducting material (usu. hardened carbon) for making or breaking contact; fixed contact that bears on slip ring of dynamo. 5. Short sharp encounter, skirmish. 6. **brush'wood**, cut or broken twigs etc.; undergrowth, thicket; **brush'work**, painter's (style of) manipulation. **brush** *v.* Sweep or scrub, put in order, remove, with brush; graze or touch in passing; ~ **aside, away**, (fig.) ignore, pass over; ~ **off**, dismiss, rebuff; ~**-off** (*n.*) curt dismissal; ~ **up**, furbish, renew one's memory of; **brush'up** (*n.*). **brushed** (*adj.*) (esp. of fabric) With nap raised by brushing. **brush'y** *adj.* (**brush·i·er, brush·i·est**).

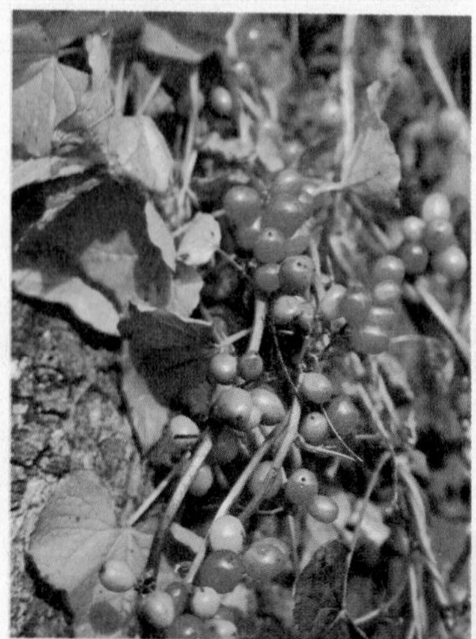

brusque (brŭsk) *adj.* Blunt, offhand, abrupt.

Brus·sels (brŭs'elz). (Fr. *Bruxelles*) Capital city of Belgium; ~ **carpet**, carpet with back of strong linen thread and pile of wool; ~ **lace**, rich lace with appliqué design, as first made in Brussels in 18th c.; ~ **sprouts**, edible bud-bearing cabbage (*Brassica oleracea gemmifera*), producing buds like small cabbages in the axils of its leaves; its buds.

Left: Tamus communis, *called black* ***bryony,*** *carries elliptical scarlet berries in the Fall. These are poisonous and larger than the berries of white bryony which is of another genus.*

Below: The Grande Place, ***Brussels,*** *has many noble buildings. The 13th-century meeting place of the Estates General and several guildhalls border the square, which is nowadays the site of a bird market.*

brut (broōt) *adj.* (of wine) Dry, unsweetened. [Fr.]

bru·tal (broō'tal) *adj.* Savagely cruel, coarse, sensual. **bru'tal·ly** *adv.* **bru·tal·i·ty** (broōtăl'ĭtē) *n.* (pl. **-ties**). **bru'tal·ize** *v.t.* & *v.i.* (**-ized, -iz·ing**).

brute (broōt) *adj.* 1. (of beast) Not possessing the capacity to reason. 2. Stupid, sensual, beastlike, cruel, or passionate; ~ **force**, unreasoning force. **brute** *n.* Brute beast, lower animal; brutal, brutelike person; lower nature in man. **brut'ish** *adj.* **brut'ish·ly** *adv.* **brut'ish·ness** *n.*

Bru·tus[1] (broō'tus). Legendary founder of the British people, according to myth a great-grandson of AENEAS; brought a group of the Trojans to England, founded Troynovant or New Troy (later called London), and was a progenitor of a line of kings.

Bru·tus[2] (broō'tus), **Lucius Junius** (d. 508 B.C.). Legendary First Consul of Rome, and leader in the expulsion of the Tarquins.

Bru·tus[3] (boō'tus), **Marcus Junius** (85–42 B.C.). Roman soldier; joined the conspirators who assassinated Julius Caesar in hope of restoring republican government.

Bry·an (brī'an), **William Jennings** (1860–1925). American lawyer and political leader; three times a candidate for the presidency; advocate of free coinage of silver; a prosecuting attorney in the famous trial of John Scopes for teaching evolution.

Bry·ant (brī'ant), **William Cullen** (1794–1878). American poet, newspaper owner, and editor; author of the poems "Thanatopsis," "To a Waterfowl," etc.

Bryce (brīs) **Canyon National Park.** National park in S. Utah noted for its colorful rock pinnacles and canyons.

Bryn·hild (broōn'hĭld) = BRUNHILD.

bry·o·ny (brī'onē) *n.* (pl. **-nies**). Either of two European climbing plants: **black** ~ (*Tamus communis*), dark shining green, without tendrils; **white** ~ (*Bryonia dioica*), rough textured and light colored, with conspicuous coiled tendrils.

bry·o·phyte (brī'ofīt) *n.* Member of the Bryophyta, a group of plants comprising the liverworts and mosses. **bry·o·phyt·ic** (brīofĭt'ĭk) *adj.*

bry·o·zo·an (brīozō'an) *adj.* & *n.* (Member) of the Bryozoa, a phylum

Bryce Canyon *National Park, Utah, established as a national monument and a sanctuary for many species of animal and bird life.*

James Buchanan, 15th President of the U.S.A. (1857–61), whose attempts to avert the conflict between North and South over slavery dominated his term in office.

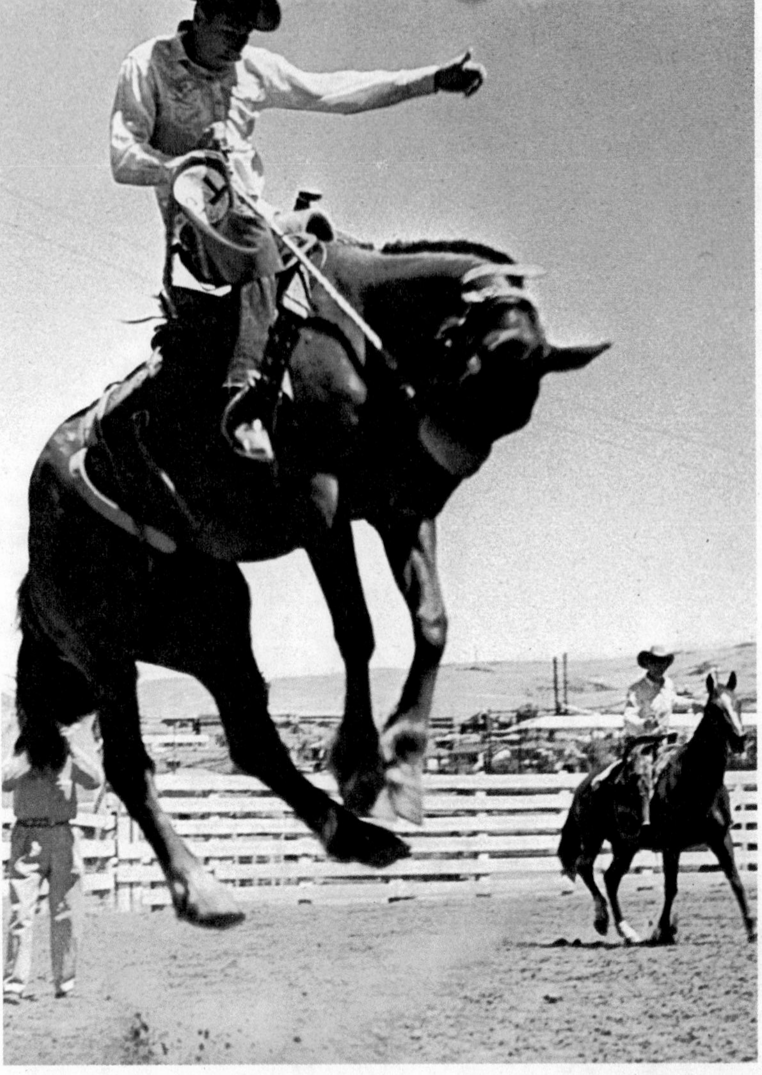

*Cowboys ride **bucking** broncos into submission, a test of courage and horsemanship. The taming of wild horses is a traditional activity in the western states of the U.S.A.*

of aquatic animals that form colonies of small polyps.

B.S. *abbrev*. Bachelor of Science.

B.S.A. *abbrev*. Boy Scouts of America.

B.Sc. *abbrev*. Bachelor of Science.

bsh. *abbrev*. Bushel, bushels.

bskt. *abbrev*. Basket.

Bt. *abbrev*. Baronet.

Btu, B.T.U., B.t.u. *abbrevs*. British thermal unit(s).

bub·ble (bŭb′*e*l) *n*. 1. Spherical or hemispherical envelope of liquid (or solidified liquid, as glass) enclosing air etc. 2. Unsubstantial or visionary project, enterprise, etc. 3. Sound or appearance of boiling; ~ **chamber**, (phys.) container of superheated liquid for detection of ionizing particles; ~ **gum**, chewing gum that can be blown into bubbles. **bubble** *v.i.* (**-bled, -bling**). Send up, rise in, make the sound of, bubbles.

bub·bly (bŭb′lē) *adj*. (**-bli·er, -bli·est**). Full of bubbles. ~ *n*. (slang) Champagne.

bu·bo (bū′bō) *n*. (pl. **-boes**). Inflamed swelling in glandular part esp. groin or armpit.

bu·bon·ic (būbŏn′ĭk, bo͞o-) *adj*. Characterized by buboes; ~ **plague**, disease characterized by these and by fever and prostration, carried by rats and transmitted to man by fleas.

buc·ca·neer (bŭk*a*nēr′) *n*. Pirate, esp. one who preyed upon Spanish shipping in the West Indies in 17th c.; unscrupulous adventurer. ~ *v.i.* Act as buccaneer. [Fr. *boucanier* f. *boucaner* to cure meat on a *boucan* (i.e. barbecue), a Tupi wd.]

Bu·ceph·a·lus (būsĕf′*alus*). Favorite war horse of Alexander the Great.

Bu·chan·an (būkăn′*a*n), **James** (1791–1868). Fifteenth president of U.S., 1857–61.

Bu·cha·rest (būk*e*rĕst′, bo͞o -, bū′k*e*rĕst, bo͞o′-). (Rumanian *Bucuresti*) Capital city of Rumania.

Bu·chen·wald (bo͝ok′*e*nwawld; *Ger.* bo͞o′χenvahlt). Village in E. Germany; site of notorious Nazi concentration camp during World War II.

buck[1] (bŭk) *n*. (pl. **bucks**, collect. **buck**). Male of fallow deer, reindeer, chamois, hare, rabbit; dandy; ~ **fever**, nervousness of inexperienced hunter at first chance to shoot; **buck′shot**, large lead shot for shotgun shells; **buck′skin**, (leather made of) buck's skin; (pl.) breeches of this; **buck′thorn**, thorny shrub esp. of genus *Rhamnus*; **buck′tooth**(**ed**), (having) projecting tooth. ~ *adj*. (slang) Male. **buck′er** *n*.

buck[2] (bŭk) *v*. (of horse) Jump vertically with back arched and feet drawn together.

buck[3] (bŭk) *v*. (slang) Oppose; ~ **up**, become or make vigorous or cheerful.

buck[4] (bŭk) *n*. Body of cart; chiefly in combination, as **buck′board**, plank slung upon wheels, light vehicle with body consisting of this.

buck[5] (bŭk) *n*. (slang) Dollar.

buck[6] (bŭk) *n*. Sawbuck; padded block in gymnasium for vaulting; **buck′saw**, saw for cutting firewood, with blade set across wooden frame.

buck[7] (bŭk) *n*. Counter placed before a poker player to mark him as the next dealer; **pass the** ~,

The **Great Buddha,** Kamakura, Japan. Wherever Buddhism has spread in Asia, temples house the dominating images of various Buddhas, Bodhisattvas and saints.

Buckingham Palace, London residence of the British Royal Family, was bought in 1762 by George III. It was rebuilt by John Nash. Queen Victoria was first sovereign to live there.

(slang) shift responsibility (*to*).

Buck (bŭk), **Pearl** (1892–1973). American novelist; awarded Nobel Prize for literature, 1938; author of *The Good Earth*, which won the Pulitzer Prize, 1932, and *Dragon Seed*, etc.

buck·et (bŭk′ĭt) *n.* 1. Vessel for collecting, holding, or carrying water etc.; amount contained in this (also **buck′etful**); ~ **brigade**, line of persons passing buckets of water from pond etc. to put out a fire (also fig.). 2. Anything resembling this; (esp.) compartment of water wheel; scoop of dredger. 3. ~ **seat**, seat with high rounded or molded back, as in sports cars; ~ **shop**, fraudulent firm of stockbrokers that speculates on its own account without regard for its clients' interests.

Buck·ing·ham (bŭk′ĭngam, -hăm), **George Villiers, 1st Duke of** (1592–1628). Favorite of James I of England.

Buck·ing·ham (bŭk′ĭngam, -hăm) **Palace.** Official London residence of the British sovereign.

buck·le (bŭk′el) *n.* Clasp usu. with hinged tongue for securing strap, belt, etc.; ornament for shoe etc. resembling this. ~ *v.* (**-led, -ling**). Fasten with buckle; (cause to) give way, crumple up, under pressure; ~ **down** (**to**), set about, get to work, start vigorously.

buck·ram (bŭk′ram) *n.* Coarse linen or cotton fabric stiffened with glue, used in linings and for binding books.

buck·wheat (bŭk′hwēt, -wēt) *n.* Cereal plant (*Polygonum fagopyrum*), with seed used for fodder and flour; ~ **cake**, pancake made of this flour.

bu·col·ic (būkŏl′ĭk) *adj.* Of shepherds, pastoral, rustic; a pastoral poem.

bud[1] (bŭd) *n.* 1. Projection at end of shoot or axil of leaf, protected by scales which are altered leaves, forming rudiment of shoot, foliage, or flower; leaf or flower not fully open; ~ **scale**, altered leaf protecting a bud. 2. (zool.) Asexual reproductive growth attached to parent and developing into new individual esp. in coelenterates. 3. **nip in the** ~, (fig.) stop (something) before it is fully developed. **bud** *v.* (**bud·ded, bud·ding**). 1. Put forth buds; begin to grow or develop. 2. Graft a bud on to another plant.

bud[2] (colloq.) = BUDDY.

Bu·da·pest (bo͞o′dapĕst, bū′-; *Hung.* bo͞o′dapĕsht). Capital city of Hungary, orig. consisting of two towns, Buda on right bank of river Danube and Pest on left.

Bud·dha (bo͞o′da, bo͝od′a). "Enlightened one," name applied esp. to Siddartha Gautama (*c*560–*c*480 B.C.), son of the rajah of the Sakya tribe (hence also called *Sakyamuni*, "sage of the Sakyas"; as a young man he abandoned his home in Nepal and renounced the world; practiced an extreme asceticism, preached, and became the founder of Buddhism.

Bud·dhism (bo͞o′dĭzem, bo͝od′ĭz-) *n.* System founded by the Buddha, orig. practiced chiefly in India; it was in decline there by the 4th C. A.D. but was diffused over China, Japan, and central and SE. Asia; there are two principal schools, MAHAYANA and THERAVADA (Hinayana); chief doctrines: the principal cause of suffering is desire; and the suppression of desire and consequently of suffering can be obtained by discipline and ultimately rewarded by NIRVANA. **Bud′dhist** *n.* & *adj.* **Bud·dhis′tic** *adj.*

bud·dle·ia (bŭd′lēa, bŭdlē′a) *n.* Shrub or tree of genus *B*~, often having honey-scented flowers. [Adam *Buddle* (d. 1715), Engl. botanist]

bud·dy (bŭd′ē) *n.* (pl. **-dies**). (colloq.) Brother; companion, friend (freq. as form of address). [Childish pronunciation of *brother*]

budge (bŭj) *v.* (**budged, budg·ing**). Move in the slightest degree, stir.

budg·er·i·gar (bŭj′erēgar) *n.* A parakeet (*Melopsittacus undulatus*), native to Australia and having green, yellow, or blue plumage, freq. kept as pet; abbrev. **bu′dgie** (bŭj′ē).

budg·et (bŭj′ĭt) *n.* 1. (archaic) Contents of a bag or bundle (chiefly fig. of news etc.). 2. Annual estimate of revenue and expenditure. 3. Amount of money required or available. 4. *attrib.* Inexpensive. **budg′et·ar·y** *adj.* **budget** *v.* (**-et·ed, -et·ing**). ~ **for**, allow or arrange for in budget. **budg′et·er** *n.*

Bue·na Vis·ta (bwā′na vēs′ta). Historic battlefield near Saltillo, NE. Mexico, where U.S. troops under Zachary Taylor defeated the Mexicans under Santa Anna, 1847, ending the northern campaign in the Mexican War.

Bue·nos Ai·res (bwā′nos ar′ēz, ir′ĭs; *Sp.* bwĕ′naws ī′rĕs). Capital city and chief port of Argentina.

buff (bŭf) *n.* 1. Stout velvety dull-yellow leather of buffalo, elk, or ox hide; **in (the)** ~, naked. 2. Dull-yellow color of buff. **buff** *adj.* Made of, colored like, buff. ~ *v.t.* Polish (metal) with buff, make (leather) velvety like buff. **buf′fer** *n.*

Buf·fa·lo (bŭf′alō). Port city on Lake Erie in W. New York State; site of 1901 Pan-American Exposition, at which President McKinley was assassinated.

buf·fa·lo (bŭf′*a*lō) *n.* (pl. **-loes, -los**, collect. **-lo**). Ox, esp. of one of three species: *Bison bison* of N. Amer., *Bubalus bubalis* of Asia, and *Syncerus caffer*, of S. Africa; ~ **chips**, dried dung of buffalo etc. as fuel; ~ **grass**, prairie grass (*Sesleria dactyloides*).

Buf·fa·lo (bŭf′*a*lō) **Bill.** Popular nickname of William Frederick Cody (1846–1917), Amer. frontiersman, scout, and showman, credited with legendary exploits against Indians and bandits and with killing buffalo to provide meat to workmen building the transcontinental railroad.

buff·er (bŭf′*er*) *n.* 1. Apparatus for deadening by springs or padding, or sustaining by strength of beams etc.; a heavy impact esp. of railroad cars or engines. 2. Shield or device preventing contact or interaction (also fig.); ~ **state**, small country lying between two larger possible belligerents. 3. (chem.) Substance or mixture that in solution resists change in acidity on addition of a small amount of acid or alkali. ~ *v.t.* Protect with a buffer; cushion; (chem.) treat with a buffer.

buf·fet[1] (bŭf′ĭt) *n.* Blow with the hand; blow of fate etc. ~ *v.* (**-fet·ed, -fet·ing**). Strike with the hand; force, struggle, contend (*with* waves etc.); strike against repeatedly. **buf′fet·er** *n.*

In Asia the **buffalo** has long been domesticated for draft work and milk, but the wild Cape buffalo of South Africa is described by many hunters as the most unpredictable and dangerous of wild animals.

buf·fet[2] (b*u*fā′, bo͞o–; *Brit.* bo͞o′fā, bŭf′ĭt) *n.* (pl. **-fets** pr. -fāz; *Brit.* -fāz, -fĭts). 1. Sideboard with drawers and cupboard, for china, glass, etc. 2. Table or counter from which food or refreshments are served; service from this or from sideboard where guests help themselves; party in which food is served in this way.

Buf·fet (büfā′), **Bernard** (1928–). French artist, painter, and lithographer.

buf·fle·head (bŭf′*e*lhĕd) *n.* (also ~ **duck**) Small N. Amer. duck (*Bucephala albeola*).

buf·foon (bŭfo͞on′) *n.* (usu. contempt.) Wag, clumsy jester, mocker. **buf·foon′er·y** *n.* **buf·foon′ish** *adj.*

bug (bŭg) *n.* 1. Hemipterous insect; any small insect. 2. (colloq.) Microorganism, (esp.) virus; (fig.) craze. 3. (slang) Defect in machine etc. 4. (slang) Concealed microphone. ~ *v.t.* (**bugged, bug·ging**). (slang) 1. Equip with alarm or concealed microphone. 2. Annoy.

bug·a·boo (bŭg′*a*bo͞o) *n.* (pl. **-boos**) = BUGBEAR.

bug·bear (bŭg′bār) *n.* Fancied object of fear; imaginary terror; (archaic) hobgoblin.

bug·gy (bŭg′ē) *n.* (pl. **-gies**). Light two-wheeled vehicle; four-wheeled vehicle, often hooded, drawn by one or two horses.

bu·gle (bū′g*e*l) *n.* Brass instrument like small trumpet used for military signals. ~ *v.* (**-gled, -gling**). Sound bugle, sound (call) on a bugle. **bu′gler** *n.*

bu·gloss (bū′glŏs) *n.* Any of several plants related to borage, esp. species of *Echium*, as **viper's** ~ (*E. vulgare*).

buhl (bo͞ol) = BOULLE.

build (bĭld) *v.* (**built, build·ing**). Construct by putting parts of material together; make one's house or nest; make gradually; base *on*, rely *on*; ~ **up**, establish, make, or accumulate gradually; strengthen; praise; surround or cover with houses etc.; ~**-up** (*n.*) (colloq.) publicity (campaign); preparation; extravagant praise. **build** *n.* Proportions of human body.

build·er (bĭl′d*er*) *n.* (esp.) Master builder, contractor for building houses.

build·ing (bĭl′dĭng) *n.* (esp.) House, edifice; ~ **blocks**, small solid shapes, as child's toy for building; interrelated pieces, ideas, etc.

built (bĭlt) *adj.*: see BUILD; (esp.) ~**-in**, forming integral part of structure, as in *built-in furniture;* ~**-up**, increased in height, thickness, etc., by addition of parts; (of area) covered with houses etc.

1

2

3

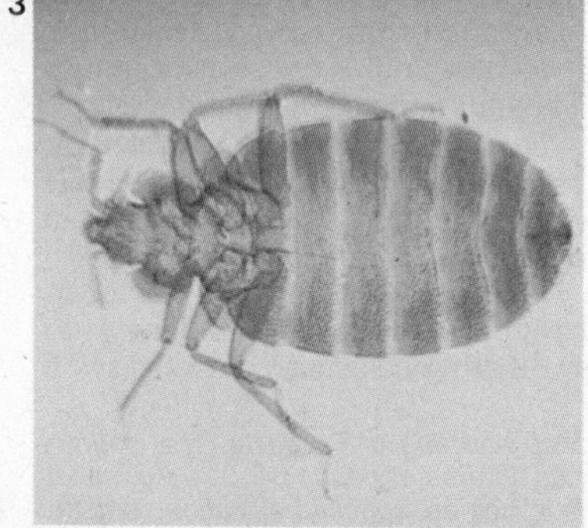

4

5

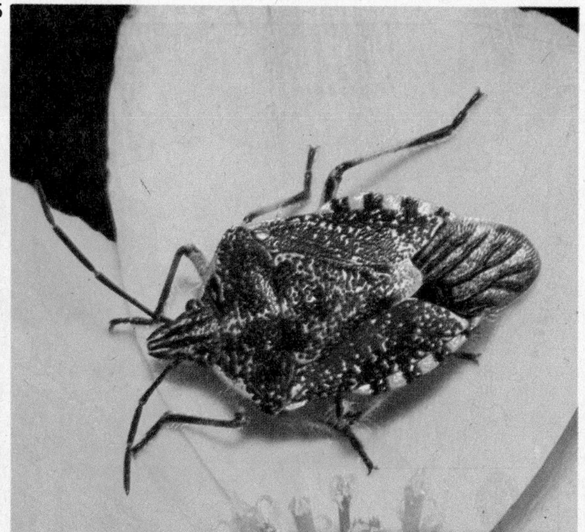

Only those insects in the order Hemiptera are properly called ***bugs*** *but the name is widely used for any small insect. A bug has a jointed beak for piercing and sucking blood or plant juices. Typically it has a smooth body, 2 pairs of wings, long legs and many have a repulsive smell. 1. A red assassin preys on insects and bites man. 2. Left to right are bed-bug, capsid, shield-bug, frog-hopper, pond-skater, mealy-bug, and assassin. 3. The bed-bug cannot fly, having wing pads only. 4. The stink-bug. 5. The shield-bug.*

Bu·jum·bu·ra (bo͞ojo͞omboor′-*a*). Capital of Burundi at the northern end of Lake Tanganyika.

bulb (bŭlb) *n.* 1. Globular base of the stem of certain plants, such as lily, onion, etc., consisting of thick fleshy scales and sending roots downward and leaves etc. upward; leaf bud detaching itself from stem and becoming separate plant; (anat.) roundish swelling of any cylindrical organ, as of hair root. 2. Dilated part of glass tube; electric lamp; bulb-shaped swelling of rubber tube. ~ *v.i.* Swell into bulb(s). **bulb·ar** (bŭl′b*e*r, -bar̄), **bulbed** *adjs.*

bulb·ous (bŭl′b*u*s) *adj.* Of, having, like, springing from, a bulb.

bul·bul (bo͝ol′bo͝ol) *n.* Any of several Asian songbirds of the family Pycnonotidae.

Bul·finch (bo͝ol′fĭnch), **Thomas** (1796–1867). American mythologist and author of *The Age of Fable*, better known as "Bulfinch's Mythology."

Bul·gar (bŭl′g*e*r, bo͝ol′gar̄) *adj.* & *n.* (Native, inhabitant) of Bulgaria.

Bul·gar·i·a (bŭlgar̄′ē*a*, bo͝ol-). Balkan republic (until 1946 a kingdom), with a population largely descended from a people related to the Huns and Avars and speaking a Slavonic language; capital, Sofia.

Bul·gar·i·an (bŭlgar̄′ē*a*n, bo͝ol-) *adj.* Of Bulgaria or its people or language. ~ *n.* Bulgarian person or language.

bulge (bŭlj) *n.* Convex part, irregular swelling, tendency to swell out, on surface; outward swell on ship's hull below waterline; (fig.) temporary increase in volume or numbers. ~ *v.* (**bulged, bulg·ing**). Swell outward irregularly; extend (bag etc.) by stuffing it. **bulg′y** *adj.* **bulg′i·ness** *n.* [L. *bulga* knapsack]

Bulge (bŭlj), **Battle of the.** Last German counteroffensive of World War II, during December 1944 and January 1945, in which the Allies were victorious; so named because the combat line formed a large bulge into Belgium.

bulk (bŭlk) *n.* 1. Cargo; in ~, loose, not in packages; in large quantities (so ~ **buying** etc.). 2. Large shape, body, person. 3. Size, magnitude; great size; mass, large mass; greater part or number *of.* ~ *v.i.* Seem in respect of size or importance.

bulk·head (bŭlk′hĕd) *n.* Upright partition dividing watertight compartments of ship; such a compartment in ship, aircraft, or train; partition dividing engine from body in motor vehicle.

bulk·y (bŭl′kē) *adj.* (**bulk·i·er, bulk·i·est**). Large, voluminous. **bulk′i·ly** *adv.* **bulk′i·ness** *n.*

bull[1] (bo͝ol) *n.* Papal edict. [L. *bulla* seal]

bull[2] (bo͝ol) *n.* 1. Uncastrated male bovine animal; male of elephant, whale, seal, and other large animals. 2. (astron.) the **B**~: see TAURUS. 3. (stock exch.) Speculator who buys low in expectation of a rise in prices or in order to effect such a rise; ~ **market**, one with rising prices. 4. (slang) Lies, nonsense, baloney. 5. **bull′dog**, (*v.t.*) throw (a steer) by grasping the horns and twisting the head; (*adj.* & *n.*) tenacious and courageous (person); dog of powerful and courageous large-headed smooth-haired breed; **bull′doze**, clear (ground etc.) with bulldozer; make *way* forcibly (also fig.); intimidate, coerce; **bull′dozer**, powerful tractor with broad vertical blade in front for clearing ground etc.; **bull′fight**, Spanish spectacle of baiting a bull with horsemen (picadors), footmen (banderilleros), and a swordsman (matador) who finally kills it; similar sport in Mexico, Portugal, and S. France, in which bull is not killed; **bull′fighter, bull′fighting** *ns.*; **bull′finch**, strong-beaked, handsome-plumaged songbird (*Pyrrhula pyrrhula*); **bull′frog,** large frog esp. of genus *Rana* with loud bellowing note; **bull′head**, small fish with large head, esp. any of several catfish (genus *Ictalurus*) and freshwater sculpins (genus *Cottus*); **bull′headed**, stubborn; **bull′pen**, (baseball) area where relief pitchers warm up; **bull′ring**, arena for bullfight; ~**′s-eye**, boss of glass formed at center of sheet of blown glass; hemispherical piece or thick disk of glass; hemispherical lens; lantern with such a lens; small circular window; central area of target; hit on this part; ~ **terrier**, dog of heavily built, smooth-haired usu. white breed. **bull′ish** *adj.* Like a bull; (of stock market or prices) tending to rise. **bull′ish·ly** *adv.* **bull′ish·ness** *n.* **bull′-like** *adj.*

Bull (bo͝ol), **John:** see JOHN[1] Bull.

bul·let (bo͝ol′ĭt) *n.* Missile of lead etc., spherical or conical, used in small arms.

Map and flag of ***Bulgaria.*** *The country has an area of nearly 43,000 sq. miles. It is still an agricultural nation, but the Communist regime has developed the country's extraction and manufacturing industries rapidly. Below right: the capital city, Sofia.*

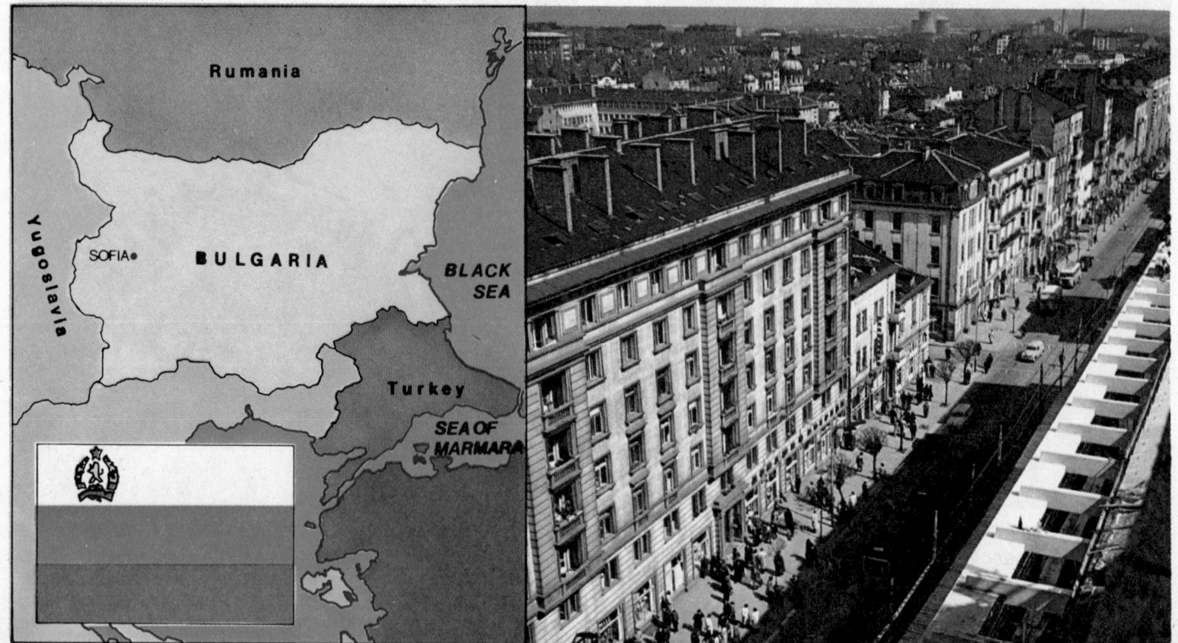

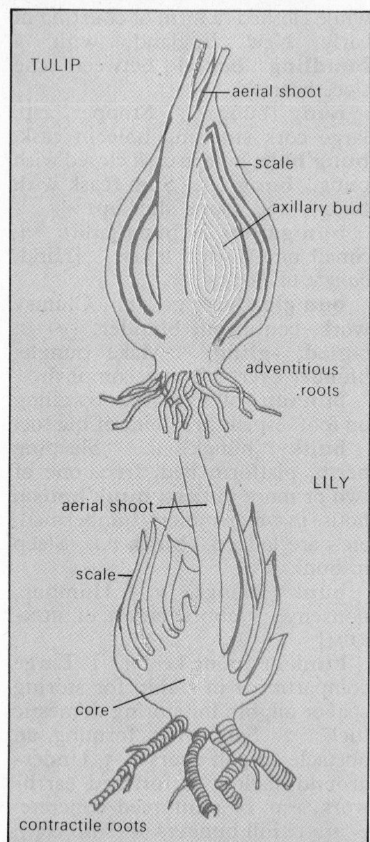

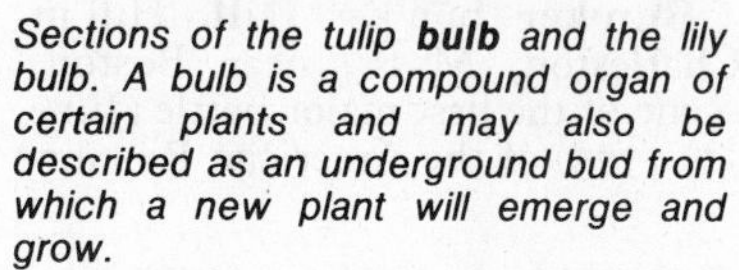
*Sections of the tulip **bulb** and the lily bulb. A bulb is a compound organ of certain plants and may also be described as an underground bud from which a new plant will emerge and grow.*

bul·le·tin (bo͞ol′*e*tĭn) *n.* Short official statement of news or on a matter of public interest; special broadcast report of news, weather, etc.; periodical published by an organization or society; ~ **board**, board mounted on a wall on which notices may be posted.

bul·lion (bo͞ol′y*o*n) *n.* Gold and silver before (or as valued apart from) coining or manufacturing.

bull·ock (bo͞ol′*o*k) *n.* Castrated bull, ox.

Bull (bo͞ol) **Run.** Creek in NE. Virginia near Manassas, scene of two important Civil War battles (1861 and 1862) in which the Confederates defeated the Union forces.

bul·ly[1] (bo͞ol′ē) *n.* (pl. **-lies**). One who oppresses or dominates by (threat of) superior force. ~ *v.t.* (**-lied, -ly·ing**). Persecute, oppress, tease, physically or morally; frighten *into* or *out of*; play the bully. ~ *adj.* & *int.* (colloq.) Excellent, splendid.

bul·ly[2] (bo͞ol′ē) **beef.** Canned or pickled beef.

bul·rush (bo͞ol′rŭsh) *n.* Kind of tall rush (*Scirpus lacustris*); reed mace; (in the Bible) papyrus of Egypt.

1 

2 

*1. A **bull** of good pedigree and championship quality is of great value as a progenitor of stock. 2. The British **bulldog** was bred from a strain that was admired for its courage in seizing the muzzle of a bull in a fight and hanging on however much it was hurt. The bulldog was aided in this by the way its jaws 'lock', making it difficult for it to let go. 3. The **bullfinch** has a thicker head and neck than other finches. 4. The **bullfrog** grows slowly through the tadpole stage, taking 3 years to mature.*

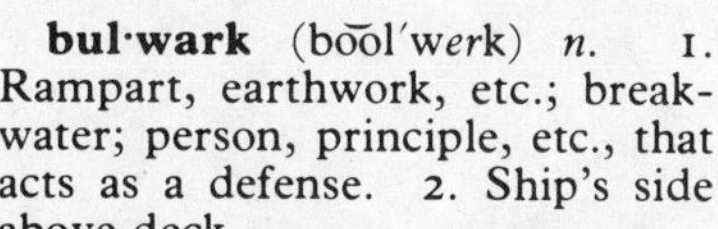

bul·wark (bo͞ol′w*e*rk) *n.* 1. Rampart, earthwork, etc.; breakwater; person, principle, etc., that acts as a defense. 2. Ship's side above deck.

bum[1] (bŭm) *n.* (chiefly Brit. slang) Buttocks; **bum′boat**, boat, plying to ships in port or off shore with fresh provisions.

bum[2] (bŭm) *n.* (colloq.) 1. Lazy and dissolute person; loafer, tramp. 2. Enthusiast of a particular recreational activity, as a **beach ~. bum** *adj.* Worthless, poor, wretched. ~ *v.* (**bummed, bum·ming**). Loaf or wander (*around*); lead life of a bum; cadge. **bum′mer** *n.*

bum·ble (bŭm′b*e*l) *v.i.* (**-bled, -bling**). Make buzzing or humming sound, as a bee; **bum′blebee**, large bee of genus *Bombus*, with a loud hum.

bum·bling (bŭm′blĭng) *adj.* 1. Buzzing. 2. Bungling, incompetent.

3, 4 

bum·mer (bŭm′*er*) *n.* (slang) 1. Error, failure. 2. Unpleasant experience, esp. with a drug.

bump (bŭmp) *v.* 1. Push, throw down, impinge violently, strike solidly (*against, into, on*). 2. ~ **into**, (colloq.) meet by chance; ~ **off**, (slang) murder. **bump** *n.* 1. Dull-sounding blow, knock, collision; swelling caused by this. 2. Protuberance; (phrenol.) prominence on skull, faculty supposed to be indicated by it. 3. Irregularity in aircraft's motion; rising current of air causing this. **bump′y** *adj.* (**bump·i·er, bump·i·est**).

bump·er (bŭm′p*er*) *n.* 1. Full glass of wine etc. 2. (slang) Anything (as harvest, theater audience) unusually large or abundant. 3. Horizontal bar attached to front and back of a vehicle to take the first shock of collision.

bump·kin (bŭmp′kĭn) *n.* Country lout, awkward or bashful fellow.

bump·tious (bŭmp′sh*us*) *adj.* Self-assertive, offensively conceited.

bun (bun) *n.* 1. Small soft bread roll, often sweetened or spiced, or with raisins, currants, etc; **hot cross ~**, spiced bun marked with icing in form of cross and eaten (esp. hot) on Good Friday. 2. Hair coiled at back of head in shape of bun.

bunch (bŭnch) *n.* Cluster of things growing or fastened together; lot, collection; company, band. **bunch′y** *adj.* (**bunch·i·er, bunch·i·est**). **bunch** *v.* Make into bunch(es), gather (fabric) thickly into folds, come, cling, crowd, together.

bunch·ber·ry (bŭnch′bĕrē) *n.* (pl. **-ries**). Dwarf cornel (*Cornus canadensis*), which bears densely clustered red berries.

Bunche (bŭnch), **Ralph Johnson** (1904–71). American statesman and undersecretary of the United Nations, 1954–71.

bun·dle (bŭn′d*el*) *n.* Collection of things fastened together; sets of sticks, rods, etc., bound up; set of parallel fibers, nerves, etc. ~ *v.* (**-dled, -dling**). Tie in, make *up* into, bundle; throw confusedly *in* any receptacle; go, put, or send hurriedly or unceremoniously *out*, *off*, etc.; ~ **up**, dress warmly. **bundle** *v.i.* Sleep or lie in one bed while clothed (a form of courting in early New England, with a **bundling board** between the sweethearts).

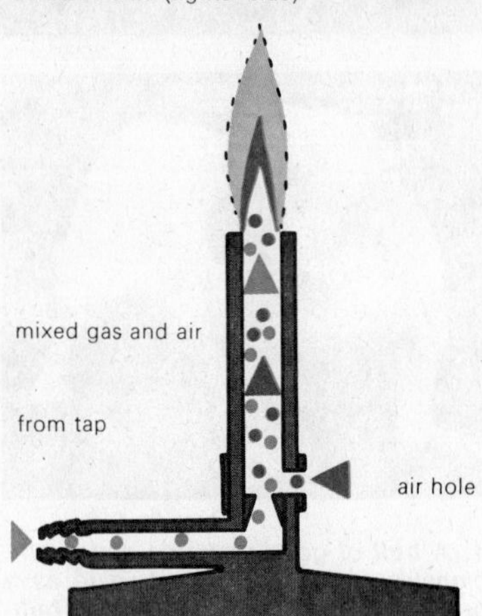

Mixing air and gas in a ratio of approximately 2½:1, a ***bunsen*** *burner completely burns the gas to produce a hot smokeless flame that gives little light. Robert von Bunsen invented the burner in 1855.*

bung (bŭng) *n.* Stopper, esp. large cork stopping hole in cask; **bung′hole**, hole in cask closed with bung. **bung** *v.t.* Stop (cask with bung); stop, close, shut up.

bun·ga·low (bŭng′g*a*lō) *n.* Small one-storied house. [Hind. *bangla* of Bengal]

bun·gle (bŭng′g*el*) *n.* Clumsy work, confusion, blunder. ~ *v.* (**-gled, -gling**). Make bungle; blunder over, fail to accomplish.

bun·ion (bŭn′y*on*) *n.* Swelling on foot, esp. at first joint of big toe.

bunk[1] (bŭngk) *n.* Sleeping berth, platform bed, freq. one of two or more in tiers; **bunk′house**, house in which miners, lumbermen, etc., are lodged. **bunk** *v.i.* Sleep in bunk.

bunk[2] (bŭngk) *n.* Humbug, nonsense. [abbreviation of BUNKUM]

bunk·er (bŭng′k*er*) *n.* 1. Large compartment in a ship for storing coal or oil; bin for storing domestic fuel. 2. Sand trap forming an obstacle on golf course. 3. Underground shelter or fortified earthwork, esp. of reinforced concrete. ~ *v.* 1. Fill bunkers of (ship etc.), fuel. 2. (golf) Hit into bunker.

Bun·ker (bŭn′k*er*) **Hill.** Hill in Charleston, Mass., near Boston, scene of the first major battle (June 17, 1775) of the American Revolu-

The ***bunker*** *remains one of the more irritating obstacles on a golf course. It is usually constructed as a sand-filled hollow.*

1 2 3 4 5 Atomic generator

*A **buoy** may be designed as an aid to navigation, as a mooring for a boat or as a marker for an underwater hazard. Top: A small permanent navigation buoy near Manacles Rocks off the Lizard, Cornwall, U.K. 1. A mooring buoy. 2. A light buoy. 3. A light buoy equipped with a bell. 4. A whistle buoy. 5. A light buoy powered by an atomic generator.*

tion; the British captured the hill but suffered heavy losses.

bun·kum (bŭng′kum) *n.* Humbug, clap-trap. [*Buncombe* county in N. Carolina; around 1820 Felix Walker, Congressman for this district, insisted on making an unnecessary speech in Congress "for Buncombe"]

bun·ny (bŭn′ē) *n.* (pl. **-nies**). Childish or pet name for rabbit.

Bun·sen (bŭn′sen), **Robert Wilhelm von** (1811–99). German chemist, credited with the invention of the ~(**gas**) **burner**, which produces a very hot, nonluminous flame by the mixture of air with the stream of gas before it is lighted.

bunt[1] (bŭnt) *v.* (baseball) Tap or push (a pitched ball), with hands apart on bat, so that ball does not roll far. ~ *n.* Such a hit; a ball so hit.

bunt[2] (bŭnt) *n.* Cavity, baggy part, of fishing net, sail, etc.

bunt·ing[1] (bŭn′tĭng) *n.* Bird of subfamily Emberizinae, allied to finches.

bunt·ing[2] (bŭn′tĭng) *n.* Worsted or cotton material of open weave used for flags; flags (esp. of ship) collectively; streamers etc. used as festive decorations.

Bun·yan[1] (bŭn′yan), **John** (1628–88). English Nonconformist preacher; author of the allegory *Pilgrim's Progress*.

Bun·yan[2] (bŭn′yan), **Paul.** Legendary American lumberjack of the NW. forests; of gigantic size and appetites, he is the subject of many comic "tall tales."

buoy (bōō′ē, boi) *n.* (pl. **buoys**). Anchored float marking a channel or indicating position of something, e.g., wreck, reefs; **life**~, float that can support person in water. **buoy** *v.t.* 1. (usu. with *up*) Keep afloat; bring to surface of water; sustain, uplift. 2. Mark with buoy(s).

buoy·an·cy (boi′ansē, bōō′yan-) *n.* Capacity for floating, tendency to float in water or air; (fig.) elasticity, recuperative power.

buoy·ant (boi′ant, bōō′yant) *adj.* Apt to float, rise, keep up, or recover; able to keep things up; light-hearted.

bur, burr (bẽr) *ns.* 1. Clinging hooked fruit or flower head; hence, person hard to shake off. 2. Knob or knot in wood. 3. Rotary cutting tool for attaching to a drill. 4. See BURR def. 3.

Bur·bage (bẽr′bĭj), **Richard** (*c*1567–1619). English actor and theater manager, part owner of the Globe Theatre; acted principal parts in plays by Shakespeare, Jonson, and Beaumont and Fletcher.

Bur·bank (bẽr′băngk), **Luther** (1849–1926). American horticulturist; developed new and improved varieties of plants.

bur·ble (bẽr′bel) *n.* Murmurous noise. ~ *v.* (**-bled, -bling**). Speak or say murmurously.

bur·bot (bẽr′bot) *n.* (pl. **-bots,** collect. **-bot**). Eel-like flat-headed bearded fresh-water fish (*Lota lota*).

bur·den[1] (bẽr′den) *n.* 1. Load; obligation; bearing of loads; obligatory expense. 2. (archaic **bur·then** pr. bẽr′dhen) Ship's carrying capacity, tonnage. ~ *v.t.* Load; encumber; oppress.

bur·den[2] (bẽr′den) *n.* Refrain, chorus of song; drone of a bagpipe. [var. of BOURDON]

bur·den·some (bẽr′densom) *adj.* Oppressive, wearying. **bur′-den·some·ly** *adv.* **bur′den·-some·ness** *n.*

bur·dock (bẽr′dŏk) *n.* Coarse weedy plant (*Arctium lappa*), with prickly flower heads and dock-like leaves.

bu·reau (būr′ō) *n.* (pl. **-reaus, -reaux**). 1. Chest of drawers; (chiefly Brit.) writing desk or table with drawers. 2. Office, esp. of government department.

bu·reauc·ra·cy (byurŏk′rasē) *n.* (pl. **-cies**). Government by bureaus, centralization; body of officials. **bu·reau·crat** (būr′akrăt) *n.* **bu·reau·crat·ic** (būrakrăt′ĭk) *adj.* **bu·reau·crat′i·cal·ly** *adv.*

bu·rette, bu·ret (byurĕt′) *ns.* Graduated glass tube with tap at lower end for delivering measured small quantities of liquid in chemical analysis.

burg (bẽrg) *n.* (colloq.) Town.

bur·gee (berjē′, bẽr′jē) *n.* Small swallow-tailed pendant used by yachts etc., usu. as distinguishing flag.

bur·geon (bẽr′jon) *v.i.* Put forth, spring forth as, young shoots, bud, begin to grow.

bur·gess (bẽr′jĭs) *n.* 1. (hist.) Member of lower house of colonial legislature of Virginia or Maryland. 2. (hist.) Member of English Parliament representing a town, borough, or university.

burgh·er (bẽr′ger) *n.* 1. (hist.) Member of merchant class of a medieval city. 2. Solid middle-class citizen.

bur·glar (bẽrg′ler) *n.* One who enters building as trespasser and commits or intends to commit a theft. **bur·glar·i·ous** (berglār′ēus) *adj.* **bur′gla·ry** *n.*

bur·gle (bẽr′gel) *v.* (**-gled, -gling**). (colloq.) Commit burglary; rob by burglary.

bur·go·mas·ter (bẽr′gōmăster, -mahs-) *n.* Mayor of Dutch, Flemish, Austrian, or German town.

bur·goo (bẽr′goo, bergoo′) *n.* (southern U.S.) Thick, spicy stew of mixed meats and vegetables.

Bur·gun·dy (bẽr′gundē). (Fr. *Bourgogne*) Region, formerly an ancient kingdom, later duchy and province, of SE. France; any of the wines produced there, including Beaune, Chambertin, Pommard (red), and Chablis and Montrachet (white); similar wine made elsewhere.

bur·i·al (bĕr′ēal) *n.* Burying, esp. of dead body.

Burke[1] (bẽrk), **Edmund** (1729–1797). English statesman and political and philosophical writer.

Burke[2] (bẽrk), **John** (1787–1848). Irish-born genealogical and heraldic writer, first compiler of *Burke's Peerage*, officially entitled *Peerage and Baronetage* (1826), issued annually since 1847.

burl (bẽrl) *n.* Knot in wool, cloth, or wood; overgrown knot in walnut etc., used in veneering.

bur·lap (bẽr′lăp) *n.* Coarse canvas of jute, used for sacks.

bur·lesque (berlĕsk′) *adj.* Imitating derisively; bombastic, mock serious; caricaturing, parodying (esp. literary or dramatic work). ~ *n.* Literary or dramatic burlesque work or performance; bombast, mock seriousness; derisive imitation; vaudeville frequently featuring striptease. ~ *v.* Make or perform burlesque (of), caricature, travesty.

bur·ley, Bur·ley (bẽr′lē) *ns.* Light tobacco grown esp. in Kentucky.

bur·ly (bẽr′lē) *adj.* (**-li·er, -li·est**). Large and sturdy. **bur′li·-ness** *n.*

Bur·ma (bẽr′ma). Republic, established in 1948, occupying the NW. portion of the peninsula projecting south from Asia between India and China; capital, Rangoon. **Bur·mese** (bermēz′, -mēs′) *adj.* & *n.* (pl. **-mese**).

Bur·ma (bẽr′ma) **Road.** Seven-hundred-mile road between China and Burma used as a supply route by the Allies during World War II.

burn (bẽrn) *v.* (**burned** or **burnt, burn·ing**). Consume, be consumed, waste, by fire; blaze or smolder; injure by burning; brand; utilize the nuclear energy of (uranium etc.); feel intense heat or emotion; ~ **off,** burn vegetation on land to clear it for cultivation. **burn** *n.* Sore, mark, made by burning; burned area in forest etc. **burn′er** *n.*, device for burning; part of stove or apparatus that shapes the flame or emits the heat.

bur·net (bẽr′nĭt) *n.* Brown-flowered plant of genus *Sanguisorba* or genus *Poterium.*

Bur·ney (bẽr′nē), **Frances** *or* **Fanny** (*Madame D'Arblay*) (1752–1840). English novelist, originator of the simple novel of home life.

burn·ing (bẽr′nĭng) *adj.* That burns; flagrant; hotly discussed, exciting; ~**-bush,** "the bush that burned and was not consumed" (Exod. 3); any of various shrubs or plants with scarlet berries or foliage turning red in autumn etc.

bur·nish (bẽr′nĭsh) *v.* Polish by friction; take a polish.

bur·noose, bur·nous (bernōōs′, bẽr′nōōs) *ns.* Arab or Moorish hooded cloak.

Burns (bẽrnz), **Robert** (1759–1796). Scottish poet, many of

Hinayana Buddhism was introduced to ***Burma*** *in 1044 by her ruler, Anawratha, who ran an immense program of temple building. Temples such as this (facing page) are found in most Burmese towns. Below: In Rangoon a child, dressed for a festival, prays.*

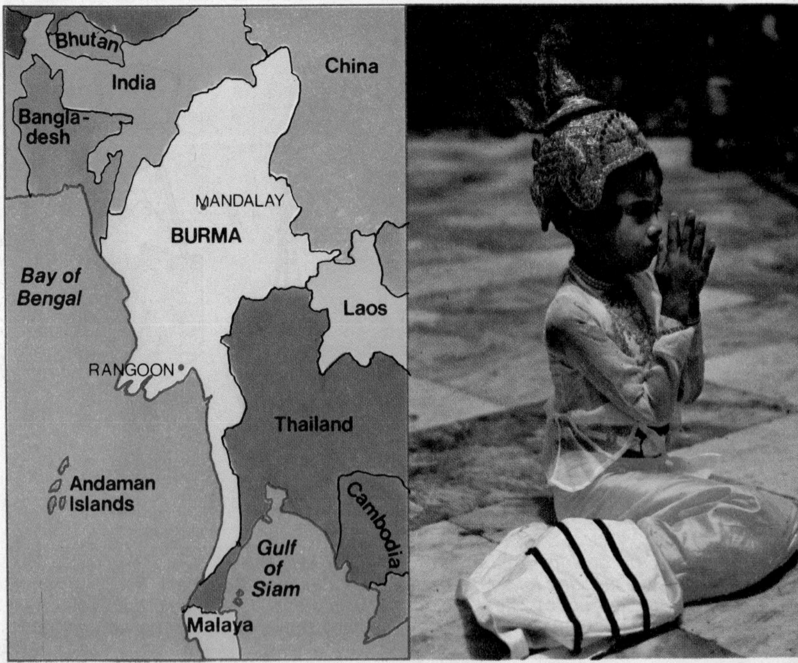

whose poems are written in Lowland Scots.

Burn·side (bẽrn′sīd), **Ambrose Everett** (1824–81). Union general during Civil War; relieved of command and resigned commission after being blamed for failure to lead aggressively; became governor of and senator from Rhode Island after the war; **burnsides**, full side whiskers worn with a mustache but with the chin kept clean shaven, as worn by General Burnside.

burnt (bẽrnt) *adj.*: see BURN; (esp., of pigment) calcined to a deeper color *e.g.*, ~ **sienna,** ~ **umber**; (of color) of a deeper shade; ~ **offering**, sacrifice offered by burning.

burp (bẽrp) *n.* & *v.* (colloq.) (Cause to) belch.

burr (bẽr) *n.* 1. Rough edge left on cut metal etc. 2. Small drill for cutting into tooth or bone. 3. (also **bur**) Rough sounding of letter *r.* ~ *v.* 1. Pronounce with burr; speak with rough or indistinct articulation. 2. Make burring sound.

Burr (bẽr), **Aaron** (1756–1836).

*From this cottage in Alloway, Strathclyde, Scotland, **Robert Burns** used to go to work on his father's farm. Burns's use of Lowland dialect brought a lively freshness to his poems.*

*A Navajo cemetery in Arizona where a man has been **buried** with the bones of his horse and his saddle placed on top of the grave. Originally semi-nomadic, the Navajo have become farmers and weavers.*

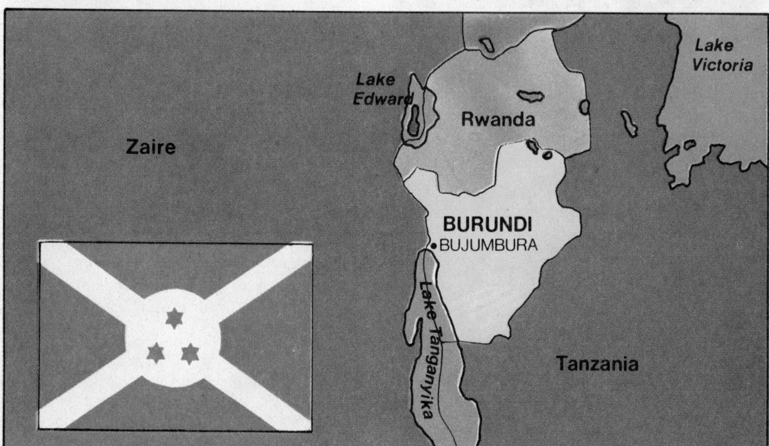

*Near a village in **Burundi,** east central Africa, a girl bears on her head a traditional decorative gift of split leaves in a basket. The map shows the relationship of Burundi (formerly called Urundi), an independent republic since 1962, to its much larger neighbors, Zaire and Tanzania. The area of the country is 10,700 sq. miles and its population about 4 million.*

Vice President of the U.S. under Thomas Jefferson, 1801–5; killed Alexander Hamilton in a duel, 1804; tried for conspiring to seize territory from Spanish America and create a republic in the Southwest; acquitted, 1807.

bur·ro (bẽr′ō, boor′ō, bŭr′ō) *n.* (pl. **-ros**). Small donkey, esp. one used as pack animal.

bur·row (bẽr′ō, bŭr′ō) *n.* Hole or excavation in ground in which rabbits, foxes, etc., live. ~ *v.* Make, live in, burrow; make by excavating; hide oneself, move, *into, under*. **bur′row·er** *n.*

bur·sa (bẽr′sa) *n.* (pl. **-sae** pr. -sē, **-sas**). (physiol.) Synovial sac between joints or between muscles, skin, etc., and bones, for lessening friction. **bur′sal** *adj.*

bur·sar (bẽr′ser, -sâr) *n.* Treasurer, esp. of a college or university. **bur·sar·i·al** (bersâr′ēal) *adj.* **bur′sar·ship** *n.*

bur·si·tis (bersī′tĭs) *n.* Inflammation of a bursa.

burst (bẽrst) *v.* (**burst, burst·ing**). Fly violently asunder, give way suddenly; explode; rush, move, appear, violently or suddenly; speak, utter, be uttered, explosively. ~ *n.* Bursting, split; explosion, outbreak; spurt; continuous gallop. **burst′ing** *adj.* (esp.) Full to overflowing.

bur·then (bẽr′dhen): see BURDEN[1], 2.

Bur·ton[1] (bẽr′ton), **Sir Richard Francis** (1821–90). English adventurer, Orientalist, and Arabic scholar; the first Englishman to reach Mecca; translator of the *Arabian Nights*.

Bur·ton[2] (bẽr′ton), **Robert** (1577–1640). English clergyman, scholar, and writer; author of the *Anatomy of Melancholy*.

Bu·run·di (berŭn′dē, bo͝oro͞on′dē). Republic on E. side of Lake Tanganyika; established 1962; capital Bujumbura.

bur·y (bĕr′ē) *v.t.* (**bur·ied, bur·y·ing**). 1. Deposit in, commit to, earth, tomb, or sea; perform burial rites over; put under ground. 2. Put away, forget; consign to obscurity; hide in earth, cover up, submerge; plunge (head *in* hands etc.).

bus (bŭs) *n.* (pl. **bus·es, bus·ses**). Long motor vehicle for carrying passengers; **bus′boy**, waiter's assistant; **bus stop**, place at which bus, following a fixed route, makes a regular or scheduled stop.

bus·by (bŭz′bē) *n.* (pl. **-bies**). Tall fur cap of hussars and guardsmen in British army.

bush (bo͝osh) *n.* Woody plant with numerous stems of moderate length; clump of shrubs; woodland, unsettled or remote area; luxuriant growth of hair etc.; **bush′buck**,

Large areas of semi-desert, the ***bush*** *is characterized by coarse scrub vegetation in Australia, where this type of land is also called the outback. In South Africa it is described as veldt.*

This traditional samurai dress embodies the spirit of ***bushido,*** *the Japanese code of ethics which demands absolute obedience from the samurai warriors.*

Mostly found in the arid western regions of the U.S.A., the flat–topped ***butte*** *is formed by erosion of the surrounding plains and is a striking feature of this desert area.*

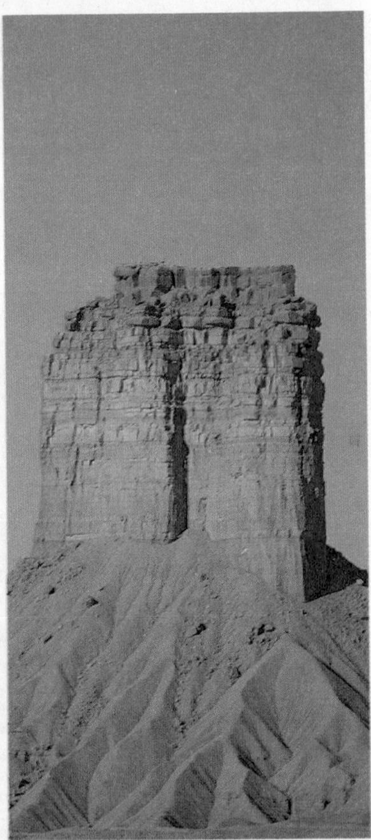

small African antelope of genus *Tragelaphus*, dwelling in forests and swamps, esp. common bushbuck (*T. scriptus*); **bush league**, (baseball) minor league; **bush'man**, member, language, of aboriginal tribe of S. Africa; (chiefly Australian) dweller in Australian bush; **bush'master**, very large venomous viper (*Lachesis mutus*) of tropical America; **bush'whacker**, backwoodsman. **bush** *v.i.* Grow, branch like a bush. **bushed** *adj.* (colloq.) Exhausted.

bush·el (bo͝osh'*e*l) *n.* U.S. dry measure = 4 pecks = 2,150.42 cubic inches.

Bu·shi·do, bu·shi·do (bo͞o'-shēdaw') *ns.* Code of honor and morals evolved by the samurai of Japan. [Jap., = "military knight way"]

bush·ing (bo͝osh'ĭng) *n.* Metal lining for axle hole etc.; box or bearing in which shaft revolves; perforated plug.

bush·y (bo͝osh'ē) *adj.* (**bush·i·er, bush·i·est**). Abounding in bushes; growing thickly.

busi·ness (bĭz'nĭs) *n.* 1. Task, duty, province; errand; agenda. 2. Serious occupation, work; habitual occupation, profession; trade, commercial transactions; commercial house, firm; ~ **end**, (colloq.) working end of object, opp. handle; **busi'nesslike**, systematic, practical; **busi'nessman**, fem. **busi'nesswoman**, one engaged in business or commerce. 3. (theatr.) Action, dumb show. 4. (contempt.) Process, concern, affair, thing.

bus·kin (bŭs'kĭn) *n.* 1. Boot reaching to calf or knee. 2. Thick-soled boot lending height to ancient Athenian tragic actor; (fig.) tragedy.

bust[1] (bŭst) *n.* 1. Sculpture of person's head and upper portion of body. 2. Upper front of body, esp. woman's bosom.

bust[2] (bŭst) *v.* (slang) Burst. ~ *adj.* (slang) Broke, without money. ~ *n.* (slang) Burst, (esp.) spree; ~**-up**, quarrel.

bus·tard (bŭs'*te*rd) *n.* Large swift-running bird of genus *Otis*.

bus·tle[1] (bŭs'*e*l) *v.* (**-tled, -tling**). Bestir oneself, make show of activity, hurry *about*; make (others) hurry or work hard. ~ *n.* Excited activity, fuss.

bus·tle[2] (bŭs'*e*l) *n.* Pad or framework puffing out top of woman's skirt at the back.

bus·y (bĭz'ē) *adj.* (**bus·i·er, bus·i·est**). Occupied, working, engaged, with intention concentrated; unresting, always employed, stirring; fussy, meddlesome, prying; (excessively) full of detail; **bus'ybody**, meddlesome person, mischief maker. **bus'i·ly** *adv.* **bus'y** *v.t.* (**bus·ied, bus·y·ing**). Occupy, keep busy.

but (bŭt) *prep.* Without, apart from. ~ *adv.* Merely. ~ *conj.* On the other hand; except; unless; yet.

bu·ta·di·ene (būt*a*dī'ēn, -dīēn') *n.* Highly unsaturated carbon (C_4H_6), gaseous at ordinary temperatures, used in manufacture of synthetic rubber.

bu·tane (bū'tān) *n.* Colorless hydrocarbon gas (C_4H_{10}), used compressed in cylinders as a fuel, refrigerant, etc.

butch (bo͞och) *n.* (slang) Tough youth or man; mannish lesbian; short haircut, crew cut.

butch·er (bo͝och'*er*) *n.* One who slaughters animals for food, dealer in meat; person who causes or delights in bloodshed; **butch'erbird**, kind of shrike. **butcher** *v.t.* Slaughter in the manner of a butcher (lit. and fig.).

butch·er·y (bo͝och'*e*rē) *n.* (pl. **-er·ies**). Butcher's trade; needless or cruel slaughter.

but·ler (bŭt'l*er*) *n.* Male servant in charge of plate, table, wine cellar, etc., head servant.

But·ler[1] (bŭt'l*er*), **Samuel** (1612–80). English poet and satirist; author of *Hudibras*.

But·ler[2] (bŭt'l*er*), **Samuel** (1835–1902). English critic and novelist; author of the Utopian novel *Erewhon* and an autobiographical novel, *The Way of All Flesh*.

butt[1] (bŭt) *n.* Wine or ale cask (holding 108–40 gallons); a unit of volume equal to 126 gallons; any barrel.

butt[2] (bŭt) *n.* 1. Thicker end, esp. of tool or weapon. 2. Stub of cigar or cigarette; (slang) cigarette. 3. (slang) Buttocks, rear end.

butt[3] (bŭt) *n.* 1. Mound behind target; shooting range; target. 2. End, aim, object *of* (ridicule etc.); object of teasing and ridicule.

butt[4] (bŭt) *v.* Push with the head; ~ **in**, intervene, meddle. **butt** *n.* Butting, push with the head. **butt'er** *n.*

Butte (būt). Mining city in SW. Montana; situated over extremely large mineral deposits, especially copper.

butte (būt) *n.* Isolated abrupt flat-topped hill.

but·ter (bŭt'*er*) *n.* Fatty pale yellow substance made from cream by churning, used for spreading on bread and in cooking; substance of similar consistency or look (as **peanut** ~); ~ **and eggs, toadflax**; ~ **bean**, dried seed of white varieties of lima bean, used as vegetable; **but'tercup**, any of various kinds of ranunculus with yellow cup-shaped flowers; **but'terfingers, but'terfingered**, (person) inclined to drop things; **but'terfish**, GUNNEL[1]; also any of several related fishes; **but'termilk**, sour milk remaining after butter has been churned out. **but'ternut**, (large oily fruit of) N. Amer. white walnut tree (*Juglans cinerea*); **but'terscotch**, syrup, sauce, flavoring, or candy made chiefly of brown sugar and butter; **but'terwort**, violet-flowered fleshy-leaved, bog plant (*Pinguicula vulgaris*). **butter** *v.t.* Spread, cook, with butter; ~ **up**, flatter.

but·ter·fly (bŭt'*er*flī) *n.* (pl. **-flies**). 1. Diurnal lepidopterous insect (cf. MOTH) with knobbed

*Women wore the **bustle** around 1870. It was a modification of the hooped crinoline and comprised a pad or framework that pulled out a woman's skirt at the back.*

*The **bustard,** extinct in Great Britain, is now found only in southern Europe, North Africa and Australia. A male has a wingspan of up to 8 ft. and may be about 4 ft. from beak to tail.*

antennae, carrying the wings erect when at rest. 2. Vain or frivolous person; trifler, esp. **social** ~. 3. (swimming) Stroke in which the arms are lifted out of the water simultaneously.

but·ter·y (bŭt′erē) *adj.* Of, resembling, containing, covered in, butter.

but·tock (bŭt′*o*k) *n.* One of the two protuberances of the rump; (usu. pl.) rump.

but·ton (bŭt′*o*n) *n.* Knob or disk attached to garment etc. to serve as fastening when pressed through loop or buttonhole, or for ornament; bud; unopened mushroom; small rounded body; terminal knob (on foil etc.), knob, handle, catch, as on electric bell; **but′tonhole,** slit through which button passes; flower(s) for wearing in buttonhole in lapel of coat; (*v.t.*) sew with buttonhole stitch; seize, detain (reluctant listener); **but′tonhole stitch,** looped stitch used for edging buttonholes; **but′tonhook,** small hook for pulling button through buttonhole in boots etc. **but′tonwood**: see SYCAMORE. **button** *v.* Furnish with button(s); fasten (often *up*) with button(s). **but′ton·er** *n.* **but′ton·less, but′ton·like** *adjs.*

but·tress (bŭt′rĭs) *n.* Support built against wall etc., prop; buttress-like projection of hill. ~ *v.* Support with buttress, by argument etc.

bux·om (bŭk′s*o*m) *adj.* (of woman) Plump of figure; full-bosomed. **bux′om·ness** *n.*

buy (bī) *v.t.* (**bought, buy·ing**). Obtain in exchange for money or other consideration; gain over by bribery; ~ **in,** purchase stock or interest in; buy back for the original owner at auction by naming higher price than the highest offered; ~ **off,** get rid of by payment, bribe; ~ **up,** buy as much as possible of. **buy** *n.* Purchase; **good** ~, bargain; useful purchase. **buy′er** *n.* (esp.) Purchasing agent for a retail store.

buzz (bŭz) *n.* Hum of bee etc., confused low sound like this; ~ **saw,** circular saw; **buzz′word,** pseudo-technical catchword or slogan. **buzz** *v.* Make buzz; move *about* busily; (of aircraft) warn, annoy, etc., by flying fast and close to; ~ **off,** (slang) go away.

buz·zard (bŭz′*e*rd) *n.* 1. Name of various kinds of hawk of genus *Buteo* and family Cathartidae. 2. Turkey buzzard.

Buz·zards (bŭz′*e*rdz) **Bay.** 1. Inlet of the Atlantic Ocean in SE. Massachusetts. 2. Resort town near the entrance to the inlet.

buz·zer (bŭz′*e*r) *n.* (esp.) Any electric signaling device that makes a buzzing sound.

B.V. *abbrev.* Blessed Virgin.

B.W.I. *abbrev.* British West Indies.

by (bī) *prep.* 1. Near to, beside; (of compass point) slightly inclining to (as *N. by E.*, between N. and NNE.); ~ **oneself,** alone. 2. Along,

Generally speaking, ***butterflies*** *are distinguished from moths by the butterfly's clubbed antennae and its diurnal habit. Below: An Australian big greasy butterfly (Cressida cressida). The male is more colorful than the female. Bottom left: A black-veined white butterfly (Aporia crataegi). Below: A male diadem butterfly (Hypolimnas misipus).*

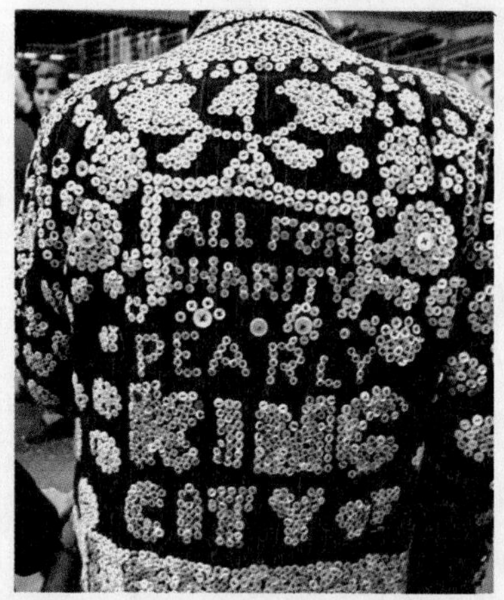

*Pearly **buttons** adorn the suits of the pearly kings and queens of London, U.K. The tradition and some of the costumes have been handed down by costermongers since the 1880s.*

*Below right: the rough-legged **buzzard** migrates from the Arctic, where it preys on ptarmigan and other small birds, to N. Europe and N. America. Both the rough-legged buzzard and the lizard buzzard (above) sight their prey, including fledgling birds and small rodents, while hovering.*

via, past. 3. During. 4. Through the agency, means, etc., of; (of animals) having as sire. 5. As soon as, not later than. 6. According to. 7. After, succeeding. 8. To the extent of. 9. In respect of. 10. (in oaths etc.) In the belief of. ~ *adj.* 1. Side, out of the way, devious, as **by'path, by'road, by'way**. 2. Collateral, side; **by'play**, action, usu. dumb show, carried on aside, esp. on stage; **by-product**, substance etc. produced incidentally in making something else. 3. Additional, subsidiary; **by'word**, proverb. **by** *adv.* Near; aside, in reverse; past; ~ **and** ~, before long; ~ **and large**, on the whole; **by'stander**, spectator.

bye (bī) *n.* Position of player in round of a tournament not paired with an opponent and thus advanced to the next round; hence, **draw a** ~.

bye-bye (bī'bī') *int.* (colloq. and nursery var. of) GOODBYE.

Bye·lo·rus·sia, Be·lo·rus·sia (byĕlōrŭsh'*a*, bĕl-). White Russia, one of the constituent republics (properly *Byelorussian, Belorussian Soviet Socialist Republic*) of the U.S.S.R., including former provinces of Minsk, Vitebsk, and Mogilov; capital, Minsk. **Bye·lo·rus'sian, Be·lo·rus'sian** *adjs.* & *ns.* (Native, language) of Byelorussia; White Russian.

by·gone (bī'gawn, -gŏn) *adj.* Past, departed; antiquated. **by'gones** *n.pl.* Past, past offenses.

by·law (bī'law) *n.* Regulation made by local government, corporation, etc.

by·pass (bī'păs) *n.* 1. Secondary pipe or channel conveying gas or

*Espousal by the English Romantic poet, **Lord Byron,** of the Greek nationalist cause led him to adopt their national costume in which he was shown in this portrait by T. Phillips.*

*Under Justinian, who reigned 527–565, the **Byzantine Empire,** (green areas in map at right) was at its most productive phase. The Empire's characteristic art reached its zenith shortly after Justinian's reign. Above right and facing page: The Basilica of St. Mark's, Venice, shows the force of this style.*

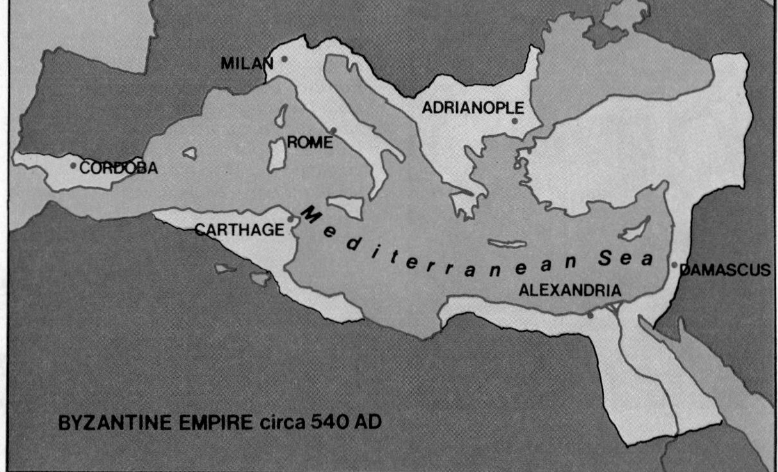

*Istanbul, Turkey, formerly called **Byzantium** and Constantinople, the capital of the Byzantine Empire to which it gave its name. The city is famed for its works of art of the period.*

liquid around fixture etc.; alternative passage for blood during surgical operation on heart; (elect.) shunt. 2. Road designed to relieve congestion by providing an alternative route for through traffic, esp. around a city. ~ *v.t.* (**-passed** or **-past, -passing**). Furnish with a bypass; make detour around (town etc.) (also fig.). **by′passed** *adj.*

Byrd (bērd), **Richard Evelyn** (1888–1957). Amer. polar explorer; made first flight over N. Pole (1926) and over S. Pole (1929).

By·ron (bīr′on), **George Gordon, 6th Baron** (1788–1824). English Romantic poet, whose poetry exerted great influence on the Romantic movement; he joined the Greek insurgents in 1823, and died of fever at Missolonghi, Greece. **By·ron·ic** (bīrŏn′ĭk) *adj.* **By·ron′i·cal·ly** *adv.*

Byz·an·tine (bĭz′antēn, -tīn, bĭzăn′tĭn) *adj.* Of Byzantium or the Byzantine Empire; of the style of art and architecture typical of this, characterized esp. by use of the round arch, circle, dome, and cross, and by rich mosaic ornament; ~ **Empire**, eastern part of Roman Empire, esp. after collapse of Western Empire in 476, with its capital at Constantinople until this city was captured by the Turks in 1453. **Byzantine** *n.* Native, inhabitant, of Byzantium or the Byzantine Empire. ~ *adj.* Complicated, underhand.

By·zan·ti·um (bĭzăn′tēum, -shēum). Original name of CONSTANTINOPLE.

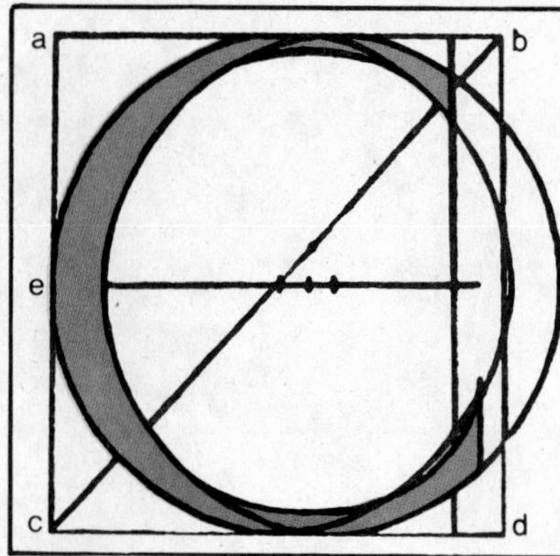

How the form of the letter **C, c** has evolved through the ages—from the Phoenician to the Anglo-Saxon. The letter corresponds to the Semitic 'gimel', probably derived from an early sign for camel, and the Greek gamma.

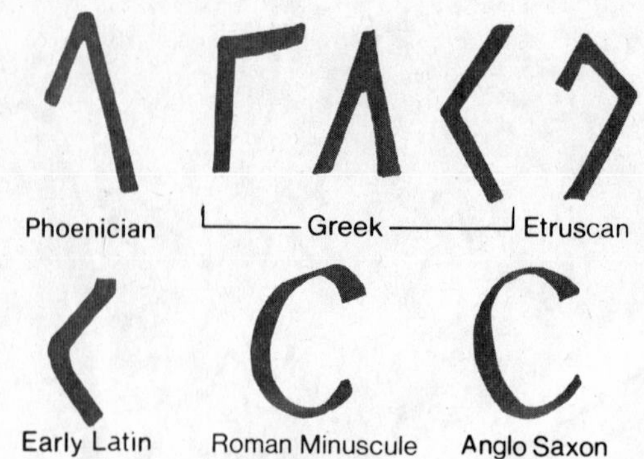

C, c (sē) (pl. **C's**, **c's** or **Cs**, **cs**). 1. Third letter of modern English and ancient Roman alphabet, deriving its form from Gk. *gamma* (*Γ*). 2. Third in series, order, or class. 3. **C**, (mus.) name of the key-note in the natural major scale and the corresponding minor scales; name of these scales. 4. Roman numeral symbol for 100.

C *abbrev.* Celsius; centigrade; coulomb(s).

c. *abbrev.* Carat; cent(s); century; chapter; circa (also *c*, *ca.*); cubic.

CA *abbrev.* California.

Ca *symbol.* Calcium.

ca. *abbrev.* Circa.

Caa·ba (kah'b*a*) = KAABA.

CAB, C.A.B. *abbrevs.* Civil Aeronautics Board.

cab (kăb) *n.* 1. Hackney carriage, esp. of brougham or hansom shape; taxicab; **cab'stand**, place where cabs are authorized to wait. 2. Driver's compartment in locomotive, truck, etc.

ca·bal (k*a*băl') *n.* Secret intrigue; conspiratorial group of plotters; clique, faction. ~ *v.i.* (**-balled, -bal·ling**). Combine in cabal, intrigue privately. [f. CABALA]

cab·a·la (kăb'*a*l*a*, k*a*bah'-) *n.* 1. Jewish oral tradition handed down from Moses to the rabbis of the Mishna and Talmud, or the pretended tradition of the mystical interpretation of the Old Testament. 2. Mystery; esoteric doctrine. **cab'a·lism, cab'a·list** *ns.* **cab·a·lis·tic** (kăb*a*lĭs'tĭk), **cab·a·lis'ti·cal** *adjs.* **cab·a·lis'ti·cal·ly** *adv.* [Heb. *ḳabbālāh* traditional law]

ca·bal·le·ro (kăb*a*lyār'ō, -lār'ō; *Sp.* kahvahlyĕ'raw) *n.* (pl. **-le·ros** pr. -lyār'ōz, -lār'ōz; *Sp.* -lyĕ'raws). Spanish gentleman; (southwest) horseman, lady's escort or admirer.

cab·a·ret (kăb*a*rā') *n.* 1. Small night club; restaurant with entertainment provided by live performers. 2. Entertainment provided in restaurant etc. while guests are at table.

cab·bage (kăb'ĭj) *n.* Any of various kinds of green vegetable (esp. of *Brassica oleracea*), with compact globular heart or head of unexpanded leaves; ~ **butterfly**, one of several white butterflies of the family Pieridae whose green larvae feed on cabbage; ~ **palm, tree**, any of various trees with edible cabbagelike terminal buds (esp. the W. Ind. *Roystonea oleracea*); ~ **rose**, double rose with large round compact flowers (esp. *Rosa centifolia*).

cab·ba·la (kăb'*a*l*a*, k*a*bah'-) = CABALA.

cab·by (kăb'ē) *n.* (pl. **-bies**). (colloq.) Cab driver.

Cab·ell (kăb'*e*l), **James Branch** (1879–1958). Amer. essayist and novelist; best known for his novel *Jurgen.*

ca·ber (kā'b*er*) *n.* Roughly trimmed young pine trunk used in Sc. Highland sport of **tossing the** ~. [Gael. *cabar* pole]

cab·in (kăb'ĭn) *n.* 1. Small rude dwelling. 2. Room or compartment in ship for sleeping or eating in; officer's or passenger's room; compartment in aircraft; ~ **boy**, boy waiting on officers or passengers on ship; ~ **cruiser**, power-driven pleasure boat with cabin for living in.

Ca·bin·da (k*a*bēn'd*a*). Territory of Angola on the Atlantic Coast of Africa, between Zaire and the Congo Republic.

cab·i·net (kăb'*i*nĭt) *n.* 1. (archaic) Small private room, closet. 2. Case with drawers, shelves, etc., for keeping valuables or displaying objects. 3. (Group of) persons appointed by president, prime minister, etc., to act as his or her council of advisers and serve as executives of various departments of government. 4. **cab'inetmaker**, craftsman skilled in making fine furniture of wood; **cab'inet-making, cab'inetwork**.

ca·ble (kā'b*e*l) *n.* 1. Strong thick rope of hemp or wire; (naut.) studded link chain attached to an anchor; measurement of distance at sea, = 720 feet (262.8 m). 2. Any insulated conductor of electricity orig. the conductor of a submarine

The ***cabbage butterfly*** *Pierisrapae regarded throughout North America as a serious pest attacking cabbage crops, was introduced in about 1860.*

telegraph. 3. = CABLEGRAM. 4. **~-stitch**, any of various twisted ropelike stitches in knitting and embroidery. 5. ~ **car**, car on ~ **railway** worked by cable and stationary engine; car hanging from and traveling along an overhead cable; **ca'blelaid**, (of rope) made of three hawser-laid ropes laid up left-handed; **cable TV**, television programs broadcast via coaxial cable or by air to a community antenna. **cable** *v.* (**-bled, -bling**). 1. Furnish, fasten with cable. 2. Transmit (message), communicate by cable.

ca·ble·gram (kā'belgrăm) *n.* Telegraph message transmitted by submarine cable.

cab·o·chon (kăb'oshŏn) *n.* Gem, polished, not cut into facets, circular or elliptical in shape with domed top.

ca·boo·dle (kabōō'del) *n.* (colloq.) **the whole** (**kit and**) ~, the whole lot.

ca·boose (kabōōs') *n.* 1. Galley on ship's deck. 2. Last car on freight train, containing crew's kitchen and sleeping quarters.

Cab·ot (kăb'ot), **John** (*c*1450–1498). Venetian navigator in the service of England; discovered Labrador in 1497 with his son

*Born in Genoa, **John Cabot** is shown here embarking from Bristol in search of the North West Passage to India. He and his son failed to find it but discovered Newfoundland.*

Sebastian (1477–1557); ~ **Strait**, channel connecting the Gulf of St. Lawrence with the Atlantic Ocean.

Ca·bral (kabrahl'), **Pedro Alvares** (1460–1526?). Portuguese navigator; discovered Brazil, 1500, and claimed it for Portugal.

Ca·bri·ni (kabrē'nē), **Saint Frances Xavier** ("Mother Cabrini") (1850–1917). Founder of Missionary Sisters of the Sacred Heart; first American canonized, 1946.

cab·ri·ole (kăb'rēōl) *n.* Kind of curved leg in 17th- and 18th-c. furniture, esp. that of Chippendale style.

cab·ri·o·let (kăbrēolā') *n.* Light two-wheeled hooded one-horse carriage. [Fr., f. *cabriole* goat's leap]

ca·ca·o (kakā'ō, -kah'ō) *n.* (pl. **-ca·os**). Seed of a tropical Amer. tree (*Theobroma cacao*), from which cocoa and chocolate are prepared; the tree itself (also ~ **tree**).

cac·cia·to·re (kăchatōr'ē, -tōr'ē) *adj.* Stewed with herbs, tomatoes, and other seasonings.

cach·a·lot (kăsh'alŏt, -lō) *n.* Sperm whale.

cache (kăsh) *n.* Hiding place for treasures, ammunition, provisions, etc., esp. as used by explorers; the stores hidden. ~ *v.t.* (**cached, cach·ing**). Place in cache.

ca·chet (kăshā', kăsh'ā) *n.* Stamp, seal, distinguishing mark, commemorative design; prestige.

cach·in·nate (kăk'ināt) *v.i.* (**-nat·ed, -nat·ing**). Laugh loudly. **cach·in·na·tion** (kăkinā'shon) *n.*

ca·cique (kasēk') *n.* W. Ind. and Latin Amer. Indian chief; Spanish or Latin Amer. local political boss.

cack·le (kăk'el) *n.* Clucking of hen after laying; noisy, inconsequent talk; shrill laugh. ~ *v.i.* (**-led, -ling**). Make cackle; talk glibly and noisily.

cac·o·dyl (kăk'odĭl) *n.* (chem.) The radical dimethyl arsenic ($As(CH_3)_2$). [Gk. *kakōdēs* stinking]

cac·o·e·thes (kăkoē'thēz) *n.* Mania or incurable itch (for doing something unwise); ~ **scribendi**, compulsion to write (books, poetry, etc.). [L., f. Gk. *kakos* bad, ugly; *ēthos* disposition]

ca·cog·ra·phy (kakŏg'rafē) *n.* Bad handwriting or spelling. **ca·cog'ra·pher** *n.* **cac·o·graph·ic** (kăkogrăf'ĭk), **cac·o·graph'i·cal** *adjs.* **cac·o·graph'i·cal·ly** *adv.*

cac·o·mis·tle (kăk′*o*mĭs*e*l) *n.* Small raccoon-like carnivore of Mexico and SW. U.S. (*Bassariscus astutus*), with bushy black-and-white ringed tail, also called ring-tailed cat.

ca·coph·o·ny (k*a*kŏf′*o*nē) *n.* (pl. **-nies**). Ugly sound, dissonance, discord. **ca·coph′o·nous** *adj.* **ca·coph′o·nous·ly** *adv.*

cac·tus (kăk′t*u*s) *n.* (pl. **-tus·es, -ti** pr. -tī). Plant of the family Cactaceae, flourishing in arid districts of the Western Hemisphere, having a thick fleshy stem adapted for retaining moisture (usu. with spines, rarely with leaves) and bearing brilliantly colored flowers. **cac·toid** (kăk′toid) *adj.*

cad (kăd) *n.* Ungentlemanly man, esp. in behavior toward women. **cad′dish** *adj.*

ca·dav·er (k*a*dăv′*er*) *n.* Corpse. **ca·dav′er·ic, ca·dav′er·ous** *adjs.* [L.]

cad·die, cad·dy[1] (kăd′ē) *ns.* (pl. **-dies**). Attendant who carries golfer's clubs etc. ~ *v.i.* (**-died, -dy·ing**). Act as caddie. [f. CADET]

cad·dis (kăd′ĭs) *n.* **cad′disfly**, feebly flying freq. nocturnal insect of order Trichoptera, with membranous or hairy wings, living near water; **cad′disworm**, larva of caddisfly etc., living in water and making cylindrical case of sticks, stone, shells, etc., used as bait for fishing.

cad·dy[2] (kăd′ē) *n.* (pl. **-dies**). Small box or other container, esp. one for holding tea. [Malay *kati*, weight of 1⅓ lb. (603 g)]

ca·dence (kā′d*e*ns) *n.* Rhythm; measured movement, esp. of sound; falling tone, esp. of voice at end of period; intonation; (mus.) close of musical movement or phrase. **ca′denced** *adj.*

ca·den·za (k*a*dĕn′z*a*) *n.* (mus.) Elaborate passage for solo instrument (or, less freq., voice) at close of movement or between two parts of movement, sometimes improvised by performer.

ca·det (k*a*dĕt′) *n.* 1. (archaic) Younger son or brother. 2. Student in a military school, training to be an officer.

cadge (kăj) *v.* (**cadged, cadg·ing**). Get by begging.

Cad·il·lac (kăd′*i*lăk), **Sieur Antoine de la Mothe** (1658–1730). French army officer and administrator in America; founder of French settlement in Detroit, 1701; governor of Louisiana, 1713–1716.

Cá·diz (kā′dĭz, k*a*dēz′). Seaport in SW. Spain, on the Atlantic Ocean near Gibraltar.

cad·mi·um (kăd′mē*u*m) *n.* (chem.) Soft bluish-white metallic element resembling tin, used in various alloys and as a protective coating on iron and steel; symbol Cd, at. no. 48, at. wt. 112.40; ~ **yellow**, cadmium sulfide, an intense yellow pigment.

Cad·mus (kăd′m*u*s). (Gk. legend) Founder of Thebes in Boeotia, reputed to have introduced the alphabet into Greece; slew a dragon and sowed its teeth in the earth, from which armed men sprang up and slew one another until only five survived, with whom he founded Thebes. **Cad·me·an** (kădmē′*a*n) *adj.*

ca·dre (kăd′r*e*, kah′dr*e*) *n.* Framework, scheme; (mil.) permanent nucleus of regiment; in Communist countries, = CELL, def. 6.

ca·du·ce·us (k*a*dōō′sē*u*s, -dū′-, -sh*u*s) *n.* (pl. **-ce·i** pr. -sēī, -shī). Ancient Greek or Roman herald's wand; esp. the wand of Mercury, usu. represented with two serpents twined around it; similar staff used as a symbol of the medical profession.

ca·du·cous (k*a*dōō′k*u*s, -dū′-) *adj.* Fleeting, perishable; (biol., of organs and parts) shed when their work is done. **ca·du·ci·ty** (k*a*dōō′sĭtē, -dū′-) *n.*

cae·cil·i·an (sēsĭl′ē*a*n) *adj.* & *n.* (zool.) (Member) of the Apoda (see APODAL).

cae·cum (sē′k*u*m) = CECUM.

Caed·mon (kăd′m*o*n) (7th c.). English monk; said by Bede to have received in a vision the power of song and put into English verse passages from the Scriptures.

Cae·li·an (sē′lē*a*n). One of the seven Hills of Rome.

Cae·no·zo·ic (sēn*o*zō′ĭk) = CENOZOIC.

Cae·sar (sē′z*er*). Cognomen of the Roman dictator Caius JULIUS CAESAR, used as title by the Roman emperors from Augustus to Hadrian, and subsequently by the emperor's heir presumptive. **Cae·-**

*Few of the **cactus** family are useful to man, but they are cultivated for their beauty and curious shapes. 1. The Saguabo cactus in Tucson Mountain Park, Arizona. 2. The orchid or epiphyllum cactus. 3. The golden ball* (Echinocactus grusonii) *growing near the Mediterranean.*

1

2

3

sar·e·an, Cae·sar·i·an (sĭzăr'ēan) *adjs.* Of Caesar or the Caesars; ~ **section**, operation of cutting through walls of the mother's abdomen to deliver a child, as was done, acc. to Pliny, at the birth of Julius Caesar.

Cae·sa·re·a (sĕzarē'a, sĕs-). Ancient seaport built by Herod the Great; capital of Roman Palestine.

cae·si·um (sē'zēum) = CESIUM.

cae·su·ra, ce·su·ra (sĭzhoor'a, -zoor'a, -zūr'a) *ns.* (pl. **-su·ras, -su·rae** pr. -zhoor'ē, -zoor'ē, -zūr'ē). (Gk. and Rom. pros.) Break between words within a metrical foot; (modern pros.) pause about the middle of metrical line. **cae·su'ral** *adj.*

ca·fé (kăfā', ka-) *n.* Coffeehouse, restaurant, bar; ~ **au lait**, coffee mixed with about an equal quantity of hot milk; the brownish-cream color of this.

caf·e·te·ri·a (kăfetēr'ēa) *n.* Restaurant in which customers take their food from a counter and carry it to a table for eating.

caf·feine, caf·fein (kăfēn', kăf'ēn) *ns.* Vegetable alkaloid crystallizing in white silky needles, found in leaves and seeds of coffee and tea plants etc. (and hence in these beverages); used in medicine as a cardiac stimulant and as a diuretic.

caf·tan (kăf'tan, kăftăn') *n.* Long girdled tunic worn in eastern countries; woman's long loose dress.

cage (kāj) *n.* 1. Fixed or portable enclosure, of wire or with bars, esp. for confining birds or beasts. 2. Any cagelike frame or device; elevator car. ~ *v.t.* (**caged, cag·ing**). Place or keep in cage.

cage·y (kā'jē) *adj.* (**cag·i·er, cag·i·est**). (colloq.) Wary, noncommittal.

Ca·glios·tro (kălyaws'trō), **Count Alessandro** (1743–95). Name assumed by Giuseppe Balsamo, a notorious adventurer, magician, and charlatan born at Palermo.

Ca·ho·ki·a (kahō'kēa) **Mounds.** Archaeological site of a group of pre-Colombian Indian mounds in SE. Illinois.

ca·hoots (kah ōōts') *n.pl.* (colloq.) **in** ~ (**with**), in collusion, league, questionable company (with).

Cai·a·phas (kā'afas, kī'-), **Joseph.** Jewish high priest from 18(?) to 36 A.D., president of the council that condemned Jesus Christ (Matt. 26).

cai·man, cay·man (kā'man) *ns.* (pl. **-mans**). Any of several tropical Amer. saurians (most of genus *Caiman*) resembling alligators and crocodiles.

Cain (kān). Eldest son of Adam and Eve, who became the first murderer when he killed his brother Abel out of jealousy (Gen. 4); murderer, fratricide; **raise** ~, (colloq.) make a disturbance, create trouble.

Cai·no·zo·ic (kīnozō'ĭk) = CENOZOIC.

ca·ique, ca·ïque (kah-ēk') *ns.* Light narrow rowboat used in the Middle East; small Levantine sailing vessel.

cairn, carn (kārn) *ns.* 1. Pyramid of stones as memorial, landmark, etc. 2. (also **Cairn terrier**) Small terrier (named from being used to hunt among cairns) with longish body, short legs, and shaggy coat, developed in Scotland.

Cai·ro (kī'rō). Capital city of Egypt, situated on the Nile about 100 miles (160 km) from its mouths. [Arab. *alkāhira* the victorious (conjuncture)]

cais·son (kā'son, -sŏn) *n.* 1. Ammunition chest or wagon. 2. Large watertight chamber used in laying foundations under water; buoyant chamber attached to side of ship engaged in raising wreck; boat-shaped vessel used as dock gate; ~ **disease**, disorder caused by working under high atmospheric pressure, in which bubbles of nitrogen released from body fluids if pressure is reduced too rapidly collect in joints and blood vessels; the bends.

cai·tiff (kă'tĭf) *n.* & *adj.* (archaic) Base, despicable (person); coward(ly).

caj·e·put, caj·u·put (kăj'eput, -pōōt) *ns.* E. Ind. tree of genus *Melaleuca*; (also ~ **oil**) aromatic oil obtained from this, used as stimulant, antispasmodic, and sudorific. [Malay *kayu* wood, *puteh* white]

ca·jole (kajōl') *v.t.* (**-joled, -jol·ing**). Persuade or soothe by flattery, deceit, etc. **ca·jol'er·y** *n.* (pl. **-er·ies**).

Ca·jun, Cai·jan (kā'jun) *ns.* (sometimes taken to be offensive) Louisiana native descended from French exiles from Acadia; their patois or dialect. [alteration of Acadian]

cake (kāk) *n.* 1. Flat, thin mass of fried or baked batter or dough. 2. Baked sweetened mixture of flour and other ingredients, as butter,

*Hunters of the spectacled **cayman** in the Amazon region have reduced its numbers to a point where the reptile is in danger of extinction. Its powerful jaws are equipped with conical teeth.*

*It is still possible to see a few **caiques** rigged for sail in the Levant, but many are now equipped with diesel engines and are in everyday service as ferries.*

eggs, spices, currants, raisins, etc. 3. Flattish compact mass of other food (as fish etc.) or of any compressed substance, as soap, wax, tobacco. 4. **cake′walk**, (orig.) a promenade of black American origin in which a prize of a cake was given for the most graceful and intricate steps; popular stage dance developed from these steps. **cake** *v.* (**caked, cak·ing**). Form into compact flattish mass.

Cal. *abbrev.* California.

cal. *abbrev.* Calorie, caliber, calendar.

cal·a·bash (kăl′*a*băsh) *n.* Any of various gourds or pumpkins, the shells of which are used for holding liquids etc.; the vessel made from such a shell; ~ **tree,** tropical Amer. and W. Ind. tree *Crescentia*, bearing a large oval or globular fruit with a hard shell.

cal·a·boose (kăl′*a*bo͞os, kăl*a*-bo͞os′) *n.* (colloq.) Prison.

Ca·la·bri·a (k*a*lā′brē*a*). Region in SW. Italy.

ca·la·di·um (k*a*lā′dē*u*m) *n.* Any of various widely cultivated tropical Amer. plants of the genus *Caladium*, esteemed for their ornamental leaves.

Ca·lais (kălā′, kăl′ā). Seaport in N. France, opposite Dover, England.

cal·a·man·co (kăl*a*măng′kō) *n.* (pl. **-cos**). Glossy Flemish woolen cloth, checkered on one side, much used in 18th c.

cal·a·man·der (kăl′*a*mănd*e*r) *n.* Extremely hard cabinet wood of Ceylon and India, from the tree (related to ebony) *Diospyros quaesita*.

cal·a·mine (kăl′*a*mīn, -mĭn) *n.* 1. Carbonate of zinc ($ZnCO_3$). 2. Pink powder containing zinc carbonate and ferric oxide, used in skin lotions and ointments.

*The South American **calceolaria** is grouped in the Scrofulariaceae family and is native to Central and South America. C. arachnoidea is illustrated.*

ca·lam·i·ty (k*a*lăm′ĭtē) *n.* (pl. **-ties**). Adversity, deep distress; grievous disaster; **C ~ Jane,** nickname of Martha Jane Burke (*née* Canary, ?1852–1903), Amer. frontierswoman and markswoman; applied to a prophet of disaster. **ca·lam′i·tous** *adj.* **ca·lam′i·tous·ly** *adv.*

cal·car·e·ous (kălkār′ē*u*s) *adj.* Of, containing, calcium carbonate or limestone.

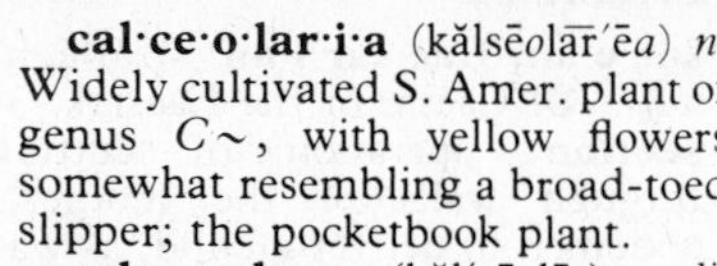

cal·ce·o·lar·i·a (kălsēolār′ē*a*) *n.* Widely cultivated S. Amer. plant of genus *C*~, with yellow flowers somewhat resembling a broad-toed slipper; the pocketbook plant.

cal·ce·o·late (kăl′sēolāt) *adj.* (bot.) Slipper-shaped.

cal·ci·cole (kăl′s*ĭ*kōl) *n.* Plant or animal inhabiting a soil with free calcium carbonate (or, in wider sense, soils rich in calcium).

cal·cic·o·lous (kălsĭk′*o*l*u*s) *adj.*

cal·cif·er·ous (kălsĭf′*e*r*u*s) *adj.* Yielding or containing chalk or calcium carbonate.

cal·ci·fy (kăl′sĭfī) *v.* (**-fied, -fy·ing**). Convert, be converted, into chalk or calcium carbonate; harden by deposit of calcium salts; petrify. **cal·ci·fi·ca·tion** (kălsĭfĭkā′sh*o*n) *n.*

cal·cine (kăl′sīn, -sĭn) *v.* (**-cined, -cin·ing**). Reduce to quicklime or friable substance by heating strongly; desiccate; refine by consuming grosser part; burn to ashes. **cal·ci·na·tion** (kălsĭnā′sh*o*n) *n.* Process of calcining.

cal·cite (kăl′sīt) *n.* (min.) Crystalline calcium carbonate, widely distributed in nature as marble, limestone, etc.

cal·ci·um (kăl′sē*u*m) *n.* (chem.) Silver-white malleable light metal, an element in the alkaline earth group (symbol Ca, at. no. 20, at. wt. 40.08), widely distributed in nature as limestone or chalk (~ **carbonate,** $CaCO_3$); ~ **carbide,** compound of calcium and carbon (CaC_2), produced by intense heating of limestone and coke in an electric

*This Jain temple is one of the glories of **Calcutta,** capital of W. Bengal and its most important manufacturing city and port. It stands on the Hooghly River 86 miles inland.*

*American sculptor **Alexander Calder** created the first mobiles. He also made stationary forms that he called stabiles. In this sculpture the two themes are mixed.*

*San Francisco is one of the largest cities in **California**. It lies on hilly coastland close to the San Andreas fault.*

furnace and yielding acetylene gas on treatment with water; ~ **hypochlorite**, chloride of lime or bleaching powder ($CaOCl_2$), used as disinfectant; ~ **oxide**, (CaO) quicklime.

calc·spar (kălk'spa̅r) *n.* (min.) Crystalline from of calcium carbonate (limestone).

cal·cu·la·ble (kăl'kyu*l*abel) *adj.* That may be reckoned, measured, computed, or relied upon. **cal·cu·la·bil·i·ty** (kălkyula-bĭl'ĭtē) *n.*

cal·cu·late (kăl'kyulāt) *v.* (**-lat·ed, -lat·ing**). Compute by figures; ascertain beforehand by exact reckoning; plan deliberately; (dial.) suppose, believe; (usu. pass.) arrange, adapt, *for*, *to*; **calculating machine**, machine that performs arithmetical processes. **cal'cu·lat·ed** *adj.* (esp.) Fit, suitable *to* do.

cal·cu·la·tion (kălkyulā'shon) *n.* (Result got by) calculation; forecast.

cal·cu·la·tor (kăl'kyulāter) *n.* (esp.) Set of tables for use in calculating; calculating machine.

cal·cu·lous (kăl'kyulus) *adj.* Of, suffering from, calculus or stone. [L., = small stone used in reckoning on abacus]

cal·cu·lus (kăl'kyulus) *n.* (pl. **-li** pr. -lī, **-lus·es**). 1. (med.) Stone, concretion in some part of the body. 2. (math.) Particular method of calculation, esp. DIFFERENTIAL and INTEGRAL calculus.

Cal·cut·ta (kălkŭt'a). City and port in India, capital of W. Bengal; **Black Hole of** ~: see BLACK *adj.*

Cal·der (kawl'der), **Alexander** (1898–1976). Amer. sculptor, famous for mobiles.

Cal·de·rón de la Bar·ca (kahl'-derŏn dĕla ba̅r'ka), **Pedro** (1600–1681). Spanish dramatist and poet, author of over 120 plays.

cal·dron (kawl'dron) = CAULDRON.

Cal·e·do·ni·a (kăledō'nēa). (poet. and rhet.) Scotland, the Scottish Highlands.

Cal·e·do·ni·an (kăledō'nēan) *adj.* Of Scotland; ~ **Canal**, 60-mile-long (96.6 km) ship canal from Inverness on the E. coast of Scotland to Fort William on the W. coast, connecting the North Sea with the Atlantic Ocean. **Caledonian** *n.* Native, inhabitant, of Scotland.

cal·en·dar (kăl'ender) *n.* 1. System by which the beginning, length, and subdivision of civil year is fixed, esp. the GREGORIAN ~; ~ **month**, one of the 12 months into which year is divided by calendar, as opp. to lunar MONTH; **Jewish** ~; see JEWISH. 2. Table(s) showing months, weeks and festivals, etc., of a given year or years. 3. Register, list, esp. of canonized saints, prisoners for trial, or documents chronologically arranged with summaries. **calendar** *v.t.* Register, enter in list; arrange, analyze, and index (documents).

cal·en·der (kăl'ender) *n.* Machine in which cloth, paper, etc., is pressed under rollers to glaze or smooth it. ~ *v.t.* Press in calender.

cal·ends (kăl'endz) *n. pl.* First day of month in Roman calendar.

cal·en·ture (kăl'encher, -choor) *n.* Tropical fever or delirium.

calf[1] (kăf, kahf) *n.* (pl. **calves** pr. kăvz, kahvz). 1. Young of bovine animal, esp. domestic cow, for first year; young of elephant, whale, etc.; **golden** ~: see Exod. 32; wealth as an object of worship; ~ **love**, immature romantic affection, puppy love. 2. Leather made from skin of domestic calf. 3. (naut.) Floating piece of ice detached from glacier, iceberg, or floe.

calf[2] (kăf, kahf) *n.* (pl. **calves** pr. kăvz, kahvz). Fleshy back part of shank of leg; part of stocking covering this.

Cal·gar·y (kăl'gerē). City in Alberta, Canada; center of cattle-raising region; site of annual ~ **stampede**, or rodeo.

Cal·houn (kălho͞on'), **John Caldwell** (1782–1850). Vice president of the U.S. under John Quincy Adams and Andrew Johnson, 1825–1832; as S. Carolina member of Congress, was a champion of slavery; U.S. Secretary of War, 1817–25, Secretary of State, 1844–1845.

Cal·i·ban (kăl'ĭbăn). Character in Shakespeare's *Tempest*, a "savage and deformed slave."

cal·i·ber, esp. Brit. **cal·i·bre** (kăl'iber) *ns.* 1. Internal diameter of gun or any tube; diameter of bullet or shell. 2. Degree of personal capacity or ability, or of merit or importance. [Arab. *qalib* mold]

cal·i·brate (kăl'ibrāt) *v.t.* (**-brat·ed, -brat·ing**). Find caliber of; calculate irregularities of (tube, gauge) before graduating; graduate (a gauge) make allowance for irregularities. **cal·i·bra·tion** (kălibrā'shon), **cal'i·bra·tor** *ns.*

cal·i·bre (kăl'iber) = CALIBER.

cal·i·co (kăl'ikō) *n.* (pl. **-coes, -cos**). Coarse cotton cloth usually printed with bright designs; (Brit.) plain white unprinted bleached or unbleached cotton cloth. ~ *adj.* Of, like calico; variegated, piebald, esp. ~ **cat.** [*Calicut*, town on Malabar coast]

Calif. *abbrev.* California.

Cal·i·for·nia (kălifo̅r'nya, -nēa). State on Pacific coast of U.S., admitted to the Union in 1850; capital, Sacramento; **Gulf of** ~, inlet of the Pacific Ocean between the Lower California peninsula and Mexico, also called the Sea of

Cortez. **Cal·i·for'nian** *adj.* & *n.*

cal·i·for·ni·um (kăl*i*fōr'nē*u*m) *n.* (chem.) Transuranic element; symbol Cf. at. no. 98, principal isotope at. wt. 244.

Ca·lig·u·la (k*a*lĭg'y*u*l*a*), **Gaius Caesar.** Roman emperor 37–41 A.D.; notorious for his cruelty and vices.

cal·i·pash (kăl'*i*păsh, kăl*i*păsh') *n.* Dull green gelatinous substance beneath a turtle's upper shell.

cal·i·pee (kăl'*i*pē, kăl*i*pē') *n.* Light yellow gelatinous substance inside a turtle's lower shell.

cal·i·per (kăl'*i*p*er*) *n.* (usu. pl.) 1. Compasses with bowed legs for measuring diameter of convex bodies, or with turned out points for measuring cavities. 2. (also ~ **brake**) Brake, esp. on bicycle, of two blocks worked through pivot to grip rim of wheel; brake of similar principle on automobile, in which two pads grip revolving disk. ~ *v.t.* Measure with calipers.

ca·liph (kā'lĭf, kăl'ĭf) *n.* (in certain Muslim countries) Chief civil and religious ruler, as successor of Muhammad. **ca·liph·ate** (kă'l*i*fāt, -fĭt, kăl'*i*-) *n.* [Arab. *ḵalīfa* successor]

cal·is·then·ics (kăl*i*sthĕn'ĭks) *n.pl.* Simple gymnastic exercises for health and general physical well-being.

calk (kawk) *n.* Sharp iron piece to prevent horseshoe or boot from slipping. ~ *v.t.* Provide with calk.

call (kawl) *v.* 1. Cry, shout, speak loudly; utter characteristic note; cry *out, to;* read *out* (names of those on list); name (suit as trumps, at cards); pay brief visit (*at* house, *on* person) in order to speak, deal, etc.; communicate by radio or telephone. 2. Summon; summon or nominate by divine authority into the Church. 3. Name, describe as; consider, regard as. 4. ~ **down**, reprimand; ~ **for**, order; demand; need; go and fetch; ~ **forth**, elicit; ~ **off** (a project), cancel it; ~ **on**, invoke, appeal to; ~ **out**, summon (troops) esp. to aid civil authorities; summon (workers) to strike; shout or utter loudly; ~ **up**, imagine; ring (on telephone); summon to serve in army etc. **call** *n.* 1. Shout, cry; special cry of bird etc., imitation of, instrument for imitating, this; signal on bugle etc. 2. Short formal or business visit. 3. Invitation, summons; duty, need, occasion; demand, claim. 4. Telephone conversation. 5. Demand for money, esp. for unpaid capital from company shareholders; (Stock Exch.) option of claiming stock at given date. 6. ~ **girl**, prostitute accepting appointments by telephone; ~ **name**, name adopted by a citizens' band radio operator for use in transmissions; ~ **sign**, identifying signal of a radio station.

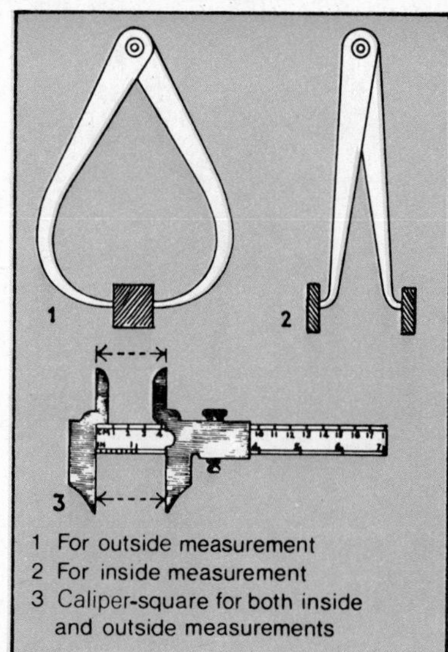

1
2
3
1 For outside measurement
2 For inside measurement
3 Caliper-square for both inside and outside measurements

Calipers, for measuring the width of an object, are of various designs. 1. Calipers for outside measurement. 2. Calipers for inside measurement. 3. Calibrated calipers for both measurements.

cal·la (kăl'*a*) *n.* 1. (also ~ **lily**) Tropical plant (*Zantedeschia aethiopica*), widely cultivated indoors for its pure white showy spathe and yellow spadix. 2. Aquatic plant (genus *C*~) of N. Europe and eastern N. America.

call·er (kaw'l*er*) *n.* (esp.) Person paying a call or visit; person who initiates telephone call.

cal·lig·ra·phy (k*a*lĭg'r*a*fē) *n.* (Art of) beautiful handwriting. **cal·lig'ra·pher, cal·lig'ra·phist** *ns.* **cal·li·graph·ic** (kăl*i*grăf'ĭk) *adj.*

call·ing (kaw'lĭng) *n.* (esp.) Occupation, profession, trade; persons following a particular occupation; ~ **card**, small card bearing a person's name, address, etc., used for social or business purposes.

Cal·li·o·pe (k*a*lī'*o*pē). (Gk. and Rom. myth.) Muse of eloquence and epic poetry. [Gk. *kalliope* beautiful voiced]

cal·li·o·pe (k*a*lī'*o*pē, kăl'ēōp) *n.* Set of steam whistles producing musical notes, played by a keyboard like that of an organ.

cal·li·per (kăl'*i*p*er*) = CALIPER.

Cal·lis·the·nes (k*a*lĭs'th*e*nēz). 4th c. B.C. Greek philosopher and chronicler of Alexander the Great.

Cal·lis·to (k*a*lĭs'tō). 1. (Gk. myth.) Daughter of Lycaon, loved by Zeus and punished for her unchastity by being turned into a bear; she and her son were transformed into constellations. 2. (astron.) Constellation URSA Major.

cal·los·i·ty (k*a*lŏs'ĭtē) *n.* (pl. **-ties**). Abnormal hardness and thickness of skin; hardened insensible part, lump.

cal·lous (kăl'*u*s) *adj.* 1. Hardened, hard (of parts of skin). 2. Unfeeling, insensible. **cal'lous·ly** *adv.* **cal'lous·ness** *n.*

cal·low (kăl'ō) *adj.* 1. Unfledged; downy like young birds. 2. Raw, inexperienced. **cal'low·ness** *n.*

cal·lus (kăl'*u*s) *n.* (pl. **-lus·es**). Thickened part of skin or soft tissue; bony material formed while bone fracture heals; (bot.) new tissue, usu. more or less corky, covering a wound.

calm (kahm) *n.* Stillness, serenity; windless period. ~ *adj.* Tranquil, quiet; windless; undisturbed; unabashed, impudent. **calm'ly** *adv.* **calm'ness** *n.* **calm** *v.* Make calm; pacify; ~ **down**, become calm.

cal·o·mel (kăl'*o*mĕl, -m*e*l) *n.* Mercurous chloride (HgCl), a heavy white powder used as a purgative and fungicide.

cal·o·rie (kăl'*o*rē) *n.* 1. (also **kilogram** or **large** ~) Standard unit of heat, amount required to raise the temperature of one kilogram (one liter) of water one degree centigrade; unit for measuring the heat and other energy produced by the metabolism of food. 2. (also **gram** or **small** ~) Amount of heat required to raise one gram (one cu. cm) of water one degree centigrade.

ca·lor·ic (k*a*lōr'ĭk, -lăr'-) *adj.* Of calories; of heat.

cal·o·rif·ic (kăl*o*rĭf'ĭk) *adj.* Of, producing heat.

cal·o·rim·e·ter (kăl*o*rĭm'*e*t*er*) *n.* Apparatus for measuring heat. **cal·o·ri·met·ric** (kăl*o*rĭmĕt'rĭk), **cal·o·ri·met'ri·cal** *adjs.* **cal·o·ri·met'ri·cal·ly** *adj.*

cal·trop (kăl'tr*o*p) *n.* 1. (hist.) 4-spiked iron ball thrown on ground to impede cavalry horses. 2. of various plants that have spiny burs or bracts.

cal·u·met (kăl'y*u*mĕt, kăly*u*mĕt') *n.* Long-stemmed ornamental pipe used by N. Amer. Indians for ceremonial purposes, esp. used as symbol of peace or friendship (the *peace pipe*).

ca·lum·ni·ate (k*a*lŭm'nēāt) *v.t.* (**-at·ed, -at·ing**). Slander. **ca·lum·ni·a·tion** (k*a*lŭmnēā'sh*o*n) *n.*

cal·um·ny (kăl'*u*mnē) *n.* (pl. **-nies**). Malicious misrepresentation; false report; slander.

Cal·va·ry (kăl'v*e*rē). Hill near Jerusalem on which Jesus Christ was crucified. [L. *calvaria* skull, transl. of GOLGOTHA in Matt. 27]

calve (kăv, kahv) *v.i.* (**calved, calv·ing**). Give birth to calf; (of glacier, iceberg, etc.) throw off masses of ice.

*The site of **Calvary** is uncertain, but the scholar Charles Gordon in the 19th century proposed a low hill outside the Damascus Gate of Jerusalem. The painting of Jesus crucified on Calvary is by Bramantino.*

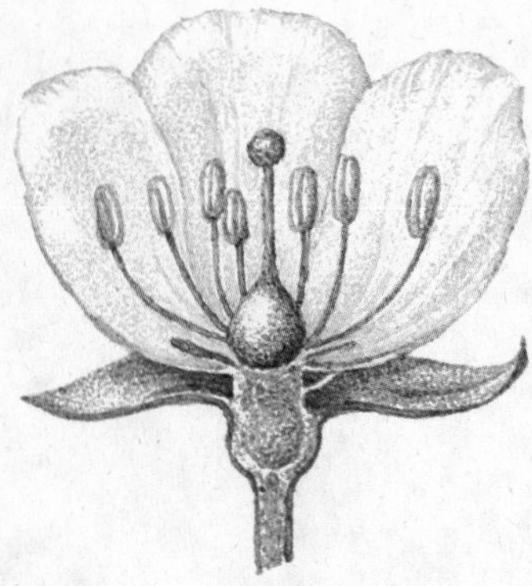

The leaf-like protective parts of a flower are collectively a ***calyx.*** *This consists of modified petals, usually green but in lilies the same color as the flower itself.*

A few Bactrian ***camels*** *(foreground) are found wild in Turkestan and Mongolia. Bactrian camels are superb beasts for the desert. Each can carry about 800 lbs for nearly 30 miles in a day. The Arabian camel (background) is a riding camel valued for its speed and endurance.*

Cal·vin (kăl′vĭn), **John** (1509–1564). French theologian and reformer; settled in Geneva, 1536; wrote *Institutes of the Christian Religion* (1535), in which he expounded his doctrine of original sin, of predestination and election; his dogma is held by the continental Reformed Churches and forms the basis of Scottish Presbyterianism.

Cal·vin·ism (kăl′vinĭzem) *n.* Tenets and doctrines of CALVIN and his followers and of the Calvinistic Churches, whose distinguishing doctrines, usu. called **the five points of ~**, are election or predestination, limited atonement, total depravity, irresistibility of grace, and the perseverance of the saints. **Cal′vin·ist** *n.* & *adj.* Follower of Calvin, adherent of Calvinism. **Cal·vin·is·tic** (kălvinĭs′tĭk), **Cal·vin·is′ti·cal** *adjs.* Pertaining to, characteristic of, Calvinism.

Ca·lyp·so (kalĭp′sō). (Gk. legend) In the *Odyssey*, a nymph who kept ODYSSEUS seven years on her island, Ogygia.

ca·lyp·so (kalĭp′sō) *n.* (pl. **-sos**). Spontaneous topical, often humorous, W. Ind.. song or chant with African rhythm.

ca·lyp·tra (kalĭp′tra) *n.* (bot.) Hood or cover, esp. hood of spore case in mosses. [Gk. *kaluptra* veil]

ca·lyx (kālĭks, kăl′ĭks) *n.* (pl. **ca·lyx·es, cal·y·ces** pr. kăl′isēz, kā′li-). (bot.) Whorl of floral parts, often leaflike, forming outer protective envelope of flower.

cam (kăm) *n.* Portion of revolving shaft or wheel bearing against, and shaped so as to impart a particular type of motion to, a lever or other movable part of a machine; **cam′shaft**, shaft bearing cam(s).

ca·ma·ra·de·rie (kahmarah′-derē) *n.* Intimacy, mutual trust, and sociability of comrades. [Fr.]

cam·ber (kăm′ber) *n.* Slight convexity of upper surface, arched form (of road, ship's deck, airplane wing, etc.); setting of automobile wheels closer together at the bottom than at the top. ~ *v.* Have, construct with, camber.

Cam·ber·well (kăm′berwĕl, -wel) **beauty.** Species of butterfly (*Nymphalis antiopa*). [*Camberwell*, borough of London]

cam·bi·um (kăm′bēum) *n.* (bot.) Layer of cells from which annual growth of woody tissue and bark takes place.

Cam·bo·di·a (kămbō′dēa, -bōd′ya): see KAMPUCHEA.

Cam·bri·a (kām′brēa). Ancient or poetic name for Wales. **Cam′-bri·an** *adj.* & *n.* 1. Welsh(man). 2. (geol.) (Of) the earliest period or system of the Paleozoic era. [Latinized f. *Cymry* Welshman]

cam·bric (kām′brĭk) *n.* Fine white linen or cotton fabric of plain weave. [*Kamerijk*, Fl. name of *Cambrai*, where linen cambric was made]

Cam·bridge[1] (kām′brĭj). City in Cambridgeshire on River Cam, England, about 50 miles (80.5 km) NE. of London; site of Cambridge University, which was first organized in 1209 and recognized by a royal writ in 1230.

Cam·bridge[2] (kām′brĭj). City in Massachusetts on the Charles River opposite Boston; site of Harvard University, founded in 1636.

cam·el (kăm′el) *n.* 1. Large ruminant quadruped of genus *Camelus* with long neck, cushioned feet, and either two humps (**Bactrian** ~) or one (**dromedary** ~) which store food, closely related to the llama and alpaca, used as beast of burden in arid regions; **~'s hair, cam′elhair**, hair of this animal, woven into a soft, warm, lightweight, usu. long-piled fabric; imitation of this fabric, usu. fawn or light tan. **camel's-hair brush**, artist's paintbrush usu. made of squirrel hair. 2. Float for increasing buoyancy of ship or raising sunken ship. 3. Shade of fawn.

ca·mel·lia (kamēl′ya, -mē′lēa) *n.* Flowering evergreen shrub of genus *C*~ of the tea family, chiefly native of China and Japan; also called japonica. [Joseph *Kamel* (1661–1706), Moravian Jesuit who described botany of island of Luzon in the Philippines]

ca·mel·o·pard (kamĕl′opărd) *n.* (archaic) Giraffe.

Cam·e·lot (kăm′elŏt). In Arthurian legend, the place where King Arthur held his court, stated by Malory to be Winchester.

Cam·em·bert (kăm′embār) *n.* Rich soft dessert cheese made near the village of Camembert in Normandy; cheese of similar type.

cam·e·o (kăm′ēō) *n.* (pl. **cam·e·os**). 1. Small piece of relief carving in stone (onyx, agate, etc.), freq. with two layers of different colors, the lower of which serves as background. 2. (fig.) Short literary sketch etc., small well-defined acting part.

cam·er·a (kăm′era, kăm′ra) *n.* Apparatus for taking photographs, consisting essentially of a box holding at one end a plate or film which is sensitized so as to retain the image projected through a lens at the other; (television) apparatus which forms the image and converts it into electrical impulses. **cam′eraman** *n.* (esp.) One who operates a motion-picture camera. [L., = "vaulted room"]

cam·er·lin·go (kămerlĭng′gō) *n.* (pl. **-gos**). The cardinal who serves as the Pope's chamberlain and financial secretary, highest officer

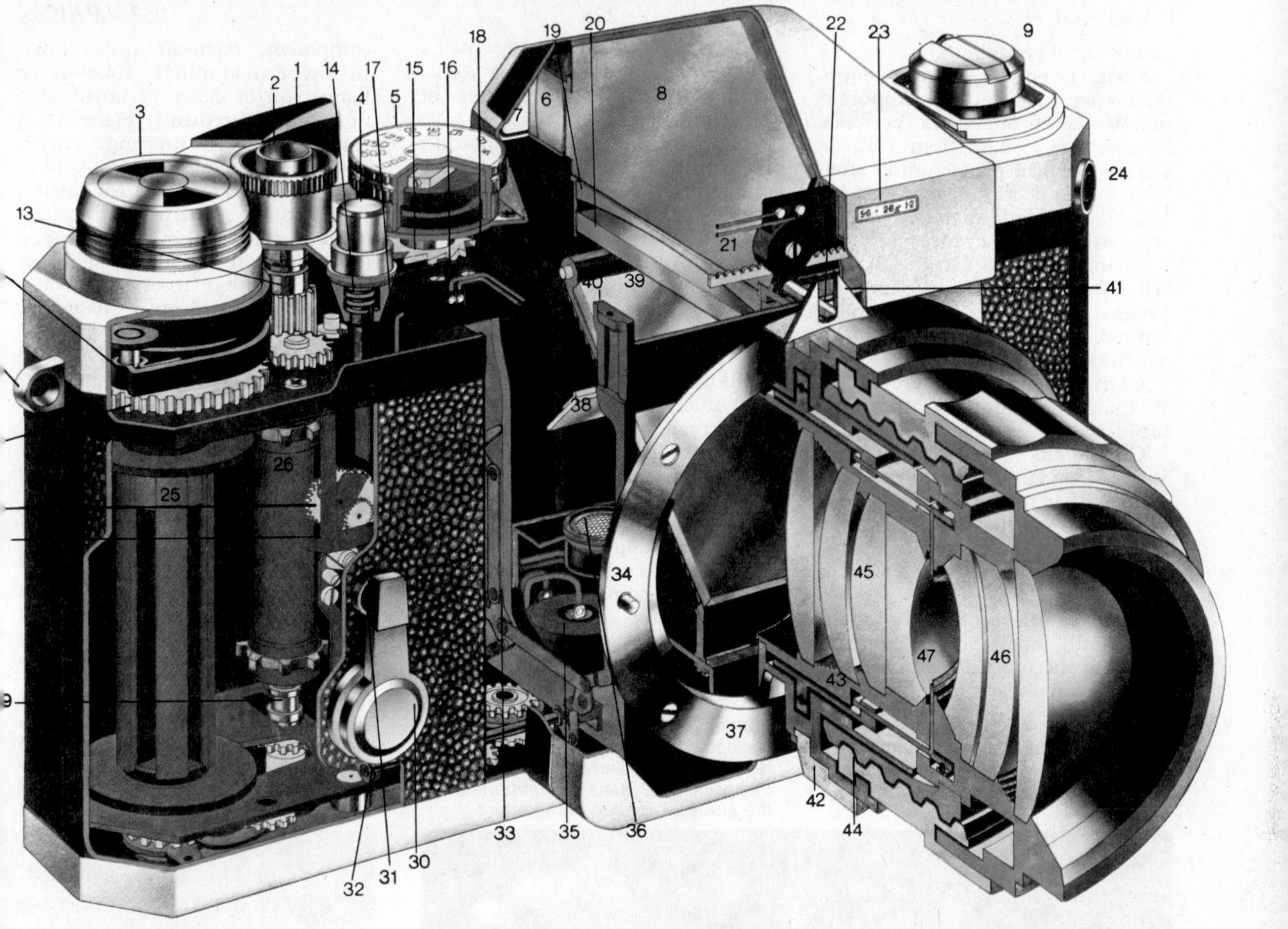

The highly developed mechanism of a modern ***camera*** *offers great advantages of speed and variety of adjustment over the ponderous cameras of the early days of photography. But photographers still depend on delicate control of the effects of light on silver compounds to produce a picture. The camera has proved its worth in recording memorable events.*

1. rewind lever
2. shutter release button
3. frame counter
4. depth of field preview button
5. shutter speed dial
6. eyepiece optics
7. viewfinder
8. pentaprism
9. rewind lever
10. strap lug
11. main spring
12. film transport gear train
13. shutter release axle
14. return spring
15. shutter speed ratchet
16. meter
17. meter inputs
18. meter inputs
19. field lens
20. focusing screen
21. diaphragm variable resistance
22. coupling prong
23. max. aperture setting (here f.2)
24. synchronization coupling
25. film take-up spool
26. filmtransport sprocket
27. self timer movement
28. self timer escape lever
29. shutter release lever
30. self timer lever
31. self timer release button
32. diaphragm stop-down linkage
33. diaphragm stop-down linkage
34. diaphragm stop-down pin
35. mallory cell
36. cadmium disulphide (CDS) cell
37. lens mounting ring
38. CDS incident light 45 mirror
39. main reflex mirror
40. main reflex mirror axle
41. diaphragm coupling
42. diaphragm ring
43. lens mounting
44. focusing ring
45. rear lens group (4 elements, 3 groups)
46. front lens group (3 elements, 3 groups)
47. iris diaphragm

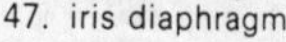

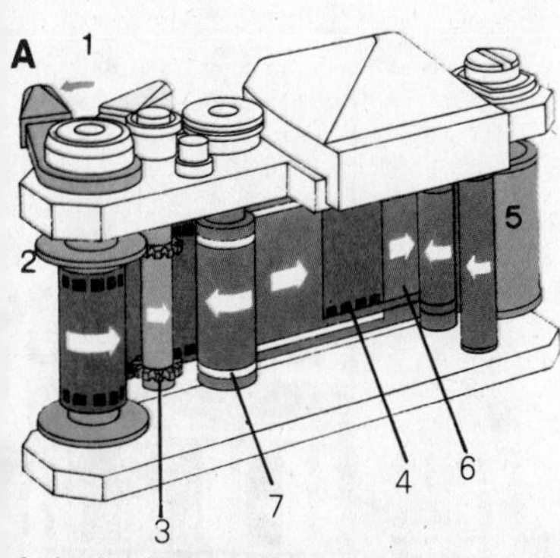

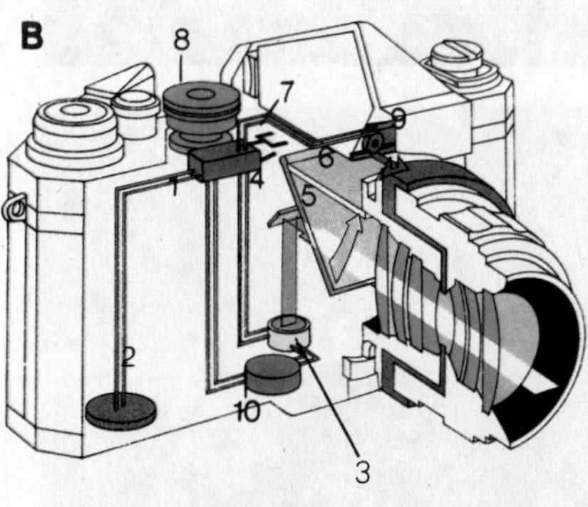

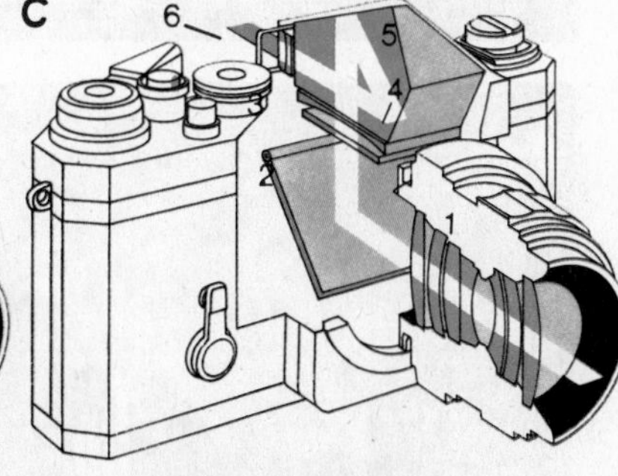

A. In this film transport and shutter system the film is shown dark green, the transport in light green, and the shutter blinds in dark blue and brown. 1. Shutter-cocking lever and film wind in wound-on position. 2. Film take-up spool. 3. Transport sprocket. 4. Film. 5. Film cassette. 6. First shutter blind. 7. Second shutter blind.

B. On an SLR, a 'match needle' through the lens light-metering system. 1. Meter. 2. Setting for the meter in relation to the film speed scale. 3. Photocell reacts to light to move the needle. 4. Mirror reflecting light to the photocell. 5. A semi-opaque mirror through which light reaches 4. 6. The same as 5 but shown retracted. 7. The indicator needle seen through the viewfinder. 8. Shutter speed dial controls the centering of the needle in a claw, and modifies the aperture of the lens. 9. Variable resistor transmits the adjustment of 8 to the lens. 10. Mercury battery to power the system.

C. The reflex viewing system. 1. The parts of the camera lens. 2. Reflex mirror. 3. Focusing screen. 4. Field lens. 5. Pentaprism. 6. Eyepiece.

in the papal household.

Cam·e·roun, Cam·e·roon (kămerōōn′, kămrōōn′). Republic on W. coast of Africa between Nigeria and Congo; from 1884 to 1916 a German protectorate; after World War I administered under League of Nations (later U.N.) trusteeship by France (*French Cameroons*) and Great Britain (*British Cameroons*); became a Federal Republic in 1960–1, and a United Republic in 1972; capital, Yaoundé.

cam·i·sole (kăm′ĭsōl) *n.* Woman's underbodice, often embroidered or trimmed with lace.

Cam·o·ëns (kăm′ōĕns), **Luiz Vaz de** (1524–80). Portuguese poet, author of the "Lusiads," an epic poem on the descendants of Lusus, the legendary hero of Portugal, and on the exploits of Vasco da GAMA.

cam·o·mile, cham·o·mile (kăm′omīl, -mēl) *ns.* Aromatic creeping herb (*Anthemis nobilis*) with downy leaves and yellow or white daisy-like flowers of which a tea is made and used as a tonic, shampoo, etc.; ~ **tea**, brew of camomile flowers.

Ca·mor·ra (kamōr′a, -mār′a). In the 19th c., a secret society practicing violence and extortion in Naples and Neapolitan cities. **Ca·mor′rist** *n.*

cam·ou·flage (kăm′oflahzh) *n.* Disguising, disguise, of objects used in war, as guns, ships, factories, etc., by means of boughs, obscuring outlines by netting and paint of various colors, etc.; deception of any kind whereby an object is concealed or made to look like something else. ~ *v.t.* (**-flaged, -flag·ing**). Conceal by or as by camouflage.

camp[1] (kămp) *n.* 1. Place where troops are lodged in tents etc. or received for training. 2. Temporary quarters of nomads, gypsies, travelers; (persons) camping out. 3. (fig.) Body of adherents. 4. ~ **chair**, portable folding chair; **camp′fire**, fire in camp or encampment, open-air fire; **camp follower**, nonmilitary follower or hanger-on of camp or army (also fig.); **camp′ground**, place for a camp or camp meeting; **camp meeting**, religious meeting held in open air or in a tent and usu. lasting several days. **camp** *v.* Encamp, lodge in camp; (also ~ **out**) lodge in tent or in the open, take up quarters; station (troops) in camp.

camp[2] (kămp) *adj.* (slang) 1. Affected, outlandish. 2. Homosexual, effeminate. ~ *v.* (slang) (also ~ **it up**) Behave, do, in a camp way.

Cam·pa·gna (kahmpahn′ya). Rich level district of Italy SE. of river Tiber, extending from the sea on the W. to the Sabine Hills.

cam·paign (kămpān′) *n.* 1. Series of military operations in a definite theater or with one objective or constituting the whole or a distinct part of a war. 2. Organized course of action, esp. in politics, as before an election etc. ~*v.i.* Serve in a campaign. **cam·paign′er** *n.*

*Below: The stick insect in naturally **camouflaged** by its color, that matches the privet leaves on which it feeds, and by its shape that imitates the privet stems.*

*Bottom: The ruins of Pompeii, an ancient city of Italy, in the **Campania** region, a few miles south of Mt. Vesuvius. The ruins are important for the study of Roman architecture.*

*Below: In St. Mark's Square in Venice stands the great **campanile** that is the focal point of the old city. Rebuilt early this century after it had collapsed, it stands 320 ft. high.*

Cam·pa·ni·a (kămpā'nēa). SW. region of Italy. **Cam·pa'ni·an** *adj.* & *n.*

cam·pa·ni·le (kămpanē'lē) *n.* (pl. **-ni·les, -ni·li** pr. -nē'lē). Bell tower, esp. one detached from main building.

cam·pa·nol·o·gy (kămpanŏl'ojē) *n.* The subject of bells (casting, ringing, etc.). **cam·pa·nol'o·gist, cam·pa·nol'o·ger** *ns.*

cam·pan·u·la (kămpăn'yula) *n.* Herbaceous plant of genus *C*~, with bell-shaped, usu. blue or white, flowers.

Camp·bell (kăm'bel), **Mrs. Patrick** (1867–1940). Original name, Beatrice Stella Tanner; English stage actress; appeared in *The Second Mrs. Tanqueray*, *Hedda Gabler*, *Pygmalion*; famous for her correspondence with George Bernard Shaw.

camp·er (kăm'per) *n.* Trucklike vehicle outfitted as living quarters for camping or long excursions.

cam·phor (kăm'fer) *n.* Translucent waxy crystalline substance with strong characteristic smell and bitter taste, obtained from a species of laurel growing in Japan, China, etc., also made synthetically from turpentine; used in pharmacy, as insect repellent, and in manufacture of film, plastics, explosives, etc. **cam·phor·ic** (kămfŏr'ĭk, -får'-) *adj.* **cam·phor·ate** (kăm'forāt) *v.t.* (**-rat·ed, -rat·ing**). Impregnate or treat with camphor.

cam·pi·on (kăm'pēon) *n.* Any of various plants of genus *Lychnis*, with red, pink, or white flowers.

Cam·pi·on (kăm'pēon), **Thomas** (1567–1620). English physician, poet, and musician.

Cam·po·bel·lo (kămpobĕl'ō). Island off the SW. coast of New Brunswick, Canada; summer home of President Franklin D. Roosevelt.

cam·pus (kăm'pus) *n.* Grounds of a college or university, open space between or around the buildings; (transf.) college or university life or people. [L., = "field"]

Cam·ranh (kăm'rahn) **Bay.** Arm of the South China Sea off the SE. coast of Vietnam.

Ca·mus (kămü'), **Albert** (1913–1960). French Existentialist novelist and playwright; one of the leaders of the French Resistance in World War II; author of *The Plague*, *The Stranger*, etc.; won Nobel Prize for literature, 1957.

can[1] (kăn) *n.* Small sealed metal container, usu. tin-clad steel or aluminum, in which food or drink is preserved; ~ **of worms**, complex situation or problem. **can** *v.t.* (**canned, can·ning**). Preserve in a can; (slang) dismiss from a job. **canned** *adj.* Preserved in a can; (slang, of music etc.) recorded; (slang) dismissed from one's job.

can[2] (kăn, unstressed kan) *v. auxil.* (neg. **can·not** contraction **can't** (kănt, kahnt); past t. and conditional **could** (kŏŏd); defective parts supplied from *be able to*). Be able to; have the right to; (colloq.) be permitted to, may.

Can. *abbrev.* Canada.

Ca·naan (kā'nan). Biblical name of esp. western part of region later called Palestine, promised by God to Abraham (Gen. 12). **Ca'naan·ite** *adj.* & *n.*

Can·a·da (kăn'ada). Member State of the British Commonwealth, occupying the N. half of the N. Amer. continent (with the exception of Alaska); the second largest country in the world; discovered by Cabot in 1497, occupied by the French in 1534, and ceded to Gt. Britain in 1763; the provinces of Canada were united as the Dominion of Canada in 1867; capital, Ottawa; ~ **balsam**, oleoresin obtained from a pine (*Abies balsamea*), used for mounting microscope slides; ~ **goose**, wild goose (*Branta canadensis*) of N. America; ~ **jay**, bold, noisy, gray jay (*Perisoreus canadensis*) of north-

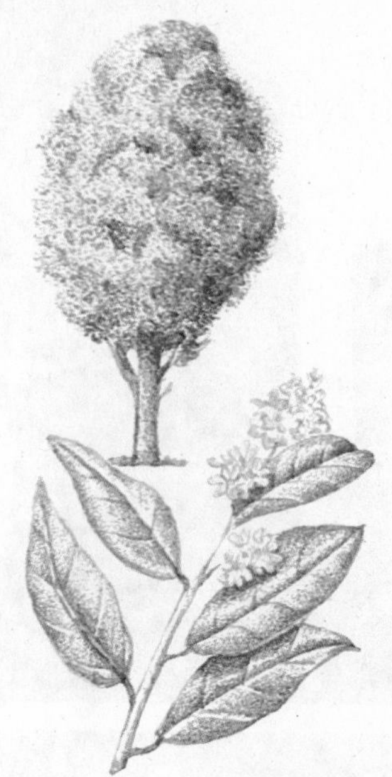

The **camphor** *tree (Cinnamomum camphor) is native to Japan. Natural camphor can be produced by using the wood in a special distillation process.*

Above: There are several species of **campion.** *One of the same family is the gillyflower with which the Elizabethans used to flavor their wine and beer.*

Top: Named after their resemblance to bells, the flowers of the Campanulaceae family include the bluebell and **Campanula** *portenschlagiana, illustrated here.*

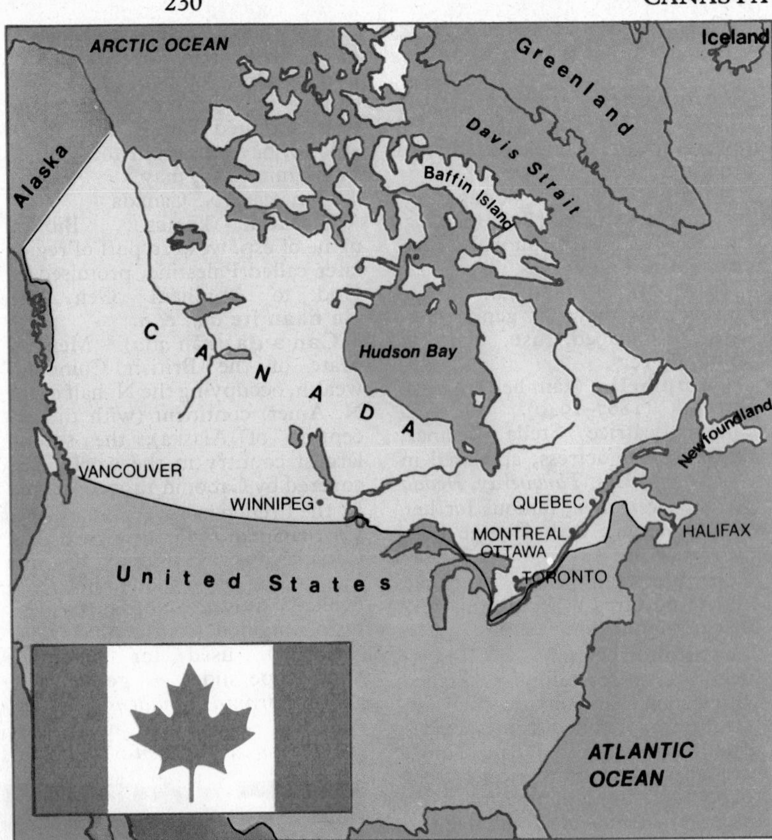

Canada covers an area of about 3,850,000 sq. miles. Top right: The map and the maple leaf flag. Top left: The City Hall, Toronto. The St. Lawrence Seaway, linking the Great Lakes with the sea, has increased Toronto's importance as a commercial and wholesale center of Canada. Above: The province of Ontario has outstanding scenery, including the Kakabeka Falls. Right: Combines harvest Canada's prairie wheat.

ern N. America. **Ca·na·di·an** (k*a*nā′dē*a*n) *adj.* & *n.*

Ca·na·di·an (k*a*nā′dē*a*n) **Falls.** Part of Niagara Falls separated from the American Falls by Goat Island; also called "Horseshoe Falls"; **Canadian River**, river flowing from N. New Mexico to the Arkansas River.

ca·naille (k*a*nāl′, -nī′) *n.* Rabble. [Fr.]

ca·nal (k*a*năl′) *n.* 1. Duct in plant or animal body for food, liquid, air, etc. 2. Artificial waterway for inland navigation or for irrigation. 3. (astron.) One of the faint markings resembling straight lines observed on the surface of the planet Mars.

Ca·na·let·to (kăn*a*lĕt′ō), **Giovanni Antonio Canal** (1697–1768). Venetian painter and etcher, known esp. for his paintings of buildings and views of Venice.

ca·nal·ize (k*a*năl′īz, kăn′*a*līz) *v.t.* (**-ized, -iz·ing**). 1. Furnish with canals; convert (river) into canal by straightening course, making locks, etc. 2. Direct (energies, wealth, etc.) into a particular course or channel. **ca·nal·i·za·tion** (k*a*nălīz-ā′sh*o*n) *n.*

Can·an·dai·gua (kăn*a*ndā′gw*a*), **Lake.** One of the Finger Lakes in W. New York State.

can·a·pé (kăn′*a*pē, -pā) *n.* A cracker or small piece of bread, toast, or pastry on which food is served as an appetizer. [Fr.]

ca·nard (k*a*nârd′, -nār′) *n.* False or unfounded story, slanderous rumor. [Fr., = "duck," "false report"]

Ca·nar·y (k*a*nār′ē). Island (**Grand ~**, *Gran Canaria*) off NW. coast of Africa; **~ Islands, Canaries**, the group to which it belongs, in Spanish possession. [L. *canaria* (*insula*) (isle) of dogs]

ca·nar·y (k*a*nār′ē) *n.* (pl. **-nar·ies**). 1. Sweet white wine from the Canary Islands, resembling sherry. 2. Songbird (*Serinus canarius*), orig. brought from the Canary Islands and commonly kept in captivity; the wild canary, or serin, is greenish above and yellow below, but the cage breed is mainly yellow (**~ yellow**).

ca·nas·ta (k*a*năs′t*a*) *n.* Card game for two to six persons, played with two standard 52-card packs and four jokers, related to rummy;

meld of seven cards. [prob. f. Span. *canastra* "basket" (from the many cards, or "basketful" of cards, used) ult. f. Gk. *kanastron*]

Ca·nav·er·al (kanăv'eral), **Cape.** Cape on E. central coast of Florida, location of John F. Kennedy Space Center and Patrick Air Force Base.

Can·ber·ra (kăn'běra, -bera). Capital of the Commonwealth of Australia, in SE. New South Wales.

can·can (kăn'kăn) *n.* High-kicking dance performed by women. [Fr.]

can·cel (kăn'sel) *v.* (**-celed, -cel·ing; -celled, -cel·ling**). Obliterate, annul, make void, countermand; neutralize, balance, make up for; (print.) delete, omit; (arith. etc.) strike out (same factor) from numerator and denominator, from two sides of equation, etc.; (of items) neutralize or balance each other (also ~ **out**). **can·cel·la·tion** (kănselā'shon) *n.* (print.) Deletion, omission.

Can·cer (kăn'ser). The Crab, a constellation; 4th sign (♋) of the zodiac, which the sun enters at the summer solstice; **Tropic of ~**, northern TROPIC.

can·cer (kăn'ser) *n.* Malignant tumor; (fig.) a continuously increasing or spreading evil. **can'cer·ous** *adj.* [L., = "crab," f. resemblance of swollen veins around tumor to crab's limbs]

can·croid (kang'kroid) *adj.* Crablike; like cancer. ~ *n.* A skin cancer.

can·de·la (kăndē'la) *n.* (abbr. cd) Unit of luminous intensity, = CANDLE, def. 2.

can·de·la·brum (kăndelah'brum, -lăb'rum, -lā'brum) *n.* (pl. **-bra** pr. -bra, **-brums**). Large, branched candlestick.

can·des·cence (kănděs'ens) *n.* Bright glow, as of white-hot metal. **can·des'cent** *adj.* Glowing (as) with white heat.

can·did (kăn'dĭd) *adj.* Unbiased; not censorious; frank; (photog.) not posed; ~ **camera**, small camera for taking unposed or informal snapshots. **can'did·ly** *adv.* **can'did·ness** *n.* [L. *candidus* white]

can·di·date (kăn'dĭdāt, -dĭt) *n.* One who seeks or is put forward for election or for appointment to an office or honor; one who undergoes a test or examination; one thought likely to gain any position. **can·di·da·cy** (kăn'dĭdasē) *n.* [L. *candidatus* one aspiring to an office (who was clothed in white toga)]

Can·dide (kăndēd'). Hero of a satirical novel by Voltaire, whose travels and misadventures mock the optimistic philosophy that "all is for the best in this best of all possible worlds"; hence, any innocent optimist.

can·died (kăn'dēd) *adj.*: see CANDY; (esp.) preserved by impregnating and coating with sugar.

can·dle (kăn'del) *n.* 1. Cylinder of wax, tallow, etc., enclosing wick, for giving light. 2. Unit of luminous intensity equal to $\frac{1}{60}$ of the luminous intensity of one sq. cm. of a black body heated to 1773.5°C; candlepower; **can'dlelight**, light of candles; any artificial light; **can'dlepower**, illuminating power of electric light etc., formerly measured in terms of the light of a standard candle; **can'dlestick**, holder for candle(s); **can'dlewick**, wick of a candle; (material with raised usu. tufted pattern in) thick soft yarn.

Can·dle·mas (kăn'delmas, -măs) *n.* The religious festival in honor of the presentation of the infant Jesus in the temple, Feb. 2. [Mass at which candles for the coming year are blessed]

can·dor, Brit. **can·dour** (kăn'der) *ns.* Fairness, impartiality; openness, frankness.

can·dy (kăn'dē) *n.* (pl. **-dies**). Confection or food with sugar or other sweeteners, flavored or filled with or partly composed of chocolate, fruit, peppermint, etc.; a small shaped piece of this; ~ **stripe,**

Venetian scene, one of many of the city painted by Giovanni Antonio Canal (1677–1768), commonly known as ***Canaletto.*** *English visitors to Venice were his foremost patrons.*

Planned by Walter Burley Griffin of Chicago, ***Canberra,*** *Australia's capital city, was founded in 1913. The Australian parliament first met there in 1927. Previously, the Australian capital had been Melbourne.*

-striped, pattern(ed) in alternate stripes of white and color; ~ **striper**, (slang) volunteer hospital worker, usu. young girl (from striped uniforms worn by these volunteers). **candy** *v.* (**-died, -dy·ing**). Preserve, cook, coat with sugar or syrup; form into crystals. [Fr. *sucre candi*, f. Arab.-Pers. *qand* crystallized sugar cane juice, ult. f. Sansk. *khaṇd* broken crystallized sugar]

can·dy·tuft (kăn′dētŭft) *n.* Herbaceous cruciferous plant of genus *Iberis*, with white, pink, or purple flowers in flat corymbs or tufts. [*Candia* the island of Crete]

cane (kān) *n.* Hollow, jointed stem of reeds and grasses, or solid stem of slender palms; walking stick; rod for flogging; stem of raspberry and similar plants; **cane′brake**, tract of land thickly overgrown with canes; **cane sugar**, sugar obtained from the sugar cane as contrasted with beet sugar. **cane** *v.t.* (**caned, can·ing**). Beat with cane; fit (seat of chair) with (braided) cane. **can′ing** *n.*

ca·nine (kā′nīn) *adj.* Of, as of, a dog or dogs; ~ **tooth**, one of the four strong pointed teeth between incisors and molars, eyetooth. **canine** *n.* Canine tooth.

can·is·ter (kăn′ĭst*er*) *n.* Small case or box, usu. of metal, for keeping dry foods, shot, etc. [Gk. *kanastron* wicker basket]

can·ker (kăng′k*er*) *n.* 1. Ulcerous sore (also ~ **sore**) of the mouth and lips; ulcerous disease of animals; disease of fruit trees; (also **can′kerworm**) caterpillar of a moth destroying leaves or buds. 2. Corrupting influence. **can′ker·-ous** *adj.* **canker** *v.t.* Consume with canker; infect, corrupt. [as CANCER]

can·na (kăn′*a*) *n.* Tropical plant of genus *C*~ now cultivated widely, with bright yellow, red, or orange flowers and ornamental foliage.

can·na·bis (kăn′*a*bĭs, k*a*nah′-) *n.* Hemp. esp. *C*~ *sativa* or *C. indica*; preparation of hemp plant as drug; see MARIJUANA, HASHISH.

Can·nae (kăn′ē). (It. *Canne*) Ancient town in SE. Italy, scene of a defeat of the Romans by Hannibal in the Second Punic War, in 216 B.C.

can·nel (kăn′*e*l) *n.* (also ~ **coal**) Coal with high gas content which burns with smoky flame and can be lit by a match.

Cannes (kăn, kănz). Mediterranean seaport and resort town in SE. France; site of annual film festival.

can·ni·bal (kăn′ĭb*a*l) *n.* Person who eats human flesh; animal that eats its own species. ~ *adj.* Of, having, these habits. **can′ni·bal·-ism** *n.* **can·ni·bal·is·tic** (kănĭbalĭs′tĭk) *adj.* [Span. *Canibales*, variant form of *Caribs*]

can·ni·bal·ize (kăn′ĭb*a*līz) *v.t.* (**-ized, -iz·ing**). Take parts from (machine) as spares for others.

can·ni·kin (kăn′*i*kĭn) *n.* Small can or cup; wooden bucket.

can·non (kăn′*o*n) *n.* Piece of ordnance; mounted gun for firing heavy projectiles; aircraft's automatic shell-firing gun; **can′non-ball**, round projectile fired by cannon; **cannon fodder**, (fig.) men regarded merely as material to be consumed in war. **cannon** *v.i.* Fire, bombard (with) cannon; cannonade.

can·non·ade (kăn*o*nād′) *n.* Continuous gunfire. ~ *v.* (**-ad·ed, -ad·ing**). Fire continuously; bombard.

can·not (kăn′ŏt, -*o*t, kănŏt′, k*a*-): see CAN[2].

can·ny (kăn′ē) *adj.* (**-ni·er, -ni·est**). Shrewd; worldly-wise; thrifty; circumspect; sly. **can′ni·ly** *adv.* **can′ni·ness** *n.*

ca·noe (k*a*nōō′) *n.* Small light keelless boat propelled by paddle(s). ~ *v.i.* (**-noed, -noe·ing**). Paddle or propel canoe; travel by canoe.

can·on[1] (kăn′*o*n) *n.* 1. Church decree; ~ **law**, official body of laws governing a Christian church; (R.C.) ecclesiastical law as set down by the pope and the councils. 2. General rule, fundamental principle, axiom; standard of judgment or authority, test, criterion. 3. Collection or list of books of the Bible accepted by the Christian churches as genuine and inspired. 4. Portion of the Mass between the Sanctus and the Lord's Prayer, containing the words of consecration. 5. List of recognized genuine works of a particular author, e.g. *the Hawthorne canon.*

These ***cannon*** *were used at the Battle of Gettysburg which was fought in 3 days in July 1863 and is regarded as the major turning point of the American Civil War.*

Below: A member of the mustard family, ***candytuft*** *is a popular border plant in gardens. It is low growing and comes in a range of several colors.*

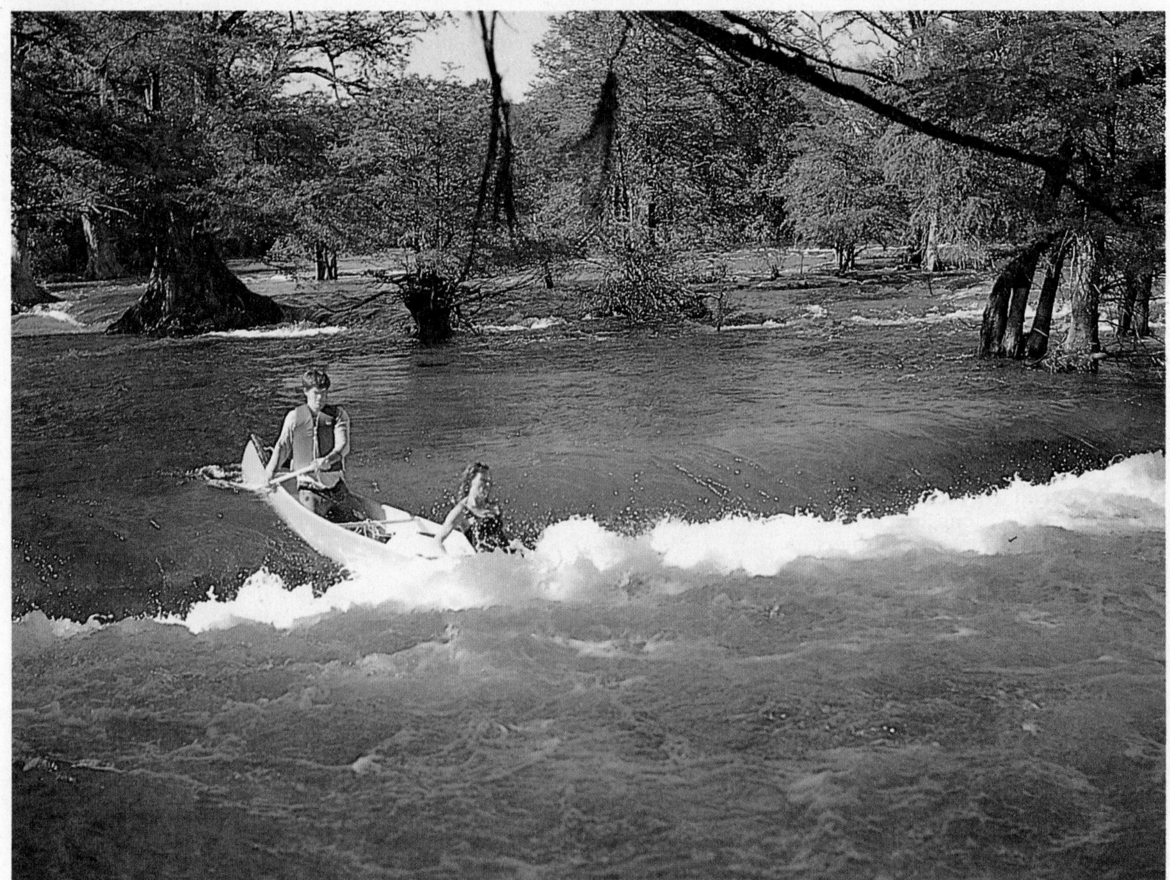

***Canoeing** on the Guadalupe River in Texas. The modern lightweight canoes and kayaks were developed in the 1930s and the sport has been increasing in popularity since then.*

ca·non[2] (kăn′*o*n) *n.* 1. Member of a religious community bound by vows and living under common rules. 2. One of a chapter of priests serving in a cathedral or collegiate church.

cañ·on (kăn′y*o*n): see CANYON.

ca·non·i·cal (k*a*nŏn′ĭk*a*l) *adj.* 1. Of, required or abiding by canon law; ~ **hours**, (R.C. and some Episcopal Churches) special prayers and psalms appointed to be read by priests etc. at certain hours of the day: matins and lauds, prime, tierce, sext, nones, vespers, and compline. 2. Included in the canon of Scripture. 3. Authoritative, standard, accepted. 4. Of a cathedral chapter or a member of it. **ca·non′i·cal·ly** *adv.* **ca·non′i·cals** *n.pl.* Canonical dress.

can·on·ist (kăn′*o*nĭst) *n.* Canon lawyer.

can·on·ize (kăn′*o*nīz) *v.t.* (**-ized, -iz·ing**). Admit formally to calendar of saints; regard as a saint; sanction by authority of Church. **can·on·i·za·tion** (kăn*o*nīzā′sh*o*n) *n.*

can·on·ry (kăn′*o*nrē) *n.* (pl. **-ries**). Benefice, status, etc., of a canon.

Ca·no·pic (k*a*nō′pĭk) *adj.* Of the town of Canopus; ~ **vase**, Egyptian vase with a lid in the form of a human head, used for holding the entrails of embalmed bodies.

Ca·no·pus (k*a*nō′p*u*s). 1. (Gk. myth.) Helmsman of Menelaus who died in Egypt on the return from Troy. 2. Town in ancient Egypt named after him. 3. (astron.) Bright star Alpha in the southern constellation Argo, the second brightest star in the sky.

can·o·py (kăn′*o*pē) *n.* (pl. **-pies**). Covering suspended or held over throne, bed, person, etc.; part of parachute that fills with air when released from its packing; (fig.) any overhanging shelter; the sky etc. ~ *v.t.* (**-pied, -py·ing**). Supply, be, a canopy to. [Gk. *kōnōpeion* mosquito net (*kōnōps* gnat)]

Ca·nos·sa (k*a*nŏs′*a*). Castle and village in Tuscany where in 1077 the Holy Roman Emperor Henry IV submitted to the penance and humiliation imposed on him by Pope Gregory VII.

cant[1] (kănt) *n.* Bevel, oblique face, slope, slant; sloping or tilted position. ~ *v.* 1. Bevel; slope, slant, tilt. 2. Throw, jerk. 3. (naut.) Swing around.

cant[2] (kănt) *n.* Jargon of class, profession, sect, etc.; temporary catchwords; words used for fashion without being meant; unreal use of words implying piety; hypocrisy. ~ *v.i.* Use cant.

can't: see CAN[2].

can·ta·bi·le (kahntah′bĭlā) *adj.* & *n.* (Music) in a smooth flowing style, songlike, melodious. [It.]

can·ta·loupe, can·ta·loup (kăn′t*a*lōp) *ns.* Small, round, ribbed, delicate-flavored variety of melon with reddish-orange flesh, developed in Italy; a similar variety of muskmelon. [*Cantalupo*, castle near Rome]

can·tan·ker·ous (kăntăng′k*e*r*u*s) *adj.* Ill-tempered, quarrelsome. **can·tan′ker·ous·ly** *adv.* **can·tan′ker·ous·ness** *n.*

can·ta·ta (k*a*ntah′t*a*) *n.* Choral work, either a short oratorio or a short lyric drama set to music but not intended for acting.

can·teen (kăntēn′) *n.* 1. Provision and liquor shop in barracks, camp, post exchange; place of relaxation and entertainment maintained by civilian group for armed forces personnel; refreshment room in factory or office building. 2. Soldiers', campers', hikers' water flask.

can·ter (kăn′t*er*) *n.* Easy gallop. ~ *v.* Go, make (horse) go, at this pace. [shortened f. CANTERBURY gallop]

Can·ter·bur·y (kăn′t*er*bĕrē). Cathedral city in SE. England, see of the archbishop and primate of all England; the shrine of Thomas à Becket (St. Thomas of Canterbury), who was murdered in the cathedral, was in pre-Reformation times a favorite object of pilgrimage; ~ **bell**, kind of campanula (f. bells of pilgrims' horses); (Brit.) ~ **gallop, pace, trot**, etc., the easy pace of the mounted pilgrims to Canterbury.

can·thar·i·des (kănthăr´idēz) *n.pl.* (sing. **-thar·is** pr. -thăr´ĭs). Dried Spanish flies (*Lytta* (*Cantharis*) *vesicatoria*), formerly used in medicine and as an aphrodisiac, usu. SPANISH fly.

can·ti·cle (kăn´tĭkel) *n.* Hymn; one of the hymns, mostly taken from the Scriptures, used in church services, as the *Benedicite*, *Nunc Dimittis*, *Te Deum;* **Canticles**, Song of Solomon.

can·ti·le·ver (kăn´tĭlēver, -lēver) *n.* (archit., eng.) Beam or girder fixed at one end to a pier or wall and free at the other, long bracket; ~ **bridge**, bridge composed of girders projecting from piers and meeting midway between them or carrying intermediate sections. **can′ti·le·vered** *adj.* Projecting like, supported by, a cantilever.

can·tle (kăn´tel) *n.* Rear portion of saddle.

can·to (kăn´tō) *n.* (pl. **-tos**). Division of long poem.

Can·ton (kăntŏn′, kăn´tŏn), known as Guang´zhou. City of S. China on the Chu-Kiang River; the capital of Kwangtung Province. **Can·ton·ese** (kăntonēz′, -nēs′, kăn′tonēz, -nēs) *adj.* & *n.* (Native, inhabitant, dialect) of Canton.

can·ton (kăn´ton, -tŏn, kăntŏn´) *n.* Subdivision of a country; one of the sovereign states of the Swiss federation. **can′ton·al** *adj.* **canton** *v.t.* 1. Divide into cantons. 2. Quarter (troops).

can·ton·ment (kăntŏn´ment, -tōn´-; *Brit.* kăntōōn´ment) *n.* Temporary lodging assigned to troops; temporary military station.

can·tor (kăn´ter, -tor) *n.* 1. Synagogue official, the chief singer of the liturgy. 2. Leader or chief singer of a church choir.

Ca·nuck (kanŭk´) *n.* (offensive slang) Canadian, esp. French Canadian.

Ca·nute, Cnut (kanōōt´, -nūt´). Danish king of England, 1016–35.

can·vas (kăn´vas) *n.* 1. Strong unbleached plain-woven cloth of hemp, flax, or other coarse yarn, for sails, tents, etc.; open kind of this, usu. flax or cotton, for tapestry, embroidery, etc.; **under** ~, in tent(s); with sails spread. 2. (also **artists'** ~) Canvas prepared for painting on by coating with size, white lead, etc.; hence, a painting, picture (lit. and fig.). 3. Sail, sails collectively. 4. **can′vasback**, N. Amer. duck (*Aythya valisineria*) (from the color of its gray-and-white mottled back feathers).

can·vass (kăn´vas) *v.* 1. Discuss thoroughly. 2. Solicit votes, solicit votes from; ascertain sentiments or opinion of; ask custom of. **can′vass·er** *n.* **canvass** *n.* Solicitation of votes, opinions, etc. [f. CANVAS, the original sense being "toss in a sheet etc.," and hence "shake up, agitate," etc.]

can·yon (kăn´yon) *n.* Deep gorge or ravine with steep sides formed by river cutting through soft rock. [Span. *cañon* tube, f. L. *canna* reed]

Can·yon de Chel·ly (kăn´yon de shā´) **National Park.** An area in NE. Arizona reserved to protect ruins of ancient Indian cliff dwellings.

caou·tchouc (kow´chōōk, kowchōōk´) *n.* Natural rubber (see RUBBER[1] *n.* def. 3). [Fr., f. Carib]

cap (kăp) *n.* 1. Covering for the

The ancient town of ***Canterbury,*** *U.K., is dominated by the 235-ft. 15th-century tower of the cathedral. The illustration shows the church as seen from the south-west.*

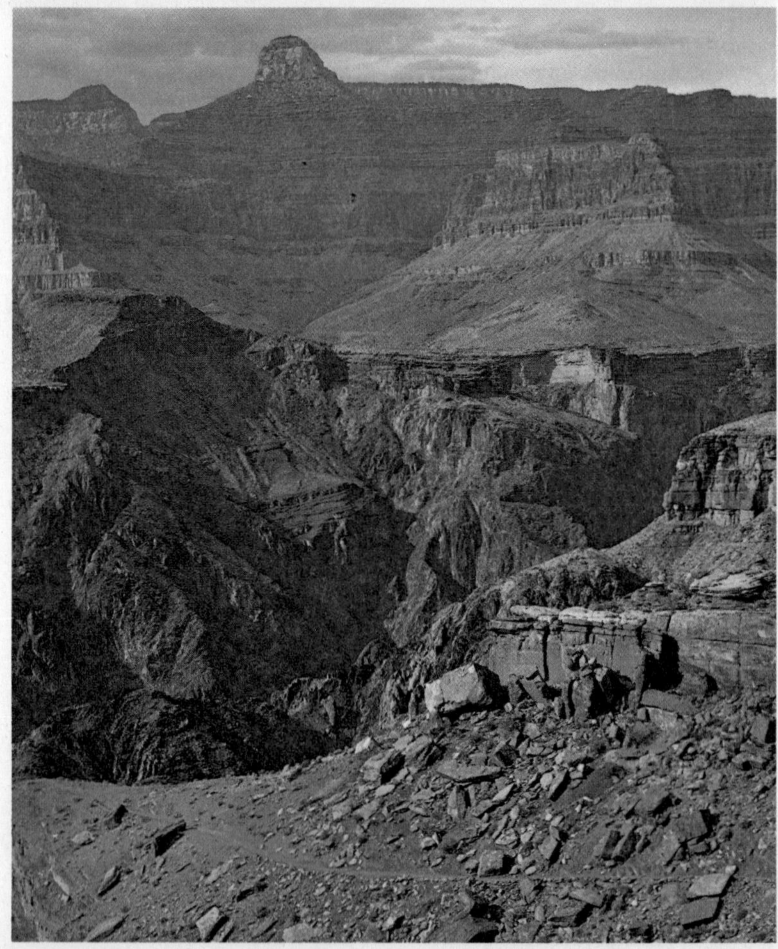

One of the most impressive of all ***canyons,*** *the Grand Canyon, N.W. Arizona, was gouged nearly one mile deep by the Colorado River. The canyon is about 217 miles long.*

head, esp. close-fitting and usu. soft and brimless; ~ **in hand**, (fig.) humbly, in supplication. 2. Special headdress denoting rank, occupation, membership in a particular group, etc.; ~ **and bells**, jester's insignia; ~ **and gown**, mortarboard and cassocklike gown worn at academic processions, college commencement, etc. 3. Mortarboard. 4. Caplike covering, as of mushroom, toe of shoe, etc. 5. (also **percussion** ~) Cap-shaped piece of copper lined with explosive, for igniting explosive in firearms etc.; paper percussion cap of toy pistol. **cap′ful** *n.* **cap** *v.t.* (**capped, cap·ping**). 1. Put cap upon. 2. Form or serve as cap of; overlie, cover; complete, supply finishing touches. 3. (colloq.) Surpass; follow with another (story etc.).

cap. *abbrev.* Capital (city); capital (letter).

ca·pa·bil·i·ty (kāpabĭl′ĭtē) *n.* (pl. **-ties**). Power *of, for, to*; undeveloped faculty.

ca·pa·ble (kā′pabel) *adj.* 1. Susceptible. 2. ~ **of**, having the power or fitness for; wicked enough for. 3. Able, gifted, competent. **ca′pa·bly** *adv.*

ca·pa·cious (kapā′shus) *adj.* Roomy. **ca·pa′cious·ly** *adv.* **ca·pa′cious·ness** *n.*

ca·pac·i·tance (kapăs′ĭtans) *n.* (elect.) Ratio of change in electric charge to corresp. change in potential; ability to store an electric charge. **ca·pac′i·tive** *adj.*

ca·pac·i·tate (kapăs′ĭtāt) *v.t.* (**-tat·ed, -tat·ing**). Render capable; make legally competent.

ca·pac·i·tor (kapăs′ĭter) *n.* Device that stores electricity during part of an operation, usu. consisting of conductors separated by insulator; formerly called CONDENSER.

ca·pac·i·ty (kapăs′ĭtē) *n.* (pl. **-ties**). 1. Ability to contain or receive; cubic content, volume. 2. (fig.) Mental power; faculty, talent; capability, opportunity, *to, of*, etc.; relative character (as *in his ~ as critic*); legal competency. 3. Maximum number or amount that can be contained, produced, etc.; **to** ~, to the limit.

cap-a-pie, cap-à-pie (kăpapē′) *advs.* From head to foot.

ca·par·i·son (kapăr′ĭson) *n.* Horses' trappings; equipment, outfit. ~ *v.t.* Put caparison upon.

cape[1] (kāp) *n.* Short sleeveless cloak, either as separate garment or as fixed or detachable part of longer cloak or coat. **caped** *adj.*

cape[2] (kāp) *n.* Promontory.

Cape (kāp), **The.** Cape Cod; the Cape of Good Hope; **C~ Cod**, peninsula in SE. Massachusetts famous as a summer resort. ~ **Dutch**, early form of Afrikaans; ~ **gooseberry**, tropical Amer. plant (*Physalis peruviana*) with yellow flowers and berries; ~ **of Good Hope**, promontory near southern extremity of Africa; ~ **Hatteras**, promontory of Hatteras Island off the coast of North Carolina; **cape′-skin**, soft leather made from sheepskin (orig. from S. Afr. sheepskin).

Cape Bret·on (kāp′ brĭt′on, brĕt′-) **Island.** Island off NE. Nova Scotia, Canada.

Ca·pek (chah′pĕk), **Karel** (1890–1938); Czech novelist and playwright; author of the play *R.U.R.*, the novel *War with the Newts*, etc.

Ca·pel·la (kapĕl′a). Star of first magnitude in the constellation Auriga.

ca·per[1] (kā′per) *n.* Bramblelike S. European shrub (*Capparis spinosa*); (pl.) its flower buds, pickled for use in sauces.

ca·per[2] (kā′per) *n.* Capering

*The city of **Cape Town,** founded by Jan van Riebeeck in 1652, spreads from the shore of Table Bay to the foot of Table Mountain. The wisp of cloud on the plateau is called the 'tablecloth'.*

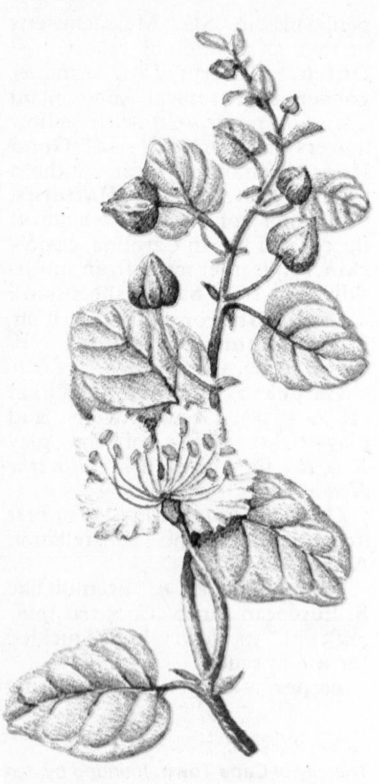

*The flower buds of the **caper** briar are pickled and used in piquant sauces, generally served with meat dishes. The plant is cultivated in Southern Europe and the U.S.*

*The largest game bird in Europe, the **capercaillie** became extinct in Scotland, where it had been a native but was reintroduced there from Scandinavia.*

*The **Capitol** in Washington, D.C., where the U.S. Congress meets, was begun in 1793 and completed 70 years later when the statue 'Freedom' was mounted on the cupola.*

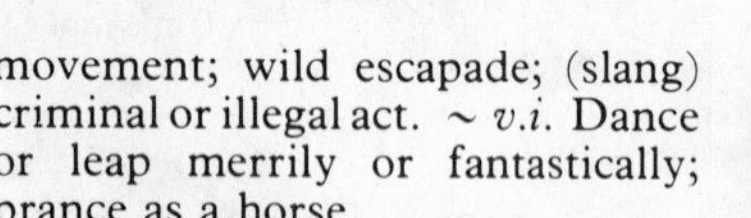

movement; wild escapade; (slang) criminal or illegal act. ~ *v.i.* Dance or leap merrily or fantastically; prance as a horse.

cap·er·cail·lie (kăp*e*rkāl′yē) *n.* Wood grouse (*Tetrao urogallus*), the largest European gallinaceous bird. [Gael. *capull coille* horse of the wood]

Ca·pet (kăp′ĭt, kā′pĭt). French dynasty founded by Hugo Capet in 987, which ruled until 1328, when it was succeeded by the House of Valois.

Cape (kāp) **Town.** Legislative capital of the Republic of S. Africa.

Cape Ver·de (kāp vĕr′dē) **Islands.** Two groups of islands, Windward and Leeward, about 400 miles W. of Senegal, formerly a Portuguese possession; independent 1975.

cap·il·lar·y (kăp′*i*lĕrē) *adj.* 1. Of, or resembling, hair. 2. Having very minute or hairlike internal diameter. 3. Of capillaries. 4. ~ **attraction**, effect of surface tension of liquid that wets material of fine tube in raising liquid inside tube to a level higher than that outside; ~ **repulsion**, corresponding effect of surface tension of liquid that does not wet tube in depressing level inside tube. **capillary** *n.* (pl. **-lar·ies**). One of the hairlike vessels joining arteries and veins in which the blood is brought into effective contact with the tissues.

cap·i·tal[1] (kăp′ĭt*a*l) *n.* Head of pillar or pilaster, wider than the shaft and usu. ornamented.

cap·i·tal[2] (kăp′ĭt*a*l) *adj.* 1. Involving loss of life; punishable by death; ~ **punishment**, punishment by death for a crime. 2. Chief; important, leading, first-class. 3. (chiefly Brit. colloq.) Excellent, first-rate. 4. Original, principal, of money capital. 5. ~ **letter**, one of the form and size used at beginning of name, sentence, etc., majuscule. **capital** *n.* 1. Chief town of country, state, etc., usu. the seat of government. 2. Stock of company with which it enters business and on which dividends are paid; (econ.) accumulated wealth of individual, community, etc., used as fund for starting fresh production; wealth of any kind used in producing more wealth; ~ **gain**, profit from sale of investments or property; hence ~ **gains tax;** ~ **goods**, goods for use in producing commodities, opp.

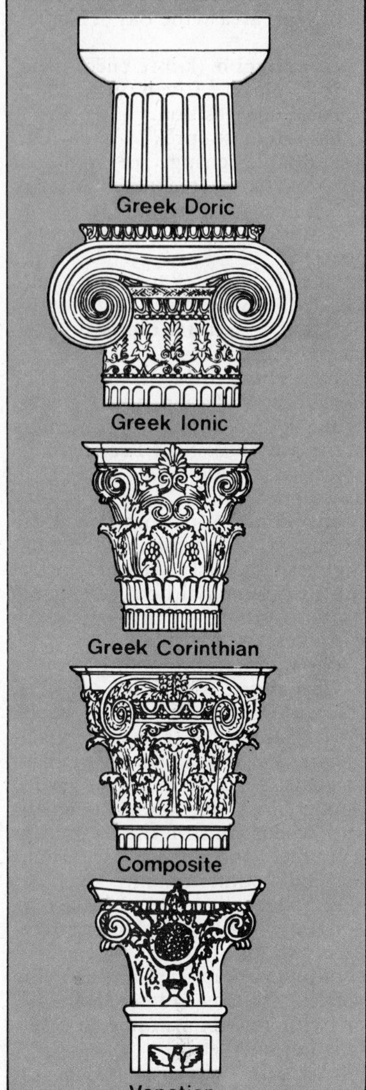

The capping member of a column, the ***capital,*** *is at the point where the weight of the roof is transferred to the column; therefore it must be strong. Left: The temple of Olympian Zeus, in Athens, has capitals of the Corinthian order.*

consumer goods. 3. Capitalists or employers of labor collectively. 4. Capital letter.

cap·i·tal·ism (kăp´ĭt*a*lĭz*e*m) *n.* Economic system by which ownership of capital or wealth, the production and distribution of goods, and the reward of labor are entrusted to private enterprise. **cap'i·tal·ist** *n.* Private owner or holder of capital, esp. in large amounts; one who has capital available for employment in finance or industry. **cap·i·tal·is·tic** (kăpĭt*a*lĭs´tĭk) *adj.* **cap'i·tal·ize** *v.t.* (**-ized, -iz·ing**). Convert into, use as, capital; compute or realize present value of (income). **cap·i·tal·i·za·tion** (kăpĭt*a*lĭzā´sh*o*n) *n.*

cap·i·ta·tion (kăpĭtā´sh*o*n) *n.* (Levying of) tax or fee of so much a head; a per capita or poll tax.

Cap·i·tol (kăp´ĭt*o*l). 1. Great national temple of ancient Rome, dedicated to Jupiter Optimus Maximus, on the Saturnian or Tarpeian (afterward called Capitoline) Hill; the hill itself, one of the seven Hills of ancient Rome. 2. Building in Washington, D.C., occupied by the U.S. Congress; the building in which a state legislature meets.

ca·pit·u·late (k*a*pĭch´*u*lāt) *v.i.* (**-lat·ed, -lat·ing**). Surrender on terms; (loosely) give up, acquiesce.

ca·pit·u·la·tion (k*a*pĭch*u*lā´sh*o*n) *n.* 1. Summary, outline. 2. Agreement, conditions. 3. Surrender on terms, agreement containing such terms.

ca·pit·u·lum (k*a*pĭch´*u*l*u*m) *n.* (pl. **-la** pr. -l*a*). 1. (physiol.) Protuberance of bone received into a hollow portion of another bone. 2. (bot.) Close head of sessile flowers.

ca·pon (kā´pŏn, -p*o*n) *n.* Castrated rooster. **ca·pon·ize** (kāp*o*nīz) *v.t.* (**-ized, -iz·ing**).

Ca·po·te (k*a*pō´te, **Truman** (1924–1984). American novelist and short story writer; author of *Other Voices, Other Rooms; The Grass Harp; Breakfast at Tiffany's; In Cold Blood*, etc.

Cap·pa·do·cia (kăp*a*dō´sh*a*). Ancient region of eastern Asia Minor, now central Turkey. **Cap·pa·do'cian** *adj.* & *n.*

Ca·pri (k*a*prē′, kah′prē). Island and resort area in the Bay of Naples, Italy.

ca·pric·ci·o (k*a*prē′chēō, -chō) *n.* (pl. **-ci·os**). Lively, usu. short, musical composition.

ca·price (k*a*prēs′) *n.* Unaccountable change of mind or conduct; fancy, freak; inclination to these; (mus.) capriccio. [It. *capriccio* suddenly start, app. f. *capra* goat]

ca·pri·cious (k*a*prĭsh′*u*s) *adj.* Guided by whim; inconstant, irregular. **ca·pri′cious·ly** *adv.* **ca·pri′cious·ness** *n.*

Cap·ri·corn (kăp′r*i*kōrn). The Goat, a constellation; 10th sign (♑) of the zodiac, which the sun enters at the winter solstice; **Tropic of ~**, southern TROPIC. [L. *caper* goat, *cornu* horn]

cap·ri·ole (kăp′rēōl) *n.* 1. Leap or caper. 2. (in manège) Horse's high leap and kick, with all four feet off the ground, without advancing. ~ *v.i.* (**-oled, -ol·ing**). Make a capriole.

caps. *abbrev.* Capital letters.

Cap·si·an (kăp′sēan) *adj.* & *n.* (Of) a Stone Age culture of N. Africa. [f. *Capsa* (gafsa), Tunisia]

cap·si·cum (kăp′s*i*k*u*m) *n.* Plant of genus *C~*, the common garden pepper, with very pungent capsule and seeds; fruit of these, used as condiment and as a digestive stimulant and counterirritant.

cap·size (kăp′sīz, kăpsīz′) *v.* (**-sized, -siz·ing**). Upset, overturn, esp. on water.

cap·stan (kăp′st*a*n) *n.* Revolving vertical cylinder rotated manually or by motor, for winding in cable, hoisting sails, etc.

cap·sule (kăp′s*u*l, -sūl) *n.* 1. (physiol.) Membranous envelope. 2. (bot.) Dry seedcase opening when ripe by parting of valves. 3. (med.) Gelatine envelope enclosing drug or other medicinal substance.

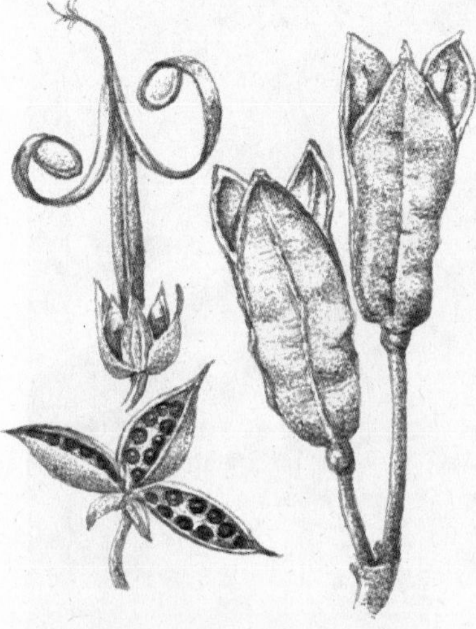

*Characteristic of multicarpel plants, a **capsule** opens by one of several means to scatter its seeds. In the campion, the apical teeth part. The iris capsule splits along its longitudinal valves.*

4. Airtight cap or seal for bottle etc. 5. Detachable nose cone of rocket or cabin of spacecraft for carrying instruments or astronauts. ~ *adj.* Compact, consise; summary. **cap·su·lar** (kăp′s*u*l*e*r, -sy*u*-), **cap·su·late** (kăp′s*u*lāt, -sy*u*-), **cap′su·lat·ed** *adjs.* **cap·sul·ize** (kăp′s*u*līz, -sy*u*-) *v.t.* (**-ized, -iz·ing**). Condense (information etc.).

Capt. *abbrev.* Captain.

cap·tain (kăp′tĭn) *n.* 1. Chief, leader; great soldier, strategist, experienced commander. 2. (mil.) Army, Air Force, or Marine Corps officer, of rank just below major and above first lieutenant, normally commanding company or troop; (nav.) officer of rank between commander and commodore (or rear admiral), officer commanding warship; master of merchant ship; pilot of civil aircraft. 3. Leader of team in game or sport. **cap′tain·cy, cap′tain·ship** *ns.* **captain** *v.t.* Be captain of; lead.

cap·tion (kăp′sh*o*n) *n.* Heading of chapter, section, newspaper article, etc.; wording under illustration; title, descriptive passage, dialogue, etc., inserted in (silent) motion picture. ~ *v.t.* Provide with caption.

cap·tious (kăp′sh*u*s) *adj.* Disposed to finding fault or criticizing; perplexing; deceptive. **cap′tious·ly** *adv.* **cap′tious·ness** *n.*

cap·ti·vate (kăp′tĭvāt) *v.t.* (**-vat·ed, -vat·ing**). Fascinate, charm. **cap·ti·va·tion** (kăptĭvā′sh*o*n) *n.* **cap′ti·vat·ing** *adj.* **cap′ti·vat·ing·ly** *adv.*

cap·tive (kăp′tĭv) *adj.* & *n.* (Person, animal) taken prisoner, kept in confinement, unable to escape; (of, like) prisoner. **cap·tiv·i·ty** (kăptĭv′ĭtē) *n.*

cap·tor (kăp′t*e*r) *n.* One who takes a captive.

cap·ture (kăp′ch*e*r) *n.* Capturing; thing or person captured. ~ *v.t.* (**-tured, -tur·ing**). Take prisoner; seize as prize; (phys., of atomic particle, atom, or nucleus) acquire an additional particle; (astron., of star or planet) bring (object) within its gravitational field.

Cap·u·chin (kăp′y*u*chĭn, -shĭn) *n.* 1. Franciscan friar of the new rule of 1528. 2. Woman's garment of cloak and hood. 3. ~ **monkey**, Central and S. Amer. monkey of genus *Cebus*, with black hair like a cowl at back of head.

cap·y·ba·ra (kăpĭbär′*a*) *n.* Large tailless semiaquatic rodent (*Hydrochoerus capybara*), allied to guinea pig, of tropical S. America.

car (kär) *n.* Wheeled vehicle, (poet.) chariot; automobile; any wheeled vehicle running on tracks

*About 1 yard long, the **capybara** lives in South America. It is at home in water, where it is prey to the cayman, and on land it can run swiftly. It has a horse-like gait.*

*The typical organ-grinder's monkey, the **capuchin monkey** thrives in captivity. In its wild state it lives in large groups in the trees of tropical South America.*

__Cappadocia__ extended across the high plateau region of Turkey, from the Black Sea to the Taurus Mountains. Right: A villager descends a ladder from his house in a rock village.

The dream of a machine-driven **car** *became a practical reality when Karl Benz (1844–1929) developed a gasoline engine and fitted it to a car in 1885. The model illustrated here was built 4 years later. Its single-cylinder 4-stroke engine was mounted in the rear of the vehicle. The lack of a radiator meant that the water boiled away rapidly.*

or cables, as **cable ~, railroad ~, street′car**; special type of railroad car, as **dining car, sleeping car**, etc.; part of airship or balloon holding passengers; enclosure for passengers, as an **elevator car; car coat**, short coat designed esp. for car drivers; **car′hop**, (colloq.) waiter at drive-in restaurant; **car pool**, (arrangement by) group of commuters who take turns driving group to work or share expenses of car; **car′port**, roofed open shelter for automobile; **car′sick**, nauseated from motion of automobile; **car′sickness** (*n.*).

ca·ra·ba·o (kārabah′ō) *n.* (pl. **-ba·os**). (Philippines) Water BUFFALO.

car·a·bin (kăr′abĭn), **car·a·bine** (kăr′abīn, -bēn) = CARBINE.

car·a·bi·neer, car·a·bi·nier (kărabinēr′) = CARBINEER.

car·a·cal (kăr′akal) *n.* Kind of lynx (*Felis caracal*) of N. Africa and SW. Asia, with reddish fur and black-tipped ears and tail; pelt of this animal. [Turk. *kara* black *kulak* ear]

Car·a·cal·la (kărakăl′a). Marcus Aurelius Antoninus Bassianus (188–217), Roman emperor 211–17.

ca·ra·ca·ra (kārakār′a) *n.* Any of various long-legged carrion hawks of southern U.S. and Central and S. Amer., (esp. *Caracara cheriway*) called **Audubon's ~.**

Ca·ra·cas (karah′kas). Capital of Venezuela, 8 (13 km) miles south of the Caribbean.

car·a·cole (kăr′akōl) *n.* Horseman's half-wheel to right or left, succession of such turns to right and left alternately. ~ *v.i.* (**-coled, -col·ing**). Execute caracole(s).

car·a·cul (kăr′akul) = KARAKUL.

ca·rafe (karăf′, -rahf′) *n.* Glass bottle for water or wine at table. [Fr., ult. f. Arab. *ġarrāfa* drinking vessel]

car·a·mel (kăr′amel, -mĕl, kār′mel) *n.* Brown substance obtained by heating sugar or syrup and used for coloring spirits etc.; brown color of this; candy made of or flavored with this.

car·a·mel·ize (kăr′amelīz, kār′me-) *v.* (**-ized, -iz·ing**). Make (sugar) into caramel; (of sugar) turn brown when heated.

car·a·pace (kăr′apās) *n.* Upper body shell of tortoises and crustaceans.

car·at (kăr′at) *n.* 1. Measure of weight, about 200 milligrams, for precious stones. 2. See KARAT.

Ca·ra·vag·gio (kăravah′jō), **Michelangelo da** (1573–1610). Italian painter noted for his realistic treatment of traditional themes.

car·a·van (kăr′avăn) *n.* 1. Company of merchants, pilgrims, etc., in the East or in N. Africa, traveling together for security, esp. through desert; group of vehicles traveling together. 2. Covered cart or carriage, as house on wheels of gypsy, traveling showman, etc. 3.

'The Sacrifice of Isaac'. (Uffizi, Florence) by ***Michelangelo da Caravaggio*** *(1573–1610), who revolutionized Italian painting with his realism and conception of color.*

(Brit.) Trailer. ~ *v.i.* (**-vaned** or **-vanned, -van·ing** or **-van·ning**). Travel, live, in a caravan. [Pers. *kārwān*]

car·a·van·sa·ry (kăr*a*văn′s*e*rē), **car·a·van·sa·rai** (kăr*a*văn′s*e*rī, -rā) *ns.* (pl. **-sa·ries**). Eastern inn with large courtyard where caravans put up.

car·a·vel, car·a·velle (kăr′*a*vĕl) *ns.* (hist., also **carvel**) Small, light, fast sailing ship, chiefly Spanish or Portuguese, of 15th-17th centuries.

car·a·way (kăr′*a*wā) *n.* Umbelliferous plant (*Carum carvi*) with small aromatic seedlike fruits, ~ **seeds**, used in cooking, etc.

car·bide (kar̄′bīd) *n.* Compound of carbon with a metal; esp. **calcium** ~: see CALCIUM, and **iron** ~, (Fe_3C) an important constituent of steel.

car·bine (kar̄′bīn, -bēn) *n.* Kind of short rifle orig. introduced for cavalry use; also **carabin, carabine.**

car·bi·neer (kar̄b*i*nēr′) *n.* Soldier armed with a carbine; also **carabineer, carabinier.**

car·bo·hy·drate (kar̄bōhī′drāt) *n.* One of a group of compounds of carbon, hydrogen, and oxygen in which the last two elements are present in the same proportions as in water; including sugars, starches, and cellulose and forming an important part of the structure of plant material and of the food of man and other animals.

car·bol·ic (kar̄bŏl′ĭk) *adj.* ~ **acid**: see PHENOL.

car·bon (kar̄′b*o*n) *n.* 1. (chem.) Element occurring in two crystalline forms (diamond and graphite) and an amorphous form (charcoal), and in combination in all organic compounds; symbol C, at. no. 6, at. wt. 12.011. 2. (elect.) Rod of carbon used in arc lamps. 3. Carbon paper; carbon copy. 4. ~ **copy**, copy made with carbon paper; (fig.) exact copy; ~ **cycle**, (biol.) cycle in which carbon dioxide is absorbed from the atmosphere by plants and replaced mainly by respiration of plants and animals and by decay of organic matter; (astron.) cycle of thermonuclear reactions in which carbon acts as a catalyst in the conversion of hydrogen into helium, the energy released being held to be the source of that radiated by sun and stars; ~ **dioxide**, compound (CO_2) of carbon with oxygen, a colorless odorless gas formed by combustion of carbon, breathed out by animals, formed during fermentation, etc.; ~ **14**, long-living radioactive isotope of mass number 14, the regular decay rate of which makes RADIOCARBON dating possible; ~ **monoxide**, highly poisonous inflammable colorless odorless gas (CO), formed by the incomplete combustion of carbon or carbon compounds, as in charcoal stoves, gasoline engines, etc; ~ **paper**, thin paper, coated on one side with a colored wax preparation, which when it is inserted between two sheets of paper causes anything written on the upper sheet to appear also on the lower one; ~ **tetrachloride**, poisonous, noninflammable, volatile liquid used as fire extinguisher, solvent, or cleaning fluid.

The principal coal measures were laid down in the ***carboniferous*** *period which lasted from about 345 million to 280 million years ago. Ferns such as this Alcthopeteris lanchitica, shown here fossilized, were prolific.*

car·bo·na·ceous (kar̄b*o*nā′sh*u*s) *adj.* Of, like, coal or charcoal; consisting of or containing carbon.

car·bo·na·do (kar̄b*o*nā′dō, -nah′dō) *n.* (pl. **-does, -dos**). Dark opaque variety of diamond found in Brazil, used as an abrasive etc.

car·bon·ate (kar̄′b*o*nāt, -nĭt) *n.* Salt of carbonic acid. **car·bon·ate** (kar̄′b*o*nāt) *v.t.* (**-at·ed, -at·ing**). Form into a carbonate; charge with carbon dioxide gas.

car·bon·ic (kar̄bŏn′ĭk) *adj.* Of carbon; ~ **acid**, compound (H_2CO_3) of carbon dioxide and water.

car·bon·if·er·ous (kar̄b*o*nĭf′-*e*r*u*s) *adj.* Producing, containing carbon or coal; **C~**, (geol.) of the period or system of the Upper Paleozoic between Devonian and Permian, containing workable coal on at least three continents. **Car·bon·if'er·ous** *n.* Carboniferous period or system.

car·bon·ize (kar̄'bonīz) *v.t.* (**-ized, -iz·ing**). Reduce to charcoal or coke by burning off superfluous material. **car·bon·i·za·tion** (kar̄bonīzā'shon) *n.*

Car·bo·run·dum (kar̄borŭn'-dum) *n.* (trademark) SILICON carbide.

car·box·yl (kărbŏk'sil) *n.* (chem.) Univalent radical, COOH, characteristic of most organic acids.

car·boy (kăr'boi) *n.* Large globular wicker-covered glass bottle for holding acids or other corrosive liquids. [Pers. *ḳarāba* large flagon]

car·bun·cle (kar̄'bŭngkel) *n.* 1. (archaic) Deep red cabochon garnet. 2. Painful, pus-producing localized inflammation of the skin and subcutaneous tissue. **car·bun·cu·lar** (kar̄bŭng'kyuler), **car'-bun·cled** *adjs.*

car·bu·ret (kar̄'burāt, -byu-, -rĕt) *v.t.* (**-ret·ed, -ret·ing**, Brit. **-ret·ted, -ret·ting**). Combine chemically with carbon or hydrocarbons.

car·bu·re·tor (kar̄'burāter, -byu-) *n.* (in gasoline engines) Apparatus for impregnating air with fine particles of fuel and thus preparing the explosive mixture for the cylinders.

car·bu·rize (kar̄'burīz, -byu-) *v.t.* (**-rized, -riz·ing**). Cause carbon to penetrate (surface of solid steel) in order to harden it.

car·cass (kar̄'kas) *n.* 1. Dead body (of human body now only in contempt or ridicule); (butchering, cooking) dead body of beast or bird without head, limbs, or organs. 2. Worthless remains; skeleton, framework (of house, ship, tire, etc.).

Car·cas·sonne (kărkăsawn'). City in S. France; site of ancient fortifications, medieval castle, and 12-arch bridge.

car·cin·o·gen (kar̄sĭn'ojen) *n.* Cancer-producing substance or agent. **car·cin·o·gen·ic** (kar̄sinō-jĕn'ĭk) *adj.*

car·ci·no·ma (kar̄sinō'ma) *n.* (pl. **-mas, -ma·ta** pr. -mata). (path.) Cancer, esp. of epithelial origin.

card[1] (kar̄d) *n.* Toothed instrument or wire brush for combing wool, flax, cotton, hemp, etc., raising nap on cloth etc. ~ *v.t.* Prepare (wool etc.) for spinning by combing out impurities and straightening the fibers with cards.

card[2] (kar̄d) *n.* 1. Thin, flat, usu. rectangular, piece of stiff paper or pasteboard used for various purposes, as for greetings, invitation, identity, membership, credit, program, etc. 2. (also **playing ~**) One of a pack of small oblong pieces of pasteboard used in playing games, consisting (except in some special games) of 52 cards divided into 4 suits; (pl.) card-playing, game(s) with cards; **in the ~s**, (fig.) likely, possible. 3. (colloq.) Amusing person, jokester. 4. **card'board**, pasteboard for cutting cards from, making boxes, etc.; **card case**, case for carrying calling or credit cards; **card catalog**, catalog, usu. library catalog, with items entered on separate cards; **card'shark**, a professional card player who cheats; also **card'sharp, card'sharper.**

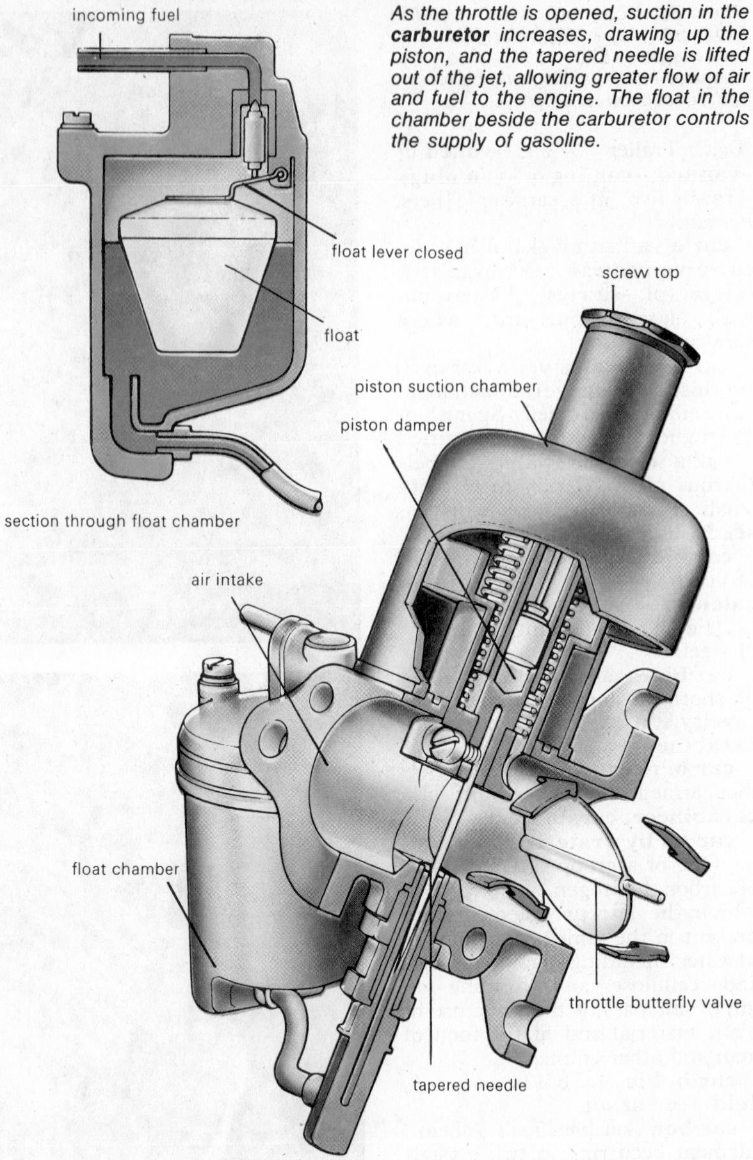

car·da·mom (kar̄'damom), **car·da·mon** (kar̄'damon) *ns.* Spice consisting of seed capsules of various species of the E. Ind. and Chinese genera *Amomum* and *Elettaria*, used as a medicine, in curries etc.

As the throttle is opened, suction in the ***carburetor*** *increases, drawing up the piston, and the tapered needle is lifted out of the jet, allowing greater flow of air and fuel to the engine. The float in the chamber beside the carburetor controls the supply of gasoline.*

car·di·ac (kar̄'dēăk) *adj.* 1. Of the heart. 2. (anat.) Of, adjoining, the upper orifice of the stomach.

Car·diff (kar̄'dĭf). Seaport and capital city of Wales.

car·di·gan (kar̄'digan) *n.* Sweater or knitted woolen jacket opening down the front. [f. 7th Earl of *Cardigan*, distinguished in the Crimean War]

car·di·nal (kar̄'dinal) *adj.* 1. On which something hinges; fundamental, important; ~ **number**, number that answers the question "how many" (*one, two, three*, etc.); ~ **point**, any of the four chief points of the compass; ~ **virtue**, one of the four "natural" virtues: justice, prudence, temperance, and fortitude. 2. Of the color of a cardinal's robes, scarlet. **car'di·nal·ly** *adv.* **cardinal** *n.* 1. (**C~**) One of the ecclesiastical princes of the R.C. Church who constitute the Sacred College or College of Cardinals and whose duty it is to elect the Pope. 2. (hist.) Woman's cloak, orig. of scarlet cloth with hood. 3. (also ~ **grosbeak**) N. Amer. crested grosbeak (*Richmondena cardinalis*), with scarlet plumage. 4. ~ **flower**, N. Amer. flower, the scarlet lobelia; ~ **red**, bright scarlet-red color, from the color of a cardinal's robes. **car·di·nal·ate** (kār′d*i*n*a*lāt, -lĭt) *n.* The College of Cardinals; the position, rank, title, etc. of a Roman Catholic cardinal.

cardio- *prefix.* Of the heart.

CARE (kār) *abbrev.* Cooperative for American Relief Everywhere, private organization established after World War II to assist needy people in foreign countries.

care (kār) *n.* (Occasion for) solicitude, anxiety; serious attention; heed, caution, pains; charge, protection; things to be done or seen to; **care′free**, free from anxiety; **care′taker**, person hired to take charge, as of house during owner's absence, of school or factory buildings, etc.; **caretaker government**, temporary government; **care′worn**, worn by anxiety and trouble. **care** *v.i.* (**cared, car·ing**). Feel concern or interest *for*, *about*; feel regard, deference, affection *for*, be concerned *whether*, etc.; be willing or desire *to*; ~ **for**, look after.

ca·reen (k*a*rēn′) *v.* 1. Turn (ship) on one side for cleaning, caulking, etc.; (cause to) heel over. 2. Move rapidly and in uncontrolled manner; lurch; swerve.

The map shows the area of the Atlantic Ocean called the ***Caribbean.*** *Its islands, the West Indies, consist of a chain of young mountain tops formed by recent geological activity.*

Bahamas
Cuba
Cayman Islands
Jamaica
Haiti
Dominican Rep
Puerto Rico
Guadeloupe
CARIBBEAN SEA
Barbados
Trinidad
Pacific Ocean

ca·reer (k*a*rēr′) *n.* 1. Swift course; impetus. 2. Course or progress through life, esp. when publicly conspicuous or successful; development and success of party, principle, etc.; course of professional life or employment, way of making livelihood. **career** *v.i.* Go swiftly or wildly.

ca·reer·ist (k*a*rēr′ĭst) *n.* Person (esp. holder of public office, government employee, etc.) who is mainly intent on personal advancement. **ca·reer′ism** *n.*

care·ful (kār′f*u*l) *adj.* Painstaking, watchful, cautious; done with, showing, care. **care′ful·ly** *adv.*

care·less (kār′lĭs) *adj.* Unconcerned, light-hearted; inattentive, negligent, thoughtless; inaccurate. **care′less·ly** *adv.* **care′less·ness** *n.*

ca·ress (k*a*rĕs′) *n.* Fondling touch. ~ *v.t.* Bestow caress(es) on; pet.

car·et (kăr′ĭt) *n.* Mark (‸) placed below line in writing to indicate where something is to be inserted. [L., = "is wanting"]

car·go (kār′gō) *n.* (pl. **-goes, -gos**). Freight carried on ship, plane, etc.

Car·ib (kăr′ĭb) *n.* (pl. **-ibs**, collect. **-ib**). One of the native Amer. Indian peoples of northern S. America and the W. Indies; their language.

Car·ib·be·an (kăr*i*bē′*a*n, k*a*rĭb′ē-) *adj.* ~ **Sea**, sea lying between the W. Indies and the mainland of Central and S. America. ~ *n.* Caribbean Sea.

Car·i·boo (kăr′*i*bo͞o) **Mountains.** Part of the Rocky Mountain range in E. British Columbia, Canada.

car·i·bou (kăr′*i*bo͞o) *n.* (pl.

One of the finch family, the ***cardinal grosbeak*** *or redbird is a North American song-bird. Varieties in the north are scarlet, farther south they may be gray and red.*

Non-migratory woodland ***caribou*** *are found throughout the boreal forest of N. America. Barren-ground caribou range the Arctic tundra.*

-bous, collect. **-bou**). Any of several large arctic Amer. deer of the genus *Rangifer*, related to the reindeer, both sexes having antlers.

car·i·ca·ture (kăr'ikacher, -choor) *n.* Grotesque or ludicrous representation of person or thing by emphasis on characteristic or striking features. ~ *v.t.* (**-tured, -tur·ing**). Represent in caricature. **car'i·ca·tur·ist** *n.*

car·ies (kār'ēz, -ēēz, kăr'-) *n.* (pl. **-ies**). Decay (of teeth or bones). **car·i·ous** (kār'ēus, kăr'-) *adj.* Decayed.

car·il·lon (kăr'ilŏn, -lon) *n.* Set of bells sounded either from keyboard or mechanically.

ca·ri·na (karī'na, -rē'-) *n.* (pl. **-nas, -nae** pr. -nē). (bot., zool.) Structure in form of keel or ridge. **car·i·nat·ed** (kăr'inātĭd) *adj.* Having a keellike part. **car·i·na·tion** (kărinā'shon) *n.*

Car·lisle (kārlīl', kār'līl). Scottish border town in NW. England; once an important Roman town; place of imprisonment of Mary, Queen of Scots, 1568.

Car·lo·ta (kārlō'ta, -lŏt'a) (1840–1927). Original name, Marie Charlotte Amelie; wife of Archduke Maximilian of Austria; empress of Mexico, 1864–67.

Car·lo·vin·gi·an (kārlovĭn'-jēan): see CAROLINGIAN.

Carls·bad (kārlz'băd) **Caverns National Park.** Region in SE. New Mexico containing a series of limestone caves.

Carls·ru·he (kārlz'rooe): = KARLSRUHE.

Car·lyle (kārlīl'), **Thomas** (1795–1881). Scottish literary critic, historian, and writer on social and political problems.

Car·mel (kārmĕl'), **Mount.** Ridge across NW. Israel to the Mediterranean.

Car·mel·ite (kār'melīt) *adj.* & *n.* (Member) of order of mendicant friars (White Friars) originating in a colony founded in the 12th c. on Mount Carmel by Berthold, a Calabrian; (member) of a community of nuns of this order.

car·min·a·tive (kārmĭn'atĭv, kār'minā-) *adj.* & *n.* (Drug) curing flatulence.

car·mine (kār'mĭn, -mīn) *n.* & *adj.* (Colored like, color of) a crimson red pigment obtained from cochineal.

car·nage (kār'nĭj) *n.* Great slaughter.

car·nal (kār'nal) *adj.* Sensual; sexual; worldly. **car·nal·i·ty** (kārnăl'ĭtē) *n.* **car'nal·ly** *adv.*

Car·nar·von (kārnār'von), **George Edward Stanhope Molyneux Herbert, 5th Earl of,** (1866–1923). English Egyptologist and collaborator with Howard Carter in excavating near Thebes; co-discoverer of tomb of Tutankhamen.

car·na·tion[1] (kārnā'shon) *n.* 1. Light rosy pink or bright red color. 2. Flesh tints in a painting; the representation of naked flesh. ~ *adj.* Deep red.

car·na·tion[2] (kārnā'shon) *n.* Widely cultivated Eurasian plant (*Dianthus caryophyllus*) having fragrant white, pink, or red flowers with fringed petals; its flower.

car·nau·ba (kārnaw'ba, -now'-) *n.* Brazilian wax palm; its yellowish wax.

Car·ne·gie (kārnā'gē, kār'ne-), **Andrew** (1835–1919). Scottish-born American owner of iron and steel works etc., famous for his philanthropy.

car·nel·ian (kārnēl'yan) *n.* (also **cornelian**) Red or reddish variety of chalcedony used in jewelry.

car·ni·val (kār'nival) *n.* 1. Last three days or last week before Lent; festivities during this season. 2. Riotous revelry, feasting, merry-making. 3. Traveling amusement show having side shows, game booths, and merry-go-round, Ferris wheel, or other rides. [Fr., f. It. *carnevale* Lenten season, f. L. *caro carn–* flesh and *levare* put away]

car·ni·vore (kār'nivōr, -vōr) *n.* Member of the Carnivora, a large order of mammals including many (cats, dogs, seals, etc.) that feed on other animals, having usu. sharp incisors and well-developed canine teeth; animal that feeds on other animals. **car·niv·o·rous** (kārnĭv'-erus) *adj.*

car·ob (kăr'ob) *n.* Mediterranean evergreen tree (*Ceratonia siliqua*) bearing edible seed pods whose seeds are said to have been the original karat weight used by goldsmiths.

car·ol (kăr'ol) *n.* Joyous song, esp. Christmas hymn. ~ *v.* (**-oled, -ol·ing**, Brit. **-olled, -ol·ling**). Sing joyfully, sing carols.

Car·o·le·an (kărolē'an) *adj.* = CAROLINE.

Car·o·li·na (kărolī'na). (hist.) English colony in N. Amer., first settled in 1653, named after Charles II of England; divided into what became the present NORTH and SOUTH CAROLINA in 1729; (also **the ~s**) North and South Carolina.

Car·o·line (kăr'olĭn) *adj.* Of, pertaining to, Charles I or Charles II of England. **Car·o·lin·i·an** (kărolĭn'ēan) *adj.* & *n.*

Car·o·line (kăr'olīn, -lĭn) **Islands.** Archipelago in the W. Pacific Ocean, part of the present (United Nations') Trust Territory of the Pacific Islands, under U.S. administration; scene of several World War II battles.

Car·o·lin·gi·an (kărolĭn'jēan) *adj.* Of CHARLEMAGNE; of the line of French kings descended from him; ~ **Empire**, empire acquired by Charlemagne early in 9th c. and regarded by him as a revival of the Roman Empire; at its greatest extent it comprised France (except Brittany), Germany, the Low Countries, N. and central Italy, Bohemia, and Croatia, its capitals being Aix-la-Chapelle (Aachen) and Rome; ~ **Renaissance**, revival of art and letters, imitation of classical antiquity, fostered by Charlemagne; ~ **script**, rounded script adopted in Carolingian period. Also **Carlovingian.**

car·o·tene (kăr'otēn) *n.* (chem.) Red or orange-yellow crystalline hydrocarbon ($C_{40}H_{56}$) contained in carrots, tomatoes, and many other vegetables, important source of vitamin A. **ca·rot·e·noid** (karŏt'-enoid) *adj.* & *n.* (Of) a pigment, resembling carotene, found in plants and animals.

ca·rot·id (karŏt'ĭd) *adj.* & *n.* (Of, near) one of the two main arteries in the neck, which in mammals carry blood to the face and cerebral hemispheres.

Facing page: The king of ***carnivorous*** *beasts that feed on other animals, a lion in a game reserve in Mozambique, Africa, relishes the zebra he has killed. In plant life, the counterparts of the carnivors are insectivorous plants like the Venus's fly-trap (below), structured to trap and digest insects.*

ca·rouse (k*a*rowz′) *n.* Drinking bout. ~ *v.i.* (**-roused, -rous·ing**). Engage in carouse, drink deep. **ca·rous′al** *n.* [Ger. *gar aus* (*trinken*) drink to the bottom]

car·ou·sel, car·rou·sel (kăr*u*-sĕl′, -zĕl′, kăr′*u*sĕl, -zĕl) *ns.* Merry-go-round.

carp[1] (kârp) *n.* (pl. **carps**, collect. **carp**). Fresh-water fish (*Cyprinus carpio*) commonly bred in ponds; other fish of genus *Cyprinus* or *Carassius*, which includes goldfish, silverfish, etc.

carp[2] (kârp) *v.i.* Talk querulously, find fault. **carp′ing** *adj.* (esp.) Captious.

Car·pa·thi·an (kârpā′thē*a*n) **Mountains.** (also **Carpathians**) Mountain system between Poland and Czechoslovakia.

car·pel (kâr′pel) *n.* (bot.) One of the units of which a compound ovary is composed. **car·pel·lar·y** (kâr′pelĕrē) *adj.*

car·pen·ter (kâr′pent*e*r) *n.* Worker who builds or repairs wooden structures, esp. houses and ships; ~ **ant**, ant of the genus *Camponotus*, nesting and boring in decaying trees and dead wood; ~ **bee**, solitary bee of the genus *Xylocopidae*, nesting in wood. **carpenter** *v.* Do, make by, carpenter's work. **car·pen·try** (kâr′pentrē) *n.*

car·pet (kâr′pĭt) *n.* Thick fabric for spreading on floor or stair, freq. patterned in colors, and made by knotting short lengths of yarn on to the warp threads of a fabric during weaving, or by same means as tapestry, or by various mechanical weaving processes; covering or expanse of grass, flowers, etc., resembling a carpet; **on the car·pet**, being reprimanded; under discussion; **car′petbag**, traveling bag, made of carpet fabric; **car′pet-bagger**, after the Civil War, a Northerner who went into the South to make money or gain political power; a meddler in the politics of a locality with which he has no genuine connection; **carpet sweeper**, household implement with revolving brush for sweeping carpets. **car′pet·ing** *n.* **car′pet·less** *adj.* **carpet** *v.t.* Cover with, as with a carpet.

car·pus (kâr′p*u*s) *n.* (pl. **-pi** pr. -pī). (anat.) Set of bones (eight in man) connecting forearm to hand; wrist. **car·pal** (kâr′p*a*l) *adj.* & *n.* (Bone) of the carpus.

car·ra·geen (kăr′*a*gēn, -jēn) *n.* (also ~ **moss**) Seaweed (*Chondrus crispus*) yielding, when dried and boiled, a jelly used for food and in medicine. [*Carragheen* near Waterford in Ireland]

car·rel (kăr′*e*l) *n.* Small alcove in or near library stacks for use by individual reader.

car·riage (kăr′ĭj) *n.* 1. Conveying, transport; cost of conveying. 2. Manner of carrying; bearing, deportment. 3. Wheeled vehicle for persons; esp. four-wheeled private vehicle with two or more horses. 4. Wheeled support of gun; wheeled framework of vehicle apart from body; (mech.) sliding etc. part of machinery for shifting position of other parts. 5. (Brit.) Railway passenger car.

car·ri·er (kăr′ē*e*r) *n.* 1. One who or that which carries; person plying for hire with cart, truck, etc., for carrying goods, packages, etc. 2. Person or animal carrying disease germs. 3. (colloq.) Aircraft carrier. 4. ~ **pigeon**: see PIGEON; ~ **wave**, radio wave whose modulations carry communication signals.

car·ri·on (kăr′ē*o*n) *n.* Dead putrefying flesh.

Car·roll (kăr′*o*l), **Lewis.** Pseudonym of Charles Lutwidge Dodgson (1832–98); English mathematician; author of *Alice's Adventures in Wonderland* (1865), *Through the Looking-Glass* (1872), *The Hunting of the Snark* (1876), etc.

car·rot (kăr′*o*t) *n.* Umbelliferous plant (*Daucus carota*) with large tapering root; orange-red, fleshy, sweet root of cultivated varieties of this, used as vegetable; ~ **top**, (slang) person with red hair. **car′rot·y** *adj.*

car·ry (kăr′ē) *v.* (**-ried, -ry·ing**). 1. Convey, transport, bear; conduct; be the bearer of; push (process, principle, etc.) to specified point. 2. Support, hold up; hold (oneself etc.) in specified way; have about the person ready for use. 3. Have specified range; (of sound) penetrate, travel; (golf, etc.) cross, pass over. 4. Succeed in establishing, passing, electing, etc. 5. Capture, take by storm. 6. (arith.) Transfer (figure) to column of higher notation. 7. Have as result or corollary, involve. 8. ~ **away**, inspire, transport, deprive of self-

Situated near Tunis, N. Africa, ***Carthage*** *stood near the ruins of Utica, a Phoenician city. The prosperity of Carthage lay in the energy of her sea-going merchants.*

*Principles of **cartography** were understood as early as 2500 B.C., when Babylonians drew maps on clay tablets. Later map-makers made more accurate charts to which they added figurative embellishments.*

control; **carrying charge**, interest on unpaid balance of charge account or installment payments; **carry forward**, (arith.) transfer (figure) to top of new page or column; **carry off**, remove from life; win; make brave show of (event etc.); **carry on**, advance (process) a stage; continue; manage; go on with what one is doing; (colloq.) behave strangely, flirt, have amorous intrigue; **carry-on**, (luggage) bag, suitcase, small enough to be kept by airplane passenger during flight; **carry out**, put in practice; **carry over**, carry forward; **carry-over**, a sum so transferred; goods kept over for later use; **carry through**, bring safely out of difficulties; complete. **carry** *n.* 1. (golf) Ball's flight. 2. Portage between rivers etc. 3. Range (of gun, sound, etc.).

Car·son (kär′s*o*n), (**Christopher**) **"Kit"** (1809–1868). Amer. frontiersman, Indian agent, and scout; **Carson City**, capital of Nevada, in the SW.

cart (kärt) *n.* Two- or four-wheeled vehicle used in farming and for carrying heavy goods; two-wheeled one-horse vehicle for driving in; **put the ~ before the horse**, reverse proper order, confuse effect with its cause; **cart′-wheel**, wheel of a cart; (slang) silver dollar or other large coin; lateral somersault, with arms and legs extended like spokes of a wheel. **cart** *v.* Carry in a cart; convey, transport. **cart′er** *n.*

Car·ta·ge·na (kärt*a*jē′n*a*; *Span.* kärtahā′n*a*). Seaport in SE. Spain, on the Mediterranean.

carte blanche (kärt′ blănch′, blahnch′; *Fr.* kărt blahnsh′) *n.* (pl. **cartes blanches**, pr. kärts′ blănch′, blahnch′; *Fr.* kărt blahnsh′). Full discretionary power. [Fr., = "blank card"]

car·tel (kärtĕl′, kär′t*e*l) *n.* 1. Written challenge, as for duel. 2. Manufacturers' combine to control production, marketing, and price.

Car·ter[1] (kär′t*er*), **Howard** (1873–1939). English archaeologist; co-discoverer with Lord Carnarvon of tomb of Tutankhamen, 1922.

Car·ter[2] (kär′t*er*), (**James Earl, Jr.**) **"Jimmy"** (1924–). Thirty-ninth president of the U.S., 1977–81.

Car·te·sian (kärtē′zh*a*n) *adj.* & *n.* (Follower) of DESCARTES or his philosophy or mathematical methods; **~ coordinates**, system of locating a point in a plane by its distance from each of two perpendicularly intersecting axes, or in space by its distance from three mutually perpendicular axes.

Car·thage (kär′thĭj). Ancient city near Tunis on N. coast of Africa, founded by the Phoenicians; destroyed during the PUNIC Wars, and rebuilt by Augustus.

Car·tha·gin·i·an (kärth*a*jĭn′ēan) *adj.* Of Carthage. **~** *n.* Native, inhabitant, of Carthage.

Car·thu·sian (kärthōō′zh*a*n) *adj.* & *n.* (Member) of order of monks founded in Dauphiné, France, in 1086 by St. Bruno, and remarkable for the severity of their rule. [*Chatrousse*, place of the first monastery]

Car·tier (kärtyā′), **Jacques** (1491–1557). French explorer of Canada; claimed the St. Lawrence River valley for France in 1534.

car·ti·lage (kär′t*i*lĭj) *n.* Elastic flexible tissue that forms the skeleton of young vertebrates and (except for some parts near the joints) changes later into bone; structure composed of this; flexible connecting tissue. **car·ti·lag·i·nous** (kärt*i*lăj′*i*n*u*s) *adj.*

car·tog·ra·phy (kärtŏg′r*a*fē) *n.* Map drawing. **car·tog′ra·pher** *n.* **car·to·graph·ic** (kärt*o*grăf′ĭk) *adj.*

car·ton (kär′t*o*n) *n.* 1. Small white disk in bull's-eye of target. 2. Cardboard box; its contents.

car·toon (kärtōōn′) *n.* 1. Preliminary drawing on stout paper as design for painting of same size or for tapestry, mosaic, etc. 2. Humorous or topical drawing in newspaper etc.; **~ strip**, series of small drawings depicting events usu. concerning some central character, freq. serial. 3. (in motion

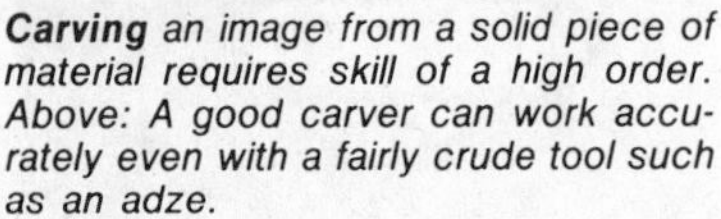

Carving an image from a solid piece of material requires skill of a high order. Above: A good carver can work accurately even with a fairly crude tool such as an adze.

*The Sisters' Peaks in the **Cascade Range** of Oregon. First explored in 1806 by Lewis and Clark, the range is a major tourist attraction with its magnificent scenery.*

pictures, also **animated** ~) Drawings photographed in series to give illusion of movement.

car·touche (kārtōōsh′) *n.* (archit.) Scroll ornament, e.g. volute of Ionic capital; tablet imitating, drawing of, scroll with rolled up ends, usu. bearing inscription; (archaeol.) oval containing hieroglyphic names and titles of Egyptian kings etc.

car·tridge (kār′trĭj) *n.* 1. Case containing explosive charge and (for small arms) bullet or shot; ~ **belt**, belt with pockets for cartridges; ~ **clip**, device for holding cartridges conveniently for use in automatic rifle, pistol, etc. 2. Small container.

car·un·cle (kăr′ŭngk*e*l, k*a*rŭng′-) *n.* 1. Fleshy excrescence, as turkey's wattles. 2. Small hard outgrowth formed on seeds of certain plants, e.g. castor-oil plant.

Ca·ru·so (k*a*rōō′sō), **Enrico** (1873–1921). Italian operatic tenor.

carve (kārv) *v.* (**carved, carv·ing**). Cut; produce by cutting; change by cutting *into*; cover or adorn *with* cut figures, designs, etc.; slice (meat, fowl) into portions at or for table; subdivide; **carving** *n.*, carved work, carved figure or design; **carving knife**, long knife for carving meat.

car·vel (kār′vel) *n.* 1. (hist.) = CARAVEL. 2. ~**-built**, (of boat) with planks flush with the side.

Car·ver[1] (kār′v*er*), **George Washington** (1864–1943). Amer. educator and agriculturist; born of slave parents; Teacher at Tuskegee Institute from 1896; best known for his agricultural research, esp. on industrial use of the peanut.

Car·ver[2] (kār′v*er*), **John** (1576–1621). First governor of Plymouth Colony in America, 1620–1.

car·y·at·id (kărēăt′ĭd) *n.* (pl. **-at·ids, -at·i·des** pr. -ăt′ĭdēz). Female figure used as column to support entablature. [Gk. *Caryatis*, a priestess of Artemis at Caryae in Laconia]

car·y·op·sis (kărēŏp′sĭs) *n.* (pl. **-ses**, pr. -sēz, **-si·des** pr. -sĭdēz). (bot.) One-seeded indehiscent fruit with pericarp fused to seed coat, as in wheat and barley.

Cas·a·blan·ca (kăs*a*blăng′k*a*). Seaport of NW. Morocco on the Atlantic; site of World War II conference between Winston Churchill and Franklin D. Roosevelt, 1943.

Ca·sals (k*a*sălz′, -sahlz′), **Pablo** (1876–1973). Spanish cellist, in Puerto Rico from 1956.

Cas·a·no·va (kăs*a*nō′v*a*, kăz-). Giovanni Jacopo Casanova de Seingalt (1725–98). Italian adventurer, author of memoirs, in French, describing his escapades and amours throughout Europe.

Cas·bah (kăz′b*a*, -bah, kahz′-), **The.** Native quarter of several north African cities, especially Algiers.

cas·cade (kăskād′) *n.* Waterfall, one section of large broken waterfall; wavy fall of lace etc. ~ *v.i.* (**-cad·ed, -cad·ing**). Fall in or like cascade.

Cas·cade (kăskād′) **Range.** Northern part of the Sierra Nevada mountains from northern California through western Washington.

cas·car·a (kăskăr′*a*) *n.* [also ~ **sa·gra·da** (s*a*grah′d*a*, -grā-)] (Extract of) bark of a Californian buckthorn, *Rhamnus purshiana*, used as a laxative or cathartic. [Span., = "sacred bark"]

case[1] (kās) *n.* 1. Instance of thing's occurring; state of affairs; circumstances; **in** ~, if (something should happen); **in any** ~, no matter what happens. 2. (med.) Condition of disease in a person; instance of disease; (fig. slang) as, (*someone's*) *a* (*mental*) ~. 3. (law) Cause, suit, for trial; statement of facts drawn up for consideration of higher court; cause that has been decided. 4. (gram.) In inflected languages, form of substantive, pronoun, or adjective expressing its relation to other words in sentence; in uninflected languages, this relation apart from form. 5. ~ **history**, (record of) information about patient etc.; ~ **law**, law based on judicial decision and precedent rather than on statute. **case′work**, social work done by personal study, handling of cases (individuals or families), hence **case′worker**.

case[2] (kās) *n.* Thing to contain or hold something else; box, chest, sheath, etc.; outer protective and covering part; box or chest with its contents; (print.) shallow wooden tray for holding type, divided into compartments to take the various letters of the alphabet; **lower** ~, case usu. holding letters other than capitals; hence (in) small letters; **upper** ~, case holding large or

Below: There are several standard sizes of **casks.** Most are made to store wine, spirits or beer. A cooper shapes oak staves so that they are wider in the middle than at their ends. He fits them into a truss at each end and heats the wood so that it will bend. Then he hammers hoops into place. Left: A butt is tapped in a wine cellar.

capital letters etc., hence, (in) capital letters; **case'harden,** harden surface of, esp. give steel surface to (iron etc.) by carbonizing; (fig.) make callous; **case-knife,** knife worn in sheath. **case** *v.t.* (**cased, cas·ing**). 1. Put into, protect with a case. 2. (slang) Examine (house etc.) in planning a crime.

ca·sein (kā'sēn, -sēĭn, kāsēn') *n.* A protein, one of the constituents of milk, coagulated by acids, and forming the basis of cheese.

case·ment (kās'ment) *n.* Metal or wooden hinged frame with glass, forming window or part of one; (poet.) window.

Case·ment (kās'ment), **Sir Roger David** (1846–1916). British diplomat and Irish nationalist; executed for treason after seeking German aid for Irish independence during World War I.

Ca·ser·ta (kazēr'ta). City near Naples, Italy; Mediterranean headquarters of the Allies during World War II; site of surrender in 1945 of German forces that fought in Italy and Yugoslavia.

cash (kăsh) *n.* Ready money; coins and banknotes; ~ **crop,** crop grown for sale; ~ **flow,** movement of money as affecting liquidity of firm etc., or as a measure of profitability; ~ **register,** till for recording and adding amounts put into it. **cash** *v.t.* Give or obtain cash for (check, money order, etc.); ~ **in one's chips,** settle accounts in game of poker; (slang) die.

cash·ew (kăsh'oo͞, kashoo͞') *n.* Large tree (*Anacardium occidentale*) of W. Indies etc., cultivated for its kidney shaped edible nut (~ **nut**). [Port. *caju,* f. Tupi (*a*) *caju*]

cash·ier[1] (kăshēr') *n.* One in charge of cash of bank or other business firm, paying and receiving money etc.; one in retail store etc. who receives customers' payments.

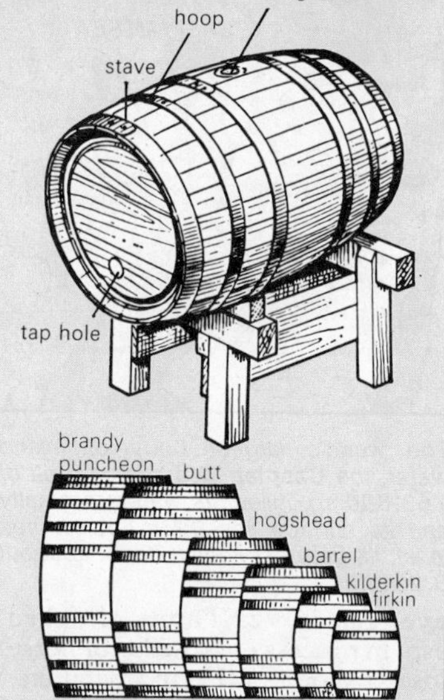

cash·ier[2] (kăshēr') *v.t.* Dismiss from service; fire.

cash·mere (kăzh'mēr, kăsh'-) *n.* Material woven from fine soft wool found beneath the hair of goats of Kashmir and Tibet; woolen fabric imitating this.

cas·ing (kā'sĭng) *n.* (esp.) = CASE[2]; framework; outer covering of a tire for car, bicycle, etc.

ca·si·no (kasē'nō) *n.* (pl. **-nos**). 1. Public room or house for entertainment, esp. gambling. 2. (also **cassino**) Card game in which each player tries to win cards by matching those exposed on the table, points being scored for winning the greatest number of cards, one for the greatest number of spades, two for ten of diamonds (**big ~**), and one for two of spades (**little ~**). [It., = "little house"]

cask (kăsk, kahsk) *n.* Barrel used esp. for beer, wine, and cider; contents or capacity of cask.

cas·ket (kăs'kĭt, kahs'-) *n.* 1. (archaic) Small, often ornamental, box for holding jewels or other valuables. 2. Coffin.

Cas·lon (kăz'lon), **William** (1692–1766). English type founder; hence, applied to style of type orig. cut at his foundry.

Cas·par (kăs'per). One of the three Magi.

The **cashew** nut of the S. American tree *Anacardium occidentale* has several uses. It is a nourishing food in itself when roasted and its oil is excellent for cooking.

Cas·pi·an (kăs′pēan) **Sea.** Inland sea between Europe and Asia; the largest inland body of water in the world, often classified as a salt lake.

casque (kăsk) *n.* (hist., poet.) Helmet.

Cas·san·dra (kasăn′dra). (Gk. myth.) Daughter of Priam, king of Troy; she was loved by Apollo, who gave her the gift of prophecy and when she deceived him ordained that her prophecies, though true, should not be believed.

Cas·satt (kasăt′), **Mary** (1845–1926). Amer. impressionist painter in France; best known for paintings of mothers and children.

cas·sa·va (kasah′va) *n.* 1. Plant of genus *Manihot*, widely cultivated in tropical America and Africa for its fleshy tuberous roots. 2. Nutritious starch obtained from its roots, used to make tapioca and as a staple in the tropics.

cas·se·role (kăs′erōl) *n.* Heat-proof vessel in which food is baked and served; food cooked in this. [Fr., = "stew pan"]

cas·sette (kasĕt′, kă-) *n.* Light-proof container for photographic film; closed container of magnetic tape for tape recorder; ~ **player**, machine for playing this; **video** ~, for recording television program.

cas·sia (kăsh′a, kăs′ēa) *n.* 1. Coarse kind of cinnamon, esp. the bark of *Cinnamonum cassia*; this tree. 2. Plant of genus *C*~ of warm climates, yielding senna leaves; any medicinal preparation from these.

Cas·si·no (kasē′nō). Town in central Italy near Naples; Benedictine monastery stands above the town, on Monte Cassino; site of World War II battles in which Allies gained victory in push toward Rome.

Cas·si·o·pe·ia (kăsēopē′a). 1. (Gk. myth.) Wife of Cepheus, king of Ethiopia, mother of Andromeda; she boasted herself more beautiful than the Nereids, thus incurring the wrath of Poseidon. 2. (astron.) Northern constellation between Cepheus and Perseus.

cas·sit·er·ite (kasĭt′erīt) *n.* Stannic dioxide, TINstone.

Cas·sius Lon·gi·nus (kăsh′us lŏnjī′nus), **Gaius** (d. 42 B.C.). Roman general; conspired with others to assassinate Julius Caesar.

cas·sock (kăs′ok) *n.* Long close-fitting tunic, usu. black, buttoning up to the neck and reaching to the feet, worn by clergy.

cas·so·war·y (kăs′owĕrē) *n.* (pl. **-war·ies**). Large flightless running bird of genus *Casuarius*, related to ostrich, found in Australia, New Guinea, etc. [Malay *kasuari*]

cast (kăst, kahst) *v.* (**cast, cast·ing**). 1. Throw, cause to fall or drop; ~ **anchor**, let it down; ~ **an**

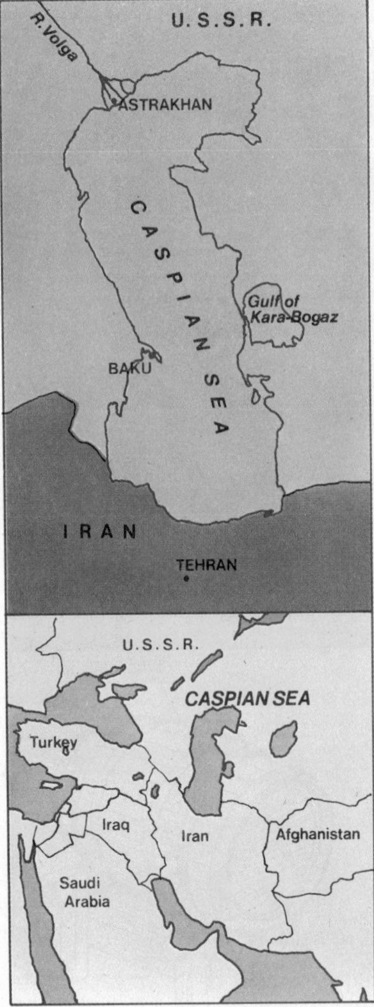

*The world's largest body of inland water, the **Caspian Sea** has an area of 163,800 sq. miles. Its waters are salty and its surface lies 92 ft. below sea level. Its greatest known depth is about 3,200 ft.*

eye, glance. 2. Throw off, shed, esp. in process of growth; (of horse) lose (a shoe). 3. Form (metal etc.) into desired shape by melting and pouring into a mold; found; ~ **iron**: see IRON; ~**-iron** (*adj.*), made of cast iron; hard, very strong, unadaptable. 4. Arrange (facts *into* a shape, actors *for* parts in play). 5. ~ **about**, look about, search here and there, *for*; ~ **adrift**, leave to drift; ~ **ashore**, leave behind on seashore; ~ **away**, reject; (pass., of ship, sailor, etc.) be wrecked; **cast′away**, person shipwrecked or cast adrift or rejected; **cast down**, depress; **cast off**, throw away, abandon; (print.) estimate printed length or size of (MS.); **cast′off** (*n.*) thing discarded; (print.) estimated length. **cast** *n.* 1. Throw of missile, fishing line, sounding lead, etc.; throw of dice, number thrown. 2. Model, shape, made by running molten metal or pressing soft substance into a mold; the mold itself; plaster copy of sculpture

*Top: The **cassowary** bird is aggressive if provoked and it is a formidable fighter. Above: Its neck is unfeathered and its head carries a horny casque.*

made thus. 3. Earth excreted by earthworm; undigested food thrown up by bird. 4. Set of actors taking the parts in a play. 5. Twist, inclination; slight squint. 6. Tinge, hue. **cast′er**[1] *n.*

Cas·ta·gno (kahstahn′yō), **Andrea del** (1423–1457). Italian Florentine realistic painter.

cas·ta·net (kăstanĕt′) *n.* Small concave shell of ivory or hard wood used to make rattling sound as accompaniment to dancing, a pair being held in the palm of the hand and clapped together with the

Castles *were generally built on sites against which it would be hard to launch an attack, and many dominated a feature of importance. Top: The castle of San Angelo in Rome commands the bridge over the River Tiber. Above: Dover Castle dominates the town.*

fingers.

caste (kăst, kahst) *n.* One of the four major hereditary classes (BRAHMAN, KSHATRIYA, VAISYA, and SUDRA) into which Hindu society is divided, each separated from the others by restrictions on occupation, marriage, and social intercourse; any social class rigidly separated from others by occupation, heredity, etc.; social status conferred by class (**lose ~**, lose prestige); **~ system**, social system based on caste. **caste'less** *adj.*

cas·tel·lat·ed (kăs'telātĭd) *adj.* Built like a castle, having battlements; castlelike. **cas·tel·la·tion** (kăstelā'shon) *n.*

cast·er[2], **cas·tor**[2] (kas'ter, kahs'-) *ns.* 1. Small solid wheel and swivel on leg of piece of furniture for moving it without lifting. 2. Small vessel with perforated top for sprinkling pepper, sugar, flour, etc.

cas·ti·gate (kăs'tĭgāt) *v.t.* (**-gat·ed, -gat·ing**). Chastise, punish. **cas·ti·ga·tion** (kăstĭgā'shon), **cas'ti·ga·tor** *ns.*

Cas·tile (kăstēl'). Central part of Spain, an ancient kingdom; **~ soap**, fine hard white or mottled soap made with olive oil and soda. **Cas·til·i·an** (kăstĭl'yan) *adj.* & *n.* (Native, inhabitant) of Castile; (of) the language of Castile, literary Spanish.

cast·ing (kăs'tĭng, kahs'-) *adj.* **~ vote**, (f. obs. sense of cast = "turn the scale") vote that decides between two equal parties. **casting** *n.* (esp.) 1. Piece of metal or other substance shaped by melting and pouring into a mold; this process of manufacture; DIE-[1] def. 3, SAND-, PRESSURE **~**: see these words. 2. = CAST *n.* def. 2.

Since he rose to power in Cuba in 1959, ***Fidel Castro*** *has worked towards close ties with Communist nations in Europe. He is seen here inspecting machines in Czechoslovakia.*

cas·tle (kăs'el, kah'sel) *n.* 1. Large fortified building or set of buildings; dwelling that was once fortified; (colloq.) palace. 2. (hist.) Small wooden tower used in war etc. and borne on elephant's back or ship's deck. 3. (chess) = ROOK[2]. 4. **~(s) in the air, in Spain**, daydream(s), visionary project or scheme. **castle** *v.i.* (**-tled, -tling**). (chess) Move king two squares toward one of the rooks and (in the same move) this rook to the square next past the king.

Cas·tor (kăs'ter, kahs'-). (Gk. myth.) One of the twin sons (**~ and Pollux**) of Tyndareus and Leda, and half brother of Helen. 2. (astron.) More northerly of the two bright stars in the constellation Gemini.

cas·tor[1] (kăs'ter, kahs'-) *n.* 1. Reddish-brown unctuous bitter substance obtained from anal glands of beaver and used in perfumery and formerly in medicine. 2. (archaic) Hat (orig. one of beaver or imitation beaver).

cas·tor[2] (kăs'ter, kahs'-) = CASTER[2].

cas·tor (kăs'ter, kahs'-) **oil.** Pale yellow nauseous acrid oil obtained from seeds of **Castor-oil plant** (*Ricinus communis*), used as purgative and lubricant.

cas·trate (kăs'trāt) *v.t.* (**-trat·ed, -trat·ing**). Remove testicles of, geld; deprive of vigor; expurgate (book). **cas·tra·tion** (kăstrā'shon) *n.*

cas·tra·to (kăstrah'tō, ka-) *n.* (pl. **-ti** pr. -tē). Adult male singer retaining boy's voice as a result of castration. [It.]

Cas·tro (kăs′trō), **Fidel** (1927–). Cuban revolutionary and premier (since 1959).

cas·u·al (kăzh′ōōal) *adj.* Accidental; irregular; undesigned, coming by chance or accident; unmethodical, careless; unconcerned, uninterested; (of clothes) informal. **cas′u·al·ly** *adv.* **cas′u·al·ness** *n.*

cas·u·al·ty (kăzh′ōōaltē, kăzh′-al-) *n.* (pl. **-ties**). Accident, mishap, disaster; killed, wounded, or injured person; (pl.) list or number of such persons.

cas·u·ist (kăzh′ōōĭst) *n.* Person (orig. a theologian) who reasons subtly in matters of conscience and conduct; hence, disparagingly, a disingenuous hairsplitter. **cas·u·ist·ry** (kăzh′ōōĭstrē) *n.*

ca·sus bel·li (kā′sus bĕl′ī, kăs′us; *Lat.* kah′sōōs bĕl′ē) (pl. **ca·sus bel·li**). Cause of war, act justifying or regarded as reason for war. [L.]

CAT *abbrev.* Clear-air turbulence.

cat (kăt) *n.* 1. Small domesticated furry carnivorous quadruped (*Felis domesticus*), kept to destroy mice and as pet; **wild′cat**: see WILD. 2. Any member of the genus *Felis*, which includes lions, tigers, panthers, etc. 3. Catlike animal of other species, as *civet cat, polecat*, etc. 4. (colloq.) Spiteful or gossiping woman. 5. (naut.) Cathead, beam projecting from bows of ship, for raising the anchor, or carrying it suspended, so called because in early times the ring to which the anchor was drawn commonly hung from an ornament, often an animal mask. 6. Cat-o′-nine-tails (see below). 7. Caterpillar tractor. 8. (slang) Jazz musician or devotee; a man. 9. **~-and-dog**, very quarrelsome (life etc.); **cat′bird**, N. Amer. songbird (*Dumetella carolinensis*) having gray plumage; **cat burglar**, one who enters house by climbing to upper story; **cat′call**, shrill call or whistle expressing disapproval; (*v.*) make catcalls, receive with catcalls; **cat′fish**, any fish of the group Siluridae, including the bullhead, most of which live in fresh water and have barbels around the mouth; **cat′head**: see sense 5 above; **cat′mint**, (archaic) catnip, esp. as a tea; **cat′nap**, short light sleep taken sitting in chair etc.; **cat′nip**, aromatic labiate plant with pale-blue flowers (*Nepeta cataria*) to which cats are strongly attracted; small bag of this for cats to play with; **cat-o′-nine-tails**, whip of nine knotted cords formerly used in military and naval punishments; **cat′s-cradle**, child's game with players lifting intertwined string from fingers in such a way as to form new patterns; **cat′s-eye**, precious stone resembling cat's eye with contracted pupil, a hard chalcedonic quartz from Ceylon, Malabar, etc.; playing marble made of or resembling this; small round reflector on vehicles, along roads, etc., to aid in night driving; **cat′s-paw**, (colloq.) person used as tool by another; **cat(′s) whisker**, fine usu. copper wire placed in contact with sensitive spot in crystal wireless receiver; **cat′tail**, reedlike marsh plant (*Typha latifolia*) with flowers in tall cylindrical spikes; **cat′walk**, narrow bridge or footway giving access to machinery etc.

cat *v.* (**cat·ted, cat·ting**). (naut.) Raise (anchor) to cathead.

cat. *abbrev.* Catalog.

cata- *prefix.* Down from, down to, against, in opposition to, mis-.

ca·tab·o·lism (katăb′olĭzem) *n.* Phase of metabolism in which complex compounds break into simpler ones. **cat·a·bol·ic** (kătabŏl′ĭk) *adj.*

cat·a·chre·sis (kătakrē′sĭs) *n.* Perversion, improper use, of words, either for rhetorical effect or from ignorance.

cat·a·clysm (kăt′aklĭzem) *n.* Deluge, esp. the Flood; sudden convulsion or alteration of conditions, political, social, etc., upheaval. **cat·a·clys·mal** (kătaklĭz′-mal), **cat·a·clys′mic** *adjs.*

cat·a·comb (kăt′akōm) *n.* Subterranean cemetery (orig. that under the basilica of St. Sebastian near Rome, supposed burying place of Peter and Paul); (pl.) subterranean galleries made by Jews and early Christians in and near Rome, with recesses in the sides for tombs;

*The domestic **cat** evolved from a civet-like creature that lived in the Miocene period some 20 million years ago. 1. The European wild cat has tabby markings, and some people believe that it mated with an African cat to produce the domestic variety. The wild cat has a rather bigger and flatter head than the domestic cat. 2. The Russian Blue cat has a remarkably thick double coat. It is*

3

5

4

6

extensively bred in the U.S. 3. The grey tabby cat almost died out in Great Britain during the 1939–45 war but the breed was revived by importing a good strain. 4. The Siamese cat was bred from a strain said to have been brought to Europe from Bangkok in 1884. It has a raucous call. 5. The Australian wild cat, carnivorous marsupial unrelated to true cats. 6. The Manx cat, sometimes called a rumpie, has no tail. The breed is reputed to come from the Isle of Man, but tailless breeds are found in many countries, including China and the U.S.S.R.

similar works elsewhere. [LL. *catacumbas*, name given to the catacomb under St. Sebastian; origin unknown]

ca·tad·ro·mous (k*a*tăd′rom*u*s) *adj.* (of fish) Descending to lower reaches of river, or to sea, to spawn.

cat·a·falque (kăt′*a*fălk, -fawk, -fawlk) *n.* Platform or base upon which a deceased person lies in state; open hearse.

Cat·a·lan (kăt′*a*lăn, kăt*a*lăn′) *adj.* & *n.* (Native, inhabitant) of Catalonia; (of) the dialect of Provençal (or langue d'oc) spoken in Catalonia.

cat·a·lep·sy (kăt′*a*lĕpsē) *n.* Muscular rigidity and lack of sensation and awareness, often associated with epilepsy, hysteria, or schizophrenia. **cat·a·lep·tic** (kăt*a*lĕp′tĭk) *adj.*

Cat·a·li·na (kăt*a*lē′n*a*) **Island.** Island and resort area off the coast of California near Los Angeles.

cat·a·log, cat·a·logue (kăt′*a*lawg, -lŏg) *ns.* Complete list, usu. alphabetical or arranged under headings, and often with descriptive or other particulars. ~ *v.* (**-loged, -log·ing, -logued, -logu·ing**). Enumerate, enter, in a catalog.

Cat·a·lo·ni·a (kăt*a*lō′nē*a*, -ny*a*). (Span. *Cataluña*) NE. part of Spain, formerly a province.

ca·tal·pa (k*a*tăl′p*a*, -tawl′-) *n.* Tree of genus *C*~ with large simple leaves and trumpet-shaped flowers, native to N. America, W. Indies, Japan, and China.

ca·tal·y·sis (k*a*tăl′ĭsĭs) *n.* (pl. **-ses** pr. -sēz). Facilitation of a chemical reaction by the presence of an added substance that is itself not consumed in the reaction. **cat·a·lyze** (kăt′*a*līz) *v.t.* (**-lyzed, -lyz·ing**). **cat·a·lyt·ic** (kăt*a*lĭt′ĭk) *adj.* & *n.*

cat·a·lyst (kăt′*a*lĭst) *n.* Substance causing catalysis.

cat·a·ma·ran (kăt*a*m*a*răn′) *n.* Raft or float of logs tied together, with longest one in middle; sailing boat with twin hulls. [Tamil *katta-maram* tied tree]

cat·a·mite (kăt′*a*mīt) *n.* Boy kept by a pederast. [L. *Catamitus*, corrupt form of *Ganymēdes* Ganymede]

cat·a·mount (kăt′*a*mownt) *n.*: see MOUNTAIN lion.

cat·a·pult (kăt′*a*pŭlt, -p͝olt) *n.*

*The principle of the **catamaran** has long been known, but not until modern materials, light and strong enough to withstand heavy seas, were available, could an ocean catamaran be built.*

*The mobile **catapult** was one of many siege engines designed for commanders who encountered the problems of capturing walled cities and strong fortresses.*

*The **caterpillar** tractor performs far more efficiently on heavy ground or in light soil where ordinary tractor tires either bog or cannot grip.*

1. Ancient military engine worked with lever and ropes for hurling stones etc. 2. (chiefly Brit.) Slingshot. 3. Mechanism for launching aircraft from deck of ship. ~ *v.* Shoot with catapult; hurl as from catapult; launch with catapult.

cat·a·ract (kăt´*a*răkt) *n.* 1. Waterfall, esp. large precipitous fall or series of falls; downpour, rush of water. 2. Progressive opacity of lens of eye, resulting, unless treated, in impairment of vision and eventual blindness.

ca·tarrh (k*a*tar´) *n.* Inflammation of mucous membrane, esp. of nose, throat, and bronchial tubes, causing increased flow of mucus. **ca·tarrh'al, ca·tarrh'ous** *adjs.*

cat·ar·rhine (kăt´*a*rīn) *adj.* & *n.* (Animal) of one of the two divisions of the suborder Anthropoidea, distinguished from the PLATYRRHINE by having the nostrils close together and directed downward, and including the Old World monkeys, the anthropoid apes, and man.

ca·tas·tro·phe (k*a*tăs´tr*o*fē) *n.* Dénouement of dramatic piece; disastrous end, overthrow, calamitous fate; event subverting order or system of things. **cat·a·stroph·ic** (kăt*a*strŏf´ĭk) *adj.* **cat·a·stroph'i·cal·ly** *adv.*

cat·a·to·ni·a (kăt*a*tō´nē*a*) *n.* (path.) Schizophrenia marked by negativism and mutism with intervals of catalepsy and occas. violence. **cat·a·ton·ic** (kăt*a*tŏn´ĭk) *adj.* & *n.*

cat·boat (kăt´bōt) *n.* Broad-beamed sailboat with mast well forward and rigged with one sail.

catch (kăch) *v.* (**caught, catch·ing**). 1. Capture, lay hold of, seize; be entangled, take hold; hit; come level with, make up arrears (also ~ **up**); intercept (ball etc.) in motion, esp. take hold of (ball thrown) before it reaches ground; be in time for (train etc.); check suddenly. 2. Surprise, detect. 3. Ignite, be ignited (also ~ **fire**). 4. Receive, incur, be infected with. 5. Grasp with senses or mind; arrest, captivate, arrest attention of; take by surprise, trick, deceive. **catch'-all**, receptacle to catch or include various items (also fig.); **catch'-penny**, got up merely to sell, without concern for quality, cheap; **catch-22**, (colloq.) conflicting or self-contradictory regulations producing frustration [f. *Catch-22*, novel (1961) by Joseph Heller, Amer. author b. 1923]; **catch'-word**, word so placed as to attract attention, as word at head of entry in dictionary etc.; word caught up and repeated, esp. in politics etc. **catch** *n.* 1. Act of catching; amount or number of fish caught; device for fastening or restraining something; chance of, success in, catching ball, as in baseball; thing or person caught or worth catching. 2. Something designed to deceive or trip up; unforeseen difficulty or awkwardness; hidden trap; surprise. 3. (mus.) Round, sometimes devised to produce punning or other humorous verbal combinations.

catch·er (kăch´*er*) *n.* (esp.) Baseball player behind home plate who directs pitcher, catches pitches that go past batter, etc.

catch·ing (kăch´ĭng) *adj.* (esp.) Infectious; captivating.

catch·ment (kăch´m*e*nt) *n.* Catching and collection of rainfall over a natural drainage area; basin, reservoir for collecting or draining water; the water so collected.

catch·y (kăch´ē) *adj.* (**catch·i·er, catch·i·est**). (colloq.) Attractive; (of tune etc.) easily remembered.

cat·e·chism (kăt´*e*kĭz*e*m) *n.* Treatise for instruction by question and answer, esp. on religious doctrine.

cat·e·chize (kăt´*e*kīz) *v.t.* (**-chized, -chiz·ing**). Instruct by question and answer, or by the use of a catechism; put questions to,

examine. **cat·e·chist** (kăt´*e*kĭst) *n.*

cat·e·chu·men (kăt*e*kū´m*e*n) *n.* Christian convert under instruction before baptism; neophyte.

cat·e·gor·i·cal (kăt*e*gŏr´ĭk*a*l, -găr´-) *adj.* Unconditional, absolute; explicit, direct; ~ **imperative**, (Kantian ethics) an absolute and universally binding moral law. **cat·e·gor´i·cal·ly** *adv.*

cat·e·go·ry (kăt´*e*gōrē, -gōrē) *n.* (pl. **-ries**). 1. Class, division. 2. In Aristotle, one of a possibly exhaustive set of classes among which all things might be distributed.

cat·e·nar·y (kăt´*e*nĕrē; *Brit.* k*a*tē´n*e*rē) *adj.* & *n.* (pl. **-nar·ies**). (Like) curve formed by uniform chain hanging freely from two points not in one vertical line.

cat·e·nate (kăt´*e*nāt) *v.t.* (**-nat·ed, -nat·ing**). Connect like links of chain. **cat·e·na·tion** (kăt*e*nā´sh*o*n) *n.*

ca·ter (kā´t*e*r) *v.i.* Purvey food; provide amusement etc. *for*; provide anything desired *to*. **ca´ter·er** *n.*

cat·er·pil·lar (kăt´*e*pĭl*e*r, kăt´*er*-) *n.* 1. Larva of butterfly, moth, sawfly, resembling a worm but possessing several pairs of legs, strong jaws, and short antennae and feeding on leaves, fruit, or other succulent parts of plants. 2. **C**~ (trademark) Tractor equipped with endless articulated steel bands carrying treads passing around two or more wheels. [OF. *chatepelose* hairy cat]

cat·er·waul (kăt´*er*wawl) *n.* Cry of cat in heat, similar squalling sound. ~ *v.i.* Make caterwaul.

cat·gut (kăt´gŭt) *n.* Dried and twisted intestines of sheep, horse, etc. (not cat), used for strings of musical instruments, tennis rackets, etc., and for sutures in surgical operations.

ca·thar·sis (k*a*thăr´sĭs) *n.* (pl. **-ses** pr. -sēz). 1. (med.) Purgation. 2. (with ref. to Aristotle's *Poetics*) Purification of emotions by vicarious experience, esp. through the drama. 3. (psychotherapy) Relieving of neurotic state by reenacting or relating an experience of strong emotional character that has undergone repression.

ca·thar·tic (k*a*thăr´tĭk) *adj.* Effecting catharsis; purgative; cleansing. ~ *n.* Purgative medicine.

Ca·thay (kăthā´). (archaic and poet.) CHINA.

The larval stage of the life of a butterfly is called a ***caterpillar.*** *In many cases the caterpillar has a body larger than that of the moth or butterfly it will become. The energy built up during this stage, by a tremendous rate of eating, is required to sustain the insect during the great changes it will experience at the pupal stage.*

ca·the·dral (k*a*thē´dr*a*l) *n.* Principal church of diocese, containing bishop's *cathedra* or throne. ~ *adj.* Ranking as a cathedral, containing or belonging to a cathedral.

Cath·er (kăth´*er*), **Willa Sibert** (1873–1947). Amer. novelist, author of *My Antonia, One of Ours, Death Comes for the Archbishop,* etc.; awarded Pulitzer Prize, 1922.

Cath·er·ine[1] (kăth´*e*rĭn, kăth´rĭn) "the Great" (1729–96). Empress of Russia 1762–96; by birth a German, Princess Sophia of Anhalt-Zerbst; married the Russian heir; six months after his accession (as Peter III) he was forced to abdicate and was murdered, whereupon Catherine became Empress.

Cath·er·ine[2] (kăth´*e*rĭn, kăth´rĭn), **St.** (d. 307). Legendary saint and martyr of Alexandria; she was beheaded, after other methods of putting her to death, including that of the wheel, had failed; ~ **wheel,** (orig.) instrument of torture consisting of four wheels armed with knives and teeth turning different ways; now, a kind of firework that rotates while burning.

Ca·the·rine[3] **de Mé·di·cis** (kăth´*e*rĭn d*e* mĕd´ĭsēz, kăth´rĭn, mĕd´ĭchēz) (1519–89). Wife of Henry II of France; regent of France (1547–59) during the minority of her son, Charles IX.

Căth·erine[4] **of Ar·a·gon** (kăth´*e*rĭn *o*v ăr´*a*g*o*n, -gŏn, kăth´rĭn) (1483–1536). Daughter of Ferdinand and Isabella of Spain; married Arthur, prince of Wales 1501, and, after his death, became the first wife of his younger brother Henry VIII 1509; divorced by Henry 1526, on ground that her first marriage made her second invalid.

cath·e·ter (kăth´ĭt*er*) *n.* Slender, flexible tube for introducing into a body channel to withdraw excess fluid or sample for analysis, esp. urine from the bladder. **cath·e·ter·ize** (kăth´ĭterīz) *v.t.* (**-ized, -iz·ing**). Use a catheter on.

cath·ode (kăth´ōd) *n.* (elect.) Negatively charged electrode; ~ **ray,** beam of electrons issuing from cathode of electrical discharge tube (~ **ray tube**).

cath·o·lic (kăth´*o*lĭk, kăth´lĭk) *adj.* 1. Universal, of universal interest or use; all-embracing, of wide sympathies. 2. **C~ Church,** (*a*) the whole body of Christians; (*b*) after the separation of Eastern and Western Churches, the Western or Latin Church; (*c*) after the Reformation, claimed as its exclusive title by that part of the Western Church that remained under Roman obedience, but (*d*) held by Anglicans to include the Church of England. 3. Of or belonging to any of these churches, esp. = Roman Catholic (see ROMAN def. 6). 4. **His C~ Majesty,** title of former kings of Spain. **C~** *n.* Member of a Catholic church, esp. Roman Catholic. **ca·thol·i·cal·ly** (k*a*thŏl´ĭklē) *adv.* **ca·thol·i·cism** (k*a*thŏl´ĭsĭz*e*m), **cath·o·lic·i·ty** (k*a*thŏ-lĭs´ĭtē) *ns.* **ca·thol·i·cize** (k*a*thŏl´-

The late Middle Ages produced a spate of ***cathederal*** *building throughout Europe. Top: the cathedral at Wells, Somerset U.K., is one of the finest of these. Its style shows the progression of changes in Gothic taste from the late 12th to the 15th centuries. Above: St. Patrick's Cathedral, New York, was designed by James Renwick and dedicated in 1879.*

ĭsīz) *v.t.* & *v.i.* (**-cized, -ciz·ing**).

cat·i·on (kăt′īon) *n.*: see ION. **cat·i·on·ic** (kătīŏn′ĭk) *adj.* [Gk., = "going down"]

cat·kin (kăt′kĭn) *n.* Deciduous spike, usu. of unisexual apetalous flowers, of willow, birch, etc.

Ca·to (kā′tō), **Marcus Porcius.** Name of two Romans: (1) "Cato the Elder" or "Cato the Censor" (239–149 B.C.), famous for his opposition to the lax morals and luxury of the Romans and for his insistence that "Carthage must be destroyed"; author of a treatise *De Agri Cultura*, the oldest extant literary prose work in Latin; (2) his great-grandson "Cato the Younger" (95–46 B.C.), also a man of unbending character; chief political antagonist of Julius Caesar.

Cats·kill (kăt′skĭl) **Mountains.** Low mountain range and resort area in SE. New York State.

cat·sup (kăt′s*u*p, kăch′*u*p, kĕch′-) *n.* Var. of KETCHUP.

cat·tle (kăt′*e*l) *n.* Bovine domestic animals (steers, cows, etc.) raised for meat, milk, etc.; ~ **prod**, prod to drive cattle, now esp. an electric one; ~ **rustler**, marauder who steals cattle.

catt·ley·a (kăt′lē*a*, kătlē′*a*, -lā′*a*) *n.* Orchidaceous Central Amer. and Brazilian plant of genus *C*~ with violet, pink, or yellow flowers. [William *Cattley* (d. 1832), English patron of botany]

cat·ty (kăt′ē) *adj.* (**-ti·er, -ti·est**). Spiteful, malicious; gossipy. **cat′ti·ly** *adv.* **cat′ti·ness** *n.*

Ca·tul·lus (k*a*tŭl′*u*s), **Gaius Valerius** (87–54? B.C.). Roman poet.

Cau·ca·sian (kawkā′zh*a*n, -sh*a*n, -kăzh′*a*n, -kăsh′*a*n) *adj.* & *n.* 1. (Native, inhabitant, language) of the Caucasus. 2. Caucasoid.

Cau·ca·soid (kaw′k*a*soid) *adj.* & *n.* (Member) of the light-skinned division of mankind found esp. in Europe, N. Africa, and SW. Asia; Caucasian.

*Several trees produce **catkins.** They are flowers borne by deciduous trees such as the beech, hazel and willow.*

*Holstein dairy **cattle** originated in northern Holland and are now being farmed in arid areas of Arizona where use of the feedlotting process allows successful milk production.*

Cau·ca·sus (kaw′k*a*s*u*s). Mountain range between Black Sea and Caspian Sea; region of the U.S.S.R. between these two seas.

cau·cus (kaw′k*u*s) *n.* (pl. **-cus·es**). Political party meeting to decide policy or select candidates; policy meeting.

cau·dal (kaw′d*a*l) *adj.* Of, at, like, tail. **cau·date** (kaw′dāt) *adj.* Tailed; of the order Caudata. **cau′dat·ed** *adj.*

cau·dil·lo (kawdēl′yō, -dē′ō; *Sp.* kowdhēl′yaw, -dhē′yaw) *n.* (pl. **-dil·los** pr. -dēl′yōz, -dē′ōz; *Sp.* -dhēl′yaws, -dhē′yaws). (in Spanish-speaking countries) Military dictator. [Span., = "leader"]

caught (kawt): see CATCH.

caul (kawl) *n.* Amnion or inner membrane enclosing fetus; part of this enclosing child's head at birth.

caul·dron (kawl′dr*o*n) *n.* Large kettle (usu.) with hoop handle and removable lid.

cau·li·flow·er (kaw′lĭflow*e*r, kŏl′ĭ-) *n.* Cultivated plant of genus *Brassica* with young inflorescence forming close white fleshy edible head; ~ **ear**, (prize fighter's) ear thickened and distorted by blows.

cau·line (kaw'lĭn, -līn) *adj.* (bot.) Of, growing on, a stem.

caulk (kawk) *v.t.* Stop up seams of (ship etc.), as with oakum and melted tar.

caus·al (kaw'zal) *adj.* Of, acting as, expressing, due to, a cause or causes; of the nature of cause and effect. **cau·sal·i·ty** (kawzăl'ĭtē) *n.* (pl. **-ties**). Being, having, a cause; relation of cause and effect, doctrine that everything has cause(s).

cau·sa·tion (kawzā'shon) *n.* Causing; relation of cause and effect. **caus·a·tive** (kaw'zatĭv) *adj.* Acting as cause (*of*); (gram.) expressing a cause or causation.

cause (kawz) *v.t.* (**caused, caus·ing**). Be the cause of, make (something) happen; induce, make (person *to* do, thing to be done). ~ *n.* 1. What produces an effect, what gives rise to any action, phenomenon, or condition; person or other agent bringing something about; ground or reason for action; motive; **First C~**, original cause or creator of the universe. 2. (law etc.) Ground for legal action; lawsuit; side of question or controversy expressed by a person or party; goal, or principle pursued with dedication; subject of concern.

cause cé·lè·bre (kawz selĕb're, -lĕb'; *Fr.* kōz sālĕb're) (pl. **causes cé·lè·bres** pr. kawz selĕb'rez, -lĕbz'; *Fr.* kōz sālĕb're). Lawsuit or scandal exciting much public interest. [Fr.]

cause·way (kawz'wā) *n.* Raised road across low or wet place or piece of water.

caus·tic (kaw'stĭk) *adj.* 1. Burning, corrosive, destroying organic tissue; ~ **soda**, sodium hydroxide. 2. Bitter, cutting, sarcastic. 3. (optics) Formed by intersection of rays from one point reflected or refracted from a curved surface. **caustic** *n.* Caustic substance. **caus'ti·cal·ly** *adv.* **caus·tic·i·ty** (kawstĭs'ĭtē) *n.*

cau·ter·ize (kaw'terīz) *v.t.* (**-ized, -iz·ing**). Sear with hot iron or caustic, esp. in treatment of wounds etc. **cau·ter·i·za·tion** (kawterĭzā'shon) *n.*

cau·tion (kaw'shon) *n.* 1. Warning; (colloq.) extraordinary, strange person or thing. 2. Avoidance of rashness, attention to safety. ~ *v.t.* Warn; admonish.

cau·tion·ar·y (kaw'shonĕrē) *adj.* Conveying a warning or admonition.

cau·tious (kaw'shus) *adj.* Disposed to or exhibiting caution. **cau'tious·ly** *adv.* **cau'tious·ness** *n.*

cav·al·cade (kăvalkād', kăv'alkād) *n.* Ceremonial procession, esp. on horseback; colorful procession or pageant.

cav·a·lier (kăvalēr', kăv'alēr) *n.* 1. Horseman. 2. Courtly gentleman, gallant, esp. as escorting a lady. 3. (**C~**) Adherent of Charles I of England; Royalist. ~ *adj.* 1. Careless in manner, offhand; haughty, supercilious. 2. Royalist. **cav·a·lier'ly** *adj.* & *adv.*

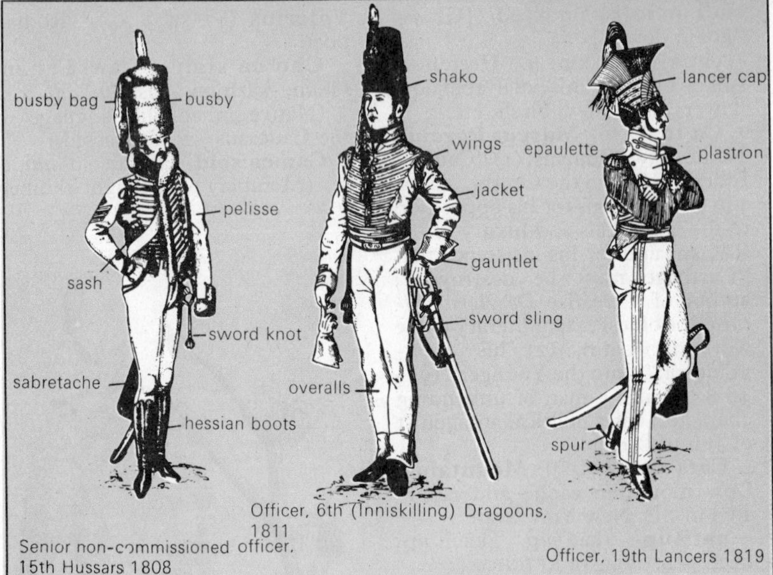

*Top: 'The Laughing Cavalier' by Franz Hals, painted in 1624, captures the spirit of élan that most people associate with **cavaliers** of the 17th century. Their taste for luxury is reflected in their rich dress.*

*Above: The **cavalry's** dash later found expression in the splendor of formal uniforms. These often copied the fashion of admired opponents, as with the British Lancers' adoption of Polish Lancers' caps.*

cav·al·ry (kăv'alrē) *n.* (pl. **-ries**). Horse soldiers, mounted troops; troops formerly mounted but now equipped with tanks or armored cars; ~ **twill**, strong material in double twill used for clothing. **cav'al·ry·man** *n.* (pl. **-men**).

cave (kāv) *n.* Hollow place opening more or less horizontally under the ground or into side of hill; ~ **man**, prehistoric man living in cave; person resembling prehistoric man in behavior, crude, rough man; ~ **in**, collapse (of earth etc. over hollow place), yield to pressure from outside or above; (fig.) yield to pressure, submit, give in; smash in; also **cave-in** (*n.*).

ca·ve·at (kā′vēăt, kăv′ē-, kah′vēaht) *n.* 1. (law) Formal notice by interested party to court requesting postponement of proceedings until he is heard. 2. Warning, caution. [L., = "let him beware"]

ca·ve·at emp·tor (kā′vēăt ĕmp′tōr, kăv′ē-, kah′vēaht). "Let the buyer beware," legal principle that the seller is not responsible for the quality of his merchandise unless he supplies a written warranty. [L.]

Cav·ell (kăv′*e*l), **Edith Louisa** (1865–1915). English nurse; shot by the Germans during World War I for aiding the escape of Allied soldiers from Belgium to Holland.

cav·en·dish (kăv′*e*ndĭsh) *n.* Tobacco softened, sweetened with molasses, and pressed into cakes.

Cav·en·dish (kăv′*e*ndĭsh), **Henry** (1731–1810). English natural philosopher; discovered the composition of water and air and the density of the earth; experimented in electricity.

cav·ern (kăv′*e*rn) *n.* (Vast) underground cave, hollow place. **cav·ern·ous** (kăv′*e*rn*u*s) *adj.*

cav·i·ar, cav·i·are (kăv′ēar̄, kăvēar̄′) *ns.* Roe of sturgeon and other large fish, pressed and salted, and eaten as a delicacy or a relish.

cav·il (kăv′*i*l) *v.i.* (**-iled, -il·ing**, Brit. **-illed, -il·ling**). Raise trivial objection. ~ *n.* Quibbling objection; caviling.

cav·i·ta·tion (kăvĭtā′sh*o*n) *n.* Successive formation and collapse of bubbles in liquids by mechanical forces, as from a ship's propeller.

cav·i·ty (kăv′ĭtē) *n.* (pl. **-ties**). Empty space within solid body, hollow place; pitted or decayed area in tooth.

ca·vort (k*a*vōrt′) *v.i.* Prance, caper, frolic.

Ca·vy (kā′vē) *n.* (pl. **-vies**). Large rodent of S. Amer. genus *Cavia*, including guinea pigs. [*cabiai*, native name in Fr. Guiana]

caw (kaw) *n.* Cry of crow, raven, etc.; sound resembling this. ~ *v.i.* Utter caw.

Cax·ton (kăks′t*o*n), **William** (1422?–91). First English printer; published first book printed in English; established a press at Westminster, 1477–91, from which he issued about 80 books, many of them his own translations of French romances.

cay (kā, kē) *n.* Small, low islet or reef of sand, rocks, etc., esp. off coast of Latin America.

Cay·enne (kīĕn′, kā-). Capital of French Guiana, on ~ **Island**.

cay·enne (kīĕn′, kā-) *n.* (also ~ **pepper**) Very hot pungent reddish powder obtained from seeds of plants of genus *Capsicum*, used as a condiment.

cay·man (kā′m*a*n) = CAIMAN.

Cay·man (kā′m*a*n) **Islands.** British dependency of three islands in the Caribbean; capital, Georgetown on Grand Cayman.

Ca·yu·ga (kāū′g*a*, kī-), **Lake.** One of the Finger Lakes in W. New York State.

cay·use (kī′o͞os, kīūs′) *n.* Amer. Ind. pony; (dial.) horse. [Name of Amer. Ind. tribe]

C.B. *abbrev.* Citizen's band (radio).

CBC *abbrev.* Canadian Broadcasting Company.

cc, c.c. *abbrevs.* Cubic centimeter.

CCC *abbrev.* Civilian Conservation Corps.

C.D., CD *abbrevs. Corps diplomatique* (diplomatic corps); Civil Defense.

Cd *symbol.* Cadium.

Cdr., CDR *abbrevs.* Commander.

Ce *symbol.* Cerium.

C.E. *abbrev.* Church of England; civil engineer; chemical engineer; Common Era.

cease (sēs) *v.* (**ceased, ceas·ing**). Abstain *from* continuing (action etc.); stop; come, bring, to an end; **~-fire**, (mil.) signal to cease firing; cessation of shooting or fighting. **cease** *n.* Ceasing (now only in **without** ~, incessantly). **cease′less** *adj.* Not ceasing. **cease′less·ly** *adv.*

Ce·cil·ia (sĭsēl′y*a*) **St.** (d. 230 A.D.). Roman martyr; patron saint of music and musicians; commemorated Nov. 22.

ce·cum, cae·cum (sē′k*u*m) *ns.* (pl. **-ca** pr. -k*a*). Any tube with one closed end in the structure of an animal, esp. that arising from the colon and ending at the vermiform appendix in mammals.

*Spelunking, the exploration of **caves** as a sport, can involve various skills including climbing and diving and is becoming increasingly popular. The scientific study of caves is called speleology.*

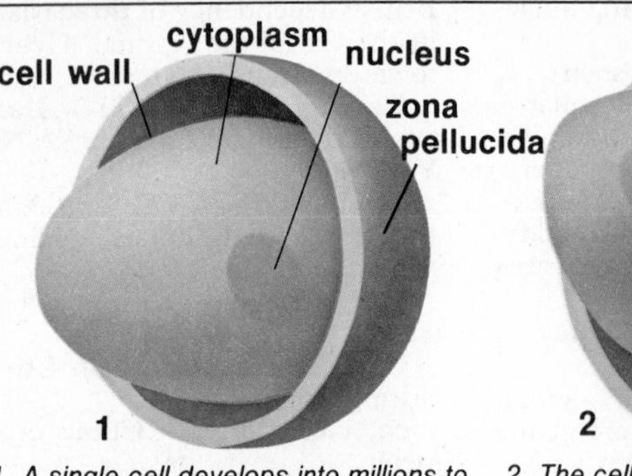

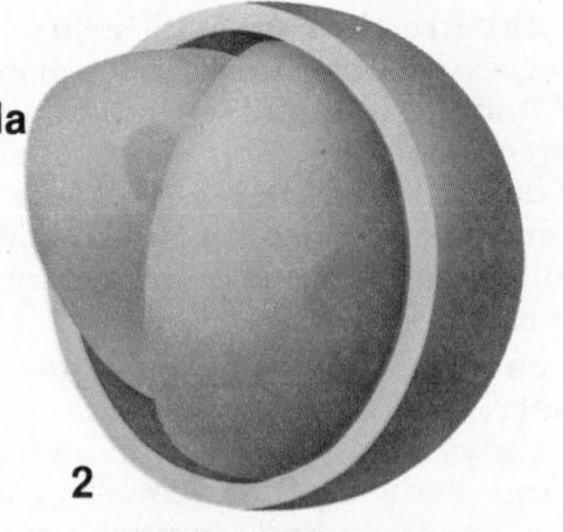

1. A single cell develops into millions to build a child's body. The fertilized egg is in one cell, its wall, holding cytoplasm and nucleus, is protected by a zona pellucida membrane.

2. The cell divides into 2 exactly similar cells after a life of some 30 hours.

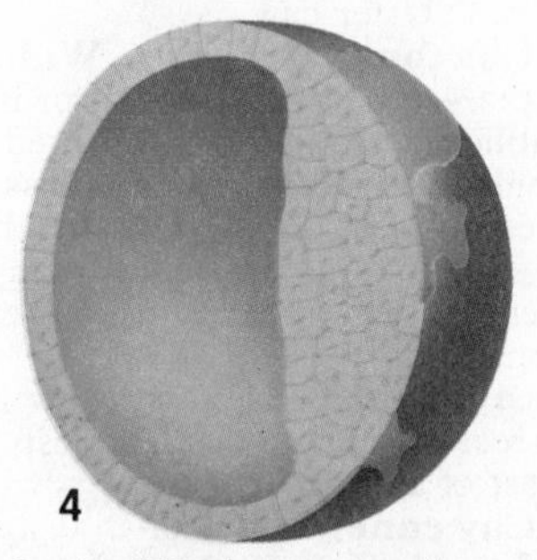

3. By the third day there are a few score cells in the zona pellucida.

4. On the fifth day some cells congregate to start embryo and others to become the placenta. The zona pellucida disintegrates.

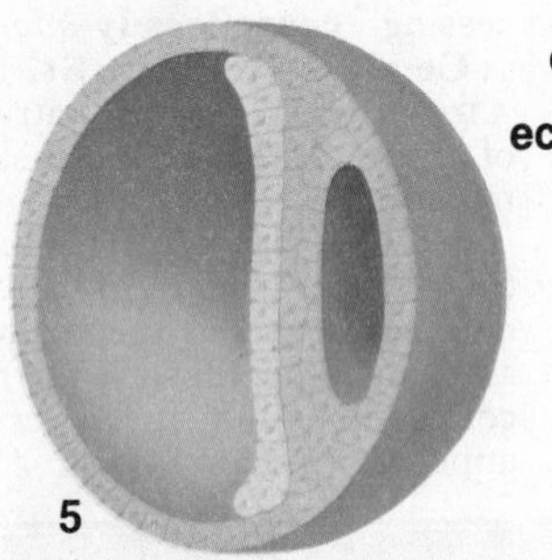

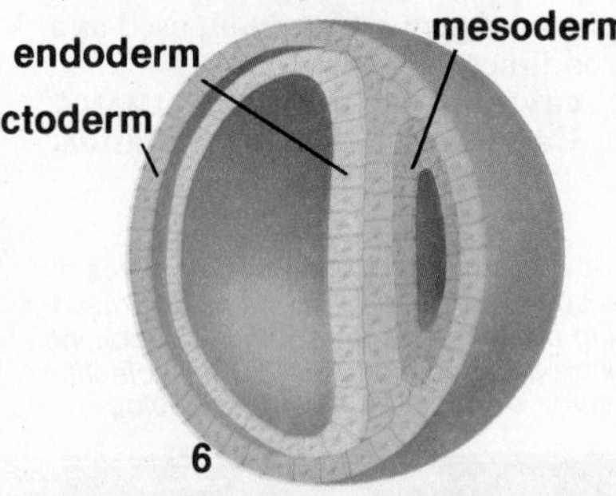

5. 14 days after fertilization a double disk begins to develop.

6. At about 20 days, another layer is added, this time of different cells. The ectoderm becomes the embryo's skin and brain, the endoderm its digestive tract, liver and lungs, and the mesoderm its heart, blood, bones, kidneys and muscles.

*Above: The growth of the **cedar** is always fairly slow in height, up to 14 ins. a year; but after 2 years, growth in girth is quick. Many huge and apparently ancient cedars were planted in the past 150 years.*

*Above: One of the earliest of spring flowers seen in Great Britain is the lesser **celandine.** Very common, it is found blooming in shady places from March to May. Its fruit is of massed carpels.*

ce·dar (sē′d*er*) *n.* Coniferous evergreen Old World tree of genus *Cedrus*; similar tree of genus *Juniperus* or *Thuja*; their aromatic wood highly resistant to insect and rot.

Ce·dar (sē′d*er*) **Rapids.** Industrial city in E. Iowa on the Cedar River.

cede (sēd) *v.t.* (**ced·ed, ced·-ing**). Give up, grant, admit; surrender (territory).

ce·dil·la (sĭdĭl′*a*) *n.* Mark written under letter *c* thus (ç) to show that it is sibilant.

ceil·ing (sē′lĭng) *n.* 1. Interior upper surface of a room. 2. (aeron.) Altitude beyond which a given aircraft cannot climb and at which only one speed of flight is possible; (meteor.) height of the lowest cloud or fog layer obscuring sky. 3. Upper limit of prices, wages, etc.

cel·an·dine (sĕl′*a*ndīn, -dēn) *n.* Either of two Old World yellow-flowered plants, the **greater** ~ (*Chelidonium majus*) and the **lesser** ~ (*Ranunculus ficaria*), also known as pilewort; a N. Amer. jewelweed (*Impatiens capensis*) with crimson-spotted orange flowers.

Cel·e·bes (sĕl′*e*bēz). Island of Indonesia, now Sulawesi. **C~ Sea**, the part of the western Pacific Ocean between Sulawesi and Mindanao Islands.

cel·e·brant (sĕl′*e*br*a*nt) *n.* Officiating priest, esp. at Eucharist; participant in any celebration.

cel·e·brate (sĕl′*e*brāt) *v.* (**-brat·ed, -brat·ing**). 1. Perform (religious ceremony etc.) publicly and duly; officiate at Eucharist. 2. Observe, honor (festival, event) with rites, festivities, etc. 3. Publish abroad, praise, extol. **cel′e·brat·-ed** *adj.* Famed, renowned. **cel·e·-bra·tion** (sĕl*e*brā′sh*o*n) *n.*

ce·leb·ri·ty (s*e*lĕb′rĭtē) *n.* (pl. **-ties**). 1. Being famous. 2. Celebrated person.

ce·ler·i·ty (s*e*lĕr′ĭtē) *n.* Swiftness.

cel·er·y (sĕl′*e*rē) *n.* Umbelliferous plant (*Apium graveolens*) cultivated for its blanched edible stalks.

1

2

3

***Ceilings** may reflect the structure or the style of a building. Top left: The 17th-century ceilings of Sudbury Hall, Derbyshire, U.K., are of the Caroline period. The ceiling paintings were commissioned from the Frenchman, Louis Laguerre. Top right: In the vaulting of the roof of Norwich Cathederal, U.K. the builders achieved a sublime decorative effect with the revealed structural members. Left: The lead ceiling of Wolsey's closet at Hampton Court, London, is an heraldic expression of Tudor ambition. Right: Ceilings at Badminton House, Gloucestershire (now Avon), are the work of Robert Adam.*

ce·les·ta (selĕs′ta) *n.* Musical instrument consisting of metal plates struck with hammers played from a keyboard.

ce·les·tial (selĕs′chal) *adj.* 1. Of the sky; ~ **equator**, great circle of celestial sphere, formed by plane cutting through Earth's center at right angles to its axis (so called because when sun is at the equator, day and night are of equal length); ~ **guidance**, guidance system for spacecraft or missile that navigates automatically by reference to celestial bodies; ~ **sphere**, imaginary sphere on which the heavenly bodies appear to lie, having its center at the center of the Earth (or at the point where the observer stands) and an infinite radius. 2. Heavenly, divine; divinely good, beautiful, etc. 3. Chinese; **C~ Empire,** (transl. of native title) the former Chinese Empire. **ce·les′tial·ly** *adv.*

cel·i·bate (sĕl′*i*bĭt, -bāt) *n.* & *adj.* (Person) remaining unmarried, abstaining from sexual relations, esp. by religious vow. **cel·i·ba·cy** (sĕl′*i*basē) *n.*

cell (sĕl) *n.* 1. Hermit's one-roomed dwelling. 2. Single person's small room in monastery etc.; similar small, confining room in prison or other place of detention. 3. (biol.) Unit of structure of living matter, mass of protoplasm bounded by a membrane (~ **wall**) and usu. containing a nucleus. 4. (zool.) Small container of earth, silk, wax, etc., in which larva or pupa develops, esp. in comb of social insects, e.g. bees. 5. (elect.) Voltaic apparatus with only one pair of metallic elements, unit of battery. 6. (fig.) Small group or single person working in factory, particular district, etc., as nucleus of political, esp. revolutionary, activity; headquarters of such group etc.

cel·la (sĕl′*a*) *n.* (pl. **cel·lae** pr. sĕl′ē). (Gk. and Rom. antiq.) Principal chamber of temple.

cel·lar (sĕl′*er*) *n.* Underground room or vault, used for storage, etc; wine cellar, stock of wines. **cel·lar·age** (sĕl′*er*ĭj) *n.* Fee for storage in cellar; cellar space.

cel·lar·et (sĕl*er*ĕt′) *n.* Case or sideboard for holding bottles of wine etc.

Cel·li·ni (ch*e*lē′nē), **Benvenuto** (1500–71). Florentine goldsmith and sculptor, famous also for his *Autobiography*.

cel·lo, ’cel·lo (chĕl′ō) *ns.* (pl. **-los**). Instrument of the violin family, four-stringed and held upright on floor by seated player, lower in tone than viola and higher than double bass, having very wide range. **cel′list, ’cel′list** *ns.*

cel·lo·phane (sĕl′*o*fān) *n.* Thin transparent material made of cellulose and used as wrapping etc.

cel·lu·lar (sĕl′y*u*l*er*) *adj.* Of, having, consisting of, cells; porous.

cel·lule (sĕl′ūl) *n.* Small cell.

Cel·lu·loid (sĕl′y*u*loid) *n.* (trademark) Solid inflammable material consisting essentially of soluble cellulose nitrate and camphor, used in the manufacture of photographic film and many other items.

cel·lu·lose (sĕl′y*u*lōs) *n.* (chem.) Carbohydrate that forms chief constituent of cell walls of all plants and of textiles such as cotton and linen. ~ **acetate**, acetic ester of cellulose, used to make rayon, plastics, etc.; ~ **nitrate**, nitric ester of cellulose, a constituent of smokeless gunpowders and of cordite, celluloid, etc. **cel·lu·lo·sic** (sĕly*u*lōsĭk) *adj.*

Cels. *abbrev.* Celsius.

Cel·si·us (sĕl′sē*u*s, -shē-, -sh*u*s), **Anders** (1701–44). Swedish astronomer; inventor of the centigrade scale for measuring temperature; hence = CENTIGRADE (abbreviated C).

Celt (sĕlt, kĕlt) *n.* 1. Member of one of the ancient peoples of W. Europe; Gaul. 2. One of the peoples speaking languages related to those of the ancient Gauls, including Bretons, Cornish, Welsh, Irish, Manx, and Gaels.

celt (sĕlt) *n.* Prehistoric bronze, stone, or iron ax.

Cel·tic (sĕl′tĭk, kĕl′-) *adj.* Of the Celts; of the branch of the Indo-European family of languages spoken by the ancient Celts or their modern representatives; ~ *n.* Celtic language. **Cel·ti·cism** (sĕl′tĭsĭz*e*m, kĕl′-) *n.*

The salt-cellar by ***Benvenuto Cellini*** *shows the figures of Neptune and Earth worked in gold and enamels. The piece was made for Francis I, King of France, who became Cellini's patron in 1540.*

The Christian ***Celts*** *of Ireland adopted Gallic drystone walling techniques and the oversailing vault when they built small churches, such as the Oratory of Gallus at Dingle in County Kerry.*

ce·ment (sĭmĕnt′) *n.* Any compound substance, esp. of lime or other stone, ground to powder and mixed with water, which hardens rapidly into stony consistency, used for binding together stones or bricks, covering floors, walls, etc.; similar substance mixed with sand and gravel etc. to form concrete; plastic material for filling tooth cavities; any adhesive material used to mend small articles of glass, china, etc.; (fig.) link or bond of union. ~ *v.t.* Unite firmly with or as with cement; coat or line with cement. **ce·men·ta·tion** (sēmĕntā′sh*o*n) *n.*

cem·e·ter·y (sĕm′ĭtĕrē) *n.* (pl. **-ter·ies**). Place for burying the dead, graveyard.

cen·o·taph (sĕn′*o*tăf) *n.* Sepulchral monument to person whose body is buried elsewhere.

Ce·no·zo·ic (sēn*o*zō′ĭk, sĕn*o*-) *adj.* & *n.* (geol.) (Of) the era or group of systems following the Mesozoic and including the present era, characterized by the first appearance of birds and mammals; sometimes = TERTIARY.

cen·ser (sĕn′s*er*) *n.* Vessel in which incense is burned.

cen·sor (sĕns*er*) *n.* 1. (Rom. antiq.) Either of two magistrates

*From the Parthenon, Athens, this figure of a **centaur** triumphing over a dead Lapith portrays the violence embodied in the fabulous creature. The Lapiths of Thessaly suffered attacks by savage mountain tribes, represented here by the centaur.*

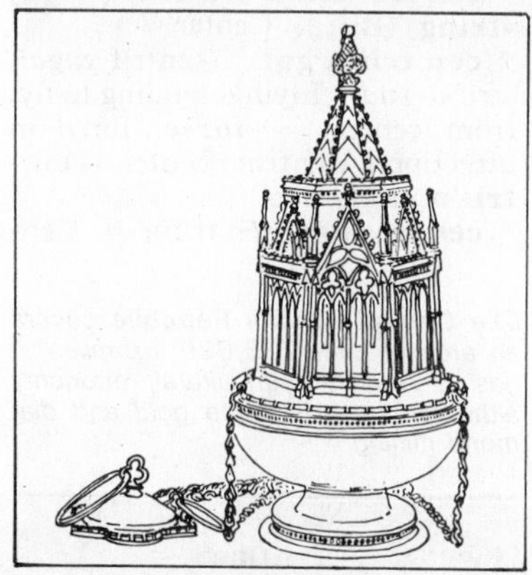

*The use of incense to promote a sense of worship has a long history. The **censer** in which the incense smoulders is often of intricate pierced metal to allow smoke to escape.*

*Growing in open, dry ground, the common **centaury** bears clusters of pink flowers in late summer. It grows to a height of 12–18 ins., and may have tonic properties.*

who drew up the register or census of citizens and supervised public morals; hence, any person supervising or criticizing the morals and conduct of others. 2. Official inspecting books, letters, newspapers, etc., to ensure that they contain nothing immoral, seditious, or unacceptable to military or other authorities. **cen′sor·ship** *n.* **cen′sor** *v.t.* Act as censor to; make excisions or changes in for reasons of morality, national security, politics, etc. **cen′sor·a·ble** *adj.*

cen·so·ri·al (sĕnsōr′ēal, -sōr′-) *adj.* Of a censor; censorious.

cen·so·ri·ous (sĕnsōr′ēus, -sōr′-) *adj.* Severely critical, faultfinding. **cen·so′ri·ous·ly** *adv.* **cen·so′ri·ous·ness** *n.*

cen·sure (sĕn′sher) *n.* Expression of disapproval or blame, reprimand. ~ *v.t.* (**-sured, -sur·ing**). Criticize harshly and unfavorably. **cen′sur·a·ble** *adj.*

cen·sus (sĕn′sus) *n.* (pl. **-sus·es**). 1. Official counting of population with various statistics. 2. (Rom. antiq.) Registration of citizens and property for taxation.

cent (sĕnt) *n.* 1. **percent′**, (often written $^{0}{}_{0}$), for (in, to) every 100, esp. in stating rates of interest etc. 2. $\frac{1}{100}$ of various monetary units, esp. the dollar, Netherlands florin, etc; coin worth one cent, penny.

cent. *abbrev.* Century.

cen·taur (sĕn′tōr) *n.* 1. (Gk. myth.) Fabulous creature with head, trunk, and arms of man joined to body and legs of horse. 2. **the C~**, (astron.) the southern constellation Centaurus.

cen·tau·ry (sĕn′tōrē) *n.* (pl. **-ries**). Any of various plants of the genus *Centaurium* (including *C. pulchellum* and *C. umbellatum*), whose medicinal properties were supposed to have been discovered by Chiron the Centaur; American knapweed (*Centaurea americana*).

cen·ta·vo (sĕntah′vō) *n.* (pl. **-vos** pr. -vōz, -vōs). $\frac{1}{100}$ of a peso or similar unit of currency in various republics of S. America and elsewhere; a coin of this denomination.

cen·te·nar·i·an (sĕntenār′ēan) *adj.* & *n.* (Person) 100 years old or more.

cen·te·nar·y (sĕn′tenĕrē; *Brit.* sĕntĕn′erē, -tē′nerē) *adj.* & *n.* (pl. **-nar·ies**). (Of) 100 years; (celebration of) 100th anniversary.

cen·ten·ni·al (sĕntĕn′ēal) *adj.* Of, having lived or lasted, completing, 100 years; of the 100th anniversary. ~ *n.* 100th anniversary.

cen·ter, Brit. **cen·tre** (sĕn′ter) *ns.* 1. Middle point of circle, sphere, line, etc.; middle point or part of anything; point, line, upon which a body turns or revolves. 2. Point of concentration, attraction, or dispersion, nucleus, source; place, building(s), etc., forming central point or main area (as **civic ~, health ~**). 3. Person, thing, occupying central position; (football etc.) player in middle of line or field of players; (pol.) persons of moderate opinions. 4. **~ of attraction**, (phys. etc.) point to which bodies tend by gravity etc.; point or object drawing general interest; **~ of gravity**, point about which all parts of a body exactly balance each other, so that if this point is supported the body remains at rest. 5. **cen′terboard**, plate lowered through slot in keel of sailboat to increase stability and check leeway; **cen′terfold**, two-page spread at middle of magazine; **cen′terpiece**, flower arrangement or other ornament for center of dining table. **cen′ter·less, cen′tric, cen·tri·cal** (sĕn′trĭkal) *adjs.*

center *v.* (**-ered, -er·ing**). Be concentrated, have center *in*, *on*, *at*, etc.; place in or as in center; (football etc.) pass (ball) to or from center.

cen·tes·i·mal (sĕntĕs′imal) *adj.* Reckoning, reckoned, by $\frac{1}{100}$.

cen·ti- *prefix.* $\frac{1}{100}$ of.

cen·ti·grade (sĕn′tigrād) *adj.* Divided into 100 degrees; (abbreviated C) of, measured by, **C～ scale**, temperature scale, invented by CELSIUS, in which the freezing point and the boiling point of water are taken as 0 degrees and 100 degrees respectively (Celsius is now the preferred term in technical use).

cen·ti·gram, *Brit.* **cen·ti·gramme** (sĕn′tigrăm) *ns.* (abbreviated cg) $\frac{1}{100}$ of a gram.

cen·ti·li·ter, Brit. **cen·ti·li·tre** (sĕn′tilēter) *ns.* (abbreviated cl) $\frac{1}{100}$ of a liter.

cen·time (sahntēm′) *n.* $\frac{1}{100}$ of a franc or similar unit of currency; a coin of this denomination.

cen·ti·me·ter, Brit. **cen·ti·me·tre** (sĕn′timēter) *ns.* (abbreviated cm) $\frac{1}{100}$ of a meter, or 0.3937 (nearly $\frac{2}{5}$) of an inch; **～-gram-second**, (abbreviated CGS, cgs) applied to a system of units of measurement based on the centimeter, gram, and second as units of length, mass, and time.

cen·ti·pede (sĕn′tipēd) *n.* Wingless wormlike animal of the class Chilopoda, having many segments and a pair of legs attached to each segment.

cen·tral (sĕn′tral) *adj.* Of, in, at, from, containing, the center; leading, principal, dominant; **～ bank**, main bank of a country, responsible for influencing the conduct of all other banks and financial institutions in pursuance of the government's monetary policy; **～ heating**, heating of building from a central source, as by circulating hot water, steam, or air through pipes or vents; **C～ Powers**, (before 1914) Germany and Austria-Hungary; (during World War I) these two countries plus Bulgaria and Turkey. **cen·tral·i·ty** (sĕntrăl′ĭtē) *n.* (pl. **-ties**). **cen′tral·ly** *adv.*

***Centrifugal** force is utilized by industry, sciences, and also in the entertainment industry. Here, patrons on this ride feel themselves flung outwards by the force.*

Cen·tral (sĕn′tral) **African Republic.** Republic between Cameroon Republic and Sudan, formerly a French colony; capital, Bangui.

Cen·tral (sĕn′tral) **America.** Region of the Western Hemisphere between Mexico and Colombia.

cen·tral·ism (sĕn′tralĭzem) *n.* Centralizing system. **cen′tral·ist** *adj.* & *n.*

cen·tral·ize (sĕn′tralīz) *v.* (**-ized, -iz·ing**). 1. Come, bring, to a center. 2. Concentrate (administrative powers) in single center instead of distributing them among local departments; bring (country etc.) under this system. **cen·tral·i·za·tion** (sĕntralīzā′shon) *n.*

cen·tre (sĕn′ter) *n.* & *v.* (**-tred, -tring**) (Brit.). Center.

cen·trif·u·gal (sĕntrĭf′yugal, -trĭf′u-) *adj.* Flying, tending to fly, from center; **～ force**, force in direction away from center. **cen·trif′u·gal·ly** *adv.*

cen·tri·fuge (sĕn′trifūj) *n.* Cen-

*The **centipede** (below) lives under a stone or in the bark of a tree. It preys on earthworms and insects. In the tropics some varieties may grow to nearly 8 ins. long.*

*The **Central African Republic** covers an area of over 238,000 sq. miles. It has a mainly agricultural economy although there is some gold and diamond mining.*

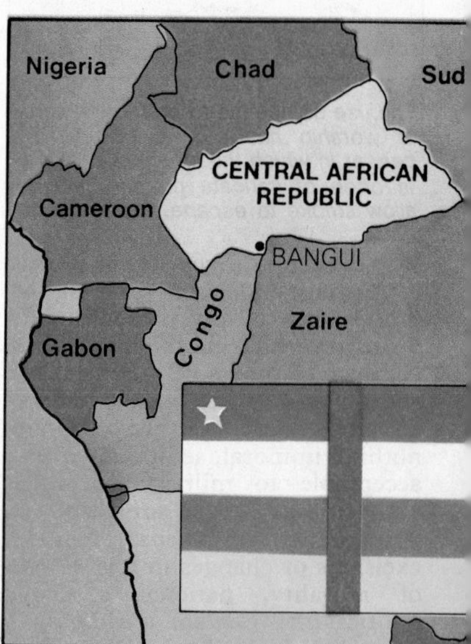

Lower left: A ***cephalopod*** *(Verania sigula) uses its powerful arms to attack another mollusk. Top left: The Octopus vulgaris is found in the Mediterranean Sea and the Atlantic. It has 8 arms with rows of suckers on each, and grows to about 10 ft. in diameter. Below right: the nautilus has survived 200 million years in this form. Its shell has many chambers or septa, the largest of which is inhabited by the animal.*

trifugal machine, esp. one for separating cream from milk, or for drying objects, by rotary motion. ~ *v.t.* (**-fuged, -fug·ing**). Subject to action of a centrifuge. **cen·trif·u·ga·tion** (sĕntrĭfy*u*gā′shon, -trĭf*u*-) *n.*

cen·trip·e·tal (sĕntrĭp′*e*tal) *adj.* Tending toward the center.

cen·tu·ri·on (sĕntoor′ē*o*n, -tūr′-) *n.* (Rom. antiq.) Commander of a century.

cen·tu·ry (sĕn′ch*u*rē) *n.* (pl. **-ries**). 1. (Rom. antiq.) Company in army, orig. of 100 men; each of the 193 political divisions by which the Roman people voted. 2. 100 years, esp. each successive period of 100 years reckoning from a fixed date, e.g. the assumed date of Christ's birth; ~ **plant**, plant of the genus *Agave*, esp. *A. americana*, supposed to flower once in 100 years, but often flowering after only five.

ce·phal·ic (s*e*făl′ĭk) *adj.* Of, in, the head; ~ **index**, number indicating the ratio of transverse to longitudinal diameter of skull.

ceph·a·lo·pod (sĕf′*a*lopŏd) *n.* Animal of the class Cephalopoda, the most highly organized class of Mollusca, characterized by head with tentacles attached and including octopus, squid, etc.

ceph·a·lo·tho·rax (sĕf*a*lōthōr′-ăks, -thōr′-) *n.* (pl. **-tho·rax·es, -tho·ra·ces** pr. -thōr′*a*sēz, -thōr′-). (zool.) In some arthropods, part of body formed by fusion of head and thorax.

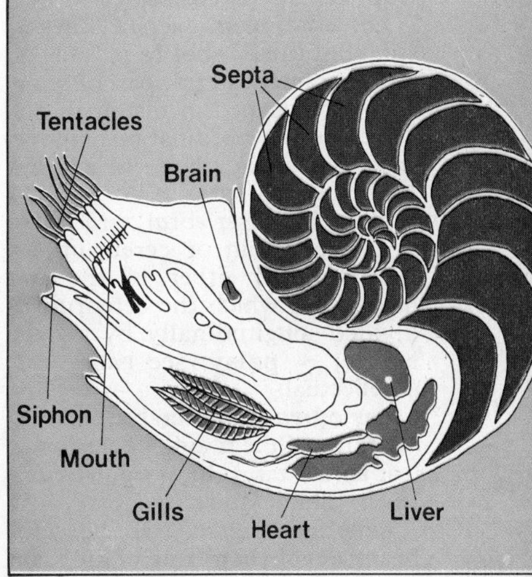

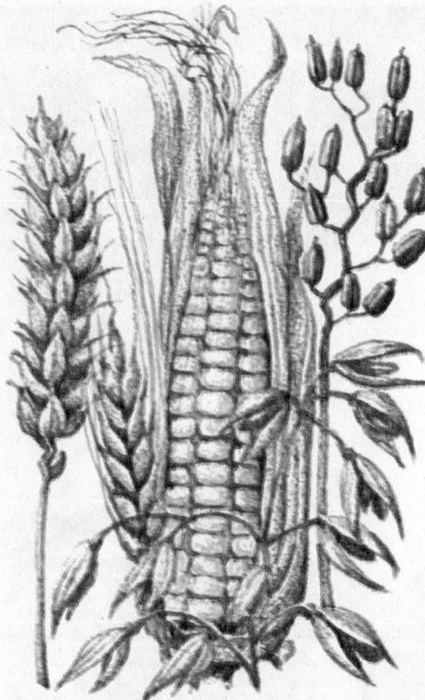

Left: Grain being loaded on ship. Above: ***Cereal*** *crops were developed from grasses, the first probably being wheat. This was not grown in America where maize predominated. Barley was used for bread until the 16th century. Rye was grown on land too poor for wheat.*

ce·ram·ic (serăm′ĭk) *adj.* Of (the art of) pottery; of (making of) substances etc. produced by firing of minerals, esp. clay, at very high temperatures. **ceramic** *n.*; product produced by ceramics. **ce·ram′ics** *n.* Ceramic art. **cer·a·mist** (sĕr′amĭst) *n.*

Cer·ber·us (sẽr′berus). (Gk. myth.) The three-headed (acc. to Hesiod, 50-headed) dog guarding the entrance to Hades.

cere (sẽr) *n.* Naked waxlike membrane at base of beak in some birds.

ce·re·al (sẽr′ēal) *adj.* Of an edible grain, as wheat, oats, or corn. ~ *n.* (freq. pl.) (Any) grain or grassy plants cultivated for their seed as human food; an article of food (esp. as breakfast dish) made from cereal. [f. CERES]

cer·e·bel·lum (sĕrebĕl′um) *n.* (pl. **-bel·lums, -bel·la** pr. -bĕl′a). Little brain, posterior part of brain, highly developed in mammals and concerned in coordination of movement and maintenance of equilibrium; see BRAIN.

cer·e·bral (sĕr′ebral, serē′-) *adj.* 1. Of the brain or cerebrum; ~ **hemisphere**, either of the two halves into which the cerebrum is divided longitudinally by a deep fissure; ~ **palsy**: see PALSY. 2. Intellectual.

cer·e·bra·tion (sĕrebrā′shon) *n.* Working of the brain. **cer·e·brate** (ser′ebrāt) *v.i.* (**-brat·ed, -brat·ing**). Think (about).

cerebro- *prefix.* Of the cerebrum; **cerebrospi′nal**, of the brain and spinal cord; **cerebrospi′nal fluid**, solution of salts and protein filling cavities of brain and spinal cord; **cerebrospi′nal meningitis**, inflammation of the meninges of brain and spinal cord.

cer·e·brum (sĕr′ebrum) *n.* (pl. **-brums, -bra** pr. -bra). Great brain, convoluted mass of tissue forming the anterior and, in the higher vertebrates, largest part of the brain, in man filling nearly the whole skull; see BRAIN.

cere·cloth (sẽr′klawth, -klŏth) *n.* (pl. **-cloths** pr. -klawdhz, -klŏdhz, -klawths, -klŏths). Waxed cloth, esp. for wrapping the dead.

cere·ment (sẽr′ment, sĕr′ement) *n.* (usu. pl.). Cerecloth.

cer·e·mo·ni·al (sĕremō′nēal) *adj.* With or of ritual or ceremony, formal. ~ *n.* System of rites; formalities proper to any occasion; observance of convention. **cer·e·mo′ni·al·ly** *adv.*

cer·e·mo·ni·ous (sĕremō′nēus) *adj.* Accompanied with rites; according to prescribed or customary formalities; punctilious in observing formalities. **cer·e·mo′ni·ous·ly** *adv.* **cer·e·mo′ni·ous·ness** *n.*

cer·e·mo·ny (sĕr′emōnē) *n.* (pl. **-nies**). 1. Outward rite or observance; solemnity; empty form. 2. Usage of courtesy, politeness, or civility; formalities, observance of conventions; **stand on** ~, insist on punctilious observance of formalities.

Ce·res (sẽr′ēz). 1. (Rom. myth.) Goddess of agriculture, identified by the Romans with DEMETER and in this later cult worshipped as corn and earth goddess. 2. (astron.) Largest of the asteroids.

ce·rise (serēs′, -rēz′) *n.* & *adj.* Moderate to deep red, cherry red.

ce·ri·um (sẽr′ēum) *n.* (chem.) Element of rare-earth group, resembling iron in color and luster; symbol Ce, at. no. 85, at. wt. 140.12.

cer·met (sẽr′mĕt) *n.* Alloy of ceramic substance with metal.

cert. *abbrev.* Certificate; certified.

cer·tain (sẽr′tin) *adj.* 1. Settled, fixed, unfailing; unerring, reliable; sure to happen; sure *to* do; indubitable, indisputable. 2. Convinced, confident (*of, that*); sure. 3. That might but need not be specified; occas., that it would not be polite to specify; of positive yet restricted amount, degree, etc.; a particular, a definite (person etc.). 4. **for** ~, for a certainty.

cer·tain·ly (sẽr′tinlē) *adv.* 1. Indubitably; infallibly; confidently; admittedly. 2. (in answers) I admit it; of course; no doubt, yes.

cer·tain·ty (sẽr′tintē) *n.* (pl. **-ties**). Thing certain or sure; being certain.

cer·tif·i·cate (sertĭf′ikĭt) *n.* Document formally attesting a fact, esp. the bearer's status, acquirements, fulfillment of conditions, right to company shares, etc. **cer·tif·i·cate** (sertĭf′ikāt) *v.t.* (**-cat·ed, -cat·ing**). Furnish with, license by, certificate. **cer·ti·fi·ca·tion** (sẽrtĭfikā′shon) *n.*

cer·ti·fy (sẽr′tifī) *v.t.* (**-fied, -fy·ing**). 1. Attest formally, declare by certificate; (chiefly Brit.) declare by certificate (of doctor etc.) to be insane; **certified public accountant**, accountant holding legal certificate of professional competence. 2. Inform certainly, assure. **cer′ti·fi·a·ble** *adj.* (esp. of lunatic or lunacy). **cer′ti·fi·a·bly** *adv.*

cer·ti·o·ra·ri (sẽrshēorãr′ī) *n.* Writ from higher court calling for records of case tried in lower court. [LL., = "to be informed," occurring in original writ]

cer·ti·tude (sẽr′tĭtōōd, -tūd) *n.* Feeling certain, conviction; freedom from doubt.

ce·ru·le·an (serōō′lēan) *adj.* Deep blue; sky blue; ~ **blue**, pigment of this color prepared from cobalt.

ce·ru·men (serōō′men) *n.* Yellow waxy secretion in the external canal of the ear. **ce·ru′mi·nous** *adj.*

Cer·van·tes (servăn′tēz; *Sp.* thĕrvahn′tĕs), **Miguel de** (1547–1616). Spanish novelist and dramatist, author of *Don Quixote* (1605–15).

cer·vi·cal (sẽr′vĭkal) *adj.* (anat.)

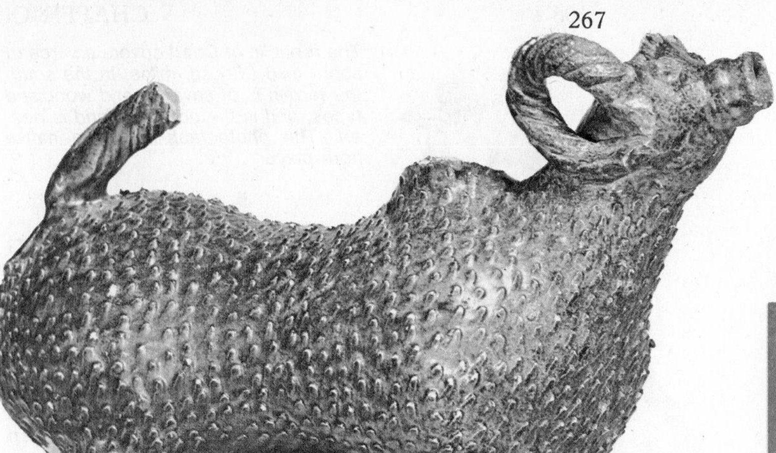

The rich variety of **ceramics** is the product of local materials, skills and tastes. Left: A ram-shaped aquamanile of buffware with a green glaze is decorated with pellets. It was found near Scarborough, Yorkshire, U.K., where it was made in the late 13th century. Below: This painted Ancient Greek vase was probably produced in the 6th century BC.

Above: Greek potters produced work of great variety. These storage jars may have been used for keeping grain or olives. The wide necks of the jars would leave the contents accessible to a scoop or ladle. Left: A Chinese neolithic jar painted in a monochrome design, part of which is linear, dark on a light ground, and part in reverse, light on a dark ground, showing an advanced grasp of decorative techniques with simple color. Right: A porcelain figure made in England at the Chelsea works, c. 1765. Underneath, it bears the gold anchor mark of the maker. Its modeling and many colored glazes make it a fine quality piece.

'A Man with a Pipe' was painted by ***Paul Cézanne*** *a Neo-Impressionist of genius. While he was no theorist, his remark that painters should look for the cone, sphere and cube in Nature was taken as law by Cubists.*

In common with many of the Fringilla genus, the ***chaffinch*** *is useful as an eater of weed seeds. Chaffinches of northern areas migrate to the Mediterranean in fall.*

The republic of ***Chad*** *covers an area of about 496,000 sq. miles. In the south the terrain is of savanna and woodland types, and in the north the land is desert. The photograph shows a native horn player.*

Of the neck; of the cervix of an organ.

cer·vine (sẽr′vīn) *adj.* Of, like, deer.

cer·vix (sẽr′vĭks) *n.* (pl. **cer·vix·es, cer·vi·ces** pr. sẽr′visēz, servī′-). (anat.) Neck; necklike structure, esp. neck of the uterus.

ce·si·um, cae·si·um (sē′zē*u*m) *ns.* (chem.) Rare alkali metal element discovered spectroscopically by Bunsen in 1861; symbol Cs, at. no. 55, at. wt. 132.9054. [L. *caesius* bluish-gray, f. the distinctive lines in its spectrum]

ces·sa·tion (sĕsā′sh*o*n) *n.* Ceasing, pause.

ces·sion (sĕsh′*o*n) *n.* Ceding, giving up.

cess·pool (sĕs′po͞ol) *n.* Well sunk to receive sewage etc., retaining solid matter and allowing liquid to escape; (fig.) any filthy or morally corrupt place.

ce·ta·cean (sĭtā′sh*o*n) *adj.* & *n.* (Member) of the Cetacea, an order of marine mammals, including whales, dolphins, porpoises, etc. **ce·ta′ceous** *adj.* [Gk. *kētos* whale]

Cey·lon (sĭlŏn′). Name until 1972 of SRI LANKA. **Cey·lo·nese** (sēl*o*nēz′, -nēs′) *adj.* & *n.* (pl. **-nese**).

Cé·zanne (sĕzăn′), **Paul** (1839–1906). French painter, central figure of the movements known as Impressionism and Post-Impressionism.

Cf. *symbol.* Californium.

cf. *abbrev.* Compare. [L. *confer* compare]

C.G. *abbrev.* Coast Guard; commanding general; consul general.

Cg. *abbrev.* Centigram(s).

c.g. *abbrev.* Center of gravity.

cgs, c.g.s., CGS *abbrevs.* Centimeter-gram-second.

Ch. *abbrev.* Chaplain; chapter; China; Chinese; Church.

Chab·lis (shăblē′) *n.* Dry white wine produced near Chablis, in N. Burgundy, France.

cha·conne (shăkŭn′, -kŏn′) *n.* Old stately Spanish dance; instrumental composition in $\frac{3}{4}$ time with an unchanging harmonic pattern against which the upper parts are varied (cf. PASSACAGLIA, which it resembles).

Chad (chăd). Republic of N. central Africa extending from Lake Chad across the E. Sudan; capital, Ndjaména (formerly Fort Lamy); **Lake C~**, lake in N. central Africa bordered by Chad, Niger, and Nigeria, from 5,000 to 10,000 square miles (12,500 to 25,000 sq. km) in area, depending on rainfall. **Chad′i·an** *adj.* & *n.*

Chad·wick (chăd′wĭk), **Sir James** (1891–1974). English physicist; discovered the neutron, carried on research on radioactivity and nuclear fission; Nobel Prize for physics 1935.

chafe (chāf) *v.* (**chafed, chaf·ing**). 1. Rub (skin etc.) to restore warmth or sensation; rub so as to abrade or injure the surface. 2. Irritate; show irritation, fume, fret. ~ *n.* Rubbing; chafing.

chaf·er (chā′f*e*r) *n.* Large slow-moving beetle, esp. COCKCHAFER.

chaff (chăf, chahf) *n.* 1. Husks of grain separated by threshing or winnowing; chopped hay and straw for feeding cattle. 2. Refuse, worthless stuff. 3. Teasing; banter. ~ *v.* Tease, make fun of.

chaf·fer (chăf′*e*r) *n.* & *v.* Haggle, bargain.

chaf·finch (chăf′ĭnch) *n.* European songbird (*Fringilla coelebs*)

The fiercest of the ***cetaceans,*** *the killer whale hunts in packs of up to 50 strong. Top right: A common dolphin. Below: A common porpoise.*

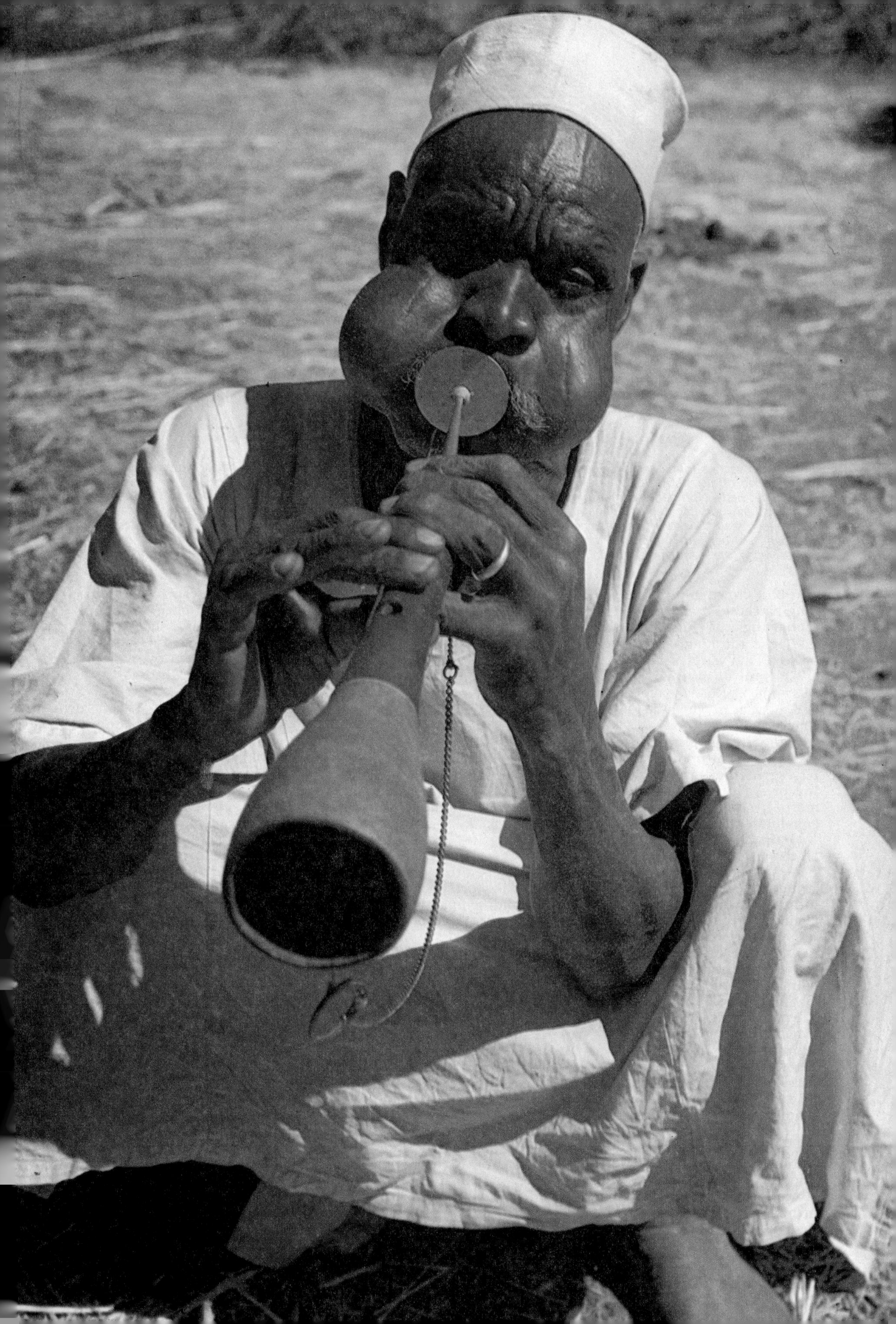

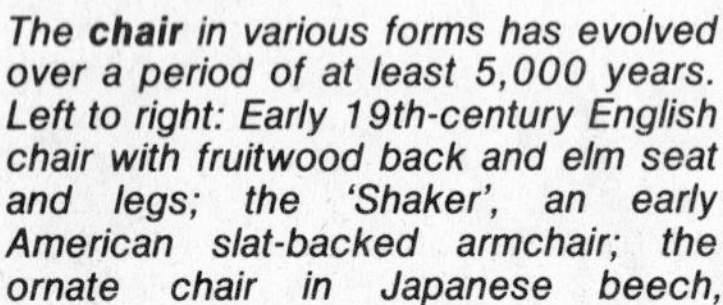

The ***chair*** *in various forms has evolved over a period of at least 5,000 years. Left to right: Early 19th-century English chair with fruitwood back and elm seat and legs; the 'Shaker', an early American slat-backed armchair; the ornate chair in Japanese beech,*

1730 (Temple Newsam House, Leeds), bearing the label of Giles Grendey of London, was part of a suite made for a Spanish nobleman. Left: An ancient Egyptian child's chair and footstool. Furniture was sometimes entombed with its illustrious owner on his death.

with blue crown in male and white wing patches.

chaf·ing (chā′fĭng) **dish.** Dish set above a heating device to cook or keep food warm at table.

Cha·gall (shahgahl′), **Marc** (1887–1985). Russian impressionist and cubist artist who lived mostly in France and U.S.

cha·grin (sh*a*grĭn′) *n.* Acute disappointment, mortification. ~ *v.t.* (**-grined** or **-grinned, -grin·ing** or **-grin·ning**). Vex acutely, mortify, by thwarting or disappointment.

chain (chān) *n.* 1. Flexible string of connected metal links. 2. (pl.) Fetters, bonds; confinement, restraint. 3. Personal ornament in form of chain around neck. 4. Connected course, train, or series (of events, objects, mountains, etc.); series of branch businesses. 5. Surveyor's measuring rod of 100 jointed iron rods called links; the length of this, 66 ft. (24.1 m). 6. (chem.) Atoms (usu. of carbon) joined in series in a molecule. 7. ~ **armor**, armor of interlaced links or rings, mail; ~ **gang**, gang of convicts chained together at work etc.; ~**letter**, letter of which the recipient is asked to make copies to be sent to a specified number of others, these being asked to do the like in their turn; ~ **link fence**, fence of linked thick steel wires; ~ **mail**, chain armor; ~ **reaction**, chemical reaction forming intermediate products that react with the original substance and are repeatedly renewed; (phys.) self-sustaining nuclear reaction, as a series of fissions; ~**saw**, power saw with teeth on endless chain; ~**-smoker**, one who lights another cigarette etc. from the stump of the last smoked; ~**-smoke** (*v.*); ~**-smoking**; ~ **stitch**, embroidery or crochet stitch resembling links of a chain; ~ **store**, one of a series of retail stores belonging to one firm and selling the same goods. **chain** *v.t.* Secure, confine, with chain.

chair (chār) *n.* 1. Seat for one person; movable, usu. four-legged, seat with rest for the back. 2. Seat, position, of authority, state, or dignity; seat occupied by person presiding at meeting etc.; seat, office, of mayor, university professor, etc. 3. (hist.) Sedan. 4. (slang) Electric chair. 5. ~**lift**, series of chairs on endless cable for carrying passengers up mountain etc. **chair** *v.t.* Act as chairman of, preside over, (meeting).

chair·man (chār′m*a*n) *n.* (pl. **-men** pr. -m*e*n). (fem. formerly **chair·wom·an**, pr. chār′wŏŏmĭn; pl. **-wom·en** pr. -wĭmĭn) Person chosen to preside over meeting, permanent president of committee, board, etc. **chair′man·ship** *n.* Office etc. of chairman.

chair·per·son (chār′pẽrs*o*n) *n.* Chairman or chairwoman.

chaise (shāz, shĕz) *n.* 1. Light open carriage for one or two persons, esp. a two-wheeled one drawn by one horse. 2. Chaise longue.

chaise longue (shāz lawng′, chāz, shĕz) (pl. **chaise longues**, *Fr.* **chaises longues**). Kind of long low chair with seat long enough to support sitter's outstretched legs. [Fr.]

chal·ced·o·ny (kălsĕd′*o*nē, kăl′s*e*dōnē) *n.* (pl. **-nies**). Precious or semiprecious stone, a cryptocrystalline form of silica with waxlike luster; including agate, cornelian, onyx, etc.

Chal·cis (kăl′sĭs). Ancient Greek city on Euboea Island; invasion point for campaign against Greece by Persians; scene of death of Aristotle.

Chal·de·a (kăldē′*a*). Country of the Chaldeans, freq. identified in the Old Testament with Babylonia.

Chal·de·an (kăldē′*a*n) *adj.* & *n.* (Member) of a Semitic people originating from Arabia, who settled in the neighborhood of Ur and were later merged with the Babylonians; (of) their language.

cha·let (shălā′, shăl′ā; *Fr.* shălā′) *n.* (pl. **cha·lets** pr. shălāz′, shăl′āz; *Fr.* shălā′). Swiss peasant's wooden house or cottage; villa or vacation cottage built in this style.

Cha·lia·pin (shahlyah′pĭn), **Fyodor Ivanovich** (1873–1938). Russian-born French operatic basso and concert singer.

chal·ice (chăl′ĭs) *n.* Goblet,

eucharistic wine cup; cup-shaped blossom.

chalk (chawk) *n.* Opaque white soft earthy limestone, consisting largely of calcium carbonate; used for burning into lime, making cement, and for writing etc. on blackboards or other **chalk'boards**; colored preparation of similar texture used for drawing etc.; **chalk stripe, -striped,** (with) pattern of thin white stripes on dark ground; **chalk talk,** (slang) lecture, talk, illustrated by drawings or diagrams on blackboard. **chalk** *v.t.* Rub, mark, draw, write, etc., with chalk; ~ **it up (to),** charge it (to) (person etc.); ~ **up,** score, register (success). **chalk'y** *adj.* (**chalk·i·er, chalk·i·est**). Abounding in, white as, chalk. **chalk'i·ness** *n.*

chal·lah (χah'la; *Heb.* χahlah') *n.* (pl. **chal·lahs**; *Heb.* **chal·loth** pr. χahlawt'). Loaf of bread, usu. braided before baking, specially prepared for the Jewish Sabbath. [Heb.]

chal·lenge (chăl'ĭnj) *n.* 1. Demand to respond, explain, justify, esp. sentry's demand for password etc. 2. (law etc.) Exception taken (to a prospective juror, a vote, etc.). 3. Summons to trial or contest, esp. duel; defiance. 4. Stimulating problem, demanding task. ~ *v.t.* (**-lenged, -leng·ing**). 1. Call to account. 2. Take exception to; dispute, deny. 3. Claim (attention, admiration, etc.). 4. Invite to play against, fight duel, etc.; defy. **chal'lenge·a·ble** *adj.* **chal'leng·er** *n.*

chal·lis, chal·lie (shăl'ē) *ns.* Lightweight soft clothing fabric.

Châ·lons (shălawṅ'). Place on the Marne, France, scene of the defeat of the Huns under Attila in 451 A.D. by the Romans and Visigoths.

cham·ber (chām'ber) *n.* 1. Room, esp. bedroom (poet. or archaic); (also **burial** ~) compartment or cavity used for burial; (pl.) judge's room for hearing cases etc. not needing to be taken in court. 2. (Hall used by) deliberative or judicial body, one of the houses of a legislature; ~ **of commerce,** association to promote and protect business and commercial interests locally. 3. (also ~ **pot**) Toilet pan or pot used in bedroom etc. for urination and defecation. 4. Cavity in animal body; enclosed space in mechanism, esp. part of gun bore in which charge is placed; in a revolver, each compartment of a cylinder holding a cartridge. 5. **cham'bermaid,** housemaid who cleans and straightens up bedrooms, now chiefly in hotels; **chamber music,** classical music for small instrumental groups; chamber orchestra, small orchestra.

***Marc Chagall** is famous for his paintings such as 'L'Anniversaire' (The Birthday) shown above. He was also an accomplished stage designer.*

cham·ber·lain (chām'berlĭn) *n.* Officer managing household of sovereign or nobleman; chief steward; high-ranking officer of a royal court; (Brit.) officer receiving rents and revenues of a municipality; treasurer.

Cham·ber·lain (chām'berlĭn), **(Arthur) Neville** (1869–1940). British prime minister 1937–40; followed policy of appeasement toward Germany and Italy until 1939.

Cham·ber·tin (shahṅbĕrtăṅ) *n.* Dry red wine produced near Chambertin in Burgundy, France.

Cham·bord (shahṅbōr'). Village in the Loire valley in N. central France, famous for its Renaissance chateau built by Francis I.

cha·me·le·on (kamē'lēon, -mēl'yon) *n.* Saurian reptile of the genus *Chamaeleo*, small lizardlike creature with power of changing color of skin to suit surroundings;

*The sure-footed **chamois** ascends mountains to the snow-line in summer and returns to wooded regions in the winter.*

(fig.) variable or inconstant person. [Gk. *khamaileōn*, lit. = "ground lion"]

cham·fer (chăm′*fer*) *n.* Oblique surface produced by beveling square edge or corner. ~ *v.t.* Give chamfer to; make oblique; flute.

cham·ois (shăm′ē) *n.* (pl. **cham·ois, cham·oix** pr. shăm′ēz). 1. Capriform antelope (*Rupicapra rupicapra*) found in mountain ranges of Europe and Asia. 2. Soft pliable washable leather from skin of goats, sheep, deer, and split hides of other animals.

cham·o·mile (kăm′*o*mīl, -mēl) = CAMOMILE.

Cha·mo·nix (shămawnē′). Valley and ski-resort area in E. France near Mont Blanc.

champ[1] (chămp), **chomp** (chŏmp) *vbs.* Munch (fodder) noisily; bite hard upon (bit); making chewing action or noise; ~ **at the bit**, be impatient.

champ[2] (chămp) *n.* (colloq.) Champion.

cham·pagne (shămpān′) *n.* Sparkling white wine bottled before fermentation has ceased, made in region of Champagne, France; similar wine made elsewhere.

cham·pi·on (chăm′pēon) *n.* 1. Fighting man, combatant; person who fights, argues, etc., for another or for a cause. 2. Person (esp. boxer, athlete), animal, plant, etc., that has defeated, or been judged superior to, all competitors. **cham′pi·on·ship** *n.* **cham′pi·on** *adj.* That is a champion. **champion** *v.t.* Fight for, maintain the cause of.

Cham·plain (shămplān′), **Samuel de** (1567?–1635). French explorer of the St. Lawrence River and of the area from Great Lakes to E. Canada; founded Quebec, 1608; governor of New France, 1633–5; **Lake Champlain**, lake and resort area between the borders of New York and Vermont.

champ·le·vé (shahṅl*e*vā′) *adj.* & *n.* (Enamelwork) of which the metal ground is hollowed out and the spaces filled with enamel (cf. CLOISONNÉ). [Fr., = "field removed"]

Cham·pol·lion (shahṅpawlyawṅ′), **Jean François** (1790–1832). French Egyptologist; found key to deciphering hieroglyphics from study of Rosetta Stone.

Chanc. *abbrev.* Chancellor; chancery.

chance (chăns, chahns) *n.* 1. Unpredictable way in which things occur; fortune; casual or fortuitous circumstance or occurrence, accident. 2. Possibility, probability, of anything happening. 3. Absence of design or assignable cause, fortuity. 4. **by** ~, as it happens or happened; without design; **the main** ~: see MAIN[1]; **take one's chances**, take what may befall one; seize one's opportunity. **chance** *adj.* Happening by chance, fortuitous. ~ *v.* (**chanced, chanc·ing**). Happen by chance; take the risk of, hazard; ~ **on, upon**, meet or find by accident.

chan·cel (chăn′s*e*l, chahn′-) *n.* Part of church near altar, reserved for clergy, choir, etc., and freq. enclosed by a railing or lattice. [L. *cancelli* lattice bars]

chan·cel·ler·y (chăn′s*e*l*e*rē, -sl*e*rē, chahn′-) *n.* (pl. **-ler·ies**). Position, staff, department, official residence, of chancellor; office or building of embassy, consulate, or legation.

chan·cel·lor (chăn′s*e*l*e*r, -sl*e*r, chahn′-) *n.* 1. **Lord (High) C~, C~ of England**, highest officer of the British Crown, presiding in House of Lords, a member of the Cabinet, and the highest judicial functionary in England. 2. **C~ of the Exchequer**, highest finance minister of British Government and a member of the Cabinet. 3. Judge of a court of equity in some U.S. states. 4. Head of certain universities. 5. In Germany, Austria, etc., chief minister of state. **chan′cel·lor·ship** *n.*

*Temperature, light and emotional stimuli govern the color changing facility of the **chameleon.** Below (from top): Jackson's chameleon, flap-necked chameleon and the common chameleon.*

Facing page: a chameleon shoots out its long, sticky-tipped tongue to catch a grasshopper; the tongue will rapidly retreat with the victim trapped on it.

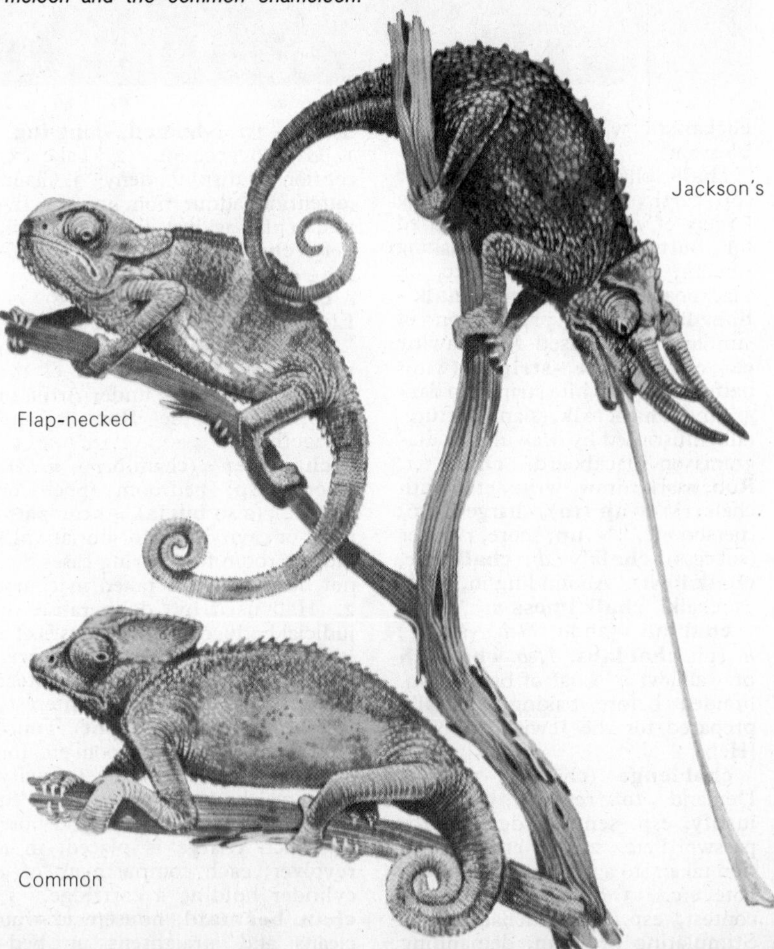

Renaissance artists and founders contributed a variety of forms and materials for the perfection of the ***chandelier,*** *derived from the simple suspended candleholder in early churches.*

Chan·cel·lors·ville (chăn′sel-erzvĭl, -slerz-, chahn′-). Town in NE. Virginia; site of a Civil War Confederate victory in which the Union's Gen. Hooker failed to break through Lee's lines; Gen. "Stonewall" Jackson was killed during this battle.

chan·cer·y (chăn′serē, chahn′-) *n.* (pl. **-cer·ies**). 1. (Brit.) Lord Chancellor's court. 2. A court in equity. 3. Office attached to embassy or consulate.

chan·cre (shăng′ker) *n.* Syphilitic ulcer. **chan′crous** *adj.*

chanc·y (chăn′sē, chahn′-) *adj.* (**chanc·i·er, chanc·i·est**). Uncertain, risky.

chan·de·lier (shăndelēr′) *n.* Ornamental branched hanging support for a number of light bulbs, candles, etc.

chan·dler (chănd′ler, chahnd′-) *n.* Dealer in candles, oil, soap, paint, and groceries; maker or seller of candles; **ship('s)** ~: see SHIP. **chan′dler·y** *n.*

change (chānj) *n.* 1. Alteration; substitution of one for another; variation, variety. 2. What may be substituted for another of the same kind, esp. in ~ **of clothes** etc. 3. Lower coins or bills given for equal value of higher ones; money returned as balance of that given in payment. 4. Any of the various orders in which a peal of bells is or may be rung; **ring the ~s**, go through all the changes in ringing a peal of bells; vary ways of putting or doing thing. 5. ~ **of life**, menopause. **change** *v.* (**changed, chang·ing**). 1. Take another instead of; resign, get rid of, *for*; give or get smaller or foreign coins or bills for; put on different clothes; put fresh clothes or coverings on (e.g., ~ **a baby**, replace used diaper with clean one); go from one to another; change trains; give and receive, exchange. 2. Make or become different; ~ **one's mind**, change one's purpose or opinion. 3. ~ **off**, take turns, alternate. **change′ful, change′less** *adjs.*

change·a·ble (chān′jabel) *adj.* Irregular, inconstant. **change·a·bil·i·ty** (chānjabĭl′ĭtē) *n.*

change·o·ver (chānj′ōver) *n.* Change from one system or situation to another.

chan·nel (chăn′el) *n.* 1. Natural or artificial bed of running water; comparatively narrow body of water joining two large bodies; **the C~**, the English Channel. 2. Tube or tubular passage for fluids. 3. (fig.) Course in which anything moves, direction; medium of transmission, communication, etc. 4. Band of frequencies sufficiently wide for transmission of radio or television signal. 5. Groove; flute. ~ *v.t.* (**-neled, -nel·ing**, Brit. **-nelled, -nel·ling**). Form channel(s) in, groove; cut out (way etc.); (fig.) direct, as in ~ **one's energies**.

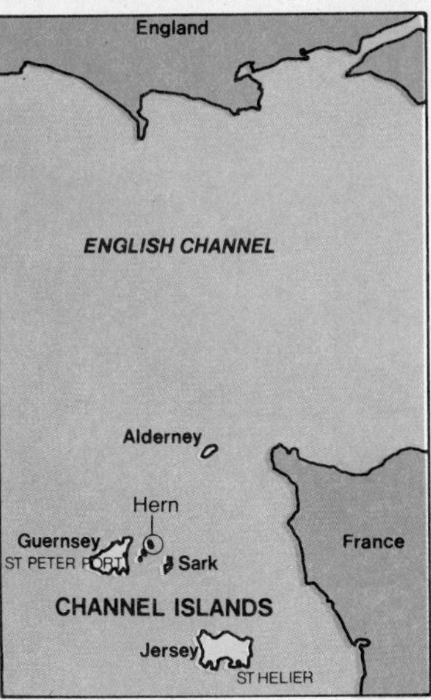

The ***Channel Islands*** *are known to the French as 'Iles Normandes'. The 4 main islands, Jersey, Guernsey, Alderney and Sark, total 75 sq. miles in area.*

Charlie Chaplin *in one of his earliest films, 'The Champion' (1915). He began his career when only seven in a clog-dancing act.*

Chan·nel (chăn′el) **Islands.** Group of nine small British islands in the English Channel off the coast of Normandy, of which the largest are Jersey, Guernsey, and Alderney.

chan·nel·ize (chăn′elīz) *v.* (**-ized, -iz·ing**). Channel.

chan·son de geste (shahṅsawṅ de zhĕst′) (pl. **chan·sons de geste** pr. shahṅsawṅ de zhĕst′). One of a group of French historical verse romances, mostly connected with Charlemagne, composed in the 11th–13th centuries; this genre of medieval French epic poem.

chant (chănt, chahnt) *n.* 1. Song.

2. Short musical passage in two or more phrases each beginning with reciting note, for singing to unmetrical words (psalms, canticles). 3. Measured monotonous song, musical recitation of words; sing-song intonation. ~ *v.* Sing; utter musically; intone, sing to a chant. **chant′er** *n.*

chan·teuse (shăntōōs′, -tōōz′; *Fr.* shahṅtöz′) *n.* (pl. **-teuses** pr. -tōō′sĭz, -zĭz; *Fr.* -töz′). Female singer of popular songs, esp. in night clubs.

chant·ey (shăn′tē, chăn′-) *n.* (pl. **-eys**). Sailors' song, esp. one sung in rhythm to hauling up sails, turning capstan, etc.

chan·ti·cleer (chăn′tĭkl ēr, shăn′-) *n.* Domestic rooster, used as proper name in medieval fables.

chan·try (chăn′trē, chahn′-) *n.* (pl. **-tries**). Endowment for priest(s) to say masses for founder's soul; altar or chapel so endowed.

Cha · nu · kah (χah′nōōkah, -n*u*ka, hah′-; *Heb.* χahnōōkah′) = HANUKKAH.

cha·os (kā′ŏs) *n.* 1. Formless void, abyss from which cosmos was created. 2. Utter confusion. **cha·ot·ic** (kāŏt′ĭk) *adj.* **cha·ot′i·cal·ly** *adv.*

chap[1] (chăp) *n.* Fissure in skin caused by exposure to cold, dampness, wind, etc. ~ *v.* (**chapped, chap·ping**). Crack, cause to crack, in fissures.

chap[2] (chăp, chŏp) = CHOP[2].

chap[3] (chăp) *n.* (colloq.) Man, boy, fellow.

chap·ar·ral (shăp*e*răl′) *n.* Dense tangled shrubs, esp. such as abounds on poor soil in the SW. U.S. and Mexico.

chap·book (chăp′bōōk) *n.* Small pamphlet of popular tales, ballads, poems, or religious tracts of the kind formerly sold by peddlers (chapmen).

cha·peau (shăpō′) *n.* (pl. **-peaux, -peaus** pr. -pōz′). (colloq.) Hat. [Fr.]

chap·el (chăp′*e*l) *n.* 1. Place of Christian worship smaller than and subordinate to a church, as one attached to a college, hospital, home, etc.; compartment or cell of cathedral etc. separately dedicated and with its own altar. 2. Private place of worship. 3. Chapel service. 4. Print shop, printing house; body of printers. [L. *cappella* dim. of *cappa* cape; first chapel was sanctuary in which St. Martin's sacred cloak was kept]

chap·er·on, chap·er·one (shăp′*e*rōn) *ns.* Married or mature woman accompanying young unmarried woman for sake of propriety on public occasions etc. ~ *v.t.* Act as chaperon to. **chap′-er·on·age** *n.* [Fr., orig. sense "hood"]

chap·fall·en (chăp′fawl*e*n) *adj.* With jaw hanging down, dejected.

chap·lain (chăp′lĭn) *n.* Priest of chapel, clergyman officiating in private chapel or institution, on board ship, or for military unit, etc. **chap′lain·cy** *n.*

chap·let (chăp′lĭt) *n.* 1. Wreath of flowers, leaves, gems, etc., for head. 2. String of prayer beads one-third of length of rosary; string of beads as necklace. 3. Anything resembling string of beads.

Chap·lin (chăp′lĭn), **Charles Spencer ("Charlie")** (1889–1977). English-born motion picture actor, producer, director, and writer, in America 1913–52, best known for his comic roles in silent films, esp. portraying "the little tramp."

chap·man (chăp′m*a*n) *n.* (pl. **-men** pr. -m*e*n). (Brit. hist.) Peddler, hawker.

chaps (chăps, shăps) *n.pl.* Stout leather trousers without seat worn over regular trousers by cowboys as protection against thorns and bushes. [Short for Mex. Span. *chaparreras*]

chap·ter (chăp′t*e*r) *n.* 1. Main division of a book or treatise (abbreviated *c.*, *cap.*, *ch.*, or *chap.*); (fig.) limited subject, piece of narrative, etc.; ~ **and verse**, exact reference. 2. General meeting or assembly of canons of cathedral or members of religious or knightly order for consultation and transaction of affairs; body of persons constituting this, esp. canons of cathedral; local branch of an organization, as of a society or fraternity.

char[1] (chār) *n.* (Brit. colloq.) Charwoman. ~ *v.i.* (**charred, char·ring**). Act as charwoman.

char[2] (chār) *v.* (**charred, char·ring**). Burn to charcoal; scorch; blacken with fire.

char[3], **charr** (chār) *ns.* (pl. **chars, charrs**, collect. **char, charr**). Trout of genus *Salvelinus*, found in mountain lakes.

char·ac·ter (kăr′ĭkt*e*r) *n.* 1. Distinctive mark, brand; graphic sign or symbol, esp. graphic symbol standing for sound, syllable, or notion, used in writing or printing; handwriting, printing; cabalistic sign or emblem. 2. Characteristic, esp. (pl.) distinguishing features of species or genus; sum of distinguishing features of individual etc., mental and moral qualities; such qualities strongly developed or strikingly displayed; reputation, (good) repute. 3. Personage, personality; imaginary person created by novelist or dramatist or played by actor; (colloq.) odd or eccentric person; ~ **actor**, one who plays pronounced or eccentric characters. **char′ac·ter·less** *adj.*

char·ac·ter·is·tic (kărĭkt*e*rĭs′-tĭk) *adj.* Distinctive, displaying the character of. ~ *n.* 1. Characteristic trait, mark, or quality. 2. (math.) Whole number in logarithm. **char·ac·ter·is′ti·cal·ly** *adv.*

char·ac·ter·ize (kăr′ĭkt*e*rīz) *v.t.* (**-ized, -iz·ing**). Describe character of; describe *as*; be characteristic of, impart character to. **char·ac·ter·i·za·tion** (kărĭkt*e*rīzā′shon) *n.*

cha·rade (sh*a*rād′; *Brit.* sh*a*rahd′) *n.* Game of guessing word, phrase, or book, song, motion picture, etc. title from written or

***Chaparral** country provides food for an abundance of wildlife during the brief wet season. In late summer, sudden fires create the right climate for germinating this typically dense scrub.*

*The **Charge of the Light Brigade** in the Battle of Balaclava, Crimean War, 1854, depicted by R. Caton Woodville. The cavalry charge cost the British 40 per cent casualties.*

acted clue given for each syllable, or word, or the whole; (fig.) absurd pretense. [Provençal *charrado* chatter]

char·coal (chār′kōl) *n.* Product of destructive DISTILLATION of wood or black residue of partly burned wood, bones, coal, etc.; porous, capable of reduction to powder, and (when pure) consisting wholly of carbon; ~ **gray**, a dark gray color.

chard (chārd, shārd) *n.* (also **Swiss** ~) Variety of beet with large succulent leaves used as a vegetable.

charge (chārj) *n.* 1. Quantity of anything that receptacle, piece of mechanism, etc. receives at one time; quantity of explosive for a gun or for one firing in blasting. 2. Electrical energy present in a proton or electron; such energy imparted to an object; accumulation of chemical energy in storage battery etc. available for conversion into electrical energy; NEGATIVE, POSITIVE ~: see these words; (slang) thrill, pleasure. 3. Responsibility, care, custody; task, duty; thing or person entrusted to another. 4. Price for services or goods; expenses; liability to pay money laid upon person; ~ **account**, credit account at store etc., permitting customer to receive goods in advance of billing; ~ **card** or **plate**, small metal or plastic CREDIT card, usu. valid for only one store or chain. 5. Precept, mandate, order; official instruction by judge to jury, bishop to clergy, etc. 6. Accusation, esp. that upon which prisoner is brought up for trial. 7. Impetuous attack; (mil.) signal for charge. **charge** *v.* (**charged, charg·ing**). 1. Fill to full or proper extent; fill *with*; impart electrical energy to (object), generate charge in (battery etc.). 2. Burden, entrust, *with*; command, order, enjoin, exhort or instruct formally or officially. 3. Bring accusation against. 4. Subject or make liable to financial obligation or liability; demand as price or sum (*for*). 5. Make violent onset, attack or assail impetuously. **charge′a·ble** *adj.*

char·gé d'af·faires (shārzhā′-dafār′, shār′zhā; *Fr.* shărzhā dăfĕr′) *n.* (pl. **char·gés d'af·faires** pr. shārzhāz′ dafār′, shār′zhāz; *Fr.* shărzhā dăfĕr′). 1. Ambassador's deputy. 2. Low-ranking diplomatic officer or envoy serving in a country to which an ambassador or other high-ranking diplomat is not sent.

charg·er (chār′jer) *n.* (esp.) Horse ridden in charging enemy; horse ridden by officer in the field.

char·i·ot (chăr′ēot) *n.* Light two-wheeled horse-drawn vehicle used in ancient warfare and racing. **char·i·ot·eer** (chărēotēr′) *n.* Chariot driver.

cha·ris·ma (karĭz′ma) *n.* Divine gift or talent; capacity to inspire followers with devotion and enthusiasm. **char·is·mat·ic** (kărĭzmăt′-ĭk) *adj.*

char·i·ta·ble (chăr′itabel) *adj.* Liberal in giving to the poor; connected with such giving; inclined to judge favorably of persons, acts, etc. **char′i·ta·bly** *adv.* **char′i·ta·ble·ness** *n.*

char·i·ty (chăr′itē) *n.* (pl. **-ties**). 1. Christian love of fellow men; kindness, affection. 2. Disposition to judge leniently of character, acts, etc., of others. 3. Beneficence, liberality to the poor, almsgiving, alms; bequest, foundation or institution for the benefit of others, esp. the poor or helpless.

char·la·tan (shār′latan) *n.* Imposter in medicine, quack; pretender to knowledge or skill, pretentious imposter. **char′la·tan·ism, char′la·tan·ry** *ns.* [It. *ciarlare* patter]

Char·le·magne (shār′lemān). Charles the Great (742–814), king of the Franks 768–814; crowned by the Pope as Holy Roman Emperor (as Charles I), 800.

Char·le·roi (shărlerwah′). City in S. central Belgium; site of first battle of World War I, 1914.

Charles[1] (chārlz), **"the Great"**: see CHARLEMAGNE.

Charles[2] (chārlz) (1500–58). King of Spain (as Charles I) 1516–1556 and Holy Roman Emperor (as Charles V) 1519–56 during the Reformation; abdicated the Imperial crown in favor of his brother Ferdinand and the crown of Spain in favor of his son Philip II.

Charles[3] (chārlz). Name of two kings of Gt. Britain: **Charles I** (1600–49), succeeded his father James I in 1625; his conflict with Parliament led to the English Civil War; beheaded in 1649; **Charles II** (1630–85) son of Charles I, became king at the Restoration, 1660; ~ **River**, short river flowing into Boston harbor and separating Boston and Cambridge, Massachusetts; named after Charles I of England.

Charles[4] (chārlz) (1948–). Prince of Wales; eldest son of Queen Elizabeth II of the United Kingdom.

Charles[5] (chārlz) (1682–1718). King of Sweden (as Charles XII) 1697–1718; a great military commander; defeated Peter the Great at Narva, 1700, but was in turn totally defeated at Poltava, 1709.

Charles[6] (chārlz) (1403–61). King of France (as Charles VII), 1422–61; defeated English at Orleans, 1429, with help of Joan of Arc.

Charles Mar·tel (chārlz′ mār-tĕl′) (689?–741). Ruler of Frankish Empire; defeated the Muslims at Tours, 732; grandfather of CHARLEMAGNE.

Charles's Law (chārlz′ez). (phys.) Law that volume of gas at constant pressure expands in proportion to absolute temperature. [Jacques *Charles*, Fr. physicist (1746–1823)]

Charles·ton[1] (chārlz′ton, chārls′ton). Capital of West Virginia, in the W. central part.

Charles·ton[2] (chārlz′ton, chārls′ton). Seaport in SE. South Carolina. ~ *n.* Fast dance characterized by side kicks from the knee, popular in the 1920's; ~ *v.i.* Dance this.

char·ley (chār′lē) **horse.** Stiffness or cramp of muscles, esp. in the thigh, from overexertion or injury.

char·lock (chār′lok) *n.* Wild mustard (*Brassica kaber*), a yellow-flowered annual weed.

Char·lotte (shār′lot). Industrial city in SW. North Carolina.

char·lotte (shār′lot) *n.* Dessert pudding of sponge cake or bread with filling of stewed fruits, custard, whipped cream, etc.; ~ **russe**, mold of whipped cream or custard surrounded by ladyfingers.

Char·lotte A·ma·lie (shār′lot amahl′yĕ). Formerly, St. Thomas; the capital of the U.S. Virgin Islands on the S. part of St. Thomas Island.

Char·lottes·ville (shār′lotsvĭl). City in central Virginia; site of Monticello, the home of Thomas Jefferson, and Ash Lawn, home of James Monroe.

charm (chārm) *n.* 1. Word(s), act, or object having or supposed to have magic or occult power or influence; talisman; amulet; trinket worn on bracelet etc. 2. Quality, attribute, feature, etc., exciting love or admiration; (pl.) beauty. ~ *v.t.* Bewitch, influence, by or as by charm or magic; endow with magic power or virtue; captivate, delight. **charmed** *adj.* (esp.) Bewitched; possessed of magic power or influence; protected, fortified, by a spell or charm. **charm′er** *n.* **charm′ing** *adj.* Fascinating; very pleasing, delightful. **charm′ing·ly** *adv.*

char·nel (chār′nel) **house.** House or vault in which dead bodies or bones are piled.

Cha·rol·lais, Cha·ro·lais (shărolā′) *ns.* Kind of beef cattle. [name of hills near Charolles, NW. of Lyons, France]

Char·on (kăr′on, kār′-). (Gk. myth.) Ferryman who conveyed the souls of the dead across the Styx to Hades.

charr (chār) = CHAR.[3]

chart (chārt) *n.* 1. Map, esp. one for navigators, showing depth of sea, rocks, channels, coasts, anchorages, etc. 2. Record (by means of curves etc. on graph) of fluctuations of temperature, prices, population, etc.; any sheet with information arranged in tabular form. ~ *v.t.* Make chart of, map.

char·ter (chār′ter) *n.* 1. Written grant of privileges, rights, etc., by sovereign or legislature, esp. creating or incorporating city, college, bank, or other public or private corporation. 2. Written instrument, contract, deed, etc. 3. Privilege; publicly conceded right; **Great C~**: see MAGNA CHARTA; **People's C~**: see CHARTIST. 4. ~ **flight**, flight in which entire plane or block of seats thereon is booked by an organized group of passengers. **charter** *v.t.* 1. Grant charter to; privilege, license. 2. Hire or lease (a vehicle, ship, or plane).

Chart·ist (chār′tĭst) *n.* Member of English political reforming body, chiefly of working classes, active 1837–48, whose aims were embodied in the People's Charter, demanding adult male suffrage, annual parliaments, and equal electoral districts. **Chart′ism** *n.*

Char·tres (shār′tre, shārt; *Fr.* shărtr). City in N. central France famous for its 13th c. Gothic cathedral.

char·treuse (shārtrooz′; for def. 2 sometimes shārtroos′) *n.* 1. Green or yellow liqueur of brandy and aromatic herbs, made by monks of Grande Chartreuse, the chief Carthusian monastery, near Grenoble, France. 2. Color of green chartruese, pale apple green.

char·wom·an (chār′wooman) *n.* (pl. **-wom·en** pr. -wĭmĭn). (Brit.) Woman hired by the day or hour for cleaning.

char·y (chār′ē) *adj.* (**char·i·er, char·i·est**). Cautious, wary; fastidious, shy; careful (*of*); frugal, sparing (*of*).

Cha·ryb·dis (karĭb′dĭs). (Gk. legend) Dangerous whirlpool in a narrow channel (later identified with the Strait of Messina, where there is no whirlpool), opposite the cave of SCYLLA.

chase[1] (chās) *n.* 1. Pursuit; **the** ~, (the sport of) hunting. 2. Hunting ground; unenclosed park (now mainly in place-names). 3. Hunted animal; quarry. ~ *v.t.* (**chased, chas·ing**). Pursue; drive *from*, *out of*, etc.; (colloq.) try to obtain. **chas′er** *n.* (esp.) 1. Hunter, pursuer. 2. Small drink of water, beer, etc. taken after hard liquor.

chase[2] (chās) *n.* (print.) Frame holding composed type for page or sheet.

chase[3] (chās) *v.t.* (**chased, chas·ing**). Engrave (metal), esp. with ornament.

Chase (chās), **Salmon P(ortland)** (1808–73). Amer. statesman and lawyer; gained prominence for defending fugitive slaves; U.S.

*Three impressions of **Charles I** in a painting by Sir Anthony Van Dyck. The king was beheaded outside the Banqueting Hall in Whitehall in 1649. He said he was 'a martyr of the people'.*

*The 16th-century **Château Chenonceaux** in the Loire, France, is an example of the 'château de plaisance', a stately home, evolving from the 'château fort', a strongly fortified medieval castle.*

senator, 1849–55, 1860; governor of Ohio, 1855–9; as secretary of the Treasury, 1861–4, he originated national banking system; chief justice of the U.S. Supreme Court, 1864–73.

chasm (kăz′*e*m) *n.* Deep fissure, cleft, or gap; break, hiatus; wide and profound difference of feelings, interests, etc.

chas·sis (shăs′ē, chăs′ē, -ĭs) *n.* (pl. **chas·is** pr. shăs′ēz, chăs′ēz). Frame of gun carriage; frame of motor vehicle, aircraft, etc., with its engine, as dist. from the body; body or cabinet of machine, electronic device, etc.

chaste (chāst) *adj.* (**chast·er, chast·est**). Not having had premarital or extramarital sexual intercourse, virtuous, continent; undefiled, pure; decent; modest, free from excess. **chaste′ly** *adv.* **chaste′ness** *n.* **chas·ti·ty** (chăs′tĭtē) *n.* State or quality of being chaste; ~ **belt**, device designed to prevent a woman from having sexual intercourse.

chas·ten (chā′s*e*n) *v.t.* 1. Discipline, correct by suffering. 2. Make chaste in style etc., refine; temper, subdue.

chas·tise (chăs′tīz, chăstīz′) *v.t.* (**-tised, -tis·ing**). Punish; beat. **chas·tise′ment** *n.*

chas·u·ble (chăz′y*u*b*e*l, -*u*b*e*l, chăs′-) *n.* Sleeveless vestment worn over all by priest at Mass.

chat[1] (chăt) *n.* & *v.i.* (Indulge in) familiar and easy talk. **chat′ty** *adj.* **chat′ti·ly** *adv.* **chat′ti·ness** *n.*

chat[2] (chăt) *n.* Any of various birds known for their chattering call, as the N. Amer. *Icteria virens* (also called **yellow-breasted** ~).

châ·teau (shătō′) *n.* (pl. **-teaus, -teaux** pr. -tōz). Castle, large mansion or country house, in France.

Cha·teau·bri·and (shătōbrēahn′), **François René, Vicomte de** (1768–1848). French author, diplomat, and political leader; one of the pioneers of the French romantic movement; author of *Le Génie du Christianisme* (1802) and several romances; **Chateaubriand** *n.* A thick slice of broiled tenderloin with sauce, named in his honor.

Châ·teau-Thier·ry (shăt′ōtĕr′ē; *Fr.* shătō tyĕrē′). Town on the Marne in N. France; site of heavy fighting during World War I, 1918.

chat·e·laine (shăt′*e*lān) *n.* 1. Mistress of castle or country house. 2. Chain(s) holding keys, watch, scissors, etc., formerly worn hanging from woman's girdle or belt.

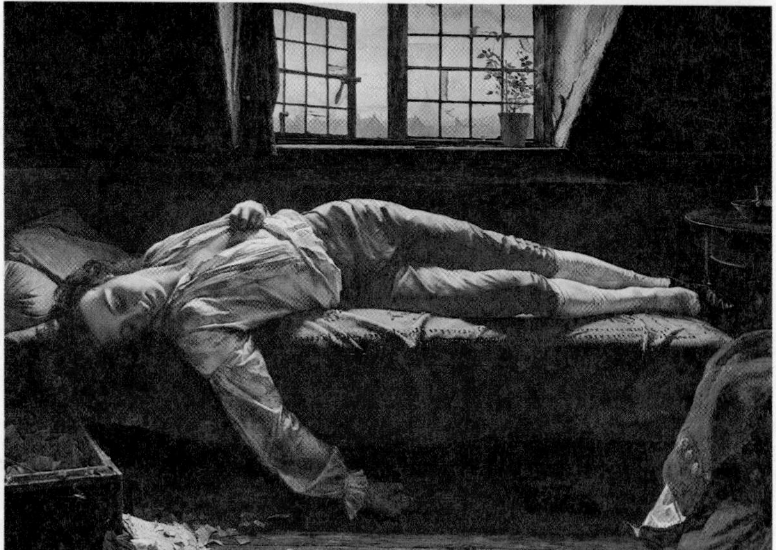

*'Death of Chatterton' (Tate, London) by Henry Wallace. When only 17, the poet **Thomas Chatterton** killed himself with arsenic in a London attic in 1770.*

Chat·ta·hoo·chee (chăt*ah*hōō′chē). River in NE. Georgia flowing 436 miles (696 km) to the Flint River at the Florida border.

Chat·ta·noo·ga (chăt′*a*nōō′g*a*). Industrial city on the Tennessee River in SE. Tennessee; site of several Civil War battles.

chat·tel (chăt′*e*l) *n.* (law) Property of every kind except real estate; (pl.) goods, possessions; (rhet.) slave.

chat·ter (chăt′*er*) *v.i.* 1. (of birds) Utter rapid series of short notes, esp. of sounds approaching those of human voice. 2. (of persons) Talk quickly, incessantly, foolishly, or inopportunely. 3. (of teeth etc.) Rattle together. ~ *n.* Sound of chattering; incessant trivial talk; **chat′terbox**, talkative person, esp. child. **chat′ter·er** *n.*

Chat·ter·ton (chăt′*er*t*o*n), **Thomas** (1752–70). English poet who fabricated a number of poems purporting to be the work of an imaginary 15th-c. Bristol poet, Thomas Rowley.

Chau·cer (chaw′s*er*), **Geoffrey** (1340?–1400). English poet, author of the *Canterbury Tales*. **Chau·ce·ri·an** (chawsēr′ē*a*n) *adj.* After the manner of Chaucer. *n.* Scholar specializing in the writings of Chaucer.

chauf·feur (shō′f*er*, shōfēr′) *n.* Paid driver of private automobile.

Chau·tau·qua (sh*a*taw′kw*a*). Town in SW. New York; site of a popular adult summer recreation and educational program inaugurated in 1874.

chau·vin·ism (shō′vĭnĭz*e*m) *n.* Militant and boastful patriotism; MALE chauvinism. **chau′vin·ist** *adj.* & *n.* **chau·vin·is·tic** (shōvĭnĭs′tĭk) *adj.* [f. Nicolas *Chauvin*, French veteran soldier of First Republic and Empire whose demonstrative loyalty was celebrated and at length ridiculed]

chaw (chaw) *n.* & *v.* (dial.) Chew.

cheap (chēp) *adj.* 1. Not costly; costing less than the usual price, rate etc.; worth more than its cost; (of money) obtainable at low rate of interest. 2. Costing little trouble, labor, etc. 3. Worthless; made light of, brought into contempt by being made too familiar; common, vulgar, immoral. 4. ~ **shot**, (slang) unfair, unkind, remark or action; **cheap'skate**, (slang) stingy person, penny pincher; **cheap, cheap'ly** *advs.* **cheap'ness** *n.*

cheap·en (chē'pen) *v.* Make or become cheap, depreciate.

cheat (chēt) *n.* 1. Fraud, deception, imposition. 2. Swindler; deceiver, impostor. ~ *v.* Deceive, trick (*out of* something); deal fraudulently; beguile (time, fatigue, etc.) **cheat'er** *n.*

check[1] (chěk) *int.* (chess) Call notifying opponent that his or her king is exposed. ~ *n.* 1. (chess) Position of king when exposed to direct attack. 2. Sudden arrest in career or onward course; rebuff, repulse; sudden stoppage or pause. 3. Restraint on action or conduct. 4. Control securing accuracy, agreement, etc.; token, ticket, of identification for baggage, coat left in baggage room, coatroom, etc.; restaurant bill; counter used in card games, chip. 5. Symbol (✓) to indicate verification, enumeration, or agreement. ~ *v.* 1. (chess) Place in check. 2. Suddenly arrest motion of; stop. 3. Restrain, curb. 4. Test (figures etc.) by comparison etc., examine accuracy of; correspond, agree upon comparison; ~ **in, out**, record arrival or departure (of). 5. ~ **list**, list of items to be compared, scheduled, purchased, supervised, etc.; ~ **off**, check items in such a list; **check'-off**, deduction of union dues by an employer from a worker's paycheck; **check'out**, counter or desk where payment is made in self-service store; **check'point**, point were traffic and travelers are checked, as at national border; **check'up**, examination (esp. medical), scrutiny. **check'er** *n.* [OF. *eschec*, f. Arab., f. Pers. *shāh* king]

check[2] (chěk) *n.* Pattern of (crosslines forming) small squares, like chessboard; fabric woven or printed with this. **checked** *adj.*

check[3] (chěk), Brit. **cheque** *ns.* Written order to bank to pay sum of money to bearer or named person; form on which this is written; **check'book**, book of such forms issued to customer of bank; **check'ing account**, bank account for meeting current expenditure, drawn on by check.

check·ers (chěk'erz) *n.pl.* (usu. considered sing.) Game played by two persons on checkerboard with 24 pieces that are moved diagonally; **check'erboard**, game board with 64 squares of alternating colors, on which chess and checkers are played. **check'er** *v.* Mark like checkerboard; **check'ered**, (fig.) undergoing varied fortunes.

check·mate (chěk'māt) *n.* 1. (chess) Position in which king cannot be extricated from check, move which brings this about. 2. Final defeat; deadlock. ~ *v.t.* (**-mat·ed, -mat·ing**). Give checkmate to; foil, stop, or defeat utterly. [OF. *eschec mat* (see CHECK[1]) f. Arab. *shāh māt* (the chess) king is dead]

Ched·dar, ched·dar (chěd'*er*) *ns.* (also ~ **cheese**) Any of several types of smooth, hard yellow cheese varying from mild to sharp in flavor, orig. made near Cheddar, a village in England.

cheek (chēk) *n.* 1. Side wall of mouth, side of face below eye; **cheek'bone**, bone forming lower boundary of eye orbit. 2. (colloq.) Impudence; cool confidence, effrontery.

cheek·y (chē'kē) *adj.* (**cheek·i·er, cheek·i·est**). (colloq.) Impudent. **cheek'i·ly** *adv.* **cheek'i·ness** *n.*

cheep (chēp) *v.i.* & *n.* (Utter) shrill feeble sound as of young bird.

*Painting of **Geoffrey Chaucer,** whose 'Canterbury Tales' vividly portrayed pilgrims from London to the shrine of St. Thomas à Becket in Canterbury.*

cheer (chēr) *n.* 1. Shout of encouragement or applause; **three ~s**, successive united hurrahs. 2. Frame of mind (only in phrases, as **be of good ~**). 3. (archaic) Food. **cheer** *v.* 1. Comfort, gladden; **~ up**, comfort, be comforted. 2. Incite, urge *on*, by shouts etc.; **cheer'leader**, one who leads organized cheering, esp. at games; also fig. 3. Applaud; shout for joy. **cheers** (chērz) *int.* Exclamation used as toast.

cheer·ful (chēr'ful) *adj.* In good spirits; pleasant; willing, not reluctant. **cheer'ful·ly** *adv.* **cheer'ful·ness** *n.*

cheer·i·o (chēr'ēō, chērēō') *int.* & *n.* (pl. **cheer·i·os**). (chiefly Brit. colloq.) Goodby.

cheer·less (chēr'lĭs) *adj.* Gloomy, dreary. **cheer'less·ly** *adv.* **cheer'less·ness** *n.*

cheer·y (chēr'ē) *adj.* (**cheer·i·er, cheer·i·est**). Lively, genial. **cheer'i·ly** *adv.* **cheer'i·ness** *n.*

cheese[1] (chēz) *n.* 1. Food made of the curd of milk, separated from the whey and pressed into a close mass; mass of this, usu. wheel-shaped, cylindrical, or globular, with a hardened outer layer or rind. 2. **cheese'burger**, hamburger with cheese on it; **cheese'cake**, cake made of cottage or cream cheese, etc., with eggs, sugar, milk, flavoring; (slang) display of scantily clad shapely female body in photographs, advertisements, etc.; **cheese'cloth**, thin cotton cloth (of the kind) in which curds are pressed for cheese. **chees'y** *adj.*

cheese[2] (chēz) *v.imp.* (slang) Stop. **~ it**, look out; run away.

chee·tah, che·tah (chē'ta) *ns.* Large, tawny, spotted member of cat family (*Acinonyx jubatus*), of Africa and S. Asia, with non-retractile claws; the fastest four-legged animal. [Hindi *chītā*, f. Sansk. *chitraka*]

chef (shĕf) *n.* Cook, esp. head cook.

chef-d'oeu·vre (shĕdö'vre) *n.* (pl. **chefs-d'oeuvre** pr. shĕdö'vre). Masterpiece. [Fr.]

Che·khov (chĕk'awf, -ŏf; *Russ.* chĕ'χŏf), **Anton Pavlovich** 1860–1904). Russian dramatist and novelist, author of *The Seagull*, *Uncle Vanya*, *The Cherry Orchard*, and other plays, and of numerous short stories.

che·la[1] (chā'lah) *n.* (Buddhism) Novice qualifying for initiation; pupil of a guru.

che·la[2] (kē'la) *n.* (pl. **-lae** pr. -lē). Prehensile claw of crabs, lobsters, scorpions, etc.

che·late (kē'lāt) *adj.* & *n.* (chem.) (Compound) with cyclic structure looping around central metal ion and attached at two or more points. **~** *v.i.* (**-lat·ed, -lat·ing**). Combine with (substance) to form chelate

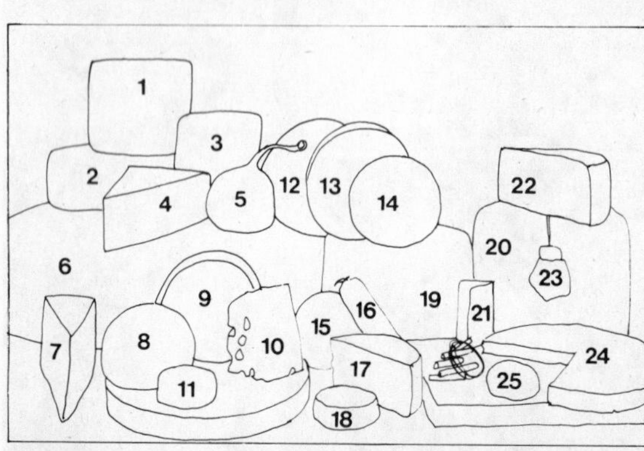

*Displayed is a variety of **cheeses.** Cheeses are in general classified according to consistency (soft to hard), manufacturing method (acid or rennet curd) and degree of ripening.*

1 Cheshire
2 Double Gloucester
3 Stilton
4 Gruyere
5 Provolone
6 Emmental
7 Sage Derby
8 Edam
9 Bel Paese
10 Cut of Emmental
11 Tom Savoie
12 Gouda
13 Caerphilly
14 Port Salut
15 Provolone (unwrapped)
16 Smoked Cheese (Austrian)
17 Roquefort
18 Camembert
19 English Cheddar
20 Farmhouse Cheddar
21 Cut of Coloured Cheshire
22 Leicester
23 Mozzarella
24 Whole Brie
25 Nucatall

Left: On Founders Day at the Royal Hospital, ***Chelsea,*** *London, U.K., Chelsea Pensioners parade for inspection. The home for 'worthy old soldiers broken in the wars' was founded by Charles II and completed in 1692. The bemedaled scarlet-uniformed military veterans remain a conspicuous part of the London scene. A fine gold Chelsea plate (above) made in Chelsea in 1770.*

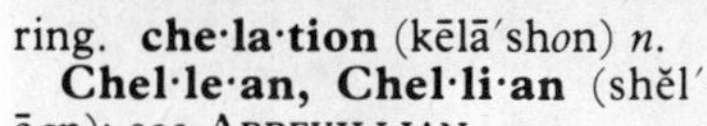

ring. **che·la·tion** (kēlā′sh*o*n) *n.*

Chel·le·an, Chel·li·an (shĕl′ēan): see ABBEVILLIAN.

Chel·sea (chĕl′sē). Borough (with Kensington) of London, associated with artists and writers.

chem·i·cal (kĕm′ĭk*a*l) *adj.* Of, made by, relating to, chemistry; ~ **engineering**, industrial application of chemistry; ~ **warfare**, use in war of chemical substances other than explosives, esp. poison gases, for purpose of injuring the enemy. **chemical** *n.* Substance obtained by or used in chemical processes. **chem′i·cal·ly** *adv.*

chem·i·lum·i·nes·cence (kĕmĭloōm*i*nĕs′*e*ns) *n.* Emission of light in chemical reaction. **chem·i·lu·mi·nes′cent** *adj.*

che·min de fer (sh*e*măn d*e* fār′; *Fr.* shmăṅ d*e* fĕr′). Form of baccarat. [Fr., = "railroad," so called from the speed of the game]

che·mise (sh*e*mēz′) *n.* Woman's shirtlike undergarment; dress hanging straight from shoulders.

chem·ist (kĕm′ĭst) *n.* 1. Scientist specializing in chemistry. 2. (Brit.) Pharmacist.

chem·is·try (kĕm′ĭstrē) *n.* (pl. **-tries**). Science of the composition of substances and their combination and change under various conditions; **inorganic** ~, chemistry of the elements other than carbon; **organic** ~, formerly, chemistry of substances found in organic structures; now, chemistry of compounds of carbon, whether natural or synthetic; **physical** ~, study of the physical aspects of chemistry.

chem·nitz (kĕm′nĭts) = KARL MARX STADT.

che·mo·ther·a·py (kēmōthĕr′*a*pē, kĕm*e*-) *n.* Treatment of disease by chemical substances that act on microorganisms or malignant tissue. **che·mo·ther·a·peu·tics** (kēmōthĕr*a*pū′tĭks, kĕm*e*-), **che·mo·ther′a·pist** *ns.*

che·nille (sh*e*nēl′) *n.* Yarn with pile protruding all around it; fabric of this or of tufted fabric, used for bedspreads, rugs, etc. [Fr., = "caterpillar"]

Chen·nault (sh*e*nawlt′), **Claire Lee** (1890–1958). U.S. Air Force general during World War II; air adviser to Chiang Kai-shek, 1937; formed the "Flying Tigers," a volunteer air corps, to help defend China and protect the Burma Road in World War II.

Che·ops (kē′ŏps) (2900?–2877 B.C.). Fourth dynasty Egyptian king; constructed Great Pyramid.

cheque (chĕk) *n.* (Brit.) Var. of CHECK[3].

Cher·bourg (shār′boorg; *Fr.* shĕrboōr′). Seaport and naval base in NW. France.

cher·chez la femme (shĕrshā′ lă făm′). Look for the woman (freq. facet., implying that the key to a problem etc. is a woman). [Fr.]

cher·ish (chĕr′ĭsh) *v.t.* Foster, nurse; value, keep in the memory or heart, cling to.

Cher·o·kee (chĕr′*o*kē, chĕr*o*kē′) *adj.* & *n.* (pl. **-kees**, collect. **-kee**). (Member) of an Iroquoian-speaking tribe of N. Amer. Indians formerly occupying North Carolina and N. Georgia, now settled primarily in Oklahoma.

che·root (sh*e*roōt′) *n.* Thin, untapered, dark cigar open at both ends.

cher·ry (chĕr′ē) *n.* (pl. **-ries**). Pulpy fruit of certain species of *Prunus*, esp. of the cultivated tree, *P. cerasus*; (wood of) tree bearing this; ~ **picker**, (esp.) type of crane, usu. mobile, for raising and lowering worker by means of a maneuverable boom; **cher′rystone (clam)**, small clam, a half-grown quahog. **cherry** *adj.* Red.

Cherry *tree with its blossom and fruit. Cherries belong to the large group of trees with a single seed enclosed in a stone, in turn enclosed in an edible fruity tissue.*

chert (chĕrt) *n.* (geol.) Form of amorphous silica found in several varieties, e.g. flint.

cher·ub (chĕr′*u*b) *n.* (pl. for 1 **cher·u·bim** pr. chĕr′*u*bĭm,

Above: Late 17th-century carved oak ***chest*** *with arcaded front and gadrooned (convex-fluted) drawer at the base. Right: Highboy chest of draws, c. 1770.*

'The Calling of St. Peter and St. Andrew' (National Gallery, London) by Caravaggio is an example of ***chiaroscuro,*** *the disposition of light and shade in a painting, from the Italian 'chiaro' (light) and 'oscuro' (shade).*

-*yu*bĭm; for 2 **cher·ubs**). 1. Order of angels (see ANGEL), gifted esp. with knowledge. 2. Representation of one of the cherubim in art, usu. as a winged child, or child's head with wings and no body; beautiful child. **che·ru·bic** (ch*e*rōō'bĭk, chĕr'*u*-) *adj.* [Heb. *k^erūb*]

cher·vil (chẽr'vĭl) *n.* Garden herb (*Anthriscus cerefolium*) with aromatic leaves used in salads, soups, etc.

Ches·a·peake (chĕs'*a*pēk) **Bay.** Large inlet of the Atlantic Ocean about 200 miles (321.9 km) long, between Maryland and Virginia.

Chesh·ire (chĕsh'*er*, -ẽr). English county of N. Midlands, bordering on Wales; **grin like a ~ cat,** grin broadly (explained as ref. to Cheshire cheeses made in shape of cat, or to lion rampant on Cheshire inn signs); **~ cheese,** kind of hard, yellow cheese made orig. in Cheshire.

chess (chĕs) *n.* Game played by two persons on board divided into 64 squares, each player having 16 pieces or "men" (a king, a queen, two bishops, two knights, two rooks, and eight pawns), the object being to CHECKMATE the opponent's king; **chess'board,** board on which chess is played, the same as a checkerboard: **chess'man,** one of the pieces used in the game.

chest (chĕst) *n.* 1. Large strong box; box for sailor's belongings. 2. Treasury of institution; fund kept in this. 3. Case of some commodity, esp. tea. 4. **~ of drawers,** piece of furniture with set of drawers. 5. Part of human or animal's body enclosed by ribs and breastbone, and containing heart and lungs.

ches·ter·field (chĕs'*ter*fēld) *n.* Kind of overcoat, usually with a velvet collar. [f. a 19th-c. earl of *Chesterfield*]

Ches·ter·field (chĕs'*ter*fēld), **Philip Dormer Stanhope, 4th Earl of** (1694–1773). British statesman and diplomat, chiefly remembered for his *Letters* to his son.

Ches·ter·ton (chĕs'*ter*t*o*n), **G(ilbert) K(eith)** (1874–1936). English author of essays, novels, verse, etc.

chest·nut (chĕs'nŭt) *n.* 1. Tree of the genus *Castanea* of the N. Hemisphere, bearing a large edible nut enclosed in a prickly pericarp or burr; this nut; the American chestnut, *C. dentata,* has been almost exterminated by a blight caused by a parasitic fungus. 2. = horsechestnut: see HORSE. 3. (colloq.) Stale anecdote or joke. 4. Chestnut color; chestnut-colored horse. ~ *adj.* Of chestnut color, varying from bright to dark reddish brown.

chest·y (chĕs'tē) *adj.* (**chest·i·er, chest·i·est**). (colloq.) Having a large chest; (colloq.) proud, conceited; (of voice) have a low register.

chev·a·lier (shĕv*a*lẽr', sh*e*văl'-yā) *n.* Horseman, knight (hist. or archaic); member of certain orders of knighthood, or of French Legion of Honor; soldier cadet of old French nobility.

chev·i·ot (shĕv'ēot, chĕv'-) *n.* (One of) a breed of sheep with short, thick wool originally raised in the Cheviot Hills on the border between England and Scotland; fabric made from its wool.

chev·ron (shĕv'r*o*n) *n.* Bent bar of inverted **V** shape as heraldic device, architectural ornament, etc.; distinguishing mark of this shape on sleeve of noncommissioned officers, policemen, etc., stripe.

Chev·y (chĕv'ē) **Chase.** 1. Skirmish, celebrated in a ballad of

15th-c. origin, beteen Percy, Earl of Northumberland, and his Scottish neighbor "the doughty Douglas"; both were killed in the fight. 2. Town in Maryland, residential suburb of Washington, D.C.

chew (cho͞o) *v.* Work about between teeth, grind to pulp or indent with repeated biting; chew tobacco; turn over in mind, meditate *on* or *over*; ~ **the cud**, (of ruminant animals) bring back half-digested food into mouth for further chewing; ~ **the fat**, (slang) talk informally; **chewing gum**, preparation of flavored hardened secretion of spruce tree, or similar insoluble substance, used for chewing (see also CHICLE). **chew** *n.* Act of chewing; quid of tobacco.

Chey·enne (shīĕn′, -ăn′) *n.* (pl. **-ennes**, collect. **-enne**). (Member of) an Algonquin tribe of N. Amer. Indians formerly inhabiting central Minnesota and North and South Dakota, now settled mainly in Montana and Oklahoma; ~, capital of Wyoming, in the SE. part.

chi (kī) *n.* Twenty-second letter of Greek alphabet (X, χ), = *ch*; ~**-rho**, monogram of chi and rho, first two letters of Gk. *Christos* (= Christ), ☧, used on altar cloths, vestments, etc., as monogram and symbol for Christ.

Chiang Kai-shek (chyahng′

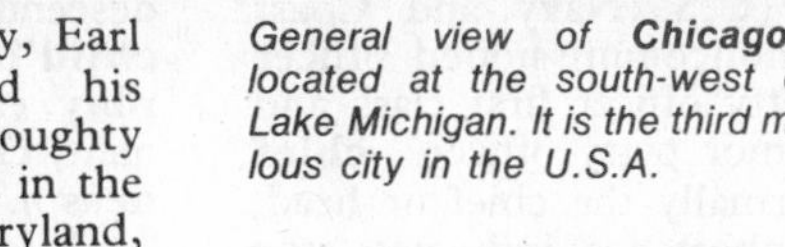

General view of **Chicago,** Illinois, located at the south-west corner of Lake Michigan. It is the third most populous city in the U.S.A.

kī shĕk′, chăng′). Chiang Chung-cheng (1887–1975), Chinese general and statesman; president of the Republic of China from 1943; withdrew government to Taiwan, 1949.

Chi·an·ti (kēahn′tē) *n.* Dry red wine produced in or near the Chianti Mountains in Tuscany, Italy.

chi·a·ro·scu·ro (kēăr*o*skūr′ō, -skoor′ō), **chi·a·ro·o·scu·ro** (kēăr̄ōōskūr′ō, -skoor′ō) *ns.* (pl. **-ros**). Treatment of light and shade in painting, esp. when strongly contrasted. [It., = "bright dark"]

chi·as·mus (kīăz′m*u*s) *n.* (pl. **-mi** pr. -mī). (rhet. etc.) Inversion in a second phrase of the order followed in first, e.g. *He saved others; himself he cannot save.* [Gk. *chiasmos* arrangement like letter chi, χ]

chic (shēk, shĭk) *n.* Sophistication in dress and manner; stylishness. ~ *adj.* Stylish, in the fashion.

Chi·ca·go (shĭkah′gō, -kaw′-). The third largest city in the U.S., on Lake Michigan in N. Illinois; important port and distribution

A ruin similar to those found at **Chichén-Itzá,** the ancient Mayan city founded by the Mayan people who were later invaded by the Itzá. By the mid 15th century the city was virtually uninhabited.

center; commercial and financial center of the midwest; known for large grain and livestock market and meat-packing plants.

chi·cane (shĭkān′) *n.* Chicanery. ~ *v.* (**-caned, -can·ing**). Use chicanery; cheat.

chi·can·er·y (shĭkā′n*e*rē) *n.* (pl. **-er·ies**). Trickery, deception; underhand dealing; sophistry.

Chi·chén-It·zá (chēchĕn′ētsah′, chē′chĕnēt′s*a*). Village in Yucatan, Mexico; famous as site of Mayan ruins.

chi·chi (shē′shē, shēshē′) *n.* & *adj.* Fussily ornamented, showy, (thing); affected (manner).

chick (chĭk) *n.* Chicken; young bird before or after hatching; (slang) young woman; **chick′-weed**, weed of genus *Stellaria.*

chick·a·dee (chĭk′*a*dē) *n.* Any of several small gray N. Amer. titmice of the genus *Parus* (esp. *P. atricapillus*), the common black-capped chickadee of northeastern U.S. and Canada.

Chick·a·mau·ga (chĭk*a*maw′-g*a*). Town near Chickamauga Creek in NW. Georgia; site of a defeat of Union troops under Gen.

Rosecrans by Confederate troops under Gen. Bragg during Civil War.

chick·en (chĭk'*en*) *n.* 1. Young bird, esp. of domestic fowl; flesh of domestic fowl as food. 2. (colloq.) Youthful person. 3. (slang, as adjective) Cowardly. 4. ~ **feed,** (colloq.) something trivial, esp. small amount of money; **~-hearted,** (slang) timorous, cowardly; ~ **pox,** mild eruptive disease with some resemblance to smallpox, chiefly affecting children. **chicken** *v.i.* (slang) Abstain through cowardice (also ~ **out**).

chick·pea (chĭk'pē) *n.* Dwarf pea (*Cicer arietinum*), widely esteemed as food, esp. in S. European and Latin American cuisine.

chic·le (chĭk'*el*) *n.* Gumlike substance obtained from the sapodilla (*Sapota zapotilla*) used for making chewing gum. [Nahuatl *tzictli*]

chic·o·ry (chĭk'*er*ē) *n.* 1. (bot.) Any plant of the genus *Cichorium.* 2. Species of this (*C. intybus*) with long smooth blanched leaves eaten as salad; its root, ground and roasted as addition to or substitute for coffee.

chide (chīd) *v.* (**chid·ed, chid, chid·den, chid·ing**). Scold. **chid'er** *n.* **chid'ing·ly** *adv.*

chief (chēf) *n.* 1. Head, leader, ruler, of body of people, esp. of clan, tribe, etc.; superior officer, head of department. 2. **C~ Executive,** President of the U.S.; ~ **justice,** presiding judge over a

__Chicory__ plant in flower. The two main species of the plant, native to Europe, are relished as salads. The root of Cichorium intybus is ground as a coffee additive or substitute.

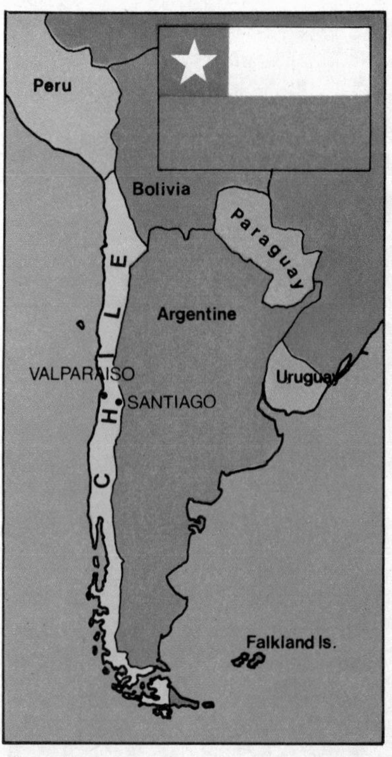

court with several judges, esp. the Supreme Court of the U.S.; **C~ of Staff,** senior officer of a service, as of U.S. Army; (l.c.) senior officer in command of a general staff; senior staff officer at or higher than division level; ~ **petty officer,** (U.S. Navy and Coast Guard) noncommissioned officer above petty officer first class and below senior petty officer. **chief** *adj.* Formally the chief or head; first in importance, influence, etc.; prominent, leading. **chief·dom** (chēf'd*o*m) *n.* **chief'ly** *adv.* & *adj.* Above all; mainly but not exclusively.

chief·tain (chēf'tĭn) *n.* Military leader (poet.); chief of clan or tribe.

chif·fon (shĭfŏn', shĭf'ŏn) *n.* Diaphanous fabric of fine hard-twisted yarn (silk, nylon, etc.). ~ *adj.* (cooking) Having a light, fluffy consistency, esp. as made with beaten egg whites (~ **pie**).

chif·fo·nier, chif·fon·nier (shĭf*o*nēr') *ns.* High chest of drawers, usu. with a mirror.

chig·ger (chĭg'*er*) *n.* Larva of a parasitic mite of the family Trombidiidae, which causes violent itching in human skin.

chi·gnon (shēn'yŏn, shēnyŏn') *n.* Coil of hair worn at back of head by women.

chig·oe, chig·o (chĭg'ō) *ns.* Small tropical flea (*Tunga penetrans*), the fertile female of which burrows under human skin.

Chi·hua·hua (chĭwah'wah, -w*a*) *n.* Very small smooth-haired dog of Mexican breed. [*Chihuahua,* city and State of Mexico]

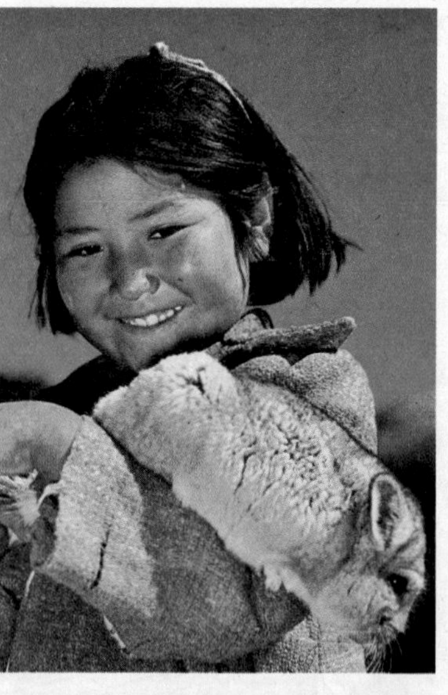

Above: A girl in __Chile__ with her pet chinchilla. Left: Map of Chile, S. American republic on the Pacific coast. The country is narrow, averaging only 110 miles in width, but it extends about 2,650 miles in length.

chil·blain (chĭl'blān) *n.* Inflammatory itching swelling on hand, foot, etc., caused by exposure to cold and poor circulation.

child (chīld) *n.* (pl. **chil·dren** pr. chĭl'drĭn). Young human being; immature person; offspring; descendant, follower, product (*of*); **child'birth,** parturition; **child's play,** easy task; **with child,** pregnant; **child'less** *adj.* **child'less·ness** *n.*

child·hood (chīld'ho͝od) *n.* Time from birth to puberty; **second ~,** dotage.

child·ish (chīl'dĭsh) *adj.* Of, proper to, a child; not befitting an adult. **child'ish·ly** *adv.* **child'ish·ness** *n.*

child·like (chīld'līk) *adj.* Having the good qualities of a child, as innocence, frankness, etc.

Chil·e (chĭl'ē; *Sp.* chē'lĕ). S. Amer. Republic lying between the Andes and the Pacific; discovered by Spanish adventurers in the 16th c. and remained under Spanish rule until 1818; capital, Santiago. **Chil'e·an** *adj.* & *n.*

chil·i (chĭl'ē) *n.* (pl. **chil·ies**), **chil·li** (chĭl'ē) *n.* (pl. **-lies**), **chil·e** (chĭl'ē) *n.* Dried pod of kinds of capsicum, acrid, pungent and of deep red color, used to make cayenne pepper; chili con carne; chili sauce; ~ **con carne,** Mexican

Above right: Former __Chief Executive__ of the U.S.A. Gerald Ford who replaced Richard Nixon after Watergate forced his resignation. Ford remained in office for 2 years.
Right: Sorting and drying green __chillis__ in Sri Lanka. This pungent spice gradually changes color as it dries in the hot sun.

stew of chili-flavored minced beef, beans, onions, etc.; ~ **sauce**, sauce made from tomatoes with chilies and other spices. [Nahuatl]

chill (chĭl) *n.* 1. Cold sensation, lowered temperature of body, feverish cold. 2. Unpleasant coldness of air, water, etc. 3. Depressing influence; coldness of manner. ~ *adj.* Lacking warmth. ~*v.* 1. Make, become, cold; deaden, blast, with cold; keep (meat or other food) at low temperature but without freezing. 2. Depress, dispirit.

chil·ly (chĭl′ē) *adj.* (**-li·er, -li·est**). Rather cold; not genial, cold-mannered. **chill′i·ness** *n.*

chime (chīm) *n.* Set of tuned bells, series of sounds given by this; harmony, melody, rhythm; agreement, correspondence. ~ *v.* (**chimed, chim·ing**). 1. Make (bell) sound; ring chimes, ring chimes on; show (hour) by chiming. 2. Harmonize, agree (*with*); ~ **in**, join in harmoniously; break into a conversation.

Chi·me·ra, Chi·mae·ra (kī-mēr′*a*, kĭ-). (Gk. myth.) Fire-breathing monster with lion's head, goat's body, and serpent's tail, killed by Bellerophon.

chi·me·ra, chi·mae·ra (kī-mēr′*a*, kĭ-) *ns.* (pl. **-ras**). Grotesque monster; thing of hybrid character, fanciful conception; organism formed by grafting etc. from tissues of different genetic origin. **chi·mer·i·cal** (kīmĕr′ĭk*a*l, -mēr′-, kĭ-) *adj.* **chi·mer′i·cal·ly** *adv.*

chim·ney (chĭm′nē) *n.* (pl. **-neys**). Flue carrying off smoke or steam of fire, furnance, etc.; part of flue above roof; glass tube enclosing flame of a lamp; natural vent of volcano etc.; narrow cleft by which cliff may be climbed; ~ **corner**, warm seat within old-fashioned fireplace; ~ **piece**, mantel; decoration over a fireplace; ~ **pot**, earthenware or metal pipe at top of chimney; ~ **sweep**, person whose trade it is to clean soot from chimneys.

chimp (chĭmp) *n.* (colloq.) Chimpanzee.

chim·pan·zee (chĭmpănzē′, chĭmpăn′zē) *n.* African ape of genus *Pan*, allied to gorilla, bearing the closest resemblance to man of any of the surviving anthropoids. [native W. African name]

chin (chĭn) *n.* Front of lower jaw. ~ *v.* (**chinned, chin·ning**). Lift (oneself), while hanging by the hands from a horizontal bar above, until chin is at height of bar; (colloq.) chatter, gossip.

Chi·na (chī′n*a*). Large country of E. Asia with a civilization dating from the 3rd millennium B.C., governed during most of its history by emperors of numerous (often rival) dynasties; after a revolution (in 1911) a republic was proclaimed

*Of surviving anthropoids the **chimpanzee** is most like man and endowed with considerable intelligence. In trees the chimpanzee swings from branch to branch with great agility.*

*A small rodent resembling a rabbit but with smaller ears, the **chinchilla** is about 14 ins. long. Chinchilla fur, particularly that of the Peruvian or royal chinchilla, is highly valued.*

*The **chipmunk,** the striped squirrel of N. America, is 4 to 6 ins. long, it is a good swimmer as well as climber. The chipmunk's call is a shrill 'chip-chip' sound.*

(1912); Communist forces obtained control 1949, and Chiang Kai-shek withdrew the government of the **Republic of China** to TAIWAN, leaving mainland China to the Communists who proclaimed the **People's Republic of China**; capital, Beijing; **Chi′naman**, (usually derog.) Chinese; **China syndrome**, theoretical condition in which uncontrollable radioactive material, as from a damaged atomic reactor, would burn a hole through Earth, as from the U.S. to China. [ult. origin unknown; not the native name; found in Sansk. *c* 1st c.]

chi·na (chī′n*a*) *n.* Very hard fine semitransparent porcelain of the hard paste kind, orig. manufactured in China; ~ **clay**, kaolin. ~ *adj.* Of china. [orig. *China-ware*, ware from China]

Chi·na·town (chī′n*a*town). Part of an Occidental city inhabited chiefly by Chinese people.

chinch (chĭnch) *n.* (dial.) Bedbug.

chin·chil·la (chĭnchĭl′*a*) *n.* Small S. Amer. squirrellike rodent of genus *C*~; fine soft grayish fur of one species, *C. laniger* of Peru and Chile.

chine (chīn) *n.* Backbone; animal's backbone or cut of meat from it; ridge or crest.

Chi·nese (chīnēz′, -nes′) *adj.* Of China or its people or language; ~ **checkers**, game in which marbles are moved from hole to hole across a board; ~ **lantern**, collapsible lantern of thin colored paper; ~-**restaurant syndrome**, gastric discomfort and faintness from reaction to monosodium glutamate often used in Chinese cooking; ~ **Wall**: see GREAT Wall of China; ~ **white**, pigment, zinc oxide. **Chinese** *n.* (pl. same) Chinese person or language.

Ch'ing (chĭng). Manchu dynasty that ruled in China 1644–1912.

Chink (chĭngk) *n.* (derog.) Chinese.

chink[1] (chĭngk) *n.* Narrow opening, esp. one that lets light, air, etc., through.

chink[2] (chĭngk) *v.* (Cause to) make sound as of glasses or coins striking together. ~ *n.* Chinking sound.

chin·ka·pin (chĭng′k*a*pĭn): = CHINQUAPIN.

chi·no (chē′nō) *n.* (pl. **-nos**). Cotton twill cloth, usu. khaki-colored; (pl.) trousers made of it.

chi·noi·se·rie (shēnwŏz*e*rē′, -wŏz′*e*rē) *n.* Imitation of Chinese motifs in furniture etc.

Chi·nook (shĭnōōk′, -nŏŏk′, chĭ-) *n.* (pl. **-nooks,** collect. **-nook**). 1. (Member of) N. Amer. Ind. tribe orig. inhabiting region around Columbus river in Oregon; their language. 2. (also ~ **jargon**)

Above: The Great Wall of **China,** thought by many to be the most ambitious building project in history, stands as a reminder of China's past. It was built from the 3rd century B.C. as a defensive fortification against northern barbarians and extends about 1500 miles from the Gulf of Chihli on the Yellow Sea to central Asia. Left: Map and flag of China. Communist forces won control in 1949 and proclaimed the country the People's Republic of China. The country has the world's largest population and covers a vast area exceeding 3½ million sq. miles. Below left: a principal street in Beijing, the capital, with cyclists predominating. Below: Joe Fei, a 12th-century hero.

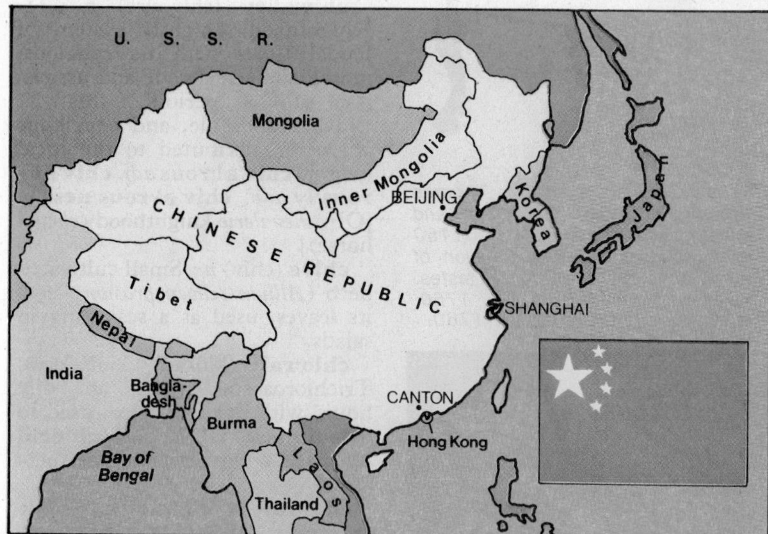

Jargon of English, French, and Indian words, formerly used by traders and Indians from Oregon to Alaska. 3. Warm, moist wind blowing from the sea on the Washington and Oregon coasts; warm, dry wind from the Rocky Mountains.

chin·qua·pin (chĭng'kapĭn) *n.* Shrubby chestnut (*Castanea pumila*) of U.S., bearing small edible nuts; evergreen (*Castanopsis chrysophylla*) of Pacific coast; the nut of either of these.

chintz (chĭnts) *n.* Orig., painted or stained calico from India; now cotton cloth printed with bright-colored designs. **chintz'y** *adj.* (**chintz·i·er, chintz·i·est**). (esp.) Cheap; gaudy. [Hind. *chīnt*, f. Sansk. *chitra* variegated]

chi·o·no·dox·a (kīonōdŏk'sa) *n.* Blue-flowered liliaceous plant of genus *C*~ from Crete and Asia Minor, blooming in early spring; glory of the snow. [Gk. *khiōn* snow + *doxa* glory]

chip (chĭp) *n.* 1. Thin piece cut from wood or broken from stone etc.; in gem cutting, piece chipped off weighing less than ¾ carat. 2. (pl.) (Brit.) French fried potatoes; **potato ~s**, thin fried slices of potato sold in packages. 3. Counter used in games of chance; **let the ~s fall where they may**, no matter what the cost (or incidental damage); no matter who is offended; **when the chips are down**, at a critical point. 4. Flaw or slight fracture caused by chipping. 5. Small square of semiconductor used to make integrated circuit. 6. ~ **off the (old) block**, child resembling father; ~ **on one's shoulder**, grievance; belligerent mood; ~ **shot**, (golf) short, slightly lofted approach shot. **chip** *v.* (**chipped, chip·ping**). Cut (wood), break (stone, crockery), at surface or edge; cut or break *off*; be susceptible to breakage at edge; make chip shot; ~ **in**, (colloq.) interrupt; contribute.

chip·munk (chĭp'mŭngk) *n.* Small striped rodent (*Tamias striatus*) of eastern N. Amer., resembling a squirrel but living on the ground; any similar rodent of genus *Eutamias* of western N. Amer. or N. Asia. [Amer. Ind.]

Chip·pen·dale (chĭp'endāl), **Thomas** (1718–79). London cabinetmaker; his business was carried on by his son **Thomas** (1749–1822); hence (as *n.*) style of furniture, characterized by flowing lines and rococo ornamentation, made by Chippendale.

chi·rop·o·dy (kĭrŏp'odē, shĭ-, kī-) *n.* Treatment of feet. **chi·rop'o·dist** *n.*

chi·ro·prac·tic (kīr'oprăktĭk, kīroprăk'-) *n.* & *adj.* (Of) manipulation of the spinal column as method of treating disease. **chi·ro·prac·tor** (kīr'oprăkter) *n.*

The style established by ***Thomas Chippendale*** *in his 'Gentleman and Cabinet-Maker's Director' lasted 150 years. His designs were a fusion of Queen Anne and Georgian tastes. Above: A Chippendale chair c. 1760. Top: A dressing table, also c. 1760.*

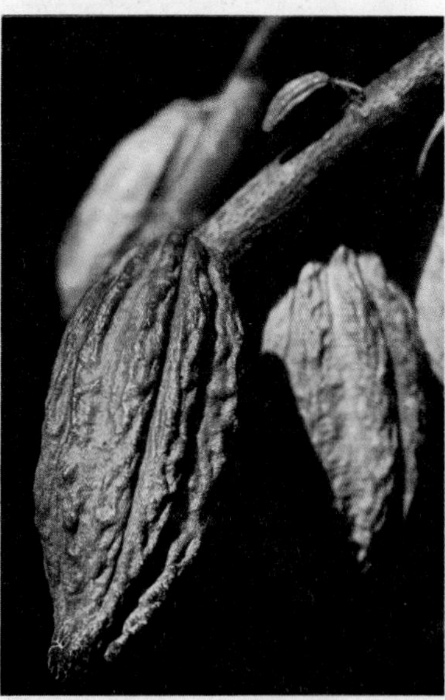

The cacao bean is the source of ***chocolate.*** *The bean is the fruit of the Theobroma cacao tree which grows in the tropics. The bean is fermented, cured, roasted and ground to a paste.*

chirp (chĕrp) *n.* Short sharp thin note as of small bird. ~ *v.* Utter chirp.

chis·el (chĭz'el) *n.* Cutting tool with square beveled metal end, worked by pressure or by blows of a mallet or hammer. ~ *v.t.* (**-eled, -el·ing**). Cut, shape, with chisel; (slang) defraud, cheat *out of*. **chis'eled** *adj.* (esp., of features) Sharply defined. **chis'el·er** *n.*

Chis·holm (chĭz'om) **Trail.** Former trail (1867–*c*1887) for driving cattle from San Antonio, Texas, to the railhead at Abilene, Kansas; the first major trail of this kind and the subject of cowboy songs and legend.

chit[1] (chĭt) *n.* Young child, esp. a girl.

chit[2] (chĭt) *n.* Check, bill, as for food or drink. [Anglo-Ind.]

chit·chat (chĭt'chăt) *n.* Light conversation; gossip.

chi·tin (kī'tĭn) *n.* Organic substance forming part of exoskeleton of arthropods. **chi'tin·ous** *adj.*

chit·ling (chĭt'lĭn, -lĭng), **chit·lin** (chĭt'lĭn), **chit·ter·ling** (chĭt'erlĭng, chĭt'lĭn) *ns.* Small intestines of pigs, cooked for food.

chiv·al·ry (shĭv'alrē) *n.* 1. Knighthood; knightly system of feudal times with its religious, moral, and social code and usages; **Age of C~**, period of this. 2. Brave, honorable, and courteous character attributed to the ideal knight. **chiv'al·rous** *adj.* **chiv'al·rous·ly** *adv.* **chiv'al·rous·ness** *n.* [OF. *chevalerie* knighthood (*cheval* horse)]

chive (chīv) *n.* Small cultivated herb (*Allium schoenoprasum*); **~s**, its leaves, used as a seasoning in salads.

chlo·ral (klōr'al, klôr'-) *n.* Trichloroacetaldehyde, an oily liquid with pungent odor, used to manufacture DDT and **chloral hydrate**, a hypnotic and anesthetic.

chlo·rate (klōr'āt, klôr'-) *n.* Salt of chloric acid ($HClO_3$).

chlo·ride (klōr'īd, klôr'-) *n.* Simple compound of chlorine with a metal or organic radical.

chlo·rine (klōr'ēn, klôr'-) *n.* (chem.) Nonmetallic element, a yellowish-green, heavy, chemically active gas with irritating smell and powerful bleaching and disinfecting qualities; symbol Cl, at. no. 17, at. wt. 35.453. **chlo·rin·ate** (klōr'ĭnāt, klôr'-) *v.t.* (**-at·ed, -at·ing**). Treat or act upon with chlorine; sterilize (drinking water) thus. **chlo·rin·a·tion** (klōrĭnā'shon, klôr-) *n.*

chlo·rite (klōr'īt, klôr'-) *n.* Hydrous silicate mineral, usu. green, often found with and resembling mica.

chlo·ro·form (klōr'ofôrm,

klōr′-) *n.* Colorless liquid with etherlike odor and pungent sweetish taste; formerly used as a general anesthetic. ~ *v.t.* Administer chloroform to.

chlo·ro·phyll, chlo·ro·phyl (klōr′*o*fĭl, klōr′-) *ns.* Coloring matter of leaves and other green parts of plants etc.

chlo·ro·plast (klōr′*o*plăst, klōr′-) *n.* Plastid containing chlorophyll, in cells of algae and higher plants.

chlo·ro·sis (klōrō′sĭs, klōr-) *n.* Greensickness, anemic disease of girls about age of puberty.

chlor·prom·a·zine (klōrprō′m*a*zēn, klōr-) *n.* Bitter drug used as sedative and against vomiting.

chlor·tet·ra·cy·cline (klōr′tĕtr*a*sī′klēn, klōr′-) *n.* Yellow crystalline antibiotic trademarked as Aureomycin and used to treat a variety of infections.

chock (chŏk) *n.* Block of wood, wedge. ~ *v.t.* Make fast, wedge, with chocks. ~ *adv.* Closely, tightly; **~-a-block, ~-full,** stuffed, crammed.

choc·o·late (chŏk′*o*lĭt, chaw′k*o*-, chŏk′lĭt, chawk′-) *n.* Paste or cake of seeds of cacao roasted, ground, sweetened, and flavored with vanilla etc.; drink made with this; candy covered with or made of chocolate; chocolate color. ~ *adj.* Covered with or made of or with chocolate; brown. [Nahautl *chocolatl* (not f. *cacao* or *cocoa*)]

Choc·taw (chŏk′taw) *n.* (pl. **-taws,** collect. **-taw**). (Member of) a tribe of N. Amer. Indians formerly living in S. Mississippi and Alabama, now chiefly settled in Oklahoma; language of this tribe.

choice (chois) *n.* Act, power, right, etc., of choosing; what is chosen; variety to choose from; elite. ~ *adj.* (**choic·er, choic·est**). Of picked quality, exquisite; carefully chosen.

choir (kwīr) *n.* 1. Group of singers performing or leading in musical parts of church service; choral society, company of singers. 2. Chancel; part of church assigned to choir (**choir loft**); **choir′-master,** director, trainer, of a choir.

choke (chōk) *n.* 1. Narrowed or constricted part of mechanism. 2. (Device operating) valve that partly closes air inlet of gasoline engine. 3. (elect.) Coil having low resistance and large inductance inserted in circuit to impede and smooth out changes in, or change phase of, current. **choke′cherry,** (astringent fruit of) N. Amer. cherry (esp. *Prunus virginiana*); **choke′damp,** carbon dioxide in coal mines etc. **choke** *v.* (**choked, chok·ing**). Suffocate; stop breath of; suffer temporary stoppage of breath; become speechless from anger etc.; smother, stifle; block up wholly or partly; ~ **back,** suppress (tears); ~ **off,** deter, dissuade; ~ (up), (colloq.) become incapacitated, perform ineptly (through fear etc.). **chok′er** *n.* (esp.) High stand-up collar; woman's close-fitting necklace etc.

chol·er (kŏl′*er*) *n.* 1. (hist.) One of the four cardinal humors, bile. 2. (poet., archaic) Anger.

chol·er·a (kŏl′*era*) *n.* (also **Asiatic** ~) Infectious and freq. fatal disease with violent vomiting and diarrhea, cramps, and collapse.

The Mormon Tabernacle ***Choir*** *in rehearsal at the Mormon Tabernacle in Salt Lake City, Utah, an imposing building with 6 spires. The 375 trained choir members are standing below the great organ in the temple.*

chol·er·ic (kŏl′erĭk, kolĕr′-) *adj.* Irascible, hot-tempered; (archaic) characterized by choler, or bile.

cho·les·ter·ol (kolĕs′terōl, -rawl, -rōl) *n.* Steroid alcohol ($C_{27}H_{45}OH$) present in animal cells and body fluids.

chomp (chŏmp) *v.* Var. of CHAMP[1].

Chong·qing (chawng′chŏng′) = CHUNGKING.

choose (cho͞oz) *v.* (**chose, cho·-sen** pr. chō′zen, **choos·ing**). Select out of greater number; make choice *between*; select as; decide, think fit, be determined *to* do; (theol.) destine to be saved. **choos′y, choos′ey** *adjs.* (**choos·i·er, choos·i·est**). Fastidious, fussy. **choos′i·ness** *n.*

chop[1] (chŏp) *v.* (**chopped, chop·ping**). Cut by a blow or blows, as with hatchet or ax; cut small; cut short (words etc.); (tennis etc.) make short heavy edgewise blow, strike (ball) thus. ~ *n.* Chopping; chopping stroke; slice of meat, esp. lamb or pork, usu. including a rib; short broken motion (of waves etc.); **chop′house**, restaurant specializing in steaks and chops. **chop′per** *n.* 1. Person or thing that chops. 2. (slang) Helicopter. **chop′py** *adj.* (**chop·pi·er, chop·-pi·est**). (of waves, their motion, etc.) Short and broken.

chop[2] (chŏp), **chap**[2] (chăp, chŏp) *ns.* (usu. pl.) Jaws of animal etc.; **lick one's ~s**, show relish or anticipation; **chop′fallen**, var. of chapfallen.

chop[3] (chŏp) *v.i.* (**chopped, chop·ping**). Change direction suddenly, swerve, as a ship in the wind.

Cho·pin (shō′păn; *Fr.* shaw-păṅ′), **Frédéric François** (1810–1849). Polish pianist; lived in France from 1829; composer of a large number of piano compositions.

chop·stick (chŏp′stĭk) *n.* One of a pair of small sticks of ivory, bone, wood, etc., held between thumb and fingers of one hand and used by Chinese, Japanese, and Koreans in eating. [Pidgin English (*chop* = quick + *stick*) equivalent of Chin. *k'wai-tsze* "nimble ones"]

*The **Christmas Cactus,** native to Brazil, has become a popular house plant for its striking red flowers. In its natural habitat it grows on trees and shrubs in shady positions.*

*Originating in China, the **chow** has a double-layer coat of soft underhair and straight outer fur. The dog stands 18-20 ins. high at the shoulder.*

chop su·ey (chŏp′ so͞o′ē). Chinese-American dish of meat or chicken, bean sprouts, etc. served with rice. [Chin. *tsa-sui* = "mixed bits"]

cho·ral[1] (kōr′al, kōr′-) *adj.* Of, sung by, a choir or chorus; spoken by group of voices. **cho′ral·ly** *adv.*

cho·ral[2], **cho·rale** (korăl′, -rahl′) *ns.* (Metrical hymn set to) simple tune, usu. sung in unison.

chord[1] (kōrd) *n.* 1. String of musical instrument (poet.); also fig. of mind, emotions, etc. 2. (math.) Straight line joining extremities of arc.

chord[2] (kōrd) *n.* (mus.) Group of notes sounded together, combined according to a harmonic system.

chor·date (kōr′dāt) *adj.* & *n.* (zool.) (Member) of the phylum Chordata; (organism) possessing at some stage of its life history a notochord, i.e. a rod of tissue lying along the back below the nerve cord.

chore (chōr, chōr) *n.* Routine, minor, or unpleasant task; daily domestic or farming task, such as washing dishes, feeding livestock, etc.

cho·re·a (korē′*a*, kō-, kaw-) *n.* Disease, esp. of children, characterized by involuntary movements of muscles; St. Vitus's dance. [L. *chorea Sancti Viti* dance of St.

*A cry of 'k'chuf' gives the **chough** its name. It is an insectivor capable of acrobatic flight. Other than at the mating season, choughs congregate in flocks of about 100.*

Vitus]

cho·re·og·ra·phy (kōrēŏg′rafē, kōr-) *n.* Arrangement of the dancing in a ballet; art of dancing. **chor·e·og′ra·pher** *n.* Designer of the dancing in a ballet. **chor·e·o·graph·ic** (kōrēográf′ĭk, kōr-) *adj.*

cho·ric (kōr′ĭk, kōr′-) *adj.* Of, like, CHORUS, def. 1.

cho·rine (kōr′ēn, kōr′-) *n.* (slang) Chorus girl.

cho·ri·on (kōr′ēŏn, kōr′-) *n.* Outermost membrane enveloping fetus before birth; membrane around egg of certain insects.

chor·is·ter (kōr′ĭster, kōr′-kār′-) *n.* Member of (usu. male) choir, esp. boy.

cho·roid (kōr′oid, kōr′-) *n.* & *adj.* (Of) the vascular membrane lining the eyeball between sclerotic coat and retina.

chor·tle (chōr′tel) *v.i.* (**-tled, -tling**) & *n.* Chuckle. [portmanteau word invented by Lewis Carroll, perh. f. *chuckle* + *snort*]

cho·rus (kōr′us), kōr′-) *n.* (pl. **-rus·es**). 1. (Gk. antiq.) Organized band of singers and dancers in religious festivals and dramatic performances, in Attic tragedy representing interested spectators and employed to explain the action, express sympathy with characters, and draw morals; song(s) sung by these. 2. Adaptation of this in other drama. 3. Band of singers, choir; group of singers or dancers in musical comedy etc. 4. Thing sung by many at once, simultaneous utterance; refrain of song, in which audience joins; main part of popular song as dist. from introductory verse; musical composition, usu. in four parts, for a considerable number of voices; **in ~**, in unison. 5. **~ girl**, female member of chorus in musical comedy etc. **chorus** *v.* (**-rused, -rus·ing**). Sing, speak, say, in chorus.

cho·sen (chō′zen): see CHOOSE.

Chou En-lai (jō′ĕnlī′) (1898–1976). Chinese Communist statesman; prime minister of Chinese People's Republic, 1949–76.

chough (chŭf) *n.* Old World bird (*Pyrrhocorax pyrrhocorax*) of crow family, with red feet and bill.

chow (chow) *n.* 1. (slang) Food. 2. Dog of Chinese breed, with short thick coat and black tongue.

chow·chow (chow′chow) *n.* Relish of chopped vegetables pickled in mustard.

chow·der (chow′der) *n.* Thick soup of clams or fish and vegetables, usually in a milk base. [app. orig. in Brittany, France, in phr. *faire la chaudière* = to supply a pot etc. for cooking a stew]

chow mein (chow mān′, show). Chinese-American dish of stewed vegetables and meat, chicken, or shrimp served with fried noodles. [Chin. *ch'ao mein* = "fried flour"]

*Holman Hunt (1827–1910) painted **Christ** as 'The Light of the World'. The picture became an extremely popular devotional work, intended to portray Christ offering his light to man.*

*The tradition of sending **Christmas cards** began in the mid-19th century, one of the most recent accretions to the ancient festival. Illustrated is a 19th century card showing a scene enacted by children's peg dolls.*

*Helleborous niger or **Christmas rose** is an evergreen plant of the Ranunculaceae family. It is used medicinally but has some highly poisonous substances.*

chres·tom·a·thy (krĕstŏm′athē) *n.* (pl. **-thies**). Collection of choice passages.

Christ (krīst). Messiah or Lord's Anointed of Jewish prophecy; (title, now treated as proper name, given to) JESUS, regarded by Christians as fulfilling this prophecy. [L. *Christus* f. Gk. *khristos* anointed one (*khriō* anoint) transl. of Heb.; see MESSIAH]

chris·ten (krĭs′en) *v.* 1. Admit or initiate into Christian Church by baptism; give name to at baptism. 2. Name, dedicate (ship etc.) with ceremony like baptism; name, give name to.

Chris·ten·dom (krĭs′endom) *n.* Christians collectively; the Christian world.

Chris·tian[1] (krĭs′chan) *adj.* Believing, professing, or belonging to, religion of Christ; resembling Christ or following or exemplifying his teaching; **~ era**: see ERA; **~ name**, name given at christening; first name; **~ Science, Scientist**, (person believing in) principles formulated by Mrs. EDDY, esp. that matter is an illusion and bodily disease an error of the mind, to be cured by teaching the patient the truth as revealed in the teaching and healing of Christ. **Christian** *n.* Christian person.

Chris·tian[2] (krĭs′chan), **Fletcher** (fl. 1789). Leader of mutiny against Captain Bligh of the Bounty, 1789; with other mutineers fled to and founded colony on Pitcairn Island.

Chris·tia·ni·a (krĭschēăn′ēa, -tē-, -ah′nēa) *n.* (skiing) Turn made from a crouching position to change direction or stop short. [former name of OSLO]

Chris·ti·an·i·ty (krĭschēăn′ĭtē) *n.* 1. Christian faith, doctrines of Christ and his apostles; Christian spirit or character. 2. Christendom.

Chris·tie[1] = CHRISTIANIA.

Chris·tie[2] (krĭs′tē), **Agatha Mary Clarissa** (*née* Miller; Lady Mallowan) (1891–1976). English author of mystery novels and plays.

Christ·mas (krĭs′mas). Festival of nativity of Christ, observed Dec. 25, as time of festivity and rejoicing; **Father ~**, (Brit.) Santa Claus or a similar personification of Christmas as a benevolent old man bringing gifts to children; **~ cactus**, spineless cactus (*Zygocactus truncatus*) of Brazilian rain forests, used as a house plant for its brilliant red flowers; crab cactus; **~ card**, card sent with greetings at Christmas; **~ Day**, Dec. 25; **~ Eve**, the night of Dec. 24; **~ pudding**, (Brit.) plum pudding eaten at Christmas; **~ rose**, white-flowered winter-blooming Euro-

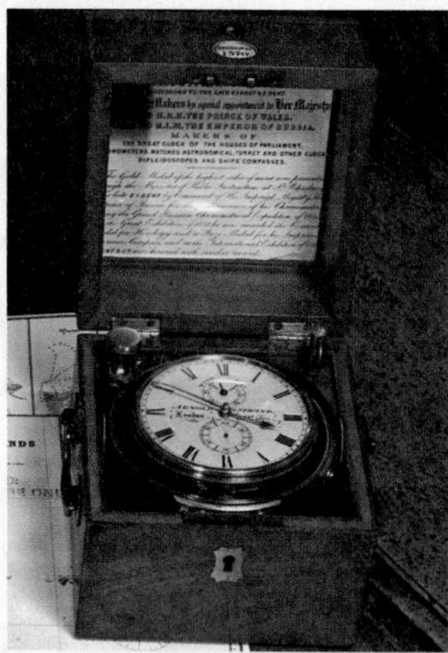

*The first accurate **chronometer** was made by Robert Hooke and became an essential instrument in navigation. He made it possible by improving the design of watch mechanisms. Today chronometers are driven by electricity.*

pean species of hellebore (*Helleborus niger*); ~ **stocking**, one hung up by children on Christmas Eve for Santa Claus to fill with candy and presents; ~**tree**, small evergreen or artificial tree decorated with ornaments, lights, etc., during the Christmas season.

Chris·tophe (krēstawf′), **Henri** (1767–1820). Haitian revolutionary leader; proclaimed King Henry I, 1811; his cruelty caused rebellion and he killed himself with a silver bullet.

Chris·to·pher (krĭs′tofer), **Saint.** Third c. legendary Christian martyr; according to tradition, devoted himself to charitable work of carrying wayfarers across a river where there was no bridge; patron saint of travelers, ferrymen, etc.

Chris·ty (krĭs′te) *n.* (pl. **-ties**) = CHRISTIANIA.

chro·mate (krō′māt) *n.* Salt of chromic acid.

chro·mat·ic (krōmăt′ĭk) *adj.* 1. Of, produced by, color; full of bright color; ~ **aberration**, failure of different colors to come to same focus after refraction. 2. (mus.) Including notes that do not belong to the diatonic scale of the prevailing key; ~ **scale**, full series of notes (12 to an octave, each note differing by a semitone from the next) on which Western music is normally based. **chro·mat′i·cal·ly** *adv.*

chro·ma·tic·i·ty (krōmatĭs′ĭtē) *n.* Quality of a color measured optically.

chro·ma·tin (krō′matĭn) *n.* (biol.) Part of cell tissue containing DNA, which can be stained readily when immersed in dye.

chro·ma·tog·ra·phy (krōmatŏg′rafē) *n.* (chem.) Process of separating components of a mixed solution by slow passage through a tube or over adsorbing material, making use of differences of partition, adsorption, ion exchange, etc.; **gas** ~, analogous process using carrier gas as moving phase to carry gaseous or vaporized sample. **chro·ma·to·graph·ic** (krōmatogrăf′ĭk), **chro·ma·to·graph′i·cal** *adjs.* **chro·ma·to·graph′i·cal·ly** *adv.*

chrome (krōm) *n.* 1. Chromium. 2. (also ~ **yellow**) Yellow pigment and color obtained from lead chromate ($PbCrO_4$). 3. Chromium compound used in dyeing and tanning. ~ *v.t.* (**chromed, chrom·ing**). Treat with chromium solution.

chro·mic (krō′mĭk) *adj.* Applied to compounds of chromium in which this element is trivalent; ~ **acid**, acid (CrO_3, strictly the anhydride of the acid) known only in solution and in form of its salts; ~ **oxide**, chromium sesquioxide (Cr_2O_3), a green powder used in metallurgy and as a pigment.

chro·mi·um (krō′mēum) *n.* (chem.) Metallic element remarkable for the brilliant red, yellow, or green color of its compounds; symbol Cr, at. no. 24, at. wt. 51.996; widely applied in electroplating and in a variety of alloys, the chief being with iron and steel, to which it imparts hardness and stainlessness.

*The resting stage in the metamorphosis of a butterfly and some other insects occurs while the creature is protected by a **chrysalis.** Illustrated here is a butterfly emerging into adult life.*

chro·mo·some (krō′mosōm) *n.* (biol.) One of the rodlike structures that occur in pairs in the cell nucleus of an animal or plant and, hence, in every developed cell; they carry genes in linear order and are usu. constant in number for each species (the human cell nucleus has 23 pairs); **X** ~, one of the sex chromosomes, usu. occurring in pairs in the female, singly in the male; **Y** ~, sex chromosome occurring only in the male. **chro·mo·so·mal** (krōmosō′mal) *adj.*

chro·mo·sphere (krō′mosfēr) *n.* Red gaseous envelope around a star. **chro·mo·spher·ic** (krōmosfĕr′ĭk) *adj.*

chro·mous (krō′mus) *adj.* Applied to compounds of chromium in which this element is divalent.

Chron. *abbrev.* Chronicles (Old Testament).

chron·ic (krŏn′ĭk) *adj.* (of diseases etc.) Lasting a long time; (of invalid) having such disease;

(transf.) continuous, constant; (colloq.) bad, intense, severe. **chron'i·cal·ly** *adv.*

chron·i·cle (krŏn'ĭkel) *n.* Detailed and continuous register of events in order of time; record, register; (*1st* and *2nd Book of the*) **Chronicles,** two historical books of Old Testament. ~ *v.t.* (**-cled, -cling**). Enter or record in a chronicle. **chron'i·cler** *n.*

chron·o·graph (krŏn'ográf, -grahf) *n.* Instrument recording time with extreme accuracy; stop-watch.

chro·nol·o·gy (kronŏl'ojē) *n.* (pl. **-gies**). Computation of time, assignment of events, etc., to their correct date, arrangement in order of time; chronological table or list. **chron·o·log·i·cal** (krŏnolŏj'ĭkal) *adj.* **chron·o·log'i·cal·ly** *adv.*

chro·nom·e·ter (kronŏm'eter) *n.* Timepiece adjusted to keep accurate time in all variations of temperature, used for determining position at sea or in the air and for other exact observations. **chron·o·met·ric** (krŏnomĕt'rĭk), **chron·o·met'ri·cal** *adjs.* Of chronometry. **chro·nom'e·try** *n.* Accurate time measurement.

chrys·a·lis (krĭs'alĭs) *n.* (pl. **-es** or **chrysalides** pr. krĭsăl'idēz). Inactive state into which larva of most insects passes before becoming imago or perfect insect; hard sheath or case enclosing larva at this stage.

chrys·an·the·mum (krĭsăn'themum) *n.* Composite plant of genus *C*~; cultivated species of this, having showy flowers and blooming in autumn.

Chrys·os·tom (krĭs'ostom, krĭsŏs'tom), **St. John** (*c*345–407). Patriarch of Constantinople (398–404); commemorated Jan. 27.

chtho·nic (thŏn'ĭk) *adj.* (of deities etc.) Dwelling in or beneath surface of the earth.

chub (chŭb) *n.* Thick fat coarse-fleshed European and Caspian river fish of carp family (*Leuciscus cephalus*); any of various other fishes, such as the American ~ and whitefish (*Coregonus*).

chub·by (chŭb'ē) *adj.* (**-bi·er, -bi·est**). Plump, round-faced.

Found in south-west North America the ***chuckwalla*** *grows up to 20 inches in length. When threatened it moves into a rock crevice and inflates its body size which makes it difficult to dislodge.*

chub'bi·ness *n.* [f. CHUB]

chuck¹ (chŭk) *v.* 1. Tap lightly *under the chin.* 2. Fling, throw, toss, carelessly or easily (*away*); ~ **it,** (colloq.) cease, give up; ~ **out,** discard, throw out; force out, eject. **chuck** *n.* Act of chucking; jerk, toss, bump.

chuck² (chŭk) *n.* 1. Cut of beef extending from neck to ribs, incl. shoulder piece. 2. Part of lathe etc. that holds rotating workpiece or tool.

chuck³ (chŭk) *n.* (colloq.) Wood-chuck.

chuck·le (chŭk'el) *v.i.* (**-led, -ling**) & *n.* (Make) suppressed and inarticulate sound(s) expressing mirth, exultation, etc.

chuck·le·head·ed (chŭk'elhĕdĭd) *adj.* (colloq.) Stupid.

chuck (chŭk) **wagon.** Wagon equipped with cooking utensils and food for serving meals to workers at a ranch, lumber camp, etc.

chuck·wal·la (chŭk'wahla) *n.* Lizard (*Sauromelus ohesus*) resembling the iguana, found in arid areas of SW. U.S. and Mexico.

chug (chŭg) *n.* & *v.i.* (**chugged, chug·ging**). (Make) repeated plunging or explosive sound (esp.

1

2

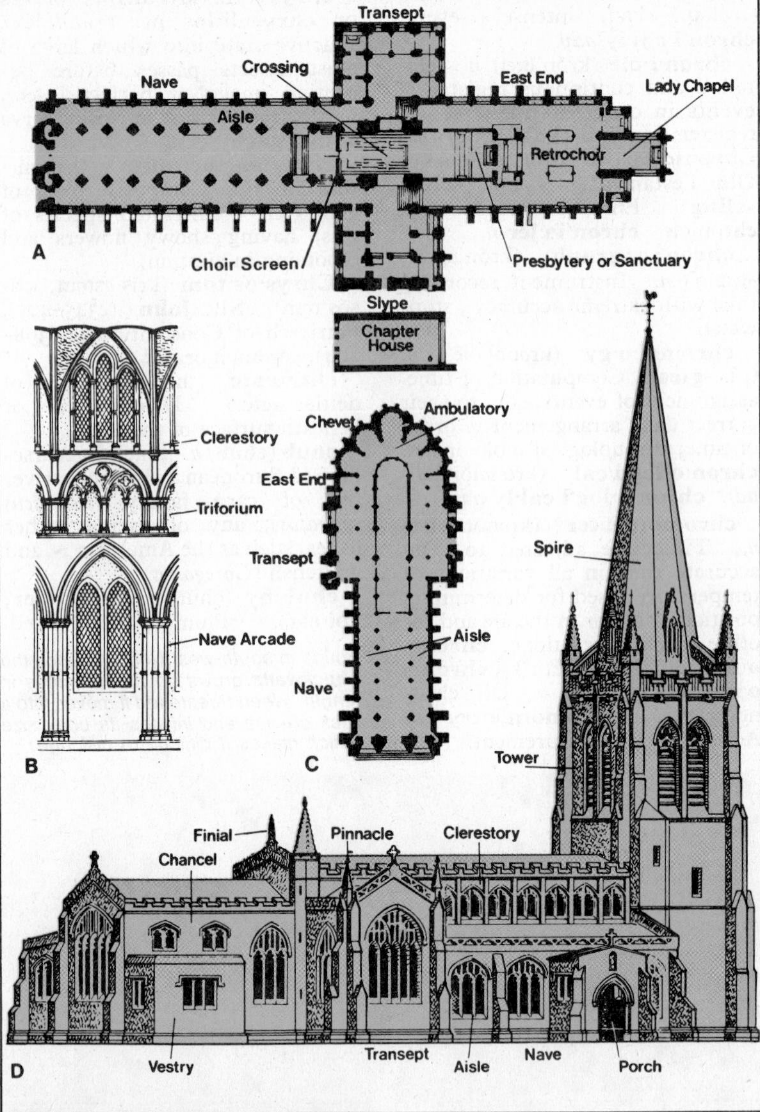

3

4

5

*1. The **church** of St. Lawrence, Bradford-on-Avon, Wiltshire, U.K., is a rare building dating from before the Norman Conquest. 2. This church sits on a cliff at the entrance to Roosevelt National Forest, Colorado. 3. Some representative layouts of cathedrals and churches. A. Plan of Winchester Cathedral. B. Bay of the nave, Salisbury Cathedral. C. Plan of Rheims Cathedral N. France. D. Typical large English parish church. 4. A stave church built in Oslo, Norway. 5. White spired church in Lexington, Massachusetts. 6. A modern church in St. Louis, Missouri.*

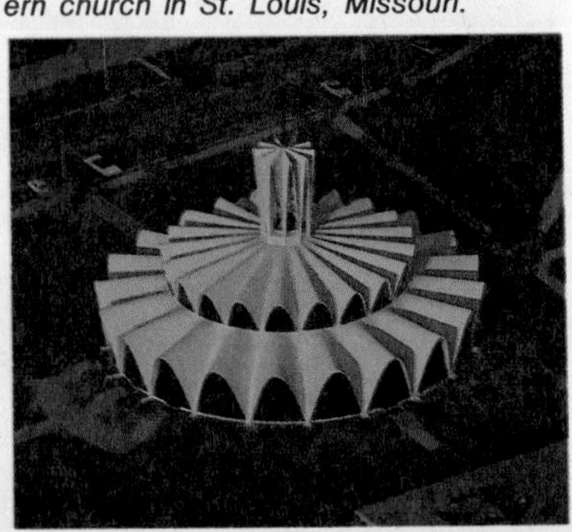

of machine).

chuk·ka (chŭk′*a*) **boot.** Ankle-high leather boot, as originally worn for polo.

chuk·ker, chuk·kar (chŭk′*er*) *ns.* Each of the 7½-minute periods into which a game of polo is divided. [Hind. *chakkar*, f. Sansk. *chakra* wheel]

chum[1] (chŭm) *n.* (colloq.) Intimate friend or companion. ~ *v.i.* (**chummed, chum·ming**). Be close friends *with*; share the same room.

chum[2] (chŭm) *n.* Chopped or ground bait thrown into the water to bring fish to the place where one is fishing. ~ *v.i.* To fish with such bait.

chum·my (chŭm′ē) *adj.* (**-mi·er, -mi·est**). (colloq.) Intimate, sociable.

chump (chŭmp) *n.* (colloq.) Blockhead; dupe.

Chung·king (chōōng′kĭng′, jōōng′gĭng′). City in SE. Szechwan Province, SW. China, on the Yangtze River.

chunk (chŭngk) *n.* Thick lump cut or broken off anything.

church (chĕrch) *n.* 1. Building for public Christian worship. 2. **the C** ~, the Christian community; any branch or distinct part of this. 3. Clergy and officers of the Church; clerical order or profession. 4. Congregation of Christians locally organized for religious worship etc.; **church′man, church′woman**, member of a church; clergyman. 5. **Church of England**, English branch of the Western Church, which at the Reformation repudiated the Pope's authority and asserted that of the sovereign over ecclesiastical as well as temporal matters in his dominions; **Church of Jesus Christ of Latter-day Saints**, official name of the MORMON Church; **church′warden**, (Anglican and Episcopalian) one of the (usu. two) lay officers of a church elected annually to manage various parochial offices, etc.; clay pipe with very long stem; **church′-yard**, enclosed area around a church, esp. as used for burials.

Church·ill (chĕr′chĭl), **Sir Winston Leonard Spencer** (1874–1965). British statesman, orator, and historian; prime minister 1940–5; 1951–5; rallied and led the United Kingdom during World War II.

churl (chĕrl) *n.* Rude, boorish person; peasant; niggardly person. **churl′ish** *adj.* **churl′ish·ly** *adv.* **churl′ish·ness** *n.*

churn (chĕrn) *n.* Vessel or machine for making butter, in which milk or cream is shaken, beaten, or otherwise agitated so as to separate the globules of fat from the serous parts. ~ *v.* Shake (milk, cream) in churn into butter; make (butter) thus; stir (liquid) about, make it froth; (of sea etc.) wash to and fro, seethe; ~ **out**, (fig.) produce in quantity.

chute[1] (shōōt) *n.* 1. Smooth rapid descent of water over slope. 2. Sloping channel, slide, for conveying things to lower level, for sliding down into water, etc.

chute[2] (shōōt) *n.* (colloq.) Parachute.

chut·ney (chŭt′nē) *n.* (pl. **-neys**). Strong pungent relish of fruits, vinegar, sugar, spices, etc. [Hind. *chatnī*]

chutz·pa (χōōt′sp*a*) *n.* (slang) Shameless audacity. [Yiddish]

CIA, C.I.A. *abbrevs.* Central Intelligence Agency.

ciao (chow) *int.* (informal) Goodby; hello. [It.]

ci·bo·ri·um (sĭbōr′ē*um*, -bŏr′-) *n.* (pl. **-bo·ri·a** pr. -bōr′ē*a*, -bŏr′-). 1. (eccles. archit.) Canopy, canopied shrine. 2. Covered chalice for holding consecrated wafers of the Eucharist.

ci·ca·da (sĭkā′d*a*, -kah′-) *n.* (pl. **-das, -dae** pr. -dē). Plant-sucking insect, usu. large, the male of which makes shrill sound from two tympanic structures on the abdomen.

cic·a·trix (sĭk′*a*trĭks, sĭkā′-) *n.* (pl. **cic·a·tri·ces** pr. sĭk*a*trī′sēz, sĭkā′tr*i*-). 1. Scar of healed wound. 2. (bot.) Mark left where leaf or branch has been detached.

Cic·er·o (sĭs′*e*rō), **Marcus Tullius** (106–43 B.C.). Roman republican statesman and orator. **Cic·er·o′ni·an** (sĭs*e*rō′nē*a*n) *adj.*

ci·ce·ro·ne (sĭs*e*rō′nē, chĭch-) *n.* (pl. **-nes, -ni** pr. -nē). Guide who

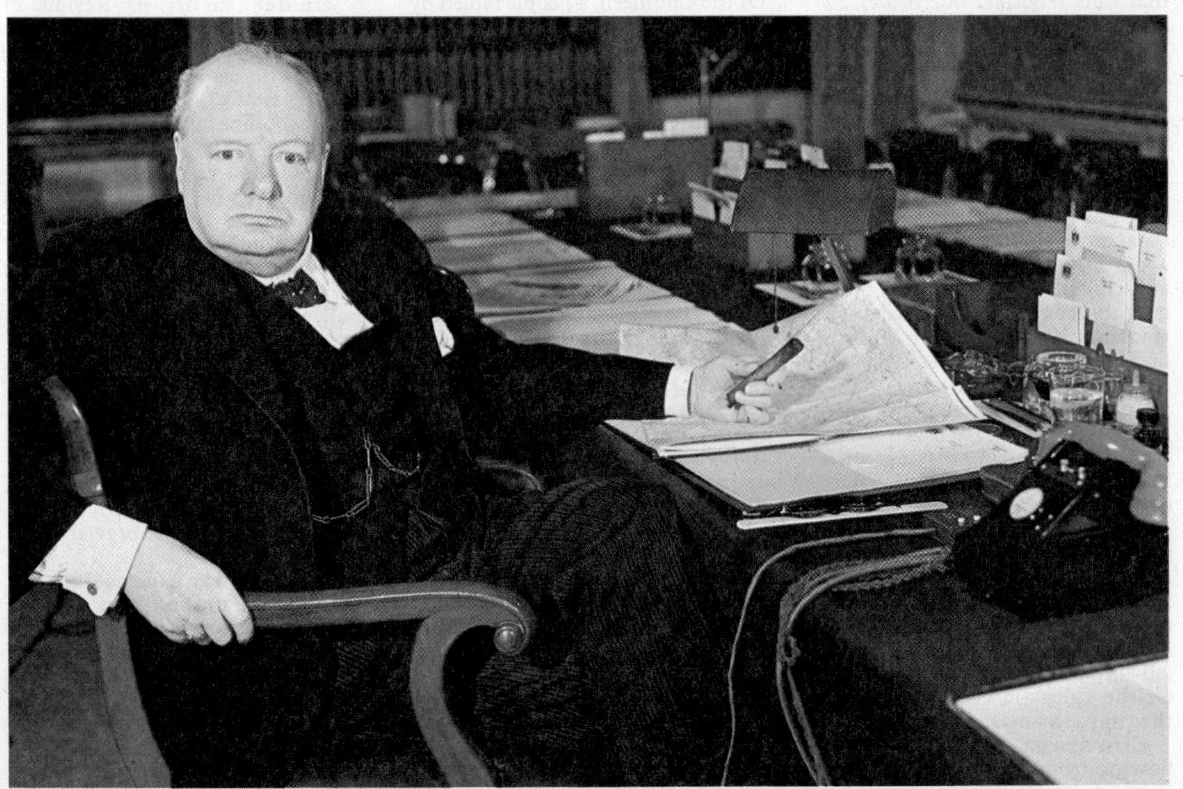

***Sir Winston Churchill** photographed at his desk in 10 Downing Street after the announcement of the Allies' Victory in Europe in the 1939–45 war. Later in 1945, Sir Winston and the Conservatives lost to Labour in the general election.*

understands and explains antiquities etc.

Cid (sĭd; *Sp.* thēd), **El.** Title in Spanish literature of Ruy Diaz, count of Bivar, 11th-c. champion of Christianity against the Moors. [Arab. *sayyid* lord]

-cide *suffix.* Forming nouns meaning (1) person or substance that kills (*regicide, insecticide*); (2) killing of (*homicide, suicide*).

ci·der (sī′d*er*) *n.* Juice pressed from apples; a beverage of this, which may be either unfermented (**sweet** ~) or fermented (**hard** ~); ~ **press**, press for crushing apples and extracting juice. [Heb. *šēkār* strong drink]

ci·gar (sĭgar̄′) *n.* Compact roll of tobacco leaves for smoking.

cig·a·rette, cig·a·ret (sĭg*a*rĕt′, sĭg′*a*rĕt) *ns.* Small cylinder of finely cut tobacco rolled in thin paper for smoking; similar cylinder of other finely cut plant leaves etc. for smoking, as a **marijuana** ~; ~ **holder**, mouthpiece holding cigarette.

cil·i·a (sĭl′ē*a*) *n.pl.* (sing. **cil·i·um** pr. sĭl′ē*u*m). 1. Eyelashes; delicate hairs resembling eyelashes on edge of leaf, insect's wing, etc. 2. Hairlike vibrating organs on animal and some vegetable tissues, serving as chief means of locomotion for many lower animals living in water. **cil·i·ar·y** (sĭl′ēĕrē), **cil·i·ate** (sĭl′ēĭt, -āt) *adjs.* Of the Ciliata, a class of protozoa that move by means of cilia.

Cim·ar·ron (sĭm′*a*rŏn). River flowing from NE. New Mexico to

Found throughout tropical and temperate regions, the ***cicada*** *makes its characteristic shrill call by vibrating membranes on the forepart of the abdomen. Only males make the sound, the females are mute.*

the Arkansas River in NE. Oklahoma.

Cim·me·ri·an (sĭmēr′ē*a*n) *adj.* Of the Cimmerii, a people fabled by the ancients (and mentioned in Homer) as living in perpetual darkness; gloomy, dark. ~ *n.* One of the Cimmerii.

C. in C. *abbrev.* Commander in Chief.

cinch (sĭnch) *n.* 1. Girth for a saddle or pack. 2. (slang) Safe or easy thing; dead certainty. ~ *v.* 1. Fix saddle securely with girth. 2. Bind, grip securely; (slang) make sure of, be deciding factor of.

cin·cho·na (sĭnkō′n*a*) *n.* S. Amer. tree or shrub of genus *C*~ with fragrant white or pink flowers; ~ **bark**, bark of certain species of this containing quinine and other related alkaloids and used as tonic and febrifuge; drug prepared from it. [named by Linnaeus in honor of countess of *Chinchon* (Spain), who when vice-queen of Peru was cured of a fever by cinchona bark in 1638 and brought a supply to Europe in 1640]

Cin·cin·nat·i (sĭnsinăt′ē). Industrial city on the Ohio River in SW. Ohio.

Cin·cin·na·tus (sĭnsinā′t*u*s), **Lucius Quinctius.** Roman who, acc. to tradition, was called in 458 B.C. from farming to deliver the Roman army from the peril in which it stood in its conflict with the Aequians; often referred to as a model of simple virtue.

cinc·ture (sĭngk′ch*er*) *n.* Girdle, belt, border; ring at top and bottom of column dividing shaft from capital and base. ~ *v.t.* (**-tured, -tur·ing**). Girdle, gird.

cin·der (sĭn′d*er*) *n.* Residue of burned material; (pl.) ashes; ~ **block**, concrete building block made with cement and cinders; ~ **path, track**, footpath, running track, of fine cinders. **cin′der·y** *adj.*

Cin·der·el·la (sĭnderĕl′*a*). Heroine of a fairy tale who, treated as a drudge by her mean stepmother and stepsisters, was transformed by her fairy godmother into a richly dressed guest at the court ball, where she met the handsome prince whom she eventually married; hence, girl who achieves sudden recognition or wealth. ~ *adj.* Achieving sudden wealth, fame, etc.; going from rags to riches.

cin·e·ma (sĭn′*e*m*a*) *n.* Motion picture; motion-picture theater; (also **the** ~) films collectively, esp. as an art form. [abbreviation of *cinematograph*]

cin·e·mat·ic (sĭn*e*măt′ĭk) *adj.* Appropriate to the cinema.

cin·e·ma·tog·ra·phy (sĭn*e*m*a*tŏg′r*a*fē) *n.* Art, technique of motion-picture photography. **cin·e·ma·tog′ra·pher** *n.* **cin·e·mat·o·graph·ic** (sĭn*e*măt*o*grăf′ĭk) *adj.* **cin·e·mat·o·graph′ic·al·ly** *adv.* [Gk. *kinēma* movement,

Above left: In the market at Kano, Nigeria, **cigarette** sellers make their wares in sight of their customers, using mounds of home-grown tobacco blended to local tastes. Above: Machines that make filter-tip cigarettes roll a double cigarette with a large filter in the center. A rotary knife cuts it in two. In this way the machine produces 2,500 cigarettes per minute.

One of the forerunners of the **cinema,** the zoōpraxiscope projected animated pictures on to a screen. Eadweard Muybridge (1830–1904), who changed his name to James Muggeridge, invented the machine in 1881. He specialised in studies of movement, taking many photographs of the gaits, walking or running, of both humans and animals.

graphō write, record]

cin·é·ma vé·ri·té (sĭn′ema vĕrĭtā′). Documentary style films using realistic techniques to avoid artificiality and present the appearance of real life. [Fr.]

cin·er·ar·i·a (sĭnerār′ēa) *n.* Any of several potted plants derived from a perennial herb (*Senecio cruentus*) of the Canary Islands, with white, red, blue, or purple flowers. [L. *cinerarius* of ashes, from the ash-colored down on the leaves]

cin·na·bar (sĭn′abār) *n.* Red crystalline form of mercuric sulphide (HgS), esp. as pigment; vermilion.

cin·na·mon (sĭn′amon) *n.* Yellowish-brown, aromatic inner bark of an E. Ind. tree (*Cinnamomum zeylanicum*), dried in the sun and used as a spice; the tree itself. ~ *adj.* Cinnamon-colored.

cin·que·cen·to (chĭngkwĭchĕn′tō) *n.* (Style of art and architecture of) the 16th c. in Italy.

cinque·foil (sĭngk′foil) *n.* 1. Plant of genus *Potentilla*, with compound leaves each of five leaflets. 2. (archit.) 5-cusped ornament in an arch or circle.

Cinque (sĭngk) **Ports.** Five ports of SE. England, orig. Hastings, Sandwich, Dover, Romney, and Hythe, to which were added Winchelsea and Rye, on the Strait of Dover and the North Sea, which defended the coast and furnished the chief part of the English navy in the 13th c. and in return were granted special privileges by Edward the Confessor, most of which they kept until the 1830's.

CIO, C.I.O. *abbrevs.* Congress of Industrial Organizations.

ci·pher (sī′fer) *n.* 1. Arithmetical symbol or character (0) of no value by itself, which when placed after any figure (or series of figures) in a whole number increases its value tenfold, and when placed before a figure in decimal fractions decreases its value in the same proportion. 2. Person or thing of no importance or worth, nonentity. 3. (rare) Any Arabic numeral. 4. Secret or disguised manner of writing; anything so written; key to this. 5. Device of intertwined initials or other letters, monogram. ~ *v.* 1. Do arithmetic; calculate. 2. Put into secret writing. [Arab. *ṣifr* zero]

cir·ca (sẽr′ka) *prep.* About. [L.]

cir·ca·di·an (serkā′dēan, sẽrkadē′-) *adj.* Of physiological activity occurring approximately every twenty-four hours.

Cir·cas·sian (serkăsh′an, -kăs′-ēan) *adj.* & *n.* (Member, language) of a group of tribes of the Caucasus, some of whom moved into Turkish territory in 19th c., whose women were remarkable for their beauty. [Russ. *Cherkés*, tribe calling themselves Adighe]

Cir·ce (sẽr′sē). (Gk. legend) Enchantress dwelling on island of Aeaea, who transformed all who drank of her cup into swine; in the *Odyssey* she detained Odysseus and his men for a year. **Cir·ce·an, Cir·cae·an** (sersē′an) *adjs.* Of, pertaining to, Circe; bewitching.

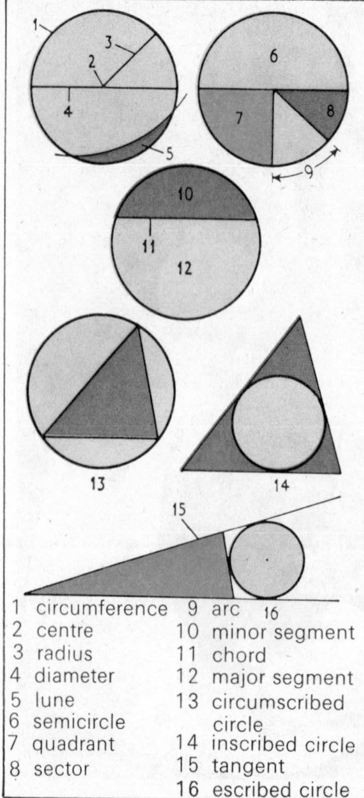

*The geometry of the Ancient Greeks examined the properties of the **circle**, some of which are illustrated here. The circle has posed for mathematicians many of their hardest problems.*

cir·cle (sẽr′kel) *n.* 1. (Line enclosing) plane figure with circumference everywhere equidistant from center; **great ~ (of a sphere)**, circle on surface of sphere, whose plane passes through center of sphere. 2. Anything shaped like a circle, ring; curved tier of seats at theater etc.; **dress ~**, lowest (and most expensive) of these in a theater, in which evening dress was once required; **upper ~**, circle next above dress circle. 3. Period, cycle, round; completed chain or sequence of events, parts, etc., esp. of consequences that react upon and intensify their causes (often **vicious ~**); (logic) fallacious reasoning, by which a proposition is used to establish a conclusion and is itself proved by means of the conclusion it has established (also **vicious ~**). 4. Persons grouped around center of interest; set, coterie, class; society. **circle** *v.* (**-cled, -cling**). 1. (poet.) Encompass. 2. Make circuit of; move in a circle.

cir·clet (sẽr′klĭt) *n.* Small circle; circular band, esp. of gold, jewels, etc., worn on head, arm, etc.

cir·cuit (sẽr′kĭt) *n.* 1. Line enclosing an area, distance around; area enclosed; journey around; roundabout way or journey. 2. Journey of judges, preachers (called **~ riders**), etc. through certain areas for purpose of holding courts of justice, preaching and performing religious ceremonies, etc. at various places in succession. 3. Number of theaters etc. under one control. 4. (elect.) Course or path of an electric current; **~ breaker**, device for interrupting electric circuit to prevent excessive current from causing damage or fire. **cir′cuit·ry** *n.* Plan, components of electric circuit; system of such circuits.

cir·cu·i·tous (serkū′itus) *adj.* Going a long way around, indirect. **cir·cu′i·tous·ly** *adv.* **cir·cu′i·tous·ness, cir·cu′i·ty** *ns.*

cir·cu·lar (sẽr′kyuler) *adj.* Of the form of, pertaining to, moving in, passing over, a circle; **~ saw**, power saw in form of revolving toothed disk. **cir·cu·lar·i·ty** (sẽrkyulăr′ĭtē) *n.* **cir′cu·lar·ly** *adv.* **circular** *n.* Advertisement, notice, etc. for mass distribution. **cir′cu·lar·ize** *v.t.* (**-ized, -iz·ing**). Advertise, notify by circulars.

cir·cu·late (sẽr′kyulāt) *v.* (**-lat·ed, -lat·ing**). 1. Move, pass through a circuit, circuitous course, system of pipes, etc.; (of blood) flow from heart through arteries and

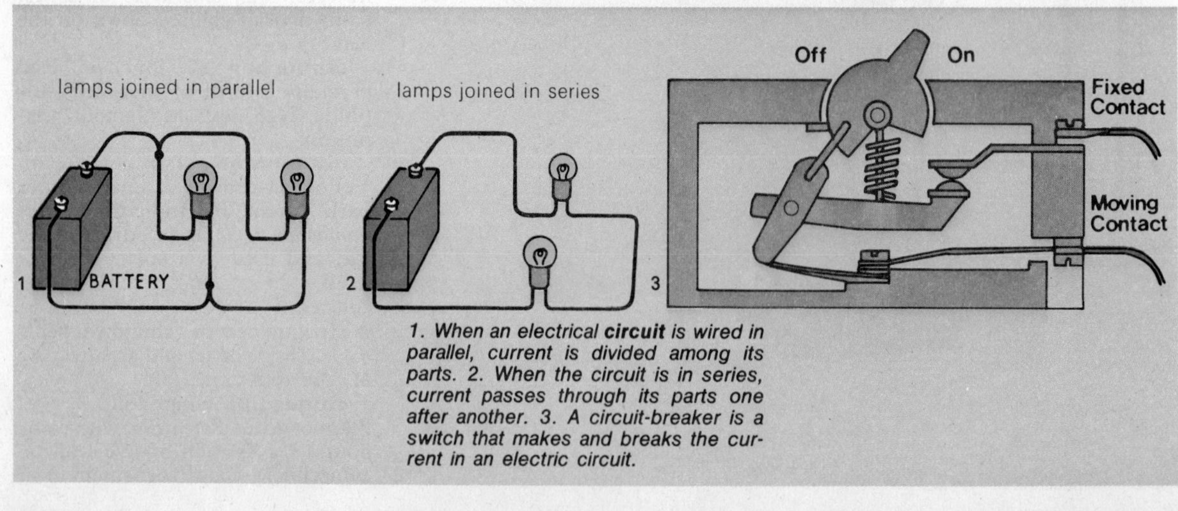

*1. When an electrical **circuit** is wired in parallel, current is divided among its parts. 2. When the circuit is in series, current passes through its parts one after another. 3. A circuit-breaker is a switch that makes and breaks the current in an electric circuit.*

*A principal attraction of the **circus** is seen in demonstrations of man's dominance of wild animals much stronger than himself. The trainer's skill and his understanding of the animals result in some exciting circus acts.*

capillaries and back through veins to heart. 2. Pass from place to place, from person to person, etc.; (of newspaper etc.) pass into hands of readers. 3. Put into circulation, cause to circulate; **circulating library**, library from which books are circulated among subscribers.

cir·cu·la·tion (sẽrkyulā'shon) *n.* 1. Movement of blood from and back to heart; movement to and fro. 2. Transmission, distribution (of news, books, money, etc.); number of copies sold, esp. of newspapers.

cir·cu·la·to·ry (sẽr'kyulatōrē, -tōrē) *adj.* Of circulation of the blood etc.

circum- *prefix.* Around, about.

cir·cum·am·bi·ent (sẽrkumăm'bēent) *adj.* Surrounding (esp. of air or other fluids). **cir·cum·am'bi·ence** *n.*

cir·cum·cise (sẽr'kumsīz) *v.t.* (**-cised, -cis·ing**). Cut off foreskin of (as Jewish or Muslim rite, or surgically), remove clitoris of. **cir·cum·ci·sion** (sẽrkumsĭzh'on) *n.*

cir·cum·fer·ence (serkŭm'ferens) *n.* Encompassing boundary, esp. of figure enclosed by curve, as circle; distance around. **cir·cum·fer·en·tial** (serkŭmferĕn'shal) *adj.*

cir·cum·flex (sẽr'kumflĕks) *n.* A mark (ˆ, in Greek ˜) placed over vowel to indicate contraction, length, or special quality; also circumflex accent.

cir·cum·fuse (sẽrkumfū') *v.t.* (**-fused, -fus·ing**). Pour or diffuse around; surround *with*, bathe. **cir·cum·fu·sion** (sẽrkumfū'zhon) *n.*

cir·cum·lo·cu·tion (sẽrkumlōkū'shon) *n.* Use of many words where few would do; evasive talk; roundabout expression. **cir·cum·loc·u·to·ry** (sẽrkumlŏk'yutōrē, -tōrē) *adj.*

cir·cum·nav·i·gate (sẽrkumnăv'ĭgāt) *v.t.* (**-gat·ed, -gat·ing**). Sail around. **cir·cum·nav·i·ga·tion** (sẽrkumnăvĭgā'shon), **cir·cum·nav'i·ga·tor** *ns.*

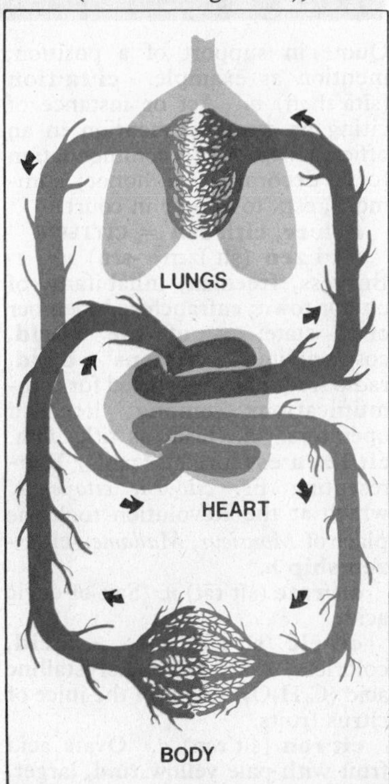

*The heart controls blood **circulation.** It sends blood to the lungs for aeration. This returns to the heart and is pumped to the limbs, and returns to the heart through the veins.*

cir·cum·po·lar (sẽrkumpō'ler) *adj.* Around, about, near, a (terrestrial or celestial) pole; (astron., of star etc.) describing its whole diurnal circle above the horizon.

cir·cum·scribe (sẽr'kumskrīb) *v.t.* (**-scribed, -scrib·ing**). 1. Draw line around; encompass. 2. Mark out or define limits of; confine, restrict. 3. (geom.) Describe (figure) about another so as to touch it at certain points without cutting it. **cir·cum·scrip·tion** (sẽrkumskrĭp'shon) *n.* Circumscribing; circular inscription around coin, seal etc.

cir·cum·so·lar (sẽrkumsō'ler) *adj.* Situated near, moving around, the sun.

cir·cum·spect (sẽr'kumspĕkt) *adj.* Cautious, wary; taking everything into account. **cir'cum·spect·ly** *adv.* **cir·cum·spec'tion** *n.*

cir·cum·stance (sẽr'kumstăns, -stans) *n.* 1. (pl.) Time, place, manner, cause, occasion, etc., surroundings, of an act; external conditions affecting or that might affect an agent. 2. (pl.) Material welfare, means. 3. Detail in narrative. 4. Formality, ceremony. 5. Incident, occurrence, fact. 6. Comparable or important thing or fact. ~ *v.t.* (**-stanced, -stanc·ing**). Place in particular circumstance or relation.

cir·cum·stan·tial (sẽrkumstăn'shal) *adj.* 1. Of or dependent on circumstances; ~ **evidence**, indirect evidence from circumstances affording a certain presumption or capable of only one explanation. 2. Adventitious, accidental; incidental. 3. Full of, particular as to, details. **cir·cum·stan'tial·ly** *adv.*

cir·cum·vent (sẽrkumvĕnt', sẽr'kumvĕnt) *v.t.* Entrap; outwit; avoid, evade. **cir·cum·ven'tion** *n.*

cir·cus (sẽr'kus) *n.* (pl. **-cus·es**). 1. Rounded or oval arena lined with tiers of seats, and often covered by a tent (~ **tent**), for equestrian and other exhibitions; entertainment given in this, consisting usu. of acrobatics, clown acts, feats of horsemanship, and performances by animals; traveling show of riders, acrobats, etc., and their equipment. 2. (Rom. antiq.) Large

The citron was the first of the **citrus** *fruits to be introduced into the Mediterranean. During the crusades others were adopted from the Arabs and grown in Europe. Later, they were introduced to the New World.*

oval or oblong building surrounded with rising tiers of seats for public spectacles and horse or chariot races. 3. (Brit.) Open usu. circular space in town with streets converging on it, traffic circle. 4. (colloq.) Excitement, fun, uproar.

cirque (sẽrk) *n.* (geol.) Bowl-shaped hollow at head of valley or on mountain slope, partly enclosed by steep walls and formed orig. by glacier.

cir·rho·sis (sĭrō′sĭs) *n.* Disease of liver, most frequent among heavy drinkers, marked by progressive destruction and regeneration of liver cells and increased connective tissue, causing portal blockage and hypertension, and eventual liver failure. **cir·rhot·ic** (sĭrŏt′ĭk) *adj.*

cir·ri·ped (sĭr′*i*pĕd) *n.* (zool.) Member of the Cirripedia, subclass of Crustacea comprising marine animals esp. the barnacles, usu. with shelly plates strengthening the carapace and feathery legs that protrude from the shell valves to collect food. ~ *adj.*

cir·ro·cu·mu·lus (sĭrōkū′myu-lus) *n.* (meteor.) Form of usu. high cloud consisting of roundish fleecy cloudlets in contact with one another, mackerel sky.

cir·ro·stra·tus (sĭrōstrā′t*u*s, -străt′*u*s) *n.* (meteor.) Thin usu. high cloud consisting of horizontal or inclined sheets attenuated upward into light cirri.

cir·rus (sĭr′*u*s) *n.* (pl. **cir·ri** pr. sĭr′ī, **cir·rus**). 1. (zool.) Slender filamentary process or appendage. 2. (meteor.) Form of cloud, usu. high, with diverging filaments or wisps, often resembling curl or lock of hair or wool.

cis- *prefix.* On this side of.

cis·al·pine (sĭsăl′pīn, -pĭn) *adj.* On this (usu. = the Roman) side of the Alps; ~ **Gaul**, the part of ancient Gaul S. of the Alps, northern Italy.

cis·lu·nar (sĭslōō′n*e*r) *adj.* Between Earth and moon.

Cis·ter·cian (sĭstẽr′sh*a*n) *n.* & *adj.* (Member) of the contemplative monastic order founded by reformist Benedictines at Cîteaux near Dijon, France, in 1098. [L. *Cistercium* Cîteaux]

cis·tern (sĭs′t*e*rn) *n.* Artificial reservoir for storing water, usu. tank for catching and holding rain water.

cit·a·del (sĭt′*a*dĕl, -del) *n.* Fortress, esp. one guarding or commanding a city; any strongly protected place.

cite (sīt) *v.t.* (**cit·ed, cit·ing**). 1. Summon to appear in court. 2. Quote in support of a position; mention as example. **ci·ta·tion** (sītā′sh*o*n) *n.* Act or instance of citing or quoting; mention in an official dispatch, recommendation for a decoration or honor; summons, esp. to appear in court.

cith·er, cith·ern = CITTERN.

cit·i·zen (sĭt′ĭz*e*n, -s*e*n) *n.* 1. Burgess, freeman, inhabitant, of city or town; enfranchised member of a state; ~ **of the world**, cosmopolitan; **citizens' band**, radio frequencies reserved for communications among licensed operators. 2. (hist., as title; fem. **cit·i·zen·ess** pr. sĭt′ĭzenĭs) Representing Fr. *citoyen, citoyenne*, which at the Revolution took the place of *Monsieur, Madame*. **cit′i·zen·ship** *n.*

cit·rate (sĭt′rāt) *n.* Salt of citric acid.

cit·ric (sĭt′rĭk) *adj.* ~ **acid**, colorless, sharp-tasting crystalline acid ($C_6H_7O_7$) found in the juice of citrus fruits.

cit·ron (sĭt′r*o*n) *n.* Ovate acid fruit with pale yellow rind, larger,

The nocturnal **civet** *is catlike but not related to the cat family. There are many species of civet in the Old World. Near their genitals they have scent glands which produce a powerful musky odor. Derivatives of this substance are used as fixatives for certain perfumes.*

less acid, and thicker skinned than lemon; tree (*Citrus medica*) bearing this.

cit·ron·el·la (sĭtrŏnĕl′*a*) *n.* Fragrant grass (*Cymbopogon nardus*) of S. Asia yielding a fragrant oil used in insect repellents and perfumery; this oil.

cit·rus (sĭt′r*u*s) *n.* Fruit of genus *C*~ including citron, orange, lime, lemon, and grapefruit. ~ *adj.*

cit·tern (sĭt′*e*rn), **cith·er** (sĭth′*er*), **cith·ern** (sĭth′*e*rn) *ns.* Stringed musical instrument somewhat like lute but with flat back, usu. played with plectrum, common in times of Chaucer and Shakespeare.

cit·y (sĭt′ē) *n.* (pl. **cit·ies**). 1. (loosely) Important town; (in England) town created city by charter, in early times esp. one containing a cathedral; town of greater importance, or size, or with wider municipal powers, than those called simply towns; **Celestial C~, Holy C~, C~ of God,** Paradise; **Eternal C~, C~ of the Seven Hills,** Rome; **Holy C~,** (esp.) Jerusalem; **~-state**, one of the small autonomous republics of ancient Greece; any small sovereign state consisting of an autonomous city and its dependencies. 2. (in England) **the C~ (of London),** that part of London within the ancient boundaries under the jurisdiction of the Lord Mayor and Corporation; esp. the part of this near the Stock Exchange and Bank of England, the center of financial and commercial activity; ~ **editor**, one who deals with local news; ~ **hall**, municipal offices or (fig.) municipal officials; ~ **manager**, official directing administration of a city.

Ci·u·dad Juá·rez (syōōdahd′ hwah′rĕs): see JUAREZ.

Ci·u·dad Tru·ji·llo (syōōdahd′ trōōhē′yō): see SANTO DOMINGO.

civ·et (sĭv′ĭt) *n.* 1. Yellowish or brownish substance, unctuous and smelling strongly of musk, obtained from anal glands of civet cat or related species. 2. Carnivorous quadruped of family Viverridae yielding this, esp. the central African ~ **cat** (*Civettictis civetta*), between fox and weasel in appearance.

civ·ic (sĭv′ĭk) *adj.* Of, proper to, citizens; of a city, municipal; of citizenship, civil. **civ′ics** *n.* Science of civic affairs.

civ·il (sĭv′*i*l) *adj.* 1. Of citizens or citizen community. 2. Of, becoming, befitting, a citizen; polite, obliging. 3. Nonmilitary; nonecclesiastical, secular; (law) not criminal or political. 4. ~ **defense**, protection of civil population against air raids or other enemy action; ~ **disobedience**, refusal to obey the laws as part of a political campaign; ~ **engineering**: see engineer; ~ **law**, law pertaining to the private rights and remedies of a citizen (cf. CRIMINAL law); law of Roman citizens; Roman law as a whole, esp. as received in Western Christendom in and after Middle Ages; ~ **liberty**, freedom

Founded in 1718 New Orleans is the largest ***city*** *in Louisiana. Famous as the home of jazz and for its annual Mardi Gras, it is of economic importance to the U.S.A. as the main port trading with Latin America.*

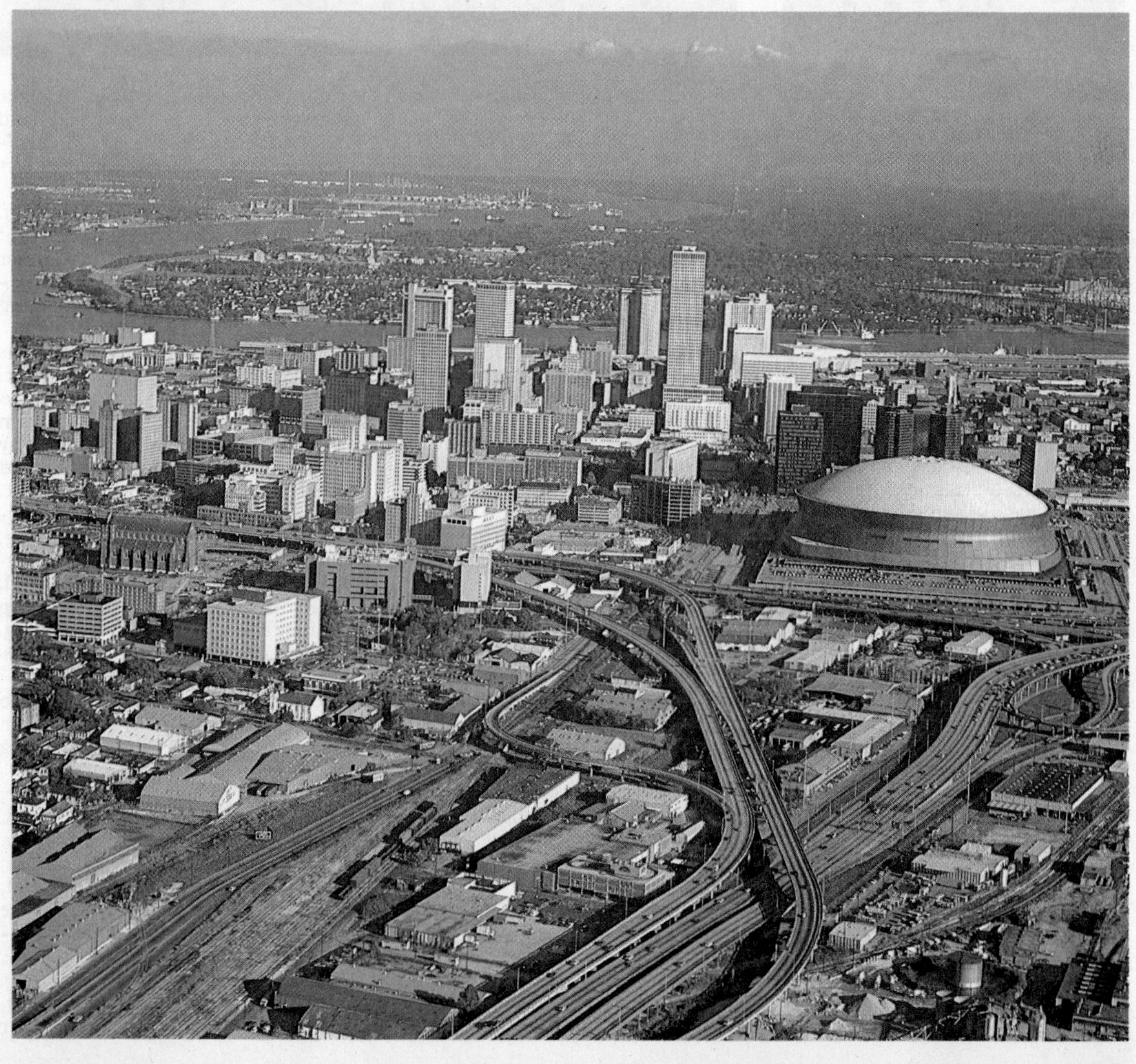

Early in the 18th century J. C. Denner invented the **clarinet** in Nuremburg, Germany. Some authorities believe his clarinet is an improved version of the chalumeau, a stopped pipe only 8 ins. long.

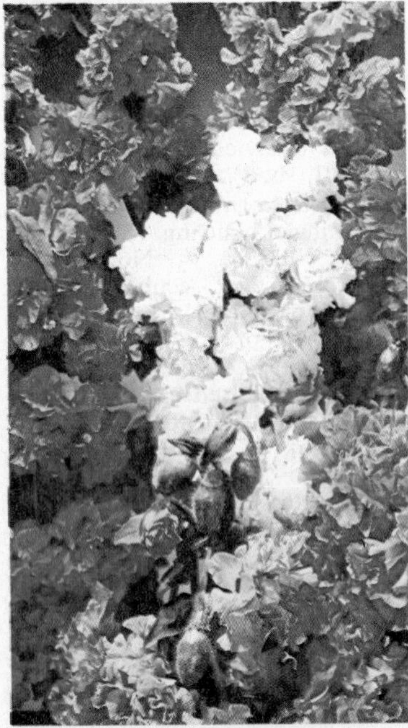

In cultivating **clarkia,** various reds can be obtained, from pale pink to dark red. The effect of the double-flowered variety is more colorful in masses but the individual flowers are less delicate.

The memorial at Gettysburg commemorates the death of over 40,000 men who died in what proved to be one of the bloodiest battles of the U.S. **Civil War.**

guaranteed by the laws of a nation to its citizens to exercise the rights of free speech, thought, and action; ~ **list**, in Gt. Britain and other countries, the yearly funds provided by the legislature for the household and personal expenses of the monarch, royal family, etc.; ~ **proceedings**, legal proceedings aimed at the redress of wrong; ~ **rights**, rights to personal liberty; rights of all to equality as citizens; ~ **servant**, official or employee in civil service; ~ **service**, administrative service of state, including all government departments and public offices (excluding armed forces); persons employed in this; **C~ War**, (i) (U.S. hist.) war between the Union (the North) and the CONFEDERACY (the South) from 1861–5, also called War of the Secession and War Between the States; the conflict grew out of sectional disputes over slavery in the South, the introduction of slavery into new states and territories, and the claim that states had the right to secede from the Union; when eleven southern states seceded (1860–1) and formed the Confederacy, war began, ending in complete defeat for the South, re-admission of the eleven states into the Union, and the abolition of slavery. (ii) (Engl. hist.) Struggle between Royalists and Parliament, 1642–51. (iii) (Span. hist.) Struggle between Fascist and Republican factions, 1936–9. ~ **war**, war between factions or regions of a country. **civ'il·ly** *adv.* **ci·vil·i·ty** (sĭvĭl'ĭtē) *n.* (pl. **-ties**). Politeness.

ci·vil·ian (sĭvĭl'yan) *adj.* & *n.* (Person) not of one of the armed services.

civ·i·li·za·tion (sĭvĭlīzā'shon) *n.* Making or becoming civilized; stage, esp. advanced stage, in social development. **civ·i·lize** (sĭv'ĭlīz) *v.t.* (**-lized, -liz·ing**). Bring out of barbarism; instruct in the arts of life; refine, enlighten.

civ·vies (sĭv'ēz) *n.pl.* (colloq.) Civilian clothes.

CJ *abbrev.* Chief Justice.

cl *abbrev.* Centiliter(s).

cl. *abbrev.* 1. Centiliter(s). 2. Class; classification. 3. Clause.

clack (klăk) *n.* Sharp sound as of boards struck together; noise or clatter of human tongues. ~ *v.i.* Chatter, prate; make clack.

clad (klăd): see CLOTHE. **clad'·ding** *n.* Coating or covering applied to surface of object, building, etc.; application of this.

claim (klām) *v.t.* Demand as one's due; represent oneself as having; demand recognition of the fact that; profess; deserve, assert. ~ *n.* 1. Demand for something as due; right, title, *to*; right to make demand *on*. 2. Piece of land allotted, esp. for mining. **claim'·ant** *n.* One who makes or enters a claim.

clair·voy·ance (klārvoi'ans) *n.* Supposed supernatural faculty of seeing what is removed in time or space from natural sight. **clair'·voy'ant** *adj.* & *n.* (Person) having clairvoyance.

clam (klăm) *n.* Any of various bivalve shellfish, esp. the N. Amer. hard or round clam (*Venus mercenaria*), and soft or long clam (*Mya arenaria*), found abundantly on sandy or muddy shores and esteemed as food; (slang) silent, uncommunicative person. **clam'·bake** *n.* Social gathering for eating, esp. clams and other shellfish, outdoors. **clam** *v.i.* (**clammed, clam·ming**). Dig for clams; ~ **up** (slang) become silent, cease talking. [orig. *clamshell*; ult. f. Ger. *klam* press or squeeze together]

clam·ber (klăm'ber) *v.i.* Climb with hands and feet; climb with difficulty or labor. ~ *n.* Climbing thus.

clam·my (klăm'ē) *adj.* (**-mi·er, -mi·est**). Moist and cold. **clam'mi·ly** *adv.* **clam'mi·ness** *n.*

clam·or (klăm'er) *n.* Shouting; loud appeal, complaint, or demand; confused noise. ~ *v.i.* Make clamor *for*, *against*, etc. **clam'or'·ous** *adj.* **clam'or·ous·ly** *adv.* **clam'or·ous·ness** *n.*

clamp (klămp) *n.* Brace, clasp, or band for strengthening other materials or holding things together; appliance or tool with opposite sides connected by screw for holding or compressing. ~ *v.t.* Strengthen, fasten, with clamp(s); ~ **down** (**on**), (fig.) become (more) strict (about), put a stop to.

clam·shell (klăm'shĕl) *n.* 1. Shell of a clam. 2. Bucket for dredging, made of two scoops hinged together at the top and opening at the bottom.

clan (klăn) *n.* 1. Group of persons descended from same ancestor and associated together, esp. in Scottish Highlands; **clans'-man**, (fellow) member of a clan. 2. Family holding together; coterie, set. **clan'nish** *adj.* **clan'nish·ly** *adv.* **clan'nish·ness** *n.*

clan·des·tine (klăndĕs'tĭn) *adj.* Surreptitious, secret, underhand. **clan·des'tine·ly** *adv.*

clang (klăng) *n.* Loud resonant metallic sound. ~ *v.* Make, cause to make, this sound.

clang·or (klăng'*er*, klăng'g*er*) *n.* Succession of loud metallic ringing noises. **clan'gor·ous** *adj.*

clank (klănk) *n.* Sharp abrupt sound, as of heavy pieces of metal struck together. ~ *v.* Make, cause to make, this sound.

clap[1] (klăp) *n.* 1. Loud explosive noise as of thunder; peal. 2. Sound made by striking palms of hands together; act of doing this as applause. ~ *v.* (**clapped, clap·ping**). 1. Make clap; signify applause, delight, etc., with clap; applaud with claps. 2. Slap with palm of hand, in approval or encouragement; apply, place, set, quickly or energetically; put (*in* prison); ~ **eyes on**, catch sight of; ~ **into** (jail), put swiftly into.

clap[2] (klăp) *n.* (vulg. slang) Gonorrhea.

clap·board (klăb'*er*d, klăp'bōrd, -bōrd) *n.* Long narrow board with one edge thicker than the other, used to cover outside walls of houses by nailing horizontally so that the thick edge overlaps the narrow edge of the board beneath it. ~ *v.t.* Cover with clapboards.

clap·per (klăp'*er*) *n.* (esp.) Tongue or striker of bell.

clap·trap (klăp'trăp) *n.* Language used or sentiments expressed only to gain applause; pretentious but empty assertions; nonsense.

claque (klăk) *n.* Body of hired applauders in theater etc.; group of fawning admirers.

Clar·en·don (klăr'*e*nd*o*n), **Edward Hyde, Earl of** (1609–74). English statesman and historian; lord chancellor under Charles II; author of *The True Historical Narrative of the Rebellion and Civil Wars in England*, from the profits of which a new printing house, which bore his name, was built for the Oxford University Press.

clar·et (klăr'ĭt) *n.* Red wine from Bordeaux; color of this, dark reddish purple; (slang) blood; ~ *adj.* Claret-colored.

clar·i·fy (klăr'*i*fī) *v.* (**-fied, -fy·ing**). Make clear; free from impurities, make transparent (liquid, butter, etc.); become or be made clear or pure. **clar·i·fi·ca·tion** (klăr*i*fĭkā'sh*o*n) *n.*

clar·i·net (klărĭnĕt') *n.* Woodwind single-reed instrument with range of about 3½ octaves from C♯ or D below middle C, having cylindrical tube with bell-shaped end, and played with fingers on holes and keys.

Chemistry ***class*** *in progress. Many educationalists consider a critical factor to be the average number of pupils per school class; an excessive number may thwart the individual child.*

clar·i·on (klăr'ēon) *n.* Shrill narrow-tubed trumpet formerly used in war; sound of trumpet, any similar rousing sound. ~ *adj.* Loud and clear, like a clarion.

clar·i·ty (klăr'ĭtē) *n.* 1. Clearness to the eye. 2. Clearness and freedom from ambiguity in verbal expression.

Clark (klārk), **George Rogers** (1752–1818). Amer. frontiersman; led many raids against Indians in Indiana, Kentucky, Illinois area; frontier military leader during Revolutionary War; his brother, **William** (1770–1838), Amer. military officer and explorer; co-leader with Meriwether Lewis of the Lewis and Clark Expedition (see LEWIS[3]).

clark·i·a (klār'kē*a*) *n.* Annual plant of genus *C*~ of western N. America with white, pink, or purple flowers. [W. *Clark*, see prec.]

clar·y (klār'ē) *n.* (pl. **clar·ies**). Aromatic herb (*Salvia sclarea*), native to S. Europe, Syria, etc., and having bluish-white flowers; other species of same genus.

clash (klăsh) *n.* 1. Loud broken sound as of collision, striking weapons or cymbals, bells rung together. 2. Encounter, conflict; disagreement. ~ *v.* 1. Make clash. 2. Conflict, disagree, be at variance *with*; (of colors) be discordant.

clasp (klăsp, klahsp) *n.* 1. Contrivance of two interlocking parts for fastening; **tie** ~, ornament for neatly holding a necktie against shirt front. 2. Embrace; grasp or joining of hands. **clasp** *v.* 1. Fasten with or as clasp. 2. Encircle, hold closely, embrace; grasp (another's hand); join (hands) by interlocking fingers.

class (klăs, klahs) *n.* 1. Rank, order, of society; class system. 2. (slang) Elegance, excellence. 3. Division of students taught together or considered of same standing; their time or place of meeting, the instruction given to them; (colleges) all students of the same standing, who enter together, graduate together, etc., *class of 1978*, those who were graduated in that year. 4. Division grouping, according to merit or quality. 5. Number of individuals having some character or feature in common; (biol.) division of animals or plants below phylum, subdivided into orders, families, genera, species. 6. ~**-action suit**, legal action against a single party taken on behalf of a group of individuals with the same complaint; ~ **conscious**, conscious of belonging to a particular class, often with implication of hostility to other classes; ~ **consciousness**; ~ **struggle**, in Marxism, the struggle for economic and political power between the bourgeoisie, or capitalists, and the

The ideals of symmetry and simplicity intrinsic in ***Classicism*** *are seen in the Philadelphia City Hall which is at the centre of Penn Square, named for William Penn the founder and planner of this elegant city.*

proletariat, or workers; ~ **system**, division of society into classes. **class** *v.t.* Assign to class. **class'less** *adj.* (of a society) Not recognizing, not having, class distinctions.

clas·sic (klăs'ĭk) *adj.* 1. Of avowed excellence. 2. Of the ancient Greek and Latin authors; of Greek and Roman antiquity. 3. (opp. ROMANTIC) In the classic style, simple, harmonious, proportioned, and finished. 4. Having literary or historic associations. 5. Of simple style that endures despite changes of fashion. ~ *n.* 1. Writer or artist, work, of acknowledged excellence. 2. Ancient Greek or Latin writer; (pl.) studies of these.

clas·si·cal (klăs'ĭk*a*l) *adj.* 1. = CLASSIC *adj.*; constituting a model. 2. Of ancient Greek or Latin standard authors or art; learned in, studying, or based on these. 3. In, following, the restrained style of classical antiquity; (in the arts) traditional. 4. (of physics etc.) Based on theories etc. established before the discovery of quantum theory, relativity, etc. **clas'si·cal·ly** *adv.*

clas·si·cism (klăs'ĭsĭz*e*m) *n.* Following of classic(al) style; classical scholarship. **clas'si·cist** *n.*

clas·si·fy (klăs'ĭfī) *v.t.* (**-fied, -fy·ing**). Arrange in classes, assign to a class; **classified**, (of official documents) belonging to a class, e.g. secret or confidential, that only specified persons may see. **clas·si·fi·ca·tion** (klăsĭfĭkā'sh*o*n) *n.*

class·y (klăs'ē) *adj.* (**class·i·er, class·i·est**). (slang) Stylish, elegant; superior, excellent.

clat·ter (klăt'*er*) *n.* Rattling sound, as of many plates struck together; noisy talk, confused din of voices. ~ *v.* Make clatter, cause to rattle.

Clau·di·us (klaw'dē*u*s) (10 B.C.–54 A.D.). Tiberius Claudius Drusus Nero Germanicus, Roman emperor 41–54 A.D.

clause (klawz) *n.* 1. (gram.) Subordinate part of sentence including subject and predicate and forming part of a compound or complex sentence. 2. Single proviso in treaty, law, contract, or other document. **claus'al** *adj.*

Clau·se·witz (klow'zevĭtz), **Karl von** (1780–1831). Prussian army officer; writer on military science.

claus·tro·pho·bi·a (klawstr*o*fō'bē*a*) *n.* Pathological fear of confined places. **claus·tro·pho'bic** *adj.* 1. Suffering from

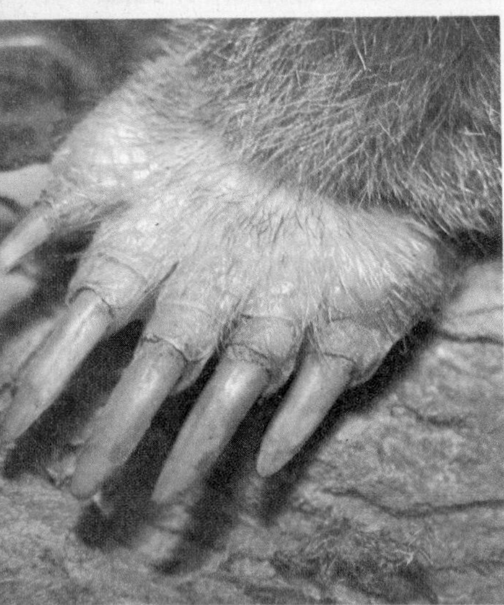

A mechanically valuable adjunct to the paws of many animals, ***claws*** *may be used to rend, scrape or pare. Illustrated here, the mole's claws, curved outwards on the forepaws, are ideal for digging.*

Above: The plasticity of ***clay*** *allows a potter to 'throw' a pot on a wheel turned by treadle or electric motor. Potters have used a wheel for their work since c. 4,000 B.C.*

claustrophobia. 2. Inducing claustrophobia.

clav·i·chord (klăv'ĭkōrd) *n.* Musical instrument resembling square piano, with keyboard and strings struck by tangents, the earliest keyboard instrument with strings, appearing in mid-14th c.

clav·i·cle (klăv'ĭk*e*l) *n.* Collarbone. **cla·vic·u·lar** (kl*a*vĭk'-y*u*l*er*) *adj.*

clav·ier, **klav·ier** (kl*a*vēr') *ns.* (Instrument with) keyboard, esp. before introduction of piano.

claw (klaw) *n.* Pointed horny nail of beast's or bird's foot; foot so armed; pincers of shellfish; (contempt.) hand; mechanical or other contrivance for grappling, tearing, etc.; ~ **hammer**, hammer with one end bent and split, for extracting nails. **claw** *v.* Scratch, tear, seize, pull toward one, with claws or nails.

clay (klā) *n.* 1. Stiff viscous earth consisting chiefly of aluminum silicate and forming with water a tenacious paste, which can be molded, or dried and baked into bricks, pottery, tiles, etc.; **feet of** ~, (fig.) fundamental weakness in person of supposed merit (cf. Dan. 2); ~ **pigeon**, clay disk thrown or ejected from trap as a flying target for trapshooting. 2. Earth; earth as the material of the human body, hence, the body. **clay'ey** *adj.*

Clay (klā), **Henry** (1777–1852). Amer. lawyer, statesman, and U.S. senator; Secretary of State, 1825–1829; sought to avert the Civil War by the Compromise of 1850; known as the "Great Pacificator" and "Great Compromiser."

clay·more (klā'mōr, -mōr) *n.* Two-edged broadsword formerly used by Scottish Highlanders. [Gael. *claidheamb mòr* great sword]

clean (klēn) *adj.* 1. Free from anything contaminating or from dirt; free from weeds, barnacles, etc.; free from defects; (of paper) blank; (of typescript, printer's proof, etc.) free from corrections; not smudged; (of nuclear devices) producing relatively little fallout; (of fuel) not polluting the air; ~ **room**, any enclosed area where air is kept free of all contaminants, as for carrying on certain scientific experiments, medical treatments, etc.; **come** ~, (colloq.) confess. 2. Free from moral stain, as in ~ **record**; free from ceremonial defilement or of disease; (of beasts etc.) fit for food. 3. Neatly made, not unwieldy, trim; neat; unencumbered, unobstructed. 4. Entire, complete, total; ~ **sweep**, complete victory over all other contestants or in all contests. **clean·ly**[1] (klēn'lē) *adv.* **clean'ness** *n.* **clean** *adv.* Completely; absolutely. ~ *v.* Make clean; make oneself clean; ~ **out**, empty, strip; ~ **up**, clean, make tidy, clear up; (slang) earn or win large amount. **clean** *n.* Cleaning.

The sensitive 'touch' of the **clavichord's** *keyboard and the delicacy of its tone won it a place high in the affections of composers of the 15th to 18th centuries.*

clean·er (klē'n*er*) *n.* (esp.) Person employed to clean house etc.; (freq. pl.) drycleaner.

clean·ly[2] (klĕn'lē) *adj.* Habitually neat and clean, attentive to cleanness. **clean'li·ness** *n.*

cleanse (klĕnz) *v.t.* (**cleansed, cleans·ing**). 1. Make clean. 2. Purify; free from guilt.

clear (klēr) *adj.* 1. Unclouded, transparent, not turbid; lustrous; unspotted; (of soup) strained to remove particles. 2. Distinct, intelligible; manifest. 3. Discerning, penetrating; confident, certain. 4. Easily audible. 5. Without reduction, net; free *of*, whole, complete; open, unobstructed; unengaged, free; not encumbered by debt; ~**-cut** (*adj.*) defined or formed sharply; evident, distinct. **clear** *adv.* Clearly; quite; apart, without contact. ~ *n.* (esp.) **in the** ~, free, esp. from imputation of guilt. **clear** *v.* 1. Make, become, clear. 2. Free from imputation of guilt, from suspicion, etc. 3. Free or rid *of*; remove; depart; (become) empty. 4. Free from contact or entanglement; pass without entanglement, contact, or collision. 5. Settle (debt etc.); free from debt; satisfy requirements, obligations, examination, etc.; (naut.) free (ship) by paying all dues; (of ship) sail. 6. Make (sum of money) as net gain. 7. Get approval of (proposal etc.). 8. ~ **away**, remove, remove remains of meal from table, (of mist etc.) disappear; ~ **off**, get rid of, melt away, (of intruders) go away; ~ **out**, empty, make off; ~ **up**, solve (mystery), make tidy, (of weather etc.) grow clear.

clear·ance (klēr'*a*ns) *n.* 1. Clearing; removal of obstructions; passing of checks through clearing house; (certificate of) clearing of ship at custom house. 2. Clear space; room to pass. 3. ~ **sale**, store's sale of merchandise at reduced prices in order to get rid of superfluous stock.

clear·ing (klēr'ĭng) *n.* (esp.) Piece of land cleared for cultivation; ~ **house**, institution or office where banks exchange checks and drafts and settle accounts; agency for collecting and distributing information etc.

clear·ly (klēr'lē) *adv.* Distinctly; manifestly; undoubtedly.

clear·ness (klēr'nĭs) *n.* Transparency; distinctness; freedom from obstruction.

cleat (klēt) *n.* Wedge; projecting piece bolted on spar, gangway, etc., to give footing or prevent rope from slipping; piece of metal, rubber, etc., fastened to sole of shoe to prevent slipping; wedge-shaped or other projecting piece of wood or metal for fastening ropes to, etc.

cleav·age (klē'vĭj) *n.* Cleaving; being cleft; way or line in which anything tends to split; property (of minerals and rocks) of splitting readily in certain directions; (colloq.) cleft between woman's

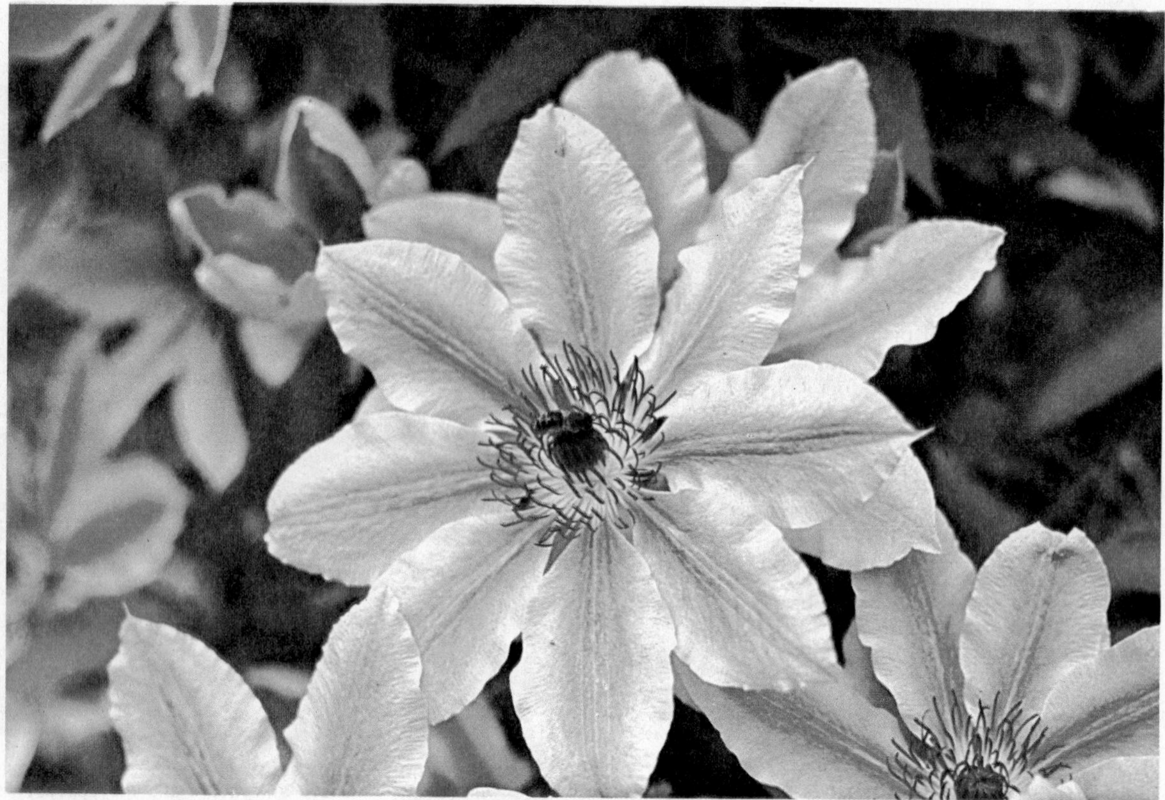

breasts, revealed by low-cut dress.

cleave[1] (klēv) *v.* (**cleft** pr. klĕft or **cleaved** or **clove** pr. klōv, **cleft** or **cleaved** or **clo·ven** pr. klō′v*e*n, **cleav·ing**). Split; chop, break, or come apart, esp. along grain or line of cleavage; make way through (water, air, etc.). **cleav′er** *n.* (esp.) Butcher's heavy axlike knife or hatchet.

cleave[2] (klēv) *v.i.* (**cleaved** or archaic **clave** pr. klāv, **cleaved, cleav·ing**). Stick fast, adhere *to* (archaic); be faithful.

clef (klĕf) *n.* Symbol on musical staff to indicate pitch of notes; **bass ~**, symbol that locates the F next below middle C; **treble ~**, symbol that locates the G above middle C.

cleft[1] (klĕft) *n.* Space or division made by cleaving; fissure, split.

cleft[2] (klĕft) *adj.*: see CLEAVE[1]; (esp.) **~ palate**, malformation of palate with longitudinal gap in middle or on either side of roof of mouth.

clem·a·tis (klĕm′*a*tĭs, kl*e*mah′-tĭs, -măt′ĭs) *n.* Twining shrub of genus *C~* having flowers with showy calyx and no corolla.

Cle·men·ceau (klĕm*e*nsō′), **Georges** (1841–1929). French statesman; premier 1906–9 and 1917–20; chairman of the Versailles Peace Conference.

clem·en·cy (klĕm′*e*nsē) *n.* (pl. **-cies**). Mildness of temper or weather; mercy.

Clem·ens (klĕm′*e*nz), **Samuel Langhorne**: see Mark TWAIN.

Above: A favorite climbing plant in gardens, ***clematis*** *is of a large genus with many varieties. Shown here is a popular clematis called Nellie Moser.*

Clem·ent (klĕm′*e*nt). Name of several popes and bishops of Rome including **~ I**, bishop of Rome during the late 1st c. and reputedly third successor to Saint Peter; **~ V** (1264–1314), Pope (1305–14), he removed the seat of papacy from Rome to Avignon, France, in 1309; **~ VII** (1478–1534), Pope (1523–1534), a Medici and cousin of Pope Leo X; he refused to sanction the divorce of Henry VIII of England in 1534.

cle·ment (klĕm′*e*nt) *adj.* Mild, showing mercy.

clench (klĕnch) *v.* Fix securely, make fast, as with nails; clinch (a nail etc.); close (teeth, fingers) tightly; grasp firmly. **~** *n.* Clenching, being clenched.

Cle·o·pa·tra (klē*o*păt′r*a*, -pah′-tr*a*, -pā′-) (68–30 B.C.). Queen of Egypt; daughter of Ptolemy Auletes, king of Egypt; wife of Ptolemy III, her brother; mistress of Julius Caesar, who restored her to her throne in 47 B.C. after her expulsion by Pothinus; mistress of Mark Antony; in the war between Antony and Augustus, the defection of her fleet at the battle of Actium (31 B.C.) hastened Antony's defeat; to escape being carried captive to Rome, she took her own life. The granite obelisks known as **~'s Needles** have no connection with the queen, but were originally erected at Heliopolis by Thothmes III *c*1475 B.C.

clep·sy·dra (klĕp′sĭdr*a*) *n.* (pl. **-dras, -drae** pr. -drē). Ancient time-measuring device worked by flow of water, also called "water clock." [Gk. *kleptō* steal *hudōr* water]

clere·sto·ry (klēr′stōrē, -stōrē) *n.* (pl. **-ries**). Upper part of wall of nave, choir, and transepts of cathedral or large church, and containing windows.

cler·gy (klēr′jē) *n.* (pl. **-gies**, collect. **-gy**). 1. The clerical order; all persons ordained for religious service; clergymen. 2. **without benefit of ~**, (colloq.) without being married; **cler′gyman**, member of the clergy.

cler·ic (klĕr′ĭk) *n.* Clerical man, clergyman. [Gk. *klērikos* f. *klēros* lot, inheritance, as used (e.g.) in Acts I:17]

cler·i·cal (klĕr′ĭk*a*l) *adj.* 1. Of the clergy, a clergyman, or clergymen. 2. Of, made by, a clerk or office worker; **~ error**, error in writing anything out. **clerical** *n.* Clergyman.

cler·i·cal·ism (klĕr′ĭk*a*lĭzem) *n.* (esp.) Clerical rule or influence. **cler′i·cal·ist** *n.*

clerk (klērk; *Brit.* klärk) *n.* 1. (archaic) Clergyman. 2. Officer in charge of records, accounts, etc., of any department, court, corporation, etc. 3. Office worker who makes written records, keeps accounts, attends to correspondence, files, etc. 4. Salesperson in

The ambition and charm of ***Cleopatra*** *quickly became legendary, capturing the imagination of writers over many centuries. Left: Cleopatra and the Roman, Antony, are in love in Shakespeare's play about them.*

Erosion of a shore can produce a ***cliff.*** *The sea undercuts the rock. It then dashes fallen boulders against the base of the cliff, continuing the work of erosion.*

a store. **clerk'ship** *n.* **clerk** *v.i.* (colloq.) Act as clerk.

Cleve·land[1] (klēv'l*a*nd). Industrial city and port on Lake Erie in NE. Ohio.

Cleve·land[2] (klēv'l*a*nd), (**Stephen**) **Grover** (1837–1908). Twenty-second and 24th president of U.S., 1885–9 and 1893–7.

clev·er (klĕv'*er*) *adj.* Adroit, neat in movement; talented; ingenious. **clev'er·ly** *adv.* **clev'er·ness** *n.*

clev·is (klĕv'ĭs) *n.* U-shaped piece of metal with holes at the ends through which a bolt or pin is run, used to attach a whiffletree, plow, etc.

clew (kloo͞) *n.* 1. Ball of thread or yarn; such a ball used as guide through maze or labyrinth (in many mythological or legendary stories). 2. (naut.) Small cords suspending hammock; lower corner of square sail, after corner of fore-and-aft sail, to which are fastened tacks and sheets for extending and securing it. 3. Clue. ~ *v.t.* (naut.) Draw lower ends of (sails) *up* to upper yard or mast for furling.

cli·ché (klēshā', klĭ-) *n.* Stereotyped or hackneyed phrase or expression.

click (klĭk) *n.* 1. Slight sharp hard nonringing sound as of dropping latch etc.; ~ **beetle**, adult wireworm or other beetle of family Elateridae, which when turned over rights itself by jumping with a click. 2. (phon.) Class of sharp nonvocal sounds occurring in certain African languages, formed by suction, with sudden withdrawal of tongue from contact with part of mouth. **click** *v.* Make click; (slang) secure one's object; be a great success; get on friendly terms (*with* person of opposite sex).

cli·ent (klī'*e*nt) *n.* 1. (Rom. antiq.) Plebeian under protection of noble; (archaic) dependent, hanger-on. 2. One employing services of lawyer; employer of services of any professional or business man; customer.

cli·en·tele (klī*e*ntĕl', klē-, klēahn-) *n.* Body of clients, customers, or patrons.

cliff (klĭf) *n.* Steep rock face; **cliff'hanger**, story, contest, etc. with outcome in suspense.

cli·mac·ter·ic (klīmăk't*e*rĭk, klīmăktĕr'ĭk) *n.* & *adj.* (Constituting) a crisis, critical; esp. (occurring at) period of life (45–60) at which vital forces begin to decline; menopause.

cli·mate (klī'mĭt) *n.* (Region with specified) prevailing conditions of temperature, rainfall, humidity, wind, etc.; (fig.) prevailing mental or moral attitude etc. **cli·mat·ic** (klīmăt'ĭk) *adj.* **cli·mat'i·cal·ly** *adv.*

cli·ma·tol·o·gy (klīm*a*tŏl'*o*jē) *n.* Study of climates. **cli·ma·to·log·i·cal** (klīm*a*tolŏj'ĭk*a*l) *adj.*

cli·max (klī'măks) *n.* 1. Culmination, apex. 2. Orgasm. 3. (ecol.) State of equilibrium reached by plant and animal community. **cli·mac·tic** (klīmăk'tĭk) *adj.*

climb (klīm) *v.* 1. Ascend, mount, go *up*, esp. with help of hands; ~ **down**, descend similarly; (fig.) retreat from position taken up, give in. 2. (of sun, aircraft, etc.) Gain height. 3. (of plants) Creep up by aid of tendrils or by twining. 4. Slope upward. 5. Rise by effort in social rank, intellectual or moral power, etc. **climb** *n.* Climbing; place climbed or to be climbed.

Robert Clive went to India for the East India Company in 1743. He joined the Company's army in 1744. His victories at Pondicherry (1748), Arcot (1751) and Plassey (1757) consolidated British power in India.

climb·er (klī'mer) *n.* (esp.) Mountaineer; climbing plant; one who attempts to rise to higher social standing.

clime (klīm) *n.* (poet.) Region; climate.

clinch (klĭnch) *n.* 1. (naut.) Way of fastening large ropes with half hitch; clinched part of rope; anything that grips. 2. Struggle or scuffle at close quarters; (boxing) grappling at close quarters. 3. (slang) Close embrace. ~ *v.* 1. Clench. 2. Drive home, make conclusive, confirm, establish. 3. Embrace closely.

clinch·er (klĭn'cher) *n.* (esp.) Remark, argument, reason that settles a matter.

cling (klĭng) *v.i.* (**clung** pr. klŭng, **cling·ing**). Adhere *together*, remain in one body or in contact, resist separation; adhere *to*; remain faithful *to*; **cling'stone** (**peach**), variety in which flesh adheres to stone.

clin·ic (klĭn'ĭk) *n.* 1. Teaching of medicine or surgery at the bedside; class, institution, so taught or conducted. 2. Institution or center for giving medical advice or treatment; medical offices of several specialists working cooperatively. 3. Center that offers counsel or instruction in fields other than medicine. **cli·ni·cian** (klĭnĭsh'an) *n.*

clin·i·cal (klĭn'ĭkal) *adj.* Of, at, the sickbed (esp. of lectures, teaching); dispassionate; ~ **medicine**, observation and treatment of patients as distinct from theoretical study of medical science; ~ **thermometer**, one for taking patient's temperature. **clin'i·cal·ly** *adv.*

clink[1] (klĭngk) *n.* Sharp, abrupt, clear ringing sound, as of small metallic objects or glasses struck together. ~ *v.* Make clink.

clink[2] (klĭngk) *n.* (slang) Prison, jail. [proper name of a former prison in London]

clink·er[1] (klĭng'ker) *n.* (colloq.) Mistake, error.

clink·er[2] (klĭng'ker) *n.* 1. Very hard pale-yellow paving brick; brick with surface vitrified by great heat. 2. Mass of bricks fused by excessive heat; hardened mass formed by fusion of earthy impurities of burned coal, limestone, etc., slag; mass of hardened volcanic lava.

Clin·ton (klĭn'ton), **George** (1739–1812). First governor of New York State, 1777–95, 1801–4; vice president of the U.S. under Thomas Jefferson and James Madison, 1805–12; his nephew, **De Witt**, (1769–1828), Amer. lawyer and statesman, U.S. senator 1802–1803; governor of New York State, 1817–21, 1825–28.

Cli·o (clī'ō). (Gk. and Rom. myth.) Muse of epic poetry and history. [Gk. *kleiō* celebrate]

clip[1] (klĭp) *n.* Appliance for holding things together, or for attachment to objects; set of cartridges held together at base or packed in special container for insertion into magazine of repeating firearm; piece of jewelry for clipping on; **clip'board**, board with spring clip for holding papers etc. **clip** *v.t.* (**clipped, clip·ping**). Grip tightly, grasp; fasten with clip(s).

clip[2] (klĭp) *n.* Clipping, shearing; quantity of wool clipped from sheep, flock, etc.; (colloq.) rate of speed, rapid pace; (colloq.) smart blow; ~ **joint**, (slang) bar, club, etc. charging exorbitant prices. **clip** *v.* (**clipped, clipped** or **clipt, clip·ping**). 1. Cut with shears or scissors; trim, make tidy, thus; cut off part of (hair, wool) thus; remove hair or wool of (sheep etc.) thus; pare edge of (coin); remove small piece of (ticket) to show that it has been used; cut short. 2. (colloq.) Move quickly, run. 3. (colloq.) Hit smartly. 4. (slang) Overcharge.

clip·per (klĭp'er) *n.* (esp.) 1. Instrument for clipping hair. 2. Ship with forward-raking bows and aft-raking masts. 3. Aircraft esp. for transoceanic flights.

clip·ping (klĭp'ĭng) *n.* (esp.) Small piece clipped off, as shred of cloth; (also **press** ~) item clipped from newspaper etc.

clique (klēk, klĭk) *n.* Small exclusive party, set, coterie. **cliqu'ish, cliqu'ey, cliqu'y** *adjs.*

clit·o·ris (klĭt'orĭs, klī'to-) *n.* Rudimentary erectile organ of female genitals, homologue of penis.

Clive (klīv), **Robert, Baron Clive of Plassey** (1725–74). English soldier and statesman in the service of the East India Company; avenged the Black Hole of Calcutta at the battle of Plassey, 1757; became governor of Bengal, 1758.

clo·a·ca (klōā'ka) *n.* (pl. **-cae** pr. -sē). 1. Sewer. 2. Common excretory cavity at end of intestinal canal in birds, reptiles, etc. **clo·a'cal** *adj.*

cloak (klōk) *n.* Loose usu. sleeveless outer garment; (fig.) covering, pretense, pretext; ~-**and-dagger**, involving esp. dramatic events of intrigue and espionage; **cloak'room**, room in which coats, hats, etc., may be left temporarily, as in a theater, school, etc. **cloak** *v.t.* Cover with, wrap in, cloak; conceal, disguise.

clob·ber (klŏb'er) *v.t.* (slang) Thrash; defeat decisively; criticize severely.

cloche (klōsh, klawsh, klŏsh) *n.* 1. Bell-shaped glass vessel for

*The urge to **climb** to the top of natural obstacles, such as mountains, is one experienced by adventurous people of many ages, but it was not until the 19th century that the urge developed into a sport of international dimensions.*

Before the mid-17th century the ***clock*** *was an inaccurate instrument for measuring time. This highly wrought silver and gilt case is by Hans Conrad Breghtel, c. 1600 (left).*
As the skills of the clock-makers grew, some produced elaborate astrological timekeepers (above left) showing the relationship of the planets, as in this clock in Prague in Czechoslovakia. The invention of the pendulum by Galileo was adopted by clock-makers after the mid-17th century. This winged lantern clock has a pendulum with a bob shaped like an anchor (far left).
By the late 17th century, cabinet-makers and clock-makers joined their crafts to make fine long-case clocks. This one is by A. C. Cooper, and was made c. 1850 (above).

covering plants, food, etc. 2. Woman's close-fitting, bell-shaped hat.

clock[1] (klŏk) *n.* 1. Time-measuring instrument consisting of train of wheels set in motion by weights, spring, electricity, etc., actuating and regulated by a pendulum, balance wheel, quartz crystal, etc., and recording hours, minutes, etc., usu. by movement of hands on a dial or displayed figures; clocklike device showing readings on a dial; **against the ~**, against a time limit; **put the ~ back**, move hands of clock to earlier position; (fig.) revert to earlier state of affairs. 2. Downy seed head of dandelion etc. 3. **~ watcher**, employee who watches assiduously for time of end of working day; **clock'wise**, moving like hands of a clock, in curve from left to right as seen from center; **clock'work**, mechanism of clock, mechanism similar to this for driving toys etc.; (attrib.) regular, mechanical, driven by clockwork; **like clockwork**, regularly, automatically. **clock** *v.* Time by the clock; attain (time or speed) in a race; register on clock or dial; **~ in, out**, register arrival, departure at factory, office, etc. by means of a time clock.

clock[2] (klŏk) *n.* Ornamental pattern on side of stocking or sock near the ankle.

clod (klŏd) *n.* Lump of earth etc.; blockhead; **clod'hopper**, bumpkin, lout. **clod'dish** *adj.* **clod'dish·ly** *adv.* **clod'dish·ness** *n.* **clod'dy** *adj.* (**-di·er, -di·est**).

clog (klŏg) *n.* 1. Block of wood fastened to animal's leg to impede motion; encumbrance, hindrance. 2. Heavy wooden-soled shoe. ~ *v.* (**clogged, clog·ging**). 1. Fetter or confine with clog; be encumbrance to, burden, impede, hamper. 2. Stop up; fill up with impeding matter; cease to function or function badly from being stopped up.

cloi·son·né (kloizonā', klaw-) *adj.* & *n.* (Enamel) of which different colors have been applied between thin metal plates laid on edge on foundation (cf. CHAMPLEVÉ).

clois·ter (kloi'ster) *n.* 1. Convent, monastery. 2. Covered walk or arcade of monastery, college, large church, often running around open court of quadrangle with plain wall on outer side and colonnade or windows on inner. **clois'tered** *adj.* Monastic; sheltered; secluded. **clois·tral** (kloi'stral) *adj.*

clone (klōn) *n.* 1. (bot.) Group of cultivated plants the individuals of which are transplanted parts of one original seedling or stock. 2. (biol.) Individual or group of individuals produced asexually from and genetically identical with one ancestor. ~ *v.t.* (**cloned, clon·ing**). Propagate as clone.

close[1] (klōs) *adj.* 1. Narrow, confined, contracted; covered, concealed; secret; niggardly; restricted. 2. Near; dense, compact; in or nearly in contact; fitting exactly; intimate; nearly equal; concentrated. 3. Sultry; ill-ventilated. 4. (of vowel) Pronounced with tongue near the palate. 5. **~ call**, (colloq.) narrow escape from death; **close'fisted**, niggardly; **close harmony**, singing of parts within octave or twelfth; **close-hauled**, (naut.) with sails hauled close, so as to sail as near the wind as possible; **close-mouthed**, reticent; **close order**, (mil.) arrangement of men in line with only slight gaps between them; **close quarters**, immediate contact with opponent or enemy; uncomfortable proximity; **close shave**, (fig.) narrow escape from accident; **close-up**, (phot.) picture taken at close range or with a telephoto lens so as to show persons etc. on large scale. **close'ly** *adv.* **close'ness** *n.* **close** *adv.* So as to be close. ~ *n.* Enclosed space; precincts of cathedral; (Scottish) narrow lane or alley.

close[2] (klōz) *v.* (**closed, clos·ing**). 1. Shut; (of place of business etc.) declare, be declared, not open; **closed circuit**, (elect.) circuit providing uninterrupted endless path for the flow of current; (television) circuit transmitting signal to restricted set of receivers;

*The Chinese produced **cloisonné** enameled work, such as this early Ming twin-cylinder case, of outstanding craftsmanship. The reservoirs of enamel are on a copper base.*

*By the 11th century the **cloister** had become an established part of the monastery. This fine Romanesque cloister is in St. Trophine's Church at Arles in France.*

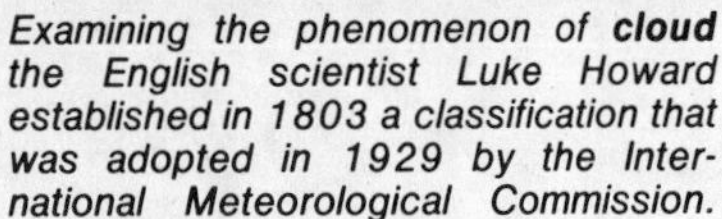

*Examining the phenomenon of **cloud** the English scientist Luke Howard established in 1803 a classification that was adopted in 1929 by the International Meteorological Commission.*

Top: Cirrus is a high cloud of feathery, delicate plumes. It often portends fine weather. Left: Altocumulus is a low cloud formation arranged in thick rolling masses. Above: Nimbus is a low, rain-bearing cloud. In its towering development cumulonimbus may assume an anvil shape and produce thunderstorms.

closed season, period during which it is unlawful to take certain specified game or fish; **closed shop**, industrial or other concern in which the employees are obliged to belong to one particular trade union. 2. Be boundary of, conclude; bring or come to an end; complete, settle. 3. Bring or come into contact; close gap(s) in rank, series, etc.; come within striking distance, grapple *with*; (naut.) approach, come alongside of. 4. ~ **down**, close finally, end business etc.; (of transmitting) cease to broadcast; ~ **in**, enclose, come nearer; **close'out**, sale of goods when a firm is going out of business or discontinuing certain kinds of merchandise; **close up**, block, fill, fill gaps (in), coalesce; move closer to; shut (place of business, etc.). **close** *n.* Conclusion, end.

clos·et (klŏz'ĭt) *n.* Small room (archaic); small storage room, cabinet; toilet. ~ *adj.* Not public, secret. ~ *v.t.* Shut up or detain in private room as for conference etc.

clo·sure (klō'zh*er*) *n.* 1. Closing, closed condition. 2. Var. of CLOTURE.

clot (klŏt) *n.* Mass of material stuck together; semisolid lump of coagulated liquid, esp. blood. ~ *v.* (**clot·ted, clot·ting**). Form into clots; **clotted cream**, thick cream obtained by scalding milk.

cloth (klawth, klŏth) *n.* (pl. **cloths** pr. klawdhz, klawths, klŏdhz, klŏths). (Piece, used for any purpose, of) woven or felted stuff; covering for table, esp. at meals; woolen woven fabric as used for clothes; ~ **of gold, silver**, tissue of gold or silver threads interwoven with silk or wool; **the** ~, the clergy.

clothe (klōdh) *v.t.* (**clothed** or **clad, cloth·ing**). Provide with clothes, put clothes upon; cover like or as with clothes or a cloth.

clothes (klōz, klōdhz) *n.pl.* Wearing apparel, dress; **clothes'-bag, clothes'basket**, bag, basket, for dirty or newly washed linen; **clothes'horse**, frame on which laundry is hung for drying; person overly concerned with dressing fashionably; **clothes'line**, rope, wire, etc. for hanging wash up to dry; **clothes'pin**, forked peg or clip for fastening wash to clothesline.

cloth·ier (klōdh'y*er*, -ē*er*) *n.* One who makes or sells clothing or cloth.

cloth·ing (klō'dhĭng) *n.* (esp.) Clothes collectively.

Clo·tho (klō'thō). (Gk. myth.) One of the three Fates, who spun the thread of life.

clo·ture (klō′cher) *n.* In legislative bodies, decision by vote or under rules to end debate and vote on the question. ~ *v.t.* (**-tured, -tur·ing**). Apply cloture to (motion, speakers, etc.).

cloud (klowd) n. 1. Visible mass of condensed water vapor floating in air at some distance above general surface of ground; **in the ~s**, deep in reverie, dreamy, impractical; **on ~ nine**, (slang) extremely happy. 2. Unsubstantial or fleeting thing; mass of smoke or dust; local dimness or obscurity in otherwise clear or transparent thing; innumerable body of insects, birds, horsemen, arrows, moving together; obscurity, anything obscuring or concealing; (anything causing) state of gloom, trouble, suspicion, etc.; darkening of countenance; **under a ~**, under suspicion; out of favor; deep in reverie, dreamy, impractical. 3. **cloud′burst**, violent rainstorm; **cloud chamber**, (phys.) apparatus containing water vapor, esp. one through which charged particles are passed and become identifiable after condensation of vapor. **cloud** *v.* Overspread, darken, with clouds, gloom, or trouble; variegate with vague patches of color or opacity; become overcast or gloomy. **cloud′less** *adj.* **cloud′less·ly** *adv.* **cloud′y** *adj.* (**cloud·i·er, cloud·i·est**). **cloud′i·ly** *adv.* **cloud′i·ness** *n.*

*The **clown** often combines the skills of juggler, acrobat and knockabout comedian. Above: The traditional white-faced make-up derives from the clown's origins in the harlequinade.*

clout (klowt) *n.* 1. (archaic and dial.) Patch; cloth; rap, knock, blow. 2. (colloq.) Influence (esp. political). ~ *v.t.* (archaic and dial.) Mend, patch; cuff heavily.

clove[1] (klōv) *n.* One of the small bulbs making up compound bulb of garlic, shallot, etc.

clove[2] (klōv) *n.* Dried flower bud of a tropical tree (*Eugenia aromatica*), used as a pungent aromatic spice; the tree itself; ~ **pink**, clove-scented species of pink (*Dianthus caryophyllus*), the original of the carnation and other cultivated forms. [Fr. *clou de girofle*; *girofle* was orig. name of the spice; *clou* (L. *clavus* nail) was used of it with ref. to its shape]

clove (klōv) **hitch.** Way of fastening rope around spar etc., formed by passing rope around twice in such a way that both ends pass under center part of loop in front. [old past part. of CLEAVE[1]]

clo·ven (klō′ven) *adj.*: see CLEAVE[1]; (esp.) ~ **hoof**, divided hoof of ruminant quadrupeds, ascribed in pagan mythology to Pan, and thence in Christian mythology to the Devil.

clo·ver (klō′ver) *n.* Any plant of the genus *Trifolium*, having compound leaves with usu. three leaflets and tight heads of small flowers; largely cultivated for fodder; **in ~**, in ease and luxury; **clo′verleaf**, highway interchange resembling four-leaf clover.

Clo·vis I (klō′vĭs) (466?–511). King of the Franks, 481–511; overthrew Romans; endeavored to unite all Franks into one kingdom.

clown (klown) *n.* 1. Rustic, lout. 2. Jester, esp. in pantomime or circus with loose baggy garments and painted face. ~ *v.* Play the clown, act like a clown, perform farcically.

clown·ish (klow′nĭsh) *adj.* Of or like a clown; rustic, boorish. **clown′ish·ly** *adv.* **clown′ish·ness** *n.*

cloy (kloi) *v.t.* Satiate, weary, by richness, sweetness, or excess.

club (klŭb) *n.* 1. Heavy stick with one thick end, esp. as weapon; stick with crooked (and usu. thickened) end used in various games, esp. golf. 2. (Playing card with) black trefoil(s); (pl.) suit of these cards. 3. Association of

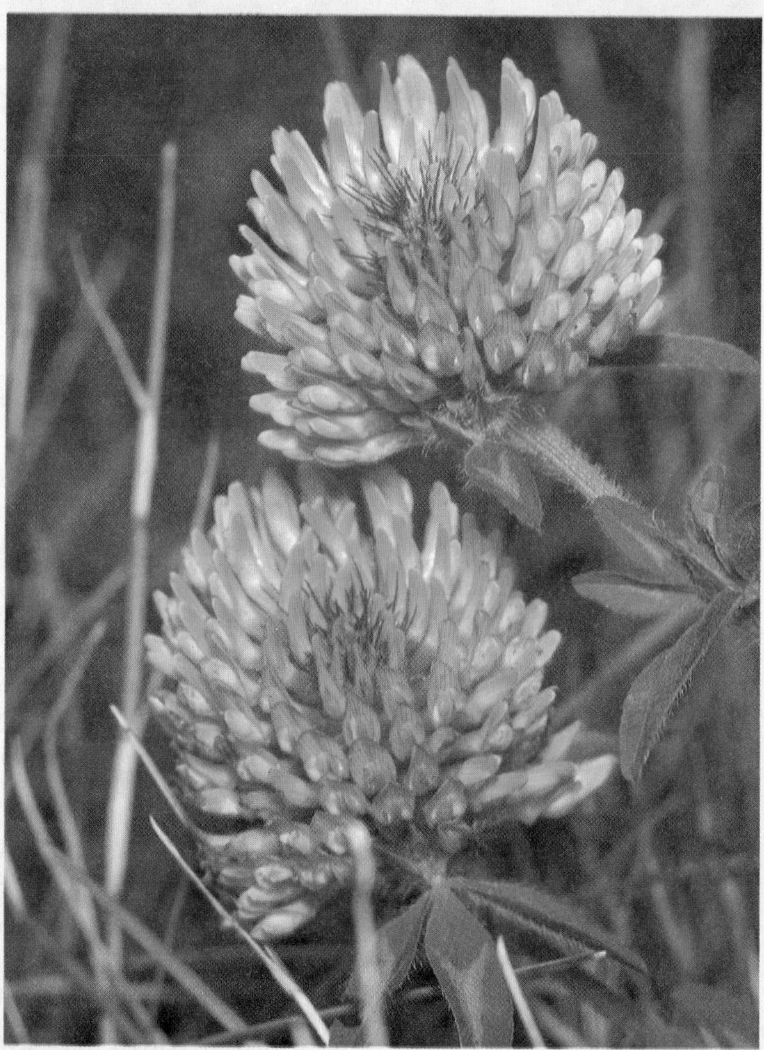

*Originating in Europe, with over 300 known species, **clover** is now grown as fodder throughout the temperate regions of the world.*

*The River **Clyde** flows for about 100 miles to pour into the sea through the Firth of Clyde. On its north bank lies Clydebank, an area important for ship-building.*

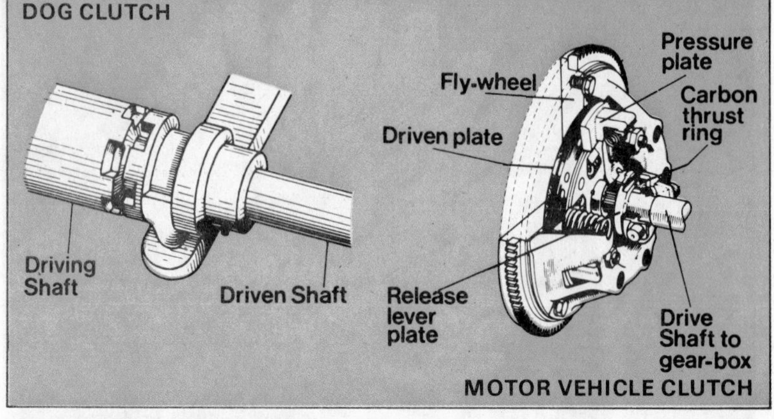

*It is common practice to use a **clutch** to connect the drive wheels of a vehicle with the engine. The operation of a clutch allows the driver to apply the engine power to the wheels gradually.*

persons with some common interest meeting periodically; body of persons combined for social purposes and having premises for meals, temporary residence, etc.; **club'house**, premises used by club. 4. **club'foot**, any of various (usu. congenital) distortions giving foot a stunted lumpy appearance; **club moss**, herb (*Lycopodium clavatum*) with clublike upright fertile spikes of spore cases; any species of evergreen plant *Lycopodium*; **club sandwich**, one containing three layers of bread (often toasted) with two fillings; **club soda**: see SODA. **club** *v.* (**clubbed, club·bing**). 1. Beat with club; use butt of (gun) as club. 2. (archaic) Bring, come, into a mass. 3. Combine *together*, or *with* others, in joint action.

cluck (klŭk) *n.* 1. Abrupt hollow guttural sound made by hen desiring to sit or calling her brood together; any similar sound. 2. Dull-witted person. ~ *v.i.* Make cluck.

clue (klo͞o) *n.* Anything that points the way, indicates a solution, or puts one on track of a discovery; sentence or phrase indicating word(s) to be inserted in crossword puzzle; clew.

clump (klŭmp) *n.* Cluster *of* trees or shrubs; cluttered mass; lump. ~ *v.* Tread or move heavily and clumsily; plant in clump; keep or mass together. **clump'y** *adj.* (**clump·i·er, clump·i·est**).

clum·sy (klŭm'zē) *adj.* (**-si·er, -si·est**). Awkward in movement or shape, ungainly; ill-contrived; tactless. **clum'si·ly** *adv.* **clum'si·ness** *n.*

clus·ter (klŭs'ter) *n.* Group of similar things, esp. such as grow together, bunch; swarm, group, of persons, stars, etc. ~ *v.* Bring, come, into cluster; be in cluster.

clutch[1] (klŭch) *v.* Seize eagerly, grasp tightly; snatch *at*. ~ *n.* 1. Tight grasp; (pl.) grasping hands, cruel grasp. 2. (mech.) Device enabling engine or driving parts of machine to be connected to or disconnected from the driven parts; (also ~ **pedal**) pedal operating this. 3. Small purse or handbag without a strap or handle. 4. (esp. sports) Critical moment or situation.

clutch[2] (klŭch) *n.* Set of eggs; brood of chickens.

clut·ter (klŭt'*er*) *n.* Crowded confusion, confused mass. ~ *v.t.* Litter, strew untidily *with*, crowd with disorderly assemblage of things.

Clyde (klīd). River in SW. Scotland flowing north to the Firth of Clyde; **Firth of** ~, an inlet of the Atlantic Ocean in SW.

Above: The ***coach*** *and harness collection kept in the Royal Mews at Buckingham Palace, London, is one of the finest. It includes this so-called glass coach.*

The stage coach was much used as a form of public transport in 18th and 19th century England. Right: The Victorian Royal Mail coach had space for passengers and baggage on top.

Scotland.

Clydes·dale (klīdz′dāl) *n.* One of a breed of large, powerful draft horses orig. bred in the Clyde River valley, Scotland.

clys·ter (klĭs′t*e*r) *n.* (archaic) Enema.

Cly·tem·nes·tra (klītemnĕs′-tr*a*). (Gk. legend) Daughter of Tyndareus, king of Sparta, and Leda; wife of AGAMEMNON.

Cm *symbol.* Curium.

cm, cm. *abbrevs.* Centimeter(s).

Cmdr. *abbrev.* Commander.

CNO *abbrev.* Chief of Naval Operations.

Cnut (k*e*nōōt′, -nūt′) = CANUTE.

CO *abbrev.* Commanding officer; conscientious objector; Colorado.

Co *symbol.* Cobalt.

Co. *abbrev.* Company; county.

co- *prefix.* 1. Jointly, mutually; joint, mutual. 2. (math.) Of the complement; complement of.

c/o *abbrev.* Care of.

coach (kōch) *n.* 1. Large closed carriage with four wheels. 2. Railroad passenger car. 3. Low-priced class of passenger accommodation on train or plane. 4. Bus, esp. a long-distance one. 5. Private tutor preparing candidate for examination; instructor or trainer of athletic team; trainer of singers, actors, etc. 6. **coach′man**, driver of coach or carriage; **coach′work**, (Brit.) bodywork. **coach** *v.* Train, tutor; study *with* a tutor.

co·ad·ju·tor (kōăj′*uter*, kō*a*jōō′-t*e*r) *n.* Helper, assistant, esp. one assisting a bishop.

co·ag·u·late (kōăg′y*u*lāt) *v.t.* (**-lat·ed, -lat·ing**). Convert, be converted, from fluid to more or less solid state; clot, curdle, set.

co·ag′u·lant *n.* Coagulating agent. **co·ag·u·la·tion** (kōăgy*u*lā′sh*o*n) *n.* **co·ag′u·la·ble** *adj.*

coal (kōl) *n.* Black or blackish sedimentary rock consisting mainly of carbonized plant tissue, found in seams or beds and used as fuel; (pl.) pieces of coal; pieces of glowing, burned, or charred coal, wood, etc; **carry ~s to Newcastle**, bring superfluous goods etc.; **haul over the ~s**, reprimand; **~-black**, completely black; **~ dust**, powdered coal; **~ field**, district with series of coal strata; **~ gas**, mixture of gases (mainly hydrogen and methane) produced by destructive distillation of coal and used for lighting and heating; ~ **mine**, mine in which coal is dug; ~ **oil**, kerosene; ~ **tar**, thick black viscous liquid, a product of destructive distillation of coal, used to make dyes, drugs, paint, roofing, organic chemicals, etc.

coal·er (kō'l*er*) *n.* Ship, train, truck carrying or supplying coal.

co·a·lesce (kō*a*lĕs') *v.i.* (**-lesced, -lesc·ing**). Come together and form one; combine in coalition. **co·a·les'cence** *n.* **co·a·les'cent** *adj.*

co·a·li·tion (kō*a*lĭsh'*o*n) *n.* Union, fusion; (government by) temporary combination of political parties. **co·a·li'tion·ist** *n.* & *adj.*

coam·ing (kō'mĭng) *n.* (naut.) Raised border around hatches and scuttles etc. to keep out water.

coarse (kōrs, kōrs) *adj.* Common, inferior; rough, loose, or large in texture, grain, or features; not delicate, unrefined; vulgar; obscene. **coarse'ly** *adv.* **coarse'ness** *n.* **coars'en** (kōr's*e*n, kōr'-) *v.t.* & *v.i.* Make, become, coarse.

coast (kōst) *n.* 1. Border of land near sea, seashore; **the ~ is clear**, the danger is over, the way is open; **C~ Guard**, military service under the Dept. of Transportation in peacetime, when it is responsible for protecting lives and property at sea, enforcing revenue, immigration, and navigation laws, and maintaining aids to navigation; in wartime it may aid the U.S. Navy with convoy duty, amphibious landing operations, etc.; (~ **guard**) any similar naval or military organization or (also **coast'guardsman**) member of such an organization; **coast'line**, configuration of coast. 2. Downhill ride on bicycle etc. without pedaling, or in car etc. with engine idling or not running. **coast'ward, coast'wards** *advs.* **coast'wise** *adj.* & *adv.* **coast** *v.i.* 1. Sail along coast, trade between ports on same coast. 2. Slide downhill on sled etc.; ride downhill on bicycle without pedaling, or in car with engine idle or off.

coast·al (kōs't*a*l) *adj.* Of, on, pertaining to, the coast.

coast·er (kōs't*er*) *n.* 1. (esp.) Vessel employed in coasting. 2. Small dish or mat placed under a glass to protect table top. 3. Person who coasts.

coat (kōt) *n.* 1. Sleeved outer garment opening at the front and covering the body from the shoulders to the waist or below. 2. Natural covering compared to garment; beast's hair, fur, etc.; covering membrane etc. of organ; skin, rind, husk; layer of bulb etc.; covering of paint etc. laid on at one time. 3. ~ **hanger**, shaped frame, hanging by central hook, on which coat etc. is draped; ~ **of arms**, tabard or surcoat blazoned with heraldic arms; heraldic insigne; **coat'tail**, hanging part of back of a man's jacket or coat; **on someone's coattails**, undeservedly benefiting from another's progress etc. **coat'less** *adj.* **coat** *v.t.* Provide with coat; cover with surface layer or coating.

*The intelligent and lively **coati** is found in the forests of Central and South America. Its partly prehensile tail helps it to keep its balance when climbing trees.*

co·a·ti (kōah'tē) *n.* (pl. **-tis**). (also **co·a·ti-mun·di** pr. kōah'tēmŭn'dē) Amer. plantigrade carnivorous mammal of the genus *Nasua*, resembling civet and raccoon, with long flexible snout and long tail.

coat·ing (kō'tĭng) *n.* (esp.) Layer of paint etc.; material for coats.

co·au·thor (kōaw'th*er*, kō'aw-) *n.* & *v.t.* (Be) joint author (of).

coax (kōks) *v.* Persuade by blandishments, wheedle; manipulate (tool etc.) gently.

co·ax·i·al (kōăk'sē*a*l), **co·ax·al** (kōăk's*a*l) *adjs.* (math.) Having a common axis; ~ **cable**, high-frequency television, telephone, and telegraph cable comprising an enclosed and insulated conducting tube surrounding a central insulated conducting core.

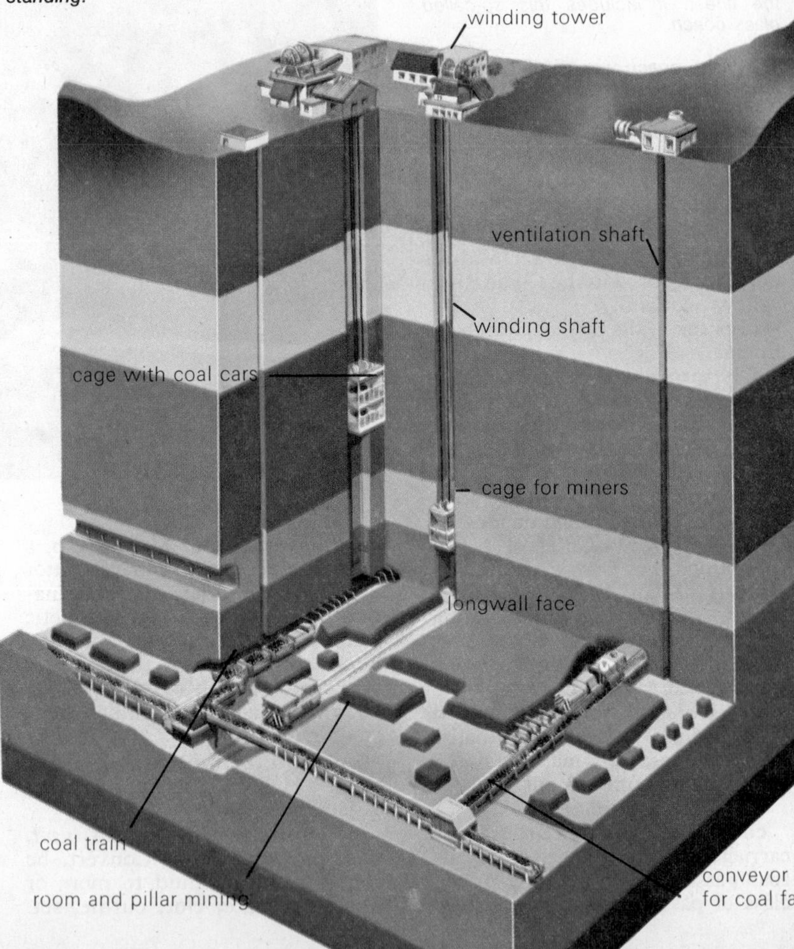

*Below: Air circulates around a **coal mine** by means of a large fan which sucks used air out, drawing fresh air down another shaft. In this mine the roof is held up by 'posts' of coal left standing.*

Opposite: Self-propelling roof-support systems are applied in the 'short wall' mining technique at Corrimal mine in New South Wales, Australia, and elsewhere.

*Found in Africa and Asia, the **cobra** is a highly poisonous snake. The king cobra may grow to 18 ft. in length. It is the smaller Egyptian cobra that is used by snake charmers.*

cob (kŏb) *n.* 1. Male swan. 2. Stout short-legged riding horse. 3. Roundish lump of coal etc. 4. Corncob.

co·balt (kō´bawlt) *n.* 1. (chem.) Silver-white malleable slightly magnetic metallic element; symbol Co, at. no. 27, at. wt. 58.9332; radioactive form of this, extensively used in radiotherapy. 2. Deep blue pigment (~ **blue**), a mixed oxide of cobalt and aluminum. [Ger. *kobold* goblin haunting mines]

co·bal·tite (kō´bawltīt, kōbawl´-tīt) *n.* Silver-white mineral with brilliant metallic luster.

Cobb (kŏb), **Ty**(**rus**) **Raymond** (1886–1961), "the Georgia Peach." Baseball player for Detroit and Philadelphia; established many batting, scoring, and base-stealing records.

cob·ble[1] (kŏb´*el*) *n.* (also **cob´-blestone**) Water-worn rounded stone, esp. of suitable size for paving. **cobble** *v.t.* (**-bled, -bling**). Pave with cobblestones.

cob·ble[2] (kŏb´*el*) *v.t.* (**-bled, -bling**). Make or mend (shoes or boots); make clumsily, bungle.

cob·bler (kŏb´l*er*) *n.* 1. One whose business is mending shoes. 2. (archaic) Clumsy workman or mender, botcher. 3. Iced drink or punch of wine or liquor, sugar, and lemon. 4. Deep-dish fruit pie with thick top crust.

co·bel·lig·er·ent (kōbelĭj´*er*ent) *adj.* & *n.* (Nation) waging war along with another.

Co·blenz (kō´blĕnts). City at the junction of the Rhine and Moselle Rivers in West Germany.

COBOL (kō´bōl, -bawl) *n.* Computer language for writing programs, esp. in business operations that process large amounts of uniformly related data. [*co*(mmon) *b*(usiness) *o*(riented) *l*(anguage)]

co·bra (kō´br*a*) *n.* Venomous snake of genus *Naja*, found in S. Asia and Africa, able to dilate its neck into a hoodlike shape when excited; esp. the **king** ~ or HAMADRYAD of India (*N. hannah*), largest of all venomous snakes, which may attain a length of more than 15 feet (5.5 m). [Port. *cobra de capello* snake with hood (L. *colubra* snake)]

cob·web (kŏb´wĕb) *n.* 1. Web or fine network spun by spider for capture of its prey; single thread of this. 2. Anything frail or flimsy; any musty accumulation, obstruction, etc., which ought to be swept away, like dusty cobwebs in a neglected room. **cob´web·by** *adj.*

co·ca (kō´k*a*) *n.* S. Amer. shrub (*Erythroxylon coca*) with leaves containing cocaine and related alkaloids; dried leaves of this chewed by people of the Andes as a stimulant.

co·caine, co·cain (kōkān´, kō´kān) *ns.* Alkaloid obtained from coca leaves and young twigs, used as local anesthetic, stimulant, etc. **co·cain·ism** (kōkā´nĭz*e*m, kō´k*a*-) *n.* (Chronic condition produced by) habitual use of cocaine.

coc·cus (kŏk´*u*s) *n.* (pl. **coc·ci** pr. kŏk´sī). Spherical bacterium.

coc·cyx (kŏk´sĭks) *n.* (pl. **coc·cy·ges** pr. kŏk´sĭjēz, **coc·cix·-es**). Small triangular bone ending spinal column in man and some apes; analogous part in birds etc. **coc·cyg·e·al** (kŏksĭj´ēal) *adj.* [Gk. *kokkux* cuckoo (f. resemblance to cuckoo's bill)]

Co·chin (kō´chĭn´). City in SW. India on the Malabar coast; founded by Vasco de Gama, 1502, first European settlement in India.

Co·chin-Chi·na (kō´chĭn-chī´-n*a*, kŏch´ĭn). Former French colony, part of Indochina; now part of Vietnam.

coch·i·neal (kŏch*i*nēl´, kŏch´-*i*nēl) *n.* Red dye prepared from dried bodies of the female of the insect *Dactylopius coccus*, found on cactuses in Mexico etc.; this insect.

Co·chise (kōchēs´, -chēz´) (1815?–1874). Amer. Apache chief and Indian leader.

coch·le·a (kŏk´lēa, kō´klē*a*) *n.* Spiral cavity of internal ear. [L., = "snail"]

cock[1] (kŏk) *n.* 1. Male of common domestic fowl (*Gallus domesticus*); male of other birds. 2. Spout, short pipe, with device for controlling flow of liquid or gas; lever in firearm raised ready to be released by trigger; cocked position or state; way of cocking hat to side; **at full** ~, with cock raised ready for firing. 3. ~**-and-bull story**, incredible tale; **cock´fighting**, setting cocks to fight as sport; **cock of the walk**, (fig.) leader, head, chief person; **cocks´comb**, cock's crest. **cock** *v.* 1. Raise cock or hammer of (gun) in readiness for firing. 2. Erect, stick, or tilt *up* jauntily or defiantly; ~ **one's ears**, listen attentively; ~ **one's hat**, set it jauntily on one side; turn up brim of hat.

*The **cockatoo** is a crested parrot found in Australia. There are several varieties, their plumage ranging from white, yellows and pinks to black.*

cock[2] (kŏk) *n.* Small conical heap of hay or straw in field. ~ *v.t.* Heap (hay or straw) in cocks.

cock·ade (kŏkād´) *n.* Rosette etc. worn in hat as badge. **cock·ad´ed** *adj.*

cock·a·leek·ie (kŏk*a*lē´kē) *n.* Scotch cream soup of chicken and leeks.

cock·a·ma·mie (kŏk*a*mā´mē, kŏk´*a*mā-) *adj.* (slang). 1. Worthless, fake. 2. Nonsensical, absurd.

cock·a·too (kŏk´*a*tōō, kŏk*a*tōō´) *n.* (pl. **-toos**). Any of various parrots of the genus *Kakatoe*, of Australia and E. Ind. islands, with movable crest or tuft of feathers on head. [Malay *kakatua*]

cock·a·trice (kŏk´*a*trĭs) *n.* Mythical monster, half cock and half serpent, supposedly able to kill with a glance.

cock·chaf·er (kŏk´chāf*er*) *n.* Large European pale-brown beetle (*Melolontha melolontha*), flying by night with loud whirring sound.

Cock·croft (kŏk´krawft, -krŏft), **Sir John Douglas** (1897–1967). British physicist; joint winner of Nobel Prize for physics, 1951, for pioneer work on transmutation of atomic nuclei by artificially accelerated atomic particles.

cocked (kŏkt) *adj.*: see COCK[1] *v.*; ~ **hat**, hat with very wide brim permanently turned up at two or three places, esp. a three-cornered hat; tricorn.

cock·er·el (kŏk´*er*el, kŏk´*r*el) *n.* Young rooster.

cock·er (kŏk´*er*) **spaniel.** (Breed of) small dog with drooping ears and long, silky, slightly waved thick coat.

cock·eyed (kŏk′īd) *adj.* (slang) Cross-eyed; askew, crooked; (fig.) absurd; drunk.

cock·horse (kŏk′hors) *n.* Anything a child rides astride upon; rocking horse.

cock·le[1] (kŏk′*e*l) *n.* Plant (*Lychnis* or *Agrostemma githago*) with reddish-purple flowers and capsules of numerous black seeds, growing as weed in grain fields.

cock·le[2] (kŏk′*e*l) *n.* Bivalve mollusk of genus *C*~, esp. *C. edule*, common on sandy coasts and used for food; the shell or a valve of the shell, of this; (**warm**) **the ~s of the heart**, (delight) one's feelings; **cock′leshell**, shell of cockle; small frail boat. **cockle** *v.* (**-led, -ling**). Wrinkle, pucker.

cock·ney (kŏk′nē) *n.* (pl. **-neys**). (often **C**~) Native of the East End of London (strictly, one born within the sound of Bow Bells); London East End dialect. ~ *adj.* Of, characteristic of, cockneys. [orig. meaning "cock's egg," prob. a small or misshapen egg; later, "townsman"]

cock·pit (kŏk′pĭt) *n.* 1. Pit or enclosed area for cockfights; arena of any struggle. 2. (naut.) Open space or well in after part of small vessel, for helmsman, crew, etc. 3. Place for pilot etc. in fuselage of aircraft; place for driver in racing car.

cock·roach (kŏk′rōch) *n.* Nocturnal voracious dark-brown beetle-like insect of the order Blattaria, esp. of genus *Blatta* or *Periplaneta*, infesting kitchens etc.

cock·sure (kŏk′shoor′) *adj.* Absolutely certain *of*, *about*; self-confident, dogmatic, presumptuous. **cock′sure′ness** *n.*

cock·tail (kŏk′tāl) *n.* 1. Any of various chilled mixed drinks of liquor with fruit juice, bitters, or other flavorings; ~ **party**, party, usu. in the late afternoon or early evening before dinner, at which alcoholic drinks and canapés are served; ~ **shaker**, tall cuplike shaker with top, in which cocktails are vigorously shaken to mix them. 2. Appetizer such as cold seafood, fruit pieces, juice, etc. **cocktail** *adj.* Of, for a cocktail party, as ~ *dress*.

The tricorne or ***cocked hat*** *was first worn in Europe in the mid-18th century and taken up by American settlers until replaced by the top hat in the 19th century.*

cock·y (kŏk′ē) *adj.* (**cock·i·er, cock·i·est**). Cheerfully self-confident; conceited. **cock′i·ly** *adv.* **cock′i·ness** *n.*

co·co (kō′kō) *n.* (pl. **-cos**). (also **coconut palm**) Tropical palm tree (*Cocos nucifera*) producing the coconut.

co·coa (kō′kō) *n.* Powder produced by crushing and grinding

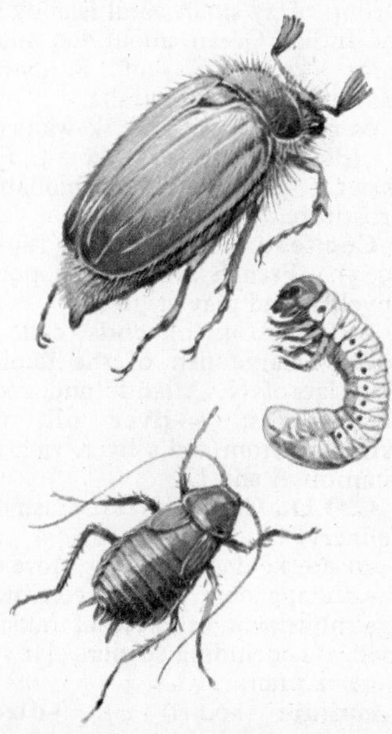

The ***cockchafer*** *is a large beetle often found on the leaves of European oaks in the day, and flying noisily at dusk. Left: the male is at the top of the illustration, the female below. Below: There are about 1,200 species of* ***cockroach***, *an orthopterous insect found in most parts of the world and especially abundant in the tropics.*

cacao seeds; beverage made by combining this powder with milk or water and sugar; ~ **bean**, cacao seed; ~ **butter**, fatty matter obtained from cacao seed. [corruption of CACAO, confused with COCO]

co·co·nut (kō′konŭt) *n.* Large ovate brown hard-shelled fruit of the coconut palm, with edible white lining and milky fluid (~ **milk**) filling the hollow center; ~ **fiber**, fiber of outer husk of coconut; ~ **palm** = COCO.

co·coon (kokōōn′) *n.* Case of silky thread spun by larvae of many insects to protect them in chrysalis state, esp. that spun by silkworm and used as source of silk; (fig.) protective covering. [Fr. *cocon*, f. mod. Provençal *coucoun* eggshell, cocoon, dim. of *coca* shell]

Co·cos (kō′kŏs, -kōs) **Islands.** Group of 27 small coral islands in the Indian Ocean, about 700 miles (1127 km) SW. of Sumatra; administered by Australia.

co·cotte (kōkŏt′; *Fr.* kawkawt′) *n.* (pl. **-cottes** pr. -kŏts′; *Fr.* -kawt′). (archaic) Fashionable prostitute.

Coc·teau (kŏktō′), **Jean** (1891–1963). French avant-garde poet, novelist, and playwright.

cod (kŏd) *n.* (pl. **cods**, collect. **cod**). Large fish of the family Gadidae of N. Atlantic and connected seas; ~**-liver oil**, oil extracted from cod's liver, rich in vitamins A and D.

C.O.D., COD *abbrevs.* Cash on delivery.

co·da (kō′da) *n.* (mus.) More or less independent passage concluding movement or piece of music; (ballet) concluding section. [It., f. L. *cauda* tail]

cod·dle (kŏd′el) *v.t.* (**-dled, -dling**). 1. Treat indulgently, baby. 2. Cook in water just below boiling point.

Most spiders have 3 pairs of spinnerets on their abdomens. With one pair they spin a special silk for their ***cocoons.*** *Their eggs are protected in the cocoon until hatched.*

code (kōd) *n.* 1. Systematic collection or digest of laws, rules and regulations, etc. 2. Set of conventional symbols used in transmitting messages by flags, telegraph, etc.; system, set, of words, figures, groups of letters, etc., used for other words or phrases, to ensure secrecy or brevity in messages or as system of reference; system of symbols used in computer etc.; also transf.; ~ **book**, list of signals, symbols, etc. used in a code; ~ **name**, ~ **number**, word or symbol, number, used for secrecy or convenience instead or ordinary name; **genetic** ~: see GENETIC. **code** *v.t.* (**cod·ed, cod·ing**). Convert into a code. **cod′er** *n.*

co·deine (kō′dēn) *n.* Alkaloid narcotic derived from opium, used as an analgesic, to relieve coughing, etc. [Gr. *kōdeia* poppy head]

co·dex (kō′dĕks) *n.* (pl. **co·di·ces** pr. kō′dĭsēz, kŏd′ĭ-). Manuscript volume, esp. of ancient texts.

codg·er (kŏj′er) *n.* (colloq.) Old man.

cod·i·cil (kŏd′isĭl) *n.* Supplement to will or agreement, altering, explaining, or revoking original contents. **cod·i·cil·la·ry** (kŏdisĭl′erē) *adj.*

cod·i·fy (kŏd′ifī, kō′di-) *v.t.* (**-fied, -fy·ing**). Reduce to a code or system. **cod·i·fi·ca·tion** (kŏdifĭkā′shon, kōdi-) *n.*

Co·dy (kō′dē), **William Frederick**: see BUFFALO BILL.

co·ed, co-ed (kō′ĕd, kōĕd′) *adjs.* Coeducational. ~ *n.* (colloq.) Girl or woman student in coeducational institution.

co·ed·u·ca·tion (kōĕjōōkā′shon) *n.* Education of both sexes together. **co·ed·u·ca′tion·al** *adj.*

co·ef·fi·cient (kōefĭsh′ent) *n.* (algebra) Number placed before and multiplying known or unknown quantity; (phys.) number expressing amount of some change or effect under certain conditions of temperature, pressure, etc. as ~ *of expansion.*

coe·la·canth (sē′lakănth) *n.* Fish of family Coelacanthidae with fleshy fin bases and narrow symmetrical tail, believed extinct since Cretaceous period until specimens (*Latimeria chalumnae*) were found in SE. Afr. seas in 1938 and later.

coe·len·ter·ate (sēlĕn′terāt, -rĭt) *adj.* & *n.* (Member) of phylum Coelenterata, comprising aquatic animals (mostly marine, including jellyfish, sea anemones, and corals) that have an intestinal canal but no separate true body cavity, usu. with

The abundant ***cod*** *is one of the foremost food fish of the seas. Cod are bottom feeders, eating mollusks, squid and small fish. Illustrated below, is an Australian reef cod.*

__Coelenterates__ are the lowest form of animal life that has definite tissue. The phylum includes polyps, corals and jellyfish such as the one—catylerhiza tuberculata—illustrated here.

stinging cells and showing radial symmetry.

coe·lom (sē′lom) *n.* (pl. **coe·loms, coe·lo·ma·ta** pr. sēlō′m*a*t*a*, -lŏm′*ata*). (zool.) Body cavity or space between intestinal canal and body wall.

co·e·qual (kōē′kw*a*l) *adj.* & *n.* Equal. **co·e′qual·ly** *adv.*

co·erce (kōẽrs′) *v.* (**-erced, -erc·ing**). Constrain into obedience etc.; use, secure by, force. **co·er·cion** (kōẽr′sh*o*n) *n.* Constraint, compulsion, government by force. **co·er·cive** (kōẽr′sĭv) *adj.*

co·es·sen·tial (kōĭsĕn′sh*a*l) *adj.* Of the same substance or essence.

Coeur d'Alene (kẽr d*a*lān′). Lake and resort area in N. Idaho.

Coeur de Lion (kẽr d*e* lēawṅ′). Lionhearted, epithet of RICHARD I.

co·e·val (kōē′v*a*l) *adj.* & *n.* (Person) of equal antiquity, of same age; contemporary. **co·e′val·ly** *adv.*

co·ex·ist (kōĭgzĭst′) *v.i.* Exist together or *with.* **co·ex·ist′ence** *n.* (esp. pol.) Peaceful existence side by side of nations professing different ideologies.

co·ex·ten·sive (kōĭkstĕn′sĭv) *adj.* Extending over same space, time, or scope.

C. of C. *abbrev.* Chamber of Commerce.

cof·fee (kaw′fē, kŏf′ē) *n.* Dark brown, slightly stimulating drink made from the shrub *Coffea arabica* by roasting and grinding its seeds and brewing them in boiling water;

Specimens of the __coelacanth,__ for long believed extinct, have been caught since a 5-ft. specimen was discovered in 1938. About 40 coelacanths have been found near Madagascar. The fish thrived in the Devonian period.

these seeds, the powder made by grinding them; the shrub itself, a native of eastern Asia and Africa, bearing fragrant white flowers and red fleshy berries each containing two seeds (~ **beans**); cup of coffee; light brown color; **cof′feecake,** cake or sweetened bread to be eaten with coffee, often containing raisins, nuts, or bits of candied fruit and covered with sugar or icing; **coffee grounds**, granular sediment in coffee after brewing; **cof'feehouse**, restaurant selling coffee etc., esp. in 17th and 18th c. when they were frequented for political and literary conversation etc.; **coffee klatsch, coffee klatch** (also **kaffee klatsch**), informal social gathering for coffee and conversation; **coffee mill**, contrivance for grinding roasted coffee beans; **cof'feepot**, percolator; pot in which coffee is made or served; **coffee shop**, small restaurant, esp. at a motel or hotel; **coffee table**, small low table. [Arab. *ḳahwa* the drink]

cof·fer (kaw'f*er*, kŏf'*er*) *n.* 1. Box, esp. strongbox for valuables etc.; funds; treasury. 2. (archit.) Sunk panel in ceiling or soffit. 3. (also **cof'ferdam**) Caisson. **coffer** *v.t.* Ornament with coffers.

cof·fin (kaw'fĭn, kŏf'ĭn) *n.* 1. Oblong box in which corpse is buried or cremated. 2. Horse's hoof; ~ **bone**, small spongy bone in horse's hoof, last phalangeal bone of foot. **coffin** *v.t.* Enclose in or as in coffin.

C. of S. *abbrev.* Chief of Staff.

cog (kŏg, kawg) *n.* One of a series of projections on wheel, bar, etc., transmitting or receiving motion by engaging with corresponding projections on another wheel etc.; ~ **railway**, (also **rack railway**) railway with a cogged center rail that engages with center cogwheel on locomotive, which thereby has enough traction to climb steep grades; **cog'wheel**, toothed wheel, wheel with cogs.

co·gent (kō'jent) *adj.* Forcibly convincing. **co'gen·cy** *n.* **co'gent·ly** *adv.*

cog·i·tate (kŏj'ĭtāt) *v.* (**-tat·ed, -tat·ing**). Ponder, meditate. **cog'i·ta·tor** *n.* **cog·i·ta·tion** (kŏjĭtā'sh*o*n) *n.* **cog'i·ta·tive** *adj.*

co·gnac (kōn'yăk, kŏn'-) *n.* Brandy produced in the vicinity of Cognac in western France. [*Cognac*, town in Charente]

cog·nate (kŏg'nāt) *adj.* 1. Descended from a common ancestor, esp., in Roman law; akin in origin, allied, related. 2. (of languages) Of the same linguistic stock; (of words) having the same root or origin, representing the same original word. ~ *n.* Cognate person; cognate word. **cog·na·tion** (kŏgnā'sh*o*n) *n.* Cognate relationship.

cog·ni·tion (kŏgnĭsh'*o*n) *n.* Action or faculty of knowing or acquiring knowledge (including sensation, conception, etc.) as dist. from feeling and volition. **cog·ni·tive** (kŏg'nĭtĭv) *adj.*

cog·ni·za·ble (kŏg'nĭz*a*bel, kŏgnī'z*a*-) *adj.* Perceptible, knowable; within jurisdiction of a court etc.

cog·ni·zance (kŏg'nĭz*a*ns) *n.* 1. Being aware; notice. 2. (Right of) dealing with a matter legally or judicially. 3. Distinguishing device or mark. **cog'ni·zant** *adj.* Having or taking cognizance; (philos.) having cognition.

cog·no·men (kŏgnō'm*e*n) *n.* (pl. **-no·mens, -nom·i·na** pr. -nŏm'-*i*n*a*). 1. Third or family name of Roman citizen, as Caius Julius *Caesar*; additional name or epithet bestowed on individual; nickname. 2. Family name; surname; name.

co·gno·scen·ti (kŏnyoshĕn'tē, kŏgno, kŏno-) *n.pl.* (sing. **-te** pr. -tē). Persons of superior taste or knowledge, connoisseurs. [It.]

co·hab·it (kōhăb'ĭt) *v.i.* Live together as husband and wife (freq. of persons not legally married). **co·hab'it·ant, co·hab·i·ta·tion** (kōhăbĭtā'sh*o*n) *ns.*

Co·han (kō'hăn), **George M(ichael)** (1878–1942). Amer. vaudeville performer, actor, songwriter, playwright, and producer; best known for his songs "I'm a Yankee Doodle Dandy," "You're a Grand Old Flag," "Give My Regards to Broadway," "Over There," etc.

co·heir (kō'âr'), **co·heir·ess** (kō'âr'ĭs) *ns.* Joint heir, masculine and feminine.

co·here (kōhēr') *v.i.* (**-hered, -her·ing**). Stick together, remain united; be consistent, well-knit.

co·her·ent (kōhēr'*e*nt) *adj.* Cohering; consistent, not rambling or inconsequent. **co·her'ent·ly** *adv.* **co·her'ence, co·her'en·cy** *ns.*

co·he·sion (kōhē'zh*o*n) *n.* Cohering; tendency to remain united; (chem.) molecular force of attraction between similar kinds of molecules (opp. ADHESION). **co·he·sive** (kōhē'sĭv) *adj.*

co·hort (kō'hŏrt) *n.* One of the ten divisions of a Roman legion, consisting of 300 to 600 men; band of warriors; group; (colloq.) associate, companion.

coif (koif) *n.* (hist.) Close cap covering top, back, and sides, of

*A **cog railway** carries tourists to the summit of Mt. Washington in New Hampshire's White Mountains. The center cog provides additional traction for the train.*

*Below: The evergreen bush that bears the **coffee** bean was probably native to Ethiopia. It grows well on well-drained volcanic soils that have over 15 ins. rainfall.*

Facing page: The husk of the coffee bean is chaffed in a simple machine. The beans are roasted before use so that the oil may be released and imparted to the eventual brew.

2
BENTALL

head.

coif·feur (kwahfēr′) *n.* (fem. **coif·feuse** pr. kwahföz′) Hairdresser. [Fr.]

coif·fure (kwahfūr′) *n.* Way hair is dressed; hair style.

coil (koil) *n.* Length of rope etc. wound continuously around one point; anything arranged thus; such arrangement; one turn of anything coiled; (elect.) helically-wound wire serving as conductor. ~ *v.* Dispose, wind, into circular or spiral shape.

coin (koin) *n.* Piece of metal of definite weight and value, made into money by being stamped with official device; coined money, money in circulation. ~ *v.t.* 1. Make (money) by stamping metal; make (metal) into coin. 2. Turn into money; ~ **money**, (colloq.) make or gain money quickly. 3. Fabricate, invent (esp. new word or phrase).

coin·age (koi′nĭj) *n.* (Right of) coining; coins collectively, currency; invention, fabrication; coined word.

co·in·cide (kōĭnsīd′) *v.i.* (**-cid·ed, -cid·ing**). Fall together and agree in position; (geom.) occupy same portion of space; occur at, occupy, same space of time; be identical, agree exactly.

co·in·ci·dence (kōĭn′sĭd*e*ns) *n.* (Instance of) coinciding; notable concurrence of events or circumstances without apparent causal connection. **co·in′ci·dent, co·in·ci·den·tal** (kōĭnsĭdĕn′t*a*l) *adjs.* **co·in·ci·den′tal·ly** *adv.*

co·i·tus (kō′ĭt*u*s, kōē′-) *n.* Insertion of penis into vagina and (usu.) ejaculation of semen. [L.]

coke[1] (kōk) *n.* Compact form of impure carbon obtained from coal by heating out of contact with air, used for smelting metals, for foundry work, as a fuel, etc. ~ *v.t.* (**coked, cok·ing**). Convert (coal) into coke.

coke[2] (kōk) *n.* (slang) Cocaine.

Coke (ko͝ok), **Sir Edward** (1552–1634). English jurist and adherent of common law; first Lord Chief Justice of England; prosecuted Essex and Raleigh, and Gunpowder Plot conspirators.

Col. *abbrev.* Colonel; Colorado.

col. *abbrev.* College; collegiate; colony; color; column.

co·la[1] (kō′l*a*) = KOLA.

co·la[2] (kō′l*a*) *n.* Any carbonated soft drink flavored with a syrup made from kola nuts or seeds.

col·an·der (kŭl′*a*nd*e*r, kŏl′-) *n.* Perforated container for straining water from foods after washing or cooking.

Col·bert (kawlbĕr′), **Jean Baptiste** (1619–83). French statesman; economic adviser to Louis XIV; founded the French

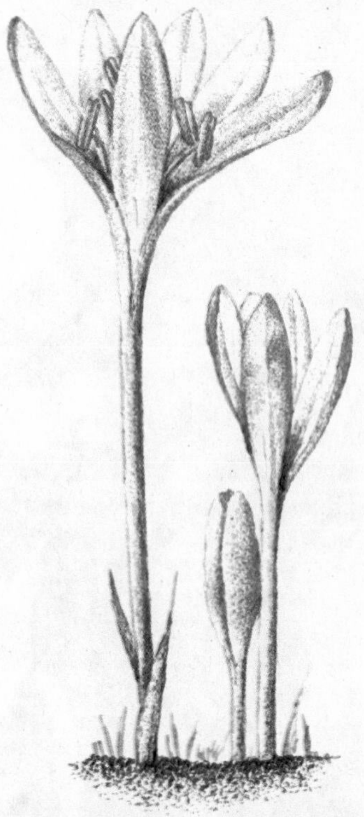

*The **Colchicum** autumnale (autumn crocus) is one of several species of crocus-like plants cultivated for pink, white or purple tube-shaped flowers. The stem contains a substance used to treat rheumatism and gout.*

*The oldest British footguards regiment, the **Coldstream Guards** was founded in 1659 at Coldstream in Scotland. The Coldstreams, prominent ceremonial troops, are highly trained infantrymen.*

*Works by the English Romantic poet **Samuel Taylor Coleridge** include 'The Rime of the Ancient Mariner' and 'Kubla Khan'. The latter was written under the influence of opium, to which he became addicted.*

The giant Roman amphitheater the ***Coliseum,*** *completed in A.D. 82, held about 50,000 spectators who watched gladiatorial combats from marble piers protected from the rain by movable awnings.*

Academies of Literature, Science, and the Fine Arts.

col·chi·cine (kŏl´chĭsēn, -sĭn, kŏl´kĭ-) *n.* Alkaloid ($C_{22}H_{25}O_6N$) derived from colchicum, used in plant breeding etc.

col·chi·cum (kŏl´chi*k*um, kŏl´-*ki*-) *n.* Liliaceous plant of genus *C*~ including autumn crocus; dried corm or seed of this, containing colchicine.

Col·chis (kŏl´kĭs). Ancient region on the Black Sea S. of the Caucasus Mountains; famous in Greek legend as the land of the Golden Fleece and the home of MEDEA.

cold (kōld) *adj.* 1. Of low temperature, esp. when compared with human body or with usual temperature; relatively without heat, not heated, having been allowed to cool; feeling cold. 2. Without ardor, friendliness, or affection; undemonstrative; apathetic; chilling, depressing; **leave** (**person**) ~, fail to excite him. 3. (of colors) Suggesting a cold or sunless day, esp. containing blue or gray. 4. (of hunting scent) Not strong, faint. 5. (in children's games) Far from the object sought, or from finding or guessing. 6. (colloq.) Unconscious. 7. **~-blooded**, (of fish and reptiles as dist. from other vertebrates) having blood whose temperature varies with that of the external air or water; (of persons, actions) unimpassioned, cool; unfeeling, callous; deliberately cruel; **in ~ blood**, without human feelings, deliberate and cruel; **~ cream**, cosmetic for skin; **~ cuts**, sliced cold cooked meats; **~ duck**, drink made by combining sparkling burgundy and champagne; **have, get, ~ feet**, (slang) become afraid; (**give the**) **~ shoulder**, (treat with) intentional coldness or indifference, snub; **~-shoulder** (*v.t.*); **~ sore**, sore caused by virus infection around the mouth, usu. accompanying a fever or head cold; **~ sweat**, simultaneous chill and perspiring as a result of shock, pain, fear, nervousness, etc.; **~ turkey**, (slang) abrupt withdrawal of narcotics from an addict; **~ war**, unfriendly relations between nations characterized by hostile propaganda etc. and threat of actual war; **~ water**, unheated water; chilled water; **throw ~ water on**, disparage, discourage. **cold'ly** *adv.* **cold'ness** *n.* **cold** *n.* 1. Prevalence of low temperature in the atmosphere; cold weather; sensation produced by loss of heat from the body. 2. Inflammatory condition of mucous membrane of nose and throat, with catarrh and freq. hoarseness and cough (freq. **head ~, ~ in the head**).

Cold·stream (kōld´strēm) **Guards.** British regiment of guards of the royal household; formed in 1659 at Coldstream on the Tweed, a river in Scotland.

cole (kōl) *n.* (rare exc. in comb.) Cabbage; see RAPE[2]; **cole'slaw**, salad of shredded raw cabbage with dressing.

co·le·op·ter·ous (kōlēŏp´t*e*r*u*s, kŏlē-) *adj.* Of the Coleoptera or beetles, a large order of insects having the front pair of wings converted into hard sheaths that cover the other pair when not in use.

co·le·op·tile (kōlēŏp´tĭl, kŏlē-) *n.* (bot.) Hollow organ produced by germinating grasses, inside which the first leaf makes its way to the ground surface.

Cole·ridge (kōl´rĭj), **Samuel Taylor** (1772–1834). English romantic poet and literary critic, one of the Lake poets (see LAKE[1]); author of "The Ancient Mariner," "Kubla Khan," "Christabel," etc.

Co·lette (kōlĕt´, kŏ-), **Sidonie Gabrielle** (1873–1954). French music hall performer and novelist; author of *Chéri*, *Gigi*, etc.

Col·fax (kōl´făks), **Schuyler** (1823–85). Vice president of the U.S. under Ulysses S. Grant, 1869–73.

col·ic (kŏl´ĭk) *n.* Severe spasmodic pain in belly and bowels. **col'ick·y** *adj.*

Col·i·se·um, Col·os·se·um (kŏl*i*sē´*u*m). 1. Amphitheater in Rome, begun by Vespasian in 72 A.D.; scene of gladiatorial combats and the martyrdom of many Christians. 2. (**c**~) Amphitheater for public entertainment, sports, etc.

co·li·tis (k*o*lī´tĭs) *n.* Inflammation of membrane of large intestine.

coll. *abbrev.* College; colloquial.

col·lab·o·rate (k*o*lăb´*o*rāt) *v.i.* (**-rat·ed, -rat·ing**). Work in combination (*with*) esp. on literary or artistic production; cooperate treasonably with the enemy (esp. in countries occupied by the Germans in World War II). **col·lab·o·ra·tion** (k*o*lăb*o*rā´sh*o*n) *n.* **col·lab·o·ra'tion·ist** *n.* Treacherous collaborator. **col·lab'o·ra·tor** *n.*

Schools such as Eton in Berkshire were called **colleges.** This indicated that the establishment provided secondary education — a social privilege in the U.K. until the 19th century.

The **collie,** a sheep-dog which is renowned for its loyalty and intelligence, has been used to herd sheep for over 300 years.

col·lage (k*o*lahzh′, kō-) *n.* Art form in which pieces of paper and other materials and objects are glued to the pictorial surface; such a work of art.

col·la·gen (kŏl′*a*j*e*n) *n.* Protein found in animal tissue and bone, which yields gelatin on boiling. **col·la·gen·ic** (kŏl*a*jĕn′ĭk) *adj.*

col·lapse (k*o*lăps′) *n.* 1. Falling in, sudden shrinking together, giving way; failure, breakdown. 2. Prostration by loss of nervous or muscular power; breakdown of mental energy, sudden loss of courage, spirits, etc. ~ *v.* (**-lapsed, -laps·ing**). 1. Fall together, give way, by external pressure, cave in; contract. 2. (Cause to) fail, break down, or come to nothing. **col·laps·i·bil·i·ty** (k*o*lăpsĭbĭl′ĭtē) *n.* **col·laps′i·ble** *adj.* Made to collapse or fold together.

col·lar (kŏl′*er*) *n.* 1. Part of garment encircling neck or forming turned-back upper border near the neck; band (often separate) of linen, lace, etc., worn around neck and completing upper part of costume. 2. Ornamental chain forming part of insigne of order of knighthood; band around neck of dog or other animal for identification or ornament; part of harness of draft animal, fitting over lower part of neck. 3. Restraining or connecting band, ring, pipe, etc., in machines etc. 4. **col′larbone**, bone connecting breastbone with shoulder blade, clavicle. **collar** *v.t.* Seize (person) by the collar, capture; (slang) lay hold of, seize, arrest (felon).

col·late (kŏlāt′, kō-, kŏl′āt, kō′lāt) *v.t.* (**-lat·ed, -lat·ing**). 1. Compare carefully and exactly (esp. copy of text *with* other or the original); (bookbinding) verify order of sheets of printed book by signatures; assemble in proper numerical or logical sequence. 2. Admit (a cleric) *to* a benefice.

col·lat·er·al (k*o*lăt′*e*ral) *adj.* 1. Situated or running side by side, parallel; subordinate but from same source; contributory; connected but aside from main subject, course, etc. 2. (opp. LINEAL) Descended from same stock but in a different line. ~ *n.* Collateral kinsman; security pledged as guarantee of repayment of loan. **col·lat′er·al·ly** *adv.*

col·la·tion (kŏlā′sh*o*n, kō-) *n.* 1. Collating; comparison; description of book or manuscript by signatures, list of contents, etc. 2. Light meal permitted on fast days; any light meal.

col·league (kŏl′ēg) *n.* Fellow member of a profession, faculty, staff, etc.; associate.

col·lect[1] (kŏl′ĕkt) *n.* Short prayer before the epistle in a communion service as appointed for particular day or season.

col·lect[2] (k*o*lĕkt′) *v.* Bring or come together, accumulate; gather (money) from a number of people, for charity, as taxes, etc.; make collection of (curiosities, rare books, etc.); regain control of, concentrate, recover (one's faculties etc., also oneself); (colloq.) call for and take away. **col·lect′ed** *adj.* (esp.) Bound together or similarly and sold as a single book or set, as ~ *works* of an author; not distracted, cool. **col·lect′ed·ly** *adv.* **col·lect′ed·ness** *n.*

col·lec·tion (k*o*lĕk′sh*o*n) *n.* 1. Collecting; money collected. 2. Set of things gathered together.

col·lec·tive (k*o*lĕk′tĭv) *adj.* Constituting a collection, gathered into one or into a whole, aggregate; of, from, a number of individuals taken or acting together, as in *people's* ~; common; ~ **bargaining**, negotiation between employer and union representatives to determine wages, hours, benefits, working conditions, etc.; ~ **farm**, in U.S.S.R., farm or group of farms organized as a unit and worked by a community under state supervision; ~ **noun**, singular noun (such as *class, jury*) used to denote a collection or number of individuals; ~ **security**, security for nations, obtained by trusting in united strength of an international organization for peace or of a group of allied nations; ~ **unconscious**: see UNCONSCIOUS. **col·lec'tive·ly** *adv.* **col·lec'tive** *n.* Collective noun; collective farm. **col·lec'-tiv·ism** *n.* Theory or practice of collective ownership or control of all means of production, esp. of land, by the whole community or nation. **col·lec'tiv·ist** *adj.* & *n.* **col·lec'tiv·ize** *v.t.* (**-ized, -iz·ing**). **col·lec·ti·vi·za·tion** (kolĕktĭvīzā'-shon) *n.*

col·lec·tor (kolĕk'ter) *n.* One who collects, esp. scientific specimens, curiosities, works of art, etc.; one who collects money for overdue bills, taxes, etc.

col·leen (kŏl'ēn, kŏlēn') *n.* (colloq.) Irish girl. [Ir. *caile* countrywoman]

col·lege (kŏl'ĭj) *n.* 1. Organized body of persons performing certain functions and sometimes possessing special rights and privileges; **Electoral C~**: see ELECTOR; **C~ of Cardinals**, body of all cardinals of the Roman Catholic Church, who constitute the pope's council and elect to the papacy. 2. Independent corporation of scholars within, or in connection with, a university (Brit.); similar organization outside a university; university; any school of higher education granting the bachelor's degree in liberal arts or science. 3. Building of a college. **col·le·gian** (kolē'jan -jēan) *n.* Member of a college. **col·le·giate** (kolē'jĭt) *adj.* Of, constituted as, a college; ~ **church**, church endowed for a body corporate or chapter but with no bishop's see; (Scotland) church under joint pastorate.

col·len·chy·ma (kolĕng'kima) *n.* (bot.) Tissue consisting of cells with local cellulose thickening on their walls, usu. developed near surface of young stems and leaves and strengthening these.

col·lide (kolīd') *v.i.* (**-lid·ed, -lid·ing**). Come forcibly into contact (*with*), strike or dash together; be in conflict, clash.

col·lie (kŏl'ē) *n.* Sheep dog of a Scotch breed, with long hair, pointed nose, and bushy tail.

col·lier (kŏl'yer) *n.* 1. Coal miner. 2. Coal ship. **col'lier·y** *n.* (Brit.) (pl. **-lier·ies**). Coal mine.

col·li·mate (kŏl'imāt) *v.t.* (**-mat·ed, -mat·ing**). Adjust (telescope) so that line of sight is in correct position; place (telescopes, lenses, etc.) with optical axes in same line; (of lens etc.) make (rays of light) parallel. **col·li·ma·tor** (kŏl'imāter) *n.* Small telescope with cross hairs at its focus, used for adjusting line of sight of larger instrument, such as surveyor's transit. **col·li·ma·tion** (kŏlimā'-shon) *n.*

Col·lins[1] (kŏl'ĭnz), **Michael** (1890–1922). Irish revolutionary leader, active in Sinn Fein movement and Irish Volunteers military group; minister of finance and commander of military forces of Irish Free State; mortally wounded in repelling an attack of irregulars.

Col·lins[2] (kŏl'ĭnz), (**William**) **Wilkie** (1824–89). English novelist; author of *The Moonstone* (1868), considered by many to be one of the first English detective novels.

col·li·sion (kolĭzh'on) *n.* Colliding; violent encounter of moving body, esp. car, ship, or train, with another; clash, clashing; ~ **course**, course bound to end in collision.

col·lo·cate (kŏl'okāt) *v.t.* (**-cat·ed, -cat·ing**). Place together, arrange. **col·lo·ca·tion** (kŏlokā'shon) *n.*

col·lo·di·on (kolō'dēon) *n.* Colorless syrupy liquid, a solution of pyroxylin in ether and alcohol, drying rapidly in air, and used for covering photographic plates, wounds, burns, etc.

col·logue (kolōg') *v.i.* (**-logued, -logu·ing**). Talk confidentially; (dial.) conspire.

col·loid (kŏl'oid) *adj.* Gluey; ~ **substance, tissue**, etc., (path.) gelatinous substance produced in certain forms of tissue degeneration. **colloid** *n.* (chem.) Suspension of finely divided solid in a liquid, etc. forming a system that does not separate on standing.

col·loi·dal (kŏloi'dal) *adj.*

colloq. *abbrev.* Colloquial.

col·lo·qui·al (kolō'kwēal) *adj.* Of or in talk, conversational; belonging to familiar, not formal or elevated, speech. **col·lo'qui·al·-ism** *n.* **col·lo'qui·al·ly** *adv.*

col·lo·quy (kŏl'okwē) *n.* (pl. **-quies**). Conversation, esp. a formal one; conference.

col·lo·type (kŏl'otīp) *n.* Planographic printing process used mainly for fine reproduction work; print so made.

col·lu·sion (kolōō'zhon) *n.* Fraudulent secret understanding. **col·lu·sive** (kolōō'sĭv) *adj.* **col·-lu'sive·ly** *adv.*

Colo. *abbrev.* Colorado.

col·o·cynth (kŏl'osĭnth) *n.* Bitter apple (*Citrullus colocynthis*), a plant of the gourd family, bearing fruit about size of orange with light spongy extremely bitter pulp; purgative drug prepared from this.

Co·logne (kolōn). (Ger. *Köln*) Industrial city on the lower Rhine in West Germany; famous since the Middle Ages for its cathedral; (also **eau de ~, c~**) toilet water made of aromatic oils and alcohol, first

The magnificent Gothic cathedral in ***Cologne*** *is one of the finest of its type in the world. The city, now the cultural and economic center of the Rhineland, was founded by the Romans.*

manufactured at Cologne.

Co·lom·bi·a (k*o*lŭm′bē*a*). Republic in NW. South America; under Spanish rule until 1819, when a republic was established by Simon BOLIVAR, consisting of the territories now known as Colombia, Panama, Venezuela, and Ecuador; Venezuela and Ecuador seceded in 1830 and Panama in 1903; capital, Bogotá. **Co·lom′bi·an** *adj.* & *n.*

Co·lom·bo (k*o*lŭm′bō). Capital city of Sri Lanka.

Co·lon (kōlŏn′). Port city of Panama on the Caribbean.

co·lon[1] (kō′l*o*n) *n.* (pl. **-lons, -la** pr. -l*a*). Greater part of large intestine, extending from cecum to rectum. **co·lon·ic** (kōlŏn′ĭk) *adj.*

co·lon[2] (kō′l*o*n) *n.* (pl. **-lons**). Punctuation mark (:), used esp. before illustration or quotation.

Co·lón (kawlawn′) **Archipelago**: see GALAPAGOS ISLANDS.

colo·nel (kẽr′n*e*l) *n.* 1. Officer in command of a regiment, ranking above lieutenant colonel and below brigadier general. 2. Honorary state title, as a **Kentucky ~. colo′nel·cy** *n.*

co·lo·ni·al (k*o*lō′nē*a*l) *adj.* Of a colony; (hist.) of the thirteen British colonies of America that became the original thirteen states of the United States; (of architecture, etc.) of the period during which these states were still colonies; **C~ Office**, department of British Government in charge of colonies, now merged with Commonwealth Relations Office. **colonial** n. Native, inhabitant, of a colony. **co·lo′ni·al·ism** *n.*

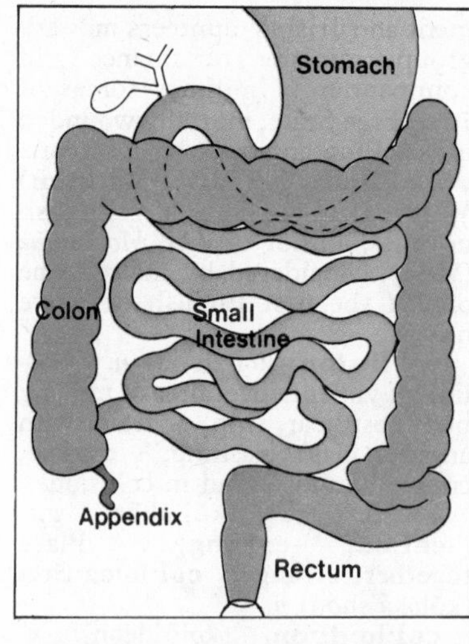

*One of the functions of the **colon** is to store waste products until they are ready to be passed from the body. The various medical problems associated with the colon include colitis and cancer.*

col·o·nist (kŏl′*o*nĭst) *n.* Settler in, founder, or inhabitant of, a colony.

col·o·nize (kŏl′*o*nīz) *v.* (**-nized, -niz·ing**). Establish colony in; establish in a colony; form or establish a colony or settlement. **col·o·ni·za·tion** (kŏl*o*nīzā′sh*o*n) *n.*

col·on·nade (kŏl*o*nād′) *n.* Row of columns at regular intervals supporting a roof.

col·o·ny (kŏl′*o*nē) *n.* (pl. **-nies**). 1. (Gk. hist.) Independent city founded by emigrants; (Rom. hist.) settlement of Roman citizens (usu. veteran soldiers) in conquered territory, where they acted as a garrison. 2. Settlement, settlers, in new country remaining subject to or connected with parent nation; territory so peopled or belonging to a nation by conquest or annexation. 3. Number of people of one nationality or occupation forming a community in a city. 4. (biol.) Aggregate of individual animals or plants forming physiologically connected structure or (more loosely) living close together. 5. **C~**, one of the 13 original colonies that became U.S. states.

col·o·phon (kŏl′*o*fŏn) *n.* 1. Inscription or device at end of book or manuscript, containing title, scribe's or printer's name, date, place of printing. 2. Publisher's emblem or trademark placed usually on title page of book.

col·or (kŭl′*e*r), Brit. **col·our** (kŭl′*er*) *ns.* 1. Quality or wavelength of light emitted or reflected from an object, determined by the physical configuration of the emitting or reflecting surface and the quality of the incident light (if any); sensation produced by stimulation of optic nerve by particular light vibrations. 2. Particular hue, one of the constituents into which white or colorless light can be decomposed; mixture of these, including black (in which rays of light are wholly absorbed) and white (in which they are wholly reflected); **primary ~**, (physiol.) one of the three colors (red, green, and violet), combinations of which give rise to sensations of all others; (in paint-

*The state of **Colorado** has its western half in the Rocky Mountains. Its most famous feature is the Grand Canyon. Seen here is a cliff palace of the Pueblo Indians in the Mesa Verde.*

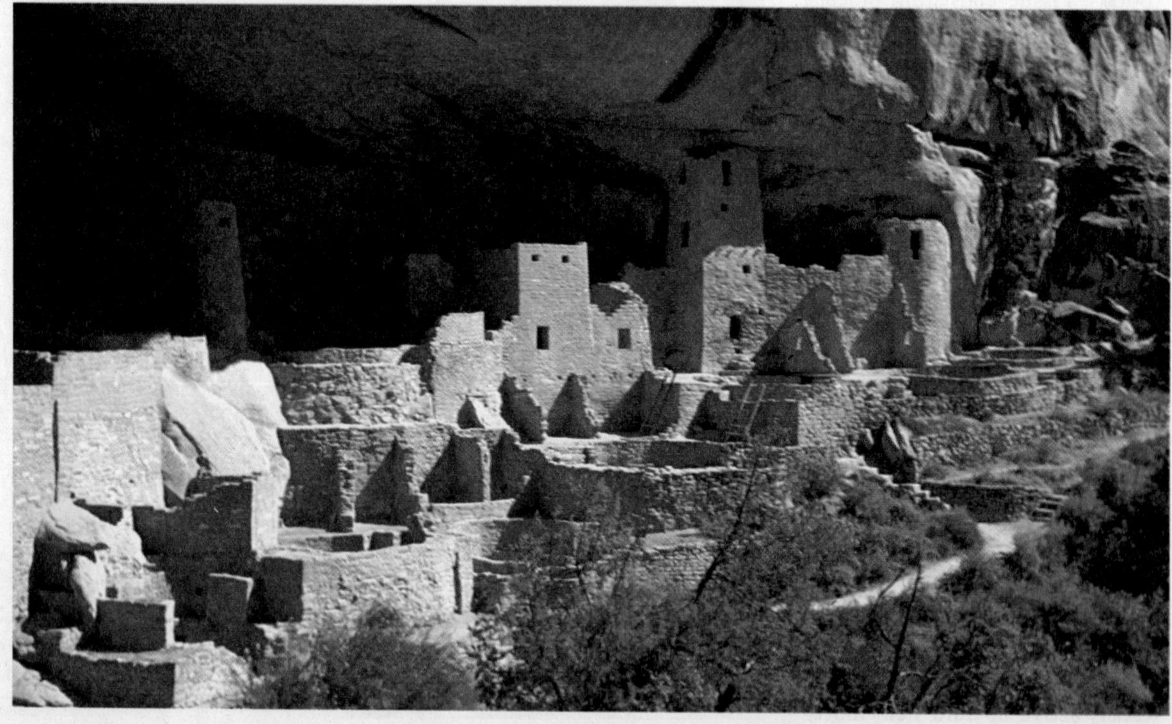

ing) red, blue, or yellow, which may be mixed to produce all other colors; **secondary** ~, one produced (as green, purple) by mixing two primary colors. 3. Complexion of a member of a black race. 4. Complexion, ruddy hue of cheeks, etc. 5. Representation of color in painting; coloring. 6. (pl.) Colored ribbon, emblem, badge, etc. worn as symbol of party, organization, athletic team, etc.; flag, ensign, or standard of regiment or ship. 7. Pigment, paint; colored material etc. 8. Outward appearance, semblance; pretext, show of reason; tone, character, kind, shade of meaning; (mus.) timbre, variety of expression, etc. 9. **local** ~, see LOCAL; ~ **bar**, legal or social distinction between white and other races; ~ **blind**, unable to see, or to distinguish between, certain colors; also fig., of races; ~ **line**, social demarcation between white and nonwhite persons; ~ **scheme**, systematic arrangement of colors or colored items. **color** *v.* Give color to; paint, stain, dye; give a distinctive character or quality to; influence; modify; distort; misrepresent; take on color; blush. **col′ored** *adj.* (of persons) Not white, wholly or partly of black descent.

Col·o·rad·o (kŏl*o*răd´ō, -rah´dō). Rocky Mountain state in W. central U.S., admitted to the Union in 1876, named after the ~ **River**, which rises there and flows into the Gulf of California; capital, Denver; ~ **beetle**, potato beetle; **C~ Desert**, arid region in SE. California and NW. Mexico; **C~ Springs**, resort city in central Colorado and site of U.S. Air Force Academy.

col·or·a·tion (kŭl*o*rā´sh*o*n) *n.* Coloring; arrangement of colors; natural, esp. variegated, color of living things.

col·o·ra·tu·ra (kŭl*e*r*a*toor´*a*, -tūr´*a*, kŏl-, kōl-) *n.* Florid ornament, freq. extempore, in singing; (also ~ **soprano**) (singer with) high flexible voice capable of this. [It., = "colored (music)"]

*The **Colorado Beetle** (above) is found in western N. America and attacks the leaves of potato plants. By the 1870s it had become a widespread pest. It is orange-red in color with black stripes and is 3/8 ins. long.*

col·or·ful (kŭl*e*rful) *adj.* Full of color; vivid. **col′or·ful·ly** *adv.* **col′or·ful·ness** *n.*

col·or·im·e·ter (kŭl*o*rĭm´*eter*) *n.* Instrument for determining, specifying, or measuring (intensity of) color.

col·or·ing (kŭl´erĭng) *n.* (esp.) Style in which a thing is colored, or in which artist uses color; complexion.

col·or·ist (kŭl′erĭst) *n.* Painter skillful in coloring.

col·or·less (kŭl′*er*lis) *adj.* Without color; pale; dull; wanting in character or vividness; neutral, indifferent. **col′or·less·ly** *adv.* **col′or·less·ness** *n.*

co·los·sal (kolŏs′*al*) *adj.* Of, like a colossus; gigantic; (colloq.) magnificent. **co·los′sal·ly** *adv.*

Col·os·se·um (kŏlosē′*u*m) = COLISEUM.

co·los·sus (kolŏs′*us*) *n.* (pl. **-los·si** pr. -lŏs′ī, **-los·sus·es**). Gigantic statue; huge dominating figure, thing, person, like the statue at Rhodes which was thought to have stood astride the harbor; **C ~ of Rhodes,** bronze statue of the god Apollo, said to have been 120 ft. (36.5 m) high; erected in 280 B.C.; it was shattered by an earthquake in 224 B.C. and the fragments, which lay about the harbor for centuries, were regarded as one of the Seven Wonders of the World.

co·los·to·my (kolŏs′t*o*mē) *n.* (pl. **-mies**). (surg.) (Formation of) an artificial excretory opening from the colon through the abdominal wall.

co·los·trum (kolŏs′tr*u*m) *n.* First milk secreted by mammal after parturition and lasting for a few days.

Colt (kōlt) *n.* (trademark) Kind of revolver. [f. Samuel *Colt* (1814–1862), Amer. inventor]

colt (kōlt) *n.* Young male of horse; (colloq.) inexperienced or frisky youth; **colts′foot,** common Old World weed (*Tussilago farfara*) with yellow flowers appearing before the heart-shaped leaves. **colt′ish** *adj.*

Co·lum·ba (kolŭm′b*a*), **St.** (521–97). Irish monk and missionary to northern Picts; founded the monastery of Iona, Scotland.

Co·lum·bi·a[1] (kolŭm′bē*a*). Poetic name for America; ~, capital of South Carolina, in the central part. [f. COLUMBUS]

Co·lum·bi·a[2] (kolŭm′bē*a*) **River.** River flowing from SE. British Columbia, Canada, and through the NW. U.S. 1,200 (1931 km) miles to the Pacific Ocean; it forms most of the border between Washington and Oregon.

Col·um·bine (kŏl′*u*mbīn). Character in Italian comedy, the mistress of Harlequin.

col·um·bine (kŏl′*u*mbīn) *n.* Plant (*Aquilegia canadensis*), the inverted flower of which, with its horned nectaries, resembles five pigeons clustered together. [L. *columba* dove]

co·lum·bi·um (kolŭm′bē*u*m) *n.* (formerly) Niobium.

Co·lum·bus (kolŭm′b*u*s), **Christopher** (*c*1451–1506). Genoese navigator who prevailed upon Ferdinand and Isabella of Spain to bear the expenses of an expedition of discovery and set out on his first voyage in 1492; generally credited with discovery of New World; first discovered the Bahamas (Oct. 12, 1492) and Cuba, and on his third voyage (1498) landed near the mouth of the Orinoco in S. America; ~, industrial city and the capital of Ohio, in the central part; ~ **Day,** once Oct. 12, now the second Monday in October, a legal holiday in U.S. celebrating the discovery of the New World by Columbus.

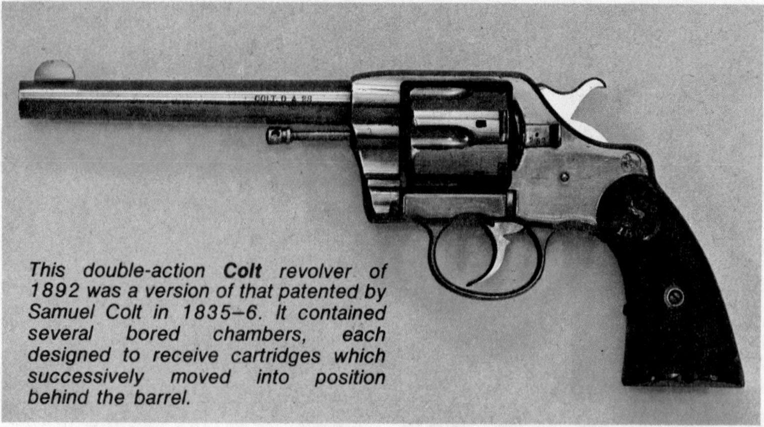

*This double-action **Colt** revolver of 1892 was a version of that patented by Samuel Colt in 1835–6. It contained several bored chambers, each designed to receive cartridges which successively moved into position behind the barrel.*

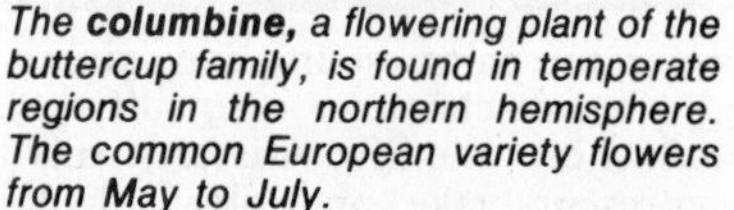

*The **columbine,** a flowering plant of the buttercup family, is found in temperate regions in the northern hemisphere. The common European variety flowers from May to July.*

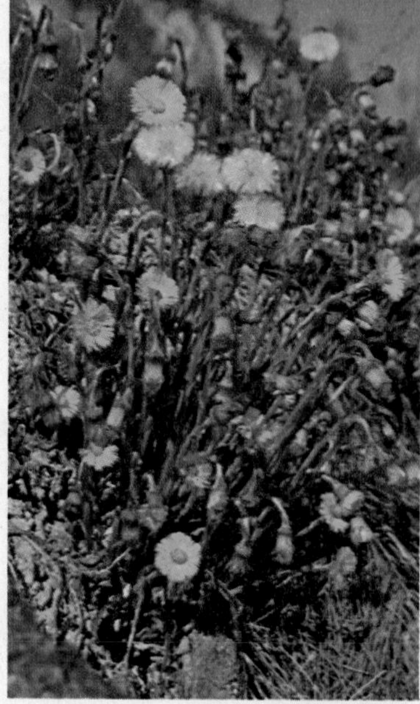

*The **coltsfoot,** a prolific weed of Britain and Europe, has leaves that were used in herbal tobacco and cigarettes, and smoked as a remedy for asthma and coughs.*

col·umn (kŏl′*u*m) *n.* 1. (archit.) Long cylindrical of slightly tapering body usu. supporting roof or arch or standing alone as monument. 2. Natural column-shaped formation, esp. of igneous rock; anything resembling a column in shape or function; upright mass of air, liquid, smoke, etc. 3. One of the narrow vertical divisions of a sheet of paper, page of book, etc., used for lists of figures, names, etc., or for convenience in arranging printed matter on a wide page; esp. such a division of a newspaper, the printed matter filling it, a newspaper article. 4. Formation of troops, armored vehicles, etc., in which the elements are placed one behind the other as dist. from *line* in which they are abreast. **col′umned** *adj.*

co·lum·nar (kolŭm′n*er*) *adj.* Like a column; in columns.

col·um·nist (kŏl′*u*mnĭst, -mĭst) *n.* Writer who regularly writes a newspaper or magazine column.

col·za (kŏl′z*a*) *n.* Plant of the mustard family; RAPE[2].

com- *prefix.* With.

co·ma[1] (kō′m*a*) *n.* (pl. **-mas**). (path.) Deep unconsciousness;

Nelson's **Column** in London's Trafalgar Square reaches a height of nearly 185 ft. including the 17 ft.-high statue of the admiral at the top. At its base are four bronze lions by Sir Edwin Landseer.

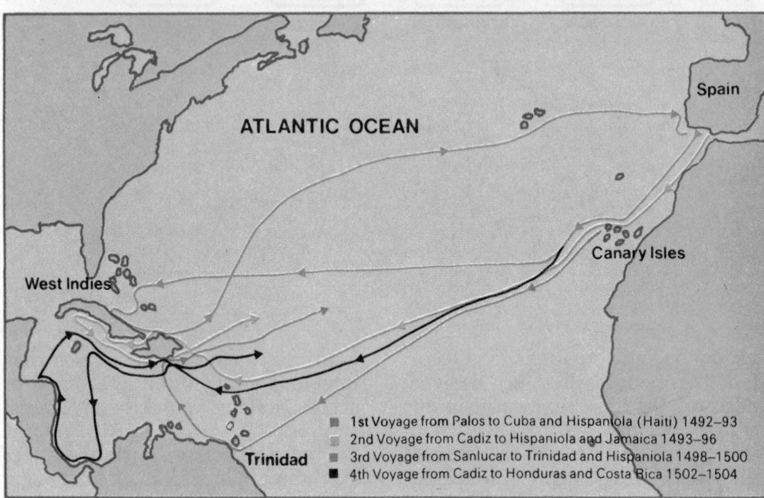

Christopher Columbus, *the discoverer of the New World, believed that by sailing west he could reach the Orient. After much difficulty he obtained the patronage of the Spanish king and queen and set out in 1492 on the first of four voyages (left) in the 'Santa Maria', seen here in replica (above left).*

(loosely) stupor, lethargy. **co·ma·tose** (kō'matōs, kŏm'*a*-) *adj.* In a state of coma; drowsy, lethargic.

co·ma[2] (kō'm*a*) *n.* (pl. **-mae** pr. -mē). (astron.) Nebulous envelope surrounding nucleus of comet. [Gk. *komē* hair]

Co·man·che (k*o*măn'chē) *adj.* & *n.* (pl. **-ches**, collect. **-che**). (Member, language) of a N. Amer. Indian people formerly ranging from Wyoming to Texas, now chiefly in Oklahoma.

comb (kōm) *n.* 1. Strip of bone, metal, etc., with indentations forming series of teeth, or with teeth inserted, used for disentangling, cleaning, and arranging hair, or to keep it in place. 2. Any of various things of similar appearance or function: instrument with several rows of teeth for carding wool or flax. 3. Red fleshy indented or serrated crest or caruncle on head of domestic fowl, esp. male. 4. Honeycomb. ~ *v.* Draw comb through (hair), dress (wool, flax) with comb; (of wave) curl over; search or examine closely.

com·bat (kŏm'băt, kŭm'-) *n.* Battle, fight; struggle; conflict; ~ **fatigue** = BATTLE fatigue. **combat** (k*o*mbăt', kŏm-) *v.* (**-bat·ted, -bat·ting**). Do battle; fight with; oppose.

com·bat·ant (k*o*mbăt'*a*nt, kŏm'b*a*t*a*nt, kŭm'-) *n.* One who fights. ~ *adj.* Fighting.

com·bat·ive (k*o*mbăt'ĭv, kŏm'b*a*tĭv, kŭm'-) *adj.* Pugnacious. **com·bat'ive·ly** *adv.* **com·bat'ive·ness** *n.*

com·bi·na·tion (kŏmbĭnā'sh*o*n) *n.* 1. Combining; combined state; group or set of things combined; sequence of letters or numbers that open a combination lock. 2. ~ **lock**, lock that can be opened only by specific sequence of movements.

com·bi·na·tive (kŏm'b*i*nātĭv, k*o*mbī'n*a*-) *adj.* Combining; of combination.

com·bine (k*o*mbīn') *v.* (**-bined, -bin·ing**). 1. Join together, unite; come together; unite for common purpose, cooperate; **combined operations**, operations in which army, naval, and air forces are combined; **combining form**, (gram.) special form of word used in compounds or derivatives. 2. Enter into chemical union (*with*); **combining weight**: see EQUIVALENT. **combine** (kŏm'bīn) *n.* Combination of persons in business, politics, etc., esp. to control prices or obstruct course of trade; harvesting

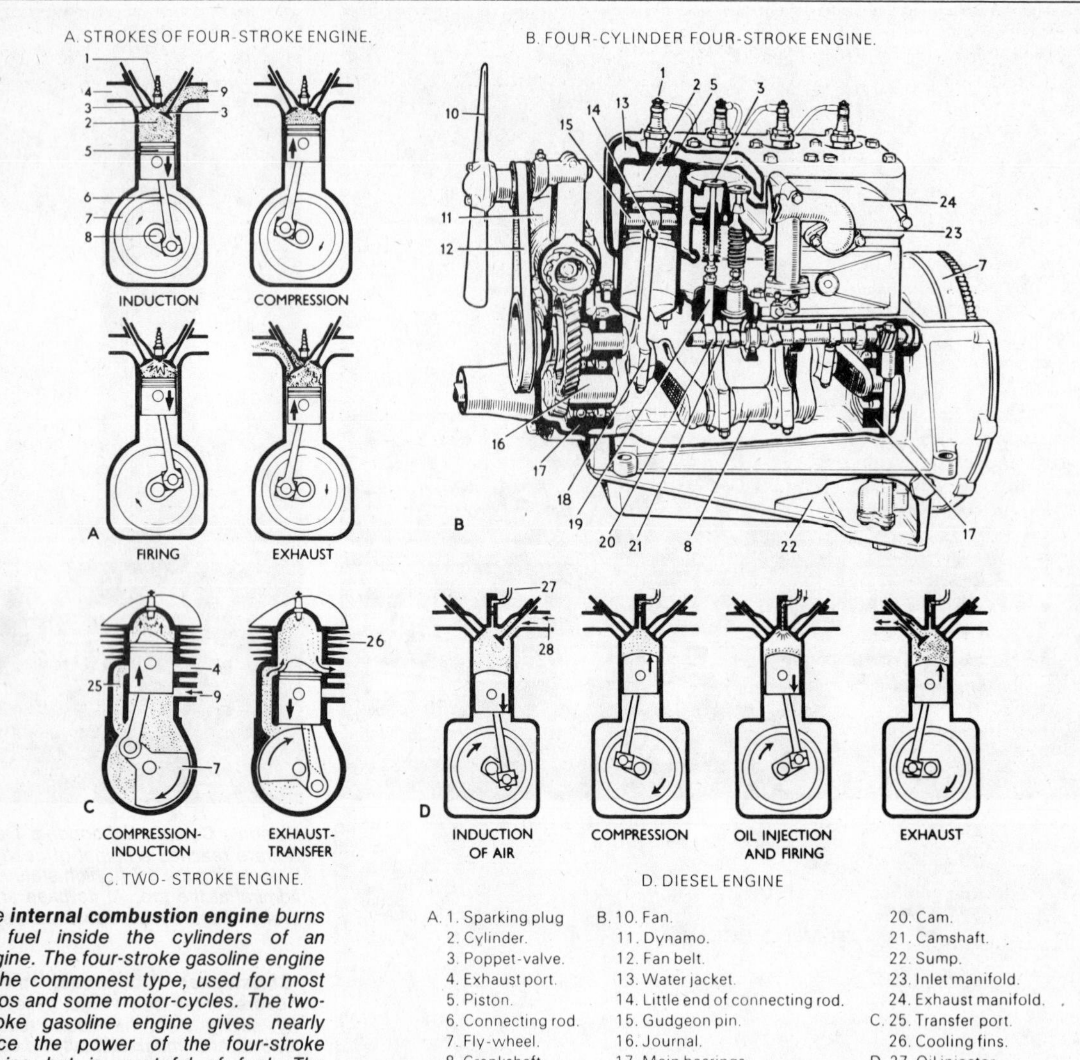

*The **internal combustion engine** burns its fuel inside the cylinders of an engine. The four-stroke gasoline engine is the commonest type, used for most autos and some motor-cycles. The two-stroke gasoline engine gives nearly twice the power of the four-stroke engine but is wasteful of fuel. The diesel engine is used in heavy machinery, locomotives and trucks.*

A. 1. Sparking plug
2. Cylinder.
3. Poppet-valve.
4. Exhaust port.
5. Piston.
6. Connecting rod.
7. Fly-wheel.
8. Crankshaft.
9. Inlet port.

B. 10. Fan.
11. Dynamo.
12. Fan belt.
13. Water jacket.
14. Little end of connecting rod.
15. Gudgeon pin.
16. Journal.
17. Main bearings.
18. Big end of connecting rod.
19. Tappet.
20. Cam.
21. Camshaft.
22. Sump.
23. Inlet manifold.
24. Exhaust manifold.

C. 25. Transfer port.
26. Cooling fins.

D. 27. Oil injector.
28. Air inlet port.

machine reaping and threshing in one operation. **com·bin′a·ble** *adj.*

comb·ings (kō′mĭngz) *n.pl.* (esp.) Hairs, wool, etc. combed off.

com·bo (kŏm′bō) *n.* (slang) 1. Small jazz band. 2. Sandwich with combination of fillings. 3. Any combination, as of clothes, colors, etc.

com·bus·ti·ble (kombŭs′tĭbel) *adj.* & *n.* (Matter, thing) capable of burning; excitable, inflammable.

com·bus·tion (kombŭs′chon) *n.* Consumption or destruction by fire; development of light and heat accompanying chemical combination; oxidation of organic material; **internal ~ engine**, engine in which the motive power is produced by the combustion and expansion of a mixture of gasoline or oil vapor and air inside the cylinders.

come (kŭm) *v.i.* (**came, come, com·ing**). 1. Move or start toward, arrive at, a point, time, or result; be brought; fall, land (*on*); **~ into view**, become visible. 2. Occur, fall; happen; issue; be derived, descend; (of time etc.) arrive in due course; become, get to be; turn out to be. 3. Traverse, accomplish (a distance). 4. (vulg.) Experience sexual orgasm. 5. **~ across**, meet with; **~ across** (**with**), hand over; **~ along**, make haste; **~ around**, revive, regain consciousness, become agreeable; **~ at**, reach, discover, get access to; **~ back**, return; recur to memory; **come′-back** (*n.*), retaliation, retort; return, recovery, reinstatement; **come by**, obtain; **come down**, extend downward *to*; be handed down; fall, be humbled; **come forward**, present oneself before the public etc.; **come in**, enter building or room; finish in a specified place (in race etc.); come into power or office; be received as income; become seasonable or fashionable; serve a purpose, find a place; **come into**, receive, esp. as heir; **come off**, become detached; occur; succeed; **come on**, advance; continue to progress, thrive, develop; come upon the stage or scene; (slang) make an initial impression; **come out**, emerge from contest, examination, etc.; (of sun etc.) emerge from clouds, begin to shine; come into public view, become public, be published; appear or be found by computation etc.; develop, display itself; make debut on stage or in society; **come out with**, utter; **come to**, revive; **come to pass**, happen; **come up**, come to higher situation in life; come close *to*; arise as subject of attention, discussion, etc.; rise to level or height of; **come up with**, catch up; produce. **come** *int.* Expression of annoyance, as in **~ now**. **come′down** *n.* Fall from dignity, prosperity, etc. **come-on** *n.* (slang) Inducement, lure; inviting look.

co·me·di·an (komē′dēan) *n.* Comic actor or entertainer; (archaic) writer of comedies; person who always jokes or tries to amuse.

co·me·di·enne (k*o*mēdēĕn′) *n. fem.* **co·me′dic** *adj.*

com·e·do (kŏm′*e*dō) *n.* (pl. **-dos, com·e·do·nes** pr. kŏm*e*dō′nēz). (med.) Skin blemish, blackhead.

com·e·dy (kŏm′*e*dē) *n.* (pl. **-dies**). Drama of light, amusing, and often satirical character, with a happy conclusion to its plot; branch of drama that adopts a humorous or familiar style and depicts laughable characters and incidents; life, or an incident in it, regarded as a comic spectacle.

come·ly (kŭm′lē) *adj.* (**-li·er, -li·est**). Pleasant to look at. **come′-li·ness** *n.*

Co·me·ni·us (k*o*mē′nē*u*s), **John Amos** (1592–1670). Czech theologian and educator; known for innovations in teaching methods, esp. for languages.

com·er (kŭm′*er*) *n.* 1. One who arrives (as **late ~**, etc.); **all ~s**, any who apply, take up challenge, etc. 2. (colloq.) Promising person or thing.

co·mes·ti·ble (k*o*mĕs′tĭb*e*l) *n.* (usu. pl.) Thing to eat.

com·et (kŏm′ĭt) *n.* Celestial body with starlike nucleus and a train or tail of light moving about sun in elliptical or parabolic orbit. **com′et·ar·y, co·met·ic** (k*o*mĕt′ĭk) *adjs.* [Gk. *komētēs* long-haired (star)]

com·fit (kŭm′fĭt, kŏm′-) *n.* Piece of candy containing nut or piece of fruit.

com·fort (kŭm′f*ert*) *n.* 1. Relief in affliction, consolation; person who consoles one or saves one trouble; cause of satisfaction. 2. Well-being, being comfortable; thing that produces or ministers to enjoyment and content. ~ *v.t.* Soothe in grief, console; make comfortable. **com′fort·ing, com′fort·less** *adjs.* **com′fort·ing·ly** *adv.*

com·fort·a·ble (kŭmf′t*a*b*e*l, kŭm′f*ert*ab*e*l) *adj.* Affording consolation; attended with or ministering to comfort or physical well-being; in a state of tranquil enjoyment and content, at ease. **com′-fort·a·bly** *adv.* **com′fort·er** *n.* 1. One who comforts; **the C~**, the Holy Spirit. 2. Quilted coverlet.

com·frey (kŭm′frē) *n.* (pl. **-freys**). Any of several bristly Old World plants of the genus *Symphytum*, with rough leaves and bell-shaped flowers.

com·fy (kŭm′fē) *adj.* (**-fi·er, -fi·est**). (colloq.) Comfortable.

com·ic (kŏm′ĭk) *adj.* Of comedy; mirth provoking, laughable or meant to be so, facetious, burlesque, funny; ~ **strip**, set of drawings, usu. broadly humorous, forming part of a series appearing regularly in a ~ **section** of a newspaper. **comic** *n.* Comic actor, performer, strip, or magazine; ~ **book**, children's magazine consisting of stories in comic-strip form.

com·i·cal (kŏm′ĭk*a*l) *adj.* Mirth provoking, laughable; odd, queer. **com·i·cal·i·ty** (kŏmĭkăl′ĭtē) *n.* **com′i·cal·ly** *adv.*

Com·in·form (kŏm′ĭnfōrm). International communist information bureau established 1947 and dissolved 1956.

com·ing (kŭm′ĭng) *adj.* 1. Next, approaching. 2. Promising success or fame in the future. ~ *n.* Approach, advent, arrival.

The first **commando** *troops fought during the Boer War in South Africa. The commandos below are U.S. Marines surveying a map before a survival course.*

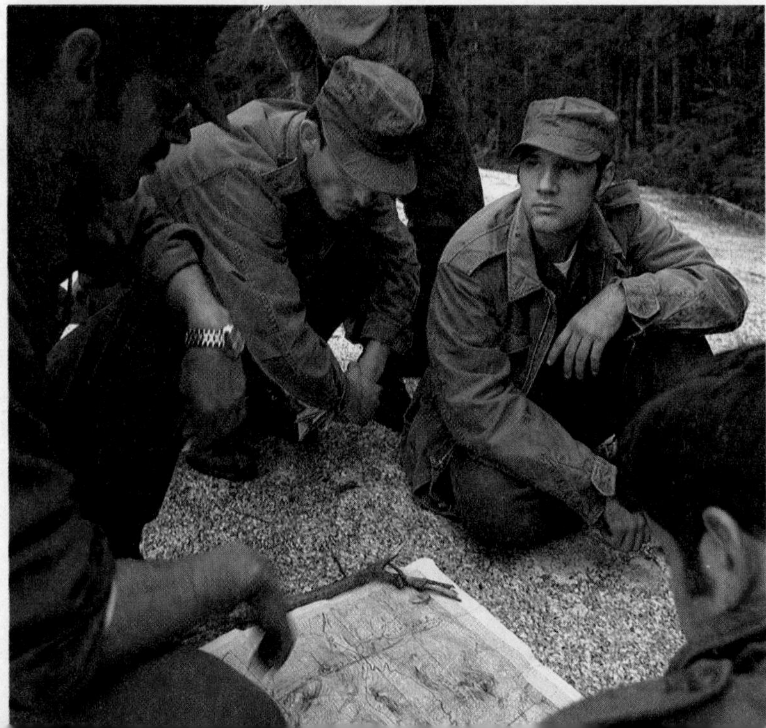

Com·in·tern (kŏm′ĭntērn). Third Communist International, founded at Moscow in March 1919; formally dissolved June 1943.

com·i·ty (kŏm′ĭtē) *n.* (pl. **-ties**). Courtesy; civility; ~ **of nations**, friendly and courteous recognition by nations of laws and usages of other nations; (loosely) nations observing this.

com·ma (kŏm′*a*) *n.* 1. Punctuation mark (,) used to separate smallest parts of a sentence, also used to separate figures etc.; (mus.) minute interval or difference of pitch; caesura. 2. (also ~ **butterfly**) Butterfly (*Polygonia comma*) with white comma-shaped mark on underside of wings.

com·mand (k*o*mănd′, -mahnd′) *n.* 1. Order, bidding. 2. Exercise or tenure of authority, esp. military; body of troops, district, ship, etc. under commander; **high ~**, highest military leadership during military operations. 3. Control, mastery, possession; ~ **performance**, performance given at the request of a head of state; (joc.) any performance given on request of person in authority. **command** *v.* 1. Order, bid. 2. Have authority over or control of, be supreme; be in command (of). 3. Restrain, master; have at disposal or within reach; demand and obtain; dominate (position etc.) from superior height, look down over.

com·man·dant (kŏm′*a*ndănt, -dahnt, kŏm*a*ndănt′, -dahnt′) *n.* Commanding officer, esp. one holding special command, of depot, particular force, etc.

com·man·deer (kŏm*a*ndēr′) *v.* Force (men) into, seize (stores) for, military service; take arbitrary possession of.

com·mand·er (k*o*măn′d*er*, -mahn′-) *n.* One who commands; one who has command of a ship, naval officer ranking next below captain; **c~ in chief**, chief commander of all military forces of a nation (in the U.S. the president); officer commanding a major armed force.

com·mand·ing (k*o*măn′dĭng, -mahn′-) *adj.* Ruling, controlling; nobly dignified; ~ **officer**, officer in command.

com·mand·ment (k*o*mănd′-m*e*nt, -mahnd′-) *n.* Divine command, esp. (**C~**) one of the **Ten Commandments**, precepts delivered by God to Moses (Exod. 20).

com·man·do (k*o*măn′dō, -mahn′-) *n.* (pl. **-dos, -does**). Small fighting unit for quick raids on enemy-held territory; member of such a unit.

comme il faut (kŭm ēl fō′) *adj. phr.* According to etiquette, proper. [Fr.]

com·mem·o·rate (komĕm´erāt) *v.t.* (**-rat·ed, -rat·ing**). Celebrate in speech or writing; preserve in memory by some celebration; by a memorial of. **com·mem·o·ra·tion** (komĕmerā´shon) *n.* **com·mem·o·ra·tive** (komĕm´eratĭv) *adj.*

com·mence (komĕns´) *v.* (**-menced, -menc·ing**). Begin; come into existence. **com·mence′ment** *n.* Beginning; ceremony of conferring academic degrees or diplomas; ~ **day**, day on which such a ceremony takes place.

com·mend (komĕnd´) *v.t.* Entrust, commit (archaic exc. in, e.g., ~ **one's soul to God**); praise, extol; recommend (a person).

com·mend·a·ble (komĕn´dabel) *adj.* Praiseworthy. **com·mend′a·bly** *adv.*

com·men·da·tion (kŏmendā´shon) *n.* Praise; act of commending person to another's favor.

com·mend·a·to·ry (komĕn´datōrē, -tōrē) *adj.* Serving to praise or recommend.

com·men·su·ra·ble (komĕn´serabel, -she-) *adj.* Measurable by the same standard; properly proportioned; fitting; divisible without remainder by the same quantity. **com·men·su·ra·bil·i·ty** (komĕnserabĭl´ĭtē, -she-) *n.* **com·men′su·ra·bly** *adv.*

com·men·su·rate (komĕn´serĭt, -she-) *adj.* Coextensive; proportionate; corresponding in extent or degree, as in ~ **with one's ability.** **com·men′su·rate·ly** *adv.*

com·ment (kŏm´ĕnt) *n.* Explanatory or critical note or remark; expository or critical matter; criticism. ~ *v.i.* Write explanatory or critical notes *on*; make comments or remarks (*on*).

com·men·tar·y (kŏm´entĕrē) *n.* (pl. **-tar·ies**). Expository treatise; series of running comments on book, speech, performance, public event, etc.; comment, remark.

com·men·ta·tor (kŏm´entāter) *n.* Writer or speaker of commentary; one who analyzes news events on radio or television.

com·merce (kŏm´ers) *n.* 1. Buying and selling of merchandise, esp. on a large scale between different countries or districts, comprising all forms of trade and ancillary services such as banking, insurance, and transportation. 2. Social intercourse.

The ***Common Market*** *or European Economic Community has its headquarters in Brussels. It was founded in 1958 with the aim to increase trade among its members.*

com·mer·cial (komẽr´shal) *adj.* Of, engaged in, bearing on, commerce; ~ **traveler**, traveling salesperson. **commercial** *n.* Advertisement broadcast on radio or television. **com·mer′cial·ism** *n.* **com·mer′cial·ize** *v.t.* (**-ized, -iz·ing**). **com·mer′cial·ly** *adv.*

com·mie (kŏm´ē) *n.* (slang) (freq. **C**~) Communist.

com·mi·na·tion (kŏmĭnā´shon) *n.* Formal denunciation; threatening, esp. of divine punishment.

com·min·gle (komĭng´gel) *v.t.* (**-gled, -gling**). Mingle or mix together.

com·mi·nute (kŏm´inōōt) *v.t.* (**-nut·ed, -nut·ing**). Reduce to minute particles; divide into small portions; **comminuted fracture**, fracture producing multiple fragments. **com·mi·nu·tion** (kŏminōō´shon) *n.*

com·mis·er·ate (komĭz´erāt) *v.* (**-at·ed, -at·ing**). Feel, show, express pity for; condole *with*. **com·mis·er·a·tion** (komĭzerā´shon) *n.* **com·mis′er·a·tive** *adj.*

com·mis·sar (kŏm´ĭsār, kŏmĭsār´) *n.* (until 1946) Head of government department (commissariat) of U.S.S.R. or its constituent republics.

com·mis·sar·i·at (kŏmĭsār´ēat) *n.* 1. Department (esp. military) for

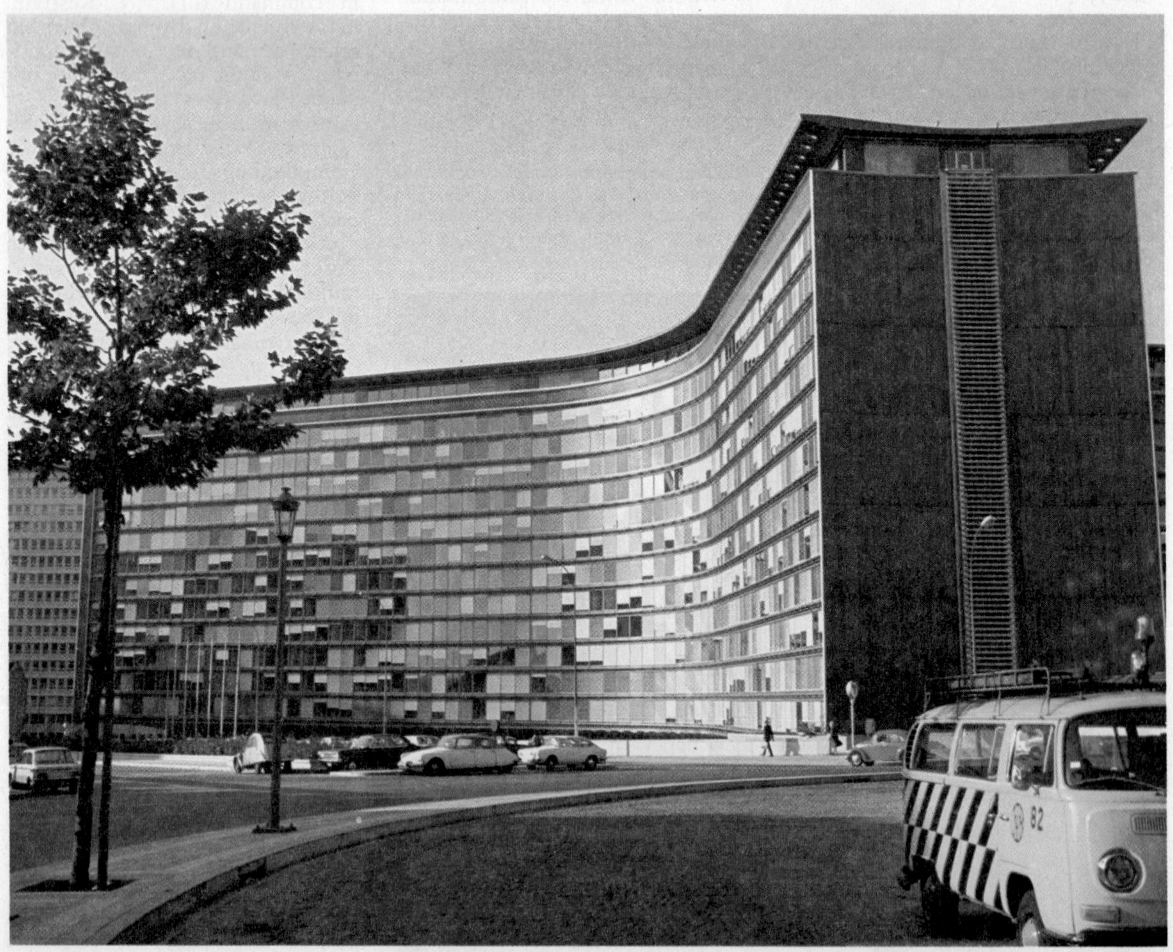

supply of food etc. 2. (until 1946) Department of Civil Service of U.S.S.R.

com·mis·sar·y (kŏm′ĭsĕrē) *n.* (pl. **-sar·ies**). 1. Deputy, delegate. 2. Officer charged with supply of food etc. for body of soldiers. 3. Supermarket and department store for personnel on military base. 4. Employees' lunchroom, cafeteria at factory, office, etc.

com·mis·sion (k*o*mĭsh′*o*n) *n.* 1. Authoritative charge or direction; authority, esp. delegated authority, body of persons having authority, to act in some specified capacity, investigate some specified question, etc. 2. Warrant conferring authority, warrant by which officer in armed services exercises command; office conferred by such a warrant. 3. Being authoritatively entrusted or given in charge; **in ~**, (of a ship of war) manned, armed, and ready for sea; in working order; ready; in service; **out of ~**, not in service; not in working order. 4. Charge entrusted to anyone to perform; order given to artist, writer, etc. for a particular piece of work. 5. Authority to act as agent for another in trade or business; system of trading in which dealer (**~ merchant**) acts as agent for another, receiving a percentage as remuneration; the percentage of the amount involved paid to the agent. **commission** *v.t.* Empower by commission; give (officer) command of ship; order (ship) prepared for active service; assume command of (ship); give (artist etc.) a commission; order (work of art etc.) as a commission. **com·mis′sioned** *adj.* (esp.) (of officer) Holding rank by commission.

com·mis·sion·er (k*o*mĭsh′*o*n*e*r) *n.* One appointed by or a member of a commission; representative of supreme authority in district, department, etc.; official at head of government department etc.; **High C~**, chief officer of British colonial territory; chief representative of British Commonwealth country.

com·mis·sure (kŏm′ĭshoor) *n.* Joining, seam; joint between two bones; line where lips, eyelids, meet; band or bundle of white or gray nerve substance connecting hemispheres of brain, parts of cerebrum and cerebellum, two sides of spinal cord, etc.

com·mit (k*o*mĭt′) *v.t.* (**-mit·ted, -mit·ting**). 1. Entrust, consign, for treatment or safe keeping, consign officially *to*, place in, custody, prison, etc.; refer (bill etc.) to committee. 2. Perpetrate (crime, blunder). 3. Involve, compromise; engage or pledge by implication (*to*). 4. **~ to memory**, memorize; **~ to writing** or **paper**, write down. **com·mit′ment** *n.* (esp.) Engagement; thing undertaken, responsibility. **com·mit′tal** *n.* Committing, consigning, esp. committing to prison; committing of body to grave at burial; reference to committee; committing of oneself.

*In radio and television the **commentator** on sporting or other events is usually an expert in his field. Here Milton Berle and a commentator discuss the finer points of golf.*

com·mit·tee (k*o*mĭt′ē) *n.* Body of persons appointed for special function by (and usu. out of) larger body; **joint ~**, one composed of members nominated by two or more distinct bodies; **standing ~**, one that is permanent during the existence of the appointing body; **in ~**, (of a bill) under consideration by a legislative committee.

com·mode (k*o*mōd′) *n.* Chest of drawers, chiffonier; chair or box containing chamber pot; toilet; stand or cupboard containing wash basin.

com·mo·di·ous (k*o*mō′dē*u*s) *adj.* Roomy. **com·mo′di·ous·ly** *adv.* **com·mo′di·ous·ness** *n.*

com·mod·i·ty (k*o*mŏd′ĭtē) *n.* (pl. **-ties**). Useful thing; article of trade, esp. product as opp. to service, often a grain traded on a **commodities market.**

com·mo·dore (kŏm′*o*dōr, -dōr) *n.* Naval officer ranking above captain and below rear admiral; as courtesy title, senior captain when three or more ships cruise together; president of yacht club etc.

com·mon (kŏm′*o*n) *adj.* 1. Possessed or shared alike by both or all; belonging to more than one; belonging to all mankind alike; general; public. 2. Of ordinary occurrence and quality; usual, frequent, undistinguished, ordinary; of little value, inferior; low class, vulgar. 3. (math.) Of a number or quantity, belonging equally to two or more quantities. 4. (gram., logic) Of a noun, name, etc., applicable to every individual or species of a class or genus; of either gender or sex. 5. (mus. etc.) (of time, measure) Consisting of two or four beats in a bar. 6. **~ carrier**, transportation company recognized by law as bound to serve the public; **~ denominator**, (math.) common multiple of denominators of several fractions; (colloq.) common feature of members of a group; **C~ Era**, Christian Era; **~ ground**, basis for argument etc. accepted by both sides; **~ law**, body of unwritten law originating in England, based on court decisions, custom, or usage in contrast to statutory law; **~-law husband, wife**, one established by common law, usu. as a result of couple living as man and wife for a specified length of time without a recognized marriage ceremony; **C~ Market**, European Economic Community; **C~ Prayer**, liturgy or form of public service prescribed by Church of England and first set forth in the Book of Common Prayer of 1549; **~ sense**, normal understanding, good practical sense in everyday affairs; **~ stock**, shares in capital of corporation or company that have exclusive claim on all income and assets after all other obligations are paid; cf. preferred stock (see

The Chamber of the U.K. parliament, the ***House of Commons*** *was originally a chapel with the altar at the end where the Speaker now sits. Government and Opposition sit facing each other on the benches.*

Communication *forms a vital part of our lives. The rapid technological progress made this century enables us to receive information as it is happening. Sophisticated video cameras greatly improve news coverage today.*

PREFER). **com'monweal,** (archaic) commonwealth; public welfare. **common** *n.* 1. Land belonging to or used by local community as a whole; (often) **~s** (pl. used as sing. or pl.). 2. **in ~**, in joint use, shared; **in ~ with**, in the same way as, like.

com·mon·al·ty (kŏm′*o*nal*t*ē) *n.* (pl. **-ties**). General body of the community, the common people as dist. from those of rank or in authority; general or universal body.

com·mon·er (kŏm′*oner*) *n.* One of the common people, one below the rank of a noble.

com·mon·ly (kŏm′*o*nlē) *adv.* Usually, frequently.

com·mon·place (kŏm′*o*nplās) *n.* Opinion or statement generally accepted; ordinary topic; anything common and trite; **~ book**, personal journal in which quotable passages, comments, and literary excerpts are written. **commonplace** *adj.* Lacking originality, trivial, hackneyed.

com·mons (kŏm′*o*nz) *n.pl.* 1. Common people; **House of C~**, representatives of counties, boroughs, etc., forming the lower house of Parliament of the United Kingdom and of Canada; building where these meet. 2. Provisions shared in common, esp. in monastic house, college, etc.

com·mon·wealth (kŏm′*o*n-wĕlth) *n.* 1. Body politic, independent community; republican or democratic nation. 2. **the C~**, (also **C~ of Nations**, formerly **British C~ of Nations**), the association of the United Kingdom and its dependencies and certain former colonies that are now self-governing sovereign nations; **C~**

*The opening of CHOGM (**Commonwealth** Heads of Government Meeting) in September 1981. Forty-four member countries (most were former British colonies) participated. CHOGM is held biennially in a Commonwealth capital.*

Day, (formerly Empire Day) a day celebrating the British Commonwealth, now celebrated on the Queen's official birthday. 3. **the C~**, (Engl. hist.) the parliamentary government between the execution of Charles I in 1649 and the Restoration in 1660; under Oliver CROMWELL until 1658, then under his son, Richard. See Lord PROTECTOR. 4. **C~ of Australia**, title of the federated states of AUSTRALIA.

com·mo·tion (kəmō'shən) *n.* Physical disturbance; bustle, confusion; public disorder.

com·mu·nal (kəmū'nəl, kŏm'yə-) *adj.* Of or for a commune or community; for common use.

com·mu·nal·ism (kəmū'nəlĭzəm, kŏm'yə-) *n.* Principle of communal organization of society; theory of government by local autonomy. **com·mu'nal·ist** *n.* **com·mu·nal·is·tic** (kəmūnəlĭs'tĭk, kŏmyə-) *adj.*

com·mune[1] (kŏm'ūn) *n.* 1. Smallest local political division for administrative purposes in France, Belgium, etc. 2. **C~**, revolutionary committee that governed Paris from 1789–95 and played a leading part in the Reign of Terror; (also) revolutionary government set up in Paris from March 18 to May 28, 1871. 3. Small group of persons (not all of one family) sharing living accommodations and goods, often composed of members who adhere to a distinct social or religious ideology. 4. KIBBUTZ.

com·mune[2] (kəmūn') *v.i.* (**-muned, -mun·ing**). Converse intimately, exchange thoughts and feelings *with*; receive Holy Communion.

com·mu·ni·cant (kəmū'nĭkənt) *n.* 1. One who receives or is entitled to receive Holy Communion. 2. One who communicates.

com·mu·ni·cate (kəmū'nĭkāt) *v.* (**-cat·ed, -cat·ing**). 1. Impart, transmit (*to*). 2. Receive, administer, Holy Communion (to). 3. Exchange, express thoughts, feelings, etc; transmit (by speech, writing, etc.). 4. (of spaces, rooms, etc.) Have common door or opening (*with*).

com·mu·ni·ca·tion (kəmūnĭkā'shən) *n.* Imparting (esp. news); information given; exchange of messages etc.; access or means of

*Students hold an anti-Iran rally in Washington. The **commotion** of public demonstration has become a traditional way for people to express political views.*

access, passage, connection by railroad, road, telegraph, etc., between places; (mil., pl.) connection between base and front.

com·mu·ni·ca·tive (kəmū'nĭkətĭv) *adj.* Ready to impart; open; talkative.

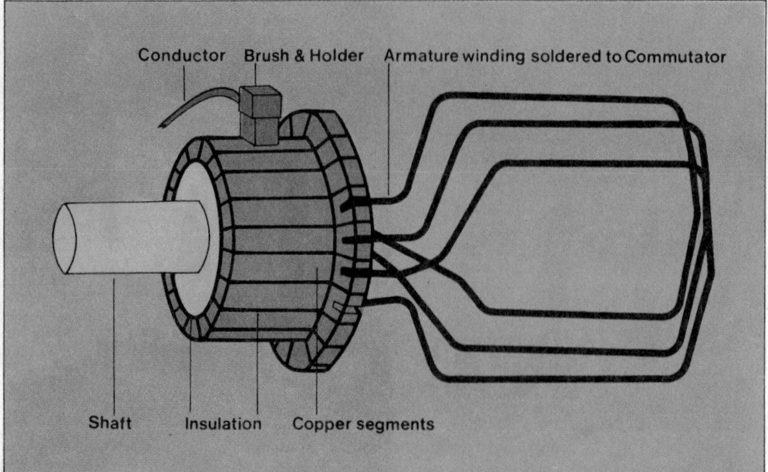

*The **commutator,** a component of electric motors, consists of a drum of copper segments, insulated from each other, which is in contact with carbon brushes.*

com·mu·ni·ca·tor (ko*m*ū′n*i*kāt*er*) *n.* Person, thing, that communicates.

com·mun·ion (ko*m*ūn′yo*n*) *n.* Sharing, participation; fellowship (esp. between branches of Catholic Church); body professing one faith; (**Holy**) **C**~, Eucharist; elements of the Eucharist, as in **receive C**~.

com·mu·ni·qué (ko*m*ūn*i*kā′, ko*m*ū′n*i*kā) *n.* Official announcement or report.

com·mu·nism (kŏm′y*u*nĭzem) *n.* 1. Order of society in which property is owned in common. 2. (usu. **C**~) Order of society in which the means of production, distribution, and exchange are owned in common and each member is to work according to his capacity and be paid according to his needs; this as the professed aim of political parties that derive their doctrines from MARX, ENGELS, and LENIN. 3. Doctrines and activities of these parties regarded as an international movement (**international** ~ or **C**~). 4. Social order established in Russia by the Bolshevik party under Lenin after the revolution of 1917 (**Soviet** ~); similar social order established elsewhere. **com′mu·nist** *adj.* & *n.* (Advocate) of communism. **com·mu·nis·tic** (kŏmy*u*nĭs′tĭk) *adj.*

Com·mu·nism (kŏm′y*u*nĭzem), **Mount.** Formerly Stalin Peak, 24,500 ft. (8,942 m), in the Pamir Range; the highest mountain in the Soviet Union.

com·mu·ni·ty (ko*m*ū′nĭtē) *n.* (pl. **-ties**). 1. Joint or common ownership, liability, etc. 2. Identity of character, quality in common. 3. Social intercourse; life in association with others; body of people organized into political, municipal, or social unity; body of persons living (amid larger group) in same locality, or with common race, religion, pursuits, etc. 4. Body of persons living together and practicing community of goods. 5. (ecol.) Association of organisms in a given area. 6. ~ **college**, public college serving residents of local area; ~ **property**, property of wife and/or husband deemed by law of some states to be jointly owned.

com·mu·nize (kŏm′y*u*nīz) *v.t.* (**-nized, -niz·ing**). Make common property; make communistic.

com·mut·a·ble (ko*m*ū′t*a*bel) *adj.* 1. Exchangeable, convertible into money value. 2. (of a prison sentence) Subject to reduction of severity of punishment. **com·mut·a·bil·i·ty** (ko*m*ūt*a*bĭl′ĭtē) *n.*

com·mu·ta·tion (kŏmy*u*tā′sho*n*) *n.* Commuting; ~ **ticket**, reduced-rate ticket for commuter.

com·mu·ta·tive (ko*m*ū′t*a*tĭv) *adj.* Relating to or involving substitution or interchange.

com·mu·ta·tor (kŏm′y*u*tāt*er*) *n.* Device for changing course of electric current; ring-shaped fitting on dynamo or electric motor providing the brushes with a series of separate connections with different parts of the armature during each revolution and so enabling a dynamo to generate, or a motor to utilize, a direct current.

com·mute (ko*m*ūt′) *v.* (**-mut·ed, -mut·ing**). 1. Exchange, change, interchange; redeem obligation by money payment; change (punishment etc.) *for* (*to, into*) less severe one, or a fine; change (one kind of payment) *into, for,* another. 2. Travel daily to and from work by any means of conveyance. **com·mut′er** *n.*

Co·mo (kō′mō). Lake and resort city in N. Italy, on the Swiss border.

Com·o·ro (kŏm′*o*rō) **Islands.** Group of islands off the E. coast of Africa between Mozambique and Madagascar; under French rule 1886–1975; became independent July 6, 1975; capital, Moroni. **Co·mo·ran** (ko*m*ō′ran) *adj.* & *n.*

comp. *abbrev.* Comparative; complete; compound.

com·pact[1] (kŏm′păkt) *n.* Agreement or contract between parties.

com·pact[2] (ko*m*păkt′) *adj.* Closely or neatly packed together; dense, solid; condensed, terse. **com·pact′ly** *adv.* **com·pact′ness** *n.* **compact** (kŏm′păkt) *n.* Small case containing mirror and face powder, for carrying in handbag. **compact** (ko*m*păkt′) *v.t.* Join firmly together; consolidate; compress, condense; devise, compose.

com·pan·ion[1] (ko*m*păn′yo*n*) *n.* 1. One who accompanies or associates with another; associate *in*, sharer *of*. 2. Person paid to live with another as a friend or equal rather than as a servant. 3. Thing that matches another; one of a pair. ~ *v.* Accompany; associate with. **com·pan′ion·a·ble** *adj.* Sociable. **com·pan′ion·a·bly** *adv.* **com·pan′ion·a·ble·ness** *n.*

com·pan·ion[2] (ko*m*păn′yo*n*) *n.* (naut.) Raised frame on quarter-deck for lighting cabins etc. below; **compan′ionway**, stairway from ship's deck to area, cabins below. [Du. *kompanje* quarter-deck, corresp. to It. (*camera della*) *compagna* pantry, caboose]

com·pan·ion·ship (ko*m*păn′yo*n*shĭp) *n.* Fellowship.

com·pa·ny (kŭm′p*a*nē) *n.* (pl. **-nies**). 1. Companionship; the society *of* others. 2. Number of individuals assembled together, person(s) with whom one usually associates; guests. 3. Body of persons combined or incorporated for a common (esp. commercial) object; medieval trade guild, or a corporation historically representing this. 4. Association formed to carry on some commercial or industrial undertaking; partner or partners not named in title of firm (abbreviated Co.). 5. Troupe of actors or other performers. 6. (mil.) Subdivision of a regiment or battalion, usu. commanded by captain. 7. (naut.) Entire crew of ship. 8. ~ **union**, workers' union within a given company, unconnected with a trade union, and closely associated with the employers; **keep** ~ (**with**), be a friend (*of*); carry on courtship; **part** ~, cease associating (*with*).

com·pa·ra·ble (kŏm′p*e*r*a*bel, kŏm′pr*a*-) *adj.* That may be compared (*with*), worthy to be compared (*to*). **com·pa·ra·bil·i·ty**

__Communism,__ a form of government which is based on the abolition of capitalism in favor of state ownership and the power of the worker. Facing page: Chinese Army Guardsman on duty at a state visit to Beijing.

This 16th century Italian **compass** is typical of the type used by European mariners from the 12th century. The compass was invented by the Chinese.

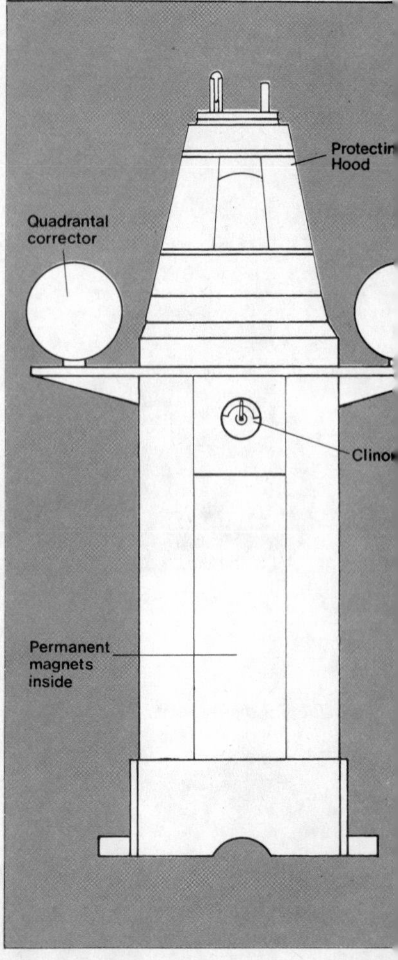

The binnacle, in which the ship's **compass** stands, is fitted with compensating magnets and pieces of iron to reduce deviation from Magnetic North.

(kŏmp*e*r*a*bĭl'ĭtē, kŏmpr*a*-), **com'pa·ra·ble·ness** *ns.* **com'pa·ra·bly** *adv.*

com·par·a·tive (k*o*mpăr'*a*tĭv) *adj.* 1. Of or involving comparison, esp. of different branches of a study, as ~ **anatomy.** 2. (gram., of an inflectional form of adjective or adverb, as *higher, faster*) Expressing a higher degree of the quality etc. denoted by the positive form (e.g. *high, fast*) of the word. 3. Estimated by comparison. **com-par'a·tive·ly** *adv.* **comparative** *n.* (gram.) (Word in) the comparative degree.

com·pare (k*o*mpār') *v.* (**-pared, -par·ing**). Liken, pronounce similar (*to*); estimate the similarity of (one thing *with, to,* another; two things together); bear comparison (*with*). ~ *n.* Comparison (chiefly in **beyond, without,** ~).

com·par·i·son (k*o*mpăr'ĭs*o*n) *n.* Comparing; simile, illustration by comparing; (gram.) **degrees of** ~, positive, comparative, and superlative of adjectives or adverbs (as *fast, faster, fastest*).

com·part·ment (k*o*mpārt'm*e*nt) *n.* Space separated by partitions; watertight division of ship. **com-part·men·tal** (k*o*mpārtmĕn't*a*l, kŏm-) *adj.* **com·part·men'tal·ize** *v.t.* (**-ized, -iz·ing**). Separate into compartments (esp. fig.) **com-part·men·tal·i·za·tion** (k*o*mpārt-mĕnt*a*lĭzā'sh*o*n, kŏm-) *n.*

com·pass (kŭm'p*a*s, kŏm'-) *n.* 1. (often pl., also **pair of compasses**) Instrument for taking measurements and describing circles, consisting of two legs connected at one end by movable joint. 2. Circumference, boundary; area, extent; range. 3. Instrument for determining magnetic meridian, or one's direction or position with respect to it, consisting of a magnetized needle turning freely on a pivot; **box the** ~: see BOX[2]; GYRO, PRISMATIC, ~: see these words; **point of the** ~, any of the 32 equidistant points marked in a circle on the ~ **card,** (also ~ **rose**) disk to which the magnetized needle (usu.) is attached with its pivot at the center of the circle. **compass** *v.t.* 1. Go around; hem in. 2. Contrive, devise; accomplish, achieve.

com·pas·sion (k*o*mpăsh'*o*n) *n.* Pity accompanied by a desire to spare or succor.

com·pas·sion·ate (k*o*mpăsh'-*o*nĭt) *adj.* Feeling or showing compassion; granted out of compassion. **com·pas'sion·ate·ly** *adv.* **com-pas'sion·ate·ness** *n.*

com·pat·i·ble (k*o*mpăt'ĭb*e*l) *adj.* Mutually tolerant; accordant, consistent, congruous. **com·pat·i-bil·i·ty** (k*o*mpătĭbĭl'ĭtē), **com-pat'i·ble·ness** *ns.* **com·pat'i·bly** *adv.*

com·pa·tri·ot (k*o*mpā'trēot) *n.* Fellow citizen of a country. **com-pa'tri·ot·ism** *n.*

com·peer (kŏm'pēr, k*o*mpēr') *n.* (literary) Equal, peer; comrade.

com·pel (k*o*mpĕl') *v.t.* (**-pelled, -pel·ling**). Constrain, force; bring about by force. **com·pel'ling** *adj.* (esp.) Arousing strong interest, respect, etc. **com·pel'la·ble** *adj.* **com·pel'la·bly** *adv.*

com·pen·di·ous (k*o*mpĕn'dē*u*s) *adj.* Brief but comprehensive. **com·pen'di·ous·ly** *adv.* **com-pen'di·ous·ness** *n.*

com·pen·di·um (k*o*mpĕn'-dē*u*m) *n.* (pl. **-di·ums, -di·a** pr. -dē*a*) (also **com·pend** pr. kŏm'-pĕnd). Abridgement; summary;

concise and comprehensive account or treatise.

com·pen·sate (kŏm′pensāt) *v.* (**-sat·ed, -sat·ing**). Counterbalance; make amends; recompense; provide with mechanical compensation, make up for (variations in a pendulum etc.); neutralize; (psychol.) counterbalance defect by development of some other characteristic. **com·pen·sa·tion** (kŏmpensā′shon) *n.* Compensating; recompense, amends. **com·pen′sa·tive** (kŏm′pensātĭv, kompĕn′sa-), **com·pen·sa·to·ry** (kompĕn′satōrē, -tōrē) *adjs.* **compensatory damages,** (law) sum awarded to plaintiff as recompense for injury. **com′pen·sa·tor** *n.*

com·pete (kompēt′) *v.i.* (**-pet·ed, -pet·ing**). Strive (*with* another, *for* or *in* something), vie (*with*), contend (*for*). **com·pet·i·tive** (kompĕt′ĭtĭv) *adj.* **com·pet′i·tive·ly** *adv.* **com·pet′i·tive·ness** *n.* **com·pet′i·to·ry** *adj.* **com·pet′i·tor** *n.*

com·pe·tence (kŏm′petens), **com·pe·ten·cy** (kŏm′petensē) *ns.* (pl. **-cies**). Sufficiency of means for living; ability (*to* do, *for* a task); (of court, magistrate, etc.) legal capacity, right to take cognizance.

com·pe·tent (kŏm′petent) *adj.* Adequate, sufficient; properly or legally qualified; belonging *to*, permissible, admissible. **com′pe·tent·ly** *adv.*

com·pe·ti·tion (kŏmpetĭsh′on) *n.* Act of competing (*for*) by examination etc.; rivalry in marketplace; striving for business; contest esp. for supremacy or prize.

Com·piègne (kawṅpyĕn′ye). City in N. France near Paris, on the Oise River; site of capture of Joan of Arc by English; World War I armistice, 1918, and armistice between France and Germany, 1940, signed nearby.

com·pi·la·tion (kŏmpilā′shon) *n.* Compiling; thing compiled.

com·pile (kompīl′) *v.t.* (**-piled, -pil·ing**). Collect (materials) into a volume; make up (volume) of such materials. **com·pil′er** *n.*

com·pla·cen·cy (komplā′sensē), **com·pla·cence** (komplā′sens) *ns.* (pl. **-cies**). Tranquil pleasure; self-satisfaction. **com·pla′cent** *adj.* **com·pla′cent·ly** *adv.*

com·plain (komplān′) *v.i.* Express dissatisfaction or discontent; let it be known that one is suffering (from illness etc.); make formal complaint of grievance *to* or *before* competent authority. **com·plain′er** *n.* **com·plain′ant** *n.* One who complains; plaintiff; one who makes a formal charge in a court. **com·plain′ing·ly** *adv.*

com·plaint (komplānt′) *n.* 1. Utterance of grievance. 2. Formal accusation; plaintiff's case in civil action. 3. Subject, ground, of complaint. 4. Bodily ailment.

com·plai·sance (komplā′sans, -zans, kŏm′plazans) *n.* Obligingness; deference. **com·plai′sant** *adj.*

com·ple·ment (kŏm′plement) *n.* 1. What completes; (gram.) word or words that complete a predicate; (math.) angular amount that, with another angle, adds up to 90°. 2. Full quantity or number required, esp. full number of ship officers and crew. ~ *v.t.* Complete; form complement to.

com·ple·men·tal (kŏmplemĕn′tal) *adj.* Forming a complement, completing. **com·ple·men′tal·ly** *adv.*

com·ple·men·ta·ry (kŏmplemĕn′terē, -trē) *adj.* Forming a complement, completing; (of two or more things) mutually complementing each other; ~ **angle,** either of two angles that together make 90°.

com·plete (komplēt′) *adj.* Having all its parts; entire; finished, thorough, unqualified; (archaic, of persons) accomplished. **com·plete′ly** *adv.* **com·plete′ness** *n.* **complete** *v.t.* (**-plet·ed, -plet·ing**). Finish; make whole or perfect; make up the amount of. **com·ple′tion** *n.*

com·plex (kŏm′plĕks) *n.* 1. Whole consisting of several parts. 2. (psychol.) Group of related ideas or memories of strongly emotional character that have undergone repression; (loosely) fixed mental tendency or obsession; inferiority ~; see INFERIOR; Oedipus ~: see OEDIPUS. **complex** (komplĕks′, kŏm′plĕks) *adj.* Consisting of parts, composite; complicated; ~ **number,** (math.) an expression $(a + bi)$ in which a and b are real numbers and $i^2 = -1$; (gram.) ~ **sentence,** one containing subordinate clause(s). **com·plex′ly** *adv.* **com·plex′ness** *n.* **com·plex′i·ty** *n.* (pl. **-ties**).

com·plex·ion (komplĕk′shon) *n.* Natural color, texture, and appearance of skin (esp. of face); character, aspect. **com·plex′ioned** *adj.* Having a (specified) complexion (as *fair-complexioned*).

com·pli·ance (komplī′ans) *n.* Action in accordance with request, demand, etc.; submission; **in ~ with,** in recognition of; according to. **com·pli′an·cy** *n.*

com·pli·ant (komplī′ant) *adj.* Disposed to comply, yielding. **com·pli′ant·ly** *adv.*

com·pli·cate (kŏm′plĭkāt) *v.t.* (**-cat·ed, -cat·ing**). Mix up *with* in intricate or involved way; make complex or intricate. **com′pli·cat·ed·ly** *adv.* **com′pli·cat·ed·ness** *n.* **com·pli·ca′tion** (kŏmplĭkā′shon) *n.* Involved condition; entangled state of affairs; complicating circumstance.

com·plic·i·ty (komplĭs′ĭtē) *n.* (pl. **-ties**). Partnership in an evil action.

com·pli·ment (kŏm′pliment) *n.* Polite expression of praise, act equivalent to this; (pl.) formal greetings. ~ (kŏm′plimĕnt, -ment) *v.t.* Pay compliment to (person *or* something); present *with* as mark of courtesy. **com·pli·men·ta·ry** (kŏmplimĕn′terē) *adj.* Expressive of, conveying, compliment; (of

*Drawing **compasses** are used in engineering and architectural draftsmanship for accurate measurements. Screws adjust compass to required diameter. Dividers measure off the distances.*

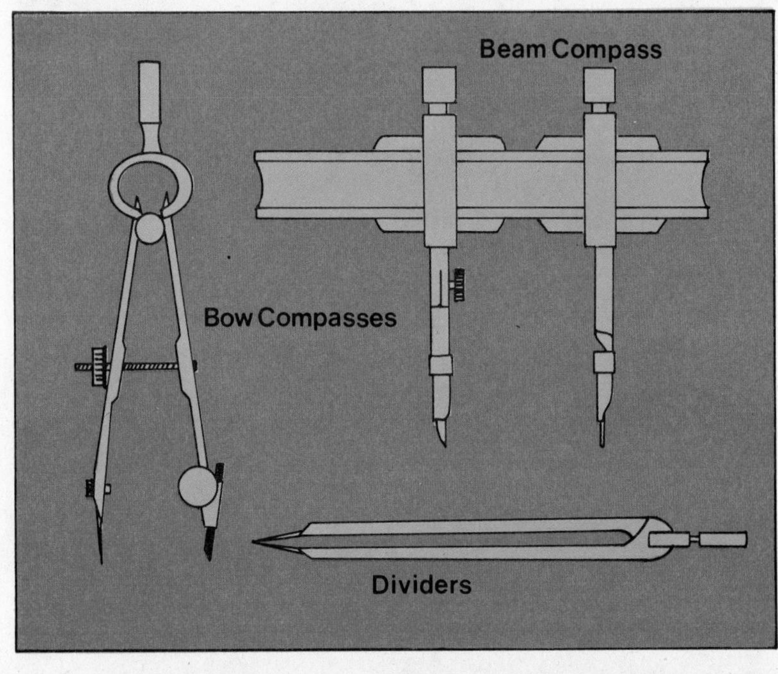

tickets etc.) presented without charge as a courtesy. **com·pli·men·tar·i·ly** (kŏmplimĕn′terilē) *adv.*

com·ply (komplī′) *v.i.* (**-plied, -ply·ing**). Act in accordance (*with*). **com·pli′er** *n.*

com·po·nent (kompō′nent) *adj.* Contributing to the composition of a whole. ~ *n.* Component part.

com·port (kompōrt′) *v.* Conduct, behave (oneself); (literary) agree, correspond *with.* **com·port′ment** *n.*

com·pose (kompōz′) *v.t.* (**-posed, -pos·ing**). 1. Make up, constitute. 2. Construct in words; produce in literary form; (mus.) invent and put into proper form; set to music. 3. (print.) Set up (type); set up in type; **composing room**, room in which type is set up; **composing stick**, compositor's metal or wooden tray of adjustable width in which type is set. 4. Put together so as to form a whole; arrange artistically. 5. Settle, arrange; adjust (oneself, one's features, etc.) in specified or understood manner, or for specified purpose; tranquilize. **com·posed′** *adj.*

com·pos·er (kompō′zer) *n.* One who composes (usu. music).

com·pos·ite (kompŏz′ĭt) *adj.* 1. Made up of various parts, compound; ~ **material**, material made of constituents that remain recognizable. 2. (archit., **C**~) Of the 5th classical order, of Ionic and Corinthian mixed. 3. (bot.) Of the natural order Compositae, in which what is pop. called the flower is a close head of many small flowers sessile on a common receptacle and surrounded by a common involucre of bracts, as daisy, dandelion, etc. **com·pos′ite·ly** *adv.* **com·pos′ite·ness** *n.* **composite** *n.* Composite thing or plant.

com·po·si·tion (kŏmpozĭsh′on) *n.* 1. Putting together; formation, construction. 2. Art of literary production; composing of music. 3. Setting up of type. 4. Arrangement (of the parts of a picture etc.); thing composed; piece of music or writing. 5. Compromise; agreement for paying, payment, esp. agreement by which creditor accepts portion of debt from debtor; sum of money paid thus.

com·pos·i·tor (kompŏz′ĭter) *n.* (see COMPOSE *v.* def. 3) Typesetter.

com·post (kŏm′pōst) *n.* Mixture of decaying organic material, such as leaves and dung, for fertilizer. ~ *v.t.* Treat with, make into, compost.

com·po·sure (kompō′zher) *n.* Tranquil demeanor, calmness.

com·pote (kŏm′pōt) *n.* Fruit stewed or cooked in syrup; long-stemmed dish for serving candy, nuts, etc.

com·pound[1] (kompownd′) *v.* 1. Mix; combine (verbal elements) into word; make up (a composite whole). 2. Settle (matter) by mutual concession, (debt) by partial payment or lump sum etc.; condone (liability, offense) for money etc.; come to terms *with* (person). 3. Compute (interest) on both principal and accrued interest. **compound** (kŏm′pownd, kŏmpownd′) *adj.* Make up of several ingredients, consisting of several parts, combined, collective; (zool., bot.) consisting of a combination of organisms or simple parts; ~ **eye**, (in insects and crustaceans), eye consisting of numerous minute simple eyes bound together; ~ **fracture**, fracture of bone associated with skin wound; ~ **interest**: see INTEREST; ~ **leaf**, leaf in which blade is divided to form two or more leaflets on a single stalk; ~ **number**, quantity involving different units of measure, as 2 pecks and 3 quarts; ~ **sentence**, one containing two or more independent clauses but no dependent clause. **compound** (kŏm′pownd) *n.* 1. (mainly fig.) Mixture of elements; compound thing, esp. word. 2. (chem.) Substance that

*The sunflower is a **composite** flower of the order Asterales which contains some 20,000 species. The plant is shown here in cross-section in various stages of flowering and in full bloom. Other Compositae are chrysanthemums and marigolds.*

Many branches of science and industry have benefited from the application of ***computers.*** *Although they are unable to 'think', they give immediate recall of vital information, enabling a business to operate much more efficiently.*

consists of elements chemically united in fixed proportions and has properties different from those of its components.

com·pound² (kŏm′pownd) *n.* Houses, huts, etc., enclosed by a barrier for protection, segregation, or imprisonment. [perh. f. Malay *kampong*]

com·pre·hend (kŏm′prĭhĕnd) *v.t.* Grasp mentally, understand; include, take in. **com·pre·hend·i·ble** (kŏmprĭhĕn′dĭbel) *adj.* **com·pre·hend′ing·ly** *adv.*

com·pre·hen·si·ble (kŏmprĭhĕn′sĭbel) *adj.* That may be understood, or comprised. **com·pre·hen·si·bil·i·ty** (kŏmprĭhĕnsĭbĭl′ĭtē) *n.* **com·pre·hen′si·bly** *adv.*

com·pre·hen·sion (kŏmprĭhĕn′shon) *n.* Understanding; inclusion.

com·pre·hen·sive (kōmprĭhĕn′sĭv) *adj.* 1. Of understanding. 2. Including much, as in ~ **education,** ~ **treatment. com·pre·hen′sive·ly** *adv.* **com·pre·hen′sive·ness** *n.*

com·press (komprĕs′) *v.t.* Squeeze together; force into smaller volume, condense. **com·pressed′** *adj.* **com·pres′sive, com·pres′si·ble** *adjs.* **com·pres·si·bil·i·ty** (komprĕsĭbĭl′ĭtē) *n.* **compress** (kŏm′prĕs) *n.* Soft pad of gauze etc. for compressing artery etc.; wet cloth applied to relieve inflammation.

com·pres·sion (komprĕsh′on) *n.* Act of compressing or state of being compressed; in internal combustion engines, act of compressing the explosive mixture after admission to the engine and before combustion. ~ **ratio,** (in internal combustion engines) ratio of volume of fuel mixture when compressed by engine to its volume at entry.

com·pres·sor (komprĕs′er) *n.* Mechanical device for reducing the volume taken up by a quantity of gas.

com·prise, comprize (komprīz′) *vbs.t.* (**-prised, -pris·ing; -prized, -priz·ing**). Include, consist of; contain.

com·pro·mise (kŏm′promīz) *n.* Settlement of dispute by mutual concession; adjustment of conflicting opinions, courses, etc., by modification of each. ~ *v.* (**-mised, -mis·ing**). Settle (dispute) by mutual concession; make compromise; bring under suspicion, into danger, by indiscreet action. **com′pro·mis·er** *n.*

comp·trol·ler (kontrō′ler) *n.* Var. of controller (see CONTROL), retained in some official titles.

com·pul·sion (kompŭl′shon) *n.* Constraint, obligation; (psychol.) strong, usu. irresistible urge to act in a certain way, esp. against one's better judgment.

com·pul·sive (kompŭl′sĭv) *adj.* Tending to compel; (psychol.) done under stress of compulsion, as in ~ **behavior. com·pul′sive·ly** *adv.*

com·pul·so·ry (kompŭl′serē) *adj.* Enforced, obligatory; compelling, coercive. **com·pul′so·ri·ly** *adv.*

com·punc·tion (kompŭngk′shon) *n.* Pricking of conscience; uneasiness caused by regret or guilt. **com·punc′tious** *adj.* **com·punc′tious·ly** *adv.*

com·pute (kompūt′) *v.* (**-put·ed, -put·ing**). Reckon; determine (an amount or number) by mathematics. **com·put′a·ble** *adj.* **com·put·a·bil·i·ty** (kompūtabĭl′ĭtē), **com·pu·ta·tion** (kŏmpyutā′shon) *ns.*

com·put·er (kompū′ter) *n.* Person who computes; electronic apparatus for performing high-speed mathematical and logical operations, storing, processing, retrieving, and transmitting coded data, etc.; **analog** ~, one using physical quantities (voltage,

*The **conch** shell is broadly triangular in shape and has a wide lip. The spider conch (right) with its underside (below right) belongs to the genus Lambis and is found in tropical seas of the eastern hemisphere.*

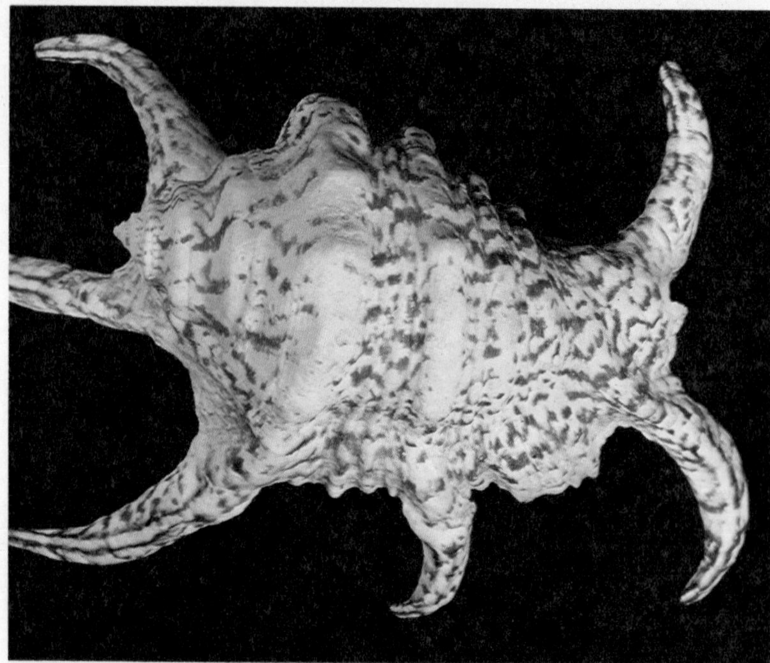

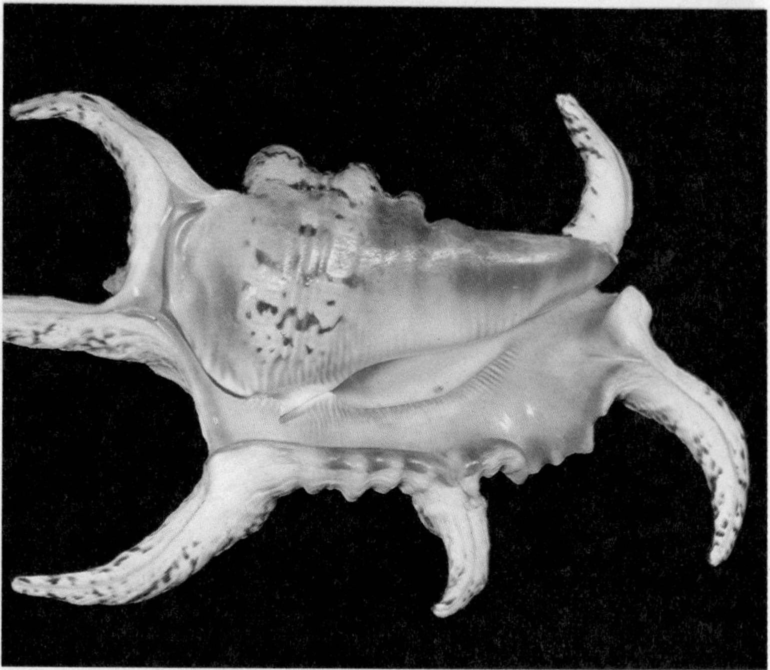

weight, length) to represent data; **digital** ~, one operating with data represented by digits, usu. in binary system; ~ **program**, plan or set of coded instructions for processing data by computer; ~ **programmer**, person trained to write computer programs. **com·pu′ter·ize** *v.t.* (**-ized, -iz·ing**). Equip with, perform by, produce by computer. **com·pu·ter·i·za·tion** (kompūterīzā′shon) *n.*

com·rade (kŏm′răd) *n.* Friend, companion, associate in work or play or fighting, equal with whom one is on familiar terms; (as title) used by socialists, communists, etc., before surname. **com′rade·li·ness** *n.* **com′rade·ly** *adv.* **com′rade·ship** *n.*

Com·sat, COM·SAT (kŏm′săt) *abbrev.* Communications satellite; corporation set up by U.S. government to manage such satellites.

Com·stock[1] (kŭm′stŏk, kŏm′-), **Anthony** (1844–1915). Amer. reformer; secretary of militant Society for the Suppression of Vice, 1873–1915.

Com·stock[2] (kŭm′stŏk, kŏm′-) **Lode.** Gold and silver lode discovered by Amer. prospector, Henry Comstock, 1859, in W. Nevada, site of Virginia City.

Comte (kawnt), **Auguste** (1798–1857). French mathematician and philosopher, founder of the positivist system (see POSITIVISM). **Comt′ism, Comt′ist** *ns.* **Com′ti·an** *adj.*

con[1] (kŏn) *v.t.* (**conned, con·ning**). Peruse, scrutinize, learn (by heart).

con[2] (kŏn) *v.t.* (**conned, con·ning**). Direct steering of (ship) from commanding position on shipboard.

con[3] (kŏn) *n.* (attrib.) Confidence, esp. in ~ **game, man**: see CONFIDENCE. **con** *v.t.* (**conned, con·ning**). Swindle by confidence trick.

con[4] (kŏn) *adv.* & *n.* (Argument) against a proposition etc.; **pros and ~s**, arguments for and against.

con[5] (kŏn) *n.* (slang) Convict; ex-convict.

con-[6] *prefix.* With.

Con·a·kry (kŏnakrē′). Capital and Atlantic seaport of the Republic of Guinea, in the SW.

con bri·o (kŏn brē′ō, kōn). (mus.) With spirit. [It.]

con·cat·e·nate (konkăt′enāt) *v.t.* (**-nat·ed, -nat·ing**). Link together (fig.) ~ *adj.* **con·cat·e·na·tion** (konkătenā′shon) *n.*

con·cave (kŏnkāv′, kŏn′kāv) *adj.* Having outline or surface curved like interior of circle or sphere (cf. CONVEX); hollow. **con·cave′ly** *adv.* **concave** (kŏn′kāv) *n.* Concave surface or line. **con·cave′ness** *n.* **con·cave′ly** *adv.* **con·cav·i·ty** (konkăv′ĭtē) *n.* (pl. **-ties**). Being concave; concave surface; hollow, cavity.

concavo- *prefix.* Concavely, concave and ..., as ~**-concave**, concave on both surfaces, as certain lenses; ~**-convex**, concave on one side, convex on the other.

con·ceal (konsēl′) *v.t.* Keep secret; hide. **con·ceal′er, con·ceal′ment** *ns.* **con·ceal′a·ble** *adj.*

con·cede (konsēd′) *v.t.* (**-ced·ed, -ced·ing**). Admit, allow, grant. **con·ced′er** *n.*

con·ceit (konsēt′) *n.* 1. Personal vanity. 2. Fanciful notion, far-fetched comparison, etc. **con·ceit′ed** *adj.* Vain. **con·ceit′ed·ly** *adv.* **con·ceit′ed·ness** *n.*

con·ceiv·a·ble (konsē′vabel) *adj.* That can be (mentally) conceived. **con·ceiv′a·bly** *adv.* **con·ceiv·a·bil·i·ty** (konsēvabĭl′ĭtē), **con·ceiv′a·ble·ness** *ns.*

con·ceive (konsēv′) *v.* (**-ceived, -ceiv·ing**). 1. Become pregnant (with). 2. Form in the mind, imagine; fancy, think. 3. Formulate, express in words, etc. **con·ceiv′er** *n.*

con·cen·trate (kŏn′sentrāt) *v.*

(**-trat·ed, -trat·ing**). Bring to or toward a common center; focus (attention), keep mind or attention intently fixed (*on*); increase strength of (solution etc.) esp. by evaporation of solvent etc.; **con·centrated,** (fig.) intense. **concentrate** *n.* Concentrated substance. **con·cen·tra·tion** (kŏnsentrā´shon) *n.* ~ **camp,** camp in which large numbers of people, esp. political prisoners, are detained by force, esp. any of the camps established by the Nazis in World War II for the detention, persecution, and mass execution of Jews and other non-Aryans, civilian war prisoners, etc.

con·cen·tric (konsĕn´trĭk) *adj.* Having a common center. **con·cen´tri·cal** *adj.* **con·cen´tri·cal·ly** *adv.* **con·cen·tric·i·ty** (kŏnsĕn-trĭs´ĭtē) *n.*

con·cept (kŏn´sĕpt) *n.* Idea of a class of objects, general notion.

con·cep·ta·cle (kŏnsĕp´takel) *n.* (bot.) Hollow organ of some algae and fungi within which sexual organs are formed.

con·cep·tion (konsĕp´shon) *n.* Conceiving; thing conceived; idea. **con·cep´tion·al** *adj.* Of, like, a conception or idea.

con·cep·tive (konsĕp´tĭv) *adj.* Conceiving; of conception.

con·cep·tu·al (konsĕp´chōōal) *adj.* Of mental conceptions. **con·cep´tu·al·ly** *adv.*

con·cep·tu·al·ism (konsĕp´-chōōalĭzem) *n.* 1. (philos.) Doctrine that universals have reality only as mental concepts. 2. (psychol.) Doctrine that the mind is capable of forming ideas corresponding to abstract and general terms. **con·cep´tu·al·ist** *n.* **con·cep·tu·al·is·tic** (konsĕpchōōalĭs´-tĭk) *adj.*

con·cern (konsērn´) *v.t.* Relate to, affect; interest (oneself). **con·cerned´** *adj.* (esp.) Involved; troubled. **con·cern´ing** *prep.* Regarding, relating to. **concern** *n.* Relation, reference; interest, solicitous regard, anxiety; matter that affects one; business establishment, firm.

con·cert (kŏn´sert) *n.* 1. Agreement; union by mutual agreement. 2. Combination of voices or sounds. 3. Musical entertainment; ~ **grand,** grand piano of largest size for concerts. 4. **in** ~, acting together. **concert** (konsērt´) *v.t.* Arrange, plan by mutual agreement. **con·cert´ed** *adj.* Contrived, prearranged; done in concert. **con·cert´ed·ly** *adv.*

con·cer·ti·na (kŏnsertē´na, -cher-) *n.* Small, hexagonal accordion with bellows and buttons for keys.

con·cer·to (konchĕr´tō, -chēr´-) *n.* (pl. **-tos, -ti** pr. -tē). Musical composition, usu. in sonata form with three or four movements, for a solo instrument (or, rarely, more than one) accompanied by orchestra.

con·ces·sion (konsĕsh´on) *n.* 1. Conceding; thing conceded; esp. grant of land or franchise by a government, company, or person for a special use or purpose. 2. Space within premises, e.g., **carnival** ~, for a subsidiary business. **con·ces·sion·ar·y** (kon-sĕsh´onĕrē) *adj.* & *n.* (pl. **-ar·ies**).

con·ces·sion·aire (konsĕsho-nār´), **con·ces·sion·er** (konsĕsh´o-ner) *ns.* Holder or operator of concession.

con·ces·sive (konsĕs´ĭv) *adj.* Of, tending to, concession.

conch (kŏngk, kŏnch) *n.* (pl. **conchs** pr. kŏngks, **con·ches** pr. kŏn´chĭz). 1. Shellfish; (now usu.) large gastropod, esp. Strombidae; the Queen Conch (*strombus gigas*); shell of mollusk, esp. spiral shell of any large gastropod; such a shell used as a trumpet, esp. (Rom. myth.) of Triton. 2. External ear, its central concavity.

con·chif·er·ous (kŏngkĭf´erus) *adj.* Shell-bearing.

con·chol·o·gy (kŏngkŏl´ojē) *n.* Study of shells and shellfish. **con·chol´o·gist** *n.*

con·cierge (kŏnsyĕrzh´) *n.* In France etc., doorkeeper, porter, of apartment house, hotel, etc.

con·cil·i·ar (konsĭl´ēer) *adj.* Of a council. **con·cil´i·ar·ly** *adv.*

con·cil·i·ate (konsĭl´ēāt) *v.t.* (**-at·ed, -at·ing**). Gain (goodwill, esteem, etc.) by acts that pacify, soothe, etc.; gain over, overcome distrust or hostility of. **con·cil·i·a·tion** (konsĭlēā´shon) *n.* Reconcilement; use of conciliatory measures. **con·cil´i·a·to·ri·ness, con·cil´i·a·tor** *ns.* **con·cil´i·a·tive, con·cil´i·a·to·ry, con·cil´i·a·ble** *adjs.* **con·cil´i·a·to·ri·ly** *adv.*

con·cise (konsīs´) *adj.* Brief and comprehensive in expression. **con·cise´ly** *adv.* **con·cise´ness** *n.*

con·clave (kŏn´klāv, kŏng´-) *n.* Meeting place, assembly, of cardinals for election of pope; private assembly.

con·clude (konklōōd´) *v.* (**-clud·ed, -clud·ing**). Bring to an end, make an end; come to an end; settle, arrange (treaty etc.); infer; come to a conclusion; resolve. **con·clud´er** *n.*

con·clu·sion (konklōō´zhon) *n.* Termination; final result; inference; decision; (logic) proposition deduced from previous ones, esp. last of three forming a syllogism; settling, arrangement (*of* peace etc.).

con·clu·sive (konklōō´sĭv) *adj.* Decisive, convincing. **con·clu´sive·ly** *adv.* **con·clu´sive·ness** *n.*

con·coct (konkŏkt´) *v.t.* Make up by mixing variety of ingredients; fabricate. **con·coc·tion** (konkŏk´-shon), **con·coct´er** *ns.* **con·coc´tive** *adj.*

con·com·i·tance (konkŏm´-ĭtans), **con·com·i·tan·cy** (kon-kŏm´ĭtansē) *ns.* (pl. **-cies**). Being concomitant, coexistence, esp. of body and blood of Christ in each of Eucharistic elements.

con·com·i·tant (konkŏm´ĭtant) *adj.* Going together, accompanying. ~ *n.* Accompanying state, quality, thing, etc. **con·com´i·tant·ly** *adv.*

Con·cord[1] (kŏng´kerd). Capital of New Hampshire, in the S. central part.

Con·cord[2] (kŏng´kerd). Town in E. Massachusetts, near Boston; site of an early Revolutionary War battle, 1775.

con·cord (kŏn´kōrd, kŏng´-) *n.* Agreement, harmony, between persons or things; treaty.

con·cord·ance (konkōr´dans) *n.* 1. Agreement, harmony. 2. Alphabetical arrangement of chief words or subjects occurring in a book (esp. the Bible) or in an author's works, with citations of passages concerned.

con·cord·ant (konkōr´dant) *adj.* Agreeing, harmonious. **con·cord´ant·ly** *adv.*

con·cor·dat (kŏnkōr´dăt) *n.* Formal agreement, esp. between pope and secular government for settlement and control of ecclesiastical affairs.

con·course (kŏn´kōrs, -kōrs, kŏng´-) *n.* 1. Flocking together; crowd, confluence; assemblage. 2. Large main hall, or central open area, as at a railroad station; broad thoroughfare, avenue.

con·crete (kŏn´krēt, kŏnkrēt´) *adj.* 1. (gram., of noun) Denoting a thing as opp. to a quality, state, or action; not abstract. 2. Existing in material form, real. 3. Made of concrete. **con·crete´ly** *adv.* **con·crete´ness** *n.* **concrete** *n.* 1. Concrete thing. 2. Composition of broken stone, sand, gravel, etc., formed into a mass with cement and used for building, paving, etc. **concrete** (kŏnkrēt´) *v.* (**-cret·ed, -cret·ing**). 1. Form into a mass, solidify. 2. Treat, build, pave, etc., with concrete.

con·cre·tion (konkrē´shon) *n.* Coalescence; concrete mass, esp. (path.) hard morbid formation in body, stone; (geol.) mass formed by aggregation of solid particles, usu. around a nucleus. **con·cre´tion·ar·y** *adj.*

con·cu·bi·nage (konkū´binĭj) *n.* Cohabiting of man and woman not legally married; being, having, a concubine.

con·cu·bine (kŏng´kyubīn, kŏn´-) *n.* Woman who cohabits with man to whom she is not married; (among polygamous

The Andean ***condor*** *is the world's largest flying bird and the Californian species (above) is one of the rarest. It feeds near open coastland. Each female lays a single egg in a year. It is now a protected species in the U.S.A.*

peoples) secondary wife, usu. of inferior status.

con·cu·pis·cence (konkū′-pĭsens) *n.* Sexual appetite. **con·cu′pis·cent** *adj.* Lustful, eagerly desirous.

con·cur (konkẽr′) *v.i.* (**-curred, -cur·ring**). Coincide; cooperate; agree, express agreement, (*with*). **con·cur′rence, con·cur′ren·cy** *ns.* (pl. **-cies**).

con·cur·rent (konkẽr′ent, -kŭr′-) *adj.* 1. Running together, going on side by side, occurring together; meeting in or tending to same point. 2. Cooperating; agreeing. **con·cur′rent·ly** *adv.*

con·cus·sion (konkŭsh′on) *n.* 1. Violent shaking; shock. 2. Injury caused, esp. to brain, by shock of heavy blow, fall, etc. **con·cus·sive** (konkŭs′ĭv) *adj.*

con·demn (kondĕm′) *v.t.* 1. Censure, blame; bring about conviction of. 2. Give judicial sentence against, find guilty; sentence (*to* death etc.); (fig., esp. pass.) doom *to* some (unkind) fate or condition. 3. Pronounce unfit for use or consumption. 4. Take title to (property) for public use. **con·demn·er** (kondĕm′er) *n.* **con·dem·na·ble** (kondĕm′nabel) *adj.* **con·demn′ing·ly** *adv.*

con·dem·na·tion (kŏndĕmnā′-shon, -dem-) *n.* Censure; condemning; state of being condemned; ground for condemning. **con·dem·na·to·ry** (kondĕm′-natōrē, -tōrē) *adj.*

con·den·sa·tion (kŏndĕnsā′-shon, -den-) *n.* Condensing; condensed mass; liquid formed by condensed gas or vapor.

con·dense (kondĕns′) *v.* (**-densed, -dens·ing**). 1. Increase density of, reduce in volume; compress, thicken, concentrate; **condensed milk**, milk thickened by evaporation and sweetened. 2. Compress into few words. 3. Reduce, be reduced, from form of gas or vapor to liquid.

con·dens·er (kondĕn′ser) *n.* (esp.) 1. (elect.) Capacitor. 2. Lens, system of lenses, for concentrating light.

con·de·scend (kŏndĭsĕnd′) *v.i.* Deign, stoop; be condescending, waive one's superiority. **con·de·scend′ing** *adj.* (esp.) Making a show of condescension, patronizing. **con·de·scend′ing·ly** *adv.* **con·de·scend′ence** *n.*

con·de·scen·sion (kŏndĭsĕn′-shon) *n.* Affability to inferiors; patronizing manner.

con·dign (kondīn′) *adj.* (of punishment) Adequate, appropriate, deserved. **con·dign′ly** *adv.*

con·di·ment (kŏn′diment) *n.* Something used to give additional flavor to food, as ketchup, mustard, or spice.

con·di·tion (kondĭsh′on) *n.* 1. Stipulation; thing upon fulfillment of which depends that of something else. 2. (pl.) Circumstances, esp. those essential to a thing's existence. 3. State of being; **in ~, out of ~**, in good, bad, training and health. **condition** *v.t.* 1. Stipulate; agree by stipulation (*to*). 2. Subject to as a condition. 3. Bring into (good) condition (*for*). 4. Train to adopt certain habits etc. **con·di′tioned** *adj.* (esp.) **~ reflex**, reflex or reflex action, which through habit or training has been induced to follow a stimulus that is not naturally associated with it.

con·di·tion·al (kondĭsh′onal) *adj.* 1. Not absolute; dependent. 2. (gram.) Of a clause, mood, conjunction, phrase, expressing or introducing a condition. **con·di′tion·al·ly** *adv.*

con·dole (kondōl′) *v.i.* (**-doled, -dol·ing**). Express sympathy (*with* person *upon* loss etc.). **con·dol′er, con·do·lence** (kondō′lens), **con·dole′ment** *ns.* **con·do·la·to·ry** (kondō′latōrē, -tōrē) *adj.*

con·dom (kŏn′dom, kŭn′-) *n.* Contraceptive or prophylactic sheath worn on penis during sexual intercourse.

con·do·min·i·um (kŏndomĭn′-ēum) *n.* Apartment house etc. in which each dwelling unit is individually owned; apartment so owned.

con·done (kondōn′) *v.t.* (**-doned, -don·ing**). Forgive;

overlook (offense) with forgiveness; give tacit approval to. **con·do·na·tion** (kŏndōnā'shon), **con·don'er** *ns.*

con·dor (kŏnder, -dōr) *n.* Large S. Amer. vulture (*Vultur gryphus*) with blackish plumage and fleshy excrescence falling over bill; **California ~**, great Californian vulture (*Gymnogyps californianus*) somewhat resembling this.

con·duce (kondōōs', -dūs') *v.i.* (**-duced, -duc·ing**). (usu. of events) Lead, contribute, *to.* **con·duc'er, con·du'cive·ness** *ns.* **con·du·cive** (kondōō'sĭv, -dū'-) *adj.*

con·duct (kondŭkt') *v.* 1. Lead, guide *to.* 2. Direct (orchestra, concert, etc.); manage (business etc.). 3. Behave (*oneself*). 4. (phys.; of a body) Convey (some form of energy, as heat, electricity, etc.) through its particles, transmit. **con·duct** (kŏn'dŭkt) *n.* Manner of conducting (any business etc., or oneself), behavior. **con·duct'i·ble** *adj.* **con·duct·i·bil·i·ty** (kondŭktibĭl'ĭtē, kŏn-) *n.*

con·duct·ance (kondŭk'tans) *n.* (elect.) Conducting power of a given conductor.

con·duc·tion (kondŭk'shon) *n.* Conducting (of liquid through a pipe etc.); transmission (of heat, electricity, etc.).

con·duc·tive (kondŭk'tĭv) *adj.* Having the property of conducting some form of energy, esp. electricity. **con·duc·tiv·i·ty** (kŏndŭktĭv'ĭtē) *n.* (pl. **-ties**).

con·duc·tor (kondŭk'ter) *n.* (fem. **-tress** pr. -trĭs). 1. Leader, guide; manager. 2. Director of orchestra or chorus, who indicates to the performers the rhythm, expression, etc., by motions of a baton or the hands. 3. Person in charge of a train or bus. 4. Thing that conducts or transmits (some form of energy).

con·duit (kŏn'dōōĭt, -dū-, -dĭt) *n.* Channel or pipe for conveying water or other liquids; tube or duct for enclosing electric wires and cable.

con·dyle (kŏn'dīl, -dil) *n.* (anat.) Rounded process at end of bone, forming articulation with another bone. **con·dy·loid** (kŏn'diloid) *adj.*

cone (kōn) *n.* 1. Solid of which the base is a circle (or other curved figure) and the summit a point, and every point in the intervening surface is in a straight line between the vertex and the circumference of the base; any conical mass. 2. Fruit of pine or fir, a dry, scaly multiple fruit, more or less cone-shaped, formed by hard persistent imbricated scales covering naked seeds. 3. Cone-shaped object; marine shell of genus *Conus* of gastropods; cone-shaped volcanic peak; (physiol.) one of the minute cone-shaped bodies that form, with rods, one of the layers of nerve elements in the retina. 4. **cone'-flower**, garden plant of genus *Rudbeckia*, esp. the black-eyed Susan (*R. hirta*), native to N. America. **cone** *v.t.* (**coned, con·ing**). Shape into a cone.

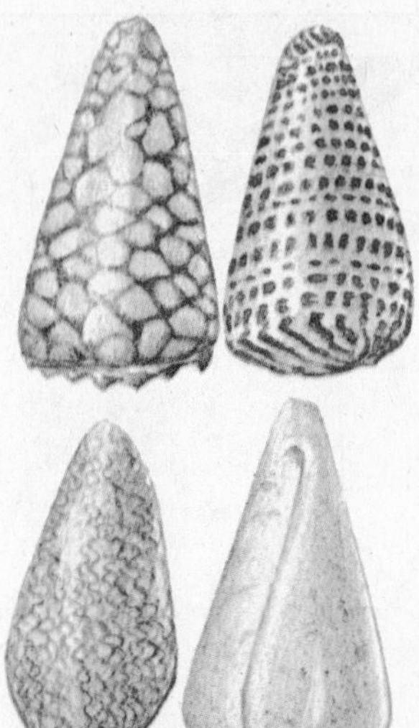

*The **cone** shellfish feeds on worms and mollusks. Its shell is conical in shape. At one time sea-cone shells were much sought by collectors, particularly that of the rare glory-of-the-sea cone.*

Con·es·to·ga (kŏnestō'ga) *n.* (Member of) tribe of N. Amer. Indians formerly inhabiting parts of Pennsylvania and Maryland; Huron Indian name for the Susquehanna river; **~ Valley**, Susquehanna river valley; **~ wagon**, heavy, broad-wheeled, Pennsylvania Dutch freight wagon, later adapted by pioneers for westward travel. [*Conestoga* (= "place of muddy water"), Pennsylvania]

co·ney (kō'nē, kŭn'ē) *n.* (pl. **-neys**) = CONY.

*This **cone-flower** of the genus Rudbeckia is one of 25 annual, biennial and perennial species. Many have segmented leaves and yellow flowers with brown or black disks, and are native to N. America.*

Co·ney (kō'nē) **Island.** Amusement resort on the Atlantic Ocean in S. Brooklyn, New York City.

con·fab (kŏn'făb) *n.* (slang) Confabulation. ~ *v.i.* (**-fabbed, -fab·bing**). (slang) Confabulate.

con·fab·u·late (konfăb'yulāt) *v.i.* (**-lat·ed, -lat·ing**). Converse, chat. **con·fab·u·la·tion** (konfăbyulā'shon) *n.*

con·fec·tion (konfĕk'shon) *n.* 1. Mixing, compounding. 2. Medicinal preparation compounded with sweetening; sweet

*The **Conestoga Wagon** was the prototype of those used by the American pioneers to transport their possessions to the West. The floor was curved to prevent any movement as they travelled the rough trails.*

preparation, as a bonbon. **con·fec·tion·ar·y** (k*o*nfĕk′sh*o*nĕrē) *adj.*

con·fec·tion·er (k*o*nfĕk′sh*o*n*er*) *n.* Maker or seller of candy, pastry, etc. **con·fec·tion·er·y** (k*o*nfĕk′sh*o*nĕrē) *n.* (pl. **-er·ies**). Things made or sold by a confectioner; confectioner's shop; confectioner's art.

con·fed·er·a·cy (k*o*nfĕd′*e*r*a*sē, -fĕd′r*a*-) *n.* (pl. **-cies**). 1. League, alliance; league for unlawful or evil purpose; conspiracy. 2. Body of allies, esp. union of states; (**Southern**) **C~**, Confederate States of America.

con·fed·er·ate (k*o*nfĕd′*e*rĭt, -fĕd′rĭt) *adj.* Allied; **C~ States** (of America), confederacy of 11 Southern states that seceded from the U.S. in 1860–1 and fought the Civil War against the Union: Alabama, Arkansas, Florida, Georgia, Louisiana, Mississippi, North Carolina, South Carolina, Tennessee, Texas, Virginia. **confederate** *n.* 1. Accomplice. 2. **C~**, supporter of the Confederate States of America. **confederate** (k*o*nfĕd′*e*rāt) *v.* (**-at·ed, -at·ing**). Bring, come, into alliance (*with*). **con·fed·er·a·tion** (k*o*nfĕd*e*rā′sh*o*n) *n.* (Union formed by) confederating.

con·fer (k*o*nfẽr′) *v.* (**-ferred, -fer·ring**). 1. Grant, bestow (title, degree, favor, etc., *on*). 2. Converse, take counsel (*with*) **con·fer′ment** *n.* Bestowing, granting. **con·fer′ra·ble** *adj.*

con·fer·ence (kŏn′f*e*r*e*ns, -fr*e*ns) *n.* 1. Consultation; meeting, for consultation or discussion. 2. Association of athletic teams, schools, or churches.

con·fess (k*o*nfĕs′) *v.* Acknowledge, own, admit; make formal confession of guilt (to police, court, etc.) or of sins, esp. to a priest; (of priest) hear confession of (a penitent). **con·fess·ed·ly** (k*o*nfĕs′ĭdlē) *adv.*

con·fes·sion (k*o*nfĕsh′*o*n) *n.* Acknowledgment, admission (of fact, guilt, etc.); acknowledgment of sin (as by individual penitent to a priest); thing confessed; **C~ (of Faith)**, formulary in which Church or body of Christians sets forth religious doctrines that it considers essential; creed.

con·fes·sion·al (k*o*nfĕsh′*o*n*a*l) *adj.* Of confession. ~ *n.* Cabinet or stall in which priest hears confession.

con·fes·sor (k*o*nfĕs′*er*) *n.* 1. One who makes confession. 2. One who avows his religion in the face of persecution but does not suffer martyrdom. 3. Priest who hears confession.

con·fet·ti (k*o*nfĕt′ē) *n.pl.* (usu. considered sing.) Small pieces of colored paper tossed into the air at celebrations, at bride and groom at

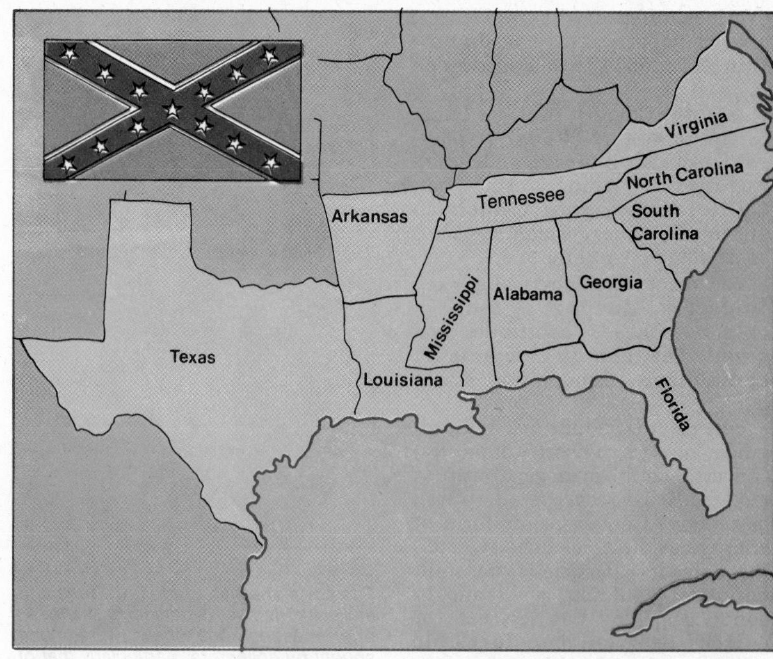

During the American Civil War 11 southern states banded together to form the ***Confederate States****. They wanted to retain state rights, as against a centralized authority in Washington. A confederation is usually a league or form of union between independent states.*

weddings, etc. [It., = "sweetmeats"]

con·fi·dant (kŏn′fĭdănt, -dahnt, kŏnfĭdănt′, -dahnt′) *n.* (fem. **-dante**). One to whom private matters or secrets are entrusted or confided.

con·fide (k*o*nfīd′) *v.* (**-fid·ed, -fid·ing**). Repose confidence *in*; impart (secret *to*); entrust (*to*); ~ **in**, talk confidentially to.

con·fi·dence (kŏn′fĭd*e*ns) *n.* 1. Firm trust; assured expectation. 2. Boldness, fearlessness; impudence, presumption. 3. Imparting of private matters; thing so imparted. 4. ~ **game**, (also **con game**) swindle worked by gaining the confidence or trust of a credulous person; ~ **man**, (also **con man**) one who practices this.

con·fi·dent (kŏn′fĭd*e*nt) *adj.* Trusting, fully assured; bold; impudent. **con′fi·dent·ly** *adv.*

con·fi·den·tial (kŏnfĭdĕn′sh*a*l) *adj.* Spoken, written, in confidence; entrusted with secrets or private matters. **con·fi·den′tial·ly** *adv.*

con·fig·u·ra·tion (k*o*nfĭgy*u*rā′sh*o*n) *n.* Mode of arrangement, conformation, outline; (astron.) relative position of planet or other celestial bodies. **con·fig·u·ra′tion·al** *adj.*

con·fine (kŏn′fīn) *n.* (usu. pl.) Border, boundaries, limit. **confine** (k*o*nfīn′) *v.t.* (**-fined, -fin·ing**). Keep *within*, *to*, limits; imprison, immure; (pass.) be in childbirth. **con·fine·ment** (k*o*nfīn′m*e*nt) *n.* Imprisonment; restriction, limitation; childbirth. **con·fin′a·ble** *adj.*

con·firm (k*o*nfẽrm′) *v.t.* 1. Establish more firmly; ratify; corroborate; establish, encourage (person *in* opinion etc.). 2. Administer religious rite of confirmation to. **con·firm′a·ble, con·firm·a·to·ry** (k*o*nfẽr′m*a*tōrē, -tōrē-), **con·firm′a·tive** *adjs.*

con·fir·ma·tion (kŏnf*e*rmā′sh*o*n) *n.* 1. Confirming, corroboration. 2. Rite administered to baptized persons esp. at age of discretion in various Christian Churches. 3. Rite by which Jewish child, after a prescribed course of study, is admitted to adult status in some sections of the Jewish community; see BAR MITZVAH, BAT MITZVAH.

con·fis·cate (kŏn′fĭskāt) *v.t.* (**-cat·ed, -cat·ing**). Appropriate to the public treasury by way of penalty; seize as by authority, appropriate summarily. **con·fis·ca·tion** (kŏnfĭskā′sh*o*n), **con·fis·ca·tor** (kŏn′fĭskāt*er*) *ns.* **con·fis·ca·to·ry** (k*o*nfĭs′k*a*tōrē, -tōre) *adj.*

con·fla·gra·tion (kŏnfl*a*grā′sh*o*n) *n.* Great and destructive fire.

con·flict (kŏn′flĭkt) *n.* Fight, struggle; collision; clashing (*of* opposed principles etc.). ~ (k*o*nflĭkt′) *v.i.* Struggle; clash, be incompatible.

con·flu·ence (kŏn′flo͞o*e*ns) *n.* Flocking or flowing together, esp. joining of two or more streams etc.

con·flu·ent (kŏn′flo͞o*e*nt) *adj.* Flowing together, uniting. ~ *n.* Stream uniting with another. **con′flu·ent·ly** *adv.*

con·form (k*o*nfōrm′) *v.* Form according to, agree with, a pattern;

*Traffic **congestion,** both human and vehicular, is becoming an increasing headache for town planners as urban populations continue to grow and people go on buying cars.*

make similar (*to*); adapt *oneself to*; comply with, be conformable (*to*). **con·form'er** *n.*

con·form·a·ble (konfŏr'mabel) *adj.* Similar (*to*); consistent, adapted (*to*); tractable. **con·form·a·bil·i·ty** (konfŏrmabĭl'ĭtē) *n.* **con·form'a·bly,** *adv.*

con·for·ma·tion (kŏnfŏrmā'shon) *n.* 1. Conforming, adaptation. 2. Manner in which thing is formed, structure.

con·form·ist (konfŏr'mĭst) *n.* One who conforms to practices of a group, society, etc.

con·form·i·ty (konfŏr'mĭtē) *n.* (pl. **-ties**). Likeness (*to, with*); compliance (*with, to*).

con·found (konfownd') *v.t.* 1. Defeat utterly, discomfit (archaic); overthrow, defeat (plan, hope); (bibl.) put to shame. 2. Throw into perplexity; throw into disorder; mix up; confuse (in idea). 3. Damn, esp. in mild oath (as ~ *it*). **con·found'ed·ly** *adv.* Damnably.

con·frere (kŏn'frār) *n.* Fellow member of profession etc.

con·front (konfrŭnt') *v.t.* Meet face to face, stand facing; be opposite to; face in hostility or defiance; oppose; bring (person) face to face *with* (accusers etc.); compare. **con·fron·ta·tion** (kŏnfrontā'shon), **con·front'ment** *ns.*

Con·fu·cius (konfū'shus) (*c*550–478 B.C.). Chinese philosopher and teacher; famous for his sayings relating mainly to temporal and secular matters. **Con·fu·cian** (konfū'shan) *adj.* & *n.* (Follower) of Confucius. **Con·fu'cian·ism** *n.* Ethical system based on teachings of Confucius, emphasizing virtue, justice, and devotion to family and the spirits of one's ancestors; political and cosmological system that evolved in China during the Han dynasty (206 B.C.–220 A.D.), which regarded the emperor and hierarchy of officials as divinely appointed, and social relations as governed by the rules of Confucius. [Latinized f. Chin. *K'ung-fu-tzŭ* or *K'ung-fu-tse* K'ung the master (or philosopher)]

con fuo·co (kŏn fwō'kō, kōn). (mus.) With fire. [It.]

con·fuse (konfūz') *v.t.* (**-fused, -fus·ing**). Throw into disorder; mix up in the mind; abash, perplex. **con·fus·ed·ly** (konfū'zĭdlē, -fūzd'-) *adv.* **con·fus'ed·ness** *n.* **con·fus'ing·ly** *adv.*

con·fu·sion (konfū'zhon) *n.* Confusing; confused state; tumult.

con·fute (konfūt') *v.t.* (**-fut·ed, -fut·ing**). Convict (person) of error by proof, refute (argument). **con·fu·ta·tion** (kŏnfyootā'shon) *n.*

con·ga (kŏng'ga) *n.* (pl. **-gas**). Latin-Amer. dance in which dancers form a long winding line (~ **line**) behind a leader.

con·geal (konjēl') *v.* Solidify, as by freezing or cooling; coagulate. **con·geal'a·ble** *adj.* **con·geal'ment** *n.*

con·gen·ial (konjēn'yal) *adj.* Kindred, sympathetic (*with, to*); suited, agreeable (*to*). **con·ge·ni·al·i·ty** (konjēnēăl'ĭtē) *n.* **con·gen'ial·ly** *adv.*

con·gen·i·tal (konjĕn'ĭtal) *adj.* Existing before or at birth; dating from birth (esp. of defects, diseases, etc.). **con·gen'i·tal·ly** *adv.*

con·ger (kŏng'ger) *n.* (also ~ **eel**) Large species of eel of the family Congridae, esp. *Conger oceanicus* of Atlantic waters.

con·ge·ries (kŏnjēr'ēz, kŏn'je-) *n.* (considered sing. or pl.). Collection; mass, heap.

con·gest (konjĕst') *v.* Accumulate to excess; affect with congestion. **con·ges'ted** *adj.* Overcrowded; filled. **con·ges'tive** *adj.* (med.) Overcharged with blood.

con·ges·tion (konjĕs'chon) *n.* 1. Congested or overcrowded condition, as of population, traffic, etc. 2. (med.) Abnormal accumulation of blood in an organ etc.

con·glom·er·ate (konglŏm'erĭt) *adj.* Gathered together into more or less rounded mass, clustered; (geol., of rock) formed of pebbles or gravel cemented together. ~ *n.*

1. Conglomerate rock. 2. Company consisting of number of subsidiary units in unrelated industries. ~ (konglŏm′erāt) *v.* (**-at·ed, -at·ing**). Collect into a coherent mass. **con·glom·er·a·tion** (konglŏmerā′shon) *n.*

Con·go (kŏng′gō). Second largest river of Africa, 2,900 mi. (4,640 km), flowing from Zambia in central Africa into Atlantic; area surrounding it; **Belgian** ~, former name of ZAIRE; **People's Republic of the C**~, country in W. Africa bordering on the Atlantic; the former French Congo; member of the French Community; capital, Brazzaville. **Con·go·lese** (kŏnggolēz′, -lēs′) *adj.* & *n.*

con·gou (kŏng′gōō) *n.* Kind of black China tea. [Chin. *kung-fu* (*ch'a*) labor (tea)]

con·grat·u·late (kongrăch′ulāt) *v.t.* (**-lat·ed, -lat·ing**). Address (person) with expression of sympathetic joy (*on* something); ~ **oneself**, think oneself fortunate. **con·grat′u·lant** *adj.* & *n.* **con·grat′u·la·tor** *n.* **con·grat·u·la·tion** (kongrăchulā′shon) *n.* Congratulating; (pl.) congratulatory expressions (also as *int.*) **con·grat·u·la·to·ry** (kongrăch′ulatōrē, -tōre) *adj.*

con·gre·gate (kŏng′gregāt) *v.* (**-gat·ed, -gat·ing**). Collect, gather, into a crowd or mass.

con·gre·ga·tion (kŏnggregā′shon) *n.* 1. Collection into a body or mass; assemblage. 2. General assembly of a group; body of assembled people. 3. Body of persons assembled for religious worship or habitually attending a particular place of worship. **con·gre·gant** (kŏng′gregant), **con′gre·ga·tor** *ns.*

con·gre·ga·tion·al (kŏnggregā′shonal) *adj.* 1. Of a congregation. 2. **C**~, of or adhering to Congregationalism.

Con·gre·ga·tion·al·ism (kŏnggregā′shonalĭzem) *n.* System of ecclesiastical polity regarding all legislative, disciplinary, and judicial functions as vested in the individual church or local congregation of believers; referring to doctrine of Congregational Christian Church. **Con·gre·ga′tion·al·ist** *n.*

con·gress (kŏng′grĭs) *n.* Coming together, meeting. 2. Formal meeting of delegates for discussion, esp. of envoys or persons engaged in special studies. 3. **C**~, national legislative body of U.S. consisting of the Senate and the House of Representatives; legislative body of certain other republics; session of this; **con′gressman, con′gresswoman**, member of U.S. Congress, esp. of the House of Representatives; **Congress of Racial Equality**, organization founded in 1942 in U.S., dedicated to ending racial segregation, improving social conditions, etc.; abbrev. CORE. **con·gres·sion·al** (kongrĕsh′onal) *adj.* Of a congress; of Congress.

Con·greve (kŏn′grēv, kŏng′-), **William** (1670–1729). English writer of Restoration comedies; author of *Love for Love*, *The Way of the World*, etc.

con·gru·ence (kŏng′grōōens) *n.* Agreement, consistency. **con′gru·en·cy** *n.* (pl. **-cies**). Congruence; (math.) relation between two numbers which, when divided by a third (the *modulus*), give the same remainder.

con·gru·ent (kŏng′grōōent) *adj.* Suitable; accordant (*with*); (math.) having congruency; (of triangles etc.) equal in all respects, capable of exact superposition. **con′gru·ent·ly** *adv.*

con·gru·ous (kŏng′grōōus) *adj.* Accordant, conformable (*with*); fitting. **con·gru·i·ty** (kongrōō′ĭtē, kŏn-) *n.* (pl. **-ties**).

con·ic (kŏn′ĭk) *adj.* Cone-shaped; of a cone; ~ **section**, figure (circle, ellipse, parabola, or hyperbola) formed by intersection of a

The river Congo (facing page) is the second largest in Africa and contains over 4,000 islands and some 8,000 miles of natural waterways. Congo (below) is a relatively poor country with most of its population engaged in subsistence agriculture. It has a hot and humid climate. Fishing is carried out in primitive boats by tribes living along the river (left).

*The **conifer** is mostly an evergreen tree or shrub, native to the northern hemisphere, whose seeds form a cone. The Norway spruce (above) and Scots Pine (right) are common in parts of western Europe with long winters and a high rainfall.*

plane and a right circular cone. **con'ics** *n.* Branch of geometry dealing with cones and conic sections.

con·i·cal (kŏn'ĭk*a*l) *adj.* Cone-shaped; of or relating to a cone.

co·ni·fer (kŏn'ĭf*er*, kō'nĭ-) *n.* Cone-bearing tree or shrub. **co·nif·er·ous** (k*o*nĭf'*er*us, kō-) *adj.*

con·jec·tur·al (k*o*njĕk'ch*era*l) *adj.* Involving, given to, conjecture. **con·jec'tur·al·ly** *adv.*

con·jec·ture (k*o*njĕk'ch*er*) *n.* Inference based on evidence that is not complete, guessing. ~ *v.* (**-tured, -tur·ing**). Guess; make a guess. **con·jec'tur·a·ble** *adj.* **con·jec'tur·er** *n.*

con·join (k*o*njoin') *v.* Join; combine. **con·joint'** *adj.* **con·joint'ly** *adv.*

con·ju·gal (kŏn'j*u*g*a*l) *adj.* Of marriage; of husband or wife in their relation to each other. **con'ju·gal·ly** *adv.* **con·ju·gal·i·ty** (kŏnj*u*găl'ĭtē) *n.*

con·ju·gate (kŏn'j*u*gāt) *v.* (**-gat·ed, -gat·ing**). 1. (gram.) Inflect (verb) in voice, mood, tense, number, person. 2. Unite; join in conjugation. **conjugate** (kŏn'j*u*gĭt, -gāt) *adj.* Joined together; coupled; (gram.) derived from same root; (math.) joined in a reciprocal relation; (bot. etc.) fused. ~ *n.* Conjugate word or thing. **con'ju·ga·tive** *adj.* **con'ju·ga·tor** *n.*

con·ju·ga·tion (kŏnj*u*gā'sh*o*n) *n.* 1. Joining together; (biol.) fusion of two (apparently) similar cells for reproduction. 2. (gram.) Scheme of verbal inflection. **con·ju·ga'tion·al** *adj.*

con·junct (k*o*njŭngkt', kŏn'-jŭngkt) *adj.* Joined together; associated. **con·junct'ly** *adv.*

con·junc·tion (k*o*njŭngk'sh*o*n) *n.* 1. Union, connection; **in ~**, together (*with*). 2. (astron.) Apparent proximity of two heavenly bodies. 3. Combination of events or circumstances. 4. (gram.) One of the parts of speech; an uninflected word used to connect other words, phrases, clauses, or sentences. **con·junc'tion·al** *adj.* **con·junc'tion·al·ly** *adv.*

con·junc·ti·va (kŏnjŭngktī'v*a*) *n.* (pl. **-vas, -vae** pr. -vē). Mucous membrane lining inner eyelid and reflected over front of eyeball. **con·junc·ti·vi·tis** (k*o*njŭngktĭvī'-tĭs) *n.* (med.) Inflammation of conjunctiva.

con·junc·tive (k*o*njŭngk'tĭv) *adj.* 1. Serving to join or unite. 2. (gram.) Of the nature of, acting as, a conjunction; uniting sense as well as construction (cf. DISJUNCTIVE). ~ *n.* Conjunctive word. **con·junc'tive·ly** *adv.*

con·junc·ture (k*o*njŭngk'ch*er*) *n.* Combination of events, posture of affairs.

con·ju·ra·tion (kŏnj*e*rā'sh*o*n) *n.* Solemn appeal, incantation, conjuring.

con·jure (kŏn'j*er*, k*o*njoor', kŭn'j*er*) *v.* (**-jured, -jur·ing**). 1. Constrain (spirit) to appear by invocation. 2. Effect, bring *out*, convey *away*, by juggling; juggle; produce magical effects by natural means, perform marvels; ~ **up**, cause to appear to the mind or fancy.

con·jur·er, con·jur·or (kŏn'-j*u*r*er*, kŭn'-) *ns.* One who practices legerdemain.

conk (kŏngk, kawngk) *v.t.* (slang) Hit on the head. ~ **out** (slang) Break or fail (of a machine); faint, go to sleep, be drained of energy.

con mo·to (kŏn mō'tō, kōn). (mus.) With spirited movement. [It.]

Conn. *abbrev.* Connecticut.

con·nect (k*o*nĕkt') *v.* Join; link together in sequence or order; associate in occurrence or action; (pass.) have to do *with*; associate mentally; unite *with* others by family relationship, common aims, etc.; join on (*with*); run in connection (*with*); **connecting rod**, rod connecting rotating with reciprocating parts of an engine, esp. rod connecting piston with crankshaft in automobile. **con·nec'tor, con·nect'er** *ns.* **con·nect'ed·ly** *adv.* **con·nect'ed·ness** *n.*

Con·nect·i·cut (k*o*nět'*i*k*u*t). New England state of U.S., one of the original 13 states of the Union (1788); capital, Hartford; ~ **River**, largest river in New England, flowing 345 mi. (555.2 km) S. from the Canadian border of New Hampshire, forming the New Hampshire-Vermont boundary, and then flowing through Massachusetts and Connecticut into Long Island Sound at New Haven.

con·nec·tion, (Brit.) **con·nex·ion** (k*o*něk'sh*o*n) *ns.* 1. Connecting, being connected; connecting part or thing; (mech.) joint between members. 2. Relation of thought etc.; personal relation or intercourse; business relationship. 3. Person related by family or marriage; influential friend or acquaintance. 4. Meeting of one means of transport (as railroad train) by another at appointed time and place to take on the passengers; train etc. meeting another thus. 5. Means of communication, as in *telephone* ~. 6. (slang) Narcotics dealer or purchase. **con·nec'tion·al** *adj.*

con·nec·tive (k*o*něk'tĭv) *adj.* Serving, tending, to connect; ~ **tissue**, fibrous tissue connecting and supporting organs of the body. **con·nec'tive·ly** *adv.* **con·nec·tiv·i·ty** (kŏněktĭv'ĭtē) *n.*

conn·ing (kŏn'ĭng) **tower.** Pilothouse of warship; superstructure on submarine in which periscope is mounted and from which steering, firing, etc. are directed when the submarine is on or near the surface. [CON² *v.*]

con·niv·ance (k*o*nī'v*a*ns) *n.* Conniving; tacit permission.

con·nive (k*o*nīv') *v.i.* (**-nived, -niv·ing**). Wink *at* (what one ought to oppose); cooperate secretly, conspire. **con·niv'er** *n.*

con·nois·seur (kŏn*o*sẽr', -soor') *n.* Critical judge (*of, in,* matters of taste). **con·nois·seur'ship** *n.*

con·note (k*o*nōt') *v.t.* (**-not·ed, -not·ing**). (of words) Imply in addition to the primary meaning; (of facts etc.) imply as a consequence or condition. **con·no·ta·tion** (kŏn*o*tā'sh*o*n) *n.* **con·no·ta·tive** (kŏn'*o*tātĭv, k*o*nō'ta-) *adj.* **con'no·ta·tive·ly** *adv.*

con·nu·bi·al (k*o*nōō'bē*a*l, -nū'-) *adj.* Of marriage; of husband or wife; married. **con·nu'bi·al·ly** *adv.* **con·nu·bi·al·i·ty** (k*o*nōō-bēăl'ĭtē, -nū-) *n.* (pl. **-ties**).

con·quer (kŏng'k*e*r) *v.* Overcome by force; get the better of; acquire, subjugate. **con'quer·or** *n.* **con'quer·ing, con'quer·a·ble** *adjs.* **con'quer·ing·ly** *adv.*

con·quest (kŏn'kwěst, kŏng'-) *n.* Subjugation, conquering; conquered territory; person whose affections have been won.

Con·rad (kŏn'răd), **Joseph** (1857–1924). Pen name of Teodor Josef Konrad Korzeniowski, English writer born in Poland; wrote novels and short stories about seafaring life; author of *Lord Jim*, *The Heart of Darkness*, etc.

Con·rail (kŏn'rāl) *abbrev.* Consolidated Rail Corporation, a U.S. government-sponsored railroad network.

Cons. *abbrev.* Constable; consul.

con·san·guin·e·ous (kŏnsăng-gwĭn'ē*u*s) *adj.* Of the same blood, akin. **con·san·guin·i·ty** (kŏnsăng-gwĭn'ĭtē) *n.* Blood relationship. **con·san·guine** (kŏnsăng'gwĭn) *adj.* **con·san·guin'e·ous·ly** *adv.*

con·science (kŏn'sh*e*ns) *n.* Moral sense of right and wrong as regards things for which one is responsible; faculty or principle pronouncing upon moral quality of one's own actions or motives; **in all** ~, in reason or fairness; ~ **money**, money paid or used to relieve conscience; ~**-stricken**, overcome with remorse. **con'science·less** *adj.*

con·sci·en·tious (kŏnshēěn'-sh*u*s) *adj.* Obedient to conscience, scrupulous; ~ **objector**, one who for moral or religious reasons, refuses participation in military service. **con·sci·en'tious·ly** *adv.* **con·sci·en'tious·ness** *n.*

con·scious (kŏn'sh*u*s) *adj.* Aware, knowing; with mental faculties awake or active; self-conscious; (of actions etc.) realized by the performer thereof. **con'scious·ly** *adv.* **con'scious·ness** *n.* State of being conscious; totality of person's thoughts and feelings, or of a class of these; perception (*of, that*).

con·script¹ (kŏn'skrĭpt) *adj.* ~ **fathers**, (Rom. hist.) collective title of Roman senators.

con·script² (kŏn'skrĭpt) *n.*

*The **conning tower** is designed to house sophisticated radio and radar antennae. The nuclear powered submarine U.S.S. Finback can stay submerged indefinitely.*

Recruit enrolled by conscription; draftee. **conscript** (k*o*nskrĭpt′) *v.t.* Enroll by conscription, draft. **con·scrip·tion** (k*o*nskrĭp′sh*o*n) *n.* Compulsory enrollment of soldiers into military service.

con·se·crate (kŏn′s*e*krāt) *v.t.* (**-crat·ed, -crat·ing**). Set apart as sacred (*to*); devote *to* (purpose); sanctify. **con′se·cra·tor, con′se·crat·er** *ns.*

con·se·cra·tion (kŏns*e*krā′sh*o*n) *n.* Act of consecrating, dedication, esp. of church, churchyard, etc.; ordination to sacred office, esp. of bishop; devotion *to* (purpose). **con·se·cra·to·ry** (kŏn′s*e*kr*a*tōrē, -tōrē) *adj.*

con·sec·u·tive (k*o*nsĕk′y*u*tĭv) *adj.* Following in succession without interruption. **con·sec′u·tive·ly** *adv.* **con·sec′u·tive·ness** *n.*

con·sen·su·al (k*o*nsĕn′shōō*a*l) *adj.* Relating to or involving consent. **con·sen′su·al·ly** *adv.*

con·sen·sus (k*o*nsĕn′s*u*s) *n.* (pl. **-sus·es**). General agreement (*of* opinions etc.).

con·sent (k*o*nsĕnt′) *v.i.* Express willingness (*to*), agree (*to, that,* etc.). ~ *n.* Voluntary agreement, compliance; permission; **con·sent′er** *n.*

con·se·quence (kŏn′s*e*kwĕns, -kw*e*ns) *n.* 1. Thing or circumstance that follows as a result (of something preceding); logical inference. 2. Importance, moment; social distinction, rank, as a *person of* ~.

con·se·quent (kŏn′s*e*kwĕnt, -kw*e*nt) *n.* Event etc. following another (without implication of causal connection); (logic) second part of conditional proposition, dependent on antecedent; (math.) second term of a ratio. ~ *adj.* Following (*on*) as a result; following logically; logically consistent.

con·se·quen·tial (kŏns*e*kwĕn′sh*a*l) *adj.* 1. Following as a result or inference. 2. Having consequence, important. **con·se·quen′tial·ly** *adv.* **con·se·quen·ti·al·i·ty** (kŏns*e*kwĕnshēăl′ĭtē) *n.*

con·se·quent·ly (kŏn′s*e*kwĕntlē, -kw*e*nt-) *adv.* & *conj.* As a result; therefore.

con·ser·van·cy (k*o*nsẽr′v*a*nsē) *n.* (pl. **-cies**). Careful use of natural resources.

con·ser·va·tion (kŏns*e*rvā′sh*o*n) *n.* Preservation, esp. of natural resources; ~ **of energy**, principle that energy is never consumed, that the total quantity of energy in the universe remains constant even though energy may change form. **con·ser·va′tion·ist** *n.* One who advocates conservation, esp. of natural resources. **con·ser·va′tion·al** *adj.*

con·ser·va·tive (k*o*nsẽr′v*a*tĭv) *adj.* 1. Preservative, keeping or tending to keep intact or unchanged. 2. Disliking great change; (pol.) favoring maintenance of existing institutions; **C~ party**, one of the main parties in Gt. Britain. 3. (of estimate etc.) Moderate, cautious, low. **conservative** *n.* Conservative person; person who holds conservative political views. **con·ser′va·tive·ly** *adv.* **con·ser′va·tism, con·ser′va·tive·ness** *ns.*

con·ser·va·tor (kŏn′s*e*rvāt*e*r, k*o*nsẽr′v*a*-) *n.* Preserver, guardian; (law) guardian; keeper.

con·ser·va·to·ry (k*o*nsẽr′v*a*tōrē, -tōrē) *n.* (pl. **-ries**). 1. Music school. 2. Small greenhouse.

con·serve (kŏn′s*e*rv, k*o*nsẽrv′) *n.* (usu. pl.) Jam made from two or more fruits stewed in sugar. ~ (k*o*nsẽrv′) *v.t.* (**-served, -serv·ing**). Keep from harm; protect; preserve. **con·serv′a·ble** *adj.* **con·serv′er** *n.*

con·sid·er (k*o*nsĭd′*e*r) *v.* Contemplate mentally; weigh the merits of; reflect, reckon with, make allowance for; be of opinion; regard as.

con·sid·er·a·ble (k*o*nsĭd′*e*r*a*b*e*l) *adj.* Worth considering; notable, important; much, not small. **con·sid′er·a·bly** *adv.*

con·sid·er·ate (k*o*nsĭd′*e*rĭt) *adj.* Thoughtful for others. **con·sid′er·ate·ly** *adv.* **con·sid′er·ate·ness** *n.*

con·sid·er·a·tion (k*o*nsĭd*e*rā′sh*o*n) *n.* 1. Considering; meditation; **take into** ~, consider. 2. Fact, thing, regarded as a reason; **in** ~ **of,** in return for, on account of. 3. Compensation, reward; (law) thing given, done, as equivalent by person to whom a promise is made. 4. Thoughtfulness for others.

con·sid·er·ing (k*o*nsĭd′*e*rĭng) *prep.* Taking into account, in view of; (ellipt., colloq.) considering the circumstances.

con·sign (k*o*nsīn′) *v.t.* Hand over, deliver, *to*; transmit, send by rail etc., *to*; entrust to another's care; set apart for special use; commit irrevocably. **con·sign′a·ble** *adj.* **con·sign·ee** (kŏnsīnē′, -sī-, k*o*nsī-), **con·sign·or** (k*o*nsī′n*e*r, kŏnsīnōr′) *ns.*

con·sign·ment (k*o*nsīn′m*e*nt) *n.* Consigning; goods consigned to an agent for sale; **on** ~, (sent to a retailer) to be paid for when sold, or returned if not sold.

The present day need for ***conservation*** *of natural resources has led to a number of experiments using wind power for the generation of electricity. There has so far been little significant commercial success.*

Episcopal ***consecration*** *by Pope Paul VI in St. Peter's, Rome. The consecration of bishops in the Roman Catholic Church necessitates an elaborate ceremony.*

*The frigate **U.S.S. Constitution** was launched in 1797 and had an illustrious career until condemned as unseaworthy in 1828. Nicknamed 'Old Ironsides', it is open to the public in Boston.*

con·sist (konsĭst′) *v.i.* Be composed *of*; be comprised or contained *in*; agree, harmonize, *with*.

con·sis·ten·cy (konsĭs′tensē), **con·sis·tence** (konsĭs′tens) *ns.* (pl. **-cies**). 1. Degree of density, esp. of thick liquids; firmness, solidity. 2. Being consistent.

con·sis·tent (konsĭs′tent) *adj.* 1. Compatible (*with*), not contradictory. 2. Constant to same principles of thought or action. **con·sis′tent·ly** *adv.*

con·sis·to·ry (konsĭs′torē) *n.* (pl. **-ries**). 1. Senate in which pope, presiding over whole body of cardinals, deliberates on affairs of the Church. 2. Religious court or governing body of clergy or lay members. **con·sis·to·ri·al** (kŏnsĭstōr′ēal, -tōr′-), **con·sis·to′ri·an** *adjs.*

con·so·la·tion (kŏnsolā′shon) *n.* Alleviation of grief or disappointment; consoling circumstance; ~ **prize**, one given to competitor who has not won a main prize.

con·sol·a·to·ry (konsŏl′atōrē, -tōrē, -sō′la-) *adj.* Tending or designed to console.

con·sole¹ (konsōl′) *v.t.* (**-soled, -sol·ing**). Bring consolation to. **con·sol′ing·ly** *adv.* **con·sol′a·ble** *adj.* **con·sol′er** *n.*

con·sole² (kŏn′sōl) *n.* 1. Decorative bracket supporting a cornice, shelf, art object, etc; ~ **table**, table supported by bracket against a wall. 2. Cabinet for radio, television set, etc. 3. Ensemble of keyboards, stops, etc., of organ, esp. when separate from body of instrument, as in electric organ. 4. Control panel for electrical or mechanical equipment.

con·sol·i·date (konsŏl′ĭdāt) *v.* (**-dat·ed, -dat·ing**). 1. Solidify, strengthen. 2. Combine (territories, companies, debts, statutes, etc.) into one whole. **con·sol·i·da·tion** (konsŏlĭdā′shon), **con·sol′i·da·tor** *ns.*

con·som·mé (kŏnsomā′) *n.* Clear soup made from meat, poultry, or vegetable stock.

con·so·nance (kŏn′sonans), **con·so·nan·cy** (kŏn′sonansē) *ns.* (pl. **-cies**). Recurrence of same or similar consonant sounds in words or syllables, assonance; (mus.) sounding together of notes in harmony; consonant interval; agreement, harmony.

con·so·nant¹ (kŏn′sonant) *adj.* Agreeable *to*, consistent *with*; harmonious; agreeing in sound; (mus.) making concord. **con′so·nant·ly** *adv.*

con·so·nant² (kŏn′sonant) *n.* Sound in speech, other than a vowel, produced by a complete momentary stoppage or by partial stoppage or constriction of the air stream in some part of the mouth cavity or by the lips as it passes from the lungs; letter or symbol representing such a sound. **con·so·nan·tal** (kŏnsonăn′tal) *adj.* [L. *consonantem* (*litteram*); the name is due to the erroneous view that a consonant can only be sounded along with a vowel]

con sor·di·no (kŏn sōrdē′nō, kōn). (mus.) With the mute or damper. [It.]

con·sort (kŏn′sōrt) *n.* 1. Husband or wife; **king, prince** ~, (titles sometimes given to) husband of reigning queen; **queen** ~, king's wife. 2. Ship sailing in company with another. 3. Companion; partner. 4. (mus.) Group of performers or instruments. **consort** (konsōrt′) *v.* Associate; keep company, (*with*); agree, harmonize, (*with*).

con·sor·ti·um (konsōr′shēum, -tēum) *n.* (pl. **-ti·a** pr. -shēa -tēa, **-ti·ums**). Association of business, banking, or manufacturing organizations for an activity requiring large amounts of capital or other resources.

con·spec·tus (konspĕk′tus) *n.* (pl. **-tus·es**). General or comprehensive survey; summary.

con·spic·u·ous (konspĭk′ūus) *adj.* Clearly visible, striking to the eye; attracting notice, remarkable. **con·spic'u·ous·ness** *n.* **con·spic'u·ous·ly** *adv.*

con·spir·a·cy (konspĭr'asē) *n.* (pl. **-cies**). Conspiring; combination for unlawful, treacherous, or evil purpose; plot. **con·spir·a·tor** (konspĭr'ater) *n.* **con·spir·a·to·ri·al** (konspĭratōr'ēal, -tŏr'-) *adj.* **con·spir·a·to'ri·al·ly** *adv.*

con·spire (konspīr') *v.* (**-spired, -spir·ing**). Combine for unlawful, treacherous, or evil purpose, esp. treason, murder, sedition; combine, concur (*to* do); plot, devise. **con·spir'er** *n.*

con·sta·ble (kŏn'stabel, kŭn'-) *n.* 1. Chief officer or governor of royal household, administration, or military forces. 2. Officer of the peace in rural area; (*Brit.*) policeman or policewoman. **con'sta·ble·ship** *n.* [L. *comes stabuli* count of the stable]

Con·sta·ble (kŭn'stabel, kŏn'-), **John** (1776–1837). English landscape painter.

con·stab·u·lar·y (konstăb'yulĕrē) *adj.* Of constables. ~ *n.* (pl. **-lar·ies**). Body of constables; district under a constable. **con·stab·u·lar** (konstăb'yuler) *n.*

Con·stance (kŏn'stans). City in SW. West Germany on Lake Constance; site of Council of Constance, 1414–18, which ended the Great Schism; **Lake** ~, (German name, *Bodensee*) lake bounded by West Germany, Switzerland, and Austria.

con·stan·cy (kŏn'stansē) *n.* Firmness, endurance; faithfulness; unchangingness.

con·stant (kŏn'stant) *adj.* Unmoved, resolute; faithful; unchanging; unremitting. ~ *n.* (math. etc.) Quantity that does not vary; numerical quantity expressing relation, property, etc., that remains the same for the same substance under all conditions.

con·stant·an (kŏn'stantăn) *n.* Alloy of copper and nickel.

Con·stan·tine I (kŏn'stantēn, -tīn) (274–337), **"the Great."** Roman emperor (306–37); converted to Christianity, which he made the state religion; in 328 transferred the capital of the empire to Byzantium, which he renamed Constantinople.

Con·stan·ti·no·ple (kŏnstăntĭnō'pel). Former name of ISTANBUL, capital of Turkey until 1923; the Roman city of Byzantium under CONSTANTINE I.

con·stant·ly (kŏn'stantlē) *adv.* Always; often.

con·stel·la·tion (kŏnstelā'shon) *n.* 1. Number of fixed stars grouped within outline of an imaginary figure as viewed from the Earth; (colloq.) group of distinguished persons. 2. (astrology) Relative position of stars, esp. at time of a person's birth, considered as influencing future events.

con·ster·na·tion (kŏnsternā'shon) *n.* Amazement and terror such as to prostrate one's faculties, dismay.

con·sti·pa·tion (kŏnstipā'shon) *n.* Condition of bowels in which defecation is irregular and difficult. **con·sti·pate** (kŏn'stipāt) *v.t.* (**-pat·ed, -pat·ing**). Affect with constipation.

con·stit·u·en·cy (konstĭch'ōōensē) *n.* (pl. **-cies**). Body of voters who elect a representative member; place, residents in place, so represented.

con·stit·u·ent (konstĭch'ōōent) *adj.* Composing, making up, a whole; appointing, electing; able to form or alter a (political) constitution. ~ *n.* 1. Component part. 2. One represented by an agent, elected official, etc.

con·sti·tute (kŏn'stĭtōōt, -tūt) *v.t.* (**-tut·ed, -tut·ing**). 1. Appoint (person) to office, dignity, etc., of; establish, found, give legal form to (assembly, institution, etc.). 2. Frame, form (by combination of elements); make up, be components of.

con·sti·tu·tion (kŏnstĭtōō'shon, -tū'-) *n.* 1. Act, mode, of constituting; way in which thing is constituted; esp. character of body in regard to health, strength, vitality, etc.; condition of mind, disposition. 2. Mode in which nation etc. is organized; body of fundamental principles according to which a nation etc. is governed; **the C**~, Constitution of the U.S. framed at Philadelphia in 1787 and ratified 1788, together with subsequent amendments. 3. **U.S.S. C**~, 44-gun frigate used by Amer. navy in War of 1812, popularly known as "Old Ironsides."

con·sti·tu·tion·al (kŏnstĭtōō'shonal, -tū'-) *adj.* 1. Of, inherent in, affecting, the bodily or mental constitution. 2. Belonging to the very constitution of anything; essential. 3. Of, in harmony with, authorized by, the political constitution; adhering to the political constitution; ~ **monarchy**, monarchy limited by constitutional forms. **constitutional** *n.* (colloq.) Walk taken for health's sake. **con·sti·tu'tion·al·ism, con·sti·tu'tion·al·ist, con·sti·tu·tion·al·i·ty** (kŏnstĭtōōshonăl'ĭtē, -tū-) *ns.* **con·sti·tu'tion·al·ly** *adv.*

con·strain (konstrān') *v.t.* Compel; bring about by compulsion; confine forcibly, imprison. **constrained'** *adj.* Forced, embarrassed. **con·strain'ed·ly** (konstrā'nĭdlē), **con·strain'ing·ly** *advs.* **con·strain'a·ble** *adj.* **con·strain'er** *n.*

con·straint (konstrānt') *n.* Compulsion; confinement; restraint of natural feelings, constrained manner.

con·strict (konstrĭkt') *v.t.* Contract, compress; cause (organic tissue) to contract. **con·stric'tion** *n.* **con·stric'tive** *adj.*

*The Roman emperor, **Constantine**, under whose reign the empire became Christian, was commemorated by this arch in Rome which was completed in A.D. 312.*

A ***container*** *ship, like this converted C-2 'Warrior' at San Juan, Puerto Rico, is designed to receive containers prepacked with cargo. This has proved an economical method of marine transportation.*

con·stric·tor (k*o*nstrĭk′t*er*) *n.* 1. Muscle that draws together or narrows a part. 2. Snake, such as boa or python, that coils around and crushes its prey.

con·struct (k*o*nstrŭkt′) *v.t.* Fit together, frame, build; (gram.) combine (words) syntactically; (geom.) draw, delineate. ~ (kŏn′strŭkt) *n.* Anything constructed. **con·struc′tor, con·struct′er** *ns.*

con·struc·tion (k*o*nstrŭk′sh*o*n) *n.* 1. Act, mode, of constructing; thing constructed. 2. (gram.) Syntactical connection betweeen verbs and their objects or complements, prepositions and their objects, etc. 3. Construing, explanation (of words); interpretation. 4. ~ **gang**, workers engaged in construction project. **con·struc′tion·al** *adj.* Of, engaged in, construction; structual.

con·struc·tion·ist (k*o*nstrŭk′sh*o*nĭst) *n.* One who interprets a law or body of laws in a specified way.

con·struc·tive (k*o*nstrŭk′tĭv) *adj.* 1. Intending to be helpful (esp. as opp. to DESTRUCTIVE). 2. Of construction, structural. 3. (law) Inferred, based on interpretation. **con·struc′tive·ly** *adv.* **con·struc′tive·ness** *n.*

con·strue (k*o*nstrōō′) *v.* (**-strued, -stru·ing**). Combine (words) grammatically; interpret; analyze grammatically and/or translate literally.

con·sub·stan·tial (kŏns*u*bstăn′sh*a*l) *adj.* Of the same substance, esp. of the three Persons of the Trinity. **con·sub·stan·ti·al·i·ty** (kŏns*u*bstănshēăl′ĭtē) *n.* **con·sub·stan′tial·ly** *adv.*

con·sub·stan·ti·ate (kŏns*u*bstăn′shēāt) *v.* (**-at·ed, -at·ing**). Unite in one substance. **con·sub·stan·ti·a·tion** (kŏns*u*bstănshēā′sh*o*n) *n.* Lutheran doctrine that body and blood of Christ exist together with bread and wine in Eucharist (dist. from TRANSUBSTANTIATION).

con·sul (kŏn′s*u*l) *n.* 1. (Rom. hist.) Either of two annually elected magistrates exercising supreme authority under the Republic. 2. One of three chief magistrates of French Republic (1799–1804), and of whom the **First C~**, Napoleon Bonaparte, had all the real power. 3. Foreign service officer stationed in a country abroad to promote trade, protect rights of fellow citizens in residence there, etc.; ~ **general**, consular officer of highest rank. **con′sul·ar** *adj.*

con·sul·ate (kŏn′s*u*lĭt) *n.* Office of consul and consular staff.

con·sult (k*o*nsŭlt′) *v.* Take counsel (*with*); seek information or advice from; take into consideration; **consulting chemist, engineer, firm**, etc., person or concern whose business is giving professional advice. **consulting physician** etc., physician etc. to whom others may refer their patients for advice. **con·sult·ant** (k*o*nsŭl′t*a*nt) *n.* **con·sul·ta·tion** (kŏns*u*ltā′sh*o*n) *n.* Act of consulting; deliberation; conference. **con·sul·ta·tive** (k*o*nsŭl′t*a*tĭv) *adj.* **con·sul·ta·to·ry** (k*o*nsŭl′t*a*tōrē, -tôrē) *adj.* **con·sult′er** *n.*

con·sume (k*o*nsōōm′) *v.* (**-sumed, -sum·ing**). Use up; eat, drink, up; burn up; spend, waste; waste away; **con·sumed′**, eaten up *with.* **con·sum′a·ble** *adj.*

con·sum·er (k*o*nsōō′m*er*) *n.* One who consumes; one who buys goods or services; customer; buyer; ~ **goods**, goods that directly satisfy human wants through their consumption or use, such as food and clothing; ~ **price index**, index of changes in cost of goods and services to a typical consumer based on their cost at an arbitrarily chosen period; also called "cost-of-living index."

con·sum·mate (k*o*nsŭm′ĭt,

kŏn′sumĭt) *adj.* Complete, perfect. **consummate** (kŏn′sumāt) *v.t.* (**-mat·ed, -mat·ing**). Accomplish, complete (esp. marriage by sexual intercourse). **con·sum·ma·tion** (kŏnsumā′shon) *n.* Completion; desired end, goal; perfection; perfected thing; physical completion of marriage.

con·sump·tion (konsŭmp′shon) *n.* 1. Consuming; destruction; waste; amount consumed. 2. Wasting disease, esp. pulmonary tuberculosis.

con·sump·tive (konsŭmp′tĭv) *adj.* 1. Tending to consume. 2. Having a tendency to, affected with, pulmonary tuberculosis. ~ *n.* Consumptive person. **con·sump′tive·ly** *adv.*

con·tact (kŏn′tăkt) *n.* State, condition, of touching; (math.) meeting of curves or surfaces so as to have tangents or tangent planes in common; (elect.) junction or touching surface of two conductors or ends of conducting wire through which a current passes; (usu. pl.) friendly or business relationships, persons with whom one comes into touch; acquaintance, esp. one useful in business; (med.) person who has been exposed to contagious disease; **come into ~ with,** come across, meet; **make, break ~,** complete, interrupt electric circuit; **~ lens,** small lens worn on eyeball. **contact** *v.t.* Get into touch with (person).

con·ta·gion (kontā′jon) *n.* Communication of disease by direct or indirect contact; contagious disease; moral corruption; contagious influence.

con·ta·gious (kontā′jus) *adj.* Communicating disease or corruption by contact; (of diseases) communicable by contact; (fig.) catching, infectious. **con·ta′gious·ly** *adv.* **con·ta′gious·ness** *n.*

con·tain (kontān′) *v.t.* 1. Have, hold, as contents; comprise, include; (of a measure) be equal to; (geom.) enclose, form boundary of; (of numbers) be divisible by (number) without remainder. 2. Restrain; (mil.) hold (enemy force) in position so that it cannot operate elsewhere; (fig.) keep within limits. **con·tain′ment** *n.* esp. **~ building,** that housing nuclear reactor and associated equipment in nuclear power station. **con·tain′er** *n.* (esp.) Receptacle of standardized design for transportation of freight; so **~ ship,** etc., one carrying freight in containers. **con·tain′a·ble** *adj.* **con·tain·er·ize** (kontā′nerīz) *v.t.* (**-ized, -iz·ing**). Pack into, transport in, sealed, reusable containers. **con·tain·er·i·za·tion** (kontānerīzā′shon) *n.*

con·tam·i·nate (kontăm′ināt) *v.t.* (**-nat·ed, -nat·ing**). Pollute, infect. **con·tam·i·na·tion** (kontămĭnā′shon) *n.*

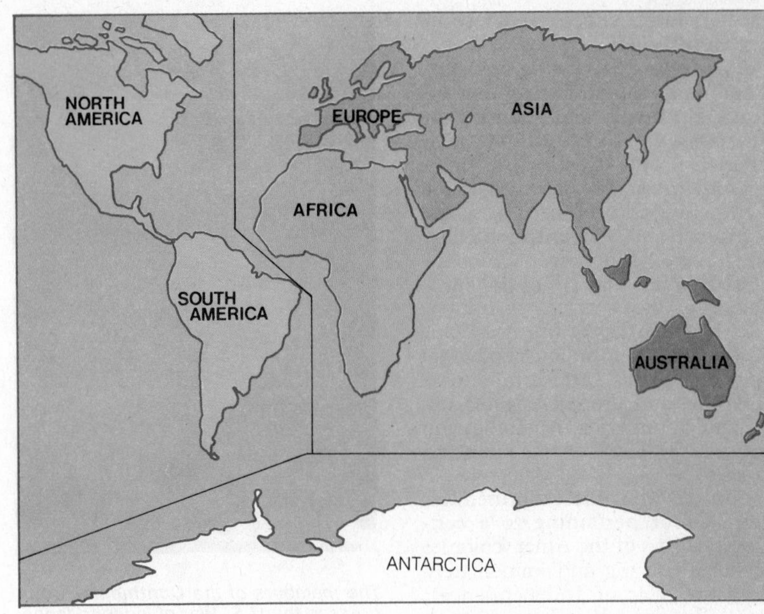

The world's ***continents*** *— Europe, Asia, Africa, North and South America, Australia and Antarctica — vary enormously in size. Two-thirds of the continental land surface is in the northern hemisphere.*

con·temn (kontĕm′) *v.t.* Despise, treat with disregard. **con·temn·er** (kontĕm′er, -tĕm′ner), **con·tem·nor** (kontĕm′ner) *ns.*

con·tem·plate (kŏn′templāt) *v.* (**-plat·ed, -plat·ing**). Gaze upon; view mentally; expect; intend, purpose; meditate. **con·tem·pla·tion** (kŏntemplā′shon), **con′tem·pla·tor** *ns.*

con·tem·pla·tive (kontĕm′platĭv, kŏn′templā-) *adj.* Meditative, thoughtful; (of life or monastic order) devoted to meditation. ~ *n.* Contemplative person. **con·tem′pla·tive·ly** *adv.* **con·tem′pla·tive·ness** *n.*

con·tem·po·ra·ne·ous (kontĕmporā′nēus) *adj.* Existing, occurring, at the same time (*with*); of the same period. **con·tem·po·ra′ne·ous·ly** *adv.* **con·tem·po·ra·ne·i·ty** (kontĕmperanē′ĭtē), **con·tem·po·ra′ne·ous·ness** *ns.*

con·tem·po·rar·y (kontĕm′porĕrē) *adj.* Belonging to the same time; equal in age; modern, esp. of art, furniture, etc. ~ *n.* (pl. **-rar·ies**). Contemporary person or thing.

con·tempt (kontĕmpt′) *n.* Act, mental attitude, of despising; condition of being despised; willful disobedience to or disrespect for legislative body or court of law. **con·tempt′i·ble** *adj.* Deserving contempt, despicable. **con·tempt·i·bil·i·ty** (kontĕmptibĭl′ĭtē), **con·tempt′i·ble·ness** *ns.* **con·tempt′i·bly** *adv.*

con·temp·tu·ous (kontĕmp′chōōus) *adj.* Showing contempt (*of*); scornful; insolent. **con·temp′tu·ous·ly** *adv.* **con·temp′tu·ous·ness** *n.*

con·tend (kontĕnd′) *v.* Strive; fight; struggle *with*; compete, be in rivalry; argue (*with*); maintain (*that*). **con·tend′er** *n.*

con·tent[1] (kŏn′tĕnt) *n.* 1. Containing capacity; volume; amount contained or yielded. 2. (often pl.) What is contained; esp. things contained or treated of in writing or document; **table of ~s,** listing of chapters, subjects, etc. included in a book or document. 3. Constituent elements of a conception; substance (of art etc., as opp. to *form*).

con·tent[2] (kontĕnt′) *n.* State or feeling of being satisfied. ~ *adj.* Satisfied; willing (*to* do). ~ *v.t.* Satisfy; **~ oneself,** be satisfied (*with*). **con·tent′ed** *adj.* **con·tent′ed·ly** *adv.* **con·tent′ed·ness, con·tent′ment** *ns.*

con·ten·tion (kontĕn′shon) *n.* Strife, controversy; rivalry; assertion made in arguing; point disputed.

con·ten·tious (kontĕn′shus) *adj.* Quarrelsome; involving contention. **con·ten′tious·ly** *adv.* **con·ten′tious·ness** *n.*

con·ter·mi·nous (kontĕr′minus) *adj.* Having a common boundary (*with*); coextensive. **con·ter′mi·nous·ly** *adv.*

con·test (kŏn′tĕst) *n.* Contending; competition. **contest** (kontĕst′) *v.* Dispute; contend or compete for. **con·test′a·ble** *adj.* **con·test′ant** *n.* One who contests. **con·test′er, con·tes·ta·tion** (kŏntĕstā′shon) *ns.*

con·text (kŏn′tĕkst) *n.* Whole structure of connected passage in relation to any of its parts; parts that immediately precede or follow a written or spoken passage and determine its meaning. **con·tex-**

tu·al (kontĕks'chŏŏal) *adj*. **con·tex'tu·al·ly** *adv*.

con·tig·u·ous (kontĭg'ūus) *adj*. Touching, adjoining; neighboring. **con·tig'u·ous·ly** *adv*. **con·tig'u·ous·ness** *n*. **con·ti·gu·i·ty** (kŏntigū'ĭtē) *n*. (pl. **-ties**).

con·ti·nent[1] (kŏn'tinent) *adj*. Temperate, characterized by sexual restraint; able to control bladder and bowel functions. **con'ti·nent·ly** *adv*. **con·ti·nence** (kŏn'tinens) *n*.

con·ti·nent[2] (kŏn'tinent) *n*. One of the main continuous bodies of land on Earth's surface (now usu. reckoned as Europe, Asia, Africa, N. and S. America, Australia, and Antarctica); **the C~**, the mainland of Europe.

con·ti·nen·tal (kŏntinĕn'tal) *adj*. Of or pertaining to a continent; (hist.) of the Amer. colonies or states (during and immediately after the War of Independence); **C~ Congress**, either of two assemblies of representatives from the Amer. colonies during the Revolutionary era: the first, meeting in 1774, voiced grievances against the British Crown; the second, convened first in 1775, established the Continental army, issued the Declaration of Independence, and served as the government until 1789, when the U.S. Constitution came into effect; **~ divide** (also **C~ Divide** in N. Amer.), divide separating river systems that flow to opposite sides of a continent; **~ drift**, (geol.) slow movement of the continents away from a single land mass to their present positions; **~shelf**, sloping platform around continent, outside which the ocean bed descends steeply. **continental** *n*. 1. Native or inhabitant of a continent, esp. Europe. 2. (hist.) Soldier of the Continental army in Revolutionary War.

con·tin·gen·cy (kontĭn'jensē) *n*. (pl. **-cies**). 1. Being contingent; contingent event etc., chance occurrence; thing incident to another. 2. Emergency, as in *~ plan*.

con·tin·gent (kontĭn'jent) *adj*. 1. Of uncertain occurrence. 2. True only under existing conditions; nonessential; conditional, dependent *on* some prior occurrence or condition. **con·tin'gent·ly** *adv*. **contingent** *n*. 1. Contingent thing. 2. Troops contributed to form part of military or naval force (also fig.).

con·tin·u·al (kontĭn'ūal) *adj*. Always continuing, incessant; very frequent. **con·tin'u·al·ly** *adv*.

con·tin·u·ance (kontĭn'ūans) *n*. Continuing in existence or operation, duration.

con·tin·u·a·tion (kontĭnūā'shon) *n*. 1. Carrying on, resumption. 2. That by which anything is continued, continuing addition.

The members of the ***Continental Congress*** *in the U.S. War of Independence (1774–83) met in this hall in Philadelphia as representatives of the people of the colony states, later the United States of America.*

con·tin·u·a·tive (kontĭn'ūātĭv, -atĭv) *adj*.

con·tin·ue (kontĭn'ū) *v*. (**-ued, -u·ing**). 1. Go or keep on with; not cease; maintain. 2. Remain in existence. 3. Resume. **con·tin'u·a·ble** *adj*. **con·tin'u·er** *n*.

con·ti·nu·i·ty (kŏntĭnōō'ĭtē, -nū'-) *n*. (pl. **-ties**). 1. Being continuous; unbroken series, succession; close relationship, logical sequence, of ideas. 2. Script or scenario for motion picture, or for television or radio program.

con·tin·u·ous (kontĭn'ūus) *adj*. Connected, unbroken, in time or sequence; **~ wave**, (phys.) electromagnetic wave of constant amplitude; (esp. of lasers) not pulsed. **con·tin'u·ous·ly** *adv*.

con·tin·u·um (kontĭn'ūum) *n*. (pl. **-tin·u·a** pr. -tĭn'ūa, **-tin·u·ums**). Continuous series or whole, as *space-time ~*.

con·tort (kontŏrt') *v.t*. Twist, distort.

con·tor·tion (kontŏr'shon) *n*. Twisting; twisted state. **con·tor'tion·ist** *n*. Person who performs gymnastic exercises involving contorted postures.

con·tour (kŏn'toor) *n*. Outline of figure, object, coast, etc.; (also **~ line**) line representing horizontal contour of Earth's surface at given elevation; **~ map**, one containing **~ lines**; **~ plowing**, plowing along lines of constant elevation to minimize erosion; **contour** *v.t*. Mark with contour lines.

con·tra (kŏn'tra) *prep*. Against. ~ *adv*. Against (a proposition, etc.); on the contrary. [CON[4]]

contra- *prefix*. Against; in names of mus. instruments and organ stops, denoting a pitch of an octave below.

con·tra·band (kŏn'trabănd) *n*. Prohibited traffic, smuggling; smuggled goods. ~ *adj*. Forbidden to be imported or exported; concerned with contraband. **con'tra·band·ist** *n*.

con·tra·bass (kŏn'trabās) *n*. (mus.) Double bass. **con'tra·bass·ist** *n*.

con·tra·cep·tion (kŏntrasĕp'shon) *n*. Prevention of conception or impregnation. **con·tra·cep'tive** *adj*. & *n*.

con·tract (kŏn'trăkt) *n*. 1. Mutual agreement between parties, nations, etc., esp. business agreement for supplying goods or performing work at specified price. 2. Agreement enforceable by law; department of law relating to contracts; formal agreement for marriage. 3. (in game of bridge) Undertaking by declarer to make so many tricks; **~ bridge**: see BRIDGE[2]. **contract** (kontrăkt') *v*. 1. Enter into business or legal arrangement. 2. Form (friendship, habit); incur (disease, liability). 3. Draw together; make or become smaller; (gram.) shorten (word) by combination or elision. **con·tract·i·bil·i·ty** (kontrăktabĭl'ĭtē) *n*. **con·tract'i·ble** *adj*.

con·trac·tile (kontrăk'til, -tīl) *adj*. Capable of, producing, contraction. **con·trac·til·i·ty** (kŏntrăktĭl'ĭtē) *n*.

con·trac·tion (kontrăk'shon) *n*. Contracting; contracted word. **con·trac'tion·al, con·trac'tive** *adjs*.

con·trac·tor (kŏn'trăkter, kontrăk'-) *n*. 1. One who undertakes a contract, esp. in building and related trades. 2. Contracting muscle.

con·trac·tu·al (kontrăk'chōōal) *adj*. Of (the nature of) a contract. **con·trac'tu·al·ly** *adv*.

con·tra·dict (kŏntradĭkt') *v.t*. Deny (statement); deny words of (person); be contrary to; imply a denial of. **con·tra·dict'a·ble** *adj*. **con·tra·dic·tor, con·tra·dict'er** *ns*.

con·tra·dic·tion (kŏntradĭk'shon) *n*. Verbal denial; direct opposition; statement contradicting another; inconsistency; **~ in terms**, plainly self-contradictory statement or words.

con·tra·dic·to·ry (kŏntradĭk'terē) *adj*. Making denial; mutually opposed or inconsistent. **con·tra·dic'to·ri·ly** *adv*. **con·tra·dic'to·ri·ness, con·tra·dic'to·ry** *ns*.

con·tra·dis·tinc·tion (kŏntradĭstĭngk'shon) *n*. Distinction by contrast.

con·tral·to (kontrăl'tō, -trahl'-) *n*. (pl. **-tos, -ti** pr. -tē). Lowest female voice; singer with such voice; musical part for this.

con·trap·tion (kontrăp′shon) *n.* (colloq.) Contrivance or device.

con·tra·pun·tal (kŏntrapŭn′tal) *adj.* Of, in, counterpoint. **con·tra·pun′tal·ly** *adv.* **con·tra·pun′tist** *n.* One skilled in counterpoint.

con·tra·ri·e·ty (kŏntrarī′itē) *n.* (pl. **-ties**). Opposition in nature, quality, or action; disagreement, inconsistency.

con·tra·ri·wise (kŏn′trĕrēwīz, kontrār′-) *adv.* On the other hand; in the opposite way; perversely.

con·tra·ry (kŏn′trĕrē) *adj.* 1. Opposed in nature or tendency (*to*); (of wind) impeding, unfavorable. 2. Perverse, self-willed. 3. Opposite in position or direction. **con′trar·i·ly** *adv.* **contrary** *adv.* In opposition (*to*). **con′tra·ri·ness** *n.* **contrary** *n.* (pl. **-ries**). Opposite; object, fact, or quality that is the very opposite of something else; **on the ~**, (corroborating a denial expressed or understood); **to the ~**, to the opposite effect (contradicting something that has been said or assumed).

con·trast (kŏn′trăst) *n.* Juxtaposition showing striking differences; comparison clearly revealing differences or opposing qualities; person or thing of most opposite qualities; (photog. etc.) differentiation between tones. **contrast** (kontrăst′) *v.* Set (two things, one *with* another) in opposition, so as to show their differences; show striking difference on comparison *with*. **con·trast′a·ble, con·trast′·ive** *adjs.*

con·tra·vene (kŏntravēn′) *v.t.* (**-vened, -ven·ing**). Infringe (law); dispute (statement); conflict with. **con·tra·ven·tion** (kŏntravĕn′shon), **con·tra·ven′er** *ns.*

con·tre·temps (kŏn′tretahṅ) *n.* (pl. **-temps** pr. -tahṅz). Unlucky accident; embarrassing or inopportune occurrence.

con·trib·ute (kontrĭb′ūt, -yut) *v.* (**-ut·ed, -ut·ing**). Pay, furnish (*to* common fund etc.), give or pay jointly with others; **~ to**, have a part or share in producing; provide (literary work). **con·trib·u·tor** (kontrĭb′yuter) *n.* **con·trib·u·tor·y** (kontrĭb′yutōrē, -tōrē) *adj.* **contributory negligence**, negligence on the part of a person injured that has helped to bring about the injury.

con·tri·bu·tion (kŏntribū′shon) *n.* Contributing; something contributed; payment in aid of common fund or collection.

con·trite (kontrīt′, kŏn′trīt) *adj.* Crushed in spirit by a sense of sin, completely penitent; (of action) arising from contrition. **con·trite′ly** *adv.* **con·trite′ness** *n.*

con·tri·tion (kontrĭsh′on) *n.* Being contrite, penitence.

con·triv·ance (kontrī′vans) *n.* 1. Contriving. 2. Deceitful practice. 3. Invention; inventive capacity; thing contrived; mechanical device.

con·trive (kontrīv′) *v.t.* (**-trived, -triv·ing**). Devise, plan, skillfully; bring to pass, manage (thing, *to* do etc.). **con·triv′er** *n.* **con·triv′a·ble** *adj.*

con·trol (kontrōl′) *n.* 1. Controlling; function or power of directing and regulating. 2. Restraint; check; standard of comparison for checking inferences from experiment etc. 3. Controller; (spiritualism) personality or spirit alleged to control medium's words and actions. **~** *v.t.* (**-trolled, -trol·ling**). Exercise restraint or direction over; command, dominate, regulate; hold in check; check, verify; **~ tower**, tower at an airport from which air traffic is directed by radar and radio. **con·trol′ler** *n.* One who controls, esp. one who checks expenditures, as of a public office or business; **air traffic control(ler)**, system, person(s), that direct(s) air traffic over a wide area. **con·trol′ler·ship** *n.*

con·tro·ver·sial (kŏntrovēr′shal, -sēal) *adj.* Of, open to, given to, controversy. **con·tro·ver′sial·ist** *n.* **con·tro·ver′sial·ly** *adv.*

con·tro·ver·sy (kŏn′trovērsē) *n.* (pl. **-sies**). Disputation, quarrel, esp. prolonged public debate or argument.

con·tro·vert (kŏn′trovērt, kŏntrovērt′) *v.t.* Call in question, dispute truth of. **con·tro·vert′i·ble** *adj.* **con·tro·vert′i·bly** *adv.*

con·tu·ma·cious (kŏntoomā′shus, -tyoo-) *adj.* Insubordinate, disobedient. **con·tu·ma′cious·ly** *adv.* **con·tu·ma′cious·ness** *n.* **con·tu·ma·cy** (kŏn′toomasē, -tyoo-) *n.* (pl. **-cies**).

con·tu·me·ly (kŏn′toomelē, -tyoo, kontoo′-, -tŭ′, kŏn′tumlē) *n.* (pl. **-lies**). Rudeness, insolence; insulting remark or act. **con·tu·me·li·ous** (kŏntoomē′lēus, -tyoo-) *adj.* **con·tu·me′li·ous·ly** *adv.*

con·tuse (kontooz′, -tūz′) *v.t.* (**-tused, -tus·ing**). Bruise. **con·tu·sion** (kontoo′zhon, -tū′-) *n.*

co·nun·drum (konŭn′drum) *n.* Riddle, puzzle.

con·va·lesce (kŏnvalĕs′) *v.i.* (**-lesced, -lesc·ing**). Regain health. **con·va·les·cence** (kŏnvalĕs′ens) *n.* Gradual recovery of health after illness.

con·va·les·cent (kŏnvalĕs′ent) *adj.* Recovering from illness. **~** *n.* Convalescent person; **~ home,**

*The **Continental Divide** in North America runs along the top of the Rocky Mountain range providing drainage to the east and west of the continent. In South America the Andes perform the same function.*

The ***convent,*** *the communal establishment in which nuns live after they have taken their religious vows, traditionally provides seclusion from the outside world. Some enclosed communities receive no visitors.*

hospital, nursing home, hospital, for such persons.

con·vec·tion (kŏnvĕk′shŏn) *n.* (phys.) Conveyance of heat by movement of gas or fluid; ~ **heater**, appliance that warms room by convection. **con·vec′tor** *n.* **con·vec′tion·al** *adj.*

con·vene (kŏnvēn′) *v.* (**-vened, -ven·ing**). Assemble; convoke; summon (person *before* tribunal). **con·ven′er** *n.*

con·ven·ience (kŏnvēn′yens) *n.* 1. Suitableness; commodiousness; material advantage; personal comfort or ease; advantage. 2. Useful appliance; (Brit.) lavatory; (pl.) material comforts. **con·ven·ient** (kŏnvēn′yent) *adj.* Fit, suitable; not troublesome; (colloq.) conveniently near. **con·ven′ient·ly** *adv.*

con·vent (kŏn′vĕnt) *n.* Religious community (usu. of women, cf. MONASTERY) living together; building occupied by this.

con·ven·ti·cle (kŏnvĕn′tĭkel) *n.* (hist.) Clandestine religious meeting, esp. of nonconformists or dissenters.

con·ven·tion (kŏnvĕn′shŏn) *n.* 1. Convening. 2. Formal assembly for deliberation or legislation on important matters; esp. **political ~s**, which meet to nominate candidates for public office and to establish party platforms. 3. Assembly of delegates or representatives, conference. 4. Agreement; in diplomacy, less formal or less important agreement than treaty, such as the GENEVA Convention. 5. General agreement or consent (often implicit) as foundation of usage etc., rule or practice based on this; accepted usage that has become artificial and formal; (pl., in game of bridge etc.) standard methods of bidding, leading, etc.

con·ven·tion·al (kŏnvĕn′shŏnal) *adj.* Depending on convention(s), not natural, not spontaneous; usual, expected; (of weapons) other than nuclear. **con·ven′tion·al·ly** *adv.* **con·ven′tion·al·ism, con·ven′tion·al·ist** *ns.* **con·ven·tion·al·i·ty** (kŏnvĕnshŏnăl′ĭtē) *n.* (pl. **-ties**).

con·verge (kŏnvẽrj′) *v.i.* (**-verged, -verg·ing**). (of lines etc.) Tend to meet in a point or line; approach nearer together; (math., of series) approximate in sum of its terms toward a definite limit. **con·ver·gence** (kŏnvẽr′jens)

This vintage automobile is one of the earliest ***convertibles,*** *with a top that may be folded back, lowered or removed. The soft top, however, gives little protection in an accident.*

n. **con·ver′gen·cy** *n.* (pl. **-cies**). **con·ver′gent** *adj.*

con·ver·sant (k*o*nvẽr′s*a*nt) *adj.* Well acquainted (*with*). **con·ver′sance** *n.* **con·ver′san·cy** *n.* (pl. **-cies**). **con·ver′sant·ly** *adv.*

con·ver·sa·tion (kŏnv*e*rsā′sh*o*n) *n.* 1. Talk, interchange of thoughts and words. 2. ~ **piece**, something that serves as a topic of conversation because of its unusualness etc.

con·ver·sa·tion·al (kŏnv*e*rsā′sh*o*n*a*l) *adj.* In the manner of, pertaining to, conversation. **con·ver·sa′tion·al·ly** *adv.* **con·ver·sa′tion·al·ist** *n.*

con·verse[1] (k*o*nvẽrs′) *v.i.* (**-versed, -vers·ing**). Talk.

con·verse[2] (kŏn′vẽrs) *adj.* Opposite, contrary. ~ *n.* Opposite; (logic) converted proposition; statement etc. derived from another by transposition of two important antithetical members, e.g. *he is brave but not good* is the converse of *he is good but not brave.* **con·verse·ly** (k*o*nvẽrs′lē, kŏn′vẽrs-) *adv.*

con·ver·sion (k*o*nvẽr′zh*o*n, -sh*o*n) *n.* Converting; being converted; (football) play for points after touchdown; point made by kick or two points made by pass on this play. **con·ver′sion·al, con·ver·sion·ar·y** (k*o*nvẽr′zh*o*nĕrē, -sh*o*-) *adjs.*

con·vert (k*o*nvẽrt′) *v.* 1. Change (*into*). 2. Cause to turn (*to* opinion, faith, etc.); turn to godliness; (logic) transpose (subject and predicate). 3. (football) Make point after touchdown. ~ (kŏn′vẽrt) *n.* Person converted, esp. to religious faith or life.

con·vert·i·ble (k*o*nvẽr′tĭb*e*l) *adj.* That may be converted; (econ., of a currency) that may be freely converted into gold or another currency. **con·vert·i·bil·i·ty** (k*o*nvẽrt*i*bĭl′ĭtē) *n.* **con·vert′i·ble** *n.* Automobile having folding roof.

con·vex (kŏnvĕks′, kŏn′vĕks) *adj.* Curved like outside of circle or sphere, reverse of CONCAVE. **con·vex·i·ty** (k*o*nvĕk′sĭtē) *n.* (pl. **-ties**). **con·vex′ly** *adv.*

con·vey (k*o*nvā′) *v.t.* Transport, carry; transmit; impart, communicate (idea, meaning); (law) transfer, make over (property) by deed or legal process. **con·vey′a·ble** *adj.*

con·vey·ance (k*o*nvā′*e*ns) *n.* 1. Carrying; transmission; communication. 2. (Document effecting) transference of property. 3. Means of conveying, esp. a vehicle.

con·vey·or, con·vey·er (k*o*nvā′*er*) *ns.* (esp.) Mechanical device (usu. in form of endless belt or band) for conveying materials or items, esp. those in process of manufacture (also ~ **belt**).

con·vict (k*o*nvĭkt′) *v.t.* Prove guilty (*of* offense); declare guilty by verdict of jury or decision of judge; (theol.) impress (person) with sense of error. ~ (kŏn′vĭkt) *n.* Condemned criminal serving prison sentence. **con·vic′tive** *adj.* **con·vic′tive·ly** *adv.*

con·vic·tion (k*o*nvĭk′sh*o*n) *n.* Convicting; being convicted; verdict of guilty; being convinced, firm belief.

con·vince (k*o*nvĭns′) *v.t.* (**-vinced, -vinc·ing**). Firmly persuade (*of, that*). **con·vin′ci·ble** *adj.* **con·vinc′ing·ly** *adv.* **con·vinc′ing·ness** *n.* Open to conviction.

con·viv·i·al (k*o*nvĭv′ē*a*l) *adj.* Sociable, jovial; of, befitting, a feast; festive. **con·viv′i·al·ly** *adv.* **con·viv·i·al·i·ty** (k*o*nvĭvēăl′ĭtē) *n.*

con·vo·ca·tion (kŏnv*o*kā′sh*o*n) *n.* Calling together; assembly, esp. ecclesiastical or academic assembly. **con·vo·ca′tion·al** *adj.*

con·voke (k*o*nvōk′) *v.t.* (**-voked, -vok·ing**). Call together; summon to assemble.

con·vo·lute (kŏn′v*o*lo͞ot) *adj.* Rolled up together, coiled, twisted; complicated or involved. ~ *n.* Coil. **convolute** *v.* (**-lut·ed, -lut·ing**). **con′vo·lut·ed** *adj.* **con·vo·lu·tion** (kŏnv*o*lo͞o′sh*o*n) *n.*

con·vol·vu·lus (k*o*nvŏl′vy*u*l*u*s) *n.* (pl. **-lus·es, -li** pr. -lī). Plant of genus *C*~ with twining stem and trumpet-shaped flowers, bindweed.

con·voy (kŏn′voi, k*o*nvoi′) *v.t.* (of warship or aircraft) Escort (usu. merchant or passenger vessel); escort with armed force. **con′voy** *n.* 1. Convoying. 2. Company, supply of provisions, etc., under escort; number of merchant ships under escort or sailing in company; number of vehicles traveling in company, esp. with military or police protection.

con·vulse (k*o*nvŭls′) *v.t.* (**-vulsed, -vuls·ing**). Shake violently; throw into convulsions (usu. pass.); cause to be violently seized with laughter (usu. pass.).

con·vul·sion (k*o*nvŭl′sh*o*n) *n.* 1. (usu. pl.) Violent irregular motion of limb or body due to involuntary contraction of muscles (esp. as disorder of infants); (pl.) violent fit of laughter. 2. Violent social or political agitation; violent physical disturbance, esp. earthquake etc.

con·vul·sive (k*o*nvŭl′sĭv) *adj.* Attended or affected with, producing, resembling, convulsions. **con·vul′sive·ly** *adv.*

co·ny, co·ney (kō′nē) *ns.* (pl. **co·nies, co·neys**). 1. Rabbit (now retained mainly as name for the fur). 2. = PIKA.

coo (ko͞o) *v.* Make soft murmuring sound of, or as of, doves; say cooingly. ~ *n.* Cooing sound. **coo′ing·ly** *adv.*

cook (ko͝ok) *v.* Prepare food, prepare (food) by application of heat; undergo cooking; concoct (a dish or meal); (slang) tamper with, falsify (accounts etc.), esp. in ~ **the books; cook′book**, book of recipes

The **convolvulus** *or morning glory grows in both tropical and temperate areas and has colorful trumpet-shaped flowers. The seeds of two of its species are the source of an hallucinogenic drug.*

The barrel **cooper,** above, is seen shaping the sides of barrel staves. Making barrels is a skilled job. They are durable and easy to use, but heavy and costly. They are mostly used for whiskey and beer.

and directions for cooking; **cook'house**, building or place for cooking, esp. for camp, ranch, etc. **cook one's goose**, ruin one's chances; **cook'out**, party, picnic, at which cooking is done outdoors; **cook up** (colloq.) plan (scheme), contrive. **cook'stove**, stove for cooking. **cook** *n.* One who cooks food.

Cook (ko͝ok), **James** (1728–79). (**"Captain Cook"**). English navigator and explorer esp. of the Pacific and Australasia; first European discoverer of Hawaiian Islands, 1778; **Cook Islands**, group of islands in the S. Pacific Ocean, self-governing in association with New Zealand; **Cook Strait**, strait separating North and South Islands, New Zealand.

cook·er (ko͝ok'*er*) *n.* Appliance or vessel for cooking; **pressure ~**: see PRESSURE. **cook'er·y** *n.* Art, practice, of cooking.

cook·ie, cook·y (ko͝ok'ē) *ns.* (pl. **cook·ies**). 1. Small thin crisp cake made from sweet stiff dough. 2. (slang) Person, e.g. *tough, smart ~*, etc.

cool (ko͞ol) *adj.* 1. Moderately cold. 2. Unexcited, calm; lacking zeal, lukewarm; wanting cordiality. 3. Calmly audacious or impudent. 4. (colloq.) Applied complacently or emphatically to a large sum of money, e.g. *it cost me a ~ thousand.* 5. (of jazz music) Restrained or relaxed in style. **cool'ly** *adv.* **cool'ness** *n.* **cool** *n.* Cool place or state; (slang) composure, calm. ~ *v.* Make or become cool; **~ one's heels**, be kept waiting. **cool'ish** *adj.*

cool·ant (ko͞o'l*a*nt) *n.* Cooling agent; (esp.) fluid applied to edge of a cutting tool to lessen friction; cooling medium in internal combustion engine, nuclear reactor, etc.

The **coot,** a duck-like water-dwelling bird, is found in larger inland waters and streams. This African species, the crested coot (Fulica cristata), is distinguished by two red knobs on its forehead.

cool·er (ko͞o'l*er*) *n.* Device or container in which anything is cooled or kept cool; portable ice chest; (slang) jail.

Coo·lidge (ko͞o'lĭj), **(John) Calvin** (1872–1933). Governor of Massachusetts, 1919–20; vice president under Harding, 1921–3; 30th president of the U.S., 1923–9; succeeded to presidency on Harding's death, then elected to a full term.

coo·lie (ko͞o'lē) *n.* Unskilled Oriental laborer.

coon (ko͞on) *n.* 1. (colloq.) = RACCOON. 2. (derog.) Black person.

coop (ko͞op) *n.* Cage or enclosure for poultry or small animals; place of confinement; **fly the ~**, escape from confinement, flee. **coop** *v.* 1. Put in coop; confine narrowly (also **~ up**). 2. (slang, esp. said of police) Sleep while on duty.

co-op (kō'ŏp) *n.* (colloq.) Cooperative.

coop·er (ko͞o'p*er*) *n.* Maker of casks and other wooden vessels formed of staves and hoops. ~ *v.t.* Make or repair (casks). **coop'er·age** *n.* Cooper's work or workshop.

Coo·per (ko͞o'p*er*), **James Fenimore** (1789–1851). Amer. novelist; author of *The Last of the Mohicans, The Pathfinder, The Deerslayer,* etc.

co·op·er·ate (kōŏp'*er*āt) *v.i.* (**-at·ed, -at·ing**). Work together (*with* person *in* a work, *to* an end); concur in producing an effect. **co·op'er·a·tor** *n.* **co·op·er·a·tion** (kōŏp*er*ā'sh*o*n) *n.* Working together to same end; cooperative.

co·op·er·a·tive (kōŏp'*er*atĭv) *adj.* Of cooperation, cooperating; willing to cooperate; **~ apartment**, apartment house jointly owned by owners of its individual apartments; apartment in such a building; **~ farm, society, store**, one in which profits are shared (often in form of dividends on purchases) by all contributing members. **cooperative** *n.* Cooperative store, apartment, or other enterprise.

co-opt (kōŏpt') *v.t.* 1. Elect into body by votes of existing members. 2. Preempt; appropriate. **co-op·ta·tion** (kōŏptā'sh*o*n), **co-op'tion** *ns.* **co-op·ta·tive** (kōŏp'*t*atĭv), **co-op·tive** (kōŏp'tĭv) *adjs.*

co-or·di·nate (kōôr'd*i*nĭt, -nāt) *adj.* Equal in rank, degree, or importance; (gram.) of equal value, as *~ phrases, clauses.* **co·or'di·nate·ly** *adv.* **co·or·di·nate** (kōôr'd*i*nĭt, -nāt) *n.* Coordinate thing, esp. (math.) each of a system of two or more magnitudes used to define position of point, line, or plane, by reference to fixed system of lines, points, etc. **co·or·di·nate** (kōôr'd*i*nāt) *v.t.* (**-nat·ed, -nat·ing**). Make coordinate; bring (parts) into proper relation.

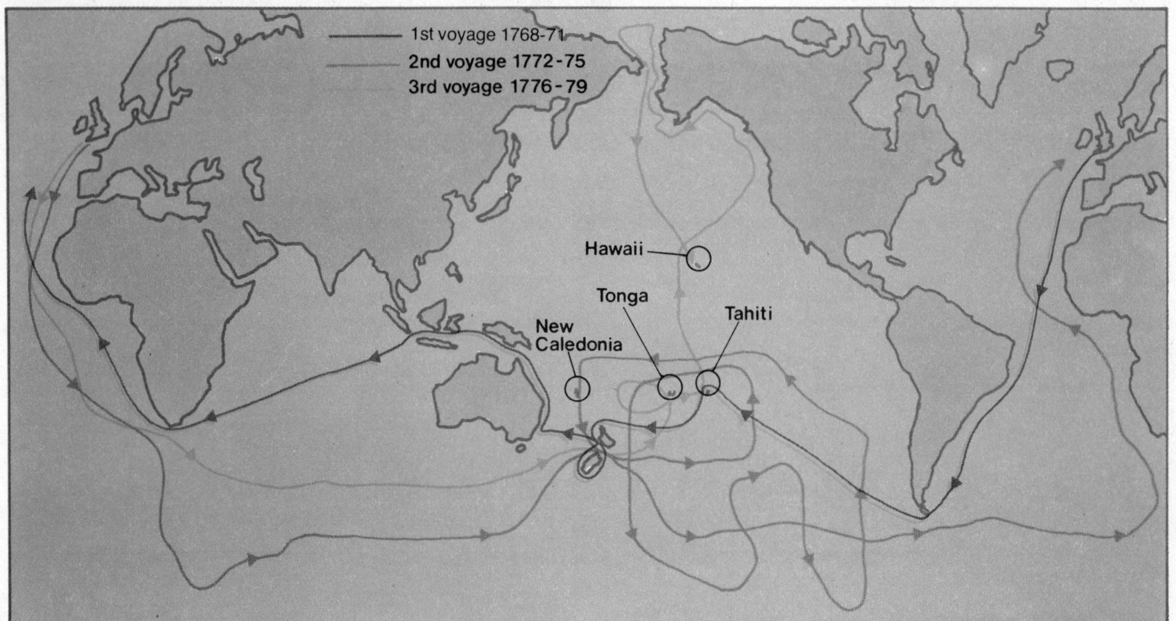

*Captain James **Cook** (above) was a great English maritime explorer who discovered the east coast of Australia. The first of his three voyages (top) began in 1768. Cook was killed by natives in Hawaii in 1779 during a voyage with the aim of discovering a north-west passage between the Pacific and Atlantic oceans.*

***Calvin Coolidge** was the 30th president of the U.S.A. President Harding's sudden death thrust him into office and he was elected in his own right in 1924.*

co·or·di·na·tion (kōōrdinā′shon), **co·or′di·na·tor** *ns.* **co·or·di·na·tive** (kōōr′dinatĭv, -nātĭv) *adj.*

Coos (kōōs) **Bay.** Inlet of the Pacific Ocean in SW. Oregon; port city on this inlet.

coot (kōōt) *n.* Any of various swimming and diving birds of genus *Fulica,* esp. *F. americana* of the New World and *F. atra* of the Old World, inhabiting edges of lakes and rivers; **old ~**, (colloq.) foolish or stubborn old man.

cop[1] (kŏp) *n.* (spinning) Roll of yarn wound upon spindle in such a way that it needs no support.

cop[2] (kŏp) *n.* (slang) Policeman. ~ *v.t.* (**copped, cop·ping**). (slang) Catch, capture; steal; **~ a plea**: see PLEA; **~ out** (slang) back out (of obligation). **cop′out** *n.* (slang) Act of copping out.

co·pal (kō′pal, -păl) *n.* Hard translucent odoriferous resin obtained from various tropical trees and used to make a fine transparent varnish. [Mex. Spanish from Nahuatl *copalli* incense]

Co·pán (kawpahn′). Site of a ruined Mayan city in W. Honduras.

co·part·ner (kōpart′ner, kō′-part-) *n.* Partner, sharer, associate. **co·part′ner·ship** *n.*

cope[1] (kōp) *n.* Long semicircular cloak without sleeves or armholes worn by clergy in procession. ~ *v.t.* (**coped, cop·ing**). Furnish with cope; cover (wall etc.) with coping.

cope[2] (kōp) *v.i.* (**coped, cop·ing**). Contend in well-matched struggle *with*; grapple successfully; deal competently (*with*), esp. in everyday affairs.

co·peck (kō′pěk) *n.* Var. of

***Copper** is found in a free metallic state in nature and was first used by neolithic man. Later it was extracted from ores. The ancient Egyptians and Sumerians made utensils, jewelry and decorative objects of copper, such as this panel from Sumeria (top). Copper is used in whisky distillers (above) to resist corrosion.*

KOPECK.

Co·pen·ha·gen (kōpenhā´gen, -hah´-, kō´penhā-, -hah-). (Dan. *Köbenhavn*) Capital city of Denmark.

Co · per · ni · cus (kopēr´nikus, ko-), **Nicolaus** (1473–1543). Latinized name of Mikolaj Kopernik, Polish astronomer, who demonstrated that the planets revolve on their own axes and move in orbits around the sun. **Co·per´-ni·can** *adj.* & *n.*

Co·pia·pó (kawpyahpaw´). Volcano, 19,950 ft. (6,081 m) in N. central Chile.

co·pi·lot (kō´pīlot) *n.* Second pilot in airplane; (fig.) right-hand man.

cop·ing (kō´pĭng) *n.* Top course of masonry or brickwork in wall or roof, usu. sloping.

co·pi·ous (kō´pēus) *adj.* Plentiful; full of matter, thoughts, or words. **co´pi·ous·ly** *adv.* **co´pi·ous·ness** *n.*

Cop·land (kōp´land), **Aaron** (1900–). Amer. composer of symphonies, chamber music, etc.

Co·pley (kŏp´lē), **John Singleton** (1738–1815). Amer. artist known for his portraits; settled in England, 1775.

co·pol·y·mer (kōpŏl´imer) *n.* Polymer of two or more different monomers. **co·pol·y·mer·ize**

(kōpŏl′*i*merīz) *v.* (**-ized, -iz·ing**). **co·pol·y·mer·i·za·tion** (kōpŏl*i*merīzā′sh*o*n) *n.*

cop·per[1] (kŏp′*er*) *n.* 1. (chem.) Malleable ductile metallic element of yellowish-red color having high electrical conductivity; symbol Cu, at. no. 29, at. wt. 63.546. 2. Coin made of copper or copper alloy. ~ **beech**, variety of European beech (*Fagus sylvatica cuprea*) with copper-colored leaves; **cop′perhead**, venomous snake (*Ankistrodon contortrix*) of eastern U.S., so called from reddish-brown color of top of head; (fig., usu. **Copperhead**) Northern sympathizer with the South during the Civil War; **cop′perplate**, polished plate of copper on which design is engraved or etched for printing, print from this; (of handwriting) neat, careful; **cop′persmith**, worker in copper. **copper** *v.t.* Cover or coat with copper. **cop′per·y** *adj.* (esp.) Copper-colored. [L. *cuprum*, f. *Cyprium* (*aes*) Cyprian (metal)]

cop·per[2] (kŏp′*er*) *n.* (slang) Policeman; law enforcement officer.

cop·ra (kŏp′r*a*, kō′pr*a*) *n.* Dried kernels of coconut from which coconut oil is extracted, used in manufacture of margarine, candles, etc.

cop·roph·a·gous (kŏprŏf′*a*gus) *adj.* (of beetles) Dung-eating.

copse (kŏps) *n.* Thicket of low trees and shrubs.

Copt (kŏpt) *n.* 1. Native Egyptian descendant of ancient Egyptians. 2. Member of the Coptic Church. [Arab. *al-kibt* f. Coptic *gyptios*, f. Gk *Aiguptios* Egyptian]

Cop·tic (kŏp′tĭk) *adj.* Of Coptic or the Copts. ~ *n.* Language of the Copts, surviving only in the liturgy of the ~ **Church**, the native Christian church of Ethiopia and Egypt.

cop·u·la (kŏp′y*u*l*a*) *n.* (pl. **-las, -lae** pr. -lē). (logic, gram.) Verb *be* or verb with similar function employed merely as sign of predication. **cop′u·lar** *adj.*

cop·u·late (kŏp′y*u*lāt) *v.i.* (**-lat·ed, -lat·ing**). Unite in copulation. **cop·u·la·tion** (kŏpy*u*lā′sh*o*n) *n.* Physical union between male and female animals, as in act of procreation.

cop·u·la·tive (kŏp′y*u*l*a*tĭv, -lā-) *adj.* Serving as copula, connecting subject and predicate; relating to sexual intercourse. **cop′u·la·tive·ly** *adv.* **copulative** *n.* Copulative conjunction or particle.

cop·y (kŏp′ē) *n.* (pl. **cop·ies**). 1. Reproduction (of writing, picture, etc.); imitation; specimen of penmanship written after a model. 2. One of the written or printed specimens of the same writing or work. 3. (archaic) Original from which a copy is made; esp. specimen of penmanship to be copied. 4. Manuscript or other matter prepared for printing; material for a story; text of advertisement. 5. **cop′ybook**, book, containing copies for learners to imitate; (*attrib.*) conventional, commonplace; **cop′yboy**, office boy in newspaper office; **cop′ycat**, (colloq.) one who copies another; **copy desk**, desk, office, where newspaper is edited and prepared for printing; **copy editor, cop′y-reader**, one who prepares a manuscript for publication esp. correcting spelling, punctuation, etc.; **cop′ywriter**, one who writes advertisements. **copy** *v.* (**cop·ied, cop·y·ing**). Transcribe (*from* original); make copy of; imitate. **cop′y·ist** *n.* One who makes written copies.

cop·y·right (kŏp′ērīt) *n.* Sole legal right to produce or reproduce a literary, dramatic, musical, or artistic work, by making copies or performance or any other means; ~ **library**, national or major library entitled to receive copies of all or specific collections of books copyrighted in a country, as the Library of Congress in the U.S.; ~ **union**, international union established by the Berne Convention of 1886, whereby each member country undertakes to give to foreign authors the same rights and

__Coptic__ art shows a variety of influences from India, Syria, Mesopotamia, Byzantium and Egypt. It is highly stylized but with a remarkable sense of color. This brightly colored mural with its flat figures is from Ethiopia.

*The **coracle** is still used in Wales as a river fishing boat. Its frame was originally made of woven canes and reeds, but it now has a canvas and tar covering.*

copyright protection its own authors receive. **copyright** *adj.* Protected by copyright. ~ *v.t.* Protect (book etc.) by copyright; secure copyright for.

co·quet (kōkĕt′) *v.i.* (**-quet·ted, -quet·ting**). Play the coquette; flirt (*with*); dally, trifle, *with*. **co·quet·ry** (kō′kĭtrē, kōkĕt′rē) *n.* (pl. **-ries**). Coquettish behavior or act; coquetting, trifling. **co·quette′** *n.* Woman who (habitually) trifles with the affections of men, flirt. **co·quet′tish** *adj.* **co·quet′tish·ly** *adv.*

Cor. *abbrev.* Corinthians (New Testament).

cor·a·cle (kŏr′*a*kel, kăr′-) *n.* Small boat of wickerwork covered with waterproof canvas. [Welsh *corwgl* f. *cwrwg* = Ir. *curach* boat]

cor·a·coid (kŏr′*a*koid, kăr′-) *adj.* Beaked like a crow. ~ *n.* Short projection of the scapula in vertebrates.

cor·al (kŏr′*a*l, kăr′-) *n.* 1. Hard calcareous substance consisting of the continuous skeleton secreted by many kinds of submarine coelenterate polyps for their support and habitation, found growing on sea bottom or in extensive accumulation (~ **reef**). 2. Piece of coral as ornament etc. 3. Unimpregnated roe of lobster (so called from color when boiled). 4. One of the individual animals that secrete ~. 5. **C~ Gables**, city on Biscayne Bay in SE. Florida; ~ **reef**, see sense 1; **C~ Sea**, area of Pacific Ocean with many coral reefs between New Guinea and N.E. Australia; site of an important U.S. naval victory (1942) over the Japanese in World War II. ~ **snake**, any of several venomous snakes of southern U.S. and tropical America of the genus *Micrurus*, having brilliant red, black, and yellow colors. **coral** *adj.* Of (the color of) coral, reddish-pink. **cor·al·loid** (kŏr′*a*loid, kăr′-) *adj.* Like or akin to coral.

cor·al·line (kŏr′*a*lĭn, -līn, kăr′-) *adj.* Coral red; corallike. ~ *n.* Seaweed of genus *Corallina* with calcareous jointed stem; any of various plantlike compound animals.

cor·bel (kŏr′b*e*l) *n.* Projection of stone, timber, etc., jutting out from wall to support weight; short timber laid longitudinally under beam or girder to shorten its unsupported span. ~ *v.t.*(**-beled, -bel·ing**, Brit. **-belled, -bel·ling**). **cor′beled** *adj.* [OF. *corbel* raven]

Cor·cy·ra (kŏrsī′r*a*): see CORFU.

cord (kŏrd) *n.* 1. (Piece of) string made from several twisted strands. 2. (anat.) Flexible cord-shaped structure of tissue fiber; SPINAL ~, VOCAL ~; see these words. 3. Raised cordlike rib on cloth, ribbed fabric, esp. corduroy; (pl.) clothing made of this fabric. 4. Measure of cut wood for fuel, usu. 128 cu. ft. (3.63 cu. m). **cord** *v.t.* Bind or fasten with cord(s).

cord·age (kŏr′dĭj) *n.* Cord or ropes collectively, esp. in rigging of a ship.

cor·date (kŏr′dāt) *adj.* Heart-shaped.

cord·ed (kŏr′dĭd) *adj.* Bound, furnished, with cords; ribbed, twilled.

cor·dial (kŏr′j*a*l; *Brit.* kŏr′dē*a*l) *adj.* 1. That stimulates the heart. 2. Hearty, sincere; warm, friendly. ~ *n.* Liqueur. **cor·dial·i·ty** (kŏrjăl′ĭtē) *n.* **cor′dial·ly** *adv.*

cor·dil·le·ra (kŏrdĭlyār′*a*, kŏrdĭl′*era*) *n.* One of a parallel series of mountain ridges, esp. in the Andes and Mexico; chain of mountains, esp. a principal range; **C~s**, name given to many ranges; the entire complex of ranges of western America from Alaska to Cape Horn.

cord·ite (kŏr′dīt) *n.* Smokeless explosive powder of nitrocellulose, nitroglycerine, and petrolatum, usu. pressed into rods of varying length and thickness.

Cór·do·ba (kŏr′do*ba*, kŏrdō′-; *Sp.* kŏr′dawvah). City of S. Spain on river Guadalquivir; Moorish capital 756–1236.

cor·do·ba (kŏr′do*ba*, -v*a*) *n.* Principal monetary unit of

*Reef-forming **coral** (facing page) can only thrive in the clear waters of tropical seas where the temperature never falls below 70°F. The Great Barrier Reef, (below) off the east coast of Australia, is the largest single system of coral reefs in the world.*

Nicaragua, = 100 centavos.

cor·don (kōr′dŏn) *n.* 1. (archit.) String-course, projecting (usu. flat) band of stone on face of wall. 2. Line of troops consisting of men placed at intervals to prevent passage; line or circle of police or other persons. 3. Ornamental cord or braid worn as badge of honor; ~ **bleu** (kōrdawṅ blö′), blue ribbon worn formerly by Knights of the Holy Ghost, the highest order under the Bourbons; hence, person of eminence, (esp.) first-class cook.

cor·do·van (kōr′dovan) *n.* Kind of soft leather, hence ~ **shoes**.

cor·du·roy (kōr′duroi, kōrdu-roi′) *n.* 1. Cotton fabric with ridges in the pile; (pl.) corduroy trousers. 2. Corduroy road. ~ *adj.* Made of corduroy, ribbed like corduroy; ~ **road**, road of tree trunks or logs laid transversely across swamp or miry ground.

CORE (kōr, kōr) *abbrev.* Congress of Racial Equality.

core (kōr, kōr) *n.* 1. Dry horny capsule embedded in pulp and containing seeds of apple, pear, etc. 2. Central portion cut out, as of rock in boring. 3. Central part of different character from what surrounds it; (esp.) assemblage of soft iron layers in center of electro-magnet or induction coil; central cord of conducting wires in telegraph etc. cable; part of center of nuclear reactor that contains fissionable fuel; unit of magnetic material in a computer. 4. Innermost part, center, heart, of anything. **core** *v.t.* (**cored, cor·ing**). Remove core from.

co·re·li·gion·ist (kōrĭlĭj′onĭst) *n.* Adherent of same religion.

co·re·op·sis (kōrēŏp′sĭs, kōr-) *n.* Composite plant of genus *C*~ cultivated for its handsome daisy-like yellow or variegated flowers.

co·re·spond·ent (kōrĭspŏn′dent, kōr-, kār-) *n.* (law) Man or woman proceeded against together with RESPONDENT in a divorce suit.

Cor·fu (kōr′fōō, -fū). One of the Ionian islands off the W. coast of Greece, anciently called Corcyra.

cor·gi (kōr′gē) *n.* (also **Welsh** ~) Dog of short-legged breed with foxlike head.

co·ri·an·der (kōrēăn′der, kōr-, kār-) *n.* Herb (*Coriandrum sativum*) of S. Europe, Levant, etc., with compound leaves and globose aromatic fruit (~ **seed**) used as flavoring and condiment.

Cor·inth (kōr′ĭnth, kār′-). City of Greece in the NE. Peloponnesus on an inlet (**the Gulf of** ~) of the Ionian Sea; notorious in ancient times for luxury and profligacy.

Co·rin·thi·an (korĭn′thēan) *adj.* 1. Of Corinth or its people. 2. (archit.) Of the Corinthian order. 3. (archaic) Given to elegant dissipation, profligate. 4. ~ **order**, (archit.) most ornate of the Greek orders, with bell-shaped capital adorned with rows of acanthus leaves giving rise to volutes and helices. **Corinthian** *n.* 1. Native, inhabitant, of Corinth; (**Epistle to the**) ~**s**, either of two books of New Testament, epistles of St. Paul to the Church at Corinth. 2. (archaic) Profligate.

Cor·i·o·la·nus (kōrēolā′nus, kār-), **Gaius Marcius.** Legendary Roman patrician and general of the first half of the 5th c. B.C., prosecuted for aspiring to become tyrant, and exiled; whereupon he joined the Volscians and led them against Rome, but on the entreaties of his mother, Veturia, he spared the town and withdrew to Antium, where he was murdered by the Volscians.

Cork (kōrk). Largest county of Republic of Ireland; county seat of this county.

cork (kōrk) *n.* 1. Bark of the cork oak (*Quercus suber*), which grows to a thickness of 1 to 2 in. (2.6 to 5.1 cm) and is very light, tough, and elastic; the tree itself. 2. Piece of cork used as float for fishing line,

*The **Corinth Canal** crosses the isthmus of Corinth and joins the Gulf of Corinth with the Saronic Gulf. Opened in 1893, it has cut the distance between the Adriatic and Piraeus by 200 miles.*

*The **cork** tree (left), although native to the Mediterranean area is now cultivated in India and the west of the U.S.A. The outer bark is removed, boiled and stacked in strips (above).*

etc. 3. Cylindrical or tapering piece of cork used as stopper for a bottle, cask, etc.; similar stopper of other substance. 4. (bot.) Tissue forming outer division of bark in higher plants and consisting of closely packed air-containing cells nearly impervious to air and water. 5. ~ **oak**, tree (*Quercus suber*); **cork'screw**, instrument for drawing corks from bottles, usu. consisting of a piece of steel twisted into a spiral with sharp point and transverse handle; (*adj.*) spirally twisted; (*v.*) twist spirally, (cause to) proceed spirally; **cork-tipped**, (cigarette) with band of corklike substance at one end; **cork** *adj.* Made of cork. ~ *v.t.* Stop, stop *up*, with or as with cork; blacken with burnt cork.

cork·age (kōr'kĭj) *n.* Corking, uncorking, of bottles; restaurant's charge for opening and serving each bottle of wine or liquor not bought on the premises.

corked (kōrkt) *adj.* 1. (of wine) Tasting of the cork, spoiled by an unsound cork into which the wine penetrates. 2. (of face and hands) Blackened with burnt cork as part of theatrical make-up. 3. Sealed in (bottle).

cork·er (kōr'ker) *n.* (slang) Something that precludes further discussion; excellent person or thing. **cork'ing** *adj.* & *adv.* (slang) Excellent.

corm (kōrm) *n.* (bot.) Swollen base of stem containing food reserves, occurring in some monocotyledonous plants, such as crocus.

cor·mo·rant (kōr'merant, -rănt) *n.* Large, lustrous, black, voracious sea bird, e.g. *Phalacrocorax aurities*; (pl.) family to which this belongs. [med. L. *corvus marinus* sea raven]

corn[1] (kōrn) *n.* 1. Any of several varieties of a tall cereal plant (*Zea mays*) widely cultivated for food and oil, with seeds or kernels on large ears, some varieties of which are also called maize or Indian corn; ears of this plant; the kernels. 2. (Brit.) Any of several cereal plants, esp. wheat or (in Scotland) oats. 3. (slang) Anything old-fashioned, trite, or sentimental. **corn'y**, *adj.* (**corn·i·er, corn·i·est**). 4. **corn'ball**, (slang) corny; **C~ Belt**, area in U.S. Middle West noted for raising corn and corn-fed livestock, esp. Indiana, Illinois, and Iowa; **corn bread**, bread made from cornmeal; **corn'cob**, woody core of ear of corn; **corncob pipe**, tobacco pipe made from corncob; **corn'crib**, building for storing ears of corn, with ventilated sides; **corn'fed**, fed on corn; (fig.) husky, innocent, and provincial; **corn'flakes**, breakfast cereal made of toasted flaked and flavored corn; **corn'flower**, name of various plants, esp. the blue-flowered *Centaurea cyanus*, or bachelor's button; **Corn Laws**, (Brit. hist.) series of British laws restricting the importation of grain, repealed 1846; **corn'meal**, meal made of corn; **corn pone** (Southern U.S.) corn bread made without milk or eggs; **corn silk**, silky fibers in corn husk; **corn'stalk**, stalk of corn; **corn syrup**, sweet syrup made from corn; **corn whiskey**, whiskey distilled from corn.

corn[2] (kōrn) *n.* Horny induration of cuticle with hard center and root sometimes penetrating deep into subjacent tissue, caused by undue pressure, chiefly of shoes on feet.

corn[3] (kōrn) *v.* Sprinkle, preserve (meat) with salt; **corned beef**, beef so preserved.

cor·ne·a (kōr'nēa) *n.* Transparent horny part of anterior covering of eyeball. **cor'ne·al** *adj.*

Cor·neille (kōrnā'), **Pierre** (1606–84). French dramatist, author of classical tragedies *Le Cid*, *Horace*, etc.

cor·nel (kōr'n*e*l) *n.* Any tree, shrub, or plant of the genus *Cornus*, including the dogwood and bunchberry.

cor·nel·ian (kōrnēl'y*a*n) *n.* Var. of CARNELIAN.

cor·ne·ous (kōr'nē*u*s) *adj.* Made of horn, hornlike.

cor·ner (kōr'n*e*r) *n.* 1. Angular meeting place of converging sides or edges, projecting angle, esp. where two streets meet; hollow angle enclosed by meeting walls etc.; **drive into a ~**, force into difficult position from which there is no escape. 2. Secluded, secret, or remote place; region, quarter; extremity or end of the earth. 3. Buying up all or most of any stock or commodity, in order to profit by raising its price. 4. **cor'nerstone**, one of those forming corner angle of wall; (fig.) indispensable thing or part. **corner** *v.* 1. Furnish with corners. 2. Set in corner; drive into corner (esp. fig.). 3. (of vehicle etc.) Go around a corner. 4. Force (dealers) or control (commodity) by means of corner (sense 3); form corner *in* (stock or commodity). **cor'nered** *adj.*

cor·net (kōrnĕt' for def. 1; kōr'nĭt for def. 2) *n.* 1. Brass musical instrument of trumpet class with valves operated by pistons for producing additional notes; cornet player. 2. Conically rolled piece of paper for candy, nuts, etc. **cor·net'ist, cor·net'tist** *ns.*

cor·nice (kōr'nĭs) *n.* (archit.) Horizontal molded projection crowning or finishing (part of) building etc., esp. uppermost member of entablature, surmounting the frieze; ornamental molding around wall of room just below ceiling.

Cor·nish (kōr'nĭsh) *adj.* Of Cornwall. ~ *n.* Ancient Celtic language of Cornwall.

cor·nu·co·pi·a (kōrn*u*kō'pē*a*) *n.* Horn of plenty, represented as a goat's horn overflowing with flowers, fruit, corn, etc. **cor·nu·co'pi·an** *adj.* Overflowingly abundant. [L. *cornu copiae* = "horn of plenty," the horn of the goat Amalthea by which the infant Zeus was suckled]

Corn·wall (kōrn'wawl; *Brit.* kōrn'w*a*l). County in the extreme SW. of England.

Corn·wal·lis (kōrnwaw'lĭs, -wŏl'ĭs), **Charles** (1738–1805). First Marquis Cornwallis, 1792; English major general; commanded British troops in America during the Revolutionary War; surrendered to George Washington at Yorktown, 1781, ending the war; later became successful British governor general and commander in chief in India, then Viceroy of Ireland.

co·rol·la (k*o*rŏl'*a*) *n.* (bot.) Whorl of floral leaves (petals) forming inner envelope of flower, and usu. its most conspicuous part.

cor·ol·lar·y (kōr'*o*lĕrē, kār'-) *n.* (pl. **-lar·ies**). Proposition appended to one already demonstrated, as self-evident inference from it; immediate deduction; natural consequence, result. [L. *corollarium* money paid for a chaplet, gratuity]

co·ro·na (k*o*rō'n*a*) *n.* (pl. **-nas, -nae** pr. -nē). 1. Circle of light seen around and close to luminous body, esp. sun or moon, caused by diffraction by water droplets in thin cloud (cf. HALO); **solar ~**, rarefied gaseous envelope of sun, visible as radiating white light during total solar eclipse; (elect.) luminous appearance around conductor accompanying ionization of surrounding gas. 2. Circular candleholder hung from ceiling. 3. (archit.) Member of cornice, with broad vertical face, usu. of considerable projection. 4. (anat., zool.) Any of various crownlike parts of body. 5. (bot.) Crownlike appendage on inner side of corolla in daffodil and other flowers. 6. Long cigar with blunt tip.

Co·ro·na·do (kōr*o*nah'dō, kōr-), **Francesco Vasquez de** (1510–1554). Spanish explorer of the southwestern U.S. and Central America; discovered the Grand Canyon, explored California Peninsula, and followed course of Rio Grande River.

cor·o·nal (kōr'*o*n*a*l, kār'-, k*o*rō'n*a*l) *adj.* 1. (anat.) ~ **suture**, transverse suture of skull between frontal bone and parietal bones. 2. (bot.) Of a corona.

cor·o·nar·y (kōr'*o*nĕrē, kār'-) *adj.* 1. (of vessels, ligaments, nerves, etc.) Encircling parts like a crown; (of parts) connected with these. 2. (of arteries, veins) Supplying blood to the heart; ~ **occlusion, thrombosis**, throm-

*The **cornet** has been superseded by the trumpet in modern usage although it is still popular with military and brass bands as a solo instrument. It first appeared in Europe in the 1820s.*

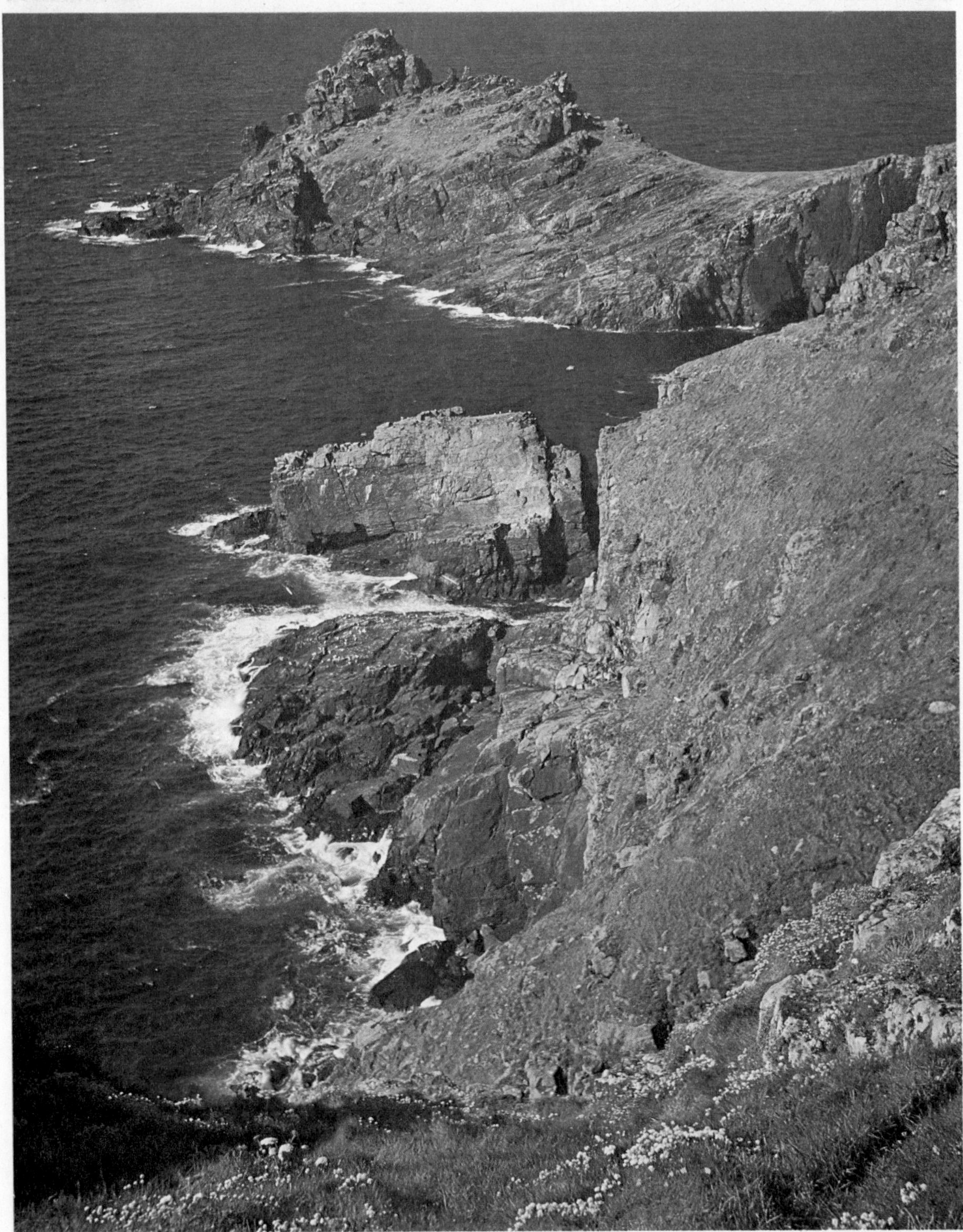

*The county of **Cornwall** in the south-west extremity of England has an attractive coastal landscape and a mild climate. It is a popular tourist area, with long stretches of its coast unspoilt.*

bosis occurring in a coronary artery. **coronary** *n.* (pl. **-nar·ies**). (esp.) Coronary thrombosis; (loosely) heart attack.

cor·o·na·tion (kŏronā′shon, kăr-) *n.* Ceremony of crowning sovereign or sovereign's consort.

cor·o·ner (kŏr′oner, kăr′-) *n.* Public official whose chief duty is to investigate deaths thought to be caused by other than natural causes.

cor·o·net (kŏr′onĭt, kăr′-, kŏro-nĕt, kăr-) *n.* 1. Small crown, esp. crown denoting dignity inferior to sovereign's, worn by nobility and varying in form according to rank. 2. Decorative fillet or wreath, esp. as part of woman's headdress; garland for the head. **cor′o·net·ed, cor′o·net·ted** *adjs.* Wearing a coronet; esp., belonging to the peerage.

Co·rot (kawrō′, ko-), **Jean Baptiste Camille** (1796–1875). French landscape painter.

corp. *abbrev.* Corporal, corporation.

cor·po·ral[1] (kŏr′peral, -pral) *adj.* Of the human body; personal, bodily; as in ~ **punishment**, that inflicted on the body; flogging. **cor·po·ral·i·ty** (kōrperăl'ĭtē) *n.* Material existence; body.

cor·po·ral² (kōr'p*e*ral, -pr*a*l) *n.* Fine linen cloth on which consecrated elements are placed during Mass.

cor·po·ral³ (kōr'p*e*ral, -pr*a*l) *n.* Noncommissioned officer ranking below sergeant; **the little C~**, nickname of Napoleon I.

cor·po·rate (kōr'perĭt, -prĭt) *adj.* Forming a body politic or corporation; forming one body of many individuals; of, belonging to, a body politic. **cor'po·rate·ly** *adv.*

cor·po·ra·tion (kōrperā'sh*o*n) *n.* 1. Body corporate legally authorized to act as a single individual; business so organized. 2. Body created for governmental purposes; agency of government. **cor·po·ra·tive** (kōr'porātĭv, -p*o*ratĭv, -pr*a*tĭv) *adj.*

cor·po·re·al (kōrpōr'ēal, -pōr'-) *adj.* Bodily; material; tangible. **cor·po're·al·ly** *adv.*

cor·po·sant (kōr'pozănt) *n.* St. Elmo's fire; see ELMO, ST.

corps (kōr, kōr) *n.* (pl. **corps** pr. kōrz, kōrz). 1. Army corps; body of troops for special service. 2. Body of persons in common organization; **corps de ballet,** members of ballet company who perform as a group and do not have solo rôles.

corpse (kōrps) *n.* Dead (usu. human) body.

cor·pu·lent (kōr'py*u*lent) *adj.* Bulky (of body); fat. **cor'pu·lence, cor'pu·len·cy** *ns.*

cor·pus (kōr'p*u*s) *n.* (pl. **-po·ra** pr. -p*o*ra). 1. Body, collection, of writings. 2. (physiol.) Structure of special character or function in animal body. 3. ~ **callosum,** band of tissue connecting hemispheres of brain; ~ **delicti** (L., = "body of the crime"), material evidence that a crime has been committed; (pop.) body of murdered person; ~ **juris,** body of law; ~ **luteum,** structure formed in ovary of mammals after ovulation.

Cor·pus Chris·ti¹ (kōr'p*u*s krĭs'tē). Feast of the Blessed Sacrament or body of Christ, the Thursday after Trinity Sunday.

Cor·pus Chris·ti² (kōr'p*u*s krĭs'tē, -tī). Seaport and industrial city in SW. Texas, on the Gulf of Mexico.

cor·pus·cle (kōr'p*u*sel, -pŭs-), **cor·pus·cule** (kōrpŭs'kūl) *ns.* 1. Minute body forming distinct part of organism; (esp.) one of the minute rounded or disklike bodies constituting a large part of the blood of vertebrates. 2. (phys. chemistry) Discrete particle, such as a proton, electron, or atom. **cor·pus·cu·lar** (kōrpŭs'ky*u*ler) *adj.*

cor·ral (korăl') *n.* Enclosure for horses, cattle, etc; defensive enclosure of wagons in encampment; enclosure for capturing wild animals. **corral** *v.t.* (**-ralled, -ral·ling**). Drive (animals) into and confine in corral; (slang) capture, obtain.

cor·rect (korĕkt') *adj.* True, accurate; right, proper (of conduct, manners, etc.), in accordance with a good standard (of taste etc.). **cor·rect'ly** *adv.* **cor·rect'ness** *n.* **correct** *v.t.* 1. Set right, amend; substitute right for (wrong); mark errors on (student's paper, printer's proof-sheet, etc.) for amendment. 2. Admonish (person); cure (person) of fault; punish (person, fault). 3. Counteract, neutralize, (hurtful qualities). 4. Bring (result of mathematical or physical observation or calculation) into accordance with certain standard conditions; eliminate aberration etc. from lens etc. **cor·rect'a·ble** *adj.* **cor·rec'tor** *n.*

cor·rec·tion (korĕk'sh*o*n) *n.* 1. Correcting. 2. Thing substituted for what is wrong. 3. Punishment. **cor·rec'tion·al** *adj.*

cor·rec·tive (korĕk'tĭv) *adj.* & *n.* (Thing) serving, tending, to correct or counteract what is harmful. **cor·rec'tive·ly** *adv.*

Cor·reg·gio (korĕj'ēō). Antonio Allegri (1494–1534), called "Il Correggio" from the place of his birth in Lombardy, an Italian painter famous for his chiaroscuro.

Cor·reg·i·dor (korĕg'ĭdōr, -dōr). Island in the Philippines at the entrance to Manila Bay; site of World War II battle, 1942, in which Amer. forces under Gen. MacArthur surrendered to Japanese; in 1945 Amer. forces under MacArthur invaded island and overcame Japanese.

cor·re·late (kōr'*e*lāt, kār'-) *n.* Each of two things so related that one implies or is complementary to the other; each of two related things viewed in reference to the other. **correlate** *v.* (**-lat·ed, -lat·ing**). Have a mutual relation (*with, to*); bring (thing) into such relation

*The Rockefeller Center in New York City reflects the **corporate** image of one of the most powerful business trusts in the world. Rockefeller's Standard Oil Company was the first corporation in the U.S.A.*

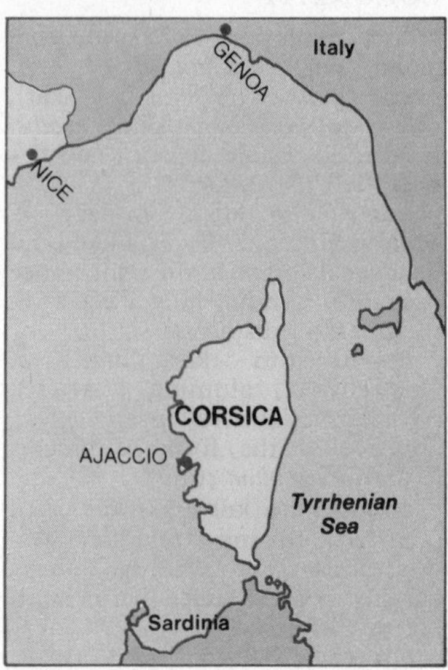

Corsica, the fourth largest island in the Mediterranean, is a 'département' of France. It is 100 miles south-east of France and 50 miles west of Italy. Left: View of Calvi, a favorite tourist resort. Above: Map of Corsica.

(*with* another). **cor·re·la·tion** (kŏrelā′shon, kăr-) *n.*

cor·rel·a·tive (korĕl′atĭv) *adj.* 1. Having a mutual relation (*with, to*); analogous. 2. (gram., of words) Corresponding with each other and regularly used together each in one member of compound or complex sentence (e.g. *either—or*; *so—as*). ~ *n.* Correlative word or thing. **cor·rel′a·tive·ly** *adv.* **cor·rel·a·tiv·i·ty** (korĕlatĭv′ĭtē) *n.*

cor·re·spond (kŏrespŏnd′, kăr-) *v.i.* 1. Be congruous, in harmony (*with, to*); be similar, analogous (*to*); agree in amount, position, etc. (*to*). 2. Communicate by interchange of letters (*with*). **cor·re·spond′ing·ly** *adv.*

cor·re·spond·ence (kŏrespŏn′dens, kăr-) *n.* 1. Agreement, harmony. 2. Communication by letters; letters; ~ **course, school**, one instructing by correspondence.

cor·re·spond·ent (kŏrespŏn′dent, kăr-) *n.* One who writes letter(s) to another; person employed to contribute news, articles, etc., to newspaper etc., esp. from a distant place or on a particular subject; person etc. with regular business relations with another (esp. in foreign country). ~ *adj.* Corresponding.

cor·ri·dor (kŏr′ĭder, -dŏr, kăr′-) *n.* 1. Main passage in large building, on which many rooms open; outside passage connecting parts of building; hallway; aisle. 2. Strip of territory of one country running through another territory to give access e.g. to the sea; **air** ~, route to which aircraft are restricted; **Polish C**~, strip that ran through Prussia from Poland to the Baltic at Danzig, created by the Treaty of Versailles (1919).

cor·ri·gen·dum (kŏrĭjĕn′dum, kăr-) *n.* (pl. **-da** pr. -da). Thing to be corrected (esp. mistake in printed book); (pl.) list of items to be corrected.

cor·ri·gi·ble (kŏr′ĭjibel, kăr′-) *n.* Capable of being corrected; open or receptive to correction.

cor·rob·o·rate (korŏb′erāt) *v.t.* (**-rat·ed, -rat·ing**). Confirm, support, or strengthen (other evidence, a statement, etc.); attest the truth of. **cor·rob·o·ra·tive** (korŏb′orātĭv, -eratĭv), **cor·rob·o·ra·to·ry** (korŏb′oratōrē, -tōrē) *adjs.* **cor·rob·o·ra·tion** (korŏborā′shon), **cor·rob·o·ra·tor** (korŏb′orāter) *ns.*

cor·rode (korōd′) *v.* (**-rod·ed, -rod·ing**). (of rust, chemical agents, etc.) Wear away, destroy gradually; become destroyed thus; decay. **cor·rod′i·ble** *adj.* **cor·ro·sion** (korō′zhon), **cor·ro′sive·ness** *ns.* **cor·ro·sive** (korō′sĭv) *adj.* & *n.* **cor·ro′sive·ly** *adv.*

cor·ru·gate (kŏr′ugāt, kăr′-) *v.* (**-gat·ed, -gat·ing**). Contract into wrinkles or folds; mark with, bend into, parallel folds or ridges. **cor′ru·gat·ed** *adj.* (esp.) ~ **iron**, galvanized sheet iron or steel bent into a series of parallel ridges and grooves, used for roofing etc.; ~ **cardboard**, type of ridged cardboard used for packing. **cor·ru·ga·tion** (kŏrugā′shon, kăr-) *n.*

cor·rupt (korŭpt′) *adj.* Rotten, decomposed (archaic); debased in character, depraved, wicked; perverted or influenced by bribery; (of language, texts, etc.) vitiated by errors or alterations. **cor·rupt′ly** *adv.* **cor·rupt′ness** *n.* **corrupt** *v.* Infect, taint; bribe; destroy purity of (text, language); make, become, corrupt. **cor·rup′tive** *adj.*

cor·rupt·i·ble (korŭp′tibel) *adj.* Liable to corruption, perishable; capable of moral corruption. **cor·rupt·i·bil·i·ty** (korŭptibĭl′ĭtē) *n.* **cor·rupt′i·bly** *adv.*

cor·rup·tion (korŭp′shon) *n.* Decomposition; moral deterioration; use of corrupt practices; bribery etc.; perversion (of language etc.) from original state.

cor·sage (kŏrsahzh′) *n.* Bodice of woman's dress; fresh flower(s) worn by a woman on bodice, shoulder, or wrist.

cor·sair (kŏr′săr) *n.* Mediterranean privateer, esp. of Barbary; corsair's ship.

cor·set (kŏr′sit) *n.* Closely fitting foundation garment, usu. stiffened and freq. laced to give support around waist and hips, worn esp. by women; stays. ~ *v.t.* Fit with corset; (fig.) constrict.

cor·se·tier, cor·se·tière (kŏrsetēr′) *ns.* Corset maker or fitter.

Cor·si·ca (kŏr′sĭka). Island off the W. coast of Italy, belonging to France; capital, Ajaccio.

Cor·si·can (kŏr′sĭkan) *adj.* Of Corsica or its people. ~ *n.* Native, inhabitant, of Corsica; **the** ~, Napoleon I, born at Ajaccio in Corsica.

cor·tege, cor·tège (kŏrtĕzh′, -tāzh′) *ns.* Train of attendants; procession, esp. a funeral procession.

Cor·tés (kŏrtĕz′), **Hernando** (1485–1547). Spanish explorer and conquistador, conqueror of the Aztecs and colonial administrator of New Spain.

cor·tex (kŏr′tĕks) *n.* (pl. **-ti·ces** pr. -tĭsēz, **-tex·es**). 1. (bot.) Inner bark. 2. (anat.) Layer of gray matter on surface of brain; outer part of kidney; outer portion of suprarenal gland. **cor′ti·cal** *adj.*

cor·ti·cate (kōr′tĭkĭt, -kāt), **cor·ti·cat·ed** (kōr′tĭkātĭd) *adjs.* Having bark or a cortex. **cor·ti·cose** (kōr′tĭkōs) *adj.*

cor·ti·sone (kōr′tĭsōn, -zōn) *n.* Steroid hormone ($C_{21}H_{28}O_5$) found in adrenal cortex; similar substance prepared synthetically, used in treatment of diseases.

co·run·dum (korŭn′dum) *n.* Crystallized alumina (Al_2O_3), translucent mineral used as an abrasive in the form of emery. [Tamil *kurundum* ruby]

cor·us·cate (kōr′uskāt, kār′-) *v.i.* (**-cat·ed, -cat·ing**). Sparkle, flash. **cor·us·ca·tion** (kōruskā′shon, kār-) *n.* **co·rus·cant** (korŭs′kant, kōr′us-, kār′-) *adj.*

cor·vette (kōrvĕt′) *n.* 1. (hist.) Flush-decked warship with one tier of guns. 2. Fast, lightly armed warship, smaller than a destroyer, used esp. for convoy work.

cor·vine (kōr′vīn, -vĭn) *adj.* Of, akin to, raven or crow.

Cor·y·don (kōr′ĭdon, -dŏn, kār′-). Name given by Theocritus and Virgil to a shepherd; hence, shepherd or rustic in pastoral poetry.

cor·ymb (kōr′ĭmb, -ĭm, kār′-) *n.* (bot.) Inflorescence; raceme in which lower flower stalks are longer than upper ones, so that flowers form a flat or slightly convex head.

cor·y·phée (kōr′ifā, kār′-) *n.* Leader of *corps de ballet.*

co·ry·za (korī′za) *n.* (path.) Inflammation of nasal mucous membrane and sinuses; cold in the head.

cos[1] (kŏs, kaws) *n.* (also ~ **lettuce**): see ROMAINE. [introduced from *Cos*, island in Aegean]

cos[2] *abbrev.* Cosine.

co·sec *abbrev.* Cosecant.

co·se·cant (kōsē′kant, -kănt) *n.* (trig., function of angle in right-angled triangle) Secant of complement of given angle (abbrev. cosec).

cosh (kŏsh) *n.* (chiefly Brit.) Blackjack. ~ *v.t.* Strike with cosh.

co·sig·na·to·ry (kōsĭg′natōrē, -tōrē) *n.* (pl. **-ries**) & *adj.* (Person) signing jointly with others.

co·sine (kō′sīn) *n.* (trig., function of angle in right-angled triangle) Sine of complement of given angle (abbrev. cos).

cos·met·ic (kŏzmĕt′ĭk) *adj.* Designed to beautify hair, skin, or complexion; (of surgery etc.) improving or modifying the appearance. ~ *n.* Cosmetic preparation. **cos·me·ti·cian** (kŏzmetĭsh′an) *n.* Cosmetic specialist. **cos·met′i·cal·ly** *adv.*

cos·mic (kŏz′mĭk) *adj.* Of the universe or cosmos; ~ **dust,** minute particles of matter in or from outer space; ~ **rays,** high-energy radiation originating in outer space. **cos′mi·cal·ly** *adv.*

cos·mog·o·ny (kŏzmŏg′onē) *n.* (pl. **-nies**). (Theory of) the origin of the universe. **cos·mo·gon·ic** (kŏzmogŏn′ĭk), **cos·mo·gon′i·cal** *adjs.* **cos·mog′o·nist** *n.*

cos·mog·ra·phy (kŏzmŏg′rafē) *n.* (pl. **-phies**). Description, mapping, study of general features of universe or Earth. **cos·mog′ra·pher** *n.* **cos·mo·graph·ic** (kŏzmogrăf′ĭk), **cos·mo·graph′i·cal** *adjs.*

cos·mol·o·gy (kŏzmŏl′ojē) *n.* Study, philosophy, of the universe as an ordered whole. **cos·mo·log′i·cal** *adj.* **cos·mol′o·gist** *n.*

cos · mo · naut (kŏz′monawt, -nŏt) *n.* (Russian) astronaut.

cos·mo·pol·i·tan (kŏzmopŏl′ĭtan) *adj.* 1. Belonging to all parts of the world; free from local, provincial, or national limitations or prejudices. 2. (of a city) Containing people from many parts of the world. ~ *n.* Citizen of the world, one without national attachments or prejudices. **cos·mo·pol′i·tan·ism** *n.*

cos·mop·o·lite (kŏzmŏp′olīt) *n.* Cosmopolitan.

cos·mos[1] (kŏz′mos, -mōs) *n.* Universe as an ordered whole; ordered system of ideas etc., sum total of experience; (astron.) all stars in existence, all the galaxies.

cos·mos[2] (kŏz′mos, -mōs) *n.* (pl. **-mos, -mos·es**). Composite tropical Amer. plant of genus *C*~, cultivated for its rose, scarlet, and purple flowers.

Cos·sack (kŏs′ăk, -ak, kaw′săk) *n.* Member of a tribe in imperial Russia who were allowed privileges by the Czars, including autonomy for their settlements in S. Russia (esp. Ukraine) and Siberia in return for service in protecting the frontiers; one of the descendants of these, noted for warlike qualities and horsemanship. ~ *adj.* Of the Cossacks. [Turk. *quzzāq*, seceder, adventurer (first used of an unrelated non-Russian nomadic people of S. Siberia, the Kazakhs)]

cost (kawst, kŏst) *n.* Price (to be) paid for thing; expenditure of time, labor, etc.; loss, penalty, detriment; (pl.) law expenses, esp. those allowed by court etc. against losing party; ~ **accounting**, accounting system indicating costs and (esp.) overhead expenses in a business; ~ **of living**, cost of basic necessities of life; ~**-of-living index**: see CONSUMER PRICE INDEX. **cost** *v.* (**cost, cost·ing**). 1. Be acquirable at, involve expenditure of; result in the loss of. 2. Estimate or fix cost of production.

co-star (kō′stār) *n.* Motion picture, stage, or television star appearing with other star(s). ~ (kō′stār′) *v.* (**-starred, -star·ring**). Perform with, include, co-star(s).

Cos·ta Ri·ca (kŏs′ta rē′ka, kaws′ta, kōs′ta). Republic of

***Cosmetics** have been used since earliest times to enhance the face or body, and in some primitive cultures as warpaint. This child from Sierra Leone (facing page) is participating in a tribal ceremony. Below: Japanese geisha girls with their white faces.*

Costa Rica is a republic in Central America on the narrow isthmus joining North and South America. Coffee, drying in the sun (above), is the country's largest export. Above right: Map and flag of Costa Rica.

*History enthusiasts wearing the **costume** of the Minutemen re-enact their roles as ever-ready militia defending Concord, Massachusetts, from the depredations of the British army.*

southern Central America between Panama and Nicaragua; until 1821 part of Spanish-American dominions; capital, San José.

cos·tate (kŏs′tāt) *adj.* Ribbed, having ribs.

cos·ter (kŏs′ter, kaws′-), **cos·ter·mon·ger** (kŏs′termŭngger, -mŏng-, kaws′-) *ns.* (Brit.) Man who sells fruit, fish, etc., from barrow, cart, or stand in street (esp. in London).

cos·tive (kŏs′tĭv, kaws′-) *adj.* Constipated; causing constipation. **cos′tive·ly** *adv.* **cos′tive·ness** *n.*

cost·ly (kawst′lē, kŏst′-) *adj.* (**-li·er, -li·est**). High-priced; resulting in great loss or sacrifice. **cost′li·ness** *n.*

cos·tume (kŏs′tōōm, -tūm) *n.* 1. Mode or fashion of personal attire and dress of a particular nation, class, or period; this as worn on the stage, to a ~ **ball** or ~ **party**, etc.; ~ **drama, play**, dramatic piece in which actors wear costume of some past period. 2. Complete set of outer garments; garments suitable for a special occasion or season. 3. ~ **jewelry**, artificial or semiprecious jewelry worn as fashion accessory. **costume** (kŏstōōm′, -tūm′, kŏs′tōōm, -tūm) *v.t.* (**-tumed, -tum·ing**). Provide with costume.

cos·tum·er (kŏstōō′mer, -tū′-) *n.* Maker of, dealer in, costumes.

co·sy (kō′zē): see COZY.

cot[1] (kŏt) *n.* Small shelter; (poet.) little cottage.

cot[2] (kŏt) *n.* Lightweight, narrow bed of canvas stretched on a collapsible frame. [f. Hind. *khāṭ* bedstead, bier]

co·tan·gent (kōtăn′jent, kō′tăn-) *n.* (trig., function of angle in right-angle triangle) Tangent of complement of given angle.

cote (kōt) *n.* Shed, stall, shelter, esp. for animals or birds.

Côte d'A·zur (kawt d'ăzür′). Mediterranean coast of France, esp. the eastern end, famous as a summer resort area.

co·te·rie (kō′terē) *n.* Circle, set, of persons associated by exclusive interests; select circle in society. [Fr., orig. association of country people, f. *cotier* cottager]

co·ter·mi·nous (kōtĕr′minus), **co·ter·mi·nal** (kōtĕr′minal) *adjs.* = CONTERMINOUS. **co·ter′mi·nous·ly** *adv.*

co·til·lion (kōtĭl′yon, ko-) *n.* Dance with elaborate series of steps and figures, with giving of favors and changes of partner; coming-out party. [Fr. *cotillon* petticoat]

co·to·ne·as·ter (kotō′nēăster, kŏt′onēster) *n.* Deciduous or evergreen shrub or small tree of genus *C*~ with white or pinkish flowers and usu. red or orange berries.

Co·to·pax·i (kōtopăk′sē). Active volcano in the Cordillera Real, Ecuador; probably the highest active volcano in the world.

Cots·wold (kŏts′wōld, -wold) *adj.* Of the Cotswold Hills. ~ *n.* (Breed of) long-wooled sheep originally developed in the Cotswolds. ~ **Hills**, (also ~**s**) area, range of hills in SW. England.

cot·tage (kŏt′ĭj) *n.* 1. Small, simple dwelling in village or rural area; one-story house. 2. Small house used for vacations. 3. ~ **cheese**, soft white cheese made from curds; ~ **industry**, industry carried on by workers in their homes. **cot′tag·er** *n.* One who lives in a cottage.

cot·ter (kŏt′er) *n.* Key, wedge, bolt, for inserting through a slot to hold parts of machinery, etc. together; (also ~ **pin**) a split cotter that opens at one end to fasten securely.

cot·ton[1] (kŏt′on) *n.* White downy fibrous substance covering seeds of cotton plant, used for making thread, cloth, etc.; cotton plant; thread spun, cloth made, from cotton; ~ **candy**, mass of fluffy spun sugar for eating; ~ **gin**, machine for separating cotton from its seeds; ~ **grass**, species of grass-like bogplants of the genus *Eriophorum*, with heads of long white silky hairs; **cot′tonmouth**, venomous snake (*Ankistrodon piscivorus*), about 6 ft. (1.83 m) long of low-lying swampy areas in southeastern U.S.; water moccasin; **cotton plant**, plant of genus *Gossypium*, yielding cotton; **cot′tonseed**, seed of cotton plant, furnishing oil (**cottonseed oil**) and cattle fodder; **cot′tontail**, any of several N. Amer. rabbits of genus *Sylvilagus*, with a white fluffy tail; **cot′tonwood**, any of various N. Amer. species of poplar, with seeds surround by cottonlike tufts. **cot′ton·y** *adj*. [Arab. *kutkn*]

cot·ton[2] (kŏt′*o*n) *v.i.* (colloq.) Be drawn *to*; ~ **(on) to**, understand, agree to, like (idea etc.).

cot·y·le·don (kŏt*i*lē′d*o*n) *n*. Primary leaf in embryo of higher plants, seed leaf. **cot·y·le′don·ous** *adj*. Having cotyledons.

couch[1] (kowch) *n*. Long upholstered seat with a back and freq. with raised ends, sofa. ~ *v*. 1. Lie, esp. in lair (of animals); crouch; lie in wait. 2. Lower (spear) to position of attack. 3. (embroidery) Stitch thick thread on surface of material by means of fine thread. 4. Express *in* language, words, terms, etc.

couch[2] (kowch, ko͞och) *n*. (usu. ~ **grass**) Species of grass (*Agropyron repens*) with long creeping underground stems, a common and troublesome weed, also called *twitch grass*. [var. of QUITCH]

couch·ant (kow′ch*a*nt) *adj*. (her., of animals) Lying with body resting on legs and head lifted.

Cou·é (ko͞oā′), **Émile** (1857–1926). French psychotherapist, advocate of a system of autosuggestion. **Cou·é·ism** (ko͞oā′ĭz*e*m, ko͞o′ā-) *n*.

Cottonfields in Alabama (above left) are usually planted and harvested annually. The plant is then processed and the ***cotton*** *fibers separated from the seed (below left). Next, the fiber is baled, usually in packages, ready for transportation (below right). The principal cotton-growing countries are U.S.A., U.S.S.R., China, India and Brazil.*

*A boxer may deliver a **counter-punch** while parrying his opponent's blow. This match for the world heavyweight title in New York was won by Joe Frazier against Jimmy Ellis.*

cou·gar (ko͞o′g*er*) *n.* (pl. **-gars**, collect. **-gar**). Mountain lion (cf. LION). [Fr., repr. Guarani *guaçu ara*]

cough (kawf, kŏf) *v.* Expel air from lungs with violent effort and characteristic noise produced by abrupt opening of glottis, in order to remove obstruction or relieve irritation in air passages; ~ **out, up**, eject by, say with, cough; ~ **up**, (slang) bring out, produce (esp. money). **cough** *n.* Act of coughing; tendency to cough; condition of respiratory organs resulting in coughing.

could (ko͝od): see CAN².

cou·loir (ko͞olwar̄′) *n.* Deep mountain gorge or gully. [Fr., *couler*, flow, f. L. *colare*, strain, filter]

cou·lomb (ko͞o′lŏm, ko͞olŏm′) *n.* Quantity of electricity conveyed in 1 second by current of 1 ampere (abbrev. C). [f. COULOMB]

Cou·lomb (ko͞o′lŏm, ko͞olŏm′; *Fr.* ko͞olawṅ′), **Charles Augustin de** (1736–1806). French physicist, experimented with electricity, magnetism, etc.; inventor of method of measuring the quantity of electricity.

coun·cil (kown′s*i*l) *n.* 1. Ecclesiastical assembly for regulating doctrine or discipline in church; (New Testament) Jewish Sanhedrin. 2. Advisory or deliberative assembly. 3. (Governmental) assembly or group acting in deliberative, advisory, or supervisory capacity. 4. ~ **of war**, assembly of military or naval officers called to consult with general etc., usu. in special emergency (freq. fig.). 5.

coun′cilman, coun′cilwoman, member of town or city council.

coun·ci·lor (kown′s*i*l*er*, -sl*er*) *n.* Official member of a council.

coun·sel (kown′s*e*l) *n.* 1. Consultation; advice; **keep one's (own)** ~, be reticent about one's intention or opinions. 2. Lawyer or legal advisers in cause, esp. a court case. **counsel** *v.t.* (**-seled, -sel·ing**, Brit. **-selled, -sel·ling**). Advise; recommend. **coun·se·lor** (kown′s*e*l*er*, -sl*er*) *n.* Adviser in school, college, camp, or other institution; (also ~**-at-law**) attorney.

count¹ (kownt) *v.* 1. Enumerate, reckon (*up*); repeat numerals in order; include, be included, in reckoning; ~ **down** (**count′down** *n.*) count in reverse from a given number to zero, usu. in seconds, to mark lapse of time before an event, esp. firing of explosive or missile, launching of spacecraft etc. 2. ~ **out**, count while taking from a stock; declare (boxer) to have lost fight by counting ten seconds before he rises to resume fight; (colloq.) remove from consideration, exclude. 3. Esteem, account, consider; be reckoned; enter into account or reckoning; ~ **on**, depend or rely on, expect with assurance. **count** *n.* 1. Counting; sum total. 2. (boxing) Counting of ten seconds (time allowed for boxer who has been knocked down to rise and resume fighting or be declared loser). 3. (textiles) Number indicating the fineness of yarn, usu. based on the length of yarn that amounts to a given weight. 4. (law) Each charge in an indictment. **count′a·ble** *adj.*

count² (kownt) *n.* (in some European countries) Nobleman corresp. to English *earl*.

coun·te·nance (kown′t*e*n*a*ns) *n.* Expression of face; face; composure; moral support. ~ *v.t.* (**-nanced, -nanc·ing**). Sanction; encourage.

count·er¹ (kown′t*er*) *n.* (esp.) 1. Small usu. round piece of metal, ivory, etc., used for keeping count in games of chance, esp. cards; imitation coin. 2. Banker's or merchant's table; table or flat surface on which money is counted, business is transacted, or food and drink are served; **under the** ~, clandestinely (esp. illegally).

count·er² (kown′t*er*) *n.* 1. Part of horse's chest between shoulders and under neck. 2. (naut.) Curved part of stern of ship. 3. Depressed part of face of printing type, coin, or medal. 4. (fencing) Circular parry, parry in which hand retains same position while point describes circle. 5. (boxing) Blow delivered while receiving or parrying another. 6. (shoemaking) Stiff material forming back part of shoe or boot around the heel. ~ *adj.* Opposed; opposite. ~ *adv.* In the opposite direction; contrary. ~ *v.* Oppose, contradict, controvert; meet with counter move; (boxing) give return blow while receiving or deflecting opponent's blow.

counter- *prefix.* 1. Against, opposite. 2. In reversal. 3. In reciprocation or reply. 4. As opposite member or constituent. 5. With contrary action etc. 6. (mus.) = CONTRA-.

coun·ter·act (kownt*e*răkt′, kown′t*e*răkt) *v.t.* Hinder, defeat, by contrary action; neutralize. **coun·ter·ac′tion** *n.* **coun·ter·ac′tive** *adj.*

coun·ter·at·tack (*v.* kownt*e*r*a*tăk′; *n.* kown′t*e*r*a*tăk). Attack in reply to enemy's attack.

coun·ter·bal·ance (kown′t*e*r-băl*a*ns) *n.* Weight balancing another. **counterbal′ance** *v.t.* (**-anced, -anc·ing**). Act as counterbalance to.

coun·ter·claim (kown′t*e*rklām) *n.* Claim set up against another; claim by defendant in suit. **counterclaim′** *v.* Claim against plaintiff or prior claim.

coun·ter·clock·wise (kownt*e*r-klŏk′wīz) *adv.* & *adj.* Moving in curve from right to left as seen from center, i.e. opposite to the hands of a clock.

coun·ter·cul·ture (kown′t*e*r-kŭlch*er*) *n.* Mode of life of persons deliberately rejecting established social values and practices.

coun·ter·es·pi·o·nage (kown-terĕs'pēonahzh, -nĭj) *n.* Espionage to detect and frustrate an enemy spy system.

coun·ter·feit (kown'terfĭt) *adj.* & *n.* (Thing) made in imitation, not genuine (esp. money bill or coin). ~ *v.t.* Make a counterfeit of (esp. bill or coin); imitate fraudulently; resemble closely. **coun'ter·feit·er** *n.*

coun·ter·in·tel·li·gence (kown-terĭntĕl'ĭjens) *n.* = COUNTER-ESPIONAGE.

coun·ter·ir·ri·tant (kownter-ĭr'ĭtant) *n.* (med.) Thing used to produce surface irritation and thus counteract symptoms of disease (also fig.).

coun·ter·mand (kownter-mănd', -mahnd', kown'termănd, -mahnd) *v.t.* Revoke (command); recall by contrary order; cancel order for. **coun'termand** *n.* Order revoking previous one.

coun·ter·march (*n.* kown'ter-march; *v.* kowntermarch', kown'-termarch). (Cause to) march in contrary direction.

coun·ter·pane kown'terpān) *n.* Coverlet, bedspread.

coun·ter·part (kown'terpart) *n.* Duplicate; person, thing, forming natural complement to another.

coun·ter·plot (kown'terplŏt) *n.* Plot contrived to defeat another. **counterplot** (kownterplŏt', kown'-terplŏt) *v.* (**-plot·ted, -plot·ting**). Frustrate by, devise, counterplot.

coun·ter·point (kown'terpoint) *n.* (mus.) Melody added as accompaniment to given melody; art of adding one or more melodies as accompaniment to given melody according to certain fixed rules; this style of composition.

coun·ter·poise (kown'terpoiz)

Launch pad 39–A at the John F. Kennedy Space Center, Cape Canaveral, Florida. The space shuttle awaits the ***countdown*** *which will activate the vast propulsion turbines to thrust the shuttle into space.*

In the Christian church an ecumenical or general ***council*** *is a meeting of the bishops of the entire church. The Second Vatican Council was convened by Pope John XXIII in 1962 and continued by Pope Paul VI.*

*The present day **counties** of Great Britain evolved from the ancient shires of the 10th century, which remained virtually unchanged until the 19th century when the Local Government Act of 1888 established county councils, each with an administrative area. The function of county councils is to provide local services.*

n. Counterbalancing weight; thing of equivalent force etc. on opposite side; equilibrium. ~ *v.t.* (**-poised, -pois·ing**). Counterbalance; compensate; bring into, keep in, equilibrium.

coun·ter·ref·or·ma·tion (kownterrĕfermā′shon) *n.* Reformation running counter to another; **C~ R~**, (hist.) reformation in the R. C. Ch. during the latter part of the 16th c, after the Protestant Reformation, initiated by the Council of TRENT².

coun·ter·rev·o·lu·tion (kown′terrĕvoloō′shon) *n.* Revolution reversing results of previous revolution. **coun′ter·rev·o·lu′tion·ar·y** *adj.* & *n.* (pl. **-aries**).

coun·ter·sign¹ (kown′tersīn) *n.* Watchword, password, given to person on guard.

coun·ter·sign² (kown′tersīn, kowntersīn′) *v.t.* Add signature to (document already signed); ratify. **coun·ter·sig·na·ture** (kowntersĭg′nacher, kown′tersig-) *n.*

coun·ter·sink (kown′tersĭngk, kowntersĭngk′) *v.t.* (**-sank, -sunk, -sink·ing**). Bevel off (top of hole) to receive head of screw or bolt; sink (screwhead) in such hole, so as to lie flush with surface. **coun′ter·sunk** *adj.* (esp., of screw) With head beveled for this purpose.

coun·ter·spy (kown′terspī) *n.* (pl. **-spies**). Spy engaged in counterespionage.

coun·ter·ten·or (kown′tertĕner) *n.* (mus.) (Part for, singer with) male voice above that of tenor.

coun·ter·vail (kowntervāl′) *v.t.* Counterbalance; avail against.

count·ess (kown′tĭs) *n.* Wife, widow, of count or (in Gt. Britain) earl; lady ranking with count or earl in her own right.

count·ing (kown′tĭng) **house.** Building, room, devoted to keeping accounts.

count·less (kownt′lĭs) *adj.* Too many to count.

coun·tri·fied (kŭn′trĭfīd) *adj.* Rural, rustic; unsophisticated.

coun·try (kŭn′trē) *n.* (pl. **-tries**). 1. Region; territory of nation; land of person's birth, citizenship, etc., fatherland. 2. Rural districts as opp. to towns; rest of a land as opp. to capital; ~ **club**, suburban club for golf, tennis, other sports, social activities, etc.; ~ **cousin**, relation of countrified manners or appearance; ~ **gentleman**, owner of an estate in the country; ~ **house**, house in country, esp. residence of country gentleman; ~ **music**, simple music, usu. with sentimental lyrics, originating in the southern U.S., based on folk and cowboy songs, spirituals and gospel music, and blues, usu. sung to the accompaniment of such instruments as guitar, banjo, mandolin, and fiddle; **coun'tryside**, rural district, its inhabitants.

coun·try·man (kŭn'trĭm*a*n) *n.* (pl. **-men** pr. -m*e*n). (fem. **coun·try·wom·an** pr. kŭn'trĭwo͝o-m*a*n, pl. **-wom·en** pr. -wĭmĭn) 1. Person of one's own (or a specified) country. 2. Person living in rural parts.

coun·ty (kown'tē) *n.* (pl. **-ties**). 1. Administrative division of a state. 2. Territorial division of Gt. Britain and Ireland exercising administrative, judicial, and political functions. 3. People of county. 4. ~ **agent**, official who represents federal and state governments in advising residents of rural regions on farming practices, agricultural marketing, home economics, etc.; ~ **court,** county judicial court; ~ seat, town in which business of county is transacted.

coup (ko͞o) *n.* (pl. **coups** pr. ko͞oz). Notable or successful stroke or move; a coup d'état; ~ **d'état,** sudden and decisive political stroke, esp. violent or illegal change of government; ~ **de grâce,** finishing stroke; deathblow administered to dying person.

coupe (ko͞op), **cou·pé** (ko͞opā') *ns.* Four-wheeled closed carriage with inside seat for two and outside seat for driver; closed two-door automobile with a sloping back.

cou·ple (kŭp'*e*l) *n.* Pair; wedded or engaged pair; pair of partners in dance; two. ~ *v.* (**-pled, -pling**). Fasten, link, together; connect (device) to other mechanism; connect (railroad cars) by a coupling; unite, bring together, in pair(s); associate in thought or speech; copulate. **cou·pler** (kŭp'l*e*r) *n.* (esp.) Device for coupling two railroad cars; contrivance for connecting two keyboards in an organ etc. so they both sound when one is played.

cou·plet (kŭp'lĭt) *n.* 1. Pair of successive lines of verse, esp. when rhyming together and of same length. 2. Two similar things; pair.

cou·pling (kŭp'lĭng) *n.* (esp.) Chain or link connecting two railroad cars, etc.; act of coupling.

cou·pon (ko͞o'pŏn, kū'-) *n.* Detachable part of ticket, advertisement, or other certificate entitling holder to some refund, gift, bond interest, service, etc., or as inquiry form, entry form for a competition, etc.

cour·age (kẽr'ĭj, kŭr'-) *n.* Bravery, boldness; fortitude.

cou·ra·geous (k*u*rā'j*u*s) *adj.* Brave, fearless. **cou·ra'geous·ly** *adv.* **cou·ra'geous·ness** *n.*

Cour·bet (koorbĕ'), **Gustave** (1819–77). French painter associated with realist school.

cou·ri·er (kẽr'ē*e*r, koor'-) *n.* Special messenger.

course (kōrs, kōrs) *n.* 1. Onward movement; line or direction taken or planned; career; habitual or ordinary manner of procedure. 2. Ground on which race is run etc.; golf links; line to be taken in race. 3. Watercourse. 4. Planned or prescribed series of actions or proceedings, as of lectures, study, diet, etc. 5. Each of successive divisions of meal, consisting of one dish or several. 6. (building) Single continuous layer of bricks, stones, etc., of same height throughout; row of slates, tiles, etc. 7. (naut.) Sail attached to lower yards of ship. 8. **in due** ~, in the natural order; **in the** ~ **of,** during; **of** ~, naturally, inevitably. **course** *v.* (**coursed, cours·ing**). Pursue (game, esp. hares) with hounds; run about, run. **cours'er** *n.* (poet). Swift horse.

court[1] (kōrt, kōrt) *n.* 1. Open area surrounded by walls of buildings; confined yard opening off street; enclosed quadrangle, open or covered, plot of ground marked off for games (as for basketball, tennis, etc.). 2. Sovereign's residence; his establishment and retinue; the body of courtiers; sovereign and his counselors as ruling power. 3. Formal assembly held by sovereign at his residence. 4. Assembly of judges or other persons acting as tribunal, e.g. *Court of Appeals*, to hear and determine any cause; place in which justice is administered; session of judicial assembly; **out of** ~, without a legal trial. 5. Attention paid to one whose favor, affection, or interest is sought. 6. **court'house,** building in which courts of law are held; seat of government of a county; **court-martial** (pl. ~**s-martial**), trial of military personnel of any rank, conducted by officers, for offenses against military law; **court-martial** (*v.t.*) (**-tialed, -tial·ing**), try by court martial; **court'room,** room where sessions of a law court are held; **court'yard,** open space surrounded by walls or buildings.

court[2] (kōrt, kōrt) *v.* Pay court (to); try to win favor or affection (of); try to attract sexually; seek to win (applause etc.); invite, tempt.

cour·te·ous (kẽr'tē*u*s) *adj.* Polite, kind, considerate, in manner or address. **cour'te·ous·ly** *adv.* **cour'te·ous·ness** *n.*

cour·te·san, cour·te·zan (kōr'-t*e*z*a*n, kẽr', -zăn) *ns.* Prostitute or kept woman, esp. one associating with men of rank or wealth. [It. *cortigiana*, orig. woman attached to the court]

cour·te·sy (kẽr't*e*sē) *n.* (pl. **-sies**). Courteous behavior or disposition; courteous act.

cour·ti·er (kōr'tē*e*r, kōr'-) *n.*

*The **courtyard** was a common feature of the grand houses of Tudor and Stuart England, such as Lacock Abbey in Wiltshire. In ancient times both the Greeks and Romans built their villas around a courtyard.*

Attendant at, frequenter of, sovereign's court.

court·ly (kōrt'lē) *adj.* (**-li·er, -li·est**). Polished, refined, in manners; obsequious, flattering. **court'li·ness** *n.*

court·ship (kōrt'shĭp, kōrt'-) *n.* (Period of) courting.

cous·cous (kōōs'kōōs) *n.* N. Afr. dish of crushed grain steamed with meat and vegetables. [Arab. *kuskus*, f. *kaskasa* bruise, pound small]

cous·in (kŭz'ĭn) *n.* 1. Child of one's uncle or aunt (also **first** ~); **second** ~, one's parent's first cousin's child. 2. Member of kindred group. **cous'in·ly** *adv.* & *adj.*

Cous·teau (kōōstō'), **Jacques** (1910–). French undersea explorer; developer of scuba-diving apparatus.

cou·ture (kōōtoor', -tūr') *n.* Fashionable dressmaking or designing; clothes made thus. **cou·tu·ri·er** (kōōtoor'ēā, -ēer, -toor'yā) *n.* (fem. **-tu·ri·ère** pr. -toor'ēer, -ēār) Fashion designer.

co·va·lence (kōvā'lens) *n.* (chem.) Covalent bond (see VALENCE); electrons forming this; number of covalent bonds an atom can form. **co·va'lent** *adj.* **co·va'lent·ly** *adv.*

cove[1] (kōv) *n.* Small bay; sheltered recess; (archit.) concave arch, curved junction of wall with ceiling. ~ *v.t.* (**coved, cov·ing**). Arch; slope inward.

cove[2] (kōv) *n.* (Brit. slang) Fellow, chap.

cov·en (kŭv'en, kō'ven) *n.* Assembly of witches.

cov·e·nant (kŭv'enant) *n.* Compact, bargain; (law) formal, sealed contract, clause of this; (bibl.) compact between God and the Israelites. ~ *v.* Make covenant (with). **cov·e·nan·tal** (kŭvenăn'tal) *adj.* **cov'e·nan·ter** *n.*

Cov·en·try (kŭv'entrē). City in central England noted for its modern cathedral; **send (person) to** ~, (chiefly Brit.) refuse to associate with or speak to him or her.

cov·er (kŭv'er) *v.t.* 1. Put or lay something over; put covering on. 2. Be over whole top of. 3. (of stallion etc.) Copulate with. 4. Conceal or shield; have gun, pistol, etc., trained on. 5. Include, provide for. 6. Extend or stretch over; traverse (distance). 7. Defray (expense etc.); protect by insurance; report for newspaper etc. 8. **covered wagon**, large wagon with

Couture *houses, where clothes are specially designed and tailored for wealthy and fashion-conscious clients. New fashions originate in spring and fall 'collections' where models show the clothes to the press and public (above). In this painting (right) clients are seen ordering clothes at the house of Paquin, Paris, in 1907.*

arched canvas top, used by Amer. pioneers going west during the 19th c.; **covering letter**, one sent along with another document to explain it. **cov′er·ing** *n.* (esp.) Cover.

cover *n.* 1. Thing that covers; lid; binding of book, either board of this; wrapper, envelope, of letter. 2. Protection; shelter. 3. Screen, pretense, esp. for a spy. 4. Woods or undergrowth sheltering game, covert. 5. ~ **charge**, fixed charge for entertainment added to cost of food and drink at a night club; ~ **crop**, crop grown to protect soil from leaching or eroding or to enrich soil. **cov·er·age** (kŭv′erĭj, kŭv′rĭj) *n.*

Cov·er·dale (kō′verdāl, kŭv′-), **Miles** (1488–1568). English Protestant bishop; made first English translation of the entire Bible and Apocrypha (from German and Latin versions).

cov·er·let (kŭv′erlĭt) *n.* Bedspread.

cov·ert[1] (kŭv′ert, kō′vert) *n.* 1. Shelter, esp. thicket hiding game; ~ **cloth**, twilled cloth of cotton, woolen, or worsted material having a speckled appearance and used for coats and suits. 2. One of the feathers covering the bases of a bird's wing and tail feathers.

cov·ert[2] (kō′vert, kŭv′ert) *adj.* Concealed, hidden, secret, disguised. **cov′ert·ly** *adv.* **cov′ert·ness** *n.*

cov·er·ture (kŭv′ercher) *n.* Covering; condition of married woman under husband's protection.

*The **covert** feathers on the wings of a bird cover the base of the primary and secondary flight feathers and the tail feathers. They are small and soft, and have a protective function.*

cov·et (kŭv′ĭt) *v.t.* Desire eagerly and wrongfully (usu. what belongs to another), as in Tenth Commandment: "Thou shalt not covet. . . ." **cov′et·a·ble** *adj.*

cov·et·ous (kŭv′ĭtus) *adj.* Eagerly desirous (*of*); grasping, avaricious. **cov′et·ous·ly** *adv.* **cov′et·ous·ness** *n.*

cov·ey (kŭv′ē) *n.* (pl. **-eys**). Brood of partridges; family, party, set.

cow[1] (kow) *n.* Female of any bovine animal, esp. of the domestic species (*Bos taurus*); female of elephant, moose, whale, seal, etc.; (slang) fat, slovenly woman; **cow′-bird**, any of various American blackbirds, esp. *Molothrus ater*, that lay their eggs in other birds' nests; **cow′boy**, man, formerly on horseback, who drives and tends cattle on a ranch, esp. in the western U.S.; man who demonstrates at rodeos the skills of cowboys, including feats of horsemanship, cattle

*A **cowboy** shows his bulldogging style at a rodeo as he tackles a writhing steer. Rodeos test the individual skills of cowboys to the limit.*

In the milk of the **cow,** sugar, cream and protein content are about equal. It is less creamy than goat's milk and less sweet than ass's milk. With cows bred for milk, efforts are made to increase cream content.

The **cowslip** is a primrose with fragrant yellow flowers, which blooms in early spring. The marsh marigold, which grows in swamps, is called a cowslip in N. America.

roping, etc.; (slang) reckless automobile driver; **cow'catcher**, frame fixed in front of locomotive or streetcar to remove cattle and other obstructions from tracks; **cow'hand**, cowboy; **cow'herd**, one who herds or tends cattle; **cow'hide**, (leather, whip, made of) cow's hide; **cow'lick**, habitually protruding lock of hair; **cow'poke**, (colloq.) cowboy; **cow'pox**, vaccine disease appearing as bluish or livid vesicles on teats of cows; **cow'puncher**, (colloq.) cowboy.

cow[2] (kow) *v.t.* Intimidate.

cow·ard (kow'*erd*) *adj.* & *n.* Fainthearted, pusillanimous (person). **cow'ard·ly** *adv.* **cow'ard·li·ness** *n.* [OF. *coard*, f. L. *cauda* tail]

Cow·ard (kow'*erd*), **Noël** (1899–1973). English playwright, actor, composer of light music, and librettist.

cow·ard·ice (kow'*er*dĭs) *n.* Faintheartedness.

cow·er (kow'*er*) *v.i.* Crouch, esp. in fear. **cow'er·ing·ly** *adv.*

cowl (kowl) *n.* 1. Monk's hooded garment; hood of this. 2. Hood-shaped covering (freq. turning with wind) of top of chimney or ventilating shaft to assist ventilation. **cowled** *adj.*

cowl·ing (kow'lĭng) *n.* Metal housing or cover for an airplane engine.

Cow·per (ko͞o'p*er*, kou'-), **William** (1731–1800). English lyric poet and hymn writer.

cow·rie, cow·ry (kow'rē) *ns.* (pl. **-ries**). Porcelainlike shell of small gastropod (*Cyprea moneta*) of Indian Ocean, used as money in parts of Africa and southern Asia; this animal, or any gastropod (or shell) of genus *Cyprea*, of oval shape, with undeveloped spine and narrow aperture as long as shell. [Hind. *kauri*]

cow·slip (kow'slĭp) *n.* 1. Wild plant (*Primula veris*) growing in pastures etc. and flowering in spring, with drooping umbels of fragrant yellow flowers. 2. MARSH marigold.

cox (kŏks) *n.* (pl. **cox·es**) & *v.* (Act as) coxswain.

cox·a (kŏk'*s*a) *n.* (pl. **cox·ae** pr. kŏk'sē). Hip; (zool.) similar joint in insects etc.

cox·comb (kŏks'kōm) *n.* Conceited dandy; fop. **cox'comb·ry** *n.* (pl. **-ries**). Foppery; pretension of manner. [= *cock's comb*]

cox·swain (kŏk'*s*ĭn, -swān) *n.* Helmsman of boat; person on board ship in charge of ship's boat and crew. [f. *cock* = cockboat + *swain*]

coy (koi) *adj.* Shy, esp. affectedly or archly so. **coy'ly** *adv.* **coy'ness** *n.*

coy·o·te (kīō'tē, kī'ōt) *n.* (pl. **-o·tes** pr. -ō'tēz, -ōts; collect. **-o·te**). Wolflike animal (*Canis latrans*) of western N. Amer.; (slang) sneaky, contemptible person. [Mex. Sp. f. Nahautl *coyotl*]

coy·pu (koi'po͞o) *n.* (pl. **-pus**, collect. **-pu**) = NUTRIA.

coz·en (kŭz'ĭn) *v.t.* (archaic) Cheat, swindle (*out of*); beguile (*into*). **coz'en·age** *n.*

co·zy, co·sy (kō'zē) *adjs.* (**-zi·er, -zi·est, -si·er, -si·est**). Comfortable, snug. ~ *n.* (pl. **-zies, -sies**). Covering of (padded) material to retain heat in a teapot. **co'zi·ly** *adv.* **co'zi·ness** *n.*

cp. *abbrev.* Compare.

C.P. *abbrev.* Communist Party; Common Prayer; command post.

c.p. *abbrev.* Candlepower.

C.P.A. *abbrev.* Certified public accountant.

CPFF *abbrev.* Cost plus fixed fee.

Cpl *abbrev.* Corporal.

CPO *abbrev.* Chief petty officer.

cps *abbrev.* Cycles per second.

Cr *symbol.* Chromium.

crab (krăb) *n.* 1. Any of various decapod crustaceans, mostly of the group Brachyura, with abdomen short and bent under thorax, the first legs being pincers, esp. edible species found on or near seacoasts. 2. **the C** ~: see CANCER. 3. Cross, peevish person. 4. Machine (orig. with claws) for hoisting heavy weights. 5. (pl.) Lowest throw of a pair of dice, in most games, two. 6. (rowing) **catch a** ~, make faulty stroke by which oar becomes jammed under water. 7. ~ **grass**, annual creeping grass infesting lawns; ~ **louse**, parasitical insect (*Phthirus pubis*) infesting human body. **crab** *v.* (**crabbed, crab·-ing**). 1. Catch or hunt crabs. 2. (Cause to) move sideways or on oblique course. 3. (colloq.) Criticize adversely; complain; interfere with. **crab'ber** *n.* **crab'by** *adj.* (**-bi·er, -bi·est**). Morose; irritable. **crab'bi·ly** *adv.* **crab'bi·ness** *n.*

crab (krăb) **apple.** Wild apple (*Malus coronaria*), or a cultivated variety having similar sour, harsh, astringent quality.

crab·bed (krăb'ĭd) *adj.* Ill-tempered; perverse; complicated; difficult to interpret; (of handwriting) hard to decipher. **crab'bed·ly** *adv.* **crab'bed·ness** *n.*

crack (krăk) *v.* 1. (Cause to)

*The **coyote,** which is noted for its mournful howls, is found on the plains of N. America. It is an intelligent animal with a reputation for cunning and swiftness.*

make sharp or explosive noise; utter (joke). 2. Break with sudden sharp report; break without complete separation of parts; collapse, break down; break open (a safe) in order to steal the contents. 3. Render (voice) dissonant; (of voice) become dissonant. 4. Split up (petroleum etc.) by heat and catalysts to produce lighter hydrocarbons (as gasoline). 5. (slang) **get cracking,** start; **crack up,** suffer breakdown; have a fit of laughing; crash automobile. 6. **crack'brained,** crazy. **crack** *n.* 1. Sudden sharp noise, as of whip, rifle, thunder; sharp blow; **have a ~ at,** (colloq.) make an attempt at. 2. Instant; break (*of* dawn, day). 3. Fissure formed by breakage; partial fracture (the parts still cohering); narrow opening formed by breaking; = CHINK[1]. 4. (slang) Sharp, cutting, or witty remark, also **wise'crack; crack'pot,** eccentric or impractical (person). **crack** *adj.* (colloq.) First-rate.

cracked (krăkt) *adj.* (esp., slang) Crazy.

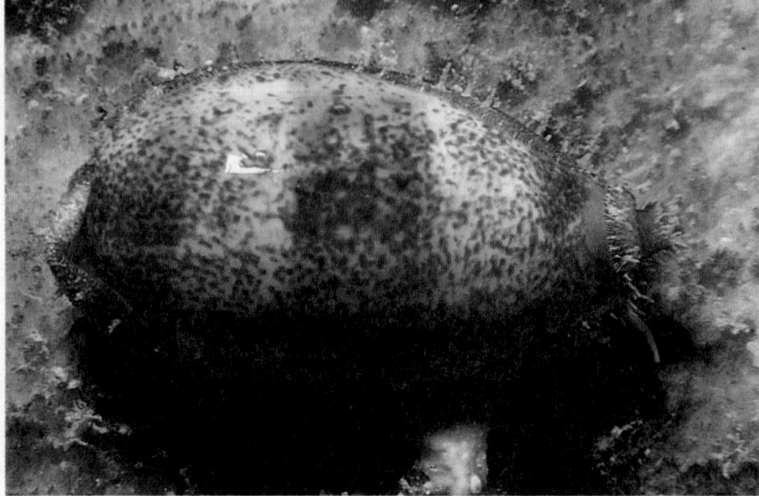

*The **cowrie** shell, usually found in warm waters, has been used as currency for many centuries. The dowry for a bride in West Africa was once set at 100,000 cowries.*

crack·er (krăk'*er*) *n.* (esp.) 1. Instrument for cracking, esp. nutcracker. 2. Thin crisp biscuit or wafer, usu. made of unleavened dough. 3. (southern U.S. derog.) Poor white, esp. in Georgia and Florida. 4. (pl., as pred. adj.; slang) Crazy.

crack·er·jack (krăk'*er*jăk) *n.* & *adj.* (slang) Exceptionally fine or splendid (person or thing).

crack·le (krăk'*el*) *v.i.* (**-led, -ling**). Emit slight continuous cracking sound. ~ *n.* 1. Crackling. 2. China or pottery glaze with minute cracks all over surface. **crack·ly** (krăk'lē) *adj.* (**-li·er, -li·est**).

crack·ling (krăk'lĭng) *n.* (esp.) Crisp skin of roast pork.

*Appetizing cooked **crab,** Fisherman's Wharf, San Francisco. Crabs range from species the size of a pea to the giant crab with legs spanning over 8 ft. The fiddler crab has an enormous claw which it waves to attract females. Hermit crabs can withdraw inside the discarded shells of univalves.*

Cra·cow (krā'kow, krah'kow): see KRAKOW.

-cracy *comb. form.* Government, ruling body, influential class, etc. (*bureaucracy, aristocracy*).

cra·dle (krā'*del*) *n.* 1. Small, low bed for infant, esp. one on rockers; (fig.) place in which thing is nurtured in earliest stage; **~ song,** lullaby. 2. Framework resembling

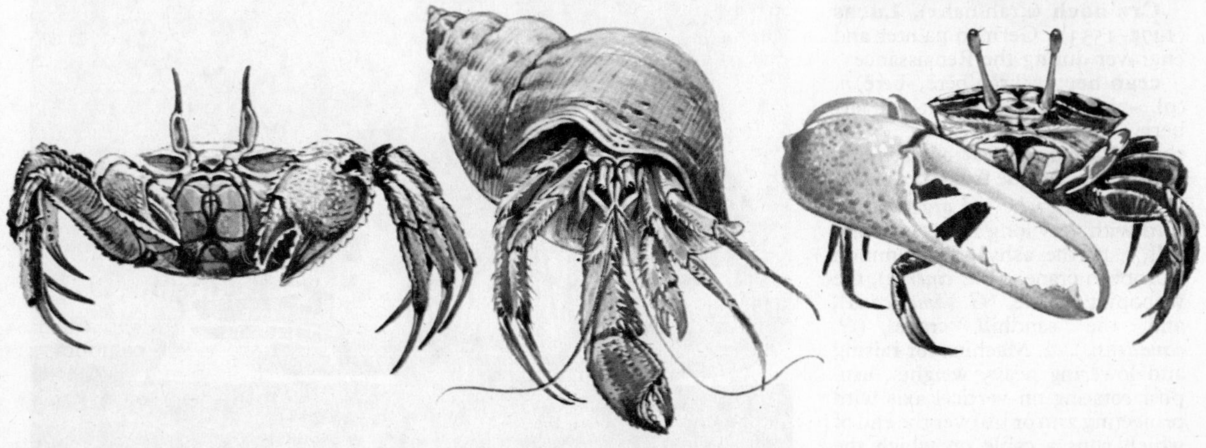

cradle, esp. stage suspended from scaffolding for manual workers; framework on which ship rests during construction or repairs; light wooden frame attached to scythe to catch grain and lay it flat as it is cut; protective or supporting framework for injured limb etc.; support for telephone receiver not in use; (mining) trough on rockers in which gold-bearing material is shaken in water to separate the gold. **cradle** *v.t.* (**-dled, -dling**). Place in cradle; contain or shelter as cradle; reap (grain) with scythe fitted with cradle.

craft (krăft, krahft) *n.* 1. Skill; cunning, deceit. 2. Art, trade; members of a trade. 3. (pl. same) Boat, vessel; aircraft, spacecraft. **crafts'man** *n.* (pl. **-men**) (also **craftsperson**). One who practices a craft, artisan; skilled person. **crafts'man·ship** *n.*

craft·y (krăf'tē, krahf'-) *adj.* (**craft·i·er, craft·i·est**). Cunning, artful, wily. **craft'i·ly** *adv.* **craft'i·ness** *n.*

crag (krăg) *n.* Steep projecting rock forming part of cliff or headland. **crag'gy** *adj.* (**-gi·er, -gi·est**). **crag'gi·ness** *n.*

cram (krăm) *v.* (**crammed, cram·ming**). 1. Fill overfull; force (*into, down*); stuff (*with* food); eat greedily. 2. (colloq.) Prepare intensively for examination; learn (subject) by intensive study. **cram'mer** *n.*

cramp[1] (krămp) *n.* Sudden painful involuntary contraction of muscles from chill, slight strain, etc.; **writer's ~**: see WRITER. **cramp** *v.t.* 1. Affect with cramp. 2. Confine narrowly; restrict.

cramp[2] (krămp) *n.* Metal bar with bent ends for holding masonry etc. together; frame with movable part (also **~ iron**) that can be fixed for pressing pieces of wood etc. together for joining; restraint. **cramp** *v.t.* Fasten with cramp.

cram·pon (krăm'pŏn), **cram·poon** (krămpōōn') *ns.* Iron spike attached to boot for climbing over ice etc.; grappling iron.

Cra·nach (krah'nahx), **Lucas** (1472–1553). German painter and engraver during the Renaissance.

cran·ber·ry (krăn'bĕrē, -berē) *n.* (pl. **-ries**). Small bright-red tart berry, fruit of N. Amer. dwarf shrub (*Vaccinium macrocarpon*); **~ sauce**, sauce made from this berry.

crane (krān) *n.* 1. Large wading bird with very long legs, neck, and bill, esp. the ashy-gray common European crane (*Grus cinerea*), the whooping crane (*G. americana*), and the sandhill crane (*G. canadensis*). 2. Machine for raising and lowering heavy weights, usu. post rotating on vertical axis with projecting arm or jib over the end of which runs a cable on which the

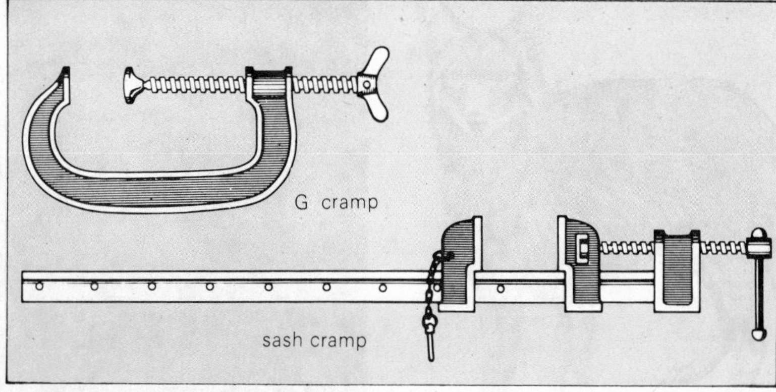

Cramps *are used for holding together parts of a brick wall, masonry or lengths of timber. The G cramp for smaller work has an adjustable screw. The sash cramp moves on a metal bar.*

Cranberry *vines are flooded to prevent crops being blighted by frost. The bulk of the harvest is canned for sauce to be added as a relish to meat dishes, especially turkey.*

An electric transporter ***crane.*** *Transporter cranes are used for shifting bulk cargoes on a large scale; those shown (at Birkenhead, U.K.) are designed for unloading.*

Crafts *are still carried out in many countries without the aid of sophisticated machinery. These copper pots, displayed here in a market at Bahrain, are made by individual craftsmen employing traditional methods.*

An Australian brolga (left) and the rare American whooping ***crane,*** *now almost extinct. The common crane (Grus grus) is over 3½ ft. from beak to tail, is migratory and inhabits marshland.*

weight may be suspended. 3. ~ **fly,** two-winged long-legged fly of genus *Tipula*, daddy-longlegs; **cranesbill,** species of wild geranium (from the long slender beak of the fruit). **crane** *v.* (**craned, cran·ing**). Stretch (neck), stretch neck like crane.

Crane[1] (krān), (**Harold**) **Hart** (1899–1932). Amer. poet, author of "The Bridge" etc.

Crane[2] (krān), **Stephen** (1871–1900). Amer. novelist, short-story writer, and war correspondent in Cuba and Greece, 1896–8; best known for his novel *The Red Badge of Courage*, a realistic account of the common man under fire in the Civil War, and his short stories "The Open Boat," "The Bride Comes to Yellow Sky," and "The Blue Hotel."

cra·ni·al (krā'nē*a*l) *adj.* Of the cranium; ~ **index,** ratio of length of skull to its width, multiplied by 100; ~ **nerve,** any member of 12 pairs of nerves attached to brain and serving regions of head and neck.

cra·ni·um (krā'nē*u*m) *n.* Skull.

crank[1] (krăngk) *n.* Part of axis bent at right angles for converting reciprocal into circular motion, or vice versa; **crank'case,** case covering crankshaft of reciprocating engine; **crank'shaft,** shaft driven by crank. **crank** *v.* 1. Bend in shape of crank; attach crank to. 2. (also ~ **up**) Start (engine) by turning crank.

crank[2] (krăngk) *n.* Eccentric person, esp. one enthusiastically possessed by idea etc; grouchy person. **crank'y** *adj.* (**crank·i·er, crank·i·est**). (esp.) Ill-tempered. **crank'i·ly** *adv.* **crank'i·ness** *n.*

cran·ny (krăn'ē) *n.* (pl. **-nies**). Chink, crevice. **cran'nied** *adj.*

crap[1] (krăp) *n.* (vulgar) 1. Feces. 2. Nonsense; junk, rubbish. ~ *v.i.* (**crapped, crap·ping**). (vulgar) Defecate. **crap'py** *adj.* (**-pi·er, -pi·est**).

crap[2] (krăp) *v.i.* (**crapped, crap·ping**). Make losing throw of 2, 3, or 12 in craps. ~ *n.* Such a throw; ~ **game,** game of craps; ~ **out,** be unsuccessful, withdraw from game etc.

crap·pie (krăp'ē) *n.* Either of two sunfishes, **black** ~ (*Pomoxis nigromaculatis*) and **white** ~ (*P. annularis*) good game and eating fishes.

craps (krăps) *n.* (usu. considered sing.) Game of chance played with two dice; **shoot** ~, play this game; **crap'shooter,** one who plays craps.

crap·u·lent (krăp'y*u*lent) *adj.* Given to, suffering from effect of, resulting from, overdrinking or overeating. **crap'u·lence** *n.* **crap'u·lous** *adj.*

crash[1] (krăsh) *n.* Loud noise as of hard body or bodies broken by violent percussion, or of thunder, loud music, etc.; violent percussion or breakage; crashing of aircraft, car, etc.; (fig.) sudden ruin or collapse, esp. financial; (attrib. or as adj.) rapid, intensive (*course, program,* etc.); ~ **dive** (*n.*), ~**-dive** (*v.i.*) (**-dived, -div·ing**), (of submarine) (make) sudden and steep dive; ~ **helmet,** helmet worn as protection in case of crashing; ~ **landing,** emergency aircraft landing that damages aircraft; so ~**-land** (*v.i.*); ~ **pad,** (slang) place to sleep, esp. in emergency. **crash** *v.* Make a crash; move, go, drive, throw, with a crash; (of aircraft) fall, cause to fall, violently to earth; (cause car etc. to) come violently into collision with vehicle or obstacle; (fig.) fail, esp. financially; (colloq.) attend (a party) without invitation.

crash[2] (krăsh) *n.* Coarse woven fabric of linen or cotton. [Russ. *krashenina* colored linen (*kráska* color, dye)]

crass (krăs) *adj.* Thick, gross;

The bright blue meadow ***crane's-bill*** *which grows 1 to 2 ft. high is one of numerous types of crane's-bill. The multi-flowered varieties (geraniums) are often cultivated.*

Crater Lake, formed in the collapsed crater of the extinct volcano Mt. Mazama. It is notable for its vivid blue water and Wizard Island, a volcanic cone rising from its depths.

(fig.) gross; grossly stupid; unfeeling, unsensitive. **crass'ly** *adv.* **crass'ness** *n.*

Cras·sus (krăs'*us*), **Marcus Licinius** (*c*112–53 B.C.). Roman general, member of 1st TRIUMVIRATE.

crate (krāt) *n.* Large wooden or wicker container for shipping or storing, esp. fragile goods; (slang) aircraft, vehicle (esp. old one). ~ *v.t.* (**crat·ed, crat·ing**). Pack in crate.

cra·ter (krā'*ter*) *n.* 1. Bowl- or funnel-shaped hollow at top or side of volcano from which eruption takes place; bowl-shaped cavity, esp. that formed by exploding shell or bomb, meteor, etc.

Cra·ter (krā'*ter*) **Lake.** Lake, 2,000 ft. (610 m) deep, in the center of extinct volcano in SW. Oregon.

cra·vat (kr*a*văt') *n.* 1. (archaic) Ornamental band with long flowing ends, or handkerchief tied, with bow in front, around neck outside shirt collar. 2. Scarf or necktie. [Fr. *cravaté* f. Croatian *Hrvat* Croat]

crave (krāv) *v.* (**craved, crav·ing**). Long for; beg, long, *for*. **crav'er** *n.* **crav'ing** *n.* Strong desire, intense longing.

cra·ven (krā'v*e*n) *adj.* & *n.* Cowardly, abject (person). **cra'ven·ly** *adv.* **cra'ven·ness** *n.*

craw (kraw) *n.* Crop of bird or insect; stomach of animal; **stick in one's** ~, be objectionable, be unacceptable.

craw·fish (kraw'fĭsh) *n.* (pl. **-fish·es,** collect. **-fish**): see CRAYFISH.

crawl[1] (krawl) *n.* Pen or enclosure in shallow water for fish, turtles, etc. [Dutch KRAAL]

crawl[2] (krawl) *v.* Move slowly with body on or close to ground,

***Top:** Inside the **crater** of a volcano on Vulcano, the southernmost of the Lipari Isles off Sicily. These islands were, with Etna, the first to which the word 'volcano' was applied and were said to be the seat of Vulcan, the Roman god of fire. **Right:** Mt. Kilimanjaro, the highest mountain in Africa, now extinct as a volcano.*

or on hands and knees; walk, move, slowly; creep abjectly; swim with crawl; swarm *with* crawling things; feel creepy sensation. ~ *n.* Crawling; (also **Australian** ~), fast swimming stroke in which arms execute alternate overarm movements and legs are kicked rapidly; ~ **space**, shallow space in a building, too low for person to stand in, but useful for storage, access to ducts etc. **crawl'er** *n.*

cray·fish (krā'fĭsh) *n.* (pl. **-fish·es**, collect. **-fish**). Any small lobsterlike freshwater crustacean of the genera *Astacus* and *Cambarus*; similar crustacean, esp. the spiny lobster.

cray·on (krā'ŏn, -*o*n) *n.* Stick of colored wax, charcoal, or chalk for drawing; drawing in crayons. ~ *v.t.* Draw with crayon(s).

craze (krāz) *v.* (**crazed, craz·ing**). 1. Drive, become insane or obsessed (usu. in past part.). 2. Produce small cracks in (glaze of pottery); have such cracks. ~ *n.* Mania; fad.

cra·zy (krā'zē) *adj.* (**-zi·er, -zi·est**). Mad, demented; insane; uncontrolled; extremely eager; (colloq.) foolish, wild, incredible, etc.; (colloq.) infatuated, enthusiastic (*about, for*). ~ **quilt**, patchwork quilt. **cra'zi·ly** *adv.* **cra'zi·ness** *n.*

Cra·zy (krā'zē) **Horse** (1849?–1877). Indian name, Tashunca-Uitco; Oglala Sioux chief and leader at the battle of Little Big Horn in which Gen. Custer was killed; surrendered and killed resisting imprisonment.

creak (krēk) *v.i.* & *n.* (Make) harsh shrill grating noise as of ungreased hinge etc. **creak'y** *adj.* (**creak·i·er, creak·i·est**). Tending to creak, full of creaks; frail; dilapidated; decrepit. **creak'i·ly** *adv.*

cream (krēm) *n.* 1. Fatty part of milk, which gathers on top, and by churning is made into butter. 2. Food like or made of cream; attrib., (of soup or sauce) containing milk or cream; (of candy, cookie, etc.) with creamy filling. 3. Creamlike substance, esp. cosmetic. 4. Best or choicest part of anything. 5. Part of liquid that gathers on top. 6. Cream color, yellowish-white. 7. ~ **of tartar**: see TARTAR. 8. ~ **pie, puff**, etc., pie, pastry, cake, etc. filled with cream or creamy custard etc.; ~ **cheese**, soft rich cheese made of unskimmed milk and cream; ~ **sherry**, full-bodied mellow sherry. **cream'y** *adj.* (**cream·i·er, cream·i·est**). **cream'i·ly** *adv.* **cream** *v.* Form cream or scum; cause (milk) to cream; take cream from (milk); take best part of; add cream to; treat (skin) with cosmetic cream; work (butter etc.) into creamy consistency; (slang) beat thoroughly, defeat decisively.

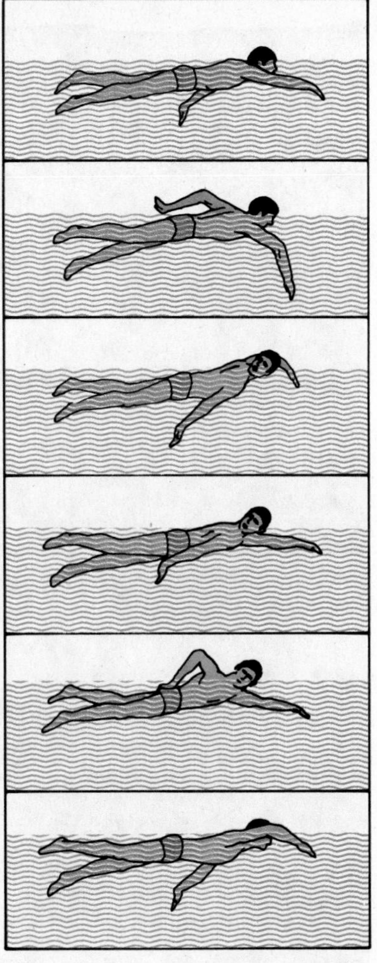

The ***crawl*** *style in swimming was developed by the Australian champion swimmer, Richard Cavill, who broke the world record for 100 yards in 1902 using this stroke. He combined an alternating over-arm movement with the rapid vertical action of the legs known as the flutter kick. The style was further refined by American swimming coaches who slightly altered the leg action.*

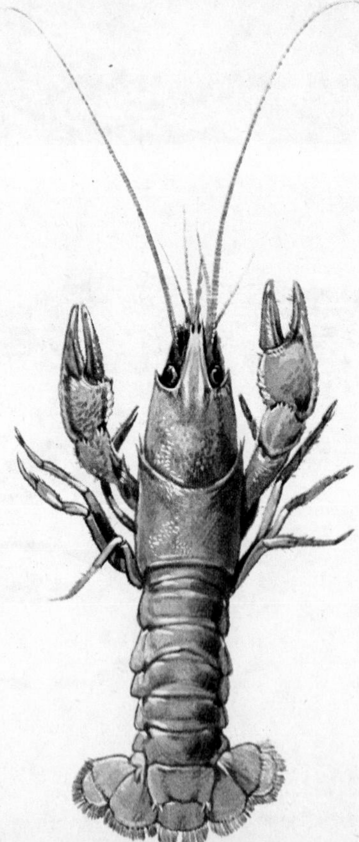

There are two families of ***crayfish,*** *the Astacidae and the Parastacidae, the former found in the northern, the latter in the southern, hemisphere. Some species are edible.*

cream·er (krē'm*e*r) *n.* Machine for separating cream from milk; small pitcher for cream. **cream·er·y** (krē'm*e*rē) *n.* (pl. **-er·ies**). Butter (and cheese) factory; store where milk, cream, etc., are sold.

crease (krēs) *n.* 1. Line caused by folding; fold; wrinkle. 2. (hockey) Area in front of goal. ~ *v.* (**creased, creas·ing**). Make creases in; fall into creases. **creas'er** *n.*

cre·ate (krēāt') *v.* (**-at·ed, -at·ing**). 1. Bring into existence, give rise to; originate; design. 2. Constitute, invest (person) with rank. **cre·a·tive** (krēā'tĭv) *adj.* **cre·a'tive·ly** *adv.* **cre·a'tive·ness, cre·a·tiv·i·ty** (krēātĭv'ĭtē) *ns.*

cre·a·tine (krē'*a*tēn, -tĭn) *n.* Amino acid found in muscles of vertebrates.

cre·a·tion (krēā'sh*o*n) *n.* 1. Creating; **the C**~, God's primal act of bringing the world or universe into existence. 2. All created things. 3. Production of human intelligence or power, esp. of the imagination.

cre·a·tor (krēā't*e*r) *n.* One who creates; **the C**~, God.

crea·ture (krē'ch*e*r) *n.* Created thing; animate being; animal (often as distinct from man); human being, person.

crèche (krĕsh, krāsh) *n.* 1. Tableau of the Nativity scene. 2. Foundling home.

cre·dence (krē'd*e*ns) *n.* 1. Belief. 2. (also ~ **table**) Small table or shelf on which Eucharistic elements are placed before consecration.

cre·den·tial (krĭdĕn'sh*a*l) *n.* (usu. pl.) Letter(s) of introduction; evidence of qualifications or authority, usu. in written form, as a diploma or certificate; (colloq.) experience.

cred·i·ble (krĕd'*i*b*e*l) *adj.* Believable, worthy of belief. **cred·i·bil·i·ty** (krĕd*i*bĭl'ĭtē), **cred'i·ble·ness** *ns.* **cred'i·bly** *adv.*

cred·it (krĕd'ĭt) *n.* 1. Belief, trust. 2. Good reputation; power derived from this; acknowledgment of merit; source of commendation or honor. 3. Trust in person's ability and intention to pay at some

Wistaria, a quick-growing and hardy deciduous shrub, is among the most popular and decorative ***creepers.*** *It is named after an American anatomist, Caspar Wistar.*

future time; reputation of solvency and probity in business; (bookkeeping) acknowledgment of payment by entry in account, sum entered on credit side of account; **letter of ~**, banker's etc. document authorizing person to draw money from writer's correspondent in another place; **~ card**, card authorizing purchase of goods or services on credit; **~ rating**, estimate of person's or firm's ability to pay; **~ union**, cooperative organization that makes small loans to its members at low interest rates. 4. Value of course of study in school or college in reckoning progress toward diploma or degree; certificate or record of successful completion of course of study. 5. (usu. pl.) List of acknowledgments giving name(s) of person(s) responsible for work on film etc. **credit** *v.t.* 1. Believe. 2. Carry to credit side of account; give credit or acknowledgment to; **~ with**, give credit for.

cred·it·a·ble (krĕd′ĭtabel) *adj.* That brings credit or honor. **cred′it·a·bly** *adv.* **cred·it·a·bil·i·ty** (krĕdĭtabĭl′ĭtē), **cred′it·a·ble·ness** *ns.*

cred·it·or (krĕd′ĭter) *n.* One who gives credit for money or goods; one to whom debt is owing.

cre·do (krē′dō, krā′-) *n.* (pl. **-dos**). Creed, esp. Apostles' Creed and Nicene Creed, which begin in Latin *credo* (= "I believe"); musical setting for these.

cred·u·lous (krĕj′ulus) *adj.* Too ready to believe; characterized by or arising from readiness to believe. **cre·du·li·ty** (kredōō′lĭtē, -dū′-), **cred′u·lous·ness** *ns.* **cred′u·lous·ly** *adv.*

creed (krēd) *n.* Brief formal summary of Christian doctrine, esp. Apostles' Creed and Nicene Creed; confession of faith; system of belief.

Creek (krēk) *n.* (pl. **Creeks**, collect. **Creek**). (Member of) a N. Amer. Ind. tribe formerly inhabiting parts of Georgia, Alabama, and northern Florida, now mainly settled in Oklahoma. [transl. Algonkin *maskoki* creeks]

creek (krēk, krĭk) *n.* 1. Brook, stream. 2. (Brit.) Narrow inlet of seacoast or tidal estuary.

creel (krēl) *n.* Large wicker basket for fish; angler's fishing basket.

creep (krēp) *v.i.* (**crept, creep·ing**). 1. Crawl; move timidly, slowly, or stealthily; proceed, exist, abjectly. 2. (of plants) Grow along ground, wall, etc.; **creeping Jenny** = moneywort (see MONEY). 3. (of flesh) Have a tingling sensation creeping over it (as result of fear, repugnance, etc.). 4. (of metal rails etc.) Move gradually forward under recurrent pressure; (of hot metal) extend slowly under tension; (of liquid) spread upward in crystals on side of vessel. **creep** *n.* 1. Creeping; creeping action of metal etc. 2. **the ~s**, (colloq.) nervous shrinking or shiver of dread or horror. 3. (slang) Obnoxious person.

creep·er (krē′per) *n.* (esp.) Plant that creeps along ground or up wall etc.; person, animal that creeps; kind of grapnel for dragging ground under water; bird that creeps on trees, esp. **brown ~** (*Certhia familiaris*).

creep·y (krē′pē) *adj.* (**creep·i·er, creep·i·est**). Having or producing a creeping of the flesh, frightening, repugnant; given to creeping. **creep·y-crawl·y** (krē′pē kraw′lē) *adj.* & *n.* (Insect, worm, etc.) producing creeping sensation. **creep′i·ly** *adv.* **creep′i·ness** *n.*

cre·mate (krē′māt, krĭmāt′) *v.t.* (**-mat·ed, -mat·ing**). 1. Consume (esp. corpse) by fire. 2. (slang) Beat thoroughly; defeat decisively. **cre·ma·tion** (krĭmā′shon), **cre′ma·tor** *ns.*

cre·ma·to·ri·um (krēmatōr′ēum, -tōr′-, krĕma-) *n.* (pl. **-to·ri·ums, -to·ri·a** pr. -tōr′ēa, -tōr′-). Establishment for cremation.

cre·ma·to·ry (krē′matōtē, -tōrē, krĕm′a-) *n.* (pl. **-ries**). Crematorium. **~** *adj.* Of cremation.

crème (krĕm, krēm, krām) *n.* Syrupy liqueur; **~ de cacao**, sweet chocolate-flavored liqueur; **~ de menthe**, sweet green liqueur flavored with mint; **~ de la ~**, (fig.) the best of anything.

Cre·mo·na (krĭmō′na). Town in Lombardy, Italy, where the craft of violin-making reached its height in 17th and early 18th centuries; hence, violin made there.

cre·nate (krē′năt), **cre·nat·ed** (krē′nātĭd) *adjs.* (bot., zool.) With notched or scalloped edge. **cre·na·tion** (krĭnā′shon) *n.*

cre·na·ture (krē′nacher, krĕn′a-) *n.* Notch or scalloped projection on edge of leaf etc.

cren·el·at·ed, *Brit.* **cren·el·lat·ed** (krĕn′elātĭd) *adjs.* Having battlements. **cren·el·a·tion** (krĕnelā′shon) *n.*

Cre·ole (krē′ōl) *n.* 1. Descendant of European settlers or slaves in W. Indies. 2. Descendant of early French or Spanish settlers in Louisiana etc.; (hist.) American-born black as dist. from an imported African slave. **~** *adj.* Born and naturalized in W. Indies etc., but of European or black descent.

Cre·on (krē′ŏn). (Gk. myth.) 1. King of Thebes and successor to Oedipus. 2. King of Corinth, father of CREUSA.

cre·o·sote (krē′osōt) *n.* Brown oily liquid, a mixture of phenols obtained from coal tar (formerly from wood tar) having antiseptic properties and used esp. for preservation of timber and as a disinfectant; **~ bush**, evergreen shrub (*Larrea tridentata*) found in N. Mexico and S. Texas. **creosote** *v.t.* (**-sot·ed, -sot·ing**). Coat with creosote.

crepe (krāp) *n.* Light, thin textile fabric with crinkled surface produced chemically or by twisting the yarn; black band of this displayed or worn on the sleeve or hat as sign of mourning; rubber rolled into thin sheets with crinkled surface; **~ de Chine** (shēn), fine silk crepe; ~ **paper**, thin crinkled paper; ~ **sole**, shoe sole of rubber crepe; **crêpe** (pr. also krĕp) **Su·zette** (sōōzĕt′), small dessert pancake served flambé.

crep·i·tate (krĕp′ĭtāt) *v.i.* (**-tat·ed, -tat·ing**). Make crackling sound. **crep·i·ta·tion** (krĕpĭtā′-sh*o*n) *n.* (med.) Grating sound made by ends of bone rubbing together; rattle of breath as heard in pneumonia etc.

crept (krĕpt): see CREEP.

cre·pus·cu·lar (krĭpŭs′ky*u*l*er*) *adj.* Of twilight; (zool.) appearing, active, at twilight.

cres., cresc. *abbrevs.* Crescendo.

cre·scen·do (krĭshĕn′dō) *adv.*, *n.* (pl. **-dos**, *It.* **-di** pr. -dē) & *adj.* (mus.) (Passage performed) with gradually increasing volume, indicated thus <; also fig. [It.]

cres·cent (krĕs′*e*nt) *n.* 1. Waxing moon, between new moon and full; concavo-convex figure of moon during first or last quarter, esp. when very new or very old. 2. Representation of this shape, esp. as badge of Turkish sultans; Turkish power (hist.); Muslim religion. 3. Anything crescent-shaped. ~ *adj.* 1. Increasing; waxing. 2. Crescent-shaped.

cre·sol (krē′sōl, -sawl, -sŏl) *n.* Any of three isomeric methyl phenols present in wood and coal tar and forming chief constituents of creosote.

cress (krĕs) *n.* Any of various cruciferous plants, usu. with pungent edible leaves, esp. WATERCRESS.

Cres·si·da (krĕs′ĭd*a*). In medieval legends of the Trojan War, the daughter of Calchas, a priest; she was faithless to her lover Troilus, a son of Priam.

crest (krĕst) *n.* 1. Comb, tuft, on bird's or animal's head; erect plume or other ornament on top of helmet or headdress. 2. (her.) Device (orig. borne by knight on his helmet) above shield and helmet in coat of arms, or used separately, as on seal, notepaper, etc. 3. Top of helmet; helmet, headpiece; summit, top, esp. of hill or mountain. 4. Ridge forming top of anything, esp. of roof or wave; surface line of neck in animals, mane; (anat.) ridge along surface of bone. 5. **crest′-fallen**, with drooping crest; abashed, disheartened. **crest** *v.* 1. Form into crest. 2. Reach crest or summit of. **crest′ed** *adj.*

cre·ta·ceous (krĭtā′sh*u*s) *adj.* Of (the nature of) chalk; **C**~ (geol.) of the last period of the Mesozoic. **Cre·ta′ceous** *n.* Cretaceous period or system.

Crete (krēt). Aegean island belonging to Greece. **Cre′tan** *adj.* & *n.* (Native, inhabitant) of Crete.

cre·tin (krē′tĭn) *n.* One suffering from cretinism; idiot. **cre′tin·ism** *n.* Idiocy combined with arrested and deformed physical development, and caused by thyroid deficiency. **cre′tin·ous** *adj.* [Swiss Fr. *crestin* Christian, in sense of "(barely) human creature"]

cre·tonne (krĭtŏn′, krē′tŏn) *n.* Strong unglazed cotton or linen fabric with printed pattern.

Cre·u·sa (krēōō′s*a*). (Gk. legend) 1. Daughter of Creon, king of Corinth; when she was about to marry Jason, she put on a garment given her by Medea which was poisoned and set her body on fire. 2. Daughter of Priam king of Troy, and wife of Aeneas.

cre·vasse (kr*e*văs′) *n.* Deep fissure in a glacier; crack in a levee or dike.

crev·ice (krĕv′ĭs) *n.* Narrow opening, fissure, esp. in rock, building, etc.

*The **Cretaceous** period was between 65 and 136 million years ago. Reptiles predominated. Towards the end of this era, the reptile population declined, and smaller mammals began to develop. The forms of Cretaceous reptiles are known from fossil remains: the tyrannosaurus and triceratops are both dinosaurs; the pteranodon was a giant winged lizard or pterodactyl (a toothed bird), the ichthyornis was a smaller toothed bird; the ornithomimus was a small ostrich-like animal; and the triconodont was a hairy primitive mammal, which was two feet long and probably carnivorous.*

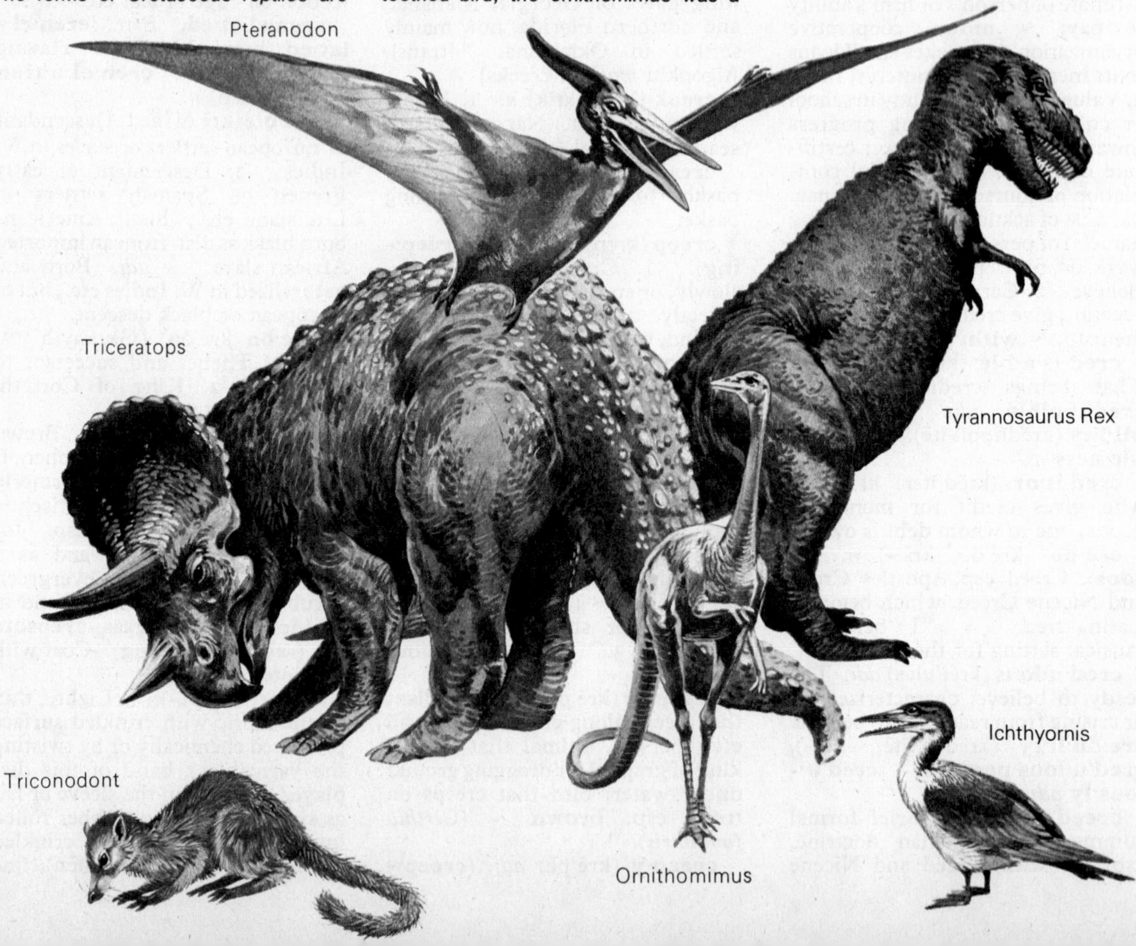

crew (kro͞o) *n.* Group of people working together; group of people manning ship, aircraft, train, etc.; sometimes, men manning ship, excluding officers; associated body, company, of persons; set, gang, mob; ~ **cut**, man's closely cropped haircut. **crew′man** *n.* (pl. **-men**). **crew** *v.* Supply or act as crew (for).

crew·el (kro͞o′el) *n.* Thin, loosely twisted worsted yarn used for embroidery; ~ **work**, decorative embroidery employing this yarn.

crib (krĭb) *n.* 1. Barred receptacle for fodder etc. 2. Cabin, hovel; (slang) living quarters. 3. Child's bed with barred or latticed sides. 4. Framework lining shaft of mine; heavy crossed timbers used in foundations in loose soil etc. 5. Set of cards in cribbage made up from discards from players' hands. 6. (colloq.) Plagiarism; translation. 7. (also ~ **sheet**) Set of answers for illegitimate use by students. **crib** *v.t.* (**cribbed, crib·bing**). 1. Confine in small space. 2. Furnish (cowshed etc.) with cribs. 3. Pilfer; plagiarize; cheat (on student examination).

crib·bage (krĭb′ĭj) *n.* Card game for two, three, or four persons, played with pack of 52 cards and a board of 61 holes on which points are scored with pegs, five or six cards being dealt to each player and the dealer having in addition the CRIB (see def. 5).

crib·ri·form (krĭb′ri fôrm) *adj.* (anat., bot.) Perforated with numerous small holes.

Crich·ton (krī′ton), **James** (1560–85). Scottish intellectual prodigy said to have disputed on scientific questions in 12 languages; **Admirable** ~, nickname given to him; hence, any very versatile person.

crick[1] (krĭk) *n.* Painful spasm of muscles of neck, back, etc., sudden stiffness.

crick[2] (krĭk) *n.* (dial.) Creek.

The Australian crested pigeon, also known as the 'top-knot' pigeon. ***Crests*** *are used, by the male birds particularly, in amorous and aggressive display. Combs and wattles have the same function.*

Crick (krĭk), **Francis Harry Compton** (1916–). British biochemist; co-discoverer (with J. D. WATSON) of DNA molecular structure; awarded Nobel Prize for medicine, 1962.

crick·et[1] (krĭk′ĭt) *n.* Orthopterous jumping insect of genus *Acheta* or related genera, esp. the common American **field** or **black** ~ (*A. assimilis*) and the **house** ~ (*A. domestica*) living in hearths and other warm places, and producing a characteristic shrill noise by rubbing parts of forewings together.

crick·et[2] (krĭk′ĭt) *n.* Outdoor game, popular in Gt. Britain, played with bats, ball, and two wickets by two sides of 11 players each, in which the batsman (one at each wicket) defends his wicket against the ball and scores by runs made between the wickets after the

Crete *is the 5th largest island in the Mediterranean. During the Bronze-Age rule of Minos, the palaces of Knossos and Phaistos were built. Crete is rich in minerals as well as archeological relics.*

*The derivation of the word **cricket** and the evolution of the game in England are not known with certainty, but cricket has been played since at least the 16th century. Top right: The Marylebone Cricket Club (M.C.C.), seen in this early 19th century color lithograph, was founded in 1788. Top left: A test match between Australia and the West Indies.*

*About 700 species of **crinoid** are known. The feathery tentacles are lined with tiny hairs to sweep food to the mouth.*

ball has been struck by the bat; **not** ~, (chiefly Brit., colloq.) unsporting, unfair. **cricket** *v.i.* Play cricket. **crick'et·er** *n.*

cri·coid (krī'koid) *adj.* Ring-shaped. ~ *n.* (anat.) Cartilage of this shape forming lower and back part of larynx.

cri·er (krī'*er*) *n.* (esp.) (hist.) (also **town** ~) Person employed to shout out public announcements in the street.

crime (krīm) *n.* Act punishable by law; evil act, sin; unjust, senseless act or condition; ~ **of passion**, crime (esp. murder) resulting from sexual jealousy; ~ **wave**, sudden brief increase in number of crimes committed.

Cri·me·a (krīmē'*a*). Peninsula of U.S.S.R. lying between Sea of Azov and Black Sea. **Cri·me'an** *adj.* ~ **War**, war fought chiefly in the Crimea, 1854–6, in which Russia was defeated by Turkey, France, and Gt. Britain, both sides sustaining heavy losses.

crim·i·nal (krĭm'ĭn*a*l) *adj.* Of (the nature of) crime; concerned with crime or its punishment; guilty of crime; ~ **conversation**, (archaic) adultery; ~ **law, proceedings**, those involving crime and its punishment (cf. CIVIL law). **crim'i·nal·ly** *adv.* **criminal** *n.* Person guilty or convicted of crime. **crim·i·nal·i·ty** (krĭmĭnăl'ĭtē) *n.* (pl. **-ties**).

crim·i·nate (krĭm´ĭnāt) *v.t.* (**-nat·ed, -nat·ing**). Charge with crime; prove guilty of crime; incriminate. **crim·i·na·tion** (krĭmĭnā´shon) *n.* **crim·i·na·tive** (krĭm´ĭnātĭv), **crim·i·na·to·ry** (krĭm´ĭnatōrē, -tōrē) *adjs.*

crim·i·nol·o·gy (krĭmĭnŏl´ojē) *n.* Scientific study of crime. **crim·i·nol´o·gist** *n.* **crim·i·no·log·i·cal** (krĭmĭnolŏj´ĭkal) *adj.*

crimp (krĭmp) *v.t.* 1. Compress into pleats or folds, frill; wrinkle or crumple minutely. Cause (flesh of newly caught fish) to contract and become firm by gashing. ~ *n.* Fold, crease; (fig.) **put a ~ in,** interfere with.

crim·son (krĭm´zon, -son) *adj.* & *n.* (Of) deep red color inclining toward purple. ~ *v.* Make, become, crimson.

cringe (krĭnj) *v.i.* (**cringed, cring·ing**). Cower; bow servilely; behave obsequiously. ~ *n.* Fawning obeisance.

cri·nite (krī´nīt) *adj.* (bot., zool.) Hairy.

crin·kle (krĭng´kel) *v.* (**-kled, -kling**) & *n.* Wrinkle. **crin´kly** *adj.* (**-kli·er, -kli·est**).

cri·noid (krī´noid, krĭn´oid) *adj.* & *n.* (Echinoderm) usu. with stalked and rooted calyxlike body; sea lily.

crin·o·line (krĭn´olĭn, -lēn) *n.* Stiff fabric of horsehair etc. formerly used for skirts; petticoat of this, or hooped petticoat, used to expand skirt of woman's dress.

crip·ple (krĭp´el) *n.* Lame person. ~ *v.t.* (**-pled, -pling**). Lame; disable, impair.

cri·sis (krī´sĭs) *n.* (pl. **-ses** pr. -sēz). Turning point, esp. of disease; moment or brief period of danger or suspense.

crisp (krĭsp) *adj.* Hard or firm but fragile, brittle; bracing; brisk, decisive; (of hair etc.) closely curling. **crisp´ly** *adv.* **crisp´ness** *n.* **crisp** *n.* Anything dried or shriveled by frying, roasting, etc. ~ *v.* Make or become crisp. **crisp´y** *adj.* (**crisp·i·er, crisp·i·est**). **crisp´i·ness** *n.*

cris·pa·tion (krĭspā´shon) *n.* Crisping, curling, undulation; slight contraction (esp. of skin in "goose flesh").

criss·cross (krĭs´kraws, -krŏs) *n.* Crossing lines, currents, etc.; network of intersecting lines. ~ *adj.* In crossing lines. ~ *adv.* Crosswise. ~ *v.* Mark with crisscross lines; cross repeatedly. [orig. *Christ's cross*]

cris·tate (krĭs´tāt), **cris·tat·ed** (krĭs´tātĭd) *adjs.* Crested, like a crest.

cri·te·ri·on (krītēr´ēon) *n.* (pl. **-te·ri·a** pr. -tēr´ēa, **-te·ri·ons**). Principle, rule, standard, by which thing is judged.

crit·ic (krĭt´ĭk) *n.* One who pronounces judgment; censurer; judge of literary, dramatic, or artistic works; one skilled in textual criticism.

crit·i·cal (krĭt´ĭkal) *adj.* 1. Censorious, faultfinding; skillful, engaged, in criticism; belonging to criticism; providing textual criticism. 2. Relating to crisis; involving risk or suspense. 3. (math., phys.) Marking transition from one state, property, condition, etc., to another; (of nuclear reactor) maintaining self-sustaining chain reaction; ~ **angle,** (optics) largest angle at which light rays passing through a dense medium can strike the face of a rarer medium and pass into it (i.e. be refracted; if the angle exceeds this, they will be totally reflected); ~ **mass,** amount of fissile material required to sustain chain reaction; ~ **point,** temperature for any gas above which it cannot be liquefied by compression (also ~ **temperature**). **crit´i·cal·ly** *adv.* **crit´i·cal·ness** *n.*

crit·i·cism (krĭt´ĭsĭzem) *n.* Criticizing; work of a critic; critical essay or remark; science dealing with text, character, composition, and origin of literary documents; **higher ~,** criticism, other than verbal or textual (**lower ~**), of the Bible; **textual ~,** criticism that seeks to ascertain the genuine text and meaning of a literary work.

crit·i·cize (krĭt´ĭsīz) *v.* (**-cized, -ciz·ing**). Discuss critically; censure, find fault (with). **crit´i·ciz·a·ble** *adj.* **crit´i·ciz·er** *n.*

cri·tique (krĭtēk´) *n.* Critical essay or notice; criticism.

croak (krōk) *n.* Deep hoarse sound made by frog or crow; sound resembling this. **croak´y** *adj.* (**croak·i·er, croak·i·est**). **croak** *v.* 1. Utter croak; utter dismally; forebode evil. 2. (slang) Die.

croak·er (krō´ker) *n.* Any of N.

*The **cricket** of the insect family Gryllidae is best recognized by its sound. There are about 1,400 known species. Their adaptations range from soil-burrowing to arboreal.*

Amer. marine fishes of the family Sciaendae that make drumming sounds.

Croat (krōt, krō'ăt) *n.* Native, inhabitant, of Croatia; descendant of Slavonic tribe which occupied that country in 7th c.; their language; Serbo-Croatian. **Cro·a·tia** (krōā'sh*a*). District of Yugoslavia. **Cro·a'tian** *adj.* Of Croatia or the Croats. ~ *n.* Croat; language of the Croats.

Cro·ce (krō'chĕ), **Benedetto** (1866–1952). Italian philosopher and historian.

cro·chet (krōshā'; *Brit.* krō'shā, -shē) *n.* Kind of knitting done with a hooked needle (~ **hook**); material so made. ~ *v.t.* (**-cheted** pr. -shād'; *Brit.* -shād, -shēd; **-chet·ing** pr. -shā'ĭng; *Brit.* -shāĭng, -shēĭng). Do crochet work; make of crochet.

crock[1] (krŏk) *n.* Earthen pot or jar; broken piece of earthenware, potsherd; (slang, fig.) pot full of lies, rubbish, or nonsense.

crock[2] (krŏk) *n.* (chiefly Brit. slang) Broken down or disabled person or thing.

crocked (krŏkt) *adj.* (slang) Drunk.

crock·er·y (krŏk'erē) *n.* Earthenware vessels, esp. for domestic use.

Crock·ett (krŏk'ĭt), **(David) "Davy"** (1786–1836). Amer. frontiersman; member of U.S. House of representatives from Tennessee, 1827–31, 1833–5; joined Texan forces and was killed at the Alamo, 1836.

croc·o·dile (krŏk'odīl) *n.* 1. Large amphibious thick-skinned long-tailed saurian reptile of *Crocodilus* or related genera, esp. *C. acutus*, the American crocodile, and *C. niloticus*, the crocodile of the Nile; tanned skin of this. 2. ~ **bird**, Egyptian black-headed plover (*Pluvianus aegyptius*), a small bird with lavender and cream plumage and black-and-white markings, which eats crocodile's insect parasites; ~ **tears**, (from the ancient belief that the crocodile wept while devouring its victim) hypocritical tears or sympathy. **croc·o·dil·i·an** (krŏk*o*dĭl'ēan) *adj.* & *n.*

cro·cus (krō'k*u*s) *n.* (pl. **-cus·es, -ci** pr. -kē, -kī, -sī). Hardy dwarf plant with corm (genus *C*~), cultivated for its brilliant, usu. yellow or purple, flowers, appearing in early spring or in autumn.

Croe·sus (krē's*u*s) (6th c. B.C.). King of Lydia, famous for his riches; hence, a very rich man.

croft (krawft, krŏft) *n.* Enclosed piece of (usu. arable) land; small agricultural holding worked by peasant tenant, esp. in Scottish Highlands. **croft'er** *n.*

crois·sant (krwahsahṅ') *n.* (pl. **-sants** pr. -sahṅ'). Buttery, flaky, crescent-shaped bread roll. [Fr.]

Cro-Mag·non (krōmăg'n*o*n, -măn'y*o*n). Cave in Dordogne, France, where remains of *Homo sapiens* were found in 1868 among deposits of upper paleolithic age; applied to a group of mankind (persisting in mesolithic and neolithic times) with long heads, low foreheads, very broad faces, deep-set eyes, and tall stature.

Crom·well[1] (krŏm'w*e*l, -wĕl, krŭm'-), **Oliver** (1599–1658). Leader of the parliamentary troops in the English Civil War; Lord PROTECTOR of England, 1653–8.

Crom·well[2] (krŏm'w*e*l, -wĕl, krŭm'-), **Thomas, Earl of Essex** (1485?–1540). Adviser and agent of Henry VIII and Cardinal Wolsey in Protestantizing England, political matters, etc.; executed for treason.

crone (krōn) *n.* Withered old woman; old ewe.

Cro·nus (krō'n*u*s, krŏn'*u*s). (Gk. myth.) One of the Titans and father of Zeus, by whom he was dethroned as ruler of the universe.

cro·ny (krō'nē) *n.* (pl. **-nies**). Intimate friend.

crook (kro͝ok) *n.* 1. Shepherd's staff, with one end curved or hooked, for catching sheep's leg; bishop's or abbot's pastoral staff; anything hooked; hook; curve, bend. 2. (colloq.) Dishonest person, esp. swindler or thief. ~ *v.* Bend, curve.

crook·ed (kro͝ok'ĭd) *adj.* Not straight, bent, angled, twisted; deformed; bent with age; not straightfoward, dishonest. **crook'ed·ly** *adv.* **crook'ed·ness** *n.*

croon (kro͞on) *n.* Low monoto-

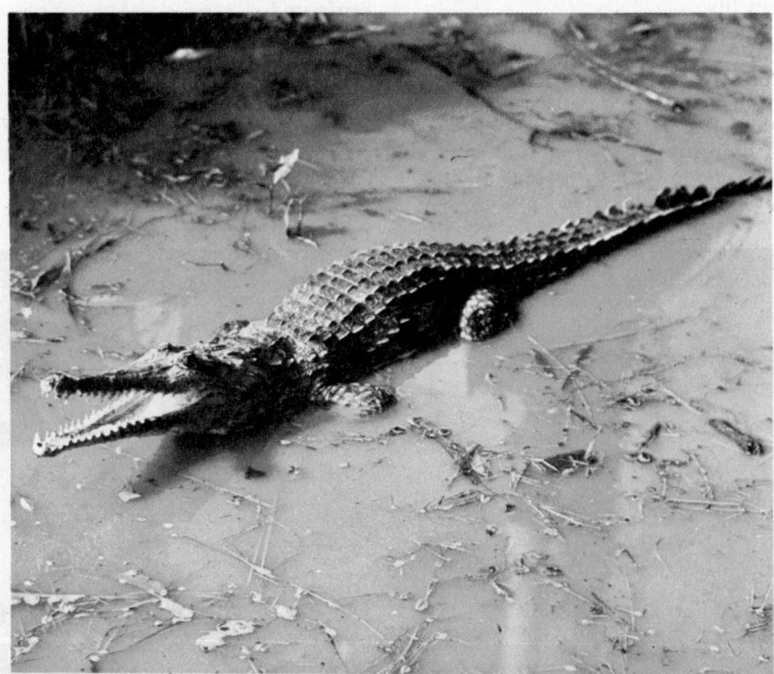

There are 13 recorded species of ***crocodile.*** *Right: The Australian freshwater crocodile (Crocodilus johnstoni) and below the estuarian species (C. porosus). Most crocodiles live in freshwater and young hatch from eggs.*

Crochet *first became popular in the 19th century and was perfected as a craft in Ireland, where it was introduced as relief work during the potato famine. The exquisite quality compares with Venetian lace.*

Oliver Cromwell *and his New Model Army at Dunbar in a painting by A. C. Gow. The execution of Charles I in 1649 brought unrest in Scotland. Cromwell won the battle of Dunbar on 3 September 1650.*

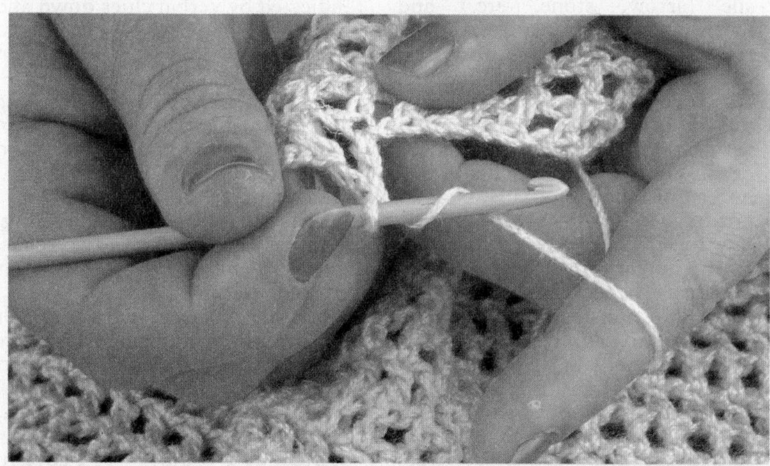

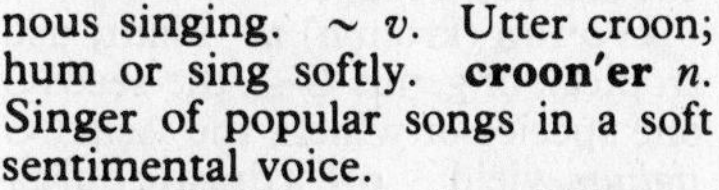

Thomas Cromwell *in a portrait by Holbein. His role in negotiating the necessary Reformation legislation for Henry VIII has been disputed; he has been both credited as author and dismissed as mere instrument.*

nous singing. ~ *v.* Utter croon; hum or sing softly. **croon'er** *n.* Singer of popular songs in a soft sentimental voice.

crop (krŏp) *n.* 1. Pouchlike enlargement of gullet in birds, where food is prepared for digestion. 2. Stock, handle, of whip; (also **hunting** ~) short whip with loop instead of lash. 3. Produce of cultivated plants, esp. cereals; agricultural produce; season's total yield (of cereal etc.). 4. Cropping of hair; style of wearing hair cut short; piece cropped or cut off anything. ~ *v.* (**cropped, crop·ping**). 1. Cut off; cut short; (of animals) bite off (tops of plants). 2. Gather, reap. 3. Trim, cut off unwanted part(s), esp. of photograph. 4. Raise crop on; bear a crop. 5. ~ **up**, turn up unexpectedly; come to surface; ~ **out**, appear.

crop·per (krŏp'*er*) *n.* (esp.) 1. (slang) Sharecropper. 2. (slang) Heavy fall (**come a** ~; also fig.).

cro·quet (krōkā'; *Brit.* krō'kā, -kē) *n.* 1. Game played on lawn, in which wooden balls are driven with wooden mallets through hoops fixed in the ground. 2. Croqueting a ball in this game. ~ *v.t.* (**-queted** pr. -kād'; *Brit.* -kād, -kēd;

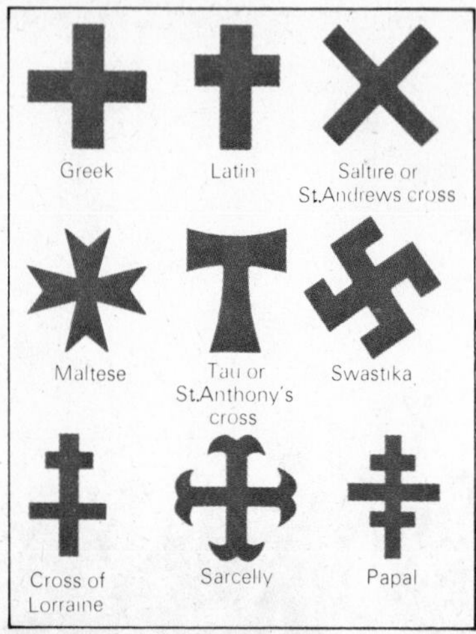

1

2

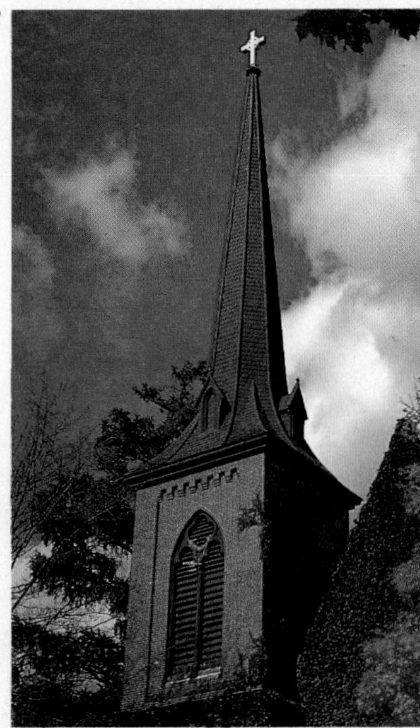

The ***cross*** *has developed complex symbolic meanings, combining religious and non-religious ideas of love and comfort with more militant connotations. Stone crosses marked routes as on Bodmin Moor, Cornwall, U.K. (1) and others were symbols of peace and security. (2) Spire of St. Peter's Episcopal Church, Concord, New Hampshire.*

-quet·ing pr. -kā′ĭng; *Brit.* -kāĭng, -kēĭng). Drive away (another ball) by striking one's own ball placed in contact with it.

cro·quette (krōkĕt′) *n.* Fried patty, usu. breaded, of minced fish, meat, potatoes, etc.

cro·sier, cro·zier (krō′zh*er*) *ns.* Pastoral staff or crook of bishop or abbot.

cross (kraws, krŏs) *n.* 1. Stake (usu. with transverse bar) used by the ancients for crucifixion, esp. (**the C~**) that on which Christ was crucified; model of this as religious emblem; sign of cross made with right hand as religious act; staff surmounted with cross and borne before archbishop or in processions. 2. Trial, affliction; annoyance. 3. Cross-shaped thing or mark; southern constellation (**Southern C~**) within Antarctic Circle, with four bright stars roughly in shape of cross; cross-shaped decoration; **fiery ~**: see FIERY. 4. Intermixture of breeds; animal etc. resulting from this; mixture, compromise, *between* two things. 5. Thing that crosses. **cross′wise, cross′ways** *advs.* **cross** *v.* 1. Place crosswise. 2. Make sign of cross on or over. 3. Draw line across; write across (what is already written, a letter). 4. Go across; bestride; carry, move, across; meet and pass. 5. Thwart; defy. 6. Crossbreed; cross-fertilize. ~ *adj.* 1. Passing from side to side, transverse; intersecting; ~ **reference**, reference from one part of book etc. to another; ~ **section**, cutting across; section made by plane cutting any solid transversely; typical representation of constituents of a thing or group. 2. Contrary, opposed. 3. (colloq.) Peevish, out of humor. **cross′ly** *adv.* In a cross or peevish way. **cross′ness** *n.*

cross- *comb. form.* **cross′bill**, bird of genus *Loxia* (one of the finches), with mandibles curved so as to cross each other when bill is closed; **cross′bones**, figure of two thighbones laid across each other, usu. under skull as emblem of death; **cross′bow**, bow fixed across wooden stock, with groove for missile (arrow, stone, etc.) and mechanism for drawing back and releasing string; **cross′bowman** (*n.*); **cross′bred**, hybrid (animal etc.); **cross′breed**, (cause to) produce hybrid; **cross-check**, verify, verification, by alternative method; **cross-country**, across fields etc. instead of following roads; **cross′-cut**, diagonal cut; **cross′cut saw**, saw for making crosscut; **cross-examine**, examine by questions designed to check answers of previous questions; esp. so examine (witness who has already given evidence for other side) in court of law; **cross-examination, cross-examiner** (*ns.*); **cross-eyed**, having squint in which eyes are turned inward; **cross-fertilize**, fertilize (plant) with gamete from another; **cross-grained**, (of wood) with grain running irregularly or in crossing directions; (fig.) perverse, intractable; **cross′hatch**, shade (drawing, engraving, etc.) with intersecting series of parallel lines; **cross-legged**, with legs crossed; with one leg laid across the other; **cross′patch**, ill-tempered person; **cross-pollinate**, pollinate from one plant to another; (**be at**) **cross-purposes**, (having) contrary or conflicting purposes; **cross′roads**, intersection of two roads; (fig.) critical turning point; **cross-stitch**, needlework stitch of two straight stitches crossing each other; **cross′tie**, (esp. railroads) transverse connecting piece (of timber etc.); **cross′town** (*adj.*), lying, leading, going, across a town; **cross′tree**, one of the horizontal transverse timbers bolted to mast of ship; **cross′word** (**puzzle**), puzzle that is solved by filling in words indicated by verbal clues down and across a pattern of numbered squares.

crosse (kraws, krŏs) *n.* Implement used in lacrosse for catching and throwing ball, consisting of long shank curved around at end with net stretched across part. [Fr.: see LACROSSE]

cross·ing (kraw′sĭng, krŏs′ĭng) *n.* (esp.) Intersection of two roads, railroads, etc.; place where street is crossed.

crotch (krŏch) *n.* Fork of tree or bough; fork of human body where legs join trunk; corresponding part of garment.

crotch·et (krŏch′ĭt) *n.* 1. (mus.) Quarter note. 2. Whimsical fancy. **crotch′et·y** *adj.* Peevish. **crotch′et·i·ness** *n.*

cro·ton (krō′ton) *n.* Plant, usu. tropical, of genus *C~*, the seeds of one species of which, the Asian *C. tiglium*, yield ~ **oil**, a drastic purgative. [Gk. *kroton* sheep tick, croton, so called from shape of seeds]

crouch (krowch) *v.i.* Stoop, bend, esp. timidly or servilely; (of animals) lie close on ground, when about to pounce on prey, or from fear. ~ *n.* Action or position of crouching.

croup[1] (kro͞op) *n.* Inflammatory

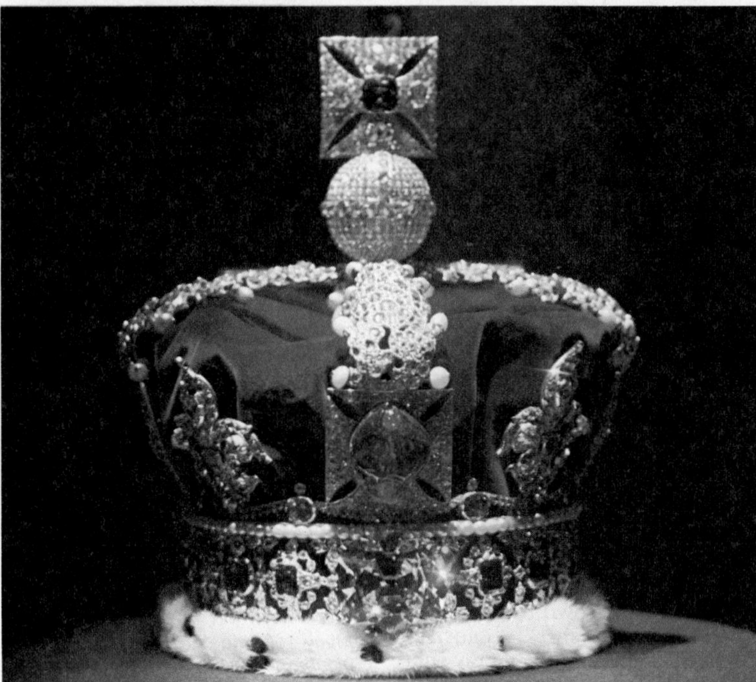

***Crowns** have consisted of oak leaves and acorns and of the world's most precious gems and metals. Two regal crowns are shown here. Above: · A crown of the former Shah of Persia. Above Right: The English Imperial State Crown made for Queen Victoria in 1838.*

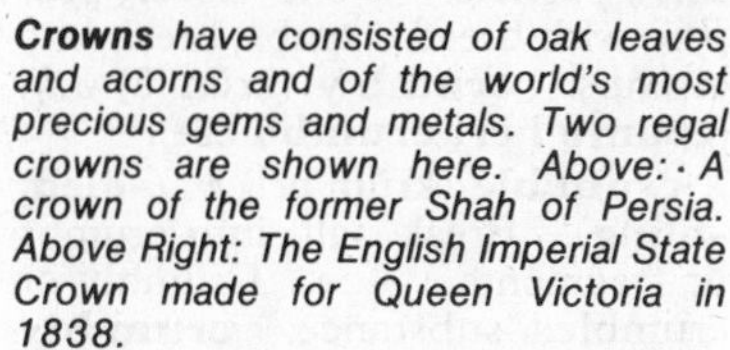

disease in larynx and trachea of children, marked by hard cough and difficulty in breathing.

croup² (kroo͞p) *n.* Rump, hind-quarters, esp. of horse.

crou·pi·er (kroo͞′pēer, -pēā) *n.* One who rakes in (with a ~**'s stick**) and pays out money at gambling table. [Fr., orig. = "one who rides behind on the croup"]

crou·ton (kroo͞′tŏn, kroo͞tŏn′) *n.* Small piece of fried or toasted bread used for garnishing or served with soup. [Fr.]

Crow (krō) *n.* Member, language, of tribe of N. Amer. Indians formerly inhabiting region between Platte and Yellowstone rivers; now settled mainly in Montana.

crow¹ (krō) *n.* 1. Bird of genus *Corvus* with glossy black feathers and raucous call. 2. (also **crow′-bar**) Metal bar, usu. with beaklike end, used as lever. 3. ~**'s-foot**, wrinkle at outer corner of human eye; ~**'s-nest**, barrel or protected platform fixed at masthead of sailing vessel for lookout; **as the ~ flies**, in a straight line; **eat ~**, submit to humiliation, be forced to admit that one is wrong.

*An Australian **crow** (Corvus cecilae), usually seen in large numbers except when breeding. Like the raven (C. coronides), from which it can be distinguished by its call, it consumes enormous quantities of insects.*

crow² (krō) *n.* Crowing of cock; joyful cry. ~ *v.i.* Utter crow; exult loudly; boast.

crowd (krowd) *n.* Throng, dense multitude; (colloq.) clique, set, lot; large number (of things). ~ *v.* 1. Collect in a crowd; fill, occupy, cram (*with*); fill (places etc.) as crowd does; force one's way *into*, *through*, etc. (confined space etc.); ~ **out**, exclude by crowding. 2. (naut.) Press or hasten on; ~ **(on) sail**, hoist large amount of sail to increase speed.

crown (krown) *n.* 1. Wreath of flowers etc. worn on head, esp. as emblem of victory. 2. Sovereign's head-covering of gold etc. and jewels; (also the **C**~; fig.) king or queen, regal power, supreme governing power in a monarchy. 3. Crown-shaped ornament. 4. Any of various coins orig. stamped with a crown; former silver coin of Gt. Britain worth five shillings. 5. Top part, esp. of skull; whole head. 6. Upper part of cut gem above girdle; highest or central part of arch or arched structure; top part of hat; part of tooth projecting from gum, artificial replacement of this. 7. ~ **colony**, colony with legislation

under control of sovereign, usu. administered by an appointed governor; ~ **glass**, kind of thick glass without lead or iron, made in circular sheets by blowing and whirling; formerly used for window panes; kind of optical glass with low refractive index; ~ **jewels**, jewels forming part of the emblems and symbols of a sovereign or royal family; ~ **prince**, heir apparent or designate to throne; ~ **princess**, wife of crown prince; female heir presumptive; ~ **vetch**, Old World plant (*Coronilla varia*) with compound leaves and pink flowers, naturalized in the U.S. **crown** *v.t.* 1. Place crown on; invest with regal crown or dignity; (fig.) reward; (slang) hit on the head. 2. Occupy the head of, form chief ornament to; put finishing touch to; bring (efforts) to happy issue. 3. (checkers) Make (piece) king, by putting another piece on top; (dentistry) fit crown to (tooth).

cro·zier (krō′zh*er*) = CROSIER.

CRT *abbrev.* Cathode ray tube.

cru·cial (kroo͞′sh*al*) *adj.* 1. Decisive, critical. 2. Cross-shaped.

cru·ci·ate (kroo͞′shēāt, -ĭt) *adj.* (zool., bot.) Cross-shaped; overlapping.

cru·ci·ble (kroo͞′sĭb*el*) *n.* Vessel (usu. of earthenware) withstanding great heat, and used for fusing metals etc.; hollow at bottom of furnace to collect molten metal; (fig.) severe test or trial.

cru·cif·er·ous (kroo͞sĭf′*er*us) *adj.* 1. Wearing, adorned with, a cross. 2. (bot.) Of the family Cruciferae, having flowers with four equal petals arranged crosswise.

cru·ci·fix (kroo͞′sĭfĭks) *n.* Figure of Christ on the Cross; (erron.) cross.

cru·ci·fix·ion (kroo͞sĭfĭk′sh*o*n) *n.* Crucifying; **the C~**, the crucifying of Christ; picture of this.

cru·ci·form (kroo͞′sĭfôrm) *adj.* Cross-shaped, esp. of church with transepts.

cru·ci·fy (kroo͞′sĭfī) *v.t.* (**-fied, -fy·ing**). Put to death by fastening to a cross; (fig.) mortify (passions, sins, flesh); (colloq.) persecute, treat with gross injustice.

crud (krŭd) *n.* (slang) 1. (Coating or deposit of) filth, impurities, etc. 2. Dirty, unpleasant, disgusting person. 3. Any illness, imagined or real, esp. a skin disease. **crud′dy** *adj.* (**crud·di·er, crud·di·est**).

crude (kroo͞d) *adj.* In the natural or raw state; unripe; unpolished, lacking refinement; rude, blunt. ~ *n.* (also ~ **oil**) Unrefined petroleum. **crude′ly** *adv.* **crude′ness, cru·di·ty** (kroo͞′dĭtē) *ns.*

cru·el (kroo͞′*el*) *adj.* Liking to inflict pain; indifferent to pain of others; painful, distressing. **cru′el·ly** *adv.* **cru′el·ness** *n.* **cru·el·ty** (kroo͞′*el*tē) *n.* (pl. **-ties**).

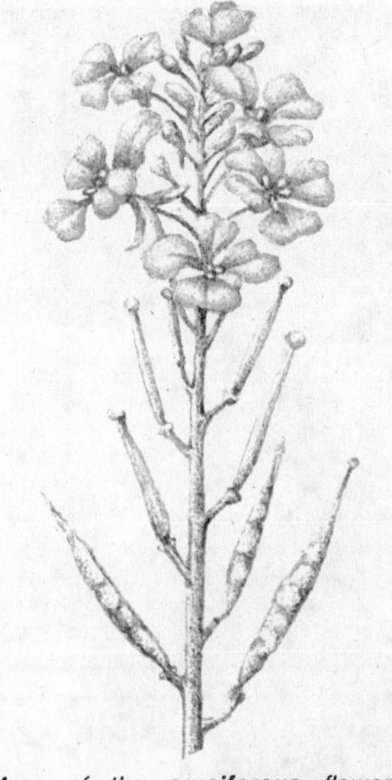

Many of the ***cruciferous*** *flowering plants commonly referred to as the 'cabbage' family, are sweet-scented, and a large number, like sea-kale, radishes, and cress, are edible and highly nutritious. They are found mainly in temperate regions.*

The ***crucifix,*** *as a central emblem of the Christian religion, has developed elaborate forms in the hands of craftsmen. That shown is silver and enamel, early 20th century.*

cru·et (kroo͞′ĭt) *n.* Small glass bottle with stopper for vinegar, oil, etc., for use at table.

cruise (kroo͞z) *v.* (**cruised, cruis·ing**). 1. Sail about, making for no particular port or calling at series of ports; sail for pleasure; (of naval vessel) sail in specified area for protection of shipping etc. 2. Travel at cruising speed. 3. Drive at random, esp. slowly, as patrolling car, taxi looking for fare, etc. 4. Cruise in (specified area). 5. ~ **missile**, low-flying jet-powered radar-controlled guided missile; **cruis′ing speed**, normal, economical traveling speed of vehicle or aircraft. **cruise** *n.* Cruising voyage.

cruis·er (kroo͞′z*er*) *n.* 1. Warship adapted for cruising, faster and less heavily armored and having less firepower than battleship. 2. (also **cabin** ~) Motorboat with cabin.

crul·ler (krŭl′*er*) *n.* Crisp doughnut, often in a twisted shape.

crumb (krŭm) *n.* Small fragment, esp. of bread, such as breaks or falls off by rubbing etc.; (fig.) small particle. ~ *v.t.* Cover, prepare with bread crumbs; break into crumbs. **crumb·y** (krŭm′ē) *adj.* (**crumb·i·er, crumb·i·est**).

crum·ble (krŭm′b*el*) *v.* (**-bled, -bling**). Break, fall, into crumbs or fragments. ~ *n.* Crumbly or crumbled substance. **crum·bly** (krŭm′blē) *adj.* (**-bli·er, -bli·est**). Apt to crumble.

crum·my (krŭm′ē) *adj.* (**-mi·er, -mi·est**). (slang) Shabby; cheap, inferior, worthless; inadequate; nasty.

crum·pet (krŭm′pĭt) *n.* (chiefly Brit.) Soft muffinlike bread cooked on griddle and eaten toasted.

crum·ple (krŭm′p*el*) *v.* (**-pled, -pling**). Crush together or *up* into creased state; ruffle, wrinkle; become creased; give way, collapse.

crunch (krŭnch) *v.* Crush with teeth, esp. noisily; grind under foot (gravel etc.); make one's way thus. ~ *n.* Crunching (noise); (colloq.) crisis. **crunch′y** *adj.* (**crunch·i·er, crunch·i·est**). Making a crunching sound.

crup·per (krŭp′*er*, kroo͝p′-) *n.* Strap buckled to back of saddle and passing under horse's tail; hindquarters of horse.

cru·sade (kroo͞sād′) *n.* 1. (freq. **C**~) One of several military expeditions undertaken by the Christians of Europe in the 11th, 12th, and 13th centuries to recover the Holy Land from the Muslims; in the **First C**~ (1096–9) the crusaders captured Jerusalem and set up a kingdom there; the **Third C**~ (1189–91), in which Richard I of England, the Holy Roman Emperor Frederick Barbarossa, and Philip Augustus of France took

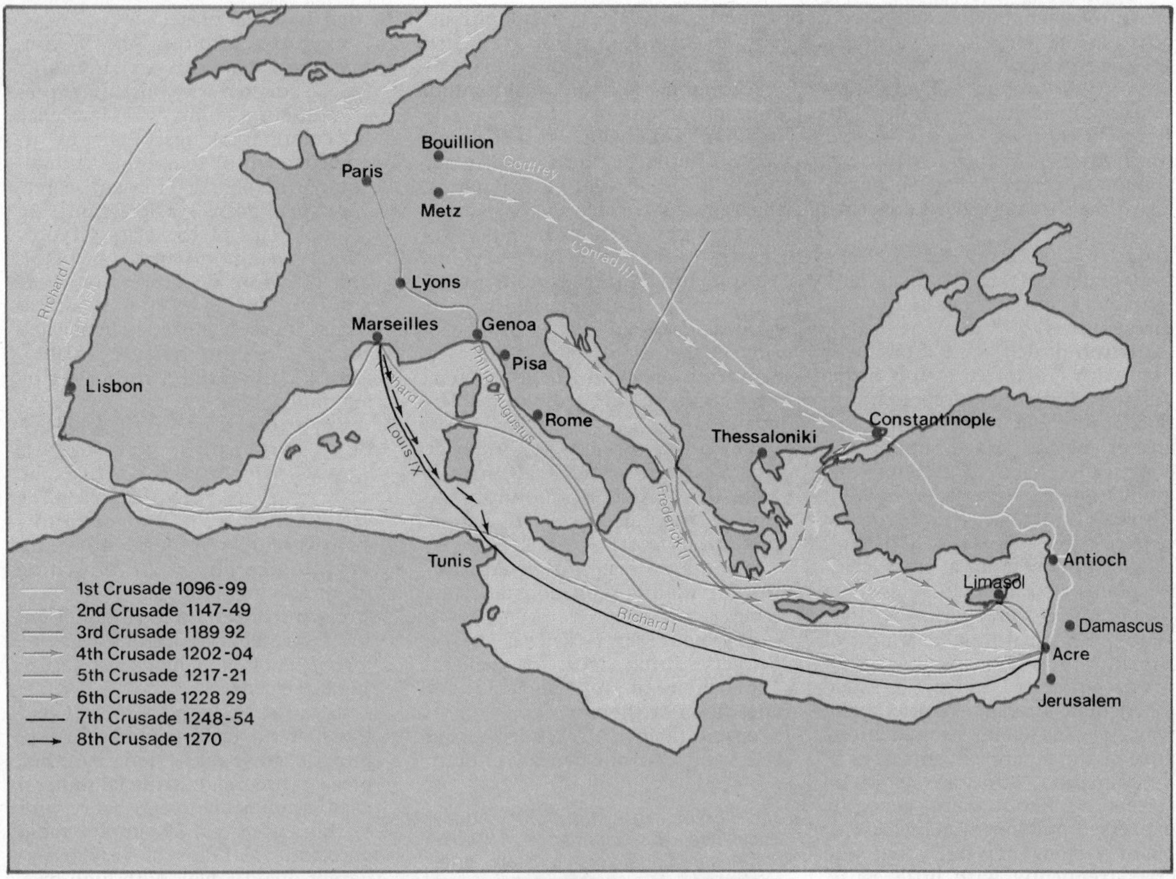

*The **crusades** had public and private purposes, the former in terms of the Christian church's aim to recover the Holy Land from the Muslims; the latter in that the individual could atone for his sins by making the pilgrimage to the Holy Land.*

*Seen here is US **cruiser,** California. Cruisers are warships built for high speed, long range travel. They are smaller than aircraft carriers, bigger than destroyers.*

part, resulted in the capture of Acre and the establishment of a Latin kingdom in the East; in the **Sixth C~** (1228–9) Jerusalem was recaptured but finally lost; the other crusades were all unsuccessful; **Children's C~**, crusade of about 500,000 unarmed children who set out in 1212 from France and Germany to recover Jerusalem. 2. Any holy war undertaken with papal sanction; (fig.) aggressive movement against public evil etc. **crusade** *v.i.* (**-sad·ed, -sad·ing**). Engage in crusade. **cru·sad'er** *n.*

crush (krŭsh) *v.* Compress, be compressed, with violence, so as to break, bruise, etc.; crease; pulverize by application of pressure; (fig.) subdue, overwhelm. ~ *n.* 1. Act of crushing. 2. Crowded mass (esp. of persons). 3. Drink, dish prepared by crushing berries or fruit. 4. (colloq.) (Object of) infatuation; **have, get, a ~ on,** (slang) form a passionate attachment to (a person).

Cru·soe (kro͞o'sō), **Robinson**: see ROBINSON CRUSOE.

crust (krŭst) *n.* Hard outer part of bread; similar casing of anything, e.g., harder layer over soft snow; hard dry scrap of bread; pastry shell, pastry under (**bottom ~**) or covering (**top ~**) pie; hard dry formation, scab, on skin; (geol.) outer portion of earth; coating, deposit, on surface of anything; deposit of tartar etc., on inside of wine bottle; hard external covering of animal or plant, such as crustaceans and lichens; (slang) insolence, gall. **crust** *v.* Cover with, form into, crust; become covered with crust. **crust'ed** *adj.* Having a crust; (of wine) having deposited a crust, as old port etc.

crus·ta·cean (krŭstā′shan) *adj.* & *n.* (Arthropod) of the class Crustacea, including crabs, lobsters, shrimps, etc., mostly aquatic, freq. with hard shell and many legs.

crus·ta·ceous (krŭstā′shus) *adj.* Crustlike; having a hard covering; crustacean.

crust·y (krŭs′tē) *adj.* (**crust·i·er, crust·i·est**). Crustlike, hard; irritable, curt. **crust′i·ly** *adv.* **crust′i·ness** *n.*

crutch (krŭch) *n.* 1. Staff (now usu. with crosspiece at top fitting under armpit) for lame person; support, prop, esp. with forked top; any of various forked supports or contrivances. 2. Anything that gives support.

crux (krŭks) *n.* (pl. **crux·es, cru·ces** pr. kroo′sēz). Difficult matter, puzzle; point at issue; critical point, vital moment.

cru·zei·ro (kroozār′ō) *n.* (pl. **-ros**). Principal monetary unit of Brazil, = 100 centavos.

cry (krī) *n.* (pl. **cries**). 1. Loud inarticulate utterance of grief, pain, fear, joy, etc.; loud excited utterance of words; appeal, entreaty. 2. Proclamation of wares sold in streets. 3. Public voice, generally expressed opinion; watchword. 4. Fit of weeping; **cry′baby**, one who cries frequently with little cause. 5. Yelping of hounds, pack of hounds; **in full cry**, in full pursuit. **cry** *v.* (**cried, cry·ing**). 1. Utter cry or cries; utter loudly; exclaim. 2. Announce for sale; make public announcement of. 3. Weep. 4. (colloq.) Complain. 5. **a far ~**, a very different matter. **cry′ing** *adj.* (esp., of evils) Calling for notice, flagrant, as *a crying shame.*

cry·o·gen (krī′ojen) *n.* Refrigerant for achieving very low temperatures. [Gr. *kruos* frost]

cry·o·gen·ics (krīojĕn′ĭks) *n.* (usu. considered sing.) Branch of physics dealing with very low temperatures and their effects. **cry·o·gen′ic** *adj.* **cry·o·gen′i·cal·ly** *adv.*

cry·o·lite (krī′olīt) *n.* Fluoride of sodium and aluminum (Na_3AlF_6) used in aluminum refining and electrical insulation. [Gk. *kruos* frost]

cry·o·stat (krī′ostăt) *n.* Apparatus for maintaining constant low temperature.

cry·o·sur·ger·y (krīosēr′jerē) *n.* Surgery using local or general application of intense cold for anesthesia or therapy.

crypt (krĭpt) *n.* Underground cell, vault, esp. one beneath church, used as burial place.

The ***crypt*** *of Mottisfont Abbey, Hampshire, U.K. founded c. 1200 by the Austin Canons, an austere order originating in Northern Italy and Southern France in the 11th century.*

cryp·tic (krĭp′tĭk) *adj.* Secret, mystical; obscure in meaning; (zool.) adapted for concealment, as **~ coloring**, animal's resemblance in color, markings, etc., to its environment or to another animal.

crypto- *prefix.* Hidden; secret.

cryp·to·gam (krĭp′togăm) *n.* (bot.) Plant of the class Cryptogamia having no stamens or pistils and therefore no flowers or seeds and reproducing by spores, such as ferns, mosses, algae, lichens, and fungi. **cryp·to·gam·ic** (krĭptogăm′ĭk), **cryp·tog·a·mous** (krĭptŏg′amus) *adjs.*

cryp·to·gram (krĭp′togrăm), **cryp·to·graph** (krĭp′tograf, -grahf) *ns.* Anything written in code or cipher. **cryp·tog·ra·pher** (krĭptŏg′rafer) *n.* **cryp·to·graph·ic** (krĭptogrăf′ĭk) *adj.* **cryp·tog′ra·phy** *n.* Art of writing in, or solving, ciphers.

cryp·to·mer·i·a (krĭptomēr′ēa) *n.* Evergreen coniferous tree (*C. japonica*) of N. China and Japan, Japanese cedar.

crys·tal (krĭs′tal) *n.* 1. Clear transparent icelike mineral, esp. pure quartz (**rock ~**); piece of this; piece of natural or artificial mineral used in contact with another or with a thin wire as a simple radio detector. 2. Glass of very transparent quality, usu. with high proportion of lead oxide; fine cut glass; anything made of this; watch glass. 3. (chem. etc.) Form in which atoms and molecules of many elements and compounds regularly aggregate, with definite internal structure and external form of solid enclosed by a number of symmetrically arranged plane faces. 4. **~ gazing**, concentrating the gaze on ball of rock crystal or glass for purpose of inducing a hallucinatory vision of distant or future events; (fig.) trying to predict the future. **crystal** *adj.* Made of, like, clear as, crystal. **crys·tal·line** (krĭs′talĭn, -līn) *adj.* Made of, like, clear as, crystal; having crystal form; **~ lens**, transparent body in eye enclosed in membranous capsule behind iris, acting as principal agent in focusing rays of light on retina.

crys·tal·lize (krĭs′talīz) *v.* (**-lized, -liz·ing**). 1. Form into crystals or (fig.) definite or permanent state. 2. Coat with, melt on, sugar.

crys·tal·log·ra·phy (krĭstalŏg′rafē) *n.* Branch of science dealing with structure, classification, and

Most ***crustaceans*** *have claws or pincers with which to defend themselves, and when caught can escape by casting off the leg which is grasped. This leaf-crab, so-called because of its leaf-like shape, is a sea crustacean found near the Atlantic coast of Europe.*

Crystal or cut-glass making evolved from about 1600 when a glass-maker in Prague used crystal and jewel cutting techniques on glass.

Picasso's 'Girl with a Mandolin' (1910). The Cubist structuring of the subject does not prevent identification. The emphasis by some Cubists was on light and shade rather than on color as evident in this reproduction.

properties of crystals. **crys·tal·log'ra·pher** *n.* **crys·tal·lo·graph·ic** (krĭstalogrăf'ĭk) *adj.*

crys·tal·loid (krĭs'taloid) *adj.* & *n.* (Substance) of crystalline structure, esp. substance capable, in solution, of passing through membranes (as dist. from COLLOID).

Crys·tal (krĭs'tal) **Palace.** Large building of iron frames and glass walls built to house exhibition in London in 1851; similar building that housed exhibition of New York City World's Fair of 1853.

C.S. *abbrev.* Chief of Staff; Christian Science; Christian Scientist; Civil Service.

Cs *symbol.* Cesium.

C/S *abbrev.* Cycles per second.

C.S.A. *abbrev.* Confederate States of America.

CST *abbrev.* Central Standard Time.

CT *abbrev.* Connecticut.

C.T. *abbrev.* Central Time.

Ct. *abbrev.* Connecticut.

ct. *abbrev.* Carat; cent; county.

ctr. *abbrev.* Center.

cu. *abbrev.* Cubic.

cub (kŭb) *n.* 1. Young of fox; young of bear or other wild beast. 2. Inexperienced youth; ~ **reporter**, apprentice newspaper reporter. 3. **C~ Scout,** member of junior division of the Boy Scouts.

Cu·ba (kū'ba). Largest of the W. Ind. islands, discovered by Columbus in 1492; formerly a part of the Span.-Amer. dominions; freed from Spanish rule by U.S. forces in Spanish American War (1898) and proclaimed an independent republic in 1902; dictatorship government of Fulgencio Batista overthrown by coup led by Fidel Castro, 1959, who established communistic government in alliance with U.S.S.R.; capital, Havana; ~ **li·bre** (lē'bre). Drink of rum, cola, and lemon or lime juice. **Cu'ban** *adj.* & *n.* (Native, inhabitant) of Cuba.

cub·by·hole (kŭb'ēhōl) *n.* Small or snug room, compartment, niche, cupboard, etc.

cube (kūb) *n.* 1. Regular solid figure contained by six equal squares; anything of this shape. 2. (math.) Third power of a quantity; ~ **root,** number or quantity which when cubed produces given number or quantity. **cube** *v.t.* (**cubed, cub·ing**). 1. Find cube of (number), find cubic content of. 2. Cut into small cubes. 3. Tenderize (meat) by slashing the fibers in a pattern of squares; ~ **steak,** thin slice of cubed beef, usu. broiled in a pan.

cu·beb (kū'bĕb) *n.* Pungent spicy berry of Javanese climbing shrub (*Piper cubeba*), formerly used in medicinal cigarettes.

cu·bic (kū'bĭk) *adj.* Cube-shaped; of three dimensions, solid; involving cube of a quantity; ~ **content,** volume (of solid) expressed in cubic feet, meters, etc.; ~ **foot, inch,** etc., volume of a cube whose edge is one foot, inch, etc. **cu'bi·cal** *adj.* **cu'bi·cal·ly** *adv.*

cu·bi·cle (kū'bĭkel) *n.* Small sleeping compartment; any small partitioned space, esp. for study or work purposes.

cu·bi·form (kū'bĭfōrm) *adj.* Cube-shaped.

Cub·ism (kū'bĭzem) *n.* Phase of Post-Impressionist art, initiated *c*1907 by Picasso and Braque, in which objects were reduced to cubic and other geometrical forms. **cub'ist** *n.* & *adj.* **cu·bis·tic** (kūbĭs'tĭk) *adj.*

cu·bit (kū'bĭt) *n.* Ancient measure of length, 17 to 21 in. **cu'bi·tal** *adj.* 1. Of the length of a cubit. 2. Of the forearm or corresponding part in

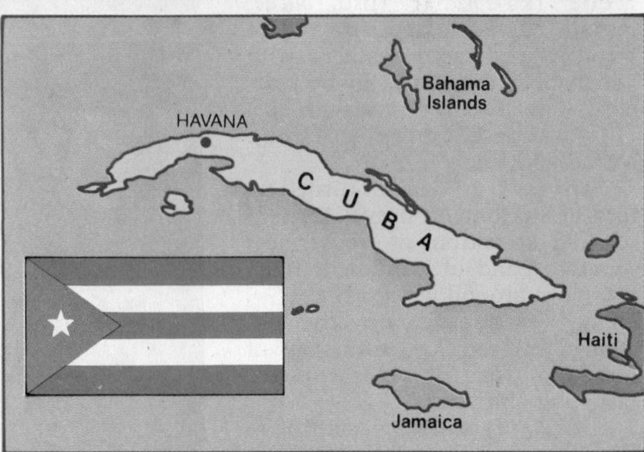

***Cuba's** population is multi-racial but wholly Spanish-speaking. The mainly agricultural economy is based on sugar, tobacco, coffee, fruit, and cattle. Cuba has rich mineral reserves, particularly of iron ore. Cuba is important as the closest Communist country to the U.S.A.*

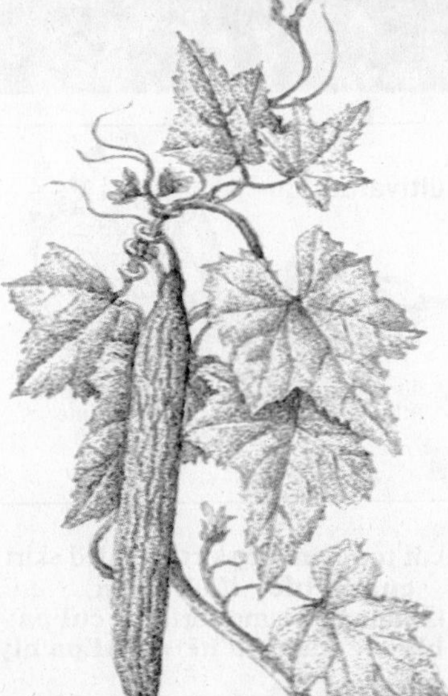

*The cultivation of the **cucumber** is believed to have started in S. Asia and its use certainly spread to the Ancient Greeks and Romans from India. The plant trails or climbs.*

animals. [L. *cubitum* length of forearm (*cubitus* elbow)]

cu·boid (kū′boid) *adj.* Cube-shaped, like a cube; of the ~ **bone. cuboid** *n.* Solid resembling cube, with rectangular faces not all equal; (also ~ **bone**) one of the bones of the foot, between heel bone and fourth and fifth metatarsal bones.

cuck·ing (kŭk′ĭng) **stool.** (hist.) Chair in which nagging women, dishonest tradesmen, etc. were tied and exposed to public ridicule or ducked in water.

cuck·old (kŭk′old) *n.* Husband of unfaithful wife. ~ *v.t.* Make a cuckold of. [OF. *cucu* cuckoo]

cuck·oo (kōō′kōō, kŏŏk′ōō) *n.* (pl. **-oos**). Migratory bird of family Cuculidae with characteristic note or cry, esp. yellow-billed cuckoo (*Coccyzus americanus*) and black-billed cuckoo (*C. erythrophthalmus*); characteristic two-note call or cry of this bird; ~ **clock**, clock in which hours are sounded by imitation of cuckoo's call; **cuck′oo-flower**, lady's smock (*Cardamine pratensis*), plant with pale lilac flower, blooming in spring. **cuckoo** *adj.* (slang) Crazy; foolish. [OF. *cuca* imit. of bird's cry]

cu·cum·ber (kū′kŭmber) *n.* 1. Creeping plant (*Cucumis sativus*) widely cultivated for its long fleshy fruit; the fruit of this, commonly eaten as salad. 2. (also ~ **tree**), N. Amer. tree (*Magnolia acuminata*), also called cucumber magnolia, with fruit resembling small cucumbers.

cud (kŭd) *n.* Food that ruminating animal brings back from first stomach into mouth and chews at leisure; a quid of chewing tobacco; **chew one's ~**, ruminate, ponder.

cud·dle (kŭd′el) *v.* (**-dled,**

*The early history of **cultivation** and how suitable kinds of seed were developed and propagated is little known. Today advanced techniques are used to evolve crops resistant to pests, adapted to particular conditions and high-yielding. 1. Flax drying near Foxton, New Zealand. 2. Sugar beet on peatland in Lancashire, U.K.*

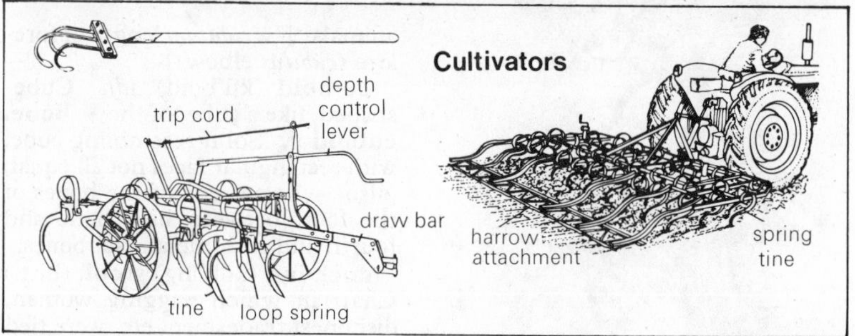

-dling). Hug gently, fondle; lie close and snug; nestle together; curl oneself *up*. ~ *n.* Act of cuddling. **cud·dle·some** (kŭd′elsom), **cud·dly** (kŭd′lē) *adjs.* (**-dli·er, -dli·est**). Pleasant to cuddle.

cudg·el (kŭj′el) *n.* Short thick stick used as weapon. ~ *v.t.* Beat with cudgel; (fig.) rack (one's brains).

cue[1] (kū) *n.* Last word or words of a speech in a play, serving as signal to another actor to enter or speak; similar guide to musical performer; sign or intimation when or how to speak or act etc. ~ *v.t.* (**cued, cu·ing, cue·ing**). Give cue to; ~ **in**, insert cue for; (slang) inform.

cue[2] (kū) *n.* 1. (usu. *queue*) Pigtail. 2. Long tapering rod of wood tipped with leather, with which balls are struck in billiards etc.; ~ **ball**, ball struck with cue. ~ *v.t.* (**cued, cu·ing, cue·ing**). Strike with cue.

cuff[1] (kŭf) *n.* Band or turned up fold at bottom of sleeve; turned-up fold at bottom of trouser leg; separate band of (stiffened) linen etc. worn around wrist; **off the** ~, (slang) extempore; **on the** ~, (slang) on credit; ~ **link**, pair of linked buttons or ornaments for fastening shirt cuff.

cuff[2] (kŭf) *n.* Blow with open hand. ~ *v.t.* Strike thus.

cui·rass (kwĭrăs′) *n.* Body armor, breastplate and backplate fastened together. **cui·ras·sier** (kwĭrasēr′) *n.* Cavalryman wearing cuirass.

cui·sine (kwĭzēn′) *n.* Style of cooking; food cooked (in a given style).

cuisse (kwĭs) *n.* (hist., usu. pl.) Thigh armor.

cul-de-sac (kŭl′desăk, ko͝ol′-kŭldesăk′, -ko͝ol-) *n.* Dead-end street. [Fr., "bottom of the sack"]

cu·let (kū′lĭt, kŭl′ĭt) *n.* Horizontal face forming bottom of brilliant cut gem.

cu·li·nar·y (kū′lĭnĕrē, kŭl′ĭ-) *adj.* Pertaining to, fit for a kitchen or cooking.

cull (kŭl) *v.t.* Pick out from others; select; gather; kill surplus (animals, as deer, seals, etc.). ~ *n.* Act of culling; something picked out from others, usu. as inferior.

culm[1] (kŭlm) *n.* Waste and coal dust from anthracite mines; inferior anthracite coal.

culm[2] (kŭlm) *n.* (bot.) Stem of plant, esp. jointed, usu. hollow, stem of grasses.

cul·mi·nant (kŭl′mĭnant) *adj.* At, forming, the top; culminating; highest. **cul·mi·nate** (kŭl′mĭnāt) *v.t.* (**-nat·ed, -nat·ing**). Reach its highest point; (astron.) be on the meridian. **cul·mi·na·tion** (kŭlmĭnā′shon) *n.*

cu·lottes (ko͞o′lŏts, kū′-, ko͞olŏts′, kū-) *n.pl.* Women's trousers cut to resemble skirt; divided skirt.

cul·pa·ble (kŭl′pabel) *adj.* Criminal, blameworthy. **cul·pa·bil·i·ty** (kŭlpabĭl′ĭtē) *n.* **cul′pa·bly** *adv.*

cul·prit (kŭl′prĭt) *n.* Person charged with a crime or offense; guilty person; wrongdoer. [orig. in 17th c. legal phrase to prisoner pleading "Not Guilty"; prob. abbreviation of Anglo-Fr. *Cul-*

pable: prest d'averrer etc. (You are) guilty: (I am) ready to prove etc.]

cult (kŭlt) *n.* System or community of religious worship and ritual, esp. one with rites centering around sacred symbols; devotion, homage, to person or thing; object of such devotion; group bound together by devotion to an idea, interest, object, etc.

cul·ti·vate (kŭl'tĭvāt) *v.t.* (**-vat·ed, -vat·ing**). 1. Till; break up (ground) with cultivator to prepare for planting; grow, tend (crops, flowers, etc.). 2. Improve, develop (person, mind, etc., esp. in past part.); pay attention to, cherish; seek the acceptance or good will of. **cul·ti·va·ble** (kŭl'tĭv*a*b*e*l) *adj.* Capable of being cultivated. **cul·ti·va·tion** (kŭltĭvā'sh*o*n) *n.* Cultivating, cultivated state.

cul·ti·va·tor (kŭl'tĭvāt*er*) *n.* 1. Tiller, farmer. 2. Agricultural implement for breaking up ground and uprooting weeds between growing plants.

cul·ture (kŭl'ch*er*) *n.* 1. Tillage; rearing, production (of trees, crops, animals, etc.); (biol.) artificial development of bacteria etc. in specially prepared media; bacteria etc. so produced. 2. Improvement or refinement of mind, manners, etc., by education and training; condition of being thus trained and refined, esp. in the arts. 3. Particular form or type of intellectual development or civilization; ~ **shock**, state of confusion in people who abruptly come into contact with a cultural environment completely different from that to which they are accustomed. **cul·tur·al** (kŭl'ch*u*r*a*l) *adj.* (esp.) ~ **revolution**, movement and vast purge in People's Republic of China, begun in 1965, seeking to restore original purity of Maoist doctrine. **cul'tur·al·ly** *adv.* **culture** *v.t.* (**-tured, -tur·ing**). Cultivate (esp. fig.); (biol.) make a culture of (bacteria etc.); **cultured pearl,** pearl formed by oyster after artificial insertion of foreign body.

Cumberland Gap *was of strategic importance during the U.S. Civil War and was alternately held by Federal and Confederate troops.*

cul·vert (kŭl'v*er*t) *n.* Channel, conduit, carrying water across, under road, canal, etc.

cum (kŭm, ko͝om) *prep.* With; plus; ~ ***gra·no sa·lis*** (kŭm grā'nō sā'lĭs; *Lat.* ko͝om grah'nō sah'lĭs), with skepticism (L., = "with a grain of salt"); **cum lau·de** (ko͝om low'dā, -dē, -d*e*, kŭm law'dē) with honor; used on diplomas to indicate graduation with high rank. Cf. MAGNA CUM LAUDE; SUMMA CUM LAUDE. [L.]

cum. *abbrev.* Cumulative.

cum·ber (kŭm'b*er*) *v.t.* Hamper, hinder; burden. **cum'ber·some** *adj.* Unwieldly, clumsy. **cum'ber·some·ly** *adv.* **cum'ber·some·ness** *n.*

Cum·ber·land (kŭm'b*er*l*a*nd). River flowing from E. Kentucky through Tennessee and Kentucky to the Ohio River; **C~ Gap**, pass through the Cumberland Mountains at the border of Kentucky, Tennessee, and Virginia, used by Daniel Boone and early settlers; **C~ Road**, first national highway in the U.S., started 1811, from Cumberland, Md., to Vandalia, Ill.

cum·brous (kŭm'br*u*s) *adj.* Cumbersome. **cum'brous·ly** *adv.* **cum'brous·ness** *n.*

cum·in, cum·min (kŭm'ĭn) *ns.* Umbelliferous plant (*Cuminum cyminum*) of the parsley family; aromatic seeds of this plant, used as a condiment.

cum·mer·bund (kŭm'*er*bŭnd) *n.* Broad, pleated waist sash worn as part of men's formal dress. [Hind. *kamar-band* loin band]

Cum·mings (kŭm'ĭngz), **Edward Estin** (until the 1930s preferred the lower-case **e. e. cummings**) (1894–1962). Amer. poet; used unique typography and punctuation to indicate rhythmic pattern and meaning in his poetry.

cu·mu·late (kū'my*u*lāt) *v.* (**-lat·ed, -lat·ing**). Accumulate. **cu·mu·la·tion** (kūmy*u*lā'sh*o*n) *n.*

cu·mu·la·tive (kū'my*u*l*a*tĭv) *adj.* Tending to accumulate; increasing in force etc. by successive additions. **cu'mu·la·tive·ly** *adv.* **cu'mu·la·tive·ness** *n.*

Cultivators *take many forms, and may be simple hand-held hoes, or mechanized ploughs driven by tractors.*

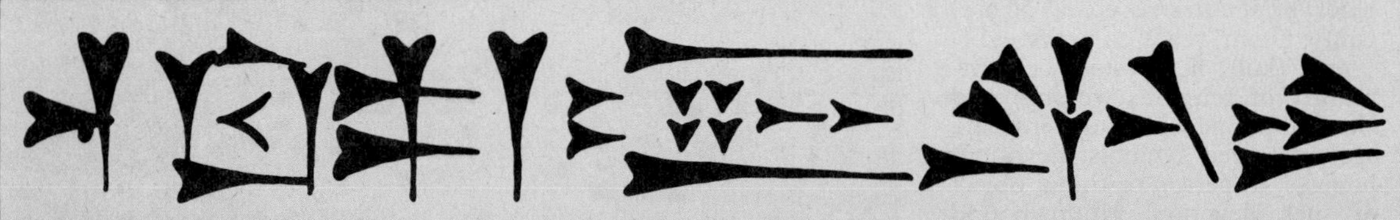

***Cuneiform** lettering is the earliest known form of writing and was used by the Mesopotamians in the 4th and 3rd millennia BC. Many of the characters are purely pictorial.*

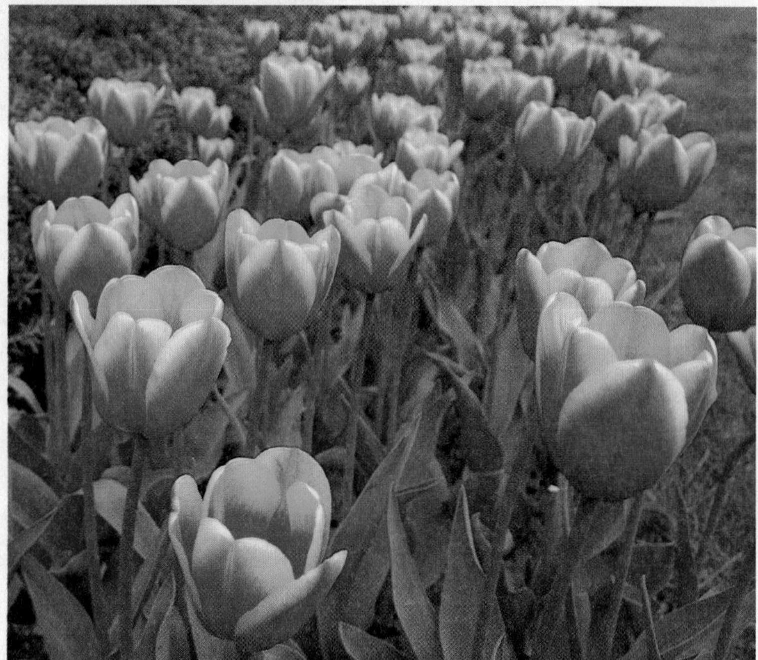

*Tulips in Augusta, Maine, U.S.A. The colorful **cup**-shaped blossom of the tulip makes it a world-wide favorite with horticulturists.*

cu·mu·lo·nim·bus (kūmy*u*lō-nĭm′b*u*s) *n.* (pl. **-bus**). (meteor.) Type of ~ dense cloud, a tall voluminous mass, present in thunderstorms.

cu·mu·lus (kū′my*u*l*u*s) *n.* (pl. **-lus**). (meteor.) Form of CLOUD, usu. low, consisting of rounded masses heaped up on nearly horizontal base, frequent in summer skies.

cu·ne·ate (kū′nēĭt, -āt) *adj.* Wedge-shaped.

cu·ne·i·form (kūnē′ĭf ôrm, kū′nē-) *adj.* Wedge-shaped; composed of wedge-shaped or arrowhead marks used in ancient inscriptions of Assyria, Babylonia, Persia; ~ **bone,** wedge-shaped bone. **cuneiform** *n.* Cuneiform characters or writing impressed in clay in ancient times.

cun·ning (kŭn′ĭng) *n.* Skill, dexterity; skill in deceit or evasion. ~ *adj.* Possessed of or displaying cunning; (colloq.) quaintly pretty. **cun′ning·ly** *adv.* **cun′ning·ness** *n.*

cunt (kŭnt) *n.* (vulg.) 1. Female pudendum. 2. Applied abusively to woman.

cup (kŭp) *n.* 1. Any drinking vessel with or without handle and stem; (esp. in modern use) a small drinking vessel with a handle and having a flat bottom; ornamental cup or other vessel as prize for race or other contest. 2. Rounded cavity, as socket of certain bones, cup-shaped hardened involucre of an acorn, calyx of flower, cup-shaped blossom, etc. 3. Cupful; (as measure in recipes) half pint, 8 fluid ounces; (fig.) something to be partaken of, experience, portion, lot; (pl.) potations; **in one's ~s,** drunk; **one's ~ of tea,** (colloq.) what interests or suits one. 4. Beverage of wine, cider, fruit juice, etc., sweetened and flavored, and usu. iced; **cup′-bearer**, one who serves wine, esp. officer of royal or noble household; **cup′cake,** small cake baked in cup-shaped container and serving one person. **cup** *v.* (**cupped, cup·ping**). Take or contain as in a cup, make or be cup-shaped. **cup′ful** *n.*

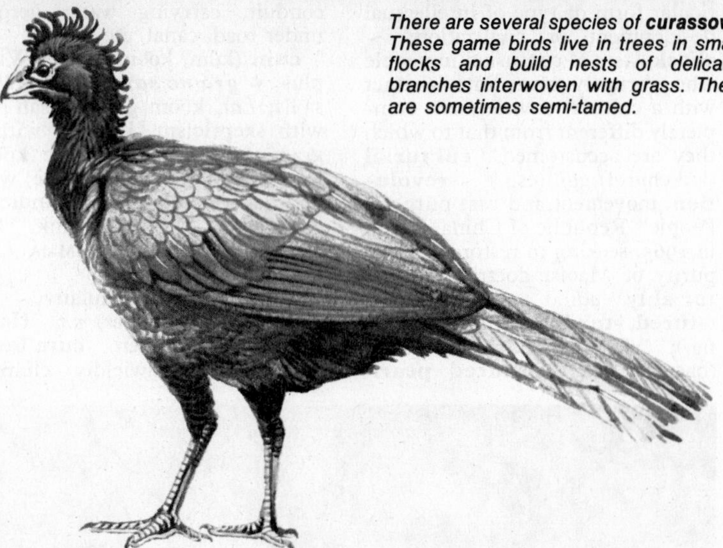

*There are several species of **curassow.** These game birds live in trees in small flocks and build nests of delicate branches interwoven with grass. They are sometimes semi-tamed.*

cup·board (kŭb′*e*rd) *n.* Recess or structure, usu. with shelves and door, for storage of dishes and food.

Cu·pid (kū′pĭd). (Rom. myth.) God of love, son of Venus; identified with the Greek Eros; often represented as a beautiful naked boy with wings, carrying bow and arrows. **~'s bow,** (line or shape resembling) the double-curved bow of Cupid. [L. *cupido* desire, love]

cu·pid·i·ty (kūpĭd′ĭtē) *n.* Greed of gain, avarice.

cu·po·la (kū′p*o*l*a*) *n.* 1. Dome forming the roof of a building or part of a building; diminutive dome above a roof; ceiling of dome. 2. Furnace for melting metals for casting (formerly with dome leading to chimney, now often without dome).

cu·pric (kū′prĭk, ko͞o′-) *adj.* (chem.) Containing copper in bivalent state.

cu·prous (kū′pr*u*s, ko͞o′-) *adj.* (chem.) Containing copper in univalent state.

cu·pule (kū'pūl) *n.* (bot., zool.) Cup-shaped organ, receptacle, etc.

cur (kẽr) *n.* Worthless, lowbred, or snappish dog; mongrel; surly, ill-bred, or cowardly fellow.

Cu·ra·çao (kūr'*a*sō, koor'*a*sow). Dutch island in Caribbean off the NW. coast of Venezuela; main island of the Netherlands Antilles; capital: Willemstad; **curaçao** *n.* Liqueur flavored with peel of bitter oranges, first produced in Curaçao.

cu·ra·cy (kūr'*a*sē) *n.* (pl. **-cies**). Curate's office, duties, or term of office.

cu·ra·re, cu·ra·ri (ky*u*rār'ē, k*u*-) *ns.* Blackish-brown resinous bitter poisonous substance extracted from S. Amer. tropical plants (esp. *Strychnos toxifera*), used by Indians to poison their arrows, and consisting of various alkaloids that block the action of the motor nerves on skeletal muscle. [corrupt. of *wurali*, native Carib name]

cu·ras·sow (kūr'*a*sō, ky*u*răs'ō) *n.* Any of several long-tailed tropical Amer. game birds of the family Cracidae, related to domestic fowl and pheasants.

cu·rate (kūr'ĭt) *n.* 1. (chiefly Brit.) Clergyman who assists or is deputy of a vicar or rector. 2. (archaic) Clergyman in charge of a parish; parish priest.

cur·a·tive (kūr'*a*tĭv) *adj.* & *n.* (Thing) tending to cure (esp. disease).

cu·ra·tor (ky*u*rā'ter, kūr'ā-) *n.* Person in charge, manager, of museum, library, etc. **cu·ra·to·ri·al** (kūr*a*tōr'ē*a*l, -tōr'-) *adj.* **cu·ra'tor·ship** *n.*

curb (kẽrb) *n.* 1. Chain, strap, passing under lower jaw of horse, used as check; (fig.) check, restraint. 2. Hard swelling on back of horse's hind leg. 3. Concrete or stone edging along the side of a street and forming part of the gutter. ~ *v.t.* Apply curb to; restrain.

cur·cu·ma (kẽr'ky*u*m*a*) *n.* Tuberous plant of genus *C*~ yielding arrowroot, turmeric, etc. [Arab. *kurkum* saffron, turmeric]

curd (kẽrd) *n.* (often pl.) Coagulated substance formed (naturally or artificially) by action of acids on milk, made into cheese or eaten as food; anything resembling this. **curd'y** *adj.* (**curd·i·er, curd·i·est**).

cur·dle (kẽr'd*e*l) *v.* (**-dled, -dling**). Congeal, form into curd; ~ **the blood**, horrify, terrify.

cure (kūr) *n.* 1. Remedy; course of medical or other treatment (esp. of specified kind); successful medical treatment, restoration to health; ~**-all** (*n.*) panacea. 2. Spiritual charge or care of parishioners etc.; parish etc. **cure** *v.* (**cured, cur·ing**). Restore to health; remedy (an evil). 2. Preserve (meat, fruit, hides) by salting, drying, smoking, etc. 3. Render (substance) harder or more durable. **cur'a·ble** *adj.* **cur·a·bil·i·ty** (kūr*a*bĭl'ĭtē) *n.*

cu·ré (ky*u*rā', kūr'ā) *n.* Parish priest in France etc.

cu·ret, cu·rette (ky*u*rĕt') *ns.* Sugeon's small scoop-like instrument. **curet** *v.t.* Scrape with curet. **cu·ret·tage** (kūr*e*tahzh', kūr'*e*tahzh) *n.* Process of curetting, esp. tissue from the uterus.

cur·few (kẽr'fū) *n.* 1. Medieval regulation for extinction of fires at fixed hour in evening (orig. for prevention of conflagrations); hour for this, bell announcing it. 2. Signal or time after which all inhabitants, or specified groups (as young people), must be indoors.

cu·ri·a (kūr'ē*a*, koor'-) *n.* (pl. **cu·ri·ae** pr. kūr'ēē, -ī, koor'ēī). 1. (Rom. hist.) One of the ten divisions of each of the three ancient Roman tribes; building belonging to such division, serving primarily for worship. 2. Senate house at Rome; senate of ancient Italian towns. 3. Court of justice, esp. under feudal organization. 4. (**C**~) Papal court, government departments of the Vatican. **cu'ri·al** *adj.*

cu·rie (kūr'ē) *n.* Unit of radioactivity equal to 3.7×10^{10} disintegrations per second. [f. CURIE]

Cu·rie (kūr'ē, kyŏorē'), **Marie** (1867–1934). Original name, Marja Sklodowska; Polish-born French physical chemist; discovered polonium and radium, isolated radium from pitchblende, and investigated radioactivity; was awarded Nobel Prize for physics, with her husband, Pierre, 1903, and Nobel Prize for chemistry, 1911; died of leukemia caused by radiation; her husband, **Pierre Curie** (1859–1906), French chemist, conducted research on magnetism; worked on radioactivity with his wife Marie and was awarded Nobel Prize for physics with her, 1903; their daughter,

*The **cupola** is the small dome most usually seen at the top of a large domed structure. In the Italian town of Alverobella in Apulia, however, all the houses are built with cupolas in stone and without cement.*

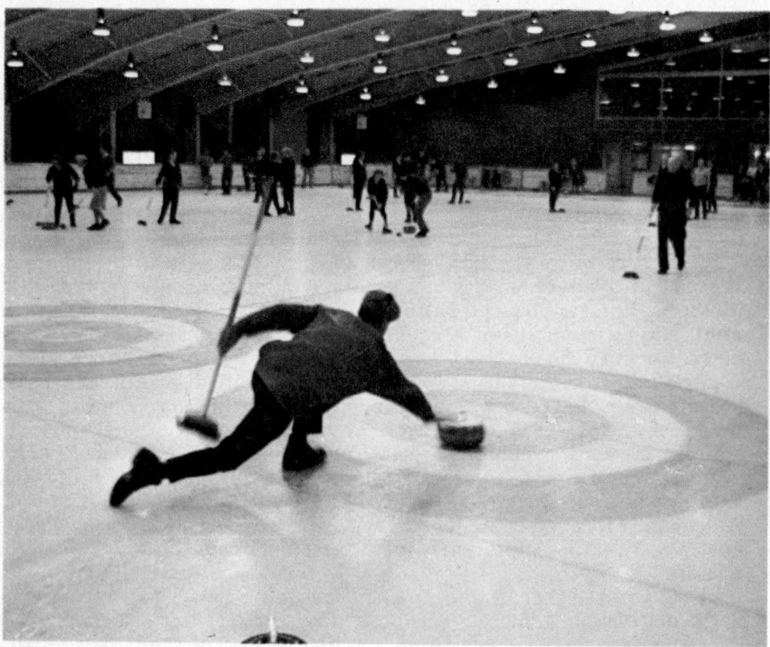

Two Bruegel paintings have been used as evidence that **curling,** a Scottish game, originated in Holland. But, Holland has no granite curling-stones.

Irene Curie (1897–1956), physicist, shared Nobel Prize with her husband, Frederic Joliot (later Joliot-Curie), 1935, in chemistry, for synthesis of new radioactive elements.

cu·ri·o (kūr'ēō') *n.* (pl. **-os**). Curious object of art or piece of bric-a-brac.

cu·ri·o·sa (kūrēō'sa) *n.pl.* Curiosities, esp. books, pamphlets, etc. dealing with unusual subjects; erotica.

cu·ri·os·i·ty (kūrēŏs'ĭtē) *n.* (pl. **-ties**). 1. Inquisitiveness; desire to know. 2. Strangeness; strange or rare object.

cu·ri·ous (kūr'ēus) *adj.* 1. Inquisitive; eager to learn. 2. Strange, surprising. **cu'ri·ous·ly** *adv.* **cu'ri·ous·ness** *n.*

cu·ri·um (kūr'ēum) *n.* (chem.) Radioactive metallic transuranic element; symbol Cm, at. no. 96, principal isotope at. wt. 242. [f. CURIE]

curl (kērl) *n.* Spiral or convolute lock of hair; anything spiral or incurved; act of curling; state of being curled. ~ *v.* 1. Bend, coil, into spiral or curved shape; move in spiral or curved form. 2. Play at CURLING. **curl'er** *n.* (esp.) Pin, clip, etc., for curling the hair. **curl'y** *adj.* (**curl·i·er, curl·i·est**). **curl'i·ness** *n.*

cur·lew (kēr'lo͞o) *n.* (pl. **-lews**, collect. **-lew**). Wading shore bird of the genus *Numenius*, esp. the long-billed curlew (*N. americanus*), with long slender curved bill.

curl·i·cue (kēr'lĭkū) *n.* Decorative curl or twist.

curl·ing (kēr'lĭng) *n.* (esp.) 1. Scottish game played on ice with large stones that are hurled along a rink toward a tee; ~ **stone**, oblate stone used in this, of polished granite, and not more than 36 in. in circumference or 50 lb. in weight, with an iron or wooden handle on the upper surface. 2. ~ **iron**, tongs for curling the hair.

cur·mudg·eon (kermŭj'on) *n.* Churlish or miserly fellow. **cur·mudg'eon·ly** *adv.*

cur·rant (kēr'ant, kŭr'-) *n.* 1. Small seedless raisin grown in California and eastern Mediterranean regions, used in cooking. 2. Small red, black, or greenish fruit of any of various prickly shrubs of genus *Ribes* having a sour taste and used for making jelly. 3. Shrub bearing such fruit. [orig. *raisins of Corauntz* (Corinth)]

cur·ren·cy (kēr'ensē, kŭr'-) *n.* (pl. **-cies**). 1. Time during which thing is current; (of money) circulation; (of words, ideas, etc.) prevalence. 2. Money in actual use in a country; **hard, soft,** ~: see HARD, SOFT.

cur·rent (kēr'ent, kŭr'-) *adj.* In general circulation or use; popular, in vogue; (of time) now passing; belonging to, of the current time. **cur'rent·ly** *adv.* **current** *n.* 1. Running stream; water, air, etc., moving in given direction. 2. Course, tendency (of events, opinions, etc.). 3. Transmission of electricity, electricity transmitted, through a body.

cur·ri·cle (kēr'ĭkel, kŭr'-) *n.* Light open two-wheeled carriage drawn by two horses abreast.

cur·ric·u·lum (kurĭk'yulum) *n.* (pl. **-lums, -la** pr. -*la*). 1. Course (of study); all courses offered by a school or college; series of courses leading to a particular degree or certificate. 2. ~ **vitae,** brief account of one's career; resumé. **cur·ric'u·lar** *adj.* [L.]

cur·ri·er (kēr'ēer, kŭr'-) *n.* One who dresses and colors tanned leather.

Cur·ri·er (kēr'ēer, kŭr'-) **and Ives** (īvz). **Nathaniel Currier** (1813–88) and **James Merritt Ives** (1824–95). Partners in an Amer. lithographing company famous for vivid prints depicting Amer. events, life, and people.

cur·ry[1] (kēr'ē, kŭr'ē) *n.* (pl. **-ries**). Curry powder; dish of meat, fish, fruit, or vegetables, cooked with curry powder and usu. served with rice; ~ **powder**, preparation of turmeric and strong spices for making curries. **curry** *v.t.* (**-ried, -ry·ing**). Make into curry; season with curry powder. [Tamil *kari* sauce]

cur·ry[2] (kēr'ē, kŭr'ē) *v.t.* (**-ried, -ry·ing**). 1. Rub down or dress (horse etc.) with comb; dress (tanned leather) by soaking, scraping, beating, coloring, etc.; ~ **favor** (orig. *favel*, f. OF. *fauvel* chestnut horse), ingratiate oneself (*with* person) by officious courtesy etc.; **cur'rycomb**, comb for currying horses etc.; (*v.t.*) curry.

The **curlew** (Numenius arquata) is 1½–2 ft long with a bill 5–7 ins. Species are found in Europe, America, Africa, and Australia. They perform strange dances and have odd courtship rites.

*The **custard apple** is the name used for the fruit of some trees in the genus Anona. Other varieties may be called sweetsops and bullock's hearts.*

curse (kẽrs) *n.* 1. Utterance (by deity or person invoking deity) supposed or intended to consign person or thing to destruction, divine vengeance, etc.; formal ecclesiastical censure, sentence of excommunication. 2. Profane oath, imprecation. 3. Evil inflicted in response to curse; great evil, bane. ~ *v.* (**cursed, curst, curs·ing**). Utter curse against; excommunicate; afflict *with*; utter curses; swear profanely.

curs·ed (kẽr'sĭd) *adj.* (esp.) Damnable, abominable. **curs'ed·ly** *adv.* **curs'ed·ness** *n.*

cur·sive (kẽr'sĭv) *adj.* & *n.* (Writing) done in a flowing style, with the characters joined together.

cur·so·ri·al (kersōr'ēal, -sōr'-) *adj.* (zool., of birds etc.). Having limbs adapted for running.

cur·so·ry (kẽr'serē) *adj.* Hasty, superficial. **cur'so·ri·ly** *adv.* **cur'so·ri·ness** *n.*

curt (kẽrt) *adj.* Discourteously brief; terse, concise. **curt'ly** *adv.* **curt'ness** *n.*

cur·tail (kertāl') *v.t.* Cut short. **cur·tail'ment** *n.*

cur·tain (kẽr'tĭn) *n.* 1. Suspended cloth used as screen esp. at window; screen separating state of theater from auditorium; (fig.) = IRON curtain. 2. Partition, cover, in various technical senses; (mil.) barrage. 3. (pl., colloq.) The end. 4. ~ **call**, call for actor to appear before curtain after play or scene of play to take bow and receive applause; ~ **raiser**, short opening piece performed before principal play in theater; ~ **rod**, horizontal rod from which curtain is hung. **curtain** *v.t.* Furish, cover, shut *off*, with curtains.

Cur·tis (kẽr'tĭs), **Charles** (1860–1936). Vice president of the U.S. under Herbert Hoover, 1929–1933.

Cur·tiss (kẽr'tĭs), **Glen Hammond** (1878–1930). Amer. aviation pioneer; designer and manufacturer of engines, motorcycles, speedboats, and airplanes; accomplished first U.S. airplane flight of 1 mi. distance, 1908; held early airplane speed records; developed hydroplane and flying boat.

curt·sy, curt·sey (kẽrt'sē) *ns.* (pl. **-sies, -seys**). Feminine bow of respect or salutation, made by placing one foot behind the other and bending the knees so that trunk is lowered (usu. **make a** ~). ~ *v.i.* (**-sied, -sy·ing, -sey·ing**). Make curtsy (*to* person).

cur·va·ture (kẽr'vacher) *n.* Curving; curved form; (geom.) amount or rate of deviation (of curve) from straight line or curved surface from plane.

curve (kẽrv) *n.* 1. Line of which no part is straight, locus traced by moving point, the direction of whose motion continuously changes or deviates from a straight line; curved form or thing; (on graph or diagram) line drawn from point to point so as to represent diagrammatically a continuous variation of quantity, force, etc. 2. (baseball) (also ~ **ball**) pitched ball that curves as it approaches the batter. ~ *v.* (**curved, curv·ing**). Bend or shape so as to form curve; make, travel in a curve; (baseball) pitch a curve ball to.

cur·vet (kervĕt', kẽr'vĭt) *n.* Horse's leap from rearing position, with hind legs outstretched before forelegs reach ground. ~ *v.i.* (**-vet·ted, -vet·ed, -vet·ting, -vet·ing**). (of horse or rider) Make curvet.

cur·vi·lin·e·ar (kẽrvĭlĭn'ēer) *adj.* Contained by, consisting of, curved line(s). **cur·vi·lin'e·ar·ly** *adv.*

cu·sec (kū'sĕk) *n.* Unit of flow of liquids, one cubic foot per second.

Cush (kŭsh). Oldest son of Ham; **land of C**~, ancient legendary region in Africa, identified with Ethiopia, settled by descendants of Cush.

Cush·ing (kŏŏsh'ĭng), **Harvey William** (1869–1939). Amer. physician specializing in brain surgery; awarded Pulitzer Prize, 1925.

cush·ion (kŏŏsh'on) *n.* 1. Case of cloth etc. filled with soft material or air, for sitting, kneeling, or reclining on or against. 2. Elastic lining or rim of inner side of billiard table, from which the balls rebound; soft buffer; body of air or stream as buffer or support. ~ *v.* Furnish, protect, with cushions; (fig.) protect against shock, mitigate effects of.

cush·y (kŏŏsh'ē) *adj.* (**cush·i·er, cush·i·est**). (slang; of job, task, etc.) Easy, pleasant, well paid. [Hind. *khush* pleasant]

cusp (kŭsp) *n.* Apex, peak; (geom.) point at which two branches of curve meet and stop; (archit.) projecting point between small arcs in tracery; (astrol.) initial point of house; (bot.) pointed end, esp. of leaf. **cus·pate** (kŭs'pĭt, -pāt), **cusped** (kŭspt), **cus·pi·date** (kŭs'pĭdāt), **cus'pi·dat·ed** *adjs.*

cus·pi·dor (kŭs'pĭdōr) *n.* Spittoon.

cuss (kŭs) *v.* (colloq.) Curse. ~ *n.* (colloq.) Curse; person (esp. an odd or perverse one). **cuss'ed·ness** *n.* Peversity.

cus·tard (kŭs'terd) *n.* Dish of beaten eggs and milk, baked or cooked; ~ **apple**, fruit of S. Amer. and W. Ind. tree (*Anona reticulata*) with dark brown rind and yellowish pulp like custard in appearance and flavor.

Cus·ter (kŭs'ter), **William Armstrong** (1839–76). Amer. army officer; Union general and cavalry hero during Civil War; active on western patrol duty and in Indian fighting; killed with all of his troops by Sioux Indians led by Sitting Bull and Crazy Horse at battle of Little Big Horn, 1876, famous as "Custer's Last Stand."

cus·to·di·al (kŭstō'dēal) *adj.* Relating to custody.

cus·to·di·an (kŭstō'dēan) *n.* Guardian, keeper, esp. of public building etc.

cus·to·dy (kŭs'todē) *n.* (pl. **-dies**). Guardianship, care; imprisonment, legal detention.

cus·tom (kŭs'tom) *n.* 1. Usual practice; (law) established usage having the force of law. 2. (pl.) Duty levied on imports from foreign countries; **Customs**, government agency collecting such duties; **custom(s) house**, office (esp. in seaport) at which customs are collected. 3. Business patronage, as of a store; **custom-made clothes**, clothes made to measure (so **~-made suit** etc.). 4. **~-built**, (*adj.*) built to customer's order.

cus·tom·ar·y (kŭs'tomĕrē) *adj.* Usual; (law) subject to, held by, custom (of a property etc.). **cus·tom·ar·i·ly** (kŭstomĕr'ĭlē, kŭs'tomĕr-) *adv.*

cus·tom·er (kŭs'tomer) *n.* Buyer, purchaser; patron, shopper; (slang) (**cool, tough, ugly**, etc. ~), person to be dealt with.

cut (kŭt) *v.* (**cut, cut·ting**). 1. Penetrate, wound, with edged instrument (also fig.); divide with knife etc. (*in, into*, pieces etc.); detach by cutting; carve (meat). 2. Cross, intersect; pass *across, through*, etc.; (slang) leave, go quickly. 3. Reduce by cutting (hair etc.); reduce (wages, price, time, etc.); shape, fashion, by cutting; edit (film); (motion pictures) make quick transition *to* next shot. 4. Perform, execute, make, as **~ a caper, figure**, etc. 5. Divide (pack of cards) into two or more parts and combine them into new order to prevent cheating or before drawing cards to select dealer or partners, etc. 6. (tennis) Strike ball across its line of flight so as to impart spin etc; (baseball) swing (*at* a pitched ball). 7. Renounce acquaintance of (person), decline to recognize him or her; absent oneself from, avoid, renounce. 8. Have (tooth) appear through gum. 9. **~ corners**, pass around corner(s) closely or go over them; (fig.) take unorthodox course, omit details to save time; act illegally; **~ down**, bring or throw down by cutting; reduce (expenses etc.); **~ in**, enter abruptly, interpose, supersede a partner during a dance; obstruct path of vehicle by moving sharply in front of it after overtaking; **~ it out** (slang) stop, cease; **~ off**, remove by cutting; bring to an end; intercept, interrupt (supplies, communications); exclude (*from*); obstruct path of oncoming vehicle by moving out from one's own side of the road; **~ out**, remove by cutting; outdo or supplant (rival); shape by cutting (out of a piece); form, fashion (esp. fig. in past part.); disconnect; (slang) leave, depart; separate (cattle) from herd, select; **have one's work ~ out**, have a difficult task; **~ up**, cut in pieces; (slang) criticize severely; (boxing) lacerate

*The **cuttlefish** is a salt-water invertebrate related to the octopus and sometimes confused with the squid; its distinguishing feature is the cuttlebone. There are about 100 species inhabiting mainly shallow coastal waters. The eggs of the common cuttlefish (above) are laid on pieces of coral, plants or on the tubes of marine worms.*

(opponent's face); play pranks; behave in a silly manner. 10. **~ and dried**, (of opinions etc.) ready-made, lacking freshness; **cut'away**, man's formal coat cut to taper toward the tails; **cut'back** (*n.*), reduction of expenditures etc., pruning; **cut'off**, shorter channel or route cutting off bend etc., bypass; **cut'out**, device for automatically disconnecting (electric circuit etc.); **cut'purse** (archaic) thief; **cut'throat** (*n.*) murderer; bloodthirsty ruffian; (*adj.*) intensive, merciless; **cut'worm**, caterpillar that cuts off young plants level with ground. **cut** *n.* 1. Act of cutting; stroke, blow, with knife, sword, whip; act, speech, deeply wounding the feelings; excision of a part; reduction in wages, prices, time, etc. 2. Particular stroke in tennis or baseball (see *v.* def. 6). 3. Avoiding, renouncing of acquaintance. 4. Passage or way across, esp. as opposed to going round about (**short'cut**). 5. Way something is cut. 6. Wound made by cutting; incision, slash. 7. Passage, channel, opening. 8. Engraved plate or wood block used for printing. 9. Piece, esp. of meat, cut off. 10. (slang) Share (of profit etc.). 11. Unexcused absence from school or a particular class. 12. **a ~ above**, (colloq.) Slightly better than.

cu·ta·ne·ous (kūtā'nēus) *adj.* Of the skin.

cute (kūt) *adj.* (**cut·er, cut·est**). Affectedly clever or pretty, precious; (colloq.) pleasingly personable and pert; shrewd. **cute'ly** *adv.* **cute'ness** *n.*

cut·i·cle (kū'tĭkel) *n.* Epidermis or other superficial skin; dead skin at base of fingernail or toenail; (bot.) continuous layer of impervious material secreted by cells of epidermis. **cu·tic·u·lar** (kūtĭk'yuler) *adj.*

cut·ie (kū'tē) *n.* (slang) Attrac-

Several kinds of small vessel are referred to as ***cutters.*** *That shown, a gaff cutter, was quite fast and used as an auxiliary to a war fleet or in the prevention of smuggling.*

The ***cyclamen*** *originated in the Mediterranean region. Of the 15 or so species,* ***Cyclamen Indicum*** *has become the most popular as a hardy indoor plant.*

tive young woman; cute person.

cu·tis (kū′tĭs) *n.* (pl. **-tes** pr. -tēz, **-tis·es**). (anat.) True skin or dermis.

cut·lass, cut·las (kŭt′l*a*s) *ns.* Short sword with slightly curved blade, esp. that formerly used by sailors.

cut·ler (kŭt′l*er*) *n.* One who makes or deals in knives and similar utensils. **cut·ler·y** (kŭt′lerē) *n.* Trade of cutler; things made or sold by cutlers; household knives, forks, and spoons.

cut·let (kŭt′lĭt) *n.* 1. Thinly sliced meat, esp. lamb or veal, suitable for frying or broiling. 2. Small flat croquette of minced meat, fish, or fowl.

cut·ter (kŭt′*er*) *n.* 1. Person, thing, that cuts; cutting part of machine. 2. Boat belonging to ship of war, fitted for rowing and sailing; small single–masted vessel rigged like sloop but with running bowsprit; fast armed motorboat used by the Coast Guard; small light sleigh, usu. drawn by one horse.

cut·ting (kŭt′ĭng) *n.* (esp.) 1. Excavation, as of high ground for railroad, road, etc. 2. Piece cut from plant for propagation. ~ *adj.* (esp.) That wounds the mind or feelings. **cut′ting·ly** *adv.*

cut·tle·fish (kŭt′*e*lfĭsh) *n.* (pl. **~fishes**, collect. **~fish**). Squid-like cephalopod of genus *Sepia*, esp. *S. officinalis*, which when pursued ejects black fluid from a sac and darkens water.

Cu·vi·er (ko͞o′vēā, ko͞ovyā′), **Georges Léopold Chrétien Fréderic Dagobert** (1769–1832). French naturalist; a founder of comparative anatomy and paleontology.

CWO *abbrev.* Chief warrant officer.

cwt. *abbrev.* Hundredweight.

-cy *suffix.* Forming nouns indicating: condition or quality (*vagrancy, idiocy*); rank or office (*presidency*).

cy·an (sī′ăn, -*a*n) *adj.* & *n.* (Greenish blue) color.

cy·an·ic (sīăn′ĭk) *adj.* 1. Blue. 2. ~ **acid,** colorless poisonous pungent volatile unstable liquid (HCNO).

cy·a·nide (sī′*a*nīd) *n.* Salt of hydrocyanic acid (HCN), compound of cyanide group CN with organic radical, as **potassium** ~ (KCN); ~ **process,** extraction of gold and silver from ore with dilute solution of sodium cyanide.

cy·an·o·gen (sīăn′*o*j*e*n) *n.* Colorless inflammable highly poisonous gas (C_2N_2).

cy·a·no·sis (sī*a*nō′sĭs) *n.* (path.) Blueness of skin caused by presence of large quantities of deoxygenated blood in its minute vessels. **cy·a·not·ic** (sī*a*nŏt′ĭk) *adj.*

Cyb·e·le (sĭb′*e*lē). (myth.) Anatolian mother-goddess, worshipped esp. in Phrygia and later in Greece with her consort Attis.

cy·ber·na·tion (sīb*e*rnā′sh*o*n) *n.* Control by machines.

cy·ber·net·ics (sīb*e*rnĕt′ĭks) *n.* Theory, study, of communication and control in living organisms and machines.

cy·cad (sī′kăd) *n.* (bot.) Plant of family Cycadaceae, related to conifers, but resembling palms, the trunk of which yields sago. **cyc·a·da·ceous** (sĭk*a*dā′sh*u*s) *adj.*

Cyc·la·des (sĭk′l*a*dēz). Circular group of Greek islands in the S. Aegean. **Cy·clad·ic** (sĭklăd′ĭk, sī-) *adj.*

cy·cla·mate (sī′kl*a*māt, sĭk′l*a*-) *n.* Salt of cyclohexylsulphamic acid ($C_6H_{11}\cdot NH\cdot SO_3H$), with sweetening properties.

cy·cla·men (sī′kl*a*m*e*n, sĭk′l*a*-) *n.* Primulaceous plant of genus *C*~ with fleshy rootstocks, cultivated for its early-blooming flowers; pinkish red color.

cy·cle (sī′k*e*l) *n.* 1. Recurrent period (of events, phenomena, etc.); period of a thing's completion; (phys. etc.) recurring series of operations or states; one complete oscillation; esp. (elect.) short form for ~ **per second,** frequently of an alternating current or potential (abbrev. c/s and cps). 2. Complete set or series; series of poems or songs dealing with central event, character, or idea. 3. (colloq.) Motorcycle, bicycle, or tricycle. ~ *v.i.* (**-cled, -cling**). 1. Move in cycles. 2. Ride cycle.

cy·clic (sī′klĭk, sĭk′lĭk), **cy·cli·**

cal (sī'klĭk*a*l, sĭk'lĭ-) *adjs.* 1. Recurring in cycles; belonging to a definite chronological cycle. 2. Of a cycle of mythic and heroic stories. 3. (bot., of flower) With its parts arranged in whorls. 4. (math.) Of a circle or cycle. 5. (chem., *-ic*) With the constituent atoms in a ring formation.

cy·clist (sī'klĭst) *n.* Rider of a cycle.

cy·cloid (sī'kloid) *n.* Curve traced in space by point in circumference or on radius of a circle as the circle rolls along a straight line. **cy·cloi'dal** *adj.*

cy·clom·e·ter (sīklŏm'*e*t*e*r) *n.* 1. Instrument for measuring circular arcs. 2. Apparatus attached to wheel of bicycle etc. for measuring distance traversed.

cy·clone (sī'klōn) *n.* 1. System of winds rotating rapidly around region of low barometric pressure, usu. accompanied by heavy rain and severe storm conditions. 2. Loosely, any severe storm, such as TORNADO. **cy·clon·ic** (sīklŏn'ĭk) *adj.*

Cy·clo·pe·an (sīkl*o*pē'*a*n, sīklō'pē-) *adj.* 1. Of, like, a Cyclops; huge. 2. Applied to an ancient style of masonry of immense irregular stones, found in Greece, Italy, etc., and anciently supposed to be the work of the Cyclops.

cy·clo·pe·di·a, cy·clo·pae·di·a (sīkl*o*pē'dē*a*) *ns.* = ENCYCLOPEDIA. **cy·clo·pe'dic, cy·clo·pae'dic** *adjs.*

Cy·clops (sī'klŏps) *n.* (pl. **Cy·clo·pes** pr. sīklō'pēz, **Cy·clops, Cy·clop·ses** pr. sī'klŏpsĭz). (Gk. myth.) One of a race of one-eyed giants who inhabited an island and forged thunderbolts for Zeus.

cy·clo·ra·ma (sīkl*o*răm'*a*, -rah'm*a*) *n.* Circular panorama; curved back of stage.

cy·clo·tron (sī'kl*o*trŏn, sĭk'l*o*-) *n.* (phys.) Apparatus for accelerating charged atomic particles, moving in a widening spiral, by passing them repeatedly through the same electromagnetic field.

cyg·net (sĭg'nĭt) *n.* Young swan.

cyl·in·der (sĭl'ĭnd*e*r) *n.* 1. (geom.) Solid or surface generated by straight line moving parallel to a fixed straight line and tracing a closed curve, esp. a circle, with one of its points. 2. Roller-shaped body, hollow or solid. 3. Cylindrical part of various machines, esp. chamber in which liquids or gases can exert pressure on a moving piston; roller used in printing to receive impression, carrying printing plates, etc.; ~ **lock,** one operated by revolving one barrel inside another.

cy·lin·dri·cal (sĭlĭn'drĭk*a*l) *adj.* Cylinder-shaped.

cy·ma (sī'm*a*) *n.* (pl. **-mae** pr. -mē, **-mas**). (archit.) Molding with double continuous curve.

cym·bal (sĭm'b*a*l) *n.* One of a pair of concave brass or bronze plates, stuck together to make ringing sound or singly with drumstick etc.

cyme (sīm) *n.* (bot.) Inflorescence in which primary axis bears single terminal flower that develops first, system being continued by axes of secondary and higher orders. **cy·mose** (sī'mōs, sīmōs') *adj.*

Cym·ric (kĭm'rĭk, sĭm'rĭk), **Kym·ric** (kĭm'rĭk) *adjs.* Of or pertaining to the Cymry. ~ *ns.* The Celtic languages of the Welsh, Cornish, and Bretons. [Welsh *Cymru* Wales, *Cymry* the Welsh]

Cym·ry, Cym·ri (kĭm'rē, sĭm'rē), **Kym·ry** (kĭm'rē) *ns.* Branch of the Celtic people, comprising the Welsh, Cornish, and Bretons.

Cyn·e·wulf (kĭn'*e*wŏŏlf). Anglo-Saxon poet of the latter part of the 8th c.

This mobile home has been wrecked by the force of a ***cyclone*** *passing through the area. Millions of dollars worth of damage occurs each year in cyclone areas.*

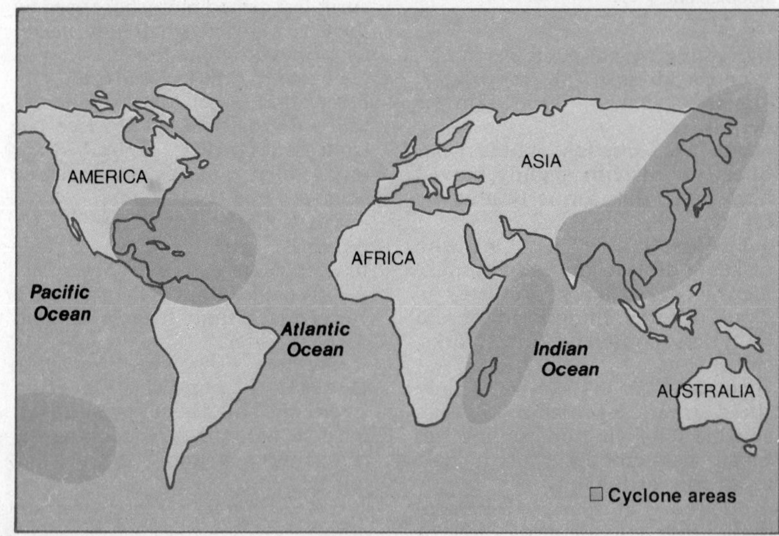

Tropical ***cyclones*** *usually occur towards the end of the hot season. The winds spiral inwards and attain speeds of 100 m.p.h. or more and are accompanied by torrential rains. This type of storm may also be called a typhoon or hurricane.*

The various evergreen trees known as ***cypresses*** *are indigenous to southern Europe, Asia, and North America. Right: The Italian cypress (Cupressus sempervirens) Left: Louisiana cypress trees on the Grant Canal.*

cyn·ic (sĭn′ĭk) *n.* 1. (**C~**) Philosopher of an ancient Greek sect, founded by Antisthenes, whose teachings showed contempt for ease, wealth, and the enjoyments of life. 2. One who sarcastically discredits the sincerity or goodness of human motives and actions. ~ *adj.* 1. (**C~**) Of, characteristic of, Cynic philosophers. 2. Cynical. **cyn′i·cal** *adj.* Incredulous of human goodness; sneering. **cyn′i·cal·ly** *adv.* **cyn·i·cism** (sĭn′ĭsĭzem) *n.* [Gk. *kuōn kunos* dog, nickname for cynic]

cy·no·sure (sī′noshoor, sĭn′*o*-) *n.* Center of attraction or admiration. [Gk. *Kunosoura* (lit., = "dog's tail") constellation Ursa Minor, containing polestar]

Cyn·thi·a (sĭn′thē*a*). (Gk. and Rom. myth.) Artemis, said to have been born on Mt. Cynthus. [L. *Cynthia* (*dea*) the Cynthian goddess]

cy·pher (sī′f*er*) (Brit.) = CIPHER.

cy·press (sī′prĭs) *n.* Coniferous tree of genus *Cupressus*, esp. the Monterey cypress (*C. macrocarpa*) of the Southwest, with hard durable wood and dense dark foliage; its wood; the bold cypress (*Taxodium distichum*) of southeastern U.S. and Mexico is not a true cypress.

Cyp·ri·an (sĭp′rēan) *adj.* & *n.* 1. Cypriote. 2. (archaic) Licentious (person).

cyp·ri·noid (sĭp′rĭnoid, sĭprī′-noid) *adj.* & *n.* (Fish) resembling or allied to carp, of the division Cyprinoidea.

Cyp·ri·ote (sĭp′rēōt, -*o*t), **Cyp·ri·ot** (sĭp′rēot) *adjs.* & *ns.* (Native, inhabitant, Greek dialect) of Cyprus.

Cy·prus (sī′pr*u*s). Island in E. Mediterranean famous in ancient times for worship of Aphrodite; captured by the Turks 1570; from 1878 administered by Gt. Britain; taken over as British colony 1914; republic since 1960; member State of the British Commonwealth; ethnically divided into 82% Greek and 18% Turkish population; capital, Nicosia.

Cyr·e·na·ic (sĭrenā′ĭk, sīr*e*-) *adj.* & *n.* (Philosopher) of the hedonistic school of Aristippus of Cyrene.

Cyr·e·na·i·ca (sĭrenā′ĭk*a*, sīr*e*-). District of NE. Libya.

Cy·re·ne (sīrē′nē). Ancient

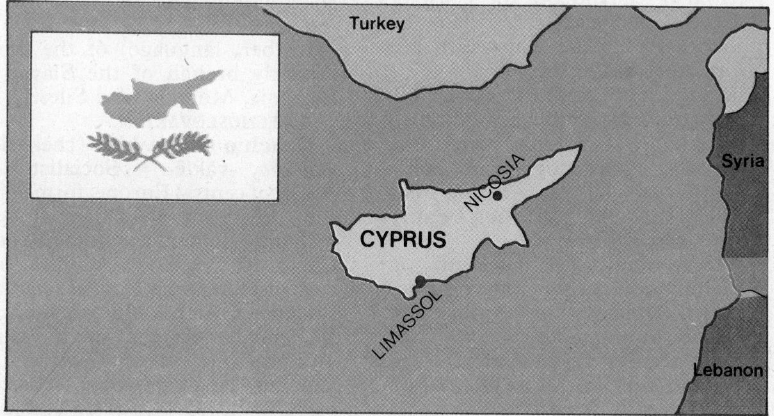

The Mediterranean island of ***Cyprus*** *has a mixed community of both Greek and Turkish 'Cypriots', each with differing religions. Above left: A woman basket-weaver at Mesoyi.*

Above: Prague, Old Town Square. ***Czechoslovakia*** *is rich in its historical associations, particularly in its architecture. Its mineral resources include silver-mines. Both industry and agriculture are important.*

Greek colony in what is now Libya.

Cyr·il (sĭr′ĭl), **Saint** (827–69). Greek Christian theologian; apostle to Slavs; reputed inventor of Cyrillic alphabet in which he and his brother, Methodius, translated the Gospels.

Cy·ril·lic (sĭrĭl′ĭk) *adj.* & *n.* (Of) the alphabet, based on Greek uncials, used by Slavonic peoples of the Eastern Church, attributed to St. CYRIL (who in fact devised the GLAGOLITIC alphabet); now used with modifications for Russian, Bulgarian, some other Slavic languages, and other languages in the U.S.S.R.

Cy·rus (sīr′*u*s), "the Great," d. 529 B.C. Founder of the Persian Empire; subdued the Greek cities of Asia Minor and conquered the Babylonians.

cyst (sĭst) *n.* (biol.) Hollow organ, bladder, etc., in animal or plant, containing liquid secretion; (path.) sac containing morbid matter, parasitic larva, etc.; cell containing embryo etc. **cyst′ic** *adj.* Of the urinary bladder; of the gall bladder; of the nature of a cyst; ~ **fibrosis**, hereditary disease affecting mucous glands, usu. appearing in young children and interfering with digestion and respiration.

cys·ti·tis (sĭstī′tĭs) *n.* Inflammation of the bladder.

Cyth·er·a (sĭth′*er*a). (mod. Gk. *Kithira*) Island off the coast of the Peloponnese, sacred to the goddess Aphrodite, who was thence surnamed Cytherea.

cyto-, cyt- *comb. forms.* Cell.

cy·tol·o·gy (sītŏl′*o*jē) *n.* Branch of biology concerned with the structure, physiology, and reproduction of cells. **cy·to·log·i·cal** (sīt*o*lŏj′ĭk*a*l) *adj.* **cy·to·log′i·cal·ly** *adv.* **cy·tol′o·gist** *n.*

cy·to·plasm (sī′t*o*plăz*e*m) *n.* Protoplasmic content of a cell other than the nucleus. **cy·to·plas·mic** (sīt*o*plăz′mĭk) *adj.*

CZ *abbrev.* Canal Zone.

czar, (zar̄), **cza·ri·na** (zahrē′n*a*): see TSAR etc.

czar·das (char̄′dahsh) *n.* Hungarian dance with slow start and quick wild finish.

Czech (chĕk) *adj.* & *n.* 1. (Member, language) of the most westerly branch of the Slavs, of Bohemia, Moravia, and Silesia. 2. = CZECHOSLOVAKIAN.

Czech·o·slo·va·ki·a (chĕk*o*slovah′kē*a*, -văk′ē*a*). Socialist Republic of central Europe; formed by the Treaty of Versailles (1919), including Bohemia, Moravia, and the northern Slavs of the old Austro-Hungarian Empire; capital, Prague. **Czech·o·slo·vak** (chĕk*o*-slō′vahk, -văk), **Czech·o·slo·va·ki·an** *adjs.* & *ns.* (Native, inhabitant, language) of Czechoslovakia.

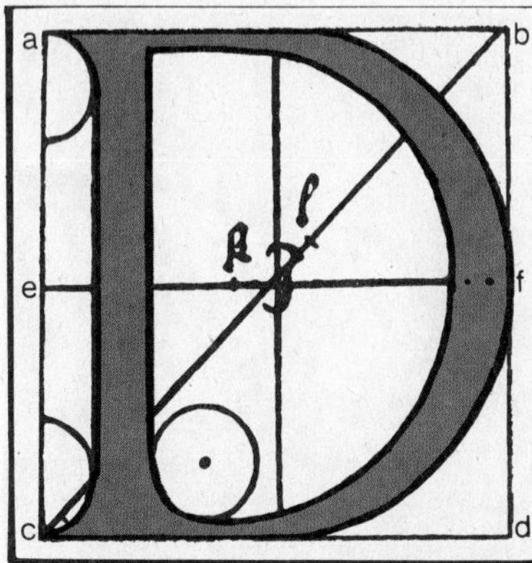

The present form of the letter **D** is a direct derivation of the north Semitic daleth and the Greek delta. In Greece the letter was also used as a geographical term for the delta of a river. In Latin the D took on its present rounded form. Left: Durer's drawing of the letter D.

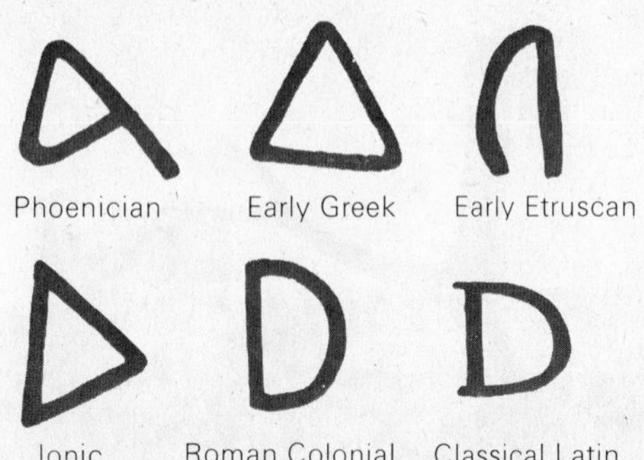

D, d (dē) (pl. **D's, d's** or **Ds, ds**). 1. Fourth letter of modern English and ancient Roman alphabet, corresponding to Greek *delta* (Δ, δ), and Phoenician and Hebrew *daleth* (ד), representing a voiced dental (or in English rather alveolar) stop consonant. 2. Fourth in serial order; classification indicating a low grade; **D-layer**, lowest stratum of the ionosphere. 3. **D**, (mus.) second note of natural scale (C major); scale or key with this note for tonic. 4. Roman numeral for 500. 5. **D**, symbol for day on which a military operation is timed to begin (= *day*, used before date is divulged, preceding days being designated as D-1, D-2, etc.); hence, **D-day**, applied esp. to June 6, 1944, day on which British, Canadian, and American forces landed in N. France. 6. **3 D**, three-dimensional. 7. Deuterium.

D. *abbrev.* December; Democrat; Doctor; Dutch.

d. *abbrev.* Date; daughter; day; died.

D.A. *abbrev.* Department of Agriculture; District Attorney.

DAB *abbrev.* Dictionary of American Biography.

dab[1] (dăb) *n.* Slight or undecided but sudden blow; brief application of soft or moist thing to surface without rubbing; moisture, color, etc., so applied. ~ *v.* (**dabbed, dab·bing**). Make dab(s) at; make dab (*at*); apply briefly without rubbing.

dab[2] (dăb) *n.* Small flatfish (*Limanda limanda*), like flounder.

dab·ble (dăb′*el*) *v.* (**-bled, -bling**). 1. Wet intermittently, slightly, or partly; soil, splash; move (with hands, bill, etc.) in shallow water, liquid, mud, etc., with splashing. 2. Engage in desultory or dilettante way (*in*). **dab′bler** *n.*

da ca·po (dah kah′pō). (mus.) Repeat from beginning. [It.]

Dac·ca (dăk′*a*). Capital of Bangladesh, situated in the E. central part of the country.

dace (dās) *n.* (pl. **daces**, collect. **dace**). Any of several freshwater minnows of the family Cyprinidae, as the redside ~ (*Clinostomus elongatus*) and the redbellied ~ (*Chiosomus erythrogaster*).

The **dace** (also called the dare or dart) is found in Europe and Siberia, inhabiting fairly fast-flowing rivers. It is a quick and elegant swimmer rarely more than 12 ins. long.

Da·chau (dah′kow; *Ger.* dah′xow). City near Munich, West Germany; site during World War II of infamous Nazi concentration camp.

dachs·hund (dŏks′ho͝ont, -ho͝ond, dăk′s*u*nd, dăsh′*u*nd) *n.* Small dog of German breed with short crooked legs and very long body. [Ger., = "badger-dog"]

Da·cron (dā′krŏn, -kr*o*n, dăk′rŏn, -r*o*n) *n.* (trademark) Synthetic textile fiber resistant to stretching and wrinkling.

dac·tyl (dăk′t*i*l) *n.* Metrical foot of one long and two short, or one accented and two unaccented syllables (— ⏑ ⏑); (zool.) finger; toe; digit. **dac·tyl·ic** (dăktĭl′ĭk) *adj.* & *n.* (Verse consisting) of dactyl(s). [Gk. *daktulos* finger (f. resemblance to its three bones)]

dad (dăd), **da·da** (dă′dă), **dad·dy** (dăd′ē) *ns.* (pls. **dads, da·das, dad·dies**). (colloq.; childish or familiar) Father (esp. as vocative); **daddy-longlegs**, arachnid having a compact body and long, slender legs.

Da·da (dah′dah) *n.* International movement in painting and literature initiated 1916 in Zurich, repudiating tradition, culture, and reason. **Da′da·ism** *n.* Dada move-

Man Ray's 'Pisces', **Dada** emerged as a reaction to the horror of the 1914–18 war and was founded on the absurd and random. It began in Zurich, while a similar movement started in New York.

ment; its doctrine. **Da'da·ist** *n.* [Fr. *être sur son dada*, ride one's hobby horse]

da·do (dā'dō) *n.* (pl. **-does, -dos**). 1. Block forming body of pedestal, between base and crown. 2. Lower part of interior wall, of different material or color from upper part.

Daed·a·lus (dĕd'*a*lus; *Brit.* dē'd*a*-). (Gk. myth.) Skillful artisan who constructed the Cretan labyrinth; he was imprisoned in Crete with his son ICARUS but escaped to Sicily on wings that he made. **Dae·da·li·an, Dae·da·le·an** (dĭdā'lē*a*n, -dāl'y*a*n) *adjs.* Intricate, labyrinthine. [Gk. *daidalos* cunning one]

dae·mon (dē'm*o*n) = DEMON 1.

daf·fo·dil (dăf'*o*dĭl) *n.* Yellow-flowered bulbous plant (*Narcissus pseudo-narcissus*) blooming in early spring; pale yellow color. ~ *adj.* Pale yellow.

daf·fy (dăf'ē) *adj.* (**-fi·er, -fi·est**) (colloq.) Silly, foolish; daft.

daft (dăft, dahft) *adj.* Foolish, reckless, wild, crazy, daffy.

dag·ger (dăg'*er*) *n.* Short two-edged pointed weapon, like small sword, for thrusting and stabbing; (print.) mark like dagger, obelisk (†); **double** ~ (‡).

da·go (dā'gō) *n.* (pl. **-gos, -goes**). (contempt.) Spaniard, Portuguese, or esp. Italian. [app. f. Span. *Diego* = James]

da·guerre·o·type (d*a*gĕr'*o*tīp, -ē*o*tīp) *n.* (Photograph taken by) early photographic process in which image was taken on silvered copper plate sensitized by iodine, and developed by exposure to mercury vapor. ~ *v.t.* Photograph by this process. [name of inventor, Louis *Daguerre* (1787–1851)]

Salvador Dali is probably the best-known, if not the most respected, painter of the Surrealist movement. His meticulous technique is evident in 'Persistence of Memory', heightening the effect of horror and nightmare.

dahl·ia (dăl'y*a*, dahl'-; *Brit.* dāl'y*a*) *n.* Plant of genus *D*~, native to Mexico and Central America, widely cultivated for its many-colored single and double flowers. [f. A. *Dahl* (d. 1789), Swedish botanist]

Da·ho·mey (d*a*hō'mē; *Fr.* dăawmā'). Former name of BENIN.

Dail Eire·ann (doil ār'*a*n). House of Representatives of the Republic of Ireland. [Ir., = "assembly of Ireland"]

dai·ly (dā'lē) *adv.* Every day or weekday; from day to day, constant(ly). ~ *adj.* Done, occurring, published, etc., daily; ~ **bread**, one's necessary food or livelihood; ~ **double**, in horse racing, system of betting whereby a bet on the results of two consecutive races is placed in a special pool; ~ **dozen**, series of physical exercises to be done every day. **daily** *n.* (pl. **-lies**). Daily newspaper.

Daim·ler (dīm'l*er*), **Gottlieb** (1834–1900). German engineer and automotive pioneer; invented early internal combustion engine.

dain·ty (dān'tē) *n.* (pl. **-ties**). Choice morsel, delicacy. ~ *adj.* (**-ti·er, -ti·est**). Choice; prettily neat; fastidious, of delicate tastes and sensibility. **dain'ti·ly** *adv.* **dain'ti·ness** *n.*

dai·qui·ri (dī'k*e*rē, dăk'*e*rē) *n.* Iced cocktail of rum, lime juice, lemon, and sugar.

dair·y (dār'ē) *n.* (pl. **dair·ies**). Room or building for keeping milk and cream and making butter etc.; store in which milk, cream, etc., are sold; department of farm or farming concerned with production of milk, butter, and cheese; dairy farm; ~ **farm**, farm producting chiefly milk, butter, etc.; **dair'ymaid**, woman employed at dairy; **dair'yman** (pl. **-men**), dealer in milk etc.

da·is (dā'ĭs, dī'ĭs, dās) *n.* Raised platform, esp. at one end of hall, for speaker's lectern, high table, throne, etc.

dai·sy (dā'zē) *n.* (pl. **-sies**). 1. Any of various related plants with rayed flowers, esp. *Chrysanthemum leucanthemum*, native of Eurasia but naturalized throughout N. Amer., whose flowers have yellow rays and a yellow disk at the center; also called "oxeye daisy." 2. Small European wild and garden flower, *Bellis perennis*, with yellow disk and white rays; ~ **chain**, chain of daisies threaded together. 3. **push up the daisies**, (slang) be dead and

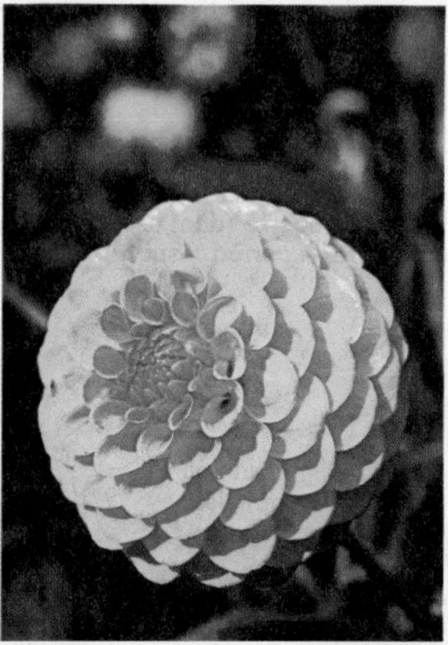

__Dahlias__ when first introduced to Europe were 7–8 ft. high with yellow centers, and red rays. Since then numerous varieties have been developed, double and single, and some a mere 18 ins. tall.

buried.

Da·kar (dahkar′). Capital and largest city of Senegal, on the Atlantic.

Da·ko·ta (d*a*kō′t*a*). Former territory of U.S., organized in 1889 into the states of NORTH DAKOTA and SOUTH DAKOTA. ~ *adj.* & *n.* (Member, language) of a Siouan-speaking group of N. Amer. plains Indians, generally called Sioux and formerly living in the area of North and South Dakota; **Dakota River**: see JAMES RIVER 1.

Da·la·dier (dălădyā′), **Edouard** (1884–1970). French statesman; premier 1933–4, 1938–40.

Da·lai La·ma (dah′lī lah′m*a*). Grand Lama, chief lama of Tibet.

dale (dāl) *n.* Valley.

Da·li (dah′lē), **Salvador** (1904–). Spanish surrealist artist; settled in U.S. 1940.

Dal·las[1] (dăl′*a*s). Second largest city in Texas, in the NE part.

Dal·las[2] (dăl′*a*s), **George Mifflin** (1792–1864). Vice president of U.S. under James Knox Polk, 1845–9.

dal·ly (dăl′ē) *v.* (**-lied, -ly·ing**). Be evasive *with* person or business; idle, loiter, delay; flirt, play, esp. amorously. **dal·li·ance** (dăl′ē*a*ns, dăl′y*a*ns) *n.*

Dal·ma·tia (dălmā′sh*a*). Province of Yugoslavia on the Adriatic coast; formerly (until 1918) province of the Austro-Hungarian Empire.

Dal·ma·tian (dălmā′sh*a*n) *adj.* Of Dalmatia or its people. ~ *n.* 1. Native, inhabitant, of Dalmatia. 2. Dog with short-haired white coat with black or brown spots, of a breed supposed to have originated in Dalmatia.

Dal·ton (dawl′t*o*n), **John** (1776–1844). English physicist and chemist, who formulated the atomic theory and table of atomic weights. **dal′ton·ism** (sometimes **D**~) *n.* Congenital color blindness, esp. inability to distinguish green from red, so called after John Dalton, who was so affected. **dal·ton·ic** (dawltŏn′ĭk) *adj.*

dam[1] (dăm) *n.* Barrier constructed across stream etc. to hold back water and raise its level, form

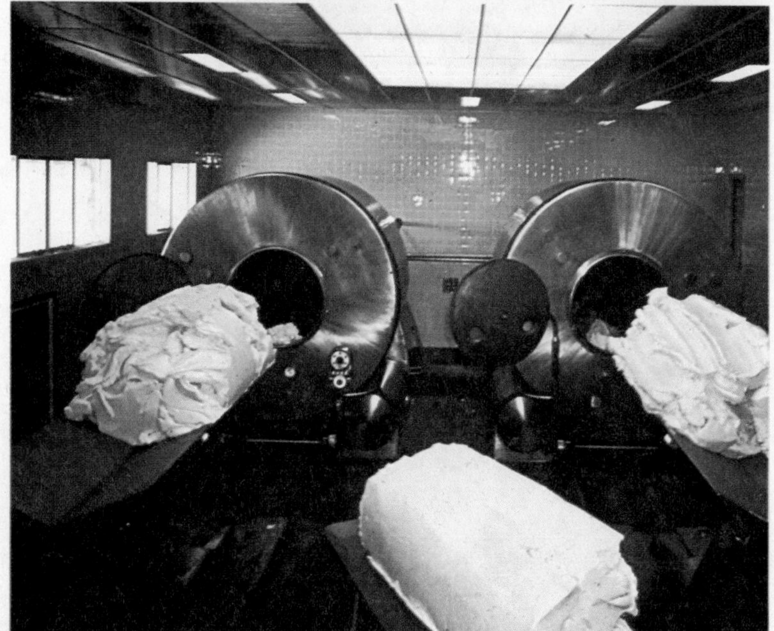

Many animals provide milk suitable for human consumption, but modern __dairy__ farming is based on the cow as source of milk, butter, cream, and cheese. Advanced mechanization has made a naturally self-sufficient branch of farming highly productive and hygienic. Top: Herring-bone milking sheds in New Zealand. Left: Collective butter-making.

a reservoir, or prevent flooding; barrier constructed in stream by beavers. ~ *v.t.* (**dammed, dam·ming**). Furnish or confine with dam; block *up*, obstruct.

dam[2] (dăm) *n.* Mother (usu. of quadruped).

dam·age (dăm'ĭj) *n.* 1. Harm; injury impairing value or usefulness. 2. (law, pl.) Sum of money claimed or adjudged in compensation for loss or injury; (slang) cost. ~ *v.t.* (**-aged, -ag·ing**). Injure (usu. thing) so as to diminish value; detract from reputation of (person etc.). **dam'age·a·ble** *adj.*

dam·a·scene (dăm'*a*sēn, dăm*a*-sēn') *v.t.* (**-scened, -scen·ing**). 1. Produce watered or striped pattern in (sword, armor, etc.) by hammering on steel in which the iron or carbon particles have separated into patches or bands during cooling. 2. Inlay (steel or iron surface) with designs in gold or silver. [f. DAMASCUS]

Da·mas·cus (d*a*măs'k*u*s). (Arab. *Esh Sham*) Capital city of Syria in the SW. part; an ancient city, famous in the Middle Ages for its silks and steel, esp. for sword blades, hence ~ **steel**.

dam·ask (dăm'*a*sk) *n.* 1. Reversible figured fabric in which the design is executed in a different weave from the background in such a way that the two weaves appear on the face and on the back in exchanged positions, orig. of silk,

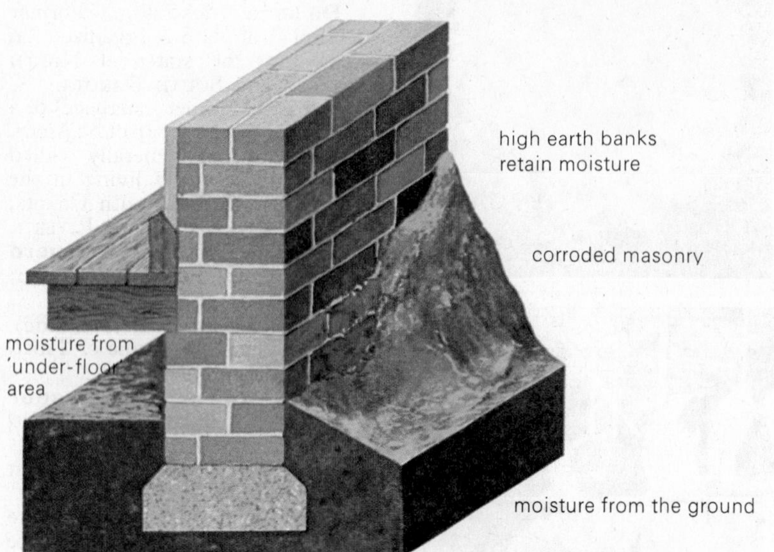

rising damp

Various methods of combating rising ***damp*** *have been developed. A special problem has been to devise ways of protecting old buildings with no built-in damp course. Strips of impermeable material are inserted between layers of bricks, silicone solutions are injected into the bricks, water is syphoned off in pipes, and copper strips, embedded in the walls and earthed, prevent water rising by inhibiting osmotic pressure.*

felt or sheeting — silicone penetration — syphonage

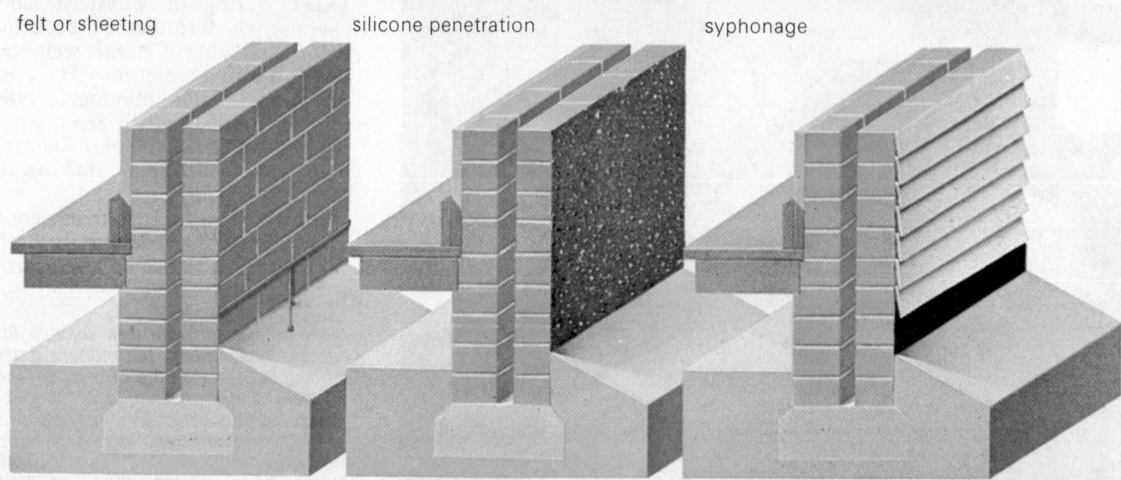
electro-osmosis — vertical damp proofing course — vertical damp proof course weather-boarding

*Above: The **Kariba Dam** in Zimbabwe under construction. Right: The Eucumbene Dam in New South Wales, Australia. The building of dams has been practiced for many thousands of years. More recently dams have been used for large scale irrigation and for hydro-electricity generation.*

later of linen, cotton, etc. 2. Steel manufactured at Damascus; combination of iron and steel with wavy pattern on surface (see DAMASCENE). 3. ~ **rose**, species of rose native to Asia (*Rosa damascena*), to which many garden varieties belong. **damask** *adj.* Made of or resembling damask fabric or steel. ~ *v.t.* 1. Weave with figured designs. 2. Damascene; ornament with pattern. [f. DAMASCUS]

dame (dām) *n.* 1. Woman (archaic or poet.; also slang). 2. Title formerly given to the mistress of a household, woman in authority, etc.; (Brit.) **D** ~, title of woman of rank of Knight (used as prefix corresp. to *Sir*).

Da·mi·en (dā′mēen), **Father** (1840–89). Orig. name, Joseph de Veuster; Belgian R.C. missionary; devoted his life to care of lepers on Molokai Island, Hawaii, and died of the disease.

damn (dăm) *v.* (**damned, damn·ing**). 1. Condemn, censure; condemn (play etc.) as a failure; bring condemnation on, be the ruin of. 2. Doom to hell; cause damnation of; curse. ~ *n.* Uttered curse; negligible amount (**not worth a** ~, worthless). ~ *int.* Exclamation of annoyance.

dam·na·ble (dăm′nabel) *adj.* Deserving damnation; hateful, annoying. **dam′na·bly** *adv.*

dam·na·tion (dămnā′shon) *n.* Damning; (condemnation to) eternal punishment in hell.

dam·na·to·ry (dăm′natōrē, -tōrē) *adj.* Conveying, causing, censure or damnation.

damned (dămd) *adj.* (esp.) Damnable, detestable; **the D** ~, souls in hell. **damned** *adv.* Damnably. **damned·est** (dăm′dĭst) *n.* **one's** ~, one's utmost.

dam·ni·fy (dăm′nĭfī) *v.t.* (**-fied, -fy·ing**). (law) Cause damage or loss to.

Dam·o·cles (dăm′*o*klēz). (Gk. legend) Flatterer who extolled the happiness of Dionysius, tyrant of Syracuse; but Dionysius, to show how precarious a ruler's happiness was, seated him at a banquet with a sword suspended over his head by a hair; hence, **sword of** ~, imminent danger, esp. in midst of prosperity. **Dam·o·cle·an** (dăm*o*-klē′*a*n) *adj*.

Da·mon (dā′m*o*n). (Gk. and Rom. legend) Syracusan whose friend Phintias was sentenced to death; Damon posted his life as bail for Phintias, who came back at the last moment and saved him; hence, ~ **and Pythias** (erron. for Phintias), faithful friends.

damp (dămp) *n*. 1. Moisture in air, on surface, or diffused through solid. 2. Dejection, chill, discouragement. ~ *adj*. Slightly wet; moist, humid; ~**-dry** (*v.t.*), dry (laundry) partially, leaving slightly moist. **damp′ly** *adv*. **damp′ness** *n*. **damp** *v.t*. 1. Stifle, choke, dull; extinguish; (mus. etc.) stop vibrations of (string etc.), furnish (piano strings) with dampers; (phys.) cause decrease in amplitude of radio waves etc. 2. Dampen. 3. Moisten, make damp.

damp·en (dăm′p*e*n) *v*. 1. Make or become damp, moisten. 2. Stifle, choke, extinguish. 3. Discourage, depress (hopes etc.).

damp·er (dăm′p*er*) *n*. 1. Person or thing that depresses. 2. Small cloth- or felt-covered pad in piano resting against string to prevent it from vibrating except when key is struck or pedal depressed. 3. Adjustable plate in flue controlling combustion by regulating or stopping draft.

Dam·rosch (dăm′rŏsh), **Walter Johnson** (1862–1950). German-born Amer. conductor and composer.

dam·sel (dăm′z*e*l) *n*. (archaic and literary) Young unmarried woman; **dam′selfly**, insect of order Odonata resembling dragonfly but with wings usu. held together over the body while resting.

dam·son (dăm′z*o*n, -s*o*n) *n*. Small dark purple plum (*Prunus insititia*) introduced in very early times into Italy and Greece from Syria; tree bearing this. [L. (*prunum*) *Damascenum* (plum) of Damascus]

Dan (dăn). 1. Hebrew patriarch, son of Jacob and Bilhah (Gen. 30); tribe of Israel traditionally descended from him. 2. City in the extreme north of Canaan.

Dan. *abbrev*. Danish.

Da·na (dā′n*a*), **Richard Henry** (1815–82). Amer. lawyer, sailor, and author; wrote *Two Years Before the Mast*.

Dan·a·ë (dăn′*a*ē) (Gk. myth.) Daughter of Acrisius, king of Argos; an oracle foretold that she would bear a son who would kill her father; he therefore imprisoned her in a tower, but Zeus visited her there in the form of a shower of gold and she conceived PERSEUS, who after many adventures killed Acrisius by accident.

Dan·a·id (dăn′āĭd) *n*. (Gk. myth.) Any of the 50 daughters of Danaus, king of Argos; all except one, Hypermnestra, murdered their husbands on the wedding night and were condemned in Hades to carry water in sieves or bottomless vessels.

Da·nang (dahnahng′, d*a*năng′). Port city in Vietnam on South China Sea.

dance (dăns, dahns) *v*. (**danced, danc·ing**). Move rhythmically with glides, leaps, etc., usu. to music, alone or with partner or in a set; perform (dance); jump about, skip, move in lively way; bob up and down on water etc. ~ *n*. 1. Dancing motion; definite succession or arrangement of steps and rhythmical movements in dancing; music for this. 2. Dancing party. 3. ~ **of death**, allegorical representation (common in Middle Ages) of Death leading all sorts and conditions of men in a dance to the grave; **St. Vitus'** ~, chorea. **danc′er** *n*. (esp.) One who dances professionally in public.

dan·de·li·on (dăn′d*e*līon) *n*. Common composite plant (*Taraxacum officinale*), abundant as a weed, with widely toothed leaves and large yellow flower on naked hollow stalk, succeeded by globular head of seeds. [Fr. *dent de lion* lion's tooth]

dan·der (dăn′d*er*) *n*. (colloq.) Temper, anger, indignation; **get one's** ~ **up**, become or make angry.

Dan·die Din·mont (dăn′dē dĭn′mŏnt). Terrier of short-legged, long-bodied, rough-coated breed

There are many species of ***dandelion*** *and they are found in many parts of the world. Unpopular with gardeners as lawn 'weeds', they are nevertheless useful plants; the leaves serve for salads, the roots for medicinal purposes.*

As a means of expression, the ***dance*** *is universal, although its types and styles are infinitely diverse, some having religious or tribal significance. Below: In the Western world ballroom dancing developed from the less sedate forms of peasant dances. Facing page: Bhutanese folk dancers.*

This 17th or 18th century painting, probably French, shows ***Daphne,*** *daughter of the river god Ladon, escaping from Apollo. Another suitor, Leucippus, was slain by her nymphs.*

from Scottish borders. [name of a character in Sir W. Scott's *Guy Mannering*, who kept a special breed of terriers]

dan·druff (dăn′dr*u*f) *n.* Dead skin in small scales among the hair, scurf.

dan·dy (dăn′dē) *n.* (pl. **-dies**). 1. Man paying excessive attention to elegance in dress etc. 2. Anything superlatively fine, neat, or dainty. 3. (naut.) Sloop with mizzen lugsail on jiggermast aft. ~ *adj.* (**-di·er, -di·est**). Foppish; (colloq.) splendid, first-rate. **dan′dy·ish** *adj.* **dan′dy·ism** *n.* [orig. Sc., perh. f. name *Andrew*]

Dane (dān) *n.* 1. Native of Denmark. 2. (hist.) Viking. 3. **Great** ~, dog of large powerful short-haired breed, of type between mastiff and greyhound.

Dane·law, Dane·lagh (dān′law) *ns.* (hist.) Part of NE. England occupied by the Danes in the 9th and 10th centuries; (erron.) body of laws established by these Danish invaders and settlers.

dan·ger (dān′j*er*) *n.* Liability or exposure to harm, risk, peril (*of*); thing that causes peril. **dan′ger·ous** *adj.* **dan′ger·ous·ly** *adv.*

dan·gle (dăng′g*e*l) *v.* (**-gled, -gling**). Hang loosely, swaying to and fro; hold or carry (thing) swaying loosely; keep (hopes, expectations, etc.) hanging uncertainly (*before* person); hang *after* or *about* a person; **dan′gling participle**, participle or participial phrase, usu. at the opening of a sentence, that is not clearly connected with the sentence element that it was supposed to modify, as *sleeping deeply* in the sentence *Sleeping deeply, the tiger's skin was singed by the fire.*

Dan·iel (dăn′y*e*l). Hebrew prophet, captive at Babylon, who interpreted the dreams of Nebuchadnezzar and was delivered by God from the lions' den into which he had been thrown by Darius; book of Old Testament bearing his name.

Dan·ish (dā′nĭsh) *adj.* & *n.* (Language) of Denmark or the Danes; ~ **pastry**, piece of light pastry topped with icing, bits of dried fruit, nuts, etc.

dank (dăngk) *adj.* Unpleasantly damp; wet and chilly. **dank′ness** n.

D'An·nun·zio (d*a*nŭn′zēō; *It.* dahnōōn′tsyō), **Gabriele** (1863–1938). Italian poet, author, aviator, and politician.

dan·seur (*Fr.* dahṅsör′) *n.* (pl. **-seurs** pr. *Fr.* -sör′). Male ballet dancer.

dan·seuse (*Fr.* dahṅsöz′) *n.* (pl. **-seuses** pr. *Fr.* -söz′). Female ballet dancer.

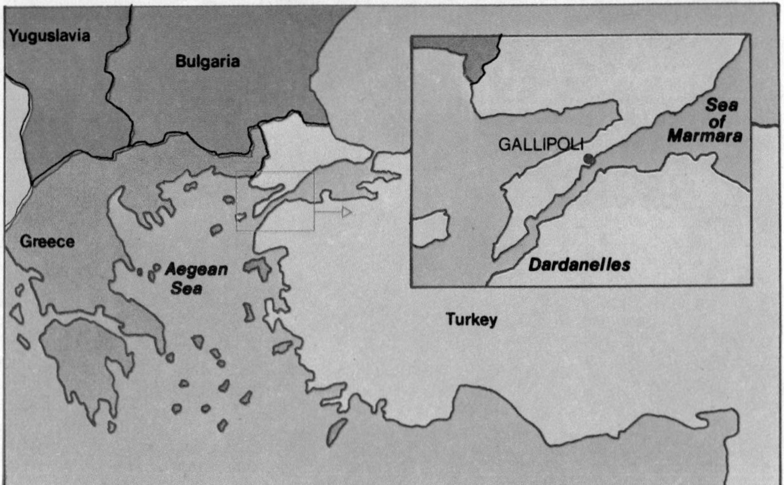

The ***Dardanelles*** *was the setting of the legend of Hero and Leander. In modern times, as the only access between the Black Sea and the Mediterranean, the Dardanelles has great strategic and commercial importance.*

Dan·te Al·i·ghie·ri (dahn′tĕ ahlēgyār′ē) (1265–1321). Italian poet, probably born at Florence, author of *Divina Commedia*, a philosophical poem comprising the "Inferno," "Purgatorio," and "Paradiso"; in his visit to Hell and Purgatory Dante has the poet Virgil for a guide; there he sees and converses with his former friends or foes; in "Paradiso" the poet encounters the lady whom he once loved, Beatrice, now an angel. **Dan·tesque** (dăntĕsk′) *adj.* Of, after the manner of, Dante.

Dan·ton (dăn′t*o*n; *Fr.* dahṅtawṅ′), **Georges Jacques** (1759–1794). French statesman of the Revolution; member of the Convention and the first (Dantonist) Committee of Public Safety; he came into conflict with ROBESPIERRE and was guillotined.

Dan·ube (dăn′ūb) (Ger. *Donau*). European river about 1,700 miles (2,736 km) long, rising in Black Forest of SW. West Germany and flowing into the Black Sea at the SE. coast of Rumania.

Dan·zig (dăn′sĭg; *Ger.* dahn′tsĭx) (Polish *Gdansk*). Baltic city and port of Poland, near mouth of Vistula.

Daph·ne (dăf′nē). (Gk. myth.) Nymph who was turned into a laurel bush to save her from the pursuit of Apollo.

daph·ne (dăf′nē) *n.* Flowering shrub of genus *D*~.

dap·per (dăp′*er*) *adj.* Neat, smart, in appearance or movement.

dap·ple (dăp′*e*l) *v.* (**-pled, -pling**). Variegate, become variegated, with rounded spots or patches of color or shade. ~ *adj.* Dappled; ~**-gray**, (horse) of gray dappled with darker spots. **dapple**

n. Dappled effect; dappled horse etc. **dap′pled** *adj.*

D.A.R. *abbrev.* Daughters of the American Revolution.

Dar·da·nelles (dārdanĕlz′). Narrow strait between Europe and Asiatic Turkey, anciently called the Hellespont; scene of unsuccessful attack on Turkey by British and French troops in 1915.

dare (dār) *v.* (**dared, dar·ing**). 1. Venture (to), have boldness or courage or impudence (to); attempt, take the risks of. 2. Defy, challenge (person) *to* thing, *to* do. 3. **dare′-devil**, reckless (person). **dar′ing** *n.* (esp.) Adventurous courage. **dar′ing** *adj.* (esp.) Adventurous, bold. **dar′ing·ly** *adv.*

Dare (dār), **Virginia** (1587?–?). First child born in America of English parentage at the colony of *Roanoke Island*, all traces of which disappeared.

Dar es Sa·laam (dār ēs salahm′). Former capital and largest city of Tanzania, on the NE coast.

Dar·i·en (dār′ēĕn, -ēen). Region of eastern Panama; **Gulf of ~**, bay in the Caribbean between NE. Panama and NW. Colombia; **Isthmus of ~**, former name of Isthmus of PANAMA.

Da·ri·us (darī′us), "the Great" (558?–486 B.C.). King of Persia, 521–486 B.C.; extended the Persian Empire and began the great war between the Persians and the Greeks; his army was defeated at MARATHON (490 B.C.).

Dar·jee·ling (dārjē′lĭng). Resort city in NE. India, in the foothills of the Himalayas. **~ tea**, fine black tea grown there.

dark (dārk) *adj.* 1. Characterized by (absolute or relative) absence of light; unilluminated; gloomy, somber. 2. (of color) Approaching black in hue; deep in shade; (of complexion etc.) brown, not fair. 3. Evil, wicked; dismal; sullen; obscure; secret; unenlightened. 4. **D~ Ages**, (formerly =) Middle Ages; (now usu.) approx. 5th–8th centuries A.D., or from fall of Rome to coronation of Charlemagne. **D~ Continent**, Africa; **~ horse**, horse about whose racing powers little is known; person of unknown capacities; relatively unknown political candidate who may receive more votes than originally expected; **dark′room**, room from which daylight is excluded and which is lighted when desired by a type of colored light that does not appreciably affect sensitive photographic materials. **dark** *n.* Absence of light; nightfall; dark color; **~ adaptation**, reflex adjustment of eyes to low light intensity; **be in the ~**, lack knowledge. **dark′ish** *adj.*

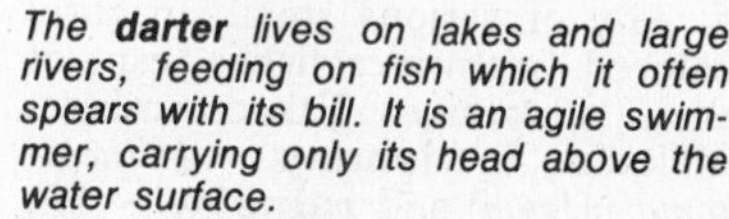

*The **darter** lives on lakes and large rivers, feeding on fish which it often spears with its bill. It is an agile swimmer, carrying only its head above the water surface.*

dark′ly *adv.* **dark′ness** *n.*

dark·en (dār′ken) *v.* Make or become dark.

dar·ling (dār′lĭng) *n.* & *adj.* Loved, best loved, lovable (person or animal).

Darm·stadt (dārm′stăt; *Ger.* dārm′shtaht). City in W. central West Germany.

darn[1] (dārn) *v.t.* Mend (esp. knitted fabric) by interweaving yarn with needle across hole; embroider with darning stitch. **~** *n.* Darned place in cloth. **darn′er** *n.* **darn′ing** *n.* (esp.) **~ needle**, long, large-eyed needle for darning.

darn[2] (dārn) *n.* & *v.t.* Damn (as mild imprecation). **darned** *adj.* & *n.* Damned.

*Many small towns dot the **Darjeeling** area of north east India (left). High mountain ranges and deep-cut river valleys characterize the area, which is noted for its fine teas.*

*A young **danseuse**, or ballerina, in classic pose (right). They are often seen as the embodiment of elegance, conveying human experience and emotion in a tangible form.*

Dar·row (dăr′ō), **Clarence Seward** (1857–1938). Amer. lawyer and social reformer; defense counsel in many celebrated cases, including the SCOPES case.

dart (dart) *n.* 1. Pointed missile thrown by hand, esp. light javelin; arrow; light pointed missile thrown at target; (pl.) game played with darts of this kind. 2. Tapering stitched fold in garment. 3. Sudden rapid motion. ~ *v.* 1. Throw (missile). 2. Emit suddenly and sharply, shoot out; spring or start with sudden rapid motion, shoot. **dart′er** *n.* (esp.) 1. = ANHINGA. 2. Any of various small, brightly colored freshwater fishes, esp. of the subfamily Etheostominae, including the **johnny** ~ (*Etheostoma nigrum*) and **rainbow** ~ (*E. caeruleum*), any of various perch of the family Percidae.

Dart·moor (dart′moor). Barren heath district in Devon, England; prison located there.

Dart·mouth (dart′m*u*th) **College.** Private, orig. men's, now coed, college at Hanover, N.H., dating from 1769.

Dar·von (dar′vŏn) *n.* (trademark) Dextropropoxyphene, a nonnarcotic compound, $C_{22}H_{29}NO_2$, used as an analgesic.

Dar·win[1] (dar′wĭn), **Charles Robert** (1809–82). English naturalist; author of *On the Origin of Species by means of Natural Selection* (1859), in which he propounded the theory of evolution by mutation and natural selection of those organisms best adapted to their environment. **Dar·win·i·an** (darwĭn′ēan) *adj.* & *n.* **Dar′win·ism** *n.*

Dar·win[2] (dar′wĭn). Capital city of Northern Territory of Australia on the Timor Sea; named after Charles DARWIN[1]

dash (dăsh) *v.* 1. Shatter *to pieces*; knock, drive, throw, thrust, *away, off*, etc.; fling, drive, splash, *against, into, upon*. 2. Bespatter *with* water etc. 3. Frustrate; discourage. 4. Put *down* on paper, throw *off* (drawing, composition) hastily and vigorously. 5. Damn (as mild imprecation, esp. in ~ **it all**). 6. Fall, move, throw oneself, with violence; come into collision *against, upon*; ride, run, drive, *up*, move about, behave, with spirit or display. 7. **dash′board,** orig. board in front of wagon to protect driver etc. from being splashed by mud and water from road; now board or panel in front of driver of car or of airplane pilot carrying indicators, gauges, etc. **dash** *n.* 1. Violent blow, impact, or collision; violent throwing and breaking of water etc., upon anything; sound of dashing. 2. Splash of color; infusion, touch, tinge. 3. Hasty pen stroke; punctuation mark used to indicate break in sense, parenthesis, omitted letters or words, etc., or in Morse code. 4. Rush, onset, sudden advance; (capacity for) vigorous action; showy appearance or behavior. 5. (colloq.) Dashboard.

dash·er (dăsh′*er*) *n.* (esp.) Contrivance for agitating cream in churn or ice cream freezer.

da·shi·ki (d*a*shē′kē) *n.* Loose, brightly colored shirt for men, orig. from western Africa.

dash·ing (dăsh′ĭng) *adj.* (esp.) Spirited, lively; showy. **dash′ing·ly** *adv.*

Dasht-i-Ka·vir (dahsht′ē kahvēr′). (also called Kavir Desert) Great salt desert in central Iran.

Dasht-i-Lut (dahsht′ē loot′). (also called Lut Desert) Large stone and sand desert in E. Iran.

das·tard (dăs′t*e*rd) *n.* Base or despicable coward, esp. one who commits malicious or brutal act. **das′tard·ly** *adj.* **das′tard·li·ness** *n.*

dat. *abbrev.* Dative.

da·ta (dā′t*a*, dăt′*a*, dah′t*a*) *n.pl.* (sing. **da·tum** pr. dā′t*u*m, dăt′*u*m, dah′t*u*m). (often construed as sing.) 1. Things known or granted;

Bowerman's Nose, a rock outcrop on ***Dartmoor,*** *U.K., a high granite plateau of heath and woodland, in Devon. Dartmoor has tin, iron, and copper mines and china clay quarries.*

Date *palms from Majorca, Spain. The tree grows to a height of 100 ft. and is native between North Africa and Asia Minor. It was first introduced to America by the Spanish.*

assumptions or premises from which inferences may be drawn. 2. Facts, statistics, etc. arranged for analysis or computation. 3. ~ **bank**, place where organized data are stored in large amounts, available for use or computer analysis; ~ **processing**, automatic, high-speed performance of operations on data by computer.

date[1] (dāt) *n.* Fruit of the ~ **palm**, (*Phoenix dactylifera*) an oblong berry, growing in large clusters, with single hard seed or stone and sweet pulp, an important article of food in W. Asia and N. Africa; the tree itself. [Gk. *daktulos* finger]

date[2] (dāt) *n.* Specification in document, letter, book, inscription, of time (and often place) of execution, writing, publication, etc.; specified time (month, day of month, year) at which anything takes place or is to take place; season, period; (colloq.) engagement, person with whom one has social engagement; period to which something ancient belongs; duration, term of life or existence; **out of date**, obsolete, antiquated; **up to date**, up to the knowledge, standard, requirements, of the time; in fashion; **date'line**, line in newspaper at head of dispatch, special article, etc., giving date and place of writing; **International Date Line**, line in Pacific Ocean (approx. meridian of 180° from Greenwich, England) at which calendar day is reckoned to begin and end, so that at places east and west of it the date differs by a day. **date** *v.* (**dat·ed, dat·ing**). Mark (letter etc.) with date; refer (event) to a time; count time, reckon (*from*); bear date, be dated; have origin *from*; be or become or make recognizable as of a past or particular period; (colloq.) make, have, social engagement with. **date'less** *adj.* Undated.

Michelangelo's ***'David'*** *(1501–4) expresses the Florentine Republic's self-confidence. The sculpture's classical proportions are in the tradition of Giotto.*

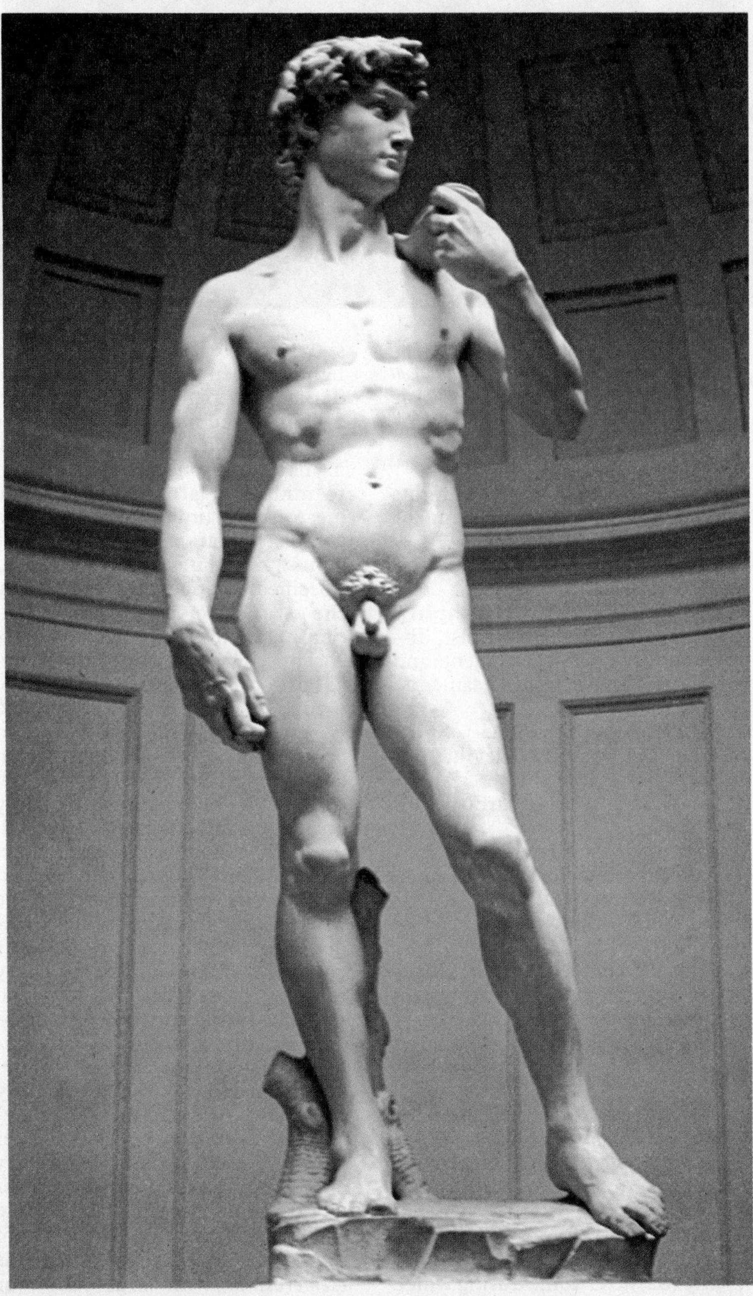

da·tive (dā'tĭv) *adj.* (gram.) Of the case chiefly denoting the indirect object. ~ *n.* (Word in) dative case.

da·tum (dā'tum, dăt'um, dah'-tum) *n.* Sing. of DATA. [L., = "(thing) given"]

da·tu·ra (datoor'a, -tūr'a) *n.* Poisonous plant of genus *D*~.

daub (dawb) *v.* 1. Coat (wall etc.) *with* plaster, clay, etc.; smear (surface); lay *on* (greasy or sticky stuff); soil, bedaub. 2. Paint coarsely and inartistically, apply (paint) crudely and clumsily. ~ *n.* 1. Material for daubing walls etc.; clay or mud mixed with stubble or chaff, daubed on laths to make walls etc. 2. Patch or smear of paint, grease, etc. 3. Clumsy coarse painting. **daub'er** *n.* Soft rounded mass used to apply ink, color, etc., to a surface in printing, painting on china, etc.

Dau·det (dōdā'), **Alphonse** (1840–97). French novelist, author of *Tartarin de Tarascon.*

daugh·ter (daw'ter) *n.* Female child in relation to her parent(s); female descendant, female member *of* family, race, etc.; woman as spiritual or intellectual descendant of some person or thing; also transf.; ~**-in-law**, son's wife, (pl. ~**s-in-law); D**~**s of the American Revolution**, patriotic society formed 1890. **daugh'ter·ly** *adj.*

Dau·mier (dōmyā'), **Honoré** (1808–79). French painter and caricaturist.

daunt (dawnt) *v.t.* Discourage, intimidate. **daunt'less** *adj.* Intrepid; persevering. **daunt'less·ly** *adv.* **daunt'less·ness** *n.*

dau·phin (daw'fĭn) *n.* (hist.) Orig. title of lords of Viennois, France, whose coat of arms bore three dolphins; (from 1349 to 1830) title of the eldest son of the king of France.

Da·vao (dahvow'). Seaport on Mindanao in the Philippines; **D**~ **Gulf**, inlet on the SE. coast of Mindanao.

dav·en·port (dăv'enpōrt, -pōrt) *n.* 1. (Brit.) Small ornamental writing desk. 2. Large sofa. [prob. from desk maker's name].

Da·vid[1] (dā'vĭd). Second king of Judah; slayer of a Philistine,

traditionally GOLIATH; on the death of Saul became king of Judah and later of the whole of Israel; father of King Solomon and reputed author of many of the Psalms.

Da·vid[2] (dahvēd′), **Jacques Louis** (1748–1825). French painter of classical and historical subjects.

da Vin·ci: see LEONARDO DA VINCI.

Da·vis[1] (dā′vĭs), **Jefferson** (1808–89). Amer. Army officer and political leader; U.S. secretary of war, 1853–7; U.S. senator from Mississippi, 1847–51, 1857–61; president of the Confederate States of America, 1861–5; arrested for treason after Civil War but prosecution proceedings dropped; retired to his estate, Beauvoir, near Biloxi, Mississippi.

Da·vis[2] (dā′vĭs), **Richard Harding** (1864–1916). Amer. war correspondent, novelist, and editor.

Da·vis (dā′vĭs) **Cup.** Trophy awarded to the nation whose team is the winner of the annual International Lawn Tennis Championship competition; it was donated in 1900 by Dwight F. Davis (1879–1945), Amer. politician.

Da·vis·son (dā′vĭsǝn), **Clinton Joseph** (1881–1958). Amer. physicist; worked on electricity, magnetism, radiant energy, and discovered diffraction of electrons; shared Nobel Prize for physics, 1937.

dav·it (dăv′ĭt, dā′vĭt) *n.* Crane at ship's bow for hoisting anchor clear of side; one of pair of uprights curved at top for suspending or lowering ship's boat.

***Dawn** over Baja California, Mexico. The colors of dawn are those of sunset in the reverse order; they are colder and clearer because of reduced dust content in the atmosphere.*

Da·vos (dah′vōs). Resort center in E. Switzerland.

Da·vy (dā′vē), **Sir Humphry** (1778–1829). English chemist, discoverer of 12 chemical elements and inventor of an early safety lamp (~ **lamp**) for miners.

Da·vy Jones (dā′vē jōnz′). Spirit of the sea, sailors' devil; **~'s locker**, bottom of the sea, esp. as grave of those who are drowned or die at sea.

daw (daw) jackdaw: see JACK.

daw·dle (daw′dǝl) *v.* (**-dled, -dling**). Idle, dally; **~ away**, waste (time). **dawdle** *n.* Act of dawdling.

Dawes (dawz), **Charles Gates** (1865–1951). Amer. statesman; vice president of the U.S. under Calvin Coolidge, 1925–9; shared Nobel Prize for peace, 1925.

dawn (dawn) *n.* First light, daybreak; rise or incipient gleam of anything. **~** *v.i.* Begin to appear to grow light; **~ on,** begin to be perceptible to.

Daw·son (daw′sǝn) **Creek.** Starting point of Alaska Highway in E. British Columbia, Canada.

day (dā) *n.* 1. Time during which sun is above horizon, interval of light between successive periods of darkness or night; dawn; daylight. 2. Time occupied by Earth in one revolution on its axis, 24 hours; 24 hours reckoned from midnight to midnight; **sidereal ~**, actual mean solar time required for a complete rotation of the Earth; 23 hours, 56 minutes, 4.09 seconds. 3. Specified or appointed day; **carry the ~**, be victorious. 4. Period, time, era; lifetime, span of existence; period of power or influence. 5. Part of day allotted for work. 6. **~ by ~, ~ after ~, from ~ to ~, every ~**, with daily repetition or progress. 7. **~ bed**, couch convertible into or used as a bed; **day′book**, book in which daily business transactions are recorded; (business) diary or memo book; appointment book; **day′break**, dawn; **day-care center**, place where infants and preschool children are looked after while their parents work; **day coach**, ordinary railroad passenger car with no sleeping or other special accommodations; **day′dream**, dream (indulged in) while awake; **day labor**, labor hired by the day (**day laborer**); **day′light (saving) time**, time one or more hours later than STANDARD time for a country or region, usu. adopted for summer months to add hours of daylight to the working day. **day lily**, any of several liliaceous plants of genus *Hemerocallis* with large yellow or orange flowers lasting only for a day; **day nursery**, nursery where pre-school children are cared for during day; **day school**, private school for pupils (**day students**) living at home; **day′time**, time of daylight.

Day (dā), **Benjamin Harrison** (1810–89). Amer. newspaperman; founded *New York Sun*, 1833, first one-cent newspaper; his grandson, **Clarence Shepard, Jr**., (1874–1935), Amer. writer, best known for *Life With Mother* and *Life with Father*.

Day·ak (dī′ăk, -*a*k) *n*. Var. of DYAK.

Day-Lew·is (dā′lo͞oĭs), **Cecil** (1904–72). English poet (also detective novelist, pseudonym, *Nicholas Blake*); poet laureate 1968–72.

day·light (dā′līt) *n*. Light of day; dawn; openness, publicity; visible interval, as between boats in race; clear understanding (**see ~**); **~-saving time**, one hour or more later than the standard time for a region or locality, usu. used during summer to give working day more daylight; **beat the daylights out of,** (colloq.) beat (someone) into a state of unconsciousness.

Day·to·na (dātō′n*a*) **Beach.** Resort city in E. Florida noted for its beautiful beach; site of International Speedway.

daze (dāz) *v.t.* (**dazed, daz·ing**). Stupefy, bewilder. **~** *n*. Dazed state. **daz′ed·ly** *adv*.

daz·zle (dăz′*e*l) *v.t.* (**-zled, -zling**). Confuse, dim sight of, (eye, person) with excess of light, intricate motion, incalculable number, etc.; confound, surprise, by brilliant display. **~** *n*. Glitter; bright confusing light. **daz′zler** *n*. **daz′zling·ly** *adv*.

dB *abbrev*. Decibel(s).

DC, D.C., dc, d-c, d.c. *abbrevs*. 1. (**DC, D.C.**) District of Columbia. 2. Direct current.

D.C.M. *abbrev*. (Brit.) Distinguished Conduct Medal.

D.D. *abbrev*. Doctor of Divinity.

D.D.S. *abbrev*. Doctor of Dental Science; Doctor of Dental Surgery.

DDT *abbrev*. Colorless, crystalline, and water-insoluble solid $(ClC_6H_4)_2$ $CHCCl_3$, used as a contact insecticide. [*D*(ichlor) *d*(iphenyl) *t*(richlorethane)]

DE *abbrev*. Delaware.

de- *prefix*. 1. Down; away; completely. 2. Un- (in this sense a living prefix in English).

de·ac·ces·sion (dēăksĕsh′*o*n) *v.t.* Remove (artifact, art, books, etc.) from the collection of a museum, library, etc. to sell, exchange, or make space for new acquisitions, etc.

dea·con (dē′k*o*n) *n*. 1. Kind of minister or officer of early church; in the Roman Catholic, Greek Orthodox, and Anglican churches, member of the clergy ranking just below priest. 2. In Protestant churches, lay official who assists the minister in various duties. **dea·con·ess** (kē′k*o*nĭs) *n.fem*. Woman with functions analogous to deacon's.

dead (dĕd) *adj*. 1. That has ceased to live. 2. Benumbed, insensible; without spiritual life; **~ to**, unconscious or inappreciative of, hardened against. 3. Obsolete; past; not effective. 4. Inanimate. 5. Extinct; dull, lusterless; without force; muffled; inactive, idle. 6. Unconnected to source of electrical power. 7. Abrupt; complete, unrelieved, exact; absolute. 8. (slang) Exhausted, tired out; **~ to the world**, fast asleep. 9. **~ ball**, (sports) ball out of play; **~ end**, closed end of any passage road etc., through which there is no way (also fig.); **dead′eye**, (naut.) round flat three-holed block for extending shrouds; (slang) expert marksman; **dead′fall**, trap for large game with weighted board or heavy log that falls on the quarry; **dead′head**, (colloq.) nonpaying theatergoer, passenger, etc.; streetcar, railroad car, etc. carrying no passengers or freight; dull, sluggish, or stupid person; **dead heat**, race in which two or more competitors cross finish line at same time; **dead letter**, unclaimed or undelivered letter at post office; **dead′line**, time limit etc. for finishing a piece of work; **dead′lock**, complete stoppage, standstill; state of affairs from which further progress is impossible; **dead man's throttle, brake**, etc. (on locomotives etc.) throttle that must be pressed down for engine to work, so that train etc. stops if engineer or operator loses grasp of it; **dead march**, march-like funeral music; **dead nettle**, nonstinging plant of genus *Lamium* with leaves like nettle's; **dead′pan**, (slang) expressionless; **dead reckoning**, (naut. and aeronaut.) estimation of ship's or aircraft's position from log, compass courses, etc., and not from observations; **dead shot**, unerring marksman; **dead soldier**, (slang) empty whiskey or beer bottle; **dead weight**, heavy inert weight, weight of dead body or lifeless matter; **dead′wood**, wood no longer alive; useless person(s) or thing(s). **dead** *n*. 1. **the ~**, dead person or persons; all who have ever died. 2. Dead period or time; time of intensest stillness, darkness, cold, etc. (*of* night, winter). **~** *adv*. Profoundly; absolutely, completely; **~ against**, directly opposite or opposed to; **dead′beat** (*n*.) person who does not pay his or her just debts.

A one-handed ***deaf-and-dumb alphabet*** *is used in the U.S.A. and Ireland, and with some variations in parts of Europe. The U.K. and Australia use the two-handed system shown here.*

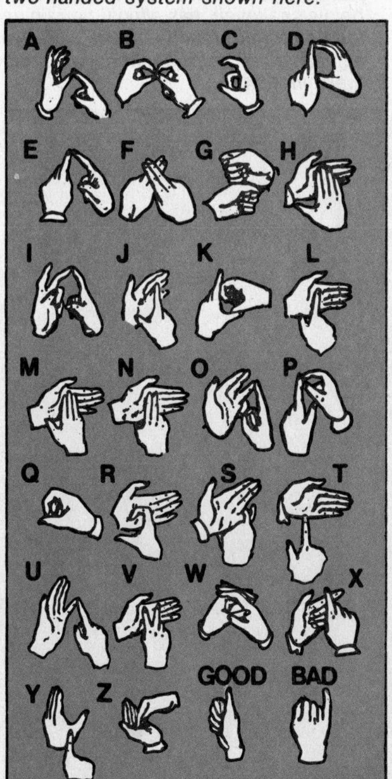

dead·en (dĕd′*e*n) *v*. Deprive of, lose, vitality, force, brightness, feeling, etc.; make insensible *to*.

dead·ly (dĕd′lē) *adj*. (**-li·er, -li·est**). 1. Causing fatal injury; of poisonous nature; implacable, mortal, to the death. 2. (of sin) Entailing spiritual death, mortal; **~ sins**, the seven sins of pride, lust, covetousness, envy, gluttony, anger, and sloth. 3. Resembling death; intense. **dead′li·ness** *n*. **dead′ly** *adv*. As if dead; extremely.

Dead (dĕd) **Sea.** Salt lake or inland sea between Israel and Jordan with intensely bitter water, into which river Jordan flows; **~ Scrolls**, large collection of Hebrew and Aramaic parchment scrolls, including parts of most books of Old Testament, found (1947–) in caves NW. of Dead Sea, apparently stored there by a community that lived at Qumran *c*135 B.C.–70 A.D.

deaf (dĕf) *adj*. 1. Wholly or partly without hearing. 2. Insensible *to*; not giving ear *to*; uncompliant. 3. **~-mute**, person unable to hear or speak, often communicating by **~-and-dumb alphabet**, a system of signs made with the hands. **deaf′ly** *adv*. **deaf′ness** *n*.

deaf·en (def′*e*n) *v.t.* Deprive of hearing by noise, stun with noise.

deal[1] (dēl) *n*. **a great** (or **good**) **~**, a large (or fairly large) amount; (adverbially) by much, considerably.

deal[2] (dēl) *n.* Sawn fir or pine wood (11 in. wide, 2½ in. thick, and 12 ft. long); wood in this form; fir or pine wood.

deal[3] (dēl) *n.* 1. Distribution, sharing; dealing of cards; turn to deal cards. 2. Business transaction, bargain; secret agreement in business or politics; **Fair D~**, policy of social improvement introduced by the presidential administration of Harry S. TRUMAN; **New D~**, program of social and economic reform of the presidential administration of Franklin D. Roosevelt from 1932 on. **deal** (dēl) *v.* (**dealt** pr. dĕlt, **deal·ing**). 1. Distribute, give *out*, among several. 2. Distribute cards to players for a game or round; give (card, hand, etc.) to player. 3. Associate *with*; do business (*with* person, *in* goods); occupy oneself, grapple by way of discussion or refutation, take measures, *with*; behave (*well, honorably, cruelly*, etc., *with* or *by* person). 4. (slang) Buy and sell drugs, as hallucinogens, narcotics, etc., without legal authorization. **deal'er** *n.* 1. Trader in a particular class of goods. 2. Player dealing at cards. 3. (slang) One who engages in illegal buying and selling of drugs. **deal'ing** *n.*

dean (dēn) *n.* 1. Official in charge of a university or college faculty or with specified administrative responsibilities; **~'s list**, listing by a school or college of students with high academic standing. 2. Head of chapter of collegiate or cathedral church. 3. Senior member of a particular group, profession, etc.; doyen. [L. *decanus* one set over ten (monks)]

dear (dēr) *adj.* 1. Beloved, loved (now often merely polite and part of ordinary formula at beginning of most letters); precious in one's regard, to which one is attached; **D~ John letter**, (slang) letter received by a man from his girlfriend or fiancée informing him that she is discontinuing their relationship. 2. Costly. **dear** *n.* Dear one, charming person or thing. **~** *adv.* At a high price; fondly. **dear'ly** *adv.* **dear'ness** *n.* **dear** *int.* Exclamation expressing surprise, distress, sympathy, etc. (**~ ~!, oh ~!, ~ me!**).

dearth (dērth) *n.* Scanty supply *of*.

death (dĕth) *n.* 1. Dying; final cessation of vital functions; being dead; cause or occasion of death; **put to ~**, execute; **talk to ~**, (colloq.) overdo discussion of a subject so that it becomes tiresome and boring. 2. Being or becoming spiritually dead; end, extinction, destruction. 3. **death'bed**, bed on which person dies; **deathbed statement** or **confession**, one made during the last hours of life; **death'blow**, blow that causes death; **death mask**, cast taken from person's face after death; **death penalty**, capital punishment; **death rate**, proportion of deaths usu. estimated per 1,000 of population per annum; **death rattle**, rattling sound in throat of dying person, caused by partial stoppage of air passage by mucus; **death's-head**, (figure or representation of) human skull, esp. as emblem of mortality; **death's-head moth**, large Old World hawk moth (*Acherontia atropos*) with markings resembling skull on thorax; **death'trap**, place etc. that is unwholesome or dangerous; **death warrant**, warrant for execution of death sentence (also fig.); **death'watch**, vigil kept beside dying, condemned, or dead person; **deathwatch beetle**, small beetle (*Xestobium rufovillosum*), which makes noise like watch ticking, formerly supposed to portend death, the larva of which bores in old wood; insect making similar sound; **death wish**, (psychol.) alleged inborn tendency of organisms to seek death, capable of being directed against the self or others.

death·less (dĕth'lĭs) *adj.* Immortal. **death'less·ly** *adv.* **death'less·ness** *n.*

death·ly (dĕth'lē) *adj.* Deadly; gloomy, pale, etc., as death. **~** *adv.* To a degree resembling death.

The ***death's-head*** *hawk moth, found in Europe, North Africa, and Asia. It has a wing-span of about 5 ins. It eats honey, imitating the noise of the queen bee on entering the hive.*

Death Valley, *California, the lowest point of the American continent (282 ft. below sea level), has almost no rain and temperatures reach 130°F. It was named after gold seekers who died there in 1849.*

*The furniture beetle, the **deathwatch** beetle, destroys hardwood timber in old houses, particularly oak and chestnut. It has a characteristic tapping noise which is heard particularly during the mating season in April and May.*

Death (dĕth) **Valley.** Desert in E. California and W. Nevada that includes the point with the lowest altitude (280 ft., 85 m, below sea level) in the Western Hemisphere; ~ **National Monument**, tourist and resort area of Death Valley, noted for ancient pictographs and unique geological formations.

deb (dĕb) *n.* (colloq.) Debutante.

de·ba·cle (d*e*bah'k*e*l, -băk'*e*l) *n.* 1. (geol.) Sudden deluge of water, breaking down barriers and carrying stones and other debris with it, esp. the breakup of ice on northern rivers. 2. Sudden and overwhelming collapse, rout, ruin. [Fr., = "breakup of ice in river"]

De Ba·key (d*e*bā'kē), **Michael Ellis** (1908–). Amer. surgeon and educator; pioneer in heart surgery.

de·bar (dĭbar̄') *v.t.* (**-barred, -bar·ring**). Exclude *from* admission or right, esp. of lawyer; hinder or prohibit. **de·bar'ment** *n.*

de·bark (dĭbar̄k') *v.* Disembark. **de·bar·ka·tion** (dēbar̄kā'sh*o*n) *n.*

de·base (dĭbās') *v.t.* (**-based, -bas·ing**). Lower in quality, value, or character; depreciate (coin) by mixture of alloy or otherwise. **de·base'ment** *n.*

de·bat·a·ble (dĭbā't*a*b*e*l) *adj.* Questionable, subject to dispute or debate.

de·bate (dĭbāt') *v.* (**-bat·ed, -bat·ing**). Contest, fight for (archaic); dispute about, discuss, (question); engage in (formal) argument or discussion (of), esp. in legislative or other assembly; consider, ponder; **debating society**, society whose members meet for practice in debating. **de·bat'er** *n.* **debate** *n.* Controversy; discussion; public argument.

de·bauch (dĭbawch') *v.t.* Pervert from virtue or morality; make intemperate or sensual; seduce; vitiate (taste, judgment). ~ *n.* Bout or habit of sensual indulgence. **de·bauch·ee** (dĭbawchē', -shē'), **de·bauch·er·y** (dĭbaw'cher*ē*) *ns.*

de Beau·voir (d*e* bōvwar̄'), **Simone** (1908–1986). French writer and one of the founders of the existentialist movement.

de·ben·ture (dĭbĕn'ch*er*) *n.* 1. Voucher or certificate acknowledging indebtedness by the signer. 2. Certificate issued by a custom house providing for refund of a tariff or other tax. 3. (also ~ **bond**) Fixed-interest bond of a private business or governmental agency or corporation, secured only by the credit of the issuer.

de·bil·i·tate (dĭbĭl'ĭtāt) *v.t.* (**-tat·ed, -tat·ing**). Enfeeble (constitution etc.). **de·bil·i·ta·tion** (dĭbĭlĭtā'sh*o*n) *n.* **de·bil·i·ta·tive** (dĭbĭl'ĭtātĭv) *adj.*

de·bil·i·ty (dĭbĭl'ĭtē) *n.* (pl. **-ties**). Feebleness (of health, purpose, etc.).

deb·it (dĕb'ĭt) *n.* Item of debt; entry in account of sum owing; side of account (left-hand) in which these entries are made; ~ **card**, credit card by which bills are paid by direct deduction from the payer's bank account. **debit** *v.t.* Charge (person) *with* sum; enter (sum) *against* or *to* person.

deb·o·nair, deb·o·naire (dĕb*o*nar̄') *adjs.* Suave, urbane; genial, pleasant. **deb·o·nair'ly** *adv.*

de·bouch (dĭbo͞osh', -bowch') *v.i.* Issue from ravine, wood, etc., into open ground. **de·bouch'ment** *n.*

de·brief·ing (dēbrē'fĭng) *n.* Interrogation, discussion, after completion of mission etc. **de·brief'** *v.t.*

de·bris (d*e*brē', dā'brē) *n.* Scattered fragments, wreckage, drifted accumulation.

Debs (dĕbz), **Eugene Victor** (1855–1926). Amer. labor leader; organized Social Democratic Party of America, 1879, and was 5 times Socialist candidate for president; indicted and convicted of violation of Espionage Act, 1918, but released from prison, 1921, by order of President Harding.

debt (dĕt) *n.* Money, goods, or service, owing; being under obligation to pay something; **national** ~, total financial obligations of a country; ~ **of honor**, debt, usu. of sum lost in gambling, not legally enforceable.

debt·or (dĕt'*er*) *n.* One who owes money, or an obligation or duty.

de·bunk (dĭbŭngk') *v.t.* Remove the false sentiment from (person, cult, etc.); expose (false claim etc.).

De·bus·sy (dĕbūsē', dā'būsē, d*e*bū'sē), **Claude** (1862–1918). French composer of symphonic poems, piano compositions, and the opera *Pelléas et Mélisande*.

de·but (dābū', dĭ-, dā'bū, dĕb'ū) *n.* First appearance, on stage etc. as performer, or in society.

deb·u·tante, déb·u·tante (dĕb'y*u*tahnt) *ns.* Young woman making first appearance in society.

De·bye (dĕbī'), **Peter Joseph Wilhelm** (1884–1966). Dutch-born Amer. physicist; researched molecular structure and developed theory of specific heat; awarded Nobel Prize for chemistry, 1936.

Dec. *abbrev.* December.

dec. *abbrev.* Deceased; decimeter.

dec-, deca- *comb. forms.* Ten, ten times.

dec·ade (dĕk'ād) *n.* Set, series, of ten; period of ten years.

dec·a·dence (dĕk'*a*d*e*ns) *n.* Falling away, declining (from former excellence, vitality, prosperity, etc.), esp. of morals or period of art or literature after a culmination.

dec·a·dent (dĕk'*a*d*e*nt) *adj.* In a state of decay or decline; of morals, literature, art, etc., belonging to a decadent age. ~ *n.* Decadent writer or artist. **dec'a·dent·ly** *adv.*

de·caf·fein·ate (dēkăf'ĭnāt, -ēĭnāt) *v.t.* (**-at·ed, -at·ing**). Remove caffeine from or reduce quantity of caffeine in (coffee).

dec·a·gon (dĕk'*a*gŏn) *n.* Plane figure with ten sides and ten angles. **de·cag·o·nal** (dekăg'*o*n*a*l) *adj.*

dec·a·gram (dĕk'*a*grăm) *n.*

(abbrev. dkg) Unit of grams.

dec·a·he·dron (dĕkahē´dron) *n.* (pl. **-drons, -dra** pr. -dra). Ten-sided solid. **dec·a·he´dral** *adj.*

de·cal·ci·fy (dēkăl´sĭfī) *v.t.* (**-fied, -fy·ing**). Deprive of lime or calcareous matter. **de·cal·ci·fi·ca·tion** (dēkălsĭfĭkā´shon) *n.*

dec·a·li·ter (dĕk´alēter) *n.* (abbrev. dkl) Ten liters.

Dec·a·logue, Dec·a·log (dĕk´a-lawg, -lŏg) *ns.* (also **d**~) The Ten Commandments (Exod. 20).

De·cam·er·on (dĭkăm´erŏn), **The.** Work by BOCCACCIO, written between 1348 and 1358, containing 100 tales told in ten days by a party of seven young ladies and three young men who had fled from the plague in Florence.

dec·a·me·ter (dĕk´amēter) *n.* (abbrev. dkm) Ten meters.

de·camp (dĭkămp´) *v.i.* Break up or leave camp; go away suddenly, abscond. **de·camp´ment** *n.*

de·cant (dĭkănt´) *v.t.* Pour off (clear liquid of solution) by gently inclining vessel without disturbing sediment; pour (wine) similarly from bottle into decanter; pour or empty out. **de·cant´er** *n.* Stoppered glass vessel in which decanted wine etc. is brought to table.

de·cap·i·tate (dĭkăp´ĭtāt) *v.t.* (**-tat·ed, -tat·ing**). Behead. **de·cap·i·ta·tion** (dĭkăpĭtā´shon) *n.*

dec·a·pod (dĕk´apŏd) *n.* Ten-footed crustacean.

de·car·bon·ize (dēkar´bonīz), **de·car·bu·rize** (dēkar´burīz) *vbs.t.* (**-ized, -iz·ing, -rized, -riz·ing**). Remove carbon from, esp. carbon deposit from (internal combustion engine). **de·car·bon·i·za·tion** (dēkarbonīzā´shon) *n.*

dec·a·syl·la·ble (dĕk´asĭlabel) *n.* (Metrical line) of ten syllables.

de·cath·lon (dĭkăth´lŏn) *n.* Athletic contest comprising ten different track and field events.

De·ca·tur (dĭkā´ter), **Stephen** (1779–1820). Amer. naval officer; victorious in battles against Tripoli, 1803–4, and during War of 1812; famous for his toast, "——our country right or wrong."

de·cay (dĭkā´) *v.* 1. Deteriorate; lose quality; decline in power, wealth, beauty, etc.; (phys.) diminish in intensity; (of radioactive particles etc.) disintegrate *into* different particles etc. ~ **heat**, heat produced by radioactive decay. 2. Rot, cause to deteriorate. ~ *n.* Act, process of decaying.

Dec·can (dĕk´an) **Plateau.** Triangular plateau of most of peninsula of India.

de·cease (dĭsēs´) *n.* (legal or formal) Death. ~ *v.i.* (**-ceased, -ceas·ing**). Die. **de·ceased´** *adj.* & *n.* Dead (person).

de·ce·dent (dĭsē´dent) *n.* (legal) Deceased person.

de·ceit (dĭsēt´) *n.* Trick or ploy to mislead or to persuade of what is false; falseness. **de·ceit´ful** *adj.* **de·ceit´ful·ly** *adv.* **de·ceit´ful·ness** *n.*

de·ceive (dĭsēv´) *v.* (**-ceived, -ceiv·ing**). Persuade of what is false, mislead; disappoint (hopes etc.). **de·ceiv´er** *n.* **de·ceiv´ing·ly** *adv.*

de·cel·er·ate (dēsĕl´erāt) *v.* (**-at·ed, -at·ing**). Decrease speed or velocity (of). **de·cel·er·a·tion** (dēsĕlerā´shon), **de·cel´er·a·tor** *ns.*

De·cem·ber (dĭsĕm´ber). Twelfth month of Gregorian (tenth of Julian) calendar, with 31 days. [L. *decem* ten]

De·cem·brist (dĭsĕm´brĭst) *n.* (hist.) One of those who in Dec. 1825 tried to raise revolt against Tsar Nicholas I of Russia.

de·cen·cy (dē´sensē) *n.* (pl. **-cies**). Propriety of behavior or demeanor; compliance with recognized notions of modesty or delicacy, freedom from impropriety; respectability; (pl.) decent or becoming acts or observances, outward conditions of decent life.

de·cen·ni·al (dĭsĕn´ēal) *adj.* Of ten-year period; recurring in ten years. **de·cen´ni·al·ly** *adv.* **de·cen·ni·um** (dĭsĕn´ēum) *n.* (pl. **-cen·ni·ums, -cen·ni·a** pr. -sĕn´ēa). Period of ten years.

de·cent (dē´sent) *adj.* 1. Seemly, not immodest, obscene, or indelicate; respectable. 2. Fair, tolerable, passable; (colloq.) kind, not severe or censorious. **de´cent·ly** *adv.*

de·cen·tral·ize (dēsĕn´tralīz) *v.t.* (**-ized, -iz·ing**). Divide and distribute (government, organization, etc.) among local centers. **de·cen·tral·i·za·tion** (dēsĕntralīzā´shon) *n.*

de·cep·tion (dĭsĕp´shon) *n.* Deceiving, being deceived; trick, sham.

de·cep·tive (dĭsĕp´tĭv) *adj.* Apt to deceive, easily mistaken. **de·cep´tive·ly** *adv.* **de·cep´tive·ness** *n.*

deci- *prefix.* One-tenth of.

dec·i·bar (dĕs´ibar) *n.* (meteor.) One-tenth of a BAR[2].

dec·i·bel (dĕs´ibĕl) *n.* Unit (= $\frac{1}{10}$ of a bel) used in comparison of levels of power in electrical communications circuit(s) or of intensities of sounds (abbrev. dB).

de·cide (dĭsīd´) *v.* (**-cid·ed, -cid·ing**). Settle (question, issue, dispute) by giving victory to one side; give judgment (*between, for, against,* etc.); bring, come, to a resolution or decision. **de·cid´a·ble** *adj.* **de·cid´ed** *adj.* (esp.) Definite, unquestionable; (of persons) of clear opinions or vigorous initiative; not vacillating. **de·cid´er** *n.* **de·cid´ed·ly** *adv.*

de·cid·u·ous (dĭsĭj´ōōus) *adj.* Shed periodically or normally; (of plant) shedding its leaves annually.

dec·i·gram (dĕs´igrăm) *n.* (abbrev. dg) One-tenth of a gram.

dec·i·li·ter (dĕs´ilēter) *n.* (abbrev. dl) One-tenth of a liter.

de·cil·lion (dĭsĭl´yon) *n.* 1. Eleventh power of a thousand (1 followed by 33 zeros). 2. (Brit.) Tenth power of a million (1 followed by 60 zeros).

dec·i·mal (dĕs´imal) *adj.* Of 10th parts, of the number ten; proceeding by tens; ~ **fraction,** fraction whose denominator is some power of 10, esp. such a fraction written to right of the units figure after the ~ *point,* and denoting tenths, hundredths, thousandths, etc.; ~ **point,** period at the left of a decimal fraction; ~ **system,** system of weights and measures in which each denomination is ten times the value of that immediately below it. **decimal** *n.* Decimal fraction. **dec´i·mal·ly** *adv.* **dec·i·mal·ize** (dĕs´imalīz) *v.t.* (**-ized, -iz·ing**). Express as decimal; convert to decimal system. **dec·i·mal·i·za·tion** (dĕsimalīzā´shon) *n.*

dec·i·mate (dĕs´imāt) *v.t.* (**-mat·ed, -mat·ing**). Put to death one in ten of; destroy $\frac{1}{10}$ of; kill or destroy large part of. **dec·i·ma·tion** (dĕsimā´shon) *n.*

dec·i·me·ter (dĕs´imēter) *n.* (abbrev. dm) One-tenth of a meter.

de·ci·pher (dĭsī´fer) *v.t.* Convert (what is written in cipher) into ordinary writing; make out, interpret, by means of key; make out meaning of. **de·ci´pher·a·ble** *adj.* **de·ci´pher·ment** *n.*

de·ci·sion (dĭsĭzh´on) *n.* Settlement (*of*), conclusion, formal judgment; making up one's mind, resolve; resoluteness, decided character.

de·ci·sive (dĭsī´sĭv) *adj.* Deciding, conclusive; decided; displaying ability to make decisions; unmistakable, unquestionable. **de·ci´sive·ly** *adv.* **de·ci´sive·ness** *n.*

deck[1] (dĕk) *n.* 1. Platform of planks or wood-covered iron extending from side to side of ship or part of it (in large ships **main, middle, lower** ~**s,** also **upper** ~ above main); planking of bridge etc.; one of several floors or levels; **clear the** ~**s,** make ready to fight, as by getting rid of unneeded gear; make ready for some activity or work, as by eliminating obstacles; ~ **chair,** folding canvas chair of the kind used on passenger ships; ~ **hand,** sailor who works on deck;

*Scrubbing the **decks** of the 'Mayflower II', a replica of the ship which carried the Pilgrim Fathers to America in 1620; the 'Mayflower II' made the journey in 1957 for the 350th anniversary of the settlement of Virginia.*

deck'house, room erected on upper deck of ship; **hit the deck**, (slang) get out of bed; fall, be pushed, or drop (oneself) to the ground or floor; **on deck**, (colloq.) ready for action; on hand; (baseball) next in order. 2. Pack of playing cards.

deck[2] (dĕk) *v.t.* 1. Array, adorn. 2. Cover as or with deck, furnish with deck. 3. (colloq.) Knock down (person, beast) with blow of fist etc.

deck·le (dĕk'*e*l) *n.* Frame in papermaking machine for limiting size or width of sheet; ~ **edge**, rough uncut edge of paper formed by deckle; ~**-edged** (*adj.*) having such an edge, as handmade paper.

de·claim (dĭklām') *v.* Speak or utter rhetorically; recite; deliver impassioned rather than reasoned speech.

dec·la·ma·tion (dĕkl*a*mā'sh*o*n) *n.* Act or art of declaiming; rhetorical exercise, set speech; impassioned speech, harangue. **de·claim'er** *n.* **de·clam·a·to·ry** (dĭklăm'*a*tōrē, -tōrē) *adj.*

de·clar·ant (dĭklār'*a*nt) *n.* One who makes legal declaration, esp. of becoming citizen of a country.

dec·la·ra·tion (dĕkl*a*rā'sh*o*n) *n.* Stating, announcing, openly, explicitly, or formally; emphatic, solemn or legal assertion or proclamation; public statement as embodied in document, instrument, or public act; (law) plaintiff's statement of claim; simple affirmation sometimes allowed in lieu of oath or solemn affirmation; creation or acknowledgment of trust or use in writing; (cards) in bridge, a bid, esp. final bid naming trump suit; **D~ of Independence:** see INDEPENDENCE; ~ **of war**, formal announcement by one nation of commencement of hostilities against another.

de·clare (dĭklār') *v.* (**-clared, -clar·ing**). 1. Make known, proclaim publicly, formally, or explicitly; pronounce to be; acknowledge possession of (dutiable goods); ~ **war**, formally proclaim beginning of hostilities. 2. (law) Make declaration. 3. (cards) In bridge, name trump suit or "no-trump" with final bid. **de·clar'a·ble, de·clar·a·tive** (dĭklăr'*a*tĭv), *adjs.* **de·clar·a·to·ry** (dĭklăr'*a*tōrē, -tōrē) *adj.* **de·clar'er** *n.*

dé·clas·sé (dāklăsā', -kl*a*-) (fem. **-sée**) *adj.* Having sunk in the social scale.

de·clas·si·fy (dēklăs'*i*fī) *v.t.* (**-fied, -fy·ing**). Cease to designate (information etc.) as secret.

de·clen·sion (dĭklĕn'sh*o*n) *n.* 1. Declining or deviating from vertical or horizontal position. 2. Decrease; decline, deterioration, decay. 3. (gram.) Variation of form of noun, adjective, or pronoun, constituting its cases; class in which noun etc. is grouped according to its inflections; declining. **de·clen'sion·al** *adj.*

The source and meaning of much **decoration** *lies in religious beliefs. The Mirror Room, Castle Linderhof, Bavaria (facing page) shows lavishness of decoration for social ends. Above: Detail from the mural, 'Great Tenochtitlan' (1945), by Diego Rivera, in the Palacio Nacional, Mexico City.*

dec·li·na·tion (dĕkl*i*nā'sh*o*n) *n.* 1. Slope, inclination, from vertical or horizontal position; decline; deviation. 2. (astron.) Angular distance of heavenly body from celestial equator. 3. (also **magnetic** ~) Deviation of magnetic needle from true north-and-south line, variation. 4. Declining, refusal.

de·cline (dĭklīn') *n.* 1. Sinking; gradual loss of vigor or excellence; decay; deterioration; wasting disease; downward movement in price or value. 2. Setting, last part of course, of sun, (fig.) of life, etc. ~ *v.* (**-clined, -clin·ing**). 1. Have downward inclination; bend down, bow down, droop. 2. (of sun, day, life, etc.) Draw to end of its course. 3. Fall off, decay, decrease, deteriorate. 4. Turn away from, refuse, withhold oneself from (discussion, challenge, etc.); not accept, refuse politely. 5. (gram.) Inflect, recite cases of. **de·clin'er** *n.*

de·clin'a·ble *adj.* (gram.) That can be declined.

de·cliv·i·ty (dĭklĭv'ĭtē) *n.* (pl. **-ties**). Downward slope; hollow.

de·coct (dĭkŏkt') *v.t.* Make decoction of. **de·coc·tion** (dĭkŏk'sh*o*n) *n.* (Liquor obtained by) boiling substance in liquid so as to extract soluble parts.

de·code (dĭkōd') *v.t.* (**-cod·ed, -cod·ing**). Decipher (coded message).

dé·colle·tage (dāk*o*ltahzh', dĕk*o*le-) *n.* (Exposure of neck and shoulders by) low-cut neck of dress. **dé·colle·té** (dāk*o*ltā', dĕk*o*le-) *adj.* (of dress) Low-necked; (of person) wearing low-necked dress. [Fr.]

de·com·mis·sion (dēk*o*mĭsh'*o*n) *v.t.* Withdraw (ship etc.) from

active service.

de·com·pose (dēkompōz′) *v.* (**-posed, -pos·ing**). 1. Separate or resolve into constituent parts or elements. 2. Disintegrate, break up; rot. **de·com·po·si·tion** (kēkŏmpozĭsh′on) *n.*

de·com·press (dēkomprĕs′) *v.t.* 1. Relieve pressure on (person who has been in compressed air) by means of air lock. 2. Reduce compression in (vehicle engine) thus making engine easier to start. **de·com·pres·sion** (dēkomprĕsh′on) *n.;* ~ **sickness,** caisson disease.

de·con·gest·ant (dēkonjĕs′tant) *adj.* & *n.* (Drug etc.) that relieves congestion.

de·con·tam·i·nate (dēkontăm′ĭnāt) *v.t.* (**-nat·ed, -nat·ing**). Rid (person, area, etc.) of contamination, esp. from poison gas, radioactivity; etc. **de·con·tam·i·na·tion** (dēkontămĭnā′shon) *n.*

de·con·trol (dēkontrōl′) *v.t.* (**-trolled, -trol·ling**) & *n.* Release from (esp. government) control.

dé·cor, de·cor (dākōr′, dĭ-, dā′kōr) *ns.* Scenery and furnishings, decorative style, of home, room, stage set, etc.

dec·o·rate (dĕk′erāt) *v.t.* (**-rat·ed, -rat·ing**). 1. Furnish with ornamental accessories; hang (streets etc.) with flags etc.; paint, paper, etc. (room, house); serve as adornment to. 2. Confer medal, honor, etc. upon. **dec·o·ra·tive** (dĕk′eratĭv, dĕk′ra-, -erā-) *adj.* **dec′o·ra·tive·ly** *adv.* **dec′o·ra·tive·ness** *n.*

dec·o·ra·tion (dĕkorā′shon) *n.* (esp.) 1. Decorating. 2. (pl.) Flags etc. put up on festive occasion. 3. Medal etc., conferred and worn as mark of honor; **D~ Day** = MEMORIAL Day.

dec·o·ra·tor (dĕk′orāter) *n.* Interior decorator.

dec·or·ous (dĕk′orus, -kōr′-) *adj.* Not violating good taste or propriety, dignified and decent. **dec′o·rous·ly** *adv.*

de·co·rum (dĭkōr′um, -kōr′-) *n.* Seemliness, propriety, etiquette; particular usage required by politeness or decency.

de·cou·page, dé·cou·page (dākōōpahzh′) *ns.* Decoration of surfaces with paper cutouts.

de·coy (dē′koi, dĭkoi′) *n.* 1. Enclosed place, pond, etc., into which wildfowl may be lured and caught. 2. Living or artificial bird or other animal used to entice game, esp. wild ducks, into shooting range or a trap; (fig.) person or thing used to decoy others. **de·coy** (dĭkoi′) *v.t.* Entice into place of capture, esp. with decoy; allure *into, out of, away,* etc., ensnare.

de·crease (dĭkrēs′) *v.* (**-creased, -creas·ing**). Lessen, diminish. **decrease** (dē′krēs; dĭkrēs′) *n.* Diminution, lessening.

de·cree (dĭkrē′) *n.* 1. Ordinance or edict set forth by authority; edict or law of ecclesiastical council; one of eternal purposes, will, of God, Providence, Nature, etc. 2. Judgment of court of equity, admiralty, probate, or divorce; in divorce cases, order of court declaring nullity or dissolution of marriage; ~ **nisi**: see NISI. **decree** *v.t.* (**-creed, -cree·ing**). Ordain by decree.

dec·re·ment (dĕk′rement) *n.* Decrease, amount lost by diminution or waste (opp. *increment*).

de·crep·it (dĭkrĕp′ĭt) *adj.* Wasted, worn out, enfeebled with age and infirmities. **de·crep·i·tude** (dĭkrĕp′ĭtōōd, -tūd) *n.*

de·cres·cent (dĭkrĕs′ent) *adj.* Waning, decreasing (usu. of moon).

de·cre·tal (dĭkrē′tal) *n.* Papal decree; **D~s**, collection of such decrees, forming part of canon law.

de·crim·i·nal·ize (dēkrĭm′ĭnalīz) *v.t.* (**-ized, -iz·ing**). Abolish or reduce criminal penalties for (specific crime, esp. use or possession of marijuana).

de·cry (dĭkrī′) *v.t.* (**-cried, -cry·ing**). Disparage, cry down.

de·cum·bent (dĭkŭm′bent) *adj.* Reclining; prostrate; (bot., zool.) lying along ground, lying flat on surface. **de·cum′bent·ly** *adv.*

de·cus·sate (dĭkŭs′āt, -ĭt) *adj.* X-shaped; (bot.) with pairs of opposite leaves etc. each at right angles to pair below. **decussate** (dĭkŭs′āt, dĕk′usāt) *v.* (**-sat·ed, -sat·ing**). Arrange, be arranged thus, intersect. **de·cus·sa·tion** (dēkusā′shon, dĕku-) *n.*

ded·i·cate (dĕd′ĭkāt) *v.t.* (**-cat·ed, -cat·ing**). Devote (*to* God etc.) with solemn rites; give up, devote (*to* person, purpose); inscribe (book, music, etc.) *to* patron or friend. **ded·i·ca·to·ry** (dĕd′ĭkatōrē, -tōrē) *adj.* **ded·i·ca·tion** (dĕdĭkā′shon) *n.* (esp.) Dedicatory inscription. **ded′i·ca·tor** *n.*

de·duce (dĭdōōs′, -dūs′) *v.t.*

(**-duced, -duc·ing**). 1. Trace course of, bring down (record etc.) *from* or *to* particular period; trace derivation or descent of. 2. Derive as conclusion *from* something already known; infer. **de·duc'i·ble** *adj.*

de·duct (dĭdŭkt') *v.t.* Take away, put aside (amount etc.) *from.* **de·duct'i·ble** *adj.*

de·duc·tion (dĭdŭk'shon) *n.* 1. Deducting; amount deducted, as in *income tax* ~. 2. Deducing; inference by reasoning from generals to particulars (opp. INDUCTION); thing deduced.

de·duc·tive (dĭdŭk'tĭv) *adj.* Of, reasoning by, deduction. **de·duc'tive·ly** *adv.*

deed (dēd) *n.* 1. Thing done by intelligent or responsible agent; act of bravery, skill, etc., feat, performance, doing. 2. (law) Written instrument purporting to effect some legal disposition, and sealed and delivered by disposing party (in practice now always signed also but not always delivered). ~ *v.t.* Convey or transfer by deed.

dee·jay (dē'jā) (slang) = DISC jockey.

deem (dēm) *v.t.* Believe, consider, judge, count.

de-em·pha·size (dēĕm'fasīz) *v.t.* (**-sized, -siz·ing**). Remove emphasis from. **de-em·pha·sis** (dēĕm'fasĭs) *n.* (pl. **-ses** pr. -sēz).

deep (dēp) *adj.* 1. Extending far down from top, or far in from surface or edge. 2. (fig.) Hard to fathom; profound, not superficial, penetrating. 3. Heartfelt; absorbing; absorbed; intense, vivid, extreme. 4. Not shrill; low-pitched, full-toned. 5. ~ **freeze**, refrigerator in which food can be quickly frozen and stored for long periods (**Deep'freeze**, trademark); ~**-sea** (*adj.*), of the deeper part of the sea, some way from shore; ~ **set** (*adj.*), deeply placed; well established; ~ **space**, regions beyond solar system. **deep'ly** *adv.* **deep'ness** *n.* **deep** *n.* 1. (poet.) **the** ~, the sea. 2. Deep part of the sea; abyss, pit, cavity; mysterious region of thought or feeling. ~ *adv.* Deeply; far down or in; ~**-freeze** (*v.t.*), freeze food quickly; (colloq.) store away (damaging information) to prevent discovery; ~**-fry** (*v.t.*), fry by immersion in a deep pan of hot oil or fat; ~**-rooted**, having deep roots; (fig.) not easily eradicated; ~**-seated**, having its seat far below surface; not superficial; ~ **-six** (*v.t.*), (slang) discard, throw away, jettison. **deep'en** *v.* Make, become, deep or deeper.

Above left: Red ***deer.*** *Below left: Fallow deer. Above right: Reindeer. Below right: Roe deer. Deer are woodland creatures found in Europe, Asia, America, and northern Africa. Speed and highly developed senses protect them from danger. The species differ in their habits.*

Deep (dēp) **South.** South-eastern states of the U.S., particularly the former Confederate states of South Carolina, Georgia, Alabama, Mississippi, and (often) Louisiana.

deer (dēr) *n.* (pl. **deer**, sometimes **deers**). Ruminant quadruped of family Cervidae, most of the males of which have deciduous branching antlers; Amer. species include **white-tailed ~, black-tailed ~**, ELK, MOOSE, and CARIBOU; Old World species include **fallow, red, roe** ~ (see FALLOW[2]; RED; ROE[1]); ~ **fly**, any of several blood-sucking flies of the genus *Chrysops* with dark wing markings; **deer'hound**, large rough greyhound of Scottish breed; **deer park**, park where deer are kept; **deer'skin**, (made of) deer's skin; **deer'stalker**, one who stalks deer; cloth cap with peak before and behind.

de·face (dĭfās') *v.t.* (**-faced, -fac·ing**). Disfigure; mar, spoil appearance of; make illegible. **de·face'ment** *n.*

de fac·to (dē făk'tō, dā) *adj.* & *adv. phr.* In fact, whether by right or not. [L.]

de·fal·cate (dĭfăl'kāt, -fawl'-) *v.i.* (**-cat·ed, -cat·ing**). Embezzle or misuse funds; misappropriate property in one's charge. **de·fal·ca·tion** (dēfălkā'shon, -fawl-) *n.*

de·fame (dĭfām') *v.t.* (**-famed, -fam·ing**). Attack the good

*Most countries today spend millions of dollars on elaborate **defense** weapons and on training forces to use them. The development since the 1939–45 war of guided missiles for defense is an example of progress in this field.*

reputation of, speak ill of. **def·a·ma·tion** (dĕfamā'shon) *n.* **de·fam·a·to·ry** (dĭfăm'atōrē, -tōrē) *adj.* **de·fam'er** *n.*

de·fault (dĭfawlt') *n.* Want, absence; failure to act or appear; neglect; failure to pay. ~ *v.* 1. Make, be guilty of, default; fail to appear in court; fail to pay money due. 2. Declare (party) in default and give judgment against him or her. **de·fault'er** *n.*

de·feat (dĭfēt') *v.t.* Win victory over, conquer, in battle or other contest; frustrate, baffle; (law) annul. ~ *n.* Act or instance of defeating or being defeated; frustration.

de·feat·ism (dĭfē'tĭzem) *n.* Disposition, conduct, of one who accepts defeat as inevitable. **de·feat'ist** *n.* & *adj.*

def·e·cate (dĕf'ekāt) *v.* (**-cat·ed, -cat·ing**). Clear of dregs, refine, purify; get rid of, purge away, (dregs, excrement, sin); void feces. **def·e·ca·tion** (dĕfekā'shon) *n.*

de·fect (dē'fĕkt, dĭfĕkt') *n.* Lack of something essential to completeness; shortcoming, failing; blemish; amount by which thing falls short. **de·fect** (dĭfĕkt') *v.i.* Desert, esp. *to* another cause, country, etc. **de·fec·tion** (dĭfĕk'shon), **de·fec'tor** *ns.*

de·fec·tive (dĭfĕk'tĭv) *adj.* Having defect(s); incomplete; faulty; wanting or deficient *in*; (gram.) not having all usual inflected forms. ~ *n.* (esp.) **mental** ~, mentally defective person. **de·fec'tive·ly** *adv.* **de·fec'tive·ness** *n.*

de·fend (dĭfĕnd') *v.* 1. Ward off attack from; keep safe; protect (*against, from*). 2. Uphold by argument, speak or write in favor of; (law) make defense in court; (of counsel) appear for defendant, conduct defense of. **de·fend'a·ble** *adj.* **de·fend'er** *n.*

de·fend·ant (dĭfĕn'dant) *n.* Person sued in court of law. ~ *adj.* That is a defendant.

de·fend·er (dĭfĕn'der) *n.* One who defends; holder of championship etc. defending the title; **D~ of the Faith** (L. *Fidei Defensor*), title borne by English sovereigns since Henry VIII, on whom it was conferred in 1521 by Pope Leo X as reward for writing against Luther.

de·fen·es·tra·tion (dēfĕnestrā'shon) *n.* Throwing out of a window.

de·fense (dĭfĕns') *n.* 1. Defending from, resistance against, attack. 2. Thing that defends; means of resisting or warding off attack; military resources of a country; (pl.) fortifications. 3. Justification, vindication; speech or writing used to this end; (law) denial or charge by accused party, defendant's pleading or proceedings. 4. ~ **mechanism**, (psychol.) dynamic mental system serving to protect the conscious personality against disruptive unconscious impulses. **de·fense'less** *adj.* **de·fense'less·ly** *adv.*

de·fen·si·ble (dĭfĕn'sĭbel) *adj.* Easily defended (in war or argument); justifiable. **de·fen·si·bil·i·ty** (dĭfĕnsĭbĭl'ĭtē) *n.* **de·fen'si·bly** *adv.*

de·fen·sive (dĭfĕn'sĭv) *adj.* Serving, used, done, for defense; protective; not aggressive. **de·fen'sive·ly** *adv.* **defensive** *n.* State or position of defense.

de·fer[1] (dĭfẽr') *v.* (**-ferred, -fer·ring**). 1. Put off, postpone; procrastinate, be dilatory. 2. Exempt from military service temporarily. 3. **deferred payment**, payment by installments; with payments or benefits withheld until a future date. **de·fer·ral** (dĭfẽr'al), **de·fer'ment, de·fer'rer** *ns.*

de·fer[2] (dĭfẽr') *v.t.* (**-ferred, -fer·ring**). Submit or make concessions in opinion or action *to* (person etc.).

def·er·ence (dĕf'erens) *n.* Compliance with advice etc. of one superior in wisdom or position; respect, manifestation of desire to comply, courteous regard; **in ~ to,** out of respect for. **def·er·en·tial** (dĕferĕn'shal) *adj.* **def·er·en'tial·ly** *adv.*

def·er·ent (dĕf'erent) *adj.* Conveying away.

de·fi·ance (dĭfī'ans) *n.* Challenge to fight or maintain cause, assertion, etc.; open disobedience or disregard.

de·fi·ant (dĭfī'ant) *adj.* Expressing defiance. **de·fi'ant·ly** *adv.*

de·fi·cien·cy (dĭfĭsh'ensē) *n.* (pl. **-cies**). Being deficient; want, lack; thing wanting; amount by which thing, esp. revenue, falls short; ~ **disease**, disease caused by lack in diet of necessary elements, esp. vitamins. **de·fi·cient** (dĭfĭsh'ent) *adj.* Incomplete, defective, wanting *in*; insufficient in quantity, force, etc. **de·fi'cient·ly** *adv.*

def·i·cit (dĕf'ĭsĭt) *n.* Amount by which anything, esp. sum of money, is too small; excess of liabilities over assets or of expenditure over income.

def·i·lade (dĕfĭlād') *v.t.* (**-lad·ed, -lad·ing**). Secure (fortress) against enfilading fire. ~ *n.* Act or operation of defilading.

de·file[1] (dĭfīl', dē'fīl) *n.* Narrow way along which troops can march only in file; narrow pass or gorge. ~ *v.i.* (**-filed, -fil·ing**). March in files, by files.

de·file[2] (dĭfīl') *v.t.* (**-filed, -fil·ing**). Make dirty, befoul; pollute, corrupt; desecrate, profane; make ceremonially unclean. **de·file'ment** *n.*

de·fine (dĭfīn') *v.t.* (**-fined, -fin·ing**). Settle limits of; make clear, esp. in outline; set forth essence of, declare exact meaning of; characterize, constitute definition of. **de·fin'a·ble** *adj.* **de·fin'a·bly** *adv.*

def·i·nite (dĕf'ĭnĭt) *adj.* With exact limits; determinate, distinct, precise, not vague; ~ **article**: see ARTICLE. **def'i·nite·ly** *adv.* Clearly, plainly; yes indeed; without fail. **def'i·nite·ness** *n.*

def·i·ni·tion (dĕfĭnĭsh'on) *n.* 1.

Defining; statement of precise nature of thing or meaning of word. 2. Making or being distinct, degree of distinctness of details in a photograph, film, television picture, etc.

de·fin·i·tive (dĭfĭn'ĭtĭv) *adj.* Decisive, unconditional, final; authoritative (~ **edition**). **de·fin'i·tive·ly** *adv.* **de·fin'i·tive·ness** *n.*

de·flate (dĭflāt') *v.* (**-flat·ed, -flat·ing**). 1. Let air etc. out of (tire, balloon, etc.). 2. Reduce (inflated currency); practice deflation. 3. Lower (person's spirits, confidence, etc.).

de·fla·tion (dĭflā'sh*o*n) *n.* 1. Deflating, esp. situation in any country where prices generally are falling relatively to costs of production, giving rise to losses and unemployment. 2. Lowering (person's spirits, confidence, etc.). **de·fla'tor** *n.* **de·fla'tion·ar·y** *adj.*

de·flect (dĭflĕkt') *v.* Bend or turn aside; bend (ray of light) from straight line. **de·flec'tive, de·flect'a·ble** *adjs.* **de·flec'tor** *n.*

de·flec·tion (dĭflĕk'sh*o*n) *n.* Deflecting; (esp.) turning of magnetic needle or recording needle of galvanometer away from its zero.

def·lo·ra·tion (dĕflorā'sh*o*n, dēflo-) *n.* Deflowering.

de·flow·er (dĭflow'*er*) *v.t.* Deprive of virginity; ravage, spoil; strip of flowers.

The Ballet Scene from Meyerbeer's 'Roberto il Diavolo' by ***Edgar Degas.*** *The Impressionist painter's compositions were influenced by the then new techniques of photography. Degas excelled in ballet and circus portrayal.*

De·foe (defō'), **Daniel** (1660?–1731). English journalist and novelist; author of *Robinson Crusoe, Moll Flanders,* etc.

de·fog (dēfawg', -fŏg') *v.t.* (**-fogged, -fog·ging**). Eliminate condensation, fog, etc. from (mirror, car window, etc.). **de·fog'ger** *n.*

de·fo·li·ant (dĭfō'lēant) *n.* Spray or dust to defoliate plants.

de·fo·li·ate (dēfō'lēāt) *v.t.* (**-at·ed, -at·ing**). Remove leaves from, esp. as military tactic. **de·fo·li·a·tion** (dēfōlēā'sh*o*n), **de·fo'li·a·tor** *ns.*

de·for·est (dēfōr'ĭst, -fär'-) *v.t.* Clear of forest. **de·for·est·a·tion** (dēfōrĭstā'sh*o*n, -fär-) *n.*

De For·est (dĭ fōr'ĭst, fär'-), **Lee** (1873–1961). Amer. inventor; called "the father of radio"; worked on wireless telegraphy, radiotelephony, sound-on-film, television, etc.

de·form (dĭfōrm') *v.t.* Deface; put out of shape, misshape (esp. in past part.). **de·form'a·ble** *adj.*

de·for·ma·tion (dēfōrmā'sh*o*n, dĕf*er*-) *n.* Disfigurement; change for the worse; perverted form.

de·form·i·ty (dĭfōr'mĭtē) *n.* (pl. **-ties**). Being deformed, ugliness, disfigurement; malformation (esp. of body or limb).

de·fraud (dĭfrawd') *v.t.* Cheat. **de·fraud'er** *n.*

de·fray (dĭfrā') *v.t.* Settle; satisfy by payment; bear or pay (costs etc.). **de·fray'ment** *n.* **de·fray'a·ble** *adj.* **de·fray'al** *n.*

de·frock (dĭfrŏk') = UNFROCK.

de·frost (dĭfrawst', -frŏst') *v.* Remove frost from; thaw, esp. frozen food.

defs. *abbrev.* Definitions.

deft (dĕft) *adj.* Dextrous, esp. in manual skill. **deft'ly** *adv.* **deft'ness** *n.*

de·funct (dĭfŭngkt') *adj.* Dead; no longer existing.

de·fuse (dēfūz') *v.t.* (**-fused, -fus·ing**). 1. Remove fuse from (explosive). 2. Reduce likelihood of trouble arising from (crisis etc.).

de·fy (dĭfī') *v.t.* (**-fied, -fy·ing**). 1. Challenge to combat (archaic); challenge *to* contest or trial of skill. 2. Resist boldly or openly, set at naught; (of things) be beyond power of.

deg. *abbrev.* Degree.

De·gas (dāgah', dā'gah), **Hilaire Germain Edgar** (1834–1917). French Impressionist painter and sculptor, known especially for his paintings of the ballet and of horses.

De Gaulle (d*e* gōl', gawl'), **Charles** (1890–1970). French general and statesman; head of the "Free French" movement after the occupation of France by Germans in 1940 and of the French Provisional Government, 1944–5; premier of France, 1958–9; president 1945–6 and 1959–69.

de·gauss (dēgows′) *v.t.* Demagnetize; esp. render (ship) immune to magnetic mines or (television receiver) to magnetic interference. [see GAUSS]

de·gen·er·ate (dĭjĕn′erĭt) *adj.* Having lost qualities proper to race or kind, sunk from former excellence, debased, degraded; (biol.) having reverted to lower type. **de·gen·er·a·cy** (dĭjĕn′erasē) *n.* **degenerate** *n.* Degenerate person or animal. **degenerate** (dĭjĕn′erāt) *v.i.* (**-at·ed, -at·ing**). Become degenerate. **de·gen′er·ate·ly** *adv.* **de·gen′er·ate·ness** *n.* **de·gen·er·a·tive** (dĭjĕn′erātĭv, -era-) *adj.*

de·gen·er·a·tion (dĭjĕnerā′shon) *n.* Becoming degenerate; (path.) morbid disintegration of tissue or change in its structure.

de·glu·ti·nate (dēglōō′tinăt) *v.t.* (**-nat·ed, -nat·ing**). Extract gluten from (flour etc.). **de·glu·ti·na·tion** (dēglōōtinā′shon) *n.*

de·grade (dĭgrād′) *v.* (**-grad·ed, -grad·ing**). 1. Reduce to lower rank or office. 2. Bring into dishonor or contempt; lower in character or quality, debase. 3. (chem.) Break down (molecule); (phys.) reduce (energy) to a form less capable of transformation. 4. (geol.) Wear down (rocks etc.) by surface abrasion or disintegration. **de·grad′a·ble** *adj.* **deg·ra·da·tion** (dĕgradā′shon) *n.* **de·grad′ed·ly** *adv.* **de·grad′ed·ness, de·grad′er** *ns.*

de·gree (dĭgrē′) *n.* 1. Thing placed like step in series; stage in ascending or descending scale or process; **by ~s**, gradually. 2. Stage in direct line of descent. 3. Relative social or official rank; relative condition or state. 4. Stage in intensity or amount; (criminal law) distinctive grade of crime (**murder in the first ~**, homicide premeditated or resulting from commission of grave crime; **in the second ~**, unpremeditated, or resulting from commission of lesser crime); **third ~**: see THIRD. 5. Academic title conferred by college or university to student who has completed course of study or (**honorary ~**) on person of distinction as honor; (freemasonry) each step of proficiency in order, conferring successively higher rank. 6. (gram.) Stage (positive, comparative, superlative) in comparison of adjective or adverb. 7. (geom. etc.) Unit of angular measurement (symbol °), angle equal to $\frac{1}{90}$ right angle, arc of $\frac{1}{360}$ circumference of circle; esp. $\frac{1}{360}$ of Earth's circumference, = 60 minutes; (thermometry) unit of temperature, varying according to scale employed; (mus.) (interval between) successive notes forming a scale.

Detail from 'Dante and Virgil in the Underworld' (Louvre, Paris) painted by ***Ferdinand Delacroix*** *(1799–1863), notable for his symbolic use of color.*

de·hisce (dĭhĭs′) *v.i.* (**-hisced, -hisc·ing**). Gape; (bot., of seed vessel etc.) burst open. **de·his′cence** *n.* **de·his′cent** *adj.*

de·hu·man·ize (dēhū′manīz, dēū′-) *v.t.* (**-ized, -iz·ing**). Divest of human characteristics. **de·hu·man·i·za·tion** (dēhūmanīzā′shon, dēū-) *n.*

de·hu·mid·i·fy (dēhūmĭd′ifī, dēū-) *v.t.* (**-fied, fy·ing**). Remove moisture from. **de·hu·mid·i·fi·ca·tion** (dēhūmĭdĭfĭkā′shon, dēū-) **de·hu·mid′i·fi·er** *ns.*

de·hy·drate (dēhī′drāt) *v.* (**-drat·ed, -drat·ing**). (chem.) Deprive of, lose, water or its constituent elements; dry completely, desiccate (foods). **de·hy·dra·tion** (dēhīdrā′shon) *n.*

de·ice (dēīs′) *v.t.* (**-iced, -ic·ing**). Remove, prevent formation of, ice on (airplane, windshield, etc.). **de·ic′er** *n.* Device or substance for deicing.

de·i·fy (dē′ifī) *v.t.* (**-fied, -fy·ing**). Make a god of; make godlike; regard as a god, worship. **de·if·i·ca·tion** (dēifĭkā′shon) *n.*

deign (dān) *v.* Think fit,

condescend (*to*); condescend to give, vouchsafe.

de·i·on·ize (dēī'onīz) *v.t.* (**-ized, -iz·ing**). Remove ions or ionic constituents from (water etc.). **de·i·on·i·za·tion** (dēīonīzā'shon) *n.*

de·ism (dē'ĭzem) *n.* Belief in the existence of a god without accepting revelation; natural religion. **de'ist** *n.* **de·is·tic** (dēĭs'tĭk) *adj.* **de·is'ti·cal·ly** *adv.*

de·i·ty (dē'itē) *n.* (pl. **-ties**). 1. Divine status, quality, or nature; a god. 2. (**the**) **Deity**, God.

dé·jà vu (dāzhah vōō'; *Fr.* dĕzhăvū'). Feeling of having previously experienced what is happening but has not actually been experienced before. [Fr., = "already seen"]

de·ject (dĭjĕkt') *v.t.* Dispirit, depress. **de·ject'ed·ly** *adv.* **de·jec·tion** (dĭjĕk'shon) *n.*

de ju·re (dē joor'ē) *adj.* & *adv. phr.* Rightful, by right. [L.]

Dek·ker (dĕk'er), **Thomas** (1570?–1632). (also **Deck·er**) English Elizabethan dramatist, author of *The Honest Whore, The Shoemaker's Holiday*, etc.

Del. *abbrev.* Delaware.

del. *abbrev.* Delegate.

De·la·croix (delăkrwah'), **Ferdinand Victor Eugène** (1799–1863). French Romantic painter.

Del·a·ware[1] (dĕl'awār) *n.* (Member, language) of an Algonquian-speaking group of N. Amer. Ind. tribes living in the Delaware River Valley and the New Jersey area.

Del·a·ware[2] (dĕl'awār). Mid-Atlantic state of U.S.; one of original 13 states and second smallest; capital, Dover; ~ **Bay**, inlet of Atlantic between Delaware and New Jersey; ~ **River**, river flowing S. from Catskill Mts. to Delaware Bay, forming several state borders along its course; ~ **Water Gap**, gorge in E. Pennsylvania formed by this river.

De La Warr (dĕl'awār), **Baron** (1577–1618). (**Thomas West**) Lord Delaware; English colonial administrator in Amer.; governor and captain general of Virginia colony, 1610; arrived in time to prevent abandonment of Jamestown by settlers.

de·lay (dĭlā') *n.* Delaying; procrastination; hindrance to progress. ~ *v.* 1. Postpone, defer, put off; hinder. 2. Loiter, be tardy; wait. 3. **delayed-action,** (attrib.) of a device etc. that operates after a lapse of time. **de·lay'er** *n.*

The 16th-century observatory, Jantar Mantar, ***Delhi.*** *Once the capital of the Mogul empire, Delhi is rich in historical monuments. The city is the 7th on the site, built between 1638 and 1658 during the reign of Shah Jahan.*

de·le (dē'lē) *v.t.* (**-led, -le·ing**). (print.) Delete indicated letter, word, etc. (usu. written ₰).

de·lec·ta·ble (dĭlĕk'tabel) *adj.* Delightful, pleasant. **de·lec·ta·tion** (dēlĕktā'shon) *n.* Enjoyment. **de·lec'ta·bly** *adv.*

del·e·gate (dĕl'egāt, -gĭt) *n.* Deputy, commissioner; elected representative sent to conference. **del·e·gate** (dĕl'egāt) *v.t.* (**-gat·ed, -gat·ing**). Depute, send as representative; commit (authority etc.) to agent. **del·e·ga·tion** (dĕlegā'shon) *n.* Entrusting of authority to deputy; body of delegates; members of legislature representing particular political unit. **del·e·ga·cy** (dĕl'egasē) *n.* (pl. **-cies**).

de Les·seps (de lĕs'eps), **Ferdinand Marie, Vicomte** (1805–94). French diplomat; promoted building of Suez Canal; president of French construction company that worked on it, 1881–8, but gave up because of financial and political difficulties.

de·lete (dĭlēt') *v.t.* (**-let·ed, -let·ing**). Strike out, obliterate (letter, word, passage, etc.). **de·le·tion** (dĭlē'shon) *n.*

del·e·te·ri·ous (dĕletēr'ēus) *adj.* Noxious, harmful. **del·e·te'ri·ous·ly** *adv.* **del·e·te'ri·ous·ness** *n.*

Delft (dĕlft). Town in Nether-

***Delicatessens** sell fine food and delicacies for the table. Usually one finds gourmet treats and specialized ethnic foods.*

lands; hence, kind of pottery (also **delft ware**) produced there, usu. with white glaze on which a decoration is painted in blue.

Del·hi (dĕl′ē, -hī). Third largest city in India, located in N. part, capital from 1912–31; a union territory of N. India, see NEW DELHI.

del·i (dĕl′ē) *n.* (pl. **del·is** pr. dĕl′ēz). (colloq.) Delicatessen.

de·lib·er·ate (dĭlĭb′erĭt) *adj.* Intentional; considered, not impulsive; slow in deciding, cautious; leisurely, not hurried. **de·lib′er·ate·ly** *adv.* **de·lib′er·ate·ness** *n.* **deliberate** (dĭlĭb′erāt) *v.* (**-at·ed, -at·ing**). Consider, think carefully; take counsel, consult, hold debate.

de·lib·er·a·tion (dĭlĭberā′shon) *n.* Careful consideration; discussion, debate; care, avoidance of impulsiveness, slowness of movement.

de·lib·er·a·tive (dĭlĭb′erātĭv, -era-) *adj.* Of, appointed for purpose of, deliberation or debate. **de·lib′er·a·tive·ly** *adv.*

del·i·ca·cy (dĕl′ĭkasē) *n.* (pl. **-cies**). 1. Fineness of texture, substance, outline, etc., or of feeling or observation. 2. Frailty; susceptibility to injury or disease; need of care in handling. 3. Refinement, sense of what is becoming or modest; regard for feelings of others. 4. Choice or dainty item of food. 5. Delicate trait; nicety.

del·i·cate (dĕl′ĭkĭt) *adj.* 1. Palatable, dainty (of food); sheltered, luxurious, (of life, upbringing, etc.). 2. Fine of texture, soft, slender, slight; of exquisite quality of workmanship; (of color) subdued. 3. Subtle. 4. Easily injured; liable to illness. 5. Requiring careful handling (lit. and fig.). 6. Subtly sensitive; finely skillful; avoiding the offensive or immodest, considerate. **del′i·cate·ly** *adv.* **del′i·cate·ness** *n.*

del·i·ca·tes·sen (dĕlĭkatĕs′en) *n.* (Store selling) foods ready for serving or nearly so, such as salads, cooked meats, sandwiches, etc.

de·li·cious (dĭlĭsh′us) *adj.* Highly delightful, esp. to taste, smell, or sense of humor. **de·li′cious·ly** *adv.* **de·li′cious·ness** *n.*

de·light (dĭlīt′) *n.* Being delighted; thing affording delight. ~ *v.* Give great pleasure or enjoyment to; rejoice, be highly pleased. **de·light′ful** *adj.* **de·light′ful·ly** *adv.* **de·light′ful·ness** *n.*

De·li·lah (dĭlī′la). Woman who betrayed Samson, her lover, to the Philistines by having his hair shorn as he was sleeping (Judges 16); hence, seductive treacherous woman.

de·lim·it (dĭlĭm′ĭt) *v.t.* Determine limits or boundary of. **de·lim·i·ta·tion** (dĭlĭmĭtā′shon) *n.*

de·lin·e·ate (dĭlĭn′ēāt) *v.t.* (**-at·ed, -at·ing**). Show by drawing or description, portray. **de·lin·e·a·tion** (dĭlĭnēā′shon), **de·lin′e·a·tor** *ns.*

de·lin·quen·cy (dĭlĭng′kwensē) *n.* (pl. **-cies**). Being a delinquent; neglect or violation of duty; guilt; act of delinquency, offense, misdeed. **de·lin·quent** (dĭlĭng′kwent) *adj.* Defaulting, guilty. ~ *n.* Delinquent person. **de·lin′quent·ly** *adv.*

del·i·quesce (dĕlĭkwĕs′) *v.i.* (**-quesced, -quesc·ing**). Become liquid, dissolve in moisture absorbed from the air; (fig.) melt away. **del·i·ques′cence** *n.* **del·i·ques′cent** *adj.*

de·lir·i·ous (dĭlēr′ēus) *adj.* Affected with delirium, temporarily or apparently mad, raving; wildly excited, ecstatic; betraying delirium or ecstasy. **de·lir′i·ous·ly** *adv.* **de·lir′i·ous·ness** *n.*

de·lir·i·um (dĭlēr′ēum) *n.* (pl. **-i·ums, -i·a** pr. -ēa). Disordered state of mind with incoherent speech, hallucinations, and frenzied excitement; great excitement, ecstasy; ~ **tremens** (trē′mĕnz), form of delirium with terrifying delusions, to which heavy drinkers are liable.

De·li·us (dē′lēus, dēl′yus), **Frederick** (1862–1934). English composer of songs, concertos, choral works, etc.

de·liv·er (dĭlĭv′er) *v.t.* 1. Rescue, save, set free (*from*). 2. Assist (female) in giving birth; assist in the birth of; (also **be delivered of**) give birth to. 3. Unburden *oneself of* opinion, thought, etc., in discourse. 4. Give *up, over,* abandon, resign, hand on *to* another; distribute (letters, packages, etc.) to addressee or purchaser; present, render, (account); (law) hand over formally (esp. deed to grantee or third party). 5. Launch, aim (blow, ball, attack). 6. Utter, pronounce openly or formally (speech, judgment, etc.).

de·liv·er·ance (dĭlĭv′erans) *n.* Rescue, esp. from bondage or danger; emphatically or formally delivered opinion, esp. jury's verdict.

de·liv·er·y (dĭlĭv′erē, -lĭv′rē) *n.* (pl. **-er·ies**). 1. Childbirth. 2. Surrender (*of*); handing over (esp. of letters or goods). 3. (law) Formal handing over of property; formal transfer of deed to grantee or third party. 4. Delivering (blow, ball, etc.); action shown in doing this. 5. Uttering of speech etc.; manner of doing this.

dell (dĕl) *n.* Small hollow or valley, usu. wooded.

del·la Rob·bia (dĕla rō′bēa, rŏb′ēa), **Luca** (1400–82). Florentine sculptor famous for his work in terracotta; his terracotta process, which was inherited by the della Robbia family, is characterized by

*The excavations at **Delphi**, begun in 1892, uncovered temples, treasuries, sculptures and fragmented frescoes of the 6th–4th centuries B.C. Inscriptions give praise to Apollo.*

the use of white figures against a usu. blue background.

De·los (dē′lŏs, dĕl′ōs). Island in the Aegean, one of the Cyclades; supposed to have been raised from the sea by Poseidon and anchored to the bottom of the sea by Zeus; an important center of the worship of Apollo. **De·li·an** (dē′lē*a*n, dēl′y*a*n) *adj*.

de·louse (dēlows′) *v.t.* (**-loused, -lous·ing**). Clear of lice.

Del·phi (dĕl′fī). Greek town on slopes of Mt. Parnassus, with ancient sanctuary and oracle of Apollo. **Del·phi·an** (dĕl′fē*a*n), **Del·phic** (dĕl′fĭk) *adjs*. Of Delphi or the Delphic Apollo or oracle; obscure and ambiguous like the oracle's responses.

del·phin·i·um (dĕlfĭn′ē*u*m) *n*. Ranunculaceous plant of genus *D*~ including larkspur, with handsome irregular-shaped blue or pink flowers, (esp.) cultivated species or variety of this. [Gk. *delphinion* larkspur, dim. of *delphin* dolphin]

del·ta (dĕl′t*a*) *n*. 1. Fourth letter of Greek alphabet Δ, δ (corresponding to *d*). 2. Triangular tract of sand, gravel, and silt enclosed and traversed by the diverging mouths of a river. 3. ~ **ray**, one of the rays of low penetrative power produced by particles emitted by radium, polonium, uranium, etc., consisting of low-velocity electrons knocked from an atom during a collision with some other particle; ~ **wing**, triangular sweptback wing of highspeed aircraft; airplane with such a wing.

del·toid (dĕl′toid) *adj*. Triangular; like river delta; ~ **muscle**, large triangular muscle forming prominence of shoulder and serving to lift upper arm. **deltoid** *n*. Deltoid muscle.

de·lude (dĭlo͞od′) *v.t.* (**-lud·ed, -lud·ing**). Mislead, deceive; cause to believe what is not true.

del·uge (dĕl′ūj) *n*. Great flood, inundation; heavy fall of rain; flood of words etc.; **the D**~, the great flood in the time of Noah. **deluge** *v.t.* (**-uged, -ug·ing**). Flood, inundate. [L. *diluvium* flood]

de·lu·sion (dĭlo͞o′zh*o*n) *n*. False impression or opinion, esp. as symptom or form of madness. **de·lu′sion·al, de·lu·sive** (dĭlo͞o′sĭv), **de·lu·so·ry** (dĭlo͞o′s*e*rē) *adjs*. **de·lu′sive·ly** *adv*. **de·lu′sive·ness** *n*.

de·luxe (d*e*lo͝oks′, -lŭks′) *adj.phr.* Luxurious, sumptuous; of superior kind. ~ *adv.phr.* [Fr.]

delve (dĕlv) *v*. (**delved, delv·ing**). Dig (archaic or dial.); (fig.) make laborious research in documents etc.

Dem. *abbrev*. Democrat.

de·mag·net·ize (dēmăg′n*e*tīz) *v.t.* (**-ized, -iz·ing**). Deprive of magnetic quality. **de·mag·net·i·za·tion** (dēmăgn*e*tĭzā′sh*o*n) *n*.

dem·a·gogue, dem·a·gog (dĕm′*a*gawg, -gŏg) *ns*. Leader of popular faction, or of mob; agitator appealing to passions and prejudices of mob; (hist.) popular leader, orator who espoused people's cause against other parties in country. **dem·a·gog·ic** (dĕm*a*gŏj′ĭk, -gŏg′-) *adj*. **dem·a·gog·y** (dĕm′*a*gōjē, -gawjē, -gŏjē), **dem·a·gog·uer·y** (dĕm′*a*gawg*e*rē, -gŏg*e*rē) *ns*.

de·mand (dĭmănd′, -mahnd′) *n*. 1. Authoritative or peremptory request or claim; what is demanded; legal claim. 2. Call for commodity by consumers; urgent or pressing claim or requirement; **on** ~, as soon as the demand is made, esp. for payment of a bill. **demand** *v.t.* 1. Ask for with legal right or authority; (law) make formal claim to; ask for peremptorily or urgently; require, have need of. 2. Ask to know, authoritatively or formally.

de·mand·ing (dĭmăn′dĭng) *adj*. 1. Trying or exacting in demands. 2. Requiring great skill, care, effort, etc.

de·mar·ca·tion, de·mar·ka·tion (dēmar̄kā′sh*o*n) *ns*. Marking of boundary or limits of anything. **de·mar·cate** (dĭmar̄′kāt, dē′mar̄-) *v.t.* (**-cat·ed, -cat·ing**).

dé·marche (dāmar̄sh′, dĭ-) *n*. (diplomacy) Political step or proceeding, esp. one involving a change in a course of policy or action. [Fr.]

de·ma·te·ri·al·ize (dēm*a*tēr′ē*a*līz) *v*. (**-ized, -iz·ing**). Make, become, nonmaterial or spiritual.

de·mean[1] (dĭmēn′) *v.refl.* Behave, conduct, *oneself* (in specified way). **de·mean′or** *n*. Bearing, outward behavior.

de·mean[2] (dĭmēn′) *v.t.* Lower in dignity, reputation, etc.; lower or humble *oneself*.

de·ment·ed (dĭmĕn′tĭd) *adj*. Crazed, mad; affected with dementia. **de·ment′ed·ly** *adv*.

de·men·tia (dĭmĕn′sh*a*, -shē*a*) *n*. Insanity characterized by failure or loss of mental powers and caused by disease in or injury to the brain; ~ **praecox** (prē′kŏks), schizophrenia.

de·mer·it (dĭmĕr′ĭt) *n*. Quality deserving blame or punishment; censurable conduct; want of merit; fault, defect.

de·mesne (dĭmān′, -mēn′) *n*. 1. (law) Possession and use of one's own land. 2. Domain; landed property, estate; grounds belonging to estate or mansion.

De·me·ter (dĭmē′t*e*r). (Gk.

myth.) Goddess of agriculture, the daughter of Cronus and mother of Persephone; identified by the Romans with CERES.

demi- *prefix*. Half, semi-.

dem·i·god (dĕm′ēgŏd) *n*. Partly divine being, son of god and mortal, or deified man.

dem·i·john (dĕm′ējŏn) *n*. Large bottle with bulging body and narrow neck and usu. cased in wickerwork. [corrupt. of Fr. *dame-Jeanne* Dame Jane]

de·mil·i·ta·rize (dēmĭl′ĭtarīz) *v.t.* (**-rized, -riz·ing**). Do away with military organization or control of; **demilitarized,** (of area) containing no armed forces. **de·mil·i·ta·ri·za·tion** (dēmĭlĭtarīzā′-shon) *n*.

De Mille[1] (de mĭl′), **Agnes** (1909–). Amer. choreographer; greatly influenced style of Amer. musical comedy.

De Mille[2] (de mĭl′), **Cecil B(lount)** (1881–1959). Amer. movie producer and director esp. noted for films on historic subjects.

dem·i·mon·daine (dĕmēmŏn-dān′, -mŏn′dān) *n*. Woman of the demimonde.

dem·i·monde (dĕm′ēmŏnd) *n*. Class of women on outskirts of society, of doubtful reputation and standing, esp. because of sexual promiscuity.

de·min·er·al·ize (dēmĭn′eralīz) *v.t.* (**-ized, -iz·ing**). Remove mineral content from.

de·mise (dĭmīz′) *v*. (**-mised, -mis·ing**). 1. Convey, grant, (estate) by will or lease; transmit (title etc.) by death or abdication. 2. Die, decease. ~ *n*. 1. Conveyance or transfer of estate by will or lease; transference of sovereignty, as by death or deposition of sovereign. 2. Decease, death.

dem·i·sem·i·qua·ver (dĕmē-sĕm′ēkwāver) (stress variable) *n*. (mus., chiefly Brit.) Note half as long (𝅘𝅥𝅯 𝅀) as semiquaver.

dem·i·tasse (dĕm′ĭtăs, -tahs) *n*. (Small cup of) strong black coffee served after dinner.

dem·i·urge (dĕm′ēĕrj) *n*. (often **D**~) (in Platonic philosophy) Creator of material world; (in Gnostic and other systems) a being subordinate to Supreme Being; occas., author of evil. **dem·i·ur·gic** (dĕmēĕr′jĭk) *adj*. [Gk. *dēmiourgos* craftsman (*dēmios* of the people, *-ergos* working)]

de·mo·bi·lize (dēmō′bĭlīz) *v.t.* (**-lized, -liz·ing**). Release from mobilized condition; disband (troops, ships, etc.). **de·mo·bi·li·za·tion** (dēmōbĭlīzā′shon) *n*.

de·moc·ra·cy (dĭmŏk′rasē) *n*. (pl. **-cies**). 1. Form of government in which power resides in the people as a whole, and is exercised either directly by them or by their elected representatives; nation having this form of government. 2. Society, condition of individual equality and respect.

dem·o·crat (dĕm′okrăt) *n*. 1. Advocate of democracy. 2. **D**~, member of DEMOCRATIC Party.

dem·o·crat·ic (dĕmokrăt′ĭk) *adj*. 1. Of, like, practicing, advocating, democracy. 2. Of the Democratic Party; **D**~ **Party,** political party that claims JEFFERSON[1] for its founder and opposes the (present-day) REPUBLICAN Party, so called since *c*1828, but previously known, at various times, as Anti-Federalist, Republican, and Democratic-Republican. **dem·o·crat′i·cal·ly** *adv*. **de·moc·ra·tize** (dĭmŏk′ratīz) *v*. (**-tized, -tiz·ing**). **de·moc·ra·ti·za·tion** (dĭmŏkrĭtīzā′shon) *n*.

De·moc·ri·tus (dĭmŏk′rĭtus) (5th c. B.C.). Greek philosopher ("the laughing philosopher"), regarded, with Leucippus, as founder of ATOMISM. **De·moc·ri·te·an** (dĭmŏkrĭtē′an) *adj*.

de·mod·u·late (dēmŏj′ulāt, -mŏd′yu-) *v.t.* (**-lat·ed, -lat·ing**). (radio) Extract modulating signal from (modulated wave). **de·mod·u·la·tion** (dēmŏjulā′shon, -mŏdyu-) *n*.

de·mog·ra·phy (dĭmŏg′rafē) *n*. Study of statistics of births, deaths, disease, etc., as illustrating conditions of life in communities. **de·mog′raph·er** *n*. **de·mo·graph·ic** (dēmograf′ĭk, dĕmo-) *adj*. **de·mo·graph′i·cal·ly** *adv*.

dem·oi·selle (dĕmwahzĕl′, -wa-) *n*. 1. Young lady. 2. (zool.) Numidian crane (*Anthropoides virgo*) with long feathers and white plumes behind the eyes [Fr., = "damsel"]

de·mol·ish (dĭmŏl′ĭsh) *v.t.* Pull or throw down (building); destroy, make an end of; consume, eat up. **dem·o·li·tion** (dĕmolĭsh′on) *n*.

de·mon, dae·mon (dē′mon) *ns*. 1. (esp. in Gk. myth.) Supernatural being, intermediate between gods and man; spirit, genius. 2. Evil spirit, devil; cruel, malignant, destructive, or terrible person; evil passion or agency personified. 3. Person exhibiting great energy, zeal, etc. **de·mon·ic** (dĭmŏn′ĭk), **de·mon′i·cal** *adjs*.

de·mon·e·tize (dēmŏn′etīz, -mŭn′-) *v.t.* (**-tized, -tiz·ing**). Withdraw from use as money; deprive of its status as money. **de·mon·e·ti·za·tion** (dēmŏnetī-zā′shon, -mŭn-) *n*.

de·mo·ni·ac (dĭmō′nēăk, dē-monī′ăk) *adj*. Possessed by a demon or evil spirit; of demoniacal possession; of or like demons; devilish; frenzied. ~ *n*. One possessed by a demon. **de·mo·ni·a·cal** (dē-monī′akal) *adj*. Demoniac.

de·mon·ic (dĭmŏn′ĭk) *adj*. Demoniac; fiendish.

de·mon·ism (dē′monĭzem) *n*. Belief in the power of demons.

de·mon·ol·o·gy (dēmonŏl′ojē) *n*. Study of beliefs about demons.

de·mon·stra·ble (dĭmŏn′strabel) *adj*. Capable of being shown or logically proved. **de·mon′stra·bly** *adv*. **de·mon·stra·bil·i·ty** (dĭmŏnstrabĭl′ĭtē) *n*.

dem·on·strate (dĕm′onstrāt) *v*.

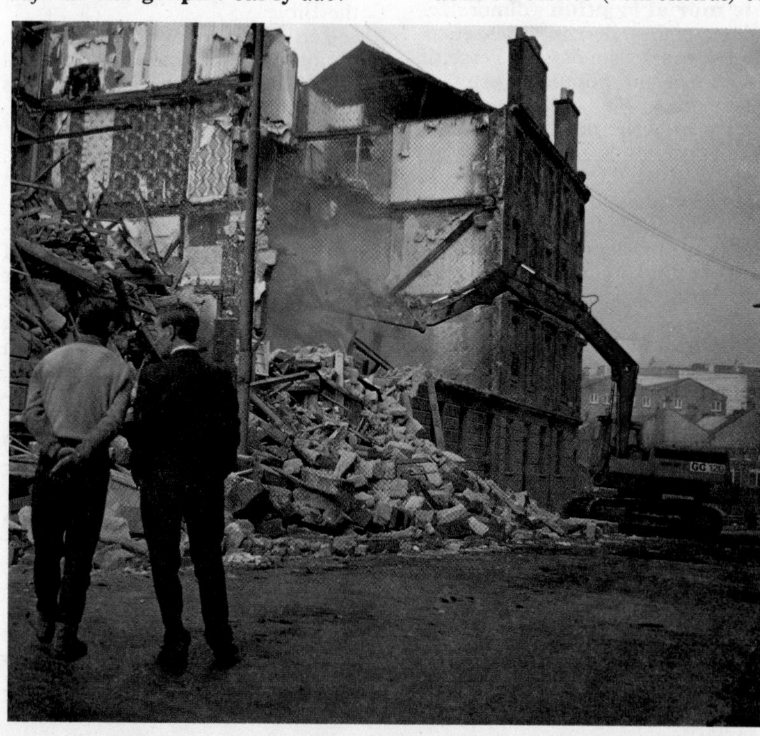

*Techniques of **demolition** and preservation of buildings have improved during the 20th century, but the disappearance of landmarks has brought public opposition.*

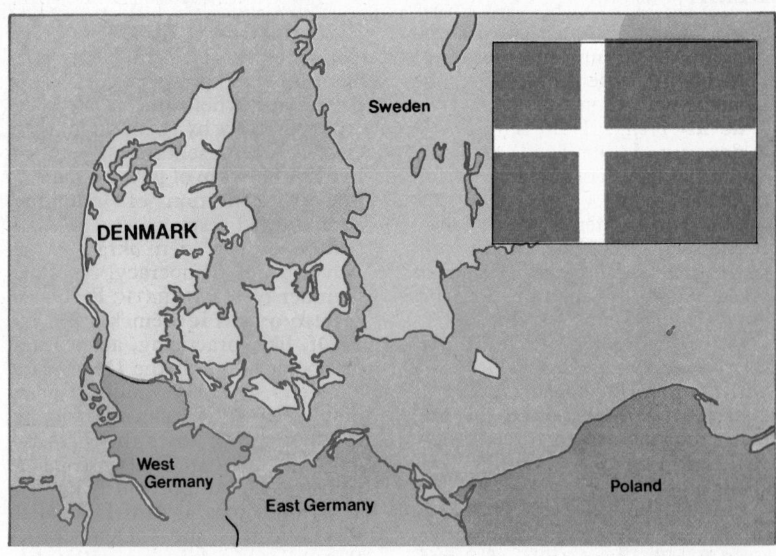

***Denmark** is strategically positioned between the Baltic and North Seas.*

(**-strat·ed, -strat·ing**). 1. Show, display (feelings etc.). 2. Describe and explain by help of specimens or experiments; act as demonstrator. 3. Establish truth of by argument or deduction; prove. 4. Make, take part in, public demonstration.

dem·on·stra·tion (dĕm*o*nstrā′sh*o*n) *n.* 1. Outward exhibition, display *of*; (mil.) show of military force or offensive movement; public manifestation (usu. mass meeting or march) of interest or sympathy with some cause etc. 2. Demonstrating, clear or indubitable proof, argument(s) proving an assertion etc.; exhibition and explanation of specimens or experiments as method of instruction in science or art.

de·mon·stra·tive (dĭmŏn′str*a*tĭv) *adj.* 1. Serving to point out or exhibit, esp. (gram.) of certain adjectives and pronouns. 2. Demonstrating logically or conclusively; serving as proof *of*; evident or provable by demonstration. 3. Given to or marked by outward exhibition or expression of feelings etc. **de·mon′stra·tive·ly** *adv.* **de·mon′stra·tive·ness** *n.*

dem·on·stra·tor (dĕm′*o*nstrāt*er*) *n.* One who demonstrates; sample used in a demonstration; one who takes part in public demonstration.

de·mor·al·ize (dĭmōr′*a*līz, -mār′-) *v.t.* (**-ized, -iz·ing**). Corrupt morals of, deprave; destroy discipline, courage, powers of endurance, etc., of (esp. troops). **de·mor·al·i·za·tion** (dĭmōr*a*lĭzā′sh*o*n, -mār-), **de·mor′al·i·zer** *ns.*

De·mos (dē′mŏs) *n.* Personification of the populace, esp. in a democracy.

De·mos·the·nes (dĭmŏs′th*e*nēz) (384–322 B.C.). Athenian orator, who roused the Athenians to the danger of the subjugation of Greece by Philip of Macedon.

de·mote (dĭmōt′) *v.t.* (**-mot·ed, -mot·ing**). Reduce to lower rank or class. **de·mo·tion** (dĭmō′sh*o*n) *n.*

de·mot·ic (dĭmŏt′ĭk) *adj.* Of the common people; esp. as epithet of popular simplified form of writing used in ancient Egypt from *c*700 B.C. until 5th C. A.D. (as dist. from *hieratic*); of the popular form of modern Greek. ~ *n.* Demotic writing; demotic Greek.

de·mul·cent (dĭmŭl′s*e*nt) *adj.* & *n.* Soothing (medicine).

de·mur (dĭmēr′) *v.i.* (**-murred, -mur·ring**). Make difficulties, raise scruples or objections *to, at*; (law) put in a demurrer. ~ *n.* Objecting, objection. **de·mur′ral** *n.* Act of demurring.

de·mure (dĭmūr′) *adj.* (**-mur·er, -mur·est**). Sober, serious, composed; affectedly or constrainedly modest or decorous. **de·mure′ly** *adv.* **de·mure′ness** *n.*

de·mur·rage (dĭmēr′ĭj) *n.* (Compensation for) detention of ship, railroad freight car, etc., by loader or unloader beyond time agreed upon.

de·mur·rer (dĭmēr′*er*) *n.* 1. Person who demurs; objector. 2. (law) Pleading that allegedly true statements of the opposition in a lawsuit fail to sustain claim on which they are based. 3. Objection; exception taken to anything.

de·my·thol·o·gize (dēmĭthŏl′*o*jīz) *v.* (**-gized, -giz·ing**). Remove mythical elements (from); reinterpret mythological elements in the Bible.

den (dĕn) *n.* Wild beast's lair; hiding place of thieves etc.; small room in which person secludes himself or herself to work etc.

Den. *abbrev.* Denmark.

de·nar·i·us (dĭnār′ē*u*s) *n.* (pl. **-nar·i·i** pr. -nār′ēī). Ancient Roman silver coin.

de·na·tion·al·ize (dēnăsh′*o*n*a*līz) *v.t.* (**-ized, -iz·ing**). Deprive of nationality; destroy independent or distinct nationality of; make (institution etc.) no longer national; transfer (enterprise, industry) from national to private ownership. **de·na·tion·al·i·za·tion** (dēnăsh*o*n*a*lĭzā′sh*o*n) *n.*

de·nat·ur·al·ize (dēnăch′*era*līz) *v.t.* (**-ized, -iz·ing**). Alter or pervert the nature of, make unnatural; deprive of status and rights of natural subject or citizen. **de·nat·ur·al·i·za·tion** (dēnăch*era*lĭzā′sh*o*n) *n.*

de·na·ture (dēnā′ch*er*) *v.t.* (**-tured, -tur·ing**). Change nature or properties of; render unfit to drink or eat, esp. by adding methanol to ethyl alcohol so it cannot be drunk. **de·na′tu·rant** *n.* Substance used as denaturing agent. **de·na·tur·a·tion** (dēnāch*e*rā′sh*o*n) *n.*

de·na·zi·fi·ca·tion (dēnahts*i*fĭkā′sh*o*n, -năts*i*-) *n.* (after World War II) Eradication of Nazi influence in Germany; removal of Nazis from positions of responsibility in German public life. **de·na·zi·fy** (dēnah′tsifī, -năt′s*i*-) *v.t.* (**-fied, -fy·ing**).

den·drite (dĕn′drīt) *n.* 1. (Stone or mineral with) natural treelike marking. 2. Branching process of nerve cell. **den·drit·ic** (dĕndrĭt′ĭk) *adj.*

den·dro·chro·nol·o·gy (dĕndrōkr*o*nŏl′*o*jē) *n.* Study of chronology from evidence of annual growth rings in (ancient) trees and timber. **den·dro·chron·o·log·i·cal** (dĕndrōkrŏn*o*lŏj′ĭk*a*l) *adj.*

den·drol·o·gy (dĕndrŏl′*o*jē) *n.* Study of trees. **den·drol′o·gist** *n.* **den·dro·log·ic** (dĕndr*o*lŏj′ĭk), **den·dro·log′i·cal** *adjs.*

den·gue (dĕng′gā, -gē) *n.* Virulent tropical and subtropical epidemic infectious disease characterized by fever, rash, excruciating pains in joints, and great prostration and debility. [prob. orig. Swahili *dinga*, associated with Span. *dengue* prudery, with ref. to stiffness in patient's neck and shoulders]

de·ni·a·ble (dĭnī′*a*b*e*l) *adj.* That can be denied.

de·ni·al (dĭnī′*a*l) *n.* Refusal of request; self-denial; contradiction, statement that thing is not true or existent; disowning, disavowal (*of* person).

de·nier (d*e*nēr′) *n.* Unit of weight used to estimate the fineness of silk or synthetic yarn (based on a length of 450 meters of yarn weighing 50 milligrams).

den·i·grate (dĕn′*i*grāt) *v.t.* (**-grat·ed, -grat·ing**). Blacken; defame. **den·i·gra·tion** (dĕn*i*grā′-

sh*o*n) *n.*

den·im (dĕn′ĭm) *n.* Twill cotton fabric used for overalls, work clothes, etc.; (pl.) overalls, trousers, etc. made of this. [f. Fr. (*serge*) *de Nîmes* (serge) of Nîmes in S. France]

den·i·zen (dĕn′ĭzen) *n.* Inhabitant, occupant (*of* place); (Brit.) foreigner admitted to residence and certain rights; naturalized foreign animal or plant. **den′i·zen·ship** *n.*

Den·mark (dĕn′mark̄). Kingdom of N. Europe, consisting of the islands of Zealand, Funen, Lolland, etc. between the North and Baltic seas, the peninsula of Jutland, and the outlying Baltic island of Bornholm; capital, Copenhagen; ~ **Strait**, channel between Greenland and Iceland connecting Arctic and Atlantic.

de·nom·i·nate (dĭnŏm′*i*nāt) *v.t.* (**-nat·ed, -nat·ing**). Give name to, call or describe as.

de·nom·i·na·tion (dĭnŏm*i*nā′sh*o*n) *n.* 1. Name, designation; esp. characteristic or class name; class, kind, with specific name. 2. Class of units in numbers, weights, money, etc. 3. Religious sect. **de·nom·i·na′tion·al** *adj.* Of, like, a religious denomination; sectarian. **de·nom·i·na′tion·al·ly** *adv.*

de·nom·i·na·tive (dĭnŏm′*i*nātĭv, -*i*natĭv) *adj.* Serving as, giving, a name.

de·nom·i·na·tor (dĭnŏm′*i*nāt*er*) *n.* (arith. etc.) Number written below line in fraction, giving quantity that divides the numerator; parts into which integer is divided; **common** ~, denominator common to a number of fractions; (freq. fig.) common feature of members of a group.

de·no·ta·tion (dēnōtā′sh*o*n) *n.* 1. Denoting; expression by marks or symbols; mark by which thing is made known or indicated; designation. 2. Meaning, signification a word or expression usually elicits; (logic) what word denotes, as dist. from *connotation*, aggregate of objects of which word may be predicated.

de·no·ta·tive (dē′nōtātĭv, dĭnō′-t*a*-) *adj.* Denoting. **de′no·ta·tive·ly** *adv.*

de·note (dĭnōt′) *v.t.* (**-not·ed, -not·ing**). 1. Mark out, distinguish, be the sign of; indicate, give to understand; signify, stand as name for (cf. CONNOTE); (logic) designate, be a name of, be predicated of.

de·noue·ment, dé·noue·ment (dānōōmahṅ′) *ns.* Unraveling of plot or complications, final solution, in play, novel, etc. [Fr.]

de·nounce (dĭnowns′) *v.t.* (**-nounced, -nounc·ing**). 1. Prophesy (woe, vengeance), proclaim as threat or warning. 2. Inform against, accuse. 3. Inveigh against. 4. Give notice of termination of (armistice, treaty, etc.). **de·nounce′ment, de·nounc′er** *ns.*

dense (dĕns) *adj.* (**dens·er, dens·est**). 1. Closely compacted in substance; crowded together. 2. Crass, stupid. **dense′ly** *adv.* **dense′ness** *n.*

den·si·ty (dĕn′sĭtē) *n.* (pl. **-ties**). 1. Closeness of substance; crowded state; (photog.) opaqueness of developed film in negative. 2. Stupidity, crassness. 3. (phys.) Degree of consistency of body etc. expressed as weight per unit of volume.

dent (dĕnt) *n.* Hollow or impression in surface such as is made by blow with blunt instrument. ~ *v.* Make dent in; receive dent in.

den·tal (dĕn′t*a*l) *adj.* Of tooth, teeth, or dentistry; (of consonant) pronounced with tip of tongue against front upper teeth; ~ **floss**, soft thread, waxed or unwaxed, used to clean between teeth; ~ **hygienist**, assistant to a dentist,

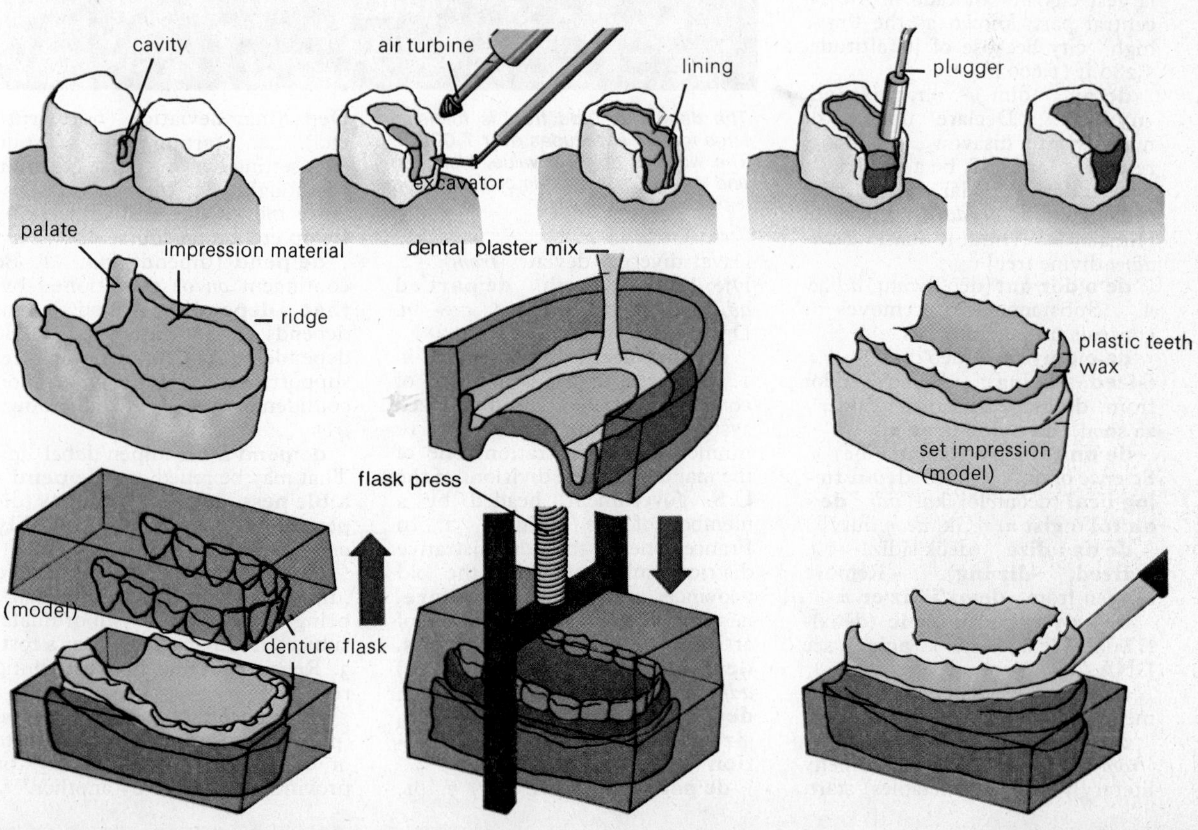

Tooth-filling and plate-making in modern ***dentistry.*** *The top diagrams show a drill cleaning out the cavity and surrounding area; the hole is then lined and plugged with a mixture of dental amalgam. Below: The construction of dentures.*

Plastic teeth are set in wax on a plaster model of the palate. After pressing, the teeth and model are held in the plaster while acrylic resin is pressed in and heated to 'cure' the plate.

esp. in cleaning patients' teeth; ~ **surgeon**, dentist specializing in surgery involving the teeth and associated oral areas. **dental** *n.* Dental consonant.

den·tate (dĕn'tāt) *adj.* Toothed; edged with toothlike projections. **den·ta·tion** (dĕntā'sh*o*n) *n.*

den·ti·cle (dĕn'tĭk*a*l) *n.* Small tooth, or toothlike projection. **den·tic·u·lar** (dĕntĭk'y*u*l*er*), **den·tic'u·late** *adjs.* **den·tic·u·la·tion** (dĕntĭky*u*lā'sh*o*n) *n.*

den·ti·frice (dĕn'tĭfrĭs) *n.* Preparation for cleaning teeth.

den·tine (dĕn'tēn, dĕntēn'), **den·tin** (dĕn'tĭn) *ns.* Hard dense tissue forming main part of teeth. **den'tin·al** *adj.*

den·tist (dĕn'tĭst) *n.* One who treats diseases and malformations of teeth and repairs, extracts, or replaces defective teeth. **den'tist·ry** *n.*

den·ti·tion (dĕntĭsh'*o*n) *n.* Teething; characteristic arrangement of teeth in animal.

den·ture (dĕn'ch*er*) *n.* One or more artificial teeth.

de·nude (dĭnōōd', -nūd') *v.t.* (**-nud·ed, -nud·ing**). Make naked; strip *of*; (geol.) lay (rock etc.) bare by removal of what lies above. **de·nu·da·tion** (dēnōōdā'sh*o*n, -nū, dĕny*u*-) *n.*

de·nun·ci·a·tion (dĭnŭnsēā'sh*o*n) *n.* Denouncing; invective. **de·nun·ci·a·tive** (dĭnŭn'sēātĭv), **de·nun·ci·a·to·ry** (dĭnŭn'sē*a*tōrē, -tôrē) *adjs.*

Den·ver (dĕn'v*er*). Capital and largest city in Colorado in the N. central part; known as the "mile high" city because of its altitude, 5,280 ft (1,609 m).

de·ny (dĭnī') *v.t.* (**-nied, -ny·ing**). Declare untrue or nonexistent; disavow, repudiate; refuse; ~ **oneself**, be abstinent.

de·o·dar (dē'*o*där) *n.* Large cedar (*Cedrus deodara*), native of Himalayas. [Hind. f. Sansk. *devadāru* divine tree]

de·o·dor·ant (dēō'd*er*ant) *adj.* & *n.* (Substance) that removes or conceals unwanted odors.

de·o·dor·ize (dēō'd*er*īz) *v.t.* (**-ized, -iz·ing**). Remove odor from. **de·o·dor·i·za·tion** (dēōd*er*ĭzā'sh*o*n), **de·o'dor·iz·er** *ns.*

de·on·tol·o·gy (dēŏntŏl'*o*jē) *n.* Science of duty, ethics. **de·on·to·log·i·cal** (dēŏnt*o*lŏj'ĭk*a*l) *adj.* **de·on·tol'o·gist** *n.* [Gk. *deon* duty]

de·ox·i·dize (dēŏk'sĭdīz) *v.t.* (**-dized, -diz·ing**). Remove oxygen from. **de·ox'i·diz·er** *n.*

de·ox·y·ri·bo·nu·cle·ic (dēŏxĭrī'bōnōōklē'ĭk, -nū-) **acid**: see DNA.

dep. *abbrev.* Depart; department; deposit; deputy.

de·part (dĭpärt') *v.* 1. Go away (*from*), take one's leave (chiefly literary); (esp. in timetables) start, leave; diverge, deviate (*from*). 2. Die; leave by death. **de·part'ed** *adj.* Bygone; deceased. ~ *n.* Deceased person.

de·part·ment (dĭpärt'm*e*nt) *n.* 1. Separate division or part of complex whole or organized system; (esp.) division of state or municipal administration; one of the major executive divisions of the U.S. government, headed by a member of the cabinet. 2. In France, one of the administrative districts substituted for the old provinces in 1790. 3. ~ **store**, large store selling a variety of articles, organized in departments. **de·part·men·tal** (dēpärtmĕn't*a*l) *adj.* **de·part·men'tal·ly** *adv.* **de·part·men'tal·ize** *v.t.* (**-ized, -iz·ing**). **de·part·men·tal·i·za·tion** (dēpärtmĕnt*a*lĭzā'sh*o*n) *n.*

de·par·ture (dĭpär'ch*er*) *n.* 1. Departing; deviation (*from* truth etc.). 2. Starting, esp. of train etc.; setting out on course of action or thought. 3. (navigation) Distance moved due east or west by a ship etc. on its course.

*The **deodar** or 'god tree' is found in large forests at altitudes over 7,000 ft. The wood is of great value. Light red and durable, it is used in cabinet work; it polishes very highly.*

de·pend (dĭpĕnd') *v.i.* 1. Be contingent *on* or conditioned by; **that depends**, (colloq.) that depends on circumstances. 2. Be dependent; rely for maintenance, support, etc. (*on*); rely, reckon confidently (*on*). 3. Hang down *from*.

de·pend·a·ble (dĭpĕn'd*a*b*e*l) *adj.* That may be relied on. **de·pend'a·ble·ness, de·pend·a·bil·i·ty** (dĭpĕnd*a*bĭl'ĭtē) *ns.* **de·pend'a·bly** *adv.*

de·pend·ence, de·pend·ance (dĭpĕn'd*e*ns) *ns.* 1. Depending (*on*); being conditioned, subordinate, subject. 2. Living at another's cost. 3. Reliance, confident trust; thing relied on.

de·pend·en·cy (dĭpĕn'd*e*nsē) *n.* (pl. **-cies**). Something subordinate or dependent, esp. country or province controlled by another.

de·pend·ent, de·pend·ant (dĭpĕn'dent) *adjs.* Depending (*on*); contingent, subordinate, subject; maintained at another's cost; (gram., of clause etc.) in subordinate relation to sentence or word. ~ *n.* One who depends on another for support; retainer, servant. **de·pend'ent·ly, de·pend'ant·ly** *advs.*

de·per·son·al·ize (dēpẽr'sonalīz) *v.t.* (**-ized, -iz·ing**). Deprive of personality; make impersonal. **de·per·son·al·i·za·tion** (dēpẽrsonalīzā'shon) *n.*

de·pict (dĭpĭkt') *v.t.* Represent in picture, sculpture, words; portray, describe. **de·pic·tion** (dĭpĭk'shon) *n.*

dep·i·late (dĕp'ilāt) *v.t.* (**-lat·ed, -lat·ing**). Remove hair from. **dep·i·la·tion** (dĕpilā'shon) *n.* **de·pil·a·to·ry** (dĭpĭl'atōrē, -tōrē) *adj.* & *n.* (pl. **-ries**) (Substance) capable of removing hair.

de·plane (dēplān') *v.* (**-planed, -plan·ing**). Disembark from an airplane.

de·plete (dĭplēt') *v.t.* (**-plet·ed, -plet·ing**). Empty out; exhaust. **de·ple·tion** (dĭplē'shon) *n.*

de·plore (dĭplōr', -plōr') *v.t.* (**-plored, -plor·ing**). Bewail, grieve over, regret; be scandalized by. **de·plor'a·ble** *adj.* **de·plor'a·bly** *adv.* **de·plor·a·bil·i·ty** (dĭplōrabĭl'ĭtē, -plōr-), **de·plor'a·ble·ness** *ns.*

de·ploy (dĭploi') *v.* (mil.) Spread out from column into line; arrange in, take up, battle formation; move strategically. **de·ploy'ment** *n.*

de·plume (dēplōōm') *v.t.* (**-plumed, -plum·ing**). Pluck, strip of feathers.

de·po·lar·ize (dēpō'lerīz) *v.t.* (**-ized, -iz·ing**). Deprive of polarity, reverse or destroy effect of polarization. **de·po·lar·i·za·tion** (dēpōlerīzā'shon) *n.*

de·po·lit·i·cize (dēpolĭt'ĭsīz) *v.t.* (**-cized, -ciz·ing**). Make nonpolitical; remove from political activity or influence.

de·pon·ent (dĭpō'nent) *adj.* (of Latin or Gk. verb) Passive in form but active in meaning (so called from idea that these verbs had laid aside their passive meaning). ~ *n.* 1. Deponent verb. 2. Person making deposition on oath or giving written testimony for use in court etc.

de·pop·u·late (dēpŏp'yulāt) *v.t.* (**-lat·ed, -lat·ing**). Reduce population of. **de·pop·u·la·tion** (dēpŏpyulā'shon), **de·pop'u·la·tor** *ns.*

de·port (dĭpōrt', -pōrt') *v.t.* 1. Bear, conduct, *oneself*; behave. 2. Carry away, remove; esp. expel, banish (alien), hence **de·por·ta·tion** (dēpōrtā'shon, -pōr-), **de·por·tee** (dēpōrtē', -pōr-) *ns.*

de·port·ment (dĭpōrt'ment, -pōrt'-) *n.* Bearing, demeanor, manners.

de·pose (dĭpōz') *v.* (**-posed, -pos·ing**). 1. Remove from office; dethrone. 2. Bear witness under oath *that*, testify, esp. in writing. **de·pos'a·ble** *adj.* **de·pos'er** *n.*

de·pos·it (dĭpŏz'ĭt) *n.* 1. Thing stored or entrusted for safekeeping; sum placed in bank; sum required and paid as pledge for performance of contract, part payment of price etc. 2. Layer of precipitated or deposited matter, natural accumulation. ~ *v.t.* 1. Lay or set down, place in more or less permanent position of rest; lay (eggs); (of water or other natural agencies) leave (matter) lying, form as natural deposit. 2. Store or entrust for keeping (esp. sum of money in bank); pay as pledge for fulfillment of contract or further payment.

de·pos·i·tar·y (dĭpŏz'ĭtĕrē) *n.* (pl. **-tar·ies**). Person to whom thing is entrusted; depository, sense 1.

dep·o·si·tion (dĕpozĭsh'on) *n.* 1. **D**~, taking down of the body of Christ from the cross; representation of this in art. 2. Deposing from office. 3. (Giving of) sworn evidence, esp. written statement. 4. Depositing.

de·pos·i·tor (dĭpŏz'ĭter) *n.* Person who deposits money etc. **de·pos·i·to·ry** (dĭpŏz'ĭtōrē, -tōrē) *n.* (pl. **-ries**). 1. Storehouse; repository. 2. = DEPOSITARY.

de·pot (dē'pō; mil. & *Brit.* dĕp'ō) *n.* 1. (mil.) Place for stores; headquarters of regiment; station for assembling and drilling recruits. 2. Place where goods are deposited or stored; warehouse. 3. Railroad or bus station.

de·prave (dĭprāv') *v.t.* (**-praved, -prav·ing**). Make bad, deteriorate, pervert, corrupt, esp. in moral character or habits. **dep·ra·va·tion** (dĕpravā'shon) *n.* **de·praved'** *adj.*

de·prav·i·ty (dĭprăv'ĭtē) *n.* (pl. **-ties**). Moral corruption, viciousness, abandoned wickedness.

Known as St. Charles until 1858, ***Denver,*** *Colorado, was an early stopping place for traders and explorers. The surrounding high mountains are popular with skiers.*

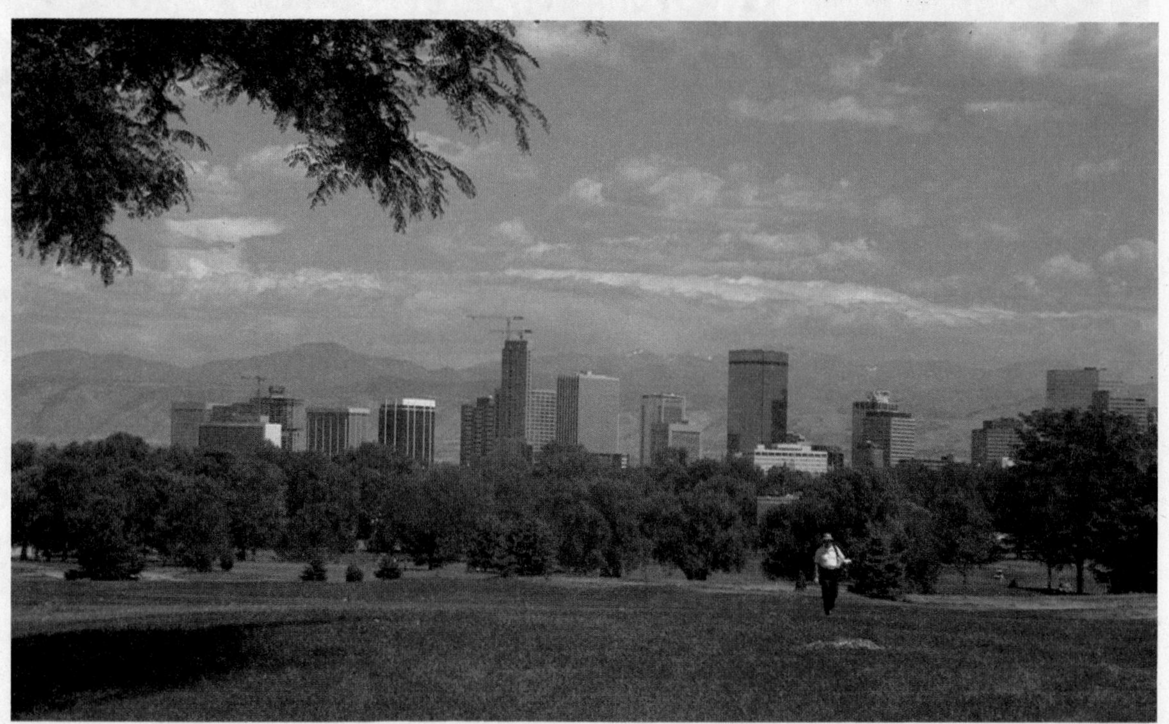

dep·re·cate (dĕp′rekāt) *v.t.* (**-cat·ed, -cat·ing**). Plead against, express earnest disapproval of. **dep·re·ca·tion** (dĕprekā′shon), **dep′re·ca·tor** *ns.* **dep·re·ca·tive** (dĕp′rekātĭv, -katĭv), **dep·re·ca·to·ry** (dĕp′rekatōrē, tōrē) *adjs.*

de·pre·ci·ate (dĭprē′shēāt) *v.* (**-at·ed, -at·ing**). 1. Diminish in value; lower market price of; reduce purchasing power of (money). 2. Disparage, belittle. **de·pre′ci·a·tor** *n.*

de·pre·ci·a·tion (dĭprēshēā′shon) *n.* Depreciating, being depreciated; (allowance made in accounting and taxation valuations, etc., for) wear and tear.

dep·re·da·tion (dĕpredā′shon) *n.* (usu. pl.) Spoliation, ravages.

de·press (dĭprĕs′) *v.t.* Press down, lower; bring low, humble; reduce activity of (esp. trade); dispirit, deject; **depressed area**, area of economic depression.

de·pres·sant (dĭprĕs′ant) *adj.* & *n.* (med.) Lowering, sedative (drug etc.).

de·pres·sion (dĭprĕsh′on) *n.* 1. Lowering, sinking; depressed or sunken formation or surface, hollow, low place. 2. (astron. etc.) Angular distance of star or other object below horizon (as opp. to *elevation* above it). 3. Lowering in quality, vigor, value, or amount, esp. of business activity; **Great D ~**, economic crisis marked by low industrial and business activity and severe unemployment in the U.S. and abroad, dating from about Oct. 1929, when stock prices plummeted, through the 1930s. 4. Lowering of barometric or atmospheric pressure; (meteorol.) center of minimum pressure, or system of winds around it. 5. Being depressed in spirits, dejection; (path.) state of reduced vitality.

de·pres·sive (dĭprĕs′ĭv) *adj.* That depresses; involving (esp. mental) depression. **de·pres′sive·ly** *adv.*

de·pres·sor (dĭprĕs′er) *n.* (esp.) Muscle depressing or pulling down part to which it is attached; (med.) instrument for pressing down some part of organ, esp. a **tongue ~**.

dep·ri·va·tion (dĕprivā′shon) *n.* Loss, being deprived (*of*); taking away of rank or office.

de·prive (dĭprīv′) *v.t.* (**-prived, -priv·ing**). 1. Strip, bereave, debar from enjoyment, *of*; **deprived child**, one lacking due parental care. 2. Depose from office.

de pro·fun·dis (dā prōfōōn′dĭs). Psalm 130, beginning thus in Latin (= "Out of the depths (have I cried)"); cry from depths of suffering or sin.

de·pro·gram (dēprō′grăm, -gram) *v.t.* Induce (person) by strong argument to leave cult whose doctrines he or she has accepted. **de·pro′gram·mer** *n.* **de·pro′gram·ming** *adj.* & *n.*

dept. *abbrev.* Department; deputy.

depth (dĕpth) *n.* 1. Being deep; measurement from top down, from front to back, or from surface inward. 2. Profundity, abstruseness; sagacity; intensity (of feelings, colors, silence, etc.). 3. Deep part of sea or any body of water (usu. pl.); (pl.) lowest part of pit, cavity, etc.; abyss (usu. pl.), lowest or inmost part; low moral condition; middle (of winter, night); deep region of thought, feeling, or being. 4. **in ~**, comprehensive(ly), thorough(ly); **out of one's ~**, in water too deep to stand in; (fig.) engaged in a matter beyond one's understanding; **~ charge**, any explosive device designed for use against underwater targets, esp. submarines.

dep·u·ta·tion (dĕpyutā′shon) *n.* Body of persons appointed to go on mission on behalf of others; delegation.

de·pute (dĭpūt′) *v.t.* (**-put·ed, -put·ing**). Commit (task, authority) to substitute; appoint as one's substitute.

dep·u·tize (dĕp′yutīz) *v.* (**-tized, -tiz·ing**). Appoint, serve as deputy.

dep·u·ty (dĕp′yutē) *n.* (pl. **-ties**). 1. Person appointed to act for another or others, substitute, lieutenant; deputy sheriff. 2. Mem-

*The **Derby**, one of the world's most prestigious horse races, has been run at Epsom, U.K. since 1780 and is for three-year-old colts and fillies. Here, the horses round Tattenham Corner.*

ber of certain legislative assemblies; **Chamber of Deputies**, lower house in some countries' legislatures. **deputy** *adj.* Deputed; acting instead of, or as subordinate to, as in ~ *sheriff*.

De Quin·cey (dĭ kwĭn'sē), **Thomas** (1785–1859). English essayist etc., author of *Confessions of an English Opium Eater* (1822).

de·rac·i·nate (dĭrăs'ināt) *v.t.* (**-nat·ed, -nat·ing**). Tear up by the roots.

de·rail (dĭrāl') *v.t.* Cause (train etc.) to leave rails. **de·rail'ment** *n.*

de·range (dĭrānj') *v.t.* (**-ranged, -rang·ing**). Throw into confusion; disorganize; cause to act irregularly; make insane. **de·range'ment** *n.*

Der·by (dēr'bē; *Brit.* dār'bē). 1. City and county seat of Derbyshire, England; **the** ~, annual horse race, for 3-year-olds, founded 1780 by 12th earl of Derby, at Epsom Downs, in Surrey, England; **The Kentucky** ~, annual horse race for 3-year-olds, founded 1875, at Churchill Downs, in Louisville, Kentucky; any of various other races or contests such as a **roller d**~, in which two teams of roller skaters compete on a circular track.

der·by (dēr'bē; *Brit.* dār'bē) *n.* (pl. **-bies.**) Stiff felt hat with rounded crown and narrow brim, bowler.

der·e·lict (dĕr'elĭkt) *adj.* & *n.* 1. Abandoned, ownerless (thing, esp. ship at sea). 2. (Person) abandoned by society.

der·e·lic·tion (dĕrelĭk'shon) *n.* 1. Forsaking, abandonment; being abandoned; retreat of sea exposing new land. 2. Morally wrong or reprehensible abandonment or neglect (*of* duty etc.); failure in duty, delinquency.

de·ride (dĭrīd') *v.t.* (**-rid·ed, -rid·ing**). Laugh to scorn. **de·ris·i·ble** (dĭrĭz'ĭbel) *adj.*

de ri·gueur (de rēgēr'). Required by etiquette. [Fr.]

de·ri·sion (dĭrĭzh'on) *n.* Ridicule, mockery.

de·ri·sive (dĭrī'sĭv) *adj.* Scoffing; mocking; provoking derision. **de·ri'sive·ly** *adv.*

deriv. *abbrev.* Derivation, derivative.

der·i·va·tion (dĕrivā'shon) *n.* Obtaining from a source; extraction, descent; formation of word from word or root, tracing or statement of this.

de·riv·a·tive (dĭrĭv'atĭv) *adj.* & *n.* (Thing, word, etc.) of derived character or nature, derived from another or from a source, not primitive or original. **de·riv'a·tive·ly** *adv.*

de·rive (dĭrīv') *v.* (**-rived, -riv·ing**). Get, obtain (*from* a source); have one's or its origin etc. *from*; gather, deduce, *from*; (pass., refl.) be descended or have one's origin *from*; (pass., of words) be formed *from*; trace, show, assert, descent or origin or formation of (person, thing, word) *from*.

der·ma[1] (dēr'ma) = DERMIS.

der·ma[2] (dēr'ma) *n.* Fowl or beef intestine used as a casing for certain dishes, esp. **stuffed** ~, or kishke, consisting of a seasoned mixture of flour, onion, and suet stuffed into the casing and then roasted.

der·ma·ti·tis (dērmatī'tĭs) *n.* Inflammation of the dermis.

der·ma·tol·o·gy (dērmatŏl'ojē) *n.* Science of the skin, its nature, diseases, etc. **der·ma·to·log·i·cal** (dērmatolŏj'ĭkal) *adj.* **der·ma·tol'o·gist** *n.*

der·mis (dēr'mĭs) *n.* (anat.) True skin, layer of tissue beneath epidermis. **der'mal** *adj.*

der·o·gate (dĕr'ogāt) *v.i.* (**-gat·ed, -gat·ing**). 1. Detract, make improper or injurious abatement, *from*. 2. Do something unsuited to one's rank or position.

der·o·ga·tion (dĕrogā'shon) *n.* Lessening or impairment *of* law, position, dignity, etc.; deterioration, debasement.

de·rog·a·to·ry (dĭrŏg'atōrē, -tōrē), **de·rog·a·tive** (dĭrŏg'atĭv) *adjs.* Tending to detract *from*, involving impairment, disparagement, or discredit, *to*; lowering, unsuited to one's dignity or position. **de·rog·a·to·ri·ly** (dĭrŏgatōr'ilē, -tōr'-) *adv.*

Three Frenchmen on 11 March 1962 set a new world record for highland parachute-dropping by their ***descent*** *into the crater of Mt. Kilimanjaro in Tanzania (over 19,000 ft).*

der·rick (dĕr'ĭk) *n.* Contrivance for hoisting or moving heavy weights; spar or boom set up obliquely on shipboard, with foot lashed, pivoted, or socketed to deck; kind of crane with jib pivoted to foot of central post, so as to take various angles with perpendicular; any outstanding jib or arm with pulley at end; framework over deep bore, as that of an oil well, for supporting drilling equipment and for hoisting or lowering. [orig. = hangman, the gallows, f. surname of hangman at Tyburn *c*1600]

der·ri·ère (dĕrēār') *n.* Buttocks; rump; rear.

der·rin·ger (dĕr'ĭnjer) *n.* Short-barreled pocket pistol. [named after its inventor, gunsmith Henry *Deringer* (1786–1868)]

der·vish (dēr'vĭsh) *n.* Member of any of various orders of Muslim ascetics, some of whom dance, whirl, chant, or sing as part of their religious devotions. [f. Pers. *darwīsh* poor]

de·sal·i·nate (dēsăl'ināt) *v.t.* (**-nat·ed, -nat·ing**). Desalinize. **de·sal·i·na·tion** (dēsălinā'shon) *n.*

de·sa·lin·ize (dēsăl'inīz) *v.t.* (**-ized, -iz·ing**). Remove salt from (esp. sea water).

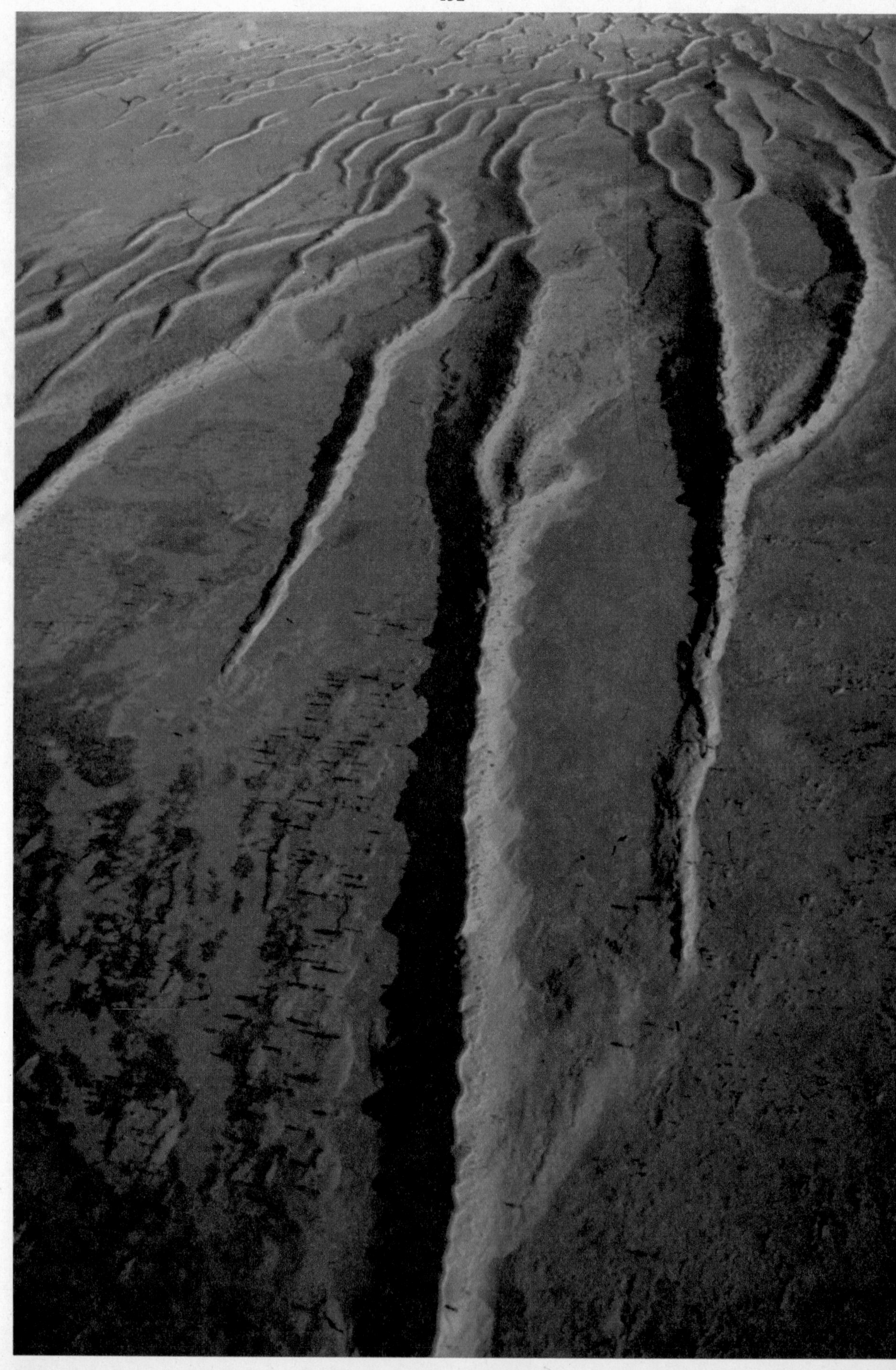

*Left: The **Simpson Desert,** in the Northern Territory, Australia. Above: White Sands, New Mexico. The former is uninhabited and consists of scrub and sand dunes. The latter, an extensive area of gypsum sand, supports plant and animal life.*

des·cant (dĕs′kănt) *n.* 1. Song containing a fixed melody and a subordinate melody added above; the added melody. 2. (fig.) Amplification of a subject, discursive comment on it. **descant** (dĕskănt′, dĭs-) *v.i.* 1. Talk at large, dwell freely, *upon.* 2. Sing a descant.

Des·cartes (dākart′), **René** (1596–1650). French mathematician, physicist, and philosopher; author of *Le Discours de la Méthode* (1637), in which he expounded a quasimechanical conception of the universe, which he reduced to space, matter, and motion, operating under mathematical laws. **Car·te·sian** (kar-tē′zhan) *adj.*

de·scend (dĭsĕnd′) *v.* 1. Come or go down, fall, sink; have downward extension, direction, or slope; come or go down (hill, steps, etc.). 2. Make excursion or attack, fall violently *on* (also transf.). 3. Come down ideally, mentally, or morally; proceed to something subsequent in time or order, or from general to particular; stoop. 4. Be transmitted by inheritance *from,* pass; **be descended from,** be derived by generation from (person, family, etc.).

de·scend·ant (dĭsĕn′dant) *n.* ~ (**of**), person or thing descended (from).

de·scend·ent (dĭsĕn′dent) *adj.* 1. Moving down. 2. Proceeding from a source or ancestor.

de·scent (dĭsĕnt′) *n.* 1. Descending, downward motion; downward slope; a way down. 2. Sudden attack. 3. Decline, sinking in scale, fall. 4. Being descended, lineage; transmission of property, title, or quality, by inheritance.

de·scribe (dĭskrīb′) *v.t.* (**-scribed, -scrib·ing**). 1. Set forth in words; recite characteristics of; qualify *as.* 2. Mark out, draw (esp. geom. figure); move in, pass or travel over (a certain course or distance). **de·scrib′a·ble** *adj.*

de·scrip·tion (dĭskrĭp′shon) *n.* Describing, verbal portrait or portraiture of person, object, or event, more or less complete definition; sort, kind.

de·scrip·tive (dĭskrĭp′tĭv) *adj.* Serving to describe; consisting chiefly of description. **de·scrip′·tive·ly** *adv.*

de·scry (dĭskrī′) *v.t.* (**-scried, -scry·ing**). Catch sight of, succeed in discerning.

des·e·crate (dĕs′ekrāt) *v.t.* (**-crat·ed, -crat·ing**). Deprive of sacred character; outrage, profane (something sacred). **des·e·cra·tion** (dĕsekrā′shon), **des′e·crat·er, des′e·cra·tor** *ns.*

de·seg·re·gate (dēsĕg′regāt) *v.t.* (**-gat·ed, -gat·ing**). Reunite (persons, classes, etc.) hitherto segregated; esp. abolish racial segregation in (schools etc.). **de·seg·re·ga·tion** (dēsĕgregā′shon) *n.*

de·sen·si·tize (dēsĕn′sĭtīz) *v.t.* (**-tized, -tiz·ing**). Reduce sensitiveness of (esp. sensitized photographic material). **de·sen·si·ti·za·tion** (dēsĕnsĭtīzā′shon), **de·sen′si·tiz·er** *ns.*

de·sert[1] (dezert′) *n.* 1. Deserving, being worthy of reward or punishment; (usu. pl.) that in conduct or character which deserves recompense; merit, worth. 2. (usu. pl.) Due reward or recompense (good or evil).

Left: A late 18th or early 19th century ***desk*** *by Thomas Chippendale the Younger, at Stourhead, Wiltshire, U.K. Chippendale's work provides an excellent example of Regency furniture. Right: An 18th century English desk and stand of beechwood, lacquered in China. The two desks shown here are pointers to the multiplicity of desk forms developed.*

des·ert[2] (dĕz′*e*rt) *n.* Desolate, barren, waterless and treeless region; ~ **rat**: see JERBOA; **D~ Rats**, (colloq.) soldiers of 7th (British) armored division, whose divisional sign was a jerboa, and who took part in World War II desert campaign in N. Africa (1941–1942). **desert** *adj.* Uninhabited, desolate; uncultivated; barren.

de·sert[3] (dĭzẽrt′) *v.* 1. Abandon, give up (thing); depart from (place, haunt); forsake (person or thing having claims on one). 2. Forsake one's post or duty, esp. leave service in the armed forces without official approval and with the intention of never returning. **de·sert′er, de·ser′tion** *ns.*

de·serve (dĭzẽrv′) *v.* (**-served, -serv·ing**). Be entitled by conduct or qualities to (good or bad); have established claim to be *well* or *ill* treated at the hands *of*. **de·serv′ing** *adj.* 1. Meritorious. 2. Worthy (*of* praise, censure, etc.). **de·served′** *adj.* **de·serv′ed·ly, de·serv′ing·ly** *advs.*

des·ha·bille (dĕz*a*bēl′, dĕs-) = DISHABILLE. [Fr.]

des·ic·cant (dĕs′*i*k*a*nt) *adj.* & *n.* (Substance) capable of drying.

des·ic·cate (dĕs′*i*kāt) *v.t.* (**-cat·ed, cat·ing**). Exhaust of all moisture, dry, dry up (esp. articles of food for preservation). **des·ic·ca·tion** (dĕs*i*kā′sh*o*n), **des′ic·ca·tor** *ns.* **des·ic·ca·tive** (dĕs′*i*kātĭv) *adj.*

de·sid·er·ate (dĭsĭd′*e*rāt) *v.t.* (**-at·ed, -at·ing**). Long for; feel the want of. **de·sid·er·a·tion** (dĭsĭd*e*rā′sh*o*n) *n.*

de·sid·er·a·tive (dĭsĭd′*e*rātĭv, -*e*ratĭv) *adj.* 1. Of desire. 2. (gram.) Formed from another verb to express desire of doing act thereby denoted.

de·sid·er·a·tum (dĭsĭd*e*rah′t*u*m, -rā′-) *n.* (pl. **-ta** pr. -t*a*). Something wanting and required or desired.

de·sign (dĭzīn′) *n.* 1. Plan or scheme to be carried out; end in view; purpose, intention; contrivance in accordance with a preconceived plan; scheme of attack *upon*. 2. Preliminary sketch for a work of art; plan for a building, machine, or any composite structure; combination of parts in a whole; general idea, construction, plot, etc.; faculty of evolving these; pattern, outline of decoration etc.; **industrial** ~, art of making designs for objects that are to be produced by machine. **design** *v.* 1. Form plan or scheme for; contrive; purpose, intend, have in view. 2. Set apart in thought for use *as*, or *for* advantage of. 3. Make preliminary sketch for (work of art etc.); plan construction of. **de·sign′ed·ly** *adv.* On purpose, intentionally. **de·sign′er** *n.* **de·sign′ing** *adj.* (esp.) Crafty, artful, scheming.

des·ig·nate (dĕz′ĭgnĭt, -nāt) *adj.* (placed after noun) Appointed or nominated but not yet installed. **des·ig·nate** (dĕz′ĭgnāt) *v.t.* (**-nat·ed, -nat·ing**). Specify, particularize; serve as name or distinctive mark of; style, describe as; appoint to office. **~d hitter**, 10th player on a team, who bats in regular rotation but does not field, replacing at bat one who fields but does not bat. **des·ig·na·tion** (dĕzĭgnā′sh*o*n) *n.* Appointing to office; name, description, title.

de·sir·a·ble (dĭzīr′*a*b*e*l) *adj.* Worthy of, arousing, desire; advisable. ~ *n.* Desirable thing or person. **de·sir·a·bil·i·ty** (dĭzīr*a*bĭl′ĭtē), **de·sir′a·ble·ness** *ns.* **de·sir′a·bly** *adv.*

de·sire (dĭzīr′) *n.* 1. Feeling or emotion directed to attainment or possession of something expected to give pleasure or satisfaction; sensual appetite, lust. 2. Expression of desire, request. 3. Object of desire. ~ *v.t.* (**-sired, -sir·ing**). Long for, crave, wish; ask for; pray, entreat, command.

de·sir·ous (dĭzīr′*u*s) *pred. adj.* Wishful, desiring, (*to* do); ambitious, having the desire, (*of*).

de·sist (dĭzĭst′, -sĭst′) *v.i.* Cease (*from*).

desk (dĕsk) *n.* 1. Piece of furniture for reading or writing at, having as its essential feature a board etc. that serves as a rest for books and papers, and often drawers etc. for writing materials. 2. Section responsible for particular subject or operation within an organization, such as *the Mideast desk* of the U.S. Department of State; editorial subdivision of newspaper office, e.g. *the city desk*.

Des Moines (d*e* moin′). Capital of Iowa in the S. central part on the **Des Moines River**, which flows from SW. Minnesota and joins the Mississippi in Iowa.

des·o·late (dĕs′*o*lĭt) *adj.* Left alone, solitary; uninhabited, deserted; dreary, dismal, forlorn. **des′o·late·ness** *n.* **des·o·late** (dĕs′*o*lāt) *v.t.* (**-lat·ed, -lat·ing**).

Depopulate, devastate; render wretched and comfortless.

des·o·la·tion (dĕsolā´shon) *n.* Devastation; dreary barrenness; desolate place, dreary waste or ruin; solitariness; grief, wretchedness.

des·ox·y·ri·bo·nu·cle·ic (dĕs-ŏksĭrībōnōōklē´ĭk, -nū-) **acid**: see DNA.

de·spair (dĭspār´) *n.* Loss, utter want, of hope; what causes despair. ~ *v.i.* Lose, be without, hope. **de·spair´ing** *n.* **de·spair´ing·ly** *adv.*

des·patch = DISPATCH.

des·per·a·do (dĕsperah´dō, -rā´-) *n.* (pl. **-does, -dos**). Desperate, dangerous criminal, esp. of the old West.

des·per·ate (dĕs´perĭt) *adj.* 1. Leaving little or no room for hope; extremely dangerous or serious; hopelessly or extremely bad, extreme. 2. Reckless from despair; staking all on a small chance. **des´per·ate·ly** *adv.* **des´per·ate·ness, des·per·a·tion** (dĕsperā´shon) *ns.*

des·pi·ca·ble (dĕs´pĭkabel, dĭs-pĭk´a-) *adj.* Vile, contemptible. **des´pi·ca·bly** *adv.*

de·spise (dĭspīz´) *v.t.* (**-spised, -spis·ing**). Look down on, think scornfully or slightingly of.

de·spite (dĭspīt´) *prep.* In spite of. **de·spite´ful** *adj.* **de·spite´ful·ly** *adv.* (archaic).

de·spoil (dĭspoil´) *v.t.* Plunder, spoil, rob, deprive. **de·spoil´er, de·spoil´ment** *ns.*

de·spo·li·a·tion (dĭspōlēā´shon) *n.* 1. Act of despoiling or plundering. 2. Condition of being despoiled or plundered.

de·spond (dĭspŏnd´) *v.i.* Lose heart, be dejected. ~ *n.* Despondency (archaic; only in **slough of D**~ in John Bunyan's allegory *Pilgrim's Progress*, 1678). **de·spond·en·cy** (dĭspŏn´densē), **de·spond´ence** *ns.* Condition of having lost heart, dejection. **de·spond´ent** *adj.* **de·spond´ent·ly, de·spond´ing·ly** *advs.*

des·pot (dĕs´pot, -pŏt) *n.* Absolute or tyrannical ruler; tyrant, oppressor. **des·pot·ic** (dĕspŏt´ĭk) *adj.* **des·pot´i·cal·ly** *adv.*

des·pot·ism (dĕs´potĭzem) *n.* Arbitrary rule; despotic state.

des·sert (dezērt´) *n.* Last course of lunch or dinner, usu. a sweet food as fruit, pie, cake, ice cream, etc.; (Brit.) course of fruit, nuts, etc., served after sweet course at end of dinner; ~ **fork,** ~ **spoon**, etc., those used for dessert. [Fr., f. *desservir* clear the table]

des·ti·na·tion (dĕstĭnā´shon) *n.* Place to which person or thing is bound.

des·tine (dĕs´tĭn) *v.t.* (**-tined, -tin·ing**). Appoint, foreordain, devote, set apart (*to, for*).

des·ti·ny (dĕs´tinē) *n.* (pl. **-nies**). 1. What is destined to happen, fate. 2. Power that foreordains, overruling or invincible necessity.

des·ti·tute (dĕs´tĭtōōt, -tūt) *adj.* Without resources, in want of

A starboard quarterbow view of the Spruance class ***destroyer*** *U.S.S. Elliott. Launched in 1974, it was built by Ingells Shipbuilding Co.*

necessaries; devoid *of*. **des·ti·tu·tion** (dĕstĭtōō´shon, -tū´-) *n.*

de·stroy (dĭstroi´) *v.t.* Pull down, demolish; make useless, spoil utterly; kill.

de·stroy·er (dĭstroi´er) *n.* (esp.) One of a class of small fast warships armed with guns, torpedoes, depth charges, etc., used for escort work, attacking submarines, etc.; ~ **escort**, warship smaller than a destroyer, used to convoy merchant ships and in submarine warfare.

de·struct·i·ble (dĭstrŭk´tibel) *adj.* Able to be destroyed. **de·struct·i·bil·i·ty** (dĭstrŭktibĭl´ĭtē) *n.*

de·struc·tion (dĭstrŭk´shon) *n.* Destroying, being destroyed; what destroys, cause of ruin.

de·struc·tive (dĭstrŭk´tĭv) *adj.* Destroying, causing destruction; (of criticism etc.) negative, not constructive. **de·struc´tive·ly** *adv.* **de·struc´tive·ness, de·struc´tor** *ns.*

des·ue·tude (dĕs´wĭtōōd, -tūd) *n.* Passing into, state of, disuse.

des·ul·to·ry (dĕs´ultōrē, -tōrē) *adj.* Skipping from one thing to another, disconnected, unmethodical. **des´ul·to·ri·ly** *adv.* **des´ul·to·ri·ness** *n.* [L. *desultor* circus rider]

de·tach (dĭtăch´) *v.t.* Unfasten and separate (*from*); (mil., nav.) separate and send off (part from main body) for special purpose or mission. **de·tach'a·ble** *adj.* **de·tach·a·bil·i·ty** (dĭtăch*a*bĭl'ĭtē) *n.*

de·tached (dĭtăcht') *adj.* 1. Separate; unattached, standing apart. 2. Disinterested, feeling no personal involvement. **de·tach'ed·ly** *adv.* **de·tach'ed·ness** *n.*

de·tach·ment (dĭtăch'm*e*nt) *n.* 1. Detaching. 2. Number of troops, ships, etc., detached from main body for employment on separate service etc. 3. Standing aloof from objects or circumstances, withdrawal from association with surroundings; aloofness from worldly concerns etc.

de·tail (dĭtāl', dē'tāl) *n.* 1. Dealing with things item by item; minute account, number of particulars. 2. Item, small or subordinate particular; minor decoration in building, picture, etc., way of treating this. 3. (mil. etc.) Distribution of orders of the day; selecting and dispatching; small party selected and dispatched for particular service or duty. **detail** (dĭtāl') *v.t.* 1. Give particulars of, relate or enumerate in detail. 2. (mil.) Select and dispatch for special duty. **de·tailed** (dĭtāld', dē'tāld) *adj.* (esp.) Related or described in detail.

de·tain (dĭtān') *v.t.* 1. Keep in confinement or under restraint. 2. Withhold (esp. what is due); keep from proceeding, keep waiting. **de·tain'ment** *n.*

de·tain·ee (dĭtānē', dē-) *n.* Person detained.

de·tain·er (dĭtā'n*e*r) *n.* (law) (Wrongful) withholding of another's property; writ by which person already arrested may be detained pending action.

de·tect (dĭtĕkt') *v.t.* Find out, discover (person) in possession of some quality or performance of some act; discover presence, existence, or fact of (something apt to elude observation). **de·tect'a·ble** *adj.* **de·tec'tion** *n.* Detecting, esp. of criminals.

de·tec·tive (dĭtĕk'tĭv) *n.* Person, esp. policeman, employed in investigating criminal etc. activities; ~ **story**, story in which interest is centered in a crime and the detection of the criminal. **detective** *adj.* Employed in, relating to, serving for, detection.

de·tec·tor (dĭtĕk't*e*r) *n.* (esp.) Instrument for detecting any thing or action liable to escape observation.

de·tent (dĭtĕnt') *n.* Pawl; mechanism acting as a checking or detaining device.

dé·tente, de·tente (dātahnt') *ns.* (diplomacy) Relaxing of strained relations between two nations. [Fr.]

de·ten·tion (dĭtĕn'sh*o*n) *n.* Detaining, being detained; arrest, confinement, esp. temporary custody while awaiting trial; ~ **center, house**, disciplinary institution for juvenile offenders.

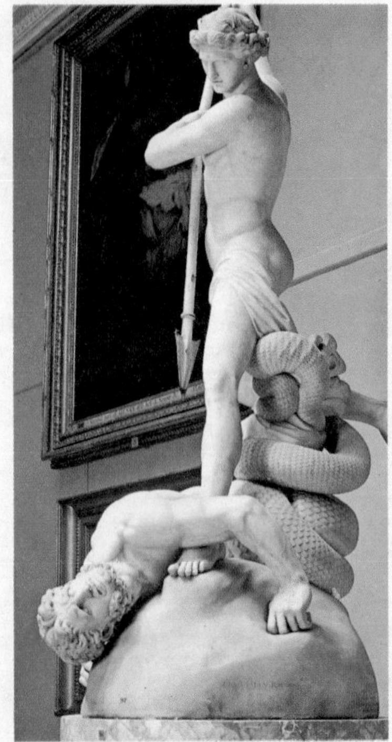

'St. Michael and Satan' by John Flaxman, an 18th-century English sculptor. The personification of the ***devil*** *as half-man, half-serpent is unusual.*

de·ter (dĭtēr') *v.t.* (**-terred, -ter·ring**). Discourage or restrain by fear or by consideration of danger or trouble. **de·ter'ment** *n.*

de·ter·gent (dĭtēr'j*e*nt) *n.* Water-soluble cleansing substance, a wetting agent and emulsifier, prepared from chemical compounds instead of the fats and oils used to make soap.

de·te·ri·o·rate (dĭtēr'ēorāt) *v.* (**-rated, -rat·ing**). Make, grow, worse. **de·te·ri·o·ra·tion** (dĭtērēorā'sh*o*n) *n.* **de·te'ri·o·ra·tive** *adj.*

de·ter·mi·na·ble (dĭtēr'm*i*n*a*bel) *adj.* Capable of being determined; liable to be terminated. **de·ter'mi·na·bly** *adv.*

de·ter·mi·nant (dĭtēr'm*i*n*a*nt) *adj.* & *n.* Determining, decisive, conditioning, defining (agent, element, word, etc.); (math.) square array of quantities representing the sum of the products of all possible sets of factors taking one from each row and one from each column, the signs of these products being determined by the direction of the diagonals joining at their factors.

de·ter·mi·nate (dĭtēr'm*i*nĭt) *adj.* Limited, definite, distinct, finite, definitive. **de·ter'mi·nate·ly** *adv.* **de·ter'mi·nate·ness** *n.*

de·ter·mi·na·tion (dĭtērm*i*nā'sh*o*n) *n.* 1. Decision, settlement, (*of* controversy, suit, etc.); conclusion, opinion, sentence. 2. Fixing, delimitation, definition, settlement, (*of* anything); exact ascertainment. 3. Fixed direction, decisive bias; settling of purpose; fixed purpose or intention; resoluteness.

de·ter·mi·na·tive (dĭtēr'm*i*nātĭv, -n*a*tĭv) *adj.* & *n.* (Thing) serving to determine. **de·ter'mi·na·tive·ly** *adv.* **de·ter'mi·na·tive·ness** *n.*

de·ter·mine (dĭtēr'mĭn) *v.* (**-mined, -min·ing**). 1. (esp. law) Bring, come, to an end. 2. Settle, decide, as judge or arbiter; come to conclusion, give decision; be decisive factor in regard to. 3. Ascertain precisely, fix. 4. Give an aim to, direct, impel *to*; decide (person) *to* do; resolve. **de·ter'mined** *adj.* (esp.) Resolute, unflinching.

de·ter·min·ism (dĭtēr'm*i*nĭz*e*m) *n.* Philosophical doctrine that human action is not free but necessarily determined by motives, regarded as external forces acting on the will. **de·ter'min·ist** *n.* **de·ter·min·is·tic** (dĭtērm*i*nĭs'tĭk) *adj.*

de·ter·rent (dĭtēr'*e*nt, -tŭr'-, -tĕr'-) *adj.* That deters. ~ *n.* Something that deters; (sep.) nuclear weapon(s), deterring enemy from attacking, hence, **nuclear** ~. **de·ter'rence** *n.*

de·test (dĭtĕst') *v.t.* Abhor, dislike intensely. **de·test'a·ble** *adj.* **de·test'a·ble·ness** *n.* **de·test'a·bly** *adv.* **de·tes·ta·tion** (dētĕstā'sh*o*n) *n.* Abhorrence; detested person or thing.

de·throne (dēthrōn') *v.t.* (**-throned, -thron·ing**). Depose. **de·throne'ment** *n.*

det·o·nate (dĕt'*o*nāt) *v.* (**-nat·ed, -nat·ing**). (Cause to) explode with loud report. **det·o·na·tion** (dĕt*o*nā'sh*o*n) *n.*

det·o·na·tor (dĕt'*o*nāt*e*r) *n.* Detonating contrivance, esp. fuse, percussion cap, etc., as part of bomb or shell.

de·tour (dē'toor, dĭtoor') *n.* Deviation, roundabout way, digression; byroad used temporarily while main route is unusable, being repaired, etc.

de·tox·i·fy (dētŏk's*i*fī) *v.t.* (**-fied, -fy·ing**). Remove poison or effects of poison from. **de·tox·i·fi·ca·tion** (dētŏks*i*fĭkā'sh*o*n) *n.*

de·tract (dĭtrăkt') *v.* Take away (*much, something,* etc.) *from*; ~ **from**, diminish, lessen in value, depreciate. **de·trac'tion, de·trac'tor** *ns.* **de·trac'tive** *adj.*

de·train (dētrān') *v.* Discharge (troops etc.), alight, from railroad train.

det·ri·ment (dĕt'r*i*m*e*nt) *n.* Harm, damage. **det·ri·men·tal**

(dĕtrimĕn′tal) *adj.* Harmful, causing loss or damage. **det·ri·men′tal·ly** *adv.*

de·tri·tion (dĭtrĭsh′on) *n.* Wearing away by rubbing.

de·tri·tus (dĭtrī′tus) *n.* Matter produced by detrition, esp. gravel, sand, clay, etc., eroded and washed away by action of water.

De·troit (dĭtroit′). City in SE. Michigan, on the ~ **River**; a center of automobile production.

de trop (de trō′). Not wanted, Unwelcome, superfluous. [Fr.]

de·tu·mes·cence (dētōōmĕs′-ens, -tū-) *n.* Subsidence from swelling, esp. contraction of swollen organ or part to normal size.

deuce[1] (dōōs, dūs) *n.* 1. The two at dice or cards. 2. (tennis) State of score when the two sides or players each have 40 points in a game (or 5 or more games) and either must gain 2 points (or games) in succession to win.

deuce[2] (dōōs, dūs) *n.* Plague, mischief; the Devil; **play the ~ with**, spoil, ruin.

deu·ced (dōō′sĭd, dū′-, dōōst, dūst) *adj.* & *adv.* Confounded(ly); extreme(ly). **deu′ced·ly** *adv.*

de·us ex ma·chi·na (dē′ōōs ĕks mah′kĭnah). Power, event, that comes in nick of time to solve difficulty, providential interposition, esp. in novel or play. [L., = "god from the machinery" (by which in ancient theater gods were shown in the air)]

Deut. *abbrev.* Deuteronomy.

deu·te·ri·um (dōōtēr′ēum, dū-) *n.* Isotope of hydrogen, present to extent of about 1 part in 6000 in ordinary hydrogen; symbol D, at. no. 1, at. wt. 2.013; ~ **oxide** (D_2O), heavy water (see HEAVY *adj.*). [Gk. *deuteros* second]

deu·ter·on (dōō′terŏn, dū′-) *n.* Nucleus of DEUTERIUM atom.

Deu·ter·on·o·my (dōōterŏn′-omē, dū-). Fifth book of the Old Testament, stating the law of Moses completely for the second time. [Gk. *deuteronomiom* 2nd book of law, from a mistranslation of Hebrew words (Deut. 17:18) meaning "a copy or duplicate of this law"]

Deut·sche (doi′che) **mark** (pl. **mark**, Eng. **marks**). Monetary unit of West Germany, = 100 pfennig.

dev. *abbrev.* Deviation.

De·va (dā′va). (Hindu myth.) Divinity, one of the good spirits. [Sansk., = "god"]

De Va·le·ra (dĕ valār′a, -lēr′a), **Ea·mon** (1882–1975). American-born prime minister of Republic of Ireland 1937–48, 1951–4, 1957–9, president 1959–73.

de·val·ue (dēvăl′ū), **de·val·u·ate** (dēvăl′ūāt) *vbs.t.* (**-val·u·ed, -val·u·ing; -at·ed, -at·ing**). Deprive of value; effect devaluation of (currency). **de·val·u·a·tion** (dēvălūā′shon) *n.* (esp.) Reduction of official value of currency in terms of gold or another currency.

De·va·na·ga·ri (dāvanah′gerē). Formal alphabet in which Sanskrit, Hindi, and other languages of India are written. [Sansk.]

dev·as·tate (dĕv′astāt) *v.t.* (**-tat·ed, -tat·ing**). Lay waste, ravage. **dev·as·ta·tion** (dĕvastā′-shon), **dev′as·ta·tor** *ns.* **dev′as·ta·ting** *adj.* (esp., fig.) Very effective; astounding. **dev′as·tat·ing·ly** *adv.*

de Ve·ga (de vā′ga), **Lope** (1562–1635). Spanish poet and playwright; founder of Spanish national drama.

de·vel·op (dĭvĕl′op) *v.* 1. Unfold, bring out all that is potentially contained in; bring or come forth from latent or elementary condition, make or become manifest; realize potentialities of (land), esp. by converting it for residential or industrial purposes. 2. (mus.) Elaborate (a theme), unfold its qualities, reveal its possibilities by modification of melody, harmony, rhythm, etc. 3. (photog.) Render visible (latent image produced by actinic action on sensitive surface) by chemical treatment. 4. Make or become fuller, more elaborate or systematic, more active, bigger; make progress; come or bring into maturity. 5. Bring or come to light; make, become known.

de·vel·op·er (dĭvĕl′oper) *n.* 1. (esp.) Chemical agent for developing photographs. 2. (real estate) Subdivider of tracts for new home building.

de·vel·op·ment (dĭvĕl′opment) *n.* Act or process of developing, as the development of an organism etc.; developed product etc.; (mus.) in sonata or similar composition, the second section of a movement, containing elaborations on the theme(s) stated in the first section; housing subdivision. **de·vel·op·men′tal** *adj.* **de·vel·op·men′tal·ly** *adv.*

de·vi·ant (dē′vēant) *adj.* & *n.* (Thing or person) that deviates from what is considered normal state or behavior. **de′vi·ance, de′vi·an·cy** *ns.*

de·vi·ate (dē′vēāt) *v.i.* (**-at·ed, -at·ing**). Turn aside (*from*); digress.

de·vi·a·tion (dēvēā′shon) *n.* (esp.) Deflection of ship's compass needle by iron in ship etc.; divergence. **de·vi·a′tion·ism** *n.* **de·vi·a′tion·ist** *adj.* & *n.*

de·vice (dĭvīs′) *n.* 1. (pl.) Fancy, will, desire (only in **leave, left, to one's own devices**). 2. Arrangement, contrivance, expedient; something designed to perform special (esp. mechanical or electrical) function. 3. Design, figure; emblematic or heraldic design; motto.

dev·il (dĕv′il) *n.* 1. **the D~**, Satan; in Jewish and Christian theology, the supreme spirit of evil, tempter and spiritual enemy of man, represented as a person, usu. with cloven hoofs, horns, and a tail. 2. Demon; heathen god, esp. malignant or evil deity, unclean spirit by which demoniacs were supposed to be possessed; one of the host of Satan, supposed to have their abode in hell. 3. Malignantly wicked or cruel person; energetic, clever, knavish, etc., person; poor wretch, luckless person (usu. **poor ~**). 4. Printer's apprentice (hist.). 5. Personified evil quality; temper, fighting spirit. 6. **Tasmanian ~**: see TASMANIAN. 7. Any of various instruments or machines, esp. with sharp teeth or spikes, for destructive use. 8. **a ~ of a**, a confounded, very violent; **like the ~**, with the violence, energy, etc., attributed to the devil; **between the ~ and the deep sea**, in an unpleasant dilemma; **go to the ~**, go to ruin or perdition; **the ~ to pay**, much trouble, violence. 9. **dev′ilfish**, any of several rays of the family Mobulidae, esp. of the genus *Manta*, e.g. the **devil ray**, inhabiting warm seas and having winglike pectoral fins spreading to about 20 feet and hornlike fleshy protuberances on the head; **devil-may-care** (*adj.*), wildly reckless; careless and rol-

Sandy beaches, where coins are easily lost, provide a profitable hunting ground for some-one with patience and a metal ***detector***.

licking; **devil's advocate** = PROMOTER FIDEI; one who advocates an opposing cause, esp. for argument; **devil's bit**, applied to several American plants, including the blazing-stars (*Liatris*), because of their bitter taste; esp. the devil's bit, *Chamaelirium luteum*. **devil's food cake**, rich chocolate cake. **Devil's Island**, former French penal colony; one of the Safety Islands, off the coast of French Guiana; **devil** *v.* (**-iled, -il·ing, -illed, -il·ling**). 1. Work as printer's apprentice. 2. Prepare (food) by chopping finely and adding mustard, pepper, and other strong seasoning; hence **~ed eggs**.

dev·il·ish (dĕv´ĭlĭsh) *adj.* Like, worthy of, the devil, fiendish; extreme, excessive. **dev'il·ish·ly** *adv.* **dev'il·ish·ness** *n.*

dev·il·ment (dĕv´ĭlment) *n.* Mischief, wild spirits.

dev·il·try (dĕv´ĭltrē) *n.* (pl. **-tries**). Diabolical art, magic; the devil and his works; wickedness, cruelty; reckless mischief, daring, or hilarity.

de·vi·ous (dē´vēus) *adj.* Winding or straying, circuitous, erratic; erring. **de'vi·ous·ly** *adv.* **de'vi·ous·ness** *n.*

***Dhows** are used in trading voyages in the Arabian Sea and on the east coast of Africa. The most common type has a single mast and is a small, although seaworthy, vessel.*

de·vise (dĭvīz´) *v.t.* (**-vised, -vis·ing**). 1. Plan, invent; plot, scheme. 2. (law) Assign or give (now only real property) by will. ~ *n.* (law) Testamentary disposition of real property, clause in will conveying this. **de·vi·see** (dĭvīzē´, dĕvĭ-) *n.* Person to whom property is devised.

de·vi·tal·ize (dēvī´talīz) *v.t.* (**-ized, -iz·ing**). Make lifeless or effete. **de·vi·tal·i·za·tion** (dēvītalīzā´shon) *n.*

de·void (dĭvoid´) *adj.* Destitute, empty, *of*.

dev·o·lu·tion (dĕvoloo´shon) *n.* 1. Descent through a series of changes; descent of property by natural or due succession. 2. (biol.) Degeneration (now rare). 3. Delegation of work or power.

de·volve (dĭvŏlv´) *v.* (**-volved, -volv·ing**). Pass on, delegate (duty, work), fall, descend, *upon* (deputy, or one who must act for want of others).

Dev·on (dĕv´on) *n.* County of SW. England; (one of) a breed of reddish cattle developed there; ~, island in Northwest Territories, Canada, S. of Ellesmere Island.

De·vo·ni·an (dĭvō´nēan) *adj.* & *n.* 1. (Native, inhabitant) of Devon. 2. (geol.) (Of) the period or system of the Paleozoic era, occurring from 350,000,000 to 400,000,000 years ago, between Silurian and Carboniferous.

Dev·on·shire (dĕv´onshēr, -sher) = DEVON; ~ **cream**, thick clotted cream prepared by slow scalding.

de·vote (dĭvōt´) *v.t.* (**-vot·ed, -vot·ing**). Consecrate, dedicate, give up exclusively *to*. **de·vot'ed** *adj.* (esp.) Zealously attached, loyal or faithful. **de·vot'ed·ly** *adv.*

dev·o·tee (dĕvotē´, -tā´, dĭvō-) *n.* Votary *of*, one devoted *to*; zealously or fanatically pious person.

de·vo·tion (dĭvō´shon) *n.* 1. Devoutness; religious worship or observance; (pl.) prayers, worship. 2. Enthusiastic addiction, attachment, or loyalty (*to*). **de·vo′tion·al** *adj.* **de·vo′tion·al·ly** *adv.*

de·vour (dĭvowr′) *v.t.* 1. Eat up voraciously, as a beast of prey, prey upon; eat greedily; eat ravenously or barbarously. 2. Consume recklessly; waste, destroy. 3. Engulf; take in greedily with eyes, ears, etc.; engross the attention of. **de·vour′er** *n.* **de·vour′ing·ly** *adv.*

de·vout (dĭvowt′) *adj.* Earnestly religious, reverent; earnest, sincere. **de·vout′ly** *adv.* **de·vout′ness** *n.*

dew (do͞o, dū) *n.* 1. Vapor condensed in small drops on cool surfaces on or near the ground, when nocturnal radiation has cooled the lower layer of the atmosphere. 2. Anything resembling this, as something refreshing, moist, or pure. 3. Any beaded or glistening moisture, esp. tears, sweat. 4. **dew′berry**, trailing plant of genus *Rubus*, which includes the blackberries; fruit of this plant; **dew′ claw**, rudimentary inner toe on inside of dog's leg, higher than other toes and not touching the ground; **dew′drop**, drop of moisture condensed in form of dew; **dew point**, temperature at which atmosphere becomes saturated with water vapor by cooling. **dew′y** *adj.* (**dew·i·er, dew·i·est**). **dew′i·ly** *adv.* **dew′i·ness** *n.* **dew** *v.t.* Bedew, moisten.

Dew·ey[1] (do͞o′ē, dū′ē), **George** (1837–1917). Amer. naval officer; destroyed Spanish ships in Manila Bay, 1898, during Spanish-American War.

Dew·ey[2] (do͞o′ē, dū′ē), **John** (1859–1952). Amer. pragmatic philosopher, author, and educator.

Dew·ey[3] (do͞o′ē, dū′ē), **Melvil** (1851–1931). Amer. librarian; devised decimal system (~ **Decimal System**) of classifying books for library indexing and display.

dew·lap (do͞o′lăp, dū′-) *n.* Fold of loose skin hanging from throat esp. in cattle. **dew′lapped** *adj.*

DEW line. Distant early warning line (see DISTANT).

dex·ter (dĕk′st*er*) *adj.* Of, on, the right-hand side (but in heraldry = on right side of shield from wearer's point of view, i.e. on spectator's left); opp. SINISTER.

dex·ter·i·ty (dĕkstĕr′ĭtē) *n.* Manual or mental adroitness, skill.

dex·ter·ous (dĕk′str*u*s, -st*er*us), **dex·trous** (dĕk′str*u*s) *adjs.* 1. Handling things neatly; skillful. 2. Mentally adroit; clever. 3. Right-handed. **dex′ter·ous·ly** *adv.* **dex′ter·ous·ness** *n.*

dex·trin (dĕk′strĭn) *n.* (chem.) Gummy substance, used as adhesive, into which starch is converted by dilute acids or alkalis, heat, etc.

dex·trose (dĕk′strōs) *n.* Glucose in animal and vegetable tissue, synthesized from starch.

dex·trous: see DEXTEROUS.

D.F.C. *abbrev.* Distinguished Flying Cross.

dg *abbrev.* Decigram(s).

dho·ti (dō′tē) *n.* (pl. **-tis**). Loin cloth worn by Hindus.

dhow (dow) *n.* Lateen-rigged Arab vessel.

di-[1] *prefix.* Two-, twice-, double-.

di-[2], **dia-** *prefixes.* Through, throughout, thorough(ly), apart, across.

di·a·be·tes (dī*a*bē′tĭs, -tēz) *n.* Disease (in medicine called **diabetes mellitus**) characterized by excessive discharge of glucose-containing urine, with thirst and emaciation, caused by failure of the pancreas to secrete an adequate amount of insulin and the consequent excessive accumulation of glucose in the blood; ~ **insipidus**, disease characterized by discharge of large quantities of urine, but not involving sugar metabolism, caused by disorder of pituitary gland.

di·a·bet·ic (dī*a*bĕt′ĭk) *adj.* Of, suffering from, diabetes. ~ *n.* Diabetic person.

di·a·bol·ic (dī*a*bŏl′ĭk), **di·a·bol·i·cal** (dī*a*bŏl′ĭk*a*l) *adjs.* Of, having to do with, under the influence of, the devil; devilish, inhumanly wicked. **di·a·bol′i·cal·ly** *adv.*

di·ab·o·lism (dīăb′*o*lĭzem) *n.* Sorcery, witchcraft; devilry; worship of the devil.

di·a·crit·i·cal (dī*a*krĭt′ĭk*a*l) *adj.* Distinguishing, distinctive; ~ **sign, mark**, one used to indicate different sounds of a letter, as accent, dieresis, etc.

di·a·dem (dī′*a*dĕm) *n.* Crown; jeweled or plain band worn around head as badge of royalty; sovereignty. **di·a·demed** (dī′*a*dĕmd) *adj.*

di·aer·e·sis (dīĕr′*e*sĭs) *n.* (pl. **-ses** pr. -sēz). Var. of DIERESIS.

Dia·ghi·lev (dyah′gĭlĕf), **Sergei Pavlovich** (1872–1929). Russian ballet impresario; founder (1909) of the Russian ballet company that revived the art of ballet in W. Europe.

di·ag·nose (dī′*a*gnōs, -nōz, dī*a*gnōs′, -nōz′) *v.t.* (**-nosed, -nos·ing**). Form a diagnosis of (a disease).

di·ag·no·sis (dī*a*gnō′sĭs) *n.* (pl. **-ses** pr. -sēz). Identification of disease by investigation of symptoms and history; formal statement of this.

di·ag·nos·tic (dī*a*gnŏs′tĭk) *adj.* Of, assisting, diagnosis. ~ *n.* Diagnosis; symptom. **di·ag·nos′ti·cal·ly** *adv.* **di·ag·nos·ti·cian** (dī*a*gnŏstĭsh′*a*n) *n.*

di·ag·o·nal (dīăg′*o*n*a*l) *adj.* Extending, as a line etc., from one angle to a nonadjacent angle of a

Devonshire's *mild, wet climate and large areas of highland have encouraged farming. Dairy cattle, as here at Exmoor, U.K. are important; Devonshire clotted cream is famous.*

rectilineal figure or solid, or from one corner of anything to the opposite corner; having an oblique direction; marked with diagonal lines. **di·ag'o·nal·ly** *adv.* **diagonal** *n.* Diagonal line, part, row, etc.

di·a·gram (dī'*a*grăm) *n.* 1. (geom.) Figure composed of lines, illustrating definition or aiding in proof etc. 2. Illustrative figure giving the general scheme or outline of an object and its parts. 3. Graphic representation of the course or results of an action or process. ~ *v.* (**-gramed, -gram·ing, -grammed, -gram·ming**). Make a diagram of. **di·a·gram·mat·ic** (dī*a*gr*a*măt'ĭk) *adj.* **di·a·gram·mat'i·cal·ly** *adv.*

di·al (dī'*a*l) *n.* 1. Sundial. 2. Surface of clock or watch bearing graduations and figures marking hours etc.; circular plate marked with figures etc. and fitted with movable index finger; rotatable ring of numbers and letters on telephone (~ **telephone**) used to make calls; ~ **tone,** steady humming sound given over telephone to show that caller may start to dial. **dial** *v.t.* (**-aled, -al·ing, -alled, -al·ling**). Measure, indicate (as) with dial; make telephone call by rotating a dial.

dial. *abbrev.* Dialect; dialectal; dialectic; dialectical.

di·a·lect (dī'*a*lĕkt) *n.* Form of speech peculiar to a district, class, etc.; subordinate variety of a language with distinguishing vocabulary, pronunciation, or idioms. **di·a·lec'tal** *adj.* **di·a·lec'tal·ly** *adv.* **di·a·lec·tol·o·gy** (dī*a*lĕktŏl'*o*jē) *n.*

di·a·lec·tic (dī*a*lĕk'tĭk) *adj.* Logical; of disputation. ~ *n.* 1. (freq. pl.) Art of critical examination into truth of opinion; investigation of truth by discussion; logical disputation. 2. Criticism dealing with metaphysical contradictions and their solutions, esp., in Hegelian philosophy, the stages of thesis, antithesis, and synthesis representing the process of thought developing toward completion **di·a·lec·ti·cian** (dī*a*lĕktĭsh'*a*n) *n.*

di·a·lec·ti·cal (dī*a*lĕk'tĭk*a*l) *adj.* 1. = DIALECTIC *adj.* 2. *Of* DIALECTIC *n.* (def. 2); ~ **materialism,** theory propagated by Karl Marx and Friedrich Engels, acc. to which political events are regarded as arising from a conflict of social forces (the "class struggle") produced by people's material needs, and history as a series of contradictions and their solutions (the thesis, antithesis, and synthesis of Hegelian philosophy). 3. = dialectal: see DIALECT. **di·a·lec'ti·cal·ly** *adv.*

di·a·logue (dī'*a*lawg, -lŏg) *n.* 1. Conversation; literary work in form of conversation between two or more persons; conversational part of novel or play. 2. Exchange of ideas, esp. on political or diplomatic issue.

di·al·y·sis (dīăl'ĭsĭs) *n.* (pl. **-ses** pr. -sēz). (chem.) Separation of soluble crystalloid substances in mixture from colloid by diffusion through semipermeable membrane; (med.) similar process used in purifying blood. **di·a·lyze** (dī'*a*līz) *v.t.* (**-lyzed, -lyz·ing**).

diam. *abbrev.* Diameter.

di·a·mag·net·ic (dī*a*măgnĕt'ĭk) *adj.* (of substance, as bismuth, zinc, copper, lead, or tin) Tending to become magnetized in the presence of a magnetic field so that it lies with its long axis at right angles to the field. **di·a·mag·net·ism** (dī*a*măg'n*e*tĭz*e*m) *n.*

di·am·e·ter (dīăm'*e*t*e*r) *n.* 1. (geom.) Straight line passing through center of circle or sphere and terminated at each end by its circumference or surface, or through center of any conic section, or through middle points of system of parallel chords in curve of any

Hardest of all minerals, the ***diamond*** *is cut by craftsmen. Low-grade diamonds have industrial uses. It was not until the mid-18th century that the art of cutting was developed to the standard seen in this ruby and diamond set (above), completed in 1816 for Louis XVIII of France. Top: A cutter at work.*

order; line passing from side to side of any body through center. 2. Transverse measurement, width, thickness; unit of measurement of lineal magnification of an object.

di·a·met·ri·cal (dīamĕt′rĭkal), **di·a·met·ric** (dīamĕt′rĭk) *adjs.* 1. Of, along, a diameter. 2. (of opposition, difference, etc.) Direct, complete, like that between opposite ends of diameter. **di·a·met′ri·cal·ly** *adv.*

dia·mond (dī′mond, dī′a-) *n.* 1. Very hard and brilliant precious stone, colorless or variously tinted, consisting of pure carbon crystallized in regular octahedrons and allied forms. 2. Glittering particle or point. 3. Glass cutting tool of small diamond set in handle. 4. Diamond-shaped figure, rhombus, or square, placed with diagonals vertical and horizontal; (playing card with) red diamond-shaped figure(s); (pl.) suit of these cards. 5. (baseball) Figure formed by the 4 bases; infield. 6. (print.) Size of type ($4\frac{1}{2}$ point). 7. **black ~**, variety of dark-colored diamond; (pl.) coal; **dia′mondback**, any of several large, venomous rattlesnakes with diamond-shaped markings on the back, including the **diamondback-terrapin** (*Malaclemys*), *Crotalus adamanteus* of SE. U.S., and *C. atrox* of SW. U.S. and Mexico; **diamond cut**, cut with facets like a diamond; **Diamond Head**, promontory on SE. coast of Oahu, Hawaii; **diamond wedding**, 60th anniversary of wedding. **diamond** *adj.* Made of, set with, diamond(s); rhombus-shaped. ~ *v.t.* Adorn with or as with diamonds.

Di·an·a (dīăn′a). (Rom. myth.) Goddess of hunting, chastity, and the moon; later regarded as identical with ARTEMIS; hence, huntress; (poetic) the moon.

di·an·thus (dīăn′thus) *n.* (pl. **-thus·es**). Flowering plant of genus *D*~ of the order Caryophyllaceae, including pinks and carnations.

di·a·pa·son (dīapā′zon, -son) *n.* 1. Fixed standard of musical pitch; ~ **normal**, pitch in which the A above middle C is set at 435 vibrations per second. 2. One of the chief foundation stops in an organ (**open** ~ and **stopped** ~) extending through whole compass of the instrument.

dia·per (dī′per, dī′a-) *n.* 1. Fabric woven with small simple diamond pattern; towel etc. of this, esp. absorbent cloth folded and worn around a baby's waist and bottom. 2. Ornamental design of diamond reticulations. ~ *v.t.* 1. Weave, decorate with diamond-shaped pattern. 2. Put diaper on a baby.

di·aph·a·nous (dīăf′anus) *adj.* Transparent or translucent; vague, indistinct.

di·a·pho·ret·ic (dīaforĕt′ĭk) *adj.* & *n.* (Drug, treatment) inducing perspiration.

di·a·phragm (dī′afrăm) *n.* 1. Muscular partition, convex toward thorax, separating thorax from abdomen in mammals, which contracts and becomes flatter when air is breathed in, thus increasing the capacity of the thorax; (zool., bot.) partition in certain shells, gastropods, plant tissues, etc. 2. Thin lamina or plate used as partition etc.; thin rubber or plastic contraceptive cap fitted over cervix; vibrating membrane or disk in acoustic instrument (telephone, loudspeaker, etc.); mechanism consisting of set of plates for varying effective aperture of lens of camera etc. **di·a·phrag·mat·ic** (dīafrăgmăt′ĭk) *adj.*

di·ar·rhe·a (dīarē′a) *n.* Excessive looseness of bowels. **di·ar·rhe′al, di·ar·rhe′ic** *adjs.*

di·a·ry (dī′arē) *n.* (pl. **-ries**). Daily record of events etc.; book etc. prepared for this or for noting future engagements. **di′a·rist** *n.* One who keeps a diary.

Di·as·po·ra (dīăs′pera) *n.* Dispersion of the Jews, after the Exile, among Gentile nations; Jews so dispersed.

di·a·stase (dī′astās) *n.* (chem.) Enzyme formed in germinating seeds and having property of converting starch into sugar.

di·as·to·le (dīăs′tolē) *n.* Dilation or relaxation of heart, rhythmically alternating with systole. **di·a·stol·ic** (dīastŏl′ĭk) *adj.*

di·as·tro·phism (dīăs′trofĭzem) *n.* Geological process that deforms the Earth's crust, thereby creating continents, mountains, faults etc. **di·a·stroph·ic** (dīastrŏf′ĭk) *adj.*

di·a·ther·mic (dīathėr′mĭk) *adj.* Of diathermy.

di·a·ther·my (dī′athėrmē), **di·a·ther·mi·a** (dīathėr′mēa) *ns.* Therapeutic use of low-voltage alternating electric currents of very high frequency to produce heat in parts of body below surface.

di·a·tom (dī′atŏm, -tom) *n.* Microscopic unicellular alga with silicified cell wall, existing in great numbers in sea and fresh water, and often forming extensive fossil deposits. **di·a·to·ma·ceous** (dīatomā′shus) *adj.* Containing or consisting of diatoms or their siliceous remains.

di·a·tom·ic (dīatŏm′ĭk) *adj.* (chem.) Consisting of two atoms;

Dice were used in the 2nd millenium B.C. and have been used ever since in games of chance. This painting of dice players is by a French painter, Georges de la Tour.

containing two replaceable atoms of hydrogen.

di·a·ton·ic (dīatŏn´ĭk) *adj.* (mus., of scale) Proceeding by notes proper to its key without chromatic alteration; (of melody etc.) constructed from such a scale.

di·a·tribe (dī´atrīb) *n.* Piece of bitter criticism, invective, denunciation. [Gk. *diatribē* wearing away (of time), discourse]

Di·az (dē´az; *Port.* dē´azh), **Bartholomeu** (1450?–1500). Portuguese navigator and explorer; sailed around Africa; discovered Cape of Good Hope.

di·az·o (dīăz´ō) **compound.** Organic compound, esp. one of those derived from aromatic hydrocarbons containing the characteristic group –N=N–, and forming the basis of a large group of dyestuffs (*azo dyes*).

di·bas·ic (dībā´sĭk) *adj.* Containing two replaceable hydrogen atoms.

dice (dīs) *n.pl.*: see DIE[1]; any game of chance using dice, esp. craps. **no ~**, (slang) no use, success, or luck. **dice** *v.* (**diced, dic·ing**). 1. Gamble, win or lose (money), with dice. 2. Cut (food) into small cubes.

di·ceph·a·lous (dīsĕf´alus) *adj.* Having two heads.

di·chot·o·my (dīkŏt´omē) *n.* (pl. **-mies**). 1. Division into two; classification into two groups; something paradoxical or ambivalent. 2. (bot., zool.) Form of

In Roman times the ***dictator*** *was an official who was given extraordinary powers in times of crisis. Here two 20th-century dictators, Mussolini and Hitler, meet at Florence Railway Station in October 1940.*

branching in which each successive axis divides into two. **di·chot´o·mous** *adj.* **di·chot´o·mize** *v.* (**-mized, -miz·ing**).

di·chro·ic (dīkrō´ĭk), **di·chro·it·ic** (dīkrōĭt´ĭk) *adjs.* Having two colors; esp. (of doubly refracting crystals) showing different colors when viewed in different directions, (of solutions) showing essentially different colors at different concentrations. **di·chro·ism** (dī´krōĭzem) *n.*

di·chro·mat·ic (dīkrōmăt´ĭk) *adj.* Having two colors, esp. (zool.) having two color phases in the adult stage.

di·chro·mic (dīkrō´mĭk) *adj.* Of, including, (only) two colors; esp., of vision of color-blind persons, including only two of the three primary colors.

dick (dĭk) *n.* (slang) Detective.

dick·cis·sel (dĭksĭs´el) *n.* A bunting (*Spiza americana*), U.S. bird with brownish back, yellowish breast, and black-patched throat.

dick·ens (dĭk´ĭnz) *n.* **the ~**, (colloq.) the deuce. [app. alliterative substitute for *devil*]

Dick·ens (dĭk´ĭnz), **Charles John Huffam** (1812–70). English novelist (pseudonym *Boz*), some of whose work, e.g. *Oliver Twist* and *Bleak House*, exposed social evils; creator, esp. in *Pickwick Papers*, of many humorous characters. **Dick·en·si·an** (dĭkĕn´zēan) *adj.*

dick·er (dĭk´er) *v.i.* Trade by barter; haggle; vacillate.

dick·ey (dĭk´ē) *n.* (pl. **-eys**). 1. Small bird (also **dick´eybird**). 2. False shirt front.

Dick·in·son (dĭk´ĭnson), **Emily (Elizabeth)** (1830–86). Amer. poet; all six volumes of her poetry were published posthumously.

di·cot·y·le·don (dīkŏtĭlē´don) *n.* Flowering plant with two cotyledons; see COTYLEDON. **di·cot·y·le´don·ous** *adj.*

dict. *abbrev.* Dictation; dictionary.

Dic·ta·phone (dĭk´tafōn) *n.* (trademark) Machine that records words spoken into it and subsequently reproduces them for transcription.

dic·tate (dĭk´tāt, diktāt´) *v.* (**-tat·ed, -tat·ing**). 1. Say or read aloud (matter to be written down). 2. Prescribe, lay down authoritatively (terms, thing to be done); lay down the law, give orders. **dic·ta·tion** (dĭktā´shon) *n.* **dictate** (dĭk´tāt) *n.* Directive, command; authoritative direction (usu. of reason, conscience, nature, etc.).

dic·ta·tor (dĭk´tāter, dĭktā´-) *n.* 1. Absolute ruler of a nation; person with absolute authority in any sphere. 2. One who dictates for transcription. **dic·ta´tor·ship** *n.* Rule of dictator.

The 19th-century English novelist ***Charles Dickens*** *achieved fame and fortune at the early age of 24 when his comic masterpiece 'The Pickwick Papers' was published.*

dic·ta·to·ri·al (dĭktatōr′ēal, -tōr′-) *adj.* Of a dictator; imperious, overbearing. **dic·ta·to′ri·al·ly** *adv.* **dic·ta·to′ri·al·ness** *n.*

dic·tion (dĭk′shon) *n.* 1. Choice of words and phrases, verbal style, in speech or writing. 2. Manner of speaking, elocution; enunciation of words.

dic·tion·ar·y (dĭk′shonĕrē) *n.* (pl. **-ar·ies**). Book dealing, usu. in alphabetical order, with the individual words of a language or some specified subject etc., setting forth their spelling, pronunciation, meaning, inflections, history, etymology, equivalents in another language, etc., or some of these; also, book of reference on any subject with items arranged in alphabetical order.

dic·tum (dĭk′tum) *n.* (pl. **-tums, -ta** pr. -ta). 1. Formal saying, pronouncement; (law) expression of judge's opinion on matter of law, not being the formal resolution or determination of a court. 2. Current saying; maxim.

did (dĭd): see DO.

di·dac·tic (dīdăk′tĭk) *adj.* Meant to instruct; (of persons) too much inclined to instruct, tending to lay down the law. **di·dac′ti·cal·ly** *adv.* **di·dac′ti·cism** *n.*

did·dle (dĭd′el) *v.* (**-dled, -dling**). 1. (Brit. slang) Cheat, swindle. 2. Waste time. **did′dler** *n.*

Di·de·rot (dē′derō), **Denis** (1713–84). French philosopher, dramatist, and critic; one of the founders of the *Encyclopédie.*

did·n't (dĭd′ent). Contraction of *did not.*

Di·do (dī′dō). Legendary daughter of a Tyrian king; fled to Africa after the death of her husband Sycheaus and is reputed to have founded the city of Carthage.

di·do (dī′dō) *n.* (pl. **-does, -dos**). (colloq.) Antic, caper, prank.

di·dym·i·um (dīdĭm′ēum, dĭ-) *n.* Rare metal, formerly supposed to be an element and given symbol Di and subsequently separated into the elements neodymium and praseodymium. [Gk. *didumos* twin, from its being always found with lanthanum]

die[1] (dī) *n.* 1. (pl. **dice** pr. dīs, freq. used as sing.) Small cube with faces marked with 1–6 spots, thrown from box or hand in games of chance; (pl.) game played with

A ***dicotyledon*** *is a plant whose seed holds two seed-leaves or embryos. Ranunculus, above, is a typical dicotyledon.*

these; **the ~ is cast**, the irrevocable decision has been made. 2. Small cubical piece of anything. 3. Engraved stamp for impressing design etc. upon softer material, as in coining etc.; **~ casting**, casting obtained from metal mold(s); process of making such castings. 4. (mech.) Cutting device in a press or stamping machine.

die[2] (dī) *v.i.* (**died, dy·ing**). 1. Cease to live, expire. 2. Suffer spiritual death. 3. Suffer as in death; **be dying for, to**, desire keenly or excessively; **die laughing**, be exhausted by laughing. 4. Lose vital force, decay; come to an end, cease to exist; (of fire etc.) go out; (also **~ out**) disappear, be forgotten. 5. **~ away**, languish; **die'hard**, stubbornly conservative person.

Die·fen·bak·er (dē'fenbāker), **John George** (1895–1979). Canadian prime minister, 1957–63.

diel·drin (dēl'drĭn) *n.* Crystalline, water-insoluble insecticide.

di·e·lec·tric (dīĭlĕk'trĭk) *adj.* & *n.* Insulating, nonconducting (medium or substance).

Dien Bien Phu (dyĕn'byĕn'foo'). Village in NW. Vietnam near border of Laos; site of victory of Vietminh forces over French army, 1954, during war between France and Indochina.

di·er·e·sis, di·aer·e·sis (dīĕr'esĭs) *ns.* (pl. **-ses** pr. -sēz). Sign (¨) placed over vowel indicating that it is to be pronounced separately, as in *naïve*.

die·sel (dē'zel) *n.* (also **~ engine**) Internal combustion engine in which air is first drawn into the cylinder and compressed so highly that the heat generated is sufficient to ignite the oil subsequently injected; vehicle driven by this; **~ fuel**, petroleum fraction used as fuel in diesel engines. [f. inventor, Rudolf *Diesel* (1858–1913), German engineer]

***Diet** differs from country to country because of the varying foodstuffs available. In India and many other eastern countries rice is the staple food, and lack of animal protein often results in under-nourishment.*

di·et[1] (dī'ĭt) *n.* Conference, congress, on national or international business; legislature; **D~ of Worms**, that convened in 1521 at Worms, Germany, at which Luther was condemned as a heretic.

di·et[2] (dī'ĭt) *n.* Way of feeding; prescribed type, quantity, etc. of food, regimen; one's habitual food. **~** *v.* (**di·et·ed, di·et·ing**). Keep to special diet; attempt to lose weight by special diet.

di·e·tar·y (dī'etĕrē) *n.* (pl. **-tar·ies**). Allowance or character of food. **~** *adj.* Of diet or a dietary.

di·e·tet·ic (dīetĕt'ĭk), **di·e·tet·i·cal** (dīetĕt'ĭkal) *adjs.* Of diet, of the regulation of kind and quantity of food; specially prepared or processed for restrictive diets; containing little sugar, starch, etc. **di·e·tet'ics** *n.pl.* (usu. considered sing.). Part of medicine dealing with regulation of diet.

di·eth·yl·stil·bes·trol (dīĕth'ilstĭlbĕs'trōl, -trawl, -trŏl) *n.* White, crystalline solid almost insoluble in water, a synthetic estrogen.

di·e·ti·tian, di·e·ti·cian (dīetĭsh'an) *ns.* Person versed in dietetics.

dif·fer (dĭf'er) *v.i.* Be unlike, be distinguishable *from*; be at variance, disagree (*with, from*).

dif·fer·ence (dĭf'erens, dĭf'rens) *n.* 1. Being different, dissimilarity; point in which things differ; quantity by which amounts differ, remainder after subtraction; **split the ~**, come to compromise; **what's the ~?** (colloq.) Is it important? What does it matter? 2. Disagreement in opinion, dispute, quarrel.

dif·fer·ent (dĭf'erent, dĭf'rent) *adj.* Differing; distinct; out of the ordinary. **dif'fer·ent·ly** *adv.*

dif·fer·en·tial (dĭferĕn'shal) *adj.* 1. Of, exhibiting, depending on, a difference; differing according to circumstances; constituting a specific difference, relating to specific differences. 2. (math.) Relating to differentiation or to infinitesimal differences. 3. **~ calculus**, (math.) method of calculation devised by Leibniz (1677), treating of infinitesimal differences between consecutive values of continuously varying quantities; **~ gear**, arrangement of gears connecting two shafts or axles in the same line and enabling one shaft to revolve faster than the other when required (e.g. in an automotive vehicle when turning a corner).

***Diesel** engines are used where economy and durability are more important than high performance. Locomotives, tractors, taxis, cargo ships, and construction plants have used diesel engines increasingly since the 1939–45 war.*

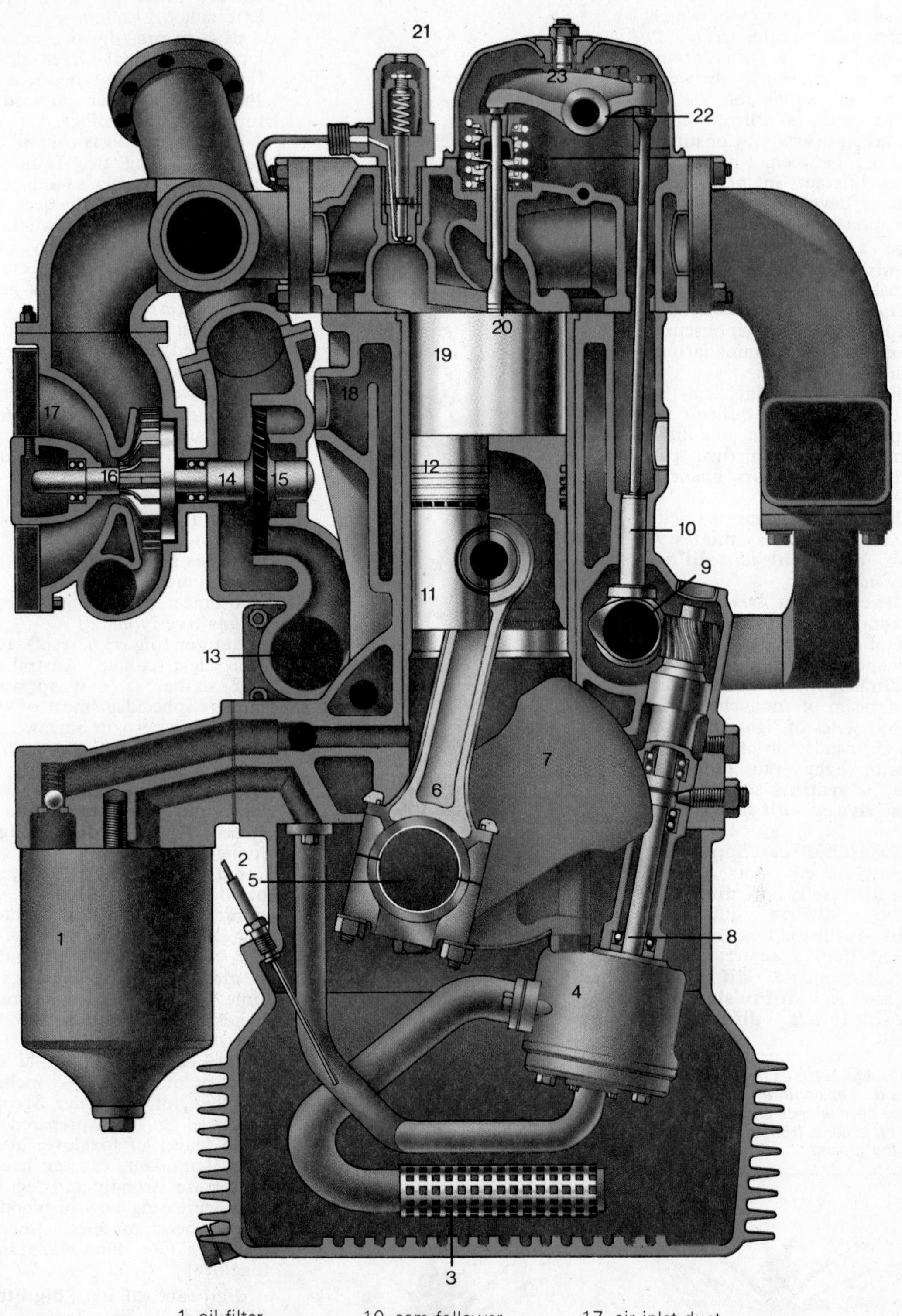

1 oil filter
2 dipstick
3 oil scavenge pipe
4 oil pump
5 crankshaft
6 connecting rod
7 crankshaft web
8 oil pump drive
9 camshaft
10 cam follower
11 piston
12 oil scraper and compression rings
13 turbocharger exhaust duct
14 turbocharger spindle
15 turbocharger turbine
16 compressor
17 air inlet duct
18 water galleries
19 cylinder bore
20 inlet valve
21 injector
22 rocker shaft
23 rocker

dif·fer·en′tial·ly *adv.* **differential** *n.* 1. (math.) Each of the infinitesimal differences of which the differential calculus treats. 2. Differential gear. 3. Difference or amount of difference between things that are comparable.

dif·fer·en·ti·ate (dĭfĕrĕn′shēāt) *v.* (**-at·ed, -at·ing**). 1. Constitute difference between; make or become different in process of growth or development, esp. by modification for special function or purpose. 2. Discriminate between, distinguish. **dif·fer·en·ti·a·tion** (dĭfĕrĕnshēā′sh*o*n) *n.*

dif·fi·cult (dĭf′*ĭ*kŭlt, -k*u*lt) *adj.* Hard to do, troublesome; obscure, perplexing; unaccommodating, stubborn.

dif·fi·cul·ty (dĭf′*ĭ*kŭltē, -k*u*l-) *n.* (pl. **-ties**). Being difficult to accomplish, understand, etc.; difficult thing or question; (usu. pl.) embarrassment of affairs, financial trouble.

dif·fi·dence (dĭf′ĭd*e*ns) *n.* Self-distrust, excessive modesty, shyness. **dif′fi·dent** *adj.* **dif′fi·dent·ly** *adv.*

dif·fract (dĭfrăkt′) *v.t.* (optics) Deflect and break up (beam of light) at edge of opaque body or through narrow aperture or slit. **dif·frac·tion** (dĭfrăk′sh*o*n) *n.* Breaking up thus of beam of monochromatic light into series of light and dark spaces or bands, or of white or composite light into series of spectra; ~ **grating**: see GRATING. **dif·frac′tive** *adj.* **dif·frac′tive·ly** *adv.*

dif·fuse (dĭfūs′) *adj.* Spread out, not concentrated; not concise, wordy. **dif·fuse′ly** *adv.* **dif·fuse′ness** *n.* **diffuse** (dĭfūz′) *v.* (**-fused, -fus·ing**). Disperse or be dispersed from a center; spread widely, disseminate. **dif·fu·sion** (dĭfū′zh*o*n) *n.* **dif·fu′sive** *adj.* **dif·fu′sive·ly** *adv.* **dif·fu′sive·ness** *n.*

***Digger wasps,** such as the Crabro hunt flies and Lepidoptera ammonphila, crush the head or neck of their prey and carry it off either in flight or by dragging it over the ground.*

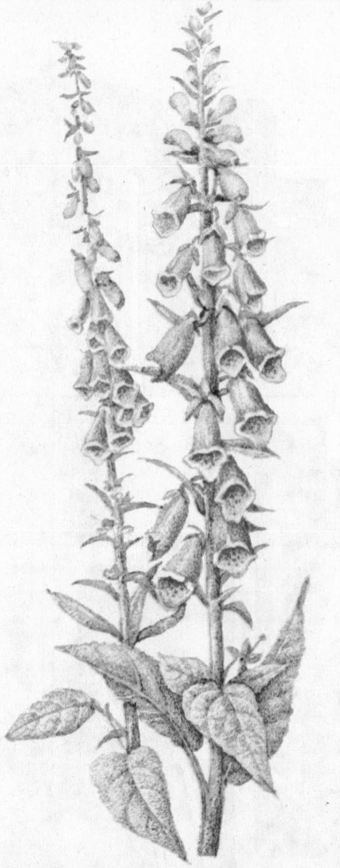

*The **digitalis** or common foxglove is found in Europe and in the Mediterranean region. It is used to produce a drug of the same name which stimulates the heart and slows the heartbeat.*

dig (dĭg) *v.* (**dug, dig·ging**). Turn up (ground) with spade or other tool, or with snout or claws; break up and turn over (soil); excavate; thrust or plunge (something) *in, into,* stab, prod; give (person) sharp nudge (*in ribs* etc.); (slang) understand, appreciate, experience; ~ **in,** (esp.) entrench; (colloq.) begin hard work; ~ **out,** get, find, make, by digging, discover by research; ~ **up,** get out of ground etc. by digging; excavate; break up and loosen soil of; find. **dig** *n.* 1. Piece of digging; archaeological excavation. 2. Thrust, poke; (fig.) gibe. 3. (pl., Brit. colloq.) Lodgings.

di·gam·ma (dīgăm′*a*) *n.* Sixth letter of original Greek alphabet (F, ϝ, prob. pronounced like English *w*), later disused but important in philology.

di·gas·tric (dīgăs′trĭk) *n.* (anat.) Muscle having two bellies with intervening tendon. ~ *adj.* Of the digastric muscle of the neck.

di·gest (dī′jĕst) *n.* 1. Methodical compendium or summary, esp. of body of law. 2. Periodical containing condensed versions of articles etc. **digest** (dĭjĕst′, dī-) *v.* 1. Reduce into systematic (and usu. condensed) form, classify; arrange methodically in mind, ponder over. 2. Reduce (food) in stomach and intestines to assimilable form; (of food) undergo digestion. **di·gest·i·bil·i·ty** (dĭjĕst*ĭ*bĭl′ĭtē, dī-) *n.* **di·gest′i·ble** *adj.*

di·ges·tion (dĭjĕs′ch*o*n, -jĕsh′-, dī-) *n.* Digesting of food; power of digesting.

di·ges·tive (dĭjĕs′tĭv, dī-) *adj.* Of, promoting, digestion. ~ *n.* Substance promoting digestion. **di·ges′tive·ly** *adv.*

dig·ger (dĭg′*er*) *n.* (esp.) 1. One who digs; (colloq.) Australian or N.Z. soldier. 2. ~ **wasp,** wasp of family Sphecidae, most of which build their nests in burrows.

dig·gings (dĭg′ĭngz) *n.pl.* 1. (often construed as sing.) Place where digging is done. 2. Material taken out of an excavation. 3. (chiefly Brit., also **digs**) Lodgings, living quarters.

dig·it (dĭj′ĭt) *n.* 1. (zool., anat., or joc.) Finger or toe. 2. Each numeral below 10 (orig. counted on fingers); each Arabic numeral from 0 to 9. **dig′it·al** *adj.* Using digits; ~ **clock,** ~ **watch,** one that shows time by displayed digits, not by hands; ~ **computer**: see COMPUTER.

dig·i·tal·is (dĭjĭtăl′ĭs, -tā′lĭs) *n.* 1. Plant of genus *D*~, including foxglove, of the order Scrophulariaceae. 2. Drug prepared from dried leaves of foxglove, used as heart stimulant, causing heart to beat more strongly and regularly, thus increasing flow of blood and resting heart muscles. [mod. L. transl. of Ger. *Fingerhut* thimble, foxglove]

dig·i·tate (dĭj′ĭtāt), **dig·i·tat·ed** (dĭj′ĭtātĭd) *adjs.* (zool., bot.) Having separate fingers or toes; with deep radiating divisions. **dig·i·ta·tion** (dĭjĭtā′sh*o*n) *n.*

dig·ni·fy (dĭg′n*ĭ*fī) *v.t.* (**-fied, -fy·ing**). Make worthy or illustrious; confer dignity on. **dig′ni·fied** *adj.* Stately, marked by dignity, majestic.

dig·ni·tar·y (dĭg′nĭtĕrē) *n.* (pl. **-tar·ies**). Person holding high rank or office.

dig·ni·ty (dĭg′nĭtē) *n.* (pl. **-ties**). 1. Worth, nobleness, excellence; high estate, position, or estimation; high or honorable office, rank, or title. 2. Proper stateliness, elevation of aspect, manner, or style; gravity.

di·graph (dī′grăf, -grahf) *n.* Pair of letters expressing one sound, as *sh.*

di·gress (dĭgrĕs′, dī-) *v.i.* Diverge from the track, stray; depart from main subject temporarily. **di·gres·sion** (dĭgrĕsh′*o*n, dī-) *n.* **di·gres·sive** (dĭgrĕs′ĭv, dī-) *adj.*

di·he·dral (dīhē′dr*a*l) *adj.* Having two plane faces; ~ **angle,** angle formed by intersecting planes or surfaces. **dihedral** *n.* Dihedral angle; upward (**positive** ~) or downward (**negative** ~, also called **anhedral**) inclination of aircraft wing from true horizontal.

di·hy·dric (dīhī′drĭk) *adj.* Having two hydroxyl groups.

dike, dyke (dīk) *ns.* 1. Ditch; any water course or channel. 2. Low wall, esp. of earth; embankment, long ridge, dam, against flooding by sea, rivers, etc.; raised causeway. ~ *v.t.* (**diked, dik·ing, dyked, dyk·ing**). Provide, protect with dike(s).

Di·lan·tin (dĭlăn′tĭn, dī-) *n.* (trademark) Drug that arrests epileptic convulsions.

di·lap·i·date (dĭlăp′ĭdāt) *v.* (**-dat·ed, -dat·ing**). Bring, come, into disrepair or decay. **di·lap·i·da·tion** (dĭlăpĭdā′sh*o*n) *n.*

di·late (dīlāt′, dī′lāt) *v.* (**-lat·ed, -lat·ing**). Make or become wider or larger; expand, widen, enlarge; expatiate, speak or write at length. **di·la·tion** (dīlā′sh*o*n), **dil·a·ta·tion** (dĭl*a*tā′sh*o*n, dīl*a*-) *ns.*

dil·a·to·ry (dĭl′*a*tōrē, -tōrē) *adj.* Tending to, designed to cause, given to, delay. **dil′a·to·ri·ly** *adv.* **dil′a·to·ri·ness** *n.*

di·lem·ma (dĭlĕm′*a*) *n.* Argument forcing opponent to choose one of two alternatives (the *horns* of the dilemma), both unfavorable to him or her; position involving choice between two evils.

dil·et·tante (dĭl*e*tănt′, -tahnt′, dĭl′*e*tănt, -tahnt, dĭl*e*tăn′tē, -tahn′tē) *n.* (pl. **-tantes, -tan·ti** pr. -tăn′tē, -tahn′tē). Lover of the fine arts; (now usu.) one who is interested in an art or science merely as a pastime and without serious study. ~ *adj.* Of, like, a dilettante. **dil·et·tan′tish** *adj.* **dil·et·tant′ism** *n.*

The raised causeway or ***dike*** *is most common in areas of flat land surrounded by water where there is particular danger of flooding. This dike and highway in Holland also serves as a dam and crosses the Ijsselmeer.*

dil·i·gence (dĭl′ĭj*e*ns) *n.* Persistent effort or work; industrious character.

dil·i·gent (dĭl′ĭj*e*nt) *adj.* Hard working, steady in application, industrious; attentive to duties. **dil′i·gent·ly** *adv.*

dill (dĭl) *n.* Umbelliferous annual yellow-flowered herb (*Anethum graveolens);* its leaves or seed; ~ **pickle,** cucumber pickled with dill.

dil·ly·dal·ly (dĭl′ēdălē) *v.i.* (**-lied, -ly·ing**). (colloq.) Vacillate; loiter; waste time.

dil·u·ent (dĭl′ūent) *adj.* Diluting. ~ *n.* Diluting agent.

di·lute (dĭlōōt′, dī-) *v.t.* (**-lut·ed, -lut·ing**). Reduce strength of (fluid) by adding water or other solvent; water down. **di·lute** (dĭlōōt′, dī-, dī′lōōt) *adj.* Weakened by addition of water; watery, watered down.

di·lu·tion (dĭlōō′sh*o*n, dī-) *n.* Act of diluting; state of being diluted; diluted substance.

dim (dĭm) *adj.* (**dim·mer, dim·mest**). Deficient in brightness or clearness; obscure; indistinct; (of person) mentally dull.

Top: sexual ***dimorphism*** *in animals is the difference in appearance between male and female of one species, shown here in Mearn's quail.*

Left: The Australian ***dingo*** *shuns human settlements and hunts mostly at night.*

dim′ly *adv.* **dim′ness** *n.* **dim** *v.* (**dimmed, dim·ming**). 1. Become, make, dim; becloud; outshine. 2. Lower automobile headlight beams, using a **dimmer**, a rheostat for dimming; **dim-out**, reduced artificial lighting in streets etc. during wartime (as dist. from *blackout*) or as result of reduced power.

dim., dimin. *abbrevs.* Diminuendo; diminutive.

dime (dīm) *n.* U.S. coin of value of one-tenth of a dollar, or 10 cents; **a ~ a dozen**, commonplace; **~ novel**, melodramatic novel of adventure or romance of a kind that formerly sold for 10 cents; **~ store**: see FIVE-AND-TEN.

di·men·sion (dĭmĕn′shon) *n.* 1. Measurable extent of any kind; (usu. pl.) measurement, measure, size. 2. Magnitude, or extension, in a particular direction; **fourth ~**, imaginary direction in which matter is supposed to extend in addition to the three dimensions (length, breadth, and thickness) of Euclidean geometry. 3. (alg.) Each of the (unknown or variable) qualities contained in a product as factors of it. **di·men′sion·al** *adj.*

dim·e·ter (dĭm′ĭter) *n.* Verse of two measures (a measure having one foot in some meters and two in others).

di·min·ish (dĭmĭn′ĭsh) *v.* Make, cause to appear, grow, less or smaller; lessen in importance, estimation, or power; **law of diminishing returns**, (econ.) principle that expenditure of labor or capital beyond a certain point does not produce proportionate return. **di·min′ished** *adj.* (esp. mus., of an interval) Less by a semitone.

di·min·u·en·do (dĭmĭnūĕn′dō) *adv., n.* (pl. **-dos**), & *adj.* (mus.) (Passage played) with gradually decreasing volume, indicated thus >.

dim·i·nu·tion (dĭmĭnōō′shon, -nū′-) *n.* Diminishing, reduction; (mus.) repetition of a passage in shorter notes than those previously used.

di·min·u·tive (dĭmĭn′yutĭv) *adj.* 1. Minute, tiny. 2. (gram.) Indicating smallness, familiarity, lovableness, etc. (used of such affixes as *-let, -kin, -ling* and of words formed with them, e.g. *ringlet, lambkin, duckling*). **di·min′u·tive·ly** *adv.* **di·min′u·tive·ness** *n.* **diminutive** *n.* Diminutive word or term; small person or thing.

dim·mer (dĭm′er): see DIM.

di·mor·phic (dĭmŏr′fĭk) *adj.* (bot., zool.) Occurring in two distinct forms in same species, individual, etc. **di·mor′phism** *n.* **di·mor′phous** *adj.*

dim·ple (dĭm′pel) *n.* Small hollow or dent in body, esp. in cheek or chin; slight surface depression or indentation resembling this. ~ *v.* (**-pled, -pling**). Mark with dimples, break into dimples or ripples.

din (dĭn) *n.* Continued confused loud noise. ~ *v.* (**dinned, din·ning**). Make din; utter continuously so as to deafen or weary; **~ into**, make (person) understand by continuous repetition.

di·nar (dĭnar′) *n.* Principal monetary unit of various countries in Middle East and N. Africa.

dine (dīn) *v.* (**dined, din·ing**). Take dinner; entertain at dinner; **dining car**, railroad car in which complete meals are served; **dining room**, room in which principal meals are taken.

din·er (dī′ner) *n.* 1. One who dines. 2. Dining car; inexpensive restaurant with long counter and booths built from or shaped like railroad car.

Din·e·sen (dĭn′ĭsen), **Isak** (1885–1962). Pen name of Baroness Karen Dinesen Blixen; Danish writer residing for many years in Kenya.

din·ette (dīnĕt′) *n.* Small room or alcove for informal meals; set of table and chairs used there.

din·ghy (dĭng′gē) *n.* (pl. **-ghies**). Small rowboat, inflatable rubber boat. [Hind. *dīngī* small boat]

din·gle (dĭng′gel) *n.* Deep dell or

hollow, usu. shaded with trees.

din·go (dĭng′gō) *n.* (pl. **-goes**). Wild or semidomesticated dog of Australia (*Canis dingo*), usu. reddish brown and with bushy tail. [Native name]

din·gy (dĭn′jē) *adj.* (**-gi·er, -gi·est**). Dull-colored, grimy, dirty; shabby; worn. **din′gi·ly** *adv.* **din′gi·ness** *n.*

din·ky (dĭng′kē) *adj.* (**-ki·er, -ki·est**). (colloq.) Small; insignificant.

din·ner (dĭn′*er*) *n.* Chief meal of day, eaten at midday or in the evening; formal meal or banquet in honor of some person, event, etc.; ~ **jacket**, man's short jacket for formal or semiformal evening wear; ~ **pail**, vessel in which worker carries his or her, usu. hot, dinner or lunch; **din′nerware**, china, glasses, etc. for use at **dinner table**. **din′ner·less** *adj.*

di·no·saur (dī′n*o*sōr) *n.* Any of the extinct saurian reptiles (orders Saurischia and Ornithischia) of the Mesozoic era, some of which were of gigantic size; **D~ National Monument**, area in NE. Utah reserved to protect fossil remains of prehistoric animals. [Gk. *deinos* terrible, *sauros* lizard]

dint (dĭnt) *n.* 1. **by ~ of**, by force of, through the persistence or vigor of. 2. Dent. ~ *v.t.* Make dent or dents in.

di·oc·e·san (dīŏs′*e*s*a*n, -z*a*n) *adj.* Of a diocese. ~ *n.* Bishop of diocese.

di·o·cese (dī′*o*sĭs, -sēz, -sēs) *n.* District under pastoral care of a bishop.

Dinosaurs *of species as small as chickens and others that were the largest known land beasts lived for 100 million years before they became extinct for unknown reasons at the end of the Cretaceous period about 80 million years ago.*

Di·o·cle·tian (dī*o*klē′sh*a*n) (245–313). Caius Aurelius Valerius Diocletianus, Roman emperor 284–305; during his reign the Christians were severely persecuted.

di·ode (dī′ōd) *n.* Any electronic device that limits current flow to one direction.

di·oe·cious (dīē′sh*u*s) *adj.* (bot.) Having the male and female flowers on separate plants.

Di·og·e·nes (dīŏj′*e*nēz) (*c*400–*c*325 B.C.). Greek Cynic philosopher; exponent of asceticism.

Di·o·ny·si·us (dīonĭs′ē*u*s, -nĭsh′-) **of Hal·i·car·nas·sus** (hăl*i*kārnăs′*u*s). First c. B.C. Greek historian; wrote history of Rome.

Di·o·ny·sus, Di·o·ny·sos (dī*o*nī′s*u*s). (Gk. myth.) Son of Zeus and Semele; god of wine and of orgiastic religion celebrating the fertility of nature; identified by the Romans with Bacchus. **Di·o·ny·sian** (dīonĭsh′*a*n, -nĭs′ē) *adj.*

di·op·ter (dīŏp′ter) *n.* Unit for expressing the power of a lens, equal to the reciprocal of its focal length in meters.

di·op·tric (dīŏp′trĭk), **di·op·tri·cal** (dīŏp′trĭkal) *adjs.* Of refraction, refractive; of dioptrics. **di·op′tri·cal·ly** *adv.* **di·op′trics** *n.* Branch of optics dealing with refraction.

di·o·ra·ma (dīorăm′a, -rah′ma) *n.* Small-scale representation of scene with objects etc. in front of painted background, viewed through aperture at the front; hence, small-scale model. **di·o·ram′ic** *adj.*

Di·os·cu·ri (dīoskūr′ī, -ŏs′kyurī) (Gk. myth.) Twin sons of Zeus, CASTOR and POLLUX.

di·ox·ide (dīŏk′sīd) *n.* (chem.) Oxide of an element in which two atoms of oxygen are united to one of the element.

dip (dĭp) *v.* (**dipped, dip·ping**). 1. Put or let down temporarily or partially into liquid or the like; dye thus; make (candle) by dipping wick in melted tallow or wax; wash (sheep, cattle, etc.) in vermin-killing liquid. 2. Obtain or take *up* by dipping. 3. Lower (flag etc.) for an instant. 4. Go under water and emerge quickly. 5. Put hand, ladle, etc., *into* to take something out. 6. Sink or drop down through small space, or below particular level, as if dipping into water; have downward inclination. 7. Look cursorily or skippingly *into*. ~ *n.* 1. Dipping; quantity dipped up; brief swim; plunge or immersion. 2. (astron. etc.) Apparent depression of horizon because of observer's elevation; MAGNETIC inclination; downward slope of surface, esp. of stratum or vein. 3. Hollow depression. 4. Candle made by dipping. 5. Sheep-dip. 6. Creamy mixture for scooping with crackers etc. 7. **dip′stick**, rod for measuring depth of liquid, esp. of oil in crankcase.

diph·the·ri·a (dĭfthēr′ēa, dĭp-) *n.* Acute, highly infectious disease characterized by inflammation of a mucous surface (usu. that of the throat), and by an exudation forming a firm pellicle or false membrane. **diph·ther·ic** (dĭfthĕr′ĭk, dĭp-), **diph·the·rit·ic** (dĭftherĭt′ĭk, dĭp-), **diph·the′ri·al** *adjs.*

diph·thong (dĭf′thawng, -thŏng) *n.* 1. Union of two vowels pronounced as one syllable. 2. (pop.) Ligature, as *æ*.

diph·thong·ize (dĭf′thawngīz, -thŏng-, dĭp′-) *v.t.* (**-ized, -iz·ing**). Develop diphthong from single vowel. **diph·thong·i·za·tion** (dĭfthawngĭzā′shon, -thŏng-, dĭp-) *n.*

dipl. *abbrev.* Diplomat(ic).

diplo- *comb. form.* Double.

*The big-horned sheep in this **diorama** feature above the snow-covered peaks in the background, but the viewer still gains an impression of the area that these animals inhabit*

dip·loid (dĭp′loid) *adj.* & *n.* (biol.) (Organism, cell, nucleus) with chromosomes in homologous pairs.

di·plo·ma (dĭplō′ma) *n.* 1. Document issued by school or university conferring a degree or attesting to satisfactory completion of a course of study. 2. Document conferring honor or privilege. [Gk., = "folded paper," "letter of recommendation"]

di·plo·ma·cy (dĭplō′masē) *n.* Management of international relations by negotiation; skill in conduct of international intercourse; adroitness, skill, in dealing with others.

dip·lo·mat (dĭp′lomăt) *n.* One officially engaged in diplomacy; adroit negotiator; extremely tactful person.

dip·lo·mate (dip′lomāt) *n.* Holder of diploma, esp. a physician who has been certified in a medical specialty.

dip·lo·mat·ic (dĭplomăt′ĭk) *adj.* Of the management of international relations; tactful, discreet; ~ **corps**, group of diplomats accredited to a government; ~ **immunity**, exemption of diplomatic staff etc. abroad from arrest, taxation, etc. **dip·lo·mat′i·cal·ly** *adv.* **diplomatic** *n.*

di·pole (dī′pōl) *n.* 1. (phys., chem.) Object oppositely charged at two points or poles. 2. (electronics) (also ~ **antenna**) Radio or television antenna consisting of two parallel rods extending straight outward in different directions. **di·po·lar** (dīpō′ler) *adj.* Having two poles, as a magnet.

dip·per (dĭp′er) *n.* 1. Any of various birds that dip or dive in water, esp. the water ouzel (*Cinclus mexicanus*) of western N. Amer. 2. Utensil for dipping up water, esp. long-handled ladle. 3. **(Big) D~**, constellation of 7 bright stars in Ursa Major; **Little D~**, similar group of 7 stars in Ursa Minor.

dip·so·ma·ni·a (dĭpsomā′nēa) *n.* Morbid craving for alcohol. **dip·so·ma′ni·ac** *n.* **dip·so·ma·ni·a·cal** (dĭpsomanī′akal) *adj.*

dip·ter·an (dĭp′teran) *adj.* & *n.* (Two-winged fly) of the order Diptera.

dip·ter·ous (dĭp′terus) *adj.* (entom.) Two-winged; (bot.) having two winglike appendages or processes, as some seeds.

dip·tych (dĭp′tĭk) *n.* 1. Ancient hinged two-leaved writing tablet with inner sides waxed. 2. Painting, esp. altarpiece, on two panels hinged together.

dir. *abbrev.* Director.

dire (dīr) *adj.* (**dir·er, dir·est**). Dreadful, calamitous; indicating disaster; urgent. **dire′ly** *adv.*

di·rect (dĭrĕkt′, dī-) *v.* 1. Address (letter etc. *to* person or place); utter, write, *to* or to be conveyed *to*. 2. Control; govern the movements of. 3. Turn straight *to* something; tell (person) the way *to*. 4. (of adviser or principle) Guide. 5. Order (person) *to* do, (thing) *to be* done; give orders; be director of (film etc.). ~ *adj.* 1. Straight, not devious or crooked; (of light etc.) coming straight from the source, without reflection, refraction, etc.; moving, proceeding, situated, at right angles to given surface etc.; straightforward, uninterrupted; (of succession) in an unbroken line from father to son. 2. Going straight to the point, unambiguous, straightforward; upright, downright. 3. Immediate, without intermediation; (of speech etc.) in form in which it was uttered, not reported in third person. 4. ~ **action**, action taking effect without intermediate instrumentality; esp., exertion of pressure on community by strikes, demonstrations, etc.; ~ **current**, (abbreviated DC, D.C., dc, d.c.) electric current flowing through circuit in one direction only; ~ **hit**, one right on the target (esp. of bombing); ~ **mail**, mail, generally made up of advertising, requests for contributions, etc., sent directly to those who are expected to buy, contribute, etc. ~ **object**: see OBJECT; ~ **opposite**, exact opposite; ~ **tax(ation)**, tax(ation) levied directly on a person's income or property (rather than on commodities). **di·rect′ness** *n.* **direct** *adv.* By direct route; without intermediaries.

di·rec·tion (dĭrĕk′sh*o*n, dī-) *n.* 1. Directing; esp., management, administration; directorate. 2. Instruction how to proceed or act, or how to find some person etc. 3. Course pursued by moving body; point to or from which person or thing moves or looks; scope, sphere, subject; ~ **finder**, radio receiving apparatus so constructed as to indicate direction from which signals are coming.

di·rec·tion·al (dĭrĕk′sh*o*nal, dī-) *adj.* (esp., radio) Sending signals in one direction only.

di·rec·tive (dĭrĕk′tĭv, dī-) *adj.* Giving guidance. ~ *n.* Statement setting forth policy etc. for guidance of others, esp. subordinates.

The common European ***dipper*** *resembles the wren in shape and stance but is much larger. It is a solitary bird and keeps to the same stretch of mountain stream.*

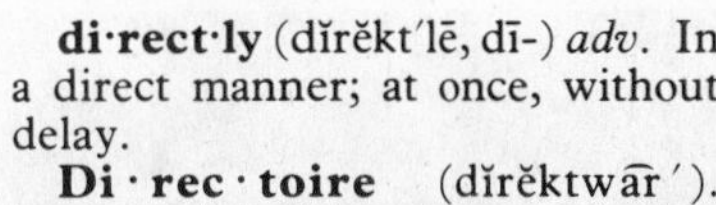

di·rect·ly (dĭrĕkt′lē, dī-) *adv.* In a direct manner; at once, without delay.

Di·rec·toire (dĭrĕktwăr′). Executive body in France during part of the revolutionary period (Oct. 1795–Nov. 1799), consisting of five members called directors. ~ *adj.* Of, imitating, the dress, furniture, etc., of this period in France, characterized by extravagance of design and imitation of Greek and Roman styles.

di·rec·tor (dĭrĕk′t*e*r, dī-) *n.* (esp.) Superintendent, manager, esp. member of board of directors of company; person responsible for directing cast and supervising a play or making of a film; conductor of an orchestra or chorus. **di·rec·to·ri·al** (dĭrĕktōr′ēal, -tōr′-, dī-) *adj.*

di·rec·tor·ate (dĭrĕk′t*e*rĭt, dī-) *n.* Office of director; group of directors.

di·rec·to·ry (dĭrĕk′t*e*rē, -trē, dī-) *n.* (pl. **-ries**). Book containing lists of inhabitants of districts, telephone subscribers, members of professions, etc., with various details.

dirge (dĕrj) *n.* 1. (obs.) Traditional ecclesiastical name (orig. *dirige*) for the Office of the Dead. 2. Song of mourning or lament for the dead; funeral hymn. [orig. *dirige*, first word of L. antiphon *Dirige, Domine, Deus meus, in conspectu tuo viam meam,* "Direct, O Lord, my God, my way in thy sight," taken from Ps. 5]

dir·i·gi·ble (dĭr′ĭj*i*b*e*l, d*i*rĭj′*i*-) *n.* Steerable balloon or airship.

dirk (dĕrk) *n.* Kind of dagger, esp. that worn by a Scottish Highlander. ~ *v.t.* Stab with dirk.

dirn·dl (dĕrn′d*e*l) *n.* Dress with tight bodice and full skirt; full skirt with tight waistband.

dirt (dĕrt) *n.* 1. Unclean matter such as soils things by adhering to them; mud; anything worthless or unclean. 2. Earth, soil; material from which metallic ore etc. is separated, esp. alluvial deposit, hence **pay** ~, gravel containing gold, (fig.) profit. 3. Foul talk or action. 4. **eat** ~, submit to degrading treatment; ~**-cheap**, as cheap as dirt, exceedingly cheap; ~ **road**, road, one with natural earth surface; ~ **track**, race track with dirt surface; track of cinders etc. for motorcycle racing.

dirt·y (dĕr′tē) *adj.* (**dirt·i·er, dirt·i·est**). 1. Soiled with dirt, muddied; mixed with dirt; that soils or befouls; **wash one's ~ linen in public**, talk openly about quarrels at home etc.; (of nuclear device) producing relatively large amount of fallout. 2. Morally unclean; obscene, as in ~ **joke**; dishonorably sordid, base, or corrupt; repulsive, despicable; ~ **pool,**

(slang) unfair or unsportsmanlike behavior; ~ **shame**, very unfortunate or disappointing event. 3. (of weather) Foul, (at sea) wet and squally. 4. (of color) Inclining to, with some tinge of, black, brown, or dark gray. **dirt'i·ly** *adv.* **dirt'i·ness** *n.* **dirt'y** *v.* (**dirt·ied, dirt·y·ing**). Make, become, dirty.

dis- *prefix.* Asunder, away, apart or between; un-, not, the reverse of.

dis·a·bil·i·ty (dĭs*a*bĭl'ĭtē) *n.* (pl. **-ties**). Thing, want, that prevents one's doing something, esp. legal disqualification; physical incapacity caused by injury or disease.

dis·a·ble (dĭsā'b*e*l) *v.t.* (**-bled, -bling**). 1. Incapacitate; cripple. 2. Disqualify legally.

dis·a·buse (dĭs*a*būz') *v.t.* (**-bused, -bus·ing**). Undeceive, disillusion.

Physical handicaps impose some limitations upon the lives of the ***disabled.*** *Imaginative training, such as teaching this child archery, creates new fields of choice.*

di·sac·cha·ride (dīsăk'*a*rīd) *n.* Carbohydrate, such as sucrose, that yields two monosaccharide molecules when hydrolyzed.

dis·ad·van·tage (dĭs*a*dvăn'tĭj, -vahn'-) *n.* Unfavorable condition or circumstance; loss or injury to interest, credit, reputation. **dis·ad·van·ta·geous** (dĭsădv*a*ntā'j*u*s) *adj.* **dis·ad·van·ta'geous·ly** *adv.*

dis·ad·van·taged (dĭs*a*dvăn'tĭjd, -vahn'-) *adj.* Placed in unfavorable social and economic conditions.

dis·af·fect·ed (dĭs*a*fĕk'tĭd) *adj.* Estranged, unfriendly, alienated. **dis·af·fect'** *v.t.* **dis·af·fec'tion** *n.*

dis·af·firm (dĭs*a*fe͞rm') *v.t.* (law) Annul, reverse (decision etc.); deny, contradict; repudiate (agreement etc.).

dis·a·gree (dĭs*a*grē') *v.i.* (**-greed, -gree·ing**). 1. Differ, be unlike, not correspond; differ in opinion, dissent, quarrel. 2. (of food etc.) Be unsuitable, have bad effects. **dis·a·gree'ment** *n.*

dis·a·gree·a·ble (dĭs*a*grē'*a*b*e*l) *adj.* 1. Not to one's taste, unpleasant. 2. Unamiable, bad-tempered. **dis·a·gree'a·bly** *adv.*

dis·al·low (dĭs*a*low') *v.t.* Refuse to sanction, accept as reasonable, or admit; prohibit. **dis·al·low'ance** *n.*

dis·ap·pear (dĭs*a*pe͞r') *v.i.* Cease to be visible; cease to exist or be known; die away gradually. **dis·ap·pear'ance** *n.*

dis·ap·point (dĭs*a*point') *v.t.* Not fulfill desire or expectation of; frustrate, thwart. **dis·ap·point'ing·ly** *adv.* **dis·ap·point'ment** *n.* Disappointing; being disappointed; person or thing that disappoints.

dis·ap·pro·ba·tion (dĭsăpr*o*bā'sh*o*n) *n.* Disapproval.

dis·ap·prove (dĭs*a*pro͞ov') *v.* (**-proved, -prov·ing**). Have, express, unfavorable opinion (*of*). **dis·ap·prov'al** *n.* **dis·ap·prov'ing·ly** *adv.*

dis·arm (dĭsa͞rm') *v.* 1. Deprive of weapons or means of defense; reduce (armed service), be reduced, to peace footing; abandon or cut down military establishment. 2. Deprive of power to injure; pacify hostility or suspicions of, conciliate. **dis·arm'ing** *adj.* **dis·arm'ing·ly** *adv.*

dis·ar·ma·ment (dĭsa͞r'm*a*m*e*nt) *n.* Reduction or abolition of a country's military forces and weapons of war.

dis·ar·range (dĭs*a*rānj') *v.t.* (**-ranged, -rang·ing**). Put into disorder, disorganize. **dis·ar·range'ment** *n.*

dis·ar·ray (dĭs*a*rā') *n.* & *v.t.* (Throw into) disorder, confusion.

dis·ar·tic·u·late (dĭsa͞rtĭk'y*u*lāt) *v.* (**-lat·ed, -lat·ing**). Disjoint.

dis·as·sem·ble (dĭs*a*sĕm'b*e*l) *v.t.* (**-bled, -bling**). Take (machine etc.) to pieces.

dis·as·ter (dĭzăs't*e*r, -zahs'-) *n.* Sudden or great misfortune. **dis·as·trous** (dĭzăs'tr*u*s, -zahs'-) *adj.* **dis·as'trous·ly** *adv.*

dis·a·vow (dĭs*a*vow') *v.t.* Refuse to avow, own, or acknowledge, repudiate, disown. **dis·a·vow'al** *n.*

dis·band (dĭsbănd') *v.* Break up, disperse. **dis·band'ment** *n.*

dis·bar (dĭsba͞r') *v.t.* (**-barred, -bar·ring**). Expel (lawyer) from the legal profession. **dis·bar'ment** *n.*

dis·be·lieve (dĭsbĭlēv') *v.* (**-lieved, -liev·ing**). Refuse credence to; not believe *in.* **dis·be·lief** (dĭsbĭlēf') *n.*

dis·bur·den (dĭsbe͞r'd*e*n) *v.t.*

*Jesus Christ's 12 **disciples** at 'The Last Supper': a painting by Leonardo da Vinci. They received Christ's training and teaching. Peter was recognized as their leader and the founder of the Christian church.*

Relieve of a burden; get rid of (burden).

dis·burse (dĭsbẽrs′) *v.* (**-bursed, -burs·ing**). Expend; defray; pay out money. **dis·burse′ment** *n.* Money expended.

disc (dĭsk) *n.* 1. see DISK. 2. Phonograph record; ~ **jockey**, person who selects and introduces phonograph records for radio show, discotheque, etc.

dis·card (dĭskārd′) *v.* 1. Throw out, reject (card) from hand at cards; esp. play (card not of trump suit) when unable to follow suit. 2. Cast aside, give up. ~ (dĭs′kārd) *n.* Discarding at cards; thing (esp. card) discarded.

dis·cern (dĭsẽrn′, -zẽrn′) *v.* Recognize, perceive distinctly (with mind or senses). **dis·cern′ing** *adj.* Having quick or true insight, penetrating. **dis·cern′ment** *n.*

dis·charge (dĭschārj′) *v.* (**-charged, -charg·ing**). 1. Unload; rid of charge or load; fire off (firearm); rid, rid itself, of electric charge. 2. Relieve *of*, release *from*, obligation etc.; dismiss from service; release from custody; send away, let go. 3. Send forth, emit; let fly, fire off; give, find, vent; (med.) emit (fluid etc.). 4. Cancel (order of court); pay, perform (debt, duty, vow). ~ (dĭs′chārj, dĭschārj′) *n.* Discharging or being discharged; certificate of this; (med.) fluid etc. discharged.

dis·ci·ple (dĭsī′pel) *n.* 1. One of Christ's personal followers, esp. one of the 12 Apostles; any early believer in Christ. 2. Follower, adherent, of any leader of thought, art, etc. **dis·ci′ple·ship** *n.*

dis·ci·pli·nar·i·an (dĭs*i*pl*i*nār′-ēan) *n.* Maintainer of (esp. strict) discipline.

dis·ci·pli·nar·y (dĭs′*i*pl*i*nĕrē) *adj.* Of, promoting, discipline.

dis·ci·pline (dĭs′*i*plĭn) *n.* 1. Branch of instruction; mental and moral training. 2. Trained condition; order maintained among persons under control or command, as pupils, soldiers, etc.; system for maintenance of order. 3. Control exercised over members of church and their conduct, as by censure, excommunication, etc. 4. Correction, chastisement; mortification of flesh by penance; whip, scourge. ~ *v.t.* (**-plined, -plin·ing**). Bring under control, train to obedience and order.

dis·claim (dĭsklām′) *v.* 1. Renounce legal claim to; renounce claim. 2. Disown, disavow; deny, repudiate. **dis·claim′er** *n.* Act of disclaiming, renunciation, disavowal.

dis·close (dĭsklōz′) *v.t.* (**-closed, -clos·ing**). Uncover, expose to view; make known, reveal. **dis·clo·sure** (dĭsklō′zh*er*) *n.* Disclosing; thing disclosed.

dis·co (dĭs′kō) *n.* (pl. **-cos**). (colloq.) DISCOTHEQUE. ~ *adj.* Of or pertaining to amplified music, strobe lights, dancing, style of dress, etc. at a discotheque.

dis·cob·o·lus (dĭskŏb′*o*l*u*s) *n.* (pl. **-li** pr. -lī, -lē). Thrower of discus.

dis·coid (dĭs′koid) *adj.* Disk-shaped; (bot., of composite flowers) having disk only, with no ray.

dis·col·or (dĭskŭl′*er*) *v.* Change or spoil the color of, stain, tarnish; become stained, tarnished, etc. **dis·col·or·a·tion** (dĭskŭlerā′sh*o*n) *n.*

dis·com·bob·u·late (dĭsk*o*m-bŏb′y*u*lāt) *v.t.* (**-lat·ed, -lat·ing**). (colloq.) Disturb, disconcert.

dis·com·fit (dĭskŭm′fĭt) *v.t.* 1. (archaic) Defeat in battle. 2. Thwart, disconcert; make uneasy, embarrass. **dis·com·fi·ture** (dĭs-kŭm′fĭch*er*) *n.*

dis·com·fort (dĭskŭm′f*er*t) *n.* Uneasiness of body or mind; want of comfort. ~ *v.t.* Make uneasy.

dis·com·pose (dĭsk*o*mpōz′) *v.t.* (**-posed, -pos·ing**). Disturb composure of, ruffle, agitate. **dis·com·po·sure** (dĭsk*o*mpō′zh*er*) *n.*

dis·con·cert (dĭsk*o*nsẽrt′) *v.t.* Perturb, upset; embarrass.

dis·con·nect (dĭsk*o*nĕkt′) *v.t.* Sever the connection of or between. **dis·con·nect′ed** *adj.* (esp., of speech or writing) Incoherent, jerky. **dis·con·nect′ed·ly** *adv.* **dis·con·nect′ed·ness** *n.*

dis·con·so·late (dĭskŏn′s*o*lĭt) *adj.* Forlorn, inconsolable, unhappy, disappointed. **dis·con′so·late·ly** *adv.* **dis·con′so·late·ness** *n.*

dis·con·tent (dĭsk*o*ntĕnt′) *n.* Dissatisfaction, want of contentment; grievance. ~ *v.t.* (usu. in past part.) Make dissatisfied. **dis·con·tent′ed** *adj.*

dis·con·tin·ue (dĭsk*o*ntĭn′ū) *v.* (**-tin·ued, -tin·u·ing**). Cause to cease, break off; give up, leave off. **dis·con·tin′u·ance** *n.*

dis·con·tin·u·ous (dĭsk*o*ntĭn′-ū*u*s) *adj.* Not continuous. **dis·con·tin′u·ous·ly** *adv.* **dis·con·ti·nu·i·ty** (dĭskŏntĭnōō′ĭtē, -nū′-) *n.* (pl. **-ties**).

dis·cord (dĭs′kōrd) *n.* 1. Disagreement, variance, strife. 2. Harsh noise, clashing sounds. 3. (mus.) Want of harmony between notes sounded together. **dis·cord′ant** *adj.* **dis·cord′ant·ly** *adv.* **dis·cord′ance** *n.* **discord** (dĭs-kōrd′) *v.i.* Disagree; be different, inconsistent, or discordant.

dis·co·theque, dis·co·thèque

(dĭs′kotĕk, dĭskotĕk′, -kō-) *ns.* Night club where amplified recorded music is played for dancing.

dis·count (dĭs′kownt) *n.* Deduction from nominal value or price; deduction from amount of bill etc.; discounting; **at a ~**, below the usual price; **~ house**, store selling goods below list price. **discount** (dĭs′kownt, dĭskownt′) *v.t.* 1. Give or receive value (after deduction of discount) of bill of exchange before it is due. 2. Leave out of account; lessen, detract from; allow for exaggeration in; take (news, event) into account beforehand, thus lessening its effect or interest.

dis·coun·te·nance (dĭskown′tenans) *v.t.* (**-nanced, -nanc·ing**). Refuse to countenance, discourage, show disapproval of.

dis·cour·age (dĭskẽr′ĭj, -kŭr′-) *v.t.* (**-aged, -ag·ing**). Deprive of courage, confidence, or energy; deter *from*; discountenance. **dis·cour′age·ment** *n.* **dis·cour′ag·ing·ly** *adv.*

dis·course (dĭs′kōrs, -kōrs) *n.* Talk, conversation; dissertation, treatise, sermon. ~ (dĭskōrs′, -kōrs′) *v.* (**-coursed, -cours·ing**). Talk, converse; hold forth in formal speech or writing on a subject.

dis·cour·te·ous (dĭskẽr′tēus) *adj.* Rude, uncivil. **dis·cour′te·ous·ly** *adv.* **dis·cour·te·sy** (dĭskẽr′tesē) *n.* (pl. **-sies**).

dis·cov·er (dĭskŭv′er) *v.t.* 1. (archaic) Disclose. 2. (chess) Give (check) by removing one's own obstructing man. 3. Find out; obtain sight or knowledge of for first time; notice. **dis·cov′er·er** *n.*

dis·cov·er·y (dĭskŭv′erē) *n.* (pl. **-er·ies**). Discovering; thing discovered.

dis·cred·it (dĭskrĕd′ĭt) *n.* Loss of repute, thing involving this; doubt, distrust. ~ *v.t.* Refuse to believe; bring disrepute or disbelief upon.

dis·cred·it·a·ble (dĭskrĕd′ĭtabel) *adj.* Bringing discredit, shameful. **dis·cred′it·a·bly** *adv.*

dis·creet (dĭskrēt′) *adj.* Prudent; cautious in speech or action. **dis·creet′ly** *adv.*

dis·crep·an·cy (dĭskrĕp′ansē) *n.* (pl. **-cies**). Want of agreement, variance, inconsistency. **dis·crep′ant** *adj.* **dis·crep′ant·ly** *adv.*

dis·crete (dĕskrēt′) *adj.* Separate, individually distinct, discontinuous. **dis·crete′ly** *adv.* **dis·crete′ness** *n.*

dis·cre·tion (dĭskrĕsh′on) *n.* 1. Liberty or power of deciding or acting as one thinks fit. 2. Discernment, prudence, judgment. **dis·cre′tion·ar·y** *adj.*

dis·crim·i·nate (dĭskrĭm′ĭnāt) *v.* (**-nat·ed, -nat·ing**). Constitute, set up, observe, a difference between, distinguish *from, between*; make a distinction; observe distinctions carefully; give unfair treatment on the basis of prejudice. ~ **against**, be prejudiced against, (esp. people of other races, religions, nationalities, etc.). **dis·crim′i·nat·ing** *adj.* Discerning, acute. **dis·crim·i·na·tion** (dĭskrĭmĭnā′shon) *n.* **dis·crim′i·na·tive** *adj.* **dis·crim′i·na·tive·ly** *adv.*

dis·cur·sive (dĭskẽr′sĭv) *adj.* 1. Rambling, digressive, expatiating. 2. Proceeding by reasoning or argument, not intuitive. **dis·cur′sive·ly** *adv.* **dis·cur′sive·ness** *n.*

dis·cus (dĭs′kus) *n.* Heavy disk now usu. weighing about 4½ pounds (2 kg), thrown for distance in athletic competitions; field event of throwing this.

dis·cuss (dĭskŭs′) *v.t.* Examine by argument, debate; speak, write, or treat of; talk over. **dis·cus·sion** (dĭskŭsh′on), **dis·cus′sant** *ns.*

dis·dain (dĭsdān′) *v.t.* Scorn; regard with contempt; consider beneath oneself or one's notice. ~ *n.* Scorn, contempt. **dis·dain′ful** *adj.* **dis·dain′ful·ly** *adv.*

dis·ease (dĭzēz′) *n.* Morbid condition of body or plant, or some part of it; (specific) disorder, illness; deranged, depraved, or morbid condition of mind etc. **dis·eased′** *adj.*

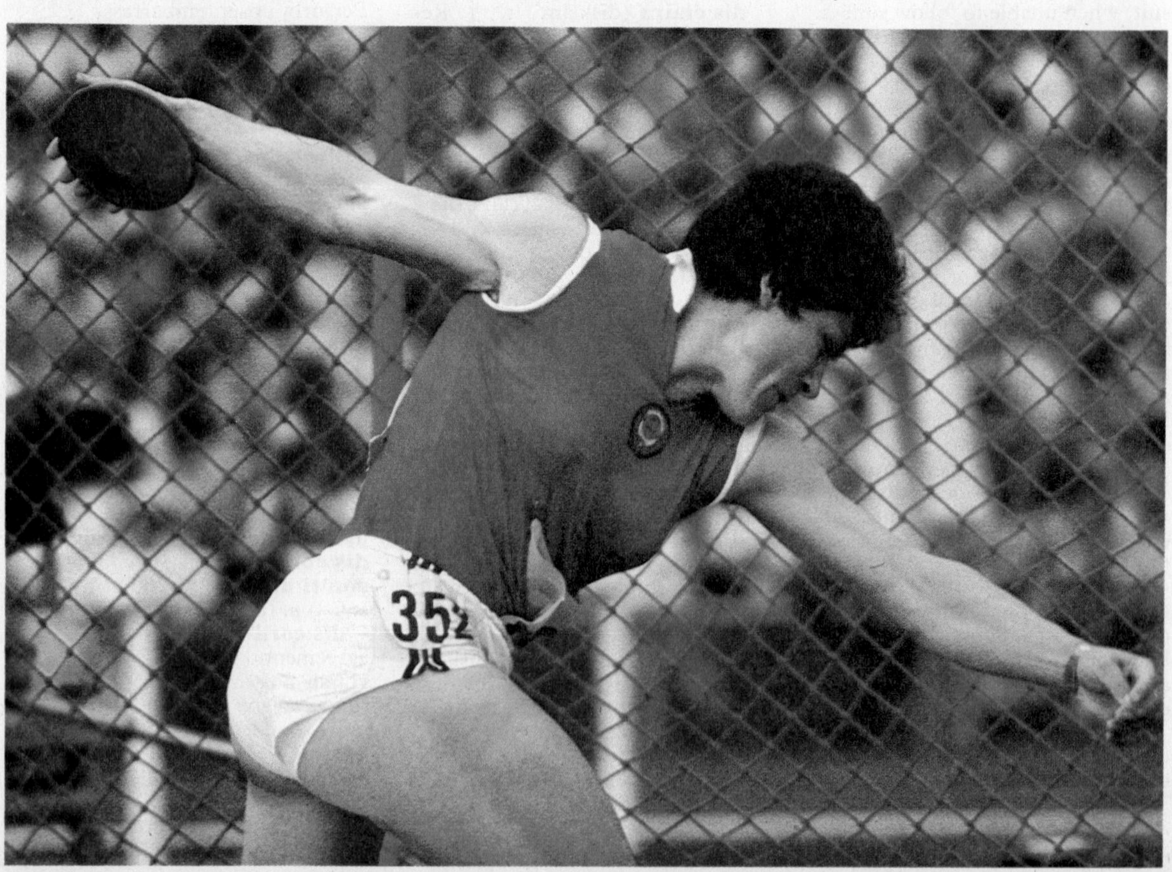

*The **discus** was thrown in the ancient Olympics and has been in the modern Olympic Games since 1896. Here, Faina Melinki competes in the 1972 women's discus at Munich.*

dis·em·bark (dĭsĕmbärk′) *v.* Put, go, ashore. **dis·em·bar·ka·tion** (dĭsĕmbärkā′sh*o*n) *n.*

dis·em·bar·rass (dĭsĕmbăr′*a*s) *v.t.* Free from embarrassment, rid or relieve (*of*). **dis·em·bar′rass·ment** *n.*

dis·em·bod·y (dĭsĕmbŏd′ē) *v.t.* (**-bod·ied, -bod·y·ing**). Separate, free (soul from body, or idea from form in which it is embodied).

dis·em·bow·el (dĭsĕmbow′*e*l) *v.t.* (**-eled** or **-elled, -el·ing** or **-el·ling**). Remove entrails of.

dis·em·broil (dĭsĕmbroil′) *v.t.* Extricate from confusion or entanglement.

dis·en·chant (dĭsĕnchănt′, -chahnt′) *v.t.* Free from enchantment or illusion. **dis·en·chant′ment** *n.*

dis·en·cum·ber (dĭsĕnkŭm′b*er*) *v.t.* Free from encumbrance.

dis·en·fran·chise (dĭsĕnfrăn′chīz) *v.t.* (**-chised, -chis·ing**) = DISFRANCHISE.

dis·en·gage (dĭsĕngāj′) *v.t.* (**-gaged, -gag·ing**). 1. Detach, liberate, loosen; come apart, break contact. 2. Release from engagement, obligation, friendship, etc. **dis·en·gaged′** *adj.* (esp.) Unoccupied; at liberty. **dis·en·gage′ment** *n.*

dis·en·tan·gle (dĭsĕntăng′g*e*l) *v.* (**-gled, -gling**). Extricate, free from complications; unravel, untwist. **dis·en·tan′gle·ment** *n.*

dis·es·tab·lish (dĭsĕstăb′lĭsh) *v.t.* Deprive of established character; esp. deprive (church) of state connection and support. **dis·es·tab′lish·ment** *n.*

dis·es·teem (dĭsĕstēm′) *n.* Lack of esteem.

di·seur (dēzör′) *n.* [fem. ***di·seuse*** (dēzöz′)] Person (usu. professional entertainer) who recites monologues. [Fr.]

dis·fa·vor (dĭsfā′v*er*) *n.* Dislike, disapproval; being disliked.

dis·fig·ure (dĭsfĭg′y*er*) *v.t.* (**-ured, -ur·ing**). Mar appearance of; deform. **dis·fig′ure·ment** *n.*

dis·fran·chise (dĭsfrăn′chīz) *v.t.* (**-chised, -chis·ing**). Deprive of rights and privileges of citizenship, esp. the right to vote, or of some franchise or privilege previously enjoyed. **dis·fran′chise·ment** *n.*

dis·gorge (dĭsgôrj′) *v.* (**-gorged, -gorg·ing**). Vomit forth (what has been swallowed, lit. and fig.); discharge, spew, pour forth.

dis·grace (dĭsgrās′) *n.* 1. Loss of favor, downfall from position of honor; shame. 2. Cause of reproach. ~ *v.t.* (**-graced, -grac·ing**). Dismiss from favor, degrade from position; bring shame or discredit upon, be a disgrace to. **dis·grace′ful** *adj.* **dis·grace′ful·ly** *adv.* **dis·grace′ful·ness** *n.*

dis·grun·tled (dĭsgrŭn′t*e*ld) *adj.* Discontented, displeased.

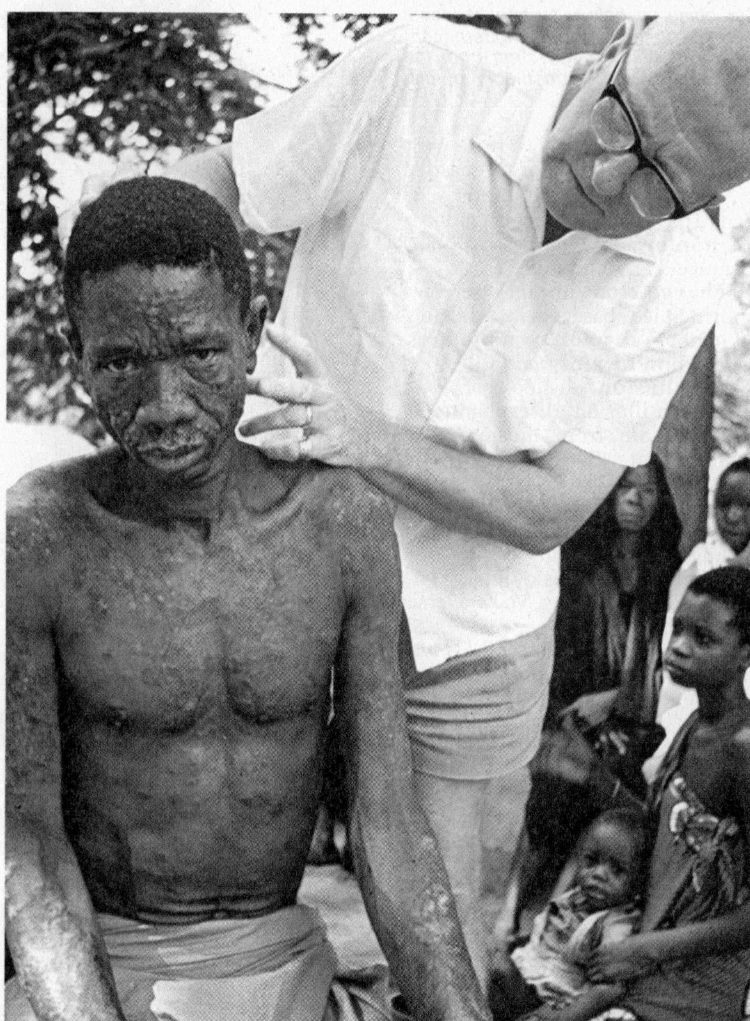

*Leprosy is a **disease** which is most prevalent in low-lying tropical or subtropical areas. Today, the use of sulphone drugs arrests the infection and produces improvement in the patient in most cases.*

dis·guise (dĭsgīz′) *v.t.* (**-guised, -guis·ing**). Conceal identity of by changing personal appearance or dress; dress *as* someone, *in* some garb; alter appearance of (anything) so as to mislead or deceive; conceal or cloak real character, state, or identity of. ~ *n.* Use of changed dress or appearance for sake of concealment; disguised condition; garb used to deceive; pretense.

dis·gust (dĭsgŭst′) *n.* Loathing, nausea, repugnance, strong aversion, or indignation in. **dis·gust′ing** *adj.* **dis·gust′ing·ly** *adv.*

dish (dĭsh) *n.* 1. Shallow flat-bottomed vessel for holding food. 2. Food served on or contained in dish; variety or article of food; (slang) attractive woman. 3. Anything dish-shaped or concave, esp. as receptacle. 4. **dish′cloth, dish′rag**, cloth for washing dishes and plates; **dish′pan**, basin to wash dishes in; **dish′washer**, person who washes dishes, esp. one hired to do so in restaurant; machine for washing dishes etc. automatically; **dish′water**, water in which dishes have been washed. **dish** *v.* Put (food) into dish ready for serving; ~ **out**, distribute, esp. indiscriminately; ~ **up**, serve, serve meal; (fig.) present (facts, arguments, etc.).

dis·ha·bille (dĭs*a*bēl′) *n.* Being negligently or partly dressed; undress; lounging attire.

dis·har·mo·ny (dĭs-här′m*o*nē) *n.* (pl. **-nies**). Discord, dissonance. **dis·har·mo·ni·ous** (dĭs-härmō′nē*u*s) *adj.*

dis·heart·en (dĭs-här′t*e*n) *v.t.* Make despondent, rob of courage. **dis·heart′en·ing** *adj.*

di·shev·eled (dĭshĕv′*e*ld) *adj.* With disordered hair; (of hair) loose, disordered; untidy, unkempt. **di·shev′el·ment** *n.* **di·shev·el** *v.t.* (**-eled** or **-elled, -el·ing** or **-el·ling**).

dis·hon·est (dĭsŏn′ĭst) *adj.* Not honest; fraudulent; insincere. **dis·hon′est·ly** *adv.* **dis·hon′es·ty** *n.* (pl. **-ties**).

dis·hon·or (dĭsŏn′*er*) *n.* Dis-

*Scrubbing up before surgery prevents infection during or after it. Modern techniques of **disinfection** stem from the discovery of the germ theory of disease.*

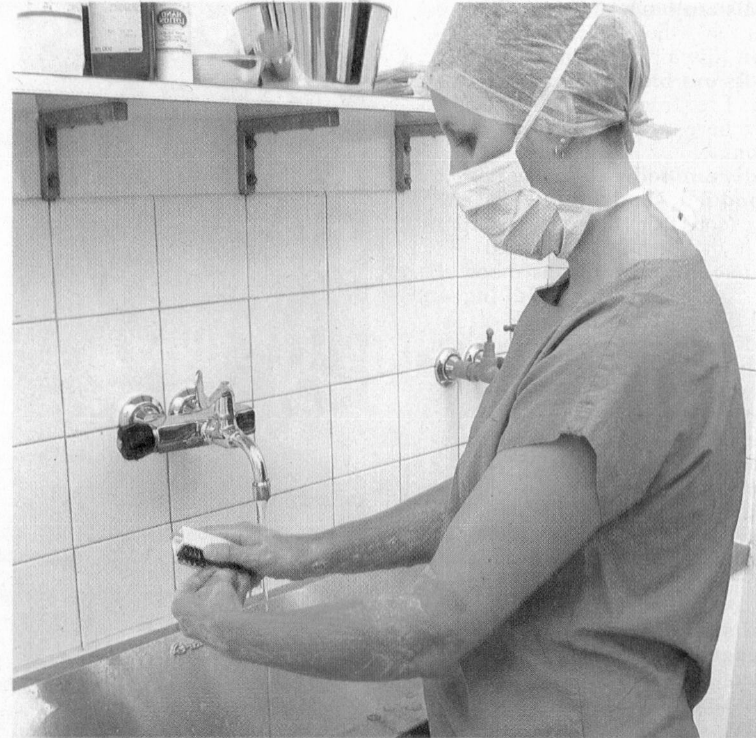

grace. ~ *v.t.* 1. Treat with indignity; violate honor or chastity of. 2. Bring dishonor upon. 3. Fail to pay (bill or other obligation). **dis·hon′or·a·ble** *adj.* Involving disgrace, ignominious, as in ~ **discharge** from military service; unprincipled, base; against dictates of honor. **dis·hon′or·a·ble·ness** *n.* **dis·hon′or·a·bly** *adv.*

dis·il·lu·sion (dĭsĭlo͞o′zh*o*n) *v.t.* Free from illusion, disenchant. ~ *n.* Freedom from illusion, disenchantment. **dis·il·lu′sion·ment** *n.*

dis·in·cli·na·tion (dĭsĭnklĭnā′sh*o*n) *n.* Want of inclination, willingness, or liking.

dis·in·cline (dĭsĭnklīn′) *v.t.* (**-clined, -clin·ing**). Make averse or unwilling.

dis·in·fect (dĭsĭnfĕkt′) *v.t.* Cleanse from infection, destroy germs of disease in. **dis·in·fect′ant** *adj.* & *n.* Disinfecting (agent).

dis·in·gen·u·ous (dĭsĭnjĕn′ū*u*s) *adj.* Insincere, not candid or frank. **dis·in·gen′u·ous·ly** *adv.* **dis·in·gen′u·ous·ness** *n.*

dis·in·her·it (dĭsĭnhĕr′ĭt) *v.t.* Deprive or dispossess of right to inherit. **dis·in·her′i·tance** *n.*

dis·in·te·grate (dĭsĭn′t*e*grāt) *v.* (**-grat·ed, -grat·ing**). Separate into component parts; deprive of, lose, cohesion. **dis·in·te·gra·tion** (dĭsĭnt*e*grā′sh*o*n) *n.*

dis·in·ter (dĭsĭntẽr′) *v.t.* (**-terred, -ter·ring**). Exhume, esp. a corpse from place of burial; unearth. **dis·in·ter′ment** *n.*

dis·in·ter·est (dĭsĭn′t*e*rĭst, -trĭst) *n.* Impartiality, disinterestedness; absence of interest. **dis·in·ter·est·ed** (dĭsĭn′t*e*rĕstĭd, -trĭstĭd) *adj.* Not influenced by self-interest or partiality; (colloq.) not interested. **dis·in′ter·est·ed·ly** *adv.* **dis·in′ter·est·ed·ness** *n.*

dis·in·tox·i·ca·tion (dĭsĭntŏksĭkā′sh*o*n) *n.* (med.) Freeing a person from effects of poison in his or her body, as an addict from a drug.

dis·join (dĭsjoin′) *v.t.* Separate, disunite.

dis·joint (dĭsjoint′) *v.t.* Dislocate; disturb working or connection of; separate at the joints. **dis·joint′ed** *adj.* (esp. of speech etc.) Incoherent, desultory. **dis·joint′ed·ly** *adv.* **dis·joint′ed·ness** *n.*

dis·junc·tive (dĭsjŭngk′tĭv) *adj.* Disjoining, involving separation; (logic) alternative; involving choice between two propositions etc.; (gram., of conjunction) expressing an alternative, contrast, or opposition between the clauses it connects. **dis·junc′tive·ly** *adv.* **disjunctive** *n.* Disjunctive proposition or conjunction.

disk, disc (dĭsk) *ns.* Thin circular plate; round, flat (or apparently flat) object, as **sun's** ~; round flattened part in body, plant, etc.; ~ **brake**, automobile etc. brake using disk-shaped friction surfaces; ~ **harrow**, harrow with concave disks set at an angle; ~ **jockey**: see DISC jockey.

dis·like (dĭslīk′) *v.t.* (**-liked, -lik·ing**) Not like; have aversion or objection to. ~ *n.* Aversion.

dis·lo·cate (dĭs′lōkāt, dĭslō′-) *v.t.* (**-cat·ed, -cat·ing**). Put out of joint; displace, shift, disturb. **dis·lo·ca·tion** (dĭslōkā′sh*o*n) *n.*

dis·lodge (dĭslŏj′) *v.t.* (**-lodged, -lodg·ing**). Remove, turn out, from position. **dis·lodg′ment** *n.*

dis·loy·al (dĭsloi′*a*l) *adj.* Unfaithful; untrue to allegiance. **dis·loy′al·ly** *adv.* **dis·loy′al·ty** *n.* (pl. **-ties**).

dis·mal (dĭz′m*a*l) *adj.* Depressing, miserable, somber, dreary. **Dismal Swamp**, swamp in SE. Virginia and NE. North Carolina, about 600 sq. miles. **dis′mal·ly** *adv.* **dis′mal·ness** *n.* [orig. noun, = "unlucky days"; OF. *dis mal* f. L. *dies mali* ill days (the medieval calendar recognized two of these in each month)]

dis·man·tle (dĭsmăn′t*e*l) *v.t.* (**-tled, -tling**). Strip of equipment, furniture, etc.; take apart, tear down; deprive of defense. **dis·man′tle·ment** *n.*

dis·may (dĭsmā′) *n.* Consternation; utter loss of moral courage or resolution in prospect of danger or difficulty. ~ *v.t.* Rouse dismay in; reduce to despair.

dis·mem·ber (dĭsmĕm′b*e*r) *v.t.* Tear or cut limb from limb; divide into parts or sections so as to destroy integrity. **dis·mem′ber·ment** *n.*

dis·miss (dĭsmĭs′) *v.t.* 1. Send away, disperse, disband; allow to go; send away from one's presence. 2. Discharge from employment, service, school, etc. 3. Put out of one's thoughts. 4. Have done with, bring to an end. 5. (law) Send out of court, refuse further hearing to (case etc.). **dis·miss′al** *n.*

dis·mount (dĭsmownt′) *v.* Alight, cause to alight, from horseback, etc.; unseat, unhorse; remove (thing) from its mount.

Dis·ney (dĭz′nē), **Walt(er) Elias** (1901–66). Amer. cartoonist, film director and producer; creator of animated cartoons, esp. Mickey Mouse. **Dis′neyland**, an amusement park (California); (fig.) any land of make-believe. **Dis′neyworld**, an amusement park (Florida); (fig.) any land of make-believe.

dis·o·be·di·ence (dĭs*o*bē′dē*e*ns) *n.* Being disobedient, withholding of obedience. **dis·o·be′di·ent** *adj.* Refusing or failing to obey; stubborn, intractable. **dis·o·be′di·ent·ly** *adv.*

dis·o·bey (dĭs*o*bā′) *v.* Disregard orders, break rules; fail or refuse to obey.

***Disneyland** amusement park in Anaheim, south-west California, was planned by **Walt Disney** and opened in 1955. It is dominated by Sleeping Beauty's castle. Along the drawbridge are Snow White and the Seven Dwarfs.*

dis·o·blige (dĭsoblīj′) *v.t.* (**-bliged, -blig·ing**). Refuse, neglect, to act in accord with the wishes of; (regional) inconvenience. **dis·o·blig′ing** *adj.* **dis·o·blig′-ing·ly** *adv.*

dis·or·der (dĭsōr′der) *n.* 1. Want of order, confusion. 2. Tumult, riot, commotion. 3. Ailment, disease. ~ *v.t.* Disarrange, throw into confusion; put out of health, upset. **dis·or′der·ly** *adj.* 1. Untidy, confused. 2. Irregular, unruly, riotous; violating public order or morality; ~ **house,** brothel; place used illegally for gambling. **dis·or′der·li·ness** *n.*

dis·or·gan·ize (dĭsōr′ganīz) *v.t.* (**-ized, -iz·ing**). Destroy system etc. of; throw into confusion. **dis·or·gan·i·za·tion** (dĭsōrganĭ-zā′shon) *n.*

dis·o·ri·ent (dĭsōr′ēent, -ōr′-), **dis·o·ri·en·tate** (dĭsōr′ēentāt, -ōr′-) *vbs.t.* (**-tat·ed, -tat·ing**). Confuse (person) as to his or her bearings (also fig.). **dis·o·ri·en·-ta·tion** (dĭsōrēentā′shon, -ōr-) *n.*

dis·own (dĭsōn′) *v.t.* Refuse to recognize, repudiate, disclaim; renounce allegiance to.

Many birds, like the peacock, ***display*** *their plumage in courtship or sometimes as a gesture of aggression. Here a cock fans his tail before the hen, strutting, quivering and uttering loud screams.*

dis·par·age (dĭspăr′ĭj) *v.t.* (**-aged, -ag·ing**). Bring discredit on, lower; speak slightingly of, depreciate. **dis·par′age·ment** *n.* **dis·par′ag·ing·ly** *adv.*

dis·pa·rate (dĭs′perĭt, dĭspăr′-) *adj.* Essentially different, diverse in kind, incommensurable, without relation. **dis′pa·rate·ly** *adv.* **dis′-pa·rate·ness** *n.*

dis·par·i·ty (dĭspăr′ĭtē) *n.* (pl. **-ties**). Inequality, difference, incongruity.

dis·pas·sion·ate (dĭspăsh′onĭt) *adj.* Free from emotion, calm, impartial. **dis·pas′sion·ate·ly** *adv.* **dis·pas′sion·ate·ness, dis·-pas′sion** *ns.*

dis·patch, des·patch (dĭspăch′) *vbs.* 1. Send off to destination or for purpose. 2. Give death blow to, kill. 3. Get (task, business) promptly done; settle, finish off; eat (food, meal) quickly. ~ *n.* 1. Sending off. 2. Putting to death. 3. Prompt settlement of business; promptitude, efficiency, rapidity. 4. Written message; official communication, esp. military or diplomatic. 5. News story sent to newspaper by reporter or correspondent.

dis·pel (dĭspĕl′) *v.t.* (**-pelled, -pel·ling**). Dissipate, disperse.

dis·pen·sa·ble (dĭspĕn′sabel) *adj.* That which may be done without, unimportant; that which can be dispensed or administered.

dis·pen·sa·ry (dĭspĕn′serē) *n.* (pl. **-ries**). 1. Place where something (esp. medicine) is dispensed. 2. Public or charitable institution where medicines are dispensed and medical advice is given.

dis·pen·sa·tion (dĭspensā′shon, -pĕn-) *n.* 1. Distributing, dealing out. 2. Ordering, management, esp. the divine ordering of worldly affairs; special dealing of Providence with community or person; (theol.) religious order or system as part of a progressive revelation adapted to particular nation or age, as **Mosaic** ~. 3. Exemption from penalty or duty laid down in ecclesiastical etc. law; granting of

***Benjamin Disraeli,** the British statesman, adversary of Gladstone, was noted as prime minister for his tact in dealing with Queen Victoria and for his vigorous foreign policy.*

license by pope, archbishop, or bishop, to a person to do what is forbidden by ecclesiastical law.

dis·pense (dĭspĕns′) *v.* (**-pensed, -pens·ing**). 1. Distribute, deal out; administer (sacrament, justice). 2. Make up (medicine) according to prescription or formula. 3. Grant dispensations; release *from* obligation. 4. ~ **with,** relax, give exemption from (rule); annul binding force of (oath); render needless; do without. **dis·pen′ser** *n.*

dis·perse (dĭspẽrs′) *v.* (**-persed, -pers·ing**). Scatter; drive, go, throw, send, in different directions; rout, dispel, be dispelled; send to, station at, different points; put in circulation, disseminate; (of gases or liquids) diffuse; (optics) spread (beam of light) so as to produce spectrum. **dis·per′sal** *n.* **dis·per′sive** *adj.* **dis·per·sion** (dĭspẽr′zhon, -shon) *n.* (esp. chem.) Suspension of particles in a medium, as in homogenized milk, smog, or emulsions; **The D**~: see DIASPORA.

dis·pir·it (dĭspĭr′ĭt) *v.t.* Make despondent, depress. **dis·pir′it·ed·ly** *adv.*

dis·place (dĭsplās′) *v.t.* (**-placed, -plac·ing**). 1. Shift from proper position; remove from office. 2. Oust, take the place of; put something else in the place of; replace. 3. **displaced person,** one removed from his home country by military or political pressure; orig., civilian deported from a German-occupied country to work in Germany during World War II and thereafter homeless.

dis·place·ment (dĭsplās′ment) *n.* 1. Displacing, being displaced; amount by which thing is shifted from its place; ousting, replacement. 2. Amount or weight of fluid displaced by body floating or immersed in it.

dis·play (dĭsplā′) *v.t.* Exhibit, expose to view, show; show ostentatiously; reveal, betray, allow to appear. ~ *n.* Displaying; exhibition, show; ostentation; specialized pattern of behavior by which birds communicate with each other; (print.) selection and arrangement of types to attract attention; (also ~ **type**) large, attention-attracting type.

dis·please (dĭsplēz′) *v.t.* (**-pleased, -pleas·ing**). Offend, annoy, make indignant or angry; be disagreeable to; **be displeased** (*at, with*), disapprove, be indignant or dissatisfied. **dis·pleas′ing·ly** *adv.*

dis·pleas·ure (dĭsplĕzh′er) *n.* Displeased feeling, dissatisfaction, disapproval, anger.

dis·pos·a·ble (dĭspō′zabel) *adj.* That can be disposed of or disposed, (of article) designed to be thrown away after use.

dis·pos·al (dĭspō′zal) *n.* Disposing of, getting rid of; settling, dealing with; bestowal, assignment; sale; control, management (usu. **at one's** ~); placing, disposition, arrangement.

dis·pose (dĭspōz′) *v.* (**-posed, -pos·ing**). 1. Place suitably, in particular order, in proper positions. 2. Bring (person, mind) into certain state; incline, make willing or desirous, *to*; give (thing) tendency *to*. 3. Determine course of events. 4. ~ **of,** do what one will with, regulate; get off one's hands, stow away, settle, finish, kill, demolish; sell.

dis·po·si·tion (dĭspozĭsh′on) *n.* 1. Setting in order, arrangement, relative position of parts. 2. Plan; stationing of troops for attack, defense, etc. 3. Ordinance, dispensation. 4. Bestowal by deed or will. 5. Control, disposal. 6. Temperament, natural tendency; inclination *to*.

dis·pos·sess (dĭspozĕs′) *v.t.* Oust, dislodge; deprive *of*. **dis·pos·ses·sion** (dĭspozĕsh′on) *n.*

dis·proof (dĭsproo͞f′) *n.* Refutation, thing that disproves.

dis·pro·por·tion (dĭsprop̄ōr′shon, -pōr′-) *n.* Want of proportion. **dis·pro·por′tion·ate** *adj.* Wanting proportion; relatively too large or too small. **dis·pro·por′tion·ate·ly** *adv.*

dis·prove (dĭspro͞ov′) *v.t.* (**-proved, -prov·ing**). Prove false, show fallacy of, refute.

dis·pu·ta·ble (dĭspū′tabel) *adj.* Open to question, uncertain. **dis·pu′ta·bly** *adv.*

dis·pu·tant (dĭspū′tant, dĭs′pyu-) *adj.* & *n.* (Person) who disputes or engages in controversy.

dis·pu·ta·tion (dĭspyutā′shon) *n.* Debate, discussion; academic exercise in which parties formally sustain, attack, and defend a question or thesis. **dis·pu·ta′tious** *adj.* **dis·pu·ta′tious·ly** *adv.* **dis·pu·ta′tious·ness** *n.*

dis·pute (dĭspūt′) *v.* (**-put·ed, -put·ing**). Argue, hold disputation; have altercation; controvert, call in question; contend for. ~

The referees' decisions in football and other sports can cause ***dissent*** *or disagreement between the referee and the players. Here the Manchester City team disputes the referee's decision in a game against Arsenal in the U.K.*

n. Controversy, debate; heated contention, quarrel.

dis·qual·i·fy (dĭskwŏl′ĭfī) *v.t.* (**-fied, -fy·ing**). Make unfit, disable; declare unqualified or ineligible (esp. to hold place or prize won in contest). **dis·qual·i·fi·ca·tion** (dĭskwŏlĭfĭkā′shon) *n.* (esp.) Thing that disqualifies.

dis·qui·et (dĭskwī′ĭt) *v.t.* Deprive of peace, worry. **dis·qui·e·tude** (dĭskwī′ĭtōōd, -tūd) *n.* Anxiety, unrest.

dis·qui·si·tion (dĭskwĭzĭsh′on) *n.* Formal discourse, treatise, or dissertation.

Dis·rae·li (dĭzrā′lē), **Benjamin, 1st Earl of Beaconsfield** (1804–1881). British statesman, prime minister 1868 and 1874–80; author of *Coningsby* (1844) and other novels.

dis·re·gard (dĭsrĭgârd′) *v.t.* Pay no attention to; ignore; treat as of no importance. ~ *n.* Indifference, neglect.

dis·re·pair (dĭsrĭpâr′) *n.* Bad condition for want of repairs.

dis·rep·u·ta·ble (dĭsrĕp′yutabel) *adj.* Discreditable; of bad repute, not respectable in character or appearance. **dis·rep′u·ta·ble·ness** *n.* **dis·rep′u·ta·bly** *adv.*

dis·re·pute (dĭsrĭpūt′) *n.* Disgrace, discredit.

dis·re·spect (dĭsrĭspĕkt′) *n.* Want of respect, rudeness. **dis·re·spect′ful** *adj.* **dis·re·spect′ful·ly** *adv.* **dis·re·spect′ful·ness** *n.*

dis·robe (dĭsrōb′) *v.* (**-robed, -rob·ing**). Divest of robe or garment; undress.

dis·rupt (dĭsrŭpt′) *v.t.* 1. Interrupt flow, continuity, procedure of. 2. Cause disorder in, throw into confusion. 3. Shatter, separate forcibly. **dis·rup′tion** *n.* **dis·rup′tive** *adj.* **dis·rup′tive·ly** *adv.*

dis·sat·is·fy (dĭssăt′ĭsfī) *v.t.* (**-fied, -fy·ing**). Fail to satisfy, make discontented. **dis·sat·is·fac·tion** (dĭssătĭsfăk′shon) *n.*

dis·sect (dĭsĕkt′, dī-) *v.t.* Cut up, esp., cut up (animal body, plant, etc.) to display position, structure, and relation of internal parts; analyze, examine or criticize minutely. **dis·sec′tion** *n.*

dis·sem·ble (dĭsĕm′bel) *v.* (**-bled, -bling**). Feign, pretend; disguise, conceal one's opinions, intentions, etc., under feigned guise. **dis·sem′bler** *n.*

dis·sem·i·nate (dĭsĕm′ināt) *v.t.* (**-nat·ed, -nat·ing**). Scatter abroad, sow in various places; (pass., of disease) dispersed or spread throughout organ, tissue, or whole body. **dis·sem·i·na·tion** (dĭsĕminā′shon), **dis·sem′i·na·tor** *ns.*

dis·sen·sion (dĭsĕn′shon) *n.* Discord arising from difference in opinion.

dis·sent (dĭsĕnt′) *v.i.* Refuse to assent; disagree; think differently, express different opinion (*from*); differ in religious opinion, differ from doctrine or worship of established church. ~ *n.* (Expression of) difference of opinion; refusal to accept doctrines of established church; nonconformity. **dis·sent′er** *n.* (esp.) Member of dissenting church or sect. **dis·sen·tient** (dĭsĕn′shent) *adj.* & *n.*

dis·ser·ta·tion (dĭsertā′shon) *n.* Spoken or written discourse treating a subject at length, esp. substantial written treatise by university doctoral candidate.

dis·serv·ice (dĭssẽr′vĭs) *n.* Rendering of ill service or ill turn; injury, detriment.

dis·sev·er (dĭsĕv′er) *v.* Sever, divide.

dis·si·dence (dĭs′ĭdens) *n.* Disagreement, dissent.

dis·si·dent (dĭs′ĭdent) *adj.* Disagreeing, dissenting. ~ *n.* One who disagrees; dissenter.

dis·sim·i·lar (dĭsĭm′iler) *adj.* Unlike (*to*). **dis·sim·i·lar·i·ty** (dĭsĭmilăr′ĭtē) *n.* (pl. **-ties**). **dis·sim′i·lar·ly** *adv.*

dis·si·mil·i·tude (dĭssĭmĭl′ĭtōōd, -tūd) *n.* Unlikeness.

dis·sim·u·late (dĭsĭm′yulāt) *v.* (**-lat·ed, -lat·ing**). Dissemble (feelings etc.); be hypocritical. **dis·sim·u·la·tion** (dĭsĭmyulā′shon), **dis·sim′u·la·tor** *ns.*

dis·si·pate (dĭs′ipāt) *v.* (**-pat·ed, -pat·ing**). Dispense, dispel (cloud, vapor, etc.); bring or come to nothing; squander, fritter away (money, time, etc.). **dis′si·pat·ed** *adj.* (esp.) Given to dissipation, dissolute.

dis·si·pa·tion (dĭsipā′shon) *n.* 1. Dissipating; wasteful expenditure *of.* 2. (Frivolous) amusement. 3. Dissolute indulgence in pleasure or vice; intemperance.

dis·so·ci·ate (dĭsō′sēāt, -shē-) *v.t.* (**-at·ed, -at·ing**). Disunite, sunder, cut off from association or society; (chem.) decompose, esp. by heat. **dis·so·ci·a·tion** (dĭsōsēā´-shon, -shē-) *n.* (esp.) Disintegration *of* personality or consciousness; (path.) state of mind in which two or more personalities exist in the same person. **dis·so′ci·a·tive** *adj.*

dis·so·lute (dĭs´olōōt) *adj.* Lax in morals, licentious. **dis′so·lute·ly** *adv.* **dis′so·lute·ness** *n.*

dis·so·lu·tion (dĭsolōō´shon) *n.* 1. Disintegration, decomposition. 2. Undoing or relaxation of any tie or bond; formal dismissal of assembly or legislature. 3. Death; coming, being brought, to an end; disintegration, disorganization.

dis·solve (dĭzŏlv´, -zawlv´) *v.* (**-solved, -solv·ing**). 1. Liquefy; (fig.) lose composure (~ **in(to) laughter, tears**); (phys., of liquid) mix with (a solid, another liquid, or a gas) without chemical action so as to form a homogeneous liquid or solution; (of substance) mix thus *in* a liquid. 2. Bring to naught, destroy; become faint, melt *away*. 3. Disperse; bring (meeting, assembly, legislature), come, to an end. 4. (motion pict., television) Change (picture) gradually by fading out one scene while next scene fades in over it. ~ *n.* (motion pict., television) Scene transition made by dissolving.

dis·so·nant (dĭs´onant) *adj.* Discordant, harsh toned, incongruous. **dis′so·nant·ly** *adv.* **dis′so·nance** *n.*

dis·suade (dĭswād´) *v.t.* (**-suad·ed, -suad·ing**). Advise (person) against; divert *from* course by persuasion or influence. **dis·sua·sion** (dĭswā´zhon) *n.* **dis·sua·sive** (dĭswā´sĭv) *adj.* **dis·sua′sive·ly** *adv.*

dis·syl·la·ble = DISYLLABLE.

dist. *abbrev.* District; distance; distant.

dis·taff (dĭs´tăf, -tahf) *n.* 1. Cleft staff about 3 ft. long on which wool or flax was wound for spinning by hand; corresponding part of hand-turned spinning wheel. 2. Woman's work. 3. Female sex. ~ **side**, female branch of family.

dis·tance (dĭs´tans) *n.* 1. Being far off, remoteness; extent of space between, interval. 2. Aloofness; **keep one's** ~, avoid familiarity. 3. Distant point; remote field of vision; distant part of landscape. 4. Being apart in time; extent of this interval. **distance** *v.t.* (**-tanced, -tanc·ing**). Place, make seem, far off; leave far behind in race or competition.

dis·tant (dĭs´tant) *adj.* 1. Far away; specified distance away (*from*); remote, far apart, in position, time, resemblance, etc.; ~ **early warning line**, also DEW line, radar system in N. Amer. for advance detection of aircraft or missile attack. 2. Reserved, cool, not intimate. **dis′tant·ly** *adv.*

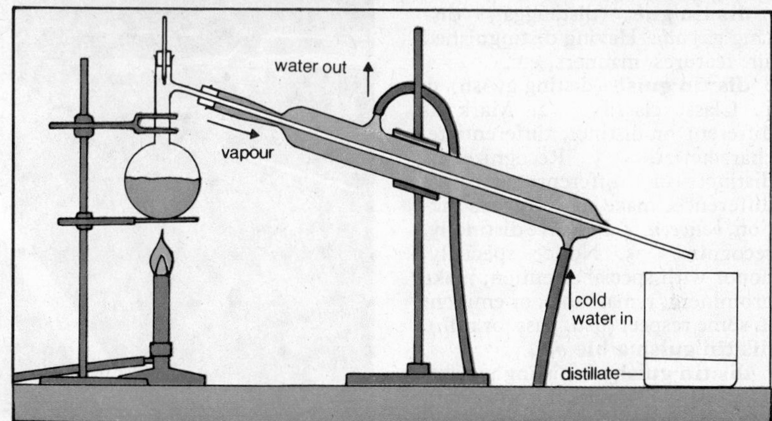

*The most important industrial applications of **distillation** concern petroleum and the production of alcohol and alcoholic 'spirits'. However, aromatic plants, such as lavender being distilled here, and other flowers and herbs are evaporated and condensed to produce perfumed essence. Distillation of the most simple kind occurs in a Liebig condenser.*

dis·taste (dĭstāst´) *n.* Dislike, repugnance, slight aversion (*for*). **dis·taste′ful** *adj.* Disagreeable, repellent (*to*). **dis·taste′ful·ly** *adv.* **dis·taste′ful·ness** *n.*

dis·tem·per (dĭstĕm´per) *n.* 1. Derangement, ailment, of body or mind. 2. Disease of dogs characterized by vomiting, fever, cough, and loss of strength; any of various diseases of other animals.

dis·tend (dĭstĕnd´) *v.* Swell out by pressure from within. **dis·ten·si·ble** (dĭstĕn´sĭbel) *adj.* **dis·ten·sion, dis·ten·tion** (dĭstĕn´shon) *ns.*

dis·till (dĭstĭl´) *v.* 1. Trickle down; issue, give forth, in drops, exude. 2. Vaporize substance by means of heat, and then condense the vapor by cooling it, so as to obtain the substance or part of it in concentrated or purified state; extract essence of, transform or convert, make or produce, drive *off*, by distillation; undergo distillation.

dis·til·la·tion (dĭstĭlā´shon) *n.* (esp.) Extraction of spirit or essence of any substance by first converting into vapor and then condensing the vapor; **destructive** ~, decomposition of substance by strong heat in a retort, and collection of volatile matters evolved; **fractional** ~, separation by distillation of two or more liquids having different boiling points, utilizing the fact that the first portion or fraction of the distillate has a higher proportion of the more volatile liquid than later

The angle from which this photograph was taken has produced a ***distortion*** *of both man and oars, so that they seem out of proportion. This gives the composition greater impact.*

fractions.

dis·till·er (dĭstĭl′*er*) *n.* (esp.) One who distills, esp. alcoholic liquors. **dis·till′er·y** *n.* (pl. **-er·ies**). Business, plant for distilling alcoholic liquors.

dis·tinct (dĭstĭngkt′) *adj.* 1. Not identical, separate, individual; different in quality or kind, unlike. 2. Clearly perceptible, plain, definite; unmistakable, decided, positive. 3. Unusual or notable. **dis·tinct′ly** *adv.* **dis·tinct′ness** *n.*

dis·tinc·tion (dĭstĭngk′sh*o*n) *n.* 1. Making of a difference; discrimination; difference made. 2. Being different. 3. Thing that differentiates; mark, name, title. 4. Showing of special consideration, mark of honor. 5. Distinguished character, excellence, eminence; individuality.

dis·tinc·tive (dĭstĭngk′tĭv) *adj.* Distinguishing, characteristic. **dis·tinc′tive·ly** *adv.* **dis·tinc′tive·ness** *n.*

dis·tin·gué (dĭstănggā′, dĭstăng′gā) *adj.* Having distinguished air, features, manners, etc.

dis·tin·guish (dĭstĭng′gwĭsh) *v.* 1. Class, classify. 2. Mark as different or distinct, differentiate, characterize. 3. Recognize as distinct or different; perceive difference, make or draw distinction, *between*. 4. Perceive distinctly, recognize. 5. Notice specially, honor with special attention; make prominent, remarkable, or eminent in some respect (usu. pass. or refl.). **dis·tin′guish·a·ble** *adj.*

dis·tin·guished (dĭstĭng′gwĭsht) *adj.* (esp.) Remarkable (*for, by*); eminent, famous, of high standing; **D~ Flying Cross**, (abbrev. D.F.C.) U.S. military decoration for distinguished heroism or achievement in aerial combat; **D~ Service Cross**, (abbrev. D.S.C.) U.S. Army decoration for exceptional heroism in combat; **D~ Service Medal**, (abbrev. D.S.M.) U.S. military decoration for distinguished performance in carrying out great responsibility.

dis·tort (dĭstôrt′) *v.t.* Put out of shape, make crooked or unshapely; misrepresent; give a false meaning to. **dis·tort′ed·ly** *adv.*

dis·tor·tion (dĭstôr′sh*o*n) *n.* Distorting, being distorted; faulty transmission or reproduction of sound.

dis·tract (dĭstrăkt′) *v.t.* Divert, draw away (mind, attention); draw in different directions, divide or confuse the attention of; bewilder, perplex; drive mad, infuriate. **dis·tract′ed·ly, dis·tract′ing·ly** *advs.*

The ***District of Columbia*** *is the seat of the U.S. national government and its territory is the City of Washington. The Capitol building is seen here from Pennsylvania Avenue.*

dis·trac·tion (dĭstrăk′sh*o*n) *n.* 1. Diversion of mind or attention; something that distracts or diverts; amusement. 2. Lack of concentration. 3. Confusion, perplexity, dissension; frenzy, madness; **to ~**, to degree approaching madness.

dis·trait (dĭstrā′) *adj.* [fem. ***dis·traite*** (dĭstrāt′)] Worriedly inattentive, absent-minded, anxiously preoccupied.

dis·traught (dĭstrawt′) *adj.* Violently agitated; emotionally upset to point of derangement.

dis·tress (dĭstrĕs′) *n.* 1. Severe pressure or strain of pain, sorrow, etc., anguish, affliction; damage or danger to ship; exhausted or distressed condition; misfortune, calamity; **~ signal**, signal of ship in distress. 2. (law) Legal seizure and detention of property against payment of debt. **dis·tress′ful** *adj.* **dis·tress′ful·ly** *adv.* **distress** *v.t.* Subject to severe strain, exhaust, afflict; vex, make anxious or unhappy. **dis·tress′ing** *adj.* **dis·tress′ing·ly** *adv.*

dis·trib·ute (dĭstrĭb′ūt) *v.t.* (**-ut·ed, -ut·ing**). 1. Deal out, give share of to each of a number; spread abroad, scatter, put at different points; divide into parts, arrange, classify; (logic) use (term) in its full extension, so that it includes every individual of the class. 2. Promote, sell, and ship (merchandise). **dis·trib′u·tor** *n.* (esp.) 1. Device distributing electric current in proper sequence to spark plugs. 2. Business firm or person engaged in distribution.

dis·tri·bu·tion (dĭstrĭbū′sh*o*n) *n.* 1. Distributing, being distributed. 2. (esp., econ.) Dispersal among consumers effected by commerce; extent to which individuals or classes share in aggregate products of community. 3. Way in which a particular character is spread over members of a class, usually represented graphically by a ~ **curve**. **dis·tri·bu′tion·al** *adj.*

dis·trib·u·tive (dĭstrĭb′y*u*tĭv) *adj.* 1. Of, concerned with, produced by, distribution. 2. (logic, gram.) Referring to each individual of a class, not to the class collectively. ~ *n.* (gram.) Distributive word. **dis·trib′u·tive·ly** *adv.*

dis·trict (dĭs′trĭkt) *n.* Territory marked off for special administrative or judicial purpose; assigned sphere of operations; tract of country with common characteristics, region; ~ **attorney**, (abbrev. D.A.) public prosecutor of a judicial district. **district** *v.t.* Divide into districts.

Dis·trict (dĭs′trĭkt) **of Columbia.** (abbrev. D.C.) Federal District of the U.S., coextensive with the capital city of Washington.

dis·trust (dĭstrŭst′) *n.* Want of trust; doubt, suspicion. ~ *v.t.* Have no confidence in, doubt, suspect. **dis·trust′ful** *adj.* **dis·trust′ful·ly** *adv.* **dis·trust′ful·ness** *n.*

dis·turb (dĭstẽrb′) *v.t.* Agitate, trouble, disquiet, unsettle; perplex.

dis·turb·ance (dĭstẽr′b*a*ns) *n.* Interruption of tranquility, agitation; tumult, uproar, outbreak.

dis·turbed (dĭstẽrbd′) *adj.* (esp.) Emotionally or mentally unstable.

di·sul·fide (dīsŭl′fīd) *n.* Sulfide containing two atoms of sulfur.

dis·un·ion (dĭsūn′y*o*n) *n.* Separation, want of union, dissension. **dis·u·nite** (dĭsūnīt′) *v.t.* (**-nit·ed, -nit·ing**). **dis·u·ni·ty** (dĭsū′nĭtē) *n.* (pl. **-ties**).

dis·use (dĭsūs′) *n.* State of not being used or of being no longer in use. **dis·used** (dĭsūzd′) *adj.*

di·syl·la·ble, dis·syl·la·ble (dī′sĭl*a*b*e*l, dĭsĭl′-) *ns.* Word, metrical foot, of two syllables. **di·syl·la·bic, dis·syl·la·bic** (dĭsĭlăb′ĭk, dīsĭ-) *adjs.*

ditch (dĭch) *n.* Long narrow excavation, esp. to hold or conduct water or serve as boundary; watercourse. ~ *v.* Make or repair ditches; provide with ditches; run, drive (vehicle) into ditch or off track or road; (slang) bring (aircraft) down into sea in emergency; (slang) get rid of; leave in the lurch.

dith·er (dĭdh′*er*) *n.* State of agitation or indecision. ~ *v.* Be in a dither.

dith·y·ramb (dĭth′*i*răm, -rămb) *n.* 1. (Gk. antiq.) Wild choric hymn (orig. in honor of Dionysus) from which Greek tragedy is believed to have evolved. 2. Vehement or inflated poem, speech, or writing. **dith·y·ram·bic** (dĭth*i*răm′bĭk) *adj.* & *n.*

dit·to (dĭt′ō) *n.* (pl. **-tos**). (abbrev. do, symbol ″, known as ~ **mark**) The aforesaid, the same thing (used in accounts and lists, or colloq.); duplicate, similar thing. **ditto** *v.t.* (**-toed, -to·ing**). Agree with, endorse opinion of; make copies. ~ *adv.* As before, likewise. [It. *ditto* (now *detto*) said, aforesaid]

dit·ty (dĭt′ē) *n.* (pl. **-ties**). Short simple song.

dit·ty (dĭt′ē) **bag, ditty box.** Sailor's bag for holding odds and ends; box for same purpose.

di·u·re·sis (dīy*u*rē′sĭs) *n.* Passing of urine in large amounts. **di·u·ret·ic** (dīy*u*rĕt′ĭk) *adj.* & *n.* (Substance) stimulating kidneys to secrete urine.

di·ur·nal (dīẽr′n*a*l) *adj.* Occupying one day (chiefly of apparent motion of heavenly bodies); performed, happening, recurring, every day; of the day as dist. from the night; (zool.) active in daytime. **di·ur′nal·ly** *adv.*

Div. *abbrev.* Divine; Divinity.

div. *abbrev.* Divided; dividend; division; divisor; divorced.

di·va (dē′v*a*) *n.* (pl. **-vas, -ve** pr. -vĕ). Great woman singer; prima donna.

di·va·lent (dīvā′l*e*nt) = BIVALENT.

di·van (dĭvăn′, -vahn′, also for def. 2 dī′văn) *n.* 1. (in Muslim countries) Council chamber; seat used by Sultan or administrator, when holding audience. 2. Long backless couch, usu. against wall of room, and furnished with cushions. [Pers. *dīwān* account book, court, council, couch]

dive (dīv) *v.i.* (**dived, dove, div·ing**). Plunge, esp. head foremost, into water etc.; go down or out of sight suddenly, dart; plunge hand *into* water, vessel, pocket; plunge *into* subject; (of aircraft etc.) descend steeply and fast; (of

Political ***disturbance*** *and demonstrations have become a familiar feature of modern life in most countries of the world. Here, Cambodian students protest in 1970.*

*The **diver** has an awkward gait on land but can slide below the water with barely a ripple. It is noted for its eerie cries during the breeding season.*

*Competition swimmers always begin their races by **diving** into the water (above) while high diving is an Olympic competition. Top: Skin-diving has become a popular pastime for amateurs who spear fish, and for professional and amateur photographers.*

submarine) submerge; **~-bomb** (*v.*) attack from aircraft with bombs released at end of steep dive; **~ bomber**, aircraft performing in this manner; **div'ing bell**, open-bottomed bell-like vessel, supplied with air under pressure, in which person can be let down into deep water; **diving helmet**, headgear of diving suit; **diving suit**, air- and water-tight garment (esp. with lead-soled boots and glass-fronted helmet, and apparatus for pumping in air) in which person can go down into deep water and remain there for some time. **dive** *n.* 1. Diving; plunge, precipitate fall. 2. (slang) Disreputable or cheap night-club, bar, etc. 3. (slang) Deliberate attempt by boxer to lose by feigned knockout, esp. in **take a ~**.

div·er (dī'v*er*) *n.* (esp.) One who dives for pearls, to examine and repair sunken vessels or to recover valuable cargo.

di·verge (dĭvẽrj', dī-) *v.* (**-verged, -verg·ing**). Proceed in different directions from point or from each other; deviate; cause (lines, rays) to diverge; (math.) of a series, approach in its sum to an indefinitely great amount when a large number of terms is taken. **di·ver'gence** *n.* **di·ver'gent** *adj.* **di·ver'gent·ly** *adv.*

di·vers (dī'v*e*rz) *adj.* (literary) Sundry, several, various.

di·verse (dĭvẽrs', dī-, dī'vẽrs) *adj.* Unlike in nature or qualities; varied, changeful. **di·verse'ly** *adv.* **di·verse'ness** *n.*

di·vers·i·fy (dĭvẽr'sĭfī, dī-) *v.t.* (**-fied, -fy·ing**). Make diverse, vary, modify, variegate; extend (activity of a business) into various fields; spread (investment) over several products or enterprises, esp. to guard against loss. **di·ver·si·fi·ca·tion** (dĭvẽrsĭfĭkā'sh*o*n, dī-) *n.*

di·ver·sion (dĭvẽr'zh*o*n, -sh*o*n, dī-) *n.* 1. Deflecting, deviation. 2. Diverting of attention; maneuver to secure this; feint. 3. Recreation, pleasant distraction, pastime.

di·ver·si·ty (dĭvẽr'sĭtē, dī-) *n.* (pl. **-ties**). Being diverse, unlikeness; different kind; variety.

di·vert (dĭvẽrt', dī) *v.t.* Turn aside from (proper) direction or course; ward off; draw off attention of, distract; entertain, amuse. **di·vert'ing** *adj.* **di·vert'ing·ly** *adv.*

di·ver·tic·u·li·tis (dīv*e*rtĭky*u*-lī'tĭs) *n.* Inflammation of a DIVERTICULUM, esp. in the colon.

di·ver·tic·u·lum (dīv*e*rtĭk'y*u*-l*u*m) *n.* (pl. **-la** pr. -l*a*). (anat.) Blind tubular side branch of cavity or passage.

di·ver·tisse·ment (dĭvẽr'tĭs-m*e*nt; *Fr.* dēvĕrtēsmahṅ') *n.* (pl. **-ments** pr. -m*e*nts; *Fr.* -mahṅ'). Short ballet; performance given between acts or longer pieces.

di·vest (dĭvĕst', dī-) *v.t.* Unclothe; strip *of* garment etc.; deprive, rid, *of* (property). **di·vest'-ment, di·ves'ture** *ns.*

di·vide (dĭvīd') *v.* (**-vid·ed, -vid·ing**). 1. Separate into parts or smaller groups, split, break up; mark out actually or mentally into parts; make classification in, distinguish kinds of; sunder, part. 2. Cause to disagree; set at variance. 3. Distribute, deal out, (*among, between*); share *with* others. 4. (math.) Find how many times a number is contained in another; (of number or quantity) be contained exact number of times in (another). **~** *n.* Ridge separating 2 watersheds; **Great D~**, in the Rocky Mountains, the divide of Continental

U.S.; (fig.) dividing line, esp. between life and death.

div·i·dend (dĭv′ĭdĕnd) *n.* 1. (math.) Number to be divided by another (the *divisor*). 2. Share of profits for stockholder, etc.; (colloq.) something extra, bonus.

di·vid·er (dĭvī′d*er*) *n.* (esp., pl., also **pair of ~s**) Compasses having a screw fastened to one leg and passing through the other, used for measuring small intervals, and for dividing straight lines etc. into any desired number of equal parts; simple pair of compasses with steel points.

div·i·na·tion (dĭv*i*nā′sh*o*n) *n.* Divining; insight into or discovery of unknown or future by supernatural means; skillful forecast, good guess.

di·vine[1] (dĭvīn′) *v.* (**-vined, -vin·ing**). Make out by inspiration, magic, intuition, or guessing; foresee, predict, conjecture; practice divination; **divining rod**, dowsing rod. **di·vin′er** *n.*

di·vine[2] (dĭvīn′) *adj.* 1. Of, from, like, God or a god; ~ **right of kings**, that claimed according to doctrine that kings derive their power from God, unlimited by any rights of their subjects. 2. Devoted or addressed to God; sacred; ~ **service**, public worship of God. 3. Superhumanly excellent, gifted, or beautiful. **di·vine′ly** *adv.*

divine *n.* Person (usu. cleric) skilled in divinity, theologian.

di·vin·i·ty (dĭvĭn′ĭtē) *n.* (**-ties**). 1. Being divine; deity; **D**~, God; godhead. 2. Object of adoration, adorable being. 3. Theology.

di·vis·i·ble (dĭvĭz′*i*b*e*l) *adj.* Capable of being divided; (math.) ~ **by**, containing (a number) some number of times without remainder. **di·vis·i·bil·i·ty** (dĭvĭz*i*bĭl′ĭtē) *n.*

di·vi·sion (dĭvĭzh′*o*n) *n.* 1. Dividing, being divided; severance, separation; distribution, sharing; ~ **of labor**, division of work into (types of) tasks, each performed by particular person or group. 2. Disagreement, discord. 3. (math.) Process of dividing number by another; **long** ~, method in which each stage of the process is written down (adopted esp. when divisor is greater than 12), opp **short** ~ in which the quotient is set down directly. 4. Dividing line, boundary. 5. Part, section; administrative, judicial, political, or other, division of country, territory, district, etc. 6. Definite part, under single command, of army, fleet, or air force; unit of an army intended to be capable of independent operations, varying in size and composition, but usually consisting of three infantry regiments and an artillery regiment, as well as various supporting units; (also) specialized arm of military force, as **armored** ~. 7. (bot.) Major classificatory grouping = PHYLUM; (zool.) subsidiary category between major groups, e.g. between phylum and class. **di·vi′sion·al** *adj.*

di·vi·sor (dĭvī′z*er*) *n.* Number by which another (the *dividend*) is to be divided; number that divides another without remainder, factor.

di·vorce (dĭvōrs′, -vо̄rs′) *n.* Legal dissolution of marriage; (fig.) complete separation, disunion of things closely connected. ~ *v.t.* (**-vorced, -vorc·ing**). Legally dissolve marriage between; separate by, obtain divorce *from* (spouse); put away, repudiate; dissolve (union); sever. **di·vor·cé** (dĭvōrsā′, -vо̄r-, -vōr′sā, -vо̄r′-) *n.* (fem. **di·vor·cee, di·vor·cée** pr. dĭvōrsē′, -sā′, -vо̄r-, -vōr′sē, -sā, -vо̄r′-) Divorced person. **di·vorce′ment** *n.*

div·ot (dĭv′*o*t) *n.* (golf) Piece of turf cut out by player's club when striking the ball.

di·vulge (dĭvŭlj′) *v.t.* (**-vulged, -vulg·ing**). Let out, reveal. **di·vulge′ment, di·vul′gence** *ns.*

*The **Great Divide** in North America is the continuous range of mountains that divides the continent's principal drainage into eastward and westward flowing patterns.*

Dix·ie (dĭk′sē). 1. Southern U.S., the South; **Dix′iecrat** (*n.*) Member of dissenting group of southern Democratic politicians during 1940s who opposed racial integration and formed States' Rights Party in 1948; **Dix′ieland** (*n.*), style of instrumental jazz with strong 2-beat rhythm and group and solo improvisation. 2. (**"Dixie"**) Popular marching song (prob. composed by Dan Emmett, 1859) sung by Confederate soldiers in the Amer. Civil War. [origin doubtful; perh. f. *dixie* (Fr. *dix* ten), a 10-dollar note issued in Louisiana before the Civil War]

diz·zy (dĭz′ē) *adj.* (**-zi·er, -zi·est**). Giddy, dazed, unsteady, tottering, confused; making giddy; whirling rapidly. **diz′zi·ly** *adv.* **diz′zi·ness** *n.* **dizzy** *v.t.* (**-zied, -zy·ing**). Make dizzy, bewilder.

D.J., DJ *abbrevs.* Disc jockey.

Dja·kar·ta (jakär′ta). City and seaport of NW. Java, capital of Indonesia.

Dji·bou·ti (jĭbo͞o′tē). Republic in NE. Africa on Gulf of Aden, formerly French territory of Afars and Issas; capital and port city of this republic.

djin, djinn: see JINN.

dkg *abbrev.* Decagram(s).

dkl *abbrev.* Decaliter(s).

dkm *abbrev.* Decameter(s).

dl *abbrev.* Deciliter(s).

D.Lit. *abbrev.* Doctor of Literature.

D.Litt. *abbrev.* Doctor of Letters.

DM, Dm *abbrevs.* Deutsche mark.

dm *abbrev.* Decimeter(s).

DNA *abbrev.* Deoxyribonucleic or desoxyribonucleic acid, any of the class of nucleic acids present in the chromosomes of higher organisms and storing genetic information.

D.N.B. *abbrev.* (Brit.) Dictionary of National Biography.

do (do͞o) *v.* (**did, done, do·ing**). 1. (*v.t.*) Perform, effect, execute; complete; produce, make; operate on, deal with; put forth, exert; (colloq.) provide (food etc.) for; tour, visit as a tourist; swindle. 2. (*v.i.*) Act, proceed; perform deeds; fare, get on; be suitable, suffice. 3. Used as auxiliary verb esp. in questions, as *do you know?*, negative or emphatic statements, as *I did not know*; *I do know*, and urgent requests, as *do come!* 4. Used as substitute for verb just used, to avoid repetition, as *I wanted to see him, and I did* (i.e. saw him). 5. With noun of action as object, = cognate verb of action; e.g. **do repairs**, repair things; **do battle**, fight. 6. **done!**, I accept (offer, bet, etc.); **have to do with**, be concerned or connected with, have dealings with; **it isn't done**, it is forbidden by custom or propriety; **nothing** etc. **doing**, nothing etc. happening or going on; (colloq.) announcement of refusal, failure, etc.; **do away (with)**, abolish; **do by**, treat, deal with, in specified way; **do for**, (colloq.) do housecleaning for; ruin, destroy; exhaust; **do in**, (slang) kill; exhaust; **do or die**, be undeterred by danger; **do time, do** (10 etc.) **years**, undergo imprisonment; **do to, unto**, do by; **do up**, restore, repair; wrap up (package); **do with**, find sufficient; (colloq.) be pleased to have, need; **do without**, dispense with. 7. **do-gooder**, (usu. derog.) well-meaning but unrealistic social reformer etc.; **do-it-yourselfer**, amateur craftsman or home handyman etc. **do** *n.* (slang) Party, entertainment; **dos and don'ts**, rules. **do′a·ble** *adj.* **do′er** *n.*

do *abbrev.* Ditto.

D.O. *abbrev.* Doctor of Optometry; Doctor of Osteopathy.

D.O.A. *abbrev.* Dead on arrival.

dob·bin (dŏb′ĭn) *n.* Draft or farm horse. [pet form of *Robert*]

Do·ber·man pin·scher (dō′berman pĭn′sher). German hound with smooth, short, usu. black coat. [*Dobermann*, name of breeder; Ger. *pinscher* terrier]

doc (dŏk) *n.* (slang) 1. Doctor. 2. Word of address to person whose name is unknown to speaker.

do·cent (dō′sent) *n.* University lecturer not a regular faculty member; lecturer or guide in a museum.

doc·ile (dŏs′ĭl) *adj.* Teachable; submissive; easily managed. **do·cil·i·ty** (dŏsĭl′ĭtē, dō-) *n.*

dock[1] (dŏk) *n.* Species of *Rumex*, coarse weedy herbs with clusters of inconspicuous greenish flowers, and large leaves.

*The **dock** is a common weed or pasture plant of the family that includes the common sorrel and the sheep's sorrel; both have a characteristic acidic taste. It has large leaves and is wind-pollinated.*

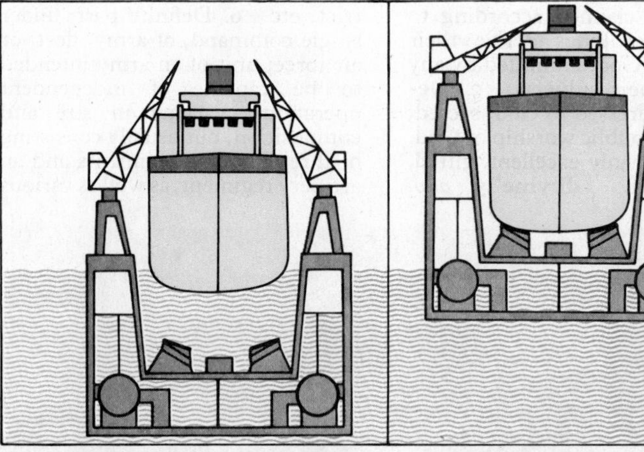

***Floating docks** are used to repair large ships where there are no suitable dry docks. They are submerged when the ship docks and are raised as the water is pumped out.*

***Djakarta**, the largest city and capital of Indonesia, lies at the mouth of the Chiliwong River and has a population of nearly 4 million. One of its most impressive structures is this freedom statue.*

*The first London **docks** were built early in the 19th century to relieve congestion at the port of London. They were dug out of the marshes of the Isle of Dogs.*

dock² (dŏk) *n.* Solid fleshy part of animal's tail. ~ *v.t.* Cut short (animal's tail, person's hair, etc.); withhold part of (the wages) of (an employee).

dock³ (dŏk) *n.* 1. Pier, wharf; platform for loading or unloading ships, trucks, etc.; usu. artificial enclosure for ships with means for regulating depth of water; **dry** ~, dock from which water can be pumped out, leaving vessel dry for repairs; **floating dry** ~, floating structure usable as dry dock. 2. (pl.) Range of docks with wharves, warehouses, offices, etc.; dockyard. 3. **dock'yard**, enclosure for building and repairing ships, preparing and collecting ships' stores, etc. **dock** *v.* 1. Bring (ship), come, into dock. 2. Join (spacecraft) to another, become joined, in space.

dock⁴ (dŏk) *n.* Enclosure in criminal court where defendant stands or sits.

dock·et (dŏk'ĭt) *n.* 1. Abstract, summary (hist.). 2. (law) Memorandum or register of legal judgments; list of cases for trial or of persons with cases pending. 3. Label, ticket affixed to package listing contents, directions, etc. ~ *v.t.* (**-et·ed, -et·ing**). Make abstract of and enter in docket; enter (case) in docket.

doc·tor (dŏk'ter) *n.* 1. (archaic) Teacher, eminently learned man. 2. (used as prefix to name, usu. abbrev. Dr.) Holder of highest academic degree awarded by college or university in any discipline; esp., doctor of medicine; (pop.) any medical practitioner. 3. Any of various mechanical appliances for removing defects, regulating, adjusting, etc. **doc'tor·al** *adj.* **doctor** *v.t.* Give, receive medical treatment; adulterate, falsify.

doc·tor·ate (dŏk'terĭt) *n.* Doctor's degree.

doc·tri·naire (dŏktrinār') *n.* One who holds some doctrine or theory and tries to apply it without allowing for circumstances; pedantic theorist. ~ *adj.* Of, like, a doctrinaire; theoretical, impractical. **doc·tri·nair'ism** *n.* [*Doctrinaire*, name of a Fr. political party, 1815]

doc·trine (dŏk'trĭn) *n.* What is taught, body of instruction; religious, political, scientific, etc., belief, dogma, or tenet; **Monroe D**~: see MONROE.

***Dry docks** are essential for repairing areas below the waterline of boats and ships. This huge cargo ship has recently had its rudder and stern painted.*

doc·u·ment (dŏk′y*u*m*e*nt) *n.* Something written, inscribed, etc., that furnishes evidence or information on any subject, as manuscript, deed to property, etc. ~ *v.t.* Prove or support by documentary evidence; furnish or provide with documents or evidence. **doc·u·men·ta·tion** (dŏky*u*mĕntā′sh*o*n) *n.*

doc·u·men·ta·ry (dŏky*u*mĕn′t*e*rē) *adj.* Of documents; (of film) dealing with real happenings or circumstances, not fiction. ~ *n.* (pl. **-ries**). Documentary film.

dod·der[1] (dŏd′*er*) *n.* Slender leafless parasitic vine of genus *Cuscuta* with twining threadlike stems.

dod·der[2] (dŏd′*er*) *v.i.* Tremble, shake, with frailty. **dod′der·er** *n.* **dod′der·ing** *adj.* Mentally feeble or inept, futile.

dodeca- *prefix.* Twelve-.

do·dec·a·gon (dōdĕk′*a*gŏn) *n.* Plane figure of 12 angles and sides.

do·dec·a·he·dron (dōdĕk*a*hē′dr*o*n) *n.* (pl. **-drons, -dra** pr. -dr*a*). Solid figure of 12 faces.

Do·dec·a·nese (dōdĕk*a*nēs′, nēz′, dōd*e*-). Group of 12 Greek islands in SE. Aegean between Turkey and Crete.

do·dec·a·syl·la·ble (dōdĕk*a*sĭl′-

Howard Chandler Christy's 'Signing of Constitution' shows the importance, practical and symbolic, that is attached to **documents.** *Most documents receive less ceremony, but to individuals they can be very important.*

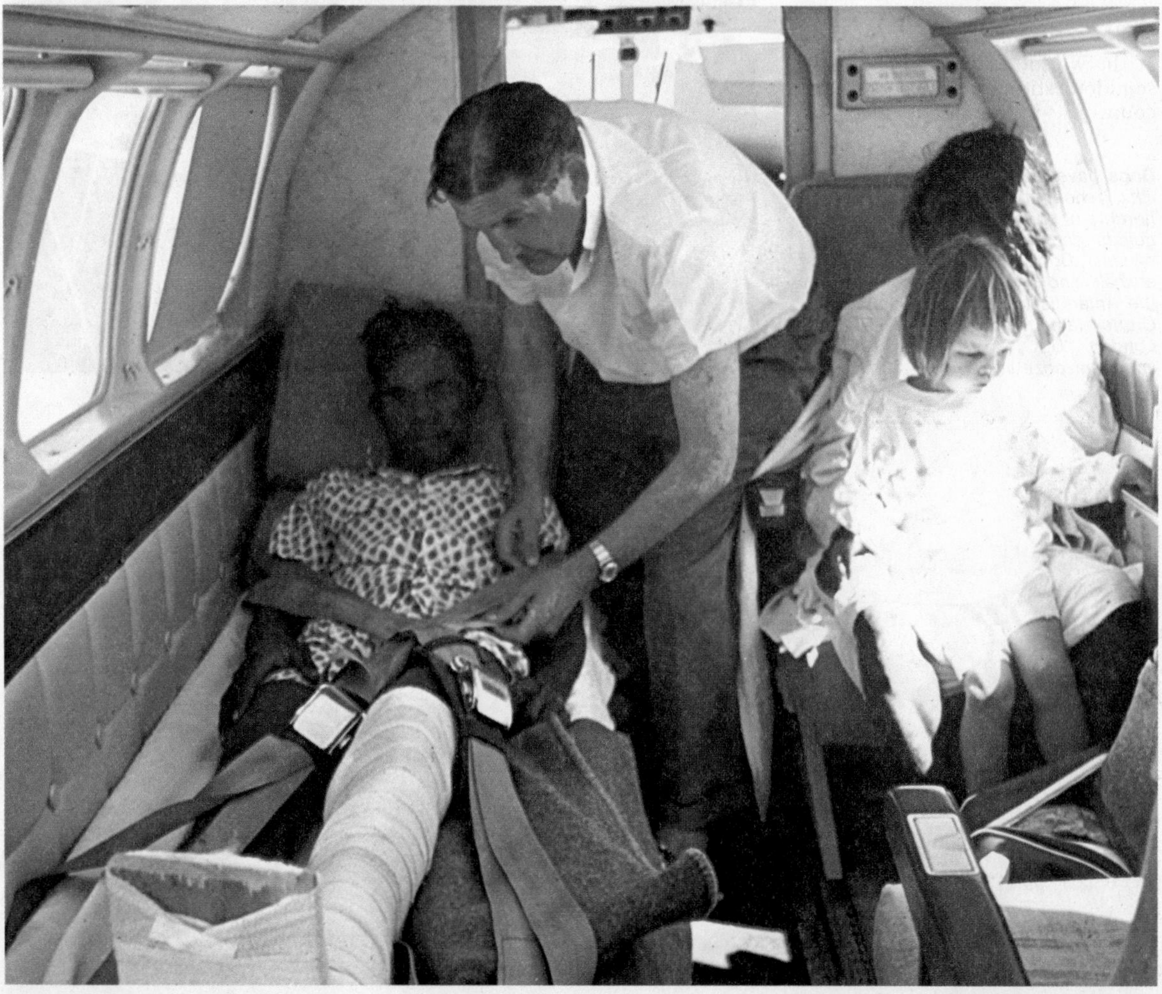

The **flying doctor** *service is used in the sparsely populated areas of the Australian outback for bringing medical aid to outlying farms. Most homesteads are in radio contact with the service's headquarters.*

abel) *n.* (pros.) Line of 12 syllables.

dodge (dŏj) *v.* (**dodged, dodg·ing**). Move to and fro, change position, shuffle; move quickly *around*, *about*, *behind*, obstacle so as to elude pursuer, blow, etc.; avoid, elude, by change of position, shifts, etc. ~ **n.** Dodging, quick side movement; trick, artifice; (colloq.) clever expedient, contrivance, etc. **dodg'er** *n.*

Dodg·son (dŏj'son), **Charles Lutwidge**: see CARROLL.

do·do (dō'dō) *n.* (pl. **-dos, -does**). 1. Extinct bird (*Raphus cucullatus*) with massive clumsy body and wings too small for flight, formerly inhabiting Mauritius. 2. Hopelessly old-fashioned person; dullard. [Port. *doudo* simpleton]

DOE *abbrev.* Department of Energy.

doe (dō) *n.* (pl. **does**, collect. **doe**). Female of deer; female of certain other animals, as hare, kangaroo, etc.; **doe'skin**, skin of doe, kind of leather made from this.

does (dŭz) *v.* Third pers. sing. pres. tense of DO. **does'n't**, contraction of *does not*.

doff (dŏf, dawf) *v.t.* Take off (hat, clothing); lift, tip (hat) in salutation.

dog (dawg, dŏg) *n.* 1. Carnivorous quadruped of the genus *Canis*, found wild in various parts of the world, and domesticated or semidomesticated in almost all countries, in numerous races or

***Dogs** have been used since the Neolithic period, in hunting and tracking, as herders of sheep and cattle, as guards, guides and domestic pets and companions. Dogs have been used as pack animals and are here being trained in the Antarctic to carry loaded sleds. In Crufts famous dog show, held in London, U.K., a whippet wins an important prize in 1973.*

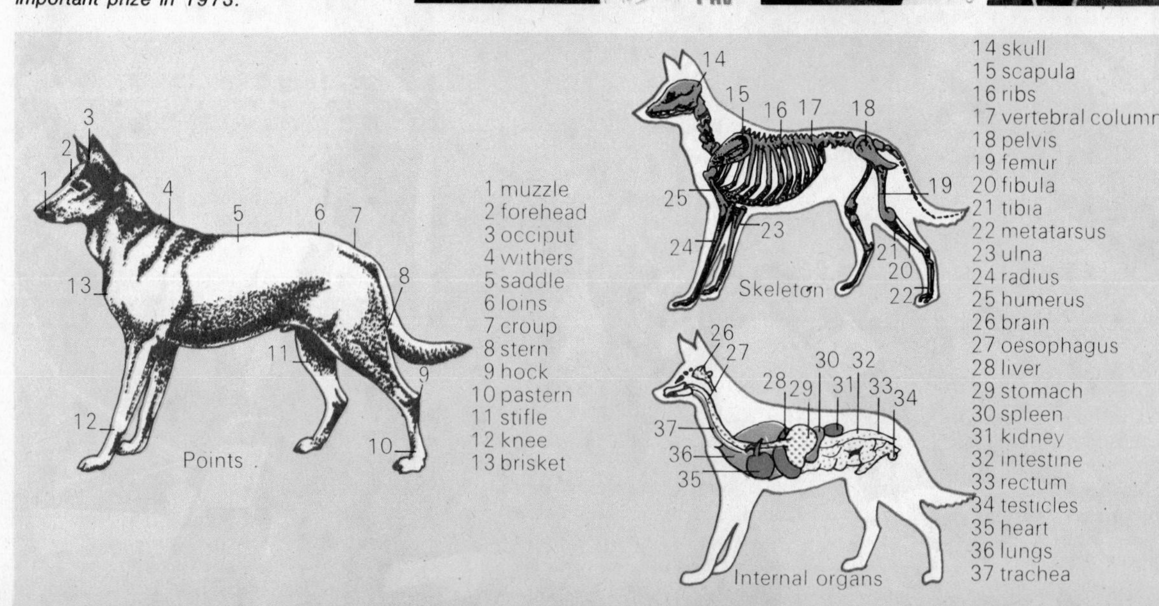

*The **dodo** was exterminated by man in the 17th century. Its large clumsy body and friendly disposition were thought to denote stupidity and it was easily captured and killed.*

breeds varying greatly in shape, size, and color. 2. Male of this animal, or of fox or wolf. 3. (slang) Unattractive woman; (also **gay ~**) gay or jovial fellow; **dirty ~**, (slang) despicable person. 4. Any of various mechanical devices, usu. having a tooth or claw for gripping or holding. 5. Firedog, andiron. 6. **die like a ~**, die miserably or shamefully; **~ in the manger**, one who prevents others from enjoying what is useless to him or her; **a ~'s life**, a life of misery, or of miserable subserviency; **a hair of the ~ that bit you**, more drink to take off effects of drunkenness; **to the ~s**, to destruction or ruin. 7. **dog'bane**, any plant of family Apocynaceae, with milky juice and a bitter root; **dog biscuit**, hard biscuit for feeding dogs; **dog'cart**, two-wheeled cart drawn by a horse and having two transverse seats back to back (the rear one orig. made to shut so as to form a box for dogs); small cart drawn by dog; **dog'catcher**, person appointed to round up stray dogs or cats for the municipal pound; **dog collar**, collar for dog's neck; (slang) clergyman's stiff white collar fastening at back of neck; straight high close-fitting collar, esp. jeweled one; **dog days**, period during part of July and August about time when Sirius, the dog star, rises and sets with the sun; considered from ancient times the hottest and most unwholesome period of the year; **dog-eared**, (of book) having leaves turned down at corner, or crumpled; **dog'fight**, fight between dogs; general melee; melee between aircraft; **dog'fish**, any of several small sharks, esp. genus *Mustelus* or *Squalus*, found in Atlantic and Pacific waters; **dog'house**, dog's kennel; **in the doghouse**, (slang) in disgrace; **dog'leg**, something bent or angled like a dog's hind leg; **dog paddle**, swimming stroke like dog's, with all four limbs submerged and paddling alternately; **Dog Star**, Sirius; **dog tag**, metal identification disk for dog or (esp. military) person; **dog-tired**, tired out, extremely tired; **dog'tooth**, canine tooth; **dog'-tooth violet**, N. Amer. spring-flowering plant of genus *Erythronium*, esp. *E. americanum*, with yellow flowers with reddish spots; also called *adder's tongue* and *trout lily*; **dog'trot**, easy steady trot like a dog's; **dog'watch**, (naut.) each of the two short watches between 4 and 8 p.m. (of two, instead of four, hours each); **dog'wood**, (also **flowering dogwood**) eastern N. Amer. tree (*Cornus florida*) with very small greenish flowers surrounded by large white (occas. pink) bracts, and with bright red berries and colorful leaves in autumn; any of several other trees and shrubs of genus *Cornus*; **dog'-gish, dog'like** *adjs.* **dog** *v.t.* (**dogged, dog·ging**). Follow closely, pursue, track; (mech.) grip with dog; **~ it**, (slang) pretend to work, slight duty.

doge (dōj) *n.* (hist.) Chief magistrate of republics of Venice and Genoa.

*The **dog-tooth violet** is not, in fact, a violet but belongs to the lily family. It grows in temperate regions of the northern hemisphere and has lily-like flowers on long stems.*

*Flowering **dogwood** (Cornus florida), a North American species, is widely grown as an ornamental for its showy bracts (modified leaves) under the tiny flowers.*

dog·ged (daw'gĭd, dŏg'ĭd) *adj.* Obstinate, tenacious, persistent, unyielding. **dog'ged·ly** *adv.* **dog'ged·ness** *n.*

dog·ger·el (daw'g*e*rel, dŏg'*e*r-) *adj.* & *n.* Trivial or irregular (verse).

dog·gone (dawg'gŏn', dŏg'-) *adj., adv., v.t.* & *int.* Mild expletive; pesky, annoying. [euphemism for Goddamn]

dog·gy, dog·gie (daw'gē, dŏg'-) *ns.* (pl. **-gies**). (nursery) Dog; **~ bag**, (colloq.) small bag offered by restaurant for taking home uneaten food. **dog'gy** *adj.* (**-gi·er, -gi·est**). Of dogs; devoted to dogs.

do·gie, do·gy (dō'gē) *ns.* (Western U.S.) Stray or motherless calf.

dog·ma (dawg'm*a*, dŏg'-) *n.* (pl. **-mas, -ma·ta** pr. -m*a*ta). Principle, tenet, doctrinal system, esp. as laid down by authority of church; principle, belief, statement of ideas considered as absolute truth.

dog·mat·ic (dawgmăt'ĭk, dŏg-), **dog·mat·i·cal** (dawgmăt'ĭk*a*l, (dŏg-) *adjs.* 1. Of, based on, dogmas; **~ theology**: see THEOLOGY. 2. Asserting dogmas or opinions, esp. arrogantly. **dog·mat'i·cal·ly** *adv.* **dog·mat'ics** *n. pl.* (usu. considered sing.). Study of arrangement and statement of religious doctrines.

dog·ma·tize (dawg'm*a*tīz, dŏg'-) *v.* (**-tized, -tiz·ing**). Make positive unsupported assertions, speak authoritatively; express (principle etc.) as a dogma. **dog'-ma·tism, dog'ma·tist** *ns.*

Do·ha (dō'h*a*). Capital of Qatar on Persian Gulf.

doi·ly (doi′lē) *n.* (pl. **-lies**). 1. (archaic) Small napkin used at dessert. 2. Small decorative mat of lace etc. to protect or adorn furniture. [fabric named f. 17th-c. inventor]

do·ing (do͞o′ĭng) *n.* Action, responsibility, conduct; (pl.) events, activities.

do-it-your·self (do͞o′ĭty*er*sĕlf′) *adj.* Intended to be built or operated by a person without professional experience.

dol. *abbrev.* Dollar(s)

dol·ce (dōl′chā) *adv.* (mus.) Sweetly, softly. [It.]

dol·drums (dōl′dr*u*mz, -dŏl′) *n. pl.* 1. Dullness, dumps, depression; **in the** ~, (of ship) becalmed. 2. Region near equator where meeting of trade winds produces light baffling winds, sudden storms, and calms. [prob. f. *dull*, the geog. sense being prob. due to misunderstanding of phrase **in the** ~]

*The **doll** may be the oldest toy in the world. In Ancient Greek and Roman periods dolls were made of wood, ivory and burnt clay. By the end of the 18th century wax and porcelain dolls became popular and were often magnificently dressed in the fashions of the day. Today dolls are made in a variety of materials, including cloth, plastics, and rubber.*

dole (dōl) *n.* 1. (archaic) Lot, destiny. 2. Charitable distribution; charitable gift; portion sparingly dealt out; (chiefly Brit. colloq.) unemployment benefit; **on the** ~, receiving this. **dole** *v.t.* (**doled, dol·ing**). Deal *out* sparingly.

dole·ful (dōl′f*u*l) *adj.* Dreary, dismal; sad, discontented, melancholy. **dole′ful·ly** *adv.* **dole′ful·ness** *n.*

dol·i·cho·ce·phal·ic (dŏl*i*kōsefăl′ĭk) *adj.* Long-headed; with breadth of skull less than $\frac{4}{5}$ of length.

doll (dŏl) *n.* Small model of human figure, esp. as toy; pretty child; (slang) pretty but vacuous woman; (slang) very attractive person; ~ *v.* ~ **up**, dress finely. [shortened pet form of *Dorothy*]

dol·lar (dŏl′*er*) *n.* 1. (orig.) Name for the German thaler and also for the Spanish piece of eight (peso) current in Spanish America and used in British N. Amer. colonies. 2. Principal monetary unit (symbol $) of U.S., Canada, Australia, and other countries, equals 100 cents. [orig. *daler*, f. *Joachimstaler*, coin from silver mine in Joachimstal, Bohemia (Ger. *tal* valley); symbol $ a modification of P[s], Mex. abbreviation for pesos or piastres]

dol·lop (dŏl′*o*p) *n.* (colloq.) Large clumsy or shapeless lump, serving, or portion.

dol·ly (dŏl′ē) *n.* (pl. **-lies**). 1. (Pet name for) doll. 2. Mobile platform on casters or wheels for moving heavy loads, a motion-picture or television camera about a set, etc.

Dol·ly Var·den (dŏl′ē vär′d*e*n). Trout (*Salvelinus malma*) of northwestern N. Amer.; (also ~ **hat**) woman's large hat with brim loop-

ing at one side, trimmed with flowers etc. [name of character in Dickens's *Barnaby Rudge*]

dol·man (dōl′m*a*n, dawl′-, dŏl′-) *n.* (pl. **-mans**). 1. Long Turkish robe open in front. 2. Hussar's uniform, elaborately decorated capelike jacket. 3. Woman's cloak or coat with capelike sleeves; ~ **sleeve**, loose sleeve like that of dolman, cut in one piece with body of garment.

dol·men (dōl′m*e*n, dawl′-, dŏl′-) *n.* Megalithic burial chamber, large flat stone laid horizontally upon upright ones. [Fr., prob. f. Cornish *tolmên*, lit. "hole of stone"]

do·lo·mite (dō′l*o*mīt, dŏl′*o*) *n.* 1. (chem.) Double carbonate of calcium and magnesium occurring as crystal or in white or colored granular masses; rock of this. 2. Dolomite mountain, esp. (**Dolomites**) those of the southern Tyrol. [Dieudonné Gratet de *Dolomieu* (1750–1801), French mineralogist]

do·lor·ous (dō′lor*u*s, dŏl′-) *adj.* (usu. poet.) Distressing, painful; doleful; distressed. **do′lor·ous·ly** *adv.*

dol·phin (dŏl′fĭn, dawl′-) *n.* 1. Cetaceous mammal of many species all of family Delphinidae, the best-known of which are the common dolphin (*Delphinus delphis*), resembling a porpoise but with longer and more slender snout, and the bottlenosed dolphin (*Tursiops truncatus*). 2. Either of two iridescent fishes of the genus *Coryphaena*, found in tropical waters.

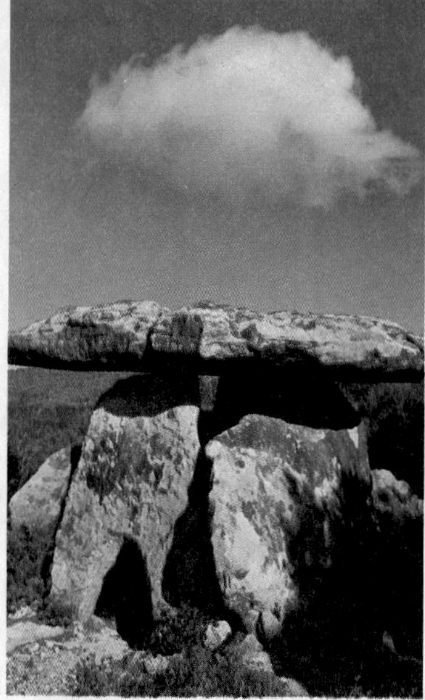

***Dolmens,** megalithic tombs found in Europe, were built chiefly in the Neolithic and Chalcolithic periods. This one is at Grandmont, near Lodève in Hérault, France.*

dolt (dōlt) *n.* Stupid person. **dolt′ish** *adj.* **dolt′ish·ly** *adv.* **dolt′ish·ness** *n.*

Dom. *abbrev.* Dominican.

dom. *abbrev.* Dominion; domestic.

-dom *suffix.* Forming nouns, denoting rank, condition, domain, as *earldom, freedom, kingdom* or collective nouns as *officialdom.*

do·main (dōmān′) *n.* 1. Estate, lands, dominions; district under rule; realm, sphere of influence; scope, field, province, of thought or action; **eminent** ~, government's power of controlling or confiscating private property for public use, subject to compensation. 2. (phys., in ferromagnetic materials) Aggregation of atoms or ions that behaves as an elementary magnet, all the ions in a domain having the axes of their permanent magnetic moment aligned in the same direction.

dome (dōm) *n.* 1. (poet.) Stately building, mansion. 2. Rounded vault forming roof, with circular, elliptical, or polygonal base; natural vault, canopy (of trees, sky, etc.); rounded summit of hill etc.; (slang) the head. ~ *v.t.* (**domed, dom·ing**). Cover with, shape as, dome. **domed** *adj.* Vaulted, domelike; having a dome or domes. [Fr., f. It. *duomo* cathedral, dome, f. L. *domus* house]

Domes·day (dōōmz′dā, dōmz′-) **Book.** Written record of census and survey of lands of England, their extent, value, ownership, etc., made by order of William the Conqueror in 1086. [pop. name (= Doomsday) given to the book as final authority]

*The many varieties of **dolphin** are found in tropical and temperate seas. They have a reputation for intelligence and are gregarious mammals that move about in schools.*

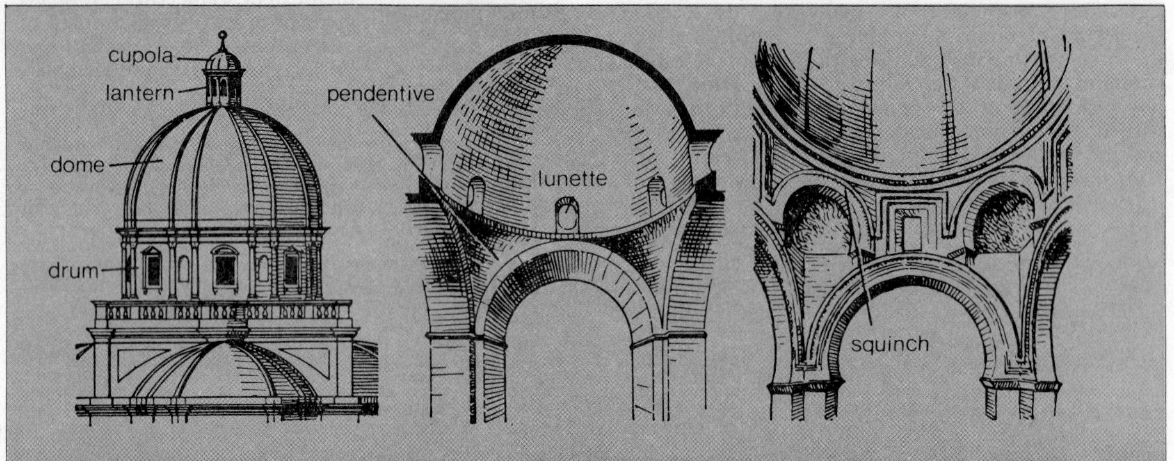

*The **dome** spans a large open area within a building, uncluttered by roof supports. The Romans established its popularity as an architectural feature and it was their example that influenced architects from the Renaissance onwards. Top left: The dome of St. Peter's, Rome, designed by Michelangelo. Top right: Part of the interior of the dome at St. Peter's.*

do·mes·tic (domĕs'tĭk) *adj.* 1. Of the home, household, or family affairs; of one's own country, not foreign; native, homemade; ~ **science**, study of household management. 2. (of animals) Tame, kept by or living with people. 3. Housekeeping; fond of home, domesticated. **domestic** *n.* Household servant. **do·mes'ti·cal·ly** *adv.*

do·mes·ti·cate (domĕs'tĭkāt) *v.t.* (**-cat·ed, -cat·ing**). Naturalize; attach to home and its duties (esp. in the past part.); tame and bring under control (animals), accustom to live near people; civilize. **do·mes'ti·ca·ble** *adj.* **do·mes·ti·ca·tion** (domĕstĭkā'sh*o*n) *n.*

do·mes·tic·i·ty (dōmĕstĭs'ĭtē) *n.* (pl. **-ties**). Domestic character; home life or devotion to it; (pl.) domestic affairs.

dom·i·cile (dŏm'ĭsīl, dō'mĭ-) *n.* Residence; home; (law) place of permanent or legal residence. ~ *v.* (**-ciled, -cil·ing**). Establish, settle, in a place.

dom·i·nant (dŏm'*i*n*a*nt) *adj.* 1. Ruling, prevailing, most influential; occupying commanding position. 2. (mus.) Of the dominant; (of chord) having dominant for its root. 3. (biol., of inherited character) That is apparent in offspring when an opposite character is also inherited (opp. RECESSIVE). ~ *n.* Dominant thing or constituent; (esp., mus.) 5th note of ascending scale; reciting note in ecclesiastical modes, usu. 5th from final; (biol.) dominant character. **dom'i·nance, dom'i·nan·cy** *ns.* **dom'i·nant·ly** *adv.*

dom·i·nate (dŏm'*i*nāt) *v.* (**-nat·ed, -nat·ing**). Have commanding influence over; be the most influential or conspicuous; (of height) overlook; occupy commanding position. **dom·i·na·tion** (dŏm*i*nā'sh*o*n) *n.* 1. Ascendancy, sway, control. 2. (pl.) Fourth order of angels (see ANGEL). **dom'i·na·tor** *n.*

dom·i·neer (dŏm*i*nēr') *v.i.* Act imperiously, tyrannize (*over*), be overbearing. **dom·i·neer'ing** *adj.* **dom·i·neer'ing·ly** *adv.*

Dom·i·nic (dŏm'*i*nĭk), **St.** Domingo de Guzman (1170–1221),

Spanish-born priest active in France; founder (in 1215) of an order of preaching friars (Dominicans).

Dom·i·ni·ca (domĭn′ĭka, dŏmi-nē′-). Island in the West Indies, formerly in British possession; member of the West Indies Associated States; capital, Roseau.

Do·min·i·can[1] (domĭn′ĭkan) *adj.* Of St. Dominic or the order of friars founded by him. ~ *n.* Dominican friar, black friar.

Do·min·i·can[2] (domĭn′ĭkan) *n.* & *adj.* (Native, inhabitant) of the Dominican Republic.

Do·min·i·can[3] (domĭn′ĭkan) **Republic.** Republic (since 1844) occupying the E. two-thirds of the W. Indian island of Hispaniola, formerly part of the Spanish Empire; capital, Santo Domingo.

do·min·ion (domĭn′yon) *n.* 1. Rule, sovereignty, control; (law) right of possession, ownership. 2. Domains of feudal lord; territory of sovereign or government. 3. **D** ~, former title of any of the self-governing nations within the British Commonwealth.

dom·i·no (dŏm′ĭnō) *n.* (pl. **-noes, nos**). 1. Loose hooded cloak, app. of Venetian origin, worn at masquerades with small mask over upper part of face; person wearing this. 2. One of a number (usu. 28) of rectangular pieces of ivory, wood, etc., usu. black, and with upper side equally divided into two squares, each either blank or marked with pips, so as to present all possible combinations from double blank to double 6; (pl.) game played with these (usu.) by placing corresponding ends in contact; ~ **theory**, theory that political event etc. in one place will cause similar events in others, like row of falling dominoes.

don[1] (dŏn) *n.* 1. Spanish title prefixed to Christian names; Spanish gentleman, Spaniard; distinguished person. 2. (Brit. colloq.) Head, fellow, or tutor of college, esp. at Oxford or Cambridge. [Span., f. L. *dominus* lord]

don[2] (dŏn) *v.t.* (**donned, don·ning**). Put on (garment).

Do·na·tel·lo (dŏnatĕl′ō) (1386–1466). Italian sculptor, famous esp. for his bronze *David* in Florence.

do·na·tion (dōnā′shon) *n.* Bestowal, presenting; thing presented, gift (esp. money given to institution). **do·nate** (dō′nāt, dōnāt′) *v.t.* (**-nat·ed, -nat·ing**). Make donation of; give, grant. **do′na·tor** *n.*

done (dŭn) *v.* Past part. of DO; ~ **for**, doomed, ruined, exhausted, dying; ~ **in**, very tired.

do·nee (dōnē′) *n.* Recipient of gift.

dong (dŏng) *n.* (pl. **dong**). Principal monetary unit of Vietnam.

Don·i·zet·ti (dŏnĭzĕt′ē), **Gaetano** (1797–1848). Italian composer of operas.

Don Ju·an (dŏn wahn′; *Brit.* dŏn jo͞o′an). Legendary Spanish nobleman of dissolute life; hence, rake, libertine.

don·key (dŏng′kē, dŭng′-) *n.* (pl. **-keys**). Domesticated ass, descended from the wild *Equus asinus*; stupid person; ~ **engine**, small steam engine, usu. for subsidiary operations on board ship; ~**-work**, (colloq.) drudgery.

Donne (dŭn), **John** (1573–1631). Dean of St. Paul's; preacher and metaphysical poet; author of satires, epistles, and elegies.

Don·ner (dŏn′er) **Pass**, in the Sierra Nevada, named for a party of westward migrants (including families named Donner) who, in 1846, were driven to cannibalism when they became stalled by winter snows.

*The **Dominican Republic,** an independent state in the West Indies, has a population of over 4 million. Below (bottom): Its capital, Santo Domingo, has dry winters, wet summers and frequent earthquakes.*

***Donatello** was the greatest Florentine sculptor before Michelangelo and a most influential artist of the Renaissance. This gilt terracotta is of the 'Virgin and Child'.*

don·nish (dŏn′ĭsh) *adj.* Like a university don; pedantic, erudite, bookish.

Don·ny·brook (dŏn′ēbro͝ok). Town near Dublin, Ireland; ~ **Fair**, annual fair formerly held there; hence, **d**~, uproar, brawl, free-for-all.

do·nor (dō′n*er*) *n.* 1. Giver; contributor of money, work of art, etc. 2. (med.) Person, animal, from whose body biological material is removed, as blood for transfusion (**blood** ~), organ (**heart** ~), or tissue (**tissue** ~), for transplantation to another person, etc.

Don Qui·xo·te: see QUIXOTE.

don't (dōnt). Contraction of do not.

do·nut = doughnut: see DOUGH.

doo·dad (do͞o′dăd) *n.* (colloq.) Fancy article; trivial ornament; gadget.

doo·dle (do͞o′d*e*l) *n.* Aimless scrawl made by a person while his attention is otherwise engaged; quick, inartistic sketch. ~ *v.t.* (**-dled, -dling**). Make a doodle.

doom (do͞om) *n.* 1. Fate, lot, (usu. evil) destiny; ruin, death. 2. Unfavorable sentence or judgment. 3. Last Judgment (chiefly in **day of** ~); **dooms'day**, day of judgment; **till doomsday**, to the end of the world, forever. **doom** *v.* Pronounce sentence against; condemn *to* some fate, *to* do; consign to misfortune or destruction (esp. in past part.).

door (dōr, dōr) *n.* 1. Movable barrier of wood or other material, turning on hinges or sliding in groove etc., and serving to close or open passage into building, room, etc.; doorway; means of entrance or exit; **at death's** ~, on the point of dying; **lay, lie, at the** ~ **of**, impute, be imputable, to. 2. **door'bell**, bell to be rung from outside to gain admission; **door'jamb**, one of two vertical members framing a door and supporting the lintel; **door'keeper**, person who guards door, porter, janitor; **door'knob**, knob for turning to release latch of door; **door'man**, doorkeeper, esp. of apartment building; **door'mat**, mat placed at door for wiping shoes on entering; **door'nail**, large nail driven through door and clinched so as to be not reusable; hence **dead as a** ~; **door'step**, step at threshold of door; **door'way**, opening or passage that door serves to close or open; **door'yard**, yard in front of door or house.

dop·ant (dō′p*a*nt) *n.* Substance added to a semiconductor to change its electrical properties.

dope (dōp) *n.* 1. Thick liquid used as lubricant etc; varnish, esp. that applied to cloth parts of model planes and (formerly) airplanes to keep them taut and airtight. 2. (slang) Narcotic; drug administered to horse etc. before race to improve or spoil its performance; ~ **fiend**, (slang) drug addict; (slang) information, esp. **inside** ~. 3. (slang) Stupid person. **dope** *v.t.* (**doped, dop·ing**). Drug; doctor; apply dope to (airplane fabric etc.). **dop'ey, dop'y** *adj.* (**dop·i·er,**

*The first **doors** made of rigid and permanent materials were often of bronze or stone, but the wooden door is the oldest and most common in antiquity. Since earliest times doors and doorways have been decorative features. Below left: Front door, Ham House, London, U.K. Bottom left: Chinese door at Claydon House. Below: St. Patrick's Cathedral, N.Y.*

dop·i·est). (slang) Heavy or stupefied, as if drugged; stupid. [app. f. Du. *doop* sauce]

Dop·pel·gäng·er (dŏp′*e*lgăng-*er*), **dou·ble·gang·er** (dŭb′*e*lgăng-*er*) *ns.* Wraith, ghostly double that haunts the living person. [Ger.]

Dop·pler (dŏp′l*er*), **Johann** (1803–53). Austrian physicist; ~ **effect**, apparent increase (or decrease) in frequency of electromagnetic and sound waves when source and observer move closer to each other (or farther apart).

Do·ré (dawrā′), **Paul Gustave** (1833–83). French artist; famous for his scriptural paintings and illustrations of Dante, Milton, etc.

Do·ri·an (dōr′ē*a*n, dōr′-) *adj.* Of DORIS or the Dorians; ~ **mode**, (mus.) ancient Greek mode, reputedly simple and solemn in character; first of ecclesiastical modes. **Dorian** *n.* Native, inhabitant, of Doris.

Dor·ic (dōr′ĭk, dŏr′-) *adj.* 1. Dorian. 2. (archit.) Of the Doric order, oldest, strongest, and

The ***dormouse,*** *which resembles a small squirrel in appearance and way of life, hibernates from mid-October to mid-April. It feeds on insects and forages only at night.*

simplest of the Greek orders of architecture, characterized by heavy fluted columns, having saucer-shaped capitals and no base. ~ *n.* 1. Doric dialect of ancient Greece. 2. Doric architecture.

Do·ris (dōr′ĭs, dōr′-). Small country in ancient Greece, S. of Thessaly, the home of the Dorians.

dor·mant (dōr′m*a*nt) *adj.* Sleeping; inactive as in sleep; with animation or development suspended; not active, in abeyance; (bot., esp. of seeds and buds) in state of suspended growth; (her., of beast) with head resting on paws. **dor′man·cy** *n.*

dor·mer (dōr′m*er*) *n.* (also ~ **window**) Projecting vertical window in sloping roof.

dor·mi·to·ry (dōr′mĭtōrē, -tōrē) *n.* (pl. **-ries**). 1. Residence hall or hostel esp. at college or university. 2. Sleeping room with several beds and sometimes cubicles.

dor·mouse (dōr′mows) *n.* (pl. **-mice** pr. -mīs). Small Old World hibernating rodent akin to mouse but resembling squirrel in form and habit.

dor·sal (dōr′s*a*l) *adj.* (anat., bot., zool.) Of, on, near, the back; ~ **fin**, main fin on dorsal surface of fishes etc. **dor′sal·ly** *adv.*

do·ry[1] (dōr′ē, dōr′ē) *n.* (pl. **-ries**). (also **John D**~) European sea fish (*Zeus faber*) used as food. [Fr. *dorée* gilded]

do·ry[2] (dōr′ē, dōr′ē) *n.* (pl. **-ries**). Small flat-bottomed fishing boat with high sides.

dos·age (dō′sĭj) *n.* Giving of medicine in doses; size of dose; amount of x-rays etc. applied at one time.

dose (dōs) *n.* 1. Amount of medicine etc. given or prescribed to be given at one time. 2. (phys.) Amount of radiation received by person or thing exposed to it. ~ *v.t.* (**dosed, dos·ing**). Give medicine to (person). **dos′er** *n.*

do·sim·e·ter (dōsĭm′*e*t*er*) *n.* De-

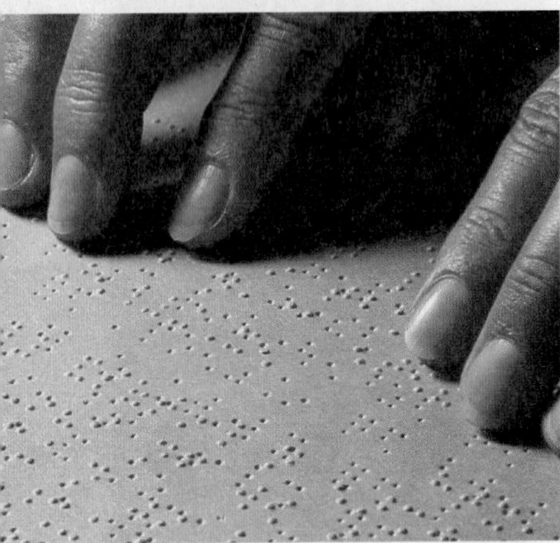

Dots *take on many forms: in morse code (top) a dot is a short audible signal; in braille (above) it is a raised area that may be felt by the reader.*

The **double bass,** *which measures about 6 ft. in height, was largely ignored by early composers. It was brought to prominence by Beethoven and later composers who recognized its unique qualities.*

vice to measure amount of radiation absorbed. **do·sim′e·try** *n.*

Dos Pas·sos (dōs păs′ōs), **John Roderigo** (1896–1970). Amer. novelist; author of the trilogy *U.S.A.* etc.

dos·si·er (daws′yā, dŏs′-, -ēā) *n.* Set or file of documents relating to a particular person or happening.

Dos·to·ev·sky, Dos·to·ev·ski (dŏstoyĕf′skē, dŭs′-, -toiĕf′-), **Feodor Mikhailovich** (1821–81). Russian novelist; author of *Crime and Punishment*, *The Idiot*, *The Brothers Karamazov*, etc.

DOT *abbrev.* Department of Transportation.

dot[1] (dŏt) *n.* Small spot, speck, roundish pen mark; period, point over *i* or *j*, point used as diacritical mark; (in Morse code) small mark or signal shorter than dash; (mus.) point placed after note or rest, lengthening it by half its value; point over or under note indicating that it is *staccato*; **on the ~**, punctually; **dot** *v.t.* (**dot·ted, dot·ting**). Mark with dot(s); place dot over (letter *i*, note in music) or after (musical note). **dotted line,** line of dots or dashes to follow in drawing etc., or on document to receive signature; hence, **sign on the dotted line,** agree formally. **dot′ter** *n.*

dot[2] (dŏt) *n.* Woman's marriage portion; dowry. [Fr.]

dot·age (dō′tĭj) *n.* Impaired intellect, esp. through old age; second childhood, senility.

dot·ard (dō′t*e*rd) *n.* Senile person.

dote (dōt) *v.i.* (**dot·ed, dot·ing**). 1. Be silly, infatuated, or feeble-minded, esp. from age. 2. Concentrate one's affections, bestow excessive fondness, *on.* **dot′er** *n.* **dot′ing·ly** *adv.*

dot·tle, dot·tel (dŏt′*e*l) *ns.* Plug of tobacco left unsmoked in pipe.

dot·ty (dŏt′ē) *adj.* (**-ti·er, -ti·est**). Feeble-minded, half idiotic. **dot′ti·ness** *n.*

Dou·ai (dōōā′). Town in N. France; ~ (usu. **Douay**) **Bible, version,** English translation of the Latin Vulgate Bible used in R.C. Church; the New Testament was published at Rheims in 1582 and the Old Testament at Douai in 1609–10.

dou·ble (dŭb′*e*l) *adj.* 1. Consisting of two members, things, or sets combined; twofold; forming a pair; folded, bent; stooping much; having some part double; (of flowers) having number of petals multiplied by conversion of stamens and carpels into petals. 2. Having twofold relation or application; dual; ambiguous. 3. Twice as much or as many (*of*); of twofold or extra size, strength, value, etc. (mus., of instruments etc.) an octave lower in pitch (from the fact that a pipe, string, etc., of double length gives a note an octave lower). ~ *adv.* To twice the amount etc.; two together. ~ *adj.* or *adv.* in comb.: **~-acting,** acting in two ways, directions, etc., **~ agent,** one spying for two rival parties; **~-barreled,** (of gun) with two barrels; **~ bass,** largest and lowest-pitched instrument of violin class, with four strings usu. tuned a fourth apart; ~ **bed**, bed for two people; ~ **boiler**, saucepan with detachable upper compartment in which food is slowly cooked by water boiling in the lower; **~-breasted**, (of coat etc.) having the two fronts overlapping across the breast; ~ **chin**, chin with fold of flesh underneath; ~ **cross**, (slang) treachery to both parties, esp. by pretended collusion with each, betrayal by acting in contradiction to agreement; **~-cross** (*v.t.*) betray thus; **~-dealing**, duplicity, deceit; (*adj.*) deceitful; **~-dealer**; **~-decker**, bus with two decks; sandwich with three slices of bread and two layers of filling; **~-dipper**, retired soldier, airman, etc., working on salary from federal government while also drawing pension; ~ **eagle**, (hist.) 20-dollar gold piece; **~-edged**, with two cutting edges; (fig., of argument etc.) telling against as well as for one; ~ **figures**, number between nine and 100; **dou′bleheader**, two games in succession on same day between the same teams; **double helix**, pair of parallel helices with common axis, esp. in structure of DNA molecule; **double-jointed**, having joints that allow unusual bending movements of limb etc.; **double-knit**, jersey-like fabric knitted double with the two surfaces locked together; **double-park**, park (vehicle) alongside another already parked parallel to curb; **double play** (baseball) play in which two runners are put out; **double pneumonia**, pneumonia affecting both lungs; **double-quick**, very quick(ly); **double standard**, rule etc. applied more strictly to some persons than to others; esp. one applied more strictly to women than to men in sexual morals; **double star** = BINARY STAR; **double-stopping**, (mus.) simultaneous sounding of notes on two strings of instrument of violin class; **double take**, delayed reaction to situation etc. immediately after one's first reaction; **double-talk**, language (usu. deliberately) ambiguous; gibberish; **double-talk** (*v.i.*); **dou′blethink**, conscious belief in contradictory ideas at the same time [word coined by George Orwell in *1984*]; **double time**, (mil.) marching pace of 180 steps per minute; **double-tonguing**, rapid vibratory motion of tongue in producing staccato or rapidly repeated notes on flute, clarinet, etc. **dou′bly** *adv.* **double** *n.* 1. Double quantity; twice as much or as many; **on the** ~, quickly; (mil.) running. 2. (bridge) Call by declarer's opponent involving doubling of score for tricks and a bonus to the declarer if he or she wins. 3. Counterpart or duplicate of thing or person. 4. (pl.) Game (tennis, handball, etc.) with two players on each side. 5. Lodging with double bed. 6. Double shot of whiskey etc. **double** *v.* (**-bled, -bling**). 1. Make or become double, increase twofold, multiply by two; amount to twice as much as; (mus.) add same note in lower or higher octave to; call a double (at bridge). 2. Bend, turn, over upon itself; clench (fist); ~ **up**, (cause to) bend into stooping or curled up position; become folded; share living, sleeping quarters with. 3. (naut.) Get around (headland). 4. Turn sharply, reverse.

dou·ble en·ten·dre (dŭb′el ahntahn′dre, -tahnd′). Ambiguous expression, phrase with two meanings, one usu. risqué; use of such phrases. [Fr., obs. (now *double entente*)]

dou·blet (dŭb′lĭt) *n.* 1. (hist.) Man's close-fitting jacket with or without sleeves (14th–18th centuries). 2. Pair; one of a pair; one of two words of same derivation but different form or sense.

dou·ble·ton (dŭb′elton) *n.* (cards) Two cards only of a suit, in one hand.

dou·bloon (dŭblo͞on′) *n.* (hist.) Spanish gold coin (orig. two pistoles).

doubt (dowt) *n.* Feeling of uncertainty (*about*), undecided frame of mind, inclination to disbelieve; uncertain state of things; **give** (person) **benefit of the** ~, assume innocence rather than guilt when evidence is contradictory or inconclusive; **no** ~, certainly, admittedly; **without** ~, certainly. **doubt** *v.* Be in doubt or uncertainty (about); call in question; mistrust. **doubt′a·ble** *adj.* **doubt′er** *n.* **doubt′ing·ly** *adv.*

doubt·ful (dowt′ful) *adj.* Of uncertain meaning, character, truth, or issue; undecided, ambiguous, questionable; uncertain, hesitating. **doubt′ful·ly** *adv.* **doubt′ful·ness** *n.*

doubt·less (dowt′lĭs) *adv.* Certainly; no doubt. **doubt′less·ly** *adv.*

douche (do͞osh) *n.* Jet of liquid applied to body externally or internally for cleansing or for medicinal purpose; application of liquid in this manner; instrument for such application. ~ *v.* (**douched, douch·ing**). Administer douche to, take douche.

Ramblers, such as the rose ***Dorothy Perkins,*** *flower mainly on new canes, the previous year's cane having been cut down in the Fall after flowering.*

The design of London's famous red ***double-decker*** *omnibuses has evolved from the early 1900s. Originally they were roofless with an uncovered stairway to the upper deck.*

Newly hatched chickens are covered with fine soft **down.** Later this will be replaced by the adult feathers, but some down will remain in the underplumage.

Dover is famous for its high chalk cliffs and owes its importance to its nearness to the French coast. Dover Castle is one of England's best-preserved medieval fortresses.

dough (dō) *n.* Mass of flour or meal kneaded into paste ready to be baked into bread etc.; any soft pasty mass; (slang) money; **dough'boy**, (esp. in World War I) infantry soldier; **dough'nut**, small, usu. ring-shaped, cake of dough fried in deep fat. **dough'y** *adj.* (**dough·i·er, dough·i·est**).

dough·ty (dow'tē) *adj.* (**-ti·er, -ti·est**). (usu. joc.) Valiant, stout-hearted. **dough'ti·ly** *adv.* **dough'ti·ness** *n.*

Doug·las[1] (dŭg'las), **Stephen Arnold** (1813–61). Amer. political leader; U.S. senator from Illinois, 1847–61; best known for his series of debates with Abraham Lincoln, 1858; defeated for presidency by Lincoln, 1860.

Doug·las[2] (dŭg'las) **fir.** Very tall evergreen tree of northwestern N. Amer., *Pseudotsuga taxifolia* or *P. menziesii*, grown for lumber. [named f. David *Douglas* (1798–1834) Scottish botanist in Amer.]

Doug·lass (dŭg'las), **Frederick** (1817?–95). Original name, Frederick Augustus Washington Bailey; Amer. black abolitionist, lecturer, editor, and statesman.

Dou·kho·bors (do͞o'kōbo͞rz): see DUKHOBORS.

dour (dowr, door) *adj.* Stern, forbidding; gloomy. **dour'ly** *adv.* **dour'ness** *n.*

douse (dows) *v.t.* (**doused, dous·ing**). 1. Extinguish (fire, light). 2. Immerse; drench, soak.

dove (dŭv) *n.* Bird of family Columbidae (see PIGEON), esp. the **tur'tledove** (*Streptopelia turtur*) of Europe and the MOURNING ~ of N. Amer.; symbol of gentleness or innocence; messenger of peace and deliverance (Gen. 8); darling; **~-(color)**, warm gray with tinge of pink or lavender; **dove'cot(e)**, structure for housing pigeons. **dov'ish** *adj.*

Do·ver (dō'ver). Seaport on E. coast of Kent in England on **Strait(s) of ~**, strait at E. end of English Channel between SE. coast of England and N. France; **White Cliffs of ~**, chalk cliffs lining Dover coast; **Dover**, capital of Delaware in E. central part.

dove·tail (dŭv'tāl) *n.* Tenon shaped like dove's spread tail or reversed wedge, fitting into corresponding mortise and forming joint; such joint. ~ *v.* Put together with dovetails; fit together compactly.

dow·a·ger (dow'ajer) *n.* Woman with title or property derived from her late husband; matron of high social standing.

dow·dy (dow'dē) *adj.* (**-di·er, -di·est**). (of clothes) Shabby, unfashionable; (of woman) shabbily or unfashionably dressed. **dow'di·ly** *adv.* **dow'di·ness** *n.* **dowdy** *n.* (pl. **-dies**). Dowdy woman.

dow·el (dow'el) *n.* Headless pin of wood, metal, etc., fastening together two pieces of wood, stone, etc. ~ *v.t.* (**-eled, -el·ing** or **-elled, -el·ling**). Fasten with dowel(s).

dow·er (dow'er) *n.* Widow's share for life of husband's estate; property or money brought by wife to husband, dowry; endowment, gift of nature, talent. ~ *v.t.* Give dowry to; endow *with* talent etc.

Dow-Jones (dow' jōnz') **average.** Index of the relative price of stocks based on the current average price of certain industrial and other stocks, published by Dow-Jones & Co., publishers of the *Wall Street Journal*.

down[1] (down) *n.* Open high land (often pl.); treeless undulating chalk upland of S. England.

down[2] (down) *n.* First fine soft covering of young birds; bird's underplumage, used for stuffing pillows, jackets, etc.; fine soft hair, esp. first hair on face; soft hair on fruit etc.; any feathery or fluffy substance. **down'y** *adj.* (**down·i·er, down·i·est**).

*Above: The **dove** has been semi-domesticated in Europe since the Middle Ages and reared as a source of food. The hundreds of species include the turtledove (top). All doves pair for life and both sexes share in rearing young.*

down[3] (down) *adv.* 1. From above, to lower place, to ground; to place regarded as lower; into helpless position; with current or wind; as initial cash payment at time of purchase (so ~ **payment**). 2. In lower place; in fallen posture, prostrate; at low level, in depression, humiliation, etc.; lower in price. 3. From higher to lower point in series or order; from earlier to later time; into quiescence. 4. **be ~ on**, be opposed to, disapprove of; **come ~ on**, pounce on; treat severely; **go ~**, be swallowed; find acceptance; (of ship) sink; (of sun etc.) set. 5. **~ and out**, (boxing) unable to resume the fight; (transf.) defeated; destitute (person); **~ east**, New England, esp. Maine; **down'hearted, down in the mouth**, dispirited; **down south**, in, into, the southern states; **down-to-earth**, practical, realistic; **down'trodden**, (fig.) oppressed; **down under**, at or to the Antipodes, in Australia etc. **down** *prep.* Downward along, through or into; from top to bottom of; at a lower part of; with (the wind, current, etc.); **down'stage**, at, toward, front of stage; **downstream'**, in direction of current, toward mouth, of river; **downtown'**, into the (business part of) town; (situated) in more central part of town. **down** *adj.* Directed downward; **down'beat** (mus.) (1) accented beat; downward stroke of conductor's baton to indicate the first beat of a measure; (2) depressed, gloomy; **on the down'grade**, (fig.) deteriorating; **down'grade** (*v.t.*), lower in status etc.; **down payment**: see *adv.*, sense 1; **down'range**, (of a missile) away from the launch pad and toward the target; **down'shift**, (of automobile transmission) shift into a lower gear. **down** *v.t.* (colloq.) Put, throw, knock, gulp, etc., down. **~** *n.* Reverse of fortune; throw in wrestling etc.; (football) one of a series of four plays in which the team must advance the ball at least ten yards.

down·cast (down'kăst, -kahst) *adj.* (of looks) Directed downward; dejected.

down·fall (down'fawl) *n.* Fall (of rain etc.); fall from prosperity, ruin.

down·hill (down'hĭl') *adj.* Sloping down; declining. **~** *adv.* In descending direction; on a decline.

Down·ing (dow'nĭng) **Street.** Street in London containing official residence of Prime Minister (no. 10), hence, the British Government. [Sir George *Downing* (*c*1624–1684), British diplomat]

down·pour (down'pōr, -pōr) *n.* Heavy fall of rain etc.

down·right (down'rīt) *adj.* Plain, definite, straightforward, blunt; out-and-out. **~** *adv.*

Thoroughly, positively, quite.

Down's (downz) **syndrome**: see MONGOLISM.

down·stairs (down'stārz') *adv.* Down the stairs. **down'stairs** *adj.* & *n.* (Of, in) lower floor of house etc.

down·trod·den (down'trŏden) *adj.* Crushed by oppression or tyranny.

down·ward (down'werd) *adj.* & *adv.* Toward what is lower or inferior. **down'wards** *adv.*

dow·ry (dow'rē) *n.* (pl. **-ries**). Portion woman brings to her husband on marriage.

dows·er (dow'zer) *n.* Person who attempts to locate underground water or minerals by holding in both hands a forked stick etc., which is supposed to dip abruptly when it is over the right spot. **dows'ing** *n.* Searching for water etc., thus ~ **rod**, forked stick etc. used by dowser, divining rod.

dox·ol·o·gy (dŏksŏl'ojē) *n.* (pl. **-gies**). Hymn of praise to God, esp. short hymn used at conclusion of psalm, canticle, etc. **dox·o·log·i·cal** (dŏksolŏj'ĭkal) *adj.*

dox·y (dŏk'sē) *n.* (pl. **dox·ies**). (archaic) Beggar's wench, paramour; prostitute.

doy·en (doi'en, doiĕn') *n.* (fem. **doy·enne** pr. doiĕn'). (chiefly Brit.) Senior member *of* a body, esp. senior ambassador at a court.

Doyle (doil), **Sir Arthur Conan** (1859–1930). British physician and novelist, famous for his "Sherlock Holmes" detective stories.

doz. *abbrev.* Dozen.

doze (dōz) *v.i.* (**dozed, doz·ing**). Sleep lightly, be half asleep; ~ **off**, fall lightly asleep. **doze** *n.* Short light sleep. **doz'er** *n.* **doz·y** *adj.* (**doz·i·er, doz·i·est**).

doz·en (dŭz'en) *n.* (pl. **-ens**, following a numeral **-en**). Twelve; set of twelve: **baker's** ~, thirteen.

D.P., DP *abbrevs.* Displaced person.

dpt. *abbrev.* Department

Dr. *abbrev.* Doctor; drive (of street names).

dr. *abbrev.* Debit; debtor; drachma(s); dram(s).

drab (drăb) *adj.* (**drab·ber, drab·best**) & *n.* (Of) dull light brown color; dull, monotonous. **drab'ly** *adv.* **drab'ness** *n.*

drach·ma (drăk'ma) *n.* (pl. **-mas, -mae** pr. -mē, **-mai** pr. mī). 1. Principal monetary unit of Greece. 2. Coin and weight of ancient Greece.

Dra·co (drā'kō), **Dra·con** (drā'kon). Chief magistrate (archon) at Athens in 621 B.C., said to have established a severe code of laws.

Dra·co·ni·an (drākō'nēan), **Dra·co·nic** (drākŏn'ĭk) *adjs.* Of Draco or his code of laws; rigorous, harsh, cruel.

*In Christian Europe **dragons** symbolized sin and paganism. One of the legendary saints who fought them was St. Michael, seen here in a painting by Fouquet.*

draft (drăft, drahft) *n.* 1. (Selection of) detachment of men from larger body for special duty; contingent; reinforcement; member of such detachment; conscription for military service; men conscripted for military service; ~ **dodger**, one evading conscription. 2. Drawing of money by written order; bill or check drawn, esp. by one branch of bank on another. 3. Sketch of work to be executed. 4. Rough copy of document. 5. Current of air in room etc. 6. Drawing, traction; drawing of net for fish; catch of fish at one drawing. 7. Single act of drinking, amount so drunk; dose of liquid medicine. 8. Depth of water ship draws or requires to float her. 9. Drawing of liquor from vessel; ~ **beer**, beer drawn from cask, not bottled; **beer on** ~, beer in tapped cask. **draft** *v.t.* 1. Draw off (part of larger body, esp. of troops) for special purpose: conscript. 2. Prepare, make rough copy of (document, report, etc). **draft·ee', draft'er** *ns.* **draft'a·ble** *adj.*

drafts·man (drăfts'man, drahfts'-) *n.* (pl. **-men** pr. -men). One employed to make drawings, plans, or sketches: one skilled in drawing or designing. **drafts'man·ship** *n.*

drag (drăg) *v.* (**dragged, drag·ging**). 1. Pull along with force, difficulty, or friction; allow (feet, tail, etc.) to trail; ~ **anchor**, trail anchor along the bottom, owing to force of wind or current. 2. Extend (conversation etc.) tediously. 3. Trail, go heavily; ~ **on**, continue tediously. 4. Search bottom of (water) with grapnels, nets, etc. (*for*). 5. Retard (wheel, vehicle) by applying a drag to it (see *n.* def. 3 below). **drag** *n.* 1. Rough sledge; large four-horse coach like stagecoach. 2. Net drawn over bottom of water to enclose all fish; (also **drag'net**, which also has fig. sense of systematic large-scale roundup of criminals); apparatus for dredging bottom of rivers or pools. 3. Iron brake for retarding vehicle downhill; obstruction to progress. 4. Strong smelling lure for hounds in lieu of fox; hunt with hounds following this. 5. Slow motion; impeded progress; (aeron.) atmospheric resistance. 6. (slang) Transvestite clothing; puff on a cigarette; boring thing or person; influence to get special privilege. 7. ~ **race**, race to determine car with fastest acceleration from a standstill; ~ **strip**, straight, short paved road or strip for drag races; **main** ~, main street.

drag·gle (drăg'el) *v.* (**-gled, -gling**). Make wet, limp, and dirty, by trailing; hang trailing.

drag·o·man (drăg'oman) *n.* (pl. **-mans, -men**). Interpreter (and guide), esp. in Arabic, Turkish, or Persian. [Arab. *tarjumān* interpreter]

drag·on (drăg'on) *n.* 1. Mythical monster like crocodile or snake with large claws, usu. winged, and often breathing fire. 2. (archaic) Large serpent. 3. Lizard of genus *Draco*, with broad winglike membrane on each flank. 4. **drag'on-fly** (pl. **-flies**), insect of order Odonata with long body, prominent eyes, and elaborately veined membranous wings usu. spread while resting, freq. brightly colored, and capable of rapid darting flight (also called "(devil's) darning needle").

dra·goon (dragōōn') *n.* Cavalryman, orig. of mounted 17th and 18th c. infantry armed with a kind of carbine called a *dragoon*, now of certain European cavalry regiments historically representing these. ~ *v.t.* Persecute, oppress; force *into* course by persecution. [Fr. *dragon* carbine, so named as breathing fire]

drain (drān) *v.* Draw (liquid) *off*, *away*, by conduit, drainpipes, etc.; drink (liquid), empty (vessel), to the dregs; dry (land etc.) by providing channels for the escape of the water in it; (of river) carry off superfluous water of (district); trickle *through*, flow gradually *away*; become rid of moisture by its gradual flowing away; **drain'pipe**, large pipe used for draining. **drain** *n.* Channel carrying off liquid, artificial conduit for water, sewage, etc.; (surg.) tube for drawing off discharge from abscess etc.; constant outlet, withdrawal, demand, or expenditure. **drain'er** *n.*

*The **dragonfly**, found in most parts of the world, is especially common in the tropics. It is probably the most powerful flying insect and flies at 60 m.p.h.*

*The **drawbridge** over the Wilamette River in Portland, Oregon. The raising and lowering requires immense power and equally strong stability from the supporting structure.*

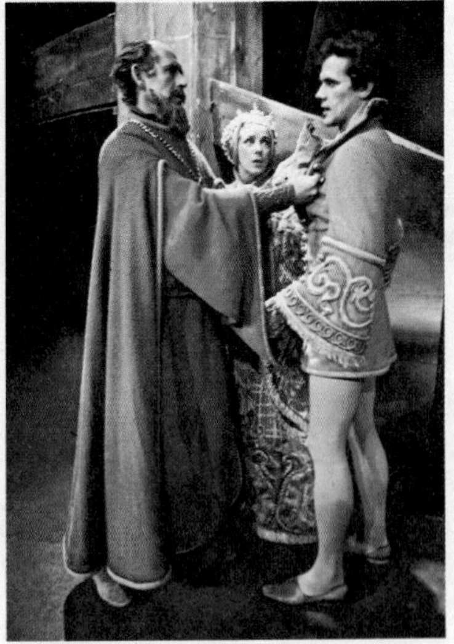

*English **drama** reached its height in Elizabethan times in the works of Shakespeare. Here Australian actors are taking part in a production of Richard II.*

drain·age (drā′nĭj) *n.* Draining; system of drains; what is drained off, sewage.

drake[1] (drāk) *n.* Mayfly of genus *Ephemera* used in fishing.

drake[2] (drāk) *n.* Male duck.

Drake (drāk), **Sir Francis** (1540?–96). English navigator, privateer, and admiral; plundered West Indies and W. coast of South Amer.; first Englishman to circumnavigate globe in his ship, *Golden Hind*; brought home first unsuccessful colonists from Virginia with potatoes and tobacco; commanded a division of English fleet which decisively defeated the Spanish Armada, 1588; **Drake Passage**, strait between Cape Horn and South Shetland Island connecting S. Atlantic and S. Pacific oceans.

dram (drăm) *n.* 1. One-sixteenth of an ounce. 2. (abbrev. dr.) Apothecaries' weight of 60 grains. 3. Small draft of liquor; bit.

dra·ma (drah′m*a*, drăm′*a*) *n.* Stage play, motion picture, or television program presenting story in dialogue; dramatic art, composition and presentation of plays; series of events having the unity and progress of a play and leading to final catastrophe or consummation.

Dram·a·mine (drăm′*a*mēn) *n.* (trademark) Antihistamine used to counteract motion sickness.

dra·mat·ic (dr*a*măt′ĭk) *adj.* Of, like, drama; theatrical; sudden, striking, impressive. **dra·mat′i·cal·ly** *adv.*

dram·a·tis per·so·nae (drăm′*a*tĭs pers*ō*′nē, drah′m*a*-). (List of) characters in a play.

dram·a·tist (drăm′*a*tĭst, drah′m*a*-) *n.* Writer of dramas or dramatic poetry.

dram·a·tize (drăm′*a*tīz, drah′m*a*-) *v.* (**-tized, -tiz·ing**). Convert (novel etc.) into play; admit of such conversion; impart dramatic character to. **dram·a·ti·za·tion** (drăm*a*tīzā′sh*o*n, drahm*a*-) *n.*

dram·a·turge (drăm′*a*tẽrj, drah′m*a*-), **dram·a·tur·gist** (drăm′*a*tẽrjĭst, drah′m*a*-) *ns.* Dramatist. **dram·a·tur·gic** (drăm*a*tẽr′jĭk, drahm*a*-) *adj.* **dram·a·tur·gy** (drăm′*a*tẽrjē, drah′m*a*-) *n.*

drape (drāp) *v.* (**draped, drap·ing**). Cover, hang, adorn, with cloth etc.; (of clothes, hangings etc.) arrange; hang in graceful folds. ~ *n.* Curtain; way in which cloth, clothes, etc. fall or hang. **drap′a·ble, drape′a·ble** *adjs.*

drap·er (drā′p*e*r) *n.* (Brit.) Retailer of cloth and piece goods. **dra′per·y** *n.* (pl. **-per·ies**). 1., Cloth, textile fabrics. 2. Arrangement of clothing in sculpture etc.; clothing or hangings disposed in folds.

dras·tic (drăs′tĭk) *adj.* Acting strongly, vigorous, violent. **dras′ti·cal·ly** *adv.*

drat (drăt) *int.* Curse. **drat′ted** *adj.*

draught (drăft) (chiefly Brit.) = DRAFT.

Dra·vid·i·an (dr*a*vĭd′ē*a*n) *adj.* & *n.* (Member) of a people of S. India and Ceylon (including Tamils and Kanarese); (of) any of the languages spoken by these people. **Dra·vid′ic** *adj.* [f. *Dravida*, old province of S. India]

draw (draw) *v.* (**drew, drawn, draw·ing**). 1. Pull; pull after one; contract, distort (features etc.); haul *in* (net); bend (bow); pull at; pull (curtain, drapes, blind) open or shut. 2. Attract, bring to one; take in; attract attention or custom; induce *to* do; be attracted, assemble, *around*, *together*, etc. 3. Extract; pull out (sword, handgun, or other weapon from sheath or holster); take out sword, handgun, etc.; pull or take one from a number of things so as to decide something by chance (esp. in ~ **lots** etc.); obtain by lot; haul up (water) from well; bring out (liquid, blood) from vessel, body; take, get, from a source; (also ~ **out**) encourage (person) to talk, reveal information,

*The principal element of **drawing** is the line. In recent times the line has been conceived of as an autonomous element of form, independent of representation, as in this study for the dirt cart by William Dobell, left. Below left, a Michelangelo drawing.*

etc.; deduce, infer; extract something from, empty, drain; disembowel; (cards) cause (trumps etc.) to be played. 4. Protract, stretch, elongate; make (wire) by pulling piece of metal through successively smaller holes; (naut., of sail) swell out with wind. 5. Trace, delineate, make (picture), represent (object), by drawing lines; use pencil, pen, etc. thus; describe in words; practice delineation; frame (document) in due form, compose; formulate, institute (comparisons, distinctions); write out (bill, check, draft, *on* bank etc.); make call *on* person, his faith, memory, etc., *for* money or service. 6. Make way, move, *toward*, *near*, *off*, etc.; (racing) get farther *away* to the front, come *level*, gain *on*. 7. (of ship) Require (a depth of water) to float. 8. End (game, battle) as a tie; (abs.) succeed in doing this. 9. ~ **back**, withdraw from undertaking; ~ **in**, entice, persuade to join; (of train or vehicle) = PULL in; ~ **off**, withdraw; ~ **on**, allure; approach, draw near; ~ **out**, lead out, detach, or array (as troops); prolong; elicit; induce to talk, reveal talent etc.; elongate; (of train or vehicle) = PULL out; ~ **up**, come up *with*, *to*; stop before finish line; bring (troops), come, into regular order; compose (documents etc.); ~ **oneself up**, assume stiff attitude. 10. **draw'string**, string that can be pulled to tighten mouth of bag, waist of garment, etc. **draw** *n.* Act of drawing, esp. pull; thing that draws business, attention, etc.; drawing of lots; raffle; drawn game; act of drawing a handgun from holster etc.

draw·back (draw'băk) *n.* 1. Refund, esp. as discount on taxes, duties, or price of goods or services for large or favored users. 2. Thing that qualifies satisfaction; disadvantage.

draw·bridge (draw'brĭj) *n.* Bridge across moat, river, etc., made to be raised, lowered, or moved to one side to prevent passage over it, or to be raised to permit passage of boat or ship.

draw·er (draw'er, drōr) *n.* 1. One who draws. 2. Box-shaped receptacle sliding in and out of special frame, or of table etc.; (pl.) chest of drawers. 3. (pl.) Underpants.

draw·ing (draw'ĭng) *n.* (esp.) Art of representing by line; delineation by means of pen or pencil or other pointed instrument; product of this, sketch; ~ **board**, board for

stretching drawing paper on; **on the ~ board**, undergoing preparation; incompletely designed; ~ **card**, entertainer etc. attracting large audience or many clients.

draw·ing (draw´ĭng) **room.** 1. Room for reception of company. 2. Private room on railroad train. [earlier *withdrawing room*]

drawl (drawl) *v.* Speak slowly, with prolonged or diphthongized vowels. ~ *n.* Regional accent of one who drawls; drawling, slow utterance. **drawl'ing·ly** *adv.*

drawn (drawn) *adj.*: see DRAW *v.*; (esp.) ~ **butter**, butter melted and clarified, often with herbs.

dray (drā) *n.* Low cart without sides for heavy loads; ~ **horse**, draft horse; **dray'man** (pl. **-men**), driver of dray.

dread (drĕd) *v.* Be in great fear of; shrink from, look forward to with terror; fear greatly; be afraid (*to* do). ~ *n.* Great fear; object of fear or awe. ~ *adj.* Greatly feared, dreadful.

dread·ful (drĕd´ful) *adj.* Terrible, awe-inspiring; troublesome, disagreeable; very bad; **penny ~**, (chiefly Brit.), cheap sensational story of crime and horror. **dread'ful·ly** *adv.* **dread'ful·ness** *n.*

dread·nought, dread·naught (drĕd´nawt) *ns.* Heavily armed battleship. [f. *D*~, name of first

*Nowadays, the wooden ox **dray** is more an historical piece than a useful farm implement. This dray can be seen in San Fernando de Espana Mission, California.*

such Brit. battleship, launched 1906]

dream (drēm) *n.* Train of thoughts, images, or fancies passing through mind during sleep; conscious indulgence of fancy, reverie; thing of dreamlike beauty, charm, goodness, etc. **dream'less, dream'like** *adjs.* **dream** *v.* (**dreamed** or **dreamt** pr. drĕmt, **dream·ing**). 1. Have visions etc. in sleep; see hear, etc., in sleep. 2. Imagine as in a dream; think possible; (with negative) so much as contemplate possibility *of*, have any conception *of*; ~ **up**, (colloq.) conceive, devise (idea or plan). 3. Fall into reverie; form imaginary visions of; be inactive or unpractical. **dream'er** *n.* (esp.) Impractical person.

dream·land (drēm´lănd) *n.* Ideal or imaginary land; utopia.

dream (drēm) **world.** 1. World of fantasy or illusion. 2. Condition of preoccupation with unworldly pursuits.

dream·y (drē´mē) *adj.* (**dream·i·er, dream·i·est**). 1. Full of dreams; given to reverie, fanciful, impractical; dreamlike, vague, misty. 2. (colloq.) Marvelous, wonderful. **dream'i·ly** *adv.* **dream'i·ness** *n.*

drear·y (drēr´ē) *adj.* (**drear·i·er, drear·i·est**). Dismal, gloomy, dull. **drear'i·ly** *adv.* **drear'i·ness** *n.*

dredge[1] (drĕj) *n.* Apparatus for bringing up oysters, specimens, etc., clearing out mud etc., from river or sea bottom, or obtaining ores from alluvial deposits. ~ *v.* (**dredged, dredg·ing**). Bring *up*, clear *away*, *out*, with dredge; clean out (harbor, river) with dredge; use dredge. **dredg'er**[1] *n.*

dredge[2] (drĕj) *v.t.* (**dredged, dredg·ing**). Sprinkle with flour or other powder; sprinkle (flour etc.) *over*. **dredg'er**[2] *n.* Box with perforated lid for sprinkling flour etc.

dreg (drĕg) *n.* (usu. pl.) Sediment, grounds, lees; worthless part, refuse.

Drei·ser (drī´zer, -ser), **Theodore (Herman Albert)** (1871–1945). Amer. novelist and editor; author of *An American Tragedy* etc.

drench (drĕnch) *n.* 1. Dose of medicine, esp. for animal. 2. Soaking; downpour. ~ *v.t.* 1. Force (animal) to take dose of medicine. 2. Steep, soak. 3. Wet all over with falling liquid.

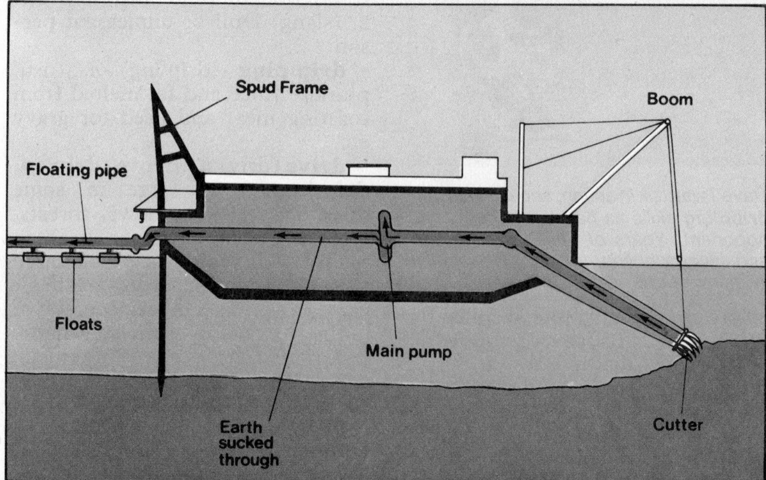

Mechanical ***dredgers*** *used for land reclamation and in mining minerals are of two types. One uses a bucket or ladder, the other (left center) a suction or hydraulic pump. Left: Tin dredge at work, Thailand.*

Dres·den (drĕz′den). City in East Germany on the Elbe; famous for Baroque architecture, art, and museums; almost totally destroyed by Allied air raids during World War II; ~ **china**, porcelain made near Dresden.

dress (drĕs) *n.* Clothing, esp. the visible part of it, costume; woman's gown; frock; external covering, outward form; **full** ~, that worn on formal occasions; **evening** ~, that worn at dinners or evening parties; **morning** ~, men's formal daytime wear; ~ **circle**: see CIRCLE *n.*; ~ **coat**, swallow-tailed coat for evening dress; **dress′maker**, woman who makes women's dresses, **dress′-making**, (*n*); **dress rehearsal**, final rehearsal, in costume, of play etc. **dress** *v.* 1. (mil.) Correct alignment of (companies etc. or men in line); come into correct place in line etc. 2. Array, clothe; provide oneself with clothes; put on one's clothes; put on evening dress; ~ **up**, clothe oneself, clothe elaborately or in masquerade. 3. Deck, adorn (ship with flags, store window with items for sale, etc.). 4. Treat (wound), apply dressing to. 5. Subject to cleansing, trimming, smoothing, etc; brush, comb, do up (hair); curry (horse, leather); finish surface of (textile fabrics, stone for building); prepare, cook (food); manure (ground), esp. in **top dressing**.

dres·sage (drĕsahzh′, dre-) *n.* Training of horse in obedience and deportment; execution by horse of precise movements in response to its rider.

dress·er[1] (drĕs′er) *n.* (esp.) Person who helps actor or actress to dress for part.

dress·er[2] (drĕs′er) *n.* Chest of drawers, esp, with mirror, in bedroom.

dress·ing (drĕs′ĭng) *n.* (esp.) 1. Seasoning, sauce, etc. used in cooking. 2. Stuffing for poultry etc. 3. Manure etc. spread over land. 4. Remedies, bandages, etc., with which wound is dressed. 5. ~ **down**, scolding; ~ **gown**, garment worn while making toilet or in dishabille; ~ **room**, room for dressing, applying make-up, etc., in home or theater; ~ **table**, table with mirror, drawers, etc., for use while dressing.

Dresden, *the most beautiful baroque city in Germany, was destroyed by air raids during the 1939–45 war. Much has been rebuilt, including this wooden bridge leading to the Crown Gate.*

dress·y (drĕs′ē) *adj.* (**dress·i·er, dress·i·est**). Fond of, smart in, dress; (of clothes) stylish; elaborate. **dress′i·ness** *n.*

drib·ble (drĭb′el) *v.* (**-bled, -bling**). 1. Flow, let flow, in drops or trickling stream; drool, slobber. 2. (basketball, soccer, etc.) Work (ball) forward with series of short bounces, kicks, etc. ~ *n.* Small trickling or barely continuous stream; act of dribbling.

drib·let (drĭb′lĭt) *n.* Small amount or portion.

dried (drīd) *adj.*: see DRY *v.*; (esp., of food) with moisture removed as method of preservation.

dri·er (drī′*er*) *n.* Substance mixed with oil paints to expedite drying; dryer.

drift (drĭft) *n.* 1. Being driven by current; slow course or current; ship's deviation from course due to currents; aircraft's deviation due to wind etc. 2. Natural or unperceived progress, tendency. 3. Purpose, meaning (as in the ~ **of an argument** etc.), tenor, scope. 4. Shower, driving mass; accumulation of snow, sand, etc. heaped up by wind. 5. (geol.) Anything transported and deposited by wind, water, or ice, esp. rock debris left by a glacier. 6. (mining) Horizontal passage following vein of mineral. 7. ~ **anchor**, floating frame keeping ship's head to wind in gale or when dismasted; ~ **ice**, detached drifting pieces of ice; ~ **net**, large net for catching fish, extended by weights at bottom and floats at top and allowed to drift with tide; **drift′wood**, wood drifting on, or cast ashore by, water. **drift** *v.* Be carried by or as by current of air or water; (of current) carry; go passively or aimlessly; pile, be piled by wind, into drifts, cover with drifts.

Dave Twardzik in action, showing his deft ***dribbling*** *skills as he tries to outwit his opponent. Years of hard work go into acquiring dribbling, a ball skill essential in many sports.*

drift·er (drĭf′t*er*) *n.* 1. (esp.) Vagabond, vagrant; person who drifts from place to place, job to job, etc. 2. Boat used in fishing with drift net.

drill[1] (drĭl) *n.* 1. Contrivance (steel tool, machine, etc.) for boring holes in metal, stone, sinking oil-wells, etc; ~ **press**, drilling machine used primarily on metals. 2. Shellfish that bores into shells of oysters. 3. Military exercise or training, hence, **drill′master**; rigorous discipline, exact routine. **drill** *v.* 1. Bore with drill etc. 2. Train in, perform, military movements and exercise; train rigorously and exactly; impart (knowledge etc.) by training in memorizing, repetition, etc. **drill′er** *n.*

drill[2] (drĭl) *n.* 1. Small furrow, ridge, for sowing seed in; row of plants sown in it. 2. Machine for sowing seed in drills. ~ *v.t.* Sow (seed) in rows; plant (ground) in drills.

dri·ly (drī′lē) *adv.* Var. of DRYLY.

drink (drĭngk) *v.* (**drank, drunk** or **drank, drink·ing**). 1. Take (liquid) through mouth and throat into stomach, swallow; swallow contents of (cup etc.); swallow liquid; (of plants, porous substances, etc.) absorb (moisture). 2. Take *in*, esp. with eyes or ears, with eager delight. 3. Drink alcoholic liquor; indulge in alcohol to excess, tipple; honor (toast etc.) by drinking *to*; ~ **to**, pledge, toast. **drink** *n.* Liquid drunk; beverage; intoxicating liquor; excessive indulgence in this, intemperance; glass or portion of liquor; **the** ~, (slang) the sea. **drink′er** *n.*

drink·a·ble (drĭng′k*a*bel) *adj.* Fit to drink.

drip (drĭp) *v.* (**dripped** or **dript, drip·ping**). Fall, let fall, in drops; let drops fall, be so wet as to shed drops; ~ **coffee**, coffee made by allowing boiling water to drip slowly through finely ground coffee beans; ~**-dry**, (of fabric, clothes) that will dry when hung up to drip, without wringing or ironing; ~ **grind**, fine-ground coffee beans for drip coffee. **drip** *n.* 1. Act of dripping; dripping liquid; (med.) continuous slow introduction of fluid into vein etc. 2. (slang) Dull or unpleasant person.

drip·ping (drĭp′ĭng) *n.* (usu. plural) Juice and fat melted from roasting meat and used for gravy etc.

drive (drīv) *v.* (**drove, driv·en, driv·ing**). 1. Urge in some direction, esp. by blows, threats, violence, etc.; chase or frighten (game, wild beasts, etc.) from large area into small in order to kill or capture. 2. Direct course of (animal drawing vehicle, vehicle, locomotive, etc.); convey in vehicle; act as driver of vehicle; travel in car at one's disposal; ~**-in**, (bank, restaurant, etc.) that can be used without alighting from car. 3. Impel forcibly, compel. 4. Cause to move, carry along, throw, propel, send, (thing) in some direction; (golf) strike (ball), strike ball with driver; force (stake, nail, etc.) *into* ground etc. with blow. 5. Bore (tunnel, horizontal cavity). 6. Aim blow or missile (*at*). 7. (of steam or other power) Set or keep (machinery) going. 8. Strive energetically toward objective; work hard. 9. Move along impelled by current, wind, etc.; ~ **at**, have for one's aim; allude to. **drive** *n.* 1. Excursion in vehicle. 2. Driving of game, enemy, etc. 3. Forcible blow, stroke, or hit at baseball etc. (in baseball also **line** ~); (golf) hit made with a driver. 4. Energy, push; energetic campaign. 5. (psychol.) Inner urge, motive principle. 6. Driving part of machinery; transmission of power to wheels of vehicle esp. through ~ **shaft**. 7. (also **drive′way**) Private road to house, garage, etc.

driv·el (drĭv′el) *n.* Silly nonsense, twaddle. ~ *v.i.* (**-eled, -el·ing** or **-elled, -el·ling**). Run at mouth or nose like child; talk childishly or idiotically. **driv′el·er, driv′el·ler** *ns.*

driv·er (drī′v*er*) *n.* 1. One who drives; ~**'s seat**, seat for driver;

(fig.) position of power. 2. (golf) Wooden-headed club (also called number 1 wood) used to send ball a long distance, esp. from tee.

drive (drīv) **wheel.** Wheel communicating motion to other wheels in machinery; large wheel of locomotive, to which power is transmitted through connecting rod to crank; wheel of vehicle to which driving power is applied.

driz·zle (drĭz′*el*) *v.i.* (**-zled, -zling**) & *n.* Rain in fine, dense, spraylike drops. **driz′zly** *adj.*

drogue (drōg) *n.* 1. Canvas cone open at both ends with a hoop at larger end, used as sea anchor; lighter form of this towed by aircraft to serve for target practice. 2. Parachute or cone used to reduce speed of aircraft etc.

droll (drōl) *adj.* Whimsically amusing; amusingly odd. **drol′ly** *adv.* **droll′ness** *n.* **droll′er·y** *n.* Droll action(s) or humor.

drom·e·dar·y (drŏm′*e*dĕrē, drŭm′-) *n.* (pl. **-dar·ies**). One-humped domesticated camel, used as beast of burden in N. Africa etc.; also called "Arabian camel."

drone (drōn) *n.* 1. Male of honey bee, which does not work; lazy idler, sluggard. 2. Continued deep monotonous sound, as of humming or buzzing. 3. Open bass pipe of bagpipe, emitting one continuous tone; tone emitted by this. ~ *v.* (**droned, dron·ing**). Buzz like bee or bagpipe; talk, utter, monotonously.

drool (drōōl) *v.i.* & *n.* Drivel; (show) excessive pleasure; water at the mouth, as in expectation of pleasure.

droop (drōōp) *v.* Hang down, incline, as from weariness or exhaustion; (of eyes) be turned down, with lowered eyelids; languish, flag; become dejected, lose heart; let (head, eyes, etc.) droop. ~ *n.* Drooping attitude; loss of spirit, fall of tone. **droop′y** *adj.* (**droop·i·er, droop·i·est**). **droop′i·ness** *n.*

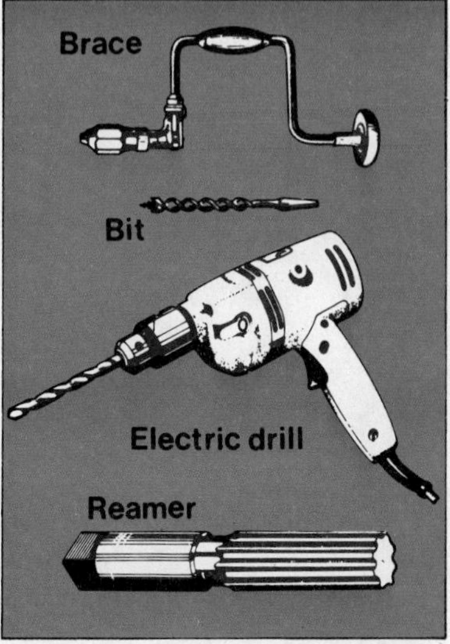

Hand drills *with bits are used by carpenters and workers in light materials. The small electric-powered hand drill has largely replaced the type rotated by hand.*

drop (drŏp) *n.* 1. Small quantity of liquid that falls, hangs, trickles down, or detaches itself in spherical or pear-shaped form; teardrop, drop of rain, blood, dew, etc.; very small quantity, esp. small quantity of drink; (pl.) medicinal preparation to be administered in drops. 2. Candy lozenge. 3. Fall, dropping, descent; abrupt fall in level of surface; depth to which anything sinks; distance through which anything falls; **~-off**, steep descent, cliff; a decline; **~-off charge**, extra fee for returning (esp.) a rented car at a depot other than that at which it was rented. 4. Curtain let down before stage between acts or scenes of play etc. (also ~ **curtain**). 5. Trapdoor on gallows, which is let fall from under feet of person to be hanged. 6. Slot through which something is deposited, as mail; repository. 7. Material, persons, etc., dropped by parachute. **drop** *v.* (**dropped** or **dropt, drop·ping**). 1. Fall in drops; give off drops, drip; fall vertically, like a single drop; descend abruptly; fall, sink to ground. 2. Cease, lapse, fall through; fall in direction, amount, degree, etc. 3. Allow oneself to fall *behind, to the rear*, etc. 4. Come down *on* forcibly. 5. Let fall, shed, in drops; let fall like a drop or drops; let fall (words etc.) casually; send (letter etc.); (of animals) give birth to (young); (slang) lose, part with (money). 6. Fell, bring down, with blow, shot, etc. 7. Set down, from ship or vehicle. 8. Omit (esp., letter etc. in pronunciation). 9. Let droop; lower (voice). 10. Break off acquaintance or association with; ~ **in**, (esp.) pay casual visit; ~ **off**, (esp.) fall asleep; become less numerous etc.; ~ **out**, (esp.) withdraw. 11. ~ **kick**, (football) kick made by dropping ball and kicking it as it begins to bounce; **drop′-out**, one who withdraws from course of study, conventional way of life, etc.

drop·let (drŏp′lĭt) *n.* Little drop.

drop·per (drŏp′*er*) *n.* Device for administering liquid in drops; also

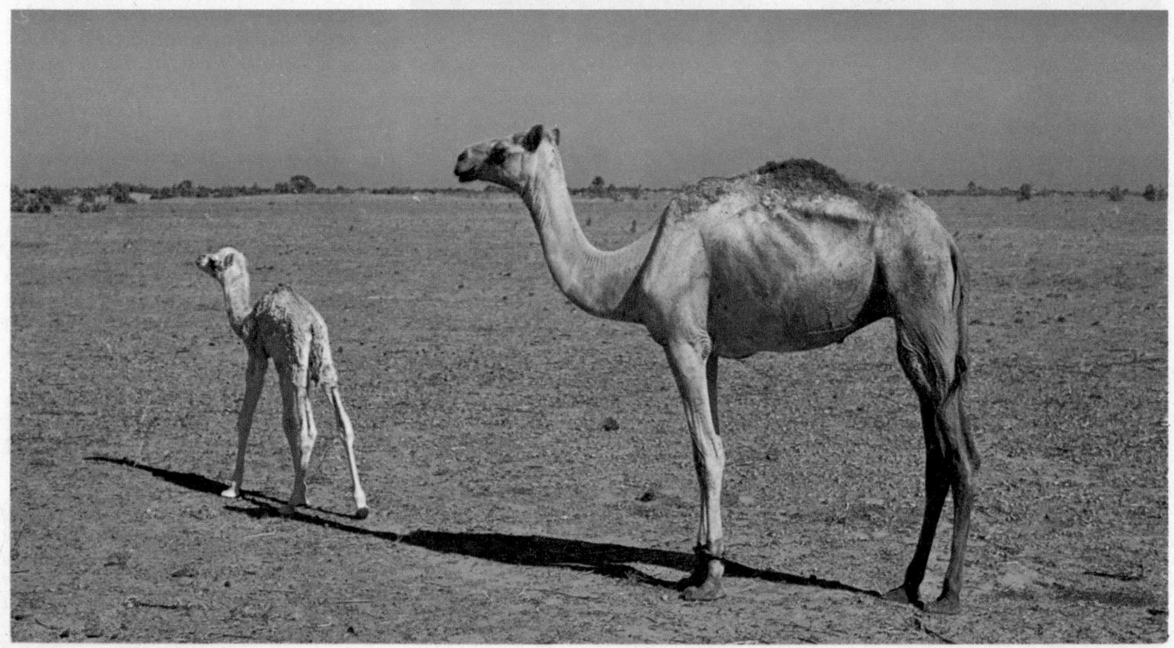

Dromedary *with its young. It is a one-humped variety of camel used in the African and Arabian deserts to carry burdens or for riding. It is a swift traveller.*

called **eye′dropper, medicine dropper**.

drop·ping (drŏp′ĭng) *n.* That which drops or falls in drops, as melted wax, etc.; (pl.) dung of animals or birds.

drop·sy (drŏp′sē) *n.* Accumulation of watery fluid in serous cavities or connective tissues of body. **drop′si·cal, drop′sied** *adjs.*

drosh·ky (drŏsh′kē, drawsh′-) *n.* (pl. **-kies**). Russian low four-wheeled open carriage.

dro·soph·i·la (drosŏf′ĭla) *n.* (pl. **-las, -lae** pr. -lē). Fruit fly of genus *D*~, much used in genetic research.

dross (draws, drŏs) *n.* Scum thrown off from metal in melting; foreign matter mixed with any substance; worthless stuff, refuse, rubbish. **dross′y** *adj.* (**dross·i·er, dross·i·est**). **dross′i·ness** *n.*

drought (drowt), **drouth** (drowth) *ns.* Continuous dry weather, lack of rain; dearth, scarcity.

drove (drōv) *n.* 1. Herd, flock, being driven or moving together; crowd, multitude, large number. 2. Mason's broad-faced chisel.

drov·er (drō′ver) *n.* One who drives cattle or sheep in droves to market; cattle dealer.

drown (drown) *v.* Suffocate by submersion, flood, drench; overcome (grief etc.) with or in drink; overpower (sound) by greater loudness.

drowse (drowz) *v.* (**drowsed, drows·ing**). Doze; be half asleep; pass *away* (time etc.) in drowsing. ~ *n.* Half-asleep condition.

drow·sy (drow′zē) *adj.* (**-si·er, -si·est**). Heavy with sleepiness; half asleep; soporific; sluggish, lethargic. **drow′si·ly** *adv.* **drow′si·ness** *n.*

drub (drŭb) *v.t.* (**drubbed, drub·bing**). Cudgel, thrash, belabor; defeat decisively. **drub′bing, drub′ber** *ns.*

drudge (drŭj) *n.* Servile worker, slave, hack; hard toiler. ~ *v.i.* (**drudged, drudg·ing**). Perform mean or servile tasks; work hard or laboriously, toil. **drudg′er·y** *n.* (pl. **-er·ies**).

drug (drŭg) *n.* Medicinal substance; (esp.) narcotic; (also **dangerous ~, hard ~**) one that causes euphoria in the taker and predisposes him to addiction, esp. preparation or extract of opium or coca; ~ **addict**, person addicted to one of these; ~ **on the market**, commodity no longer in demand, unsalable thing; **drug′store**, store where prescribed drugs are dispensed and where medicines, toilet articles, stationery, newspapers, light refreshments, etc. are sold; **drug traffic**, commercial sale of drugs, forbidden by law. **drug** *v.t.* (**drugged, drug·ging**). Administer drug, esp. narcotic, to; add drug to (food or drink).

drug·gist (drŭg′ĭst) *n.* Pharmacist.

dru·id, Dru·id (drōō′ĭd) *ns.* (fem. **-id·ess** pr. -ĭdĭs). One of an order of priests among the Celts in ancient Gaul and Britain who appear in Irish and Welsh legend as magicians. **dru·id·ic** (drōōĭd′ĭk) *adj.* **dru′id·ism** *n.* Religious system of Druids.

drum (drŭm) *n.* 1. Percussive musical instrument consisting of hollow cylindrical or hemispherical frame with tightly stretched mem-

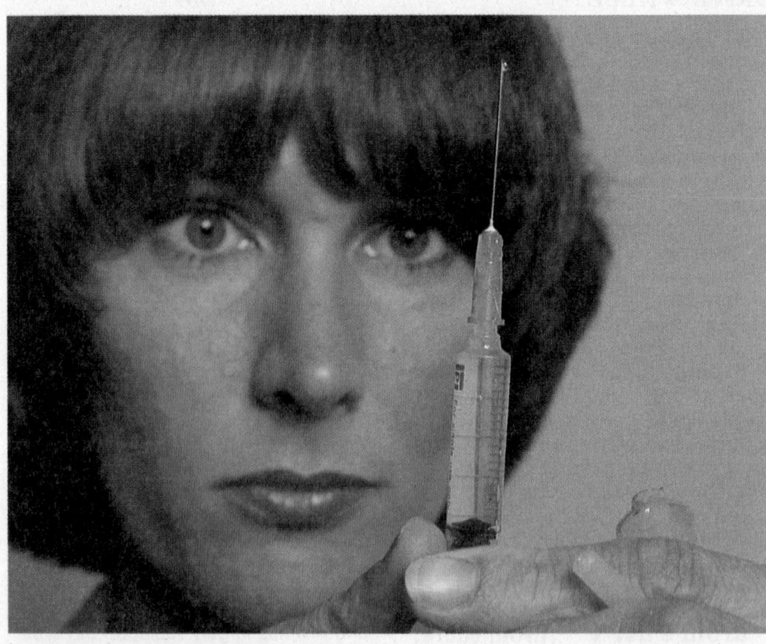

***Drugs** are used in treating, preventing and diagnosing diseases. A nurse is shown expelling air from a syringe prior to administering a drug by injection.*

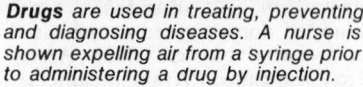

*The **drosophila** or fruit-fly is often used in scientific experiments on breeding because of its speed of reproduction and its four large paired chromosomes.*

***Drought** is the most serious physical hazard to agriculture in most parts of the world. This skull is of an animal killed by drought. Efforts to make rain by seeding clouds have had only limited success.*

The ***drum,*** *essential to most orchestras and jazz bands (right), is still widely associated with magic in some societies. Above: The Embu tribesmen from Mount Kenya use it as an accompaniment to ritualistic dances. The drum is also associated with military music.*

brane at one or both ends, which is struck to produce sound; sound of this; **bass ~**, large drum with 2 heads struck sideways simultaneously to make a loud, low sound; **ket'tledrum**, cauldron-shaped drum that can be tuned to produce note of definite pitch. 2. Drum-shaped thing, as cylinder wound with cable, wire, etc; barrel-like metal receptacle for oil etc.; (archit.) solid part of Corinthian and composite capitals; block of stone forming one section of shaft of column; cylindrical structure supporting dome. 3. = *drumfish* (see def. 4 below). 4. **drum'beat,** sound of a drum; **drum'fire,** rapid heavy gunfire; **drum'fish,** any of various Amer. fishes (*Sciaenops ocellata, Pogonias cromis,* etc.) making a drumming noise; see CROAKER. **drum'head,** stretched skin or membrane of drum; circular top of capstan, into which capstan bars are fixed; **drumhead court-martial**, court-martial (hist. held around an upturned drum) for summary treatment of offenses during military operations; **drum major,** person who leads marching band; **drum majorette**, girl or woman accompanying marching band and twirling baton etc.; **drum'stick,** stick often with padded knob at one end for beating drum; lower part of leg of cooked poultry, so called from its shape. **drum** *v.* (**drummed, drum·ming**). 1. Play the drum; beat, tap, or thump, continuously on something; (of bird, insect) make loud hollow noise with quivering wings. 2. Summon, beat *up*, as by drumming; (colloq.) obtain (custom, customers) by canvassing etc.; solicit orders; drive *out* of regiment etc. publicly by beat of drum, so as to heighten disgrace; din *into* (person). **drum'mer** *n.* 1. Player of drum. 2. Traveling salesman.

drunk (drŭngk) *adj.:* see DRINK *v.*; (esp.) intoxicated. ~ *n.* Drinking bout; drunken person; alcoholic. **drunk'ard** *n.* Sot; habitually drunken person. **drunk'en** *adj.* Often drunk; caused by or exhibiting drunkenness. **drunk'en·ly** *adv.* **drunk'en·ness** *n.*

drupe (dro͞op) *n.* Fleshy or pulpy fruit having single hard stone, as peach, plum, cherry. **dru·pa·ceous** (dro͞opā'shus) *adj.* Bearing drupes.

Druse (dro͞oz) *n.* Member of Muslim political and religious sect in Syria and Lebanon, believing in transmigration, and holding the 6th Fatimate Caliph, Hakim Biamrillahi, to be a divine incarnation. [Arab *durūz*, prob. f. *Isma'īl al-Darazī* (the tailor), their founder]

dry (drī) *adj.* (**dri·er, dri·est**). 1. Free from moisture, not wet or moist; deficient in rain, not rainy; dried, desiccated, parched; thirsty, causing thirst; not yielding water etc., (of cows etc.) not yielding milk. 2. Not under, in, or on water; not submerged. 3. (of bread etc.) Without butter or the like. 4. Solid, not liquid; (of measures etc.) relating to non-liquids. 5. (of wines etc.) Not sweet or fruity. 6. Favoring or enforcing prohibition of alcoholic liquor. 7. Feeling or showing no emotion; stiff, cold; caustically witty; uttered in, using, matter-of-fact tones without air of pleasantry. 8. ~ **battery**, battery consisting of dry cells; ~**-bulb thermometer**, one of a pair of thermometers in hygrometer of which one has dry and other wet bulb; ~**cell**, (electr.) voltaic cell whose contents are made non-spillable by use of some absorbent substance or having electrolyte in form of moist paste; ~**-clean** (*v.t.*) clean (clothes etc.) with chemical solvent having no or little water; ~ **cleaner**, shop that dry-cleans; ~ **dock**: see DOCK[3]; ~ **farming**, various methods of arable farming designed to conserve moisture in dry areas: ~ **fly**, (angling) artificial fly resting lightly on water; ~ **goods**, clothing, textiles, and related articles of trade; **D ~ Ice**, (trademark) solid carbon dioxide, which passes directly from a solid to a gas at −78.5°C., absorbing a great amount of heat, making it useful as refrigerant; ~ **measure**, system of units for measuring dry quantities, esp. for grain, fruits, etc.; ~ **plate**, (photog.) sensitized plate that does not require immersion before exposure; **dry'point**, strong pointed tool for scratching design (without use of acid) on copper plate from which prints are taken; process of engraving thus, print so produced; ~ **rot**, decayed condition, caused by various fungi, of unventilated timber, in which it becomes dry, light, and friable; ~ **run**, (colloq.) rehearsal; (mil.) practice exercise without ammunition; ~ **spell**, period of little or no rain; ~ **wall**, (stone) wall without mortar; **dry'wall** (*n.* & *adj.*), (of) wall construction with plasterboard, plywood, etc., without plaster; **dry well**, drainage hole filled with loose stones, for collecting and dispersing rainwater etc. **dry·a·ble** *adj.* **dry'ly, dri'ly** *advs.* **dry'ness** *n.* **dry** *v.* (**dried, dry·-ing**). Make or become dry by wiping, evaporation, draining, etc.; ~ **up**, make, become, utterly dry; cease to yield water or milk; (slang) cease talking.

dry·ad (drī'ăd) *n.* (pl. **-ads, -a·des** pr. *-adēz*). Wood-nymph.

Dry·den (drī'*d*en), **John** (1631–1700). English poet, dramatist, critic; translator of Virgil, Horace, Ovid, etc.

dry·er (drī'*er*) *n.* Thing, person that dries, esp. appliance to dry clothers, hair, etc.; drier.

D.S.C., DSC *abbrevs.* Distinguished Service Cross.

D.S.M., DSM *abbrevs.* Distinguished Service Medal.

DST *abbrev.* Daylight-saving time.

d.t., d.t.'s *abbrevs.* Delirium tremens.

Du. *abbrev.* Dutch.

du·al (dōō'*a*l, dū'-) *adj.* Of two; twofold, divided in two; double; having a double nature or character. **du·al·i·ty** (dōōăl'ĭtē, dū-) *n.*

du·al·ism (dōō'*a*lĭzem, dū'-) *n.* 1. Being dual. 2. Theory or system of thought recognizing two independent principles; (philos.) doctrine that mind and matter exist as distinct entities (opp. MONISM and PLURALISM); doctrine that there are two independent principles, good and evil. **du'al·ist** *n.* & *adj.* **du·al·is·tic** (dōō*a*lĭs'tĭk, dū-) *adj.*

dub[1] (dŭb) *v.t.* (**dubbed, dub·-bing**). 1. Make (person) into *a knight* by striking shoulder with sword. 2. Invest with (new title); name, nickname. 3. Smear leather with grease. 4. (golf) Hit a ball ineffectually. ~ *n.* (esp.) Poor golfer; clumsy person.

dub[2] (dŭb) *v.t.* (**dubbed, dub·-ing**). Add sound effects or new

*Typical **drupes,** or fleshy fruits with one or more seeds each surrounded by a hard layer, are cherries and walnuts. In raspberries small drupes are clustered together.*

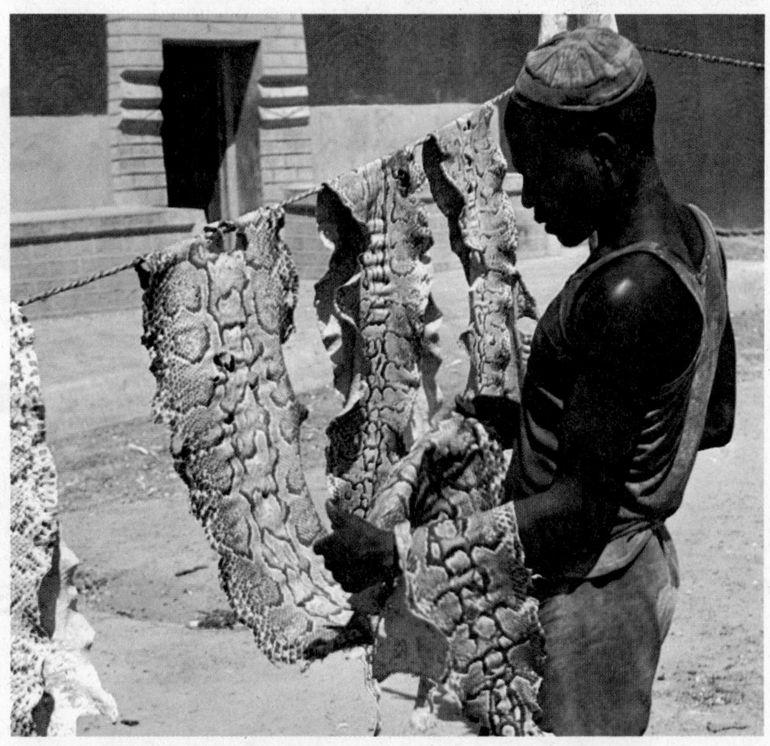

*The **drying** of snake or crocodile skins in Nigeria is achieved by simply exposing the skin to the sun's heat. The dried skins are then despatched for manufacture into handbags, shoes etc.*

sound track, esp. in a different language, to (film); insert (sound effects) *in* film or radio or television production.

du·bi·e·ty (do͞obī′etē, dū-) *n.* (pl. **-ties**). Feeling of doubt.

du·bi·ous (do͞o′bēus, dū′-) *adj.* Doubtful; of questionable or suspected character. **du′bi·ous·ly** *adv.* **du′bi·ous·ness** *n.*

Dub·lin (dŭb′lĭn). Capital of the Republic of Ireland, port on the Irish Sea; formerly capital of all Ireland.

Du Bois (do͞o bois′), **W(illiam) E(dward) B(urghardt)** (1868–1963). Amer. sociologist, educator and writer; a founder of the NAACP, 1910.

Du·brov·nik (do͞obrawv′nĭk). Port city and resort on Dalmatian coast of Yugoslavia.

Du·buf·fet (dübüfĕ′), **Jean** (1901–). French sculptor and painter.

du·cal (do͞o′kal, dū′-) *adj.* Of, like, bearing title of, duke.

duc·at (dŭk′ĭt) *n.* (hist.) Gold coin of varying value formerly current in most European countries; (hist.) Italian silver coin; (colloq.) coin, (pl.) cash.

Duc·cio di Buo·nin·se·gna (do͞ot′chaw dē bwawnĕnsĕ′nyah) (1255?–1319). Ital. painter and founder of the Sienese school.

duch·ess (dŭch′ĭs) *n.* Wife or widow of duke; lady holding title to a duchy in her own right.

duch·y (dŭch′ē) *n.* (pl. **duch·ies**). Territory of reigning duke or duchess.

duck[1] (dŭk) *n.* (pl. **ducks**, collect. **duck**). 1. Any of several kinds of swimming bird of the family Anatidae found all over the world, esp. domesticated form of mallard or wild duck; female of this (male being DRAKE[2]); flesh of this bird. 2. **dead ~**, person or cause certain to fail; **lame ~**, elected official completing remaining term after an election in which he was not reelected; **~s and drakes**, game of making flat stone skip over surface of water; **duck′bill, ~-billed platypus**: see PLATYPUS; **duck′board**, narrow path of wooden slats laid on muddy ground; **duck′pin**, short bowling pin; **duck soup**, (slang) easy task; **duck′weed**, any plant of genus *Lemna*, floating on still water and covering surface like a green carpet.

duck[2] (dŭk) *n.* Strong untwilled linen or cotton fabric for clothing, sails, etc.; (pl.) clothing, esp. trousers of this.

duck[3] (dŭk) *v.* Plunge, dive, dip head, under water and emerge; bend quickly, bob, to avoid blow etc; plunge (person) momentarily *in, under* water; lower (head) suddenly. **~** *n.* Quick dip below water in bathing; lowering of head.

duck·ing (dŭk′ĭng) *n.* Immersion in water, or wetting by submersion; **~ stool**, chair in which scolds, dishonest tradesmen, etc., were tied and ducked in water as a punishment.

duck·ling (dŭk′lĭng) *n.* Young duck; **ugly ~**: see UGLY.

duct (dŭkt) *n.* Conduit, tube, for conveying liquid; conduit for electric cable; (physiol.) tube or canal conveying secretions or lymph in animal body; (bot.) vessel of plant's vascular tissue holding air, water, etc. **duct′less** *adj.* (of gland) Having no ducts, containing secretion that passes directly from cells to blood; endocrine. **duct** *v.t.* Convey through a duct.

duc·tile (dŭk′tĭl, -tīl) *adj.* 1. (of metal) Malleable, flexible, not brittle; (tech.) capable of being drawn into wire, tough. 2. Plastic; pliable, pliant. **duc·til·i·ty** (dŭktĭl′ĭtē) *n.*

dud (dŭd) *n.* 1. (slang) (pl.) Clothes. 2. Shell etc. that fails to explode; futile plan or person.

dude (do͞od, dūd) *n.* (slang) Exaggeratedly fastidious or foppish person; dandy, swell; (also) any male; **~ ranch**, cattle ranch converted into resort for visitors, with facilities for riding etc.

dudg·eon (dŭj′on) *n.* (usu. **high ~**) Resentment, feeling of offense.

due (do͞o, dū) *adj.* 1. Owing, payable, as a debt or obligation; that ought to be given or rendered (*to*); fitting, proper, rightful. 2. To be ascribed or attributed *to* (cause, agent, etc.). 3. Under engagement or contract to be ready, be present, or arrive (at defined time). **~** *adv.* (with ref. to points of compass) Straight, exactly, directly. **~** *n.* 1. Person's right, what is owed him; what one owes. 2. (usu. pl.) Fee or charge for membership, as in a club, etc.; **pay one's ~s**, (slang) gain experience through trouble.

du·el (do͞o′el, dū′-) *n.* Fight with deadly weapons between two persons, in presence of two observers (*seconds*), to settle quarrel; any contest between two parties, persons,

*Some of the many species of **duck** have considerable commercial value. The eider duck, which breeds in Iceland and Scotland, is raised for its down, and ducks have been reared for food for hundreds of years.*

animals, causes. ~ *v.i.* (**-eled, -el·ing** or **-elled, -el·ling**). Fight duel. **du'el·ist, du'el·er** *ns.*

du·en·na (dōōĕn'*a*, dū-) *n.* Older woman acting as governess and chaperon to girl(s) (orig. and esp. in Spanish family); chaperon.

du·et (dōōĕt', dū-) *n.* (mus.) (Composition for) two voices or instruments.

duf·fel, duf·fle (dŭf'*el*) *ns.* Coarse woolen cloth with thick nap; camper's change of clothes or personal effects; ~ **bag**, cylindrical canvas bag; ~ **coat**, coat made of duffel, esp. one with hood and toggle fastenings. [f. *Duffel* in Brabant]

duf·fer (dŭf'*er*) *n.* (colloq.) Inefficient or stupid person, novice, beginner.

dug (dŭg) *n.* Udder, breast, or teat of female mammal.

du·gong (dōō'gŏng) *n.* Large aquatic herbivorous mammal, *D~ dugon*, of tropical Asian coasts. [Malay *duyong*]

dug·out (dŭg'owt) *adj.* Hollowed out by digging. ~ *n.* 1. Canoe made of hollowed out tree trunk. 2. Underground shelter esp. for troops in trenches. 3. Roofed, sunken shelter at side of baseball field for players not on the field.

dui·ker (dī'*ker*) *n.* (pl. **-kers**, collect. **-ker**). Small African antelope (genus *Cephalophus*) with short backward-pointing horns; so called from its habit of diving suddenly into the bush. [Du. *duiker* diver]

duke (dōōk, dūk) *n.* 1. In Gt. Britain and some other countries, hereditary noble ranking next below prince; **royal** ~, duke who

The Carolina **wood duck** is one of the most brilliantly colored of all ducks. The white markings highlight and accentuate the duck's lines and features.

is a member of royal family, taking precedence of other dukes. 2. In some parts of Europe, sovereign prince, ruler of duchy. 3. (slang) Hand, fist. **duke'dom** *n.* Duchy; office or dignity of duke.

Du·kho·bors (dōō'kōbŏrz), **Du·kho·bor·tsy** (dōōkōbŏrt'sē) *ns.pl.* Members of a Russian Christian sect who rejected authority of church and state, were persecuted for refusing to pay taxes or perform military service, and migrated to Saskatchewan and British Columbia, Canada, in 1899.

The **duiker** or duikerbok is a small antelope that inhabits forest and brush country in Africa. It has a habit of diving into and threading its way through thick bush.

[Russ., = "spirit wrestler"]

dul·cet (dŭl'sĭt) *adj.* Sweet, soothing (esp. of sounds).

dul·ci·mer (dŭl'sim*er*) *n.* Musical instrument in which metallic strings of graduated length are stretched over a trapezoidal sounding board and struck with hammers held in the hands; similar folk instrument played by plucking strings.

dull (dŭl) *adj.* 1. Slow of understanding, stupid; lacking sensibility or keenness of perception; (of pain etc.) not keen or intense. 2. Slow, heavy, drowsy; stagnant, sluggish; listless, not lively or cheerful, depressed; causing depression or boredom. 3. Not sharp or keen; not clear, vivid, or intense; obscure, muffled, flat, insipid; (of weather) overcast, gloomy. ~ *v.* Make or become dull, sluggish, inert, etc.; blunt; make or become dim or indistinct. **dull'ard** *n.* Dull or stupid person, dunce. **dul'ly** *adv.* **dull'ness, dul'ness** *ns.*

dulse (dŭls) *n.* Edible species of reddish-brown seaweed (*Rhodymenia palmata*).

du·ly (dōō'lē, dū'-) *adv.* Rightly, properly, fitly; sufficiently; punctually.

Du·mas (dōōmah', dū-), **Alexandre.** (1) "Dumas *père*" (1802–70), French dramatist and prolific writer of swashbuckling historical novels including *The Three Musketeers*, *The Count of Monte Cristo*; (2) "Dumas *fils*," his natural son **Alexandre** (1824–95), French dramatist, author of *La Dame aux Camélias* etc.

dumb (dŭm) *adj.* 1. Destitute

of faculty of speech. 2. Temporarily bereft of speech from astonishment, shock, etc.; remaining persistently silent; refusing to speak. 3. (of actions) Not attended with speech. 4. Not emitting or attended with sound; silent, mute; not having some quality, property, etc., usual in things of the name. 5. Foolish, stupid (prob. after Ger. *dumm*). 6. **dumb′bell**, short bar with heavy knob at each end, used in pairs for exercising muscles; object of this shape; **dumb cluck**, (slang) stupid person; **dumb show**, pantomime; communication by gestures; **dumb′waiter**, small elevator for conveying food etc. between floors. **dumb′ly** *adv*. **dumb′ness** *n*.

dum·dum (dŭm′dŭm) *n*. (also ~ **bullet**) Soft-nosed bullet that expands on impact. [*Dum-Dum*, town and arsenal near Calcutta]

dum·found, dumb·found (dŭm′fownd′) *vbs.t.* Strike dumb, confound, nonplus.

dum·my (dŭm′ē) *n*. (pl. **-mies**). 1. (bridge) Hand turned up and played by declarer; person holding this hand. 2. Person taking no real part, or present only for show, figurehead, mere tool; ~ **corporation**, corporation set up to mask real aims (usu. illegal or unethical) of its promoters. 3. Counterfeit object, sham package, etc. 4. Man's figure used as target; manikin; imitation ammunition used in training. 5. (colloq.) Stupid person. ~ *adj*. That is a dummy, sham.

*Sand **dunes** are most commonly found in deserts and on sea coasts. They may range in height from a few feet to more than 300 feet, particularly, as here, in the Sahara Desert.*

dump (dŭmp) *n*. Rubbish heap, place where garbage or refuse is deposited; temporary depot, pile, of ammunition, equipment, etc.; (colloq.) unpleasant or dreary place; (pl. colloq.) low spirits. ~ *v*. Deposit, unload, put down (rubbish); let fall with a bump; send (goods unsalable at high price in home market) to foreign market for sale at low price; sell or otherwise dispose of unwanted merchandise or possessions at a loss; (colloq.) abandon.

dump·ling (dŭm′plĭng) *n*. Ball of dough cooked in stew, boiled with beef, etc., or sweetened and baked with fruit inside.

dump·y (dŭm′pē) *adj*. (**dump·i·er, dump·i·est**). Short and stout.

dun[1] (dŭn) *adj*. Of dull grayish-brown color; (of horse) of golden sand-colored body with black mane and tail; (poet.) dark, dusky. ~ *n*. Dun color; dun horse.

dun[2] (dŭn) *v.t.* (**dunned, dun·ning**). Importune for payment of debt; pester.

dunce (dŭns) *n*. One slow at learning, dullard; ~**'s cap**, cone-shaped paper cup formerly put on head of dunce at school. [John Duns Scotus, whose followers were ridiculed by 16th-c. reformers and humanists as enemies of learning]

dun·der·head (dŭn′derhĕd) *n*. Blockhead; dunce. **dun′der·head·ed** *adj*.

dune (dōōn, dūn) *n*. Mound or ridge of drifted sand; ~ **buggy** = BEACH buggy.

dung (dŭng) *n*. Manure; excrement of animals (rarely of man); moral filth; ~ **beetle**, any of various beetles that breed in dung; **dung′hill**, heap of dung; foul or infamous place. **dung** *v.t.* Manure (field).

dun·ga·ree (dŭnggarē′, dŭng′garē) *n*. Sturdy, usu. blue, denim

*Some species of **dung** beetle knead animal dung into balls which they roll along the ground and into a hollow. The dung is for their own consumption or is collected for their brood.*

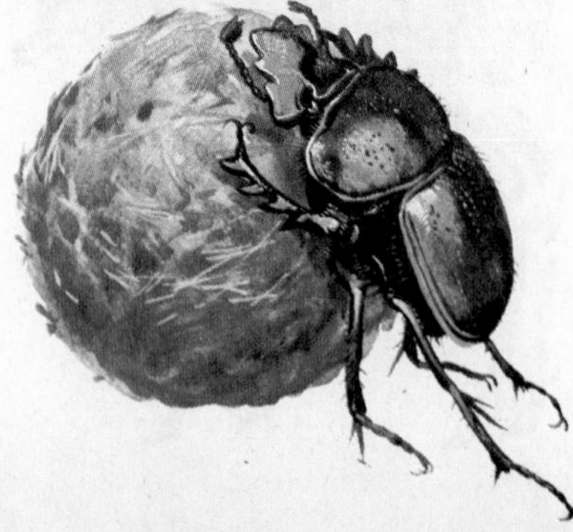

fabric; (pl.) trousers or overalls of this.

dun·geon (dŭn′jon) *n.* Strong dark cell; subterranean place of confinement.

dunk (dŭngk) *v.t.* 1. Dip (bread, cake, doughnut, etc.) into soup, coffee, etc. while eating. 2. (colloq.) Shoot (basketball) through basket from above, hence ~ **shot.** 3. Submerge in water or other liquid.

Dun·kirk (dŭn′kẽrk), *Fr.* **Dun·kerque** (dŏnkĕrk′). Seaport in NE. France on North Sea; scene of heroic British troop evacuation May 29–June 3, 1940, during World War II; any similar withdrawal, crisis, etc.

dun·lin (dŭn′lĭn) *n.* Small reddish-backed migratory wading bird (*Erolia alpina*), allied to sandpiper, abundant on sea coasts of Europe and northern N. Amer.; also called red-backed sandpiper.

dun·nage (dŭn′ĭj) *n.* Light material, as brushwood, mats, etc., stowed under or among cargo to prevent damage; miscellaneous baggage.

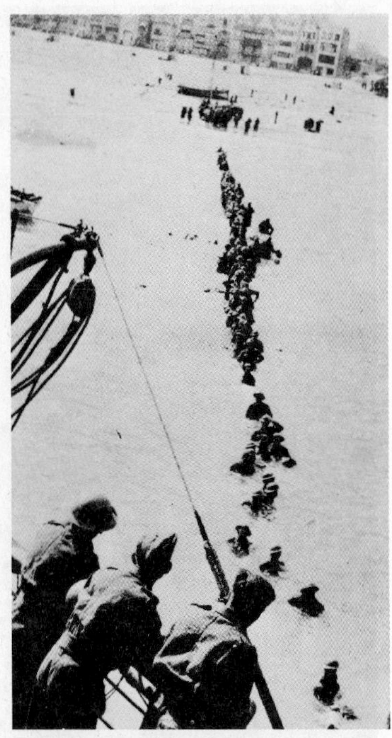

*The evacuation of British forces from the beaches and harbor of **Dunkirk** in 1940 during the 1939–45 war involved the use of naval ships and many small civilian craft.*

*The small **dunlin,** about 8 ins. long, breeds around the North Pole and northern Europe, and winters further south towards the Equator. The curved beak probes for food.*

__Dummies__ stored in a factory (below) look rather like merchandise in a human spare parts store. These dummies will finish up in a store window, displaying the latest clothes.

du·o (dōō′ō, dū′ō) *n.* (pl. **du·os**). 1. (mus.) Duet. 2. Couple or pair.

du·o·dec·i·mal (dōōodĕs′*i*mal, dū-) *adj.* Of 12 or twelfths, proceeding by twelves.

du·o·dec·i·mo (dōōodĕs′*i*mō, dū) *n.* (abbreviated 12mo) Page or book size (5 × 7¾ in.; 12.7 × 19.7 cm) of a book formed by folding a single printed sheet into 12 leaves; book composed of pages of this size.

du·o·de·num (dōōodē′n*u*m, -ŏd′*e*-, dū-) *n.* (pl. **du·o·de·na** pr. dōōodē′n*a*, -ŏd′*e*, dū-, **du·o·de·nums**). (anat.) First portion of small intestine immediately below stomach. **du·o·de′nal** *adj.* [L. *duodeni* 12 at once (f. its being about 12 in. long)]

dup. *abbrev.* Duplicate.

dupe (dōōp, dūp) *n.* Victim of deception; person easily fooled, gull. **dup′er·y** *n.* (pl. **-er·ies**). **dupe** *v.t.* (**duped, dup·ing**). Cheat, make a fool of.

du·ple (dōō′p*e*l, dū′-) *adj.* (mus., of time) Having two beats in bar; (math., of proportion) in which one quantity is double the other.

du·plex (dōō′plĕks, dū′-) *adj.* Of two elements; twofold; (also ~ **apartment**) One on two connected floors; house for two families.

du·pli·cate (dōō′pl*i*kĭt, dū′-) *adj.* 1. With two corresponding parts; existing in two examples. 2. Doubled; twice as large or as many. 3. Exactly like thing already existing. ~ *n.* One of two things exactly alike; exact copy; second copy, with equal legal force, of letter or document; **in** ~, in two exactly corresponding copies or parts. ~ (dōō′pl*i*kāt, dū′-) *v.t.* (**-cat·ed, -cat·ing**). 1. Double, multiply by two. 2. Make in duplicate; make exact copy of; produce copies of; repeat. **du·pli·ca·tion** (dōōpl*i*kā′sh*o*n, dū-) *n.*

du·pli·ca·tor (dōō′pl*i*kāt*e*r,

*Works by **Albrecht Dürer** consist of woodcuts, engravings, paintings and drawings. His widest influence was felt through his brilliant woodcuts and engravings. 'Hands', illustrated here, is one of his drypoint drawings.*

dū'-) *n.* Machine (mimeograph etc.) for producing copies of documents.

du·plic·i·ty (dōōplĭs'ĭtē, dū-) *n.* (pl. **-ties**). Double-dealing, deceitfulness; deception.

dur·a·ble (door'*a*b*e*l, dūr'-) *adj.* Lasting, not transitory; resisting wear, decay, etc.; ~ **goods**, manufactured products, as cars, appliances, etc., that can be used over a period of time; ~ **press** = PERMANENT press. **du·ra·bil·i·ty** (door*a*bĭl'ĭtē, dūr-) *n.*

du·ra ma·ter (door'*a* mā't*e*r). (anat.) Dense tough membrane enveloping brain and spinal cord. [med. L. transl. of Arab anatomical term, = "hard mother," so called because it was supposed to give rise to all membranes of body]

du·ra·men (d*u*rā'm*e*n, dy*u*-) *n.* Dense inner part of tree trunk, heartwood.

dur·ance (door'*a*ns, dūr'-) *n.* Forced confinement, imprisonment, esp. (literary) **in ~ vile**.

Du·rant (d*u*rănt'), **Will(iam) James** (1885–1981). Amer. educator; with his wife, **Ariel** (1898–1981), wrote popular works on philosophy and history, notably the multivolume *Story of Civilization.*

du·ra·tion (d*u*rā'sh*o*n, dy*u*-) *n.* Continuance in time; time during which thing, action, or state continues.

Dur·ban (dẽr'b*a*n). Port city on E. coast of Republic of South Africa.

Dü·rer (door'*e*r, dūr'-), **Albrecht** (1471–1528). German Renaissance engraver and painter; famous for his line engravings and woodcuts.

du·ress (d*u*rĕs', dy*u*-, door'ĭs, dūr'-) *n.* Forcible restraint, imprisonment; constraint illegally exercised to force person to perform some act, compulsion.

Dur·ham (dẽr'*a*m). 1. County in NE. England; its county seat; (one of) a breed of Shorthorn beef cattle orig. developed in this county. 2. City in North Carolina, site of Duke University.

dur·ing (door'ĭng, dūr'-) *prep.* Throughout, at some point in, the continuance of.

Durr·en·matt (door'*e*nmaht), **Friedrich** (1921–). Swiss novelist and playwright.

durst (dẽrst) *v.* (archaic) Past tense of DARE, before expressed or implied infinitive without *to.*

du·rum (door'*u*m, dūr'-) *n.* Species of wheat (*Triticum durum*) with hard seeds, used chiefly for pasta.

***Durham Cathedral,** one of Britain's finest Norman buildings, was begun in 1093 and the Galilee Chapel was added in 1176. There were later additions in the 13th and 15th centuries.*

dusk (dŭsk) *n.* Shade, gloom; darker stage of twilight. ~ *adj.* (poet.) Dusky.

dusk·y (dŭs'kē) *adj.* (**dusk·i·er, dusk·i·est**). Shadowy, dim; dark-colored. **dusk'i·ly** *adv.* **dusk'i·ness** *n.*

Düs·sel·dorf (dōōs'*e*ldôrf; *Ger.* düs'*e*ldôrf). Industrial city on Rhine River in West Germany.

dust (dŭst) *n.* 1. Earth or other solid matter in minute and fine state of subdivision, in particles small and light enough to be easily raised and carried in cloud by wind; cloud of dust; **bite the ~**, fall to the ground killed or wounded; **dry as ~**, extremely boring, pedantic; **throw ~ in person's eyes**, deceive him. 2. What anything is reduced to by disintegration or decay, esp. remains of dead body; person's mortal remains. 3. **dust'-bin**, (Brit.) trash can, garbage can; **dust bowl**, area made desert by

*Top: **Dusk** in Yellowstone National Park sees a young deer make its way to water. Above: In strong winds, dunes of sand can easily be transformed into **dust** storms, sometimes erasing all visibility.*

deforestation, drought, and dust storms; **dust devil,** small column-like whirlwind of dust; **dust jacket,** paper jacket covering hardcover book; **dust'man,** (Brit.) person who collects and carts away refuse etc.; **dust'pan,** utensil into which dust is swept from floor etc.; **dust storm,** severe dust-filled windstorm, esp. in arid region, during drought; **dust'up,** (colloq.) quarrel, fight. **dust** *v.* 1. Sprinkle with dust or powder, (cooking) flour, sugar, etc.; make dusty; sprinkle (powder etc.). 2. Clear of dust by brushing, wiping, etc.; clear away (dust etc.); clear furniture etc. of dust.

dust·er (dŭs'tėr) *n.* 1. Cloth or brush for dusting furniture etc. 2. Smock; woman's loose-fitting dresslike housecoat.

dust·y (dŭs'tē) *adj.* (**dust·i·er, dust·i·est**). Full of dust, strewn with dust; finely powdered like dust; ~ **miller,** any of several plants with gray or white leaves covered with dustlike down, esp. the beach wormwood (*Artemisia stelleriana*) and *Lychnis coronaria,* or mullein pink. **dust'i·ly** *adv.* **dust'i·ness** *n.*

Dutch (dŭch) *adj.* 1. Of the Netherlands or its language or people; coming from the Netherlands; characteristic of the Dutch. 2. (hist.) Of Germany, German; Teutonic; **High ~**, of the southern Germans, High German; **Low ~**, of the northern Germans, of the northern and northwest parts, including the Netherlands and Flanders. 3. **go ~**, have each person pay his or her own expenses; **in ~**, (colloq.) in trouble, out of favor; **~ courage**, (colloq.) courage from intoxicants and therefore not lasting; **~ door**, door with upper and lower halves that can be opened independently; **~ elm disease**, fatal disease of elm trees, caused by a fungus *Ceratocystis ulmi*, first found in the Netherlands; **~ metal**, alloy of copper and zinc made in leaf form in imitation of gold leaf; **~ oven**, (1) metal box of which open side is turned toward fireplace, for roasting meat etc.; (2) large, heavy, usu. cast-iron pot with close-fitting lid, for cooking roasts, etc.; **~ treat**, party, date, etc. in which each person pays for or contributes his or her own share; **~ uncle**, (colloq.) severe and candid critic. **Dutch** *n.* 1. (collect.) People of the Netherlands. 2. Language of the Netherlands, a Germanic dialect that has not undergone the High German consonant mutation (second sound shift). 3. (obs.) German language; **High ~** = HIGH GERMAN; **Low ~** = LOW GERMAN; **Pennsylvania ~**, (German as spoken by) descendants of 17th and 18th c. German and Swiss immigrants into Pennsylvania. **Dutch'man** *n.* (pl. **-men**). 1. Native, inhabitant, of the Netherlands. 2. Dutch ship; **Flying ~**, legendary spectral ship condemned with all her crew to sail the seas for ever, and supposed to be seen near the Cape of Good Hope. 3. (hist.) German. 4. **Dutchman's breeches**, a wildflower (*Dicentra cucullaria*) so called from the shape of its flower, which resembles breeches hanging upside down.

***Dutch** customs, culture and landscape have been magnificently recorded by such artists as Rembrandt, Vermeer and Van Gogh. This painting, 'The Lacemaker', is by Jan Vermeer.*

du·te·ous (do͞o'tēus, dū'-) *adj.* (poet.) Dutiful, obedient. **du'te·ous·ly** *adv.* **du'te·ous·ness** *n.*

du·ti·a·ble (do͞o'tēabel, dū'-) *adj.* Subject to import tax.

du·ti·ful (do͞o'tĭful, dū'-) *adj.* Regular or willing in obedience and service. **du'ti·ful·ly** *adv.* **du'ti·ful·ness** *n.*

du·ty (do͞o'tē, dū'-) *n.* (pl. **-ties**). 1. Action and conduct owed to deference, respect, custom, etc. 2. Payment to public revenue levied on imports. 3. Action, act, due in way of moral or legal obligation. 4. Business, office, function, performance of or engagement in these

(**on, off,** ~, actually so engaged or not); (eccles.) performance of church services; ~ **officer**, (mil. etc.) person left in charge when others are absent. 5. Measure of engine's effectiveness in units of work done per unit of fuel.

du·um·vir (dōōŭm´vėr, dū-) *n.* (Rom. hist.) One of a pair of coequal magistrates and functionaries in Rome and her colonies. **du·um′vir·ate** *n.*

Du·va·lier (dōōvahlyā´; *Fr.* düvályā´), **François** (1907–71). Commonly called "Papa Doc"; president and dictator of Haiti, 1957–71.

D.V.M. *abbrev.* Doctor of Veterinary Medicine.

Dvo·rak (dvōr´zhahk, -zhăk), **Anton(in)** (1841–1904). Czech composer of symphonies, Slavic dances, operas, etc.

*The **Dyaks** of the Borneo forests, once headhunters and cannibals, are extremely fond of ornaments, as can be seen in the large metal earrings worn by the womenfolk.*

dwarf (dwōrf) *n.* (pl. **dwarfs, dwarves** pr. dwōrvz). 1. Person, animal, or plant, much below ordinary size of species. 2. (also ~ **star**) One of the class of smaller stars of greater density as dist. from the larger diffuse stars or "giants." 3. (Teutonic, esp. Scand., myth.) Small manlike, often ugly, creature living underground. **dwarf** *adj.* Undersized; puny, stunted. ~ **cornel**: see BUNCHBERRY. **dwarf′ish** *adj.* **dwarf′ish·ness** *n.* **dwarf′ism** *n.* (med.) Condition of being considerably undersized. **dwarf** *v.t.* Stunt in growth, intellect, etc.; make to look small by contrast or distance.

dwell (dwĕl) *v.i.* (**dwelt, dwelled, dwell·ing**). 1. Continue, remain, for a time (archaic); have one's abode, live (in house, country, etc.). 2. ~ **on**, spend time upon, linger over in thought; treat at length. **dwell′er** *n.* Inhabitant, resident.

dwell·ing (dwĕl´ĭng) *n.* (esp.) Place of residence, house; ~ **place**, dwelling.

dwin·dle (dwĭn´dėl) *v.i.* (**-dled, -dling**). Become smaller, shrink, waste away; lose importance, decline; degenerate.

dwt. *abbrev.* Pennyweight.

Dy *symbol.* Dysprosium.

dy·ad (dī′ăd) *n.* The number two; group of two, couple, pair.

Dy·ak (dī′ăk) *n.* Member, language, of an aboriginal tribe of Borneo.

dyb·buk (dĭb′*u*k) *n.* (pl. **dyb·-buks,** *Heb.* **dyb·bu·kim** pr. dĭbo͝okēm′). (Jewish folklore) Malevolent spirit (of dead person) that enters living person's body and controls it until exorcised.

dye (dī) *v.* (**dyed, dye·ing**). Color, stain, tinge; impregnate with color, fix a color in the substance of; make (thing) specified color; **dyed in the wool**: see WOOL. **dy′er** *n.* One who dyes clothes etc. **dye** *n.* Color produced by or as by dyeing; tinge, hue; matter used for dyeing, coloring matter in solution. **dye′stuff,** material used as or producing a dye.

dy·ing: see DIE[2]

dyke: see DIKE.

dy·nam·ic (dīnăm′ĭk) *adj.* Of force producing motion; of force in action or operation, active; potent, energetic; of dynamics; (philos.) relating to the reason of existence of an object of experience; accounting for matter, or mind, as merely the action of forces. **dy·nam′ics** *n.pl.* Branch of physics treating of the behavior of matter under the action of force; branch of any science considering force or forces; moving forces, physical or moral, in any sphere. **dy·nam′i·cal·ly** *adv.*

dy·na·mism (dī′n*a*mĭzem) *n.* Philosophical system or theory explaining phenomena of universe by some immanent force or energy. **dy·na·mis·tic** (dīn*a*mĭs′tĭk) *adj.*

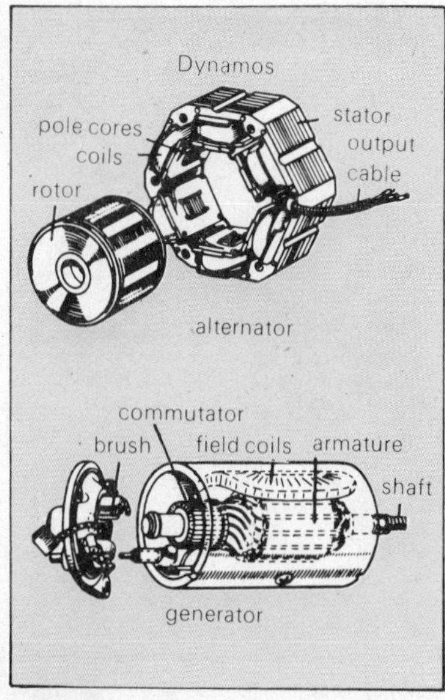

The constituents of a ***dynamo:*** *an alternator (above) and a generator (below). A dynamo is used to convert mechanical energy into electrical energy.*

dy·na·mite (dī′n*a*mīt) *n.* High explosive of nitroglycerine contained in some absorbent substance. ~ *v.t.* (**-mit·ed, -mit·ing**). Set charge of dynamite to, blow up with dynamite. **dy′na·mit·er** *n.* [named by Alfred Nobel (1833–96), the inventor, f. Gk. *dunamis* force]

dy·na·mo (dī′n*a*mō) *n.* (pl. **-mos**). Machine converting mechanical into electrical energy by rotating coils of copper wire in a magnetic field. [short for *dynamo-electric machine*]

dy·na·mom·e·ter (dīn*a*mŏm′-*e*t*e*r) *n.* Instrument for measuring energy.

dy·nast (dī′năst, -n*a*st; *Brit.* also dĭn′ăst) *n.* Ruler, member of dynasty. **dy·nas·ty** (dī′n*a*stē; *Brit.* also dĭn′*a*stē) *n.* (pl. **-ties**). Line of hereditary rulers. **dy·nas·tic** (dīnăs′tĭk; *Brit.* also dĭnăs′tĭk) *adj.* **dy·nas′ti·cal·ly** *adv.*

dyne (dīn) *n.* (phys.) Absolute unit of force in the cgs system, force that, acting on a mass of 1 gram, will make it move 1 cm per second faster in every second.

dys- *prefix.* Bad; difficult.

dys·en·ter·y (dĭs′*e*ntĕr′ē) *n.* Disease with inflammation of mucous membrane and glands of large intestine, and mucous and bloody evacuations.

dys·lex·i·a (dĭslĕk′sē*a*) *n.* Partial word blindness, impairment of ability to read due to impaired neural function. **dys·lex′ic** *adj.*

dys·pep·si·a (dĭspĕp′se*a*) *n.* Indigestion. **dys·pep·tic** (dĭspĕp′tĭk) *adj.* & *n.*

dysp·ne·a (dĭspnē′*a*) *n.* (med.) Difficult or labored breathing.

dys·pro·si·um (dĭsprō′zē*u*m, -zhē-) *n.* (chem.) Element of rare-earth group; highly magnetic; symbol Dy, at. no. 66, at. wt. 162.50. [mod. L., f. Gk. *dusprositos* hard to get at]

dys·tro·phy (dĭs′tr*o*fē) *n.* (path.) Imperfect nutrition; disorder characterized by weakness and wasting esp. of muscles (**muscular** ~).

dz. *abbrev.* Dozen, dozens.

Dyeing *fabric involves primitive methods in some parts of Africa. Below: Pits are used for indigo dyeing in Nigeria. Facing page: In the dyeworks in Fez, Morocco, more up-to-date methods are used.*

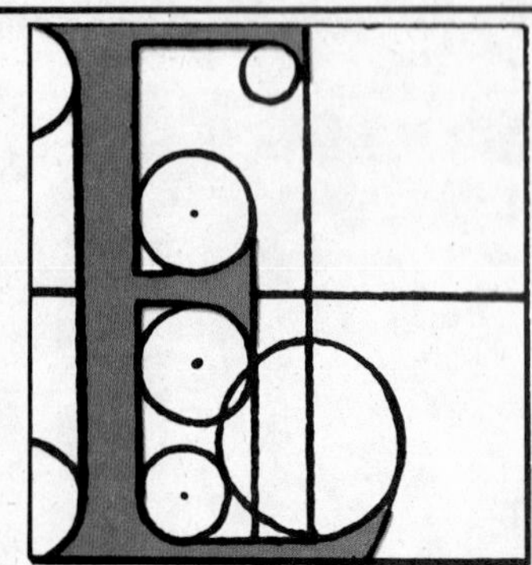

How the form of the letter ***E, e*** *5th letter of the modern English and ancient Roman alphabet, has developed through the ages. The letter has Semitic, Greek and Latin derivations.*

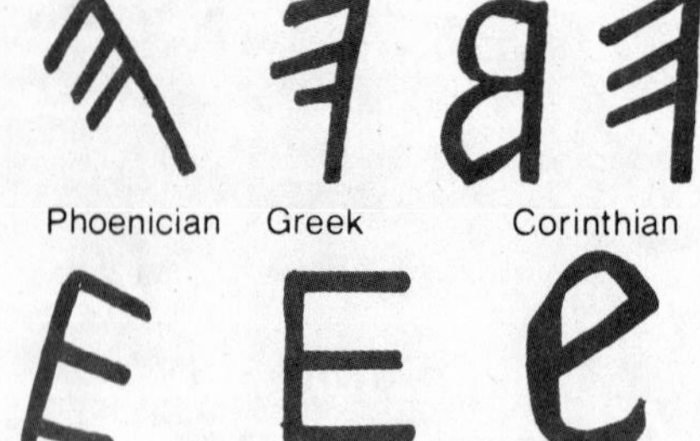

E, e (ē) (pl. **E's, e's** or **Es, es**). 1. Fifth letter of modern English and ancient Roman alphabet, representing Semitic Ǝ, which orig. expressed a sound like that of *h* but was adopted by the Greeks as a vowel. 2. Fifth in a series or row. 3. **E,** (mus.) third note of natural scale (C major); scale or key with this for tonic. 4. **E-layer,** stratum of ionosphere some 60 mi. (100 km) above the Earth, transparent to shortwave radio waves and reflecting back long wave ones.

E *abbrev.* 1. East(ern). 2. (physics) Energy. 3. English.

e *abbrev.* 1. East(ern). 2. Electron. 3. (baseball) Error. 4. (math.) Number having value of approximately 2.7182818 ..., used as base of natural system of logarithms.

E. *abbrev.* 1. Earl. 2. Earth. 3. East(ern). 4. Easter. 5. Engineer(ing). 6. English.

e. *abbrev.* 1. Engineer(ing). 2. Eldest. 3. (baseball) Error.

ea. *abbrev.* Each.

each (ēch) *adj.* Every (one) taken separately; ~ **other,** (used as a compound reciprocal pronoun) one another. ~ *adv.* To, from, or for each. ~ *pron.* Each one.

ea·ger (ē′gėr) *adj.* Strongly desirous; keen, impatient. **ea′ger·ly** *adv.* **ea′ger·ness** *n.*

ea·gle (ē′gel) *n.* 1. Any of a number of large birds of prey of family Accipitridae, noted for keen vision and powerful flight, incl. the 2 N. Amer. species *Aquila chrysaëtos*, the bald eagle, and *Haliaeetus leucocephalus*, the golden eagle. 2. Representation or figure of the eagle, esp. as symbol of the U.S. (astron.) Northern constellation *Aquila*. 3. (hist.) Coin bearing

Left: The ***golden eagle,*** *the best-known of these large birds of prey, inhabits mountainous or rocky regions of N. America, Europe, and Asia. Below: The huge wing-span of a wedge-tailed eagle from Australia.*

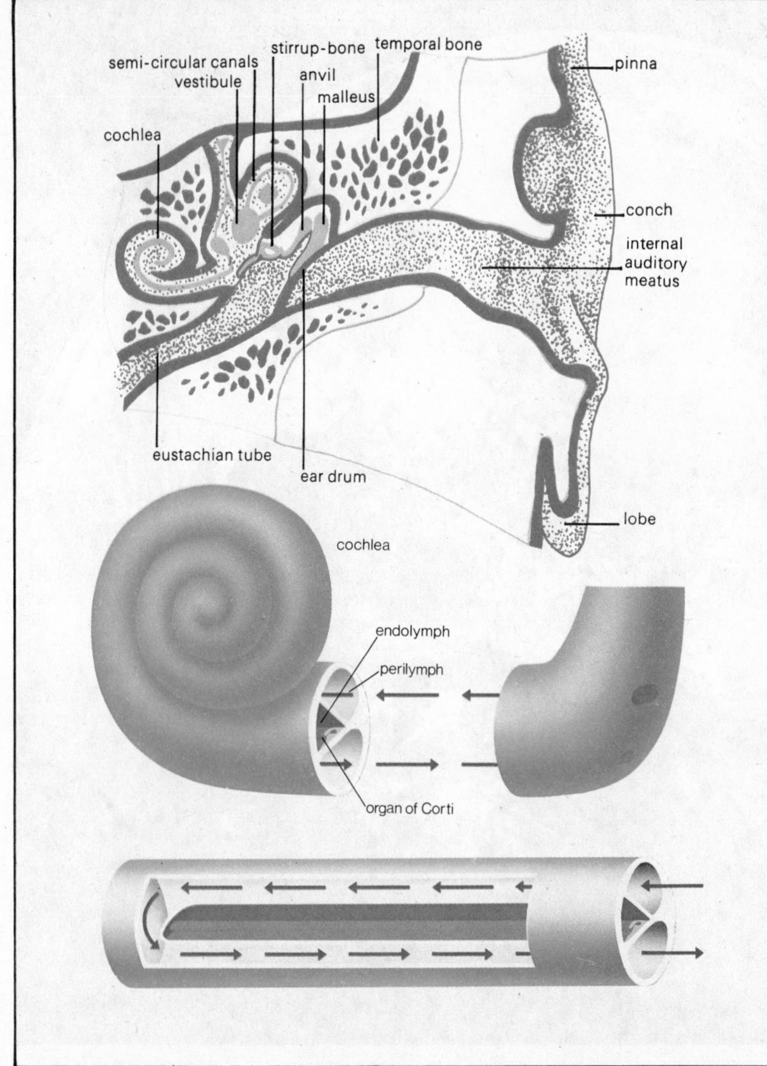

The human ***ear*** *has three parts: the outer ear or auricle; the middle ear, joined to the outer ear by a canal and containing three bones, the malleus (hammer), incus (anvil), and stapes (stirrup), and the eustachian tube which allows air to pass from the nose, and finally the inner ear, vital for balance as well as sound perception, the cochlea being concerned with the latter.*

image of eagle; 10-dollar gold coin (**double** ~, 20-dollar). 4. (golf) Score of two under par on any hole. 5. ~**-eyed**, keen-sighted.

ea·glet (ē′glĭt) *n.* Young eagle.

Ea·kins (ā′kĭnz), **Thomas** (1844–1916). Amer. painter and sculptor.

ear[1] (ēr) *n.* 1. Organ of hearing in man and animals, esp. the external part of this. 2. Sense of hearing; faculty of discriminating sounds, esp. that of recognizing musical intervals; listening, attention. 3. Earlike object; handle of pitcher etc.; projection on side of anything serving as handle, support, etc. 4. **be all** ~**s**, listen attentively; **turn a deaf** ~, disregard request etc. 5. **ear′ache**, pain in internal ear; **ear′drum**, tympanum; **ear′mark**, mark, usu. a notch, in ear of sheep etc. as sign of ownership; (*v.t.*) mark (animals) thus, mark (anything) as one's own, assign (fund etc.) for some purpose; **ear′muff**, either of a pair of coverings for the ears worn as protection against the cold; **ear′phone**, one of pair of telephone or radio receivers attachable to listener's ears; **ear′ring**, ornament worn in or on lobe of ear; **ear′shot**, hearing distance; **ear′splitting**, very loud; **ear trumpet**, trumpet-shaped tube held to ear by partly deaf persons to enable them to hear better; **ear′wax**, cerumen.

ear[2] (ēr) *n.* Grain-bearing spike, head, of corn, containing its flowers or seeds.

Ear·hart (âr′härt), **Amelia** (1898–1937?). Amer. aviator; first woman to fly across Atlantic, 1928; lost on flight over Pacific, 1937.

earl (ērl) *n.* British nobleman ranking between marquis and viscount. **earl′dom** *n.*

ear·ly (ēr′lē) *adj.* (**-li·er, -li·est**). Absolutely or relatively near the beginning of a portion of time; of, in, the first part of the morning, the year, etc.; ~ **bird**, (joc.) person who is early or arises early in the morning; ~ **on**, at an early stage. ~ *adv.* At an early time.

earn (ērn) *v.t.* Obtain as reward of labor or merit. **earn′ings** *n.pl.* Money earned.

ear·nest[1] (ēr′nĭst) *n.* Money

There are 1,200 species of ***earwig,*** *and modern communications are spreading them throughout the world. They are characterized by a pair of horny forceps.*

The ***earth,*** *taken from 'Apollo II', July 1969. The earth's movement round the sun is dictated by the forces of the solar system. The attraction of the earth for the sun is mirrored by the moon's attraction for the earth.*

paid as part payment to confirm contract etc.; foretaste, presage, token (of what is to come).

ear·nest² (ẽr′nĭst) *adj.* Serious, zealous, not trifling; ardent. **ear′nest·ly** *adv.* **ear′nest·ness** *n.* **ear′nest** *n.* Complete seriousness; **in ~**, serious(ly), not jesting(ly).

Earp (ẽrp), **Wyatt** (1849–1929). Amer. frontier law officer.

earth (ẽrth) *n.* 1. Ground; soil, esp. as suited for cultivation; dry land; (also **E ~**) planet on which we dwell, the world; the present abode of man, as dist. from heaven or hell. 2. Hole or hiding place of fox, badger, etc.; **run to ~**, (fig.) find by searching. 3. (Brit. elect.) GROUND¹. 4. (chem.) Any of certain naturally occurring metallic oxides. 5. **earth′ling**, inhabitant of Earth; **earth mother**, (myth.) spirit symbolizing earth; (fig.) sensual and maternal woman;

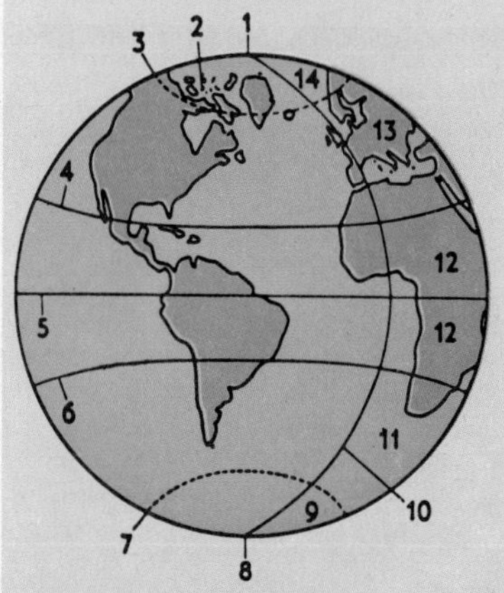

1. North Pole. 2. North Magnetic Pole. 3. Arctic Circle. 4. Tropic of Cancer. 5. Equator. 6. Tropic of Capricorn. 7. Antarctic Circle. 8. South Pole. 9. South Frigid Zone. 10. Meridian of Greenwich. 11. South Temperate Zone. 12. Torrid Zone. 13. North Temperate Zone. 14. North Frigid Zone.

earth′nut, (plant having) edible roundish tubers, roots, or pods; **earth science**, any of several sciences, including geology, physical geography, and others that deal with the earth and any of its phenomena; **earth′shaking**, having great impact on basic beliefs, theories, attitudes, etc.; **earth′work**, bank or mound of earth as rampart or fortification; **earth′worm**, annelid worm (of various genera) that subsists on soil. **earth** *v.* Cover (roots of plants *up*) with heaped-up earth.

earth·en (ẽr′then, -dhen) *adj.* Made of earth; made of baked clay. **earth′enware** *n.* (Vessels etc. made of) baked clay, esp. coarse porous kinds fired at relatively low temperature as dist. from porcelain (also attrib.).

earth·ly (ẽrth′lē) *adj.* (**-li·er, -li·est**). Of the earth, terrestrial; **no ~ use** etc., (colloq.) no use etc., at all. **earth′li·ness** *n.*

earth·quake (ẽrth′kwāk) *n.* Convulsion of earth's surface caused by volcanic activity or faults in the earth's crust; (fig.) any disturbance or upheaval.

earth·y (ẽr′thē, -dhē) *adj.* (**earth·i·er, earth·i·est**). Like, of, earth or soil; grossly material, coarse. **earth'i·ness** *n.*

ear·wig (ēr'wĭg) *n.* Insect of the order Dermaptera and, in the U.S., family Labiidae with about 20 species, having large terminal forceps, formerly held to penetrate into head through ear; kind of small centipede.

ease (ēz) *n.* Freedom from pain or trouble; freedom from constraint; relief from pain; facility; **at ~**, (mil. etc.) stand in relaxed attitude, with hands behind back and feet apart. ~ *v.t.* (**eased, eas·ing**). Relieve from pain, trouble, etc.; give mental ease to; relax, adjust (what is too tight); (naut.) slacken (rope, sail, speed, etc.); move gently or gradually; relax or cease one's efforts; ~ **off, up**, become less burdensome, take things easy.

ea·sel (ē'zel) *n.* Frame to support picture (esp. while artist is at work on it) etc. [Du. *ezel* = Ger. *esel* ass]

ease·ment (ēz'ment) *n.* 1. (archaic) Advantage, convenience; something serving as convenience, as shed, farm building, etc., accommodation in house. 2. (law) Acquired right or privilege of using something not one's own (e.g. right of way).

east (ēst) *adv.* Toward, in, the east. ~ *n.* 1. Point of horizon where sun rises at equinox; this direction. 2. Cardinal point of the compass 90° to the right of north. 3. (usu. **the E~**) That part of a country, district, etc. which lies to the east; part of world lying east of Europe, the Orient; Communist countries of Asia and eastern Europe; states of U.S. bordering on the Atlantic esp. N. of Maryland; New England. ~ *adj.* Toward, in, the east; (of wind) blowing from the east; **E~ Berlin**: see BERLIN; **E~ Cape**, easternmost point of Papua New Guinea; easternmost point of New Zealand; former name of Cape Dezhnev; **E~ China Sea**, arm of Pacific between E. coast of China and Ryukyu Islands; **E~ Germany**, German Democratic Republic: see GERMANY; **E~ India Company**, company of British merchants trading with the East Indies, incorporated in 1600; **E~ Pakistan**, former name of BANGLADESH; **E~ River**, strait connecting Upper New York Bay and Long Island Sound, separating Manhattan and Long Island; **E~ Side**, part of Manhattan, N.Y.C., E. of Fifth Ave. **east·ward** (ēst'werd) *adj., adv.,* & *n.* **east'ward·ly** *adj.* & *adv.* **east'wards** *adv.*

East·er (ēs'ter) *n.* Christian festival commemorating the resurrection of Christ, and observed by the Western Churches on the first Sunday after the calendar full moon falling on or next after Mar. 21; (also **Eastertide**) week commencing with this day; ~ **egg**, colored egg or egg-shaped candy used as Easter gift or ornament.

Eas·ter (ēs'ter) **Island.** Pacific island west of Chile, discovered by the Dutch navigator Roggeveen on Easter Day, 1722, noted esp. for its monolithic statues.

east·er·ly (ēs'terlē) *adj.* In the east; (of wind) blowing from the east. ~ *adv.* Toward the east. ~ *n.* East wind.

east·ern (ēs'tern) *adj.* Of the east; oriental; lying or directed toward the east; (poet.) in, coming from, the east; **E~**, of the East i.e. of Communist countries; **E~ Church**, ORTHODOX Church; **E~ Empire**: see ROMAN Empire; **E~ Hemisphere**: see HEMISPHERE; **E~ Shore**, parts of Maryland and Virginia E. of Chesapeake Bay. **east·ern·most** (ēs'ternmōst) *adj.* **east'ern·er** *n.* (also **E~**) Native, inhabitant, of the east, esp. of eastern U.S.

East (ēst) **Indies.** Islands off the SE. coast of Asia, formerly including India and the Malay peninsula. **East Indian** *adj.* & *n.* (Native, inhabitant) of the East Indies.

eas·y (ē'zē) *adj.* (**eas·i·er, eas·i·est**). 1. Free from pain, worry, or constraint. 2. Conducive to ease or comfort. 3. Causing little discomfort, difficulty, or obstruction; compliant; easily obtained; loosely fitting; **of ~ virtue**, (of woman) sexually promiscuous. 4. **~ chair**, padded or stuffed chair with arms; ~ **does it**, go carefully; **ea'sy-going**, relaxed and casual; tolerant;

*These statues on **Easter Island** are made from compressed volcanic ash. Those found have varied in height from 3 to 36 ft.*

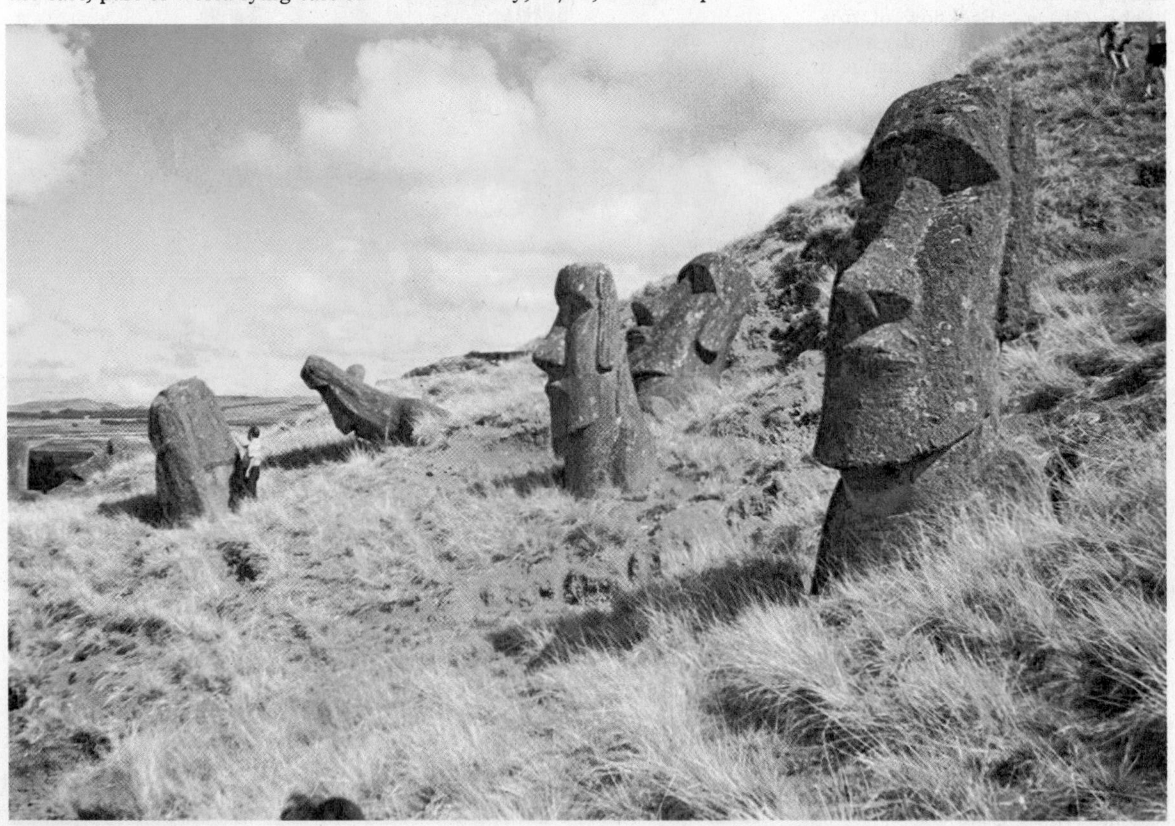

easy mark, (colloq.) person or thing easily overcome, persuaded, etc.; **easy money**, money obtained or obtainable without hard work or difficulty. **eas′i·ly** *adv.* **eas′i·ness** *n.* **easy** *adv.* In an easy manner, at leisurely pace; **~!**, (move) gently!; **take it ~**, proceed comfortably, do no more than one must.

eat (ēt) *v.* (**ate, eat·en, eat·ing**). 1. Take into mouth, masticate, and swallow as food, swallow (soup etc.); consume food, take a meal; **~ one's words**, retract them in humiliating manner; **~ out**, take a meal elsewhere than at home; **~ out of person's hand**, be tamely or completely submissive to him. 2. Devour, consume, prey upon; (of frost, rust, etc.) destroy slowly and gradually; make (hole, passage), make a way, by fretting or corrosion; **what's eat′ing you?**, (colloq.) why are you angry, worried, etc.?; **eat away** or **~ into**, destroy gradually. **eats** *n.* (slang) Food. **eat′a·ble** *adj.* **eat′a·bles** *n.pl.* Articles of food.

eat·er·y (ē′terē) *n.* (pl. **-er·ies**). (slang) Restaurant, diner, etc.

eau de Cologne (ō de kolōn′): see COLOGNE.

eaves (ēvz) *n.pl.* (orig. sing.) Overhanging edge of roof.

eaves·drop (ēvz′drŏp) *v.i.* (**-dropped, -drop·ping**). Stand close to walls of house under eaves to listen to secrets; listen secretly to private conversation. **eaves′-drop·per** *n.*

ebb (ĕb) *n.* Backflow of tide, return of tidewater toward sea (also **~ tide**); decline, decay, change to worse state, point of decline or depression. **ebb** *v.i.* Flow back, recede; flow away; decay, decline.

eb·on (ĕb′on) *adj.* & *n.* (poet.) (Made of, black as) ebony.

eb·on·ite (ĕb′onīt) *n.* Vulcanite.

eb·on·y (ĕb′onē) *n.* (pl. **-on·ies**). Hard heavy black wood obtained from various tropical trees, esp. various species of *Diospyros* of Ceylon, Madagascar, and Coromandel; tree yielding this. **~** *adj.* Made of, black as, ebony; intensely black.

E·bro (ē′brō). Longest river in Spain, 575 mi. (920 km), flowing SE. from Cantabrian Mountains in N. to Mediterranean.

e·bul·lient (ĭbŭl′yent, ĭbo͝ol′-) *adj.* Boiling; exuberant, enthusiastic. **e·bul′lience, e·bul′lien·cy** *ns.* **e·bul′lient·ly** *adv.*

eb·ul·li·tion (ĕbulĭsh′on) *n.* Boiling; effervescence; sudden outburst (*of* violence, passion, etc.).

Ebony *wood has been highly valued since classical times for actual and legendary properties. Left: Tree and fruit of one of the species Diospyros, from which ebony is obtained.*

EC *abbrev.* European Community.

ec·ce ho·mo (ĕch′ā hō′mō, ĕk′sē, ĕk′ā). Representation of Christ wearing crown of thorns. [L., = "behold the man," words used by Pontius Pilate to present Christ, crowned with thorns, to his accusers. (John 19)]

ec·cen·tric (ĭksĕn′trĭk, ĕk-) *adj.* 1. Not concentric to, with axis, point of support, etc., otherwise than centrally placed; not centrally placed or passing through center; (of orbital motion, curve, etc.) not circular, deviating from a circle; moving in eccentric orbit. 2. Irregular, capricious, odd, whimsical. **ec·cen′tri·cal·ly** *adv.* **ec·cen·tric·i·ty** (ĕksĕntrĭs′ĭtē) *n.* (pl. **-ties**). **eccentric** *n.* 1. Eccentric disk on revolving shaft, with connecting rods etc., for changing rotating into backward and forward motion. 2. Eccentric person.

Eccl., Eccles. *abbrevs.* Ecclesiastes (Old Testament).

Ec·cle·si·as·tes (ĭklēzĭăs′tēz). Book of Old Testament traditionally ascribed to Solomon.

ec·cle·si·as·tic (ĭklēzēăs′tĭk) *n.* Clergyman, priest.

ec·cle·si·as·ti·cal (ĭklēzēăs′tĭkal) *adj.* Of Church or clergy.

Carved ***ebony*** *table and candlestands, Ham House, London, U.K. The wood is hard, deep in colour and easy to polish: such things as black piano keys and knife handles are made of it.*

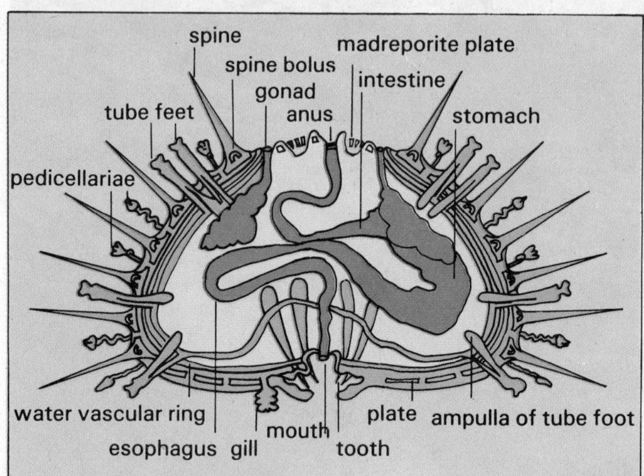

***Echinoderm** comes from a Greek word meaning 'prickle-skinned', and is used for a large group of sea-dwelling creatures. The five extant forms are the sea-urchin (see top, above left, and above right), the starfish or sea-star (see top), the brittle-star, the feather-star and sea-lily, and the sea-cucumber. Their symmetry is striking.*

ec·cle·si·as'ti·cal·ly *adv.*

Ec·cle·si·as·ti·cus (ĭklēzēăs′-tĭk*u*s). Book of the Apocrypha, otherwise known as "The Wisdom of Jesus the son of Sirach," containing moral and practical maxims.

ec·dys·i·ast (ĕkdĭz′ēăst, -*a*st) *n.* Stripteaser.

ec·dy·sis (ĕk′dĭsĭs) *n.* (pl. **-ses** pr. -sēz). (zool.) Casting of outer skin or shell.

ECG *abbrev.* Electrocardiogram.

ech·e·lon (ĕsh′*e*lŏn) *n.* 1. Steplike formation of troops or airplanes in parallel units, each with its front clear of that in advance; any similar formation. 2. Grade, rank. [Fr. *échelle* ladder]

e·chid·na (ĭkĭd′n*a*) *n.* Spiny anteater (*Tachyglossus aculeatus*), an egg-laying burrowing nocturnal mammal, with long extensile tongue for eating ants, native to Australia, N.Z., etc.: see ANT.

e·chi·no·derm (ĭkī′n*o*dẽrm, ĕk′-ĭn*o*-) *n.* Member of the class Echinodermata (sea urchins, starfish, etc.), some species of which have skin studded with spines or hard plates.

e·chi·noid (ĭkī′noid, ĕk′ĭ-) *adj.* Resembling the *Echinus*, a genus of sea urchins. ~ *n.* Any of the sea urchins (Echinoidea), a large group of marine animals with usu. globular or heart-shaped calcareous skeleton of interlocking plates; fossilized member of this group.

ech·o (ĕk′ō) *n.* (pl. **ech·oes**). Repetition of sound produced by reflection of sound waves from something denser than air, usu. from a rigid and approx. vertical surface; secondary sound constituted by reflected waves; reflection of radar wave; (fig.) repetition or close imitation, enfeebled reproduction; close or obsequious imitator or adherent; **echoloca'tion**, location of objects by reflected sound. **echo** *v.* (**ech·oed, ech·o·ing**). (of place) Resound with echo; (of sounds) be repeated by echoes, reverberate, resound; repeat (sound) by or like echo; repeat (another's words), imitate words or opinions of.

e·cho·ic (ĕkō′ĭk) *adj.* (of word etc.) Echoing the sound that it denotes; onomatopoeic.

é·clair (āklār′, ĭ-, ā′klār) *n.* Small finger-shaped pastry filled with cream or custard and usu.

Despite rich mineral and agricultural resources, the majority of the people of ***Ecuador*** *remain poor, many continue to wash their clothes in the rivers (right). Map and flag (below).*

iced.

é·clat (āklah′) *n.* Conspicuous success, acclaim; brilliance of achievement.

ec·lec·tic (ĭklĕk′tĭk, ĕ-) *adj.* & *n.* 1. (Philosopher, esp. of antiquity) not belonging to any recognized school but selecting such doctrines as pleased him in every school. 2. (Person) borrowing freely from various sources, not exclusive in opinion, taste, etc. **ec·lec′ti·cal·ly** *adv.* **ec·lec·ti·cism** (ĭklĕk′tĭsĭzem, ĕ-) *n.*

e·clipse (ĭklĭps′) *n.* 1. Partial or total interception of light of sun by passage of moon between it and the earth (~ **of the sun, solar** ~); partial or total obscuration of moon by the Earth's shadow (~ **of the moon, lunar** ~); similar obscuration of a satellite by another planet. 2. Obscuration, obscurity, loss of brilliance or splendor. **eclipse** *v.t.* (**e·clipsed, e·clips·ing**). (of moon) Cause eclipse of the sun from a portion of the Earth; usu. pass., (of sun) have light so intercepted, (of moon) be obscured by Earth's shadow; deprive of luster, outshine, surpass.

e·clip·tic (ĭklĭp′tĭk) *n.* Great circle of celestial sphere, apparent orbit of sun (so called because eclipses happen only when moon is on or very near this line).

ec·logue (ĕk′lawg, -lŏg) *n.* Short poem, esp. pastoral dialogue.

E.C.M. *abbrev.* European Common Market.

e·co·cide (ē′kosīd, ĕk′*o*-) *n.* Destruction of the natural environment, as by discharge of pollutants etc.

ecol. *abbrev.* Ecological; ecology.

e·col·o·gy (ĭkŏl′ojē) *n.* Branch of biology dealing with relations of living organisms to their surroundings, their habits, modes of life, populations, etc. **ec·o·log·i·cal** (ĕkolŏj′ĭk*a*l, ēk*o*-) *adj.* **ec·o·log′i·cal·ly** *adv.* **e·col′o·gist** *n.*

econ. *abbrev.* Economic(s); economy.

e·con·o·met·rics (ĭkŏn*o*mĕt′rĭks) *n.* Branch of economics concerned with application of mathematical economics by use of statistics. **e·con·o·met′ric, e·con·o·met′ri·cal** *adjs.* **e·con·o·me·tri·cian** (ĭkŏn*o*metrĭsh′*a*n), **e·con·o·met′rist** *ns.*

e·co·nom·ic (ēk*o*nŏm′ĭk, ĕk*o*-) *adj.* Of economics, maintained for profit; practical, utilitarian. **e·co·nom′i·cal** *adj.* 1. Saving, thrifty; not wasteful (of). 2. Economic. **e·co·nom′i·cal·ly** *adv.* **e·co·**

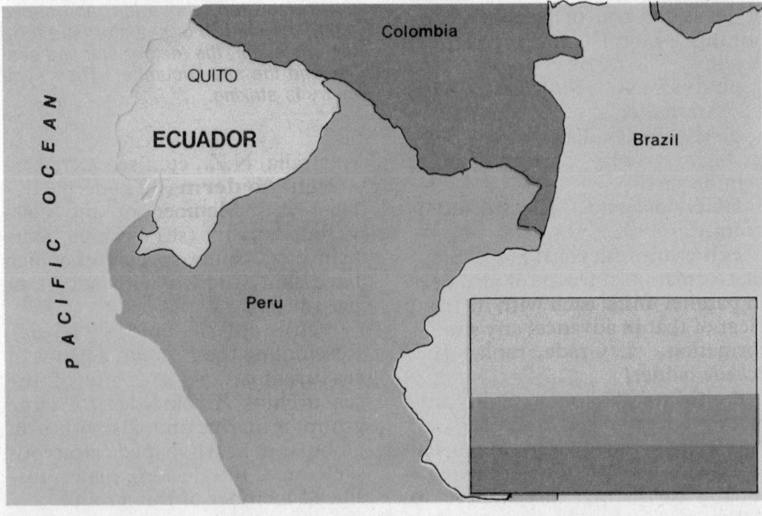

nom'ics *n.pl.* Science relating to the production and distribution of material wealth; condition of country with regard to material prosperity.

e·con·o·mist (ĭkŏn′*o*mĭst) *n.* One expert in economics or political economy.

e·con·o·mize (ĭkŏn′*o*mīz) *v.* (**-mized, -miz·ing**). Use economically; practice economy; reduce expenditure.

e·con·o·my (ĭkŏn′*o*mē) *n.* (pl. **-mies**). 1. Administration of concerns and resources of any community; art or science of such administration; **political ~**, former name for ECONOMICS, now applied esp. to analysis of problems of economic policy of governments. 2. Careful management of resources, so as to make them go as far as possible; frugality, thrift; a saving. ~ *adj.* Economical, thrifty.

e·co·sys·tem (ē′kōsĭst*e*m, ĕk′ō-) *n.* System comprising living organisms together with their physical environment.

ec·ru (ĕk′ro͞o, ā′kro͞o) *adj.* & *n.* (Of) grayish to pale yellow, light tan color.

ec·sta·sy (ĕk′st*a*sē) *n.* (pl. **-sies**). Exalted state of feeling, rapture, transport, esp. of delight; state of rapture in contemplation of divine things; poetic frenzy.

ec·stat·ic (ĕkstăt′ĭk, ĭk-) *adj.* Of, producing, subject to, ecstasy. ~ *n.* One subject to ecstasy.

ecto- *prefix.* Outer, external.

ec·to·blast (ĕk′t*o*blăst) *n.* (physiol.) Outer membrane of a cell.

ec·to·derm (ĕk′t*o*dẽrm) *n.* (embryol.) Outermost of three layers of cells formed by embryo at early stage, layer from which skin and nervous system are developed.

-ectomy *comb. form.* Removal of a part by surgery, as in *appendectomy, hysterectomy.*

ec·top·ic (ĕktŏp′ĭk) *adj.* (path.) In an abnormal place, as an ~ **pregnancy**, one in which the fertilized ovum develops outside the uterus.

ec·to·plasm (ĕk′t*o*plăz*e*m) *n.* 1. (biol.) Clear viscid outer layer of cytoplasm in an animal cell. 2. (spiritualism) Supposed emanation from body of medium.

Ec·ua·dor (ĕk′w*a*dōr). Republic in northwest S. Amer.; capital, Quito.

ec·u·men·i·cal (ĕky*u*mĕn′ĭk*a*l) *adj.* Of or representing the whole Christian world; seeking worldwide Christian unity, as an ~ **council**; worldwide. **ec·u·men′i·cal·ism, ec·u·me·nic·i·ty** (eky*u*m*e*nĭs′ĭtē), **ec′u·me·nism, ec·u·men′i·cism** *ns.* **ec·u·men′i·cal·ly** *adv.*

ec·ze·ma (ĕk′s*e*m*a*, ĕg′z*e*-, ĭgzē′-) *n.* (path.) Inflammation of skin, with redness, itching, and lesions that discharge serous matter. **ec·zem·a·tous** (ĭgzĕm′*a*t*u*s) *adj.*

-ed[1] *suffix.* Forming past tense and past participle of most verbs (*borrowed, moaned, slipped*).

-ed[2] *suffix.* Forming adjectives from nouns indicating having, characterized by, provided with, wearing, etc. (*striped, whiskered*).

ed. *abbrev.* Edited (by), edition, editor.

EDC *abbrev.* European Defense Community.

Ed.D. *abbrev.* Doctor of Education.

Ed·da (ĕd′*a*). 1. (also **Elder, Poetic,** ~) Collection (*c*1200) of ancient Old Norse poems on mythical or traditional subjects. 2. (also **Younger, Prose,** ~) Miscellaneous manual of Icelandic poetry with quotations and prose paraphrases, partly by the Icelandic historian Snorri Sturlason (*c*1230).

ed·dy (ĕd′ē) *n.* (pl. **-dies**). Circular current in water, small whirlpool; similar unsteady or swirling motion of air, wind, fog, dust, etc. ~ *v.i.* (**-died, -dy·ing**). Whirl around, move, in eddies.

Ed·dy (ĕd′ē), **Mrs. Mary Baker Glover** (1821–1910). American founder of the Church of Christ, Scientist (the Christian Science movement).

e·del·weiss (ā′d*e*lvīs, -wīs) *n.* Alpine plant (*Leontopodium alpinum*) with white flower, growing in rocky places. [Ger. *edel* noble, *weiss* white]

e·de·ma (ĭdē′m*a*) *n.* Abnormal accumulation of fluid in tissue; dropsy.

E·den[1] (ē′d*e*n). (also **Garden of** ~) Abode of Adam and Eve at their creation, Paradise; (transf.) delightful abode, state of supreme happiness. [Heb. *éden*, orig. = "delight"]

E·den[2] (ē′d*e*n), **(Robert) Anthony, 1st Earl of Avon** (1897–1977). British statesman; prime minister 1955–7.

An ***eddy,*** *known in the region as the 'Dust Devil', funnels dust up to great heights in Tanzania, Africa. Such swirling motions can be caused either on land or water.*

e·den·tate (ĭdĕn′tāt) *adj.* & *n.* (Animal) belonging to mammalian order Edentata, having no teeth or very simple teeth without enamel (sloths, great anteaters, armadillos, aardvarks, etc.); lacking teeth.

edge (ĕj) *n.* 1. Thin sharpened side of cutting instrument or weapon; sharpness given to blade by whetting; (fig.) effectiveness, trenchancy (of speech etc.); **be on** ~, be excited or irritable; **set person's teeth on** ~, jar his or her nerves or sensibilities. 2. Crest of ridge; line at which 2 surfaces

Eclipses *have been watched and recorded since ancient times. Modern astronomers can predict precisely future eclipses and calculate the dates of past ones. A total eclipse of the sun allows observation of stars near the sun and of its outer layers.*

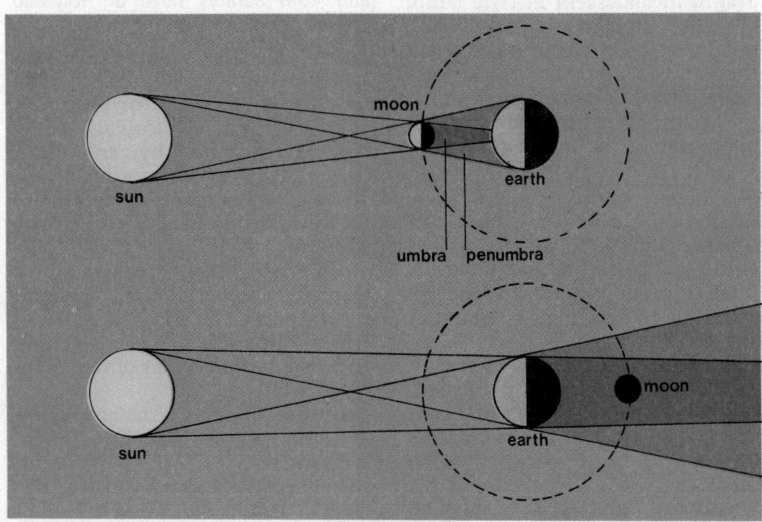

meet abruptly; (fig.) perilous or critical position or moment. 3. One of narrow surfaces of thin flat object; rim (of vessel); one of the 3 surfaces of book left uncovered by binding. 4. Boundary of any surface, border, brink (of precipice). 5. (colloq.) Advantage, superiority. ~ *v.* (**edged, edg·ing**). 1. Give an edge to, sharpen. 2. Border; furnish with edging. 3. Move edgewise; advance (esp. obliquely) by repeated almost imperceptible degrees; move (thing, oneself) thus, nudge on.

edge·wise (ĕj′wīz), **edge·ways** (ĕj′wāz) *advs.* With edge foremost or turned toward spectator; edge to edge; (moving) with edge foremost; **get (word) in** ~, manage to speak in interval of loquacious person's talk.

edg·ing (ĕj′ĭng) *n.* (esp.) Border, fringe, etc., on garment, border (of grass etc.) around flower beds or lawn; lace etc. made to be sewn to edge of garment.

edg·y (ĕj′ē) *adj.* (**edg·i·er, edg·i·est**). Sharp-edged; tense, nervous; irritable.

ed·i·ble (ĕd′ĭbel) *adj.* & *n.* (Thing) fit to be eaten, eatable. **ed·i·bil·i·ty** (ĕdĭbĭl′ĭtē), **ed′i·ble·ness** *ns.*

e·dict (ē′dĭkt) *n.* What is proclaimed by authority; order issued by sovereign to subjects; **E~ of Nantes**: see NANTES.

ed·i·fice (ĕd′ĭfĭs) *n.* Building, esp. large and stately one.

ed·i·fy (ĕd′ĭfī) *v.t.* (**-fied, -fy·ing**). Benefit spiritually, strengthen, support; instruct, improve. **ed·i·fi·ca·tion** (ĕdĭfĭkā′shon) *n.*

Ed·in·burgh (ĕd′inbĕrō, -bŭrō; *Brit.* ĕd′ĭnbr*u*). Capital of Scotland, situated on the Firth of Forth; capital of Scottish kingdom, 1436–1707.

Ed·i·son (ĕd′ĭs*o*n), **Thomas Alva** (1847–1931). American inventor of the microphone, phonograph, incandescent electric lamp, alkaline storage battery, etc.; obtained over 1,000 patents on these and on improvements, devices dealing with dynamos, motors, the telegraph, the mimeograph, photography, motion pictures, etc.

ed·it (ĕd′ĭt) *v.t.* Prepare edition of (book, article, etc.); collate (material chiefly provided by others) for publication; act as editor of; assemble and integrate final (film, sound track, tape recording) by cutting, combining, and splicing.

e·di·tion (ĭdĭsh′*o*n) *n.* Form in which literary work is published; whole number of copies of book, newspaper, etc., printed from same set of types and issued at same time.

ed·i·tor (ĕd′ĭt*e*r) *n.* One who edits; one who supervises newspaper or periodical, or section of newspaper etc. **ed′i·tor·ship** *n.*

Edinburgh Castle *and Princes Street Gardens. From the castle the Royal Mile runs down to the Palace of Holyrood House and ruins of the 12th and 13th century nave of Holyrood Abbey.*

ed·i·to·ri·al (ĕdĭtōr′ē*a*l, -tōr′-) *adj.* Of, written by, an editor. ~ *n.* Newspaper, magazine article written by or expressing opinion of its editor or publisher. **ed·i·to′ri·al·ly** *adv.*

Ed · mon · ton (ĕd′m*o*nt*o*n). Capital of Alberta, Canada, in S. central part on North Saskatchewan River; important transportation and distribution center of Canadian Northwest.

E·dom (ē′d*o*m). Ancient region of Asia S. of the Dead Sea. **E′dom·ite** n. (Member) of an ancient people traditionally descended from Esau, living in Edom.

Downtown ***Edmonton,*** *in Alberta, Canada. Edmonton is the commercial hub of the Canadian northwest, particularly for agricultural and oil-based industries.*

EDP *abbrev.* Electronic data processing.

EDT, E.D.T. *abbrevs.* Eastern Daylight Time.

educ. *abbrev.* Education(al).

ed·u·ca·ble (ĕj′*u*kabel, ĕd′y*u*-) *adj.* Capable of being educated or trained. **ed·u·ca·bil·i·ty** (ĕj*u*ka-bĭl′ĭtē, ĕdy*u*-) *n.*

ed·u·cate (ĕj′*u*kāt, ĕd′y*u*-) *v.t.* (**-cat·ed, -cat·ing**). Bring up from childhood, so as to form habits, manners, intellectual aptitudes, etc.; instruct, provide schooling for; train, discipline, so as to develop some special aptitude, taste, or disposition. **ed′u·ca·tor** *n.*

ed·u·ca·tion (ĕj*u*kā′sh*o*n, ĕdy*u*-) *n.* Systematic instruction, schooling, or training in preparation for life or some particular task; scholastic instruction; bringing up. **ed·u·ca′tion·al** *adj.* ~ **television**, television program(s) produced for educational purposes. **ed·u·ca′-tion·al·ly** *adv.* **ed·u·ca′tion·al·ist** *n.* One who studies the science or methods of education.

ed·u·ca·tive (ĕj′*u*kātiv, ĕd′y*u*-) *adj.* Of education; educating; bearing on, conducive to, education.

e·duce (ĭdōōs′, ĭdūs′) *v.t.* (**e·duced, e·duc·ing**). Bring out, elicit, develop, from latent, rudimentary, or potential condition; infer; extract. **e·duc′i·ble** *adj.*

In 1877 ***Thomas Alva Edison*** *applied for a U.S. patent for his phonograph (below), which consisted of a tin-foil covered cylinder and a hand crank. He later produced a motor-driven cylinder player. Right: The original Edison light bulb. Left: The first commercial light bulb.*

Education *today still concerns itself with the basic lessons, despite having moved very much into the computer age. Audio-visual aids and computers are now an integral part of education.*

e·duc·tion (ĭdŭk′sh*o*n) *n.*

Ed·ward[1] (ĕd′w*e*rd). Name of two kings of the English before the Norman Conquest; ~ **the Confessor**, son of Ethelred the Unready, reigned 1042–66; last Anglo-Saxon king of England; ~ **the Martyr**, reigned 975–9, assassinated by order of his stepmother.

Ed·ward[2] (ĕd′w*e*rd). Name of six kings of England since the Norman Conquest and two of the United Kingdom: **Edward I** (1239–1307), son of Henry III; king of England 1272–1307; conquered Wales and attempted the conquest of Scotland; **Edward II** (1284–1327), succeeded his father Edward I in 1307; continued the attempted conquest of Scotland but was

***Edward VI,** when he was 13, painted by a follower of Hans Holbein, c. 1550. His reign as King of England (1547–53) was rife with faction fights.*

***Edward VII** in a painting by Sir Luke Fildes. After the long reign of his mother, Queen Victoria, he succeeded to the U.K. throne in 1901 aged 60.*

defeated by Robert Bruce at Bannockburn (1314); murdered in 1327; **Edward III** (1312–77), son of Edward II, reigned 1327–77; the Hundred Years War against France began in his reign, and he gained temporarily the duchy of Aquitaine by the Treaty of Bretigny (1360); **Edward IV** (1442–83), the first Yorkist king; descended from Edward III; reigned 1461–83; defeated the Lancastrians in the Wars of the Roses; **Edward V** (1470–83), son of Edward IV; king in 1483, in which year he was deposed; **Edward VI** (1537–53), son of Henry VIII and Jane Seymour; reigned 1547–53; **Edward VII** (1841–1910), son of Queen Victoria; king of the United Kingdom 1901–10; **Edward VIII** (1894–1972); succeeded his father, George V, 1936; abdicated same year to marry Amer. divorcée Wallis Warfield Simpson.

Ed·ward·i·an (ĕdwôr′dēan, -wâr′-) *adj.* & *n.* (Person) belonging to, characteristic of, or following styles and views of reign of Edward VII of the United Kingdom.

Ed·wards (ĕd′werdz), **Jonathan** (1703–58). Amer. Congregational clergyman and Calvinist theologian; known for powerful emotional sermons such as "Sinners in the Hands of an Angry God."

E.E. *abbrev.* Electrical engineer(ing).

EEC *abbrev.* European Economic Community.

EEG *abbrev.* Electroencephalogram.

eel (ēl) *n.* (pl. **eels,** collect. **eel**). 1. Any of numerous small-finned and soft-finned snakelike fishes of the order Anguilliformes (or Apodes), the fresh-water forms of which migrate to the Sargasso Sea to spawn. 2. Any of various other fishes resembling eels in shape. 3. **electric** ~: see ELECTRIC; **eel′-grass,** any of several submerged aquatic plants of genus *Zostera* of coastal areas, with grasslike leaves; **eel′worm,** any of various wormlike often microscopic animals of the phylum Nematoda, some of which are parasitic on crops.

e'er (âr) *adv.* (poet.) = EVER.

ee·rie, ee·ry (ēr′ē) *adjs.* (**ee·ri·er, ee·ri·est**). Gloomy, strange, weird. **ee′ri·ly** *adv.* **ee′ri·ness** *n.*

ef·face (ĭfās′) *v.t.* (**-faced, -fac·ing**). Rub out; obliterate, wipe out; reduce *oneself* to insignificance, be humble. **ef·face′a·ble** *adj.* **ef·face′ment** *n.*

ef·fect (ĭfĕkt′) *n.* 1. Result, consequence; efficacy; combination of color or form in picture, landscape, etc.; (pl.) lighting, appropriate sounds, etc., in play etc.; phenomenon. 2. (pl.) Property, goods. 3. Being operative; operative influence; **take** ~, become operative, come into force. 4. Impression produced on spectator, hearer, etc. 5. **in** ~, virtually, for practical purposes. **effect** *v.t.* Bring about, accomplish. **ef·fec′tive** *adj.* 1. Having an effect; that is actually brought to bear on an object; coming into effect, becoming operative. 2. Powerful in effect; striking. 3. Functioning, operative. 4. Actual, existing. **ef·fec′tive** *n.* Combat-ready soldier. **ef·fec′tive·ly** *adv.* **ef·fec′tive·ness** *n.*

ef·fec·tu·al (ĭfĕk′cho͞oal) *adj.* Answering its purpose; valid. **ef·fec′tu·al·ly** *adv.*

ef·fec·tu·ate (ĭfĕk′choōāt) *v.t.* (**-at·ed, -at·ing**). Bring to pass, accomplish. **ef·fec·tu·a·tion** (ĭfĕk-choōā′shon) *n.*

ef·fem·i·nate (ĭfĕm′ĭnĭt) *adj.* Womanish, unmanly. **ef·fem′i·nate·ly** *adv.* **ef·fem·i·na·cy** (ĭfĕm′ĭnasē) *n.*

ef·fen·di (ĭfĕn′dē) *n.* (pl. **-dis**). Former Turkish title of respect for officials etc.

ef·fer·ent (ĕf′erent) *adj.* (physiol.) Conveying outward; (of nerves) conveying impulses from central nervous system to muscles and glands.

ef·fer·vesce (ĕfervĕs′) *v.i.* (**-vesced, -vesc·ing**). Give off bubbles of gas, esp. as result of chemical action; bubble. **ef·fer·ves′cence** *n.* **ef·fer·ves′cent** *adj.*

ef·fete (ĭfēt′) *adj.* Exhausted, worn out; feeble, incapable; decadent. **ef·fete′ness** *n.*

ef·fi·ca·cious (ĕfĭkā′shus) *adj.* (of instrument, method, action) Producing, sure to produce, intended or appropriate effect. **ef·fi·ca′cious·ly** *adv.* **ef·fi·ca′cious·ness, ef·fi·ca·cy** (ĕf′ĭkasē) (pl. **-cies**) *ns.*

ef·fi·cient (ĭfĭsh′ent) *adj.* Making, causing to be; productive of effects; effective, operative; skilled, capable. **ef·fi′cient·ly** *adv.* **ef·fi·cien·cy** (ĭfĭsh′ensē) *n.* (pl. **-cies**). State or quality of being efficient; (phys.) ratio of energy or work produced to that expended.

ef·fi·gy (ĕf′ĭjē) *n.* (pl. **-gies**). Portrait, image; rough representation of hated person; **burn (hang) in ~**, burn (or hang) image of hated person as expression of anger, disdain, ridicule.

ef·flo·resce (ĕflorĕs′) *v.i.* (**-resced, -resc·ing**). 1. Blossom, flower (lit. and fig.). 2. (chem., of crystals or salts) (Come to surface and) turn to fine powder on exposure to air; (of surface) become covered with powdery saline crust. **ef·flo·res′cence** *n.* **ef·flo·res′cent** *adj.*

ef·flu·ence (ĕf′loōens, ĕfloō′-) *n.* Flowing out; what flows out, emanation.

ef·flu·ent (ĕf′loōent, ĕfloō′-) *adj.* Flowing forth. ~ *n.* Stream flowing from larger stream, reservoir, lake, etc.; outflow from septic tank etc.

ef·flu·vi·um (ĭfloō′vēum) *n.* (pl. **-vi·a** pr. -vēa). Barely visible or invisible outflow of gas or particulate matter, esp. one that is offensive or noxious. **ef·flu′vi·al** *adj.*

ef·flux (ĕf′lŭks) *n.* Flowing out (of liquid, air, gas); that which flows out.

ef·fort (ĕf′ert) *n.* Strenuous exertion; display of power, achievement.

ef·fort·less (ĕf′ertlĭs) *adj.* Requiring, making little or no effort; easy. **ef′fort·less·ly** *adv.* **ef′fort·less·ness** *n.*

ef·fron·ter·y (ĭfrŭn′terē, ĕ-) *n.* (pl. **-ter·ies**). Shameless audacity; impudent boldness.

ef·ful·gent (ĭfŭl′jent) *adj.* Radiant. **ef·ful′gent·ly** *adv.* **ef·ful′gence** *n.*

ef·fuse (ĭfūz′) *v.t.* (**-fused, -fus·ing**). Pour forth; spread out.

ef·fu·sion (ĭfū′zhon) *n.* Pouring forth; outpouring, as of emotions, words, etc.

ef·fu·sive (ĭfū′sĭv) *adj.* Exuberant, unduly demonstrative. **ef·fu′sive·ly** *adv.* **ef·fu′sive·ness** *n.*

eft (ĕft) *n.* Newt.

Eg. *abbrev.* Egypt(ian).

e.g. *abbrev.* *Exempli gratia* (L., = "for example").

e·gal·i·tar·i·an (ĭgălĭtār′ēan) *adj.* & *n.* (Person) asserting equality of mankind, esp. in political or social life.

egg[1] (ĕg) *n.* 1. (pop.) More or less spheroidal body, containing germ of new individual within a shell or membrane, deposited externally (laid) by female of some animals esp. birds, reptiles, fishes, and insects; esp., domestic fowl's egg as article of food. 2. (zool.) Non-motile cell produced by female, capable, usu. after fertilization by a sperm, of developing into a new individual; ovum. 3. (**have** or **put**) **all one's ~s in one basket**, (risk) all on a single venture; **bad ~**, person who comes to no good; **good ~**, (slang) nice person. 4. **egg′beater**, device for beating eggs, mixing cake batter, etc.; (slang) helicopter; **egg′cup**, cup-shaped vessel to hold boiled egg in shell for eating; **egg foo yong** (or **young**), Chinese dish of eggs beaten and cooked with bean sprouts, onions, celery, and gingerroot, combined with minced meat, fish, or poultry; **egg′head**, (slang) intellectual, highbrow; **egg′nog**, drink of milk or cream, beaten eggs, sugar, and nutmeg, usu. mixed with

Below: Easter ***eggs*** *by Fabergé (1846–1920); the turn-of-the-century work of this Russian jeweller and goldsmith is highly valued. Bottom: Two blackbird's eggs. The colored shells serve to camouflage the eggs from predators.*

*The **egret** is found in N. America, Asia, and Australia. The popularity of the dorsal plumes (ospreys) that the egret sports when breeding brought one species close to extinction.*

liquor; **egg′plant**, perennial plant (*Solanum melongena*) cultivated for its edible fruit, served as a vegetable; ovoid fruit of this plant, aubergine; **egg roll**, Chinese dish of egg pastry rolled into oblong casings that are stuffed with minced meat or seafood and chopped vegetables and browned in deep fat; **eggs Benedict**, poached eggs on toasted English muffins and ham, topped with hollandaise sauce; **egg′shell**, shell of egg; freq. as type of anything frail or fragile; **egg tooth**, protuberance on bill sheath of embryo bird, reptile, etc., for cracking its shell.

egg[2] (ĕg) *v.t.* Incite, encourage, urge (*on*).

eg·lan·tine (ĕg′lantĭn, -tēn): see SWEETbrier.

e·go (ē′gō, ĕg′ō) *n.* (pl. **e·gos**). 1. (metaphys.) Conscious thinking subject as opp. to *non-ego* or object; the self. 2. (psychol.) That part of the mind which is organized and has a sense of individuality (thus used by Freud to distinguish it from the primitive, impersonal, unconscious part which he called the *id*); ~ **trip**, (colloq.) activity etc. devoted entirely to one's own interests or feelings. [L., = "I"]

e·go·cen·tric (ēgōsĕn′trĭk, ĕgō-) *adj.* Centered in the ego; self-centered, egoistic. **e·go·cen·tric·i·ty** (ēgōsĕntrĭs′ĭtē, ĕgō-) *n.*

e·go·ism (ē′gōĭzem, ĕg′ō-) *n.* 1. (ethics) Theory that regards self-interest as foundation of morality. 2. Regard to one's own interest, systematic selfishness; selfish aims or purposes; self-opinionatedness. **e′go·ist** *n.* **e·go·is·tic** (ēgōĭs′tĭk, ĕgō-), **e·go·is′ti·cal** *adjs.* **e·go·is′ti·cal·ly** *adv.*

e·go·ma·ni·a (ēgōmā′nēa, -mān′ya, ĕgō-) *n.* Morbid egotism. **e·go·ma′ni·ac** *n.*

e·go·tism (ē′gotĭzem, ĕg′o-) *n.* Practice of talking about oneself excessively; boasting; self-conceit. **e′go·tist** *n.* **e·go·tis·tic** (ēgotĭs′tĭk, ĕgo-), **e·go·tis′ti·cal** *adjs.* **e·go·tis′ti·cal·ly** *adv.*

e·gre·gious (ĭgrē′jus) *adj.* Glaringly bad, blatant, **e·gre′gious·ly** *adv.* **e·gre′gious·ness** *n.* [L. *egregius*, lit. "towering above the flock" (*grex* flock)]

e·gress (ē′grĕs) *n.* (Right or liberty of) going out; (astron.) end of eclipse or occultation; exit.

e·gret (ē′grĭt, ĭgrĕt′, ĕg′rĭt) *n.* Any of several herons having long ornamental drooping plumes during breeding season, esp. the American egret (*Casmerodius albus egretta*), the snowy egret (*Leucophoyx thula*), and the reddish egret (*Dichromanassa rufescens*).

E·gypt (ē′jĭpt). Arab Republic of Egypt, a country in NE. Africa bounded on N. by the Mediterranean and on E. by the Red Sea; capital Cairo; **Ancient** ~, civilization in the Nile valley from the Stone Age until the Roman period; ruled by successive dynasties until conquest by Alexander the Great in 332 B.C.; after periods of Greek and Roman domination it passed to the Byzantine Empire (395–642); the ancient culture died out after the Arab conquest, and Egypt became a province of the Ottoman Empire 1517–1879, then a British protectorate 1914–22.

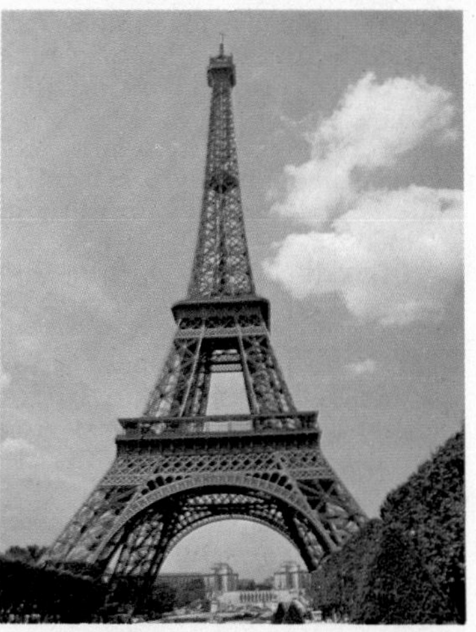

*Built when France led the world in the development of iron and steel buildings, and initially a subject of protest, the **Eiffel Tower** remains a prominent feature of Paris. It now serves also as a T.V. transmitter.*

E·gyp·tian (ĭjĭp′shan) *adj.* Of Egypt or its people or language. ~ *n.* 1. Egyptian person. 2. Language of the ancient Egyptians together with its descendant, Coptic, which is still used in the liturgies of the Coptic Church; one of the Hamitic group of languages.

E·gyp·tol·o·gy (ējĭptŏl′ojē) *n.* Study of Egyptian antiquities. **E·gyp·tol′o·gist** *n.*

eh (ā) *int.* Ejaculation of inquiry or surprise, or inviting assent.

EHF *abbrev.* Extremely high frequency.

Ehr·lich (ār′lĭx), **Paul** (1854–1915). German bacteriologist;

*The Republic of Ireland or **Eire** constitutes the major part of the second largest of the British Isles. The history of this mainly agricultural island has been turbulent.*

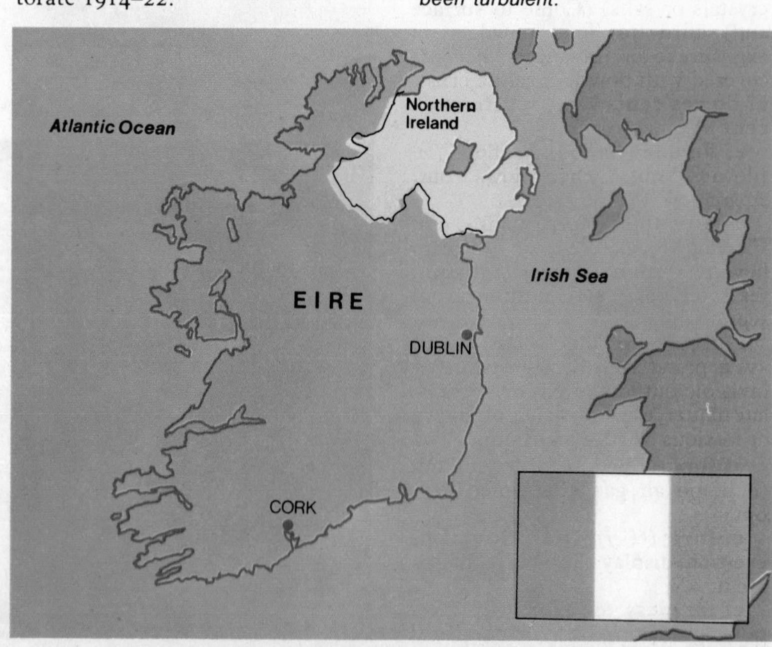

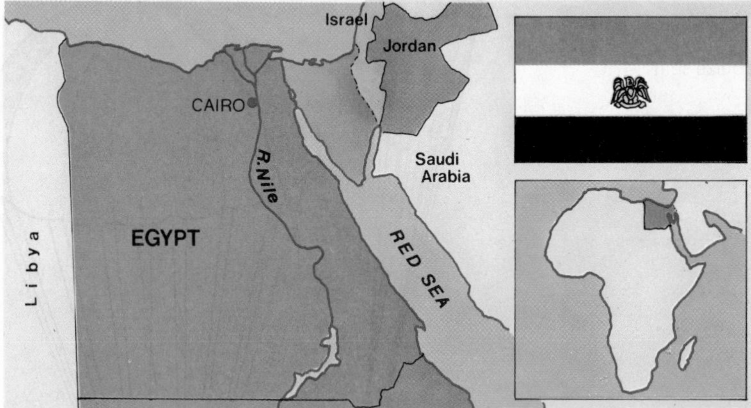

Above: sculpture of man with harpoon.

*The central geographical feature of **Egypt** is the Nile whose fertile valley forms the most populous area of the country and whose seasonal flooding dictated the patterns of agriculture until modern systems of irrigation were developed. The chief cash crop is cotton. Egypt's rich and ancient history has been extensively preserved in monuments and artifacts thanks to the dry climate. Top left: The Sphinx of Hatshepsut at Memphis.*

pioneer in bacteriology, immunology, and chemotherapy; discoverer of salvarsan; shared Nobel Prize for medicine and physiology 1908.

ei·der (ī′d*er*) *n.* Any of several sea ducks of N. hemisphere, esp. of genus *Somateria*, having valuable down; **ei′derdown**, small soft feathers from breast of eider duck; soft quilt, orig. one stuffed with eiderdown.

ei·det·ic (īdĕt′ĭk) *adj.* (psychol., of mental image) Vivid or lifelike, often unreal, esp. of images experienced in childhood. **ei·det′i·cal·ly** *adv.*

Eif·fel (ī′fel) **Tower.** Iron tower, 984 ft. (300 m) high, originally built for the Exposition of 1889 by A. G. Eiffel in Paris, France.

eight (āt) *adj.* One more than seven ~ *n.* One more than seven; symbol for this (8, viii, or VIII); anything in the form 8, esp. skating figure; card with eight pips; eight o'clock; size etc. indicated by 8; set of eight things or persons, esp. a rowing crew; **eight′ball**, black pool ball bearing the number 8; (slang) clumsy person, bungler; **behind the eightball**, (slang) at a disadvantage; in trouble; **~-track** (*n.*), magnetic tape cartridge, esp. one having eight parallel tracks of prerecorded music or sound.

eight·een (ā′tēn′) *adj.* & *n.* One more than 17 (18, xviii, or XVIII). **eight·eenth** (ā′tēnth′) *adj.* & *n.*

eighth (ātth) *adj.* Next after seventh. ~ *n.* Eighth part (see PART[1] def 1); eighth thing etc.

eight·y (ā′tē) *adj.* Eight times 10 in number. ~ *n.* (pl. **eight·ies**). Cardinal number 8 times 10 (80, lxxx, or LXXX); set of 80 things or persons; **eight′ies**, numbers etc. from 80 to 89; these years of century or life. **eight·i·eth** (ā′tēĭth) *adj.* & *n.*

Ein·stein (īn′stīn; *Ger.* īn′shtīn), **Albert** (1879–1955). German-born Amer. theoretical physicist; explained Brownian motion and the photoelectric effect, investigated atomic spectra; most famous for his revolutionary theory of the nature of space and time, known as the theory of RELATIVITY, which upset the Newtonian conception of the universe.

ein·stein·i·um (īnstī′nē*u*m) *n.* (chem.) Transuranic element, symbol E, at. no. 99, principal isotope at. wt. 253.

Eir·e (ār′*e*, īr′*e*). Former and Gaelic name for the Republic of IRELAND.

Ei·sen·how·er (ī′zenhow*er*),

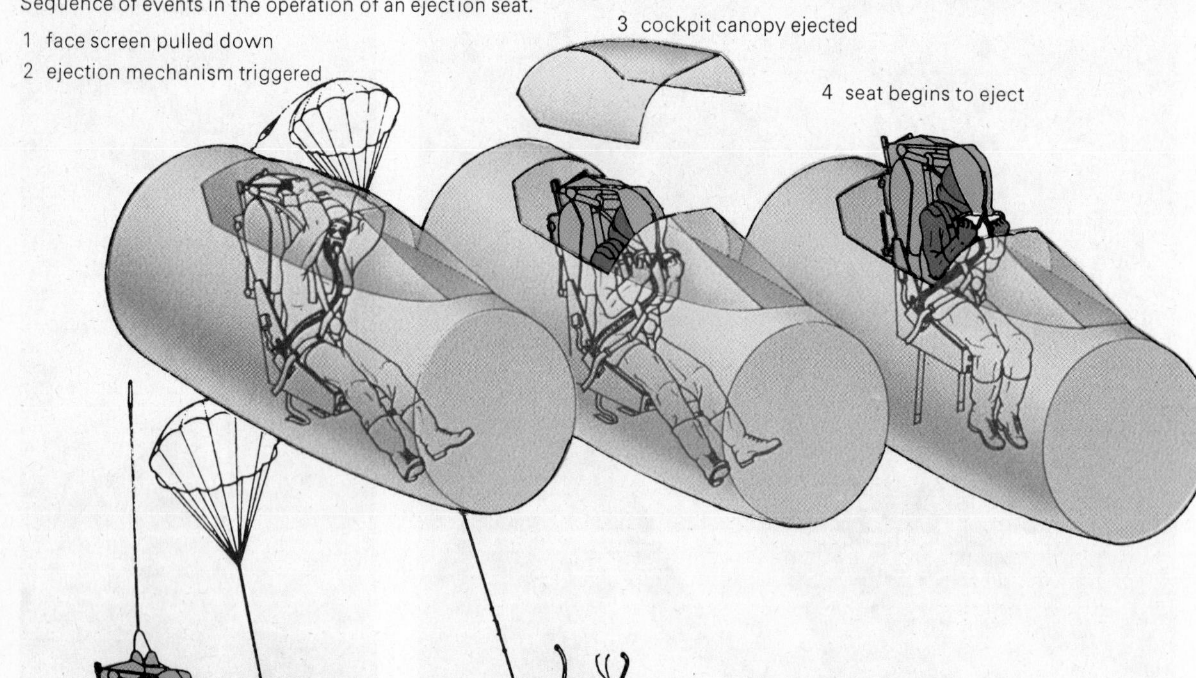

***Ejection** seats equipped with parachutes to control their rate of fall, were first considered by Leonardo da Vinci about 1500. In the 18th century, balloonists made jumps using something like an umbrella; the first folding parachute was used in America in 1880. A modern ejection seat with a parachute which opens automatically was not perfected until after the development of high-speed aircraft.*

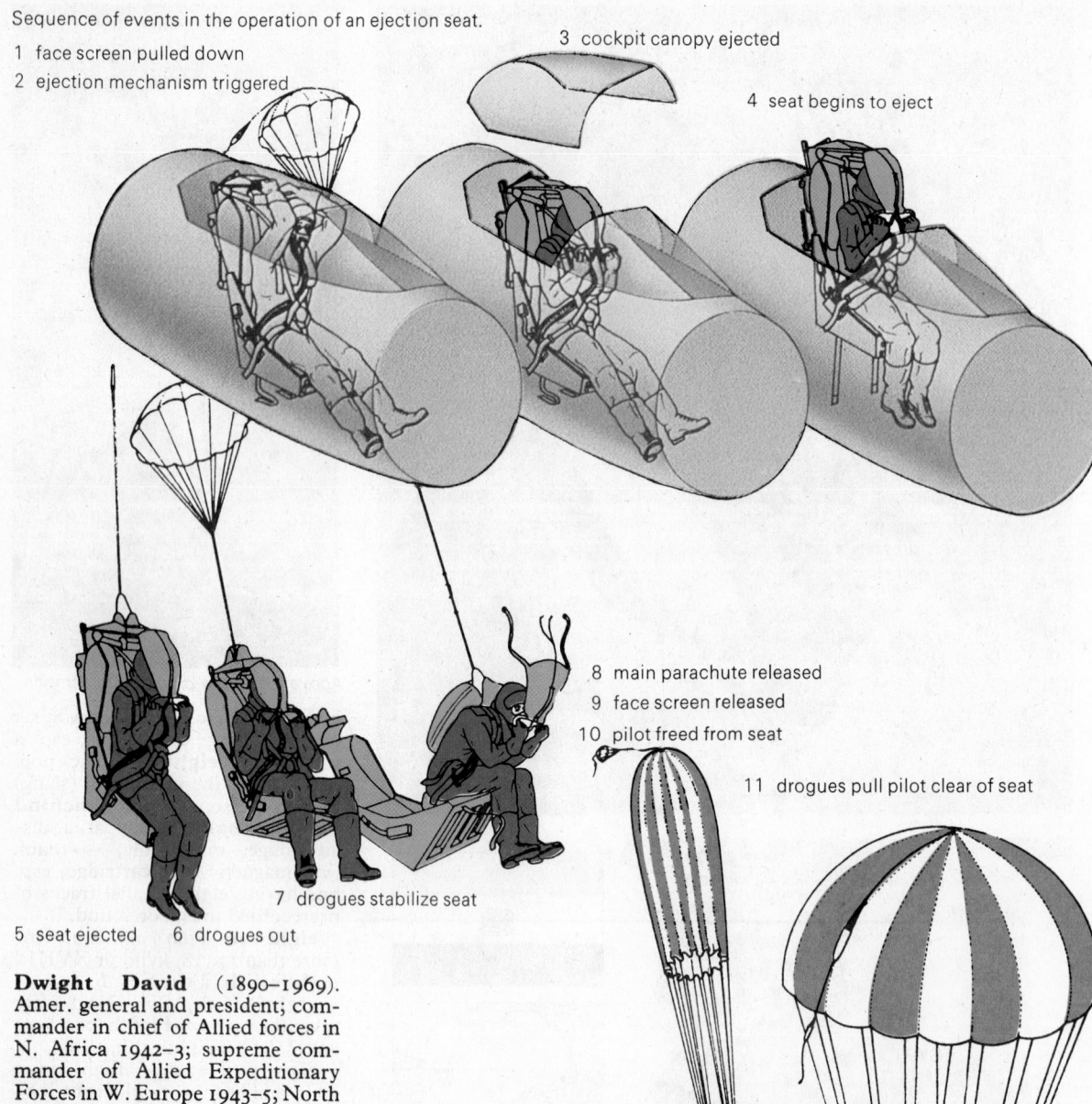

Dwight David (1890–1969). Amer. general and president; commander in chief of Allied forces in N. Africa 1942–3; supreme commander of Allied Expeditionary Forces in W. Europe 1943–5; North Atlantic supreme commander 1950–2; 34th president of the U.S. 1953–61.

ei·ther (ē′dher, ī′-) *adj.* & *pron.* Each of two; one or the other of two. ~ *adv.* Introducing first of alternatives (**either** ... **or** ...); (in neg. or interrog. sentences) any more than the other, as *if you do not go, I shall not* ~.

e·jac·u·late (ĭjăk′yulāt) *v.t.* (**-lat·ed, -lat·ing**). 1. Utter suddenly. 2. Eject (fluids, esp. semen) from body. **e·jac·u·la·tion** (ĭjăkyulā′shon) *n.* **e·jac·u·la·to·ry** (ĭjăk′yulatōrē, -tōrē) *adj.*

e·ject (ĭjĕkt′) *v.t.* 1. Expel, evict (*from* place, office, etc.). 2. Throw out from within; emit. **e·jec′tion** *n.* ~ **seat,** escape seat designed to eject with its occupant from an aircraft in emergencies and parachute to earth. **e·jec′tor** *n.*

eke[1] (ēk) *v.t.* (**eked, ek·ing**). ~ **out,** supplement with great effort, strain to supply deficiencies of; contrive to make (livelihood) or support (existence) by various makeshift means.

eke[2] (ēk) *adv.* (archaic) Also.

EKG *abbrev.* Electrocardiogram.

e·kis·tics (ĭkĭs′tĭks) *n.pl.* (usu. considered sing.). Study of human settlements and their planning and development. **e·kis′tic, e·kis′ti·cal** *adjs.* **e·kis·ti′cian** *n.*

el. *abbrev.* Elevation.

e·lab·o·rate (ĭlăb′orĭt) *adj.* Carefully or minutely worked out; highly finished. **e·lab′o·rate·ly** *adv.* **e·lab′o·rate·ness** *n.* **elab·orate** (ĭlăb′orāt) *v.t.* (**-rat·ed, -rat·ing**). Work out with care in detail; develop thoroughly; create; add details in writing or speech. **e·lab·o·ra·tion** (ĭlăborā′shon) *n.*

E·laine (ĭlān′). In Arthurian legend, the name of two women who loved Lancelot; one died of unrequited love, the other was the mother of Galahad by him.

E·lam·ite (ē′lamīt) *adj.* & *n.* (Native, inhabitant, language) of Elam, an ancient country of Mesopotamia with its capital at Susa (now Shush, in Iran).

é·lan (ālahn′) *n.* Vivacity, dash; style, flair.

e·land (ē′land) *n.* (pl. **e·lands**, collect. **e·land**). Either of two large heavily built African antelopes of genus *Taurotragus*, with spirally twisted horns.

élan vi·tal (*Fr.* ālahṅ vētăl′). In the philosophy of Henri Bergson, the life force or mysterious vital principle, basis of an organism's physical form, growth, and development.

e·lapse (ĭlăps′) *v.i.* (**e·lapsed, e·laps·ing**). (of time) Pass, slip away.

e·las·mo·branch (ĭlăz′mobrăngk) *n.* (pl. **-branchs** pr. -brăngks). (zool.) Any cartilaginous fish (shark, ray, skate, etc.).

e·las·tic (ĭlăs′tĭk) *adj.* 1. Spontaneously resuming its normal bulk or shape after having been contracted, dilated, or distorted; buoyant, springy; flexible, accommodating. 2. (of fabric etc.) Containing, made of, thin strips or threads of rubber usu. covered with woven material, or made of elasticized material. ~ *n.* Elastic fabric, elastic cord or string. **e·las′ti·cal·ly** *adv.* **e·las·tic·i·ty** (ĭlăstĭs′- Treat or weave (yarn or cloth) to give it elastic properties.

e·las·to·mer (ĭlăs′tomer) *n.* Synthetic rubber or plastic resembling rubber. **e·las·to·mer·ic** (ĭlăstomĕr′ĭk) *adj.*

e·late (ĭlāt′) *v.t.* (**-lat·ed, -lat·ing**). Raise spirits of, encourage, excite. **e·la′tion** *n.*

El·ba (ĕl′ba). Italian island off the W. coast of Italy, the place of Napoleon's first exile (1814–15).

*Top: 'The **Election;** Chairing the Member', by William Hogarth (1697–1764), a satirical comment on political elections. Above: Delegates demonstrate at a Republican Party national convention during the U.S. presidential election campaign, 1968. The basis of the franchise and electoral traditions and methods vary from country to country.*

el·bow (ĕl′bō) *n.* Outer part of joint between fore- and upper arm; elbow-shaped bend or corner in river, road, etc.; short piece of pipe bent at an angle to join two straight pieces; **out at the ~s**, ragged, poor; **up to the ~s**, busily, fully engaged *in*; ~ **grease**, vigorous rubbing, hard work; ~ **macaroni**, short-cut tubular macaroni, dried in small, curved pieces; **el′bowroom**, sufficient space to move or work in. **elbow** *v.* Thrust, jostle, (as) with the elbows.

El·brus (ĕl′brōōs), **Mount.** (also **El·bo·rus**) Highest mountain in Europe, 18,480 ft. (5,636 m), in the Caucasus range of Georgian U.S.S.R.

El Cap·i·tan (ĕl kăpĭtăn′, kahpētahn′). Peak, 7,564 ft. (2,307 m), in Yosemite National Park in the Sierra Nevadas, California.

eld·er[1] (ĕl′der) *n.* Low tree or shrub of genus *Sambucus*, with clusters of small white flowers and red, purple, or black berries; **el′derberry**, elder; its fruit, used esp. to make **elderberry wine.**

eld·er[2] (ĕl′der) *adj.* Senior (of relations, or of 2 indicated persons); ~ **statesman**, retired statesman etc. whose advice is available. **elder** *n.* 1. (pl.) Persons of greater age. 2. (chiefly hist.) Member of senate, governing body, or class, of men venerable for age. 3. (eccles.) One of a body of laymen assisting in the management of church affairs, having pastoral or teaching functions etc.

eld·er·ly (ĕl′derlē) *adj.* Somewhat old; past middle age.

eld·est (ĕl′dĭst) *adj.* Oldest, esp. first-born or oldest surviving (member of family, son, daughter, etc.).

El Do·ra·do, El·do·ra·do (ĕldorah′dō, -rā′-). Legendary country or city abounding in gold, jewels, etc., believed by 16th-c. explorers to exist in Spanish Amer.; hence, any place of fabulous wealth, opportunity, etc., esp. California during the gold rush. [Span., = "the gilded"]

El·e·at·ic (ĕlēăt′ĭk) *adj.* Of, pertaining to, a school of Greek philosophers of the 6th c. B.C. founded by PARMENIDES and his successor Zeno at Elea in Lucania.

el·e·cam·pane (ĕlĕkămpān′) *n.* Perennial Eurasian plant (*Inula helenium*) with large yellow flowers and bitter aromatic leaves and root, formerly used as tonic etc.

e·lect (ĭlĕkt′) *adj.* 1. Chosen; choice. 2. (theol.) Chosen by God, esp. for salvation or eternal life. 3. (usu. following n.) Elected but not yet installed in office, as *president-elect*. ~ *v.t.* Choose, choose (person) by vote; (of God) choose (persons) for salvation etc.; choose to study (a course).

e·lec·tion (ĭlĕk′sh*o*n) *n.* Choosing, esp. by vote; public vote.

e·lec·tion·eer (ĭlĕksh*o*nēr′) *v.i.* Work on behalf of a political candidate, party, etc. in an election.

e·lec·tive (ĭlĕk′tĭv) *adj.* 1. Appointed or filled by, (of authority) derived from, election; having power of electing by vote; pertaining to, based on, system or principle of election. 2. (of courses in university etc.) Optional. ~ *n.* Elective course.

e·lec·tor (ĭlĕk′t*er*) *n.* Person with right to vote in election; member of **Electoral College**, elected by the voters of the 50 states and the District of Columbia and responsible for election of the president and vice president of the U.S.; **Elector**, one of the German princes of the Holy Roman Empire entitled to take part in electing the emperor. **e·lec′tor·al** *adj.*

e·lec·tor·ate (ĭlĕk′terĭt) *n.* 1. (hist.) Territory of German elector. 2. Whole body of qualified voters.

E·lec·tra (ĭlĕk′tr*a*). (Gk. myth.) Daughter of Agamemnon and Clytemnestra; urged her brother Orestes to kill Clytemnestra and Aegisthus in revenge for murder of Agamemnon; ~ **complex**, (psychol.) counterpart in females of OEDIPUS complex, daughter's feeling of attraction toward father and hostility toward mother.

e·lec·tric (ĭlĕk′trĭk) *adj.* Of, charged with, worked by, capable of developing, electricity; electrifying, thrilling; ~ **blue**, brilliant light blue; ~ **chair**, chair in which persons condemned to death are executed by electrocution; ~ **circuit**, system of conductors through which electric energy is conveyed; ~ **current**, flow of electricity through conducting body from positive to negative pole, or from high to low potential; ~ **eel**, large S. Amer. fresh-water eellike fish (*Electrophorus electricus*), capable of giving electric shock; ~ **eye**: see PHOTOELECTRIC; ~ **ray**, RAY[2] of family Torpedinidae that emits electric discharges to numb or kill its prey; ~ **shock**, effect on animal body of sudden discharge of electricity; ~ **spark**, luminous discharge over gap in electric circuit. **e·lec′tri·cal** *adj.* Relating to, connected with, of nature of, electricity; electric. **e·lec′tri·cal·ly** *adv.*

e·lec·tri·cian (ĭlĕktrĭsh′*a*n, ē-) *n.* Person who makes, installs, repairs, or operates electrical apparatus or wiring.

e·lec·tric·i·ty (ĭlĕktrĭs′ĭtē, ē-) *n.* Form of energy present in PROTON or ELECTRON, energy associated with the displacement or movement of CHARGE.

e·lec·tri·fy (ĭlĕk′trĭfī) *v.t.* (**-fied, -fy·ing**). 1. Charge with electricity; pass electric current through; subject to electric shock; convert (railroad, factory, etc.) to use of electric power. 2. Startle, rouse, excite, as with electric shock. **e·lec·tri·fi·ca·tion** (ĭlĕktrĭfĭkā′sh*o*n) *n.* **e·lec′tri·fi·er** *n.*

electro- *comb. form.* Of, pertaining to, caused by electricity (*electrodynamic, electrolysis, electrotype*).

e·lec·tro·car·di·o·gram (ĭlĕktrōkar′dēogrăm) *n.* (abbrev. ECG or EKG) Record of sequence of electrical waves generated at each beat of heart, used in diagnosis of heart disorders. **e·lec·tro·car′di·o·graph** *n.* Instrument applied to body for taking such records.

e·lec·tro·chem·is·try (ĭlĕktrōkĕm′ĭstrē) *n.* Branch of chemistry concerned with relation between chemical changes and electrical phenomena. **e·lec·tro·chem′i·cal** *adj.* **e·lec·tro·chem′i·cal·ly** *adv.*

e·lec·tro·cute (ĭlĕk′tr*o*kūt) *v.t.* (**-cut·ed, -cut·ing**). Put to death, execute, by powerful electric current; kill by electricity. **e·lec·tro·cu·tion** (ĭlĕktr*o*kū′sh*o*n) *n.*

e·lec·trode (ĭlĕk′trōd) *n.* Conductor or semiconductor by which

*An **electric** bell: An electromagnet pulls an iron armature so that an attached bob strikes a gong. The armature's movement breaks the current; the armature is forced back by a spring, thus reconnecting the circuit.*

*An **electrolyte** solution is used in electroplating, a method of giving objects a thin coating of metal. A bath in the electrolyte, with an electric current passed through, plates the immersed article.*

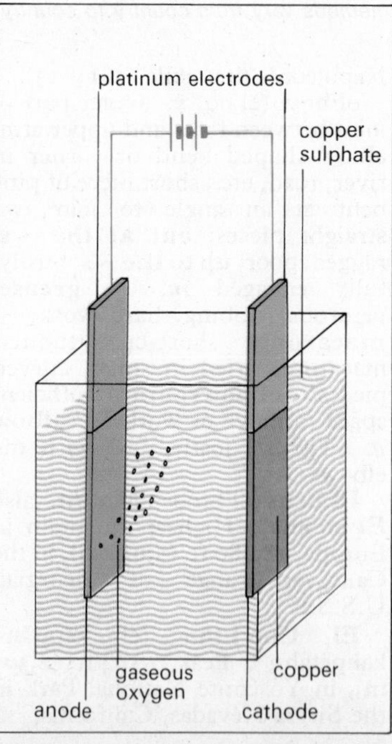

1. Alternating current. 2. Earth. 3. Cell. 4. Switch. 5. Wires joining. 6. Wires to pass without joining. 7. Fuse. 8. Resistor. 9. Variable resistor. 10. Coil. 11. Ammeter. 12. Voltmeter. 13. Amplifier. 14 Capacitor. 15. Anode. 16. Diode. 17. Transistor. 18. Transformer.

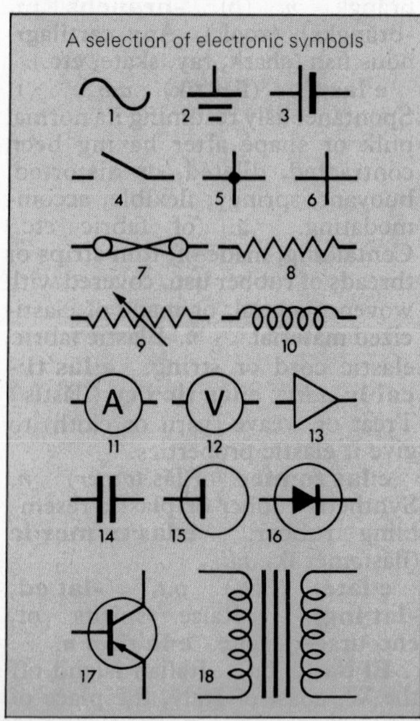

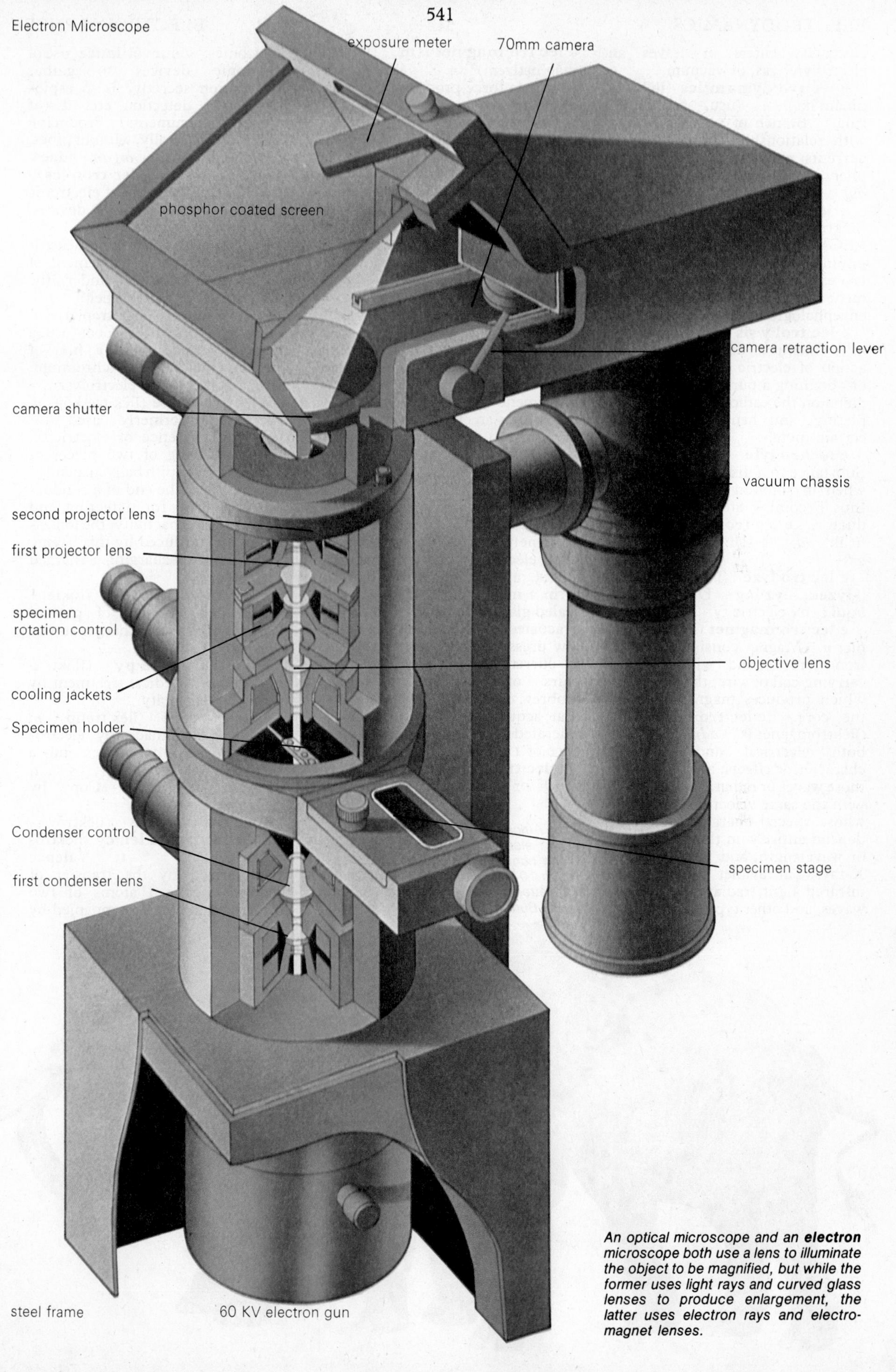

*An optical microscope and an **electron** microscope both use a lens to illuminate the object to be magnified, but while the former uses light rays and curved glass lenses to produce enlargement, the latter uses electron rays and electro-magnet lenses.*

electricity enters or leaves an electrolyte, gas, or vacuum.

e·lec·tro·dy·nam·ics (ĭlĕktrōdīnăm´ĭks) *n.* (usu. considered sing.) Branch of physics dealing with relationships among electric currents, magnets, and mechanical phenomena. **e·lec·tro·dy·nam´ic** *adj.*

e·lec·tro·en·ceph·a·lo·gram (ĭlĕktrōĕnsĕf´*a*lo̤grăm) *n.* (abbrev. EEG) Record of minute electrical impulses inside the brain. **e·lec·tro·en·ceph´a·lo·graph** *n.* Instrument for producing an electroencephalogram.

e·lec·trol·y·sis (ĭlĕktrŏl´ĭsĭs, ē-) *n.* Chemical decomposition by action of electric current; method of obtaining a purified deposit of a metal on the cathode, as in electroplating, and hence of purifying certain metals.

e·lec·tro·lyte (ĭlĕk´tr*o*līt) *n.* Substance that dissociates into ions when in solution or when fused, thus becoming an electrical conductor. **e·lec·tro·lyt·ic** (ĭlĕktr*o*lĭt´ĭk) *adj.* **e·lec·tro·lyt´i·cal·ly** *adv.*

e·lec·tro·lyze (ĭlĕk´tr*o*līz) *v.t.* (**-lyzed, -lyz·ing**). Decompose (a liquid) by electricity.

e·lec·tro·mag·net (ĭlĕktrōmăg´nĭt) *n.* Magnet consisting of soft iron core wound with current-carrying coil of wire, the current in which produces magnetization of the core. **e·lec·tro·mag·net·ic** (ĭlĕktrōmăgnĕt´ĭk) *adj.* Having both electrical and magnetic character or effects; applied esp. to those waves or radiations that travel with the same velocity as light and whose special character seems to depend entirely on their frequency or wavelength, and which include X-rays, ultraviolet visible, and infrared light, radiant heat, radio waves, and other types of radiation.

e·lec·tro·mag·net·ism (ĭlĕktrōmăg´n*e*tĭzem) *n.* (Study of) magnetic force produced by means of electricity.

e·lec·trom·e·ter (ĭlĕktrŏm´ĭt*er*, ē-) *n.* Instrument for detecting and measuring the magnitude of an electric charge, current, or voltage.

e·lec·tro·mo·tive (ĭlĕktr*o*mō´tĭv) *adj.* Of, pertaining to, producing electric current; ~ **force**, (abbrev. emf) force set up by difference of potential in an electric circuit, usu. measured in volts.

e·lec·tron (ĭlĕk´trŏn) *n.* (phys.) Elementary particle with an indivisible charge of negative electricity, one or more of which surround the nucleus of each atom and give it its chemical properties and the movement of which, when free, constitutes an electric current; **free** ~, electron freed from its bound state within the atom; ~ **lens**, device producing system of electric and magnetic fields capable of focusing a stream of electrons; ~ **microscope**, microscope with extremely high magnification, using electrons focused by magnetic lenses rather than visible light to form a magnified image; ~ **tube**, sealed glass tube, either completely evacuated or containing gas under low pressure, used to control flow of current between one or more pairs of electrodes; ~**-volt**, (abbrev. eV) unit of energy equal to that acquired by an electron accelerated through a potential difference of 1 volt.

e·lec·tron·ic (ĭlĕktrŏn´ĭk, ē-) *adj.* 1. Of or relating to electrons or electronics; ~ **surveillance**, use of electronic devices to gather information secretly, as in espionage, crime detection, etc. 2. (of musical instruments) Producing sound electronically, without pipes, strings, etc., esp. ~ *organ*. **e·lec·tron´i·cal·ly** *adv.* **e·lec·tron´ics** *n.* 1. Science, technology of electronic phenomena. 2. Electronic devices, industry or business.

e·lec·tro·pho·re·sis (ĭlĕktrōforē´sĭs) *n.* (phys.) Movement of particles in a fluid under the influence of an electric field.

e·lec·tro·plate (ĭlĕk´tr*o*plāt) *v.t.* (**-plat·ed, -plat·ing**). Coat (usu. a metallic surface) with a film of another metal (e.g. chromium, silver, or nickel) by electrolysis.

e·lec·tro·scope (ĭlĕk´tr*o*skōp) *n.* Instrument formerly used for detecting presence of electricity, freq. consisting of two pieces of gold leaf or two pith balls suspended together from the end of a conductor, now used for detecting and measuring radioactivity, the ionization of air produced by this having the effect of discharging a charged electroscope.

e·lec·tro·stat·ics (ĭlĕktr*o*stăt´ĭks) *n.* Branch of physics dealing with electric charges at rest. **e·lec·tro·stat´ic** *adj.*

e·lec·tro·ther·a·py (ĭlĕktrōthĕr´*a*pē) *n.* Medical treatment by means of electricity.

e·lec·tro·type (ĭlĕk´tr*o*tīp) *n.* Printing plate made by electrolytically depositing copper onto a mold of wax or lead. ~ *v.t.* (**-typed, -typ·ing**). Copy by electrotype.

e·lec·tro·va·lence (ĭlĕktrōvā´lens), **e·lec·tro·va·len·cy** (ĭlĕktrōvā´lensē) *ns.* 1. Valence characterized by the transfer of electrons between atoms of two different elements accompanied by

*The African **elephant** (left) and the Indian elephant. The former has been much hunted for its tusks, which may reach 10 ft. long and 220 lbs in weight. The latter is used as a working animal in India, Burma, and Thailand.*

formation of ions. 2. Number of charges an atom acquires or loses as the result of such a transfer of electrons. **e·lec·tro·va'lent** *adj.*

el·ee·mos·y·nar·y (ĕlemŏs'-ĭnĕrē, -mŏz'-, ĕlēe-) *adj.* Of, dependent on, charity; charitable.

el·e·gant (ĕl'egant) *adj.* 1. Tastefully ornate in dress; graceful; tasteful, refined; of refined luxury. 2. Excellent, first-rate. **el'e·gance** *n.* **el'e·gant·ly** *adv.*

el·e·gi·ac (ĕlejī'ak, -ăk, ĭlē'jēăk) *adj.* Appropriate to elegies; mournful; (of meter, couplet) consisting of dactylic hexameter and pentameter.

el·e·gy (ĕl'ejē) *n.* (pl. **-gies**). Song of lamentation, esp. for the dead; poem, poetry, in elegiac meter. **el·e·gize** (ĕl'ejīz) *v.* (**-gized, -giz·ing**). Write elegy, write elegy upon.

el·e·ment (ĕl'ement) *n.* 1. Component part; constituent; resistance wire carrying the current in an electric heater etc. 2. In ancient and medieval philosophy, one of the four substances (earth, water, air, fire) of which all material bodies were held to be compounded; now, (pl.) atmospheric agencies or powers; (fig.) person's etc. ordinary range of activity, surroundings in which one feels at home. 3. (chem.) Any of over 100 different substances that have never been separated into simpler substances by chemical means and that alone or in combination constitute all matter; they are distinguished from each other by the number of electrons in their atoms outside the atomic nucleus (see PERIODIC law). 4. (pl.) Rudiments of learning; first principles of an art or science.

el·e·men·tal (ĕlemĕn'tal) *adj.* 1. Of all or any of the four elements (see ELEMENT def. 2); of the powers or agencies of nature. 2. Of the nature of an ultimate constituent, simple, uncompounded; basic, constituent.

el·e·men·ta·ry (ĕlemĕn'terē, -trē) *adj.* 1. Rudimentary, introductory; simple. 2. Fundamental, essential, irreducible; ~ **particle**, (phys.) one smaller than an atom; ~ **school**, the first six to eight grades of school, where young children receive basic education. **el·e·men'ta·ri·ly** *adv.* **el·e·men'-ta·ri·ness** *n.*

e·len·chus (ĭlĕng'kus) *n.* (pl. **-chi** pr. -kī, -kē). Logical refutation; **Socratic** ~, Socratic method of eliciting truth by short question and answer.

el·e·phant (ĕl'efant) *n.* (pl. **-phants,** collect. **-phant**). 1. Huge four-footed thick-skinned mammal of the order Proboscidea, with long curving ivory tusks and a prehensile trunk or proboscis (only two

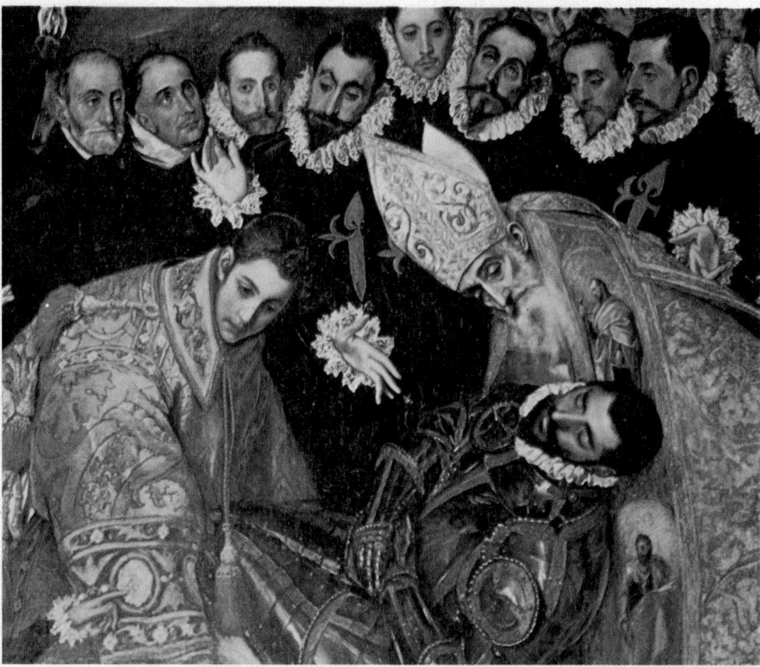

'The Burial of Count Orgaz', a painting by ***El Greco*** *(1541–1614). El Greco used color in his works to heighten emotional impact. His output was large and his way of life, when he settled in a Spanish castle, luxurious.*

species, the Indian and the African, now exist). 2. ~ **seal** or **sea** ~, either of 2 species of seal of genus *Mirounga* (the large *M. leonina* of S. hemisphere and the smaller *M. angustirostris* of N. Amer. Pacific coast) with prolonged snout in male.

el·e·phan·ti·a·sis (ĕlefantī'asĭs) *n.* Tropical disease, caused by a nematode parasite, resulting in gross enlargement of legs etc. and thickening of skin.

el·e·phan·tine (ĕlefăn'tĭn, -tīn, -tēn) *adj.* Of elephants; elephant-like; clumsy, ponderous.

elev. *abbrev.* Elevation.

el·e·vate (ĕl'evāt) *v.t.* (**-vat·ed, -vat·ing**). Lift up; hold up; raise (eyes etc.), direct upward; exalt in rank etc.; raise morally or intellectually; (gunnery) raise axis of (gun etc.). **el'e·vat·ed** *adj.* (esp.) 1. Elated, exhilarated. 2. (also ~ **railroad**) Railroad supported on pillars or arches above street level; (also ~ **train**) train on such railroad.

el·e·va·tion (ĕlevā'shon) *n.* 1. Elevating, being elevated. 2. Swelling; rising ground, eminence. 3. Angle with horizon (esp. of gun); (astron.) angular distance of heavenly body above horizontal plane (as opp. to *depression*, below it). 4. Height above a given level, esp. that of sea; height, loftiness, grandeur, dignity. 5. Drawing of building made in projection on vertical plane, as dist. from ground plan.

el·e·va·tor (ĕl'evā'ter) *n.* (esp.) 1. Muscle that raises limb etc. 2. Machine for hoisting grain, usu. a bucket conveyor; large building (containing such machines) for storing grain. 3. Apparatus for raising and lowering people or things to other floor of building. 4. (aeron.) Movable stabilizing surface on an airplane, usu. hinged to tail, where it functions like a horizontal rudder and makes the craft go up or down.

e·lev·en (ĭlĕv'en) *adj.* Amounting to 11. ~ *n.* One more than 10; symbol for this (11, xi, or XI); 11 o'clock; size etc. indicated by 11; set of 11 things or persons, esp. forming football team.

e·lev·enth (ĭlĕv'enth) *adj.* Next after 10th; ~ **hour**, latest possible time (Matt. 20). **eleventh** *n.* Eleventh part (see PART[1]); 11th thing etc.

elf (ĕlf) *n.* (pl. **elves** pr. ĕlvz). One of a class of supernatural beings, in early Teutonic belief supposed to be of dwarfish form and to have magic powers; mischievous creature; dwarf, little creature. **elf·in** (ĕl'fĭn) *adj.* Of elves, elflike; diminutive; fairy-like, full of strange charm. **elf'ish** *adj.* **elf'ish·ly** *adv.* **elf'ish·ness** *n.*

El Fai·yum (ĕl fīyo͞om'). City in N. Egypt, in bed of ancient lake noted for abundant archaeological objects.

El·gin (ĕl'gĭn, -jĭn) **Marbles.** Collection of Greek sculptures chiefly of the school of Phidias and from the Parthenon, acquired by the 7th Earl of Elgin and sold by him to the British Government in 1816; now in the British Museum.

El Grec·o (ĕl grĕk'ō), **Domeni-**

kos **Theotokopoulos** (1541–1614). Crete-born Spanish painter, esp. of religious pictures and portraits. [Span., = "the Greek"]

e·lic·it (ĭlĭs′ĭt) *v.t.* Draw forth (what is latent or potential); educe (truths etc.) *from* data; extract, (information, response, etc.) *from* person. **e·lic·i·ta·tion** (ĭlĭsĭtā′shon), **e·lic′i·tor** *ns.*

e·lide (ĭlīd′) *v.t.* (**e·lid·ed, e·lid·ing**). Omit, slur over (vowel, syllable) in pronunciation.

el·i·gi·ble (ĕl′ĭjibel) *adj.* Fit to be chosen, qualified (*for* office etc.); acceptable, suitable (esp. as husband or wife). **el·i·gi·bil·i·ty** (ĕlĭjibĭl′ĭtē) *n.* **el′i·gi·bly** *adv.*

E·li·jah (ĭlī′ja). Hebrew prophet of 9th c. B.C.; raised the dead son of the widow of Zarephath; was carried to heaven in a chariot of fire (1 Kings 17–2 Kings 2).

e·lim·i·nate (ĭlĭm′ĭnāt) *v.t.* (**-nat·ed, -nat·ing**). Remove, get rid of (esp. waste matter from body or tissues by excretion); expel, exclude; (alg.) get rid of (quantities) from equation; get rid of (unknown quantities) in simultaneous equations by combining equations. **e·lim·i·na·tion** (ĭlĭmĭnā′shon), **e·lim′i·na·tor** *ns.*

El·i·ot[1] (ĕl′ēot, ĕl′yot), **George.** Pen name of Mary Ann Cross (1819–80), *née* Evans; English novelist; author of *Adam Bede, The Mill on the Floss, Silas Marner, Middlemarch,* etc.

El·i·ot[2] (ĕl′ēot, ĕl′yot) **T(homas) S(tearns)** (1888–1965). American-born Brit. poet, critic, and playwright; author of the poems "The Waste Land," "Four Quartets," etc.; Nobel Prize for literature 1948.

Elizabeth I *by Gheeraerts the Younger, c 1592. Her reign was complicated by religious conflict and lack of an heir but British influence increased with victory over the Spanish.*

E·li·sha (ĭlī′sha). Hebrew prophet; disciple and successor of Elijah.

e·li·sion (ĭlĭzh′on) *n.* Suppression or slurring of letter (esp. vowel) or syllable in pronouncing.

e·lite, é·lite (ĭlēt′, ā-) *ns.* Choice part, best (*of*); select group or class; typewriter type with 12 characters to the inch. **e·lit′ism** *n.* Advocacy of or reliance on leadership or dominance of a select group. **e·lit′ist** *n.* & *adj.*

e·lix·ir (ĭlĭk′ser) *n.* 1. (alchemy) Preparation designed to change base metals into gold or to prolong life indefinitely; universal remedy for disease. 2. Sweetened aromatic solution of water and alcohol used as flavoring for medicine. [Arab. *al-iksīr*, prob. f. late Gk. *xērion* desiccative powder for wounds]

E·liz·a·beth (ĭlĭz′abeth). Name of two English queens: **Elizabeth I** (1533–1603), daughter of Henry VIII and Anne Boleyn; queen of England 1558–1603; **Elizabeth II** (1926–), daughter of George VI,

Elizabeth II *in 1953, the year of her coronation in the U.K. As a constitutional monarch, she has few of the direct powers enjoyed by Elizabeth I; she is detached from political factions.*

Elm *trees, found chiefly in the N. Hemisphere, are popular as ornamental and shade trees. American or white elm and English or Wych elm are both susceptible to attack by fungus known as Dutch elm disease. Few elms now remain in U.K.*

queen of the United Kingdom 1952– . **E·liz·a·be·than** (ĭlĭzabē′than, -bĕth′an) *adj.* & *n.* (Person, writer) of the time of Queen Elizabeth I or (occas.) II.

elk (ĕlk) *n.* (pl. **elks**, collect. **elk**). 1. Either of two large N. Amer. deer (*Cervus canadensis,* also called wapiti, or *Cervus nannodes,* the tule elk), both of western U.S. and Canada, having basically brown hair and a nearly black mane and, in mature males, widely branched antlers of six or seven points. 2. (Brit.) = MOOSE. 3. **elk′hound,** hunting dog of Scandinavian breed with thick gray coat and tail curled over back. 4. **E~,** *n.* Member of fraternal organization, Benevolent and Protective Order of Elks.

ell (ĕl) *n.* L-shaped room; wing of building at right angle to main structure.

el·lipse (ĭlĭps′) *n.* Plane closed curve in which the sum of the distances of any point from the two foci is a constant quantity; figure produced when a cone is cut obliquely by a plane making a smaller angle with the base than the side of the cone makes with the base. **el·lip·tic** (ĭlĭp′tĭk), **el·lip·ti·cal** (ĭlĭp′tĭkal) *adjs.* **el·lip′ti·cal·ly** *adv.*

el·lip·sis (ĭlĭp′sĭs) *n.* (pl. **-ses** pr. -sēz). 1. (gram.) Omission from sentence of word(s) needed to complete grammatical construction but not necessary for understanding (as *Coming?* for *Are you coming?*). 2. Series of marks (... or * * *) used in printing and writing to indicate omission of word(s), as in a long quotation.

el·lip·soid (ĭlĭp′soid) *n.* Solid formed by rotating an ellipse about an axis through its foci or the perpendicular bisector of this. **el·lip·soi′dal** *adj.*

El·lis (ĕl′ĭs) **Island.** Island in New York harbor, belonging to U.S. Government, major U.S. immigration center (1892–1943), now part of the Statue of Liberty National Monument.

El·li·son (ĕl′ĭson), **Ralph (Waldo)** (1914–). Amer. writer; best known for his novel, *Invisible Man.*

elm (ĕlm) *n.* Large tree of genus *Ulmus,* usually with doubly serrated leaves, rough bark, and arching branches, widely planted as a shade tree; wood of such trees.

El·mo (ĕl′mō), **St.** (pop.) St. Peter González (*c*1190–1246), Spanish Dominican preacher who became patron saint of seamen; **St. ~'s fire,** luminous electrical discharge sometimes seen on ship during storm, interpreted as sign of St. Elmo's protection, or sometimes of impending disaster, also called corposant.

El Mor·ro (ĕl mŏr′ō) **National Monument.** Area in W. New Mexico reserved for protection of cliff-dweller ruins and sandstone rock bearing inscriptions of Spanish explorers.

el·o·cu·tion (ĕlokū′shon) *n.* Manner, style, art, of vocal production and delivery, esp. of public speaking. **el·o·cu′tion·ar·y** *adj.* **el·o·cu′tion·ist** *n.*

E·lo·him (ĕlōhĭm′, ĕlō′hĭm; *Heb.* ĕlawhēm′). Hebrew name for God.

E·lo·hist (ĕlō′hĭst) *n.* Author(s) of those parts of the Hexateuch where God is referred to as *Elohim* rather than *Yahweh.* **El·o·his·tic** (ĕlōhĭs′tĭk) *adj.*

e·lon·gate (ĭlawng′gāt, -lŏng′-, ē′lawng-, -lŏng-) *v.* (**-gat·ed, -gat·ing**). Lengthen, prolong; have slender or tapering form. ~ *adj.* (bot., zool.) Long in proportion to its breadth; slender, tapering.

e·lon·ga·tion (ĭlawnggā′shon, -lŏng-, ē-) *n.* Lengthening; extension.

e·lope (ĭlōp′) *v.i.* (**e·loped, e·lop·ing**). Run away from home for secret marriage, (*with* lover); (of couple) run away together to get married. **e·lope′ment** *n.*

el·o·quence (ĕl′okwens) *n.* Fluent, forcible, and apt use of language; rhetoric. **el′o·quent** *adj.* **el′o·quent·ly** *adv.*

El Pas·o (ĕl păs′ō). City in W. Texas on Rio Grande opposite Ciudad Juarez, Mexico.

El Sal·va·dor (ĕl săl′vadŏr). Republic in W. Central America, on Pacific; capital, San Salvador.

else (ĕls) *adv.* (following indef. or interrog. pron.) Besides, as *anything ~, who ~?*; instead, as *what ~ could I say?*; otherwise, if not, as *run, or ~ you will be late.* **else·where** (ĕls′hwār, ĕls′wār) *adv.* In, to, some other place, at some other point.

El·si·nore (ĕlsĭnŏr′). Seaport in Denmark; setting of Shakespeare's play, *Hamlet.*

e·lu·ci·date (ĭlōō′sĭdāt) *v.t.* (**-dat·ed, -dat·ing**). Throw light upon, clear up, explain. **e·lu·ci·da·tion** (ĭlōōsĭdā′shon) *n.*

e·lude (ĭlōōd′) *v.t.* (**e·lud·ed, e·lud·ing**). Escape by dexterity or stratagem (blow, danger, etc.); slip away from (person, pursuit, etc.); evade. **e·lu·sion** (ĭlōō′zhon) *n.* **e·lu·sive** (ĭlōō′sĭv) *adj.* **e·lu′sive·ly** *adv.* **e·lu′sive·ness** *n.*

el·ver (ĕl′ver) *n.* Young eel.

E·ly·sée (ālēzā′). Official residence of French president, on the Champs Elysées, Paris.

E·ly·si·um (ĭlĭz′ēum, ĭlĭzh′-, ĭlē′zhē-). (Gk. myth.) Abode of the blessed after death; hence, place, state, of ideal or perfect happiness. **E·ly·sian** (ĭlĭzh′an, ĭlē′zhan) *adj.* **~ fields,** Elysium.

el·y·tron (ĕl′ĭtrŏn) *n.* Outer hard wing case of coleopterous insect.

em (ĕm) *n.* 1. Letter M, m. 2. (print.) Measure equivalent to 12 points; also, the square of the body size of any type used as a unit of measure, as of the length of a dash.

em- = EN-.

e·ma·ci·ate (ĭmā′shēāt) *v.t.* (**-at·ed, -at·ing**). Make thin, as by starvation or illness. **e·ma·ci·a·tion** (ĭmāshēā′shon) *n.*

em·a·nate (ĕm′anāt) *v.i.* (**-nat·ed, -nat·ing**). Issue, originate (*from* source, person, etc.); proceed, issue, flow forth (*from*). **em·a·na·tive** (ĕm′anātĭv) *adj.*

em·a·na·tion (ĕmanā′shon) *n.*

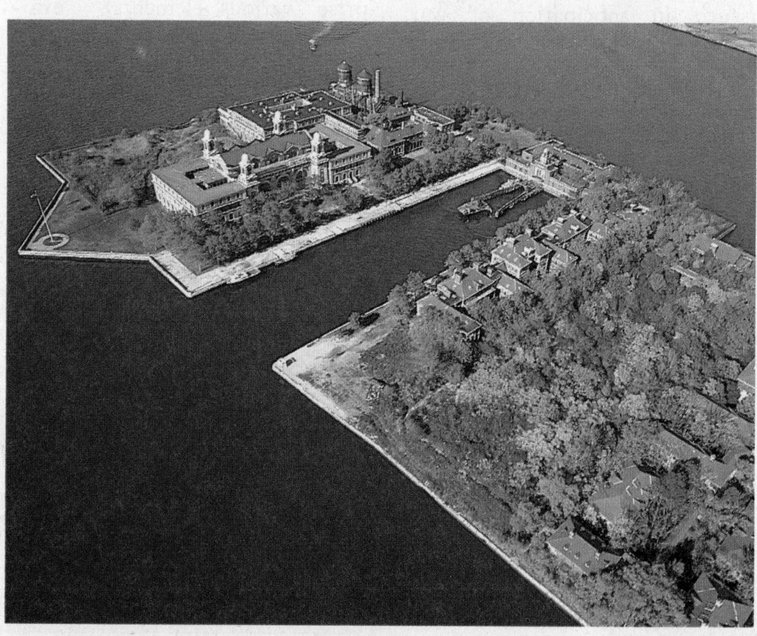

***Ellis Island,** in Upper New York Bay, was reopened to the public in 1976 after a checkered history in which it was used as a ballast dump and detention center.*

(esp.) 1. Something emitted or radiated (*from*). 2. (chem.) Radioactive gas produced by radioactive decay of a solid, e.g. radon.

e·man·ci·pate (ĭmăn′sĭpāt) *v.t.* (**-pat·ed, -pat·ing**). 1. Set free from control, or from legal, social, or political restraint; esp., set free (slave). 2. (Rom. law) Release (child, wife) from power of *pater familias*. **e·man′ci·pa·tor** *n.*

e·man·ci·pa·tion (ĭmănsĭpā′shon) *n.* Setting free, esp. from slavery, intellectual or moral fetters, or legal disabilities; **E∼ Proclamation,** (U.S. hist.) proclamation issued by President Lincoln on Jan. 1, 1863, freeing slaves in all areas still in rebellion against the Union.

e·mas·cu·late (ĭmăs′kyulāt) *v.t.* (**-lat·ed, -lat·ing**). Castrate; weaken, make effeminate; enfeeble, impoverish (language); weaken (literary composition) by removing what is supposed to be indecorous or offensive. **e·mas·cu·la·tion** (ĭmăskyulā′shon) *n.* **e·mas′cu·la·tive, e·mas·cu·la·to·ry** (ĭmăs′kyulatōrē, -tōrē) *adjs.* **emasculate** (ĭmăs′kyulĭt) *adj.* Castrated; effeminate.

em·balm (ĕmbahm′) *v.t.* Preserve (corpse) from decay by treatment with preservatives; preserve, cherish the memory of; endow with balmy fragrance. **em·balm′er, em·balm′ment** *ns.*

em·bank (ĕmbăngk′) *v.t.* Shut in, confine (river etc.) by banks, raised stone structure, etc. **em·bank′ment** *n.* 1. Mound, bank, etc., for confining river etc. 2. Long earthen bank or mound supporting roadway.

em·bar·go (ĕmbar′gō) *n.* (pl. **-goes**). Order forbidding ships of foreign power to enter, or any ships to leave, ports of a country, usu. issued in anticipation of war; suspension of (branch of) commerce; stoppage, prohibition. ∼ *v.t.* (**-goed, -go·ing**). Lay (vessel, trade) under embargo.

em·bark (ĕmbark′) *v.* 1. Put, go, on board ship (*for* destination). 2. Set out (*on, upon,* undertaking etc.). **em·bar·ka·tion** (ĕmbarkā′shon) *n.*

em·bar·rass (ĕmbăr′as) *v.t.* 1. Encumber, hamper, impede; (pass.) be in difficulties from want of money, encumbered with debts. 2. Perplex, throw into doubt or difficulty; cause to feel self-conscious or ashamed; complicate (question etc.). **em·bar·rassed·ly** (ĕmbăr′astlē, -asĭdlē), **em·bar′rass·ing·ly** *advs.* **em·bar′rass·ment** *n.* Embarrassed state or condition.

em·bas·sy (ĕm′basē) *n.* (pl. **-sies**). Ambassador's function or office; ambassador's residence; mission to foreign government headed by ambassador.

em·bat·tle (ĕmbăt′el) *v.t.* (**-tled, -tling**). 1. Arrange in battle order; prepare for battle. 2. Fortify against attack. **em·bat′tled** *adj.* Arranged or ready for battle.

em·bed (ĕmbĕd′) *v.t.* (**-bed·ded, -bed·ding**). Fix firmly in surrounding mass; (of mass) surround thus.

em·bel·lish (ĕmbĕl′ĭsh) *v.t.* Beautify, adorn; add to, heighten (narrative) with fictitious additions. **em·bel′lish·ment** *n.*

em·ber (ĕm′ber) *n.* (usu. pl.) Small piece of live coal or wood in dying fire; smoldering ash.

em·bez·zle (ĕmbĕz′el) *v.t.* (**-zled, -zling**). Divert to one's own use (money etc.) in violation of trust or official duty. **em·bez′zle·ment** *n.*

em·bit·ter (ĕmbĭt′er) *v.t.* Make bitter (now usu. fig.); exasperate (person, feeling). **em·bit′ter·ment** *n.*

em·bla·zon (ĕmblā′zon) *v.t.* Inscribe or portray conspicuously, as on heraldic shield; adorn *with* heraldic devices etc.; celebrate, extol. **em·bla′zon·ment** *n.* **em·bla′zon·ry** *n.* = BLAZONRY.

em·blem (ĕm′blem) *n.* Symbol, typical representation; type, personification (*of* a quality); heraldic device, or other figured object as distinctive badge of person, family, etc.

em·blem·at·ic (ĕmblemăt′ĭk), **em·blem·at·i·cal** (ĕmblemăt′ĭkal) *adjs.* Serving as type or emblem (*of*). **em·blem·at′i·cal·ly** *adv.*

em·bod·y (ĕmbŏd′ē) *v.t.* (**-bod·ied, -bod·y·ing**). 1. Invest or clothe (spirit) with body; give concrete form to (what is abstract or ideal); be embodiment or expression of. 2. Unite into one body; incorporate; include, comprise (various elements). **em·bod′i·ment** *n.*

An ***embryo*** *develops from the fusion of 2 cells, the male spermatozoon and the female ovum or egg, each of which has equal influence on the resulting individual, although these influences are far from fully understood.*

em·bold·en (ĕmbōl′den) *v.t.* Make bold, encourage (*to* do).

em·bo·lism (ĕm′bolĭzem) *n.* Blockage of blood vessel by blood clot, air bubble, fat globule, etc.

em·bon·point (ahṅbawṅpwăṅ′) *n.* (Fr.) Plumpness; stoutness.

em·boss (ĕmbaws′, -bŏs′) *v.t.* Carve, mold, in relief; cause figures etc. to stand out on (surface). **em·boss′ment** *n.*

em·bou·chure (ahmbushoor′, ahm′bushoor) *n.* 1. Mouth of river. 2. Mouthpiece of wind instrument. 3. Manner of applying the lips and tongue to wind instrument's mouthpiece.

em·brace (ĕmbrās′) *v.t.* (**-braced, -brac·ing**). 1. Clasp (person) in arms, usu. as sign of fondness or friendship (also abs.); clasp, enclose. 2. Accept eagerly, avail oneself of (offer, opportunity, etc.); adopt (course of action, party, opinion, etc.). 3. Include, comprise; take in with eye or mind. ∼ *n.* Folding in the arms. **em·brace′ment** *n.*

em·bra·sure (ĕmbrā′zher) *n.* Beveling off of wall at sides of door or window, so that inside profile of window is larger than that of outside; opening in wall or parapet for gun, widening from within.

em·broi·der (ĕmbroi′der) *v.t.* Ornament (cloth etc.; or abs.) with needlework; work in needlework; embellish (narrative) with rhetorical ornament or fictitious additions. **em·broi·der·y** (ĕmbroi′derē, -drē) *n.* (pl. **-der·ies**).

em·broil (ĕmbroil′) *v.t.* Bring (affairs, narrative, etc.) into state of confusion; involve (person) in hostility (*with* another). **em·broil′ment** *n.*

em·bry·o (ĕm′brēō) *n.* (pl. **-os**). 1. (biol.) Organism in its early stages of development, as the young before birth or emergence from egg. 2. (bot.) Rudimentary plant contained in seed. 3. Thing in rudimentary stage. ∼ *adj.* Undeveloped, immature. **em·bry·on·ic** (ĕmbrēŏn′ĭk) *adj.*

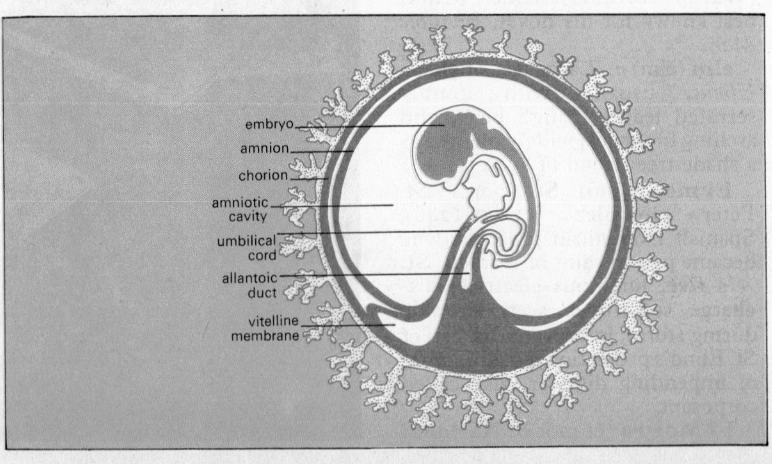

The structure of a human ***embryo.*** *In modern research on transmission of hereditary characteristics, the sciences of genetics and embryology are closely linked.*

The ***emperor*** *penguin, near Little America, Antarctica. The penguin is a flightless seabird. It uses its wings as paddles, to walk, and to fight. It breeds in large 'rookeries'.*

em·bry·ol·o·gy (ĕmbrēŏl′*o*jē) *n.* Branch of biology dealing with the formation, early stages, and development of embryos. **em·bry·ol′o·gist** *n.* **em·bry·o·log·i·cal** (ĕmbrē*o*lŏj′ĭk*a*l) *adj.*

em·cee (ĕm′sē′) *n.* Master of ceremonies. ~ *v.* (**-ceed, -cee·ing**). Act as master of ceremonies (for).

e·mend (ĭmĕnd′) *v.t.* Correct; esp., remove errors from (text of book etc.). **e·men·da·tion** (ēmĕndā′sh*o*n, ĕmen-), **e·men·da·tor** (ē′mendāt*e*r) *ns.* **e·mend·a·to·ry** (ĭmĕn′d*a*tōrē, -tōrē) *adj.*

em·er·ald (ĕm′*e*rald) *n.* 1. Bright green precious stone, variety of beryl found chiefly in S. Amer., Siberia, and India. 2. ~ **cut**, (of gem) type of step cut with beveled corners; ~ **green**, vivid green; **E~ Isle**, island of Ireland (from its greenness).

e·merge (ĭmẽrj′) *v.i.* (**e·merged, e·merg·ing**). Come up out of liquid; come into view, issue (*from* enclosed space, state of suffering, etc.); rise into notice (*from* obscurity etc.); (of fact etc.) come out as a result of investigation or discussion. **e·mer′gence** *n.* **e·mer′gent** *adj.*

e·mer·gen·cy (ĭmẽr′j*e*nsē) *n.* (pl. **-cies**). Situation or sudden occurrence demanding immediate action; (attrib.) used, arising, etc., in an emergency.

e·mer·i·tus (ĭmĕr′ĭt*u*s) *adj.* Retired with honorary title corresponding to that held before retirement, as **professor** ~. [L., = "that has served his time"]

Em·er·son (ĕm′*e*rs*o*n), **Ralph Waldo** (1803–82). Amer. poet and essayist; leader of transcendentalist philosophy; called "The Sage of Concord"; wrote *Essays First and Second Series, Nature,* etc.

em·er·y (ĕm′*e*rē, ĕm′rē) *n.* Coarse corundum, used for polishing metals, stones, glass, etc.; ~ **board**, emery-coated nail file; ~ **cloth, paper, wheel**, cloth, paper, wheel, coated with emery powder; ~ **powder**, ground emery.

e·met·ic (ĭmĕt′ĭk) *adj.* & *n.* (Medicine) that causes vomiting.

emf, EMF *abbrevs.* Electromotive force.

em·i·grate (ĕm′ĭgrāt) *v.i.* (**-grat·ed, -grat·ing**). Leave one's country to settle in another. **em·i·grant** (ĕm′ĭgr*a*nt) *adj.* & *n.* **em·i·gra·tion** (ĕmĭgrā′sh*o*n) *n.*

é·mi·gré (ĕm′ĭgrā) *n.* Emigrant, esp. one who fled his or her country during a revolution. [Fr.]

em·i·nence (ĕm′ĭn*e*ns) *n.* 1. Rising ground. 2. Distinguished superiority. 3. **E~**, in R.C. Church, title of honor borne by cardinals.

em·i·nent (ĕm′ĭn*e*nt) *adj.* Exalted, distinguished; (of qualities) remarkable in degree; signal, noteworthy; ~ **domain**: see DOMAIN. **em′i·nent·ly** *adv.*

e·mir (ĕmēr′) *n.* 1. Arab chieftain prince, or governor. 2. Title given to descendants of Muhammad; title of Muslim rulers. **e·mir·ate** (ĕmēr′āt, -ĭt) *n.* Rank, office, or domain of an emir. [Arab. '*amīr* commander]

em·is·sar·y (ĕm′ĭsĕrē) *n.* (pl. **-sar·ies**). Person sent on mission, to gain information, adherents, etc.

e·mis·sion (ĭmĭsh′*o*n) *n.* Giving of or out; what is emitted; discharge. **e·mis·sive** (ĭmĭs′ĭv) *adj.* **em·is·siv·i·ty** (ĕmĭsĭv′ĭtē) *n.* (phys.) Power of a surface to radiate heat, light, etc.

e·mit (ĭmĭt′) *v.t.* (**e·mit·ted, e·mit·ting**). Give out, send forth (light, heat, sound, opinion, etc.).

Em·man·u·el (ĭmăn′ū*e*l): see IMMANUEL.

e·mol·li·ent (ĭmŏl′y*e*nt) *adj.* & *n.* (Substance) having power of softening or relaxing living animal tissues.

e·mol·u·ment (ĭmŏl′y*u*m*e*nt) *n.* Fee from office or employment, salary.

e·mo·tion (ĭmō′sh*o*n) *n.* Agitation or disturbance of mind, vehement or excited mental state; feeling. **e·mo′tion·less** *adj.*

e·mo·tion·al (ĭmō′sh*o*n*a*l) *adj.* Of the emotions; liable to emotion. **e·mo′tion·al·ism** *n.* **e·mo′tion·al·ly** *adv.*

e·mo·tive (ĭmō′tĭv) *adj.* Of, tending to excite, emotion. **e·mo′tive·ly** *adv.*

Emp. *abbrev.* Emperor; empire; empress.

em·pan·el (ĕmpăn′*e*l): see IMPANEL.

em·pa·thy (ĕm′p*a*thē) *n.* Ability to identify oneself mentally with a person or thing and so understand his feelings or its meaning. **em·path·ic** (ĕmpăth′ĭk) *adj.* [transl. of Ger. *Einfühlung* (*ein-* in, *fühlen* feel)]

em·pen·nage (ahmp*e*nahzh′) *n.* Arrangement of stabilizing surfaces in the tail assembly of an airplane.

em·per·or (ĕm′p*e*r*e*r) *n.* Ruler of an empire (title); (hist., esp.) sovereign of Roman or Byzantine Empire or head of Holy Roman Empire; ~ **butterfly**, any of several richly colored butterflies of the family Nymphalidae, such as the tawny emperor (*Asterocampa*

*The **Empire State Building** rising above the New York skyline. Completed in 1931, it was the first skyscraper to be so high (1,250 ft.). The Roman **Empire.** Numerous empires have risen and fallen, encouraging cyclical theories of history. Their organization has differed considerably.*

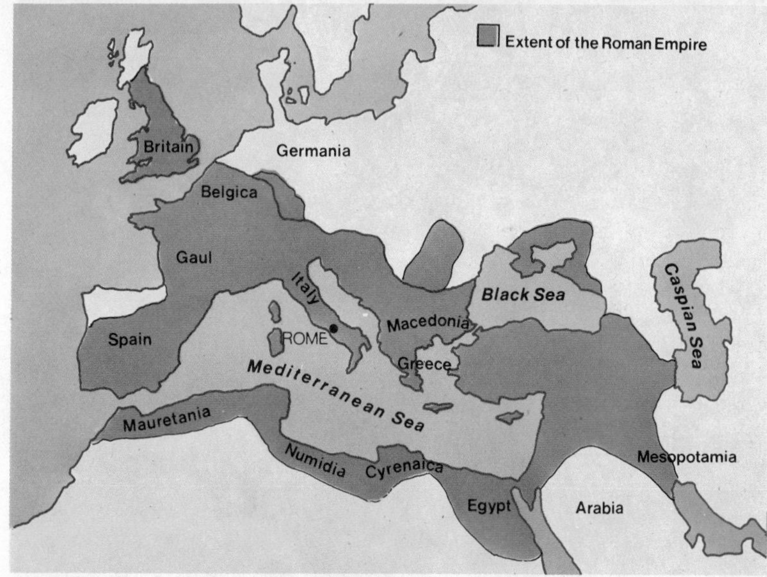

clyton), having orange-tawny wings with dark brown markings; ~ **penguin**, largest known species of penguin of the Antarctic.

em·pha·sis (ĕm´fasĭs) *n.* (pl. **-ses** pr. -sez). Stress on word or phrase to indicate special significance or importance; vigor, intensity, of expression, feeling, action, etc.; importance assigned to fact, idea, etc.; prominence.

em·pha·size (ĕm´fasīz) *v.t.* (**-sized, -siz·ing**). Lay stress on (word, fact, etc.).

em·phat·ic (ĕmfăt´ĭk) *adj.* (of language, tone, gesture) Forcibly expressive; (of words etc.) bearing stress; (of person) expressing oneself with emphasis; (of actions) forcible, significant. **em·phat´i·cal·ly** *adv.*

em·phy·se·ma (ĕmfĭsē´ma) *n.* (path.) Abnormal distention of the air cells of the lungs, causing impairment in breathing.

em·pire (ĕm´pīr) *n.* Political unit consisting of several territories, states, peoples, etc., ruled by an emperor or empress. 2. Powerful organization under control of one individual, family, corporation, etc.; the **E~**, (esp.) (i) the Holy Roman Empire (see ROMAN); (ii) the British Empire; (iii) (period of) reign of Napoleon I as Emperor of the French, 1804–15, also called **First E~** to distinguish it from the **Second E~** of Napoleon III, 1852–70. 3. (attrib.) **E~** (ahṅpēr´), of, in the style of, the First French Empire, (of furniture) having long straight lines and details from classical and ancient Egyptian art, (of women's dress) having very high waist, low neck, and flowing skirt; (less freq.) of the Second Empire; **E~ State**, nickname for state of New York; **E~ State Building**, one of the world's tallest buildings, 1,250 ft. (381 m), located on Fifth Ave. in New York City.

em·pir·ic (ĕmpĭr´ĭk) *adj.* Empirical. ~ *n.* 1. Person believing practical experience is sole source of knowledge, as scientist relying solely on observation and experiment. 2. Untrained practitioner, quack.

em·pir·i·cal (ĕmpĭr´ĭkal) *adj.* 1. Based, acting, on observation and experiment, not on theory. 2. (chem.) ~ **formula**, simplest formula of a compound, indicating only the numerical ratios of the atoms present in the molecule of the compound but not necessarily their actual number and not implying its molecular structure. **em·pir´i·cal·ly** *adv.*

em·pir·i·cism (ĕmpĭr´ĭsĭzem) *n.* 1. Use of empirical methods. 2.

(philos.) Belief that experience is the sole source of knowledge. 3. Practice of medicine without regard for scientific knowledge; quackery. **em·pir'i·cist** *n.*

em·place·ment (ĕmplās'ment) *n.* Situation; placing; platform for mounting heavy guns.

em·ploy (ĕmploi') *v.t.* Apply (thing) to definite purpose, devote (effort, thought, etc.) to object; make use of (time etc.); use services of (person) in professional capacity or for some special work or business; find work or occupation for (person, his or her bodily or mental powers). ~ *n.* Being employed, esp. for wages; employment, occupation, profession, business.

em·ploy·ee, em·ploy·e (ĕm-ploi'ē, ĕmploiē') *ns.* Person employed for wages.

em·ploy·er (ĕmploi'*er*) *n.* (esp.) One who employs servants, workmen, etc., for wages; company that employs workers.

The **emu** *is, apart from the ostrich, the largest living bird. It inhabits open country, nesting in shallow pits in the ground. Numerous eggs are incubated by the cock. Its diet consists of fruits, roots, and herbage.*

em·ploy·ment (ĕmploi'm*e*nt) *n.* (esp.) Regular occupation or business, trade, profession; state of being employed; number of people gainfully employed; ~ **agency**, business that finds employers or employees for those seeking them.

em·po·ri·um (ĕmpōr'ē*u*m, -pōr'-) *n.* (pl. **-po·ri·ums, -po·ri·a** pr. -pōr'ē*a*, -pōr'ē*a*). 1. Center of trade; marketplace. 2. Large store; department store.

em·pow·er (ĕmpow'*er*) *v.t.* Authorize, license (*to* do); enable.

em·press (ĕm'prĭs) *n.* Wife, widow of emperor; woman ruling an empire.

emp·ty (ĕmp'tē) *adj.* (**-ti·er, -ti·est**). 1. Containing nothing; void, devoid, (*of*); vacant, unoccupied; without anything to carry; (colloq.) hungry. 2. Frivolous, foolish; unsatisfactory, vain; **~-handed**, bringing no gift, carrying nothing away; **~-headed**, frivolous, witless; **~-nester**, (colloq.) married person whose children have grown and left home or who never had children. **emp'ti·ly** *adv.* **emp'ti·ness** *n.* **empty** *n.* (pl. **-ties**). Empty truck, freight car, etc.; empty box, bottle, etc., that has contained something. ~ *v.* Remove contents of; transfer (contents of one thing *into* another); (of river etc.) discharge itself (*into*); become empty.

em·py·re·an (ĕmp*i*rē'*a*n, -pī-, ĕmpĭr'ē*a*n) *adj.* & *n.* (Of) the highest reaches of heaven, as (in ancient cosmology) the sphere of fire, or as the abode of God. **em·py·re'al** *adj.*

EMU *abbrev.* Electromagnetic unit.

e·mu (ē'mū) *n.* Large flightless Australian bird (*Dromaius novaehollandiae*), allied to cassowary, with long drooping feathers.

em·u·late (ĕm'y*u*lāt) *v.t.* (**-lat·ed, -lat·ing**). Try to equal or excel; rival; imitate zealously. **em·u·la·tion** (ĕmy*u*lā'sh*o*n), **em'u·la·tor** *ns.* **em'u·la·tive** *adj.*

em·u·lous (ĕm'y*u*l*u*s) *adj.* Zealously or jealously imitative (*of*); desirous (*of* renown etc.); actuated by spirit of rivalry. **em'u·lous·ly** *adv.*

e·mul·si·fy (ĭmŭl'sĭfī) *v.t.* (**-fied, -fy·ing**). Convert into emulsion. **e·mul'si·fi·er** *n.*

e·mul·sion (ĭmŭl'sh*o*n) *n.* Suspension of small globules of one liquid in another with which the first will not mix; this as pharmaceutical preparation, cosmetic, lubricant, paint, etc.; (photog.) light-sensitive coating on film. **e·mul'sive** *adj.*

en (ĕn) *n.* 1. Letter N, n. 2. (print.) Measure equivalent to half an em.

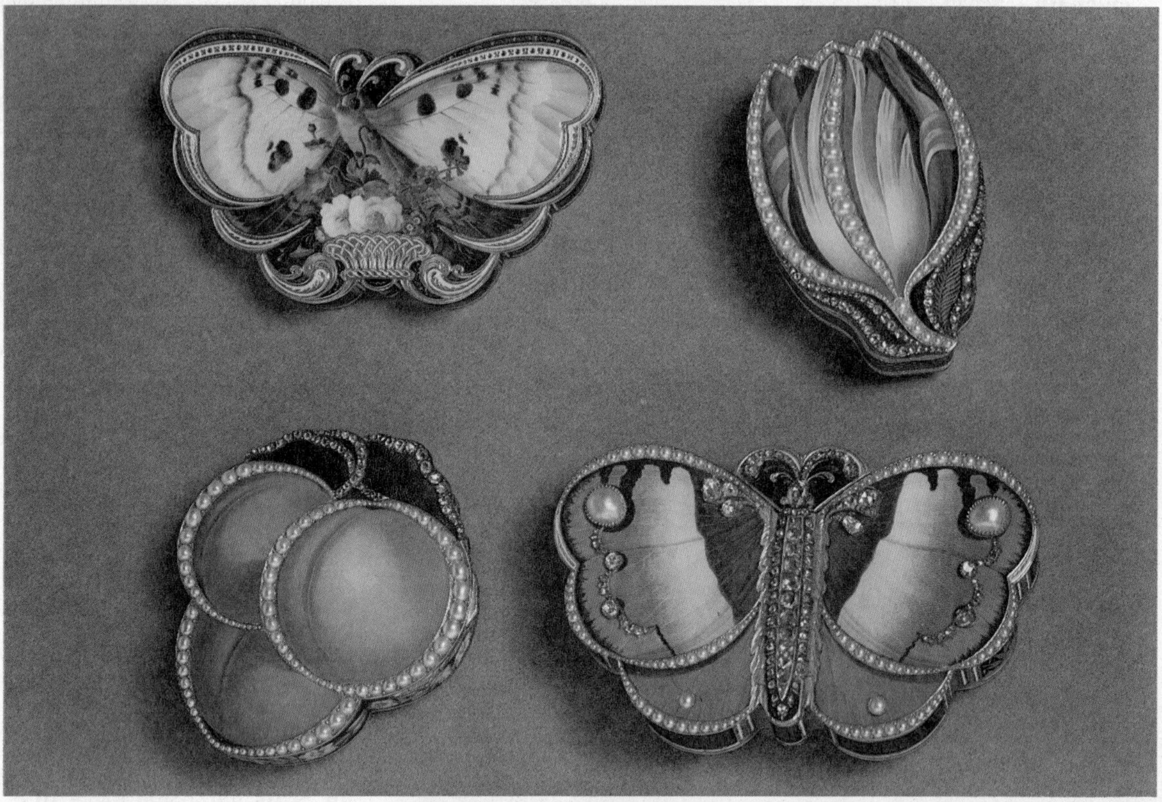

Enamelled and jewelled boxes, c. 1820, Swiss. Placed against a ground of precious metal, ***enamel*** *has great brilliance of color and it has been used to enrich such work.*

Encaging *an animal generally means something far more humane than it did some years ago. Zoos and animal parks have realized contact between viewer and animal is of prime importance.*

en-, em- *prefixes.* In, into, on.

-en *suffix.* Forming: (1) verbs from adjectives to indicate being, becoming, or causing to be (*deepen, shorten, weaken*) or verbs from nouns to indicate coming to have, causing to have (*lengthen, heighten*); (2) adjectives from nouns to indicate consisting of, made of, or like (golden, wooden); (3) past participles of strong verbs (*frozen*); (4) pl. nouns (*brethren*); (5) diminutives (*children, chicken*).

en·a·ble (ĕnā′b*e*l) *v.t.* (**-bled, -bling**). Authorize, empower (*to* do); supply with means *to* (do).

en·act (ĕnăkt′) *v.t.* 1. Make (bill) into legislative act, pass (bill) in legislature. 2. Act out (a play, the part of, etc.). **en·act′ment, en·ac′tor** *ns.*

e·nam·el (ĭnăm′*e*l) *n.* 1. Colored glass, powdered and fused, used as decoration for gold, silver, or copper, or for painting. 2. Hard oil paint, freq. containing varnish, which renders it glossy; any smooth and lustrous surface coloring. 3. Calcified substance forming glossy coating of teeth. ~ *v.t.* Inlay, encrust, cover, with enamel; variegate like enamel work.

en·am·or, Brit. **en·am·our** (ĕnăm′er) *vbs.t.* Inspire with love, make fond (*of*; usu. pass.).

en·cage (ĕnkāj′) *v.t.* (**-caged, -cag·ing**). Confine (as) in cage.

en·camp (ĕnkămp′) *v.* Set up or live in camp; lodge in open in tents etc. **en·camp′ment** *n.* (esp.) Place where troops are encamped; temporary quarters of nomads etc.

en·case (ĕnkās′) *v.t.* (**-cased, -cas·ing**). Put into case; surround as with case.

-ence *suffix.* Forming nouns from adjectives ending in *-ent* to indicate action or quality (*reminiscence, congruence*).

en·ceinte (ahṅsăṅt′) *adj.* (of woman) Pregnant.

en·ceph·a·li·tis (ĕnsĕf*a*lī′tĭs) *n.* (path.) Inflammation of the brain; **lethargic** ~ (or ~ **lethargica**), infectious form of this due to a virus, usu. accompanied by extreme drowsiness; sleeping sickness.

en·chain (ĕnchān′) *v.t.* Chain up, fetter.

en·chant (ĕnchănt′, -chahnt′) *v.t.* Bewitch; charm, delight. **en·chant′er, en·chant′ress, en·chant′ment** *ns.* **en·chant′ing·ly** *adv.*

en·chi·la·da (ĕnchĭlah′d*a*) *n.* Tortilla with meat etc. and chili sauce.

en·ci·pher (ĕnsī′f*er*) *v.t.* Write (message etc.) in cipher.

en·cir·cle (ĕnsẽr′k*e*l) *v.t.* (**-cled, -cling**). Surround, encompass; form a circle around.

encl. *abbrev.* Enclosed; enclosure.

en·clave (ĕn′klāv) *n.* Territory surrounded by territory of another country; minority culture or other group existing within a group.

en·close (ĕnklōz′) *v.t.* (**-closed, -clos·ing**). 1. Surround (with walls, forces, etc.) so as to prevent free access; fence in; shut up *in*. 2. Shut up in receptacle (esp. something along *with* letter in envelope); bound on all sides, contain; surround, hem in on all sides.

en·clo·sure (ĕnklō′zh*er*) *n.* Enclosing; enclosing fence etc.; enclosed place; document etc. enclosed with letter in envelope.

en·code (ĕnkōd′) *v.t.* (**-cod·ed, -cod·ing**). Put (message) into code or cipher; encipher. **en·cod′er** *n.*

en·co·mi·um (ĕnkō′mē*u*m) *n.* (pl. **-mi·ums, -mi·a** pr. -mē*a*). Formal or high-flown expression of praise; eulogy, panegyric.

en·com·pass (ĕnkŭm′p*a*s) *v.t.* Surround, form circle about; comprise; include. **en·com′pass·ment** *n.*

en·core (ahng′kōr, -kōr, ahn′-) *n.* & *int.* (Call for performance to be repeated) again, once more; repetition or additional item given in response. ~ *v.t.* Demand encore of (song, performer, etc.).

en·coun·ter (ĕnkown′t*er*) *v.t.* 1. Meet as adversary, confront in battle. 2. Meet, fall in with, esp. casually; experience (opposition etc.). ~ *n.* Meeting in combat or casually; ~ **group**, small group of persons who meet to improve their self-awareness and responsiveness through therapy that involves open expression of emotions.

en·cour·age (ĕnkẽr′ĭj, -kŭr′-) *v.t.* (**-aged, -ag·ing**). Inspire with courage, embolden; stimulate by assistance, reward, approval, etc.; allow or promote continuance or progress of. **en·cour′age·ment** *n.* **en·cour′ag·ing** *adj.* **en·cour′ag·ing·ly** *adv.*

en·croach (ĕnkrōch′) *v.i.* Intrude usurpingly (*on*). **en·croach′ment** *n.*

en·crust (ĕnkrŭst′) = INCRUST.

en·cum·ber (ĕnkŭm′b*er*) *v.t.* Hamper *with* burden; burden with obligations, debts, etc.

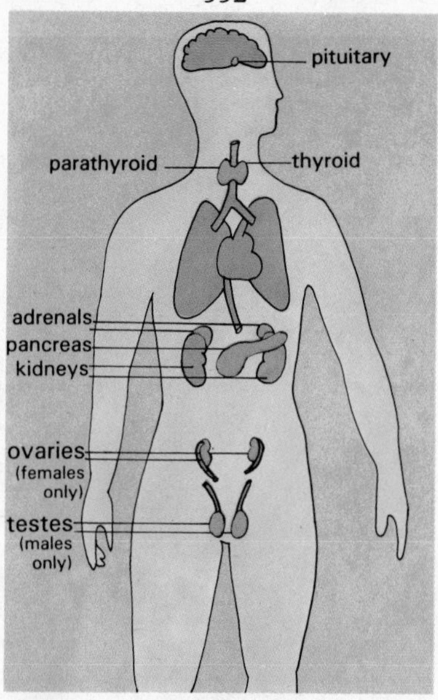

***Endocrine** glands, with the exception of the pancreas which secretes insulin, release hormones into the bloodstream. The pituitary gland controls other glands shown in the diagram.*

en·cum·brance (ĕnkŭm′br*a*ns) *n.* 1. Burden; impediment. 2. Claim or lien upon property.

-ency *suffix.* Forming nouns indicating quality (*efficiency*) or state (*presidency*), but not action (cf. -ENCE).

ency., encyc., encycl. *abbrevs.* Encyclopedia.

en·cyc·li·cal (ĕnsĭk′lĭk*a*l, -sī′-klĭ-) *adj.* & *n.* (Letter, esp. issued by pope) intended for extensive circulation and dealing with matters of doctrine.

en·cy·clo·pe·di·a (ĕnsīklopē′dē*a*) *n.* Reference work containing extensive information on all branches or one particular branch of knowledge, usu. in alphabetical or topical order. **en·cy·clo·pe′dic** *adj.* **en·cy·clo·pe′dist** *n.* [pseudo-Gk. *egkuklopaideia*, spurious f. *egkuklios paideia* all-around education, the arts and sciences considered essential to a liberal education]

en·cyst (ĕnsĭst′) *v.t.* Enclose in or become a cyst.

end (ĕnd) *n.* 1. Extreme point or outermost part, utmost limit; one of the extremities of line or of greatest dimension of object; surface bounding thing at either extremity; piece broken off etc., remnant; (naut.) last length, short length, of rope or cable. 2. Limit, close, conclusion, of period of time, action, process, series, discourse, book, etc.; latter or concluding part; termination of existence, destruction; death; ultimate state or condition. 3. Event, issue; intended result, aim, purpose; object for which thing exists or is designed. 4. **be at, come to, an** ~, be, become, exhausted; be completed; end; **be at the** ~ **of**, have no more of; **bring to an** ~, exhaust, complete, end; **keep one's** ~ **up**, (colloq.) bear one's part, acquit oneself well; **make both** ~**s meet**, live within one's income; **no** ~, (colloq.) vast quantity or number *of*; immensely; **on** ~, resting on its end, upright; consecutively; **put an** ~ **to**, put a stop to; ~ **to** ~, with ends in contact, lengthwise. 5. ~ **game**, (chess) last stage in game when few pieces are left; ~ **man**, man at either end of row of minstrels, playing bones or tambourine and contributing comic effects; ~ **organ**, any specialized structure forming the peripheral terminus of nerve fibers having either motor or sensory functions; ~ **papers**, blank leaves at beginning and end of book, esp. the first

*The **endoplasm** is the central granular fluid in the protoplasm of an amoeba, which consists also of an outer plasma membrane and a layer of clear ectoplasm just beneath that.*

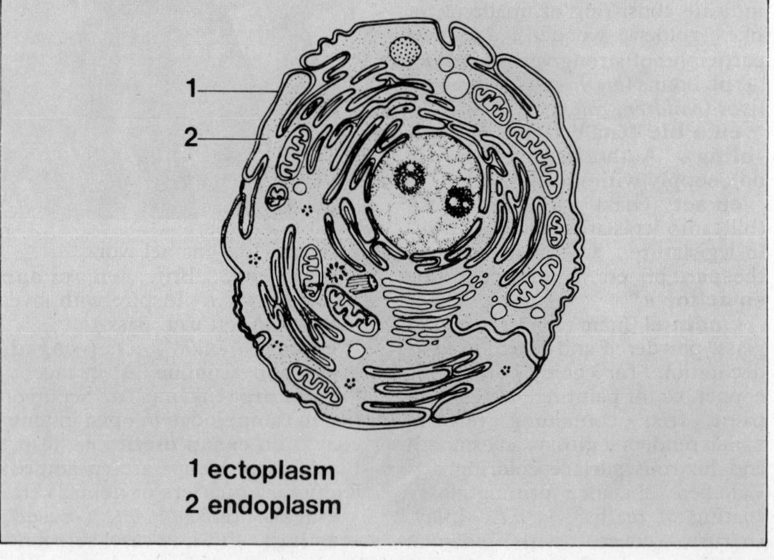

and last, which are pasted to the binding; ~ **product**, finished article as opposed to raw material; ~ **table**, small table to be placed at the end of a sofa or beside a chair. **end** *v.* Bring to an end; put an end to, destroy; come to an end; result *in*; ~ **by** (**doing**), come ultimately to (doing); ~ **up**, conclude, finish.

en·dan·ger (ĕndān′*jer*) *v.t.* Cause danger to. **en·dan′gered** *adj.* In danger of extinction, esp. ~ **species**, plant, animal, bird, etc., threatened with extinction because of destruction of environment etc.

en·dear (ĕndēr′) *v.t.* Render dear (*to*). **en·dear′ing·ly** *adv.* **en·dear′ment** *n.* (esp.) Action or utterance expressing affection.

en·deav·or (ĕndĕv′*er*) *v.* Try (*to* do); strive. ~ *n.* Attempt, effort.

en·dem·ic (ĕndĕm′ĭk) *adj.* Regularly found among (specified) people or in (specified) country or district as a disease. **en·dem′i·cal·ly** *adv.* **en·dem′ic** *n.* Endemic plant or animal; endemic disease.

end·ing (ĕn′dĭng) *n.* (esp.) Concluding part (of book, story, etc.); (gram.) inflectional or formative suffix.

en·dive (ĕn′dīv) *n.* 1. Plant (*Cichorium endivia*), the lacy leaves of which are used in salads; variety of this, ESCAROLE. 2. Variety of common chicory, (*Cichorium intybus*), whose long, narrow leaves are bleached in cultivation and used for salads.

end·less (ĕnd′lĭs) *adj.* Infinite; eternal; incessant. **end′less·ly** *adv.* **end′less·ness** *n.*

endo- *prefix.* Within.

en·do·car·di·um (ĕndōkar′dē*u*m) *n.* (pl. **-di·a** pr. -dē*a*). (physiol.) Smooth membrane lining cavities of heart. **en·do·car·di·tis** (ĕndōkardī′tĭs) *n.* Inflammation of the endocardium.

en·do·carp (ĕn′d*o*karp) *n.* (bot.) Inner layer of pericarp, lining seed chamber, fleshy (as in orange), membranous (as in apple), or hard (as in peach).

en·do·crine (ĕn′d*o*krĭn, -krīn, -krēn) *adj.* & *n.* (Gland) pouring its secretions into the blood or lymph, ductless (gland).

en·do·cri·nol·o·gy (ĕndōkrĭn-ŏl′*o*jē) *n.* Branch of medicine dealing with the endocrine glands and their secretions. **en·do·cri·nol′o·gist** *n.*

en·do·derm (ĕn′d*o*derm) *n.* (physiol.) Innermost layer of cells of embryo, from which alimentary system is developed.

en·do·der·mis (ĕnd*o*der′mĭs) *n.* (bot.) Cylinder of tissue 1 cell thick lying between cortex and conducting tissues.

en·dog·a·my (ĕndŏg′*a*mē) *n.* Custom of marrying only within one's own clan, tribe, caste, etc. **en·dog′a·mous** *adj.*

*When European man arrived in North America, it was estimated that there were 60,000,000 bison; by 1900 they had become an **endangered species.** Desperate action saved it from extinction.*

***Endive** was supposedly introduced to Europe from the East Indies or Egypt. It is cultivated for culinary purposes and bleached while growing to prevent the leaves from tasting bitter.*

en·dog·e·nous (ĕndŏj′*e*n*u*s) *adj.* Growing or originating from within.

en·do·plasm (ĕn′d*o*plăz*e*m) *n.* (biol.) Granular fluid cytoplasm contained within ectoplasm in an animal cell. **en·do·plas·mic** (ĕnd*o*plăz′mĭk) *adj.*

en·dorse (ĕndōrs′) *v.t.* (**-dorsed, -dors·ing**). 1. Write on back of (document), esp. sign one's name (as payee etc.) on (bill, check, etc.); make (check etc.) payable *to* another by endorsement. 2. Confirm, vouch for (statement, opinion); express approval of (thing, person, etc.). **en·dorse′ment** *n.*

en·do·sperm (ĕn′d*o*sperm) *n.* (bot.) Albumen enclosed with embryo in many seeds. **en·do·sper·mic** (ĕndōsper′mĭk) *adj.*

en·do·the·li·um (ĕndōthē′lē*u*m) *n.* (pl. **-li·a** pr. -lē*a*). Layer of cells lining blood vessels etc.

en·do·ther·mic (ĕndōther′mĭk) *adj.* (chem.) Occurring or formed with absorption of heat.

en·dow (ĕndow′) *v.t.* Give, bequeath, permanent income to (person, institution, etc.); enrich *with* (privileges etc.); furnish *with* (quality, ability, etc.). **en·dow′ment** *n.*

en·dur·ance (ĕndoor′*a*ns, -dūr′-) *n.* 1. Act, power, or quality of withstanding fatigue, stress, pain, etc. 2. Fact or state of persevering; lasting or continuing.

en·dure (ĕndoor′, -dūr′) *v.* (**-dured, -dur·ing**). 1. Undergo (pain etc.); submit to; bear (*to* do); tolerate (thing, person). 2. Last.

Types of ***energy:*** *Top left: Muscular energy; Alan Pascoe jumping hurdles. Bottom left: Nuclear energy; research workers handle isotopes, using mechanical hands from behind protective barriers. Top right: Potential kinetic energy — the Victoria Falls, between Zambia and Zimbabwe. Bottom, far right: A drainage windmill at Horsey, Norfolk, U.K. Bottom, near right: Two of the many large generators in the Foster Dam, Oregon.*

end·ways (ĕnd'wāz), **end·wise** (ĕnd'wīz) *advs.* With end toward spectator or uppermost or foremost; end to end.

En·dym·i·on (ĕndĭm'ēon). (Gk. myth.) Shepherd, the most beautiful of men, of whom Selene (the Moon) became enamored.

ENE, E.N.E., e.n.e. *abbrevs.* East-northeast.

-ene *comb. form.* (chem.) Used to form names of unsaturated hydrocarbons (*benzene, ethylene*).

en·e·ma (ĕn'ema) *n.* (med.) Injection of fluid into the rectum, esp. as laxative; fluid injected in this manner.

en·e·my (ĕn'emē) *n.* (pl. **-mies**). 1. Hostile person; opponent, antagonist; opposing person, influence, etc. 2. (Member of) hostile army or nation; hostile force; nation at war with another. ~ *adj.* Of a hostile force or nation; hostile.

en·er·get·ic (ĕnerjĕt'ĭk) *adj.* Strenuously active; forcible, vigorous; powerfully operative. **en·er·get'i·cal·ly** *adv.*

en·er·gize (ĕn'erjīz) *v.t.* (**-gized, -giz·ing**). Supply with energy; activate; charge. **en'er·giz·er** *n.*

en·er·gy (ĕn'erjē) *n.* (pl. **-gies**). 1. Force, vigor (of speech, action, person, etc.); active operation; power actively exerted, (pl.) individual capacity to produce effect. 2. (phys.) Power of doing work possessed at any instant by a body or system of bodies; **conservation of** ~: see CONSERVATION; **kinetic** ~, power of doing work possessed by moving body by virtue of its motion; **potential** ~, body's power of doing work by virtue of stresses resulting from its relation to other bodies; **mass-**~, energy that all bodies possess in virtue of their mass, and of which a small portion is released (as radiations etc.) in radioactivity and other types of atomic disintegration. 3. Fuel and other sources of such energy used for the operation of machinery etc.

en·er·vate (ĕn'ervāt) *v.t.* (**-vat·ed, -vat·ing**). Weaken physically, debilitate; deprive of strength or vitality. **en·er·va·tion** (ĕnervā'shon) *n.*

en·fant ter·ri·ble (ahṅfahṅ tĕrē'ble). Child who embarrasses his or her elders by untimely remarks (also transf.). [Fr.]

en·fee·ble (ĕnfē'bel) *v.t.* (**-bled, -bling**). Make feeble. **en·fee'ble·ment** *n.*

en·fi·lade (ĕn'filād, -lahd, ĕnfilād', -lahd') *n.* Fire from guns etc. sweeping line from end to end. ~ *v.t.* (**-lad·ed, -lad·ing**). Subject (troops etc.) to enfilade.

en·fold (ĕnfōld') *v.t.* Wrap up (*in, with*); clasp, embrace.

en·force (ĕnfōrs', -fōrs') *v.t.* (**-forced, -forc·ing**). Compel (performance of action, observance of law, etc.). **en·force'ment** *n.* **en·force'a·ble** *adj.*

en·fran·chise (ĕnfrăn'chīz) *v.t.* (**-chised, -chis·ing**). 1. Set free as from bondage. 2. Admit to full rights of citizenship, esp. voting rights. **en·fran·chise·ment** (ĕnfrăn'chīzment, -chĭz-) *n.*

Eng. *abbrev.* England; English.

eng. *abbrev.* Engine; engineer(ing).

en·gage (ĕngāj') *v.* (**-gaged, -gag·ing**). 1. Bind by contract or promise (esp. of marriage); pledge oneself. 2. Hire (employee); contract beforehand to occupy (position, office, etc.). 3. Attract, charm. 4. Fasten, attach; (mech.) mesh or interlock (*with*), fit into corresponding part. 5. Hold fast, attract (attention etc.); employ, occupy (person, his powers, thought, etc.); embark *in*, enter upon, action, business, etc. 6. Bring, come, into conflict *with* enemy; attack, enter into combat with. **en·gaged'** *adj.* (esp.) Betrothed; occupied; in use. **en·gage'ment** *n.*

en·gag·ing (ĕngā'jĭng) *adj.* (esp.) Winning, attractive. **en·gag'ing·ly** *adv.*

En·gels (ĕng'elz), **Friedrich** (1820–95). German socialist leader and writer; settled in England 1849; collaborated with Karl Marx in producing the *Communist Manifesto*, 1848.

en·gen·der (ĕnjĕn'der) *v.* Beget (now only fig.); give rise to, bring about.

en·gine (ĕn'jin) *n.* 1. Machine consisting of several parts working together to produce given physical effect; esp., machine consisting of oscillating or reciprocating parts that converts the chemical energy of fuel into mechanical power in a useful form; locomotive; ~ **room**, room containing (esp. ship's) engine. 2. (hist.) Machine used in warfare, esp. of large size (e.g. catapult, battering ram).

en·gi·neer (ĕnjinēr') *n.* 1. One skilled in the construction and maintenance of works of public utility such as roads and bridges (**civil** ~), or in the design, construction, and maintenance of machines (**mechanical** ~), or in the production and transmission of electrical energy and the manufacture of electrical apparatus

*The **steam engine** was developed from the first inefficient pumping machine of 1700. James Watt improved on this model in the 18th century but only in the 19th was a way found of using steam to provide locomotive power.*

*A surveyor at work during the construction of a main road in Australia. **Engineering** requires wide-ranging technical knowledge that enables the engineer to communicate and work with other specialists.*

England is the largest, richest, and most populous unit of the United Kingdom. Its countryside is varied. Above: Coniston Water in the Lake District. Right: The West Gate, Canterbury, an ancient entrance to one of England's most historic cities.

(**electrical** ~). 2. One who designs and constructs military works for attack or defense. 3. One who has charge of steam engine (also **stationary** ~); operator of locomotive. **engineer** *v.* 1. Act as engineer; construct, manage (work), as engineer. 2. Contrive, arrange, bring about. **en·gi·neer′·ing** *n.* Science, profession, of engineer; work done by engineer.

Eng·land (ĭng′gl*a*nd). Kingdom occupying, together with Wales, the southern part of Gt. Britain; capital, London; (pop.) Gt. Britain; the United Kingdom of Gt. Britain and Northern Ireland.

Eng·lish (ĭng′glĭsh) *adj.* Of England or its people or language; ~ **Channel**, channel between S. coast of England and N. coast of France; ~ **horn**, double-reed woodwind musical instrument, similar to the oboe but larger and pitched ⅕ lower; **Eng′lishman, Eng′lishwoman**, English person; ~ **sonnet**: see SONNET. **English** *n.* 1. (collect.) English people. 2. Language of the English, member of the western branch of the Germanic family of languages, orig. the dialect of the Angles, later including all dialects of the vernacular whether Anglian or Saxon, and including **Old** ~, Anglo-Saxon, *c*5th c. to *c*1100, **Middle** ~, *c*1100 to *c*1500, and **Modern** ~, *c*1500– ; **American** ~, the variety of English spoken in U.S.; **Canadian** ~, English language as spoken and written in Canada, having elements of English pronunciation and vocabulary and showing strong U.S. influence; **King's** (**Queen's**) ~, correct grammatical English; (**in**) **plain** ~, (in) plain intelligible words. 3. (print.) Size of type (14 point). 4. (sometimes **e**~) (billiards, bowling, etc.) Spinning motion given to a ball by striking it on the side or letting it go with a quick twist. 5. ~ **muffin**, round, rather flat yeast roll, baked on a griddle, and toasted after being split with fork; ~ **setter**, any of a breed of setter of medium size and having flat, silky white coat with black or brownish markings and feathery hair on the tail and backs of legs; ~ **sparrow**: see HOUSE sparrow; ~ **walnut**, walnut tree (*Juglans reglia*) of Asia, cultivated in S. Europe and California on a commercial basis for its large edible nuts.

en·gorge (ĕngôrj′) *v.t.* (**-gorged, -gorg·ing**). 1. Devour greedily. 2. (pass.) Be crammed; (path.) be congested with blood. **en·gorge′ment** *n.*

engr. *abbrev.* Engineer(ing); engraved; engraver; engraving.

en·grave (ĕngrāv′) *v.t.*

(**-graved, -grav·ing**). Inscribe, ornament (hard surface) *with* incised marks; carve (design, letters, etc.) *upon* surface; cut (design etc.) on metal plate or wood block for printing; (fig.) impress deeply (*upon* memory etc.). **en·grav'er** *n.*

en·grav·ing (ĕngrā'vĭng) *n.* (esp.) Print made from engraved plate; copy of painting etc. made by this means; art of imparting designs to plates or blocks in such a way that prints may be taken from them, esp. by incising lines (**line ~**); this and numerous other hand and mechanical processes collectively.

en·gross (ĕngrōs') *v.t.* Occupy entirely or exclusively, monopolize (person, his attention, etc.). **en·gross'ment** *n.*

en·gulf (ĕngŭlf') *v.t.* Plunge into, swallow up (as) in, gulf; surround. **en·gulf'ment** *n.*

en·hance (ĕnhăns', -hahns') *v.* (**-hanced, -hanc·ing**). Heighten, intensify (qualities, powers, etc.); exaggerate; increase in price or value. **en·hance'ment** *n.*

e·nig·ma (enĭg'ma) *n.* (pl. **-mas, -ma·ta** pr. -mata). Riddle; puzzling person or thing. **en·ig·mat·ic** (ĕnĭgmăt'ĭk), **en·ig·mat'i·cal** *adjs.* **en·ig·mat'i·cal·ly** *adv.*

en·join (ĕnjoin') *v.t.* 1. Prescribe, impose (action, conduct, *on* person); command. 2. Prohibit, restrain (esp. by legal injunction).

en·joy (ĕnjoi') *v.t.* 1. Find pleasure in; **~ oneself**, experience pleasure, be happy. 2. Use, possess, or experience with delight, take delight in; have use or benefit of. **en·joy'a·ble** *adj.* **en·joy'a·bly** *adv.* **en·joy'ment** *n.*

en·kin·dle (ĕnkĭn'del) *v.t.* (**-dled, -dling**). Cause (flame, passions, war, etc.) to blaze up.

en·lace (ĕnlās') *v.t.* (**-laced, -lac·ing**). Encircle tightly; enfold; entwine. **en·lace'ment** *n.*

en·large (ĕnlarj') *v.* (**-larged, -larg·ing**). 1. Make, become larger, extend limits of, increase size, amount, or number of; (phot.) make picture larger than original negative. 2. Extend range or scope of, widen (ideas, sympathies, etc.); expatiate *upon.* **en·large'ment** *n.* **en·larg'er** *n.* Photographic apparatus for enlarging or reducing negatives or positives.

en·light·en (ĕnlī'ten) *v.t.* Instruct, inform (*on* subject); free from prejudice or superstition. **en·light'en·ment** *n.* **the E~**, (after Ger. *Aufklärung*) an 18th c. philosophical movement characterized by a reliance on reason and directed to freeing religion and morals from tradition and prejudice.

en·list (ĕnlĭst') *v.* 1. (Persuade to) enter military service voluntarily; enroll (volunteer); hence enlistee' *n.* and **enlisted man** or **woman**, as opp. to *draftee.* 2. Secure cooperation or support of (*in* enterprise etc.). **en·list'ment** *n.*

*This mule deer, **ensnared** in a rope net, will be released by its captors, trained wildlife officers, at a location better suited to its longterm survival. This particular operation involved many mule deer.*

en·liv·en (ĕnlī'ven) *v.t.* Animate, make lively; brighten. **en·liv'en·ment** *n.*

en masse (ahn măs', ĕn; *Fr.* ahṅ măs'). In a mass; in one body, all together. [Fr.]

en·mesh (ĕnmĕsh') *v.t.* Entangle (as) in net; involve. **en·mesh'ment** *n.*

en·mi·ty (ĕn'mĭtē) *n.* (pl. **-ties**). Hatred; state of hostility.

en·no·ble (ĕnnō'bel) *v.t.* Invest with nobility; add to the honor of. **en·no'ble·ment** *n.*

en·nui (ahnwē', ahn'wē) *n.* Boredom.

e·nor·mi·ty (ĭnôr'mĭtē) *n.* (pl. **-ties**). Monstrous wickedness; crime, monstrous offense.

e·nor·mous (ĭnôr'mus) *adj.* Very large. **e·nor'mous·ly** *adv.* **e·nor'mous·ness** *n.*

e·nough (ĭnŭf') *adj., n.,* & *adv.* Adequate or sufficient (in quantity, number, or degree).

e·now (ĭnow') *adj., n.,* & *adv.* (poet.) Enough.

en·plane (ĕnplān') *v.i.* (**-planed, -plan·ing**). Go on board an airplane.

en·quire (ĕnkwīr'), **en·quir·y** (ĕnkwīr'ē, ĭn'kwerē): see INQUIRE, INQUIRY.

en·rage (ĕnrāj') *v.t.* (**-raged, -rag·ing**). Make furious.

en·rap·ture (ĕnrăp'cher) *v.t.* (**-tured, -tur·ing**). Delight intensely.

en·rich (ĕnrĭch') *v.t.* Make rich; make better or finer. **en·rich'ment** *n.*

en·roll, en·rol (ĕnrōl') *vbs.* (**-rolled, -roll·ing**). Write (name), inscribe name of (person) on roll or list, esp. of school etc.; incorporate (person) as member (*in* club etc.); record; enlist. **en·roll'ment, en·rol'ment** *ns.*

en route (ahn ro͞ot', ĕn; *Fr.* ahṅ ro͞ot'). On or along the way. [Fr.]

Ens. *abbrev.* Ensign.

en·sconce (ĕnskŏns') *v.t.* (**-sconced, -sconc·ing**). Establish (*in* concealed, secure, comfortable, etc., position).

en·sem·ble (ahnsahm'bel, -sahmb') *n.* Thing viewed as whole; woman's outfit of harmonizing items; = CHORUS *n.* def. 3; (mus.) united performance of group of voices or instruments in concert. [Fr.]

en·shrine (ĕnshrīn') *v.t.* (**-shrined, -shrin·ing**). Enclose (relic etc.) in or as in shrine; cherish as sacred. **en·shrine'ment** *n.*

en·shroud (ĕnshrowd') *v.t.* Cover completely, hide from view.

en·sign (ĕn'sīn; *naut.* ĕn'sin) *n.* 1. Conventional sign, emblem; esp., badge or symbol of dignity or office. 2. (chiefly naut.) Standard, banner, flag. 3. (U.S. Navy and Coast Guard) Commissioned officer of lowest rank, below a lieutenant, junior grade.

en·si·lage (ĕn'sĭlĭj) = SILAGE.

en·sile (ĕnsīl', ĕn'sīl) *v.t.* (**-siled, -sil·ing**). Put (fodder) into silo; preserve (fodder) in silo.

en·slave (ĕnslāv') *v.t.* (**-slaved, -slav·ing**). Make slave of, reduce to slavery. **en·slave'ment** *n.*

en·snare (ĕnsnār') *v.t.* (**-snared, -snar·ing**). Entrap.

en·sue (ĕnso͞o') *v.* (**-sued, -su·ing**). Happen afterward; result (*from, on*).

en·sure (ĕnshoor') *v.t.* (**-sured, -sur·ing**). 1. Make certain; secure, guarantee (thing *to, for*, person, etc.). 2. Insure.

-ent *suffix.* Forming adjectives denoting existence of action (*consequent, effluent*) and nouns denoting agent (*coefficient, president*), usu. from verbs.

en·tab·la·ture (ĕntăb'lacher) *n.* (archit.) Part of classical order above column, including architrave, frieze, and cornice.

en·tail (ĕntāl') *n.* Act of entailing property; entailed estate. **~** *v.t.* 1. Limit the inheritance (of property) to a specific, unalterable succession of heirs, so that inherited property cannot be bequeathed at pleasure by any succeeding one; bestow (thing) as inalienable possession. 2. Impose (expense, duty, *on* person); necessitate. **en·tail'ment** *n.*

en·tan·gle (ĕntăng'gel) *v.t.* (**-gled, -gling**). Catch in snare or among obstacles; involve in difficulties; make tangled or intricate. **en·tan'gle·ment** *n.*

En·teb·be (ĕntĕb'ē). Former capital of Uganda from 1896–1962,

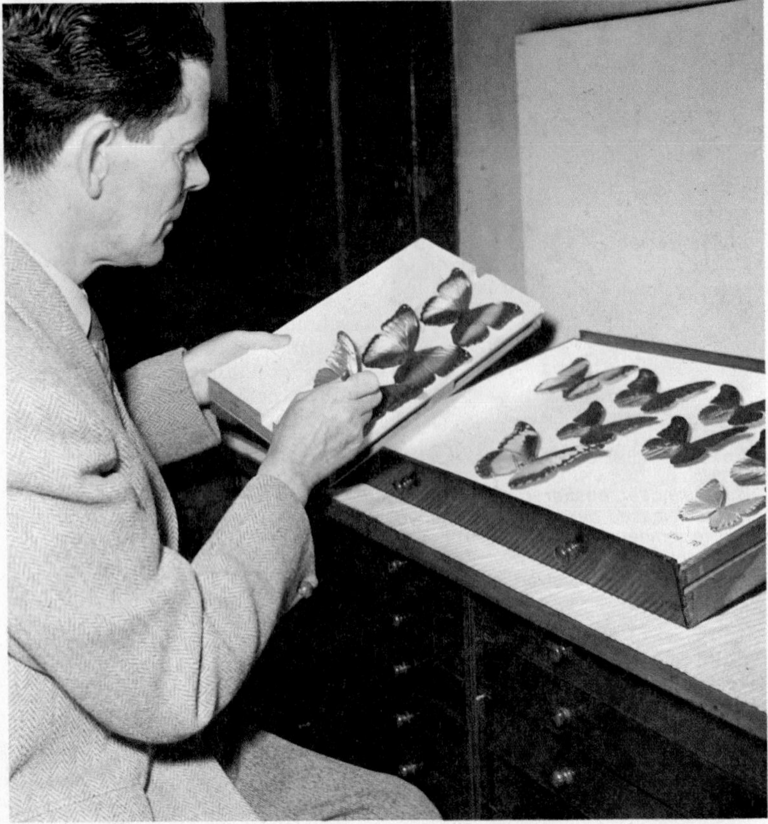

Transferring Blue Morphone butterflies from the setting block to a showcase. ***Entomology*** *is a vast subject: insects outnumber all other forms of animal life and their embryology, biology, etc. are highly complex.*

in the S. part on Lake Victoria.

en·tente (ahntahnt′; *Fr.* ahṅtahṅt′) *n.* (pl. **-tentes** pr. -tahnts′; *Fr.* -tahṅt′). (diplom.) Friendly understanding or, usu. informal, agreement between nations for cooperative policy or action; group of nations; **Triple E~**, that between England, France, and Russia (1908); **E~ Cordiale**, that formed between Gt. Britain and France in 1904. [Fr.]

en·ter (ĕn′ter) *v.* 1. Go, come, in; come upon stage; **~ for**, undertake to compete in (race etc.); **~ into**, engage in, form part of, bind oneself by (contract, treaty, etc.). 2. Go, come, into; penetrate; begin (period of time). 3. Become member of (society or organized body). 4. Put (name) on list, (fact etc.) into description or record, etc.; admit, procure admission for, as pupil, member of club etc.; **~ a judgment, writ, protest**, present or submit a judgment etc. for consideration, esp. officially.

en·ter·ic (ĕntĕr′ĭk) *adj.* Of the intestines; **~ fever**, typhoid. **enteric** *n.* Enteric fever. **en·ter·i·tis** (ĕnterī′tĭs) *n.* (Acute) inflammation of intestinal tract.

en·ter·prise (ĕn′terprīz) *n.* Undertaking, esp. bold or difficult one; courage, readiness to engage in enterprises; initiative; business venture; **private ~**, economic activity under private control. **en′ter·pris·ing** *adj.* Energetic, full of initiative.

en·ter·tain (ĕntertān′) *v.t.* 1. Occupy (person etc.) agreeably, amuse. 2. Receive as guest, show hospitality to (also abs.). 3. Admit to consideration, harbor, cherish (idea, opinion, proposal, etc.). **en·ter·tain′er** *n.* Person who entertains, esp. comedian, popular singer, etc. **en·ter·tain′ing** *adj.* **en·ter·tain′ing·ly** *adv.*

en·ter·tain·ment (ĕntertān′ment) *n.* (esp.) Amusement; public performance.

en·thrall, en·thral (ĕnthrawl′) *vbs.t.* (**-thralled, -thrall·ing**). Enslave; charm. **en·thrall′ment, en·thral′ment** *ns.*

en·throne (ĕnthrōn′) *v.t.* (**-throned, -thron·ing**). Place (king etc.) on throne, esp. as formal induction; exalt, revere. **en·throne′ment** *n.*

en·thuse (ĕnthōōz′) *v.* (**-thused, -thus·ing**). Show, evoke enthusiasm in.

en·thu·si·asm (ĕnthōō′zēăzem) *n.* 1. (archaic) Poorly regulated or misdirected religious emotion; extravagant or false confidence in divine inspiration or favor. 2. Rapturous intensity of feeling *for* a person, cause, pursuit, etc.; passionate eagerness; object of this.

en·thu·si·ast (ĕnthōō′zēăst) *n.* One who is full of enthusiasm; follower, fan. **en·thu·si·as·tic** (ĕnthōōzēăs′tĭk) *adj.* **en·thu·si·as′ti·cal·ly** *adv.*

en·tice (ĕntīs′) *v.t.* (**-ticed, -tic·ing**). Attract, esp. insidiously or adroitly, by offer of pleasure or advantage. **en·tice′ment** *n.*

en·tire (ĕntīr′, ĕn′tīr) *adj.* Whole, complete; not broken; not castrated; all of one piece, continuous; pure, unmixed.

en·tire·ly (ĕntīr′lē) *adv.* Wholly; solely.

en·tire·ty (ĕntīr′tē) *n.* (pl. **-ties**). Completeness; whole, sum total; **in its ~**, in its complete form, as a whole.

en·ti·tle (ĕntī′tel) *v.t.* (**-tled, -tling**). 1. Give (person, book, etc.) the title of. 2. Give (person etc.) a right (*to* a thing, *to* do). **en·ti′tle·ment** *n.*

en·ti·ty (ĕn′titē) *n.* (pl. **-ties**). 1. A thing's existence, as dist. from its qualities or relations. 2. Something that has a real existence.

en·tomb (ĕntōōm′) *v.t.* Place in tomb; serve as tomb for. **en·tomb′ment** *n.*

en·to·mol·o·gy (ĕntomŏl′ojē) *n.* Branch of zoology dealing with insects. **en·to·mo·log·i·cal** (ĕntomolŏj′ĭkal) *adj.* **en·to·mol′o·gist** *n.*

en·tou·rage (ahntōōrahzh′) *n.* Persons surrounding or attending on a superior; surroundings. [Fr.]

en·tr'acte (ahn′ trăkt, -trahkt, ahntrăkt, -trahkt′) *n.* (Performance in) interval between acts of play; music etc. for this. [Fr.]

en·trails (ĕn′trālz, -tralz) *n.pl.* Internal organs, esp. the intestines; viscera; inner parts (*of* the Earth etc.).

en·train (ĕntrān′) *v.* 1. Put, go, on a train. 2. (of a liquid) Trap bubbles.

en·trance[1] (ĕn′trans) *n.* 1. Coming or going in; coming of actor upon stage; entering *into*, *upon* (office etc.). 2. Right of admission; fee paid on admission. 3. Door, passage, etc., one enters by.

en·trance[2] (ĕntrăns′, -trahns′) *v.t.* (**-tranced, -tranc·ing**). Throw into trance; overwhelm (*with* joy, fear); fascinate, enchant.

en·trant (ĕn′trant) *n.* One who enters room, profession, etc., or *for* (race etc.).

en·trap (ĕntrăp′) *v.t.* (**-trapped, -trap·ping**). Catch in or as in trap; beguile (*into* doing).

en·treat (ĕntrēt′) *v.t.* 1. Ask earnestly (*to* do). 2. (archaic) Treat, deal with, in specified manner. **en·treat·y** (ĕntrē′tē) *n.* (pl. **-treat·ies**). Earnest request.

en·tre·chat (ahn′treshah; *Fr.* ahṅtreshă′) *n.* (ballet) Leap during which dancer crosses the feet a number of times, often with a beating motion. [Fr.]

en·tree, en·trée (ahn′trā) *ns.* 1. Right or privilege of admission. 2. (usu.) Main course; dish served before main course, esp. between fish and meat courses (in formal dining).

en·trench (ĕntrĕnch′) *v.t.* 1. Surround, fortify, with trench (freq. fig.). 2. Establish firmly in defensible position. **en·trench′ment** *n.*

en·tre nous (ahntre nōō′). Between ourselves; in private. [Fr.]

en·tre·pre·neur (ahntreprenēr′, -noor′) *n.* 1. Organizer, manager, of (esp. musical) entertainments; manager. 2. One who undertakes an enterprise. **en·tre·pre·neur′i·al** *adj.*

en·tro·py (ĕn′tropē) *n.* (phys.) Measure of the degree of molecular disorder existing in a system, also determining how much of the system's thermal energy is unavailable for conversion into mechanical work, expressed as a thermodynamic function.

en·trust (ĕntrŭst′) *v.t.* Charge (person) *with* (duty, object of care); confide (duty etc. *to* person etc.).

en·try (ĕn′trē) *n.* (pl. **-tries**). 1. Coming or going in; coming (of actor) upon stage; ceremonial entrance; **~-level (job),** generally low paying (work for beginners in a factory etc.), but offering opportunity to acquire skills and earn promotion. 2. Place of entrance; door, gate, entrance hall, etc. 3. Entering or registering in list, record, ledger, etc. or in dictionary, encyclopedia, etc.; **double ~**, of bookkeeping in which every credit item of one account in ledger is entered to debit of another. 4. One item so entered; registered as competitor, participant (in race etc.).

en·twine (ĕntwīn′) *v.t.* (**-twined, -twin·ing**). Twine or twist together, with, or around.

e·nu·mer·ate (ĭnōō′merāt, ĭnū′-) *v.t.* (**-at·ed, -at·ing**). Count; mention (number of things or persons) separately; specify. **e·nu·mer·a·tion** (ĭnōōmerā′shon, ĭnū-) *n.* **e·nu·mer·a·tive** (ĭnōō′merātĭv, -mera-, ĭnū′-) *adj.*

e·nun·ci·ate (ĭnŭn′sēāt) *v.t.* (**-at·ed, -at·ing**). Express (proposition, theory) definitely; proclaim; pronounce (articulate sounds). **e·nun·ci·a·tion** (ĭnŭnsēā′shon), **e·nun′ci·a·tor** *ns.*

en·u·re·sis (ĕnyurē′sĭs) *n.* (path.) Involuntary passing of urine.

en·vel·op (ĕnvĕl′op) *v.t.* Wrap up; cover; enclose; (mil.) surround. **en·vel′op·ment, en·vel′op·er** *ns.*

en·ve·lope (ĕn′velōp, ahn′-) *n.* 1. Wrapper, covering; folded and gummed cover for letter; fabric enclosing gasbag of airship. 2. (bot.) Calyx or corolla, or both together. 3. (math.) Line or curve tangent to each line or curve of a given family.

en·vi·a·ble (ĕn′vēabel) *adj.* Likely to arouse envy; highly desirable. **en′vi·a·bly** *adv.*

en·vi·ous (ĕn′vēus) *adj.* Full of envy; feeling envy *of.* **en′vi·ous·ly** *adv.*

en·vi·ron·ment (ĕnvī′ronment, -vī′ern-) *n.* Surroundings, surrounding objects, region, conditions, or influences. **en·vi·ron·men·tal** (ĕnvīronmĕn′tal, -vīern-) *adj.*

en·vi·ron·men·tal·ist (ĕnvī′ronmĕnt′alĭst) *n.* Person working for protection of the environment from pollution, exhaustion of natural resources, adverse effects of rapid population growth, etc. **en·vi·ron·men′tal·ism** *n.*

en·vi·rons (ĕnvī′ronz, -vī′ernz, ĕn′veronz) *n.pl.* Outskirts, surrounding districts, of town etc.

en·vis·age (ĕnvĭz′ĭj) *v.t.* (**-aged, -ag·ing**). Think of as likely in the future; imagine; visualize.

en·vi·sion (ĕnvĭzh′on) *v.t.* Picture in one's mind; foresee.

en·voi, en·voy[1] (ĕn′voi, ahn′-)

Always popular with both children and adults, Mickey Mouse and his friends at Disneyland seem to know what ***entertainment*** *is all about. The unique Disney characters have seen many forms of entertainment come and go.*

ns. Concluding stanza, esp. of ballade dedicating poem to a patron, serving as a summation etc.

en·voy[2] (ĕn′voi, ahn′-) *n.* Public minister, now esp., diplomatic minister ranking below ambassador and above chargé d'affaires; messenger, representative.

en·vy (ĕn′vē) *n.* (pl. **-vies**). Mortification, ill will, or longing occasioned by another's good fortune; object of this. ~ *v.t.* (**-vied, -vy·ing**). Feel envy of (person, his advantages). **en′vy·ing·ly** *adv.*

en·zyme (ĕn′zīm) *n.* Protein catalyst of a specific biochemical reaction. **en·zy·mic** (ĕnzī′mĭk, -zĭm′ĭk) *adj.*

E·o·cene (ē′osēn) *adj.* & *n.* (geol.) (Of) the 2nd epoch or system of the Tertiary period.

e.o.m. *abbrev.* End of the month.

e·on (ē′on, ē′ŏn) *n.* Immeasurably long period; an age of the universe; longest division of geologic time, including 2 or more eras.

The final scene from 'The Fall of the Roman Empire' (1964). The cinema has developed a modern form of ***epic,*** *a large-scale narrative film of heroic or semi-legendary events and people.*

-eous *suffix.* Forming adjectives meaning "of the nature of" (*ligneous* like wood, *vitreous* like glass).

EPA *abbrev.* Environmental Protection Agency.

ep·arch (ĕp′ārk) *n.* Governor or bishop of eparchy. **ep′ar·chy** *n.* 1. Subdivision of modern Greece. 2. Diocese of Greek Orthodox Church.

ep·au·let, ep·au·lette (ĕp′ulĕt, -lĭt, ĕpulĕt′) *ns.* Ornamental shoulder piece of uniform.

e·pee, é·pée (āpā′, ā′pā) *ns.* Fencing sword with bowl-shaped guard and long, thin, blunt-tipped, 3-sided blade having no cutting edge. **é·pée′ist** *n.*

e·pergne (ĭpērn′, āpārn′) *n.* Large (esp. branched) ornamental dish (for fruit, flowers, etc.) for centerpiece of dining table.

Eph. *abbrev.* Ephesians (New Testament).

e·phah, e·pha (ē′fa) *ns.* Unit of dry measure used by ancient Hebrews, equal to slightly more than a bushel.

e·phed·rine (ĭfĕd′rĭn, ĕf′edrēn, -drĭn) *n.* Alkaloid drug used to relieve asthma, allergies, etc.

e·phem·er·a (ĭfĕm′era) (pl. **-er·as, -er·ae** pr. -erē), **e·phem·er·on** (ĭfĕm′erŏn) (pl. **-er·ons, er·a** pr. -era) *ns.* Short-lived insect of order Ephemeroptera; commonest of the mayflies, insect with delicate lacy wings and three long tail filaments, found near water; hence, short-lived thing; thing of transitory usefulness.

e·phem·er·al (ĭfĕm′*e*ral) *adj.* 1. (of insects etc.) Living for a day or a few days. 2. Short-lived, transitory.

e·phem·er·is (ĭfĕm′*e*rĭs) *n.* (pl. **eph·e·mer·i·des** pr. ĕf*e*mĕr′ĭdēz). Table showing predicted positions of heavenly body for every day during given period; astronomical almanac.

E·phe·sian (ĭfē′zh*a*n) *adj.* Of Ephesus. ~ *n.* Native, inhabitant, of Ephesus; (**Epistle to the**) **~s,** book of New Testament ascribed to St. Paul, an epistle to the Christians at Ephesus.

Eph·e·sus (ĕf′*e*s*u*s). One of the principal Ionian cities on the Aegean coast of Asia Minor (now several miles inland); site of the Temple of Artemis.

epi- *prefix.* Upon, at, on the ground or occasion of, in addition.

ep·ic (ĕp′ĭk) *adj.* Of, in, that species of poetical composition celebrating in continuous narrative achievements of heroic personage(s) of history or tradition; such as is described in epic poetry, of heroic type or scale; heroic or majestic; ~ **dialect**, dialect in which Greek epic poems were written. **epic** *n.* Epic poem; composition comparable to epic poem; subject worthy of epic treatment.

ep·i·carp (ĕp′ĭkārp) *n.* (bot.) Outermost layer, skin, of fleshy fruit.

ep·i·cene (ĕp′ĭsēn) *adj.* 1. (L. and Gk. gram.) Denoting either sex without change of gender. 2. For, used by, both sexes; having characteristics of both sexes; effeminate or unmanly. ~ *n.* Epicene person.

ep·i·cen·ter (ĕp′ĭsĕnt*e*r), **ep·i·cen·trum** (ĕpĭsĕn′tr*u*m) *ns.* (pl. **-trums, -tra** pr. -tr*a*). Point on earth's surface directly above place where earthquake originates. **ep·i·cen′tral** *adj.*

ep·i·cure (ĕp′ĭkūr) *n.* One who cultivates discriminating taste in food and drink. **ep′i·cur·ism** *n.* [f. EPICURUS].

Ep·i·cu·re·an (ĕpĭkyur*ē*′*a*n, -kūr′ē-) *adj.* & *n.* 1. (Follower) of Epicurus. 2. (**e**~) (Person) devoted to pleasures, esp. refined sensuous enjoyment. **Ep·i·cu·re′an·ism, ep·i·cu·re′an·ism** *ns.*

Ep·i·cu·rus (ĕpĭkūr′*u*s) (341–270 B.C.). Athenian philosopher who held that the highest good was calmness of mind and freedom from pain, and rejected the idea of an afterlife and of the influence of gods in human affairs.

ep·i·cy·cle (ĕp′ĭsīk*e*l) *n.* 1. (geom.) Small circle rolling on the circumference of a greater one. 2. (hist., in ancient astronomy) Circle having its center on the circumference of a greater circle, used in the Ptolemaic system to represent

*An **epigraph,** inscription, on a tombstone. Although perhaps a sombre study, the scrutiny of memorial inscriptions has yielded much historical information.*

the revolutions of the planets. **ep·i·cy·clic** (ĕpĭsī′klĭk, -sĭk′lĭk) *adj.*

Ep·i·dau·rus (ĕpĭdōr′*u*s). Ancient Greek town on E. coast of Argolis; site of well-preserved ancient theater.

ep·i·dem·ic (ĕpĭdĕm′ĭk) *adj.* & *n.* (Disease) spreading rapidly through a community for a period (cf. ENDEMIC). **ep·i·dem′i·cal** *n.* **ep·i·dem′i·cal·ly** *adv.*

ep·i·de·mi·ol·o·gy (ĕpĭdēmēŏl′*o*jē) *n.* Science of epidemics.

ep·i·der·mis (ĕpĭdėr′mĭs) *n.* 1. (physiol.) Outer nonvascular layer of skin of animals, cuticle; outer animal integument of shell. 2. (bot.) Outermost cell layer in plants before secondary growth begins. **ep·i·der′mal, ep·i·der′mic, ep·i·der′moid** *adjs.*

*An **epergne** — a branched, ornamental centre-piece for the table — was used to hold desserts. The name may derive from the French word 'épargne' which means saving.*

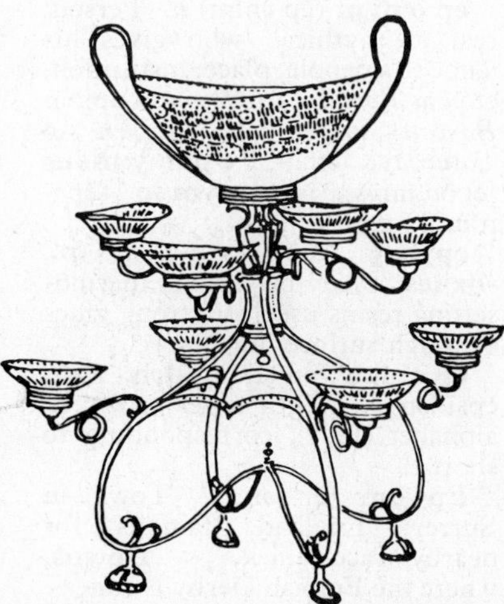

ep·i·gas·tri·um (ĕpĭgăs′trē*u*m) *n.* (pl. **-tri·a** pr. -trē*a*). Part of abdomen immediately over stomach. **ep·i·gas′tric** *adj.*

ep·i·glot·tis (ĕpĭglŏt′ĭs) *n.* (pl. **-glot·tis·es, -glot·i·des** pr. -glŏt′ĭdēz). Erect cartilage at root of tongue, depressed in act of swallowing to cover glottis.

ep·i·gram (ĕp′ĭgrăm) *n.* Short poem ending in witty or ingenious turn of thought; pointed saying or mode of expression. **ep·i·gram·mat·ic** (ĕpĭgr*a*măt′ĭk) *adj.* **ep·i·gram·mat′i·cal·ly** *adv.* **ep·i·gram·ma·tist** (ĕpĭgrăm′*a*tĭst) *n.*

ep·i·graph (ĕp′ĭgrăf, -grahf) *n.* Inscription on stone, statue, coin, etc.; motto. **ep·i·graph·ic** (ĕpĭgrăf′ĭk) *adj.*

ep·i·lep·sy (ĕp′ĭlĕpsē) *n.* Symptom of nervous disorder generally involving recurrent temporary loss of consciousness with or without convulsions, automatic movements, muscular spasms, etc. **ep·i·lep·tic** (ĕpĭlĕp′tĭk) *adj.* Of, subject to, epilepsy. ~ *n.* Epileptic person.

ep·i·logue, ep·i·log (ĕp′ĭlawg, -lŏg) *ns.* Concluding part of, short addition to, literary work; speech, short poem, addressed by actor to spectators at end of play.

ep·i·neph·rine (ĕpĭnĕf′rĭn, -rēn) *n.* 1. Adrenal hormone that raises blood pressure. 2. Isolated or synthesized preparation of this for heart stimulant, treatment of asthma, etc.

E·piph·a·ny (ĭpĭf′*a*nē) *n.* (pl. **-nies**). Christian festival commemorating the manifestation of Christ to the Gentiles in the persons of the Magi, observed on Jan. 6.

e·piph·a·ny (ĭpĭf′*a*nē) *n.* 1. Revelation or manifestation of a divine being. 2. Sudden revelation or recognition of the essential nature of something.

ep·i·phyte (ĕp′ĭfīt) *n.* Plant growing on another (usu. deriving only support, not nutrition, from it); vegetable parasite on animal body. **ep·i·phyt·ic** (ĕpĭfĭt′ĭk) *adj.*

Epis. *abbrev.* Epistle; Episcopal(ian).

Episc. *abbrev.* Episcopal(ian).

e·pis·co·pa·cy (ĭpĭs′k*o*p*a*sē) *n.* (pl. **-cies**). Government of church by bishops; the bishops collectively.

e·pis·co·pal (ĭpĭs′k*o*p*a*l) *adj.* Of bishop(s); **E~ Church** (also Protestant Episcopal Church) church body in the U.S. separate since 1789 but orig. part of Church of England and still in communion with it and close to it in practices and doctrine. **e·pis′co·pal·ly** *adv.*

e·pis·co·pa·lian (ĭpĭskopāl′yan, -pā′lēan) *adj.* & *n.* (Adherent) of episcopacy; **E∼**, (member) of Episcopal Church. **e·pis·co·pa′lian·ism, E·pis·co·pa′lian·ism** *ns.*

e·pis·co·pate (ĭpĭs′kopĭt, -pāt) *n.* Office, see, tenure, of bishop; the bishops collectively.

ep·i·si·ot·o·my (ĭpēzēŏt′omē) *n.* (pl. **-mies**). (surg.) Incision of the vulva to facilitate childbirth.

ep·i·sode (ĕp′ĭsōd, -zōd) *n.* 1. Incidental narrative, digression, in poem, story, etc.; incidental happening or series of events in history of a country or in person's life, as in **psychotic ∼**, temporary insanity; separately presented section of a serial novel, radio or television drama, etc. 2. In Gk. tragedy, interlocutory (orig. interpolated) parts between 2 choric songs. 3. (mus.) Intervening passage. **ep·i·sod·ic** (ĕpĭsŏd′ĭk, -zŏd′-) *adj.*

Epist. *abbrev.* Epistle.

e·pis·te·mol·o·gy (ĭpĭstemŏl′ojē) *n.* (pl. **-gies**). Theory of method or grounds of knowledge. **e·pis·te·mo·log·i·cal** (ĭpĭstemolŏj′ĭkal) *adj.*

e·pis·tle (ĭpĭs′el) *n.* 1. Letter; (esp.) letter from apostle, forming part of canon of Scripture; **E∼**, extract from one of these read as part of Communion service. 2. Literary work, usu. in verse, in form of letter.

e·pis·to·lar·y (ĭpĭs′tolĕrē) *adj.* Of, carried on by, suited to, letters.

ep·i·style (ĕp′ĭstīl) *n.* (archit.) Architrave.

ep·i·taph (ĕp′ĭtăf, -tahf) *n.* Inscription upon tomb; brief composition expressed as if for inscribing on tombstone.

ep·i·tha·la·mi·on (ĕpĭthalā′mēon) (pl. **-mi·a** pr. -mēa), **ep·i·tha·la·mi·um** (ĕpĭthalā′mēum) (pl. **-mi·ums, -mi·a** pr. -mēa) *ns.* Nuptial song or poem.

ep·i·the·li·um (ĕpĭthē′lēum) *n.* (pl. **-li·ums, -li·a** pr. -lēa). (biol.) Layer of cells that covers the body surface or lines a cavity that communicates with it. **ep·i·the′li·al** *adj.*

ep·i·thet (ĕp′ĭthĕt) *n.* Adjective expressing quality or attribute; this as term of abuse or profanity; significant appellation or characterization that comes to substitute for name of person, as *Honest Abe* for Abraham Lincoln, or *The Melancholy Dane* for Hamlet. **ep·i·thet·ic** (ĕpĭthĕt′ĭk), **ep·i·thet′i·cal** *adjs.*

e·pit·o·me (ĭpĭt′omē) *n.* Summary, abstract, of book; condensed account; (fig.) thing representing entire class or type; embodiment. **e·pit′o·mize** *v.t.*

*The Owen Stanley Range, New Guinea. **Equatorial** rain forests, large, dense, richly diverse forests dependent on heavy rainfall and high temperatures, are found in central Africa, Malaysia, Indonesia, and the Amazon Basin.*

(**-mized, -miz·ing**).

e plu·ri·bus u·num (ē ploor′ĭbus ū′num, ōō′num). Out of many, one; the motto of the U.S. [L.]

ep·och (ĕp′ok; *Brit.* ē′pok) *n.* (Beginning of) era in history, science, life, etc.; division of a geological period. **ep′och·al** *adj.* **ep′och·al·ly** *adv.*

ep·o·nym (ĕp′onĭm) *n.* Person, real or mythical, who gives his name to a people, place, institution, etc., as *Romulus* for *Rome*, Captain *Boycott* to *boycott*, *Saturn* to *Saturday*, etc. **e·pon·y·mous** (ĕpŏn′imus), **ep·o·nym·ic** (ĕponĭm′ĭk) *adjs.*

ep·ox·y (ĕpŏk′sē, ĭ-) *n.* (pl. **-ox·ies**). Any of various thermosetting resins used for strong glues or tough surface finishes.

ep·si·lon (ĕp′sĭlŏn, -lon; *Brit.* ĕpsī′lon) *n.* Fifth letter of Greek alphabet (Ε, ϵ), corresponding to short *e*.

Ep·som (ĕp′som). Town in Surrey, England, famous for nearby race track, **∼ Downs**, where the English Derby is run; **∼ salt(s)**, bitter crystalline salt, magnesium sulphate, used as a cathartic, orig. prepared from Epsom mineral waters.

eq. *abbrev.* Equal; equation; equivalent.

eq·ua·ble (ĕk′wabel, ē′kwa-) *adj.* Uniform, even, not easily disturbed. **eq·ua·bil·i·ty** (ĕkwabĭl′ĭtē, ēkwa-) *n.* **eq′ua·bly** *adv.*

e·qual (ē′kwal) *adj.* The same in number, size, value, degree, etc.; having strength, courage, ability, etc., adequate *to* (occasion etc.); uniform in operation, action, etc.; evenly balanced; **∼ sign**, symbol (=) used, esp. in equations, to indicate that the terms it separates are logically or mathematically equal; **∼ time**, (pol.) principle that different points of view should be allowed equal time in debate; (esp. radio and television) principle that station must give equal broadcast time to all political candidates or parties if it gives to one. **equal** *n.* Person equal to another in rank etc.; (pl.) equal things. **∼** *v.t.* (**e·qualed, e·qualled, e·qual·ing, e·qual·ling**). Be equal to.

e·qual·i·tar·i·an (ēkwŏlĭtār′ēan) *adj.* & *n.* Egalitarian.

e·qual·i·ty (ĭkwŏl′ĭtē) *n.* (pl. **-ties**). Condition of being equal; equal footing.

e·qual·ize (ē′kwalīz) *v.t.* (**-ized, -iz·ing**). Make (thing etc.) equal (to, with). **e·qual·i·za·tion**

Show-jumping is an exhilarating form of ***equestrian*** *skill, requiring close co-operation between horse and rider and a certain amount of natural talent in both.*

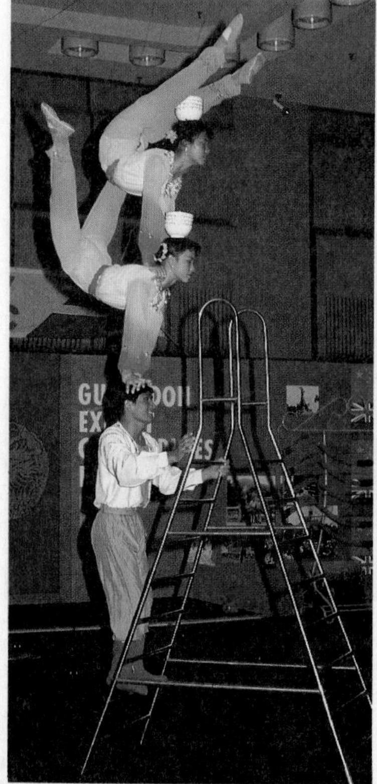

Chinese ***equilibrists*** *(balance artists) performing at a Chinese fair exhibition. The Chinese are noted for their balancing skills.*

(ēkwalīzā′shon) *n.* **e′qual·iz·er** *n.* (slang) Pistol.

e·qual·ly (ē′kwalē) *adv.* In an equal degree; in equal shares; uniformly.

e·qua·nim·i·ty (ēkwanĭm′ĭtē, ĕkwa-) *n.* Evenness of mind or temper; composure; resignation.

e·quate (ĭkwāt′) *v.t.* (**e·quat·ed, e·quat·ing**). State equality of (thing *to*, *with*, another); treat as equivalent.

e·qua·tion (ĭkwā′zhon, -shon) *n.* 1. Make equal, balancing; equilibrium, equality. 2. (math.) Formula affirming equivalence of 2 quantitative expressions, which are connected by the sign =. 3. (chem.) Expression representing chemical reaction quantitatively by means of symbols.

e·qua·tor (ĭkwā′ter) *n.* (astron., also **celestial** ~): see CELESTIAL; (geog.) great circle of the earth equidistant from poles; similar circle on any spherical body; **magnetic** ~, irregular line around earth near equator on which the angle of magnetic dip is zero.

e·qua·to·ri·al (ēkwatōr′ēal, -tōr′-, ĕkwa-) *adj.* Of, near, the equator. **e·qua·to′ri·al·ly** *adv.*

E·qua·to·ri·al (ēkwatōr′ēal, -tōr′-, ĕkwa-) **Guinea.** Republic in W. Central Africa, on the Atlantic; established 1959; capital, Malabo.

e·ques·tri·an (ĭkwĕs′trēan) *adj.* 1. Of, skilled in, horseback riding; mounted on horse; (of statue) representing person on horseback. 2. (Rom. antiq.) Of the order of *Equites* or knights. ~ *n.* Rider, performer, on horseback.

e·ques·tri·enne (ĭkwĕstrēĕn′) *n.* Horsewoman.

equi- *comb. form.* Equal.

e·qui·an·gu·lar (ēkwēăng′gyuler) *adj.* Having equal angles.

e·qui·dis·tant (ēkwĭdĭs′tant) *adj.* Separated by equal distance(s); parallel.

e·qui·lat·er·al (ēkwĭlăt′eral) *adj.* Having all the sides equal, as in ~ **triangle.**

e·quil·i·brate (ĭkwĭl′ĭbrāt) *v.* (**-brat·ed, -brat·ing**). Cause (2 things) to balance; balance; be or keep in equilibrium; counterpoise. **e·qui·li·bra·tion** (ēkwĭlĭbrā′shon) *n.*

e·quil·i·brist (ĭkwĭl′ĭbrĭst) *n.* Tightrope walker, acrobat.

e·qui·lib·ri·um (ēkwĭlĭb′rēum) *n.* (pl. **-ri·ums, -ri·a** pr. -rēa). State of equal balance between opposing forces or powers; balance, stability; mental or emotional balance or stability.

e·quine (ē′kwīn) *adj.* Of, like, a horse.

e·qui·noc·tial (ēkwĭnŏk′sh*a*l) *adj.* 1. Of, at, or near time of equinox, as ~ **winds;** ~ **line**, celestial equator. 2. At, near, the equator. **equinoctial** *n.* Equinoctial line; (pl.) equinoctial gales.

e·qui·nox (ē′kwĭnŏks, ĕk′wĭ-) *n.* Time when the sun crosses the equator and day and night are equal, occurring twice yearly, on March 20 or 21 (**vernal** ~) and Sept. 22 or 23 (**autumnal** ~); either of the two points at which the sun's path crosses the equator.

e·quip (ĭkwĭp′) *v.t.* (**e·quipped, e·quip·ping**). Furnish (ship, army, person, *with* requisites); provide (*oneself* etc.) for journey etc.

equip. *abbrev.* Equipment.

eq·ui·page (ĕk′wĭpĭj) *n.* Requisites for undertaking; outfit for journey etc.; carriage and horses with attendants. **e·quip·ment** (ĭkwĭp′m*e*nt) *n.* Equipping, being equipped, manner in which person or thing is equipped; outfit, warlike apparatus, necessaries for expedition, voyage, etc.

e·qui·poise (ē′kwĭpoiz, ĕk′wĭ-) *n.* Equilibrium; counterpoise, balancing force or thing.

e·qui·po·ten·tial (ēkwĭp*o*tĕn′sh*a*l) *adj.* & *n.* (phys.) (Surface, line, etc.) such that the potential of a force is the same or constant at all its points.

eq·ui·ta·ble (ĕk′wĭt*a*b*e*l) *adj.* Fair, just; (of claims etc.) valid in equity as dist. from law. **eq′ui·ta·bly** *adv.* **eq′ui·ta·ble·ness** *n.*

eq·ui·ta·tion (ĕkwĭtā′sh*o*n) *n.* Riding on horseback; horsemanship.

eq·ui·ty (ĕk′wĭtē) *n.* (pl. **-ties**). 1. Fairness, impartiality. 2. Recourse to general principle of justice to correct or supplement provisions of law; system of law existing side by side with common and statute law, and superseding these when they conflict with it. 3. Equitable right, right recognizable by court of equity. 4. Value of business, property, etc. after all mortgages, liabilities, charges, etc. are satisfied.

equiv. *abbrev.* Equivalent.

e·quiv·a·lent (ĭkwĭv′*a*l*e*nt) *adj.* 1. Equal in value; having equal or corresponding import or meaning; that is virtually the same thing, tantamount; corresponding. 2. (chem.) ~ **weight** (also **combining weight**), that amount of an element, by weight, that will combine with or replace 1 unit weight of hydrogen. **equivalent** *n.* Equivalent thing, amount, word, etc.; (chem.) see *adj.* above. **e·quiv′a·lence, e·quiv′a·len·cy** *ns.*

e·quiv·o·cal (ĭkwĭv′*o*k*a*l) *adj.* Of double meaning, ambiguous; of uncertain nature; undecided; questionable, suspicious. **e·quiv′o·cal·ly** *adv.* **e·quiv′o·cal·ness** *n.*

e·quiv·o·cate (ĭkwĭv′*o*kāt) *v.i.* (**-cat·ed, -cat·ing**). Use ambiguous words to conceal truth; hedge. **e·quiv·o·ca·tion** (ĭkwĭv*o*kā′sh*o*n), **e·quiv′o·ca·tor** *ns.*

Er *symbol.* Erbium.

-er[1] *suffix.* Forming nouns from nouns, adjectives, and verbs meaning: (1) person or animal that does (*lover, maker*) or person or thing that is or has (*foreigner, fiver, four-wheeler*); (2) instrument,

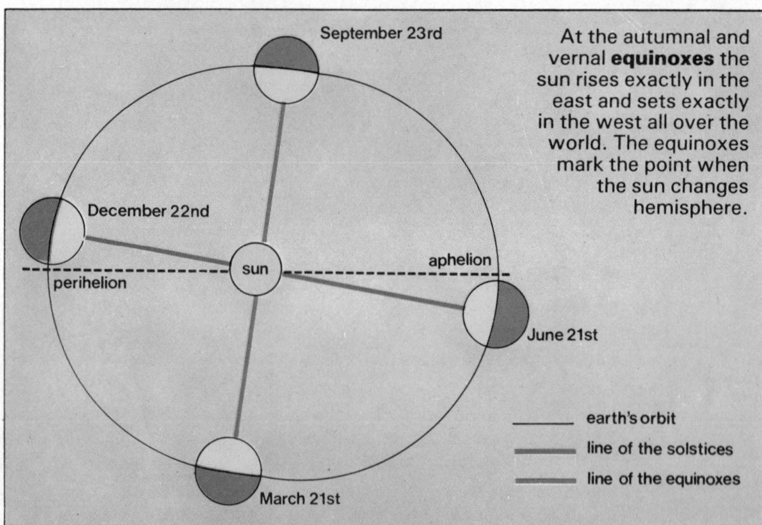
September 23rd
At the autumnal and vernal **equinoxes** the sun rises exactly in the east and sets exactly in the west all over the world. The equinoxes mark the point when the sun changes hemisphere.
December 22nd
sun
aphelion
perihelion
June 21st
earth's orbit
line of the solstices
line of the equinoxes
March 21st

'Erasmus Writing' (1523), one of Hans Holbein's most notable portraits. A leading critic of the Catholic Church, ***Erasmus*** *never shared Luther's extreme views, but their public disagreement did credit to neither position.*

*The stoat or **ermine,** the latter name strictly applicable only to the animal in its winter coat. In more southern latitudes the coat does not become entirely white. The fur is valued.*

machine, occurrence, action, etc. (*poker, computer, eye-opener, header*); person concerned with thing (*geographer, outfielder*); (3) person belonging to a place etc. (*New Yorker, Vermonter*).

-er[2] *suffix.* Forming comparatives of adjectives and adverbs (*wider, faster*).

ERA *abbrev.* Equal Rights Amendment (proposed for U.S. Constitution, prohibiting discrimination based on sex).

e·ra (ēr´*a*, ĕr´*a*) *n.* 1. System of chronology starting from some particular point of time (as the **Christian** ~, from the date of the birth of Jesus Christ; the **Muslim** ~, from the year of Muhammad's flight from Mecca (622), etc.); initial point in such system. 2. Historical period; period in individual's life, in some continuous process, etc.; major division of geological time, usu. comprising several periods.

e·rad·i·cate (ĭrăd´ĭkāt) *v.t.* (**-cat·ed, -cat·ing**). Remove all traces of; annihilate; erase. **e·rad´i·ca·ble** *adj.* **e·rad·i·ca·tion** (ĭrădĭkā´sh*o*n) *n.*

e·rase (ĭrās´) *v.t.* (**e·rased, e·ras·ing**). Rub out; obliterate. **e·ras´er** *n.* That which erases, esp., preparation of rubber or similar substance for rubbing out writing etc. **e·ra·sure** (ĭrā´sh*e*r, -zh*e*r) *n.* Process of erasing; word etc. rubbed out.

E·ras·mus (ĭrăz´m*u*s), **Desiderius** (1466–1536), orig. name Geert Geerts. Dutch theologian, scholar, and humanist; prepared the way for the Reformation by his version of the New Testament and his condemnation of Church abuses in *Moriae Encomium* (*The Praise of Folly*).

Er·a·to (ĕr´*a*tō). (Gk. and Rom. myth.) Muse of love, erotic poetry, and mime.

er·bi·um (ēr´bē*u*m) *n.* (chem.) Metallic element of rare-earth group, occurring in gadolinite etc.; symbol Er, at. no. 68, at. wt. 167.26. [f. *Ytterby* in Sweden, where found]

ere (ār) *prep.* & *conj.* (poet., archaic). Before (in time).

Er·e·bus (ĕr´*e*b*u*s). (Gk. myth.) Place of darkness between earth and Hades; ~ **Mount**, active volcano, 13,202 ft. (4,027 m), on Ross Island, Antarctica.

E·rech·the·um (ĭrĕk´thē*u*m). Temple of Erechtheus, legendary founder and king of Athens, on the Acropolis, erected 421–407 B.C.

e·rect (ĭrĕkt´) *adj.* Upright, not stooping; vertical; (of hair etc.) rigid and upright, bristling; (of part of the body) enlarged and rigid, esp. from sexual excitement. **e·rect´ly** *adv.* **e·rect´ness** *n.* **erect** *v.t.* Raise, set upright; build; assemble or form *into*; establish.

e·rec·tile (ĭrĕk´t*i*l, -tīl) *adj.* Capable of being erected; ~ **tissue**, tissue in various parts of animals capable of being distended with blood and becoming rigid under excitement.

e·rec·tion (ĭrĕk´sh*o*n) *n.* Erecting; building, structure; erect state of penis or clitoris.

e·rec·tor (ĭrĕk´t*e*r) *n.* Person, thing, that erects; muscle that holds up or causes erection of a body part.

er·e·mite (ĕr´*e*mīt) *n.* Recluse, hermit.

erg (ērg) *n.* (phys.) Amount of work done when a force of 1 dyne acts over a distance of 1 centimeter.

er·go (ēr´gō, ĕr´-) *adv.* Therefore. [L.]

er·gos·ter·ol (ērgŏs´t*e*rōl, -rawl, -rŏl) *n.* Sterol that, when exposed to ultraviolet radiation, gives a mixture of compounds including vitamin D, found in yeasts and fungi and present in small quantities in the fats of plants and animals.

er·got (ēr´g*o*t, -gŏt) *n.* Diseased condition of seed of rye and other grasses; dark violet hardened mycelium of the fungus (*Claviceps purpurea*) causing this, used medically to control hemorrhage or contract uterus. **er´got·ism** *n.* Disease of grasses consisting in formation of ergot; diseased condition of man or animals caused by eating grain or grasses infected with ergot and characterized by lameness and gangrene.

Er·ics·son (ēr´ĭks*o*n), **Leif** (lēf; *Icel.* lāv). Son of ERIC THE RED, first European discoverer of N. Amer., c1000 A.D., founded settlement in VINLAND, prob. Newfoundland.

Er·ic (ĕr´ĭk) **the Red.** Tenth c. Icelandic explorer; discovered, settled, and named Greenland.

Er·ie (ēr´ē) *n.* 1. (Member of) an Iroquoian tribe of N. Amer. Indians formerly inhabiting the region around Lake Erie; **Lake** ~, fourth largest of the Great Lakes, on the boundary between the U.S. and Canada; ~ **Canal**, canal extending 363 mi. from Albany to Buffalo, N.Y., connecting the Hudson River to Lake Erie, now part of N.Y. State Barge Canal system. 2. Shipping and industrial city in NW. Pennsylvania, on Lake Erie.

Er·in (ĕr´ĭn, ēr´-, ār´-). Ancient name or Ireland, now only poetical.

Er·i·tre·a (ĕrĭtrē´*a*). Province of Ethiopia, on the Red Sea; formerly an Italian colony.

er·mine (ēr´mĭn) *n.* (pl. **-mines,** collect. **-mine**). 1. (in U.S.) Any of various weasels. 2. Carnivorous mammal of weasel family (*Mustela erminea*), inhabiting northern European countries, with reddish-brown fur above and white beneath in summer and (in northern regions) white in winter, except for black tip of tail; stoat. 3. Fur of the ermine.

e·rode (ĭrōd´) *v.t.* (**e·rod·ed, e·rod·ing**). (of acids, water currents, etc.) Eat away, destroy surface of.

e·rog·e·nous (ĭrŏj´*e*n*u*s) *adj.* Of, giving rise to, sexual desire.

E·ros (ĕr´ŏs, ēr´-). (Gk. myth.) God of love, son of Aphrodite; identified by the Romans with Cupid.

e·ros (ĕr´ŏs, ēr´-) *n.* Earthly or sexual love. (opp. AGAPE[1]).

e·ro·sion (ĭrō´zh*o*n) *n.* Eroding; (geol.) wearing away of earth's surface by wind, water, or ice (cf. ABRASION). **e·ro·sive** (ĭrō´sĭv) *adj.*

e·rot·ic (ĭrŏt´ĭk) *adj.* Of sexual love. **e·rot·i·ca** (ĭrŏt´ĭk*a*) *n.pl.* Erotic writings, pictures, etc. **e·rot·i·cism** (ĭrŏt´ĭsĭz*e*m), **er·o·tism** (ĕr´*o*tĭz*e*m) *ns.* **e·rot´i·cal·ly** *adv.*

err (ēr, ĕr) *v.i.* Make mistakes; be incorrect; sin.

er·rand (ĕr´*a*nd) *n.* Short journey on which person is sent to carry message etc.; business on which one is sent, object of journey.

er·rant (ĕr´*a*nt) *adj.* Roaming in quest of adventure (esp. in **knight** ~); wandering; straying from the proper course, opinion, conduct, etc. **er´ran·cy** *n.*

__Erosion__ in areas altered by man, such as this farmland in Wyoming, is usually the result of overgrazing or removal of surface vegetation.

er·ra·tic (ĭrăt′ĭk) *adj.* Wandering; (of diseases, pains, etc.) moving from one part to another; irregular or uncertain in movement, having no fixed course, eccentric in conduct, habit, or opinion. **er·rat′i·cal·ly** *adv.*

er·ra·tum (ĭrah′t*u*m, ĭrăt′*u*m) *n.* (pl. **-ta** pr. -t*a*). Error in printing or writing, esp. (usu. pl.) list of errors and corrections attached to book.

er·ro·ne·ous (ĭrō′nēus) *adj.* Mistaken, incorrect. **er·ro′ne·ous·ly** *adv.*

er·ror (ĕr′*er*) *n.* Mistake; condition of erring in opinion, wrong opinion; transgression; (math. etc.) quantity of deviation from correct or accurate result, determination, etc.; (baseball) any mistaken play by a fielder in catching or throwing that permits a runner to be safe when he could have been put out.

Erse (ẽrs) *adj.* & *n.* Irish Gaelic, formerly applied also to the Gaelic of Scotland. [var. of *Irish*]

erst (ẽrst) *adv.* (archaic) Formerly, of old; first. **erst·while** (ẽrst′hwīl, -wīl) *adv.* & *adj.* Erst, former.

e·ruc·ta·tion (ĭrŭktā′sh*o*n) *n.* Belching; eruptive action of volcano; emission of gas from stomach. **eruct** *v.i.*

er·u·dite (ĕr′y*u*dĭt, ĕr′*u*-) *adj.* Learned. **er′u·dite·ly** *adv.* **er·u·di·tion** (ĕry*u*dĭsh′*o*n, ĕr*u*-) *n.*

e·rupt (ĭrŭpt′) *v.* Break out or through; (of volcano) emit rocks, lava, ash, or gases, (of geyser) spurt water; (of teeth) break through gums; (of rash) appear on skin.

e·rup·tion (ĭrŭp′sh*o*n) *n.* Erupting; outbreak of volcano, ejection of hot water from geyser, etc.; breaking out of rash etc.; also (fig.) of war, passion, mirth, etc.

e·rup·tive (ĭrŭp′tĭv) *adj.* Bursting forth; tending to burst forth; of, formed by, forced up by, volcanic eruption. **e·rup′tive·ly** *adv.*

-ery *suffix.* Forming nouns meaning class of persons or things (*citizenry, greenery*); condition (*slavery*); place or occupation (*brewery, eatery*); derogation (*trumpery, popery, foolery*).

er·y·sip·e·las (ĕrĭsĭp′*e*l*a*s) *n.* Acute inflammation of lymphatic vessels of the skin, caused by streptococcal infection.

er·y·the·ma (ĕrĭthē′m*a*) *n.* Superficial blotchy redness of skin, as caused by sunburn or chemical poisoning.

e·ryth·ro·cyte (ĭrĭth′r*o*sīt) *n.* Red blood cell.

The __eruption__ of a volcano at Vestmannaeyjar, Iceland, 24 January 1973. Eruptions are produced by gases. The lava, which solidifies when it cools, is a compound, differing between volcanoes, but the rock is usually basalt.

Es *symbol.* Einsteinium.

-es[1] Plural ending for nouns ending with a sibilant.

-es[2] Ending, third person sing. pres. ind., for verbs ending with a sibilant or *-o*.

E·sau (ē′saw). Elder son of Isaac and Rebecca; sold his birthright to his brother Jacob for a mess of pottage (Gen. 25).

es·ca·late (ĕs′k*a*lāt) *v.* (**-lat·ed, -lat·ing**). Increase or develop by degrees; intensify (esp. a war). **es·ca·la·tion** (ĕsk*a*lā′sh*o*n) *n.*

es·ca·la·tor (ĕs′k*a*lāt*er*) *n.* Moving stairway (with stairs linked to an endless belt).

es·cal·lop, es·cal·op (ĕskŏl′*o*p, -kăl′-) *ns.* 1. = SCALLOP *n.* def. 1. 2. Thin slice of meat for frying or baking.

es·ca·pade (ĕs′k*a*pād, ĕsk*a*pād′) *n.* Breaking loose from restraint; carefree, reckless adventure; fling, caper.

es·cape (ĕskāp′) *v.* (**-caped, -cap·ing**). 1. Gain liberty by fleeing, get free from detention,

__Eschscholtzia,__ or Californian poppy. Several varieties of different colors of this sun-loving poppy are cultivated in dry spots. There is a dwarf species (E. caespitosa).

This __escarpment,__ in the Zion National Park, Utah, is a sheer drop of several hundred feet, clearly dividing mountain and valley.

control, oppression, etc.; (of fluids etc.) issue, find a way out; (of words etc.) issue unawares from (person, his lips). 2. Get off safely, go unhurt or unpunished; get clear away from (person, his grasp, etc.); avoid; elude notice or recollection of. **escape** *n.* Act of escaping; fact of having escaped; leakage (of gas etc.); outlet; FIRE escape; ~ **clause,** clause in a contract absolving a contracting party from a particular obligation in specified circumstances; ~ **chute,** slide opening automatically from airplane for emergency exit; ~ **hatch,** means of emergency exit (from submarine etc. or fig.); ~ **velocity,** minimum velocity needed for an object to escape from a gravitational field, as that of a spacecraft from Earth's gravity; ~ **wheel,** toothed wheel in escapement.

es·cap·ee (ĕskāpē′) *n.* One who has escaped.

es·cape·ment (ĕskāp′mĕnt) *n.* Outlet; mechanism in watch or clock or other timing device, intervening between motive power and regulator, and alternately checking and releasing the train, causing intermittent impulse to be given to regulator.

es·cap·ism (ĕskā′pĭzem) *n.* Tendency to escape from realities of life into fantasy, amusements, etc. **es·cap′ist** *adj.* & *n.*

es·ca·role (ĕs′karōl) *n.* Variety of ENDIVE, *Cichorium endivia*, used in salads.

es·carp·ment (ĕskârp′ment) *n.* Steep bank immediately in front of and below rampart; similar natural formation.

-escence *suffix.* Forming nouns corresponding to adjectives ending in *-escent* (*deliquescence, effervescence*).

-escent *suffix.* Forming adjectives denoting beginning of a state or variation of color etc. (*deliquescent, iridescent*).

es·cha·tol·o·gy (ĕskatŏl′ojē) *n.* Branch of theology concerned with death, judgment, heaven, and hell. **es·cha·to·log·i·cal** (ĕskatolŏj′ĭkal) *adj.*

es·cheat (ĕschēt′) *n.* (law) Reversion of fief to feudal lord when tenant died without leaving qualified successor; lapsing of land to crown, nation, or lord of manor on owner's dying intestate without heirs; property so lapsing or reverting. ~ *v.* Confiscate; hand over (property) as an escheat; revert by escheat.

es·chew (ĕschōō′) *v.t.* Avoid, abstain from (particular kind of conduct, food, etc.). **es·chew′al, es·chew′er** *ns.*

esch·scholt·zi·a (ĕshōlt′sēa) *n.* Californian herbaceous plant of genus **E**~ of the poppy family, the best known species being *E. californica*, California poppy, which has finely divided glaucous leaves and large bright yellow flowers with saffron-colored center. [J. F. von *Eschscholtz* (1793–1831), Ger. botanist]

es·cort (ĕs′kôrt) *n.* Body of armed men or women acting as guard to persons, baggage, etc.; person(s) accompanying another on journey for protection or guidance, or for courtesy's sake; ship(s), aircraft, etc., so employed. ~ (ĕskôrt′) *v.t.* Act as escort to.

es·cri·toire (ĕskrētwâr′) *n.* Writing desk with drawers etc.

es·cu·do (ĕskōō′dō) *n.* (pl. **-dos**). 1. Principal monetary unit of Portugal, = 100 centavos. 2. Principal monetary unit of Chile, = 100 centesimos.

es·cutch·eon (ĕskŭch′on) *n.* 1. Shield or shieldlike emblem bearing a coat of arms. 2. Plate on ship's stern bearing its name and home port.

Es·dras (ĕz′dras). Name of first two of the books of the Apocrypha; the first is mainly a compilation from Chronicles, Nehemiah, and Ezra, and the second is a record of angelic revelations.

ESE, E.S.E., e.s.e. *abbrevs.* East-southeast.

-ese *suffix.* Forming adjectives and nouns (pl. same) f. names of foreign countries and cities (*Japanese, Viennese*), meaning (inhabitant or language) of; or f. nouns or names of writers (*officialese, Dreiserese*), meaning style of writing.

Es·ki·mo, Es·qui·mau (ĕs′kimō) *ns.* (pl. **-mos,** collect. **-mo;** pl. **-maux** pr. -mōz, collect. **-mau**). (Member of a) people inhabiting

Arctic coastal regions from Greenland to Alaska and NE. Siberia; their language; ~ **dog**, breed of powerful dog with long hair, used by the Eskimos as sled dog.

e·soph·a·gus (ĭsŏf′*agus*) *n.* (pl. **-gi** pr. -gī, -jī). Canal leading from mouth to stomach; gullet.

es·o·ter·ic (ĕs*o*tĕr′ĭk) *adj.* (of philosophical doctrine etc.) Meant for, intelligible to, the initiated only; (of disciples) initiated; private, confidential. **es·o·ter′i·cal·ly** *adv.*

ESP *abbrev.* Extrasensory perception.

esp. *abbrev.* Especially.

es·pa·drille (ĕs′p*a*drĭl) *n.* Rope-soled canvas shoe.

es·pal·ier (ĕspăl′y*er*, -yā) *n.* Framework on which fruit trees or ornamental shrubs are trained; tree so trained.

es·pe·cial (ĕspĕsh′*al*) *adj.* Preeminent, exceptional; particular; belonging chiefly to one person, thing, etc. **es·pe′cial·ly** *adv.*

Es·pe·ran·to (ĕsp*e*rahn′tō, -răn′-) *n.* & *adj.* (Of) an artificial language invented (1887) for universal use by a Polish physician, Dr. Ludovik Lazarus Zamenhof, with vocabulary consisting of roots common to the chief European languages with endings normalized. **Es·pe·ran′tist** *n.* [pen name, Dr. *Esperanto* (= "hopeful one"), of its inventor, f. L. *spero* hope]

*A team of **Eskimo dogs** pull a sled across the Antarctic ice to the runway at McMurdo Station. In Arctic regions also these dogs are invaluable. They travel in areas that would be impassable for motor transport.*

es·pi·o·nage (ĕs′pē*o*nahzh, -nĭj, -nahj, ĕspē*o*nahzh′) *n.* Practice of spying or using spies.

es·pla·nade (ĕspl*e*nahd′, -nād′) *n.* Level piece of ground or pavement used for public promenade, esp. along a shore.

es·pouse (ĕspowz′) *v.t.* (**-poused, -pous·ing**). 1. (usu. of man) Marry; give (woman) in marriage (*to*). 2. Adopt, support (cause, opinion, etc.) **es·pou·sal** (ĕspow′-*zal*) *n.*

es·pres·so (ĕsprĕs′ō) *n.* Coffee made under steam pressure; device for making this.

es·prit (ĕsprē′) *n.* Sprightliness, wit; ~ **de corps**, spirit of devotion to and enthusiasm for group one belongs to. [Fr.]

es·py (ĕspī′) *v.t.* (**-pied, -py·ing**). Catch sight of; detect.

Esq., Esqr. *abbrevs.* Esquire.

-esque *suffix.* Forming adjectives meaning "in the manner of" (*picturesque, arabesque, Giottesque*).

Es·qui·line (ĕs′kwĭlīn). One of the Seven Hills of Rome.

Es·qui·mau: see ESKIMO.

es·quire (ĕs′kwīr, ĕskwīr′) *n.* 1. (hist. archaic) Young man of gentle birth attending on knight; squire. 2. Man belonging to higher order of English gentry, ranking immediately below knight. 3. Courtesy title appended to a man's name in formal use (esp. of a lawyer) and (abbreviated Esq.) in addressing letters etc. where no prefixed title is used. [L. *scutarius* shield bearer]

-ess *suffix.* Forming nouns denoting females (*lioness, goddess, actress*).

es·say (ĕs′ā; for def. 1. also ĕsā′) *n.* 1. Attempt (*at*). 2. Literary composition of moderate length on any subject. ~ (ĕsā) *v.t.* Try, test (person, thing); attempt. **es′say·ist** *n.* Writer of essays.

es·sence (ĕs′*e*ns) *n.* 1. Existence, entity (now usu. spiritual or immaterial). 2. Absolute being, reality underlying phenomena; that by which anything subsists, foundation of being. 3. All that makes a thing what it is; intrinsic nature as a thing in itself; (loosely) most important indispensable quality or constituent element of anything. 4. Extract obtained by distillation etc. from plant, medicinal, odoriferous, or nutritious substance, etc.; alcoholic solution containing volatile elements to which perfume, flavor, etc., are due; perfume.

Es·sene (ĕs´ēn, ĕsēn´) *n.* Member of an ascetic Jewish sect living as a community in Palestine from 2nd C. B.C. to 2nd C. A.D.

es·sen·tial (ĭsĕn´shal) *adj.* 1. Of, constituting, a thing's essence; that is such in essence; indispensable, necessarily implied; absolutely necessary. 2. That is or is like, an essence or extract; ~ **oil**, volatile oil obtained by distillation and marked by characteristic odor etc. of substance from which it is extracted. **essential** *n.* Indispensable element. **es·sen·ti·al·i·ty** (ĭsĕnsheăl´ĭtē) *n.* **es·sen´tial·ly** *adv.*

-est[1] *suffix.* Forming superlatives of adjectives and adverbs (*widest, fastest*).

-est[2] *suffix.* Forming archaic 2nd person sing. of verbs (*knowest*).

est. *abbrev.* Estimate(d); estate; established.

estab. *abbrev.* Established.

es·tab·lish (ĕstăb´lĭsh) *v.t.* Set up on permanent basis; settle; secure permanent acceptance for; place beyond dispute; make state institution of (particular religion or Church).

es·tab·lish·ment (ĕstăb´lĭshment) *n.* Establishing; Church system established by law, established Church; organized body of men maintained for a purpose, as army, navy, civil service; staff of servants, etc.; public institution, house of business; household; **the E~**, those with (official or unofficial) authority or influence, regarded as having joint interest in resisting change.

es·tate (ĕstāt´) *n.* 1. (chiefly archaic) State, condition; worldly standing, fortune, etc.; status, degree of rank; **man's, woman's ~**, manhood, womanhood. 2. Order, class of citizens as part of body politic and as sharing directly or indirectly in government; **fourth ~**, politically powerful group other than the three estates in Britain or pre-revolutionary France (bishops, nobles, and commons), hence, the public press. 3. Whole of one's wealth, property, possessions, etc., esp. left by a deceased person; large piece of rural or residential land, usu. with a large house; **real ~**, property in land and buildings; **real ~ agent**, person, company, conducting business in sale of buildings and land.

es·teem (ĕstēm´) *v.t.* Think highly of; consider. ~ *n.* Favorable opinion, regard, respect.

es·ter (ĕs´ter) *n.* Any of a class of organic compounds formed by the interaction of an acid and an alcohol with the elimination of water; used as solvents, flavoring essences, etc., and in many chemical processes.

'Bathers', an ***etching*** *by Rembrandt (1606–69). As in line-engraving, the lines to be printed are incised, rather than left in relief, as in wood-engraving. Etching has been practiced in N. Europe since at least the 15th century.*

Es·ther (ĕs´ter). Beautiful Jewish queen of Persia who saved her people from massacre; book of Old Testament containing the story of Esther.

es·thete = AESTHETE.

es·thet·ic = AESTHETIC.

es·ti·ma·ble (ĕs´timabel) *adj.* Worthy of esteem.

es·ti·mate (ĕs´timĭt, -māt) *n.* Approximate judgment (of number, amount, etc.); quantity assigned by this; statement of sum for which one offers to undertake specified work; judgment of character or qualities. ~ (ĕs´timāt) *v.t.* (**-mat·ed, -mat·ing**). Form estimate of; fix by estimate *at* (so much); form an opinion of. **es´ti·ma·tor** *n.*

es·ti·ma·tion (ĕstimā´shon) *n.* Judgment of worth; opinion, judgment; esteem.

es·ti·val: see AESTIVAL.

Es·to·ni·a (ĕstō´nēa). Former country in NE. Europe along Baltic Sea; once part of the Russian Empire; proclaimed an independent republic 1918; incorporated in the Soviet Union 1940 as a constituent republic (properly *Estonian Soviet Socialist Republic*); capital, Tallinn. **Es·to´ni·an** *adj.* & *n.* (Native, inhabitant, language) of Estonia.

es·top (ĕstŏp´) *v.t* (**-topped, -top·ping**). (law) Stop, bar, hinder; (refl. and pass.) be precluded by one's own previous act or declaration from doing etc. **es·top·pel** (ĕstŏp´el) *n.* Being estopped.

es·trange (ĕstrānj´) *v.t.* (**-tranged, -trang·ing**). Cause (person) to turn away in feeling or affection; make hostile or indifferent. **es·trange´ment** *n.*

es·tro·gen (ĕs´trojen) *n.* Any of several hormones produced esp. by the ovary, capable of developing and maintaining female characteristics of body.

es·trus (ĕs´trus) *n.* Periodic sexual excitement and readiness for mating in female animals; rut.

es·tu·ar·y (ĕs´chōōĕrē) *n.* (pl. **-ar·ies**). Tidal mouth of river; inlet of sea extending inland to a river. **es·tu·ar·ine** (ĕs´chōōarĭn, -rĭn) *adj.*

ETA *abbrev.* Estimated time of arrival.

e·ta (ā´ta, ē´-) *n.* Eighth (later seventh) letter of Greek alphabet (H, η), transliterated in English by long *e* (ē).

é·ta·gère (ātăzhār´) *n.* Vertical series of open shelves, supported by legs at the corners, for knicknacks, plants, etc.

et al. *abbrev.* *Et alii* (L., = "and others").

etc. *abbrev.* Et cetera.

et cet·er·a (ĕt sĕt′*er*a, sĕt′r*a*). And the rest, and so on. **et·cet′er·as** *n.pl.* Extras, additional odds and ends. [L.]

etch (ĕch) *v.* Portray by drawing with an **etching needle** on a metal plate previously coated with a wax and resin mixture (the *ground*) and immersing in acid, which corrodes the parts laid bare by the needle; make (print) from plate thus prepared; copy (picture) by this process; practice this craft. **etch′er** *n.* **etch′ing** *n.* Print made from an etched plate; art, process, of etching.

ETD *abbrev.* Estimated time of departure.

e·ter·nal (ĭtẽr′n*a*l) *adj.* Without beginning or end, that always (has existed and always) will exist; (colloq.) incessant, too frequent; **E∼ City**, Rome; ∼ **triangle**, (emotional relationships in) group of two women and a man or two men and a woman. **e·ter′nal·ize** *v.t.* (**-ized, -iz·ing**). **e·ter′nal·ly** *adv.*

e·ter·ni·ty (ĭtẽr′nĭtē) *n.* (pl. **-ties**). Being eternal; infinite (esp. future) time; the future life; tediously long time.

-eth[1] *suffix*: see -TH.

-eth[2] *suffix.* Forming archaic 3rd pers. pres. sing. of verbs (*findeth, doeth*).

eth·ane (ĕth′ān) *n.* Colorless odorless gas (C_2H_6), a constituent of natural gas used as a fuel, refrigerant, etc.

eth·a·nol (ĕth′*a*nōl, -nawl, -nŏl) *n.* = ETHYL alcohol.

Eth·el·red (ĕth′*e*lrĕd) (*c*968–1016), "the Unready" (= "without counsel"). King of the English 979–1016; son of Edgar and father of Edward the Confessor.

e·ther (ē′th*er*) *n.* 1. Clear sky, upper regions of space beyond Earth's atmosphere. 2. Hypothetical substance of great elasticity and subtlety formerly postulated by the wave theory of light as permeating the whole of space, esp. as medium of propagation of radio waves etc. 3. (chem.) Colorless volatile liquid $(C_2H_5)_2O$ with a characteristic aromatic odor obtained by distillation of alcohol with sulfuric acid and used as a solvent for the extraction of oils, fats, waxes, etc., and as an anesthetic; any of a large class of compounds of similar composition.

e·the·re·al (ĭthẽr′ē*a*l) *adj.* 1. Light, airy; heavenly; of unearthly delicacy of substance, character, or appearance. 2. Of, like, ether. **e·the·re·al·i·ty** (ĭthẽrēăl′ĭtē) *n.* **e·the′re·al·ly** *adv.*

eth·ic (ĕth′ĭk) *n.* Principle or body of principles of right or good conduct. **eth·i·cal** (ĕth′ĭk*a*l) *adj.* Relating to, treating of, morals or ethics; moral, honorable; (of drug etc.) available only on doctor's prescription. **eth′i·cal·ly** *adv.*

eth·ics (ĕth′ĭks) *n.pl.* 1. (as sing.) Science of morals, study of principles of human duty; treatise on this. 2. (as pl.) Moral principles; rules of conduct.

E·thi·o·pi·a (ēthēō′pē*a*). (hist.) Region on the upper Nile; (in modern usage) a country in NE. Africa SW. of Red Sea and Gulf of Aden; capital, Addis Ababa; after being converted to Christianity in 4th c., the country was cut off from European influences by Muslim dominion; rediscovered by Portuguese in 16th c.; Italians invaded and annexed the country in 1935, but were driven out in 1941 and Emperor Haile Selassie I was reinstated; he was deposed in 1974. **E·thi·o′pi·an** *adj.* Of, pertaining to, Ethiopia. ∼ *n.* Native, inhabitant, of Ethiopia; (hist.) African.

E·thi·op·ic (ēthēŏp′ĭk, -ō′pĭk) *adj.* & *n.* (Of) an ancient Semitic language (Ge′ez) of Ethiopia surviving in the liturgical language of the Christian Church of Ethiopia.

eth·nic (ĕth′nĭk) *adj.* Originating from a national, linguistic, racial, etc., group sharing distinctive cultural characteristics. ∼ *n.* Member of ethnic group.

eth·nic·i·ty (ĕthnĭs′ĭtē) *n.* Condition of belonging to a particular ethnic group; ethnic feeling, pride.

eth·nog·ra·phy (ĕthnŏg′r*a*fē) *n.* Scientific description of races of men. **eth·nog′ra·pher** *n.* **eth·no·graph·ic** (ĕthn*o*grăf′ĭk), **eth·no·graph′i·cal** *adjs.* **eth·no·graph′i·cal·ly** *adv.*

eth·nol·o·gy (ĕthnŏl′*o*jē) *n.* Science of races and peoples, their relations to one another, distinctive physical and other characteristics, etc. **eth·no·log·i·cal** (ĕthn*o*lŏj′ĭk*a*l) *adj.* **eth·no·log′i·cal·ly** *adv.* **eth·nol′o·gist** *n.*

e·thol·o·gy (ēthŏl′*o*jē) *n.* Study of animal behavior. **e·tho·log·i·cal** (ēth*o*lŏj′ĭk*a*l) *adj.* **e·thol′o·gist** *n.*

__Ethiopia__ is a huge mountain plateau divided by the Great Rift Valley, through which runs a chain of lakes. The population is of diverse ethnic origin: the Amhara and Tigreans are of Hamitic-Semitic origin and are Coptic Christians; the Galla (right: Galla child) are of Hamitic origin, and may be Christians or Muslims; the Falashas are Jews.

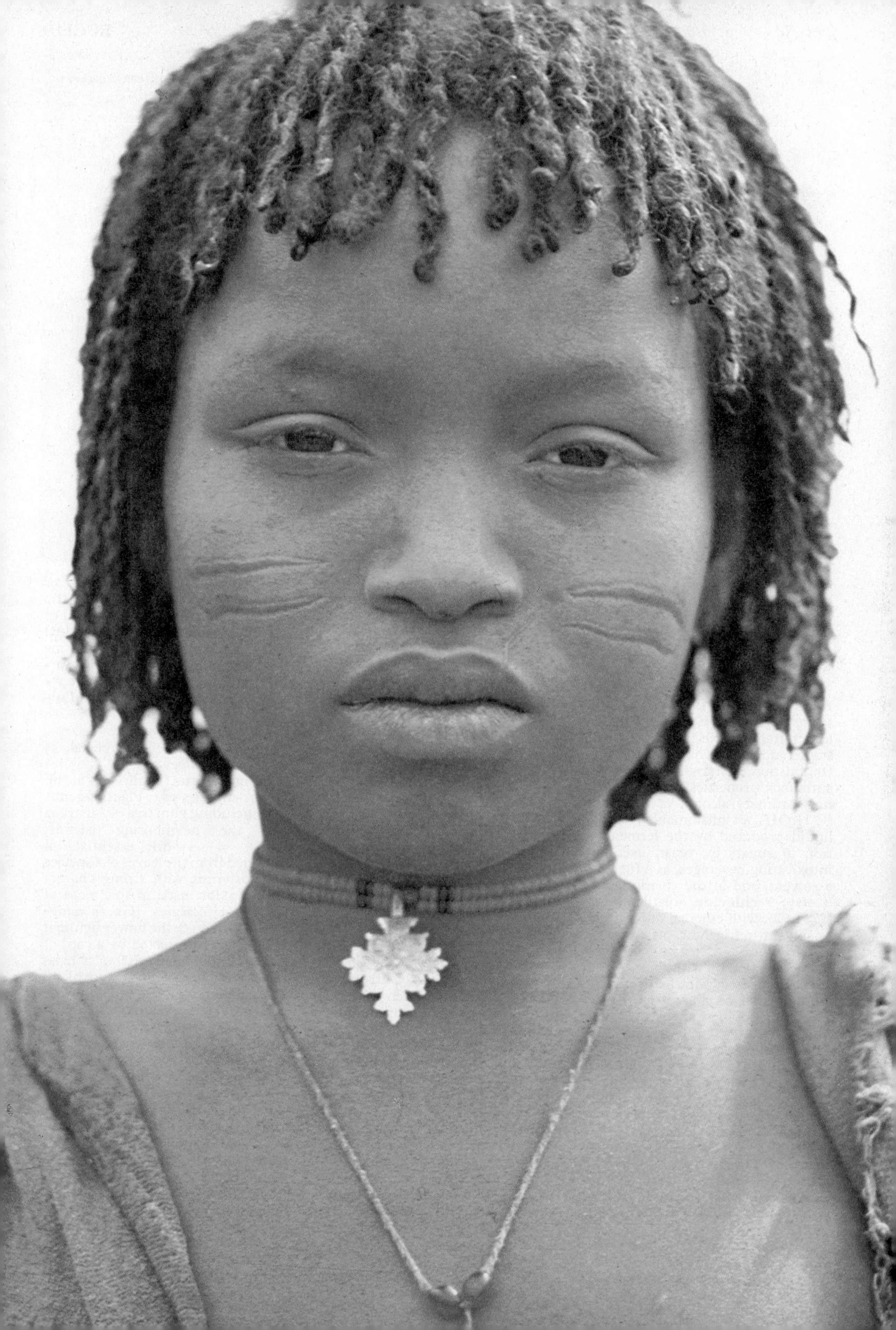

*Left: An **Etruscan** skyphos or cup c. 300 B.C. The origin of the Etruscans is not known — possibly they came from Asia Minor. Etruria was rich, thanks to fertile soil and iron- and copper-mines. The three periods of its art were influenced by Asia, Greece, and Rome.*

e·thos (ē´thŏs) *n.* 1. Characteristic sentiment, attitude, etc. of community, people, or system. 2. Underlying principle of a literary or other movement, statement, work of art, etc.

eth·yl (ĕth´*i*l) *n.* 1. (chem.) Alkyl radical having two carbon atoms (C_2H_5). 2. (**E ~**) (trademark) lead tetraethyl, $Pb(C_2H_5)_4$, a substance added to gasoline to improve combustion, thereby increasing its antiknock properties. 3. ~ **alcohol**, ordinary alcohol or **ethanol** (C_2H_5OH), an inflammable volatile liquid produced by the fermentation of sugars by yeast, used in intoxicating beverages, as a fuel, as a solvent, and in the chemical industry; ~ **chloride**, volatile liquid (C_2H_5Cl), with ethereal odor, used as solvent, refrigerant, etc.

eth·yl·ene (ĕth´*i*lēn) *n.* Inflammable gas (C_2H_4) with faint sweet smell used as an anesthetic and as a color enhancer for citrus fruits; ~ **glycol**, colorless slightly viscous liquid used as antifreeze in car engines, for deicing aircraft, etc.

e·ti·o·late (ē´tēolāt) *v.t.* (**-lat·ed, -lat·ing**). Render (plant etc.) pale and colorless by excluding light; blanch; give sickly hue to (person). **e·ti·o·la·tion** (ētē*o*lā´shon) *n.*

e·ti·ol·o·gy (ētēŏl´*o*jē) *n.* Assignment of a cause; philosophy of causation; (med.) science of the cause of disease. **e·ti·o·log´i·cal** (ētēŏlŏj´ĭk*a*l) *adj.* **e·ti·o·log´i·cal·ly** *adv.*

et·i·quette (ĕt´ĭkĭt, -kĕt) *n.* Conventional rules of personal behavior in polite society; ceremonial of court; unwritten professional code of behavior.

Et·na (ĕt´n*a*), **Mount.** Highest active volcano in Europe (altitude 10,758 ft., 3,279 m), in E. Sicily.

E·ton (ē´t*o*n). ~ **College**, English private school for boys near Windsor, founded 1440; ~ **collar**, broad stiff white collar overlapping the lapels, worn with an ~ **jacket**, short black waist-length jacket (formerly worn by younger boys at Eton), worn open in front. **E·to·ni·an** (ētō´nē*a*n) *adj.* & *n.*

E·trus·can (ĭtrŭs´k*a*n) *adj.* & *n.* (Member, language) of the earliest historical inhabitants of Etruria, an ancient country between the Arno and Tiber rivers (approximately modern Tuscany), who there developed a system of powerful city-states and a flourishing civilization.

et seq. *abbrev.* (pl. **et seqq., et sqq.**). *Et sequentia* (L., = "and what follows").

-ette *suffix.* Forming nouns meaning small (*kitchenette*), imitation (*leatherette*), or female (*suffragette, usherette*).

é·tude (ā´to͞od, -tūd) *n.* Short musical composition or exercise.

ETV *abbrev.* Educational television.

et·y·mol·o·gy (ĕt*i*mŏl´*o*jē) *n.* (pl. **-gies**). Account of, facts relating to, origin and development of word(s); branch of linguistic science concerned with this; part of grammar treating of individual words and their formation and inflections; abbrev. *etym.* **et·y·mo·log·i·cal** (ĕt*i*m*o*lŏj´ĭk*a*l) *adj.* **et·y·mo·log´i·cal·ly** *adv.* **et·y·mol´o·gist** *n.*

Eu *symbol.* Europium.

eu- *prefix.* Well; beneficial, as in *eugenics, eulogy*.

eu·ca·lyp·tus (ūk*a*lĭp´t*u*s) *n.* (pl. **-ti** pr. -tī, **-tus·es**). Plant of genus **E ~** including gum tree of Australia and the neighboring islands; (pop.) = ~ **oil**, essential oil obtained from the leaves of a species of eucalyptus with strong characteristic odor, used in treatment of respiratory diseases. [Gk. *eu kaluptos* well covered, the flower before it opens being protected by a cap]

Eu·cha·rist (ū´kerĭst) *n.* Christian sacrament of body and blood of Christ, in which bread and wine are partaken of; consecrated elements, esp. bread. **Eu·cha·ris·tic** (ūkerĭs´tĭk), **Eu·cha·ris´ti·cal** *adjs.* [Gk. *eukharistia* thanksgiving (*kharizomai* offer willingly)]

eu·chre (ū´k*er*) *n.* Card game for two, three, or four persons, played with pack of 32 cards (the 2, 3, 4, 5, 6, of each suit being rejected), in which, if a player fails to take three tricks, he or his side is said to be "euchred," and the other side gains two points. ~ *v.t.* (**-chred, -chring**). Gain advantage over (opponent) by his failure to take three tricks; (fig.) outwit.

Eu·clid (ū´klĭd) (*c*300 B.C.).

Mathematician of Alexandria, author of the first systematic treatise on geometry (the *Elements*). **Eu·clid·e·an, Eu·clid·i·an** (ūklĭd′ēan) *adjs.* Of Euclid; ~ **geometry**, geometry based on his postulates; ~ **space**, kind of space for which his postulates are valid (in which, e.g., a straight line may be produced to infinity).

eu·gen·ics (ūjĕn′ĭks) *n.pl.* (usu. considered sing.) (Study, science, of) improving (esp. human) species by selective breeding.

Eu·gé·nie (üzhānē′) (1826–1920). Full name, Eugénie Marie de Montijo de Guzmán; wife of Napoleon III, and empress of France, 1853–71.

eu·lo·gize (ū′lojīz) *v.t.* (**-gized, -giz·ing**). Extol, praise. **eu′lo·gist** *n.* **eu·lo·gis·tic** (ūlojĭs′tĭk) *adj.*

eu·lo·gy (ū′lojē) *n.* (pl. **-gies**). Speech, writing, in commendation or praise.

Eu·men·i·des (ūmĕn′ĭdēz). (Gk. myth.) (Euphemistic name for) the Furies. [Gk., = "kindly ones"]

eu·nuch (ū′n*u*k) *n.* Castrated man, esp. one employed in harem or (in Oriental courts and under Roman Empire) in affairs of state.

eu·on·y·mus (ūŏn′*i*m*u*s) *n.* Shrub, tree, or vine of genus **E**~, of which many species are cultivated for decorative foliage or berries. [Gk. *euonumos* well-named, lucky (*onoma* name)]

A gorge of the ***Euphrates*** *near Malatya, Turkey. The river rises in the Turkish Armenian highlands and its course is about 1,700 miles. It is not generally navigable.*

The ***euonymus*** *may be deciduous or evergreen and its many species grow throughout the northern temperate zone. The flowering of the euonymus was said to foreshadow the arrival of the plague.*

eu·phe·mism (ū′fem*ĭ*zem) *n.* Substitution of mild or vague expression for harsher or more offensive one; expression thus substituted. **eu·phe·mis·tic** (ūfemĭs′tĭk) *adj.* **eu·phe·mis′ti·cal·ly** *adv.*

eu·pho·ny (ū′fonē) *n.* (pl. **-nies**). Pleasing sound; quality of having this. **eu·phon·ic** (ūfŏn′ĭk), **eu·pho·ni·ous** (ūfō′nē*u*s) *adjs.* **eu·pho′ni·ous·ly** *adv.*

eu·pho·ri·a (ūfōr′ē*a*, ūfōr′-) *n.* Sense, feeling, of well-being; bliss; exaggerated sense of well-being with no basis in reality. **eu·phor′ic** *adj.*

Eu·phra·tes (ūfrā′tēz). River of SW. Asia, flowing 1,739 mi., (2,799 km) through E. Turkey and Iraq to join the Tigris and then the Persian Gulf.

Eu·phros·y·ne (ūfrŏs′ĭnē). (Gk. myth.) One of the Graces.

eu·phu·ism (ū′fūĭzem) *n.* Affectedly elegant style of language, originally the literary style used by imitators of John Lyly, known for its elaborate alliteration, antitheses, and long strings of similes. **eu′phu·ist** *n.* **eu·phu·is·tic** (ūfūĭs′tĭk), **eu·phu·is′ti·cal** *adjs.* [f. *Euphuēs* (Gk., = "well-endowed"), chief character in two of Lyly's works]

Eur. *abbrev.* Europe(an).

Eur·a·sian (yo͞orā′zh*a*n) *adj.* Of mixed European and Asian parentage; of Europe and Asia. ~ *n.* Eurasian person.

Eur·at·om (yo͞orăt′*o*m) *n.* Organization formed by France, the Netherlands, West Germany, Belgium, and Luxembourg in 1957 to coordinate development of atomic energy.

eu·re·ka (yo͞orē′k*a*) *int.* & *n.* Exclamation of exultation, "I have found it!" [Gk. *heurēka* (*heuriskein* find) uttered by Archimedes when, while bathing, he discovered means

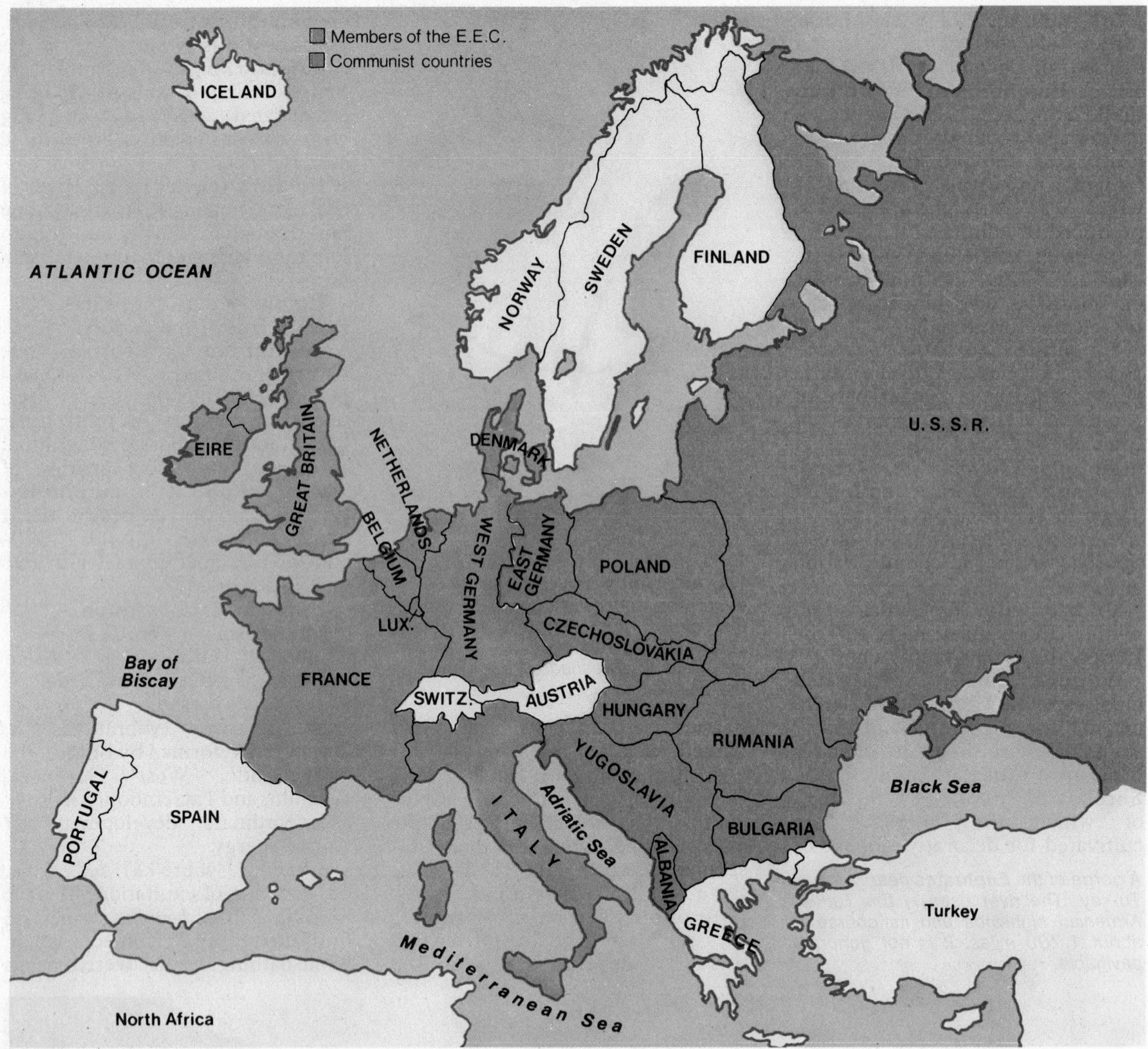

of determining volume of irregular solid by measuring its displacement of water; he was thus able to determine the proportion of base metal in Hiero's golden crown]

eu·rhyth·mics (yo͝orĭdh′mĭks) *n.* (considered sing. or pl.) System (founded by Swiss composer Émile Jaques-Dalcroze, 1865–1950) of expressing musical rhythm in bodily movement.

Eu·rip·i·des (yo͝orĭp′ĭdēz) (*c*485–*c*406 B.C.). Greek tragedian; author of *Alcestis, Medea, The Trojan Women, etc.*

Euro- *comb. form.* Europe; European.

Eu·ro·com·mu·nism (ūrōcŏm′yunĭzem) *n.* (Policies of) Communist parties in W. Europe alleged to differ significantly from policies of the Soviet Union.

Eu·ro·dol·lars (ūr′odŏlerz) *n.pl.* Dollars held in bank in Europe etc., not in U.S.

Eu·ro·pa (yo͝orō′pa). (Gk. myth.) Daughter of Agenor, king of Phoenicia; was wooed and abducted to Crete by Zeus, who took the form of a beautiful white

***Europe** is the smallest continent except for Australia. The distinction between Asia and Europe was made in the 5th century B.C., apparently first by the Assyrians, when Asia was regarded as the land of the rising sun and Europe as that of the setting sun.*

bull.

Eu·rope (ūr′op). Continent of N. hemisphere, western part of the Eurasian or Old World land mass, bordering on the Atlantic Ocean; about 3,700,000 sq. mi.

Eu·ro·pe·an (ūropē′an) *adj.* Of Europe or its people; ~ **Economic Community**, economic association established in 1957, consisting of Belgium, France, Italy, Luxembourg, the Netherlands, West Germany, and (1973) Denmark, the Republic of Ireland, Greece, Spain, Portugal and the United Kingdom; also called "Common Market"; ~ **plan**, hotel rate covering room and service but not meals (opp. AMERICAN plan). **European** *n.* European person.

eu·ro·pi·um (yo͝orō′pēum) *n.* (chem.) Rare-earth element; symbol Eu, at. no. 63, at. wt. 151.96. [f. EUROPE]

Eu·rus (ūr′us). (Gk. and Rom. myth.) God of E. or SE. wind.

Eu·ryd·i·ce (yo͝orĭd′ĭsē). (Gk. myth.) Wife of ORPHEUS.

Eu·sta·chi·us (ūstā′kēus), **Bartolommeo** (d. 1574). Italian anatomist. **Eu·sta·chian** (ūstā′shan, -kēan) *adj.* ~ **tube**, pharyngo-tympanic tube, passage communicating between the middle ear (tympanic cavity) and the back of the throat (larynx), and serving to equalize air pressure on both sides of the eardrum.

eu·tec·tic (ūtĕk′tĭk) *adj.* & *n.* (Of) a mixture whose constituents are in such proportions as to melt and solidify at one temperature like a pure substance.

Eu·ter·pe (ūtĕr′pē). (Gk. and Rom. myth.) Muse of music and lyric poetry.

eu·tha·na·sia (ūthanā′zha, -zhēa, -zēa) *n.* Gentle and easy death; bringing about of this for merciful reasons, esp. in case of incurable and painful disease.

eu·troph·ic (ūtrŏf′ĭk, ūtrō′fĭk) *adj.* Designating a pond, lake, etc., in which nutrients accumulate in abundance, supporting heavy growth of plant life that causes oxygen deficiency and hence extinction of animal life in the water. **eu·troph·i·ca·tion** (ūtrofĭkā′shon), **eu·tro·phy** (ū′trofē) *ns.*

eV, Ev *abbrevs.* Electron volt.

EVA *abbrev.* (astronautics) Extravehicular activity.

e·vac·u·ate (ĭvăk′ūāt) *v.t.* (**-at·ed, -at·ing**). 1. Empty (esp. stomach or other bodily organ *of* contents); discharge excrement etc. 2. Withdraw troops, inhabitants, from (place); remove (person) esp. from a place considered dangerous. **e·vac·u·a·tion** (ĭvăkūā′shon) *n.*

e·vac·u·ee (ĭvăkūē′) *n.* Person evacuated from place of danger etc.

e·vade (ĭvād′) *v.t.* (**e·vad·ed, e·vad·ing**). Escape, avoid, elude (attack, pursuit, etc.); avoid doing (duty etc.), answering (question), yielding to (argument etc.), esp. by trickiness or cleverness while complying with rules, laws, etc.; baffle. **e·vad′er** *n.*

e·val·u·ate (ĭvăl′ūāt) *v.t.* (**-at·ed, -at·ing**). Ascertain amount or value of; appraise; estimate. **e·val·u·a·tion** (ĭvălūā′shon) *n.*

ev·a·nesce (ĕvanĕs′) *v.i.* (**-nesced, -nesc·ing**). Fade out of sight; disappear.

ev·a·nes·cent (ĕvanĕs′ent) *adj.* Quickly fading or vanishing away; transitory; fleeting. **ev·a·nes′cence** *n.* **ev·a·nes′cent·ly** *adv.*

e·van·gel (ĭvăn′jel) *n.* (archaic) Christian gospel; one of the four Gospels of the New Testament. [Gk. *euaggelion* (reward for bringing) good news]

*Painted porcelain plate: 'The Temptation of Adam'. The Biblical story of the world's genesis neatly explains the hard lot of woman as the result of **Eve's** weakness towards the serpent.*

e·van·gel·i·cal (ēvănjĕl′ĭkal, ĕvan-) *adj.* 1. Of, according to, the teaching of the Christian gospel. 2. (often **E**~) Protestant, (esp.) of the school of Protestants maintaining that the essence of the gospel consists in the doctrine of salvation by faith and grace and denying that either sacraments or good works have any saving efficacy. ~ *n.* Member of evangelical Church.

e·van·gel′i·cal·ism *n.* **e·van·gel′i·cal·ly** *adv.*

e·van·gel·ism (ĭvăn′jelĭzem) *n.* Zealous preaching or promulgation of the gospel.

e·van·ge·list (ĭvăn′jelĭst) *n.* 1. (usu. cap.) One of the writers of the 4 Gospels of the New Testament: Matthew, Mark, Luke, or John. 2. Preacher of the gospel; now usu., layman doing home missionary work. **e·van·ge·lis·tic** (ĭvănjelĭs′tĭk) *adj.*

e·van·gel·ize (ĭvăn′jelīz) *v.t.* (**-ized, -iz·ing**). Preach gospel to, win over to Christian faith. **e·van·gel·i·za·tion** (ĭvănjelīzā′shon) *n.*

Ev·ans (ĕv′anz), **Mary Ann.** Real name of George ELIOT[1].

e·vap·o·rate (ĭvăp′orāt) *v.* (**-rat·ed, -rat·ing**). Turn from solid or liquid into vapor; pass away like vapor; remove liquid part of by heating or drying; lose liquid by evaporation; **evaporated milk**, concentrated unsweetened milk prepared by evaporation. **e·vap·o·ra·tion** (ĭvăporā′shon), **e·vap′o·ra·tor** *ns.*

e·va·sion (ĭvā′zhon) *n.* Act, means, of evading; subterfuge. **e·va·sive** (ĭvā′sĭv) *adj.* Seeking to evade, addicted to evasion; tending to evasion. **e·va′sive·ly** *adv.* **e·va′sive·ness** *n.*

Eve (ēv). Name given by Adam to his wife (Gen. 3), the first woman; hence, woman.

eve (ēv) *n.* 1. (poet. and archaic) Evening. 2. Evening or day before saint's day, holiday, etc., or before any date or event; time immediately preceding.

*Lake Everard, a salt lake in South Australia. The **evaporation** of water is so fast that only salt is left. The water vapor produced by evaporation from all over the world's surface is vital to the earth's atmosphere.*

For 70 years, ***Mount Everest,*** *at 29,028 ft. the world's highest mountain, has challenged climbers. For most of the time, it is swathed in the clouds that rise from the plains of India.*

e·ven[1] (ē′vėn) *n.* (poet. and archaic) Evening; **e′vensong,** Evening Prayer; **e′ventide,** (archaic) evening.

e·ven[2] (ē′vėn) *adj.* 1. Level; smooth; uniform in quality; in same plane or line *with.* 2. Equally balanced, impartial; equal in number or amount; **get ~ (with),** take one's revenge (on). 3. (of temper etc.) Equable, unruffled; **e′venhanded,** equitable; fair; impartial. 4. (of numbers) Integrally divisible by 2; (of sums of money etc.) expressible in integers, tens, etc. (opp. ODD); **~ money,** equal stakes in betting. **even** *v.t.* Make even. **e′ven·ly** *adv.* **e′ven·ness** *n.*

e·ven[3] (ē′vėn) *adv.* Inviting comparison of an assertion, negation, etc., with a less strong one that might have been made, as *I never ~ opened the book* (much less read it), *does he ~ suspect* (not to say realize) *the danger?, she sings ~ better than he does* (though he sings very well), etc.; (archaic) exactly, just.

eve·ning (ēv′nĭng) *n.* Close of day, esp. time between sunset and bedtime; closing or declining period of life etc.; **~ dress**: see DRESS; **~ gown,** woman's formal dress, usu. floor-length, for wear in the evening; **E~ Prayer,** (Anglican Ch.) evening service that is read or sung; **~ primrose**: see PRIMROSE: **~ star,** Venus (occas. also Jupiter or Mercury) when seen in the west after sunset.

e·vent (ĭvĕnt′) *n.* 1. (Actual or contemplated) fact of a thing's happening; thing that happens, esp. important thing. 2. Any of several possible mutually exclusive occurrences, one of which will happen under stated conditions; something on issue of which money is staked; one of the items in a sports program. 3. Result, outcome; **in any ~, at all ~s,** in any case. **e·vent′ful** *adj.* 1. Having many events. 2. Significant; important.

e·ven·tu·al (ĭvĕn′chōōal) *adj.* That will happen in certain circumstances; ultimately resulting. **e·ven′tu·al·ly** *adv.* **e·ven·tu·al·i·ty** (ĭvĕnchōōăl′ĭtē) *n.* (pl. **-ties**). Possible event.

e·ven·tu·ate (ĭvĕn′chōōāt) *v.i.* (**-at·ed, -at·ing**). Turn out; result (*in*); happen, come to pass.

ev·er (ĕv′*er*) *adv.* 1. Always, at all times, as in **~ after, ~ since; forev′er,** for all future time, incessantly. 2. (with negatives, or in interrogative, hypothetical, or conditional sentences) At any time; by any chance, at all. 3. Added for emphasis to *before* etc., or following interrogative pronouns, adverbs, etc., to intimate that the speaker has no notion what the answer will be. 4. **~ so,** (colloq.) very.

Ev·er·est (ĕv′*er*ĭst), **Mount.** Highest mountain of the world (29,028 ft., 8,848 m), in the

Himalayas on the border of Nepal and Tibet. [f. Sir George *Everest* (1790–1866), surveyor general of India]

ev·er·glade (ĕv′ĕrglād) *n.* Marshy tract of land mostly under water and covered in places with tall grass; **The Everglades**, large swampy region of S. Florida including the Everglades National Park, abundant in tropical and subtropical wildlife and plants.

ev·er·green (ĕv′ĕrgrēn) *adj.* Always green or fresh; (of trees etc.) having green leaves all year round and in some cases for several years (the leaves of one season remaining on the tree until those of the next are completely formed). ~ *n.* Evergreen tree or shrub.

ev·er·last·ing (ĕverlăs′tĭng, -lah′stĭng) *adj.* Lasting forever; lasting long; lasting too long, repeated too often; (of plants) keeping their shape and color when dried. ~ *n.* 1. Eternity; **the E~**, God. 2. Everlasting flower.

ev·er·more (ĕvermōr′, -mōr′) *adv.* Constantly; always in future.

eve·ry (ĕv′rē) *adj.* 1. Each; all taken separately. 2. **eve′rybody,** every person; **everybody else,** every other person; **eve′ryday,** occurring daily, worn or used on ordinary days, commonplace; **eve′ryone,** each (*of*), each person, everybody; **eve′rything,** all things, thing of first importance; **eve′ryway,** in every way, in every respect; **eve′rywhere,** in every place.

Eve·ry·man (ĕv′rēmăn) *n.* Ordinary or typical person. [Name of leading character in 15th c. morality play]

e·vict (ĭvĭkt′) *v.t.* Expel (tenant) by legal process. **e·vic′tion** *n.*

ev·i·dence (ĕv′ĭdens) *n.* 1. Being evident, clearness; **in ~**, present; prominent, conspicuous. 2. Indication, mark, sign, (*of* something); ground for belief, testimony or facts tending to prove or disprove something. 3. Information (personal testimony, production of material objects, etc.) given in legal investigation to establish a fact or point in question; statements etc. admissible as testimony in court of law; **turn state's ~**, (Brit.) **turn Queen's (King's) ~**, (of accomplice or sharer in crime) offer himself as witness for prosecution against other persons implicated. **evidence** *v.t.* (**-denced, -denc·ing**). Serve to indicate; attest; show clearly. **ev·i·dent** (ĕv′ĭdent) *adj.* Obvious to eyes or mind, clear, plain. **ev′i·dent·ly** *adv.* **ev·i·den·tial** (ĕvĭdĕn′shal) *adj.*

e·vil (ē′vil) *adj.* Bad, harmful, wicked; boding ill; **the E~ One**, the Devil; **e′vildoer**, person who does evil; **evil eye**, malicious or envious look, superstitiously believed to do material harm; supposed faculty of inflicting injury by a look; **evil-minded**, having evil ideas, thoughts, plans, etc. **evil** *n.* Evil thing; sin; harm, mischief. **e′vil·ly** *adv.*

e·vince (ĭvĭns′) *v.t.* (**e·vinced, e·vinc·ing**). Show, indicate (quality etc.); exhibit, demonstrate (quality). **e·vin′ci·ble** *adj.*

e·vis·cer·ate (ĭvĭs′erāt) *v.t.* (**-at·ed, -at·ing**). Disembowel; remove entrails of; (fig.) remove a vital part. **e·vis·cer·a·tion** (ĭvĭserā′shon) *n.*

e·voke (ĭvōk′) *v.t.* (**e·voked, e·vok·ing**). Call up, elicit (spirit, feeling, memory, etc.). **ev·o·ca·tion** (ĕvokā′shon) *n.* **e·voc·a·tive**

*The devil personified during Independence Day celebrations in Liberia, Africa. In Jewish and Christian theology, the Devil, Satan, is the supreme spirit of **evil** that tempts man.*

(ĭvŏk′ativ, ĭvō′ka-) *adj.* **e·vok′er** *n.*

ev·o·lu·tion (ĕvoloō′shon, ēvo-) *n.* 1. Appearance (of events etc.) in due succession. 2. Development, detailed working out, of what is implicitly or potentially contained in an idea or principle; development from rudimentary to mature or complete state. 3. Origination of species of animals and plants by process of development from earlier forms; the theory of this origination. **ev·o·lu′tion·al, ev·o·lu′tion·ar·y** *adjs.* **ev·o·lu′tion·ism, ev·o·lu′tion·ist** *ns.*

e·volve (ĭvŏlv′) *v.* (**e·volved, e·volv·ing**). 1. Unfold, open out; set forth in due sequence; develop, deduce (theory, facts, etc.). 2. Produce, give off (heat etc.). 3. Develop by natural process from rudimentary to more highly organized condition; produce or modify by evolution.

ev·zone (ĕv′zōn) *n.* Member of select Greek infantry regiment.

EW *abbrev.* Enlisted woman; enlisted women.

ewe (ū) *n.* Female sheep.

ew·er (ū′er) *n.* Large wide-mouthed pitcher or water jug.

ex[1] (ĕks) *prep.* 1. Without. 2. Out of. 3. Of particular college class without having graduated with it.

ex[2] (ĕks) *n.* (colloq.) Former occupant of specific position etc., esp. former spouse.

Ex. *abbrev.* Exodus (Old Testament).

ex- *prefix.* 1. (with verbs) Out of; thoroughly. 2. (with adjectives) Without, deprived of. 3. (with nouns) Former (as *ex-president*).

ex·ac·er·bate (ĭgzăs′erbāt) *v.t.* (**-bat·ed, -bat·ing**). Aggravate (pain, anger, etc.); irritate. **ex·ac·er·ba·tion** (ĭgzăserbā′shon) *n.*

ex·act[1] (ĭgzăkt′) *adj.* Precise, rigorous; accurate, strictly correct; ~ **sciences**, those that admit of absolute precision in results, e.g., physics and chemistry. **ex·act′ness, ex·ac·ti·tude** (ĭgzăk′tĭtood, -tūd) *ns.*

ex·act[2] (ĭgzăkt′) *v.t.* Demand and enforce payment of (money etc.); insist upon (act, conduct); require urgently. **ex·ac′tion** *n.* Exacting; thing etc. exacted.

ex·act·ing (ĭgzăk′tĭng) *adj.* 1. Making very severe demands; stringent. 2. Requiring great attention, effort, or care.

ex·act·ly (ĭgzăkt′lē) *adv.* (esp., as answer or confirmation) Quite so, just as you say.

ex·ag·ger·ate (ĭgzăj′erāt) *v.t.* (**-at·ed, -at·ing**). Magnify beyond limits of truth; intensify, aggravate; make (physical features etc.) of abnormal size. **ex·ag′ger·at·ed·ly** *adv.* **ex·ag·ger·a·tion** (ĭgzăjerā′shon), **ex·ag′ger·a·tor** *ns.* **ex·ag·ger·a·tive** (ĭgzăj′erātĭv, -eratĭv) *adj.*

ex·alt (ĭgzawlt′) *v.t.* Raise, place high in rank, power, etc.; praise, extol; dignify, ennoble. **ex·al·ta·tion** (ĕgzawltā′shon, -zal-) *n.* Raising, lifting up; elation, rapturous emotion.

ex·am (ĭgzăm′) *n.* (colloq.) Examination.

ex·am·i·na·tion (ĭgzămĭnā′shon) *n.* 1. Investigation by inspection or experiment, minute inspection; investigation; scrutiny. 2. Testing of knowledge or ability of pupils etc. by oral or written questions; ~ **paper**, paper of questions to be answered; written answers to these questions. 3. Formal interrogation, esp. of witness or accused person; **cross-**~: see CROSS-. **ex·am·i·na′tion·al** *adj.*

ex·am·ine (ĭgzăm′ĭn) *v.* (**-ined, -in·ing**). Investigate; scrutinize; test, esp. test knowledge or capacity of, by questions; interrogate formally, esp. witness or accused person in court of law; inquire *into*. **ex·am·i·nee** (ĭgzămĭnē′), **ex·am′in·er** *ns.*

ex·am·ple (ĭgzăm′pel, -zahm′-) *n.* 1. Typical instance, fact, thing, person, illustrating or forming particular case of general principle, rule, state of things, etc.; specimen of workmanship etc. 2. Warning to others. 3. Precedent. 4. Action or conduct as object of imitation.

ex·arch (ĕk′sark) *n.* 1. Governor of province in Byzantine Empire. 2. (Eastern Orthodox Church) Bishop ranking between patriarch and metropolitan; patriarch's deputy. **ex·ar·chate** (ĕk′sarkāt, ĕksar′-) *n.*

ex·as·per·ate (ĭgzăs′perāt) *v.t.* (**-at·ed, -at·ing**). Irritate; provoke (person). **ex·as·per·a·tion** (ĭgzăsperā′shon) *n.*

exc. *abbrev.* Except; *excudit* (L., = engraved this).

Ex·cal·i·bur (ĕkskăl′ĭber). (Arthurian legend) Name of King ARTHUR'S[1] magic sword, which he drew easily from a rock where it was held fast, and which was returned on his death to the Lady of the Lake.

ex ca·the·dra (ĕks kathē′dra,

Forms of man during his ***evolution.*** *The earth is believed to be 5,000–6,000 million years old, while man's traces go back 1–3 million years. During the last 2 stages of the Tertiary period a group of apes, called Australopithecines, emerged; these may have been direct, tool-making ancestors of Homo erectus. Human fossils are usually named after their place of discovery, e.g.,*

A giant ***excavator*** *for opencast lignite mining. In the late 19th century steam shovels were used to move earth. The diesel engine has made possible the use of a wide number of specialized types of machine.*

kăth´ĭdr*a*). Authoritative(ly), official(ly), said esp. of papal pronouncements; **speak ~**, (of the pope) pronounce an infallible judgment on matter of faith or morals. [L., = "from the chair"]

ex·ca·vate (ĕks´k*a*vāt) *v.t.* (**-vat·ed, -vat·ing**). Make hollow; make (hole etc.) by digging; dig out (soil) leaving a hole; unearth, get out, uncover, by digging. **ex·ca·va·tion** (ĕksk*a*vā´sh*o*n), **ex´ca·va·tor** *ns.*

ex·ceed (ĭksēd´) *v.* Do more than is warranted by (one's authority, rights, etc.); be greater than (quantity, thing, *by* so much); surpass; be preeminent. **ex·ceed´ing** *adj.* **ex·ceed´ing·ly** *adv.*

ex·cel (ĭksĕl´) *v.* (**-celled, -cel·ling**). Surpass; be preeminent.

ex·cel·lence (ĕk´sel*e*ns) *n.* Surpassing merit; thing in which person etc. excels.

Ex·cel·len·cy (ĕk´sel*e*nsē) *n.* (pl. **-cies**). Title of ambassadors, bishops, archbishops, governors, and some other high officers.

ex·cel·lent (ĕk´sel*e*nt) *adj.* Preeminent; very good. **ex´cel·lent·ly** *adv.*

Steinheim and Neanderthal. The latter was living at the beginning of the last Ice Age; at the same time Modern Man, Homo sapiens, Cro-Magnon, was evolving, seemingly independently. Mesolithic and Neolithic are types of Modern Man.

Neanderthal man

Cro Magnon

Mesolithic

Neolithic

ex·cel·si·or (ĭksĕl′sēer) *n.* Short thin shavings of soft wood for stuffing, packing, etc. ~ *adj.* (L.) Always upward; higher; used as motto on the New York State seal.

ex·cept[1] (ĭksĕpt′) *v.* Exclude (thing) from enumeration, statement, etc.

ex·cept[2] (ĭksĕpt′), **ex·cept·ing** (ĭksĕp′tĭng) *preps.* & *conjs.* Not including; but, save, with the exception of; (archaic) unless.

ex·cep·tion (ĭksĕp′shon) *n.* Excepting; thing excepted, thing that does not follow the rule; (law) objection to ruling of court; **the ~ proves the rule**, the excepting of some cases shows that the rule exists, or that it applies to those not excepted; **take ~**, object *to.*

ex·cep·tion·al (ĭksĕp′shonal) *adj.* Forming an exception; unusual. **ex·cep′tion·al·ly** *adv.*

ex·cerpt (ĕk′serpt) *n.* Extract from book etc. ~ (ĭksẽrpt′) *v.t.* Extract, quote, (passage *from* book etc.)

ex·cess (ĭksĕs′, ĕk′sĕs) *n.* 1. (usu. pl.) Overstepping limits of moderation; (esp.) intemperance in eating or drinking. 2. Fact of exceeding;

A painting of the ***execution*** *of Charles I outside the Banqueting Hall, Whitehall, in 1649. He was the only English king to have been tried and sentenced to death by his subjects.*

amount by which one quantity exceeds another; exceeding of proper amount or degree; ~ **baggage,** luggage over the weight or total dimensions ordinarily carried free and for which a passenger must pay an extra charge; ~ **profits tax**, tax levied on business profits in excess of average profits of a standard period. **ex·ces·sive** (ĭksĕs′ĭv) *adj.* **ex·ces′-sive·ly** *adv.*

ex·change (ĭkschānj′) *v.* (**-changed, -chang·ing**). Give, receive, (thing) in place of (*for*) another; interchange (blows, words, glances, etc.). ~ *n.* 1. Act, process, of exchanging; exchanging of coin, notes, bank deposits, etc., for their equivalent in another country's money; (also ~ **rate, rate of ~**) price at which another country's money may be bought; difference between this and par. 2. Building where merchants, stock-brokers, etc., assemble to transact business. 3. (also **telephone ~**) Center to which local telephone lines are connected and through which communication between individual telephones is effected.

ex·change·a·ble (ĭkschān′jabel) *adj.* That may be exchanged (*for*). **ex·change·a·bil′i·ty** *n.*

ex·cheq·uer (ĕks′chĕker, ĭks chĕk′-) *n.* 1. Brit. government department of public service charged with the collection and care of revenue. 2. Formerly a Brit. court dealing with matters of revenue etc. 3. Royal or national treasury (esp. Brit.); money of private person, society, etc. [Fr. *eschequier* f. med. L. *scaccarium* chessboard, from use of table with checkered cloth for accounts]

ex·cise[1] (ĕk′sīz, -sīs) *n.* Duty or tax levied on goods and commodities produced or sold within the country and on various licenses etc.

ex·cise[2] (ĭksīz′) *v.t.* (**-cised, -cis·ing**). Cut out or away (passage of book, limb, organ, etc.). **ex·ci·sion** (ĭksĭzh′on) *n.*

ex·cite (ĭksīt′) *v.t* (**-cit·ed, -cit·ing**). Set in motion, stir up, rouse (feelings, faculties, etc.); provoke, bring about, stimulate (action, active condition); arouse (a person) sexually; move (person) to strong emotion, stir up to eager tumultuous feeling. **ex·cit'a·ble** *adj.* (esp., of persons) Easily excited. **ex·cit·a·bil·i·ty** (ĭksītabĭl'ĭtē), **ex·ci·ta·tion** (ĕksītā'shon) *ns.* **ex·cit'ed·ly** *adv.* **ex·cite·ment** (ĭksīt'ment) *n.*

excl. *abbrev.* Exclamation; excluding; exclusive.

ex·claim (ĭksklām') *v.* Cry out, esp. from pain, anger, delight, etc.; utter thus.

ex·cla·ma·tion (ĕksklamā'shon) *n.* Exclaiming; words exclaimed; interjection; ~ **mark,** ~ **point,** punctuation mark (!) used after exclamation. **ex·clam·a·to·ry** (ĭksklăm'atōrē, -tōrē) *adj.*

ex·clude (ĭksklōōd') *v.t.* (**-clud·ed, -clud·ing**). Shut out (*from* place, society, privilege, etc.); prevent the occurrence of, make impossible; leave out, not include. **ex·clu·sion** (ĭksklōō'zhon) *n.*

ex·clu·sive (ĭksklōō'sĭv) *adj.* 1. Shutting out; not admitting *of*; desirous of excluding others, (of social group etc.) chary of admitting others, select; (of news, goods, etc.) not to be had, not published, elsewhere; (of terms etc.) excluding all but what is specified; employed, followed, to the exclusion of all else. 2. (quasi-*adv.*) ~ **of,** not including, not counting. **ex·clu'sive·ly** *adv.* **ex·clu'sive·ness** *n.*

ex·com·mu·ni·cate (ĕkskomū'nĭkāt) *v.t.* (**-cat·ed, -cat·ing**). (eccles.) Cut off (person) from participation in sacrament, or from all communication with Church. **ex·com·mu·ni·ca·tion** (ĕkskomūnĭkā'shon), **ex·com·mu'ni·ca·tor** *ns.* **ex·com·mu'ni·ca·tive, ex·com·mu'ni·ca·to·ry** *adjs.*

ex·co·ri·ate (ĭkskōr'ēāt, -skōr'-) *v.t.* (**-at·ed, -at·ing**). 1. Remove part of skin of (person etc.) by abrasion etc.; strip, peel off (skin). 2. Denounce; upbraid; berate harshly. **ex·co·ri·a·tion** (ĭkskōrēā'shon, -skōr-) *n.*

ex·cre·ment (ĕk'skrement) *n.* Waste matter discharged from the body, esp. feces. **ex·cre·men·tal** (ĕkskremĕn'tal) *adj.*

ex·cres·cence (ĭkskrĕs'ens) *n.* Abnormal or morbid outgrowth on animal or vegetable body (also fig.).

ex·cres·cent (ĭkskrĕs'ent) *adj.* Growing abnormally, redundant.

ex·cre·ta (ĭkskrē'ta) *n.pl.* Waste expelled from body, esp. feces and urine.

ex·crete (ĭkskrēt') *v.t.* (**-cret·ed, -cret·ing**). (of animals, plants, etc.) Separate and expel (waste matters) from system. **ex·cre'tion** *n.* **ex·cre'tive, ex·cre·to·ry** (ĕk'skretōrē, -tōrē) *adjs.*

ex·cru·ci·ate (ĭkskrōō'shēāt) *v.t.* (**-at·ed, -at·ing**). Torture physically or mentally. **ex·cru'ci·at·ing·ly** *adv.* **ex·cru·ci·a·tion** (ĭkskrōōshēā'shon) *n.*

ex·cul·pate (ĕk'skŭlpāt, ĭkskŭl'-) *v.t.* (**-pat·ed, -pat·ing**). Free from blame; clear (*from* charge etc.). **ex·cul·pa·tion** (ĕkskŭlpā'shon) *n.* **ex·cul·pa·to·ry** (ĭkskŭl'patōrē, -tōrē) *adj.*

ex·cur·sion (ĭkskẽr'zhon, -shon) *n.* 1. Journey or ramble from any place with intention of returning to it; pleasure trip, esp. one taken by a number of persons; ~ **fare,** reduced rate for a round-trip ticket on a train, bus, etc., usu. with time limits for departure and return; ~ **flight,** trip by airplane to specified place(s), for which limited group of individuals pay excursion fare. 2. Sortie, military raid (obs. exc. in *alar(u)ms and ~s*). 3. (astron.) Deviation from regular path or course. **ex·cur'sion·ist** *n.* One who makes pleasure excursion.

ex·cur·sive (ĭkskẽr'sĭv) *adj.* Desultory; erratic, digressive, in writing or speech. **ex·cur'sive·ly** *adv.* **ex·cur'sive·ness** *n.*

ex·cuse (ĭkskūz') *v.t.* (**-cused, -cus·ing**). 1. Attempt to clear (person) from blame without denying or justifying his imputed action; seek to remove or extenuate blame of (acknowledged fault); serve as excuse for. 2. Obtain exemption or release for, set free, (person) from task, duty, obligation. 3. Accept apology for, overlook, condone; pardon faults of, regard indulgently; dispense with. 4. ~ **me,** used as apology for lack of ceremony, interruption, etc., or as polite way of disputing statement; ~ **oneself,** ask permission to leave. **ex·cus'a·ble** *adj.* **excuse** (ĭkskūs') *n.* Apology offered, exculpation; ground of this; plea for release from duty etc.

ex·e·cra·ble (ĕk'sekrabel) *adj.* Abominable. **ex'e·cra·bly** *adv.*

ex·e·crate (ĕk'sekrāt) *v.* (**-crat·ed, -crat·ing**). Express, feel, abhorrence for; utter curses. **ex·e·cra·tion** (ĕksekrā'shon), **ex'e·cra·tor** *ns.*

ex·ec·u·tant (ĭgzĕk'yutant) *n.* One who executes, performer (esp. of music).

ex·e·cute (ĕk'sekūt) *v.t.* (**-cut·ed, -cut·ing**). 1. Carry (plan, command, law, will, judicial sentence) into effect; perform (action, operation, etc.); make (legal instrument) valid by signing, sealing, etc.; discharge (office, function). 2. Carry out design for (product of art or skill); perform (musical composition). 3. Inflict capital punishment on.

ex·e·cu·tion (ĕksekū'shon) *n.* Executing; manner of executing; effective action; infliction of capital

The ornate New York ***Stock Exchange,*** *commercial and financial focal point of the western world, dominates Wall Street.*

punishment. **ex·e·cu′tion·er** *n.* One who carries out a capital sentence.

ex·ec·u·tive (ĭgzĕk′y*u*tĭv) *adj.* Pertaining to, having function of, executing; concerned with executing laws, decrees, and sentences; ~ **order**, president's order on administrative matter not requiring legislation; ~ **session**, private legislative session to deal with executive business; hence, private meeting. **executive** *n.* 1. Executive branch of government. 2. Person holding executive position in business etc.; executive official.

ex·ec·u·tor (ĭgzĕk′y*u*ter) *n.* 1. One who carries out or performs. 2. Person appointed by testator to execute his will; **literary** ~, person entrusted with papers and unpublished works of writer. **ex·ec·u·to·ri·al** (ĭgzĕky*u*tōr′ē*a*l, -tōr′-) *adj.* **ex·ec′u·tor·ship** *n.*

ex·ec·u·trix (ĭgzĕk′y*u*trĭks) *n.* (pl. **ex·ec·u·tri·ces** pr. ĭgzĕky*u*trī′sēz, **ex·ec·u·trix·es**). Female executor.

ex·e·ge·sis (ĕks*e*jē′sĭs) *n.* (pl. **-ses** pr. -sēz). Critical exposition, interpretation, esp. of Scripture. **ex·e·get·ic** (ĕks*e*jĕt′ĭk), **ex·e·get′i·cal** *adjs.* **ex·e·get′i·cal·ly** *adv.*

ex·e·gete (ĕk′s*e*jēt) *n.* Person skilled in exegesis.

ex·em·plar (ĭgzĕm′pl*e*r, -plär) *n.* Worthy model; pattern; typical example.

ex·em·pla·ry (ĭgzĕm′pl*e*rē) *adj.* Fit to be imitated; illustrative; (of penalty, damages) serving as a warning. **ex·em′pla·ri·ly** *adv.* **ex·em′pla·ri·ness** *n.*

ex·em·pli·fy (ĭgzĕm′plĭfī) *v.t.* (**-fied, -fy·ing**). Illustrate by example; be example of. 2. Make official copy of; make attested copy of (public document).

ex·empt (ĭgzĕmpt′) *adj.* Freed *from* allegiance or liability to; ~ **from**, not liable, exposed, or subject to (charge, duty, etc.). ~ *n.* Exempted person. ~ *v.t.* Grant to (person) immunity or freedom *from*. **ex·emp′tion** *n.*

ex·e·quies (ĕk′s*e*kwēz) *n.pl.* Funeral rites.

ex·er·cise (ĕk′s*e*rsīz) *n.* 1. Employment (of organ, faculty, power, right); practice (of virtues, profession, functions, religious rites). 2. Exertion of muscles, limbs, etc., esp. for health's sake; (pl.) military drill, athletics, etc. 3. Bodily, mental, or spiritual training; task set for this purpose; composition etc. assigned to pupils at school; piece of music etc. designed to afford practice to learners. 4. Ceremony on some special occasion. ~ *v.* (**-cised, -cis·ing**). Employ (faculty, right, etc.); train (person etc.); tax the powers of; discharge (functions); take, give (dog etc.), exercise.

Exercise *takes many forms. It can be passive and relaxing, or strenuous and exhausting. Modern man seems obsessed with fitness, evidenced by the many gyms and fitness records available.*

ex·ert (ĭgzērt′) *v.t.* Exercise, bring to bear (quality, force, influence); ~ **oneself**, use efforts or endeavors, strive. **ex·er·tion** (ĭgzēr′sh*o*n) *n.* Exerting; vigorous action, effort.

ex·e·unt (ĕk′sē*u*nt). (stage direction) They (2 or more actors) leave the stage. [L., = "they go out"]

ex·ha·la·tion (ĕks-h*a*lā′sh*o*n) *n.* Exhaling; what is exhaled.

ex·hale (ĕks-hāl′, ĕks′hāl) *v.* (**-haled, -hal·ing**). Give off, be given off, in vapor, evaporate; breathe out.

ex·haust (ĭgzawst′) *v.* 1. Draw off (air); empty (vessel) of contents. 2. Consume entirely; use, account for, the whole of; treat or study (subject etc.) so as to leave nothing further to be explained or discovered. 3. Drain (person etc.) of strength, resources, etc.; tire out. **ex·haust′i·ble** *adj.* **ex·haust·i·bil·i·ty** (ĭgzawst*i*bĭl′ĭtē) *n.* **exhaust** *n.* Expulsion or exit of vaporous waste material from an engine; fumes or gases expelled thus; (also ~ **pipe**) pipe by which they escape.

ex·haus·tion (ĭgzaws′ch*o*n) *n.* (esp.) Total loss of energy.

ex·haus·tive (ĭgzaws′tĭv) *adj.* (esp.) Comprehensive, exhausting a subject. **ex·haus′tive·ly** *adv.* **ex·haus′tive·ness** *n.*

ex·hib·it (ĭgzĭb′ĭt) *v.t.* Show, display; submit (document) for inspection; manifest (quality); show publicly. ~ *n.* 1. (law) Document or thing formally introduced as evidence in court. 2. Thing, collection of things, sent by person, firm, etc., to exhibition, or on permanent show in museum etc. **ex·hib′it·er, ex·hib′i·tor** *ns.*

ex·hi·bi·tion (ĕksĭbĭsh′*o*n) *n.* Showing, exhibiting, display; public display (of works of art, manufactured articles, etc.), place where this is held.

ex·hi·bi·tion·ism (ĕksĭbĭsh′*o*nĭz*e*m) *n.* Tendency toward display, extravagant behavior; (psychol.) compulsive indecent exposure. **ex·hi·bi′tion·ist** *n.*

ex·hil·a·rate (ĭgzĭl′*e*rāt) *v.t.* (**-rat·ed, -rat·ing**). Enliven, invigorate, gladden (person, spirits). **ex·hil·a·ra·tion** (ĭgzĭl*e*rā′sh*o*n) *n.*

ex·hort (ĭgzôrt′) *v.t.* Admonish earnestly; urge (*to*). **ex·hor·ta·tion** (ĕgzôrtā′sh*o*n, ĕksôr-) *n.* **ex·hor′ta·tive** *adj.*

ex·hume (ĭgzōōm′, -zūm′, ĕks hūm′) *v.t.* (**-humed, -hum·ing**).

Dig out (something buried), unearth. **ex·hu·ma·tion** (ĕks-hūmā'-shon) *n.*

ex·i·gen·cy (ĕk'sĭjensē), **ex·i·gence** (ĕk'sĭjens) *ns.* (pls. **-cies, -genc·es**). 1. Quality or state of being urgent. 2. (usu. **~cies**) Demand or need that is an essential of a situation, condition, etc. **ex'i·gent** *adj.* Urgent, pressing; exacting.

ex·ig·u·ous (ĭgzĭg'ūus, ĭksĭ'-) *adj.* Scanty, small. **ex·ig·u·i·ty** (ĕksĭgū'itē), **ex·ig'u·ous·ness** *ns.*

ex·ile (ĕg'zīl, ĕk'sīl) *n.* 1. Banishment; long absence from one's country; **the E~**, esp., captivity of Jews in Babylon in 6th c. B.C. 2. Exiled person; one living in a foreign country. **exile** *v.t.* (**-iled, -il·ing**). Banish (*from*).

ex·ist (ĭgzĭst') *v.i.* Have objective being; have being in specified place or under specified conditions; occur, be found; live; continue in being.

ex·ist·ence (ĭgzĭs'tens) *n.* Being, existing; life; mode of existing; all that exists; existing thing.

ex·ist·ent (ĭgzĭs'tent) *adj.* Existing, actual, current.

ex·is·ten·tial (ĕgzĭstĕn'shal, ĕksĭs-) *adj.* Of or relating to existence; (logic, of a proposition) predicating existence; of existentialism. **ex·is·ten'tial·ism** *n.* Philosophic theory emphasizing existence of the individual as free and responsible agent determining his own development. **ex·is·ten'tial·ist** *adj.* & *n.*

ex·it[1] (ĕg'zĭt, ĕk'sĭt) *n.* Departure of actor from stage (also fig.); death; going out or forth, liberty to do this; way out.

ex·it[2] (ĕg'zĭt, ĕk'sĭt) *v.i.* (stage direction) Goes off stage. [L., = "goes out"]

ex li·bris (ĕks lē'brĭs, lĭb'rĭs). From the library of (person whose name follows); as used on bookplates. [L.]

exo- *prefix.* Outside; external.

ex·o·crine (ĕk'sokrĭn, -krēn, -krīn) *adj.* & *n.* (Gland) secreting externally, through a duct.

Exod. *abbrev.* Exodus (Old Testament).

ex·o·der·mis (ĕksōdēr'mĭs) *n.* Outer layer of blastoderm.

Ex·o·dus (ĕk'sodus). Second book of Old Testament, relating departure of Israelites from Egypt.

ex·o·dus (ĕk'sodus) *n.* Departure, esp. in considerable numbers; the **E~**, departure of Israelites from Egypt under the leadership of Moses.

ex of·fi·ci·o (ĕks ofĭsh'ēō). By virtue of one's office. [L.]

ex·og·a·mous (ĕksŏg'amus) *adj.* Following the custom compelling man to marry outside his own tribe or group. **ex·og'a·my** *n.*

ex·og·e·nous (ĕksŏj'enus) *adj.* Growing or originating externally.

ex·on·er·ate (ĭgzŏn'erāt) *v.t.* (**-at·ed, -at·ing**). Exculpate; free (person) *from* (blame etc.); release (person *from* duty etc.). **ex·on·er·a·tion** (ĭgzŏnerā'shon) *n.*

ex·oph·thal·mos, ex·oph·thal·mus (ĕksŏfthăl'mos) *ns.* Abnormal protrusion of eyeball, caused by injury or disease. **ex·oph·thal'mic** *adj.*

ex·or·bi·tant (ĭgzōr'bĭtant) *adj.* Grossly excessive (of price, demand, ambition, person). **ex·or'bi·tance** *n.* **ex·or'bi·tant·ly** *adv.*

ex·or·cise, ex·or·cize (ĕk'sōrsīz, -ser-) *vbs.t.* (**-cised, -cis·ing, -cized, -ciz·ing**). Expel (evil spirit *from, out of*, person or place) by invocation or use of holy name; clear (person, place, *of* evil spirits). **ex·or·cism** (ĕk'sōrsĭzem, -ser-), **ex'or·cist** *ns.*

ex·o·skel·e·ton (ĕksōskĕl'eton) *n.* External skeleton, as of insect, crustacean, etc.

ex·o·sphere (ĕk'sōsfēr) *n.* Outermost layer of atmosphere, beginning at 300–600 mi. above the Earth.

ex·o·ter·ic (ĕksotĕr'ĭk) *adj.* (of doctrines, mode of speech, etc.) Intelligible to outsiders; (of disciples) not admitted to esoteric teaching; commonplace, ordinary, popular. **ex·o·ter'i·cal·ly** *adv.*

ex·o·ther·mic (ĕksōthēr'mĭk), **ex·o·ther·mal** (ĕksōthēr'mal) *adjs.* (chem.) Liberating, as opposed to absorbing, heat.

ex·ot·ic (ĭgzŏt'ĭk) *adj.* (of plants, words, fashions) Introduced from abroad; strange, bizarre; **~ dancer**, striptease, belly dancer, nude or partially clothed dancer, etc. **exotic** *n.* Exotic plant (also fig.).

exp. *abbrev.* Expenses; experiment(al); export; express.

ex·pand (ĭkspănd') *v.* 1. Spread out flat or smooth; unfold, open out; swell, increase in bulk. 2. Expound, write out, in full (what is condensed or abbreviated, algebraic expression, etc.). 3. Become genial or talkative, throw off reserve. **ex·pand'a·ble** *adj.* & *n.* **ex·pan·si·ble** (ĭkspăn'sĭbel) *adj.*

ex·panse (ĭkspăns') *n.* Wide area or extent; expansion.

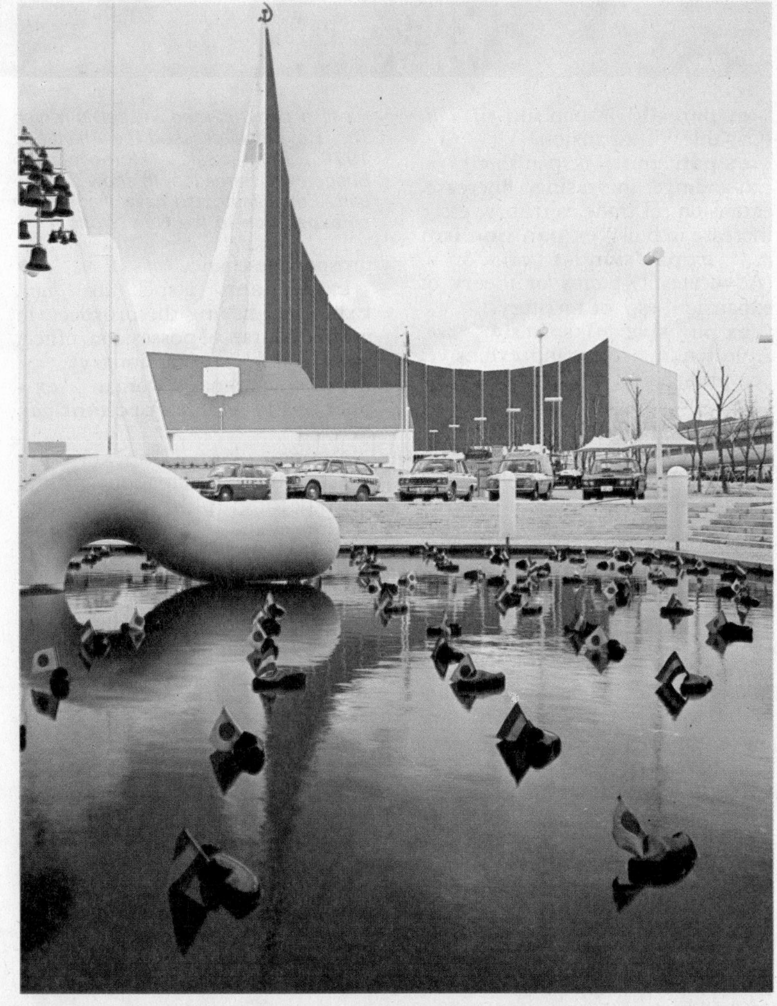

Expo 70, Japan, the U.S.S.R. Pavilion. Large international industrial ***exhibitions*** *with ancillary attractions stem largely from The Great Exhibition held in London, U.K. in 1851.*

*Ra II, a papyrus-reed vessel in which Thor Heyerdahl crossed the Atlantic in 1970 from Safi, Morocco, to Bridgetown, Barbados, to show that the early Egyptians could have made such an **expedition** to the New World.*

ex·pan·sile (ĭkspăn′sĭl, -sīl) *adj.* (Capable) of expansion.

ex·pan·sion (ĭkspăn′shon) *n.* Expanding; increasing, increase, extension (of trade, territory, etc.); increase in bulk. **ex·pan′sion·ism** *n.* **ex·pan′sion·ist** *adj.* & *n.* (Advocate of) policy or theory of expansion, esp. of territory.

ex·pan·sive (ĭkspăn′sĭv) *adj.* Able, tending, to expand; extensive; comprehensive; (of persons, feelings, speech) effusive. **ex·pan′sive·ly** *adv.* **ex·pan′sive·ness** *n.*

ex par·te (ĕks pār′tē). (law) On, in interests of, one side only; made or said thus.

ex·pa·ti·ate (ĭkspā′shēāt) *v.i.* (**-at·ed, -at·ing**). Speak, write, copiously (*on* subject). **ex·pa·ti·a·tion** (ĭkspāshēā′shon) *n.*

ex·pa·tri·ate (ĕkspā′trēāt) *v.t.* (**-at·ed, -at·ing**). Banish; (*refl.*) withdraw from one's country, renounce one's citizenship. **ex·pa·tri·a·tion** (ĕkspātrēā′shon) *n.* **ex·pa·tri·ate** (ĕkspā′trēĭt, -āt) *adj.* & *n.* Expatriated (person); (person) living in a foreign country.

ex·pect (ĭkspĕkt′) *v.t.* Look forward to, regard as likely; look for, anticipate coming of (person or thing); (colloq.) think, suppose. **ex·pect′er** *n.*

ex·pect·an·cy (ĭkspĕk′tănsē) *n.* (pl. **-cies**). State of expectation; prospect, esp. of future possession; prospective chance (*of*).

ex·pect·ant (ĭkspĕk′tant) *adj.* Expecting; having the prospect, in normal course, of possession, office, etc.; (law) reversionary; ~ **mother**, pregnant woman. **ex·pect′ant·ly** *adv.* **ex·pec′tant** *adj.* & *n.*

ex·pec·ta·tion (ĕkspĕktā′shon) *n.* Awaiting; anticipation; ground for expecting; (pl.) prospects, esp. of inheritance; being expected; thing expected.

ex·pec·to·rate (ĭkspĕk′terāt) *v.t.* (**-rat·ed, -rat·ing**). Eject (phlegm or other material) from lung airways by coughing; spit. **ex·pec·to·ra·tion** (ĭkspĕk′terāshon) *n.* **ex·pec·to·rant** (ĭkspĕk′terant) *adj.* & *n.* (Medicine) promoting expectoration.

ex·pe·di·ent (ĭkspē′dēent) *adj.* Advantageous, suitable; politic rather than just. **ex·pe′di·ent·ly** *adv.* **ex·pe′di·ence, ex·pe′di·en·cy** *ns.* **expedient** *n.* Contrivance, device; means to an end.

ex·pe·dite (ĕk′spedīt) *v.t.* (**-dit·ed, -dit·ing**). Speed up, facilitate progress of (measure, process, etc.); dispatch (business).

ex·pe·di·tion (ĕkspedĭsh′on) *n.* 1. Warlike enterprise; journey, voyage, excursion, for definite purpose; body of persons, fleet, etc., sent out for warlike or other definite purpose. 2. Promptness, speed. **ex·pe·di′tion·ar·y** *adj.*

ex·pe·di·tious (ĕkspedĭsh′us) adj. Doing, done, speedily; suited to speedy performance. **ex·pe·di′tious·ly** *adv.* **ex·pe·di′tious·ness** *n.*

ex·pel (ĭkspĕl′) *v.t.* (**-pelled, -pel·ling**). Eject (*from*) by force; turn out (person *from* community, school, etc.).

ex·pend (ĭkspĕnd′) *v.t.* Spend (money, time, care, etc.); use up; consume. **ex·pend′a·ble** *adj.* That can be expended or spared; (mil.) that may be sacrificed in order to accomplish an objective.

ex·pend·i·ture (ĭkspĕn′dĭcher) *n.* Laying out, spending; consuming; amount expended.

ex·pense (ĭkspĕns′) *n.* Expenditure cost; (pl.) outlay in performing one's job etc.; reimbursement of this.

ex·pen·sive (ĭkspĕn′sĭv) *adj.* Costly. **ex·pen′sive·ly** *adv.*

ex·pe·ri·ence (ĭkspēr′ēens) *n.* 1. Actual observation of facts or events; knowledge resulting from this. 2. Event that affects one; fact, process, of being so affected. ~ *v.t.* (**-enced, -enc·ing**). Meet with, feel, undergo (pleasure, treatment, fate, etc.); learn, find. **ex·pe′ri·enced** *adj.* (esp.) Having experience, wise or skillful through experience. **ex·pe·ri·en·tial** (ĭkspēr̄ēĕn′sh*a*l) *adj.* **ex·pe·ri·en′tial·ly** *adv.*

ex·pe·ri·ment (ĭkspĕr′ĭm*e*nt, -spēr′-) *n.* Action or operation undertaken in order to discover something unknown, test hypothesis, illustrate known fact, etc.; method etc. adopted in uncertainty whether it will answer the purpose. ~ (ĭkspĕr′ĭmĕnt, -spēr′-) *v.i.* Conduct experiment (*on, with*).

ex·per·i·men·tal (ĭkspĕrĭmĕn′t*a*l, -spēr-) *adj.* 1. Based on, derived from, experience; empirical. 2. Based on experiment; of, used in, experiments. **ex·per·i·men′tal·ly** *adv.*

ex·pert (ĕk′spērt, ĭkspērt′) *adj.* Trained by practice, skillful (*at, in*). **ex·pert′ly** *adv.* **ex·pert′ness** *n.* **expert** (ĕk′spērt) *n.* Person having special skill or knowledge (freq. attrib.).

ex·pert·ise (ĕkspērtēz′) *n.* Expert skill or knowledge.

ex·pi·ate (ĕk′spēāt) *v.t.* (**-at·ed, -at·ing**). Pay penalty of, make amends or atonement for (sin). **ex·pi·a·ble** (ĕk′spē*a*b*e*l), **ex·pi·a·to·ry** (ĕk′spē*a*tōrē, -tōrē) *adjs.* **ex·pi·a·tion** (ĕkspēā′sh*o*n), **ex′·pi·a·tor** *ns.*

ex·pi·ra·tion (ĕksp*e*rā′sh*o*n) *n.* 1. Breathing out. 2. Termination (of period of time, something made to last a certain time); ending. **ex·pir·a·to·ry** (ĕkspīr′*a*tōrē, -tōrē) *adj.*

ex·pire (ĭkspīr′) *v.* (**-pired, -pir·ing**). 1. Breathe out. 2. Die; (of fire etc.) die out. 3. (of period) Come to an end; (of law, patent, etc.) become void, reach its term.

ex·plain (ĭksplān′) *v.* Give details of; make plain or intelligible; give explanation; interpret; make clear cause, origin, or reason of, account for; ~ **away**, modify, do away with, by explanation; ~ **oneself**, make one's meaning clear, give account of one's motives or intentions.

ex·pla·na·tion (ĕkspl*a*nā′sh*o*n) *n.* Explaining, esp. with view to mutual understanding or reconciliation; statement, circumstance, that explains.

ex·plan·a·to·ry (ĭksplăn′*a*tōrē, -tōrē) *adj.* Serving, meant, to explain. **ex·plan·a·to′ri·ly** *adv.*

ex·ple·tive (ĕk′splĕtĭv) *adj.* Serving to fill out; (of words etc.) serving to fill out sentence, metrical line, etc. ~ *n.* Expletive word or phrase, esp. exclamation; oath, esp. an obscene or profane one.

ex·pli·ca·ble (ĕk′splĭk*a*b*e*l, ĭksplĭk′-) *adj.* That may be explained.

ex·pli·cate (ĕk′spl*i*kāt) *v.t.* (**-cat·ed, -cat·ing**). 1. Develop (notion, principle, proposition). 2. Explain; interpret (text). **ex′pli·ca·tive, ex′pli·ca·to·ry** *adjs.*

ex·plic·it (ĭksplĭs′ĭt) *adj.* Stated in detail, leaving nothing merely implied; definite; (of persons) outspoken. **ex·plic′it·ly** *adv.* **ex·plic′it·ness** *n.*

ex·plode (ĭksplōd′) *v.* (**-plod·ed, -plod·ing**). 1. Bring into disrepute, expose hollowness of (theory, belief, etc.). 2. (Cause to) go off with loud noise; (of gunpowder etc.) expand violently with loud report under influence of suddenly developed internal energy; (of shell, etc.) burst from similar cause; (of boiler etc.) burst from excessive pressure of steam inside it. 3. Give vent suddenly to

Above right: Miners ***explode*** *copper deposits at Bougainville Island so that the ore can be easily removed. Right: An explosion during a military exercise.*

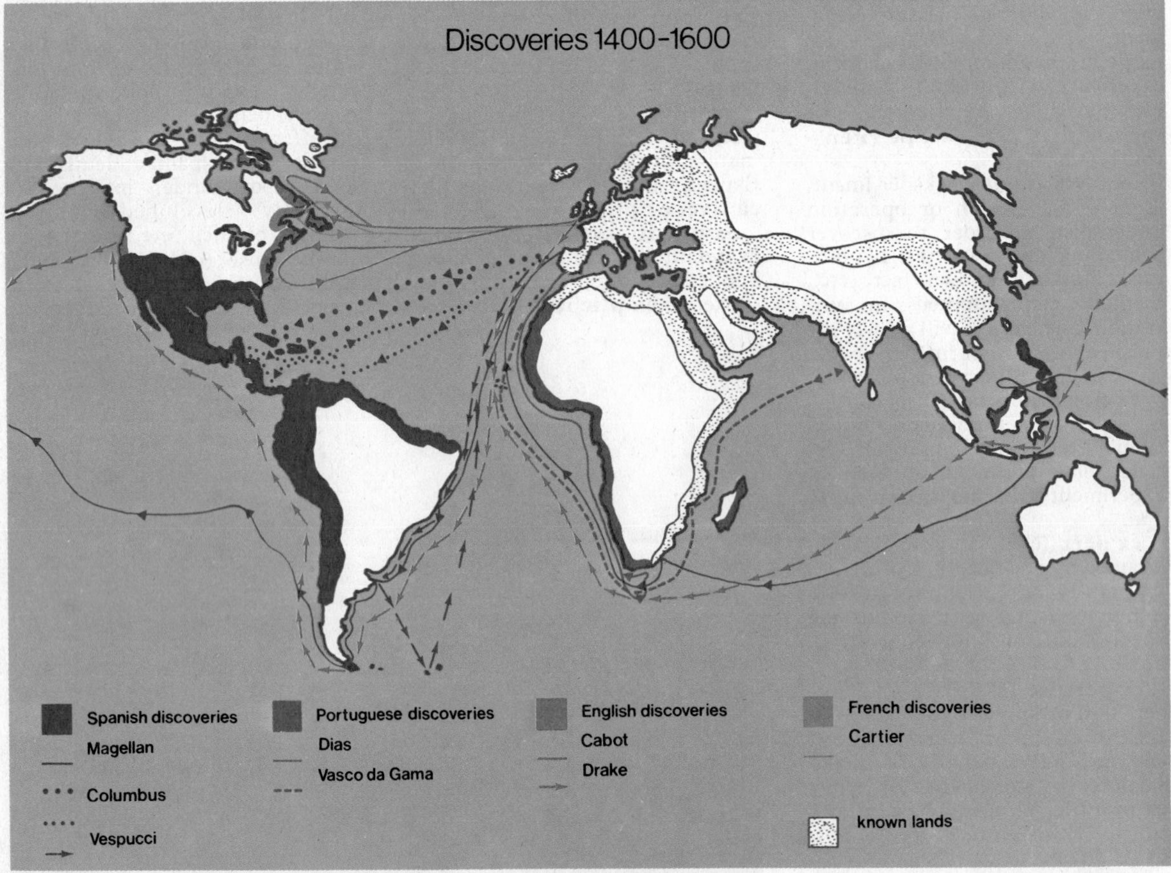

emotion. 4. (of population etc.) Increase suddenly or rapidly.

ex·plod·ed (ĭksplō′dĭd) *adj.* (esp., of diagram etc.) Showing components of a machine etc. separately but retaining their relative positions (as in ~ **view**).

ex·ploit[1] (ĕk′sploit, ĭksploit′) *n.* Heroic or spectacular feat.

ex·ploit[2] (ĭksploit′) *v.t.* Work, turn to account (mine etc.); make use of (person etc.), esp. unfairly or selfishly. **ex·ploit′a·ble** *adj.* **ex·ploi·ta·tion** (ĕksploitā′shon) *n.*

ex·plore (ĭksplōr′, -splōr′-) *v.t.* (**-plored, -plor·ing**). 1. Investigate (condition, fact); examine, pry into; probe, examine by touch (wound etc.). 2. Search into, examine region, place, etc. by going through it; go into, range over, for purpose of discovery. **ex·plo·ra·tion** (ĕksplorā′shon), **ex·plor′er** *ns.* **ex·plor′a·tive, ex·plor′a·to·ry** *adjs.*

ex·plo·sion (ĭksplō′zhon) *n.* Exploding; resulting noise, detonation; sudden marked increase, esp. **population** ~; outburst (of anger etc.).

ex·plo·sive (ĭksplō′sĭv) *adj.* Tending to drive something forth with violence and noise; tending to explode or cause explosion; of, like, explosion; (of consonant) produced by explosion of breath, stopped. **ex·plo′sive·ly** *adv.* **ex·plo′sive·ness** *n.* **explosive** *n.* 1. Explosive

Map of routes of ***exploration.*** *The motives for exploration include economic necessity and pure curiosity, personal ambition and the desire of a country for expansion. It is from Europe that the history of exploration emanates, for it was Europeans who stretched the world map consistently by sea and land.*

agent or compound; **high** ~, kind having violent and shattering effect and used not as propellant but in shells, bombs, etc. 2. Explosive consonant.

ex·po·nent (ĭkspō′nent; for def. 2 also ĕk′spōnent) *n.* 1. Person or thing that sets forth or interprets; type, representative. 2. (alg.) Index; symbol denoting number of times particular quantity is to be taken as factor to produce the power indicated. **ex·po·nen·tial** (ĕkspōnĕn′shal) *adj.* (esp., math.) Involving the unknown quantity as (part of) an exponent. ~ *n.* Exponential quantity or function.

ex·port (ĭkspōrt′, -spōrt′, ĕk′spōrt, -spōrt) *v.t.* Send out (goods) to another country. **ex·port′a·ble** *adj.* **ex·por·ta·tion** (ĕkspōrtā′shon, -spōr-) *n.* **export** (ĕk′spōrt, -spōrt) *n.* Exported article; (usu. pl.) (amount exported; exportation.

ex·pose (ĭkspōz′) *v.t.* (**-posed, -pos·ing**). 1. Leave, place, in unsheltered or unprotected position; (fig.) lay open, subject (*to* risk etc.). 2. Exhibit, display; disclose (secret, project, etc.); unmask, show up (fault, guilty person, etc.). 3. (photog.) Subject (sensitized surface of film etc.) to action of actinic rays.

ex·po·sé (ĕkspōzā′) *n.* Statement of facts; showing up (of discreditable thing). [Fr.]

ex·po·si·tion (ĕkspozĭsh′on) *n.* 1. Exposure; exhibition. 2. Setting forth, description; explanation; commentary. 3. (mus.) Presentation of principal theme(s).

ex·pos·i·tor·y (ĭkspŏz′ĭtōrē, -tōrē) *adj.* Descriptive; explanatory.

ex post fac·to (ĕks′ pōst făk′tō). Acting retrospectively or retroactively. [L., = "from what is made (i.e. enacted) afterward"]

ex·pos·tu·late (ĭkspŏs′chulāt) *v.i.* (**-lat·ed, -lat·ing**). Reason earnestly against something; make (esp. friendly) remonstrance. **ex·pos·tu·la·tion** (ĭkspŏschulā′shon) *n.* **ex·pos′tu·la·to·ry** *adj.*

ex·po·sure (ĭkspō′zher) *n.* 1. Exposing, being exposed; (time taken in) exposing of photographic film etc.; area of film exposed for a single photograph. 2. (of building etc.) Aspect. 3. Frequent public appearance, as on television. 4. Condition of being exposed in helpless state to natural elements; **indecent** ~, intentional act of publicly and indecently exposing one's body; ~ **meter**, photo-

electric device indicating correct length of time for film etc. to be exposed.

ex·pound (ĭkspownd′) *v.t.* Set forth in detail (doctrine etc.); explain, interpret.

ex·press[1] (ĭksprĕs′) *adj.* 1. (of likeness) Exact; definitely stated, not merely implied. 2. Done, made, sent, for special purpose; ~ **highway**, major highway of four or more traffic lanes with limited access and no or very few crossroads, traffic lights, etc., esp. for high-speed travel over long distances; ~ **train**, fast train stopping only at a few important stations (orig., train run expressly to convey

*'Madonna', a lithograph by Edvard Munch (1863–1944). Munch was a leading exponent of **Expressionism,** a movement in art which set out to express human emotions rather than to portray the physical world.*

passengers to a particular place); so ~ **bus** etc. 3. (to be delivered) By fastest means (so ~ **letter, air** ~, etc.). **ex·press′ly** *adv.* **express** *adv.* With speed; by express messenger, train, etc. **express** *n.* Express train or bus etc.; company for transporting packages etc.; ~ **agent**, agent of express company. **express** *v.t.* Send by express (delivery).

ex·press[2] (ĭksprĕs′) *v.t.* 1. Press, squeeze, or wring out; emit, exude, as if by pressure. 2. Represent by drawing etc. or by figures or other symbols; represent in language, put into words; (*refl.*) put one's thought into words; manifest, reveal, communicate (feelings, personal qualities, etc.).

ex·pres·sion (ĭksprĕsh′on) *n.* Expressing; wording, diction, word, phrase; (alg.) collection of symbols together expressing algebraical quantity; expressive quality; aspect (of face), intonation (of voice), etc.; manner of musical performance suited to bringing out feeling of passage; (painting etc.)

mode of expressing character. **ex·pres′sion·less** *adj.* Lacking expression; impassive.

ex·pres·sion·ism (ikspre̊sh′*on*ĭzem) *n.* (freq. cap.) Movement in art, literature, and music in late 19th and early 20th centuries seeking to express emotional experience rather than impressions of the physical world. **ex·pres′sion·ist** *adj.* & *n.* **ex·pres·sion·is·tic** (ĭksprĕsh*o*nĭs′tĭk) *adj.* **ex·pres·sion·is′ti·cal·ly** *adv.*

ex·pres·sive (ĭksprĕs′ĭv) *adj.* Of expression, serving to express; full of, emphatic in, expression; significant. **ex·pres′sive·ly** *adv.* **ex·pres′sive·ness** *n.*

ex·press·way (ĭksprĕs′wā) *n.* Express highway; see EXPRESS[1].

ex·pro·pri·ate (ĕksprō′prēāt) *v.t.* (**-at·ed, -at·ing**). Deprive of, take away (property), esp. for public use; take and use (another's work, idea, etc.) as one's own. **ex·pro·pri·a·tion** (ĕksprōprēā′sh*o*n) *n.*

ex·pul·sion (ĭkspŭl′sh*o*n) *n.* Expelling.

ex·punge (ĭkspŭnj′) *v.t.* (**-punged, -pung·ing**). Erase, omit, strike out.

ex·pur·gate (ĕk′sp*e*rgāt) *v.t.* (**-gated, -gat·ing**). Purify (book etc.) by removing objectionable matter; clear away (such matter). **ex·pur·ga·tion** (ĕksp*e*rgā′sh*o*n), **ex′pur·ga·tor** *ns.*

ex·qui·site (ĕkskwĭz′ĭt, ĕk′skwĭzĭt) *adj.* Of consummate excellence or beauty; acute; keen. **ex·qui′site·ly** *adv.* **ex·qui′site·ness** *n.*

ext. *abbrev.* Extension; external; extra; extract.

ex·tant (ĕk′st*a*nt, ĭkstănt′) *adj.* Still existing (esp. of documents etc.).

ex·tem·po·re (ĭkstĕm′p*e*rē) *adv.* & *adj.* (Spoken, done) without preparation; offhand. **ex·tem·po·ra·ne·ous** (ĭkstĕmp*e*rā′nē*u*s) *adj.* **ex·tem·po·ra′ne·ous·ly** *adv.* **ex·tem·po·rar·y** (ĭkstĕm′p*e*rĕrē) *adj.*

ex·tem·po·rize (ĭkstĕm′p*e*rīz) *v.* (**-rized, -riz·ing**). Compose, produce, speak extemporaneously. **ex·tem·po·ri·za·tion** (ĭkstĕmp*e*rĭzā′sh*o*n) *n.*

ex·tend (ĭkstĕnd′) *v.* 1. Place (esp. body, limbs, etc.) at full length. 2. Reach, cause to reach (*to* point, *over, across,* etc., space). 3. Prolong (period); enlarge (scope, meaning, of word, etc.). 4. (mil.) Spread out, cause (line etc.) to spread out, into open order with regular intervals between men. 5. Tax powers of (horse, athlete, etc.) to the utmost. 6. Stretch forth (hand, arm); accord (kindness, patronage, *to*). 7. (law) Seize (land etc.) for debt. **ex·tend′ed** *adj.* ~ **care**, nursing care given at home or in nursing homes to persons unable to care for themselves; ~ **family**, family unit consisting of parents, children, and other near relatives, all living in close proximity. **ex·tend′i·ble, ex·tend′a·ble, ex·ten′si·ble** *adjs.* **ex·tend·i·bil·i·ty** (ĭkstĕndĭbĭl′ĭtē), **ex·tend′er** *ns.*

ex·ten·sile (ĭkstĕn′sĭl, -sīl) *adj.* Capable of being stretched out or protruded.

ex·ten·sion (ĭkstĕn′sh*o*n) *n.* Extending; extent, range; prolongation, enlargement; additional part, building, line, etc. (of railroad, plan, theory, etc.); subsidiary telephone; (**university**) ~ **course**, one offered away from the campus.

ex·ten·sive (ĭkstĕn′sĭv) *adj.* Large; far-reaching, comprehensive; (of agricultural production) cultivating vast areas with a minimum of labor and expense. **ex·ten′sive·ly** *adv.* **ex·ten′sive·ness** *n.*

ex·ten·sor (ĭkstĕn′s*e*r, -sōr) *n.* Muscle serving to extend or straighten out any part of body (opp. FLEXOR).

ex·tent (ĭkstĕnt′) *n.* 1. Space over which thing extends; width of application, scope. 2. (law) Writ for creditor's temporary seizure, (of lands etc.).

ex·ten·u·ate (ĭkstĕn′ūāt) *v.t.* (**-at·ed, -at·ing**). Lessen seeming magnitude of (guilt, offense) by partial excuse, as in **extenuating circumstances. ex·ten·u·a·tion** (ĭkstĕnūā′sh*o*n) *n.*

ex·te·ri·or (ĭkstēr′ē*e*r) *adj.* Outer, situated or coming from without; ~ **angle**, that between any side of a polygon and adjacent side produced. **ex·te′ri·or·ly** *adv.* **exterior** *n.* Outward aspect or demeanor; (film) outdoor scene.

ex·ter·mi·nate (ĭkstēr′m*i*nāt) *v.t.* (**-nat·ed, -nat·ing**). Destroy utterly, root out (species, race, etc.). **ex·ter·mi·na·tion** (ĭkstērmĭnā′sh*o*n), **ex·ter′mi·na·tor** *ns.*

ex·tern (ĕk′stērn) *n.* Person having some association with an institution but not living in it, esp. a nonresident physician in a hospital.

ex·ter·nal (ĭkstēr′n*a*l) *adj.* Situated outside; (of remedies etc.) applied to outside of body; consisting in outward acts or appearances; belonging to external world of things or phenomena, considered as outside the perceiving mind; arising, acting, from without, connected with, referring to, what is outside; ~ **evidence**, evidence derived from source independent of the thing discussed. **ex·ter·nal·i·ty** (ĕkstērnăl′ĭtē) *n.* (pl. **-ties**). **ex·ter′nal·ly** *adv.* **ex·ter′nals** *n.pl.* Outward features or aspect; external circumstances; nonessentials.

ex·ter·nal·ize (ĭkstēr′n*a*līz) *v.t.* (**-ized, -iz·ing**). Give, attribute, external existence to. **ex·ter·nal·i·za·tion** (ĭkstērn*a*lĭzā′sh*o*n) *n.*

ex·tinct (ĭkstĭngkt′) *adj.* (of fire etc.) No longer burning; (of volcano) that has ceased eruption; (of life, hope, etc.) quenched; (of family, class, species) that has died out.

ex·tinc·tion (ĭkstĭngk′sh*o*n) *n.* Extinguishing; making, being, becoming, extinct. **ex·tinc′tive** *adj.*

ex·tin·guish (ĭkstĭng′gwĭsh) *v.t.* Put out, quench (light, hope, life, etc.); eclipse, obscure (person) by superior brilliance.; wipe out (debt). **ex·tin′guish·a·ble** *adj.*

ex·tin·guish·er (ĭkstĭng′gwĭsh*e*r) *n.* (esp.) Hollow conical cap for

After the hard work of training, and the tensions of competition, the winner has the right to ***exult*** *and be jubilant. Below, an exultant marathon runner (Robert de Castella) holds up his medal.*

extinguishing light of candle etc.; FIRE extinguisher.

ex·tir·pate (ĕk′sterpāt, ĭkstėr′-) *v.t.* (**-pat·ed, -pat·ing**). Root out, destroy. **ex·tir·pa·tion** (ĕksterpā′shon), **ex′tir·pa·tor** *ns.*

ex·tol, ex·toll (ĭkstōl′) *vbs.t.* (**-tolled, -tol·ling**). Praise enthusiastically. **ex·tol′ler** *n.*

ex·tort (ĭkstort′) *v.t.* Obtain (money, promise, etc.) by violence, intimidation, abuse, etc. (*from*).

ex·tor·tion (ĭkstor′shon) *n.* Extorting, esp. of money; illegal exaction. **ex·tor·tion·ate** (ĭkstor′shonĭt) *adj.* Using, given to, extortion; (of prices etc.) exorbitant. **ex·tor′tion·ist** *n.*

ex·tra (ĕk′stra) *adj.* Additional; larger than its name indicates; beyond what is anticipated; of superior quality. ~ *adv.* More than usually; additionally. ~ *n.* Extra thing, one for which extra charge is made; special or additional issue of newspaper; (film) actor hired to play a very minor part, as in crowd scene.

extra- *prefix.* Situated outside of a thing, not coming within its scope.

ex·tract (ĕk′străkt) *n.* 1. (chem.) Preparation containing active principle of substance in concentrated form obtained by treatment with a solvent (usu. followed by evaporation of solvent). 2. Passage copied from book etc., excerpt, quotation. ~ (ĭksträkt′) *v.t.* 1. Copy out (passage in book etc.); make extracts from (book etc.) 2. Take out by force (tooth, anything firmly fixed); draw forth (money, admission, etc.) against person's will. 3. Obtain (juices etc.) by suction, pressure, distillation, etc.; derive (pleasure etc. *from*); deduce (principle etc. *from*). 4. (math.) Find (root of a number). **ex·trac′tive** *adj.* & *n.* **ex·trac′tor** *n.*

ex·trac·tion (ĭksträk′shon) *n.* 1. Extracting. 2. Lineage; origin; descent, as *of Indian* ~.

ex·tra·cur·ric·u·lar (ĕkstrakurĭk′yuler) *adj.* Not included in the curriculum.

ex·tra·dite (ĕk′stradīt) *v.t.* (**-dit·ed, -dit·ing**). Give up (fugitive, criminal) to the proper authorities in another jurisdiction (state or country).

ex·tra·di·tion (ĕkstradĭsh′on) *n.* Delivery of fugitive or criminal to authorities of country, state, etc. in which crime was committed.

ex·tra·ga·lac·tic (ĕkstragalăk′tĭk) *adj.* Situated outside the galaxy.

ex·tra·ju·di·cial (ĕkstrajoo͞dĭsh′al) *adj.* Not belonging to the case before the court; (of opinion, confession, etc.) not made in court; outside ordinary course of law or justice. **ex·tra·ju·di′cial·ly** *adv.*

ex·tra·le·gal (ĕkstralē′gal) *adj.* Beyond legal authority; unregulated by law.

ex·tra·mar·i·tal (ĕkstramăr′ĭtal) *adj.* (of a sexual relationship) Outside marriage, adulterous.

ex·tra·mu·ral (ĕkstramūr′al) *adj.* Outside the walls or boundaries of a school, city, etc.

ex·tra·ne·ous (ĭkstrā′nēus) *adj.* Of external origin; foreign *to* (object to which it is attached etc.); not belonging (*to* matter in hand, class); unessential; irrelevant. **ex·tra′ne·ous·ly** *adv.* **ex·tra′ne·ous·ness** *n.*

ex·traor·di·nary (ĭkstror′dinĕrē, ĕkstraor′-) *adj.* Out of the usual course; exceptional, surprising; unusually great; (of officials etc.) additional, specially employed. **ex·traor·di·nar′i·ly** *adv.*

ex·trap·o·late (ĭksträp′olāt) *v.* (**-lat·ed, -lat·ing**). (math.) Calculate, from known terms, a series of other terms that lie outside the range of the known terms (also fig.). **ex·trap·o·la·tion** (ĭksträpolā′shon) *n.*

ex·tra·sen·so·ry (ĕkstrasĕn′serē) *adj.* (of perception) Made otherwise than by the known sense organs.

ex·tra·ter·res·tri·al (ĕkstraterĕs′trēal) *adj.* (Originating) outside the Earth or its atmosphere.

ex·tra·ter·ri·to·ri·al (ĕkstratĕrĭtōr′ēal, -tor′-) *adj.* Located outside of territorial boundaries; of the privilege extended to ambassadors of being regarded as outside the territory, and therefore free from the jurisdiction, of the power to which they are sent; of a country's rights of jurisdiction over all its subjects abroad. **ex·tra·ter·ri·to·ri·al·i·ty** (ĕkstratĕrĭtōrēăl′ĭtē, -tor-) *n.*

ex·trav·a·gance (ĭksträv′agans) *n.* Being extravagant; absurd statement or action; unreasonably costly item.

ex·trav·a·gant (ĭksträv′agant) *adj.* Immoderate; exceeding the bounds of reason; profuse, wasteful; (of price etc.) exorbitant. **ex·trav′a·gant·ly** *adv.*

ex·trav·a·gan·za (ĭksträvagăn′za) *n.* Extravagant or fantastic entertainment.

ex·tra·ve·hic·u·lar (ĕkstravēhĭk′yuler) *adj.* Outside a vehicle, esp. (also ~ **activity**) of an astronaut's activity (exploration, repair, etc.) conducted outside a space vehicle while in flight.

ex·tra·vert (ĕk′stravert) *n.* Var. of EXTROVERT.

ex·treme (ĭkstrēm′) *adj.* (**-trem·er, -trem·est**). 1. Outermost; farthest from center; situated at either end. 2. Utmost. 3. ~ **unction**, (R.C. Ch.) sacrament in which a priest anoints and prays for the recovery and salvation of a person who is critically ill or injured. 4. (of actions, measures, etc.) Severe, stringent; (of opinions, persons, etc.) going to great lengths, not moderate. **ex·treme′ly** *adv.* **ex·treme′ness** *n.* **extreme** *n.* 1. **in the** ~, extremely. 2. Thing at either end of anything; esp. (pl.) things as remote or as different as possible; excessive degree. 3. (logic) Major or minor term in syllogism; (math.) first or last term of ratio or series.

ex·treme·ly (ĭkstrēm′lē) **high frequency.** Any radio frequency in the highest range, between 30,000 and 300,000 megahertz.

ex·trem·ist (ĭkstrē′mĭst) *n.* One who holds extreme views or advocates extreme measures. **ex·trem′ism** *n.*

ex·trem·i·ty (ĭkstrĕm′ĭtē) *n.* (pl. **-ties**). 1. Extreme point; very end; (pl.) hands and feet. 2. Extreme adversity, embarrassment, etc.; (usu. pl.) extreme measure(s).

ex·tri·cate (ĕk′strĭkāt) *v.t.* (**-cat·ed, -cat·ing**). Disentangle, release (*from* confinement, difficulty, etc.). **ex·tri·ca·ble** (ĕk′strĭkabel, ĭkstrĭk′-) *adj.* **ex·tri·ca·tion** (ĕkstrĭkā′shon) *n.*

ex·trin·sic (ĭkstrĭn′zĭk, -sĭk) *adj.* Lying outside, not belonging, (*to*); operating from without; not inherent or essential. **ex·trin′si·cal·ly** *adv.*

ex·tro·vert (ĕk′strovert, -strō-) *n.* (psychol.) One whose thoughts and activities are directed to things outside the self (opp. INTROVERT). **ex·tro·ver·sion** (ĕkstrōver′zhon, -shon, ĕk′strōver-, -stro-) *n.* **ex·tro·ver′sive** *adj.*

ex·trude (ĭkstroo͞d′) *v.* (**-trud·ed, -trud·ing**). 1. Thrust out (*from*). 2. Shape (metal, plastics, etc.) by forcing through die. 3. Protrude. **ex·trus′ive** *adj.* 1. Tending to extrude. 2. (geol.) Forced out as molten matter through the Earth's crust. **ex·tru·sion** (ĭkstroo͞′zhon) *n.*

ex·u·ber·ant (ĭgzoo͞′berant) *adj.* Luxuriant, prolific; effusive; copious; full of high spirits or joyous abandon. **ex·u′ber·ant·ly** *adv.* **ex·u′ber·ance** *n.*

ex·ude (ĭgzoo͞d′) *v.* (**-ud·ed, -ud·ing**). Ooze out, give off (moisture etc.) like sweat. **ex·u·da·tive** (ĭgzoo͞′datĭv, ĕk′sūdā-) *adj.* **ex·u·da·tion** (ĕksūdā′shon, ĕksu-, ĕgzu-), **ex·u·date** (ĕk′sūdāt, -su-, ĕg′zu-) *ns.*

ex·ult (ĭgzŭlt′) *v.i.* Rejoice exceedingly; triumph (*over*). **ex·ul·ta·tion** (ĕgzŭltā′shon, ĕksŭl-) *n.* **ex·ult′ant** *adj.* **ex·ult′ant·ly** *adv.*

ex·urb (ĕk′serb, ĕg′zerb) *n.* Community outside city or town, esp. prosperous and fashionable area beyond suburbs.

ex·ur·ban·ite (ĕkser′banīt, ĕgzer′-) *n.* Person who lives in an exurb.

ex·ur·bi·a (ĕkser′bēa, ĕgzer′-) *n.*

Exurbs collectively, region beyond suburbs.

eye (ī) *n.* 1. Organ of sight; iris of this; region of the eyes; eye as possessing power of vision; sense of seeing; look, glance, gaze; attention, regard; estimation, opinion, judgment; **have an ~ for**, be capable of perceiving or appreciating; **in the ~ of**, in the direction of (the wind); **keep an ~ on**, direct one's attention (lit. or fig.) to; **make ~s at**, look amorously at, ogle; **see ~ to ~**, agree entirely (*with*); **set ~s on**, catch sight of; **with an ~ to**, with a view to. 2. Thing like eye; spot on peacock's tail, wing of insect etc.; one of three spots at end of coconut; hole in needle for thread etc., hole in tool or implement for insertion of some other object; metal loop used with hook for fastening dress etc.; loop of cord or rope; undeveloped bud of plant; center of flower; leafbud of potato etc. 3. **eye'ball**, eye within lids and socket; **eye'bolt**, bolt, bar, with circular hole through head; **eye'brow**, fringe of hair along upper orbit of eye; **eye catcher**, (colloq.) something that particularly attracts one's attention; **eye'dropper**, dropper for administering medicines to the eye; **eye'ful**, (slang) remarkable or attractive sight, esp. attractive woman; **eye'glass**, lens for assisting defective sight; monocle; (pl.) pair of these lenses worn in frame that passes over nose and over or around the ears; **eye'hole**, cavity or socket of eye; hole to look through; **eye'lash**, hair, row of hairs, on edge of eyelid; **eye'lid**, one of movable folds of skin with which eyes are covered or uncovered; **eye'liner**, cosmetic applied as line around eye; **eye'opener**, enlightening or surprising circumstance etc.; alcoholic drink, esp. in morning; **eye'piece**, lens(es) at eye end of telescope etc.; **eye'shade**, device to protect eyes from strong light; **eye shadow**, cosmetic applied to eyelids or around the eyes; **eye'sight**, power, faculty, of seeing; **eye'sore**, ugly object, thing that offends the sight; **eye'strain**, weariness of eyes from excessive or incorrect use; **eye'tooth**, pointed tooth just under eye, in upper or lower jaw, upper canine tooth; **eye'wash**, lotion for eye; (slang) humbug, blarney; **eye'witness**, one who can bear witness from his own observation. **eye** *v.t.* (**eyed, ey·ing**). Observe, watch.

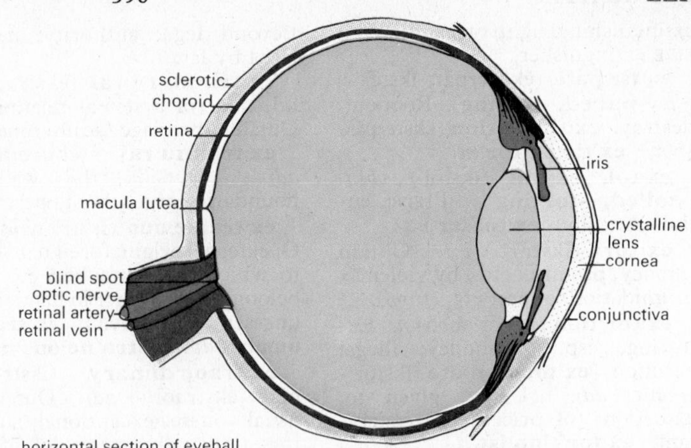

*In order to see properly, not only a functioning **eye** is required but an intact nervous system to convey the impulses from the eye to the right part of the brain for interpretation.*

eye·let (ī'lĭt) *n.* Small hole in cloth, sail, etc., for lace, ring, rope, etc.; loophole; small eye.

ey·rie, ey·ry (ār'ē, ēr'ē, īr'ē) *ns.* (pl. **-ries**). Var. of AERIE.

E·ze·ki·el (ĭzē'kēel, -kyel). Hebrew major prophet of 6th c. B.C.; book of Old Testament containing his prophecies.

Ez·ra (ĕz'ra). Hebrew scribe and priest of 5th c. B.C.; book of Old Testament dealing with the return of the Jews from Babylon and the rebuilding of the Temple.

*In Zaire, an African fishing-eagle nests in his remote **eyrie.** Eagle species build their large nests of twigs at high altitudes on ledges of mountains or cliffs.*

*Model Jane Seeney shows how important the **eyes** are to appearance, and how **eye shadow** can enhance their effect on the viewer, creating a stunning impression.*

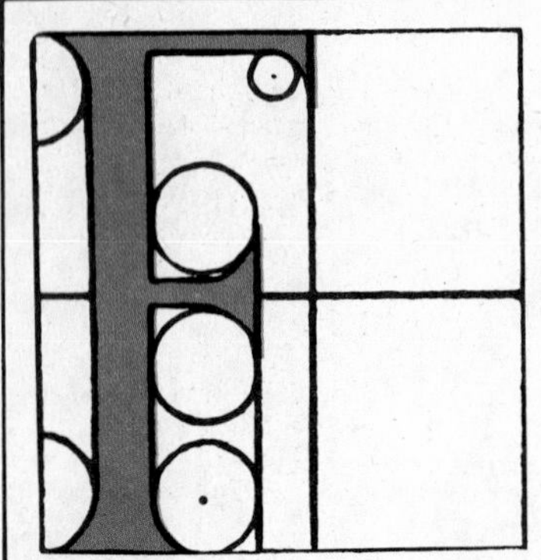

*The illustrations show how the written forms of the letter **F, f** have developed through the ages. It is the 6th letter of the Modern English and ancient Roman alphabet. In the earliest Latin, the two letters w h were used to signify the f sound. The elongated small f probably first came into use when early scribes, writing at speed, joined it to the preceding and following letters.*

Phoenician Early Greek Early Etruscan

Classical Latin Anglo-Saxon Italian (italic)

F, f (ĕf) (pl. **F's, f's** or **Fs, fs**). 1. Sixth letter of modern English and ancient Roman alphabet, representing Semitic *waw* (= *w, u*) and preclassical Greek digamma (*F*) and pronounced in English as a voiceless labiodental spirant. 2. **F,** (mus.) fourth note of natural scale (C major); scale or key with this note for tonic. 3. **F-layer**, highest stratum of the ionosphere, approximately 120–250 mi. (190–400 km) above the Earth.

F *abbrev.* Fahrenheit; farad(s).

f *abbrev.* (photog.) Focal length (used with numbers to indicate ratio of focal length of lens to diameter of stop); frequency; farad; (music) forte.

f. *abbrev.* Feminine, female; farad; following; foot; folio; (music) forte; franc(s); from.

FAA *abbrev.* Federal Aviation Agency.

Fa·bi·an (fā'bēan) *adj.* 1. Of, like, Quintus Fabius Maximus (d. 203 B.C.), Roman general who harassed Hannibal in the second Punic War by avoiding major battles while weakening the enemy by cutting off supplies; hence, cautious in strategy, avoiding direct confrontation. 2. Of the ~ **Society**, society of English socialists advocating Fabian policy rather than immediate revolutionary action, founded 1884. **Fabian** *n.* Member of the Fabian Society. **Fa'bi·an·ism** *n.*

fa·ble (fā'bel) *n.* 1. Story, esp. of supernatural character, not founded on fact; (collect.) myths, legendary tales. 2. Short story, esp. with animals for characters, conveying a moral. ~ *v.* (**-bled, -bling**). (archaic and poet.) Tell fictitious tales; state fictitiously; **fabled** *adj.* celebrated in fable, fictitious; unreal.

fab·ric (făb'rĭk) *n.* Thing put together; edifice, building; frame, structure; construction, texture, tissue; woven material.

fab·ri·cate (făb'rĭkāt) *v.t.* (**-cat·ed, -cat·ing**). 1. Construct, manufacture, esp. by joining components together. 2. Invent (fact), forge (document). **fab·ri·ca·tion** (făbrĭkā'shon), **fab'ri·ca·tor** *ns.*

fab·u·list (făb'yulĭst) *n.* Composer of fables; liar.

fab·u·lous (făb'yulus) *adj.* Celebrated in fable; incredible; (colloq.) wonderful. **fab'u·lous·ly** *adv.* **fab'u·lous·ness** *n.*

fac. *abbrev.* Facsimile; faculty; factory.

fa·çade, fa·cade (fasahd', fă-)

*The origins of fable are lost in the mists of time. Aesop's **fable** of the 'Fox and the Grapes', depicted here on an 18th century French tapestry, was one of those included in the 'Fables' of La Fontaine.*

ns. Face of building, esp. the principal front; hence, frontal appearance of anything (also fig.).

face (fās) *n.* 1. Front of head from forehead to chin; ~ **to** ~, confronted; ~ **to** ~ **with**, confronting; **fly in the** ~ **of**, openly disobey. 2. Expression of countenance; grimace. 3. Composure, coolness, effrontery. 4. Outward show; aspect; surface; front, facade; right side, obverse; dial of clock etc.; working surface of implement etc.; each surface of solid; (also **type** ~) part of type or plate that takes the ink; style or design of this; **lose** ~, be humiliated; lose one's good name; **on the** ~ **of it**, to judge by appearance; obviously, plainly; **put a new** ~ **on**, alter aspect of; **save** ~, save one's good name. 5. ~ **card**, one of a pack of playing cards on which a human face is represented; the king, queen, or knave; **face'cloth**, cloth for washing the face; **face-lift**, face lifting; (fig.) improvement in appearance; **face lifting**, operation for tightening the skin of the face to remove wrinkles etc.; **face-saving**, serving to keep one from being humiliated; **face value**, nominal value as stated on coin, note, etc.; (fig.) apparent value. **face** *v.* (**faced, fac·ing**). 1. Meet confidently or defiantly; not shrink from, stand fronting; ~ **the music**, not quail at moment of trial or punishment. 2. Present itself to; look, have face or front, in special direction; front toward, be opposite to; (mil.) turn in special direction. 3. Cover part of (garment) with another material, esp. at edge, trim, turn up *with*; cover (surface) with layer of other material; dress surface of. 4. (ice hockey etc.) Start play by dropping (puck, etc.) between sticks of two opposing players (also ~ **off**). **faced** *adj.*

face·less (fās'lĭs) *adj.* (esp.) Anonymous, characterless, without identity. **face'less·ness** *n.*

fac·et (făs'ĭt) *n.* One side of many-sided body, esp. of cut gem; one segment of compound eye. ~ *v.t.* (**-et·ed, -et·ing**, Brit. **-et·ted, -et·ting**). Cut facets on.

The magnificent Gothic ***façade*** *of Orvieto cathedral in Italy shows the pointed arches, stone lace-work and stained-glass windows characteristic of the Gothic style. The cathedral was begun in 1290 A.D.*

fa·ce·tious (fasē′sh*u*s) *adj.* Joking, esp. in forced or trivial way. **fa·ce′tious·ly** *adv.* **fa·ce′tious·ness** *n.*

fa·cial (fā′sh*a*l) *adj.* Of the face. ~ *n.* Beauty treatment for the face, often including a facial massage.

fac·ile (făs′īl; *Brit.* also făs′īl) *adj.* Easily done or won; working easily, ready, fluent; of easy temper, flexible. **fac′ile·ly** *adv.*

fa·cil·i·tate (fasĭl′ĭtāt) *v.t.* (**-tat·ed, -tat·ing**). Make easy, promote, help forward (action or result). **fa·cil·i·ta·tion** (f*a*sĭlĭtā′sh*o*n) *n.*

fa·cil·i·ty (f*a*sĭl′ĭtē) *n.* (pl. **-ties**). Being easy, absence of difficulty; unimpeded opportunity; ease or readiness of speech etc.; pliancy; (slang) toilet; (pl.) amenities, services.

fac·ing (fā′sĭng) *n.* (esp.) Something with which garment is faced, as cuffs and collar of jacket; coating of different material, esp. of stone etc., on wall.

fac·sim·i·le (făksĭm′*i*lē) *n.* Exact copy, esp. of writing, printing, picture, etc. ~ *v.t.* (**-led, -le·ing**). Make facsimile of.

fact (făkt) *n.* 1. Thing certainly known to have occurred or be true; datum of experience; thing assumed as basis for inference; what is true or existent; reality; **~s of life,** (colloq.) facts of sex and reproduction. 2. Evil deed, crime (in **before, after, the** ~). **fact′ful** *adj.*

fac·tion (făk′sh*o*n) *n.* Self-interested, turbulent, or unscrupulous party, esp. in politics; minority group within a larger group. **fac′tion·al, fac′tious** *adjs.* **fac′tious·ly** *adv.* **fac′tious·ness** *n.*

fac·ti·tious (făktĭsh′*u*s) *adj.* Produced artificially; contrived; not natural. **fac·ti′tious·ly** *adv.* **fac·ti′tious·ness** *n.*

fac·tor (făk′t*er*) *n.* 1. Agent; firm, person granting short-term business loans accepting accounts receivable as security. 2. (math.) One of two or more numbers etc. that, when multiplied together, give a given number, expression, etc. 3. Circumstance, fact, influence, contributing to result. 4. (biol.) Gene or other agent transmitted from parent to offspring and influencing or determining a hereditary character. ~ *v.t.* Resolve into factors or components.

fac·to·ri·al (făktōr′ē*a*l, -tōr′ē-)

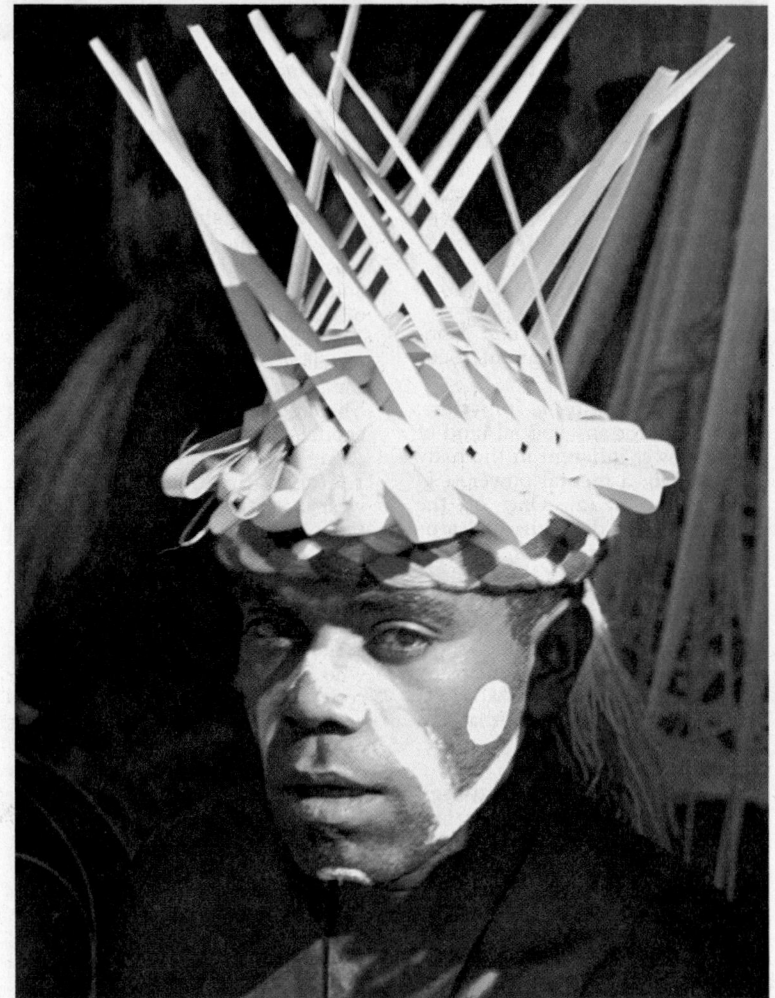

The Melanesian tribal dancer in New Caledonia, W. Pacific, has a traditional pattern painted on his ***face.*** *Decoration or masking of the face is customary in tribal ritual throughout the world.*

adj. Of a factor or a factorial. ~ *n.* (math.) Product of series of factors in arithmetical progression; product of integer multiplied by all lower integers.

fac·to·ry (făk′terē, -trē) *n.* (pl. **-ries**). Building or group of buildings with equipment for manufacturing goods.

fac·to·tum (făktō′tum) *n.* Man of all work.

fac·tu·al (făk′chōōal) *adj.* Concerned with, of the nature of, facts. **fac′tu·al·ly** *adv.*

fac·ul·ty (făk′ultē) *n.* (pl. **-ties**). 1. Aptitude for any special kind of action; power inherent in the body or an organ; a mental power (e.g. will, reason). 2. One of the departments or divisions of learning at a university or college; teaching staff of any of these; entire teaching staff of a school, body of teachers; members of a learned profession, esp. medicine. 3. Liberty to do something given by law or a superior; authorization.

fad (făd) *n.* Fashion that has wide but brief popularity, craze. **fad′dish** *adj.* **fad′dist** *n.*

fade (fād) *v.* (**fad·ed, fad·ing**). Droop, wither; (cause to) lose freshness or color; disappear gradually; (of sound) grow faint, die *away, out*; (of brake) gradually lose power; ~ **in, out, up**, gradually increase or decrease brightness, intensity, or distinctness of (motion picture, sound, etc.).

*The Krupp **factory** at Essen, West Germany, was the center of the German munitions industry from the late 19th century to the end of the 1939–45 war.*

fae·ces (fē′sēz) = FECES.

Fa·en·za (fahĕn′za). City in N. Italy, 19 mi. (30.5 km), SW. of Ravenna; gained renown in 15th and 16th centuries for production of ceramic Faenza ware or faïence.

Faer·oe (fār′ō) **Islands.** Group of self-governing Danish islands in the N. Atlantic between the Shetland Islands and Iceland; capital, Thorshaven.

fag (făg) *v.* (**fagged, fag·ging**). 1. (of occupation) Tire, make weary. 2. (in certain British boys' schools, of seniors) Require menial tasks of (juniors); (of juniors) do menial tasks for seniors. 3. (slang) Faggot. ~ *n.* 1. Drudgery; unwelcome task; exhaustion. 2. (in certain British boys' schools) Junior who has to fag. 3. (slang) Cigarette; ~ **end**, inferior or useless remnant of anything, esp. of cigar or cigarette; extreme end.

fag·got (făg′ot) *n.* (slang) Male homosexual (freq. **fag**).

Fa·gin (fā′gĭn). Corrupt old man who teaches young children to steal. [from a character in Dickens's *Oliver Twist*]

fag·ot (făg′ot) *n.* Bundle of sticks or twigs bound together as fuel; bundle of iron or steel rods bound together for reheating or welding. ~ *v.* Bind in fagot(s); make fagots.

Fahr·en·heit (făr′enhīt), **Gabriel Daniel** (1686–1736). Prussian physicist; popularized use of mercurial thermometer and devised temperature scale; hence as *adj.*, (abbreviated F, Fahr., Fah) according to the Fahrenheit scale; ~ **thermometer, scale**, etc., one with 32° and 212° as freezing and boiling points of water.

fa·ïence (fāahns′, fī-) *n.* Painted and glazed earthenware, majolica. [Fr., = *Faenza*, Italy, site of factory]

fail (fāl) *n.* **without** ~ (emphasizing injunction or promise), for certain, irrespective of hindrances. ~ *v.* 1. Be or become deficient; die away; flag, break down; disappoint hopes of, be of no help; **~-safe**, (of mechanism, nuclear devices, etc.) revert, in event of breakdown, to condition involving no danger. 2. Be wanting or deficient *in.* 3. Fall short in performance or attainment; not succeed (*in* doing, *to* do); come to nothing; become bankrupt; be rejected, reject, as candidate; be unsuccessful in (examination, course, etc.).

fail·ing (fā′lĭng) *n.* (esp.) Foible, shortcoming, weakness. ~ *prep.* In default of.

faille (fīl, fāl) *n.* Delicately ribbed cloth woven of silk, cotton, or rayon.

fail·ure (fāl′yer) *n.* Nonoccur-

***Fairs** have traditionally been held at established times and places for the exchange of goods. Top: Nowadays international exhibitions, such as the Brussels Fair of 1958, are often called fairs although no selling takes place. Above: Sideshows and amusements, such as the roundabout accompany the business of buying and selling at a fun fair.*

rence, nonperformance; running short; breaking down; ill success; insolvency; unsuccessful person, thing, or attempt.

fain (fān) *pred. adj.* (archaic) Willing, ready *to*; obliged *to*. ~ *adv.* Gladly, willingly (as in **would** ~).

faint (fānt) *adj.* 1. Sluggish; timid; feeble; dim, indistinct, pale. 2. Giddy or languid with fear, hunger, etc., inclined to faint; dizzy and weak; **faint′hearted**, timid, cowardly; **faint′heartedly** (*adv.*), **faint′heartedness** (*n.*) **faint′ly** *adv.* **faint′ness** *n.* **faint** *v.i.* 1. (archaic) Lose heart or courage, flag. 2. Lose consciousness. ~ *n.* Fainting fit.

fair[1] (fār) *n.* Periodical gathering for sale of goods, often with shows and entertainments, at fixed place and time; trade show; (also **country** ~) exhibition of farm products, farm animals, etc. in competition at **fair′ground.**

fair[2] (fār) *adj.* 1. Beautiful; pleasing at first sight or hearing. 2. (of complexion etc.) Light, not dark; ~**-haired**, blond; ~**-haired boy**, (colloq.) young man who is looked upon with favor by superior, or who tries to gain favor. 3. Free from blemish; clear, clean; just, equitable. 4. Of moderate quality; not bad, pretty good. 5. Favorable, promising; gentle; unobstructed; ~**-spoken**, speaking or spoken politely or in a convincing way. 6. ~ **ball**, (baseball) ball batted inside the foul lines; ~ **copy**, copy of document etc. made from corrected rough copy or after final correction; ~ **play**, equal conditions for all; ~ **shake**, (slang) honest or just treatment; equal chance; ~**-trade law**, federal or state law permitting manufacturer and retailer to set minimum prices on trademarked products; **the** ~ **sex**, women; **fair′way**, navigable channel, usual course of vessel(s); (golf) short-grassed part of course between tee and green; **fair-weather**, fit only for fine weather (freq. fig. of inconstant friends). **fair** *n.* What is fair. **fair′ish** *adj.* **fair′ness** *n.* **fair** *adv.* In a fair manner; **bid** ~ **to do**, show promise of doing.

Fair·banks (fār′băngks). Chief city of central Alaska at the junction of Tanana and Chena Rivers, 250 mi. (402 km) N. of Anchorage; northern terminus of railroad to Seward and Alaska Highway.

fair·ing (fār′ĭng) *n.* (eng.) Shielding around struts of aircraft, supports of bridge, etc., reducing resistance to air or water; streamlining.

fair·ly (fār′lē) *adv.* In a fair manner; utterly, completely; rather, tolerably.

Fair (fār) **Oaks.** Site of Civil War battle of 1862, also called "Seven Pines," 6 mi. E. of Richmond, Va.; Union troops led by George B. McClellan repulsed Confederate forces under Joseph E. Johnston.

fair·y (fār′ē) *n.* (pl. **fair·ies**). 1. Small supernatural being with magical powers; **fair′yland**, country of fairies, enchanted land of fancy; **fairy ring** (on grass), circular band of darker grass caused by fungi or a ring of mushrooms growing in grass, pop. attributed to fairy dancing; **fairy tale**, story about fairies; unreal or incredible story; falsehood. 2. (slang) Male homosexual. **fairy** *adj.* Of fairies; imaginary, fictitious; fairylike, beautiful and delicate or small.

fait ac·com·pli (fāt *a*kŏmplē′; *Fr.* fĕt ăkawṅplē′) (pl. **faits ac·com·plis** pr. fāt *a*kŏmplēz′; *Fr.* fĕz ăkawṅplē′). Accomplished fact. [Fr.]

faith (fāth) *n.* 1. Reliance, trust, *in*; belief founded on authority; (theol.) belief in religious doctrines, esp. such as affects character and conduct, spiritual apprehension of divine truth apart from proof. 2. System of religious belief; things (to be) believed. 3. Duty of fulfilling trust, promise, etc.; observance of this; loyalty, fidelity; **good** ~, honesty of intention; **bad** ~, intent to deceive. 4. ~ **cure, healing**, cure, healing, by power of faith, not drugs etc.

faith·ful (fāth′ful) *adj.* Showing faith; loyal, constant (*to*); conscientious; trustworthy; true to fact, the original, etc., accurate. ~ *n.* (collect., **the** ~) True believers; practicing members of a religious faith, esp. Christians or Muslims. **faith′ful·ly** *adv.* **faith′ful·ness** *n.*

faith·less (fāth′lĭs) *adj.* (esp.) Perfidious, false to promises; unreliable. **faith′less·ly** *adv.* **faith′less·ness** *n.*

fake (fāk) *v.t.* (**faked, fak·ing**). Counterfeit; feign; make presentable or specious; contrive out of poor material; tamper with, contrive, in order to deceive. ~ *n.* (freq. attrib.) Piece of faking; faked thing.

fa·kir (făkēr′, fah-, fā′ker) *n.* Muslim (or Hindu) religious mendicant, devotee. [Arab. *faḳir* poor man]

Fa·lang·ist (falăn′jĭst) *n.* & *adj.* (Member) of the ruling party in Spain under General Franco, orig. founded (1933) as a Fascist movement. [Span. *falange* phalanx]

fal·cate (făl′kāt) *adj.* (anat., bot., zool.) Sickle-shaped.

fal·con (fawl′kon, făl′-, faw′kon) *n.* Small diurnal bird of prey of genus *Falco*, with short hooked beak and powerful claws; one of these trained to hunt other birds or game, usu. the peregrine falcon (*F. peregrinus*). **fal′con·er** *n.* Keeper and trainer of hawks; one who hunts with hawks. **fal′con·ry** *n.* Hawking; breeding and training of hawks.

Falk·land (fawk′land) **Islands.** Group of British islands in the S. Atlantic, off the SE. coast of Argentina.

fall (fawl) *v.i.* (**fell, fall·en, fall·ing**). 1. Descend freely, drop, lose high position; become detached and drop off; hang down; (of speech etc.) issue from; (of the young of animals) be born. 2. Sink, descend to lower level; decline; slope; subside, diminish; (of river etc.) discharge itself *into*; (of face) show sudden dismay; (of eyes) be lowered. 3. Cease to stand; come, be brought, (suddenly) to the ground; prostrate oneself; succumb to attack or opposing force; yield to temptation; drop down wounded or dead, die by violence; stumble, be drawn or forced, *into* (danger etc.). 4. (of missile, sight, light, etc.) Take direction, be directed; settle; have its situation *in* certain place, *on* certain object etc.; (of choice, lot, etc.) light *upon*; be allotted or apportioned; come as burden or duty. 5. Come by chance into certain position etc.; come naturally. 6. Pass suddenly, accidentally, or in the course of events, into a certain condition, become (as ~ **asleep, silent**, etc.). 7. Come to pass, befall; come in due course; (of season etc.) occur at stated time, within certain limits etc. 8. With preps.: ~ **all over oneself**, show great enthusiasm; ~ **behind**, be outstripped by; ~ **for**, (colloq.) be captivated by, be enamored of; ~ **into**, take one's place in (line etc.); engage, enter upon (talk etc.); drop into (habit); ~ **on**, make hostile descent or attack on; ~ **to**, take to, begin; ~ **under**, be classified among; be subjected to (observation etc.). 9. With advs.: ~ **away**, desert, revolt; apostatize; decay, vanish; ~ **back**, retreat, give way; ~ **back on**, have recourse to; ~ **behind**, lag; ~ **flat**, (colloq.) fail to create the desired impression; ~ **in**, (mil.) take, cause to take, places in line; give way inward; ~ **in with**, happen to meet; accede to, agree with (views etc.); ~ **off**, withdraw, decrease, degenerate; ~ **out**, quarrel; (mil.) leave the ranks; ~ **short**, be or become insufficient; (of missile) not go far enough; ~ **through**, miscarry, fail; ~ **to**, begin eating or fighting. 10. ~ **guy**, (slang) person who is easily deceived, dupe; person to blame, scapegoat; **fall′out**, airborne radioactive refuse of a nuclear explosion; **falling star**: see STAR. **fall** *n.* 1. Falling; what falls, esp. amount of rain etc. 2. Autumn; season of year

Fairies, as imaginary creatures with powers of good and evil, have formed part of the folk-lore of all civilizations. This watercolor by Edmund Dulac shows popular fairytale characters.

*The **falcon** is one of the most widely distributed of all bird species, some of which are called hawks, kestrels and merlins. The hooded Saker falcon (below) is specially bred for hunting. Other common species are shown on the facing page.*

merlin
gyr
rock dove
hobby
peregrine swooping on rock-dove
caracara
prairie falcon
lanner

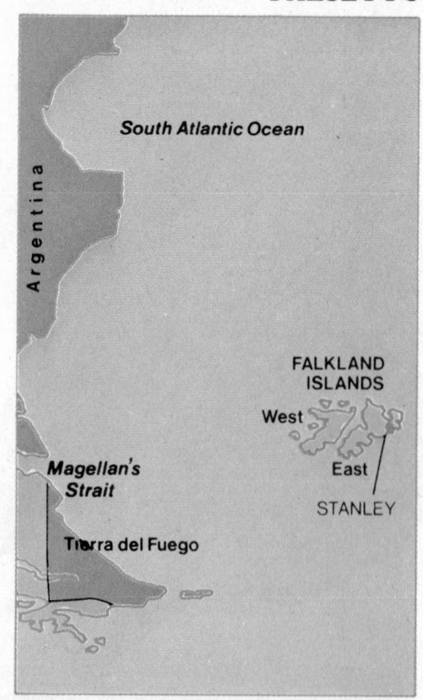

*The **Falkland Islands,** off the southern tip of South America, have a population of 2,100. The people are of British origin and their principal occupation is sheep-farming. Above: General view and map of the islands.*

*One of the most spectacular ways to break a **fall** is with parachutes. These three parachutes control the fall of Apollo 16, 27 April 1972, carrying three astronauts.*

between summer and winter, popularly reckoned in N. hemisphere as comprising the months September, October, and November, but astronomically as lasting from autumnal equinox (Sept. 22 or 23) to winter solstice (Dec. 21 or 22); (fig.) season of incipient decay. 3. (freq. pl.) Cataract, cascade; ~ **line**, line joining waterfalls on parallel rivers, usu. demarking mountains from a coastal plain. 4. Downward trend, amount of descent. 5. Thow in a wrestling bout. 6. (naut.) Hoisting tackle. 7. Succumbing to temptation; **the F~ (of man)**, Adam's sin of eating the forbidden fruit and the consequent loss of man's innocence and of grace.

Fal·la (fah'ya), **Manuel de** (1876–1946). Spanish composer, noted esp. for instrumental music; his works include the opera *La Vida Breve* and the ballets *Wedded by Witchcraft* and *The Three-Cornered Hat*.

fal·la·cy (făl'asē) *n.* (pl. **-cies**). Misleading argument, sophism; (logic) material or formal flaw that vitiates a syllogism; delusion, error; unsoundness, delusiveness. **fal·la·cious** (falā'shus) *adj.* **fal·la'cious·ly** *adv.* **fal·la'cious·ness** *n.*

fall·en (faw'len) *adj.* see FALL; (esp., of woman) unchaste (archaic).

fal·li·ble (făl'ĭbel) *adj.* Liable to error or be erroneous. **fal·li·bil·i·ty** (fălĭbĭl'ĭtē) *n.* **fal'li·bly** *adv.*

Fal·lo·pi·an (falō'pēan) **tube.** Either of the pair of oviducts in humans and other mammals. [discovered by G. *Falloppio*, Italian physician (1523–62)].

fal·low[1] (făl'ō) *adj.* (of ground) Ploughed and tilled but left unseeded during a growing season. ~ *v.t.* Plough and break up (land) for sowing or to destroy weeds.

fal·low[2] (făl'ō) *adj.* Of pale brownish or reddish yellow (now only in ~ **deer**, species of Eurasian deer (*Dama dama*) smaller than the red deer and usu. dappled).

Fal·mouth (făl'muth). Resort town in SE. Massachusetts near E. shore of Buzzards Bay; former whaling town; site of Woods Hole Oceanographic Institute.

false (fawls) *adj.* (**fals·er, fals·est**). 1. Erroneous; not true or correct. 2. Lying, deceitful; treacherous, unfaithful *to*; deceptive; spurious, sham, artificial. 3. Improperly so called, pseudo-; substituted for, supplementing. 4. ~ **alarm**, alarm given without good cause, either to deceive or under misapprehension of danger; **under ~ colors**, under a flag one has no right to (freq. fig.); ~ **dawn**, transient light in east, freq. preceding true dawn by about an hour; ~ **Solomon's-seal**, any of several wildflowers of the genus *Smilacina*, esp. *S. racemosa* of eastern N. America; ~ **start**, wrong start (esp. in racing); ~ **step**, stumble; transgression. **false'ly** *adv.* **false'ness, fal·si·ty** (fawl'sĭtē) (pl. **-ties**) *ns.* **false** *adv.* **play ~**, cheat or betray.

false·hood (fawls'ho͝od) *n.* Falsity; something untrue; contrariety to fact; lying, lie(s).

fal·set·to (fawlsĕt'ō) *n.* Voice or register above the natural range esp. in men, singer with such voice. ~

adj. & *adv.*

fal·si·fy (fawl´sĭfī) *v.t.* (**-fied, -fy·ing**). Fraudulently alter (document); misrepresent; counterfeit, forge. **fal·si·fi·ca·tion** (fawlsĭfĭkā´shon) *n.*

Fal·staff (fawl´stăf, -stahf), **Sir John.** Fat convivial good-humored braggart in Shakespeare's *Henry IV* and *Merry Wives of Windsor.* **Fal·staff·i·an** (fawlstăf´ēan) *adj.*

fal·ter (fawl´ter) *v.* Stumble, stagger, go unsteadily; stammer, speak hesitatingly; waver, lose courage, flinch. **fal'ter·ing·ly** *adv.*

fame (fām) *n.* Public recognition, renown; reputation, good reputation; renown, celebrity. ~ *v.t.* (**famed, fam·ing**). (pass.) Be renowned. **famed** *adj.* Famous, much spoken of.

fa·mil·ial (famĭl´yal, -ēal) *adj.* Of, occurring in, characteristic of (members of) a family.

fa·mil·iar (famĭl´yer) *adj.* 1. Extremely friendly, intimate (*with*); closely acquainted *with* (some subject). 2. Well-known, no longer novel, (*to*); common, current, usual. 3. Unceremonious, free, overfree; amorously or sexually intimate (*with*). **fa·mil'iar·ly** *adv.* **fa·mil'iar** *n.* 1. (R.C. Ch.) Person rendering domestic services in household of pope or bishop; (hist.) officer of Inquisition, chiefly employed in arresting and imprisoning accused. 2. Intimate friend or associate.

fa·mil·i·ar·i·ty (famĭlēăr´ĭtē) *n.* (pl. **-ties**). Close intercourse, intimacy *with* (person, subject); amorous intimacy, (pl.) caresses etc.; unceremoniousness, treating of inferiors or superiors as equals.

fa·mil·iar·ize (famĭl´yerīz) *v.t.* (**-ized, -iz·ing**). Make (thing) well known; make well acquainted or at home *with.* **fa·mil·iar·i·za·tion** (famĭlyerĭzā´shon) *n.*

fam·i·ly (făm´ĭlē, făm´lē) *n.* (pl. **-lies**). 1. Members of household, parents, children, etc.; set of parents and children, or of relations, whether living together or not; person's children. 2. All descendants of common ancestor, house, lineage; group of peoples from common stock. 3. Group of objects, languages, etc., distinguished by common features; (biol.) grouping above *genus* and below *order.* 4. ~ **man,** man with family, domestic person; ~ **planning,** birth control; ~ **tree,** genealogical chart; **in the ~ way,** pregnant.

fam·ine (făm´ĭn) *n.* Extreme scarcity of food in district etc.; dearth of something specified; hunger, starvation.

fam·ish (făm´ĭsh) *v.* Reduce, be reduced, to extreme hunger.

fa·mous (fā´mus) *adj.* Celebrated (*for*); well-known. **fa'mous·ly** *adv.*

fan[1] (făn) *n.* 1. Winnowing machine. 2. Instrument, usu. folding and sector-shaped when spread out, on radiating ribs, for agitating air to cool face; anything so spread out, as bird's tail, wing, leaf, kind of ornamental vaulting; rotating apparatus giving current of air for ventilation, etc.; (in windmill) small rudderlike vane for keeping sails at right angles to the wind; ~ **belt,** belt driving radiator fan on car engine; **fan'jet,** jet engine with additional thrust from cold air drawn in by fan; **fan'light,** fan-shaped window; **fan'tail,** fan-shaped tail or end; kind of pigeon, goldfish, etc. with fan-shaped tail; overhang at stern of ship. **fan** *v.* (**fanned, fan·ning**). 1. Winnow (grain); winnow away (chaff). 2. Sweep *away* (as) by wind from fan; move (air) with fan; drive current of air (as) with fan upon, to cool (face etc.) or to kindle (flame); (of breeze) blow gently on, cool. 3. Spread *out* in fan shape. 4. Increase (love, interest, etc.).

fan[2] (făn) *n.* Devotee of specified amusement, or of a particular person or thing; **fan'dom** (*n.*), fans collectively; **fan mail,** letters from fans. [abbrev. of *fanatic*]

fa·nat·ic (fanăt´ĭk) *n.* & *adj.* (Person) filled with excessive or unreasoning enthusiasm, esp. in religion. **fa·nat'i·cal** *adj.* **fa·nat'i·cal·ly** *adv.* **fa·nat·i·cism** (fanăt´ĭsĭzem) *n.*

fan·ci·er (făn´sēer) *n.* Connoisseur of some article or animal (as **bird-~, rose-~**).

fan·ci·ful (făn´sĭful) *adj.* Indulging in fancies, whimsical, capricious; fantastically designed, ornamented, etc.; imaginary, unreal. **fan'ci·ful·ly** *adv.* **fan'ci·ful·ness** *n.*

fan·cy (făn´sē) *n.* (pl. **-cies**). 1. Delusion; unfounded belief. 2. Faculty of calling up things not present, of inventing imagery; mental image; supposition resting on no solid grounds, arbitrary notion. 3. Caprice, whim; individual taste, inclination; **take a ~ to,** have a passing liking or taste for; **~-free,** carefree, without commitment or (esp. romantic) attachment. 4. **fancy** *adj.* (**-ci·er, -ci·est**). Ornamental, not plain; parti-

*The **fallow deer** is commonly kept on estates and in parks and zoos, but is still found wild in Europe and elsewhere. The males remain apart from females and young except during the breeding season.*

colored (of flowers etc.); capricious, whimsical, extravagant; based on imagination, not fact; (of animal) bred for particular points or qualities; ~ **dress**, fanciful costume, esp. representing historical or fictitious character etc., worn for party or ball; **fan'cywork**, ornamental needlework etc. **fancy** *v.t.* (**-cied, -cy·ing**). 1. Picture to oneself; conceive, imagine; be inclined to suppose, rather think. 2. (colloq.) Have good conceit of (*oneself* etc.); take a fancy to, like. 3. Breed, grow (animals, plants) in order to develop particular points or qualities.

fan·dan·go (făndăng'gō) *n.* (pl. **-gos**). Lively Spanish dance in ¾ time; tune for this.

fan·fare (făn'fa̅r) *n.* Short showy or ceremonious sounding of trumpets, bugles, etc.

fang (făng) *n.* Canine tooth, esp. of dogs and wolves; serpent's venom tooth.

fan·ny (făn'ē) *n.* (pl. **-nies**). (colloq.) Buttocks.

fan·ta·si·a (făntā'zh*a*, -zhē*a*, făntazē'*a*) *n.* Musical composition in which form is subservient to fancy.

fan·ta·size (făn't*a*sīz) *v.* (**-sized, -siz·ing**). Have fantasy or fanciful vision (of). **fan·ta·sist** (făn't*a*sĭst, -zĭst, făntā'zhĭst) *n.*

fan·tas·tic (făntăs'tĭk) *adj.* Extravagantly fanciful; grotesque or quaint in design etc.; (colloq.) very great; remarkable. **fan·tas'ti·cal** *adj.* **fan·tas'ti·cal·ly** *adv.* **fan·tas'ti·cal·ness** *n.*

fan·ta·sy (făn't*a*sē, -zē) *n.* (pl. **-sies**). Image-making faculty, esp. when extravagant or visionary; mental image; fantastic design; fantasia; whimsical speculation.

FAO *abbrev.* Food and Agriculture Organization (of the United Nations).

far (fa̅r) *adv.* At a great distance, a long way off; to a great distance or advanced point; by a great interval, by much; **as ~ as**, right to, not short of; **as ~ as, so ~ as, in so ~ as**, to whatever extent; **by ~**, by a large amount; **how ~**, to what extent; **so ~**, to such a distance, up to now; **far'away**, remote, long past; (of look etc.) absent, dreamy; **far between**, infrequent; **far-fetched**, (of simile, illustration, etc.) studiously sought out, strained; **far-flung**, widely extended; widely distributed; **far-gone**, advanced; very ill, very drunk, much in debt, etc.; **far-off**, remote; **far-out**, (slang) unusual, different; avant garde; extreme; **far-reaching**, widely applicable; carrying many consequences; **far'seeing**, prescient, prudent; **far'sighted**, farseeing; seeing distant things more clearly than near ones. **far** *adj.* (**far·ther** or **fur·ther, far·thest** or **fur·thest**). Distant, remote; **F~ East**, Asia, esp. China and Japan; **F~ West**, regions in Rocky Mountains and along Pacific coast.

far·ad (făr'*a*d, -ăd) *n.* Unit of capacitance, capacitance of a capacitor in which a charge of 1 coulomb raises the potential difference between the plates by 1 volt (abbreviated f or f.). [f. FARADAY]

Far·a·day (făr'*a*dā, -dē), **Michael** (1791–1867). English physicist and chemist; famous for his discovery of electric and magnetoelectric induction and for his work on electrolysis.

farce (fa̅rs) *n.* Dramatic work with sole object of exciting laughter; this species of drama; absurdly futile proceeding, pretense, mockery. **far'ci·cal** *adj.* **far'ci·cal·ly** *adv.*

fare (fa̅r) *v.i.* (**fared, far·ing**).

In Western society nowadays the ***family*** *usually means a husband and wife and their children. It has gradually excluded other relatives. One such 'nuclear' family is depicted in this painting by Picasso of the Soler family.*

1. Journey, go, travel (poet.). 2. Happen, turn out; get on *well, ill,* etc., have specified luck. 3. Be entertained, be fed, feed oneself, *well,* etc. ~ *n.* 1. Cost of passenger's transportation; passenger transported for a fee. 2. Food provided.

fare·well (fārwĕl') *int.* Goodby. ~ *n.* Leave-taking, parting good wishes.

fa·ri·na (farē'na) *n.* Fine meal made from grain and other starchy plant products, used as a cereal, in cooking, etc. **far·i·na'ceous** *adj.* Made from, resembling starch; mealy, powdery.

farm (fārm) *n.* Tract of land used for cultivation; also tract of water used for breeding oysters etc.; ~ **hand**, worker on farm; **farm'house**, house of farm; **farm'stead**, farm with buildings on it; **farm team**, (baseball) minor league team associated with major league team, used to train players; **farm'yard**, enclosure attached to farmhouse. **farm** *v.* 1. Cultivate, till; till the soil, be a farmer. 2. Take proceeds of (tax, office, etc.) on payment of fixed sum; let (*out*) proceeds of (tax etc.) to person for fixed sum; arrange for (work) to be performed by other than principal contractor. 3. (baseball) Assign

Michael Faraday, *the 19th-century English scientist, was early in his career an assistant to Sir Humphrey Davy. His important work on electrical and magnetic phenomena was carried out in this laboratory at the Royal Institute.*

Farmers *in long-settled districts generally take a pragmatic view of environment and land use, striving to reach a balance between the two. Leaving vegetation along streams is one way of maintaining a balance.*

1

2

3

*The **farming** of land and the breeding of livestock are as old as history. Both provide man with essential foods which he either uses himself or trades in return for other necessary commodities. 1. The cultivated fields in the Cotswolds in England are devoted to mixed farming. 2. The farmhouse is occupied by either the farmer himself or his tenant. Farm workers live in other cottages on the farm or in houses in nearby villages. 3. Traditional **farming** methods in the U.S.A. still see some farmers shepherding their flocks.*

A sow and her piglets, soon after **farrowing.** The piglets are born blind, covered with soft white fur. In a few days the eyes open and the fur largely disappears. Many religious taboos cover pigs.

(player) to farm team (used with *out*).

farm·er (fa͞r´m*er*) *n.* One who farms (esp. land); ~ **cheese,** pressed cheese of a consistency like dry cottage cheese.

far·o (fa͞r´ō, făr´ō) *n.* Gambling game in which players bet on the order in which certain cards will appear when taken singly from top of pack. [f. PHARAOH]

Far·oe Islands: see FAEROE ISLANDS.

far·ra·go (*f*arah´gō, -rā´-) *n.* (pl. **-goes**). Medley, confused mixture. [L., = "mixed fodder" (*far* corn)]

Far·ra·gut (făr´*agut*), **David Glasgow** (1801–70). American admiral for Union forces during Civil War; captured New Orleans (1862) and Forts Morgan and Gaines (1864) on Mobile Bay.

far·ri·er (făr´ēer) *n.* One who shoes horses. **far´ri·er·y** *n.* (pl. **-er·ies**).

far·row (făr´ō) *n.* Giving birth to, litter of, pigs. ~ *v.* Produce (pigs).

fart (fa͞rt) *v.i.* (vulg.) Emit wind from anus. ~ *n.* (vulg.) Such emission.

far·ther (fa͞r´dh*er*) *adv.* & *adj.* (To or at a point that is) more distant; further. **far´ther·most** *adj.* **far´thest** *adj.* & *adv.*

far·thing (fa͞r´dhĭng) *n.* Former British coin, one quarter of an old penny; very small amount.

F.A.S. *abbrev.* Free alongside ship.

fas·ces (făs´ēz) *n.pl.* (usu. considered sing.) Bundle of wooden symbol of official authority in ancient Rome, carried before Roman consul or other high official; this as emblem of Italian fascists. [L. pl. of *fascis* bundle]

fas·ci·a (făsh´ē*a*) *n.* (pl. **fas·ci·ae** pr. făsh´ēē). 1. (archit.) Long flat surface of wood or stone under eaves or cornice. 2. (anat.) Thin sheet of connective tissue separating muscle layers and ensheathing muscle bundles. 3. Stripe, band. **fas´ci·al** *adj.*

fas·ci·cle (făs´ĭk*e*l) *n.* 1. One part of book published in installments. 2. (bot. etc.) Bunch, bundle. **fas·cic·u·lar** (*f*asĭk´y*u*l*er*), **fas·cic·u·late** (*f*asĭk´y*u*lĭt, -lāt), **fas·cic´u·lat·ed** *adjs.* **fas·cic·u·la·tion** (*f*asĭkyulā´sh*o*n) *n.*

fas·ci·nate (făs´*i*nāt) *v.t.* (**-nat·ed, -nat·ing**). Deprive (victim) of power of escape or resistance by one's look or presence (esp. of serpents); attract irresistibly, enchant, charm. **fas´ci·nat·ing** *adj.* **fas´ci·nat·ing·ly** *adv.* **fas·ci·na·tion** (făs*i*nā´sh*o*n), **fas´ci·na·tor** *ns.*

fas·cism (făsh´ĭz*e*m) *n.* (often **F**~) Principles and organization of Italian nationalist anticommunist dictatorship (1922–43); system of extreme right wing or authoritarian views. **fas´cist** *adj.* & *n.* (freq. **Fas´cist**). [see FASCES]

fash·ion (făsh´*o*n) *n.* 1. Make, shape; style, pattern, manner; **after, in, a** ~, tolerably, somehow or other, not too well. 2. Prevailing custom, esp. in dress; **the** ~, mode of dress, speech, etc., adopted in society for time being; person, thing, temporarily admired or discussed; **man** etc. **of** ~, person of social standing, moving in and conforming with upper-class society; ~ **plate,** (obs.) engraved, often colored picture of person(s) wearing clothes of latest designs; (fig.) person wearing such clothes. **fashion** *v.t.* Give shape to, form, mold.

3

4

*Women's **fashions** have often reflected the social climate of their particular age. The soft diaphanous garments of the 1820s (1) reflected the spirit of post-revolutionary Europe and the slender gowns of the 1900s (2) a reaction against stiff Victorian clothes. The emphasis throughout the 1930s was on slim hips (3) while during the 1939–45 war a broad-shouldered, short skirted look prevailed (4).*

fash·ion·a·ble (făsh′onabel) *adj.* Following, suited to, the fashion; characteristic of, treating of, patronized by, persons of fashion. **fash′ion·a·ble·ness** *n.* **fash′ion·a·bly** *adv.*

fast[1] (făst, fahst) *v.i.* 1. Abstain from all or some kinds of food as religious observance, a sign of mourning, protest, etc. 2. Go without food. ~ *n.* Act of fasting; season or day appointed for fasting; going without food; ~ **day**, day appointed for fasting.

fast[2] (făst, fahst) *adj.* 1. Firmly fixed or attached; (of friends) steadfast; (of color etc.) not fading or washing out. 2. Rapid, quick-moving; producing quick movement; (of watch etc.) more advanced than the true time; (photog., of lens) transmitting a large amount of light; (of flim) very sensitive to light; (of persons) dissipated (see below); **fast′back,** automobile with back sloping in continuous line; such a back; **fast-food,** (of restaurants, sandwich shops, etc.) where food is quickly prepared and served; **fast one,** (colloq.) shrewd or unscrupulous action; **fast-talk,** (colloq.) persuade by rapid or deceitful talk. **fast** *adv.* 1. Firmly; fixedly; tightly; securely. 2. (archaic and poet.) Close *beside, upon,* etc. 3. Quickly; in quick succession; **live** ~, live in a dissipated way; expend much energy in short time.

fas·ten (făs′*en*, fah′s*en*) *v.* 1. Make fast, attach, fix; secure by some tie or bond; become fast. 2. Direct (look, thoughts, etc.) keenly *on*; fix (nickname etc.) *on*; ~ **on**, lay hold of, single out for attack, seize on (pretext). **fas′ten·er, fas′ten·ing** *ns.*

fas·tid·i·ous (făstĭd′ēus) *adj.* Easily disgusted, exacting in taste, hard to please. **fas·tid′i·ous·ly** *adv.* **fas·tid′i·ous·ness** *n.*

fast·ness (făst′nĭs, fahst′-) *n.* (esp.) Stronghold, fortress.

fat (făt) *adj.* (**fat·ter, fat·test**). 1. Fed up for slaughter, fatted; well-fed, plump; corpulent; thick, substantial. 2. Greasy, oily, unctuous. 3. Fertile, rich; abundant; (slang, of actor's part) offering abundant opportunity for skill, display, etc. 4. **fat′back**, fat off the back of a hog, usu. dried and cured with salt; **fat cat**, (slang) wealthy person, esp. as contributor of money; **fat chance**, (slang) very little chance; **fat farm**, (colloq.) place where people undergo special regimens of exercise and diet to lose weight; **fat′head**, (slang) stupid person; **fatheaded**, (*adj.*) stupid. **fat** *n.* 1. Fat part of anything; (colloq.) best or richest part; **live off the ~ of the land**, have the best of everything. 2. Oily substance composing fat parts of animal bodies; (chem.) one of the organic compounds of which animal fats are composed, glyceryl ester of a fatty acid. **fat** *v.* (**fat·ted, fat·ting**). Fatten; **kill the fatted calf** (Luke 15), receive returned prodigal with joy; (extended) celebrate. **fat′ly** *adv.* **fat′ness** *n.*

fa·tal (fā′t*al*) *adj.* 1. Like fate, inevitable, necessary; of, appointed by, destiny. 2. Fateful, important, decisive. 3. Destructive, ruinous, ending in death; deadly, sure to kill. **fa′tal·ly** *adv.*

*Post-war **fashion** has ventured into a wide variety of styles, some of them bizarre and highly impractical. 1. Hot pants, usually worn with boots, had a short life in the early 1970s. 2. Balmain's evening dress of 1972 was traditionally feminine. 3. The space-age plastic 'garments' produced in Paris were part of the fashion revolution.*

fa·tal·ism (fā'talĭzem) *n.* Belief that all events are predetermined by arbitrary decree; submission to all that happens as inevitable. **fa'tal·ist** *n.* **fa·tal·is·tic** (fātalĭs'tĭk) *adj.* **fa·tal·is'ti·cal·ly** *adv.*

fa·tal·i·ty (fătăl'ĭtē, fa-) *n.* (pl. **-ties**). 1. Subjection to, supremacy of, fate; predestined liability to disaster; fatal influence. 2. Misfortune, calamity; death by accident, in war, etc.

fate (fāt) *n.* 1. Power predetermining events unalterably from eternity; (myth.) goddess of destiny; **the Fates,** (Gk. myth.) the 3 Greek goddesses of destiny, Clotho, Lachesis, and Atropos; (Scand. myth.) Norns. 2. What is destined to happen; appointed lot of person etc.; ultimate condition, destiny; death, destruction, ruin. ~ *v.t.* (**fat·ed, fat·ing**). (usu. pass.) Preordain; **fated,** doomed to calamity.

fate·ful (fāt'ful) *adj.* Prophetic; fraught with destiny, important, decisive; controlled by, showing power of, fate. **fate'ful·ly** *adv.* **fate'ful·ness** *n.*

fa·ther (fah'dher) *n.* 1. Male parent; father-in-law; stepfather; man who has adopted a child; progenitor, forefather. 2. Originator, designer, early leader; one who deserves filial reverence; religious teacher or counselor; **Fathers (of the Church)**, Christian writers of first 5 centuries. 3. **the F~**, God; (theol.) first person of the Trinity. 4. (eccles.) Confessor, spiritual director; priest belonging to religious order or congregation; superior of monastic house; **the Holy F~**, the Pope. 5. Venerable person, god; oldest member, doyen; (pl.) leading men, elders. 6. **~-in-law** (pl. **~s-in-law**), father of one's wife or husband; **fa'therland,** one's native country; **the Fatherland,** Germany. **fa'ther·less, fa'ther·ly** *adjs.* **fa'ther·hood** *n.* **father** *v.t.* Beget, be the father of; originate (statement etc.); be the author, of; govern paternally; fix paternity of (child, book, etc.) *on.*

fath·om (fădh'om) *n.* (pl. **-oms,** collect. **-om**). Measure of 6 ft. (1.83 m) chiefly used in marine soundings. ~ **v.t.** Measure with fathom line, sound (depth of water); (fig.) get to the bottom of, comprehend. **fath'om·less** *adj.* That cannot be fathomed, of measureless depth; that cannot be understood.

fa·tigue (fatēg') *n.* 1. Weariness after exertion. 2. Weakness in metals etc. caused by cyclic variations in stress. 3. Task etc. that wearies; (also ~ **duty**) soldier's menial or manual duty, sometimes allotted as punishment; **fatigues** (fatēgz') (*n.pl.*), (mil.) uniform worn by soldiers while engaged in non-military duties. **fatigue** *v.t.* (**-tigued, -tigu·ing**). Cause fatigue to, exhaust.

Fat·i·ma (făt'ĭma, fah'tēmah) (606?–632). Daughter of Muhammad by his first wife. **Fat·i·mid** (făt'ĭmĭd), **Fat·i·mite** (făt'ĭmīt) *ns.* (Person) descended from Fatima and her husband Ali; (member) of Muslim dynasty ruling part of N. Africa, Egypt, and Syria, 908–1171.

fat·ten (făt'en) *v.* Make fat (esp.

animals for slaughter); grow fat; enrich (purse).

fat·ty (făt'ē) *adj.* (**-ti·er, -ti·est**). 1. Like fat, greasy. 2. Consisting of fat, adipose; with morbid deposition of fat; ~ **degeneration**, morbid condition that begins in individual cells and results in deposits of fat in the tissues. 3. (chem.) ~ **acid**, one of a series of acids of the general formula CnH_2nO_2, of which some members occur in or are derived from natural fats. **fatty** *n.* (pl. **-ties**). Fat person.

fat·u·ous (făch'o͞o*u*s) *adj.* Vacantly silly, purposeless, idiotic. **fat'u·ous·ly** *adv.* **fat'u·ous·ness, fa·tu·i·ty** (fato͞o'ĭtē, -tū'-) *ns.* (pl. **-ties**).

fau·bourg (fō'boor, -boorg) *n.* Suburb, esp. of Paris. [Fr.]

fau·cet (faw'sĭt) *n.* Device for letting liquid flow from a pipe, barrel, cask, etc.

Faulk·ner (fawk'n*er*), **William** (**Cuthbert**) (1879–1962). American novelist and short-story writer; famous for *Sartoris, The Sound and the Fury, Absalom, Absalom!, Light in August*, etc.; awarded Nobel Prize for literature (1949) and Pulitzer Prize (1955, and 1963 posthumously).

fault (fawlt) *n.* 1. Defect, imperfection, blemish, of character, structure, appearance, etc.; **to a** ~, excessively. 2. Transgression, offense; thing wrongly done; (tennis, etc.) ball wrongly served; **double** ~, two consecutive faults; **find** ~ **with**, criticize unfavorably, complain of, hence **fault'finder, fault'finding** (*ns.*). 3. Culpability, responsibility for something wrong; defect causing specified evil. 4. (hunting) Loss of the scent by dogs; **at** ~, at a loss, in the wrong. 5. Flaw in ice; (geol.) place or line where rocklayers have fractured and moved out of alignment; ~ **plane**, plane of a fault, surface along which rocks on one side of a fault have moved relatively to those on the other. **fault** *v.* Cause fault in (strata etc.); show fault; find fault with. **fault'less** *adj.* **fault'less·ly** *adv.* **fault'y** *adj.* (**fault·i·er, fault·i·est**). **fault'i·ly** *adv.* **fault'-i·ness** *n.*

faun (fawn) *n.* (Rom. myth.) One of the rural deities represented with horns, pointed ears, and tail of goat, and later also with goat's legs like satyrs, with whom they were associated. [f. FAUNUS]

fau·na (faw'n*a*) *n.* (pl. **-nas, -nae** pr. -nē). Animals or animal life of a region or period. [L. *Fauna*, rural goddess, sister of FAUNUS]

Fau·nus (faw'n*u*s). (Rom. myth.) God or demigod of nature and fertility worshipped by shepherds and farmers and identified with the Greek PAN.

Faust (fowst), **Johann.** Wandering astrologer and magician who lived in Germany *c*1488–1541 and was reputed to have sold his soul to the Devil; hero of dramas by Marlowe and Goethe. **Faust'i·an** *adj.*

Fauve (fōv) *adj.* & *n.* (sometimes **f**~) (Member) of group of French painters in early 1900s who used vivid colors and distorted images in their works. **Fauv'ism, Fauv'ist** *ns.*

faux pas (fō pah') (pl. **faux pas** pr. fō pahz'). Error in manners; breach of etiquette; indiscretion. [Fr.]

fa·vor (fā'v*er*) *n.* 1. Friendly regard, goodwill; approval; good graces; kindness beyond what is due, partiality, too lenient or generous treatment; aid, furtherance; **in** ~ **of**, on behalf or in support of; on the side of; to the advantage or account of. 2. Thing given or worn as mark of favor; small gift distributed at a party, e.g., knickknack, paper hat; knot of ribbons, rosette, badge. 3. (archaic) Looks, countenance. 4. (pl.) Permission for sexual intimacy. **favor** *v.t.* 1. Look kindly upon, approve; treat kindly, countenance; indulge, oblige, *with*. 2. Treat with partiality; be propitious or advantageous to; aid, support. 3. (colloq.) Resemble in face or feature. 4. (journalese) Choose to wear. **fa'-vored** *adj.* **most favored nation clause**, clause in trade agreement giving special advantages with regard to import duties, permission to trade, etc., to a particular nation; hence, **most** ~ **nation; well-, ill-favored**, having handsome, ugly, features.

fa·vor·a·ble (fā'vor*a*bel) *adj.* Propitious; encouraging, approving; promising, auspicious; helpful, suitable (*to*). **fa'vor·a·bly** *adv.* **fa'vor·a·ble·ness** *n.*

fa·vor·ite (fā'verĭt) *adj.* Preferred above others; ~ **son**, person preferred as political candidate by delegates from his own state; chosen as intimate by king or superior and unduly favored. ~ *n.* Favorite person or thing; **the** ~, (racing, sports) competitor generally favored as being most likely to win. **fa'vor·it·ism** *n.* (esp.) Favoring one person or group unfairly.

Fawkes (fawks), **Guy** (1570–1606). English Roman Catholic, who, with other conspirators, planned to blow up the Houses of Parliament and assassinate the king on Nov. 5, 1605 (Gunpowder Plot) in retaliation for increasing repression of Roman Catholics; he was arrested on Nov. 4 and hanged; **Guy** ~ **day**, (in Britain) Nov. 5, anniversary of this plot, celebrated with fireworks and burning of Fawkes in effigy.

fawn[1] (fawn) *n.* 1. Young deer, esp. one less than 1 year old. 2. Color of this, light yellowish brown. ~ *adj.* Fawn-colored.

*The **FBI** division of the U.S. Department of Justice investigates violations of Federal law including espionage, kidnapping and fraud against the government. Some of their medical and scientific equipment is shown below.*

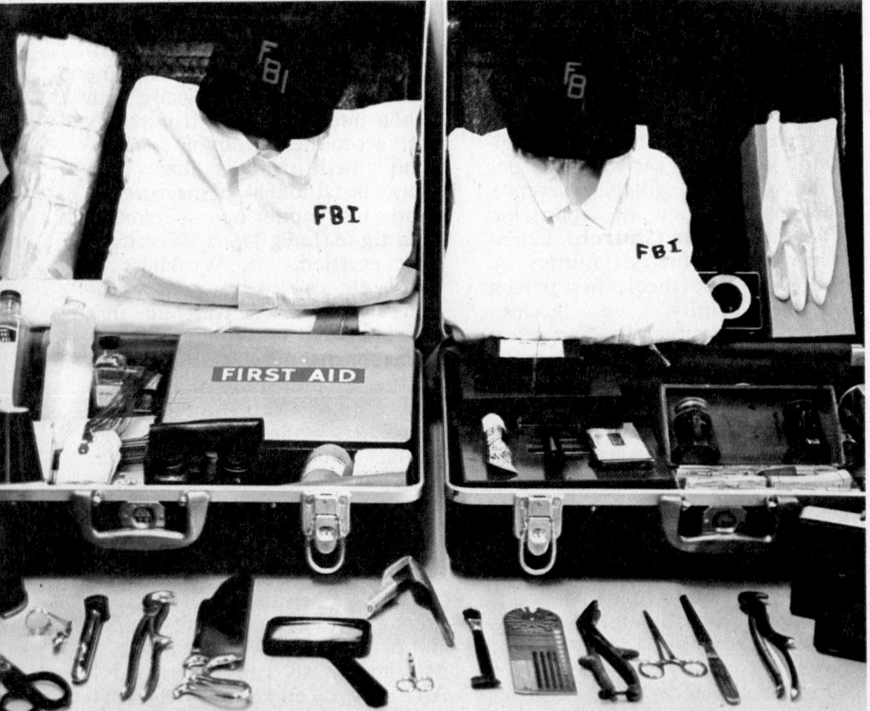

*The **feathers** of many birds, such as this red-sided parrot (above), are brilliantly colored, and have often been used by women as a fashion accessory. The different parts of a feather are shown on the right.*

fawn[2] (fawn) *v.i.* (of animal, esp. dog) Show affection by tail-wagging, groveling, etc.; (of persons) behave servilely, cringe. **fawn'er** *n.* **fawn'ing·ly** *adv.*

fay (fā) *n.* Fairy; sprite or elf.

faze (fāz) *v.t.* (**fazed, faz·ing**). (also **feaze**) (colloq.) Disconcert, perturb.

FBI, F.B.I. *abbrevs.* Federal Bureau of Investigation.

FCC, F.C.C. *abbrevs.* Federal Communications Commission.

F.D. *abbrev.* Fire department; Fidei Defensor.

FDA, F.D.A. *abbrevs.* Food and Drug Administration.

FDIC, F.D.I.C. *abbrevs.* Federal Deposit Insurance Corporation.

Fe. *symbol.* Iron.

fe·al·ty (fē'altē) *n.* (pl. **-ties**). Feudal tenant's or vassal's fidelity to his lord; acknowledgment or obligation of this.

fear (fēr) *n.* Emotion caused by impending danger or evil; state of alarm; dread *of, that*; dread and reverence; anxiety for the safety *of*; **for ~ of**, in order to avoid or prevent; **no fear!**, it is not likely; **without ~ or favor**, impartially. **fear** *v.* Be afraid; be afraid of; hesitate *to* do, shrink from *doing*; revere (God); apprehend, expect uneasily; be afraid *that*. **fear'less** *adj.* Feeling no fear, brave. **fear'less·ly** *adv.* **fear'less·ness** *n.*

fear·ful (fēr'ful) *adj.* 1. Terrible, awful; (by exaggeration) annoying etc. 2. Frightened, timid; apprehensive *of*; reverential. **fear'ful·ly** *adv.* **fear'ful·ness** *n.*

fear·some (fēr'som) *adj.* Appalling; awesome. **fear'some·ly** *adv.* **fear'some·ness** *n.*

fea·si·ble (fē'zibel) *adj.* Practicable, possible; capable of being done or accomplished; (loosely) likely, probable. **fea·si·bil·i·ty** (fēzibĭl'ĭtē) *n.* (pl. **-ties**).

feast (fēst) *n.* 1. Religious anniversary appointed to be observed with rejoicing; **movable ~**, feast (as Easter etc.) of which date varies from year to year. 2. Sumptuous meal, esp. one given to number of guests and of public nature; (fig.) gratification, rich treat, to senses or mind. **feast** *v.* Partake of feast, fare sumptuously; regale.

feat (fēt) *n.* Noteworthy act, esp. deed of valor; act of dexterity or strength, surprising trick.

feath·er (fĕdh'er) *n.* 1. One of the appendages growing from a bird's skin, usu. consisting of a central horny shaft fringed on either side with a vane of barbs forming rounded outline at end; (collect.) plumage; **birds of a ~**, people of the same kind or character; **~ duster**, brush for light dusting, made of feathers. 2. Piece(s) of feather attached to base of arrow or dart to direct flight; plume worn in hat etc.; very light object; **a ~ in one's cap**, something one may be proud of. 3. Tuft or ridge of upright hair, as on leg or tail of some dogs; featherlike flaw in gem. 4. (rowing) Action of feathering (see *v.* sense 2). 5. **~ bed**, mattress stuffed with feathers; **feath'er-bedding**, keeping people on payroll to do unnecessary jobs or restricting production; **feath'er-brain**, silly person; **feath'er-brained**, silly; **feath'erstitch**, zigzag embroidery stitch; **feath'er-weight**, very light or insignificant thing or person; boxer of weight between bantamweight and lightweight. **feath'ered, feath'er·less, feath'er·y** *adjs.* **feather** *v.* 1. Furnish, adorn, line, coat etc. with feathers; form featherlike covering or adornment for; **~ one's nest**, enrich oneself. 2. Float, move, wave, like feathers; turn (oar), turn oar as it leaves water, so that it passes through air horizontally edgeways; rotate (blades of propeller) so that they are parallel to direction of motion.

feath·er·ing (fĕdh'erĭng) *n.* (esp.) Plumage; feathers of arrow; feathery structure or marking.

fea·ture (fē'cher) *n.* 1. (usu. pl.) Part(s) of the face, esp. with regard to shape and visible effect. 2. Distinctive or characteristic part of a thing, part that arrests attention;

distinctive or prominent article in newspaper; feature film or program; **fea'ture·less** *adj.* **feature** *v.t.* (**-tured, -tur·ing**). Stand as distinctive mark upon; portray, sketch prominent points of; make attraction or special feature of; (of film) give prominence to (actor etc.), as **featured player** etc.

feaze (fēz, fāz) = FAZE.

Feb. *abbrev.* February.

feb·ri·fuge (fĕb'rifūj) *n.* & *adj.* (Medicine) that reduces fever.

fe·brile (fē'bril, fĕb'ril) *adj.* Of fever, feverish.

Feb·ru·ar·y (fĕb'rooĕrē) *n.* (pl. **-ar·ies**). Second month of Gregorian (12th of Julian) calendar, with 28 days except in leap year, when it has 29; ~ **revolution**: see Russian REVOLUTION. [L. *februa*, Roman festival of purification held on 15th of this month]

fe·ces, fae·ces (fē'sēz) *ns.pl.* Excrement; waste matter discharged from bowels. **fe'cal** *adj.*

feck·less (fĕk'lĭs) *adj.* Feeble, futile, inefficient. **feck'less·ly** *adv.* **feck'less·ness** *n.*

fe·cund (fē'kund, -kŭnd, fĕk'und, -ŭnd) *adj.* Prolific, fertile; productive. **fe·cun·di·ty** (fĭkŭn'dĭtē) *n.*

fe·cun·date (fē'kundāt, fĕk'un-) *v.t.* (**-dat·ed, -dat·ing**). Make fruitful.

fed[1] (fĕd) *adj.* see FEED; (esp.) ~ **up**, (slang) surfeited, disgusted

The Capitol, seen here from its grounds in late Fall, stands in the ***Federal district*** *known as the District of Columbia, the seat of Federal government in the U.S.A.*

(*with*), bored.

fed[2] (fĕd) *n.* (freq. **Fed**) (colloq.) Official of the federal government, esp. a law enforcement officer.

Fed. *abbrev.* Federal.

fed·a·yeen (fĕdahyēn') *n.pl.* 1. Arab guerrillas operating against Israel. 2. Iranian guerrillas, having left-wing political sympathies, active from about 1970 and important in the 1979 revolution.

fed·er·al (fĕd'eral, fĕd'ral) *adj.* 1. Of the form of government in which two or more states form a political unity but remain independent in internal affairs; of such political unity, as dist. from the separate states composing it; **F~ district**, area in some countries reserved for national capital, such as the District of Columbia; **F~ Republic of Germany**: see GERMANY. 2. Favoring strong central government; of the Union or its troops, in the U.S. Civil War. **fed'er·al·ism** *n.* 1. Federal system of government or organization. 2. Support or advocacy of such a system. 3. (**F~**) Principles of the Federalist Party. **fed'er·al·ist** *adj.* & *n.* **Federalist Party**, (hist.) group that advocated adoption of U.S. Constitution; later, a political party favoring strong centralized U.S. government. **fed·er·al·is·tic** (fĕderalĭs'tĭk, fĕdral-) *adj.* **fed'er·al·ize** *v.t.* (**-ized, -iz·ing**). 1. Bring (states) together in a federal union. 2. Put under jurisdiction of a federal government. **fed·er·al·i·za·tion** (fĕderalĭzā'shon, fĕdra-) *n.*

fed·er·ate (fĕd'erāt) *v.* (**-at·ed, -at·ing**). Bind together in league for some common object; organize on federal basis. ~ (fĕd'erĭt), **fed·er·a·tive** (fĕd'erātĭv, -erativ) *adjs.*

fed·er·a·tion (fĕderā'shon) *n.* Federating; federated society, esp. federal group of states.

fe·do·ra (fĭdōr'a, -dŏr'a) *n.* Low soft felt hat with curled brim and crown creased lengthways. [*Fédora*, title of 1882 play (pop. in U.S. in 1883) by Fr. playwright Victorien Sardou]

fee (fē) *n.* 1. (hist.) Fief; feudal benefice. 2. (law) Estate of inheritance in land; estate held in fee, lordship; **in** ~, as one's absolute and rightful possession; ~ **simple**, estate in land in which the inheritor has unqualified ownership and right of disposition; **in ~ simple**, in absolute possession; ~ **tail**, estate in land limited to some particular class of heirs of person to whom it is granted. 3. Sum payable to public officer for performing his or her function; sum paid or due to professional, performer, etc., for service or performance; entrance money for contest, school, society, etc. **fee** *v.t.* Pay fee to.

fee·ble (fē'bel) *adj.* (**-bler, -blest**). Weak, infirm; wanting in energy, force, or effect; dim, indistinct. **fee'ble·ness** *n.* **fee'bly** *adv.*

fee·ble·mind·ed (fē'belmīn'dĭd) *adj.* Lacking normal mental ability; of lower than average intelligence; stupid. **fee'ble·mind'ed·ness** *n.*

feed (fēd) *v.* (**fed, feed·ing**). 1. Supply with food; put food into mouth of; graze (cattle); deal out (fodder) to animals; take food, eat; serve as food for. 2. Gratify (vanity, eyes, etc.), comfort (person) *with* hope, etc. 3. Nourish, make grow. 4. Keep (reservoir, fire, etc.) supplied; supply (machine) with material to work on; supply (material) *to* machine; (basketball, hockey, etc.) give (ball, puck, etc.) to; (theatr. slang) give (actor) cues, opportunities for jokes, etc. 5. **feed'back**, (electr.) return of a fraction of the output signal from one stage of a circuit, amplifier, etc., to the input of the same or a preceding stage; (transf.) modification of a process etc. by its own effects; information; **feed'pipe**, pipe conveying material, water, etc. to where it is needed. **feed** *n.* 1. Act of feeding; giving of food; **off one's ~**, with no appetite. 2. Pasturage, grain crops; horse's allowance of oats etc.; fodder; **feed'lot**, place where cattle etc. are fattened with extra food before slaughtering. 3. (colloq.) Meal, feast.

feed·er (fē'der) *n.* (esp.) 1. Tributary stream. 2. Hopper or feeding apparatus in machine. 3. (freq. attrib.) Railroad line, air service, etc. linking outlying districts with main line or service.

feel (fēl) *v.* (**felt, feel·ing**). 1. Explore by touch; search (*about*) with hand *for*; try to ascertain by touch *whether, if, how*; **~ one's way**, find one's way by groping, (also fig.); **~ out**, try to get information from or about by devious means. 2. Perceive by touch; have sensation of touch. 3. Be conscious of (sensation, emotion, conviction); be consciously; experience, undergo consciously; be affected by, behave as if conscious of; **~ like**, (colloq.) have inclination for; **~ up to**, (colloq.) be ready for, capable of, or ready to. 4. Be emotionally affected by; have sympathy *with*, compassion *for*; have vague or emotional conviction (*that*). 5. Be realized as; seem, produce impression of being. **feel** *n.* Sense of touch; testing by touch; sensation characterizing something; **have a ~ for**, be endowed with inborn ability or awareness.

feel·er (fē'ler) *n.* (esp.) 1. (pop.) Organ in certain animals for testing things by touch or searching for food. 2. (fig.) Tentative proposal or hint designed to test probable response.

feel·ing (fē'lĭng) *n.* (esp.) 1. Sense of touch; physical sensation. 2. Emotion; (pl.) susceptibilities, sympathies; readiness to feel, tenderness for others' sufferings. 3. Consciousness *of*; conviction not based solely on reason; sentiment. 4. (art etc.) General emotional effect produced. **~** *adj.* (esp.) Sensitive, sympathetic; showing emotion. **feel'ing·ly** *adv.*

feet (fēt): see FOOT.

feign (fān) *v.* 1. Fabricate (excuse, story, accusation). 2. Represent falsely; imitate deceptively; pretend.

feint (fānt) *n.* Sham attack (blow, cut, thrust, etc.) to divert attention or deceive opponent; pretense. **~** *v.i.* Make feint.

feist·y (fīs'tē) *adj.* (**feist·i·er, feist·i·est**). Aggressive, exuberant; touchy.

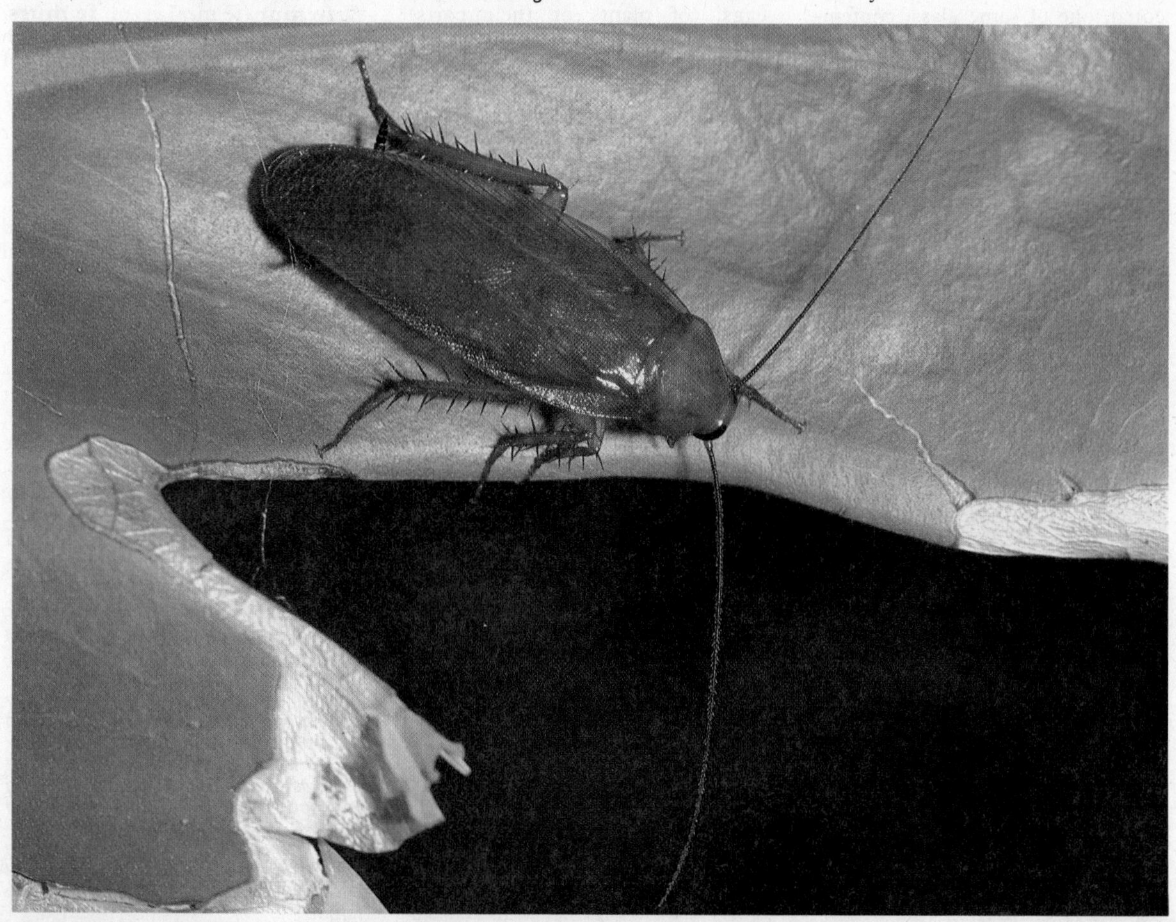

*The **feelers** on this American cockroach (Periplaneta americana), act as sensory organs that aid in the detection of food, especially when the cockroach is active at night.*

feld·spar (fĕld´spār, fĕl´-), **fel·spar** (fĕl´spār) *ns.* Any of a group of minerals, esp. aluminosilicates of potassium, sodium, and calcium, usu. white or flesh colored, occurring in crystals and in granite and other primary rocks; used in ceramic and enameling processes.

fe·lic·i·tate (fĭlĭs´ĭtāt) *v.t.* (**-tat·ed, -tat·ing**). Congratulate (*on*). **fe·lic·i·ta´tion** *n.*

fe·lic·i·tous (fĭlĭs´ĭt*us*) *adj.* Strikingly apt in expression or manner (of words, action, etc., or of person). **fe·lic´i·tous·ly** *adv.*

fe·lic·i·ty (fĭlĭs´ĭtē) *n.* (pl. **-ties**). 1. Being happy, intense happiness. 2. Happy faculty in expression, appropriateness.

fe·line (fē´līn) *adj.* 1. Of cats; catlike. 2. Stealthy, sly. ~ *n.* Member of Felidae or cat family. **fe·lin·i·ty** (fĭlĭn´ĭtē) *n.*

fell[1] (fĕl) *adj.* Fierce, ruthless, terrible, destructuve.

fell[2] (fĕl) *v.* 1. Strike (person, animal) down by blow or cut. 2. Cut down (tree). 3. Stitch (edge of seam) so that it lies flat. ~ *n.* Amount of timber cut in a season.

fel·lah (fĕl´*a*) *n.* (pl. **fel·lahs, fel·la·hin, fel·la·heen** pr. fĕlahhēn´). Egyptian peasant. [Arab. *fellāh* = "husbandman"]

fel·low (fĕl´ō) *n.* 1. One associated with another, comrade. 2. Counterpart, match; other of equal, one of same class, contemporary. 3. (Brit.) Incorporated member of college or collegiate foundation; graduate student holding grant on condition of pursuing specified branch of study. 4. Member of learned society. 5. Man; boy. 6. (attrib.) Belonging to same class; associated in joint action; in same relation to same object; ~ **creature**, person or animal also created by God; ~ **traveler**, (esp.) noncommunist who sympathizes with aims and general policy of Communist Party.

fel·low·ship (fĕl´ōshĭp) *n.* 1. Participation, sharing, community of interest. 2. (also **good** ~) Companionship, friendliness. 3. Body of associates, company; fraternity; brotherhood. 4. Graduate scholarship or grant at a college or university.

fe·lon (fĕl´*on*) *n.* One who has committed felony. ~ *adj.* (poet.) Cruel, wicked, murderous. **fe·lo·ni·ous** (felō´nē*us*) *adj.* Criminal; (law) of, involving, of the nature of felony. **fe·lo´ni·ous·ly** *adv.*

fel·o·ny (fĕl´*o*nē) *n.* (pl. **-nies**). Grave indictable offense, such as murder, rape, larceny.

fel·spar: see FELDSPAR.

felt[1] (fĕlt) *n.* Fabric made by shrinking and rolling wool, fur, etc. so that the fibers interlock; ~**-(tip[ped]) pen**, pen with felt point. **felt** *v.* Make into felt; mat together, become matted; cover with felt.

felt[2] (fĕlt): see FEEL.

fem. *abbrev.* Female, feminine.

fe·male (fē´māl) *adj.* 1. Of the sex that bears offspring or produces eggs; (of plants or their parts) fruit-bearing. 2. Of women; of female animals or plants. 3. (of part of machinery etc.) Designed to receive corresponding male part. ~ *n.* Female person or animal; woman, girl. **fe´male·ness** *n.*

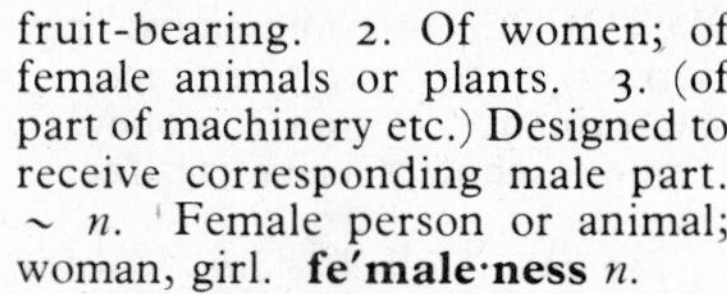

fem·i·nine (fĕm´*i*nĭn) *adj.* 1. Of women; womanly; womanish. 2. (gram.) Of gender to which appellations of females belong; (of ending) proper to this gender. 3. Gentle, delicate. 4. (pros.) ~ **ending**, ending of line of verse with last stress on penult; ~ **rhyme**, in Fr. verse, one ending in mute *e* (a common feminine suffix); hence, rhyme of two syllables of which second is unstressed. **fem´i·nine·ly** *adv.* **feminine** *n.* (gram.) (Word having) feminine gender. **fem´i·nine·ness, fem·i·nin·i·ty** (fĕm*i*nĭn´ĭtē) *ns.*

fem·i·nism (fĕm´*i*nĭz*e*m) *n.* Advocacy of extended recognition of claims and achievements of women; advocacy of women's rights. **fem´i·nist** *adj.* & *n.* **fem·i·nis·tic** (fĕm*i*nĭs´tĭk) *adj.*

fem·i·nize (fĕm´*i*nīz) *v.* (**-nized, -niz·ing**). Make, become, feminine. **fem·i·ni·za·tion** (fĕm*i*nĭzā´sh*o*n) *n.*

femme fa·tale (fĕm fatăl´, -tahl´, fahm). Woman whose seductive charms lead men on and cause dangerous situations. [Fr., = "fatal woman"]

fe·mur (fē´m*er*) *n.* (pl. **fe·murs; fem·o·ra** pr. fĕm´*er*a). 1. Thigh bone. 2. One of upper portions of an insect leg. **fem·o·ral** (fĕm´*er*al) *adj.*

fen (fĕn) *n.* Low marshy or flooded tract of land.

fence (fĕns) *n.* 1. Bulwark (archaic); hedge, wall, railing, etc., keeping out intruders from field etc.; **sit on the** ~, remain neutral in contest, be undecided in opinion. 2. Guard, guide, or gauge, regulating movements of tool or machine. 3. Receiver, then seller, of stolen goods. **fence** *v.* (**fenced, fenc·ing**). 1. Practice swordplay or art of fencing; use sword scientifically; ~ **with**, parry, try to evade (question, questioner). 2. Screen, shield, protect (*from, against*); keep *off* or *out*; surround (as) with fence, enclose. 3. Deal in stolen goods. **fenc´er** *n.* (esp.) One who fences with a foil.

fenc·ing (fĕn´sĭng) *n.* 1. Railing; fences; material for fences. 2. Sport or art of attack and defense with the

The crystalline minerals of the ***feldspar*** *group are usually white or pink in color. They are used in the manufacture of porcelain and glass and as a source of semi-precious stones.*

The art of ***fencing*** *was developed by the Italians in the 16th century when they produced the rapier. It was perfected in the 17th century at the court of Louis XIV of France. Modern fencing is based on the movements worked out then. 1. U.S.S.R. and Hungary compete in the Munich Olympics. 2. The lunge and return to guard. 3. The eight defensive positions. 4. The parts of the target.*

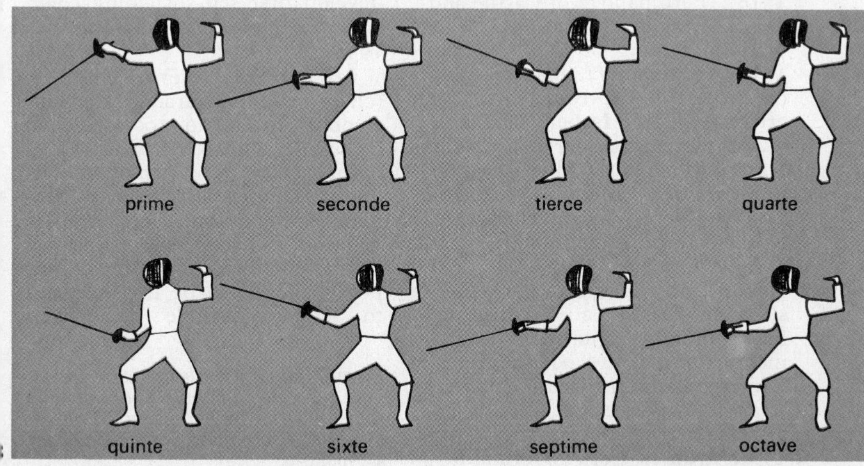
prime
seconde
tierce
quarte
quinte
sixte
septime
octave

4

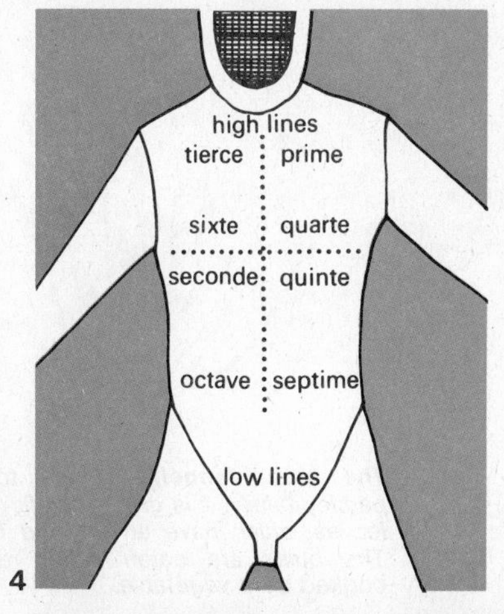
high lines
tierce
prime
sixte
quarte
seconde
quinte
octave
septime
low lines

épée, foil, or saber.

fend (fĕnd) *v.* Ward *off*; provide *for* (usu. *oneself*).

fend·er (fĕn´d*e*r) *n.* Thing used to keep something off, prevent collision, etc.; guard; metal frame around hearth to prevent falling coals from rolling into room; (naut.) piece of old cable, matting, old tires, etc., hung over vessel's side; part of automobile body over, framing, or near each wheel to protect body from mud etc.

fe·nes·trate (f*e*nĕs´trāt, fĕn´*e*s-trāt) *adj.* Having small perforations or openings like windows. **fe·nes·trat·ed** (f*e*nĕs´trātĭd, fĕn´*e*strā-) *adj.*

fen·es·tra·tion (fĕn*e*strā´sh*o*n) *n.* (esp.) 1. Arrangement of windows in building. 2. (surg.) Perforation esp. of bony labyrinth of ear to restore hearing.

Fe·ni·an (fē´nē*a*n, fēn´y*a*n) *adj.* & *n.* (hist.) 1. (pl.) Legendary group of heroic Irish warriors of the 2nd and 3rd centuries. 2. (Member) of secret organization formed by Irish in New York City in the middle of the 19th c. to overthrow British rule in Ireland. **Fe´ni·an·ism** *n.* [OIr. *féne* the ancient Irish people, confused with *fiann* warriors defending Ireland under Finn and other legendary kings]

fen·nel (fĕn´*e*l) *n.* Fragrant yellow-flowered perennial umbellifer (*Foeniculum vulgare*) native to Europe whose seeds are used as flavoring; the seeds of this; the stalks of this.

fen·u·greek (fĕn´y*u*grēk) *n.* Leguminous plant (*Trigonella foenum-graecum*) with seeds used as flavoring; the seeds of this.

feoff (fēf): see FIEF.

feoff·ee (fĕfē´) *n.* Person to whom feoffment is granted.

*The herb, **fennel,** belongs to the parsley family. It is grown chiefly for its leaves which have an aniseed flavor. The bulbs are eaten either raw or cooked as a vegetable.*

1 2

3 4

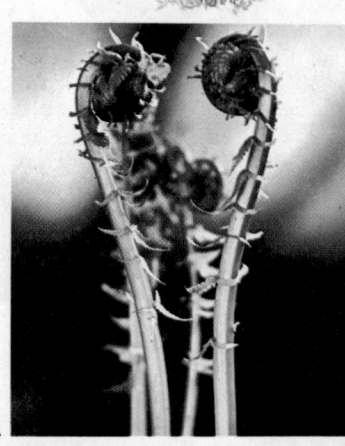

__Ferns__ are mostly perennial herbs and grow mainly in moist shady places in all parts of the world. Fern trees which have shrubby roots or woody trunks are tropical species found in southern Asia, Indonesia and Australasia. 1. The Ponga Fern, New Zealand. 2. Prickly Shield Fern. 3. Fern Tree, Australia. 4. Fern Fiddleheads.

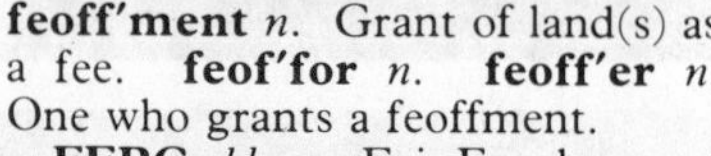

feoff´ment *n.* Grant of land(s) as a fee. **feof´for** *n.* **feoff´er** *n.* One who grants a feoffment.

FEPC *abbrev.* Fair Employment Practices Committee.

fe·ral (fēr´*a*l, fĕr´-) *adj.* Wild, untamed, uncultivated; brutal; (zool.) escaped from captivity and reverted to wild state.

Fer·di·nand (fēr´d*i*nănd) (1452–1516). Ferdinand V of Castile and II of Aragon, known as "The Catholic"; king of Sicily (1468–1516), of Aragon (1479–1516), and of Naples (1504–16); joint sovereign with wife Isabella of Castile (1474–1504); conquered Granada (1492), Spain's last Moorish kingdom; funded Columbus's expedition to New World; established Spanish Inquisition (1478).

fer·ment (fēr´m*e*nt) *n.* 1. Leaven; any fermentative agent, such as yeast. 2. Fermenting, fermentation; agitation, excitement, tumult. ~ (fērmĕnt´) *v.* Undergo, subject to, fermentation; (make) effervesce; excite, stir up, foment.

fer·men·ta·tion (fērmĕntā´-sh*o*n) *n.* Process like that induced by yeast on dough or sugar solutions, with effervescence, evolution of heat, and change of properties; agitation, excitement. **fer·ment·a·tive** (f*e*rmĕn´t*a*tĭv) *adj.*

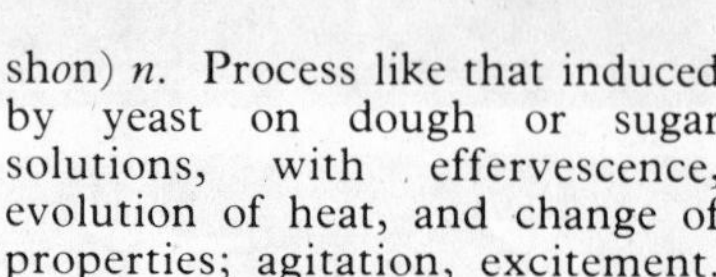

Fer·mi (fēr´mē; *It.* fĕr´mē), **Enrico** (1901–54). Italian atomic and nuclear physicist, living in U.S. from 1939; he helped to develop first self-sustaining chain reaction; Nobel Prize for physics 1938.

fer·mi·um (fēr´mē*u*m) *n.* (chem.) Transuranic element, symbol Fm, at. no. 100, principal isotope at. wt. 256. [f. FERMI]

fern (fērn) *n.* Any of various flowerless, seedless plants, freq. with feathery fronds, of the order Filicales; ~ **seed**, supposed seed (actually spores) of the fern, once pop. believed to be invisible and to render invisible those who

__Fermentation__ vats take many forms. Top: Ornate copper vats at the Carlsberg Brewery, Denmark. Bottom: Massive concrete vats for brewing beer in Australia.

*At Dover harbor one **ferry** backs in while another loads cars on deck. Ferries are used extensively in the English Channel to carry, not only goods and passengers, but also cars, to ports on the European continent.*

carried it. **fern'y** *adj.* (**fern·i·er, fern·i·est**). **fern'er·y** *n.* (pl. **-er·ies**). Place where ferns are grown; collection of ferns.

fe·ro·cious (ferō'sh*u*s) *adj.* Fierce, savage, cruel. **fe·ro'cious·ly** *adv.*

fe·roc·i·ty (ferŏs'ĭtē) *n.* Ferocious character or act.

-ferous *suffix.* Forming adjectives (usu. with intermediate -i-) with sense bearing, having, as in *coniferous.*

fer·ret[1] (fĕr'ĭt) *n.* Half-tamed variety of Old World polecat (*Mustela putorius*), kept for driving rabbits from burrows, killing rats, etc.; also, **black-footed ~** (*Mustela nigripes*), a rare and endangered animal of Western N. Amer. ~ *v.* 1. Hunt with ferrets; clear out (holes, ground), take or drive away (rabbits etc.), with ferrets. 2. Rummage; search *out.*

fer·ret[2] (fĕr'ĭt) *n.* Stout cotton or silk tape for edging or binding fabric. [It. *fioretti* floss silk (L. *flos* flower)]

ferri- *prefix.* (chem.) Containing iron in the ferric or trivalent state.

fer·ric (fĕr'ĭk) *adj.* 1. Of iron. 2. (chem.) Applied to compounds of trivalent iron, e.g. ~ **oxide** (Fe_2O_3).

Fer·ris (fĕr'ĭs) **wheel.** Giant revolving vertical wheel suspending passenger seats on its rim, an amusement ride at fairs etc. [G. W. G. *Ferris* (1859–96), Amer. engineer]

fer·rite (fĕr'īt) *n.* 1. (chem.) Compound formed from ferric oxide and a basic oxide or from ferric hydroxide and a base, esp. magnetic substance used in high-frequency electrical components. 2. (metall.) Soft allotrope of pure iron; solid solution based on this allotrope.

ferro- *comb. form.* 1. Of, containing, iron. 2. (chem., in names of compounds) Containing iron in the ferrous or bivalent state.

fer·ro·mag·net·ic (fĕrōmăgnĕt'ĭk) *adj.* Possessing the property shown by iron, cobalt, nickel, and their alloys, of having a large magnetic permeability and retaining magnetization in the absence of an external magnetic field. **fer·ro·mag'net·ism** *n.*

fer·ro·man·ga·nese (fĕrōmăng'ganēs, -nēz) *n.* Alloy of manganese and iron used in making alloy steels.

fer·ro·type (fĕr'otīp) *n.* Photographic process producing print on thin iron plate; such photograph;

*The **ferret** is said to have been brought to Europe from North Africa by the Romans and has been used for hunting since that time. It is a domesticated form of the polecat.*

Fertilizers, *either natural or chemical, are used where soil is either poor or impoverished. Where large areas of land are under cultivation, as here in Australia, aerial crop-dusting is employed.*

tintype.

fer·rous (fĕr′*u*s) *adj.* (chem.) Of or containing iron, esp. in the bivalent state, e.g. ~ **oxide** (FeO).

fer·rule (fĕr′*u*l, -o͞ol) *n.* Metal ring or cap strengthening end of stick or tube; ring or band holding parts together; one of several small rings through which line runs on fishing rod.

fer·ry (fĕr′ē) *n.* (pl. **-ries**). Place where boats pass to and fro over river etc., to transport passengers, cars, or freight; ferryboat; ferryboat landing; short-distance transportation service, esp. one connecting main-line services; **fer′ryboat**, boat used for ferrying; **fer′ryman**, man who owns or operates a ferry. **ferry** *v.* (**-ried, -ry·ing**). Transport (person, car, freight, etc.) across a body of water; (of boat) pass to and fro, over river, lake, etc.; transport from place to place, esp. on regular service; deliver, transport (vehicle) under its own power.

fer·tile (fẽr′t*i*l; *Brit.* fẽr′tīl) *adj.* Bearing abundantly, fruitful; (of seed or egg etc.) capable of developing into a new individual; **F~ Crescent**, semicircle of formerly fertile land from Israel to the Tigris River and the Persian Gulf. **fer·til·i·ty** (fẽrtĭl′ĭtē) *n.*

fer·til·ize (fẽr′t*i*līz) *v.t.* (**-ized, -iz·ing**). 1. Make fertile, enrich (esp. soil); make productive. 2. (biol.) Make (ovum etc., female individual or organ) fruitful by introduction of sperm, pollen, etc. **fer·til·i·za·tion** (fẽrt*i*līzā′sh*o*n) *n.* Fertilizing; (biol.) fusion of male reproductive cell with female one. **fer′til·iz·er** *n.* (esp.) Manure; chemical compound, usu. containing nitrogen, phosphorus, or potassium, used to increase fertility of soil.

fer·ule (fĕr′*u*l, -o͞ol) *n.* Cane, rod, or stick used for punishing children.

fer·vent (fẽr′v*e*nt) *adj.* 1. Hot, glowing. 2. Ardent, intense. **fer′ven·cy** *n.* **fer′vent·ly** *adv.*

fer·vid (fẽr′vĭd) *adj.* 1. Hot, glowing. 2. Fervent; impassioned. **fer′vid·ly** *adv.* **fer′vid·ness** *n.*

fer·vor (fẽr′v*e*r) *n.* 1. Intense heat. 2. Vehemence, passion, zeal.

fes·cue (fĕs′kū) *n.* Grass of genus *Festuca*, valuable as pasturage.

fes·tal (fĕs′t*a*l) *adj.* Of a feast; festive; joyous. **fes′tal·ly** *adv.*

The ***Edinburgh Festival*** *offers a variety of cultural events, mostly in music and drama, for a period of 3 weeks in the Fall. Here a tattoo is performed in front of Edinburgh Castle.*

fes·ter (fĕs′t*e*r) *v.* (of wound or sore) Generate matter, ulcerate; (of poison, disease, grief) cause suppuration, rankle; putrefy, rot; cause festering in. ~ *n.* Festering condition.

fes·ti·val (fĕs′tĭv*a*l) *adj.* Of, befitting, a feast or feast day. ~ *n.* Time of festive celebration; merry-making; (periodic) series of performances (of music, drama, films, etc.).

fes·tive (fĕs′tĭv) *adj.* Of a feast or festival; joyous. **fes′tive·ly** *adv.*

fes·tiv·i·ty (fĕstĭv′ĭtē) *n.* (pl. **-ties**). Gaiety, rejoicing; festive celebration; (pl.) festive proceedings.

fes·toon (fĕstōōn′) *n.* Chain of flowers or leaves, or ribbons etc., hung in curve between 2 points; carved or molded representation of this. ~ *v.* Adorn (as) with, form into, festoons. **fes·toon′er·y** *n.*

Fest·schrift (fĕst′shrĭft) *n.* (pl. **-schrift·en** pr. -shrĭft*e*n, **-schrifts**). (also l.c.) Collection of writings in honor of eminent scholar. [Ger., = "festival writing"]

F.E.T. *abbrev.* Federal Excise Tax.

fe·tal (fē′t*a*l) *adj.* Of, pertaining to, or like a fetus.

fetch (fĕch) *v.* 1. (Go for and) bring back (person or thing); (now rare) cause to come, draw forth (blood, tears, etc.). 2. Bring in, realize, sell for (a price). 3. Heave (sigh); draw (breath); deal (blow). **fetch′ing** *adj.* Attractive, taking. **fetch** *n.* Act of fetching.

fete, fête (fāt, fĕt) *ns.* Festival; elaborate party, dinner, or entertainment; bazaar or fair. ~ *v.t.* (**fet·ed, fet·ing, fêt·ed, fêt·ing**). Entertain, honor, or celebrate with a fete.

fet·id, Brit. **foet·id** (fĕt′ĭd, fē′tĭd) *adjs.* Stinking. **fet′id·ly** *adv.* **fet′id·ness** *n.*

fet·ish (fĕt′ĭsh, fē′tĭsh) *n.* 1. Inanimate object worshipped by primitive peoples for its supposed inherent magical powers or as being inhabited by a spirit; anything irrationally reverenced. 2. (psych.) Abnormal stimulus, or object, of sexual desire. **fet′ish·ism, fet′ish·ist** *ns.* **fet·ish·is·tic** (fĕtĭshĭs′tĭk) *adj.* [Port. *feitiço* charm. f. L. *facticius* factitious]

fet·lock (fĕt′lŏk) *n.* Part of horse's leg where tuft of hair grows behind pastern joint; this tuft of hair.

fe·tor (fē′t*e*r) *n.* Stench.

fet·ter (fĕt′*e*r) *n.* Shackle for feet; bond; (pl.) captivity; check, restraint. ~ *v.t.* Bind (as) with fetters; impede, restrain.

fet·tle (fĕt′*e*l) *n.* Condition, trim (only in **in fine** etc. ~).

fet·tu·ci·ni (fĕt*u*chē′nē) *n.* (considered sing. or pl.). Pasta in narrow strips, cooked and served with a sauce.

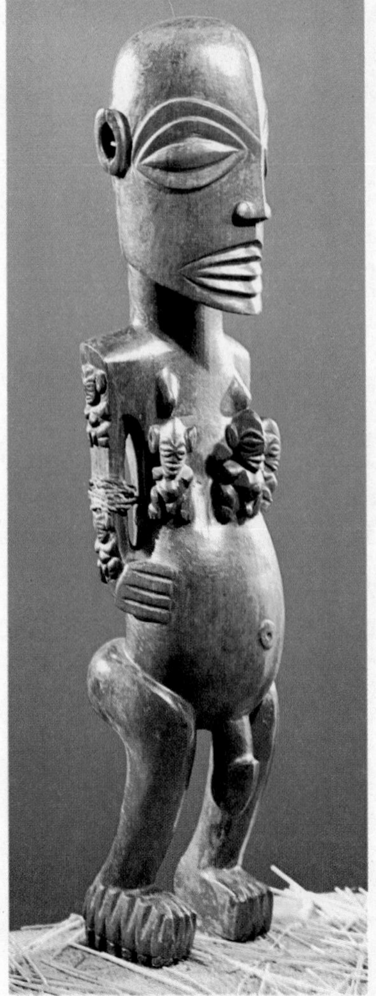

*This **fetish** is from Rarotonga, in the Cook Islands in the south-west Pacific Ocean. It is an ironwood image of the god, Te Rango, and his 3 sons.*

*The **feverfew** thrives in ordinary soil and in open positions. It was formerly used for medicinal purposes, but can also be a troublesome weed.*

fe·tus, foe·tus (fē′t*u*s) *ns.* (pl. **-tus·es**). Unborn or unhatched offspring, esp. human embryo more than eight weeks after conception.

feud (fūd) *n.* Lasting mutual hostility, esp. between two clans or families, with murderous assaults in revenge for previous injury. ~ *v.i.* Engage in feud.

feu·dal (fū′d*a*l) *adj.* Of a fief; of, resembling, according to, the feudal system; ~ **system**, medieval European economic and social system based on relation of superior and vassal arising from holding of lands in feud; system by which land was held in return for services, including military service, homage, etc. to a superior. **feu′dal·ly** *adv.* **feu′dal·ism, feu′dal·ist** *ns.* **feu·dal·is·tic** (fūd*a*lĭs′tĭk) *adj.*

fe·ver (fē′v*e*r) *n.* 1. Abnormally high body temperature; reaction of the body to a general infection, characterized by raised temperature, restlessness, panting, thirst, and wasting; any of a group of diseases, each caused by a specific agent, in which this reaction occurs; ~ **therapy**, artificial production of state of fever in order to raise body temperature to a point lethal to certain organisms of disease. 2. Nervous excitement, agitation.

fe·ver·few (fē′v*e*rfū) *n.* Feathery-leaved perennial plant (*Chrysanthemum parthenium*) allied to the camomile, formerly used as a febrifuge. [L. *febris* fever, *fugare* drive away]

fe·ver·ish (fē′v*e*rĭsh) *adj.* Having symptoms of fever; excited, fitful, restless; of or like fever; causing, infected by, fever. **fe′ver·ish·ly** *adv.* **fe′ver·ish·ness** *n.*

few (fū) *adj.* Not many but more than one; ~ **and far between**, infrequent; **have a** ~, (colloq.) take several alcoholic drinks; **quite a** ~, a fair number (of); **some** ~, no great number (of). **few** *n.* Few persons or things; **the** ~, the minority, the elect, etc. **few′ness** *n.*

fey (fā) *adj.* 1. (Sc.) Fated to die, at point of death; having visionary power, like person about to die. 2. Affected; whimsical.

fez (fĕz) *n.* Muslim man's red felt cap like truncated cone, with long black tassel from top, formerly Turkish national headdress. [Turk., perh. f. Fez, town in Morocco.]

ff *abbrev.* (music) Fortissimo.

ff. *abbrev.* Folios; following pages etc.

FHA *abbrev.* Federal Housing Administration.

fi·an·cé, fem. **fi·an·cée** (fēahnsā′, -ahn′sā) *ns.* One's betrothed.

fi·as·co (fēăs′kō, -ah′skō) *n.* (pl. **-coes, -cos**). Complete failure or

*Another name for violin is fiddle. Though most violins are played in an orchestra, occasionally a **fiddler** will entertain drinkers in a restaurant or bar.*

breakdown; ignominious result. [It., = "bottle" (unexplained allusion)]

fi·at (fī′at, fē′-, -ăt) *n.* Authorization; decree, order; ~ **money**, paper money made legal tender by government fiat and not backed by gold or silver. [L. *fiat* be it done]

fib (fĭb) *n.* & *v.i.* (**fibbed, fib·bing**). (Tell) venial or trivial falsehood; lie. **fib′ber** *n.*

fi·ber, Brit. **fi·bre** (fī′ber) *ns.* Threadlike cell or filament forming, with others, animal or vegetable tissue or textile substance; substance consisting of fibers; fibrous structure; fibrous substance fit for textile fabrics; small root or twig; **fi′berboard**, stiff board made of wood fibers; **fi′berglass** (also **Fiberglas** [trademark]), glass in fibrous form woven into textiles or used for packing, insulation, etc.; plastic reinforced with this; ~ **optics**, transmission of images through glass etc. fibers by total internal reflection. **fi·bri·form** (fī′brifōrm, fĭb′ri-) *adj.*

fi·bril (fī′bril, fĭb′ril) *n.* 1. Small fiber; subdivision of fiber. 2. Ultimate subdivision of root.

fi·bril·la·tion (fībrilā′shon, fĭbri-) *n.* Formation of fibers or fibrils; (path.) quivering movement in fibrils of muscle or nerve.

fi·brin (fī′brĭn) *n.* Insoluble protein formed from fibrinogen during blood clotting, and polymerizing to form the network of the clot. **fi′brin·ous** *adj.*

fi·brin·o·gen (fībrĭn′ojen) *n.* Soluble protein in blood plasma, precursor of fibrin.

fibro- *comb. form.* Fiber.

fi·broid (fī′broid) *adj.* (chiefly path.) Resembling fiber or fibrous tissue; (of disease) characterized by formation or inflammation of connective tissue. ~ *n.* Fibroid uterine tumor.

fi·bro·sis (fībrō′sĭs) *n.* (path.) Fibroid degeneration; development of fibrous tissue in organ.

fi·brous (fī′brus) *adj.* Of, resembling, fiber(s).

fib·u·la (fĭb′yula) *n.* (pl. **-lae** pr. -lē, **-las**). (anat.) Slender bone on outer side of leg between knee and ankle. **fib′u·lar** *adj.*

-fic *suffix.* Forming (usu. with intermediate -i-) adjectives with sense of producing, making (*beatific, pacific, scientific*).

F.I.C.A. *abbrev.* Federal Insurance Contributions Act.

fiche (fēsh, fĭsh) *n.* Microfiche.

fick·le (fĭk′el) *adj.* Inconstant, changeable. **fick′le·ness** *n.*

fic·tion (fĭk′shon) *n.* 1. Feigning, invention; thing feigned or imagined, invented statement or narrative; literature consisting of such narrative, esp. novels. 2. Conventionally accepted falsehood; **legal** ~: see LEGAL. **fic′tion·al** *adj.* **fic′tion·al·ly** *adv.* **fic·tion·al·ize** (fĭk′shonalīz) *v.t.* (**-ized, -iz·ing**). Make into fiction.

fic·ti·tious (fĭktĭsh′us) *adj.* Counterfeit, not genuine; (of name or character) feigned, assumed; imaginary, unreal; of fiction; constituted or regarded as such by (legal or conventional) fiction. **fic·ti′tious·ly** *adv.* **fic·ti′tious·ness** *n.*

fic·tive (fĭk′tĭv) *adj.* Creating, created, by imagination; of fiction or its creation.

fid·dle (fĭd′el) *n.* 1. (colloq.) Violin; **play first, second,** ~, take leading, subordinate, position. 2. (naut.) Rack, guardrail, etc. to keep things from rolling off table. 3. **fiddlededee′!**, nonsense!; **fiddle-faddle**, trifling talk or action, trivial matters; (*int.*) nonsense! (*v.i.*) fuss, trifle; **fid′dlestick**, violin bow; **fiddlesticks!**, nonsense!; ~ *int.* nonsense! **fiddle** *v.* (**-dled, -dling**). 1. Play the fiddle; play (tune) on fiddle. 2. Be idle or frivolous; make aimless movements or changes (*with*); fritter *away*. 3. Cheat, swindle; falsify (accounts).

fid·dler (fĭd′ler) *n.* (esp.) 1. Player on fiddle. 2. ~ **crab**, any of several small, burrowing crabs of the genus *Uca*, in coastal regions, the male of which has one of its claws much enlarged.

Fi·de·i De·fen·sor (fī′dēī dĭfĕn′-sōr). Defender of the Faith; title of English sovereigns since Henry VIII, who received it from Pope Leo X in 1521 as a reward for writing against Luther. [L.]

fi·del·i·ty (fĭdĕl′ĭtē, fī-) *n.* (pl. **-ties**). Faithfulness, loyalty (*to*); strict conformity to truth or fact, exact correspondence to the original.

fidg·et (fĭj′ĭt) *n.* 1. Bodily uneasiness seeking relief in spasmodic movements (freq. **the** ~**s**); restless mood. 2. Person who fidgets. 3. Fidgeting. ~ *v.* Move restlessly (*about*); be uneasy, worry; make (person) uncomfortable, worry. **fidg′et·y** *adj.* **fidg′et·i·ness** *n.*

fi·du·cial (fĭdōō′shal, -dū′-) *adj.* 1. Of, of the nature of, trust or reliance. 2. (surveying etc., of line, point, etc.) Assumed as fixed basis of comparison.

fi·du·ci·ar·y (fĭd ōō′shēērē, -dū′-, -sherē) *adj.* Of trust or trustee(ship); held or given in trust; ~ **bond**, bond posted as surety by a fiduciary as administrator of an estate. **fiduciary** *n.* (pl. **-ar·ies**). Trustee of property, securities, etc.

fief (fēf) *n.* Feudal estate; fee.

field (fēld) *n.* 1. (Piece of) ground, esp. one used for tillage or pasture; tract abounding in some natural product, as coal, oil, diamonds. 2. Ground on which battle is fought; scene of campaign or military operations; **in the** ~, (esp.) engaged in military operations; working with agents, customers, etc. away from home office; **leave the** ~ **open**, abstain from interference or competition; **play the** ~, (colloq.) avoid exclusive commitment to one person etc. 3. Ground for playing football, cricket, etc.; (baseball) outfield. 4. Those who take part in outdoor contest or sport; all competitors in race etc., or all except the favorite; in horse races, those entries that are treated as a single entry in pari-mutuel betting. 5. Large stretch, expanse, of sea, ice, snow, etc. (also fig.). 6. Surface on which something is portrayed; (her.) surface of escutcheon or of one of its divisions; ground of flag, picture, etc. 7. Area or sphere of action, operation, investigation, etc.; space or range within which objects are visible through optical instrument; **magnetic** ~, region in which magnetic properties can be detected. 8. (attrib.) (of animals, plants, etc.) Growing or living in a field or fields; wild; (of investigation, study, etc.) carried out on the spot, not in laboratory, classroom, or office; ~ **artillery**, light and mobile artillery for use in the field, so ~ **gun;** ~ **day**, day devoted to outdoor games, sports, activities, athletic competitions, etc.; ~ **events**, throwing and jumping events of a track meet, as opp. to the running events; ~ **glasses**, portable lightweight binocular telescope for outdoor use; ~ **goal**, (basketball) score of two points, made by tossing ball through basket during regular play; (football) score of three points, made by kicking the ball from field; ~ **hand**, hired farm worker; ~ **hockey**, game played on field between goals, using ball and curved sticks; ~ **hospital**, temporary hospital near battlefield; ~ **marshal**: see MARSHAL; ~ **officer**, army officer above rank of captain and below that of general; **field'stone**, stone as it naturally occurs in fields, esp. when used for building; **field test**, test of a product, process, etc., by subjecting it to actual working conditions; **field work**, field investigation, study, etc. (see above). **field** *v.* Act as a fielder in baseball, cricket, etc.; stop (and return) ball; put (team) into field. **field'er** *n.*

***Field glasses** or binoculars are used in many outdoor activities. In sports like horse racing and baseball where the spectator may be some distance from the action, they are essential.*

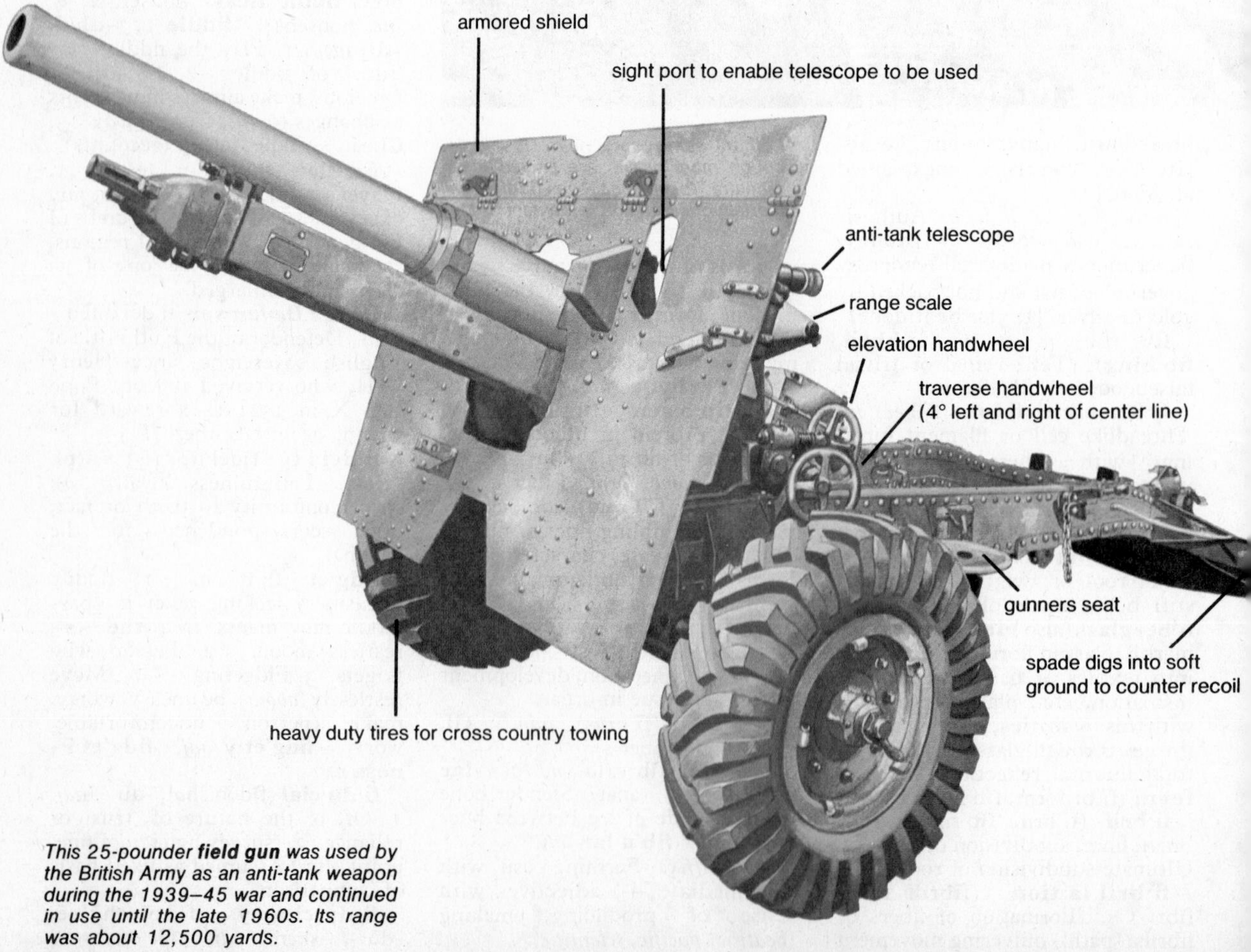

armored shield
sight port to enable telescope to be used
anti-tank telescope
range scale
elevation handwheel
traverse handwheel (4° left and right of center line)
gunners seat
spade digs into soft ground to counter recoil
heavy duty tires for cross country towing

*This 25-pounder **field gun** was used by the British Army as an anti-tank weapon during the 1939–45 war and continued in use until the late 1960s. Its range was about 12,500 yards.*

Field[1] (fēld), **Cyrus West** (1819–92). Amer. financier who promoted and backed construction of first underwater transatlantic cable (1854); first message was transmitted between England and U.S. on Aug. 16, 1858.

Field[2] (fēld), **Eugene** (1850–95). Amer. journalist and poet noted for children's verse; wrote "Wynken, Blynken, and Nod," "Little Boy Blue," "The Little Peach," etc.

field·fare (fēld′fār) *n.* Species of Old World thrush (*Turdus pilaris*) having brown and gray plumage.

Field·ing (fēl′dĭng), **Henry** (1707–54). English novelist; author of *Joseph Andrews*, *Tom Jones*, etc.

Fields (fēldz), **W(illiam) C(laude) Dunkenfield** (1880–1946). Amer. vaudeville and motion picture actor.

fiend (fēnd) *n.* (usu. cap.) The Devil; evil spirit, demon; person of superhuman wickedness (esp. cruelty or malignity); one addicted esp. to drugs); one obsessed with a hobby, job, etc. **fiend′ish** *adj.* **fiend′ish·ly** *adv.* **fiend′ish·ness** *n.*

fierce (fērs) *adj.* Violent in hostility, angrily combative; of formidably violent and intractable temper; raging, vehement; ardent, eager. **fierce′ly** *adv.* **fierce′ness** *n.*

fi·er·y (fī′erē, fīr′ē) *adj.* (**-er·i·er, -er·i·est**). 1. Consisting of or flaming with fire. 2. Looking like fire, blazing red; (of eyes) flashing, ardent. 3. Hot as fire; acting like fire, producing burning sensation. 4. ~ **cross**, wooden

Field events, *particularly throwing contests, were a part of the original Olympic Games as played in Greece. Jumping events include high jump, broad jump and triple jump.*

cross with arms charred or dipped in blood, formerly sent among Scottish Highland clans as a call to arms; burning cross used by Ku Klux Klan as symbol or emblem. 5. Eager, pugnacious, spirited; excitable; tempestuous. **fi′er·i·ly** *adv.* **fi′er·i·ness** *n.*

fi·es·ta (fēĕs′ta) *n.* (in Spain etc.) Religious or other festival.

fife (fīf) *n.* Small shrill-toned instrument of flute kind, used chiefly to accompany drum in military music. ~ *v.* (**fifed, fif·ing**). Play fife; play (air etc.) on fife. **fif′er** *n.*

FIFO *abbrev.* First in first out (method of inventory valuation under which the price of merchandise sold and used is based on the cost of the earliest acquisitions and the value of the remaining merchandise is based on the cost of the most recent acquisition).

fif·teen (fĭf′tēn′) *adj.* Amounting to 15. ~ *n.* One more than 14 (15, xv, or XV). **fif′teenth′** *adj.* & *n.*

fifth (fĭfth *adj.* Next after fourth; **F~ Amendment**, amendment to the U.S. Constitution providing that no one may be held for a serious crime unless indicted, nor be tried twice for the same offense, nor be forced to testify against himself or herself, nor deprived of life, liberty, or property without due process of law; **F~ Avenue**, one of the principal streets of New York, noted for its fine stores; ~ **column**, orig. the column of supporters that Gen. Mola declared himself to have in Madrid, when he was besieging it in the Spanish Civil War, in addition to the 4 columns of his army outside the city; hence, organized body sympathizing with and working for enemy within a country at war; ~ **columnist**, member of such a body; **taking the F~**, refusing to testify on the grounds that to do so might incriminate oneself; ~ **wheel**, superfluous person or thing. **fifth** *n.* Fifth part; fifth thing etc.; fifth grade in school; (mus.) interval of which the span involves five alphabetical names of notes, harmonic combination of notes thus separated. **fifth′ly** *adv.* In the fifth place.

fif·ty (fĭf′tē) *adj.* Amounting to 50. ~ *n.* (pl. **-ties**). Cardinal number, 5 times 10 (50, l, or L); **fifties**, numbers etc. from 50 to 59; these years of century or life; **fifty-fifty**, (colloq.) half-and-half (i.e. 50% each), equally; equal. **fif′ti·eth** *adj.*

fig[1] (fĭg) *n.* 1. (usu. ~ **tree**) Broad-leaved tree (esp. *Ficus carica*) bearing soft pear-shaped multiple fruit eaten fresh or dried; this fruit. 2. Anything valueless, as in *I don't care a* ~. 3. ~ **leaf**, leaf of a fig tree; stylized representation of such a leaf, esp. as used on statues to conceal the genitals; something designed to hide whatever might be thought in questionable taste (see Gen. 3); ~ **marigold**, any of various South African plants of the genus *Mesembryanthemum* having fleshy leaves and brilliant blooms of various colors; **fig·wort** (fĭg'wẽrt, -wõrt), herb of genus *Scrophularia* (esp. *S. lanceolata*).

fig[2] (fĭg) *n.* Dress, array; condition, form.

fig. *abbrev.* Figure(s); figurative(ly).

fight (fīt) *v.* (**fought** pr. fawt, **fight·ing**). Contend in battle or single combat (*against*, *with*); strive to overcome (disease, fire, fear, etc.); maintain (cause, suit at law, quarrel) against opponent; contend over (question), win one's way by fighting; contend with in battle or duel, or with the fists; set on (cocks, dogs) to fight; ~ **back**, resist; ~ **for**, fight on behalf of (person, beliefs, etc.) or to secure (thing); ~ **off**, repel with effort; ~ **it out**, settle by fighting; ~ **shy of**, keep aloof from; **fighting chance**, chance of succeeding by great effort; **fighting cock**, gamecock trained to fight; **fighting fish**, Siamese fish of genus *Betta* (esp. *B. splendens*). **fight** *n.* Action of fighting; battle; combat, esp. pugilistic or unpremeditated, between two or more persons, animals or parties; strife, conflict; appetite or ability for fighting, as in *he has ~ in him yet*; **running** ~, fight kept up while one party flees and one pursues; **show** ~, not yield tamely.

fight·er (fī'ter) *n.* One who fights; fast warplane designed for aerial combat rather than for bombing; ~**-bomber**, military aircraft combining functions of a fighter and a bomber.

fig·ment (fĭg'ment) *n.* Invented statement; thing with no existence except in imagination.

fig·ur·al (fĭg'yeral) *adj.* Of human or animal figures or their pictorial representation.

fig·ur·a·tion (fĭgyurā'shon) *n.* 1. Determination to a certain form; the resulting form. 2. Allegorical or figurative representation. 3. (mus.) Use of florid counterpoint.

fig·ur·a·tive (fĭg'yeratĭv) *adj.* 1. Representing by a figure or emblem; of pictorial or plastic representation. 2. (of speech etc.) Using metaphors, metaphorical, not literal; metaphorically so called; abounding in, addicted to, figures of speech. **fig'ur·a·tive·ly** *adv.* **fig'ur·a·tive·ness** *n.*

fig·ure (fĭg'yer; *Brit.* fĭg'er) *n.* 1. External form, shape; (geom.) definite form constituted by line or lines enclosing superficial space, or by surface or surfaces enclosing space of three dimensions; bodily shape; person considered with regard to visible form or appearance; person as contemplated mentally. 2. Conspicuous appearance, as in *cut a fine* ~; (archaic) importance, distinction. 3. Image, likeness; representation of human form in sculpture, painting, etc. 4. Diagram, illustration; pattern, design; (dancing) evolution or movement of dance or dancer, division of set dance; (skating) movement, series of movements, beginning and ending at center. 5. Numerical system, esp. one of the ten Arabic numerals; amount, number, sum, expressed in figures. 6. (rhet.) Form of expression deviating from normal order or use of words used to give variety, force, etc., e.g., hyperbole, metaphor, etc. (also ~ **of speech**); (logic) particular form of syllogism according to position of middle term; (mus.) brief melodic or rhythmic formula out of which longer passages are developed. 7. **fig'urehead**, ornamental carving, usu. bust or full-length figure, over ship's prow; nominal leader, president, etc., without real authority or influence. **figure** *v.* (**-ured, -ur·ing**). 1. Represent in diagram or picture; picture mentally, imagine; embellish with design or pattern, esp. (mus.) with accompaniment in quicker time. 2. Mark with (numerical) figures; (mus.) write

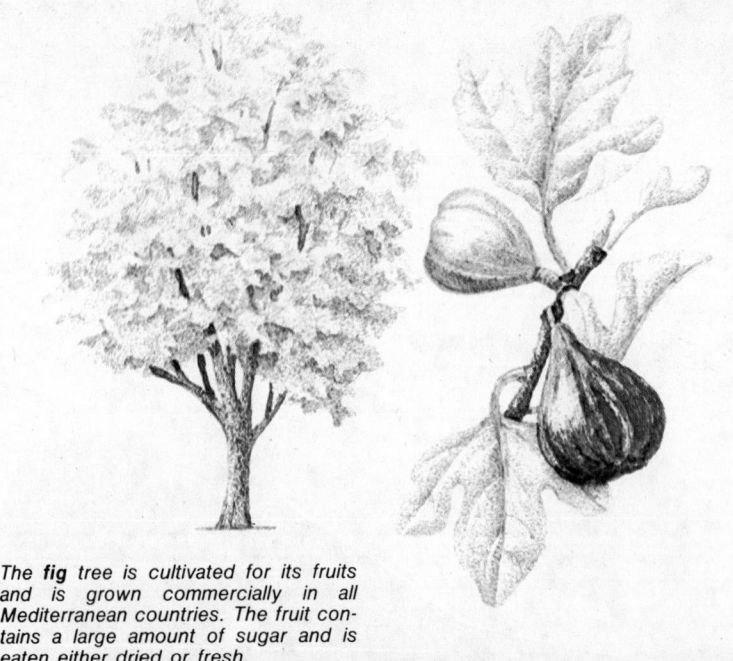

*The **fig** tree is cultivated for its fruits and is grown commercially in all Mediterranean countries. The fruit contains a large amount of sugar and is eaten either dried or fresh.*

*Animals rarely **fight** or attack their own species. They display aggression, however, when guarding their territory or their young, and when competing for a mate. In many instances such displays follow a ritualistic pattern.*

Porcelain **figurines,** which were both delicate and durable, were produced in England and Europe from the early 1700s. This was because of the addition of bone to the china clay. This Derby figurine was made about 1755.

This flamboyant **figurehead,** (left) the Ajax, is from a ship of the early 19th century. Figureheads originally had religious or military significance and were lavishly painted and decorated.

Filigree metalwork, with its open, lace-like effect, has an ancient and widespread history. There are numerous examples from ancient Greece, Egypt, and Rome. This dagger is of Italian origin.

figures over or under (bass) to indicate harmony. 3. Use figures in arithmetic; work out (sum); (colloq.) calculate, reckon, estimate; ~ **on**, rely on, count on.

fig·ur·ine (fĭgyurēn′) *n.* Small modeled or sculpted figure, statuette.

Fi·ji (fē′jē). 1. Principal island of ~ **Islands**, an archipelago of about 250 islands in the S. Pacific; in British possession from 1874; republic, member of Brit. Commonwealth, 1970; capital, Suva. 2. Native, language, of Fiji or the Fiji Islands. **Fi·ji·an** (fē′jēan, fĭjē′-) *adj.* & *n.*

fil·a·gree (fĭl′agrē) = FILIGREE.

fil·a·ment (fĭl′ament) *n.* Slender threadlike body (esp., in animal and vegetable structures, one consisting of a row of cells); (bot.) part of stamen supporting anther; fine, not easily fusible metallic conductor in electric light bulb, vacuum tube, etc., heated or made incandescent by current. **fil·a·men·ta·ry** (fĭlamĕn′terē), **fil·a·men′tous** *adjs.*

fi·lar·i·a (fĭlār′ēa) *n.* (pl. **-lar·i·ae** pr. -lār′ēē). Parasitic nematode worm esp. of genus *Filaria*, infesting vertebrates, including man. **fi·lar′i·al, fi·lar′i·an** *adjs.*

fil·a·ri·a·sis (fĭlarī′asĭs) *n.* Disease caused by filarial worms when they infest lymph tissue.

fil·bert (fĭl′bert) *n.* (Nut of) cultivated hazel (*Corylus maxima*). [Fr. *noix de filbert*, from being ripe near St. Philibert's day, Aug. 20]

filch (fĭlch) *v.t.* Steal, pilfer.

file[1] (fīl) *n.* Instrument usu. of steel with one or more surfaces covered with numerous small raised cutting edges or teeth, for abrading, reducing, or smoothing surfaces. ~ *v.t.* (**filed, fil·ing**). Smooth, reduce surface of, with file; ~ **away, off**, remove with file.

file[2] (fīl) *n.* Receptacle, etc. that keeps documents for preservation and reference; folder or other device for holding papers for reference; set of papers so kept; series of issues of newspaper in order. ~ *v.t.* (**filed, fil·ing**). Place (papers) on file or among public records.

file[3] (fīl) *n.* (mil.) Line of soldiers or vehicles one behind the other; row of persons or things one behind the other; (chess) one of the 8 lines of squares extending across board from player to player; **in** ~, one behind the other; **rank and** ~: see RANK[1]; **on** ~, stored in file. **file** *v.* (**filed, fil·ing**). March in file.

fi·let (fĭlā′, fĭl′ā; *Brit.* fĭl′ĭt) *n.* (pl. **fi·lets** pr. fĭlāz′, fĭl′āz; *Brit.* fĭl′ĭts). 1. Net with square mesh, used for curtains etc. 2. = FILLET def. 2.

fi·let mi·gnon (fĭlā′mĭnyŏn′) (pl. **fi·lets mi·gnons** pr. fĭlā′-mĭnyŏnz′). Small round cut of beef tenderloin.

fil·i·al (fĭl′ēal) *adj.* Of, befitting, a son or daughter.

fil·i·bus·ter (fĭl′*i*bŭst*er*) *n.* 1. Adventurer who engages in a private military action against a foreign country; (hist.) piratical adventurer pillaging Spanish W. Indian colonies in 17th c.; member of bands of adventurers organizing revolutionary expeditions from U.S. to Central America and Spanish W. Indies, 1850–60. 2. Obstructionist, obstruction, in legislative assembly, esp. one who or that which employs prolonged speeches; long obstructive speech or series of speeches in a legislature. ~ *v.* Conduct a legislative filibuster. [Du. *vrijbuiter* freebooter]

fil·i·gree (fĭl′*i*grē) *n.* Ornamental work of fine gold or silver wire formed into delicate tracery; fine metal openwork; anything delicate resembling this. ~ *v.t.* (**-greed, -gree·ing**). Decorate or form into filigree.

fil·ing (fī′lĭng) *n.* (esp., usu. pl.) Particle(s) rubbed off by file.

Fil·i·pi·no (fĭl*i*pē′nō) *n.* (pl. **-nos**). Native, inhabitant, of Philippine Islands.

fill (fĭl) *v.* 1. Make or become full (*with*); stock abundantly, occupy whole capacity or extent of, pervade; satisfy, satiate; (of wind) cause (sails) to swell; (of sail) become full of wind; (of dentist) block up (cavity) with cement etc.; (poker) complete (flush, full house, etc.) by drawing card(s). 2. Hold (position), discharge duties of (office); occupy (vacant time); appoint holder of (vacant post). 3. Adulterate; add a foreign substance. 4. ~ **in**, complete (outline); act as substitute; add what is wanted to complete (unfinished document, blank check, etc.); (slang) inform (person) more fully; ~**-in** (*n.*), person or thing that substitutes or replaces, usu. temporarily; (colloq.) short summary of basic facts; ~ **out**, enlarge, become enlarged; ~ **up**, fill completely; fill tank of vehicle with gasoline; supply vacant parts or places or deficiencies in; grow full. **fill′er** *n.* Trivial news item designed primarily to fill space in newspapers; substance used to fill spaces left in construction; person or substance that fills. **fill** *n.* Full supply of drink or food (only in **drink, eat, have**, etc., **one's** ~); enough to fill something.

fil·let (fĭl′ĭt; for def. 2 of *n.* & *v.* also fĭlā′, fĭl′ā) *n.* 1. String, narrow band of any material, bound around head to confine hair, for ornament, etc.; band, bandage; thin narrow strip of anything. 2. (also **filet**) Piece of boneless meat or fish. 3. (archit.) Narrow flat band separating two moldings; small band between flutes of column; raised rim or edge on any surface; (bookbinding) plain line impressed on cover, tool for making this. ~ *v.t.* 1. Bind (hair etc.) with fillet; encircle with ornamental band. 2. Divide (fish or meat) into fillets; remove bones from.

Filberts fruit best in well-drained soil and in full sun. These hazelnut plantations are in Turkey which, with Italy and Spain, is a leading commercial producer of the hazelnut.

fill·ing (fĭl′ĭng) *adj.* & *n.* (esp.) Cement etc. inserted into cavity of tooth; ~ **station**, retail establishment selling gasoline to motorists.

fil·lip (fĭl′*i*p) *n.* Sudden release of finger or thumb when it has been bent and checked by thumb or finger; slight smart stroke thus given; stimulus, incentive. ~ *v.* Propel (coin, marble, etc.) with a fillip; stimulate; strike slightly and smartly; make a fillip.

Fill·more (fĭl′mōr, -mŏr), **Millard** (1800–74). Vice president of U.S., 1849–50; 13th president of U.S., 1850–3.

fil·ly (fĭl′ē) *n.* (pl. **-lies**). Female colt; (slang) lively young woman.

film (fĭlm) *n.* 1. Thin skin, plate, coating, or layer; slight veil or covering of haze, mist, etc.; fine thread or filament; morbid growth on eye; growing dimness in eyes of dying person. 2. (phot.) Thin strip of material (esp. cellulose acetate) coated with light-sensitive emulsion for exposure in camera; piece of this for one exposure, or roll sufficient for a series. 3. Story, incident, etc., recorded on film in motion pictures; (pl.) cinema industry. 4. **film′dom**, motion picture business or the people who work in it; **film′goer**, one who goes to the cinema; **film pack**, cut photographic films arranged in pile in case or holder for daylight loading or changing; **film′strip**, series of transparencies for projection. **film′y** *adj.* (**film·i·er, film·i·est**). 1. Of or resembling a film; transparent, gauzy. 2. Covered by or as if by a film; hazy, blurred. **film′i·ness** *n.* **film** *v.* 1. Cover, become covered, (as) with film. 2. Photograph (scene, story, etc.) for a movie; make a movie.

fil·ter (fĭl′t*er*) *n.* Contrivance for freeing liquid from suspended impurities by passing it through stratum of sand, fiber, charcoal, etc.; porous substance used for this purpose; combination of electric circuits designed to suppress unwanted frequencies; (phot.) screen (usu. of colored glass or gelatine) for absorbing light of certain colors; ~ **paper**, unsized paper for filtering liquids; ~ **tip, -tipped**, (cigarette or cigar) with mouthpiece that filters the smoke. **filter** *v.* Pass (liquid etc.), flow, through filter; make way *through, into*, etc.; (of news etc.) leak *out*, come *through*; obtain by filtering. **fil′ter·a·ble, fil′tra·ble** *adjs.*

filth (fĭlth) *n.* Foul or dirty matter; corruption, pollution, obscenity; foul language. **filth'y** *adj.* (**filth·i·er, filth·i·est**). ~ **lucre**, dishonorable gain; money. **filth'i·ly** *adv.* **filth'i·ness** *n.*

fil·trate (fĭl'trāt) *n.* Filtered liquid. ~ *v.* (**-trat·ed, -trat·ing**). Filter. **fil·tra·tion** (fĭltrā'sh*o*n) *n.*

fin (fĭn) *n.* 1. Membranous appendage extending from body of fish, cetaceans, etc. for propelling and steering; (slang) hand. 2. Small projecting surface on various parts of aircraft etc. for ensuring stability. 3. (slang) Five-dollar bill.

Fin. *abbrev.* Finland; Finnish.

fin. *abbrev.* Financial; finance.

fi·na·gle (fĭnā'g*e*l) *v.* (**-gled, -gling**). (colloq.) Use, get by, trickery; wangle. **fi·na'gler** *n.*

fi·nal (fī'n*a*l) *adj.* 1. At the end, coming last, ultimate; putting an end to doubt etc., conclusive, definitive, unalterable. 2. Concerned with end or purpose. **fi'nal·ly** *adv.* **final** *n.* (sing. or pl.) Last or deciding heat, game, or series; last examination in academic course; last edition of newspaper in a given day. **fi'nal·ist** *n.* Competitor in final.

fi·na·le (fĭnăl'ē, -nah'lē) *n.* (mus.) Last movement of instrumental composition; music bringing act of opera to a close; last scene, closing part, of drama etc., conclusion, end.

fi·nal·i·ty (fĭnăl'ĭtē) *n.* (pl. **-ties**). Being final; conclusiveness; final act, state, or utterance.

fi·nal·ize (fī'n*a*līz) *v.t.* (**-ized, -iz·ing**). Put in final form; approve final form of; complete (agreement etc.).

fi·nance (fĭnăns', fī'năns) *n.* 1. (pl.) Pecuniary resources of nation, company, person, etc. 2. Management of (esp. public) revenue; money management; ~ **company**, company that makes loans to businesses and consumers. **finance** *v.t.* (**-nanced, -nanc·ing**). Furnish with finances, or money; find capital for.

fi·nan·cial (fĭnăn'sh*a*l, fī-) *adj.* Of finance(s). **fi·nan'cial·ly** *adv.*

fin·an·cier (fĭn*a*nsēr', fī-, -năn-) *n.* One skilled in raising and controlling capital for investment; one skilled in or conducting financial operations.

finch (fĭnch) *n.* Any of numerous small birds of the family Fringillidae, including the bullfinch, bunting, canary, cardinal, and grosbeak, having short conical beak used for cracking seeds.

find (fīnd) *v.t.* (**found** pr. fownd, **find·ing**). 1. Come across, fall in with, light upon; meet with, obtain, get (usu. something desirable or needful); gain, recover, use of; perceive, recognize; acknowledge or discover to be. 2. Discover by search; recover (something lost); succeed in obtaining; summon up (courage, resolution, etc.); reach, obtain, attain, as if by effort; ascertain, discover, by mental effort, calculation, study, etc.; ~ **one's bearings**, discover one's location, esp. point or (fig.) condition from which to continue; ~ **one's way**, contrive to reach one's destination; go, be brought, to place, position, etc., in spite of difficulties, inexperience, etc.; ~ **oneself**, discover one's vocation or true self. 3. (law) Determine and declare (person) *guilty* or *innocent*; agree upon (verdict); ascertain validity of (indictment etc.). 4. Supply, provide, furnish. 5. ~ **out**, discover; devise; solve. **find** *n.* Finding, discovery; what is found.

find·er (fīn'd*e*r) *n.* Person, thing, that finds; small telescope attached to large one to find object; (photog.) viewfinder.

fin de siè·cle (făn d*e* syĕ'kl*e*). Characteristic of end of 19th c.; decadent. [Fr.]

find·ing (fīn'dĭng) *n.* (esp.) Verdict, decision (of court, jury, etc.); conclusion after examining; (pl.), small articles, tools, etc., supplied by workmen; verdict or decision reached after judicial proceeding.

fine[1] (fīn) *n.* 1. End (now only in **in** ~, to sum up, finally). 2. Sum of money fixed as penalty for offense. ~ *v.* (**fined, fin·ing**). Punish by a fine.

*The true **finch** is restricted to 125 species. The name, however, is often used to refer to any small, seed-eating bird, including waxbills, buntings, and weavers. This one is the Bicheno or banded finch.*

fine[2] (fīn) *adj.* (**fin·er, fin·est**). 1. Of high quality; clear, pure, refined; (of gold or silver) containing specified proportion of pure metal. 2. Delicate, subtle; exquisitely fashioned; (of feelings) elevated. 3. Of slender thread; in small particles; thin; sharp. 4. Capable of delicate perception or discrimination; perceptible only with difficulty. 5. Excellent, of striking merit, good, satisfactory, fortunate, of good effect (often iron.); well-conceived or expressed; of handsome appearance or size, dignified; refined; (of weather) bright, free from rain; ornate, showy, smart; fastidious, dainty, flattering, complimentary. 6. ~ **arts**: see ART[1]; ~**-drawn**, subtle; extremely thin; ~ **hand**, devious method of manipulating people or events; cunning; subtle; **fine'spun**, delicate, flimsy; excessively subtle; **go over** (or **through**) **with a fine-tooth(ed) comb**, make detailed search or investigation. **fine'ly** *adv.* **fine'ness** *n.* **fine** *adv.*

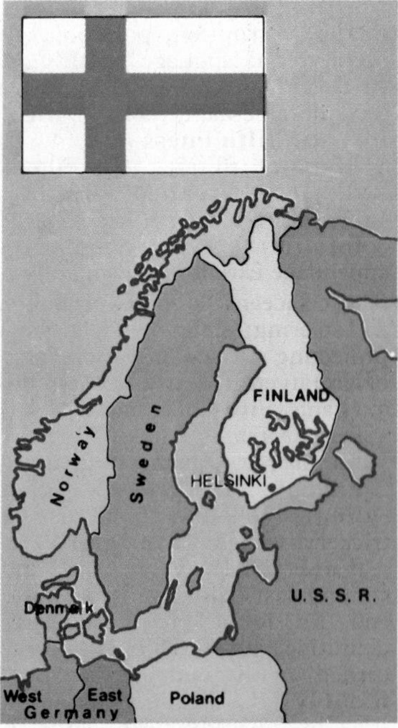

*The republic of **Finland** in northern Europe has a population of 4½ million, most of whom live in southern areas near the Gulf of Finland, although there are some Lapps in the Arctic north. Seventy per cent of the land is forest. Above left: Floating logs and timber stacks on Lake Saimaa. Above right: Map and flag of Finland.*

With only a small margin of time or space, as **to cut ~. fine** *v.* (**fined, fin·ing**). Make, become clearer, finer, etc.

fin·er·y (fī′nerē) *n.* (pl. **-er·ies**). Showy dress or decoration.

fi·nesse (fĭnĕs′) *n.* 1. Delicate manipulation, subtle discrimination; artfulness, cunning strategy. 2. (bridge) Playing lower card in hope of taking trick, while holding higher card of same suit (not in sequence). ~ *v.* (**-nessed, -ness·ing**). Use finesse; trick *into* etc. by finesse; make finesse, play (card) by way of finesse, in bridge.

fin·ger (fĭng′ger) *n.* 1. One of five terminal members of hand, or four excluding thumb (usu. numbered first to fourth, starting from that next to thumb); **have a finger in**, be concerned in; **lay, keep one's fingers crossed**, wish for good luck etc. or hope that nothing bad may occur; **put one's finger on**, point with precision to; **turn, twist, around one's (little) finger**, cajole; persuade easily. 2. Part of glove made to receive a finger. 3. Measure, breadth of a finger; small quantity of liquor. 4. Fingerlike object or projection. 5. **fin′gerboard**, part of neck of violin, guitar, etc., on to which strings are pressed when stopped by fingers; **finger bowl**, bowl for rinsing fingers at table after a meal; **Finger Lakes**, group of long, narrow glacial lakes in central and W. New York resort region; **fin′gernail**, horny covering of upper surface of tip of finger; **finger paint**, paint of jellylike consistency, used esp. by children and applied to damp paper with fingers or entire hand; **finger painting**, (1) creation of a painting with finger paints; (2) painting created with finger paints; **finger-paint** (*v.t.*); **fin′gerprint**, impression of tip of finger, esp. as means of identification; **fin′gertip**, end of finger; **have at one's fingertips**, be versed in, know familiarly; **finger wave**, hair wave made by dampening the hair and shaping with comb and fingers. **finger** *v.t.* 1. Touch with, turn about in, the fingers. 2. Play upon (musical instrument) with fingers; (mus.) mark (music) with figures indicating finger with which note is to be played. 3. (slang) Indicate (victim or criminal to police).

fin·ger·ing (fĭng′gerĭng) *n.* (esp.) Proper method of using fingers in playing music; marks on music indicating this.

fin·ger·ling (fĭng′gerlĭng) *n.* Fish of about 1 finger's length or any young fish less than 1 year old.

fin·i·al (fĭn′ēal) *n.* Ornament finishing off apex of roof, gable, spire, etc.; similar ornament used on top of cabinet etc.

fin·i·cal (fĭn′ĭkal) = FINICKY. **fin′i·cal·ly** *adv.* **fin′i·cal·ness** *n.*

fin·ick·y (fĭn′ĭkē) *adj.* Overnice, precise, fastidious; difficult to please; fussy.

fi·nis (fĭn′ĭs, fēnē′, fī′nĭs) *n.* (at end of book or motion picture) End; end of anything.

fin·ish (fĭn′ĭsh) *n.* Last stage, termination; what serves to give completeness; accomplished or completed state; style of finishing (esp. furniture); surface coating or texture; final coat of paint etc.; (**fight**) **to a** ~, (fight) till one party is completely worsted. **finish** *v.* Bring to an end, come to the end

*Left-hand **fingerprints.** Fingerprinting is used chiefly in criminal investigation as a means of identification. There is about one chance in 64 thousand million of two people having identical fingerprints.*

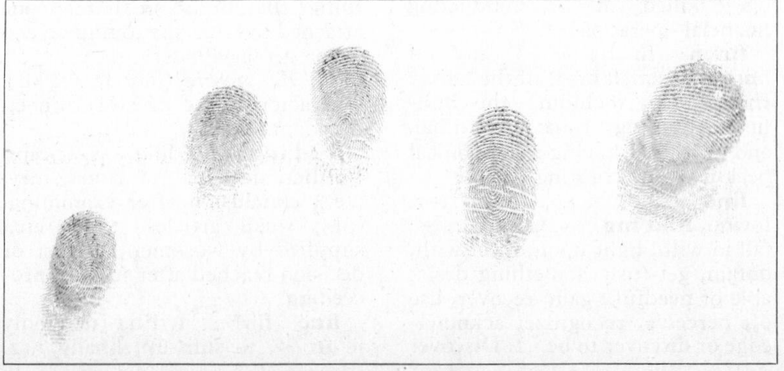

of, complete; consume, get through, the whole or remainder of; ~ **off,** kill, dispatch, overcome completely; perfect, put final or finishing touches on; complete education of; reach the end, cease, leave *off*; end *in* something or *by* doing; with, complete one's use of or association with; **fin'ishing touch(es),** step(s) that complete or perfect the making of something. **fin'ish·er** *n.* (esp.) Workman or machine doing last operation in manufacture.

fi·nite (fī'nīt) *adj.* Bounded, limited; not infinite; (gram., of verb) limited by number and person, not infinitive. **fi'nite·ly** *adv.* **fi'nite·ness** *n.*

fink (fĭngk) *n.* 1. Strikebreaker, esp. a professional one. 2. Informer. 3. Unpleasant person.

Fin·land (fĭn'l*a*nd). Country of NE. Europe situated on the gulfs of Finland and Bothnia; captured by Russia from Sweden in 1809; since 1917 an independent republic; capital, Helsinki.

Finn[1] (fĭn) *n.* Native of Finland. **Finn'ish** *adj.* & *n.* (Language) of Finland.

Finn[2] (fĭn). Principal hero of a cycle of Irish legends; son of Cumal and father of Ossian; supposed to have lived in the 3rd c. A.D.

Finn. *abbrev.* Finnish.

fin·nan had·die (fĭn'*a*n hăd'ē). Haddock cured with smoke. [app. f. name of river *Findhorn*, confused with *Findon*, village in Kincardineshire, Scotland]

Finno- *prefix.* Finnish; **~-Ugrian, -Ugric,** (of) a subfamily of the Uralic languages spoken in Hungary, Lapland, Finland, and some adjacent parts of U.S.S.R.

fiord = FJORD.

fir (fẽr) *n.* 1. (also ~ **tree**) Evergreen coniferous tree of genus *Abies*, esp. **balsam** ~ (*Abies balsamea*), the common eastern Christmas tree; various other genera of evergreen trees with needles arranged singly on the shoots.

fire (fīr, fī'*er*) *n.* 1. Natural agency or active principle operative in combustion; flame, incandescence; volcanic heat; state of ignition; **catch, take,** ~, begin to burn; **on** ~, burning; **set** ~ **to, set on** ~, cause to burn, kindle. 2. Burning fuel in grate, furnace, etc. 3. Destructive burning, esp. of building, forest, etc., conflagration. 4. Luminosity, glow, like that of fire; **St. Elmo's** ~: see ELMO. 5. Burning heat, fever. 6. Burning passion; fervor, enthusiasm; liveliness and warmth of imagination, poetic inspiration. 7. Discharge of firearms; **line of** ~, path of bullet etc.; **open** ~, begin firing; **under**

__Fiords__ are formed by the sinking of the land or the rise of sea-level leading to the flooding of mountainous coastal valleys. Fiords, like this one in New Zealand, are found also in Scotland, Alaska, Iceland, and Norway.

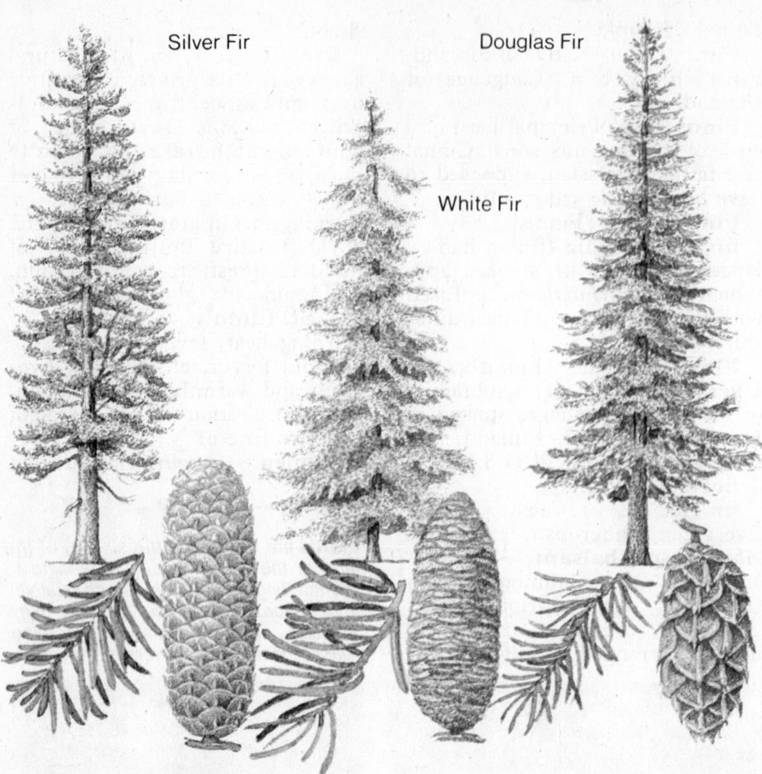

*The **fir** tree differs from the pine in that its leaves are short and are borne separately along the twigs. The silver fir is found in Britain and central Europe where it forms large forests. The Colorado (white) fir is often used for planting in parks. The Douglas fir and some spruces are mistakenly called firs.*

~, being shot at. 8. ~ **alarm**, automatic arrangement for giving notice of outbreak of fire; **fire'arm**, (usu. pl.) weapon from which missiles are propelled by gunpowder or other explosive; **fire'ball**, large luminous meteor, lightning in globular form; **fire'base**, military base near front line, giving support to advancing troops with artillery, rockets, etc.; **fire'boat**, boat with fire-fighting equipment, used in waterfront areas; **fire'bomb**, incendiary bomb; **fire'box**, fuel chamber of steam boiler; **fire'brand**, piece of burning wood; person who stirs up strife or mischief; **fire'break**, strip of land cleared, burned, or plowed to stop the advance of a fire through a forest, across a prairie, etc.; **fire'brick**, brick capable of withstanding great heat, used in furnaces etc.; **fire'bug**, (colloq.) incendiary, pyromaniac, arsonist; **fire'cracker**, cylinder of paper or cardboard containing an explosive and having a fuse that can be lit to cause an explosion (usu. for fun); **fire'damp**, explosive mixture of methane and air formed in coal mines; **fire'dog**, andiron; **fire door**, fire-resistant door, usu. metal, designed to check spreading of fire; **fire-eater**, entertainer who pretends to eat flames; vigorous or combative person; (colloq.) fireman; **fire engine**, vehicle carrying apparatus and firemen for extinguishing fires; **fire escape**, metal stairway on outside of building, movable ladder, or other apparatus for emergency exit to escape from fire; **fire extinguisher**, portable container from which a chemical can be discharged to extinguish fire; **fire fight**, (mil.) preliminary encounter or skirmish before a major battle; **fire fighter**, person employed by fire department to fight fires; **fire'fly**, beetle capable of emitting light (any of about 2,000 species); **fire'guard**, protective screen placed in front of fireplace to catch sparks and to prevent injury to people; **fire hose**, hose for extinguishing fire; **fire'house**, headquarters where on-duty firemen stay and fire-fighting equipment is stored; **fire insurance**, insurance against loss by fire; **fire irons**, implements for tending fireplace, usu. shovel, tongs, and poker; **Fire Island**, 30-mi.-long barrier beach and summer resort off S. central Long Island, N.Y., between Great South Bay and Atlantic Ocean; **fire'light**, light given by fire; **fire'lock**, flintlock; **fire'man**, firefighter; tender of furnace or fire of steam engine; stoker; **fire'place**, grate or hearth for fire in room etc.; **fire'plug**, hydrant for drawing water from a water main to extinguish fires; **fire'power**, (mil.) amount of accurate fire that a weapon or military unit is capable of delivering; **fire'proof**, capable of withstanding fire or preventing damage by fire; not inflammable; **fire-resistant**, able to resist but not completely to prevent destruction by fire; less than fireproof; **fire screen**, fireguard; **fire'side**, space around fireplace; home life; **fire storm**, large and intense fire, often following atomic explosion, in which mass of rising hot air creates strong rush of winds that feed and spread the flames; **fire'trap**, structure that is dangerous in case of fire because of inflammable materials and inadequate escape routes; **fire truck**, fire engine; **fire walk**, ceremony of walking barefoot over hot stones, ashes, etc., as religious rite or ordeal; hence, **fire walker**; **fire watcher**, person detailed to detect and report fires; **fire'water**, (slang) strong whiskey; **fire'weed**, any of various plants springing up in newly burned areas, esp. *Epilobium angustifolium*, also called willow herb, with showy purplish-pink flowers; **fire'wood**, wood for fuel; **fire'work**, contrivance or apparatus for producing spectacular colored lights, smoke, and noise by use of combustibles, explosives, etc.; (pl.) pyrotechnic display. **fire** *v.* (**fired, fir·ing**). 1. Set fire to with intention of destroying; kindle (explosives). 2. Catch fire; become heated or excited; redden; (of internal combustion engine) have gaseous mixture ignite. 3. Bake (pottery, bricks) in a kiln. 4. Supply (furnace, engine) with fuel. 5. Cause (explosive) to explode; shoot, discharge gun, etc.; (of gun etc.) go off; propel (missile) from gun etc. 6. (slang) Discharge from a job, dismiss (person). 7. ~ **away**, begin, go ahead; ~ **up**, show sudden anger; **firing line**, line of guns, men engaged in firing on enemy or at a target; **firing squad**, squad of soldiers detailed to shoot condemned person.

firm[1] (fẽrm) *n.* Company, usu. not a corporation, for carrying on business, commercial house.

firm[2] (fẽrm) *adj.* Of solid or compact structure; fixed, stable; steady, not shaking; established, immutable; (of offer etc.) not liable to cancellation after acceptance; steadfast, unflinching, resolute; constant *to*; (of prices, goods) maintaining their level or value. **firm'ly** *adv.* **firm'ness** *n.* **firm** *adv.* Firmly (chiefly in **hold** ~, **stand** ~). **firm** *v.* Solidify, compact; make, become firm.

fir·ma·ment (fẽr'm*a*ment) *n.* Vault or expanse of the heavens.

first (fẽrst) *adj.* 1. Earliest in time or order; foremost in position,

2

4

*There is particular danger of **fire** where highly inflammable liquids such as oil are involved. Despite stringent safety precautions, explosions do occur, such as this one on an oil rig in the Gulf of Mexico in 1970 (1). The most devastating fires, however, have been bushfires where the spread of flames can be uncontrollably fast and where fire will leap hundreds of yards at a time. This bushfire was in Zambia (2). Fireworks displays show how fire can be harnessed (3) but often controls are needed, such as here in the Bronx (4).*

rank, or importance; coming next after specified or implied time; (mus., of part) highest or chief part for a certain voice or instrument in concerted music; that performs such a part; **in the ~ place**, to begin with; first; **(the) ~ thing**, as the first thing that is done. 2. **~ aid**, assistance given to injured before medical treatment is available; **~ class**, set of persons or things grouped together as better than others; best level of accommodations on train, plane, ship, in hotel, etc.; **~-class** (*adj.*) being first class, of best quality, very good; (*adv.*) by first class; with best accommodations, care, etc.; **~ cousin**, child of one's uncle or aunt; **~-day cover**, envelope bearing stamp(s) postmarked on day of first issue; **~ floor**, ground floor; (chiefly Brit.) floor above ground floor; **~ form**, lowest class in Brit. school; **~ fruit**, (usu. pl.) first products of agriculture for season, esp. as offered to God; first products of work etc.; **first'hand**, direct, without intermediate agency; **first lady**, wife of the president; wife of governor, mayor, etc.; foremost woman in any art or profession; **first lieutenant**, commissioned officer next above a second lieutenant and below a captain; **first mate**, ship's officer next in rank beneath the captain; **first name** (*n.*), **first-name** (*adj.*), given name, Christian name; **first-night(er)**, (habitual frequenter of) first performance of play etc.; **first offender**, offender against whom no previous conviction is recorded; **first person**, (gram.) form of pronoun (*I*, *we*) or verb (*am*, *are*) referring to the speaker or speakers; **first-rate**, of the highest quality; excellent; **first sergeant**, noncommissioned officer in the U.S. Army and Marine Corps, next in rank beneath sergeant major; **first-string**, (colloq.) made up of regular players on a team, as in baseball; **first** *n.* First day (*of* month); first or lowest gear of an automotive vehicle or bicycle; (pl.) best quality (of certain articles of commerce); **the ~**, person or thing first mentioned; **at ~**, at the beginning; **from ~ to last**, throughout; **from the ~**, from the beginning. **first** *adv.* Before anyone or anything else; before some specified or implied event, time, etc., in preference, rather; for the first time; **~ and last**, taking one thing with another, on the whole; **first'born**, eldest (child).

first·ling (fẽrst'lĭng) *n.* (usu. pl.). First result of anything; first offspring.

first·ly (fẽrst'lē) *adv.* (only in enumerating) In the first place, first.

firth (fẽrth) *n.* Arm of sea; estuary.

fis·cal (fĭs'kal) *adj.* Of public revenue; financial. **fis'cal·ly** *adv.*

fish[1] (fĭsh) *n.* (pl. **fish·es**, collect. **fish**). 1. (pop.) Animal living exclusively in water; (strictly) one of class of vertebrate aquatic animals having gills throughout life and usu. fins. 2. Flesh of fish as food; **other ~ to fry**, (colloq.) more important business to attend to; **~ and chips**, fried fish and fried chipped potatoes; **fish cake**, small cake of shredded fish and mashed potato. 3. (colloq.) Person, fellow, of specified kind, as **poor ~, queer ~**. 4. **the Fishes**: see PISCES. 5. **fish'bowl**, glass bowl in which live fish are kept; **~ hawk**, osprey; **fish'hook**, barbed hook used for catching fish; **fish'monger**, (chiefly Brit.) dealer in fish; **fish'pond**, pond in which fish are kept; **fish story**, (colloq.) exaggerated or unbelievable story; **fish'tail**, shaped like tail of a fish; **fish'wife**, woman selling fish; loud abusive woman, termagant. **fish** *v.* Catch or try to catch fish; search *for* something in or under water; collect (pearls, coral) from bottom of sea; try to catch fish in (pool etc.); draw *out of* water, pocket, etc., draw *out*; seek by indirect means or artifice *for* (secrets, compliments, etc.); get (fact, opinion, secret) *out*; **fish in troubled waters**, make one's profit out of disturbances; **fishing rod**, long tapering usu. jointed rod to which line is attached for catching fish.

fish[2] *n.* 1. (naut.) Piece of curved wood, used to strengthen mast or yard. 2. (also **fish'plate**) Flat plate of steel, wood, etc., strengthening beam or joint; one of two plates bolted together through ends of two rails on railroad to cover and strengthen joint.

fish·er (fĭsh'*er*) *n.* 1. Fisherman (archaic). 2. Carnivorous mammal (*Martes pennanti*) of northern N. Amer., like a weasel but larger and having dark brown-black fur. **fish'er·man** *n.* (pl. **-men**). Man who lives by fishing; angler; fishing boat. **fish'er·y** *n.* (pl. **-er·ies**). Business or occupation of catching fish etc.; fishing ground; fish hatchery; right of fishing.

fish·y (fĭsh'ē) *adj.* (**fish·i·er, fish·i·est**). 1. Like fish; smelling or tasting like fish. 2. (slang) Of dubious character, questionable. **fish'i·ly** *adv.* **fish'i·ness** *n.*

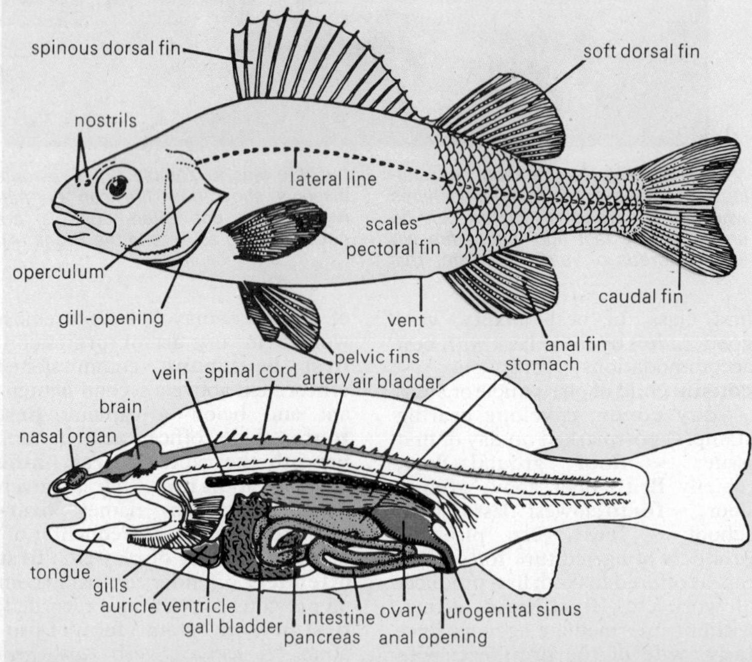

The decorative ***firefish*** *(Pterois volitans) (above left) has venomous fin spines which can produce painful puncture wounds. Left: The external and internal organs of a* ***fish.*** *The grouper (facing page) lives mainly in tropical waters and is one of the prime food fishes. The jewfish is one of the largest and best known of the species, as is the Nassau grouper which changes color.*

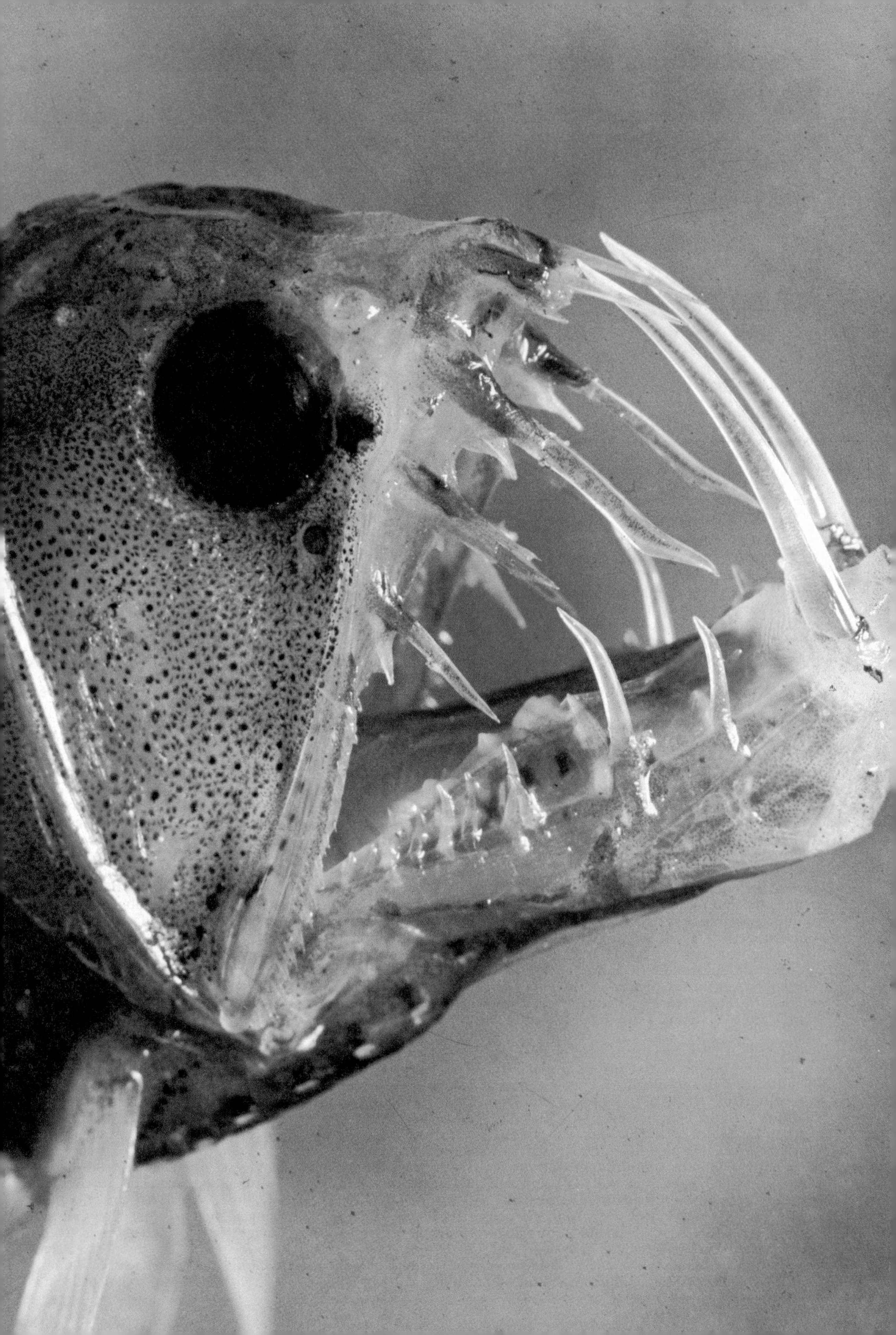

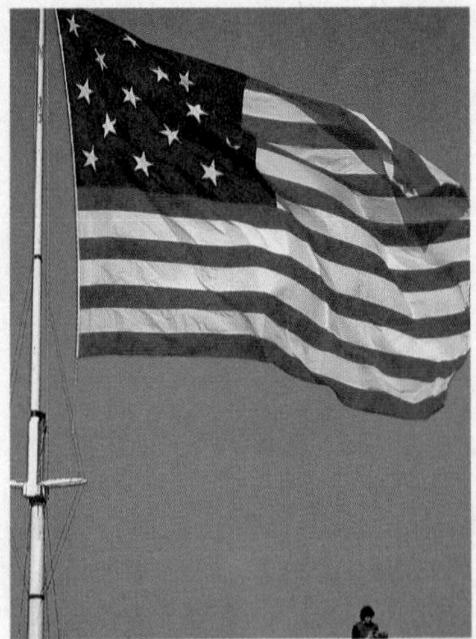

*Many **flags** have undergone changes as their nations have altered in structure and makeup. The American flag is no exception. Left: an early version of the stars and stripes. Right: A giant colonial stars and stripes flying over Fort McHenry in Marylands takes viewers back many years.*

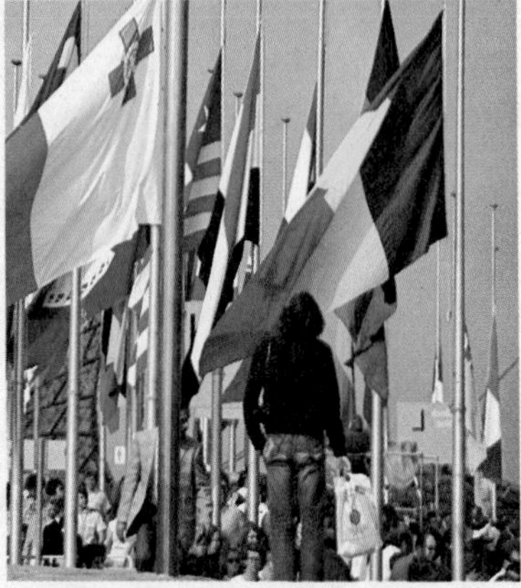

Fisk (fĭsk), **James** (1834–72). Amer. financier and stock market speculator; became wealthy in Erie Railroad and gold price fixing dealings; tried to corner gold market (Black Friday, Sept. 1869) but failed when government intervened.

Fiske (fĭsk), **Minnie Maddern Davey** (1865–1932). Amer. actress; appeared in many Ibsen plays.

fissi- *prefix*. Cleft, divided.

fis·sile (fĭs'*i*l, -īl) *adj*. 1. Cleavable, tending to split. 2. Capable of undergoing NUCLEAR fission. **fis·sil·i·ty** (fĭsĭl'ĭtē) *n*.

fis·sion (fĭsh'*o*n) *n*. 1. (biol.) Division of cell or organism into new cells or organisms, as mode of asexual reproduction. 2. NUCLEAR fission. **fis'sion·a·ble** *adj*. Capable of undergoing nuclear fission.

fis·sure (fĭsh'*er*) *n*. Opening, usu. long and narrow, made by splitting or separation of parts; (anat.) groove, furrow dividing an organ into lobes etc., esp. in the brain. ~ *v*. (**-sured, -sur·ing**). Split.

fist (fĭst) *n*. Clenched hand, esp. as used in boxing. **fist'ful** *n*. Handful. **fist'ic** *adj*. Pugilistic.

fis·ti·cuffs (fĭs'tĭkŭfs) *n.pl*. Fighting with the fists; boxing.

fis·tu·la (fĭs'ch*u*la) *n*. (pl. **-las, -lae** pr. -lē). Long pipe-like ulcer with narrow mouth; suppurating canal; passage made surgically. Pipelike. **fis'tu·lar, fis'tu·lous** *adjs*.

fit[1] (fĭt) *n*. Paroxysm, or one of recurrent attacks, of periodic or constitutional ailment; sudden transitory attack of some illness; sudden seizure, with loss of consciousness or convulsions, of hysteria, apoplexy, fainting, paralysis, or epilepsy; violent outburst (of laughter, rage, etc.), capricious impulse, mood; **by ~s and starts**, spasmodically; **have ~s, throw a ~**, (colloq.) become very angry or excited.

fit[2] (fĭt) *adj*. (**fit·ter, fit·test**). Well adapted or suited (*for, to*); good enough *for*; becoming, proper, right; qualified, competent, worthy (*to*); in suitable condition, ready, *to* do, *for*; in good athletic condition or health, as in **~ as a fiddle. fit** *v*. (**fit, fit·ted, fit·ting**). Be in harmony with, become, befit; be of right measure, shape, and size for (esp. of dress); fill up, exactly correspond to, make to do this; make suitable, adapt, *for, to*: make competent *for, to*; supply, furnish (ship etc.) *with*; **~ out, up**, equip. **fit** *n*. Way thing fits.

fit·ful (fĭt'f*u*l) *adj*. Characterized by irregular fits of activity or strength; spasmodic, changing, capricious. **fit'ful·ly** *adv*. **fit'ful·ness** *n*.

fit·ness (fĭt'nĭs) *n*. Being fit; moral worthiness; propriety.

fit·ter (fĭt'*er*) *n*. (esp.) 1. Mechanic who installs or adjusts parts of machine or other equipment. 2. Tailor or dressmaker who alters garments.

fit·ting (fĭt'ĭng) *n*. (esp., usu. pl.) Fixtures; furniture; apparatus. ~ *adj*. (esp.) Becoming, proper, right. **fit'ting·ly** *adv*. **fit'ting·ness** *n*.

Fitz·ger·ald[1] (fĭtsjĕr'*a*ld), **Edward** (1809–83). English scholar; famous for his poetic translation of the *Rubáiyát of Omar Khayyám*.

Fitz·ger·ald[2] (fĭtsjĕr'*a*ld), **F(rancis) Scott (Key)** (1896–1940). Amer. novelist and short-story writer; author of the novels *The Great Gatsby, The Last Tycoon, Tender Is the Night*, etc. and many stories of the jazz age.

five (fīv) *adj*. Amounting to five, **~-finger exercise**, piano exercise for practicing all fingers, keeping them on same five notes all the time; **F~ Nations**, powerful confederacy of five Iroquoian Indian tribes in western New York, first formed *c*1570 and consisting of the Senecas, Cayugas, Onondagas, Oneidas, and Mohawks; **F~-year plan**, scheme for economic development over a period of five years, orig. that begun in U.S.S.R. in 1928. **five** *n*. One more than four; symbol for this (5, v, or V); card, die face, or domino with five pips; five o'clock; size etc. indicated by five; set of five things or persons. **five'fold** *adj*. & *adv*.

five-and-ten(-cent store), five-and-dime, dime (ten-cent) store. Store selling variety of inexpensive articles, orig. priced at 5 or 10 cents.

fiv·er (fī'v*er*) *n*. (slang) Five-dollar bill.

fix (fĭks) *v*. 1. Make firm or stable, fasten, secure, implant; direct steadily, set (eyes, attention, etc.) *on*; (of object) attract and hold (attention etc.); make (eyes, features), or become, rigid; deprive of, lose, volatility or fluidity, congeal; make (color, photographic image) fast; **~ with one's eyes**, direct steady gaze upon. 2. Place definitely or permanently, station, establish; settle one's choice, decide *on*; assign precise position of; refer (thing, person) to definite place or time; determine incidence of (liability etc.); settle, determine, specify (price, date, place); arrest changes or development in, settle permanent form of (language etc.); arrange, get ready, put in order (also ~ **up**); ~ **it**, arrange matters. **fix** *n*. Dilemma, position hard to escape from; position determined by bearings or astronomical observations; (slang) addict's dose of drug; (slang) correction. **fix'er** *n*. 1. One who or that which fixes. 2. (colloq.) Person who exerts influence or pays bribes to affect results, as in arranging outcome of sports events. 3. (slang) Person who arranges illegal sale of narcotics to users.

fix·a·tion (fĭksā'sh*o*n) *n*. 1. Fixing, being fixed. 2. (psycho.) Persistent attachment to a person or object, esp. when developed early in life in association with great pleasure, sorrow, fear, etc., and continuing as neurotic or immature behavior.

fix·a·tive (fĭk'*s*atĭv) *adj*. Tending to fix. ~ *n*. Fixative substance, esp. with which drawing or watercolor, film, etc. is coated to prevent blurring or evaporation.

fixed (fĭkst) *adj*. 1. Immovable; stationary; ~ **satellite**, earth satellite that remains over a specific location on Earth's surface; ~ **star**: see STAR. 2. Steady; unyielding; resolute. 3. (chem.) Nonvolatile, used of oils. 4. Not affected by fluctuation or change; unvarying. 5. (colloq.) Situated as regards money etc. 6. (slang) With results dishonestly planned beforehand. **fix·ed·ly** (fĭk'sĭdlē) *adv*. In fixed manner, intently. **fix'ed·ness** *n*.

fix·ings (fĭk'sĭngz) *n.pl*. Necessary apparatus or equipment; accessories, adjuncts, trimmings.

fix·i·ty (fĭk'sĭtē) *n*. (pl. **-ties**). Fixed state; stability, permanence.

fix·ture (fĭks'ch*e*r) *n*. Thing fixed or fastened in position; (law) article of accessory character annexed to houses or lands; person or thing confined to or established in one place.

fizz (fĭz) *n*. Hissing or spluttering sound; effervescence; (colloq.) champagne; any effervescing drink. **fizz'y** *adj*. (**fizz·i·er, fizz·i·est**). **fizz** *v.i*. Make hissing or spluttering sound; effervesce.

fiz·zle (fĭz'*e*l) *v.i*. (**-zled, -zling**). Hiss or splutter feebly; ~ **out**, come to lame conclusion, fail. **fizzle** *n*. Hissing, spluttering; (colloq.) failure, fiasco.

fj·ord (fyōrd) *n*. Long narrow arm of sea between high cliffs, as in Norway.

FL *abbrev*. Florida.

fl. *abbrev*. Florin(s); floruit.

Fla. *abbrev*. Florida.

flab (flăb) *n*. (colloq.) Flabby, fat flesh.

flab·ber·gast (flăb'*e*rgăst) *v.t*. Dumbfound, overwhelm with astonishment.

flab·by (flăb'ē) *adj*. (**-bi·er, -bi·est**). Lacking firmness; flaccid, soft; feeble; ineffectual; fat. **flab'bi·ly** *adv*. **flab'bi·ness** *n*.

flac·cid (flăk'sĭd) *adj*. Hanging or lying loose or wrinkled, limp, flabby; drooping. **flac·cid·i·ty** (flăksĭd'ĭtē) *n*. **flac'cid·ly** *adv*.

flag[1] (flăg) *n*. Any of various monocotyledonous plants with bladed or sword-shaped leaves, esp. of the genus *Iris*, mostly growing in moist places; **blue** ~ (*Iris versicolor*) of N. Amer. **sweet** ~, (*Acorus calamus*) plant with aromatic rhizome.

flag[2] (flăg) *n*. Flat slab of any fine-grained rock that can be split into flagstones; (also **flag'stone**) flat stone suitable for paving. **flag** *v.t*. (**flagged, flag·ging**). Pave with flags.

flag[3] (flăg) *n*. Piece of bunting or other material attached by one edge to staff or halyard and used as standard, ensign, or signal; (naut.) flag carried by flagship as emblem of admiral's rank afloat; plate attached to taxicab meter and lowered to start meter when vehicle is engaged; flag used to indicate start or finish of race; distinctly colored or shaped tail of deer, dog, etc.; **black** ~, flag used as ensign by pirates; also, that formerly hoisted at prison to announce execution of criminal; **quarantine** ~, yellow flag (see below); **white** ~, plain white flag used in token of truce or surrender; **yellow** ~, flag displayed by ship with infectious

*The **flag** or iris is one of the world's most popular and varied garden flowers. The yellow or water flag is a swamp plant found in Eurasia and North Africa; the blue flag occupies similar areas in North America.*

disease on board, hospital ship, or ship in quarantine; ~ **of convenience**, foreign flag under which ship is registered to avoid certain taxes, duties, etc.; ~ **captain**, captain of flagship; **F ~ Day**, June 14, annual holiday celebrating the adoption by Congress of the official U.S. flag (1777); **flag'man** (pl. **-men**), signaler at races etc.; **flag officer**, admiral, vice-admiral, or rear admiral; **flag'pole**, pole on which flag is hoisted; **flag'ship**, ship having fleet or squadron commander on board and flying that officer's flag; **flag'staff**, flagpole. **flag** *v.t.* (**flagged, flag·ging**). Place flag on or over; mark out with flags; inform, warn, communicate, by flag signals; ~ **down**, bring to a stop thus.

flag[4] (flăg) *v.i.* (**flagged, flag·ging**). Hang down, flap loosely; droop, fade, become limp; lag, lose vigor, grow languid; fall off in interest.

flag·el·lant (flăj'*e*lant, fl*a*jĕl'-) *n.* & *adj.* (One) who scourges himself, esp. as religious discipline or penance.

flag·el·late[1] (flăj'*e*lāt) *v.t.* (**-lat·ed, -lat·ing**). Scourge, whip. **flag·el·la·tion** (flăj*e*lā'sh*o*n), **flag'el·la·tor** *ns.*

fla·gel·lum (fl*a*jĕl'*u*m) *n.* (pl. **-gel·la** pr. -jĕl'*a*, **-gel·lums**). (zool., bot.) Microscopic lashlike appendage, esp. one used for locomotion. **flag·el·late**[2] (flăj'*e*lĭt, -lāt, fl*a*jĕl'ĭt) *adj.* & *n.* (Protozoan) having one or more flagella. **fla·gel·li·form** (fl*a*jĕl'*i*fōrm) *adj.*

flag·eo·let (flăj*o*lĕt', -lā') *n.* Small flute blown at end.

flag·on (flăg'*o*n) *n.* Large vessel, usu. with handle, spout, and lid, to hold wine or liquor; large bottle for wine etc., often of flattened globular shape, usu. holding about twice as much as ordinary bottle.

fla·grant (flā'gr*a*nt) *adj.* (of offense or offender) Glaring, notorious, scandalous. **fla'gran·cy** *n.* **fla'grant·ly** *adv.*

fla·gran·te de·lic·to (fl*a*grăn'tē dĭlĭk'tō) = *in flagrante delicto.*

flail (flāl) *n.* Threshing implement, wooden staff at end of which a heavy stick hangs swinging. ~ *v.* Beat or strike (as) with flail; wave wildly or erratically.

The ***flame-thrower*** *has been an effective weapon in war since 1915 and is used mainly to force the enemy out of cover. Here, British troops use a pack-type flame-thrower.*

flair (flār) *n.* Instinctive discernment, selective instinct for what is good, paying, etc.

flak (flăk) *n.* Antiaircraft fire; (fig. slang) barrage of criticism, opposition, abuse, etc. [Ger., f. initial letters of *Fl*ieger*a*bwehr*k*anone A.A. gun]

flake[1] (flāk) *n.* Frame or rack for drying fish etc.; small platform hung over ship's side for workmen to stand on.

flake[2] (flāk) *n.* Small light fleecy mass, esp. of snow; thin broad piece peeled off surface; natural division of fish flesh; (archaeol.) piece of hard stone chipped off core for use as tool. ~ *v.* (**flaked, flak·ing**). Fall like, sprinkle as with, snow; take, come, *away, off*, in flakes. **flak'y** *adj.* (**flak·i·er, flak·i·est**). 1. (esp., of pastry) Consisting when baked of thin delicate flakes or layers. 2. (slang) Very unconventional or odd; eccentric. **flak'i·ness** *n.*

flam[1] (flăm) *n.* Hoax, trick, deception; FLIMFLAM.

flam[2] (flăm) *n.* Drumbeat made by hitting the drumhead with both sticks in rapid succession.

flam·bé (flahmbā') *adj.* (of food) Served flaming in ignited liquor, esp. brandy.

flam·beau (flăm'bō) *n.* (pl. **-beaux, -beaus** pr. -bōz). Torch, esp. of several thick waxed wicks.

flam·boy·ant (flămboi'*a*nt) *adj.* 1. (archit.) Characterized by wavy flamelike lines: of the style prevalent in France in 15th and first half of 16th centuries. 2. Florid, floridly decorated; gorgeously colored; ornate. **flam·boy'ance** *n.*

flame (flām) *n.* 1. Vapor heated to point of combustion, ignited gas; portion of this, often spire-like or tonguelike; (pl.) fire; visible combustion; **flame'out**, failure of jet engine because of poor combustion or failure in fuel supply; **flame'-thrower**, (Ger. *flammenwerfer*), machine of war with reservoir from which long spray of flame can be ejected. 2. Bright light; brilliant coloring; flame-red. 3. Passion, esp. of love; (slang) sweetheart. **flame** *v.* (**flamed, flam·ing**). 1. Emit flames, blaze. 2. (of passion) Burst out; (of persons) break *out*, blaze *up*, into anger. 3. Glow like or as with flame; shine brightly. 4. Move as or like flame.

fla·men·co (fl*a*mĕng'kō) *n.* (pl. **-cos**). Spanish gypsy style of singing or dancing; song or dance in this style.

flam·ing (flā'mĭng) *adj.* Very hot; bright-colored; very bright; highly colored, exaggerated, startling.

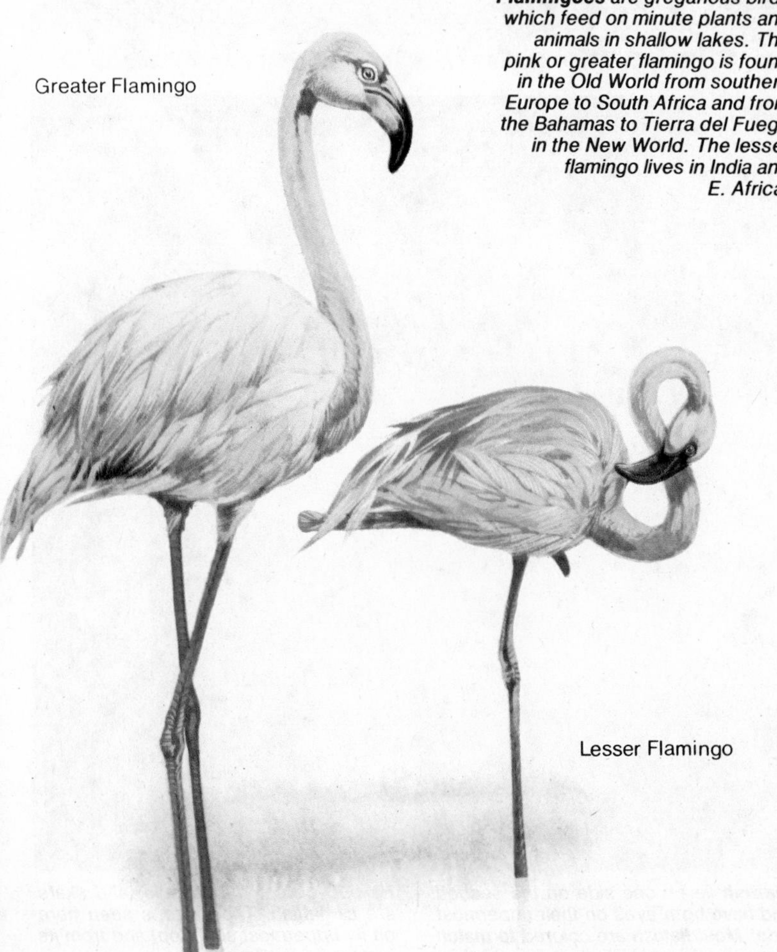

***Flamingoes** are gregarious birds which feed on minute plants and animals in shallow lakes. The pink or greater flamingo is found in the Old World from southern Europe to South Africa and from the Bahamas to Tierra del Fuego in the New World. The lesser flamingo lives in India and E. Africa.*

fla·min·go (fl*a*mĭng´gō) *n.* (pl. **-gos, -goes**). Wading bird of the widely distributed family Phoenicopteridae with reddish-orange plumage, extremely long legs and neck, and heavy bent bill.

flam·ma·ble (flăm´*a*bel) *adj.* Easily set on fire, inflammable. **flam·ma·bil·i·ty** (flăm*a*bĭl´ĭtē) *n.*

flan (flăn, flahn) *n.* Molded custard with burnt caramel topping.

Flan·ders (flăn´d*e*rz). Ancient countship now a region divided between Belgium, France, and Holland; also, the area of Belgium comprising the provinces of **East** ~ and **West** ~.

flange (flănj) *n.* Projecting flat rim, collar, or rib, used to strengthen an object, attach it to another, etc. ~ *v.t.* (**flanged, flang·ing**).

flank (flăngk) *n.* 1. Fleshy or muscular part of side between ribs and hip. 2. Side of building, mountain, etc.; (mil.) extreme left or right side of army or body of troops. 3. Slice of meat from animal flank, often ~ **steak. flank** *v.t.* Guard, protect, strengthen, on flank; menace or attack flank of; be posted or situated at flank of; (pass.) have at flanks or sides.

flan·nel (flăn´*e*l) *n.* Light soft woolen fabric, usu. without nap; (pl.) underclothing of flannel; (pl.) garments, esp. trousers, of flannel. ~ *v.t.* Wrap in flannel; polish with flannel.

flap (flăp) *v.* (**flapped, flap·-**

ping). 1. Strike with something broad and flexible. 2. Swing or sway about, flutter, oscillate; move (wings), (of wings) move, up and down; beat the wings. ~ *n.* 1. Light blow with something broad; motion of something broad and loose, as wing, etc. 2. Broad hanging piece hinged or attached by one side only, as leaf of table, piece of cloth covering opening of pocket, etc.; movable section on wing or tail of aircraft, used to modify lift or drag. 3. (slang) State of agitation or fuss.

flap·jack (flăp′jăk) *n.* Pancake.

flap·per (flăp′*er*) *n.* (esp.) 1. Broad fin; flipper. 2. (colloq.) Young woman of the 1920s, esp. one having bold manners and dressing unconventionally.

flare (flār) *v.* (**flared, flar·ing**). 1. (Cause to) widen or spread (gradually) outward, as the sides of a ship, a skirt, etc.; **flared** (*adj.*) widening thus. 2. Burn with spreading unsteady flame; shine like such flame; glow as with flame; **flare up**, burst into sudden blaze or anger. **flare** *n.* 1. Dazzling irregular light; unshaded flame in open air; sudden outburst of flame; combustible material burned as signal or guide in fog, at night, etc.; bright light dropped from aircraft to illuminate target etc.; (photog.) fogging caused by internal reflection within a lens; **flare′-up** (*n.*) (1) sudden blaze of flame; (2) sudden outburst of rage, violence, illness, etc. 2. Gradual widening or spreading of ship's sides, skirt, etc.

flash (flăsh) *n.* 1. Sudden quick transitory blaze; time occupied by this, instant; brief outburst, transitory display; superficial brilliance, ostentation; (photog.) artificial light illuminating subject briefly during exposure; ~ **in the pan**, ignition of gunpowder in pan of old gun without discharge of missile; (fig.) abortive effort or outburst. 2. Flashlight. 3. (also **news** ~) Very brief, important news report. 4. **flash′back**, (motion pictures, novels, etc.) Recapitulation of earlier scene, episode beginning with sudden change to an earlier point of time; **flash′bulb**, electric bulb that briefly emits dazzling light when ignited, for taking photographs; **flash card**, any of a group of cards having words, numbers, or pictures flashed individually by teacher in front of class for quick answers during a drill; **flash′cube**, small cube containing four flashbulbs and rotating automatically when a photograph is taken with the camera into which it is plugged; **flash flood**, sudden localized flooding occurring after heavy rain in the immediate area; **flash gun**, synchronized photographic apparatus that simul-

***Flatfish** lie on one side on the seabed and have both eyes on their uppermost side. Most flatfish are colored to match the ground on which they lie and they are found in warm and temperate seas. Halibut, plaice, turbot, sole, and skate are all flatfish. The skate is seen here on its uppermost side (top) and from its underside (bottom).*

taneously discharges a flashbulb and works camera shutter; **flash'light**, small, portable electric light operated by dry batteries; (photog.) brief burst of dazzling light from a photographic lamp; **flash'over**, electric spark or arc appearing suddenly across surface of insulating material; **flash point**, temperature at which vapor given off by oil etc. will ignite; **flash'tube**, gaseous discharge tube used in an electronic flash and producing short, intense bursts of light. **flash** *adj.* 1. (archaic) Connected with thieves, tramps, etc., or their jargon. 2. Showy; sudden, brief. **flash** *v.* 1. Break suddenly into flame or light; give out flame or sparks; emit or reflect light, gleam; send, reflect, like a flash or in flashes; cause to flash. 2. Burst suddenly into view or perception; move swiftly. 3. Express or communicate quickly. 4. (colloq.) Make ostentatious show (of possessions). 5. (slang) Show (a gun, badge, etc.). 6. Protect joints of roofing etc. with flashing. 7. (slang) Expose part(s) of body to public view. **flash'er** *n.*

flash·ing (flăsh'ĭng) *n.* Strip of metal to prevent flooding or leakage at joint of roofing etc.

flash·y (flăsh'ē) *adj.* (**flash·i·er, flash·i·est**). Brilliant but shallow or transitory; cheaply attractive; showy, gaudy; given to display. **flash'i·ly** *adv.* **flash'i·ness** *n.*

flask (flăsk, flahsk) *n.* 1. (hist., usu. **powder ~**) Leather or metal case for carrying hunter's etc. supply of gunpowder. 2. Narrow-necked bulbous bottle. 3. Pocket bottle of metal or glass.

flat[1] (flăt) *n.* (chiefly Brit.) Apartment.

flat[2] (flăt) *adj.* (**flat·ter, flat·test**). 1. Horizontal, level; spread out, lying at full length. 2. Even, smooth, unbroken, without projection; with broad level surface and little depth. 3. Unqualified, plain, downright. 4. Dull, lifeless, monotonous; dejected, without energy; (of drink) that has lost its effervescence or flavor, insipid, stale; (of paint) without luster; (photog.) wanting in contrast. 5. Below the true pitch; **B ~, E ~**, etc. (written B♭ etc.; see *n.* below, sense 5), a semitone lower than B, E, etc. 6. (of price, rate, etc.) Unvarying, fixed, uniform; not varying with changed conditions. 7. **flat'bed**, truck or trailer with body in the form of a platform or shallow box; **flat'boat**, flat-bottomed boat for transport in shallow water; **flat'car**, railroad freight car without sides or top; **flat'fish**, any of numerous fishes, including halibut, flounder, turbot, and sole, having a compressed body and both eyes on the uppermost side; **flat'foot(ed)**, (having) foot not normally arched at instep; hence, (fig.) heavy, clumsy; (slang) police officer; **Flat'head**, (member of) one of several N. Amer. Ind. tribes of the NW. coast thought to flatten their children's heads; (member of) the Salishan tribe of Montana; **flat'iron**, iron for pressing clothes (now usu. of one heated from below, not within); **flat-out** (*adj.*) (colloq.) thorough, absolute; **flat race**, horse race over clear and level dirt track (opp. to STEEPLECHASE); **flat'ware**, table utensils such as knives, forks, and spoons; **flat'worm**, any of the tapeworms, flukes, etc. **flat'ly** *adv.* **flat'ness** *n.* **flat** *adv.* Downright, positively, plainly; fully, quite; **~ out, ~-out**, = ALL out. **flat** *n.* 1. What is flat; flat surface or part, esp. broad surface of blade as opp. to edge; inside of open hand; (often pl.) level country; low lying marshy land, swamp; (usu. pl., also **mud ~s**) level ground over which tide flows, or which is covered by shallow water. 2. (theatr.) Section of scenery mounted on frame. 3. Shallow box for plant seedlings. 4. Deflated automobile tire. 5. (mus.) Note lowered by a semitone below usual pitch; sign (♭) indicating this lowering, placed before note that is to be flattened or forming part of key signature; **double ~** (♭♭), sign indicating that note must be lowered two semitones; **two ~s, three ~s**, etc., key indicated by two, three, etc., flats in key signature. **flat** *v.* (**flat·ted, flat·ting**). Make flat.

flat·ten (flăt'en) *v.t.* Make flat; **~ out**, (esp.) bring (flight of aircraft) parallel with ground after diving.

flat·ter (flăt'*er*) *v.t.* Court, fawn upon; praise or compliment unduly or insincerely; gratify vanity or self-esteem of, make feel honored or distinguished; please (usu. **oneself**) with belief, idea, suggestion, *that;* exaggerate good points of, represent too favorably. **flat'ter·er, flat'ter·y** *ns.* **flat'ter·ing·ly** *adv.*

flat·u·lent (flăch'*u*lent) *adj.* Generating gas or air in the alimentary canal; caused by, attended with, troubled with, accumulation of this; (fig.) inflated, puffed up, windy, pretentious. **flat'u·lence** *n.* **flat'u·lent·ly** *adv.*

fla·tus (flā'*tus*) *n.* Gas, air, in stomach or bowel.

Flau·bert (flōbār'), **Gustave** (1821–80). French realistic novelist; author of *Madame Bovary, Salammbô*, etc.

flaunt (flawnt) *v.* Wave proudly; display oneself or one's finery; show off, parade. **flaunt'ing·ly** *adv.*

flau·tist (flow'ĭst, flaw'-) *n.* Flute player; flutist.

fla·vin (flā'vĭn) *n.* Any of a group of yellow pigments found in

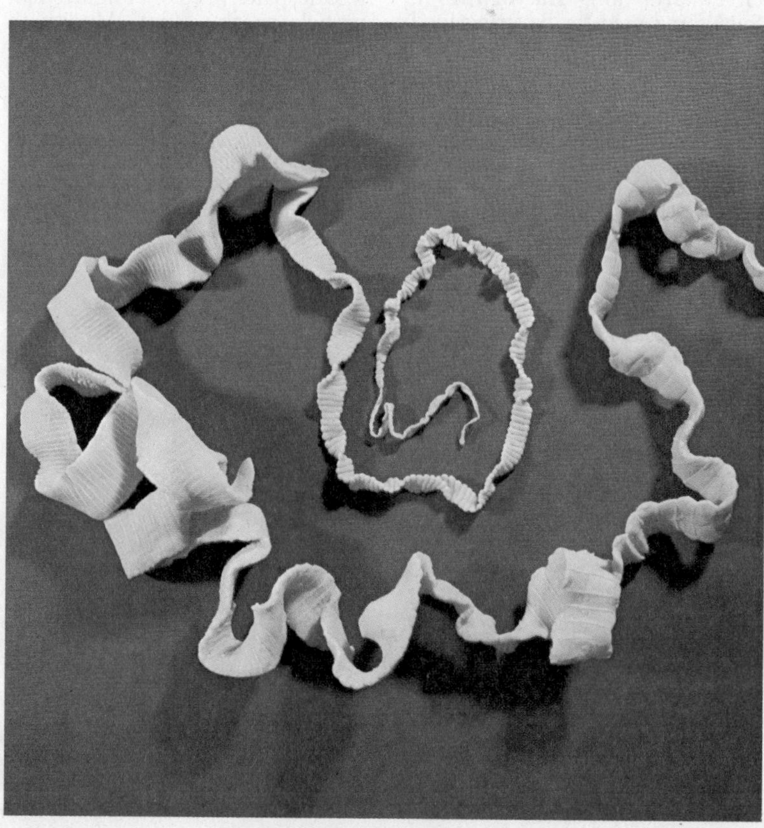

Flatworms like this beef tapeworm, are small slender parasites which dwell in or on the bodies of other animals or plants. This tapeworm is parasitic in man.

Flax produces two kinds of yarn. One is very fine and is used for high-quality linen and lace. The coarser kind is mainly used for making rope. Linseed oil, from the seed, is used in paint and varnishes.

Fleabane plants are characterized by their white or purplish flower heads and orange centers; all are reputed to repel fleas.

plants and animals and used as dyes and antiseptics.

fla·vor (flā′*ver*) *n.* Distinctive taste; undefinable characteristic quality. **fla′vor·ful, fla′vor·less, fla′vor·some** *adjs.* **flavor** *v.t.* Give flavor to. **fla′vor·ing** *n.* Something used for flavoring food or drink.

flaw[1] (flaw) *n.* Crack, breach, rent; imperfection, blemish; invalidating defect in legal document etc. ~ *v.* Crack, damage, mar. **flaw′less** *adj.* **flaw′less·ly** *adv.* **flaw′less·ness** *n.*

flaw[2] (flaw) *n.* Squall of wind; short storm.

flax (flăks) *n.* Blue-flowered plant (*Linum usitatissimum*) cultivated for its seeds (linseed) and for textile fiber obtained from the stem of the plant; dressed or undressed flax fibers; cloth made from these, linen; **flax′seed**, linseed. **flax′en** *adj.* Of flax; (of hair) colored like dressed flax, pale yellow.

flay (flā) *v.t.* Strip off skin or hide of; (fig.) criticize severely; fleece, charge extortionately; peel off (skin, bark, peel).

flea (flē) *n.* Small wingless insect of order Siphonapter, well known for its biting propensities and powers of jumping, feeding on human and other blood; **flea′bag**, (joc.) old worn-out horse; cheap hotel; **flea′bane**, any of various plants of the genus *Erigeron*, having daisylike flowers of several colors, reputed to repel fleas; **~-bitten**, bitten by or infested with fleas; (colloq.) showing wear or heavy use; seedy, disreputable; ~ **market**, shop or market, usu. having numerous separate tables, stalls, etc., selling antiques, secondhand merchandise, etc.

fleck (flĕk) *n.* Spot in the skin, freckle; patch of color or light; small particle, speck. ~ *v.t.* Mark with flecks, dapple, variegate.

fled (flĕd): see FLEE.

fledge (flĕj) *v.t.* (**fledged, fledg·ing**). Provide with feathers or plumage, wing for flight; cover as with feathers or down; feather (arrow).

fledg·ling (flĕj′lĭng) *n.* Young bird just fledged.

flee (flē) *v.* (**fled, flee·ing**). Run away, seek safety in flight; vanish, cease, pass away; run away from, leave abruptly; shun.

fleece (flēs) *n.* Woolly covering of sheep or similar animal; quantity of wool shorn from sheep at one time; thing like a fleece, white cloud, falling snow, etc.; **Golden**

*The **fleece** of sheep bred mainly for wool yields about 15 lbs per animal; in Britain, where the emphasis is on mutton, woolly breeds only give about 10 lbs. Shearing (facing page) takes place once a year, and the fleece, which should come off in one piece, is rolled up and graded (below). In Australia and New Zealand it takes about 5 minutes to shear a sheep.*

PREVENT BUSH FIRES

F~: see GOLDEN. **fleec'y** *adj.* (**fleec·i·er, fleec·i·est**). **fleece** *v.t.* (**fleeced, fleec·ing**). 1. (rare) Shear (sheep). 2. Strip of money, property, etc.; plunder, rob heartlessly. 3. Overspread as with fleece.

fleet[1] (flēt) *n.* Navy, number of warships under one command; number of ships or boats sailing in company; number of boats, vehicles, etc. forming, owned, or operated as a group or unit; ~ **admiral**, highest ranking officer of U.S. Navy, next above admiral, and wearing five stars.

fleet[2] (flēt) *n.* (Brit. archaic or dial.) Inlet.

fleet[3] (flēt) *adj.* Swift, nimble. **fleet'ly** *adv.* **fleet'ness** *n.*

fleet[4] (flēt) *v.i.* Glide away, vanish, be transitory; pass rapidly, slip *away*; move swiftly, fly. **fleet'ing** *adj.* **fleet'ing·ly** *adv.* **fleet'ing·ness** *n.*

Flem, Flem. *abbrevs.* Flemish.

Flem·ing[1] (flĕm'ĭng) *n.* Native, inhabitant, of Flanders.

Flem·ing[2] (flĕm'ĭng), **Sir Alexander** (1881–1955). Brit. bacteriologist; the chief discoverer of PENICILLIN.

***Alexander Fleming** accidentally discovered the antibiotic, penicillin, when he was cultivating bacteria responsible for boils, and found his culture spoilt by a blue-green mold. Fleming was awarded the Nobel Prize in 1945.*

Flem·ish (flĕm'ĭsh) *adj.* Of Flanders or its people or language. ~ *n.* 1. (collect.) People of Flanders. 2. Language of Flanders.

*The major **Flemish** artist of the 15th century was Jan van Eyck who perfected the use of oil as a medium in painting. His brilliant use of color and realistic detailing are evident in this painting, 'Arnolfini Marriage'.*

flense (flĕns) *v.t.* (**flensed, flens·ing**), also **flench** (flĕnch). Strip (blubber) from (whale, seal).

flesh (flĕsh) *n.* 1. Soft substance, esp. muscular parts, of animal body between skin and bones; ~ **and blood**, human body or its material; mankind; human nature with its emotions and infirmities; (as *adj.*) actually living, not supernatural or imaginary; **one's own ~ and blood**, near relations, descendants. 2. Pulpy substance of fruit or plant. 3. Plumpness, fat; **lose, put on, ~**, grow thin, fat. 4. Tissue of animal bodies (sometimes excluding fish and fowl) as food; meat. 5. Visible surface of human body, with ref. to color or appearance. 6. Whatever has corporeal life; the body (now only in biblical allusions); man's physical nature; the sensual appetites; **in the ~**, in bodily form, in life; in person; **sins of the ~**, unchastity. 7. **~-color(ed)**, (of the) color of Caucasian skin, yellowish-pink; ~ **fly**, insect of family Sarcophagidae, which deposits eggs in dead flesh; **flesh'-pots**, (with ref. to Exod. 16) places offering licentious high living, luxuries; **flesh wound**, wound not reaching bone or vital organ. **flesh** *v.t.* Incite (hound etc.) by taste of blood; initiate in bloodshed.

flesh·ly (flĕsh'lē) *adj.* (**-li·er, -li·est**). 1. Carnal, lascivious, sensual. 2. Mortal, material; not divine or spiritual; worldly. **flesh'li·ness** *n.*

flesh·y (flĕsh'ē) *adj.* (**flesh·i·er, flesh·i·est**). Plump, fat; (of fruit etc.) pulpy; like flesh. **flesh'i·ness** *n.*

fleur-de-lis, fleur-de-lys (flẽr de lē', floor, lēs'; *Fr.* flör delēs') *ns.* (pl. **fleurs-de-lys** pr. flẽr de lēz', floor; *Fr.* flör de lēs'). Iris flower; heraldic lily; royal arms of France, resembling three petals of an iris tied together.

flew (flōō): see FLY[2].

flex (flĕks) *v.t.* Bend; esp. bend (joint or limb) by action of flexor muscles.

flex·i·ble (flĕk'sibel) *adj.* That will bend without breaking, pliable, pliant; easily led, manageable; adaptable, versatile; supple, complaisant. **flex·i·bil·i·ty** (flĕksibĭl'ĭtē) *n.* **flex'i·bly** *adv.*

flex·ion (flĕk'shon) *n.* Bending, bent state (esp. of limb or joint).

flex·or (flĕk'ser) *n.* Muscle producing flexion in any part of body (opp. EXTENSOR).

flex·ure (flĕk'sher) *n.* Bending, curvature, bent state.

flick (flĭk) *n.* 1. Light sharp blow with whiplash etc. shot out and withdrawn, or with fingernail; sudden movement, jerk; quick turn of wrist, as in bowling or batting; slight sharp cracking sound. 2. (orig. Brit. slang) Motion picture. ~ *v.* Strike with a flick; dash or jerk *away, off*; give a flick with; throw (ball etc.) with a flick of the wrist; flutter, twitch.

flick·er[1] (flĭk′*er*) *v.i.* Quiver, vibrate; wave to and fro, flutter; flash up and die away alternately; burn fitfully or unsteadily. ~ *n.* Flickering movement; wavering or rapidly fluctuating light or flame.

flick·er[2] (flĭk′*er*) *n.* Large N. Amer. woodpecker of genus *Colaptes* with spotted breast and brown back.

fli·er, fly·er (flī′*er*) *ns.* Bird etc. that flies; animal, vehicle, etc., going with exceptional speed; (usu. **flyer**) airplane pilot; (colloq.) speculation, business risk; handbill.

flight[1] (flīt) *n.* 1. (Manner of) flying; swift movement, esp. through the air; swift passage (of time); soaring, excursion, sally (*of* wit, fancy, ambition, etc.). 2. Migration, migrating body, flock, of birds or insects; number of warplanes forming a subdivision of a squadron; volley *of* arrows etc. 3. Distance that bird, aircraft, or missile can fly. 4. Airplane trip; scheduled airplane; (mil.) planes flying in formation. 5. Series (*of* stairs etc.) mounting between landings, or without change of direction. 6. Feather etc. on arrow or dart. 7. ~ **bag**, small lightweight bag in which airline passengers carry personal items; ~ **deck**, deck of aircraft carrier for taking off and landing of aircraft; ~ **line**, section of airfield where planes are parked and serviced; ~ **path**, locus of center of gravity of airplane while airborne; ~ **recorder**, device in aircraft recording details of flight; ~ **strip**, landing strip for emergency use by airplanes; ~**-test**, (*v.*), test (airplane) when in the air.

flight[2] (flīt) *n.* Running away, fleeing; hasty retreat; absconding; **put to** ~, rout; **take (to)** ~, run away.

flight·less (flīt′lĭs) *adj.* (of bird etc.) Unable to fly.

flight·y (flī′tē) *adj.* (**flight·i·er, flight·i·est**). Guided by whim or fancy, fickle; unstable, irresponsible; dim-witted. **flight′i·ly** *adv.* **flight′i·ness** *n.*

flim·flam (flĭm′flăm) *n.* Nonsense; humbug; deception, swindle, confidence game.

flim·sy (flĭm′zē) *adj.* (**-si·er, -si·est**). Easily destroyed, frail, slightly put together; paltry, trivial; frivolous, superficial. **flim′si·ly** *adv.* **flim′si·ness** *n.* **flim′sy** *n.* Thin kind of paper, esp. that used for carbon copies; carbon copy.

flinch (flĭnch) *v.i.* Give way, draw back, shrink (*from* something as dangerous, painful, or difficult); wince.

fling (flĭng) *v.* (**flung, fling·ing**). 1. Rush, go angrily or violently. 2. Throw, cast, hurl; throw with violence, or hostile intent, hurl as missile; extend (arms) with sudden movement; cast (glance etc.); throw *into* (prison etc.); (of wrestler or ridden horse) throw to the ground; launch (troops etc.) *on* enemy, *against* fortress, etc. ~ *n.* 1. Throw, cast. 2. Vigorous dance in which arms and legs are flung about (esp. **Highland** ~). 3. Spell of indulgence in pleasure; esp. in **have a** ~. 4. Attempt, esp. in **take a ~ at.**

flint (flĭnt) *n.* Hard stone of nearly pure silica found in roundish nodules, usu. steely gray and encrusted with white, and having the property of giving off sparks when struck with steel; piece of this used with steel to kindle flame, fire powder in flintlock gun, etc.; piece of hard alloy used to produce spark in cigarette lighter etc.; pebble or

*This **flight recorder,** known as the 'red egg', converts information on an aircraft's flight into digital form and records it on stainless steel wire. Its case can withstand extremes of pressure and temperature.*

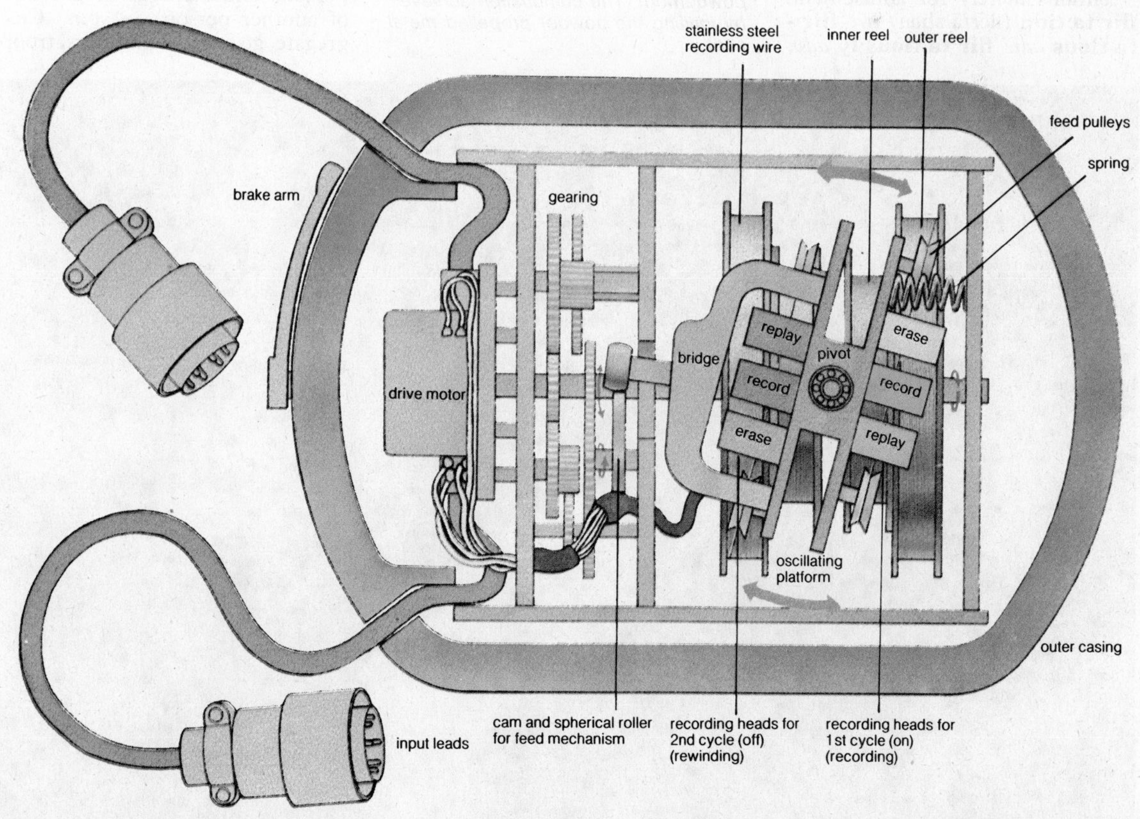

nodule of flint flaked or chipped by prehistoric man to form a tool or weapon; ~ **glass**, pure lustrous glass, orig. made with ground flint; **flint'lock**, (gun with) lock in which flint struck against hammer produces sparks which ignite priming. **flint'y** *adj.* (**flint·i·er, flint·i·est**). **flint'i·ly** *adv.* **flint'i·ness** *n.*

flip[1] (flĭp) *n.* Mixture of beer, or usu. liquor, sweetened and heated with hot iron rod; mixed drink with wine or liquor, egg, etc.

flip[2] (flĭp) *v.* (**flipped, flip·ping**). Propel, strike, with fillip or flick; make, move with, flip; (slang) react strongly or enthusiastically; ~ **one's lid,** ~ **out**, lose self-control. **flip** *n.* Fillip, flick; ~ **side**, (colloq.) reverse side of phonograph record.

flip[3] (flĭp) *adj.* (**flip·per, flip·pest**). Flippant, glib.

flip·pant (flĭp'*a*nt) *adj.* Lacking in gravity; treating serious subjects with unbecoming levity, disrespectful. **flip'pan·cy** *n.* **flip'pant·ly** *adv.*

flip·per (flĭp'*er*) *n.* Limb used to swim with, e.g., forelimb of cetacean, any limb of seal, walrus, turtle; wing of penguin; (pl.) rubber etc. devices attached to the feet for underwater swimming.

flirt (flẽrt) *v.* 1. Flit, dart. 2. Play at courtship *with*; trifle, toy *with*. ~ *n.* 1. Sudden jerk; quick motion quickly checked. 2. Man who pays, or usu. woman who invites or accepts, amorous attentions merely for amusement. **flir·ta·tion** (flẽrtā'sh*o*n) *n.* **flir·ta'tious** *adj.* **flir·ta'tious·ly** *adv.*

flit (flĭt) *v.i.* (**flit·ted, flit·ting**). 1. Move, dart about rapidly. 2. Fly lightly and swiftly; make short and swift flights. ~ *n.*

flitch (flĭch) *n.* 1. Salted or cured side of bacon. 2. Slice cut lengthwise from tree trunk; strengthening plate on beam, girder, etc. ~ *v.t.* Cut into flitches.

flit·ter (flĭt'*er*) *v.i.* Flit about, flutter.

fliv·ver (flĭv'*er*) *n.* (slang) Old or cheap automobile, usu. a Model-T Ford.

float (flōt) *v.* 1. Rest, drift, on surface of liquid; (of stranded vessel) get afloat; be suspended freely *in* liquid; move or be suspended in air as if buoyed up; hover *before* eye or mind; (of currency) (allow to) fluctuate in regard to exchange rate. 2. Launch (scheme, enterprise, etc.), be launched. 3. Cover with liquid, inundate; (of water etc.) support, bear along (object); set afloat; waft through air. ~ *n.* 1. Floating object; raft; cork supporting fishing line and dipping when fish bites; cork etc. supporting edge of fishing net; hollow metallic ball regulating water level in boiler or tank; watertight structure attached to seaplane to give it buoyancy when resting on surface of water. 2. Cold soft drink with ball of ice cream floating on top. 3. Large flat vehicle or platform on wheels carrying an exhibit in parade etc. 4. Tool for smoothing plaster. 5. (commerc.) Sum representing outstanding checks in process of collection.

float·er (flō'ter) *n.* 1. One who floats. 2. One who drifts from place to place, job to job, etc.

float·ing (flō'tĭng) *adj.* (esp.) 1. Having little attachment, disconnected; (of kidney etc.) displaced, out of the normal position; ~ **rib**, rib (in man, one of the two lower pairs) not attached to breastbone in front. 2. (commerc.) In circulation; (of capital) available for use; (of debt) short-term. 3. Fluctuating; variable; not settled in definite state or place. 4. ~ **(dry) dock**: see DOCK[3].

floc·cu·lant (flŏk'y*u*l*a*nt) *n.* Chemical agent for causing suspended particles to form flocculent masses.

floc·cu·lent (flŏk'y*u*l*e*nt) *adj.* Like tufts of wool; in, showing, tufts. **floc'cu·lence** *n.*

flock[1] (flŏk) *n.* Lock, tuft, of wool, cotton, etc.; material for quilting and stuffing made of wool refuse or shredded cloth; powdered wool or felt applied to paper, cloth, etc. to produce a pattern or texture.

flock[2] (flŏk) *n.* 1. Large assembly of people. 2. Number of animals of one kind (now esp. birds) feeding or traveling in company; number of domestic animals (now only sheep or goats) kept together. 3. Congregation, esp. in relation to its minister; (occas.) any body of persons under charge or guidance of another person. ~ *v.i.* Congregate, go in great numbers, troop.

*A well-preserved **flintlock** pistol and powderhorn. The combustion achieved by igniting the powder propelled metal shot.*

*The lobster trap **float** (above) is used to provide buoyancy to the trap. There is a multitude of fishing floats. The Sunderland flying boat (right) floats on the water when at rest. Flying boats are mainly used where there are few conventional landing strips, but plenty of calm water.*

floe (flō) *n.* Sheet of floating ice.

flog (flŏg) *v.t.* (**flogged, flog·ging**). 1. Beat with stick, whip, etc. 2. (slang) Sell. **flog'ger** *n.*

flood (flŭd) *n.* Flowing in of tide; flowing water, river, stream, sea (poet.); irruption of water over land, inundation (**the F ~**, the great deluge recorded in Genesis as occurring in time of Noah); outpouring of water; torrent, downpour (also fig. as **~ of abuse, ~ of tears**); **flood'gate**, gate that can be opened or closed to admit or exclude water, esp. floodwater; lower gate of lock; sluice; **flood'light**, artificial light flooding surface of building etc. more or less uniformly; (*v.t.*) light thus; **flood plain**, plain near a river, subject to flooding; **flood tide**, high tide; (fig.) peak, climax. **flood** *v.* Inundate, cover with a flood; irrigate; deluge with water; (of rain) fill (river) to overflowing; become flooded; come in floods or great quantities; drive *out* by floods.

floor (flōr, flo͞r) *n.* 1. Layer of boards, brick, etc., on which people tread in room, lower surface of interior of room; bottom of sea, cave, etc.; lowest boundary or part. 2. (in legislative assemblies etc.) Part of house where members sit and from which they speak; hence, in parliamentary proceedings, the right of speaking. 3. Set of rooms etc. on same level in building, story. 4. Level area; platform or leveled space for threshing etc. 5. Bottom price or limit, in law, at an auction, etc. 6. **floor'board**, one of the boards of a floor, esp. in a boat; (often pl.) the floor of a car; **floor leader**, person appointed by a political party to direct its activities on the floor of legislative body; person at convention who directs campaign of candidate seeking nomination; **floor manager**, stage manager of television production; **floor'shift**, automobile gearshift lever set in floor; **floor show**, entertainment presented in night club etc.; **floor'walker**, (formerly) department store sales supervisor. **floor** *v.t.* 1. Furnish with floor; pave; serve as floor of. 2. Bring to floor or ground, knock down; confound, nonplus; get the better of.

***Flint** was first used by primitive man for making knives, spearheads and other tools and weapons since it broke easily into flakes and fragments. It is an excellent building material because of its durability.*

***Floods** have always been a part of the natural order, and in many ancient civilizations were put to good use as a means of supplying nutrients to the land. Modern man, however, sees floods in a destructive light. Right: Floodwaters spilling across roads in Bonsale, California. Middle: Farmland submerged under water at least 10 ft. deep. Bottom: Floods tore through these grain elevators in the Mid-West, ruining the crop. Flood control is a problem that has confronted man for many years, and still no real solution is in sight.*

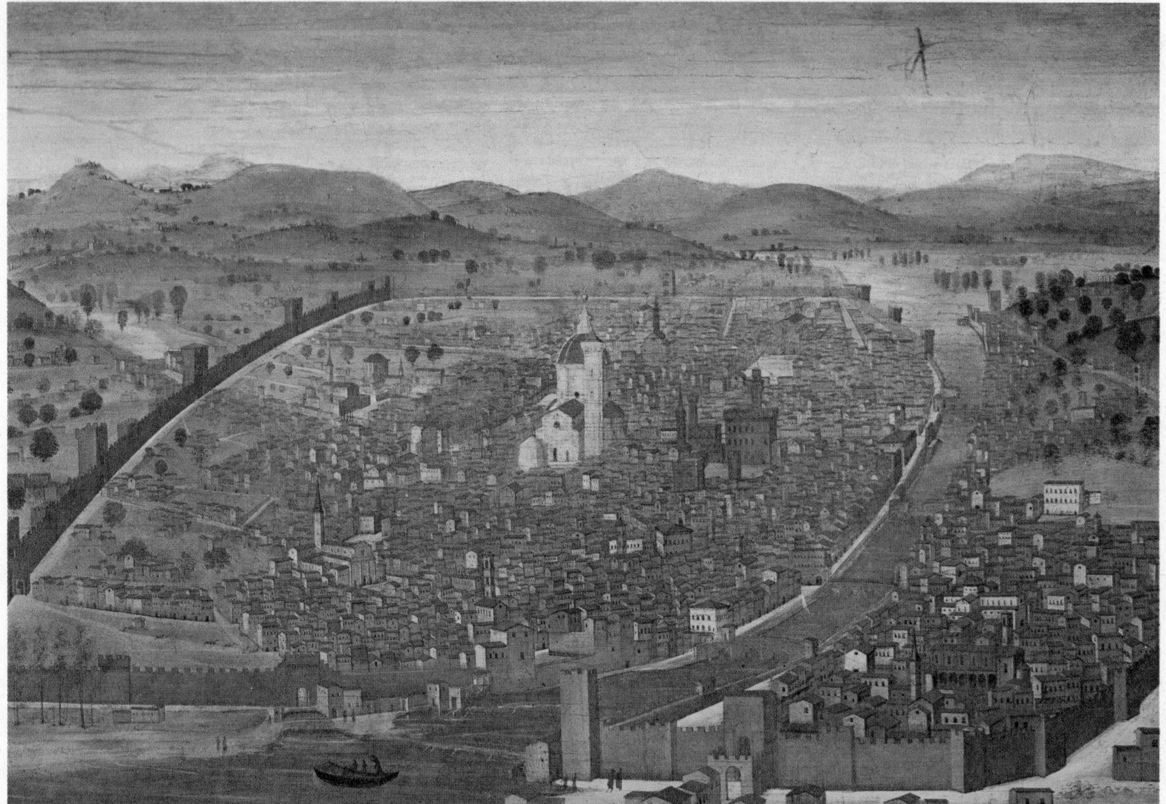

*15th century **Florence** was the center of Italian art and culture and the birthplace of the Renaissance. The city contains some of the finest works of that period, many of them housed in the Palazzo Pitti.*

floo·zy (flo͞o′zē) *n.* (pl. **-zies**). Cheaply and flashily dressed woman of loose morals; a prostitute.

flop (flŏp) *v.* (**flopped, flop·ping**). Sway about heavily and loosely, flap; move clumsily or heavily, or with sudden bump or thud; (slang) fail. ~ *n.* Flopping motion, sound made by it; (slang) failure. **flop′py** *adj.* (**-pi·er, -pi·est**). Inclined to flop.

flop·house (flŏp′hows) *n.* Low-grade rooming house or hotel chiefly for indigent men.

flop·o·ver (flŏp′ōv*e*r) *n.* Continuous vertical motion on television screen, caused by poor reception.

Flo·ra (flōr′*a*, flo͞r′*a*). (Rom. myth.) Goddess of flowers and spring.

flo·ra (flōr′*a*, flo͞r′*a*) *n.* (pl. **flo·ras, flo·rae** pr. flōr′ē, flo͞r′ē). (List of) plants of particular region or epoch. **flo′ral** *adj.* Of flora(s); of flower(s). **flo′ral·ly** *adv.* [f. FLORA]

Flo·ré·al (flawrāahl′). Eighth month (Apr. 20–May 19) in French Revolutionary calendar.

Flor·ence (flo͞r′ens, fla͞r′-). Central Italian city in Tuscany on the Arno River at the foot of the Apennines; major cultural and artistic center in W. Europe during 14th–16th centuries, esp. in development of Italian Renaissance.

Flor·en·tine (flo͞r′entēn, -tīn, fla͞r′-) *adj.* Of Florence. ~ *n.* Native, inhabitant, of Florence.

flo·res·cence (fl*o*rĕs′*e*ns) *n.* Period or state of blossoming. **flo·res′cent** *adj.*

flo·ret (flōr′ĭt, flo͞r′-, fl*o*rĕt′) *n.* (bot.) One of the small flowers making up a composite flower; small flower.

flo·ri·bun·da (flōr*i*bŭn′d*a*, flo͞r-) *n.* Plant (esp. kind of rose) bearing flowers in dense clusters.

flo·ri·cul·ture (flōr′*i*kŭlch*e*r, flo͞r′-) *n.* Cultivation of flowers. **flo·ri·cul·tur·ist** (flōr*i*kŭl′ch*e*rĭst, flo͞r-) *n.*

flor·id (flo͞r′ĭd, fla͞r′-) *adj.* (obs.) Profusely adorned as with flowers; elaborately ornate; ostentatious, showy; ruddy, flushed, high-colored. **flor′id·ly** *adv.*

Flor·i·da (flo͞r′ĭd*a*, fla͞r′-). Southeasternmost U.S. state, extending as a peninsula between the Atlantic and the Gulf of Mexico; 27th state to join Union (1845); capital Tallahassee; ~ **Keys,** chain of small islands extending from S. tip of Florida 150 mi. (242 km) SW. to Key West; ~ **Straits,** straits between the Florida Keys and Cuba connecting the Gulf of Mexico with the Atlantic Ocean. **Flo·rid′i·an, Flor′i·dan** *adjs.* & *ns.*

flor·in (flo͞r′ĭn, fla͞r′-) *n.* 1. Brit. coin, former 2-shilling piece. 2. Monetary unit of various European and South African countries. 3. (hist.) Gold coin first issued at Florence in 1252; any of various other gold coins formerly current in Europe. [OF. f. L. *flos flor-* flower, because the orig. florin was stamped with a lily]

flo·rist (flo͞r′ĭst, fla͞r′-) *n.* One who (raises and) sells flowers and ornamental plants.

flo·ru·it (flōr′ŭĭt, flo͞r′-, -o͝oĭt) *n.* Period (failing exact dates of birth and death) at which person was alive or worked (abbrev. fl.). [L., = "flourished"]

floss (flaws, flŏs) *n.* Rough silk enveloping silkworm cocoon; untwisted or loosely twisted filaments of silk used for needlework. **floss′y** *adj.* (**floss·i·er, floss·i·est**).

flo·ta·tion (flōtā′sh*o*n) *n.* Floating; launching of a company or enterprise; ~ **collar,** circular inflated tube attached to space vehicle after landing in water.

flo·til·la (flōtĭl′*a*) *n.* Small fleet; fleet of boats or small ships; (U.S. Navy) unit of two or more squadrons of small warships.

flot·sam (flŏt′s*a*m) *n.* Wreckage found floating (cf. JETSAM).

flounce[1] (flowns) *v.i.* (**flounced, flounc·ing**). Go with agitated or violent motion, flop, plunge, throw the body about. ~ *n.* Fling, jerk, of body or limb.

flounce[2] (flowns) *n.* Ornamental

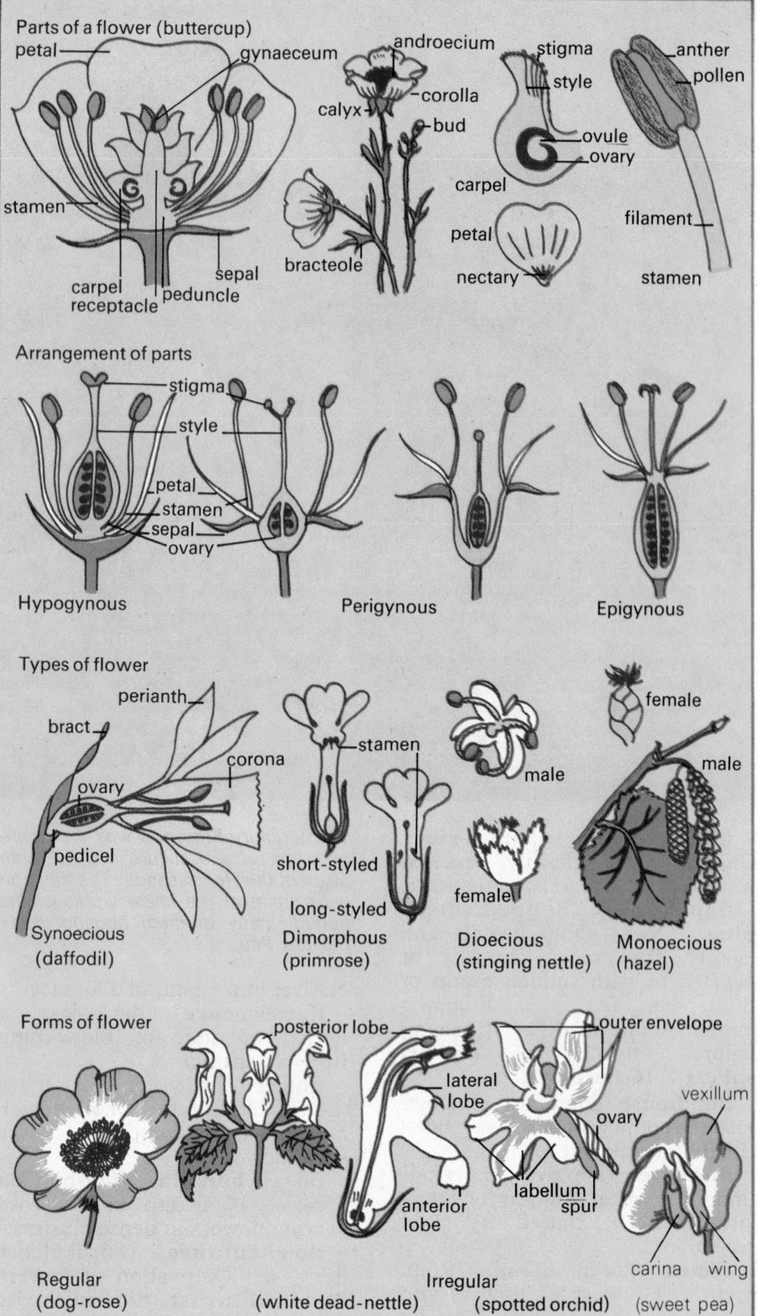

*The **flower** of a plant is responsible for the production of seeds. Certain parts of the flower, like the stamens and the carpels, are concerned only with reproduction. Other parts, like the petals and sepals, are protective or serve to attract insects to the flowers. Flowering plants of many different kinds have been cultivated by man because of their beauty and their decorative qualities.*

strip gathered and sewn by upper edge around woman's skirt etc. and with lower edge hanging. ~ *v.t.* Trim with flounces.

floun·der[1] (flown′dėr) *n.* (pl. **-ders**, collect. **-der**). Small edible flatfish, esp. the **winter** ~ (*Pseudopleuronectes americanus*) of N. Atlantic waters.

floun·der[2] (flown′dėr) *v.i.* Struggle or plunge (as) in mud or wading; make mistakes, manage affair badly or with difficulty.

flour (flowr, flow′ėr) *n.* Finer part of meal (of wheat or other grain) obtained by grinding and sifting; wheat meal as dist. from that of other grain; fine soft powder, esp. that obtained by grinding seeds, farinaceous roots, etc. ~ *v.t.* Sprinkle with flour; grind into flour; **flour mill**, mill for making flour (dist. from *gristmill*). **flour′y** *adj.* [form of FLOWER; orig. sense "finest part"]

flour·ish (flĕr′ĭsh, flŭr′-) *v.* 1. Grow vigorously; thrive, prosper, be successful; be in one's prime. 2. Embellish with flourishes. 3. Show ostentatiously; wave (weapon) about; throw (limbs) about. ~ *n.* Ornament of flowing curves about letter or word in handwriting; rhetorical embellishment, florid expression; ostentatious waving of weapon etc.; (mus.) fanfare of brass instruments, esp. to announce distinguished person's approach; florid passage, profuse ornamentation; short extemporized sequence of notes as prelude.

flout (flowt) *v.* Mock, insult, express contempt for by word or act; scoff *at*. **flout′er** *n.*

flow (flō) *v.i.* 1. Glide along as a stream; (of blood etc.) circulate; (of persons, things) come, go, in numbers; (of talk, literary style, etc.) move easily; (of garment, hair, etc.) hang easily, undulate; result *from*. 2. Gush out, spring; (of blood) be spilled; run full, be in flood; (of wine etc.) be poured out without stint. ~ *n.* Flowing movement in stream; amount that flows; flowing liquid; outpouring, stream, continuous supply; rise of tide; ~ **chart,** ~ **diagram**, schematic representation of a sequence of operations, procedures, etc., in manufacturing, computer use, etc.

flow·er (flow′ėr) *n.* 1. (bot.) Reproductive organ in plant containing one or more pistils or stamens or both, and usu. a corolla and calyx; (pop.) colored (i.e. not green) part of plant from which seed or fruit is later developed; blossom; flowering plant. 2. (pl., chem. etc.) Pulverulent form of substance, esp. powder formed by sublimation. 3. Pick or choice *of*; best part, choicest embodiment *of*. 4. State of blooming; prime. 5. ~ **children**, young people of 1960s living a Bohemian life and carrying flowers as symbols of peace and love; ~ **girl**, very young girl in wedding procession walking in front of bride and carrying flowers; ~ **head**, cluster of florets giving effect of single flower; **flow′erpot**, pot holding soil in which plant may be set; **flower show**, competitive or other exhibition of flowers etc. **flow′ered, flow′er·less, flow′er·ing** *adjs.* **flower** *v.* Produce flowers; be in full bloom; bring into flower; decorate with flowers or floral design; develop fully, reach maturity or peak, flourish.

flow·er·y (flow′ėrē) *adj.* Abounding in flowers; full of fine words, compliments, figures of speech, etc. **flow′er·i·ness** *n.*

flow·ing (flō′ĭng) *adj.* (esp., of style) Fluent, easy; (of lines) smoothly continuous. **flow′ing·ly**

adv.

flown (flōn): see FLY[2].

fl. oz. *abbrev.* Fluid ounce.

flu (flo͞o) *n.* Influenza.

flub (flŭb) *v.* (**flubbed, flub·bing**). Botch, bungle. ~ *n.* Something flubbed.

fluc·tu·ate (flŭk'cho͞oāt) *v.i.* (**-at·ed, -at·ing**). Vary irregularly, rise and fall, be unstable; vacillate, waver. **fluc·tu·a·tion** (flŭkcho͞oā'shon) *n.*

flue (flo͞o) *n.* Smoke duct in chimney; channel for conveying heat.

flu·en·cy (flo͞o'ensē) *n.* Smooth easy flow, esp. in speech; ready utterance.

flu·ent (flo͞o'ent) *adj.* 1. Flowing (easily); liable to change. 2. (of motion, curves, etc.) Graceful, easy; (of speech, style) copious, coming easily, ready; expressing oneself quickly and easily. **flu'ent·ly** *adv.*

fluff (flŭf) *n.* Light feathery stuff such as separates from dressed wool etc.; soft fur; soft downy mass or bunch; (slang) mistake, blunder, esp. by actor in speech. ~ *v.t.* Make into fluff; shake *up* or *out* into fluffy mass; (slang) make mistake, blunder; bungle. **fluff'y** *adj.* (**fluff·i·er, fluff·i·est**).

flu·id (flo͞o'ĭd) *adj.* Consisting of particles that move freely among themselves and yield to the slightest pressure; moving readily, not solid or rigid, not stable; ~ **dram**, $\frac{1}{8}$ fluid ounce; ~ **drive**, transmission of automobile power between two rotors with vanes operating in oil, permitting smooth starts; ~ **ounce**: see OUNCE[1]. **fluid** *n.* Fluid substance (gas or liquid); liquid constitutent or secretion. **flu·id·i·ty** (flo͞oĭd'ĭtē), **flu'id·ness** *ns.*

flu·id·ics (flo͞oĭd'ĭks) *n.pl.* (usu. considered sing.) Technique of using small interacting flows and fluid jets for amplification, switching, etc.

fluke[1] (flo͞ok) *n.* 1. Flatfish, esp. the common FLOUNDER. 2. One of the class Trematoda of parasitic flatworms infesting the liver of sheep and cattle (so called from resemblance to flounder).

fluke[2] (flo͞ok) *n.* Broad flattened barbed extremity of the arm of an anchor; barbed head of lance, harpoon, etc.; either of the two sections of a whale's large triangular tail.

fluke[3] (flo͞ok) *n.* Unexpected or undeserved success. ~ *v.* (**fluked, fluk·ing**). Make a fluke; get by a fluke. **fluk'y** *adj.* (**fluk·i·er, fluk·i·est**). **fluk'i·ness** *n.*

flume (flo͞om) *n.* Artificial channel conveying water for industrial use, to carry logs, etc.; ravine with stream. ~ *v.* Convey down a flume.

flum·mer·y (flŭm'erē) *n.* (pl. **-mer·ies**). Orig. a jellylike food made by straining boiled, slightly fermented oatmeal; any of various soft, bland foods, e.g. custard; empty compliments, trifles, nonsense. [Welsh *llymru*]

flum·mox (flŭm'oks) *v.t.* (slang) Confound, bewilder, disconcert.

flung (flŭng): see FLING.

flunk (flŭngk) *v.* (colloq.) Fail, esp. in an examination; reject or fail (a student or candidate); ~ **out**, be dismissed from school etc. because of academic failure.

flun·ky (flŭng'kē) *n.* (pl. **-kies**). (orig. Sc.) Liveried servant, footman (usu. contempt.); lackey; servile aide; toady.

fluo·res·cence (flo͞orĕs'ens, flo-; *Brit.* flo͞oorĕs'ens) *n.* Colored luminosity produced in some materials by direct action of (esp. violet and ultraviolet) light rays, X-rays, and other invisible radiations; property of converting ultraviolet light and other invisible radiations into visible light by absorption and reemission. **fluo·resce'** *v.i.* (**-resced, -resc·ing**). **fluo·res'cent** *adj.*

fluor·i·da·tion (floorĭdā'shon, flōr-, flo͝r-) *n.* (esp.) Addition of traces of fluoride to water supply with the object of reducing the incidence of dental caries. **fluor·i·date** (floor'ĭdāt, flōr'-, flo͝r'-) *v.t.* (**-dat·ed, -dat·ing**).

flu·o·ride (floor'īd, flōr'-, flo͝r'-; *Brit.* flo͞o'orīd) *n.* Salt of hydrofluoric acid, compound of fluorine with another element or organic radical.

fluo·rine (floor'ēn, -ĭn, flōr'-, flo͝r'-; *Brit.* flo͞o'orēn, -rĭn) *n.* (chem.) Pungent corrosive gaseous element of pale greenish-yellow color, extremely active chemically; symbol F, at. no. 9, at. wt. 18.99840.

fluor·o·scope (floor'oskōp, flōr'-, flo͝r'-; *Brit.* flo͞o'oroskōp) *n.* Apparatus incorporating a fluorescent screen, used for viewing objects by means of X-rays.

flur·ry (flĕr'ē, flŭr'ē) *n.* (pl. **-ries**). 1. Gust, squall; light snowfall, not enough to cover ground; snow shower. 2. Commotion, excitement; nervous hurry, agitation. ~ *v.t.* (**-ried, -ry·ing**). Confuse by haste or noise, agitate.

flush[1] (flŭsh) *v.* Take wing and fly away; cause (birds) to do this, put up; (fig.) bring into the open. ~ *n.* Bird or flock of birds suddenly taking flight.

flush[2] (flŭsh) *v.* 1. Spurt, rush out; cleanse (drain etc.) by flow of water; flood. 2. (Cause to) glow with warm color; (of blood) rush into and redden face; (of face) become red or hot, blush; inflame with pride or passion. ~ *n.* 1. Rush of water; sudden abundance; cleansing of drain by flushing. 2. Rush of emotion, elation produced by it or by victory etc. 3. Freshness, vigor. 4. Rush of blood to face, reddening caused by this or by fever.

flush[3] (flŭsh) *adj.* 1. Full to overflowing, in flood. 2. (usu. pred.) Having plentiful supply of

***Flowers** are typically bright colored in an effort to attract insects — often essential in pollination. Masses of flowers, as on this dogwood, increase the chance of success.*

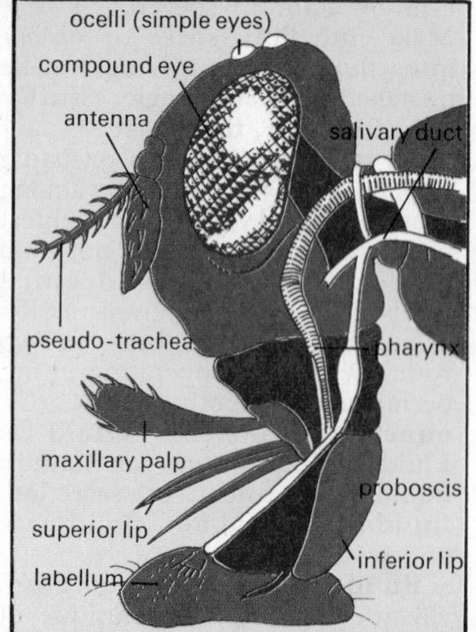

*The best known and most widespread of flies is the common **house fly,** the head of which appears above right. It is prolific and the female deposits from 500 to 2,000 eggs after copulation. It is an offensive pest which is capable of transmitting diseases to man and domestic animals. Other species of flies include the robber fly (top), consuming a moth it has captured in mid-air. Flies differ from all other insects in possessing only one pair of functional wings. The others are reduced to club-like balances.*

money etc. 3. Even, in same plane; level *with*; without projections or raised edges. ~ *v.t.* Level; fill in (joint) level with surface.

flush[4] (flŭsh) *n.* (cards) Hand of cards all of one suit, or including prescribed number of one suit.

flus·ter (flŭs′t*er*) *v.* Confuse; make nervous; be agitated, bustle. ~ *n.* Flurry, flutter, agitation.

flute (flo͞ot) *n.* 1. Musical instrument of woodwind family, a wooden or silver tube without a reed; the modern type is played horizontally and has a mouth hole at the side and holes stopped by keys, and its range is 3 octaves above middle C. 2. Organ stop with flutelike tone. 3. Semicylindrical vertical groove in pillar; similar groove or channel elsewhere, e.g., in frills. ~ *v.* (**flut·ed, flut·ing**). 1. Play flute; play on flute. 2. Make flutes or grooves in. **flut′ing** *n.* **flut′ist** *n.* Player of flute.

flut·ter (flŭt′*er*) *v.* 1. Flap wings, flap (wings), without flying or in short flights; come or go with quivering motion; go about restlessly, flit, hover; quiver, vibrate; (of pulse) beat feebly and irregularly; move (flag, fan, etc.) irregularly. 2. Tremble with excitement, be agitated; agitate, ruffle; throw into confusion or agitation. ~ *n.* Fluttering; tremulous excitement; stir, sensation; (colloq.) small bet (on horse etc.).

flu·vi·al (flo͞o′vē*a*l) *adj.* Of, found in, river(s).

flux (flŭks) *n.* 1. Flowing; continued flow or flood. 2. Continuous succession of changes of condition, composition, etc. 3. (phys.) Rate of flow of matter or energy; amount of light incident on a given area in a given time; total amount of magnetic or electric field passing through a given area. 4. (archaic) Morbid or excessive discharge of blood or excrement, as in **bloody** ~, dysentery. 5. Substance mixed with metal etc. to facilitate soldering and to remove oxides; substance used to make colors fusible in enameling etc. ~ *v.* 1. Issue in a flux; flow copiously.

***Flycatchers** of the Old World, such as the paradise flycatcher, have an upright stance and make short erratic flights to catch passing insects. New World or 'tyrant' flycatchers are the most aggressive of American perching birds.*

*The limbs of **flying lemurs** have gliding membranes which enable the animal to glide through the air for several yards. The flying lemur resembles a squirrel.*

***Flying fish** execute a rapid glide, rather than a true flight, and take to the air in shoals, often to escape a pursuing enemy. Their take-off speed is about 40 m.p.h.*

2. Make fluid, melt; fuse; treat with flux.

flux·ion (flŭk′shon) *n.* Flowing; continuous change. **flux′ion·al, flux′ion·ar·y** *adjs.*

fly[1] (flī) *n.* (pl. **flies**). Two-winged insect, esp. of the order Diptera; winged insect, as caddis fly; natural or artificial fly used as bait in fishing; ~ **in the ointment**, disturbing condition in otherwise workable scheme; **fly′blow,** (*n.*) egg or larva of blowfly, esp. as maggot in meat etc.; (*v.t.*) deposit eggs in, taint; **fly′blown**, so tainted; **fly book**, case for keeping angler's flies in; **fly′catcher**, any of various birds of the New World family Tyrannidae or the Old World family Muscicapidae that characteristically dart out from a perch to catch flying insects; **fly fishing, fly casting**, technique of angling with fly as lure; **fly′paper**, paper treated with preparation for catching or poisoning flies; **fly′-speck**, tiny spot made by excrement of a fly; any insignificant spot; **fly′weight**, boxer of lightest weight.

fly[2] (flī) *v.* (**flew**, for baseball def. **flied, flown, fly·ing**). 1. Move through air with wings; travel, convey, by aircraft etc., (of aircraft etc.) travel through air or space; pilot (aircraft); make (pigeon, hawk) fly; make (kite) rise and stay aloft; pass or rise quickly through air; jump clear over or *over* fence, etc.; ~ **high**, be ambitious; be successful for the moment; **high-flown**, exalted; turgid, bombastic. 2. (of flag, hair, garment, etc.) Flutter, wave; set or keep (flag) flying. 3. Travel swiftly, rush along, pass rapidly; hasten; be driven or forced off suddenly; (baseball) hit a fly ball; **let ~**, discharge (missile); shoot, use strong language, *at*; ~ **at**, attack violently. 4. Run away, flee, flee from. 5. **fly′by**, (often ceremonial) flight by aircraft past a given point, usu. at low altitude; (of a spacecraft) close approach to a planet etc. for observation; **fly-by-night**, transitory, unstable, of dubious character; **fly-by-wire** (of model aircraft), controlled electrically by a wire tether; **fly the coop**, (colloq.) escape, depart suddenly.

fly *n.* (pl. **flies**). 1. Fold on garment, esp. on front of trousers, to contain or cover fastening; tent fly. 2. Part of flag farthest from staff; breadth of flag from staff to

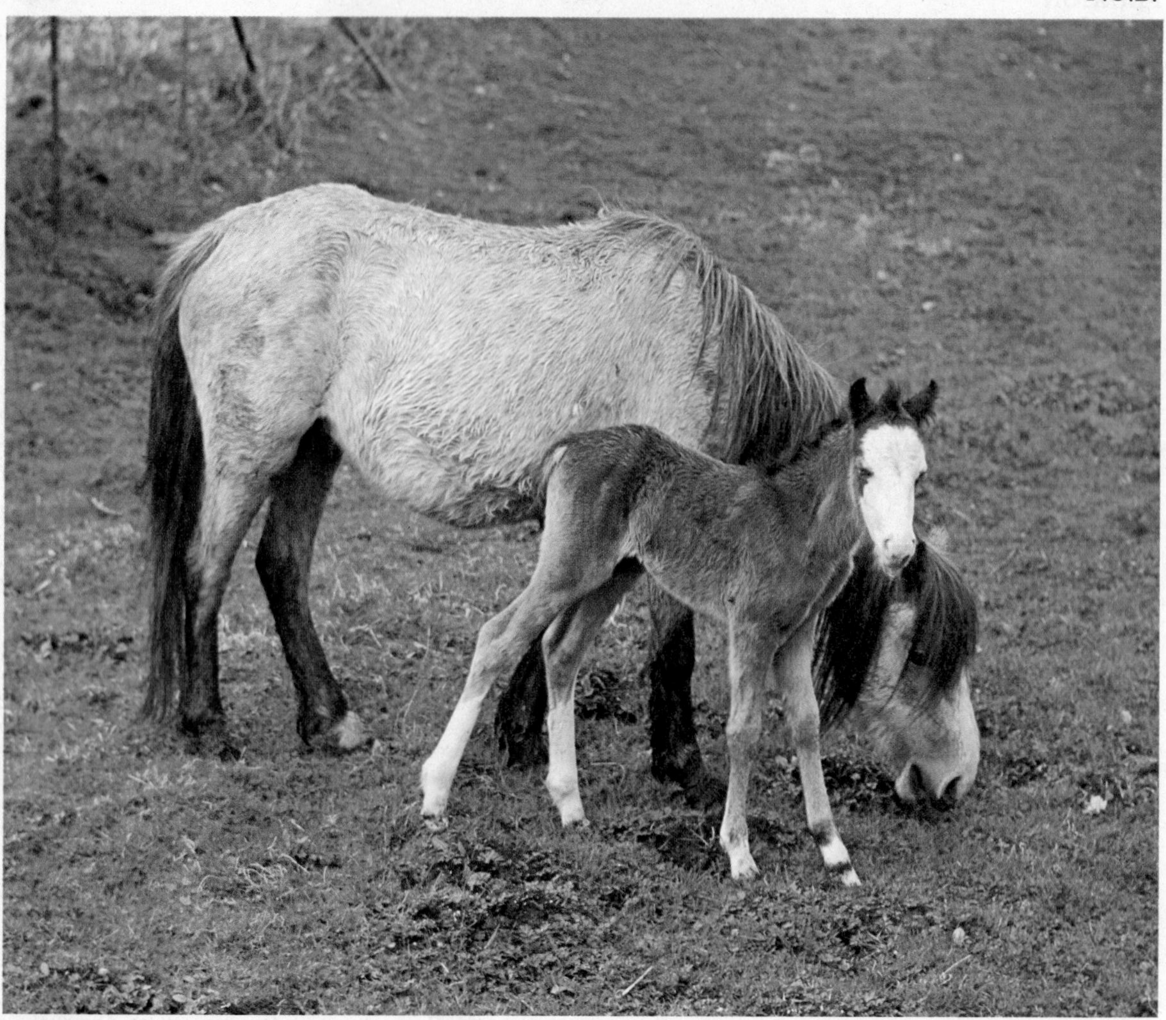

end. 3. (theatr., pl.) Space over proscenium, including upper mechanism and galleries on each side from which it is worked. 4. Speed-regulating device, usu. of vanes on rotating shaft, for regulating striking mechanism of clock etc. flywheel etc. for regulating speed of machinery. 5. ~ **ball**, (baseball) ball batted high in air, esp. to the outfield; **fly'leaf** (pl. **-leaves**), blank leaf at beginning or end of book; **fly'wheel**, wheel with heavy rim on revolving shaft, for regulating motion of machinery or accumulating power.

fly·er: see FLIER.

fly·ing (flī'ĭng) *adj.* 1. That flies. 2. Floating loosely, fluttering, waving; hanging loose. 3. Traveling or passing swiftly; ~ **start**, start of a race in which starting point is passed at full speed. 4. ~ **buttress**, (archit.) buttress slanting from pier etc. to wall and usu. carried on arch for taking thrust of roof or vault; ~ **colors**, high success, triumph; ~ **doctor**, doctor who visits patients in remote areas, esp. Australian outback, by aerial ambulance; **F ~ Dutchman**: see DUTCH; ~ **fish**, fish of two

A mare is generally mated to a stallion in spring or early summer and gives birth to a ***foal*** *about 11 months later. The foal gets to its legs about half an hour after birth.*

genera (*Dactylopterus* and *Exocetus*), found in warm seas, which can rise into air by means of enlarged winglike pectoral fins; ~ **fox**, fruit-eating bat of genus *Pteropus*, found in tropical Africa, Asia, and Australia; ~ **jib**, light sail set before jib on the jib boom; ~ **saucer**, unidentified disk- or saucer-shaped object reported as appearing in the sky; ~ **squirrel**, any of several squirrels, esp. of genera *Pteromys* and *Glaucomys*, which can glide through air by means of extension of skin connecting fore and hind limbs. **flying** *n.* Act or process of moving through the air; flight; ~ **boat**, seaplane with boatlike hull; ~ **machine**, airplane, esp. an early type or model.

FM *abbrev.* Frequency modulation.

Fm *symbol.* Fermium.

F number. Ratio of focal length to the aperture diameter of a camera lens.

foal (fōl) *n.* Young of horse, ass, etc., colt or filly. ~ *v.* Give birth to (foal).

foam (fōm) *n.* 1. Collection of small bubbles formed in liquid by agitation, fermentation, etc.; froth of saliva or perspiration. 2. (poet.) Sea. 3. Rubber or plastic material in form of cellular mass; ~ **rubber**, light, firm rubber with high content of air, used for cushions, mattresses, etc. **foam** *v.i.* Emit foam, froth at the mouth; (of water etc.) froth, gather foam, run foaming *along, down, over*, etc.; (of cup, etc.) be filled with foaming liquid. **foam'y** *adj.* (**foam·i·er, foam·i·est**).

fob[1] (fŏb) *n.* 1. Small pocket for watch etc. formerly made in waistband of trousers. 2. Short chain or ribbon attached to watch, to be worn outside pocket for display. 3. Ornament attached to watch chain for display.

fob[2] (fŏb) *v.t.* (**fobbed, fob·bing**). Cheat, take in; palm (something inferior) *off on* person; put (person) *off with* something inferior.

f.o.b., F.O.B. *abbrevs.* Free on

board (i.e., price quoted includes delivery onto a carrier at a specified point but not the carrier's charges).

fo·cal (fō'kal) *adj.* Of, situated or collected at, a focus; ~ **distance** or **length**, distance between center of lens or mirror and its focus; ~ **plane**, plane parallel with that of lens, passing through the focus; ~ **point**, center of action or attention; FOCUS.

fo'c's'le (fōk'sel): see FORECASTLE.

fo·cus (fō'kus) *n.* (pl. **-cus·es, -ci** pr. -sī). 1. (geom.) One of the points from which the distances to any point of a given curve are connected by a linear relation. 2. (optics etc.) Point at which rays meet after being refracted or reflected; point from which rays appear to proceed; point at which object must be situated in order that image produced by lens may be clear and well defined; adjustment (of eye or eyeglass) necessary to produce a clear image. 3. Principal seat of disease; center of activity. ~ *v.t.* Converge, make converge, to a focus; adjust focus of (lens, eye); bring into focus.

fod·der (fŏd'er) *n.* Feed for livestock, esp. hay, straw, cornstalks, etc. ~ *v.t.* Give fodder to.

foe (fō) *n.* Enemy, adversary, opponent.

foe·tid = FETID.

foe·tus = FETUS.

fog (fŏg, fawg) *n.* 1. Thick mist or cloud of minute water droplets suspended in atmosphere at or near earth's surface; obscurity caused by this; **fog'horn**, sounding instrument for warning ships in fog. 2. (photog.) Opaque cloudy patch on developed negative. **fog** *v.* (**fogged, fog·ging**). Envelop (as) with fog; bewilder, perplex; (photog.) cause fog on (negative); become enveloped in fog.

fog·gy (fŏg'ē, faw'gē) *adj.* (**-gi·er, -gi·est**). Thick, murky; of, like, infested with, fog; obscure, dull, confused; beclouded, indistinct. **fog'gi·ly** *adv.* **fog'gi·ness** *n.*

fo·gy, fo·gey (fō'gē) *ns.* (pl. **-gies, -geys**). (usu. **old** ~) Person with antiquated ideas.

foi·ble (foi'bel) *n.* 1. Weak point; weakness of character; quality on which one mistakenly prides oneself. 2. (fencing) Pliant part of sword blade from middle to point.

foil[1] (foil) *n.* 1. Metal hammered or rolled into thin sheet; sheet of this formerly placed behind glass of mirror to produce reflection; thin leaf of metal placed under precious stone to increase its brilliance, or under transparent substance to make it look like precious stone. 2. Anything serving to set off another thing by contrast, esp. a person. ~ *v.t.* Set off by contrast.

foil[2] (foil) *v.* Beat off, repulse; frustrate, parry, baffle.

foil[3] (foil) *n.* Blunt-edged fencing sword with flat guard and blunt-tipped point.

foist (foist) *v.t.* Introduce surreptitiously or unwarrantably *into* or *in*; palm (*off*) *on*.

fol. *abbrev.* Folio, following.

fold[1] (fōld) *n.* Enclosure for sheep; flock of sheep; (fig.) Church, body of believers. ~ *v.t.* Shut up (sheep etc.) in fold.

fold[2] (fōld) *n.* Doubling of folded object; hollow between two thicknesses, in mountain, etc.; coil of serpent etc.; folding; line made by folding; (geol.) bend in strata. ~ *v.* 1. Double (flexible thing) over upon itself; ~ **over, together**; bend portion or (thing) *back, down*; become, be able to be, folded; ~ **up**, make more compact by folding; (colloq.) fail; **fold'away**, designed to be folded and stored out of the way when not in use, as *foldaway cot;* **folding door**, door in two parts (often themselves consisting of hinged leaves that fold up when door is open) hung on opposite jambs, so that edges meet when door is closed; **fold'out**, large insert in book or magazine folded so as to fit within the pages. 2. Wind, clasp (arms etc.) *around*; interlace (arms), clasp (one's) hands; swathe, envelop; embrace *in* arms, *to* breast. **fold'er** *n.* (esp.) Folded circular etc.; cover or holder for loose papers.

*These dancers in South Korea perform a traditional **folk dance.** Such dances reveal something of the life and culture of a country, and of how war and other events have influenced it. Some such dances are purely recreational.*

-fold *suffix.* Multiplied by, as *sevenfold.*

fo·li·age (fō'lēĭj) *n.* Leaves, leafage.

fo·li·ate (fō'lēĭt, -āt) *adj.* Leaf-like; having leaves; having specified number of leaflets. ~ (fō'lēāt) *v.* (**-at·ed, -at·ing**). Split into laminae; decorate with foils; number leaves (not pages) of (volume) consecutively. **fo·li·a·tion** (fōlēā'shon) *n.*

fo·lic (fō'lĭk, fŏl'ĭk) *adj.* Of, involving, folic acid; ~ **acid**, vitamin of the B group, deficiency of which in people is associated with anemia.

fo·li·o (fō'lēō) *n.* (pl. **-li·os**). 1. Leaf of paper, parchment, etc., numbered only on front; two opposite pages of ledger etc. used concurrently in bookkeeping; page of ledger etc. used for both sides of account; page number of printed book; number of words (in U.S. usu. 100, in England usu. 72 or 90) taken as unit in reckoning length of document. 2. Sheet of paper folded once; volume of the largest common size, made up of sheets of paper folded once. ~ *adj.* Formed of sheets or a sheet folded once; folio size.

folk (fōk) *n.* (pl. **folks**, sometimes **folk**). 1. People; ethnic group; race. 2. (usu. pl.) People in general; people of specified class; relatives. 3. (attrib.) Of the people; ~ **dance**, (music for) traditional dance of popular origin in a nation or region; ~ **etymology**, popular perversion of a word to make it seem derived from familiar elements, as *cole slaw* into *cold slaw*, *chaise longue* into *chaise lounge*, or *foxglove* into *folk's-glove*; **folk'lore**, traditional beliefs, customs, etc., of the people; study of these; hence **folk'lorist; folk mass**, liturgical mass with folk music instead of conventional church music; **folk medicine**, traditional medicine developed by people isolated from modern practices, relying esp. on vegetable remedies; **folk music**, music arising from common people of a nation or region, usu. orally transmitted and anonymous; **folk rock**, style of music combining elements of rock-'n'-roll and folk music; **folk singer**, singer of either kind of folk song; **folk song**, song belonging to the folk music of a people, or one composed in deliberate imitation of such a song; **folk'ways**, (sociol. etc.) traditional patterns of behavior common to members of a particular culture or society. **folk·sy** (fōk'sē) *adj.* (**-si·er, -si·est**). Sociable, friendly, informal; resembling folk art.

foll. *abbrev.* Following.

fol·li·cle (fŏl'ĭkel) *n.* 1. (anat.) Small sac; secretory gland of this shape; minute pit in which hair root grows; **Graafian** ~: see GRAAF. 2. (bot.) Fruit that consists of a single carpel and splits open along ventral suture only. **fol·li·cu·lar** (folĭk'yuler), **fol·lic'u·lat·ed** *adjs.*

fol·low (fŏl'ō) *v.* 1. Go or come after (moving thing or person); pursue; go along (path); come after, come next, in order or time; ~ **the leader**, game in which each player must move as leader does; ~ **one's nose**, go straight on; be guided by instinct; ~ **one's star(s)**, pursue what one believes is one's destined success. 2. Accompany, serve, attend upon; go as person's attendant; go after as admirer; be consequence of; result (from). 3. Strive after, aim at. 4. Take as guide or leader; take as rule; conform to; practice (profession etc.); ~ **the sea**, be a sailor. 5. Keep up with mentally; grasp the meaning of; grasp argument, meaning, etc. 6. ~ **through**, (golf, baseball, etc.) carry stroke through to fullest possible extent after striking ball; ~**-through** (*n.*); ~ **up**, pursue steadily; add another blow etc. to (previous blow etc.); (fig.) prosecute (suggestion etc.) to a conclusion; ~**-up** (*n.*).

fol·low·er (fŏl'ōer) *n.* (esp.) Adherent, disciple.

fol·low·ing (fŏl'ōĭng) *n.* (esp.) Body of adherents, followers. ~ *adj.* (esp.) Now to be mentioned; coming next. ~ *prep.* After.

fol·ly (fŏl'ē) *n.* (pl. **-lies**). 1. Foolishness; foolish act, idea, etc. 2. (pl. considered as sing.) Theatrical revue featuring glamorous female performers. 3. Costly enterprise deemed useless or foolish; **Seward's** ~, U.S. purchase of Alaska from Russia for $7 million, arranged by Secretary of State William SEWARD in 1867.

fo·ment (fōmĕnt') *v.t.* 1. Bathe with warm or medicated lotions; apply warmth to. 2. Foster, stimulate, instigate (sentiment, conduct, sedition, etc.). **fo·men·ta·tion** (fōmĕntā'shon) *n.* (Application of) warm or medicated substance for fomenting purposes.

fond (fŏnd) *adj.* Tender, loving; doting; (archaic) foolishly credulous; ~ **of**, full of love for, much inclined to. **fond'ly** *adv.* **fond'ness** *n.*

fon·dle (fŏn'del) *v.* (**-dled, -dling**). Touch or stroke lovingly; toy amorously.

fon·due (fŏndōō', fŏn'dōō; *Fr.* fawn̄dü') *n.* (cookery) Hot melted cheese flavored with wine, beer, etc., into which pieces of bread are dipped.

font (fŏnt) *n.* 1. Receptacle, usu. of stone, for baptismal water; receptacle for holy water; oil reservoir of lamp. 2. (of type) Complete assortment of one size and style.

Fon·taine·bleau (fŏn'tĭnblō; *Fr.* fawn̄tĕnblō'). French town on Seine River, 35 mi. SSE. of Paris in Fontainebleau Forest; chateau there was former residence of French monarchs, now a summer home of country's presidents; Edict of NANTES revoked there (1685).

fon·ta·nel, fon·ta·nelle (fŏntanĕl') *ns.* Membrane-covered space in bony vault of skull where union of the bones is incomplete at birth, normally closing in infancy.

fon·ti·na (fŏntē'na) *n.* Type of Italian cheese made from ewe's milk.

Foo·chow (fōō'chow'; *Chin.* fōō'jō'). Province of SE. China.

food (fōōd) *n.* Substance taken into the body to maintain life and growth; solid substance used thus (opp. drink); (particular kind of) edibles (also transf. and fig.); ~ **chain**, (ecol.) series of organisms in which each eats a smaller and is in turn eaten by a larger; ~ **processor**, kitchen appliance for preparing foods by grinding, shredding, etc.; ~ **stamps**, stamps given or sold below face value by federal government to poor persons and redeemed at face value for food; **food'stuff**, material for food; (pl.) articles of food in bulk.

fool (fōōl) *n.* Silly person, simpleton; dupe; professional jester in medieval great household; **play the** ~, blunder, trifle; indulge in buffoonery; **fool'proof**, so plain that even a fool cannot misunderstand; (of machines etc.) not apt to be injured by misuse; **fool's cap**, fantastic cap, usu. with bells, worn by medieval jester; dunce's conical paper cap; **fools'cap**, long sheet of writing or printing paper

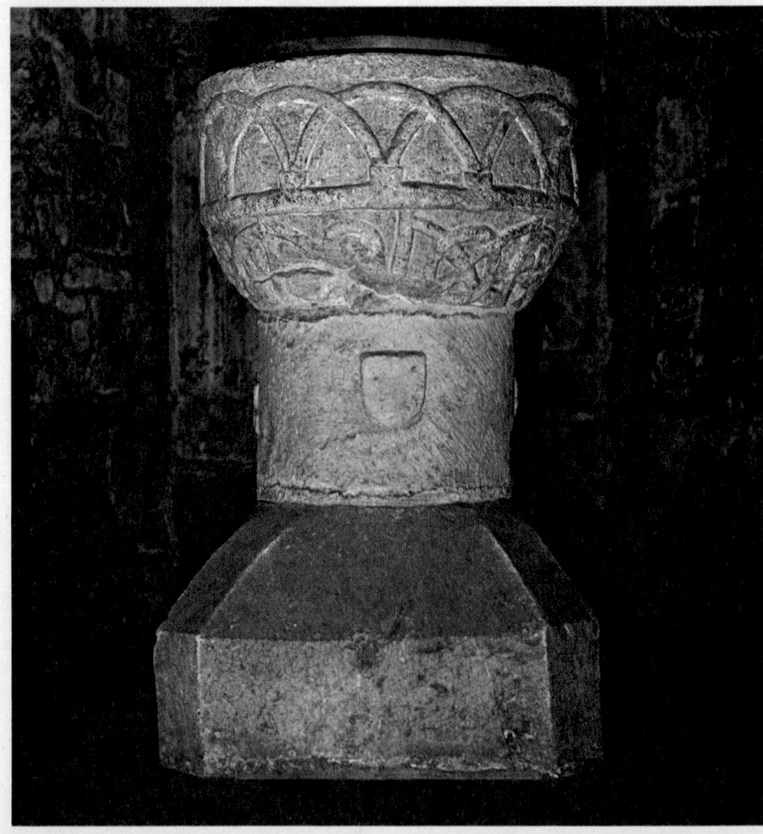

*The baptismal **font** is normally placed near the west end of the church. Its name comes from the Latin word for 'stream'. This magnificent Norman font is at Torpenhow church, near Wigton, Cumbria, U.K.*

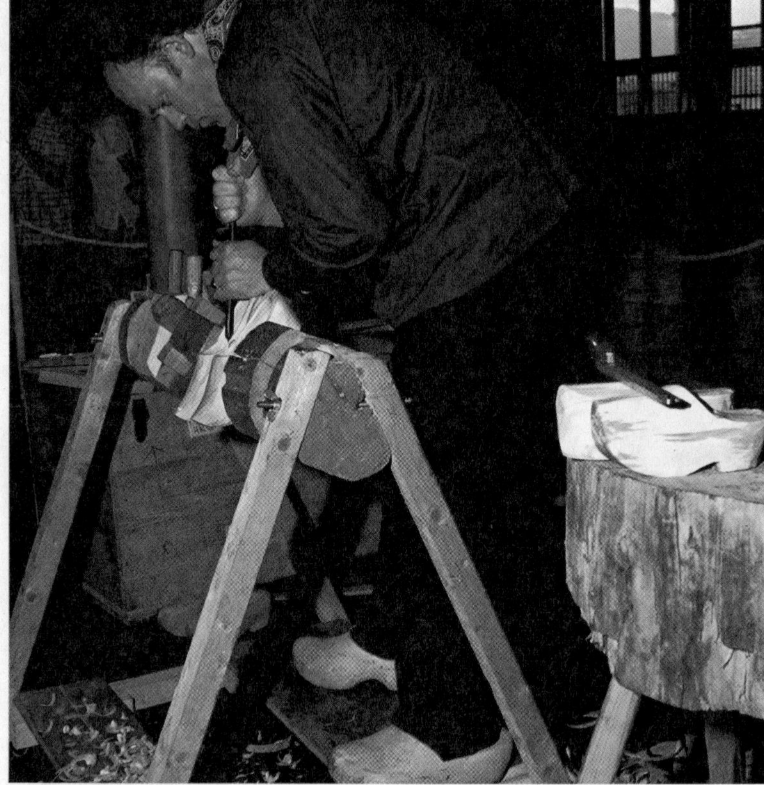

One of the earliest and most practical forms of **footwear** was the wooden shoe or clog which is still worn in rural France, Belgium, the Netherlands, and Germany. It was particularly suitable for walking over wet or muddy ground.

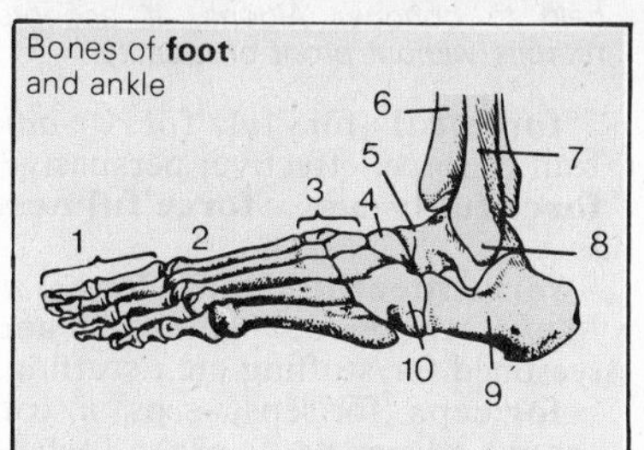

1 phalanges 6 fibula
2 metatarsus 7 lateral malleolus
3 navicular 8 heel bone
4 talus 9 cuboid bone
5 tibia (3, 4, 5, 9, 10 – tarsus)

13 × 16 inches (381–432 × 305–343 mm) (from watermark of fool's cap on some old paper); **fool's errand**, fruitless errand; **fool's gold**, iron pyrites, sometimes mistaken for gold; also fig.; **fool's paradise**, illusory happiness. **fool·er·y** (fo͞o′lerē) *n.* **fool·ish** (fo͞o′lĭsh) *adj.* **fool′ish·ly** *adv.* **fool′ish·ness** *n.* **fool** *adj.* That is a fool. **fool** *v.* Play the fool; cheat (person) *out of*; throw *away* foolishly; make a fool of, dupe, play tricks on; ~ **around**, spend time aimlessly; flirt, philander; ~ **with**, play aimlessly with, meddle with. [OF. *fol* mad f. L. *follis* bellows, empty-headed person]

fool·har·dy (fo͞ol′hârdē) *adj.* (**-di·er, -di·est**). Foolishly venturesome, delighting in needless risks. **fool′har·di·ness** *n.*

foot (fo͝ot) *n.* (pl. **feet**). 1. Lowest part of leg beyond ankle; this as organ of locomotion; **on** ~, walking, not riding; **put one's** ~ **down**, take up firm position (fig.); **put one's** ~ **in it, put one's** ~ **in one's mouth**, blunder; **under** ~, beneath the foot or feet; in the way; into state of subjection or inferiority. 2. End of bed, grave, etc., toward which feet are placed; part of stocking etc. covering foot. 3. Metrical unit, division of line, with varying number of syllables, one of which is accented. 4. Linear measure of 12 inches. 5. Lower (usu. projecting) part of object, base. 6. (zool.) Organ of locomotion or attachment of some invertebrates, e.g., mussels. 7. Bottom (of hill, stairs, page, etc.). 8. ~**-and-mouth (disease)**, contagious fever, caused by a filtrable virus, of horned cattle and other animals, with ulcerating vesicles in mouth, near hoof, etc.; **foot′ball**, Amer. game played with an ellipsoid ball on a field 100 yards long by two teams of 11 players, who seek to get and hold the ball and by running and passing advance over the others' goal line; the ball used in this game; see also SOCCER; **foot′-bridge**, bridge for foot passengers; **foot-candle**, unit of illumination, equal to the illumination of a surface at a uniform distance of 1 ft. from a symmetrical point source of 1 candela; **foot′fall**, sound of footsteps; **foot′hill**, lower hill at foot of mountain or mountain range; **foot′hold**, place just wide enough for a foot to be placed on when climbing etc.; small but secure position gained in a business etc.; **foot′lights**, row of lights along front of stage on level with actors' feet; **foot′locker**, small trunk for personal belongings, esp. for a soldier to keep at the foot of bunk; **foot-loose**, free, unhampered by ties or obligations; **foot′man**, liveried servant attending carriage, waiting at table, and answering door; **foot′note**, note inserted at foot of page; **foot′pad**, (hist.) unmounted highwayman or street robber; **foot′path**, path for pedestrians; **foot-pound**, work done when a force of 1 pound moves its point of application 1 foot in the line of action of the force; **foot′print**, impression left by foot; **foot′race**, race between persons on foot; ~ **soldier**, infantryman; **foot′sore**, having sore feet, esp. from walking; **foot′step**, tread; noise made by treading; **foot′stool**, low stool for resting feet on; **foot′wear**, shoes, boots, slippers, etc., collectively; **foot′work**, manner of using feet in sports, dancing, etc.; agility. **foot′less** *adj.* **foot′age** *n.* Number of linear feet of material, motion picture film, etc. **foot** *v.* (**foot·ed, foot·ing**). Traverse on foot (rare); put foot to (stocking); add up or *up* (account); pay (bill).

foot·ing (fo͝ot′ĭng) *n.* Foothold; secure position; conditions, relations, position, status, in which person is toward others.

foot·sie, foot·sy (fo͝ot′sē) *ns.* (pl. **-sies**). Amorous play with the feet; **play** ~ **with**, carry this on; cooperate secretly.

fop (fŏp) *n.* Dandy. **fop′per·y** *n.* **fop′pish** *adj.* **fop′pish·ly** *adv.* **fop′pish·ness** *n.*

for (fôr, unstressed fer) *prep.* In place of, as in *b. stands* ~ *born*; in exchange against, *sold* ~ *$2*; in defense or favor of; in the interest of, to reach, obtain, etc., *went* ~ *a taxi, sailed* ~ *Bermuda*; as regards (esp. with words implying fitness), as *fit* ~ *nothing*; because of, on account of; corresponding to, ~ *every enemy he has 50 friends*; considering the nature of, *cool* ~ *a summer day*; during, to the extent of, *wait* ~ *years, walk* ~ *3 miles.* **for** *conj.* (introducing new sentence etc. containing reason for believing what has been previously stated) Seeing that, since; because.

fo·ra: see FORUM.

for·age (fôr′ĭj, fär′-) *n.* Food for horses and cattle, fodder. ~ *v.*

Henry Ford's famous 'Model T' car, seen here in a 4-seater tourer version of 1915, was designed for the mass market. Between 1908 and 1927, 15 million were produced.

The French Foreign Legion was set up in 1831 as a means of organizing former soldiers and political refugees to help to conquer Algeria. It accepts recruits without proof of identity.

(**-aged, -ag·ing**). Collect forage from, ravage; search for forage or (fig.) *for* anything, rummage; supply with forage; get by foraging. **for′ag·er** *n*.

fo·ra·men (forā′men) *n*. (pl. **-ram·i·na** pr. -răm′*ina*, **-ra·-mens**). Orifice, hole, passage in a bone or anatomical structure.

for·ay (fŏr′ā, făr′-) *n*. Incursion, raid. ~ *v.i.* Go on, make, foray.

for·bear[1] = FOREBEAR.

for·bear[2] (fōrbār′) *v*. (**-bore, -borne, -bear·ing**). Abstain or refrain from or *from*; not use or mention; be patient. **for·bear′-ance, for·bear′er** *ns*.

for·bid (ferbĭd′, fōr-) *v.t.* (**-bade** or **-bad, -bid·den** or **-bid, -bid·ding**). Command not *to* do, not *to* go to (place); not allow (person etc. something; person or thing to exist or happen); prevent; **Forbidden City**, Lhasa in Tibet, which foreigners were forbidden to enter; also walled area of Peking containing the imperial palace of the former Chinese Empire. **for·-bid′ding** *adj*. Repellent, of uninviting appearance. **for·bid′-ding·ly** *adv*.

force (fōrs, fōrs) *n*. 1. Strength, violence, intense effort; strength exerted on an object, coercion; ~ **play**, (baseball) put out a baserunner by touching foot to base or home plate. 2. Military strength; body of armed men, army; body of police; **in** ~, in great numbers; (pl.) troops. 3. Mental or moral strength; power to convince, vividness of effect; binding power, validity; real import, precise meaning; **in** ~, in operation, valid. 4. (phys.) Measurable and determinable influence inclining body to motion, intensity of this; (formerly) cause of any class of physical phenomena (e.g. of heat or motion) conceived as inherent in matter; (fig.) agency likened to these. **force** *v.t.* 1. Constrain, compel; put strained sense upon (words); (cards) compel (player) to trump or reveal his or her strength, compel player to play (certain card); compel (person) *to* do, *into* doing, *into* specified action; strain to the utmost; (baseball) compel base runner (by a hit) to vacate base only to be put out at the next base; ~ **out**, (make) such a hit; ~ **play**, putting out such a runner; ~ **(in)**, cause a run to be scored by passing the batter when bases are full; ~ **person's hand**, compel him to act prematurely or adopt policy unwillingly; ~ **the pace**, adopt high speed in race to tire adversary out quickly. 2. Overpower, capture, make way through, break open (stronghold, defenses, pass, lock, door) by force; drive by force; propel against resistance; effect, produce, by effort; take by force, extort, wring; impose, press, (thing) *on* person. 3. Artificially hasten maturity of (plant etc.). **forced** *adj*. (esp.) ~ **landing**, unavoidable landing of aircraft in an emergency; ~ **march**, march requiring special effort by troops etc. **forc′ed·ly** *adv*.

force·ful (fōrs′f*u*l, fōrs′-) *adj*. Full of force; effective; persuasive. **force′ful·ly** *adv*. **force′ful·ness** *n*.

force·meat (fōrs′mēt, fōrs′-) *n*. Meat chopped, spiced, and seasoned for stuffing etc.; stuffing.

for·ceps (fōr′sĕps, -s*e*ps) *n*. (pl. **-ceps, -ci·pes** pr. -s*i*pēz). Instrument like pincers, for seizing and holding objects (esp. in surgery); (zool. etc.) clasping organ resembling forceps (esp. in insects).

for·ci·ble (fōr′s*i*bel, fōr′-) *adj*. Done by, involving, force; powerful; convincing. **for′ci·ble·ness** *n*. **for′ci·bly** *adv*.

ford (fōrd, fōrd) *n*. Shallow place where river etc. can be crossed by wading or in wheeled vehicle. ~ *v.t.* Wade or drive across (river etc.). **ford′a·ble** *adj*.

Ford[1] (fōrd, fōrd), **Gerald R(andolph)** (born Leslie Lynch King, later renamed after stepfather) (1913–). Appointed vice president of U.S. (1973–4) after resignation of Spiro Agnew; became 38th president of U.S. (1974–7) upon resignation of Richard Nixon.

Ford[2] (fōrd, fōrd), **Henry** (1863–1947). Amer. founder and president (1903–19, 1943–5) of one of world's largest automobile manufacturing plants, Ford Motor Co. in Detroit, Mich.; emphasized the economy of mass production; introduced profit sharing in company (1914).

fore[1] (fōr, fŏr) *adj.* Situated in front. ~ *n.* Fore part, bow of ship; **to the** ~, ready at hand, conspicuous; into, toward prominence.

fore[2] (fōr, fŏr) *adv.* ~ **and aft**, at bow and stern; lengthwise in ship; ~**-and-aft** (*adj.*) (of rigging) with sails set lengthwise as in a schooner.

fore[3] (fōr, fŏr) *int.* (golf) Warning cry to person in line of flight of the ball.

fore- *prefix.* In front; beforehand, in advance; anticipatory, precedent.

fore·arm[1] (fōr′ārm, fŏr′-) *n.* Arm from elbow to wrist or fingertips.

fore·arm[2] (fōrārm′, fŏr-) *v.t.* Arm beforehand.

fore·bear (fōr′bār, fŏr′-) *n.* Forefather; ancestor.

fore·bode (fōrbōd′, fŏr-) *v.t.* (**-bod·ed, -bod·ing**). Betoken, portend; have presentiment of (a misfortune). **fore·bod′ing** *adj.* & *n.* Presage, omen, presentiment (esp. of evil or misfortune). **fore·bod′ing·ly** *adv.*

fore·brain (fōr′brān, fŏr′-): see BRAIN.

fore·cast (fōr′kăst, -kahst, fŏr′-) *v.t.* (**-cast** or **-cast·ed, -cast·ing**). Estimate, conjecture, calculate beforehand. ~ *n.* Conjectural estimate, calculation of future thing, esp. of coming weather.

fore·cas·tle (fōk′s*e*l, fōr′kăs*e*l, -kahs*e*l, fŏr′-), **fo′c’s’le** (fōk′s*e*l) *ns.* Forward part of upper deck of a ship; crew’s quarters in this or in special superstructure at bow of a merchant ship; (hist.) short raised deck at ship’s bow.

fore·close (fōrklōz′, fŏr-) *v.* (**-closed, -clos·ing**). 1. Bar, preclude, prevent; shut out from enjoyment of. 2. (mortgage law) Bar (person entitled to redeem) upon nonpayment of money due; bar (right of redemption); take away power of redeeming (mortgage). **fore·clo·sure** (fōrklō′zh*e*r, fŏr-) *n.*

fore·court (fōr′kōrt, fŏr′kōrt) *n.* Enclosed space, courtyard before building; (tennis, handball, etc.) part of court nearest net or wall.

fore·doom (fōrdōōm′, fŏr-) *v.t.* Doom beforehand; condemn beforehand *to*; foreordain, predestine.

fore·fa·ther (fōr′fahdh*e*r, fŏr′-) *n.* (chiefly pl.) Ancestor, progenitor.

fore·fin·ger (fōr′fĭngg*e*r, fŏr′-) *n.* Finger next to thumb, index finger.

fore·foot (fōr′fo͝ot, fŏr′-) *n.* (pl. **-feet**). 1. One of animal’s front feet. 2. (naut.) Foremost part of keel.

fore·front (fōr′frŭnt, fŏr′-) *n.* Very front, foremost part; foremost position.

fore·go (fōrgō′, fŏr-) *v.* (**-went, -gone, -go·ing**). Precede in place or time; **foregoing**, previously mentioned; **foregone conclusion**, decision or opinion formed before case is argued or full evidence known; result that can be or could have been foreseen.

fore·ground (fōr′grownd, fŏr′-) *n.* Part of view, esp. in picture, nearest observer; most conspicuous position.

fore·hand (fōr′hănd, fŏr′-) *n.* Part of horse in front of rider; (tennis etc.) forehand stroke. ~ *adj.* (tennis etc.) (of stroke) Made with palm of hand turned forward; foremost, leading; prior (Cf. BACKHAND).

fore·head (fōr′ĭd, fär′-, -hĕd) *n.* Part of face above eyebrows and between temples.

for·eign (fōr′ĭn, fär′-) *adj.* 1. Belonging to, proceeding from, other persons or things; alien *from* or *to*; irrelevant, dissimilar, inappropriate, *to*; introduced from outside (esp. ~ **body** in the eye, tissues, etc.); situated outside, coming from another culture, area, etc. 2. Outside the country, not in one’s own land; of, in, characteristic of, coming from, dealing with, some country not one’s own. 3. **F~ Legion**: see LEGION. **for′eign·er, for′eign·ness** *ns.*

fore·knowl·edge (fōr′nŏlĭdj, fŏr′-, fōrnŏl′-, fŏr-) *n.* Prior knowledge; prescience.

fore·leg (fōr′lĕg, fŏr′-) *n.* Animal’s front leg.

fore·limb (fōr′lĭm, fŏr′-) *n.* Front limb of animal.

fore·lock[1] (fōr′lŏk, fŏr′-) *n.* Lock of hair growing just above forehead.

fore·lock[2] (fōr′lŏk, fŏr′-) *n.* (chiefly naut.) Wedge put through hole in bolt to keep it in place; linchpin.

fore·man (fō′m*a*n, fŏr′-) *n.* (pl. **-men**). Chairman and spokesman of jury; principal workman superintending others.

fore·mast (fōr′măst, -mahst, fŏr′-) *n.* Forward lower mast of ship.

fore·most (fōr′mōst, fŏr′-) *adj.* Most advanced in position, front; most notable, best, chief. ~ *adv.* Before anything else in position; in the first place.

fore·noon (fōr′no͞on, fŏr′-) *n.* Part of day between sunrise and noon.

fo·ren·sic (forĕn′sĭk) *adj.* 1. Of, used in, legal proceedings; ~ **medicine**, application of medical knowledge to legal, esp. criminal, problems. 2. Of, used in, debate or argument; rhetorical. **fo·ren′sics** *n.* (pl. considered as sing.) Study, art, of formal debate and argument. **fo·ren′si·cal·ly** *adv.*

fore·or·dain (fōrōrdān′, fŏr-) *v.t.* Predestinate, appoint beforehand. **fore·or·di·na·tion** (fōrōrd*i*nā′sh*o*n, fŏr-) *n.*

fore·play (fōr′plā, fŏr′-) *n.* Stimulation preceding sexual intercourse.

fore·run (fōrrŭn′, fŏr-) *v.t.* (**-ran, -run, -run·ning**). Be precursor of, foreshadow. **fore·run′ner** *n.*

fore·sail (fōr′sāl, fŏr′-; naut. fōr′s*e*l, *f*ŏr′-) *n.* Principal sail on foremast; in square-rigged vessel, lowest square sail; in fore-and-aft rigged, triangular sail before mast.

fore·see (fōrsē′, fŏr-) *v.t.* (**-saw, -seen, -see·ing**). See or realize beforehand.

fore·shad·ow (fōrshăd′ō, fŏr-) *v.t.* Prefigure, serve as type or presage of; warn of beforehand.

fore·short·en (fōrshōr′t*e*n, fŏr-) *v.t.* Show, portray, (object) with the apparent shortening due to visual perspective; (of visual perspective) cause (object) to appear shorter in directions not lying in plane perpendicular to line of sight.

fore·sight (fōr′sīt, fŏr′-) *n.* Foreseeing, prevision; care for the future.

fore·skin (fōr′skĭn, fŏr′-) *n.* Prepuce.

for·est (fōr′ĭst, fär′-) *n.* Large tract covered with trees and undergrowth; ~ **ranger**, person caring for or supervising (esp. public or national) forest.

fore·stall (fōrstawl′, fŏr-) *v.t.* 1. (hist.) Buy up (goods) in order to profit by enhanced price; prevent sales at (fair, market) thus.

Most temperate ***forests*** *in Europe and North America have been reduced by agriculture over the centuries. In Rumania, however, forests occupy 27 per cent of the land.*

*This **forge** at Brandeston, U.K. with furnace, anvil and bellows, was once the workshop of a blacksmith. Forging metals into a desired shape is now done with sophisticated machinery.*

2. Anticipate in action; take precautionary measures.

for·est·er (fŏr′ester, făr′-) *n.* 1. Person in charge of forest, or of growing timber; person trained in forestry. 2. Dweller in forest; bird or beast of forest.

for·es·try (fŏr′estrē, făr′-) *n.* Wooded country, forests; science and art of managing forests.

fore·taste (fōr′tāst, fŏr′-) *n.* Partial enjoyment or suffering (*of*) in advance. ~ *v.t.* (**-tast·ed, -tast·ing**). Taste beforehand, anticipate enjoyment etc. of.

fore·tell (fōrtĕl′, fŏr-) *v.t.* (**-told, -tell·ing**). Predict, prophesy; presage, be precursor of.

fore·thought (fōr′thawt, fŏr′-) *n.* Previous contriving, deliberate intention; provident care.

fore·to·ken (fōrtō′ken, fŏr-) *v.t.* Portend, point to. ~ (fōr′tōken, fŏr′-) *n.*

for·ev·er (forĕv′er) *adv.* For all (future) time, incessantly; (colloq.) for a very long time.

for·ev·er·more (forĕvermōr′, -mŏr′) *adv.* For all future time.

fore·warn (fōrwŏrn′, fŏr-) *v.t.* Warn beforehand.

fore·word (fōr′wērd, fŏr′-, -werd) *n.* Preface; introduction, esp. to a book.

for·feit (fŏr′fĭt) *n.* Thing lost owing to crime or fault; penalty for breach of contract or neglect, fine; trivial fine for breach of rules in games etc.; article surrendered by player in game of **forfeits** to be redeemed by performing ludicrous task; forfeiture. **forfeit** *adj.* That has been lost or given up as penalty. ~ *v.t.* Lose right to, be deprived of, have to pay, as penalty of crime, neglect, etc., or as necessary consequence of something. **for·fei·ture** (fŏr′fĭcher) *n.*

for·fend (fŏrfĕnd′) *v.t.* (archaic) Avert, keep away, prevent; defend; forbid.

for·gath·er (fŏrgădh′er, fŏr-) *v.i.* Assemble, meet together, associate; meet accidentally *with*.

forge[1] (fōrj, fŏrj) *n.* Blacksmith's hearth or fireplace with bellows, smithy; furnace or hearth for melting or refining metal, workshop containing this. ~ *v.* 1. Shape by heating in forge and hammering. 2. Fabricate, invent (tale, lie); make in fraudulent imitation, esp. imitate (signature etc.) in writing in order to pass it off as genuine; commit forgery. **forg′er** *n.*

forge[2] (fōrj, fŏrj) *v.i.* (**forged, forg·ing**). Make way, advance, gradually or with difficulty; ~ **ahead**, take lead in race etc., get start; make good progress.

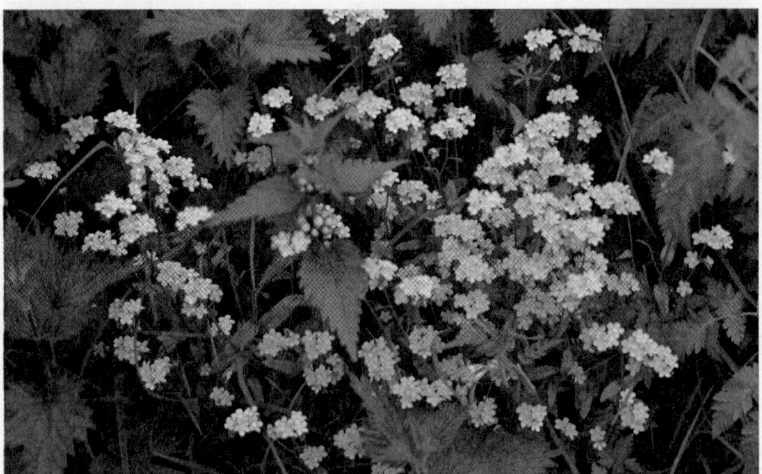

*The **forget-me-not** is native to temperate regions and common in Europe, northern Asia, North America, Australia and New Zealand. The five-petalled flowers are usually sky-blue.*

for·ger·y (fōr′jerē, fŏr′-) *n.* (pl. **-ger·ies**). Forging, counterfeiting, or falsifying, of document; spurious thing, esp. document or signature.

for·get (fergĕt′) *v.* (**-got, -got·ten, -get·ting**). Lose remembrance of or *about*; neglect; inadvertently omit to bring, mention, attend to, etc.; put out of mind, cease to think of; disregard, overlook, slight; ~ **oneself**, neglect one's own interests; act unbecomingly, presumptuously, or unworthily; ~**-me-not**, plant of genus *Myosotis* (esp. *M. scorpioides*) with small yellow-eyed blue flowers. **for·get′ful** *adj.* **for·get′ful·ly** *adv.* **for·get′ful·ness** *n.*

for·give (fergĭv′) *v.t.* (**-gave, -giv·en, -giv·ing**). Absolve, excuse from payment of (debt etc.); give up resentment against, pardon (offender). **for·giv′a·ble** *adj.* **for·give′ness** *n.* **for·giv′ing** *adj.* **for·giv′er** *n.*

for·go (fŏrgō′, fŏr-) *v.t.* (**-went, -gone, -go·ing**). Abstain from, go without, let go, omit to take or use, relinquish.

fork (fŏrk) *n.* 1. Pronged agricultural instrument for digging, lifting, carrying, or throwing. 2. Two-, three-, or four-pronged instrument used to hold food while it is cut, convey it to mouth, etc., and in cooking. 3. Two-pronged steel instrument giving musical note when struck, tuning fork. 4. Stake with forked end; forking, bifurcation, e.g., that of diverging roads, rivers, etc.; forked part of bicycle frame in which wheel revolves. 5. **fork′lift**, vehicle with fork in front for lifting and carrying loads. **fork** *v.* Form fork; have or develop branches; lift, carry, dig, throw, with fork; ~ **over**, (slang) hand over, pay. **forked** *adj.* Having a fork or fork-like branches.

for·lorn (fŏrlŏrn′) *adj.* Desperate, hopeless; abandoned, forsaken; (poet.) deprived *of*; in pitiful condition, of wretched appearance. **for·lorn′ly** *adv.* **for·lorn′ness** *n.*

form (fōrm) *n.* 1. Shape, arrangement of parts, visible aspect (esp. apart from color); shape of body; body in respect to outward shape and appearance. 2. Mode in which thing exists or manifests itself; species, kind, variety; (gram.) one of various modes of spelling, inflection, etc., under which word may appear, external characteristics of words, as dist. from their meaning. 3. One of the numbered classes or grades in British schools and some U.S. private schools. 4. Arrangement and style in literary or musical composition; orderly arrangement of parts. 5. Set or customary method or procedure; set or fixed order of words etc.; document with blanks to be filled up. 6. Formality, mere piece of ceremony, as a ~ **letter**, one printed in many copies to be sent to a number of people; behavior according to rule or custom; **good, bad,** ~, behavior satisfying or offending current ideals. 7. Condition of health and training; good spirits. 8. (print.) Body of type secured in chase for printing at one impression; film material arranged for making plate, etc. 9. Lair or nest in which hare rests. **form** *v.* Fashion, mold; assume shape, become solid; mold by discipline, train, instruct; embody, organize, *into* company etc.; frame, make, produce; articulate (word); conceive (idea, judgment); develop (habit); contract (alliance); be material of, make up, make *one* or *part of*; (mil.) draw up in order, assume specified formation.

-form *suffix.* Forming adjectives (1) having the form of (*cruciform, cuneiform*); (2) indicating number of forms (*uniform, multiform*).

for·mal (fōr′mal) *adj.* 1. Of the form or constitutive essence of a thing, essential; of the outward form, shape, appearance, or external qualities; (logic) concerned with the form, not the matter, of reasoning. 2. That is such in form; that is according to recognized forms, or the rules of art or law; valid by virtue of its form, explicit and definite, not merely tacit. 3. Ceremonial, required by convention; perfunctory, having the form without the spirit; observant of forms, precise; excessively regular or symmetrical, stiff, methodical. **for′mal·ly** *adv.*

form·al·de·hyde (fōrmăl′dehīd, fer-) *n.* Colorless gas (CH_2O) with a characteristic pungent odor, used in solution as preservative, disinfectant etc.

for·mal·ism (fōr′malĭzem) *n.* Strict observance of forms; excessive regularity or symmetry. **for′mal·ist** *n.* **for·mal·is′tic** *adj.*

Forsythias, also called 'golden bells', flourish in gardens of all temperate regions. Their bright yellow flowers appear in early spring, often before the leaves unfold.

for·mal·i·ty (fōrmăl′ĭtē) *n.* (pl. **-ties**). Conformity to rules, propriety; ceremony, elaborate procedure; formal or ceremonial act, requirement of etiquette or custom; being formal, precision of manners, stiffness of design.

for·mal·ize (fōr′malīz) *v.t.* (**-ized, -iz·ing**). Give definite shape or legal formality to; make ceremonious, precise, or rigid; imbue with formalism.

for·mat (fōr′măt) *n.* Shape and size (of book etc.); style of arrangement etc.

for·ma·tion (fōrmā′shon) *n.* Forming, being formed; thing formed; arrangement of parts, structure; (mil.) disposition of troops, formal stationing or arrangement of number of ships, aircraft, etc.; (geol.) assemblage of rocks or series of strata having some common characteristic.

form·a·tive (fōr′matĭv) *adj.* Serving to form, of formation; (gram., of suffixes etc.) used in forming words. ~ *n.* Formative element of a word.

for·mer (fōr′mer) *adj.* Of the past or an earlier period; **the** ~, the first or first mentioned of two (freq. with ellipsis of *n.*; opp. LATTER). **for′mer·ly** *adv.*

form·fit·ting (fōrm′fĭtĭng) *adj.* Adhering closely to the body; designed to reveal or suggest rather than conceal.

For·mi·ca (fōrmī′ka, fer-) *n.* (trademark) Hard durable plastic laminate used esp. as decorative surfacing material.

for·mi·da·ble (fōr′mĭdabel, fōrmĭd′-) *adj.* To be dreaded; likely to be hard to overcome, resist, or deal with. **for′mi·da·ble·ness** *n.* **for′mi·da·bly** *adv.*

form·less (fōrm′lĭs) *adj.* Shapeless, without determinate or regular form.

For·mo·sa (fōrmō′sa). Former name of TAIWAN; ~ **Strait**, strait of the China Sea between Taiwan and the People's Republic of China. [Port. name, f. L. *formosus* beautiful]

for·mu·la (fōr′myula) *n.* (pl. **-las, -lae** pr. -lē, -lī). 1. Set form of words in which something is defined, stated, etc., or which is prescribed for use on ceremonial occasion etc.; conventional usage or belief. 2. Recipe; prescription; (math.) rule or principle expressed in algebraic symbols; (chem.) expression of constituents of compound in symbols and figures; tabulation of facts etc. in symbols and figures. 3. Class or specification of a racing car. **for·mu·lar·ize** (fōr′myulerīz) *v.t.* (**-ized, -iz·ing**).

for·mu·late (fōr′myulāt) *v.t.* (**-lated, -lat·ing**). Reduce to, express in, a formula; set forth systematically. **for·mu·la·tion** (fōrmyulā′shon) *n.*

for·ni·cate (fōr′nĭkāt) *v.i.* (**-cat·ed, -cat·ing**). Commit fornication. **for·ni·ca·tion** (fōrnĭkā′shon) *n.* Voluntary sexual intercourse between a man and a woman not married to each other. **for′ni·ca·tor** *n.*

for·sake (fōrsāk′) *v.t.* (**-sook** pr. -so͝ok, **-sak·en, -sak·ing**). Give up, break off from, renounce; withdraw one's help etc. from: desert, abandon.

for·swear (fōrswār′) *v.* (**-swore, -sworn, -swear·ing**). Abjure, renounce on oath; ~ **oneself**, swear falsely, perjure oneself; commit perjury; **forsworn′**, perjured.

for·syth·i·a (fōrsĭth′ēa, fer-) *n.* Ornamental spring-flowering shrub of genus *F*~ with bright yellow bell-shaped flowers. [f. W. *Forsyth* (1737–1804), English botanist]

fort (fōrt, fōrt) *n.* Fortified place, usu. single building or set of connected military buildings; trading station (hist., orig. fortified); **hold the** ~, act as temporary substitute; cope with emergency.

fort. *abbrev.* Fortification.

forte[1] (fōrt, fōrt, fōr′tā, -tē; fencing fōrt, fōrt) *n.* Person's stong point; (fencing) strong part of sword blade, from hilt to middle.

for·te[2] (fōr′tā) *adv.* (mus.) Loudly; **double** ~, very loudly; ~ **piano**, loudly then immediately softly. **forte** *adj.* & *n.* Loud (passage). [It.]

The silent guns of Fort McHenry, in Maryland guard its perimeters. Other U.S. **fortifications** are much more active.

The **Roman forum,** of which only the ruins remain, was located between the Capitoline and Palatine hills. It was the center of life in ancient Rome.

forth (fōrth, fōrth) *adv.* Forward (now only in **back and ~**, to and fro); onward in time (now only in **from this time ~** etc.); forward into view; out, away, from home, etc.; **and so ~**, and so on, and the like.

forth·com·ing (fōrth′kŭm′ĭng, fōrth′-) *adj.* About or likely to come forth; approaching; available when wanted.

forth·right (fōrth′rīt, fōrth′-) *adj.* Proceeding straight ahead; straightforward, frank, candid, outspoken, unswerving; decisive. **forth·right′** *adv.* Straight ahead.

forth·with (fōrthwĭth′, -wĭdh′, fōrth-) *adv.* Immediately, without delay.

for·ti·fi·ca·tion (fōrt*ĭ*f*ĭ*kā′sh*o*n) *n.* 1. Fortifying. 2. Defensive work, wall, earthwork, tower, etc.

for·ti·fy (fōr′t*ĭ*fī) *v.* (**-fied, -fy·ing**). Strengthen structure of; impart vigor or strength or endurance to, encourage; provide with defensive works; erect fortifications; strengthen (wine etc.) with alcohol; add nutrients to (food).

for·tis·si·mo (fōrtĭs′ĭmō) *adv., n.* (pl. **-mos, -mi** pr. -mē) & *adj.* (mus.) (Passage performed) very loud(ly).

for·ti·tude (fōr′tĭtōōd, -tūd) *n.* Courage in pain or adversity.

Fort Knox (nŏks). Military reservation in N. central Kentucky, SSW. of Louisville; site of U.S. gold bullion depository since 1936.

Fort Mc·Hen·ry (m*a*kĕn′rē) **National Monument.** Harbor fort and surrounding 43 acres in Baltimore, Md., established as national monument in 1925; attack on fort by British (1814) inspired Francis Scott Key to compose "The Star Spangled Banner."

fort·night (fōrt′nīt, -nĭt) *n.* (chiefly Brit.) Period of two weeks. **fort′night·ly** *adj.* & *adv.* (Happening, appearing) once every two weeks.

FOR·TRAN (fōr′trăn) *n.* Computer programming language used chiefly for scientific and mathematical calculations. [*for*mula *tran*slation]

for·tress (fōr′trĭs) *n.* Military stronghold, esp. strongly fortified town fit for large garrison.

Fort Sum·ter (sŭm′t*e*r) **National Monument.** Fort in Charleston harbor, SE. South Carolina, attacked and conquered by Confederate forces on Apr. 12, 1861, in opening battle of Civil War.

for·tu·i·tous (fōrtōō′ĭt*u*s, -tū′-) *adj.* Due to or characterized by chance, accidental, casual. **for·tu′i·tous·ly** *adv.* **for·tu′i·tous·ness** *n.* **for·tu′i·ty** *n.* Fortuitousness; a chance occurrence; accident.

for·tu·nate (fōr′ch*u*nĭt) *adj.* Favored by fortune, lucky, prosperous. **for′tu·nate·ly** *adv.* Luckily, successfully.

for·tune (fōr′ch*u*n) *n.* 1. Chance as a power in people's affairs; freq. personified as goddess with wheel, betokening vicissitude, as emblem; **soldier of ~**: see SOLDIER. 2. Luck, good or bad, falling to anyone in life or particular affair; destiny; what is to befall in future (chiefly in **tell person his ~**); **for'tune-teller**, one who professes to foretell the future. 3. Good luck; prosperity, prosperous condition, wealth; large sum of money; **make (one's) ~**, become rich, prosper; **~ hunter**, person seeking rich spouse.

for·ty (fŏr'tē) *adj.* Amounting to forty; **~-five** (*n.*) .45-caliber revolver; **~-niner**, one who went to California in the gold rush of 1849; **~ winks**, nap. **forty** *n.* (pl. **-ties**). Cardinal number, four times ten (40, xl, or XL); **for'ties**, numbers etc. from 40 to 49; these years of century or life. **for'·ti·eth** *adj.* & *n.*

fo·rum (fŏr'*u*m, fŏr'-) *n.* (pl. **fo·rums**; **fo·ra** pr. fŏr'*a*, fŏr'*a*). (Rom. antiq.) Public place or marketplace of city; in ancient Rome, place of assembly for judicial and other public business; place of public discussion; court, tribunal (freq. fig.).

for·ward (fŏr'w*e*rd) *adj.* 1. (naut.) Belonging to fore part of ship. 2. Lying in front, or in direction of movement; onward or toward the front; **~ pass**, (football) pass thrown forward toward or over line of scrimmage; opp. LATERAL pass. 3. Advanced, progressing to maturity or completion. 4. Precocious, presumptuous, pert. **for'ward·ly** *adv.* **for'ward·ness** *n.* **forward, for'wards** *advs.* 1. Toward the future, continuously onward; toward the front, in the direction one is facing; with continuous forward motion; in advance, ahead; to the front, into prominence; onward so as to make progress; **bring forward**, draw attention to; **bring, carry forward**, (bookkeeping) transfer entry to next page or column; **come forward**, offer oneself for task, position, etc.; **put forward**, suggest, allege; **put oneself forward**, make oneself conspicuous. 2. (naut.) To, at, in, fore part of ship. **forward** *n.* (basketball, soccer, hockey, etc.) Player in the front line usu. for offense. **forward** *v.t.* Help forward, promote; send (letter etc.) on to another stipulated destination; (loosely) dispatch (goods etc.). **for'ward·er** *n.* (usu. **freight ~**) Person or agency that forwards; esp. one handling freight or getting goods to their destination.

fosse, foss (fŏs, faws) *ns.* Ditch; moat.

fos·sil (fŏs'*i*l) *adj.* Of the nature of a fossil. **~** *n.* Thing found in strata of earth recognizable as remains of plant or animal of former geological period or as showing vestiges of animal or vegetable life

*A **fossil** may be in the form of the actual remains of a creature or plant or it may be the impression left by that object in rock, as with this brachiopod found in limestone.*

of such period; (person or thing) belonging to the past, antiquated, incapable of further growth or progress. **fos·sil·ize** (fŏs'*i*līz) *v.t.* (**-ized, -iz·ing**). **fos·sil·i·za·tion** (fŏs*i*līzā'sh*o*n) *n.*

fos·ter (faw'st*e*r, fŏs't*e*r) *v.t.* Bring up, rear, tend with affectionate care; encourage or harbor (feeling); (of circumstances) be favorable to. **~** *adj.* Having a specified relation, not by blood but in virtue of nursing or bringing up (**~** *brother*, *child*, *daughter*, *father*, *mother*, etc.); concerning care of orphans etc. (**~** *care*, **~** *home*). **fos'ter·ling** *n.* Foster child.

Fos·ter (faw'st*e*r, fŏs't*e*r), **Stephen (Collins)** (1826–64). Amer. songwriter best known for contributions to music of black minstrel troupes; wrote "My Old Kentucky Home," "Massa's in the Cold, Cold Ground," "O Susanna," "Old Black Joe," etc.; elected to American Hall of Fame (1940).

fought: see FIGHT.

foul (fowl) *adj.* 1. Offensive to the senses, loathsome, stinking; dirty, soiled; charged with noxious matter. 2. Clogged, choked; (of ship's bottom etc.) overgrown with weeds, barnacles, etc. (hence **foul'·ing** (*n.*), such an incrustation). 3. Morally polluted, obscene, disgustingly abusive; unfair, against rules of game etc.; (of weather) wet, rough, stormy; (of wind) contrary; (naut.) embarrassed, entangled, in collision, etc. 4. **~ ball**, (base-

ball) any batted ball going outside foul lines; ~ **line**, (baseball) either of the lines between home plate and 1st base and home plate and 3rd base and prolonged into the outfield; (basketball) line from which free throws are made; **foul′-mouthed′**, given to obscene or abusive speech; **foul play**, unfair play in games; unfair or treacherous dealing, esp. involving murder. **foul′ly** *adv*. **foul′ness** *n*. **foul** *n*. Something foul; (sports) action contrary to rules, usu. against opponent's body; (boxing) blow struck low or otherwise illegally; (baseball) foul ball. **foul** *adv*. In a foul or irregular way. ~ *v*. Make or become foul; entangle, become entangled; collide with; hit foul ball, commit foul (blow) against; ~ **out**, (baseball) hit foul fly ball that is caught; ~ **up**, (colloq.) botch, bungle, mess up; ~**-up**, (colloq.) confusion arising from ineptitude or mechanical breakdown.

fou·lard (fo͞olärd′) *n*. Thin soft smooth material, usu. silk, cotton, or rayon and with a small printed design; a necktie, scarf, etc. of this.

found[1] (fownd) *v*. Lay base of (building etc.); be original builder, begin building, of (town, edifice); set up, establish (esp. with endowment), originate, initiate, (institution); construct, base (tale, one's fortunes, rule, etc.) *on* some ground, support, principle, etc.; rely, base oneself, (of argument etc.) be based, *on*. **found′er**[1] *n*.

found[2] (fownd) *v.t*. Melt and mold (metal), fuse (materials and glass); make (thing of molten metal, glass) by melting. **found′er**[2] *n*.

found[3]: see FIND.

foun·da·tion (fowndā′shon) *n*. 1. Establishing, constituting on permanent basis, esp. of endowed institution; funds given for permanent support of hospital, school, etc.; organization established by endowment to promote arts, science, education, etc. 2. Solid ground or base, natural or artificial, on which building rests; lowest part of building, usu. below ground level; basis, groundwork, underlying principle; body or ground on which other parts are overlaid. 3. (cosmetics) Base. 4. ~ **garment**, woman's supporting undergarment, e.g., corset or girdle.

found·er[1,2] (fown′dėr): see FOUND[1, 2].

found·er[3] (fown′dėr) *v*. 1. (of earth, building, etc.) Fall down or in, give way; (of horse) collapse, fall lame, stumble etc.; (of ship) fill with water and sink. 2. Cause (horse, ship) to founder. ~ *n*. Inflammation of horse's hoof from overwork.

found·ling (fownd′lĭng) *n*. Deserted infant of unknown parents.

found (fownd) **object.** Object picked up by chance and kept as or as part of a work of art.

*Builders of early artificial **fountains** may have been symbolizing their belief in the sanctity of springs of water. The 18th century fountain illustrated is one of Rome's many public fountains.*

found·ry (fown′drē) *n*. (pl. **-ries**). Factory in which molten metal castings are produced.

fount[1] (fownt) *n*. (poet. or rhet.) Spring, source, fountain.

fount[2] (fownt, fŏnt) *n*. (chiefly Brit.) = FONT def. 2.

foun·tain (fown′tĭn) *n*. Spring, esp. as the source of a river etc.; jet of water made to spout, structure provided for it; structure for constant supply of drinking water; soda fountain; **foun′tainhead**, original source; **fountain pen**, pen containing reservoir of ink.

four (fōr, fōr) *adj*. Amounting to four; ~ **figures**, 1,000 (dollars etc.) or over; ~**-flush**, (poker) flush containing only four (instead of five) cards; **four′flusher**, (slang) pretender, humbug; **Four Freedoms**: see FREEDOM; **Four-H club, 4-H club**, club sponsored by U.S. Department of Agriculture to instruct young people in agriculture and citizenship (improving head, hearts, hands, and health); ~**-handed**, (of games) played by, requiring four players; (of piano music) composed, arranged for, four hands, as a duet; **the F~ Hundred**, most exclusive social set, orig. that of New York (which *c*1890 was supposed to consist of about this number of people); ~**-in-hand**, vehicle with four horses driven by one person; necktie tied in a slipknot with long ends hanging and overlapping; ~**-letter word**, any of several monosyllabic English words dealing with sex or excrement and generally regarded as vulgar or obscene; ~**-o'-clock**, plant (*Mirabilis jalapa*) native to tropical Amer. and with flowers opening about four p.m.; also, prairie wildflower (*M. nyctaginea*); **four′poster**, bed having four tall corner posts (to support canopy and curtains); **four′score**, 80; **four′-square**, square-shaped; solidly based, steady, forthright, honest; **four-wheel**, (vehicle) with four wheels, esp. **four-wheel drive**, (vehicle) with power transmitted to all four wheels. **four** *n*. One more than three; symbol for this (4, iv, or IV); card, die face, or domino with four pips; four o'clock; size etc. indicated by 4; **on all fours**, crawling on hands and knees. **four′fold** *adj*. & *adv*. In four parts; four times as much.

Fou·rier[1] (foor′ēā, fooryā′), **(François Marie) Charles** (1772–1837). French Utopian socialist writer. **Fou·ri·er·ism** (foor′ēerĭzem) *n*. Communistic system for the reorganization of society devised by Fourier under which the population was to be grouped in *phalansteries*, socialistic groups of about 1,800 persons holding property in common.

Fou·rier[2] (foor'ēā, fooryā'), **Baron Jean Baptiste Joseph** (1768–1830). French mathematician and physicist; received title of baron from Napoleon Bonaparte (1808).

four·some (fōr'som, fōr'-) *adj*. Consisting of, involving four persons together. ~ *n*. Golf match or other game between two pairs of players; company or party of four persons.

four·teen (fōr'tēn', fōr'-) *adj*. & *n*. One more than thirteen (14, xiv, or XIV). **four'teenth'** *adj*. & *n*. ~ **of July**, French annual holiday in celebration of fall of Bastille, 1789.

fourth (fōrth, fōrth) *adj*. Next after third. ~ *n*. 1. Fourth part (see PART[1] def. 1), quarter. 2. (mus.) Interval of which the span involves four alphabetical names of notes; harmonic combination of two notes thus separated. 3. Fourth thing etc.; **the F~**, the 4th of July, annual holiday celebrating the signing of the Declaration of Independence (1776), also called Independence Day; ~ **class**, class of mail consisting of merchandise or certain printed matter and sent at lowest rate; ~ **dimension**: see DIMENSION; ~ **estate**: see ESTATE. 4. Fourth grade in school. 5. (in motor vehicle) Fourth gear.

fo·ve·a (fō'vēa) *n*. (pl. **-ve·ae** pr. -vēē). (anat.) Small pit or cuplike depression in bone or organ; ~ **centralis**, small depression in macula lutea of retina, spot where vision is most acute.

fowl (fowl) *n*. (pl. **fowls**, collect. **fowl**). 1. Any bird(s) used as food or hunted as game; birds (rare exc. in **wild'fowl**); flesh of birds as food. 2. (also **domestic** ~) Domestic chicken of genus *Gallus*; its flesh as food. ~ *v.i.* Catch, hunt, shoot, or snare wildfowl; **fowl'ing piece**, light shotgun for shooting birds. **fow'ler** *n*.

Fow·ler (fow'ler), **Henry Watson** (1858–1933). English lexicographer; with his brother F. G. Fowler, wrote *The King's English* (1906) and compiled *The Concise Oxford Dictionary of Current English* (1911); author of *A Dictionary of Modern English Usage* (1926).

fox (fŏks) *n*. (pl. **fox·es**, collect. **fox**). 1. Flesh-eating quadruped of the dog family, esp. the red foxes (Vulpes) and the gray foxes (Urocyon) having elongated pointed muzzle, upright ears, and long bushy tail; proverbial for cunning; crafty person. 2. **Fox**, tribe of N. Amer. Indians; member of this tribe. 3. **fox'fire**, phosphorescence from decaying wood; **fox'glove**, tall plant of genus *Digitalis*, esp. European *Digitalis purpurea*, the leaves of which yield digitalis, with drooping, tubular

*The wide demand for the eggs and meat of the domestic **fowl** led to the development of new breeds to meet the conditions of intensive production after the 1939–45 war.*

*The canny **fox** is a skillful hunter and makes a difficult prey for those who hunt it. The red fox, found in much of Eurasia, North Africa, and North America, is hunted for pleasure. Silver and black foxes are color phases occasionally found in a red fox's litter. In North America they are bred for the value of their fine quality pelts.*

purple or white flowers; also, the N. Amer. **false ~s** (Geradia) with bright yellow flowers. **fox'hole,** (mil.) small pit in ground used by soldier as shelter on battlefield; (fig.) place of refuge or concealment; **fox'hound**, kind of hound bred and trained to hunt foxes; **fox hunt**, chase, hunting of, fox with hounds; **fox'tail**, species of grass with soft brushlike spikes of flowers, esp. *Alopecurus pratensis*; **fox terrier**, small terrier with smooth or rough (wire-haired) short hair, usu. white with black markings, of a kind bred for unearthing foxes, but kept chiefly as pets; **fox trot**, ballroom dance in $\frac{4}{4}$ time based on slow or quick steps. **fox** *v.* Trick, outwit; be sly and crafty; outfox; (loosely) impede, ruin plans of, etc.

fox·y (fŏk'sē) *adj.* (**fox·i·er, fox·i·est**). 1. Crafty, cunning. 2. Fox-colored, reddish brown.

foy·er (foi'*er*) *n.* Lobby or entrance hall of a theater, hotel, etc; vestibule or entrance hall of a home or apartment.

f.p., fp *abbrevs.* Forward pass, freezing point.

FPC *abbrev.* Federal Power Commission.

fpm *abbrev.* Feet per minute.

FPO *abbrev.* Fleet post office.

fps *abbrev.* Foot-pound-second.

f.p.s. *abbrev.* Feet per second.

Fr *symbol.* Francium.

Fr. *abbrev.* Father (priest), French, franc(s).

fr. *abbrev.* Fragment, franc(s), from.

Fra (frah) *n.* Brother (title of a friar). [It.]

fra·cas (frā'k*a*s; *Brit.* frăk'*a*s) *n.* (pl. same). Noisy quarrel, row, brawl.

frac·tion (frăk'sh*o*n) *n.* 1. Numerical quantity that is not an integer, one or more aliquot parts of unit or whole number; small piece or amount, scrap; **proper (improper) ~**, fraction in which numerator is less than (greater than or equal to) denominator. 2. Portion separable by fractionation. **frac'tion·al** *adj.* **frac'tion·al·ly** *adv.*

frac·tion·ate (frăk'sh*o*nāt) *v.t.* (**-at·ed, -at·ing**). Separate (mixture) by distillation or otherwise into portions of differing properties. **frac·tion·a·tion** (frăksh*o*nā'sh*o*n) *n.*

frac·tious (frăk'sh*u*s) *adj.* Unruly, cross, peevish. **frac'tious·ly** *adv.* **frac'tious·ness** *n.*

frac·ture (frăk'ch*er*) *n.* 1. Breaking, breakage or crack, esp. of bone or cartilage; **compound ~**, fracture of bone with breaking of skin; **simple ~**, breaking of bone but not of skin. 2. Characteristic appearance of fresh surface of mineral broken with hammer. ~ *v.* (**-tured, -tur·ing**). Cause fracture in, be fractured; break continuity of.

frag (frăg) *v.t.* (**fragged, frag·ging**). Attack (esp. unpopular commander) with a grenade.

frag·ile (frăj'*i*l) *adj.* Easily snapped or shattered; weak, perishable; of delicate frame or constitution. **fra·gil·i·ty** (fr*a*jĭl'ĭtē) *n.*

frag·ment (frăg'm*e*nt) *n.* Part broken off, detached piece; isolated or incomplete part, remainder of lost or destroyed whole; esp. extant remains or unfinished portion of writing or work of art. **frag·men·tar·y** (frăg'm*e*ntĕrē) *adj.* **frag·men·ta·tion** (frăgm*e*ntā'sh*o*n) *n.* Separation into fragments; ~ **bomb**, one designed to disintegrate into small fragments on explosion. **fragment** (frăg'mĕnt) *v.* Break or separate into fragments.

Fra·go·nard (frăg*o*nār'), **Jean Honoré** (1732–1806). French engraver and painter.

fra·grant (frā'gr*a*nt) *adj.* Sweet smelling. **fra'grance** *n.* Quality of being fragrant; perfume.

frail[1] (frāl') *n.* Rush basket for holding fruit, esp. dried fruit as figs, raisins, etc.; quantity of fruit contained in a frail, usu. 50–75 lbs.

frail[2] (frāl) *adj.* Fragile; morally weak, unable to resist temptation. **frail·ty** (frāl'tē) *n.* (pl. **-ties**). Liability to err or yield to temptation; fault, weakness, foible.

frame (frām) *n.* 1. Construction, constitution, build; established order, plan, system. 2. Temporary state (*of* mind). 3. Framed work or structure; human or animal body; skeleton of building; underlying support or essential substructure of

*The growing use of steel and other alloys in the building industry has led to an examination of new ways of constructing **frames** to provide great strength and rigidity with lightness so that few interior supports are needed. The geodesic dome, built of triangular sections, and double grids offers solutions to the problem of strength versus weight.*

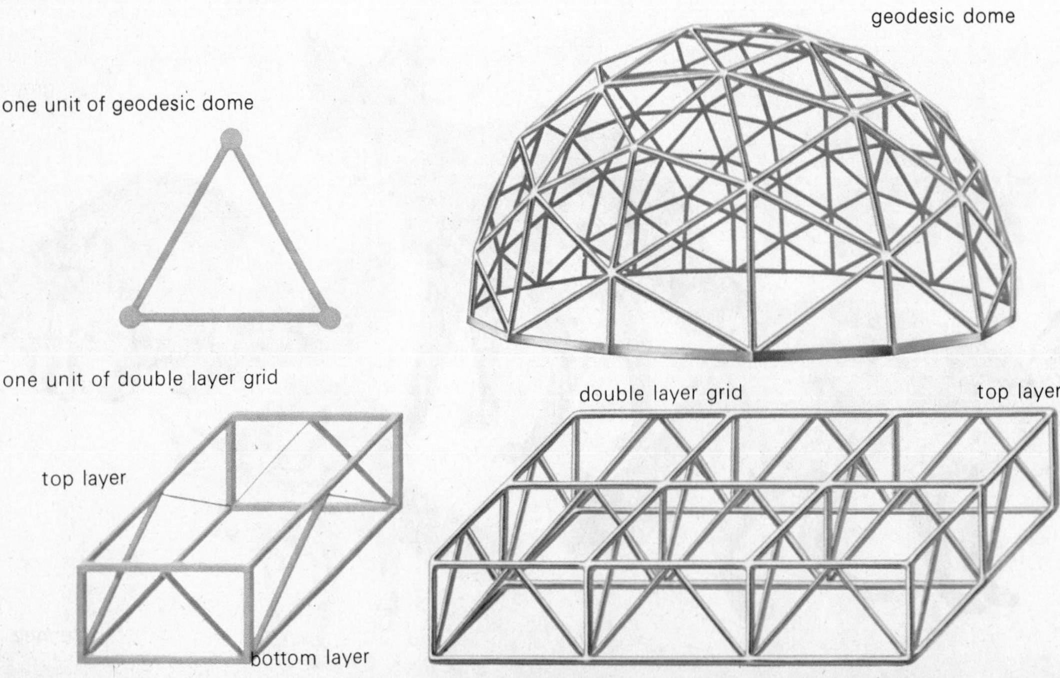

anything. 4. Case or border enclosing picture, pane of glass, etc. 5. (gardening) Glazed structure protecting plants from cold. 6. Rigid part of bicycle; skeleton of motor vehicle etc. supporting machinery and body. 7. (bowling) Any of ten divisions of game. 8. Each separate picture on a motion-picture film. 9. Single complete picture transmitted in series of lines by television. 10. (pool, etc.) Triangular rack in which balls are set up; the balls as set up; round of play required to pocket them all. 11. ~ **house**, house of wooden framework covered with boards etc; ~ **of reference**, characteristic of perception whereby objects are correctly localized in space; standard governing perceptual or logical evaluation; ~**-up**, (colloq.) conspiracy, trumped-up case or charge; **frame'work**, frame, substructure, upon or into which anything may be put. **frame** *v.* (**framed, fram·ing**). 1. Shape, direct, dispose, to a purpose; adapt, fit, *to*, or *into*. 2. Construct by combination of parts or adaptation to design; contrive, devise, invent, compose, express; articulate (words); conceive, imagine. 3. Set in frame; serve as frame for. 4. (slang) Concoct false charge or rig evidence against, make victim of frame-up.

franc (frăngk) *n.* Principal monetary unit of France, Belgium, Switzerland, and certain other countries, usu. = 100 centimes; (hist.) any of various gold and silver coins. [Fr., perh. f. *Francorum Rex* king of the Franks, legend on earliest coin so called]

France[1] (frăns, frahns). Republic of W. Europe; the monarchial system of government was overthrown during the French Revolution (1789–93), and the First Republic lasted until Napoleon founded the First Empire in 1804; the monarchy was restored in 1814 and lasted until 1848 when the Second Republic was formed, which became the Second Empire under Napoleon III in 1852; Napoleon was deposed in 1870 and the Third Republic established; this lasted until the occupation of France by the Germans (1940) during World War II; after the liberation of France (1945) the republic was restored and the Constitution of the Fourth Republic was in force from 1945 until Oct. 1958, when a new constitution established the Fifth Republic; capital, Paris.

France[2] (frăns, frahns), **Anatole.** Pseudonym of Jacques Anatole Thibault (1844–1924), French satirical writer.

fran·chise (frăn'chīz) *n.* 1. (chiefly hist.) Legal immunity or exemption from some burden or jurisdiction; privilege or exceptional right, granted to person,

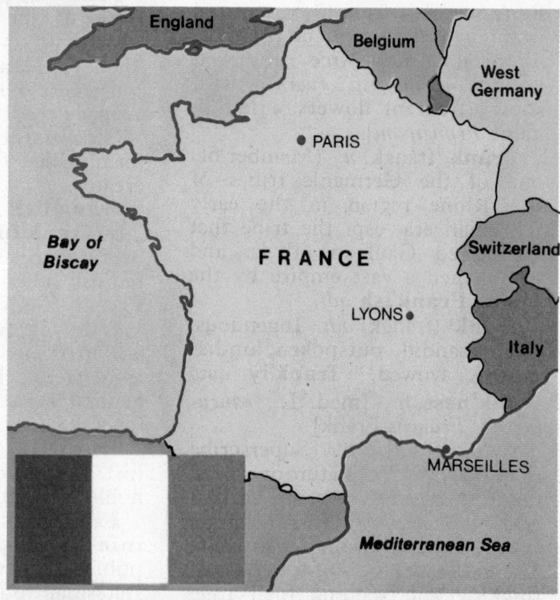

The large area covered by ***France,*** *about 212,660 sq miles, includes a wide variety of landforms. Upper Left: The Alps in the south east, photographed through a glaciated valley to Col D'Iseran, form a border with Italy. Lower left: Avignon, a town in the Rhône Valley, was first established in Roman times. Below: Map of France.*

corporation, etc.; right to distribute, sell company's products or services in particular area, often under the company's name and with its advice and direction. 2. Full membership of corporation or nation, citizenship. 3. Right of voting at public elections, esp. for member of legislative body; principle of qualification for this. ~ *v.t.* (**-chised, -chis·ing**). Give franchise to.

Fran·cis of As·si·si (frăn′sĭs *o*v *a*sē′zē, frahn′-) **St.** Giovanni Francesco Bernardone (1181?–1226). Italian friar; founded *c*1209 an order of friars, whose rules require chastity, poverty, and obedience, and lay special stress on preaching and ministration to the sick. **Fran·cis·can** (frănsĭs′k*a*n) *adj.* & *n.* (Member) of the order founded by St. Francis (also called *Minorites, Gray Friars*).

fran·ci·um (frăn′sē*u*m) *n.* (chem.) Radioactive metallic element of short life, the heaviest member of the alkali metal series; symbol Fr, at. no. 87, principal isotope at. wt. 223. [f. *France*, because its existence was first reported by a Frenchwoman, Mlle. M. Perey]

Fran·co (frăng′kō), **Generalissimo.** Francisco Franco Bahamonde (1892–1975), Spanish political leader; leader (caudillo) of the Empire, chief of the State, and head of the Falangist party 1939–75.

Franco- *prefix.* French and —, as ~*-German.*

Fran·co·phile (frăng′k*o*fīl), **Fran·co·phobe** (frăng′k*o*fōb) *ns.* One who loves, hates, the French.

fran·gi·pan·i (frănj*i*păn′ē, -pah′nē) *n.* (pl. **-pan·is, -pan·i**) [also **fran·gi·pane** (frăn′j*i*pān)] 1. Kind of filling for pastry made with almonds, sugar, and cream. 2. Perfume made from flowers of red jasmine or imitation of this. 3. Tropical Amer. tree, the red jasmine (*Plumeria rubra*), with showy fragrant flowers. [family name *Frangipani*]

Frank (frăngk) *n.* (Member of) one of the Germanic tribes of the Rhine region in the early Christian era, esp. the tribe that conquered Gaul in 6th c. and established a vast empire by the 9th c. **Frank′ish** *adj.*

frank[1] (frăngk) *adj.* Ingenuous, open, candid, outspoken; undisguised, avowed. **frank′ly** *adv.* **frank′ness** *n.* [med. L. *francus* free, f. *Francus* Frank]

frank[2] (frăngk) *v.t.* Superscribe (letter etc.) with signature or official mark to ensure its being carried without charge, send free of charge; **frank′ing privilege**, perquisite granted to members of Congress of franking and sending mail free.

The rich white and yellow flowers of the Hawaiian **frangipani** *fill the long summer days and nights with a scent that pervades every nook and cranny. It is even packaged into aerosol cans.*

frank *n.* (hist.) Franking signature, franked cover.

frank[3] (frăngk) *n.* (colloq.) Frankfurter.

Frank·en·stein (frăng′k*e*nstīn). Hero of the novel *Frankenstein* (1818) by Mary Wollstonecraft Shelley; he is a medical student who constructs a human monster that eventually destroys him, whence **~'s monster**, thing that becomes formidable to or destroys its creator.

frank·furt·er (frăngk′f*e*rt*e*r) *n.* (also **frank′furt**). Smoked beef or beef and pork sausage made in long, reddish links, orig. associated with Frankfurt, Germany; hot dog.

frank·in·cense (frăng′kĭnsĕns) *n.* Aromatic gum resin obtained from trees, chiefly E. African, of genus *Boswellia* and burned as incense.

frank·lin (frăngk′lĭn) *n.* (Brit. hist.) Landowner of free but not noble birth in 14th–15th centuries.

Frank·lin (frăngk′lĭn), **Benjamin** (1706–90). Amer. writer, publisher, inventor, scientist, and statesman; publisher of *The Pennsylvania Gazette* (1730–48) and a collection of wit and morality, *Poor Richard's Almanack* (1732–57); author of *Autobiography*, published with inaccuracies in 1791 and 1817, corrected and reissued in 1868; colonial emissary to Europe; member of the Second Continental Congress (1775); drafter and signer of the Declaration of Independence; signer of the Treaty of Paris (Sept. 3, 1783) with Great Britain, ending the Revolutionary War; ambassador to France (1776–85); member of the Constitutional Convention (1787); experimenter with electricity and optics; inventor of the lightning rod, bifocal glasses, improved cast-iron heating stove, etc.

fran·tic (fran′tĭk) *adj.* Wildly excited, beside oneself with rage, pain, grief, etc.; showing frenzy, uncontrolled. **fran′ti·cal·ly, fran′tic·ly** *advs.*

Franz Jo·sef (frahns′ jō′sĭf, frănz′ jōzĭf; *Ger.* frănts′ yō′zĕf) (1830–1916). Emperor of Austria (1848–1916); king of Hungary (1867–1916); concluded Triple Alliance with Germany and Italy (1883); assassination of his nephew and heir Archduke Francis Ferdinand at Sarajevo (June 28, 1914) precipitated World War I.

frap·pé (frăpā′), **frappe** (frăp) *ns.* 1. Milk shake. 2. Frozen fruit-flavored dessert. 3. Liqueur poured over crushed ice.

frat (frăt) *n.* (slang) College or high school fraternity.

fra·ter (frā′t*er*) *n.* Comrade, brother, esp. in a religious order.

fra·ter·nal (fr*a*tẽr′n*a*l) *adj.* (As) of brothers, brotherly; ~ **order**, friendly or charitable society, brotherhood; ~ **twins**, twins not necessarily of same sex and freq. bearing merely fraternal resemblance, resulting from fertilization of two ova, not one (opp. IDENTICAL).

fra·ter·ni·ty (fr*a*tẽr′nĭtē) *n.* (pl. **-ties**). 1. Being fraternal, brotherliness; brotherhood. 2. Body or order of men organized for religious or devout purposes; body of men associated by some tie or common interest, or of same class, occupation, etc.; social association of male students of school, college, or university.

frat·er·nize (frăt′*er*nīz) *v.t.* (**-nized, -niz·ing**). Associate (*with*, together, etc.), make friends, behave as intimates; cultivate friendly relations *with* (troops or inhabitants of enemy country). **frat·er·ni·za·tion** (frăt*er*nīzā′sh*o*n) *n.*

frat·ri·cide (frăt′rĭsīd) *n.* Killing of one's brother; one who commits fratricide. **frat·ri·cid·al** (frătrĭsī′d*a*l) *adj.*

fraud (frawd) *n.* Criminal deception, using of false representations to obtain unjust advantage or injure another; dishonest trick or stratagem; dishonest contrivance or person; impostor, humbug.

fraud·u·lent (fraw′j*u*l*e*nt) *adj.* Guilty of, of the nature of, characterized or effected by, fraud. **fraud′u·lence** *n.* **fraud′u·lent·ly** *adv.*

fraught (frawt) *adj.* Stored, equipped, *with* (poet.); ~ **with**, (fig.) involving, attended with, threatening (danger, woe, etc.); full of (meaning etc.).

fray[1] (frā) *n.* Noisy quarrel, brawl; fight, conflict.

fray[2] (frā) *v.* Wear away by rubbing; unravel edge or end of; become ragged at edge (also fig.).

Fra·zer (frā′z*er*), **Sir James George** (1854–1941). Scottish anthropologist, author of *The Golden Bough*.

fraz·zle (frăz′*e*l) *n.* Worn or exhausted state. ~ *v.* (**-zled, -zling**). To fray; become frayed or worn out.

FRB *abbrev.* Federal Reserve Board.

freak (frēk) *n.* 1. Caprice, vagary; capriciousness. 2. Product of sportive fancy; eccentric person; (also ~ **of nature**) monstrosity, abnormally developed individual; very unusual or irregular thing or occurrence. 3. (slang) Narcotics user; fanatical devotee (of music, food, etc.). ~ *v.* (usu. ~ **out**) (slang) (Cause to) undergo narcotic etc. hallucinations or wild excitement, adopt unconventional life style. **freak′out** *n.* Such experience. **freak′ish, freak′y** *adjs.* **freak′ish·ly** *adv.* **freak′ish·ness** *n.*

freck·le (frĕk′*e*l) *n.* Spotted pigmentation of skin, produced esp. by ultraviolet light, and probably serving as a protection to the tissues; (pl.) number of such spots on various parts of the body, caused by exposure to sun. ~ *v.* (**-led, -ling**). Spot, be spotted, with freckles. **freck′ly** *adv.*

Fred·er·ick[1] (frĕd′rĭk, -*e*rĭk). (Ger. **Friedrich**) Name of 3 Holy Roman Emperors; **Frederick I** (1121?–90), "Barbarossa" (= "Redbeard"); emperor 1155–90; king of Germany 1152–90; king of Italy 1155–90; **Frederick II** (1194–1250), emperor 1220–50; **Frederick III** (1415–93), emperor 1440–1493.

Fred·er·ick[2] (frĕd′rĭk, -*e*rĭk). (Ger. **Friedrich**) Name of 3 kings of Prussia: **Frederick I** (1657–1713), reigned 1701–13; **Frederick II** (1712–86), "the Great"; engaged in wars against Austria and France and raised Prussia to the rank of a powerful state; **Frederick III** (1831–88), German emperor 1888.

Fred·er·icks·burg (frĕd′rĭksbẽrg). Industrial city in NE. Virginia on Rappahannock River, 41 mi. SW. of Alexandria, where Confederate army under Robert E.

The austerity of the rule imposed by ***St. Francis of Assisi*** *on himself and members of his order, the Franciscans, is symbolized in the devotional picture by Francisco de Zurbaran.*

As Caudillo of Spain, ***Generalissimo Franco*** *ruled his nation as a dictator. In 1937 Franco reduced his country's political parties to one, the Falangist party.*

Lee defeated Union forces led by Burnside (Dec. 11–15, 1862) during Civil War.

free (frē) *adj.* (**fre·er, fre·est**). 1. Not in bondage to another, having personal rights and social and political liberty; (of nation, its citizens, etc.) subject neither to foreign dominion nor to despotic government, having national and civil liberty. 2. At liberty, not in custody or confinement; without ties, obligations, or constraint upon one's action; released or exempt from work or duty; not constrained or timid; not fettered in judgment; (of literary composition etc.) not observing strict laws of form; (of translation) not adhering strictly to original. 3. Allowable or allowed (*to* do); unobstructed; clear *of, from*; not fixed or fastened; not in contact; (chem.) uncombined. 4. Spontaneous, gratuitous, willing; lavish, frank, unreserved; forward, familiar. 5. Released or exempt *from*; possessed of certain exclusive rights or privileges; not subject to tax, toll, duty, trade restrictions, fees, etc.; provided without payment. 6. ~**-and-easy**, unconstrained, unaffected, unconventional; ~ **association**, undirected mental activity like that of reverie or dreams; this as a method of psychoanalysis; **free'board**, part of ship's side between line of flotation and deck level; **free'-born**, born a free person (not a slave); born to the conditions and privileges of citizenship; **free city**, independent city-state under international protection; (hist.) medieval independent city-state in Germany and Italy; **free enterprise**, (system, doctrine, of) competitive private businesses operating for profit with a minimum of governmental interference; **free fall**, part of fall in parachute descent before parachute opens; fall of a body due entirely to the pull of gravity; **free flight**, flight of aircraft or rocket without power or control; **free-for-all**, fight in which all and sundry engage promiscuously; **free'hand**, (of drawing) done without guiding instruments, measures, or other artificial aid; **free-handed**, open-handed, generous; **free'hold**, (estate held by) tenure in fee simple or for term of life; held by freehold, **free'holder**, possessor of freehold estate; **free kick**, (soccer) kick allowed without interference, as penalty for infraction of rules by the other side; **free lance**, writer or artist who sells his or her work or services to a variety of employers or for short periods of time; person working for himself and not for an employer; **free-living**, given to self-indulgence; **free'load** (*v.*) (**-load·ed, -load·ing**), (slang) sponge; eat, drink, be

The development of parachute design has encouraged the daring practice of ***free fall*** *parachuting. Here a team of free fallers glide into position for a linked-hands formation high above Geneva.*

entertained, etc., at others' expense; **free'loader** (*n.*) person who habitually freeloads; **free love**, sexual relations irrespective of marriage; **free'man**, one who is not a slave or serf, or not subject to tyranny or usurped dominion; one who has full rights and privileges of citizenship; **free'mason**, member of secret international fraternity for mutual help and brotherly feeling, called **Free and Accepted Masons**, having elaborate ritual and system of secret signs (the original **freemasons** were probably skilled masons emancipated and moving from place to place for erection of important buildings in and after 14th c., the *accepted masons* being honorary members (orig. supposed to be eminent for architectural or antiquarian learning) who began to be admitted early in 17th c.); **free'-masonry**, system and institutions of Freemasons; secret or tacit brotherhood, instinctive sympathy; **free on board**, (abbrev. f.o.b.) (of goods) with all charges paid for delivery when put on board ship or other means of conveyance; **free port**, port open to all commercial vessels to load and unload in, (also) port, or zone within a port, where imports and exports are exempt from customs duty; **free school**, school charging no fees; (1960s) school organized as alternative to public and private schools, with unconventional teaching methods and curriculum; **free silver**, free coinage of silver usu. at fixed ratio with gold; political theory favoring this; **free'standing**, (of sculpture, column, etc.) not supported by structural framework; **Free State**, state prohibiting slavery before the

Civil War; **free'stone**, fine-grained sandstone or limestone that can easily be cut or sawn; kind of peach etc. in which when ripe the stone is loose; **free'thinker**, one who refuses to submit his reason to control of authority in matters of religious belief; rationalist, deist, etc.; so **free thought**; **free trade**, trade left to its natural course without customs duties to restrict imports or protect home industries; **free university**, (1960s) informal organization of college students offering unconventional courses and methods, analogous to free school; **free verse**, verse without metrical pattern or fixed or predictable rhythm; **free'way**, expressway; **free'wheeling**, (of) device that permits vehicle to coast with wheels disengaged from driving mechanism; (fig., colloq.) irresponsible, independent, heedless; **free will**, unconstrained choice; (belief in) power of directing one's own actions without constraint by necessity or fate; **free world**, non-communist countries' collective name for themselves. **free'ly** *adv.* **free** *adv.* Freely; without cost or payment. ~ *v.t.* (**freed, free·ing**). 1. Make free, set at liberty. 2. Relieve *from*, rid or ease *of*; clear, disengage, disentangle; **freed'man**, emancipated slave.

free·boot·er (frē'bo͞oter) *n.* (lit. and fig.) Pirate, piratical adventurer.

free·dom (frē'dom) *n.* 1. Personal liberty, exemption or release from slavery or imprisonment; civil liberty, independence; liberty of action; power of self-determination, independence of fate or necessity; **Four Freedoms**, those propounded by President F. D. Roosevelt in 1941 (freedom of speech and worship, freedom from want and fear). 2. Frankness, outspokenness; undue familiarity; facility, ease, in action; boldness of conception. 3. Exemption *from* defect, disadvantage, burden, etc.

free·si·a (frē'zhēa, -zēa, -zha) *n.* Iridaceous bulbous plant of genus *F*~, of S. Africa, allied to gladiolus and cultivated for its ornamental and perfumed flowers. [F. H. T. *Freese* (d. 1876), German physician]

freeze (frēz) *v.* (**froze, fro·zen, freez·ing**). 1. (impers.) To have the temperature such that water becomes ice. 2. Be converted into or covered with ice; become hard or rigid as result of cold; become fastened *to*, *together*, by freezing or action of frost; ~**on to**, (colloq.) take or keep tight hold of. 3. Be affected by, feel, extreme cold; die by frost; be devoid of heat; be chilled or immobilized by fear etc. 4. Cause to congeal, change (fluid) to solid by diminution of heat, cause ice to form on; congeal (the blood) as if by frost, with terror etc.; chill (feelings etc.), paralyze (powers etc.); stiffen, harden, injure, kill, etc., by chilling; preserve (meat etc.) by freezing; make (assets etc.) unrealizable, peg or stabilize (prices, wages, etc.); (fig.) become stuck or fixed (by heat, friction, etc.); ~**-dry** (*v.t.*) freeze material and dry it by evaporation of ice under high vacuum; **freezing point**, temperature at which water freezes, temperature at which given liquid freezes; **freeze out**, exclude from business, society, etc., by competition, boycotting, etc.; **freeze over**, cover or (esp. of pond, river, etc.) become covered with ice (colloq., **till hell freezes over** = forever). **freeze** *n.* State, coming, period, of frost; freezing of assets etc. **freez'er** *n.* Person or thing that freezes, esp. refrigerated room or compartment for keeping food frozen; deep-freeze.

freez·ing (frē'zĭng) *adj.* (esp.) Very cold; (of manner) chilling; distant. **freez'ing·ly** *adv.*

freight (frāt) *n.* Cargo transported by a vessel or vehicle, esp. by a commercial carrier; commercial transportation of goods; charge for this; load, burden, freight train; ~ **car**, railroad car for carrying freight, esp. a boxlike car for this; ~ **train**, railroad train made up of freight cars. **freight** *v.t.* Load with goods for transport; transport, convey commercial cargo.

freight·age (frā'tĭj) *n.* Commercial transportation of goods; the charge for this; cargo.

freight·er (frā'ter) *n.* Shipper

The purple of the ***freesia*** *illustrated here is only one of the wide variety of colors commonly found in this fragrant flower, which is a hybrid.*

The shipment of ***freight*** *overland and by sea is now frequently organized in a system using modular containers which are moved by purpose-built trucks, cranes and ships.*

*One of the key events of the **French Revolution** was the storming of the Tuileries Palace on 10 August 1792, here depicted dramatically by the painter Bertaux. For a time, the palace became a prison for Louis XVI.*

*The **French bean** grows well in soils of most kinds, provided they are not too heavy or too acid. The plant requires warm soil for germination.*

of cargo; cargo ship, freight-carrying aircraft.

French (frĕnch) *adj.* Of France or its people or language; ~ **and Indian War**, 1754–60, war in America in which French and their Indian allies opposed the English; ~ **bean**, (chiefly Brit.) kidney or haricot bean (*Phaseolus vulgaris*) used as culinary vegetable both in unripe sliced pods and in ripe seeds; ~ **bread**, bread of flour, water, and yeast baked in long crusty loaves; ~ **Community**, association formed in 1958 of France, her departments and territories overseas, and former French territories that chose to maintain association after achieving independence; ~ **cuff**, shirt cuff of double thickness and fastened with a cuff link; ~ **door**, door having glass panes from top to bottom, usu. hung in pairs; ~ **dressing**, salad dressing of vinegar and oil usu. seasoned; ~ **fries**, French-fried slices of potato; ~ **fry** (*v.*) (**fried, fry·ing**) fry in deep fat; ~ **Guiana**, French overseas department in NE. South Amer., bounded by Brazil on E. and S. and Surinam on W.; capital Cayenne; ~ **horn**: see HORN[1] def. 3; **take ~ leave**, depart, go away without notice; **French′man, French′woman**, French person; **French Polynesia**, French overseas territory in the S. Pacific Ocean, encompassing the Marquesa, Society, Gambier, Tuamotu, and other island groups; capital Papeete on Tahiti, Society Islands; **French Revolution**, revolution in which the French monarchy was overthrown and the First Republic established; the First Republic lasted from 1789–99, when Napoleon gained control; **French seam**, seam in which raw edges of cloth are enclosed; **French toast**, sliced bread dipped in egg-and-milk batter and lightly fried; **French window** = French door. **French** *n.* 1. (collect.) People of France. 2. Language of France, one of the descendants of Latin; **Old ~**, French from *c*9th to *c*13th (or sometimes 16th) century.

fre·net·ic (frenĕt′ĭk) *adj.* Frantic; frenzied. **fre·net′i·cal·ly** *adv.*

fren·zy (frĕn′zē) *n.* (pl. **-zies**). Delirious fury or agitation. **fren′zied** *adj.*

freq. *abbrev.* Frequent(ly).

*Italian artists of the Renaissance carried **fresco** painting to its highest stage of achievement. 'The Creation of Adam', a detail from Michelangelo's frescos in the Sistine chapel in the Vatican is considered a masterpiece.*

fre·quen·cy (frē′kwensē) *n.* (pl. **-cies**). 1. Frequent occurrence; being repeated at short intervals. 2. (physiol.) Number of pulsebeats per minute. 3. (phys., acoustics, etc.) Rate of recurrence of a repeated event, e.g., a vibration; (elect.) number of complete cycles per second of an alternating current or potential; such currents are classified as: **audio** ~ (AF) frequency within the audible range, 30 Hz–20 kHz; **high** ~, (HF) used of frequencies above the audible range, esp. those used for radio communication; **low** ~, (LF) used of audio frequencies as dist. from radio (and see below); **radio** ~, (RF) frequency suitable for radio transmission, above 10^4 Hz and below 3×10^{12} Hz approx., subdivided into **low** ~ (LF) 30–300 kHz, **medium** ~ (MF) 3×10^5–3×10^6 Hz, **very high** ~ (VHF) 30–300 MHz, **ultra-high** ~ **(UHF)** 3×10^8–3×10^9 Hz; ~ **modulation**: see MODULATE. 4. (statistics) Ratio of number of actual to number of possible occurrences of an event.

fre·quent (frē′kwent) *adj.* Often occurring or appearing; happening in close succession, constant. **fre′quent·ly** *adv.* **frequent** (frēkwĕnt′, frē′kwĕnt) *v.t.* Go often or habitually to. **fre·quent′er** *n.*

fres·co (frĕs′kō) *n.* (pl. **-coes, -cos**). Method of painting with powdered pigments by mixing them with water and applying them to wall or ceiling before plaster is dry; picture painted thus. ~ *v.t.* (**-coed, -co·ing**). Paint in fresco. [It., = "fresh"]

fresh (frĕsh) *adj.* 1. New, novel; not previously known, met with, used, etc.; different; recent, newly made or arrived; newly come or taken *from*; raw, inexperienced; **fresh′man**, high school, college, or university student in first year. 2. (of food) Not artificially preserved, not salted, pickled, smoked, etc., not frozen or canned; (of butter) not salted; (of water) not salt or bitter, fit for drinking; (of air etc.) pure, untainted, refreshing; **fresh·wat·er**, (*adj.*) of fresh water, not of the sea. 3. Not stale, musty, or vapid; not faded; unsullied, bright and pure in color; looking healthy or young. 4. Not weary, vigorous. 5. (slang, prob. infl. by Ger. *frech* impertinent) Presumptuous, forward. **fresh′ness** *n.* **fresh′en** *v.* **fresh** *adv.* Freshly, recently, newly. ~ *n.* 1. Fresh or early part of day etc. 2. Freshet. **fresh′ness** *n.*

fresh·et (frĕsh′ĭt) *n.* Rush of fresh water flowing into sea; overflow of river from heavy rain or melted snow.

fresh·ly (frĕsh′lē) *adv.* Recently; with unabated vigor; with fresh appearance, odor, etc.

Fres·nel (frenĕl′), **Augustin Jean** (1788–1827). French physicist; supported wave theory of light; initiated use of compound lenses in lighthouses.

fret[1] (frĕt) *n.* Ornamental pattern of continuous combinations of straight lines joined usu. at right angles; ~ **saw**, very thin saw stretched on frame for cutting thin wood in ornamental patterns; **fret′work**, (archit.) carved work in decorative patterns, esp. of intersecting lines; wood cut with fret saw into ornamental patterns. **fret** *v.t.* (**fret·ted, fret·ting**). Adorn with fretwork.

fret[2] (frĕt) *v.* (**fret·ted, fret·ting**). 1. Gnaw; wear away; eat *away*; form or make by wearing away. 2. Chafe, worry; distress oneself with regret or discontent. ~ *n.* Irritation, vexation, worry. **fret′ful** *adj.* **fret′ful·ly** *adv.* **fret′ful·ness** *n.*

fret[3] (frĕt) *n.* Bar or ridge on fingerboard of certain stringed instruments fixing positions of fingers to produce required notes.

Freud (froid), **Sigmund** (1856–1939). Austrian neurologist and founder of psychoanalysis; advocated free association of ideas as a method of treatment; stressed importance of dreams as manifestations of repressed, particularly sexual, desires. **Freud·i·an** (froi′dēan) *adj.* & *n.*

Fri. *abbrev.* Friday.

fri·a·ble (frī′abel) *adj.* Easily crumbled. **fri·a·bil·i·ty** (frīabĭl′ĭtē), **fri′a·ble·ness** *ns.*

fri·ar (frī′er) *n.* Brother or member of certain religious orders, esp. of the 4 mendicant orders, Franciscans (**Gray Friars**), Augustines (**Austin Friars**), Dominicans (**Black Friars**), and Carmelites (**White Friars**). **fri′ar·y** *n.* Monastery, fraternity, of friars.

fric·as·see (frĭkasē′, -zē′, frĭk′asē, -zē) *n.* Dish of meat, poultry, etc., cut up, braised lightly, then stewed, and served in sauce. ~ *v.t.* (**-seed, -see·ing**). Make fricassee of.

fric·a·tive (frĭk′atĭv) *adj.* & *n.* (phonet.) (Consonant) produced by friction of breath through narrow opening formed in the mouth with the tongue or lips, as *s*, *f*.

Frick (frĭk), **Henry Clay** (1849–1919). Amer. industrialist and philanthropist; instrumental in formation of U.S. Steel Corporation (1901).

fric·tion (frĭk′shon) *n.* Rubbing of one object or surface against another; (phys. etc.) resistance body meets with in moving over another; (fig.) clash of wills, temperaments, opinions, etc.; ~ **coupling**, device to transmit motion by frictional contact; ~ **tape**, strong cloth adhesive tape used esp. to insulate electrical conductors. **fric′tion·al** *adj.* **fric′tion·al·ly** *adv.*

Fri·day (frī′dē, -dā) *n.* Sixth day of the week; **Good** ~, Friday before Easter, observed by Christians in commemoration of the Crucifixion of Jesus; **man** ~, once Robinson Crusoe's devoted companion in Defoe's story, now male assistant with diverse duties (so **girl** ~). [= "day of (the goddess) Frig" (i.e. FRIGG), transl. of L. *dies Veneris* day of (the planet) Venus]

fried (frīd). Past t. and past part. of FRY[2].

friend (frĕnd) *n.* 1. Person one knows well, likes, and trusts; acquaintance or associate; stranger toward whom one wishes to express goodwill or kindly condescension. 2. Sympathizer, helper, patron; ~ **at court**, one who will use his or her influence in high places to help another. 3. One who is not an enemy, who is on same side. 4. **F**~, member of Society of Friends, Quaker; ordinary mode of address among Quakers; (**Society of**) **Friends**, the QUAKERS as a communion. **friend′less** *adj.*

friend·ly (frĕnd′lē) *adj.* Acting, disposed to act, as friend; characteristic of friends, expressing, showing, prompted by, kindness; opportune. **friend′li·ness** *n.*

friend·ship (frĕnd′shĭp) *n.* Being friends, relation between friends; friendly disposition felt or shown.

frieze[1] (frēz) *n.* Coarse woolen cloth with nap usu. on one side only.

frieze[2] (frēz) *n.* Member of entablature above architrave and below cornice; horizontal broad band of sculpture filling this; any horizontal band of painted or sculptured decoration etc. along the upper part of a wall. [Fr. *frise* f. L. *Phrygium* (*opus*) Phrygian (work)]

frig·ate (frĭg′ĭt) *n.* 1. Fast, medium-sized sailing warship of the 17th c.–19th c., usu. with raised quarterdeck and forecastle. 2. (U.S. Navy) Warship between a cruiser and destroyer in size and used mainly for escort duty. 3. ~ **bird**, large swift brown seabird (genus *Fregata*) of tropical regions, with habit of cruising near other species and snatching food from them; esp. **magnificent** ~ (*F. magnificens*) of the Forida Keys; also man-o'-war-bird.

Frig·ga (frĭg′a), **Frigg** (frĭg). (Scand. myth.) Wife of Odin and goddess of married love, the hearth, and heaven.

fright (frīt) *n.* Sudden fear, violent terror, alarm; grotesque person or thing. ~ *v.t.* (poet.) Frighten.

fright·en (frī′ten) *v.t.* Throw into a fright, terrify; drive (*away*, *out of*, *into*, etc.) by fright; **frightened at**, affected with fright of.

fright·ful (frīt′ful) *adj.* Dreadful, shocking, revolting; ugly, hideous; (slang) very great. **fright′ful·ly** *adv.* **fright′ful·ness** *n.*

frig·id (frĭj′ĭd) *adj.* 1. Intensely cold; **F**~ **Zone**, region lying within either polar circle. 2. Without ardor, apathetic; (of a woman) sexually unresponsive. 3. Formal, forced. **frig′id·ly** *adv.* **frig′id·ness, fri·gid·i·ty** (frĭjĭd′ĭtē) *ns.*

frill (frĭl) *n.* Ornamental edging of strip of material with one edge

*Left: The aggressive **frigate bird,** sometimes called the man o' war bird, forces other sea birds to disgorge their catches. Right: The bird's distinctive orange pouch turns bright red during courtship.*

gathered and the other left loose so as to give wavy or fluted appearance; natural fringe of feathers, hair etc., on bird, animal, or plant; unnecessary or superfluous ornament or convenience. ~ *v.* Furnish or decorate with frill; form frill. **frill'y** *adv.* (**frill·i·er, frill·i·est**).

fringe (frĭnj) *n.* Ornamental bordering of threads of silk, cotton, etc., either loose or formed into tassels, twists, etc.; anything resembling this, border, edging; margin, outer edge; ~ **area**, area where television reception is unsatisfactory because of distance from station, blockage, etc.; ~ **benefit**, benefit, in addition to salary, received by employee, as medical insurance, pension, etc. **fringe** *v.t.* (**fringed, fring·ing**). Adorn or encircle with fringe; serve as fringe to; **fringed gentian**: see GENTIAN.

frip·per·y (frĭp'erē) *n.* (pl. **-per·ies**). Pretentious finery, needless or tawdry adornment, esp. in dress; trifles.

frisk (frĭsk) *v.* 1. Move sportively; caper. 2. (slang) Search (person, clothing) for concealed weapon etc. ~ *n.* 1. Frolic, caper. 2. (slang) Act of frisking for weapons. **frisk'y** *adj.* (**frisk·i·er, frisk·i·est**). **frisk'i·ly** *adv.* **frisk'i·ness** *n.*

frit (frĭt) *n.* Calcined mixture of sand and fluxes prepared for melting to form glass; vitreous composition from which soft porcelain is made. ~ *v.t.* (**frit·ted, frit·ting**). Make into frit; partially fuse, calcine.

Fritch·ie (frĭch'ē), **Barbara.** Patriotic old woman who reportedly waved a Union flag from her window as Stonewall Jackson and Confederate troops marched through Frederick, Md.; subject of poem (1864) by John Greenleaf Whittier.

*Crown Imperial (left) is the popular name for the **fritillary** (Fritillaria imperialis). It is a plant that is popular in gardens for its color.*

frit·il·lar·y (frĭt'ilĕrē) *n.* (pl. **-lar·ies**). 1. Bulbous plant of the liliaceous genus *Fritillaria.* 2. Any of various butterflies of family Nymphalidae, esp. of genus *Speyeria* and *Boloria*, with spotted markings. [L. *fritillus* dicebox, with ref. to checked markings of corolla]

frit·ter[1] (frĭt'*er*) *n.* Portion of deep-fried batter, usu. containing pieces of corn, fruit, etc.

frit·ter[2] (frĭt'*er*) *v.t.* Throw *away* (time, money, energy, etc.) in trifling and wasteful way on various aims.

friv·ol (frĭv'*o*l) *v.i.* (**-oled, -ol·ing, -olled, -ol·ling**). Be a trifler, trifle.

friv·o·lous (frĭv'*o*l*u*s) *adj.* Paltry, trifling, futile; given to trifling, silly. **friv'o·lous·ly** *adv.* **friv'o·lous·ness, fri·vol·i·ty** (frĭvŏl'ĭtē) *ns.* (pl. **-ties**).

friz (frĭz) *v.* (**frizzed, friz·zing**). Curl, crisp, form into mass of small curls. ~ *n.* (pl. **friz·zes**). Frizzed state; frizzed hair, mass of curls. **friz'zy** *adj.* (**-zi·er, -zi·est**).

friz·zle (frĭz'*e*l) *v.* (**-zled, -zling**). 1. Curl (*up*) in small crisp curls. 2. Make sputtering noise in frying. **friz'zly** *adj.* (**-zli·er, -zli·est**).

fro (frō) *adv.* Away (only in **to and** ~: see TO *adv.*).

frock (frŏk) *n.* 1. Long habit with large open sleeves, the outer and characteristic dress of a monk; (fig.) priestly character. 2. Woman's or girl's dress. 3. Frock coat; man's double-breasted coat with long square tails or skirts not cut away in front.

*Apache Indians during the Crown Dance, Phoenix, Arizona. The **fringes** on the clothing are a part of their traditional garb. Many other races also make use of fringes on clothing.*

frog[1] (frŏg, frawg) *n.* Tailless chiefly aquatic amphibious animal of order Salientia, esp. the common frog (genus *Rana*) with smooth shiny skin and long powerful web-footed hind legs with which it swims and leaps; (**F** ~, contempt.) Frenchman (as eating frogs; also **frog-eater**); **frog′fish**, any of various fishes of the family Antennariidae, esp. the angler; **frog in one's throat**, hoarseness; **frog′-man**, underwater swimmer and demolition expert equipped with long rubber foot flippers like frog's hind feet.

frog[2] (frŏg, frawg) *n.* Elastic horny substance in middle of sole of horse's hoof.

frog[3] (frŏg, frawg) *n.* Attachment to or loop on belt to support or hold sword, bayonet, etc.; ornamental looped braid with a spindle-shaped knot or covered button for decoration or fastening front of garment.

frog[4] (frŏg, frawg) *n.* Grooved piece of steel on intersecting railroad tracks permitting train wheels to cross the junction.

frol·ic (frŏl′ĭk) *adj.* (archaic) Joyous, sportive. ~ *v.i.* (**-icked, -ick·ing**). Play pranks; gambol. ~ *n.* Outburst of gaiety; prank; merriment; party. **frol′ic·some** *adj.*

from (frŭm, frŏm; unstressed frəm) *prep.* Out of, indicating place etc. whence motion or action proceeds (*walked ~ the town; called ~ the window*), starting point (*~ the beginning*; *~ July*), first-named limit (*~ 10 to 20 men*), object etc. whereby distance or remoteness is reckoned (*10 miles ~ the station*; *am far ~ saying*), source (*water ~ the well*), giver, sender (*a present ~ Ann*), thing or person got rid of, avoided, etc. (*dissuade ~ folly*; *release ~ engagement*), state changed for another (*~ being*

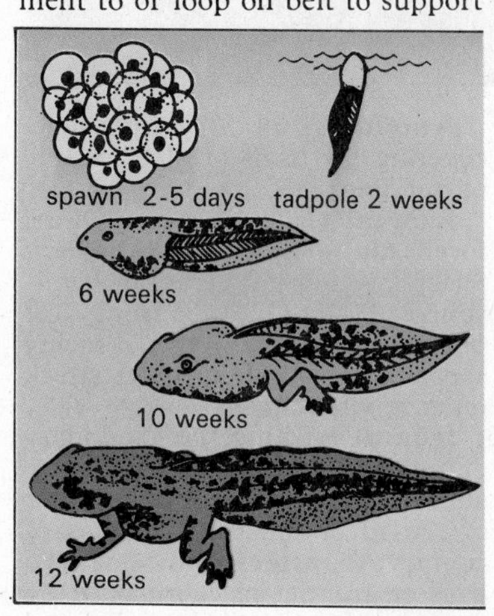

*Above: The **frog** lays its eggs as spawn in still water; here the spawn is of Rana dalmatina. Top left: The frog metamorphoses through a tadpole stage before adulthood. Below: Some of the species of frog adapted to various environments.*

*The American **Frontier** was slowly extended thanks to these hardy souls who pushed into largely virgin land, regardless of the many risks.*

attacked became the aggressor), thing distinguished (*know good* ~ *bad*), origin in place or time, with adverbs or adverbial phrases or prepositions (~ *long ago*; ~ *under the bed*).

frond (frŏnd) *n.* (bot.) Leaf of certain flowerless plants, esp. ferns; (zool.) leaflike expansion in certain seaweeds, lichens, etc.

front (frŭnt) *n.* 1. Forehead (poet.); face (archaic). 2. (mil.) Foremost line of military unit; line of battle; part of ground toward enemy; scene of actual fighting; direction toward which line faces when formed. 3. Organized body of (esp. leftist) political forces, as **popular** ~ etc. 4. (archit.) Any face of building, esp. that containing main entrance. 5. (meteor.) Forward edge of an advancing mass of warm air meeting cold, or vice versa. 6. Side or part normally nearer or toward spectator or direction of motion; part of theater where audience sits (i.e. in front of the curtain); of land area, property, town, etc. fronting ocean, lake, or river (**ocean ~, water ~, river ~, lake ~**); organization etc. serving as cover for criminal activities; breast of man's shirt. 7. (with prep.) Forward position or situation; **in ~ of**, before, in advance of; confronting. **front** *adj.* Of the front; situated in front; (phonet., of sound) in which forepart of tongue touches or is raised toward front of hard palate; **(on the) ~ burner**, (colloq.) deemed as most important, for immediate attention; **~ door**, principal entrance door of house; ~ **office**, main office, executive officers, policy makers, of an organization; ~ **page**, first page of a newspaper, esp. as containing important or remarkable news; hence **front'-page** (*adj.*), sensational; **front runner**, competitor in the lead. **front** *v.* 1. Face, look out upon; stand opposite to, confront; have front on side of (street etc.). 2. Furnish with front.

front·age (frŭn'tĭj) *n.* 1. Land abutting on street or water; land between front of building and street; extent of front; front of building. 2. Fronting in certain direction; exposure, outlook.

*While **frost** will kill the young buds and shoots of many plants, the young birch tree will survive the heavy frost that coats its branches if the buds have not yet opened.*

fron·tal[1] (frŭn'tal) *n.* Movable covering for front of altar; facade of building.

fron·tal[2] (frŭn'tal) *adj.* 1. Of the forehead; ~ **bone**; ~ **lobe**, anterior portion of cerebral hemisphere. 2. Of the front; (of portrait, painted figure, etc.) facing spectator; ~ **attack**, direct attack on enemy's front.

fron·tier (frŭntēr') *n.* Boundary of a country where its territory abuts on that of another; border of settled or inhabited regions of country; **frontiers'man**, one who lives on frontier of country, or on extreme edge of settled or inhabited districts. **frontier** *adj.* Of, on, the frontier.

fron·tis·piece (frŭn'tĭspēs, frŏn'-) *n.* 1. (archit.) Principal face of building; decorated entrance; pediment over door etc. 2. Illustration facing title page of book or one of its divisions.

front·let (frŭnt'lĭt) *n.* Band worn on forehead; phylactery; animal's forehead; cloth hanging over upper part of altar frontal.

fron·ton (frŏn'tŏn, frŏntŏn'): see JAI ALAI.

frost (frawst, frŏst) *n.* 1. Freezing temperature of atmosphere when it is below freezing point of water; frozen dew or vapor; **frost'-bite**, inflamed or gangrenous state of skin and adjacent parts produced by exposure to severe cold; **frost'-bitten**, affected with this. **frost** *v.t.* 1. Kill, injure (plants etc.), with frost. 2. Cover (as) with frost; cover (cake) with icing, ice. 3. Give roughened or finely granulated surface to (glass, metal). 4. Turn, tint strands of (hair) white or light blond. **frost'ing** *n.* (esp.) Icing for cakes.

Frost (frawst, frŏst), **Robert (Lee)** (1875–1963). American poet and winner of Pulitzer Prize (1923, 1930, 1936, 1942); author of "A

2

4

6

The edible parts of a **fruit** *may be its seed, juicy envelope or skin, or all of these. 1. The banana is eaten either unripe and green or ripe and yellow. 2. Oranges and blossom on the same tree in Florida. 3. Italians of the Chianti district grow purple grapes for making red wine. 4. Peaches require a warm, temperate climate to ripen. 5. The pineapple is low growing. 6. A pomegranate.*

Boy's Will," "North of Boston," "A Further Range," etc.

frost·y (fraws′tē, frŏs′-) *adj.* (**frost·i·er, frost·i·est**). Affected with frost, ice-cold; chilling, frigid, lacking in warmth of feeling; covered, looking as if covered, with frost.

froth (frawth, frŏth) *n.* Aggregation of small bubbles in liquid, caused by agitation, fermentation, effervescence, etc.; insubstantial or worthless thing, triviality. ~ *v.* Emit, cover with, froth; ~ **at the mouth**, emit foam of saliva, as in convulsive seizures etc.; (fig.) be enraged. **froth′y** *adj.* (**froth·i·er, froth·i·est**). **froth′i·ly** *adv.* **froth′i·ness** *n.*

frown (frown) *n.* Vertically furrowed state of brow; look expressing severity, disapproval, or deep thought. ~ *v.* Knit brows, esp. to express displeasure or concentrate attention; (of future, fate, etc.) present gloomy aspect; express disapprobation (*at, on*); express (defiance etc.) with frown.

frow·zy (frow′zē) *adj.* (**-zi·er, -zi·est**). Ill-smelling, musty; unkempt, slovenly, shabby. **frow′zi·ly** *adv.* **frow′zi·ness** *n.*

fro·zen (frō′zen) *adj.*: see FREEZE; (esp., of food) preserved by freezing; (of assets etc.) not realizable.

FRS *abbrev.* Federal Reserve System.

fruc·ti·fi·ca·tion (frŭk*tif*ikā′shon, frŏŏk-) *n.* 1. Production of fruit. 2. (bot.) Reproductive parts of plant, esp. of ferns and mosses.

fruc·ti·fy (frŭk′*ti*fī, frŏŏk′-) *v.* (**-fied, -fy·ing**). Bear fruit; make fruitful or productive.

fruc·tose (frŭk′tōs, frŏŏk′-) *n.* (chem.) Fruit sugar, levulose, occurring in sweet fruits and honey.

fru·gal (frōō′g*a*l) *adj.* Careful, sparing (*of*); economical, thrifty; sparingly used or supplied; costing little. **fru·gal·i·ty** (frōōg*a*l′ĭtē) *n.* (pl. **-ties**). **fru′gal·ly** *adv.*

fruit (frōōt) *n.* (pl. **fruits**, collect. **fruit**). 1. (now usu. pl.) Vegetable products fit for food. 2. Edible product of plant or tree, consisting of seed and its envelope, esp. when this is juicy or pulpy; (bot.) ripe seeds and structure surrounding them. 3. (chiefly bibl.) Offspring. 4. What results from action, effort, cause, etc.; issue, consequence; advantage, profit; (pl.) products, revenues. 5. ~ **bat**, tropical fruit-eating bat of suborder Megachiroptera, esp. flying fox; **fruitcake**, cake containing raisins, nuts, preserved fruits, etc.; **fruit fly**, any of numerous small flies of the family Drosophilidae whose larvae feed on fruit; **fruit salad**, mixture of various sliced or diced fruits served in their juices, syrup, etc.; **fruit tree**, tree cultivated for its fruit. **fruit** *v.* Bear, make bear, fruit.

fruit·ar·i·an (frōōtār'ēan) *n.* & *adj.* (Of) one who lives on fruit.

fruit·er (frōō'ter) *n.* 1. Tree producing fruit. 2. Ship carrying fruit.

fruit·ful (frōōt'ful) *adj.* Productive, fertile, causing fertility; productive of offspring, prolific; beneficial, remunerative. **fruit'ful·ly** *adv.* **fruit'ful·ness** *n.*

fru·i·tion (frōōĭsh'on) *n.* Enjoyment, attainment of thing desired, realization of hopes, etc.

fruit·less (frōōt'lĭs) *adj.* Not bearing fruit; yielding no profit; useless, vain. **fruit'less·ly** *adv.* **fruit'less·ness** *n.*

fruit·y (frōō'tē) *adj.* (**fruit·i·er, fruit·i·est**). Of or like fruit; (of wine) tasting of the grape.

frump (frŭmp) *n.* Plain, dull, dowdy woman. **frump'ish** *adj.* **frump'y** *adj.* (**frump·i·er, frump·i·est**).

frus·trate (frŭs'trāt; *Brit.* frŭstrāt') *v.t.* (**-trat·ed, -trat·ing**). Balk, baffle; counteract; defeat, foil. **frus·tra·tion** (frŭstrā'shon) *n.* **frus'trat·ed** *adj.*

frus·tum (frŭs'tum) *n.* (pl. **-tums, -ta** pr. -ta). Portion of regular solid left after cutting off upper part by plane parallel to base; portion between two planes either parallel or inclined to each other.

fru·ti·cose (frōō'tĭkōs) *adj.* Shrublike.

fry[1] (frī) *n.* (pl. **fry**). Young fishes, esp. just produced from spawn; young of other creatures produced in large numbers; **small ~**, young or insignificant beings, children, etc.

fry[2] (frī) *v.* (**fried, fry·ing**). Cook in hot fat or oil in frying pan; **deep-~**, cook by completely immersing in hot fat or oil in deep pan; **frying pan, fry pan**, skillet, shallow pan with long handle for frying. **fry** *n.* (pl. **fries**). Dish of fried food; social gathering at which fried food is served, as a **fish-~.**

FSLIC *abbrev.* Federal Savings and Loan Insurance Corporation.

f-stop (ĕf'stŏp) *n.* Camera lens aperture setting indicated by an f-number.

ft *abbrev.* Foot, feet.

ft. *abbrev.* Fort, fortification; foot, feet.

FTC *abbrev.* Federal Trade Commission.

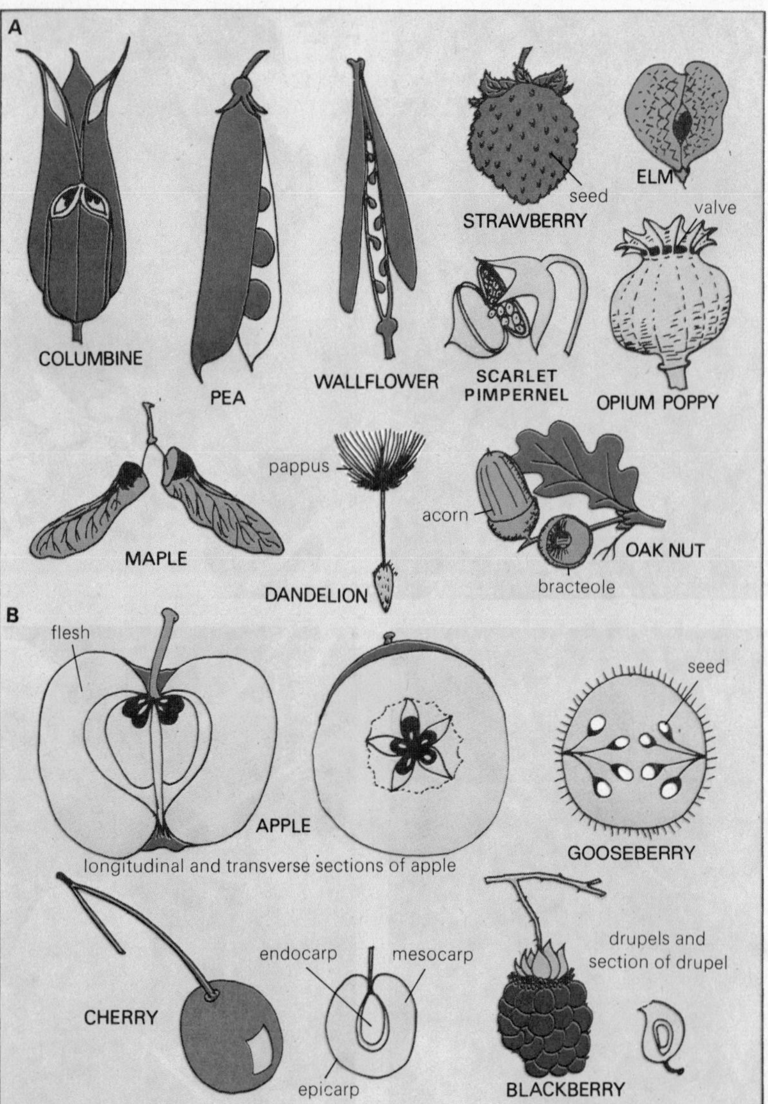

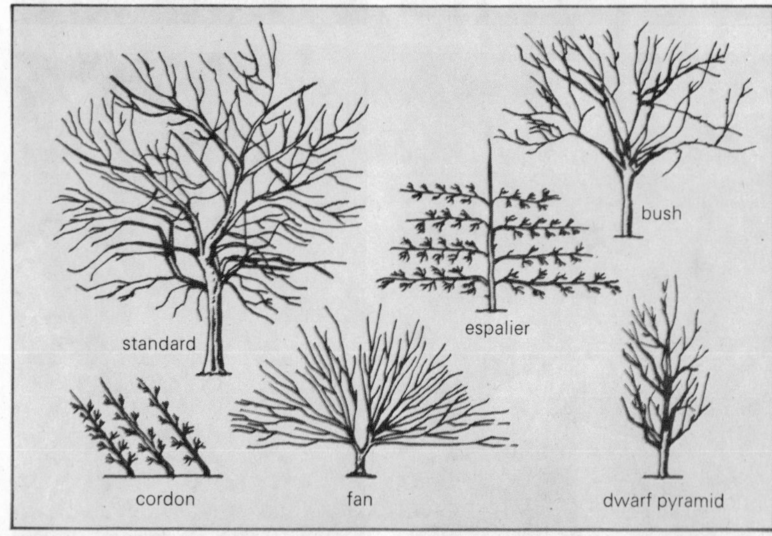

*Top: The base of a blossom develops into a **fruit** that will be of either a dry (A) or succulent (B) type. For distributing their seeds, fruits have a variety of mechanisms, those of the dry fruits being perhaps more varied. Bottom: Trees are cultivated in shapes that are convenient to the grower and that take best advantage of the tree's characteristics and of its position in the garden or orchard in relation to the sun and wind.*

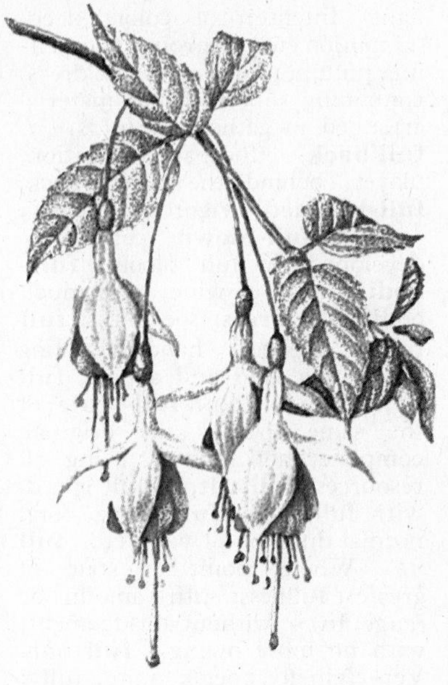

*Above: Most **fuchsias** seen in gardens are hybrids. Native to S. America, their pendulous crimson and purple flowers have made them popular ornamentals. Left: Native fuchsia of Australia.*

ft-lb *abbrev.* Foot-pound(s).

fuch·sia (fū´sh*a*) *n.* Ornamental shrub of genus *F*~ with drooping, usu. red, flowers; color of vivid purplish red. [L. *Fuchs*, 16th-c. German botanist]

fuck (fŭk) *v.* (vulg.) 1. Copulate (with). 2. Used in exclamations etc. **fuck´ing** *adj.* & *adv.* (vulg.) Used abusively or as intensive. **fuck** *n.* (vulg.) Act of copulation.

fu·cus (fū´k*u*s) *n.* (pl. **-ci** pr. -sī, **-cus·es**). Brown seaweed of genus *F*~ with flat leathery fronds.

fud·dle (fŭd´*e*l) *v.* (**-dled, -dling**). Intoxicate; stupefy, confuse. ~ *n.* Fuddled state.

fud·dy-dud·dy (fŭd´ē dŭd´ē) *n.* (pl. **-dud·dies**) & *adj.* Excessively old-fashioned or fussy (person).

fudge (fŭj) *int.* Nonsense! ~ *n.* 1. Nonsense. 2. Soft, rich candy, made by boiling together sugar, butter, milk, chocolate, and flavoring. ~ *v.* (**fudged, fudg·ing**). 1. Make up, in a makeshift or dishonest way, fake, falsify. 2. Avoid facing reality (of a situation).

fueh·rer (fūr´*er*; *Ger.* für´*er*): = FÜHRER.

fu·el (fū´*e*l, fūl) *n.* Material for fires, combustible matter; material used as source of nuclear energy; (fig.) something that feeds passion, excitement, etc; ~ **cell**, primary cell producing electricity direct from chemical reaction; ~ **injection**, direct introduction of fuel under pressure into combustion unit of internal combustion engine; ~ **oil**, heavy petroleum oil having a flash point higher than that of kerosene, used esp. in furnaces, diesels, etc; ~ **pellet**, segmented form of uranium used to create and maintain fission in nuclear power plant. **fuel** *v.* (**-eled, -el·ing, -elled, -el·ling**). Provide (ship etc.) with fuel; (of ship etc.) take in fuel; **fueling station**, port where this is done.

fu·ga·cious (fūgā´sh*u*s) *adj.* Fleeting, evanescent. **fu·gac·i·ty** (fūgăs´ĭtē) *n.* (pl. **-ties**).

fu·gi·tive (fū´jĭtĭv) *adj.* 1. Fleeing; that has taken flight (from duty, an enemy, master, etc.). 2. Fleeting, transient; (of literature) of passing interest, ephemeral, as ~ **verse**. ~ *n.* One who flees (*from*).

fugue (fūg) *n.* 1. (mus.) Polyphonic composition in which a short melodic theme is introduced by one of the parts and successively taken up by others, thereafter forming the main material of the texture. 2. (psychol.) Loss of awareness of one's identity, often coupled with disappearance from one's usual environment, and amnesia of all actions during the period.

füh·rer (fūr´*er*; *Ger.* für´*er*) *n.* 1. Leader, esp. one with the powers of a tyrant. 2. **der F**~, title assumed by Adolf HITLER as head of the German Reich. [Ger., = "leader"]

Fu·ji (fōō´jē). [also known as **Fu·ji·ya·ma** (fōōjēyah´m*a*)] Extinct volcano and Japan's highest mountain peak (12,388 ft., 3,776 m) in S. central Honshu Island, 70 mi. (113 km) WSW. of Tokyo; considered sacred by Buddhists.

Fu·jian (fōō´jahn´) = FUKIEN.

Fu·kien (fōō´kyĕn´). Maritime province of SE. China; capital Foochow.

-ful *suffix.* Forming adjectives with sense full of (*beautiful*), suggesting (*masterful, direful*), or accustomed to (*forgetful*); forming nouns with sense amount needed to fill (*spoonful, handful*).

ful·crum (fōōl´kr*u*m, fŭl´-) *n.* (pl. **-crums, -cra** pr. -kr*a*). 1. (mech.) Point against which lever is placed to get purchase or on which it turns or is supported. 2. Any means of exerting influence. [L. = "post of couch"]

ful·fill, ful·fil (fōōlfĭl´) *vbs.t.* (**-filled, -fill·ing**). Bring to consummation, carry out (prophecy, promise), satisfy (desire, prayer); perform, execute (command, law); answer (purpose), comply with (conditions); bring to an end, complete (period, work). **ful·fill´ment** *n.*

ful·gent (fŭl´j*e*nt) *adj.* Shining, brilliant.

full[1] (fōōl) *adj.* 1. Containing all it will hold, having no space empty, replete; containing abundance *of*, charged, crowded; abounding (in); replete with food. 2. ~ **of**, engrossed with, absorbed in. 3. Copious, satisfying. 4. Complete; answering in every respect to a name or description; reaching the specified or usual limit; (of moon) having disk completely illuminated; (of face etc.) entirely visible to spectator; ~ **brother, sister**, one born of same father and mother. 5. (of light) Intense; (of color) deep; (of motion etc.) vigorous. 6. Swelling, plump, protuberant; (of dress) containing superfluity of material arranged in gathers or folds. 7. **full'back**, (football) position, player, behind the quarterback; **full-blooded**, vigorous, hearty, sensual; **full-blown**, completely developed, in full bloom; **full-bodied**, esp. of wine, with much body; **full dress**: see DRESS; **full house**, (poker) hand containing three of a kind and a pair; **full nelson**: see NELSON; **full-scale**, of the same size as the original, complete; not limited, using all resources; **full tilt**, at full speed, with full force; **full time**, total normal duration of work etc. **full** *n.* Whole; point or state of greatest fullness; entire amount or range; **in ~**, without abridgement; with no more owing. **full** *adv.* Very (chiefly poet.); quite, fully; exactly; more than sufficiently; **full-fledged**, having fully developed adult plumage; (fig.) mature, having full status or position; **~-grown**, having reached maturity. **full'ness, ful'ness** *ns.*

full[2] (fo͞ol) *v.t.* Tread or beat (cloth) to cleanse and thicken it; cleanse and thicken (cloth etc.).

full·er (fo͞ol'*er*) *n.* One who fulls cloth; **~'s earth**, absorbent clay containing hydrated silica and alumina, used in fulling cloth and purifying oils and fats.

full·y (fo͞ol'ē) *adv.* Completely, without deficiency.

ful·mar (fo͞ol'm*er*) *n.* Arctic sea bird (*Fulmarus glacialis*) about size of gull, noted for its easy gliding flight by sea cliffs.

ful·mi·nant (fŭl'm*i*nant) *adj.* Fulminating; (path., of diseases or pain) developing suddenly and intensely.

ful·mi·nate (fŭl'm*i*nāt) *v.* (**-nat·ed, -nat·ing**). 1. Flash like lightning; explode, detonate. 2. Thunder forth, utter or publish (censure); issue (usu. official) censures *against*. **ful·mi·na·tion** (fŭlm*i*nā'sh*o*n) *n.* **ful·mi·na·to·ry** (fŭl'm*i*natōrē, -tōrē) *adj.* **fulminate** *n.* (also **~ of mercury**) Very sensitive explosive, Hg(ONC)$_2$, used in detonators.

ful·ness = FULLness.

ful·some (fo͞ol's*o*m) *adj.* (of flattery, servility, etc.) Cloying, excessive, disgusting by excess. **ful'some·ly** *adv.* **ful'some·ness** *n.*

Ful·ton (fo͞ol't*o*n), **Robert** (1765–1815). Amer. engineer; invented first financially profitable U.S. steamboat (1807).

fu·ma·role (fū'm*a*rōl) *n.* Hole in earth's crust near a volcano, through which gases and vapor issue.

fum·ble (fŭm'b*e*l) *v* (**-bled, -bling**). 1. Use the hands awkwardly, grope about; handle or deal with awkwardly or nervously. 2. (sports) Fail to catch or field (ball) clearly. **~** *n.* Bungling attempt. **fum'bler** *n.*

fume (fūm) *n.* (esp. pl.) Odorous smoke, vapor, or exhalation; fit of anger. **~** *v.* (**fumed, fum·ing**). 1. Treat with, emit, fumes. 2. Be pettish; chafe, fret. **fum'y** *adj.* (**fum·i·er, fum·i·est**).

fu·mi·gate (fū'm*i*gāt) *v.t.* (**-gat·ed, -gat·ing**). Apply fumes to, esp. to exterminate insects, vermin, etc.; disinfect or purify with fumes. **fu·mi·ga·tion** (fūm*i*gā'sh*o*n), **fu'mi·ga·tor** *ns.*

fun (fŭn) *n.* Sport, amusement; jocularity, drollery; **make ~ of, poke ~ at**, ridicule.

func·tion (fŭngk'sh*o*n) *n.* 1. Activity proper to person or institution; mode of action by which thing fulfills its purpose. 2. Social meeting of formal or important kind. 3. (math.) Variable quantity regarded in relation to other(s) in terms of which it may be expressed or on whose value its own depends. 4. **~ word**, (gram. jargon) word expressing chiefly grammatical relation, as preposition, conjunction,

The gliding flight of the ***fulmar*** *characterizes it as one of the 35 species of the shearwater family. Above: Fulmarus glacialis of the Arctic with its newly hatched chick was photographed in the Farne Islands.*

auxiliary verb, etc. **function** *v.i.* Fulfill a function, operate, act.

func·tion·al (fŭngk'sh*o*nal) *adj.* 1. Of a function or functions. 2. (physiol.) Of, affecting, only the functions of an organ etc., not structural or organic (esp. of diseases). 3. (math.) Of a function. 4. (of building etc.) Shaped, constructed, with regard only to its function, not to traditional or other theories of design. **func'tion·al·ism** *n.* **func'tion·al·ist** *adj.* & *n.* **func'tion·al·ly** *adv.*

func·tion·ar·y (fŭngk'sh*o*nĕrē) *n.* (pl. **-ar·ies**). One with certain functions or duties to perform, official.

fund (fŭnd) *n.* Permanent stock of something ready to be drawn upon; sum of money, esp. one set apart for a purpose; (pl.) financial resources; **mutual ~**: see MUTUAL. **fund** *v.t.* Convert (debt) into more or less permanent debt at fixed interest; furnish a fund for, pay for.

fun·da·ment (fŭn'd*a*ment) *n.* Buttocks; anus.

fun·da·men·tal (fŭnd*a*mĕn't*a*l) *adj.* 1. Of the groundwork, going to the root of the matter, serving as base or foundation; essential, primary, original; from which others are derived. 2. (mus., of a note) That is the lowest note of a chord in its original form; (of a chord) with the root as the lowest note; (of a tone) that is produced by the vibration of the whole of a sonorous body (as dist. from *harmonics*). **fun·da·men'tal, fun·da·men·tal·i·ty** (fŭndaměntăl'ĭtē) *ns.* (pl. **-ties**). Principle, rule, article, serving as groundwork of system (often pl.). **fun·da·men'tal·ly** *adv.*

fun·da·men·tal·ism (fŭndaměn'talĭzem) *n.* Strict adherence to traditional orthodox (Protestant) tenets (e.g. the literal infallibility of Scripture), held to be fundamental to Christianity; adherence to traditional beliefs of any kind. **fun·da·men'tal·ist** *adj.* & *n.*

Fun·dy (fŭn'dē), **Bay of.** Atlantic Ocean inlet approx. 100 mi. (161 km) long, in SE. Canada between New Brunswick and Nova Scotia, noted for treacherous currents and high tides (reaching up to 70 ft. (22 m) at head of bay).

fu·ner·al (fū'neral) *adj.* Of, used, carried, etc., at burial or cremation of the dead; ~ **pyre**, pile of wood etc. on which corpse is burned. **funeral** *n.* Burial of the dead with its ceremonies etc; funeral procession; funeral service; ~ **director**, person who is in charge of funeral service or funeral home; undertaker; ~ **home**, establishment where bodies are prepared for burial or cremation and funerals are conducted.

fu·ner·ar·y (fū'nerĕrē) *adj.* Of funeral or burial.

fu·ne·re·al (fūnēr'ēal) *adj.* Appropriate to funeral, gloomy, dark, mournful. **fu·ne're·al·ly** *adv.*

fun·gi·cide (fŭn'jĭsīd) *n.* Fungus-destroying substance. **fun·gi·ci·dal** (fŭnjĭsī'dal) *adj.*

fun·goid (fŭng'goid) *adj.* Funguslike.

fun·gous (fŭng'gus) *adj.* Of, caused by, fungi; having nature of a fungus.

fun·gus (fŭng'gus) *n.* (pl. **fun·gi** pr. fŭn'jī, -jē, **fun·gus·es**). Mushroom, toadstool, or one of the allied plants, including the various molds; (bot.) cryptogamous plant without chlorophyll deriving its substance from organic matter. **fun·gal** (fŭng'gal) *adj.*

fu·nic·u·lar (fūnĭk'yuler) *adj.* Of a rope or its tension; depending on or worked by a rope or cable; ~ *n.* cable railroad in which ascending and descending cars are counterbalanced.

funk (fŭngk) *n.* (colloq.) Fear, panic; dejection; coward; **blue** ~, terror. **funk** *v.* Flinch, shrink, show cowardice, fight shy of, (try to) evade; be afraid of.

fun·ky (fŭng'kē) *adj.* (**-ki·er, -ki·est**). (slang) 1. (jazz) Uncomplicated, pulsating, based on blues. 2. Strong smelling. 3. Fashionably unconventional, offbeat.

fun·nel (fŭn'el) *n.* 1. Narrowing tube, cone-shaped vessel with tube at apex, for conducting liquid, powder, etc., into small opening. Ventilating etc. shaft; smokestack of locomotive, ship, etc.

fun·ny (fŭn'ē) *adj.* (**-ni·er, -ni·est**). Causing laughter or amusement, affording fun, comical; queer, perplexing; ~ **bone**, part of elbow over which ulnar nerve passes (from peculiar sensation experienced when it is struck); ~ **farm**, (slang) mental hospital; ~ **money**, counterfeit money; money from concealed or dishonest sources. **fun'ni·ly** *adv.* **fun'ni·ness** *n.*

fur (fēr) *n.* 1. Coat of certain animals (as ermine, beaver, fox,

*Capable of reproducing asexually, **fungus** is generally parasitic and has neither roots nor flowers. Fungi are useful in the preparation of enzymes, alcohol, antibiotics, and vitamins, and are vital to the renewal of soil by assisting in the decomposition of humus. Below left: Hypholoma fasciculare. Below: Dictyophol. sp. Bottom: Amanita muscaria.*

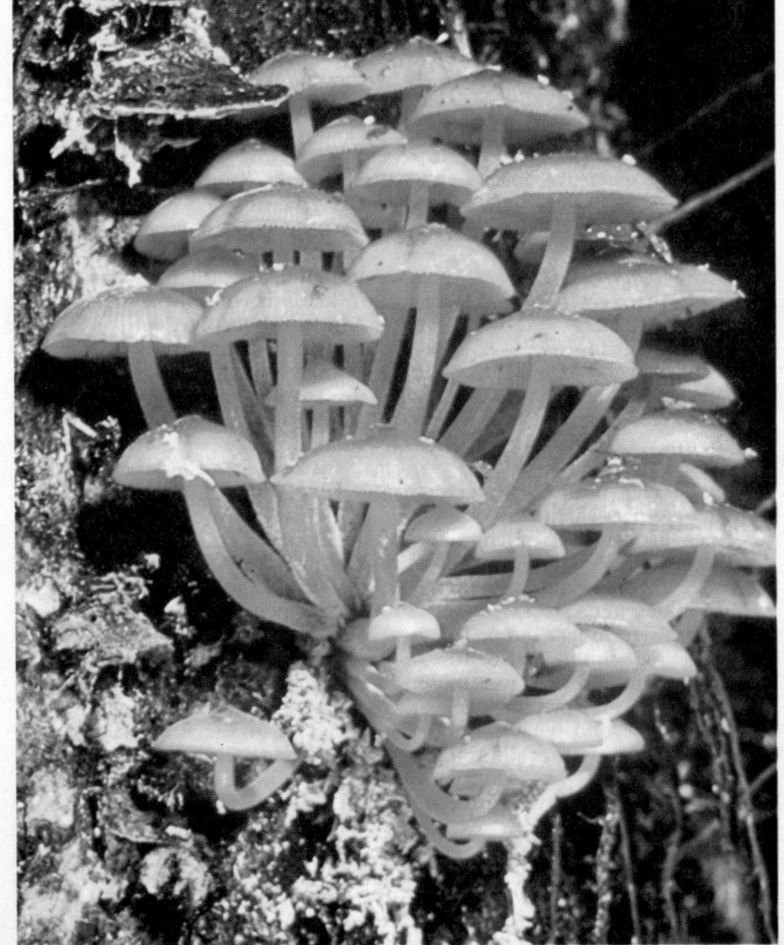

etc.); dressed coat of such animals or imitation of this, used for garments, trimming, lining, etc.; a coat, stole, etc., of this; (usu. pl.) garment(s) of or trimmed with fur. 2. Short fine soft hair of certain animals as distinct from the longer and coarser hair; (pl.) skins of such animals with the fur. **fur·ry** (fēr´ē, fŭr´ē) *adj.* (**-ri·er, -ri·est**). **fur** *v.* (**furred, fur·ring**). 1. Trim, line, cover, with fur. 2. (carpentry) Line, level (floor timbers, rafters, etc.), with FURRING.

fur. *abbrev.* Furlong.

fur·be·low (fēr´belō) *n.* Gathered strip, as a ruffle or flounce, or other trimming, esp. on 17th–18th c. dress; showy ornament. ~ *v.t.* Adorn with furbelows.

fur·bish (fēr´bĭsh) *v.t.* Polish, burnish; give new look to, renovate, revive.

fur·cate (fēr´kāt, -kĭt) *adj.* Forked, branched. ~ (fēr´kāt) *v.i.* (**-cat·ed, -cat·ing**). Branch, divide.

fu·ri·ous (fūr´ēus) *adj.* Full of fury, raging, frantic, violent; **fast and** ~, very fast, uproarious(ly), in great numbers, with rapid repetition. **fu'ri·ous·ly** *adv.*

furl (fērl) *v.* Roll up and tie (sail, flag, etc.) on yard, boom, or pole; roll or gather up, close, fold up; become furled; roll away like clouds.

fur·long (fēr´lawng, -lŏng) *n.* Measure of length, ⅛ mile or 220 yards. [OE. *furlang*, f. *furh* furrow and *lang* long]

fur·lough (fēr´lō) *n.* Leave of absence, esp. one longer than a weekend to member of armed forces; leave. ~ *v.t.* Grant furlough to.

fur·nace (fēr´nĭs) *n.* Apparatus containing chamber for combustibles in which minerals, metals, etc., may be subjected to continuous action of intense heat; device with combustion chamber for furnishing heat to a building, etc.; (fig.) hot place.

Fur·neaux (fēr´nō) **Islands.** Group of islands in Bass Strait off coast of NE. Tasmania, Australia, encompassing 900 sq. mi. (2,331 sq. kl); Flinders Island and Cape Barren Island are the largest.

fur·nish (fēr´nĭsh) *v.t.* Provide *with*; fit (house, room) with all necessary appliances, esp. movable furniture; provide, afford, yield; **fur'nishing**, (*n.*, esp. pl.) articles of furniture or other things required to furnish a house etc.

fur·ni·ture (fēr´nĭcher) *n.* Movable articles (as tables, chairs) for use or ornament in house or room; necessary equipment, as for a ship, factory, etc.

fu·ror (fūr´ōr) *n.* 1. Outburst of enthusiasm. 2. Uproar.

*When a crucible of molten metal leaves a **furnace** it has slag on its surface. The slag can be skimmed off and used elsewhere in cement-making.*

fur·ri·er (fēr´ēer, fŭr´-) *n.* Dealer in, dresser of, furs.

fur·ring (fēr´ĭng, fŭr´-) *n.* Fixing strips of wood or metal to floor timbers, rafters, etc. to form a level surface or space above which a new surface may be applied; strips of wood used for this.

fur·row (fēr´ō, fŭr´ō) *n.* Narrow trench made in earth with plow; rut, track, groove, long indentation; deep wrinkle. ~ *v.t.* Plow; make furrows, grooves, etc., in; mark with wrinkles.

fur·ther (fēr´dher) *adv.* To a greater extent, more (also **fur'thermore**); in addition; to a more advanced point in time; farther. ~ *adj.* Going beyond what exists or has been dealt with, additional; more distant. ~ *v.t.* Help on, promote, favor. **fur'ther·ance** *n.* **fur'ther·most** *adj.*

fur·thest (fēr´dhest) *adj.* & *adv.* Most distant in time or degree; farthest.

fur·tive (fēr´tĭv) *adj.* Stealthy, sly; taken secretly. **fur'tive·ly** *adv.* **fur'tive·ness** *n.*

fu·ry (fūr´ē) *n.* (pl. **-ries**). 1. Fierce passion, wild anger; fierce impetuosity or violence. 2. **F**~, (Gk. myth.) one of the snake-haired goddesses (esp. Alecto, Megaera, Tisiphone) sent from Tartarus to avenge wrong and punish crime; (fig.) avenging or tormenting spirit. 3. Virago, angry or malignant woman.

furze (fērz) *n.* Gorse.

fuse[1] (fūz) *v.* (**fused, fus·ing**). Melt with intense heat; blend, amalgamate, into whole (as) by melting. ~ *n.* Strip or wire of easily fused metal in electric circuit which melts and so interrupts the circuit if current increases beyond a certain limit. **fu'si·ble** *adj.* **fu·si·bil·i·ty** (fūzibĭl´ĭtē) *n.*

fuse[2], **fuze** (fūz) *ns.* (usu. *fuse*) Tube, casing, cord, etc., filled or saturated with combustible matter for igniting blasting charge, bomb, etc.; (usu. *fuze*) component screwed into shell, mine, etc., designed to detonate explosive charge either after an interval (**time** ~) or on impact, or when subjected to magnetic, vibratory, or other stimulation. **fuse** *v.t.* (**fused, fus·ing**). Fit fuse to.

fu·see (fūzē′) *n.* 1. Conical pulley or wheel, esp. wheel in watch or clock on which chain is wound and which equalizes power of mainspring. 2. Large-headed match for use in wind; railroad warning flare.

fu·se·lage (fū′selĭj, -ze-, -lahzh) *n.* Body or framework of airplane.

fu·sel (fū′zel, -sel,) **oil.** Mixture of several alcohols, chiefly amyl, sometimes produced, usu. in small amounts, during fermentation of alcoholic liquor and making it harmful or poisonous. [Ger. *fusel* or Du. *foezel* bad spirit]

fu·sil (fū′zil, -sil) *n.* (hist.) Light musket or firelock.

fu·sil·ier, fu·sil·eer (fūzilēr′) *ns.* (hist.) Soldier armed with a fusil; **Fusiliers,** (soldiers of) certain Brit. infantry regiments formerly armed with fusils.

fu·sil·lade (fū′silād, -lahd, -zi-) *n.* (Wholesale execution by) continous discharge of firearms.

fu·sion (fū′zhon) *n.* Fusing; fused mass; blending of different things into one; coalition; (phys.) energy-releasing union of atomic nuclei in thermonuclear reaction to form heavier nucleus.

The ambition of artists who embraced ***futurism*** *was to employ all aspects of modern life in their work. This philosophy is seen in the use of newspapers and textures in St. Etienne's 'Still Life with Lacerba'.*

fuss (fŭs) *n.* Bustle, excessive commotion, ostentatious or nervous activity; treatment of trifles as important; (colloq.) person who is always making a fuss (also **~-budget, ~ pot**). **fuss** *v.* Make fuss; busy oneself restlessly with trifles; move fussily *about*, etc., agitate, worry (person). **fuss′y** *adj.* (**fuss·i·er, fuss·i·est**). (esp.) Fastidious; meticulous.

fus·tian (fŭs′chan) *n.* 1. Thick twilled cotton cloth with short nap, usu. dyed in dark dull colors. 2. Pompous language, bombast. **~** *adj.* Made of fustian; bombastic.

fus·tic (fŭs′tĭk) *n.* Small tropical Amer. tree (*Chlorophora tinctoria*), having wood yielding a yellow dyestuff; the wood of this tree; the dye. [Arab. *fustuq* f. Gk. *pistakē* pistachio]

fus·ty (fŭs′tē) *adj.* (**-ti·er, -ti·est**). Stale-smelling, musty; stuffy; old-fashioned. **fus′ti·ness** *n.*

fut. *abbrev.* Future.

fu·tile (fū′til; *Brit.* fū′tīl) *adj.* Useless, ineffectual, vain, frivolous. **fu′tile·ly** *adv.* **fu·til·i·ty** (fūtĭl′ĭtē) *n.* (pl. **-ties**).

fu·ture (fū′cher) *adj.* That will be hereafter; of time to come; (gram., of tense) relating to time to come. **~** *n.* Time to come; what will happen in the future; person's, country's, etc., prospective condition; (gram.) future tense; (commerc., pl.) commodities and stocks sold for future delivery, contracts for these; **~ perfect,** (gram.) tense designating action completed at a certain time in the future (*will have done*); **~ shock,** disorientation and demoralization caused by too swift social and technological changes. [title of book (1970) by Alvin Toffler, Amer. author] **fu·tu·rol·o·gy** (fūcherŏl′ojē) *n.*

fu·tur·ist (fū′cherĭst) *n.* Adherent of futurism. **fu·tur·is·tic** (fūcherĭs′tĭk) *adj.* **fu′tur·ism** *n.* Artistic and literary movement begun *c*1909 in Italy, marked by violent departure from traditional methods and attempting to represent nature not in a static but in a dynamic state.

fu·tu·ri·ty (fūtoor′ĭtē, -tūr′-, -choor′-) *n.* (pl. **-ties**). Future time; future events; future condition, extent, or possibility; (also **~ race**) horse race in which horses must be entered far in advance of the running, e.g. at birth.

Fu·zhou (fo͞o′jō′) = FOOCHOW.

fuzz[1] (fŭz) *n.* Mass of fine light fluff; fibers, hairs, etc.; down, as of a peach. **fuzz′y** *adj.* (**fuzz·i·er, fuzz·i·est**). Of, covered with fuzz; frayed, fluffy; blurred, indistinct; frizzled; confused.

fuzz[2] (fŭz) *n.* (slang) Policeman; (collect.) the police.

fwd. *abbrev.* Four-wheel drive.

FY *abbrev.* Fiscal year.

-fy *suffix.* Forming verbs with sense of make, produce, or cause (*satisfy*, *solidify*, *stupefy*).

FYI *abbrev.* For your information.

Although some ***furniture*** *is still made by individual craftsmen, most is mass-produced, one group of workers completing part of the manufacture and the item being finished and assembled by hand at the end of the process.*

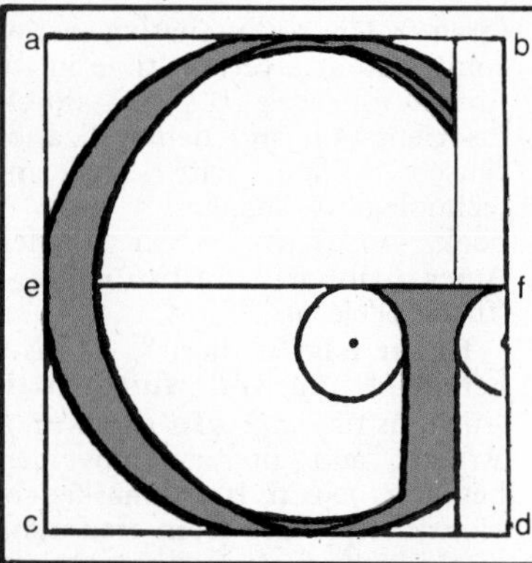

How the written form of the letter **G, g** has developed over the centuries from the apparently unrelated early Phoenician version to the Latin version in use today. Left: The G in Albrecht Durer's design of the Alphabet.

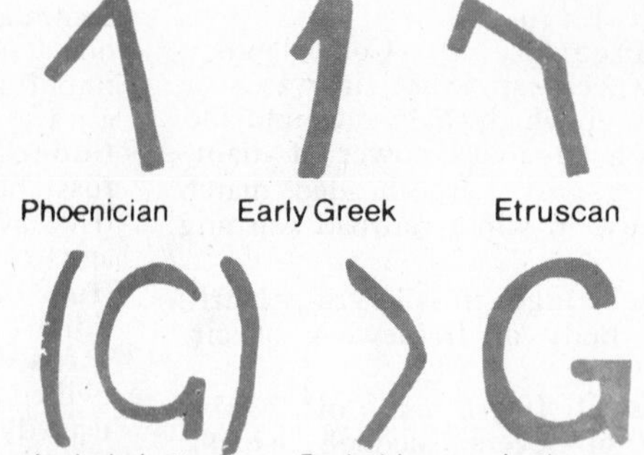

G, g (jē) (pl. **G's, g's** or **Gs, gs**). 1. Seventh letter of modern English and ancient Roman alphabet, orig. differentiated form of C, representing in English a voiced postpalatal stop (*hard g*) except in some words, chiefly of French, Latin, or Greek origin, before *e* or *i*, where it is equivalent to the composite sound (*j*). 2. **G**, (mus.) fifth note of natural scale (C major); scale or key with this note for tonic.

G *abbrev.* Gauss; giga-; (slang) $1,000.

g *abbrev.* Gram(s); acceleration due to gravity.

G. *abbrev.* German; gulf.

g. *abbrev.* Gauge; gender.

Ga *symbol.* Gallium.

Ga., GA *abbrevs.* Georgia.

G.A. *abbrev.* General Assembly.

gab (găb) *n.* (colloq.) Talk, prattle, twaddle; **gift of ~**, talent for speaking; loquacity. **gab** *v.i.* (**gabbed, gab·bing**).

gab·ar·dine (găb′*er*dēn, găb*er*dēn′) *n.* Twill woven cloth of worsted, cotton, or rayon.

gab·ble (găb′*e*l) *v.* (**-bled, -bling**). Talk volubly or inarticulately; utter too fast. **~** *n.* Rapid esp. unintelligible talk. **gab′bler** *n.*

ga·ble (gā′b*e*l) *n.* Vertical triangular upper part of wall at end of ridged roof, from level of eaves upward; triangular section over a window, door, etc. **ga′bled** *adj.*

Ga·bon (găbŏn′; *Fr.* găbawṅ′). Republic in W. Africa; formerly a territory of French Equatorial Africa; independent since 1960; capital, Libreville. **Gab·on·ese** (găb*o*nēz′, -nēs′) *adj.* & *n.*

Gab·o·ro·ne (găb*o*rō′n*e*). Capital of Botswana, in the SE. part.

Ga·bri·el (gā′brē*e*l). One of the seven archangels enumerated in the "Book of Enoch," a messenger of God (Dan. 8, Luke I); in Muslim religion, one of the 4 principal angels.

Gad (găd). Hebrew patriarch, son of Jacob and Zilpah (Gen. 30); tribe of Israel, traditionally descended from him.

gad (găd) *v.i.* (**gad·ded, gad·ding**). (usu. **~ about**) Go *about* seeking entertainment; rove, wander.

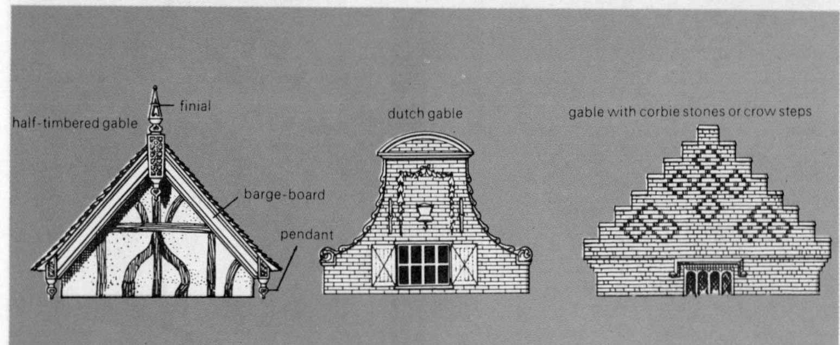

The ornamentation of the ***gables*** *of houses has long been practiced and the feature reached a new level of importance in 17th-century Dutch town houses. Here the gables rise in regular waves along the terraces of an Amsterdam street. Hooks were commonly built into the gables for the convenience of hoisting furniture in and out of windows.*

gad·a·bout (găd′*a*bowt) *adj.* & *n.* (Person) given to gadding about.

gad·fly (găd′flī) *n.* (pl. **-flies**). Fly that bites and goads cattle, esp. one of the family Tabanidae; irritating or harassing person.

gadg·et (găj′ĭt) *n.* (orig. naut.) Small fitting, contrivance, or piece of mechanism; device.

ga·doid (gā′doid) *adj.* & *n.* (Fish) of the cod family (Gadidae).

gad·o·lin·i·um (găd*o*lĭn′ē*u*m) *n.* (chem.) Metallic element of rare-earth group; symbol Gd, at. no. 64, at. wt. 157.25. [J. *Gadolin* (1760–1852), Finnish mineralogist]

Gads·den (gădz′d*e*n), **James** (1788–1858). Amer. railroad promoter and statesman; U.S. minister to Mexico, 1853–54; in 1853 he negotiated the $10,000,000 purchase (**Gadsden Purchase**) from Mexico of 29,640 sq. mi. (76,767 sq. km), in what is now New Mexico and Arizona.

Gae·a (jē′*a*). (Gk. myth.)

The red, yellow or purple flowers of the **gaillardia** make a brilliant display. In the U.S. they grow in such profusion as to warrant the name of blanket flower.

A swarm of **gadflies** can distress cattle with their stinging bites to the point where the cattle stampede. Here two gadflies feed on an animal.

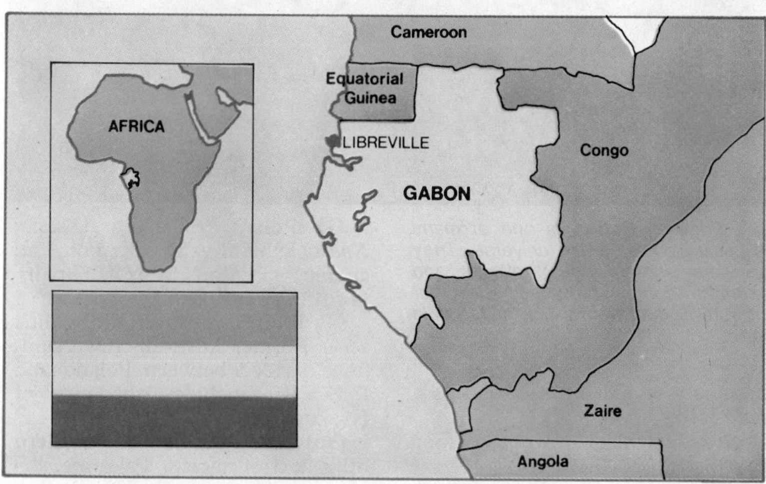

A republic of approximately 520,000 people, ***Gabon*** *has an area of 102,000 sq. miles. Until 1815, it was an infamous center of the slave trade. The late Dr. Albert Schweitzer's leper hospital was at Lambarene in western Gabon.*

Personification of the earth.

Gael (gāl) *n.* Scottish or Irish Celt. **Gael'ic** *adj.* & *n.* (Language) of the Celtic inhabitants of Scottish highlands, or of the branch of Celts including Scottish, Irish, and Manx Celts.

Gael. *abbrev.* Gaelic.

gaff (găf) *n.* 1. Barbed fishing spear; stick with iron hook for landing large fish. 2. (naut.) Spar used to extend fore-and-aft sails not set on stays; **stand the ~**, (slang) endure difficulties. **gaff** *v.t.* Seize (fish) with gaff.

gaffe (găf) *n.* Blunder, indiscreet act or remark, faux pas. [Fr.]

gaf·fer (găf'*er*) *n.* Elderly rustic, old fellow. [contr. of *godfather*, *ga-* by assoc. w. *grandfather*]

gag (găg) *n.* 1. Thing thrust into mouth to prevent speech or outcry; obstacle to or censorship of free speech; closure. 2. Joke. ~ *v.* (**gagged, gag·ging**). 1. Apply gag to; silence, deprive of free speech. 2. Joke. 3. Retch; choke.

ga·ga (gah'gah) *n.* Senile, doting; silly, inane, fatuous.

Ga·ga·rin (*ga*gar̄'ĭn), **Yuri Alekseyevich** (1934–68). Russian cosmonaut and first man to orbit Earth, 1961.

gage[1] (gāj) *n.* Pledge, thing deposited as security; (glove thrown down as, any symbol of) challenge to fight; challenge, test. ~ *v.* (**gaged, gag·ing**).

gage[2] = GAUGE.

gage[3] (gāj) = greengage: see GREEN.

gag·gle (găg'*e*l) *n.* Flock (of geese). ~ *v.i.* (**-gled, -gling**). (of geese) Make clucking sound.

gai·e·ty (gā'*e*tē) *n.* (pl. **-ties**). Being gay or merry; mirth; merry-making, festivity; bright or showy appearance.

gail·lar·di·a (gālar̄'dē*a*) *n.* Showy-flowered composite plant of genus *G~* of western N. Amer., with yellow- or red-rayed flowers. [*Gaillard* de Marentonneau, Fr. botanist]

gai·ly (gā'lē): see GAY.

gain (gān) *n.* Increase of possessions, advantage, etc., of any kind; profit, improvement; acquisition of wealth; increase in amount; (pl.) sums acquired by trade etc., emoluments, winnings. ~ *v.* Obtain, secure (desired or advantageous thing); win (sum) as profits etc.; earn; make a profit, be benefited, improve or advance *in* some respect; be enhanced *by* comparison or contrast; win (battle, victory); bring over to one's interests or views; reach, arrive at (desired place); (of clock etc.) become fast; ~ **the ear of**, get favorable hearing from; ~ **on**, get closer to (person or thing pursued); ~ **time**, obtain delay by pretexts or slow methods.

gain·ful (gān′ful) *adj.* Lucrative, remunerative; (of occupation etc.) paid. **gain′ful·ness** *n.* **gain′ful·ly** *adv.*

gain·say (gān′sā) *v.t.* (**-said, -say·ing**). Deny, contradict.

Gains·bor·ough (gānz′bĕrō, -bŭrō; *Brit.* gānz′bero, -bro), **Thomas** (1727–88). English painter; famous for portraits.

gait (gāt) *n.* Manner of walking; bearing or carriage as one walks. **gait′ed** *adj.*

gai·ter (gā′ter) *n.* Covering of cloth, leather, etc., for ankle, or ankle and lower leg.

gal (găl) *n.* (colloq.) Woman or girl.

Gal. *abbrev.* Galatians (New Testament).

gal. *abbrev.* Gallon(s).

ga·la (gā′la, găl′a, gah′la) *n.* Festive occasion, fête.

ga·lac·tic (galăk′tĭk) *adj.* (astron.) Of a galaxy; of the Milky Way.

Gal·a·had (găl′ahăd), **Sir.** In Arthurian legend, knight of immaculate purity, destined to retrieve the Holy Grail.

gal·an·tine (găl′antēn, gălantēn′) *n.* Dish of meat or fish, boned, stuffed, boiled, and served cold in aspic.

Ga·lá·pa·gos (galah′pagōs) **Islands (Colón Archipelago).** Pacific Ocean island group, a province of Ecuador, encompassing 2,966 sq. mi. (7,681 sq. km), located 650 mi. (1,046 km) W. of mainland on the equator; capital San Cristobal; famous for species of almost extinct giant tortoise; site of study of species and fossils conducted by Charles Darwin in his research on evolution.

Gal·a·te·a (gălatē′a). (Gk. myth.) Statue of a woman brought to life by Aphrodite in answer to the prayers of its sculptor, Pygmalion, who had fallen in love with it.

Ga·la·tia (galā′sha). Ancient region of central Asia Minor, centered about modern-day Ankara, Turkey.

Ga·la·tian (galā′shan) *adj.* Of Galatia. ~ *n.* One of its inhabitants, believed to have been Gauls who settled there in the 3rd c. B.C.; (**Epistle to the**) ~**s**, book of New Testament, epistle of St. Paul to the Christians of Galatia about 58 A.D.

gal·ax·y (găl′aksē) *n.* (pl. **-ax·ies**). 1. One of the independent systems of stars and other matter existing in space, esp. (**G**~) group containing the solar system. 2. **G**~, Milky Way. 3. (fig.) Brilliant company or assemblage (of). [Gk. *gala* milk]

The Edge-on ***Galaxy*** *is one of many elliptical galaxies in the universe. They are generally the largest galaxies, and seem to contain no young stars, or interstellar dust from which stars could form.*

gale[1] (gāl) *n.* (also **sweet** ~). Bog myrtle.

gale[2] (gāl) *n.* 1. Strong wind; (naut.) storm; (meteor.) wind of speed between 32 and 63 mi. per hour; ~ **warning**, notice of probability of gales issued by the weather bureau. 2. Gust, outburst, esp. of laughter.

Ga·len (gā′len). Claudius Galenus (*c*130–*c*201 A.D.), Greek physician and writer on medicine; practiced in Rome; physician to emperor Marcus Aurelius. **Ga·len·ic** (gālĕn′ĭk, ga-), **Ga·len′i·cal** *adjs.* Of, according to, Galen; (of remedies) made of vegetable, not chemical, components.

ga·le·na (galē′na), **ga·le·nite** (galē′nīt) *ns.* (min.) Lead sulfide, the common ore of lead (PbS).

Ga·li·cia[1] (galĭsh′a, -lē′shēa; *Span.* gahlē′thyah). Region and ancient kingdom of NW. Spain. **Ga·li′cian** *adj.* & *n.*

Ga·li·cia[2] (galĭsh′a; *Yid.* galĭt′sēa). Former Austrian crown land, now divided between Poland and U.S.S.R.; includes the city of Kraków.

Gal·i·lee (găl′ilē). Northern hilly part of ancient Palestine, W. of the Jordan (now in Israel); **Sea of** ~ (also called Sea of Tiberias and Lake of Gennesaret), freshwater lake in NE. Israel on Syrian border, fed by Jordan River; 696 ft. (212 m) below sea level. **Gal·i·le·an**[1] (gălilē′an) *adj.* & *n.*

Gal·i·le·o (gălilā′ō, -lē′ō). Galileo Galilei (1564–1642), Italian astronomer and physicist; discovered the four most prominent satellites of Jupiter, the libration of the moon, etc.; his observations brought him into conflict with the Inquisition and he was compelled to repudiate the Copernican theory. **Gal·i·le·an**[2] (gălilē′an) *adj.* (of telescope) Of the form invented by Galileo, a refracting telescope with

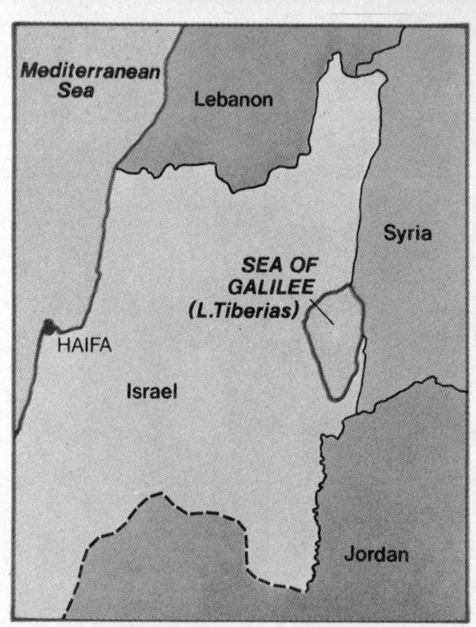

A center of Judaism after the fall of Jerusalem in A.D. 70, ***Galilee*** *became the center for Zionism in the 19th century. The Sea of Galilee is a freshwater lake.*

The Metropolitan Museum of Art, a highly respected ***gallery*** *on the corner of 5th and 82nd Streets, New York, draws viewers from many parts of the world.*

A ***gall*** *can be formed by the larvae of various insects including flies and wasps. They remain within this plant tissue for most of their life cycle and emerge when mature.*

concave eyepiece.

gall[1] (gawl) *n.* Bitter greenish secretion of the liver, bile (now only of lower animals); gallbladder and its contents; (fig.) anything bitter; asperity, rancor; impudence; **gall′bladder**, vessel containing the gall or bile; **gall′stone**, calculus or stone in gallbladder.

gall[2] (gawl) *n.* Painful swelling, pustule, blister, esp. in horse; sore produced by chafing; mental soreness or irritation; something galling or exasperating; place rubbed bare. ~ *v.* Rub sore, injure by rubbing; vex, humiliate. **gall′ing** *adj.* **gall′ing·ly** *adv.*

gall[3] (gawl) *n.* Excrescence produced on trees by deposition of the eggs of mites or insects; **gall′fly** *n.* (pl. **-flies**), insect causing galls.

Gal·la (găl′*a*) *n.* (pl. **-las**, collect. **-la**). One of a group of largely pastoral Hamitic tribes of S. Ethiopia and the Somali Republic, allied to Ethiopians in language and origin.

gal·lant (găl′*a*nt; esp. for def. 3 g*a*lănt′, -lahnt′) *adj.* 1. Fine, stately (esp. of ship, horse, etc.). 2. Brave, chivalrous. 3. Markedly attentive to women; amatory. **gal′lant·ly** *adv.* **gallant** (g*a*lănt′, -lahnt′, găl′*a*nt) *n.* Man of fashion; ladies' man; paramour. ~ (g*a*lănt′, -lahnt′) *v.* Play the gallant, flirt (with); escort.

gal·lant·ry (găl′*a*ntrē) *n.* (pl. **-ries**). 1. Bravery, dashing courage. 2. Courtliness, devotion to women; polite or amorous act or speech; conduct of a gallant.

gal·le·on (găl′ē*o*n, găl′y*o*n) *n.* (hist.) Large three-masted, multi-decked sailing ship of the 15th and 16th centuries, used as a trading ship and warship, esp. by Spain.

gal·ler·y (găl′*e*rē, găl′rē) *n.* (pl. **-ries**). 1. Covered space for walking, partly open at side; portico, colonnade; balcony; long narrow passage in thickness of wall or supported on corbels, open toward interior of building. 2. Platform projecting from inner wall of church, hall, etc., providing extra

The ***galley*** *of a ship is equipped to enable the cook to produce meals even when the ship is rolling. Top: The galley of a reconstruction of the 17th century barque, 'Mayflower'.*

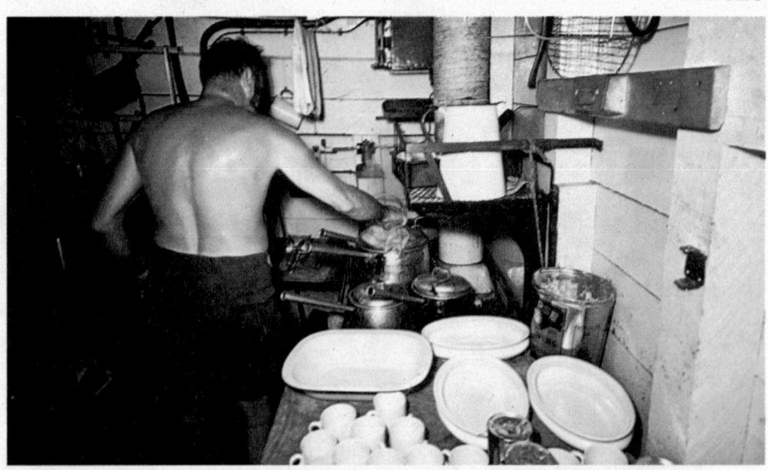

room for spectators etc. or reserved for musicians etc.; highest of such balconies in theater, containing cheapest seats; persons seated there, least refined part of audience; group of spectators at golf match etc.; **play to the ~**, appeal to lower taste. 3. Long narrow room, passage, corridor; room or building used for showing works of art. 4. (mil., mining) Underground horizontal or nearly horizontal passage. 5. Ornamental parapet or railing along edge of table, shelf, etc. **gallery** *v.* (**-ler·ied, -ler·y·ing**). Provide, pierce, etc., with gallery or galleries.

gal·ley (găl'ē) *n.* (pl. **-leys**). 1. (chiefly hist.) Low flat single-decked seagoing vessel using sails and oars, and usu. rowed by slaves or criminals (**~ slaves**). 2. Greek or Roman warship with one or more banks of oars. 3. Kitchen on ship or aircraft. 4. (print.) Oblong tray for holding type that has been set; corresponding part of composing machine. 5. (also **~ proof**) Printer's proof taken from type in galley.

Gal·lic (găl'ĭk) *adj.* 1. Of the Gauls or Gaul, Gaulish. 2. French. **Gal·li·cism, gallicism** (găl'ĭsĭzem) *ns.* 1. French idiom or phrase used in another language. 2. French characteristic, custom, etc. **gal·li·cize** (găl'ĭsīz) *v.* (**-cized, -ciz·ing**).

Gal·li·can (găl'ĭk*a*n) *adj.* & *n.* Of the French R. C. Ch.; (member) of the French Roman Catholics who maintained the right of the French Church to be in certain respects free from papal control (opp. ULTRAMONTANE). **Gal'li·can·ism** *n.*

gal·li·mau·fry (găl*i*maw'frē) *n.* (pl. **-fries**). Heterogeneous mixture, jumble, medley; hash.

gal·li·na·ceous (găl*i*nā'sh*u*s) *adj.* (zool.) Of the order Galliformes, including domestic poultry, pheasants, partridges, turkeys, etc.

Ga·lli·nas (gahyē'nahs), **Point.** Cape in N. central Colombia, northermost point of S. Amer.

gal·li·nule (găl'*i*no͞ol, -nūl) *n.* Any of various wading birds of genera *Gallinula* and *Porphyrula*, with long webless toes and glossy plumage.

Gal·lip·o·li (g*a*lĭp'*o*lē). Peninsula of European Turkey, 63 mi. (101 km) long, between the Dardanelles and the Aegean.

gal·li·um (găl'ē*u*m) *n.* (chem.) Rare bluish-white metallic element found in some zinc and aluminum minerals, remarkable for its extremely low melting point (29° C); symbol Ga, at. no. 31, at. wt. 69.72. [L. *gallus* cock, transl. of *Lecoq* de Boisbaudran, its discoverer, 1875]

gal·li·vant, gal·a·vant (găl'ĭvănt) *vbs.i.* Gad about.

gal·lon (găl'*o*n) *n.* Unit of liquid capacity equal to 4 quarts or 3.785 liters.

gal·lop (găl'*o*p) *n.* Horse's or other quadruped's fastest pace (though slower than a run) with all feet off ground together in each stride; a ride at this pace; (fig.) any speedy action. **~** *v.* Go at a gallop; make (horse etc.) gallop; read, speak, very fast; move or progress rapidly. **gal'lop·er** *n.*

Gal·lo-Ro·man (găl'ō rō'm*a*n) *adj.* & *n.* (Inhabitant) of Gaul when it formed part of Roman Empire.

gal·lows (găl'ōz) *n.pl.* (pl. **-lows·es, -lows**). (usu. considered sing.) Structure, usu. of two uprights and crosspiece, on which criminals may be hanged; similar structure for other uses; punishment of hanging; **~ bird**, person fit to be hanged; **~ humor**, grim and ironical humor.

Above: 'Nonsuch II', a reconstruction of a ***galleon,*** *undergoing sea trials off Falmouth, Cornwall, U.K. Galleons were formidable gun ships but could be outmaneuvered by smaller ships.*

Gal·lup (găl'*u*p) **poll.** Poll taken from a cross section of the inhabitants of a country or region in order to ascertain public opinion on a topic. [after G. H. *Gallup* (1901–), Amer. statistician]

gal·lus·es (găl'*u*sĭz) *n.pl.* (colloq.) Trouser suspenders.

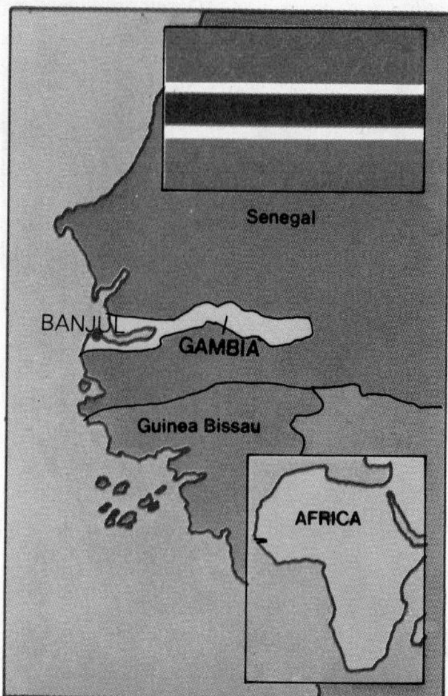

The republic of ***Gambia*** *has a population of 510,000. Most of the people are engaged in agriculture and produce the main export crops of peanuts and palm kernels. Above: Map and flag of Gambia. Left: A shark cleaned on the beach.*

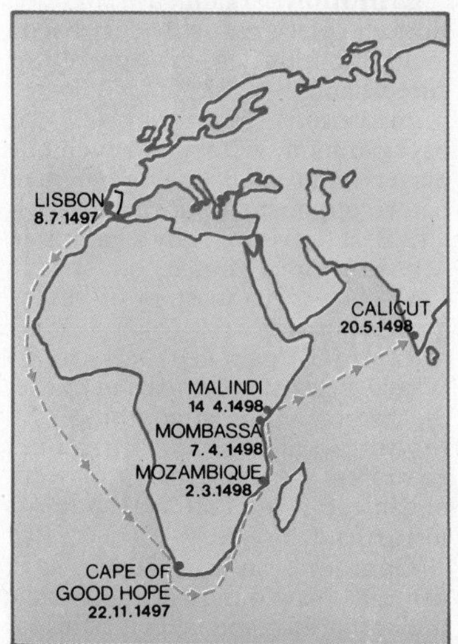

The map of the voyages of ***Vasco da Gama*** *indicates the enormous range of his achievement. He was the first European to reach India by sea when he arrived at Calicut in 1498 and again in 1503.*

gal·op (găl′*o*p) *n.* Lively 19th c. dance in 2/4 time. ~ *v.i.* Dance a galop.

ga·lore (g*a*lōr′, -lôr′) *adv.* & *n.* (In) abundance. [Ir. *go leór* to sufficiency]

ga·losh, ga·loshe (g*a*lŏsh′) *ns.* Waterproof overshoe usu. of rubber.

Gals·wor·thy (gawlz′wĕrdhē), **John** (1867–1933). English novelist and playwright; author of *The Forsyte Saga* etc.

Gal·ton (gawl′t*o*n), **Sir Francis** (1822–1911). British meteorologist and anthropologist; founded science of eugenics; his work on the markings of fingertips led to the adoption of fingerprint identification of criminals.

ga·lumph (g*a*lŭmf′) *v.i.* Go prancing exultantly. [coined by Lewis Carroll, perh. f. *gallop, triumph*]

galv. *abbrev.* Galvanized.

Gal·va·ni (gahlvah′nē), **Luigi** (1737–98). Italian scientist; discoverer of electricity produced by chemical action.

gal·van·ic (gălvăn′ĭk) *adj.* Of, produced by, suggestive of, galvanism; ~ **battery**, battery of primary cells used in galvanism.

gal·va·nism (găl′v*a*nĭzem) *n.* Direct-current electricity, usu. from a primary battery or other chemical source.

gal·va·nize (găl′v*a*nīz) *v.t.* (**-nized, -niz·ing**). 1. Stimulate to activity by or as by electricity, rouse by shock or excitement. 2. Coat iron or steel with rust-resistant zinc (usu. without the use of electricity) to protect it from rust. **gal·va·ni·za·tion** (gălv*a*nīzā′sh*o*n) *n.*

gal·va·nom·e·ter (gălv*a*nŏm′-*e*ter) *n.* Apparatus for detecting and measuring small electric currents.

Gal·ves·ton (găl′vest*o*n). Port on E. end of Galveston Island at mouth of Galveston Bay off SE. Texas.

Gal·way (gawl′wā). County of W. central Ireland; ~ **Bay**, Atlantic Ocean inlet extending 20 mi. (32 km) inland between counties Galway and Clare in W. central Ireland.

gam (găm) *n.* (slang) Person's leg, esp. a woman's attractive leg.

Ga·ma (gah′m*a*, găm′*a*), **Vasco da** (*c*1469–1524). Portuguese navigator; he was the first European to sail around the Cape of Good Hope (1497) and to reach India by sea.

Gam·bi·a (găm′bē*a*). (also **The** ~) W. African republic on river Gambia; former Brit. colony; independent, 1965; capital, Banjul. **Gam′bi·an** *adj.* & *n.*

gam·bir, gam·bier (găm′bēr) *ns.* Astringent extract of Asiatic plant (*Uncaria gambir*) used in tanning etc. [Malay *gambir*, the plant]

gam·bit (găm′bĭt) *n.* Chess opening in which player sacrifices pawn or pieces to obtain some advantage over opponent; opening move in discussion etc. [It. *gambetto* tripping up (*gamba* leg)]

'Mahatma' Gandhi, *Indian political and spiritual leader. His frail figure and advocacy of passive resistance belied his political strength and determination to liberate India from British rule.*

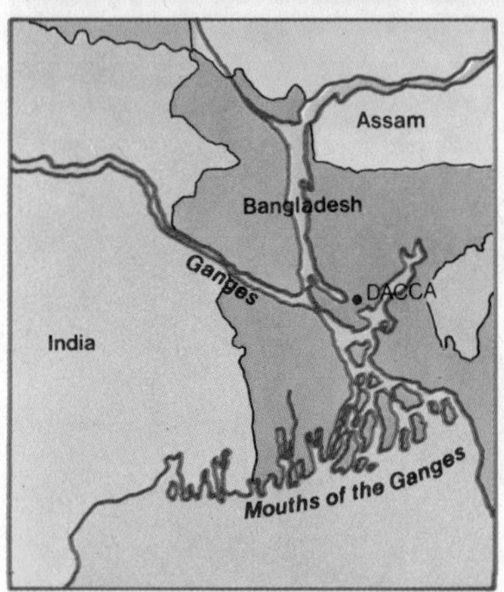

The sacred river of the Hindus, the **Ganges** *flows through the sacred city of Varanasi. Above: A funeral pyre burns on the river bank before the ashes are cast into the river. Left: The map of the Ganges shows its delta where it flows into the Bay of Bengal.*

gam·ble (găm′bel) *v.* (**-bled, -bling**). Play games of chance for money; risk, chance, take a chance *on* (freq. fig.); ~ **away**, lose by gambling. **gamble** *n.* Gambling; risky undertaking or attempt. **gam′bler** *n.*

gam·boge (gămbōj′, -bo͞ozh′) *n.* Gum resin from various Asiatic trees of genus *Garcinia*, used as pigment giving bright yellow color. [f. *Cambodia*]

gam·bol (găm′bol) *n.* & *v.i.* (**-boled, -bol·ing, -bolled, -bol·ling**). Caper; skip(ping) about.

game[1] (gām) *n.* 1. Diversion, pastime; bit of fun. 2. Contest played according to rules and decided by skill, strength, or luck; (pl., Gk. and Rom. antiq.) athletic, dramatic, and musical contests, gladiatorial etc. shows; (pl.) organized athletics in school etc. 3. Scheme, undertaking, etc., followed up like a game; (also ~ **plan**) policy, plan of action; (pl.) dodges, tricks. 4. Single round in some contests, e.g. tennis; winning score in game. 5. Person's normal standard of play; **on, off, one's ~**, playing well, badly. 6. Object of chase, animal(s) hunted; object of pursuit; (collect.) wild animals or birds hunted for sport or food, flesh of these. 7. **game′bag**, bag for holding game killed by sportsman; **game′cock**, cock bred and trained for fighting, or of breed suitable for cockfighting; ~ **fish**, any edible fish caught by anglers for sport; **game′keeper**, man employed to take care of game, prevent poaching etc; **games′manship**, art of winning unfairly but without breaking rules; **game point**, point that enables scorer to win game, as in tennis; **game theory**, mathematical analysis of conflicts in war, economics, games of skill, etc. **game** *adj.* (**gam·er, gam·est**). Pertaining to animals hunted for sport; like a gamecock, spirited; having the spirit *for*. **game′ly** *adv.* **game′ness** *n.* **game** *v.* (**gamed, gam·ing**). Play at games of chance for money, gamble; throw *away* in gambling; **gaming house**, house frequented for gambling; so **gaming table**.

game[2] (gām) *adj.* (of limb) Lame, crippled.

game·some (gām′som) *adj.* Sportive. **game′some·ly** *adv.* **game′some·ness** *n.*

game·ster (gām′ster) *n.* Gambler.

gam·ete (găm′ēt, gamēt′) *n.* Protoplasmic body capable of uniting with another to form new individual; mature sexual cell, **ga·met·ic** (gamĕt′ĭk) *adj.*

gam·in (găm′ĭn) *n.* (fem. **gam·ine** pr. gămēn′). Street urchin; waif; mischievous child. [Fr.]

gam·ma (găm′a) *n.* 1. Third letter of Greek alphabet (Γ, γ) corresponding to *g*, used in enumerations etc. 2. ~ **globulin**, globulin fraction containing many antibodies present in the original serum; ~ **rays**, electromagnetic radiations of very short wavelength emitted by radioactive substances, orig. regarded as the 3rd and most penetrating kind of rays emitted by radium (see ALPHA, BETA) but now known to be identical with very short X-rays.

gam·mon[1] (găm′on) *n.* 1. Bottom piece of side of bacon including hind leg. 2. Smoked or cured ham.

gam·mon[2] (găm′on) *n.* At backgammon, victory in which one player removes all his or her men before opponent removes any. ~ *v.t.* Beat (adversary) by a gammon.

gam·mon[3] (găm′on) *v.t.* (naut.) Lash (bowsprit) to stem of vessel. **gam′mon·ing** *n.*

gam·ut (găm′ut) *n.* (mus.) Whole series of notes used in music; (fig.) whole range of anything.

gam·y (gā′mē) *adj.* (**gam·i·er, gam·i·est**). Having flavor or scent of game, esp. kept after freshness is lost; ribald, risqué.

Gan·der (găn′der). Town in E. central Newfoundland, Canada; major fuel stop and takeoff point for transatlantic flights to Europe, and site of U.S. air base.

gan·der (găn′der) *n.* Male goose.

Gan·dhi (gahn′dē, găn′-), **Indira Nehru** (1917–1985). Prime minister of India, 1966–77; 1979–1985; daughter of Jawaharlal Nehru, Congress Party leader.

Gan·dhi (gahn′dē), **Mohandas Karamchand**, called "Mahatma" (1869–1948). Indian nationalist and spiritual leader; originator of

Below: the ***gannet*** *dives on to fish that are its prey and pursues them underwater. Tropical and sub-tropical gannets are called boobies. Left: Gannets lay their eggs on ledges and their chicks are well camouflaged.*

passive resistance as a form of political action.

gang (găng) *n.* 1. Group of workers working together; group of slaves or prisoners; band of persons acting or going about together, esp. for criminal purpose or one disapproved of by speaker. 2. Set of tools etc. arranged to work simultaneously; **chain** ~: see CHAIN; **gang'land**, domain of gangsters. **gang** *v.i.* ~ **up (on)**, (colloq.) combine (against).

Gan·ges (găn'jēz). River in NE. India flowing SE. 1,557 mi. (2,506 km) from the Himalaya Mountains to the Bay of Bengal, held sacred by Hindus.

gan·gling (găng'glĭng) *adj.* Tall, thin, and ungraceful; lanky.

gan·gli·on (găng'glē*o*n) *n.* (pl. **-gli·a** pr. -glē*a*, **-gli·ons**). 1. Enlargement or knot on nerve forming center for reception and transmission of impulses. 2. (path.) Cyst-like swelling on tendon. **gan'gli·on·at·ed, gan·gli·on·ic** (gănggleŏn'ĭk) *adjs.*

gang·plank (găng'plăngk) *n.* Movable plank usu. with cleats nailed on it for walking into or out of boat etc.

gan·grene (găng'grēn, găng-grēn') *n.* Local death and decay of body tissue caused by obstruction of the blood circulation. ~ *v.* (**-grened, -gren·ing**). Become affected, affect, with gangrene. **gan·gre·nous** (găng'gr*e*n*u*s) *adj.*

gang·ster (găng'st*er*) *n.* Member of gang of criminals. **gang'ster·ism** *n.*

gang·way (găng'wā) *n.* Passage, esp. between rows of seats; passage etc. on ship, esp. platform connecting quarterdeck and forecastle; opening in bulwarks by which ship is entered or left, bridge laid across from this to shore etc.

gan·net (găn'ĭt) *n.* (pl. **-nets**, collect. **-net**). Any of several large white seabirds of family Sulidae, with black-tipped wings and wedge-shaped tail, esp. *Monus bassanus* of N. Atlantic coastal waters.

gan·oid (găn'oid) *adj.* (of fish scales) Armorlike, covered with layers of dentine and enamel and therefore shiny; (of fish) having such scales. ~ *n.* Fish with ganoid scales, as the sturgeon, gar, etc.

Gan·su (gahn'sōō') = KANSU.

gant·let (gănt'lĭt, gawnt'-) = GAUNTLET².

gan·try (găn'trē) *n.* (pl. **-tries**). Four-footed wooden stand for barrels; structure supporting traveling crane, railroad signals, equipment to prepare rocket for launching, etc.

Gan·y·mede (găn'*i*mēd). 1. (Gk. myth.) Trojan youth, so beautiful that Zeus caused an eagle to carry him up to heaven and made him his cupbearer. 2. (astron.) Fourth and largest moon of the planet Jupiter. 3. (usu. **g**~) Young barman or waiter who serves alcoholic drinks.

GAO *abbrev.* General Accounting Office.

gaol (jāl) *n.* (Brit.) JAIL. **gaol'er** *n.*

gap (găp) *n.* Breach in hedge or wall; gorge, pass; unfilled space or interval, blank; break in continuity; wide divergence in views, sympathies, etc. **gapped'** *adj.*

gape (gāp) *v.i.* (**gaped, gap·ing**). Open mouth wide; open or be open wide, split, part asunder; stare, gaze curiously, *at*; yawn. ~ *n.* Yawn; open-mouthed stare; expanse of open mouth or beak, part of beak that opens; ~**s**, disease of poultry and some wild birds constituted by the presence of **gape'worm** (*Syngamus trachea*) in the trachea, the obstruction caused by which makes the birds gape or gasp for breath. **gap'er** *n.* **gap'ing·ly** *adv.*

gar (gar̄) *n.* (pl. **gars**, collect. **gar**). (also **gar'fish, gar'pike**) 1. Fish of family Belonidae, allied to flying fish; needlefish. 2. N. and Central Amer. fresh-water fish of the ganoid genus *Lepisosteus* with lozenge-shaped scales, bony pike; **alligator** ~, large species of this living in rivers of southern U.S. with head resembling alligator's.

G.A.R. *abbrev.* Grand Army of the Republic.

ga·rage (g*a*rahzh', -rahj'; *Brit.* găr'ĭj, -ahzh) *n.* Building or establishment for storing or repair of motor vehicles; ~ **sale**, sale, usu. in garage, of one's unwanted

The ***gar*** *or gar pike is a primitive fish found in lakes and rivers of N. America. Lurking in weeds much of the time, it rushes from cover to capture smaller fish.*

*The formal **garden** at Hampton Court, London, U.K. laid out geometrically with flower beds, gravelled or paved walks and topiary, is typical of those gardens conceived as natural cloisters for conversation.*

furniture, kitchen utensils, clothing, etc. **garage** *v.t.* (**-raged, -rag·ing**). Put (car etc.) into a garage.

garb (gārb) *n.* Dress, costume, esp. distinctive attire of one's occupation or calling; appearance. ~ *v.t.* Attire, put (esp. distinctive) clothes upon.

gar·bage (gār'bĭj) *n.* Kitchen waste; refuse; rubbish (also fig.)

gar·ban·zo (gārbăn'zō, -bahn'-) *n.* (pl. **-zos**): see CHICKPEA.

gar·ble (gār'bel) *v.t.* (**-bled, -bling**). Make (usu. unfair or malicious) selections from (facts, statements, etc.); distort; scramble. [Arab. *ḡarbala* sift, select]

Gar·ci·a Lor·ca (gārsē'*a* lōr'k*a*), **Federico** (1899–1936). Spanish poet and playwright; considered the greatest 20-c. Spanish poet, murdered by Falangists during the Spanish Civil War.

gar·çon (gărsawṅ') *n.* (pl. **-çons** pr. -sawṅ'). Waiter in French restaurant, hotel, etc. [Fr.]

Gar·da (gār'd*a*) **Lake.** Italy's largest lake, 143 sq. mi. (370 sq. km), in the N. part.

gar·dant = GUARDANT.

gar·den (gār'd*e*n) *n.* Piece of ground devoted to growing flowers, fruit, or vegetables; (pl.) ornamental grounds for public resort; ~ **party**, outdoor party or social gathering on lawn or in garden. **garden** *adj.* Of, pertaining to, or grown in a garden; ~ **variety**, (colloq.) ordinary, common. **garden** *v.i.* Cultivate, work in, a garden. **gar'den·er** *n.* One who gardens; person employed to tend garden.

gar·de·nia (gārdēn'y*a*) *n.* Tree or shrub of genus *G*~ of tropical Asia and Africa, bearing large white or yellow, usu. fragrant, flowers; flower of one of these. [Dr. Alexander *Garden* (1731–90), Scottish naturalist]

Gar·field (gār'fēld), **James Abram** (1831–81). Twentieth president of U.S., 1881; shot by Charles J. Guiteau on July 2, 1881, and died Sept. 19, 1881.

gar·fish (gār'fĭsh) *n.* (pl. **-fish·es,** collect. **-fish**) = GAR.

gar·gan·tu·an (gārgăn'cho͞o*a*n) *adj.* Enormous, gigantic. [*Gargantua*, giant king with enormous physical and intellectual appetites, the hero of Rabelais' satirical romance *Gargantua and Pantagruel*]

gar·gle (gār'gel) *v.* (**-gled, -gling**). Wash (throat or mouth) with liquid held suspended in throat and kept in motion by breath; wash mouth or throat thus. ~ *n.* Liquid used for gargling.

*The use of **gargoyles** to carry water spouts clear of the sides of medieval churches may have had the dual purpose of avoiding damp penetrating the walls and scaring demons, as at the church of Notre Dame, Paris.*

gar·goyle (gār'goil) *n.* Grotesque waterspout usu. with human or animal mouth, head, or body, projecting from gutter of (esp. Gothic) building to carry water clear of wall.

Gar·i·bal·di (găr*i*bawl'dē, -băl'-), **Giuseppe** (1807–82). Italian general and nationalist leader; hero of the RISORGIMENTO; commanded a volunteer force for Sardinia against Austria, 1859; organized expeditions by which he conquered Sicily; expelled Francis II from Naples; and finally marched (unsuccessfully) against Rome, 1860–2.

gar·ish (găr'ĭsh, gār'-) *adj.* Obtrusively bright, gaudy. **gar'·ish·ly** *adv.* **gar'ish·ness** *n.*

gar·land (gār'l*a*nd) *n.* Wreath of flowers, leaves, etc., worn on head or hung on something as decoration; distinction, prize, for victory etc.; representation of garland in metal etc.; (archaic) anthology, miscellany. ~ *v.t.* Crown with garland; deck with garlands; serve as garland to.

gar·lic (gār'lĭk) *n.* Plant of genus *Allium* (usu. *A. sativum*) with strong-smelling pungent-tasting bulbs used as a seasoning. **gar'·lick·y** *adj.*

gar·ment (gār'm*e*nt) *n.* Article of dress; (pl.) clothes.

gar·ner (gār'n*e*r) *n.* Granary.

~ *v.t.* Gather and store; acquire, collect (usu. fig.).

Gar·ner (gär′ner), **John Nance** (1868–1967). Amer. politician; speaker of the House of Representatives, 1931–3; vice president under Franklin D. Roosevelt, 1933–41.

gar·net (gär′nĭt) *n.* Vitreous mineral, occurring as a 12-sided crystal of which the deep red transparent variety is used as a gem. [med. L. *granatum* pomegranate (f. resemblance to its seeds)]

gar·nish (gär′nĭsh) *v.t.* Decorate, embellish (esp. dish for table). ~ *n.* Decorative or savory addition to dish for table. **gar′nish·er, gar′nish·ment** *ns.*

gar·nish·ee (gärnĭshē′) *v.t.* (**-nish·eed, -nish·ee·ing**). Serve notice on (person) for purpose of attaching money, such as pay, belonging to debtor; attach (money, pay) thus. ~ *n.* Person in whose hands money belonging to debtor is attached.

gar·ret (găr′ĭt) = ATTIC, def. 2.

Gar·rick (găr′ĭk), **David** (1717–1779). Actor-manager of Drury Lane Theatre, London.

gar·ri·son (găr′ĭson) *n.* Troops stationed in fortress, town, etc., to defend it; military post. ~ *v.t.* Furnish with, occupy as, garrison; place (troops, soldier) on garrison duty.

Gar·ri·son (găr′ĭson), **William Lloyd** (1805–79). Amer. abolitionist leader and editor; founder of *The Liberator*, a weekly newspaper published from 1831–65, denouncing slavery; founder, 1833, and president, 1843–65, of the American Anti-Slavery Society; editor of *Nation*, 1865–1906.

gar·rote, ga·rotte, gar·rotte (garōt′, -rŏt′) *ns.* Spanish method of capital punishment by strangulation; instrument used in it with apparatus for strangling, later with brass collar fitted with a sharp point that pierces the spinal cord; robbery performed by throttling victim. **garrote** *v.t.* (**-rot·ed, -rot·ing, -rot·ted, -rot·ting**). Execute or kill by strangulation; throttle in order to rob. **gar·rot′er** *n.*

gar·ru·lous (găr′ulus, -yulus) *adj.* Talkative, wordy. **gar′ru·lous·ly** *adv.* **gar′ru·lous·ness, gar·ru·li·ty** (garōō′lĭtē) *ns.*

gar·ter (gär′ter) *n.* Band worn above or below knee to keep stocking up or as ornament; **the G ~**, badge (dark blue velvet ribbon edged and buckled with gold, worn below knee) of highest order of English knighthood, instituted *c*1344; membership of this order, the order itself. ~ *v.t.* Fasten (stocking), encircle (leg), with garter.

garter (gär′ter) **snake.** Any of numerous small harmless N. Amer. snakes of the genus *Thamnophis*, often having longitudinal stripes along the back.

*The flowers of the **garlic** (Allium sativum) emerge from clustered bulbils. The bulb of the plant is used as a flavoring. When eaten by cattle, wild garlic (Allium vineale) spoils their milk.*

Gar·vey (gär′vē), **Marcus** (1887–1940). Jamaican-born Amer. black leader; founder of Universal Negro Improvement Association, 1914; advocate of racial separatism.

gas[1] (găs) *n.* (pl. **gas·es**). 1. Substance that is neither solid nor liquid, capable of expanding indefinitely when subjected to temperature and pressure changes and completely filling its container. 2. Substance(s) in gaseous state, (i) suitable to be burned for lighting, heating, or cooking, esp. natural gas; (ii) used as anesthetic, esp. in surgery; (iii) (esp. hydrogen or helium) used to inflate balloon etc.; (iv) producing asphyxiating, poisonous, or irritant atmosphere, esp. in warfare; **poison ~**, (coal mining) explosive mixture of firedamp with air. 3. (colloq.) Empty talk, boasting. 4. **~ bag**, bag for holding gas; empty talker; airship's gas container; **~ chamber**, place of execution by gas poisoning; **~ fitter**, one who installs and repairs gas pipes or fixtures and appliances; **gashouse**: see GASWORKS; **gas′light**, light from an incandescent mantle; **gas mantle**: see MANTLE; **gas mask**, device including respirator, worn over the face as protection against poison gas; **gas turbine**, gas-driven turbine, esp. one used to drive air compressor in jet-propelled aircraft; **gas′works, gas′house**, factory producing gas for lighting and heating. **gas** *v.* (**gassed, gas·sing**). 1. Supply, treat, with gas. 2. Project poison gas upon (enemy, place); (pass.) be poisoned with gas. 3. Talk emptily or boastfully. **gas·e·ous** (găs′ēus, găsh′us) *adj.* [wd invented by Van Helmont, Du. chemist, after Gk. *khaos* chaos]

gas[2] (găs) *n.* Gasoline; **~ pedal,**

*The discovery of large deposits of natural **gas,** most of which lie in areas remote from the industries that use it, has necessitated the building of long pipelines. Here sections of pipe are being welded together.*

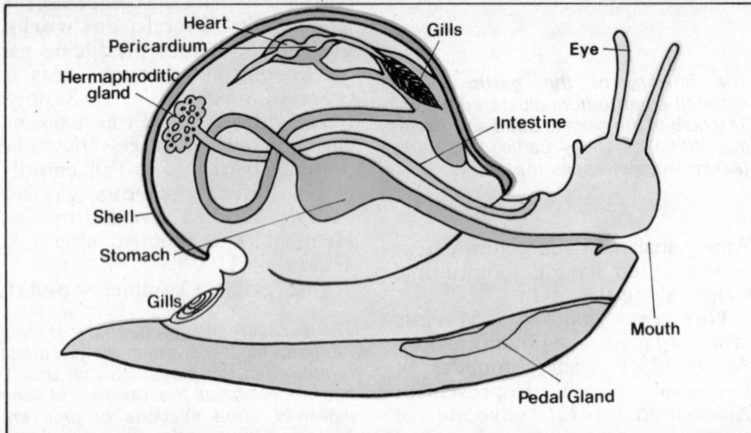

***Gastropods** represent the most numerous class in the mollusk phyllum. Top: Brown-lipped snail (Cepaea nemoralis) has the typical helical shell and broad muscular foot of most gastropods.*

Center: Cross section of a gastropod showing the unsegmented body protected by a strong shell. Bottom, right to left: the abalone inside its shell, outer shell and pearly lining.

pedal that controls supply of gasoline to internal combustion engine; ~ **station**, place where gasoline, oil, and other supplies for motor vehicles are sold and automotive maintenance services provided; filling station; service station; **step on the** ~, accelerate car by pressing harder on gas pedal; (fig.) put on speed, hurry.

Gas·con (găs′kon) *adj.* & *n.* (Native, inhabitant) of Gascony, former province of SW. France; braggart.

gas·con·ade (găskonād′) *n.* & *v.i.* (**-ad·ed, -ad·ing**). Boast.

gash (găsh) *n.* Long and deep slash, cut, or wound; cleft such as might be made by slashing cut; act of making such cut. ~ *v.t.* Make gash in; cut.

Gas·kell (găs′kel), **Mrs. Elizabeth Cleghorn** (1810–65). English novelist; author of *Cranford* etc.

gas·ket (găs′kĭt) *n.* Small cord for securing furled sail to yard; strip of hemp, asbestos, rubber, metal, etc., used for packing piston, forming water- or gas-tight joint in pipe, internal combustion engine, etc.

gas·kin (găs′kĭn) *n.* Hind thigh of horse.

gas·o·hol (găs′ohawl, -hŏl) *n.* Fuel for automobile engines, combining 90% gasoline and 10% alcohol.

gas·o·line, gas·o·lene (găsolēn′, găs′olēn) *ns.* Volatile, inflammable liquid mixture of hydrocarbons obtained by fractional distillation of petroleum and used mainly as a fuel for internal-combustion engines.

gas·om·e·ter (găsŏm′ĭter) *n.* 1. (Brit.) Fuel-gas storage container, esp. a large cylindrical tank. 2. Gas-measuring apparatus.

gasp (găsp, gahsp) *v.* Catch breath, strain *for* air or breath, with open mouth as in exhaustion or astonishment; utter with gasps. ~ *n.* Convulsive catching of breath; **at one's last** ~, at point of death (also fig.). **gasp′ing·ly** *adv.*

Gas·pé (găspā′) **Peninsula.** Peninsula of SE. Quebec, Canada, between Chaleur Bay N. of New Brunswick and the mouth of the St. Lawrence River.

gas·sy (găs′ē) *adj.* (**-si·er, -si·est**). Of, full of, like, gas; (of talk etc.) empty, verbose.

gas·tric (găs′trĭk) *adj.* Of the stomach; ~ **juice**, thin clear acid nearly colorless fluid secreted by certain stomach glands and acting as agent of digestion.

gas·tri·tis (găstrī′tĭs) *n.* Inflammation of the stomach.

gastro-, gastr- *comb. forms.* Of the stomach; **gastroenteri′tis**, inflammation affecting both stomach and intestines; **gastrointes′tinal**, of or pertaining to the stomach and intestines.

*The **gauchos** of South America have pursued an independent, robust and politically active style of life. Here a gaucho, aided by companions, ropes a steer.*

gas·tro·nome (găs'tronōm) *n.* Connoisseur of cookery; gourmet. **gas·tron·o·my** (găstrŏn'omē) *n.* Art and science of good eating. **gas·tron'o·mer, gas·tron'o·mist** *ns.* **gas·tro·nom·ic** (găstronŏm'ĭk), **gas·tro·nom'i·cal** *adjs.* **gas·tro·nom'i·cal·ly** *adv.*

gas·tro·pod (găs'tropŏd) *n.* One of the Gastropoda, a class of mollusks having the locomotive organ placed ventrally (snails, whelks, limpets, etc.).

gas·tru·la (găs'trula) *n.* (pl. **-la**). (biol.) Stage in development of embryo (typically a double-layered sac) produced by migration of cells of BLASTULA into new positions.

gat (găt) *n.* (slang.) Revolver or pistol. [short for GATLING GUN]

gate (gāt) *n.* 1. Opening in wall of city or enclosure, made for entrance and exit and capable of being closed with barrier; means of entrance or exit. 2. Barrier closing opening of wall, wooden or metal etc. framework, solid or of bars or gratings, hung on hinges, turning on pivots, or sliding; contrivance regulating passage of water or gas through a dam or conduit; (photog.) mechanism controlling passage of film behind lens; (in computers) electronic device, signal, etc., controlling passage of current, selecting signals, etc. 3. Number entering by payment at gates to see sports contest, public entertainment, etc.; amount of money thus taken. 4. ~ **crash** (*v.*) (slang) gain entrance (to party, reception, etc.) without invitation or ticket of admission; ~ **crasher** (*n.*); **gate'house** (pl. **-houses**), lodge of park etc.; (hist.) room over city gate often used as prison; room over gate of castle; **gate-leg(ged) table**, folding table with leaves supported on gate-shaped structure, which can be swung back to allow them to hang down; **gate'post**, post on which gate is hung or on which it shuts; **gate'way**, frame of or structure built over gate; any passage by which a region can be entered.

gath·er (gădh'er) *v.* 1. Bring or come together. 2. Pick or harvest (flowers, grain, etc.); pick *up* from ground; infer, deduce (*that*); ~ **way**, (of ship) begin to move. 3. Summon up (energies); gain or recover (breath); summon *up* (thoughts, strength, etc.) for an effort. 4. Draw (garment, brow) together in folds or wrinkles; pucker (part of dress) by running thread through; draw *up* (limbs, person) into smaller compass. 5. Come to a head, develop purulent swelling. **gather** *n.* (usu. pl.) Gathered part of dress. **gath'er·er** *n.* **gath'er·ing** *n.* 1. Assembly; meeting, collection, accumulation. 2. Gather in cloth or a garment.

Gat·ling (găt'lĭng) **gun.** Machine gun with cluster of barrels. [R. J. *Gatling* (1818–1903), inventor]

GATT *abbrev.* General Agreement on Tariffs and Trade (treaty to which 85 countries are parties to promote trade and economic development).

Ga·tun (gahtōōn'). Artificial lake, 164 sq. mi. (425 sq. km), created by the Gatun Dam in the northern Canal Zone, Panama.

gauche (gōsh) *adj.* Tactless; without ease or grace, socially awkward. **gauche'ly** *adv.* **gauche'ness** *n.* **gau·che·rie** (gōsherē') *n.* Gauche manners; a gauche action.

gau·cho (gow'chō) *n.* (pl. **-chos**). Cowboy of South Amer. pampas.

gaud (gawd) *n.* Showy ornament.

gaud·y (gaw'dē) *adj.* (**gaud·i·er, gaud·i·est**). Tastelessly or inappropriately showy. **gaud'i·ly** *adv.* **gaud'i·ness** *n.*

gauge (gāj) *n.* 1. Standard measure to which things must conform, as measure of capacity or contents of barrel, diameter of bullet, thickness of sheet metal, etc.; distance between rails of railroad etc. 2. Graduated instrument measuring force or quantity of rainfall, stream, tide, wind, etc.; instrument for testing and verifying dimensions of tools, wire, etc.; carpenter's adjustable tool for marking parallel lines; (print.) strip regulating depth of margin etc.; means of estimating, criterion, test.

*While President of France, **General de Gaulle** pursued a foreign policy that was often at variance with the wishes of his NATO allies. Here he is shown with a characteristic expression.*

*There are many species of **gazelle.** Most stand between two and three ft high at the shoulder. Grant's gazelle, seen here with its superb ribbed horns, was photographed in Nairobi National Park, Kenya.*

*'The Girl with a Fan' by **Paul Gauguin** shows a lingering influence of the style he adopted in 1888, requiring the use of non-naturalistic color and flat planes. His paintings were always powerfully designed.*

~ *v.t.* (**gauged, gaug·ing**). Measure exactly (esp. objects of standard size, as wire, bolts; depth of liquid content; fluctuating quantities or forces, as rainfall, wind); find capacity or content of (cask etc.) by measurement and calculation; estimate, take measure of (person, character); make uniform, bring to standard size or shape. **gaug′er** *n.*

Gau·guin (gōgăn′), (**Eugène Henri**) **Paul** (1848–1903). French painter; spent the latter part of his life in the South Sea Islands.

Gaul (gawl). 1. Roman province of W. Europe. 2. Native or inhabitant of ancient Gaul; Frenchman.

Gaul·ish (gaw′lĭsh) *adj.* Of Gaul; French. ~ *n.* Celtic language of Gaul.

gaunt (gawnt) *adj.* Lean, haggard; grim or desolate looking. **gaunt′ly** *adv.* **gaunt′ness** *n.*

gaunt·let[1] (gawnt′lĭt) *n.* 1. (hist.) Glove worn as part of armor, usu. of leather covered with steel plates; **fling, throw, down the** ~, issue challenge; **pick, take, up the** ~, accept challenge. 2. Protective glove with long wrist or flaring cuff. **gaunt′let·ed** *adj.*

gaunt·let[2] (gawnt′lĭt, gahnt′-) *n.* **run the** ~, (orig. mil.) undergo punishment of passing between two rows of men who strike one with sticks etc.; (fig.) be subjected to criticism. [Swed. *gatlopp* (*gata* lane, *lopp* course)]

Gauss (gows), **Karl Friedrich** (1777–1855). German mathematician, astronomer, and physicist.

gauss (gows) *n.* Unit of magnetic induction in cgs system, equal to the induction that exerts a force of 1 dyne on each centimeter of a straight wire carrying 1 electromagnetic unit of current when the induction is perpendicular to the wire (abbreviated G). [f. GAUSS]

Gau·ta·ma, Go·ta·ma (gaw′*tama*, gow′-). Family name of the BUDDHA.

gauze (gawz) *n.* Thin transparent fabric of silk, cotton, wire, etc.; slight haze. **gauz′y** *adj.* (**gauz·i·er, gauz·i·est**). **gauz′i·ly** *adv.* **gauz′i·ness** *n.*

gav·el (găv′*el*) *n.* Auctioneer's or judge's mallet or hammer.

ga·vi·al (gā′vēal) *n.* Long-snouted fish-eating crocodilian inhabiting S. Asia.

ga·votte, ga·vot (*ga*vŏt′) *ns.* French 18th c. peasant dance, like minuet but more lively; music for this, in common time.

G.A.W. *abbrev.* Guaranteed annual wage.

gawk (gawk) *n.* Awkward or bashful person. **gawk′i·ly** *adv.* **gawk·y** *adj.* (**gawk·i·er, gawk·i·est**). **gawk** *v.i.* Stare stupidly.

gay (gā) *adj.* 1. Mirthful, light-hearted. 2. Showy, bright-colored. 3. Dissolute, immoral. 4. (slang) Homosexual; ~ **bar**, one frequented primarily by homosexuals; ~ **rights**, claim for equal legal treatment of homosexuals in regard to employment etc. **gai′ly** *adv.* **gay′ness** *n.*

Gay (gā), **John** (1685–1732). English playwright; author of *The Beggar's Opera*.

Gay-Lus·sac (gā*lu*săk′), **Joseph Louis** (1778–1850). French chemist; **~'s Law,** (i) or law of combining volumes, statement that when gases react together there is always a simple numerical relationship between their volumes and that of the products, if gaseous (also called "law of combining volumes"); (ii) = CHARLES'S LAW.

gaz. *abbrev.* Gazette; gazetteer.

Ga·za (gah′*za*, găz′*a*). Mediterranean seaport in the Gaza Strip near SW. Israel; ~ **Strip**, W. Mediterranean coastal area bordering Israel; administered by the United Arab Republic but the subject of territorial dispute.

gaze (gāz) *v.i.* (**gazed, gaz·ing**). Look fixedly. ~ *n.* Intent look. **gaz′er** *n.*

ga·ze·bo (*ga*zē′bō) *n.* (pl. **-bos, -boes**). Structure from which an attractive view may be seen, belvedere, pavilion, etc.

ga·zelle (*ga*zĕl′) *n.* (pl. **-zelles**, collect. **-zelle**). Small graceful

soft-eyed delicately formed antelope esp. of genus *Gazella*, found in Asia and Africa. [Arab. *ḡazāl*]

ga·zette (g*a*zĕt′) *n.* Newspaper; official journal; used often in names of newspapers.

gaz·et·teer (găzetēr′) *n.* Geographical index or dictionary. [f. an early work of this kind, *The Gazetteer's or Newsman's Interpreter*]

G.B. *abbrev.* Great Britain.

G.C.M. *abbrev.* Good Conduct Medal.

G.C.T. *abbrev.* Greenwich Civil Time.

Gd *symbol.* Gadolinium.

Gdansk (gdahnsk, gdănsk). (or German, Danzig) Port city on the Gulf of Danzig in N. Poland.

Ge *symbol.* Germanium.

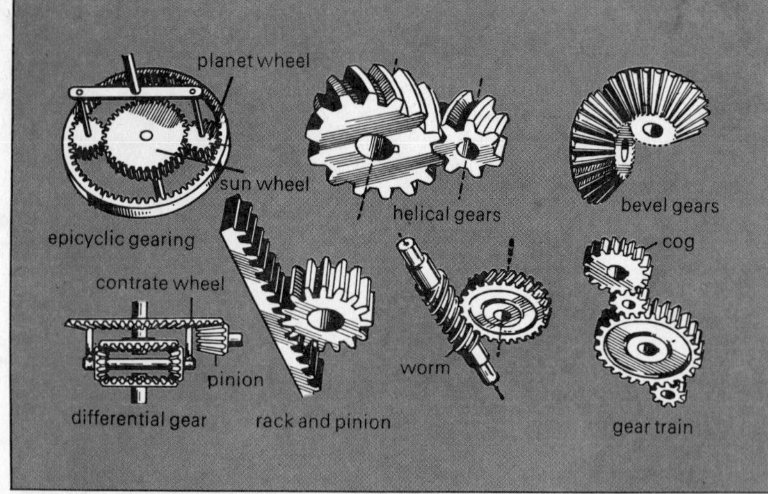

gear (gēr) *n.* 1. Equipment, apparel, etc.; harness of draft animals; apparatus, appliances, tackle, tools. 2. Combination of wheels, levers, etc.; wheels working on one another by teeth etc.; mechanical arrangement connecting motor with its work, usu. effecting a change of relative speed of revolution between driving and driven parts; **in, out of,** ~, in, out of, connection with motor; working, not working; **high, low,** ~, gear by which driven part of vehicle etc. revolves faster, slower, relatively to driving part (so *first, second, third, reverse*, etc. ~). 3. Rigging. 4. **gear′box**, in motor vehicle, the part containing the gear-changing mechanism; transmission; **gear′shift,** mechanism for changing gears in a power transmission unit, esp. in motor vehicle; **gear′wheel,** cogwheel, esp. that in bicycles, that is driven directly by pedals. **gear** *v.* Put (machinery) in gear; provide with gear; (of cogwheel) fit exactly *into*, be in gear *with*; ~ **up**, modify (production, organization) to meet more demanding requirements. **gear′ing** *n.* Manner in which a machine is geared; apparatus for transmission of motion or power from one part of a machine to another, esp. a train of toothed wheels.

geck·o (gĕk′ō) *n.* (**-os, -oes**). Any of numerous species of small lizard (family Gekkonidae), found in warm climates, with peculiar cry and (in some species) adhesive disks on the feet enabling them to climb vertical surfaces. [Malay *gēkoq*,

*Performing a sleeve dance: **geisha** girls of the Geisha Theatre, Kyoto, Japan, keep alive the arts practiced by past geishas, many of whom were influential courtesans.*

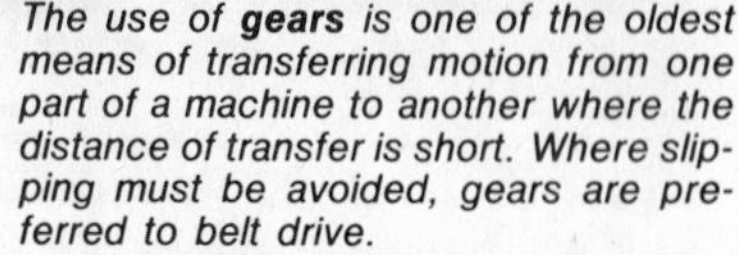

*The use of **gears** is one of the oldest means of transferring motion from one part of a machine to another where the distance of transfer is short. Where slipping must be avoided, gears are preferred to belt drive.*

imitating its cry]

gee[1] (jē) *int.* Word of command to horse etc. to go on, go faster (also ~ **up**), or turn to right. ~ *v.* (**geed, gee·ing**).

gee[2] (jē) *int.* (slang) Exclamation of surprise, discovery, etc., so **gee·whil·li·kens** (jē′hwĭl′ĭkĭnz), **gee-whiz** (jē′hwĭz′).

geese: see GOOSE.

Ge·ez, Ge′ez (gēĕz′, gā-): see ETHIOPIC.

gee·zer (gē′z*e*r) *n.* (slang) Old man, esp. an eccentric one.

ge·fil·te (g*e*fĭl′t*e*) **fish.** (Jewish cookery) Balls of boneless fish mixed with bread crumbs, egg, and seasoning, cooked in broth, and usu. served chilled.

Ge·hen·na (g*e*hĕn′*a*). Hell; place of burning, torment, or misery. [Heb. *gê-hinnōm* valley near Jerusalem where children were burned in sacrifice to Baal or Moloch]

Gei·ger (gī′g*e*r) **counter.** Instrument for detecting and counting ionizing radiation; used esp. for measuring radioactivity. [Hans *Geiger* (1882–1945), German physicist]

gei·sha (gā′sh*a*, gē′-) *n.* (pl. **-sha, -shas**). Japanese girl trained as traditional singer, dancer, and entertainer, esp. for men.

gel (jĕl) *n.* Semisolid colloidal solution. ~ *v.i.* (**gelled, gel·ling**). Form or become a gel.

gel·a·tin, gel·a·tine (jĕl′*a*tĭn) *ns.* Amorphous brittle yellowish transparent substance consisting essentially of protein, extracted from animal skins and bones, used in making soups, jellies, etc., in many photographic processes, and as the principal constituent of glue. **ge·lat·i·nize** (j*e*lăt′ĭnīz, jĕl′*a*t*i*-) *v.t.*

There are about 670 species of **gecko** found in warm climates in many parts of the world. They are small lizards with tongues that they extend to catch insects. All species have eyes without movable lids. Below: A variegated gecko with her eggs.

(**-nized, -niz·ing**). **ge·lat'i·nous** *adj*. Jellylike in consistency etc.; of gelatin.

geld (gĕld) *v.t.* (**geld·ed** or **gelt, geld·ing**). Deprive (usu. male animal) of generative power, castrate, excise testicles of. **geld'-ing** *n*. Gelded horse or other animal.

gel·id (jĕl'ĭd) *adj*. Ice-cold; cool. **gel'id·ly** *adv*.

gem (jĕm) *n*. Precious stone, esp. when cut and polished (also **gem'-stone**); object of great beauty or worth, choicest part *of*, prized possession. ~ *v.t.* (**gemmed, gem·ming**). Adorn (as) with gems.

Ge·ma·ra (gemar̄'*a*, -mōr'*a*). Later (5th c. A.D.) part of the Talmud, Aramaic commentary paragraph by paragraph on the oldest part (Mishnah). [Aram. *gemārā* completion]

Gem·i·ni (jĕm'*inī*, -nē). The Twins, a constellation also called "Castor and Pollux"; 3rd sign [♊] of the zodiac, which the sun enters about May 21. [L., = "twins"]

gem·ma (jĕm'*a*) *n*. (pl. **gem·-mae** pr. jĕm'ē). 1. (bot.) Small cellular body that separates from mother plant and starts new one, esp. in mosses, liverworts, etc. 2. (zool.) = BUD[1] def. 2.

gem·mate (jĕm'āt) *adj*. Having buds, reproducing by gemmation. ~ *v.i.* (**-mat·ed, -mat·ing**). Put forth buds, propagate by gemmation. **gem·ma·tion** (jĕmā'shon) *n*. Act, manner, of budding; arrangement of buds; reproduction by gemmae.

gem·ol·o·gy, gem·mol·o·gy (jĕmŏl'ojē) *ns*. Science or study of gems. **gem·ol'o·gist, gem·mol'-o·gist** *ns*.

ge·müt·lich (gemüt'lĭx) *adj*. Cheerful; cozy; genial.

Gen. *abbrev*. General; Genesis.

gen., genit. *abbrevs*. Genitive.

-gen *suffix*. Forming nouns with sense "that which produces" (*oxygen, hydrogen, antigen*).

gen·darme (zhahn'dar̄m) *n*. Soldier employed in police duties, esp. in France. **gen·dar·me·rie, gen·dar·mer·y** (zhahndar̄'merē) *ns*. Force of gendarmes.

gen·der (jĕn'*der*) *n*. Each of the three (or in some languages two) grammatical kinds, corresponding more or less to distinctions of sex and absence of sex (*masculine, feminine, neuter*), into which nouns are divided according to the modification they may require in words syntactically connected with them; property (in a noun) of belonging to or (in other parts of speech) of having the appropriate form to concord with a specified one of these kinds; division of words into genders as principle of grammatical classification; classification of or by sex; sex.

gene (jēn) *n.* Member of any of the pairs of factors, usu. forming segments of a chromosome at fixed positions relative to each other, that cause the development in offspring of certain characters, one member of each pair being transmitted from each parent, the pairs of genes being on pairs of chromosomes.

ge·ne·a·log·i·cal (jēnēalŏj′ĭkal, jĕnē-) *adj.* Of genealogy; tracing family descent; ~ **chart, tree,** chart like branching tree showing descent of family or of animal species. **ge·ne·a·log′i·cal·ly** *adv.*

ge·ne·al·o·gy (jēnēŏl′ojē, -ăl′-, jĕnē-) *n.* (pl. **-gies**). Account of descent from ancestor by enumeration of intermediate persons; pedigree; investigation of pedigrees; plants' or animals' line of development from earlier forms. **ge·ne·al′o·gist** *n.*

gen·er·a: see GENUS.

gen·er·al (jĕn′eral) *adj.* Completely or approximately universal, not partial or particular; of a whole territory or organization etc.; prevalent, usual; not restricted, not specialized; dealing with main elements, features, etc., with neglect of unimportant details; vague, indefinite; (mil., of officer) above rank of colonel; (appended to titles) chief, head, with unrestricted authority or sphere; **in** ~, generally; in all ordinary cases, barring special exceptions, for the most part; **G~ Assembly**, deliberative and legislative council of certain religious denominations; legislative body of various organizations, states, etc.; deliberative body of the United Nations, consisting of delegations from all members; ~ **delivery**, postal service that delivers mail to the post office, where addressee goes to collect it; ~ **election**, one in which representatives are elected by every state, constituency, etc.; **G~ headquarters**, (abbrev. GHQ) headquarters of commander in chief; ~ **hospital**, hospital for all patients, with full range of services; ~ **post office**, (loosely) chief post office in town etc. (abbreviated G.P.O.); ~ **practice, practitioner**, (work of) doctor who treats cases of all kinds; ~ **semantics**, study of how words and symbols may be used to improve human behavior; ~ **staff**, (mil.) group of officers who assist military commander in planning and administration; ~ **store**, store that retails a variety of merchandise but is not organized in separate departments; ~ **strike**, strike by workers of all or most important trades or industries; strike of working citizens as political protest etc. **general** *n.* 1. (pl.; now rare) General principles, notions, or rules. 2. Chief of certain religious orders, fraternal and charitable organizations, political groups, etc. 3. (mil.) Officer holding a rank above colonel in U.S. Army, Air Force, and Marine Corps, including **brigadier** ~, **lieutenant** ~, and **major** ~; commander of army; tactician, strategist.

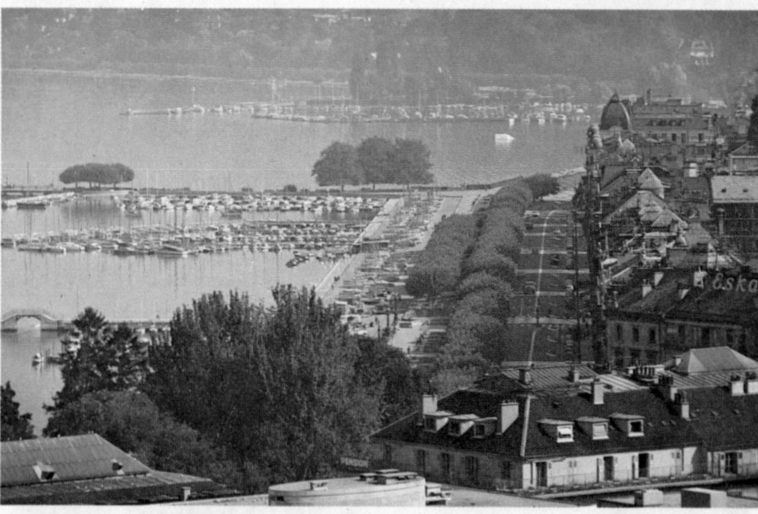

*The Swiss city of **Geneva,** a canton capital, stands on the shores of a lake of the same name. The lake is part of the River Rhône and flows out near the city. The language spoken in this area is mainly French.*

gen·er·al·is·si·mo (jĕneralĭs′imō) *n.* (pl. **-mos**). Commander in chief of the armed forces in certain countries; commander of combined forces.

gen·er·al·i·ty (jĕnerăl′ĭtē) *n.* (pl. **-ties**). 1. Being general, applicability to whole class of instances. 2. Vagueness. 3. General point, principle, law, or statement. 4. Main body, bulk, majority, *of.*

gen·er·al·i·za·tion (jĕneralĭzā′shon) *n.* (esp.) (Forming of) general notion or proposition obtained by induction.

gen·er·al·ize (jĕn′eralīz) *v.* (**-ized, -iz·ing**). 1. Reduce to general laws, form into a general notion, give a general character to, call by a general name; infer (law, conclusion) by induction; base general statement upon (facts etc.); (math., philos.) throw into general form, extend application of; form general notions by abstraction. 2. Make vague or indefinite; use generalities, speak vaguely. 3. Bring into general use. 4. **generalized,** (zool., of organ or structure) suitable for general use, not specialized (e.g. reptile's forelimb as distinct from bird's wing); (of animal) having generalized organs etc.

gen·er·al·ly (jĕn′eralē) *adv.* For the most part, extensively; in a general sense, without regard to particulars; not specially; as a general rule, commonly.

gen·er·al·ship (jĕn′eralshĭp) *n.* Office of a general; strategy, military skill; leadership, skillful management, tact, diplomacy.

gen·er·ate (jĕn′erāt) *v.t.* (**-at·ed, -at·ing**). Bring into existence, produce, evolve; (math., of point, line, surface, conceived as moving) make (line, surface, solid).

gen·er·a·tion (jĕnerā′shon) *n.* 1.

*The camouflage of the **genet** is well adapted to the dappled light that filters through the leaves of the tropical forests in which it lives.*

Procreation, propagation of species, begetting or being begotten; production by natural or artificial process. 2. Offspring of same parent or parents, regarded as single step in descent or pedigree; whole body of persons born about same time; time covered by lives of these; in reckoning historically, interval of time between birth of parents and that of their children; ~ **gap**, differences of opinion between those of different generations. **gen·er·a'tion·al** *adj*.

gen·er·a·tive (jĕn'*e*ratĭv, -ātĭv) *adj*. Of procreation; able to produce, productive. **gen'er·a·tive·ly** *adv*.

gen·er·a·tor (jĕn'erāt*er*) *n*. Begetter; apparatus for producing gases, steam, etc.; machine for converting mechanical into electrical energy, dynamo.

ge·ne·ric (j*e*nĕr'ĭk) *adj*. Characteristic of a genus or class; applied to (any individual of) a large group or class; general, not specific or special; not protected by trademark, esp. ~ **drug** (cf. PROPRIETARY); ~ **name**, (biol.) Latin name (written with capital) indicating the genus to which an animal or plant belongs and preceding the *specific name*, which indicates the species. **ge·ner'i·cal·ly** *adv*.

gen·er·ous (jĕn'*e*r*u*s) *adj*. Magnanimous, noble-minded, not mean or prejudiced; free in giving, munificent; ample, abundant, copious; (of wine, color, etc.) rich and full. **gen'er·ous·ly** *adv*. **gen·er·os·i·ty** (jĕn*e*rŏs'ĭtē) *n*. (pl. **-ties**).

Gen·e·sis (jĕn'*e*sĭs). First book of Old Testament containing account of creation of the world.

gen·e·sis (jĕn'*e*sĭs) *n*. (pl. **-ses** pr. -sēz). Origin; mode of formation or generation. [Gk., = "origin," "creation"]

gen·et (jĕn'ĭt) *n*. (Fur of) kind of civet cat (*Genetta vulgaris*), native of S. Europe, Africa, and W. Asia.

Gen·et (zh*e*nā'), **Jean** (1910–). French dramatist, poet and novelist; author of the novel *The Thief's Journal* and the plays *The Maids, The Blacks*, etc.

ge·net·ic (j*e*nĕt'ĭk) *adj*. Of, in, concerning, origin; of genetics. **ge·net'i·cal·ly** *adv*. **ge·net'ics** *n.pl*. Branch of biology concerned with natural development; study of heredity and variation; **genetic code**, system of storage of genetic information in chromosomes. **ge·net'i·cist** *n*.

Ge·ne·va (j*e*nē'v*a*). City of SW. Switzerland on the Lake of Geneva and the Rhône River; ~ **bands**, strips of white cloth suspended from the front of the collar, worn esp. by the Calvinist and Presbyterian clergy; ~ **Convention**, convention of 1864 and later, governing status of wounded, hospitals, ambulances, etc., in war; ~ **cross**, red Greek cross on a white ground used as a symbol of the Red Cross Society, as a sign of neutrality, and as identification for hospitals etc. in time of war; more commonly called the red cross; ~ **gown**, loose black, wide-sleeved clerical or academic gown, orig. worn by Calvinist clergymen in Geneva; **Lake of** ~ (also called Lake Léman), lake in SW. Switzerland covering 225 sq. mi. (583 sq. km) with southern shore in E. France. **Ge·ne·van** (j*e*nē'v*a*n) *adj*. Of Geneva; (esp.) Calvinistic.

In the 17th century Flemish artists brought to ***genre*** *painting a fresh intimacy and sensitiveness. Jan Vermeer's 'A Woman Reading a Letter' is typical of this rich vein of domestic art.*

Gen·e·vese (jĕn*e*vēz') *adj*. & *n*. (pl. **-vese**). (Native, inhabitant) of Geneva.

Gen·ghis Khan (jĕng'gĭs kahn') (1162–1227). Mongol conqueror whose empire extended from the shores of the Pacific to the northern shores of the Black Sea.

ge·nial[1] (jē'ny*a*l, -nē*a*l) *adj*. 1. Conducive to life or growth; pleasantly warm, mild. 2. Cheering, kindly, sociable. **ge'ni·al·ly** *adv*. **ge·ni·al·i·ty** (jēnēăl'ĭtē) *n*.

ge·ni·al[2] (j*e*nī'*a*l) *adj*. (anat.) Of the chin.

ge·nie (jē'nē) *n*. (pl. **-nies, -ni·i** pr. -nēī). Sprite or goblin of Arabian tales, esp. sprite who does one's bidding; jinnee.

gen·i·tal (jĕn'ĭt*a*l) *adj*. Of animal generation; ~ **stage**, (psychoanalysis) (i) of or pertaining to the focusing of sexual interest on the genitals; (ii) of or pertaining to the adult or final stage of psychosexual development, in which the individual finds satisfaction in the sexual relationship (cf. ANAL; ORAL). **gen'i·tals, gen·i·ta·lia** (jĕnĭtāl'y*a*, -tā'lē*a*) *ns. pl*. Organs of generation, esp. external.

gen·i·tive (jĕn'ĭtĭv) *adj*. (gram.) Of the case (also **possessive**) chiefly denoting relation as source, possessor, etc. ~ *n*. (Word in) genitive case. **gen·i·ti·val** (jĕnĭtī'v*a*l) *adj*.

gen·i·to·u·ri·nar·y (jĕnĭtōŭr'ĭnĕrē) *adj*. Of the genital and urinary organs.

gen·ius (jēn'y*u*s) *n*. (pl. **gen·ius·es** for defs. 1, 3, 4; **gen·i·i** pr. jē'nēī for defs. 1 & 2). 1. (Rom. myth.) Tutelary spirit of person, place, or institution; **good, evil**, ~, mutually opposed spirits by whom every person was supposed to be attended; hence, person powerfully influencing another for good or evil. 2. (Muslim myth.) Demon, supernatural being. 3. Prevalent feeling, opinions, taste, of nation, age, etc.; character, spirit, drift, method, of language, law, etc.; associations, inspirations, *of* a place. 4. Natural ability, special mental endowments; exalted intellectual power, instinctive and extraordinary imaginative, creative, or inventive capacity; person having this.

Gen·nes·a·ret (j*e*nĕs'*a*rĕt), **Lake of**: see GALILEE, Sea of.

Gen·o·a (jĕn'ō*a*). (Ital. *Genova*) City and seaport of NW. Italy on the Ligurian Sea. **Gen·o·ese** (jĕnōēz', -ēs') *adj*. & *n*. (Native, inhabitant) of Genoa.

gen·o·cide (jĕn'*o*sīd) *n*. Planned, systematic extermination of a race, ethnic group, population, etc. **gen·o·ci·dal** (jĕn*o*sī'd*a*l) *adj*.

gen·o·type (jĕn'*o*tīp) *n*. (biol.) Genetic constitution of an organism (cf. PHENOTYPE).

-genous *suffix.* Forming adjectives with sense "produced" (*nitrogenous*).

gen·re (zhahn′re) *n.* Kind, esp. of art or literature; (also ~ **painting**) portrayal of scenes from ordinary life, esp. that of a particular class, e.g. peasants.

gens (jĕnz) *n.* (pl. **gen·tes** pr. jĕn′tēz). 1. (Rom. antiq.) Clan. 2. (anthrop.) Line of descent through father. [L.]

gent (jĕnt) *n.* (colloq.) Gentleman; (slang) **G ~ s,** public toilet for men.

gen·teel (jĕntēl′) *adj.* 1. Well-bred; elegant; refined in manners etc. 2. Affectedly refined. **gen·teel′ly** *adv.*

gen·tian (jĕn′shan) *n.* Plant of the genus *Gentiana*, usu. with conspicuous blue flowers, esp. the **fringed** ~ (*G. crinita*) of eastern N. Amer., with fringed petals; and the **bottle** or **closed** ~ (*G. andrewsii*), with deep-blue blossoms that remain closed; (also ~ **root**) (pharm.) dried rhizome and roots of *G. lutea*, sometimes used as a tonic; ~ **violet**, dye, used as antiseptic. [L. f. *Gentius* king of Illyria]

gen·tile (jĕn′tīl) *adj.* & *n.* (also **G ~**) (Person) not of Jewish faith, esp. a Christian as distinguished from a Jew; (in Mormon use) non-Mormon; heathen, pagan.

gen·til·i·ty (jĕntĭl′ĭtē) *n.* (pl. **-ties**). 1. (now rare) Gentle birth, status of gentleman or lady. 2. Being genteel, esp. affectedly so.

gen·tle (jĕn′tel) *adj.* (**-tler, -tlest**). 1. Wellborn; (her.) having right to bear arms; (of birth, blood, etc.) honorable. 2. (archaic) Generous, noble, courteous. 3. Tame, quiet; easily managed; not stormy, rough, or violent; mild; moderate, gradual; kind, tender. ~ *n.* (f. obs. sense *soft* of *adj.*) Larva of bluebottle fly, used as bait by anglers. ~ *v.t.* (**-tled, -tling**). Break in or handle (horse) gently. **gen′tle·folk, gen′tle·folks** *ns.pl.* Persons of good position and family.

gen·tle·man (jĕn′telman) *n.* (pl. **-men**). 1. (Brit.) Man of gentle birth or entitled to bear arms but not included in nobility (chiefly hist.); man of gentle birth attached to household of sovereign or great person; **~-at-arms**, one of Brit. sovereign's ceremonial bodyguards. 2. Man of chivalrous instincts, fine feelings, and good breeding; man of good social position, man of wealth and leisure; (courteous synonym for) man; **gentleman's ~**, valet; **~'s agreement**, unwritten agreement binding only as a matter of honor; (ironic) illegal or unethical unwritten agreement, as to exclude minority groups from membership in clubs, to inflate prices, etc. **gen′tle·man·like** *adj.* Appropriate to, resembling, a gentleman. **gen′tle·man·ly** *adv.* Feeling, behaving, or looking like a gentleman; befitting a gentleman.

gen·tle·ness (jĕn′telnĭs) *n.* Kindliness, mildness; freedom from severity, violence, suddenness, etc.

gen·tle·wom·an (jĕn′telwŏŏman) *n.* (pl. **-wom·en** pr. -wĭmĭn). Woman of good birth or breeding, lady.

gen·tly (jĕnt′lē) *adv.* Quietly, moderately, softly, slowly; mildly, kindly.

gen·try (jĕn′trē) *n.* 1. (Brit.) People next below nobility in position and birth, esp. the upper middle class. 2. Well-bred people.

gen·u·flect (jĕn′yuflĕkt) *v.i.* Bend the knee, kneel or halfway kneel, esp. in worship or adoration. **gen·u·flec·tion** (jĕnyuflĕk′shon) *n.*

gen·u·ine (jĕn′ūĭn) *adj.* Of the original stock, purebred; really proceeding from its reputed source or author; having the supposed character, not counterfeit, properly so called. **gen′u·ine·ly** *adv.* **gen′u·ine·ness** *n.*

ge·nus (jē′nus) *n.* (pl. **gen·er·a** pr. jĕn′era, **ge·nus·es**). (logic) Class of things including subordinate kinds or species; (biol.) taxonomic category smaller than a family and larger than a species (and usu. containing several species) of animals or plants having common structural characteristics distinct from those of all other groups; (loosely) kind, class, order, tribe.

-geny *comb. form.* Forming nouns with sense of "mode of production or development of" (*ontogeny*).

Geo. *abbrev.* George.

geo- *prefix.* Of Earth (*geochronology, geophysics*).

ge·o·cen·tric (jēōsĕn′trĭk) *adj.* Considered as viewed from Earth's center; having or representing Earth as center. **ge·o·cen′tri·cal·ly** *adv.*

ge·o·chem·is·try (jēōkĕm′ĭstrē)

*The **gentian** family has many varieties that flourish in alpine and northern temperate regions. Below: In Europe the commonest of these flowers is the blue gentian (Gentiana acaulis). Left: Gentiana saponaria.*

A map, drawn in 1617 by Pieter van der Keere, of the Provinces of United Netherlands. Map-making has been to the science of **geography** what printing has been to the realm of literature.

n. Science of the chemical composition of and changes in Earth's crust. **ge·o·chem·i·cal** (jēōkĕm′ĭkal) *adj.*

ge·ode (jē′ōd) *n.* Cavity in an igneous rock that has been partly filled with minerals in well-shaped crystals. **ge·od·ic** (jēŏd′ĭk) *adj.*

ge·od·es·y (jēŏd′ĭsē) *n.* Branch of mathematics dealing with size and shape of Earth or large portions of it. **ge·o·des·ic** (jēodĕs′ĭk) *adj.* Of geodesy; **geodesic dome,** lightweight domelike structure framed with short struts that form a network of polygons; **geodesic line,** shortest possible line joining 2 points on a curved surface. **geodesic** *n.* Geodesic line. **ge·o·det·ic** (jēodĕt′ĭk), **ge·o·det′i·cal** *adjs.* **ge·o·det′i·cal·ly** *adv.*

ge·o·graph·ic (jēogrăf′ĭk), **ge·o·graph·i·cal** (jēogrăf′ĭkal) *adjs.* Of geography; ~ **mile,** 1 minute of longitude measured along the equator, equal to 1,852 m (about 6,076 ft.). **ge·o·graph′i·cal·ly** *adv.*

ge·og·ra·phy (jēŏg′rafē) *n.* (pl. **-phies**). Science of Earth's surface, form, physical features, natural and political divisions, climate, productions, population, etc.; subject matter of geography; treatise or manual of geography; features, arrangements, *of* place. **ge·og′ra·pher** *n.*

ge·o·log·i·cal (jēolŏj′ĭkal), **ge·o·log·ic** (jēolŏj′ĭk) *adjs.* Of geology; ~ **map,** map showing the formations of rock exposed at, or underlying, the surface of a region; ~ **survey,** survey that reports on the geological aspects of a country or area, as water supply, mineral deposits, etc. **ge·o·log′i·cal·ly** *adv.*

ge·ol·o·gy (jēŏl′ojē) *n.* (pl. **-gies**). Science of the formation of Earth, the strata of its crust, and their relations and changes; geological features *of* a district. **ge·ol′o·gist** *n.*

ge·o·man·cy (jē′omănsē) *n.* Divination from figure given by handful of earth thrown down, and hence from figures given by dots made at random. **ge′o·man·cer** *n.* **ge·o·man·tic** (jēomăn′tĭk) *adj.*

ge·o·met·ric (jēomĕt′rĭk), **ge·o·met·ri·cal** (jēomĕt′rĭkal) *adjs.* Of, according to, geometry; (of patterns) rectilinear or curvilinear; ~ **mean,** the *n*th root, generally positive, of the product of *n* factors; ~ **progression,** progression in which each term is a fixed multiple of the preceding one, as 1, 3, 9, 27. **ge·o·met′ri·cal·ly** *adv.*

ge·om·e·trid (jēŏm′etrĭd) *adj.* & *n.* (Member) of the family Geometridae of moths whose larvae move with a looping movement as if measuring the ground, hence called "loopers," "inchworms," or "measuring worms."

ge·om·e·try (jēŏm′etrē) *n.* (pl. **-tries**). Science of properties and relations of magnitudes in space, as lines, surfaces, solids.

ge·o·mor·phol·o·gy (jēōmōrfŏl′ojē) *n.* Branch of geology dealing with the origin, evolution, and configuration of the natural features of Earth's surface. **ge·o·mor·pho·log·i·cal** (jēōmōrfolŏj′ĭkal) *adj.* **ge·o·mor·phol′o·gist** *n.*

*The study of **geophysics** encompasses astronomy, geology, oceanography, seismology, meteorology and several other sciences. Here a technician examines meteorological instruments in a laboratory.*

ge·o·phys·ics (jēōfĭz′ĭks) *n.* Study of the physics of Earth and geological phenomena, including oceanography, seismology, meteorology, etc.; application of methods of physics to the study of Earth. **ge·o·phys′i·cal** *adj.* **ge·o·phys·i·cist** (jēōfĭz′ĭsĭst) *n.*

ge·o·pol·i·tics (jēōpŏl′ĭtĭks) *n. pl.* (treated as sing.) 1. Study of the interrelationship between geography and politics, esp. the effect of geography on a nation's domestic and foreign policies. 2. National policy based on such an interrelationship, esp. Nazi program of expansion aimed at domination of the world by Germany. **ge·o·po·lit·i·cal** (jēōpolĭt′ĭkal) *adj.*

George[1] (jōrj). Name of 6 kings of Gt. Britain: (**the four ~s**, George I–IV, of the House of Hanover, who ruled Gt. Britain from 1714–1830): **George I** (1660–1727), son of the first Elector of Hanover and great-grandson of James I, reigned 1714–27; **George II** (1683–1760), his son, reigned 1727–60; **George III** (1738–1820), grandson of George II, reigned 1760–1820; **George IV** (1762–1830), son of George III; Prince Regent 1811–20; reigned 1820–30; **George V** (1865–1936), son of Edward VII, reigned 1910–36; **George VI** (1895–1952), son of George V and brother of Edward VIII, reigned 1936–52.

*For long the patron saint of England, **St. George** was portrayed slaying evil in devotional paintings. Lack of historical substance in the legends surrounding his name led the Vatican to de-canonize him.*

George[2] (jōrj), **St.** (d. 303). Christian martyr; legendary slayer of a dragon; patron saint of England from 14th c.; **St. ~'s cross**, vertical and horizontal bars crossing in center; (her.) red cross on white ground, the national cross of England.

George·town (jōrj′town). Chief seaport and capital of Guyana.

Geor·gia[1] (jōr′ja). S. Atlantic state of U.S., founded as an English colony in 1733; one of the original 13 states of the Union (1788); capital, Atlanta. [f. name of *George II* of England]

Geor·gia[2] (jōr′ja) (Russ. *Gruziya*) District of the Caucasus, an ancient kingdom now a constituent republic (properly *Georgian Soviet Socialist Republic*) of the U.S.S.R.; capital, Tbilisi (Tiflis).

Geor·gia[3] (jōr′ja), **Strait of.** Pacific Ocean inlet 150 mi. (241 km)

*By the beginning of the Iron Age Mediterranean cultures understood some **geometry.** Craftsmen of the period incorporated geometrical patterns in their work, as in this Cypriot bowl of c. 1000–759 B.C.*

long between Canada and U.S., bounded by Vancouver Island on W., mainland British Columbia on E. and NE., and the state of Washington on the SE.

Geor·gian[1] (jŏr'jan) *adj.* Of the time of the four Georges of Gt. Britain, who ruled from 1714 to 1830.

Geor·gian[2] (jŏr'jan) *adj.* & *n.* 1. (Inhabitant) of the U.S. state of Georgia. 2. (Inhabitant, language) of Georgia in the Caucasus.

ge·ot·ro·pism (jēŏt'ropĭzem) *n.* Relation of plant growth to gravity; **positive ~**, tendency (of roots etc.) to grow towards center of Earth; **negative ~**, tendency (of stems etc.) to grow away from center of Earth. **ge·o·trop·ic** (jēotrŏp'ĭk, -trō'pĭk) *adj.* **ge·o·trop'i·cal·ly** *adv.*

Ger. *abbrev.* German; Germany.

ge·ra·ni·um (jerā'nēum) *n.* Herbaceous plant or shrub of genus *G~* of temperate regions, with red, pink, or purple, or white flowers. [Gk. *geranos* crane because the fruit resembles a crane's bill]

Two Hanoverian British monarchs. Top left: ***George II,*** *painted by John Shackleton, the king's painter. Top right:* ***George III,*** *painted by the German, Johann Zoffany, who worked mostly in England.* ***George V*** *(of the House of Windsor) is portrayed by F. O. Salisbury at a thanksgiving service. The king is with Queen Mary and followed by his sons, Prince Edward and Prince Albert.*

ger·bil, ger·bille (jĕr'bĭl) *ns.* Small burrowing rodent of Africa and Asia with long hind legs, now a popular household pet.

ger·fal·con = GYRFALCON.

ger·i·at·ric (jĕrēăt'rĭk) *adj.* Of, concerning, the health and welfare of old people. **ger·i·at'rics** *n.pl.* Branch of medicine, or of social science, dealing with geriatric problems.

germ (jĕrm) *n.* 1. Portion of organism capable of developing into a new one; embryo of seed; (fig.) seed, rudiment, elementary principle. 2. Microorganism or microbe, esp. one of those capable of causing disease. 3. **~ cell**, cell in body of an organism that is specialized for the purpose of reproduction, and, when united to one of the opposite sex, forms a new individual; gamete; **~ plasm**, nuclear part of germ cell containing hereditary material, genes and chromosomes.

Ger·man (jĕr'man) *adj.* Of Germany or its people or language; **~ Democratic Republic**: see GERMANY; **~ measles**, mild contagious disease (*rubella*) resembling measles; **~ shepherd (dog)** or **~ police dog**, large dog of a breed developed in Germany to herd sheep, wolflike in appearance and having a thick coat that may be black, brownish, black and tan, gray, or brindled, used in police work and as a guide for the blind. **German** *n.* 1. German person. 2. German language, one of the Germanic or Teutonic group, subdivided into **High ~**, group of dialects spoken in south and part of central Germany, and **Low ~**, dialects of N. Germany; **Old High ~**, High German from *c*750 to *c*1100. **Ger'man·ism, Ger'-**

Above right: After the 1939–45 war ***Germany*** *was divided into the Federal Republic of Germany, covering 95,800 sq. miles (excluding W. Berlin), and the German Democratic Republic of 41,500 sq. miles (excluding E. Berlin). Above left: A fairy-tale castle, Neuschwanstein, in Bavaria. Left: The Moselle River, Germany.*

man·ist *ns.*

ger·man (jẽr′man) *adj.* In the fullest sense of parental relationship; **brother-~**, brother having the same parents, own brother; similarly **sister-~**; **cousin-~**, child of one's father's or mother's own brother or sister; first cousin.

ger·man·der (jermăn′der) *n.* Any plant of the genus *Teucrium*, usu. aromatic and with reddish or purplish flowers.

ger·mane (jermān′) *adj.* Relevant, pertinent, *to* the matter or subject. [var. of GERMAN]

Ger·man·ic (jermăn′ĭk) *adj.* Of, pertaining to, the Teutons or their language; German. **~** *n.* Language of the Teutons, esp. in its earliest form, a branch of the Indo-European language family divided into **East ~**, Gothic and some almost lost languages as Burgundian and Vandal; **North ~**, Danish, Norwegian, Swedish, and Icelandic; **West ~**, German, English, Frisian, and Dutch.

ger·ma·ni·um (jermā′nēum) *n.* (chem.) Rare metallic element of grayish-white color; symbol Ge, at. no. 32, at. wt. 72.59. [L. *Germania* Germany]

Ger·man·y (jẽr′manē). Former state of central Europe between the Baltic Sea and the North Sea; in 1871 a confederation of German-speaking states united under the king of Prussia, who became German emperor; this Second Empire (regarded as the successor to the Holy Roman Empire) lasted until the end of World War I; it was followed by the Weimar Republic, then by the Third Empire (Third Reich) under Adolf Hitler, 1933–1945; since World War II the region has been divided between the **Federal Republic of ~** (also called West ~; capital, Bonn) and the **German Democratic Republic** (also called **East Germany**; capital, East Berlin).

ger·mi·cide (jẽr′mĭsīd) *n.* & *adj.* (Substance) having power to destroy (esp. disease) germs. **ger·mi·ci·dal** (jẽrmĭsī′dal) *adj.*

Ger·mi·nal (jẽr′mĭnal; *Fr.* zhĕrmēnăl′) *n.* Month from March 21 to April 19 in the French Revolutionary calendar.

ger·mi·nal (jẽr′mĭnal) *adj.* Of germs, of the nature of a germ; in the earliest stage of development. **ger′mi·nal·ly** *adv.*

ger·mi·nate (jẽr′mĭnāt) *v.* (**-nat·ed, -nat·ing**). Sprout, bud; cause to shoot, produce. **ger·mi·na·tion** (jẽrmĭnā′shon), **ger′mi·na·tor** *ns.* **ger′mi·na·tive** *adj.*

Ge·ron·i·mo (jerŏn′imō) (1829–1909). (Indian name Goyathlay) Amer. Apache Indian chief and leader against whites, 1885–6, in Arizona.

ger·on·toc·ra·cy (jĕrontŏk′rasē) *n.* (pl. **-cies**). Government by, governing body of, elders.

ger·on·tol·o·gy (jĕrontŏl′ojē) *n.* Study of old age, esp. conditions affecting the health of the aged. **ger·on·tol′o·gist** *n.* **ge·ron·to·log·i·cal** (jerŏntolŏj′ĭkal) *adj.*

ger·ry·man·der (jẽr′ĭmănder) *v.* Divide (a state, county, etc.) into voting districts in such a way as to give unfair advantage to one political party in elections. **~** *n.* Such manipulation. [orig. f.

Elbridge *Gerry*, governor of Massachusetts, + (sala)*mander*, from the shape of an election district formed to his advantage in 1812]

Gersh·win (gẽrsh′wĭn), **George** (1898–1937). Amer. composer of popular songs, musical comedies, symphonic jazz and orchestral works; famous for the symphony "Rhapsody in Blue," the folk opera *Porgy and Bess*, etc.; Pulitzer Prize, 1932, for musical comedy *Of Thee I Sing*.

ger·und (jĕr′*u*nd) *n.* 1. Form of Latin verb capable of being construed as noun but able to govern like verb. 2. English word with verbal ending *-ing* functioning as noun.

ge·run·dive (jerŭn′dĭv) *adj.* Of, like, the gerund. ~ *n.* Latin verbal adjective, with same suffix as gerund, expressing idea of fitness or necessity.

Ge·sell (gezĕl′), **Arnold Lucius** (1880–1961). Amer. psychologist, pediatrician and author; founder, 1911, of Yale Clinic of Child Development.

ges·so (jĕs′ō) *n.* Plaster of Paris and glue prepared for use in modeling or as ground for painting.

ge·stalt (g*e*shtahlt′, -shtawlt′) *n.* (pl. **-stal·ten** pr. -shtahl′t*e*n, -shtawl′-, **-stalts**). (psychol.) Shape or structure that as an object of perception forms a specific whole and has properties that cannot be completely deduced from a knowledge of the properties of its parts; chiefly attrib. as ~ or **G~ psychology**, theory that perceptions, reactions, etc. are gestalts. [Ger., = "form," "shape"]

Ge·sta·po (g*e*stah′pō; *Ger.* ge-shtah′pō) *n.* (pl. **-pos**). Nazi secret police. [Ger., initial letters of *Ge*heime *Sta*ats*po*lizei secret state police]

ges·ta·tion (jĕstā′sh*o*n) *n.* Carrying or being carried in womb between conception and birth; this period. **ges·tate** (jĕs′tāt) *v.t.* (**-tat·ed, -tat·ing**).

ges·tic·u·late (jĕstĭk′y*u*lāt) *v.* (**-lat·ed, -lat·ing**). Use expressive motion of limbs or body with or instead of speech; express thus. **ges·tic·u·la·tion** (jĕstĭky*u*lā′sh*o*n), **ges·tic′u·la·tor** *ns.* **ges·tic′u·la·tive, ges·tic′u·la·to·ry** *adjs.*

ges·ture (jĕs′ch*e*r) *n.* 1. Significant movement of limb or body; use of such movements as expression of feeling or rhetorical device. 2. (after Fr. *geste*) Step or move calculated to evoke response from another or convey (esp. friendly) intention. ~ *v.* (**-tured, -tur·ing**). Gesticulate.

get (gĕt) *v.* (**got** pr. gŏt or **got·ten** pr. gŏt′*e*n, **get·ting**). 1. Obtain, produce, by effort or contrivance; earn, gain, win; learn *by heart* or *rote*; obtain as result of calculation; receive as gift, wages, etc.; extract by plea, demand, inquiry, etc.; come to have; contract; have inflicted on one; receive as one's lot or penalty; procure, provide; catch (fish etc.); bring in, carry home (crop); communicate with by telephone; obtain radio signal from; succeed in bringing, placing, etc.; bring into some state; suffer injury etc.; induce, prevail upon (person) *to* do; (of animals) beget; (colloq.) puzzle, catch in argument; understand; enthrall; (in perf.) have; *have got to*, must; ~ **the best** or **worst of it**, be victorious, be defeated; ~ **it**, be punished or reprimanded; understand (something); ~ **on the brain**, be obsessed by; ~ **on one's nerves**, be irritated by; ~ **religion**, become (esp. suddenly) zealous about religion. 2. (intrans.) Succeed in coming or going *to*, *from*, *over*, *here*, etc.; (slang) be off, clear out; (with infin.) acquire habit; come to be (doing); become. 3. (with preps.): ~ **around**, cajole; evade; ~ **at**, get hold of, ascertain; (slang) tamper with, bribe, etc.; (slang) attack; ~ **into**, (colloq.) put on (shoes, clothes); ~ **off**, dismount from; obtain release from (engagement etc.); not remain on; ~ **on**, mount (horse etc.); ~ **over**, surmount (difficulty); recover from (illness, disappointment, or from surprise at); ~ **through**, bring to an end; (of bill etc.) be passed by (legislature); ~ **to**, begin (business etc.). 4. (with advs.): ~ **about**, go from place to place; begin to walk (after illness etc.); ~ **across**, (slang) reach audience, be understood or effective; ~ **along**, advance, meet with success, fare *well*, etc.; move along; manage *without* something; live harmoniously *together*, *with*; ~ **along with you!**, (colloq.) be off!; nonsense!; ~ **away**, escape; start; (imper.) leave!; ~ **back**, come home etc.; recover (lost thing); ~ **one's own back**, have one's revenge; ~ **better, well**, recover from illness; ~ **down**, dismount; depress, weary (person); ~ **in**, be elected; enter car, house, etc.; bring home (crop); fit (work etc.) into given time; succeed in placing (blow); ~

After a period of dormancy a sweet chestnut will ***germinate*** *and the seedling shoot towards light, fed by the energy stored in the endosperm or in the cotyledons. The seedling then obtains food from the soil.*

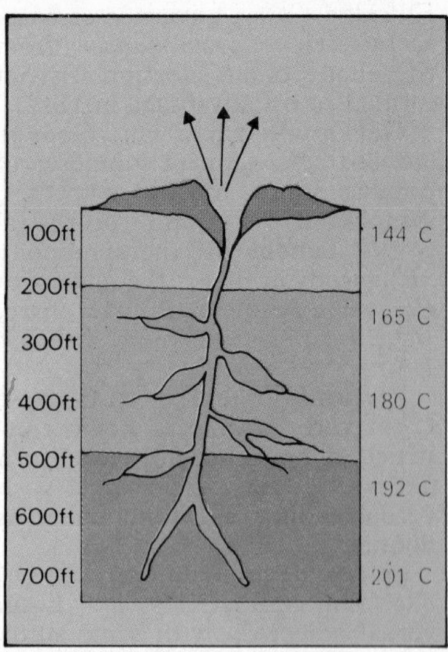

A **geyser** may send a fountain of hot water and mud as high as 200 ft. This is followed by a jet of steam, after which it is dormant for a while. Above: Water flows down the vent, is heated, and releases dissolved gases which force the water out again.

nowhere, achieve nothing; make no progress; ~ **off**, escape; start; be acquitted or pardoned, be let off *with* or *for* specified penalty; procure pardon, acquittal, or slight penalty for (person); ~ **on**, don; advance, make progress; prosper, fare; advance in time or age; ~ **out!** (imper.) leave!; nonsense!; succeed in uttering, publishing, etc.; ~ **out of**, issue or escape from; abandon (habit) gradually; evade doing; elicit (information), obtain (money) from (person); ~ **over**, bring (troublesome task etc.) to an end; get across; ~ **there**, (colloq.) succeed; reach one's goal; ~ **through**, bring to, reach, destination, establish communication, esp. by telephone or radio; (of bill etc.) be passed in a legislature; ~ **together**, collect; meet; ~ **up**, rise, esp. from bed; arrange the appearance of; make rise; produce; work up (emotion etc.); ~ **up steam**, produce enough to work engine etc.; (fig.) work oneself up into action or energy; ~ **wind of**, learn of. 5. (comb.) **get′away**, (esp.) escape of criminals; **get-together**, meeting, social gathering; **get′up**, costume; style; **get-up-and-go**, initiative; ambition. **get′ta·ble, get′a·ble** *adjs.* (esp.) Obtainable; reachable. **get** *n.* (male) animal.

Geth·sem·a·ne (gĕthsĕm′*a*nē). Garden on the Mount of Olives E. of Jerusalem, scene of the agony, betrayal, and arrest of Jesus (Matt. 26).

get·ter (gĕt′*er*) *n.* (esp.) Substance inserted into vacuum to absorb stray gases exuded into it after sealing.

Get·tys·burg (gĕt′ēzberg). Town in S. Pennsylvania, site of a decisive battle (1863) in the Civil War, in which Union forces under Meade defeated the Confederates under Lee; site of ~ **National Military Park**, national cemetery for those killed in the battle; ~ **Address**, speech by Abraham LINCOLN² at dedication of the cemetery, containing the phrase "government of the people, by the people, for the people."

GeV *abbrev.* Gigaelectron volt.

gew·gaw (gū′gaw, gōō′-) *n.* Gaudy plaything or ornament, bauble; paltry showy trifle.

gey·ser (gī′*zer*) *n.* Hot spring (usu. in volcanic area) that spouts water at more or less regular intervals. [*Geysir*, name of a hot spring in Iceland]

Gha·na (gah′*na*, găn′*a*). 1. (hist.) Medieval African kingdom in W. Sudan. 2. W. African country comprising the former Gold Coast colony, Ashanti, the Northern Territories (of the Gold Coast region), and Transvolta-Togoland; member of the British Commonwealth; independent 1957; capital, Accra. **Gha·na·ian** (gah′nē*a*n, găn′ē-) *adj.* & *n.*

ghast·ly (găst′lē, gahst′-) *adj.* (**-li·er, -li·est**). Horrible, frightful; deathlike, pallid; unpleasant, bad. ~ *adv.* (chiefly with adjectives). **ghast′li·ness** *n.*

ghat (gawt) *n.* 1. Either of 2 mountain ranges of S. India, the **Eastern G~** along the Bay of Bengal or the **Western G~** along the Arabian Sea. 2. Mountain pass, defile. 3. Passage or flight of steps leading to riverside. 4. (also **burning** ~) Hindu funeral pyre.

ghee (gē) *n.* Indian buffalo milk butter clarified to resemble oil.

Ghent (gĕnt). Manufacturing and commercial city in NW. central Belgium; Treaty of Ghent, Dec. 24, 1814, signed here ending War of 1812 between U.S. and Great Britain.

gher·kin (ger′kĭn) *n.* Young or small cucumber, used for pickling.

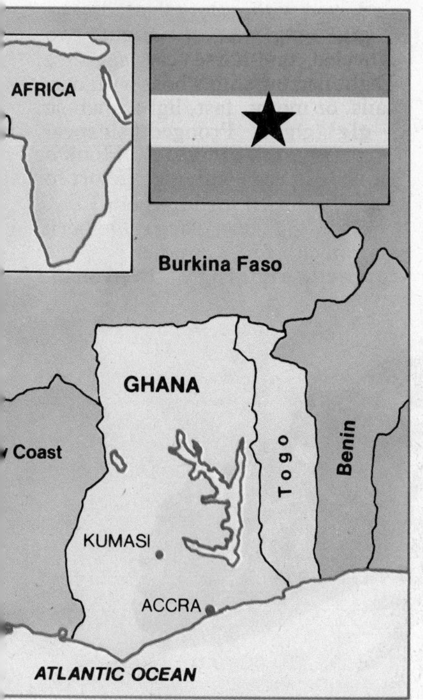

Left: The republic of ***Ghana,*** *populated by 9,600,000, has a land area of about 92,000 sq. miles. The country has rich resources of minerals and hardwoods. Above: The Ashanti, once part of an independent kingdom, are now subjects of Ghana.*

ghet·to (gĕt′ō) *n.* (pl. **-tos, -toes**). Quarter of a European city to which Jews were restricted (hist.); (esp. slum) quarter inhabited predominantly by minority group(s).

Ghi·ber·ti (gēbĕr′tē), **Lorenzo** (1378–1455). Florentine sculptor, painter and goldsmith, noted for his use of perspective and gilt bronze relief, especially in the N. and E. doors of the baptistry of Florence.

ghost (gōst) *n.* 1. Soul or spirit, as principle of life (now only in **give up the ~**, die); Spirit (of God), Holy Ghost. 2. Soul of dead person appearing to living; apparition, specter; emaciated person; shadowy outline or semblance. 3. (optics) Bright spot or secondary image in field of telescope due to defect of lens; (television) faint duplicated image not coinciding with the intended one. 4. (also **ghost-writer**) Person who writes for and gives credit of authorship to employer; **ghost′write** *v.* (**-wrote, -writ·ten, -writ·ing**). 5. **~ town**, town with few or no remaining inhabitants. **ghost** *v.i.* Act, write, as ghost (sense 4). **ghost′ly** *adj.* 1. (archaic) Spiritual; incorporeal; concerned with incorporeal matters. 2. (As) of a ghost, spectral. **ghost′li·ness** *n.*

ghoul (go͞ol) *n.* Spirit supposed in Muslim superstition to prey on corpses; person enjoying what is gruesome. **ghoul′ish** *adj.* **ghoul′ish·ly** *adv.*

GHQ *abbrev.* General Headquarters.

GI (jē′ī′) *n.* & *adj.* (pl. **GI's, GIs**). (colloq.) (Pertaining to) enlisted man in or veteran of U.S. Army (esp. one serving in World War II). [abbrev. of *g*overnment (or *g*eneral) *i*ssue]

G.I., GI, g.i. *abbrevs.* 1. Galvanized iron. 2. Government issue. 3. General issue. 4.

Gastrointestinal.

gi·ant (jī′ant) *n.* 1. Being of human form but superhuman stature; (Gk. myth.) one of the race of beings, sons of Gaea (Earth) and Uranus (Heaven) or Tartarus (Hell) who warred against and were destroyed by the gods. 2. Agency of enormous power; abnormally tall or large person, animal, or plant; person of extraordinary ability, courage, strength, etc. 3. Large diffuse star, as dist. from DWARF. 4. **Giant's Causeway**, group of basaltic columns formed in Tertiary period on N. coast of Antrim, N. Ireland.

gi·ant·ism (jī′antĭzem) *n.* Growth (esp. of bones) to abnormally large size.

Gib. *abbrev.* (colloq.) Gibraltar.

gib·ber (jĭb′er, gĭb′-) *v.i.* Speak fast and inarticulately, chatter like an ape. ~ *n.* Gibbering speech.

gib·ber·ish (jĭb′erĭsh, gĭb′-) *n.* Unintelligible speech, meaningless sounds; blundering or ungrammatical talk.

gib·bet (jĭb′ĭt) *n.* (orig.) Gallows; (later) upright post with arm on which bodies of executed criminals were hung up. ~ *v.t.* (**-bet·ed, -bet·ing**). Put to death by hanging; expose on gibbet; hand up as on gibbet; hold up to infamy or contempt.

gib·bon (gĭb′on) *n.* Long-armed, arboreal tailless ape of genus *Hylobates*, found in SE. Asia.

Gib·bon (gĭb′on), **Edward** (1737–94). English historian; author of *History of the Decline and Fall of the Roman Empire.*

gib·bous (gĭb′us) *adj.* 1. Convex, protuberant; (of moon or planet) having bright part greater than semicircle and less than circle. 2. Humped, hunchbacked. **gib′bous·ly** *adv.* **gib·bos·i·ty** (gĭbŏs′ĭtē) *n.*

gibe (jīb) *v.* (**gibed, gib·ing**). Flout, jeer, mock (*at*). ~ *n.* Taunting remark. **gib′er** *n.* **gib′ing·ly** *adv.*

gib·let (jĭb′lĭt) *n.* usu. *pl.* Heart, liver, gizzard of fowl, as removed before cooking; gizzard.

Gi·bral·tar (jĭbrawl′ter). British self-governing dependency covering 2¼ sq. mi (5.8 sq. km), and town on peninsula of S. Spain on the Strait of Gibraltar at W. entrance to Mediterranean; site of British naval and air base; **Rock of ~**, peninsular headland on the S. central coast of Spain; **Strait of ~**, 36-mi.-long strait connecting the Mediterranean Sea with the Atlantic Ocean and separating Spain and N. Africa. [Arab. *gebel-el-Tarik* hill of Tarik (a Saracen commander of the 8th c.)]

Gib·son[1] (gĭb′son) *n.* Dry martini having a small pickled onion instead of an olive or twisted lemon peel.

Gib·son[2] (gĭb′son), **Charles Dana** (1867–1944). Amer. illustrator; originator of the **Gibson girl**, idealized 1890s Amer. girl dressed in tailored blouse with puffed sleeves and long skirt.

gid·dy (gĭd′ē) *adj.* (**-di·er, -di·est**). Dizzy, disposed to fall, stagger, or spin around; making dizzy; excitable, flighty. **gid′di·ly** *adv.* **gid′di·ness** *n.* **gid′dy** *v.* (**-died, -dy·ing**). Make or become giddy.

Gide (zhēd), **André** (1869–1951). French novelist, critic, and essayist; author of *The Immoralist* etc.; Nobel Prize for literature 1947.

Giel·gud (gĭl′go͝od, gēl′-), **Sir (Arthur) John** (1904–), English actor and director of plays, films, etc.

gift (gĭft) *n.* 1. Giving; voluntary transference of property without recompense. 2. Thing given, present, donation; faculty looked upon as given by heaven etc.; natural endowment, talent; ~ **of gab**, loquacity; ~ **of tongues**: see GLOSSOLALIA. ~**-wrap** (*v.t.*) (**-wrapped** or **wrapt, -wrap·ping**), wrap (gift etc.) decoratively. **gift** *v.t.* Endow with gifts; present *with* as a gift; bestow as gift. **gift′ed** *adj.* (esp.) Naturally endowed with gifts, talented.

gig[1] (gĭg) *n.* 1. Light two-wheeled one-horse carriage. 2. Light narrow ship's boat with oars, sails, or motor; fast, light rowboat.

gig[2] (gĭg) *n.* Pronged fish spear. ~ *v.* (**gigged, gig·ging**). Hook or catch (fish etc.) with gig. [short for *fizgig*, f. Span. *fisga* harpoon]

gig[3] (gĭg) *n.* (slang) Demerit; reprimand for a soldier. ~ *v.* (**gigged, gig·ging**). Reprimand

*The name **gillyflower** is in some countries applied to stocks and pinks as well as to wallflowers. Here are pink gillyflowers (dianthus).*

*The **gila** or gila monster is one of the two poisonous lizard species. When it bites, its poison passes along grooves in its teeth into the wound.*

with a gig; give gig to.

gig[4] (gĭg) *n.* (slang) 1. Engagement for jazz musician(s). 2. Any job or task.

giga- *prefix.* One billion (abbrev. G).

gi·gan·tic (jīgăn′tĭk) *adj.* Giantlike in size, stature, etc.; abnormally large, huge. **gi·gan′ti·cal·ly** *adv.* **gi·gan·tism** (jīgăn′tĭzem, jī′găn-) *n.* Giantism.

gig·gle (gĭg′el) *v.i.* (**-gled, -gling**). Laugh continuously, not uproariously but in manner suggesting foolish levity or uncontrollable amusement. ~ *n.* Giggling laugh. **gig′gler** *n.* **gig′gly** *adj.* (**-gli·er, -gli·est**). **gig′gling·ly** *adv.*

gig·o·lo (jĭg′olō, zhĭg′-) *n.* (pl. **-los**). Man supported by mistress, esp. an older woman; professional dancing partner of woman client.

gigue (zhēg) *n.* (mus.) = JIG.

Gi·la (hē′la) **monster.** Large venomous lizard (*Heloderma suspectum*) of southwestern U.S. and N. Mexico.

gil·bert (gĭl′bert) *n.* (phys.) Unit of magnetomotive force in the cgs system, equivalent to $10 \div 4\pi$ ampere turns. [William *Gilbert* (1540–1603), English physicist]

***Gibraltar** overlooks a strait that links the Mediterranean with the Atlantic, a position which gave the peninsula a strategic importance for many centuries.*

Gil·bert[1] (gĭl′bert), **Sir Humphrey** (1539?–83). English navigator and discoverer; founded (1583) at St. John's, Newfoundland, the first British colony in N. Amer.

Gil·bert[2] (gĭl′bert), **William** (1540–1603). English physician and physicist, known as the "father of electricity"; originated the terms "electric force," "electric attraction," and "magnetic pole."

Gil·bert[3] (gĭl′bert), **William Schwenck** (1836–1911). English librettist of light satiric operas written in collaboration with Arthur Sullivan (Gilbert composed the libretto and Sullivan the music); famous for *H.M.S. Pinafore*, *The Pirates of Penzance*, *The Mikado*, etc.

Gil·bert (gĭl′bert) **Islands:** see KIRIBATI.

gild[1] (gĭld) *v.t.* (**gild·ed** or **gilt, gild·ing**). Cover with thin layer of gold laid on as gold leaf or otherwise; give, esp. deceptive, attractive appearance to; ~ **the lily**, try to improve what is already quite satisfactory. **gild′ing** *n.*

gild[2] = GUILD.

Gil·e·ad (gĭl′ēăd). Mountainous region in ancient Palestine, now NW. Jordan, E. of Jordan River between the Sea of Galilee and the Dead Sea.

gill[1] (gĭl) *n.* (usu. pl.) 1. Respiratory organ(s) in fishes and other water-breathing animals, so arranged that venous blood is exposed to aerating influence of water. 2. Wattles or dewlap of fowl. 3. Vertical radial plates on underside of mushrooms etc. 4. Flesh below person's jaws and ears. ~ *v.t.* Gut (fish); catch (fish) in a ~ **net**, fishnet set vertically in the water to entangle fish by the gills.

gill[2] (jĭl) *n.* Liquid measure = ½ pint.

gil·ly·flow·er, gil·li·flow·er (jĭl′ēflower) *ns.* 1. Any of several plants of the genus *Dianthus*, as the carnation. 2. Any of various other plants having fragrant blooms, including stock and wallflower. [OF. *girofle*, ult. f. Gk. *karuophullon* (*karuon* nut, *phullon* leaf)]

gilt (gĭlt) *adj.*: see GILD[1]. ~ *n.* Gilding; ~**-edged**, having gilded

edges, as the pages of a book; (of securities etc.) reliable, safe (not touched by market fluctuations), orig. Brit. Government stock (from being printed on gilt-edged paper).

gim·bals (jĭm′balz, gĭm′-) *n.pl.* (usu. **gimbal** in comb.) Contrivance, usu. of rings and pivots, for keeping objects such as compass or chronometer horizontal at sea.

gim·crack (jĭm′krăk) *n.* Useless article, knickknack. ~ *adj.* Showy and flimsy, worthless. **gim′crack·er·y** *n.* (pl. **-er·ies**).

gim·let (gĭm′lĭt) *n.* Small boring tool usu. with wooden crosspiece as handle and screw at pointed end; cocktail of vodka or gin, sugar, and lime juice.

gim·mick (gĭm′ĭk) *n.* (slang) Tricky device; device adopted in order to attract attention or publicity. **gim′mick·er·y, gim′mick·ry** *ns.* **gim′mick·y** *adj.*

***Giorgione,** an innovator and leader of Venetian 16th-century painters, used warm colors to create expressive atmosphere in 'The Tempest', in which a nursing woman forms a foreground to the summer storm.*

gimp (gĭmp) *n.* Silk, worsted, or cotton twist with cord or wire running through it; trimming made of this; (slang) limp; (slang) cripple.

gin[1] (jĭn) *n.* 1. Snare, net, trap. 2. Hoisting apparatus, crane; (now usu.) tripod with winch for winding rope; (mining) windlass, drum, etc., for hoisting, pumping, etc. 3. Machine (**cotton** ~) for separating seeds from cotton fibers, esp. type invented by Eli Whitney in 1793. ~ *v.t.* (**ginned, gin·ning**). Remove (seeds from cotton) with a gin.

gin[2] (jĭn) *n.* 1. Strong alcoholic liquor obtained by distilling grain and flavoring with juniper berries. 2. Similar liquor flavored with coriander, aniseed, or other aromatic agent; ~ **mill**, cheap, disreputable tavern; ~ **rummy**, form of rummy in which player with cards totaling less than ten points may end a game.

gin·ger (jĭn′jer) *n.* 1. (Tropical plant, *Zingiber officinale*, with) hot spicy root used as a flavoring and medicine, and preserved in syrup or candied as dessert. 2. Mettle, spirit; liveliness; vigor. 3. Light reddish-yellow color. 4. ~ **ale**, ginger-flavored effervescent soft drink; ~ **beer**, strong ginger ale flavored with fermented ginger, popular in England; **gin′gerbread**, cake made with molasses and

*A male **giraffe** may have a height of 18 ft. Its neck has the same seven vertebrae as other mammals, but those on the giraffe are each 15 inches long. The height is to enable these animals to obtain shoots from trees. Above: To drink from a water-hole a giraffe must spread its forelegs.*

ginger, often cut into shapes, as of a boy or girl, and decorated with colored icing; **gin′gersnap**, thin brittle cookie flavored with ginger and molasses. **ginger** *v.t.* Flavor with ginger. **gin′ger·y** *adj.*

gin·ger·ly (jĭn′*jer*lē) *adv.* & *adj.* With, showing, extreme caution so as to avoid making a noise or injuring oneself or what is touched or stepped on.

ging·ham (gĭng′*am*) *n.* Plain-woven cotton fabric of dyed yarns, often striped or checked. [Malay *ginggang* striped]

gin·gi·val (jĭnjī′*val*, jĭn′*ji*-) *adj.* Of the gums.

gin·gi·vi·tis (jĭn*ji*vī′tĭs) *n.* Inflammation of the gums.

gink·go (gĭng′kō) *n.* (pl. **-goes**). Maidenhair tree (*G~ biloba*) with wedge-shaped leaves and yellow seeds, native to China and cultivated elsewhere esp. because of its resistance to air pollution; the only living species of the order Ginkgoales, which flourished in the Mesozoic era. [Jap., f. Chin. *yin-hing* silver apricot]

gin·seng (jĭn′sĕng) *n.* (Root of) plant (*Panax*) found in N. China, Nepal, Canada, and eastern U.S., having a forked root and believed by some to have medicinal or mystic properties. [Chin. *jên shên* image of man (from forked shape of root)]

Gior·gio·ne (jôrjō′nē). **Giorgio da Castelfranco** (1477–1510), Venetian painter.

Giot·to (jŏt′ō). **Giotto di Bondone** (1266?–1337), Florentine painter, architect, and sculptor.

gip = GYP.

gip·sy = GYPSY.

gi·raffe (*ji*răf′, -rahf′) *n.* (pl. **-raffes**, collect. **-raffe**). African ruminant quadruped with remarkably long neck and forelegs, and tan skin spotted like panther's.

gir·an·dole (jĭr′*and*ōl), **gi·ran·do·la** (*ji*răn′*dola*) *ns.* 1. Revolving display, esp. of firework. 2. Branched candleholder or other support for lights. 3. Earring or pendant with large central stone surrounded by smaller ones.

gird (gẽrd) *v.t.* (**gird·ed** or **girt**, **gird·ing**). Encircle (waist, person as to waist) with belt etc., esp. to confine clothes; equip *with* sword in belt; fasten (sword etc.) on with belt; secure (clothes) on body with girdle or belt; put (cord etc.) *around*; encircle; **~ (up) one's loins**, prepare for action.

gird·er (gẽr′*der*) *n.* Beam supporting joists of floor; iron or steel beam for like use; latticed or other compound structure of steel etc. forming span of bridge, roof, etc.

gir·dle (gẽr′del) *n.* 1. Belt or cord worn around waist; elasticized corset. 2. Something that surrounds like girdle; part of cut gem dividing crown from base and held by the setting; (anat.) bony support for upper and lower limbs (**pelvic ~, pectoral ~**); ring around tree made by removal of bark. ~ *v.t.* (**-dled, -dling**). Surround with girdle; remove ring of bark from (tree), usu. to kill it.

girl (gẽrl) *n.* Female child; young unmarried woman; maidservant; (colloq.) man's sweetheart (also **best ~**); ~ **Friday**: see FRIDAY; **girl′friend**, female friend, esp. boy's or man's usual or preferred female companion; ~ **scout**, member of the **Girl Scouts**, organization founded by Juliette Low in Savannah, Ga., in 1912 to teach girls citizenship and homemaking skills, good personal habits, etc. **girl′hood** *n.* **girl′ish** *adj.* **girl′ish·ly** *adv.* **girl′ish·ness** *n.*

girt (gẽrt): see GIRD.

girth (gẽrth) *n.* 1. Leather or cloth band tightened around body of horse etc. to secure saddle etc. 2. Measurement around any more or less cylindrical thing. ~ *v.t.* Secure (saddle etc.) with girth.

Gis·card d'Es·taing (zhēskär′ dĕstăṅ′) **Valéry** (1926–). President of France 1974–1981.

gis·mo = GIZMO.

gist (jĭst) *n.* Real idea or point, substance or pith of a matter.

give (gĭv) *v.* (**gave, giv·en, giv·ing**). 1. Bestow gratuitously, hand over as present or donation; confer, grant; accord (affection, confidence, etc.); sanction marriage of (daughter etc.). 2. Deliver, hand over, without reference to ownership; put (food etc.) before one; administer (medicine); deliver (message etc.); consign, entrust; pledge, assign as guarantee (*one's word* etc.). 3. Make over in exchange or payment, pay, sell *for* price. 4. Devote, dedicate; addict. 5. Put forth (some action or effort) to affect another; deliver (judgment etc.) authoritatively; provide (party, dinner, etc.) as host. 6. Present, offer (one's hand, arm, etc.); perform or produce (play etc.). 7. Make partaker of; impart, be source of. 8. Allot; grant; assume. 9. Yield as product or result. 10. Cause or allow to have. 11. Collapse; lose firmness, yield to pressure, become relaxed; make room, shrink. 12. (of window etc.) Look, lead, *on, into.* 13. ~ **chase**, start in pursuit; ~ **ear**, listen; ~ **rise to**, occasion; ~ **way**, retire; collapse; be superseded; be dislodged; allow precedence *to*; abandon oneself *to* grief etc. 14. (with adverbs) ~ **away**, transfer by gift; hand over (bride) to bridegroom; betray or expose to ridicule or detection; distribute (prizes); ~ **back**, give (thing) again to its previous owner; ~ **forth**, emit; ~ **in**, yield, cease fighting or arguing; ~ **off**, emit (vapor etc.); ~ **out**, announce; distribute; cease or break down from exhaustion etc.; run short; ~ **over**, hand over; ~ **up**, resign, surrender, part with; deliver (fugitive etc.) into hands of pursuers etc.; abandon *oneself to* a feeling etc.; cease to have to do with; cease from effort; divulge (names of accomplices etc.); pronounce insoluble, renounce hope of. **giv′en** *adj.* ~ **name**, name given to person, hence first name, opp. surname. **giv′er** *n.* **give** *n.* Yielding to pressure, elasticity; springiness, bending, resiliency; **~-and-take**, mutual concession, compromise, exchange of talk; **give′away**, telltale disclosure; sales premium; gift; television program offering prizes to contestants.

*The role of **gladiator** (below) probably derives from the Etruscan custom of holding fights to the death at funerals, though it is mainly associated with such contests in Rome (circa 200 B.C.–400 A.D.)*

Gi·za (gē′za). City in N. Egypt on W. bank of Nile River near Cairo; the Great Pyramids and the Sphinx are 5 mi. to the W.

giz·mo, gis·mo (gĭz′mō) *ns.* (slang) Device; gadget, esp. one without a name.

giz·zard (gĭz′erd) *n.* Bird's second, or muscular, stomach for grinding food after it has been mixed in the first with gastric juice; thickened muscular stomach of some mollusks; (colloq.) stomach; **stick in one's ~**, be unwelcome or unpalatable.

Gk. *abbrev.* Greek.

gla·brous (glā′brus) *adj.* (anat. etc.) Free of hair or down, smooth-skinned.

gla·cé (glăsā′) *adj.* 1. Crusted with a glaze of sugar; candied. 2. Having a glossy, smooth surface. ~ *v.* (**-céed, -cé·ing**).

gla·cial (glā′shal) *adj.* 1. (geol.) Characterized, produced, by the presence or agency of ice; of a period during which the greater part of the N. hemisphere was covered with an ice sheet; ~ **deposit**, formation laid down by the action of ice (e.g. boulder clay, moraine, kame). 2. Resembling ice; bitterly cold. **gla′cial·ly** *adv.*

gla·ci·ate (glā′shēāt) *v.t.* Subject to, mark, polish by, glacial action; cover with a glacier. **gla·ci·a·tion** (glāshēā′shon) *n.*

gla·cier (glā′sher) *n.* Slowly moving mass of ice in high mountain valley formed by accumulation and gradual consolidation of snow on higher ground; **G~ National Park**, region in NW. Montana covering 1,560 sq. mi. (4,040 sq. km) of forests, mountains, glaciers, and lakes designated a national park in 1910.

gla·ci·ol·o·gy (glāshēŏl′ojē) *n.* Science of geological action of ice. **gla·ci·ol′o·gist** *n.*

glad (glăd) *adj.* (**glad·der, glad·dest**). Pleased; marked by, filled with, expressing, joy; giving joy; (of nature etc.) bright, beautiful; ~ **eye**, (slang) amorous glance, ogle; ~ **hand**, (colloq.) hearty welcome, esp. if overdone or insincere; ~ **rags**, (slang) best clothes, esp. evening dress. **glad′ly** *adv.* **glad′ness** *n.* **glad** *v.t.* (**glad·ded, glad·ding**). (archaic) Make glad. **glad′den** *v.t.* **glad′some** *adj.* (poet.) **glad′some·ly** *adv.* **glad′some·ness** *n.*

glade (glād) *n.* Clear open space in forest.

glad·i·a·tor (glăd′ēāter) *n.* 1. In ancient Rome, man armed with sword, club, etc., and forced to fight other men or animals in an arena for the entertainment of spectators. 2. Any person taking part in a public dispute or controversy. **glad·i·a·to·ri·al** (glădēatōr′ēal, -tōr′-) *adj.*

glad·i·o·lus (glădēō′lus) *n.* (pl. **-li** pr. -lī, -lē, **-lus, -lus·es**). Plant of iris family with sword-shaped leaves and spikes of brilliant flowers; many varieties are native to S. Africa. [L. = "little sword"]

Glad·stone (glăd′stōn), **William Ewart** (1809–98). British

*Facing page: Peaking at over 10,000 ft., the **Tasman Glacier**, the longest in New Zealand, flows from the eastern slopes of Mount Cook. Its rate of movement is as high as 20 ins. a day. The area is a popular skiing center.*
Below: Three successive phases in the development of a glacier. When a period of cold climate is prolonged, the snow line gets lower and lower and the glacial elements finally merge, flowing into a single basin.

statesman; 4 times prime minister, 1868–74, 1880–5, 1886, and 1892–1894; ~ **bag**, light leather piece of hand luggage, hinged so as to open flat into 2 approx. equal compartments.

Glag·o·lit·ic (glăgolĭt′ĭk) *adj.* & *n.* (Of) the alphabet, based on Greek minuscules, devised by St. CYRIL[2] and still used in liturgical books of the Uniats in Dalmatia. [Slav. *glagol* word]

glam·our, glam·or (glăm′*er*) *ns.* Alluring beauty or charm; attractive and exciting qualities that arouse envy; (archaic) magic, enchantment. **glam′or·ous, glam′our·ous** *adjs.* **glam′or·ize** *v.t.* (**-ized, -iz·ing**). Make glamorous. **glam·or·i·za·tion** (glămerīzā′shon) *n.* [var. of *grammar* in old sense of magic or necromancy]

glance (glăns, glahns) *v.* (**glanced, glanc·ing**). 1. (of weapon) Glide off object instead of striking it full; (of talk etc.) pass quickly *over*, glide *off* or *from*, subject. 2. (of bright object or light) Flash, dart, gleam; (of eye etc.) cast momentary look, give brief look *at*; ~ **at, over**, read cursorily. **glance** *n.* 1. Swift oblique movement or impact. 2. (Sudden movement producing) flash or gleam; brief look.

gland[1] (glănd) *n.* Organ in animal body secreting the chemical compounds required for a particular function and discharging them (usu. through a duct, but cf. ENDOCRINE ~) into the body or outside it; similar organ in plant. **glan·du·lar** (glăn′j*u*ler), **gland′less** *adjs.*

gland[2] (glănd) *n.* (mech.) Sleeve used to press a packing tight on a piston rod.

glare (glār) *v.* (**glared, glar·ing**). 1. Shine dazzlingly or disagreeably; be overly conspicuous or obtrusive. 2. Look fixedly or fiercely (*at*); express (hate etc.) by look. **glar′ing** *adj.* **glar′ing·ly** *adv.* **glare** *n.* Strong fierce light, oppressive unrelieved sunshine; tawdry brilliance; fierce or fixed look. **glar′y** *adj.* (**glar·i·er, glar·i·est**).

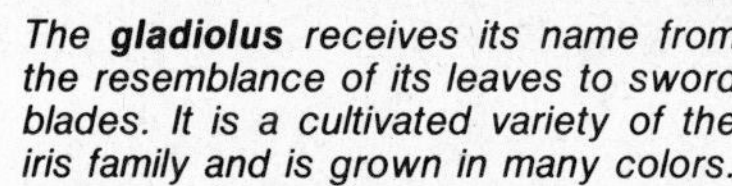

The ***gladiolus*** *receives its name from the resemblance of its leaves to sword blades. It is a cultivated variety of the iris family and is grown in many colors.*

Glas·gow (glăz′gō, glăs′-). Largest city in Scotland, situated in the SW. on the banks of the Clyde.

glass (glăs, glahs) *n.* 1. Noncrystalline solid substance, usu. transparent, lustrous, hard, and brittle, made by fusing sand (silica) with soda or potash, or both, and usu. with other ingredients, as lead oxide; ornaments, utensils, windows, etc., made of this. 2. Glass vessel esp. for drinking, amount of liquid contained in this, drink; sandglass, hourglass; window; plate of glass; looking glass; eyeglass, (pl.) spectacles; glass disk covering watch face; barometer; lens, esp. one that magnifies; (pl.) field or opera glasses. 3. ~ **blower**, one who fashions hollow and other glassware by blowing molten glass; ~ **cutter**, tool for cutting glass, glazier's diamond; ~ **eye**, false eye made of glass; **glass′ware**, articles made of glass; **glass wool**, glass in form of fine fibers for insulation, filters, etc.; **glass′wort**, any of various plants (esp. *Salicornia herbacea* and *Salsola kali*) containing large quantity of alkali, formerly burned to provide potash for glassmaking. **glass** *v.t.* Fit or cover with glass; mirror, reflect. **glass′ful** *n.* (pl. **-fuls**). Amount of fluid held in a glass.

glass·y (glăs′ē, glah′sē) *adj.* (**glass·i·er, glass·i·est**). Having

The craft of the ***glass blower,*** *who collects a ball of molten glass on the end of a tube and blows into it to fashion a hollow vessel, survives. Below: A glass blower at work in Mexico City. Below right: Most glassware is now made in automated factories. Right: The Portland Vase is a 1st-century masterpiece of Roman cameo glass. The vase was made in two layers; the outer one was delicately cut away to leave white images on a dark blue ground. It was smashed in 1845 but brilliantly restored.*

__John Glenn__ was the first U.S. astronaut to orbit the Earth, in space capsule 'Friendship', 1962. Glenn made three orbits in just under five hours, travelling at 17,545 mph.

properties of, resembling, glass; (of eye etc.) lacking fire, dull, fixed. **glass'i·ly** *adv.* **glass'i·ness** *n.*

Glas·we·gian (glăswē'j*a*n, -jē*a*n) *adj.* & *n.* (Native, inhabitant) of Glasgow.

Glau·ber (glow'b*er*), **Johann Rudolf** (1604–68). German chemist and physician; **~'s salt(s)**, sodium sulfate, used in paper and glass manufacturing and as a cathartic.

glau·co·ma (glawkō'm*a*, glow-) *n.* Eye disease characterized by increased tension and hardness of eyeball causing gradual impairment or loss of sight. **glau·co'ma·tous** *adj.*

glau·cous (glaw'k*us*) *adj.* Of dull grayish green or blue; (bot.) covered with bloom as of grapes.

glaze (glāz) *v.* (**glazed, glaz·ing**). 1. Fit (window, picture) with glass. 2. Cover (pottery etc.) with vitreous substance fixed by fusion; overlay (cloth, leather, pastry, etc.) with smooth lustrous coating; cover (eye) with a film; cover (painted surface) with thin coat of transparent color to modify tone; give glassy surface to; become glassy. ~ *n.* Vitreous composition for glazing pottery etc.; anything used to produce glazed or lustrous surface; smooth and glossy surface; thin transparent coat of color laid over another color. **glaz'ing, glaz'er** *ns.*

gla·zier (glā'zh*er*) *n.* One whose trade is to glaze windows.

gleam (glēm) *n.* Subdued or transient light; faint, temporary, or intermittent show *of* some quality etc. ~ *v.i.* Emit gleams, shine with subdued or interrupted brightness.

glean (glēn) *v.* Gather grain left by reapers; collect in small quantities; scrape together (news, facts, etc.). **glean'er, glean'ing** *ns.*

glee (glē) *n.* 1. Unaccompanied part song for three or more male voices, popular in 18th c.; ~ **club**, singing group that performs choral music. 2. Mirth; lively and manifest delight. **glee'ful** *adj.* **glee'ful·ly** *adv.*

glen (glĕn) *n.* (chiefly Sc.) Narrow valley.

Glenn (glĕn), **John H(erschel), Jr.** (1921–). First Amer. astronaut to orbit the Earth, 1962; U.S. senator from Ohio, 1975– .

glib (glĭb) *adj.* (**glib·ber, glib·best**). (of speaker, speech,

Mexican pottery in Calexico, California, showing the diverse and colorful applications of __glaze.__ Glazing serves both aesthetic and practical purposes in pottery.

etc.) Fluent, more talkative than sincere or thoughtful. **glib′ly** *adv.* **glib′ness** *n.*

glide (glīd) *v.* (**glid·ed, glid·ing**). Pass, proceed, by smooth continuous motion; go quietly or stealthily; pass gently or gradually; cause to glide; (aeron.) fly without engine power, fly in glider. ~ *n.* Act of gliding; (mus., phonet., etc.) succession of sounds, sound, made in passing from one note to another, or from one speech sound to another. **glid′er** *n.* 1. Person or thing that glides. 2. Aircraft like an airplane, but not having an engine and depending upon air currents for flight. 3. Swinging couch, generally used on porches, hung from a vertical framework with springs on links.

glim·mer (glĭm′*er*) *v.i.* Shine faintly or intermittently. ~ *n.* Feeble or wavering light; faint gleam *of* hope etc.; glimpse, half view. **glim′mer·ing** *n.*

glimpse (glĭmps) *n.* Faint and transient appearance; momentary or imperfect view of. ~ *v.t.* (**glimpsed, glimps·ing**). Catch glimpse of, see faintly or partly.

glint (glĭnt) *v.* & *n.* (Make) flash, glitter, sparkle.

glis·sade (glĭsahd′, -sād′) *n.* Controlled sliding down steep slope (esp. of ice or snow); dance step consisting of glide to right or left. ~ *v.i.* (**-sad·ed, -sad·ing**). Perform glissade.

*The man-powered launches of **gliders** in the 1890s have been superseded. Gliders now may be launched by towing them behind an aeroplane or catapulting them from the ground using an elastic rope.*

glis·san·do (glĭsahn′dō) *adv.*, *n.* (pl. **-di** pr. -dē, **-dos**), & *adj.* (music) Effect produced by blending one tone into the next, as by sliding tip or back of finger over piano keys or harp strings. [Italianized form of Fr. *glissant*, f. *glisser* slide]

glis·ten (glĭs′*en*) *v.i.* Shine fitfully; glitter, sparkle. ~ *n.*

glit·ter (glĭt′*er*) *v.i.* Shine with brilliant tremulous light, gleam, sparkle; be showy or splendid (*with* jewels etc.). ~ *n.*

gloam·ing (glō′mĭng) *n.* (chiefly Sc. or poet.) Evening twilight.

gloat (glōt) *v.i.* Feast eyes or mind lustfully, avariciously, malignantly, etc., *on* or *over*. **gloat′ing·ly** *adv.*

glob (glŏb) *n.* 1. Small drop or globule of something. 2. Rather rounded lump or mass, as of grease, clay, pudding, etc.

glob·al (glō′b*a*l) *adj.* Of the whole of a group of items, categories, etc.; of, extending over, the whole world; spherical. **glob′al·ism** *n.* Policy, attitude, etc. that encompasses the needs of the whole world rather than those of single nations. **glob′al·ist** *n.* **glob′al·ly** *adv.*

globe (glōb) *n.* Spherical body; Earth; spherical chart of Earth (**terrestrial** ~) or the constellations (**celestial** ~); golden orb as emblem of sovereignty; approximately spherical glass vessel, esp. electric light bulb or fishbowl; **globe′fish**, tropical fish (species of Tetraodontidae) able to inflate itself into globular shape; **globe′-flower**, plant (*Trollius laxus*) of family Ranunculaceae with round yellow flowers; **G~ Theatre**, London theater where many of Shakespeare's plays were originally produced; **~-trotting**, traveling through foreign countries for sightseeing; hence, **globetrotter**. **globe** *v.* (**globed, glob·ing**). Make, become, globular. **glo·boid** (glō′boid) *adj.* & *n.* **glo·bose** (glō′bōs, glōbōs′) *adj.* **glo·bos·i·ty** (glōbŏs′ĭtē) *n.*

glob·u·lar (glŏb′y*u*ler) *adj.* Globe-shaped, spherical; composed of globules. **glob′u·lar·ly** *adv.*

glob·ule (glŏb′ūl) *n.* Small spherical body, esp. of liquid; drop.

glob·u·lin (glŏb′y*u*lĭn) *n.* Protein found in animal or plant tissue.

glock·en·spiel (glŏk′*e*nshpēl, -spēl) *n.* Musical instrument, series of tuned metal bars played with hammers. [Ger., = "bell play"]

gloom (gloom) *n.* Darkness, obscurity; melancholy, despondency. **gloom′y** *adj.* (**gloom·i·er, gloom·i·est**). **gloom′i·ly** *adv.*

*The **globe-flower** grows wild in the meadows and marshes of northern temperate lands, and the species (Trollius europaeus) is cultivated in European and American gardens.*

*Native to the West Indies and tropical America, the **gloxinia** is cultivated as a pot plant for the beauty of its dark foliage as well as its richly coloured flowers. Above right: (Sinningia speciosa).*

gloom'i·ness *n.* **gloom** *v.i.* (**gloomed, gloom·ing**) Look or be gloomy.

glop (glŏp) *n.* (colloq.) Liquid or viscous substance, esp. unattractive food.

glo·ri·a (glōr'ēa, glōr'ēa) *n.* 1. (short for **G~ Patri**) Doxology beginning "Glory be to the Father"; **G~ in excelsis Deo**, doxology beginning "Glory be to God on high." 2. Aureole, halo. [L.]

glo·ri·fy (glōr'ĭfī, glōr'-) *v.t.* (**-fied, -fy·ing**). 1. Make glorious, exalt to the glory of heaven; invest with radiance; transform into something more splendid, invest (common or inferior thing) with charm or beauty. 2. Extol, laud. **glo·ri·fi·ca·tion** (glōrĭfĭkā'shon, glōr-) *n.*

glo·ri·ous (glōr'ēus, glōr'-) *adj.* Possessing glory, illustrious; conferring glory, honorable; splendid, excellent. **glo'ri·ous·ly** *adv.*

glo·ry (glōr'ē, glōr'ē) *n.* (pl. **-ries**). 1. Exalted renown, honorable fame; subject for boasting, special distinction, ornament, pride. 2. Adoring praise and thanksgiving. 3. Resplendent majesty, beauty, or magnificence; effulgence of heavenly light; imagined unearthly beauty; bliss and splendor of heaven. 4. State of exultation, prosperity, etc. 5. Circle of light around head or figure of deity or saint, aureole, halo. ~ *v.i.* (**-ried, -ry·ing**). Exult, pride oneself, *in*.

gloss[1] (glŏs, glaws) *n.* Word inserted between lines or in margin to explain word in text; comment, explanation, interpretation, paraphrase; misrepresentation of another's words; glossary, interlinear translation, or set of notes. ~ *v.* Insert glosses in (text etc.); write glosses; make comments, esp. unfavorable ones; read different sense into, explain away.

gloss[2] (glŏs, glaws) *n.* Surface shininess or luster; deceptive appearance, fair outside. ~ *v.t.* Make glossy; give specious appearance to (freq. *over*). **gloss'y** *adj.* (**gloss·i·er, gloss·i·est**). **gloss'i·ly** *adv.* **gloss'i·ness** *n.*

glos·sa·ry (glŏs'erē, glaw'serē) *n.* (pl. **-ries**). Collection of glosses; list and explanations of abstruse, obsolete, dialectal, or technical terms, partial dictionary. **glos·sar·i·al** (glŏsār'ēal, glaw-) *adj.* **glos'sar·ist** *n.*

glos·so·la·li·a (glŏsolā'lēa, glaw-) *n.* 1. Gift of tongues: see TONGUE. 2. Nonsense speech, esp. in some kinds of schizophrenia.

glot·tal (glŏt'al) *adj.* Of, produced in, the glottis; ~ **stop**, speech sound produced by sudden explosive release of breath from behind the closed glottis.

glot·tis (glŏt'ĭs) *n.* (pl. **glot·tis·es, glot·ti·des** pr. glŏt'ĭdēz). Opening at upper part of windpipe and between vocal cords, affecting modulation of voice by contracting or dilating.

Glouces·ter (glŏs'ter, glaws'-). Fishing port and summer resort 27 mi. (43 km) NE. of Boston on coast of Cape Ann, NE. Massachusetts.

glove (glŭv) *n.* Covering of leather, cotton, silk, wool, etc., for the hand, usu. with separated fingers; padded glove for boxing. ~ *v.t.* (**gloved, glov·ing**). Provide with gloves. **glov'er** *n.* Maker or seller of gloves.

glow (glō) *v.i.* Be heated to incandescence, throw out light and heat without flame; shine like thing intensely heated; show warm color; burn with bodily heat or emotional fervor. ~ *n.* Glowing state; brightness and warmth of color; ardor, passion. **glow'ing·ly** *adv.*

glow·er (glow'er) *v.i.* Stare, scowl (*at*). **glow'er·ing·ly** *adv.*

glow·worm (glō'werm) *n.* Any of various wingless insects or larvae of the Lampyridae family that emit greenish luminescence, esp. the female or larva of the firefly.

glox·in·i·a (glŏksĭn'ēa) *n.* Tropical S. Amer. plant with large bell-shaped flowers. [Benjamin Peter *Gloxin*, 18th-c. Ger. botanist]

Gluck (glo͝ok), **Christoph Willibald von** (1714–87). Bavarian composer of operas, of which *Orpheus and Eurydice* is the most famous.

glu·cose (glōō′kōs) *n.* Dextrose, grape sugar ($C_6H_{12}O_6$), occurring in many plant and fruit juices, in animal tissue fluids, and in blood.

glue (glōō) *n.* Viscous adhesive substance obtained from the hides, bones, and other waste parts of animals by boiling with suitable solvents; any similar adhesive substance; ~ **sniffing**, inhalation of fumes of plastic cement as narcotic. **glue** *v.t.* (**glued, glu·ing**). Fasten or join (as) with glue; attach tightly or closely. **glue′y** *adj.* (**glu·i·er, glu·i·est**).

glum (glŭm) *adj.* (**glum·mer, glum·mest**). Sullen, looking dejected or displeased. **glum′ly** *adv.* **glum′ness** *n.*

glut (glŭt) *v.t.* (**glut·ted, glut·ting**). Feed (person, stomach) or indulge (appetite, desire) to the full, overload with food; satiate, cloy; choke up, fill to excess; overstock (market) with goods. ~ *n.* Full indulgence; one's fill, surfeit; supply in excess of demand.

glu·te·al (glōō′tēal, glōōtē′-) *adj.* ~ **muscle**, one of the three large muscles (*gluteus maximus, medius, minimus*) forming buttock and serving to move thigh in man.

glu·ten (glōō′ten) *n.* Nitrogenous part of flour, remaining as viscid substance when starch is washed out. **glu·ti·nos·i·ty** (glōōtinŏs′ĭtē) *n.* **glu′ti·nous** *adj.* Viscid, sticky. **glu′ti·nous·ly** *adv.* **glu′ti·nous·ness** *n.*

*The wolverine (Gulo gulo) is a **glutton** and its zoological name is derived from its voracious habits. These animals are related to the weasels but are much larger.*

glut·ton (glŭt′en) *n.* 1. Excessive eater, gormandizer; (fig.) person with excessive appetite *for* some activity etc. 2. (Brit.) = WOLVERINE. **glut′ton·ize** *v.i.* (**-ized, -iz·ing**). **glut′ton·ous** *adj.* **glut′ton·ous·ly** *adv.* **glut′ton·y** *n.* (pl. **-ton·ies**).

glyc·er·ide (glĭs′erīd) *n.* (chem.) Ester of glycerin.

glyc·er·in (glĭs′erĭn), **glyc·er·ine** (glĭs′erĭn, -erēn) *ns.* Colorless sweet viscous liquid obtained as a by-product in the conversion of animal and vegetable oils and fats into soap; used as ointment, as vehicle for drugs, in manufacture of explosives, etc.

gly·co·gen (glī′kojen) *n.* Reserve carbohydrate $(C_6H_{10}O_5)_n$ of the animal cell, into which sugar is converted by insulin. **gly·co·gen·ic** (glīkojĕn′ĭk) *adj.*

gly·col (glī′kōl, -kawl, -kŏl) *n.* Any aliphatic dihydric alcohol, esp. ethylene glycol (see ETHYLENE). **gly·col·ic** (glīkŏl′ĭk) *adj.*

gm. *abbrev.* Gram(s).

G-man (jē′măn) *n.* (pl. **-men** pr. -mĕn). Agent of the Federal Bureau of Investigation. ["G" = "government"]

GMT, G.M.T. *abbrevs.* Greenwich mean time.

gnarled (năr̄ld) *adj.* (of tree) Covered with protuberances; twisted, rugged, knotted, like an old tree.

gnash (năsh) *v.* Grind, grind teeth; (of teeth) strike together.

gnat (năt) *n.* Any of various

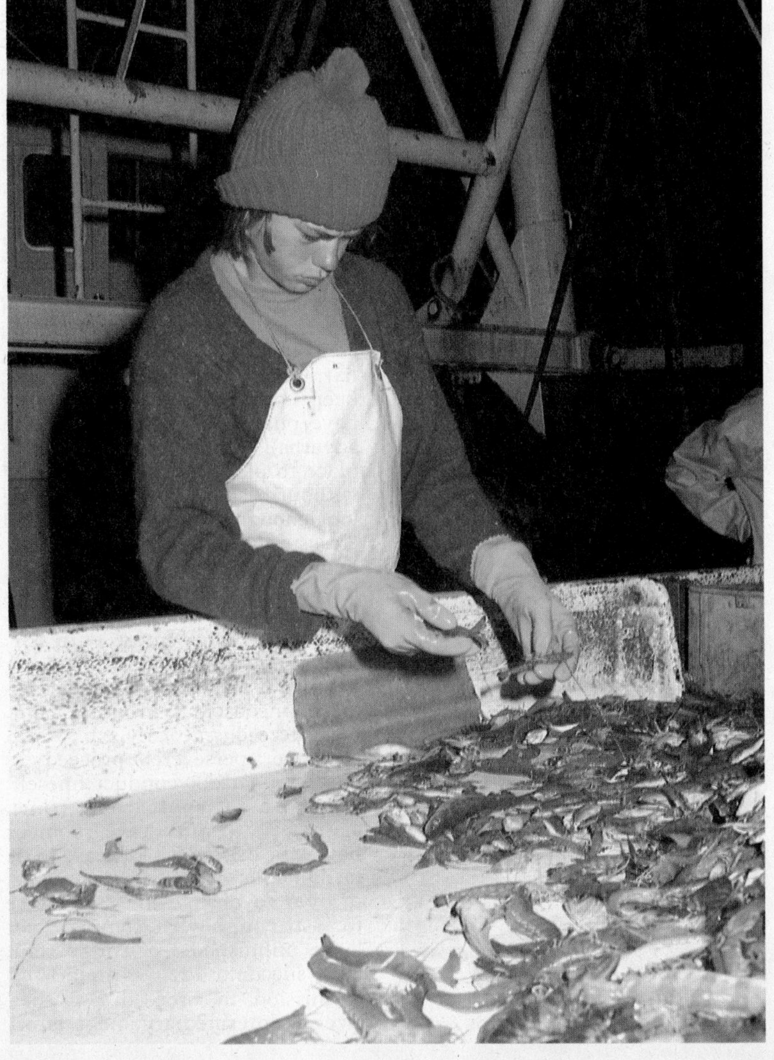

***Gloves** come in a wide variety of styles, and each is better suited to one job than another. Some are purely for dress; some serve to keep the hands warm; and here they provide protection from cuts.*

*The mountain **goat** is known for its hardiness and great agility. Like most goats it prefers an arid climate but will live in wet temperate regions quite happily.*

small 2-winged insects, esp. those that bite.

gnaw (naw) *v.* Bite persistently, wear away thus; (of pain etc.) corrode, waste away, consume, torture. **gnaw'er** *n.* **gnaw'ing·ly** *adv.*

gneiss (nīs) *n.* (geol.) Coarse-grained metamorphic rock in which the mineral grains are arranged in roughly parallel bands, usu. containing feldspar and a dark mineral and sometimes quartz.

gnome[1] (nōm) *n.* Maxim, aphorism. **gno'mic** *adj.* Of, consisting of, using, aphorisms.

gnome[2] (nōm) *n.* 1. (myth.) Supernatural dwarfish being of subterranean race guarding treasures of the earth; goblin, dwarf. 2. (colloq.) International (esp. Swiss) financier, esp. in **~s of Zurich** (with implication of sinister influence). **gnomish** (nō'mĭsh) *adj.* [f. mod. L. *gnomus* invented by Paracelsus]

gno·sis (nō'sĭs) *n.* Special knowledge of spiritual mysteries; Gnosticism.

-gnosis *comb. form.* Knowledge, recognition (*diagnosis, prognosis*).

gnos·tic (nŏs'tĭk), **gnos·ti·cal** (nŏs'tĭkal) *adjs.* Relating to intellectual or spiritual knowledge; **G~**, of the Gnostics, occult, mystic. **Gnos'tic** *n.* (hist.) Member of heretical sects of early Christians claiming to have superior knowledge of spiritual things, and interpreting sacred writings by a mystic philosophy. **Gnos·ti·cism** (nŏs'tĭsĭzem) *n.*

GNP *abbrev.* Gross national product.

gnu (noo, nū) *n.* (pl. **gnus**, collect. **gnu**). African quadruped of genus *Connochaetes*, of antelope family but resembling ox or buffalo; wildebeest.

go[1] (gō) *v.* (**went** pr. wĕnt, **gone** pr. gawn, gŏn, **go·ing**). 1. Start, depart, move, continue moving, from some place, position, time, etc. (often not specified if obvious); begin motion; travel, proceed. 2. (of line etc.) Lie, point, in certain direction. 3. Be moving, acting, in working order. 4. Make specified motion. 5. (of time) Pass, elapse. 6. (of document etc.) Have specified tenor. 7. (of verse etc.) Be adaptable *to* a tune. 8. (of events) Turn out *well, badly*, etc.; (colloq.) be permitted. 9. Get away *free, unpunished*, etc. 10. Be sold *for* sum. 11. (of money) Be spent for goods. 12. Be relinquished, abolished, or lost; die (esp. in past part.). 13. Be kept or put in certain place. 14. Reach, extend, penetrate. 15. Be allotted; tend. 16. (of number) Be capable of being contained in another either without

*The **goblet** has long been the object of elaborate workmanship. The two-handled example illustrated here was fashioned in silver gilt by Jules Barbe in the late 19th century.*

remainder or simply. 17. Pass into a (esp. undesirable) condition. 18. Bid, offer. 19. (phrases): **going to**, preparing or intending to; about to; **gone**, dead, lost, undone; **gone on**, (colloq.) infatuated with; **far gone**, in advanced stage (of disease etc.), deeply engaged or entangled. 20. (with prepositions): **~ about**, set to work at; **~ at**, attack, take in hand energetically; **~ behind**, seek out, examine grounds of (decision etc.); **~ by**, be guided by; **~ for**, fetch; be accounted as; strive to attain; be applicable to; (colloq.) be infatuated with; show interest in; (colloq.) attack; **~ into**, enter (profession etc.); take part in; investigate; **~ over**, inspect details of; rehearse, retouch; **~ through**, discuss in detail; scrutinize; perform (ceremony etc.); undergo; (of book) be published successively in (so many editions); **~ with**, be concomitant of, be associated with; harmonize with, match; (colloq.) keep company; **~ without**, not have, put up with want of. 21. (with adverbs): **~ about**, move from place to place; **~ ahead**, proceed without hesitation; **~ around**, be long enough to encompass; (of food etc.) suffice for whole party etc.; **~ around with**, (colloq.) date frequently; **~ by**, pass; **~ down**, (of ship) sink; (colloq.) find acceptance *with*; **~ in**, enter; **~ in for**, take as one's pursuit, style, etc.; **~ off**, leave the stage; explode; become unconscious in sleep, faint, etc.; succeed *well, badly*, etc.; **~ on**, continue, persevere; proceed as next step *to* do; conduct oneself; **going on to**, approaching (time, age, etc.); **~ out**, leave room or house; be extinguished; cease to be fashionable; (of workmen) strike; **~ over to**, change one's allegiance to; **~ through with**, complete, not leave unfinished; **~ under**, fail, sink, succumb. 22. **~-ahead** (*n.*) permission to proceed; **~-between**, intermediary, negotiator;

The **go-cart** is a popular hobby for children and, in its simplest form, is quite easy to make. Races add to the pleasure. Modified, motor-driven versions are also available.

*The once numerous herds of **gnu** have declined greatly. The smaller white-tailed species is now domesticated but the slightly larger brindled gnu is found in wild herds.*

~-cart, small wagon for children to ride in or to pull; light framework on casters for helping children learn to walk; handcart; small, low, racing and recreational vehicle, consisting of a framework on wheels with a driver's seat, motor, and steering wheel; **~-getter**, active, ambitious person. **go** *n.* (pl. **goes**). 1. Act of going. 2. Mettle, dash, animation. 3. Turn at doing something; attempt *at*. 4. **it's no ~**, nothing can be done; **on the ~**, in motion.

go[2] (gō) *n.* (also **I-go**) Japanese game of territorial possession, using a board of 19 parallel lines intersecting 19 others at right angles, creating 361 points of intersection on which the players' pieces, 361 stones, are placed and on which the game is played.

Go·a (gō′*a*). District on W. coast of India, administered (with Daman and Diu) by India; capital, Panaji. **Go·a·nese** (gō*a*nēz′, -nēs′) *adj.* & *n.*

goad (gōd) *n.* Spiked stick used for prodding cattle; thing that torments, incites, or stimulates. ~ *v.t.* Urge with goad; irritate; instigate, drive (*on*), by annoyance.

goal (gōl) *n.* 1. Finish line of race; object of effort or ambition; destination. 2. Posts between which ball is to be driven, kicked, etc. at soccer, football, and other games; points won by doing this; **goal′keeper, goal′tender, goal′-ie,** (soccer etc.) player stationed to protect goal; **goal line**, line (at either end of playing field) in center of which goal posts are placed.

goat (gōt) *n.* Hardy usu. horned and bearded ruminant quadruped (genus *Capra*); licentious person; fool; scapegoat; **get one's ~**, irritate a person; **the G~**: see CAPRICORN; **goat′herd**, one who tends goats; **goats′beard**, plant (*Tragopogon pratensis*), with yellow flowers; (*Aruncus dioicus*) tall plant with small white flowers; **goat′-skin**, (garment, bottle, made of) skin of goat; **goat′sucker**, any of several birds of the family Caprimulgidae, including the nighthawk and whippoorwill (formerly believed to suck the milk of goats).

goat·ee (gōtē′) *n.* Small beard on chin resembling goat's beard.

gob[1] (gŏb) *n.* (colloq.) Small lump.

gob[2] (gŏb) *n.* (colloq.) Sailor in the U.S. Navy.

gob·ble[1] (gŏb′*el*) *v.* (**-bled, -bling**). Eat hurriedly and noisily. **gob′bler**[1] *n.*

gob·ble[2] (gŏb′*el*) *v.i.* (**-bled, -bling**). (of male turkey) Make characteristic sound in throat. **gob′bler**[2] *n.* Male turkey.

gob·ble·dy·gook, gob·ble·de·gook (gŏb′*el*dēgo͝ok) *ns.* Pretentious and unintelligible jargon and circumlocution, esp. in bureaucratic writing.

Gob·e·lin (gŏb′*e*lĭn, gō′b*e*-) *adj.* Of, made at, the French government-owned tapestry factory of the Gobelins in Paris, orig. workshops owned by a 15th-c. family of dyers named Gobelin. ~ *n.* Tapestry of a kind woven there.

Go·bi (gō′bē) **Desert.** Desert in E. central Asia covering 500,000 sq. mi. (1,295,000 sq. km), mostly in Mongolian People's Republic.

gob·let (gŏb′lĭt) *n.* (archaic) Bowl-shaped drinking cup without handles; drinking vessel with a stem and base, dist. from TUMBLER.

gob·lin (gŏb′lĭn) *n.* Mischievous and ugly demon.

go·by (gō′bē) *n.* (pl. **-bies**, collect. **-by**). Small fish (esp. *Gobius*) with ventral fins joined into disk or sucker.

god (gŏd) *n.* 1. Any superhuman being worshipped as having power over nature and human fortunes, deity; **~ of fire**, Vulcan; **~ of love**, Cupid; **~ of war**, Mars; **~ of wine**, Bacchus. 2. Image, animal, or other object, worshipped as symbolizing, being the visible habitation of, or itself possessing, divine power; an idol; adored, admired, or influential person. 3. **God**, supreme being, creator and ruler of universe; **God the Father, Son, Holy Spirit**, persons of the Trinity; **God knows**, it is beyond mortal or my knowledge, I don't know; **play G~**, attempt to direct the destiny of others; **in the lap of the gods**, beyond human control at the moment; **god willing**, if circumstances allow. 4. **god′-father, god′mother, god′-parent**, sponsor, as at baptism; so **god′child, -son, -daughter**; **god′father**, (colloq.) feared and revered absolute leader, esp. of the Mafia; **God-fearing**, sincerely religious; **Godforsaken**, devoid of all merit; forlorn, dismal; **god′send**, unexpected welcome event or acquisition; **God′speed**, usu. in **wish** or **bid person Godspeed**, wish him success in journey, undertaking, etc. **god′hood** *n.* **god′like** *adj.*

god·dess (gŏd′ĭs) *n.* Female deity; ~ **of love**, Venus; ~ **of wisdom**, Minerva.

Go·dey (gō′dē), **Louis Antoine** (1804–78). Amer. publisher; founded first U.S. periodical for women, *Godey's Lady's Book*, 1830.

god·head (gŏd′hĕd) *n.* Being God or a god, divine nature, deity; **the G**~, God.

Go·di·va (godī′va). Wife of Leofric, earl of Mercia; acc. to legend, her husband had imposed a tax on the inhabitants of Coventry, England, which he jestingly promised to remit if she would ride naked through the streets at noonday; taking him at his word, she did this, having told the people to stay indoors with closed windows.

god·less (gŏd′lĭs) *adj.* Without a god; not recognizing God; impious, wicked. **god′less·ness** *n.*

god·ly (gŏd′lē) *adj.* (**-li·er, -li·est**). Religious, pious, devout. **god′li·ness** *n.*

Go·du·nov (gŏd′*u*nawf, go͝od′-), **Boris Fyodorovich** (1552–1605). Tsar of Russia, 1598–1605; his career was theme of opera by Russian composer Mussorgski, based on play by Pushkin.

God·win Aus·ten (gŏd′wĭn aws′t*e*n) = K2.

god·wit (gŏd′wĭt) *n.* One of several species of large wading birds of genus *Limosa*, like curlew but with bill slightly curved upward.

Goe·thals (gō′thalz), **George Washington** (1858–1928). U.S. army officer and engineer; chief engineer in Panama Canal construction, 1907–14; governor of Canal Zone, 1914–16.

Goe·the (gö′te), **Johann Wolfgang von** (1749–1832). German novelist, poet, and dramatist; *Faust*, a dramatic poem, and the novels *The Sorrows of Young Werther* and *Wilhelm Meister* are the most famous of his works.

Gog and Ma·gog (gŏg′ *a*n mā′gŏg). 1. Names of various people and lands in Old Testament. 2. Nations under dominion of Satan (Rev. 20) opposed to the people of God. 3. (in medieval legend) Opponents of Alexander the Great, living north of the Caucasus. 4. Names given to two giant statues standing in the Guildhall, London, from the time of Henry V (destroyed in 1666 and 1940; replaced in 1953), either (acc. to Caxton) the last two survivors of a race of giants inhabiting Britain before Roman times, or (in another account) Gogmagog, chief of the giants, and Corineus, a Roman invader.

*Completed in 1937, the **Golden Gate Bridge,** spanning the Golden Gate Strait, is unmatched for the beauty of its setting. The main span is 4,200 ft. in length.*

gog·gle (gŏg′*e*l) *v.* (**-gled, -gling**). Squint, roll eyes about; (of eyes) project, roll about; turn (eyes) sideways or from side to side. ~ *adj.* (of eyes) Protuberant, full and rolling. **gog′gles** *n.pl.* Large spectacles with shielding sidepieces for protecting eyes from glare, dust, etc.

go-go (gō′gō) *adj.* (slang) Energetic, modern, full of pep; (of a young woman) dancing solo, often partially undressed, at a discotheque.

Go·gol (gō′g*o*l), **Nikolai Vasilievich** (1809–52). Russian novelist and dramatist best known for his picaresque romance *Dead Souls* satirizing provincial Russian society.

go·ing (gō′ĭng) *n.* (esp.) Condition of ground for walking, riding, etc.; **goings-on**, behavior. **going** *adj.* ~ **concern**, business in actual, esp. successful, operation.

goi·ter, goi·tre (goi′t*e*r) *ns.* Morbid enlargement of thyroid gland, often visible as swelling in neck. **goi′trous** *adj.*

Gol·con·da (gŏlkŏn′d*a*). Old name of Hyderabad, formerly celebrated for diamonds; hence, mine of wealth, source of great riches.

gold (gōld) *n.* 1. (chem.) Metallic element, malleable, ductile, of yellow color and high specific gravity, occurring in the free state, not attacked by most acids, but dissolved by aqua regia, regarded as a precious metal, and used as a standard of value and as the international medium of exchange; symbol Au, at. no. 79, at. wt. 196.9665. 2. Coins made of gold, money in large sums, wealth; metal used for coating surface or as pigment, gilding; color of the metal; (fig.) brilliant, beautiful, or precious things, stuff, etc. 3. **gold′brick**, something worthless that appears valuable; a fraud; **gold′brick** (*v.*), (slang) swindle; seek out sinecures; shirk work; **gold′brick(er)**, (slang) one who goldbricks; **gold bug**, N. Amer.

beetle (*Metriora bicolor*) with golden luster; (slang) advocate of the gold standard, or of gold as an investment; **gold digger**, one who digs for gold; (slang) woman attaching herself to man merely for gain; **gold dust**, gold in fine particles, as often found; **gold field**, area in which gold is found; **gold foil**, gold beaten into thin sheet; **gold leaf**, sheet of beaten gold, thinner than gold foil; **gold mine**, place where gold is mined; source of wealth; **gold-plate** (*v.t.*), plate with gold; **gold rush**, rush to new gold field; **gold'smith**, worker in gold; **gold standard**, financial system of a country in which paper, silver money, etc., is redeemable on demand in gold at a fixed weight and fineness. **gold** *adj.* Wholly or chiefly of, colored like, gold; **gold'-**

*The ore in which **gold** is present is broken down mechanically and separated chemically. It may be refined by a smelting process after which it is poured into molds where it cools into ingots of standard size.*

finch, bright yellow Amer. songbird (*Spinus tristis*) with black cap and wings; also green-backed or black-backed Western species (*S. psaltria*), or the European goldfinch (*Carduelis carduelis*); **gold'fish**, golden-red Asiatic fresh-water fish (*Carrasius auratus*) of carp family.

Gold (gōld) **Coast**: see GHANA.

gold·en (gōl′den) *adj.* Made, consisting, of gold; colored, shining, like gold; precious, excellent, important; ~ **age**, (i) (Gk. and Rom. myth.) first and best age of world, in which mankind was ideally prosperous and happy; (ii) most flourishing period (of literature etc.); ~ **ager**, (colloq., often ironic) elderly retired person; ~ **chain**, laburnum; ~ **eagle**, large eagle of Northern hemisphere with golden yellow feathers on head and neck; **gold'eneye**, either of two species of duck of genus *Bucephala* with dark-and-white plumage in male and gold-colored iris of the eye; **Golden Fleece**, (Gk. legend) fleece of gold taken from the ram that bore Phrixus through the air to Colchis; it was placed in a sacred grove by Aeëtes, king of Colchis, where it was guarded by a sleepless dragon, until it was won by JASON; **Golden Gate**, entrance strait of San Francisco Bay; **Golden Horde**, (trans. of Tartar name, from richness of Batu Khan's

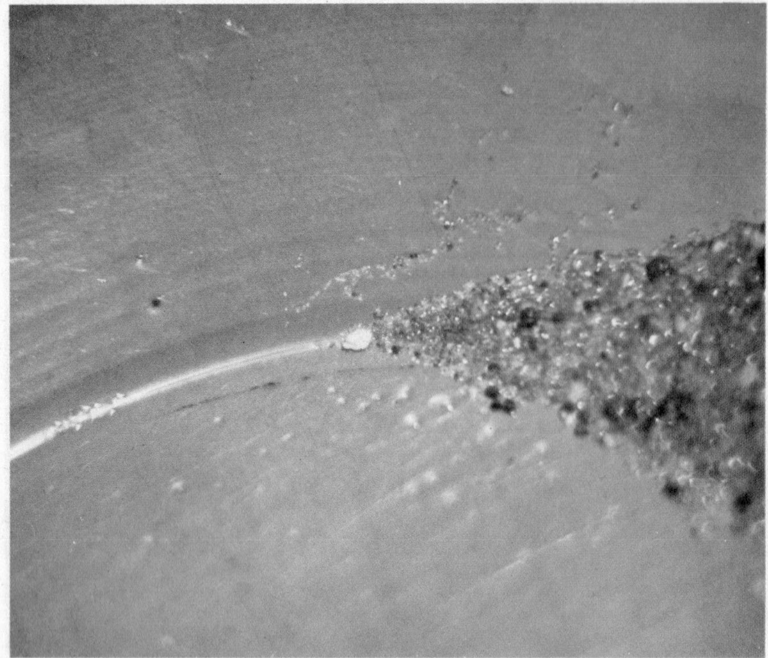

*1. Alluvial **gold** scoured into rivers is washed from lighter sand and mud in a pan. 2. Gold is smelted and cast into ingots which are then weighed. 3. Gold's malleability allows craftsmen to beat it into extremely thin sheets. They may then be laid down on any surface that requires decoration. The initial is enriched with gold leaf laid down by the limner of the Book of Kells which dates from the 8th or 9th century. 4. Gold bullion supports much currency and here a bank counts in a new deposit. 5. The workmanship of a pre-Columbian gold vase worked in the shape of a head demonstrates the malleability of gold.*

tent) Tartar horde that overran Eastern Europe in 13th c. under Batu Khan, grandson of Genghiz, and kept Russia in subjection until 1486; **G~ Horn,** curved inlet of Bosporus, forming harbor of Istanbul, Turkey; **golden mean,** moderation; course between extremes; **gold'enrod,** composite chiefly N. Amer. plant of genus *Solidago* with rodlike stem and spike of bright yellow flowers; **golden rule,** rule, *do unto others as you would have them do unto you,* from the precept in Matt. 7; **golden section,** division of a straight line into 2 parts so that the ratio of the whole line to the larger part is the same as the ratio of the larger part to the smaller; **golden wedding,** 50th anniversary of wedding.

Gold·smith (gōld′smĭth), **Oliver** (1728–74). Irish writer; author of the novel *The Vicar of Wakefield* and the comic play *She Stoops to Conquer*.

go·lem (gō′lĕm, -lem) *n.* (Jewish legend) Clay figure supernaturally brought to life; automaton, robot.

golf (gŏlf, gawlf) *n.* Game in which small hard rubber-cored ball is struck with clubs over surface of course into series of small holes on smooth greens, the aim being to hit the ball with the fewest possible strokes into any hole or all 9 or 18 holes successively; **~ club,** (premises of) association for playing golf; one of the sticks with which golf is played; **~ course, links,** tract of land on which the game is played, usu. of 9 or 18 holes arranged at intervals freq. with artificial obstacles (bunkers etc.) added; ~ **widow**, woman whose husband spends much time at golf. **golf** *v.i.* Play golf. **golf'er** *n.*

Gol·gi (gawl'jē) **apparatus, Golgi body.** (biol.) Intracellular system of membranes and vacuoles near the nucleus in cells of most animals and some plants, usu. concerned with intracellular secretion. [Camillo *Golgi* (1844–1926), Ital. physician]

Gol·go·tha (gŏl'go*tha*). Aramaic name of CALVARY (Mark 15); hence, burial place, cemetery. [Heb. *gulgōleth* skull]

Go·li·ath (golī'*a*th). Philistine giant, acc. to legend slain by DAVID[1] (1 Sam. 17), with a stone and sling.

gol·ly (gŏl'ē) *int.* (colloq. euphemism) By God (used as mild expletive).

go·losh (golŏsh'): see GALOSH.

Go·mor·rah, Go·mor·rha (gomŏr'*a*, -mar'-). Town of ancient Palestine that, along with Sodom, was destroyed by God because of the godlessness of its inhabitants (Gen. 18, 19); hence, (type of) wicked town.

Gom·pers (gŏm'p*e*rz), **Samuel** (1850–1924). British-born U.S. labor leader; president and one of organizers of American Federation of Labor, 1886–94, 1896–1924.

go·nad (gō'năd) *n.* (biol.) Organ (as testis or ovary) producing gametes. **go·nad·al** (gōnăd'*a*l) *adj.*

gon·do·la (gŏn'd*o*l*a*) *n.* Light flat-bottomed boat with cabin amidships and high point at each end, worked by one oar at stern, used on Venetian canals; basket or car suspended from balloon or airship; (also ~ **car**) flat, open railroad freight car with low sides. **gon·do·lier** (gŏnd*o*lēr') *n.* Rower or poler of gondola.

Gond·wa·na·land (gŏndwah'-n*a*lănd). Ancient land mass supposed to have existed in the southern hemisphere until late Paleozoic times, including Africa, India, Australia, and South America.

gone: see GO[1].

gon·er (gaw'n*e*r, gŏn'*e*r) *n.* (slang) Person or thing doomed, irrevocably lost, etc.

gong (gawng, gŏng) *n.* Metal disk with turned rim giving resonant note when struck with padded mallet. [Malay]

go·ni·om·e·ter (gōnēŏm'*e*t*e*r) *n.* 1. Optical instrument for measuring angles in crystals etc. 2. Apparatus for detecting direction of radio waves without the need for a rotating aerial.

gon·o·coc·cus (gŏn*o*kŏk'*u*s) *n.* (pl. **-coc·ci** pr. -kŏk'sī). Microorganism causing gonorrhea.

gon·or·rhe·a (gŏn*o*rē'*a*) *n.* Venereal disease characterized by inflammatory discharge of mucus from urethra or vagina. **gon·or·rhe'al** *adj.*

goo (gōō) *n.* (slang) Viscous or sticky substance; (fig.) sickly sentiment.

goo·ber (gōō'b*e*r) *n.* (southern U.S.) Peanut.

good (gŏŏd) *adj.* (**bet·ter, best**). Having the right qualities, adequate; expedient; morally excellent, virtuous; benevolent; well-behaved (esp. of child), not giving trouble; agreeable, advantageous; wholesome; suitable; efficient; reliable, safe; valid, sound; considerable; not less than (as in *a ~ 3 miles* etc.); **as ~ as**, practically, almost; **have a ~ mind to**, be much inclined to; **have a ~ time**, enjoy oneself; **make ~**: see MAKE[1]; **say a ~ word for**, commend, defend; ~ **afternoon, day, morning, night**, forms of salutation at meeting or parting; ~ **breeding**, good character as revealed in manners and sensitivity to others; ~ **fellow**, sociable person, agreeable companion; ~-**fellowship**, conviviality, sociability; ~ **for**, beneficial to; having good effect on; in condition to undertake or pay; (of a check) drawn for (so much); ~-**for-nothing**, worthless, useless (person); **G~ Friday**: see FRIDAY;

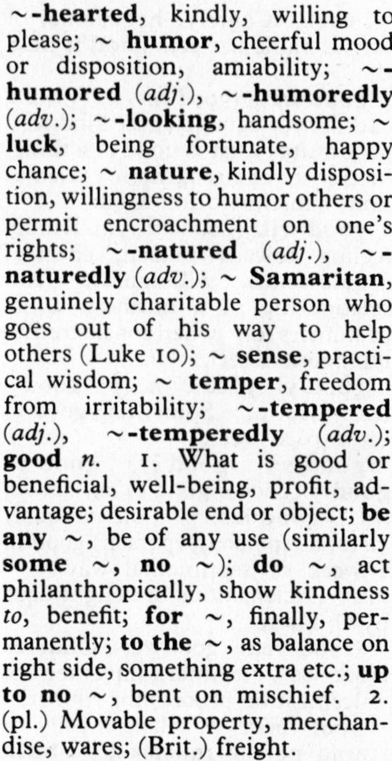

~-**hearted**, kindly, willing to please; ~ **humor**, cheerful mood or disposition, amiability; ~-**humored** (*adj.*), ~-**humoredly** (*adv.*); ~-**looking**, handsome; ~ **luck**, being fortunate, happy chance; ~ **nature**, kindly disposition, willingness to humor others or permit encroachment on one's rights; ~-**natured** (*adj.*), ~-**naturedly** (*adv.*); ~ **Samaritan**, genuinely charitable person who goes out of his way to help others (Luke 10); ~ **sense**, practical wisdom; ~ **temper**, freedom from irritability; ~-**tempered** (*adj.*), ~-**temperedly** (*adv.*); **good** *n.* 1. What is good or beneficial, well-being, profit, advantage; desirable end or object; **be any ~**, be of any use (similarly **some ~, no ~**); **do ~**, act philanthropically, show kindness *to*, benefit; **for ~**, finally, permanently; **to the ~**, as balance on right side, something extra etc.; **up to no ~**, bent on mischief. 2. (pl.) Movable property, merchandise, wares; (Brit.) freight.

good·by, good·bye (gŏŏdbī') *ints.* & *ns.* (pl. **-bys, -byes**). Expression used conventionally at parting. [contraction of *God be with you!* with *good* substituted on analogy of *good night* etc.]

Good (gŏŏd) **Hope, Cape of.** Promontory in Republic of South Africa, S. of Cape Town at tip of Africa, the foot of the continent; Vasco da Gama rounded cape in 1497 journey to India.

good·ly (gŏŏd'lē) *adj.* (**-li·er,**

The canal system of the lagoon city of Venice has a unique form of transport in the ***gondolas.*** *These fragile, light craft are maneuvered with great skill along the narrow canals.*

-li·est). Comely, handsome; of considerable size etc. **good'li·ness** *n.*

good·ness (gŏŏd'nĭs) *n.* Virtue; excellence; benevolence, kindness, generosity, what is good in a thing, its essence or strength; (in exclamations substituted for) God.

good·will (gŏŏdwĭl') *n.* Kindly feeling toward person; cheerful acquiescence, willingness; good relationship of a business to its customers (esp. when considered an intangible asset).

good·y[1] (gŏŏd'ē) *n.* (pl. **good·ies**). (usu. pl.) Something good to eat, esp. a sweet.

good·y[2] (gŏŏd'ē), **good·y-good·y** (gŏŏd'ē gŏŏd'ē) *adjs.* & *ns.* (pl. **-good·ies**). Ostentatiously virtuous (person); (person) good in a weak or sentimental way. ~ *ints.* Exclamations of delight used by children.

Good·year (gŏŏd'yēr), **Charles** (1800–60). Amer. inventor of vulcanization process for rubber.

goof (gōōf) *n.* (slang) Silly or stupid person; mistake; **~-ball**, (slang) (1) pill containing barbiturate or other drug; (2) very stupid person. **goof'y** *adj.* (**goof·i·er, goof·i·est**). **goof** *v.* Bungle, make a mistake; loaf, waste time (usu. ~ **off**); **~-off** (*n.*), one who goofs off.

goo·gol (gōō'gŏl, -gol) *n.* (math.) Number 1 followed by 100 zeros (10^{100}); **goo'gol·plex'**, number 10 raised to the googol power; 1 followed by 10^{100} zeros. [word coined by the young daughter of Edward Kasner (1878–1955), Amer. mathematician]

gook (gŏŏk) *n.* (slang) 1. Grimy goo. 2. (offensive) Oriental.

goon (gōōn) *n.* 1. (slang) Hired thug. 2. Dull or stupid person.

goose (gōōs) *n.* (pl. **geese** pr. gēs). 1. Large web-footed bird (of genus *Anser* or subfamily Anserinae), usu. between duck and swan in size; female of this; its flesh as food. 2. Simpleton. 3. Tailor's pressing iron (with handle like neck of goose). 4. **barnacle ~**: see BARNACLE; **cook one's ~**, (colloq.) ruin one's chances; **~ egg**, (colloq.) score of zero in a game or inning; **~ flesh, bumps, pimples**, rough bristling state of skin produced by cold or fright; **goose'foot**, plant of genus *Chenopodium* (from shape of leaves); **goose'neck**, pipe, lamp, etc., curved like neck of goose; **goose step**, balance step, used by some armies in marching on ceremonial parades, in which the legs are alternately advanced without bending the knees; **goose-step** (*v.i.*) (**-stepped, -step·ping**), march thus. **goose** *v.t.* (**goosed, goos·ing**). (slang) Poke (person) in sensitive part of the body, esp. the buttocks.

*The wild **goose** is a gregarious bird whose habit of making long migratory flights in 'V'-shaped formations is well known. The powerful Canada goose weighs 13 ½ lbs. Some authorities describe the Egyptian goose as a duck and it remains a borderline case. The red-breasted goose is one of several ornamental varieties. The snow goose breeds in Canada and northern U.S.A. The Chinese goose is the largest wild goose.*

goose·ber·ry (gōōs'bĕrē, -berē, gōōz'-) *n.* (pl. **-ries**). (Edible berry of) any thorny species of *Ribes*.

G.O.P. *abbrev.* Grand Old Party (U.S. Republican Party).

go·pher (gō'fer) *n.* 1. Short-tailed burrowing rodent of family Geomyidae of N. Amer. having external cheek pouches. 2. Nocturnal burrowing land tortoise of southern U.S. 3. **~ snake**, non-venomous snake (*Pituophis catenifer*) of western N. Amer. preying on gophers. 4. Ground squirrel; **~ ball**, (baseball slang)

*Several animals that imitate the burrowing habits of the **gopher** are called after it. For example (1) the gopher snake, (2) the nocturnal gopher tortoise and (4) the gopher squirrel. 3: The gopher itself is between 7 and 14 ins. long and burrows extensive tunnels which are valuable in aerating the soil but which may erode sloping ground.*

pitch easy to hit or *go for*; HOME run ball.

go·pher·wood (gō′ferwo͝od) *n.* Unidentified wood used in construction of Noah's ark (Gen. 6), supposed to be cypress.

go·ral (gōr′*a*l, gōr′-) *n.* Goatlike antelope (*Naemorhedus goral*) of E. Asia, having short backward-curving horns.

Gor·di·an (gōr′dē*a*n) *adj.* ~ **knot**, intricate knot tied by Gordius, king of Gordium in Phrygia; an oracle declared that whoever loosened it should rule Asia, and Alexander the Great, unable to undo it, cut it with his sword; hence, a difficult problem or task; **cut the ~ knot**, solve problem by bold direct action.

gore[1] (gōr, gōr) *n.* Blood shed and thickened or clotted. **gor′y** *adj.* (**gor·i·er, gor·i·est**). Covered with blood; involving bloodshed. **gor′i·ly** *adv.*

gore[2] (gōr, gōr) *n.* Wedge-shaped piece in garment, umbrella, sail, etc.; wedge-shaped strip of land. ~ *v.t.* (**gored, gor·ing**). Shape, provide, with gore.

gore[3] (gōr, gōr) *v.t.* (**gored, gor·ing**). Pierce with the horn or (rarely) tusk.

Gor·gas (gōr′g*a*s), **William**

Above and below: The Indian ***goral*** *is sometimes called the Indian antelope. It is a goat-antelope rather like a chamois and lives between 8,000 and 12,000 ft.*

Gorbachev (Gor′boh′chof) **Mikhail** (1931–). General Secretary of the Central Committee of the Communist Party of the Soviet Union (1985–).

Crawford (1854–1920). U.S. army surgeon general, 1914–18; rid Havana, Cuba, of yellow fever while chief sanitary officer there, 1898–1902, after Spanish-American War; made digging of Panama Canal possible by controlling yellow fever while chief sanitary officer, Panama Canal Commission, 1904–13.

gorge (gōrj) *n.* 1. (rhet.) Internal throat. 2. What has been swallowed, contents of stomach; act of gorging; surfeit; **one's ~ rises at**, one is disgusted or angered by. 3. (fort.) Neck of bastion or other outwork; rear entrance to a work. 4. Narrow opening between hills, rocky ravine, usu. with stream. ~ *v.* (**gorged, gorg·ing**). Feed greedily; satiate, glut; swallow, devour greedily; fill, distend, choke up.

gor·geous (gōr′j*u*s) *adj.* Richly colored, sumptuous, magnificent. **gor′geous·ly** *adv.* **gor′geous·ness** *n.*

Gor·gon (gōr′g*o*n). (Gk. myth.) One of three sisters, Stheno, Euryale, and MEDUSA (the only mortal one), with snakes for hair, whose look turned the beholder to stone; hence (**g**~), repulsive or terrifying woman.

Using its power and strength of its talons and beak, the ***goshawk*** *seizes its prey — birds, reptiles and small mammals. Goshawks of all varieties hunt by day using to advantage their phenomenal binocular vision to discover their victims.*

Gor·gon·zo·la (gŏrgonzō'la) *n.* Rich strong cheese, with veinings of bluish mold, orig. made at Gorgonzola, a village near Milan, Italy.

go·ril·la (gorĭl'a) *n.* 1. Large powerful anthropoid ape, *Gorilla gorilla*, of western equatorial Africa. 2. (slang) Brutish man; gangster.

Gor·ki, Gor·ky (gŏr'kē), **Maxim** (1868–1936). Pseudonym of Alexei Maximovich Pyeshkov, Russian writer and revolutionary; famous for his realistic short stories, dealing principally with thieves, tramps, and other outcasts.

gor·mand·ize (gŏr'mandīz) *v.* (**-ized, -iz·ing**). Eat voraciously or gluttonously. **gor'mand·iz·er** *n.*

gorse (gŏrs) *n.* Prickly yellow-flowered European shrub (*Ulex europaeus*).

gosh (gŏsh) *int.* (colloq. euphemism) By God (used as mild expletive).

gos·hawk (gŏs'hawk) *n.* Long-tailed hawk (*Accipiter gentilis*), largest of its genus, of N. N. Amer. and N. Europe.

Go·shen (gō'shen). Prosperous region of ancient Egypt on E. delta of the Nile, inhabited by Israelites from the time of Joseph until the Exodus; hence, a place of plenty (Gen. 45, Exod. 8, 9).

gos·ling (gŏz'lĭng) *n.* Young goose.

gos·pel (gŏs'pel) *n.* 1. Glad tidings (of kingdom of God) preached by Christ; religious doctrine of Christ and his apostles, Christian revelation. 2. (usu. **G~**) Record of Christ's life and teaching in first 4 books of New Testament (Matthew, Mark, Luke, John); any of these books. 3. Thing that may safely be believed; principle that one acts upon, believes in, or preaches. 4. ~ **singing**, fervent or evangelical singing, esp. as a style of jazz; ~ **singer;** ~ **truth**, truth contained in gospel; something as true as gospel. [OE. *god-spel* (*god* good, *spell* tidings)]

gos·sa·mer (gŏs'amer) *n.* Light filmy substance, spiderwebs or cobwebs floating in calm air or spread over grass; thread of this; something flimsy; delicate gauze. ~ *adj.* Light and flimsy as gossamer. [ME. *gossomer* = "goose summer," St. Martin's summer, i.e. early November, when geese were customarily eaten and gossamer is abundant]

gos·sip (gŏs'ĭp) *n.* 1. (archaic) Familiar acquaintance; (esp. woman) friend. 2. Idle talker, tattler (esp. of woman). 3. Idle talk, groundless rumors, tittle-tattle; easy unconstrained talk or writing, esp. about persons or social incidents; hence ~ **column**, column devoted to this in newspaper. **gos'sip·y** *adj.* **gos'sip** *v.i.* (**-siped, -sip·ing**). Talk idly or lightly, tattle; write in gossipy style. [orig. = sponsor at baptism, f. *God* + *sib* akin, related]

got: see GET.

Gö·te·borg (gaw'tebŏrg; *Swed.* yötebŏr'ye), **Goth·en·burg** (gŏth'enbĕrg, gŏt'-). Second largest city in Sweden, in the SW.; seaport and shipbuilding center.

Goth (gŏth) *n.* One of a Germanic tribe who in 3rd, 4th, and 5th centuries invaded both the Eastern and Western Roman Empires and founded kingdoms in Italy, France, and Spain; hence, barbarian or rude or ignorant person.

The ***gorilla*** *is the largest of the anthropoid apes, a group that also includes the chimpanzee. Only one species exists, but this is divided into three races.*

Goth. *abbrev.* Gothic.

Goth·am (def. 1 gō'tham, -tam; def. 2 gŏth'am, gō'tham). 1. Village (perh. the one of this name in Nottinghamshire, England) proverbial for folly of its inhabitants. 2. (joc.) New York City, a name first given to it in *Salmagundi*, a humorous work by Washington Irving, William Irving, and J. K. Paulding, because its inhabitants were reputed to be wiseacres. **Goth'am·ite** *n.* New Yorker.

Goth·ic (gŏth'ĭk) *adj.* 1. Of, like, the Goths; hence (fig.) barbarous, rude. 2. (archit.) Of the style of architecture prevalent in W. Europe from the 12th to the 16th c., characterized by ribbed vaults, pointed arches, clustered pillars, etc.; of the art of this period; (of script) of style used by Ulfilas (see *n.* 2 below). 3. ~ **Revival**, revival in England and U.S. of Gothic architecture in the mid-18th and esp. the 19th c.; ~ **novel,** (hist.) novel, fashionable in late 18th c., featuring mystery, horror, and sentimental romance; 20th c. popular novels resembling these. **Gothic** *n.* 1. Gothic architecture. 2. Extinct language of the Goths, one of the E. GERMANIC group of languages, known from the 4th-c. translation of parts of the Bible made by Bishop Ulfilas and from other scattered remnants.

Goths (gŏths): see OSTROGOTH and VISIGOTH.

Got·land (gŏt′land). Island in Baltic Sea off SE. coast of Sweden; early Roman and Byzantine trade center.

got·ten: see GET.

Göt·ter·däm·mer·ung (göter-dĕm′erōōng) *n.* (Ger. myth.) Twilight of the gods (see TWILIGHT).

gouache (gwahsh; *Brit.* gōō′-ahsh) *n.* (Painting in) opaque watercolor.

Gou·da (gōō′da) *n.* Flat, round, mild, pale-yellow cheese, usu. in red wax coating, and orig. made at Gouda in the W. Netherlands.

gouge (gowj) *n.* Concave-bladed chisel. ~ *v.t.* 1. Cut with gouge; cut *out* (as) with gouge; force (out, esp. person's eye with thumb) (as) with gouge; force out eye of. 2. (colloq.) Swindle. **goug′er** *n.*

gou·lash (gōō′lahsh) *n.* Hungarian stew of meat and vegetables seasoned with paprika, also **Hungarian ~**. [Magyar *gulyás-hús* (*gulyás* herdsman, *hús* meat)]

gourd (gōrd, gōrd, goord) *n.* (Large fleshy fruit of) trailing or climbing plant of family Cucurbitaceae, related to the squash and pumpkin; shell of the fruit dried and used as vessel.

gour·mand (goor′mahnd, -mand, goormahnd′) *n.* Lover of food in both quality and quantity; glutton.

gour·met (goormā′, goor′mā) *n.* Connoisseur of fine food and wine.

gout (gowt) *n.* 1. Metabolic disease characterized by painful inflammation of smaller joints, esp. that of big toe, and excessive amount of uric acid in blood. 2. Blob, clot, mass of something fluid or sticky, drop, esp. of blood. **gout′y** *adj.* (**gout·i·er, gout·i·est**). **gout′i·ness** *n.*

Gov., gov. *abbrevs.* Governor, government.

gov·ern (gŭv′ern) *v.* 1. Rule with authority; conduct policy and affairs of (nation etc.); curb, control; sway, influence; constitute law, rule, principle, etc., for, serve to decide (case); **governing board, body**, managers of hospital, school, etc. 2. (gram., esp. of verb or preposition) Have (noun, case) depending on it; be necessarily followed by (a certain case).

The ***Gothic*** *style of architecture emerged in the ambulatory of the Abbey of St. Denis, Paris, c. 1140. Its pointed arch and ribbed vaults crossed the English Channel where they found expression (top) in Gloucester Cathedral. The style was revived in the 18th century and (above) was used by architects of the British Houses of Parliament in the 19th century.*

gov·ern·ance (gŭv′ernans) *n.* Act, manner, fact, or function, of governing.

gov·ern·ess (gŭv′ernĭs) *n.* Woman employed to educate, train, and look after children of a household.

gov·ern·ment (gŭv′ernment, -erment) *n.* 1. Act, manner, fact, of governing; area under a single rule; system of governing, form of polity. 2. Body or successive bodies of persons governing a state; the state as an agent; administration or ministry; **G~ House,** official residence of governor of Brit. colony; **government issue,** (often cap.) (of) equipment issued to soldiers etc. by government. **gov·ern·men·tal** (gŭvernmĕn′tal), **gov·ern·men′tal·ly** *adv.*

gov·er·nor (gŭv′erner) *n.* 1. One who governs, ruler; official appointed to govern province, town etc.; chief executive of a U.S. state; officer commanding fortress or garrison; head, or member of governing body, of institution; ~ **general** (pl. **governors general**

or **governor generals**). 2. (chiefly Brit. slang) One's employer; one's father; sir. 3. (mech.) Automatic regulator of supply of gas, steam, etc., to machine, ensuring an even motion; device for keeping clockwork or similar machine at constant speed. **gov′er·nor·ship** *n.*

gown (gown) *n.* Loose flowing outer garment, esp. woman's dress, frock; ancient Roman toga; official or uniform robe of various types worn by judges, clergymen, members of university, etc.; **cap and ~**: see CAP[1]; **town and ~**: see TOWN. **gown** *v.t.* (chiefly in past part.) Attire in gown.

Go·ya (goi′*a*), **Francisco José de Goya y Lucientes** (1746–1828). Spanish painter, esp. of portraits; etcher of the "Disasters of War" and other series of macabre and satirical prints.

G.P. *abbrev.* General practitioner (doctor).

GPO, G.P.O. *abbrevs.* General post office; Government Printing Office.

G.P.U. (also O.G.P.U.; hist.) Soviet secret police organization (1922–34) that superseded the Cheka. [f. initials of Russ. (*O*bedinennoe) *G*osudarstvennoe *P*oliticheskoe *U*pravlenie (United State Political Directorate)]

gr. *abbrev.* Grain(s); grade; grammar; gross; group.

*Early paintings by **Goya** express a fresh delight in life through scenes of common life. At Court he painted portraits that might be honest to the point of cruelty but in this one of Countess de Gondomar he is tender.*

*Below: The State Department building in Washington D.C. **Government** is typically divided into departments to facilitate smooth operation and strategic differentiation of labor.*

*Above: Tourists passing through the main street of Lima, Peru, are offered an amazing variety of **gourds.** They range from the practical and simple to the ornate and decorative.*

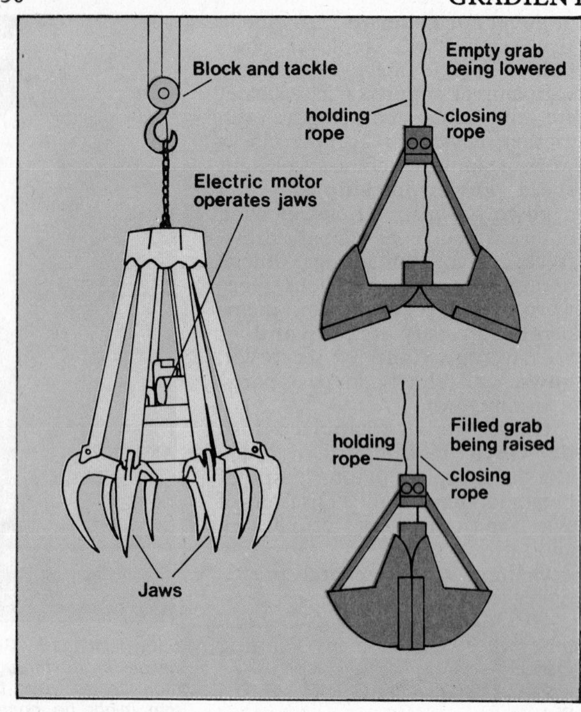

Right: The jaws of a **grab** *are held apart until they surround their load; then the jaws are closed on the load by another rope. On some the jaws are operated by means of an electric motor. Left above: A grab may be used to load harvests such as sugar cane.*

Graaf (grahf), **Regnier de** (1641–73). Dutch anatomist. **Graafian** (grah′fē*a*n) **follicle**, one of the small sacs in the ovary of mammals in which the ova are matured.

grab (grăb) *v.* (**grabbed, grab·bing**). 1. Seize suddenly, appropriate rapaciously; capture, arrest; make snatch *at*. 2. (slang) Attract, arouse interest. ~ *n.* 1. Sudden clutch, grasp, seizure, or attempt to seize; practice of grabbing, rapacious proceedings, esp. in politics or commerce. 2. (mech.) Device for clutching or gripping. 3. ~ **bag**, at bazaar, party, etc., container of articles of more or less value to be drawn blindly; any miscellaneous collection; **up for ~s**, (colloq.) readily available to first comer, or to anyone willing to work for it. **grab′ber** *n.* (esp. colloq.) One who grabs without scruple or consideration.

grace (grās) *n.* 1. Pleasing quality, attractiveness, charm, esp. that belonging to elegant proportions or ease and refinement of movement, manner, etc.; attractive feature; **with good ~**, as if willing. 2. (mus.) Embellishment of additional note(s) (~ **note**) not essential to harmony or melody. 3. (Gk. myth.) **the (three) Graces**, beautiful sister-goddesses (Aglaia, Thalia, Euphrosyne), bestowers of beauty and charm. 4. Benign regard or its manifestation on part of superior; unconstrained goodwill as ground of concession; boon; dispensation from statutes; **be in person's good ~s**, enjoy his or her favor or liking. 5. (theol.) Unmerited favor of God; divine regenerating, inspiring, and strengthening influence; condition (also **state of ~**) of being so influenced; divinely given virtue or excellence, etc.; (archaic) **year of ~**, year as reckoned from birth of Christ. 6. Favor shown by granting delay; mercy, clemency; ~ **period, days of ~**, time allowed for payment without penalty of a premium, note, etc., after it is due. 7. Short blessing or prayer of thanksgiving before or after meal. 8. **his, her, your, G~**, forms of address or description for duke, duchess, or archbishop. **grace** *v.t.* (**graced, grac·ing**). Add grace to, adorn, set off *with*; confer honor or dignity on, honor *with* title etc.; do credit to. **grace′ful** *adj.* Full of grace (sense 1). **grace′ful·ly** *adv.* **grace′ful·ness** *n.*

grace·less (grās′lĭs) *adj.* Without sense of decency; without charm or elegance. **grace′less·ly** *adv.* **grace′less·ness** *n.*

grac·ile (grăs′ĭl) *adj.* Slender, thin, lean.

gra·cious (grā′sh*u*s) *adj.* (archaic) Agreeable, pleasing; kindly, benevolent, courteous; (of God) dispensing grace, merciful, benignant. **gra′cious·ly** *adv.* **gra′cious·ness** *n.* **gracious** *int.* (ellipt. for ~ **God**, as) **good ~!, ~ me!**, exclamations of surprise.

grack·le (grăk′*e*l) *n.* Either of 2 N. Amer. blackbirds, the **common** ~ (*Quiscalus quiscula*), or the very large **boat-tailed** ~ (*Cassidix mexicanus*).

grad (grăd) *n.* (colloq.) Graduate. ~ *adj.* (colloq.) Graduate, usu. in ~ **student**.

gra·date (grā′dāt) *v.* (**-dat·ed, -dat·ing**). (Cause to) pass by imperceptible degrees from one shade of color to another; arrange in steps or grades.

gra·da·tion (grādā′sh*o*n) *n.* Stage(s) of transition or advance (usu. pl.); series of degrees in rank, merit, divergence, etc.; (pl.) such degrees; arrangement in such degrees; (fine arts) gradual passing from one shade, tone, etc., to another. **gra·da′tion·al** *adj.* **gra·da′tion·al·ly** *adv.*

grade (grād) *n.* 1. Degree in rank, proficiency, value, etc.; class of persons or things alike in these; (pupils constituting) an elementary school class; ~ **school**: see ELEMENTARY school 2. (cattle breeding) Variety produced by crossing ordinary stock with superior breed. 3. Gradient, slope; rate of ascent or descent; ~ **crossing**, place where railroad and road or two railroads cross at same level; **make the ~**, reach the proper standard, be up to the mark. 4. Rating on school assignment, examination, or course of study. **grade** *v.t.* (**grad·ed, grad·ing**). Arrange in grades, class, sort; gradate; reduce (road etc.) to easy gradients; (cattle breeding) cross with better breed. **grad′er** *n.*

gra·di·ent (grā′dē*e*nt) *n.* Amount of slope, inclination to horizontal, in road etc., measured as the ratio of the difference in elevation between two points to the horizontal distance between them (so that a slope rising 1 ft. per 10 ft. of horizontal distance has a gradient of 1 in 10).

grad·u·al[1] (grăj′ōōal) *n.* Response sung in the service of the Mass between Epistle and Gospel; book containing this and other music for the Mass. [so called because sung at altar steps; f. L. *gradus* steps]

grad·u·al[2] (grăj′ōōal) *adj.* Taking place by degrees, slowly progressive; not rapid, steep, or abrupt. **grad′u·al·ly** *adv.* **grad′u·al·ness** *n.*

grad·u·ate (grăj′ōōĭt, -āt) *n.* One who holds an academic degree; one who has been graduated from high school, elementary school, etc. ~ (grăj′ōōāt) *v.* (**-at·ed, -at·ing**). 1. Take academic degree; receive diploma for completing high school education or work at other educational institution; certify (students) as having completed education or training. 2. Mark out in degrees; arrange in gradations, apportion incidence of (tax) according to a scale; hence, **graduated income tax** etc. **grad·u·a·tion** (grăjōōā′shon), **grad′u·a·tor** *ns.*

Grae·cism (grē′sĭzem): see GRECISM.

graf·fi·to (grafē′tō) *n.* (pl. **-ti** pr. -tē). Drawing or writing scratched on wall etc., esp. on ancient walls as at Pompeii; (pl.) scribblings or drawings made on walls in public places; messages or slogans inscribed there, usu. of obscene or political nature.

graft[1] (grăft, grahft) *n.* Plant consisting of shoot or scion inserted into a stock, from which it receives sap; (surg.) piece of transplanted living tissue; process of grafting; place where graft is inserted. ~ *v.* Insert (scion) as graft; insert graft(s) upon (stock); insert graft(s); (surg.) transplant (living tissue); insert or fix *in* or *upon* so as to produce vital or indissoluble union.

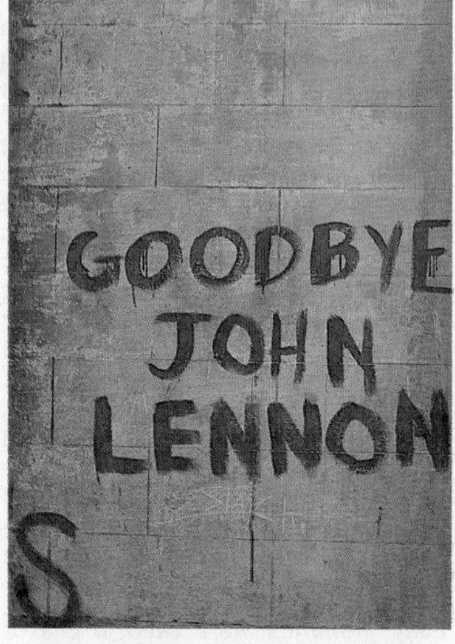

***Graffiti,** irreverent inscriptions painted on walls in public places, deal with many subjects. Graffito originally referred to a method of decoration.*

graft[2] (grăft, grahft) *n.* Obtaining of profit or advantage by dishonest means; profits so obtained. ~ *v.i.* Seek, make, graft. **graft′er** *n.*

Gra·ham[1] (grā′em), **Martha** (1894–). Amer. dancer and choreographer, a pioneer developer of modern dance.

Gra·ham[2] (grā′am), **Sylvester** (1794–1851). Amer. advocate of vegetarianism; **graham cracker,** cracker made from unbolted wheat flour (~ **flour**).

Grail (grāl) *n.* (also **holy** ~) In medieval legend, the cup or chalice that Christ used at the Last Supper and in which Joseph of Arimathaea received Christ's blood at the Cross; medieval romances tell how it was sought for by Arthur's knights.

grain (grān) *n.* 1. Fruit or seed of a cereal; (collect. sing.) wheat or the allied food grasses or their seeds after harvesting; ~ **alcohol,** ETHYL alcohol; ~ **elevator,** building in which grain is stored and handled by elevators and conveyors. 2. Small hard usu. roundish particle of sand, salt, gunpowder, etc. 3. Smallest unit of weight, 0.002285 ounce; smallest possible quantity, hence ~ **of truth** (in something). 4. (poet.) Dye, color; **in** ~, fast dyed, genuine, thorough. 5. Granular texture, roughness of surface, mottling, texture, arrangement and size of constituent particles, in flesh, skin, wood, stone, etc.; lines of rays in wood, often giving a pattern; (fig.) nature, temper, tendency. 6. **against the** ~, contrary to inclination. **grain** *v.* Form into grains; give granular surface to; remove hair from (hides); paint in imitation of grain of wood or marble. **grain′y** *adj.* (**grain·i·er, grain·i·est**).

gram[1] (grăm) *n.* Chickpea; any legume used as horse fodder.

gram[2] (grăm) *n.* $\frac{1}{1000}$ of a kilogram (abbrev. g).

Gram (grahm), **Hans Christian Joachim** (1853–1938). Danish biologist; ~**-positive,** ~**-negative,** (of organism) that does, does not, stain by Gram's method of staining bacteria for microscopic examination.

-gram[1] *suffix.* Forming nouns, indicating something written or pictured, as *telegram, diagram.*

*One of the common ways of propagating a shrub or tree is by **grafting.** A cut is made in the root stock and a new plant material, a scion, is inserted and bound in place. This may be done several ways. A cleft may be cut in the stock and a scion inserted. A cut may be mortised in a tongue shape. A bud may be grafted into stock by binding it into a slit in the bark.*

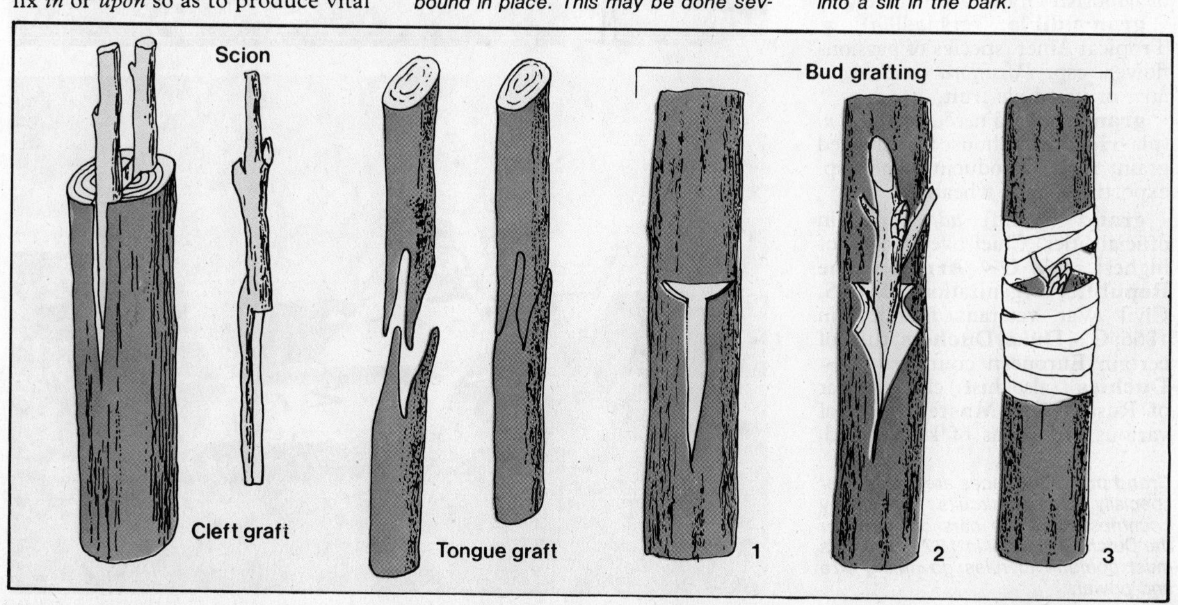

-gram[2] *suffix.* Comb. form of GRAM[2], as in *kilogram.*

gram·mar (grăm'*er*) *n.* 1. Language study dealing with inflectional forms or other means of indicating relation of words within sentence, and with rules for employing these (in early English use *grammar* meant only *Latin grammar*); treatise or book on grammar; person's manner of using grammatical forms; speech or writing regarded as good or bad by the rules of grammar, what is correct according to those rules; body of forms and usages in a language; elements, rudiments, of an art or science; **comparative ~**, study of relation between grammars of two or more languages; **historical ~**, study of historical development of the grammar of a language. 2. **~ school**, grade school; (hist.) school stressing the study of classical languages. **gram·mar·i·an** (gr*a*mār'ēan) *n.*

gram·mat·i·cal (gr*a*măt'ĭk*a*l) *adj.* Of grammar; conforming to rules of grammar; **~ gender**, gender (in most Indo-European and Semitic languages) not determined by real or attributed sex. **gram·mat'i·cal·ly** *adv.*

gramme (grăm) *n.* Brit. var. of GRAM[2].

Gram·o·phone (grăm'*o*fōn) *n.* (trademark) Phonograph, esp. of an early type.

gram·pus (grăm'p*u*s) *n.* (pl. **-pus·es**). Dolphinlike marine mammal (*Grampus griseus*); also (sometimes) KILLER whale.

Gra·na·da (gr*a*nah'd*a*; *Sp.* grahnah'dhah). Province of S. Spain on Mediterranean coast; former Moorish kingdom, 8th–15th centuries; captured in 1492 by Ferdinand and Isabella of Castile, ending Moorish power in Spain; city in S. Spain and former capital of Moorish Granada province.

gran·a·dil·la (grăn*a*dĭl'*a*) *n.* Tropical Amer. species of passionflower, esp. *Passiflora quadrangularis* or its edible fruit.

gran·a·ry (grā'n*e*rē, grăn'*e*rē) *n.* (pl. **-ries**). Storehouse for threshed grain; region producing, and esp. exporting, much wheat.

grand (grănd) *adj.* 1. (in official titles) Chief over others, of highest rank; **G~ Army of the Republic**, organization of U.S. Civil War veterans founded in 1866; **G~ Duke, Duchess**, ruler of certain European countries (**G~ Duchies**); (also, hist.) child of Tsar of Russia; **G~ Master**, head of various orders, as of knighthood, Freemasons, Oddfellows, etc.; **~ vizier**, chief minister of a Muslim country, esp. formerly of Turkish empire. 2. (law) Great, principal, chief, (opp. petty); **~ jury**: see JURY; **~ larceny**, larceny involving goods whose value is above a certain amount (see PETTY larceny;) 3. Of most or great importance; main; (mus.) full, of full dimensions, for full orchestra, in full classical form; (in Fr. phrases or imitations) great; **~ opera**: see OPERA. 4. Conducted with solemnity, splendor, etc.; fine, splendid; belonging to high society, distinguished; imposing, great and handsome; dignified, lofty in conception, treatment, or expression; morally imposing, noble, admirable; (colloq.) very satisfactory; **~ manner, style**, style and manner fitted for great subjects; **G~ Old Party** (G.O.P.), Republican Party. 5. (in names of relationships) In the second degree of ascent or descent, as **grand'-daughter, grand'son**, one's child's daughter, son; **grand'-father, grand'mother**, one's parent's father, mother; so **grand'-child, grand'parent**, etc. 6. In combinations: **grand'father clock**, eight-day clock of kind formerly in common use, with weight-and-pendulum movement and tall wooden case; **grand piano**: see PIANO[2]; **grand'sire,** (archaic) grandfather; forefather; **Grand Prix**: see separate entry; **grand slam**: see SLAM[2]; **grand'stand**, principal stand for spectators at stadium, race track, etc.; **Grand Teton**: see separate entry; **grand tour**: see TOUR. **grand'ly** *adv.* **grand'ness** *n.* **grand** *n.* 1. Grand piano; **baby ~**, small grand piano. 2. (slang) 1,000 dollars.

*Early **granaries** were sited in pits or buildings. The disadvantages of this arrangement (vulnerability to damp and rodents) were overcome by building huge concrete containers for aboveground storage.*

***Grand prix** motor races are driven over specially built circuits in many countries. Here the cars compete for the Dutch Grand Prix in 1971. The cars must conform to rules governing size and power.*

Grand (grănd) **Banks.** Shoal in Atlantic Ocean off S. and E. Newfoundland, Canada; world's greatest cod fishing area.

Grand (grănd) **Canal.** 1. Canal in NE. China extending 1,000 mi. (1,609 km) from Tientsin (Tianjin) S. to Hangchow (Hangzhou); also called "Imperial River" or "Transport River" by the Chinese. 2. Main waterway of Venice, Italy, 80 to 175 ft. (24 to 53 m) wide.

Grand (grănd) **Canyon.** NW. Arizona gorge, formed by the Colorado River, extending W. from the mouth of the Little Colorado River to Lake Mead on the Arizona-Nevada boundary; about 280 mi. (451 km) long, 4 to 18 mi. (6 to 29 km) wide, and up to 1 mi. (1.6 km) deep; ~ ~ **National Park**, park in NW. Arizona, established in 1919, covering 1,009 sq. mi. (2,613 sq. km), including part of the Grand Canyon.

Grand Cou·lee (grănd ko͞o′lē) **Dam.** Dam at the N. end of the Columbia River in the state of Washington.

gran·dee (grăndē′) *n.* Spanish or Portuguese nobleman of highest rank; person of high rank or eminence.

gran·deur (grăn′jer, -dyer) *n.* Greatness; great nobility of character; sublimity, majesty; conscious dignity; splendor.

Grand Gui·gnol (grahṅ gēnyawl′). Paris theater specializing in short sensational plays with themes of violence and bloodshed; hence, sensational, violent entertainment, incidents, etc. [f. assoc. with *Guignol*, pop. hero of Fr. puppet theaters, and perh. f. affinity with *guignon* evil]

gran·dil·o·quent (grăndĭl′o-kwent) *adj.* Pompous or bombastic in language. **gran·dil′o·quent·ly** *adv.* **gran·dil′o·quence** *n.*

gran·di·ose (grăn′dēōs) *adj.* Producing, intended or trying to produce, an impression of greatness; planned on a magnificent scale; pompous. **gran′di·ose·ly** *adv.* **gran·di·os′i·ty** *n.*

grand mal (grahn′mahl′, grăn′-măl; *Fr.* grahṅ măl′). Severe form of epilepsy (opp. PETIT MAL). [Fr.]

Grand·ma Mo·ses (grănd′mah mō zĭz). (full name, Anna Mary Robertson Moses) (1860–1961); U.S. primitive painter who began career late in life.

Grand Prix (grahṅ prē′) (pl. **Grands Prix** pr. grahṅ prē′). International horse race for three-year-olds, run annually at Longchamps, near Paris; any of various international road races for sport cars of specific engine size.

Grand Te·ton (grănd tē′tŏn). Highest peak (13,766 ft., 4,196 m) in Teton Range, NW. Wyoming; ~ ~ **National Park**, NW. Wyoming national park covering 310,358 acres (125,601 hectares) and including **Grand Teton Mountain**.

grange (grānj) *n.* 1. (Brit.) Country house with farm buildings attached. 2. (cap.) U.S. farmers' association founded in 1867; one of its lodges.

gran·ite (grăn′ĭt) *n.* Granular crystalline rock of quartz, feldspar, and mica, very abundant and used in building because of its hardness and durability; ~ **ware**, kind of pottery speckled like granite; kind of speckled enameled ironware.

gran·ny, gran·nie (grăn′ē) *ns.* (pl. **-nies**). 1. (colloq.) Grandmother; old woman; (fig.) fussy person. 2. (also **granny knot**) Square knot crossed the wrong way. **granny** *adj.* Old-fashioned, as in *granny glasses*.

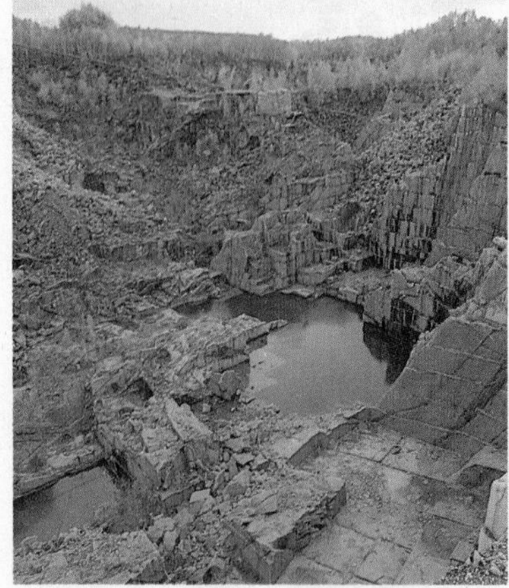

***Granite** is formed by cooling magma. It is high in quartz and feldspar, and is the most common plutonic rock of the Earth's crust.*

gra·no·la (granō′la) *n.* Dry breakfast food, a mixture of grains, nuts, fruit, etc.

grant (grănt, grahnt) *v.t.* Consent to fulfill (request etc.); concede as indulgence; allow (person) to have; give formally, transfer (property) legally; concede (proposition) as basis for argument; **take for granted**, assume. ~ *n.* Granting; formal conferment, legal assignment; thing, esp. sum of money, granted; conveyance by written instrument; **~-in-aid** (pl. **grants-in-aid**), sum granted to individual to finance university studies; **grants′manship**, (colloq.) art of gaining government grants, usu. for projects enriching the grantee more than enhancing public welfare or world of intellect; art of parlaying one grant to more, as a way of life. **gran·tee** (grăntē′, grahn-), **gran·tor** (grăn′ter, grahn′-, grăntōr′, grahn-) *ns.*

*The spectacular **Grand Canyon,** carved by the erosive powers of the Colorado River, takes on many different colors depending on the time of day and the prevailing weather. Right: Mule trains carry weary tourists along the winding slopes of the canyon.*

Starch from the bulbs of the **grape hyacinth** was once used to stiffen linen and won it the name of starch lily. The flower grows to a height of 7 ins. and blooms in spring. It is often grown as a border plant.

The **grape** harvest at Limogne, in France, is gathered in baskets to be taken from the vineyards to the presses where the juice is extracted for winemaking. Grapes were introduced into France by the Romans.

Ulysses Grant ruled the U.S.A. as President from 1869–77, during which time he advocated amnesty for Confederate leaders, and protection of civil rights of Negroes. Much of his rule was clouded by scandal.

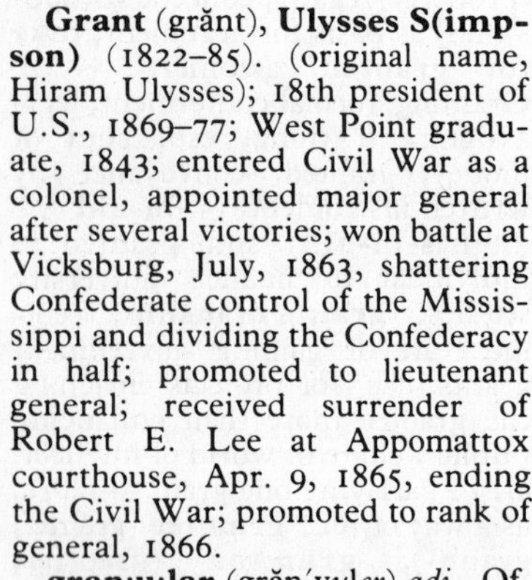

Grant (grănt), **Ulysses S(impson)** (1822–85). (original name, Hiram Ulysses); 18th president of U.S., 1869–77; West Point graduate, 1843; entered Civil War as a colonel, appointed major general after several victories; won battle at Vicksburg, July, 1863, shattering Confederate control of the Mississippi and dividing the Confederacy in half; promoted to lieutenant general; received surrender of Robert E. Lee at Appomattox courthouse, Apr. 9, 1865, ending the Civil War; promoted to rank of general, 1866.

gran·u·lar (grăn′y*u*l*er*) *adj.* Of, like, grains; with granulated surface or structure. **gran′u·lar·ly** *adv.* **gran·u·lar·i·ty** (grăny*u*lăr′ĭtē) *n.*

gran·u·late (grăn′y*u*lāt) *v.* (**-lat·ed, -lat·ing**). Form into grains; roughen surface of. **gran′u·lat·ed** *adj.* (of sugar etc.) Formed into or consisting of granules or grainlike bodies. **gran·u·la·tion** (grăny*u*lā′sh*o*n), **gran′u·la·tor** *ns.*

gran·ule (grăn′ūl) *n.* Small grain or particle.

grape (grāp) *n.* Green or purple berry growing in clusters on vine, eaten as fruit or used in making wine; **the ~**, wine; **grape′fruit**, globular fruit of tree *Citrus paradisi*, with a bitter yellow rind and acid juicy pulp, so called as growing in clusters; **grape hyacinth**, plant of genus *Muscari* with a raceme of small blue flowers; **grape′shot**, cluster of small iron balls formerly used as charge for cannon; **grape**

With more than 10,000 species, ***grass*** *has the widest distribution of the vascular plants and is one of the plant world's most adaptable groups. 1: Couch-grass shoots from long rhizomes. 2: Poa vivipara grass. 3: Rye-grass grows two feet tall. 4: Lesser quaking grass grows on roadsides and arable land. 5: The female plumes of pampas grass are used to ornament houses and gardens.*

sugar, dextrose; **grape'vine**, vine bearing grapes; (colloq.) route by which rumors pass.

graph (grăf, grahf) *n.* Diagram representing the relation between two or more variable quantities by the distance of a series of points (or a curve or other line joining these) from axes of reference, which are usu. at right angles to each other; abscissa of any point corresponding to the value of one variable and the ordinate to that of the other. ~ *v.t.* Represent (information) in a graph. [abbrev. of *graphic formula*]

-graph *suffix.* Forming nouns, denoting something written, drawn, or recorded, as *photograph, seismograph.*

graph·ic (grăf'ĭk) *adj.* Of drawing, painting, engraving, etching, etc.; vividly descriptive, lifelike; of writing; of diagrams, linear figures, or symbolic curves; ~ **arts**, reproductive arts of engraving, etching, woodcut, lithography, etc. **graph'i·cal** *adj.* **graph'i·cal·ly** *adv.*

graph·ics (grăf'ĭks) *n.pl.* (considered sing. or pl.) Design and decoration involving or accompanying printed work; use of diagrams in calculation and design; production of diagrams etc. by computer.

graph·ite (grăf'īt) *n.* Crystalline allotropic form of carbon, used in pencils, as solid lubricant, etc. **gra·phit·ic** (grafĭt'ĭk) *adj.*

graph·ol·o·gy (grăfŏl'ojē) *n.* Study of character deduced from handwriting. **graph·ol'o·gist** *n.* **graph·o·log·i·cal** (grăfolŏj'ĭkal) *adj.*

grap·nel (grăp'nel) *n.* Metal-clawed instrument thrown with rope to seize object, esp. enemy's ship; small anchor with several flukes, used for boats and balloons.

grap·ple (grăp'el) *n.* Grapnel; hold or grip (as) of wrestlers. ~ *v.* (**grap·pled, grap·pling**). Seize, fasten, (as) with grapnel; take hold of, grip, with the hands, come to close quarters with; contend in close fight, struggle *with*; ~ **with**, try to overcome, accomplish, or deal with; **grappling iron** = GRAPNEL.

grasp (grăsp, grahsp) *v.* Clutch *at*, try to seize; seize and hold firmly with hand; get mental hold of, comprehend. ~ *n.* Fast hold, grip; control, mastery; mental hold, comprehensiveness of mind. **grasp'a·ble** *adj.* **grasp'ing** *adj.* (esp.) Greedy, avaricious. **grasp'ing·ly** *adv.*

grass (grăs, grahs) *n.* Herbage in general, blades or leaves and stalks of which are eaten by horses, cattle, etc.; plant belonging to the

***Grasshoppers** have various defenses. They have remarkable powers of jumping and many are well camouflaged. Top: 5 per cent of greenleaf long-horned grasshoppers have wings. They exude a noxious smell from glands near their hind legs to repel predators. Their brilliant green color ensures the aggressors remember the results of an attack. Below; left: A bladder grasshopper looks like a leaf; right: A mating pair of green leaf grasshoppers.*

order Gramineae (in bot. use including, in popular use excluding, the cereals, reeds, and bamboos); grazing, pasture; pasture land; grass-covered ground, lawn, grass border; (slang) marijuana (as drug); **grass′hopper**, orthopterous insect (of families Tettigoniidae and Locustidae) with remarkable powers of leaping and producing a shrill chirping noise by rubbing the forewings together or with the hind legs; **grass′land**, area of grass or grasslike vegetation; prairie; **~-of-Parnassus**, any plant of the genus *Parnassia*, with wide leaves and a single pale flower; **~ roots**, (fig.) source; rank and file of political party etc. **~-roots** (*adj.*); **~ snake**, harmless common ringed snake (*Natrix natrix*) of Europe, and common green snake (*Ophiodrys vernalis*) of U.S.; **~ widow**, married woman whose husband is absent for a period. **grass′less; grass′y** *adjs.* (**grass·i·er, grass·i·est**). **grass** *v.t.* Cover with grass, grow grass on; feed grass to (animals).

grate[1] (grāt) *n.* Frame of metal bars for holding fuel in fireplace, stove, or furnace; fireplace.

grate[2] (grāt) *v.* (**grat·ed, grat·ing**). Reduce to small particles by rubbing on rough surface; have irritating effect *on*; grind (teeth); rub with harsh scraping noise *against, on* something else; sound harshly or discordantly. **grat′er** *n.* Utensil for grating cheese, vegetables, etc. **grat′ing·ly** *adv.*

grate·ful (grāt′ful) *adj.* Comforting, refreshing, agreeable; feeling or showing gratitude. **grate′ful·ly** *adv.* **grate′ful·ness** *n.*

grat·i·fy (grăt′ĭfī) *v.t.* (**-fied, -fy·ing**). Please, satisfy, delight; give free course to, indulge in (desire, feeling, impulse). **grat·i·fi·ca·tion** (grătĭfĭkā′shon) *n.*

grat′i·fy·ing *adj.* **grat′i·fy·ing·ly** *adv.*

grat·ing (grā′tĭng) *n.* Framework of parallel or crossed wooden or metal bars; (optics) (also **diffraction** ~) arrangement of parallel wires, surface of glass, etc., ruled with parallel lines, for producing spectra by diffraction.

gra·tis (grăt′ĭs, grah′tĭs, grā′-) *adv.* & *adj.* Gratuitous(ly); free(ly); without charge.

grat·i·tude (grăt′ĭtōōd, -tūd) *n.* Being thankful, appreciation of and inclination to return kindness.

gra·tu·i·tous (gr*a*tōō′ĭt*u*s, -tū′-) *adj.* Received or given free, not earned or paid for; uncalled for, unwarranted, motiveless, done or acting without good or assignable reason. **gra·tu′i·tous·ly** *adv.* **gra·tu′i·tous·ness** *n.*

gra·tu·i·ty (gr*a*tōō′ĭtē, -tū′-) *n.* (pl. **-ties**). Money present, in addition to payment due, given in recognition of services, tip.

gra·va·men (gr*a*vā′men) *n.* (pl. **-vam·i·na** pr. -văm′in*a*). (law) Essence, worst part, *of* accusation or charge.

grave[1] (grāv) *n.* Excavation to receive corpse, mound or monument over it; death; receptacle of or for what is dead; **grave′clothes**, clothes or shroud in which corpse is buried; **grave′stone** (also *headstone*), stone over grave, inscribed stone at head or foot of grave; **grave′yard**, burial ground; **graveyard shift**, (colloq.) work shift beginning at midnight; workers on this shift.

grave[2] (grāv) *adj.* (**grav·er, grav·est**). 1. Important, weighty, needing serious thought; (of faults, responsibilities, charges, etc.) serious, formidable; dignified, solemn, slow-moving, not gay; somber, plain, not showy. 2. (of sounds) Low in pitch, deep in tone; ~ **accent**, (*grave* usu. pr. grahv) accent, orig. indicating a low or falling pitch on vowel so marked; (usu. in English verse) indicating a pronounced *e* in verb ending *-ed*. **grave′ly** *adv.* **grave** *n.* Grave accent.

grave[3] (grāv) *v.t.* (**graved, grav·en** or **graved, grav·ing**). Clean (ship's wooden bottom) by burning off accretions and tarring while aground or in dry dock.

grav·el (grăv′*e*l) *n.* 1. Coarse sand and small water-worn stones, freq. with slight intermixture of clay. 2. (path.) (Disease with) aggregations of urinary crystals recognizable as masses by naked eye. **grav′el·ly** *adj.* **gravel** *v.t.* (**-eled, -el·ing, -elled, -el·ling**). 1. Pave, strew, with gravel. 2. Perplex, puzzle, nonplus.

Graves (grāvz), **Robert (Ranke)** (1895–1985). English poet, novelist, scholar; author of historical novels *I, Claudius, The Golden Fleece*, etc.

Graves′ (grāvz) **disease.** (med.) Exophthalmic goiter. [Robert James *Graves* (1796–1853), Irish physician]

grav·id (grăv′ĭd) *adj.* Pregnant; full of, distended by, ripe eggs.

grav·i·tate (grăv′ĭtāt) *v.* (**-tat·ed, -tat·ing**). Move or tend by force of gravity *toward* a body; sink (as) by gravity, tend to low level, settle down; cause to sink by gravitation; (transf.) be strongly attracted *to(ward)* some center of influence.

grav·i·ta·tion (grăvĭtā′sh*o*n) *n.* Falling of bodies to earth, or sinking to lowest level, moving or tending to center of attraction; tendency of every particle of matter toward every other particle, of which fall of bodies to earth is an instance; **law of** ~, law (formulated by Sir Isaac Newton) according to which the attractive force of bodies varies directly as their masses and inversely as the square of the distance between them. **grav·i·ta′tion·al** *adj.*

grav·i·ty (grăv′ĭtē) *n.* (pl. **-ties**). 1. Being grave, solemnity; importance, seriousness; staidness, sobriety, serious demeanor. 2. Weight; **specific** ~, relative weight of any kind of matter, expressed by ratio of weight of given volume to weight of equal volume of some substance taken as standard (usu. water for liquids and solids, hydrogen or air for gases). 3. Attractive force by which all bodies tend to move toward center of earth, degree of intensity with which body in given position is affected by this, measured by amount of acceleration produced (abbrev. g); degree of intensity with which any body is similarly attracted by any other.

*The **grave** of an admired person is usually commemorated with elaborate display but Sir Ernest Shackleton's grave in the Whaler's Cemetery on St. Georgia Island is austerely simple.*

gra·vure (gr*a*vūr′, grāv′y*er*) *n.* Photogravure; rotogravure.

gra·vy (grā′vē) *n.* (pl. **-vies**). Fat and juices exuding from meat during and after cooking; sauce for meat etc. made from these with condiments etc.; ~ **boat**, boat-shaped vessel for gravy. 2. (slang) Unearned or unexpected money or benefit; excess money; ~ **train**, (slang) sinecure; source of easy money.

gray, Brit. **grey** (grā) *adjs.* Intermediate between black and white, colored like ashes or lead, between light and dark; dull, clouded, depressing, dismal; (of horse) of dark metallic color, iron gray; (of person, hair, etc.) turning white with age etc.; ancient, immemorial; belonging to old age, experienced, mature; ~ **area**, undecided or ambiguous aspects of a matter or parts of a controversy; **gray′beard**, old man; **Gray Friar**, Franciscan, from the color of the habit; **gray matter**: see MATTER; **gray power**, political pressure of organized old or retired persons; **gray squirrel**, common squirrel (*Sciurus carolinensis*), gray or black, arboreal, with bushy tail. **gray** *n.* Gray clothes; cold sunless light; gray color, pigment, horse. ~ *v.* Become, make, gray. **gray′ish** *adj.* **gray′ly** *adv.* **gray′ness** *n.*

Gray (grā), **Thomas** (1716–71). English poet; author of "Elegy in a Country Churchyard" etc.

gray·lag (grā′lăg) *n.* Common European wild goose (*Anser anser*).

gray·ling (grā′lĭng) *n.* (pl. **-lings**, collect. **-ling**). 1. Silver-gray freshwater fish (*Thymallus*) of salmon family, with long high dorsal fin, used for food. 2. Common butterfly.

graze[1] (grāz) *v.* (**grazed, graz·ing**). Feed (esp. cattle, or *v.i.* of cattle) on growing grass etc.; feed on (grass etc.); tend grazing cattle; pasture cattle.

graze[2] (grāz) *v.* (**grazed, graz·ing**). Touch lightly in passing; abrade (skin etc.) in rubbing past; suffer slight abrasion of (part of body). ~ *n.* Grazing; abrasion caused by grazing.

Gr. Br. *abbrev.* Great Britain.

grease (grēs) *n.* Melted fat of dead animals, esp. when soft; oily or fatty matter, esp. as lubricant; oily matter in wool, uncleansed wool; ~ **gun**, kind of pump for lubricating parts of machinery with grease; ~ **monkey** (slang) mechanic who lubricates machines; garage worker; ~ **paint**, make-up for painting actors' faces etc.; **greasewood**: = CREOSOTE BUSH. **grease** (grēs, grēz) *v.t.* (**greased, greas·ing**). Anoint or lubricate with grease; ~ **person's palm**: see PALM²; **like greased lightning**, (slang) very fast.

greas·er (grē'ser, -zer) *n.* (derog.) Native Mexican, Spanish-American.

greas·y (grē'sē, -zē) *adj.* (**greas·i·er, greas·i·est**). 1. Smeared or covered with, containing, made of, like, with too much, grease; (of wool) uncleansed; ~ **spoon**, (slang) cheap and dirty restaurant. 2. Slimy or slippery with mud, moisture, etc. 3. (of manners or expression) Disagreeably unctuous. **greas'i·ly** *adv.* **greas'i·ness** *n.*

great (grāt) *adj.* 1. Large, big (freq. preceding partly synonymous adjective, as ~ **big**, ~ **thick**, etc.); (of animal etc., species or variety) larger than others; (of part of building etc.) main, principal; (of qualities, emotions, etc.) beyond the ordinary in degree or extent; **the ~ majority**, much the larger part; **Greater**, (of cities) including adjoining areas etc. 2. Important, elevated, distinguished, *the* chief, preeminent; **the G~** (following proper name), the most famous of the name, one of the great figures of history. 3. Of remarkable ability, genius, intellectual or practical qualities, loftiness or integrity of character; fully deserving the name of, (with agent nouns) doing the act much or on a large scale, as **a ~ fiasco, a ~ scoundrel**; (colloq.) highly satisfactory, fine, magnificent; (predic.) having much skill *at* or information *on*; **great'hearted** (*adj.*), noble, magnanimous, generous, courageous. 4. (with terms denoting kinship, esp. with compounds of *grand*) One degree farther removed in ascending or descending relationship; as **~-aunt, -uncle**, one's parent's aunt, uncle, **~-grandfather, -grandmother**, one's parent's grandfather, grandmother; so **~-grandchild** etc.; **~-~-grandfather** etc., one's parent's great-grandfather etc. 5. **G~ Australian Bight**, wide bay of the Indian Ocean stretching from S. to W. Australia; **G~ Barrier Reef**, largest coral formation in the world, a series of reefs extending for more than 1,250 miles (2,012.5 km) off the coast of Queensland, NE. Australia; **G~ Britain**: see BRITAIN; **~ circle**: see CIRCLE; **great'coat**, large heavy overcoat; **the Great Fire of London**, fire that in Sept. 1666 destroyed most of London; **great horned owl**: see OWL; **Great Lakes**: see separate entry; **Great Powers**, nations having great political and military influence and international importance; **great primer**: see PRIMER²; **Great Russian**, Russian language excluding Ukrainian and Byelorussian; **Great Spirit**, supreme deity of many N. Amer. Indians; **great unwashed**: see UNWASHED; **Great War**, World War I (see WORLD). **great'ness** *n.* **great** *n.* (pl. **greats**, collect. **great**). (pl.) Great persons.

Great (grāt) **Basin.** Elevated region in the W. United States covering 189,000 sq. mi. (489,510 sq. km); it includes most of Nevada and parts of Utah, California, Oregon, Idaho, and Wyoming; also includes the Great Salt Lake and Mojave Deserts, Carson Sink and Death Valley; area has no drainage to the ocean, the Great Salt Lake serving as the primary interior drainage center.

Great·er An·til·les (grā'ter ăntĭl'ēz). Caribbean island group forming part of the West Indies, consisting of Cuba, Hispaniola, Jamaica, and Puerto Rico.

*Diving birds renowned for their courtship displays, species of **grebe** are found in N. and S. America, Eurasia, Africa, Asia and Australia. Parents share in nest building and care of young.*

*Above left: A map of **Greece** and the national flag. The nation occupies 51,000 sq. miles of territory and has a population of 9 million, half of whom work in agriculture. Above right: Women hoe the parched earth of a co-operative farm. Right: The Academy in Athens, the capital. The nation is working to industrialize and many factories are being built.*

great (grāt) **horned owl.** Large N. Amer. owl (*Bubo virginianus*) with feathery projections on either side of its head.

Great (grāt) **Lakes.** Five lakes, the largest group of freshwater lakes in the world, covering almost 95,000 square mi. (152,950 km) on either side of the U.S.-Canadian border, and consisting of lakes Superior, Michigan, Huron, Erie, and Ontario.

great·ly (grāt′lē) *adv.* 1. Much, by much. 2. Nobly, loftily.

Great (grāt) **Plains.** Region of valleys and plains in central N. Amer., bounded by the base of the Rocky Mountains in the W., Canada's Laurentian Highlands in the N., and the margins of the Central Plains in the U.S.

Great (grāt) **Salt Lake.** Shallow, strongly saline lake occupying 2,000 sq. mi. (5,180 sq. km) of N. Utah near Salt Lake City in the Great Basin of the U.S.; **Great Salt Lake Desert**, flat, arid area about 110 mi. by 50 mi., (177 km by 80 km) SW. of the Great Salt Lake in N. Utah.

Great (grāt) **Smoky Mountains.** (also called **Great Smokies**) Appalachian mountain range extending along North Carolina-Tennessee boundary; highest peak, Clingmans Dome (6,643 ft., 2,025 m).

Great (grāt) **Wall of China.** (also known as *Chinese* Wall *or* Chin. *Chang-chêng*) Defensive wall in N. China, 20 to 50 ft. (6 to 15 m) high, 15 to 25 ft. (4.5 to 7 m) thick, extending 2,000 mi. (3,219 km) from Kansu province E. to the Yellow Sea; it was constructed in 3rd c. to prevent incursions from what is now called Manchuria and Mongolia.

greaves (grēvz) *n.pl.* (considered sing. or pl.) Fibrous matter or skin found in animal fat after rendering; cracklings.

grebe (grēb) *n.* (pl. **grebes**, collect. **grebe**). Any of various short-bodied almost tailless diving birds of family Podicipedidae with flattened and lobed feet set far behind.

Gre·cian (grē′sh*a*n) *adj.* Greek, Hellenic (rare exc. of architecture and facial outline); ~ **nose, profile**, nose straight in profile, continuing forehead line without a dip. ~ *n.* (rare) Native of Greece; (archaic) Greek scholar.

Gre·cism (grē′sĭz*e*m) *n.* Greek idiom, esp. as imitated in another language; Greek spirit, style, etc., imitation of these. **Gre′cize** *v.t.* (**-cized, -ciz·ing**). Make Greek in form or character.

Gre·co-Ro·man (grĕk′ō rō′-m*a*n, grē′kō-) *adj.* Of or relating to both ancient Greece and ancient Rome; of the later ancient world dominated by Rome.

Greece (grēs). Maritime country (a republic since 1973) in SE. Europe, bounded on the N. by Albania, Yugoslavia, and Bulgaria, on the S. and W. by the Ionian Sea, and on the E. by the Aegean and Turkey; capital, Athens; **Ancient** or **classical** ~, earliest great civilization of Europe, which

*At about 6,000 ft. the monastery of Mount Athos stands above a scene characteristic of north-eastern **Greece.** Limestone mountains stretch into three peninsulas of the Chalcidice, the easternmost being Mount Athos.*

developed around the shores of the Aegean, reached its peak in 5th c. B.C., and consisted of a number of city states of which Athens and Sparta became the most powerful; in 146 B.C. Greece became part of the Roman Empire; remained under the Eastern (Byzantine) Empire until overrun by Serbia during the 13th c.; was conquered by Turkey in the 14th–15th centuries and remained under Turkish rule until independence in 1821; was overrun by Germans in World War II, liberated in 1945.

greed (grēd) *n.* Insatiate longing, esp. for food or wealth. **greed'y** *adj.* (**greed·i·er, greed·i·est**). **greed'i·ly** *adv.* **greed'i·ness** *n.*

Greek (grēk) *adj.* Of, pertaining to, Greece, its inhabitants or their language; ~ **Church,** ~ **Orthodox Church**: see ORTHODOX: ~ **cross**, upright cross with limbs of equal length; ~ **god**, (fig.) paragon of male beauty. **Greek** *n.* 1. Greek person. 2. Language of the Greeks, (i) that of the classical period, a member of the Indo-Germanic family of languages, represented in classical times by four main dialects, Ionic, Attic, Aeolic, and Doric; (ii) the modern form, dating from 15th c.

Gree·ley (grē'lē), **Horace** (1811–72). Amer. journalist and politician; co-founder of the *New Yorker*, 1834, a weekly journal that later merged and became the New York *Tribune*, 1841; Republican presidential nominee, 1872, defeated by Ulysses S. Grant.

green (grēn) *adj.* 1. Of the color between blue and yellow in the spectrum, colored like grass, emerald, etc.; covered with herbage, verdant, in leaf; (of complexion) pale, sickly-hued, as in jealousy, sickness, etc.; (fig.) jealous, envious. 2. (of fruit etc.) Unripe; not withered or worn out; (of persons) immature, inexperienced, gullible; (of wood) not dried or seasoned; (of hide) not tanned. 3. **green'back**, U.S. currency note; **Greenback Party**, former U.S. political party, organized 1874, advocating greenbacks as the sole U.S. paper currency; **green bean**: see STRING bean; **green belt**, strip of land around a built-up area, kept free from building development etc.; **green cheese**, unripened cheese; very strong green-colored cheese; **green corn**: see SWEET CORN; **green-eyed**, (esp.) jealous; **green-eyed monster**, jealousy; **green flash**, rarely seen, dazzling momentary green appearance of top of sun's disk caused by refraction as sun dips below or rises above horizon; **green'gage**, green plum (f. name of Sir W. *Gage*); **green'grocer**, (Brit.) retail dealer in fruit and vegetables; so **green'grocery; green'heart**, tropical Amer. tree (*Ocotea rodiaei*), with dark, greenish, very hard wood; **green'horn**, (colloq.) inexperienced, immature person; newcomer, recent immigrant; gullible person; **green'house**, glass house for rearing delicate or tropical plants; **green light**, (fig.) permission to proceed; **green pepper**: see PEPPER def. 2; **green'room**, room in theater or television studio accommodating performers when off stage; **green salad**, salad composed wholly or almost wholly of greens; **green sickness**, chlorosis; **green'stick (fracture)**, bone fracture, esp. in children, in which one side of bone is broken and one only bent; **green'stone**, any of various eruptive rocks containing feldspar and hornblende; **green'sward**, turf; **green tea**: see TEA; **green thumb**, (colloq.) aptitude for making plants grow; **green'wood**, woodlands in summer. **green'ly** *adv.* **green'ness** *n.* **green'ish** *adj.* **green** *n.* 1. What is green; green part of anything; green color; green dye. 2. Vegetation, greenery; (pl.) leafy plants eaten as vegetables; cut leaves and branches used as decoration, esp. for Christmas. 3. (hist.) Piece of public or common grassy land; grass plot used for special purpose. 4. (golf) Area of closely mown turf around hole. ~ *v.* Become green.

Green (grēn), **William** (1873–1952). Amer. labor leader; president of American Federation of Labor, 1924–52.

green·er·y (grē'nerē) *n.* (pl. **-er·ies**). Verdure; green branches or leaves as decoration.

green·ing (grē'nĭng) *n.* Kind of cooking apple, green when ripe.

Green · land (grēn'land). Largest island in the world, 839,999 sq. mi. (2,175,597 sq. km), with only about 135,000 sq. mi. (349,650 sq. km) ice-free, in N. Atlantic NE. of N. Amer.; first colonized by Eric the Red in 985; now in Danish possession; capital, Godthaab; the only known source of cryolite, necessary in aluminum production.

Green·wich (grĕn'ĭj, -ĭch, grĭn'-; for def. 2 also grēn'wĭch).

*Below: A map of **Greenland,** the world's largest island after Australia. Its area of 840,000 sq. miles is mainly within the Arctic Circle and the population is 49,000. Most of these people work in the fish industry on the west coast. Below right: Houses of the capital, Godthaab, are wooden and have steep roofs.*

1. Borough of London, original site of the British Royal Astronomical Observatory, founded 1675 for the purpose of calculating longitude; ~ **Mean Time**, (abbrev. GMT or G.M.T.; also ~ **Time**) mean solar time of the meridian of Greenwich, England, used as a basis for calculating time, and in navigation, throughout most of the world. 2. Town in SW. Connecticut, 35 mi. (56 km) from New York City; ~ **Village**, section of lower Manhattan, New York City, frequented by artists, writers, and students.

greet (grēt) *v.t.* Accost with salutation; salute *with* words or gestures, receive on meeting or arrival *with* speech or action; (of sight etc.) meet (eye, ear). **greet'er, greet'ing** *ns.*

gre·gar·i·ous (gregār'ēus, -găr'-) *adj.* Living in flocks or communities; fond of company; of flocks or crowds. **gre·gar'i·ous·ly** *adv.* **gre·gar'i·ous·ness** *n.*

Gre·go·ri·an (grĭgōr'ēan, -gōr'-) *adj.* Pertaining to, originated by, some person named Gregory, esp. one of the popes of that name; ~ **calendar**, modified calendar, also known as the "New Style," introduced by Pope Gregory XIII in 1582 and now in use throughout most of the world; ordinary year has 365 days, and leap year of 366 days occurs when year is divisible by 4, except centenary years e.g. 2000, 2100; ~ **chant**, monodic liturgical plainsong of the R.C. Ch., founded on the "Antiphonarium," of which Pope Gregory I is presumed to have been the compiler.

Greg·o·ry[1] (grĕg'erē). Name of 16 popes: **Gregory I**, saint, pope 590–604, a zealous propagator of Christianity; sent AUGUSTINE to

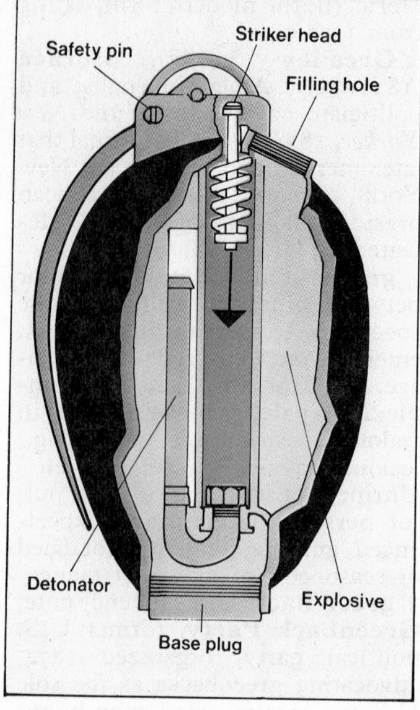

England; is presumed to have originated the GREGORIAN chant; **Gregory VII**, saint, pope 1073–85, a Benedictine monk, called Hildebrand; before his election attempted to extend the temporal power of the papacy; **Gregory XIII**, pope 1572–85, introduced the GREGORIAN calendar.

Greg·o·ry[2] (grĕg'erē), **Lady** (Isabella) Augusta (Persse) (1859?–1932). Irish dramatist; helped establish the Irish National Theater Society with W. B. Yeats and others and the Abbey Theatre in Dublin, which she directed.

*The Marriage Room at **Gretna Green,** Dumfries, Scotland, is now a place visited for the sake of its romantic associations with eloping couples in the past.*

*The modern hand **grenade** is primed with a detonator. When the safety pin is pulled free the handle is released and triggers the grenade. Its fuse delays the explosion for a fixed period of seconds.*

greige (grā, grāzh) *n.* & *adj.* (Of) color between beige and gray. [Fr. *grège* raw (silk)]

grem·lin (grĕm'lĭn) *n.* Mischievous sprite to whom mechanical defects of military airplanes were humorously attributed during World War II; mechanical trouble or its cause.

Gre·na·da (grenā'da, -nah'-). Island in the West Indies, 120 sq. mi. (193 sq. km), southernmost of the Windward Islands; with its adjacent islands, the southern Grenadines, it is an independent member (since 1974) of the Commonwealth of Nations; capital, St. George's.

gre·nade (grenād') *n.* Small explosive shell thrown by hand (**hand** ~) or shot from rifle; glass receptacle thrown to disperse chemicals for extinguishing fires etc. [Span. *granada* pomegranate]

gren·a·dier (grĕnadēr') *n.* 1. (orig.) Soldier who threw grenades (orig. four or five men in each company); later, in England, a company of the tallest and finest men in each regiment, hence **G~ Guards**, or **Grenadiers**, first regiment of British royal household infantry. 2. Deep-sea fish of family Macrouridae, related to cod, with long tapering tail; rat-tail.

gren·a·dine[1] (grĕnadēn', grĕn'adēn) *n.* Loosely-woven silk or silk-and-wool dress fabric.

gren·a·dine[2] (grĕn'adēn, grĕnadēn') *n.* French cordial syrup of pomegranates.

Gren·a·dines (grĕnadēnz', grĕn'adēnz). Chain of about 600

*Originating as a fabulous beast in legends from the eastern Mediterranean the **griffin** may have symbolized strength and attentiveness, qualities carried into heraldic usage.*

islands in the central Windward group in the E. Caribbean, between Grenada and St. Vincent.

Gresh·am's (grĕsh′amz) **Law.** (econ.) Tendency, when two or more kinds of money of equal nominal value but different intrinsic value are in circulation, for the one having the least intrinsic value to remain in circulation and for the other to be hoarded; expressed (colloq.) as "bad money drives out good." [Sir Thomas *Gresham* (1519?–1579), English financier, founder of the Royal Exchange]

Gret·na (grĕt′na) **Green.** Village in Scotland, near English border, noted as a place where eloping English couples could be quickly married (between 1754 and 1857, after which Scottish marriage laws became stricter).

grey *adj.* (chiefly Brit.) = GRAY.

Grey[1] (grā), **Lady Jane** (1537–1554). Great-granddaughter of Henry VII; proclaimed queen of England after death of Edward VI, 1553, in unsuccessful plot to alter succession to throne; she was imprisoned, refused to renounce Protestantism, and was beheaded; succeeded by Catholic queen Mary Tudor.

Grey[2] (grā), **Zane** (1875–1939). Amer. writer of adventure stories, freq. with western backgrounds; author of *Riders of the Purple Sage, The Vanishing American, West of the Pecos*, etc.

grey·hound (grā′hownd) *n.* Slender long-legged keen-sighted swift dog, now used primarily in dog racing.

grid (grĭd) *n.* 1. Grating, frame of parallel bars; gridiron. 2. Network of lines, esp. system of numbered squares printed on map and forming basis of map reference. 3. Network of wires for distributing electric current, of pipes for distributing gas, etc. 4. (elect.) Electrode in a vacuum tube that controls the flow of electrons in the tube.

grid·dle (grĭd′el) *n.* Flat pan or metal surface for cooking by dry heat; frying pan or surface; ~ **cake**, thin flat cake of batter cooked on griddle; PANCAKE.

grid·i·ron (grĭd′īern) *n.* Metal utensil with bars for supporting food to be broiled or grilled; (theatr.) structure high over stage supporting lights, mechanism for raising and lowering backdrops, etc.; football field (from the parallel yard lines).

grief (grēf) *n.* Deep or violent sorrow, keen regret; **come to ~**, meet with disaster, fail, fall.

Grieg (grēg), **Edvard Hagerup** (1843–1907). Norwegian composer noted for folk songs, Norwegian dances, and compositions for piano, orchestra and chorus.

griev·ance (grē′vans) *n.* Real or fancied ground of complaint; complaint or resentment against unjust act; hence, ~ **committee**, esp. of a labor union.

grieve (grēv) *v.* (**grieved, griev·ing**). Give deep sorrow to; feel grief. **griev′er** *n.*

griev·ous (grē′vus) *adj.* 1. Causing grief or suffering; (of pain, problems, etc.) serious, grave, dire. 2. Flagrant, heinous. **griev′ous·ly** *adv.* **griev′ous·ness** *n.*

grif·fin, grif·fon[1] (grĭf′in) *ns.* Fabulous creature with eagle's head and wings and lion's body; (her.) representation of this creature as charge or crest.

Grif·fith (grĭf′ĭth), **D. W. (David Lewelyn Wark)** (1875–1948). Amer. motion picture producer and director; famous for such cinematography innovations as the close-up shot, etc.; among his works, *The Birth of a Nation, Intolerance, Broken Blossoms.*

grif·fon[2] (grĭf′on) *n.* Kind of coarse-haired terrier-like dog of Belgian breed.

grill[1] (grĭl) *v.* Broil under grill or on gridiron; (colloq.) subject to severe questioning. ~ *n.* 1. Grilled dish; cooking surface or flame for broiling or frying; restaurant serving grilled food; **bar and ~**: see BAR[1]. **grilled** *adj.*

grille, grill[2] (grĭl) *ns.* Grating, latticed screen, esp. in window or gateway.

grim (grĭm) *adj.* (**grim·mer, grim·mest**). Stern, unrelenting, merciless, severe; of forbidding or harsh aspect; sinister, ghastly, unmirthful. **grim′ly** *adv.* **grim′ness** *n.*

gri·mace (grĭm′ĭs, grĭmās′) *n.* Wry face expressing annoyance etc. or meant to raise a laugh; affected look. ~ *v.i.* (**-maced, -mac·ing**). Make wry face.

grime (grīm) *n.* Soot, dirt, ingrained in some surface, esp. the skin. ~ *v.t.* (**grimed, grim·ing**). Blacken, befoul. **grim′y** *adj.* (**grim·i·er, grim·i·est**).

Grimm (grĭm), **Jacob Ludwig Carl** (1785–1863) and **Wilhelm Carl** (1786–1859). Brothers, famous for their research into German language, literature, and antiquities and for their collection of German folk tales (*Grimm's Fairy Tales*); **~'s Law**, statement, formulated by Jacob Grimm in 1822, of the regular changes that certain consonants of the primitive Indo-Germanic consonant system have undergone in the Germanic languages.

grin (grĭn) *v.* (**grinned, grin·ning**). Show teeth in cheerful or unrestrained or forced smile, or in sign of pain or fatuity; express (contempt, satisfaction) by grinning. ~ *n.* Act of grinning. **grin′ner** *n.*

grind (grīnd) *v.* (**ground, grind·ing**). 1. Reduce to small

Accepted as a show breed from 1886, the **Brussels griffon** is a popular dog. It should weigh between 6 and 9 lbs. and its color may be red, black or black and tan.

To the new style of 'natural' landscape gardens of the 18th century a ***grotto,*** *temple or picturesque ruin was added to lend a romantic air to the gardens. This one is at Stourhead, Wiltshire, U.K.*

particles or powder by crushing between millstones, teeth, etc.; produce (flour) by grinding; work (handmill); turn handle of (hurdy-gurdy), produce (music) from hurdy-gurdy etc.; (quasi-pass.) admit of being ground. 2. Sharpen, smooth, or fit by abrasion as in ~ **in** (valves etc.). 3. Oppress, harass with exactions; toil monotonously, study hard. 4. Rub gratingly *against*; rub (teeth) hard together. 5. **grind'stone**, thick revolving stone disk for grinding, sharpening, and polishing; kind of stone used for these; **keep one's nose to the grindstone**, work incessantly. **grind** *n.* Grinding; hard monotonous work or task; measure of size of particles obtained by grinding, as of coffee beans, *percolator grind*; (slang) student who works hard.

grind·er (grīn'd*er*) *n.* Thing, person, that grinds; molar tooth; grinding machine; (slang) sandwich, esp. hero sandwich (see HERO).

grin·go (grĭng'gō) *n.* (pl. **-gos**). (contempt.) Among Latin Americans, a U.S. citizen, esp. of Anglo-Saxon descent; any foreigner.

gri·ot (grē'*o*t) *n.* Tribal bard, singer, historian, of W. Africa.

grip (grĭp) *n.* Firm hold, tight grasp or clasp, grasping power; way of clasping hands; control, mastery, intellectual hold; power of arresting attention; part in machinery etc. that clips, part of weapon etc. that is held; small suitcase. ~ *v.* (**gripped** or **gript, grip·ping**). Seize, grasp, or hold, tightly; take firm hold; compel attention of. **grip'per** *n.*

gripe (grīp) *v.* (**griped, grip·ing**). Clutch; affect with colic pains; annoy, irritate; (slang) complain. ~ *n.* 1. Act of griping; handle of implement or weapon; (slang) complaint. 2. (pl.) Colic pains.

grippe (grĭp) *n.* Influenza.

gri·saille (grĭzī', -zāl') *n.* Method of painting in gray or grayish monochrome, freq. representing figures in relief.

gris·ly (grĭz'lē) *adj.* (**-li·er, -li·est**). Causing horror, terror, or superstitious dread. **gris'li·ness** *n.*

grist (grĭst) *n.* Grain for grinding; ground grain; ~ **for one's mill**, something useful or profitable.

gris·tle (grĭs'*e*l) *n.* Whitish tough flexible connective tissue in vertebrates; cartilage, esp. in meats. **gris'tly** *adj.* (**-tli·er, -tli·est**).

grit (grĭt) *n.* Small particles of stone or sand, esp. as causing discomfort or clogging machinery etc.; (geol.) coarse-grained sand or sandstone; grain or texture of stone; (colloq.) strength of character, pluck, endurance. ~ *v.* (**grit·ted, grit·ting**). Produce, move with, grating sound; grind (teeth). **grit'ty** *adj.* (**-ti·er, -ti·est**). **grit'ti·ness** *n.*

grits (grĭts) *n.pl.* (considered sing. or pl.). Coarsely ground grain, esp. corn; HOMINY.

griz·zle (grĭz'*e*l) *v.* (**-zled, -zling**). Make, become gray.

griz·zly (grĭz'lē) *adj.* (**-zli·er, -zli·est**). Gray, grayish, gray-haired; ~ **bear**, very large, fierce, yellowish-brown or grayish ("silvertip") bear (*Ursus horribilis*) of western N. America. ~ *n.* (pl. **-zlies**). Grizzly bear.

groan (grōn) *n.* Deep inarticulate sound expressing pain, grief, or disapproval. ~ *v.* Utter groan; utter with groans; creak, as boards, furniture, etc., with imposed weight. **groan'ing·ly** *adv.*

groat (grōt) *n.* (hist.) English silver coin worth four pence, first coined in 1351–2 and current until 1662. [MDu. *groot* great, thick (penny)]

groats (grōts) *n.pl.* (considered sing. or pl.) Hulled (sometimes also crushed) grain, esp. oats; KASHA.

gro·cer (grō's*er*) *n.* Merchant selling foodstuffs and household supplies. **gro'cer·y** *n.* (pl. **-cer·ies**). Grocer's store; (pl.) food sold there.

grog (grŏg) *n.* Drink of rum and water. [reputedly f. *grogram*, nickname (from his cloak) of Brit. Admiral Edward Vernon (1684–1757) who first had grog served in navy instead of straight rum]

grog·gy (grŏg'ē) *adj.* (**-gi·er, -gi·est**). Drunk(en); tottering; unsteady, shaky. **grog'gi·ly** *adv.* **grog'gi·ness** *n.*

groin (groin) *n.* 1. Depression between belly and thigh. 2. (archit.) Edge formed by intersecting vaults, fillet covering this. ~ *v.t.* (archit.) Build with groins. **groin'ing** *n.*

grom·met (grŏm'ĭt) *n.* Reinforced eyelet in cloth etc. to receive cord, fastener, etc.; (naut.) ring to secure edge of sail.

grom·well (grŏm'w*e*l) *n.* Any plant of genus *Lithospermum*, with hard stony seeds formerly used in medicine.

groom (grōōm) *n.* 1. One of certain officers of English Royal Household, chiefly in Lord Chamberlain's department. 2. Servant having care of horses. 3. Bridegroom; **grooms'man** (pl. **-men**), (archaic) best man or usher at wedding. **groom** *v.t.* Curry etc. (horse); give neat or attractive appearance to; train, prepare (person) for a specific role, position, etc.

groove (grōōv) *n.* Channel or hollow, esp. one made to direct motion or receive corresponding ridge; satisfactory niche; routine, undeviating course, rut; **in the ~**, (slang) performing excellently. ~ *v.* (**grooved, groov·ing**). Make groove(s) in; (slang) get along wel' *with* (person), be in the groove. **groov'y** *adj.* (**groov·i·er, groov·i·est**). (slang) In the groove, exciting, deeply satisfying.

grope (grōp) *v.i.* (**groped, grop·ing**). Feel about as in dark (*for*); search blindly; ~ **one's way**, find way by feeling, proceed tentatively. **grop'ing·ly** *adv.*

Gro·pi·us (grō'pēus), **Walter** (1883–1969). German-born Amer. architect; founded BAUHAUS school of design in Weimar in 1919.

gros·beak (grōs'bēk) *n.* Any of various finches with large strong beak, esp. those of genera *Pinicola* and *Hesperiphona*.

gros·grain (grō'grān) *n.* Corded fabric or ribbon of silk etc.; ribbon of this.

gros point (grōs'point) (pl. **gros points**). 1. Needlepoint lace with design in high relief. 2. Large embroidery cross-stitch covering two or more threads of canvas.

gross[1] (grōs) *n.* (pl. **gross**). Twelve dozen.

gross[2] (grōs) *adj.* 1. Repulsively fat; flagrant, glaring. 2. Total, without deductions, not net; ~ **national product**, total market value of goods produced and services provided in a country in one year. 3. Dense, thick; coarse, dull; coarse in manners or morals, unrefined, indecent; disgusting. ~ *v.t.* Earn a total of. **gross'ly** *adv.* **gross'ness** *n.*

gro·tesque (grōtěsk') *n.* Decoration with fantastic interweaving of human and animal forms with foliage; (pop.) comically distorted figure or design. ~ *adj.* (archit.) In the style of a grotesque; distorted, bizarre; ludicrous from incongruity, absurd. **gro·tesque'·ly** *adv.* **gro·tesque'ness** *n.* [It. *grottesca* antique work, prob. *grotta* (grotto) of ancient Roman houses, where such paintings were found]

Gro·ti·us (grō'shēus, -shus), **Hugo** (1583–1645). Dutch statesman and jurist; famous for his treatise codifying international law, the *De jure Belli et Pacis*, published in 1625.

*Commonly called the **blue gromwell**, Lithospermum purpurocaeruleum is normally found in soil rich in calcium carbonate such as chalk.*

grot·to (grŏt'ō) *n.* (pl. **-toes, -tos**). Picturesque cave; artificial ornamental cave; (geog.) cave formed by underground stream.

grouch (growch) *n.* Grumbling; complaint; sulky, grumbling mood; grumbler. **grouch'y** *adj.* (**grouch·i·er, grouch·i·est**). **grouch'i·ly** *adv.* **grouch'i·ness** *n.* **grouch** *v.i.* Grumble; be sulky.

ground[1] (grownd) *n.* 1. Bottom of sea; (pl.) dregs, esp. of coffee. 2. Base, foundation; motive, valid reason. 3. Substratum, underlying part; surface worked upon in embroidery, painting, etc.; undecorated part; prevailing color or tone; (painting) preparation spread over canvas, panel, etc., to isolate it from paint layer. 4. Surface of Earth; position, area, etc. on Earth's surface; area of special kind or use; portion of land forming person's property; space on which person etc. takes a stand (freq. fig.); (pl.) enclosed land for ornament or recreation attached to house; **above ~**, alive; **down to the ~**, (colloq.) in all respects; thoroughly; **be dashed to the ~**, (of scheme, hope) be abandoned, fail; **forbidden ~**, subject that must be avoided; **gain ~**, advance; **lose, give, ~**, retreat, decline; **run into the ~**, explain at unreasonable length; overdo; **stand, shift, one's ~**, maintain, change, one's argument or intention. 5. (elect.) Connection to earth (or some other large conducting body) as completion of circuit. 6. attrib.: (in names of birds) terrestrial, (of beasts) burrowing in or lying on ground, (of plants) dwarfish or trailing. 7. ~ **ball** (also **grounder**), (baseball) batted ball that rolls or bounces (opp. FLY ball); ~ **bass**, (mus.) theme in bass constantly repeated with varied melody or harmony above; ~ **cover**, low-growing plants used in place of grass or to control erosion; ~ **crew**, workers, mechanics, etc., who service and maintain aircraft on the ground; ~ **floor**, floor of a building at or nearly at level of outside ground; **get in on the ~ floor**, be admitted to company, scheme, etc. at its inception; **ground'hog**, woodchuck; **ground ice**, ice formed at bottom of water; **ground ivy**, common labiate plant (*Glechoma hederacea*) with bluish-purple flowers; **ground'nut**, edible tuber or underground nut of a plant, as

***Ground ivy** (Nepeta hederacea) is not related to common ivy and is a ground dweller. Its flowers are blue to purple and bloom from mid- to late summer.*

the peanut. **ground pine**, European herbaceous plant (*Ajuga chamaepitys*) with resinous smell; club moss; **ground plan**, plane drawing of divisions of building on the ground level or ground floor; outline, general design, of anything; **ground rule**, (usu. pl.) basic principle(s) of a situation; (baseball etc.) rule(s) arising from nature of playing field or location of spectators; **ground'sheet**, waterproof sheet for spreading on ground as protection against damp, as under sleeping bag etc.; **ground speed**, horizontal component of aircraft velocity relative to the earth; **ground squirrel**, gopher; **ground swell**, heavy sea swell as result of distant storm; unexpected gathering or increase of public opinion; **ground water**, water lying below Earth's surface in springs and in pores of rock; **ground'work**, foundation or basis (usu. fig.). **ground** *v.* Base, establish, *on* some fact or authority; instruct thoroughly (*in* elements of subject); prepare ground of (canvas etc. for painting); keep on the ground, prevent (aircraft pilot) from taking off or flying; run ashore, strand; (elect.) connect an electric circuit, appliance, etc. to a ground.

ground[2] (grownd): see GRIND; (esp.) ~ **glass**, glass made nontransparent by grinding or etching.

ground·ing (grown'dĭng) *n.* (esp.) Instruction in, understanding of elements of subject.

ground·less (grownd'lĭs) *adj.* Without foundation, authority, or support, unfounded. **ground'less·ly** *adv.* **ground'less·ness** *n.*

ground·sel (grownd'sel) *n.* Plant of genus *Senecio*, esp. *S. vulgaris*, common European weed with small yellow flowers.

***Groundsel** (Senecio vulgaris) grows abundantly on cultivated ground, and flowers throughout the year. It is a common weed which contains a substance poisonous to birds.*

group (groop) *n.* In fine arts, 2 or more figures or objects forming complete design or distinct part of one; number of persons or things standing near together, knot, cluster; number of persons or things belonging or classed together; **Oxford G**~: see MORAL Rearmament; ~ **captain**, officer of Brit. Royal Air Force, ranking above wing commander; ~ **insurance**, insurance covering all members of a group, usu. at lower premium rates; ~ **practice**, medical practice run by several doctors in cooperation; ~ **therapy**, (psych.) therapy in which patients are brought together to discuss their problems and assist one another. **group** *v.* Form into a group, place in a group (*with*); form into well-arranged and harmonious whole; classify. **group'ie** *n.* (slang) Young girl devotee of rock group, team, etc.; hanger-on; member of a group sharing a vacation house.

group·er (groo'p*er*) *n.* (pl. **-ers**, collect. **-er**). Any of various, often very large, marine food fishes of the family Serranidae, found esp. in tropical seas.

grouse[1] (grows) *n.* (pl. **grouse**). Name of many species of gallinaceous birds of the family Tetraonidae esp. (in Amer.) **ruffed** ~ (*Bonasa umbellus*), medium-sized, with feathered feet, the males usu. staging elaborate courtship display.

grouse[2] (grows) *v.i.* (**groused, grous·ing**) & *n.* (colloq.) Grumble; complain. **grous'er** *n.*

grout (growt) *n.* Thin fluid mortar for filling masonry joints etc. ~ *v.t.* Fill up or finish with grout or cement.

grove (grōv) *n.* Small wood; group of trees.

grov·el (grŏv'el, grŭv'-) *v.i.* (**-eled, -el·ing, -elled, -el·ling**). Lie prone, humble oneself. **grov'el·ing** *adj.* Abject, low, base. **grov'el·ing·ly, grov'el·ling·ly** *advs.*

grow (grō) *v.* (**grew** pr. groo, **grown, grow·ing**). 1. Develop or exist as living plant; germinate, sprout, spring up, be produced, come naturally into existence, arise. 2. Increase in size, height, quantity, degree, power, etc.; become gradually; **growing pains**, children's pains prob. of a rheumatic character popularly attributed to growing;

*The term **grouse** may refer to a particular British game bird, or to a wider group in the northern hemisphere, also hunted for food. 1: The spruce grouse. 2: The red grouse found in Great Britain. 3: The black grouse. 4: The sage grouse of the U.S.A., so called because its sage diet flavors its flesh.*

growing season, season (longest near equator) when rainfall and temperature permit plants to grow; **grow on**, gain more and more of (person's etc.) liking or admiration; **grow up**, advance to maturity; reach full size; (of custom) arise, become common. 3. Produce by cultivation; bring forth; let (beard etc.) grow; (pass.) be covered (*over*) with some growth. **grow'er** *n.* (esp.) Person growing produce; plant that grows in specified way.

growl (growl) *n.* Guttural sound of anger; rumble; angry murmur, complaint. ~ *v.* Utter growl, rumble, murmur angrily; utter with a growl. **growl'ing·ly** *adv.*

grown (grōn) *adj.*: see GROW; (esp.) **~-up**, (*adj.* & *n.*) adult.

growth (grōth) *n.* Growing, development, increase; what has grown or is growing; (path.) morbid formation.

grub (grŭb) *n.* 1. Larva of insect, caterpillar, maggot. 2. (slang) Food. ~ *v.* (**grubbed, grub·bing**). 1. Dig superficially; clear (ground) of roots and stumps; clear away (roots etc.); fetch *up* or *out* by digging; search, rummage. 2. Plod, toil, *on, along, away*. 3. (slang) Feed; **grub'stake** (*n.*), supplies or money advanced (orig. to mining prospector) with agreement that profits will be shared; **grub'stake** (*v.*) (**-staked, -stak·ing**), supply a grubstake. **grub'ber** *n.*

grub·by (grŭb'ē) *adj.* (**-bi·er, -bi·est**). 1. Of, infested with, grubs. 2. Dirty, grimy, slovenly. **grub'bi·ness** *n.*

Grub (grŭb) **Street.** London street (now Milton Street) inhabited in 17th c. by impoverished authors and literary hacks; hence, such writers (also attrib.).

grudge (grŭj) *v.t.* (**grudged, grudg·ing**). Be unwilling to give, grant, or allow (*to*); be unwilling *to* do. **grudg'ing·ly** *adv.* **grudge** *n.* Feeling of resentment or ill will.

gru·el (grōō'*e*l) *n.* Thin, watery porridge.

gru·el·ing, gru·el·ling (grōō'*e*-lĭng) *adjs.* & *ns.* Exhausting or punishing (experience).

grue·some (grōō'*s*om) *adj.* Grisly, disgusting. **grue'some·ly** *adv.* **grue'some·ness** *n.*

gruff (grŭf) *adj.* Surly, laconic, rough-mannered, rough-voiced. **gruff'ly** *adv.* **gruff'ness** *n.*

grum·ble (grŭm'b*e*l) *n.* Dull inarticulate sound, murmur, complaint. ~ *v.* (**-bled, -bling**). Utter grumble, murmur, growl faintly; rumble; complain; utter complainingly. **grum'bler** *n.* **grum'bling·ly** *adv.*

grump·y (grŭm'pē) *adj.* (**grump·i·er, grump·i·est**). Ill-tempered, surly. **grump'i·ly** *adv.* **grump'i·ness** *n.*

Grun·dy (grŭn'dē), **Mrs.** In Thomas Morton's English play *Speed the Plough* (1798), a neighbor who never appears but is constantly referred to ("What will Mrs. Grundy say?"); hence, symbol of conventional propriety or prudery. **Grun'dy·ism** *n.*

grun·ion (grŭn'y*o*n) *n.* Small California sea fish that comes ashore to spawn.

grunt (grŭnt) *n.* 1. Low gruff sound characteristic of hogs, any similar sound. 2. Any of several tropical marine fishes of family Pomadasyidae, which make grunting noise. ~ *v.* Utter grunt; express discontent, dissent, assent, fatigue, etc., by this; utter with grunt.

Gru·yère (grōōyār', grē-) *n.* Pale, firm, yellow cow's-milk cheese, often with small cavities, orig. made at Gruyère, Switzerland.

GSA *abbrev.* General Services Administration; Girl Scouts of America.

G-string (jē'strĭng) *n.* Narrow strip of cloth etc. covering the genitals, esp. as worn by strip teasers.

G-suit (jē'sōōt) *n.* Garment to enable flier or astronaut to withstand high acceleration.

The stage between the egg and the pupa of an insect is the ***grub*** *or larval stage. Aborigines of Australia search for bardies or witchety grubs which they eat, raw or cooked.*

Gt. Br. *abbrev.* Great Britain.

GU *abbrev.* Guam.

gua·ca·mo·le (gwahk*a*mō'lē) *n.* 1. Mexican sauce of mashed avocado, hot peppers, etc. 2. Latin Amer. salad with avocado.

Gua·da·la·ja·ra (gwahd*a*l*a*-hār'*a*). City in W. central Mexico; noted for its cathedral, university, and pottery and handicrafts.

Gua·dal·ca·nal (gwahd*a*lk*a*-năl'). Island of the Solomon group in W. Pacific; occupied by Japanese in World War II and scene of several major battles with U.S. forces, Aug. 7–Nov. 13, 1942, before Japanese evacuated, Feb., 1943.

Gua·de·loupe (gwahd*e*lōōp'). Pair of islands in the E. West Indies, which, together with their five adjacent dependencies, constitute a French overseas department; discovered by Columbus, 1493; capital Basse-Terre.

guai·a·col (gwī'*a*kōl, -kawl, -kŏl) *n.* Colorless or yellowish liquid or white crystalline solid with strong smell, obtained by distilling guaiacum resin or wood tar creosote, and used in medicine.

guai·a·cum (gwī'*a*k*u*m): see LIGNUM VITAE.

Guam (gwahm). Largest and southernmost of the Mariana Islands in the W. Pacific; ceded to U.S. by Spain in 1898; capital, Agaña.

guan (gwahn) *n.* Any of several S. Amer. gallinaceous birds allied

*The **guan** is a gregarious bird. The blue throated guan (above) lives in areas between Texas and Argentina and feeds on insects, fruit and vegetation of many kinds. Attempts have been made to domesticate the guan but they have not succeeded.*

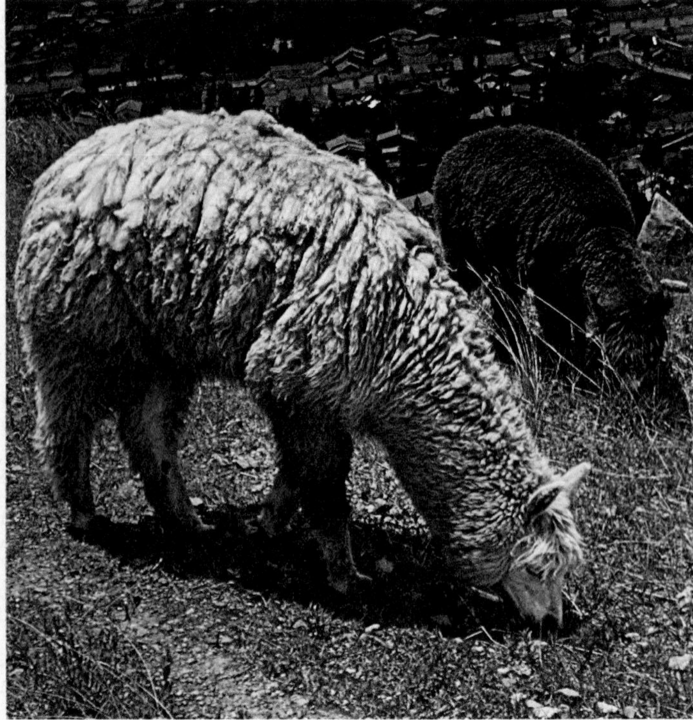

*The **guanaco** grazes the mountain slopes of the Andes. It is related to the camel and grows to a height of some 3½ ft. at the shoulder. Its hide is used to make warm clothing. The guanaco is able to drink salty water as well as fresh water when necessary.*

to curassows.

gua·na·co (gwahnah'kō) *n.* (pl. **-cos**, collect. **-co**). S. Amer. wild llama (*Lama huanacus*) with reddish-brown wool.

Gua·na·jua·to (gwahnahhwah'-tō). City in central Mexico famous for its gold and silver mines and catacombs.

Guang·dong (gwahn'do͝ong') = KWANGTUNG.

Guang·xi Zhuang (gwahng'shē jwahng') = KWANGSI-CHUANG.

Guang·zhou (gwahng'zho͞o') = CANTON.

gua·no (gwah'nō) *n.* Excrement of sea birds or bats accumulated along certain coastal or island areas and in caves, rich in phosphates and ammonia and used as manure; artificial manure, esp. that made from fish.

Guan·ta·na·mo (gwahntah'n*a*-mō). Town in SE. Cuba on ~ **Bay**, a Caribbean Sea inlet; site of U.S. naval base; Amer. forces landed here during Spanish-American War, June, 1898.

Gua·ra·ní (gwa͞ranē') *n.* (pl. **-nís, -níes**, collect. **-ní**). One of the two main divisions of the Tupi-Guaraní Indians of Bolivia, Paraguay, and S. Brazil; language of this people.

guar·an·tee (gă*r*antē') *n.* Person making guaranty or giving security; guaranty; thing given or existing as security for fulfillment of conditions or permanence etc. of something; ~ *v.t.* (**-teed, -tee·ing**). Be guarantee for, answer for due fulfillment of (contract etc.) or genuineness etc. of (article); engage *that* something has happened or will happen; secure possession of *to* person; secure *against* or *from* (risk etc.). **guar·an·tor** (găr'*a*ntōr, -t*er*) *n.*

guar·an·ty (găr'*a*ntē) *n.* (pl. **-ties**). Undertaking, esp. written, to answer for payment of debt or performance of obligation by another person; ground or basis of security; act of giving security; guarantor. ~ *v.t.* (**-tied, -ty·ing**).

guard (ga͞rd) *n.* 1. Defensive posture or motion in fencing, boxing, etc.; watch, vigilant state; **be on** ~, act as sentry etc.; **on, off, one's** ~, prepared, unprepared, against attack, surprise, etc. 2. Protector, defender, sentry; one who supervises prisoners. 3. Body of soldiers etc. serving as protectors of place or person, escort etc.; **Guards**, selected bodies of troops normally for escort or ceremonial duties, e.g. in British Army the *Royal Horse Guards*, the *Coldstream Guards*, etc. 4. Contrivance to prevent injury or accident; e.g. part of sword hilt protecting hand from injury, trigger guard, etc. 5. (sports) One who guards an opponent; (football) (one of two players having) a position on either side of the center; (basketball) (one of two players having) a position defending in back court or play-making in mid-court. 6. ~ **chain**, chain securing watch, brooch, etc.; **guard'house** (pl. **-hous·es**), building for accommodation of military guard or keeping of prisoners under guard; **guard'rail**, hand- or other rail to prevent falling, etc.; extra inner rail to keep wheel on line at railroad switches, crossings, etc.; **guard'room**, room for keeping prisoners under guard, or for military guard; **guards'man** (pl. **-men**), guard; member of U.S. National Guard; (Brit.) member of the Guards. **guard** *v.* Keep safe, stand guard over, keep (door etc.) so as to control passage; protect, defend; secure by explanations or stipulations etc. from misunderstanding or abuse; keep (thoughts, speech) in check; take precautions *against*; (sports) block or frustrate (an opponent). **guard'ed** *adj.* Cautious. **guard'ed·ly** *adv.* Cautiously.

guard·ant, gard·ant (ga͞r'd*a*nt) *adjs.* (her.) (of a beast) Having the full face toward the viewer.

guard·i·an (ga͞r'dē*a*n) *n.* Keeper, defender, protector; (law) one having custody of person or property, or both, of minor, etc.; ~ **angel**, spirit watching over person or place. **guard'i·an·ship** *n.*

Guar·ne·ri, Guar·nie·ri (gwa͞r-na͞r'ē). Name of a 17th- and 18th-c. family of Italian violin-makers of Cremona; hence, **Guar·ne·ri·us** (gwa͞rna͞r'ē*u*s), vio-

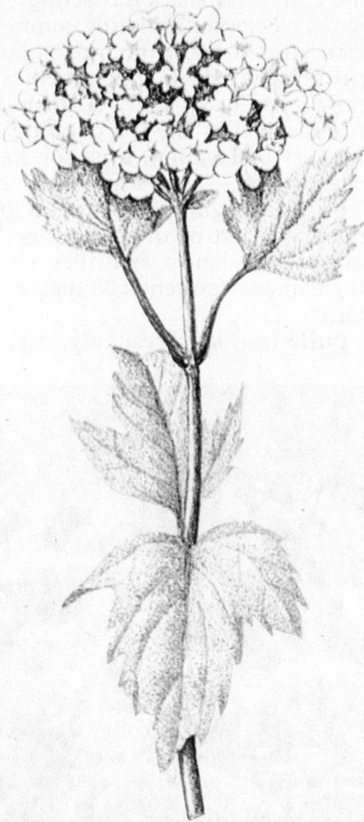

Growing in damp woodlands and in marshy ditches the ***guelder rose*** *blooms in the middle summer months. Later it bears clusters of attractive, scarlet globose fruits.*

lin made by one of this family.

Gua·te·ma·la (gwahtemah′la). Most northerly republic of Central America, bordering on Mexico; capital, Guatemala City. **Gua·te·ma′lan** *adj.* & *n.*

gua·va (gwah′va) *n.* Tree of tropical Amer. genus *Psidium* of family Myrtaceae, esp. *P. guajava;* acid fruit of this, used for making jelly etc. [Span. *guayaba,* prob. f. native Amer. name]

Gua·ya·quil (gwahyahkēl′). Largest city of Ecuador, in the SW., a seaport on mouth of Guayas River.

gu·ber·na·to·ri·al (gōōberna-tōr′ēal, -tōr′-, gū-) *adj.* Of a governor; of the office of governor.

gudg·eon[1] (gŭj′on) *n.* Small European freshwater fish (*Gobio gobio*) used as bait; gullible person.

gudg·eon[2] (gŭj′on) *n.* Pivot at end of beam, axle, etc., on which bell, wheel, etc., works; socket in which rudder works; pin holding two blocks of stone etc. together.

guel·der (gĕl′der) **rose.** Small tree or shrub (*Viburnum opulus*), native to Eurasia bearing round bunches of white flowers and small red fruit. [f. *Guelders,* town in Prussia, or *Guelderland,* province of the Netherlands]

Guelph, Guelf (gwĕlf) *ns.* 1. Member of medieval Italian party supporting the pope and the Italian city-states against the German emperor. 2. Member of a ducal family of Swabian origin established in the 9th c. [It. *Guelfo* f. MHG. *Welf,* name of the founder of the family]

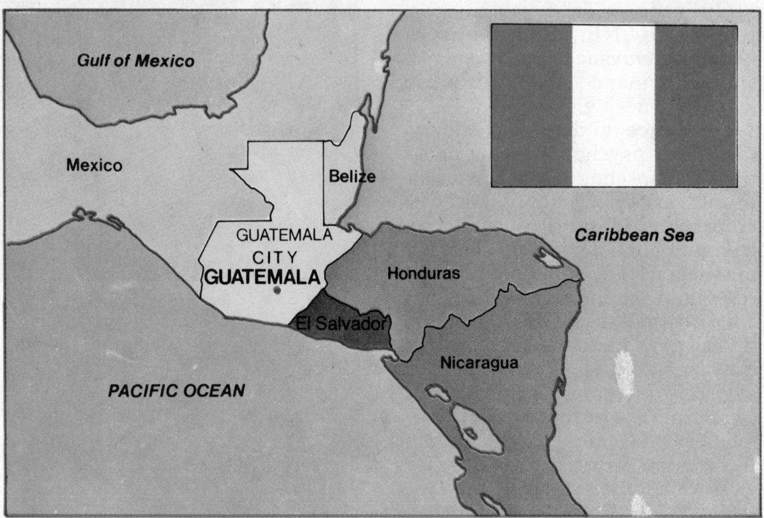

The most densely populated country of S. America, ***Guatemala*** *has a population of 5.5 million occupying its 42,000 sq. miles of land. Above: Some of the citizens carry firewood to sell in Guatemala City, the nation's capital. Center: A map of Guatemala and the national flag.*

guer·don (gēr′don) *n.* & *v.t.* (poet.) Reward, recompense.

Guer·ni·ca (gwĕr′nĭka; *Sp.* gĕrnē′kah) (also ~ **y Lu·na** pr. -ēlōō′nah). Basque town in N. central Spain; destroyed by the Condor Legion, the German air force supporting Franco's forces, in mass bombing, 1937, during Spanish civil war; the bombing is the subject of Picasso's famous mural "Guernica."

Guern·sey (gērn′zē). Second largest of the English Channel Islands; capital, St. Peter Port.

guern·sey (gērn′zē) *n.* 1. Thick knitted closely fitting wool shirt as worn by seamen. 2. **G**~ (pl. **-seys**), (one of) a breed of usu. fawn-and-white dairy cattle, orig. raised in Guernsey.

guer·ril·la, gue·ril·la (gerĭl′a) *ns.* Person engaged in irregular fighting [~ **war(fare)**] carried out by small bodies of men and women serving a patriotic or revolutionary movement; ~ **theater,** crude, quasi-impromptu playlets (on war, peace, justice, revolution, etc.) produced in the streets. [Span. *guerrilla* little war]

guess (gĕs) *v.* Estimate; think likely; form hypothesis as to, conjecture, hazard opinion about; conjecture (answer to riddle etc.) rightly; **I ~**, I feel sure, I know well. ~ *n.* Rough estimate, conjecture, hypothesis; **guess'work**, (procedure based on) guessing. **guess'er** *n.*

guess·ti·mate (*v.* gĕs'tĭmāt; *n.* gĕs'tĭmĭt, -māt) *v.* (**-mat·ed, -mat·ing**) & *n.* (slang) (Make a) rough, uninformed estimate.

guest (gĕst) *n.* Person given food or lodging at another's house etc.; person lodging at hotel, boarding-house, etc.; **paying ~**, boarder; **guest'house**, (1) separate house for guests on an estate; (2) small, informal hotel, sometimes inexpensive, sometimes luxurious.

guf·faw (gŭfaw', gu-) *n.* Loud, boisterous laugh. ~ *v.* Make, say with, guffaw.

Gug·gen·heim (go͝og'enhīm, go͞o'gen-), **Daniel** (1856–1930). Amer. industrialist and philanthropist; leading figure in copper industry; established the Guggenheim Foundation, 1924, to promote "the well-being of mankind."

Gui·a·na (gēăn'a, -ah'na, gī-). Region in NE. South Amer., including Guyana, French Guiana, and Surinam. **Gui·a·nese** (gēanēz', -nēs', gī-) *adj.* & *n.*

gui·dance (gī'dans) *n.* Guiding, direction; psychological or vocational counseling in a school or social service agency, hence ~ **counselor; inertial ~ (system)**, (computer and devices for) keeping missile, aircraft, etc., on course by responding to inertial forces.

guide (gīd) *n.* 1. One who shows the way; hired conductor of traveler, tourist, or climber; adviser; directing principle or standard; **G~** (formerly **Girl G~**) member of the Girl Guides Association, a Brit. organization for girls somewhat similar to the Girl Scouts. 2. Book of rudiments, manual; (also **guide'book**), book to inform tourists about country, city, museum, etc. 3. (mech.) Bar, rod, etc., directing motion of something; gauge etc.; controlling tool; thing marking a position or guiding the eye. 4. ~ **dog**, dog trained to guide blind person; **guide'line**, (usu. pl., often bureaucratic jargon) suggestion or indication of future action; statement of policy by some authority; directions to be followed, but without the clarity or sanction of law; **guide'post**, signpost. **guide** *v.t.* (**guid·ed, guid·ing**). Act as guide to, go before, lead, direct course of; arrange course of (events); be principle, motive, or ground, of; conduct affairs of (state etc.); **guided missile** etc., missile etc. steered by remote control or internal mechanism. **guid'er** *n.*

gui·don (gī'don; *Brit.* gē'don) *n.* Small flag or pennant, often with forked end; this as a military unit's standard; the soldier carrying such a standard.

guild (gĭld) *n.* Society for mutual aid or prosecution of common object, esp. medieval trade or craft association, acting as benefit society, promoting common trade interests of members etc.; **guild'hall**, hall in which medieval guild met; town hall; **Guildhall,** meeting hall of the Corporation of the City of London, used for state banquets etc.

guil·der (gĭl'der) *n.* Principal monetary unit of the Netherlands, the Netherlands Antilles and Surinam, = 100 cents; Netherlands florin.

guile (gīl) *n.* Treachery, deceit;

*A member of the auk family, the common **guillemot** is about 16 ins. in length. It is one of the most skilful diving birds. Above right: It nests on inaccessible cliffs. The black guillemot is a smaller bird with white wing covers.*

The West African republic of ***Guinea*** *has a population of 4.3 million inhabiting 95,000 sq. miles. The nation has the largest bauxite deposits in the world but most of the people work in agriculture.*

cunning devices. **guile'ful** *adj.* **guile'ful·ly** *adv.* **guile'ful·ness** *n.* **guile'less** *adj.* **guile'less·ly** *adv.* **guile'less·ness** *n.*

guil·le·mot (gĭl'*e*mŏt) *n.* Small northern sea bird of genus *Cepphus* with white markings on black plumage.

guil·lo·tine (gĭl'*o*tēn, gē'*o*-) *n.* 1. Instrument used in France (esp. during the Revolution) and elsewhere for beheading, consisting of heavy, sharp blade sliding between grooved posts. 2. Surgical instrument for excising tonsils etc. ~ (gĭl'*o*tēn, gē'*o*-, gĭl*o*tēn', gē*o*-) *v.t.* (**-tined, -tin·ing**). Behead with a guillotine. [J. I. *Guillotin* (1738–1814), French physician, who advocated its use in 1789]

guilt (gĭlt) *n.* Fact of having committed a specified or implied offense; criminality, culpability. **guilt'less** *adj.* Innocent (*of*). **guilt'less·ly** *adv.* **guilt'less·ness** *n.*

guilt·y (gĭl'tē) *adj.* (**guilt·i·er, guilt·i·est**). Criminal, culpable; conscious of, prompted by, guilt; having committed a particular offense; ~, **not** ~, pleas, verdicts, in criminal trials. **guilt'i·ly** *adv.* **guilt'i·ness** *n.*

Guin·ea (gĭn'ē). Republic on coast of W. Africa, formerly part of French West Africa; capital, Conakry. **Guin'e·an** *adj.* & *n.*

guin·ea (gĭn'ē) *n.* Former British gold coin, orig. of gold from Guinea and for trade with Guinea, of fluctuating value, but chiefly worth 1 pound and 1 shilling; ~ **fowl, hen**, gallinaceous bird (*Numida*, esp. *N. meleagris*) with slate-colored white-spotted plumage, native to Africa but widely domesticated; ~ **pig**, (origin of name doubtful) S. Amer. rodent (*Cavia porcellus*) now domesticated as pet, and also used as subject for laboratory experiments; (also **human** ~ **pig**) person used in an experiment; ~ **worm**, tropical parasitic nematoid worm (*Dracunculus medinensis*) infesting skin of man and horse, esp. in legs and feet, and causing sores.

Guin·ea-Bis·sau (gĭn'ē bĭsow'). Republic on coast of W. Africa, formerly Portuguese Guinea; capital, Bissau.

Guin·e·vere (gwĭn'*e*vēr). (Arthurian legend) Wife of King Arthur and mistress of Lancelot.

guise (gīz) *n.* Style of attire, garb (archaic); external appearance; semblance, assumed appearance, pretense.

gui·tar (gĭtar') *n.* Musical instrument, usu. with six strings, played with fingers or plectrum. **gui·tar'ist** *n.*

The helmeted ***guinea fowl*** *is native to Africa and Madagascar though long domesticated in Europe and the U.S.A. The* ***guinea pig*** *grows to 10 ins. in length. It is part of the diet in many S. American countries.*

Gui·zhou (gwē'jō') = KWEICHOW.

Gu·ja·rat (go͞oj*a*raht'). Region of W. India; state of W. India. **Gu·ja·ra·ti** (go͞oj*a*rah'tē) *adj.* & *n.* (Native or inhabitant, language) of Gujarat.

gulch (gŭlch) *n.* Small ravine.

gules (gūlz) *n.* & *adj.* (her.) Red.

gulf (gŭlf) *n.* 1. (geog.) Portion of sea partially enclosed by sweep of coast, and usu. narrower at mouth than bay. 2. Deep hollow, chasm, abyss; (poet.) profound depth (in river, ocean); impassable dividing line.

Gulf (gŭlf) **Intracoastal Waterway.** Inland waterway composed of rivers, bays and canals, 1,100 mi. (1,770 km), extending from NW. Florida to Brownsville, Texas.

Gulf (gŭlf) **States.** Five southern U.S. states bordering on the Gulf of Mexico: Florida, Alabama, Mississippi, Louisiana, and Texas.

Gulf (gŭlf) **Stream.** Great ocean current of warm water flowing from Gulf of Mexico parallel with Amer. coast to Newfoundland, and then E. to the N. Atlantic Current.

gull[1] (gŭl) *n.* Any of several long-winged web-footed sea birds (family Laridae), usu. white with mantle varying from pearl-gray to black, with bright-colored bill and harsh cry.

gull[2] (gŭl) *n.* & *v.t.* Dupe, fool. **gul'li·ble** *adj.* Easily cheated or duped. **gul'li·bly** *adv.* **gul·li·bil·i·ty** (gŭl*i*bĭl'ĭtē) *n.*

Gul·lah (gŭl'*a*) *n.* 1. One of a group of descendants of slaves from W. Africa, inhabiting the Sea Islands and coastal regions of South Carolina, Georgia, and N. Florida. 2. English-African patois or dialect of these people.

gul·let (gŭl'ĭt) *n.* Esophagus; (loosely) throat.

gul·ly (gŭl'ē) *n.* (pl. **-lies**). Deep ditch or channel cut by running water. ~ *v.t.* (**-lied, -ly·ing**). Make gullies in by water action.

gulp (gŭlp) *v.* Swallow (usu. *down*) hastily, greedily, or with effort; perform act of swallowing with difficulty, gasp, choke. ~ *n.* Act of gulping; effort to swallow; large mouthful. **gulp'ing·ly** *adv.*

gum[1] (gŭm) *n.* (usu. pl.) Firm fleshy integument of jaws and bases of teeth; **gum'boil**, abscess on gum. ~ *v.t.* (**gummed, gum·ming**).

gum[2] (gŭm) *n.* 1. Viscous secretion of certain trees and shrubs hardening when dry but usu. soluble in water; chewing gum. 2. (also ~ **tree**) Any tree that exudes gum, esp. eucalyptus, various species of the N. Amer. genus *Nyssa* etc.; hollowed-out log, usu. from gum tree, serving as water trough, etc. 3. ~ **arabic**: see ARABIC; **gum'drop**, small soft candy, of flavored gum arabic or gelatin, with coating of coarse sugar; **gum'shoe**, (1) rubber shoe or overshoe; (2) (slang) detective; hence **gum'shoe** (*v.*) (**-shoeing, -shoed**), (slang) move stealthily, snoop; ~ **tree**: see 2 above. **gum** *v.* (**gummed, gum·ming**). Stiffen, smear, fasten with gum; exude gum; ~ **up**, (colloq.) impede; spoil, ruin. **gum'my** *adj.* (**-mi·er, -mi·est**). Viscid, sticky, abounding in, exuding, gum.

Gum·bo (gŭm'bō) *n.* Creole patois of French W. Indies, Louisiana, etc.

gum·bo (gŭm'bō) *n.* (pl. **-bos**). Okra plant or its pods (*Hibiscus esculentus*); soup thickened with the pods of this plant; (slang) thick mud; goo.

gump·tion (gŭmp'shon) *n.* (colloq.) Resource, enterprising spirit, initiative.

gun (gŭn) *n.* Metal tube for aiming or projecting missiles utilizing the explosive force of gunpowder or some other propellant; piece of ordnance, cannon, musket, fowling piece, rifle, carbine; pistol; revolver; (slang) one who wears or uses a gun, esp. a gunfighter or professional assassin; **stick to one's ~s**, maintain one's argument; **gun'boat**, small warship carrying heavy gun(s); armed vessel of light draft, esp. for use on rivers; **gun'boat diplomacy**, diplomacy supported by use or threat of military force, esp. against a much weaker nation; **gun'cotton**, (esp. Brit.) nitrocellulose; **gun'fight**, (colloq.) fight with guns; **gun'fire**, firing of guns; **gun'man** (pl. **-men**), armed robber; professional killer; desperado; **gun'metal**, alloy of copper and 10% tin (formerly used for guns); **at gun'point**, under threat of injury by a gun; **gun'powder**, explosive of saltpeter, sulfur, and charcoal; **Gunpowder Plot**, plot to blow up

*The Australian **red gum** (Eucalyptus camaldulensis) grows to 120 ft. high. Its 12-in. leaves clothe the branches spreading from a short, stocky truck.*

***Gum** of various kinds is refined from resins and other plant materials. Right: Kauri gum in its dried form. Gum arabic is a common water-soluble gum obtained from plants of the genus Acacia.*

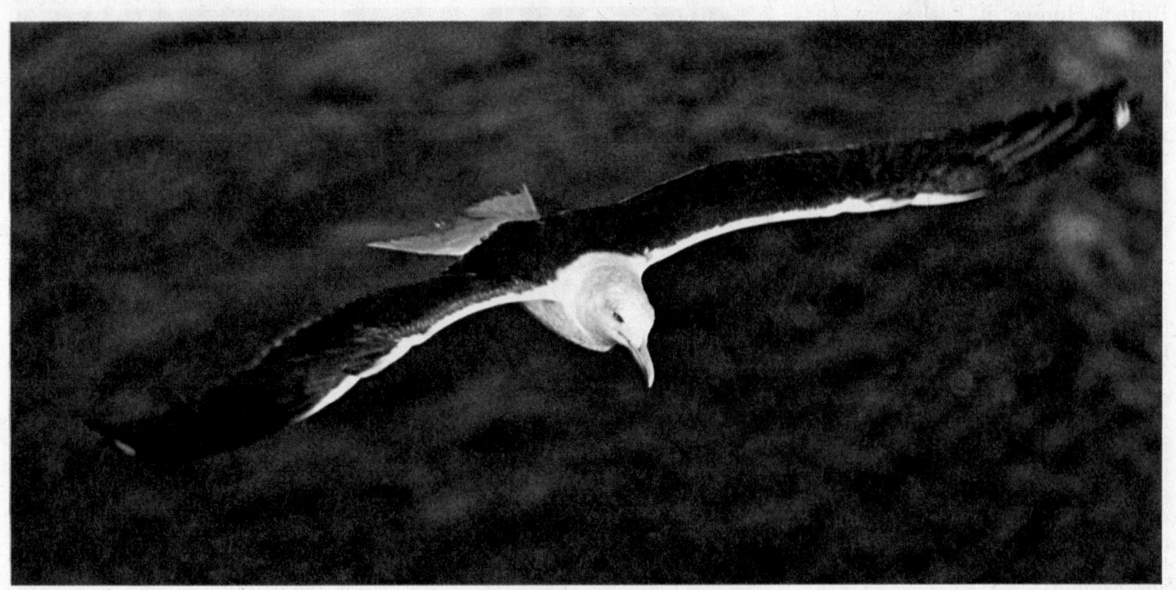

Above: The **gull** is well adapted to flight. Long narrow wings enable it to soar and glide while its webbed feet enable it to land on and maneuver in water or on land. Most gulls nest on the ground, often on ledges of cliffs or on inaccessible rocks. There are several species including 1: Black-headed. 2: Common and 3: Herring gulls.

British Houses of Parliament on Nov. 5, 1605, while the king and parliament were assembled there (see FAWKES); **gunpowder tea**, fine kind of green tea with leaves rolled up into pellets; **gun room**, room where guns are kept; compartment on Brit. warship fitted up for junior officers or as lieutenants' mess; **gun'runner, gun'running**, (person engaged in) illegal introduction of firearms into country; **gun'shot**, (1) shot fired from gun; (2) range of gun (*out of, within,* gunshot); **gun-shy**, (esp. of sporting dogs) afraid of the report of gun; **gun'slinger**, (colloq.) gunman; **gun'smith**, maker and repairer of firearms. **gun** *v.* (**gunned, gun·ning**). Shoot with gun; ~ **for**, go in search of with gun (also fig.). [perh. f. *Gunna* pet form of ON. *Gunnhildr* woman's name used as nickname for ballistae and cannon]

gun·nel[1] (gŭn'*el*) *n.* Eellike fish (*Pholis gunnellus*) of N. Atlantic.

gun·nel[2]: see GUNWALE.

gun·ner (gŭn'*er*) *n.* One who operates a gun; (naut.) warrant officer in charge of ordnance.

gun·ner·y (gŭn'*er*ē) *n.* Construction and management of guns; firing of guns; hence, ~ **officer,** ~ **sergeant**, etc.

gun·ny (gŭn'ē) *n.* (pl. **-nies**). Coarse sacking, sack, usu. of jute fiber; burlap; **gun'nysack**, sack made of burlap or gunny.

Gun·ther (go͞on'*ter*). In the Nibelungenlied, husband of Brunhilde and brother of Kriemhild, by whom he was beheaded in revenge for Siegfried's murder.

gun·wale, gun·nel[2] (gŭn'*el*) *ns.* Upper edge of ship's or boat's side.

gup·py (gŭp'ē) *n.* (pl. **-pies**). Small W. Indian fish (*Lebistes reticulatus*) freq. kept in aquaria.

gur·gi·ta·tion (gẽrjĭtā'sh*o*n) *n.* Whirling, surging, bubbling motion or sound.

gur·gle (gẽr'g*e*l) *n.* Bubbling sound as of water poured from bottle or running over stones. ~ *v.* (**-gled, -gling**). Make gurgle; utter with gurgle(s).

Gur·kha (gẽr'k*a*, goor'-) *n.* (pl. **-khas**, collect. **-kha**). One of a military people of Hindu descent and Sanskritic speech, who settled in the province of Gurkha, Nepal, in the 18th c.; one of these, or any soldier from Nepal serving in the Brit. or Indian army.

gur·nard (gẽr'n*e*rd) *n.* (pl. **-nards**). Marine fish of family Triglidae, esp. of the Old World genus *Trigla* with large spiny head, mailed cheeks, and two or three pairs of finger-shaped processes used as feelers. [OF. *gournart*, lit. = "grunter"]

gu·ru (go͞o'ro͞o, go͞oro͞o') *n.* Hindu spiritual teacher or head of religious sect; any wise leader or teacher. [Sansk.]

The butterfly ***gurnard*** *(Paratrigla vanessa) is capable of 'walking' along sandy bottoms on its three pairs of leg-like appendages in the course of its search for food.*

gush (gŭsh) *n.* Sudden or copious stream (often fig. of speech etc.); effusiveness, sentimental affectation. ~ *v.* Issue in, send forth, gush; emit (water etc.) copiously; speak, behave, with effusiveness. **gush'er** *n.* (esp.) Oil well spouting oil profusely without pumping. **gush'ing·ly** *adv.* **gush'y** *adj.* (**gush·i·er, gush·i·est**). Sentimentally effusive.

gus·set (gŭs'ĭt) *n.* Piece let into garment to strengthen or enlarge some part.

gus·sy (gŭs'ē) *v.* (**-sied, -sy·ing**). (slang) Dress elegantly, decorate, doll up, as in **all gussied up**.

gust[1] (gŭst) *n.* Sudden violent rush of wind; burst of rain, fire, smoke, sound, etc. **gust'y** *adj.* (**gust·i·er, gust·i·est**). **gust'i·ly** *adv.* **gust'less** *adj.*

gust[2] (gŭst) *n.* (archaic and poet.) Sense of taste; keen relish; flavor.

gus·ta·tion (gŭstā'sh*o*n) *n.* Tasting. **gus·ta·tive** (gŭs't*a*tĭv), **gus·ta·to·ry** (gŭs't*a*tōrē, -tōrē) *adjs.*

gus·to (gŭs'tō) *n.* Zest, enjoyment with which something is done.

gut (gŭt) *n.* 1. (pl.) Bowels or entrails (esp. of animals); (fig. and colloq.) courage, fortitude, pluck; (sing.) particular part of lower alimentary canal, intestine; **blind** ~, cecum. 2. Material for violin strings made from intestines of animals; material for fishing lines made from unspun silk substance in silkworms. 3. Narrow passage or channel. ~ *v.* (**gut·ted, gut·ting**). Take out guts of, clean, (fish); remove or destroy internal fittings of (house etc.). ~ *adj.* (slang) 1. Central, essential, as in ~ **issues.** 2. Strongly emotional, based on emotion rather than intellect, as in ~ **reaction**. 3. (college slang) Easy; ~ **course**, one requiring little or no work.

Gu·ten·berg (go͞o't*e*nbẽrg), **Johann** (*c*1398–1468). Printer in Mainz, Germany; inventor of movable printing types.

gut·ta (gŭt'*a*) *n.* (pl. **gut·tae** pr. gŭt'ē). 1. (archit.) (pl.) Drops in a row as ornament esp. in Doric architecture. 2. (med.) Drop.

gut·ta-per·cha (gŭt'*a* pẽr'ch*a*) *n.* Grayish rubberlike substance obtained from juice of various Malayan trees, esp. *Palaquium gutta*, used in electrical insulations etc.; any of these trees. [Malay *getāh* gum, *percha* name of tree]

gut·ter (gŭt'*er*) *n.* Shallow trough below eaves, channel at side of street, carrying off rain water; open conduit for outflow of fluid; groove; **in, out of, the** ~, in, out of, low, disreputable, or poverty-stricken surroundings; **gut'ter-snipe**, street urchin. **gutter** *v.* Furrow, channel; flow in streams.

gut·tur·al (gŭt'*er*al) *adj.* Of the throat; (of sounds) produced in throat, or by back of tongue and palate. ~ *n.* Guttural sound or letter. **gut'tur·al·ism** *n.* **gut'tur·al·ize** *v.t.* (**-ized, -iz·ing**). **gut'tur·al·ly** *adv.*

guy[1] (gī) *n.* Rope, chain, etc. to guide and steady thing being hoisted and lowered, or to secure or steady anything liable to shift, or to hold tent etc. in place. ~ *v.t.* (**guyed, guy·ing**). Secure with guy(s).

guy[2] (gī) *n.* (Brit.) Effigy of GUY FAWKES burned on Nov. 5; (Brit.) grotesquely dressed person, fright; man, fellow. ~ *v.t.* (**guyed, guy·ing**). Ridicule, make fun of.

Guy·a·na (gēăn'*a*, -ah'n*a*, gī-). Republic on NE. coast of South

1: The great ***guns*** *of a battleship were its principal armament. Here British Royal Marines parade beneath them. 2: An American 7-in. self-propelled gun, first made in 1962. 3: Two sub-machine guns, the lower one adapted for shooting round corners. 4: Revolvers with a powder flask and cartridge and ball ammunition.*

2

3

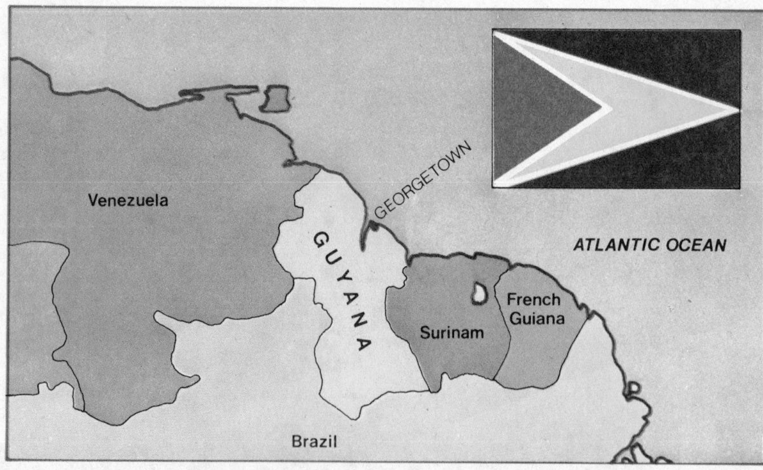

*The republic of **Guyana** has an area of 83,000 sq. miles and a population of a little under 1 million people. The most important crops of the region are rice and sugar cane grown on the narrow coastal strip. The interior is densely forested and mountainous. It is an area famous for its many great waterfalls. The country has a high temperature range and high humidity.*

Amer. (formerly **British Guiana**); capital, Georgetown. **Guy·a·nese** (gēanēz′, -nēs′, gī-) *adj.* & *n.*

guz·zle (gŭz′*e*l) *v.* (**-zled, -zling**). Drink, eat, greedily; consume in guzzling. **guz′zler** *n.*

Gwyn (gwĭn), **Nell** (1650?–87). (original name, Eleanor Gwynne) English actress and mistress of Charles II.

gym (jĭm) *n.* (colloq.) Gymnasium, gymnastics; ~ **shoes**, rubber-soled shoes worn in a gymnasium.

gym·kha·na (jĭmkah′n*a*) *n.* (chiefly Brit.) (Public place with facilities for) athletic or equestrian displays or contests; sporting event, esp. gymnastics. [mixture of *gymnastics* and Hind. *gend-khāna* ball house (racquet court)]

gym·na·si·um (jĭmnā′zē*u*m; for def. 2 also gĭmnah′zēo͞om) *n.* (pl. **-si·ums, -si·a** pr. -zē*a*, -zh*a*). 1. Place, room, or building, with equipment for gymnastics and sports. 2. European, esp. German, academic high school preparing pupils for universities.

gym·nast (jĭm′năst, -n*a*st) *n.* Expert in gymnastics.

gym·nas·tic (jĭmnăs′tĭk) *adj.* Of gymnastics. **gym·nas′ti·cal·ly** *adv.* **gym·nas′tics** *n.pl.* 1. Exercises developing the muscles, esp. such as are performed with special apparatus in gymnasium. 2. (treated as sing.) Art or practice of such exercises.

gym·no·spern (jĭm′n*o*spẽrm) *n.* (bot.) Plant having its seeds unprotected by seed vessels (opp. ANGIOSPERM). **gym·no·sper·mous** (jĭmnōspẽr′m*u*s) *adj.*

gyn. *abbrev.* Gynecology, gynecological.

gy·nan·dro·morph (gīnăn′dr*o*mōrf, jī-, jĭ-) *n.* (biol.) Individual with characters of both sexes.

gy·nan·drous (gīnăn′dr*u*s, jī-, jĭ-) *adj.* (biol.) Of mixed sex; (bot.) with stamens and pistil united in one column as in orchids.

gyn·e·col·o·gy (gīn*e*kŏl′*o*jē, jĭn*e*-, jīn*e*-) *n.* Science of diseases of women, esp. of the reproductive system. **gyn·e·co·log′i·cal** *adj.* **gyn·e·col′o·gist** *n.*

gyp, gip (jĭp) *vbs.t.* (colloq.) Cheat, swindle, defraud. ~ *n.* Swindle; cheating; cheater; swindler.

gyp·soph·i·la (jĭpsŏf′*i*l*a*) *n.* Plant of genus *G*~ with small delicate pink or white flowers and including the baby's-breath. [Gk. *gupsos* chalk, *philos* loving]

gyp·sum (jĭp′s*u*m) *n.* Hydrated calcium sulfate, mineral from which plaster of Paris is made by dehydration. **gyp·se·ous** (jĭp′sē*u*s), **gyp·sif·er·ous** (jĭpsĭf′*er*u*s) *adjs.*

gyp·sy (jĭp′sē) *n.* (pl. **-sies**). 1. Member of dark-haired tawny-skinned people (called by themselves ROMANY), originally from India, entering Europe in 14th and 15th centuries, now mainly in Europe and U.S., still somewhat maintaining nomadic ways as basket makers, horse traders, fortunetellers. etc. 2. Their language; Romany. 3. One who looks or lives like them. ~ *adj.* ~**cab**, (colloq.) taxicab operating without proper permission, license, etc.; ~ **moth**, moth (*Porthetria dispar*)

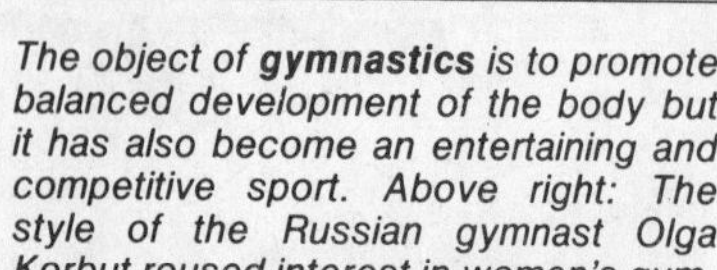

*The object of **gymnastics** is to promote balanced development of the body but it has also become an entertaining and competitive sport. Above right: The style of the Russian gymnast Olga Korbut roused interest in women's gymnastics in the 1970s. Here she performs on a balance beam. Above: A balance beam exercise — a forward walkover and a delayed somersault to the ground. Opposite: A gymnast adopts a crucifix position.*

*Chalky soils or ground that contains some mortar rubble are ideal for **gypsophilas.** They thrive best in a sunny position. The flowers are often dried and used in decorations.*

native to the Old World but introduced to Amer., whose larva is very destructive to trees.

gy·rate (jī′rāt, jīrāt′) *v.i.* (**-rat·ed, -rat·ing**). Go in circle or spiral; revolve, whirl. **gy·ra·tion** (jīrā′sh*o*n) *n.* **gy·ra·to·ry** (jī′r*a*tōrē, -tōrē) *adj.*

gyre (jīr) *n.* (lit.) Spiral, vortex; circle; spiral motion.

gyr·fal·con, ger·fal·con (jẽr′-fawlk*o*n, -faw-) *ns.* Largest of all falcons (*Falco rusticolus*), living in Arctic Amer. and Europe, with plumage in white, gray, and black phases.

gy·ro (jī′rō) *n.* (pl. **-ros**). Gyroscope; **gy′rocompass**, form of gyroscope used as a compass, mounted so that its axis remains parallel to that of the Earth.

gy·ro·plane (jī′r*o*plān) *n.* Flying machine (including the helicopter and autogyro) in which the lift is mainly provided by vanes rotating freely in a more or less horizontal plane.

gy·ro·scope (jī′r*o*skōp) *n.* Instrument to illustrate dynamics of rotating bodies; solid rotating wheel mounted in ring, with axis free to turn in any direction; form of this attached to vessels, aircraft, etc., to maintain equilibrium, measure angular velocity and acceleration, etc. **gy·ro·scop·ic** (jīr*o*skŏp′ĭk) *adj.* **gy·ro·scop′i·cal·ly** *adv.*

*Right: If the flywheel of a **gyroscope** is rotated in the direction of the arrow then a downward force T will result in a motion in the direction P. The gyroscope was used first to demonstrate the Earth's rotation. The device is used in steering and stabilizers. Below: A toy gyroscope.*

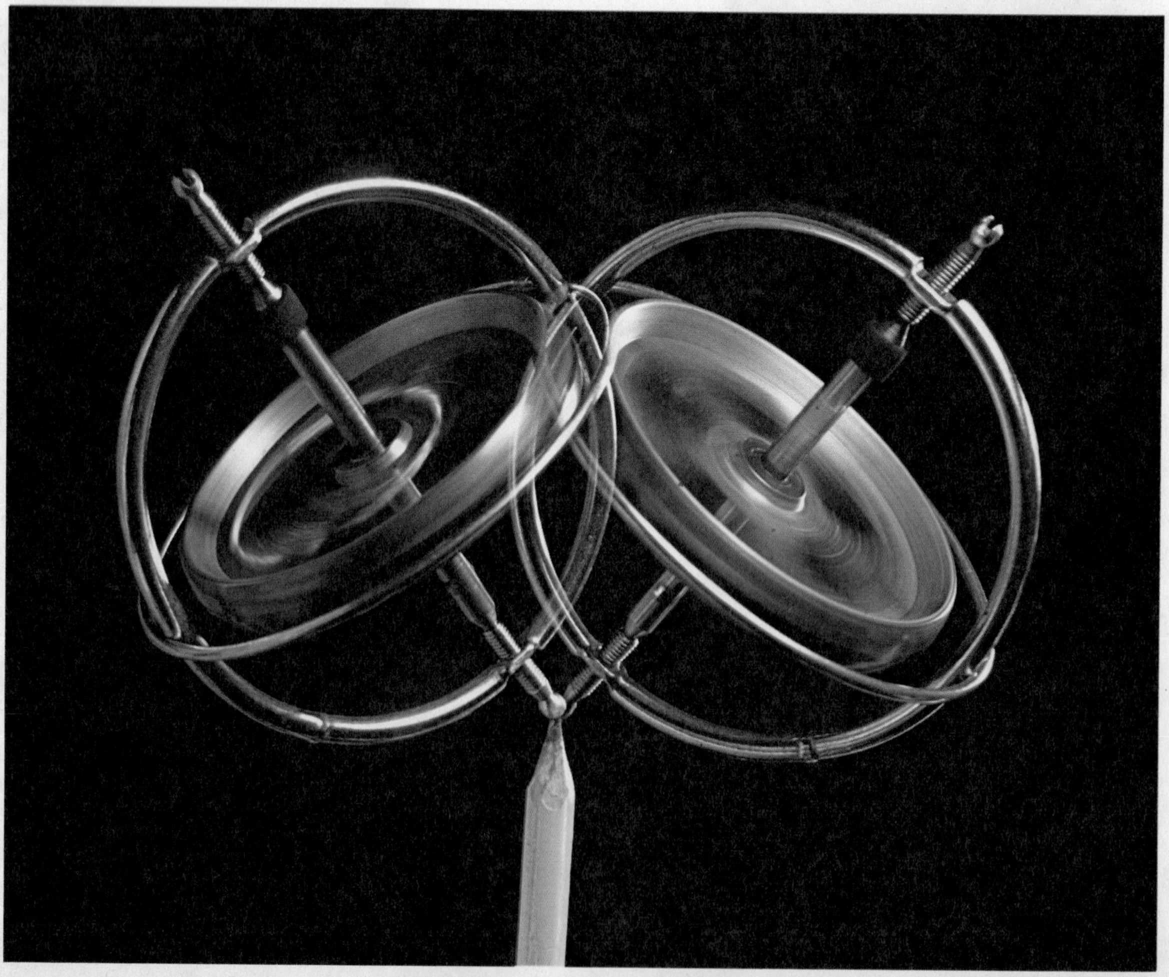

gy·ro·stat (jī′r*o*stăt) *n.* Form of gyroscope in which the wheel is fixed in a case.

gy·rus (jī′r*u*s) *n.* (pl. **gy·ri** pr. jī′rī). (anat.) Fold, convolution, esp. of brain surface.

gyve (jīv, gīv) *n.* (usu. pl.) & *v.t.* (**gyved, gyv·ing**). (archaic) Shackle, fetter, esp. for the leg.

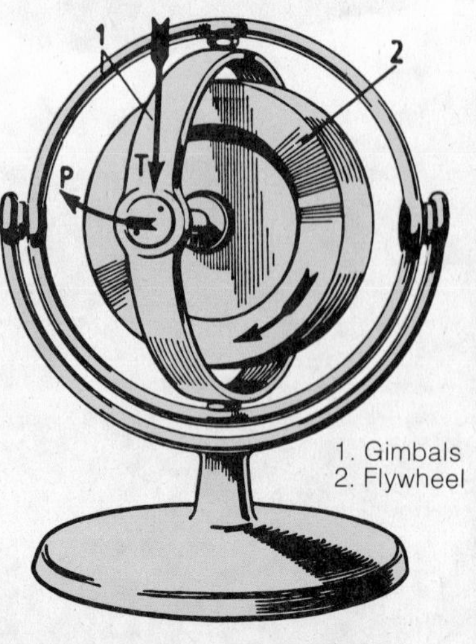

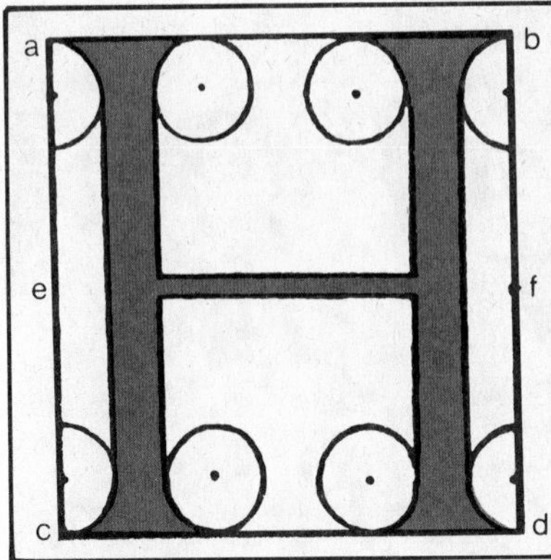

*The letter **H, h** is pronounced as an aspirate in most languages but is variously stressed. The letter and sound derive from a Semitic original which was sounded with a partial coincidence of the back of the tongue and soft palate, giving a guttural sound as used in German today. Italians do not pronounce 'h' but use it to soften attack on vowels that follow and to 'soften' other consonants, such as 'ch'.*

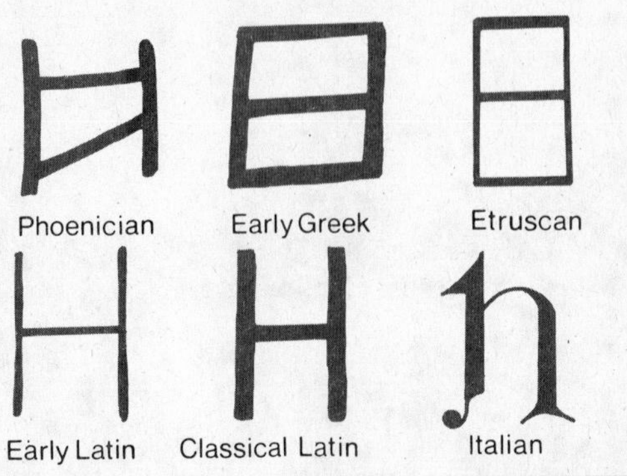

H, h (āch) (pl. **H's, h's** or **Hs, hs**). Eighth letter of modern English and ancient Roman alphabet, representing historically Semitic (laryngeal or guttural spirant, or rough aspirate), Greek H; in modern English usu. standing (except in combination with *c, g, s, t, w*) for simple aspiration or breathing, with just enough narrowing of glottis to be audible before vowel.

H *abbrev.* Hard(ness); henry(s); (slang) heroin.

H *symbol.* Hydrogen.

h. *abbrev.* Hecto-; height; high; (baseball) hit(s); hour(s); hundred.

ha[1] (hah) *int.* Exclamation of surprise, joy, suspicion, triumph, etc.

ha[2] *abbrev.* Hectare(s).

ha·be·as cor·pus (hā'bēas kôr'pus). Writ requiring a person to be brought before a judge or into court, esp. to investigate whether it has been lawful to hold him in custody. [L., = "you must have the body"]

hab·er·dash·er (hăb'erdăsher) *n.* Dealer in men's furnishings, as shirts, socks, etc.; (Brit.) dealer in sewing notions, as ribbon, tape, etc. **hab'er·dash·er·y** *n.* (pl. **-er·ies**). (Shop selling) haberdasher's goods.

ha·bil·i·ment (habĭl'iment) *n.* Attire, dress; (pl.) dress suited to particular office or occasion.

hab·it (hăb'ĭt) *n.* 1. Action or behavior so often repeated as to be almost unconscious; settled tendency or practice; mental constitution (~ **of mind**); **~-forming** (esp. of drugs etc.) addictive. 2. Dress, esp. of religious order; (also **riding** ~) costume worn by a horseback rider. **habit** *v.t.* 1. Clothe. 2. (archaic) Inhabit.

hab·it·a·ble (hăb'ĭtabel) *adj.* That can be inhabited. **hab·it·a·bil·i·ty** (hăbĭtabĭl'ĭtē), **hab'it·a·ble·ness** *ns.* **hab'it·a·bly** *adv.*

hab·it·ant (hăb'ĭtant; for def. 2 ăbētahṅ') *n.* (pl. **hab·it·ants** pr. hăb'ĭtants; for def. 2 ăbētahṅ'). 1. Inhabitant. 2. One of the (descendants of) early French settlers in Canada, Louisiana, etc., chiefly farmers.

hab·i·tat (hăb'ĭtăt) *n.* Natural home of plant or animal; habitation. [L., = "(it) inhabits"]

hab·i·ta·tion (hăbĭtā'shon) *n.* Inhabiting; place of abode.

ha·bit·u·al (habĭch'o͞oal) *adj.* Customary; constant, continual; given to (specified) habit. **ha·bit'u·al·ly** *adv.* **ha·bit'u·al·ness** *n.*

ha·bit·u·ate (habĭch'o͞oāt) *v.t.* (**-at·ed, -at·ing**). Accustom (*to*). **ha·bit·u·a·tion** (habĭcho͞oā'shon) *n.*

hab·i·tude (hăb'ĭto͞od, -tūd) *n.* Mental or bodily constitution; custom, tendency.

ha·bit·u·é (habĭch'o͞oā, -bĭch-o͞oā') *n.* Habitual visitor; frequenter of a particular place. [Fr.]

Habs·burg = HAPSBURG.

ha·chure (hăshoor', hăsh'oor) *n.* In map-drawing, one of the short lines of shading indicating differences of slope (close together for steep slopes, wider apart for gradual ones).

ha·ci·en·da (hahsēĕn'da) *n.* (pl. **-das**). In Spanish-speaking countries, an estate, plantation, or ranch, or the main house on this; ranch house.

*One of the distinguished members of the **Habsburg** family was Franz Josef, ruler of the Austro-Hungarian Empire from 1848–1916. Two years after his death the empire was dissolved.*

hack[1] (hăk) *n.* Mattock; hoe; gash, wound, or blow made by this. ~ *v.* Cut, notch, chop, etc. with a knife, pick, hoe, etc.; strike the arm or kick the shin of (an opponent in sports); deal cutting blows (*at*); emit short dry coughs (so *hacking cough*); **hack'saw**, saw with narrow blade set in a frame, for cutting metal.

hack[2] (hăk) *n.* 1. Horse let out for hire; inferior or worn-out horse; horse for ordinary riding; (hist.) hackney carriage; (colloq.) taxicab. 2. Common (esp. literary) drudge, mere scribbler. ~ *v.* Make common, hackney; ride (horse), ride on horseback, on road at ordinary pace. ~ *adj.* Of or by a hack; routine, banal.

hack·le (hăk'el) *n.* Long feathers on neck of domestic cock and other birds; (also ~ **fly**) angler's artificial fly dressed with hackle; **with ~s up**, (of cock, dog, etc.) angry, ready to fight. **hackle** *v.t.* (**-led, -ling**). Mangle, cut roughly.

hack·ney (hăk'nē) *n.* (pl. **-neys**). Horse of middle size and quality for ordinary riding; (also ~ **carriage**, ~ **coach**, etc.) carriage or coach for hire. ~ *v.t.* (**-neyed, -ney·ing**). Make common or trite by repetition (esp. in past part. **hackneyed**).

had: see HAVE.

had·dock (hăd'ok) *n.* (pl. **-docks**, collect. **-dock**). Fish (*Melanogrammus aeglefinus*) allied to cod but smaller, common in N. Atlantic etc. and much used for food.

Ha·des (hā'dēz). (Gk. myth.) Oldest name of Pluto; his kingdom, abode of departed souls; (often **h** ~) hell.

ha·dith (hahdēth'; *Brit.* hăd'ĭth) *n.* (pl. **-dith, -diths**). Body of traditions relating to Muhammad, now forming supplement to Koran (the *Sunna*).

hadj·i, haj·ji (hăj'ē) *ns.* (pl. **hadj·is, haj·jis** pr. hăj'ēz). Muslim pilgrim who has been to Mecca; **H**~, title of such.

Ha·dri·an (hā'drēan). Publius

Aelius Hadrianus (76–138 A.D.), Roman emperor 117–38; ~**'s Wall**, wall from Solway Firth to mouth of the Tyne River, in N. England; built by Hadrian to protect Roman Britain from the tribes of the north.

Built between AD 121–127, ***Hadrian's Wall*** *crosses northern England for 73 miles. The wall is at least 8 ft. thick and it was designed to stop marauders from the north. The section illustrated is in Northumberland.*

Hematite *occurs as a kidney ore, as illustrated, or in crystal, specular or oolitic forms. It receives its name from its color of dried blood in the earthy state. Crystallized it is steel gray.*

Haeck·el (hĕk′*e*l), **Ernst Heinrich** (1834–1919). German biologist and philosopher; 1st German supporter of organic evolution; advocate of MONISM.

hae·mat·ic = HEMATIC.

haem·a·tite = HEMATITE.

hae·ma·tol·o·gy = HEMATOLOGY.

hae·mo·glo·bin = HEMOGLOBIN.

hae·mo·phil·i·a = HEMOPHILIA.

haem·or·rhage = HEMORRHAGE.

haem·or·rhoid = HEMORRHOID.

ha·fiz (hah′fĭz) *n.* Muslim who knows the Koran by heart; **H**~, title of such. [Arab. *hāfiz*]

haf·ni·um (hăf′nē*u*m) *n.* (chem.) Rare metallic element, symbol Hf, at. no. 72, at. wt. 178.49, usu. found with zirconium and resembling it in properties. [*Hafnia*, L. name of Copenhagen]

haft (hăft, hahft) *n.* Handle or hilt (of dagger, knife, etc.). ~ *v.t.* Furnish with haft.

hag (hăg) *n.* 1. Ugly old woman; witch; (formerly) evil spirit in female form. 2. (also **hag′fish**) Round-mouthed eellike fish (*Myxine glutinosa*) allied to lamprey and living on dead or dying fish.

Hag·ga·dah (hagah′d*a*; *Heb.* hahgahdah′) *n.* (pl. **-doth** pr. -dōs, -dōt; *Heb.* -dawt′, **-dahs**). Legendary part of the Talmud, anecdote, parable, etc., introduced to illustrate a point of the Law; book containing the story of the Exodus and the ritual of the Seder for first night(s) of Passover.

hag·gard (hăg′*e*rd) *adj.* Worn-out or wild looking (esp. as result of fatigue, privation, worry, etc.); (of hawk) caught in its adult plumage, untamed. **hag′gard·ly** *adv.* **hag′gard·ness** *n.* **haggard** *n.* Haggard hawk.

hag·gis (hăg′ĭs) *n.* Scottish dish of the heart, lungs, and liver, of sheep etc., with salt, pepper, onions, suet, etc., and oatmeal, boiled like large sausage in the stomach of the animal.

hag·gle (hăg′*e*l) *n.* & *v.i.* (**-gled, -gling**). Dispute, wrangle (esp. *over* or *about* prices or terms).

Hag·i·og·ra·pha (hăgēŏg′r*a*f*a*, hājē-) *n.pl.* (considered sing. or pl.) Books of Jewish Scriptures not included under Law and Prophets. **hag·i·og′ra·pher** *n.* Writer of any of these, or of saints' lives. **hag·i·o·graph·ic** (hăgē*o*grăf′ĭk, hājē-) *adj.* **hag·i·og′ra·phy** *n.* Writing of lives of saints.

hag·i·ol·a·try (hăgēŏl′*a*trē, hājē-) *n.* Worship of saints.

hag·i·ol·o·gy (hăgēŏl′*o*jē, hājē-) *n.* Literature treating of lives and legends of saints.

Hague (hāg), **The.** (Du. *'s-Gravenhage*) Seat of government of the Netherlands, on the North Sea; seat of the Court of International Justice.

ha-ha[1] (hah hah′) *int.* Representation of sound of laughter.

ha-ha[2] (hah′hah) *n.* Moat or fence in a ditch bounding park or garden so as not to impair view or scenic appeal.

Hahn (hahn), **Otto** (1879–1968). German chemist; researched atomic fission; co-discoverer with Lise Meitner, of protoactinium; Nobel Prize for chemistry, 1944.

Hai·fa (hī′f*a*). Port of Israel in the NW. on Bay of Acre.

hai·ku (hī′kōō) *n.* (pl. **-ku**). (English imitation of) Japanese poem of three lines of five, seven, and five syllables respectively. [Jap. *hai*, recreation + *ku*, verse]

hail[1] (hāl) *n.* Pellets of condensed and frozen moisture falling in shower, as **hail′storm**; shower of missiles, questions, etc.; **hail′stone**, pellet of hail. **hail** *v.* 1. Precipitate in the form of hail. 2. (fig.) Pour down (words, blows, etc.).

hail[2] (hāl) *int.* of greeting; ~**-fellow (well met)**, heartily congenial man. **hail** *v.* Salute; greet (*as*); call to (ship, person) to attract attention; (of ship, person) have come *from* (place). ~ *n.* Salutation; **H**~ **Mary** = AVE MARIA.

Hai·le Se·las·sie (hī′lē s*e*lăs′ē, -lah′sē) (1892–1975). Emperor of Ethiopia 1930–74; following Italian invasion was forced to leave Addis Ababa, 1936; reinstated in capital 1941; deposed Sept. 1974.

Hai·phong (hī′fŏng′). Port of Vietnam near Gulf of Tonkin.

hair (hār) *n.* One or (collect. sing.) all of the fine filaments growing from skins of animals, esp. from human head; (of plants) cells growing from epidermis; hairlike thing; small amount; **get** (person) **by the short** ~**s**, (slang) hold so that escape is painful; have complete control over; **split ~s**, make fine or caviling distinctions; be overly precise; **to a ~**, exactly; **not turn a ~**, show no sign of exhaustion or discomposure; **hair′-ball**, ball of hair in intestines of cat or other animal that licks its fur, causing distress and often death; **hair′breadth, hairs′breadth**, minute space or distance; narrow margin; **hair′brush**, brush for hair; **hair′cut**, act or style of cutting the hair; **hair′do**, way hair is dressed; **hair′dresser**, one who cuts and styles hair; **hair′line**, edge of hair on forehead etc.; very fine line; **hair′net**, fine or loosely woven net for keeping hair in place; **hair′piece**, toupee, wig; **hair′pin**, U-shaped piece of wire etc. used for fastening up hair; **hairpin curve**, very sharp curve where road etc. doubles back; **hair-raising**, enough to make hair stand on end through fear or excitement; **hair shirt**, ascetic's or penitent's shirt of hair or wiry fabric for mortifying the flesh; **hair space**, narrowest space between words in printing; **hair′splitting**, oversubtle(ty); **hair′spray**, cosmetic liquid sprayed on hair to hold it in place; **hair′spring**, fine spring in watch, regulating balance wheel; **hair trigger**, gun trigger responding to very slight pressure (also fig. **hair-trigger** (*adj.*), of temper, nerves, balance, etc.); **hair′-weaving**, covering bald spot by interweaving matched hair with person's own hair. **hair′i·ness** *n.* **hair′less, hair′like, hair′y** *adjs.* (**hair·i·er, hair·i·est**).

Hai·ti (hā′tē). Republic occupying western part of island of Hispaniola, W. Indies; capital, Port-au-Prince. **Hai·tian** (hā′-shan, -tean) *adj.* & *n.*

haj·ji = HADJI.

hake (hāk) *n.* (pl. **hakes**, collect. **hake**). Any of several codlike food fishes of the genera *Merluccius* and *Urophycis* living in Atlantic waters from N. Carolina to Newfoundland.

ha·ken·kreuz (hah′kenkroits) *n.* (pl. **-kreu·ze** pr. -kroitse). Swastika that was used as an emblem of the Nazi party and the Third Reich. [Ger., = "hook cross"]

ha·kim, ha·keem (hahkēm′) *ns.* (esp. in Muslim countries) 1. Wise and learned man. 2. Muslim physician. [Arab. *hakīm* wise, physician]

ha·la·tion (hālā′shon, hă-) *n.* (phot.) Spreading of light beyond its proper boundaries on a developed film or plate.

hal·berd (hăl′berd, hawl′-) *n.* (hist.) Combined spear and battle-ax. **hal·berd·ier** (hălberdēr′, hawl-) *n.* Soldier or guard armed with halberd.

hal·cy·on (hăl′sēon) *n.* 1. Bird fabled by the ancients to breed in floating nest on sea at winter solstice, and to charm wind and waves into calm for the purpose, identified with the kingfisher. ~ *adj.* Calm, peaceful, quiet; prosperous; ~ **days**, 14 days of calm weather believed by ancients to occur about winter solstice; period of peace or prosperity. [Gk. *alkuōn* kingfisher]

hale[1] (hāl) *adj.* (**hal·er, hal·est**). Robust, vigorous, in good health, as in ~ **and hearty**.

hale[2] (hāl) *v.t.* (**haled, hal·ing**). Drag or draw forcibly (lit. or fig.).

Hale[1] (hāl), **Edward Everett** (1822–1909). Amer. Unitarian clergyman and author; best known for short story, "The Man Without a Country."

Hale[2] (hāl), **Nathan** (1755–1776). Amer. Revolutionary War officer and hero hanged by British as spy; his last words were: "I only regret that I have but one life to lose for my country."

Ha·le·a·ka·la (hahlēahkahlah′). Dormant volcano on E. Maui Island, Hawaii; contains largest crater in the world.

half (hăf, hahf) *n.* (pl. **halves** pr. hăvz, hahvz). One of two equal or corresponding parts into which thing is divided; halfback; one of

__Hair__ is keratin, a material which in a different form forms fingernails, feathers and reptile scales. Below: Electron microscope view of a human hair magnified 200 times. Left: Elaborate Papuan hair-style.

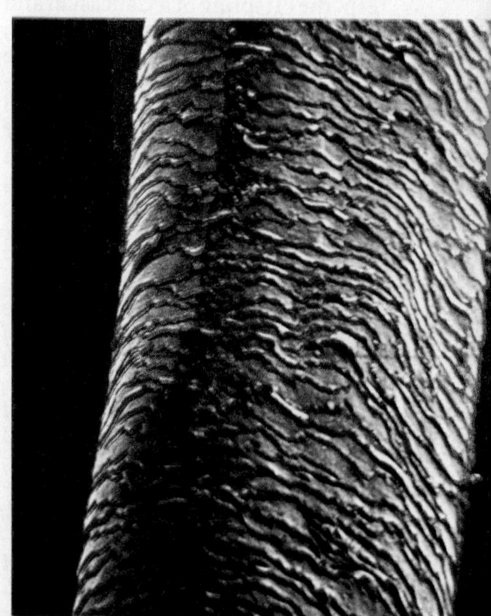

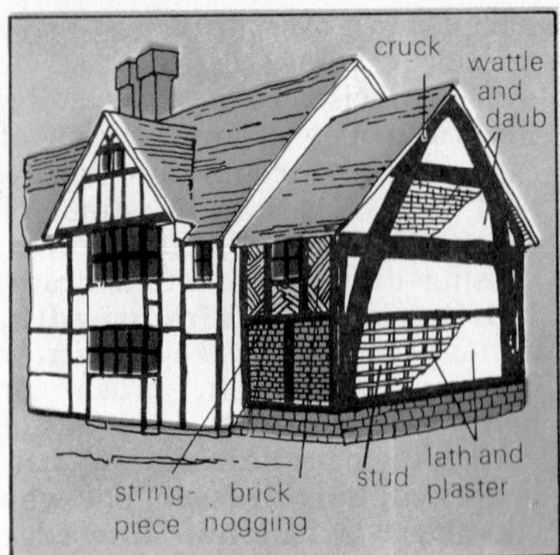

*The **half-timbered** frames of domestic houses were made of hardwoods, such as oak. The spaces between the frames were filled with a choice of materials which lent further range to individual taste.*

*The wood frames of **half-timbered** houses were cheaply made when the raw materials were plentiful up to the 1600s. The durability of these structures is seen in these houses at Stratford-upon-Avon, U.K.*

two periods game is divided into; **better** ~: see BETTER; (colloq.) wife; **go halves**, share equally (*with* person *in* thing). **half** *adj.* Forming a half. ~ *adv.* To the extent of half; (loosely) to a considerable extent; **not ~ bad**, (colloq.) not at all bad, quite good. **half** *n., adj.,* or *adv.* in comb.: **~-and-~**, (what is) half one thing and half another, esp. mixture of milk and cream; **~-assed**, (slang, vulgar) incomplete, unprepared, incompetent, unrealistic; **half′back**, (football) one of 2 players usu. flanking quarterback and fullback; (soccer, field hockey) one of 3 players behind forward line; **half-baked**, (fig.) inadequately prepared; half-witted; **half binding**, bookbinding with leather back and corners, cloth or paper sides; **half-breed**, person having parents of different races, esp. the offspring of a Caucasian and an Amer. Indian; **half brother**, brother by one parent only (so **half sister**); **half-caste**, half-breed; esp. offspring of a European and an Asiatic; **half crown**, former British silver or cupronickel coin worth two shillings and sixpence; (usu. **half a crown**) this sum; **half′hearted**, lacking courage or zeal; so **half′heartedly, half′heartedness; half hitch**: see HITCH; **half′life**, (phys.) time during which the radioactivity of a substance falls to half its original value; **half-mast, at half-mast**, (of flag) lowered to half height of mast as mark of respect for the dead or on other occasions of mourning; **half measures**, compromise, half-and-half policy etc.; **half-moon**, moon of which only half is illuminated; anything of this shape; **half nelson**: see NELSON; **half pint**, (slang) diminutive person or animal; **half-seas over**, (slang) drunk; **half sister**: see HALF BROTHER above; **half size**, any fractional size in women's clothing for short women with full figures; **half-slip**, underskirt, petticoat; **half sole**, sole of shoe between shank and toe; **half-timber(ed)**, (archit.) having walls made of timber frame with spaces filled with bricks or plaster; **half time**, (esp.) interval between two halves of play in football, basketball, etc.; **half title**, title of a book printed at head of first page of text, or title of a section of a book printed on the recto of the leaf preceding it; **half tone**, (mus.) = SEMITONE; **half′tone**, (art) tone intermediate between the extreme lights and extreme shades; (photoengraving, printing) illustration printed from a block in which the tones are broken up into small or large dots by the interposition of a glass screen, ruled with fine crosslines, between the camera and the object; this process; **half-track**, (mil.) armored vehicle with wheels in front and caterpillar treads in back; **half-truth**, statement that conveys only part of the truth, omitting some relevant facts; **half volley** (*n.*) (tennis, cricket, etc.) ball hit or returned as soon as it touches the ground; **half′way**, equidistant from 2 ends; **halfway house**, (hist.) inn midway between 2 towns etc.; home for rehabilitation of former convicts, drug addicts, etc. as they adjust to normal society; **half-witted**, imbecilic.

half·pen·ny (hā′penē, hăp′nē) *n.* (pl. **half·pen·nies** for coin, **half·pence** for amount, pr. hā′pens). (Brit.) Former bronze coin worth half a penny; this amount.

hal·i·but (hăl′ĭbut) *n.* Any of several large flat fish (*Hippoglossus vulgaris* and *H. stenolepsis*) abundant in northern seas and much used for food. [*haly* holy, *butt* flat fish (because eaten on holy days)]

Hal·i·car·nas·sus (hălĭkārnăs′-us). Ancient Greek city in SW. Asia Minor; site of tomb of Mausolus, the Mausoleum.

hal·ide (hăl′īd, -ĭd, hā′līd) *n.*

*The **hallmark** system was established in London in 1300 where it was supervised by the Goldsmith's Hall. Other countries instituted similar systems but many unofficial marks are found on their base metal wares.*

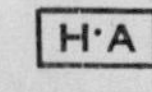

Birmingham London Sheffield Edinburgh

office marks

maker's marks

Salt derived from a halogen.

Hal·i·fax (hăl′ifăks). Capital city and port of Nova Scotia, Canada.

hal·i·to·sis (hălĭtō′sĭs) *n.* Foul breath.

hall (hawl) *n.* 1. Large public room in mansion, palace, etc.; principal living room of medieval house; common dining room in English colleges etc.; large room for public business, entrance passage of house; any corridor or passage in building. 2. Building for students on college or school campus. 3. **hall′way**, entrance hall or corridor in building.

hal·le·lu·jah, hal·le·lu·iah (hălelōō′ya) *interjs.* & *ns.* Praise ye the Lord [Heb.] [also **al·le·lu·ia** (ălelōō′ya)].

Hal·ley (hăl′ē), **Edmund** (1656–1742). English astronomer, mathematician; and inventor; ~ **'s comet**, comet with a periodicity of 76 years, the return of which in 1758 was predicted by Halley in 1682; its last appearance in the 20th c. was in 1986.

hal·liard: see HALYARD.

Hal·li·bur·ton (hăl′ibĕrton), **Richard** (1900–39). Amer. adventurer and writer; retraced routes of Cortez, Balboa, Alexander the Great, Hannibal, etc.; swam Hellespont; lost at sea in typhoon while sailing across Pacific.

hall·mark (hawl′mărk) *n.* Impression stamped on gold and silver articles in England when such articles meet established standards of purity; any mark indicating quality or excellence; any conspicuous indication of the quality or character of a thing. ~ *v.t.* Mark with hallmark. [f. Goldsmiths' *Hall*, London, where gold and silver articles were orig. appraised and stamped]

hal·low (hăl′ō) *v.t.* Make holy; honor as holy.

Hal·low·een, Hal·low·e'en (hălowēn′, hŏl-) *ns.* Eve of All Saints' Day, Oct. 31, on which children go from door to door begging treats by threatening tricks.

hal·lu·ci·nate (halōō′sināt) *v.t.* (**-nat·ed, -nat·ing**). Produce false impressions in mind of (person). **hal·lu·ci·na·tion** (halōōsinā′shon) *n.* Illusion; apparent perception of external object not actually present. **hal·lu·ci·na·to·ry** (halōō′sinatōrē, -tōrē) *adj.* **hal·lu·ci·no·gen·ic** (halōōsinojĕn′ĭk) *adj.* (esp., of drug) Inducing hallucination. **hal·lu·ci·no·gen** (halōō′sinojen, hălyusĭn′-) *n.*

ha·lo (hā′lō) *n.* (pl. **-los, -loes**). Circle of luminous or prismatically colored light seen around a celestial body or light source, esp. that around sun or moon caused by refraction through ice crystals in thin cloud; circle, ring; disk or ring of light shown around head of a sacred figure in paintings etc., nimbus; (fig.) ideal glory investing person etc. ~ *v.t.* (**-loed, -lo·ing**). Surround with halo.

hal·o·gen (hăl′ojen) *n.* (chem.) Any of the nonmetallic elements, fluorine, chlorine, bromine, iodine, and astatine.

hal·o·phyte (hăl′ofīt) *n.* Plant inhabiting salty soils.

Hals (hahls), **Frans** (*c*1584–1666). Dutch portrait and genre painter, most famous work the so-called "Laughing Cavalier."

halt[1] (hawlt) *n.* Temporary stoppage on march or journey. ~ *v.* Make a halt; (mil.) bring to a stand.

halt[2] (hawlt) *adj.* (archaic) Lame; crippled. ~ *v.i.* Walk hesitatingly; hesitate (*between*); (of speech, argument, verse, etc.) be defective. **halt′ing·ly** *adv.*

hal·ter (hawl′ter) *n.* 1. Rope, strap, with noose or headstall for horses or cattle; rope with noose for hanging person; death by hanging. 2. Woman's garment tied behind neck and across lower back, leaving arms, shoulders, and back bare. ~ *v.t.* Fasten with halter; hang (person) with halter.

hal·vah (hahlvah′, hahl′vah) *n.* Confection, orig. Turkish, of ground sesame seeds and honey.

halve (hăv, hahv) *v.t.* (**halved, halv·ing**). Divide into halves; share equally; reduce to half; (golf) play (game, hole) in same number of strokes as opponent.

hal·yard, hal·liard (hăl′yerd) *ns.* (naut.) Rope, tackle, for raising or lowering sail, yard, etc.

Ham (hăm). Second son of Noah (Gen. 10).

ham (hăm) *n.* Back of thigh; thigh and buttock; (formerly) the back of the knee; thigh of hog, esp. when dried, smoked, salted, or otherwise cured for food; (colloq.) licensed amateur radio operator; (slang) overemphatic actor (also attrib.).

ham·a·dry·ad (hămadrī′ad, -ăd) *n.* 1. (Gk. myth.) Nymph living and dying with the tree she inhabited. 2. (zool.) KING COBRA.

Ha·man (hā′man). Chief minister of Persian King Ahaseurus; when his plot against the Jews was revealed by Esther (Esther 8), he was hanged on the gallows.

Ham·burg (hăm′bĕrg; *Ger.* hahm′boorχ). City on the Elbe in northern West Germany.

ham·burg·er (hăm′bĕrger), **ham·burg** (hăm′bĕrg) *ns.* Ground or chopped meat, usu. beef; (also ~ **steak**) fried or broiled patty of this as a meat course; sandwich of this, usu. on a bun or roll. [f. *Hamburg*, Germany, where the cooked chopped steak was first popular]

Ham·e·lin (hăm′lin; Ger. hah′meln). City on the Weser in SW. West Germany; scene of legend of "Pied Piper of Hamelin."

Ham·il·ton[1] (hăm′ilton). 1. City on Lake Ontario, Canada. 2. Capital of Bermuda, W. Atlantic. 3. River flowing from S. central Labrador to Lake Melville, Canada.

Ham·il·ton[2] (hăm′ilton), **Alexander** (1755–1804). Amer. lawyer and statesman; secretary and aide-de-camp to Gen. Washington; member of Continental Congress; first U.S. secretary of the Treasury,

Halifax is the largest of Nova Scotia's cities and her busiest port. Halifax has a rich industrial life, including oil refining nearby, meat packing, sugar refining, fishing and furniture making.

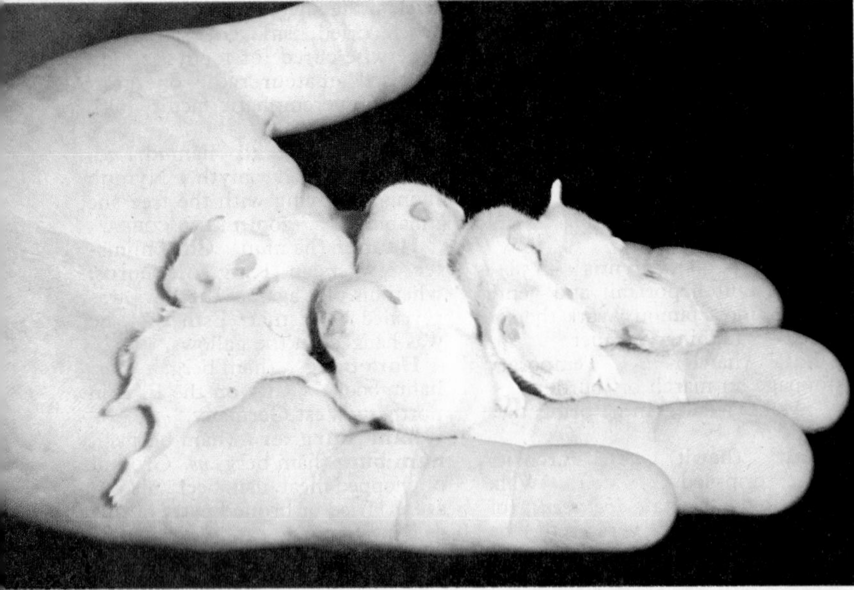

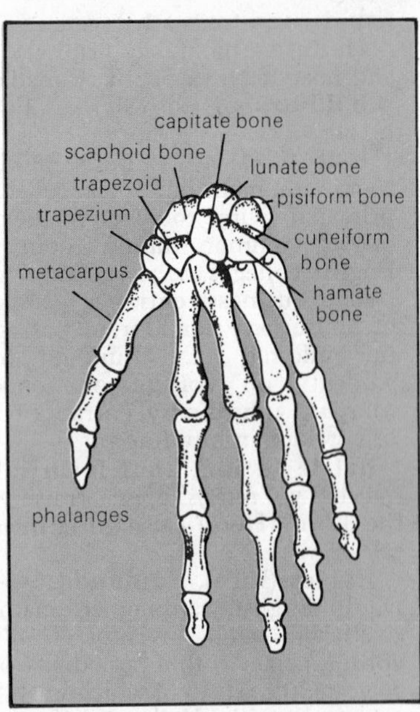

*An adult **hamster** grows to 6 ins. long. Above: A few days after birth several golden hamsters fit comfortably into the palm of a hand. Left: Native to temperate Europe and west Asia are many species, including this black bellied variety.*

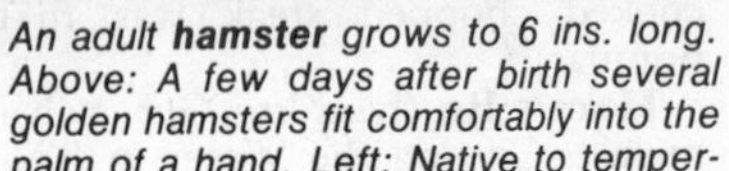

*The human **hand** has 27 bones and is constructed to enable the thumb to touch the front of each finger, a great evolutionary advance on other and clumsier primate hands.*

1789–95; planned policies establishing national fiscal system; strengthened central government; mortally wounded in duel with Aaron BURR.

Ham·ite (hăm′īt) *n.* 1. Supposed descendant of HAM. 2. Member of Egyptian, Berber, and other peoples of N. or E. Africa. **Ham·it·ic** (hămĭt′ĭk) *adj.* Of Hamites; (esp.) of the group of African languages including ancient Egyptian, Berber, Galla, etc.

Ham·let (hăm′lĭt). Legendary prince of Denmark, hero of a tragedy by Shakespeare.

ham·let (hăm′lĭt) *n.* Small village.

Ham·lin (hăm′lĭn), **Hannibal** (1809–91). Vice president of U.S. under Abraham Lincoln, 1861–5.

ham·mer (hăm′*er*) *n.* Instrument for beating, breaking, driving nails, etc., with hard solid (usu. metal) head at right angles to handle; similar contrivance, as for exploding charge in gun, striking string of piano, etc.; auctioneer's mallet used to indicate by rap that article is sold; metal ball weighing 16 pounds (7.257 kg) attached to a wire with a grip handle, used in **throwing the ~**, track-and-field contest in which this is thrown for distance; **come under the ~**, be sold by auction; **~ and tongs**, with might and main; **ham′merhead**, head of hammer; any of several large sharks of genus *Sphyrna*, with lateral extensions of the head and eyes; **ham′merlock**, (wrestling) position in which a wrestler is held with one arm bent behind his back. **hammer** *v.* Strike, beat, drive, (as) with hammer; (colloq.) inflict heavy defeat(s) on in war or games; **~ away**, work hard *at*; **~ out**, (fig.) evolve (an agreement) by long and repeated negotiations.

ham·mock (hăm′*o*k) *n.* Hanging bed of canvas etc. or netting suspended by cords at ends.

Ham·mond (hăm′*o*nd) **organ.** (trademark) Electronic organ.

Ham·mu·ra·bi (hahmo͝orah′bē), **Ham·mu·ra·pi** (hahmo͝orah′pē). (*c*18th c. B.C.) King and lawgiver of Babylonia; **Code of ~**, famous early civil and criminal legal code attributed to him.

ham·per[1] (hăm′p*er*) *n.* Large wickerwork basket, usu. with a lid.

ham·per[2] (hăm′p*er*) *v.t.* Obstruct movement of (person etc.); impede, hinder.

Hamp·ton (hămp′t*o*n) **Roads.** Channel connecting James and Elizabeth Rivers with Chesapeake Bay in SE. Virginia; scene of Civil War naval battle between MERRIMAC and MONITOR, 1862.

ham·shack·le (hăm′shăk*e*l) *v.t.* (**-led, -ling**). Hobble (horse etc.) with rope connecting head and a foreleg; hinder.

ham·ster (hăm′st*er*) *n.* Small hibernating rodent of genus *Cricetus*, with short tail, and cheek pouches; **golden ~**, species of this (*C. auratus*).

ham·string (hăm′strĭng) *n.* (in man) One of the tendons at back of knee, (in quadrupeds) great tendon at back of hock, corresponding to that of heel in man. **~** *v.t.* (**-strung, -stringed, -string·ing**). Cripple by cutting hamstring(s); hinder, hold back (person) by rules, lack of authority,

Han (hahn). Chinese dynasty, 206 B.C. to 220 A.D., when Chinese territory was expanded and unified, literature and art flourished, and Buddhism was introduced.

Han·cock (hăn′kŏk), **John** (1737–93). Amer. statesman; president of Continental Congress, 1775–7; first signer of Declaration of Independence; first governor of Massachusetts, 1780–5, and again 1787–93; **John Hancock**, (colloq.) signature.

hand (hănd) *n.* 1. Terminal part of human being's arm beyond wrist; similar part in other animals. 2. Possession, charge, authority, disposal (often pl.); agency, instrumentality (often pl.); share in the doing of something; pledge of marriage, bestowal in marriage. 3. Side (right or left), quarter. 4. Person, source, from which thing comes; person who does something, person in relation to action or in reference to skill in doing something; workman, manual worker; (pl.) ship's crew; **all ~s,** whole crew. 5. Skill; style of workmanship; style of writing; (hist.) signature. 6. Applause. 7. Handlike thing, esp. pointer of clock or watch. 8. Linear measure of horse's height = 4 inches. 9. (cards) Cards dealt to a player; player holding these; single round of game; game (of cards etc.). 10. **at ~**, close by; about to happen soon; **by ~**, by physical (as opp. to mechanical) labor; **(live) from ~ to mouth**, improvidently; **in ~**, held in the hand; at one's disposal, available; **on hand**, in one's possession; in stock; **on** (or **off**) **one's hands**, resting on (or passed from) one as a responsibility; **out of hand**, without preparation; out of control; **to hand**, within reach. 11. **change hands**, (of property) pass from one person to another; **come to hand**, turn up, be received; **keep one's hand in**, be in practice; **take in hand**, undertake; undertake to teach or train; **with a heavy hand**, oppressively; **with a high hand**, boldly, arrogantly. 12. **hands down**, easily, without effort; **hands off!**, do not touch; **hands up!**, direction to persons to hold up their hands to be robbed, to preclude resistance, etc.; **hand in** (or **and**) **glove**, intimate (*with*); **hand over hand** or **fist**, with each hand successively passing over the other, as in climbing rope; rapidly; greedily; **hand to hand**, (of conflict etc.) at close quarters. 13. In comb. = made, operated, etc., by hand and not by machinery. 14. Special comb.: **hand'bag**, purse carried by woman; **hand'ball**, game played by striking hard rubber ball by hand against a wall; **hand'bill**, printed notice circulated by hand; **hand'book**, short treatise, manual, guidebook; **hand brake**, brake operated by hand; **hand'car**, small open railroad car propelled by hand pump, used to transport track workers; **hand'cart**, cart pushed or drawn by hand; **hand'clasp**, clasping of hands of two or more persons to show friendship etc.; **hand'craft**, handicraft; **hand'cuffs**, pair of metal rings joined by short chain, for securing prisoner's hands; **hand'cuff** (*v.*) secure (person) with these; **hand glass**, small magnifying glass or mirror with handle; **hand'gun**, gun that can be held and fired with one hand; pistol, etc.; **hand grenade**, small explosive shell thrown by hand; **hand'hold**, something for the hands to grip (in climbing etc.); **hand'maid(en)**, (archaic, exc. fig.) female servant; **hand-me-down**, (colloq.) article of clothing used by one person and passed on to another, usu. member of family; anything secondhand or inferior (also *adj.*); **hand organ**, barrel organ with crank turned by hand; **hand'out**, food, money, etc., handed out to a beggar; publicity or news release handed out to the press; **hand'rail**, railing along edge of stairs etc.; **hand'shake**, shake of person's hand with one's own, as greeting; **hand'spike**, lever for shifting heavy objects, as guns, by hand; spoke of capstan or windlass; **hand'spring**, somersault in which one lands first on one's hands and then on one's feet; **turn hand'springs**, (esp.) exert special effort (for someone); **hand'work**, handiwork, handicraft; **hand'writing**, writing by hand, esp. of particular person. **hand** *v.t.* Help (person) with the hand (*into, out of*, carriage etc.); (naut.) take in, furl (sail); deliver, transfer by hand or otherwise; **~ it to**, acknowledge superiority of.

Han·del (hăn′del; *Ger.* hĕn′del) (orig. *Haendel*), **George Frederick** (1685–1759). German-born composer of operas and oratorios; settled in England in 1712 and became court composer; famous for his *Messiah, Samson, Judas Maccabaeus*, etc.

hand·ful (hănd′fo͝ol) *n.* (pl. **-fuls**). Quantity that fills the hand; small number (of men etc.); (col-

*Before more advanced implements were developed, the quill was the standard instrument used for **handwriting.***

*The influence of Buddhism is seen in Chinese art of the **Han dynasty.** Missionary contacts with India developed into broader cultural and trade contacts. This painting is a detail of one found in a Han tomb.*

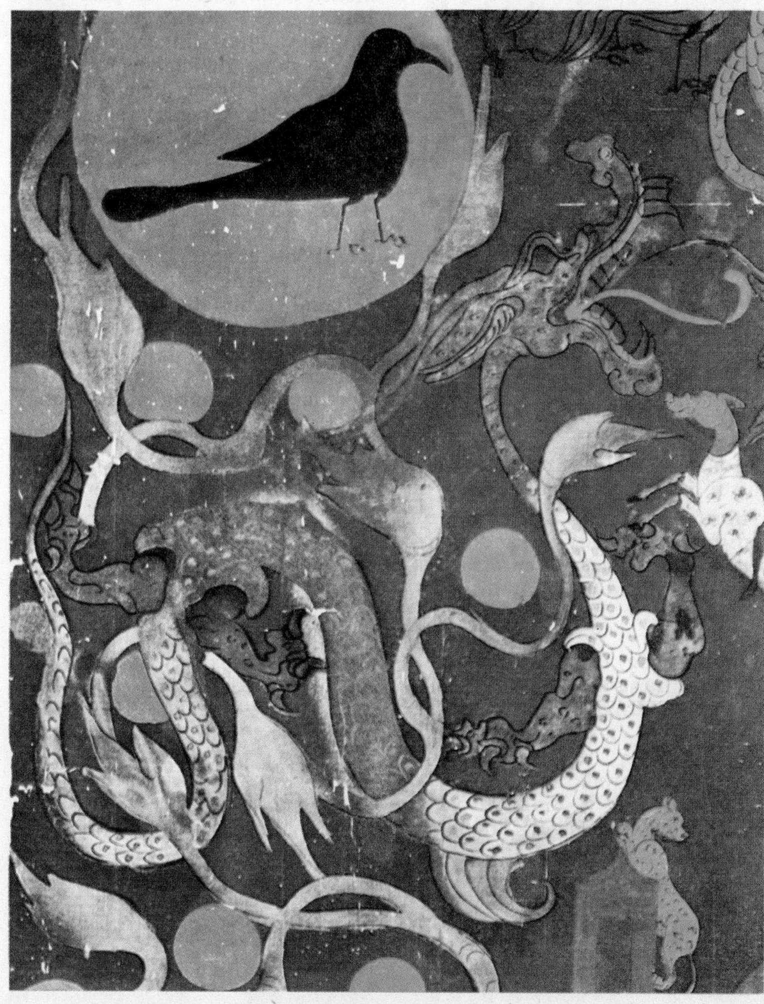

loq.) troublesome person.

hand·i·cap (hăn'dēkăp) *n.* Race or any contest of skill or strength in which to equalize chances of winning, some disadvantage in weight, score, etc. is imposed on a superior competitor, or some advantage is given to an inferior competitor; advantage given or disadvantage imposed; disability of any kind. ~ *v.t.* (**-capped, -cap·ping**). Impose handicap on (competitor); (fig., of circumstances) place (person) at a disadvantage; attempt to predict winner of horse race by comparing past performances, weights carried, etc. **hand'i·capped** *adj.* Suffering from physical or mental disability. **hand'i·cap·per** *n.* (esp.) Racetrack official who assigns weights to be carried by horses in handicap races.

hand·i·craft (hăn'dēkrăft, -krahft) *n.* Manual art or trade, as weaving, pottery, etc.; work, articles so produced. **hand'i·crafts·man**, person who practices a handicraft.

hand·i·work (hăn'dēwĕrk) *n.* Work done, thing made, by the hands or by anyone's personal agency.

hand·ker·chief (hăng'kerchĭf, -chēf) *n.* Square of linen, silk, etc., carried in pocket (**pocket-~**) for wiping nose etc.

han·dle[1] (hăn'del) *n.* That part of thing which is made to hold it by; (slang) person's name; (CB jargon) call name. **han'dlebar**, (of bicycle etc.) steering bar with handle at each end.

han·dle[2] (hăn'del) *v.t.* (**-dled, -dling**). Touch, feel with the hands; manipulate; manage (thing, person); treat; treat of; deal in (goods). **han'dler** *n.* (esp.) Person in charge of a trained animal, show dog, etc.

hand·some (hăn'som) *adj.* (**-som·er, -som·est**). Of fine form or figure; (of a man) good-looking; (of conduct etc.) generous; (of price, fortune, etc.) considerable. **hand'some·ly** *adv.* **hand'some·ness** *n.*

hand·y (hăn'dē) *adj.* (**hand·i·er, hand·i·est**). Ready to hand; convenient to handle; clever with the hands; **handyman** *n.* (hăn'dēmăn), person able to do all sorts of odd jobs.

hang (hăng) *v.* (**hung** pr. hŭng, **hanged, hang·ing**). 1. (past t. & past part. **hung**) Suspend, attach loosely (*from, to*); suspend (meat, game) to dry, age, etc.; place (picture) on wall; attach (wallpaper); suspend floating in space; rest (door on hinges) in free-swinging position; let droop; remain, be, suspended; decorate *with* (things suspended); **hanging gardens**: see BABYLON. 2. (past t. & past part. **hanged**) Suspend, be suspended, by the neck until dead (esp. as capital punishment). 3. (past t. & past part. **hung**) ~ **about** or **around** (colloq.) loiter, linger, about; ~ **back**, show reluctance to act or move; ~ **glider**, kitelike glider controlled by operator suspended in harness beneath; ~ **heavy**, (of time) pass slowly; ~ **in (there)**, persevere in troublesome situation; ~ **on**, attend carefully to (words etc.); stick closely (*to*); keep telephone connection open; persevere; (slang) wait; ~ **out**, suspend from; (slang) frequent (*at* place); ~ **together**, be coherent; ~ **up**, suspend; end telephone conversation by putting receiver back in cradle; **hung over**, (slang) suffering from a hangover. 4. **hang'dog**, base and sneaking; shamed, cringing (expression etc.); **hang'man**, one appointed to hang condemned persons; **hang'nail**, torn skin at root of fingernail; resulting soreness; **hang'out**, (colloq.) place often visited; place where one is usu. found; **hang'over**, (slang) unpleasant aftereffects of intoxication; **hang'up**, (colloq.) psychological block or fixation. **hang** *n.* Downward droop or bend; way a thing hangs; **get the ~ of**, get the knack of, understand.

hang·ar (hăng'ger, hăng'er) *n.* Building for housing aircraft.

hang·er (hăng'er) *n.* (esp.) Loop etc. by which thing is hung; coat hanger; **~-on**, sycophantic follower.

hang·ing (hăng'ĭng) *n.* (esp., pl.) Drapery with which walls etc. are hung; **a ~ matter**, action etc. punishable by capital punishment.

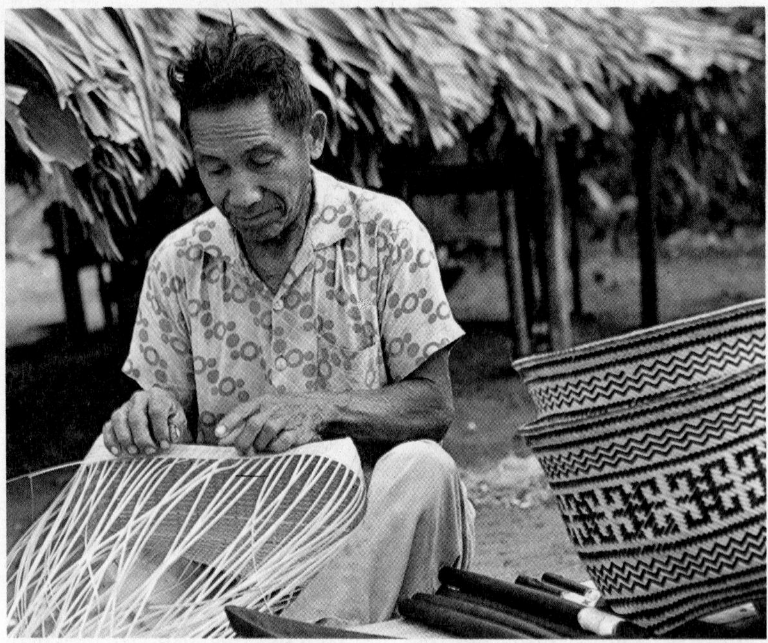

*In many communities **handicraft** is the only form of manufacture. This Guyanese craftsman weaves baskets of characteristic local patterns, using materials from the surrounding country.*

hank (hăngk) *n.* Circular loop or coil, orig. as definite length of yarn; (naut.) ring of rope, iron, etc., for fixing staysails to stays.

hank·er (hăng'ker) *v.i.* Crave, long, *after*. **hank'er·ing** *n.*

Hanks (hăngks), **Nancy**, (1783–1818). Mother of Abraham Lincoln; married Thomas Lincoln, 1806.

han·ky (hăng'kē) *n.* (pl. **-kies**). (colloq.) Handkerchief.

han·ky-pan·ky (hăng'kē păng'kē) *n.* (colloq.) Underhand dealing; mischief, deceit.

Han·ni·bal (hăn'ibal) (3rd c. B.C.). Carthaginian general; fought against Rome in second Punic War; crossed the Alps into Italy and defeated the Romans at Lake Trasimene (217 B.C.) and Cannae (216 B.C.), was eventually forced to withdraw from Italy and was defeated by Scipio in N. Africa.

Ha·noi (hănoi'). Capital of Vietnam in the NE.

Han·o·ver (hăn'ōver). (Ger. *Hannover*) Town in the north of West Germany; once capital of the country of Hanover, which was later a province of Prussia; in 1714 the elector of Hanover (Georg Ludwig) became King George I of England; **House of ~**, British royal dynasty from 1714 to the death of Queen Victoria in 1901.

Hanse (hăns) *n.* Company or guild of merchants, esp. political and commercial league (**Hanseatic League**) of Germanic towns, which flourished in the 14th and 15th centuries. **Han·se·at·ic** (hănsēăt'ĭk) *adj.* Of the German Hanse.

han·som (hăn'som) *n.* (also ~ **cab**) Cabriolet for two inside, with driver mounted behind and reins going over roof. [J. A. *Hansom* (1803–82), Engl. inventor]

Ha·nuk·kah, Cha·nu·kah (hah′nuka, -nōōkah; *Heb.* χahnōō-kah′) *ns.* Jewish festival commemorating victory of the Maccabees over the Syrians in 165 B.C. and the rededication of the Temple at Jerusalem (also called Feast of Lights, Festival of Lights).

hap·haz·ard (hăphăz′erd) *adj.* Casual; unplanned. **hap·haz′ard·ly** *adv.*

hap·less (hăp′lĭs) *adj.* Unlucky. **hap′less·ly** *adv.*

hap·loid (hăp′loid) *adj.* & *n.* (biol.) (Organism, cell) with only one set of chromosomes (half the DIPLOID complement).

hap·pen (hăp′en) *v.i.* 1. (of event) Occur. 2. Chance, have the fortune, *to* (do); come *upon* by chance. **hap′pen·ing** *n.* 1. Event. 2. Impromptu performance, or one in which audience participates. **hap·pen·stance** (hăp′enstăns) *n.* (joc.) Chance.

hap·py (hăp′ē) *adj.* (**-pi·er, -pi·est**). (esp. of circumstance) Lucky, fortunate; contented or pleased with one's lot; successful, apt, felicitous; **~-go-lucky** (*adj.*); cheerfully casual. **hap′pi·ly** *adv.* **hap′pi·ness** *n.*

Haps·burg, Habs·burg (hăps′-bĕrg; *Ger.* hahps′boorχ). German family (named after the castle of Hapsburg near Aaran in Switzerland) to which belonged the rulers of Austria and many of the Holy Roman Emperors from 1273 to 1918; branch of the family that ruled Spain from 1516 to 1700.

ha·ra-ki·ri (hăr′akēr′ē, hăr′-) *n.* Suicide by disembowelment, as formerly practiced by military (or samurai) class in Japan when in disgrace or sentenced to death. [Jap. *hara* belly, *kiri* cut]

ha·rangue (harăng′) *n.* Long, loud, or vehement address; tirade. ~ *v.* (**-rangued, -rangu·ing**). **Ha·ra·re** (Hă′ra′rē). See SALISBURY.

har·ass (hăr′as, harăs′) *v.t.* Vex by repeated attacks; trouble, worry. **har·ass′ment, har′ass·ment** *ns.*

Har·bin (hărbēn′). (Chinese **Pinkiang**) City in central Manchuria; important railroad junction and trade center.

har·bin·ger (hăr′bĭnjer) *n.* 1. (formerly) One sent to secure lodgings for army, royal train, etc. 2. Person or thing that announces another's approach, forerunner. ~ *v.t.* Announce approach of.

har·bor, Brit. **har·bour** (hăr′-ber) *ns.* Place of shelter for ships, esp. where they may lie close to and sheltered by shore, piers, etc.; shelter. ~ *v.* Give shelter to, foster, cherish (evil thoughts); come to anchor in harbor. **har′bor·age**, Brit. **har′bour·age** *ns.* (Place of) shelter.

hard (hărd) *adj.* 1. Firm, unyielding to touch, solid. 2. Difficult (*to* do); difficult to understand or explain; ~ **of hearing**, somewhat deaf. 3. Difficult to bear; unfeeling, harsh; involving undue or unfair suffering; stingy; harsh; (of liquor) distilled or with high alcoholic content; intoxicating; (of drugs) addictive. 4. In phonetics, applied to: (*a*) the letters *c, g* when they have their original guttural sounds, as in *can, get*, as dist. from the palatal and sibilant sounds, as in *center, gin*; (*b*) voiceless as dist. from voiced consonants, as *th* in *think* compared with *th* in *this*. ~ *adv.* Strenuously, severely; with difficulty; **be ~ put to it**, be in difficulties; **~ by**, close by; **~ on**, too severe in criticism or treatment; (of circumstances) bearing with undue severity on. **hard** *adj.* or *adv.* in comb.; **~-and-fast**, (of rules) strict; **hard′ball**, baseball as opp. to softball; (pol.) tough, unscrupulous machinations; **hard-bitten**, tough in fight, stubborn; **hard-boiled**, (of eggs) boiled until white and yolk are solid; hardened, callous; hardheaded; **hard cash**, cash as opp. to credit; **hard cider**, fermented apple juice; **hard coal**, anthracite; **hard core**, (fig.) irreducible nucleus or residue; **hard-core**, inveterate; constituting a difficult social problem; (of pornography) explicit and with no redeeming value; **hard currency**, currency unlikely to depreciate suddenly or fluctuate greatly in value; **hard hat**, light protective helmet worn by construction workers, baseball players, etc.; (colloq.) construction worker; any working-class conservative; **hard′-headed**, practical, not sentimental; **hard′hearted**, unfeeling; **hard-hit**, severely damaged, harmed, or troubled; **hard labor**, compulsory physical labor, as road building, stone breaking, etc., formerly imposed as part of legal punishment on criminals during imprisonment; **hard line**, unyielding adherence to firm policy; **hard-nosed** (colloq.) obdurate, uncompromising; **hard′-pan**, firm subsoil of clay, gravel, or sand; hard unbroken ground; **hard rock**, very loud rock-'n'-roll, with a heavy beat; **hard sauce**, mixture of butter and sugar often with brandy etc. added; **hard sell**, aggressive salesmanship; **hard-shell**, having a hard shell, as **hard-shell crab**, one that has not recently molted; (fig.) rigid and uncompromising in religious orthodoxy; **hard′tack**, hard biscuit made with flour and water only, ship biscuit; **hard up**, in want, esp. of money; at a loss *for*; **hard′ware**, metal goods such as small tools, nails, locks, etc.; (colloq., parts of) machine(s); items of electronic or mechanical equipment; (esp.) apparatus of a computer; **hard water**, water containing mineral, esp. calcareous, salts that decompose soap, thus making the water unsuitable for washing etc., and causing incrustations in boilers; **hard′wood**, wood of deciduous trees as opp. to pines and firs. **hard′en** *v.* Make or become hard or callous.

Har·ding (hăr′dĭng), **Warren Gamaliel** (1865–1923). Twenty-ninth president of U.S., 1921–3; senator from Ohio, 1915–21; conservative Republican; opposed League of Nations; died in office.

hard·ly (hărd′lē) *adv.* Scarcely; probably or surely not; harshly.

hard·ness (hărd′nĭs) *n.* 1. Quality or state of being hard. 2. (min.) Degree of resistance of a mineral to abrasion or scratching, expressed in terms of the following scale, known as MOHS' scale: (i) talc; (ii) gypsum; (iii) calcite; (iv) fluorite; (v) apatite; (vi) orthoclase; (vii) quartz; (viii) topaz; (ix) sapphire (corundum); (x) diamond; thus, in the description of a mineral, "H. 7.5" means that it is harder than quartz but softer than topaz. 3. Quality of water containing dissolved salts of calcium and magnesium, bicarbonates causing temporary hardness, i.e. removable by boiling, and sulfates and chlorides causing permanent hardness, i.e. not removable by boiling.

hard·ship (hărd′shĭp) *n.* Hardness of circumstance; severe

*The Market Church towering above the Marktplatz in **Hanover** was completed in 1359. It is a Gothic basilica of brick. After the town's destruction in 1939–45 war, the church became a symbol of Hanover's recovery.*

The ***hare*** *is able to run swiftly from predators. It can outdistance most when running uphill, aided by its long back legs. This illustration shows a leveret when surprised.*

suffering or privation.

har·dy[1] (hăr′dē) *adj.* (**-di·er, -di·est**). 1. Bold, audacious. 2. Robust, capable of endurance; (hort., of plants) able to grow in the open air all the year. **har′di·ly** *adv.* **har′di·ness** *n.*

har·dy[2] (hăr′dē) *n.* (pl. **-dies**). Blacksmith's bar of hard iron for cutting metal on etc.

Har·dy (hăr′dē), **Thomas** (1840–1928). English novelist and poet; author of many novels of Wessex life, including *Tess of the D'Urbervilles* (1891) and *Jude the Obscure* (1896).

hare (hăr) *n.* Quadruped (*Lepus*) resembling a rabbit but larger, with long ears and hind legs, short tail, and divided upper lip, noted for timidity and swiftness; **varying ~**: see SNOWshoe rabbit; **hare′-brained**, silly, rash, wild; **hare′-lip**, fissure of upper lip caused by arrested development of upper lip or jaw.

hare·bell (hăr′bĕl) *n.* Perennial plant (*Campanula rotundifolia*) with loose panicle of delicate blue bell-shaped flowers on slender stalk.

ha·rem (hăr′em, hăr′-) *n.* Women's part of Muslim dwelling house; its occupants, female members of Muslim family, esp. wives and concubines.

har·i·cot (hăr′ĭkō) *n.* (also **~ bean**) (chiefly Brit.) Kidney bean; any similar bean of genus *Phaseolus*, eaten as vegetable.

hark (hărk) *v.* Listen; **~ back**, (of hounds) retrace course to find scent; recall (hounds); (fig.) revert (*to* subject).

Har·lem (hăr′lem). Section of New York City at the N. end of Manhattan; founded as a village in 1658; since World War I a major black district.

har·le·quin (hăr′lekwĭn) *n.* 1. (usu. **Harlequin**) Character in Italian comedy; in English pantomime, mute character, invisible to clown and pantaloon, in particolored bespangled tights and visor, and carrying wooden sword or lath as magic wand. 2. (also **~ duck**) Northern species of duck (*Histrionicus histrionicus*) with distinctively variegated plumage. **har·le·quin·ade** (hărlekwĭnăd′, -kĭ-) *n.* Part of pantomime in which harlequin and clown play principal parts.

Har·ley (hăr′lē) **Street.** London street associated with eminent or fashionable physicians and surgeons.

har·lot (hăr′lot) *n.* (archaic) Prostitute. **har′lot·ry** *n.*

harm (hărm) *n.* Damage, hurt; mischief, injury; **out of ~'s way**, in safety. **harm** *v.t.* Do harm to; damage, injure. **harm′ful** *adj.* **harm′ful·ly** *adv.* **harm′ful·ness** *n.* **harm′less** *adj.* Doing no harm. **harm′less·ly** *adv.* **harm′less·ness** *n.*

har·mon·ic (hărmŏn′ĭk) *adj.* Harmonious, concordant; relating to harmony; (math., of quantities) with reciprocals in arithmetical progression; **~ progression**, (math.) series of numbers whose reciprocals are in arithmetical progression, as $\frac{1}{2}$, $\frac{1}{3}$, $\frac{1}{4}$, or 12, 15, 20. **har·mon′i·cal·ly** *adv.* **harmonic** *n.* Secondary tone produced by vibration of aliquot parts of sonorous body, usu. accompanying primary or fundamental tone produced by vibration of body as a whole, but sometimes produced independently, as in stringed instrument by light pressure on the string at various points etc.; (elect.) one of the component frequencies of a wave or alternating current that is an integral multiple of the fundamental frequency.

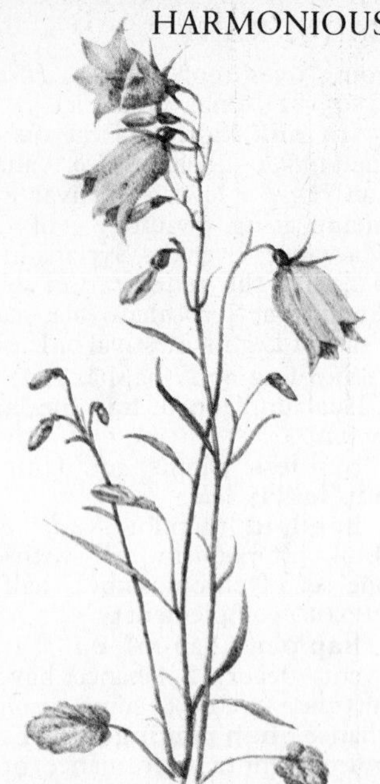

The ***harebell,*** *called a bluebell in Scotland, grows to between 10 ins. and 1 ft. tall. It thrives in open woodlands and grassy places, often in dense carpets of color.*

har·mon·i·ca (hărmŏn′ĭka) *n.* Thin rectangular box containing metal reeds, each tuned to a note, moved before mouth while air is blown or sucked through it to play tunes.

har·mo·ni·ous (hărmō′nēus) *adj.* Concordant, forming a consistent or agreeable whole; free from dissent; sweet-sounding; sing-

Thomas Hardy *was born in this brick and thatch cottage in Bockhampton, a Dorset hamlet. This author was very much influenced by 'Wessex', where he spent most of his life.*

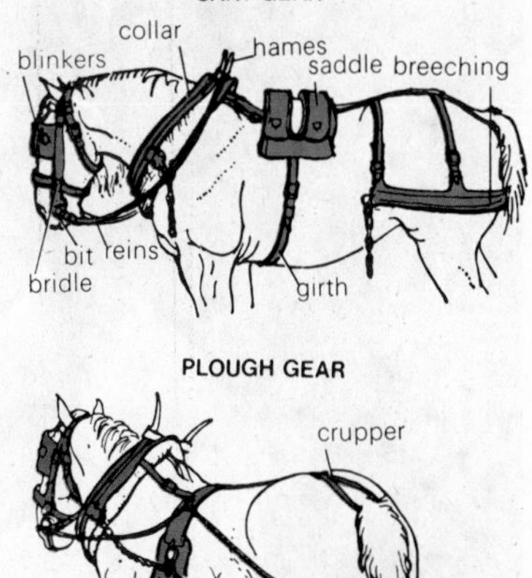

ing, playing, tunefully. **har·mo'·ni·ous·ly** *adv.*

har·mo·ni·um (har̄mō'nēum) *n.* Organlike musical instrument, in which the keys operate metal reeds, and a bellows, worked by the player's feet, supplies the wind.

har·mo·nize (har̄'monīz) *v.* (**-nized, -niz·ing**). Bring into, be in, harmony (*with*); make, be, agreeable in artistic effect; add notes to (melody) to form chords.

har·mo·ny (har̄'monē) *n.* (pl. **-nies**). 1. Combination or arrangement of parts to form consistent and orderly whole, agreement, congruity; agreeable effect of apt arrangement of parts. 2. Combination of musical notes to produce pleasing effect; combination of (simultaneous) notes to form chords, part of music dealing with formation and relation of chords. 3. Collation of parallel narratives, passages on same subject etc., esp. of the four Gospels.

har·ness (har̄'nĭs) *n.* Gear of draft horse or other animal; apparatus in loom for shifting warp threads; (hist.) defensive armor; **in ~**, in the routine of daily work. **har'ness** *v.t.* Put harness on (horse etc.); (fig.) utilize (river, waterfall, natural forces) for motive power.

Har·old (hăr'old). Name of two kings of England: **Harold I** (d. 1040), reigned 1035–40; **Harold II**, king in 1066; killed in that year at the battle of Hastings.

harp (har̄p) *n.* Stringed musical instrument, roughly triangular, with strings of graduated lengths played with fingers, and with pedals for raising tone of strings by one or 2 semitones. **~** *v.i.* Play on harp; dwell tediously *on* (subject). **harp'ist** *n.*

Har·pers (har̄'perz) **Ferry.** Town and tourist resort in NE. West Virginia; site of U.S. arsenal

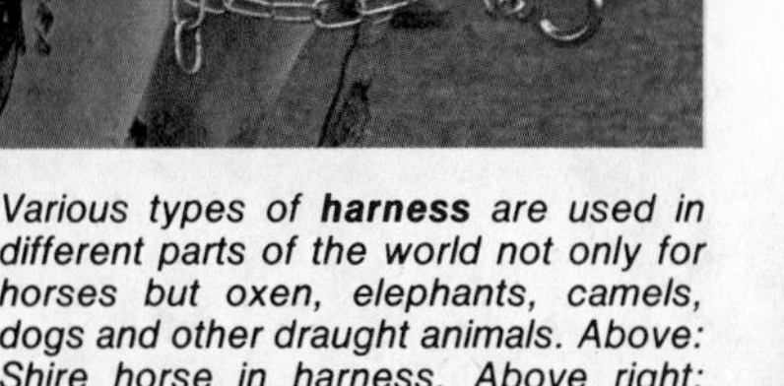
*Various types of **harness** are used in different parts of the world not only for horses but oxen, elephants, camels, dogs and other draught animals. Above: Shire horse in harness. Above right: Harness gear.*

seized by John Brown's raid in 1859.

har·poon (har̄po͞on') *n.* Barbed spearlike missile with rope attached, for catching whales and large fish; **~ gun**, gun for firing harpoon. **harpoon** *v.t.* Strike, spear, with harpoon.

harp·si·chord (har̄p'sĭkōrd) *n.* Keyboard musical instrument resembling in shape and construction the grand piano (which partly superseded it) but producing notes by means of strings plucked with quills or plectra.

Har·py (har̄'pē) *n.* (pl. **-pies**). 1. (Gk. and Rom. myth.) Rapacious monster with woman's face and body and bird's wings and claws; rapacious person. 2. **h~**, scolding, nagging woman.

har·que·bus (har̄'kwebus) *n.* (pl. **-bus·es**). (hist.) Early type of portable matchlock gun, supported on tripod by hook or on forked rest.

har·ri·dan (hăr'ĭdan) *n.* Haggard or scolding old woman.

har·ri·er[1] (hăr'ēer) *n.* One who harries.

har·ri·er[2] (hăr'ēer) *n.* 1. Hound used for hunting hare. 2. Hawk of genus *Circus*, esp. the marsh hawk (*C. cyaneus hudsonius*).

Har·ris·burg (hăr'isbērg). Capital of Pennsylvania on Susquehanna in SE. part of state.

Har·ri·son[1] (hăr'ĭson), **Benjamin** (1833–1901). Twenty-third president of U.S., 1889–93; grandson of William Henry Harrison.

Har·ri·son[2] (hăr'ĭson), **William Henry** (1773–1841). Ninth president of U.S., 1841; Amer.

*The **harp** was widely used in ancient Mediterranean and near-Eastern civilizations, although it was rare in ancient Greece and Rome. The modern harp has a full chromatic range of notes.*

general; led Americans during war against Indians, 1811–12; congressman from Ohio 1816–19; senator, 1825–8; minister to Colombia, 1828–9; died of pneumonia after one month as president.

har·row (hăr'ō) *n.* Frame with tines or disks that when dragged over soil, stirs it up, breaks clods, covers seed, etc. **~** *v.t.* Draw harrow over (land); distress painfully. **har'row·ing** *adj.* Distressing.

har·ry (hăr'ē) *v.t.* (**-ried, -ry·ing**). Ravage, waste, spoil (land); harass.

harsh (har̄sh) *adj.* Rough to the touch, taste, eye, or ear; cruel, unfeeling. **harsh'ly** *adv.* **harsh'·ness** *n.*

hart (har̄t) *n.* (pl. **harts,** collect. **hart**). Male of (esp. red) deer, esp. after fifth year; **~'s-tongue**, fern (*Phyllitis scolopendrium*) with long undivided fronds.

Harvesting may be a highly mechanized operation, or a simple hand task, as here in Amagon, Arkansas, where this couple are picking cotton.

Harte (hārt), **(Francis) Bret(t)** (1836–1902). Amer. writer of short stories and humorous verse; best known for his pieces written as a California journalist, including the short stories "The Luck of Roaring Camp" and "The Outcasts of Poker Flat."

har·te·beest (hār'tebēst, hārt'-bēst) *n.* Common antelope of genus *Alcelephas* of the Sudan and southern Africa, of reddish color with long outward curved horns and long skull.

Hart·ford (hārt'ferd). Capital of Connecticut in the central part on the Connecticut River.

har · um-scar · um (hār'um skār'um) *adj.* & *n.* Reckless (person, conduct). ~ *adv.* In reckless manner.

ha·rus·pex (harŭs'pěks, hăr'-uspěks) *n.* (pl. **ha·rus·pi·ces** pr. harŭs'pĭsēz). (Rom. antiq.) Soothsayer of Etruscan origin performing divination by inspection of entrails etc.

Har·vard (hār'verd). U.S. university at Cambridge, Massachusetts; named after clergyman John Harvard (1607–38), an English settler who left to the original college (founded 1636) his library and half his estate.

har·vest (hār'vĭst) *n.* (Season for) reaping and gathering in of grain or other products; crop gathered in one season; (fig.) product of any action; ~ **moon**, moon that is full nearest the autumn equinox (Sept. 22 or 23). **harvest** *v.t.* Reap and collect (crop) as harvest. **har'ves·ter** *n.* 1. Reaper. 2. Reaping machine (esp. reaper and binder).

Har·vey (hār'vē), **William** (1578–1657). English physician; discoverer of circulation of the blood, 1616.

Harz (hārts) **Mountains.** Mountain range and resort area of

*The swift and slender **hartebeest** lives in herds on the open plains and scrublands of Africa. Some species such as Swayne's hartebeest are rare and endangered animals.*

northern West Germany between the Elbe and the Weser.

has-been (hăz′bĭn) *n.* (colloq.) Person no longer useful, successful, or famous.

ha·sen·pfef·fer (hah′senfĕf*er*) *n.* Highly seasoned stew of rabbit meat. [Ger. *Hase* = rabbit + *pfeffer* = pepper]

hash[1] (hăsh) *n.* Dish of hashed meat and potatoes and sometimes vegetables, usually fried or baked, and often made of leftovers; old matter served up in new form; medley; ~ **mark**, (mil. slang) service stripe on sleeve of uniform; **make a ~ of**, spoil in dealing with; **settle a person's ~**, make an end of, silence, him. **hash** *v.t.* Cut (meat etc.) in small pieces.

hash[2] (hăsh) *n.* (slang) Hashish.

Hash·e·mite (hăsh′emīt) *adj.* & *n.* ~ **Kingdom of the Jordan**: see JORDAN.

Hash·i·mite (hăsh′imīt) *adj.* & *n.* (Member) of an Arab princely family claiming descent from Hashim, great-grandfather of Muhammad.

hash·ish, hash·eesh (hăsh′ēsh, hah′shēsh) *ns.* Top leaves and tender parts of common hemp, dried for smoking or chewing as narcotic; liquor prepared from this. [Arab., = "herbs"]

Hats for all occasions — from wide brimmed straw hats, to the ever-popular peaked cotton variety.

Ha·sid (hah′sĭd, hahsĭd′; *Heb.* χahsēd′) *n.* (pl. **Ha·sid·im** pr. hahsĭd′ĭm; *Heb.* χahsēdēm′). Member of Jewish sect founded in Poland in 18th c., characterized by mysticism and joyous zeal. **Ha·sid·ic** (hahsĭd′ĭk) *adj.*

hasp (hăsp, hahsp) *n.* Fastening contrivance, esp. clasp passing over staple and secured by padlock or toggle. ~ *v.t.* Fasten with hasp.

has·sock (hăs′*o*k) *n.* 1. Cushion for kneeling or use as a footstool. 2. Tuft of matted grass etc.

hast (hăst) *v.* (archaic) Second pers. sing. pres. ind. of *have.*

haste (hāst) *n.* Urgency of movement, hurry, precipitancy; **make ~**, be quick. **haste** *v.t.* (poet.) (**hast·ed, hast·ing**). Make haste. **has·ten** (hā′sen) *v.* Cause (person) to make haste; accelerate (work etc.); make haste; come or go in haste.

Has·tings (hās′tĭngz). Town on coast of Sussex, England, on the Strait of Dover, scene of the **Battle of ~**, (1066), in which the Normans, under William of Normandy, defeated the Saxons under HAROLD II.

hast·y (hās′tē) *adj.* (**hast·i·er, hast·i·est**). Hurried; speedy; rash, inconsiderate; quick-tempered; ~ **pudding**, cornmeal mush. **hast′i·ly** *adv.* **hast′i·ness** *n.*

hat (hăt) *n.* 1. Man's or woman's outdoor head covering, esp. with brim; **opera ~**, collapsible top hat worn in evening; **top ~**, man's tall silk hat. 2. **keep under one's ~**, keep confidential; **pass the ~**, solicit contributions; **talk through one's ~**, exaggerate, make unsupported assertions; **throw one's**

*The **hawthorn** is widely cultivated in Europe and North America, particularly in hedges. Its white or pink flowers, which usually grow in clusters, form into small fruit.*

~ **into the ring**, announce one's candidacy for political office. 3. **hat'band**, band of ribbon etc. around hat just above the brim; **hat trick**, (ice hockey, soccer, etc.) scoring of 3 goals by the same player in one game. **hat'ful** *n.* **hat'less** *adj.* **hat'ter** *n.* Person who makes or sells hats; **mad as a hatter**, quite mad (usu. alluding to the Mad Hatter, character in Lewis Carroll's *Alice in Wonderland*, but it may have its origin in the mercury poisoning, causing violent tremors, common among 19th c. hat makers).

hatch[1] (hăch) *n.* Lower half of divided door; aperture in door, wall, floor, or deck; (naut.) (also **hatch'way**) opening in ship's deck for lowering cargo, cover for this; floodgate; (aeron.) opening or door in aircraft or spacecraft; **down the ~**, informal drinking toast.

hatch[2] (hăch) *v.* Bring forth (young birds etc.) from egg; incubate (egg); emerge from egg; (of egg) produce young; contrive and develop (plot etc.). ~ *n.* Hatching; brood hatched. **hatch'er·y** *n.* (pl. **-er·ies**). Place for hatching eggs, esp. of fish.

hatch[3] (hăch) *v.t.* Mark with (esp. close parallel) lines, as for shading in engraving or drawing. ~ *n.* Shading line in engraving or drawing. **hatch'ing** *n.* Series of engraved or drawn lines producing effect of shading.

hatch·back (hăch'băk) *n.* Automobile with sloping rear door and window that lift as a unit.

hatch·et (hăch'ĭt) *n.* Light short-handled ax; **bury the ~**, make peace, compose a quarrel; ~ **face**, narrow sharp-featured face; ~ **job**, (colloq.) destructive criticism or gossip intended to damage the recipient; ~ **man**, (colloq.) paid killer; employee whose task it is to carry out unpleasant tasks for his employer.

hate (hāt) *n.* Hatred. ~ *v.t.* (**hat·ed, hat·ing**). Have strong dislike of; bear malice to. **hate'ful** *adj.* Exciting hatred. **hate'ful·ly** *adv.* **hate'ful·ness** *n.*

hath (hăth) *v.* (archaic) Third pers. sing. pres. ind. of *have*.

ha·tred (hā'trĭd) *n.* Active dislike; enmity, ill will.

Hat·ter·as (hăt'*e*r*a*s), **Cape.** Promontory of Hatteras Island off coast of North Carolina, part of Cape Hatteras National Seashore.

haugh·ty (haw'tē) *adj.* (**-ti·er, -ti·est**). Proud, arrogant; dignified. **haugh'ti·ly** *adv.* **haugh'ti·ness** *n.*

haul (hawl) *v.* Pull, drag, forcibly; transport by cart, wagon, truck, etc.; (naut.) turn ship's course; (of wind) shift; ~ **off**, pull arm back, prepare, to deliver blow. **haul** *n.* Hauling; distance hauled; (fig.) amount gained, acquisition, take; **long ~, short ~**, long, short, distance or period of time. **haul·age** (haw'lĭj) *n.* Fee charged for hauling.

haunch (hawnch) *n.* 1. Part of body (of man and quadrupeds) between last ribs and thigh; leg and loin of deer etc. as food. 2. Side of arch between crown and pier.

haunt (hawnt) *v.* 1. Frequent (place); frequent company of (person); (of thoughts etc.) visit (person) frequently; stay habitually. 2. (of ghosts etc.) Visit frequently with manifestations of their presence and influence; (past part.) visited, frequented, by ghosts. ~ *n.* Place of frequent resort.

Haupt·mann (howpt'mahn), **Gerhart** (1862–1946). German dramatist and novelist; Nobel Prize for literature, 1912.

Hau·sa (how's*a*, -z*a*) *n.* (pl. **-sas**, collect. **-sa**). (Member of) widespread people of the Sudan and N. Nigeria, of Bantu family with some Hamitic mixture; Hamitic language of these people, used, esp. in commerce, over much of W. Africa.

haut·boy (hō'boi, ō'-) *n.* (Old name for) OBOE; oboe player; reed stop in organ with tone like oboe.

haute cou·ture (ōt kōōtür'). High fashion; (creations of) leading fashion houses. [Fr.]

haute cui·sine (ōt kwēzēn'). Elegant style of cooking developed by French chefs. [French]

Ha·van·a (h*a*văn'*a*). Capital city of Cuba; hence, cigar of Cuban tobacco.

have (hăv) *v.* (**had** pr. hăd, **hav·ing**). 1. Possess as property or at one's disposal; possess as relative,

*The **hawk moth,** which is found in most parts of the world, pollinates flowers such as orchids and petunias. The larvae of some North American species are destructive pests to tobacco and potato crops.*

*The **hawk** occasionally destroys poultry but usually eats smaller mammals, reptiles and insects. The broad-winged hawk is about the size of a crow; the red-tailed hawk is one of the most common species; the red-shouldered hawk is reddish-brown and about 20 ins. long; and the rough-legged buzzard has fully-feathered legs and is 24 ins. long.*

adjunct, appendage, attribute, function, right, etc.; experience, suffer; ~ **on**, wear (clothing). 2. Possess as duty; be obliged. 3. Retain; entertain in the mind; show, exhibit (sentiment etc.) in action; carry on, engage in (proceeding etc.); ~ **in mind**, plan, propose; ~ **to do with**, deal with. 4. Express (*it*); assert, maintain; **will not** ~ **it**, refuse to allow or admit. 5. Come into possession of, obtain, get; (slang) deceive, take in; **I** ~ **it**, I have found a solution etc. 6. Get into specified condition, procure or oblige (to be done etc.). 7. ~ **at**, go at vigorously, attack; ~ **it**, win, have the superiority; ~ **had it**, (slang) be exhausted, defeated, etc.; ~ **it coming**, merit it; **let** (person) ~ **it**, give it to him; attack, punish, or reprimand him. **have** *v.aux.* Forming (with past part. of verb) compound tenses, pres. t. of *have* forming perfect, past t. of *have* forming past perfect. **have** *n.* One who *has*, one belonging to wealthier classes (usu. in pl., opp. to *have-nots*).

ha·ven (hā′ven) *n.* Harbor, port; refuge.

ha·ver·sack (hăv′ersăk) *n.* (Soldier's, traveler's) stout canvas bag for provisions, carried on back or over shoulder. [Ger. *habersack* (*haber* oats)]

hav·oc (hăv′ok) *n.* Devastation, destruction; **cry** ~, give signal to army to seize spoil (now only fig.); **play** ~ **with**, destroy.

haw[1] (haw) *n.* (Fruit of) hawthorn; ~**finch**, kind of finch with very thick beak (*Coccothraustes coccothraustes*).

haw[2] (haw) *n.* Third eyelid of horse, dog, etc., cartilage within inner corner of eye.

haw[3] (haw) *v.* Hesitate, esp. in speech; stammer; esp. in phrase **hem and** ~.

haw[4] (haw) *int.* Command to animal to turn left (opp. GEE[1]).

Ha·wai·i (hawī′ē, -wī′e). Formerly Sandwich Islands, now state of U.S. comprising a chain of islands in the central Pacific including Hawaii; settled by Polynesians c10th c.; discovered by Europeans under Capt. Cook 1778; annexed by U.S., 1898; admitted to the Union in 1959; capital, Honolulu. **Ha·wai·ian** (hawī′an) *adj.* & *n.* [Polynesian *Hawai′i* or *Havaiki* = Little Sava or Java, legendary home of Polynesians]

hawk[1] (hawk) *n.* Diurnal bird of prey of the order Falconiformes, esp. one of the Accipitridae or true hawks; (pol.) person advocating bellicose policies or nationalism; rapacious or aggressive person; ~**-eyed**, keen sighted; ~ **moth**, moth of family Sphingidae, noted for its hovering and darting flight; sphinx moth; **hawks' bill, hawks'-bill**, species of turtle (*Eretmochelys imbricata*) with mouth like hawk's beak, inhabiting Indian Ocean and warmer parts of Atlantic, source of tortoise shell; **hawk′weed**, yellow-flowered composite perennial plant of genus *Hieracium*. **hawk** *v.* Attack as hawk does; hunt with trained hawks.

hawk[2] (hawk) *v.t.* Peddle (wares) by crying them in the streets (also fig.). **haw′ker** *n.*

hawk[3] (hawk) *v.* Clear the throat noisily; bring (phlegm etc.) *up* from throat.

hawk[4] (hawk) *n.* Plasterer's or

*The grasses which produce **hay** are usually cut while still green. They are dried in the field and piled into haystacks, like these in Tuscany, Italy.*

mason's square board with handle underneath.

hawse (hawz) *n.* Part of ship's bows containing ~ **holes**, openings through which a hawser or cable is passed; space between head of anchored vessel and anchors; situation of cables before ship's stern when moored with two anchors out from forward, one on starboard, other on port bow.

haw·ser (haw′zer) *n.* (naut.) Large rope, small cable, now freq. of steel.

haw·thorn (haw′thōrn) *n.* Thorny shrub or small tree of genus *Crataegus*, with white, red, or pink blossom and small dark red berry; ~ **china, jar, pattern**, (china, jar, with) decoration of flowering branches of Japanese plum tree in white on dark blue ground.

Haw·thorne (haw′thōrn), **Nathaniel** (1804–64). Amer. writer of short stories and novels; among his works, *Twice-Told Tales, The Scarlet Letter*, and *The House of Seven Gables*.

hay[1] (hā) *n.* Grass, clover, alfalfa, etc., cut and dried for fodder; **make ~ while the sun shines**, seize opportunities; **hay′cock**, (chiefly Brit.) hay piled into a conical heap in a field; **hay fever**, allergy with catarrhal and freq. asthmatic symptoms, caused by pollen etc.; **hay′fork**, fork for turning over or loading hay; **hay′loft**, loft in barn for storing hay; **hay′maker**, one who lifts, tosses, and spreads hay after mowing; instrument for shaking and drying hay; (slang) powerful swinging blow; **hay′mow**, hay stored in barn; hayloft; **hay′stack**, regular pile of hay with pointed or ridged top for winter storage in the open; **hay′seed**, (slang) rustic, bumpkin; **hay′wire**, wire used to bind a bale of hay, straw, etc.; (*pred. adj.*) in disorder; distracted, crazy. **hay** *v.* Make into hay; make hay; feed hay to (animals).

hay[2] (hā) *n.* Country dance, or movement in dance, of winding or serpentine kind.

Hay·dn (hī′den), **Franz Josef** (1732–1809). Austrian-born composer of many symphonies, string quartets, masses, oratorios ("The Creation," "The Seasons"), etc.

Hayes (hāz), **Rutherford B(irchard)** (1822–93). Amer. lawyer and soldier; governor of Ohio 1868–72, 1876–7; 19th president of U.S., 1877–81, after being declared the winner over Samuel Tilden in a close and disputed election.

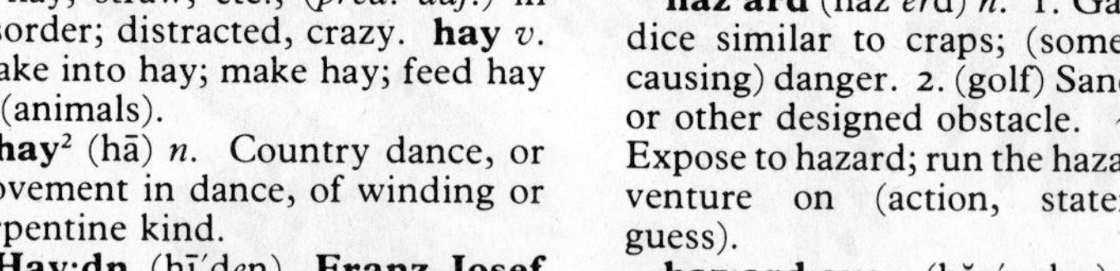

haz·ard (hăz′erd) *n.* 1. Game of dice similar to craps; (something causing) danger. 2. (golf) Sand trap or other designed obstacle. ~ *v.t.* Expose to hazard; run the hazard of; venture on (action, statement, guess).

haz·ard·ous (hăz′erdus) *adj.* Risky; dangerous; dependent on chance. **haz′ard·ous·ly** *adv.*

haze[1] (hāz) *n.* Obscuration of atmosphere at or near ground level caused by presence of visible droplets of water in the air above wet ground or by a mixing of ascending hot air and descending colder air above hot ground; (fig.) mental obscurity or confusion. ~ *v.i.* (**hazed, haz·ing**).

haze[2] (hāz) *v.t.* (**hazed, haz·ing**). 1. (naut.) Harass with overwork. 2. Bully, subject to cruel horseplay, esp. as part of initiation into college fraternity.

ha·zel (hā′zel) *n.* Bush or small tree (*Corylus*) bearing nuts; light brown color of ripe **ha′zelnut**, (esp. of eyes).

Haz·litt (hăz′lĭt), **William** (1778–1830). English critic and essayist.

ha·zy (hā′zē) *adj.* (**-zi·er, -zi·est**). Misty, vague, indistinct. **ha′zi·ly** *adv.* **ha′zi·ness** *n.*

Hb *abbrev.* Hemoglobin.

H-bomb (āch′bŏm) *n.* Hydrogen bomb.

H.C. *abbrev.* House of Commons; Holy Communion.

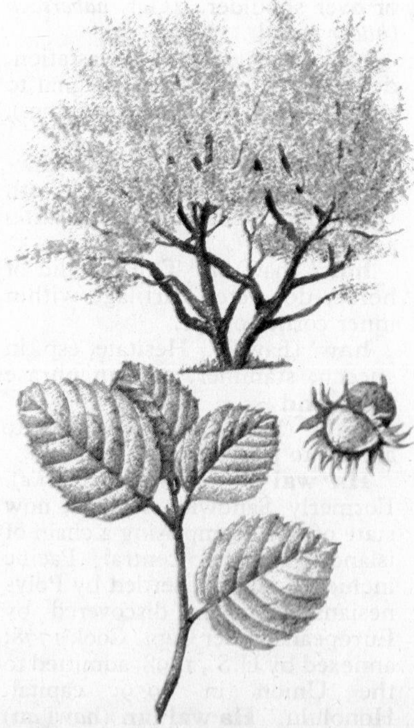

*The small trees or hairy-leaved shrubs of the **hazel** are found in temperate regions. The hazel's hard-shelled nut is edible.*

h.d. *abbrev.* Heavy duty.

HE, H.E. *abbrevs.* High explosive.

He *symbol.* Helium.

he (hē) *pron.* Third person nom. sing. masc. pronoun, denoting the male person or animal referred to. ~ *n.* Male animal; **~-man** (pl. **-men**), strong virile man.

head (hĕd) *n.* 1. Anterior part of body of animal, upper part of human body, containing mouth, sense organs, and brain; seat of intellect or imagination; headache (colloq.); image of head, esp. on one side of coin; person; individual, esp. of cattle. 2. Thing like head in form or position, e.g. cutting or striking part of tool, part of long bone next to joint, flat end of barrel or cask etc.; rounded or compact part of plant, e.g. compact mass of leaves in cabbage or lettuce, flower-buds in cauliflower, etc.; foam on top of beer; top (of staircase, page, etc.); maturated part of boil etc.; upper end; end of lake at which river enters it; end of bed etc. toward which head lies; source of river or stream; (height of) body of water kept at height for supplying mill etc., force of its fall; pressure (per unit of area) of confined body of steam etc.; front (of procession, army, etc.); front part of plow, holding the share; bows of ship; promontory; underground passage for working coal in mine. 3. Ruler, chief; headmaster or headmistress of school; position of command; main division in discourse; category; culmination, crisis. 4. (slang) Lavatory aboard naval vessel. 5. **from ~ to foot**, all over; **out of one's ~**, crazy; delirious; **over one's ~**, above one; beyond one's comprehension; **~ and shoulders** (**above** etc.), (taller etc.) by measure of head and shoulders (freq. fig.); **head'first**, (of plunge etc.) with head foremost; (fig.) precipitately; **head of hair**, hair on head, esp. when long or thick; **head over heels**, topsy-turvy, as in a somersault; deeply; **keep one's head**, keep calm; **keep one's head above water**, (fig.) keep out of debt; **lose one's head**, be beheaded; become confused, lose presence of mind. 6. **head'ache**, continuous pain in head; (colloq.) troublesome or annoying thing; **head'band**, band worn around head; **head'board**, board forming the head esp. of a bed; **head'dress**, covering esp. ornamental attire, for the head; **head'gear**, hat, cap, headdress; **head'hunting** (1) practice of primitive tribes of preserving enemies' heads as trophies; (2) similar practice of civilized hunters with animals; (3) ruthless elimination of political or business rivals; (4) (business) acquisition of (esp. executive) personnel; (5) acquisition of famous guests by ambitious hostesses; **head'land**, promontory; **head'light**, (beam from) powerful light at front of vehicle; **head'line**, line at top of front page of newspaper containing title etc. or major news story; title or subtitle in newspaper; (pl.) summary of a news broadcast; **head'lock**, wrestling hold with arm around opponent's head; **head'master, head'mistress**, director of a private school; **head-on**, (of collision etc.) with head or front of vehicle pointed directly toward or running full against something, esp. front of another vehicle; **head'phone**, (usu. pl.; radio, telephony) pair of receivers that can be held against listener's ears by band passing over head; **head'piece**, hat, helmet; **head'quarters**, (mil. etc.) commander in chief's office or place where commander's orders are issued; center of operations; **head'room**, overhead space; **head'stall**, part of bridle or halter that fits around horse's head; **head start**, early advantage or lead in competition; **head'stone**, gravestone;

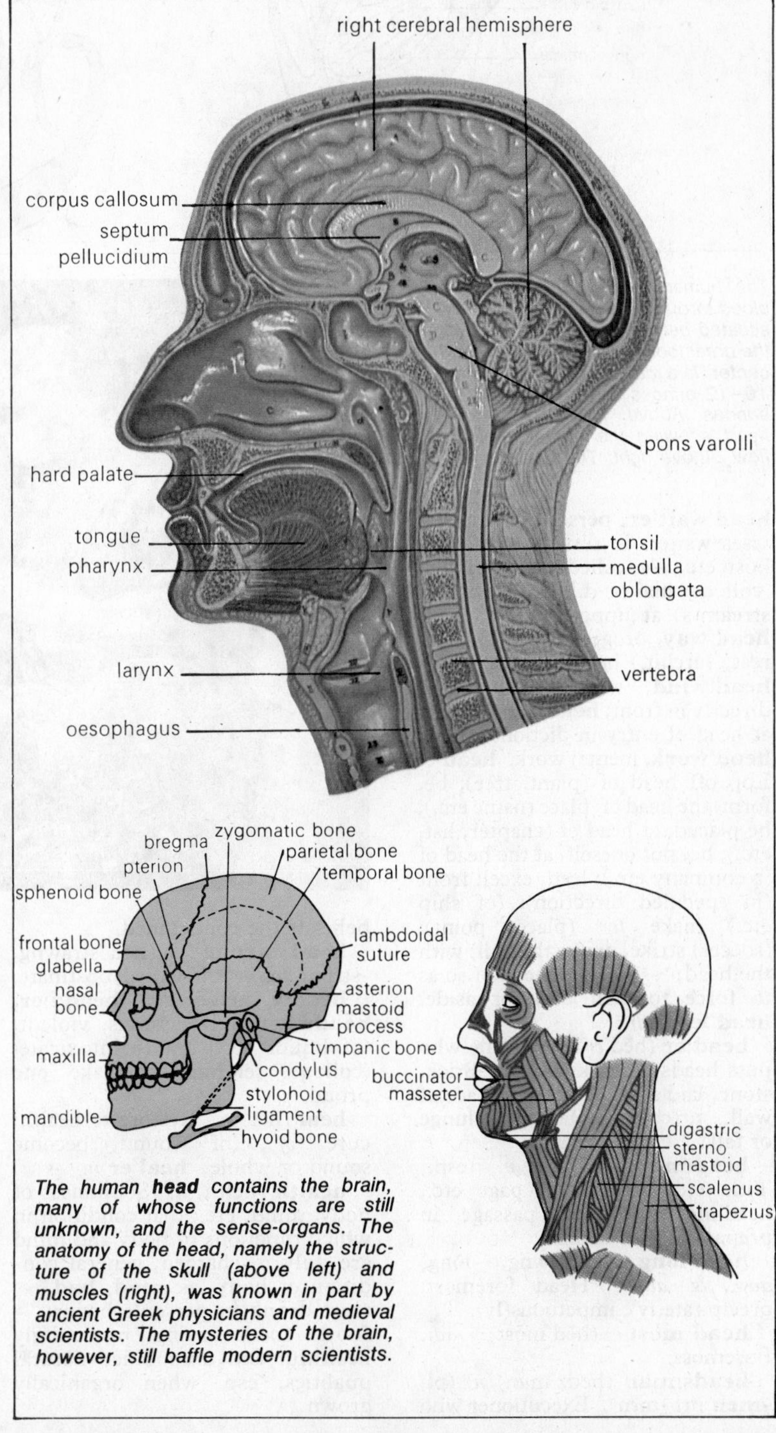

The human ***head*** *contains the brain, many of whose functions are still unknown, and the sense-organs. The anatomy of the head, namely the structure of the skull (above left) and muscles (right), was known in part by ancient Greek physicians and medieval scientists. The mysteries of the brain, however, still baffle modern scientists.*

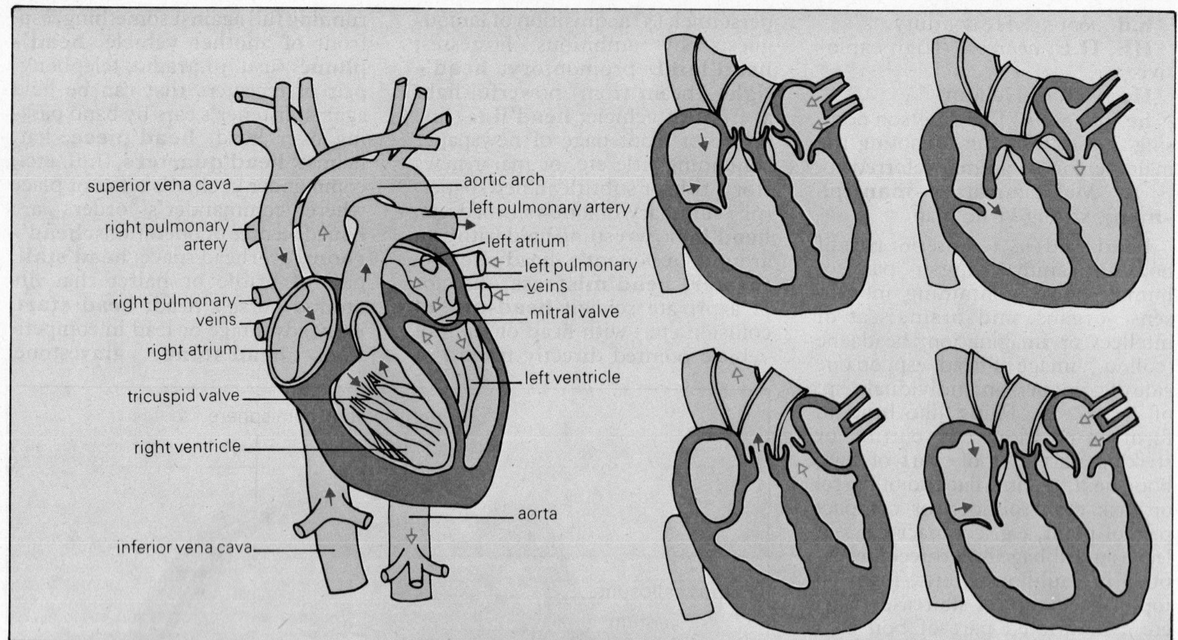

*The human **heart,** which pumps the blood through the circulatory system, is situated between the two lungs behind the breastbone and slightly to the left of center. In a man the heart weighs about 10–12 ounces and in a woman 8–10 ounces. Above: The structure of the heart showing the direction of blood flow. Above right: The heart's cycle.*

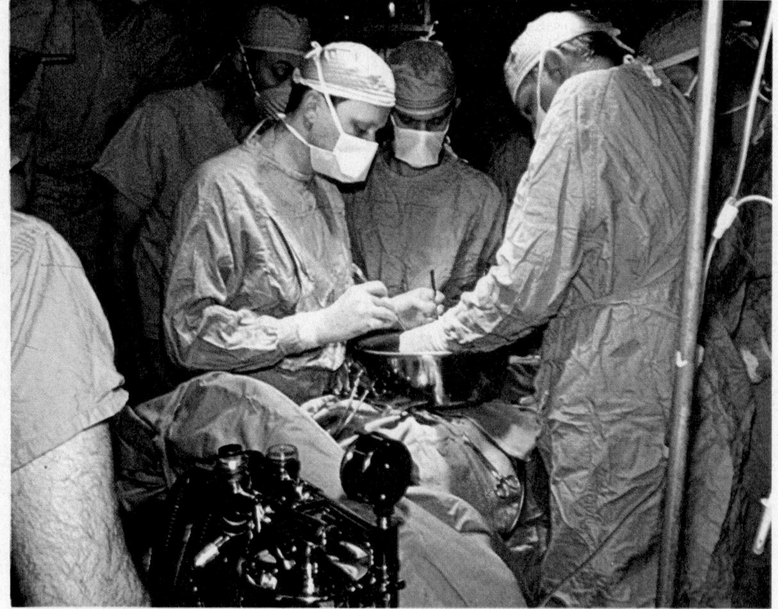

*A **heart** transplant operation involves the removal of a hopelessly diseased heart and its replacement with a sound heart from a person who has died. This transplant is being carried out in Houston, Texas.*

head'wait'er, person who supervises waiters in restaurant, acts as host, etc.; also called maître d'hôtel, (colloq.) maître d.; **head'waters**, stream(s) at upper part of river; **head'way**, progress; rate of progress; (archit.) height of arch etc.; **head'wind**, wind meeting one directly in front; **head'word**, word at head of entry in dictionary etc.; **head'work**, mental work. **head** *v.* Lop off head of (plant, tree); be, form, the head of; place (name etc.), be placed, at head of (chapter, list, etc.); be, put oneself, at the head of (a company etc.); lead; excel; front (in specified direction); (of ship etc.) make *for* (place, point); (soccer) strike, drive (the ball) with the head; ~ **off**, get ahead of so as to force to turn back or aside. **head'less** *adj.*

head·er (hĕd'*er*) *n.* 1. One who puts heads on casks etc. 2. Brick, stone, laid at right angles to face of wall. 3. (colloq.) Headfirst plunge or fall.

head·ing (hĕd'ĭng) *n.* (esp.) Title etc. at head of page etc., headline; horizontal passage in preparation for tunnel.

head·long (hĕd'lawng, -lŏng) *adv.* & *adj.* Head foremost; precipitate(ly); impetuous(ly).

head·most (hĕd'mōst) *adj.* Foremost.

heads·man (hĕdz'm*a*n) *n.* (pl. **-men** pr. -m*e*n). Executioner who beheads the condemned.

head·strong (hĕd'strawng, -strŏng) *adj.* Self-willed; obstinate.

head·y (hĕd'ē) *adj.* (**head·i·er, head·i·est**). Impetuous, violent; (of liquor etc.) apt to intoxicate; (colloq.) tending to make one proud.

heal (hēl) *v.* Restore to health; cure (*of*); (of wound) become sound or whole. **heal'er** *n.*

health (hĕlth) *n.* Soundness of body, mind, etc.; that condition in which functions of body and mind are duly discharged; general condition of body, as **good, bad** ~; toast drunk in person's honor; ~ **food**, food having particularly healthful and unmodified natural qualities, esp. when organically grown.

health·ful (hĕlth'f*u*l) *adj.* Health-giving; conducive to moral or spiritual welfare. **health'ful·ly** *adv.* **health'ful·ness** *n.*

health·y (hĕl'thē) *adj.* (**health·i·er, health·i·est**). Having good health; conducive to good health. **health'i·ly** *adv.* **health'i·ness** *n.*

heap (hēp) *n.* Group of things lying one on another; (colloq., esp. pl.) large number or amount. ~ *v.t.* Pile in a heap; load (*with*); accumulate (insults etc. *upon*).

hear (hēr) *v.* (**heard** pr. hĕrd,

hear·ing). Perceive (sound etc.), perceive sound(s), with the ear; listen, give audience, to; listen judicially to (case, plaintiff, etc.); grant (prayer); be informed; entertain notion *of*; receive letter or message *from*; **~! ~!**, exclamation expressing agreement. **hear'er** *n.*

hear·ing (hēr'ĭng) *n.* 1. Faculty of perception by means of the ear. 2. Opportunity to state one's case; listening to evidence and pleadings in a court of law; trial of a cause, esp. trial before a judge without a jury; ~ **aid**, device worn by person who is hard of hearing.

heark·en (hār'ken) *v.i.* (archaic) Listen (*to*).

hear·say (hēr'sā) *n.* What one hears (but does not know to be true), gossip.

hearse (hērs) *n.* Vehicle for conveying coffin at funeral; (formerly) framework supporting coffin at funeral, often adapted for carrying candles.

heart (hārt) *n.* 1. Hollow muscular organ that by rhythmic contraction and relaxation drives the blood through the vascular system; consisting in mammals and birds of four chambers. 2. Breast; mind; soul; seat of the emotions, esp. of love; sensibility, tenderness, feeling; courage; enthusiasm, energy. 3. Central part of anything, center, pith, core. 4. Vital part or principle. 5. Heart-shaped thing, esp. conventional symmetrical figure of two similar curves meeting in point at one end and cusp at the other; (playing card with) red heart-shaped figure(s); (pl.) suit of these cards. 6. Phrases: **break** (person's) ~, overwhelm him or her with sorrow; **cry one's ~ out**, cry violently; **eat one's ~ out**, grieve or yearn inconsolably; **have a ~!**, (colloq.) protesting appeal for sympathy; **have the ~**, be hardhearted or brave enough (*to*); **in one's ~ of ~s**, in one's inmost feelings; **have one's ~ in one's mouth**, be violently alarmed or startled; **set one's ~ on**, determine or select; **take ~**, pluck up courage. 7. With prepositions: **at ~**, in one's innermost feelings; **have at ~**, be deeply interested in; **by ~**, in, from, memory; **from (the bottom of) one's ~**, sincerely; **find in one's ~**, prevail on oneself (*to*); **near(est) one's ~**, dear(est) to one; **~-to-~**, frank, sincere; **take to ~**, be much affected in one's feelings by; **with all one's ~**, sincerely, with the utmost good will. 8. Comb.: **heart'ache**, mental anguish; **heart attack**, heart failure; **heart'beat**, pulsation of heart; **heart'break**, overwhelming distress; **heart'broken**, overwhelmed by grief; **heart'burn**, burning sensation in lower part of chest, due to putrefactive fermentation of food in stomach; **heart failure**, (med.) any derangement of heart's mechanism, not necessarily fatal; (pop.) cessation of heartbeat causing death; **heart'felt**, sincere; **heart'rending**, distressing; **hearts'ease**, pansy, esp. small wild form; **heart'sick**, despondent; **heart'warming**, moving, encouraging; **heart'wood**, dense inner part of tree trunk, containing the hardest timber.

*The **heartsease** or wild pansy grows where water is plentiful. It has oval-shaped leaves and the flowers are usually purple, blue and yellow, although there are all-white forms.*

heart·en (hār'ten) *v.* Inspirit, cheer; cheer *up*.

hearth (hārth) *n.* Floor of fireplace; floor of reverberatory furnace, of smith's forge, etc.; **hearth'stone**, stone forming hearth; soft kind of stone, rubbed with water over hearth, doorstep, etc. to whiten.

heart·i·ly (hār'tĭlē) *adv.* With good will, courage, or appetite; very.

heart·less (hārt'lĭs) *adj.* Unfeeling, pitiless, cruel. **heart'less·ly** *adv.* **heart'less·ness** *n.*

heart·y (hār'tē) *adj.* (**heart·i·er, heart·i·est**). Cordial, genial; (of feelings) sincere; vigorous; (of meals) abundant. ~ *n.* Hearty fellow, esp. sailor.

heat (hēt) *n.* 1. Being hot, high temperature; sensation, perception, of this; one of the primary sensations produced by contact with or nearness to fire or any body at a high temperature; (phys.) form of energy arising from the random molecular motion of a substance and capable of transmission by conduction or radiation. 2. Hot weather. 3. Warmth of feeling; anger; violent stage (of debate etc.); (slang) pressure, as in *the ~ is on*; (slang) police activity in searching out felons, as in *put the ~ on*. 4. = ESTRUS. 5. Single course in race or other contest. 6. **latent ~**, heat required to convert solid into liquid or vapor, or liquid into vapor (so called because it does not show its presence by an increase in temperature); **prickly ~**: see PRICKLY; **specific ~**, heat required to raise temperature of unit mass of given substance to given extent (usu. 1 degree), calculated relatively to some standard, usu. water; **~ lightning**, flashes of light without thunder, seen near the horizon on a hot summer evening; **~ of formation**, thermal change that occurs when substances chemically combine; **~ shield**, device to protect from excessive heat, esp. on spacecraft during reentry; **heat'-stroke**, prostration from excessive heat; **heat wave**: see WAVE *n.* defs. 3, 4. **heat** *v.* Make hot; inflame (blood etc.); inflame with passion; become hot. **heat'ed·ly** *adv.* Vehemently, angrily.

***Heat** is an essential ingredient of many operations, especially when it is required to melt a normally solid substance into liquid. Here workers pour gold into 100 ounce ingots.*

heat·er (hē'ter) *n.* (esp.) Any contrivance for warming up room etc.; (slang) pistol.

heath (hēth) *n.* (esp. Brit.) Barren flat waste tract of land, esp. if covered with low herbage and dwarf shrubs; plants and shrubs found on heaths, esp. low shrubs of genus *Erica*, heather.

hea·then (hē'dhen) *adj.* & *n.* (pl. **-thens, -then**). (One who is) neither Christian, Jewish, nor Muslim (in Old Testament, = gentile; hist., used also of Muslims; later restricted to holders of polytheistic religions, esp. when uncivilized); pagan. **hea'then·dom, hea'then·ism** *ns.* **hea'then·ish** *adj.*

heath·er (hĕdh'*er*) *n.* Species of plant or shrub of genus *Erica*, esp. the common heather, *Calluna vulgaris*, growing on moors and heaths, and bearing purple bell-shaped flowers in autumn; color of heather. **heath'er·y** *adj.*

heave (hēv) *v.* (**heaved, hove** (naut.) pr. hōv, **heaving**). 1. Lift (heavy thing); utter (groan, sigh) with effort; (naut. and colloq.) throw; (naut.) haul up, haul, by rope; pull (on rope etc.); ~ **to**, bring (vessel) to standstill with head to wind. 2. Rise, swell up; rise with alternate falls, as waves; pant; (colloq.) vomit. ~ *n.* Heaving; (pl.) disease of horses, "broken wind."

heav·en (hĕv'*e*n) *n.* Sky, firmament (in prose now usu. pl.); region of atmosphere in which clouds float, winds blow, and birds fly; (formerly) each of the heavenly spheres; (often cap.) supposed habitation of God and his angels, usu. placed beyond sky; God, providence; place, state, of supreme bliss. **heav·en·ward** (hĕv'*e*nw*e*rd) *adj.* & *adv.* **heav'en·wards** *adv.*

heav·en·ly (hĕv'*e*nlē) *adj.* Of heaven, divine; of the sky; of superhuman excellence. **heav'en·li·ness** *n.*

heav·i·er-than-air (hĕv'ē*er* dh*a*n âr') *adj.* (of aircraft) With weight greater than that of air it displaces, as distinct from balloons and dirigibles.

Heav·i·side (hĕv'ēsīd), **Oliver** (1850–1925). English physicist; ~ **layer**, E-layer of the ionosphere.

heav·y (hĕv'ē) *adj.* (**heav·i·er, heav·i·est**). 1. Of great weight; of great specific gravity; weighty because abundant; laden *with*; (of ordnance etc.) large; (mil.) carrying heavy arms or equipment; (of bread etc.) that has not risen properly, compact, dense. 2. Striking or falling with force or violence; (of ground etc.) clinging, difficult to travel over, dig, etc.; (of food)

difficult to digest. 3. Grave, severe; overcast, gloomy; clumsy in appearance or effect; intellectually slow; dull, tedious; oppressive, grievous; sad; despondent; doleful; drowsy; sober, serious. 4. ~**-duty**, intended to be unusually resistant to stresses in use; ~**-handed**, clumsy, oppressive; ~**-hearted**, melancholy, doleful; ~ **hydrogen** = DEUTERIUM; **heav'yset**, having a heavy, stocky build; ~ **water**, deuterium oxide (D_2O), with the same chemical properties as ordinary water, but density about 10% greater; **heav'yweight**, (colloq.) influential person; boxer of heaviest weight. **heav'i·ly** *adv.* **heav'i·ness** *n.* **heavy** *adv.* Heavily. ~ *n.* (colloq.) Villain; gangster; actor who plays a villain or gangster.

Heather is traditionally associated with the Scottish Highlands, where it was mixed with peat-mud and straw to provide thatching for the Highlanders huts; Heather is also found throughout Asia, N. America, and Africa.

Heb. *abbrev.* Hebrew; Hebrews (New Testament).

He·be (hē'bē). (Gk. myth.) Goddess of youth and spring, daughter of Zeus and Hera, and cupbearer of Olympus.

Heb·ei = HOPEI.

He·bra·ic (hĭbrā'ĭk) *adj.* Of, pertaining to, the Hebrews, or Hebrew. **He·bra'i·cal·ly** *adv.*

He·bra·ism (hē'brāĭzem, -brē-) *n.* Quality or attribute of the Hebrews; Hebrew system of thought or religion; Hebrew idiom or expression. **He'bra·ist** *n.* Hebrew scholar.

He·bra·ize (hē'brāīz) *v.* (**-ized, -iz·ing**). Translate into Hebrew; make, become, like a Hebrew.

He·brew (hē'broo) *n.* 1. Member of a Semitic people inhabiting ancient Palestine esp. before the Exile, traditionally descended from Abraham, Isaac, and Jacob; (**Epistle to the**) ~**s**, book of New Testament, traditionally included among the letters of St. Paul but now usu. held to be nonPauline. 2. Semitic language used by the Hebrews, and in which most of the books of the Old Testament were written; modern form of this, the language of modern Israel. ~ *adj.* Belonging to the Hebrews; ~ **alphabet**, Semitic alphabet of 22 letters, the vowels being indicated by a system of diacritical marks; ~ **calendar**: see JEWISH. [Aramaic *'ebrāyā*, Heb. *'ibrī* = "one from the

The Inner and Outer ***Hebrides,*** *which are also known as the Western Isles, consist of more than 500 islands, 92 of which are inhabited. The Isle of Lewis, shown here, is the main island of the Outer Hebrides.*

The ***Heaven Room*** *in Burghley House, Lincs., U.K., was painted by Antonio Verrio in 1695–6 and depicts the Greek gods on Mt. Olympus. Burghley House, one of the finest Elizabethan houses, also has a Hell Room.*

other side" (of the river)]

Heb·ri·des (hĕb′rĭdēz). Two groups of islands (**Inner** and **Outer** ~) off the NW. coast of Scotland. **Heb·ri·de·an, He·brid·i·an** (hĕbrĭd′ēan) *adjs.* (Native, inhabitant) of the Hebrides.

Hec·a·te (hĕk′atē). (Gk. myth.) Goddess, said to be of Thracian origin, daughter of Perses and Asteria; in later times identified with Artemis or Persephone, and hence regarded as presiding over witchcraft and magical rites.

heck (hĕk) *int.* (euphem.) Hell.

heck·le (hĕk′el) *v.t.* (**-led, -ling**). 1. Dress (flax etc.) with hackle. 2. Harass (performer or speaker) with gibes, interruptions, awkward questions, etc. **heck′ler** *n.*

hec·tare (hĕk′tār, -târ) *n.* (abbrev. ha) One hundred ares (2.471 acres).

hec·tic (hĕk′tĭk) *adj.* 1. (hist.) ~ **fever**, that which accompanies consumption and similar diseases, attended with flushed cheeks and hot skin; consumptive; morbidly flushed. 2. Feverishly excited or active. **hec′ti·cal·ly** *adv.*

hecto- *prefix.* One hundred times.

hec·to·gram (hĕk′tográm) *n.* (abbrev. hg) One hundred grams.

hec·to·li·ter (hĕk′tolēter) *n.* (abbrev. hl) One hundred liters.

hec·to·me·ter (hĕk′tomēter) *n.* (abbrev. hm) One hundred meters.

Hec·tor (hĕk′ter). (Gk. legend) Trojan warrior, son of Priam and Hecuba and husband of Andromache; killed by Achilles, who dragged his body three times around the walls of Troy.

hec·tor (hĕk′ter) *v.t.* Intimidate; bully. [f. HECTOR]

Hebrew *or Jewish people claim descent from Abraham and their religion is Judaism. The Wailing Wall in Jerusalem, reputedly on the site of Solomon's Temple, is now a sacred place for prayers and lamentations.*

Hedges, *like this one outside the Mormon Tabernacle in Salt Lake City, Utah, have several uses. Some are purely decorative; others are property dividers. In steeplechasing, hedges are used as fences to be jumped.*

Hec·u·ba (hĕk′yuba). (Gk. legend) Wife of Priam, king of Troy, and mother of Hector, Paris, and Cassandra, among other children.

hedge (hĕj) *n.* 1. Fence of bushes or low trees. 2. Barrier. 3. Protection against loss in gambling or speculation; **hedge′hop**: see HOP[2]; **hedge′row**, row of bushes forming hedge. **hedge** *v.* (**hedged, hedg·ing**). 1. Surround with hedge; hem *in*; make, trim, hedges. 2. Secure oneself against loss on (bet, speculation, etc.) by compensating transactions on the other side; avoid committing oneself. **hedg′er** *n.*

hedge·hog (hĕj′hŏg, -hawg) *n.* Any of several Old World insectivorous mammals of the family Erinaceidae having a back covered with dense, erectile spines and able to roll itself into a ball with these bristling in every direction; any of various animals armed with spines, such as the Amer. porcupine.

he·do·nism (hē′dənĭzəm) *n.* Doctrine or ethical theory that pleasure is the chief good, or the proper end of action. **he′do·nist** *n.* **he·do·nis·tic** (hēdənĭs′tĭk) *adj.*

hee·bie-jee·bies (hē′bē jē′bēz) *n.pl.* (slang) State of nervousness or uneasiness.

heed (hēd) *v.t.* Concern oneself about, take notice of. ~ *n.* Careful attention; esp. in **take ~, pay ~, to. heed′ful** *adj.* **heed′ful·ly** *adv.* **heed′ful·ness** *n.* **heed′less** *adj.* **heed′less·ly** *adv.* **heed′less·ness** *n.*

hee·haw (hē′haw′) *n.* Donkey's bray; loud laugh.

heel[1] (hēl) *n.* 1. Hind part of human foot below ankle; corresponding part of hind limb in quadruped, often raised above ground; (pop.) hind part of quadruped's hoof, (pl.) hind feet; **on the ~s of**, close behind, in close pursuit; **take to one's ~s, show a clean pair of ~s**, run away; **turn on one's ~**, turn sharply around. 2. Part of stocking that covers heel; part of boot or shoe that supports or raises heel; **down at ~**, (of shoes) with heel worn down; (of person) wearing such shoes, slovenly, destitute. 3. Thing like heel in shape or position, as lower rear surface of golf club, aft end of ship's keel; crusty end of loaf of bread. 4. Cad, dishonorable man. **heel** *v.* Touch ground with heel, e.g. in dancing; furnish (shoe etc.) with heel; chase or follow closely, esp. of trained dog. **heeled** *adj.* (esp. slang) Supplied with money, esp. in **well ~**.

heel[2] (hēl) *v.* (of ship etc.) Lean over owing to pressure of wind or uneven load; cause (ship) to do this. ~ *n.* (naut.) Inclination of heeling ship.

heft (hĕft) *n.* (colloq.) Weight. ~ *v.t.* Lift, esp. to judge weight.

heft·y (hĕf′tē) *adj.* (**heft·i·er, heft·i·est**). Heavy; sturdy, stalwart.

He·gel (hā′gəl), **Georg Wilhelm Friedrich** (1770–1831). German philosopher in whose system of absolute idealism pure being is regarded as pure thought, the universe as its development, and philosophy as its dialectical explication. **He·ge·li·an** (hāgā′lēən, -gē′-) *adj.* & *n.* (Follower) of Hegel or his philosophy. **He·ge′li·an·ism** *n.*

he·gem·o·ny (hĭjĕm′ənē, hĕj′-əmō-) *n.* (pl. **-nies**). Leadership; influence, esp. of one nation over others. **heg·e·mon′ic** *adj.*

He·gi·ra, He·ji·ra (hĭjīr′ə, hĕj′ərə) *ns.* Flight of Muhammad from Mecca to Medina in 622 A.D., from which the Muslim chronological era is reckoned; **h~**, any flight or exodus, esp. from danger. [Arab. *hijra* departure from one's country]

*The insect-eating **hedgehog** (above) is found throughout the whole of Europe and in Asia and Africa. It hibernates in winter and, like the African hedgehog shown here with her young, produces two litters a year.*

Hei·del·berg (hī′dəlbĕrg; *Ger.* hī′dəlbĕrχ). German university city on the river Neckar in Baden-Württemberg, West Germany; **~ man**, extinct species of man allied to Neanderthal man, and living in the Pleistocene period, a fossil jawbone of which was found near Heidelberg in 1907.

heif·er (hĕf′ər) *n.* Young cow that has not had a calf.

height (hīt) *n.* Measurement from base to top; elevation above ground or recognized level, esp. that of sea; considerable elevation; high point; top, highest point or degree; rising ground.

height·en (hī′tən) *v.* Make or become greater or higher; intensify.

Hei·ne (hī′nə), **Heinrich** (1799–1856). German lyric poet and critic.

hei·nous (hā′nəs) *adj.* Odious, atrocious. **hei′nous·ly** *adv.* **hei′nous·ness** *n.*

heir (ār) *n.* (fem. **heir·ess** pr. ār′ĭs). Person receiving or entitled to receive property or hereditary rank, title, or office of former owner, esp. upon death of the latter; **~ apparent**: see APPARENT; **~ presumptive**: see PRESUMPTIVE.

heir·loom (ār′lōōm) *n.* Piece of personal property that has been in family for generations.

He·jaz (hĕjăz′). Region on the Red Sea coast, forming with Nejd and Asir the Kingdom of Saudi Arabia.

He·ji·ra: see HEGIRA.

held: see HOLD[2].

Hel·en (hĕl′ən) (**of Troy**). (Gk. legend) Most beautiful woman of her time, daughter of Zeus and Leda; wife of Menelaus; her abduction by PARIS[2] led to the Trojan War.

Hel·e·na[1] (hĕl′ənə). Capital of Montana in the W. central part.

Hel·e·na[2] (hĕl′ənə), **St.** Mother of the Emperor Constantine; said to

The ***helicopter*** *first came into use in 1942, although the flight principles had been known for centuries. Its designer was the Russian-born American engineer, Igor Sikorsky, whose later design, the Sikorsky Sea King, is shown below. Peaceful uses for the helicopter include the transport of large materials in difficult landscapes (above right), use by police in rescue operations and short-distance taxi services between city centers and airports. During the Vietnam War, helicopters were used extensively both in combat and to recover wounded soldiers.*

Above: Four OH6 helicopters fly in formation.

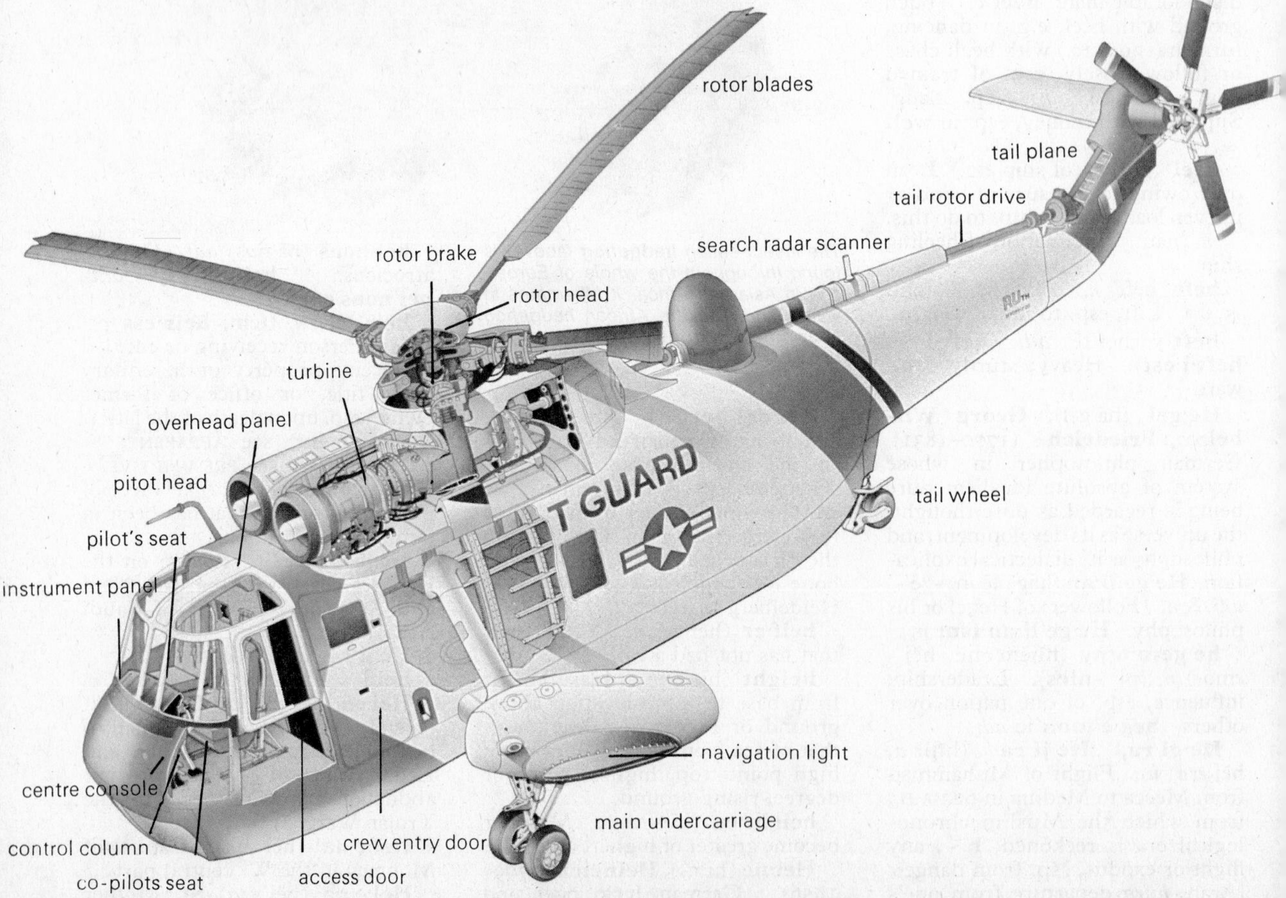

rotor blades
tail plane
tail rotor drive
search radar scanner
rotor brake
rotor head
turbine
overhead panel
pitot head
pilot's seat
instrument panel
T GUARD
tail wheel
navigation light
centre console
main undercarriage
control column
crew entry door
co-pilots seat
access door

The **heliotrope,** a herbaceous plant found in tropical or temperate regions throughout the world, is cultivated for its fragrant, purple to white clustered flowers.

have discovered the cross on which Christ was crucified; island in the S. Atlantic, the place of Napoleon's captivity (1815–21).

hel·i·cal (hĕl'ĭk*a*l) *adj.* Of or like a helix, as in ~ **gear. hel'i·cal·ly** *adv.*

Hel·i·con (hĕl'*i*kŏn, -kon). Mountain in Boeotia, Greece, sacred to the Muses.

hel·i·cop·ter (hĕl'*i*kŏpt*er*, hē'l*i*-) *n.* Aircraft lifted by rotor blades revolving horizontally.

he·li·o·cen·tric (hēlēosĕn'trĭk) *adj.* As viewed from center of sun; taking sun as center.

He·li·o·gab·a·lus (hēlēogăb'*alus*). Adopted name of Varius Avitus Bassianus, Roman emperor 218–22 A.D., famed for folly and profligacy. [Latinized f. *Elagabal*, Syro-Phoenician sun god]

he·li·o·gram (hē'lēogrăm) *n.* Message transmitted by heliograph.

he·li·o·graph (hē'lēogrăf, -grahf) *n.* Apparatus for signaling with movable mirror reflecting flashes of sunlight. ~ *v.* Communicate by heliograph.

he·li·om·e·ter (hēlēŏm'*eter*) *n.* Astronomical instrument for determining angular distance between celestial bodies (orig. for measuring diameter of sun).

He·li·op·o·lis (hēlēŏp'*o*lĭs). Ruined ancient city in N. Egypt near Cairo; the Biblical On; ancient name for BAALBEK.

he·li·o·trope (hē'lēotrōp, hĕl'-yo-; *Brit.* also hĕl'ēotrōp) *n.* 1. Plant of genus *Heliotropium* of herbs or shrubs with small clustered purple flowers, esp. *H. arborescens*; color or scent of heliotrope. 2. = BLOODstone.

he·li·o·trop·ic (hēlēotrŏp'ĭk, -trō'pik) *adj.* Phototropic. **he·li·ot·ro·pism** (hēlēŏt'r*o*pĭzem) *n.*

hel·i·pad (hĕl'*i*păd, hē'l*i*-) *n.* Area used by helicopters to take off or land.

hel·i·port (hĕl'*i*pōrt, -pōrt, hē'l*i*-) *n.* Airport for helicopter.

he·li·um (hē'lē*u*m) *n.* (chem.) Element, an inert gas occurring in small quantities in the atmosphere and in certain natural gases, and produced during radioactive decay; used, because of its lightness and noninflammability, in balloons and airships; symbol He, at. no. 2, at. wt. 4.00260.

he·lix (hē'lĭks) *n.* (pl. **hel·i·ces** pr. hĕl'ĭsēz, **he·lix·es**). 1. Spiral or coil like corkscrew; (archit. etc.) spiral ornament. 2. (anat.) Curved fold or prominence forming rim of external ear.

hell (hĕl) *n.* Abode of the dead; abode of devils and condemned spirits, figured as place of torment; place, state, of wickedness or misery; **a ~ of a**, an infernal, a very bad, great, loud, etc.; ~ **(bent)-for-leather**, at breakneck speed; **hell'cat**, (slang) spiteful or furious woman; **hell'fire**, fire of hell; **hell'hole**, any very squalid or disreputable place; **hell'hound**, fiend. **hell'ish** *adj.* **hell'ish·ly** *adv.* **hell'ish·ness** *n.*

***Hell,** as depicted by the 15th century Flemish painter, Hieronymus Bosch, is the product of his bizarre and fantastic imagination. Traditionally, the Hell to which damned souls go is made up of fire and brimstone.*

The **hellebore** is a genus of some 20 herbaceous perennials from western Asia and southern Europe. The most commonly seen variety is the Helleborus orientalis, known as the Winter or Lenten rose.

Hel·las (hĕl'*a*s). Greece; orig. the name of a district in Thessaly, but applied by the ancient Greeks to the whole of their country.

hel·le·bore (hĕl'*e*bōr, -bōr) *n.* Ancient name of various Old World plants supposed to cure madness; (bot.) species of genus *Veratrum* of N. Amer., including false hellebore (*V. viride*) having large leaves and greenish-yellow to green flowers.

Hel·lene (hĕl'ēn) *n.* Greek person. **Hel·len·ic** (h*e*lĕn'ĭk) *adj.* & *n.* (Language) of the Greeks.

Hel·len·ism (hĕl'*e*nĭzem) *n.* Greek idiom or construction; Greek character or culture, esp. that represented by ideals of the classical Greeks; Greek nationality. **Hel'len·ist** *n.* 1. Greek scholar. 2. One of the Byzantine Greeks who contributed to the revival of learning in Europe in the 15th c. 3. One who used the Greek language but was not a Greek, applied esp. to the Jews of the Diaspora. **Hel·len·is·tic** (hĕlenĭs'tĭk) *adj.* 1. Of, pertaining to, the Hellenists. 2. Of, pertaining to, Greek history, language, and culture after Alexander the Great.

Hel·len·ize (hĕl'*e*nīz) *v.* (**-ized, -iz·ing**). Make, become, Greek in form or character.

Hel·les·pont (hĕl'*e*spŏnt). Ancient name of the DARDANELLES, named after the legendary Helle, who fell into that part of the sea from the back of a ram with golden fleece and wings, which was carrying her and her brother Phrixus from Thebes to Colchis (see also GOLDEN Fleece).

Hell (hĕl) **Gate.** Narrow channel in the East River, New York City, between Long Island and Manhattan.

hell·gram·mite (hĕl′gramīt) *n.* Larva (used as fishing bait) of the dobson fly, an aquatic insect of the order Neuroptera (*Corydalus cornutus*).

hel·lion (hĕl′yon) *n.* (colloq.) Mischievous or naughty person, esp. a child or teenager.

hel·lo (hĕlō′, he-, hĕl′ō) *int.* & *n.* (pl. **-los**). Greeting.

helm (hĕlm) *n.* Tiller, wheel, by which rudder is managed; (fig.) government, guidance, leadership; **helms′man**, person who steers a ship.

hel·met (hĕl′mĭt) *n.* Defensive head cover of soldiers, firemen, football players, etc.; felt or pith hat for hot climates; (bot.) arched upper part of corolla in some flowers, esp. labiates and orchids. **hel′met·ed** *adj.*

Helm·holtz (hĕlm′hōlts), **Hermann Ludwig Ferdinand** (1821–1894). German physicist, physiologist, mathematician, and philosopher.

hel·minth (hĕl′mĭnth) *n.* Worm (esp. intestinal). **hel·min·thic** (hĕlmĭn′thĭk), **hel·min′thoid** *adjs.* **hel·min·thol·o·gy** (hĕlmĭnthŏl′ojē) *n.* Study of worms.

Hé·lo·ïse (ĕl′ōēz, ĕlōēz′) (1101–1163). Learned Frenchwoman, renowned for love affair with ABÉLARD that ended in tragic separation.

Hel·ot (hĕl′ot, hē′lot) *n.* In ancient Sparta, a descendant of the original (chiefly Messenian) inhabitants who were conquered by the Spartans and used by them as serfs.

help (hĕlp) *v.t.* Furnish (person etc.) with what he needs; further the action or purpose of; aid, assist; be of service; make easier; ~ (person) **on with his coat**, help him to put it on; ~ (person) **out**, be of assistance to; ~ (person) **to**, serve him with (food); distribute (food at meal); remedy, prevent, as *it can't be helped, he couldn't ~ being late*; (with neg.) avoid doing, as *I can't ~ hoping that ---*; ~ **oneself to**, (colloq.) take. **help** *n.* 1. Action of helping, assistance; one who or that which helps; domestic servant; employee(s). 2. Remedy. **help′er** *n.*

help·ful (hĕlp′ful) *adj.* (of person or thing) Useful, serviceable. **help′ful·ly** *adv.* **help′ful·ness** *n.*

help·ing (hĕl′pĭng) *n.* (esp.) Portion of food served.

help·less (hĕlp′lĭs) *adj.* Unable to help oneself. **help′less·ly** *adv.* **help′less·ness** *n.*

help·mate (hĕlp′māt) *n.* Helpful companion or partner, usu. husband or wife.

help·meet (hĕlp′mēt) *n.* Helpmate (f. misunderstanding of Gen. 2).

Hel·sin·ki (hĕl′sĭngkē, hĕlsĭng′-). Capital of Finland in the S. part on the Gulf of Finland.

hel·ter-skel·ter (hĕl′ter skĕl′ter) *adv.* & *adj.* In disordered haste. ~ *n.* Disordered haste.

Hel·ve·tian (hĕlvē′shan) *adj.* & *n.* Swiss. [L. *Helvetii*, a people of SE. Gaul]

hem[1] (hĕm) *n.* Border, edge, of cloth etc., esp. border made by turning in edge and sewing it down; **hem′stitch**, (hem *cloth* etc. with) kind of ornamental stitch producing openwork effect by drawing together threads of material. **hem** *v.t.* (**hemmed, hem·ming**). Turn in and sew down edge of (cloth etc.); ~ **in, about, around**, enclose, confine.

hem[2] (hĕm) *int.* Exclamation calling attention or expressing hesitation. ~ *n.* Utterance of "hem." ~ *v.i.* (**hemmed, hem·ming**). Utter "hem"; clear throat; hesitate in speech.

he·mat·ic, hae·mat·ic (hĭmăt′ĭk) *adjs.* Of or containing blood. ~ *n.* Medicine acting on the blood.

hem·a·tite, haem·a·tite (hĕm′atīt, hē′ma-) *ns.* Natural ferric oxide (Fe_2O_3), red, brown, or blackish iron ore.

he·ma·tol·o·gy, hae·ma·tol·o·gy (hēmatŏl′ojē, hĕma-) *ns.* Study of blood and its diseases.

he·ma·to·ma, hae·ma·to·ma (hēmatō′ma, hĕma-) *ns.* (pl. **-mas, -ma·ta** pr. -mata). Localized tumor or swelling filled with blood.

hemi- *prefix.* Half-, affecting one half, etc.

hem·i·he·dral (hĕmĭhē′dral) *adj.* (chem., of crystal) Having half the number of planes required by the highest degree of symmetry belonging to its system.

Hem·ing·way (hĕm′ĭngwā), **Ernest (Miller)** (1899–1961). Amer. novelist, short-story writer, and foreign correspondent; author of *The Sun Also Rises, For Whom the Bell Tolls, The Old Man and the Sea, Death in the Afternoon*, etc.; received Nobel Prize for literature, 1954.

1

2

3

Eight kings of England were called Henry. 1. ***Henry III,*** *whose inability to rule effectively led to rebellion and to Simon de Montfort's control of government. 2.* ***Henry IV,*** *son of John of Gaunt, defeated the rebel barons, Owen Glendower and Sir Henry Percy (1403) and Thomas de Mowbray (1405). 3.* ***Henry V,*** *victor of the Battle of Agincourt.*

4

5

6

*4. **Henry VI,** the last of the Lancastrians, whose mental instability and the resulting crisis in leadership led to the Wars of the Roses. 5. **Henry VII** ended the Wars of the Roses, established order at home and diplomacy in foreign affairs. 6. **Henry VIII,** one of the strongest of English monarchs, was the father of Elizabeth I.*

hem·i·ple·gi·a (hĕmĭplē′jēa, -ja) *n.* Paralysis of one side of body.

he·mip·ter·ous (hĭmĭp′terus) *adj.* Of the Hemiptera, an order of insects with wings leathery at base and membranous at tip, and mouthparts adapted to piercing and sucking. **he·mip′ter·an** *n.*

hem·i·sphere (hĕm′ĭsfēr) *n.* Half sphere; half the celestial sphere, esp. as divided by equator; (anat.) each half of cerebrum of brain; (geog.) half the Earth, esp. as divided by the equator (into **Northern** and **Southern ~s**), or (loosely) one of those containing Europe, Asia, Australia, and Africa (**Eastern ~**), and America (**Western ~**), respectively. **hem·i·spher·ic** (hĕmĭsfĕr′ĭk), **hem·i·spher′i·cal** *adjs.*

hem·lock (hĕm′lŏk) *n.* 1. Poisonous umbelliferous plant (*Conium maculatum*) with stout-branched, purple-spotted stem, finely divided leaves, and small white flowers, used as powerful sedative; poisonous potion obtained from this (believed to be the poison by which Socrates was put to death). 2. N. Amer. evergreen tree of genus *Tsuga*, esp. *T. canadensis*, from resemblance of branches to hemlock leaves.

hemo- *comb. form.* Blood.

he·mo·glo·bin, hae·mo·glo·bin (hē′moglōbĭn, hĕm′o-) *ns.* Oxygen-carrying pigment contained in the red blood cells of vertebrates.

he·mo·phil·i·a, hae·mo·phil·i·a (hēmofĭl′ēa, -fēl′ya, hĕmo-) *ns.* Constitutional, usu. hereditary, incapacity of blood to clot quickly or at all, involving risk of severe bleeding even from a slight injury. **he·mo·phil′i·ac** *n.* **he·mo·phil′ic** *adj.*

hem·or·rhage, haem·or·rhage (hĕm′erĭj, hĕm′rĭj) *ns.* Escape of blood from blood vessels.

hem·or·rhoid, haem·or·rhoid (hĕm′eroid, hĕm′roid) *ns.* (usu. in pl.) Varicose vein of anus; piles.

he·mo·stat, hae·mo·stat (hē′mostăt, hĕm′o-) *ns.* Instrument or agent used to stop flow of blood.

hemp (hĕmp) *n.* Annual herbaceous plant, *Cannabis sativa*, native of W. and central Asia, cultivated esp. for its cortical fiber; this fiber used for making cordage and woven into stout fabrics; any of several narcotic drugs, as bhang, hashish, etc., obtained from hemp; any of various other plants yielding useful fiber; ~ **agrimony**, perennial plant (*Eupatorium cannabinum*) of the daisy family, with pale purple flowers and hairy leaves. **hemp′en** *adj.*

hen (hĕn) *n.* Female of common domestic fowl; female of various other birds, or of any bird; **hen′bane**, (drug extracted from) plant (*Hyoscyamus niger*) of Europe and N. Asia, growing on waste ground, with dull yellow purple-streaked flowers, viscoid stem and leaves, unpleasant smell, and narcotic and poisonous properties; **hen′pecked**, (of husband) dominated by wife.

hence (hĕns) *adv.* 1. (archaic) From here, from this; **hence′forth′, hence′for′ward**, from this time forward. 2. As a result of this; as an inference from this; therefore.

hench·man (hĕnch′man) *n.* (pl. **-men** pr. -men). Squire, page of honor (now only hist.); trusty follower or subordinate; political supporter seeking personal gain.

hendeca- *prefix.* Eleven.

hen·dec·a·syl·lab·ic (hĕndĕkasĭlăb′ĭk) *adj.* & *n.* (Verse) of 11 syllables. **hen·dec·a·syl·la·ble** (hĕndĕk′asĭlabel, -dĕkasĭl′-) *n.* Such a verse.

Hen·driks (hĕn′drĭks), **Thomas Andrews** (1819–85). Amer. politician; U.S. vice president under Grover Cleveland, 1885.

hen·na (hĕn′a) *n.* Shrub (*Lawsonia inermis*) of N. Africa and Asia; shoots and leaves of this used as yellowish-red dye for parts of body, hair, etc. ~ *v.t.* Dye or tint with henna.

hen·o·the·ism (hĕn′othēĭzem) *n.* Belief in one god without asserting that he is the only God.

Hen·ri: see HENRY[2].

Hen·ry[1] (hĕn′rē). Name of eight kings of England: **Henry I** (1068–1135), younger son of William I, reigned 1100–35; conquered Normandy; **Henry II** (1133–89), grandson of Henry I, reigned 1154–1189; 1st of Plantagenet line; married Eleanor of Aquitaine; added Anjou and Aquitaine to the English possessions; established his rule in Ireland, and forced the king of Scotland to acknowledge him overlord of that kingdom; **Henry III** (1207–72), son of John, reigned 1216–72; **Henry IV** (1367–1413), grandson of Edward III, deposed Richard II and became first of the Lancastrian kings, 1399–1413; **Henry V** (1387–1422), son of Henry IV, reigned 1413–22; defeated the French at Agincourt, became regent of France and heir to the French throne; **Henry VI** (1421–71, son of Henry V, reigned 1422–61; during his reign the French possessions were lost and the Wars of the Roses, leading to his deposition by the Yorkists, begun; **Henry VII** (1457–1509), descended from Edward III; 1st of the Tudor line; succeeded Richard III after defeating him at Bosworth Field; reigned 1485–1509; **Henry VIII** (1491–1547), son of Henry VII, reigned 1509–47; his quarrels with the pope resulted in his establishment of the Church of England; married six times; father of Edward VI, Mary I, and Elizabeth I.

Hen·ry[2] (hĕn′rē). (Fr. *Henri*) Name of four kings of France: **Henry I** (d. 1060), reigned 1031–1060; **Henry II** (1519–59), son of Francis I, reigned 1547–59; **Henry III** (1551–89), son of Henry II and Catherine de Médicis, reigned 1574–89; **Henry IV** (1553–1610), king of Navarre, first Bourbon king of France; leader of Huguenots; reigned 1589–1610.

Hen·ry[3] (hĕn′rē), **Joseph** (1797–1878). Amer. physicist; experimented in electromagnetism; unit of induction, HENRY, named for him; first secretary and director of Smithsonian Institution, Washington, D.C., 1846.

Hen·ry[4] (hĕn′rē), **O.** (1862–1910). Pen name of William Sydney Porter, Amer. short-story writer noted for his surprise endings; among his works, "Gift of the Magi," "The Last Leaf."

Hen·ry[5] (hĕn′rē), **Patrick** (1736–99). Amer. lawyer, statesman, and Revolutionary War leader, introduced resolutions in the Virginia legislature opposing the Stamp Act; member of the Continental Congress, 1774–6; remembered for his patriotic demand for freedom from Great Britain, "Give me liberty, or give me death!"

hen·ry (hĕn′rē) *n.* (pl. **-ries, -rys**). (abbrev. H) Electromagnetic unit of inductance, the inductance of a circuit in which the variation of current at the rate of 1 ampere per second induces an electromotive force of 1 volt. [Joseph *Henry* (1797–1878), Amer. physicist]

hep (hĕp) *adj.* (slang) = HIP[4].

he·pat·ic (hĭpăt′ĭk) *adj.* Of, resembling, the liver; liver-colored, dark brownish-red.

he·pat·i·ca (hĭpăt′ĭk*a*) *n.* Any of several small plants of the genus *Hepatica*, having three-lobed leaves and lavender, white, blue, or pink flowers.

hep·a·ti·tis (hĕp*a*tī′tĭs) *n.* Inflammation of the liver.

He·phaes·tus (hĭfĕs′t*u*s). (Gk. myth.) God of fire; identified by the Romans with Vulcan.

Hep·ple·white (hĕp′*e*lhwīt, -wīt), **George** (d. 1786). English cabinetmaker; furniture made by or in the style of Hepplewhite.

hepta- *prefix.* Seven.

hep·tad (hĕp′tăd) *n.* Set, group, of seven.

hep·ta·gon (hĕp′t*a*gŏn) *n.* Plane figure of seven angles and sides. **hep·tag·o·nal** (hĕptăg′*o*n*a*l) *adj.*

hep·ta·he·dron (hĕpt*a*hē′dr*o*n) *n.* (pl. **-drons, -dra** pr. -dr*a*). Solid figure of seven faces.

hep·tam·e·ter (hĕptăm′*e*t*er*) *n.* Verse having seven metrical feet.

hep·tar·chy (hĕp′tark̄ē) *n.* (pl. **-chies**). Government by seven rulers; **H~**, seven kingdoms supposed to have been established by the Angles and Saxons in Britain.

her (hẽr) *pron.* Objective (accus.) case of SHE. ~ *poss. pron.* Possessive case of SHE used as attrib. adjective and as pred. complement; **hers** (hẽrz), belonging to, affecting, her; used also as subj. or pred. complement.

He·ra (hēr′*a*). (Gk. myth.) Daughter of Cronos and Rhea; sister and wife of Zeus; worshipped as queen of the heavens and goddess of power and riches; identified by the Romans with Juno.

Her·a·cli·tus (hĕr*a*klī′t*u*s). Greek philosopher, of the 6th c.; his melancholy views on the changing character of life led to his being known as the "weeping philosopher."

Her·a·kles, Her·a·cles (hĕr′*a*klēz) = HERCULES.

her·ald (hĕr′*a*ld) *n.* 1. Officer who made state proclamations, bore messages between princes, officiated in tournaments, arranged various state ceremonials, regulated use of armorial bearings, etc. 2. Messenger, envoy (freq. as title of newspaper); forerunner. ~ *v.t.* Proclaim the approach of; usher in.

he·ral·dic (hĕrăl′dĭk, he-) *adj.* Of heraldry.

her·ald·ry (hĕr′*a*ldrē) *n.* Science of a herald, esp. art of blazoning armorial bearings and settling right of persons to bear arms or certain bearings; armorial bearings; heraldic pomp.

herb (ẽrb, hẽrb) *n.* Plant whose stem is not woody or persistent but dies down after flowering; plant of which leaves etc. are used for medicine, scent, flavor, etc.; ~ **bennet**, yellow-flowered species of geum; ~ **Robert**, common wild species of plant *Geranium* (*G. robertianum*) with divided leaves and light reddish-purple flowers; ~ **tea**, medicinal brew of herbs.

her·ba·ceous (hẽrbā′sh*u*s, ẽr-) *adj.* Of (the nature of) herb(s).

herb·age (ẽr′bĭj, hẽr′-) *n.* Herbs collectively, esp. grass and other low-growing plants covering large extent of ground and used as pasture etc.; green succulent parts of herbaceous plants.

__Heraldic__ symbols originated as identification devices on shields during the Middle Ages, and developed into hereditary bearings used to distinguish individuals or families. These flags hang in King Henry VIII's chapel at Westminster Abbey, U.K.

her·bal (ẽr′b*a*l, hẽr′-) *adj.* & *n.* (Book with descriptions) of herbs. **herb′al·ist** *n.* One skilled in herbs or plants (now used of early botanical writers).

her·bar·i·um (hẽrbar′ē*u*m, ẽr-) *n.* (pl. **-bar·i·ums, -bar·i·a** pr.

The __Hepplewhite__ furniture of the late 18th century is characterized by a graceful Neo-classical style. This armchair is of carved mahogany and is dated c. 1780 — some years before the publication of Hepplewhite's designs.

-bār'ēa). (Book, case, room, containing) collection of dried plants.

herb·i·cide (ēr'bĭsīd, hēr'-) *n.* Any substance, esp. chemical preparation, used to kill plants.

her·biv·or·ous (hērbĭv'*erus*, ēr-) *adj.* (of animals) Feeding on plants. **her·bi·vore** (hēr'b*i*vōr, -vōr, ēr'-) *n.*

Her·ce·go·vi·na (hērts*e*gov*ē*'n*a*, -gaw'vĭ-): see HERZEGOVINA.

Her·cu·la·ne·um (hērkyulā'nē*u*m). Ancient town in Campania, Italy, buried with Pompeii in eruption of Vesuvius, 79 A.D.

Her·cu·le·an (hērky*u*lē'*a*n, -kū'lē-) *adj.* Of Hercules; strong as Hercules; difficult as his labors.

Her·cu·les (hēr'ky*u*lēz). 1. (Gk. and Rom. myth.) Hero of prodigious strength, who performed 12 immense tasks or labors imposed on him by Eurystheus, and after death was ranked among the gods; **Pillars of ~**, rocks Calpe (Gibraltar) and Abyla (Ceuta) on either side of Strait of Gibraltar, thought to have been set up by Hercules and to be supports of western boundaries of the world. 2. (astron.) Northern constellation, figured as a man kneeling on his right knee.

herd[1] (hērd) *n.* Group of animals, esp. cattle, feeding or traveling together; (contempt.) large number of people; **~ instinct**, gregariousness and mutual influence as psychological factor; **herds'man** (pl. **-men**), keeper of herds. **herd** *v.* Go, collect, in a herd (*together, with* others).

herd[2] (hērd) *v.t.* Tend (sheep, cattle). **herd'er** *n.*

here (hēr) *adv.* In this place; in this country, region, etc.; present to the sight or mind; in this life, on earth; at this juncture, at this point in action, speech, etc.; in the matter before us or in question; (with verbs of coming or bringing) to or toward this place; **~'s to,** formula in drinking toasts; **~ and there,** in various places; **~, there, and everywhere**, everywhere, all about; **neither ~ nor there,** not to the point, of no importance; **~ goes!,** (colloq.) exclamation announcing commencement of bold act; **here'abouts**, somewhere near here; **hereaf'ter**, in the future, later on; (in) the world to come; **here'by**, by this means, as a result; **herein'**, in this point, book, etc.; **hereinaf'ter**, below (in document etc.); **hereto'**, (archaic) to this matter; **heretofore'**, formerly; **hereun'der**, below (in book etc.); **hereupon'**, after this; in consequence of this; **herewith'**, with this (esp. of enclosure in letter etc.). **here** *n.* This place or point.

he·red·i·tar·y (hered'ĭtĕrē) *adj.* Descending by inheritance; transmitted from one generation to another; like, the same as, that one's parents had; of, holding position by, inheritance.

he·red·i·ty (hered'ĭtē) *n.* (pl. **-ties**). Tendency of like to beget like, property of organic beings by which offspring inherit nature and characteristics of parents or other ancestors; organic relation between successive generations; genetic constitution.

Her·e·ford (hĕr'*e*f*e*rd, hēr'f*e*rd). (One of) a breed of beef cattle originating in Herefordshire, England (red and white, with white faces).

he·re·si·arch (herē'zēārk, hĕr'*e*sē-) *n.* Leader, founder, of a heresy.

her·e·sy (hĕr'*e*sē) *n.* (pl. **-sies**). Opinion or doctrine contrary to the orthodox doctrine of the Christian Church, or to the accepted doctrine on any subject.

her·e·tic (hĕr'*e*tĭk) *n.* Holder of

***Herbs** have been used since ancient times to flavor food and also for their medicinal value. Popular herbs include parsley, mint and thyme.*

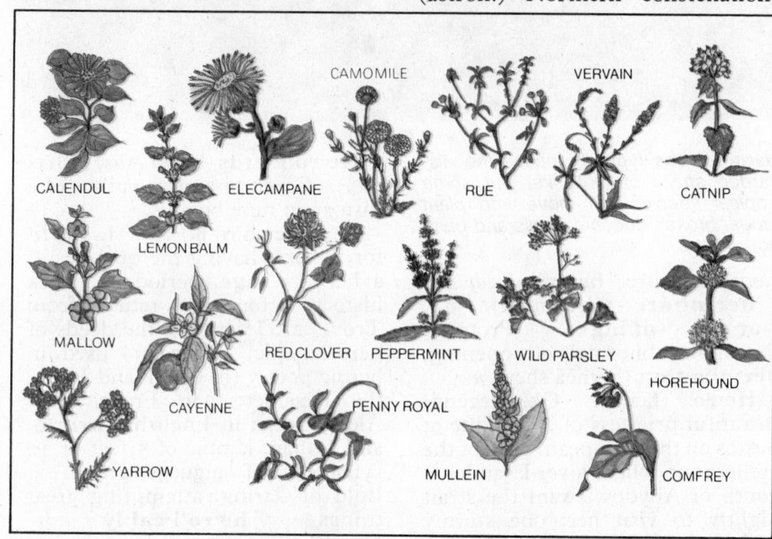

***Herbaceous** gardens, like those surrounding this French cottage in Périgord, contain flowering plants but not trees or shrubs. Most herbaceous gardens are made up of flower beds in different patterns.*

an unorthodox opinion (orig. in matter of religion). **he·ret·i·cal** (herĕt´ĭkal) *adj.*

her·it·a·ble (hĕr´ĭtabel) *adj.* That passes to heirs (opp. to movable property); transmissible from parent to child; capable of inheriting.

her·it·age (hĕr´ĭtĭj) *n.* What is or may be inherited; inherited lot or portion.

her·i·tor (hĕr´ĭter) *n.* One who inherits.

her·maph·ro·dite (hẽrmăf´rodīt) *n.* 1. Human being, animal, combining characteristics of both sexes; (zool.) animal having normally both male and female sexual organs; (bot.) plant in which same flower has both stamens and pistils. 2. Person, thing, combining opposite qualities. **her·maph·ro·dit·ic** (hẽrmăfrodĭt´ĭk) *adj.* Combining both sexes or opposite characteristics. **her·maph'ro·dit·ism** *n.* [Gk. *Hermaphroditos*, son of Hermes and Aphrodite, who became one with the nymph Salmacis]

her·me·neu·tic (hẽrmenōō´tĭk, -nū´-) *adj.* Of interpretation; interpretive; explanatory. **her·me·neu'tics** *n.pl.* Interpretation, esp. of Scripture. **her·me·neu'ti·cal** *adj.*

Her·mes (hẽr´mēz). 1. (Gk. myth.) Son of Zeus and Maia; represented as messenger of the gods, god of science, commerce, eloquence, etc., identified by the Romans with Mercury, and represented as a youth with winged rod (*caduceus*), brimmed hat (*petasus*), and winged shoes (*talaria*). 2. ~ **Trismegistus** ("thrice-greatest"), name given by Neoplatonists etc. to Egyptian god Thoth, regarded as author of all mysterious doctrines and esp. of secrets of alchemy.

her·met·ic (hẽrmĕt´ĭk) *adj.* (cap.) Of Hermes Trismegistus; of alchemy, magical, alchemical; completely sealed, airtight. **her·met'i·cal·ly** *adv.*

her·mit (hẽr´mĭt) *n.* One who from religious motives has retired into solitary life, esp. early Christian recluse; person living in solitude; ~ **crab**, crab of family Paguridae, living in mollusk's discarded shell to protect soft abdomen.

her·mit·age (hẽr´mĭtĭj) *n.* 1. Hermit's abode; solitary abode. 2. **H**~, museum of art in Leningrad, containing collections begun by Catherine the Great in 1765 and inheriting its name from the retreat in which she displayed them to her friends.

her·ni·a (hẽr´nēa) *n.* (pl. **-ni·as, -ni·ae** pr. -nēē). (path.) Tumor formed by the displacement of part of an organ so that it protrudes through the walls of its containing cavity; rupture. **her'ni·al** *adj.*

Hermit crabs *typically inhabit the discarded shells of mollusks, but some tropical species will move into plant tubes, broken coconut shells and bamboo stems.*

her·ni·ate (hẽr´nēāt) *v.i.* (**-at·ed, -at·ing**). Protrude through an abnormal body opening. **her·ni·a·tion** (hẽrnēā´shon) *n.*

He·ro (hẽr´ō). (Gk. legend) Beautiful priestess of Aphrodite at Sestos on the European shore of the Hellespont, whose lover Leander, a youth of Abydos, swam the strait nightly to visit her; one stormy night he was drowned and Hero in grief threw herself into the sea.

he·ro (hẽr´ō) *n.* (pl. **-roes**). 1. (Gk. antiq.) Man of superhuman strength, courage, or ability, favored by the gods; later regarded as intermediate between gods and men, and immortal. 2. Illustrious warrior; man of extraordinary bravery, fortitude, or greatness of soul. 3. Man forming subject of epic; chief male character in poem, play, or story; ~ **sandwich**, large sandwich, usu. a long roll sliced lengthwise and filled with a variety of sliced meats, cheeses, vegetables, pickles, etc.; ~ **worship(er)**, worship(er) of some great man or men or a personal hero.

Her·od (hĕr´od). Name of four rulers in ancient Palestine: **Herod the Great** (d. 4 B.C.), king of the Jews 40–4 B.C., **Herod Antipas**, his son, tetrarch of Galilee and Peraea 4 B.C.–39 A.D., married Herodias and had St. John the Baptist beheaded; **Herod Agrippa I**, (called "Herod" in Acts), grandson of Herod the Great, king of the Jews 41–44 A.D.; put St. James the Apostle to death; **Herod Agrippa II**, his son, king of various territories in N. Palestine 50–*c*93 A.D.; St. Paul appeared before him (Acts 25).

He·rod·o·tus (hĭrŏd´otus) (5th c. B.C.). Greek historian; author of a history in nine books.

he·ro·ic (hĭrō´ĭk) *adj.* 1. Of, fit for, a hero; having the qualities of a hero; ~ **age**, period of Greek history before the return from Troy. 2. Describing the deeds of heroes, epic; (of meter) used in heroic poetry (in Greek and Latin, the hexameter; in French, the Alexandrine; in English, German, and Italian, iambic of 5 feet or 10 syllables); (of language) grand. 3. Bold or daring, attempting great things. **he·ro'i·cal·ly** *adv.* **he·ro'ic** *n.* Grand language or sentiments.

her·o·in (hĕr´ōĭn) *n.* Drug, also called diacetylmorphine or diamorphine, prepared from morphine, which it resembles in its effects, capable of causing addiction.

her·o·ine (hĕr´ōĭn) *n.* Heroic woman; chief female character in poem, play, or story.

her·o·ism (hĕr´ōĭzem) *n.* Heroic conduct or qualities.

her·on (hĕr´on) *n.* (pl. **-ons**, collect. **-on**). One of the long-necked, long-legged wading birds of the family Ardeidae. **her'on·ry** *n.* Place where herons breed.

her·pes (hẽr´pēz) *n.* Either of 2 forms of virus affection, ~ **zoster**, shingles, an infection of the cutaneous nerves resulting in severe pain and outbreaks of small blisters related to the distribution of the nerves, and ~ **simplex**, painless form in which the blisters have no relation to the nerves of the skin.

her·pe·tol·o·gy (hẽrpetŏl´ojē) *n.* Zoology of reptiles. **her·pe·to·log·ic** (hẽrpetolŏj´ĭk), **her·pe·to·log'i·cal** *adjs.* **her·pe·tol'o·gist** *n.*

Her·rick (hĕr´ĭk), **Robert** (1591–1674). English Cavalier poet; author of *Hesperides* (1648), a collection of some 1,200 mostly idyllic nature poems.

*The **heron** is found all over the world but is most common in the tropics. It feeds on frogs, fishes and other aquatic animals. The great blue heron is a large bird with a wing span of 6 ft.; the grey or common heron is widely distributed in Europe; the boat-billed heron is a night bird, feeding in twilight hours and at night and is found in Central and South America.*

her·ring (hĕr'ĭng) *n.* Edible fish, *Clupea harengus*, of N. Atlantic, coming near coast in large shoals to spawn; **red** ~: see RED; **her'ring-bone**, (of masonry, paving) in which stones or tiles are set in zigzag pattern; (of cloth etc.) woven in zigzag pattern; **herring gull**, large gull of N. Atlantic (*Larus argentatus*), with black tips to wings.

hers (hẽrz): see HER.

Her·schel (hẽr'shel), **Sir William** (1738–1822). German-born English astronomer; discoverer of the planet Uranus.

her·self (hersĕlf') *pron.* Emphatic and reflexive form corresponding to SHE, HER.

Hertz (hẽrts; *Ger.* hĕrts), **Heinrich Rudolph** (1857–94). German physicist; demonstrated electromagnetic radio waves in 1888.

hertz (hẽrts) *n.* (pl. same; abbrev. Hz) Unit of frequency, 1 cycle per second. [f. HERTZ]

Her·ze·go·vi·na (hẽrtsegovē'na, -gaw'vĭ-). Region and former province S. of Bosnia, in Yugoslavia.

Her·zl (hĕr'tsel), **Theodor** (1860–1904). Hungarian-born Austrian Jewish writer; founder of Zionism.

He·si·od (hē'sēod, hĕs'ē-) (8th c. B.C.). Greek poet; author of *Works and Days*, descriptive of agricultural life in Boeotia, and probably of the *Theogony*, containing a mythical account of the origin of the world and the genealogy of the gods, and of a *Catalogue of Women* who, being beloved of the gods, became the mothers of heroes. **He·si·od·ic** (hēsēŏd'ĭk, hĕsē-) *adj.*

hes·i·tant (hĕz'ĭtant) *adj.* Hesitating, irresolute. **hes'i·tance** *n.* **hes'i·tan·cy** *n.* (pl. **-sies**).

hes·i·tate (hĕz'ĭtāt) *v.i.* (**-tat·ed, -tat·ing**). Show, speak with, indecision; be reluctant, *to* (do). **hes'i·tat·ing·ly** *adv.* **hes·i·ta·tion** (hĕzĭtā'shon) *n.* **hes'i·ta·tive** *adj.*

Hes·per·i·des (hĕspĕr'ĭdēz). (Gk. myth.) Three, four, or seven nymphs, daughters of Hesperus; they were guardians, with the aid of a watchful dragon, of the garden in which golden apples grew, in the Islands of the Blessed (see ISLAND).

Hesse[1] (hĕs). (Ger. *Hessen*) Former state of SW. Germany, now a province of West Germany; capital, Wiesbaden.

Hesse[2] (hĕs), **Hermann** (1877–1962). German novelist and poet; author of *Steppenwolf*, *Das Glasperlenspiel*, etc.; received Nobel Prize for literature, 1946.

Hes·sian (hĕsh'an) *adj.* Of Hesse[1]; ~ **boot**, high boot, with tassels in front at the top, first worn by Hessian troops; ~ **fly**, midge (*Phytophaga destructor*) with larva very destructive to wheat (erroneously supposed to have been carried to America by Hessian troops). **Hessian** *n.* Native or inhabitant of, soldier from, Hesse; military or political hireling, mercenary (from the Hessian mercenaries used by the British army during the Revolutionary War).

*The **herring gull** is a common N. Atlantic species, often seen feeding on the wastes of human habitation. It can be recognized by its orange-colored legs, gray mantle and black-and-white wing tips.*

hest (hĕst) *n.* (archaic) Behest.

he·tae·ra (hĭtēr'a) (pl. **-tae·ras, -tae·rae** pr. -tēr'ē), **he·tai·ra** (hĭtīr'a) (pl. **-tai·ras, -tai·rai** pr. -tīr'ī) *ns.* Courtesan, esp. in ancient Greece. **he·tae'rism, he·tai'rism** *ns.* Open concubinage; communal marriage in a tribe.

hetero- *prefix.* Other, different.

het·er·o·dox (hĕt'erodŏks) *adj.* Not orthodox. **het'er·o·dox·y** *n.*

het·er·o·dyne (hĕt'erodīn) *n.* Apparatus for, process of, converting a high-frequency radio wave to one of an audible frequency by superimposing another high-frequency wave of nearly the same period and so producing a pulsation. ~ *v.i.* (**-dyned, -dyn·ing**). Produce a heterodyne effect.

het·er·og·a·my (hĕterŏg'amē) *n.* (biol.) Alternation of differently organized generations of animals or plants, as where sexual generation alternates with parthenogenesis; condition of having, or union of, gametes of different size and structure. **het·er·og'a·mous** *adj.*

het·er·o·ge·ne·ous (hĕterojē'nēus) *adj.* Diverse in character; composed of diverse elements or substances. **het·er·o·ge'ne·ous·ly** *adv.* **het·er·o·ge'ne·ous·ness** *n.* **het·er·o·ge·ne'i·ty** *n.* (pl. **-ties**).

het·er·o·gen·e·sis (hĕterojĕn'esĭs) *n.* Birth of a living being otherwise than from parent of same kind, esp. supposed spontaneous generation from inorganic matter; alternation of generation. **het·-**

er·o·ge·net·ic (hĕterōjenĕt'ĭk) *adj.* Descended from different ancestral stock.

het·er·o·sex·u·al (hĕterosĕk'-shōōal) *adj.* Relating or belonging to the opposite sex or different sexes; sexually attracted to members of the opposite sex. ~ *n.* Heterosexual person. **het·er·o·sex·u·al·i·ty** (hĕterōsĕkshōōăl'ĭtē) *n.*

het·er·o·zy·gote (hĕterozī'gōt) *n.* Zygote resulting from fusion of unlike gametes; Mendelian hybrid containing dominant and recessive characters and therefore not breeding true. **het·er·o·zy'gous** *adj.* Bearing two dissimilar alternative genetical factors.

heu·ris·tic (hyurĭs'tĭk) *adj.* Serving to (encourage to) find out or discover.

hew (hū) *v.t.* (**hewed, hewn, hew·ing**). Chop, cut (*down, asunder*, etc.) with ax, sword, etc.; cut into shape; fell or cut (wood); cleave. **hew'er** *n.*

hex (hĕks) *v.* Practice witchcraft (on); bewitch. ~ *n.* Witch; magic spell.

hexa-, hex- *prefixes.* Six.

hex·ad (hĕk'săd) *n.* Set, group, of 6.

hex·a·gon (hĕk'sagŏn) *n.* Plane figure of six angles and sides. **hex·ag·o·nal** (hĕksăg'onal) *adj.* **hex·ag'o·nal·ly** *adv.*

hex·a·gram (hĕk'sagrăm) *n.* Figure formed by two intersecting equilateral triangles (the angular points coinciding with those of a hexagon); figure of six lines.

hex·a·he·dron (hĕksahē'dron) *n.* (pl. **-drons, -dra** pr. -dra). Solid figure of six faces. **hex·a·he'dral** *adj.*

hex·am·e·ter (hĕksăm'eter) *n.* Line of six metrical feet, esp. the **dactylic** ~ of Latin and Greek epic poetry, in which the first four feet may be dactyls or spondees, the fifth is a dactyl, and the sixth a spondee or less commonly a trochee.

hey (hā) *int.* Exclamation calling attention, or of joy, surprise, or interrogation.

hey·day (hā'dā) *n.* Prime period (of youth, vigor, prosperity, etc.).

Hey·er·dahl (hā'erdahl), **Thor** (1914–). Norwegian anthropologist who believed the first Polynesian settlers were from S. Amer.; to prove this, he sailed a balsa wood boat from Peru to island near Tahiti.

Hez·e·ki·ah (hĕzekī'ah). King of Judah in 8th–7th c. B.C.

HF, H.F., hf, h.f. *abbrevs.* High FREQUENCY.

Hf *symbol.* Hafnium.

HG, H.G. *abbrevs.* High German.

Hg *symbol.* Mercury.

hg *abbrev.* Hectogram(s).

hgt. *abbrev.* Height.

H.H. *abbrev.* His (*or* Her) Highness; His Holiness (the Pope).

HI *abbrev.* Hawaii.

H.I. *abbrev.* Hawaiian Islands.

hi (hī) *int.* Exclamation calling (colloq.) a greeting or (chiefly Brit.) attention.

hi·a·tus (hīā'tus) *n.* (pl. **-tus·es, -tus**). Break, gap, esp. in a series, account, or chain of proof; interruption or loss in time or continuity.

Hi·a·wath·a (hīawŏth'a, -waw'-tha). Indian hero in long narrative poem by Henry Wadsworth Longfellow, "The Song of Hiawatha."

hi·ba·chi (hĭbah'chē) *n.* Small charcoal-fueled grill of Japanese origin.

hi·ber·nate (hī'bernāt) *v.i.* (**-nat·ed, -nat·ing**). (of animals) Spend the winter in torpid state; (fig.) remain inactive. **hi·ber·na·tion** (hībernā'shon) *n.*

Hi·ber·ni·an (hībĕr'nēan) *adj.* & *n.* (Native, inhabitant) of Ireland. [f. L. *Hibernia* Ireland]

hi·bis·cus (hībĭs'kus, hĭ-) *n.* Malvaceous plant of genus *H*~, with large bright-colored flowers.

hic·cup, hic·cough (hĭk'ŭp, -up) *ns.* Involuntary spasm of respiratory organs, with sudden closure of glottis and characteristic sound. ~ *v.* (**-cuped, -cupped, -cup·ing, -cup·ping**). Make hiccup; say, bring out, with hiccup(s).

hick (hĭk) *n.* (colloq.) Provincial, rustic.

Hick·ok (hĭk'ŏk), **James Butler** (1837–76). (also known as **Wild Bill Hickok**) Amer. army scout and deputy U.S. marshal; toured with Buffalo Bill Cody, 1872–3.

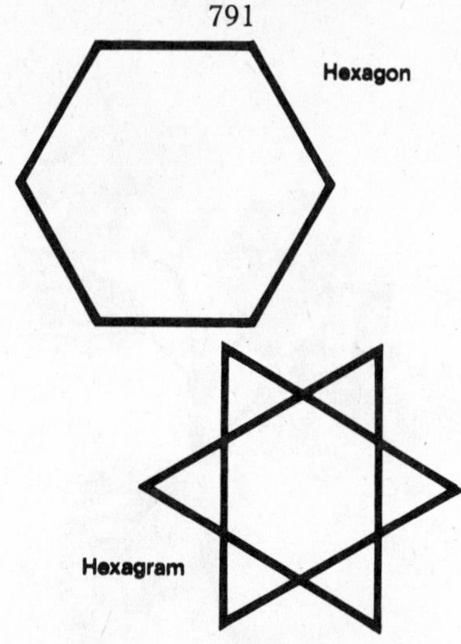

*The **hexagon** and **hexagram** are geometrical figures made up of 6 lines. The Star of David, symbol of the Jewish religion, which appears on Israel's national flag, is a hexagram.*

*Heinrich **Hertz**, the 19th-century German physicist, used this oscillator, incorporating an induction coil, to demonstrate the production and reception of electromagnetic waves. This formed the basis of radio.*

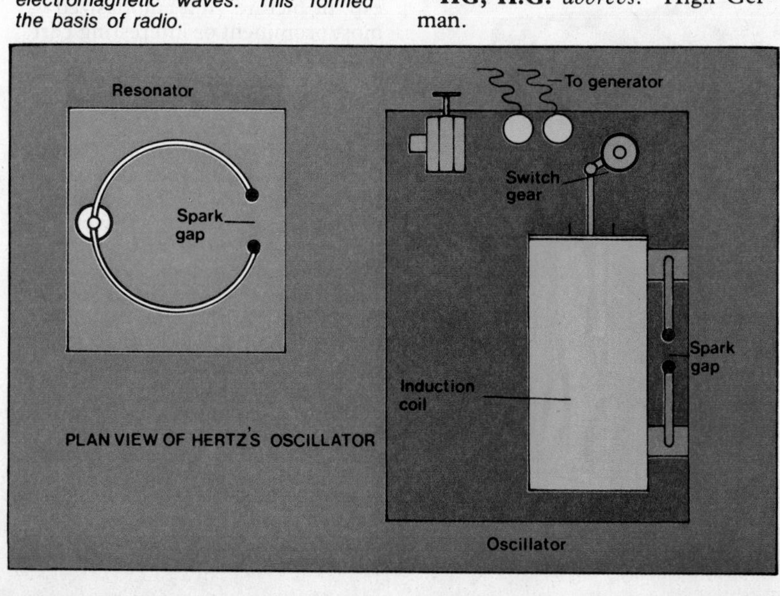

*The former German state, **Hesse**, contained Frankfurt-am-Main as one of its major cities. Goethe's birth-place, shown here, is in Frankfurt, today a thriving industrial city.*

hick·o·ry (hĭk′erē) *n.* (pl. **-ries**). N. Amer. tree (*Carya*) closely allied to walnut, with tough heavy wood bearing drupes (usu. with hard woody ring) enclosing edible nuts; wood, stick, of this; hickory nut; **Old H ~**, nickname of President Andrew JACKSON[2].

hid: see HIDE[3].

hi·dal·go (hĭdăl′gō, -dahl′-) *n.* One of the lower nobility in Spain. [Span. *hijo dalgo* son of a "somebody"]

hid·den: see HIDE[3].

hide[1] (hīd) *n.* Animal skin, raw or dressed; (joc.) human skin; **hide′bound**, (of cattle) with skin clinging closely to back and ribs as result of bad feeding; (fig.) narrow-minded, rigidly conventional.

hide[2] (hīd) *n.* (hist.) Medieval measure of land, of varying extent; orig., the amount required by one free family and its dependents, or as much as could be tilled with one plow in a year.

hide[3] (hīd) *v.* (**hid** pr. hĭd, **hid·den, hid·ing**). Put, keep, out of sight; keep (fact) secret (*from*); keep from view, obstruct the view of (without implication of intention); conceal oneself; **~-and-(go) seek**, children's game in which one player tries to find others who are hiding (also fig. of dealings with evasive person or thing); **hide′away**, hiding place; refuge; **hide′out**, hiding place.

hid·e·ous (hĭd′ēus) *adj.* Frightful, repulsive, revolting, to senses or mind. **hid′e·ous·ly** *adv.* **hid′e·ous·ness** *n.*

hid·ing[1] (hī′dĭng) *n.* (esp.) **in ~**, hidden; **~ place**, place of concealment.

hid·ing[2] (hī′dĭng) *n.* Thrashing.

hie (hī) *v.i.* (**hied, hie·ing, hy·ing**). (poet.) Go quickly (*to* etc.).

hi·er·arch (hī′erark) *n.* Chief priest; archbishop.

hi·er·ar·chy (hī′erarkē) *n.* (pl. **-chies**). 1. Each of three divisions of angels (each comprising three orders) in the system of Dionysus the Pseudo-Areopagite; the angels. 2. Priestly government; organized priesthood in successive grades; any graded organization. **hi·er·ar·chic** (hīerar′kĭk), **hi·er·ar′chi·cal** *adjs.*

hi·er·at·ic (hīerăt′ĭk, hīrăt′-) *adj.* Of the priests (esp. of ancient Egyptian cursive writing intermediate between hieroglyphic and demotic); priestly; of traditional styles of art (e.g. Egyptian, Byzantine) in which earlier types and methods are conventionally retained.

hi·er·o·glyph (hī′eroglĭf, hī′ro-) *n.* 1. Figure of an object (pictograph, ideograph, phonogram, or determinative), used to represent a word or sound or syllable in any of the pictorial systems of writing, esp. the ancient Egyptian. 2. Secret

*The **hibiscus,** which is found in tropical and semi-tropical regions, is cultivated for its attractive flowers which are large, trumpet-shaped and usually pink, red, yellow or white.*

symbol; writing difficult to make out. **hi·er·o·glyph·ic** (hīeroglĭf′ĭk, hīro-) *adj.* Of, written in, hieroglyphs; hard to decipher. **hi·er·o·glyph′ics** *n.pl.* Hieroglyphs.

hi-fi (hī′fī′) *n.* High fidelity; electronic sound reproduction system of high fidelity.

hig·gle (hĭg′el) *v.i.* (**-gled, -gling**). Haggle.

hig·gle·dy-pig·gle·dy (hĭg′eldē pĭg′eldē) *adv., adj., & n.* (In) utter confusion.

*Egyptian **hieroglyphics,** seen here on the temple of Kom-ombo in Upper Egypt, evolved about 3000 B.C. They were deciphered by the French scholar Jean-François Champollion in 1823 from the Rosetta stone.*

high (hī) *adj.* 1. Of great or specified upward extent; situated far above ground, sea level, etc., upper, inland; (of physical actions) extending to or from, performed at, a height; (of vowel sound) produced with (part of) tongue raised. 2. Of exalted rank, position, or quality; important, weighty; (of officers etc.) chief. 3. Great, intense, extreme; (of latitude) at great distance from equator; (of time) far advanced; **~ color**, fresh complexion, flush. 4. (of meat, esp. game) Slightly tainted. 5. (of sounds) Acute in pitch, shrill. 6. Extreme in opinion. 7. (colloq.) Intoxicated by alcohol or drugs. 8. **with a ~ hand**: see HAND; **on one's ~ horse**: see HORSE; **~ and dry**, (of ship) out of the water; (fig.) out of the current of events; **~ and low**, (*adv.*) everywhere; **~ and mighty**, arrogant. 9. **~ altar**, chief altar of church; **high′ball**, whiskey and soda, ginger ale, etc., served in tall glass with ice; **high′boy**, tall chest of drawers on legs; **high′brow**, (colloq.) (person) of intellectual interests; **high′chair**, infant's chair for use at meals, with long legs and usu. tray; **H ~ Church**, (party, principles of the Anglican Church) giving a high place to authority of episcopate and priesthood, saving grace of sacraments, and ritual; hence **H ~ Churchman**; **high explosive**, explosive detonating very rapidly and with powerful effect; **high′falutin(g)**, (colloq.) pretentious, bombastic; **high fidelity**, electronic reproduction of sound (as recorded, taped, or broadcast music etc.) with minimum of distortion; **high frequency**: see FREQUENCY; **High German**: see GERMAN; **high′handed**, overbearing, arbitrary; **high jinks**: see JINKS; **high life**, fashionable, luxurious living; **high′light(s)**, brightest part(s), esp. of picture etc.; emphasized or most prominent or interesting part; **highlight**, (*v.t.*) emphasize, make prominent; **High Mass**: see MASS; **high-minded**, of morally lofty character; **high noon**, exactly noon; **high-pitched**, (of sound) acute in pitch; (of roof etc.) steep; **high-pressure**, (of engine, machine, etc.) having, driven by, high pressure of steam, air, etc.; (fig.) urgent, intense, as *high-pressure salesmanship*; **high priest**, chief priest; **high relief**, sculpture in which figures etc. project more than half their thickness from background; **high-rise**, (of a building) having many stories;

*This **hibernating** dormouse spends most of the winter in a state close to death, with its body temperature near to freezing point. It relies on reserved body fat and stored food supplies to keep alive.*

high'road, (chiefly Brit.) main road; (fig.) direct or sure path or way; **high school**, secondary school that includes grades 9–12 or sometimes only 10–12; **high seas**, seas, ocean, outside territorial waters; **high-spirited**, of lofty or courageous spirit; lively; **high spirits**, elated or merry mood; **high-stepper**, horse that steps high; frequenter of fashionable society; one who lives luxuriously; **high-strung**, very sensitive or nervous; **high tea**, (Brit.) substantial early evening meal at which tea is served (usu. a hot supper that is not the main meal of the day); **high-test**, (of gasoline) vaporizing at comparatively low temperature; **high tide**: see TIDE; **high treason**: see TREASON; **high-water mark**, level reached at high tide; highest point of flood. **high** *adv.* Far up, aloft; in, to, a high degree; at a high price; for high stakes; (of sounds) at, to, a high pitch; **run ~**, (of sea) have strong current with high tide; **high'born**, of noble birth; **high-flown**, extravagant, bombastic; **high'flyer, high'flier**, (fig.) ambitious person; one who has high-flown notions. **high** *n.* High place; high level; (meteor.) region of high atmospheric pressure; (slang) intoxication by alcohol or euphoria induced by a drug; **on ~**, in a high place, in heaven.

high·lands (hī'landz) *n.pl.* (freq. **H~**). Mountainous or elevated country; esp. (**H~**) N. part of Scotland. **high'land** *adj.* **high'land·er, High'land·er** *ns.* Inhabitant of highlands, esp. (**H~**) those of Scotland.

high·ly (hī'lē) *adv.* In a high degree; at a high price or rate; honorably, favorably (as ~ *recommended*).

High·ness (hī'nĭs) *n.* Title of various princes etc., as **His, Her**, (Royal, Serene, Imperial) ~.

high·way (hī'wā) *n.* Main or principal public road connecting cities or towns; main route by land or water; **high'wayman**, (hist.) man (usu. mounted) who robbed passengers on highway.

hi·jack (hī'jăk) *v.t.* & *n.* Seize, seizure of, means of transport or goods etc. in transit. **hi'jack·er** *n.*

hike (hīk) *n.* 1. Long walk in the country for pleasure or exercise. 2. (colloq.) Increase (of prices etc.). ~ *v.* (**hiked, hik·ing**). 1. Walk vigorously or laboriously; go for long walk. 2. Raise or pull up with a jerk. 3. Increase or advance (prices etc.). **hik'er** *n.*

hi·lar·i·ous (hĭlār'ēus) *adj.* Mirthful, joyous, boisterously merry; very funny. **hi·lar'i·ous·ly** *adv.* **hi·lar'i·ous·ness** *n.* **hi·lar'·i·ty** (hĭlăr'ĭtē, -lār'-) *n.*

hill (hĭl) *n.* Natural elevation of earth's surface, small mountain; heap, mound, of sand, earth, etc.; **hill'billy**, (colloq., usu. disparaging) rustic mountaineer; **hill'billy music, song**, music, song of simple ballad type popular among such people. **hill** *v.t.* Form into hill; bank *up* (plants) with soil. **hill'y** *adj.* (**hill·i·er, hill·i·est**). **hill'i·ness** *n.*

*The **Highlands** of Scotland lie north of a line drawn from Dunbarton to Stonehaven and contain Ben Nevis, seen here, the highest mountain in the U.K. at 4,406 ft.*

Hill (hĭl), **James Jerome** (1838–1916). Amer. railroad promoter and financier; formed the Great Northern Railway, 1890; his stock market battle for control of the Northern Pacific Railroad caused the panic of 1901; he became known as "Empire Builder."

Hil·la·ry (hĭl'erē), **Sir Edmund** (1919–). N.Z. mountaineer; with Sherpa guide Tenzing Norkay, 1st to reach summit of Mount Everest, 1953.

hill·ock (hĭl'ok) *n.* Small hill or mound.

Hi·lo (hē'lō). Port and largest city of Hawaii Island, Hawaii, on the E. coast.

hilt (hĭlt) *n.* Handle of sword or dagger; handle of other weapon or tool; **to the ~**, completely.

hi·lum (hī'lum) *n.* (bot.) Mark at point of attachment of seed to seed vessel.

him (hĭm) *pron.* Objective case of HE.

H.I.M. *abbrev.* His (or Her) Imperial Majesty.

Hi·ma·la·yas (hĭmalā'az, hĭmahl'yaz). Mountain range in S. central Asia extending 1,500 mi. (2,414 km), from Jammu and Kashmir in the W., to Assam in the E.; highest peak, Mt. Everest, 29,028 ft. (8,848 m).

him·self (hĭmsĕlf') *pron.* Emphatic and reflexive form corresponding to HE, HIM.

Hi·na·ya·na (hēnayah'na) = THERAVADA. [Sansk. *hina* lesser, *yāna* vehicle]

hind[1] (hīnd) *n.* Female of (esp. red) deer, esp. in and after third year.

hind[2] (hīnd) *adj.* Situated at the back, posterior; **hind'brain**: see BRAIN; **hind'quarters**, hind legs and adjoining parts of quadruped; **hind'sight**, rear sight of a rifle; perception after the event (opp. *foresight*).

Hin·den·burg (hĭn'denbĕrg), **Paul von** (1847–1934). German general and statesman; field marshal then chief of staff during World War I; president of Weimar Republic, 1925–34; appointed Hitler as chancellor, 1933.

hind·er (hĭn'der) *v.t.* Impede, prevent.

Hin·di (hĭn'dē) *n.* 1. Group of Indo-Aryan spoken dialects including Eastern and Western Hindi. 2. Literary form of Hindustani drawing literary vocabulary from San-

*The **Himalayas** in southern Asia contain 30 of the world's highest peaks including Everest, Kanchenjunga and Nanga Parbat; the slopes and foothills provide a magnificent variety of plant and animal life.*

skrit and using the Devanagari script.

hind·most (hīnd′mōst) *adj*. Farthest behind; most remote.

hin·drance (hĭn′drans) *n*. Obstruction, prevention; obstacle.

Hin·du, (archaic) **Hin·doo** (hĭn′dōō) *ns*. One who practices Hinduism. **Hindu**, (archaic) **Hindoo** *adjs*. **Hindu Kush**, mountain range in S. Asia, extending west from the Himalayas. **Hin′du·ism** *n*. Religious and social system with adherents, esp. in India, with belief in reincarnation, worship of several gods, and caste as basis of society.

Hin·du·stan (hĭndōōstahn′, -stăn′). Persian name of India; in the stricter sense, India N. of the

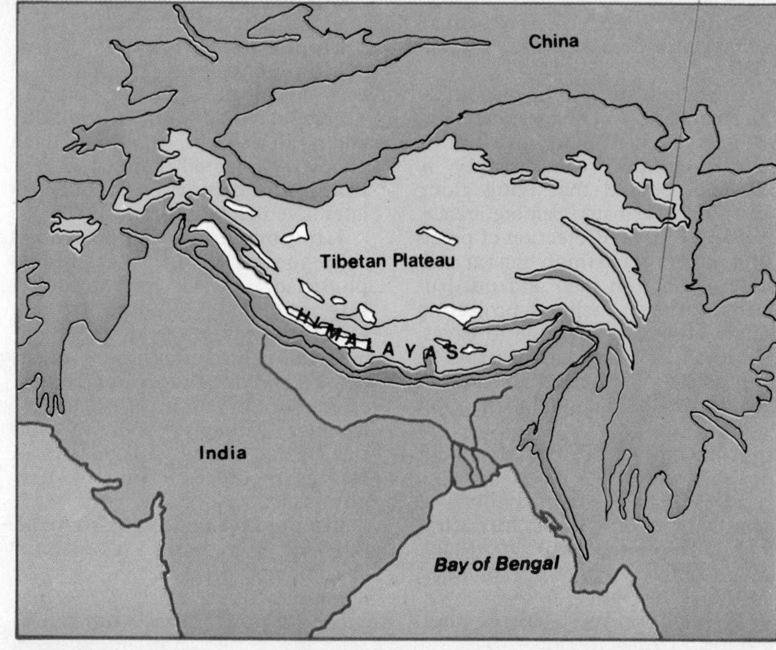

*The worship of several gods is the basis of **Hindu** religious ceremonies, such as this festival at Katmandu, Nepal. The majority of Indians still adhere to the Hindu caste system, a social as well as religious feature.*

Deccan exclusive of Bengal and Bihar. [lit., "place of the Hindus"]

Hin·du·sta·ni (hĭndōōstah'nē, -stăn'ē) *n.* Language based on Western Hindi used widely in northern India and Pakistan; (formerly) = URDU. ~ *adj.* Of Hindustan or its people; of Hindustani.

hinge (hĭnj) *n.* Movable joint, as mechanism like that by which door is hung on side post; natural joint doing similar work, as that of bivalve shell; (fig.) central principle, critical point, on which all turns; small piece of adhesive paper for mounting stamps, photographs, etc. in album. ~ *v.* (**hinged, hing·ing**). Attach (as) with hinge; (of door etc. or fig.) hang and turn *on* (post, principle, etc.). **hinge'-less** *adj.*

hin·ny (hĭn'ē) *n.* (pl. **-nies**). Offspring of female donkey by stallion.

hint (hĭnt) *n.* Slight indication; covert or indirect suggestion. ~*v.* Suggest slightly; ~ **at**, give hint of.

hin·ter·land (hĭn'terlănd) *n.* District behind that lying along coast or river bank; remote area.

hip[1] (hĭp) *n.* Projection of pelvis and upper part of thigh bone at each side of body in man and quadrupeds; (archit.) inclined projecting angle of roof from ridge to eaves; ~ **flask**, whiskey flask carried in hip pocket; ~ **pocket**, rear pocket in trousers, just behind hip. **hipped** *adj.*

hip[2] (hĭp) *n.* Fruit of (esp. wild) rose.

hip[3] (hĭp) *n.* Exclamation introducing cheer (~, ~, **hurrah**).

hip[4] (hĭp), **hep** (hĕp) *adjs.* (slang) Cognizant, wise, esp. to latest attitudes and tastes; in the know.

Hip·par·chus (hĭpar'kus). Second century B.C. Greek astronomer; originated system of trigonometry and of using latitude and longitude to locate geographical positions.

hip·pie, hip·py (hĭp'ē) *ns.* (pl. **-pies**). Member of a group of young people in the 1960s who rejected customs, career goals, dress styles, etc. of conventional society and turned to communal living, psychedelic drugs, Eastern religions, and sexual freedom.

hip·po (hĭp'ō) *n.* (pl. **-pos**). (colloq.) Hippopotamus.

hippo- *prefix.* Horse.

hip·po·cam·pus (hĭpokăm'pus) *n.* (pl. **-pi** pr. -pī). 1. (myth.) Seahorse, with 2 forefeet, and body ending in fish tail. 2. (anat.) Each of two elongated eminences (~ **major and minor**) on floor of each lateral ventricle of brain.

Hip·poc·ra·tes (hĭpŏk'ratēz) (469–399 B.C.). Most celebrated physician of Greek antiquity. **Hip·po·cra·tic** (hĭpokrăt'ĭk) *adj.* Of Hippocrates or the school of medicine named after him; ~ **oath**, oath embodying the code of medical ethics, preserved in Hippocrates' writings (though prob. of still earlier date), and still taken, in various modified forms, by new physicians.

hip·po·drome (hĭp'odrōm) *n.* (Gk. and Rom. antiq.) Course for chariot races etc.; arena, esp. for horse shows etc.

hip·po·pot·a·mus (hĭpopŏt'amus) *n.* (pl. **-mus·es, -mi** pr. -mī). Large African quadruped (*H. amphibius*) with thick heavy almost hairless body, large muzzle and short legs, inhabiting rivers, lakes, etc. [Gk. *hippos* horse, *potamos* river]

hip·py: see HIPPIE.

hip·ster (hĭp'ster) *n.* (slang) Person who is well-informed about newest ideas, styles, etc.

hir·cine (hēr'sīn, -sĭn) *adj.* Goatlike.

hire (hīr) *n.* Payment for use of thing or for personal service; use or service of for payment; ~ **on**, obtain work, esp. as laborer; ~ **out**, exchange or offer one's services for compensation. **hire** *v.t.* (**hired, hir·ing**). Employ (person) for wages; procure, grant, temporary use of (thing) for payment.

hire·ling (hīr'lĭng) *n.* (usu. contempt.) One who serves for hire.

Hi·ro·hi·to (hērōhē'tō) (1901–). Emperor of Japan 1926– ; after World War II the Japanese constitution stripped him of divine rights.

Hi·ro·shi·ma (hērōshē'ma, hĭrō'shĭ-, hĭrōsh'ĭ-). Seaport in SW. Honshu, Japan, devastated by 1st atomic bomb used in warfare, Aug. 6, 1945.

hir·sute (hēr'sōōt, hērsōōt') *adj.* Hairy, shaggy; untrimmed. **hir'-sute·ness** *n.*

his (hĭz) *poss. pron.* Possessive case of, and adjective corresponding to, HE, belonging to, affecting, him.

His·pan·ic (hĭspăn'ĭk) *adj.* Of, pertaining to, Spain, its people or their language. [L. *Hispania* the Iberian peninsula]

His·pa·nio·la (hĭspanyō'la). Island of the West Indies, E. of Cuba, covering about 30,000 sq. mi. (77,700 sq. km); divided into the Republic of HAITI in the W. part and the DOMINICAN[3] REPUBLIC in the E.

hiss (hĭs) *n.* Sharp continuous spirant sound such as is made by geese and serpents, and in pronunciation of "s"; this sound uttered in disapproval or scorn. ~ *v.* Make sound of hiss, esp. as expression of disapproval or derision; express disapproval of thus; utter with angry hiss.

hist. *abbrev.* Historian; historical; history.

his·ta·mine (hĭs'tamēn, -mĭn) *n.* Substance naturally present in the body, responsible for complex physiological phenomena, esp. in connection with work of blood vessels.

his·tol·o·gy (hĭstŏl'ojē) *n.* Study of the minute structure of organic tissues. **his·to·log'i·cal** *adj.* **his·tol'o·gist** *n.*

his·to·ri·an (hĭstōr'ean, -tōr'-, -tār'-) *n.* Writer of, person learned in, history.

his·tor·ic (hĭstŏr′ĭk, -tăr′-) *adj.* 1. Noted in history. 2. (of tenses of verb) Used in narration of past events; ~ **present**, present tense used instead of past in vivid narration. **his·tor′i·cal** *adj.* Of history; belonging to history, not legend; belonging to the past, not of the present; (of the study of a subject) based on analysis of a subject, language, etc., at successive periods of time; (of novel, picture, etc.) dealing with historical events. **his·tor′i·cal·ly** *adv.*

his·to·ric·i·ty (hĭstorĭs′ĭtē) *n.* Historic quality, character, or authenticity.

his·to·ri·og·ra·pher (hĭstŏrēŏg′rafer, -tŏr-) *n.* Writer of history, esp. official historian of a group, court, etc. **his·to·ri·og′ra·phy** *n.* (pl. **-phies**). Writing of history.

The ***hippopotamus*** *is found in Africa from the Upper Nile to South Africa. It is gregarious and comes ashore at night to graze. The smaller pygmy hippopotamus lives only on the Ivory Coast, Liberia and Sierra Leone and is a very rare and now completely protected species.*

his·to·ry (hĭs′terē, hĭs′trē) *n.* (pl. **-ries**) *n.* 1. Continuous methodical record in order of time, of important or public events; study of formation and growth of communities and nations; whole train of events connected with particular country, person, thing, etc.; past events in general, course of human affairs; **ancient** ~, history usu. reckoned as ending with fall of Roman Empire, 476 A.D.; (joc.) thing that is out of date, or long

Hippopotamus

***Adolf Hitler** in storm-trooper uniform, with his Chief-Of-Staff, Victor Lutze, at a Nazi Party rally in 1934. Hitler apparently committed suicide in 1945 when Berlin fell to the Russians.*

past. 2. Systematic account of set of natural phenomena (rare exc. in **natural** ~).

his·tri·on·ic (hĭstrēŏn´ĭk) *adj.* Of actors or acting; stagy, overly emotional or dramatic. **his·tri·on'i·cal·ly** *adv.* **his·tri·on'ics** *n.pl.* Theatricals, theatrical act; being dramatic for effect.

hit (hĭt) *v.* (**hit, hit·ting**). 1. Strike with blow or missile; direct blow *at*; (of moving body) strike; strike *against*; deliver (blow, person etc. a blow); (fig.) affect sensibly, wound; (slang) murder; **~-and-run**, of a motor accident in which driver of vehicle fails to stop; of an attack or raid of short duration by a few attackers or raiders; **~-or-miss, ~-and-miss**, (colloq.) casual, careless; **~-out**, deal vigorous blows. 2. Fall in with, suit; ~ **it off**, agree; become friends quickly (*with, together*); ~ **on**, come by chance on. **hit** *n.* Blow, stroke; stroke of sarcasm etc. (*at*); stroke of good luck; successful attempt; success; (slang) murder by a paid assassin (~ **man**); (baseball) **base** ~: see BASE[2]. **hit'ter** *n.*

hitch (hĭch) *v.* Move (thing) with jerk; shift; ~ **up**, lift, pull up, with jerk. 2. Fasten with loop, hook, etc.; become so fastened; ~ **up (horses)**, attach them to wagon. 3. (also **hitch'hike**) Travel by soliciting free rides in vehicles. **hitch** *n.* 1. Jerk, abrupt pull or push. 2. (naut.) Noose, knot, of various kinds, by which rope is caught around or temporarily made fast to something, as **half** ~, one formed by passing end of rope around its standing part and then through the bight. 3. Temporary stoppage; impediment.

hith·er (hĭdh'*er*) *adv.* To, toward, this place; ~ **and thither,** ~ **and yon**, in various directions, here and there; **hith'erto'**, up to this time; **hith'erward**, (archaic) in this direction. **hither** *adj.* Situated on this side; nearer (of two).

Hit·ler (hĭt'l*er*), **Adolf** (1889–1945). Austrian-born German political leader; founded Nationalist Socialist German Workers' Party (Nazi party) 1919–20; wrote *Mein Kampf*, 1924, describing his aims; President Hindenburg forced to name him chancellor; was granted temporary dictatorial powers by the Reichstag, 1933; combined the offices of chancellor and president upon Hindenburg's death and created the title "Der Führer" as dictator of the Third Reich, 1934–45; was committed to a fanatical policy of establishing Aryan racial supremacy involving elimination of Jews, and to the establishment of Germany as the dominant world power; broke the Treaty of Versailles, withdrew from the League of Nations, 1935, reoccupied the Rhineland, annexed Austria and Sudetenland, 1938, and Czechoslovakia, 1939; his invasion of Poland, Sept., 1939, led to onset of World War II; he committed suicide in Berlin bunker as Allies drew near. **Hit'ler·ism** *n.* **Hit'ler·ite** *adj.* & *n.*

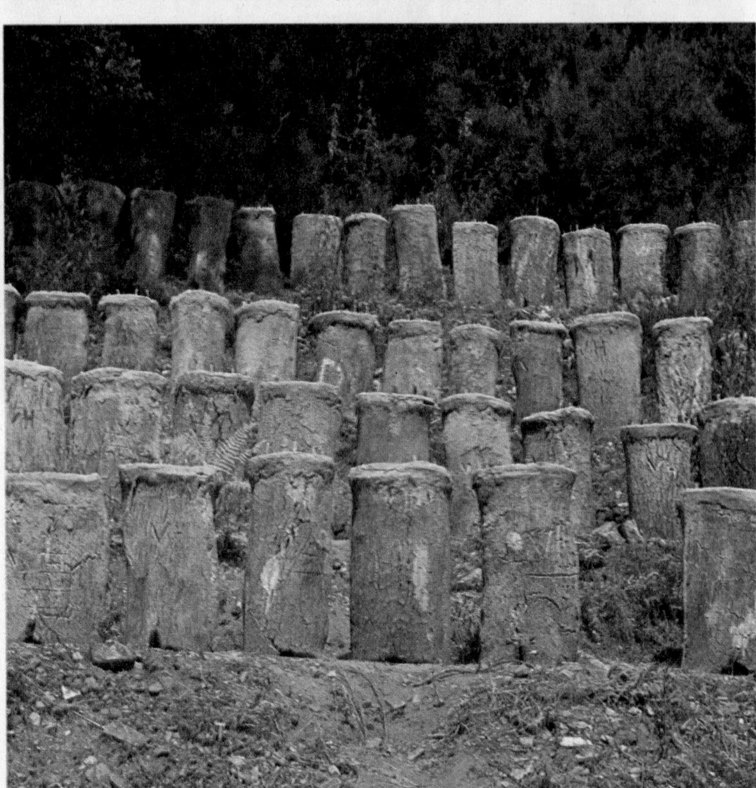

*These **hives** in Spain are made from cork and sacking. Most up-to-date commercial beekeepers, however, use wooden boxes with movable frames in which the bees build their combs.*

Hit·tite (hĭt'īt) *n.* 1. Member of an ancient people who flourished in Anatolia *c*2000–1200 B.C. and controlled N. Syria and other parts of the Near East. 2. (Old Testament) People of N. Syria, possibly descended from the Hittites of Anatolia or akin to them. 3. Language of the Hittites of Anatolia, known from Babylonian cuneiform inscriptions, related to the Indo-European family of languages. ~ *adj.* Of the Hittites or their language.

*With a population of 158,000, **Hobart,** State capital of Tasmania, Australia, is built beside the Derwent River. Its deep-water port is the export outlet for zinc, iron, apples and wool from the southern parts of the island.*

*The **hobby-horse,** associated with the traditional British Morris dance, celebrates rebirth in spring. At Padstow, Cornwall (above), similar dances are held but they are designed to eliminate evil and death and to encourage human fertility.*

hive (hīv) *n.* Habitation for bees; colony of bees living in a hive; (fig.) busy swarming place. ~ *v.* (**hived, hiv·ing**). Place (bees) in hive; enter hive, live together like bees; store, hoard up (honey etc.) in hive.

hives (hīvz) *n.pl.* (pop.) Any of various physical disorders, as skin eruptions etc.

hl *abbrev.* Hectoliter(s).

hm *abbrev.* Hectometer(s).

H.M. *abbrev.* His (or Her) Majesty.

HMO *abbrev.* Health maintenance organization.

H.M.S. *abbrev.* His (or Her) Majesty's Ship.

Ho *symbol.* Holmium.

ho (hō) *int.* Exclamation expressing surprise, admiration, triumph, derision, calling attention, etc.

hoa·gy, hoa·gie (hō′gē) *ns.* (pl. **-gies**) = HERO SANDWICH.

hoar (hōr, hōr) *adj.* Gray-haired with age; grayish white; (of things) gray with age; **hoar′frost**, frozen dew forming a white frostlike coating. **hoar** *n.* Hoariness; hoarfrost.

hoard (hōrd, hōrd) *n.* Stock, store (esp. of food, money) laid by; amassed stock of facts etc. ~ *v.t.* Amass (food, money, etc.) and put away, store *up*.

hoar·hound = HOREHOUND.

hoarse (hōrs, hōrs) *adj.* (**hoars·er, hoars·est**). (of voice) Rough, husky, croaking; (of person) having such a voice. **hoarse′ly** *adv.* **hoarse′ness** *n.* **hoars′en** *v.* Make, become, hoarse.

hoar·y (hōr′ē, hōr′ē) *adj.* (**hoar·i·er, hoar·i·est**). (of hair) Gray, white, with age; having such hair, venerable; ancient, very old; (bot., entom.) covered with short white hairs. **hoar′i·ness** *n.*

hoax (hōks) *v.t.* Deceive, take in (person) by way of joke. ~ *n.* Humorous or mischievous deception.

hob (hŏb) *n.* Part of casing of fireplace having surface level with top of grate, forming stand for kettle, pan, etc.

Ho·bart[1] (hō′bărt). Capital and a port of Tasmania.

Ho·bart[2] (hō′bărt), **Garret Augustus** (1844–99). Amer. lawyer; U.S. vice president under William McKinley, 1897–9.

Hobbes (hŏbz), **Thomas** (1588–1679). English philosopher; expounded his political philosophy, according to which man is a naturally selfish unit, in the *Leviathan* (1651).

hob·ble (hŏb′el) *v.* (**-bled, -bling**). Walk lamely, limp; proceed haltingly; cause to hobble; tie together legs of (horse etc.) to prevent it from straying etc.; tie (legs) thus. ~ *n.* Uneven or infirm gait; rope, clog, etc., for hobbling horse etc.; ~ **skirt**, type of long skirt, popular *c*1910, that was so narrow below the knee it impeded wearer in walking.

hob·ble·de·hoy (hŏb′eldēhoi) *n.* (pl. **-hoys**). Awkward, gawky adolescent boy.

hob·by[1] (hŏb′ē) *n.* (pl. **-bies**). 1. (archaic) Small horse. 2. Subject, activity, or occupation engaged in primarily for pleasure; **hob′by-horse**, stick with horse's head that children bestride as toy horse; rocking horse; favorite theme, obsession.

hob·by[2] (hŏb′ē) *n.* (pl. **-bies**). Small falcon (*Falco subbuteo*).

hob·gob·lin (hŏb′gŏblĭn) *n.* Mischievous, or sometimes evil and ugly, imp; bogey; bugbear.

*The **hockey field,** which measures 100 x 60 yards, is divided into four zones. Two teams of 11 hockey players take up different positions on the field and aim to score hits in their opponent's goal.*

hob·nail (hŏb′nāl) *n.* Heavy-headed nail, for soles of shoes and boots. **hob′nailed** *adj.* Furnished or set with hobnails.

hob·nob (hŏb′nŏb) *v.i.* (**-nobbed, -nob·bing**). Associate familiarly, as drinking companions; hold familiar conversation (*with*).

ho·bo (hō′bō) *n.* (pl. **-boes, -bos**). Migratory worker; tramp.

Hob·son's (hŏb′sonz) **choice.** No choice at all, necessity of taking what one can get. [f. Thomas *Hobson*, 1544?–1631, liveryman of Cambridge, England, who rented out his horses in rotation without allowing his customers to choose among them]

Ho Chi Minh (hō′ chē′ mĭn′) (1890–1969). Vietnamese political leader; president and major leader of North Vietnam, 1954–69, during Vietnam War. ~ **City**, former name of SAIGON.

hock[1] (hŏk) *n.* Joint of quadruped's hind leg between true knee and fetlock.

hock[2] (hŏk) *n.* (esp. Brit.) German white wine, properly that of Hochheim on the river Main.

hock[3] (hŏk) *n.* (colloq.) **in** ~, in pawn; in debt; **hock′shop**, pawnshop. **hock** *v.t.* Pawn.

hock·ey (hŏk′ē) *n.* Field game (also **field hockey**) played with a small hard ball and with sticks hooked or curved at one end between 2 teams of 11 players on each side, the object being to drive the ball through the opponents' goal; **ice** ~, form of hockey played on ice with each side having 6 players on skates and with PUCK instead of ball.

ho·cus (hō′kus) *v.t.* (**-cused, -cus·ing**, Brit. **-cussed, -cus·sing**). Take in, hoax; stupefy (person) with drugs; drug (food or esp. drink).

ho·cus-po·cus (hō′kus pō′kus) *n.* Sleight of hand, deception; typical conjuring formula. ~ *v.* (**-cused, -cus·ing**, Brit. **-cussed, -cus·sing**). Play tricks on.

hod (hŏd) *n.* 1. Builder's light open trough on staff for carrying mortar etc; ~ **carrier**, worker who carries hod. 2. Coal scuttle.

hodge·podge (hŏj′pŏj), **hotch-potch** (hŏch′pŏch) *ns.* Dish of mixed ingredients; mixture, medley.

Hodg·kin's (hŏj′kĭnz) **disease.** Disease characterized by chronic progressive enlargement and inflammation of the lymph nodes and other lymphoid tissues, esp. of the spleen and often of the kidneys and liver. [T. *Hodgkin* (1798–1866), English physician]

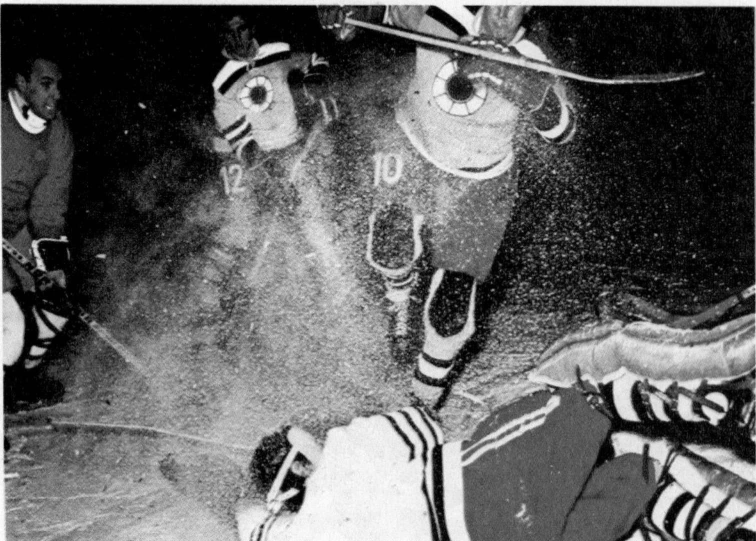

***Ice hockey** is particularly popular in North America. Two teams of 6 players on skates use sticks to hit a hard rubber disc called a puck into the opponent's goal.*

hoe (hō) *n.* Tool consisting of thin metal blade fixed transversely on long handle, for loosening soil, scraping up weeds, etc.; **hoe′cake**, thin cornmeal cake (perh. orig. baked on broad thin blade of hoe); **hoe′down**, lively dance or party featuring dancing, often square dancing; music for such dancing. **hoe** *v.* (**hoed, hoe·ing**). Weed (crops), loosen (ground), dig *up*, cut *down*, with hoe; use hoe.

Hof·manns·thal (hawf′mahns-tahl), **Hugo von** (1874–1929). Austrian poet and dramatist; a pioneer of the new Romantic movement in German drama.

hog (hawg, hŏg) *n.* Mammal of the family Suidae, including the domesticated pig, the boar, wart hog, etc.; (esp.) domestic pig weighing over 120 lbs.; (fig.) coarse, gluttonous, or filthy person; **go the whole** ~, do the thing thoroughly; **live (eat) high off (on) the** ~, (colloq.) live luxuriously or extravagantly; **hog′back**, sharply crested ridge, steep on each side and sloping gradually at each end; **hog cholera**, often fatal disease of swine; **hog′tie**, secure by tying together animal's feet or person's hands and feet; hamper, frustrate; **hog′wash**, kitchen swill etc. for hogs; (colloq.) nonsense; **hog′weed**, coarse weed of parsnip family with leaves relished by many animals; **hog-wild**, (colloq.) highly enthusiastic; lacking restraint. **hog** *v.* (**hogged, hog·ging**). Raise (back etc.), rise, archwise in center; (slang) appropriate selfishly; refuse to share. **hog′gish** *adj.* Piglike, swinish; coarsely self-indulgent or gluttonous. **hog′gish·ly** *adv.* **hog′gish·ness** *n.*

ho·gan (hō′gahn, -gan) *n.* Nava-

*The 16th-century German painter and engraver, **Hans Holbein** the Younger, is famous for his accomplished and realistic portraits. This 'Lady with a Squirrel' is the Marchioness Lady Cholmondley.*

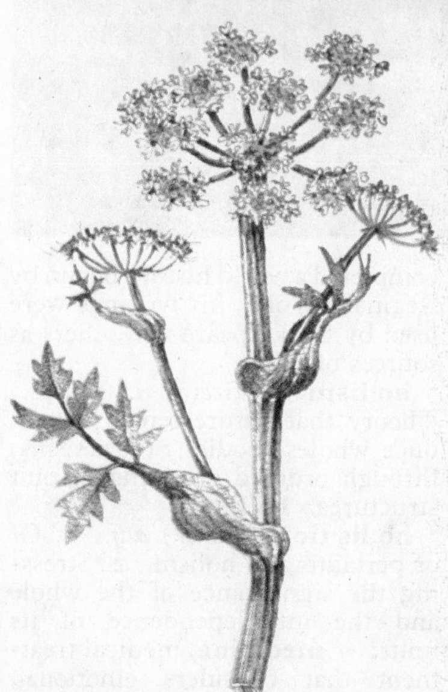

*The **hogweed** or cow parsnip grows by roadsides and in wastes and pastures. It is found in northern temperate climates and has small white or pink flowers.*

ho Indian dwelling built of branches and covered with sod or mud.

Ho·garth (hō'gärth), **William** (1697–1764). English painter and engraver of social and political caricature.

hogs·head (hŏgz'hĕd) *n.* Large cask; liquid measure of 63 gallons, although it can vary as unit of volume or capacity from 62.5 to 140 gallons.

Hoh·en·zol·lern (hō'enzŏlern; *Ger.* hō'entsawlern). German princely family of Swabian origin, from which came the kings of Prussia from 1701 to 1918 and German emperors from 1871 to 1918.

hoicks (hoiks): var. of YOICKS.

hoi pol·loi (hoi' poloi'). Majority, the masses. [Gk. = "the many"]

hoist[1] (hoist) *v.t.* Raise aloft (esp. flags); raise by means of tackle etc. ~ *n.* Hoisting, shove up; elevator esp. for things; pulley, (eng.) fixed crane.

hoist[2] (hoist) *adj.* ~ **with one's own petard**, ruined by one's own devices against others. [past part. of obs. *hoise* hoist]

hoi·ty-toi·ty (hoi'tē toi'tē) *adj.* Haughty.

hoke (hōk) *v.* (slang) Treat in falsely contrived way (usu. ~ **up**). **hoke** *n.* (slang) = HOKUM. **hok'ey** *adj.*

Hok·kai·do (hawk'kīdō'). Northernmost island of Japan in the Pacific Ocean off the E. coast of Asia covering 30,372 sq. mi. (78,663 sq. km).

ho·kum (hō'kum) *n.* Stage properties, action, etc., designed to have sentimental or melodramatic appeal; fakery; nonsense, bunkum. [perh. blending of *hocus-pocus* and *bunkum*]

Hol·bein (hōl'bīn; *Ger.* hawl'-bīn), **Hans** (1497–1543). German portrait painter; became court painter to Henry VIII of England, 1536; called "the Younger" to distinguish him from his less famous father.

hold[1] (hōld) *n.* Cavity in ship below deck, where cargo is stored.

hold[2] (hōld) *v.* (**held** pr. hĕld, **hold·ing**). 1. Keep fast, grasp; keep (oneself, one's head, etc.) in particular attitude. 2. Possess, be owner or holder or tenant of; have capacity for, contain; keep possession of (place); occupy (place, person's thoughts, etc.); engross (person, his attention); **holding company**, company controlling or holding partial or complete interest in other companies. 3. Keep (person etc.) in specified place, condition, etc.; make (person) adhere *to* (terms, promise). 4. Observe, celebrate, conduct (festival, meeting, conversation). 5. Restrain. 6. Think, believe; (of judge or court) lay down, decide (*that*); entertain specified feelings toward; **hold dear**, regard with affection. 7. Remain unbroken, not give way; keep going; (of laws, rules, etc.) be valid, apply; (archaic) stop, wait; **hold to**, adhere to (choice, purpose, etc.); **hold with**, approve of. 8. **hold one's ground, one's own**, not give way; **hold one's head high**, behave proudly; **hold up one's head**, not be downcast or ashamed; **hold water**, (fig.) be sound, bear examination. 9. **hold oneself aloof**, avoid communication with persons etc.; **hold back**, restrain; hesitate, refrain *from*; **hold down**, continue to occupy (a place or post); retain (a job); **hold forth**, (usu. contempt.) speak publicly; **hold in**, confine, keep in

North and South **Holland** are two provinces of the Netherlands, rich dairying regions also famous for their tulips (above). Haarlem and Amsterdam are in the north and The Hague and Rotterdam in the south. Above right: Typical Dutch windmill. Right: Opening bridge over the River Amstel.

check; **hold off**, delay; **hold on**, keep one's grasp on something; keep telephone line open; (colloq., imper.) stop; **hold out**, stretch forth; offer (inducement etc.); endure, persist; **hold out for**, refuse to accept anything but (specified terms etc.); **hold over**, postpone; **hold together**, (cause to) cohere; **hold up**, support; exhibit, display (esp. *to* derision etc.); arrest progress of, obstruct, delay; stop and rob; rob; **hold'up**, (*n*.), armed robbery; delay. **hold** *n*. Grasp (esp. in **take, get, keep, ~ of**); opportunity of holding, thing to hold by; means of exerting influence *on, over*.

hold·er (hōl'd*e*r) *n*. (esp.) Contrivance for holding something, as a pen, cigarette, etc.

hold·ing (hōl'dĭng) *n*. (esp.) 1. (usu. pl.) Land, stocks, capital, etc. held. 2. (sports) Illegal hampering or blocking of an opponent's movements with the hands or arms.

hole (hōl) *n*. Hollow place in solid body; deep place in stream etc.; animal's burrow; (slang) small mean abode; cavity into which ball etc. must be got in various games, esp. golf; (golf) point scored by player who gets ball from tee to hole with fewest strokes; perforation; (slang) awkward situation; **in the ~**, (slang) owing money; **make a ~ in**, use a large amount of; **pick ~s in**, find fault with. **hole** *v*. (**holed, hol·ing**). Make holes in; put into hole; hit (golf ball, or abs.) into hole; **~ up**, (slang) hide oneself.

hol·i·day (hŏl'ĭdā) *n*. 1. Day of cessation from work or of recreation; (chiefly Brit.) (usu. pl.) period of this, vacation. 2. Holy day.

ho·li·ness (hō'lēnĭs) *n*. Sanctity; (with possessive) **H ~**, title of pope.

Hol·ins·hed (hŏl'ĭnzhĕd, -ĭnshĕd) or **Hol·lings·head** (hŏl'ĭngzhĕd), **Raphael** (d. 1580). English historian; wrote *Chronicles of England, Scotland and Ireland*, 1577; completed a world history begun by Reginald Wolfe; his writings were used by Shakespeare and others as sources of plots.

ho·lism (hō'lĭz*e*m) *n*. (philos.) Theory that nature tends to produce wholes (bodies or oganisms) through ordered grouping of unit structures. **ho'list** *n*.

ho·lis·tic (hōlĭs'tĭk) *adj*. 1. Of or pertaining to holism. 2. Stressing the significance of the whole and the interdependence of its units; **~ medicine**, medical treatment that considers emotional, mental, etc., aspects, as well as physical symptoms, in treatment of patients. **ho·lis'ti·cal·ly** *adv*.

Hol·land (hŏl'*a*nd). Name of province of the Northern Netherlands, now usu. extended by foreigners to the kingdom of the NETHERLANDS. **Hol'land·er** *n.*

hol·lan·daise (hŏl'andāz, hŏlandāz') **sauce.** Sauce for fish, vegetables, etc. of butter, egg yolks, vinegar, etc. [Fr., = "Dutch"]

hol·ler (hŏl'*er*) *v.* & *n.* (Make, express with) loud cry or noise.

hol·low (hŏl'ō) *adj.* Having a hole, cavity, or depression; not solid, empty inside; empty, insincere, false. **hol'low·ly** *adv.* **hol'low·ness** *n.* **hollow** *n.* Hollow place; hole; valley, basin. ~ *adv.* Completely (esp. in *beat* ~ etc.). ~ *v.t.* Bend into hollow shape; (also ~ **out**), excavate.

hol·ly (hŏl'ē) *n.* (pl. **-lies**). Evergreen shrub (*Ilex*, esp. *I. opaca*, Amer. holly, and *I. aquifolium*, English holly) with usu. dark green tough glossy leaves, having indented edges with sharp stiff prickles at the points, and bearing bright red berries, much used for decorating houses etc. at Christmas.

hol·ly·hock (hŏl'ēhŏk) *n.* Tall plant (*Althaea rosea*) with stout stem bearing numerous large flowers of many varieties of color on very short stalks. [*holy* + *hock* mallow]

Hol·ly·wood (hŏl'ēwo͝od). Section of Los Angeles, California; center of the U.S. television and motion-picture industry, though major studios no longer are concentrated there; (fig.) the motion-picture industry, its glamour, etc.

Holmes[1] (hōmz, hōlmz), **Oliver Wendell** (1809–94). Amer. physician and man of letters; best known for his collected *Atlantic Monthly* magazine pieces, *The Autocrat at the Breakfast Table*, and the poems "Old Ironsides," "Chambered Nautilus," and "The Wonderful One-Hoss Shay"; his son, **Oliver Wendell** (1841–1935), Amer. jurist; associate justice of the U.S. Supreme Court, 1902–32; known as "the great dissenter," he believed that the law was made for society and not society for the law, and that law was based on experience, not logic.

Holmes[2] (hōmz, hōlmz), **Sherlock.** Private detective, the chief character in a number of detective stories by Sir A. Conan Doyle.

hol·mi·um (hōl'mē*u*m) *n.* (chem.) Element of yttrium-cerium group found in gadolinite; symbol Ho, at. no. 67, at. wt. 164.9340. [f. Stock*holm*, near which yttria-bearing minerals are found]

hol·o·caust (hŏl'*o*kawst, hō'l*o*-) *n.* Whole burned offering; wholesale sacrifice (fig.) or destruction, esp. by fire; **the H**~, the murder by the Nazis of over 6 million Jews.

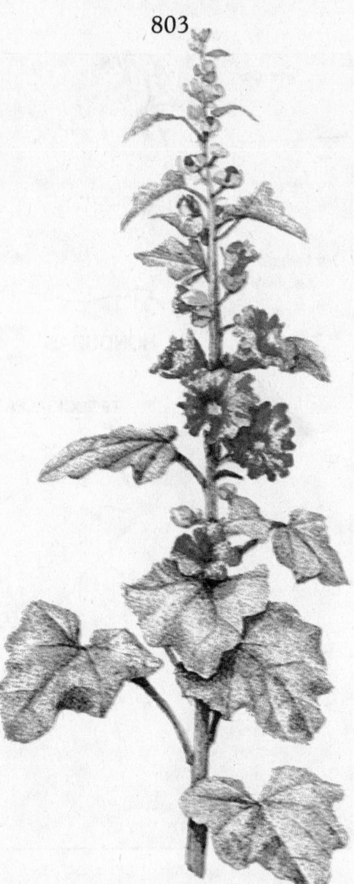

*The **hollyhock** is widely cultivated for its ornamental flowers. The stems grow from 5 to 9 ft. tall and the flowers, usually white, pink, red or yellow are 3 ins. or more across.*

ho·lo·gram (hō'logrăm, hŏl'*o*-) *n.* (phys.) 1. Pattern produced by interference between coherent light beam and light diffracted etc. from same beam by an object. 2. Photograph of such pattern which, when suitably illuminated, produces an image of the object in two or three dimensions.

hol·o·graph (hŏl'*o*grăf, -grahf, hō'l*o*-) *adj.* & *n.* (Document) written wholly in handwriting of person in whose name it appears (cf. AUTOGRAPH). **hol·o·graph·ic** (hŏlogrăf'ĭk) *adj.*

ho·log·ra·phy (hōlŏg'r*a*fē) *n.* Process or method of producing holograms.

hol·o·thu·ri·an (hŏl*o*thoor'ē*a*n, hōl*o*-), **hol·o·thu·ri·oid** (hŏl*o*thoor'ēoid) *adjs.* & *ns.* (Animal) of the Holothurioidea, a class of echinoderms including sea cucumber and characterized by elongated form, tough leathery integument, and a ring of tentacles around the mouth.

Hol·stein (hōl'shtīn). Former Danish duchy; later (after 1866) part of the province of Schleswig-Holstein, Prussia. ~ *n.* (Any of) a breed of black and white dairy cattle developed in Holstein.

hol·ster (hōl'st*er*) *n.* Leather case for pistol, fixed to saddle or worn on belt.

ho·ly (hō'lē) *adj.* (**-li·er, -li·est**). Consecrated, sacred; morally and spiritually perfect; belonging to, commissioned by, devoted to, God; of high moral excellence; **H**~ **Alliance**, that formed in 1815, after fall of Napoleon, among Russia, Austria, and Prussia ostensibly to preserve peace and justice in Europe; **H**~ **Communion**, celebration of the EUCHARIST; ~ **cross**, cross of Christ; **H**~ **Father**: see FATHER; **H**~ **Ghost**, third member of the Trinity; ~ **grail**: see GRAIL; ~ **Joe**, (naut. slang) clergyman, pious person; **H**~ **Land**, western region of PALESTINE, esp. Judea, as scene of life and death of Jesus Christ and of sacred sites, esp. the Holy Sepulcher at Jerusalem; ~ **name**, name of Jesus as object of formal devotion; ~ **orders**: see ORDER; **H**~ **Roman Empire**: see ROMAN; ~ **Rood**: see ROOD; **H**~ **Saturday**, Saturday before Easter; ~ **terror**, (slang) formidable person, embarrassing child; **H**~ **Thursday**, Thursday in Holy Week; (in the Anglican Ch.) Ascension Day; ~ **water**, water dedicated to holy uses and used for ritual purification; water blessed by priest and used in various rites and devotional acts; **H**~ **Week**, week preceding Easter Sunday; **H**~ **Writ**: see WRIT[1]. **holy** *n.* (pl. **-lies**). ~ **of holies**, inner chamber of sanctuary in Jewish temple; innermost shrine.

hom·age (hŏm'ĭj, ŏm'-) *n.* (in feudal law) Formal and public acknowledgment of allegiance to feudal superior; acknowledgment of superiority; dutiful reverence, respect.

hom·burg (hŏm'bẽrg) *n.* Man's soft felt hat with slightly curved brim and crown indented lengthwise. [*Homburg*, town in W. Germany, where first manufactured]

home (hōm) *n.* 1. Dwelling place, fixed residence of family or household; members of family collectively; private house; ~ **away from** ~, place providing homelike amenities. 2. Native land; place where thing is native or most common. 3. Institution of refuge or rest for destitute or infirm persons. 4. (in games) Goal; (baseball) home plate. 5. **at** ~, in one's own house; at one's ease; familiar *with*, *in* (subject etc.); accessible to callers. **home** *adj.* Of, connected with, home; carried on at home; proceeding from home; in the neighborhood of home; played etc. on team's own ground; carried on, produced, in one's own country; treating of domestic affairs; **home'body**, person who likes to stay at home; **home-brewed**, (beer etc.) brewed at home; **home'-**

***Honduras,** a republic in Central America, has an area of 43,227 sq. miles, and a population of 2,930,000. Most of its people are of mixed Indian-European origin. The capital is Tegucigalpa (below right). The principal exports are bananas, coffee, timber and silver.*

coming, arrival at home; **home economics**, science and art of household management, including budgeting, nutrition, child care, cooking, etc.; **home′grown**, grown or produced at home; **home guard**, volunteer armed force of civilians who protect their country while the regular army is fighting in the field; **home′land**, native land; mother country; **home′made′**, made at home or by oneself; **home′maker**, person who manages household affairs; **home plate**, base at which baseball batter stands, and that must be crossed by runner to score a run; **home′room**, room in school where a class meets daily to be checked for absences, receive special announcements, etc.; **home rule**, government of country, colony, etc. by its own citizens; **home run**, (baseball) hit that allows batter to circle bases and score a run; **home run ball**, pitch easy to hit for a home run; **home′sick**, depressed by absence from home, longing for home; **home′spun**, (plain coarse woolen cloth) spun at home; (anything) plain, homely; **home′stretch**, straight part of racetrack between final bend and finish line; **home′work**, office work, piecework, etc. done at home; esp. lessons and exercises to be done by schoolchild at home. **home** *adv.* To one's home or country, as **come, go, ~**; arrived at home; to the point aimed at, as **that hits ~**. **home′less, home′like** *adjs.* **home** *v.* (**homed, hom·ing**). 1. Go home (esp. of pigeons); (of aircraft etc.) proceed under guidance of radio signal etc. 2. Bring or send home; bring in (aircraft etc.) under guidance of radio signal etc.

home·ly (hōm′lē) *adj.* (**-li·er, -li·est**). Simple, plain; primitive; unpretending; (of persons or features) uncomely, plain. **home′li·ness** *n.*

ho·me·op·a·thy (hōmēŏp′*a*thē) *n.* System (founded *c*1796 by Samuel Hahnemann of Leipzig) of treatment of disease by drugs (usu. in minute doses) that in a healthy person would produce symptoms like those of the disease. **ho·me·o·path** (hō′mē*o*păth) *n.* **ho·me·o·path·ic** (hōmē*o*păth′ĭk) *adj.*

ho·me·o·sta·sis (hōmē*o*stā′sĭs) *n.* Tendency toward relatively stable equilibrium between interdependent elements, esp. as maintained by physiological processes. **ho·me·o·stat·ic** (hōmē*o*stăt′ĭk) *adj.*

Ho·mer[1] (hō′m*er*). Greek epic poet, of uncertain birthplace and date; traditionally believed to be the author of the *Iliad* and the *Odyssey*. **Ho·mer·ic** (hōmĕr′ĭk) *adj.* Of, in the style of, Homer or the poems attributed to him, or the legends and age of which he wrote; heroic, epic.

Ho·mer[2] (hō′m*er*), **Winslow** (1836–1910). Amer. painter and illustrator noted for realistic portrayals of outdoor life and seascapes.

hom·er[1] (hō′m*er*) *n.* Homing pigeon.

ho·mer[2] (hō′m*er*) *n.* Ancient Hebrew measure of capacity, containing 10 ephahs (prob. *c* 10 or 11 bushels dry measure or 80 to 100 gallons liquid measure). [Heb. *k̲ōmer* heap]

ho·mer[3] (hō′m*er*) *n.* HOME run.

home·stead (hōm′stĕd) *n.* House with outbuildings; farm; land claimed by a settler or squatter, esp. lot of 160 acres granted to settlers by **Homestead Act** of Congress, 1862. **homestead** *v.* Settle and farm a homestead. **home′stead·er** *n.*

home·ward (hōm′werd) *adv.* & *adj.* (Going, leading) toward home; ~ **bound**, (esp. of ship) preparing to go, on the way, home. **home′wards** *adv.*

home·y, hom·y (hō′mē) *adjs.* (**hom·i·er, hom·i·est**). Suggesting home, homelike.

hom·i·cide (hŏm′ĭsīd, hō′mĭ-) *n.* 1. One who kills a human being. 2. Killing of one human being by another; MANSLAUGHTER; MURDER; **justifiable** ~, killing of a person where no blame attaches to the killer. **hom·i·ci·dal** (hŏmĭsī′d*a*l, hōmĭ-) *adj.* Having a tendency to homicide; murderous.

hom·i·let·ics (hŏm*i*lĕt′ĭks) *n.* Art of preaching. **hom·i·let′ic** *adj.*

hom·i·ly (hŏm′*i*lē) *n.* (pl. **-lies**). Sermon; tedious moralizing discourse.

hom·ing (hō′mĭng) *adj.* Returning home; ~ **pigeon**: see PIGEON.

hom·i·nid (hŏm′*i*nĭd) *n.* & *adj.* (Member) of the human zoological family including existing and fossil man.

hom·i·ny (hŏm′*i*nē) *n.* (also ~ **grits**) Hulled and dried kernels of corn boiled with water or milk.

Ho·mo (hō′mō) *n.* Genus of primates of the family Hominidae, consisting of mankind now usu. regarded as a single species, ~ **sapiens**. [L. *homo* man, *sapiens* wise]

ho·mo (hō′mō) *n.* (pl. **-mos**). (slang) Homosexual.

homo- *prefix.* Same. [Gk. *homos*]

ho·mo·cen·tric (hōmōsĕn′trĭk) *adj.* Having same center.

ho·mo·ge·ne·ous (hōm*o*jē′nē*u*s, -jēn′y*u*s, hŏm*o*-) *adj.* Of the same kind; consisting of parts all of the same kind, uniform. **ho·mo·ge′ne·ous·ly** *adv.* **ho·mo·ge·ne·i·ty** (hōm*o*j*e*nē′ĭtē, hŏm*o*-), **ho·mo·ge′ne·ous·ness** *ns.*

ho·mo·ge·net·ic (hōm*o*j*e*nĕt′ĭk, hŏm*o*-) *adj.* Having common descent or origin.

ho·mog·e·nize (h*o*mŏj′*e*nīz) *v.t.* (**-nized, -niz·ing**). Treat (milk) so that fat globules emulsify and cream does not separate; make homogeneous.

hom·o·graph (hŏm′*o*grăf, -grahf) *n.* Word spelled like another, but of different meaning or origin. **hom·o·graph·ic** (hŏm*o*grăf′ĭk) *adj.*

ho·mol·o·gous (h*o*mŏl′*o*g*u*s) *adj.* Having the relation or relative position; corresponding; (biol., of limb or organ) similar in position and structure but not necessarily in function (cf. ANALOGOUS).

Homer *is the name given to the author/s of the Greek epic poems, the 'Iliad' and 'Odyssey'. They are believed to be compilations of earlier oral stories and were written about 850 B.C.*

hom·o·logue, hom·o·log (hŏm′*o*lawg, -lŏg) *ns.* Homologous thing.

hom·o·nym (hŏm′*o*nĭm) *n.* Word of same form as another but different sense, as *pale* "stake" and *pale* "wan"; namesake. **hom·o·nym·ic** (hŏm*o*nĭm′ĭk), **hom·on·y·mous** (h*o*mŏn′*i*m*u*s) *adjs.*

Honesty *is widely grown for its oval satin-white seed pods which are used in many flower arrangements. The best known species is also known as moonflower, money or satin flower.*

ho·mo·phile (hō′m*o*fīl) *n.* Homosexual. ~ *adj.* Advocating equal employment opportunities and other rights of homophiles.

hom·o·phone (hŏm′*o*fōn) *n.* Word having same sound as another, but of different spelling, meaning, and origin, as *sew* and *sow*. **hom·o·phon′ic** *adj.* Of same sound; (mus.) of same pitch, in unison; having one part or melody predominating. **hom·o′phon·y** *n.*

ho·mo·sex·u·al (hōm*o*sĕk′shōō*a*l) *adj.* Sexually attracted only to members of the same sex; of those who are so attracted. ~ *n.* Homosexual person. **ho·mo·sex·u·al·i·ty** (hōm*o*sĕkshōōăl′ĭtē) *n.*

ho·mo·zy·gote (hōm*o*zī′gōt) *n.* Zygote of like gametes. **ho·mo·zy′gous** *adj.*

ho·mun·cu·lus (hōmŭng′ky*u*l*u*s) *n.* (pl. **-li** pr. -lī). Little man, manikin.

hom·y: var. HOMEY.

Hon., hon. *abbrevs.* Honorary; Honorable.

Ho·nan (hō′năn′). Province of central China. ~ *adj.* Of Honan, esp. its spicy cuisine.

hon·cho (hŏn′chō) *n.* (pl. **-chos**). (slang) Leader, boss.

Hon·du·ras (hŏndoor′*a*s, -dūr′-). Republic of Central Amer. with a seaboard on the Caribbean, formerly (until 1821) part of the Spanish American dominions; capital, Tegucigalpa; **British** ~, former name of Belize; **Gulf of** ~, inlet of the Caribbean bounded by Belize, Guatemala, and Honduras. **Hon·du′ran** *adj.* & *n.*

hone (hōn) *n.* Whetstone, esp. for razors etc.; any of various stones as material for this. ~ *v.t.* (**honed, hon·ing**). Sharpen on hone.

hon·est (ŏn′ĭst) *adj.* Fair and upright in speech and act, not lying, cheating, or stealing; sincere; good, worthy; (of act etc.) showing uprightness; (of gain etc.) earned by fair means; (of things) unadulterated, genuine; (archaic, of woman) chaste, virtuous; ~ **broker**, mediator in international, industrial, etc., disputes; **make an** ~ **woman of**, marry (seduced woman); ~ **Injun**: see INJUN. **hon′est·ly** *adv.*

hon·es·ty (ŏn′ĭstē) *n.* (pl. **-ties**). 1. Uprightness, truthfulness. 2. Cruciferous plant (*Lunaria annua*) with large purple (or white) flowers and flat round semitransparent fruits.

hon·ey (hŭn′ē) *n.* (pl. **-eys**). Sweet viscid yellow fluid, nectar of flowers collected and worked up for food by bees and other insects; (fig.) sweetness; (colloq.) sweet one, sweetheart, darling; **hon′eybee**, bee that gathers and stores honey, esp. the common bee (*Apis melli-*

Honey was long used as a sweetener, especially in places where sugar-beet or sugar-cane did not grow. The bees gather nectar from flowers and store it in a **honeycomb,** which is also used to hatch the eggs of the queen-bee.

fera); **hon'eydew**, sweet sticky substance, secreted by aphides, found on leaves and stems; (also **honeydew melon**) melon, variety of *Cucumis melo*, having pale green flesh and a smooth rind; **hon'ey-suckle**, any of various vines or shrubs of the genus *Lonicera*, having fragrant yellowish, white, or pink trumpet-shaped flowers, frequent in woods; other plants of this genus. **hon'eyed** *adj*.

hon·ey·comb (hŭn'ēkōm) *n*. Beeswax structure of hexagonal cells for honey and eggs; any structure, ornament, etc. resembling this. ~ *v.t.* Fill with cavities; mark with honeycomb pattern.

hon·ey·moon (hŭn'ēmo͞on) *n*. Holiday or trip taken by newly married couple. ~ *v.i.* Spend honeymoon (*in*, *at*, place). **hon'ey·moon·er** *n*.

Hong Kong (hŏng' kŏng'). British Crown Colony, consisting of a number of islands and a part of the mainland, situated off the SE. coast of China; first occupied by Gt. Britain 1841 and formally ceded by Treaty of Nanking, 1842; capital, Victoria, is situated on the 32-sq. mi. island of Hong Kong.

honk (hŏngk, hawngk) *n*. Wild goose's cry; sound of automobile etc. horn. ~ *v.i.* Emit or give honk.

hon·ky, hon·key, hon·kie (hŏng'kē, hawng'-) *ns*. (pl. **-kies**). (slang) White person; used derog., esp. by blacks.

honk·y-tonk (hŏng'kē tŏngk, hawng'kē tawngk) *n*. (slang) Cheap, noisy nightclub, barroom, dance hall, etc.

Hon·o·lu·lu (hŏnolo͞o'lo͞o). Capital and principal port of HAWAII, on the S. coast of Oahu.

hon·or, Brit. **hon·our** (ŏn'*er*) *ns*. 1. High respect; glory; reputation, good name. 2. Nobleness of mind; allegiance to what is right or to approved standard of conduct; (of woman) chastity, reputation for this. 3. Exalted position; (with possessive) title for holder of certain offices. 4. Person, thing, that reflects honor on (*to*) another; thing conferred or done as token of respect or distinction; position or title of rank, dignity; (sports, games) right of taking first turn, beginning, etc., as having won previous game, having better record, etc.; (pl.) civilities rendered to guests etc. (**do the ~s**); **military ~s**, marks of respect paid by troops at burial of officers, statesmen, royalty, etc.; **~s of war**, privileges granted to capitulating force, as that of marching out with colors flying etc. 5. (pl., in bridge and certain other card games) Ace, king, queen, jack, and sometimes 10, of trumps or of all suits. 6. (pl.) Special distinction for proficiency beyond that required to receive an academic degree; program or course of higher or specialized studies for exceptional students. 7. **code of ~**, rules forming conventional or personal standard of conduct; **in ~ of**, in celebration of; **in ~ bound**, bound as a moral duty (*to* do); **be on one's ~**, be under moral obligation; **upon my ~**, (colloq.) **~ bright**, forms of earnest declaration. **honor** *v.t.* Respect highly; confer dignity upon; (commerc.) accept, pay (bill) when due.

hon·or·a·ble, Brit. **hon·our·a·ble** (ŏn'*e*rab*e*l) *adjs*. 1. Worthy of honor; bringing honor to its possessor; consistent with honor; upright. 2. **H~**, (abbrev. Hon.) title of younger sons of earls and children of British viscounts and barons; title of certain officials, including judges and legislators; **Right ~**, title of British peers below rank of marquis, and others. 3. (parl., in conventional use) Title of members of the British House of Commons. **hon'or·a·bly**, Brit. **hon'our·a·bly** *advs*.

Honeysuckle grows in temperate regions of both hemispheres and also in the Himalayas, South Asia and North Africa. It has fragrant flowers and is also known as woodbine.

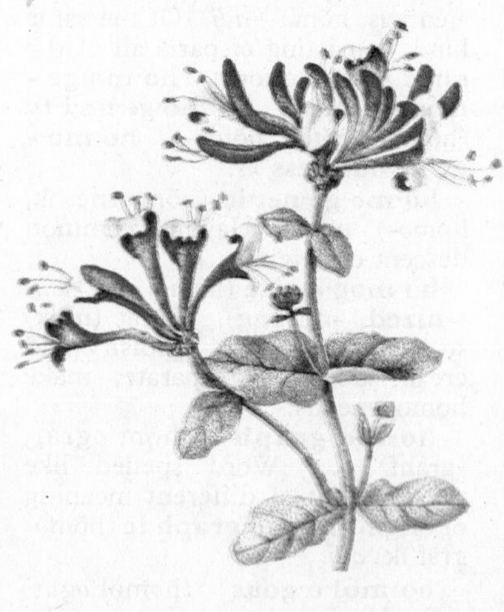

***Hong Kong** has a population of 4,250,000 people, and most speak the Cantonese dialect of Chinese. Victoria, the capital (above), has one of the finest natural harbors and is the world's largest entrepôt port. Right: Map of Hong Kong.*

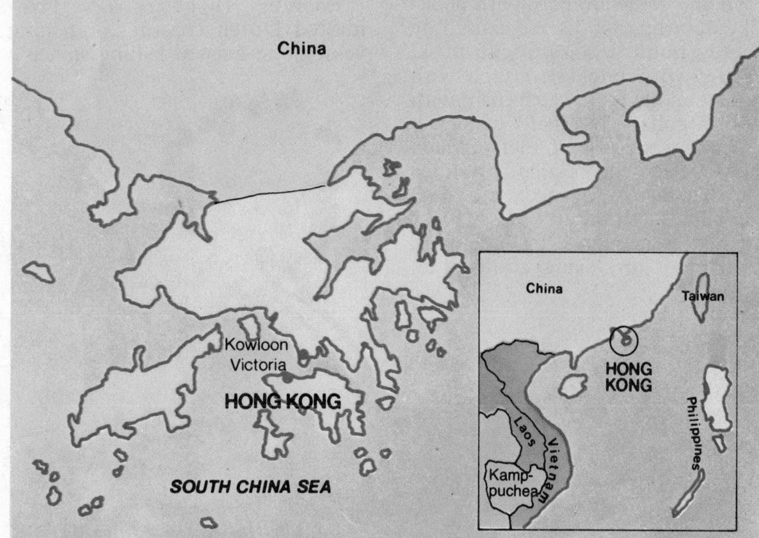

hon·o·rar·i·um (ŏnorār′ēum) *n.* (pl. **-rar·i·ums, -rar·i·a** pr. -rār′ēa). Gift of money in return for voluntary services; payment in lieu of fixed fee for professional services etc.

hon·or·ar·y (ŏn′orĕrē) *adj.* Conferred as an honor (without the usual requirements, adjuncts, etc.); holding honorary title or position without pay; (of obligations) depending on honor, not legally enforceable.

hon·or·if·ic (ŏnorĭf′ĭk) *adj.* & *n.* (Expression) implying respect.

Hon·shu (hŏn′shōō). Island of Japan in the Pacific off the E. coast of Asia; largest of Japan's main islands, 88,925 sq. mi. (230,316 sq. km.)

hooch (hōōch) *n.* (slang) Alcoholic liquor, esp. inferior or bootleg liquor. [abbreviation of Alaskan *Hoochinoo*, a tribe that made a distilled liquor]

hood[1] (hŏŏd) *n.* Covering for head and neck, whether part of cloak etc. or separate; leather covering for hawk's head; thing like hood in shape or use, as a carriage top, the cover for a stove or hearth, etc.; hinged covering over the front of a motor vehicle, covering the engine; ornamental draping of cloth hung from the shoulders of an ecclesiastical, academic, or other robe. ~ *v.t.* Cover with hood. **hood′ed** *adj.*

hood[2] (hŏŏd) *n.* (slang) Hoodlum.

Hood (hŏŏd), **Mount.** Mountain and highest peak, 11,235 ft. (3,424 m), in NW. Oregon in the Cascade Range.

-hood *suffix.* Having a specified state, condition, or quality (*childhood, falsehood*).

hood·lum (hōōd′lum, hŏŏd′-) *n.* Hooligan, thug.

hoo·doo (hōō′dōō) *n.* Voodoo; bad luck; person or thing bringing bad luck. ~ *v.t.* Bring bad luck to. [Alteration of VOODOO]

hood·wink (hŏŏd′wĭngk) *v.t.*

Deceive, humbug; (archaic) blindfold.

hoo·ey (hōō′ē) *n.* (slang) Nonsense, humbug.

hoof (hōōf, hōōf) *n.* (pl. **hoofs, hooves**, pr. hōōvz, hōōvz). Horny casing of foot of ruminants, horses, swine, and allied animals, anatomically a development of the toenail; **cloven ~**: see CLOVEN; **~-and-mouth disease**: see FOOT-and-mouth disease. **hoof** *v.* Strike with hoof; (slang) go on foot; walk; (slang) dance, esp. perform on stage as a dancer. **hoof′er** *n.* (esp.) Dancer, as a professional tap-dancer etc.

hook (hōōk) *n.* Piece of metal or other material bent back or having sharp angle, for catching hold or for hanging things upon; bent piece of wire, usu. barbed, for catching fish; leftward hooked stroke in golf; (boxing) short swinging blow with elbow bent and rigid; sharp bend, e.g. in river; curved projecting point of land; **~ and eye**, small metal hook and loop as fastening; **by ~ or (by) crook**, by fair means or foul; **off the ~**, no longer in difficulty; (of telephone receiver) not on its rest, thus preventing incoming calls; **on one's own ~**, (colloq.) on one's own account; **~-nose(d)**, (having) aquiline nose; **hook′up**, interconnection of broadcasting stations for special transmissions; **hook′worm**, any of various nematode worms infesting man and some animals, with hook-like mouthparts; disease caused by these. **hook** *v.* Grasp with hook; secure with hook(s); attach with hook (*on*, *up*, etc.); catch (fish) with hook; (golf) drive (ball) widely to left or (in the case of a left-handed player) to the right; **hook′up (with)**, fasten, connect, etc., (as) with hook. **hooked′** *adj.* Hook-shaped; having, made with, hook(s); **~ on**, (slang) addicted to.

*The **hookah** is widely used in the Middle East. The smoke is cooled by being drawn through water, which is often scented. The pipe is passed from person to person.*

hook·ah (hōōk′*a*) *n.* Oriental smoking pipe with long flexible tube, smoke being drawn through water in vase to which tube and bowl are attached. [Arab. *ḥuḳḳa* casket, hookah bottle]

Hooke (hōōk), **Robert** (1635–1703). English mathematician, physicist, and philosopher.

hook·er[1] (hōōk′*er*) *n.* Two-masted Dutch coasting or fishing vessel; one-masted fishing smack.

*The **hoopoe** is so called because of its cry. It is a little larger than a thrush and is found over most of Asia and central and southern Europe. It migrates in winter to Africa and India.*

hook·er[2] (hōōk′*er*) *n.* (slang) Prostitute.

hook·y (hōōk′ē) *n.* (colloq.) Truancy from school; **play ~**, play truant.

hoo·li·gan (hōō′l*i*g*a*n) *n.* Young rowdy; member of street gang. **hoo′li·gan·ism** *n.*

hoop[1] (hōōp) *n.* Circular band of metal, wood, etc., esp. for binding staves of casks; wooden or iron circle trundled along by child; circle of lightweight material for expanding woman's hoop skirt; circle, ring, arc; one of iron arches through which balls must be driven in croquet; **~ skirt**, long full skirt flared out into a bell shape by a series of connected hoops. **hoop** *v.t.* Bind with hoops; surround as hoop does.

hoop[2] (hōōp) *v.i.* & *n.* Whoop.

hoop·la (hōōp′lah) *n.* (colloq.) 1. Bustling activity or commotion. 2. Overblown speech or writing, usu. intended to confuse or to conceal truth.

hoo·poe (hōō′pōō) *n.* Bird, esp. S. European *Upupa epops*, with conspicuous variegated plumage and large erectile crest.

hoo·ray: see HURRAH.

hoose·gow, hoos·gow (hōōs′-gow) *ns.* (slang) Jail. [Span. Amer. *juzgao* tribunal, f. L. *judicatum* judged]

Hoo·sier (hōō′zh*er*) *n.* (Nickname for) native or inhabitant of Indiana.

hoot (hōōt) *v.* Make loud sounds, esp. of disapproval (*at*); assail (person etc.) with derisive shouts; drive (person) *out*, *off*, etc. by hooting; (of owl) utter characteristic cry; sound automobile horn, train whistle, etc.; (of horn etc.) sound. **~** *n.* Inarticulate shout, esp. of derision or disapprobation; owl's cry; **don't give, care a ~**, (slang) don't care at all; **not worth a ~**, worthless. **hoot′er** *n.*

The ***hop*** *(above), a perennial herbaceous climbing plant used for flavoring beer and ale.* ***Herbert Hoover*** *(right): The humanitarian image of him that was widespread during 1914–18 war was tarnished in the Great Depression.*

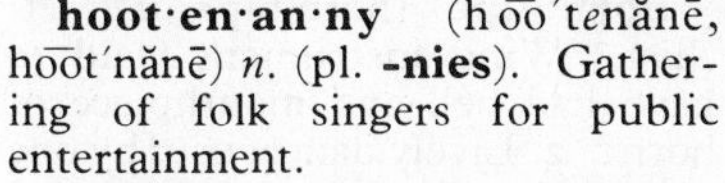

hoot·en·an·ny (ho͞o′tenănē, ho͞ot′nănē) *n.* (pl. **-nies**). Gathering of folk singers for public entertainment.

Hoo·ver[1] (ho͞o′v*er*), **Herbert Clark** (1874–1964). Amer. mining engineer, businessman, and 31st U.S. president, 1929–33; chairman of the Amer. Relief Committee, 1914–5, and Commission for Relief in Belgium, 1915–9; secretary of commerce, 1921–8; his administration was blamed by many for the Great Depression.

Hoo·ver[2] (ho͞o′v*er*) **Dam** (formerly **Boulder Dam**). Dam located on the Colorado River on the border of NW. Arizona and SE. Nevada and forming Lake Mead.

hop[1] (hŏp) *n.* Ripened cones of female hop plant, used for giving bitter flavor to beer etc. (usu. pl.); climbing perennial plant (*Humulus lupulus*) with rough lobed leaves, cultivated for green cones of broad scales borne by female; **hop′head,** (slang) drug addict. **hop** *v.* (**hopped, hop·ping**). Flavor with hops; gather hops; ~ **up,** (slang) stimulate with or as with drugs.

hop[2] (hŏp) *v.* (**hopped, hop·ping**). Spring (of person) on one foot or skip or bound on two feet; (of birds and animals) bound with both or all feet at once; hop over (ditch etc.); (of aircraft) pass low over physical features in a series of movements resembling hops, hence, **hedge-hopping**; jump on to (train etc.); **~-o'-my-thumb,** dwarf, tiny person; **hop′scotch,** child's game in which players toss a pebble into a section of diagram marked on ground, then hop through all sections of the diagram and retrieve the pebble. **hop** *n.* Hopping; spring; (colloq.) dance, esp. a student dance; distance traversed, esp. in aircraft, at one stretch, one stage of long journey, esp. by plane; ~ **skip** (or **step**), **and jump,** exercise consisting of these three movements in sequence; (fig.) short distance.

hope (hōp) *n.* Expectation and desire combined (*of, that*); ground of hope, probability; person, thing, that hope centers on; ~ **against** ~, cling to the slightest hope. **hope** *v.* (**hoped, hop·ing**). Look with expectation and desire (*for*); expect and desire.

hope·ful (hōp′f*u*l) *adj.* Feeling hope; inspiring hope, promising. ~ *n.* Promising or aspiring person. **hope′ful·ly** *adv.* With hope; (colloq.) it is to be hoped, let us hope. **hope′ful·ness** *n.*

Hop·ei (haw′pā′), **Heb·ei** (hö′bā′). Province of E. China; capital Tientsin.

hope·less (hōp′lĭs) *adj.* Feeling no hope; admitting no hope; impossible; incurable. **hope′less·ly** *adv.* **hope′less·ness** *n.*

Ho·pi (hō′pē) *n.* (pl. **-pis,** collect. **-pi**). (Member of) a Pueblo Indian tribe now inhabiting a reservation in NE. Arizona; the Uto-Aztecan language of this tribe.

Hop·kins[1] (hŏp′kĭnz), **Gerard Manley** (1844–89). English poet and Jesuit priest; he is known for his use of internal rhyme and elliptical phrasing, and as the inventor of sprung rhythm.

Hop·kins[2] (hŏp′kĭnz), **Johns** (1795–1873). Amer. financier and philanthropist; founded university and hospital bearing his name, located in Baltimore, Maryland.

hop·per (hŏp′*er*) *n.* 1. One who hops; hopping insect. 2. Inverted pyramid or cone (orig. with hopping or shaking motion) through which grain etc. passes in mill; similar contrivance in various machines etc.; barge carrying away mud etc. from dredging machine and discharging it through collapsible bottom; railroad freight car with similar device.

Hop·per (hŏp′*er*), **Edward** (1882–1967). Amer. painter.

hop·sack·ing (hŏp′săkĭng) *n.* (Coarse material of hemp and jute for making) sack in which hops are packed; woolen fabric of coarse weave with threads in pairs.

ho·ra (hōr′*a*, hōr′*a*) *n.* Traditional Israeli folk dance done in a circle; music for this dance.

Hor·ace (hōr′ĭs, hăr′-). Quintus Horatius Flaccus (65–8 B.C.), Roman poet; his work includes the *Satires, Odes, Epodes, Epistles,* and *Ars Poetica.* **Ho·ra·tian** (horā′sh*a*n) *adj.*

ho·ra·ry (hōr′*a*rē, hōr′-) *adj.* Of the hours; occurring every hour; lasting an hour.

Ho·ra·tius (horā′sh*u*s). Publius Horatius Cocles, legendary Roman hero famous for defending bridge over Tiber against the Etruscans.

horde (hōrd, hōrd) *n.* Tribe of Tartar or kindred Asiatic nomads, dwelling in tents or wagons and migrating for pasturage or for war or plunder; throng; swarm; gang, troop (usu. contempt.); **Golden H~**: see GOLDEN. [Turki *ordi, ordu* camp]

hore·hound, hoar·hound (hōr′hownd, hōr′-) *ns.* Labiate herb (*Marrubium vulgare*) with stem and leaves covered with white cottony pubescence, and aromatic bitter juice used as remedy for coughs and as a flavoring; hard candy made of this; allied herb.

ho·ri·zon (horī′zon) *n.* 1. Line at which earth and sky appear to meet; (fig.) limit of mental perception, experience, interest, etc.; **apparent, visible ~**, circle of contact with Earth's surface of a cone whose vertex is the observer's eye; **celestial, true ~**, great circle of celestial sphere, plane of which passes through center of Earth and is parallel to that of sensible horizon of a plane. 2. (geol.) Stratum or set of strata characterized by particular features, as fossils etc.

hor·i·zon·tal (hŏrĭzŏn'tal, hăr-) *adj.* Of, at, the horizon; parallel to the plane of this, at right angles to the vertical; level, flat; (of machinery etc.) having its parts working in horizontal direction; (of manufacturers, corporations, etc.) engaged in a single stage of manufacture or distribution of a product (opp. VERTICAL). **hor·i·zon'tal·ly** *adv.* **horizontal** *n.* Horizontal line, plane, etc.

hor·mone (hŏr'mōn) *n.* (physiol.) Substance secreted by a ductless gland or formed in an organ (as insulin in the pancreas, sex hormone in testis and ovary) and carried by the bloodstream to a specific organ it stimulates; similar substance prepared synthetically. **hor·mo·nal** (hŏrmō'nal) *adj.*

horn (hŏrn) *n.* 1. Hard, permanent outgrowth, freq. one of a pair, often curved and pointed, consisting of epidermal sheath about a bony core, on head of cattle, sheep, goats, and other mammals; projection on head of other animals, e.g. tentacle of snail or slug, crest of feathers on horned owl's head etc.; **pull, draw, in one's ~s,** restrain one's ardor, draw back; recant. 2. Substance of which horns consist, article made of this, as powder horn, drinking horn, etc.; **~ of plenty**, cornucopia. 3. Wind instrument orig. made of horn and more or less resembling horn in shape; (esp.) modern brass instrument such as the trumpet and **French ~**, which has an 11-ft. tube coiled in a circle and a system of valves for producing intermediate notes; **basset ~**: see BASSET HORN; **English ~**, large oboe with lower pitch than standard oboe. 4. Funnel- or trumpet-shaped part of early record players etc. for amplifying sound by resonance. 5. Instrument for sounding warning signal. 6. Horn-shaped projection; extremity of moon or other crescent; arm, branch, of bay, river, etc; **on the ~s of a dilemma**, forced to choose between two equally distasteful alternatives. 7. **horn'beam**, any of several related trees and shrubs of the family Betulaceae, including Amer. hornbeam (*Carpinus caroliniana*), having smooth, gray bark and very hard, heavy wood, and hop hornbeam (*Ostrya virginiana*) of eastern N. Amer., having fruit that resembles hops; **horn'bill**, bird (of family Bucerotidae) with hornlike excrescence on bill; **horn-rimmed**, (of eyeglasses) rimmed with horn or tortoise shell. **horn** *v.* Furnish with horns; gore with the horns; **~ in**, (slang) intrude (*on*); **horned owl**: see GREAT HORNED OWL; **horned toad**, lizard (*Phrynosoma*) of western N. Amer. with hornlike projections on its head.

Horn (hŏrn), **Cape.** Headland on an island of Tierra del Fuego, southernmost point of S. Amer.; discovered by the Dutch navigator Schouten in 1616, and named after Hoorn, his birthplace.

horn·blende (hŏrn'blĕnd) *n.* Dark brown, black, or greenish-black mineral, constituent of granite and many rocks, composed chiefly of silica, magnesia, and lime, and occurring in numerous varieties.

hor·net (hŏr'nĭt) *n.* Large insect of wasp family (esp. Eur. *Vespa crabro* and Amer. *V. maculata*), inflicting serious sting.

horn·pipe (hŏrn'pīp) *n.* 1. (hist.) Wind instrument (said to have had bell and mouthpiece of horn). 2. Lively dance, usu. by one person, associated esp. with merrymaking of sailors; music for this.

horn·y (hŏr'nē) *adj.* (**horn·i·er, horn·i·est**). Of, like, horn; abounding in horns; hard as horn, callous; (slang) sexually aroused. **horn'i·ness** *n.*

hor·o·loge (hŏr'olōj, -lŏj, hăr'-)

*A pair of magnificent **horns** characteristic of the Highland bull (below left) raised on Bodmin moor, Cornwall, U.K. Below right: The trumpet-shaped horn used for amplifying sound in early gramophones was also used in some early radios. Facing page: Tibetan musical horns are blown to announce the arrival of the new year in Katmandu.*

*The **hornbeam**, an ornamental tree of the Birch family, is found in Europe, Asia and North America. It has shaggy scaling bark and thin, translucent green leaves with hairy leaf-stalks. The European hop hornbeam, seen here, grows to about 65 ft. and produces a green fruit.*

*The **hornbill** is a tropical bird, conspicuous for its fantastic beak. Most species are forest animals living in trees. The great Indian hornbill measures about 5 ft. in length; the African ground species live mainly on open plains.*

n. Timepiece, dial, clock. **ho·rol'·o·ger** (hörŏl'ojer), **ho·rol'o·gist** *ns.* **ho·rol'o·gy** *n.* Art of measuring time or making clocks. **hor·o·log'·i·cal** *adj.*

hor·o·scope (hŏr'oskōp, hăr'-) *n.* 1. (astrol.) Observation of sky and planets at certain moments, esp. at person's birth, supposed to reveal influence on destiny; zodiacal plan showing disposition of heavens at particular moment. 2. Prediction based on such observation or plan. **hor·o·scop·ic** (hŏr'oskŏp'ĭk, -skō'pĭk, hăr-) *adj.* **ho·ros·co·py** (horŏs'kopē) *n.*

hor·ri·ble (hŏr'ibel, hăr'-) *adj.* Exciting, fit to excite, horror; hideous, shocking; unpleasant; offensive. **hor'ri·ble·ness** *n.* **hor'ri·bly** *adv.*

hor·rid (hŏr'ĭd, hăr'-) *adj.* Terrible, frightful; (poet., archaic) rough, bristling; unpleasant, very bad, objectionable. **hor'rid·ly** *adv.* **hor'rid·ness** *n.*

hor·ri·fy (hŏr'ifī, hăr'-) *v.t.* (**-fied, -fy·ing**). Excite horror in; shock; scandalize. **hor·rif·ic** (horĭf'ĭk) *adj.*

hor·ror (hŏr'er, hăr'-) *n.* Terrified shuddering; terror, fear; intense dislike (*of*); horrifying thing; **the ~s**, fit of horror or depression, esp. as in delirium tremens; **~-struck, -stricken,** shocked, horrified.

hors de com·bat (ŏr de kawṅbah'). Out of the fight.

hors d'oeu·vre (ŏr dĕrv'; *Fr.* ŏr dö'vre) (pl. **hors d'oeu·vres** pr. ŏr dĕrvz'; *Fr.* ŏr dö'vre). Canapé or appetizer served with cocktails or before a meal. [Fr.]

horse (hŏrs) *n.* (pl. **hors·es**, collect. **horse**). 1. Solid-hoofed quadruped (*Equus cabullus*) with flowing mane and tail, used as beast of burden, as draft animal, and for riding on; (esp.) adult male horse; (collect. sing.) cavalry; **hold one's ~s**, (slang) check one's impatience; **~ of a different color**, completely different thing; **on one's high ~**, putting on airs; behaving arrogantly; **on horse'back**, mounted on a horse; **straight from the horse's mouth**, (of information) from authoritative source, esp. from person concerned. 2. Upholstered vaulting block in gymnasium; frame, often with legs, on which something is supported, as **clothes'horse**; (mining) obstruction in vein. 3. **horse chestnut**, large ornamental tree (*Aesculus hippocastanum*), native to Albania, Greece, and Iran, with large digitate leaves, upright conical clusters of showy flowers, and fruit consisting of soft thick prickly husk enclosing one or two large hard smooth shining brown seeds of bitter taste; nut of this; **horse'-feathers,** (slang) something utterly insignificant; **horse'flesh**, flesh of horse, esp. as food; horses collectively, esp. racing or riding horses; **horse'fly**, any of various large flies of the family Tabanidae, the female of which sucks the blood of certain mammals; (fig.) any large variety of fly; **horse'hair**, hair from mane or tail of horse, esp. as used in upholstery; **horse'hide,** hide of a horse, leather made from this; **horse latitudes,** belt of calms at N. and S. edges of trade winds; **horse'laugh**, loud coarse laugh; **horse'leech**, large European leech (*Haemopsis sanguisuga*); **horse mackerel**, any of various fishes allied to mackerel, esp. the bluefin tuna (*Thunnus thynnus*); **horse'-**

man, horse′woman, (skilled) rider on horseback; horse breeder or trainer; owner of racing stable; **horse′manship**, art of riding, skill in riding, on horseback; **horse opera**, (slang) motion picture or play with a western U.S. setting and dealing with cowboys, Indians, land claim fights, cattle rustling, etc.; **horse′play**, rough or boisterous play; **horse′power**, (abbrev. h.p.) unit of power of 33,000 foot-pounds per minute or 745.7 watts; **horse race**, race between horses (with riders); (fig.) contest between equally matched opponents; **horse′radish**, cruciferous plant (*Armoracia rusticana*) with white flowers and broad rough leaves, whose pungent root is scraped or grated as condiment; **horse sense**, (colloq.) common sense; **horse′-shoe**, iron shoe for horse, usu. narrow iron plate bent to outline of horse's hoof; thing of this shape; (pl.) game in which horseshoes are tossed at a stake, the player encircling the stake most often with a shoe or coming closest to it being the winner; **horseshoe crab**, any of various horseshoe-shaped marine animals of eastern N. Amer., esp of the genus *Limulus*, having a long, stiff tail; **horse′tail**, tail of horse (formerly used in Turkey as standard, or as ensign denoting rank of pasha); cryptogamous plant (*Equisetum*) with hollow jointed stem and whorls of slender branches at joints; **horse′-whip**, whip for horse; (*v.t.*) chastise (person) with this; **horse′woman**: see horseman above. **horse** *v.* (**horsed, hors·ing**). Provide (person, vehicle) with horse(s); mount, ride a horse; (slang) ~ **around**, indulge in horseplay.

hors·y, hors·ey (hōr′sē) *adjs.* (**hors·i·er, hors·i·est**). Concerned with, addicted to, horse, horse-racing, or horseback riding.

hor·ta·tive (hōr′tatĭv), **hor·ta·to·ry** (hōr′tatōrē, -tōrē) *adjs.* Tending, serving, to exhort.

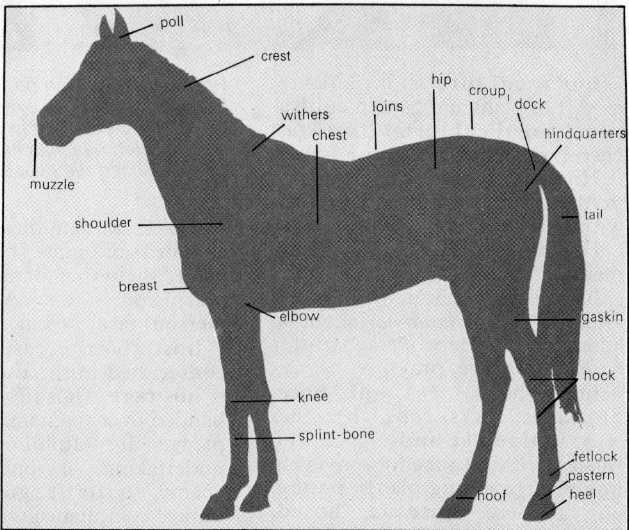

*The **horse** has been domesticated since prehistoric times, and has been used as a beast of burden, a draught animal and for riding. Above left: A dapple-grey horse. Above right: The parts of a horse. Below, left to right: Przewalski and Tarpan, earliest surviving forms of horse; and the Shire horse.*

Horus, the Egyptian god of light, had a hawk's head and his eyes were the sun and moon. According to Egyptian mythology his left eye was injured in a fight. This explained the phases of the moon.

These hounds, from the Duke of Bedford's Hunt in Wilts, U.K., are specially bred for fox-hunting — a popular sport in the 19th century and one which still flourishes today.

hor·ti·cul·ture (hŏr′tĭkŭlcher) *n.* Art of plant and garden cultivation. **hor·ti·cul·tur·al** (hŏrtĭkŭl′-cheral) *adj.* **hor·ti·cul′tur·ist** *n.*

Ho·rus (hōr′us, hŏr′-). (Egyptian myth.) God of light, represented with hawk's head.

Hos. *abbrev.* Hosea (Old Testament).

ho·san·na (hōzăn′a) *n.* (pl. **-nas**). Cry of *hosanna*, shout of adoration. [Heb. *hosha'na*, for *hoshi'ahnna* save, pray!]

hose (hōz) *n.* 1. (pl. **hose**) Stockings; socks; (obs.) breeches (esp. in **doublet and ~**). 2. (pl. **hos·es**) Flexible tube for conveying liquid for watering plants, putting out fires, etc. **hose** *v.t.* (**hosed, hos·ing**). Drench or water with hose.

Ho·se·a (hōzē′a) (8th c. B.C.). Hebrew minor prophet; book of Old Testament containing his prophecies.

ho·sier (hō′zher) *n.* Dealer in hose and knitted or woven underwear. **ho′sier·y** *n.* (esp.) Stockings and socks.

hos·pice (hŏs′pĭs) *n.* House of rest for travelers, esp. one kept by religious order; home for the destitute or sick, esp. terminally ill.

hos·pi·ta·ble (hŏs′pĭtabel, hŏspĭt′a-) *adj.* Giving, disposed to give, welcome and entertainment to strangers or guests. **hos′pi·ta·bly** *adv.*

hos·pi·tal (hŏs′pĭtal) *n.* Institution for care of the sick or wounded; **~ ship, train,** one equipped for transporting the sick or wounded.

hos·pi·tal·i·ty (hŏspĭtăl′ĭtē) *n.* (pl. **-ties**). Friendly and liberal reception of guests or strangers.

hos·pi·tal·ize (hŏs′pĭtalīz) *v.t.* (**-ized, -iz·ing**). Put (sick or injured person) into a hospital.

host[1] (hōst) *n.* Large number (*of*); (archaic) army: **Lord (God) of ~s**, frequent title of Jehovah in some Old Testament books.

host[2] (hōst) *n.* One who lodges and entertains another in his house; landlord of inn; (biol.) animal, plant, sheltering parasite or other organism. **~** *v.t.* Act as host to (person) or at (event).

host[3] (hōst) *n.* (usu. cap.) Bread consecrated in the Eucharist.

hos·tage (hŏs′tĭj) *n.* Person handed over to enemies or allies as pledge for fulfillment of any undertaking or one seized by enemy, terrorist group, etc. to induce compliance with demands.

hos·tel (hŏs′tel) *n.* Inn (archaic); inexpensive lodging for youthful travelers or other special class, YOUTH hostel.

hos·tel·ry (hŏs′telrē) *n.* (pl. **-ries**). (archaic) Inn.

host·ess (hōs′tĭs) *n.* Woman who entertains guests; one who receives or assists clients or visitors.

hos·tile (hŏs′tĭl; *Brit.* hŏs′tīl) *adj.* Of an enemy; unfriendly; opposed; **~ witness**, one who shows that he is hostile to the party calling him and is considered not to give his evidence fairly. **hostile** *n.* Hostile person, esp. N. Amer. Indian of late 19th century resisting establishment of tribal reservations. **hos′tile·ly** *adv.* **hos·til·i·ty** (hŏstĭl′ĭtē) *n.* (pl. **-ties**). Enmity; state of warfare; opposition; (pl.) acts of warfare; war.

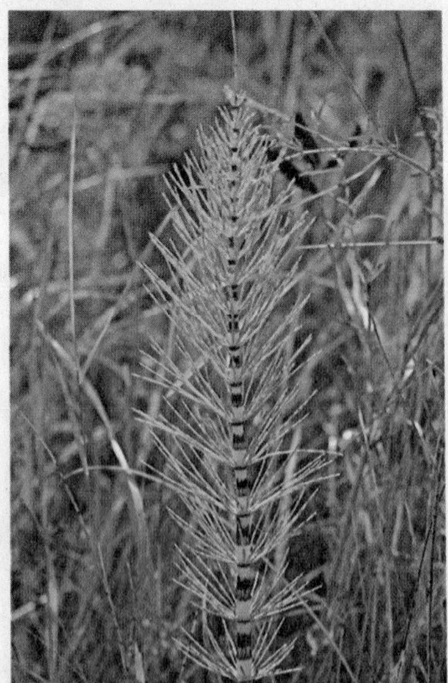

The horsetail, a rush-like plant, grows in rich moist soils in all parts of the world except Australasia. This European giant horsetail reaches well over 3½ ft. in height.

hos·tler (hŏs′ler, ŏs′-) *n.* Person who takes care of horses at an inn, stable, etc.; stableman.

hot (hŏt) *adj.* (**hot·ter, hot·test**). 1. Of a high temperature; very warm; communicating or feeling heat; producing the sensation of heat; (of pepper etc.) pungent, biting. 2. Ardent, passionate; angry; (sexually excited) exciting; (of dance music) performed with vigor, virtuosity, and excitement. 3. (hunting, of scent) Strong; (fig., of news etc.) fresh, recent; (slang, of stolen items) recently stolen or easily identifiable and so dangerous to possess. 4. **~ air,** (slang) excited or boastful talk; **hot′bed**, bed of earth heated by fermenting manure; (fig.) place very favorable to growth *of* (vice, unpopular ideas, etc.); **hot-blooded,** (fig.) ardent, passionate; **hot′box,** bearing on an axle or shaft of a railroad car overheated by too much friction; **hot′cake(s),** pan- or griddlecakes, (**sell like hot cakes,** be disposed of rapidly); **hot dog,** frankfurter or frankfurter sandwich, usu. on a soft roll; (colloq.) an exclamation of satisfaction or enthusiasm; **hot flash**, feeling of a wave of heat passing over the body, often experienced by women shortly before and during menopause; **hot'foot**, insertion and lighting of a match between the sole and upper of an unsuspecting person's shoe as a practical joke; in hot haste; **hot'head**, impetuous person; **hot'house**, heated building with glass roof and sides for growing plants out of season or in colder climate; **hot line**, direct channel of telephone or teletype communication for use by heads of government in times of crisis or emergency, specif., the U.S.–U.S.S.R. line established in 1963; **hot plate**, heated metal plate, portable heater, for cooking etc.; **hot potato**, (colloq.) thing awkward to deal with; **hot-press**, press of glazed boards and hot metal plates for smoothing paper or cloth; (*v.t.*) press (paper etc.) in this; **hot rod**, (slang) automobile, often an old one, whose engine has been modified to give extra power and speed; hence **hot-rodder**, one who drives such an automobile; **hot seat**, (slang) electric chair, (fig.) embarrassing or difficult situation; **hot'shot**, (slang) person who is or thinks he is very skillful, talented, important, etc.; **hot water**, (fig.) trouble, disgrace, scrape; **hot-water bottle**, bag (usu. rubber) for holding hot water to apply warmth esp. to the body. **hot'ly** *adv.* **hot'ness** *n.* **hot** *adv.* Hotly, eagerly, angrily. ~ *v.t.* (colloq.) Heat, warm *up*.

hotch·potch: see HODGEPODGE.

ho·tel (hōtĕl') *n.* Commercial establishment providing lodging to the general public, esp. travelers and chiefly for short stays at daily rates.

Hot (hŏt) **Springs.** City and resort in W. central Arkansas, famous for its thermal mineral springs; located within **Hot Springs National Park.**

Hot·ten·tot (hŏt'entŏt) *n.* Member of short stocky people of SW. Africa, related to Bushmen; their language; ~ **fig**, fleshy-leaved South African plant, *Mesembryanthemum edule*, with edible pulpy fruit. [Du., perh. = "stammerer"]

hound (hownd) *n.* Dog for chase, esp. one hunting by scent, of various breeds, as **blood'hound, grey'hound**, etc.; (colloq.) any dog; (slang) enthusiast (in combination, as *photography hound, coffee hound*, etc.); **the hounds**, pack of foxhounds; **hound's-tooth check**, check pattern with reversed diagonal threads giving notched effect. **hound** *v.t.* Chase (as) with hound; urge (person) *on*.

hour (owr) *n.* 1. Twenty-fourth part of day, 60 minutes; appointed or customary time; occasion; time of occupation or duty; time of day; habitual time of getting up or going to bed. 2. Prayer or office to be said at one of seven stated times of day. 3. **hour'glass**, device for measuring intervals of time, consisting of wasp-waisted reversible glass with two bulbs containing sand that takes a definite time in passing from upper to lower bulb, now practically obsolete except for measuring time required to boil an egg; **hour hand**, hand on clock etc. showing hour.

hou·ri (hoor'ē, howr'ē) *n.* (pl. **-ris**). Nymph of Muslim paradise; voluptuously beautiful woman.

__Houses__ in primitive societies make use of local, natural materials and are designed to suit not only the climate but also the community's social structure. These mud and straw-thatched houses are in Mali.

[Fr., f. Pers., f. Arab. *hūr* gazelle-like (in the eyes)]

hour·ly (owr´lē) *adj.* & *adv.* (Occurring, done, reckoned) every hour.

Hou·sa·ton·ic (hoosatŏn´ĭk). River, 148 mi. (238 km), flowing from NW. Massachusetts through Connecticut into Long Island Sound.

house (hows) *n.* (pl. **hous·es** pr. how´zĭz). 1. Building for human habitation or (usu. with defining prefix) occupation; inn, tavern; building for keeping animals or goods; (place of abode of) religious fraternity; (esp. Brit.) college in university; (boys in) boardinghouse forming part of school; (building used by) legislative or deliberative assembly; (audience in) theater etc.; household; family, dynasty; mercantile firm; **the House**, (pol.) House of Representatives; **on the house**, given by the management, free. 2. (transf.) Habitation of any animal; shell of snail, tortoise, etc., in which the animal lives or into which it retires. 3. (astrol.) Twelfth part of heavens as divided by great circles through N. and S. points of horizon; sign of zodiac considered as seat of greatest influence of a particular planet. 4. **keep house**, maintain, manage affairs of, a household; **like a house on fire, afire**, vigorously, fast; **house of cards**, house built of playing cards; (fig.) insecure thing; **house of God**, church, place of worship; **house of ill fame, ill repute**, brothel; **house-to-house**, carried on by means of visits to every house in a neighborhood. 5. attrib. (of animals) Kept in, frequenting, infesting, the house. 6. **house arrest**, detention in one's house, not in prison; **house´boat**, barge-like boat fitted up for living in; **house´boy**, boy or man as servant in house; **house´breaker**, burglar; **house´breaking**, burglary; **house´broken**, (of pets) trained not to excrete indoors; **house´coat**, woman's garment worn indoors as dressing gown or instead of a dress; **house´fly**, common fly, *Musca domestica*, infesting houses; **house´keeper**, woman managing affairs of household; person in charge of house, hotel maids, linens, etc.; **house´keeping**, domestic economy; **house´leek**, succulent herb (*Sempervivum tectorum*) with pink flowers, thick stem, and dense rosette of leaves close to root, growing on walls and roofs; hen and chickens; **house´maid**, female servant serving as maid; **housemaid's knee**, inflammation of the bursa over the kneecap due to kneeling, as from washing floors; **house´master**, master in charge of school boarding house; **house´mother**, woman in charge of a house, esp. of

*The Navajo Indians built **houses** that belied their semi-nomadic existence. They are unusual in that, unlike the homes of most wandering people, they are quite strong and permanent. They are also adapted to the hot, dry climate.*

home for orphaned etc. children; **house organ**, periodical or newsletter issued by company for employees or customers; **house party**, party of guests staying overnight or for several days; **house physician**, physician residing in hospital; **house sparrow**, small brown and gray bird (*Passer domesticus*), originally of Europe but introduced into Amer. and other parts of the world, where it readily adapted; English sparrow; **house surgeon**, surgeon residing in hospital; **house´top**, roof (esp. in **shout from the housetops**, give wide publicity to); **house´warming**, party to celebrate moving into new house; **house´work**, domestic work. **house** (howz) *v.* (**housed, hous·ing**). 1. Lodge, shelter (person etc.), store (goods), in house or as house does. 2. Provide houses for (population).

house·hold (hows´hōld) *n.* Those who live under the same roof, as a family etc.; domestic establishment; royal household; ~ **gods**, (Rom. antiq.) lares and penates; ~ **word**, familiar saying or name. **house´holder** *n.* One who occupies house as his own dwelling (esp. formerly, one thus qualified for franchise); head of household.

house·wife (hows´wīf) *n.* (pl. **-wives** pr. -wīvz). Mistress of family; married woman who supervises a household. **house´wife·ly** *adv.* **house´wif·er·y** *n.* Housekeeping; domestic economy.

hous·ing[1] (how´zĭng) *n.* (esp.) (Provision of) accommodation, houses collectively; shelter, covering; socket, casing.

hous·ing[2] (how´zĭng) *n.* Horse's or saddle's cloth covering for protection or ornament.

Hous·man (hows´m*a*n, howz´-), **A(lfred) E(dward)** (1859–1936). English classical scholar and lyric poet; author of "A Shropshire Lad" etc.

Hous·ton[1] (hūs´t*o*n). Largest city of Texas, in the SE. part; connected with Gulf of Mexico by Houston Ship Channel; a leading oil and petrochemical center.

Hous·ton[2] (hūs´t*o*n), **Sam(uel)** (1793–1863). Amer. soldier and statesman; commander in chief of Texan army in fight for independence from Mexico; defeated Santa Ana at San Jacinto, 1836; first president of Republic of Texas, 1836–8, and president again 1841–4; became senator and then governor after Texas was admitted to Union, but was deposed when he refused to support the Confederacy.

Hou·yhn·hnm (hoōĭn´ĭm, hwĭn´-, wĭn´-) *n.* One of the civilized talking horses in *Gulliver's Travels*, by Jonathan Swift. [imit. of horse's neigh]

hove: see HEAVE.

hov·el (hŭv´*e*l, hŏv´-) *n.* Open shed, mean dwelling.

hov·er (hŭv´*e*r, hŏv´-) *v.* (of

bird etc.) Hang in the air (*over*, *about*, spot); loiter *about* (person, place). ~ *n.* Hovering, state of suspense.

hov·er·craft (hŭv′*er*krăft, -krahft) *n.* Vehicle that travels over land or water on a cushion of compressed air provided by a downward blast.

how (how) *adv.* In what way; to what extent; (in indirect statement, rhet. for) that; (in relative clause) in whatever way, as; ~ **are you?**, ~ **do you do?**, what is your state of health? (freq. as form of greeting); ~ **come?**, (colloq.) why?; **here's** ~!, I drink to your good health; ~ **about?**, what about? how come?; ~ **now?**, (archaic) what is the meaning of this?; **that's a fine** ~**-d'ye'-do**, (colloq.) embarrassing situation; ~ **'sthat?** what did you say?; can you explain?; **howev'er**, in whatever way; to whatever extent; nevertheless; (archaic) in any case; **howsoev'er**, in whatsoever manner; to what extent soever; **how-to** (*adj.*), giving basic instruction in carpentry, electrical wiring, plumbing, etc., and in handicrafts.

how·dah (how′d*a*) *n.* Seat for two or more, usu. with canopy, on elephant's back. [Arab. *hawdaj* litter]

Howe (how), **Elias** (1819–67). Amer. inventor of the sewing machine, etc.

Howe (how), **Julia Ward** (1819–1910). Editor, writer, and social reformer; wrote poem "The Battle Hymn of the Republic," 1862, later set to music; supported women's suffrage, prison reform, and international peace.

How·ells (how′*e*lz), **William Dean** (1837–1920). Amer. writer, editor, and critic; editor of the *Atlantic Monthly*, 1871–81; author

1 forward car ramp
2 flexible skirt
3 skirt fingers
4 forward passenger compartment
5 12-blade lift fan
6 air intakes
7 extension shaft from turbine
8 main bevel drive gear-box
9 propeller gear-box
10 HS Dynamics propeller
11 air-conditioning packs
12 main passenger compartment
13 baggage racks
14 door to car deck
15 passenger entrance door
16 engine intakes
17 acoustic baffles
18 Marine Proteus gas-turbine
19 pylon
20 fin
21 car deck
22 rear car ramp
23 hatch to auxiliary power unit
24 crew entry ladder
25 control deck

*This British **Hovercraft** Corporation SR-N4 (bottom) weighs over 160 tons and is in regular use on cross-Channel runs. Below: Four rear-mounted gas-turbine engines each drive one lift fan and one propeller which are geared together. Air is drawn in through intakes on the top decking and bleeds into the tubular skirt and fingers to form a stable air-cushion.*

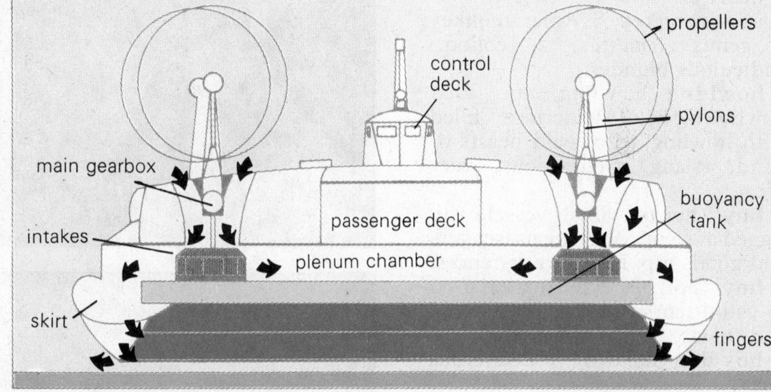

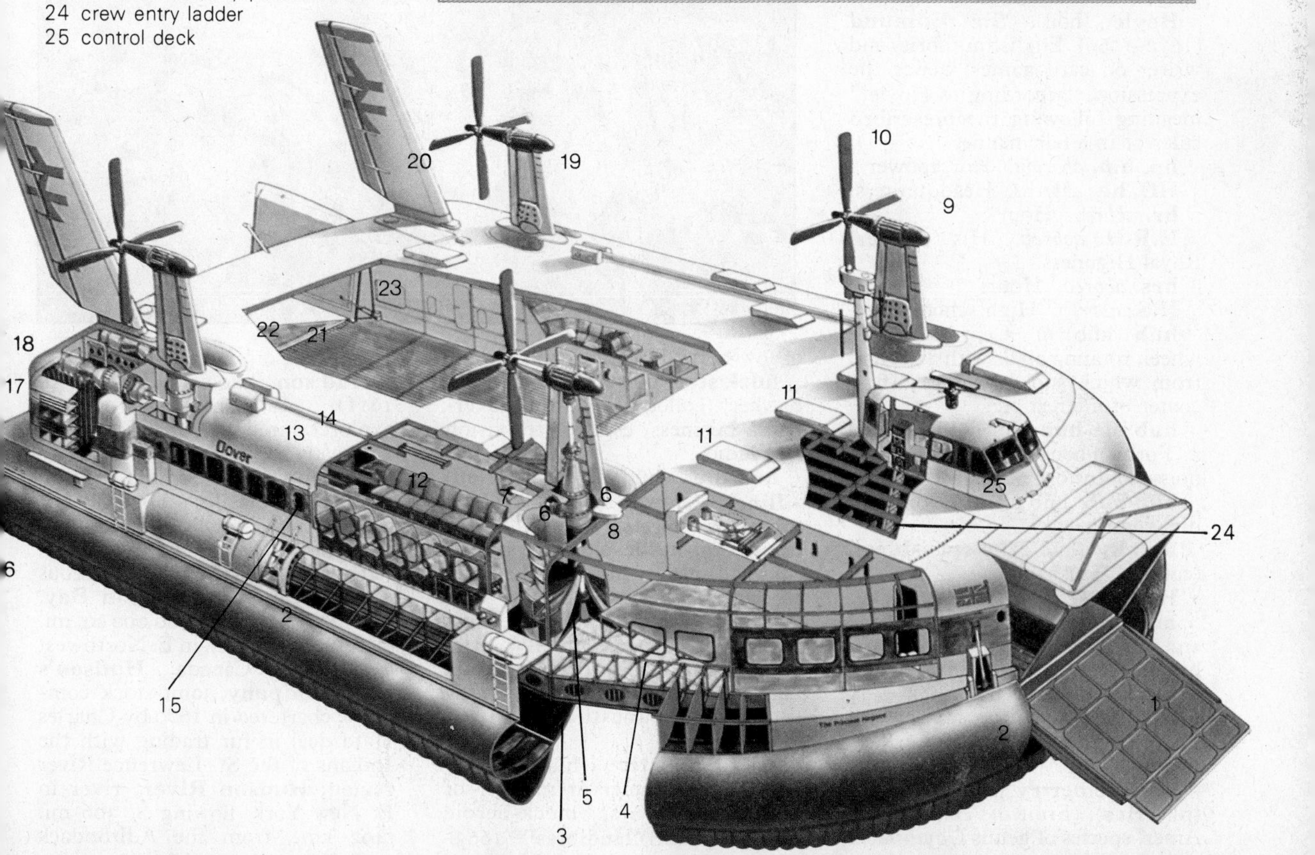

*The voyages of the English navigator **Henry Hudson** resulted in a much more accurate knowledge of North Atlantic coasts. His aim had been to find a north-west sea passage between the North Atlantic and North Pacific Oceans. In 1611, his crew mutinied and he was cast adrift to die (right).*

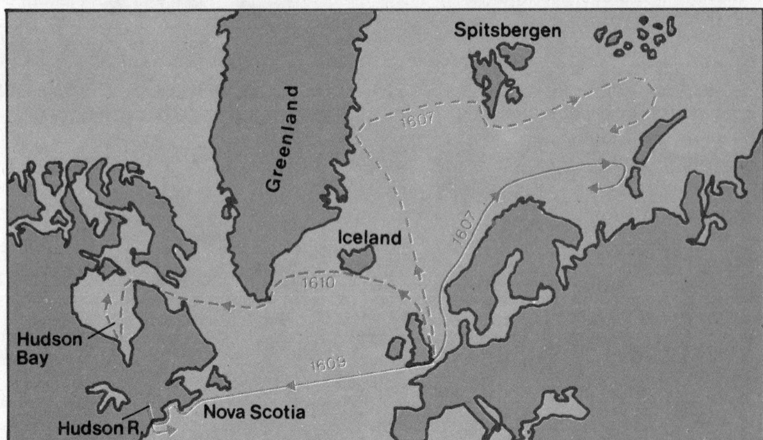

of *The Rise of Silas Lapham.*

how·itz·er (how'ĭts*e*r) *n.* Short gun for high-angle firing of shells at low velocities. [Ger. *haubitze*, f. Czech *houfnice* catapult]

howl (howl) *v.* (of animals) Utter long loud doleful cry; (of persons) utter long cry of pain, derision, etc.; utter (words) with howling; (of radio receiver) make howl. ~ *n.* Long doleful cry of dog, wolf, etc.; loud cry of pain; yell of derision; loud noise like animal's howl in radio receiver, usu. due to low-frequency oscillation.

howl·er (how'l*e*r) *n.* (esp.) 1. (also ~ **monkey**) S. Amer. monkey of genus *Alouatta*. 2. (colloq.) Ridiculous blunder.

howl·ing (how'lĭng) *adj.* That howls; (bibl., of wilderness) filled with howling, as of wild beasts or wind; (slang) tremendous, very great.

hoy[1] (hoi) *n.* Small vessel, usu. rigged as sloop, carrying passengers and goods esp. for short distances.

hoy[2] (hoi) *int.* Exclamation used to call attention, drive beasts etc., and (naut.) hail or call aloft.

hoy·den (hoi'd*e*n) *n.* Boisterous girl.

Hoyle (hoil), **Sir Edmund** (1672–1769). English authority and writer on card games; hence the expression, "according to Hoyle," meaning following the prescribed rules or in a fair manner.

hp, h.p. *abbrevs.* Horsepower.

HQ, hq. *abbrevs.* Headquarters.

hr. *abbrev.* Hour.

H.R.H. *abbrev.* His (or Her) Royal Highness.

hrs. *abbrev.* Hours.

H.S. *abbrev.* High school.

hub (hŭb) *n.* Central part of wheel, rotating on or with axle, and from which spokes radiate; (fig.) center of interest etc.

hub·ble-bub·ble (hŭb'*e*l bŭb*e*l) *n.* Form of hookah; bubbling noise; noisy confusion, hubbub.

hub·bub (hŭb'ŭb) *n.* Confused din; tumult.

hub·by (hŭb'ē) *n.* (pl. **-bies**). (colloq.) Husband.

Hu·bei: see HUPEH.

hu·bris (hū'brĭs, hōō'-) *n.* Pride and insolence. **hu·bris·tic** (hūbrĭs'tĭk, hōō-) *adj.* [Gk.]

huck·a·back (hŭk'*a*băk) *n.* Stout linen or cotton fabric with figured weave and rough surface, for towels etc.

huck·le·ber·ry (hŭk'*e*lbĕrē) *n.* (pl. **-ries**). (Fruit of) common N. Amer. species of genus *Gaylussacia* of low berry-bearing shrubs.

huck·ster (huk'st*e*r) *n.* Peddler, hawker; (colloq.) person in advertising business, esp. for television and radio.

hud·dle (hŭd'*e*l) *v.* (**-dled, -dling**). Crowd (things etc.) promiscuously *together, into*, etc.; coil *oneself up*; nestle closely *together*; (football) gather in a huddle; meet to confer or consult. ~ *n.* Confused array; jumble; densely packed group; (football) brief gathering of team around quarterback to discuss plans, signals, etc.; consultation, discussion; **go into a** ~, confer.

Hu·di·bras·tic (hūd*i*brăs'tĭk) *adj.* In the meter or manner of Samuel Butler's mock-heroic satirical poem "Hudibras" (1663–1678).

Hud·son (hŭd's*o*n), **Henry** (d. 1611). English navigator and explorer; hired by Dutch East India Company to find a NE. passage to the Orient; discovered the Hudson River, 1609, sailing his ship the *Half Moon* as far as Albany; later reached **Hudson Bay**, Canada, 1610–11; set adrift by his mutinous crew to die, 1611; **Hudson Bay**, inland sea, covering 480,000 sq. mi. (1,243,000 sq. km), in E. Northwest Territories, Canada; **Hudson's Bay Company**, joint-stock company, chartered in 1670 by Charles II to deal in fur trading with the Indians of the St. Lawrence River region; **Hudson River**, river in E. New York, flowing S. 306 mi. (492 km), from the Adirondack

Mountains to its mouth at New York City on Upper New York Bay, where it forms the boundary between New York and New Jersey; **Hudson Strait**, strait extending 450 mi. (724 km), in NE. Canada and connecting Hudson Bay to the Atlantic Ocean; navigated by Hudson, 1607–11.

hue[1] (hū) *n.* Color, tint; variety of color caused by mixture with another; **hued** *adj.*

hue[2] (hū) *n.* ~ **and cry**, clamor of pursuit or assault; outcry (*against*); proclamation for capture of criminal.

huff (hŭf) *v.* (archaic) Bully, bluster; anger; take offense; puff, blow; inflate. ~ *n.* Fit of petulance or offended dignity. **huff'ish** *adj.* **huff'ish·ly** *adv.* **huff'ish·ness** *n.*

hug (hŭg) *v.t.* (**hugged, hug·ging**). Squeeze closely in one's arms, usu. with affection; (of bear) squeeze between its forelegs; delight in, cling to (prejudices etc.); keep close to (shore etc.); **~-me-tight**, woman's close-fitting knitted woolen sleeveless jacket. **hug** *n.* Strong clasp with the arms.

huge (hūj, ūj) *adv.* Very large; (of immaterial things) great. **huge'ness** *n.* **huge'ly** *adv.*

Hughes[1] (hūz), **Charles Evans** (1862–1948). Amer. jurist and statesman; governor of New York, 1907–10; associate justice of the U.S. Supreme Court, 1910–16; secretary of State, 1921–5; member of the Hague Tribunal, 1926–30; chief justice of U.S. Supreme Court, 1930–41.

Hughes[2] (hūz), **(James) Langston** (1902–67). Amer. poet and writer about black life in America.

Hu·go (hū'gō; *Fr.* ügō'), **Victor-Marie** (1802–85). French poet, novelist, and dramatist; leader of the French Romantic movement; author of *La Légende des Siècles*, of the dramas *Ruy Blas, Hernani*, etc., and the novels *Notre Dame de Paris, Les Misérables*, etc.

Hu·gue·not (hū'genŏt) *n.* French Protestant, member of the Calvinistic or Reformed communion of France whose liberty of worship, at first denied, was defined in the Edict of Nantes (1598) and again withdrawn when the Edict was revoked (1685) by Louis XIV; to escape persecution many Huguenots then emigrated to Protestant countries, esp. England and America. [assimilation of Swiss Ger. *eidgenoss* (= confederate) to name of Geneva burgomaster *Hugues*]

hu·la (hōō'la) *n.* (also **hula-hula**) Undulating Polynesian dance pantomiming a story; rhythmic drumbeats, chants, and other music for this dance.

hulk (hŭlk) *n.* Body of dismantled, wrecked, or old ship; (hist.) this used as a warehouse or prison; unwieldy vessel; (fig.) big or clumsy person; large, awkward object. **hulk'ing** *adj.* Bulky; clumsy.

Hull (hŭl), **Cordell** (1871–1955). Amer. statesman and diplomat; U.S. secretary of State under President F. D. Roosevelt, 1933–44; awarded Nobel Prize for peace, 1945.

hull[1] (hŭl) *n.* Outer covering of fruit, esp. pod of peas and beans; (fig.) covering. ~ *v.t.* Remove hull of.

hull[2] (hul) *n.* Frame of ship.

hul·la·ba·loo (hŭl'abalōō) *n.* (pl. **-loos**). Uproar.

Hu·lun Nor (hōō'lōōn nōr'). Largest lake in Manchuria, NE. China; 35 mi. (56 km) long, and 5 mi. (8 km) wide.

hum[1] (hŭm) *v.* (**hummed, hum·ming**). Make continuous low-pitched sound, as of bee, spinning top, machinery, etc.; sing with closed lips; (colloq.) be in state of activity or bustle. ~ *n.* Humming sound.

hum[2] (hum) *int.* Exclamation expressing hesitation, dissent, etc.

hu·man (hū'man, ū'-) *adj.* Of, belonging to, man (= MAN *n.* def. 1); that is a person or consists of people; of man as opp. to God; having, showing, qualities distinctive of man; ~ **rights**, basic rights of citizens of a nation to express opinions, hold jobs, move about freely, etc., within reason, and esp. freedom to disagree with the government. **human** *n.* Human being.

hu·mane (hūmān', ū-) *adj.* Benevolent, compassionate; of or promoting human qualities of mercy, kindness, etc.; civilizing, refining. **hu·mane'ly** *adv.* **hu·mane'ness** *n.*

hu·man·ism (hū'manĭzem, ū'-) *n.* 1. Devotion to human interests. 2. (often cap.) Literary culture, esp. that of the Humanists. 3. Any of various philosophies concerned with human (not divine or supernatural) matters, or with the human race (not the individual), or with

*A ship's **hull** was made of wood until the 19th century when steel was developed. Repairs to the hull are usually carried out in dry docks or floating docks. The giant liner QE2 is seen here in dry dock.*

man as a responsible and progressive intellectual being. **hu'man·ist** *n.* 1. Student of human nature or human affairs; one versed in the humanities. 2. **H**~, one of the scholars who at the revival of learning in 14th–16th centuries devoted themselves to study of language, literature, and antiquities of Greece and Rome; later disciple of same culture. 3. Adherent of humanism (3). **hu·man·is·tic** (hūmanĭs'tĭk, ū-) *adj.*

hu·man·i·tar·i·an (hūmănĭtār'ēan, ū-) *n.* One who holds that man's duty consists in advancement of welfare of human race; one who devotes himself to welfare of mankind at large, philanthropist. ~ *adj.* Holding, concerned with, views of humanitarians. **hu·man·i·tar'i·an·ism** *n.*

hu·man·i·ty (hūmăn'ĭtē, ū-) *n.* (for def. 4 pl. **-ties**). 1. Human nature; (pl.) human attributes. 2. Human race; human beings collectively. 3. Humaneness, benevolence. 4. (pl.) Learning concerned with human culture, as literature, the arts, philosophy, etc., esp. as opposed to natural and social sciences.

hu·man·ize (hū'manīz, ū'-) *v.* (**-ized, -iz·ing**). 1. Make human, give human character to. 2. Make, become, humane.

hu·man·kind (hū'mankīnd, ū'-) *n.* Mankind.

hu·man·ly (hū'manlē, ū'-) *adv.* In a human manner; by human means; from human point of view; with human feeling.

hum·ble (hŭm'bel) *adj.* (**-bler, -blest**). Having, showing, low estimate of one's own importance; lowly condition; of modest pretensions, dimensions, etc.; **eat ~ pie**, make humble apology, submit to humiliation. **humble** *v.t.* (**-bled, -bling**). Make humble; bring low, abase. **hum'bly** *adv.* **hum'ble·ness** *n.*

Hum·boldt (hŭm'bōlt; *Ger.* hoom'bawlt), **Friedrich Heinrich Alexander von** (1769–1859). German author of the *Kosmos*, a physical description of the universe; naturalist, traveler, and statesman; explored in S. Amer. and Asia; **Humboldt** (hŭm'bōlt) **Current**, cold Pacific Ocean current flowing N. along the coast of Chile and Peru to S. Ecuador.

hum·bug (hŭm'bŭg) *n.* Sham, deception; imposter; nonsense, rubbish. ~ *v.* (**-bugged, -bug·ging**). Delude, trick (person); be, behave like, a humbug.

hum·drum (hŭm'drŭm) *adj.* & *n.* Commonplace(ness); dull(ness).

Hume (hūm), **David** (1711–76). Scottish philosopher and historian; author of *Treatise of Human Nature* and *Enquiry Concerning Human Understanding*; in his system of philosophical skepticism, human knowledge is restricted to experience of ideas and impressions, and ultimate verification of their truth or falsehood is impossible.

hu·mer·us (hū'merus) *n.* (pl. **-mer·i** pr. -merī'). Bone of upper arm in man; corresponding bone in other vertebrates. **hu'mer·al** *adj.*

hu·mid (hū'mĭd) *adj.* Moist, damp; (of air) containing much water or water vapor. **hu·mid'i·fy** *v.t.* (**-fied, -fy·ing**). **hu·mid'i·ty** *n.* Moisture, dampness; degree of moisture, esp. in atmosphere; **absolute** ~, amount of water vapor in a given volume of air (usu. in grams per cubic meter); **relative** ~, ratio between the amount actually present and the amount that would be present if the air were saturated at the same temperature.

*Many animals have developed ways of storing food for scarce times. In some animals, such as bison and camels, this storage system manifests itself as a characteristic **hump** on the animal's back.*

hu·mi·dor (hū'mĭdōr) *n.* Container for keeping cigars or tobacco moist.

hu·mil·i·ate (hūmĭl'ēāt, ū-) *v.t.* (**-at·ed, -at·ing**). Lower the dignity or self-respect of; mortify. **hu·mil'i·at·ing** *adj.* **hu·mil·i·a·tion** (hūmĭlēā'shōn, ū-) *n.*

hu·mil·i·ty (hūmĭl'ĭtē, ū-) *n.* Humbleness, meekness.

hum·ming (hŭm'ĭng) *adj.* That hums; **hum'mingbird**, any bird of Amer. (chiefly tropical) family Trochilidae, of very small size, and usu. brilliantly colored, making humming sound by rapid vibration of wings; all species feed while hovering and can fly backward.

hum·mock (hŭm'ok) *n.* Hillock, knoll; rising ground, esp. in marsh; hump or ridge of ice in ice field. **hum'mock·y** *adj.*

hu·mor, Brit. **hu·mour** (hū'mer) *ns.* 1. State of mind, mood; inclination; **out of** ~, displeased. 2. Faculty of perceiving the ludicrous; jocose imagination (less intellectual but more sympathetic than WIT[1]); comicality; facetiousness. 3. (physiol.) Transparent fluid or semifluid substance, esp. **aqueous** ~, between lens of eye and cornea, and **vitreous** ~, within eyeball. 4. (hist.) In ancient and medieval physiology, one of four chief fluids of the body (blood, phlegm, choler or bile, and melancholy or black choler) that, by their relative proportions, were supposed to determine a person's physical and mental qualities. **humor** *v.t.* Gratify, indulge, (person, taste, temper, etc.); make concessions to. **hu'mor·less** *adj.* Lacking a sense of the ridiculous.

hu·mor·al (hū'meral, ū'-) *adj.* Of the bodily humors (see HUMOR n. 4).

hu·mor·esque (hūmorĕsk', ū-) *n.* (mus.) Composition of light capricious character.

hu·mor·ist (hū'merĭst, ū'-) *n.* Facetious person; writer, performer of humorous pieces.

hu·mor·ous (hū'merus, ū'-) *adj.* Full of humor; facetious, funny. **hu'mor·ous·ly** *adv.* **hu'mor·ous·ness** *n.*

hu·mour = HUMOR.

hump (hŭmp) *n.* Protuberance, esp. on back, formed by curved spine or fleshy excrescence, as natural feature in camel, bison, etc.,

*The **humming-bird** is usually very brightly colored and in many species the tail feathers are greatly elongated. While in flight its wings beat up to 80 times per second. It is found in great numbers in the tropical forests of South America but ranges from Alaska to Tierra del Fuego. Its very long tongue probes nectar and insects from flowers.*

magnificent rivolis
lodiges racket-tail
ribbon-tailed
sword-billed
sappho comet
pucherans emerald
ruby and topaz
ruby-throated
frilled coquette

or deformity in man; rounded boss of earth etc.; **hump'back** (person having) back with a hump; **hump-back whale**, whale of genus *Megaptera*, so called because of the low hump on the back; **hump'-backed**, having such a back. **hump** *v.* Make arched or rounded; bend; (vulg.) copulate (*with*). **humped, hump'y** *adjs.* (**hump·i·er, hump·i·est**).

Hum·per·dinck (ho͝om'pe*r*-dĭngk), **Engelbert** (1854–1921). German composer famous for the fairy tale opera, *Hänsel and Gretel.*

humph (hŭmf) *int.* Exclamation of doubt or mild contempt.

Hum·phrey (hŭm'frē), **Hubert Horatio** (1911–78). Amer. politician; U.S. senator from Minnesota, 1949–64, 1970–8, and vice president under Lyndon Johnson, 1965–1969.

Hump·ty Dump·ty (hŭmp'tē dŭmp'tē). Short dumpy person; (from nursery rhyme in which name is taken to mean an egg) person or thing that once overthrown cannot be restored; (from Lewis Carroll's *Through the Looking-Glass*) person who makes words mean what he chooses.

hu·mus (hū'm*u*s, ū'-) *n.* Decayed vegetable matter, the characteristic organic constituent of the soil formed by the decomposition of plant materials.

Hun (hŭn) *n.* 1. One of the Asiatic race of warlike nomads who invaded Europe *c*375 A.D. and overran much of it under Attila in middle of 5th c. 2. (contempt.) German soldier, German (esp. during World War I). **Hun'nish** *adj.* (fig.) Barbarous, destructive.

Hu·nan (ho͞o'nahn'). Province of S. China. ~ *adj.* Of Hunan, esp. its spicy cuisine.

hunch (hŭnch) *v.t.* Bend, arch, convexly; thrust *out*, *up*, to form a hump. ~ *n.* 1. Hump; thick piece, hunk; **hunch'back(ed)**, humpback(ed). 2. Intuition, premonition.

hun·dred (hŭn'drĭd) *n.* (pl. **-dreds**, following a numeral **-dred**). 1. Cardinal number equal to ten times ten (100, c, or C); also as ordinal when followed by other numbers; hundredweight; $100 or a $100 bill; **a ~ percent**, entire(ly), complete(ly); **the ~s**, between 100 and 999. 2. (chiefly hist.) Subdivision of county or shire in England and Ireland. 3. **hun'-dredweight**, (abbrev. cwt) 100 lb.; (Brit.) 112 lb. avoirdupois. **hundred** *adj.* Amounting to 100; **H~ Days**, period between return of Napoleon I to Paris (Mar. 20, 1815) and his second abdication (June 22); **H~ Years War**, intermittent war between England and France (1337–1453), arising out of English kings' claim to French crown and during which England lost all her French lands except Calais. **hun'dred·fold** *adj.* & *adv.* **hun'-dredth** *adj.* & *n.*

***Hunger** and malnutrition are perennial problems in the over-populated under-developed countries of the Third World. These children from Nigeria have the pot-bellies and thin limbs characteristic of starvation.*

hung: see HANG.

Hun·gar·i·an (hŭnggār'ē*a*n) *adj.* Of Hungary or its people or language. ~ *n.* Hungarian person or language; MAGYAR.

Hun·ga·ry (hŭng'ge*r*ē). Country of central Europe, forming until the end of World War I the eastern division of Austro-Hungarian Empire; declared an independent republic in 1918; reconstituted as a kingdom, the functions of the monarch being exercised by a regent, in 1920; again declared a republic in 1946; proclaimed a Communist People's Republic, 1949; anti-communist uprisings began in Budapest, 1956, and were quelled by Soviet troops and tanks; capital, Budapest.

hun·ger (hŭng'g*e*r) *n.* Uneasy sensation, exhausted condition, caused by lack of food; (fig.) strong desire; ~ **strike**, refusal to take food (esp. by prisoner trying to force compliance with his demands). **hunger** *v.i.* Feel hunger; have craving (*for*, *after*).

hun·gry (hŭng'grē) *adj.* (**-gri·er, -gri·est**). Feeling hunger; showing hunger; inducing hunger; (fig.) eager, greedy; (of soil) poor, barren. **hun'gri·ly** *adv.* **hun'gri·-ness** *n.*

hunk (hŭngk) *n.* Large piece cut off; clumsy piece.

hun·ker (hŭng'k*e*r) *v.i.* Sit or squat down on the heels. **hun·kers** *n.pl.* Haunches.

hunk·y (hŭng'kē) *n.* (pl. **hunk·-ies**). (slang, derog.) Person from central or eastern Europe.

hunk·y-do·ry (hŭng'kē dōr'ē,

*The central European republic of **Hungary** has an area of 35,912 sq. miles and a population of just over 10 million people. The capital is Budapest, on the river Danube which bisects the country.*

*The end of a successful quail **hunt** for this hunter and his dog. In most parts of the U.S., hunting is governed by a system of licenses and seasons, which restricts hunting of particular species to certain times of the year.*

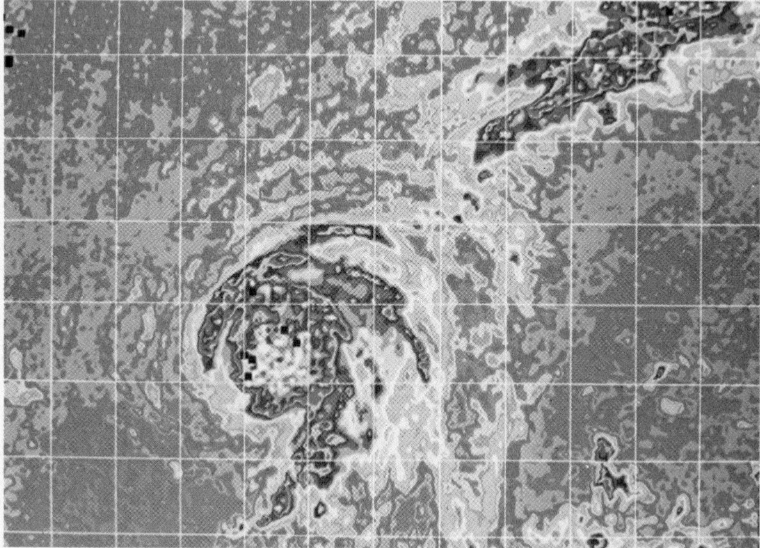

*This computer photograph is of **Hurricane Camille** which hit the Mississippi Gulf Coast in August 1969. It caused 157 deaths and the estimated damage from flooding alone was well over a hundred million (U.S.) dollars.*

-dŏr'ē) *adj.* (slang) Excellent.

Hun·nish (hŭn'ĭsh): see HUN.

hunt (hŭnt) *v.* 1. Pursue wild animals or game; chase (these) for food or sport; pursue with force, violence, or hostility; shoot (game); seek *after, for, out*; scour (district) in pursuit of game; use (horse, hounds) in hunting; **~-and-peck**, typing method involving search for each key before striking; **~ down**, bring to bay; **~ out**, track out, find by search; **~ up**, search for. 2. (elect. mech.) Be in a state of instability, oscillate, jump backward and forward. **hunt** *n.* Hunting (lit. and fig.); persons hunting with a pack.

hunt·er (hŭn'ter) *n.* (fem. of def. 1. **hunt·ress** pr. hŭn'trĭs). 1. One who hunts; **hunter's moon**, next full moon after harvest moon. 2. Horse ridden for hunting.

hunt·ing (hŭn'tĭng) *n.* Action of person or animal that hunts; chase, pursuit; **~ box**, small house used during hunting season; **~ ground**, place where one hunts (freq. fig.); **happy ~ grounds**, those expected by Amer. Indians in world to come (also fig.); **~ leopard** = CHEETAH.

hunts·man (hŭnts'man) *n.* (pl. **-men** pr. -men). Hunter; man in charge of (esp. fox-) hounds.

Hunts·ville (hŭnts'vĭl). City in N. Alabama and site of a NASA space flight center.

Hu·peh (ho͞o'pā'), **Hu·bei** (hü'-bōē'). Province of central China.

hur·dle (hēr'del) *n.* (chiefly Brit.) Portable rectangular frame for temporary fence etc.; wooden frame to be jumped over in **~ race**; (pl.) hurdle race; (hist.) frame on which traitors were dragged to execution. **hurdle** *v.* (**-dled, -dling**). Run in hurdle race; jump as over a hurdle etc. (lit. and fig.). **hur'dler** *n.* One who makes hurdles or runs in hurdle races.

hur·dy-gur·dy (hēr'dē gēr'dē) *n.* (pl. **-gur·dies**). 1. Medieval musical instrument resembling lute, sounded by rosined wheel turned with right hand and keys to "stop" strings played with left hand. 2. Any droning instrument played by turning a handle, as barrel organ.

hurl (hērl) *v.t.* Throw violently from some position; throw (missile etc.); (baseball) pitch. **~** *n.* Hurling, violent throw. **hurl'er** *n.* (baseball) Pitcher.

hurl·ing (hēr'lĭng) *n.* Irish game resembling hockey; stick used in this.

hurl·y-burl·y (hēr'lē bēr'lē) *n.* (pl. **-bur·lies**). Commotion, tumult.

Hu·ron[1] (hūr'ŏn, -on) *n.* (Member, language of) confederation of four Iroquoian-speaking Indian tribes formerly occupying the region between Lakes Huron, Erie, and Ontario.

Hur·on[2] (hūr'ŏn), **Lake.** Lake in northern U.S. and southern Canada, covering 23,010 sq. mi. (59,596 sq. km); second largest of the five Great Lakes.

hur·rah (hurah', -raw'), **hur·ray** (hurā'), **hoo·ray** (ho͞orā') *ints.* Exclamation of exultation or approbation. **~** *n.* & *v.i.* Shout hurrah etc.; **last ~**: see LAST[2] hurrah.

hur·ri·cane (hēr'ikān, hŭr'-; *Brit.* hŭr'ĭkan) *n.* 1. Violent tropical cyclone originating in the Caribbean Sea and tropical regions of the Atlantic Ocean, with heavy rains and winds exceeding 75 m.p.h. around a central calm space or "eye" that follows a N., NW., or NE. path. 2. Any storm in which wind blows with terrific violence; (meteor.) wind of 73 m.p.h. or more (force 12 in BEAUFORT SCALE); ~ **deck**, upper deck on river steamer; ~ **force**, speed of wind 73 m.p.h. or more (Beaufort Scale 12); ~ **lamp**, lamp covered by a glass chimney, orig. so as not to be extinguished by violent wind.

hur·ry (hēr′ē, hŭr′ē) *n.* Haste; eagerness to get thing done quickly; eagerness (*to* do thing); (with neg. or interrog.) need for haste; (*not*) **in a** ~, (not) readily; ~**-scurry**, (in) disorderly haste; proceed thus. **hurry** *v.* (**-ried, -ry·ing**). Carry, drive (person *away*, *along*, *into*, etc.) with haste; move, act, with great or undue haste; ~ **up**, make haste. **hur′ried·ly** *adv.* **hur′ried·ness** *n.*

hurt (hērt) *n.* Wound, material injury; harm, wrong. ~ *v.* (**hurt, hurt·ing**). Cause bodily injury or pain to; damage; inflict injury upon; distress, wound (person, his feelings, etc.); (colloq.) suffer injury or pain. **hurt′ful** *adj.* **hurt′ful·ly** *adv.* **hurt′ful·ness** *n.*

hur·tle (hēr′tel) *v.* (**-tled, -tling**). Strike together, against something else; hurl swiftly; strike *against*; move with clattering sound; come with a crash.

hus·band (hŭz′band) *n.* Man married to a woman; (archaic) prudent manager. ~ *v.t.* 1. Manage thriftily, economize; (archaic) till (ground), cultivate (plants). 2. (poet.) Provide with husband.

hus·band·ry (hŭz′bandrē) *n.* Farming; economy; conservation; careful management.

hush (hŭsh) *n.* Stillness; silence; ~ **money**, money paid to prevent disclosure or hush up something discreditable. **hush** *v.* Silence, quiet; be silent (esp. as int. **hush!**); ~ **up**, suppress public mention of. **hush′-hush′** *adj.* (colloq.) Highly confidential, very secret.

husk (hŭsk) *n.* Dry outer integument of some fruits or seeds; (fig.) worthless outside part of anything. ~ *v.t.* Remove husk from.

hus·ky[1] (hŭs′kē) *adj.* (**-ki·er, -ki·est**). 1. Of, full of, husks; dry as a husk; (of voice or person) dry, hoarse. 2. (colloq.) Rugged and strong; big, strong, and vigorous. **husk′i·ly** *adv.* **husk′i·ness** *n.* **husky** *n.* (pl. **-kies**). Strong stoutly built vigorous looking person.

hus·ky[2] (hŭs′kē) *n.* (pl. **-kies**). Eskimo dog. [app. corrupt. of *Eskimo*]

Huss (hŭs), **John** (1373–1415). Bohemian religious reformer; convicted of heresy by the Council of Constance and burned alive. **Huss′ite** *n.* Follower of Huss.

hus·sar (hoozār′, -sār′) *n.* One of a body of light horsemen organized in Hungary in 15th c.; soldier of light cavalry regiment elsewhere. [O. Serb. *husar*, f. It. *corsaro* corsair]

*The **hyacinth** has narrow, untoothed leaves at the base of the plant and fragrant flowers which are usually blue, but may be pink, white or other colors in cultivated species.*

Hus·sein I (hoosān′), **King** (1935–). King of Jordan since 1953.

hus·sy (hŭs′ē, hŭz′ē) *n.* Woman of worthless character; pert girl. [f. *housewife*]

hus·tings (hŭs′tĭngz) *n.* 1. Court formerly held in some British cities by the mayor, recorder, sheriffs or aldermen, etc. for common pleas, probate, appeals against sheriffs' decisions, etc.; platform on which mayor etc. sat for this court (obs.) 2. Platform from which (before 1872) candidates for the Brit. Parliament were nominated; (Brit.) election proceedings. 3. Any platform for political campaigning.

hus·tle (hŭs′el) *v.* (**-tled, -tling**). Push roughly, jostle; shove (person *into*, *out of*, etc.); impel unceremoniously; push roughly *against*; push one's way; hurry, bustle; (slang) get money, living etc., by dubious means. ~ *n.* Hustling. **hus′tler** *n.* Person who hustles (in good or bad senses), esp. a prostitute.

hut (hŭt) *n.* Small roughly constructed house or shelter, esp. for temporary use; (mil.) temporary wooden etc. house for troops. ~ *v.* Place (troops etc.) in huts; lodge or store in hut.

hutch (hŭch) *n.* Boxlike pen for rabbits etc.; hut; storage bin; cabinet with some open shelves.

Hutch·in·son (hŭch′ĭnson), **Anne** (1591–1643). Religious leader whose preachings conflicted with beliefs of clergymen in Massachusetts Bay Colony; expelled from colony, 1637; settled in Rhode Island; moved to New York where she was massacred by Indians.

hut·ment (hŭt′ment) *n.* Encampment of huts.

hutz·pa, hutz·pah (hoots′pa, xoots′-) = CHUTZPA.

Hux·ley[1] (hŭks′lē), **Aldous Leonard** (1894–1963). Grandson of Thomas Henry Huxley; English novelist and essayist, author of *Brave New World*.

Hux·ley[2] (hŭks′lē), **Sir Julian Sorell** (1887–1975). Biologist and writer; brother of Aldous Huxley.

Hux·ley[3] (hŭks′lē), **Thomas Henry** (1825–95). English physician and agnostic philosopher; supported Darwinism in his many popular scientific writings.

Huy·gens (hī′genz, hoi′-), **Christian** (1629–95). Dutch mathematician and astronomer; ~**'s principle**, (phys.) principle of wave propagation, according to which every point on an advancing wave front acts as a source of disturbance and sends out smaller waves, the resultant effect of which constitutes the propagation of the wave as a whole.

huz·za (huzah′) *int.*, *n.*, & *v.i.* (archaic) Hurrah.

hwy. *abbrev.* Highway.

hy·a·cinth (hīasĭnth) *n.* 1. Precious stone (in ancient times a blue gem, prob. sapphire); now, reddish-orange variety of zircon (occas. also of garnet and topaz). 2. Bulbous plant of genus *Hyacinthus* with fragrant bell-shaped flowers of various colors, esp. purplish blue; deep blue (traditional rendering of Homeric epithet applied to hair, perh. meaning dark and glossy). **hy·a·cin′thine** *adj.*

Hy·a·cin·thus (hīasĭn′thus). (Gk. myth.) Beautiful youth, beloved by Apollo and Zephyrus, accidentally killed by a quoit thrown by Apollo; from his blood Apollo caused the flower that bears his name to spring up.

Hy·a·des (hī′adēz) *n.pl.* 1. (Gk. myth.) Nymphs, daughters of Atlas, placed by Zeus among the Pleiades. 2. (astron.) Cluster of stars in the constellation of Taurus, anciently supposed to indicate rainy weather when they rose simultaneously with the sun.

hy·ae·na: see HYENA.

hy·brid (hī′brĭd) *n.* Offspring of two animals or plants of different species or varieties; (fig.) something of mixed origin or components; thing, word, composed of incongruous elements. ~ *adj.* Crossbred, mongrel; heterogeneous. **hy′brid·ism** *n.* Fact, condition, of being hybrid; crossbreeding. **hy·brid·i·ty** (hībrĭd′ĭtē) *n.*

hy·brid·ize (hī′brĭdīz) *v.* (**-ized, -iz·ing**). Subject (species etc.) to crossbreeding; produce hybrids; interbreed. **hy·brid·i·za·tion** (hībrĭdīzā′sh*o*n) *n.*

Hyde (hīd), **Edward**: see Jekyll.

Hyde (hīd) **Park.** 1. Public park of 361 acres in central London. 2. Village in SE. New York on Hudson River, home of President Franklin D. Roosevelt.

Hy·der·a·bad (hīd*e*r*a*bahd′, -băd′, hīdra-). Former state of India, in the Deccan; its capital; now in southern West Pakistan.

Hy·dra (hī′dr*a*). 1. (Gk. myth.) Many-headed snake of marshes of Lerna, whose heads grew again as they were cut off, killed by Hercules; hence, thing hard to extirpate. 2. (astron.) Southern constellation represented as water snake or sea serpent.

hy·dra (hī′dr*a*) *n.* (pl. **-dras, -drae** pr. -drē). Freshwater polyp of simple structure of genus *H*~, with tubular body and mouth surrounded by ring of tentacles with stinging thread cells.

hy·dran·gea (hīdrān′j*a*, -jē*a*) *n.* Shrub of genus *H*~, native of temperate regions of Asia and Amer., with white, blue, or pink flowers in large globular clusters.

hy·drant (hī′dr*a*nt) *n.* Pipe with nozzle to which hose can be attached, for drawing water directly from main, esp. in street, for fire fighting (also **fire ~**).

hy·drate (hī′drāt) *n.* (chem.) Compound of water with another compound. ~ *v.t.* (**-drat·ed, -drat·ing**). Combine chemically with water. **hy·dra·tion** (hīdrā′sh*o*n) *n.*

hy·drau·lic (hīdraw′lĭk, -drŏl′ĭk) *adj.* Of water (or other liquid) as conveyed through pipes or channels, esp. mechanically; (of machine or other device) operated by resistance offered when water, oil, or other liquid is forced through a pipe or orifice, as ~ **brake, crane,** etc.; (of cement

*The Saronic island of **Hydra** in the Aegean Sea supports sponge-fishing, cotton and silk-weaving, ship-building and tourism. Its chief town, which surrounds this sheltered harbor, is an artists' and writers' colony.*

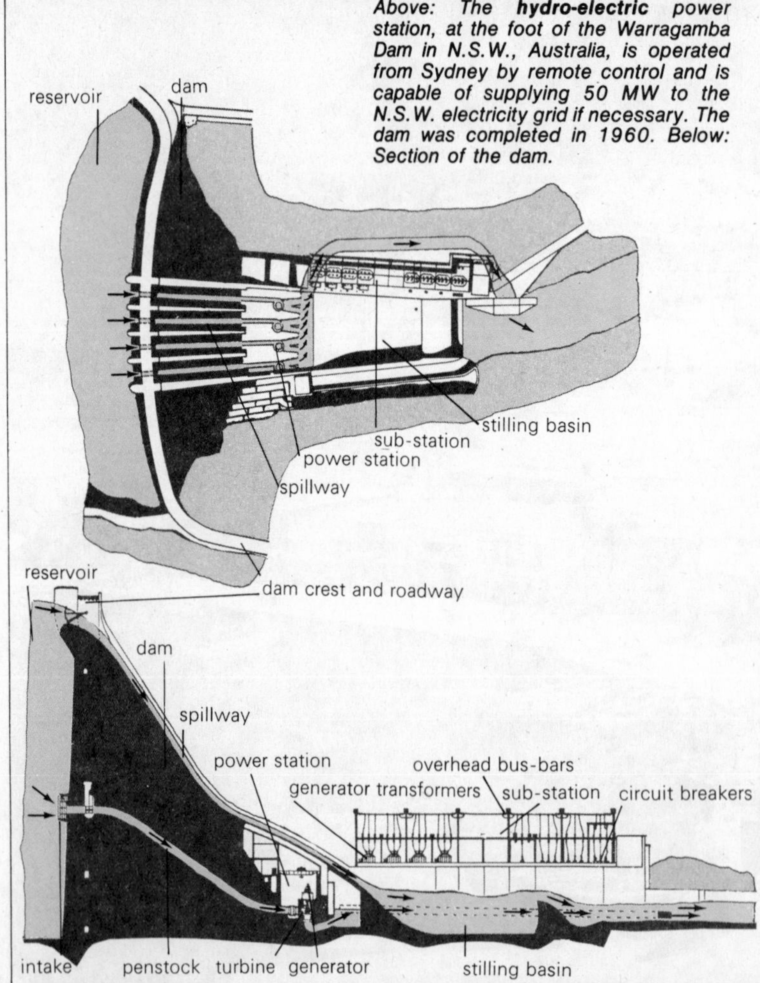

*Above: The **hydro-electric** power station, at the foot of the Warragamba Dam in N.S.W., Australia, is operated from Sydney by remote control and is capable of supplying 50 MW to the N.S.W. electricity grid if necessary. The dam was completed in 1960. Below: Section of the dam.*

etc.) hardening under water. **hy·drau'li·cal·ly** *adv.* **hy·drau'lics** *n.* Science of conveyance of liquids through pipes, etc., esp. as a motive force.

hydro- *prefix.* 1. Having to do with water. 2. (chem.) Combined with hydrogen.

hy·dro·car·bon (hīdrokar̄'bon) *n.* Chemical compound containing hydrogen and carbon only, as methane and benzene.

hy·dro·ceph·a·lus (hīdrosĕf'alus) *n.* Disease of brain, esp. in young children, with accumulation of serous fluid in cavity of cranium and consequent weakness of mental faculties; water on the brain. **hy·dro·ce·phal·ic** (hīdrosefăl'ĭk) *adj.* & *n.*

hy·dro·chlo·ric (hīdroklōr'ĭk, -klōr'-) *adj.* ~ **acid**, clear, aqueous, acidic, and poisonous solution of hydrogen chloride (HCl), which fumes in moist air, used in various industrial processes, including petroleum production, ore processing, and metal cleaning.

hy·dro·cy·an·ic (hīdrosīăn'ĭk) *adj.* ~ **acid**, highly poisonous volatile liquid (HCN), hydrogen cyanide, with smell like bitter almonds, solution of which in water is PRUSSIC *acid.*

hy·dro·dy·nam·ic (hīdrōdīnăm'ĭk), **hy·dro·dy·nam·i·cal** (hīdrōdīnăm'ĭkal) *adjs.* Of the forces acting on or exerted by liquids. **hy·dro·dy·nam'ics** *n.pl.* Science of the motion, energy, and pressure of moving fluids.

hy·dro·e·lec·tric (hīdroĭlĕk'trĭk) *adj.* Of the utilization of water power for the production of electricity; of electricity so generated.

hy·dro·foil (hī'drofoil) *n.* (Fast motorboat, seaplane, etc., with) plate or fin for lifting hull out of water at speed.

hy·dro·gen (hī'drojen) *n.* (chem.) Lightest of the elements, a colorless odorless gas that burns with pale blue, very hot flame in oxygen (or air) and combines with oxygen to form water (H_2O); symbol H, at. no. 1, at. wt. 1.0080; ~ **bomb**, immensely powerful bomb deriving its energy from the fusion at extremely high temperature of hydrogen isotopes to form helium; also called H-bomb, fusion bomb; ~ **fluoride**, colorless, highly corrosive gas (HF), anhydride of *hydrofluoric acid;* ~ **peroxide**, in its pure anhydrous state, a clear colorless syrupy liquid (H_2O_2), used in aqueous solution as an antiseptic and disinfectant. **hy·drog·e·nous** (hīdrŏj'enus) *adj.*

hy·dro·gen·ate (hī'drojenāt, hīdrŏj'e-) *v.t.* (**-at·ed, -at·ing**). Charge, cause to combine, with hydrogen; esp. combine hydrogen and unsaturated compound. **hy·-**

dro·gen·a·tion (hīdrojenā'shon, hīdrŏje-) *n.*

hy·droid (hī'droid) *adj.* & *n.* (zool.) (Animal) like, allied to, the hydra.

hy·drol·o·gy (hīdrŏl'ojē) *n.* Study of water, esp. its distribution and control. **hy·dro·log·i·cal** (hīdrolŏj'ĭkal) *adj.*

hy·drol·y·sis (hīdrŏl'isĭs) *n.* Splitting of compound substance by interaction with water. **hy·dro·lyt·ic** (hīdrolĭt'ĭk) *adj.*

hy·drom·e·ter (hīdrŏm'eter) *n.* Instrument for determining specific gravity of liquids, commonly a graduated stem with a hollow bulb and a weight at lower end, floated upright in liquid, of which specific gravity is indicated by depth to which stem is immersed. **hy·dro·met·ric** (hīdromĕt'rĭk) *adj.* **hy·drom'e·try** *n.*

hy·dro·path·ic (hīdropăth'ĭk) *adj.* Of, concerned with, hydropathy. **hy·drop·a·thy** (hīdrŏp'athē) *n.* Medical treatment by external and internal application of water; water cure.

hy·dro·pho·bi·a (hīdrofō'bēa): see RABIES.

hy·dro·phone (hī'drofōn) *n.* Instrument for the detection or monitoring of sound waves in water.

hy·dro·phyte (hī'drofīt) *n.* Aquatic plant, esp. alga.

hy·dro·plane (hī'droplān) *n.* 1. Light, fast motorboat designed to skim over surface of water. 2. Finlike horizontal device enabling submarine to submerge or rise. 3. Seaplane.

hy·dro·pon·ics (hīdropŏn'ĭks) *n.pl.* Cultivation of plants without soil, in water containing dissolved nutrients.

hy·dro·sphere (hī'drosfēr) *n.* Waters of the Earth's surface.

hy·dro·stat·ic (hīdrostăt'ĭk) *adj.* Of the equilibrium of liquids and the pressure exerted by liquids at rest; (of instruments etc.) involving pressure of liquid as source of power or otherwise, hydraulic. **hy·dro·stat'i·cal** *adj.* **hy·dro·stat'i·cal·ly** *adv.* **hy·dro·stat'ics** *n.pl.* Branch of mechanics concerned with the pressure and equilibrium of liquids at rest.

hy·dro·ther·a·peu·tic (hīdrōthĕrapū'tĭk) *adj.* Hydropathic. **hy·dro·ther'a·py** *n.* Hydropathy.

hy·drous (hī'drus) *adj.* (chem., min.) Containing water.

hy·drox·ide (hīdrŏk'sīd) *n.* (chem.) Compound containing hydroxyl.

hydroxy- *prefix.* Containing hydroxyl.

hy·drox·yl (hīdrŏk'sĭl) *n.* (chem.) Radical OH, which occurs in the structures of many chemical compounds.

hy·dro·zo·an (hīdrozō'an) *adj.* & *n.* (Member) of the Hydrozoa, a class of coelenterate animals, chiefly marine, and simple or compound, including the freshwater hydra.

hy·en·a, hy·ae·na (hīē'na) *ns.*

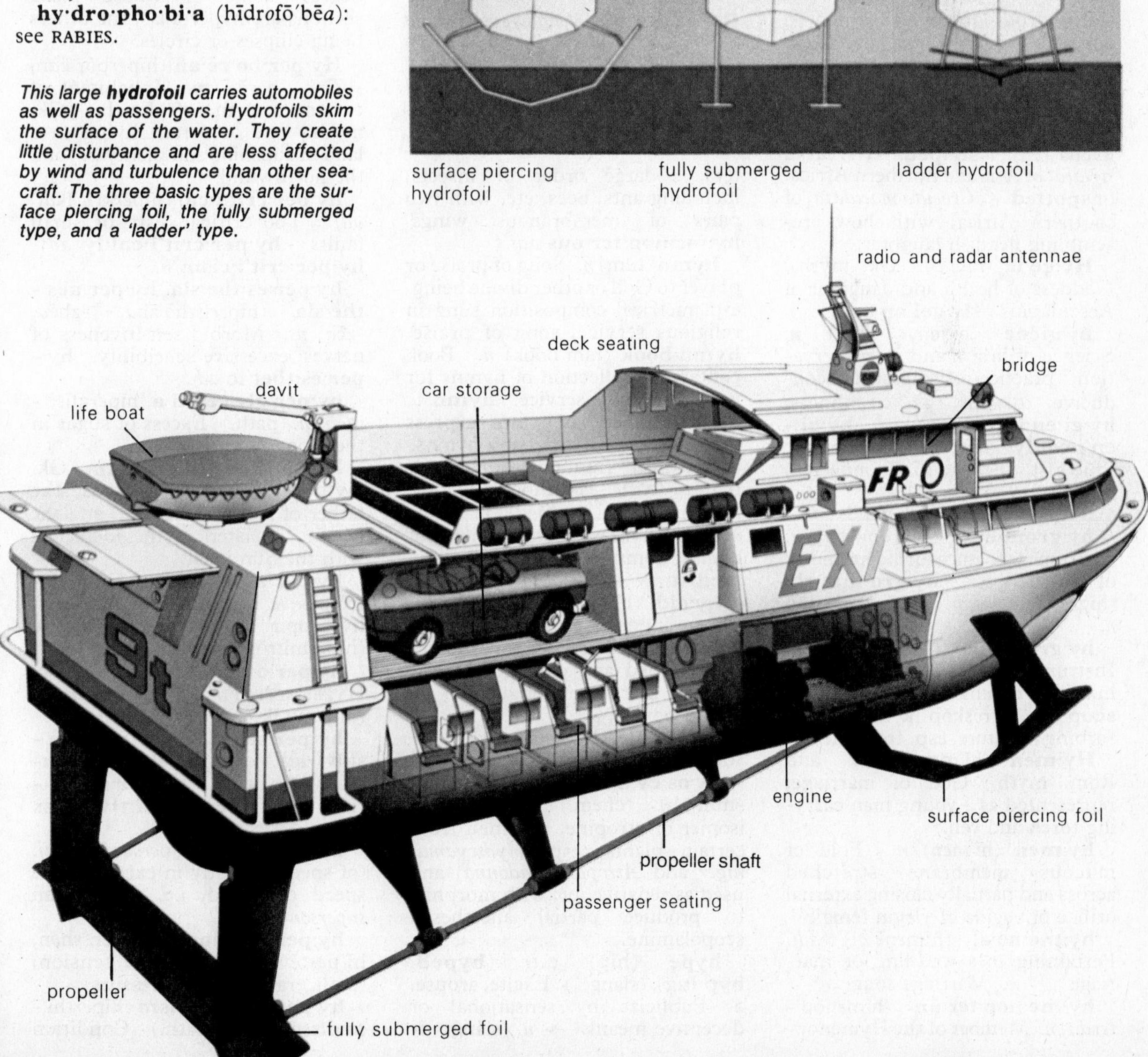

*This large **hydrofoil** carries automobiles as well as passengers. Hydrofoils skim the surface of the water. They create little disturbance and are less affected by wind and turbulence than other seacraft. The three basic types are the surface piercing foil, the fully submerged type, and a 'ladder' type.*

This spotted or laughing ***hyena*** *is found in Africa south of the Sahara. It is the most daring of the species and when food is scarce has attacked sleeping people and children.*

Carnivorous quadruped allied to dog tribe, with powerful jaws, neck, and shoulders, but low and comparatively poorly developed hindquarters; cruel, treacherous, or rapacious person; **laughing ~**, hyena (either **striped ~**, *Hyaena striata*, of Asia and northern Africa, or **spotted ~**, *Crocuta maculata*, of southern Africa) with howl resembling fiendish laughter.

Hy·ge·ia (hījē´*a*). (Gk. myth.) Goddess of health and daughter of Aesculapius. **Hy·gei´an** *adj.*

hy·giene (hī´jēn, -jēēn) *n.* Science of health and its preservation; practice of measures conducive to this, as cleanliness. **hy·gi·en·ic** (hījēēn´ĭk) *adj.* **hy·gi·en´i·cal·ly** *adv.* **hy·gi·en·ist** (hījē´nĭst, -jĕn´ĭst, hī´jē-, hījēēn´-) *n.*

hygro- *prefix.* Wet, fluid.

hy·grom·e·ter (hīgrŏm´*e*t*er*) *n.* Instrument for measuring humidity of air or gas. **hy·gro·met·ric** (hīgr*o*mĕt´rĭk) *adj.* **hy·grom´e·try** *n.*

hy·gro·scope (hī´gr*o*skōp) *n.* Instrument indicating approximate humidity of atmosphere. **hy·gro·scop·ic** (hīgr*o*skŏp´ĭk) *adj.* Absorbing moisture, esp. from the air.

Hy·men (hī´m*e*n). (Gk. and Rom. myth.) God of marriage; represented as a young man carrying torch and veil.

hy·men (hī´m*e*n) *n.* Fold of mucous membrane stretched across and partially closing external orifice of vagina of virgin female.

hy·me·ne·al (hīm*e*nē´*a*l) *adj.* Pertaining to a wedding or marriage. **~** *n.* Marriage song.

hy·me·nop·ter·an (hīm*e*nŏp´t*e*r*a*n) *n.* Member of the Hymenoptera, a large order of insects, including ants, bees, etc. with two pairs of membranous wings. **hy·me·nop´ter·ous** *adj.*

hymn (hĭm) *n.* Song of praise or prayer to God or other divine being, esp. metrical composition sung in religious service; song of praise. **hymn·book** (hĭm´bo͝ok) *n.* Book containing collection of hymns for use in religious service. **hymn** *v.* Praise (God etc.) in hymns, express (praise etc.) in hymn; sing hymns.

hym·nal (hĭm´n*a*l) *adj.* Of hymns. **~** *n.* Hymnbook.

hym·no·dy (hĭm´n*o*dē) *n.* Singing of hymns; composition of hymns; hymns collectively. **hym´no·dist** *n.*

hy·oid (hī´oid) *adj.* **~ bone,** tongue bone, between chin and thyroid cartilage, in man, horseshoe-shaped and embedded horizontally in root of tongue. **~** *n.* Hyoid bone.

hy·os·cine (hī´*o*sēn, -sĭn) = SCOPOLAMINE.

hy·os·cy·a·mine (hī*o*sī´*a*mēn, -mĭn) *n.* (chem.) Alkaloid, an isomer of atropine, obtained from certain plants (esp. *Hyoscyamus niger* and *Atropa belladonna*) and used as sedative, or, with morphia, to produce partial anesthesia; scopolamine.

hype (hīp) *v.t.* (**hyped, hyp·ing**). (slang) 1. Excite, arouse. 2. Publicize by sensational or deceptive means. **~** *n.* (slang) 1. Sensational or deceptive publicity to increase interest. 2. Drug addict, esp. user of hypodermic needle.

hyper- *prefix.* Over, above, exceeding, excessive.

hy·per·ac·tive (hīp*e*răk´tĭv) *adj.* Abnormally or too active. **hy·per·ac·tiv·i·ty** (hīp*e*răktĭv´ĭtē) *n.*

hy·per·aes·the·sia: see HYPERESTHESIA.

hy·per·bo·la (hīpĕr´b*o*l*a*) *n.* (geom.) One of the conic sections, a plane curve consisting of 2 separate, similar, equal, and infinite branches, formed by the intersection of a cone by a plane making a larger angle with the base than the side of the cone makes. **hy·per·bol·ic** (hīp*e*rbŏl´ĭk) *adj.*

hy·per·bo·le (hīpĕr´b*o*lē) *n.* (rhet.) Exaggerated statement not meant to be taken literally (*big as a house*). **hy·per·bol´i·cal** *adj.* **hy·per·bol´i·cal·ly** *adv.* **hy·per´bo·lism** *n.*

hy·per·bo·loid (hīpĕr´b*o*loid) *n.* (geom.) Solid or surface of the 2nd degree, some of whose plane sections are hyperbolas, the others being ellipses or circles.

Hy·per·bo·re·an (hīp*e*rbōr´ē*a*n, -bŏr´-, -b*o*rē´-) *n.* Inhabitant of extreme north of Earth; (Gk. myth.) one of a race living in a land of sunshine and plenty beyond the north wind.

hy·per·crit·i·cal (hīp*e*rkrĭt´ĭk*a*l) *adj.* Too critical, esp. of small faults. **hy·per·crit´i·cal·ly** *adv.* **hy·per·crit´i·cism** *n.*

hy·per·es·the·sia, hy·per·aes·the·sia (hīp*e*rĭsthē´zh*a*, -zhē*a*, -zē*a*) *ns.* Morbid sensitiveness of nerves; excessive sensibility. **hy·per·es·thet´ic** *adj.*

hy·per·gly·ce·mi·a (hīp*e*rglīsē´mē*a*) *n.* (path.) Excess of sugar in the blood.

Hy·pe·ri·on (hīpĕr´ē*o*n). (Gk. myth.) One of the Titans, the father of Aurora, the Sun, and the Moon; in later myth. identified with the Sun itself.

hy·per·me·tro·pi·a (hīp*e*rmĭtrō´pē*a*) *n.* Morbid far-sightedness; hyperopia. **hy·per·me·trop·ic** (hīp*e*rmĭtrŏp´ĭk) *adj.*

hy·per·o·pi·a (hīp*e*rō´pē*a*) *n.* HYPERMETROPIA. **hy·per·op·ic** (hīp*e*rŏp´ĭk) *adj.*

hy·per·sen·si·tive (hīp*e*rsĕn´sĭtĭv) *adj.* Excessively or abnormally sensitive. **hy·per·sen·si·tiv´i·ty, hy·per·sen´si·tive·ness** *ns.*

hy·per·son·ic (hīp*e*rsŏn´ĭk) *adj.* (of speed) Greatly in excess of the speed of sound, i.e. faster than *supersonic.*

hy·per·ten·sion (hīp*e*rtĕn´sh*o*n, hī´p*e*rtĕn-) *n.* Extreme tension; (path.) raised blood pressure.

hy·per·thy·roid·ism (hīp*e*rthī´roidĭz*e*m) *n.* (path.) Condition resulting from overactivity of thyroid gland.

hy·per·tro·phy (hīpẽr'trofē) *n.* (pl. **-phies**). Excessive development, morbid enlargement, of organ etc. (opp. ATROPHY). **hy·per·troph·ic** (hīpertrŏf'ĭk) *adj.*

hy·per·ven·ti·la·tion (hīpervĕntĭlā'shon) *n.* (med.) Abnormally rapid and deep breathing, producing carbon dioxide decrease in blood.

hy·phen (hī'fen) *n.* Sign (-) used to join two words together, to join separated syllables of word broken at end of line, or to divide word into parts. ~ *v.t.* Join (words) with hyphen. **hy·phen·ate** (hī'fenat) *v.t.* (**-at·ed, -at·ing**). Hyphen; **hyphenated**, (colloq.) of foreign birth or mixed national origin, e.g. *Irish-American*.

hyp·no·sis (hĭpnō'sĭs) *n.* (pl. **-ses** pr. -sēz). Artificially produced sleep, esp. that induced by hypnotism.

hyp·not·ic (hĭpnŏt'ĭk) *adj.* Of, producing, hypnotism; (of drugs) soporific. ~ *n.* Thing that produces sleep; person under influence of hypnotism.

hyp·no·tism (hĭp'notĭzem) *n.* (Artificial production of) state resembling deep sleep, in which subject acts only on external suggestion or direction, to which he is involuntarily and unconsciously obedient. **hyp'no·tist** *n.* **hyp'no·tize** *v.t.* (**-tized, -tiz·ing**).

hy·po (hī'pō) *n.* (pl. **-pos**). Sodium thiosulfate, $Na_2S_2O_3 . {}_5H_2O$ (incorrectly called sodium hyposulfite), used in fixing photographic negatives and prints.

hypo- *prefix.* Below, under, slightly.

hy·po·blast (hī'poblăst) *n.* Inner layer of cells in blastoderm.

hy·po·cen·ter (hī'posĕnter) *n.* Underground point of origin of an earthquake (f. EPICENTER).

hy·po·chon·dri·a (hīpokŏn'drēa) *n.* Needless or excessive anxiety about one's health.

hy·po·chon·dri·ac (hīpokŏn'drēăk) *adj.* Of, affected by, hypochondria. ~ *n.* Hypochondriac person. **hy·po·chon·dri·a·cal** (hīpokondrī'akal) *adj.* **hy·po·chon·dri'a·cal·ly** *adv.*

hy·po·cot·yl (hīpokŏt'ĭl) *n.* (bot.) Axis of seedling below seed leaves, forming anatomically a transition zone between stem and root.

hy·poc·ri·sy (hĭpŏk'risē) *n.* (pl. **-sies**). Simulation of virtue or goodness; dissimulation, pretense.

hyp·o·crite (hĭp'okrĭt) *n.* Person guilty of hypocrisy; dissembler, pretender. **hyp·o·crit·i·cal** (hĭpokrĭt'ĭkal) *adj.* **hyp·o·crit'i·cal·ly** *adv.*

hy·po·cy·cloid (hīposī'kloid) *n.* (geom.) Curve traced by a point in the circumference of a circle which rolls around the interior circumference of another circle.

hy·po·der·mic (hīpodẽr'mĭk) *adj.* (med., of drugs etc.) Introduced beneath the skin; (anat.) lying under the skin; ~ **needle, syringe**, one used in hypodermic injection. **hy·po·der'mi·cal·ly** *adv.* **hy·po·der'mic** *n.* Hypodermic injection or syringe.

hy·po·gas·tri·um (hīpogăs'trēum) *n.* Lowest region of abdomen. **hy·po·gas'tric** *adj.*

hy·po·gly·ce·mi·a (hīpōglīsē'mēa) *n.* (path.) Deficiency of sugar (glucose) in the blood.

hy·pog·y·nous (hīpŏj'inus, hĭ-) *adj.* (of stamens) Situated below pistil or ovary; (of flower) having such stamens.

hy·pos·ta·sis (hīpŏs'tasĭs, hĭ-) *n.* (pl. **-ses** pr. -sēz). (metaphys.) Underlying substance, opp. to attributes or to what is unsubstantial; (theol.) personality (of Christ), person (of the Godhead). **hy·po·stat·ic** (hīpostăt'ĭk), **hy·po·stat'i·cal** *adjs.* **hy·po·stat'i·cal·ly** *adv.*

hy·pos·ta·tize (hīpŏs'tatīz) *v.t.* (**-tized, -tiz·ing**). Make into or treat as substance; personify.

hy·pot·e·nuse (hīpŏt'en ōōs, -nūs) *n.* Side of right-angled triangle opposite the right angle.

hy·poth·e·cate (hīpŏth'ekāt, hĭ-) *v.t.* (**-cat·ed, -cat·ing**). Pledge, mortgage. **hy·poth·e·ca·tion** (hīpŏthekā'shon, hĭ-) *n.*

hy·poth·e·sis (hīpŏth'esĭs, hĭ-) *n.* (pl. **-ses** pr. -sēz). Supposition made as basis for reasoning, without reference to its truth, or as starting point for investigation; groundless assumption. **hy·po·thet·ic** (hīpothĕt'ĭk), **hy·po·thet'i·cal** *adjs.* **hy·po·thet'i·cal·ly** *adv.*

hy·poth·e·size (hīpŏth'esīz, hĭ-) *v.* (**-sized, -siz·ing**). Frame a hypothesis; assume as hypothesis.

hyp·som·e·ter (hĭpsŏm'eter) *n.* Instrument for measuring altitudes, by determining the boiling points of liquids. **hyp·so·met·ric** (hĭpsomĕt'rĭk), **hyp·so·met'ri·cal** *adjs.* **hyp·som'e·try** *n.*

hy·rax (hī'răks) *n.* (pl. **hy·rax·es, hy·ra·ces** pr. hī'rasēz). One of a small group of mammals of the order Hyracoida, the coneys, distantly related to the elephant and having plantigrade feet with hooves and including the Syrian rock rabbit and the South African rock badger.

hys·sop (hĭs'op) *n.* Small bushy aromatic herb of genus *Hyssopus*, esp *H. officinalis*, formerly used medicinally; (bibl.) plant whose twigs were used for sprinkling in Jewish rites, bunch of this used in purification.

hys·ter·ec·to·my (hĭsterĕk'tomē) *n.* (pl. **-mies**). Surgical removal of the uterus.

hys·ter·e·sis (hĭsterē'sĭs) *n.* (phys.) Lagging or retardation of an effect when the forces acting on a body are changed, esp. lagging or magnetic induction behind the magnetizing force (**magnetic** ~).

hys·te·ri·a (hĭstĕr'ēa, -stẽr'-) *n.* 1. (med., psych.) Functional disturbance of nervous system, of psychoneurotic origin. 2. Uncontrollable or excessive fear, grief, etc. **hys·ter·i·cal** (hĭstĕr'ĭkal) *adj.* **hys·ter'i·cal·ly** *adv.* **hys·ter'ics** *n.pl.* Hysterical fits or convulsions; uncontrollable fit of crying, laughing, etc.

Hz *abbrev.* Hertz.

*The rock **hyrax** lives in groups and is active by day. It is primarily a vegetarian and its natural enemies are pythons, eagles and large cats. It is most prolific in Africa.*

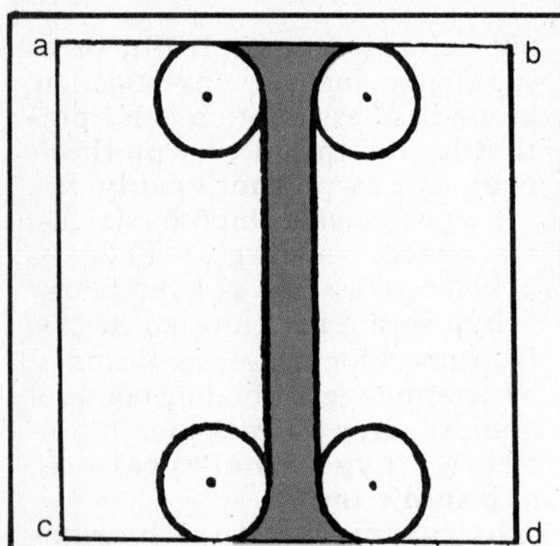

Shown here is the evolution from earliest scripts of the letter form **I, i.** In the languages of continental Europe, *i* is always used phonetically as counterpart of the English *e*. But in English the letter has two sounds — long (as in 'slide') and short (as in 'bid')

Phoenician
Cretan
Archaic Latin
Cursive Minuscule
Anglo Saxon
Roman

I[1], **i** (ī) (pl. **I's, i's** or **Is, is**). I. Ninth letter of modern English and ancient Roman alphabet, in which it was orig. used as symbol both of *i* vowel and of a consonant (orig. *y*, later, in Romanic, developing into "soft g" [j]); differentiation was finally made between these two in English *c*1630–40, the consonant being expressed by the character J, j, orig. merely a variant form of I, i. 2. Roman numeral symbol for I.

I[2] (ī) *pron.* First person nom. sing. pronoun, denoting the speaker. ~*n.* (pl. **I's**). **the I**, the ego, subject or object of self-consciousness.

I[3] *abbrev.* Interstate (highway).

I[4] *symbol.* Iodine.

I. *abbrev.* Island(s); isle(s).

i. *abbrev.* Interest; intransitive; island(s); isles.

IA, Ia. *abbrevs.* Iowa.

i·amb (ī'ăm, īămb) *n.* Metrical foot of unaccented followed by accented syllable, or of short followed by long syllable.

i·am·bic (īăm'bĭk) *adj.* Of, containing, based on, iambs.

i·am·bus (īăm'bus) *n.* (pl. **-bi** pr. -bī, **-bus·es**) = IAMB.

I·ap·e·tus (īăp'etus). I. (Gk. myth.) A Titan, father of Atlas, Prometheus, and Epimetheus; hence, regarded as progenitor of mankind. 2. (astron.) Eighth satellite of Saturn.

ib., ibid. *abbrevs. Ibidem.*

I·be·ri·a (ībēr'ēa). I. Ancient name for country comprising Spain and Portugal, and forming peninsula of extreme SW. of Europe. 2. Ancient name of GEORGIA[2] of the U.S.S.R.

I·be·ri·an (ībēr'ēan) *adj.* Of Iberia. ~ *n.* I. Inhabitant of ancient Iberian peninsula; member of short dark neolithic people, with long heads, who buried their dead and are thought to have built the cairns, dolmens, etc., found in N. Africa, Spain, France, and Gt. Britain. 2. Language of ancient Iberia, supposed to be represented by modern Basque.

i·bex (ī'bĕks) *n.* (pl. **i·bex·es, ib·i·ces**, pr. ĭb'ĭsēz, ī'bĭ-, collect. **i·bex**). Species of wild goat (genus *Capra*), with large scimitar-like horns, now rare in Alps but found in Mongolia and Ethiopia.

ib·i·dem (ĭb'īdĕm, ĭbī'dem) *adv.* (abbrev. ib., ibid.) In the same book, chapter, passage, etc. [L., = "in same place"]

i·bis (ī'bĭs) *n.* (pl. **i·bis·es** pr. ī'bĭsĭz, collect. **i·bis**). Any of a group of birds, widely distributed in warm climates, of the family Threskiornithidae, with long down-curved bills, esp. the white ibis (*Eudocimus albus*) and the glossy ibis (*Plegadis falcinellus*); **sacred** ~, white ibis, common in the Nile basin, venerated by the

The European or Alpine **ibex** *(right) lives in herds in the mountains of Europe. It has been greatly reduced in numbers and is now protected in the Italian Alps. The Pyrenean or Spanish ibex (below) is one of the critically endangered species.*

The **ibis** resembles a stork and occurs in all warm regions except the South Pacific Islands. It usually breeds in vast colonies. This new-born ibis comes from Australia.

ancient Egyptians.

-ible *suffix*. Forming adjectives with same meaning as -ABLE (*terrible, forcible, defensible*).

Ib·sen (ĭb′sen), **Henrik** (1828–1906). Norwegian poet and dramatist, famous for his *A Doll's House*, *Ghosts*, *Hedda Gabler*, etc., examining and criticizing social conventions.

-ical *suffix*. Forming adjectives corresponding to nouns or adjectives ending in *-ic* (*classical, historical*) or to nouns in *-y* (*pathological*).

Ic·a·rus (ĭk′erus, ī′ker-). (Gk. myth.) Son of DAEDALUS; tried to escape from Crete on wings made by his father, but flew so near the sun that the wax attaching his wings was melted and he fell into the Aegean Sea.

ICBM *abbrev*. Intercontinental ballistic missile.

ICC *abbrev*. Interstate Commerce Commission.

ice (īs) *n*. 1. Frozen water; water made solid by exposure to low temperature, a transparent crystalline brittle almost colorless substance; frozen surface of body of water; **break the ~**, (fig.) make a beginning, break through reserve or stiffness; **cut no ~**, have no influence or importance, achieve nothing; **on ~**, (fig.) held suspended, in reserve; absolutely certain; **on thin ~**, (fig.) in a risky situation. 2. Frozen dessert made of fruit juice, water, and sugar. 3. **I~ Age**, period during the Pleistocene, when large parts of Earth were covered by ice; **ice age**, any cold epoch with extensive glaciation; **~ ax**, ax used by mountain climbers to cut footholds in ice slopes; **~ bag**, small waterproof bag to hold ice for

The sacred **ibis** of South Arabia and Africa south of the Sahara was venerated by the ancient Egyptians and is about 30 ins. long. The scarlet ibis is found in tropical America.

Ice, in the form of glaciers like this one, is a powerful agent of erosion. Glaciers move slowly, accumulating debris and rocks which scour the landscape, creating smooth troughs.

cooling head or other part of body; **ice'berg**, floating mass of ice, a detached portion of polar ice sheet or glacier, often traveling great distances in ocean currents before it melts completely; **ice'bound**, hemmed in by ice; **ice'box**, insulated chest in which ice is put to preserve food; (colloq.) refrigerator; **ice'breaker**, boat with reinforced bow for breaking channel through ice of river, harbor, etc.; a means of breaking through reserve or stiffness; **ice'cap**, mass of thick ice covering continent, island, or other region; **ice cream**, food or dessert made from milk, cream, etc., sweetened, flavored, and frozen smooth; **ice cube**, small block of ice made in refrigerator; **ice field**, extensive sheet of floating ice; **ice floe**, flattish free mass of floating ice, smaller than an ice field; **ice hockey**: see HOCKEY; **ice'-house**, (hist.) building for storing ice; **ice'man** (pl. **ice'men**), man who sells or delivers ice; **ice milk**, ice cream made from skim milk, or with greatly reduced butterfat; **ice pick**, awl for chipping ice; **ice plant**, plant (*Mesembryanthemum crystallinum*) of S. Africa, Canary Islands, etc., with leaves covered with pellucid watery vesicles; **ice show**, entertainment by skaters on ice; **ice skate**, metal blade attached to shoe for gliding on ice; **ice-skate** (*v.i.*) (**-skated, -skat·ing**), move, glide, over ice on these; **ice water**, iced water. **ice** *v.t.* (**iced, ic·ing**). Freeze; cover (as) with ice; cool (wine) in ice; cover (cake etc.) with icing; (hockey) push (puck) out of one's own territory to far end of ice; (fig.) make secure; put on ice.

Ice·land (īs'land). Large sparsely inhabited island (39,709 sq. mi., 105,240 sq. km), in N. Atlantic between Greenland and Scandinavia; colonized by Scandinavians after 874; united with Norway 1262–4; on union of Norway and Denmark (1831), Iceland was transferred to Denmark, which conceded home rule to Iceland in 1874 and recognized it as a sovereign state, in union with Denmark, in 1918; union dissolved in 1944 when Iceland became an independent republic; capital, Reykjavik; ~ **moss**, species of edible arctic lichen (*Cetraria islandica*), having medicinal properties; **Ice'-land·er** *n.* Inhabitant, native, of Iceland.

Ice·lan·dic (īslăn'dĭk) *adj.* Of Iceland. ~ *n.* Language of Iceland, in its oldest form practically identical with Old Norse, which it still closely resembles.

I·ce·ni (īsē'nī) *n.pl.* Ancient Celtic tribe inhabiting a district in England roughly corresponding to modern Norfolk and Suffolk, who were conquered, with their queen BOADICEA, by the Romans *c*62 A.D.

I Ching (ē'jĭng'). The Book of Changes, ancient Chinese book of divination and mystical speculation adopted as one of the "Five Classics" into the Confucian canon.

ich·neu·mon (ĭknōō'mon, -nū'-) *n.* 1. N. African mongoose (*Herpestes ichneumon*). 2. ~ **fly**, member of a group of insects related to bees and wasps, whose larvae are parasitic on the larvae of other insects. [Gk. *ikhneumon* tracker]

ichthyo- *Comb. form.* (before vowel **ichthy-**) Of or like fish. [Gk. *ikhthus* fish]

ich·thy·oid (ĭk'thēoid) *adj.* Fishlike. ~ *n.* Any fishlike

*This Byzantine **icon** of the Savior was made at the beginning of the 15th century. The subject matter and artistic style were prescribed by the Eastern Church and remained unchanged for centuries.*

vertebrate.

ich·thy·ol·o·gy (ĭkthēŏl′*o*jē) *n.* Study of fishes. **ich·thy·o·log·i·cal** (ĭkthē*o*lŏj′ĭk*a*l) *adj.* **ich·thy·ol′o·gist** *n.*

ich·thy·oph·a·gous (ĭkthēŏf′*a*-g*u*s) *adj.* Fish-eating.

Ich·thy·or·nis (ĭkthēōr′nĭs) *n.* Genus of extinct toothed birds that had fishlike vertebrae.

ich·thy·o·saur (ĭk′thē*o*sōr), **ich·thy·o·saur·us** (ĭkthē*o*sōr′*u*s) *ns.* (pl. **-saurs, -saur·us·es**). Marine reptile of extinct order Ichthyosauria, with superficial resemblance to the modern dolphin.

-ician *suffix.* (comb. of *-ic* and *-ian*) Forming agent nouns denoting persons skilled in or concerned with arts or sciences having names ending in *-ic(s)* (*politician*, *logician*).

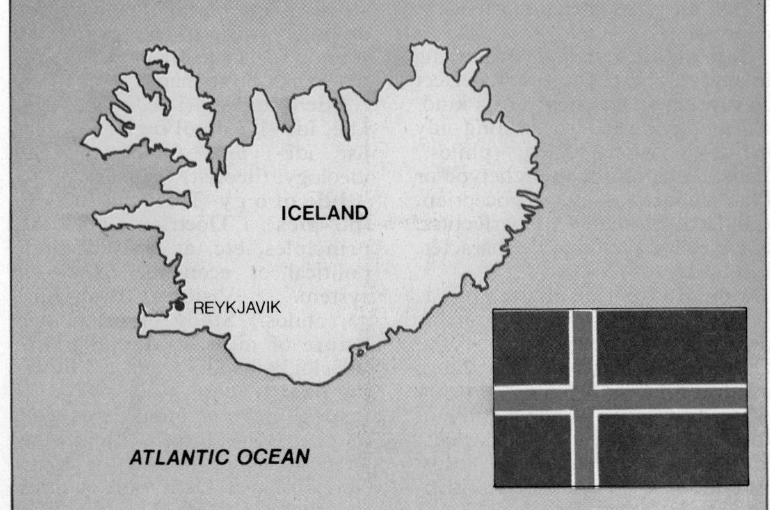

***Iceland** is a sparsely populated island republic in the North Atlantic. It contains over 100 volcanoes and earthquakes are frequent. Iceland's map and flag are shown here.*

i·ci·cle (ī′sĭk*e*l) *n.* Tapering ice formation, produced by freezing of successive drops of water trickling from the point of attachment.

ic·ing (ī′sĭng) *n.* 1. Glaze of sugar, water, white of egg, butter, flavoring, etc. for covering or decorating cakes, cookies, etc. 2. Formation of ice on aircraft, roads, etc.

ICJ *abbrev.* International Court of Justice.

ick·y (ĭk′ē) *adj.* (**ick·i·er, ick·i·est**). (slang) Repulsive, sticky; (fig.) cloyingly sentimental.

i·con (ī′kŏn) *n.* Image, picture, statue; (Eastern Churches) painting, mosaic, etc. of sacred personage, itself regarded with reverence.

i·con·ic (īkŏn′ĭk) *adj.* Of (the nature of) an image or portrait; (of statues) following a conventional type.

i·con·o·clasm (īkŏn′*o*klăz*e*m) *n.* Breaking of images. **i·con′o·clast** *n.* Breaker of images, esp. one who took part in movement in 8th and 9th centuries against use of images in religious worship in Eastern Churches; one who assails cherished beliefs and traditional institutions. **i·con·o·clas·tic** (īkŏn*o*-klăs′tĭk) *adj.*

i·co·nog·ra·phy (īk*o*nŏg′r*a*fē) *n.* (pl. **-phies**). 1. Description of a subject by drawings or figures; book containing this. 2. Subject matter of art; study of this. **i·co·nog′ra·pher** *n.* 1. Person who illustrates a subject. 2. Student of iconography. **i·con·o·graph·ic** (īkŏn*o*grăf′ĭk), **i·con·o·graph′i·cal** *adjs.*

i·co·nol·a·try (īk*o*nŏl′*a*trē) *n.* Worship of images. **i·co·nol′a·ter** *n.*

i·co·nol·o·gy (īk*o*nŏl′*o*jē) *n.* 1. Study of icons, images, and symbols. 2. Symbolical representation, symbolism. **i·con·o·log·i·cal** (īk*o*-nolŏj′ĭk*a*l) *adj.* **i·co·nol′o·gist** *n.*

i·con·o·scope (īkŏn′*o*skōp) *n.* (formerly trademark) Television camera tube generating high-velocity electron beam to scan the camera's photoemissive mosaic screen.

i·co·sa·he·dron (īkōs*a*hē′dr*o*n, īkŏs*a*-) *n.* (pl. **-drons, -dra** pr. -dr*a*). (geom.) Solid figure of 20 faces; **regular ~**, one formed by 20 equilateral triangles.

-ics *suffix.* Forming nouns (variously considered pl. or sing.) denoting sciences and systems of practical activity, facts, principles, etc. (*acoustics*, *ethics*, *tactics*).

ICU *abbrev.* Intensive care unit (in a hospital).

i·cy (ī'sē) *adj.* (**i·ci·er, i·ci·est**). Abounding in, covered with, ice; very cold. **i·ci·ly** (ī'sĭlē) *adv.* **i·ci·ness** (ī'sēnĭs) *n.*

ID *abbrev.* Idaho; identification.

I.D. *abbrev.* Identification; ~ **card**, identification card; ~ **tag, bracelet**, one showing owner's name etc.

Id., Ida. *abbrevs.* Idaho.

id (ĭd) *n.* (psychol.) Part of the mind that comprises the inherited instinctive impulses of the individual together with memories and fantasies evolved in early infancy (cf. EGO).

id. *abbrev. Idem.*

i.d. *abbrev.* Inside diameter.

I'd (īd) *contr.* I would, I should.

-id[1] *suffix.* Forming nouns denoting belonging to the family of (*Nereid*), and forming names of meteors or comets from their apparent parent constellation or comet (*Andromedid, Geminid*).

-id[2] *suffix.* (zool.) Forming nouns and adjectives indicating members of a zoological family, division, or group (*arachnid, hominid, orchid*).

-id[3] *suffix.* (chem.) Early variant of -IDE (*parotid*).

I·da (ī'da), **Mount.** 1. Mountain range in S. Phrygia, near ancient Troy, from whose summit Zeus was supposed to have watched the progress of the Trojan War; scene of the rape of GANYMEDE and the home of PARIS[2]; highest point 5,810 ft. (1,771 m). 2. Ancient name of chief mountain (Mt. Psiloriti) in Crete, where Zeus is said to have been brought up; 8,195 ft. (2,498 m) high.

-ida *pl. suffix.* (zool.) Forming names of orders and classes (*Arachnida*).

-idae *pl. suffix.* (zool.) Forming taxonomic names of families (*Canidae, Hominidae*).

I·da·ho (ī'dahō). State in northwestern U.S.; admitted to the Union in 1890; capital, Boise.

-ide *suffix.* (chem.) Forming names of simple compounds by addition to the (usu. abbrev.) name of the more electronegative element of the compound (*carbon sulfide, ferrous oxide*).

i·de·a (īdē'a) *n.* 1. Mental conception or impression; thought; motion. 2. Opinion, belief, way of thinking. 3. Intention, plan of action; supposition; fantasy. 4. (philos.) Concept of standard or principle that is desirable or ideal; (in Platonic philos.) eternal archetype or pattern from which natural objects etc. derive their being and of which they are imperfect copies; (in Descartes, Locke, et al.) immediate object of thought or mental perception; (in Kant, et al.) conception of reason transcending all experience; (in Hegel, et al.) absolute truth of which all phenomenal existence is expression.

This Polynesian ***idol,*** *carved in wood, is a representation of the sea-god Tangaroa. He is creating mankind from the human forms that grow from his body. This sculpture comes from Rurutu in the Austral Islands.*

i·de·al (īdē'al) *adj.* 1. Answering to one's highest conception; perfect or supremely excellent of its kind. 2. Embodying an idea; existing only in idea; visionary. 3. (philos.) Being, relating to, an archetype or Platonic idea. ~ *n.* 1. Conception, standard, or model of perfection. 2. Object or aim of noble character. **i·de'al·ly** *adv.*

i·de·al·ism (īdē'alĭzem) *n.* 1. Pursuit or cherishing of noble principles, purposes, etc. 2. Idealizing; representation of things in ideal form. 3. (philos.) Theory that the real is of the nature of thought or that the external object of perception consists of ideas. **i·de'al·ist** *n.* **i·de·al·is·tic** (īdēalĭs'tĭk) *adj.*

i·de·al·ize (īdē'alīz) *v.* (**-ized, -iz·ing**). Represent in ideal form or character, exalt to ideal perfection or excellence. **i·de·al·i·za·tion** (īdēalĭzā'shon) *n.*

i·de·ate (ī'dēāt, īdē'-) *v.* (**-at·ed, -at·ing**). Imagine, conceive; form ideas. **i·de·a·tion** (īdēā'shon) *n.* **i·de·a'tion·al** *adj.*

i·dée fixe (ēdā fēks') (pl. **i·dées fixes** pr. ēdā fēks'). Idea that dominates the mind, monomania. [Fr., = "fixed idea"]

i·dem (ī'dĕm, ĭd'ĕm) *pron.* (abbrev. id.) Same author; same work. [L., = "the same"]

i·den·ti·cal (īdĕn'tĭkal) *adj.* (of one thing etc. viewed at different times) Very same; (of different things) agreeing in every detail (with); (logic, math.) expressing an identity; ~ **twins**, twins resulting from fertilization of single ovum and consequently alike in all respects, including sex (opp. FRATERNAL). **i·den'ti·cal·ly** *adv.*

i·den·ti·fy (īdĕn'tĭfī) *v.* (**-fied, -fy·ing**). 1. Establish or verify the identity of. 2. Treat (thing) as identical (with); associate oneself (*with*) in feeling, interest, etc. **i·den·ti·fi·ca·tion** (īdĕntĭfĭkā'shon) *n.* **identification card**, one serving to identify bearer.

i·den·ti·ty (īdĕn'tĭtē) *n.* (pl. **-ties**). 1. Condition or fact that person or thing is itself and not something else; individuality, personality. 2. Absolute sameness; oneness; (alg.) equality of two expressions for all values of the literal quantities, equation expressing this; ~ **crisis**, (psych.) distressing emotional conflict or confusion in a person concerning his social role and true self, esp. during adolescence.

ideo- *comb. form.* Denoting idea, character (*ideogram, ideograph*).

id·e·o·gram (ĭd'ēogrăm, ī'dē-), **id·e·o·graph** (ĭd'ēogrăf, -grahf, ī'dē-) *ns.* Character (e.g., in Chinese pictorial writing, numerals, &, $, etc.) symbolizing an idea or object without expressing the sounds (as in a phonetic system) that make up its name.

i·de·o·logue (ī'dēolawg, -lŏg, ĭd'ē, īdē'-), **i·de·ol·o·gist** (īdēŏl'ojĭst, ĭdē-) *ns.* Advocate of an ideology; theorist, visionary.

i·de·ol·o·gy (īdēŏl'ojē, ĭdē-) *n.* (pl. **-gies**). 1. Doctrine, set of ideas, principles, etc. at basis of some political or economic theory or system. 2. Visionary theorizing. 3. (philos.) Study of origin and nature of ideas. **i·de·o·log·i·cal** (īdēolŏj'ĭkal, ĭdē-) *adj.* **i·de·o·log'i·cal·ly** *adv.*

ides (īdz) *n.pl.* (considered sing. or pl.) (Rom. antiq.) Eighth day after nones (15th day of Mar., May, July, or Oct.; 13th of other months); ~ **of March**, day, according to tradition, predicted as that of the assassination of Julius Caesar, hence, inauspicious day.

id est (ĭd ĕst′) (abbrev. i.e.) That is. [L.]

idio- *comb. form.* Individual, peculiar to one (*idiomatic, idiosyncrasy*).

id·i·o·cy (ĭd′ēosē) *n.* (pl. **-cies**). Mental condition of an IDIOT; extreme imbecility, utter foolishness.

id·i·om (ĭd′ēom) *n.* Language of a people, area, or country; specific character of this; form of expression peculiar to a language; characteristic mode of expression in art, music, etc. **id·i·o·mat·ic** (ĭdēomăt′ĭk) *adj.* Characteristic of a particular language; vernacular, colloquial. **id·i·o·mat′i·cal·ly** *adv.*

id·i·o·mor·phic (ĭdēomōr′fĭk) *adj.* (min.) Having its own characteristic form, esp. its characteristic crystallographic faces.

id·i·o·syn·cra·sy (ĭdēosĭng′krasē) *n.* (pl. **-sies**). Habit, mannerism, view, mode of expression, peculiar to a person; (med.) physical constitution peculiar to a person. **id·i·o·syn·crat·ic** (ĭdēōsĭnkrăt′ĭk) *adj.*

id·i·ot (ĭd′ēot) *n.* Person so deficient in mind as to be permanently incapable of rational conduct and having a mental development not exceeding that of an average normal child of two years old (the lowest grade of mental deficiency, next below IMBECILE); utter fool; ~ **box**, (slang) television set; ~ **card**, (slang) cue card for television performer; ~ **light**, (slang) warning light on automobile dashboard indicating malfunction etc. **id·i·ot·ic** (ĭdēŏt′ĭk) *adj.* **id·i·ot′i·cal·ly** *adv.*

i·dle (ī′del) *adj.* (**i·dler, i·dlest**). 1. Unoccupied; lazy, indolent; (of things) not in use or operation; (of money) not in circulation. 2. (of words, action, etc.) Worthless, insignificant, frivolous, groundless; ~ **wheel,** intermediate wheel transmitting motion between two geared wheels without changing the direction of the motion. **i′dle·ness** *n.* **i′dly** *adv.* **idle** *v.* (**i·dled, i·dling**). Be idle; pass (time etc.) *away* in idleness; saunter, loiter; (of engine etc.) run at low speed without doing any work. **i′dler** *n.*

i·dol (ī′dol) *n.* Image of deity used as object of worship; false god; person, thing, that is object of excessive devotion; (logic) false mental image or conception.

i·dol·a·ter (īdŏl′ater) *n.* (fem. **i·dol·a·tress** pr. īdŏl′atrĭs). Worshipper of idols; devoted admirer (*of*). **i·dol′a·try** *n.* (pl. **-tries**). **i·dol′a·trous** *adj.* **i·dol′a·trous·ly** *adv.*

i·dol·ize (ī′dolīz) *v.* (**-ized, -iz·ing**). Make an idol of; venerate, love, to excess; practice idolatry. **i·dol·i·za·tion** (īdolĭzā′shon) *n.*

Id·u·mae·a, Id·u·me·a (ĭdyumē′a) = EDOM. **Id·u·mae′an** *adj.* & *n.*

I·dun (ē′dhōōn), **I·dun·a** (ē′dhōōna). (Scand. myth.) Goddess of spring, wife of Bragi; she kept the apples that restored the youth of the gods.

i·dyll (ī′dĭl) *n.* Short description in verse or (**prose** ~) in prose of pastoral or charmingly simple scene or incident; episode suitable for such treatment. **i·dyl·lic** (īdĭl′ĭk) *adj.* **i·dyl′li·cal·ly** *adv.*

i.e. *abbrev. Id est* (L. that is).

-ie *suffix.* Variant of -Y[3] (*Charlie, dearie*).

IF *abbrev.* (radio) Intermediate frequency.

if (ĭf) *conj.* On the condition or supposition that; whenever; whether; even though; **as if**, as the case would be if, as though. **if** *n.* Condition, supposition; uncertain possibility.

if·fy (ĭf′ē) *adj.* (**if·fi·er, if·fi·est**). (colloq.) Uncertain, doubtful; chancy.

I·gerne: see IGRAINE.

ig·loo (ĭg′lōō) *n.* (pl. **-loos**). Eskimo dome-shaped house, esp. one built of blocks of compact snow. [Eskimo, = "house"]

Ig·na·tius[1] (ĭgnā′shus), **St.** (Ignatius Theophorus) Bishop of Antioch, martyred at Rome early in 2nd c.

Ig·na·tius[2] **Loyola** (ĭgnā′shus) **St.** (1491–1556). Spanish soldier and ecclesiastic, founder of the Society of Jesus (see JESUIT).

ig·ne·ous (ĭg′nēus) *adj.* Produced by volcanic agency; of fire, fiery.

ig·nis fat·u·us (ĭg′nĭs făch′ōōĭs) (pl. **ig·nes fat·u·i** pr. ĭg′nēz făch′ōōī). Will-o'-the-wisp, phosphorescent light (now rarely) seen on marshy ground, supposedly due to the spontaneous combustion of marsh gas (CH_4), containing traces of phosphorus compounds; delusive hope, aim, etc. [med. or mod. L., = foolish fire]

ig·nite (ĭgnīt′) *v.* (**-nit·ed, -nit·ing**). Set on fire; take fire; (chem.) heat to point of combustion or chemical change. **ig·ni·tion** (ĭgnĭsh′on) *n.* Igniting; (esp.) process or mechanism that ignites fuel in cylinder of internal combustion engine.

*The **iguana** is found in tropical America and Madagascar. It usually lives in trees but takes readily to water and feeds mainly on young leaves, flowers and fruits. Some species are hunted for their flesh.*

*The Middle Western State of **Illinois** contains one of the country's largest cities, Chicago — the center of the meat-packing industry. The city's skyline is shown here.*

ig·no·ble (ĭgnō′b*e*l) *adj.* Of low birth, position, or reputation; mean, base, dishonorable. **ig·no′ble·ness** *n.* **ig·no′bly** *adv.*

ig·no·min·y (ĭg′n*o*mĭnē) *n.* (pl. **-min·ies**). Dishonor, infamy. **ig·no·min·i·ous** (ĭgn*o*mĭn′ē*u*s) *adj.* Marked by ignominy; humiliating. **ig·no·min′i·ous·ly** *adv.*

ig·no·ra·mus (ĭgn*o*rā′m*u*s, -răm′*u*s) *n.* (pl. **-mus·es**). Ignorant person. [L., = we do not know]

ig·no·rance (ĭg′n*o*r*a*ns) *n.* Want of knowledge. **ig′no·rant** *adj.* Lacking knowledge; uninformed (*of, in*). **ig′no·rant·ly** *adv.*

ig·nore (ĭgnōr′, -nōr′) *v.t.* (**-nored, -nor·ing**). Refuse to take notice of or accept.

I·graine (ĭgrān′), **I·gerne, Y·gerne** (ĭgērn′). (Arthurian legend) Wife of Gorlois of Cornwall and mother (by Uther Pendragon) of Arthur.

i·gua·na (ĭgwah′n*a*) *n.* Any of the large tropical American lizards of the family Iguanidae; most have spiny projections along the back, and some grow to more than 5 ft. (1½ m).

IGY *abbrev.* International Geophysical Year (the 1st being the 18-month period from July 1, 1957, to Dec. 31, 1958, devoted to co-operative international geophysical studies and exploration).

IHS. First three letters of Greek ΙΗΣΟΥΣ (*Iēsous*) Jesus; often taken as initials of *J*esus *H*ominum *S*alvator "Jesus savior of men" or *I*n *H*oc *S*igno (vinces) "in this sign (thou shalt conquer)," or *I*n *H*ac (cruce) *S*alus "in this (cross) is salvation."

i·ke·ba·na (ēkĕbah′nah) *n.* Japanese art of flower arranging with strict rules emphasizing form and balance. [Jap., = living flowers]

Ikh·na·ton (ĭknah′t*o*n) = AKHNATON.

IL *abbrev.* Illinois.

il- *prefix.* Form of IN-[1, 2] before *l* (*illuminate, illogical*).

ILA *abbrev.* International Longshoremen's Association.

i·lang-i·lang (ē′lahng ē′lahng) = YLANG-YLANG.

Île-de-France (ēl d*e* frahṅs′). Region and former province of France, with Paris as capital, between rivers Seine, Oise, Marne, and Aisne.

il·e·os·to·my (ĭlēŏs′t*o*mē) *n.* (pl. **-mies**). (surg.) (Formation of) an opening from the ileum through the abdominal wall.

il·e·um (ĭl′ē*u*m) *n.* (pl. **il·e·a** pr. ĭl′ē*a*). (anat.) Third and terminal portion of small intestine, opening into large intestine. **il·e·i·tis** (ĭlēī′tĭs) *n.*

i·lex (ī′lĕks) *n.* 1. Holm oak. 2. Tree or shrub of genus *I*~ having small flowers and berrylike fruits; holly.

I.L.G.W.U. *abbrev.* International Ladies' Garment Workers' Union.

il·i·ac (ĭl′ēăk) *adj.* Of the flank or flank bone (ILIUM); but orig. of or affecting the ILEUM.

Il·i·ad (ĭl′ē*a*d). Greek epic poem attributed to Homer, describing incidents in the tenth and last year of the siege of Troy by the Greeks, esp. "the wrath of Achilles."

Il·i·um (ĭl′ē*u*m). Troy. [L. form of Gk. name *Ilion*]

il·i·um (ĭl′ē*u*m) *n.* (pl. **il·i·a** pr. ĭl′ē*a*). (anat.) Hipbone, the anterior or superior bone of the pelvis.

ilk (ĭlk) *n.* (colloq.) Family, class, or kind.

ill (ĭl) *adj.* 1. Sick; (of physical and mental health) unsound, disordered. 2. Morally bad; harmful; hostile; unkind; wretched, disastrous; ~ **fame**, bad repute; **house of** ~ **fame**, brothel; ~ **will**, animosity. 3. Unskillful; (of manners or conduct) improper. **ill** *n.* Evil, the opposite of good; harm, injury; misfortune, calamity, adversity. ~ *adv.* Badly; unfavorably; imperfectly, scarcely; ~ **at ease**, embarrassed, uneasy; ~**-advised**, imprudent; ~**-advisedly**; ~**-bred**, badly brought up, rude; ~**-considered**, unwise, not thoroughly considered; ~**-disposed**, disposed to evil, malevolent; unfavorably disposed, unsympathetic (toward); ~**-fated**, destined to, bringing, bad fortune; ~**-favored**, uncomely; displeasing, objectionable; ~**-gotten**, gained by evil or improper means; ~**-humored**, bad-tempered; ~**-judged**, unwise; ~**-natured**, bad-tempered, malevolent; ~**-starred**, born under an evil star, unlucky; ~**-suited**, inappropriate; ~**-timed**, inopportune; ~**-treat, -use**, treat badly.

Ill. *abbrev.* Illinois.

I'll (īl). *contr.* I will; I shall.

ill. *abbrev.* Illustrated; illustration; illustrator.

il·la·tion (ĭlā′sh*o*n) *n.* Deduction, conclusion; thing deduced, inference.

il·le·gal (ĭlē′g*a*l) *adj.* Not legal; contrary to law. **il·le′gal·ly** *adv.* **il·le·gal·i·ty** (ĭlēgăl′ĭtē) *n.*

il·leg·i·ble (ĭlĕj′ĭb*e*l) *adj.* Not legible. **il·leg·i·bil·i·ty** (ĭlĕjĭbĭl′ĭtē) *n.* **il·leg′i·bly** *adv.*

il·le·git·i·mate (ĭlĭjĭt′ĭmĭt) *adj.* Not legitimate; (esp.) born out of wedlock. **il·le·git′i·mate·ly** *adv.* **il·le·git′i·ma·cy** *n.* **illegitimate** (ĭlĭjĭt′ĭmāt) *v.t.* (**-mat·ed, -mat·ing**). Declare illegitimate.

il·lib·er·al (ĭlĭb′*e*r*a*l) *adj.* Narrow-minded, bigoted; stingy. **il·lib′er·al·ly** *adv.* **il·lib·er·al·i·ty** (ĭlĭb*e*răl′ĭtē) *n.* (pl. **-ties**).

il·lic·it (ĭlĭs′ĭt) *adj.* Not permitted, forbidden; unlawful, unlicensed. **il·lic′it·ly** *adv.*

il·lim·it·a·ble (ĭlĭm′ĭt*a*b*e*l) *adj.* Boundless. **il·lim·it·a·bil·i·ty** (ĭlĭmĭt*a*bĭl′ĭtē), **il·lim′it·a·ble·ness** *ns.* **il·lim′it·a·bly** *adv.*

Il·li·noi·an (ĭl*i*noi′*a*n) *adj.* Of, pertaining to the third glacial stage in N. Amer.

Il·li·nois[1] (ĭlinoi′, -noiz′). State in north-central U.S.; admitted to the Union in 1818; capital, Springfield.

Il·li·nois[2] (ĭlinoi′, -noiz′) *n.* Indian of confederacy of Algonquian tribes formerly living in Illinois and parts of Iowa and Wisconsin.

il·lit·er·ate (ĭlĭt′erĭt) *adj.* Unable to read and write; unlearned. ~ *n.* Illiterate person. **il·lit·er·a·cy** (ĭlĭt′erasē), **il·lit′er·ate·ness** *ns.*

ill·ness (ĭl′nĭs) *n.* Disease, ailment, sickness.

il·log·i·cal (ĭlŏj′ĭkal) *adj.* Devoid of, contrary to, logic. **il·log′i·cal·ly** *adv.* **il·log·i·cal·i·ty** (ĭlŏjĭkăl′ĭtē) *n.*

il·lume (ĭloom′) *v.t.* (**-lumed, -lum·ing**). (poet.) Light up, make bright.

il·lu·mi·nate (ĭloo′minăt) *v.t.* (**-nat·ed, -nat·ing**). Light up, supply with light; enlighten; throw light upon (subject); shed luster upon; decorate (buildings etc.) profusely with lights; decorate (initial letter in manuscript etc.) with gold, silver, and brilliant colors. **il·lu·mi·na·tion** (ĭloominā′shon) *n.* Act or process of illuminating; supply of light; state of being illuminated; enlightenment; decoration of lights; colored decorations in a manuscript; (optics) surface light density per unit area on an intercepting surface (see FOOT candle, LUMEN[1], LUX, PHOT). **il·lu′mi·na·tor** *n.* **il·lu·mi·na·tive** (ĭloo′minātĭv, -natĭv) *adj.*

il·lu·mine (ĭloo′mĭn) *v.t.* (**-mined, -min·ing**). Light up; enlighten spiritually; brighten. **il·lu′min·ism, il·lu′min·ist** *ns.*

illus. *abbrev.* Illustrated; illustration; illustrator.

il·lu·sion (ĭloo′zhon) *n.* Deception, delusion; physical perception of an external object involving a false belief.

il·lu·sion·ist (ĭloo′zhonĭst) *n.* 1. Conjurer, magician who produces illusions. 2. One who believes the material world is an illusion.

il·lu·sive (ĭloo′sĭv) *adj.* Deceptive. **il·lu′sive·ly** *adv.* **il·lu′sive·ness** *n.*

il·lu·so·ry (ĭloo′serē, -zerē) *adj.* Having the character of an illusion, unreal. **il·lu′so·ri·ly** *adv.* **il·lu′so·ri·ness** *n.*

il·lus·trate (ĭl′ustrāt, ĭlŭs′-) *v.t.* (**-trat·ed, -trat·ing**). Make clear, explain; make clear by examples; elucidate (description etc.) by drawings; ornament (book, newspaper etc.) with pictures etc. **il′lus·tra·tor** *n.* **il·lus·tra·tion** (ĭlustrā′shon) *n.* Illustrating; example; drawing etc. illustrating book or article in paper.

il·lus·tra·tive (ĭlŭs′tratĭv, ĭl′ustrā-) *adj.* Serving as explanation or example (*of*). **il·lus′tra·tive·ly** *adv.*

il·lus·tri·ous (ĭlŭs′trēus) *adj.* Distinguished, renowned. **il·lus′tri·ous·ly** *adv.* **il·lus′tri·ous·ness** *n.*

Il·lyr·i·a (ĭlēr′ēa). Ancient region extending along Balkan coast of Adriatic and including modern Dalmatia, Bosnia and Herzegovina, Montenegro, and part of Albania.

Il·lyr·i·an (ĭlēr′ēan) *adj.* Of Illyria. ~ *n.* Native, inhabitant, of Illyria; Indo-European language (closely related to modern Albanian) of the Illyrians.

I.L.O. *abbrev.* International Labor Organization.

I·lus (ī′lus). (Gk. legend) Founder of Troy (Gk. *Ilion*) and grandfather of Priam.

I'm (īm) *contr.* I am.

im- *prefix.* Form of IN-[1, 2] before *b, m, p.*

im·age (ĭm′ĭj) *n.* 1. Artificial imitation of external form of an object, e.g. statue; form, semblance; (esp.) figure of saint or divinity as object of religious veneration. 2. Optical appearance or counterpart of object produced by rays of light reflected from a mirror or refracted through any transparent medium. 3. Mental picture, idea, conception; general impression (of person, party, etc.) given to others. ~ *v.t.* (**-aged, -ag·ing**). Make an image of, portray; reflect, mirror; picture, imagine; describe vividly; typify.

im·age·ry (ĭm′ĭjrē) *n.* (pl. **-ries**). Images; statuary, carving; figurative illustration.

i·mag·i·na·ble (ĭmăj′inabel) *adj.* That can be imagined. **i·mag′i·na·bly** *adv.*

i·mag·i·nar·y (ĭmăj′inĕrē) *adj.* Existing only in imagination; (math.) having no real existence, but assumed to exist for a special purpose (as an ~ **number**), e.g. the square root of a negative quantity.

i·mag·i·na·tion (ĭmăjinā′shon) *n.* Imagining; mental faculty forming images of external objects not present to the senses; fancy; creative faculty of the mind.

i·mag·i·na·tive (ĭmăj′inatĭv, -nātĭv) *adj.* Of, given to using, having or showing in a high degree, the faculty of imagination. **i·mag′i·na·tive·ly** *adv.* **i·mag′i·na·tive·ness** *n.*

i·mag·ine (ĭmăj′ĭn) *v.* (**-ined, -in·ing**). Form mental image (*of*); conceive; guess, suppose, be of opinion; take into one's head.

im·ag·ism (ĭm′ajĭzem) *n.* Movement in Amer. and Brit. poetry, originating in 1912 and represented by Ezra Pound, Amy Lowell, Hilda Doolittle, and others, in revolt against romanticism and using free verse and exact visual images. **im′ag·ist** *n.*

i·ma·go (ĭmā′gō) *n.* (pl. **i·ma·goes, i·ma·gi·nes** pr. ĭmăj′inēz). 1. (entom.) Final and perfect stage of adult insect after it has undergone all its metamorphoses. 2. (psychol.) Idealized concept of a person, esp. a parent, formed in childhood and retained in the unconscious.

i·mam (ĭmahm′), **i·maum** (ĭmahm′, ĭmawm′) *ns.* 1. In Muslim communities, name given to the person who is regarded as taking Muhammad's place as leader of Islam, esp. any of 12 successive heads of Islam, beginning with Ali and his sons, recognized by the Shiites, hence, any great spiritual leader. 2. Official who leads the prayers in a mosque. 3. Any of the hereditary rulers of Yemen. **i·mam·ate** (ĭmah′māt) *n.* Office, title, of imam. [Arab. *'imam* leader f. *'amma* lead]

im·bal·ance (ĭmbăl′ans) *n.* 1. Lack of balance; disproportion; esp. state of having a disproportionately large number of one racial or ethnic group (as in a school), or

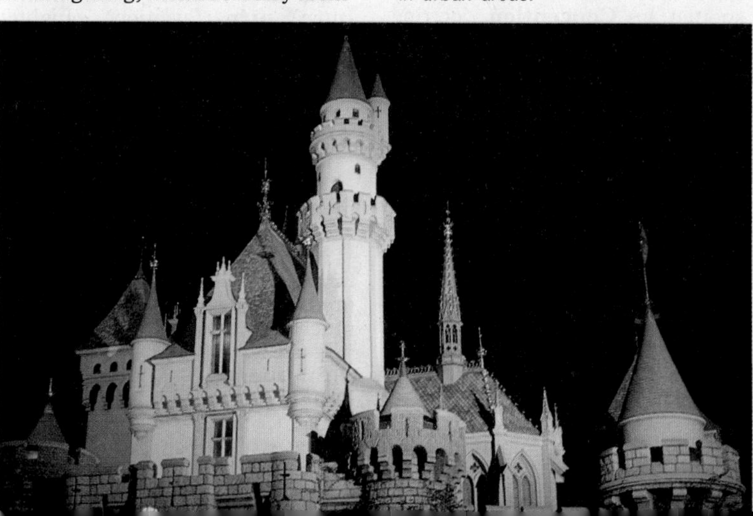

*Castle at Disneyland, L.A. Many historic monuments are **illuminated** in this way so that people can enjoy them by night. Illumination is also an important safety measure for motorists and pedestrians in urban areas.*

disproportion of men or women in a population. 2. (psychol.) Disturbance of mental or bodily equilibrium.

im·be·cile (ĭm'besĭl, -sil; *Brit.* ĭm'besēl) *n.* Adult person whose intelligence is equal to that of the average normal child between the ages of 3 and 7 years, or between 25 and 50 per cent of that of the average normal adult (see also IDIOT, MORON); person of weak intellect. ~ *adj.* Mentally weak, stupid, absurd. **im·be·cil·i·ty** (ĭmbesĭl'ĭtē) *n.*

im·bed (ĭmbĕd') = EMBED.

im·bibe (ĭmbīb') *v.t.* (**-bibed, -bib·ing**). Drink in, assimilate, (ideas etc.); drink (liquid); inhale (air etc.); absorb (moisture etc.). **im·bi·bi·tion** (ĭmbĭbĭsh'on) *n.*

im·bri·cate (ĭm'brikāt) *v.* (**-cat·ed, -cat·ing**). Arrange (leaves, scales of fish, etc.), be arranged, so as to overlap like tiles. ~ (ĭm'brikĭt, -kāt) *adj.* So arranged. **im·bri·ca·tion** (ĭmbrikā'shon) *n.*

im·bro·glio (ĭmbrōl'yō) *n.* (pl. **-glios**). 1. Confused or complicated state of affairs; difficult predicament; confused heap. 2. Misunderstanding, disagreement.

im·bue (ĭmbū') *v.t.* (**-bued, -bu·ing**). Saturate (*with*); dye (*with*); permeate, inspire (*with* feelings etc.); imbrue.

I.M.F. *abbrev.* International Monetary Fund.

im·i·ta·ble (ĭm'ĭtabel) *adj.* Capable of being imitated. **im·i·ta·bil·i·ty** (ĭmĭtabĭl'ĭtē) *n.*

im·i·tate (ĭm'ĭtāt) *v.t.* (**-tat·ed, -tat·ing**). Follow example of; mimic, copy; be like. **im·i·ta·tion** (ĭmĭtā'shon) *n.* Imitating; copy; counterfeit (freq. attrib.); **im'i·ta·tor** *n.*

im·i·ta·tive (ĭm'ĭtātĭv) *adj.* Following model or example (*of*); characterized by, consisting in, imitation; fictitious, counterfeit. **im'i·ta·tive·ly** *adv.* **im'i·ta·tive·ness** *n.*

im·mac·u·late (ĭmăk'yulĭt) *adj.* Pure, spotless; faultless; (biol.) not spotted; **I ~ Conception**, doctrine that the Virgin Mary was conceived free from taint of original sin (in 1854 declared an article of faith of Roman Catholicism). **im·mac'u·late·ly** *adv.* **im·mac'u·la·cy** *n.*

im·ma·nent (ĭm'anent) *adj.* Indwelling, inherent (*in*); (of God) permanently pervading the universe (opp. TRANSCENDENT). **im'ma·nence, im'ma·nen·cy** *ns.*

Im·man·u·el, Em·man·u·el (ĭmăn'ūel). Name of the coming Messiah as prophesied by Isaiah (Isa. 7, 8; Matt. 1), represented in Christian exegesis as being Christ. [Heb., = "God with us"]

im·ma·te·ri·al (ĭmater'ēal) *adj.* 1. Not relevant, unimportant. 2.

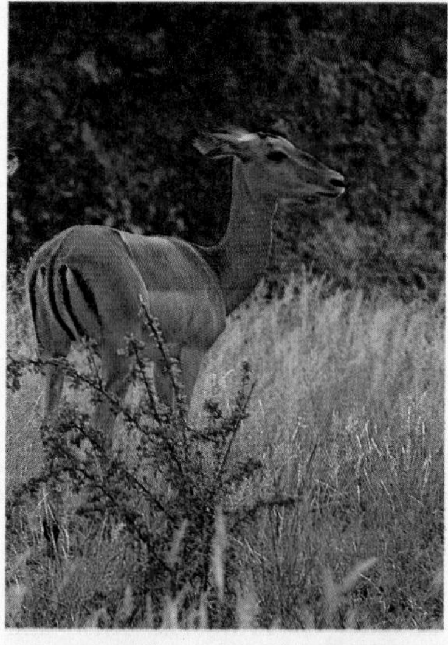

*The **Impala** is a species of African antelope which can travel at great speed and can jump up to 30 ft. in length and 10 ft. high when disturbed. Its slight build lends grace to its movements.*

Not material, incorporeal. **im·ma·te'ri·al·ism** *n.* Doctrine that there is no material world and all things exist only in the mind or have only spiritual existence. **im·ma·te'ri·al·ist** *n.* **im·ma·te·ri·a·bil·i·ty** (ĭmatērēabĭl'ĭtē) *n.*

im·ma·ture (ĭmatoor', -tūr', -choor') *adj.* Not mature, not developed fully; youthful. **im·ma·tu'ri·ty** *n.*

im·meas·ur·a·ble (ĭmĕzh'erabel) *adj.* Not measurable, immense. **im·meas'ur·a·ble·ness, im·meas·ur·a·bil·i·ty** (ĭmĕzherabĭl'ĭtē) *ns.* **im·meas'ur·a·bly** *adv.*

im·me·di·ate (ĭmē'dēĭt) *adj.* Occurring at once, without delay; of, pertaining to the present time; not separated by or not having any intervening object, agent, or medium, next, nearest; ~ **inference**, (logic) inference from single premise, without intervention of middle term. **im·me'di·ate·ly** adv. **im·me'di·ate·ness, im·me·di·a·cy** (ĭmē'dēasē) *ns.*

Im·mel·mann (ĭm'elmahn, -man) **turn.** (aviation) Fighter plane or stunt plane maneuver of half loop followed by half roll to gain altitude and reverse direction quickly. [f. Max *Immelmann*, (1890–1916) German aviator]

im·me·mo·ri·al (ĭmemōr'ēal, -mōr'-) *adj.* Ancient beyond memory; very old. **im·me·mo'ri·al·ly** *adv.*

im·mense (ĭmĕns') *adj.* Vast, huge; **im'mense·ly** *adv.* In an immense degree; (colloq.) very much. **im·men·si·ty** (ĭmĕn'sĭtē) *n.* (pl. **-ties**).

im·merse (ĭmers') *v.t.* (**-mersed, -mers·ing**). Dip, plunge (*in* liquid); put below surface of water, esp. baptize thus; bury, embed, (*in*); involve deeply, absorb, (*in* debt, difficulties, thought, etc.).

im·mer·sion (ĭmer'zhon, -shon) *n.* Immersing; baptism by plunging whole person in water; absorption (*in* thought etc.); (astron.) disappearance of celestial body into eclipse behind another or in its shadow; ~ **heater**, electrical element, usu. thermostatically controlled, immersed in water which it heats.

im·mi·grate (ĭm'igrāt) *v.* (**-grat·ed, -grat·ing**). Come as settler (*into* foreign country); **im·mi·grant** (ĭm'igrant) *adj.* & *n.* **im·mi·gra·tion** (ĭmigrā'shon) *n.*

im·mi·nent (ĭm'inent) *adj.* (Of events, esp. dangers) impending, soon to happen. **im'mi·nent·ly** *adv.* **im'mi·nence** *n.*

im·mis·ci·ble (ĭmĭs'ibel) *adj.* That cannot be mixed. **im·mis'ci·bil·i·ty** (ĭmĭsibĭl'ĭtē) *n.* **im·mis'ci·bly** *adv.*

im·mo·bile (ĭmō'bĭl, -bēl) *adj.* Immovable; not mobile; motionless. **im·mo·bil·i·ty** (ĭmōbĭl'ĭtē) *n.*

im·mo·bi·lize (ĭmō'bilīz) *v.t.* (**-lized, -liz·ing**). Fix immovably; render immobile or stationary; keep (limb, patient) restricted in movement in order to heal; restrict movement of; withdraw (specie) from circulation, holding it against bank notes to create a monetary reserve or a fixed capital. **im·mo·bi·li·za·tion** (ĭmōbilīzā'shon) *n.*

im·mod·er·ate (ĭmŏd'erĭt) *adj.* Excessive, wanting in moderation. **im·mod'er·ate·ly** *adv.* **im·mod·er·a·tion** (ĭmŏderā'shon) *n.*

im·mod·est (ĭmŏd'ĭst) *adj.* Lacking modesty; shameless; impudent. **im·mod'est·ly** *adv.* **im·mod'es·ty** *n.* (pl. **-ties**).

im·mo·late (ĭm'olāt) *v.t.* (**-lat·ed, -lat·ing**). Kill (victim) as sacrifice, as by fire; (fig.) sacrifice (thing etc. to another). **im·mo·la·tion** (ĭmolā'shon), **im'mo·la·tor** *ns.*

im·mo·ral (ĭmōr'al, -mār'-) *adj.* Not conforming to morality; morally evil; vicious, dissolute. **im·mor'al·ist** *n.* **im·mor'al·ly** *adv.* **im·mo·ral·i·ty** (ĭmorăl'ĭtē) *n.*

im·mor·tal (ĭmōr'tal) *adj.* Not mortal, not subject to death; divine; remembered or celebrated forever; everlasting, perpetual. **im·mor'tal·ly** *adv.* **immortal** *n.* Immortal being, esp. (pl.) gods of classical mythology; person, esp. author, of enduring fame; **The I ~ s**, 40 members of the Académie Française (so called because each member's place is filled as soon as he dies); picked body of 10,000 infantry forming ancient Persian royal bodyguard. **im·mor·tal·i·ty** (ĭmōrtăl'ĭtē) *n.*

im·mor·tal·ize (ĭmōr'talīz) *v.t.* (**-ized, -iz·ing**). Confer enduring fame upon; endow with endless life;

perpetuate. **im·mor·tal·i·za·tion** (ĭmōrt*a*lĭzā′sh*o*n) *n.*

im·mor·telle (ĭmōrtĕl′) *n.* Any of several flowers of papery texture retaining color and shape after being dried.

im·mov·a·ble (ĭmōō′v*a*b*e*l) *adj.* That cannot be moved, stationary; motionless; not subject to change; steadfast, unyielding; emotionless; (law, of property) consisting of land, houses, etc.; = REAL; not changing from one date to another in different years, occurring on a fixed date of the modern calendar (as an ~ **feast** or holiday). **im·mov′a·ble·ness, im·mov·a·bil·i·ty** (ĭmōōv*a*bĭl′ĭtē) *ns.* **im·mov′a·bly** *adv.* **im·mov′a·bles** *n.pl.* Immovable property.

im·mune (ĭmūn′) *adj.* Having immunity, exempt; (esp.) protected from a disease by natural resistance or inoculation; ~ **response,** ~ **reaction,** living organism's natural rejection of or reaction to foreign tissues or agents.

im·mu·ni·ty (ĭmū′nĭtē) *n.* (pl. **-ties**). 1. Freedom (from); (law) exemption (*from* taxation, jurisdiction, etc.). 2. (physiol.) That property of a living organism by which infection is resisted and overcome; **active** ~, increased resistance to an invading microbe or its products, developed in response to infection (whether a natural infection or one introduced artificially), as distinct from **passive** ~, temporary resistance acquired prenatally or by injection of antibody; **acquired** ~, immunity of an organism that manufactures, or is injected with, antibodies.

im·mu·nize (ĭm′y*u*nīz) *v.t.* (**-nized, -niz·ing**). Render immune (*against* infection). **im·mu·ni·za·tion** (ĭmy*u*nĭzā′sh*o*n) *n.*

immuno- *comb. form* (before vowel **immun-**) = immune, immunity (*immunology, immunosuppression*).

im·mu·nol·o·gy (ĭmy*u*nŏl′*o*jē) *n.* (pl. **-gies**). Study of immunity from disease and the conditions governing it. **im·mu·nol′o·gist** *n.*

im·mu·no·sup·pres·sion (ĭmy*u*nōs*u*prĕsh′*o*n) *n.* Medical suppression (as by drugs) of natural immune responses. **im·mu·no·sup·pres′sant** *n.* **im·mu·no·sup·pres′sive** *adj.*

im·mure (ĭmūr′) *v.t.* (**-mured, -mur·ing**). Enclose within walls, imprison, confine; entomb or build into a wall. **im·mure′ment** *n.*

im·mu·ta·ble (ĭmū′t*a*b*e*l) *adj.* Unchangeable; not subject to variation. **im·mu·ta·bil·i·ty** (ĭmūt*a*bĭl′ĭtē) *n.* **im·mu′ta·bly** *adv.*

Imp. *abbrev.* Emperor; empress; imperial. [L. *imperator, imperatrix*]

imp (ĭmp) *n.* Child of the devil; little devil; mischievous child.

imp. *abbrev.* (gram.) Imperative; imperfect; imperfection; imperial; import; imported; imprimatur.

im·pact[1] (ĭm′păkt) *n.* 1. Striking, collision. 2. (fig.) Influence, effect.

im·pact[2] (ĭmpăkt′) *v.t.* Press, fix, closely or firmly (*into, in*); crowd densely, wedge together. **im·pac·tion** (ĭmpăk′sh*o*n) *n.* (esp., surg.) Fracture in which broken parts are driven together so as to become locked; (dentistry) condition in which a tooth is so confined in its socket as to prevent normal growth through the gum.

*The **Impatiens** genus of plants has widespread distribution particularly in Africa, Asia and North America. The name meaning 'impatient' relates to the speed of seed dispersal.*

im·pair (ĭmpār′) *v.t.* Damage, weaken. **im·pair′ment** *n.*

im·pa·la (ĭmpăl′*a*, -pah′l*a*) *n.* (pl. **-pa·las,** collect. **-pa·la**). African antelope (*Aepyceros melampus*) with reddish coat and great leaping ability, the male having lyre-shaped, ringed horns. [f. Zulu]

im·pale (ĭmpāl′) *v.t.* (**-paled, -pal·ing**). Transfix (body etc., *with*, sharpened stake, pin, etc., esp. as form of capital punishment). **im·pale′ment** *n.*

im·pal·pa·ble (ĭmpăl′p*a*b*e*l) *adj.* Imperceptible to the touch; not easily grasped by the mind; intangible. **im·pal·pa·bil·i·ty** (ĭmpălp*a*bĭl′ĭtē) *n.* **im·pal′pa·bly** *adv.*

im·pan·el (ĭmpăn′*e*l), **em·pan·el** (ĕmpăn′*e*l) *vbs.t.* Enter on a panel for jury duty; enroll (a jury). **im·pan′el·ment** *n.*

im·part (ĭmpārt′) *v.t.* Communicate, make known, relate (news, etc. *to*); give share of, bestow.

im·par·tial (ĭmpār′sh*a*l) *adj.* Not partial, unprejudiced, fair. **im·par′tial·ly** *adv.* **im·par·ti·al·i·ty** (ĭmpārshēăl′ĭtē) *n.*

im·pass·a·ble (ĭmpăs′*a*b*e*l) *adj.* That cannot be traversed; that cannot be surmounted or overcome. **im·pass′a·ble·ness, im·pass·a·bil·i·ty** (ĭmpăs*a*bĭl′ĭtē) *ns.*

im·passe (ĭm′păs, ĭmpăs′) *n.* Deadlock, unresolvable dilemma; position from which there is no escape; road having no exit, dead end.

im·pas·si·ble (ĭmpăs′*i*b*e*l) *adj.* Incapable of feeling or emotion; incapable of suffering injury; not subject to suffering. **im·pas′si·ble·ness, im·pas·si·bil·i·ty** (ĭmpăs*i*bĭl′ĭtē) *ns.* **im·pas′si·bly** *adv.*

im·pas·sion (ĭmpăsh′*o*n) *v.t.* Stir the passions of, excite strongly (chiefly in past part.).

im·pas·sive (ĭmpăs′ĭv) *adj.* Deficient in feeling or emotion; serene; without sensation; not subject to suffering. **im·pas′sive·ly** *adv.* **im·pas′sive·ness, im·pas·siv·i·ty** (ĭmpăsĭv′ĭtē) *ns.*

im·pas·to (ĭmpăs′tō, -pah′stō) *n.* (pl. **-tos**). (paint.) Laying on of color thickly; (ceramics) enamel colors on slip standing out in relief from surface of ware.

im·pa·tiens (ĭmpā′sh*e*nz, -sh*e*ns) *n.* Any plant of the genus *I*~, including the ornamental garden balsam (*I. balsamins*) and the jewelweed. [L. impatient, because seed pods burst and scatter seeds when barely touched]

im·pa·tient (ĭmpā′sh*e*nt) *adj.* Not patient, not enduring with composure; intolerant *of*; restlessly desirous (*for* thing, *to* do). **im·pa′tient·ly** *adv.* **im·pa′tience** *n.*

im·peach (ĭmpēch′) *v.t.* Call in question, disparage (character, the credibility of, etc.); accuse (person) *of*, charge *with*; find fault with; accuse (a public official) of high crime before competent tribunal. **im·peach′ment** *n.* Calling in question; accusation and prosecution of a public official for high crime or before a competent tribunal, as the presentation of formal charges against a high public official by the lower house of a legislature for possible trial before the upper house. **im·peach′a·ble** *adj.*

im·pec·ca·ble (ĭmpĕk′*a*bel) *adj.* Faultless, irreproachable; not liable to sin. **im·pec·ca·bil·i·ty** (ĭmpĕk*a*bĭl′ĭtē) *n.* **im·pec′ca·bly** *adv.*

im·pe·cu·ni·ous (ĭmpekū′nē*u*s) *adj.* Having little or no money. **im·pe·cu·ni·os·i·ty** (ĭmpekūnēŏs′-ĭtē) *n.*

im·ped·ance (ĭmpē′d*a*ns) *n.* (elect.) Resistance of an electric circuit to the flow of alternating current.

im·pede (ĭmpēd′) *v.t.* (**-ped·ed, -ped·ing**). Retard, hinder.

im·ped·i·ment (ĭmpĕd′ĭm*e*nt) *n.* Hindrance, obstruction; (also **speech ~**) stammer, stutter.

im·pel (ĭmpĕl′) *v.t.* (**-pelled, -pel·ling**). Drive or urge forward, propel. **im·pel′lent** *n.*

im·pend (ĭmpĕnd′) *v.i.* Be imminent; be a threat or menace; hang, be suspended (*over*). **im·pend′ence, im·pend′en·cy** *ns.* **im·pend′ent** *adj.*

im·pen·e·tra·ble (ĭmpĕn′*e*tr*a*bel) *adj.* That cannot be penetrated, pierced, entered, etc.; inscrutable, unfathomable; impervious; (phys.) having that property in virtue of which 2 bodies cannot occupy same place at same time. **im·pen′e·tra·ble·ness, im·pen·e·tra·bil·i·ty** (ĭmpĕn*e*tr*a*bĭl′ĭtē) *ns.* **im·pen′e·tra·bly** *adv.*

im·pen·i·tent (ĭmpĕn′ĭt*e*nt) *adj.* Not penitent. **im·pen′i·tent·ly** *adv.* **im·pen′i·tence** *n.*

imper. *abbrev.* Imperative.

im·per·a·tive (ĭmpĕr′*a*tĭv) *adj.* 1. (gram., of verbal mood, or form belonging to it) Expressing command, request, or exhortation. 2. Commanding, peremptory; urgent; obligatory. **im·per′a·tive·ly** *adv.* **im·per′a·tive·ness** *n.* **im·per′a·tive** *n.* Imperative mood.

im·per·cep·ti·ble (ĭmp*e*rsĕp′-tĭbel) *adj.* That cannot be perceived; very slight, gradual, or subtle. **im·per·cep′ti·bly** *adv.* **im·per·cep′ti·ble·ness** *n.*

imperf. *abbrev.* (gram.) Imperfect.

im·per·fect (ĭmpẽr′fĭkt) *adj.* 1. Not fully formed or done, incomplete; faulty. 2. (gram., of tense) Implying action going on but not complete (e.g. *he is*, *he will be*, *singing*, but usu. of past time, *as he was singing*). **im·per′fect·ly** *adv.*

*A young orange grove in **Imperial Valley**. This area, once part of the Colorado Desert, has been extensively irrigated by the All-American Canal and yields a large range of agricultural produce.*

im·per·fec·tion (ĭmp*e*rfĕk′sh*o*n) *n.* Incompleteness; faultiness; fault, blemish.

im·per·fo·rate (ĭmpẽr′f*e*rĭt, -f*e*rāt), **im·per·fo·rat·ed** (ĭmpẽr′-f*e*rātĭd) *adjs.* Not perforated; (of sheet of postage stamps) without perforations.

im·pe·ri·al (ĭmpẽr′ē*a*l) *adj.* Of an empire or sovereign state ranking with an empire; of an emperor or empress; (of weights and measures) appointed by statute for use throughout the United Kingdom; hence, ~ **gallon**, Brit. gallon, equivalent to $1\frac{1}{5}$ U.S. gallon. **im·pe′ri·al·ly** *adv.*

Im·pe·ri·al (ĭmpẽr′ē*a*l) **Valley.** Agricultural area in SE. California adjacent to Mexico, once part of the Colorado Desert, irrigated by the All-American Canal; land is mostly below sea level and includes the Salton Sink.

im·pe·ri·al·ism (ĭmpẽr′ē*a*lĭz*e*m) *n.* Political or economic sway over other nations; (usu. derog.) (belief in desirability of) acquiring colonies and dependencies; principle or spirit of empire, advocacy of what are held to be imperial interests. **im·pe′ri·al·ist** *n.* & *adj.* Adherent of an emperor; advocate of imperial rule; advocate of imperialism. **im·pe·ri·al·is·tic** (ĭmpẽrē*a*lĭs′tĭk) *adj.*

im·per·il (ĭmpĕr′ĭl) *v.t.* (**-iled, -il·ing**, esp. Brit. **-illed, -il·ling**). Bring into danger.

im·pe·ri·ous (ĭmpẽr′ē*u*s) *adj.* Overbearing, domineering; urgent, imperative. **im·pe′ri·ous·ly** *adv.* **im·pe′ri·ous·ness** *n.*

im·per·ish·a·ble (ĭmpĕr′ĭsh-*a*bel) *adj.* That cannot perish. **im·per·ish·a·bil·i·ty** (ĭmpĕrĭsh-*a*bĭl′ĭtē) *n.* **im·per′ish·a·bly** *adv.*

im·per·ma·nent (ĭmpẽr′m*a*-n*e*nt) *adj.* Not permanent. **im·per′ma·nence, im·per·ma·nen·cy** *ns.*

im·per·me·a·ble (ĭmpẽr′mē-*a*bel) *adj.* That cannot be passed through; that does not permit passage of fluids. **im·per·me·a·bil·i·ty** (ĭmpẽrmē*a*bĭl′ĭtē) *n.* **im·per′me·a·bly** *adv.*

im·per·mis·si·ble (ĭmp*e*rmĭs′-ĭbel) *adj.* Not allowable.

im·per·son·al (ĭmpẽr′s*o*n*a*l) *adj.* 1. (gram., of verbs) Used only in 3rd person singular without referring to a person or definite subject; hence, used without a subject or with a merely formal one, as Engl. *it*. 2. Having no personality or personal reference or tone. **im·per′son·al·ly** *adv.* **im·per·son·al·i·ty** (ĭmpẽrs*o*năl′ĭtē) *n.*

im·per·son·ate (ĭmpẽr′s*o*nāt) *v.t.* (**-at·ed, -at·ing**). Represent in bodily form, personify; play the part of, personate; act (character). **im·per·son·a·tion** (ĭmpẽrs*o*nā′-sh*o*n), **im·per′son·a·tor** *ns.*

im·per·ti·nent (ĭmpẽr′tĭn*e*nt) *adj.* 1. Irrelevant. 2. Presumptuous; insolent, saucy. **im·per′ti·nent·ly** *adv.* **im·per′ti·nence** *n.*

im·per·turb·a·ble (ĭmp*e*rtẽr′-b*a*bel) *adj* Not excitable, calm. **im·per·turb′a·ble·ness, im·per·turb·a·bil·i·ty** (ĭmp*e*rtẽrb*a*-bĭl′ĭtē) *ns.* **im·per·turb′a·bly** *adv.*

im·per·vi·ous (ĭmpẽr′vē*u*s) *adj.* Not affording passage (*to*); (fig.) impenetrable, not affording entrance *to* (argument, feeling, etc.). **im·per′vi·ous·ly** *adv.* **im·per′vi·ous·ness** *n.*

im·pe·ti·go (ĭmpetī′gō) *n.* (pl. **-gos**). Acute inflammatory disease of skin caused by streptococcal and staphylococcal organisms, characterized by pustules chiefly on face and hands.

im·pet·u·ous (ĭmpĕch′o͞o*u*s) *adj.* Moving violently or rapidly; acting with rash or sudden energy. **im·pet′u·ous·ly** *adv.* **im·pet′u·ous·ness, im·pet·u·os·i·ty** (ĭm-pĕcho͞oŏs′ĭtē) *ns.*

im·pe·tus (ĭm′pet*u*s) *n.* (pl. **-tus·es**). Force with which a body moves; (fig.) moving force, impulse.

im·pi·e·ty (ĭmpī′etē) *n.* (pl. **-ties**). Ungodliness; want of dutifulness or reverence.

im·pinge (ĭmpĭnj′) *v.* (**-pinged, -ping·ing**). Make impact (*on, upon*); encroach; collide, strike (*against*). **im·pinge′ment** *n.*

im·pi·ous (ĭm′pē*u*s, ĭmpī′-) *adj.* Not pious, profane. **im′pi·ous·ly** *adv.*

imp·ish (ĭm′pĭsh) *adj.* Of, like,

an imp. **imp'ish·ly** *adv.* **imp'ish·ness** *n.*

im·plac·a·ble (ĭmplăk'*a*bel) *adj.* That cannot be appeased. **im·plac·a·bil'i·ty** *n.* **im·plac'a·bly** *adv.*

im·plant (ĭmplănt', -plahnt') *v.t.* Insert, infix (*in*); instill (*in* mind etc.); plant. **im·plan·ta·tion** (ĭmplăntā'sh*o*n) *n.*

im·plau·si·ble (ĭmplaw'z*i*bel) *adj.* Not plausible.

im·ple·ment[1] (ĭm'plem*e*nt) *n.* 1. Thing serving as equipment or part of outfit. 2. Tool; apparatus, utensil, instrument, etc.

im·ple·ment[2] (ĭm'plemĕnt) *v.t.* Put into effect; provide plan or procedure to do so; fulfill. **im·ple·men·ta·tion** (ĭmpl*e*mĕntā'shon) *n.*

im·pli·cate (ĭm'plĭkāt) *v.t.* (**-cat·ed, -cat·ing**). 1. (archaic) Entwine, entangle. 2. Involve, imply, as inference; involve (*in* charge, crime, etc.). **im·pli·ca·tion** (ĭmplĭkā'sh*o*n) *n.*

im·plic·it (ĭmplĭs'ĭt) *adj.* Implied though not plainly expressed; virtually contained (*in*). **im·plic'it·ly** *adv.* **im·plic'it·ness** *n.*

im·plode (ĭmplōd') *v.* (**-plod·ed, -plod·ing**). (Cause to) burst inward. **im·plo·sion** (ĭmplō'zh*o*n) *n.*

im·plore (ĭmplōr', -plōr') *v.t.* (**-plored, -plor·ing**). Beg earnestly for; entreat. **im·plor'ing·ly** *adv.*

im·ply (ĭmplī') *v.t.* (**-plied, -ply·ing**). Involve the truth of (thing not expressly asserted); mean; insinuate, hint.

im·po·lite (ĭmp*o*līt') *adj.* Uncivil, rude. **im·po·lite'ly** *adv.* **im·po·lite'ness** *n.*

im·pol·i·tic (ĭmpŏl'ĭtĭk) *adj.* Not politic; inexpedient. **im·pol'i·tic·ly** *adv.*

im·pon·der·a·ble (ĭmpŏn'der*a*bel) *adj.* Not capable of being precisely weighed, measured, or evaluated. ~ *n.* Imponderable thing.

im·port (ĭmpōrt', -pōrt') *v.t.* 1. Bring, introduce (esp. goods from foreign country *into*). 2. Imply, indicate, mean; express, make known. 3. Be of consequence. **im·por·ta·tion** (ĭmpōrtā'sh*o*n, -pōr-) *n.* Bringing in, introducing. **im·port'er** *n.* One who imports goods. **import** (ĭm'pōrt, -pōrt) *n.* 1. What is implied, meaning, importance. 2. (usu. pl.) Commodity imported.

im·por·tance (ĭmpōr't*a*ns) *n.* Being important; weight, significance; personal consequence, dignity.

im·por·tant (ĭmpōr't*a*nt) *adj.* Carrying with it great consequence (*to*), weighty, momentous; consequential. **im·por'tant·ly** *adv.*

im·por·tu·nate (ĭmpōr'ch*u*nĭt) *adj.* Persistent, pressing, in solicitation; (of affairs) urgent. **im·por'tu·nate·ness** *n.* **im·por'tu·nate·ly** *adv.*

im·por·tune (ĭmpōrtōōn', -tūn', -pōr'ch*u*n) *v.t.* (**-tuned, -tun·ing**). Solicit pressingly.

im·pose (ĭmpōz') *v.* (**-posed, -pos·ing**). 1. Place (thing) *on* (archaic); (print.) lay (pages of type) in proper order and secure them in a chase. 2. Lay (tax, duty, charge, *on*). 3. ~ **on**, take advantage of (person); practice deception upon. **im·po·si·tion** (ĭmp*o*zĭsh'*o*n), **im·pos'er** *ns.*

im·pos·ing (ĭmpō'zĭng) *adj.* Grand, impressive through size or power, majestic. **im·pos'ing·ly** *adv.*

im·pos·si·ble (ĭmpŏs'ĭbel) *adj.* Not possible; (loosely) not easy, not convenient; (colloq.) outrageous, intolerable. **im·pos·si·bil·i·ty** (ĭmpŏs*i*bĭl'ĭtē) *n.* (pl. **-ties**). **im·pos'si·bly** *adv.*

im·post[1] (ĭm'pōst) *n.* Tax, duty, tribute.

im·post[2] (ĭm'pōst) *n.* Upper course of pillar, bearing arch.

im·pos·tor (ĭmpŏs't*e*r) *n.* One who assumes a false character or passes himself off as someone else.

im·pos·ture (ĭmpŏs'ch*e*r) *n.* Fraudulent deception.

im·po·tent (ĭm'p*o*tent) *adj.* Powerless; helpless; (of males) incapable of sexual intercourse; incapable of fathering a child. **im'po·tent·ly** *adv.* **im'po·tence, im'po·ten·cy** *ns.*

im·pound (ĭmpownd') *v.t.* Shut up (cattle) in pound; shut up (person, thing) as in pound; take legal possession of; confiscate. **im·pound'ment** *n.*

im·pov·er·ish (ĭmpŏv'erĭsh) *v.t.* Make poor; exhaust strength of. **im·pov'er·ish·ment** *n.*

im·prac·ti·ca·ble (ĭmprăk'tĭk*a*bel) *adj.* Impossible in practice; impassable (of road etc.); incapable of being done. **im·prac'ti·ca·ble·ness, im·prac·ti·ca·bil·i·ty** (ĭmprăktĭk*a*bĭl'ĭtē) *ns.*

*Dog catchers **impound** dogs that are found wandering the streets. After a set waiting period those that have not been claimed are put to sleep.*

im·prac·ti·cal (ĭmprăk'tĭk*a*l) *adj.* Not practical or useful. **im·prac·ti·cal·i·ty** (ĭmpraktĭkăl'ĭtē) *n.*

im·pre·cate (ĭm'pr*e*kāt) *v.t.* (**-cat·ed, -cat·ing**). Invoke, call down, (evil *upon* person etc.). **im·pre·ca·tion** (ĭmpr*e*kā'sh*o*n) *n.* (esp.) Spoken curse. **im'pre·ca·tor** *n.* **im·pre·ca·to·ry** (ĭm'pr*e*k*a*tōrē, -tōrē) *adj.*

im·preg·na·ble (ĭmprĕg'n*a*bel) *adj.* (of fortress etc.) That cannot be taken by force; (fig.) proof against attack. **im·preg·na·bil·i·ty** (ĭmprĕgn*a*bĭl'ĭtē) *n.* **im·preg'na·bly** *adv.*

im·preg·nate (ĭmprĕg'nāt) *v.t.* (**-nat·ed, -nat·ing**). 1. Make (female) pregnant; = FERTILIZE def. 2. 2. Fill, saturate, (*with*); imbue, fill. **im·preg·na'tion** *n.*

im·pre·sa·ri·o (ĭmpr*e*sār'ēō, -sār'-) *n.* (pl. **-sa·ri·os**). Organizer of public entertainments, esp. manager of operatic or concert company.

im·press[1] (ĭm'prĕs) *n.* Stamping; mark made by seal, stamp, etc.; (fig.) characteristic mark. ~ (ĭmprĕs') *v.t.* Apply (mark etc.) with pressure, imprint, stamp, (*on*); imprint, enforce, (idea etc. *on* person, his mind); mark (thing *with* stamp etc.); affect, influence; affect (person) strongly (*with* idea etc.). **im·press'i·ble** *adj.* **im·press·i·bil·i·ty** (ĭmprĕs*i*bĭl'ĭtē) *n.*

im·press[2] (ĭmprĕs') *v.t.* Force (men) to serve in army or navy; seize (goods etc.) for public service; enlist, make use of, (thing) in argument etc. **im·press'ment** *n.*

im·pres·sion (ĭmprĕsh'*o*n) *n.* 1. Impressing (of mark); mark impressed. 2. Individual print taken from type or engraving. 3. Effect produced (esp. on mind or feelings); notion, (vague) belief, impressed on the mind.

im·pres·sion·a·ble (ĭmprĕsh´-*o*n*a*bel) *adj.* Susceptible of impressions, easily influenced.

im·pres·sion·ism (ĭmprĕsh´*o*n-ĭzem) *n.* (often cap.) Method of painting initiated *c*1870 by a school of French painters (including Manet, Monet, Pissarro, Renoir, and Degas), whose aim was to paint the momentary or transitory appearance of things, and esp. the effects of light and atmosphere, rather than form or structure; method of writing, style of music, resembling this. **im·pres′sion·ist** *n.* & *adj.* **im·pres·sion·is·tic** (ĭmprĕsh*o*nĭs´tĭk) *adj.* **im·pres·sion·is′ti·cal·ly** *adv.*

im·pres·sive (ĭmprĕs´ĭv) *adj.* Able to excite deep feeling, making deep impression on mind or senses. **im·pres′sive·ly** *adv.* **im·pres′sive·ness** *n.*

im·pri·ma·tur (ĭmprĭmā´t*e*r, -mah´-) *n.* Official license to print esp. works sanctioned by R.C. Ch.; (fig.) sanction. [mod. L., = "let it be printed"]

im·print (ĭmprĭnt´) *v.t.* Stamp (figure etc. *on*); impress (idea etc. *on*, *in* mind etc.); impress (quality etc. *on*, *in*); stamp (thing *with* figure). ~ (ĭm´prĭnt) *n.* 1. Impression, stamp. 2. Name of printer or publisher, date and place of printing or publication, at foot or back of title page or at end of book etc.

im·pris·on (ĭmprĭz´*on*) *v.t.* Put into prison; confine, shut up. **im·pris′on·ment** *n.*

im·prob·a·ble (ĭmprŏb´*a*bel) *adj.* Not likely to be true or to happen. **im·prob·a·bil·i·ty** (ĭmprŏb*a*bĭl´ĭtē) *n.* (pl. **-ties**). **im·prob′a·bly** *adv.*

im·pro·bi·ty (ĭmprō´bĭtē, -prŏb´ĭ-) *n.* Wickedness; dishonesty.

im·promp·tu (ĭmprŏmp´to͞o, -tū) *adv.* & *adj.* (Spoken, done) without preparation, extemporaneous. ~ *n.* Improvised or extemporaneous performance or composition. [L. *in promptu* in readiness]

im·prop·er (ĭmprŏp´*er*) *adj.* Inaccurate, wrong; unseemly, indecent; ~ **fraction**, fraction with numerator greater than denominator. **im·prop′er·ly** *adv.* **im·prop′er·ness** *n.*

im·pro·pri·e·ty (ĭmpr*o*prī´*e*tē) *n.* (pl. **-ties**). Incorrectness; unfitness; indecency.

im·prov·a·ble (ĭmpro͞o´v*a*bel) *adj.* That can be improved. **im·prov′a·ble·ness, im·prov·a·bil·i·ty** (ĭmpro͞ov*a*bĭl´ĭtē) *ns.*

im·prove (ĭmpro͞ov´) *v.* (**-proved, -prov·ing**). Make, become, better; make good use of; ~ **on**, produce something better than. **im·prove′ment, im·prov′er** *ns.*

im·prov·i·dent (ĭmprŏv´ĭd*e*nt) *adj.* Unforeseeing; heedless; thriftless. **im·prov′i·dent·ly** *adv.* **im·prov′i·dence** *n.*

The fortified ***Inca*** *city of Machu Picchu provided a refuge for priests and nobles after the Spanish capture of Cuzco. It was so well hidden between two mountain peaks that it was not discovered until 1911.*

im·pro·vise (ĭm´pr*o*vīz) *v.t.* (**-vised, -vis·ing**). Compose, utter, (verse, music, etc.) without preparation; provide, get up, extemporaneously. **im·prov·i·sa·tion** (ĭmprŏvĭzā´sh*on*) *n.* **im·prov·i·sa·to·ri·al** (ĭmprŏvĭz*a*tōr´ē*a*l, -tōr´-) *adj.* **im′pro·vis·er, im′pro·vi·sor** *ns.*

im·pru·dent (ĭmpro͞o´d*e*nt) *adj.* Rash, indiscreet. **im·pru′dent·ly** *adv.* **im·pru′dence** *n.*

im·pu·dent (ĭm´py*u*d*e*nt) *adj.* Shamelessly forward; unblushing; insolently disrespectful. **im′pu·dent·ly** *adv.* **im′pu·dence** *n.* **im′pu·den·cy** *n.* (pl. **-cies**).

im·pugn (ĭmpūn´) *v.t.* Assail by word, call in question (statement, action). **im·pugn′ment, im·pugn′er** *ns.*

im·pulse (ĭm´pŭls) *n.* 1. Impelling, push; (dynamics) force producing momentum; momentum thus produced; product of average value of force multiplied by time during which it acts. 2. Mental incitement; sudden tendency to act without reflection; impetus.

im·pul·sive (ĭmpŭl´sĭv) *adj.* 1. Tending to impel. 2. (of persons, conduct, etc.) Apt to be moved, prompted, by sudden impulse. **im·pul′sive·ly** *adv.* **im·pul′sive·ness** *n.*

im·pu·ni·ty (ĭmpū´nĭtē) *n.* Exemption from punishment; exemption from injury as consequence of act.

im·pure (ĭmpūr´) *adj.* Dirty; unchaste; mixed with foreign matter, adulterated; (of color) mixed with another color. **im·pure′ly** *adv.* **im·pur′i·ty** *n.* (pl. **-ties**).

im·pute (ĭmpūt´) *v.t.* (**-put·ed, -put·ing**). Attribute, ascribe, (fault etc. *to*). **im·pu·ta·tion** (ĭmpyo͞otā´sh*o*n) *n.* **im·put·a·tive** (ĭmpū´t*a*tĭv) *adj.* **im·put′a·tive·ly** *adv.*

IN *abbrev.* Indiana.

In *symbol.* Indium.

in (ĭn) *prep.* Within limits of space, time, circumstance, etc., as ~ *Europe*, ~ *Los Angeles*, ~ *a box*, ~ *the day*, ~ *the army*; **nothing, little, not much,** ~ **it**, no or little profit or advantage to be gained; no or little truth, information, etc. contained in (a rumor, message, etc.). **in** *adv.* 1. In or at a place, the right or normal state, the fashion, etc.; in season, on the inside, within; at home; in one's office; at work. 2. So as to pass within. 3. ~ **for it**, certain to meet with punishment or something unpleasant; ~ **with**, on friendly terms with. **in** *adj.* That is in; lying etc. within. ~ *n.* (pl.) ~**s and outs**, turnings to and fro (usu. fig.), details (*of* procedure etc.).

in. *abbrev.* Inch(es).

-in *suffix.* Forming names of neutral substances (*gelatin, protein*) and antibiotics (*penicillin*).

in-[1] *prefix.* In, on, into, toward, against (*insight, influx*).

in-[2] *prefix.* Not (*insane, inseparable*).

in·a·bil·i·ty (ĭn*a*bĭl´ĭtē) *n.* Being unable; lack of power or means.

in·ac·ces·si·ble (ĭn*a*ksĕs´*i*bel) *adj.* That cannot be reached; unapproachable. **in·ac·ces·si·bil·i·ty** (ĭn*a*ksĕs*i*bĭl´ĭtē) *n.* **in·ac·ces'si·bly** *adv.*

in·ac·cu·rate (ĭnăk´yerĭt) *adj.* Not accurate. **in·ac'cu·rate·ly** *adv.* **in·ac'cu·ra·cy** *n.* (pl. **-cies**).

in·ac·tion (ĭnăk´sh*o*n) *n.* Absence of action; sluggishness, inertness. **in·ac'tive** *adj.* **in·ac'tive·ly** *adv.* **in·ac·tiv·i·ty** (ĭnăktĭv´ĭtē) *n.* **in·ac·ti·vate** (ĭnăk´tĭvāt) *v.t.* (**-vat·ed, -vat·ing**).

in·ad·e·quate (ĭnăd´ekwĭt) *adj.* Not adequate; insufficient. **in·ad'e·quate·ly** *adv.* **in·ad'e·qua·cy** *n.* (pl. **-cies**).

in·ad·mis·si·ble (ĭn*a*dmĭs´*i*bel) *adj.* That cannot be admitted or allowed. **in·ad·mis·si·bil·i·ty** (ĭn*a*dmĭs*i*bĭl´ĭtē) *n.* **in·ad·mis'si·bly** *adv.*

in·ad·ver·tent (ĭn*a*dvĕr´tent) *adj.* Not properly attentive; negligent; (of actions) unintentional. **in·ad·vert'ent·ly** *adv.* **in·ad·vert'ence, in·ad·vert'en·cy** *ns.* (pl. **-cies**).

in·al·ien·a·ble (ĭnāl´yen*a*bel, -ā´lēen*a*-) *adj.* Not alienable or transferable. **in·al·ien·a·bil·i·ty** (ĭnāly*e*n*a*bĭl´ĭtē, -ā´lēen*a*-) *n.* **in·al'ien·a·bly** *adv.*

in·am·o·ra·to (ĭnăm*o*rah´tō) *n.* (pl. **-tos**) (fem. **in·am·o·ra·ta** pr. ĭnăm*o*rah´t*a*; pl. **-tas**). Lover.

in·ane (ĭnān´) *adj.* Empty, void; silly, senseless. **in·ane'ly** *adv.* **in·an·i·ty** (ĭnăn´ĭtē) *n.* (pl. **-ties**).

in·an·i·mate (ĭnăn´*i*mĭt) *adj.* Destitute of life; not endowed with animal life; spiritless, dull. **in·an'i·mate·ly** *adv.* **in·an'i·mate·ness** *n.*

in·ap·pli·ca·ble (ĭnăp´l*i*k*a*bel) *adj.* Not applicable, unsuitable (*to*). **in·ap·pli·ca·bil·i·ty** (ĭnăpl*i*k*a*bĭl´ĭtē) *n.* **in·ap'pli·ca·bly** *adv.*

in·ap·pre·ci·a·ble (ĭn*a*prē´shē*a*bel, -sh*a*bel) *adj.* Imperceptible, not worth reckoning; negligible, insignificant. **in·ap·pre'ci·a·bly** *adv.*

in·ap·pro·pri·ate (ĭn*a*prō´prēĭt) *adj.* Not appropriate. **in·ap·pro'pri·ate·ly** *adv.* **in·ap·pro'pri·ate·ness** *n.*

in·ar·tic·u·late (ĭnărtĭk´y*u*lĭt) *adj.* 1. Not jointed. 2. Not articulate; unable to speak distinctly; speechless; unable to express one's ideas. **in·ar·tic'u·late·ly** *adv.* **in·ar·tic'u·late·ness** *n.*

in·ar·tis·tic (ĭnărtĭs´tĭk) *adj.* Not following the principles of art; unskilled in art.

in·as·much (ĭn*a*zmŭch´) *adv.* ~ **as**, since, because; in so far as.

in·at·ten·tion (ĭn*a*tĕn´sh*o*n) *n.* Want of attention, heedlessness; neglect to show courtesy. **in·at·ten·tive** (ĭn*a*tĕn´tĭv) *adj.* **in·at·ten'tive·ly** *adv.* **in·at·ten'tive·ness** *n.*

in·au·di·ble (ĭnaw´d*i*bel) *adj.* That cannot be heard. **in·au·di·bil·i·ty** (ĭnawd*i*bĭl´ĭtē) *n.* **in·au'di·bly** *adv.*

in·au·gu·ral (ĭnaw´gy*u*r*a*l) *adj.* (of ceremony) Inaugurating; (of speech etc.) given by person who is being inaugurated. ~ *n.* Inaugural speech, esp. by a U.S. president.

in·au·gu·rate (ĭnaw´gy*u*rāt) *v.t.* (**-rat·ed, -rat·ing**). Admit (person) to office etc. with ceremony; enter with ceremony upon (undertaking etc.); initiate public use of (building etc.). **in·au·gu·ra·tion** (ĭnawgy*u*rā´sh*o*n) *n.*

in·aus·pi·cious (ĭnawspĭsh´*u*s) *adj.* Not of good omen; unlucky. **in·aus·pi'cious·ly** *adv.* **in·aus·pi'cious·ness** *n.*

in·board (ĭn´bōrd, -bōrd) *adv.* & *adj.* (Situated) within sides or toward center of ship or aircraft.

in·born (ĭn´bōrn) *adj.* Implanted by nature.

in·bound (ĭn´bownd´) *adj.* Inward bound (of ships, planes, etc.).

in·bred (in´bred´) *adj.* 1. Innate, inherent by nature. 2. Born of closely related parents.

in·breed·ing (ĭn´brēdĭng) *n.* Breeding from animals or persons closely related.

Inc. *abbrev.* Incorporated.

inc. *abbrev.* Incorporated; income; increase.

In·ca (ĭng´k*a*) *n.* Member of Amer. Indian Quechua-speaking people, who at the time of the Spanish expedition, which overthrew them in 1533, had a highly developed civilization and ruled a large region of N.W. South Amer., with center at Cuzco, Peru; member of its ruling class, supposedly descended from the sun; **the** ~, the emperor or chief ruler of the Incas. **In'can** *adj.* & *n.*

in·cal·cu·la·ble (ĭnkăl´ky*u*l*a*bel) *adj.* Too great for calculation; that cannot be reckoned beforehand; uncertain. **in·cal·cu·la·bil·i·ty** (ĭnkălky*u*l*a*bĭl´ĭtē) *n.* **in·cal'cu·la·bly** *adv.*

in·can·desce (ĭnk*a*ndĕs´) *v.* (**-desced, -desc·ing**). (Cause to) glow with heat. **in·can·des·cent** (ĭnk*a*ndĕs´*e*nt) *adj.* Glowing with heat; shining brightly; (of gas or electric light etc.) produced by glowing of mantle or filament raised to white heat by flame of burning gas or passage of electricity. **in·can·des'cence** *n.*

in·can·ta·tion (ĭnkăntā´sh*o*n) *n.* (Use of) magical formula; spell, charm.

in·ca·pa·ble (ĭnkā´p*a*bel) *adj.*

__Incantations__ are still used by modern witches allegedly to cast spells and charms. In this ceremony the witch holds a sword in one hand and a rope in the other.

Not capable (*of*; freq. = too honest etc. to do); not susceptible (*of* improvement etc.); without ordinary capacity or natural ability. **in·ca·pa·bil·i·ty** (ĭnkāp*a*bĭl′ĭtē) *n.* **in·ca′pa·bly** *adv.*

in·ca·pac·i·tate (ĭnk*a*păs′ĭtāt) *v.t.* (**-tat·ed, -tat·ing**). Render incapable or unfit. **in·ca·pac·i·ta·tion** (ĭnk*a*păsĭtā′sh*o*n) *n.*

in·ca·pac·i·ty (ĭnk*a*păs′ĭtē) *n.* (pl. **-ties**). Inability; disability; legal disqualification.

in·car·cer·ate (ĭnkar̄′s*e*rāt) *v.t.* (**-at·ed, -at·ing**). Imprison. **in·car·cer·a·tion** (ĭnkar̄s*e*rā′sh*o*n), **in·car′cer·a·tor** *ns.*

in·car·nate (ĭnkar̄′nĭt, -nāt) *adj.* Embodied in flesh, esp. in human form. ~ (ĭnkar̄′nāt, ĭn′kar̄-) *v.t.* (**-nat·ed, -nat·ing**). Embody in flesh; put (idea etc.) into concrete form, realize; be living embodiment of (quality). **in·car·na·tion** (ĭnkar̄nā′sh*o*n) *n.* Embodiment in (esp. human) flesh, esp. **the I~** (of Christ); personification, living type (*of* quality etc.).

in·cau·tious (ĭnkaw′sh*u*s) *adj.* Rash. **in·cau′tious·ly** *adv.* **in·cau′tious·ness** *n.*

in·cen·di·ar·y (ĭnsĕn′dēērē) *adj.* Of, guilty of, arson; causing, capable of causing, fire; (mil.) used for setting on fire enemy's property, esp. ~ **bomb**, bomb containing napalm etc. and igniting on impact; (fig.) tending to stir up strife, inflammatory.

in·cense[1] (ĭn′sĕns) *n.* Aromatic gum or other vegetable product, giving sweet smell when burned; smoke of this, esp. in religious ceremonial. ~ *v.t.* (**-censed, -cens·ing**). Fumigate with incense; burn incense to (deity etc.); suffuse with fragrance.

in·cense[2] (ĭnsĕns′) *v.t.* (**-censed, -cens·ing**). Enrage, make angry.

in·cen·tive (ĭnsĕn′tĭv) *adj.* Tending to incite. ~ *n.* Incitement, provocation, motive; (in industry) payment or concession to encourage harder work.

in·cep·tion (ĭnsĕp′sh*o*n) *n.* Beginning.

in·cer·ti·tude (ĭnser̄′tĭt ōōd, -tūd) *n.* Uncertainty.

in·ces·sant (ĭnsĕs′*a*nt) *adj.* Unceasing, continual, repeated. **in·ces′sant·ly** *adv.*

in·cest (ĭn′sĕst) *n.* Sexual intercourse between person too closely related to be legally married. **in·ces·tu·ous** (ĭnsĕs′chōō*u*s) *adj.* **in·ces′tu·ous·ly** *adv.*

inch (ĭnch) *n.* (abbrev. in.) Twelfth part of foot in measures of length; (as unit of rainfall) quantity that would cover horizontal surface to depth of 1 in.; (of atmospheric or other pressure) amount that balances weight of column of mercury 1 in. high in mercurial barometer; small amount; (pl.) stature; **by inches**, bit by bit; **every inch**, entirely; ~ **worm** = MEASURING WORM. **inch** *v.* Move by inches, edge *in, forward*, etc.

in·cho·ate (ĭnkō′ĭt) *adj.* Just begun; undeveloped.

in·ci·dence (ĭn′sĭd*e*ns) *n.* 1. Falling on, contact with, a thing; range, scope, extent, of influence; (of disease) rate, scale, frequency, of occurrence in a community. 2. (math., phys.) Falling of a line, or a thing moving in a line, upon a surface; **angle of** ~, angle that the incident line, ray, etc., makes with the perpendicular to the surface at the point of contact.

in·ci·dent[1] (ĭn′sĭd*e*nt) *adj.* 1. (of light etc.) Falling, striking, (*upon*). 2. Apt to occur, naturally attaching, (*to*).

in·ci·dent[2] (ĭn′sĭd*e*nt) *n.* Subordinate or accessory event; event, occurrence; detached event attracting general attention; distinct piece of action in play etc.

in·ci·den·tal (ĭnsĭdĕn′t*a*l) *adj.* Casual, not essential; ~ **music**, music interpolated in spoken play etc. **in·ci·den′tal·ly** *adv.* 1. By chance; casually. 2. Parenthetically; as a subordinate or casual comment.

in·cin·er·ate (ĭnsĭn′*e*rāt) *v.t.* (**-at·ed, -at·ing**). Reduce to ashes; consume by fire. **in·cin·er·a·tion** (ĭnsĭn*e*rā′sh*o*n) *n.* **in·cin′er·a·tor** *n.* (esp.) Apparatus for burning rubbish.

in·cip·i·ent (ĭnsĭp′ē*e*nt) *adj.* Beginning; in an initial stage. **in·cip′i·ent·ly** *adv.* **in·cip′i·ence, in·cip′i·en·cy** *ns.*

***Incense-burners** were widely used in the East. This pottery burner was excavated in 1972 from a 2,100-year-old tomb in China. Inside the pot were scented herbs.*

in·cise (ĭnsīz′) *v.t.* (**-cised, -cis·ing**). Make a cut in; engrave. **in·ci·sion** (ĭnsĭzh′*o*n) *n.* Cutting into a thing; cut.

in·ci·sive (ĭnsī′sĭv) *adj.* Cutting, penetrating; mentally sharp; acute, trenchant. **in·ci′sive·ly** *adv.* **in·ci′sive·ness** *n.*

in·ci·sor (ĭnsī′z*e*r) *n.* Cutting tooth, any front tooth in either jaw, between canine teeth, having sharp edge and single fang.

in·cite (ĭnsīt′) *v.t.* (**-cit·ed, -cit·ing**). Urge, stir up (person etc. *to*). **in·cite′ment** *n.*

in·ci·vil·i·ty (ĭns*i*vĭl′ĭtē) *n.* (pl. **-ties**). Rudeness, discourtesy.

in·clem·ent (ĭnklĕm′*e*nt) *adj.* (of weather etc.) Severe, esp. cold or stormy. **in·clem′en·cy** *n.* (pl. **-cies**).

in·cli·na·tion (ĭnkl*i*nā′sh*o*n) *n.* 1. Leaning, slope, slant; difference of direction of 2 lines, esp. as measured by angle between them; (of magnetic needle) = DIP *n.* def. 2; (astron.) angle between plane of a planet's orbit and that of the ecliptic. 2. Disposition, propensity (*to, for*); liking, affection (*for*).

in·cline (ĭnklīn′) *v.* (**-clined, -clin·ing**). 1. Bend (head etc.) forward or downward; lean, cause to lean, from vertical etc. 2. Dispose (person, mind, etc., *to*); be disposed; tend (*to*). 3. **inclined plane**, sloping plane (esp. as a means of reducing force needed to raise load). **incline** (ĭn′klīn) *n.* Inclined surface; slope.

in·clude (ĭnklo͞od′) *v.t.* (**-clud·ed, -clud·ing**). Comprise, embrace, as part of a whole; treat, regard, as so comprised. **in·clu·sion** (ĭnklo͞o′zhon) *n.*

in·clu·sive (ĭnklo͞o′sĭv) *adj.* Including, enclosing, comprehending; comprising; ~ **of**, embracing, comprising (something specified); (quasi- *adv.*) the term or terms named being included. **in·clu′sive·ly** *adv.* **in·clu′sive·ness** *n.*

in·cog·ni·to (ĭnkŏg′nĭtō, -kŏgnē′-) *adj.* & *adv.* With one's name, character, etc., concealed. ~ *n.* (pl. **-tos**) (fem. **in·cog·ni·ta** pr. ĭnkŏg′nĭta, -kŏgnē′-; pl. **-tas**). (Pretended identity of) person who is incognito.

in·co·her·ent (ĭnkohēr′ent, -kō-) *adj.* Not coherent. **in·co·her′ent·ly** *adv.* **in·co·her′ence** *n.* **in·co·her′en·cy** *n.* (pl. **-cies**).

in·com·bus·ti·ble (ĭnkombŭs′tĭbel) *n.* & *adj.* (Substance, object) that cannot be consumed by fire. **in·com·bus·ti·bil·i·ty** (ĭnkombŭstĭbĭl′ĭtē) *n.*

in·come (ĭn′kŭm) *n.* Periodical receipts from business, lands, work, investments, etc.; ~ **tax**, tax levied on this; **negative ~ tax**, taxation system by which credits are allowed for certain commitments and paid as supplementary income to persons for whom they exceed taxable income.

in·com·ing (ĭn′kŭmĭng) *n.* Entrance, arrival. ~ *adj.* Entering; about to enter, take office, etc.

in·com·men·su·ra·ble (ĭnkomĕn′serabel, -shera-) *adj.* Having no common measure integral or fractional (*with* another magnitude); not capable of being measured, compared *with*, or judged. **in·com·men·su·ra·bil′i·ty** *n.* **in·com·men′su·ra·bly** *adv.*

in·com·men·su·rate (ĭnkomĕn′serĭt, -sherĭt) *adj.* Out of proportion, inadequate, (*with, to*); incommensurable. **in·com·men′su·rate·ly** *adv.* **in·com·men′su·rate·ness** *n.*

in·com·mu·ni·ca·ble (ĭnkomū′nĭkabel) *adj.* That cannot be shared; that cannot be told. **in·com·mu·ni·ca·bil·i·ty** (ĭnkomūnĭkabĭl′ĭtē) *n.* **in·com·mu′ni·ca·bly** *adv.*

in·com·mu·ni·ca·do (ĭnkomūnĭkah′dō) *adj.* Without or deprived of means of communication; in solitary confinement.

in·com·mu·ni·ca·tive (ĭnkomū′nĭkātĭv, -katĭv) *adj.* Not communicative. **in·com·mu′ni·ca·tive·ly** *adv.* **in·com·mu′ni·ca·tive·ness** *n.*

in·com·pa·ra·ble (ĭnkŏm′perabel, -prabel) *adj.* Matchless; that cannot be compared. **in·com′par·a·ble·ness** *n.* **in·com′par·a·bly** *adv.*

in·com·pat·i·ble (ĭnkompăt′ĭbel) *adj.* Opposed in character, discordant; (of persons) unable to live, work, etc., together in harmony; (of drugs) not suitable for taking at the same time; inconsistent (with). **in·com·pat·i·bil·i·ty** (ĭnkompătĭbĭl′ĭtē) *n.* (pl. **-ties**). **in·com·pat′i·bly** *adv.*

in·com·pe·tent (ĭnkŏm′petent) *adj.* Not qualified or able (*to do*); not legally qualified. **in·com′pe·tent·ly** *adv.* **in·com′pe·tence, in·com′pe·ten·cy** *ns.* (pl. **-cies**).

in·com·plete (ĭnkomplēt′) *adj.* Not complete. **in·com·plete′ly** *adv.* **in·com·plete′ness** *n.*

in·com·pre·hen·si·ble (ĭnkŏmprĭhĕn′sĭbel) *adj.* That cannot be understood. **in·com·pre·hen′si·ble·ness, in·com·pre·hen·si·bil·i·ty** (ĭnkŏmprĭhĕnsĭbĭl′ĭtē) *ns.* **in·com·pre·hen′si·bly** *adv.*

in·com·press·i·ble (ĭnkomprĕs′ĭbel) *adj.* That cannot be compressed. **in·com·press·i·bil·i·ty** (ĭnkomprĕsĭbĭl′ĭtē) *n.*

in·con·ceiv·a·ble (ĭnkonsē′vabel) *adj.* That cannot be imagined. **in·con·ceiv·a·bil·i·ty** (ĭnkonsēvabĭl′ĭtē) *n.* **in·con·ceiv′a·bly** *adv.*

in·con·clu·sive (ĭnkonklo͞o′sĭv) *adj.* (of argument etc.) Not decisive or convincing. **in·con·clu′sive·ly** *adv.* **in·con·clu′sive·ness** *n.*

in·con·gru·ous (ĭnkŏng′gro͞oŭs) *adj.* Disagreeing, out of keeping, (*with*); out of place, absurd. **in·con′gru·ous·ly** *adv.* **in·con′gru·ous·ness** *n.* **in·con·gru·i·ty** (ĭnkŏnggro͞o′ĭtē) *n.* (pl. **-ties**).

A lion in the Royal National Park, Nairobi, Kenya, opens its mouth wide, displaying its menacing **incisors,** *sharp-edged cutting-teeth that can lacerate and destroy prey.*

in·con·se·quent (ĭnkŏn′sekwent) *adj.* Not following naturally, irrelevant; wanting in logical sequence; disconnected. **in·con′se·quent·ly** *adv.* **in·con′se·quence** *n.* **in·con·se·quen·tial** (ĭnkŏnsekwĕn′shal) *adj.* **in·con·se·quen′tial·ly** *adv.* Unimportant; inconsequent.

in·con·sid·er·ate (ĭnkonsĭd′erĭt) *adj.* Thoughtless, rash; lacking in regard for feelings etc. of others. **in·con·sid′er·ate·ly** *adv.* **in·con·sid′er·ate·ness** *n.*

in·con·sis·tent (ĭnkonsĭs′tent) *adj.* Not in keeping, discordant, incompatible, (*with*); acting at variance with one's own principles or former conduct. **in·con·sis′tent·ly** *adv.* **in·con·sis′ten·cy** *n.* (pl. **-cies**).

in·con·sol·a·ble (ĭnkonsō′label) *adj.* That cannot be consoled. **in·con·sol′a·bly** *adv.*

in·con·spic·u·ous (ĭnkonspĭk′ūus) *adj.* Not conspicuous; not readily seen or noticed. **in·con·spic′u·ous·ly** *adv.* **in·con·spic′u·ous·ness** *n.*

in·con·test·a·ble (ĭnkontĕs′tabel) *adj.* That cannot be disputed. **in·con·test′a·bly** *adv.*

in·con·ti·nent (ĭnkŏn′tĭnent) *adj.* Wanting in self-restraint (esp. in regard to sexual appetite); unable to hold in something; unable to control bladder and bowel functions. **in·con′ti·nence** *n.*

in·con·tro·ver·ti·ble (ĭnkŏntrovēr′tĭbel) *adj.* Not to be disputed. **in·con·tro·vert′i·bly** *adv.*

in·con·ven·ience (ĭnkonvēn′yens) *n.* Want of adaptation to personal requirement or ease; instance of this. ~ *v.t.* (**-ienced, -ienc·ing**). Put to inconvenience. **in·con·ven′ient** *adj.* Unfavorable to ease or comfort, troublesome, awkward. **in·con·ven′ient·ly** *adv.*

in·cor·po·rate (ĭnkōr′perĭt, -prĭt) *adj.* Formed into a legal corporation; merged; united. ~ (ĭnkōr′porāt) *v.* (**-rat·ed, -rat·ing**). 1. Unite; combine (ingredients) into one substance. 2. Constitute as, form into, a legal corporation; become incorporated (*with*). **in·cor·po·ra·tion** (ĭnkōrporā′shon), **in·cor′po·ra·tor** *ns.*

in·cor·po·re·al (ĭnkōrpōr′ēal) *adj.* Not composed of matter; immaterial; of immaterial beings; spiritual; (law) having no material existence. **in·cor·po′re·al·ly** *adv.*

in·cor·rect (ĭnkorĕkt′) *adj.* Not in conformity with recognized standard, or with fact; improper; erroneous. **in·cor·rect′ly** *adv.* **in·cor·rect′ness** *n.*

in·cor·ri·gi·ble (ĭnkōr′ĭjĭbel, -kăr′-) *adj.* Incurably bad or depraved. **in·cor·ri·gi·bil·i·ty** (ĭn-

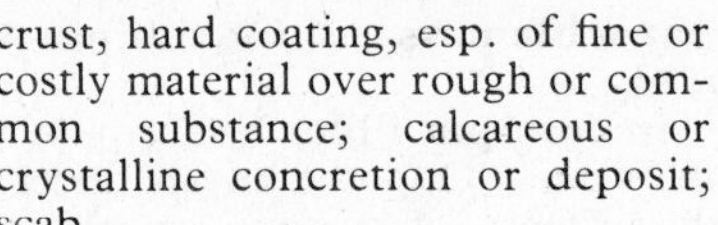

kŏrĭj*i*bĭl´ĭtē, -kār-) *n.* **in·cor′ri·gi·bly** *adv.*

in·cor·rupt·i·ble (ĭnk*o*rŭp´t*i*b*e*l) *adj.* That cannot decay; that cannot be corrupted, esp. that cannot be bribed. **in·cor·rupt·i·bil·i·ty** (ĭnk*o*rŭpt*i*bĭl´ĭtē) *n.* **in·cor·rupt′i·bly** *adv.*

in·crease (ĭnkrēs´) *v.* (**-creased, -creas·ing**). Become greater; grow in numbers, esp. by propagation; advance (*in* quality, attainment, etc.); make greater or more numerous; intensify (quality). **in·creas′ing·ly** *adv.* **increase** (ĭn´krēs) *n.* Growth, enlargement; growth in numbers; increased amount; **on the ~**, increasing.

in·cred·i·ble (ĭnkrĕd´*i*b*e*l) *adj.* That cannot be believed; hard to believe or realize. **in·cred·i·bil·i·ty** (ĭnkrĕd*i*bĭl´ĭtē) *n.* **in·cred′i·bly** *adv.*

in·cred·u·lous (ĭnkrĕj´*u*l*u*s) *adj.* Unbelieving. **in·cred′u·lous·ly** *adv.* **in·cre·du·li·ty** (ĭnkr*e*do͞o´lĭtē, -dū´-) *n.*

in·cre·ment (ĭn´kr*e*m*e*nt, ĭng´-) *n.* Increase; amount of this; profit; (math.) small amount by which variable quantity increases.

in·crim·i·nate (ĭnkrĭm´*i*nāt) *v.t.* (**-nat·ed, -nat·ing**). Charge with crime; involve in accusation. **in·crim·i·na·tion** (ĭnkrĭm*i*nā´sh*o*n) *n.* **in·crim′i·na·to·ry** *adj.*

in·crust (ĭnkrŭst´), **en·crust** (ĕnkrŭst´) *vbs.* Cover with crust; overlay (surface) with ornamental crust of precious material.

in·crus·ta·tion (ĭnkrŭstā´sh*o*n) *n.* Incrusting, being incrusted; crust, hard coating, esp. of fine or costly material over rough or common substance; calcareous or crystalline concretion or deposit; scab.

in·cu·bate (ĭn´ky*u*bāt, ĭng´-) *v.* (**-bat·ed, -bat·ing**). Sit on eggs, brood; hatch (eggs) thus or by artificial heat; subject (microorganisms) to warmth for a period. **in·cu·ba·tion** (ĭnky*u*bā´sh*o*n, ĭng-) *n.* (esp. path.) Early phase of disease after microorganisms have invaded the host and before symptoms of infection appear. **in′cu·ba·tive** *adj.*

in·cu·ba·tor (ĭn´ky*u*bāt*e*r, ĭng´-) *n.* Apparatus maintaining uniform temperature for hatching birds or growing bacterial cultures; apparatus providing controlled temperature, humidity, and oxygen to maintain infants born prematurely.

in·cu·bus (ĭn´ky*u*b*u*s, ĭng´-) *n.* (pl. **-bi** pr. -bī, **-bus·es**). Evil spirit supposed to descend on sleeping persons; nightmare; person, thing, that oppresses like nightmare.

in·cul·cate (ĭnkŭl´kāt, ĭn´kŭl-) *v.t.* (**-cat·ed, -cat·ing**). Urge, impress, persistently (*upon, in,* person, mind). **in·cul·ca·tion** (ĭnkŭlkā´sh*o*n), **in·cul′ca·tor** *ns.*

in·cul·pate (ĭnkŭl´pāt, ĭn´kŭl-) *v.t.* (**-pat·ed, -pat·ing**). Accuse, blame; involve in charge. **in·cul·pa·tion** (ĭnkŭlpā´sh*o*n) *n.* **in·cul′pa·to·ry** *adj.*

*The **incubator** is used in hospitals for the care of premature babies and others who need the maintenance of a uniform temperature and humidity. Chickens are also hatched in incubators.*

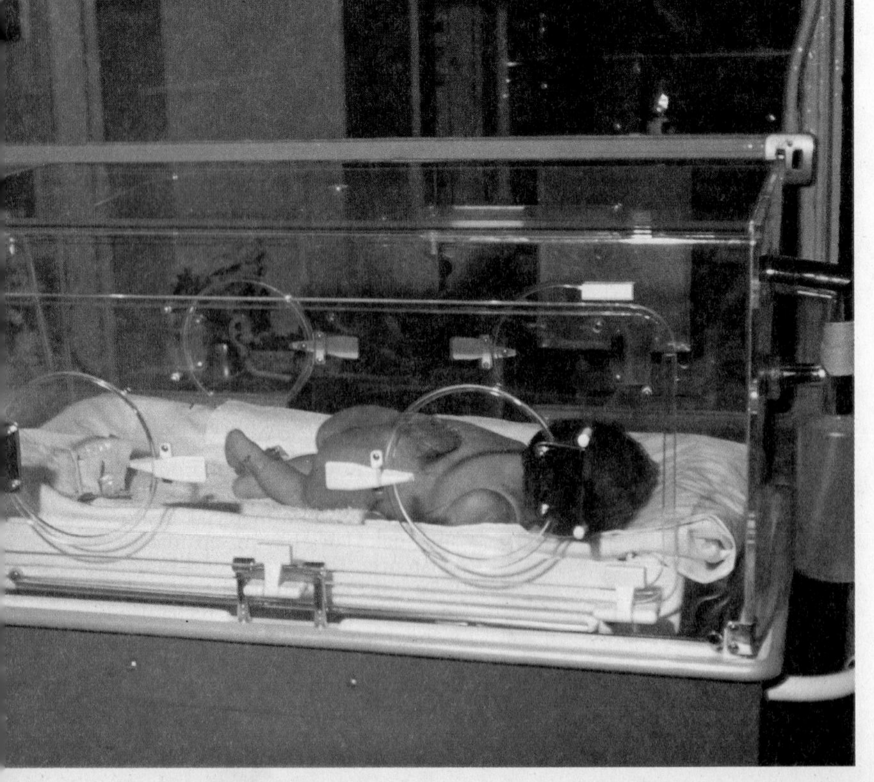

in·cum·ben·cy (ĭnkŭm´b*e*nsē) *n.* (pl. **-cies**). Office, tenure, sphere, of an incumbent. **in·cum′bent**[1] *n.* Holder of an office.

in·cum·bent[2] (ĭnkŭm´b*e*nt) *adj.* Lying, pressing, (*on*); resting *on* (person) as duty.

in·cu·nab·u·lum (ĭnkyo͞onăb´y*u*l*u*m) *n.* (pl. **-la** pr. -l*a*). Early printed book, esp. one produced before 1501. [L. *incunabula* swaddling clothes, infancy]

in·cur (ĭnkẽr´) *v.t.* (**-curred, -cur·ring**). Fall into, bring on oneself (danger, blame, etc.).

in·cur·a·ble (ĭnkūr´*a*b*e*l) *adj.* & *n.* (Person) that cannot be cured. **in·cur′a·ble·ness, in·cur·a·bil·i·ty** (ĭnkūr*a*bĭl´ĭtē) *ns.* **in·cur′a·bly** *adv.*

in·cur·sion (ĭnkẽr´zh*o*n, -sh*o*n) *n.* Hostile invasion; sudden attack.

Ind. *abbrev.* India(n); Indiana; Indies.

in·debt·ed (ĭndĕt´ĭd) *adj.* Owing money (*to*); owing gratitude (*to*). **in·debt′ed·ness** *n.*

in·de·cent (ĭndē´s*e*nt) *adj.* Immodest; offending against standards of decency. **in·de′cent·ly** *adv.* **in·de′cen·cy** *n.* (pl. **-cies**).

in·de·ci·pher·a·ble (ĭndĭsī´f*e*r*a*b*e*l) *adj.* That cannot be deciphered.

in·de·ci·sion (ĭndĭsĭzh´*o*n) *n.* Want of decision, hesitation.

in·de·ci·sive (ĭndĭsī´sĭv) *adj.* Not decisive; undecided, irresolute. **in·de·ci′sive·ly** *adv.* **in·de·ci′sive·ness** *n.*

in·de·clin·a·ble (ĭndĭklī´n*a*b*e*l) *adj.* (gram.) Having no inflections.

in·dec·o·rous (ĭndĕk´*e*r*u*s, -dĭkōr´-, -dĭkōr´-) *adj.* Improper; in bad taste. **in·dec′o·rous·ly** *adv.* **in·dec′o·rous·ness** *n.* **in·de·co·rum** (ĭndĭkōr´*u*m, -kōr´-) *n.* Lack of decorum.

in·deed (ĭndēd´) *adv.* In truth, really (freq. placed after a word to emphasize it). **~** *int.* Exclamation of surprise, contempt, etc.

in·de·fat·i·ga·ble (ĭndĭfăt´*i*g*a*b*e*l) *adj.* Unremitting, unwearying. **in·de·fat·i·ga·bil·i·ty** (ĭndĭfăt*i*g*a*bĭl´ĭtē) *n.* **in·de·fat′i·ga·bly** *adv.*

in·de·fen·si·ble (ĭndĭfĕn´s*i*b*e*l) *adj.* Admitting of no defense. **in·de·fen·si·bil·i·ty** (ĭndĭfĕns*i*bĭl´ĭtē) *n.* **in·de·fen′si·bly** *adv.*

in·de·fin·a·ble (ĭndĭfī´n*a*b*e*l) *adj.* That cannot be defined, described, or analyzed. **in·de·fin′a·bly** *adv.*

in·def·i·nite (ĭndĕf´*i*nĭt) *adj.* 1. Vague, undefined; unlimited. 2. (gram., of adjectives, pronouns, etc.) Not determining the person, thing, time, manner, etc., to which they refer; (of tenses of verbs)

denoting an action without specifying whether it is continuous or complete; ~ **article**: see ARTICLE. **in·def'i·nite·ly** *adv.* **in·def'i·nite·ness** *n.*

in·de·his·cent (ĭndĭhĭs'ent) *adj.* (bot.) Not dehiscent; (of fruit) not splitting open when mature, but liberating seed by decay.

in·del·i·ble (ĭndĕl'*i*bel) *adj.* That cannot be erased, blotted out, etc. **in·del'i·bly** *adv.*

in·del·i·cate (ĭndĕl'*i*kĭt) *adj.* Coarse, immodest. **in·del'i·cate·ly** *adv.* **in·del'i·ca·cy** *n.* (pl. **-cies**).

in·dem·ni·fy (ĭndĕm'n*i*fī) *v.t.* (**-fied, -fy·ing**). Protect, secure (*from, against,* harm or loss); secure (person) against legal responsibility (*for* actions); compensate (*for* loss, expenses incurred, etc.). **in·dem·ni·fi·ca·tion** (ĭndĕmn*i*fĭkā'sh*o*n) *n.*

in·dem·ni·ty (ĭndĕm'nĭtē) *n.* (pl. **-ties**). Security against damage or loss; legal exemption from penalties etc. incurred; compensation for loss; sum paid for this.

in·de·mon·stra·ble (ĭnde-mŏn'str*a*bel) *adj.* That cannot be proved.

in·dent (ĭndĕnt') *v.* 1. Make toothlike notches in; form deep recesses in (coastline etc.). 2. Set in (beginning of printed or written line) from margin, as for new paragraph etc. **in'dent** *n.* Indentation.

in·den·ta·tion (ĭndĕntā'sh*o*n) *n.*

*The American **War of Independence** (1775–83) was the struggle of the 13 Colonies of America for independence from British rule. Washington declared independence on July 4, 1776 although the war continued until 1783.*

Indenting; cut, notch; recess in coastline etc.

in·den·tion (ĭndĕn'sh*o*n) *n.* Indenting of line in printing or writing; indentation.

in·den·ture (ĭndĕn'ch*e*r) *n.* Any binding agreement or contract, esp. that which binds apprentice to master; formal list, certificate, etc.; indentation. ~ *v.t.* (**-tured, -tur·ing**). Bind (person) by indenture, esp. as apprentice.

in·de·pend·ence (ĭndĭpĕn'd*e*ns) *n.* Being independent; **Declaration of I ~**, proclamation by which the 2nd Continental Congress, on July 4, 1776, declared the 13 Amer. colonies to be free and independent of Gt. Britain; **I ~ Day**, July 4, an annual holiday celebrating this. **in·de·pend'en·cy** *n.* (pl. **-cies**). Independent state.

in·de·pend·ent (ĭndĭpĕn'd*e*nt) *adj.* Not depending on authority of another, autonomous, free; not depending on something else for its validity, efficiency, etc.; unwilling to be under obligation to others; not needing to earn one's livelihood; (of income etc.) sufficient to make one independent. **in·de·pend'ent·ly** *adv.* **independent** *n.* Person who acts (in politics etc.) independently of any party, group, etc.

in·de·scrib·a·ble (ĭndĭskrī-b*a*bel) *adj.* Vague, indefinite; too great, beautiful, bad, etc., to be described. **in·de·scrib·a·bil·i·ty** (ĭndĭskrīb*a*bĭl'ĭtē) *n.* **in·de·scrib'a·bly** *adv.*

in·de·struct·i·ble (ĭndĭstrŭk'-t*i*bel) *adj.* That cannot be destroyed. **in·de·struct·i·bil·i·ty** (ĭndĭstrŭkt*i*bĭl'ĭtē) *n.* **in·de·struct'i·bly** *adv.*

in·de·ter·mi·na·ble (ĭndĭtẽr'-m*i*n*a*bel) *adj.* That cannot be definitely fixed or ascertained; that cannot be settled.

in·de·ter·mi·nate (ĭndĭtẽr'm*i*-nĭt) *adj.* Not fixed in extent, character, etc.; vague; left doubtful; (math., of quantity) not limited to fixed value(s). **in·de·ter'mi·nate·ly** *adv.* **in·de·ter'mi·na·cy, in·de·ter'mi·nate·ness** *ns.* **in·de·ter·mi·na·tion** (ĭndĭtẽrm*i*nā'-sh*o*n) *n.* Want of determination; being indeterminate.

in·dex (ĭn'dĕks) *n.* (pl. **-dex·es, -di·ces** pr. -dĭsēz). 1. ~ **finger**, forefinger; (on instruments) pointer showing measurement etc.; sign, token, indication (*of* something). 2. Alphabetical list, usu. at end of book, of names, subjects, etc., with references. 3. ***I ~***, short for ***I ~ librorum prohibitorum*** (L., = "Index of prohibited books"), list formerly published by authority (abolished 1966), of books that Roman Catholics were forbidden to read, including the ***I*~ *expurgatorius*** ("Expurgatory Index"), formerly a separate list of passages to be expunged in books otherwise permitted. 4. (alg.) Exponent; ~ **number**, (statistics) number used in comparing wages, prices, etc., at a certain time with their value at a standard time; ~-**linked**, calculated in accordance with index number; (of wages, pensions, etc.) allowed to rise with rise in CONSUMER price index. **index** *v.t.* Furnish (book) with index; enter (word etc.) in index.

In·di·a (ĭn'dē*a*). 1. Large peninsula of S. central Asia, bounded on N. by Himalayas; inhabited by peoples following Hindu, Muslim, and other religions and speaking over 200 languages, esp. Hindi and Bengali in N. and Tamil and Telugu in S.; British interest began in early 17th c. with formation of East India Company; in 1858 the Brit. government took over the Company's authority and in 1877 Queen Victoria was proclaimed Empress of India; in 1947 the 15 provinces (**British** ~) and numerous native states under British protection were divided between India (see 2 below) and PAKISTAN. 2. Republic, predominantly Hindu, constituted in 1950 as a member nation of the New Commonwealth and comprising much of the N. and all the S. and central part of the peninsula; capital, New Delhi. 3. ~ **ink**, ink made from lampblack and a binding agent; ~ **paper**, thin, delicate, uncoated cream or buff paper esp. used for proofs or first impressions of engravings. [Gk. *Indos* Indus, f. Pers. *hind* = Sansk. *sindhu* river]

In·di·an (ĭn'dē*a*n) *adj.* 1. Of India or the E. Indies or their peoples. 2. Of the original inhabitants of America and the W. Indies. 3. ~ **club**, heavy bottle-shaped wooden club used in gymnastic exercises; ~ **corn**, (chiefly Brit.) maize; ~ **file**, single file (so called because N. Amer. Indians marched thus); ~ **hemp**, common HEMP; ~ **meal**, (chiefly Brit.) corn meal; ~ **Ocean**, ocean to S. of India, extending from E. coast of Africa to Malay Archipelago; ~ **paintbrush**, plant of genus *Castilleja*, common in W. America, with

1

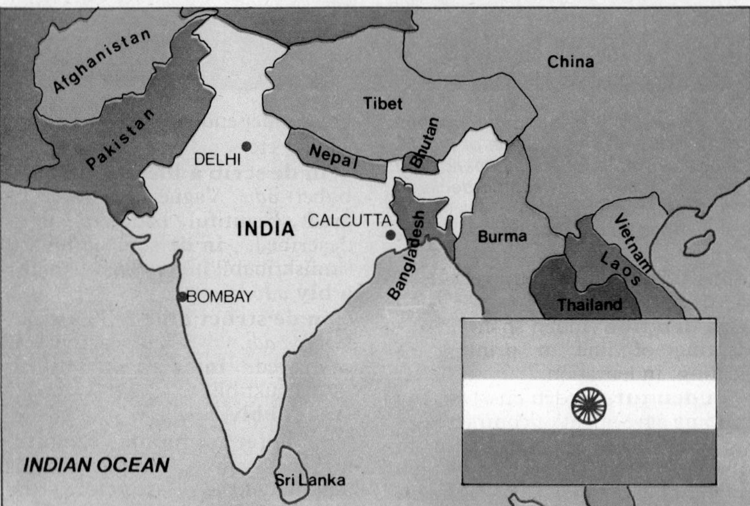

2

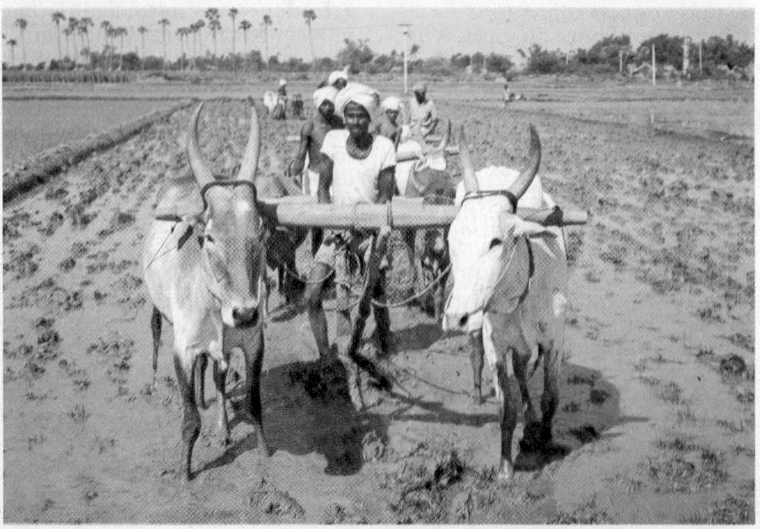

3

*The Republic of **India** occupies an area of 1,229,919 sq. miles and has a population of 586 million people. 1. Coastal craft unload their wares at Panjim, Goa, which was a Portuguese possession until 1961. 2. Map and flag of India. 3. Rice planting in Madras. India is the second-largest producer of rice. Facing page: A Delhi girl plays the sitar.*

small flowers and bright-colored bracts; ~ **pipe**, leafless saprophytic plant, *Monotropa uniflora*, with a single white flower, resembling a pipe; ~ **summer**, period of calm, dry, mild weather with hazy atmosphere, occurring in late autumn; ~ **Territory**, former U.S. territory covering 31,000 sq. mi. (80,290 sq. km); merged with Oklahoma Territory and became state of Oklahoma, 1907. **Indian** *n.* 1. Native, inhabitant of India. 2. (also called Amer. Indian, (Brit.) Red Indian, or (including Eskimos etc.) Amerind) member of any of the aboriginal N. and S. Amer. peoples who orig. migrated from Asia over the land bridge now called the Bering Strait, and were well established throughout N. and S. America *c*10,000 B.C.; they included a wide variety of cultures from nomadic hunters to builders of vast and complex city-empires (Mayan, Aztec, Inca, etc.). 3. Any or all of the languages of the Amer. Indians.

In·di·an·a (ĭndēăn′*a*). State in north-central U.S., admitted to the Union in 1816; capital, Indianapolis.

In·di·an·ap·o·lis (ĭndē*a*năp′*o*-lĭs). Capital and largest city of Indiana in the central part on the White River; site of annual ~ **500** car race.

In·di·a (ĭn′dē*a*) **rubber** = RUBBER[1] def. 3.

In·dic (ĭn′dĭk) *adj.* & *n.* (Of, pertaining to) language group comprising Sanskrit and its modern descendants.

in·di·cate (ĭn′d*i*kāt) *v.t.* (**-cat·ed, -cat·ing**). Point out, make known, show; state briefly; be a sign of, betoken; (med.) suggest, call for, (treatment). **in·di·ca·tion** (ĭnd*i*kā′sh*o*n) *n.*

in·dic·a·tive (ĭndĭk′*a*tĭv) *adj.* 1. Suggestive, giving indications, *of*. 2. (gram., of verbal mood) Stating something as objective fact, not as conception, wish, etc., of speaker. **in·dic′a·tive·ly** *adv.* **indicative** *n.* Indicative mood.

*This woman is a Hopi **Indian.** She is weaving a basket, a traditional skill amongst women of the Hopi tribe, as is the making of pots. The Hopi culture is gradually disintegrating in the face of modern trends.*

*The **Indianapolis 500** is one of the richest automobile races in the world with prizes worth more than $1 million in the 1970s. It has been held annually since 1911.*

in·di·ca·tor (ĭn′d*i*kāt*e*r) *n.* Person, thing, that points out or indicates; mechanical device indicating condition of apparatus etc. to which it is attached.

in·dict (ĭndīt′) *v.t.* Accuse (person), esp. by legal process. **in·dict·a·ble** (ĭndī′t*a*b*e*l) *adj.* Liable, rendering one liable, to be indicted. **in·dict·ment** (ĭndīt′m*e*nt) *n.* Formal accusation; (law) legal document charging a party with having committed a crime, drawn up by a prosecuting attorney and found and presented by a grand jury.

In·dies (ĭn′dēz). **the** ~, (formerly) India and adjacent regions and islands; the East Indies; the West Indies.

in·dif·fer·ence (ĭndĭf′*e*r*e*ns, -dĭf′r*e*ns) *n.* Absence of interest or attention (*to, toward*); neutrality; unimportance.

in·dif·fer·ent (ĭndĭf′*e*r*e*nt, -dĭf′-r*e*nt) *adj.* Impartial, neutral; having no inclination for or against; neither good nor bad, right nor wrong, too much nor too little, etc.; mediocre; unimportant. **in·dif′fer·ent·ly** *adv.*

in·dig·e·nous (ĭndĭj′*e*n*u*s) *adj.* Native, belonging naturally; innate, intrinsic. **in·dig′e·nous·ly** *adv.*

in·di·gent (ĭn′dĭj*e*nt) *adj.* Needy, poor. **in′di·gence** *n.*

in·di·gest·i·ble (ĭndĭjĕs′t*i*b*e*l, -dī-) *adj.* Not digestible; hard to digest. **in·di·gest·i·bil·i·ty** (ĭn-dĭjĕst*i*bĭl′ĭtē, -dī-) *n.* **in·di·ges′-tion** *n.* Difficulty in digesting food; illness, discomfort from this.

in·dig·nant (ĭndĭg′n*a*nt) *adj.* Moved by mingled anger and scorn or feeling of injured innocence.

in·dig′nant·ly *adv.*

in·dig·na·tion (ĭndĭgnā′sh*o*n) *n.* Anger excited by meanness, injustice, wickedness, or misconduct.

in·dig·ni·ty (ĭndĭg′nĭtē) *n.* (pl. **-ties**). Unworthy treatment, slight, insult.

in·di·go (ĭn′d*i*gō) *n.* (pl. **-gos, -goes**). Blue dye obtained from plants of genus *Indigofera*; plant from which this is obtained; dark blue or bluish-purple color; ~ **blue**, blue color of indigo; ~ **bunting**, brilliant blue songbird of eastern U.S., *Passerina cyanea.* [Gk. *indikon* Indian]

in·di·rect (ĭnd*i*rĕkt′, -dī-) *adj.* 1. Not straight; not going straight to the point; not directly aimed at; ~ **tax**, one paid by consumer in form of increased price for the taxed goods. 2. (gram.) ~ **object**, person, thing, affected by action of verb but not primarily acted on (e.g. *him* in *give him the book*). **in·di·rect′ly** *adv.* **in·di·rect′ness** *n.*

in·dis·creet (ĭndĭskrēt′) *adj.* Injudicious, unwary. **in·dis·creet′ly** *adv.*

in·dis·crete (ĭndĭskrēt′, -dĭs′krēt) *adj.* Not divided into distinct parts.

in·dis·cre·tion (ĭndĭskrĕsh′*o*n) *n.* Injudicious conduct; accidental or supposed accidental revelation of official secret etc.; imprudence; transgression of social morality.

in·dis·crim·i·nate (ĭndĭskrĭm′*i*nĭt) *adj.* Confused, haphazard; promiscuous; making no distinctions. **in·dis·crim′i·nate·ly** *adv.* **in·dis·crim′i·nate·ness, in·dis·crim·i·na·tion** (ĭndĭskrĭm*i*nā′sh*o*n) *ns.*

in·dis·pen·sa·ble (ĭndĭspĕn′s*a*bel) *adj.* That cannot be dispensed with, necessary; (of duty etc.) that cannot be set aside. **in·dis·pen′sa·ble·ness, in·dis·pen·sa·bil·i·ty** (ĭndĭspĕns*a*bĭl′ĭtē) *ns.*

in·dis·pose (ĭndĭspōz′) *v.t.* (**-posed, -pos·ing**). Render unfit or unable; make averse; (esp. in past part.) put out of health. **in·dis·po·si·tion** (ĭndĭsp*o*zĭsh′*o*n) *n.* Ill health, ailment, (esp. of minor kind); disinclination; aversion. **in·dis·posed′** *adj.*

in·dis·pu·ta·ble (ĭndĭspū′t*a*bel, -dĭs′py*u*-) *adj.* That cannot be disputed. **in·dis·put′a·ble·ness, in·dis·put·a·bil·i·ty** (ĭndĭspū-t*a*bĭl′ĭtē) *ns.* **in·dis·pu′ta·bly** *adv.*

in·dis·sol·u·ble (ĭndĭsŏl′y*u*bel) *adj.* Lasting, stable; that cannot be dissolved or decomposed. **in·dis·sol·u·bil·i·ty** (ĭndĭsŏly*u*bĭl′ĭtē) *n.* **in·dis·sol′u·bly** *adv.*

in·dis·tinct (ĭndĭstĭngkt′) *adj.* Not distinct; confused, obscure. **in·dis·tinct′ly** *adv.* **in·dis·tinct′ness** *n.*

in·dis·tin·guish·a·ble (ĭndĭs-tĭng′gwĭsh*a*bel) *adj.* Not distinguishable. **in·dis·tin′guish·a·bly** *adv.*

in·di·um (ĭn′dē*u*m) *n.* (chem.) Rare silver-white soft metallic element, occurring in association with zinc etc.; symbol In, at. no. 49, at. wt. 114.82. [L. *indicum* INDIGO, from two blue lines in the metal's spectrum]

in·di·vid·u·al (ĭnd*i*vĭj′ōō*a*l) *adj.* Single; particular, special; having distinct character; of a single person or thing, characteristic of an individual. ~ *n.* Single member of a class, group, or number; single human being (opp. to society, the family, etc.); (colloq.) person.

in·di·vid·u·al·ism (ĭnd*i*vĭj′ōō*a*-lĭz*e*m) *n.* 1. Individuality. 2. Independence in thought and action. 3. Social theory advocating free and independent action of individual (cf. SOCIALISM). **in·di·vid′u·al·ist** *n.* **in·di·vid·u·al·is·tic** (ĭnd*i*vĭjōō-*a*lĭs′tĭk) *adj.*

in·di·vid·u·al·i·ty (ĭnd*i*vĭjōōăl′-ĭtē) *n.* (pl. **-ties**). Separate existence; individual character, esp. when strongly marked.

in·di·vid·u·al·ize (ĭnd*i*vĭj′ōō*a*-līz) *v.t.* (**-ized, -iz·ing**). Give individual character to; specify. **in·di·vid·u·al·i·za·tion** (ĭnd*i*vĭj-ōō*a*lĭzā′sh*o*n) *n.*

in·di·vid·u·al·ly (ĭnd*i*vĭj′ōō*a*lē) *adv.* Personally, in an individual capacity; in a distinctive manner; one by one, not collectively.

in·di·vis·i·ble (ĭnd*i*vĭz′*i*bel) *adj.* Not divisible. **in·di·vis·i·bil·i·ty** (ĭnd*i*vĭz*a*bĭl′ĭtē) *n.* **in·di·vis′i·bly** *adv.*

Indo- *prefix.* Indian; Indian and —.

In·do·chi·na (ĭn′dōchī′n*a*). 1. Peninsula in SE. Asia occupied by Burma, Thailand, Malaya, Laos, Cambodia, and Vietnam. 2. (hist.) Region now occupied by Laos, Kampuchea, and Vietnam, formerly a French dependency (**French ~**). **In·do·chi·nese** (ĭn′-dōchīnēz′, -nēs′) *adj.* & *n.* (pl. **-nese**).

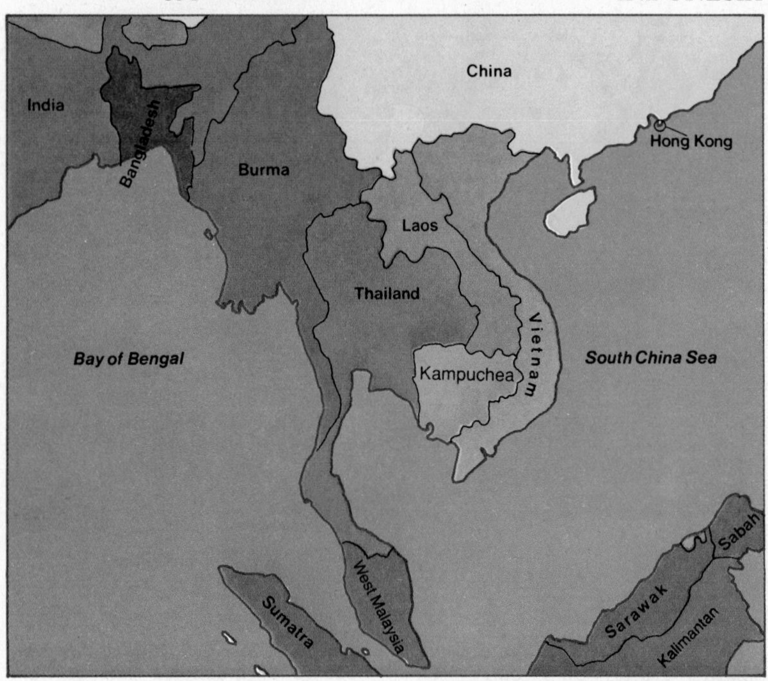

***Indo-China** was a French colony from the mid-19th century to 1954. It consisted of Laos, Kampuchea (Cambodia) and Vietnam. Today Indo-China may also include Burma, Thailand and West Malaysia.*

in·doc·tri·nate (ĭndŏk′tr*i*nāt) *v.t.* (**-nat·ed, -nat·ing**). Instruct in a doctrine, ideology, etc.; teach to accept (ideology etc.) uncritically. **in·doc·tri·na·tion** (ĭndŏktr*i*nā′-sh*o*n) *n.*

In·do-Eu·ro·pe·an (ĭn′dōūr*o*-pē′*a*n) *n.* & *adj.* (Of) the family of languages spoken over most of Europe and in Asia as far as N. India, including esp. the Indo-Iranian, Balto-Slavonic, Greek, Italic, Celtic, and Germanic groups; (member) of a people speaking one of these languages.

in·do·lent (ĭn′d*o*lent) *adj.* Slothful, lazy; (med., of tumor etc.) causing little or no pain. **in′do·lent·ly** *adv.* **in′do·lence** *n.*

in·dom·i·ta·ble (ĭndŏm′ĭt*a*bel) *adj.* Unyielding; stubbornly persistent. **in·dom′i·ta·bly** *adv.*

In·do·ne·sia (ĭnd*o*nē′zh*a*, -sh*a*, -zē*a*, -dō-). Republic of SE. Asia, comprising Sumatra, Java, S. and E. Borneo, Celebes and other islands; formerly belonging to the Netherlands and then known as the Netherlands (or Dutch) East Indies; independent since 1949; capital, Djakarta.

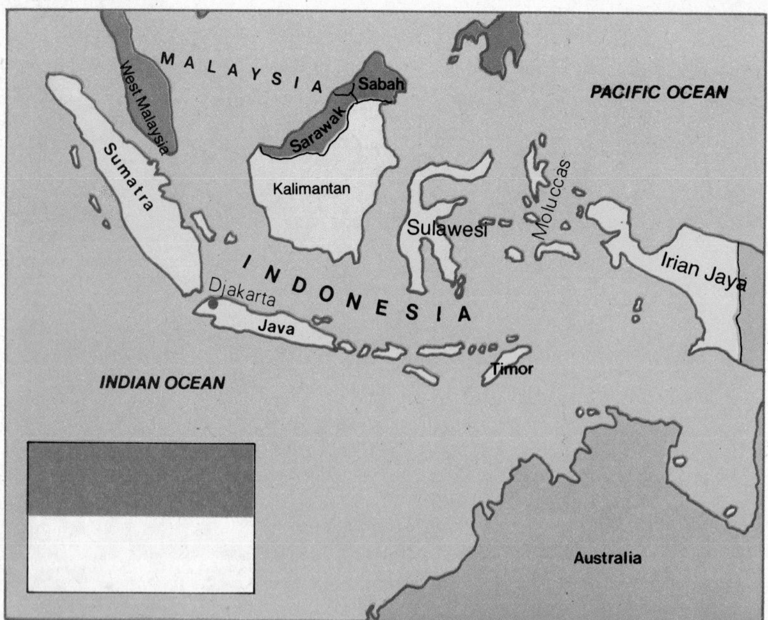

With more than 13,000 islands, the Republic of **Indonesia** extends from Sumatra (alongside Western Malaysia) to Irian Jaya — the western half of New Guinea. Above left: Map and flag of Indonesia. Above right: Rice paddies in Bali. Rice is a major crop in the area.

In·do·ne·sian (ĭndonē′zh*a*n, -sh*a*n, -zē*a*n, -dō-) *adj.* Of Indonesia or its people, esp. of Sumatra, Java, and Bali; of one of the vast number of SE. Asian languages spoken in Malay Peninsula and Archipelago. ~ *n.* Indonesian person; (esp.) one of a people forming the chief pre-Malay population of Malay Archipelago, and combining Polynesian and Mongoloid characteristics; Indonesian language; ~ **Timor,** (formerly Netherlands Timor) W. section of S. Malay Archipelago island of Timor, the largest and easternmost of the Lesser Sunda Islands; formerly Dutch-ruled, the W. half covers 5,765 sq. mi. (14,931 sq. km) and is now an Indonesian possession; the E. half is a Portuguese province.

in·door (ĭn′dōr, -dŏr) *adj.* Situated, carried on, within a house or other building. **in·doors′** *adv.* Within a house or other building.

in·dorse (ĭndŏrs′) = ENDORSE.

in·du·bi·ta·ble (ĭndōō′bĭt*a*bel, -dū′-) *adj.* That cannot be doubted. **in·du′bi·ta·bly** *adv.*

in·duce (ĭndōōs′, -dūs′) *v.t.* (**-duced, -duc·ing**). 1. Prevail on, persuade (*to*); bring about, give rise to. 2. (elect.) Produce (current) by induction. **in·duce′ment** *n.* What induces; attraction that leads one on (*to*).

in·duct (ĭndŭkt′) *v.t.* Formally place in an office or benefice; install (*into*); initiate, admit as a member; draft into military service.

in·duct·ance (ĭndŭk′t*a*ns) *n.* Setting up of a magnetic field or flux by induction.

in·duc·tion (ĭndŭk′sh*o*n) *n.* 1. Inducting. 2. Production (*of* facts) to prove general statement; inferring of general law from particular instances; **mathematical ~,** method of proving universal truth of law by showing (i) that if true in a particular case it is true in the next case, and also (ii) that it is true in a particular case. 3. (elect. etc.) Bringing about of electric or magnetic state in a body by proximity (without contact) of electrified or magnetized body; production of electric current in conductor by motion of magnet near it, or by changes in the magnetic field in which it lies due to other causes; (esp.) generation of electric current in a conductor by changes in current in a neighboring conductor; ~ **coil,** apparatus for producing electric currents by induction, consisting normally of a soft iron core, surrounded by a coil of wire (the *primary coil*), which is in turn surrounded by a second and usu. much longer coil (the *secondary coil*): when the current in the primary coil is interrupted, a current of much higher voltage than the original one is induced in the secondary coil; by using very long coils enormous voltages suitable for producing x-rays and conducting many physical and other experiments can be induced.

in·duc·tive (ĭndŭk′tĭv) *adj.* 1. (of reasoning etc.) Of, based on, induction. 2. Of electric or magnetic induction. **in·duc′tive·ly** *adv.*

in·duc·tor (ĭndŭk′ter) *n.* 1. Person who inducts, as into office. 2. Part of electric apparatus that produces induction.

in·dulge (ĭndŭlj′) *v.* (**-dulged, -dulg·ing**). Please by yielding to wishes of; yield to (desire etc.); gratify one's appetite (for); take one's pleasure freely *in.* **in·dul′gent** *adj.* **in·dul′gent·ly** *adv.*

The **Indus** River is 1,800 miles long and has a drainage basin of 450,000 sq. miles. It is navigable for small steamers as far as Hyderabad. Its principal dams are the Sukkur and the Kotri.

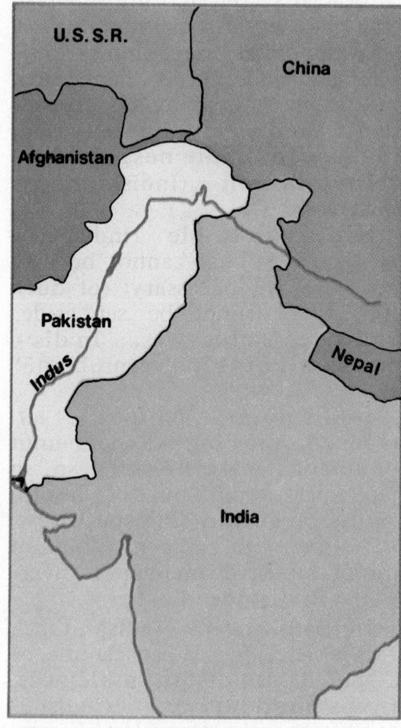

in·dul·gence (ĭndŭl′j*e*ns) *n.* 1. Indulging. 2. Privilege granted; (R.C. Ch.) remission of temporal punishment still due for sins whose eternal punishment has been remitted by sacramental absolution.

in·du·rate (ĭn′durāt, -dyu-) *v.* (**-rat·ed, -rat·ing**). Make, become, hard; make callous or un-

The ***Industrial Revolution,*** *which marked the change from domestic industry to the factory system, began in the textile industry. These workers from Wigan's cotton mills in England are shown taking their dinner hour.*

feeling; become inveterate. **in·du·ra·tion** (ĭndurā´shon) *n.* **in'du·ra·tive** *adj.*

In·dus (ĭn´dus). One of the 3 great rivers of the Indian subcontinent, rising in Himalayas of W. Tibet, flowing 1900 mi. (3059 km) NW. through Tibet, then SW. through Pakistan to Arabian Sea.

in·dus·tri·al (ĭndŭs´trēal) *adj.* Of industries; engaged in, connected with, industry; having highly developed industries; **I~ Revolution** (also **i~ r~**), rapid development of industry through employment of machinery; this development in England in late 18th and early 19th c.; **~ union**, one organized to represent all crafts and trades within an industry; **I~ Workers of the World**, (abbrev. I.W.W.) international industrial labor organization founded at Chicago in 1905 and existing until the 1920s, advocating syndicalism and international socialism. **in·dus'tri·al·ly** *adv.* **in·dus'tri·al·ism, in·dus'tri·al·ist** *ns.* **in·dus'tri·al·ize** *v.t.* (**-ized, -iz·ing**).

in·dus·tri·ous (ĭndŭs´trēus) *adj.* Diligent, hardworking. **in·dus'tri·ous·ly** *adv.*

in·dus·try (ĭn´dustrē) *n.* (pl. **-tries**). 1. Diligence; exertion, effort; systematic work; habitual employment in useful work. 2. Branch of trade or manufacture, esp. one employing much labor and capital; manufacturing in general.

-ine[1] *suffix.* Forming adjectives with sense of "pertaining to," "of the nature of" (*Alpine*, *equine*, *marine*).

-ine[2] *suffix.* Forming feminine nouns (*heroine*).

-ine[3] *suffix.* Forming (esp. abstract) nouns (*discipline*, *medicine*).

in·e·bri·ate (ĭnē´brēĭt) *adj.* Intoxicated. **~** *n.* Inebriate person, esp. habitual drunkard. **~** (ĭnē´brēāt) *v.t.* (**-at·ed, -at·ing**). Make drunk, intoxicate. **in·e·bri·a·tion** (ĭnēbrēā´shon), **in·e·bri·e·ty** (ĭnĭbrī´etē) *ns.* (Habit of) drunkenness.

in·ed·i·ble (ĭnĕd´ibel) *adj.* Not suitable as food; not edible.

in·ed·u·ca·ble (ĭnĕj´ukabel) *adj.* Incapable of being educated, esp. as a result of mental retardation.

in·ef·fa·ble (ĭnĕf´abel) *adj.* Unutterable. **in·ef'fa·bly** *adj.*

in·ef·fec·tive (ĭnĭfĕk´tĭv) *adj.* Not producing the desired effect; (of person) inefficient. **in·ef·fec'tive·ly** *adv.* **in·ef·fec'tive·ness** *n.*

in·ef·fec·tu·al (ĭnĭfĕk´chōōal) *adj.* Without effect, fruitless. **in·ef·fec'tu·al·ly** *adv.* **in·ef·fec'tu·al·ness** *n.*

in·ef·fi·cient (ĭnĭfĭsh´ent) *adj.* Not efficient; wasteful; lacking ability or competence. **in·ef·fi'cient·ly** *adv.* **in·ef·fi'cien·cy** *n.*

in·e·las·tic (ĭnĭlăs´tĭk) *adj.* Not elastic; unadaptable, unyielding. **in·e·las·tic·i·ty** (ĭnĭlăstĭs´ĭtē) *n.*

in·el·i·gi·ble (ĭnĕl´ĭjibel) *adj.* Not eligible. **in·el·i·gi·bil·i·ty** (ĭnĕlĭjibĭl´ĭtē) *n.* **in·el'i·gi·bly** *adv.*

in·e·luc·ta·ble (ĭnĭlŭk´tabel) *adj.* That cannot be avoided or overcome.

in·ept (ĭnĕpt´) *adj.* Out of place; absurd, silly; incompetent; clumsy. **in·ept'ly** *adv.* **in·ept'ness, in·ept'i·tude** *ns.*

in·e·qual·i·ty (ĭnĭkwŏl´ĭtē) *n.* (pl. **-ties**). Want of equality in magnitude, quality, rank, etc.; variableness; (of surface) irregularity.

in·eq·ui·ta·ble (ĭnĕk´wĭtabel) *adj.* Unfair, unjust. **in·eq'ui·ta·bly** *adv.* **in·eq'ui·ty** *n.* (pl. **-ties**).

in·e·rad·i·ca·ble (ĭnĭrăd´ikabel) *adj.* That cannot be erased or rooted out. **in·e·rad'i·ca·bly** *adv.*

in·ert (ĭnẽrt´) *adj.* Without inherent power of action, motion, or resistance; sluggish, slow; (chem., of gases) chemically inactive; esp., belonging to the group of gases comprising helium, neon, argon, krypton, xenon, and radon.

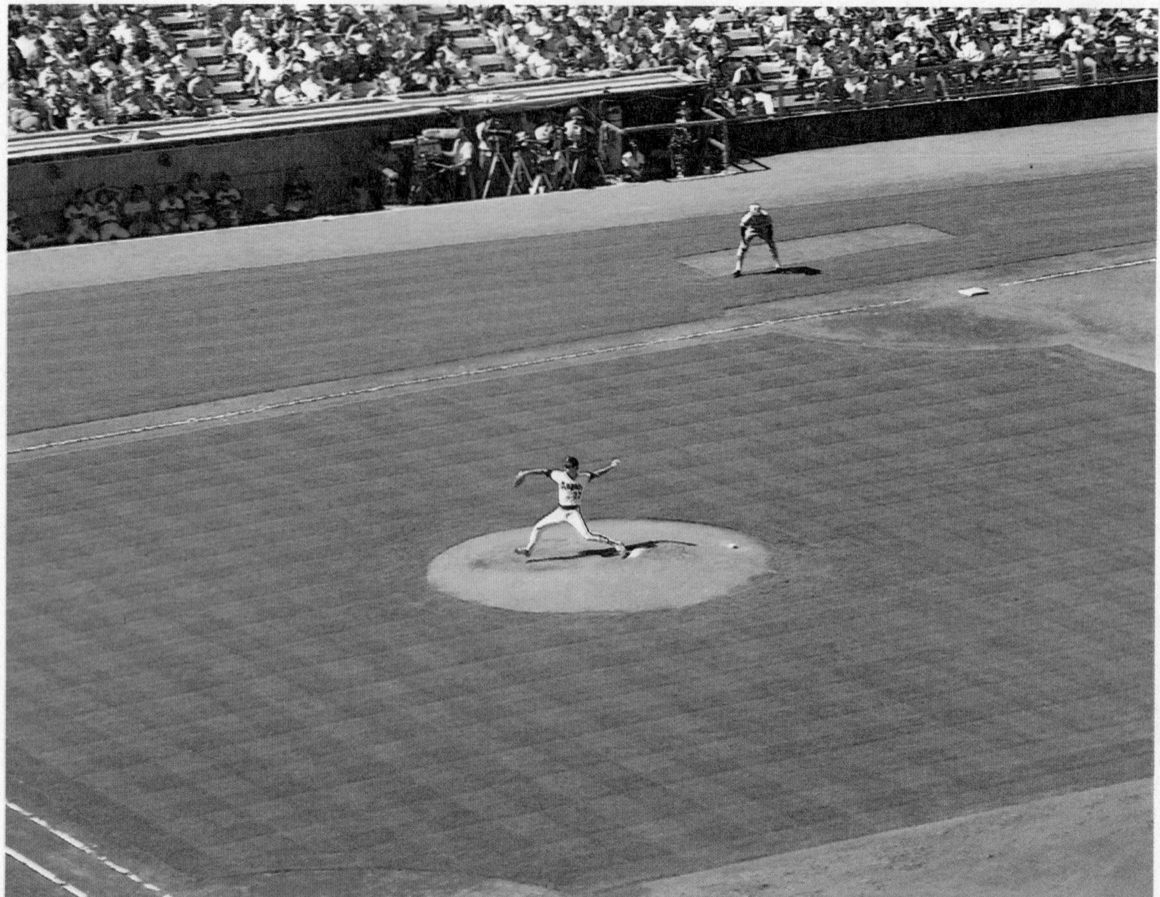

In baseball the ***infield*** *is the area of the field enclosed by the baselines. Baseball was played in America (in Philadelphia) as early as 1833 and the rules have changed very little.*

in·ert'ly *adv.* **in·ert'ness** *n.*

in·er·tia (ĭnėr'sh*a*) *n.* 1. (phys.) Property of matter by which it continues in its existing state of rest or uniform motion in a straight line unless that state is changed by an external force. 2. Inertness, sloth. **in·er'tial** *adj.* (esp.) **inertial guidance, navigation**: see GUIDANCE.

in·es·cap·a·ble (ĭnĕskā'p*a*bel) *adj.* Not to be escaped. **in·es·cap'a·bly** *adv.*

in·es·ti·ma·ble (ĭnĕs't*i*mabel) *adj.* Too great, intense, precious, etc., to be estimated. **in·es'ti·ma·bly** *adv.*

in·ev·i·ta·ble (ĭnĕv'ĭtabel) *adj.* Unavoidable, sure to happen. **in·ev'i·ta·ble·ness, in·ev·i·ta·bil·i·ty** (ĭnĕvĭtabĭl'ĭtē) *ns.* **in·ev'i·ta·bly** *adv.*

in·ex·act (ĭnĭgzăkt') *adj.* Not exact. **in·ex·act'ly** *adv.* **in·ex·act'ness, in·ex·act'i·tude** *ns.*

in·ex·cus·a·ble (ĭnĭkskū'z*a*bel) *adj.* That cannot be excused or justified. **in·ex·cus'a·bly** *adv.*

in·ex·haust·i·ble (ĭnĭgzaws't*i*bel) *adj.* That cannot be exhausted; limitless. **in·ex·haust·i·bil·i·ty** (ĭnĭgzawst*i*bĭl'ĭtē) *n.* **in·ex·haust'i·bly** *adv.*

in·ex·o·ra·ble (ĭnĕk'ser*a*bel) *adj.* Relentless. **in·ex'o·ra·bly** *adv.*

in·ex·pi·a·ble (ĭnĕks'pē*a*bel) *adj.* That cannot be expiated. **in·ex'pi·a·bly** *adv.*

in·ex·pli·ca·ble (ĭnĕks'pl*i*kabel, -ĭksplĭk'-) *adj.* That cannot be explained or accounted for. **in·ex'pli·ca·bly** *adv.*

in ex·tre·mis (ĭn ĭkstrē'mĭs; *Lat.* ĭn ĕkstrĕ'mēs). At the point of death; also fig. (L., = "in extremity")

in·ex·tri·ca·ble (ĭnĕks'tr*i*kabel, -ĕkstrĭk'-) *adj.* That cannot be unraveled, freed, or solved. **in·ex'tri·ca·bly** *adv.*

inf. *abbrev.* Infantry; (gram.) infinitive; information; [L. *infra*] below.

in·fal·li·ble (ĭnfăl'*i*bel) *adj.* Incapable of erring; unfailing. **in·fal'li·bly** *adv.* **in·fal·li·bil·i·ty** (ĭnfăl*i*bĭl'ĭtē) *n.* (esp. as attribute of the pope speaking *ex cathedra*, defined 1870 by Vatican Council).

in·fa·mous (ĭn'fam*u*s) *adj.* Of ill fame, notoriously vile; abominable. **in'fa·mous·ly** *adv.* **in'fa·my** *n.* (pl. **-mies**).

in·fan·cy (ĭn'fansē) *n.* (pl. **-cies**). 1. Early childhood, babyhood. 2. (law) = MINORITY def. 1. 3. Early stage of development.

in·fant (ĭn'f*a*nt) *n.* Child during earliest period of life; (law) = MINOR *n.* def. 1.

in·fan·ta (ĭnfăn't*a*) *n.* (hist.) Daughter of king of Spain or Portugal (usu. eldest daughter), not heir to throne. **in·fan·te** (ĭnfăn'tā, -tē) *n.* (hist.) Son (usu. second son) of king of Spain or Portugal, not heir to throne.

in·fan·ti·cide (ĭnfăn'tĭsīd) *n.* 1. Murder of infant; custom of killing newborn infants. 2. One who kills an infant.

in·fan·tile (ĭn'f*a*ntīl) *adj.* Of, as of, infants; in its infancy; childish, silly; ~ **paralysis**: see POLIOMYELITIS.

in·fan·ti·lism (ĭn'f*a*nt*i*lĭzem, ĭnfăn't*i*-) *n.* Mentally or physically undeveloped state.

in·fan·try (ĭn'f*a*ntrē) *n.* (pl. **-tries**). Foot soldiers; **in'fantry·man**, soldier of infantry regiment, trained to fight on foot, usu. equipped with light weapons.

in·farct (ĭnfârkt', ĭn'fârkt) *n.* (path.) Area of dead tissue caused by the blocking of an artery that normally nourishes it. **in·farc'tion** *n.*

in·fat·u·ate (ĭnfăch'o͞oāt) *v.t.* (**-at·ed, -at·ing**). Affect (person) with extreme folly; inspire with extravagant passion. **in·fat'u·at·ed·ly** *adv.* **in·fat·u·a·tion** (ĭnfăcho͞oā'sh*o*n) *n.*

in·fect (ĭnfĕkt′) *v.t.* Implant disease-forming microorganisms in (person, animal, plant, etc.); imbue (person *with* opinion etc.). **in·fec′tive** *adj.* **in·fec′tive·ness** *n.*

in·fec·tion (ĭnfĕk′sh*o*n) *n.* Communication of disease; diffusive influence of example, sympathy, etc.

in·fec·tious (ĭnfĕk′sh*u*s) *adj.* Infecting with disease, pestilential; (of disease) such that the infecting agent can be communicated to the environment; (of emotions etc.) apt to spread, catching. **in·fec′tious·ly** *adv.* **in·fec′tious·ness** *n.*

in·fe·lic·i·tous (ĭnfelĭs′ĭt*u*s) *adj.* Not felicitous; unfortunate; inappropriate; unhappy. **in·fe·lic′i·ty** *n.* Unhappiness; misfortune; inaptness of expression etc.

in·fer (ĭnfẽr′) *v.t.* (**-ferred, -fer·ring**). Deduce, conclude; (erron.) imply.

in·fer·ence (ĭn′fer*e*ns) *n.* Inferring; (esp., logic) forming of a conclusion from premises either by induction or deduction; thing inferred. **in·fer·en·tial** (ĭnferĕn′sh*a*l) *adj.* **in·fer·en′tial·ly** *adv.*

in·fe·ri·or (ĭnfēr′ēer) *adj.* 1. Situated below; (bot., of calyx) below ovary, (of ovary) below calyx; (print., of small letters or figures) placed lower than ordinary letters, e.g. H_2, C_n. 2. Lower in rank, quality, etc. (*to*); of poor quality. **in·fe′ri·or·ly** *adv.* **in·ferior** *n.* Person inferior to another, esp. in rank. **in·fe·ri·or·i·ty** (ĭnfēreŏr′ĭtē, -ăr′-) *n.* ~ **complex**, unconscious feeling of inferiority to others, freq. manifested in self-assertive behavior; (pop.) sense of inferiority.

in·fer·nal (ĭnfẽr′n*a*l) *adj.* Of hell; hellish, fiendish; (colloq.) abominable, confounded. **in·fer′nal·ly** *adv.*

in·fer·no (ĭnfẽr′nō) *n.* (pl. **-nos**). Hell (**The I**~, 1st part of Dante's *Divine Comedy*); scene of horror.

in·fer·tile (ĭnfẽr′t*i*l) *adj.* Not fertile. **in·fer·til·i·ty** (ĭnf*e*rtĭl′ĭtē) *n.*

in·fest (ĭnfĕst′) *v.t.* Inhabit in large numbers, overrun; swarm in or about, (place). **in·fes·ta·tion** (ĭnfĕstā′sh*o*n) *n.*

in·fi·del (ĭn′fĭd*e*l) *n.* Person with no religious beliefs; adherent of religion opposed to some particular religion, esp. to Christianity or Islam; unbeliever. ~ *adj.* Unbelieving; of unbelievers.

in·fi·del·i·ty (ĭnfĭdĕl′*i*tē) *n.* (pl. **-ties**). 1. Lack of religious beliefs or faith. 2. Disloyalty, esp. to husband or wife; adultery.

in·field (ĭn′fēld) *n.* 1. Farm land around farmhouse. 2. (baseball) Part of field enclosed within baselines; the four infielders: first, second, third basemen and shortstop. **in′field·er** *n.* (baseball) One of the infield.

in·fight·ing (ĭn′fītĭng) *n.* 1. Boxing at closer quarters than arm's length. 2. (colloq.) Internal strife between (members of) organization(s) etc. **in′fight·er** *n.*

in·fil·trate (ĭnfĭl′trāt, ĭn′fĭl-) *v.* (**-trated, -trat·ing**). Introduce (fluid) by filtration; permeate by filtration (also fig.). **in·fil·tra′tion** *n.* (esp.) Gradual penetration into territory by small groups of settlers, or into enemy ground by small parties of troops; dissemination of ideas by small group working inside political party etc.; enter an organization as a spy.

in·fi·nite (ĭn′fĭnĭt) *adj.* Boundless, endless; very great; innumerable, very many; (math., of quantity or magnitude) greater than any assignable quantity or magnitude; (of series) that may be continued indefinitely without ever coming to an end. **in′fi·nite·ly** *adv.*

in·fin·i·tes·i·mal (ĭnfĭnĭtĕs′ĭm*a*l) *adj.* & *n.* Infinitely or very small (amount). **in·fin·i·tes′i·mal·ly** *adv.*

*Foot-soldiers of the **infantry** have been the backbone of most armies throughout the ages and have a key role even in these days of highly mobile and mechanized warfare. Below Left: Historical re-enactment of Civil War infantry at rest. Below right: Infantrymen ready for deployment during the Vietnam hostilities.*

Inflatable plastic structures, ranging from furniture and houses to 'art' forms, have been developed by modern designers. This 'inflatable sculpture' is by the Swiss artist, Karl Bucher.

in·fin·i·tive (ĭnfĭn'ĭtĭv) *adj.* & *n.* (gram.) (Verb form) that expresses the verbal notion without predicating it of any subject (e.g. (*to*) *see*). **in·fin·i·ti·val** (ĭnfĭnĭtī'v*a*l) *adj.*

in·fin·i·ty (ĭnfĭn'ĭtē) *n.* (pl. **-ties**). Boundlessness; boundless number or extent; (math.) infinite quantity (symbol ∞).

in·firm (ĭnfẽrm') *adj.* Physically weak, esp. through age; (of person, mind, judgment, etc.) weak, irresolute. **in·firm'ly** *adv.* **in·fir·mi·ty** (ĭnfẽr'mĭtē) *n.* (pl. **-ties**).

in·fir·ma·ry (ĭnfẽr'm*e*rē) *n.* (pl. **-ries**). Small hospital or dispensary, esp. in school, factory, etc.

in fla·gran·te de·lic·to (ĭn fl*a*grăn'tē dĭlĭk'tō; *Lat.* ĭn flahgrahn'tĕ dĕlĭk'tō). In the very act of committing an offense. [L., = "in blazing crime"]

in·flame (ĭnflām') *v.* (**-flamed, -flam·ing**). 1. Set ablaze; catch fire. 2. Excite passionately; become excited; aggravate. 3. Cause inflammation in (body etc.); become affected with inflammation.

in·flam·ma·ble (ĭnflăm'*a*b*e*l) *adj.* Easily set on fire; flammable; easily excited. ~ *n.* (usu. pl.) Inflammable substance. **in·flam·ma·bil·i·ty** (ĭnflăm*a*bĭl'ĭtē) *n.*

in·flam·ma·tion (ĭnfl*a*mā'sh*o*n) *n.* Inflaming; (path.) condition of living tissue marked by heat, swelling, redness, and usu. pain, esp. as reaction to damage or infection.

in·flam·ma·to·ry (ĭnflăm'*a*tōrē, -tōrē) *adj.* Tending to inflame with desire or passion; (path.) of, characterized by, inflammation.

in·flate (ĭnflāt') *v.t.* (**-flat·ed, -flat·ing**). Distend with air or gas; puff up (*with* pride etc.); resort to inflation of (currency); raise (price) artificially; **inflated**, (of language) bombastic.

in·fla·tion (ĭnflā'sh*o*n) *n.* Inflating; (esp.) increase in purchasing power in relation to goods available for purchase, resulting in fall in value of money and general increase in prices. **in·fla·tion·ar·y** (ĭnflā'sh*o*nĕrē) *adj.*

in·flect (ĭnflĕkt') *v.t.* 1. Bend inward, curve. 2. (gram.) Vary termination of (word) to express grammatical relation. 3. Modulate (voice etc.). **in·flec'tion** *n.* 1. Inflecting, bending. 2. Modification of word to express grammatical relationship; inflected form of word; inflectional suffix or element. 3. Modulation of voice; change in pitch or tone. **in·flec'tive** *adj.* Of, characterized by, inflection.

in·flex·i·ble (ĭnflĕk's*i*b*e*l) *adj.* Unbendable; (fig.) unbending, rigid. **in·flex·i·bil'i·ty** *n.* **in·flex'i·bly** *adv.*

in·flict (ĭnflĭkt') *v.t.* Lay on (blow, etc.); impose (suffering, penalty, etc., *upon*). **in·flic'tion** *n.*

in-flight (ĭn'flīt) *adj.* Served, offered, etc., as food, movies, etc., on plane during flight.

in·flo·res·cence (ĭnflōrĕs'*e*ns) *n.* (bot.) Arrangement of flowers of plant in relation to axis and to each other; collective flower of plant; flowering.

in·flow (ĭn'flō) *n.* Flowing in.

in·flu·ence (ĭn'flōō*e*ns) *n.* 1. Action exercised (*on*); ascendancy, moral power (*over, with*); thing, person, exercising (usu. nonmaterial) power. 2. (astrol.) Supposed flowing from stars of ethereal fluid affecting character and destiny of man. ~ *v.t.* (**-enced, -enc·ing**). Exert influence upon, have effect upon.

in·flu·en·tial (ĭnflōōĕn'sh*a*l) *adj.* Having great influence. **in·flu·en'tial·ly** *adv.*

in·flu·en·za (ĭnflōōĕn'z*a*) *n.* Acute infectious febrile disorder, caused by a virus, occurring usu. in widespread epidemics.

in·flux (ĭn'flŭks) *n.* Flowing in, esp. of persons or things (*into* place etc.).

in·fo (ĭn'fō) *n.* (Slang) Information.

in·fold (ĭnfōld') = ENFOLD.

in·form (ĭnfôrm') *v.* 1. Inspire, imbue (person, thing, *with* quality, principle, etc.). 2. Tell (person *of* thing, *that, how*, etc.). 3. Bring charge (*against*). **in·form·ant** (ĭnfôr'm*a*nt) *n.* (esp.) One who tells or gives information.

in·form·al (ĭnfôr'm*a*l) *adj.* Not according to due form; without formality. **in·for'mal·ly** *adv.* **in·for·mal·i·ty** (ĭnfôrmăl'ĭtē) *n.* (pl. **-ties**).

in·for·ma·tion (ĭnf*e*rmā'sh*o*n) *n.* 1. Informing, telling; thing told, knowledge, items of knowledge, news; ~ **retrieval**, systematic recovery of data from memory bank of computer, files, etc. 2. (law)

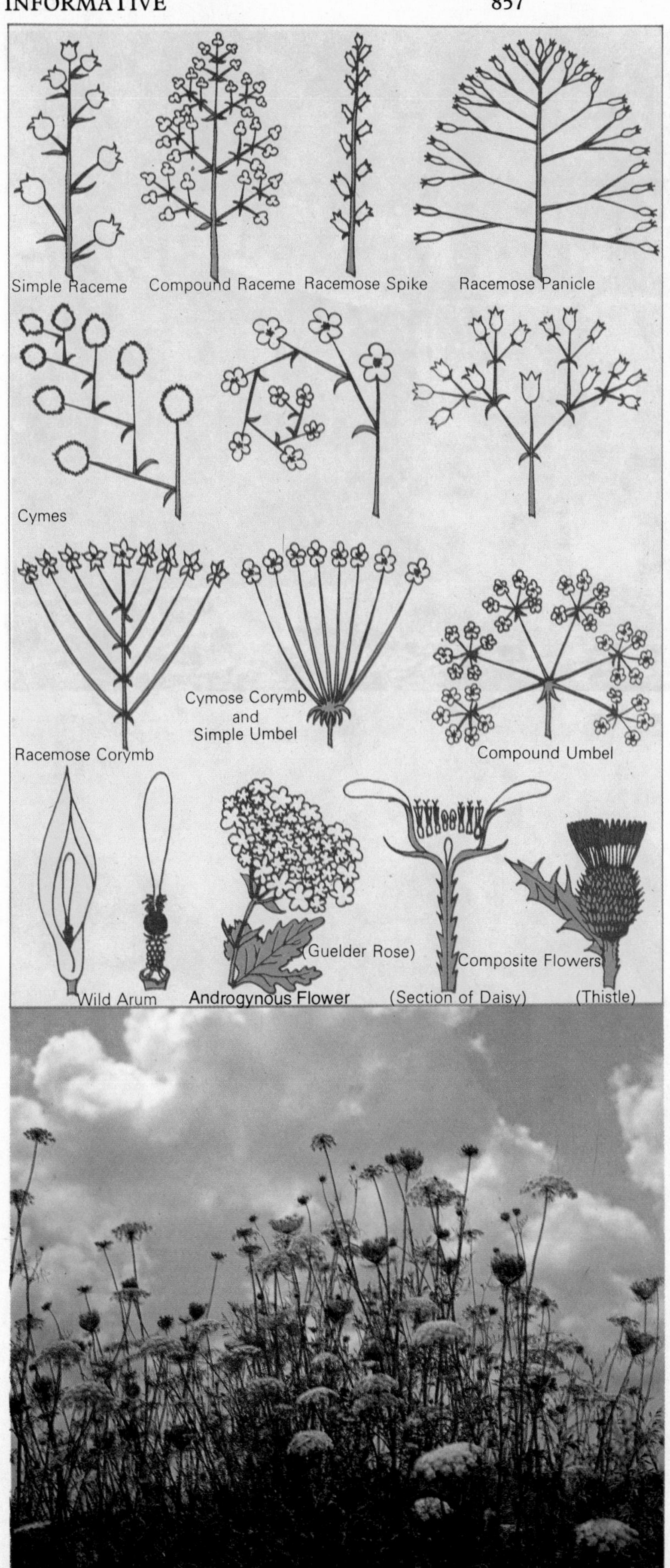

Charge, complaint, lodged with court or magistrate (*against*). **in·for·ma'tion·al** *adj.*

in·form·a·tive (ĭnfôr'matĭv) *adj.* Giving information, instructive.

in·formed (ĭnfôrmd') *adj.* Instructed, knowing the facts, educated.

in·form·er (ĭnfôr'mer) *n.* One who informs against another.

in·fra (ĭn'fra) *adv.* Below, lower down, further on (in book). [L.]

infra- *prefix.* Below.

in·frac·tion (ĭnfrăk'shon) *n.* Infringement, violation.

in·fra dig (ĭn'fra dĭg'). (chiefly Brit.) Beneath one's dignity, unbecoming. [abbrev. L. *infra dignitatem*]

in·fran·gi·ble (ĭnfrăn'jibel) *adj.* Unbreakable; inviolable.

in·fra·red (ĭnfrarĕd') *adj.* (phys.) Lying beyond the red end of the visible spectrum; of, producing, electromagnetic radiations with a wavelength longer than that of red light, perceived as heat and used in heat therapy, cooking devices, etc.

in·fra·struc·ture (ĭn'frastrŭkcher) *n.* Fixed installations and facilities necessary to support military operations, as airfields, naval bases, training establishments, supply works, etc.; supporting system of any organization.

in·fre·quent (ĭnfrē'kwent) *adj.* Not frequent. **in·fre'quent·ly** *adv.* **in·fre'quen·cy, in·fre'quence** *ns.*

in·fringe (ĭnfrĭnj') *v.t.* (**-fringed, -fring·ing**). Transgress, violate (law, oath, etc.). **in·fringe'ment** *n.*

in·fu·ri·ate (ĭnfūr'ēāt) *v.t.* (**-at·ed, -at·ing**). Fill with fury, enrage.

in·fuse (ĭnfūz') *v.* (**-fused, -fus·ing**). 1. Pour (*into*); instill (*into*). 2. Steep (herb etc.) in liquid to extract its soluble properties; undergo infusion.

in·fu·si·ble (ĭnfū'zibel) *adj.* That cannot be fused or melted. **in·fus·i·bil·i·ty** (ĭnfūzibĭl'ĭtē) *n.*

in·fu·sion (ĭnfū'zhon) *n.* Infusing; liquid extract thus obtained; infused element, admixture.

-ing[1] *suffix.* Forming nouns f. verbs, denoting action (*asking, fighting*); product (*building*); material (*clothing*).

ing[2] *suffix.* Forming pres. part. of verbs, often used as adjectives (*charming, well-meaning*).

in·gen·ious (ĭnjēn'yus) *adj.* Showing ingenuity. **in·gen'ious·ly** *adv.* **in·gen'ious·ness** *n.*

Inflorescence, *in its simplest form, is when the stem of a plant bears a series of flower stalks (peduncles) at equal distances apart and with flowers at their tips. The cow parsley (left) is an example. More complex inflorescences occur when there are secondary peduncles (above left).*

Gold, silver and steel are cast into ***ingots*** *for further processing, storage or transportation. Steel ingots can weigh more than 100 tons. These steel ingots are ready for forging at the Krupp Works, Essen, W. Germany.*

in·gé·nue (ăn′jenōō, -nū, ahn′-zhe-; *Fr.* ahṅzhānü′) *n.* (pl. **-nues** pr. -nōōz, -nūz; *Fr.* -nü′). Artless girl, esp. as stage type. [Fr.]

in·ge·nu·i·ty (ĭnjenōō′ĭtē) *n.* Cleverness, imagination, inventiveness.

in·gen·u·ous (ĭnjĕn′ūus) *adj.* Open, frank; innocent, artless. **in·gen′u·ous·ly** *adv.* **in·gen′u·ous·ness** *n.*

in·gest (ĭnjĕst′) *v.t.* Take in (food etc.) by, or as if by, swallowing. **in·ges·tion** (ĭnjĕs′chon) *n.* **in·ges′tive** *adj.*

in·glo·ri·ous (ĭnglōr′ēus, -glōr′-) *adj.* Shameful, ignominious. **in·glo′ri·ous·ly** *adv.*

in·got (ĭng′got) *n.* Mass (usu. oblong) of cast metal, esp. of gold, silver, or steel.

in·grain (ĭn′grān) *adj.* Inherent, inveterate, thorough.

in·grained (ĭngrānd′, ĭn′grānd) *adj.* Deeply rooted, inveterate; thorough.

in·grate (ĭn′grāt) *n.* Ungrateful person.

in·gra·ti·ate (ĭngrā′shēāt) *v.t.* (**-at·ed, -at·ing**). Bring *oneself* into favor *with.* **in·gra·ti·a·tion** (ĭngrāshēā′shon) *n.*

in·grat·i·tude (ĭngrăt′ĭtōōd, -tūd) *n.* Lack of gratitude.

in·gre·di·ent (ĭngrē′dēent) *n.* Component part, element, in a mixture.

in·gress (ĭn′grĕs), **in·gres·sion** (ĭngrĕsh′on) *ns.* Going in; right of entrance.

in·grow·ing (ĭngrō′ĭng) *adj.* Growing inward, esp. (of nail) growing into the flesh.

in·gui·nal (ĭng′gwinal) *adj.* Of the groin.

in·hab·it (ĭnhăb′ĭt) *v.t.* Dwell in, occupy (region, town, house, etc.). **in·hab′i·tant** *n.*

in·hal·ant (ĭnhā′lant) *n.* (esp.) Medicinal preparation for inhaling.

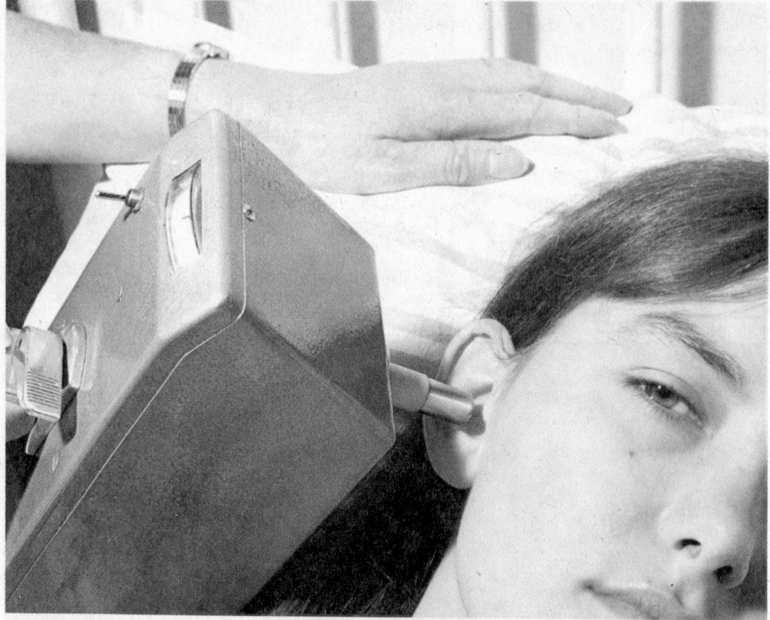

The ***infra-red*** *portion of the electromagnetic spectrum is invisible to the eye, but can be detected as a sensation of warmth. This infra-red thermometer, used in hospitals, records the temperature of an internal section of the body.*

in·ha·la·tor (ĭn′halāter) *n.* Apparatus for introducing medication or vapor into breathing passages, or for administering anesthetic.

in·hale (ĭnhāl′) *v.t.* (**-haled, -hal·ing**). Breathe in (air, gas, etc.); take (esp. tobacco smoke) into the lungs. **in·ha·la·tion** (ĭnhalā′shon) *n.*

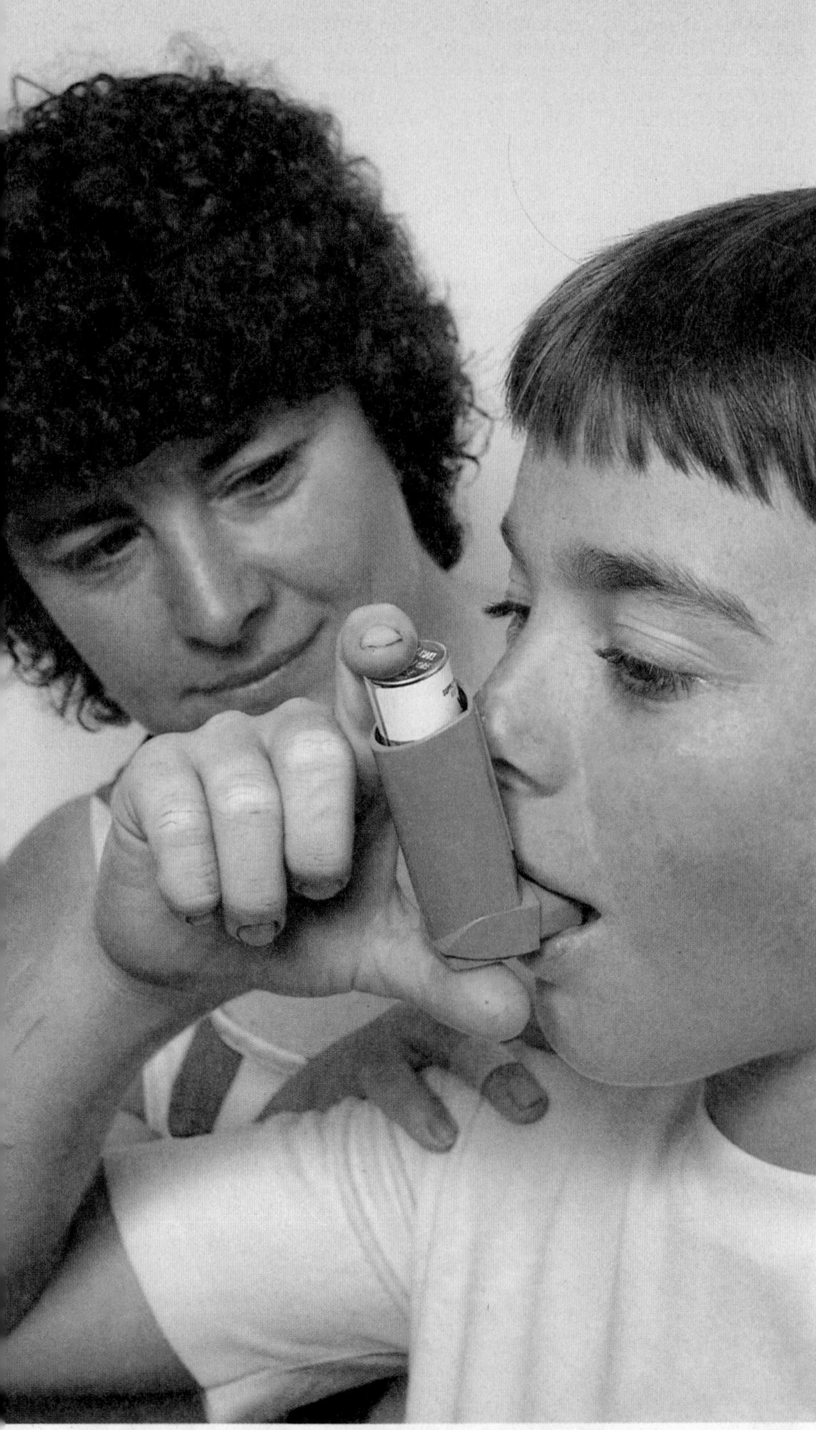

*This young asthma sufferer has to **inhale** medication to alleviate the breathing difficulties that are an inevitable part of the condition. Prolonged asthmatic attacks can be dangerous if the sufferer is weakened.*

in·hal·er (ĭnhā´l*er*) *n.* (esp.) 1. Inhalator. 2. RESPIRATOR.

in·here (ĭnhēr´) *v.i.* (**-hered, -her·ing**). (of qualities etc.) Exist, abide, *in*; (of rights etc.) be vested *in*. **in·her·ence** (ĭnhēr´*e*ns, -hĕr´-) *n.* **in·her´en·cy** *n.* (pl. **-cies**). **in·her´ent** *adj.* **in·her´ent·ly** *adv.*

in·her·it (ĭnhĕr´ĭt) *v.t.* Receive by legal descent or succession; derive (quality etc.) from one's progenitors; (abs.) succeed as heir. **in·her´i·tance** *n.* Inheriting; what is inherited; **inheritance tax**, tax on inherited property. **in·her´it·a·ble** *adj.* Capable of inheriting or of being inherited. **in·her´i·tor** *n.* **in·her·i·trix** (ĭnhĕr´ĭtrĭks) *n.fem.* (pl. **in·her·i·tri·ces** pr. ĭnhĕr´ĭtr*i*sēz, -hĕrĭtrī´-).

in·hib·it (ĭnhĭb´ĭt) *v.t.* Hinder, restrain (action, process); forbid, prohibit. **in·hi·bi·tion** (ĭnhĭbĭsh´*o*n) *n.* (esp., psychol.) Blocking of thought or action by emotional resistance.

in·hib·i·tor (ĭnhĭb´ĭt*er*) *n.* Thing that inhibits; (physiol.) substance that represses a normal physiological process or antagonizes an abnormal one; (chem.) substance that slows down or suppresses a chemical change.

in·hos·pi·ta·ble (ĭnhŏs´pĭt*a*b*e*l, -hŏspĭt´*a*-) *adj.* Not hospitable; unfriendly; (of region etc.) not affording shelter etc. **in·hos´pi·ta·bly** *adv.* **in·hos´pi·ta·ble·ness, in·hos·pi·tal·i·ty** (ĭnhŏspĭtăl´ĭtē) *ns.*

in-house (ĭn´hows´) *adj.* & *adv.* Within an organization or using its own resources (*an* ~ *editor*, ~ *project*).

in·hu·man (ĭnhū´m*a*n, ĭnū´-) *adj.* Brutal, unfeeling, barbarous; not of the ordinary human type. **in·hu´man·ly** *adv.* **in·hu·man·i·ty** (ĭnhūmăn´ĭtē) *n.* (pl. **-ties**).

in·im·i·cal (ĭnĭm´ĭk*a*l) *adj.* Hostile; harmful. **in·im´i·cal·ly** *adv.*

in·im·i·ta·ble (ĭnĭm´ĭt*a*bel) *adj.* That defies imitation. **in·im´i·ta·bly** *adv.*

in·iq·ui·ty (ĭnĭk´wĭtē) *n.* (pl. **-ties**). Unrighteousness, wickedness; gross injustice. **in·iq´ui·tous** *adj.* **in·iq´ui·tous·ly** *adv.*

in·i·tial (ĭnĭsh´*a*l) *adj.* Of, existing or occurring at, the beginning; ~ **letter**, letter standing at beginning of word. **in·i´tial·ly** *adv.* **initial** *n.* (esp. pl.) First letter(s) of person's name and surname. ~ *v.t.* (**-tialed, -tial·ing**, Brit. **-tialled, -tial·ling**). Mark, sign, with initials.

in·i·ti·ate (ĭnĭsh´ēāt) *v.t.* (**-at·ed, -at·ing**). 1. Begin, set going, originate. 2. Admit (person), esp. with introductory rites or forms (*into* society, office, secret, *in* mysteries, science, etc.). **in·i·ti·a·tion** (ĭnĭshēā´sh*o*n) *n.* **in·i·ti·a·to·ry** (ĭnĭsh´ē*a*tōrē, -tōrē) *adj.* **initiate** (ĭnĭsh´ēĭt, -āt) *adj.* & *n.* (Person) who has been initiated.

in·i·ti·a·tive (ĭnĭsh´ē*a*tĭv, ĭnĭsh´-*a*-) *n.* First step, origination; power, right, or function of originating something; esp., right of citizen(s) outside legislature to initiate legislation; **take the** ~, take the lead. **initiative** *adj.* Beginning, originating.

in·ject (ĭnjĕkt´) *v.t.* Drive, force (fluid, medicine, *into* cavity etc.) by or as by syringe or hypodermic needle; fill (cavity etc.) by injecting. **in·jec·tion** (ĭnjĕk´sh*o*n) *n.* 1. Injecting; **fuel** ~, direct introduction of fuel under pressure into combustion chamber of internal combustion engine. 2. Liquid or solution injected.

in·ju·di·cious (ĭnjo͞odĭsh´*u*s) *adj.*

Unwise, ill-judged. **in·ju·di′cious·ly** *adv.* **in·ju·di′cious·ness** *n.*

In·jun (ĭn′*j*un) *n.* (colloq.) Var. of INDIAN *n.* def 2; **honest** ~, real(ly), true, truly.

in·junc·tion (ĭnjŭnk′sh*o*n) *n.* Enjoining; directive, order; (law) court order enjoining or prohibiting a party from a course of action.

in·jure (ĭn′j*er*) *v.t.* (**-jured, -jur·ing**). Do wrong to; hurt, harm, impair. **in′jured** *adj.* Wronged; hurt; showing sense of wrong, offended.

in·ju·ri·ous (ĭnjoor′ē*u*s) *adj.* Damaging, harmful; (of language) insulting; libelous; slanderous.

in·ju·ry (ĭn′j*e*rē) *n.* (pl. **-ries**). Wrongful action or treatment; harm, damage.

in·jus·tice (ĭnjŭs′tĭs) *n.* Lack of equity, unfairness; unjust act.

ink (ĭngk) *n.* 1. Colored fluid for writing with pen on paper etc. or for printing, consisting of pigment dispersed in water (for writing inks) or in oil, resin, etc., for printing and ballpoint inks; **India** ~: see INDIA. 2. Black inky liquid secreted by cuttlefish etc. and ejected to cloud water and assist escape. 3. **ink blot**, stain of spilled ink on paper, esp. such pattern of such stain used in RORSCHACH test; **ink′well**, (formerly) container for ink fitted into hole in desk. **ink** *v.t.* mark (*in*, *over*, etc.) with ink; cover (types) with ink. **ink′y** *adj.* (**ink·i·er, ink·i·est**). Of, like ink; black or very dark; covered or stained with ink.

ink·ling (ĭngk′lĭng) *n.* Hint, slight knowledge or suspicion, (*of*).

in·laid (ĭn′lād, ĭnlād′): see INLAY.

in·land (ĭn′lănd, -l*a*nd) *n.* Interior of country. ~ *adj.* Placed in interior of country, remote from sea or border. **in′land** *adv.* In, toward, the interior.

In·land (ĭn′lănd) **Sea.** Shallow Pacific Ocean inlet extending 240 mi. (386 km), in SW. Japan; bounded on the N. by Honshu, and on the S. by Shikoku and Kyushu.

in-law (ĭn′law) *n.* Relative by marriage.

in-lay (ĭn′lā, ĭnlā′) *v.t.* (**-laid, -lay·ing**). Embed (thing *in* another) so that their surfaces are even; ornament (thing) with another inlaid. **in′lay** *n.* (pl. **-lays**). Inlaid ornament, esp. furniture or woodwork; (dentistry) large filling.

in·let (ĭn′lĕt) *n.* Small arm of sea, creek.

in lo·co pa·ren·tis (ĭn lō′kō p*a*rĕn′tĭs). In place of a parent. [L.]

in·mate (ĭn′māt) *n.* Occupant (*of* house, and esp. of a prison, asylum, etc.) esp. along with others.

in me·mo·ri·am (ĭn m*e*mōr′-ē*a*m, -mōr′-). In memory (of). [L.]

in·most (ĭn′mōst) *adj.* Most inward.

inn (ĭn) *n.* House providing lodging, food, etc., for payment, esp. for travelers; tavern; **inn′keeper**, one who keeps an inn.

in·nards (ĭn′*er*dz) *n.pl.* (colloq.) Viscera; internal bodily organs.

in·nate (ĭnāt′, ĭn′āt) *adj.* Inborn, natural. **in·nate′ly** *adv.* **in·nate′ness** *n.*

in·ner (ĭn′*er*) *adj.* Interior, internal; ~ **city**, central area of city, typically characterized by overcrowding, dilapidation, and poverty; ~ **directed**, guided by personal standards rather than external social pressure; ~ **ear**, internal part of ear comprising vestibule, semicircular canals, and cochlea; **the ~ man**, man's soul or mind; (joc.) stomach; ~ **space**, space below surface of ocean; **in′nerspring (mattress)**, having enclosed helical springs supporting padding; **inner tube**, separate inflatable rubber tube inside a pneumatic tire. **in′ner·most** *adj.* **in′ner** *n.* & *adj.*

in·ning (ĭn′ĭng) *n.* (baseball) Portion of game in which each team is at bat until it has three outs; ~**s**, (usu. considered sing.) (cricket) portion of game in which one team is at bat; ~**s**, (pl.) opportunity to perform.

In·no·cent (ĭn′*o*s*e*nt). Name of 13 popes: (esp.) **Innocent III**, pope 1198–1216; champion of supremacy of spiritual over temporal authority; proclaimer of fourth Crusade and initiator of "crusades" against ALBIGENSES; **Innocent IV**, pope 1243–54; canon lawyer, extreme supporter of papal claims to temporal authority; first bestower

*The Greenland Fishery **Inn** in King's Lynn, U.K., was built in 1605 as a merchant's house with a cruck-based roof, 17th-century wall paintings and an overhanging upper floor.*

*This 18th-century French games table has **inlays** of ivory and ebony on its tulipwood surface. Its four sides are inset with 26 Sèvres plaques mounted in ormolu.*

*In the New Guinea highlands a child is about to take part with a group of others in a ceremony of **initiation** into boyhood. One task will be to kill a pig. The cowrie shells have a sacred connotation*

Pope Innocent X (1574–1655), a lover of the arts, was the patron of the great Baroque sculptor, Bernini. This portrait of him is by the Spanish painter, Velazquez.

of red hat on Roman cardinals.

in·no·cent (ĭn′osent) *adj.* Free from moral wrong, sinless; not guilty (*of* crime etc.); simple, guileless; harmless. **in′no·cent·ly** *adv.* **innocent** *n.* Innocent person, esp. young child; simple person. **in′no·cence** *n.*

in·noc·u·ous (ĭnŏk′ūus) *adj.* Not injurious; harmless; banal; not important. **in·noc′u·ous·ly** *adv.* **in·noc′u·ous·ness, in·no·cu·i·ty** (ĭnokū′ĭtē) *ns.*

in·nom·i·nate (ĭnŏm′inĭt) *adj.* Unnamed; (anat.) ~ **bone**, hip-bone, union of three bones (ilium, ischium, and pubis).

in·no·vate (ĭn′ovāt) *v.i.* (**-vat·ed, -vat·ing**). Bring in novelties; make changes *in*. **in·no·va·tion** (ĭnovā′shon), **in′no·va·tor** *ns.*

in·nu·en·do (ĭnūĕn′dō) *n.* (pl. **-dos, -does**). Oblique hint, insinuation, allusive remark (usu. disparaging). [L., = by nodding at, pointing at, meaning (*innuere* nod at, mean)]

In·nu·it (ĭn′ūĭt) *n.* (pl. **-its, -it**). Eskimo of N. America or Greenland as distinct from those of Aleutians or Asia; tribe, language, of these Eskimos. [Eskimo, = people]

in·nu·mer·a·ble (ĭnōō′merabel, -nū′-) *adj.* Countless.

in·oc·u·late (ĭnŏk′yulāt) *v.t.* (**-lat·ed, -lat·ing**). Impregnate (person or animal) *with* agent of disease to induce milder form of it and so safeguard against further attacks. **in·oc·u·la·tion** (ĭnŏkyulā′shon) *n.*

in·of·fen·sive (ĭnofĕn′sĭv) *adj.* Unoffending; not objectionable. **in·of·fen′sive·ly** *adv.*

in·op·er·a·ble (ĭnŏp′erabel) *adj.* That cannot be operated; not curable by surgical operation.

in·op·er·a·tive (ĭnŏp′eratĭv) *adj.* Not working or taking effect.

in·op·por·tune (ĭnŏpertōōn′, -tūn′) *adj.* Unseasonable, untimely, tactless. **in·op·por·tune′ly** *adv.* **in·op·por·tune′ness** *n.*

in·or·di·nate (ĭnōr′dinĭt) *adj.* Immoderate, excessive; intemperate; disorderly. **in·or′di·nate·ly** *adv.*

in·or·gan·ic (ĭnōrgăn′ĭk) *adj.* 1. Having no organized physical structure; not existing by natural growth. 2. (chem.) Belonging to any class of substance other than organic compounds; ~ **chemistry**: see CHEMISTRY. **in·or·gan′i·cal·ly** *adv.*

in·pa·tient (ĭn′pā′shent) *n.* Patient living in a hospital during treatment.

in pet·to (ĭn pĕt′ō). (of cardinals appointed but not disclosed by the pope) Undisclosed. [It., = in the breast]

in·put (ĭn′pōōt) *n.* What is put in, esp. in economic, electrical, or industrial processes; data, programs, etc., supplied to computer; (jargon, colloq.) opinions, facts, etc., offered to decision makers.

in·quest (ĭn′kwĕst) *n.* Judicial inquiry to ascertain matter of fact, usu. before a jury; the jury itself; inquiry held by coroner's court to ascertain cause of person's death (also **coroner's** ~); also fig.

in·quire (ĭnkwīr′) *v.* (**-quired, -quir·ing**). Make search (*into* matter); seek information (*of* person, *about* thing, etc.); ask *about*, ask to be told. **in·quir′ing·ly** *adv.*

in·quir·y (ĭnkwīr′ē, ĭn′kwerē) *n.* (pl. **-quir·ies**). Asking; question; investigation.

in·qui·si·tion (ĭnkwĭzĭsh′on) *n.* 1. Search, investigation; official inquiry. 2. **I~**, (R.C. Ch.) ecclesiastical tribunal (the *Holy Office*) set up in 13th c. under Innocent III for the suppression of heresy and punishment of heretics, notorious esp. in Spain in 16th c. for its severities; finally abolished in France 1772, in Spain 1834. **in·qui·si′tion·al** *adj.*

in·quis·i·tive (ĭnkwĭz′ĭtĭv) *adj.* Inquiring, curious; prying. **in·quis′i·tive·ly** *adv.* **in·quis′i·tive·ness** *n.*

in·quis·i·tor (ĭnkwĭz′ĭter) *n.* Investigator; questioner; officer of the Inquisition.

in·quis·i·to·ri·al (ĭnkwĭzĭtōr′ēal, -tōr′-) *adj.* Of, like, an inquisitor; offensively prying. **in·quis·i·to′ri·al·ly** *adv.*

in re (ĭn rē′, rā′) = RE.

I.N.R.I. *abbrev. Iesus Nazarenus Rex Iudaeorum* (L., = Jesus of Nazareth, King of the Jews).

in·road (ĭn′rōd) *n.* (usu. pl.) Hostile incursion, raid; (fig.) encroachment.

in·rush (ĭn′rŭsh) *n.* Rushing in; influx.

in·sane (ĭnsān′) *adj.* Not sane, mad; senseless. **in·sane′ly** *adv.* **in·san·i·ty** (ĭnsăn′ĭtē) *n.* (pl. **-ties**).

in·sa·tia·ble (ĭnsā′shabel, -shēabel) *adj.* That cannot be satisfied. **in·sa·tia·bil·i·ty** (ĭnsāshabĭl′ĭtē, -shēa-) *n.* **in·sa′tia·bly** *adv.*

in·sa·ti·ate (ĭnsā′shēĭt) *adj.* Never satisfied.

in·scribe (ĭnskrīb′) *v.t.* (**-scribed, -scrib·ing**). 1. Write (words etc. *in, on*); enter name of (person) on list; dedicate (a copy of a book, photograph, etc.) (*to*) by writing one's name or a salutation on it. 2. (geom.) Trace (figure) within another so that some particular points of it lie on the boundary of that other.

in·scrip·tion (ĭnskrĭp′shon) *n.* Words inscribed, esp. on monument, coin, etc.

in·scru·ta·ble (ĭnskrōō′tabel) *adj.* That cannot be penetrated, wholly mysterious. **in·scru′ta·ble·ness, in·scru·ta·bil·i·ty** (ĭnskrōōtabĭl′ĭtē) *ns.* **in·scru′ta·bly** *adv.*

in·seam (ĭn′sēm) *n.* Inner seam of trouser leg etc.

in·sect (ĭn′sĕkt) *n.* (pop.) Small animal with body divided into segments; (zool.) arthropod of the

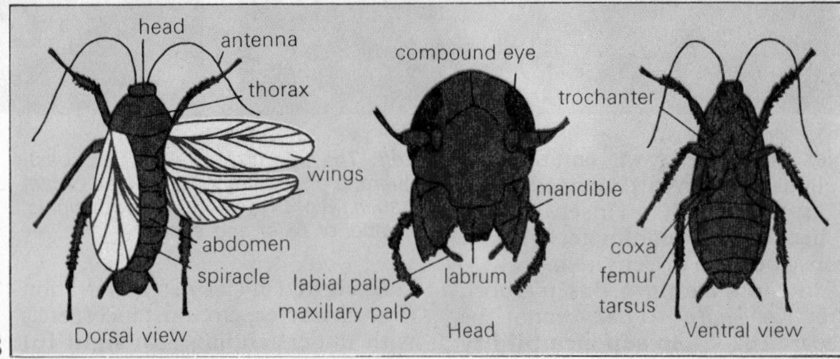

*There are an estimated 2 million described species of **insects** in the world. 1. The stick insect closely resembles the plant on which it feeds. 2. Aphids carry virus diseases from infected to healthy plants. 3. The cockroach can be a household pest. 4. The Pyrrhocorid plant bug causes discoloration of cotton lint on the plant.*

class Insecta that breathes through tracheae and has a body divided into three regions (head, thorax, and abdomen) and usu., in the adult, three pairs of legs and two pairs of wings.

in·sec·ti·cide (ĭnsĕk′tĭsīd) *n.* Preparation used for killing insects. **in·sec·ti·cid·al** (ĭnsĕktĭsī′d*a*l) *adj.*

in·sec·ti·vore (ĭnsĕk′t*i*vōr, -vōr) *n.* Insect-eating animal; member of the Insectivora, an order of primitive mammals, most members of which (e.g. mole, shrew, hedgehog) usu. feed on insects. **in·sec·tiv·o·rous** (ĭnsĕktĭv′*e*r*u*s) *adj.* Insect-eating; (of plant) having special structures for trapping and digesting insects.

in·se·cure (ĭns*e*kūr′) *adj.* 1. Unsafe; not secure; inadequately protected or guarded. 2. Lacking self-confidence; unsure; shaky. **in·se·cure′ly** *adv.* **in·se·cu′ri·ty** *n.* (pl. **-ties**).

in·sem·i·nate (ĭnsĕm′*i*nāt) *v.t.* (**-nat·ed, -nat·ing**). Sow (seed etc.) *in* (lit. and fig.); (biol.) introduce spermatozoa into (female reproductive system, or the eggs of creatures (e.g. frogs) that fertilize externally). **in·sem·i·na′tion** *n.*

in·sen·sate (ĭnsĕn′sāt, -sĭt) *adj.* Without sensibility, unfeeling; without physical sensation; unconscious. **in·sen′sate·ly** *adv.*

in·sen·si·bil·i·ty (ĭnsĕns*i*bĭl′ĭtē) *n.* (pl. **-ties**). Lack of mental feeling or emotion; indifference (*to*); unconsciousness, swoon.

in·sen·si·ble (ĭnsĕn′s*i*b*e*l) *adj.* Too small or gradual to be perceived; inappreciable; unconscious; unaware. **in·sen′si·bly** *adv.*

in·sen·si·tive (ĭnsĕn′s*i*tĭv) *adj.*

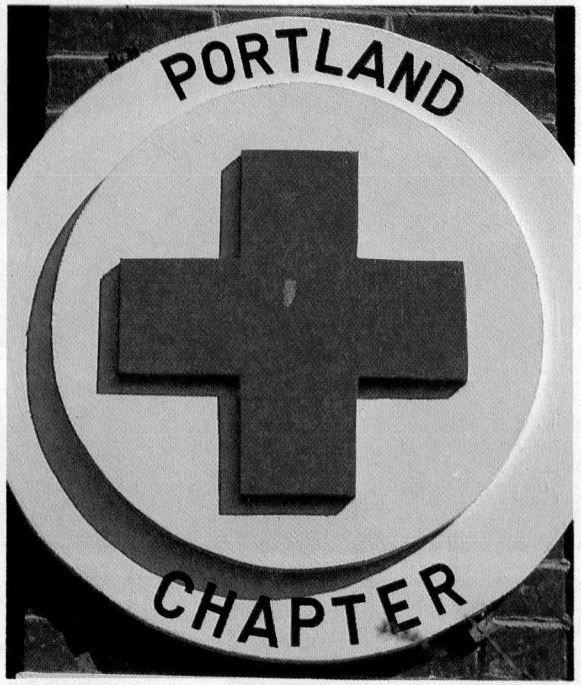

Left: The ***insignia*** *of the U.S. coastguard, a government-supervised organization. Right: the Red Cross insignia, symbol of relief and succor.*

Not sensitive (*to*); emotionless, callous. **in·sen'si·tive·ness** *n.*

in·sen·ti·ent (ĭnsĕn´shēent, -shent) *adj.* Inanimate; without consciousness or sensation.

in·sep·a·ra·ble (ĭnsĕp´*era*bel, -sĕp´r*a*-) *adj.* That cannot be separated. **in·sep·a·ra·bil·i·ty** (ĭnsĕp*era*bĭl´ĭtē, -sĕpr*a*-) *n.* **in·sep'a·ra·bly** *adv.*

in·sert (ĭnsĕrt´) *v.t.* Place, fit, thrust, (thing *in, into*, another etc.); introduce (letter, article, etc., *in, into*, written matter, newspaper, etc.). **in'sert** *n.* Thing inserted. **in·ser'tion** *n.* Inserting; thing inserted, esp. in writing or print.

in·set (ĭn´sĕt) *n.* Extra page(s) inserted in sheet or book; small map etc. inserted within border of larger; piece set into dress etc. **in·set'** *v.t.* (**-set, -set·ting**). Put in as an inset; insert.

in·side (ĭn´sīd, ĭnsīd´) *n.* 1. Inner side or surface; (of path) side next to wall or away from road; inner part, interior; ~ **out**, so that inner side becomes outer. 2. **insides** (*n.pl.*), stomach and bowels (colloq.). **in'sides', inside'** *adjs.* Situated on or in, derived from, the inside; ~ **information**, information not accessible to outsiders. **in·side'** *adv.* On or in or to the inside; (slang) in prison; ~ **of**, (colloq.) in less time than. **in'side, inside'** *preps.* On or to the inner side of, within.

in·sid·er (ĭn´sī´d*er*) *n.* One who is in some society, organization, etc.; one who has access to secret information.

in·sid·i·ous (ĭnsĭd´ēus) *adj.* Treacherous, crafty; proceeding secretly or subtly. **in·sid'i·ous·ly** *adv.* **in·sid'i·ous·ness** *n.*

in·sight (ĭn´sīt) *n.* Penetration (*into* character, circumstances, etc.) with understanding. **in·sight'ful** *adj.*

in·sig·ni·a (ĭnsĭg´nē*a*) *n.pl.* (previously pl. of **in·sig·ne** pr. ĭnsĭg´nē, now usu. considered sing., pl. **-ni·as, -ni·a**). Badge(s), distinguishing mark(s) (*of* office, honor, etc.).

in·sig·nif·i·cant (ĭnsĭgnĭf´ĭk*a*nt) *adj.* Unimportant, trifling; meaningless. **in·sig·nif'i·cant·ly** *adv.* **in·sig·nif'i·cance** *n.*

in·sin·cere (ĭnsĭnsēr´) *adj.* Not sincere. **in·sin·cere'ly** *adv.* **in·sin·cer·i·ty** (ĭnsĭnsĕr´ĭtē) *n.* (pl. **-ties**).

in·sin·u·ate (ĭnsĭn´ūāt) *v.t.* (**-at·ed, -at·ing**). Introduce gradually or subtly; convey indirectly, hint obliquely. **in·sin'u·at·ing·ly** *adv.* **in·sin·u·a·tion** (ĭnsĭnūā´sh*o*n), **in·sin'u·a·tor** *ns.* **in·sin·u·a·tive** (ĭnsĭn´ūātĭv, -ū*a*-) *adj.*

in·sip·id (ĭnsĭp´ĭd) *adj.* Tasteless; wanting in flavor; lifeless, dull, uninteresting. **in·sip'id·ly** *adv.* **in·sip'id·ness, in·si·pid·i·ty** (ĭnsĭpĭd´ĭtē) *ns.*

in·sist (ĭnsĭst´) *v.* Dwell long or emphatically (*on*); maintain positively; make a stand *on* as essential. **in·sist'ence, in·sist'en·cy** *ns.* **in·sist'ent** *adj.* **in·sist'ent·ly** *adv.*

in si·tu (ĭn sī´too͞, -tū; *Lat.* ĭn sē´too͞). In its (original) place.

in·so·bri·e·ty (ĭnsobrī´etē) *n.* Lack of sobriety; intemperance.

in·so·far (ĭnsōfăr´) *adv.* To such an extent or degree (*as*).

in·sole (ĭn´sōl) *n.* 1. Inner sole of the boot or shoe. 2. Flat piece of material worn inside shoe for warmth or comfort.

in·so·lent (ĭn´s*o*lent) *adj.* Offensively contemptuous, insulting. **in'so·lent·ly** *adv.* **in'so·lence** *n.*

in·sol·u·ble (ĭnsŏl´y*u*bel) *adj.* 1. That cannot be solved. 2. That cannot be dissolved. **in·sol'u·ble·ness, in·sol·u·bil·i·ty** (ĭnsŏly*u*bĭl´ĭtē) *ns.* **in·sol'u·bly** *adv.*

in·sol·vent (ĭnsŏl´vent) *adj.* & *n.* (Debtor) unable to pay debts. **in·sol'ven·cy** *n.*

in·som·ni·a (ĭnsŏm´nē*a*) *n.* Chronic inability to sleep. **in·som'ni·ac** *n.* & *adj.*

in·sou·ci·ant (ĭnsoo͞´sēant) *adj.* Careless, unconcerned. **in·sou'ci·ance** *n.*

in·spect (ĭnspĕkt´) *v.t.* Look closely into; examine officially. **in·spec'tion** *n.*

in·spec·tor (ĭnspĕk´t*er*) *n.* (esp.) High-ranking police officer; ~ **general**, (esp.) head of military department concerned with discipline, supply, accounts, etc. **in·spec'to·ral, in·spec·to·ri·al** (ĭnspĕktŏr´ē*a*l, -tōr´-) *adjs.* **in·spec'tor·ship** *n.*

in·spi·ra·tion (ĭnsp*i*rā´sh*o*n) *n.* 1. Drawing in of breath. 2. Inspiring; divine influence. 3. Thought etc. inspired, prompting; sudden happy idea. 4. Inspiring principle. **in·spi·ra'tion·al** *adj.*

in·spire (ĭnspīr´) *v.t.* (**-spired, -spir·ing**). 1. Breathe in, inhale. 2. Infuse thought or feeling into (person); animate (person etc. *with* feeling); infuse (feeling *into* person etc.), create (feeling *in*); suggest or prompt expression of a particular opinion etc., prompt writer or speaker to such expression. **in·spir·a·to·ry** (ĭnspīr′atōrē, -tōrē) *adj*.

inst. *abbrev*. = INSTANT[1] def. 2.

in·sta·bil·i·ty (ĭnstabĭl′ĭtē) *n*. Lack of stability.

in·stall (ĭnstawl′) *v.t.* (**-stalled, -stall·ing**). Place (person *in* office or dignity) with ceremonies; establish (*in* place, condition, etc.); place (apparatus) in position for use. **in·stal·la·tion** (ĭnstalā′shon) *n*. (Ceremony of) installing; apparatus installed. **in·stall′er** *n*.

in·stall·ment, in·stal·ment (ĭnstawl′ment) *ns*. Each of several parts, successively falling due, of a sum payable; each of several parts supplied etc. at different times; part of serial story printed in one issue; ~ **plan**, arrangement for payment in installments.

in·stance (ĭn′stans) *n*. Fact illustrating a general truth, example; particular case; (law) process, suit; **for** ~, for example; **at the** ~ **of**, at the request or suggestion of. **instance** *v.t.* (**-stanced, -stanc·ing**). (rare) Cite as an instance.

in·stant[1] (ĭn′stant) *adj*. 1. Urgent, pressing. 2. Immediate; (abbrev. inst.) of the current calendar month. 3. (of food) Processed for quick preparation. 4. ~ **replay**, immediate reshowing of short section of television broadcast, esp. of a sports event.

in·stant[2] (ĭn′stant) *n*. Precise (esp. the present) point of time; short space of time, moment. **in′stant·ly** *adv*.

in·stan·ta·ne·ous (ĭnstantā′nēus) *adj*. Occurring, done, in an instant; immediate; existing at a particular instant. **in·stan·ta′ne·ous·ly** *adv*. **in·stan·ta′ne·ous·ness** *n*.

in·state (ĭnstāt′) *v.t.* (**-stat·ed, -stat·ing**). Put in office, install.

in·stead (ĭnstĕd′) *adv*. As a substitute or alternative; in place *of*.

in·step (ĭn′stĕp) *n*. Upper surface of foot between toe and ankle; part of shoe, etc., fitting over or under this.

in·sti·gate (ĭn′stigāt) *v.t.* (**-gat·ed, -gat·ing**). Urge on, incite (person *to*); bring about by persuasion. **in·sti·ga·tion** (ĭnstigā′shon), **in′sti·ga·tor** *ns*.

in·still (ĭnstĭl′) *v.t.* (**-stilled, -stil·ling**). Put in (liquid) by drops; infuse (feeling, idea, etc.) gradually. **in·stil·la·tion** (ĭnstilā′shon) *n*.

in·stinct (ĭn′stĭngkt) *n*. Innate propensity to certain seemingly rational acts performed without conscious design; innate impulse; intuition, unconscious skill; (zool.) inborn and usually rigid pattern of behavior in animals, often in response to certain simple stimuli. **in·stinc′tive** *adj*. **in·stinc′tive·ly** *adv*.

in·sti·tute (ĭn′stĭtōōt, -tūt) *n*. Society, organization, for promotion of scientific or other object; building used by this. ~ *v.t.* (**-tut·ed, -tut·ing**). Establish, found; begin (inquiry etc.).

in·sti·tu·tion (ĭnstĭtōō′shon, -tū′-) *n*. 1. Instituting. 2. Established law, custom, or practice. 3. Organization for promotion of some public object, religious, charitable, educational, etc.; building used by this. 4. Place of confinement, mental hospital, etc. **in·sti·tu′tion·al** *adj*. **in·sti·tu′tion·al·ly** *adv*. **in·sti·tu′tion·al·ize** *v.t.* (**-ized, -iz·ing**). Make institutional; place, confine (person), in institution. **in·sti·tu′tion·al·ism** *n*.

in·struct (ĭnstrŭkt′) *v.t.* Teach (person etc. *in* subject); direct, command. **in·struc′tor** *n*.

in·struc·tion (ĭnstrŭk′shon) *n*. 1. Teaching. 2. (pl.) Directions, orders. **in·struc′tion·al** *adj*.

in·struc·tive (ĭnstrŭk′tĭv) *adj*. Tending to instruct, conveying a lesson.

in·stru·ment (ĭn′strument) *n*. 1. Thing used in performing an action; person so made use of; tool, implement, esp. for delicate or scientific work. 2. Any of several devices, esp. in an airplane or spacecraft, serving to determine position, to measure performance, direction, etc., or to maintain control of operations. 3. (also **musical** ~) Contrivance for producing musical sounds. 4. Formal, esp. legal, document.

in·stru·men·tal (ĭnstrumĕn′tal) *adj*. 1. Serving as instrument or means (*to, in*). 2. Of, arising from, an instrument. 3. (of music) Performed on or written for instruments. **in·stru·men′tal·ly** *adv*.

in·stru·men·tal·ist (ĭnstrumĕn′talĭst) *n*. Performer on musical instrument.

in·stru·men·tal·i·ty (ĭnstrumĕntăl′ĭtē) *n*. (pl. **-ties**). Agency, means.

in·stru·men·ta·tion (ĭnstrumĕntā′shon) *n*. 1. Composition or arrangement of music for instruments; (loosely) orchestration. 2. Use of mechanical instruments in industry etc.

in·sub·or·di·nate (ĭnsubōr′dinĭt) *adj*. Disobedient, rebellious. **in·sub·or·di·na·tion** (ĭnsubōrdinā′shon) *n*.

in·sub·stan·tial (ĭnsubstăn′shal) *adj*. Not real; lacking solidity or substance. **in·sub·stan·ti·al·i·ty** (ĭnsubstănshēăl′ĭtē) *n*.

in·suf·fer·a·ble (ĭnsŭf′erabel) *adj*. Unbearably arrogant, conceited, etc.; intolerable. **in·suf′fer·a·bly** *adv*.

*These tiny turtles are born with the **instinct** to head straight from the nest on the beach, into the sea. Breeding is usually an annual occurrence.*

***Insulation** for heat and sound can be carried out easily in modern buildings. A wide variety of materials is used, including porous bricks and quilted 'mattresses' of insulating material.*

in·suf·fi·cient (ĭnsufĭsh'ent) *adj.* Not sufficient, inadequate. **in·suf·fi'cient·ly** *adv.* **in·suf·fi'cien·cy** *n.* (pl. **-cies**).

in·su·lar (ĭn'suler, ĭns'yu-) *adj.* Of (the nature of) an island; of, like, islanders, esp. circumscribed, isolated, narrow-minded. **in'su·lar·ly** *adv.* **in'su·lar·ism, in·su·lar·i·ty** (ĭnsulăr'ĭtē, ĭnsyu-) *ns.*

in·su·late (ĭn'sulāt, ĭns'yu-) *v.t.* (**-lat·ed, -lat·ing**). 1. Detach (person, thing) from surroundings, isolate. 2. Isolate (thing) by interposition of nonconductors, to prevent passage of electricity, heat, or sound. **in·su·la·tion** (ĭnsulā'shon, ĭnsyu-) *n.*

in·su·la·tor (ĭn'sulāter, ĭns'yu-) *n.* That which insulates, esp. a nonconducting substance, as porcelain or glass, for insulating electric wires.

in·su·lin (ĭn'sulĭn, ĭns'yu-) *n.* 1. Hormone secreted by the islets of LANGERHANS in the pancreas of vertebrates, accelerating the passage of glucose from the blood to the tissues and promoting its storage as glycogen in the liver and muscles. 2. Preparation of this substance, used to treat diabetes.

in·sult (ĭnsŭlt') *v.t.* Treat with scornful abuse, offer indignity to; affront. **in·sult'ing·ly** *adv.* **in'sult** *n.* Insulting speech or action, affront.

in·su·per·a·ble (ĭnsōō'perabel, -pra-) *adj.* That cannot be surmounted or overcome. **in·su'per·a·bly** *adv.*

in·sup·port·a·ble (ĭnsupōr'tabel, -pōr'-) *adj.* Unbearable; unjustifiable.

in·sur·ance (ĭnshoor'ăns) *n.* Insuring; sum paid for this, premium.

in·sure (ĭnshoor') *v.t.* (**-sured, -sur·ing**). Secure payment of sum of money in event of loss of or damage to property (esp. by casualty at sea, fire, burglary, etc.), or of the death or disablement of a person, in consideration of the payment of a premium and observance of certain conditions; **the insured**, person to whom such payment is secured. **in·sur'a·ble** *adj.* **in·sur'er** *n.* One who insures in consideration of premium, underwriter.

in·sur·gent (ĭnsĕr'jent) *adj.* Rising in active revolt. ~ *n.* Rebel. **in·sur'gence, in·sur'gen·cy** *n.*

in·sur·mount·a·ble (ĭnsermown'tabel) *adj.* Not to be surmounted. **in·sur·mount'a·bly** *adv.*

in·sur·rec·tion (ĭnsurĕk'shon) *n.* Rising in open resistance to established authority; incipient rebellion. **in·sur·rec'tion·a·ry** *adj.* **in·sur·rec'tion·ist** *n.*

int. *abbrev.* Interest; interior; interjection; intransitive; international.

in·tact (ĭntăkt') *adj.* Untouched; entire; unimpaired.

in·tagl·io (ĭntăl'yō, -tahl'-) *n.* (pl. **-tagl·ios, -tagl·i** pr. -tăl'yē, -tahl'-). Engraved design; incised carving in hard material; gem with incised design (opp. CAMEO).

in·take (ĭn'tāk) *n.* Place where fluid or gas etc. is taken into channel or pipe; taking in; thing, amount, taken in.

in·tan·gi·ble (ĭntăn'jibel) *adj.* That cannot be touched; impalpable; that cannot be grasped mentally. **in·tan·gi·bil·i·ty** (ĭntănjibĭl'ĭtē) *n.* **in·tan'gi·bly** *adv.*

in·te·ger (ĭn'tejer) *n.* Whole number, undivided quantity; thing complete in itself.

in·te·gral (ĭn'tegral) *adj.* Of, necessary to the completeness of, a whole; whole, complete; (math.) of, denoted by, an integer, involving only integers; ~ **calculus**, branch of calculus dealing with integrals of functions; used also to include solution of differential equations, parts of theory of functions, etc. **in'te·gral·ly** *adv.* **in·te·gral·i·ty** (ĭntegrăl'ĭtē) *n.* **integral** *n.* (math.)

Quantity of which given function is differential or differential coefficient; equation or system of equations from which given equation or system can be derived by differentiation.

in·te·grate (ĭn′tegrāt) *v.* (**-grat·ed, -grat·ing**). Complete (imperfect thing) by addition of parts; combine (parts) into a whole; combine (religious, ethnic, etc. groups) within a system esp. as equals; cease to segregate (racially); (math.) find the integral of; indicate mean volume or total sum of (area, temperature, etc.); **~d circuit**, small chip etc. of material designed to replace conventional electric circuit of many components. **in·te·gra·tion** (ĭntegrā′shon) *n.* **in′te·gra·tive** *adj.*

in·teg·ri·ty (ĭntĕg′rĭtē) *n.* Completeness; soundness; uprightness, honesty.

in·teg·u·ment (ĭntĕg′yument) *n.* Skin, husk, rind, or other (usu. natural) covering. **in·teg·u·men·ta·ry** (ĭntĕgyumĕn′terē) *adj.*

in·tel·lect (ĭn′telĕkt) *n.* Faculty of knowing and reasoning; person(s) of great intellectual ability.

in·tel·lec·tu·al (ĭntelĕk′chooal) *adj.* Of, appealing to, requiring the exercise of, intellect; possessing a good understanding, enlightened; given to mental pursuits. **in·tel·lec′tu·al·ly** *adv.* **in·tel·lec·tu·al′i·ty** *n.* **in·tel·lec′tu·al·ize** *v.* (**-ized, -iz·ing**). **intellectual** *n.* Intellectual person.

in·tel·li·gence (ĭntĕl′ĭjens) *n.* 1. Intellect, understanding; quickness of understanding, sagacity; rational being; **~ quotient**, (abbrev. I.Q.) ratio of mental to chronological age; **~ test**, test designed to ascertain intelligence or mental age, rather than acquired knowledge, of examinee. 2. Information, news; obtaining of (esp. secret) information, persons employed in this; secret service.

in·tel·li·gent (ĭntĕl′ĭjent) *adj.* Having or showing (usu. a high degree of) understanding. **in·tel′li·gent·ly** *adv.*

in·tel·li·gent·si·a (ĭntĕlĭjĕnt′sēa, -gĕnt′-) *n. collect.* (sometimes considered sing.) Class of intellectuals within a society.

in·tel·li·gi·ble (ĭntĕl′ĭjibel) *adj.* That can be understood; comprehensible *to*; (philos.) that can be apprehended only by the intellect, not by the senses. **in·tel·li·gi·bil·i·ty** (ĭntĕlĭjibĭl′ĭtē) *n.* **in·tel′li·gi·bly** *adv.*

in·tem·per·ate (ĭntĕm′perĭt) *adj.* Immoderate, unbridled, violent; excessive in indulgence of an appetite; addicted to drinking. **in·tem′per·ate·ly** *adv.* **in·tem′per·ance** *n.*

in·tend (ĭntĕnd′) *v.t.* Purpose, design; design, destine, for a purpose; mean.

in·tend·ed (ĭntĕn′dĭd) *n.* (colloq.) Fiancé(e).

in·tense (ĭntĕns′) *adj.* Existing in a high degree, violent, vehement; having some quality in high degree; eager, ardent; feeling, apt to feel, intense emotion. **in·tense′ly** *adv.* **in·tense′ness, in·ten′si·ty** *ns.* (pl. **-ties**).

in·ten·si·fy (ĭntĕn′sĭfī) *v.* (**-fied, -fy·ing**). Render, become, intense; (phot.) increase opacity of the deposit in a negative by chemical or other means. **in·ten·si·fi·ca·tion** (ĭntĕnsĭfikā′shon) *n.*

in·ten·sion (ĭntĕn′shon) *n.* (Rare) Intensity; (logic) connotation of a term, sum of the attributes, qualities comprised in a concept.

in·ten·sive (ĭntĕn′sĭv) *adj.* Of, relating to, intensity as opp. to extent; producing intensity; making intense, esp. (gram.) giving force or emphasis; concentrated, directed to a single point, area, or subject; **~ care**, constant surveillance, by nurses and electrical etc. devices, of critically ill patients in hospital. **in·ten′sive·ly** *adv.* **intensive** *n.* (gram.) Intensive word or prefix.

in·tent[1] (ĭntĕnt′) *n.* Intention, purpose; **to all ~s and purposes**, practically, virtually.

in·tent[2] (ĭntĕnt′) *adj.* Resolved, bent (*on*); sedulously occupied (*on*); earnest, eager. **in·tent′ly** *adv.*

*The commonest example of **intaglio** is an engraved seal-ring. This beaten metal panel, however, is on a larger scale. Its delicate art nouveau design is by the Scottish artist, Margaret Macdonald, and was executed in 1898–99.*

*The **interbreeding** of different species of cattle is aimed at producing the best qualities of both breeds in one animal. The Hereford bull (left) crossed with the Friesian (right) produces this large steer (below).*

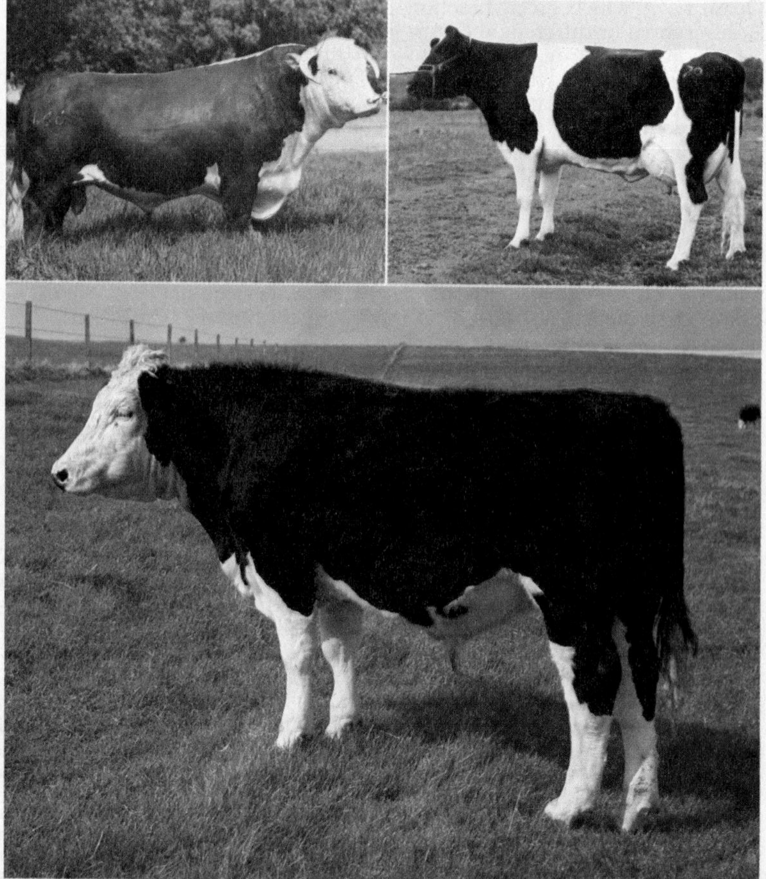

in·ten·tion (ĭntĕn'shon) *n.* Intending; thing intended, purpose; ultimate aim; (pl., colloq.) purposes in regard to proposal of marriage. **in·ten'tion·al** *adj.* Done on purpose. **in·ten'tion·al·ly** *adv.*

in·ter (ĭntẽr') *v.t.* (**-terred, -ter·ring**). Deposit (corpse etc.) in earth, tomb, etc.; bury.

inter- *prefix.* Expressing mutual or reciprocal act or relation, or with sense "among," "between."

in·ter·act (ĭnterăkt') *v.i.* Act reciprocally, act on each other. **in·ter·ac·tion** (ĭnterăk'shon) *n.* **in·ter·ac'tive** *adj.*

in·ter a·li·a (ĭn'ter ā'lēa; *Lat.* ĭn'tĕr ah'lēah). Among other things. [L.]

in·ter·breed (ĭnterbrēd') *v.* (**-bred, -breed·ing**). 1. Cross-breed. 2. Breed within a narrow range or population.

in·ter·cede (ĭntersēd') *v.i.* (**-ced·ed, -ced·ing**). Interpose on behalf of another, plead (*with* one person *for* another).

in·ter·cel·lu·lar (ĭntersĕl'yuler) *adj.* Between or among cells.

in·ter·cept (ĭntersĕpt') *v.t.* Seize, catch, stop (person, enemy aircraft, etc.) on the way from place to place; pick up (esp. enemy's) radio signal; cut off (light etc. *from*); check, stop; (math.) mark off (space) between two points etc. **in·ter·cep·tion** (ĭntersĕp'shon) *n.* **in·ter·cep'tive** *adj.* **in'tercept** *n.* (math.) Part intercepted.

in·ter·cep·tor, in·ter·cep·ter (ĭntersĕp'ter) *ns.* (esp.) Fighter plane having task of intercepting enemy planes.

in·ter·ces·sion (ĭntersĕsh'on) *n.* Interceding. **in·ter·ces·so·ry** (ĭntersĕs'erē) *adj.*

in·ter·change (ĭnterchānj') *v.* (**-changed, -chang·ing**). 1. (of 2 persons) Exchange (things) with each other. 2. Put each of (2 things) in the other's place. 3. Alternate. **in·ter·change'a·ble** *adj.* **in·ter·change'a·bly** *adv.* **in·ter·change·a·bil·i·ty** (ĭnterchānjabĭl'ĭtē) *n.* **in'terchange** *n.* Reciprocal exchange; alternation; road junction so arranged that vehicles do not cross any traffic stream.

in·ter·col·le·giate (ĭnterkolē'jĭt) *adj.* (esp. sports) Existing, carried on, between colleges.

in·ter·com (ĭn'terkŏm) *n.* System of internal communication by telephone, radio, etc., between units of an organization, offices in a building, etc.

in·ter·com·mu·ni·cate (ĭnterkomū'nĭkāt) *v.i.* (**-cat·ed, -cat·ing**). Communicate with each other; (of rooms etc.) have free passage to each other. **in·ter·com·mu·ni·ca·tion** (ĭnterkomūnĭkā'shon) *n.*

in·ter·con·ti·nen·tal (ĭnterkŏntinen'tal) *adj.* 1. Of, between, or among continents. 2. Capable of traveling between continents, as a guided missile, airplane, etc.

in·ter·cos·tal (ĭnterkŏs'tal) *adj.* Between the ribs.

in·ter·course (ĭn'terkōrs, -kõrs) *n.* 1. Social communication, dealings, between individuals; communion between man and God; communication for purposes of trade etc. between different countries etc. 2. = SEXUAL intercourse.

in·ter·cul·tur·al (ĭnterkŭl'cheral) *adj.* Between or among people of different cultures; ~ **education**, education to encourage good relations among people of different races, cultures, religions, etc.

in·ter·de·pend (ĭnterdĭpĕnd') *v.i.* Depend on each other. **in·ter·de·pend'ence, in·ter·de·pend'en·cy** *ns.* **in·ter·de·pend'ent** *adj.*

in·ter·dict (ĭnterdĭkt') *v.t.* Prohibit (action); forbid use of; restrain (*from*); forbid (thing *to* person). **in·ter·dic·tion** (ĭnterdĭk'shon) *n.* **in·ter·dic'to·ry** *adj.* **in'terdict** *n.* Authoritative prohibition; injunction; (R.C. Ch.) sentence debarring place or person from most ecclesiastical functions and privileges.

in·ter·est (ĭn'terĭst, -trĭst) *n.* 1. Legal right, claim, or share (*in* something); pecuniary stake (*in* commercial undertaking etc.). 2. Advantage, profit; self-interest. 3. Thing in which one is concerned; principle in which a party is concerned; ~ **group**, (usu. pol.) group acting together from common interest or purpose. 4. Concern, curiosity, or quality exciting them. 5. Money paid for use of money lent or for forbearance of debt; **compound** ~, interest reckoned on principal and on accumulations of interest; **simple** ~, interest reckoned on principal only. **interest** *v.t.* Cause (person) to take personal interest or share (*in*); excite curiosity or attention of; (past part.) having a private interest, not impartial or disinterested. **in'ter·est·ed·ly** *adv.* **in'ter·est·ing** *adj.* **in'ter·est·ing·ly** *adv.*

in·ter·face (ĭn'terfās) *n.* 1. Surface forming common boundary between 2 regions. 2. Place, or piece of equipment, where interaction occurs between 2 systems, processes, etc. (also fig.). **in·ter·fa·cial** (ĭnterfā'shal) *adj.*

in·ter·fere (ĭnterfēr') *v.i.*

(**-fered, -fer·ing**). Come into collision or opposition (*with*); hinder, impede; intrude; meddle; intervene; (sports) illegally obstruct an opponent's action; (phys.) produce interference with another wave; (radio) impede or distort reception.

in·ter·fer·ence (ĭnterfēr'ens) *n.* 1. Interfering. 2. (radio) Intrusion of unwanted signals, atmospherics, etc., causing poor reception of desired signals. 3. (phys.) Alternate mutual neutralization and reinforcement by two beams of sound, light, electromagnetic waves so as to produce alternation of light and dark, silence and sound, etc.

in·ter·fer·om·e·ter (ĭnterferŏm'eter) *n.* Device for measuring wavelengths, astronomical distances, etc., by means of interference phenomena.

in·ter·fer·on (ĭnterfēr'ŏn) *n.* Protein preventing development of virus in cell.

in·ter·fuse (ĭnterfūz') *v.* (**-fused, -fus·ing**). Mix; blend together; blend with each other. **in·ter·fu·sion** (ĭnterfū'zhon) *n.*

in·ter·ga·lac·tic (ĭntergalăk'tĭk) *adj.* Of or in the space between galaxies.

in·ter·gla·cial (ĭnterglā'shal) *adj.* (geol.) Occurring or formed between glacial periods.

in·ter·im (ĭn'terĭm) *n.* Intervening time. ~ *adj.* Intervening; provisional, temporary.

in·te·ri·or (ĭntēr'ēer) *adj.* Situated within; inland, remote from coast or frontier; internal, domestic (opp. *foreign*); existing in mind or soul, inward; ~ **monologue**, form of writing that represents the inner thoughts of a character. **in·te'ri·or·ly** *adv.* **interior** *n.* Interior part, inside; inland region; inside of building or room; domestic affairs of a country; **Department of the I~**, government department dealing with these; **interior decoration, design**, art, profession, of designing layout, furnishings, ornament, of the inside of buildings; ~ **decorator**.

in·ter·ject (ĭnterjĕkt') *v.t.* Throw in, interpose (remark etc.) abruptly; remark parenthetically. **in·ter·jec'to·ry** *adj.*

in·ter·jec·tion (ĭnterjĕk'shon) *n.* Exclamation, ejaculation; natural exclamation viewed as part of speech. **in·ter·jec'tion·al** *adj.* **in·ter·jec'tion·al·ly** *adv.*

This British 'Lightning', jet fighter with strong climbing power, ***intercepts*** *the Soviet long range reconnaissance aircraft 'Bear' during the exercise 'Northern Merger' in September 1974.*

in·ter·lace (ĭnterlās′) *v.* (**-laced, -lac·ing**). Bind together intricately, entangle; interweave; mingle; cross each other intricately. **in·ter·lace′ment** *n.*

in·ter·lard (ĭnterlârd′) *v.t.* Mix (writing, speech, etc., *with*).

in·ter·leave (ĭnterlēv′) *v.t.* (**-leaved, -leav·ing**). Insert leaves between leaves of (book).

in·ter·line[1] (ĭnterlīn′) *v.t.* (**-lined, -lin·ing**). Insert words between lines of (document etc.); insert (words) thus. **in·ter·lin·e·ar** (ĭnterlĭn′ēer) *adj.* Written, printed, between the lines. **in·ter·lin·e·a·tion** (ĭnterlĭnēā′shon) *n.*

in·ter·line[2] (ĭnterlīn′) *v.t.* (**-lined, -lin·ing**). Put extra lining between ordinary lining and outer material of (garment). **in′ter·lin·ing** *n.*

in·ter·lock (ĭnterlŏk′) *v.* Fit together by dovetailing, overlapping etc.; lock, clasp, within each other; connect (switches, apparatus, etc.) so they cannot be operated independently of each other.

in·ter·loc·u·tor (ĭnterlŏk′yuter) *n.* One who takes part in dialogue or conversation; performer in middle of line of minstrels at minstrel show who acts as announcer and trades jokes with the end men. **in·ter·loc·u·to·ry** (ĭnterlŏk′yutōrē, -tōrē) *adj.*

in·ter·lop·er (ĭn′terlōper) *n.* Intruder, one who (esp. for profit) thrusts himself into others' affairs; (hist.) unauthorized trader. **in·ter·lope** (ĭnterlōp′, ĭn′terlōp) *v.i.* (**-loped, -lop·ing**).

in·ter·lude (ĭn′terlōōd) *n.* 1. Any intervening period of time, episode, etc. 2. Pause between acts of play; what fills this up; (mus.) instrumental piece played between verses of hymn etc., in intervals of church service etc.

in·ter·lu·nar (ĭnterlōō′ner) *adj.* Of, pertaining to, the period of the lunar month when the moon is invisible; in the dark of the moon.

in·ter·mar·riage (ĭntermăr′ĭj) *n.* Marriage between members of different families, tribes, ethnic or religious groups, etc., or (loosely) between near relations.

in·ter·mar·ry (ĭntermăr′ē) *v.i.* (**-ried, -ry·ing**). Become connected by marriage or intermarriage (*with*).

in·ter·me·di·ar·y (ĭntermē′dēĕrē) *adj.* Acting between parties, mediatory; intermediate. ~ *n.* (pl. **-ar·ies**). Intermediary person or thing, esp. mediator.

in·ter·me·di·ate (ĭntermē′dēĭt) *adj.* Coming *between* two things, in time, place, or order. **in·ter·me′di·ate·ly** *adv.* **intermediate** *n.* Intermediate thing; (chem.) compound manufactured from a substance obtained directly from raw materials, and used as a basis for the synthesis of another product. ~ (ĭntermē′dēāt) *v.i.* (**-at·ed, -at·ing**). Act between others, mediate (*between*). **in·ter·me·di·a·tion** (ĭntermēdēā′shon), **in·ter·me′di·a·tor** *ns.*

These U.S. prisoners of war were ***interned*** *in North Vietnam by Viet Cong forces during the Vietnamese War of 1964–75. They were repatriated after the withdrawal of American troops from the peninsula.*

in·ter·ment (ĭntĕr′ment) *n.* Burial.

in·ter·mez·zo (ĭntermĕt′sō, -mĕd′zō) *n.* (pl. **-mez·zos, -mez·zi** pr. -mĕt′sē, -mĕd′zē). Short light dramatic or musical performance between acts of drama or opera; short movement connecting main divisions of large musical work.

in·ter·mi·na·ble (ĭntĕr′minabel) *adj.* Endless; tediously long. **in·ter′mi·na·bly** *adj.*

in·ter·min·gle (ĭntermĭng′gel) *v.* (**-gled, -gling**). Mix together; mingle (*with*).

in·ter·mis·sion (ĭntermĭsh′on) *n.* Pause, cessation; interval; recess; period between acts of a play or other performance.

in·ter·mit (ĭntermĭt′) *v.* (**-mit·ted, -mit·ting**). Suspend, discontinue; stop for a time (esp. of fever, pain, etc., or pulse). **in·ter·mit′tence** *n.* **in·ter·mit′tent** *adj.* **in·ter·mit′tent·ly** *adv.*

in·ter·mix (ĭntermĭks′) *v.* Mix together.

in·tern[1] (ĭntĕrn′) *v.t.* Oblige to reside within limits of country etc.; confine (esp. enemy aliens and prisoners of war) within prescribed limits. **in·tern·ee** (ĭntĕrnē′) *n.* Person interned. **in·tern′ment** *n.*

in·tern[2] (ĭn′tĕrn) *n.* Advanced student or recent graduate undergoing supervised practical training, esp. a medical student or graduate acting as assistant doctor in a hospital.

in·ter·nal (ĭntĕr′nal) *adj.* Of, situated in, the inside of, a thing; of the inner nature of a thing, intrinsic; of the domestic affairs of a country; of the mind or soul, inward, subjective; ~ **combustion engine**: see COMBUSTION; ~ **evidence**, evidence derived from what is contained in the thing itself. **in·ter′nal·ly** *adv.*

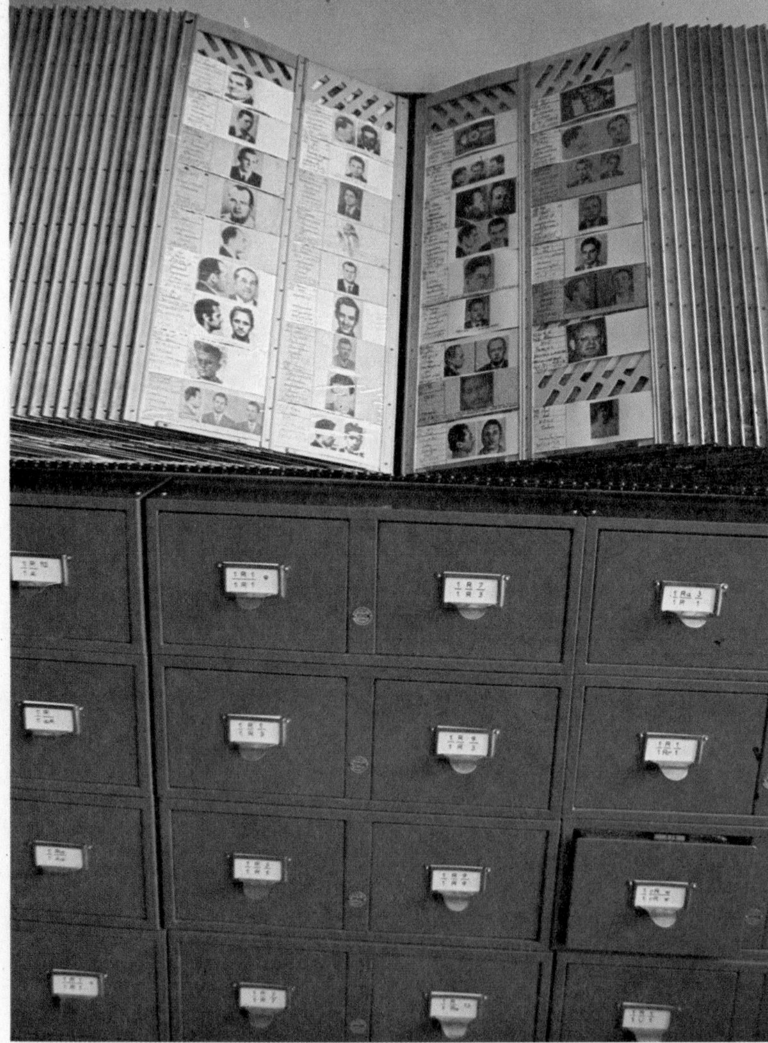

*This criminal portraits file is located in **Interpol's** Paris headquarters. Interpol provides liaison between member nations in searching for international criminals.*

in·ter·na·tion·al (ĭnternăsh′-onal) *adj.* Existing, carried on, between different nations; **I ~ Court of Justice**, judicial court of the United Nations, established in 1945; **~ law**, body of rules regarded by the nations of the world as being binding on them in their relations with each other, in peace and war; **I ~ Monetary Fund**, (abbrev. I.M.F.) organization having a monetary pool on which member nations can draw, established in 1945 to promote international trade and stabilization of currencies; **I ~ System** (of units): system based on the meter, kilogram, second, ampere, kelvin, candela, and mole. **in·ter·na′tion·al·ly** *adv.* **in·ter·na′tion·al** *n.* 1. International firm. 2. Any of various socialist or labor international organizations, esp. the following: **First I ~**, the International Working Men's Association; **Second I ~**, organization founded at Paris 1889 to celebrate 100th anniversary of French Revolution; **Third I ~** (**Communist ~**, COMINTERN, COMINFORM), founded at Moscow 1919 by delegates from 12 countries to promote communism and support the Russian Revolution, nominally dissolved 1943; **Fourth I ~**, founded 1936 by followers of Trotsky.

In·ter·na·tio·nale (ĭnternăsh-onăl′; *Fr.* ăntĕrnăsyawnăl′) *n.* Revolutionary hymn composed by Eugène Pottier in 1871 and adopted by various socialist and communist movements.

in·ter·na·tion·al·ist (ĭnter-năsh′onalĭst) *n.* One who advocates community of interests between nations. **in·ter·na′tion·al·ism** *n.*

in·ter·na·tion·al·ize (ĭnter-năsh′onalīz) *v.t.* (**-ized, -iz·ing**). Make international; esp. bring (territory etc.) under combined protection etc. of different nations. **in·ter·na·tion·al·i·za·tion** (ĭnter-năshonalīzā′shon) *n.*

in·ter·ne·cine (ĭnternē′sēn, -sīn, -nĕs′ēn, -īn) *adj.* 1. Mutually destructive; (orig.) deadly. 2. Of a struggle within a nation, organization, group, etc.

in·ter·plan·e·tar·y (ĭnterplăn′-etĕrē) *adj.* Between planets.

in·ter·play (ĭn′terplā) *n.* Operation of two things on each other; interaction.

In·ter·pol (ĭn′terpōl). International Criminal Police Commission, with headquarters in Paris.

in·ter·po·late (ĭntẽr′polāt) *v.t.* (**-lat·ed, -lat·ing**). Make insertions in (books etc.), esp. so as to give false impressions as to date etc.; introduce (words) thus; interpose (a remark); (math.) insert (intermediate term) in series. **in·ter·po·la·tion** (ĭntẽrpolā′shon), **in·ter′po·la·tor** *ns.*

in·ter·pose (ĭnterpōz′) *v.* (**-posed, -pos·ing**). Insert, make intervene, (*between*); put forth, introduce, (veto, objection, authority, etc.) by way of interference; intervene (between disputants etc.); say as an interruption; make an interruption. **in·ter·pos·al** (ĭnter-pō′zal), **in·ter·po·si·tion** (ĭnterpo-zĭsh′on) *ns.*

in·ter·pret (ĭntẽr′prĭt) *v.* Expound the meaning of (abstruse words, writings, etc.); make out the meaning of; translate; bring out the meaning of, render, by artistic representation or performance; explain, understand, in specified manner; act as interpreter. **in·ter′pre·ta·tive·ly** *adv.* **in·ter·pre·ta·tion** (ĭntẽrpretā′shon) *n.* **in·ter·pre·ta·tive** (ĭntẽr′pretātĭv), **in·ter·pre·ta′tion·al** *adjs.*

in·ter·pret·er (ĭntẽr′preter) *n.* One who interprets; one whose office it is to translate orally in their presence the words of persons speaking different languages.

in·ter·reg·num (ĭnterrĕg′num) *n.* (pl. **-reg·nums, -reg·na** pr. -rĕg′na). Period during which government has no normal ruler, esp. between end of king's reign and accession of successor; interval, pause.

in·ter·re·la·tion (ĭnterrĭlā′shon) *n.* Mutual relation. **in·ter·re·la′tion·ship** *n.*

in·ter·ro·gate (ĭntĕr′ogāt) *v.t.* (**-gat·ed, -gat·ing**). Ask questions of, esp. closely or formally. **in·ter·ro·ga·tion** (ĭntĕrogā′shon) *n.* Asking questions; interview for close questioning; question.

in·ter·rog·a·tive (ĭnterŏg′atĭv) *adj.* Of, having the form or force of, a question; of inquiry; (gram., of words) used in asking question. **in·ter·rog′a·tive·ly** *adv.* **interrogative** *n.* Interrogative pronoun, sentence, etc.

in·ter·rog·a·to·ry (ĭnterŏg′a-tōrē, -tōrē) *adj.* Of inquiry. **~** *n.* (pl. **-ries**). Question, set of questions, esp. (law) one formally put to accused person etc.

in·ter·rupt (ĭnterŭpt′) *v.t.* Break

***Interstellar** matter often gathers together in vast clouds of gas and dust to form a nebula like this one in the constellation Serpeus. This was photographed through a 200-inch telescope in California.*

in upon (action, speech, person speaking or working, etc.); break the continuity of. **in·ter·rupt′ed·ly** *adv.* **in·ter·rupt′er, in·ter·rup′tion** *ns.*

in·ter·sect (ĭntersĕkt′) *v.* Divide (thing) by passing or lying across it; (of lines etc.) cross, cut, each other. **in·ter·sec′tion** *n.* Intersecting; point, line, common to intersecting lines, planes; place where things intersect, esp. 2 or more roads.

in·ter·sperse (ĭnterspẽrs′) *v.t.* (**-spersed, -spers·ing**). Scatter, place here and there (*between, among*); diversify (thing) *with* (others so scattered). **in·ter·sper·sion** (ĭnterspẽr′zhon, -shon) *n.*

in·ter·state (ĭnterstāt′, ĭn′terstāt) *adj.* Existing, carried on, between states; **The I~**, U.S. Interstate Highway System; any of the roads of this.

in·ter·stel·lar (ĭnterstĕl′er) *adj.* Between stars.

in·ter·stice (ĭntẽr′stĭs) *n.* Intervening space; crevice. **in·ter·sti·tial** (ĭnterstĭsh′al) *adj.* Of, forming, occupying interstice(s).

in·ter·twine (ĭntertwīn′) *v.* (**-twined, -twin·ing**). Entwine; become entwined. **in·ter·twine′ment** *n.*

in·ter·ur·ban (ĭnterẽr′ban) *adj.* Located between or serving to connect cities.

in·ter·val (ĭn′terval) *n.* 1. Intervening time or space; pause; break, gap; **at ~s**, now and then, here and there. 2. (mus.) Difference of pitch between 2 sounds, in melody or harmony. 3. Distance between persons or things. [L. *intervallum* space between ramparts (*vallum* rampart)]

in·ter·vene (ĭntervēn′) *v.i.* (**-vened, -ven·ing**). Come in, as something extraneous; occur in the meantime; lie, be situated, between; (of person or thing) come between, interfere, so as to prevent or modify result etc.; (law) enter into a lawsuit as a 3rd party to protect one's interest. **in·ter·ven′er, in·ter·ve′nor, in·ter·ven·tion** (ĭntervĕn′shon) *ns.*

in·ter·view (ĭn′tervū) *n.* Meeting of persons face to face, esp. for purpose of conference; meeting between representative of press and person from whom he seeks to obtain statements for publication; published report of such meeting; meeting between candidate for employment, college admission, etc., and prospective employer, dean, etc. ~ *v.t.* Have interview with (person), esp. with view to publication of statements etc. **in′ter·view·er** *n.*

in·ter·weave (ĭnterwēv′) *v.t.* (**-wove, -wo·ven, -weav·ing**). Weave together, interlace; blend intimately.

in·tes·tate (ĭntĕs′tāt, -tĭt) *adj.* Not having made a legal will; not disposed of by legal will. ~ *n.*

Person who dies intestate. **in·tes·ta·cy** (ĭntĕs´tasē) *n.*

in·tes·tine (ĭntĕs´tĭn) *n.* (usu. pl.) Lower part of alimentary canal from pyloric end of stomach to anus; **large ~**, cecum, colon, and rectum; **small ~**, duodenum, jejunum, and ileum. **in·tes'ti·nal** *adj.*

in·ti·mate[1] (ĭn´tĭmĭt) *adj.* Close in acquaintance, familiar; essential, intrinsic; closely personal. **in'ti·mate·ly** *adv.* **in·ti·ma·cy** (ĭn´tĭmasē) *n.* (pl. **-cies**). State of being intimate; intimate act; (euphem.) sexual intercourse. **inti·mate** *n.* Intimate friend.

in·ti·mate[2] (ĭn´tĭmāt) *v.t.* (**-mat·ed, -mat·ing**). Make known; imply, hint. **in·ti·ma·tion** (ĭntĭmā´shon), **in'ti·mate·ness** *ns.*

in·tim·i·date (ĭntĭm´ĭdāt) *v.t.* (**-dat·ed, -dat·ing**). Inspire with fear, cow, esp. in order to influence conduct. **in·tim·i·da·tion** (ĭntĭmidā´shon) *n.*

in·to (ĭn´tōō, unstressed ĭn´to) *prep.* Expressing (1) motion or direction to a point within a thing, as *come ~ the house, inquire ~ the problem*; (2) change, condition, result, as *water turns ~ ice, collect them ~ heaps.*

in·tol·er·a·ble (ĭntŏl´erabel) *adj.* That cannot be endured. **in·tol'er·a·ble·ness** *n.* **in·tol'er·a·bly** *adv.*

in·tol·er·ant (ĭntŏl´erant) *adj.* Not tolerant (*of*); bigoted, prejudiced (esp. against a racial or religious group, etc.). **in·tol'er·ant·ly** *adv.* **in·tol'er·ance** *n.*

in·to·na·tion (ĭntonā´shon) *n.* (mus.) Opening phrase of a Gregorian chant, sung by priest alone or by one or a few of the choir; intoning, reciting in singing voice; utterance, production, of musical tones; modulation of voice in speaking.

in·tone (ĭntōn´) *v.t.* (**-toned, -ton·ing**). Recite, sing, utter in singing voice or with a specific intonation.

in to·to (ĭn tō´tō). Completely; altogether. [L.]

in·tox·i·cant (ĭntŏk´sĭkant) *adj.* & *n.* Intoxicating (liquor).

in·tox·i·cate (ĭntŏk´sĭkāt) *v.t.* (**-cat·ed, -cat·ing**). Make drunk; excite, exhilarate, beyond self-control. **in·tox'i·cat·ing** *adj.* **in·tox·i·ca·tion** (ĭntŏksĭkā´shon) *n.*

intra- *prefix.* On the inside, within.

in·trac·ta·ble (ĭntrăk´tabel) *adj.* Not docile, refractory; (of things) not easily dealt with. **in·trac'ta·ble·ness, in·trac·ta·bil·i·ty** (ĭntrăktabĭl´ĭtē) *ns.* **in·trac'ta·bly** *adv.*

in·tra·mus·cu·lar (ĭntramŭs´kyuler) *adj.* Within or going into a muscle.

intrans. *abbrev.* Intransitive.

in·tran·si·gent (ĭntrăn´sĭjent,

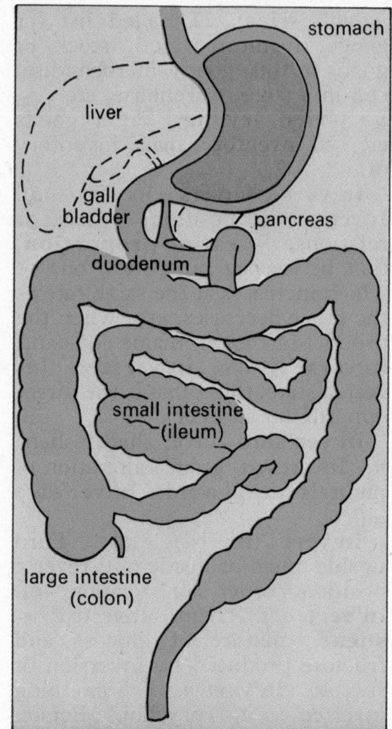

*The small **intestine** deals with the digestion of food. In the large intestine water is absorbed from undigested material and anything left passes to the rectum as waste matter.*

-zĭ-) *adj.* Uncompromising (person). **in·tran'si·gence, in·tran'si·gen·cy** *ns.* **in·tran'si·gent·ly** *adv.*

in·tran·si·tive (ĭntrăn´sĭtĭv) *adj.* & *n.* (Verb) that does not take a direct object. **in·tran'si·tive·ly** *adv.*

in·tra·state (ĭntrastāt´, ĭn´trastāt) *adj.* Within a state, esp. one of the states of U.S.

in·tra·u·ter·ine (ĭntraū´terĭn, -rīn) *adj.* Within the uterus; **~ device**, (abbrev. I.U.D.) contraceptive device so placed.

in·tra·ve·nous (ĭntravē´nus) *adj.* Within or going into a vein. **in·tra·ve'nous·ly** *adv.*

in·trep·id (ĭntrĕp´ĭd) *adj.* Fearless, brave. **in·trep'id·ly** *adv.* **in·trep·id·i·ty** (ĭntrepĭd´ĭtē) *n.*

in·tri·cate (ĭn´trĭkĭt) *adj.* Complex; involved. **in'tri·cate·ly** *adv.* **in·tri·ca·cy** (ĭn´trĭkasē) *n.* (pl. **-cies**).

in·trigue (ĭntrēg´) *v.* (**-trigued, -trigu·ing**). 1. Carry on underhand plot; employ secret influence (*with*). 2. Excite the interest or curiosity of. **~** (ĭn´trēg, ĭntrēg´) *n.* Underhand plotting or plot; secret love affair, liaison.

in·trin·sic (ĭntrĭn´sĭk, -zĭk) *adj.* Belonging naturally, inherent, essential. **in·trin'si·cal·ly** *adv.*

intro- *prefix.* To the inside.

in·tro·duce (ĭntrodōōs´, -dūs´) *v.t.* (**-duced, -duc·ing**). 1. Bring in; place in, insert; bring into use (custom, idea, etc.); usher in, bring forward, begin. 2. Make known, esp. in formal manner (person *to* another); present formally, as at court or in an assembly; make acquainted with, draw attention of (person) *to*; bring (bill etc.) before legislature. **in·tro·duc'er** *n.* **in·tro·duc·to·ry** (ĭntrodŭk´terē) *adj.*

in·tro·duc·tion (ĭntrodŭk´shon) *n.* Introducing; preliminary matter prefixed to book; introductory treatise; formal presentation.

in·tro·spect (ĭntrospĕkt´) *v.i.* Examine one's own thoughts and feelings. **in·tro·spec'tion** *n.* **in·tro·spec'tive** *adj.* **in·tro·spec'tive·ly** *adv.* **in·tro·spec'tive·ness** *n.*

in·tro·vert (ĭntrovērt´) *v.t.* 1. Turn (mind, thought) inward. 2. (zool.) Withdraw (organ etc.) within its own tube or base, like finger of glove. **in·tro·ver·sion** (ĭntrovēr´zhon, -shon, ĭn´trovēr-) *n.* **in'trovert** *n.* 1. (psych.) Person given to introversion (opp. EXTROVERT); (pop.) unsociable person, one who prefers privacy and lone pursuits. 2. (zool.) Part or organ that is turned inward upon itself.

in·trude (ĭntrōōd´) *v.* (**-trud·ed, -trud·ing**). Thrust, force, (thing *into*); force (thing *upon* person); come uninvited, thrust oneself in (*into* company, place, etc., *upon* person etc.). **in·trud'er** *n.* One who intrudes; invading enemy; burglar, one who breaks and enters.

in·tru·sion (ĭntrōō´zhon) *n.* Intruding, forcing in; forcing oneself in; (law) illegal appropriation of or entry into property of another.

in·tru·sive (ĭntrōō´sĭv) *adj.* Intruding, tending to intrude. **in·tru'sive·ly** *adv.* **in·tru'sive·ness** *n.*

in·trust (ĭntrŭst´) = ENTRUST.

in·tu·it (ĭntōō´ĭt, -tū´-, ĭn´tōō-, -tū-) *v.* Know by intuition.

in·tu·i·tion (ĭntōōĭsh´on, -tū-) *n.* Immediate apprehension by the mind without reasoning; immediate apprehension by sense; immediate insight. **in·tu·i'tion·al** *adj.*

in·tu·i·tive (ĭntōō´ĭtĭv, -tū´-) *adj.* Of, possessing, perceived by, intuition. **in·tu'i·tive·ly** *adv.* **in·tu'i·tive·ness** *n.*

in·tu·mes·cent (ĭntōōmĕs´ent, -tyōō-) *adj.* Swelling up. **in·tu·mes'cence** *n.*

in·un·date (ĭn´undāt, ĭnŭn´-) *v.t.* (**-dat·ed, -dat·ing**). Overflow, flood (*with* water etc.; also fig.). **in·un·da·tion** (ĭnŭndā´shon) *n.*

in·ure (ĭnūr´, ĭnoor´) *v.* (**-ured, -ur·ing**). Accustom, habituate; come into operation, take affect. **in·ure'ment** *n.*

in·vade (ĭnvād´) *v.t.* (**-vad·ed, -vad·ing**). Make hostile inroad into; assail; encroach upon. **in·vad'er** *n.*

in·va·lid[1] (ĭn´valĭd) *n.* & *adj.* (Person) enfeebled or disabled by illness or injury. ~ *v.t.* Lay up, disable, (person) by illness. **in'va·lid·ism** *n.*

in·val·id[2] (ĭnvăl'ĭd) *adj.* Not valid; esp., having no legal force. **in·va·lid·i·ty** (ĭnvalĭd'ĭtē) *n.* **in·val'id·ly** *adv.*

in·val·i·date (ĭnvăl'ĭdāt) *v.t.* (**-dat·ed, -dat·ing**). Make invalid. **in·val·i·da·tion** (ĭnvălĭdā'shon) *n.*

in·val·u·a·ble (ĭnvăl'ūabel) *adj.* Of value too great to be measured.

in·var·i·a·ble (ĭnvār'ēabel) *adj.* Unchangeable; always the same; (math.) constant, fixed. **in·var'i·a·ble·ness, in·var·i·a·bil·i·ty** (ĭnvārēabĭl'ĭtē) *ns.* **in·var'i·a·bly** *adv.*

in·va·sion (ĭnvā'zhon) *n.* Invading; encroachment.

in·va·sive (ĭnvā'sĭv) *adj.* That invades, esp. (med.) tending to invade healthy tissue.

in·vec·tive (ĭnvĕk'tĭv) *n.* Violent attack in words; abusive oratory.

in·veigh (ĭnvā') *v.i.* Speak violently, rail, protest loudly, *against.*

in·vei·gle (ĭnvā'gel) *v.t.* (**-gled, -gling**). Entice, seduce (*into*). **in·vei'gle·ment** *n.*

in·vent (ĭnvĕnt') *v.t.* Devise, originate; produce or construct by original thought etc.; fabricate (false story etc.). **in·ven·tion** (ĭnvĕn'shon) *n.* 1. Inventing; thing invented, contrivance. 2. Inventiveness. 3. Fictitious story. **in·ven'tive** *adj.* **in·ven'tive·ly** *adv.* **in·ven'tive·ness, in·ven'tor** *ns.*

in·ven·to·ry (ĭn'ventōrē, -tōrē) *n.* (pl. **-ries**). Detailed list (of goods, furniture, etc.); stock of goods in this; goods, merchandise, etc. in a store, warehouse, etc. ~ *v.t.* (**-ried, -ry·ing**). Enter (goods etc.) in inventory; make inventory of.

in·verse (ĭnvērs', ĭn'vērs) *adj.* Inverted in position, order, or relations; ~ **ratio, proportion,** that between 2 quantities, one of which increases at the same rate as the other decreases, esp. when the product of the 2 remains constant. **in·verse'ly** *adv.* **in'verse** *n.* Inverted state; thing that is the direct opposite (*of* another).

in·ver·sion (ĭnvēr'zhon, -shon) *n.* Inverting; (gram.) alteration of natural order of words. **in·ver'sive** *adj.*

in·vert (ĭnvērt') *v.t.* Turn upside down or inside out; reverse position, order, or relation, of. **in'vert** *adj.* (chem.) Inverted; ~ **sugar,** mixture of glucose and fructose produced by inversion of sucrose. **in'vert** *n.* 1. Something inverted. 2. (psychol.) Person whose sexual instincts are inverted, homosexual.

in·ver·te·brate (ĭnvēr'tebrĭt, -brāt) *adj.* Not having a spinal column or backbone; (fig.) lacking

The Allied ***invasion*** *of Normandy on D-Day (June 6, 1944) marked the turning point in the 1939–45 war. This painting by Barnett Freedman shows the Allied forces at Arromanches, 20 days after the landing.*

1. The ***invention*** *of the Mule spinning frame by Samuel Crompton from 1774 to 1779 combined Paul's and Arkwright's method of drawing by rollers and Hargreave's reciprocating carriage. It was capable of spinning the finest of yarns. 2. A Hammond typewriter of 1895. 3. The first practicable photographic process was invented by Louis Daguerre in 1838. Cameras like these were in wide use by 1900.*

firmness of character; (zool.) belonging to the Invertebrata, a classification of convenience that comprises all animals other than the Vertebrata, and includes principally those animals that have no notochord in any state of development. ~ *n.* Invertebrate animal.

in·vest (ĭnvĕst') *v.* 1. (rare) Clothe (person etc. *in, with*); cover; clothe, endow (person etc. *with* qualities, insignia of office etc.). 2. (mil.) Besiege, surround. 3. Employ (money in stocks, business, etc.); ~ **in,** put money into (stocks); (colloq.) lay out money, time, effort, on. **in·ves'tor** *n.*

in·ves·ti·gate (ĭnvĕs'tigāt) *v.t.* (**-gat·ed, -gat·ing**). Examine, inquire into. **in·ves·ti·ga·tion** (ĭnvĕstigā'shon), **in·ves'ti·ga·tor** *ns.* **in·ves·ti·ga·to·ry** (ĭnvĕs'tigatōrē, -tōrē), **in·ves'ti·ga·tive** *adjs.*

in·ves·ti·ture (ĭnvĕs'tĭcher) *n.* Formal investing of person (*with* office), esp. ceremony at which sovereign or his deputy confers honors; cover, garment.

in·vest·ment (ĭnvĕst'ment) *n.* 1. Investing of money; money in-

The Academy in Athens, an example of the ***Ionic*** *style of architecture developed by the ancient Greeks, but also adopted at a later date by the Romans.*

vested; property, stocks, etc. in which money is invested. 2. Investiture. 3. (mil.) Act of besieging.

in·vet·er·ate (ĭnvĕt′*e*rĭt) *adj.* Long-established; deep-rooted, obstinate. **in·vet′er·ate·ly** *adv.* **in·vet′er·a·cy** *n.*

in·vid·i·ous (ĭnvĭd′ēus) *adj.* (of conduct etc.) Giving offense, esp. by real or seeming injustice, unfair (distinction, discrimination, etc.); (of thing) likely to excite ill feeling against the possessor. **in·vid′i·ous·ly** *adv.* **in·vid′i·ous·ness** *n.*

in·vig·or·ate (ĭnvĭg′*o*rāt) *v.t.* (**-at·ed, -at·ing**). Make vigorous; animate. **in·vig·or·a·tive** (ĭnvĭg′orātĭv) *adj.* **in·vig·or·a·tion** (ĭnvĭgorā′sh*o*n) *n.*

in·vin·ci·ble (ĭnvĭn′sĭb*e*l) *adj.* Unconquerable. **in·vin·ci·bil·i·ty** (ĭnvĭnsĭbĭl′ĭtē) *n.* **in·vin′ci·bly** *adv.*

in·vi·o·la·ble (ĭnvī′*o*lab*e*l) *adj.* Safe from assault, trespass, or violation; to be kept sacred from infraction, profanation, etc. **in·vi·o·la·bil·i·ty** (ĭnvī*o*l*a*bĭl′ĭtē) *n.* **in·vi′o·la·bly** *adv.*

in·vi·o·late (ĭnvī′olĭt, -lāt) *adj.* Not violated; unbroken; unprofaned. **in·vi′o·late·ly** *adv.* **in·vi′o·late·ness, in·vi′o·la·cy** *ns.*

in·vis·i·ble (ĭnvĭz′ĭb*e*l) *adj.* That cannot be seen; not to be seen at a particular time; too small to be seen; ~ **ink**, ink that requires heat, vapor, or the like to make visible what is written in it. **in·vis·i·bil·i·ty** (ĭnvĭzĭbĭl′ĭtē), **in·vis′i·ble·ness** *ns.* **in·vis′i·bly** *adv.* **invisible** *n.*

in·vite (ĭnvīt′) *v.* (**-vit·ed, -vit·ing**). Request courteously to come (*to* dinner, *to* a party, *to* one's house, etc.); request courteously (*to* do); solicit courteously; bring on, tend to bring on (thing) unintentionally; (of thing) present inducements, attract. **in·vit′ing** *adj.* **in·vit′ing·ly** *adv.* **in·vit′ing·ness, in·vi·ta·tion** (ĭnvĭtā′sh*o*n) *ns.* **in′vite** *n.* (slang) Invitation.

in·vo·ca·tion (ĭnv*o*kā′sh*o*n) *n.* Invoking, calling upon deity in prayer; appeal to a spirit, one's muse, etc. **in·voc·a·to·ry** (ĭnvŏk′*a*tōrē, -tōrē) *adj.*

in·voice (ĭn′vois) *n.* List of goods shipped or sent, with prices and charges. ~ *v.t.* (**-voiced, -voic·ing**). Make an invoice of (goods); bill.

in·voke (ĭnvōk′) *v.t.* (**-voked, -vok·ing**). Call on (deity etc.) in prayer or as witness; appeal to (person's authority etc.); summon (spirit) by charms; ask earnestly for (vengeance, help, etc.); cite in support of one's cause.

in·vo·lu·cre (ĭn′v*o*lōōk*e*r) *n.* (bot.) Whorl of bracts surrounding inflorescence.

in·vol·un·tar·y (ĭnvŏl′*u*ntĕrē) *adj.* Done without exercise of the will, unintentional. **in·vol·un·tar·i·ly** (ĭnvŏl*u*ntĕr′*i*lē, -vŏl′*u*ntĕr-) *adv.* **in·vol′un·tar·i·ness** *n.*

in·vo·lute (ĭn′v*o*lōōt) *adj.* Involved, intricate, curled spirally; (bot.) rolled inward at the edges.

in·vo·lu·tion (ĭnv*o*lōō′sh*o*n) *n.* Involving; entanglement; intricacy; curling inward; part so curled; (math.) raising of quantity to any power.

in·volve (ĭnvŏlv′) *v.t.* (**-volved, -volv·ing**). Wrap (thing *in* another); entangle (person, thing, *in* difficulties, mystery, etc.); implicate (*in*); include (*in*); imply, entail. **in·volve′ment** *n.*

in·vul·ner·a·ble (ĭnvŭl′n*e*r*a*b*e*l) *adj.* That cannot be wounded or hurt; immune to attack. **in·vul·ner·a·bil·i·ty** (ĭnvŭln*e*r*a*bĭl′ĭtē) *n.* **in·vul′ner·a·bly** *adv.*

in·ward (ĭn′w*e*rd) *adj.* Situated within; mental, spiritual; directed toward the inside. **in′ward·ly** *adv.* Of the inside; not aloud; in mind or spirit. **in′ward·ness** *n.* Inner nature, essence. **inward, in′wards** *advs.*

i·o·dide (ī′*o*dīd) *n.* Compound of iodine with another element or radical.

i·o·dine (ī′*o*dīn, -dĭn, -dēn) *n.* (chem.) Nonmetallic element widely diffused in nature but never in the free state, used in medicine as an antiseptic; symbol I, at. no. 53, at. wt. 126.9045; tincture or solution of this in alcohol.

i·o·dize (ī′*o*dīz) *v.t.* (**-dized, -diz·ing**). Treat, combine with iodine or an iodide.

i·o (ī′ō) **moth.** Large yellow N. Amer. moth, *Automeris io*, with eyelike spots on hind wings. [f. *Io*, girl in Gk. myth loved by Zeus and tormented by the jealous Hera with a stinging gadfly (the moth's larva stings)]

i·on (ī′*o*n, ī′ŏn) *n.* (phys.) 1. Electrified particle formed when a neutral atom or group of atoms loses or gains one or more electrons, as a *cation*, with positive charge, formed by electron loss, or an *anion*, with negative charge, formed by electron gain. 2. Gaseous particle electrically charged by action of x-rays or other rays. [Gk. *ion* (thing) going]

-ion *suffix.* Forming nouns of action, condition, etc., usu. from verbs (*destruction, infection*).

I·o·ni·a (īō′nē*a*). Ancient Greek colony on W. coast of Asia Minor; Aegean coast of W. Asia Minor.

I·o·ni·an (īō′nē*a*n) *adj.* Of Ionia or its people; ~ **Islands**, group of Greek islands in the Ionian Sea; ~ **Sea**, part of Mediterranean, between Greece and S. Italy. ~ *n.* Native, inhabitant, of Ionia.

I·on·ic (īŏn′ĭk) *adj.* Of Ionia; of the Ionic dialect, order, or school; ~ **dialect**, most important of the three main branches of ancient Greek, of which ATTIC was a development; ~ **order**, (archit.) Greek order characterized by two lateral volutes of the capital.

i·on·ic (īŏn′ĭk) *adj.* Of or

pertaining to ions.

i·on·ize (ī′onīz) *v.* (**-ized, -iz·ing**). Convert into, produce ions. **i·on·i·za·tion** (īonīzā′sh*o*n) *n.*

i·on·o·sphere (īŏn′*o*sfēr) *n.* Ionized region of the upper atmosphere, from altitudes of approximately 30 to 250 mi., able to reflect radio waves for transmission around Earth.

I.O.O.F. *abbrev.* Independent Order of Odd Fellows.

i·o·ta (īō′t*a*) *n.* Tenth (later ninth) letter of Greek alphabet (Ι, ι) corresponding to *i*; insignificant part, jot, atom.

IOU, I.O.U. (īōū′) *ns.* (pl. **IOUs, I.O.U.'s**). Signed document bearing these letters followed by specified sum, constituting formal acknowledgment of debt. [= I owe you]

I·o·wa (ī′*o*w*a*). State in midwestern U.S.; admitted to the Union in 1846; capital Des Moines; ~ **River**, flows from N. Iowa to the Mississippi River in the SE.

IPA, I.P.A. *abbrevs.* International Phonetic Alphabet.

ip·e·cac (ĭp′*e*kăk), **ip·e·cac·u·an·ha** (ĭp*e*kăkūăn′*a*) *ns.* Root of S. Amer. herbaceous or shrubby plant (*Cephaëlis ipecacuanha*) which possesses emetic, diaphoretic, and purgative properties, a common ingredient of cough medicines; the plant itself

Iph·i·ge·ni·a (ĭfĭj*e*nī′*a*, -nē′*a*). (Gk. legend) Daughter of Agamemnon and Clytemnestra; she was offered by her father as a sacrifice to Artemis when the Greeks, on their way to the Trojan War, were becalmed at Aulis, but was snatched from the altar by the goddess and borne away to Tauris, where she became a priestess; she was rescued by her brother Orestes.

ip·so fac·to (ĭp′sō făk′tō). By that very fact. [L.]

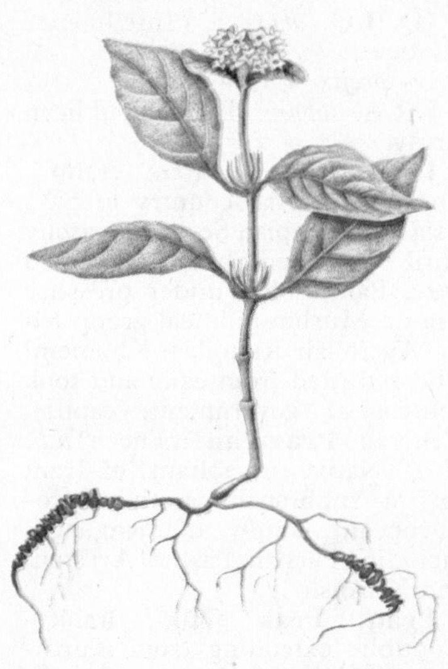

*The dried roots of the **ipecacuanha** produce a drug widely used in medicine as an emetic and as an expectorant. The plant is cultivated commercially in Brazil, Malaysia and Bengal in India.*

*An unusual perspective of Des Moines, the capital city of the state of **Iowa.** A large number of German immigrants came to Iowa in the 1850s followed by British, Irish and Scandinavians.*

IQ, I.Q. *abbrevs.* Intelligence quotient.

ir- *prefix* = IN[1,2] before *r*.

I.R.A. *abbrev.* Irish Republican Army.

I·ran (ĭrăn′, ī-; *Pers.* ērahn′). Formerly Persia; country in SW. Asia S. of Caspian Sea; a monarchy until 1979 when Shah Mohammed Reza Pahlevi left under pressure from a Muslim political group led by Ayatollah Ruhollah Khomeini who returned from exile and took control of government; capital, Teheran. **I·ra·ni·an** (ĭrā′nēan) *adj.* & *n.* (Native, inhabitant) of Iran; (of) a subbranch of the Indo-European family of languages including Persian, Pashto, Avestan, and Kurdish.

I·raq, I·rak (ĭrăk′, ĭrahk′). Republic extending from Kurdistan on N. and NE. to the Persian Gulf on the S. and SE. and from Iran in E. to Syria and the Arabian Desert on W.; formerly known as MESOPOTAMIA; freed from Turkish rule during World War I, then under a British mandate until 1932; a kingdom from 1921 until assassination of Faisal II in 1958, when it became a republic; capital, Baghdad. **I·ra·qi** (ĭrăk′ē, ĭrah′kē) *adj.* & *n.* (pl. **-qis**). (Native, inhabitant) of Iraq; (of) the modern Arabic dialect spoken in Iraq.

i·ras·ci·ble (ĭrăs′ĭbel) *adj.* Irritable, hot-tempered. **i·ras·ci·bil·i·ty** (ĭrăsĭbĭl′ĭtē) *n.*

i·rate (īrāt′, īr′āt) *adj.* Angry. **i·rate′ly** *adv.*

IRBM *abbrev.* Intermediate range ballistic missile.

ire (īr) *n.* Anger. **ire′ful** *adj.*

Ire·land (īr′land). Island in the Atlantic Ocean, to W. of Gt. Britain; made subordinate to the English legislature in 1494; in 1920 the British Parliament divided Ireland into two parts: (1) Southern Ireland, which became an independent country, since 1949 officially called the Republic of Ireland (formerly, 1921–37, the Irish Free State; 1937–49, Eire); capital Dublin; and (2) NORTHERN IRELAND.

ir·i·da·ceous (ĭrĭdā′shus) *adj.* (of plants) Of the iris kind.

ir·i·des·cent (ĭrĭdĕs′ent) *adj.* Showing colors like those of rainbow; changing color with position. **ir·i·des′cence** *n.*

i·rid·i·um (ĭrĭd′ēum, ī-) *n.* (chem.) White metallic brittle element of platinum group, used esp. to form hard, corrosion-proof alloys with platinum or osmium; symbol Ir, at. no. 77, at. wt. 192.22.

I·ris (īr′ĭs). (Gk. myth.) Goddess who acted as the messenger of the gods, and displayed as her sign the rainbow.

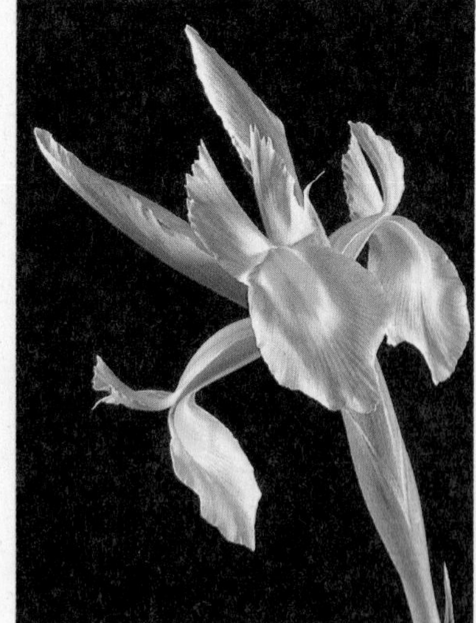

The blue flag ***Iris,*** *native to Eurasia is also found in similar habitats in North America. There are up to 300 species of Iris which has become a very popular garden flower and is used widely in Japanese floral arrangements.*

The republic of ***Iran*** *has a population of 31,960,000 people, 90% of them Muslim. Below: Map and flag of Iran. Below right: Dome of the Madrasseh Mader-E-Shah at Isfahan, the former captial of Persia and the center of the textile industry. Bottom: Weaving a Persian carpet at Nishapur.*

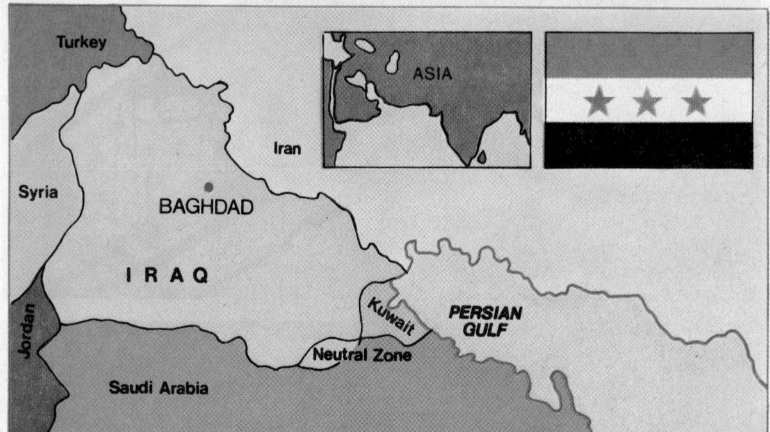

*The republic of **Iraq** is bisected by the rivers Tigris and Euphrates which water its fertile center — the site of ancient Mesopotamia. Its capital is Baghdad, and the country produces 80% of the world's supply of dates. Above: Aerial view of Kadimain mosque. Right: Map and flag of Iraq.*

i·ris (īr′ĭs) *n.* (pl. **i·ris·es, ir·i·des** pr. ĭr′ĭdēz, īr′-). 1. Circular pigmented diaphragm in anterior chamber of eye, with central aperture (the *pupil*) that admits light to the lens and contracts or expands according to intensity of light; ~ **diaphragm**, mechanical device resembling the iris, used on cameras for controlling the aperture of the lens by means of movable overlapping shutters. 2. (bot.) Plant of genus *I* ~ with tubers or bulbs, sword-shaped leaves, and showy flowers.

I·rish (īr′ĭsh) *adj.* 1. Of Ireland, its people, or language; ~ **coffee**, hot coffee and whiskey, with sugar and whipped cream; ~ **Free State**: see IRELAND; **I′rishman, I′rishwoman**, Irish person; **Irish Republican Army**, (abbrev. I.R.A.) secret Irish nationalist organization formed to oppose the British partition of Ireland and fight for the unification and independence of all Ireland; has carried out anti-British terrorist acts since the 1920s, and is now active chiefly in Northern Ireland; **Irish Sea**, sea between Ireland and England; **Irish setter**, setter having long, silky, golden red or reddish-brown hair; **Irish stew**, stew of meat (often mutton), potatoes, and onions; **Irish terrier**, breed of terrier with rough wiry coat of reddish-brown color; **Irish whiskey**: see WHISKEY; **Irish wolfhound**, wolfhound of large tall Irish breed with rough, shaggy coat. 2. Of the branch of the Celtic languages spoken in Ireland. **Irish** *n.* 1. (collect.) People of

Ireland. 2. Irish language.

I·rish·ism (īr′ĭshĭzem) *n.* Irish idiom or custom.

irk (ẽrk) *v.t.* Vex; weary, bore. **irk′some** *adj.* Tedious, annoying. **irk′some·ly** *adv.* **irk′some·ness** *n.*

IRO, I.R.O. *abbrevs.* International Refugee Organization.

i·ron (īrn, ī′ern) *n.* 1. (chem.) Abundant metallic element, widely distributed in form of ores, silver-white in color, and characterized by great tensile strength, ductility, and magnetic susceptibility; symbol Fe, at. no. 26, at. wt. 55.847; when purified and alloyed with small quantities of other materials, known as STEEL; **cast ~**, iron obtained by smelting from ores, silvery gray when clean, hard, brittle, crystalline in structure, and containing 2–5% of carbon and smaller quantities of sulfur, phosphorus, and silicon; **pig ~**, cast iron as first obtained from the smelting furnace, cast in long blocks (pigs) for convenience; **wrought ~**, highly malleable iron obtained by stirring pig iron when molten (puddling), nearly pure but always containing some slag in the form of filaments and thus showing a fibrous structure. 2. Tool, implement, instrument, made of iron, as **curling ~, grappling ~**; electric appliance with smooth flat undersurface, now usu. heated by

electricity, for smoothing out clothes, linen, etc. (for **flatiron**, see FLAT[2]); golf club with iron or steel head laid back for lofting the ball; (usu. pl.) fetters, shackles. 3. Preparation of iron used in medicine as a tonic. 4. (fig.) Type of hardness, as *man of ~, rod of ~*. 5. Phrases: **strike while the ~ is hot**, act promptly and at a good opportunity; **have many ~s in the fire**, have many undertakings afoot at the same time. 6. **I~ Age**, period in the history of a people, following the Bronze Age, characterized by use of iron implements and weapons; **i′ronbark**, any species of *Eucalyptus* with hard, rough bark; **i′ronbound**, bound with iron; (fig.) rigid, inflexible, unyielding; (of coast) rugged, rocky; **i′ronclad**, covered with, protected by, iron; **Iron Cross**, German military decoration; **iron curtain**, (fig.) barrier to passage of persons and information at western boundary of Russian sphere of influence in Europe; any similar barrier to spread of ideas etc.; **iron lung**, rigid box enclosing the body of a patient (leaving the head free) used, in the treatment of paralyzing diseases, for administering prolonged artificial respiration by means of mechanical pumps; **iron pyrites**: see PYRITES; **i′ronstone**, name of various hard iron ores; a hard white pottery; **i′ronware**, generic name for all light articles made of iron; hardware; **i′ronwood**: see HORNbeam; **i′ronwork**, iron parts of a structure; casting, moldings, etc., made of iron; **i′ronworks**, place where iron

*The **ironbark,** a native of Australia, is noted for the strength of its bark. The species shown is Eucalyptus siderophoia, the broad-leaved ironbark.*

1

3

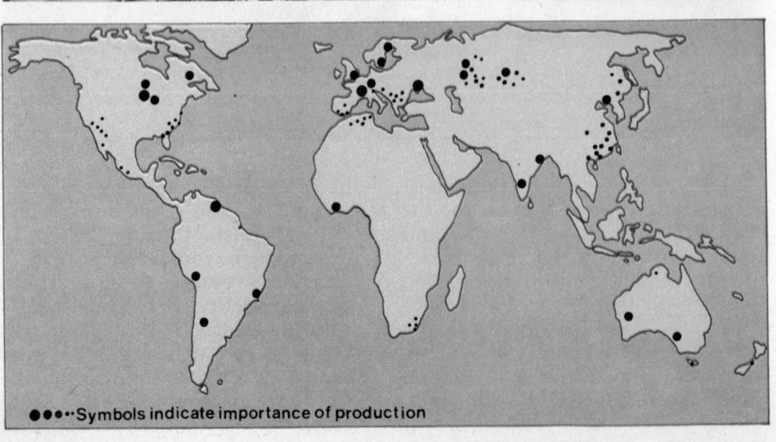

***Iron** in its pure state is a shiny silvery metal which is tough but malleable. Iron ore is smelted in blast furnaces like this one at Sheffield, U.K. to produce pig iron or cast iron (facing page). 1. The 'L' blast furnace at Sparrows Point in Maryland owned by the Bethlehem Steel Corporation is of primary economic importance to the state. 2. This map of the world's known iron ore deposits shows that the U.S.S.R. has 25% of the world's supply. 3. Lace ironwork favored for decoration in the latter part of the 19th century, is a distinctive feature of the French quarter of New Orleans.*

*A bucket wheel reclaimer working on the refined **iron ore** in Port Hedland, Western Australia. The ore is sent down conveyors to a waiting ore carrier.*

is smelted or iron goods are made. **iron** *adj.* Made of iron; hard; strong; firm, unyielding. ~ *v.t.* Shackle with irons; smooth (clothes, linen, etc.) with a hot iron; ~ **out**, (fig.) remove (difficulties etc.).

i·ron·ic (īrŏn′ĭk), **i·ron·i·cal** (īrŏn′ĭk*a*l) *adjs.* Of, using, said in, addicted to, irony. **i·ron′i·cal·ly** *adv.*

i·ron·ing (īr′nĭng, ī′*er*-) *n.* Process of smoothing (clothes etc.) with a heated iron; clothes, linen, etc. to be ironed; ~ **board**, smooth cloth-covered board on which clothes etc. are spread for ironing.

i·ro·ny[1] (ī′r*o*nē, ī′*er*nē) *n.* (pl. **-nies**). Figure of speech in which the intended meaning is the opposite of that expressed by the words used, ridicule in which laudatory expressions are used to imply condemnation or contempt; course of events, combination of circumstances, the result of which is the direct opposite of what might be expected as though due to the malice of fate, as in **life's ironies, irony of fate**; use of language that has an inner meaning for a privileged audience and an outer meaning for the persons addressed or concerned, as in **tragic irony**; **Socratic irony**, feigned ignorance as means of confuting an opponent in dispute.

i·ron·y[2] (ī′*er*nē) *adj.* Of, like, iron.

Ir·o·quoi·an (ĭr*o*kwoi′*a*n) *n.* Family of N. Amer. Indian languages spoken in the eastern U.S. and Canada by the Iroquois, Cherokee, Erie, Wyandotte, and other tribes. ~ *adj.* Of or speaking a language of this family; of the Iroquois.

Ir·o·quois (ĭr′*o*kwoi) *n.* (pl. **-quois** pr. -kwoiz, -kwoi). (Member of) any of several Iroquoian-speaking N. Amer. Indian tribes of a powerful confederacy formerly inhabiting New York State and known as the Five Nations (see FIVE).

ir·ra·di·ate (ĭrā′dēāt) *v.t.* (**-at·ed, -at·ing**). Subject to radiation, esp. of X-rays, gamma rays, or ultraviolet rays; **ir·ra·di-**

*This **iron** bridge over the River Severn was the first of its kind to be built in England. It was constructed between 1775 and 1779 by Abraham Darby and has a single arch.*

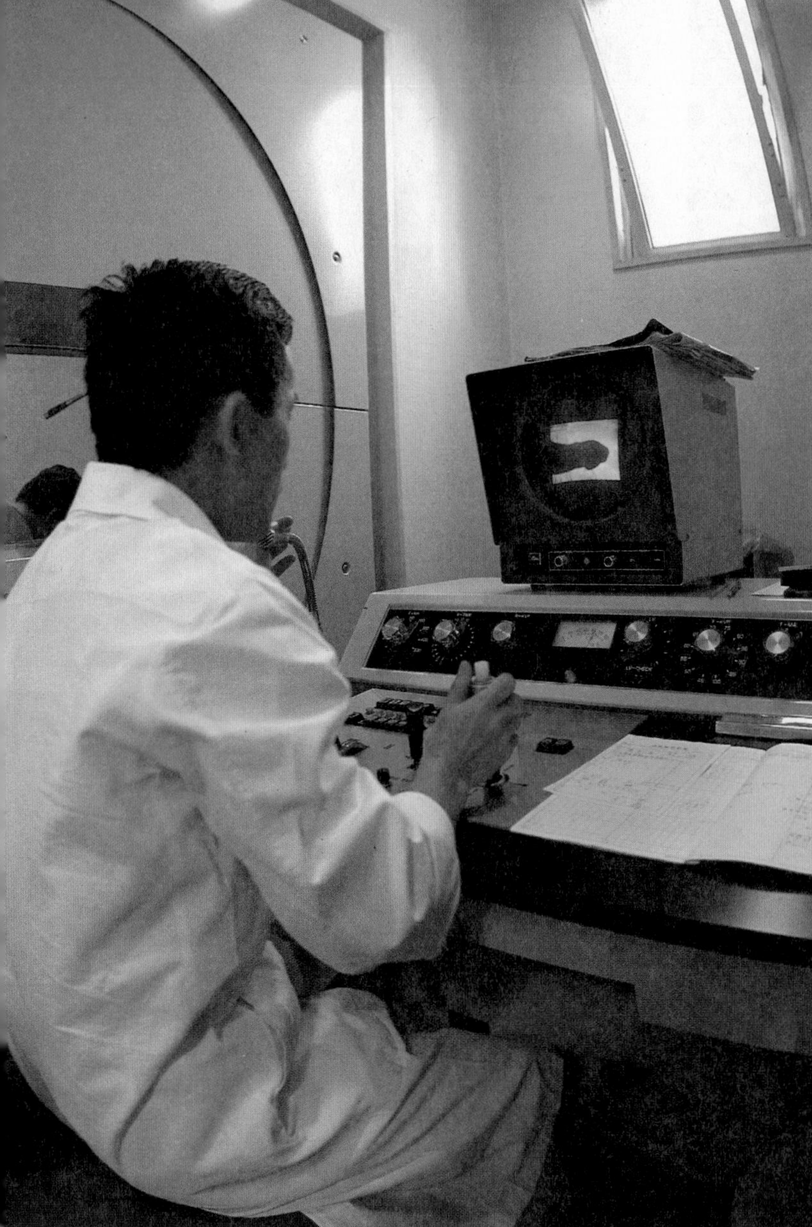

An X-ray in progress in Japan. The radiographer has to ***irradiate*** *the area intended for X-ray which is placed between an X-ray tube and a film that contains high levels of silver halide emulsion.*

a·tion (ĭrādēā′sh*o*n) *n.* **ir·ra′di·a·tive** *adj.*

ir·ra·tion·al (ĭrăsh′*o*n*a*l) *adj.* Unreasonable, illogical, absurd; not endowed with reason; (math., of roots etc.) not rational, not expressible by an ordinary (finite) fraction, proper or improper. **ir·ra·tion·al·i·ty** (ĭrăsh*o*năl′ĭtē) *n.* (pl. **-ties**). **ir·ra′tion·al·ly** *adv.*

ir·re·claim·a·ble (ĭrĭklā′m*a*b*e*l) *adj.* Not to be reclaimed or reformed. **ir·re·claim′a·bly** *adv.*

ir·rec·on·cil·a·ble (ĭrĕk*o*nsī′l*a*b*e*l) *adj.* Implacably hostile; (of ideas etc.) incompatible. ~ *n.* Person who cannot or will not compromise; idea, belief, or result that cannot be brought into harmony with others. **ir·rec·on·cil·a·bil·i·ty** (ĭrĕk*o*nsīl*a*bĭl′ĭtē), **ir·rec′on·cil·a·ble·ness** *ns.* **ir·rec′on·cil·a·bly** *adv.*

ir·re·cov·er·a·ble (ĭrĭkŭv′*era*b*e*l) *adj.* That cannot be recovered or remedied. **ir·re·cov′er·a·bly** *adv.*

ir·re·cu·sa·ble (ĭrĭkū′z*a*b*e*l) *adj.* That must be accepted.

Ir·re·den·tist (ĭrĭdĕn′tĭst) *n.* (It. politics) Advocate of recovery to Italy of all Italian-speaking districts; **i~**, (of any country) nationalist who advocates recovery of linguistically or historically related area from foreign rule. **ir·re·den′tism** *n.* [It. (*Italia*) *irredenta* unredeemed Italy]

ir·re·duc·i·ble (ĭrĭdo͞o′sĭb*e*l, -dū′-) *adj.* That cannot be brought (*to* desired condition); not capable of being reduced; ~ **minimum**, smallest amount, lowest degree, to which anything can be reduced, or point beyond which further reduction would be useless or unacceptable. **ir·re·duc′i·bly** *adv.*

ir·ref·ra·ga·ble (ĭrĕf′r*aga*b*e*l) *adj.* (of statement, argument, person) Indisputable, unanswerable. **ir·ref′ra·ga·bly** *adv.*

ir·re·fran·gi·ble (ĭrĭfrăn′jĭb*e*l) *adj.* Inviolate; not breakable; (optics) not capable of being refracted.

ir·ref·u·ta·ble (ĭrĕf′y*u*t*a*b*e*l, ĭrĭfū′t*a*-) *adj.* Not to be refuted. **ir·ref·u·ta·bil′i·ty** *n.* **ir·ref′u·ta·bly** *adv.*

ir·reg·u·lar (ĭrĕg′y*u*l*er*) *adj.* Not regular, contrary to rule, abnormal; not of symmetrical form; (of surface) uneven; uneven in duration, order, etc.; (gram.) not inflected in the usual way; (of troops) not in regular service. ~ *n.* Member of irregular military force. **ir·reg·u·lar·i·ty** (ĭrĕgy*u*lăr′ĭtē) *n.* (pl. **-ties**). **ir·reg′u·lar·ly** *adv.*

ir·rel·e·vant (ĭrĕl′*e*v*a*nt) *adj.* Not to the point; not applicable (*to* matter in hand). **ir·rel′e·vance, ir·rel′e·van·cy** *ns.* **ir·rel′e·vant·ly** *adv.*

ir·re·li·gion (ĭrĭlĭj′*o*n) *n.* Hostility to, disregard of, religion. **ir·re·li′gious·ly** *adv.*

ir·re·me·di·a·ble (ĭrĭmē′dē*a*b*e*l) *adj.* That cannot be remedied. **ir·re·me′di·a·bly** *adv.*

ir·rep·a·ra·ble (ĭrĕp′*era*b*e*l) *adj.* (of injury, loss, etc.) That cannot be rectified or made good. **ir·rep′a·ra·ble·ness** *n.* **ir·rep′a·ra·bly** *adv.*

ir·re·place·a·ble (ĭrĭplā′s*a*b*e*l) *adj.* Incapable of being replaced.

ir·re·press·i·ble (ĭrĭprĕs′*a*b*e*l) *adj.* Not to be repressed or restrained. **ir·re·press′i·bly** *adv.*

ir·re·proach·a·ble (ĭrĭprō′ch*a*b*e*l) *adj.* Free from blame, faultless. **ir·re·proach·a·bil·i·ty** (ĭrĭprōch*a*bĭl′ĭtē) *n.* **ir·re·proach′a·bly** *adv.*

ir·re·sist·i·ble (ĭrĭzĭs′t*a*b*e*l) *adj.* Too strong, convincing, charming, etc., to be resisted. **ir·re·sist·i·bil·i·ty** (ĭrĭzĭst*a*bĭl′ĭtē) *n.* **ir·re·sist′i·bly** *adv.*

ir·re·spec·tive (ĭrĭspĕk′tĭv) *adj.* ~ **of**, not taking into account, without reference to. **ir·re·spec′tive·ly** *adv.*

ir·re·spon·si·ble (ĭrĭspŏn′sĭb*e*l) *adj.* Not responsible for conduct; acting, done, without due sense of responsibility. **ir·re·spon·si·bil·i·ty** (ĭrĭspŏns*ĭ*bĭl′ĭtē) *n.* **ir·re·spon′si·bly** *adv.*

ir·re·triev·a·ble (ĭrĭtrē′v*a*b*e*l) *adj.* That cannot be retrieved. **ir·re·triev·a·bil·i·ty** (ĭrĭtrēv*a*bĭl′ĭtē) *n.* **ir·re·triev′a·bly** *adv.*

1

3

Irrigation is one of the most ancient techniques in agriculture. 1. Dams like the Burrendong Dam on the Macquarie River, Australia, conserve water for irrigation purposes. 2. A barley field being watered by a portable irrigation system.

3. Cotton is irrigated in Wee Waa, Australia from these artificial troughs. 4. Primitive forms of irrigation, as here in Iran, make use of a well and windlass to draw water.

ir·rev·er·ent (ĭrĕv´erent) *adj.* Lacking in reverence. **ir·rev´er·ent·ly** *adv.* **ir·rev´er·ence** *n.*

ir·re·vers·i·ble (ĭrĭvẽr´sibel) *adj.* Unalterable; not reversible. **ir·re·vers·i·bil·i·ty** (ĭrĭvẽrsabĭl´ĭtē) *n.* **ir·re·vers´i·bly** *adv.*

ir·rev·o·ca·ble (ĭrĕv´okabel) *adj.* Incapable of being revoked or retracted. **ir·rev·o·ca·bil·i·ty** (ĭrĕvocabĭl´ĭtē) *n.* **ir·rev´o·ca·bly** *adv.*

ir·ri·gate (ĭr´igāt) *v.t.* (**-gat·ed, -gat·ing**). (of streams etc.) Supply land with water; water (land) by system of artificial channels, ditches; (med.) wash, moisten (wound etc.) with flow of liquid. **ir·ri·ga·ble** (ĭr´igabel) *adj.* **ir·ri·ga·tion** (ĭrigā´shon) *n.*

ir·ri·ta·ble (ĭr´ĭtabel) *adj.* Quick to anger, touchy; (physiol.) (of parts of body, wounds, etc.) excessively sensitive to stimuli; (bot.) capable of responding to external stimulus. **ir·ri·ta·bil·i·ty** (ĭrĭtabĭl´ĭtē) *n.* **ir´ri·ta·bly** *adv.*

ir·ri·tant (ĭr´ĭtant) *adj.* Causing (usu. physical) irritation. ~ *n.* Substance causing irritation (also fig.).

ir·ri·tate (ĭr´ĭtāt) *v.t.* (**-tat·ed, -tat·ing**). Excite to anger, annoy; chafe, inflame, make sore (part of body etc.). **ir´ri·tat·ing** *adj.* **ir´ri·tat·ing·ly** *adv.* **ir·ri·ta·tion** (ĭrĭtā´shon) *n.*

IRS *abbrev.* Internal Revenue Service.

Ir·ving[1] (ẽr´vĭng), **Washington** (1783–1859). Amer. writer; best known for his genially satirical *History of New York ... by Diedrich Knickerbocker*, and the short stories "The Legend of Sleepy Hollow"

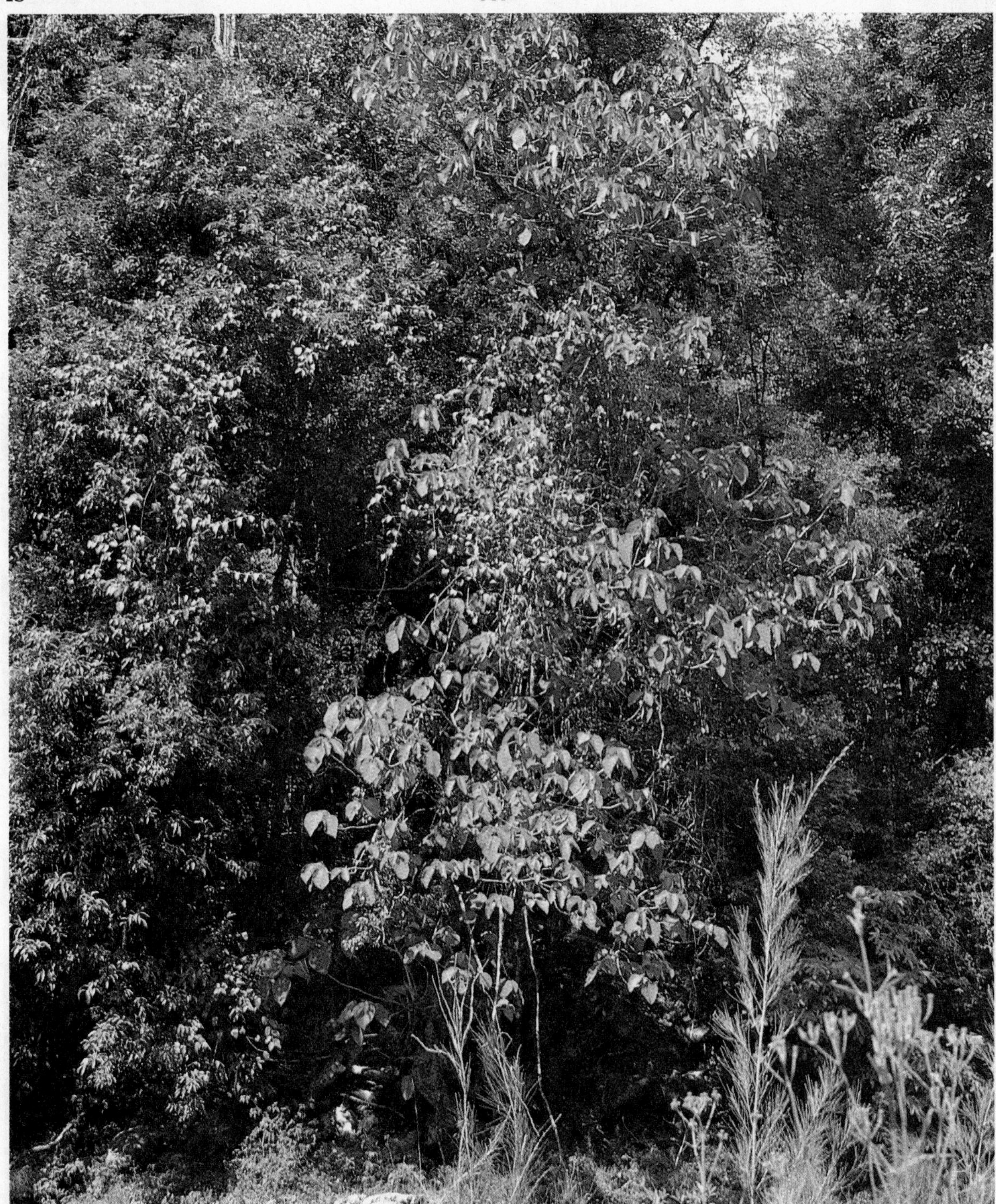

and "Rip Van Winkle."

is (ĭz). Third pers. sing. pres. ind. of BE.

Is. *abbrev.* Isaiah (Old Testament; also Isa.); Island(s).

I·saac (ī′zak). Hebrew patriarch, son of Abraham and Sarah and father of Jacob and Esau (Gen. 21 etc.).

Is·a·bel·la I (ĭzabĕl′*a*) (1451–1501). (also known as "The Catholic") Queen of Castile, 1474–1504, with her husband Ferdinand of Aragon, joint sovereign of Castile and Aragon, 1479–1504; gave aid to Columbus in his expedition to the New World.

Stinging hairs on leaves of the Giant Nettle Tree of Australia, causes an intense ***irritation*** *in the human body.*

I·sa·iah (īzā′*a*; *Brit.* īzī′*a*). Hebrew prophet who ministered in Judah in 8th c. B.C. and attacked corruption in the national life; book of Old Testament containing his prophecies.

is·chi·um (ĭs′kē*u*m) *n.* (pl. **-chi·a** pr. -kē*a*). One of the bones of the pelvis.

I·seult (ĭsōōlt′, ĭzōōlt′). (Ger. *Isolde*, Fr. *Isoud, Ysoud*) Name of two characters in medieval legend: (1) ~ **of Ireland**, daughter of the king of Ireland and wife of king Mark of Cornwall, loved by Tristram; (2) ~ **of Brittany,** ~ **of the White Hands**, daughter of the king of Brittany and wife of Tristram.

-ish *suffix.* Of the nature of; somewhat; approximately (*boyish, reddish, fortyish*).

Ish·ma·el (ĭsh′mē*a*l, -māl). Son of Abraham by Sarah's handmaid Hagar, of whom it was predicted, "His hand will be against every man, and every man's hand against him" (Gen. 16); hence, an outcast, one at war with society. **Ish′-ma·el·ite** *n.* (Member of) a desert people believed by ancient Hebrews to be descended from Ishmael; an outcast.

Ish·tar (ĭsh′tar̄). Assyrian and Babylonian equivalent of ASTARTE.

I·sis (ī′sĭs). (Egyptian myth.) Sister and wife of OSIRIS, and mother of HORUS, regarded as a nature goddess.

Is·lam (ĭs′l*a*m, ĭz′-, ĭslahm′). 1. Religion revealed through the Prophet Muhammad. 2. Muslim world. **Is·lam·ic** (ĭslăm′ĭk, -lah′-mĭk, ĭz-), **Is·lam·it·ic** (ĭsl*a*mĭt′ĭk, ĭz-) *adjs.* **Is·lam·ite** (ĭs′l*a*mīt, ĭz′-) *n.* [Arab. *'islām* resignation to will of God]

Is·lam·a·bad (ĭslah′m*a*bahd, ĭz-). Capital city of Pakistan in NW. Pakistan NE. of Rawalpindi.

is·land (ī′l*a*nd) *n.* Piece of land surrounded by water; (fig.) anything detached or isolated; (physiol.) detached portion of tissue or group of cells; **~s of Langerhans**: see LANGERHANS; **Islands of the Blest**, (Gk. and Rom. myth.) islands of the Western Ocean, abode of the favorites of the gods after death. **island** *v.t.* Make into an island; isolate.

is·land·er (ī′l*a*nd*e*r) *n.* Native or inhabitant of an island.

isle (īl) *n.* (esp. poet. or in proper name) Island (usu. small).

*The teachings of **Islam** are preserved in the Koran and the Sunna. Mecca (above) is a holy city and the birthplace of Mohammed. Right: Tunisian prayer-mats. The countries of North Africa are predominantly Muslim.*

is·let (ī′lĭt) *n.* Little island.

ism (ĭz′*e*m) *n.* Any distinctive doctrine or practice.

-ism *suffix.* Forming nouns (1) of action (*baptism*); (2) of condition or conduct (*barbarism, heroism*); (3) of system or belief (*conservatism*); (4) of peculiarity of language (*archaism, Gallicism*); (5) of pathological condition (*alcoholism, Parkinsonism*).

Is·ma·il·i (ĭsmaīl′ē, ĭz-) *n.* Member of a Muslim sect that seceded from the Shiah in 9th c. after the rejection of the claim of Isma'il, a descendant of Muhammad's son-in-law Ali, to be leader (imam) of Islam; the Ismailis now survive mainly in India, Iran, and Afghanistan, and regard the Aga Khan as their imam.

iso- *prefix.* Equal.

i·so·bar (ī′s*o*bar̄) *n.* 1. Line on map connecting places at which atmospheric pressure is the same (at given time or on the average). 2. One of two or more isotopes having the same atomic weight but different chemical properties. **i·so·bar·ic** (īsobăr′ĭk) *adj.*

I·soc·ra·tes (īsŏk′r*a*tēz) (436–338 B.C.). Athenian orator and

teacher of rhetoric.

i·so·late (ī′s*o*lāt, ĭs′*o*-) *v.t.* (**-lat·ed, -lat·ing**). Place apart or alone; (chem.) free substance from its compounds; subject (person etc.) to quarantine, separate (infectious patient) from others. **i·so·la·tion** (īsolā′sh*o*n, ĭso-) *n.*

i·so·la·tion·ist (īsolā′sh*o*nĭst, ĭso-) *n.* One who favors (political or national) isolation. **i·so·la′tion·ism** *n.*

I·sol·de (ĭsōl′d*e*, ĭzōld′) = ISEULT.

i·so·mer (īʹsomer) *n.* (chem.) One of two or more substances composed of molecules having the same kind of atoms and in the same proportions, but which, by reason of a difference in arrangement of the atoms, have different chemical and physical properties. **i·so·mer·ic** (īsomĕrʹĭk) *adj.* **i·somʹer·ism** *n.*

i·so·met·ric (īsomĕtʹrĭk), **i·so·met·ri·cal** (īsomĕtʹrĭkal) *adjs.* Of equal measure or dimensions; ~ **drawing**, engineer's or architect's drawing in which the three dimensions are represented by three sets of lines 120 apart and all measurements are on same scale (i.e. not in perspective); ~ **exercises, isometrics** (*n.pl.*) system of physical exercises in which muscles are pitted one against another or against a fixed object.

i·so·morph (īʹsomōrf) *n.* Substance or organism isomorphous with another. **i·so·mor·phic** (īsomōrʹfĭk), **i·so·morʹphous** *adjs.* Having the same form; having the property of crystallizing in the same or closely related geometric forms; (math., of groups and other systems) exactly corresponding in form and in the relations between their elements. **i·so·morʹphism** *n.*

i·so·pod (īʹsopŏd) *n.* Crustacean of large order Isopoda (including, e.g., woodlice) varying greatly in form and often parasitic.

i·sos·ce·les (īsŏsʹelēz) *adj.* (of a triangle) Having two equal sides.

i·so·therm (īʹsotherm) *n.* Line on map connecting places having the same temperature. **i·so·ther·mal** (īsotherʹmal) *adj.* & *n.*

i·so·ton·ic (īsotŏnʹĭk) *adj.* Having equal tension.

i·so·tope (īʹsotōp) *n.* One or two or more forms of an element having the same atomic number and the same chemical properties and occupying the same place in the periodic table, but differing in atomic weight and in nuclear properties such as radioactivity. **i·so·top·ic** (īsotŏpʹĭk) *adj.*

Is·ra·el[1] (ĭzʹrēel, -rā-). 1. Name given to Jacob after he wrestled with the angel (Gen. 32). 2. Hebrew nation or people traditionally descended from Jacob, whose 12 sons became founders of the 12 tribes; all the Hebrew people, the Jews. 3. Northern kingdom of the Hebrews (933–721 B.C.), opp. JUDAH. **Isʹra·el·ite** *adj.* & *n.* [Heb. = he that strives with God]

Is·ra·el[2] (ĭzʹrēel, -rā-). Independent Jewish republic in country formerly called Palestine, bordering on E. of Mediterranean Sea; established in 1948; capital Jerusalem. **Is·rae·li** (ĭzrāʹlē) *adj.* & *n.* (pl. **-lis**, collect. **-li**).

Is·ra·fel (ĭzʹrafĕl), **Is·ra·fil** (ĭzʹrafēl). In Muslim tradition, angel of music, who will sound the trumpet on the Day of Judgment.

Is·sa·char (ĭsʹakar). Hebrew patriarch, son of Jacob and Leah (Gen. 30).

Is·sei (ēsʹsāʹ) *n.* (pl. **-sei, -seis**). Japanese immigrant to U.S. or Canada; cf. NISEI and KIBEI. [Jap. = first generation]

is·sue (ĭshʹōō; *Brit.* ĭsʹū) *n.* 1. Outgoing, outflow; (med.) discharge of blood etc. 2. Place of egress; outlet. 3. Progeny, children. 4. Result, outcome. 5. Point in question; point of discussion, debate, or dispute. 6. Giving out, issuing, (*of* bills of exchange, stamps, etc.); number of coins, notes, copies of newspaper or book etc., issued at one time; ~ *v.* (**-sued, -su·ing**). 1. Go or come

*The population of **Israel** doubled in the 10 years after its foundation in 1948, as Jews from the Middle East and Central Europe flooded in. Below: The Church of the Nativity, Bethlehem. Below right: Map and flag of Israel.*

Istanbul *is Turkey's chief entry port and financial center. The Ottoman era gave the city its architectural character, with narrow streets, low buildings and many mosques. There are large foreign minorities in the city.*

out; be derived, spring, (*from*); result (*from*); end, result, (*in*). 2. Come out, be published; send forth; publish, put into circulation (notes, newspaper, book, etc.). 3. (mil.) Supply (soldier) *with* article of equipment etc. **is'su·a·ble** *adj.* **is'su·ance** *n.*

-ist *suffix.* Forming nouns (1) of agent (*plagiarist, antagonist*); (2) of adherent of creed etc. (*atheist, Methodist*); (3) of one concerned with any subject (*dentist, tobacconist*) esp. as player on musical instrument (*cellist*).

Is·tan·bul (ĭstănbo͞ol', -tahn-). City and port of Turkey on the European side of the Bosporus (orig. Byzantium, later CONSTANTINOPLE).

isth·mus (ĭs'm*u*s) *n.* (pl. **-mus·es, -mi** pr. -mī). Narrow portion of land connecting two larger bodies of land, neck of land; (anat., bot., zool.) narrow part or passage connecting two larger ones.

is·tle (ĭst'lē) *n.* Any of several plants of the genus *Agave*, yielding a tough fiber. [Mex. Span. *ixtle*]

it (ĭt) *pron.* Third person sing. pronoun denoting thing or person in question; as subject of impersonal verb expressing action or condition of things without reference to agent; as subject of verb, anticipating deferred virtual subject in apposition; as antecedent to relative of either number and any gender, separated by predicate; as indefinite object with transitive or intransitive verb; with specific but unexpressed reference: **with ~**: see WITH; as quasi-*n.*, (1) in children's games, player who must catch or find others; (2) (colloq.) the very person or thing; perfection.

i.t.a. *abbrev.* Initial teaching alphabet.

ital. *abbrev.* Italic (type).

I·tal·ian (ĭtăl'y*a*n) *adj.* Of Italy, its people, or language; (of script) = ITALIC, 1; **~ sonnet**: see SONNET.

Italian *n.* 1. Italian person. 2. Language of Italy, one of the modern descendants of Latin. **I·tal·ian·ate** (ĭtăl'y*a*nāt, -nĭt) *adj.* Of Italian form or character.

I·tal·ic (ĭtăl'ĭk, ī-) *adj.* 1. Of ancient Italy or its tribes; of the Greek colonies in southern Italy; **~ languages**, Indo-European languages of ancient Italy (Latin, Oscan, Umbrian) as a group. **I·tal·i·cism** (ĭtăl'ĭsĭz*e*m, ī-) *n.*

i·tal·ic (ĭtăl'ĭk, ī-) *adj.* 1. Of the kind of handwriting developed in Italy (opp. GOTHIC). 2. Of the kind of printing type imitating italic script, introduced by Aldus Manutius (1501), in which letters slope toward the right (now usu. employed to emphasize word(s) or distinguish word(s) from others in same context). **~** *n.* (also pl.) Italic type. **i·tal'i·cize** *v.t.* (**-cized, -ciz·ing**). Print in italics; (in writing) underline.

It·a·ly (ĭt'*a*lē). Peninsula running southward into Mediterranean from the mass of central Europe; formerly divided among various mercantile city-states or under foreign domination until unified in 19th c.; a monarchy from 1861 until 1946 when a republic was declared; capital, Rome.

itch (ĭch) *n.* Uneasy sense of irritation in skin; any of various

Italy's *main products are wine and olive oil, and its earnings from tourism are second only to those of the U.S.A. The main cities are Rome, Florence, Venice, Naples, and Milan. Its art treasures are unrivalled in the world. Below left: St. Peter's, Rome. Below right: Map and flag of Italy. Facing page: Cliffside town of Manarola, Liguria.*

contagious skin diseases marked by this sensation, eruptions, etc.; restless desire, hankering; ~ **mite**, mite causing scabies. **itch** *v.i.* Feel irritation in skin; crave uneasily; **itching palm**, avarice. **itch'i·ness** *n.* **itch'y** *adj.* (**itch·i·er, itch·i·est**).

-ite[1] *suffix.* Forming nouns meaning "person or thing belonging to or connected with" (*Trotskyite, Muscovite, anthracite, cordite, vulcanite*). [Gk. *-itēs*]

-ite[2] *suffix.* Forming adjectives (*erudite*), nouns (*appetite*), and verbs (*expedite, unite*). [L. *-itus*]

i·tem (ī'tem) *n.* Article, unit, included in enumeration; entry of this in account etc.; detail of news etc. in newspaper etc. ~ *adv.* Likewise, also, (introducing mention of item). **i'tem·ize** *v.t.* (**-ized, -iz·ing**). Set down by items; specify items of (account etc.). [L. *item* in like manner, also]

it·er·ate (ĭt'erāt) *v.t.* (**-at·ed, -at·ing**). Repeat (quoted words etc.); make (charge, assertion, etc.) repeatedly. **it·er·a·tion** (ĭterā'shon) *n.*

it·er·a·tive (ĭt'erātĭv, -eratĭv) *adj.* Repetitious; (gram., of verb) denoting repetition of action, frequentative.

Ith·a·ca (ĭth'aka). 1. (Gk. *Itháki*) Small island W. of Greece, in the Ionian Sea. 2. Island described by Homer as the kingdom of Odysseus; traditionally identified with modern Ithaca, but thought by some to be the neighboring larger island of Leukas.

i·tin·er·ant (ītĭn'erant, ĭ-) *adj.* Traveling from place to place, esp. to find work or carry out official task or duty.

*The Suribachi-**Iwo Jima** statue in Washington D.C. commemorating the battle between U.S. and Japanese troops at the Volcano Island archipelago in the western Pacific in 1945.*

i·tin·er·ar·y (ītĭn'erĕrē, ĭ-) *n.* (pl. **-ar·ies**). Route or proposed route, list of stopovers, etc.; record of travel; guidebook. ~ *adj.* Of traveling, of a route.

-itious *suffix.* Forming adjectives corresp. to nouns ending in *-ition* (*ambitious, nutritious*).

-itis *suffix.* Forming nouns indicating inflammatory diseases lit. (*appendicitis, gastritis*) and (colloq.) fig. *baseballitis.*

its (ĭts) *poss. pron.* Possessive case of IT used as attrib. adjective, belonging to, affecting, it.

it's (ĭts) *contr.* It is.

it·self (ĭtsĕlf') *pron.* Emphatic and reflexive form corresponding to IT; **by** ~, automatically; apart from its surroundings; **in** ~, viewed in its essential qualities etc.

it·sy-bit·sy (ĭt'sē bĭt'sē), **it·ty-bit·ty** (ĭt'ē bĭt'ē) *adjs.* (slang, baby talk) Tiny, insignificant.

IUD, IUCD *abbrevs.* Intrauterine (contraceptive) device.

I.V., i.v. *abbrevs.* Intravenous.

I·van (ī'van; *Russ.* ēvahn'). Name of several rulers of Russia: **Ivan I** (d. 1341), grand duke of Vladimir (1328–41); **Ivan II** (d. 1359), grand duke of Vladimir; **Ivan III** "the Great" (1440–1505), grand duke of Muscovy (1462–1505); **Ivan IV** "the Terrible" (1530–84), first tsar of Muscovy (1533–84); a successful ruler, who conquered Kazan and Astrakhan and added Siberia to his dominions; was subject to fits of rage in one of which he killed his son; **Ivan V** (1666–96), associated as tsar from 1682 with his half-brother Peter the Great; **Ivan VI** (1740–64), emperor of Russia (1740–1); imprisoned from 1742 until his death.

I've (īv) *contr.* I have.

-ive *suffix.* Forming adjectives meaning "tending to, having the nature of" (*active, evasive*), and nouns (*captive, directive*).

Ives (īvz), **James Merritt**: see CURRIER AND IVES.

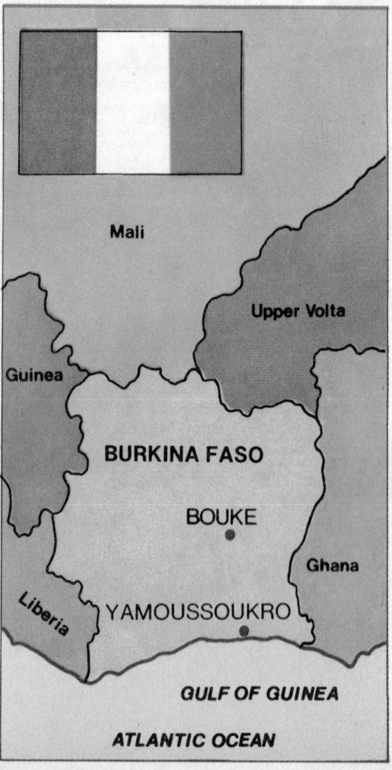

*The **Ivory Coast,** a former French colony, is one of the most stable and prosperous of the West African states. Its main products are cocoa and timber. Below: Pottery market at Adjame. Below right: Map and flag of the country.*

i·vo·ry (ī´vərē, īv´rē) *n.* (pl. **-ries**). 1. Hard white fine-grained substance (dentine of exceptional hardness) composing main part of tusks of elephant, hippopotamus, walrus, and narwhal; ~ **tower**, situation or attitude of seclusion from the world or practical affairs (esp. of intellectual seclusion). 2. Color of ivory, ivory-white. 3. (slang, pl.) Teeth; dice, piano keys.

I·vo·ry (īvərē, īv´rē) **Coast.** Republic of W. Africa, between Liberia and Ghana; formerly a French colony; independent since 1960; capital, Yamoussoukro.

i·vy (ī´vē) *n.* (pl. **i·vies**). Climbing or trailing evergreen shrub (*Hedera helix*) with dark green shining leaves, usu. five-angled; any of various other climbing or creeping plants, such as POISON ivy; **Ivy League**, association of northeastern U.S. colleges: Brown, Columbia, Cornell, Dartmouth, Harvard, Princeton, University of Pennsylvania, and Yale; (*adj.*) of or like Ivy League traditions.

***Ivory** is prized for its beauty, durability and suitability for carving. Tusks of African elephants, like this one, average about 6 ft. in length and weigh about 100 lbs. per pair. The tusks of the female Indian elephant are rarely visible.*

I·wo Ji·ma (ē´wō jē´mə, ē´wō). Middle and largest of the Japanese Volcano Islands in the Pacific Ocean, S. of Japan; scene of severe fighting during World War II, when island was completely taken by U.S. forces; returned to Japan, 1968.

I.W.W. *abbrev.* Industrial Workers of the World.

Ix·i·on (ĭk´sēən). (Gk. myth.) King of Thessaly, father of the Centaurs; tried to seduce Hera, and was condemned to be bound to a fiery wheel revolving unceasingly through the underworld.

-ize *suffix.* Forming verbs meaning (1) treat in a specified way (*patronize, monopolize*); (2) follow specified practice (*gourmandize*); (3) bring or come into specified state (*vaporize, Anglicize*); (4) treat or act according to method (*pasteurize*); (5) provide or affect with (*oxidize, magnetize*).

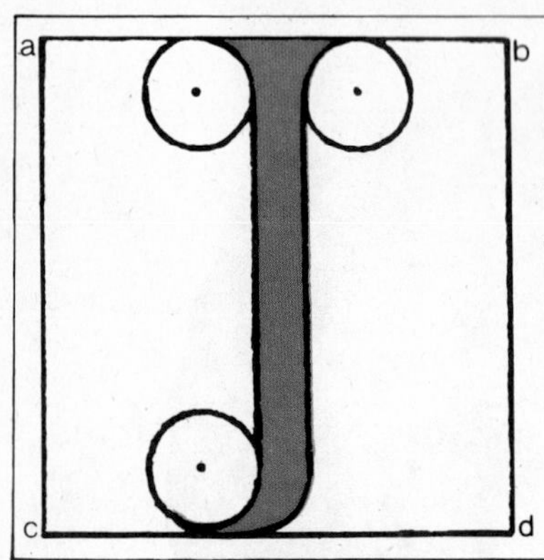

The letter J was unknown as an alphabetic character until the 14th century. The letter J emerged through the ornamental lengthening of I in medieval manuscripts particularly when it appeared as an initial or with another i. It gradually acquired the value of a consonant.

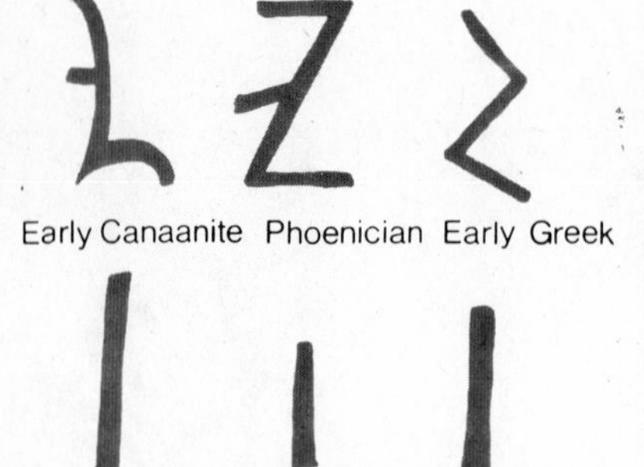

J, j (jā) (pl. **J's, j's** or **Js, js**). Tenth letter of modern English alphabet, a late modification of I; in form, i with a tail (final i was freq. written thus in manuscripts); in modern English representing a voiced composite sound (dzh), corresponding to the voiceless *tsh*.

J *abbrev.* (phys.) Joule(s).

J. *abbrev.* (cards) Jack; judge; justice.

J.A. *abbrev.* Judge Advocate.

jab (jăb) *v.t.* (**jabbed, jab·bing**). Poke roughly; stab; thrust (thing) abruptly (*into*). ~ *n.* Abrupt stabbing blow with pointed thing or fist. **jab'bing·ly** *adv.*

jab·ber (jăb'*er*) *v.* Speak volubly and with little sense; utter (words) rapidly and indistinctly; chatter, as monkeys etc. ~ *n.* Jabbering talk or sound. **jab'ber·er** *n.*

jab·i·ru (jăb'ĭrōō) *n.* Large white, wading stork, esp. *Jabiru mycteria* of tropical Amer.

jab·o·ran·di (jăb*o*răn'dē) *n.* (pl. **-dis**). Any of several tropical Amer. shrubs of genus *Pilocarpus*; dried leaflets of certain of these, esp. *P. jaborandi*, yielding pilocarpine, a sudorific.

ja·bot (zhăbō'; *Brit.* zhăb'ō) *n.* Ornamental frill on front of woman's bodice; frill on man's shirt front.

ja·ça·na (zhahs*a*nah') *n.* Tropical wading bird of family Jacanidae, including *Jaçana spinosa*, occas. in Florida and Texas, and having very long toes enabling it to walk on floating plants.

jac·a·ran·da (jăk*a*răn'd*a*) *n.* 1. Any of various tropical Amer. timber trees with heavy dark wood. 2. Tree of genus *J~*, with trumpet-shaped blue flowers.

jack (jăk) *n.* 1. (usu. **J~**) Fellow; **every man** ~, (colloq.) every individual man; STEEPLEjack; **J~ Tar, ~-tar**, sailor. 2. (cards) Playing card carrying the picture of a servant or soldier, knave. 3. Machine for lifting and supporting weights from below; part of various machines; in spinet, harpsichord, etc., wooden upright fixed to back of key lever and fitted with quill for plucking string; (elect.) device for connecting one set of wires to a corresponding set by the insertion of a single plug. 4. Male of various animals (so JACKASS); pike, esp. young or small. 5. Ship's flag, smaller than ensign, esp. one flown from jackstaff, indicating nationality; **Union J~**: see UNION. 6. (pl. construed as sing.) Game played with set of small, six-pointed metal objects. 7. (slang) Money. 8. **jack'boot**, large boot coming above knee; **jack'daw**, small Eurasian crow (*Corvus monedula*), easily tamed and taught to imitate sound of words; **Jack Frost**, frost personified; **jack'-**

***The jacana** is also called the lily-trotter or lotus bird. It has long spidery toes which are equipped with straight claws for walking on vegetation. It is found in tropical regions.*

*The **jackal** is a nocturnal animal, which often follows lions and other large cats in order to finish a carcass when the larger animal has eaten its fill. When hunting in packs it can kill antelopes and sheep.*

***Andrew Jackson,** 7th U.S. president, was elected to the Senate in 1822. His first run for office failed but he was elected in 1824 and then again in 1828 for a second term.*

hammer, pneumatic hammer; **jack-in-the-box** (pl. **-box·es**), toy figure that springs out of box when opened; **jack-in-the-pulpit** (pl. **-pul·pits**), plant (*Arisaema triphyllum*) of eastern N. America, having an upright flower spike partly enclosed by a hoodlike spathe; **jack'knife** (pl. **-knives**), large pocket clasp knife; dive in which diver touches feet or ankles with hands; **jack'knife** (*v.i.*) (**-knifed, -knif·ing**), double like folding knife; **jack'leg** (*adj.*), (slang) not trained for one's work; incompetent; makeshift; without standards; unscrupulous; **jack-of-all-trades**, (pl. **jacks-**), one who can turn his hand to anything; **~-o'-lantern** (pl. **-terns**), hollowed-out pumpkin lantern with a carved face; **jack pine**, evergreen tree (*Pinus bankstana*) of northern N. America, having short needles and numerous cones; **jack'pot**, (in poker) pool that cannot be opened until some player has two jacks or better in his hand; cumulative stakes or prize in lottery etc.; **hit the jackpot**, (slang) have sudden success; **jack rabbit**, large hare of western N. America with very long ears and legs; **jack'screw**, machine for lifting heavy loads, operated by turning screw; **jack'snipe** (pl. **-snipes**, collect. **-snipe**), small Old World species of snipe (*Lymnocryptes minima*); **jack'straw**, thin splinter of wood, plastic, etc., used in game (pl.) in which heap of these is to be removed one at a time without disturbing the others; **Jack Tar**: see def. 1; **Jack the Ripper**, undiscovered murderer of women in London (1888–91), who mutilated his victims. **jack** *v.t.* Hoist (*up*) with mechanical jack etc.; usu. **~ up**, raise (prices, confidence, in). [*Jack*, fam. form of name *John*]

jack·al (jăk'*a*l, -awl) *n.* (pl. **-als**, collect. **-al**). 1. Any of several members of the dog family found wild in Asia and Africa, living on carrion and small animals. 2. Person who does subordinate preparatory work or drudgery for another (because jackals were formerly believed to hunt up lion's prey for him). [Turk. *chakāl*]

jack·a·napes (jăk'*a*nāps) *n.* 1. (archaic) (Tame) ape or monkey. 2. Impertinent young fellow; coxcomb.

jack·ass (jăk'ăs) *n.* 1. Male ass or donkey. 2. Stupid person.

*The **Jacob's ladder** or greek valerian has loose clusters of drooping flowers, which are funnel-shaped and usually blue, violet or white. It grows up to 3 ft. tall.*

jack·et (jăk'ĭt) *n.* 1. Short coat, coatlike garment for upper part of body; **life ~**: see LIFE. 2. Any outer coat or covering, as skin of potato. 3. Outer covering around boiler etc. to protect it or cool it or keep in heat. 4. Wrapper around book. **jacket** *v.t.* Cover with jacket. **jack'et·ed, jack'et·less** *adjs.*

Jack·son[1] (jăk'son). Capital and largest city of Mississippi, in the SW. central part, on the Pearl River.

Jack·son[2] (jăk's*o*n), **Andrew** (1767–1845). "Old Hickory," U.S. soldier and politician; became national hero as a successful Indian fighter and defender of New Orleans against the British in War of 1812; seventh president of U.S. 1829–37; during his administration he introduced the spoils system, paid off the national debt, and vetoed the charter of the United States Bank.

Jack·son[3] (jăk's*o*n), **Thomas Jonathan** (1824–63). "Stonewall Jackson," Amer. general; Lee's chief assistant in Civil War; commanded Confederate troops at Bull Run and Shenandoah Valley; was accidentally killed by the fire of his own men at Chancellorsville.

Jack·son·ville (jăk's*o*nvĭl). City in NE. Florida near the mouth of the St. Johns River; Confederates used it as a base for blockade running during Civil War.

Ja·cob (jā'k*o*b). Hebrew patriarch, son of Isaac and Rebecca, younger twin brother of Esau, and traditional founder of Israel (Gen. 25–60); **~'s ladder**, ladder between earth and heaven, with angels ascending and descending, which Jacob saw in a dream at Bethel

Jacobean architecture is exemplified in Blickling Hall, Norfolk, built between 1616 and 1624. Its tall chimneys, towers at each corner, decorated stonework and symmetrical plan are typical of the Jacobean style.

(Gen. 28); hence, rope ladder with wooden rungs for ascending ship's rigging; also, blue-flowered perennial plant (*Polemonium caeruleum*) with closely pinnate leaves giving ladderlike appearance.

Jac·o·be·an (jăkobē′an) *adj.* Of the reign of James I of England (1603–25); of the style of building or furniture in England in early 17th c. [L. *Jacobus* James]

Jac·o·bin (jăk′obĭn) *n.* 1. Dominican friar, esp. French member of the order, from their 1st convent near church of St. Jacques in Paris. 2. Member of radical French political club founded 1789 in the old Jacobin convent in Paris, and responsible, under Robespierre, for the Reign of Terror; dissolved 1799. 3. Sympathizer with principles of Jacobins in French Revolution; extreme radical, revolutionary.

Jac·o·bite (jă′kobīt) *n.* Adherent of James II of England after his abdication or supporter of Stuart pretenders after revolution of 1688.

Jac·quard (jăk′ard, jăkard′; *Fr.* zhăkăr′), **Joseph Marie** (1752–1834). French inventor, improver of the loom; ~ **loom**, loom for mechanically weaving fabric of figured patterns (**jacquard**) by means of an endless belt of cards punched with holes arranged to form the required pattern.

jade[1] (jād) *n.* Poor or worn-out horse; (archaic) hussy. **jad′ed** *adj.* Worn out, weary; dulled.

jade[2] (jād) *n.* 1. Nephrite, a hard translucent light green, bluish, or whitish stone, a silicate of calcium and magnesium, used for ornaments etc. 2. Jadeite, a silicate of sodium and aluminum, closely resembling nephrite in appearance. 3. Carved piece of jadeite or nephrite. 4. (also ~ **green**) Light green. [Span. (*piedra de*) *ijada* (stone of) the colic, f. L. *ilia* flank]

jade·ite (jā′dīt). See JADE[2], def. 2.

Jaf·fa (jăf′a; *Heb.* yah′fah). City and port of Israel, combined with Tel Aviv into one municipality; (also ~ **orange**) large seedless orange grown near there.

jag[1] (jăg) *n.* Sharp projection. ~ *v.t.* (**jag·ged, jag·ging**). Cut, tear, break, in uneven manner, make indentations in. **jag·ged** (jăg′ĭd) *adj.* **jag′ged·ly** *adv.* **jag′ged·ness** *n.* **jag′gy** *adj.* (**-gi·er, -gi·est**).

jag[2] (jăg) *n.* (dial.) Small load or portion; (slang) spree, bout.

J.A.G. *abbrev.* Judge Advocate General.

Jag·an·nath (jŭg′anaht, -nawt),

*The earliest **jade** carvings in China date from about 2000 B.C. Abrasives such as quartz are used to work the stone into the intricate patterns seen on this jade bowl. In Chinese tradition the stone was 'a mirror of virtues'.*

Jag·an·na·tha (jŭganaht′ha), **Jag·ga·nath** (jŭg′anaht, -nawt). (Hindu myth.) Title of KRISHNA; = JUGGERNAUT.

jag·uar (jăg′war; *Brit.* also jăg′ūer) *n.* (pl. **-uars,** collect. **-uar**). Large carnivorous spotted feline quadruped (*Panthera onca*), of tropical America.

Jah·veh, Jah·ve (yah′vĕ, -vā), **Jah·weh, Jah·we** (yah′wĕ, -wā) = YAHWEH. **Jah·vist** (yah′vĭst), **Jah·wist** (yah′wĭst) = YAHWIST.

Jah·vis·tic (yahvĭs′tĭk), **Jah·wis·tic** (yahwĭs′tĭk) *adjs.*

jai a·lai (hī′lī, hī′alī, hīalī′). Game played in a three-wall court and similar to handball, in which players strap a long curved basket to the arm to catch a small, hard ball and throw it against the wall.

jail (jāl) *n.* Public prison for detention of persons committed by process of law; **jail′bird**, (colloq.) person who is or has been kept in jail; prisoner; **jail′break**, escape from jail; **jail′er**, person in charge of jail or prisoners in it. **jail** *v.t.* Put in jail, imprison.

Jain (jīn) *n.* Member of ascetic non-Brahminical Hindu sect, chiefly of India, established in 6th

*The **jaguar** resembles the leopard but is larger and more heavily built. It is a solitary predator and stalks animals such as deer, tapirs, fish and birds. It is swift and agile and is found in tropical America.*

c. B.C., with doctrines closely resembling those of Buddhism. **Jain′ism** *n.* [Sansk. *jina* a Buddha (*ji* conquer, overcome)]

Jai·pur (jī′poor). Commercial city in NW. India noted for its walls and fortifications.

Ja·kar·ta (j*a*kar̄′t*a*): = DJAKARTA.

ja·lop·y (j*a*lŏp′ē) *n.* (pl. **-lop·ies**). (colloq.) Old, dilapidated automobile; (transf.) battered old aircraft.

jal·ou·sie (jăl′*o*sē; *Brit.* zhăl′-ōōzē) *n.* Blind, shutter, with slats sloping upward from without. [Fr., = "jealousy"]

jam[1] (jăm) *v.* (**jammed, jam·ming**). 1. Squeeze between two surfaces or bodies; fill up, block (passage etc.) by crowding into it. 2. Wedge (part of machine) so that it cannot work; become so wedged; ~ **on**, apply (brakes) forcibly. 3. (radio etc.) Cause interference with. **jam** *n.* Crush, squeeze; stoppage (of machine etc.) due to this; crowded mass, esp. accumulation of logs in river or traffic in street etc.; (slang) awkward situation, fix; **~-packed**, very full; ~ **session**, improvised playing by group of jazz musicians.

jam[2] (jăm) *n.* Preserves made by boiling whole fruit and sugar to a thick consistency.

Ja·mai·ca (j*a*mā′k*a*). Island of 4,411 sq. mi. (11,425 sq. km) in the Caribbean Sea S. of Cuba; discovered by Columbus in 1494 and ruled by Spain until captured by England in 1655; independent since 1962; capital, Kingston. **Ja·mai′can** *adj.* & *n.*

jamb (jăm) *n.* Side post of doorway, window, etc.

jam·bo·ree (jămb*o*rē′) *n.* Noisy celebration; large rally or assembly, as of Scouts, political party, etc.

James[1] (jāmz). Name of several persons in New Testament: 1. Son of Zebedee and elder brother of St. John the Evangelist (Mark 3); one of the 12 Apostles and the first to be martyred (44 A.D.); called **St. ~ the Great** or **Greater**; commemorated July 25; patron saint of Spain. 2. Person described as brother of Jesus (cf. Mark 6, Gal. 1); traditionally identified with St. James the Less(er); a leader of the church at Jerusalem until put to death by the Sanhedrin in 62 A.D.; **(Epistle of) St. ~**, book of New Testament traditionally ascribed to him. 3. One of the 12 Apostles, son of Alphaeus; called **St. ~ the Less**; commemorated May 1.

James[2] (jāmz). Name of 7 Stuart

*Strictly speaking a **jalopy** is a dilapidated old car. This Veteran Model T Ford is a shining example of what a renovated jalopy can look like.*

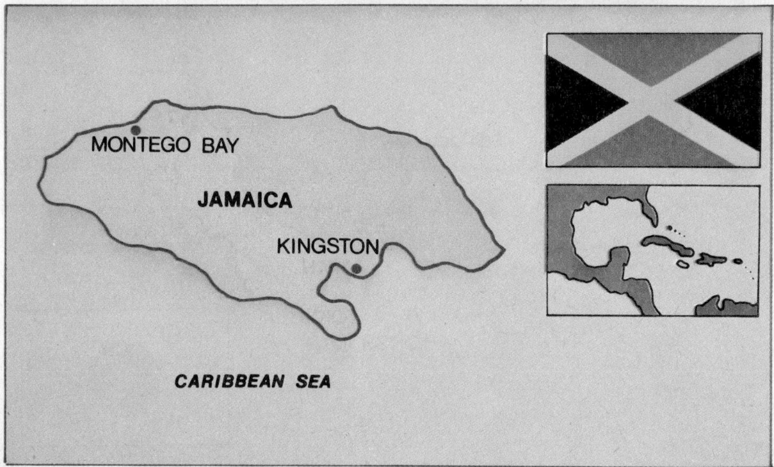

***Jamaica** has an important tourist trade and is the world's largest producer of bauxite. Coffee grown in the island's Blue Mountains is also highly prized. The country's map and flag are shown here.*

kings of Scotland: **James I** (1394–1437); son of Robert III; reigned 1406–37, held captive in England till 1424; **James II** (1430–60), his son, reigned 1437–60; **James III** (1451–88), his son, reigned 1460–1488; **James IV** (1473–1513), his son, reigned 1488–1513; married Margaret Tudor, daughter of Henry VII of England; invaded England, 1513, and was killed at Flodden Field; **James V** (1512–42), son of James IV and father of Mary Queen of Scots; reigned 1513–42; **James VI** and **VII**: see next entry.

James[3] (jāmz). Name of two Stuart kings of England and Scotland: **James I** of England and **VI** of Scotland (1566–1625), son of Lord Darnley and Mary Queen of Scots; on her abdication, became king of Scotland (1567–1625) and, on death of Elizabeth I, king of England (1603–25); patron of the King James Bible; **James II** of England and **VII** of Scotland (1633–1701), son of Charles I and grandson of James I; succeeded his brother, Charles II, 1685; had Catholic sympathies; fled to France, and was succeeded, 1688, by his Protestant son-in-law William of Orange.

James[4] (jāmz) (1688–1766). James Francis Edward Stuart, son of JAMES[3] II: see Old PRETENDER.

James[5] (jāmz), **Henry** (1843–1916). Amer. novelist living mainly in England; author of *The American, Daisy Miller, The Portrait of a Lady, The Wings of the Dove, The Turn of the Screw,* etc.

James[6] (jāmz), **Jesse Woodson** (1847–82). Amer. outlaw leader, railroad and bank robber; **James boys**, gang of outlaws led by Jesse and his brother, Frank, 1843–1915.

James[7] (jāmz), **William** (1842–1910). Amer. philosopher and psychologist, elder brother of Henry JAMES[5]; formulator of theory of pragmatism: see PRAGMATIC; author of *The Principles of Psychology, The Varieties of Religious Experience,* etc.

James·town (jāmz′town). 1. Village in E. Virginia on the James River; first permanent English settlement in America, 1607. 2. Capital of St. Helena, in the S. Atlantic off Africa.

Jam·mu and Kash·mir (jŭm′-ōō, Kăsh′mēr). Former princely State on NW. border of India, divided into two parts, 1949: the NW. controlled by Pakistan, with capital at Muzaffarabad, and the rest made an Indian State with capitals at Srinagar (in summer) and Jammu (in winter), sovereignty disputed by India and Pakistan since 1947.

Jan. *abbrev.* January.

jan·gle (jăng′gel) *v.* (**-gled, -gling**). Make harsh metallic noise; cause (bell etc.) to do this. ~ *n.* Harsh metallic noise, discordant sound. **jan′gler** *n.* **jan′gly** *adj.*

James I of England was the first of the Stuart kings and the son of Mary Queen of Scots. The Authorized Version of the Bible was published (1611) during his reign.

jan·is·sar·y (jăn′ĭsĕrē) (pl. **-sar·ies**), **jan·i·zar·y** (jăn′ĭzĕrē) (pl. **-zar·ies**) *ns.* (hist.) One of body of Turkish infantry forming sultan's guards and main fighting force of Turkish army from 14th c. to 1826. [Turk. *yeni tsheri* new soldiery]

jan·i·tor (jăn′ĭter) *n.* (fem. **jan·i·tress** pr. jăn′ĭtrĭs). Caretaker of building, office, etc. charged with maintaining and esp. cleaning it. **jan·i·to·ri·al** (jănĭtōr′ēal, -tōr′-) *adj.*

Jan·sen (jăn′sen), **Cornelius** (1585–1638). Dutch R.C. theologian and bishop of Ypres in Flanders.

Jan·sen·ism (jăn′senĭzem) *n.* Theological principles of Cornelius Jansen maintaining that the natural human will is perverse and incapable of good, capacity for the love of God can be attained only by conversion, and that God converts whom he pleases; opposed by the Jesuits and condemned as heretical by several popes esp. Clement X; flourished chiefly in France (17th and 18th centuries). **Jan′sen·ist** *n.*

Jan·u·ar·y (jăn′ūĕrē) (pl. **-ar·ies**). First month of Gregorian (11th of Julian) calendar, with 31 days. [L. *(mensis) Januarius* (month) of JANUS]

Ja·nus (jā′nus). (Rom. myth.) Ancient Italian deity, guardian of gates and doorways and of the state in time of war; represented with two faces, one at front and one at back of his head.

Jap (jăp) *n.* (slang, usu. derog.) Japanese.

Jap. *abbrev.* Japan; Japanese.

Ja·pan (japăn′). Country in W. Pacific off E. coast of Asia, consisting of four main islands covering 143,750 sq. mi. (372, 313 sq. km), Honshu, Hokkaido, Kyushu, and Shikoku; capital, Tokyo; once feudalistic society; governed by shogun (military dictator) and emperor 12th to 19th c.; 1st contact with western civilization and Christianity, 1542, but trade with foreign countries restricted to port of Nagasaki; Commodore Perry entered Tokyo Bay with Amer. fleet, 1854, securing first commercial treaty; parliamentary government retaining emperor established, 1889; after short war with China, acquired Formosa (Taiwan), Pescadores, and part of southern Manchuria; defeated Russia and gained additional terri-

***Japan,** whose map and flag appear below, is the leading trading nation in Asia. It has made an astonishing economic recovery since 1945. 1. Rice is Japan's leading crop. 2. Japanese photographic equipment being assembled in a factory. Cameras are a major export item. 3. These 'husband and wife' rocks are linked with a rope, a symbol of their unity. 4. The famous Miyajima shrine is built on stilts, so that at high tide it seems to float.*

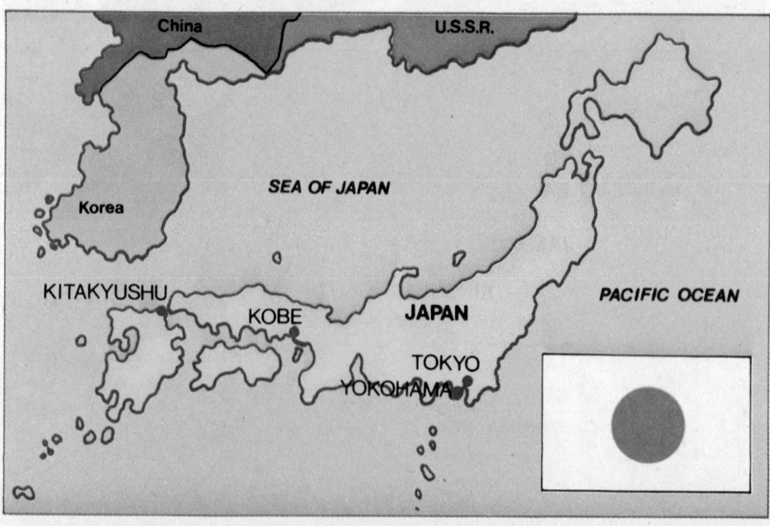

2

3

4

tory in Manchuria; joined Axis Pact, 1936; invaded China, 1937, attacked Pearl Harbor, 1941, provoking U.S. entry into World War II; surrendered 1945, after destruction of Hiroshima and Nagasaki by U.S. atomic bombs; set up new constitution with bicameral government and elected prime minister, 1947, with emperor as figurehead; large export industry includes cotton textiles, electronic instruments, steel, automobiles, and ships; **Sea of ~**, part of W. Pacific Ocean between Japan on E. and mainland Asia on W.; ~ **Trench**, depression in the Pacific Ocean off the E. coast of Japan, reaching depths over 30,000 ft. (9,144 m).

ja·pan (j*a*păn′) *n.* Hard black lacquer or enamel originating in Japan and used to produce a glossy finish; varnish, etc. in imitation of this; object decorated with this. ~ *v.t.* (**-panned, -pan·ning**). Cover with japan; make black and glossy as with japan.

Jap·a·nese (jăp*a*nēz′, -nēs′) *adj.* Of Japan, its people, or language; ~ **beetle**, bronze and green beetle (*Popillia japonica*), orig. from E. Asia but introduced into N. America, where the larvae and adults are major plant pests; ~ **cherry**, hybrid flowering cherry tree with pink or white, usu. double, flowers; ~ **iris**, tall, beardless iris (*Iris kaempferi*), native of Asia, widely cultivated for its flat, showy flowers; ~ **maple**, small tree (*Acer palmatum*) orig. of E. Asia, prized for its foliage, which is deeply lobed and which turns crimson in the fall. **Japanese** *n.* (pl. **-nese**). 1. Japanese person. 2. Language of Japan, which is agglutinative and written in Chinese ideographs with characters of a syllabary called *kana* for the agglutinative and inflectional endings. [Chinese *Jih-pun* sunrise (*jih* sun, *pun* origin)]

jape (jāp) *n.* & *v.i.* (**japed, japing**). Jest, quip, joke. **jap′er·y** *n.*

Ja·pheth (jā′fĭth). Third son of Noah (Gen. 10); traditional ancestor of the peoples living around Mediterranean. **Ja·phet·ic** (j*a*fĕt′ĭk) *adj.*

Ja·pu·rá (zhahpo͞orah′). River of S. Amer. flowing SE. 1,500 mi. (2,414 km), from the Andes Mountains in SW. Colombia to the Amazon in NW. Brazil.

jar[1] (jar̄) *n.* Harsh sound; discord; jolt; shock. ~ *v.* (**jarred, jar·ring**). 1. Make discordant sound, make grating impression (*on*, person, his ear, etc.). 2. Be at variance, disagree (*with*). **jar′ring·ly** *adv.*

jar[2] (jar̄) *n.* Cylindrical glass or pottery vessel with a wide mouth and usu. without handles; amount in this.

jar·din·iere (jar̄d*i*nēr′, zhar̄dĭnyar̄′) *n.* 1. Ornamental pot or stand for display of plants. 2. Dish of mixed vegetables served alone or as garnish with meat. [Fr.]

jar·gon[1] (jar̄′g*o*n) *n.* Unintelligible or meaningless words; technical or specialized language of a profession, group, etc.; hybrid language or dialect, patois.

jar·gon[2] (jar̄′gŏn), **jar·goon** (jar̄go͞on′) *ns.* Translucent, colorless, or smoky variety of zircon found in Sri Lanka.

jarl (yar̄l) *n.* (hist.) Scandinavian or Danish chieftain.

Jas. *abbrev.* James.

jas·mine, jas·min (jăz′mĭn, jăs′-), **jes·sa·mine** (jĕs′*a*mĭn) *ns.* Shrub of genus *Jasminum* with white or yellow salver-shaped flowers, esp. **common** or **white** ~ (*J. officinale*), and of genus *Gelsemium*, esp. **yellow** or **Carolina** jessamine (*G. sempervirens*). [Pers. *yāsimīn*]

Ja·son (jā′s*o*n). (Gk. legend) Son of Aeson, king of Iolcos; the throne was usurped by Pelias, who promised to surrender it if Jason would bring him the Golden Fleece (see GOLDEN); Jason sailed with the Argonauts and obtained the fleece with the aid of MEDEA, whom he married.

jas·per (jăs′p*e*r) *n.* Opaque variety of quartz, usu. red, yellow, or brown.

Jat (jaht, jawt) *n.* Member of an Indo-Aryan people widely distributed in NW. India.

ja·to (jā′tō) *n.* (pl. **-tos**). (aeron.) Jet-assisted takeoff; auxiliary jet engine(s) to provide temporary extra thrust at takeoff.

jaun·dice (jawn′dĭs) *n.* Yellow discoloration of skin and normally white part of eyeball due to the presence of pigments in the blood that are normally excreted in the bile, often caused by an obstructed bile duct; this condition; disordered or discolored vision as characteristic of this. **jaun′diced** *adj.* Affected with jaundice; (fig.) colored by envy, low spirits, etc.

__Jasmine__ is found in warm and temperate climates. It is a climbing shrubby plant with fragrant yellow or white flowers. It is used in the manufacture of perfume.

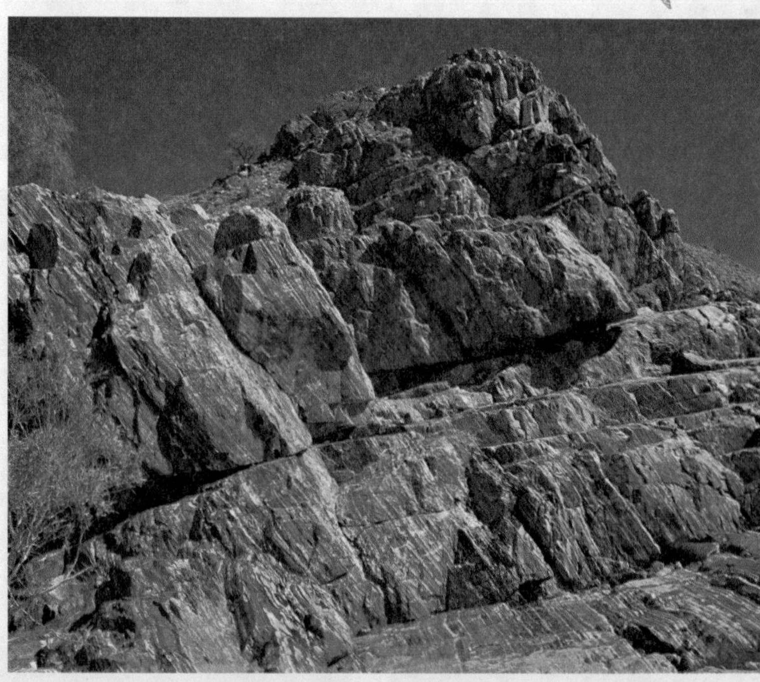

__Jasper__ is usually brick red to brownish red in color. Medicinal values attributed to it include the belief that it strengthened the stomach of the wearer. This jasper rock is in Marble Bar, Western Australia.

*The island of **Java** is the political, economic and cultural center of Indonesia. It is a region of high volcanic mountains like this one (left). Center left: Map of Java.*

jaunt (jawnt) *n.* Excursion, esp. for pleasure. ~ *v.i.* Take a jaunt.

jaun·ty (jawn′tē) *adj.* (**-ti·er, -ti·est**). Having or affecting easy sprightliness, airy self-satisfaction. **jaun′ti·ly** *adv.* **jaun′ti·ness** *n.*

Jav. *abbrev.* Javanese.

Ja·va (jah′va). Large island of Malay archipelago, first settled by Dutch in 17th c. and now part of Indonesia; ~ **man**, fossil hominid *Homo erectus* (formerly *Pithecanthropus erectus*), whose remains were first found in Java in 1891; ~ **Sea**, shallow area of the Pacific Ocean N. of the island of Java and S. of Borneo. **Jav·a·nese** (jăvanēz′, -nēs′) *adj.* & *n.* (Native, inhabitant, Malayan language) of Java.

jav·e·lin (jăv′lĭn, -elĭn) *n.* Light spear thrown with the hand.

jaw (jaw) *n.* 1. One of the bones or sets of bones forming the framework of the mouth and carrying the teeth in vertebrates; in sing. usu. = lower jaw rather than upper; (pl.) bones etc. of mouth including teeth; mouth. 2. (pl.) Structure in invertebrates analogous to vertebrates' jaws. 3. (pl.) Seizing parts of machine, e.g. vise. 4. **jaw′bone**, each of the two bones forming lower jaw in most mammals; these two combined into one in others; **jaw′-breaker**, (colloq.) word hard to pronounce; very hard round candy, often with chewing gum in the center. **jaw** *v.* (colloq.) Speak, esp. at tedious length; scold, lecture *at* (person).

jay (jā) *n.* Any of several birds of the crow family (Corvidae), often having loud, rasping calls, esp. the BLUE JAY and CANADA JAY; **Jay′-hawker**, nickname for Kansan; (sometimes **j** ~) Missouri-Kansas border fighter for abolition of slavery before and during Amer. Civil War; **jay′vee**, (colloq.) member of a junior varsity team; **jay′walker**, pedestrian who crosses street without observing regulations; so **jay′walking**.

Jay (jā), **John** (1745–1829). Amer. statesman and diplomat; president, Continental Congress, 1778–9; co-author with Hamilton and Madison of the *Federalist* articles, urging ratification of the Constitution; first chief justice of U.S. Supreme Court, 1789–95; governor of New York, 1795–1801.

Jay·cee (jā′sē′) *n.* Member of a junior chamber of commerce.

jazz (jăz) *n.* Syncopated music, of U.S. black origin, with charac-

***Javelin** throwing was a field event in the ancient Olympics as well as in the modern Games. Ruth Francis is seen here at the 1972 Olympics.*

teristic harmony and ragtime rhythm; (slang) pretentious talk, lies; nonsense; ~ **band**, orchestra playing jazz. **jazz** *v.* Play jazz; ~ **up**, (slang) enliven; make more colorful, interesting, etc. **jazz'i·ness** *n.* **jazz'i·ly** *adv.* **jazz'y** *adj.* (**jazz·i·er, jazz·i·est**).

J.C.S., JCS *abbrevs.* Joint Chiefs of Staff.

jct. *abbrev.* Junction.

JD *abbrev.* Juvenile delinquent.

J.D. *abbrev.* Doctor of Jurisprudence; Doctor of Laws; Department of Justice; juvenile delinquent.

JDL *abbrev.* Jewish Defense League.

Je. *abbrev.* June.

jea·lous (jĕl'*us*) *adj.* 1. Solicitous for preservation *of* (rights etc.); (bibl., of God) intolerant of unfaithfulness; (of inquiry etc.) vigilant. 2. Apprehensive of being displaced in the love or goodwill *of* (wife, lover, friend, etc.; also *of* supposed rival); envious (*of*). **jeal'ous·ly** *adv.* **jeal'ous·y** *n.* (pl. **-ous·ies**). Quality, state, of being jealous.

jean (jēn) *n.* Heavy twilled cotton fabric; (pl.) garment, esp. western-cut pants, of this. [prob. f. Fr. *Gênes* Genoa]

Je·bel Mu·sa (jĕb'*e*l mo͞o'sah). Mountain rising 2,775 ft. (846 m), in NW. Morocco on the Strait of Gibraltar; one of the Pillars of Hercules.

jeep (jēp) *n.* Small, strong, unadorned, all-purpose motor vehicle with four-wheel drive and ¼-ton capacity developed for the armed forces during World War II. **J~**, (trademark) similar vehicle for civil use. [said to have been f. *g p*, initials of *general purposes*]

jeer (jēr) *v.* Scoff derisively (*at*); deride. ~ *n.* Derisive taunt. **jeer'ing·ly** *adv.*

Jef·fers (jĕf'*e*rz), **(John) Robinson** (1887–1962). Amer. poet noted for narrative poems based on biblical and classical sources; author of *The Roan Stallion, Tamar and Other Poems*, etc.

Jef·fer·son[1] (jĕf'*e*rs*o*n), **Thomas** (1743–1826). Amer. statesman and diplomat; champion of states' rights; member of Continental Congress; principal drafter and a signer of the Declaration of Independence; U.S. minister to France, 1785–9, secretary of State, 1790–3, vice president, under John Adams, 1797–1801; as third elected president of U.S., 1801–9, he pushed through the Louisiana Purchase and upheld the Embargo Act.

Jef·fer·son[2] (jĕf'*e*rs*o*n) **City.** Capital of Missouri, in the central part on the Missouri River.

je·had: see JIHAD.

Je·hosh·a·phat (j*e*hŏsh'*a*făt, -hŏs'-). King of Judah, son of Asa (1 Kings 22; 2 Chron. 20).

*The Jefferson Memorial in Washington D.C. commemorates the architect of America's Declaration of Independence, **Thomas Jefferson,** 3rd president of the U.S. Dedicated in 1943 on the 200th anniversary of his birth, it lies in 18 acres of parkland.*

Je·ho·vah (j*e*hō'v*a*). 1. Name of God in Old Testament (Exod. 6; cf. YAHWEH). 2. (in Christian use) God; **~'s Witnesses**, actively evangelical sect founded *c*1879 by Charles Taze Russell (1852–1916) of Pittsburgh, Pa. and believing in the imminent arrival of the millennium. **Je·ho·vist** (j*e*hō'vĭst) = YAHWIST. **Je·ho·vis·tic** (jēhō-vĭs'tĭk) *adj.* [erron. rendering of Heb. JHVH]

Je·hu (jē'hū). King of Israel, son of Jehoshaphat, famous for furious driving of chariot (2 Kings 9).

je·june (jĭjo͞on') *adj.* Meager, not nourishing; insipid; childish; weak. **je·june'ly** *adv.* **je·june'ness** *n.*

je·ju·num (jĭjo͞o'n*u*m) *n.* (anat.) Part of small intestine between duodenum and ileum.

Je·kyll (jĕk'ĭl), **Henry.** Hero of R. L. Stevenson's story "The Strange Case of Dr. Jekyll and Mr. Hyde" (1886); handsome and well-respected, he transformed himself by a potion into the dwarfish and detestable Edward Hyde, in whom was embodied only the evil side of Jekyll; hence, **~-and-Hyde character**, dual personality.

jell (jĕl) *v.i.* (colloq.) Set as jelly; (fig.) take shape.

jel·ly (jĕl'ē) *n.* (pl. **-lies**). Soft stiffish substance, usu. semitransparent, made of gelatin or other gelatinous substance, esp. as food usu. made with meat or with fruit juices; concentrated usu. fruit-flavored preparation of this for dissolving; anything of similar consistency; **jel'lybean**, bean-shaped candy consisting of firm filling and hard sugar coating; **jel'lyfish** (pl. **-fish·es**, collect. **-fish**), any of numerous free-swimming marine coelenterates, having a jellylike body with saucer shape and long tentacles; medusa; (colloq.) spineless person; **jelly roll**, thin flat sponge cake spread with fruit jelly or jam and rolled up. **jelly** *v.* (**-lied, -ly·ing**). Make into jelly; congeal. **jel·lied** (jĕl'ēd) *adj.* Made into, set in, jelly.

je ne sais quoi (zh*e* n*e* sā kwŏ'). Indefinable esp. pleasing quality. [Fr., = "I know not what"]

Jen·ghiz Khan (jĕng'gĭz kahn'): = GENGHIS KHAN.

Jen·ner (jĕn'*e*r), **Edward** (1749–1823). English physician and pioneer of vaccination.

jen·net (jĕn'ĭt) *n.* 1. Small Spanish horse. 2. Female donkey or ass.

jen·ny (jĕn'ē) *n.* (pl. **-nies**). 1. The SPINNING JENNY. 2. Female donkey. 3. Female wren; wren. [fam. form of *Jane* or *Janet*]

jeop·ard·ize (jĕp'*e*rdīz) *v.t.* (**-ized, -iz·ing**). Endanger.

jeop·ard·y (jĕp'*e*rdē) *n.* (pl.

-ard·ies). Danger, esp. of severe loss or harm. [OF. *ieu parti* divided (i.e. even) game]

Jeph·thah (jĕf′th*a*). Judge of Israel, son of Gilead; sacrificed his daughter in consequence of a vow that if victorious against the Ammonites he would sacrifice the first living thing that met him on his return (Judges 11, 12).

Jer. *abbrev.* Jeremiah (Old Testament).

Jer·bo·a (jėrbō′*a*) *n.* Member of family of rodents including the desert rat (*Dipus*) of N. Africa, with very long hind legs and tail. [Arab. *yarbu*ʿ]

jer·e·mi·ad (jĕr*e*mī′ăd) *n.* Lamentation, doleful complaint. [f. *Jeremiah*]

Jer·e·mi·ah (jĕr*e*mī′*a*), **Jer·e·mi·as** (jĕr*e*mī*a*s) (*c*650–*c*585 B.C.). Hebrew major prophet, who saw the fall of Assyria, the vassalage of Judah in turn to Egypt and Babylon, and the destruction of Jerusalem; book of Old Testament containing his prophecies; hence, doleful person, denouncer of the times.

Je·rez (hĕrĕth′). (full name ~ **de la Frontera**) Town in Andalusia, Spain, 15 mi. W. of Cadiz; center of sherry-making industry.

Jer·i·cho (jĕr′*i*kō). Ancient city near N. end of the Dead Sea; first Canaanite city attacked and taken by Israelites (Joshua 6).

jerk[1] (jėrk) *n.* 1. Sharp sudden pull, twist, etc. 2. Involuntary spasmodic contraction of muscle. 3. (slang) Stupid, foolish, or insignificant person. ~ *v.* Pull, thrust, twist, etc., with a jerk; throw with suddenly arrested motion; move with a jerk. **jerk′y** *adj.* (**jerk·i·er, jerk·i·est**). **jerk′i·ly** *adv.* **jerk′i·ness** *n.*

jerk[2] (jėrk) *v.t.* Cure (esp. beef) by cutting in long slices and drying in sun. [Peruv. *echarqui* dried flesh]

jer·kin (jėr′kĭn) *n.* Man's close-fitting jacket, often of leather (hist.); sleeveless jacket.

jerk·wa·ter (jėrk′wawt*er*, -wŏt′*er*) *adj.* (colloq.) Absurdly unimportant and remote; insignificant.

Jer·o·bo·am (jĕr*o*bō′*a*m). Name of 2 kings in ancient Israel: (1) (10th c. B.C.) first king of northern Israel (I Kings 11–14), "a mighty man of valor," one "who made Israel to sin"; (2) (8th c. B.C.) king of Israel (2 Kings 14).

***Jerusalem,** the holy city of Jews and Christians, was divided between Jordan and Israel until Israel annexed the Jordanian part after the third Arab-Israeli War in 1967. The Mandelbaum Gate divides the old city from the new.*

jer·o·bo·am (jĕr*o*bō′*a*m) *n.* Large wine bottle, holding about ⅘ of a gallon (3l.). [f. JEROBOAM]

jer·ry-build (jĕr′ēbĭld) *v.* (**-built, -build·ing**). Build with poor and cheap materials. **jer′ry-built** *adj.*

jer·ry (jĕr′ē) **can.** Metal container esp. for fuel, holding 5 gallons.

jer·sey (jėr′zē) *n.* (pl. **-seys**). 1. Knitted pullover shirt worn for certain sports. 2. Machine-knitted fabric. 3. **J**~, (one of) a breed of small usu. buff-colored dairy cattle, producing milk of high fat content, orig. raised in Jersey, Channel Islands.

Je·ru·sa·lem (jer*o͞o*′s*a*lem). Ancient capital of Judea, the holy city of the Jews, sacred also to Christians and Muslims; capital of modern Israel; **the New** ~, the Heavenly City, the abode of God and the saints; ~ **artichoke**: see ARTICHOKE.

jes·sa·mine: see JASMINE.

Jesse (jĕs′ē). Father of David (1 Sam.).

jest (jĕst) *n.* Joke; witticism; fun; object of derision. ~ *v.i.* Joke, make jests. **jest′ing·ly** *adv.*

*The **jerboa,** a small nocturnal rodent, looks rather like a miniature kangaroo. It is found in the deserts and dry plains of Asia and North Africa. The desert jerboa (Jaculus) is found in N. Africa, and the four-toed in Egypt and Asia.*

jest·er (jĕs′t*er*) *n.* One who jests; (esp., hist.) professional entertainer maintained in court or noble household.

Jes·u·it (jĕzh′ōōĭt, jĕz′ū-, jĕz′ōōĭt) *n.* Member of the Society of Jesus, an order of R.C. priests founded 1534 in Paris by Ignatius Loyola, Francis Xavier, and others, to defend the church and propagate its faith. **Jes·u·it·i·cal** (jĕzhōōĭt′ĭ-k*a*l, jĕzū-, jĕzōō-) *adj.*

Je·sus (jē′z*u*s) (*c*4 B.C.–*c*30 A.D.). (also ~ **Christ**) Source of the Christian religion, accepted by Christians as son of God and as the Messiah; second person of the Trinity; born (traditionally at Bethlehem) of the Virgin Mary; began his public life at about 30; for some three years went about ancient Palestine, chiefly in Galilee, with a band of followers or disciples, teaching and healing; was then arrested in Jerusalem at the time of Passover, handed over to the Roman authorities, and condemned to death by crucifixion; the Christian doctrine is that after three days he rose from the dead; **Society of** ~: see JESUIT.

jet[1] (jĕt) *n.* Hard black coal taking brilliant polish; color of this, deep glossy black. ~ *adj.* (also ~**-black**) Deep glossy black.

jet[2] (jĕt) *n.* 1. Stream of water, steam, gas(es), etc., ejected from small opening; spout, nozzle, for emitting water etc. thus. 2. In aircraft, stream of gas ejected from rearward-facing nozzle and propelling the aircraft forward; aircraft propelled thus; hence ~ **plane,** ~**-propelled,** ~ **propulsion**, etc. 3. ~ **lag**, delayed bodily effects felt after long flight by jet aircraft (esp. owing to difference of local time); **jet′liner**, jet airplane in commercial passenger service; **jet′port**, airport designed for jet aircraft; **jet set**, wealthy elite making frequent air trips between social or business engagements; hence **jet setter**; **jet stream**, narrow current of strong westerly winds in upper troposphere. **jet** *v.* (**jet·ted, jet·ting**). Spout forth in jet(s).

This painting of ***Jesus*** *carrying the Cross is by El Greco. The artist's spiritual intensity is revealed in his use of strange colors, the elongation of the human figure and the juxtaposition of dark and light.*

jet·sam (jĕt′s*a*m) *n.* Goods thrown overboard from ship to lighten it, and (in mod. use) washed ashore.

jet·ti·son (jĕt′ĭs*o*n, -z*o*n) *n.* Throwing of goods overboard, esp. to lighten ship in distress. ~ *v.t.* Throw (goods) overboard thus; (fig.) abandon.

jet·ty[1] (jĕt′ē) *n.* (pl. **-ties**). 1. Pier or breakwater extending from shoreline out into the water to protect harbor or beach. 2. Landing pier; wharf.

jet·ty[2] (jĕt′ē) *adj.* Jet-black.

Jew (jōō) *n.* (fem., now considered offensive, **jew′ess**) Person of Hebrew descent; one whose religion is Judaism; (hist.) Hebrew of kingdom of Judah, as opp. to those of ten tribes of Israel; **Wandering** ~: see WANDERING; ~**-baiting**, systematic persecution of Jews; **jew′fish** (pl. **-fish·es**, collect. **-fish**), any of several large marine fishes of the family Serranidae, of tropical waters; **jews' harp, jew's-harp**, simple musical instrument consisting of flexible steel tongue affixed at one end to lyre-shaped metal frame, played by holding frame between teeth and striking free end of metal tongue with finger.

jew·el (jōō′*e*l) *n.* Ornament of precious stone(s), worn for personal adornment; precious stone; highly prized person or thing. ~ *v.t.* (**-eled, -el·ing,** Brit. **-elled, -el·ling**). Adorn, furnish, with jewels; fit (watch) with jewels for the pivot holes. **jew′el·er,** Brit. **jew′el·ler, jew′el·ry**, Brit. **jew′-el·ler·y** *ns.*

jew·el·weed (jōō′*e*lwēd) *n.* Any of several plants of the genus *Impatiens*, having yellow flowers sometimes marked with reddish brown spots.

Jew·ish (jōō′ĭsh) *adj.* Of the Jews; ~ **calendar**, lunar calendar in use among the Jews, adapted to the solar year by various expedients, having normally 12 months, but 13 months in leap years, which occur seven times in every cycle of

19 years; the years are reckoned from the Creation (3761 B.C.). ~ *n.* Yiddish. **Jew'ish·ness** *n.*

Jew·ry (jōō'rē, joor'ē) *n.* (pl. **-ries**). 1. (collect.) Jews. 2. (hist.) Jewish ghetto of medieval city.

Jez·e·bel (jěz'eběl, -bel). Ninth c. Phoenician princess, daughter of king of Tyre; queen of Israel as wife of Ahab; denounced by Elijah for introducing worship of Baal; killed when Jehu triumphed over Ahab; hence, (often **j**~) shameless or abandoned woman.

jg, j.g. *abbrevs.* Junior grade.

Jiang·i (jahn'shē') = KIANGSI.

Jiang·su (jang'sōō') = KIANGSU.

jib (jĭb) *n.* Triangular staysail from outer end of jib boom to foretop masthead in large ships, from bowsprit to masthead in smaller ones; **cut of person's** ~, his personal appearance; ~ **boom,** spar run out from end of bowsprit; projecting arm of crane. **jib** *v.* (**jibbed, jib·bing**) = JIBE[1].

jibe[1], **gybe** (jīb) *vbs.* (**jibed, jib·ing, gybed, gyb·ing**). 1. Shift a fore-and-aft sail from one side of a ship to the other. 2. Change course of a ship so that a fore-and-aft sail shifts thus.

jibe[2]: see GIBE.

jibe[3](jīb) *v.* (**jibed, jib·ing**). (colloq.) Fit or agree with.

jif·fy (jĭf'ē) (pl. **-fies**), **jiff** (jĭf) *ns.* (colloq.) Very short time, moment.

jig (jĭg) *n.* 1. Lively dance; music for this, usu. in $\frac{3}{4}$ or $\frac{6}{8}$ time. 2. (eng.) Device for holding parts in appropriate position for drilling or assembling. 3. Contrivance for separating ore by agitation. 4. **jig'saw,** machine fret saw; (also **jigsaw puzzle**) picture pasted on board etc. and cut in irregular pieces to be fitted together. **jig** *v.* (**jigged, jig·ging**). Dance a jig; bob up and down rapidly and jerkily; separate coarser and finer portions of (ore) by shaking it under water in box with perforated bottom; **in ~ time,** quickly; **the ~ is up,** (slang) success is now impossible.

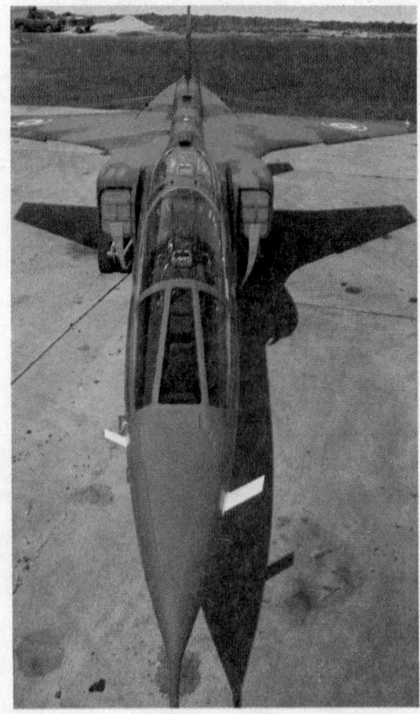

*The construction and testing of **jet planes** like Concorde and this Anglo-French Jaguar aircraft, a strike fighter, is jointly funded by France and Britain.*

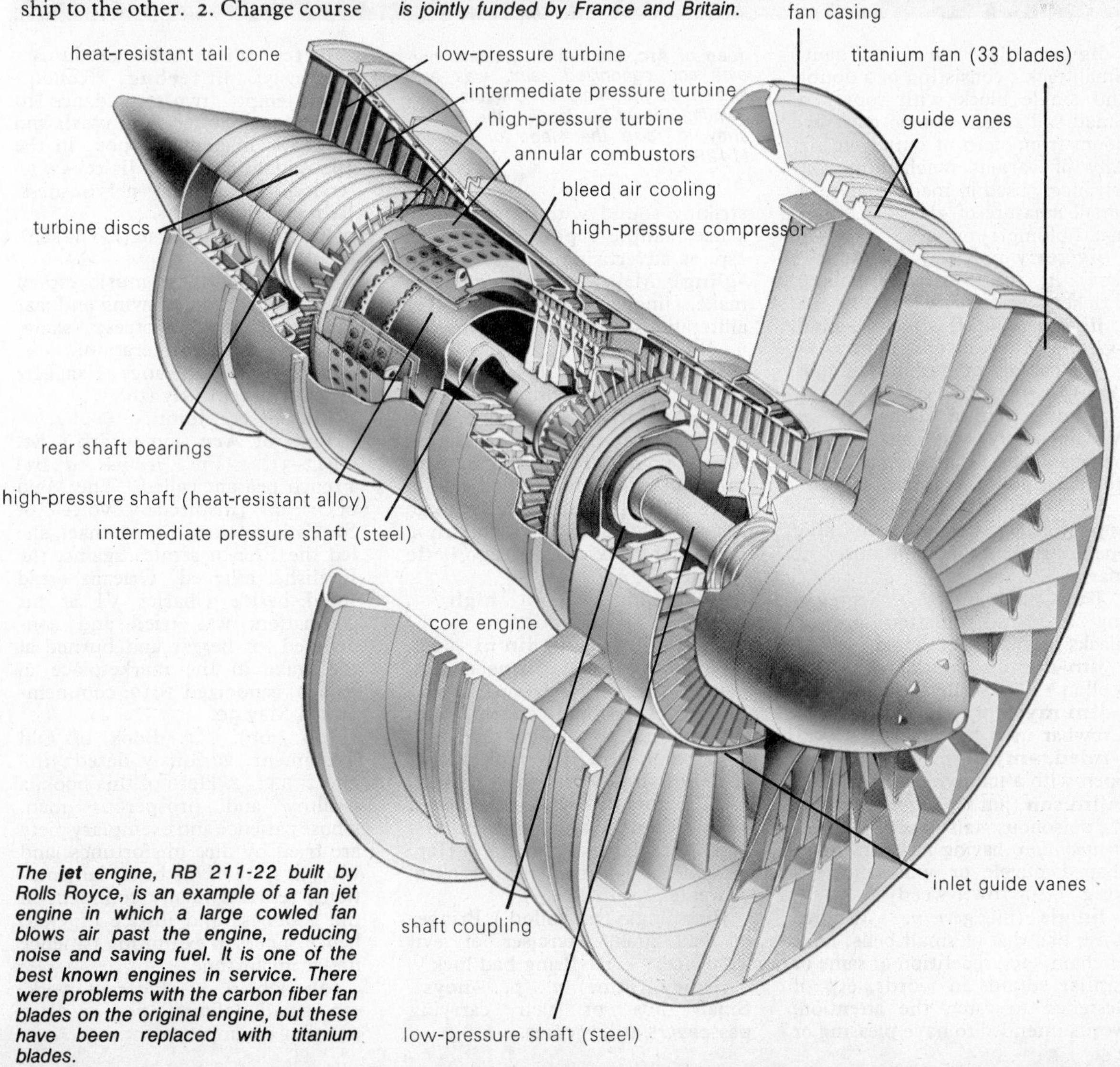

fan casing
heat-resistant tail cone
low-pressure turbine
titanium fan (33 blades)
intermediate pressure turbine
high-pressure turbine
guide vanes
annular combustors
bleed air cooling
turbine discs
high-pressure compressor
rear shaft bearings
high-pressure shaft (heat-resistant alloy)
intermediate pressure shaft (steel)
core engine
inlet guide vanes
shaft coupling
low-pressure shaft (steel)

*The **jet** engine, RB 211-22 built by Rolls Royce, is an example of a fan jet engine in which a large cowled fan blows air past the engine, reducing noise and saving fuel. It is one of the best known engines in service. There were problems with the carbon fiber fan blades on the original engine, but these have been replaced with titanium blades.*

Joan of Arc, the French national heroine and canonized saint, was also known as the Maid of Orleans. This painting shows her leading the French army to raise the siege of Orleans (1429).

jig·ger (jĭg'*er*) *n.* 1. (naut.) Small tackle consisting of a double and single block with rope. 2. Small sail rigged out on mast and boom from stern of cutter etc. 3. Any of various mechanical contrivances, used in many trades. 4. Small measure of glass for liquor, usu. holding 1½ ounces.

jig·ger·y-pok·er·y (jĭg'*er*ē pō'-*ker*ē) *n.* (pl. **-er·ies**). (colloq.) Trickery, underhand dealing.

jig·gle (jĭg'*el*) *v.t.* (**-gled, -gling**). Rock or jerk lightly. ~ *n.* Rocking or jerking motion. **jig'gly** *adj.*

ji·had, je·had (jĭhahd') *ns.* Muslim holy war against unbelievers; (fig.) campaign against a doctrine, policy, etc.; crusade.

Jil·in (chĭl'ēn') = KIRIN.

jilt (jĭlt) *v.t.* Cast off (lover) after encouragement or promise to marry.

Jim Crow (jĭm'krō'). Segregating of, discrimination against, blacks in U.S.; segregated.

jim-dan·dy (jĭm'dăn'dē) *adj.* (colloq.) Of excellent quality.

jim·my (jĭm'ē) *n.* (pl. **-mies**). Crowbar used by burglars. ~ *v.* (**-mied, -my·ing**). Force or pry open with a jimmy.

jim·son (jĭm's*o*n) **weed.** Highly poisonous tall weed (*Datura stramonium*) having large trumpet-shaped purple or white flowers. [orig. JAMESTOWN-weed]

jin·gle (jĭng'*gel*) *n.* Mingled noise like that of small bells, links of chain, etc.; repetition of same or similar sounds in words, esp. if designed to catch the attention; words intended to have pleasing or striking sound without regard to sense; simple repetitious rhyme, esp. as advertising. ~ *v.* (**-gled, -gling**). Make, cause (keys etc.) to make, a jingle; (of writing) be full of alliterations, rhymes, etc. **jin'gler** *n.* **jin'gly** *adv.*

jin·go (jĭng'gō) *n.* (pl. **-goes**). 1. **by** ~, used for emphasis or to express surprise. 2. Blatant patriot, esp. supporter of a belligerent foreign policy (from use of *by jingo* in popular Brit. music hall refrain of 1878, sung by those ready to go to war with Russia). **jin'go·ism** *n.* **jin'go·ist** *n.* & *adj.* **jin·go·is·tic** (jĭngōĭs'tĭk) *adj.*

jinks (jĭngks) *n.pl.* **high** ~, boisterous sport, frolic.

jinn, djinn (jĭn), **jin·ni** (jĭnē', jin'ē) *ns.* (pl. **jinns, djinns,** collect. **jinn, djinn**). (Islamic myth.) Spirit lower than angels, with supernatural power over men.

jin·rick·sha, jin·rick·shaw, jin·rik·i·sha (jĭnrĭk'shaw, -shah) *ns.* Light two-wheeled hooded vehicle drawn by man or men, first used in Japan *c*1870. [Jap. *jin-riki-sha* (*jin* man, *riki* strength, power, *sha* vehicle)]

jinx (jĭngks) *n.* (colloq.) Bringer of bad luck, exerciser of evil influence. ~ *v.* Bring bad luck.

jit·ney (jĭt'nē) *n.* (pl. **-neys**). Small bus or taxi carrying passengers at low rates.

jit·ter (jĭt'*er*) *v.t.* Be nervous, act nervously; **jit'terbug,** (colloq.) quick-tempo, two-step dance to swing music, often with twirls and acrobatic maneuvers, pop. in the 1940s; dancer of this. **jit'ters** *n.pl.* (colloq.) Extreme nervousness. **jit'ter·y** *adv.*

jiu·jit·su, jiu·jut·su (jōō jĭt'sōō): see JUJITSU.

jive (jīv) *n.* Swing music, esp. of the 1940s; jargon of swing and jazz musicians and devotees; (slang) deceptive talk, exaggeration. ~ *v.* (**jived, jiv·ing**). (slang) Exaggerate, talk deceptively (to).

jnt. *abbrev.* Joint.

Joan of Arc (jōn'*o*v ārk'), **St.** (1412–31). (Fr. *Jeanne d'Arc*) French peasant called "The Maid of Orleans"; inspired by "voices" of St. Catherine and St. Michael, she led the French armies against the English, relieved Orleans, and stood beside Charles VI at his coronation; was tried and condemned for heresy and burned at the stake in the marketplace in Rouen; canonized 1919; commemorated May 30.

Job (jōb). 1. Book of Old Testament, variously dated 5th–2nd c. B.C. 2. Hero of this book, a wealthy and prosperous man, whose patience and exemplary piety are tried by dire misfortunes, and who, in spite of his bitter lamentations, remains finally confident in the goodness and justice of God; hence, a person exhibiting patience under misfortune.

job (jŏb) *n.* 1. Piece of work, esp. small definite one. 2. Paid position of employment. 3. Any-

John the Baptist, *painted here by Leonardo da Vinci, was a cousin of Jesus. He preached a mission of repentance in preparation for the imminent coming of the Messiah and baptized his followers.*

thing one has to do; (colloq.) difficult task. 4. **bad, good, ~**, bad, good work, results, state of affairs, etc.; **~ lot**, miscellaneous goods sold as a single lot; **odd ~s**, miscellaneous tasks; **on the ~**, at work, in the course of doing a piece of work; (slang) attentive; alert. 5. **~ action**, organized protest, such as mass absence etc., by employees forbidden by law to strike; **~ bank**, computerized data file to help place unemployed workers in suitable jobs; **job'holder**, person having a regular job; **job printer**, printer who specializes in miscellaneous items, such as letterheads, broadsides, cards, etc.; **job shop**, employment agency that places technical specialists in short-term assignments under temporary contracts. **job** *v.* (**jobbed, job·bing**). 1. Do jobs; hire out for definite time or job. 2. Act as middleman, wholesaler, or jobber. **job'ber** *n.* 1. Person who purchases merchandise from manufacturer and sells to retailers; wholesaler. 2. One who does odd jobs or works by the job; pieceworker.

job·less (jŏb'lĭs) *adj.* Out of work. **job'less·ness** *n.*

Jo·cas·ta (jōkăs'tə). (Gk. legend) Daughter of Creon, king of Corinth; mother and wife of OEDIPUS.

jock (jŏk) *n.* 1. (colloq.) DISC jockey. 2. (slang) Male athlete. 3. **jock'strap**, support or protection for male genitals, worn esp. by athletes.

jock·ey (jŏk'ē) *n.* (pl. **-eys**). Rider in horse races; **~ cap**, cap with long peak, worn by jockeys. **jockey** *v.* (**-eyed, -ey·ing**). Ride (a horse) as its jockey; cheat, trick (*into, out of*, etc.); **~ for position**, maneuver for advantageous position (also fig.). [f. Sc. *Jock*, Jack]

jo·cose (jōkōs') *adj.* Playful, waggish. **jo·cos·i·ty** (jōkŏs'ĭtē) *n.*

joc·u·lar (jŏk'yəler) *adj.* Mirthful; humorous. **joc'u·lar·ly** *adv.* **joc·u·lar·i·ty** (jŏkyəlăr'ĭtē) *n.*

joc·und (jŏk'ənd, jō'kənd) *adj.* Merry, sprightly; pleasant. **joc'und·ly** *adv.*

jodh·purs (jŏd'perz) *n.pl.* Riding breeches reaching to the ankle, full above and tight below the knee. [f. *Jodhpur*, former state of India]

Joe Mil·ler (jō'mĭl'er). Stale joke, chestnut. [f. *Joe Miller's Jests*, a jest book (1739) by John Mottley; named after Joseph Miller (1684–1738), comedian at London's Drury Lane theater]

joe-pie (jō pī') **weed.** Any of various tall N. Amer. plants (*Eupatorium*) having whorled, toothed leaves and flat-topped clusters of small purplish, pinkish, or occas. white, flowers.

Johannesburg *in the Transvaal is the largest city in South Africa. It is the industrial center of the world's biggest gold-mining district (Witwatersrand) and a livestock and produce market.*

jog[1] (jŏg) *v.* (**jogged, jog·ging**). 1. Shake with push or jerk; nudge (person), esp. to arouse attention; stimulate (memory). 2. Move up and down with unsteady motion; run at a slow steady trot, now esp. as a regular form of exercise. **~** *n.* Shake, push; nudge; slow, steady trot. **jog'ger** *n.* (esp.) One who jogs regularly for exercise.

jog[2] (jŏg) *n.* 1. Section of a line or surface that juts out or recedes. 2. Sudden change of direction. **~** *v.* (**jogged, jog·ging**). Turn or bend abruptly.

jog·gle[1] (jŏg'el) *v.* (**-gled, -gling**). Shake, move, (as) by repeated jerks. **~** *n.* Slight shake.

jog·gle[2] (jŏg'el) *n.* Joint of two pieces of stone or timber, contrived to prevent their sliding on one another; notch in one piece, corresponding projection in the other, or small piece let in between both, for this purpose. ~ *v.t.* (**-gled, -gling**). Join by means of a joggle.

Jo·han·nes·burg (jōhăn′ĭsbērg, yōhah′nĭs-). Largest city of the Republic of South Africa.

John[1] (jŏn). Masculine proper name used in various combinations with various meanings, as ~ **Barleycorn**: see BARLEY; ~ **Bull** (from name of character representing English nation in John Arbuthnot's satire *Law is a Bottomless Pit*, 1712), personification of England, typical Englishman, represented as a stoutish red-faced farmerlike man in top hat and high boots; ~ **Doe**, name used in legal proceedings to designate an unidentified or fictitious person or any average man; ~ **Dory**, either of two fishes, *Zenopsis ocellata* or *Zeus faber* of the Atlantic, having a laterally flattened body and long dorsal spines; ~ **Hancock**, (colloq.) person's signature, see HANCOCK.

John[2] (jŏn). Name of 23 popes or antipopes, esp.: **John VIII**, pope 872–82; much involved in imperial politics; **John XXI**, pope 1276–7; identified with Petrus Hispanus, author of medical and philosophical works, and freq. referred to by chroniclers as a magician; **John XXII**, pope at Avignon, 1316–34; accused of heresy; **John XXIII**, antipope, 1410–15; **John XXIII** (Angelo Giuseppe Roncalli, 1881–1963), pope 1958–63.

John[3] (jŏn) (1167–1216). King of England; called "John Lackland" because as youngest son of Henry II he had no royal lands to maintain him; succeeded his brother Richard Coeur de Lion, 1199; alienated barons and people by bad administration and heavy taxation; was forced by barons to sign MAGNA CARTA.

John[4] (jŏn). Name of six kings of Portugal including: **John I** "the Great," reigned 1385–1433; **John II** "the Perfect," reigned 1481–95; encouraged exploration of sea route to India; **John IV** "the Fortunate," reigned 1541–56; founder of Braganza dynasty; **John VI**, reigned 1816–26.

John[5] (jŏn), **St.** Name of various saints: **St. ~ the Baptist**, son of Elizabeth and Zacharias, a priest (Luke I); preached in the wilderness; forerunner of Jesus Christ; was executed by order of Herod Antipas; **St. ~ Chrysostom**: see CHRYSOSTOM; **St. ~ of the Cross** (1542–91), Spanish mystical poet and Carmelite friar; friend of St. Theresa; canonized 1726; **St. ~ the Evangelist**: see JOHN[6].

John[6] (jŏn), **St.** Apostle, called

Andrew Johnson *was vice president when Abraham Lincoln was assassinated during the final months of the American Civil War. He became the 17th president of the U.S.A. His opponents tried to have him impeached.*

St. ~ the Evangelist or **St. ~ the Divine**; son of Zebedee, a Galilean fisherman, and brother of James; credited (prob. erron.) with authorship of fourth Gospel and APOCALYPSE, and of three epistles of New Testament; commemorated Dec. 27; fourth Gospel; any of the three epistles attributed to St. John; **St. ~'s wort**, herb or shrub of genus *Hypericum*, with oval leaves and bright yellow flowers.

john (jŏn) *n.* (slang) 1. Lavatory. 2. Man patronizing prostitute.

john·ny (jŏn′ē) *n.* (pl. **-nies**). (slang) Short gown with short sleeves and tied in the back, used by hospital patients; **john'nycake**, corn cake baked on ashes of fire or fried in pan; cornmeal pancake; **johnny-jump-up**, small type of pansy grown esp. in rock gardens; **Johnny Reb**, (colloq.) Confederate soldier in the Civil War. [pet form of *John*]

John Paul (jŏn′pawl′). Name of two popes: **John Paul I** (Albino Luciani, 1912–78) pope Aug. 26–Sept. 28, 1978; **John Paul II** (Karol Wojtyla, 1920–) pope 1978– .

John·son[1] (jŏn′sŏn), **Andrew** (1808–75). U.S. president, 1865–9; member of House of Representatives, 1843–53; Lincoln's vice president; became president after Lincoln's assassination; attempted to carry out Lincoln's Reconstruction policies after Civil War; Congress brought impeachment proceedings against him, 1868, for dismissing Secretary of War Edwin Stanton in defiance of the Tenure of Office Act, but he was acquitted by one vote.

John·son[2] (jŏn′sŏn), **Lyndon Baines** (1908–73). U.S. politician; served in Congress 1937–61; 36th president of U.S., 1963–9; vice president 1961–3; succeeded to presidency on assassination of Kennedy, then elected to a full term; his administration was best known for his social welfare programs and the escalation of the Vietnam War.

John·son[3] (jŏn′sŏn), **Richard Mentor** (1780–1850). U.S. vice president, 1837–41, under Martin Van Buren; only vice president elected by decision of the U.S. Senate, because no candidate received an electoral college majority.

John·son[4] (jŏn′sŏn), **("Dr.")**

Samuel (1709–84). English man of letters and lexicographer; famous esp. for his landmark *Dictionary of the English Language*, 1755, and conversation recorded in his friend James Boswell's *Life of Samuel Johnson*; published a critical edition of Shakespeare; wrote *Rasselas, Lives of the Poets*, etc. **John·so·ni·an** (jŏnsō´nēan) *adj.* Of Samuel Johnson; esp. of an English prose style abounding in words derived or made up from Latin, or characterized by weighty and well-balanced sentences.

Jo·hore (johōr´, -hōr´). State of Malaysia at S. end of Malay peninsula; capital, Johore Bahru.

joie de viv·re (zhwah de vē´vre). Carefree enjoyment of life. [Fr.]

join (join) *v.* 1. Put together, fasten, unite; connect (two points) by a line; unite in marriage, friendship, alliance, etc.; come together, be united. 2. Take part with others (in); come into company of (person); become member of (club etc.); take, resume, one's place in (regiment, ship, company, etc.); ~ **up**, enlist. 3. ~ **battle**, begin fighting; ~ **hands**, clasp each other's hands; (fig.) combine in action or enterprise. **join** *n.* Joint, junction.

join·er (joi´ner) *n.* (esp.) 1. (chiefly Brit.) Cabinetmaker; furniture maker. 2. (colloq.) One who joins many clubs, societies, etc.

joint[1] (joint) *n.* 1. Place at which two things are joined together; structure in animal body by which two bones are fitted together; part of stem from which leaf or branch grows; point at which, contrivance by which, two parts of artificial structure are joined, rigidly or so as to allow movement; (geol.) fracture in rock, esp. one along which there has been little or no movement. 2. One of the parts into which butcher divides carcass, esp. large cut of meat as served at table. 3. (slang) Cheap or disreputable bar, restaurant, etc.; (slang) marijuana cigarette; **out of** ~, out of place at the joint; dislocated; (fig.) disorganized; disordered. **joint** *v.t.* 1. Connect by joints. 2. Cut (meat) into joints.

joint[2] (joint) *adj.* Held or done by, belonging to, two or more persons etc. in conjunction; (of persons) sharing (*with* others in possession, action, state, etc.). **joint´ly** *adv.*

joist (joist) *n.* One of parallel horizontal beams set from wall to wall for ceiling laths or floorboards to be nailed to.

joke (jōk) *n.* Thing said or done to excite laughter; amusing or ridiculous thing, person, or circumstance; **practical** ~, trick played on person in order to have laugh at his expense. **joke** *v.i.* (**joked, jok·ing**). Make jokes, banter. **jok´ing·ly** *adv.*

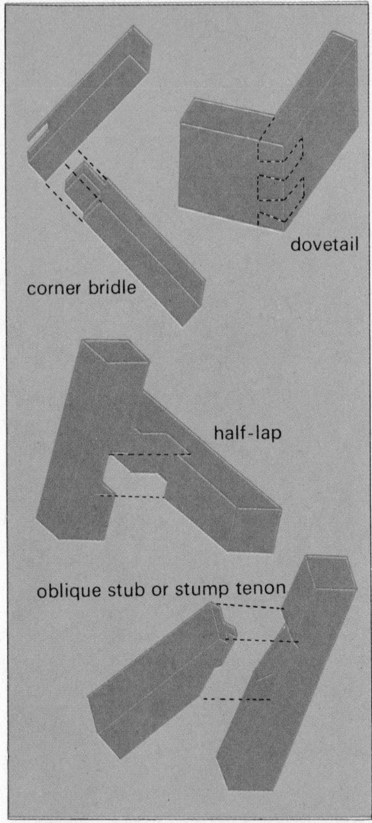

*Wooden **joints** form an essential part of standard furniture, window frames and paneled doors. There are different types of joints but all must have the qualities of strength and rigidity.*

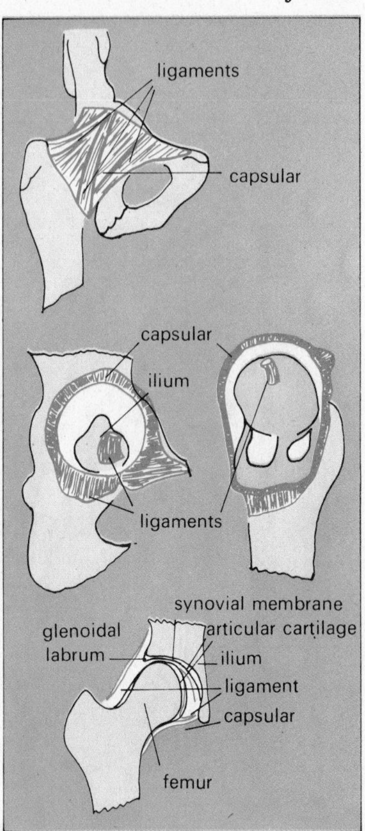

*The **hip-joint** works as a ball-and-socket joint, and has strong muscles and ligaments supporting it. Disorders affecting the joints of the body are mainly various forms of arthritis and dislocation.*

jok·er (jō´ker) *n.* 1. One who jokes; (slang) fellow. 2. (cards) Extra card, often with picture of jester, counting in some games (e.g. euchre) as a trump, in others (e.g. certain forms of poker) as any card the holder chooses to make it. 3. Clause unobtrusively inserted in legislation and affecting its operation in some way not immediately apparent; unseen difficulty.

Jo·li·et, Jol·li·et (jō´lēĕt, jōlēĕt´), **Louis** (1645–1700). French-Canadian who, with MARQUETTE, explored Mississippi River as far S. as Arkansas and returned via Illinois River to Lake Michigan; also explored Gulf of St. Lawrence, and the Hudson Bay area.

Jo·liot-Cu·rie (zhawlyō´ kürē´), **Frédéric** (orig. name **Joliot**) (1900–58) and **Irene** (1897–1956). French husband and wife physicists who discovered a synthesis of new radioactive elements; jointly awarded Nobel Prize for chemistry, 1935; wife was daughter of Pierre and Marie Curie.

jol·li·ty (jŏl´ĭtē) *n.* (pl. **-ties**). Merrymaking, gaiety.

jol·ly (jŏl´ē) *adj.* (**-li·er, -li·est**). Joyful; festive, jovial; (Brit. colloq.) very pleasant, delightful. ~ *adv.* (Brit. colloq.) 1. (with adjective or adverb) Very. 2. ~ **well**: used with verb to give emphasis. **jolly** *v.t.* (**-lied, -ly·ing**). Talk or behave agreeably to (person) in order to put or keep him in good humor. **jol´li·ly** *adv.* **jol´li·ness** *n.*

jolt (jōlt) *v.* Jar, knock, jostle, as with a blow or shove; bump into; (of vehicle) move along in a jerky or bumpy way. ~ *n.* Sudden jerk or jar, as from a blow; surprise, shock. **jolt´y** *adv.*

Jo·nah (jō´na). 1. Hebrew minor prophet; book of Old Testament bearing his name, acc. to which he fled when bidden by God to go to Nineveh and prophesy; God then sent a storm to wreck his ship, and the seamen, holding him responsible, threw him overboard; he was swallowed by a great fish and lived in its belly for three days before being cast out on dry land. 2. Person regarded as bringing bad luck to others.

Jon·a·than (jŏn´athan). Eldest son of King Saul and friend of David, killed at battle of Mount Gilboa 1 Sam. 13 etc.).

jon · a · than (jŏn´athan) *n.* Variety of red late-ripening apple.

Jones[1] (jōnz), **Anson** (1798–

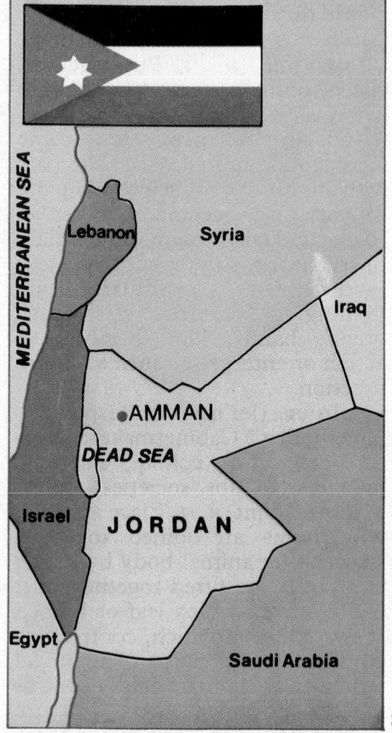

1858). President of the Republic of Texas, 1844–6.

Jones[2] (jōnz), **John Paul** (orig. name, John Paul) (1747–92). Scottish-born Amer. naval commander; when asked to surrender during the Revolutionary War battle between the British warship "Serapis" and the "Bonhomme Richard," Sept., 1779, Jones's famous reply was, "I have not yet begun to fight!"

jon·gleur (zhawṅglör′) *n.* (pl. **-gleurs** pr. -glör′). (hist.) Wandering minstrel in medieval France and England. [Fr.]

jon·quil (jŏng′kwĭl, jŏn′-) *n.* Species of narcissus (*N. jonquilla*) with long linear leaves and clusters of fragrant white and yellow flowers.

Jon·son (jŏn′son), **Ben(jamin)** (1574–1637). English poet and dramatist; author of the plays *Every Man in his Humour, Every Man out of his Humour, Volpone,* etc., and of

Jordan's *stability has been severely tested for 20 years and owes much to the skill and courage of its ruler, King Hussein. Over one third of its Arab population are Palestinian refugees. 1. Arab legionnaires. 2. The ancient forum at Jerash, built in an elliptical shape. 3. Map and flag of Jordan.*

song "Drink to Me Only with Thine Eyes." **Jon·so·ni·an** (jŏnsō′nēan) *adj.*

Jor·dan (jŏr′dan). 1. River flowing 200 mi. (322 km) southward from N. Israel through Sea of Galilee and into Dead Sea. 2. Short for **Hashemite Kingdom of the ~**, Arab nation east of the river Jordan, bordered by Israel, Syria, Iraq, and Saudi Arabia; capital, Amman. **Jor·da·ni·an** (jŏrdā′nēan) *adj.* & *n.*

Jo·seph[1] (jō′zef, -sef). Name of several persons in the Bible, esp.: 1. Son of Jacob and Rachel; sold by his brothers into captivity in Egypt, where he attained high office (Gen. 30–50). 2. Carpenter of Nazareth, husband of MARY[1]. 3. **~ of Arimathea,** Jew who buried Jesus Christ in a rock-hewn tomb; he was the subject of many legends, one being that he afterward led a mission to England and built the Christian church in England.

Jo·seph[2] (jō′zef, -sef). Name of two Holy Roman emperors: **Joseph I** (1678–1711), reigned 1705–11; **Joseph II** (1741–90), eldest son of Maria Theresa, reigned 1765–90.

Jo·se·phine (jō′zefēn, -se-). Marie Rose Joséphine Tascher de la Pagerie (1763–1814), a Creole of Martinique; wife of Vicomte Alexander Beauharnais (guillotined in 1794) and subsequently (1796) of Napoleon Bonaparte; empress of the French from 1804 until Napoleon divorced her "for reasons of state" in 1809.

josh (jŏsh) *v.* (colloq.) Poke fun at in good-natured way. **josh′er** *n.*

Josh. *abbrev.* Joshua (Old Testament).

Josh·u·a (jŏsh′o͞oa). Successor of Moses in leadership of Israel; 6th book of Old Testament telling how he conquered the land of Canaan; ~ **tree**, treelike plant (*Yucca brevifolia*) of southwestern U.S., having branches that are like outstretched arms, daggerlike leaves, and pale greenish-white blossoms.

Jo·si·ah (jōsī′*a*), **Jo·si·as** (jōsī′*a*s) (647–*c*608 B.C.). King of Judah; carried out complete religious reform based on a book of law (app. Deuteronomy) found in the Temple.

joss (jŏs, jaws) *n.* Chinese idol; ~ **house**, Chinese temple or shrine containing idols; ~ **stick**, stick of incense for burning before a joss. [app. f. Port. *deos* f. L. *deus* god]

jos·tle (jŏs′*e*l) *v.* (**-tled, -tling**). Knock or push (*against* etc.); elbow; vie with for an advantage. ~ *n.* Jostling.

jot[1] (jŏt) *n.* Small amount, whit. [Gk. *iota*, letter i, smallest in alphabet]

jot[2] (jŏt) *v.t.* (**jot·ted, jot·ting**). Write (*down*) briefly or hastily. **jot′ter** *n.*

jot·ting (jŏt′ĭng) *n.* Hastily written note.

joule (jo͞ol) *n.* (phys.) Unit of work or energy in meter-kilogram-second (MKS) system, amount of work done or heat generated by a force of 1 newton acting over a distance of 1 meter (abbrev. J); energy of 1 watt acting for 1 second. [f. JOULE]

Joule (jo͞ol), **James Prescott** (1818–89). English physicist who established the universal constant of proportionality between mechanical work and heat.

jounce (jowns) *v.* (**jounced, jounc·ing**). Bump, bounce, jolt. ~ *n.* Jouncing motion. **jounc′y** *adj.*

jour·nal (jĕr′n*a*l) *n.* 1. (in bookkeeping by double entry) Book in which each transaction is entered, with statement of accounts to which it is to be debited and credited. 2. Diary; record of daily transactions of public body or association; (naut.) ship's log; newspaper, other periodical. 3. Part of shaft or axle that rests on bearings; ~ **box**, box enclosing journal or bearings.

jour·nal·ese (jĕr′n*a*lēz′, -lēs′) *n.* Slick, superficial style of writing or new word formation characteristic of some newspapers and magazines.

jour·nal·ist (jĕr′n*a*lĭst) *n.* One who edits or esp. writes for a newspaper or magazine. **jour′nal·ism** *n.* **jour·nal·is·tic** (jĕrn*a*lĭs′tĭk) *adj.* **jour·nal·is′tic·al·ly** *adv.*

jour·ney (jĕr′nē) *n.* (pl. **-neys**) & *v.i.* (**-neyed, -ney·ing**). Travel from one place to another, esp. by land or air (dist. from *voyage*); (make) expedition to some distance.

jour·ney·man (jĕr′nēm*a*n) *n.* (pl. **-men**). Qualified artisan or workman who works for another (orig. after having completed his apprenticeship in a craft or trade).

joust (jowst, jŭst, jo͞ost), **just**[1] (jŭst, jo͞ost) *vbs.i.* & *ns.* (Engage in) combat between two knights etc. on horseback with lances; (fig.) any combat. **joust′er** *n.*

Jove (jōv). (Rom. myth.) = JUPITER.

jo·vi·al (jō′vē*a*l) *adj.* Merry; convivial. **jo′vi·al·ly** *adv.* **jo·vi·al·i·ty** (jōvēăl′ĭtē) *n.* [L. *jovialis* of Jupiter]

*A **joshua tree** in Joshua Tree National Monument, California.*

jowl (jowl) *n.* Flesh under the lower jaw, esp. when prominent; dewlap or wattle. **jowl′y** *adj.*

joy (joi) *n.* Vivid emotion of pleasure, gladness; thing that causes delight; ~ **ride**, (slang) pleasure ride in a car driven carelessly and usu. without permission of the owner (hence ~ **rider,** ~ **rid·ing**); **joy′stick**, (slang) control lever of airplane. **joy′ful** *adj.* **joy′ful·ly** *adv.* **joy′ful·ness** *n.* **joy′less** *adj.* **joy′less·ly** *adv.* **joy′less·ness** *n.* **joy·ous** (joi′*u*s) *adj.* **joy′ous·ly** *adv.* **joy′ous·ness** *n.*

Joyce (jois), **James** (1882–1941). Irish novelist and short-story writer; best known for his novels *Ulysses* (1922) and *Finnegans Wake* (1939), written in a highly allusive style employing the stream-of-consciousness technique.

JP *abbrev.* Jet propulsion.

J.P. *abbrev.* Justice of the Peace.

Jr., jr. *abbrevs.* Junior.

Juan Carlos (hwahn′ kahr′lōs) (1938–). King of Spain, Head of State (1975–).

Juan de Fu·ca (jo͞o′an de fū′k*a*; *Sp.* hwahn′ dĕ fo͞o′kah) **Strait.** Inlet of the Pacific Ocean extending 100 mi. (161 km), between Vancouver Island, Canada and NW. Washington.

Ju·an Fer·nan·dez (jo͞o′an fer-năn′dĕz; *Sp.* hwahn′ fĕrnahn′dĕth). Group of 3 volcanic islands in S. Pacific, 400 mi. (644 km) off coast of Chile, to which they belong; discovered 1563 by a Spanish pilot, Juan Fernandez.

Juá·rez[1] (wār′ĕz; *Sp.* hwah′rĕs). City in N. Mexico opposite El Paso, Texas, on the Rio Grande.

Juá·rez[2] (wār′ĕz; *Sp.* hwah′rĕs), **Benito Pablo** (1806–72). Mexican

The diamond ***jubilee*** *of Queen Victoria's reign in 1897 was celebrated with universal enthusiasm. Her reign had seen rapid industrialization and a vast increase in the wealth of Britain.*

statesman and reform leader; president of Mexico, 1857–72.

Ju·ba (jo͞o′bah). River in E. Africa flowing S. 1,000 mi. (1,609 km) from S. central Ethiopia to the Indian Ocean.

ju·bi·late (jo͞o′bĭlāt) *v.i.* (**-lat·ed, -lat·ing**). Exult, make demonstrations of joy. **ju·bi·lance** (jo͞o′bĭlans), **ju·bi·la·tion** (jo͞obĭlā′shon) *ns.* **ju′bi·lant** *adj.* **ju′bi·lant·ly** *adv.*

ju·bi·lee (jo͞o′bĭlē, jo͞obĭlē′) *n.* 1. (Jewish hist.) Year of emancipation and restoration, kept every 50 years, according to Lev. 25; (R.C. Ch.) year during which plenary indulgence may be obtained by performing certain pious acts, granted formerly at various intervals, now at any time. 2. Fiftieth anniversary as occasion for rejoicing (also **golden ~**); **silver ~**, (celebration of) 25th anniversary, **diamond ~**, of 60th. 3. Any season or occasion of celebration or rejoicing. [Heb. *yobel* ram, ram's horn trumpet, jubilee]

Ju·dae·a: see JUDEA.

Ju·dah (jo͞o′d*a*). 1. Hebrew patriarch, son of Jacob and Leah (Gen. 29); powerful tribe of Israel, traditionally descended from him. 2. Southern kingdom of the Hebrews (opp. ISRAEL[1], def. 3) established by this tribe and the tribe of Benjamin.

Ju·da·ic (jo͞odā′ĭk) *adj.* Of Judaism or Jews.

Ju·da·i·ca (jo͞odā′ĭk*a*) *n.pl.* Things pertaining to Jews or their religion, esp. books about Jewish history and culture.

Ju·da·ism (jo͞o′dēĭzem, -dā-) *n.* 1. Monotheistic religion of the Jews, based on Mosaic precepts and rabbinic teaching, with traditions, laws, and moral principles from the Old Testament and the Talmud. 2. (Conformity to) traditional ceremonies, rites, and way of life of the Jews. **Ju·da·ize** (jo͞o′dēīz, -dā-) *v.* (**-ized, -iz·ing**). Follow Jewish customs or rites; make Jewish.

Ju·das[1] (jo͞o′d*a*s). (also **~ Iscariot**) Apostle who betrayed Jesus Christ for 30 pieces of silver and afterward (acc. to Matt. 27) repented and hanged himself; hence, betrayer, traitor; **~ kiss**, act of betrayal (from kiss which Judas gave to Jesus as a signal to his captors); **~ tree**, (from legend that Judas hanged himself on tree of this kind) leguminous S. European and Asiatic tree (*Cercis siliquastrum*), with abundant purplish-pink flowers appearing in spring before the leaves; any tree of genus *Cercis*, esp. redbud.

Ju·das[2] (jo͞od*a*s). St. JUDE.

Ju·das Mac·ca·bae·us (jo͞o′d*a*s măk*a*bē′*u*s): see MACCABEES.

Jude (jo͞od), **St.** One of the 12 Apostles, also called Judas (Luke 6, John 14); usu. identified with Jude the brother of James (Jude I); martyred in Persia with St. Simon; commemorated with St. Simon, Oct. 28; **(Epistle of) ~**, last epistle of New Testament, traditionally ascribed to St. Jude.

Ju·de·a, Ju·dae·a (jo͞odē′*a*). Name in Greco-Roman times for S. part of ancient Palestine W. of the Jordan.

Judg. *abbrev.* Judges (Old Testament).

judge (jŭj) *n.* 1. Public official who hears and tries cases in court of justice; person appointed to decide dispute or contest; person who decides a question; person who is qualified to decide on merits of thing or question; **J~ Advocate General** (pl. **J~ Advocates General, J~ Advocate Generals**) major general serving as senior legal officer in the U.S. Army or Air Force. 2. Officer having temporary authority in Israel in period between Joshua and the kings; **(Book of) Judges**, seventh book of Old Testament, containing history of this period. **judge** *v.* (**judged, judg·ing**). Pronounce sentence on (person) in court of justice; try (cause); decide (question); decide, decree; form a judgment (*of*). **judge′ship** *n.*

judg·ment, judge·ment (jŭj′m*e*nt) *ns.* 1. Sentence of court of justice; misfortune viewed as sign of divine displeasure; **Last J~**, final judgment by God of all mankind; **J~ Day**, day of Last Judgment. 2. Criticism; opinion, estimate; critical faculty, discernment; good sense. **judg·men′tal** *adj.*

ju·di·ca·ture (jo͞o′dĭk*a*choor, -kāch*e*r) *n.* Administration of justice; function, authority, jurisdiction of a judge or court; body of judges; court of justice.

ju·di·cial (jo͞odĭsh′*a*l) *adj.* Of, done by, proper to, a court of law; having the function of judgment; of, proper to, a judge; expressing a judgment; impartial. **ju·di′cial·ly** *adv.*

ju·di·ci·ar·y (jo͞odĭsh′ēĕrē, -dĭsh′*e*rē) *n.* (pl. **-ar·ies**). Judges collectively; court system; the judicial branch of government. **~** *adj.* Of or pertaining to the judicial branch, court system, or judges.

ju·di·cious (jo͞odĭsh′*u*s) *adj.* Sensible, prudent; sound in discernment. **ju·di′cious·ly** *adv.* **ju·di′cious·ness** *n.*

ju·do (jo͞o′dō) *n.* Modern form of JUJITSU. **ju·do·ka** (jo͞odōkah′) (pl. **-kas, -ka**), **ju′do·ist** *ns.* Judo performer. [Jap. *jiu dō*, f. Chin. *jiu tao* soft way]

Ju·dy (jo͞o′dē). Wife of PUNCH in "Punch and Judy." [dim. of Judith]

jug (jŭg) *n.* Deep vessel for holding liquids, with handle and usu. spout; (slang) prison. ~ *v.t.* (**jugged, jug·ging**). Stew (hare, rabbit) in jug or jar (usu. in past part.); (slang) imprison. **jug′ful** *n.* (pl. **-fuls**).

Jug·ger·naut (jŭg′ernawt). (also **Jagannath**) Idol of Krishna at Puri, Orissa, annually dragged in procession in an enormous car under whose wheels devotees are said to have thrown themselves; hence (also **j**~; fig.) institution, notion, to which persons blindly sacrifice themselves or others; large overpowering force, object, etc.

jug·gle (jŭg′el) *v.* (**-gled, -gling**). Perform feats of dexterity (*with* objects tossed up); play juggling tricks with; manipulate, change the relative position of; engage in trickery with intent to cheat or deceive. **jug·gler** (jŭg′ler), **jug′gler·y** *ns.* (pl. **-gler·ies**).

Ju·go·slav (yo͞o′gōslahv), **Ju·go·sla·vi·a** (yo͞ogōslah′vēa): see YUGOSLAV(IA).

jug·u·lar (jŭg′yuler, jo͞o′gyu-) *adj.* Of the neck or throat; ~ **vein**, any of four great veins at sides of neck, an external pair conveying blood from superficial parts of head and an internal pair from inside of skull. ~ *n.* Jugular vein.

juice (jo͞os) *n.* Liquid part of vegetable or fruit; fluid part of animal body or substance; (fig.) essence, spirit, of anything; (slang) electricity, electric current.

juic·y (jo͞o′sē) *adj.* (**juic·i·er, juic·i·est**). Full of juice, succulent; (colloq.) of rich intellectual quality, interesting. **juic′i·ness** *n.* **juic′i·ly** *adv.*

ju·jit·su, ju·jut·su, (jiu·jit·soo, jiu·jut·soo, jo͞ojĭt′so͞o) *ns.* Japanese system of self-defense characterized by special holds or maneuvers that turn an opponent's strength and weight against him. [Jap. *jūjutsu*, f. Chin. *jiu shu*(*t*) soft art]

ju·ju (jo͞o′jo͞o) *n.* (W. Afr.) Charm or fetish; supernatural power attributed to this.

ju·jube (jo͞o′jo͞ob) *n.* Edible acid berrylike drupe of certain plants; thorny plant (*Zizyphus*) of S. Europe and Asia bearing this; fruit-flavored firm candy with such a berrylike shape.

juke·box, juke box (jo͞ok′bŏks) *ns.* Machine that automatically plays selected records when a coin is inserted.

Jul. *abbrev.* July.

ju·lep (jo͞o′lep) *n.* (hist.) Sweet syrupy drink, esp. as vehicle for medicine; tall drink (esp. **mint** ~) of liquor, sugar, ice, and flavoring. [Pers. *gulāb* (*gul* rose, *āb* water)]

Jul·ian[1] (jo͞ol′yan) (332–63). Flavius Claudius Julianus, Roman emperor 361–3; called Julian the Apostate because, though brought up as a Christian, he reverted to the worship of the old gods and became an opponent of Christianity.

Jul·ian[2] (jo͞ol′yan) *adj.* Of Julius Caesar; ~ **calendar**, reformed calendar introduced by him in 46 B.C. and slightly modified under Augustus, in which ordinary year has 365 days, and every fourth year is a leap year of 366 days (see also GREGORIAN).

ju·li·enne (jo͞olēēn′, zho͞o-) *adj.* Cut into long thin strips (esp. vegetables). ~ *n.* Soup or consomme containing julienne vegetables.

Jul·ius (jo͞ol′yus). Name of three popes: **Julius I**, St., pope 337–52; **Julius II** (Giuliano della Rovere, 1433–1513), pope 1503–13, statesman and patron of Michelangelo, Raphael, etc.; carried out many reforms; **Julius III** (Giovanni Maria del Monte, 1487–1555), pope 1550–5.

Jul·ius Cae·sar (jo͞ol′yus sē′zer). Gaius Julius Caesar (prob. 101–44 B.C.), Roman general and statesman; formed 1st TRIUMVIRATE, 59 B.C.; conducted the Gallic Wars from 58 to 49 B.C. and invaded Britain 55 and 54 B.C.; crossed the RUBICON in defiance of the Senate in 49 B.C., and defeated Pompey in civil war, becoming dictator; was murdered on the Ides of March 44 B.C. by a group of nobles.

Ju·ly (jo͞olī′, ju-) (pl. **-lies**). Seventh month of Gregorian (fifth of Julian) calendar, with 31 days; ~ **monarchy**, (Fr. hist.) that of Louis Philippe; ~ **revolution**, (Fr. hist.) revolution in July 1830 against Charles X, who fled into exile and was succeeded by Louis Philippe. [f. *Julius* Caesar]

jum·ble (jŭm′bel) *v.* (**-bled, -bling**). Move about in disorder; mix *up*, confuse. ~ *n.* Confused assemblage; muddle.

jum·bo (jŭm′bō) *n.* (pl. **-bos**). Big clumsy person, animal, or thing. ~ *adj.* Larger than average, oversized; ~ **jet**, large jet passenger aircraft wide enough to have two aisles. [after *Jumbo*, a large elephant exhibited by P. T. Barnum after 1882 and a feature of his circus]

jump (jŭmp) *n.* Leap, bound, spring from ground; start caused by shock or excitement; abrupt rise in amount, price, value, etc.; sudden transition, gap in series, argument, etc.; **get (have) the ~ on,** (slang) get (have) an advantage at the beginning; ~ **rope**, length of rope with handle at each end, swung over head and under feet during jumping as game or exercise; ~ **suit**, one-piece garment for whole body, orig. worn by paratroops. **jump** *v.* 1. Spring from ground etc. by flexion and sudden muscular extension of legs or (of fish) tail; move suddenly with leap or bound; start with sudden jerk from excitement, shock, etc.; rise suddenly in price, etc.; come *to* arrive *at* (conclusion) hastily; (slang) be very lively; (slang) depart abruptly, esp. without permission; **jump at**, accept (offer, bargain) eagerly; **jump on**, attack (offender etc.) crushingly with word or act. 2. Leap over; (of moving train) leave the rails; pass one piece *over* another in checkers etc., capturing it. 3. Pounce upon (thing); take summary possession of (claim abandoned or forfeited by former occupant);

***Julius Caesar's** excessive powers and almost regal honors led to the conspiracy of Brutus and Cassius who assassinated him in the Senate in 44 B.C. He was ancient Rome's outstanding statesman and general.*

jump bail, flee while free on bail; **jumping-off place**, starting point; **jump the gun**, make premature start. **jump'a·ble** *adj.* **jump'ing·ly** *adv.* **jump'y** *adj.* (**jump·i·er, jump·i·est**). (esp.) In a state of nervous excitement. **jump'i·ness** *n.*

jump·er[1] (jŭm'p*er*) *n.* 1. Person, animal, or thing that jumps. 2. Person who jumps from airplane with parachute. 3. (elect.) Short wire used to make or break a circuit.

jump·er[2] (jŭm'p*er*) *n.* Loose outer jacket or protective garment; sleeveless dress worn over a blouse or sweater; child's garment of pants and attached biblike bodice.

Jun., jun. *abbrevs.* June; junior.

junc. *abbrev.* Junction.

jun·co (jŭng'kō) *n.* (pl. **-cos**). Any of several N. and Central Amer. finches of the genus *Junco*, having black or slate-gray head and white tail feathers.

junc·tion (jŭngk'sh*o*n) *n.* Joining; joint, meeting place; esp. place, station, where railroad lines meet and unite. **junc'tion·al** *adj.*

junc·ture (jŭngk'ch*er*) *n.* Joining; place where things join; concurrence of events, state of affairs.

June (jo͞on). Sixth month of Gregorian (fourth of Julian) calendar, with 30 days; ~ **beetle,** ~ **bug**, any of various large beetles of genus *Phyllophaga* appearing in late spring; **June'berry**: see SHADbush. [L. prob. orig. f. goddess *Juno*]

Ju·neau (jo͞o'nō). Port and capital of Alaska in the SE. part near British Columbia, Canada.

Jung (yo͝ong), **Carl Gustav** (1875–1961). Swiss psychologist; orig. a follower of Freud; later founded school of analytical psychology, differing from psychoanalysis in its use of the concepts of unconscious and libido and in its advocacy of a complex classification of types of personality. **Jung·i·an** (yo͝ong'ēan) *adj.*

Jung·frau (yo͝ong'frow). Mountain in Swiss Alps 13,642 ft. (4,158 m). [Ger., = "maiden"]

jun·gle (jŭng'g*e*l) *n.* Land overgrown with tropical vegetation and trees; wild tangled mass; ~ **fever**, severe form of malarial fever. [Hind. *jangal* desert, forest]

jun·ior (jo͞on'y*er*) *adj.* Younger (esp. of son having same name as father); of less standing, of lower position; (in high schools and colleges) belonging to year below senior; ~ **college**, school offering two-year course esp. in preparation for completion at senior college; ~ **high school**, school generally including grades 7, 8, and 9; ~ **miss**: see MISS[2]; ~ **varsity**, athletic team whose members did not qualify for varsity. **junior** *n.* Junior person; (used as form of address to) male child.

The ***junk,*** *a classic Chinese sailing vessel of ancient but unknown origin, is still in wide use. Its square sails of linen or matting can be spread or closed like a Venetian blind.*

ju·ni·per (jo͞o'n*i*p*er*) *n.* Evergreen shrub of genus *Juniperus*, with prickly leaves and aromatic dark purplish berries of pungent taste.

junk[1] (jŭngk) *n.* 1. (hist.) Old cable cut up for oakum etc. 2. Discarded material, worthless rubbish. 3. (naut.) Hard salt meat. 4. (slang) Narcotic drug, esp. heroin; ~ **food**, food having low nutritive value and usually high caloric count; ~ **mail**, unsolicited advertising matter sent by postal service. **junk** *v.* (colloq.) Discard as rubbish.

junk[2] (jŭngk) *n.* Flat-bottomed sailing vessel of China seas, with square prow, prominent stem, and lugsails. [app. f. Javanese *djong*]

Jun·ker (yo͝ong'k*er*) *n.* (hist.) Young German noble; ultra-reactionary, overbearing member of Prussian aristocracy.

Jun·kers (yo͝ong'k*er*z), **Hugo** (1859–1935). German aircraft designer and engineer; built the first all-metal airplane.

jun·ket (jŭng'kĭt) *n.* Dish of sweetened and flavored curds; feast, outing; trip taken by public official on public funds. ~ *v.i.* Feast, go on a junket. **jun·ke·teer** (jŭngk*e*tēr'), **jun'ke·ter** *ns.*

junk·ie, junk·y (jŭng'kē) *ns.* (pl. **junk·ies**). (slang) Drug addict.

Ju·no (jo͞o'nō). 1. (Rom. myth.) Chief Roman goddess, wife and sister of Jupiter; worshipped esp. by women; identified with HERA. 2. (astron.) One of the asteroids.

Ju·no·esque (jo͞onōĕsk') *adj.* Resembling Juno in stately beauty.

jun·ta (ho͝on't*a*, ho͝on'-, jŭn'-, hŭn'-), **jun·to** (jŭn'tō) *ns.* (pl. **-tos**). Deliberative or administrative council in Spain or Italy; clique, faction, political or other combination of persons; group of military officers ruling a country after a coup d'etat.

Ju·pi·ter (jo͞o'pĭt*er*). 1. (Rom. myth.) Orig. a sky spirit, associated with lightning and thunderbolts; later, the chief of the gods, giver of victory, patron of the Roman state, identified with ZEUS. 2. (astron.) Largest planet in solar system, the fifth from the sun, revolving in orbit between those of Mars and Saturn, and with four large and several smaller satellites; its diameter is approx. 86,000 mi. (138,400 km), its mass over 300 times that of Earth, and its period of revolution around the sun 11.86 years.

Ju·ra (joor'*a*; *Fr.* zhürā'). System of mountain ranges between rivers Rhine and Rhone forming the frontier between France and Switzerland.

Ju·ras·sic (jo͝orăs'ĭk) *adj.* & *n.* (geol.) (Of) the middle period or system of the Mesozoic, between the Cretaceous and the Triassic (135- to 180-million years ago), when dinosaurs and the earliest mammals existed. [f. JURA]

ju·rid·i·cal (jo͞orĭd′ĭkal), **ju·rid·ic** (jo͞orĭd′ĭk) *adjs.* Of judicial proceedings; legal. **ju·rid′i·cal·ly** *adv.*

ju·ris·dic·tion (joorĭsdĭk′shon) *n.* Administration of justice; legal or other authority; extent of this, territory it extends over. **ju·ris·dic′tion·al** *adj.*

ju·ris·pru·dence (joorĭspro͞o′dens) *n.* Science, philosophy, of law; skill in law. **ju·ris·pru′dent, ju·ris·pru·den·tial** (joorĭspro͞odĕn′shal) *adjs.*

ju·rist (joor′ĭst) *n.* One versed in law, esp. an eminent judge or lawyer. **ju·ris·tic** (jo͞orĭs′tĭk), **ju·ris′ti·cal** *adjs.* Of jurist(s); legal, created by law. **ju·ris′ti·cal·ly** *adv.*

ju·ror (joor′*er*) *n.* Member of jury.

ju·ry (joor′ē) *n.* (pl. **-ries**). 1. Body of persons sworn to render verdict on question submitted to them in court of justice; **coroner's ~**, jury of persons who pronounce decision at coroner's inquest; **grand ~**, jury convened to evaluate accusations against person(s)

The Supreme Court building in Washington D.C. The court was formed in 1787 to act in cases involving interpretation of the Constitution and thus represents the apogee of ***justice.***

Composed almost entirely of gas ***Jupiter*** *has a mean diameter of 88,700 miles and orbits the sun at a mean distance of 483,310,000 miles. Here, a probe approaches Jupiter's surface.*

charged with a crime to determine whether the evidence warrants an indictment; ~ **box**, enclosure for jury in court; **ju'ryman, ju'ry-woman**, (pl. **-men, -wom·en**) member of jury; juror. 2. Body of persons judging competition etc.

just[1]: see JOUST.

just[2] (jŭst) *adj.* Equitable, fair; deserved; well-grounded; right in amount etc., proper. **just'ly** *adv.* **just'ness** *n.*

just[3] (jŭst) *adv.* Exactly; barely; merely; exactly at that moment; (colloq.) positively, quite; ~ **now**, at this moment; a little time ago.

jus·tice (jŭs'tĭs) *n.* 1. Just conduct; fairness; exercise of authority in maintenance of right; judicial proceedings; **poetic** ~, ideal justice as shown in poetry or fiction; **do** ~ **to**, treat fairly; show due appreciation of; **do oneself** ~, perform worthily of one's abilities. 2. Judge, esp. of Supreme Court; **Justice of the Peace**, (abbrev. J.P.) local magistrate having authority in limited area to hear minor cases, send others to higher courts, administer oaths, perform marriages, etc.

jus·ti·ci·a·ble (jŭstĭsh'ēa*b*el) *adj.* Subject to trial or court decision.

jus·ti·ci·ar·y (jŭstĭsh'ēĕrē, -yerē) *adj.* Of the administration of justice.

*The bark of the **jute** is processed for its fiber which is made into textiles and cordage. The fibers may reach 10 ft. in length and are separated by soaking. Jute is grown commercially chiefly in Bengal in India and Bangladesh.*

jus·ti·fy (jŭs'tĭfī) *v.t.* (**-fied, -fy·ing**). 1. Show the justice or rightness of; vindicate, be such as to justify; make good (statement etc.); adduce adequate grounds for. 2. (theol.) Declare (person) free from guilt; absolve. 3. (print.) Adjust (line of type) to fill a space neatly. **jus·ti·fi·a·ble** (jŭs'tĭfīa*b*el, jŭstĭfī'-), **jus·ti·fi·ca·to·ry** (jŭstĭf'ĭkatōrē, -tōrē, jŭs'tifikātĕrē) *adjs.* **jus'ti·fi·a·bly** *adv.* **jus·ti·fi·ca·tion** (jŭstĭfĭkā'shon) *n.*

Jus·tin·i·an (jŭstĭn'ēan). Name of two Eastern Roman emperors: **Justinian I** (483–565), called "the Great," emperor 527–65; reorganized and codified Roman law (~ **Code**); built church of St. Sophia at Constantinople; his general Belisarius recovered Africa from Vandals, occupied Rome, and overthrew the Gothic kingdom in Italy; **Justinian II** (669–711), emperor 685–95 and 704–11.

jut (jŭt) *n.* Projection; protruding point. ~ *v.i.* (**jut·ted, jut·ting**). Stick out; protrude; project. **jut'ting·ly** *adv.*

Jute (jōōt) *n.* Member of a Low German tribe that invaded Britain in 5th c. and settled in Kent, the Isle of Wight, etc. [Icel. *Iótar* people of Jutland]

jute (jōōt) *n.* Fiber from bark of Asian plants (*Corchorus capsularis* and *C. olitorius*), used for cordage, canvas, etc.; these plants. [Sansk. *juṭa, jaṭa* braid of hair]

Jut·land (jŭt'land). Peninsula that forms the continental part of Denmark and Schleswig-Holstein in West Germany.

juv. *abbrev.* Juvenile.

Ju·ve·nal (jōō'venal). Decimus Junius Juvenalis (*c*60–*c*130 A.D.), Roman satirist and poet.

ju·ven·ile (jōō'venĭl, -nīl) *adj.* Young, youthful; suited to, characteristic of, youth; ~ **delinquency**, criminal or antisocial actions by children or adolescents (~ **delinquents**); ~ **lead**, (theatr.) youthful hero's part in play; actor who takes this. **juvenile** *n.* 1. Young person. 2. Book for children. **ju·ve·nil·i·ty** (jōōvenĭl'ĭtē) *n.* (pl. **-ties**).

ju·ve·nil·i·a (jōōvenĭl'ēa, -nĭl'ya) *n.pl.* Literary or artistic works produced in youth.

jux·ta·pose (jŭkstapōz', jŭk'stapōz) *v.t.* (**-posed, -pos·ing**). Place (things) side by side. **jux·ta·po·si·tion** (jŭkstapozĭsh'on) *n.* Placing, being placed, side by side.

JV, J.V. *abbrevs.* Junior varsity.

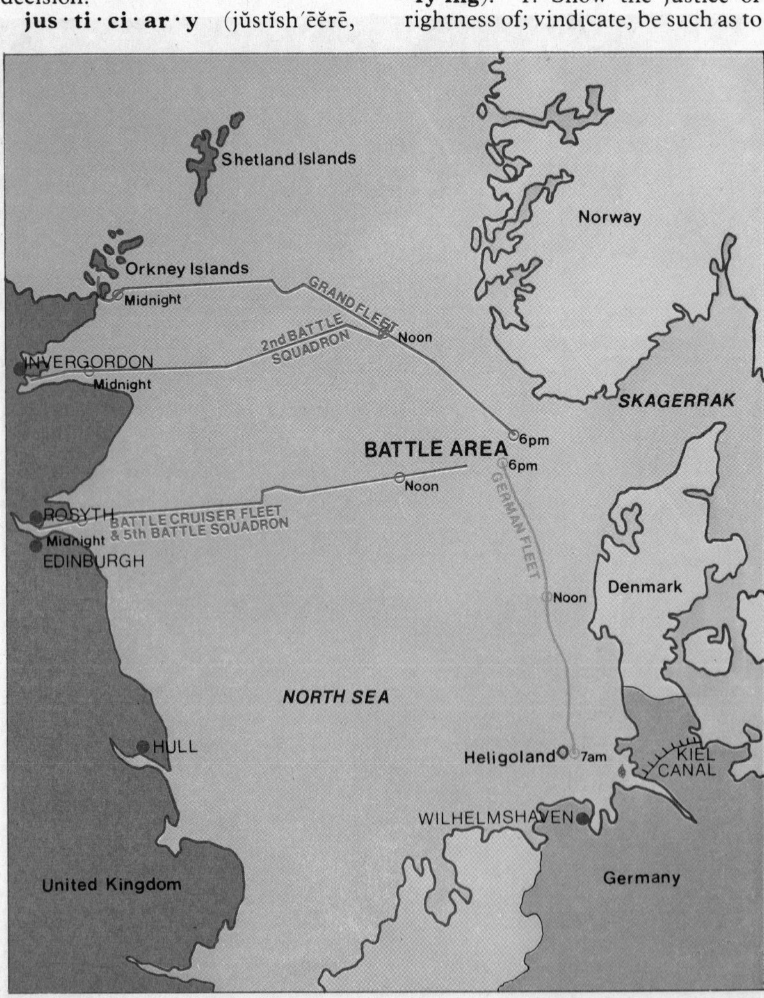

*Map shows the disposition of the opposing British and German Naval forces during the crucial **Battle of Jutland** in 1916. Despite heavy losses, the British Grand Fleet under Admiral Jellicoe remained dominant.*

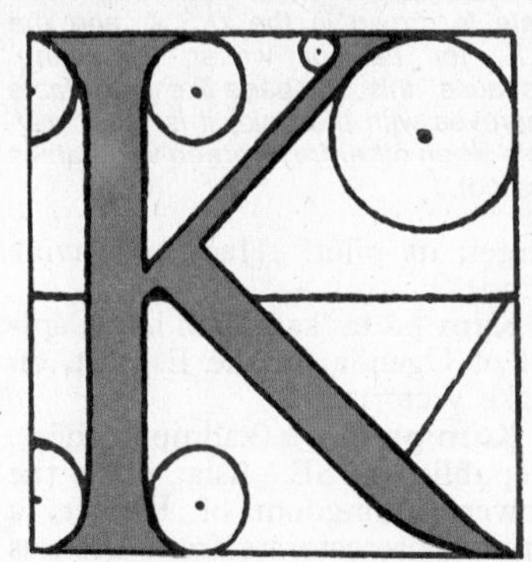

The letter K, k an aspirate glottal sound, was adopted by the Greeks from the Syriac 'kaf'. The Greeks called the letter 'kappa', meaning the hollow of the hand and perhaps for this reason placed it after the letter that means 'hand'. In classical Latin, K was used only as an abbreviation because its pronunciation was the same as the letter C.

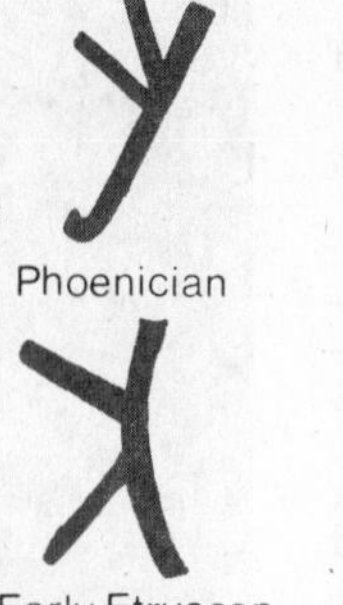

K, k (kā) (pl. **K's, k's** or **Ks, ks**). Eleventh letter of modern English alphabet, taken from Gk. κ (*kappa*), orig. ꓘ, from Phoenician and general Semitic ꓘ (*Kaph*); pronounced in modern English as a voiceless stop consonant.

K *abbrev*. Kelvin; kindergarten; (chem.) potassium; (chess) king.

K. *abbrev*. Köchel.

k. *abbrev*. Karat; kilogram(s); (chess) king.

K2. Peak of the W. Himalayas, 8,611 m (28,250 ft.) high, second highest in the world; also known as Godwin Austen.

Kaa·ba, Caa·ba (kah'b*a*) *ns*. Sacred building at Mecca, Muslim Holy of Holies containing sacred black stone.

ka·bob = KEBAB.

ka·bu·ki (kahbo͞o'kē, -k*a*-) *n*. Traditional popular Japanese drama with highly stylized song etc. acted by males only.

Ka·bul (kah'bo͝ol). Capital of Afghanistan in the E. central part; ~ **River**, chief river of Afghanistan rising W. of Kabul and flowing 360 mi. (576 km) to the Indus in Pakistan.

Kad·dish (kah'dĭsh; *Heb*. kahdēsh') *n*. (pl. **Kad·di·shim** pr. kahdĭsh'ĭm; *Heb*. kahdēshēm'). Prayer in praise of God recited during synagogue service and by mourners. [Aram. *ḳaddīš* holy]

kaf·fee klatsch (kah'fā klahch, kah'fē klăch) = COFFEE klatsch.

Kaf·fir, Kaf·ir[1] (kăf'*er*, kah'f*er*) *ns*. (pl. **-firs, -irs**, collect. **-fir, -ir**). Bantu inhabitant, language, of southern Africa (derog. as used by Arabic Muslims), non-Muslim, infidel. [Arab. *kāfir* infidel]

Kaf·ir[2] (kah'fēr, kahfēr') *n*. Member of a small group of tribes of NE. Afghanistan, prob. of Iranian origin, speaking an Indo-European language.

Kaf·ka (kahf'kah, -k*a*), **Franz** (1883–1924). Austrian novelist, born in Prague; author of *The Trial*, *The Castle*, etc. **Kaf·ka·esque** (kahfkahesk') *adj*. Resembling esp. the nightmare quality of Kafka's writings.

kail: see KALE.

kai·ser (kī'z*er*) *n*. Emperor; (hist.) German emperor; emperor of Austria; head of Holy Roman Empire; **the K**~: see WILLIAM[3].

ka·ke·mo·no (kahk*a*mō'nō; *Jap*. kahkĕmaw'naw) *n*. (pl. **-nos**; *Jap*. **-no**). Japanese vertical hanging scroll mounted on rollers, containing either text or painting on silk or paper. [Jap. *kake* hang, *mono* thing]

Ka·la·ha·ri (kahlahhar'ē) **Desert.** Large high barren plateau of

Afghanistan has a mixed population. The Kabul River leads south to the Khyber Pass — the traditional route of invaders. A unifying factor is religion: most of the people are Muslim.

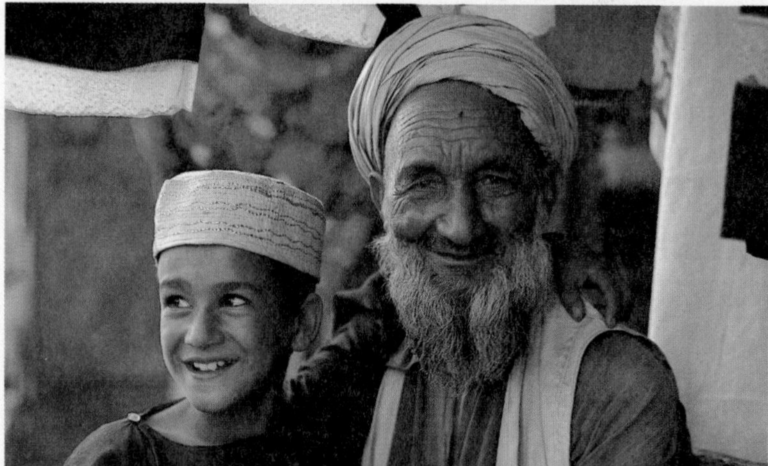

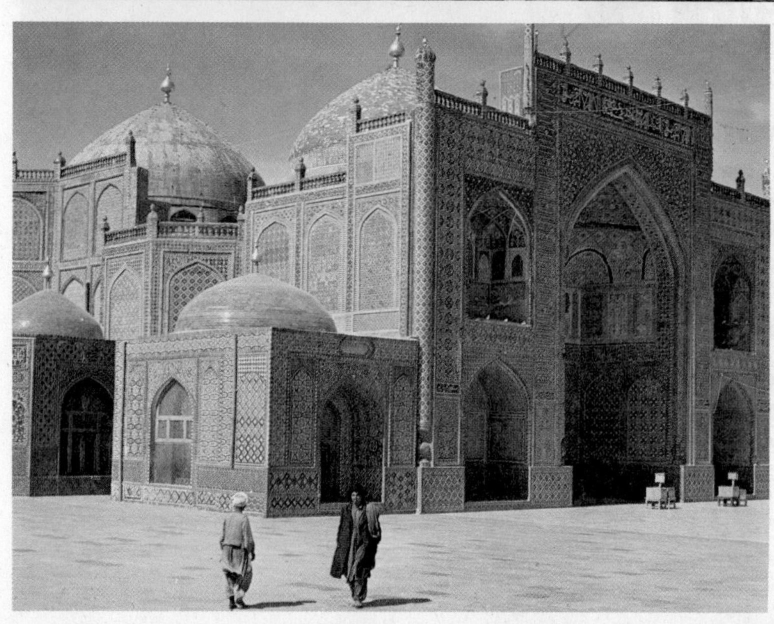

Relics of Mogul rule, as in the Mazar-i-Sharif, are still found in **Kabul** today. Babar, in the 16th century made Kabul capital of the Mogul Empire. Now the capital of Afghanistan, the city has a university and growing industries.

southern Africa, mainly in Botswana.

kale, kail (kāl) *ns.* Variety of cabbage with wrinkled leaves not forming compact head (*Brassica oleracea acephala*).

ka·lei·do·scope (kalī'doskōp) *n.* Tube through which are seen symmetrical figures, produced by reflections of pieces of colored glass, and varied by rotation of tube; (fig.) constantly changing group of bright objects; series of changing or varied objects, events, etc. **ka·lei·do·scop·ic** (kalīdoskŏp'ĭk), **ka·lei·do·scop'i·cal** *adjs.* **ka·lei·do·scop'i·cal·ly** *adv.*

kal·ends (kăl'endz): see CALENDS.

Ka·li (kah'lē). (Hindu myth.) Form of Durga, the bloodthirsty wife of Siva, represented with black body, four arms, necklace of human heads, and protruding bloodstained tongue.

Kal·muck, Kal·muk (kăl'mŭk) *ns.* 1. Member of Buddhist Mongol people of central Asia who invaded Russia in 16th and 17th centuries and settled along lower Volga. 2. Language of the Kalmucks, one of the Ural-Altaic family.

ka·long (kah'lŏng) *n.* Malay flying fox or fruit-eating bat (*Pteropus vampyrus*), the largest of the bats, having a wingspread of up to 5 ft.

Ka·ma (kah'ma). (Hindu myth.) God of love, represented as a beautiful youth riding on a sparrow and armed with bow and arrows.

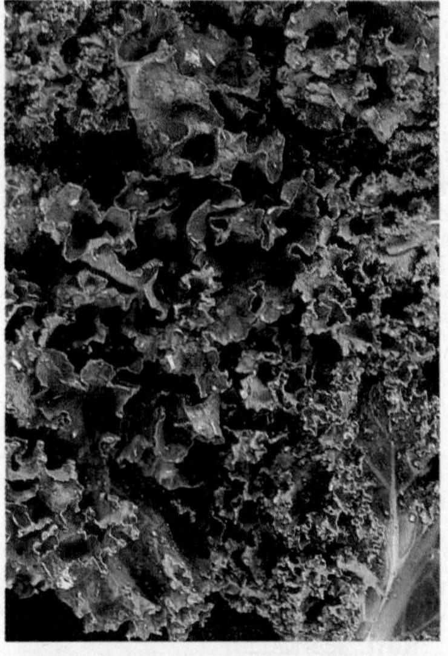

Kam·chat·ka (kahmchaht'kah). Peninsula of NE. Siberia running S. between Bering Sea and Sea of Okhotsk.

Ka·me·ha·me·ha (kamā'hamā'ha). Name of five kings of the Hawaiian Islands who reigned from 1795–1872.

ka·mi·ka·ze (kahmēkah'zē) *n.* World War II Japanese aircraft laden with explosives and deliberately crashed by its pilot on its target; its pilot. [Jap., = divine wind]

*The **Kansas State Capitol** in Topeka which is the capital of Kansas. The State was named after the Kansa or Kaw Indians, a hunting and farming people living in the area.*

__Kale__ is grown in the U.S.A. and the U.K. for Fall or winter harvesting. Because this cabbage-like vegetable improves with the cold, it is thus available when other fresh green vegetables are not.

Kam·pa·la (kahmpah'la). Capital of Uganda, in the E. part, on Lake Victoria.

Kam·pu·che·a (kahmpōō'chēa). Republic in SE. Asia; once the powerful kingdom of Khmer; a French protectorate from 1863 as part of French Indochina; gained independence during French-Indochinese war, 1953; now officially Democratic Kampuchea, capital Phnom Penh.

Ka·nak·a (kanăk'a, -nah'ka) *n.* Native of South Sea Islands. [Hawaiian, = "man"]

kan·ga·roo (kănggarōō') *n.* (pl. **-roos**, collect. **-roo**). Marsupial of genus *Macropus* with strongly developed hindquarters and great leaping power, native of Australia, Tasmania, etc.; ~ **court**, self-constituted court held by strikers, mutineers, etc.; dishonest court, esp. one determined to pronounce a person guilty regardless of the evidence; ~ **rat**, small Austral. marsupial belonging to any of several genera, esp. *Potorous* and *Bettongia*; also, Amer. pouched rodent (*Dipodomys*) of southwestern states and Mexico.

kan·ji (kahn'jē) *n.* (pl. **-ji, -jis**). Japanese writing using Chinese characters.

Kans. *abbrev.* Kansas.

Kan·sas (kăn'zas). State in central U.S., admitted to the Union in 1861; capital, Topeka; ~ **City**, large city in Missouri, on Missouri River; smaller city in Kansas, across river; ~ **River**, river draining N. part of Kansas and flowing eastward into Missouri River. **Kan'san** *adj.* & *n.*

Kan·su (kahn'sōō'). Extreme NW. province of China.

Kant (kănt; *Ger.* kahnt), **Immanuel** (1724–1804). German philosopher, founder of school of transcendental philosophy, of which one of the fundamental principles is that knowledge of the external world depends upon sense impressions coordinated or synthesized by the reason, employing such "categories" or laws of thought as quality, quantity, causation, etc. **Kant'i·an** *adj.* & *n.*

ka·o·lin, ka·o·line (kā'olĭn) *ns.* Fine white clay formed by the decomposition and weathering of feldspar in granite; used in making porcelain, as a filler for paper and textiles, etc. [Chin. *kao-ling* high hill (mountain where orig. obtained)]

Ka·pell·meis·ter (kahpĕl'mī-

Above: The ***red kangaroo,*** *a little smaller than the grey kangaroo, is the most widespread of the kangaroo family. It is seen here with a joey climbing out of the female's pouch. Below: A rufous rat kangaroo is about as large as a hare. Left: The black tree kangaroo. Left center: A red kangaroo.*

*The seed pod of the **kapok** contains a floss which is dried and cleaned to make an insulating material used to stuff sleeping bags and mattresses. Fats from the seeds are used in the manufacture of soap.*

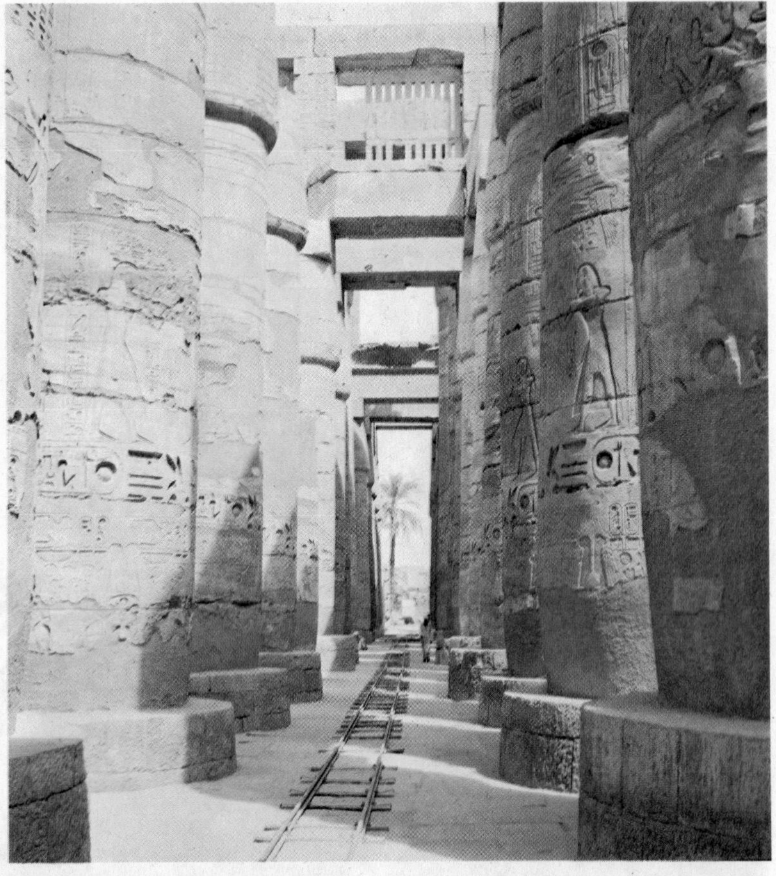

*The greatest building at **Karnak** in central Egypt is the Temple of Amon. The 134 massive columns of the hypostyle hall, seen here, are arranged in 16 rows and cover an area of 388 by 170 ft. The site is 1 mile east of Luxor.*

st*er*) *n.* (pl. **-ter**). Conductor of orchestra or choir. [Ger.]

ka·pok (kā'pŏk, kăp'*o*k) *n.* = SILK cotton from tree *Ceiba pentandra.* [Malay *kapoq*]

kap·pa (kăp'*a*) *n.* Eleventh (later tenth) letter of Greek alphabet (Κ, κ), corresponding to *k.*

ka·put (kahpo͝ot', -po͞ot') *adj.* (slang) Finished, done for. [Ger.]

Ka·ra·chi (k*a*rah'chē). Seaport and former capital of Pakistan, on an inlet of the Arabian Sea.

kar·a·kul, car·a·cul (kăr'*a*k*u*l) *ns.* Asian sheep whose young have dark curled fleece; fur, wool, made from or resembling this.

Ka·ra Kum, Qa·ra Qum (kârah ko͞om'). Flat desert region of the Turkmen Soviet Socialist Republic in the SW. Soviet Union.

kar·at (kăr'*a*t) *n.* Measure of $\frac{1}{24}$ stating fineness of gold; if e.g. the mass contains 22 parts of gold and two of alloy it is 22 karats fine, or 22-karat gold.

ka·ra·te (k*a*rah'tē) *n.* Japanese system of unarmed combat using hands etc. as weapons.

Ka·re·lia (k*a*rēl'y*a*). 1. Area of NW. U.S.S.R. between Finnish border and White Sea. 2. Autonomous republic (properly *Karelian Autonomous Soviet Socialist Republic*) of R.S.F.S.R.; capital, Petrozavodsk. **Ka·re'li·an** *adj.* & *n.*

Karl-Marx-Stadt (kârl'-mârks'shtaht'). City and textile center of East Germany, SE. of Leipzig; called Chemnitz until 1953.

Karls·bad (kârlz'bahd; *Ger.* kârls'baht). German name of *Karlovy Vary*, town in NW. Czechoslovakia; noted for its mineral springs.

Karls·ru·he (kârlz'ro͞o*e*). (also **Carlsruhe**) City in SW. West Germany on Rhine River.

kar·ma (kâr'm*a*) *n.* (Buddhism, Hinduism) Sum of person's actions in one of his successive states of existence viewed as deciding his fate in the next; destiny. **kar'mic** *adj.*

Kar·nak (kâr'năk). Village of Upper Egypt, on Nile near Luxor, containing magnificent ruins of temple of Ammon on site of ancient Thebes.

karst (kârst) *n.* Barren limestone formation with abrupt ridges, caverns, and underground streams. [*Karst*, limestone plateau in NW. Yugoslavia]

kart (kârt) *n.* Small, low-slung racing car with skeleton body.

ka·sha (kah'sh*a*) *n.* Cracked grain, esp. buckwheat, cooked until mushy; groats.

Kash·mir (kăshmēr', kăsh'mēr) = JAMMU AND KASHMIR. **Kash·mir'i** *n.* Indo-European language of Kashmir, much influenced by Sanskrit.

ka·ta·ka·na (kaht*a*kah'n*a*) *n.* Japanese set of written symbols, or syllabary.

Kat·mai (kăt'mī) **National Monument.** Area in S. Alaska at the N. end of the Alaska Peninsula covering 4,215 sq. mi. (10,917 sq. km) and including **Mount Katmai**, a volcano rising 6,715 ft. (2,047 m) and the Valley of Ten Thousand Smokes.

Kat·man·du (kahtmahndo͞o'). Capital of Nepal, in a valley of the Himalayas in the E. part.

ka·ty·did (kā'tēdĭd) *n.* Any of several large green insects of the genus *Microcentrun* and related genera, related to the grasshoppers and crickets and producing characteristic noise by stridulation [imit.]

Kau·ai (kowī'). Island in the Hawaiian group, NW. of Oahu, covering 555 sq. mi. (1,437 sq. km).

ka·va (kah'v*a*), **ka·va-ka·va** (kah'v*a* kah'v*a*) *ns.* (Intoxicating beverage prepared from dried roots of) Polynesian shrub, *Piper methysticum.*

Ka·wa·sa·ki (kahw*a*sah'kē). City and industrial center in SE. Honshu, Japan, on the W. coast of Tokyo Bay.

kay·ak (kī'ăk) *n.* Eskimo one-man canoe of light wooden framework covered with sealskins; small boat resembling this.

Ka·zakh, Ka·zak (k*a*zahk') *ns.* Member of a Turkic people of S. Siberia.

Ka·zakh·stan, Ka·zak·stan (kahzahkstahn'). Kazak(h) Soviet Socialist Republic, a constituent republic (properly *Kazakh Soviet Socialist Republic*) of U.S.S.R.; capital, Alma-Ata.

ka·zoo (k*a*zōō') *n.* Toy musical instrument into which player sings or hums.

kc, kc. *abbrevs.* Kilocycle(s).

K.C. *abbrev.* Knights of Columbus.

ke·a (kā'*a*, kē'*a*) *n.* Green parrot (*Nestor notabilis*) of a group peculiar to New Zealand mountainous areas, normally living on fruit, grubs, and carrion, but reputed to kill sheep by pecking at their flesh.

Keats (kēts), **John** (1795–1821). English lyric poet; author of "The Eve of St. Agnes," "Ode on a Grecian Urn," "Ode to a Nightingale," "Ode to Autumn," etc.

ke·bab, ka·bob (k*e*bŏb') *ns.* Oriental dish of small pieces of marinated meat, chicken, seafood, etc., often with onions, green peppers, cut tomatoes, or other vegetables grilled on skewer.

Ke·dah (kā'dah). State of Malaysia; capital, Alor Star.

Ke·dar (kē'd*er*). Son of ISHMAEL (Gen. 25), whose descendants were a tribe of nomads identified in later Jewish literature with the Arabs.

kedge (kĕj) *v.* (**kedged, kedg·ing**). (naut.) Change position of a ship by winding in hawser attached to small anchor at some distance; (of ship) move thus; move (ship) thus. ~ *n.* Small anchor for kedging.

ked·ger·ee (kĕj'*e*rē) *n.* Indian dish of rice, lentils, onions, eggs, etc.; European dish of fish, rice, eggs, and condiments.

keel (kēl) *n.* Lowest longitudinal timber of vessel, on which framework of whole is built up; similar structural member in nonwooden vessel; (poet.) ship; (in aircraft) vertical fin extending longitudinally underneath; (bot., zool.) carina; **keel'haul**, haul (person) under keel of ship as punishment. **keel** *v.* Turn (ship) keel upward; ~ **over**, turn, be turned, over, capsize; faint, drop from exhaustion, shock, etc. **keeled, keel'less** *adjs.*

Kee·ling (kē'lĭng) **Islands**: see Cocos Islands.

John Keats *(1795–1821) reading beside a window was painted by his friend Joseph Severn. Severn journeyed with Keats to Italy in 1820 and cared for him till his death. Keats' finest poems were written between 1817 and 1820.*

keen[1] (kēn) *n.* Wailing lamentation for the dead. ~ *v.* Utter a keen; bewail (person) thus; utter in wailing tone.

keen[2] (kēn) *adj.* Having sharp edge or point; sharp; (of sound, light, etc.) penetrating, vivid, strong, (of cold) intense; (of pain etc.) acute; (of person, desire, interest) eager, ardent (colloq. *on*); (of eyes etc.) sharp, highly sensitive; intellectually acute. **keen'ly** *adv.* **keen'ness** *n.*

The New Zealand ***kea*** *is a parrot whose tongue is adapted rather like a brush to collect nectar from flowers. But the kea will also eat meat when it needs alternative nourishment.*

keep[1] (kēp) *v.* (**kept, keep·ing**). 1. Pay due regard to, observe, stand by (law, promise, faith, etc.); observe, solemnize (feast etc.). 2. Guard, protect (person, fortress, etc.); have charge of; maintain in proper form and order; provide for sustenance of, maintain, support; own and manage (animals etc.); maintain (woman) as mistress, (man) as lover; have (commodity) habitually on sale. 3. Retain possession of, not lose; maintain,

The racing yacht's deep ***keel*** *is seen clearly as the vessel is lifted out of the water. The weight of the keel and the resistance of its surfaces help to stabilize the boat.*

remain, in proper or specified condition; reserve, admit of being reserved (*for* future time etc.); hide, conceal (secret etc.). 4. Detain (person *in prison* etc.); restrain (*from*); refrain *from*. 5. Continue to follow (way, course); remain in (one's bed, room, house); retain one's place in (the saddle, one's ground, etc.) against opposition; remain (indoors etc.). 6. ~ **house**: see HOUSE. 7. **keep at**, work persistently at; **keep away**, avoid coming; prevent from coming; **keep back**, hold back, retard progress of, conceal; **keep down**, hold in subjection; keep low in amount; **keep in**, confine, restrain (feelings, etc.); keep (fire) burning; **keep one's hand in**: see HAND; **keep off**, ward off, avert; stay at a distance; **keep on**, continue to use, show, etc.; continue (*doing*); **keep out**, not allow to enter; **keep to**, adhere to, confine oneself to; **keep to oneself**, avoid society; refuse to share with others; **keep together**, remain, cause to remain, together; **keep up**, prevent from sinking; maintain; keep in repair; carry on (correspondence etc.); cause (person) to be awake and up at night; bear up, not break down; proceed at equal pace *with*; **keep it up**, not slacken.

keep[2] (kēp) *n.* 1. (hist.) Tower, stronghold. 2. Maintenance, food required for this. 3. **for ~s**, (playing) seriously, intending to keep one's winnings; forever.

keep·er (kē'p*er*) *n.* One who keeps, guards, manages, etc.; custodian; mechanical device for keeping something in place.

keep·ing (kē'pĭng) *n.* (esp.) 1. Custody, charge. 2. Agreement, harmony.

keep·sake (kēp'sāk) *n.* Thing given or kept as a reminder of the giver; memento.

kees·hond (kās'hŏnd) *n.* (pl. **-hon·den** pr. -hŏnd*e*n). One of a breed of small Dutch dogs with thick black and gray hair and a tail curled up over the back.

kef·fi·yeh (kĕfē'yĕ), **kaf·fi·yeh** (kahfē'yĕ) *ns.* Bedouin Arab's kerchief worn as headdress.

keg (kĕg) *n.* Small barrel, usu. of less than 10 gallons.

Kel·ler (kĕl'*er*), **Helen (Adams)** (1880–1968). Amer. author, born in Alabama; became blind and deaf in infancy; was taught to speak, read, and use a typewriter; wrote several books, including the story of her life; traveled extensively and did much for the education of those similarly handicapped.

Kel·logg-Bri·and (kĕl'awg brēahnd', -ŏg) **Pact.** Treaty renouncing war as an instrument of national policy; signed in Paris, 1928, by representatives of 15 nations; also called "Kellogg Peace Pact." [F. B. *Kellogg* (1856–1937), U.S. secretary of state 1924–9]

Kells in the County of Meath was the seat of a 9th-century bishopric which had earlier associations with Columba. The Book of Kells is probably the finest Irish illuminated work. This page reproduced from it portrays Jesus Christ.

Kells (kĕlz), **Book of.** Illuminated manuscript of the gospels, now at Trinity College, Dublin; made perh. by Irish monks in 8th or early 9th c. [from *Kells*, town in Co. Meath, Ireland, where it was formerly kept]

kelp (kĕlp) *n.* (Any of the) large seaweeds that are burned for the potash, iodine, etc., they contain; calcined ashes of these.

Kelt (kĕlt): see CELT.

kel·vin (kĕl'vĭn) *n.* Unit of measurement in the Kelvin scale (abbrev. K). [f. KELVIN]

Kel·vin (kĕl'vĭn), **William Thomson, 1st Baron** (1824–1907). Irish-born physicist who advanced the science of thermodynamics and electricity, improved the system of electrical units, and invented several scientific instruments; **Kelvin scale**, scale of absolute temperature, in which the zero (corresponding roughly to −273 C) is the temperature at which a perfect gas would occupy zero volume if it could be cooled indefinitely, without liquefaction or solidification.

Ke·mal Pa·sha (k*e*mahl' pahshah'): see ATATÜRK.

Kem·ble (kĕm'b*e*l). Name of a family of English actors: **Charles** ~ (1775–1854); **Frances Anne ("Fanny")** ~ (1809–93), actress, his daughter; **John Philip** ~ (1757–1823), his brother; **Roger** ~ (1721–1802), actor and manager, father of John and Charles and of Mrs. Siddons.

Kem·pis (kĕm′pĭs), **Thomas à.** Thomas Hämmerken (*c*1380–1471), named from his birthplace, Kempen, near Düsseldorf; Augustinian monk, author of *De Imitatione Christi*.

ken (kĕn) *n.* Range of sight or knowledge. ~ *v.* (**kenned** or **kent, ken·ning**). (chiefly Sc.) Recognize at sight; know; understand.

Ken·ne·bec (kĕn′*e*bĕk). River in Maine flowing S. 150 mi. (241 km) from Moosehead Lake to the Atlantic Ocean.

Ken·ne·dy (kĕn′*e*dē). Name of wealthy Amer. family from Massachusetts prominent in politics, including **John Fitzgerald** (1917–1963) 35th president of the U.S. (1961–3); first Roman Catholic to hold this office; member of House of Representatives, 1947–53, and Senate, 1953–60; his term of office is noted for the formation of the Peace Corps, the Alliance for Progress aid program to Latin America, the Cuban missile crisis, in which he forced Soviet withdrawal of offensive atomic missiles, confrontation with Russians concerning the Berlin Wall, and encouragement of full civil rights for blacks; he received Pulitzer Prize, 1957, for collection of essays *Profiles in Courage*; was assassinated Nov. 22, 1963 in Dallas, Texas; 2. **Robert Francis** (1925–1968), brother of John; U.S. attorney general, 1961–4; U.S. senator from N.Y., 1965–8; assassinated June, 1968, in Los Angeles, Calif., while campaigning for presidency; 3. **Edward Moore ("Ted")** (1932–), brother of John and Robert; U.S. senator from Massachusetts, 1962– ; assistant majority leader, U.S. senate, 1969–1971; 4. **Joseph Patrick** (1888–1969), father of John, Robert, and Edward; Amer. financier and diplomat; chairman of the Securities and Exchange Commission, 1934–5; U.S. ambassador to the Court of St. James, 1937–41.

*At 43, **J. F. Kennedy** became the youngest president of the U.S.A. His foreign policy was notable for the failure in the Bay of Pigs fiasco and the success in the Cuban missile crisis in 1962.*

ken·nel (kĕn′*e*l) *n.* House, hut, for shelter of dog or dogs; place where dogs are bred or boarded. ~ *v.* (**-neled, -nel·ing**; Brit. **-nelled, -nel·ling**). Live in, go to, kennel; put into, keep in, kennel.

Ken·neth (kĕn′ĭth). Name of two Scottish kings: **Kenneth I MacAlpin** (d. *c*860), traditional founder of kingdom of Scotland; **Kenneth II** (d. 995).

ken·ning (kĕn′ĭng) *n.* Periphrastic expression used instead of simple name of thing in Old English, Old Norse, etc. poetry e.g. *whale road* = ocean, *ring-giver* = king.

Ken·ny (kĕn′ē), **Elizabeth** (1886–1952). Australian nurse who developed a method of muscle exercise and stimulation in treating paralysis caused by poliomyelitis.

ke·no (kē′nō) *n.* Gambling game resembling bingo.

ke·no·sis (kĭnō′sĭs) *n.* (theol.) Renunciation of divine nature, at least in part, by Christ in incarnation.

*The **keeper** of a zoo is responsible for maintaining the health and general welfare of the animals in his or her care.*

Kentucky, birthplace of Abraham Lincoln, was opened up by Daniel Boone and his companions in 1769. It is now the 2nd-highest producer of coal in the U.S.A. Each year in May the famous Kentucky Derby horse race is run.

Ken·tuck·y (kentŭk′ē). State in southeastern U.S., admitted to the Union in 1792; capital, Frankfort; ~ **Derby**, see DERBY. **Ken·tuck′i·an** *adj.* & *n.*

Ken·ya (kēn′ya, kĕn′-). Country of E. Africa between Ethiopia and Tanzania; former British colony, independent since 1963; capital, Nairobi; **Mount** ~, extinct volcano rising 17,040 ft. (5,197 m) in the central part S. of the equator; second highest mountain in Africa. **Ken′yan** *adj.* & *n.*

Ken·yat·ta (kĕnyah′ta), **Jo·mo** (jō′mō) (1893?–1978). Political leader of Kenya; president, 1963–1978.

kep·i (kā′pē, kĕp′ē) *n.* (pl. **kep·is**). French military cap with visor.

Kep·ler (kĕp′ler), **Johann** (1571–1630). German astronomer, whose three laws of planetary motion provided the basis for much of Newton's work.

Ke·pone (kē′pōn) *n.* (trademark) Pesticide believed to be water pollutant and source of damage to human nervous system.

kept (kĕpt): see KEEP[1]. ~ *adj.* (esp.) Supported financially in exchange for sexual favors.

ker·a·tin (kĕr′atĭn), **cer·a·tin** (sĕr′atĭn) *ns.* Protein or group of proteins found in skin, hair, nails, horns, hoofs, and feathers.

kerb (kẽrb) *n.* (Brit.) Curb.

ker·chief (kẽr′chĭf) *n.* Cloth used to cover head; (poet.) handkerchief.

kerf (kẽrf) *n.* Slit made by cutting, esp. with saw.

Ker·gue·len, Ker·gué·len (kẽr′gelĕn). Desolation Island, uninhabited subantarctic island, belonging to France, in Southern Ocean SE. of Cape of Good Hope and SW. of Australia; discovered (1772) by a Breton navigator, Yves-Joseph de Kerguélen-Trémarec.

ker·mes (kẽr′mēz) *n.* Female of insect *Kermes ilicis*, dried and used in dyeing; red dyestuff prepared from dried bodies of these.

kern[1] (kẽrn) *n.* (print.) Part of a metal type projecting beyond the body or shank, as the curled head of *f* and tail of *j*, etc.

kern[2], **kerne** (kẽrn) *ns.* (hist.) Lightly armed Irish foot soldier; peasant, boor.

Kern (kẽrn), **Jerome David** (1885–1945). Amer. composer famous for musical comedies; his songs include "Ol' Man River," "Smoke Gets in Your Eyes," "The Last Time I Saw Paris," etc.

ker·nel (kẽr′nel) *n.* Softer (usu. edible) part within hard shell of nut or stone fruit; whole seed within husk etc., e.g. grain of wheat; nucleus, center of formation (freq. fig.).

ker·o·sene, ker·o·sine (kĕr′osēn, kăr′-, kĕrosēn′, kăr-) *ns.* Fuel oil obtained by distillation of petroleum, or from coal or shale.

Ker·ry (kĕr′ē). County of the Republic of Ireland, in the SW.; hence, one of a breed of very small black dairy cattle orig. produced there; ~ **blue**, Irish breed of terrier, with silky blue-gray coat.

kes·trel (kĕs′trel) *n.* Small falcon, in U.S., the sparrow hawk (*Falco sparverius*); in the Old World *F. tinnunculus*, with habit of remaining in same place in air with head to the wind; windhover; see FALCON.

ketch (kĕch) *n.* Small two-masted sailing vessel for coastal waters.

ketch·up (kĕch′up, kăch′-), **katch·up** (kăch′up, kĕch′-), **cat·sup** (kăt′sup, kăch′up, kĕch′-) *ns.* Sauce of tomatoes (usu.), mushrooms, or walnuts, etc., with vinegar, raisins, spices, etc., used as condiment. [prob. f. Chin. *kôechiap* brine of pickled fish]

ke·tone (kē′tōn) *n.* (chem.) One of a group of organic compounds containing carbonyl group (CO) doubly united with carbon, usu. colorless volatile liquids with pungent ethereal smell, used esp. as solvents. [Ger. *keton*, modification of *acetone*]

ket·tle (kĕt′el) *n.* 1. Large vessel for boiling or stewing, usu. of metal with lid; similar but smaller vessel with spout and handle, teakettle. 2. (geol.) (also ~ **hole**) Sunken area in glacial drift, apparent result of melting of isolated mass of glacial ice. 3. **pretty** ~ **of fish**, awkward state of affairs; **ket′tledrum**: see

DRUM.

key[1] (kē) *n.* (pl. **keys**). 1. Metal instrument for moving bolt of lock forward or backward. 2. What gives or precludes opportunity for or access to something. 3. (pl., with allusion to Matt. 16) Ecclesiastical authority held to be transmitted to pope as successor of St. Peter. 4. Solution, explanation; translation of book or exercise in foreign language; book of solutions of mathematical problems etc. 5. (mus.) System of tones definitely related to each other and based on **key'note** in which a piece of music is written; (fig.) tone, style, of thought or expression (hence **keynote speech**, address, esp. at political convention, stating basic policies, principles, positions on topical issues, etc., and given by person designated as **key'noter**). 6. Wood or metal pin inserted between parts to secure them. 7. Lever pressed by finger in playing organ, piano, flute, etc.; similar lever in typewriter etc. 8. Small instrument for winding clock etc. 9. **key'board**, set of keys in piano, organ, typewriter, data processing machine, etc.; **key club**, private night club to which each member has personal door key; **key'hole**, hole by which key is put into lock; **key'note**: see sense 5; (fig.) prevailing tone or idea. **key'punch**, machine with which keyboard operator records coded data by punching holes in cards; **key ring**, ring for keeping keys on; **key signature**, (mus.) one or more flats or sharps written on the staff after the clef to give the key of a composition; **keystone**: see separate entry; **key word**, key to cipher etc. **key'less** *adj.* **key** *v.t.* (**keyed, key·ing**). Fasten (*in, on,* etc.) with pin, wedge, bolt, etc.; ~ **up**, (fig.) stimulate.

key[2] (kē) *n.* (pl. **keys**). Low offshore island or reef, of kind common in West Indies or off coast of Florida.

Key[1] (kē), **Francis Scott** (1779–1843). Amer. lawyer; wrote the poem that became lyrics of a popular song, "The Star Spangled Banner," which Congress made national anthem, 1931; Key wrote the poem after seeing the Amer. flag still flying over Fort McHenry in Baltimore following British shelling during War of 1812.

Key[2] (kē) **West.** Resort city on Key West island, Florida; southernmost U.S. city.

Keynes (kānz), **John Maynard, 1st Baron** (1883–1946). English economist. **Keynes'i·an** *adj.* & *n.*

key·stone (kē'stōn) *n.* 1. Stone at summit of arch locking the whole together; (fig.) central principle etc. on which all depends. 2. **K~ State**, nickname of PENNSYLVANIA. **keystone** *adj.* Of or pertaining to type of slapstick comedy popular in silent films (produced by Keystone Co.) depicting clownlike, inept policemen (~ **cops**).

kg, kg. *abbrevs.* Kilogram(s).

KGB, K.G.B. *abbrevs.* Secret

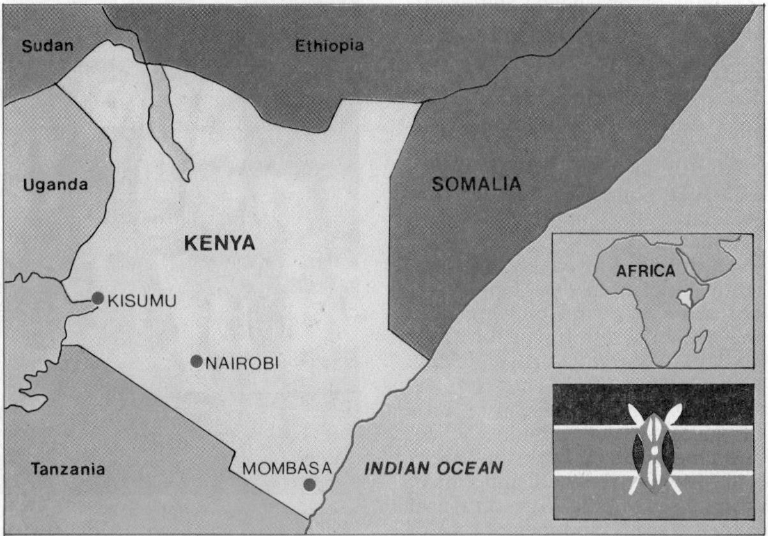

*Top: A map of **Kenya** with (inset) a location guide to show its position in Africa, and the flag of Kenya. Right: The economy of Kenya is largely based on agriculture. Cattle are raised and coffee, tea, wheat, maize and tobacco grown. Here a worker removes young shoots from tobacco plants.*

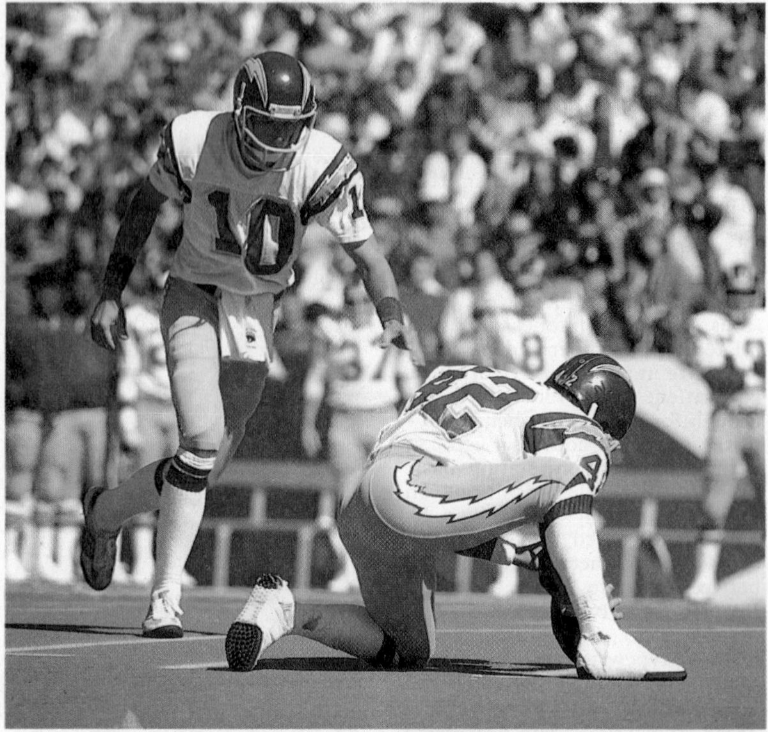

In 1912 when the rules for gridiron football were being changed to make it a less brutal game (in 1905 there had been 18 deaths) the ***kickoff,*** *previously made from center field, was moved to the kicking side's 40-yard line.*

police of U.S.S.R., which took over functions of M.V.D. in 1960. [initials of Russ. *K*omitét *G*osudárstvennoĭ *B*ezopásnosti, State security committee]

kha·ki (kăk´ē, kah´kē) *adj.* Dull brownish yellow. ~ *n.* (pl. **-kis**). Khaki fabric used in army for field uniforms. [Hind., = dusty (*khak* dust)]

kha·lif (kahlēf´, kā´lĭf, kăl´ĭf), **kha·li·fa** (kahlē´fah), **khal·i·fate** (kăl´ĭfāt, -fĭt) *ns.* = CALIPH, caliphate.

kham·sin, kam·seen, kam·sin (kăm´sĭn, kămsēn´) *ns.* Oppressive hot S. or SE. wind blowing from the Sahara across Egypt for about 50 days in March, April, and May. [Arab. *ḳamsīn* fifty]

khan[1] (kahn, kăn) *n.* (hist.) Title of successors of Genghis Khan, supreme rulers of Turkish, Tartar, and Mongol tribes and emperors of China, in Middle Ages; title of rulers, officials, and men of rank of central Asia, Afghanistan, etc. **khan'ate** *n.* [Turk., perhaps f. *khāgān* king]

khan[2] (kahn, kăn) *n.* Caravansary. [Arab., = "inn"]

Khar·toum (kartōōm´). Capital of Sudan, on Blue Nile just above junction with White Nile; besieged 1885 and captured from the British by the Mahdists; recaptured by the British under KITCHENER, 1898.

Khay·yám (kīyahm´, -yăm´), **Omar**: see OMAR KHAYYÁM.

khe·dive (k*e*dēv´) *n.* (hist.) Title of viceroy or governor of Egypt until 1914; orig. accorded to Ismail Pasha by Turkey in 1867.

Khmer[1] (kmĕr, χmār) *n.* 1. Native, inhabitant, of the ancient kingdom of Khmer in SE. Asia, which reached peak of its power in 11th c. and was destroyed by Siamese conquests in 12th and 14th centuries; native, inhabitant, of the Khmer Republic. 2. Monosyllabic language of this people, of Mon-Khmer group of Austro-Asiatic family.

Khmer[2] (kmĕr, χmār) = KAMPUCHEA.

Khru·shchev (krōōsh´chĕf, -chawf, krōōsh´-; *Russ.* χrōōsh-chawf´), **Nikita Sergeyevich** (1894–1971). Dictator and premier of U.S.S.R. 1958–64; denounced Stalin at party congresses in 1956 and 1961.

Khy·ber (kī´b*er*) **Pass.** Chief pass between Afghanistan and Pakistan.

kHz *abbrev.* Kilohertz.

KIA *abbrev.* Killed in action.

ki·ang (kēăng´) *n.* Tibetan ass (*Equus hemionus*), with thick furry coat, found at altitudes of 15,000 ft. (4,500 m) and upward.

Kiang·si (kyahng´sē´). Province of SE. China.

Kiang·su (kyahng´sōō´). Coastal province of E. China at outlet of Yangtze Kiang.

kib·ble (kĭb´*e*l) *v.t.* (**-bled, -bling**). Bruise or grind coarsely; crush into small pieces.

kib·butz (kĭbōōts´) *n.* (pl. **kib·but·zim** pr. kĭbōōtsēm´). Collective farm or settlement in Israel. [Heb.]

Ki·bei (kē´bā´) *n.* (pl. **-bei, -beis**). Native citizen of U.S., born of immigrant Japanese parents but educated in Japan. Cf. ISSEI; NISEI; SANSEI.

kib·itz·er (kĭb´ĭts*er*) *n.* (colloq.) Meddlesome person, one who gives advice gratuitously; one who watches game of cards from behind the players; meddlesome onlooker. **kib'itz** *v.*

ki·bosh (kī´bŏsh, kĭbŏsh´) *n.* (slang) **put the ~ on**, put an end to.

kick (kĭk) *n.* Act of kicking; (colloq.) power of reaction, resilience; recoil of gun when discharged; (colloq.) complaint, criticism; (slang) sharp stimulant effect, thrill; **kick'back**, (colloq.) strong reaction; (slang) payment for help in making profit, for showing favor, etc.; **kick'off**, (football) kick starting game, second half of game, or play after score is made; (colloq.) start, as of fund drive, political campaign, etc.; **kick'stand**, short metal bar on rear axle of bicycle or motorcycle, used to hold vehicle

The attack that ***Khrushchev*** *launched on Stalinism released a burst of separatist activity among the U.S.S.R.'s satellites. He survived this crisis and strengthened his position at home with a policy of decentralization of industry.*

upright when not in use; **kick starter**, pedal on motorcycle etc. for starting engine by downward push with foot. **kick** *v.* Strike out with the foot; (colloq.) show annoyance, dislike, etc. (*against, at*); strike with foot; drive, move, (thing) by kicking; (football) score (field goal or point after touchdown) by a kick; drive forcibly and contemptuously (*out* etc.); ~

*For centuries the **Khyber Pass** has provided a route to India, either for trade or for invasion. The fort (left) was garrisoned by the British whose regimental badges on plaques record their tours of duty.*

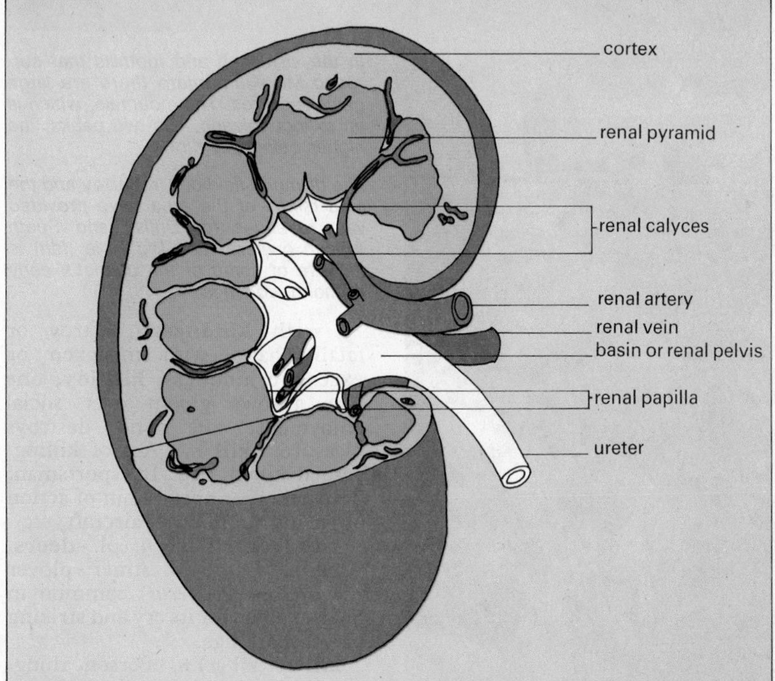

Mammals must have at least one of their two kidneys operating effectively. The human kidney is about 4 ins. x 2½ ins. Blood enters the kidney through the renal artery, is purified and then passes out through the renal vein.

about (**around**), treat person roughly or scornfully; discuss (idea) unsystematically; move idly from place to place; be unused or unwanted; **kick back**, (slang) pay kickback; **kick in,** (slang) give (one's share), esp. in money; **kick off,** (football) put ball in play by kickoff; (colloq.) start (fund drive etc.); **kick oneself**, be angry with oneself; **kick over**, (colloq.) start, or make start, running, as an internal combustion engine; **kick the bucket**, (slang) die; **kick the habit**, rid oneself of drug addiction, bad habit, etc.; **kick up**, (colloq.) raise (dust); create (fuss, noise). **kick′er** *n.*

Kick·a·poo (kĭk′*a*pōō) *n.* (Member of a) N. Amer. Indian tribe of Algonquin linguistic stock, orig. found in S. Wisconsin and N. Illinois; its language.

kid[1] (kĭd) *n.* Young of goat; leather from skin of this, used for gloves and boots; (slang) child, young person. ~ *v.i.* (**kid·ded, kid·ding**). Give birth to kid. **kid′dy, kid′die** *ns.* (pl. **-dies**). (slang) Little child.

kid[2] (kĭd) *v.* (**kid·ded, kid·ding**). (colloq.) Tease, josh.

Kidd (kĭd), **William** (*c*1645–1701). "Captain Kidd," English privateer and pirate; hanged for piracy, 1701.

kid·nap (kĭd′năp) *v.t.* (**-napped, -nap·ping, -naped, -nap·ing**). Abduct (child), carry off (person) by illegal force, esp. to hold for ransom. **kid′nap·per, kid′nap·er** *ns.*

kid·ney (kĭd′nē) *n.* (pl. **-neys**). 1. One of a pair of glandular organs in abdominal cavity of vertebrates, serving mainly to excrete nitrogenous matter from the blood; analogous organ in other animals; kidney of sheep, cattle, or pigs, as food. 2. Kind, disposition, temperament; ~ **bean**, oval-shaped edible seed of common garden bean (*Phaesolus vulgaris*); ~ **stone**, abnormal concretion formed in the kidney.

Kier·ke·gaard (kēr′k*e*gârd; *Dan.* kēr′k*e*gōr), **Sören Aabye** (suh′r*e*n aw′bü) (1813–55). Danish philosopher and theological writer.

Kiev (kē′ĕf, -ĕv). (Russ. **Kiyev**) Capital of Ukrainian S.S.R., U.S.S.R., in the SW. part on the Dnieper River.

Ki·ga·li (kēgah′lē). Capital of Rwanda, in the central part.

Ki·ku·yu (kĭkōō′yōō) *n.* (pl. **-yus**, collect. **-yu**). (Member of) an agricultural Bantu people of Kenya; their language.

Ki·lau·e·a (kēlowā′*a*). Volcanic crater on the E. side of Mauna Loa, Hawaii; world's largest active volcano, 2 mi. (3 km) wide, 4,090 ft. (1,247 m) high.

Kil·i·man·ja·ro (kĭl*i*m*a*njâr′ō). Mountain in NE. Tanzania, highest mountain in Africa (19,340 ft., 5,895 m).

kill (kĭl) *v.t.* 1. Put to death; cause the death of; perform act of killing, execute; ~ **off**, get rid of (number of animals, persons etc.) by killing; ~ **two birds with one stone**, effect two purposes at once. 2. Destroy vitality of; destroy, put an end to; consume (time) for the sake of doing so; (slang) overwhelm (person) with admiration, amusement, etc.; strike (ball in tennis etc.) so that it cannot be returned; totally defeat (bill in legislature);

In the savannah and foothills that surround ***Mt. Kilimanjaro*** *there are large game reserves. The mountain, which is an extinct volcano, has two peaks, the higher being Mt. Kibo.*

The diamond field of ***Kimberley*** *and the gold mines of the area have provided vast revenues for British and South African owners. The Big Hole (left) is the site of some of the district's early diamond workings.*

~ **with kindness**, destroy or fatally harm with mistaken or excessive kindness; **kill'joy,** one who throws gloom over social enjoyment, one who destroys pleasure. **kill** *n.* Act of killing; animal killed, esp. by sportsman; destruction or putting out of action of enemy submarine, aircraft, etc.

kill·deer (kĭl′dēr) *n.* (pl. **-deers, -deer**). Large N. Amer. plover (*Charadrius vociferus*) common in fields, known for its cry and striking breast markings.

kill·er (kĭl′*er*) *n.* Person, thing, that kills; murderous ruffian; ~ **whale**, a black and white predatory whale (*Orcinus orca*).

kill·ing (kĭl′ĭng) *n.* (esp.) Murder; kill (of animals, as by hunters); (slang) large, quick profit. ~ *adj.* 1. Fatal; exhausting. 2. (colloq.) Overwhelmingly funny.

kiln (kĭl, kĭln) *n.* Furnace, oven, for burning, baking, or drying, esp. for calcining lime, baking bricks or drying hops; ~**-dry**, (*v.t.*) dry in kiln.

ki·lo (kē′lō, kĭl′ō) *n.* (pl. **ki·los**). Kilogram.

kilo- *prefix*. One thousand times (abbrev. k).

kil·o·cy·cle (kĭl′osīkel) *n*. One thousand cycles, as unit in measuring frequency of electromagnetic waves (abbrev. kc).

kil·o·gram (kĭl′ogrăm) *n*. Unit of mass in the metric system (abbrev. kg), equal to the mass of the international prototype of the kilogram at Sèvres (approx. 2.20 lb.).

kil·o·hertz (kĭl′ohẽrts) *n*. (pl. **-hertz**). Unit of vibration frequency = 1,000 cycles per second.

kil·o·joule (kĭl′ojōōl) *n*. One thousand joules.

kil·o·li·ter (kĭl′olēter) *n*. One thousand liters (abbrev. kl).

ki·lom·e·ter (kĭl′omēter, kĭlŏm′e-) *n*. One thousand meters (abbrev. km). **kil·o·met′ric** *adj*.

kil·o·ton (kĭl′otŭn) *n*. One thousand tons; unit of explosive power equivalent to 1,000 tons of TNT.

kil·o·watt (kĭl′owŏt) *n*. One thousand watts (abbrev. kw); **~-hour**, unit of electrical energy, energy used when a rate of 1 kilowatt is maintained for 1 hour.

kilt (kĭlt) *v.t*. Tuck up (skirts) around body; gather in vertical pleats. **~** *n*. (often **kilts**) Part of Highland dress, skirt, usu. of tartan cloth, heavily pleated around back and sides, reaching from waist to knee. **kilt′ed** *adj*.

kil·ter (kĭl′ter) *n*. Good working order (**out of ~**, not working properly).

Kim·ber·ley (kĭm′berlē). Diamond mine, district, and town in N. Cape Province, S. Africa. [1st earl of *Kimberley*, colonial secretary (1871) when gold mines were taken under protection of Gt. Britain]

ki·mo·no (kĭmō′no, -nō) *n*. (pl. **-nos**). Long Japanese robe with wide sleeves; one of these, or similar robe, worn as dressing gown etc.

kin (kĭn) *n*. Ancestral stock, family; one's relatives; **kith and ~**: see KITH; **next of ~**: see NEXT. **kin** *pred. adj*. Related.

-kin *suffix*. Forming diminutive nouns (*catkin, napkin*).

kind[1] (kīnd) *n*. Class, sort, category, variety; character, quality; (archaic) nature in general; (rare) way, fashion, natural to person, etc.; **in ~**, (of payment) in goods or natural produce, not in money; (of repayment) in something of the same kind as that received; **~ of**, (colloq.) to some extent; **of a ~**, of the same group, type, etc.; similar; **of the ~**, like it.

kind[2] (kīnd) *adj*. Of gentle or benevolent nature; friendly in one's conduct *to*; (archaic) affectionate. **kind′ness** *n*.

kin·der·gar·ten (kĭn′dergārten,

*The **killer whale** is a member of the dolphin family found in seas all over the world. Unlike other whales that feed off the small shrimp, krill, the killer whale eats sharks, salmon and seals.*

*The **kimono** is actually derived from a Chinese garment and was first worn by the Japanese in about 650 A.D. It is still a popular mode of dress and has changed little.*

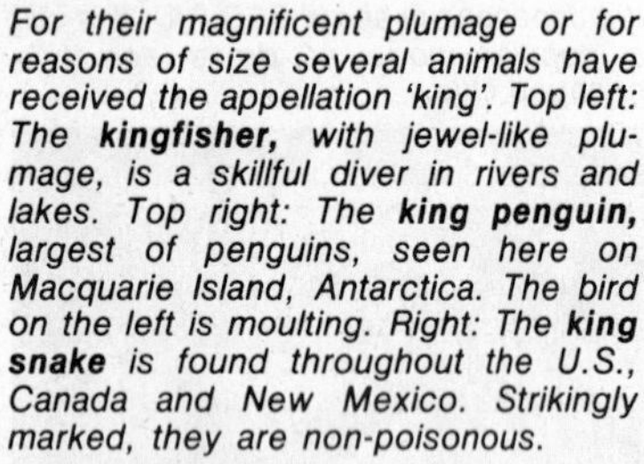

For their magnificent plumage or for reasons of size several animals have received the appellation 'king'. Top left: The ***kingfisher,*** *with jewel-like plumage, is a skillful diver in rivers and lakes. Top right: The* ***king penguin,*** *largest of penguins, seen here on Macquarie Island, Antarctica. The bird on the left is moulting. Right: The* ***king snake*** *is found throughout the U.S., Canada and New Mexico. Strikingly marked, they are non-poisonous.*

-d*e*n) *n.* School or class in a school for children under six years of age. **kin′der·gart·ner, kin′der·gar·-ten·er** *ns.* [Ger., = "children's garden"]

kin·dle (kĭn′d*e*l) *v.* (**-dled, -dling**). Set on fire, light; inflame, inspire (passion etc.); stir up (person *to*); catch fire, burst into flame; become animated, glow with passion, etc.; make, become, bright (cause to) glow. **kin′dling** *n.* (esp.) Small wood for starting fires.

kind·ly (kīnd′lē) *adv.* In a kind manner; obligingly; **take ~**, accept pleasantly; **take ~ to**, accept tolerantly. **kindly** *adj.* (**-li·er, -li·est**). Kind; pleasant, genial. **kind′li·ness** *n.*

kin·dred (kĭn′drĭd) *n.* Blood relationship; resemblance in character; one's relatives. ~ *adj.* Related by blood; allied, connected, similar.

kine (kīn). Archaic pl. of cow[1].

kin·e·mat·ic (kĭn*e*măt′ĭk), **kin·-e·mat·i·cal** (kĭn*e*măt′ĭk*a*l) *adjs.* Of motion considered abstractly without reference to force or mass. **kin·e·mat′ics** *n.* Science of kinematic motion.

kin·e·scope (kĭn′*e*skōp) *n.* 1. Cathode ray tube used as screen on which televised images are displayed. 2. Motion-picture record of a transmitted television program.

kin·es·the·sia (kĭnĭsthē′zh*a*) *n.* Sense of muscular effort in voluntary movement of body. **kin·es·-thet·ic** (kĭnĭsthĕt′ĭk) *adj.*

ki·net·ic (kĭnĕt′ĭk) *adj.* Of, due to, motion; **~ energy**: see ENERGY; **~ theory**, theory that heat, gaseous state, is due to motion of particles of matter. **ki·net′ics** *n.* Science of relations between the motions of bodies and the forces acting on them.

king (kĭng) *n.* 1. (Title of) male sovereign (esp. hereditary) ruler of independent state; **K~ of Kings**, God; title assumed by many Eastern kings; **the three kings**, wise men who came from the East to worship the newborn Christ; (**1st** and **2nd Book of the Kings**), two historical books of Old Testament, following the two Books of Samuel and covering Jewish history, esp. that of the kingdom of Judah, from the death of David to the destruction of the Temple (586 B.C.). 2. Great merchant etc.; best kind (*of* fruits, plants, animals, products, etc.); **king of beasts**, lion. 3. (chess) Piece that must be protected against checkmate; (checkers) piece that has been "crowned"; (cards) one card in each suit bearing representation of king, and usu. ranking next below ace; **king's bishop, knight, rook**, chess pieces on king's side of board at beginning of game; **king's pawn**, pawn in front of king at beginning of game. 4. **king′bird**, any of several flycatchers, esp. the eastern kingbird (*Tyrannus tyrannus*) or the western (*T. verticalis*); **king′-bolt**, main or large bolt in mechanical structure; **King Charles spaniel**, English black-and-tan toy spaniel with long silky coat and pendulous ears; **king cobra**, large, extremely venomous snake (*Ophi-*

*Top left: The **kingcup** is sometimes called a mollyblob. Here kingcups are growing on an alpine pasture, but they are frequently found in marshy ground where they flower in spring. Top right: The **King Charles spaniel** is a sporty rather than a toy breed, and weighs between 8 and 14 lbs.*

ophagus hannah) of tropical Asia, hamadryad; **king crab**, large, edible crab (*Paralithodes camtschatica*) of northern Pacific waters; HORSEshoe crab; **king'cup**, (Brit.) marsh marigold; **king'fish** (pl. **-fishes**, collect. **-fish**), name used variously for several large fish of the genus *Menticirrhus* of warm ocean waters; *Genyonemus lineatus*, marine food fish inhabiting Californian coastal waters; **king'fisher**, any of several birds of family Alcedinidae, esp. the belted kingfisher (*Megaceryle alcyon*), feeding on fish it captures by diving; **King James Bible** or **Version** = AUTHORIZED VERSION; **king penguin**, large species of penguin (*Aptenodytes petagonica*) of Antarctic regions; **king'pin**, (bowling) central or foremost pin; kingbolt; (fig.) most important person in organization etc.; **king post**, upright post from tie beam to rafter top; **king's** BENCH, ENGLISH, EVIDENCE: see these words; **king-size (bed)**, usually larger, longer than standard; 6½ by 6½ ft.; (**cigarette**) longer than standard; **king snake**, any of various medium-sized, harmless snakes (*Lampropeltis*) found from S. Canada through much of the U.S. and feeding on rats, mice, lizards, etc. **king'li·ness** *n.* **king'less, king'like** *adjs.* **king'ship** *n.* **king** *v.* (checkers) Make into a king.

King¹ (kĭng), **Martin Luther, Jr.** (1929–68). Amer. Baptist minister and civil rights leader; prominent in Montgomery, Ala. bus transportation boycott in fight for desegregation; founder of Southern Christian Leadership Conference; received Nobel Prize for peace, 1964; assassinated April, 1968, in Memphis, Tenn.

King² (kĭng), **William Lyon Mackenzie** (1874–1950). Canadian statesman; prime minister, 1921–6, 1926–30, 1935–48.

King³ (kĭng), **William Rufus DeVane** (1786–1853). Amer. politician; U.S. vice president, 1853, under Franklin Pierce.

king·dom (kĭng'dom) *n.* State with king as its head; monarchical State; territory subject to a king; spiritual reign of God, sphere of this (esp. **K ~ of Heaven**); domain; province of nature (esp. **animal, vegetable, mineral,** ~); ~ **come**, (slang) the next world; **Middle K ~**, imperial state of HONAN under Chan dynasty; **Old, Middle, New K ~**, successive periods of civilization in ancient Egypt.

king·let (kĭng'lĭt) *n.* Either of two small N. Amer. songbirds, the **golden-crowned** ~ (*Regulus satrapa*) or the **ruby-crowned** ~ (*R. calendula*), both olive green and having a bright yellow, orange, or red head marking.

king·ly (kĭng'lē) *adj.* (**-li·er, -li·est**). Fit for, appropriate to, a king; kinglike, majestic. **king'li·ness** *n.*

Kings·ton (kĭngz'ton, kĭng'ston). Chief port and capital of JAMAICA, on the SE. coast.

kink (kĭngk) *n.* Back twist in wire, chain, or rope, such as may cause obstruction or a break; tight curl; sharp twist; (fig.) mental twist, eccentricity. ~ *v.* Form a kink; cause (rope) to do this. **kink'y** *adj.* (**kink·i·er, kink·i·est**). Having kinks; (slang) eccentric, perverted.

kin·ka·jou (kĭng'kajōō) *n.* Carnivorous arboreal mammal (*Potos flavus*) of Central and S. Amer., allied to raccoon, with prehensile tail.

Kin·sey (kĭn'zē), **Alfred Charles** (1894–1956). Amer. zoologist and sociologist famous for his studies of human sexual behavior.

kins·folk (kĭnz'fōlk) *n.pl.* Relations by blood. **kins·man** (kĭnz'man) *n.* (pl. **-men** pr. -men), fem. **kins·wom·an** (kĭnz'wōōman) *n.* (pl. **-wom·en** pr. -wĭmĭn).

Kin·sha·sa (kĭn'shahsa). (formerly Léopoldville) Capital of the Republic of Zaire (the former Democratic Republic of the Congo) and major port on the Congo River, on the NW. border.

kin·ship (kĭn'shĭp) *n.* Blood relationship; similarity, alliance, in character.

ki·osk (kēŏsk', kē'ŏsk) *n.* Light open pavilion in Turkey and Iran; structure like this for sale of newspapers etc.

kip¹ (kĭp) *n.* Hide of young or small beast as used for leather.

kip² (kĭp) *n.* (chiefly Brit. slang) Rooming house; bed. ~ *v.i.* (**kipped, kip·ping**). Go to bed; sleep.

Kip·ling (kĭp'lĭng), **Rudyard** (1865–1936). English novelist and poet; born in India; famous for short stories about India, and for children's books; author of *The Jungle Book*, *Captains Courageous*, *Just So Stories*, and the poem "Gunga Din."

kip·per (kĭp'er) *n.* Male salmon in spawning season; kippered herring. ~ *v.t.* Cure (salmon, herring, etc.) by splitting open, salting, and smoking.

Kir·ghiz, Kir·giz (kērgēz') *adjs.*

*The forked tail of the swallow-tailed **kite** is clearly displayed in flight. The bird is found principally in warm marshy areas. Common kites once scavenged the streets of London.*

& *ns.* (pl. **-ghiz, -ghiz·es**). (Member) of a Turkic, mainly Muslim people of central Asia; (of) their language, one of the Ural-Altaic family; (also **Kir·ghi·zia**, pr. kĕrgē´zh*a*) constituent republic (properly *Kirghiz Soviet Socialist Republic*) of U.S.S.R., on Chinese frontier; capital, Frunze.

Ki·ri·ba·ti (kĭ´rĭbăsh). Formerly Gilbert Islands; Brit. dependency, NE. of Solomon Islands; largest island, Tarawa; became independent republic 1979.

*During the 1914–18 war **Field Marshal Kitchener** threw the weight of his influence behind a recruiting campaign that increased the British army from 20 divisions to 70 in two years.*

Ki·rin (kē̆r´ĭn). Province of NE. China.

kirk (kĕrk) *n.* (chiefly Sc.) Church.

kirsch (kĕrsh), **kirsch-was·ser** (kĕrsh´vahs*er*) *ns.* Colorless brandy made from cherries.

kish·ke (kĭsh´k*e*) *n.* Stuffed derma.

kis·met (kĭz´mĭt, kĭs´-) *n.* Destiny. [Arab. *kisma* lot, fate]

kiss (kĭs) *n.* Caress given with lips; light touch, a brushing against; any of various candies; ~ **of peace**, ceremonial kiss of worshippers in eucharistic liturgy as sign of love and union; pax; **kiss-off**, (slang) dismissal. **kiss** *v.t.* Touch with the lips, esp. in sign of affection, greeting, or reverence; touch lightly, brush against; ~ **away**, remove (tears etc.) with kisses; ~ **off**, (slang) get rid of, reject, dismiss.

kiss·er (kĭs´*er*) *n.* (slang) Face, mouth.

Kis·sin·ger (kĭs´ĭnj*er*), **Henry** (1923–). German-born Amer. political scientist; special assistant to Pres. Nixon for national security affairs; U.S. secretary of state under Presidents Nixon and Ford, 1973–1977; co-recipient of Nobel Prize for peace, 1973.

kit (kĭt) *n.* (Articles carried in) soldier's knapsack; personal equipment, esp. as packed for traveling; set of tools or other equipment; set of parts or materials to be assembled; ~ **bag**, bag, usu. cylindrical, for carrying soldier's or traveler's kit.

kitch·en (kĭch´*e*n) *n.* Part of house where food is cooked; ~ **garden**, garden for growing fruit and vegetables for table; ~ **police**, (mil.) enlisted men designated to perform menial kitchen tasks.

Kitch·en·er (kĭch´en*er*), **Horatio Herbert, Earl Kitchener of Khartoum** (1850–1916). British military leader; retook Khartoum with Anglo-Egyptian force 1898; commander in chief in Boer War, 1900–2, and in India; secretary of state for war, 1914–16.

kitch·en·ette, kitch·en·et (kĭch*e*nĕt´) *ns.* Small kitchen; alcove used as kitchen.

kite (kīt) *n.* 1. Any large hawk-like bird of family Milvinae or Elaninae with long wings and usu. forked tail. 2. Toy consisting of light wooden or plastic frame with paper or other thin material stretched over it, made to fly in strong wind at end of a long string; such a contrivance of box shape (**box-** ~) with open sides; highest or lightest sail of ship, set only in light wind. 3. Bad check or other commercial paper without value used to get money or credit. **kite** *v.* (**kit·ed, kit·ing**). 1. (Cause to) soar like kite. 2. Get money or credit through use of kites.

kith (kĭth) *n.* ~ **and kin**, friends and relatives; now freq., kinsfolk.

kitsch (kĭch) *n.* Literature, art, music, etc., having little cultural merit but produced to appeal to popular taste.

kit·ten (kĭt´*e*n) *n.* Young of cat. **kit'ten·ish** *adj.* **kitten** *v.i.* Give birth to kittens. **kit'ten·ish·ly** *adv.*

kit·ti·wake (kĭt´ēwāk) *n.* Smallest of the strictly marine gulls (*Rissa tridactyla*) of Arctic and N. Atlantic oceans, with black markings on usu. white plumage, very long wings, and very short hind toe. [imit.]

kit·ty[1] (kĭt´ē) *n.* (pl. **-ties**). Pet name for kitten.

kit·ty[2] (kĭt´ē) *n.* (pl. **-ties**). Pool or joint fund in games etc.

Kit·ty (kĭt´ē) **Hawk.** Village in eastern North Carolina; site of first successful airplane flight, by Wright Brothers on Dec. 17, 1903.

Ki·wa·nis (kĭw*a*h´nĭs). International organization (founded in Detroit, 1915) of business and professional men, with clubs chiefly in U.S. and Canada.

ki·wi (kē´wē) *n.* (pl. **-wis**). 1. New Zealand flightless nocturnal bird of family Apterygidae, with rudimentary wings and no tail; this as emblem of New Zealand. 2. Fuzzy, brown, edible fruit of a vine (*Actinidia chinensis*) native to subtropical Asia; Chinese gooseberry.

K.K.K., KKK *abbrevs.* Ku Klux Klan.

kl, kl. *abbrevs.* Kiloliter(s).

Klam·ath (klăm´*a*th) **Mountains.** Mountain range extending from NW. California into SW. Oregon; **Klamath River**, river flowing SW. 250 mi. (402 km) from Oregon through NW. California into the Pacific Ocean.

Klan (klăn) *n.* Ku Klux Klan.

*Until the early years of the 20th century the **kitchen** was the center of home management to a degree no longer experienced. Storage and preparation areas had to be large and well planned, as at Lanhydrock House, Cornwall, U.K.*

*The **kiwi** is a New Zealand flightless bird of the family Apterygidae. It is so called because of the male's shrill call. The kiwi is a shy nocturnal bird about the size of a chicken.*

kla·vier (kl*a*vēr′, klăv′ēer, klā′-vē-): see CLAVIER.

klax·on (klăk′s*o*n) *n.* (formerly trademark) (Electric) horn formerly used on automobiles.

Klee (klā), **Paul** (1879–1940). Swiss painter of abstract works of art.

Klein (klīn) **bottle.** (math.) Closed surface with only one side, formed by passing neck of bottle through side of bottle to join hole in base.

klep·to·ma·ni·a (klĕpt*o*mā′nē*a*) *n.* Irresistible impulse to steal in persons not driven to it by need. **klep·to·ma′ni·ac** *n.*

klieg (klēg) **light.** Powerful arc light used in movie making. [f. name of inventors, *Kliegl* brothers]

klip·spring·er (klĭp′sprĭng*er*) *n.* Small South African mountain antelope (*Oreotragus oreotragus*) having large ears.

Klon·dike (klŏn′dīk). Region in the Yukon Territory, NW. Canada, where gold was discovered in 1896; ~ **River**, tributary of Yukon River.

km, km. *abbrevs.* Kilometer(s).

kn *abbrev.* Knot(s).

knack (năk) *n.* Acquired faculty of doing a thing adroitly; ingenious device, habit, of action, speech, etc.

knack·wurst, knock·wurst ŏk′wẽrst, -woorst, -voorsht) *ns.* Short, thick, highly seasoned sausage, similar to frankfurter.

knap·sack (năp′săk) *n.* Soldier's or traveler's canvas or leather bag, strapped to back and used for carrying necessaries. [Low Ger.]

knap·weed (năp′wēd) *n.* Species of *Centaurea* (esp. *C. nigra*), a common weed with tough stem and light purple flowers on dark globular head.

knave (nāv) *n.* 1. Rogue. 2. (cards) Lowest picture card of each suit, jack. **knav′er·y** *n.* (pl. **-er·ies**). **knav′ish** *adj.* **knav′-ish·ly** *adv.* **knav·ish·ness** *n.*

knead (nēd) *v.t.* Work up (dough, clay, etc.) by drawing out and pressing or squeezing together; make (bread, pottery) thus; work on (muscles etc.) as if kneading, massage. **knead′er** *n.*

knee (nē) *n.* Joint between thigh and lower leg in man; area above this joint considered as place on which child or object is held; corresponding joint in animals; part of garment covering the knee; thing like knee in shape or position; **on one's** ~**s**, kneeling, esp. in supplication, worship, or submission; **bring** (person) **to his** ~**s**, reduce him to submission; ~ **breeches**, breeches reaching down to or just below knee; **knee′cap**, convex bone in front of knee joint, patella; **knee-deep, -high**, so deep or high as to reach the knees; **knee′hole**, (of writing table etc.) having hole between drawer pedestals to admit knees. **knee** *v.t.* (**kneed, knee·-ing**). Touch or poke with the knee.

kneel (nēl) *v.i.* (**knelt** pr. nĕlt or **kneeled, kneel·ing**). Fall, rest, on the knee(s), esp. in prayer or reverence (*to*).

knell (nĕl) *n.* Sound of bell, esp. of one rung solemnly after death or at funeral; (fig.) anything regarded as omen of death or ex-

*Relics of the gold rush to the **Klondyke** remain on the banks of Bonanza Creek. About 18,000 people joined the gold rush of 1896 and the sudden increase in the population of the area caused a severe food shortage.*

*The **knapsack** has become far more sophisticated in its design and material than the simple rucksack originally used as a convenient carry-all by soldiers.*

*There are several species of **knapweed** of which the commonest is probably the hardhead (Centaurea nigra). The plant grows in heavy soils among grass and it flowers in the summer.*

tinction. ~ *v.* (of bell) Ring, esp. at death or funeral; proclaim as by a knell; (fig.) sound ominously.

Knes·set, Knes·seth (knĕs′ĕt) *ns.* Israeli parliament.

knew (nōō, nū) *v.* past t. of KNOW.

Knick·er·bock·er (nĭk′*er*-bŏk*er*) *n.* 1. Descendant of original Dutch settlers of New York; New Yorker. 2. (**knickerbockers**) Loose-fitting breeches gathered in at knee. [*Knickerbocker*, pretended author of W. Irving's *History of New York*]

knick·ers (nĭk′*erz*) *n.pl.* Knickerbockers.

knick·knack, nick-nack (nĭk′-năk) *ns.* Small ornamental article, trinket, gimcrack.

knife (nīf) *n.* (pl. **knives** pr. nīvz). 1. Blade with sharpened longitudinal edge fixed in handle either rigidly or with hinge, used as cutting instrument or as weapon; sharpened cutting blade forming part of machine, as in paper cutter etc.; **under the** ~, (colloq.) undergoing surgical operation. 2. **knife edge**, edge of knife; steel wedge serving as fulcrum on which balancing beam, lever, etc. works. **knife** *v.t.* (**knifed, knif·ing**). Cut, stab, with knife; (fig.) betray, seek to defeat by underhand means.

knight (nīt) *n.* 1. (hist.) Military follower, esp. one devoted to service *of* (lady) as attendant or champion in war or tournament; (hist.) person, usu. one of noble birth who had served as page and squire, raised to honorable military rank by king or qualified person. 2. One on whom is conferred rank corresponding to medieval knight as reward for personal merit or services to crown or country. 3. Piece in game of chess, usu. shaped like horse's head. 4. ~**-errant** (pl. ~**s-errant**), medieval knight wandering in search of chivalrous adventures; (fig.) person of chivalrous or quixotic spirit; **knight-errantry** (pl. **-tries**), practice, conduct, of a knight-errant; **Knight of the Round Table**, one of King ARTHUR[1]'S knights; **Knights of Columbus**, benevolent society of R.C. men, founded in the U.S. in 1882; **knight** *v.t.* Confer knighthood on. **knight′hood** *n.* Rank, dignity, of a knight.

knight′ly *adj.*

knish (knĭsh) *n.* Dumpling of flaky dough filled with cheese, mashed potatoes, chopped meat, etc., and baked or fried.

knit (nĭt) *v.* (**knit·ted, knit·ting**). Form (close texture) by interlooping successive series of loops of yarn or thread; make (garments etc.) of this; contract (brow) in wrinkles; make, become, close or compact; unite intimately by means of common interests, marriage etc.

knit·ting (nĭt′ĭng) *n.* (esp.) Work in process of knitting; ~ **needle**, slender rod of metal, wood, plastic, etc., two or more of which are used together in knitting.

knob (nŏb) *n.* Rounded protuberance, esp. at end or on surface of thing; such handle of door or drawer. **knobbed** *adj.* **knob′by** *adj.* (**-bi·er, -bi·est**). **knob′bi·ness** *n.*

knock (nŏk) *v.* 1. Strike with hard blow; strike door, strike *at, on the door*, to gain admittances; drive (thing) *in, out, off*, etc., by striking; (of internal combustion engine etc.) make knocking, clanging noise from mechanical defect or faulty ignition; (colloq.) disparage. 2. ~ **about**, strike repeatedly, treat roughly; wander, lead irregular life; ~ **against**, collide with; ~ **down**, strike to ground with blow; take (machinery, furniture) to pieces to save space in transportation; dispose of (article *to* bidder at auction) by knock with hammer; ~ **off**, strike off with blow; leave off (work); (colloq.) dispatch (business) or compose (verses etc.) rapidly; deduct (sum from price etc.); ~ **out**, render unconscious with a blow; (boxing) defeat opponent by knocking him down for a count of ten (ten seconds); (colloq.) exhaust completely; (slang) overwhelm with feeling, emotions, laughter, etc.; (slang) produce hastily; ~ **together**, put hastily together; ~ **up**, (slang) impregnate. 3. **knock′-about**, boisterous, noisy (performance); wandering irregularly; (of clothes) suitable for rough or casual use; **knock′down**, (of blow) knocking down the opponent; (of price at auction) minimum; **knock-kneed, -knee**, (having) knees turned inward toward each other; **knock′out** (blow) that knocks boxer out; (slang) outstandingly beautiful woman or thing; **knockout drops**, drops added to drink in order to make drinker unconscious. **knock**

*The whetting and finishing of a fine edge to a **knife** requires a stone of fine grain and a skillful operator. This knife-grinder in a street in Beirut, Lebanon, works the whetstone by operating a treadle.*

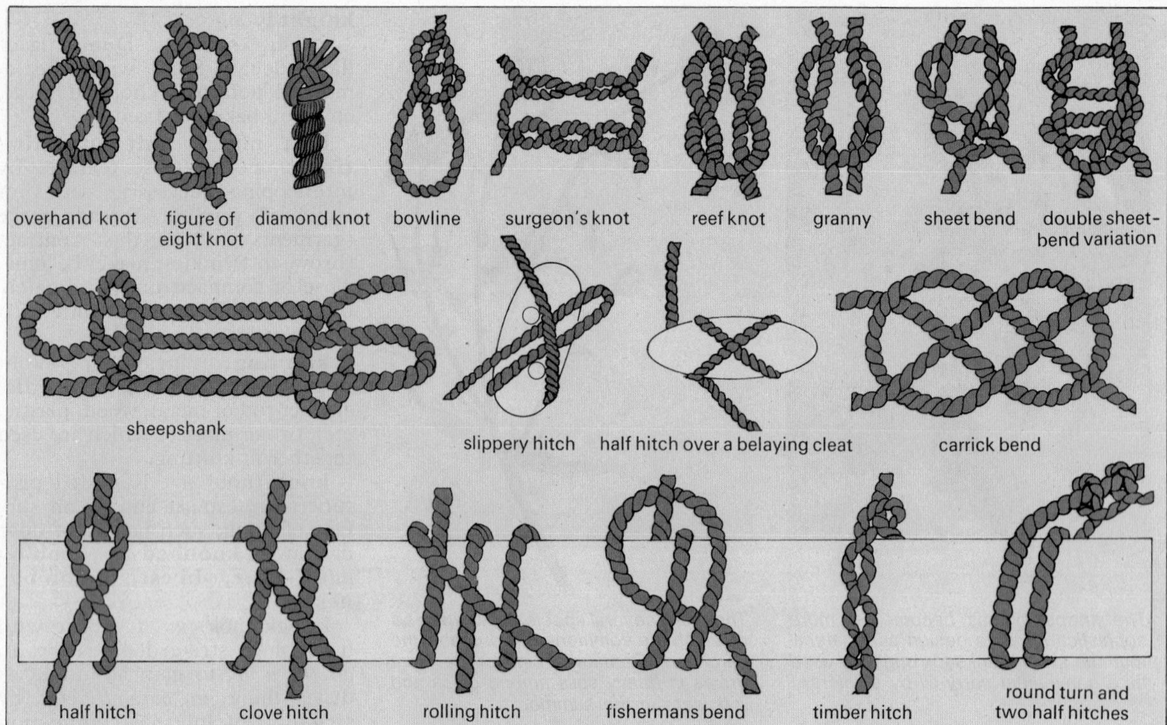

There are types of **knots** *for various functions: single knots secure the line to itself; double knots join two lines or more; securing knots attach a line to an object, such as a spar, and knots may be used to shorten a line.*

n. Blow; rap, esp. at door; thumping noise in engine etc.

knock·er (nŏk′*er*) *n.* (esp.) Appendage, usu. of iron or brass, so hinged to door that it can be struck against metal plate to call attention.

knock·wurst: see KNACKWURST.

knoll[1] (nol) *n.* Small hill, mound.

knoll[2] (nōl) *v.* (archaic) Ring (bell); (of bell) sound; knell; toll out (hours); summon by sound of bell.

Knos·sos, Cnos·sus (nŏs′*us*). Ancient city of Crete; center of the MINOAN civilization, with vast labyrinthine palace (the Palace of MINOS).

knot (nŏt) *n.* 1. Intertwining of parts of one or more ropes, strings, etc., to fasten them together; ribbon etc. so tied as ornament or adjunct to dress; string etc. entangled so it is hard to undo; that which forms or maintains union (esp. marriage); difficulty, problem. 2. (naut.) Unit of speed of 1 nautical mi. per hour (orig. measured by knots on log line; abbrev. kn). 3. Hard lump in animal body; (hard mass formed in trunk at insertion of branch, causing) round cross-grained piece in board, which may fall out, leaving **knot′hole**; node on stem of plant. 4. Group, cluster, of persons or things. 5. **knot′grass**, common weed (*Polygonum aviculare*) with intricately branched creeping stems and small pale pink flowers. **knot** *v.* (**knot·ted, knot·ting**). Tie (string etc.) in knot; entangle. **knot′ty** *adj.* (**-ti·er, ti·est**). Full of knots; (fig.) puzzling, hard to explain or solve.

knout (nowt, nōōt) *n.* & *v.t.* (Flog with) scourge formerly used as instrument of punishment in Russia, often fatal in its effects.

know (nō) *v.* (**knew** pr. nōō, nū, **known** pr. nōn, **know·ing**). 1. Recognize, identify; be able to distinguish; be acquainted with (*by sight, to speak to*, etc.); have personal experience of; be on friendly terms with; be aware of, be aware (*that, how*, etc.); be versed in; ~ **about**, have information about; ~ **better than**, be too well informed of the facts to believe; be too discreet or well behaved (*to* do): ~ **of**, be aware of; ~ **one's own mind**, not vacillate. 2. ~**-it-all**, person claiming or pretending omniscience; ~**-how**, (*n.*) practical knowledge of methods; **know-nothing**, ignorant person; **Know Nothing**, (member of) U.S. political movement in 1850s, hostile to Catholics and immigrants; **you know**, meaningless parenthesis in substandard speech. **know** *n.* **in the** ~, (colloq.) knowing (about) the thing in question or what is not generally known. **know′a·ble** *adj.* **know′er** *n.*

know·ing (nō′ĭng) *adj.* (esp.) Cunning, wide-awake. **know′-ing·ly** *adv.* In a knowing manner; consciously, intentionally.

knowl·edge (nŏl′ĭj) *n.* Knowing, familiarity gained by experience, (*of*); person's range of information; theoretical or practical understanding (*of*); the sum of what is known; **to my** ~, as far as I know. **knowl′edge·a·ble** *adj.* Well-informed, intelligent.

knuck·le (nŭk′*el*) *n.* Bone at finger joint, esp. at root of finger; projection of carpal or tarsal joint of quadruped; cut of meat consisting of this with parts above and below it; **knuck′lebone**, bone forming knuckle; limb bone with ball-like knob at joint end, this part of animal's leg as cut of meat; metacarpal or metatarsal bone of sheep etc.; **knuckle-duster** (slang): see BRASS knuckles; **knuck′lehead**, (*n.*) (colloq.) stupid, bungling person; fool. **knuckle** *v.* (**-led, -ling**). Strike, press, rub, with knuckles; place knuckles on ground when shooting a marble or, esp., shoot (marble) with thumb from knuckle of bent forefinger; ~ **down**, work hard, apply oneself diligently; ~ **under**, give in, submit.

knur (nẽr) *n.* Hard excrescence on trunk of tree; hard concretion.

knurl (nẽrl) *n.* Knot, knob; bead or ridge in metal object, esp. one of a series of ridges to aid in gripping. **knurled** *adj.*

KO, K.O., k.o. (pl. **KO's**) *abbrevs.* Knockout; knock out. **KO** *v.t.* (**KO'd, KO'ing**).

ko·a·la (kōah′*la*) *n.* Tailless arboreal marsupial (*Phascolarctos cinereus*) of the Australian region, feeding almost exclusively on the leaves of the eucalyptus tree.

Ko·be (kō′bā; *Jap.* kaw′bĕ′). City and port in S. Honshu, Japan.

Koch (kawχ), **Robert** (1843–1910). German bacteriologist and physician, famous for his work on the bacillus of tuberculosis.

Kö·chel (kö′χel) *n.* ~ **number.** Number of a composition by Mozart as listed in complete catalog of his works compiled in 19th c. by Austrian scientist Ludwig von Köchel.

Ko·di·ak (kō′dēăk). Island of Alaska SE. of the Alaska Peninsula in the Gulf of Alaska; noted for salmon fishing industry and as the habitat of the **Kodiak bear**, a large brown bear (*Ursus middendorffi*) inhabiting islands and coasts of Alaska and British Columbia, weighing up to 1500 lbs. and growing up to 9 ft.

K. of C. *abbrev.* Knights of Columbus.

Koh·i·noor, Koh-i-noor (kō′-*i*noor) *ns.* Famous Indian diamond of great size (109 karats), with history going back to 14th c.; one of the British crown jewels since annexation of Punjab, 1849. [Pers. *kōh-i-nūr*, mountain of light]

kohl (kōl) *n.* Preparation, based on powdered sulfide of lead or sulfide of antimony used to darken eyelids etc. [Arab. *kuhl*]

kohl·ra·bi (kōlrah′bē, kōl′rah-) *n.* (pl. **-bies**). Garden vegetable (*Brassica cauloropa*) of cabbage family, bulbous part of steam at ground level being edible.

Koi·ne (koinā′) *n.* Common language of the Greeks from the close of the classical period to the Byzantine era; (**k**~) language shared by various peoples; lingua franca.

*The **Komodo dragon** is the largest of the lizard species, and can weigh up to 300 lbs. It comes from Komodo Island in Indonesia.*

Ko·la (kō′l*a*). Peninsula of northwestern U.S.S.R. between Barents Sea and White Sea.

ko·la, co·la (kō′l*a*) *ns.* Either of two trees native to W. Africa and introduced into W. Indies and Brazil, (*Cola nitida* or *C. acuminata*); ~ **nut**, seed of these trees, yielding mildly stimulating extract used in beverages and medicines.

ko·lin·sky (k*o*lĭn′skē) *n.* (pl. **-skies**). Siberian mink; its fur. [Russ., f. KOLA]

kol·khoz (kawlkawz′, -χawz′) *n.* Collective farm in U.S.S.R.

Ko·mo·do (k*o*mō′dō) **dragon.** Very large monitor lizard (*Varanus komodoenis*), of the Indonesian islands of Komodo and Flores, with heavy powerful body, sometimes 15 ft. (4.5 m) long. [*Komodo*, island in Malay Archipelago]

koo·doo: see KUDU.

kook (ko͝ok) *n.* & *adj.* (slang) Crazy or eccentric (person). **kook·y, kook·ie** *adjs.* (**kook·i·er, kook·i·est**).

kook·a·bur·ra (ko͝ok*a*bŭr′*a*, ko͞o′k*a*bēr*a*) *n.* Large kingfisher (*Dacelo novaeguineae*) of S. Australia, having a raucous laughing call, also called "laughing jackass."

Koo·te·nay (ko͞o′t*e*nā). (also **Kootenai**) River flowing 407 mi. (655 km) from SE. British Colum-

*Sometimes called an Australian bear the **koala** is a marsupial. At birth, the ¾ in. long baby crawls to the mother's pouch where it remains for about 8 months. Adults can be 2 ft. 6 in. long.*

bia, Canada, through NW. Montana and N. Idaho, then N. through ~ **Lake** in British Columbia to the Columbia River.

ko·peck, ko·pek, co·peck (kō'pěk) *ns.* Russian coin = $\frac{1}{100}$ of a ruble.

Ko·ran (kōrahn', -răn, kaw-). Sacred book of Islam, in Arabic, consisting of 114 chapters of revelations orally delivered by Muhammad, collected in writing and put in order after his death by Abu Bakr; the four chief duties that it enjoins are prayer, the giving of alms, fasting, and the pilgrimage to Mecca. [Arab. *kur'ān* the reading]

Ko·re·a (kōrē'*a*, kaw-). (Chin. *Tai Han*, Jap. *Chōsen*) Country of E. Asia consisting principally of a mountainous peninsula running southward from Manchuria opposite Japan; in Japanese possession 1910–45; at end of World War II occupied by troops of U.S. (for the United Nations) and the U.S.S.R. respectively S. and N. of the 38th parallel; the **Republic of** ~ (capital, Seoul) was proclaimed in S. Korea in July 1948 and the (communist) **Democratic People's Republic of** ~ (capital, Pyongyang) in N. Korea in Sept. 1948; a war between the two lasted 1950–3, with the U.S.-led United Nations forces joining S. Korean forces and with U.S.S.R. pilots and advisors and, eventually, Chinese Communist troops, joining N. Korean forces; **Korea Strait**, channel 120 mi. (193 km) wide between South Korea and SW. Japan connecting the Sea of Japan and the East China Sea. **Ko·re'an** *adj.* & *n.* (Native, inhabitant) of Korea; (of) the agglutinative language of Korea, which is related to Japanese; ~ **War**, war between N. and S. Korea, 1950–3.

Bottom: A map of ***Korea,*** *a location map and the national flags. The divided country covers about 85,000 sq. miles. People work mostly at agriculture but also exploit mineral deposits. Below: Korean folk dancers in Seoul.*

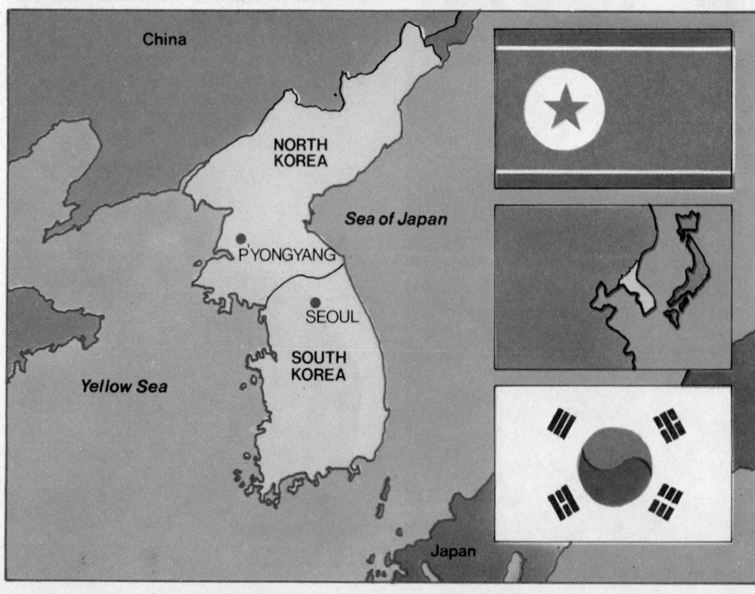

Kos·ci·us·ko (kŏsēŭs'kō, -ōōs'-; *Pol.* kawshchōōsh'kō), **Thaddeus** (1746–1817). Polish national hero, soldier, and liberal statesman; served in Revolutionary War under Washington; after the second partition of Poland, 1793, he led an uprising against Russia that failed.

ko·sher (kō'sh*er*) *adj.* (of food, or store where food is sold or used) Fulfilling requirements of Jewish dietary law. [Heb. *kāšēr* right, fit]

Kos·suth (kŏs'ōōth, -ōōt; *Hung.* kaw'shōōt), **La·jos** (lŭ'yawsh) (1802–92). Hungarian national hero and liberal statesman.

Ko·sy·gin (kawsē'gĭn), **Aleksei Nikolayevich** (1904–80). Soviet statesman; premier of U.S.S.R. 1964–80.

ko·to (kō'tō; *Jap.* kaw'taw') *n.* Japanese musical instrument with 13 long silk strings.

Kot·ze·bue (kawt's*e*bōō), **August Friedrich Ferdinand von** ~ (1761–1819), German dramatist, author of sentimental plays; **Otto von** ~ (1787–1846), his son, navigator and explorer, discoverer of **Kotzebue Sound**, inlet of NW. Alaska.

Kous·se·vitz·ky (kōōs*e*vĭt'skē), **Serge** (1874–1951). Russian-born orchestra conductor; conducted Boston Symphony Orchestra, 1924–49; organized Berkshire Music Center, Tanglewood, Mass.

Kow·loon (kow'lōōn'). City on ~ **Peninsula**, SE. China, opposite Hong Kong Island and part of the crown colony of Hong Kong.

kow·tow (kowtow', kow'tow) *n.* Chinese custom of touching ground with forehead as sign of worship or submission. ~ *v.i.* Make a kowtow; act obsequiously (*to*). [Chin. *k'o t'ou* knock head]

KP, K.P. *abbrevs.* Kitchen police.

K.P.H., k.p.h., kph *abbrevs.* Kilometers per hour.

Kr *symbol.* Krypton.

Kr., kr. *abbrevs.* Krona, krone.

kraal (krahl) *n.* South African village of huts enclosed by stockade; enclosure for cattle or sheep. [Afrikaans, f. Port. *corral*]

Krafft-E·bing (krăft'ĕb'ĭng, krahft'-; *Ger.* krahft'ā'bĭng), **Richard von** (1840–1902). German physician and psychologist; author of *Psychopathia Sexualis.*

kraft (krăft, krahft) *n.* (also ~ **paper**) Strong smooth brown wrapping paper made from unbleached sulfate wood pulp.

Kra·ka·to·a (krăk*a*tō'*a*), **Kra·ka·tau** (krahk*a*tow'). Small volcanic island of Indonesia in Sunda

Often called a laughing jackass because of its call, the ***kookaburra*** *is a type of Australian kingfisher with a thick, short beak adapted to killing reptiles and rodents.*

Strait between Java and Sumatra, scene of a great eruption in 1883.

Kra·ków (krah´kow). (English Cracow) City in S. Poland on the Vistula River.

Krem·lin (krĕm´lĭn). Fortified enclosure or citadel within Russian town or city; esp. that of Moscow, containing the old imperial palace and many public buildings, now the political and administrative center of the U.S.S.R.; hence, **the** ~, the Russian Government.

kreut·zer, kreu·zer (kroit´s*er*) *ns.* Small silver and copper coins formerly current in Germany and Austria. [Ger. *kreuz* cross]

krieg·spiel (krēg´spēl, -shpēl) *n.* War game in which blocks, flags, etc., representing troops etc. are moved about on maps.

Kriem·hild (krēm´hĭlt). In the Nibelungenlied, a Burgundian princess, wife of Siegfried and later of Etzel (Attila), whom she marries in order to be revenged on her brothers for the murder of Siegfried.

krill (krĭl) *n.* Tiny planktonic crustaceans eaten by whales etc.

kris (krĭs, krēs) *n.* Malayan dagger with wavy blade.

Krish·na (krĭsh´n*a*). (Hindu myth.) Great deity or deified hero, worshipped as incarnation of Vishnu.

kró·na, kro·na (krō´n*a*) *ns.* Principal monetary unit of Sweden (pl. **-nor** pr. -nōr) = 100 öre; of Iceland (pl. **-nur** pr. -n*er*).

kro·ne (krō´n*e*) *n.* (pl. **-ner** pr. -n*er*). 1. Principal monetary unit of Denmark and Norway = 100 öre. 2. (hist.) Austrian silver coin. 3. (hist.) German ten-mark gold piece. [Ger. and Dan., = "crown"]

Kron·shlot (krawn´shl*o*t). (formerly **Kronstadt, Cronstadt**) Russian fortress and naval base on Kotlin Island in Gulf of Finland, protecting approach to Leningrad.

Kru·ger[1] (kroo͞´g*er*; *Du.* krü´χ*er*), **Stephanus Johannes Paulus** (1825–1904). "Oom Paul," Afrikaans soldier and statesman; president of Transvaal republic 1883–1899.

Kru·ger[2] (kroo͞´g*er*) **National Park.** Park and wildlife preserve covering 8,000 sq. mi. (20,720 sq. km) in the Republic of South Africa, in the NE. part.

Krupp (krŭp; *Ger.* kroo͞p), **Alfred** (1812–87). German metallurgist, founder of steel and armament works at Essen.

kryp·ton (krĭp´tŏn) *n.* (chem.) Element, one of the inert rare gases of the atmosphere (1 part in 1,000,000 by volume); symbol Kr, at. no. 36, at. wt. 83.80. [Gk. *krupton* hidden]

KS *abbrev.* Kansas.

Kshat·ri·ya (kshăt´rē*a*) *n.* Member of second of the four Hindu castes, the military, governing, and professional caste. [Sansk., f. *kshatra* rule]

Kt. *abbrev.* Knight.

kt. *abbrev.* Karat.

Kua·la Lum·pur (kwah´l*a* lo͞ompoor´). Capital and commercial center of Malaysia, in the SW. Malay Peninsula.

Ku·blai Khan (koo͞´blī kahn´), **Ku·bla Khan** (koo͞´bl*a* kahn) (1216–94). Mongol conqueror and emperor, grandson of GENGHIS KHAN; founder of Mongol dynasty (the Yüan) in China.

ku·dos (koo͞´dōz, -dōs, -dŏs, kū´-) *n.* Glory, acclaim as a result of achievement or position; (incorrectly misconstrued as *n.pl.*)

*The **Kremlin** in Moscow covers a roughly triangular area of 90 acres. Within the walls of its cathedral square are three cathedrals and the great bell-tower of Ivan the Terrible.*

*By the 5th century A.D. **Krishna** held an established place in the Hindu pantheon as the 8th incarnation of Vishnu, one of the supreme gods. Here Krishna supports Mt. Govardhana in a painting by Ustad Sahibdin, c. 1690.*

compliments, awards.

ku·du, koo·doo (ko͞o′do͞o) *ns.* Antelope of S. and E. Africa (genus *Strepsiceros*), with vertical white stripes on body and, in the male, twisted horns.

kud·zu (ko͝od′zo͞o) *n.* Rapidly growing perennial vine (*Pueraria lobata*) native to Japan and China and later established in southern U.S.; used for food and forage and as soil stabilizer.

Ku Klux Klan (ko͞o′ klŭks′ klăn′, kū′-). 1. Secret society formed *c*1865 in southern states by Confederate officers after Civil War; quickly grew into a group aimed at reasserting white supremacy by terrorizing blacks and their defenders, the members covering themselves and their horses with white sheets. 2. Similar but more widespread organization that originated in Georgia in 1915; militantly patriotic, anti-Catholic, anti-Jewish, and anti-liberal; influential after World War I; revived 1945. [Gk. *kuklos* circle (*klan* added for effect)]

After the 1939–45 war, there was an attempt to revive the ***Ku Klux Klan*** *in the U.S.A. The attempt failed although the organization still survives despite bans placed on its activities in most States.*

kuk·ri (ko͝ok′rē) *n.* Curved knife broadening toward point, used by Gurkhas of India.

ku·lak (ko͞olăk′, -lahk′, ko͞o′lăk, -lahk) *n.* Well-to-do Russian peasant, farmer, or trader, esp. (under Soviet) peasant-proprietor tilling land for his own profit; compelled by Stalin to work for the State, 1925–35. [Russ., = "fist"]

Below: The greater ***kudu*** *survives well even in settled parts of Africa where other antelopes have died out. The lesser kudu is found only in Somaliland and Kenya.*

Kul·tur (ko͞oltoor′) *n.* Culture and civilization, esp. German, as idealized by exponents and defenders of German imperialism, esp. from 1900 to the end of World War II.

küm·mel (kĭm′*el*; *Ger.* küm′*el*) *n.* Sweet colorless liqueur flavored with caraway, anis, or cumin, orig. made in Riga.

kum·quat (kŭm′kwŏt) *n.* Any of several citrus trees (genus *Fortunella*) native of China but cultivated in California, Florida, and the Gulf states for their plum-sized, orange-like fruit.

Kun (ko͞on), **Bé·la** (bā′*la*) (1886–1945). Hungarian communist leader; head of Hungarian communist government that ruled for a few months in 1919.

kung fu (ko͞ong fo͞o′, go͞ong′). Chinese system of self-defense, similar to karate.

Kuo·min·tang (kwō′mĭntăng′, -tahng′; *Chin.* gwaw′mĭn′dahng′). Chinese nationalist radical party, founded 1905 by Sun Yat-Sen and led, after his death in 1925, by Chiang Kai-Shek; it led the revolution of 1911; was at first aided by the communists but fought them intermittently from 1927 onward; gained control over most of China and set up a government at Nanking, 1927; in 1949 it was driven out by the communists, and its government withdrew to Taiwan. [Chin., = "national people's party"]

Kurd (kẽrd, koord) *n.* One of a tall, fair-haired, long-headed nomadic people of Indo-European stock with Turkish admixture, inhabiting Kurdistan.

Kurd·ish (kẽr′dĭsh, koor′dĭsh) *adj.* Of the Kurds or their language. ~ *n.* Language of the

Kurds, a dialect of Iranian.

Kur·dis·tan (kẽrdĭstăn′, koordĭstahn′). Mountainous region of SE. Turkey, N. Iraq, and NW. Iran, inhabited chiefly by Kurds.

Ku·rile, Ku·ril (koor′ĭl, ko͞orēl′) **Islands.** Chain of small islands stretching 700 mi. (1,127 km) northward from Japan to Kamchatka; ceded by Russia to Japan, 1875; regained by Russia at end of World War II.

Ku·wait (ko͞owāt′). State on NW. coast of Persian Gulf; former British protectorate, independent since 1961; major oil-producing country; capital, Kuwait.

Kuz·netsk (ko͞oznĕtsk′) **Basin.** Industrial region in S. central U.S.S.R., important for coal and iron ore deposits.

kvass (kvahs) *n.* Russian fermented beverage similar to beer and made from infusion of rye or barley with malt.

kw *abbrev.* Kilowatt.

Kwa·ja·lein (kwah′jalēn). Island in the W. Pacific in the Marshall Islands; site of Amer. naval base.

There are no national boundaries to ***Kurdistan.*** *The area inhabited by Kurds is partly in Turkey, Iraq, Iran and Russia. Here, a Kurd leads his herd to pasture beside Lake Van in Turkey.*

Kwang·si-Chuang (kwahng′sē chwahng′; *Chin.* gwahng′sē jwahng′). Autonomous region of China, in the SE.; capital, Nanning.

Kwang·tung (kwahng′to͝ong′; *Chin.* gwahng′do͝ong′). Coastal province of SE. China.

Kwan·tung (kwahn′to͝ong′; *Chin.* gwahn′do͝ong′). Territory of S. Manchuria forming S. part of Liaotung peninsula.

Kwan Yin (kwahn′yĭn′). Female divinity worshipped by Chinese Buddhists as incarnation of mercy or compassion. [Chin., = "regard sound," i.e. listen to human cries]

kwash·i·or·kor (kwashēōr′kōr, -ker) *n.* Nutritional disease of infants and children esp. in Africa, caused by protein deficiency.

Kwei·chow (kwā′chow′; *Chin.* gwā′jō′). Province of SW. China.

KY *abbrev.* Kentucky.

ky·mo·graph, cy·mo·graph (kīmograf, -grahf) *ns.* Instrument recording variations of pressure (esp. blood pressure), pulsations, sound waves, etc. **ky·mo·graph′ic** *adj.*

Kyo·to (kyō′tō; *Jap.* kyaw′taw). (also **Kioto**) City and former capital of Japan, on S. Honshu Island.

Kyr·i·e (kẽr′ēā, kĭr′-) *n.* (also ~ **e·le·i·son** pr. ĕlā′ēsawn) Short petition beginning thus, used in Orthodox and R.C. churches esp. at beginning of mass; musical setting of this; response to commandments in communion service in Episcopal Church. [Gk. *kurie eleēson* Lord have mercy]

Kyu·shu (kū′sho͞o′). (also **Kiu·shu**) Island of Japan in the Pacific Ocean off the E. coast of Asia; third largest and farthest S. of the four main islands.

The wealth of ***Kuwait*** *lies solely in its great oil deposits. Below: the port of the same name is the best on the Persian Gulf and serves much of north Arabia. Below left: A map of Kuwait and its flag.*

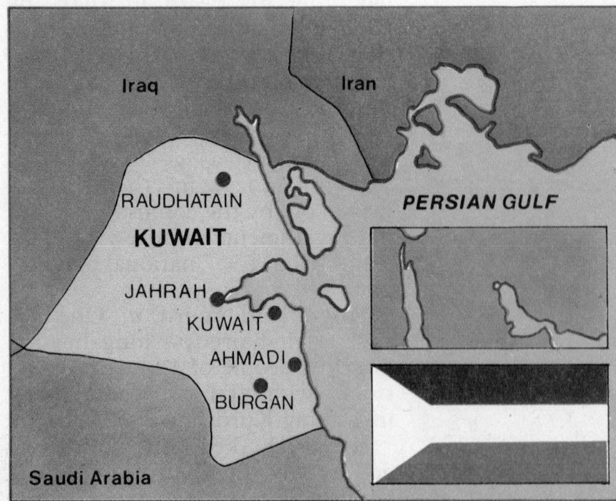

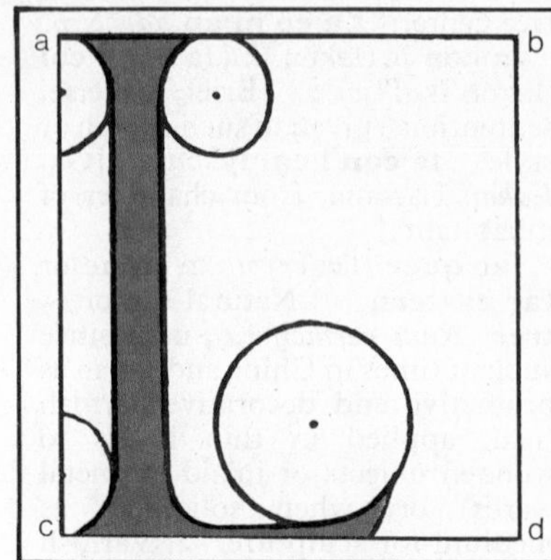

The letter ***L l,*** *a labio-palatal consonant, is derived from the 12th letter of the ancient Semitic alphabet. The Greek 'lambda' is believed to mean ox-goad, although the letter does not seem to represent the shape of goads discovered in the area. In the Roman cursive form, the horizontal line was used as a link with other letters and was not used when the letter stood alone.*

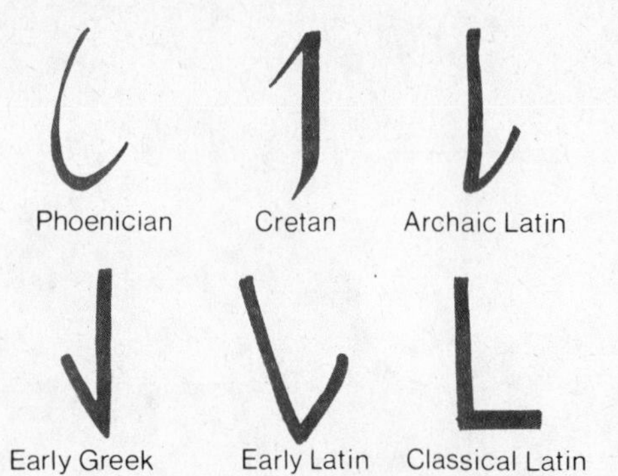

L, l (ĕl) (pl. **L's, l's** or **Ls, ls**). 1. Twelfth letter of modern English and 11th of ancient Roman alphabet, representing Greek lambda and Semitic *lamed* (of which earliest known forms are ℓ and ℓ), in modern English representing a voiced consonant formed by emission of breath at sides, or one side, of oral passage, with point of tongue in contact with gums or palate. 2. Thing shaped like L; rectangular joint of pipes etc. 3. Roman numeral symbol for 50.

L. *abbrev.* Lake; lambert; Latin; latitude.

l. *abbrev.* Left; length; line; lira, lire; liter(s).

£ Symbol for POUND[1], defs. 2 and 3.

La *symbol.* Lanthanum.

La., LA *abbrevs.* Louisiana.

L.A. *abbrev.* Los Angeles.

lab (lăb) *n.* (colloq.) Laboratory.

Lab. *abbrev.* Labrador.

la·bel (lā′bel) *n.* Slip of paper, card, linen, metal, etc., for attaching to object and indicating its nature, owner, name, destination, etc.; (fig.) short classifying phrase or name applied to persons etc. ~ *v.t.* (**-beled, -bel·ing**, Brit. **-belled, -bel·ling**). Attach label to; assign to category.

la·bi·al (lā′bēal) *adj.* 1. Of the lips; (anat., zool.) of, like, serving as, a lip, labial part, or labium; ~ **palp**, sensitive lobe near mouth of certain mollusks; jointed appendage on insect labium. 2. (phon. of sounds) Formed by complete or partial closure of lips, for example, *m, b, f.* **labial** *n.* Labial sound. **la·bi·al·ize** (lā′bēalīz) *v.t.* (**-ized, -iz·ing**).

la·bi·a ma·jo·ra (lā′bēa majōr′a, -jōr′a) (sing. **la·bi·um ma·jus** pr. lā′bēum mā′jus). (anat.) The outer folds of skin of the external female genitalia.

la·bi·a mi·no·ra (lā′bēa mĭnōr′a, -nōr′a) (sing. **la·bi·um mi·nus** pr. lābēum mī′nus). (anat.) The inner folds of skin of the external female genitalia.

la·bi·ate (lā′bēāt, -ĭt) *adj.* (bot.) With corolla or calyx divided into two parts suggesting lips; (bot., zool.) like lip or labium. ~ *n.* Labiate plant.

la·bile (lā′bĭl; *Brit.* lā′bīl) *adj.* (phys., chem.) Unstable, liable to displacement or change.

la·bi·um (lā′bēum) *n.* (pl. **-bi·a** pr. -bēa). 1. (anat., usu. in pl.) Lip(s) of female pudendum: see LABIA MAJORA and LABIA MINORA. 2. (zool.) Lower part of insect's mouth, the fused second maxillae. 3. (bot.) Lip, esp. the lower, of labiate corolla.

la·bor, Brit. **la·bour** (lā′ber) *ns.* 1. Bodily or mental toil, exertion, task; (service rendered by) laborers; working classes as a political force; **hard** ~: see HARD; ~ **of love**: see LOVE *n.*, 2; ~ **of Hercules**, task needing enormous strength etc. 2. Uterine contractions in childbirth. 3. **L** ~ **Day**, day celebrated in honor of workers, in U.S. on first Monday in September; ~ **market**, supply of unemployed labor with reference to demand for it; ~ **pains**, those preceding childbirth; ~ **party**, political party representing interests of workers; ~ **saving**, tending to reduce amount of work required to accomplish a task; ~ **union**, association of workers organized for mutual benefit and for collective bargaining with company management. **labor** *v.* 1. Exert oneself, work hard; strive (*for, to*). 2. Advance with difficulty; be troubled or impeded; suffer *under* mistake etc. 3. Elaborate, work out in detail, treat at length. **la′bored** *adj.* Showing signs of labor, not spontaneous. **la′bor·er** *n.* (esp.) Unskilled worker doing (esp. heavy) manual work.

The ***labiate*** *form of the white dead-nettle is clear. Its lower lip has lateral lobes with teeth-like features. The plant flourishes on waste ground and on roadsides, blooming in early summer and in the Fall.*

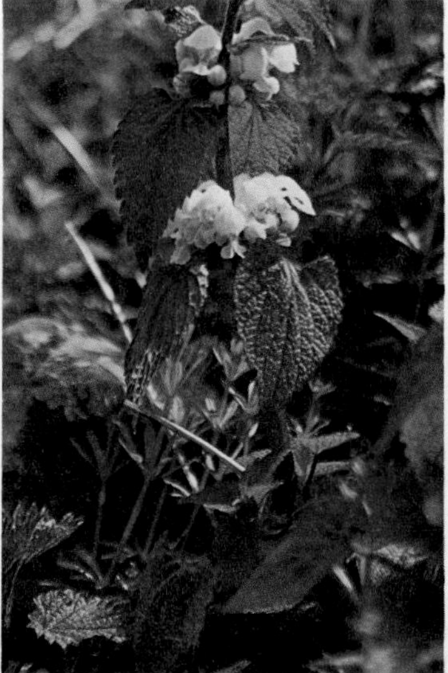

lab·o·ra·to·ry (lăb′ratōrē, -tōrē, lăb′era-; *Brit.* labŏr′aterē, -atrē) *n.* (pl. **-ries**). Room or building used for scientific experiments, tests, etc., or for the preparation of chemical substances etc.; **language** ~, room equipped with tape recorders for study of foreign languages.

la·bo·ri·ous (labōr′ēus, -bōr′-) *adj.* Hard working; showing signs of toil, not facile or fluent. **la·bo′ri·ous·ly** *adv.* **la·bo′ri·ous·ness** *n.*

Lab·ra·dor[1] (lăb′radōr). Eastern coastal part of large peninsula of extreme NE. America, between Hudson Bay and Atlantic; part of the Canadian province of Newfoundland; ~ **Current**, cold ocean current moving southward from Arctic Ocean along part of E. coast of N. America.

Lab·ra·dor[2] (lăb′radōr) *n.* (also ~ **retriever**) Dog of black- or golden-coated breed related to spaniel and setter and used for retrieving game.

la·brum (lā′brum, lăb′rum) *n.* (pl. **la·bra** pr. lā′bra). Ventral lobe of front of insect's head, covering the mouth parts.

la·bur·num (labẽr′num) *n.* Small leguminous tree or shrub of genus *L* ~ with poisonous seeds, of which the commonest species, *L. anagyroides*, has racemes of bright-yellow flowers.

lab·y·rinth (lăb′erĭnth) *n.* Complicated irregular structure with many passages hard to find way through or about without guidance,

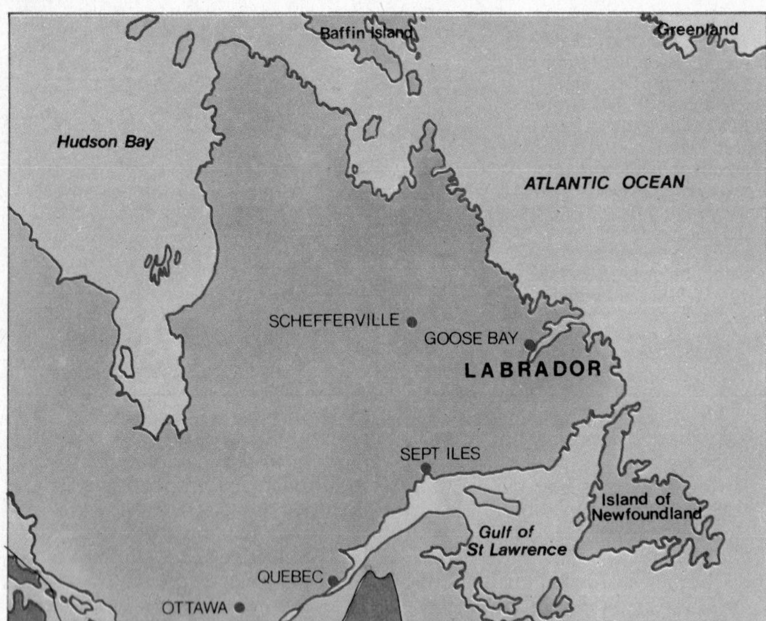

*The forbidding terrain of **Labrador** delayed its development until well into the 20th century. The potential of the Grand Falls for hydro-electric power and the discovery of huge iron deposits encouraged development.*

maze; intricate or tortuous arrangement; (anat.) complex cavity of internal ear. **lab·y·rin·thine** (lăberĭn′thĭn, -thēn) *adj.*

lac (lăk) *n.* Resinous incrustation produced on certain trees in E. Indies by the insect *Tachardia lacca* and used as varnish or as substitute for true lacquer; known, when melted and formed into thin plates, as shellac.

Lac·ca·dive (lăk′*a*dīv) **Islands.** Group of circular coral reefs in Indian Ocean about 200 miles (322 km) W. of the Malabar Coast of India; administered (with adjacent Minicoy and Amindivi Islands) by India; capital, Kozhikode.

lace (lās) *n.* 1. Cord or leather strip for fastening or tightening opposite edges of boots, shoes, etc., by help of eyelets or hooks. 2. Openwork ornamental patterned fabric of fine, usu. linen, thread, esp. that composed of needlework stitches (**needlepoint** ~), or braided with the aid of bobbins on a pillow (**bobbin** ~). 3. **lace′bark tree**, W. Indian tree (*Lagetta lintearia*) with inner bark of lace-like fibers; **lace′wing**, name given to various insects of order Neuroptera. **lac′y** *adj.* (**lac·i·er, lac·i·est**). **lace** *v.* (**laced, lac·ing**). Fasten, tighten, compress, trim, with lace(s); compress one's waist; embroider (*with* thread etc.); pass (cord etc.) through; diversify *with* streaks of color; flavor, fortify (beverage) *with* whiskey.

lac·er·ate (lăs′*e*rāt) *v.t.* (**-at·ed, -at·ing**). Mangle, tear (esp. flesh or tissues); afflict, distress (heart, feelings). **lac·er·a·tion** (lăs*e*rā′sh*o*n) *n.*

Lach·e·sis (lăk′ĭsĭs). (Gk. myth.) One of the three Fates, who, with her spindle, spun out the course of human life.

Lach·ry·ma Chris·ti (lăk′r*i*m*a* krĭs′tē). Strong sweet red wine of S. Italy. [L., = "Christ's tear"]

lach·ry·mal, lac·ri·mal (lăk′r*i*m*a*l) *adjs.* Of, for tears; ~ **gland**, (anat.) gland beneath upper eyelid secreting tears, which drain from inner corner of eye through ~ **duct** to nose; ~ **vase**, vase intended to contain tears.

lach·ry·ma·to·ry, lac·ri·ma·to·ry (lăk′r*i*m*a*tōrē, -tōrē) *adjs.* Of, for tears; causing eyes to water. ~ *n.* (pl. **-ries**). Small vial of kind found in Roman tombs and thought to be bottles meant to contain tears.

lach·ry·mose (lăk′r*i*mōs) *adj.* Tearful, given to weeping. **lach′ry·mose·ly** *adv.*

lac·ing (lā′sĭng) *n.*: see LACE def. 1.

lack (lăk) *n.* Deficiency, want, need, *of*; **for** ~ **of**, owing to want or absence of. **lack** *v.* Be without, not have, be deficient in; **lack′-luster**, (of eye etc.) dull. **lack′-ing** *adj.* Not available, inadequate.

lack·a·dai·si·cal (lăk*a*dā′zĭk*a*l) *adj.* Languidly superior, affected; feebly sentimental. **lack·a·dai′si·cal·ly** *adv.* **lack·a·dai′si·cal·ness** *n.* [archaic *lackaday, -daisy,* alack]

lack·ey (lăk′ē) *n.* (pl. **-eys**). Footman, manservant (usu. liveried); obsequious person; servant. ~ *v.t.* (**-eyed, -ey·ing**). Dance attendance on, behave servilely to.

La·co·ni·a (l*a*kō′nē*a*). Ancient territory of SW. Greece, now a department, its ancient capital, Sparta, being still the administrative center. **La·co′ni·an** *adj.* & *n.*

la·con·ic (l*a*kŏn′ĭk), **la·con·i·cal** (l*a*kŏn′ĭk*a*l) *adjs.* Brief, concise, sententious; given to such speech or style. **la·con′i·cal·ly** *adv.* [Gk. *Lakon* Laconia, from character of inhabitants]

lac·quer (lăk′*er*) *n.* 1. (**true** or **far eastern** ~) Natural sap of ~ **tree** (*Rhus vernicifera*), used since ancient times in China and Japan as protective and decorative varnish (usu. applied in thin layers to wooden objects or inlaid on metal wares) or, when solidified, as medium for sculpture. 2. Varnish imitating this, invented in Europe in 17th c. and prepared from resin lac or shellac (see LAC). **lacquer** *v.t.* Coat with lacquer.

lac·ri·mal (lăk′r*i*m*a*l) = LACHRYMAL.

la·crosse (l*a*kraws′, -krŏs′) *n.* Game (orig. of N. Amer. Indians) with ten players on each side, in which the ball is flung by and carried in netted rackets, the object being to throw the ball through the opponents' goal. [Fr., so named by Jesuit missionaries f. resemblance of racket to crosier]

lac·tate (lăk′tāt) *n.* Salt of lactic acid. ~ *v.* (**-tat·ed, -tat·ing**). Produce or secrete milk. **lac·ta·tion** (lăktā′sh*o*n) *n.*

lac·te·al (lăk′tē*a*l) *adj.* Of milk; conveying milky fluid. ~ *n.* One of the minute lymphatic vessels of the mesentery, conveying chyle to the thoracic duct.

lac·tes·cence (lăktĕs′*e*ns) *n.* Milky appearance; milky juice. **lac·tes′cent** *adj.* Milky; yielding milky juice.

lac·tic (lăk′tĭk) *adj.* (chem.) Of milk; ~ **acid**, hygroscopic acid ($CH_3CH(OH)COOH$) formed by the fermentation of sugars etc. and present in sour milk.

lac·to·pro·tein (lăktōprō′tēn, -tēĭn) *n.* Albuminous constituent of milk.

lac·tose (lăk′tōs) *n.* Milk sugar, a substance somewhat similar to cane sugar, present in milk, and manufactured by the evaporation of whey.

la·cu·na (l*a*kū′n*a*) *n.* (pl. **-nae** pr. -nē, **-nas**). Hiatus, blank, missing portion, empty part; cavity in bone, tissue, etc. **la·cu′nal, la·cu′nar, la·cu′nar·y** *adjs.*

la·cus·trine (l*a*kŭs′trĭn) *adj.* Of, dwelling or growing in, lake(s).

lad (lăd) *n.* Boy, youth, young fellow; fellow. **lad·die** (lăd′ē) *n.* (chiefly Scot.).

lad·der (lăd′*er*) *n.* Set of rungs inserted usu. in two uprights of wood or metal or in two ropes to serve as (usu. portable) means of ascending building etc.; (fig.) means of rising in the world or attaining object; ~**-back chair**, one having back formed of horizontal bars; ~

*Females of the order Mammalia **lactate** after giving birth to supply their young with sustenance. The milk they produce varies in consistency and content, and not all have nipples, i.e. monotremes.*

stitch, crossbar stitch in embroidery.

lade (lād) *v.t.* (**lad·ed, lad·en** or **lad·ed, lad·ing**). Put cargo on board (ship); ship (goods) as cargo. **lad′en** *adj.* Loaded (*with*); painfully burdened *with*. **lad′ing** *n.* **bill of** ~: see BILL[3].

la-di-da, la-de-da, lah-di-dah (lah′dēdah′) *adjs.* (colloq.) Pretentious or affected, esp. in pronunciation. [imit. of pronunciation used, f. comic song of 1880]

La·din (lahdēn′) *n.* RHAEDO-ROMANIC. [Romansh, f. L. *latinus* Latin]

La·di·no (*la*dē′nō; *Sp.* lahdē′-naw) *n.* Spanish dialect of Sephardic Jews.

Lad·is·laus (lăd′ĭslaws). Name of several kings of Hungary; **Ladislaus I, St.** (1040–95), king of Hungary 1077–95; introduced Catholicism into Croatia, which he secured for Hungary; **Ladislaus IV** (1262–90), king of Hungary 1272–90; killed after two years of civil war; **Ladislaus V (Posthumene)** (1440–57), king of Hungary and Bohemia.

la·dle (lā′del) *n.* 1. Large spoon, with cup-shaped bowl and long handle, for transferring liquid. 2. (in foundry) Receptacle for molten metal. ~ *v.t.* (**-dled, -dling**). Transfer with ladle.

La·do·ga (lah′dōgah). Largest European lake, 7,100 sq. mi. (18,389 sq. km), in U.S.S.R., near Finnish border.

*The game of **lacrosse** is played for 4 periods of 20 minutes each. The hard ball is passed from player to player by means of the crosse until a goal is scored by hurling the ball through the 6 ft. by 6 ft. goal.*

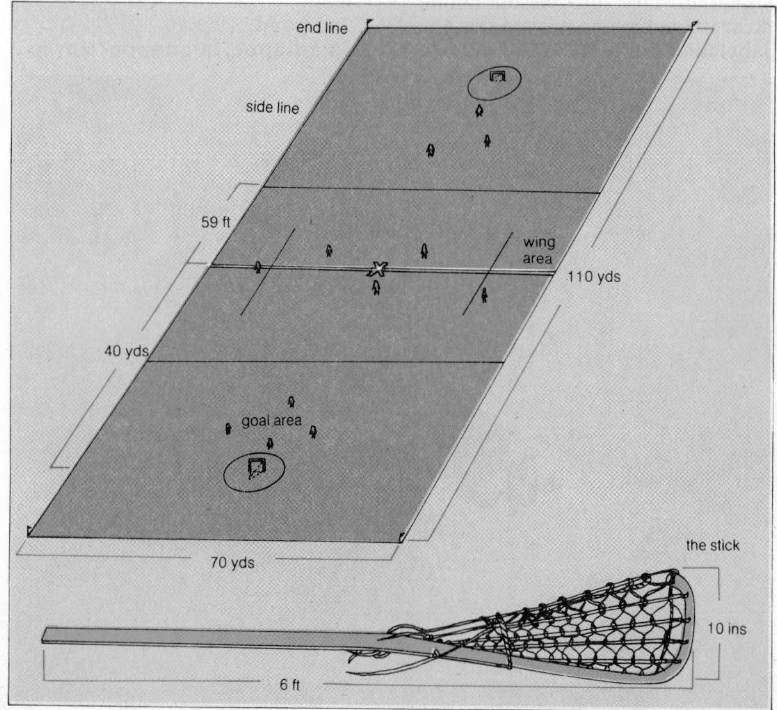

*The **lace** industry was one of the first to be automated but the individuality of handworked lace as produced by this craftswoman working with bobbins on a pillow in Brussels is much sought after by collectors.*

la·dy (lā´dē) *n.* (pl. **-dies**). 1. Woman ruling over subjects, or to whom obedience or homage is due (archaic or poet. exc. in ~ **of the manor, Our L~**, the Virgin Mary). 2. Woman to whom man is devoted, mistress. 3. Woman of good birth or breeding; ~ **of the bedchamber,** ~**-in-waiting**, lady attending a queen or princess. 4. (used courteously) Woman. 5. (Brit.) Prefixed title, part of customary appellation of marchioness, countess, viscountess, baroness; followed by Christian (and family) name of daughter of duke, marquis, or earl; followed by husband's Christian (and family) name of wife of holder of courtesy title *Lord*; followed by surname of wife of baronet or knight; **my** ~, respectful form of address to holders of title *Lady* and women judges. 6. (poet. or joc.) Wife. 7. **Ladies' Day**, day set aside for women to attend (game, entertainment) at reduced or no cost; **ladies' man**, man fond of female society; **la'dybird** (Brit.) = ladybug; **la'dybug**, coleopterous insect of family Coccinellidae, usu. reddish brown with black spots; **la'dy-finger**, finger-shaped sponge cake; **lady-killer**, man devoting himself to making conquests of women; **la'dylove**, sweetheart; **Lady of the Lake**, (in Arthurian legend) supernatural being (Morgan le Fay, Vivien, Nimue) who gave Arthur the sword Excalibur and was one of the three queens in the ship that bore him to Avalon; **Lady of the Lamp**, Florence NIGHTINGALE, so called in allusion to her visits to hospital wards at night; **lady's maid**, lady's personal maid; **lady's-slipper**, orchidaceous plant of genus *Cypripedium*; **ladies' tresses** (used with sing. or pl. verb), any of various orchids of the genus *Spiranthes*, with a spike of white flowers.

la·dy·like (lā´dēlīk) *adj.* With manners etc. of a lady; befitting a lady.

la·dy·ship (lā´dēship) *n.* (esp.) Respectful form of address to or mention of woman with title of Lady, preceded by *your* or *her*.

la·e·trile (lā´etrĭl) *n.* Drug prepared from apricot pits, used in treatment of cancer.

La·fa·yette (lăfēĕt´, lahfē-, -fā-; *Fr.* lăfăyĕt´), **Marie Joseph Paul Yves Roch Gilbert du Motier, Marquis de** (1757–1834). French general and politician; served as a major general of Amer. troops in Amer. Revolutionary War.

Above left: ***Lady's finger,*** *or kidney vetch, grows on sandy or calcareous soils. Above:* ***Lady's slipper*** *is rare and found on limestone soil.*

Laf·fitte (lahfēt´), **Jean** (1780?–1826). French pirate and smuggler in the Caribbean; aided America during War of 1812 by revealing British plans for attack on New Orleans, then helped Andrew Jackson defend city.

La Fon·taine (lă fawṅtĕn´), **Jean de** (1621–95). French poet and fabulist.

lag (lăg) *v.* (**lagged, lag·ging**). Go too slow, not keep pace, fall *behind.* ~ *n.* Delay in time; (amount of) retardation in current or movement, esp. (elect.) of current behind voltage in an alternating current circuit. **lag·gard** (lăg´erd) *n.* & *adj.* **lag'ging** *adj.*

La·gash (lā´găsh). Ancient Sumerian city in Mesopotamia, excavation of which proved that the Babylonians inherited their culture and the art of writing from the Sumerians.

la·ger (lah´ger, law´-) *n.* (also ~ **beer**) Light, orig. German, beer, distinguished from other kinds by longer fermentation at lower temperature. [Ger. *lagerbier* beer brewed for keeping]

La·ger·löf (lah´gerlöf), **Selma Ottiliana Louisa** (1858–1940). Swedish novelist; author of *Gösta Berling's Saga*; first woman to receive Nobel Prize for literature (1909).

lag·gard: see LAG.

la·gniappe, la·gnappe (lănyăp´,

There are 5,000 species of ***ladybird*** *ranging from red to yellow with black or colored spots. They are important to agriculture because they prey voraciously on harmful aphids. Right: Coccinella semptempunctata.*

The city of Venice is surrounded by a ***lagoon*** *whose waters are blocked from the open sea by sand bars and mud banks. This view of the city shows the shallow-draft gondolas well suited to the waters of the area.*

Lake Cuyamaca *in California. Recent studies have been attempting to find a way of reversing the gradual drying up process that occurs in lakes so that the water will be available to man.*

lăn′yăp) *ns.* Unexpected bonus or gratuity; something extra.

la·goon (l*a*gōōn′) *n.* Shallow stretch of salt water partly or wholly separated from sea by narrow strip of land or low sandbank or coral reef; enclosed water of atoll.

La·gos (lah′gōs, lā′gŏs). Capital city of Nigeria, in the SW., on the Gulf of Guinea.

lag (lăg) **screw.** Long, heavy wood screw with a square bolt head.

La Guar·di·a (l*a* gwâr′dē*a*), **Fiorello H(enry)** (1882–1947). American lawyer and congressman; mayor of New York City, 1934–45.

La·hore (l*a*hōr′). City in Punjab, W. Pakistan, near Indian frontier; largest in W. Pakistan after Karachi.

la·ic (lā′ĭk) *adj.* Nonclerical, lay; secular, temporal. ~ *n.* Layman. **la·i·cal** (lā′ĭk*a*l) *adj.* **la′i·cal·ly** *adv.*

la·i·cize (lā′ĭsīz) *v.t.* (**-cized, -ciz·ing**). Make lay; commit (school etc.), throw open (office), to laymen. **la·i·ci·za·tion** (lāĭsīzā′-sh*o*n) *n.*

laid (lād) *adj.*: see LAY³; **laid paper**, paper having ribs on surface caused by wires of cylinder on which it was dried.

lain: see LIE².

lair (lâr) *n.* 1. Wild beast's den. 2. Place of concealment for robbers etc. ~ *v.* Go to, rest or place in, lair.

laird (lârd) *n.* Landed proprietor in Scotland. **laird′ship** *n.*

lais·sez faire (lĕsāfâr′; *Fr.* lĕsĕfĕr′). Policy of noninterference; (orig.) freedom from government interference in economic or industrial affairs by tariffs, restrictions on individual enterprise, etc. [Fr.]

la·i·ty (lā′ĭtē) *n.* 1. Body of religious worshippers as distinguished from clergy. 2. People outside a particular profession; those lacking professional knowledge of a subject.

lake¹ (lāk) *n.* Large body of water entirely surrounded by land; **Great Lakes**: see GREAT; **Lake country, district, Lakeland, the Lakes**, region of lakes in NW. England; **lake dweller, dwelling**, (inhabitant of) primitive esp. prehistoric habitation built on piles or other support over a lake; **Lake Ijs·sel**: see IJSSELMEER; **Lake poets**, Coleridge, Southey, and Wordsworth, who lived in Lake district; **Lake Success**, village on Long Island, New York State; early headquarters of the United Nations Security Council, 1946–51.

lake² (lāk) *n.* Reddish pigment, orig. made from lac; pigment made from animal, vegetable, or coal tar coloring matter combined with metallic oxide or earth; (dyeing) any insoluble substance resulting from the chemical combination of soluble coloring matter with a mordant.

Laksh·mi (lŭksh′mē). (Hindu myth.) Wife of Vishnu and goddess of fortune or prosperity.

Lal·lan (lăl′*a*n) *adj.* Of the Lowlands of Scotland. ~ *n.* (also **Lallans**) Lowland Scots dialect, the vernacular speech of the Lowlands of Scotland, as a literary language.

Lam. *abbrev.* Lamentations (Old Testament).

lam[1] (lăm) *v.* (**lammed, lam·ming**). (slang) Thrash, hit hard with cane etc.

lam[2] (lăm) *n.* (slang) Flight, escape; **on the** ~, fleeing, hiding from the police. **lam** *v.* (**lammed, lam·ming**). Escape, flee.

la·ma (lah′m*a*) *n.* Priest or monk in Lamaism; see DALAI L~, TASHI L~. **La′ma·ism** *n.* Mahayana form of Buddhism found in Tibet, Mongolia, and nearby regions. **La′ma·ist** *n.* **la·ma·ser·y** (lah′m*a*sĕrē) *n.* (pl. **-ser·ies**). Monastery of lamas. [Tibetan *blama* (silent *b*)]

La·marck (l*a*mark′), **Jean-Baptiste Pierre Antoine de Monet, Chevalier de** (1744–1829). French botanist and zoologist, who anticipated Darwin in conceiving the idea of organic evolution, but accounted for it by the theory that acquired characteristics can be inherited by offspring.

La·marck′i·an *adj.* & *n.* **La·marck′ism** *n.* Lamarckian theory.

La·maze (l*a*mahz′) **technique.** System of prenatal training for natural childbirth emphasizing psychological and physical preparation of the expectant mother, including muscle stretching exercises.

lamb (lăm) *n.* Young of sheep; its flesh as food; young member of church flock; innocent, weak, or dear person; **the L~ (of God)**, Christ; **lamb′skin**, skin of lamb with wool on, used for clothing etc.; leather prepared from skin of lamb; **lamb's quarters** = PIG WEED. **lamb** *v.* Bring forth lamb; (pass., of lambs) be brought forth. **lamb·kin** (lăm′kĭn) *n.* Young lamb. **lamb′like** *adj.*

Lamb (lăm), **Charles** (1775–1834). English essayist and critic; author of *Essays of Elia* and, with his sister **Mary** (1764–1847), of *Tales from Shakespeare.*

lam·baste (lămbāst′) *v.t.* (**-bast·ed, -bast·ing**). (colloq.) Beat, thrash.

lamb·da (lăm′d*a*) *n.* Twelfth (later 11th) letter of Greek alphabet (Λ, λ), corresponding to *l.*

lam·bent (lăm′b*e*nt) *adj.* (of flame etc.) Playing on surface without burning it, with soft radiance; (of eyes, sky, etc.) softly radiant; (of wit etc.) gently brilliant. **lam′ben·cy** *n.* **lam′bent·ly** *adv.*

lam·bert (lăm′b*e*rt) *n.* Unit of brightness, equal to that of a perfectly diffusing surface radiating or reflecting light at the rate of one lumen per square centimeter (abbrev. L.). [J. H. *Lambert* (1728–77), German physicist]

lame (lām) *adj.* (**lam·er, lam·est**). Disabled by injury or defect in limb, esp. foot or leg; limping or unable to walk; (of argument, story, etc.) imperfect, unsatisfactory; (of meter) halting; **lame′brain**, (slang) stupid person, half-wit; **lame duck**: see DUCK[1]. **lame′ly** *adv.* **lame′ness** *n.* **lame** *v.t.* (**lamed, lam·ing**). Make lame, cripple.

la·mé (lămā′) *n.* & *adj.* (Material) with metal thread woven in.

la·mel·la (l*a*mĕl′*a*) *n.* (pl. **-mel·lae** pr. -mĕl′ē, **-mel·las**). Thin plate, scale, layer, or film, esp. of bone or tissue. **la·mel·lar** (l*a*mĕl′*er*, lăm′*eler*), **lam·el·late** (lăm′*e*lāt, -lĭt, l*a*mĕl′āt, -ĭt), **lam′el·lat·ed, la·mel·lose** (l*a*-mĕl′ōs, lăm′*e*lōs) *adjs.*

la·ment (l*a*mĕnt′) *n.* Passionate expression of grief; verse or song of mourning. ~ *v.* Express or feel grief for or about; be distressed at,

***Great Salt Lake** in northern Utah is the largest inland saline body of water in the western hemisphere. In recent years it has become a water sports venue and a wildlife reserve.*

Lambing season is usually in the spring, and the young ***lamb*** *is sold as meat between 3 and 8 months. The gestation period for ewes is 147 days. Some breeds are noted for bearing twins.*

regret; **lamented**, mourned for (esp. conventionally of the dead); **the late lamented**, (freq. iron.) the deceased.

lam·en·ta·ble (lăm′entabel, la-mĕn′-) *adj.* Deplorable, regrettable. **lam′en·ta·bly** *adv.*

lam·en·ta·tion (lămentā′shon) *n.* Lamenting, lament; *Lamentations*, poetical book of Old Testament, traditionally ascribed to Jeremiah.

la·mi·a (lā′mēa) *n.* (pl. **-mi·as, -mi·ae** pr. -mēē). (Gk. and Rom. myth.) Monster with head and breasts of a woman and body of a serpent preying on human beings and sucking children's blood. [L.]

lam·i·na (lăm′ina) *n.* (pl. **-nae** pr. -nē, **-nas**). 1. Thin plate, scale, layer, or flake, or metal, bone, membrane, stratified rock, etc. 2. (bot.) Blade of leaf. **lam′i·nar, lam·i·nate**[1] (lăm′ināt, -nĭt), **lam·i·nose** (lăm′inōs) *adjs.*

lam·i·nate[2] (lăm′ināt) *v.* (**-nat·ed, -nat·ing**). Beat or roll (metal) into thin plates; split into layers or leaves; overlay with metal plates; manufacture by placing layer on layer. **lam·i·na′tion** *n.*

lam·mer·gei·er, lam·mer·gey·er (lăm′ergīer) *ns.* Bearded vulture (*Gypaetus barbatus*), largest European bird of prey. [Ger. *lämmer* lambs, *geier* vulture]

lamp (lămp) *n.* Vessel with oil and wick for giving light; glass vessel enclosing candle, gas jet, incandescent wire, or other illuminant; device that gives radiation; (archaic) sun, moon, star; (fig.) source of spiritual or intellectual light, hope, etc.; **smell of the ~**, betray nocturnal study, be laborious in style, etc.; **lamp′-black**, pigment consisting of finely divided almost pure carbon, made from soot of burning oil or gas; **lamp′lighter**, person who lights

The Tibetan version of Buddhism is ***Lamaism,*** *which has accretions of the demonolatry of Bon, a primitive atavistic religion of the region. Below: Lamas in Bodhnath, Nepal, dance to drive away evil.*

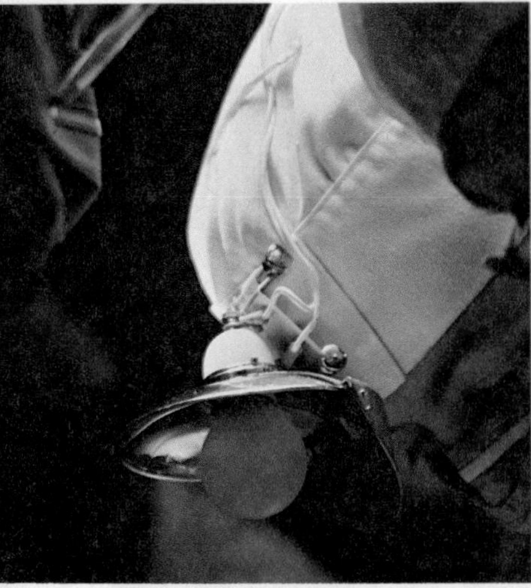

*Above: The specialized lighting requirements of the surgeon are met by having the **lamp** attached to his head, throwing a direct light on the subject. Right: The Spanish 18th-century glass oil-lamp has spouts for 4 wicks.*

*This old gas **lamp** in Providence, Rhode Island is typical of the sort used before electricity became the favored power source.*

gas street lamps; **lamp'post**, post usu. of steel or concrete supporting street lamp. **lamp** *v.* (poet.) Shine, illuminate.

lam·pi·on (lăm′pēon) *n.* Pot of usu. colored glass with oil and wick used in illuminations.

lam·poon (lămpōōn′) *n.* Virulent or scurrilous satire on individual. ~ *v.t.* Write lampoon(s) against. **lam·poon'er, lam·poon'ist** *ns.*

lam·prey (lăm′prē) *n.* (pl. **-preys**). Any of several eel-shaped aquatic vertebrates (genera *Lampetra* and *Petromyzon*) resembling fish but without scales or jaws and having suckerlike mouth.

La·na·i (lahnah′ē, lanī′). One of the Hawaiian Islands, 141 sq. mi. (365 sq. km) in area, W. of Maui.

la·na·i (lahnah′ē, lanī′) *n.* (pl. **-na·is**). Veranda. [Hawaiian]

Lan·cas·ter (lăng′kaster). Name of English royal house descended from John of Gaunt, including Henry IV, Henry V, and Henry VI; party of the red rose in the Wars of the Roses. **Lan·cas·tri·an** (lăngkăs′trēan) *n.* & *adj.*

lance (lăns, lahns) *n.* 1. Weapon with long wooden shaft and pointed steel head used by horseman in charging; similar implement for spearing fish or killing harpooned whale; ~ **corporal**, U.S. Marine Corps noncommissioned officer of lowest rank, below corporal; **lance'wood**, tough elastic kinds of W. Indian wood used for fishing rods etc. 2. Lancet. **lance** *v.t.* (**lanced, lanc·ing**). 1. (poet.) Pierce (as) with lance. 2. (surg.) Prick, cut open, with lancet.

lance·let (lăns′lĭt, lahns′-) *n.* Small marine animal of genus *Branchiostoma*, one of the lowest forms of chordate, about 50 mm long, found in sand of shallow waters throughout the world.

Lan·ce·lot (lăn′selot, -lŏt, lahn′-). (Arthurian legend) Son of King Ban of Brittany; brought up by the Lady of the Lake; most famous of Arthur's knights of the Round Table; his love affair with Queen Guinevere resulted in a war with King Arthur.

lan·ce·o·late (lăn′sēolāt, -lĭt) *adj.* Shaped like spearhead, tapered at ends.

lan·cer (lăn′ser, lahn′-) *n.* 1. Soldier of cavalry regiment orig. armed with lances. 2. (pl.) Square dance, variant of quadrille, for 8 or 16 pairs, derived from cavalry displays and in vogue in England from *c*1850 to World War I; music for this.

lan·cet (lăn′sĭt, lahn′-) *n.* 1. Fine-pointed double-edged surgical knife. 2. (also ~ **arch, window**) High narrow pointed window or arch in 12th and 13th c. Gothic architecture.

lan·ci·nat·ing (lăn′sinātĭng, lahn′-) *adj.* (of pain) Acute, shooting.

land (lănd) *n.* 1. Solid part of Earth's surface; ground, soil, expanse of country; country; landed property, (pl.) estates. 2. Any of the divisions between rifling grooves of guns. 3. ~ **bank**, bank issuing notes on security of landed property; ~ **breeze**, breeze blowing seaward from land; ~ **crab**, any of various crabs that live on land but breed in sea; **land'fall**, approach to land esp. for first time in voyage or flight; **land grant**, government grant of land, as for railroads or colleges; **land'-holder**, proprietor or (usu.) tenant of land; **land laws**, law(s) of landed property; **land'locked**, (usu. of water) almost or quite enclosed by land; **land'lady, land'lord**, person who owns land, buildings, etc. for rent to others; **land'lubber**, (naut.) person ignorant of the sea and ships; **land'mark**, object marking boundary of country, estate, etc.; conspicuous object in district etc. (orig.) esp. as guide in navigation; (fig.) notable event; **land mine**, explosive mine laid in, or dropped by parachute on, land; **Land of the Midnight Sun**, land N. of the Arctic Circle where daylight is continuous during the short summer; **Land of the Rising Sun**, Japan; **land'-office business**, (colloq.) a successful, lively business; **land'owner**, owner of land; **land-poor**, owning much land and little ready money; **Land's End**, rocky promontory in Cornwall forming westernmost point of England; **land'slide**, sliding down of mass of land, land fallen, from cliff or mountain; overwhelming majority of votes in election; **land tax**, tax on landed property; **land wind**, land breeze. **land'less** *adj.* **land** *v.* 1. Set or go ashore; disembark (*at*); set down from vehicle or aircraft. 2. Bring (aircraft) down to ground or surface of water; (of aircraft) come down thus. 3. Bring to, reach, find oneself in, a certain place, stage, or position; deal (person blow etc.); alight after jump etc. 4. Bring (fish) to land; (fig.) win (prize etc.).

Land (lănd), **Edwin Herbert** (1909–). American inventor noted for Polaroid Land camera, which develops film immediately after picture is taken.

lan·dau (lăn'daw, -dow) *n.* 1. Four-wheeled carriage with top of which front and back halves can be independently raised and lowered. 2. Motor car with collapsible top over rear seat. [*Landau*, town in Germany]

land·ed (lăn'dĭd) *adj.* Possessed of land; consisting of land.

land·grave (lănd'grāv) *n.* (hist.) Title of certain German princes; orig., count having jurisdiction over territory, and with inferior counts under him. **land·gra·vine** (lănd'-gravēn) *n.* (hist.) Wife of landgrave; woman landgrave.

land·ing (lăn'dĭng) *n.* (esp.) Place for disembarking (also ~ **place**); platform between two flights of stairs; floor, passage at top of staircase on to which rooms open; ~ **craft**, boat, often flat-bottomed and with collapsible side, for carrying troops, armored vehicles, etc., in amphibious operations; ~ **gear**, understructure of an aircraft (wheels etc.) supporting it when landing or taxiing; ~ **net**, net for landing large fish when hooked; ~ **strip**, airstrip.

land·scape (lănd'skāp) *n.* Picture etc. or part of one representing inland scenery; actual piece of such

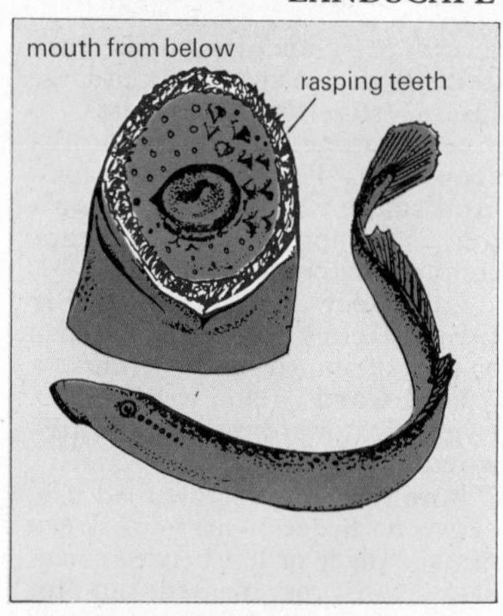

The muscular toothed tongue of the ***lamprey*** *rasps pieces of tissue from fish to which the lamprey attaches itself. Its eggs hatch in mud and the larvae stay there for 3 to 4 years before emerging as adults.*

This Pan-Am airplane carries the standard landing gear for a commercial jet of its size. The principle of retracting ***landing gear*** *into the fuselage was introduced in the 1930s and improved aircraft performance.*

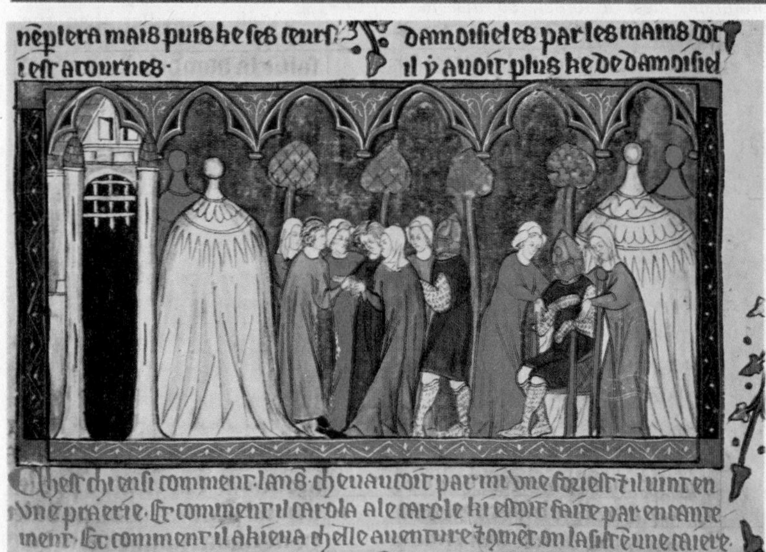

The story of ***Lancelot*** *first appears in the stories by Chrétien de Troyes in the 12th century. Right: Lancelot with dancers depicted on a 14th-century illuminated page. Lancelot was the father of Galahad, purest of knights.*

scenery; ~ **architecture, gardening**, design and layout of large spaces, suburbs, parks, etc., to produce attractive effects. **land'scap·ist** *n.* Painter of landscapes. **land'scape** *v.t.* (**-scaped, -scap·ing**). Improve by landscape architecture or gardening.

Land·seer (lănd'sēr, -syer), **Sir Edwin Henry** (1802–73). English painter of animals and portraits.

land·ward (lănd'werd) *adv.* Lying etc. toward the land. **land'-wards** *adj.*

lane (lān) *n.* Narrow road usu. between hedges; narrow street; passage made or left between rows of persons, or marked out for runners in race, streams of traffic, etc.; regular route of ships or aircraft; channel of water in icefield.

lang (lăng) *adj.* & *n.* (Scot.) Long. ~ *adv.* (Scot.) Long; **(auld) ~ syne**, (in) the old days [Scot. pronunc. of old long since]

Lang·er·hans (lăng'erhănz, -hăns; *Ger.* lahng'erhahns), **Paul** (1847–88). German pathologist; **islands (islets) of ~**, groups of small granular cells in the pancreas that secrete INSULIN.

Lang·land (lăng'land), **William** (c1330–c1400). English poet, author of *Piers Plowman*.

Lan·go·bard (lăng'gobârd) *n.* Lombard.

Lang·try (lăng'trē), **Emily Charlotte** (1853–1929). English actress; known as Lillie Langtry or "the Jersey Lily."

lan·guage (lăng'gwĭj) *n.* Whole body of words and methods of combination of words used by a section or group of people (as a nation, community, etc.); method of expression; words and their use; faculty of speech; person's style of expressing himself; professional or sectional vocabulary; literary style, wording; **bad ~**, oaths and abusive talk; **strong ~**, speech expressing vehement feelings.

langue d'oc (lahṅgdawk'). Romance dialects of S. provinces of France. [Fr. *langue* language, *oc* Provençal form of *oui* yes]

Langue·doc (lahṅgdawk'). Old province of S. France stretching from W. bank of Rhône to Pyrenees and including Cévennes and valleys of upper Loire.

langue d'oïl (lahṅgdawēl'). Romance dialects of France other than those of S. France (cf. LANGUE D'OC). [Fr. *langue* language, OF. *oïl* yes]

lan·guid (lăng'gwĭd) *adj.* Inert, lacking vigor; spiritless, apathetic; sluggish, slow-moving; faint, weak. **lan'guid·ly** *adv.* **lan'guid·ness** *n.*

lan·guish (lăng'gwĭsh) *v.i.* Grow or be feeble, lose or lack vitality; live *under* enfeebling or depressing conditions; droop, pine (*for*); affect languor or sentimental tenderness. **lan'guish·ing·ly** *adv.* **lan'guish·ment** *n.*

lan·guor (lăng'ger) *n.* Faintness, fatigue; inertia, want of alertness; soft or tender mood or effect; slackness, dullness, drooping state. **lan'guor·ous** *adj.* **lan'guor·ous·ly** *adv.*

lan·gur (lŭnggoor') *n.* Long-tailed monkey of southeast Asia, of genus *Presbytis*.

la·nif·er·ous (lanĭf'erus) *adj.* [also **la·nig·er·ous** (lanĭj'erus)]. Wool-bearing.

lank (lăngk) *adj.* Shrunken, spare; tall and lean; long and flaccid; (of hair) straight and limp, not wavy.

lank·y (lăng'kē) *adj.* (**lank·i·er, lank·i·est**). Ungracefully lean and long or tall. **lank'i·ness** *n.*

lan·ner (lăn'er) *n.* Mediterranean species of falcon, *Falco biarmicus*; (in falconry) female of this. **lan·ner·et** (lăn'erĕt) *n.* Male lanner, which is smaller than the female.

This **landscape** is typical of the environment of the beaver who favors lakes, preferably near a forest, so that its source of food and building material is readily available.

Above: The **langur** (Presbytis entellus), can leap through the tree tops for distances of up to 40 ft. On the jungle floor it moves with the gait typical of a quadruped.

lan·o·lin, lan·o·line (lăn'olĭn) *ns.* Fatty matter extracted from sheep's wool, used as basis of ointments and toilet preparations.

Lan·sing (lăn'sĭng). Capital of Michigan, in the S. central part.

lan·ta·na (lăntā'na, -tah'-) *n.* Any of several chiefly tropical plants of the genus *Lantana*, cultivated for their aromatic, brightly colored flowers.

lan·tern (lăn'tern) *n.* 1. (Lamp, either fixed or portable, often burning kerosene, with) transparent case protecting the flame. 2. (also **magic ~**) Apparatus for projecting image on screen; projector. 3. Light chamber of lighthouse. 4. **~ clock**, clock enclosed in metal case like lantern; **~ jaw**, long thin jaw giving hollow look to face, hence **~-jawed; ~ slide**, slide for projection by lantern.

lan·tha·num (lăn'thanum) *n.* (chem.) Rare-earth element found in a number of rare minerals and in monazite sand; symbol La, at. no. 57, at. wt. 138.9055. [Gk. *lanthanō* hide]

lan·yard (lăn'yerd) *n.* Short rope made fast to something (naut.); cord attached to knife, whistle, etc., to hold it or serve as handle.

La·oc·o·ön (lāŏk'ōŏn). (Gk. legend) Trojan priest; warned the Trojans against the WOODEN horse; was crushed to death with his two sons by two serpents that emerged from the sea.

La·os (lah'ōs, lā'ŏs). Former kingdom of SE. Asia, incorporated into French Indo-China, 1893; gained independence, 1950; now

This **landscape** (facing page), painted by John Constable in 1802 is of Dedham Vale, Essex. Constable, perhaps the greatest English landscape artist of the 19th century, believed that nature was the source of all originality.

*Right: A map of **Laos** with the national flag. Laos has a population of between 3 and 4 million. The administrative capital is Vientiane. Right below: A treasure house in the former royal capital, Luang Prabang.*

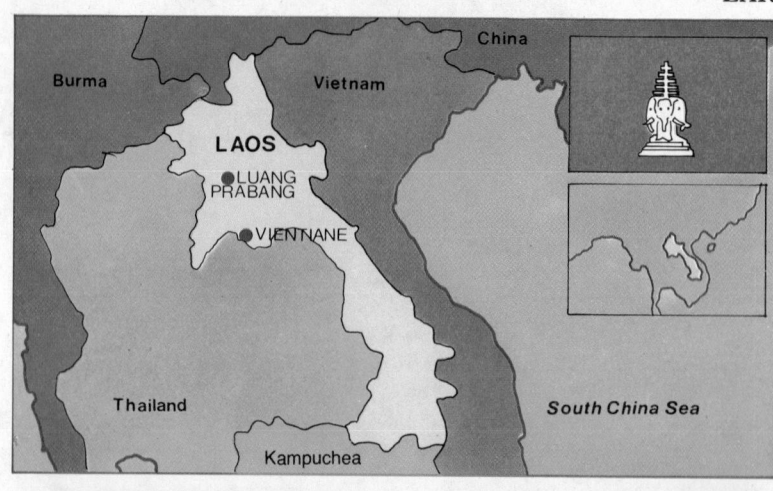

People's Democratic Republic; capital Vientiane. **La·o·tian** (lāō´sh*a*n) *adj.* & *n.*

Lao-tse, Lao-tzu, Lao-tsze (low´dzo͞o). (6th c. B.C.) Chinese philosopher and metaphysician; reputed founder of TAOISM and contemporary of Confucius.

lap[1] (lăp) *n.* Hanging part or flap of garment, saddle, etc.; front part of body from waist to knees of seated person, considered with dress as place on which child is nursed or object held; **in one's ~**, in one's charge or control; **in the ~ of luxury**, in luxurious surroundings; **lap′belt**, safety belt across lap of car driver or passenger; **lap′board**, flat board held on lap to use as table; **lap dog**, small pet dog; **lap robe**, rug to cover knees of person seated in vehicle.

lap[2] (lăp) *v.* (**lapped, lap·ping**). 1. Coil, fold, wrap (garment etc. *about, around*); enfold, swathe, *in*; surround, encircle, enfold caressingly. 2. Make overlap; project *over* something; **~ over**, overlap. 3. (racing etc.) Travel over (distance) as lap; pass (competitor) by one or more laps. **lap** *n.* Amount of overlapping, overlapping part; layer or sheet (of cotton etc. being made) wound on roller; single turn of rope, silk, thread, etc., round drum or reel; one circuit of race track.

lap[3] (lăp) *n.* Rotating disk for polishing gems or metal. **~** *v.t.* (**lapped, lap·ping**). Polish with lap.

lap[4] (lăp) *v.* (**lapped, lap·ping**). Drink by scooping with tongue; drink (*up* or *down*) greedily (also fig.); (of wavelets etc.) move, beat, with light slapping sound *against*. **~** *n.* Single act of lapping, amount taken up by it; act or sound of lapping wavelets etc.

lap·a·rot·o·my (lăp*e*rŏt´*o*mē) *n.* (pl. **-mies**). Surgical incision through abdominal walls into abdominal cavity.

La Paz (l*a* pahz´; *Port.* lah pahs´). Capital city of Bolivia.

la·pel (l*a*pĕl´) *n.* Part of front of coat etc. folded back toward shoulder. **la·pelled′** *adj.*

lap·i·dar·y (lăp´ĭdĕrē) *adj.* Concerned with stones; engraved on stone; (of style) suitable for inscriptions, monumental. **~** *n.* (pl. **-dar·ies**). Cutter, polisher, or engraver, of stones.

lap·is laz·u·li (lăp´ĭs lăz´o͞olē, -lī, lăz´ū-, lăzh´o͞o-). (min.) Sodium aluminum silicate containing sulfur, used as bright blue pigment; color of this. [L., = "stone of azure"]

Lap·ith (lăp´ĭth) *n.* (Gk. myth.) Member of a Thessalian people (*Lapithae*) who fought and defeated the Centaurs.

Lap·land (lăp´l*a*nd, -lănd). Region inhabited by Lapps, most northerly part of Scandinavia (often includes northern area of Finland and NW. U.S.S.R. lying above the Arctic Circle). **Lap′land·er** *n.* Lapp.

Lapp (lăp) *n.* Member of a small-statured Mongoloid people, largely nomadic, inhabiting Lapland. **Lap′pish** *adj.* & *n.* (Of) the language of the Lapps, one of the Finno-Ugrian family.

lapse (lăps) *n.* Slip of memory etc., slight mistake; weak or careless deviation from what is right, backsliding; decline to lower state; gliding, flow of (water etc.); passage or interval *of* time; (law) termination of right or privilege through disuse; **~ rate**, (meteor.) rate of decrease of temperature as height increases. **lapse** *v.i.* (**lapsed, laps·ing**). Fail to maintain position or state for want of effort or vigor; fall *back, away*; glide, flow, subside, pass *away*; (of estate, title, etc.) fall in, pass away, become void, revert *to* someone, by failure of conditions, heirs, etc.

lap·sus (lăp´s*u*s; *Lat.* lahp´so͞os) *n.* Slip; **~ ca·la·mi** (kăl´*a*mī; *Lat.* kah´lahmē), slip of the pen; **~ lin·guae** (lĭng´gwē; *Lat.* lĭng´gwī), slip of the tongue. [L.]

La·pu·ta (l*a*pū´t*a*). In Swift's *Gulliver's Travels*, a flying island inhabited by learned men who are absorbed in impractical philosophical and scientific speculation. **La·pu′tan** *adj.* & *n.*

lap·wing (lăp´wĭng) *n.* Bird of plover family, *Vanellus vanellus*, common in temperate parts of Old World.

lar (lar̄) *n.* (pl. **lar·es** pr. lar̄´ēz, lā´rēz, **lars**). God worshipped, together with the PENATES, by households in ancient Rome; **lares and penates**, (transf.) treasured possessions of a household.

lar·board (lar̄ʹbōrd, -bōrd; *Naut.* lar̄ʹberd) *n.* & *adj.* (naut., obs.) Left side of ship looking forward (replaced, to avoid confusion with *starboard*, by *port*).

lar·ce·ny (lar̄ʹsenē) *n.* (pl. **-nies**). (law) Felonious taking away of another's personal goods with intent to convert them to one's own use; **grand ~**, theft of property of value above that constituting petit larceny; **petit ~, petty ~**, theft of property of value below a small fixed sum. **larʹce·nous** *adj.* **larʹce·nous·ly** *adv.*

larch (lar̄ch) *n.* Deciduous coniferous tree of genus *Larix*, yielding tough timber and bark used in tanning; tamarack; wood of this.

lard (lar̄d) *n.* Internal fat of abdomen of pigs etc., esp. when rendered and clarified for use in cooking. ~ *v.t.* Insert strips of bacon in (meat etc.) before cooking; smear (as) with lard; (fig.) garnish (talk, writing) *with* particular words, expressions, etc. **lardʹy** *adj.* (**lard·i·er, lard·i·est**).

lard·er (lar̄ʹder) *n.* (chiefly Brit.) Room or cupboard for storing provisions.

La·re·do (larāʹdō). City in SW. Texas on the Rio Grande on the Mexican border.

lar·es: see LAR.

large (lar̄j) *adj.* (**larg·er, larg·est**). Of considerable or relatively great magnitude; wide in range or capacity, comprehensive; **~-scale**, extensive; made or drawn on a large scale to show detail (of maps, diagrams, etc.). **large** *n.* **at ~**, at liberty, free; (of narration etc.) at full length, with details; as a body or whole; without particularizing, without specific aim; (of representative etc.) representing nation, state, etc. as a whole, not merely a district of it. **largeʹness** *n.* **largʹish** *adj.*

Below: The **lark** nests on the ground where it is well camouflaged. The bird utters its trilling song usually while soaring and it is often silent while returning to earth.

Above: The **larch** is a swiftly growing softwood tree and, while it is a member of the pine family, it is not evergreen. Male and female cones grow side by side on the same branch.

large·ly (lar̄jʹlē) *adv.* (esp.) To a great or preponderating extent.

lar·gess, lar·gesse (lar̄jĕsʹ, lar̄ʹjĭs) *ns.* Money or gifts freely bestowed, esp. by great person on occasion of rejoicing; generous or plentiful bestowal.

lar·go (lar̄ʹgō) *adv.* & *n.* (pl. **-gos**). (mus.) (Passage, piece of music) to be rendered in slow time and with broad, dignified treatment. [It.]

lar·i·at (lărʹēat) *n.* Long rope or leather line for tethering grazing animals; lasso.

lark[1] (lar̄k) *n.* Any bird of the family Alaudidae, in which the hind claw is usu. greatly elongated; (pop.) SKYLARK; **horned ~**, a N. Amer. lark (*Eremophila alpestris*); also, any of various birds unrelated to these, as **meadʹowlark**, N. Amer. songbirds *Sturnella magna* and *S. neglecta*.

lark[2] (lar̄k) *n.* Frolic, spree; amusing incident. ~ *v.i.* Play tricks, frolic.

lark·spur (lar̄kʹspėr) *n.* Plant of genus *Delphinium* with spur-shaped calyx.

La Roche·fou·cauld (lă rawshfōōkōʹ), **François de Marsillac, duc de** (1613–80). French writer of maxims, embodying a cynical philosophy that finds in self-love the prime motive of action.

La·rousse (lărōōsʹ), **Pierre Athanase** (1817–75). French lexicographer and encyclopedist.

lar·rup (lărʹup) *v.t.* (**-rupped, -rup·ping**). (colloq.) Thrash.

Lars Por·se·na (lar̄zʹ por̄ʹsena) = PORSENA.

lar·va (lar̄ʹva) *n.* (pl. **-vae** pr. -vē). Insect from time of leaving egg until transformation into pupa; grub; immature form of other animals that undergo metamorphosis. **larʹval** *adj.* [L., = "ghost, mask"]

la·ryn·ge·al (larĭnʹjēal, lărĭnjēʹal) *adj.* Of the larynx.

lar·yn·gec·to·my (lărĭnjĕkʹtomē) *n.* (pl. **-mies**). Surgical removal of the larynx.

lar·yn·gi·tis (lărĭnjīʹtĭs) *n.* Inflammation of lining membrane of larynx.

lar·yn·gol·o·gy (lărĭnggŏlʹojē) *n.* Branch of medicine dealing with diseases of throat. **lar·yn·golʹo·gist** *n.*

la·ryn·go·scope (larĭngʹgoskōp) *n.* Mirror apparatus for inspecting larynx. **lar·yn·gos·co·py** (lărĭnggŏsʹkopē) *n.* (pl. **-pies**).

lar·yn·go·to·my (lărĭnggŏtʹomē) *n.* Surgical incision into larynx from without, esp. to provide breathing-channel.

lar·ynx (lărʹĭngks) *n.* (pl. **la·ryn·ges**, pr. larĭnʹjēz, **lar·ynx·es**). Cavity in upper part of windpipe with cartilaginous walls which, when moved by muscles, vary the tension of the vocal cords and hence the quality of the sound produced.

la·sa·gna (lazahnʹya) *n.* Dish baked of layers of flat pasta with ground meat, cheese, tomatoes, sauce, etc.

La Salle (la sălʹ; *Fr.* lă sălʹ), **René Robert Cavelier, Sieur de** (1640–87). French explorer of the Ohio and Mississippi rivers.

las·car (lăsʹker) *n.* Oriental, esp. E. Indian, sailor, employed on European ships. [Port., f. Hind., f. Arab *al-ʻaskarī* the soldier]

Las·caux (lăskōʹ). Prehistoric

Below: The **lapwing** or plover is commonly seen on the seashore or mudflats where it eats small marine invertebrates. The lapwing is also seen on inland pastures.

cave, Dordogne, S. France, containing wall paintings dating from *c*15,000 B.C.

las·civ·i·ous (lasĭv'ēus) *adj.* Lustful, wanton; inciting to lust. **las·civ'i·ous·ly** *adv.* **las·civ'i·ous·ness** *n.*

la·ser (lā'zer) *n.* Device producing an intense narrow beam of light by amplifying radiation that is within or near the frequency range of visible light. [*l*ight *a*mplification by *s*timulated *e*mission of *r*adiation]

lash (lăsh) *v.* 1. Make sudden movement of limb, tail, etc.; pour, rush, vehemently; strike violently *at*; hit or kick *out*; break *out* into excess, strong language, etc. 2. Beat with lash, flog; (of waves) beat upon; castigate in words, satirize; urge as with whip. 3. Fasten (*down, on, to,* etc.) with cord etc.; **~-up**, temporary connection of apparatus for experiment or in an emergency. **lash** *n.* 1. Stroke given with thong, whip, etc.; flexible part of whip; thong; goading influence; **the ~**, punishment of flogging. 2. Eyelash. **lash'less** *adj.*

Las Pal·mas (lahs pahl'mahs). Largest city of the Spanish Canary Islands, on the NE. coast of Grand Canary Island.

lass (lăs), **las·sie** (lăs'ē) *ns.* Girl. [chiefly Sc.]

Las·sen (lăs'en) **Peak.** Only active volcano in the continental U.S.; 10,453 feet (3,186 m), in the Cascade Range in N. California.

las·si·tude (lăs'ĭtood, -tūd) *n.* Weariness, languor; disinclination to exert or interest oneself.

las·so (lăs'ō, lăsōō') *n.* (pl. **-sos, -soes**). Rope, line of untanned hide etc., with running noose esp. for catching cattle. **~** *v.t.* (**-soed, -so·ing**). Catch with lasso.

last[1] (lăst, lahst) *n.* Shoemaker's wooden or metal model on which shoes are shaped.

last[2] (lăst, lahst) *adj.* After all others, coming out or belonging to the end; latest up to now; lowest, of least rank or estimation; only remaining; latest *to be*; least likely or willing or suitable; definitive; utmost, extreme; **~ day**, Judgment Day; end of the world; **~ ditch**, (place) of final desperate defense; **~ hurrah**, (colloq.) a final, futile political campaign; **~-in, first out**, method of evaluating business inventory on the assumption that the last lot to be received will be the first sold or used; **L~ Judgment**, God's final judgment on the world and on each person; **~ straw**, slight addition that makes something no longer bearable (as with camel's load); limit of tolerance; **L~ Supper**, supper of Jesus Christ and disciples on eve of the Crucifixion; **~ word**: see WORD; **last** *n.* Last-mentioned person or thing; last day or moments, death; last performance of certain acts; last mention; **at (long) ~**, in the end, after much delay. **last** *adv.* After all others; on the last occasion before the present; in the last place, finally. **last'ly** *adv.*

last[3] (lăst, lahst) *v.* Go on, remain unexhausted or adequate or alive; suffice; **~ out**, continue (esp. in vigor or use) at least as long as.

Las·tex (lăs'tĕks) *n.* (trademark) Yarn made of elastic rubber wound with synthetic or natural thread.

last·ing (lăs'tĭng, lahs'tĭng) *adj.* Enduring, permanent; durable. **last'ing·ly** *adv.* **last'ing·ness** *n.*

Las Ve·gas (lahs vā'gas). City and gambling resort in SE. Nevada.

Lat. *abbrev.* Latin.

lat. *abbrev.* Latitude.

Lat·a·ki·a (lătakē'a, lahtah-). Seaport of Syria, the ancient Laodicea ad Mare; fine kind of Turkish tobacco shipped from there.

latch (lăch) *n.* Door or gate fastening made of small bar falling into catch and lifted by lever, etc. from outside; small springlock of outer door catching when door is closed and worked by **latch'key** from outside; **~ onto**, (colloq.) attach oneself to; get; **latch'string**, cord passed through hole in door to open latch from outside. **latch** *v.* Fasten with latch.

late (lāt) *adj.* (**lat·er, lat·ter; lat·est, last**). 1. After the due or usual time; backward in flowering, ripening, etc.; far on in day or night, or in time; far on in a period, development, etc. 2. (usu. recently) dead; immediately preceding the present in office (as *the ~ president*); of recent date. **late'ness** *n.* **late** *adv.* After proper time; far on in time; (poet.) recently, lately; **~-comer**, (of person) recent arrival. **late** *n.* **of ~**, recently.

la·teen (lătēn') *adj.* **~ sail**, triangular sail on long yard at angle of 45 to mast; (of ship etc.) so rigged. [Fr. (*voile*) *latine* "Latin sail," because common in Mediterranean]

late·ly (lāt'lē) *adv.* Not long ago, in recent times.

La Tène (lă tĕn'). Archaeological site at E. end of Lake of Neufchâtel, Switzerland; **~ culture**, that of second Iron Age of central and W. Europe, so called because objects characteristic of it were first identified at La Tène.

la·tent (lā'tent) *adj.* Concealed; dormant; existing but not developed or manifest; **~ heat**: see HEAT. **la'ten·cy** *n.* **la'tent·ly** *adv.*

lat·er·al (lăt'eral) *adj.* Of, at, toward, from, the side(s); side-; **~ branch** (of family), branch descended from brother or sister of person in direct line; **~ pass**, (football) pass thrown parallel to line of scrimmage or backward (opp. to forward pass). **lat'er·al·ly** *adv.* **lateral** *n.* Side part, member or object, esp. lateral shoot or branch; (football) lateral pass.

Lat·er·an (lăt'eran). Site in Rome containing the basilica of St. John the Baptist (**St. John ~**) cathedral church of Rome, and the **~ Palace**, now a museum, where the popes resided until 14th c.; ~

*Below: A helium neon gas **laser** carries a television signal. Light is directed into an optical receiver (rear right) to strike a photocell, is converted to the original signal and relayed to a cathode ray tube.*

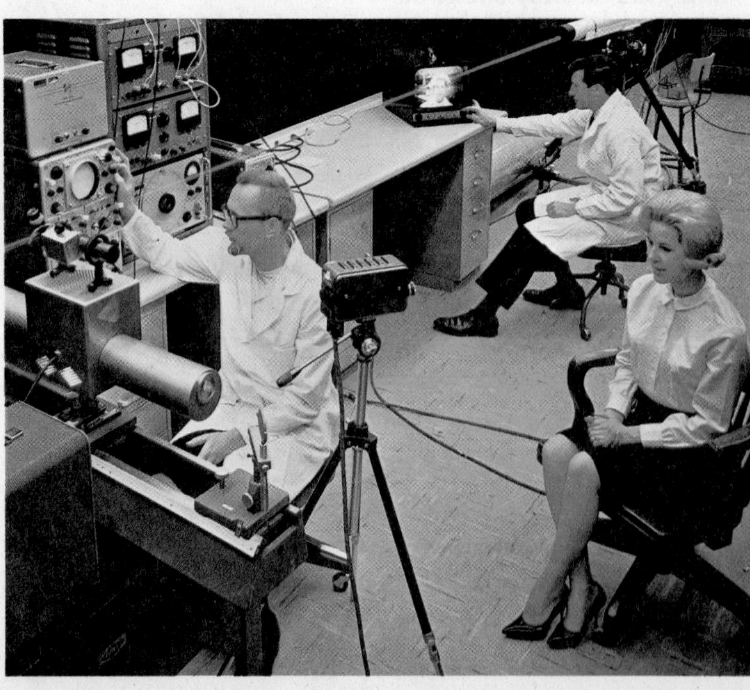

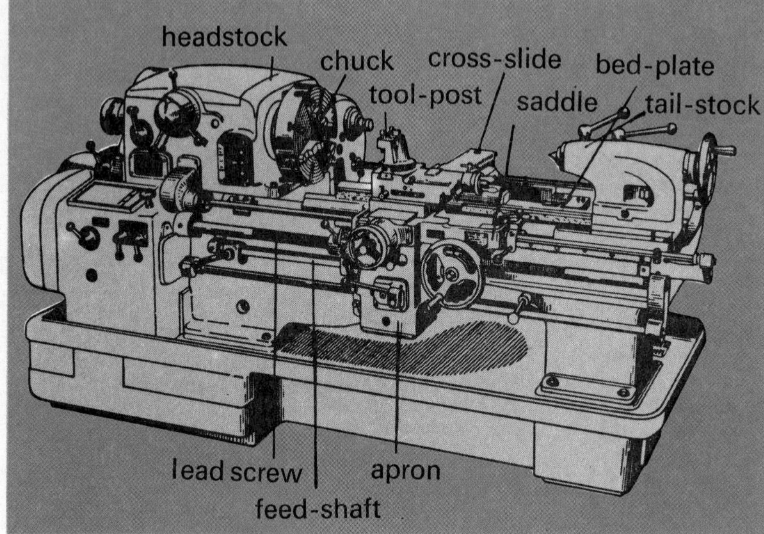

*Above: The material to be shaped on a **lathe** is secured between the headstock, using a chuck, and the tail-stock. The cutting tool may be attached to or hand-held against the tool-post.*

Council, any of the five general ecclesiastical councils or synods of the Western Church, held in St. John Lateran (1123, 1139, 1179, 1215, 1512–17); ~ **Treaty**, concordat between Italy and Holy See, signed 1929 in Lateran Palace, and recognizing as fully sovereign and independent a new (papal) State called Vatican City.

lat·er·ite (lăt′erīt) *n.* (geol.) Superficial deposit rich in iron and aluminum oxides, red or yellow in color, developed by weathering of rocks in some wet tropical climates.

la·tex (lā′tĕks) *n.* (pl. **lat·i·ces** pr. lăt′ĭsēz, **la·tex·es**). Milky fluid of a number of plants, exuding from cut surfaces and sometimes coagulating rapidly on exposure, used as the raw material of several commercial products, esp. rubber; synthetic product resembling this. [L., = "liquid"]

lath (lăth, lahth) *n.* (pl. **laths** pr. lădhz, lăths, lahdhz, lahths). Thin narrow strip of wood esp. for use as support for plaster etc. ~ *v.t.* Provide (wall, ceiling) with laths.

lathe (lādh) *n.* Machine for turning wood, metal, etc., by rotating the article to be turned against tools that cut it to the required shape.

lath·er (lădh′*er*) *n.* Froth made by agitation of mixture of soap, or other detergent, and water; frothy sweat of horse; (fig.) state of excitement, as **in a ~. lath′er·y** *adj.* **lather** *v.* Cover (esp. chin etc. for shaving) with lather; (of horse) become covered with lather; (of soap etc.) form lather.

lat·i·fun·di·um (lăt*i*fŭn′dē*u*m) *n.* (pl. **-di·a** pr. -dē*a*). (Rom. hist.) Large pastoral estate worked by slaves or poor tenants.

Lat·in (lăt′ĭn) *n.* 1. Indo-European language of ancient Latium and of the Romans, orig. that of the people of Latium (*Latini*), and spoken by the Romans, subsequently the language of R.C. Church and used generally in law and the sciences in W. Europe, that of the post-classical period being distinguished chronologically as **Late** ~ (*c*200–600 A.D.) and **Medieval** ~ (*c*600–1500 A.D.); **Low** ~, any post-classical Latin; **modern** ~, that of modern times, employed esp. in scientific descriptions and classifications; **pig** ~: see PIG; **Silver** ~, literary language and style of the century following the death of Augustus (14 A.D.); **Vulgar** ~, popular and provincial forms of Latin, esp. those from which Romance languages developed. 2. Native, inhabitant, of ancient Latium. 3. (hist.) During the Crusades, member of western nations of Europe (as dist. from "Greeks"). 4. Member of any of the Latin peoples. **Latin** *adj.* 1. Of Latium or the ancient Latins; of, written in, the Latin language. 2. Of the Latin Church. 3. Of the European peoples speaking languages descended from Latin. 4. ~ **America**, all Western Hemisphere countries S. of U.S. where Spanish or Portuguese is the chief language; ~ **Church**, Roman Catholic Church; ~ **cross**, plain cross with lower member longer than the other three; ~ **League**, (Rom. hist.) confederation of cities of Latium, merged in Roman State 338 B.C.; ~ **Quarter**, district of Paris on left or S. bank of Seine, where students and artists live and principal university buildings are situated.

Lat·in·ism (lăt′*i*nĭzem) *n.* Idiom characteristic of Latin, esp. one used in another language; conformity in style to Latin models.

Lat′in·ist *n.* Latin scholar.

Lat·in·ize (lăt′*i*nīz) *v.* (**-ized, -iz·ing**). Give Latin form to (word), put into Latin; make conformable to ideas, customs, etc., of the ancient Romans, Latin peoples, or Latin Church; use Latin forms, idioms, etc.

La·ti·no (lătē′nō) *n.* Person of Latin-American descent living in U.S.

La·ti·nus (l*a*tī′n*u*s). (Rom. legend) Eponymous hero of Latins, son of Faunus and the nymph Marica, king of Latium and father of Lavinia, whom Aeneas married.

la·tis·si·mus dor·si (l*a*tĭs′*i*m*u*s dôr′sī) (pl. **la·tis·si·mi dor·si** pr. l*a*tĭs′*i*mī dôr′sī). (also ~ **muscle**) Broad flat muscle covering lumbar region.

lat·i·tude (lăt′ĭtōōd, -tūd) *n.* 1. Breadth, width (now only joc.); scope, full extent (rare). 2. Freedom from narrowness; liberality of interpretation; tolerated variety of attitude or opinion. 3. (geog.) Angular distance on a meridian, place's angular distance on its meridian, N. or S. of equator, measured from Earth's center; (usu. pl.) regions, climes (esp. with ref. to temperature); (astron.) angular distance of heavenly body from ecliptic. **lat·i·tu′di·nal** *adj.* **lat·i·tu′di·nal·ly** *adv.*

lat·i·tu·di·nar·i·an (lătĭtōōd*i*nār′ē*a*n, -tū-) *n.* & *adj.* (One who is) tolerant; characterized by latitude of opinion, esp. in religious matters. **lat·i·tu·di·nar′i·an·ism** *n.*

La·ti·um (lā′shē*u*m). Ancient name of district of central Italy lying S. of Apennines and E. of Tiber.

La·to·na (l*a*tō′n*a*). (Rom. myth.) = LETO.

la·trine (l*a*trēn′) *n.* Communal toilet, esp. in military camp etc.

lat·ter (lăt′*er*) *adj.* Later, second (archaic); belonging to end of period, world, etc.; second-mentioned (opp. to FORMER); **~-day**, modern; **L ~ Day Saints**, the MORMONS. **latter** *n.* Second-mentioned thing or person.

lat·ter·ly (lăt′*er*lē) *adv.* Of late; toward the end of some period etc.

lat·tice (lăt′ĭs) *n.* 1. Framework of wood or other material made of laths crossed diagonally so as to form a netlike structure serving as screen, door, etc.; (also **lat′tice-work**) laths etc. so arranged. 2. Arrangement of points representing the relative position of corresponding atomic or molecular centers in the structure units of a crystal. 3. ~ **window**, one having lattice; one with small panes set in diagonally crossing strips of lead. **lat′ticed** *adj.*

Lat·vi·a (lăt′vē*a*). Area on the E. and S. shore of the Gulf of Riga; formerly a Baltic province of the Russian Empire; proclaimed an independent republic in 1918; incorporated in the U.S.S.R. in 1940 as a constituent republic (properly *Latvian Soviet Socialist Republic*); capital, Riga. **Lat'vi·an** *adj.* & *n.*

laud (lawd) *n.* 1. Praise, hymn of praise (rare). 2. **Lauds,** (R.C. Ch.) canonical HOUR joined to Matins. **laud** *v.t.* Praise, celebrate. **lau·da·tion** (lawdā'shon) *n.* **laud'a·tive, laud·a·to·ry** (law'datōrē, -tōrē) *adjs.*

laud·a·ble (law'dabel) *adj.* Commendable, praiseworthy. **laud·a·bil·i·ty** (lawdabĭl'ĭtē) *n.* **laud'a·bly** *adv.*

lau·da·num (law'danum, lawd'num) *n.* Tincture of opium. [name given by Paracelsus to a costly medicament, later transferred to preparations containing opium]

laugh (lăf, lahf) *v.* Make the sounds and the movements of face and sides by which lively amusement, sense of the ludicrous, exultation, and scorn, are instinctively expressed; have these emotions; utter laughingly; get (person) *out of* habit, belief, etc., by ridicule; (of objects etc.) be lively with play of movement or light; ridicule; ~ **away,** dismiss (subject) with a laugh; while away (time) with jests; ~ **off,** get rid of (embarrassment etc.) with a jest; ~ **out of court,** deprive of a hearing by ridicule; ~ **out of the other side of one's mouth,** change from pleasure or amusement to sorrow or vexation; ~ **up one's sleeve,** be secretly amused. **laugh** *n.* Sound or act of laughing; **have the last ~ (on),** win after apparent defeat; reverse one's fortunes successfully; trick a trickster. **laugh'a·ble** *adj.* **laugh'a·bly** *adv.* Exciting laughter, amusing.

laugh·ing (lăf'ĭng, lah'fĭng) *n.* (esp.) **no ~ matter,** serious thing, not a fit subject for laughter; ~ **gas,** nitrous oxide used as anesthetic, producing exhilarating effects when inhaled; **laugh'ing-stock,** object of general derision; **laughing** *adj.* **laugh'ing·ly** *adv.*

laugh·ter (lăf'ter, lahf'ter) *n.* Act, sound, of laughing.

launch[1] (lawnch, lahnch) *v.* 1. Hurl, discharge, send forth (missile, blow, threat, etc.); burst *into* strong language, lengthy speech, etc.; ~, **launching pad,** platform from which rocket or guided missile is launched. 2. Set (vessel) afloat, cause to slide from land or stocks into water; send off, start, on a course; initiate (an enterprise). **launch** *n.* Process of launching ship.

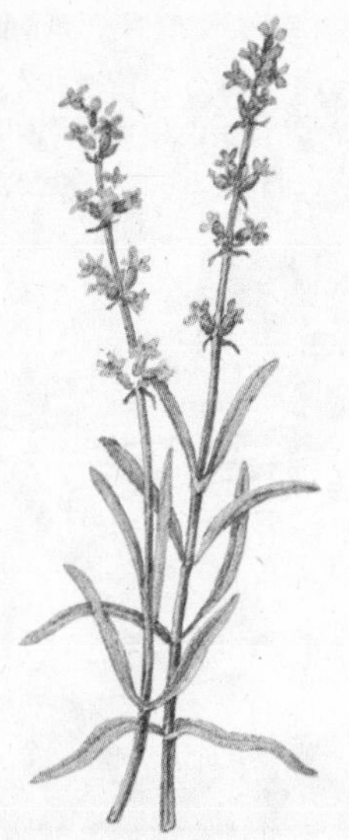

*The fragrance of **lavender** (above: L. officinalis) has earned it a place in gardens of many warm temperate countries. The flowers of L. spica are used in making lavender water.*

launch[2] (lawnch, lahnch) *n.* Large electric or steam or motorboat for passengers, pleasure trips, etc.; heavy motorboat.

laun·der (lawn'der, lahn'-) *v.* 1. Wash and iron (linen etc.); (of fabric) bear laundering (*well* etc.). 2. (slang) Pass (illicit funds) through (esp. foreign) banks to hide original ownership.

laun·der·ette (lawnderĕt', lahn-, lawn'derĕt, lahn'-) *n.* Establishment where washing machines may be used for a fee; Laundromat.

laun·dress (lawn'drĭs, lahn'-) *n.* Woman who earns her livelihood by washing clothes etc.

Laun·dro·mat (lawn'dromăt, lahn'-) *n.* (trademark) Self-service establishment equipped with coin-operated washing machines and dryers.

laun·dry (lawn'drē, lahn'-) *n.* (pl. **-dries**). Room or establishment for washing linen; batch of clothes etc. sent to or from laundry; ~ **list,** list of items sent to laundry; (colloq.) long ill-assorted list of items.

Lau·ra (lōr'a). Subject of love poems of PETRARCH, by tradition Laura de Noves (*c*1308–48), wife of Count Hugues de Sade.

lau·re·ate (lōr'ēĭt) *adj.* Wreathed with, (of wreath) consisting of, laurels; worthy of laurels as poet, orator, etc.; **Nobel ~,** recipient of any of the NOBEL prizes; **poet ~,** (England) poet receiving stipend as officer of British Royal Household, writer of poems for state occasions; (U.S.) outstanding poet receiving comparable hc from state legislature. **laureate** *n.* Poet laureate. **lau're·ate·ship** *n.*

lau·rel (lōr'el, lăr'-) *n.* 1. Bay tree (*Laurus nobilis*) (also **bay ~**); foliage of this as emblem of victory or poetic merit; **look to one's ~s,** beware of losing preeminence; **rest on one's ~s,** cease to strive for further glory. 2. Any of various trees and shrubs with leaves resembling those of bay, esp. MOUNTAIN laurel; sweet magnolia, sweet bay, ~ **oak,** N. Amer. species of oak. **laurel** *v.t.* **(-reled, -rel·ing,** Brit. **-relled, -rel·ling).** Wreathe with laurel.

Lau·rence (lōr'ens, lăr'-), **St.** (3rd c.). Roman Christian martyr; usu. represented with a gridiron, the instrument of his martyrdom.

Lau·ren·tian (lawrĕn'shan) **Mountains.** Low mountain range between the St. Lawrence River and Hudson Bay in the province of Quebec, Canada; summer and winter resort area.

*The **launch** of the Apollo 16 Saturn V spacecraft at Kennedy Space Center, Florida. This space flight was the 8th manned voyage to the moon and took place on April 16th 1972 with a crew of four on board.*

lau·rus·ti·nus (lōr*u*stī′n*u*s) *n.* Evergreen flowering shrub, *Viburnum tinus.*

la·va (lah′v*a*, lăv′*a*) *n.* Molten rock which flows down sides of volcano; solid substance this cools into.

la·va·bo (l*a*vā′bō, -vah′-) *n.* Ritual washing of celebrant's hands at offertory in Mass (accompanied by saying of Ps. 26); towel or basin used for this; washing trough in some medieval monasteries. [L., = "I will wash," first wd of Ps. 26:6]

lav·a·to·ry (lăv′*a*tōrē, -tōrē) *n.* (pl. **-ries**). 1. Room or compartment with facilities for urination and defecation. 2. Room etc. with facilities for washing face and hands.

lave (lāv) *v.t.* (**laved, lav·ing**). (poet.) Wash, bathe; wash against, flow along.

lav·en·der (lăv′*e*nd*e*r) *n.* Small lilac-flowered narrow-leaved shrub of genus *Lavandula*, native in S. Europe and N. Africa, extensively cultivated for its perfume; flowers and stalks of this laid among linen etc.; pale-blue color with trace of red; ~ **water**, perfume made from distilled lavender.

la·ver (lā′v*e*r) *n.* Any of various marine algae, esp. the edible species.

La·vin·i·a (l*a*vĭn′ē*a*). (Rom. legend) Daughter of Latinus, king of Latium, and wife of Aeneas.

lav·ish (lăv′ĭsh) *adj.* Giving or producing without stint, profuse, prodigal; very or too abundant. **lav′ish·ly** *adv.* **lav′ish·ness** *n.* **lavish** *v.t.* Bestow or spread profusely.

La·voi·sier (lăvwŏzyā′), **Antoine Laurent** (1743–94). French chemist; laid the foundations of modern chemistry by giving a correct explanation of the part played by oxygen in combustion; discovered animal metabolism.

law (law) *n.* 1. Body of enacted or customary rules recognized by a community as binding; one of these rules; their controlling influence, law-abiding state of society (freq. ~ **and order**); laws as a system or science, jurisprudence; binding injunction(s); one of the branches of the study of law, laws concerning specified department; statute and common law (opp. EQUITY); legal knowledge; judicial remedy, law courts as providing it, litigation; **the** ~, the legal profession; (colloq.) the police; **the L~ (of Moses)**: see MOSAIC law; **lay down the** ~, talk authoritatively, hector; **be a** ~ **unto oneself**, take one's own line, disregard convention; **take the** ~ **into one's own hands**, redress one's wrong by force. 2. Rule of action or procedure, esp. in an art, department of life, or game; (also ~ **of nature**), correct statement of invariable sequence between specified conditions and specified phenomenon; regularity of nature. ~**-abiding**, obedient to law; **law′breaker**, person who violates the law; **law′giver**, one who makes (esp. code of) laws; **law′maker**, one who drafts or enacts laws (often fig.); legislator; **law′man**, esp. sheriff of Old West; **law of nations**, international law, law regulating relations between countries; **law′suit**, prosecution of claim in court of law.

law·ful (law′f*u*l) *adj.* Permitted, appointed, qualified, recognized, by law. **law′ful·ly** *adv.* **law′ful·ness** *n.*

law·less (law′lĭs) *adj.* Without law, not regulated by law; regardless of, disobedient to, uncontrolled by, law; unbridled, licentious. **law′less·ness** *n.*

lawn[1] (lawn, lahn) *n.* Very fine material of plain weave, made orig. of linen, now usu. of cotton. [prob. f. *Laon* in France]

lawn[2] (lawn, lahn) *n.* Area of closely-cut grass in a garden or park, or used for a game, as *croquet*; ~ **mower**, machine for mowing lawn; ~ **tennis** = TENNIS.

Law·rence[1] (lōr′*e*ns, lar′-), **D(avid) H(erbert)** (1885–1930). English novelist and poet, author of *Sons and Lovers, Lady Chatterly's Lover*, etc.

Law·rence[2] (lōr′*e*ns, lar′-), **Ernest Orlando** (1901–58). American physicist; inventor of the cyclotron; received Nobel Prize for physics, 1939.

Law·rence[3] (lōr′*e*ns, lar′-), **T(homas) E(dward)** (1888–1935). Known as "Lawrence of Arabia"; British soldier and scholar; a leader in World War I, of guerrilla warfare against Turks, described by him in *The Seven Pillars of Wisdom.*

law·ren·ci·um (lawrĕn′sē*u*m, lahrĕn′-) *n.* (chem.) Transuranic element; symbol Lw, at. no. 103.

law·yer (law′y*e*r, loi′*e*r) *n.* Member of legal profession, esp. attorney, (Brit.) solicitor; person versed in law.

lax (lăks) *adj.* Loose, not compact; negligent, not strict, vague. **lax′ly** *adv.* **lax′ness, lax′i·ty** *ns.*

lax·a·tive (lăk′s*a*tĭv) *adj.* & *n.* (Medicine) tending to loosen the bowels.

lay[1] (lā) *n.* Short lyric or narrative poem meant to be sung; (loosely) song, poem.

lay[2] (lā) *adj.* Nonclerical, not in orders; of, done by, layman or laity; nonprofessional, not expert; (esp. with ref. to psychoanalysis) not a physician; ~ **brother, sister**, person who has taken habit and vows of religious order but is employed in manual labor and excused from other duties; **lay′man**, member of the laity; **lay reader**, layman licensed to conduct religious services.

Below: The layout of a ***lawn tennis*** *court is marked out with white lime. Below left: A men's singles match is played on one of the courts at Wimbledon during the Lawn Tennis Association Championship.*

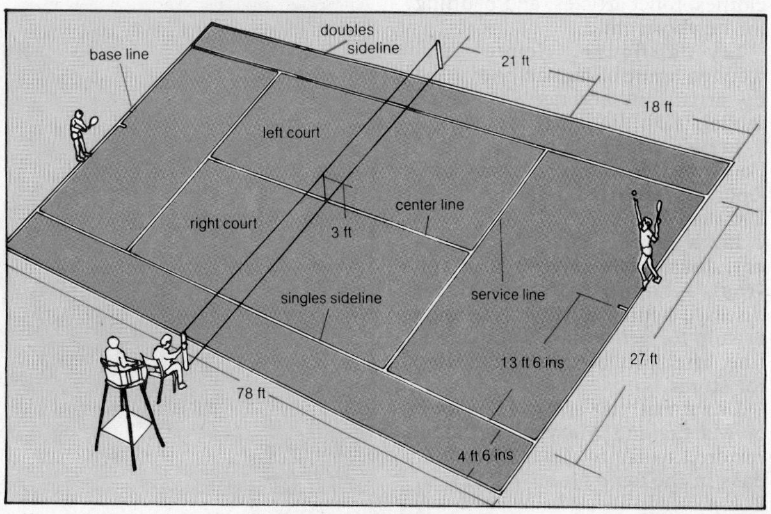

lay[3] (lā) *v.* (**laid, layed, lay·ing**). Place on a surface or in horizontal position; spread, apply (paint etc.); cause to subside (ghost, dust, storm, etc.); impose (obligation etc.); beat down (crops); set (trap) in readiness; aim (cannon); wager (stake); produce (egg); make (rope) by twisting yarn; **~-about** (*n.*), habitual loafer; **~ by, in**, store; **~ down**, relinquish (office etc.), formulate (principle), store (wine) in cellar; **~ hands on**, attack or seize, (*of* bishop) confirm or ordain; **~ off** (employee), dismiss temporarily owing to shortage of work; (slang) stop, desist; **lay'off** (*n.*); **lay on**, provide for supply of (water, electricity, etc.); **lay open**, cut open; expose; **lay out**, prepare (corpse) for burial; dispose, arrange, (site etc.); (slang) kill, knock down, exhaust, (person); **lay'out** (*n.*), (plan etc. showing) arrangement of site, printed page, etc.; **lay'over** (*n.*), stopover; **lay papers, bill** (on table), follow procedure for consideration by legislature; **lay table, breakfast**, etc., prepare for meal; **lay to**, impute to; **lay up**, save, store; put (ship or vehicle) temporarily out of active use; confine to bed through illness. **lay** *n.* Way, position, or direction in which something (esp. country) lies; (of rope) direction or amount of twist given to strands; lie; **~ of the land**, general nature of an area; (fig.) general view or prospects of a matter, the facts of the case.

lay·a·way (lā'*a*wā) **plan.** Reservation of merchandise by payment of deposit.

lay·er (lā'*er*) *n.* (esp.) 1. Stratum, thickness of matter (esp. one of several) spread over surface; **~ cake**, one made in layers with filling between. 2. (hort.) Shoot fastened into earth to establish root while attached to parent plant. 3. Oyster bed. **layer** *v.t.* Propagate in layers; (of plant) form layers.

lay·ette (lāĕt') *n.* Outfit of clothes, toilet articles, and bedding for newborn child.

lay (lā) **figure.** Jointed usu. wooden figure of human body used by artists, in absence of human model. [Du. *led* joint]

laz·ar (lăz'*er*, lā'zer) *n.* (obs.) Poor and diseased person, esp. leper; **~ house**, lazaretto. [f. LAZARUS[1]]

laz·a·ret·to (lăzerĕt'ō), **laz·a·ret, laz·a·rette** (lăzerĕt') *ns.* (pl. **-tos**). Formerly a hospital for diseased poor, esp. lepers; building or ship for performance of quarantine; after part of ship's hold used for stores.

Laz·a·rus[1] (lăz'*er*us). 1. Brother of Martha and Mary of Bethany, restored to life by Jesus after four days in the tomb (John 11, 12). 2. Beggar in the parable of the rich man and the beggar (Luke 16).

Laz·a·rus[2] (lăz'*er*us), **Emma** (1849–87). American humanitarian, poet, and philanthropist; champion of Russian Jews during their persecution, 1879–83; best remembered for her sonnet, "The New Colossus," engraved on pedestal of the Statue of Liberty and including the words "Give me your tired, your poor/Your huddled masses, yearning to be free."

laze (lāz) *v.* (**lazed, laz·ing**). (colloq.) Be lazy; pass (time) *away* in laziness.

la·zy (lā'zē) *adj.* (**la·zi·er, la·zi·est**). Averse to labor, slothful; appropriate to, inducing, indolence; (of stream) slow-moving; **la'zybones**, lazy person; **lazy Susan**, revolving tray at center of table that holds serving dishes, condiments, etc.; **lazy tongs**, arrangement of several pairs of levers crossing and pivoted at center like scissors, for picking up objects at a distance. **la'zi·ly** *adv.* **la'zi·ness** *n.*

lb. *abbrev.* Pound, pounds.

lbs. *abbrev.* Pounds.

L.C. *abbrev.* Library of Congress.

l.c. *abbrev.* *Loco citato* (L., = in the passage already quoted); lower case (of print).

LCD *abbrev.* Liquid crystal diode.

L.C.D., l.c.d. *abbrevs.* Lowest common denominator.

LCDR *abbrev.* Lieutenant commander.

L.C.M. *abbrev.* Lowest common multiple.

Ld. *abbrev.* Lord.

L-dopa (ĕl'dō'p*a*) *n.* Drug used in treating Parkinson's disease.

lea (lē, lā) *n.* (poet.) Tract of open ground, esp. grassland.

leach (lēch) *v.t.* Make (liquid) percolate through some material; subject (bark, ore) to action of percolating fluid; purge (soluble matter) *away* etc. by such means.

Lea·cock (lē'kŏk), **Stephen (Butler)** (1869–1944). English-born Canadian humorist and economist.

lead[1] (lĕd) *n.* 1. (chem.) Heavy soft easily fusible metallic element of dull bluish-gray color, usu. obtained from lead sulfide (the principal ore, PbS) by heating in a furnace; symbol Pb, at. no. 82, at. wt. 207.2; **red ~**, red oxide of lead, used as pigment and in glass-making; **white ~**, mixture of lead carbonate and lead hydroxide, used as pigment. 2. Lump of lead used in sounding depth of water. 3. (print.) Metal strip for spacing out (**lead'ing**) lines or letters of type. 4. (pl.) Strips of lead used to cover roof; piece of (esp. horizontal) lead-covered roof; lead frames holding glass of lattices or painted window. 5. (also **pencil ~**) Graphite. 6. **~ poisoning**, form of poisoning caused by absorption of lead into the system. **lead** (lĕd) *v.t.* Cover, weight, frame (panes etc.) with lead; (print.) separate lines or letters of (type) with leads; treat with lead, as in **leaded** or **unleaded** gasoline. **lead'ed, lead'less** *adjs.*

lead[2] (lēd) *v.* (**led** pr. lĕd, **lead·ing**). 1. Conduct, guide, esp. by going in front; (of commander) direct movements of; **~ the way**, act as guide or leader. 2. Conduct (person) by the hand or contact, (animal) by halter etc.; guide by persuasion; guide actions or opinions of, induce *to* do; **~ astray**, (esp.) tempt to sin etc. 3. (of road etc.) Conduct (usu. abs.) *to* place; (fig.) have as result, as in **~** *to happiness.* 4. Make (rope, water, etc.) go through pulley, channel, etc. 5. Pass, go through, spend, (life etc.). 6. Have first place in; go first; be

*The resistance of **lead** to corrosion makes it a suitable material for use as cladding on buildings where it protects the structure from the effects of the weather.*

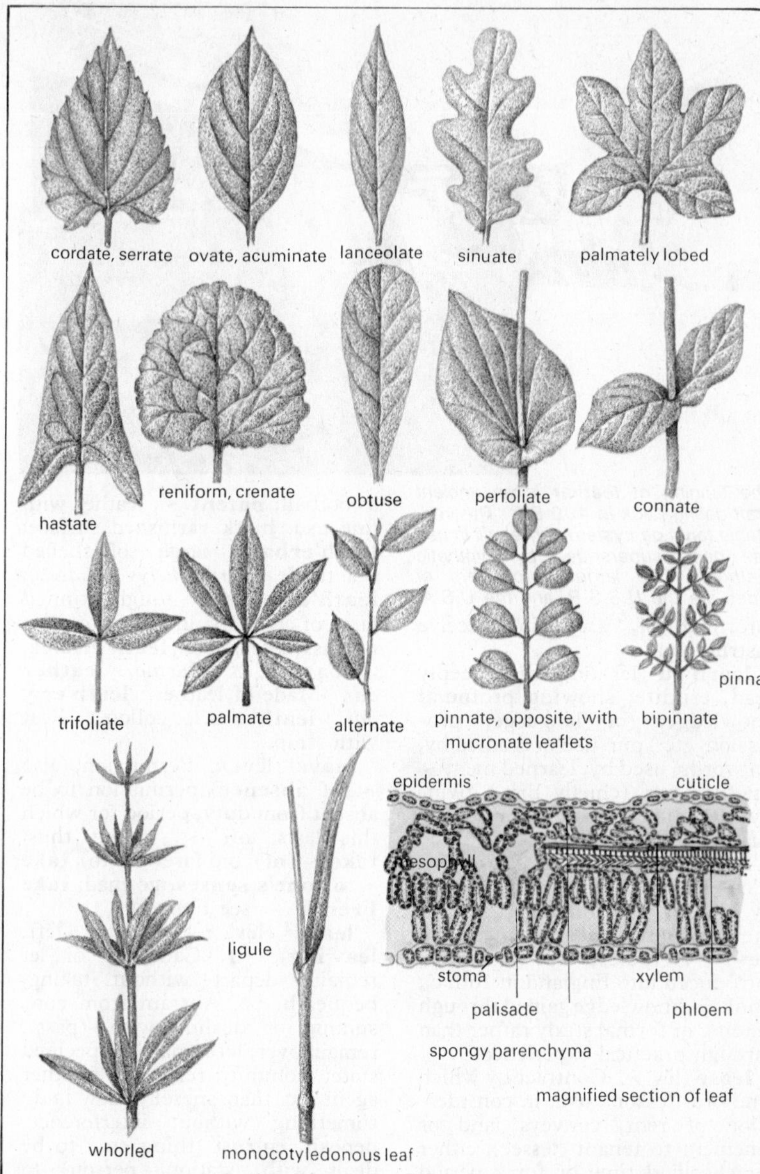

*The pattern of veins in a **leaf** is closely related to the shape of the leaf. In a monocotyledonous leaf the veins run parallel along its length. In a dicotyledonous leaf the veins are reticulate and the leaf, such as a maple, may be divided.*

first at some point in race; direct by example; be official director or spokesman of political party, team, etc.; have chief role in play etc.; take the offensive (in contest etc.). 7. (cards) Play as first card, be first player, in trick; play one of (suit) when leading; ~ **away from**, lead card of suit other than (ace or other high card) in one's hand; ~ **up to**, play card so as to elicit (specified high card, usu. ace) from an opponent's hand. 8. ~ **off**, begin (dance, conversation, etc.); (baseball) bat first in inning; **lead′off** *adj.* or *n.*; **lead on**, entice into going further than was intended; **lead up to**, form preparation for, serve to introduce, direct conversation toward (subject). 9. Ply (witness) with leading questions. **lead** (lĕd) *n.* 1. Direction given by going in front, example; leading place, leadership; (theatr.) (player of) chief part; (cards) act or right of playing first; ~ **time**, interval required between planning and starting or completing a project. 2. (elect.) Connecting wire to or from an electric device (~**-in**, wire connecting external aerial to radio receiver); channel in ice field. 3. Strap, strip of leather, etc., for leading dog.

lead·en (lĕd′en) *adj.* (As) of LEAD[1]; heavy, slow, burdensome; inert, deadening; lead colored.

lead·er (lē′der) *n.* (esp.) 1. Person or thing that guides or leads; see LOSS ~, MAJORITY ~, MINORITY ~. 2. (mus.) Conductor. 3. Shoot growing at apex of stem or principal branch. 4. (Brit.) LEADING article. 5. (print.) Line of dots or dashes to guide eye. **lead′er·less** *adj.* **lead′er·ship** *n.*

lead·ing (lē′dĭng) *n.* Guidance; direction. ~ *adj.* (esp.) ~ **article**, article in newspaper etc. in prominent position and (Brit.) expressing editorial opinion; ~ **edge**, forward edge of blade of propeller; foremost edge of aircraft wing, tail, or fin; ~ **lady, man**, actor taking chief part in play etc.; ~ **light**, prominent influential person; ~ **note**, seventh note in ascending scale, leading the ear to expect the tonic; ~ **question**, question that suggests the answer the questioner wishes to receive.

leaf (lēf) *n.* (pl. **leaves** pr. lēvz). 1. Expanded organ (usu. green) of plant springing from side of stem or branch or directly from root; (pop.) petal (esp. **rose** ~); foliage; **in** ~, with leaves out; ~ **miner**, larva of any of numerous insects digging into and feeding on leaves; ~ **mold**, soil composed chiefly of dead leaves. 2. Leaves of plant cultivated for commercial purposes, e.g., tobacco, tea. 3. Single thickness of folded paper, esp. in book; very thin sheet of metal, esp. gold or silver, or horn, marble, etc.; **turn over a new** ~, mend one's ways. 4. Slab inserted in expandable table. **leaf′age** *n.* **leaf′less** *adj.* **leaf′less·ness** *n.* **leaf′y** *adj.* (**leaf·i·er, leaf·i·est**). **leaf′i·ness** *n.* **leaf** *v.t.* ~ **through**, turn over pages.

leaf·let (lēf′lĭt) *n.* 1. (bot.) One division of compound leaf; young leaf. 2. Small leaf of paper, or sheet folded but not stitched, with printed matter, esp. for distribution.

league[1] (lēg) *n.* Measure of distance, usu. about 3 miles (4.8 km).

league[2] (lēg) *n.* Association for mutual protection and assistance or prosecution of common interests; (sports) group of teams competing chiefly against one another; **in** ~ **with**, allied with; ~ **standing**, (sports) position of team with respect to championship. **league** *v.* Join in league.

League (lēg) **of Nations.** Association of nations established in 1919 peace treaty "in order to promote international cooperation and to achieve international peace and security"; dissolved in 1946, superseded by the UNITED NATIONS.

lea·guer (lē′ger) *n.* Member of sports league, as *Little Leaguer*.

Le·ah (lē′*a*, lā′*a*). Elder daughter of Laban, and wife of Jacob (Gen. 29,30).

leak (lēk) *n.* 1. Perforation through which liquid, steam, or gas makes way into or out of vessel that is immersed in or contains it. 2. Water passing through such a perforation into a ship; liquid etc.

escaping through a flaw in a receptacle. 3. Escape of electric charge from an incompletely insulated conductor. 4. (radio) (also **grid** ~) High resistance placed in parallel with a grid condenser to prevent overaccumulation of negative charge on the grid. 5. Divulging of secret information etc.; information etc. divulged; **news** ~. **leak** *v.* Escape, allow escape of, through leak; divulge (secret information etc.); ~ **out,** become known improperly. **leak'age** *n.* **leak'y** *adj.* (**leak·i·er, leak·i·est**). **leak'i·ness** *n.*

lean[1] (lēn) *adj.* Thin, not plump; meager, of poor quality, unnutritious; unremunerative; (of meat) consisting chiefly of muscular tissue, not of fat; ~ **years,** years of scarcity. **lean** *n.* Lean part of meat.

lean[2] (lēn) *v.* (**leaned,** Brit. **leant** pr. lĕnt, **lean·ing**). Incline one's body against something for support; be or put in sloping position, *against, on;* incline body *back, forward,* etc.; stand obliquely, out of the perpendicular; rely or depend *on;* have tendency *to,* be partial *to* cause, opinion, person, etc.; ~**-to,** (*n.*) shed etc. with roof leaning against larger building or wall. **lean** *n.* Inclination, slope.

Le·an·der (lēăn'd*er*). (Gk. legend) Lover of HERO.

leap (lēp) *v.* (**leaped** or **leapt** pr. lĕpt, lēpt, **leap·ing**). 1. Jump; **leap'frog,** game in which players vault over, by placing hands upon, the bent back or shoulders of others. 2. Act hastily. **leap** *n.* Jump; thing to be jumped; ~ **in the dark,** hazardous attempt of doubtful issue; **by ~s and bounds,** with startlingly rapid progress; ~ **year,** year in which an extra day (Feb. 29) is inserted to make calendar year conform with astronomical YEAR (in Gregorian calendar it occurs every fourth year, i.e., when date is divisible by 4, but not in century years unless divisible by 400); ~ **year proposal,** proposal of marriage made by woman to man, traditionally allowable only in leap year.

Lear[1] (lēr). Legendary British king, a supposed descendant of Aeneas; subject of Shakespeare's tragedy, *King Lear.*

Lear[2] (lēr), **Edward** (1812–88). English artist and writer of nonsense verse; author and illustrator of *The Book of Nonsense* (1846), which popularized the LIMERICK, and of "The Owl and the Pussy-cat," (1871).

learn (lērn) *v.* (**learned, learnt, learn·ing**). Get knowledge of or skill in by study, experience, or being taught; commit to memory (esp. ~ **by heart** or **rote**); become aware *that, how,* etc.; be informed of, ascertain; receive instruction.

*The tanning of **leather** is an ancient craft dating back to 400 B.C. The vegetable tannage system, while still in use has been superseded by synthetic methods. The largest producers of hides are the U.S.S.R. and the U.S.A.*

learn·ed (lēr'nĭd) *adj.* Deeply read, erudite; showing profound knowledge; (of language, profession, etc.) pursued or studied by, (of words) used by, learned men; ~ **professions,** (chiefly Brit.) divinity, law, and medicine. **learn'ed·ly** *adv.* **learn'ed·ness** *n.*

learn·ing (lēr'nĭng) *n.* (esp.) (Possession of) knowledge obtained by study, esp. of language or literary or historical science; **the new** ~, studies, esp. of Greek, introduced into England in 16th c.; **book** ~, knowledge gained through reading or formal study rather than through practical experience.

lease (lēs) *n.* Contract by which landlord (lessor), usu. in consideration of rent, conveys land or tenement to tenant (lessee), either for specified time or for a period terminable at the will of either party; **lease'hold,** (real property) held by lease. **lease** *v.t.* (**leased, leas·ing**). Grant or take lease of; ~**-lend** = LEND-lease.

leash (lēsh) *n.* Thong or line by which dogs are held; LEAD[2] (*n.*). ~ *v.t.* Connect, hold in, with leash.

least (lēst) *adj.,* superl. of *little.* Smallest, slightest; **the** ~, (esp. after neg.) any, however small. ~ *n.* Least amount; **to say the** ~ **of it,** to put the case moderately; **at** ~, at all events, even if a wider statement is disputable; at the lowest computation; **(in) the** ~, in the smallest degree, at all. **least** *adv.* In the least degree.

least·wise (lēst'wīz), (dial. **least'ways**) *adv.* (colloq.) Anyway, at least.

leath·er (lĕdh'*er*) *n.* Animal skin prepared for use by tanning or similar process; article, or part of one, made of leather, piece of leather for polishing, thong; (slang) a football; **patent** ~, leather with fine usu. black varnished surface; **leath'erback,** large soft-shelled sea turtle (*Dermochelys coriacea*); **leath'erjacket,** tough-skinned larva of crane fly, injurious to roots of grass, cereals, etc.; **leath'erneck,** (slang) a U.S. Marine. **leather** *adj.* Made of leather. **leath'er·y** *adj.* **leather** *v.t.* (colloq.) Beat with strap.

leave[1] (lēv) *n.* Permission; (also ~ **of absence**) permission to be absent from duty, period for which this lasts; **on** ~, absent thus; **take ~ (of),** bid farewell (to); **take ~ of one's senses,** go mad; **take French** ~: see FRENCH.

leave[2] (lēv) *v.t.* (**left** pr. lĕft, **leav·ing**). 1. Cause to or let remain, depart without taking; bequeath. 2. Abstain from consuming or dealing with, (pass.) remain over; let remain in specified state; commit, refer, *to* another agent etc. than oneself; allow *to* do something without interference; deposit, entrust (thing etc.) to be dealt with, station (person) to discharge function, in one's absence. 3. Quit, go away from; depart; pass (object) so as to put it in specified relative direction; cease to reside at, belong to, or serve; abandon, forsake; ~ **alone,** not interfere with; ~ **behind,** go away without; leave as consequence or trace; pass; ~ **off,** discontinue; come to, make, an end; ~ **out,** omit; ~ **over,** let stand over for a time.

leave[3] (lēv) *v.i.* (**leaved, leav·ing**). Put forth leaves.

leav·en (lĕv'*en*) *n.* Substance added to dough to produce fermentation, esp. fermenting dough reserved from previous batch for this; (fig.) spreading and transforming influence (Matt. 13), tinge or admixture *of* some quality. ~ *v.t.* Ferment (dough) with leaven; permeate and transform, modify *with* tempering element.

leav·ings (lē'vĭngz) *n.pl.* What is left.

Leb·a·non (lĕb'*anon*). 1. Mountain range extending the length of Lebanon, famous in ancient times for its cedars. 2. Republic on E. coast of Mediterranean, between Israel and Syria; formerly in French-mandated territory with Syria; independent in 1944; capital, Beirut. **Leb·a·nese** (lĕb*an*ēz', -nēs') *adj.* & *n.*

Le·bens·raum (lā'bensrowm, -benz-) *n.* Area claimed by a nation etc. for its due development (also fig.). [Ger., = "living space"]

lech·er (lĕch'*er*) *n.* Fornicator, debauchee. **lech'er·ous** *adj.* Lustful. **lech'er·ous·ly** *adv.* **lech'er·y** *n.* (pl. **-er·ies**).

lec·i·thin (lĕs'*i*thĭn) *n.* (biochem.) Complex fatty substance containing phosphorus, occurring in plant and animal tissues and egg yolk; commercial preparation of this used as an emulsifying agent in foods etc.

Le Cor·bu·sier (*le* kōrbōōzyā'). Charles Edouard Jeanneret (1887–1965), French architect of Swiss birth, pioneer in international style of architecture making much use of steel and concrete.

lec·tern (lĕk't*e*rn) *n.* 1. Reading or singing desk in church, esp. that for the lessons. 2. Similar desk for lecturer etc.

lec·tion·ar·y (lĕk'sh*o*nĕrē) *n.* (pl. **-ar·ies**). Book containing, list of, portions of Scripture appointed to be read at divine service.

lec·ture (lĕk'ch*er*) *n.* Discourse before audience or class on given subject, usu. by way of instruction; lengthy admonition. ~ *v.* (**-tured, -tur·ing**). Deliver lecture(s) (*on* subject); instruct or entertain by lecture; admonish lengthily. **lec'tur·er** *n.* (esp.) Teacher in a university department. **lec'ture·ship** *n.* Position of lecturer.

Lebanon, *was considered the 'middleman' of the Arab world and tried to protect its commercial strength with political neutrality. In 1975, however, civil war broke out. Left: Dog River, just north of Beirut.*

lec·y·thus (lĕs'*i*th*u*s) *n.* (pl. **-thi** pr. -thī). (Gk. antiq.) Narrow-necked vase or flask.

led *adj.*: see LEAD[2].

Le·da (lē'd*a*). (Gk. legend) Wife of Tyndareus, king of Sparta; was loved by Zeus, who took the form of a swan; among her children were Castor and Pollux and Helen (all by Zeus), and Clytemnestra.

ledge (lĕj) *n.* Narrow horizontal surface projecting from wall etc.; shelflike projection on side of rock or mountain; ridge of rocks, esp. below water; (mining) stratum of metal-bearing rock.

ledg·er (lĕj'*er*) *n.* 1. Principal book of the set used for recording trade transactions, containing debtor and creditor accounts. 2. Horizontal timber in scaffolding, parallel to face of building. 3. Flat gravestone. 4. ~ (*adj.*) (mus.) = LEGER.

lee (lē) *n.* Shelter given by neighboring object; (also ~ **side**) sheltered side, side away from wind (opp. weather side); (attrib.)

Le Corbusier, *the French architect, town planner and painter, was one of the best-known exponents of the 'modern' movement in architecture. This church at Ronchamp, France is one of his most famous structures.*

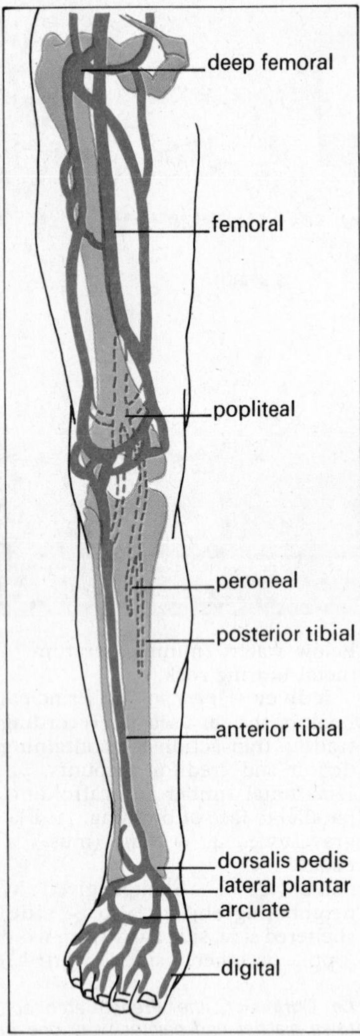

*The **leg** is the limb which supports the human body. The arteries of the leg are shown in red. The bones of the leg include the femur (the thigh bone), fibula and tibia (the bones below the knee).*

belonging to ship's lee side or to leeward of other object; **lee'board**, plank frame fixed to side of flat-bottomed sailing vessel and let down into water to diminish leeway; **lee shore**, shore to leeward of ship; **lee'way**, lateral drift of ship to leeward of desired course; **make up leeway**, (fig.) make up for loss of time or retardation of progress.

Lee[1] (lē), **Ann** (1736–84). British religious zealot; founder of first Shaker colony in America at Watervliet, N.Y., 1776.

Lee[2] (lē), **Robert E(dward)** (1807–70). American soldier, commander in chief of Confederate armies in Civil War; his father, **Henry** ("Light-Horse Harry") **Lee** (1756–1818), was an American Revolutionary War commander and statesman.

leech[1] (lēch) *n.* (obs.) Physician, healer.

leech[2] (lēch) *n.* Mainly aquatic bloodsucking worm (*Hirudo medicinalis*) formerly used medicinally for bleeding; person clinging to another, esp. draining his resources.

leek (lēk) *n.* Culinary herb (*Allium porrum*) allied to onion but with cylindrical bulbous part and broad flat leaves; this as Welsh national emblem.

leer (lēr) *v.i.* & *n.* Glance (esp. sideways) with sly, lascivious, or malign expression. **leer'ing·ly** *adv.*

leer·y (lēr'ē) *adj.* (**leer·i·er, leer·i·est**). (slang) Knowing, sly; suspicious.

lees (lēz) *n.pl.* Sediment of wine etc.; basest part, refuse.

Lee·u·wen·hoek (lā'vĕnhōōk; *Du.* lā'üwĕnhōōk), **Anton van** (1632–1723). Dutch microscopist and naturalist; using single-lens microscopes of his own making, he was the first to observe bacteria, protozoa, and other minute forms of life.

lee·ward (lē'werd; naut. lōō'werd) *adj.* & *adv.* On, toward, side sheltered from wind. ~ *n.* Leeward direction or region. **lee'-ward·ly** *adv.* (of ship) Apt to fall to leeward.

Lee·ward (lē'werd) **Islands.** Most northerly group of Lesser Antilles, in W. Indies, including Anguilla, Antigua, St. Kitts, Nevis, Montserrat, and the British Virgin Islands (these being the former **British Leeward Islands** colony) and Guadeloupe, Saba, and the U.S. Virgin Islands.

left[1] (lĕft) *adj.* Belonging to side of person's body on which the heart is and of which the hand is normally less used (opp. RIGHT); having corresponding relation to front of any object; (of bank of river etc.) on left hand of person looking downstream; ~ **hand**, hand on left side; region or direction of this side of person; ~**-hand**, placed on the left hand; ~**-hand screw**, screw with thread turning to left; ~**-handed**, using left hand more than right; for use by left-handed person; (of blow etc.) struck; made, with left hand; (fig.) awkward; ambiguous, having a contrary meaning; ~**-hander**, left-handed person or blow; ~ **turn**, turn to the left into a position at right angles with the original one; ~ **wing**, (esp.) extreme left in politics (see *n.* sense 2). **left** *adv.* On or to the left side. ~ *n.* 1. Left hand; (boxing) left-handed blow. 2. In many legislatures, members on left side of chamber, traditionally the more liberal or radical (cf. RIGHT); hence, more advanced or innovating section of any group, esp. in politics; radicals collectively. **left·ward** (lĕft'werd) *adv.* & *adj.* **left'wards** *adv.*

left[2]: see LEAVE[2].

left·ism (lĕf'tĭzem) *n.* Political views of the left (see LEFT[1] *n.* 2). **left'ist** *n.*

leg (lĕg) *n.* 1. Organ of support and locomotion in animal body; (in human) part of this from hip to ankle; artificial substitute for this. 2. Leg of animal as food. 3. (archaic) Obeisance made by drawing back one leg. 4. Support pole, prop, of machine etc.; support of chair, table, bed, etc. 5. One branch of forked object; side of triangle other than base. 6. Portion of a course, as section or

*The **Leeward Islands** in the West Indies include Antigua which was discovered by Columbus (1493) and first settled by the English in 1632. Primitive dwellings, like this straw-roofed hut, are still found in remote parts.*

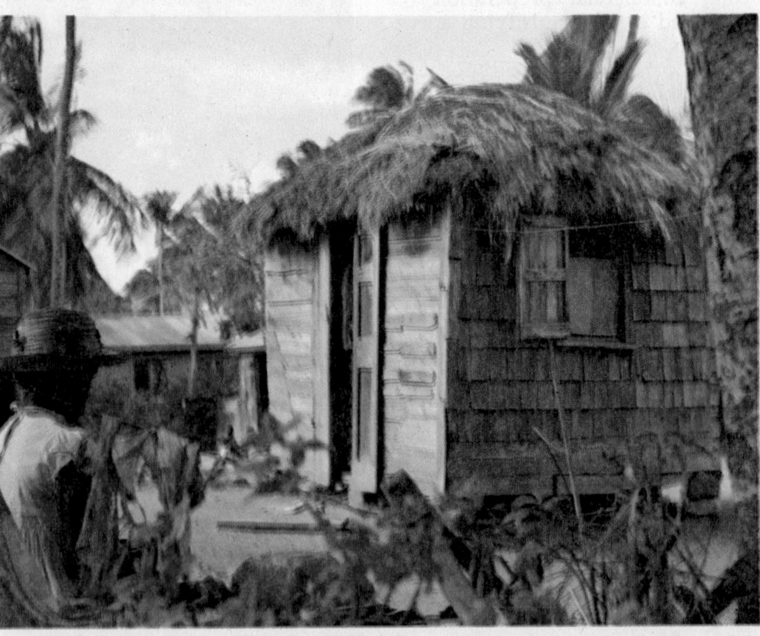

stage of journey; (naut.) run made on single tack. 7. Part of garment covering leg. 8. **feel, find, one's ~s**, get power of standing or walking (also fig.); **give a ~ up**, help to mount (horse etc.) or get over obstacle (also fig.); **on one's last ~s**, near death or end; **pull person's ~**, tease, deceive jokingly; **shake a ~**, (slang) hurry, dance; **show a ~**, get out of bed; **take to one's ~s**, run away; **walk person off his ~s**, tire him out in walking; **without a ~ to stand on**, unable to support thesis by any facts or sound reasons. 9. **~-of-mutton sleeve, sail**, etc., sleeve, sail, etc., shaped like leg of mutton; **~-pull**, (colloq.) piece of teasing; **~ rest**, support for leg of seated person. **leg** *v.i.* (**legged, leg·ging**). **~ it**, (slang) walk or run hard; go away.

leg·a·cy (lĕg′*a*sē) *n.* (pl. **-cies**). Sum of money or article bequeathed by will; material or immaterial thing handed down by predecessor.

le·gal (lē′g*a*l) *adj.* Of, based on, falling within province of, occupied with, law; required or appointed by law; recognized by law as distinct from equity; lawful; (theol.) of the Mosaic law, of salvation by works not faith; **~ fiction**, statement that is probably fictitious but admitted as true in order to enable some useful purpose, as redress of wrong etc., to be accomplished; **~ tender**: see TENDER². **le′gal·ly** *adv.*

le·gal·ism (lē′g*a*lĭz*e*m) *n.* Exaltation of law or formula, "red tape"; (theol.) preference of the law to the Gospel, doctrine of justification by works. **le′gal·ist** *n.* **le·gal·is′tic** *adj.*

le·gal·i·ty (lēgăl′ĭtē) *n.* (pl. **-ties**). Lawfulness; legalism.

leg·ate¹ (lĕg′ĭt) *n.* 1. Ecclesiastic deputed to represent pope; **~ a latere** (-ah lăt′*e*ra), one of highest class and full powers. 2. (archaic) Ambassador, delegate. **leg·a·tine** (lĕg′*a*tĭn, -tīn) *adj.* **leg′ate·ship** *n.*

le·gate² (lĭgāt′) *v.t.* (**-gat·ed, -gat·ing**). Bequeath. **le·ga·tor** (lĭgā′t*e*r, lĕg*a*tōr′) *n.*

leg·a·tee (lĕg*a*tē′) *n.* Recipient of legacy.

le·ga·tion (lĭgā′sh*o*n) *n.* Sending of legate or deputy; body of deputies; diplomatic minister and his staff (esp. when he does not rank as ambassador), his official residence; legateship.

le·ga·to (l*e*gah′tō; *It.* lĕgah′taw) *adj.* & *adv.* (mus.) Smooth(ly) and connected(ly). [It.]

leg·end (lĕj′*e*nd) *n.* 1. Traditional story popularly regarded as historical, myth; such literature or tradition; (hist.) life of saint, collection of such lives or similar stories; **Golden L~**: see GOLDEN. 2. Inscription or motto, esp. on

***Legumes** or pod-bearing plants are also known as the pea family. There are more than 12,000 species, including beans, peas, lentils and the carob tree, which has edible fruits, shown here.*

coin or medal, below picture, etc. **leg′end·ar·y** *adj.*

leg·er (lĕj′*e*r) *adj.* **~ line**, (mus.) short line added above or below staff to extend its compass.

Lé·ger (lĕzhĕ′), **Fernand** (1881–1955). French painter; known for his cubist paintings.

leg·er·de·main (lĕj*e*rd*e*mān′) *n.* Sleight of hand; trickery, sophistry. [Fr. *lèger de main* light of hand]

leg·ging (lĕg′ĭng) *n.* (usu. pl.) Outer covering of leather etc. for leg up to knee.

leg·gy (lĕg′ē) *adj.* (**-gi·er, -gi·est**). Having disproportionately long legs.

Leg·horn (lĕg′hōrn). (Ital. *Livorno*) City and seaport of Tuscany, Italy.

leg·horn (for def. 1 lĕg′hōrn; for def. 2 lĕg′*e*rn, -hōrn) *n.* 1. Fine braided straw for hats etc. imported from Leghorn, made of stems of a Mediterranean wheat (*Triticum sativum turgidum*) cut green and bleached; hat of this. 2. One of a small hardy breed of domestic poultry.

leg·i·ble (lĕj′*i*b*e*l) *adj.* Clear, easily read. **leg·i·bil·i·ty** (lĕj*i*bĭl′ĭtē), **leg′i·ble·ness** *ns.* **leg′i·bly** *adv.*

le·gion (lē′j*o*n) *n.* 1. (Rom. hist.) Division of 3,000–6,000 men, including complement of cavalry, in ancient Roman army. 2. Vast host or multitude. 3. **American L~**, national association of veterans, founded 1919; **Foreign L~**, body of foreign volunteers in modern (esp. French) army, serving in colonies or on distant expeditions; **L~ of Honor**, (Fr. *légion d'honneur*) French order of distinction conferred for civil or military services etc., founded by Napoleon I in 1802.

le·gion·ar·y (lē′j*o*nĕrē) *adj.* Of legion(s). **~** *n.* (pl. **-ar·ies**). (Rom. hist.) Soldier of a legion.

le·gion·naire (lēj*o*nār′) *n.* Member of legion, esp. French Foreign Legion or American Legion.

le·gion·naires' (lēj*o*nārz′) **disease.** Little understood, often fatal, pneumonia-like infection first identified after its eruption at an American Legion convention in Philadelphia in 1976.

leg·is·late (lĕj′ĭslāt) *v.i.* (**-lat·ed, -lat·ing**). Make laws. **leg·is·la·tion** (lĕjĭslā′sh*o*n) *n.* (Enacting of) laws. **leg′is·la·tive** *adj.* **leg′is·la·tive·ly** *adv.*

leg·is·la·tor (lĕj′ĭslāt*e*r) *n.* Lawgiver; member of legislative body.

leg·is·la·ture (lĕj′ĭslāch*e*r) *n.* Lawmaking body of a government.

le·git·i·mate (lĭjĭt′*i*mĭt) *adj.* Born in wedlock; lawful, proper, regular, conforming to standard type; logically admissible; (of sovereign's title) based on strict hereditary right; (theatr.) of stage plays not including revues, farces, etc. **le·git′i·mate·ly** *adv.* **legitimate** (lĭjĭt′*i*māt) *v.t.* (**-mated, -mat·ing**). Make legitimate by decree, enactment, or proof; justify, serve as justification for. **le·git·i·ma·tion** (lĭjĭtimā′sh*o*n), **le·git′i·ma·cy** *ns.* **le·git′i·ma·tize** *v.t.* (**-tized, -tiz·ing**). **le·git·i·mize** (lĭjĭt′*i*mīz) *v.t.* (**-mized, -miz·ing**). Make legitimate. **le·git·i·mi·za′·tion** *n.*

leg·ume (lĕg′ūm, lĭgūm′) *n.* Fruit, edible part, pod, of leguminous plant; such vegetable used for food.

le·gu·mi·nous (lĭgū′m*i*n*u*s) *adj.* (bot. etc.) Of the order Leguminosae, including peas, beans, and other pod-bearing plants.

Le Ha·vre (l*e* hah′vr*e*, -v*e*r; *Fr.*

le ah′vr*e*). City and port of N. France on English Channel.

le·i (lā′ē, lā) *n.* (pl. **le·is**). Polynesian garland of flowers etc. worn round neck. [Hawaiian]

Leib·niz (līb′nĭts; *Ger.* līp′nĭts), **Gottfried Wilhelm** (1646–1716). German mathematician and philosopher; discoverer of theory of calculus simultaneously with Newton; regarded matter as a multitude of monads, each a microcosm of the universe. **Leib·niz′i·an** (lībnĭt′sē*a*n) *adj.* & *n.*

Leices·ter (lĕs′t*er*), **Robert Dudley, Earl of** (*c*1532–88). English courtier and general, favorite of Queen Elizabeth.

Lei·den = LEYDEN.

Leif Er·ics·son (lēf ĕr′ĭks*o*n; *Icel.* lāv): see VINLAND.

leis·ter (lēs′t*er*) *n.* Pronged salmon spear. ~ *v.t.* Spear with this.

lei·sure (lē′zh*er*, lĕzh′*er*) *n.* (Opportunity *to* do, *for*, afforded by) free time, time at one's own disposal; **at** ~, not occupied; deliberately, without hurry; **at one's** ~, when one has time. **lei′sured** *adj.*

lei·sure·ly (lē′zh*er*lē, lĕzh′*er*-) *adj.* Having, acting or done at, leisure, deliberate. ~ *adv.* Deliberately, without haste.

leit·mo·tif (līt′mōtēf) *n.* (mus.) Theme associated throughout work with some person, situation, or sentiment. [Ger.]

Le·man (l*e*mahṅ′), **Lake**: see GENEVA.

Le Mans (l*e* mahṅ′). City in W. central France; site of annual 24-hour auto race.

lem·ma (lĕm′*a*) *n.* (pl. **lem·mas, lem·ma·ta** pr. lĕm′*a*t*a*). Assumed or demonstrated proposition used in argument or proof; argument or subject of literary composition; head word of dictionary entry; motto appended to picture etc.

lem·ming (lĕm′ĭng) *n.* (pl. **-mings**, collect. **-ming**). Small rodent of family Muridae inhabiting arctic and subarctic regions, of which one species, the Norway lemming (*Lemmus lemmus*), migrates in large numbers and has been reported to continue headlong into the sea and drown.

***Lemmings** inhabit the tundra or bordering regions of north Eurasia and North America. The Norway lemming is very prolific and periodically migrates in hordes towards, and often into, the sea, moving chiefly at night.*

*Flowers of the **lemon** tree have a distinctive perfume and some of these eventually form into the well-known fruit which is rich in Vitamin C. These trees flourish best in a temperate climate.*

Lem·nos (lĕm′nŏs, -nōs). Large Greek island in N. Aegean. **Lem·ni·an** (lĕm′nē*a*n) *adj.* & *n.*

lem·on[1] (lĕm′*o*n) *n.* Tree (*Citrus limon*), native of Indian Himalayas, now cultivated in U.S. and Mediterranean countries, bearing oval-seeded fruit with pale-yellow skin and acid juice; fruit of this; pale-yellow color; (fig.) defective thing or unpleasant person, esp. a car prone to breakdowns; ~ **drop**, hard lemon-flavored candy; ~ **grass**, tropical grass of genus *Cymbopogon*, yielding fragrant oil.

lem·on[2] (lĕm′*o*n) *n.* ~ **dab, sole,** kind of plaice or flounder resembling sole.

lem·on·ade (lĕm*o*nād′, lĕm′*o*nād) *n.* Drink of sweetened lemon juice and water; synthetic substitute for this.

le·mur (lē′m*er*) *n.* Nocturnal mammal of genus *L*~, allied to monkeys but with pointed muzzle, found in Madagascar. **lem·u·roid** (lĕm′y*er*oid) *adj.* [L. *lemures* spirits of the dead]

Le·na (lē′n*a*; *Rus.* lĕ′nah). River rising W. of Lake Baikal, most easterly of three great Siberian rivers, it flows 2,650 miles N. to the Laptev Sea; famous for the goldfields in its basin.

lend (lĕnd) *v.t.* (**lent** pr. lĕnt, **lend·ing**). Grant (person) use of (thing) on understanding that it or its equivalent shall be returned; let out (money) at interest, (books etc.) for hire; bestow, contribute (something of temporary service or effect); accommodate *oneself to* some policy or purpose; ~ **(an) ear, one's ears**, listen; ~ **a (helping) hand,** help; **lending library**, library that lends books, esp. for hire; **lend-lease,** arrangement (1941) whereby U.S. supplied equipment etc. to countries at war with the Axis powers, orig. as a loan in return for the use of certain bases. **lend′er** *n.*

L'En·fant (lahṅfahṅ′), **Pierre Charles** (1754–1825). French-born Amer. engineer; original designer of Washington, D.C.

length (lĕngkth, lĕngth) *n.* Thing's measurement from end to end, greatest of body's three dimensions; extent in, of, or with regard to, time; distance thing extends; long stretch or extent; piece of cloth etc. of certain length; (pros.) quantity of syllable or vowel; **at** ~, in detail or without curtailment; at last or after a long time; **at full** ~, lying stretched out; in full. **length′ways** *adv* & *adj.* **length′wise** *adv.* & *adj.*

length·en (lĕngk′th*e*n, lĕng′th*e*n) *v.* Make or become longer; (pros.) make (vowel) long.

length·y (lĕngk′thē, lĕng′thē) *adj.* (**length·i·er, length·i·est**). Of unusual length, prolix, tedious. **length′i·ly** *adv.* **length′i·ness** *n.*

le·ni·ent (lē′nēent, lēn′yent) *adj.* Tolerant, gentle, indisposed to severity; (of punishment etc.) mild. **le′ni·ent·ly** *adv.* **le′ni·ence** *n.* **le′ni·en·cy** *n.* (pl. **-cies**).

Len·in (lĕn′ĭn; *Rus.* lĕnēn′). Assumed name of Vladimir Ilyich Ulyanov (1870–1924), Russian revolutionary, exponent of doctrines of Marx, and founder of Bolshevik party; imprisoned, then exiled from Russia in 1900; returned in disguise and took part in revolution of 1905; escaped 1907 and directed revolutionary operations from abroad until 1917 when he returned to Russia and became first premier of the U.S.S.R., 1917; **Lenin Peak**, the highest mountain, 23,400 feet (7,133 m), in the Pamir Range of the Soviet Union.

*The **lemur**, a slender, large-eyed primate, is docile, gregarious and mostly nocturnal. There are about 15 species, of which the best known is the ringtailed lemur, which is active by day. Other species include the black lemur (the male only is black), the mouse lemur and the dwarf lemur.*

female
black lemur
male
ruffed lemur
fat-tailed dwarf lemur
ring-tailed lemur
mouse lemur
Verreaux's sifaka lemur
fork-crowned
lemur

Len'in·ist, Len'in·ite *adjs.* & *ns.* **Len'in·ism** *n.*

Len·in·grad (lĕn'ĭngrăd; *Rus.* lĕnĭngraht'). Russian city on an inlet of the Gulf of Finland, founded 1703 by Peter the Great and until 1918 capital of Russia; known as St. Petersburg before the Revolution and as Petrograd from 1917 until 1924, when it was renamed after LENIN.

lens (lĕnz) *n.* (pl. **lens·es**). Piece of glass etc. with two curved surfaces, or one plane and one curved, causing regular convergence or divergence of rays of light passing through it, commonly used, either singly or combined, in optical instruments, as a camera, telescope, eyeglass, etc.; (anat.) = CRYSTALline lens; one facet of compound eye; **electron ~**: see ELECTRON.

Lent (lĕnt). Period of fasting before Easter; in western Christian churches, period from Ash Wednesday to Easter eve, of which the 40 weekdays are devoted to fasting and penitence in commemoration of the fasting of Jesus in the wilderness. **Lent'en, lent'en** *adjs.* Of, in, appropriate to, Lent.

lent (lĕnt): see LEND.

len·ti·cel (lĕn'tisĕl, -sel) *n.* (bot.) Aeration pore penetrating the young cork of stems and some roots.

len·tic·u·lar (lĕntĭk'yuler) *adj.* Shaped like lentil or lens (esp. ~ **cloud**), double convex; of the lens of the eye.

len·til (lĕn'til) *n.* (Double convex seed of) leguminous plant, *Lens culinaris*, grown for food.

len·to (lĕn'tō) *adj.* & *adv.* (mus.) Slow(ly). [It.]

len·toid (lĕn'toid) *adj.* Lens-shaped.

Le·o[1] (lē'ō). The Lion, a constellation; 5th sign (♌) of the zodiac which the sun enters about July 21.

Le·o[2] (lē'ō). Name of 13 popes: **Leo I, St.,** "the Great," pope 440–61, obtained (445) recognition of the primacy of the popes in the Christian Church; **Leo IV**, pope 847–55, built the LEONINE City; **Leo X** (Giovanni de' Medici, 1475–1521), pope 1513–21, excommunicated Luther and bestowed on Henry VIII of England title of "Defender of the Faith"; **Leo XIII** (1810–1903), pope 1878–1903, issued encyclical on labor, *Rerum Novarum*; "prisoner in Vatican" for refusing to recognize Italian government.

Le·o·nar·do da Vin·ci (lēonär'dō da vĭn'chē; *It.* lēawnär'daw dah vēn'chē) (1452–1519). Italian painter, sculptor, architect, engineer, inventor, scientist; among his paintings are the mural "Last Supper" and "La Gioconda" (or "Mona Lisa"); his scientific accomplishments include originating the science of hydraulics, and significant studies in anatomy and mathematics; his notebooks contain visionary sketches for guns and

*The **lentil** is one of the oldest plants to be brought under cultivation. Its edible seed, which contains over 25% protein, is one of the most nutritious of pulses and is important in India, where it appears as 'dhal'.*

leopard

snow leopard

*The **leopard** (which is also called a panther, especially in India), is found in Africa and most of Asia. It is a solitary animal of the bush and forest and is mainly nocturnal in habit. The snow leopard, a similar feline, inhabits the mountains of central Asia.*

Leonardo da Vinci was one of the greatest of the 'universal men' produced by the Renaissance. This painting, 'The Virgin of the Rocks', has a near-duplicate, possibly the work of his pupils, in the Louvre.

cannons, airplanes, parachutes, submarines, and spiral staircases.

Le·on·ca·val·lo (lĕawnkahvah′-law), **Ruggiero** (1858–1919). Italian composer, famous for his opera *I Pagliacci*.

Le·o·nid (lē′onĭd) *n.* (pl. **Le·o·nids, Le·on·i·des** pr. lēŏn′ĭdēz). One of a shower of meteors radiating from a point in the constellation Leo, observable every November but brilliant every 33 years when Earth passes near the center of their swarm.

Le·on·i·das (lēŏn′ĭdas). King of Sparta 491–480 B.C.; hero of defense of pass of Thermopylae against invading army of Xerxes, 480 B.C.

Le·o·nine (lē′onīn) *adj.* Of, made by, a person (esp. a pope) named Leo; ~ **City**, part of Rome in which Vatican stands, walled and fortified by Leo IV; **leonine verse**, medieval form of Latin verse in hexameters or alternate hexameters and pentameters, in which final word rhymes with that immediately before the caesura; English verse in which middle and last syllables of two lines rhyme.

le·o·nine (lē′onīn) *adj.* Lionlike, of lions.

leop·ard (lĕp′erd) *n.* 1. Large chiefly nocturnal carnivore (*Felis pardus*) of cat family, with long tail and usu. dark-spotted yellowish-fawn coat, found in Africa and S. Asia, panther; **American** ~, jaguar; **black** ~, Indian species, identical except for black color; **hunting** ~, cheetah; **snow** ~, ounce; ~**'s bane**, name given to several herbaceous perennial plants of family Compositae.

Le·o·pold (lē′opōld). Name of three kings of the Belgians: **Leopold I** (1790–1865), elected king of the Belgians 1831; **Leopold II** (1835–1909), king of the Belgians 1865–1909; **Leopold III** (b. 1901), king of the Belgians from 1934 until his abdication in 1951.

Le·o·pold (lē′opōld), **Lake.** Nine hundred-square-mile (2,331 sq. km) lake in W. central Democratic Republic of the Congo.

Lé·o·pold·ville (lā′opōldvĭl): see KINSHASA.

le·o·tard (lē′otârd) *n.* Close-fitting body garment worn by acrobats, ballet dancers, etc. [f. J.

Lepidoptera, such as butterflies and moths, have four wings covered with minute scales and are often brightly colored. The order comprises more than 100,000 species. These butterflies are common European types.

Léotard, 19th-c. Fr. trapeze performer]

Le·pan·to (lĭpăn´tō; *It.* le´pahntaw), **Strait of.** Entrance to Gulf of Corinth or Lepanto, Greece; scene (1571) of naval battle in which Ottoman sea power was almost completely destroyed by an armada of the Holy League (Pope Pius V, Venice, Spain, Genoa, Savoy, and other Italian States) under Don John of Austria.

lep·er (lĕp´*er*) *n.* Person suffering from leprosy; (fig.) outcast.

lep·i·dop·ter·ous (lĕpĭdŏp´te*r*us) *adj.* Of the Lepidoptera, an order of insects comprising butterflies and moths, with two pairs of membranous wings covered with flattened scales often forming striking color patterns. **lep·i·dop´ter·ist** *n.* **lep·i·dop´ter·an** *adj.* & *n.* [Gk. *lepis* scale, *pteron* wing]

Lep·i·dus (lĕp´ĭd*u*s), **Marcus Aemilius** (d. 13 B.C.). Roman politician; member of the second TRIUMVIRATE, 43–36 B.C., after death of Julius Caesar.

lep·re·chaun (lĕp´*r*ekawn, -kŏn) *n.* Irish sprite in form of a wizened old man.

lep·ro·sy (lĕp´*r*osē) *n.* Chronic endemic bacterial disease caused by the organism *Mycobacterium leprae*, characterized by thickening and ulceration of skin with loss of sensation, and, in severe cases, deformity, blindness, and death; once incurable, now readily arrested; now occurring chiefly in tropical and eastern countries but more widely distributed in the Middle Ages; (formerly) any of various diseases causing skin lesions confused with leprosy before recognition of the organism causing it. **lep´rous** *adj.* Having, like, (as) of, leprosy.

lep·ton (lĕp´tŏn) *n.* (pl. **-ta** pr. -t*a*). (phys.) Any of a family of elementary particles whose mass is equal to or less than that of a muon.

Les·bi·an (lĕz´bē*a*n) *adj.* Of Lesbos; (often **l**~) of homosexuality in women (from the association of the island with Sappho, who was accused of this). ~ *n.* Homosexual woman. **les´bi·an·ism** *n.*

Les·bos (lĕz´bŏs, -bōs). Island in Aegean Sea, off W. coast of Turkey, inhabited from an early date by Aeolians; birthplace of Alcaeus and Sappho.

lese majesty, (lēz) **lèse ma·jes·té** (lāz mahzhĕstā´). Treason; affront to sovereign or ruler; attack on any revered person or institution; (joc.) presumptuous conduct. [Fr., f. L. *laesa majestas* injured majesty]

le·sion (lē´zh*o*n) *n.* Damage, injury; esp. (path.) morbid change in functioning or texture of organ etc.

Le·so·tho (lĕsō´thō). (formerly *Basutoland*) Kingdom, enclave within the Republic of South Africa; formerly a Brit. protectorate; capital, Maseru.

less (lĕs) *adj.* Smaller; of smaller quantity, not so much, not so much of; of lower rank etc. (rare); (preceding numeral etc.) minus, not including. ~ *n.* Smaller amount, quantity, or number. ~ *adv.* To smaller extent, in lower degree.

les·see (lĕsē´) *n.* Holder of, tenant under, lease. **les·see´ship** *n.*

less·en (lĕs´*e*n) *v.* Make or become less.

less·er (lĕs´*er*) *attrib. adj.* (superl. **least**). Not so great as the other, or the rest, minor, smaller.

Less·er (lĕs´*er*) **Antilles.** Chain of islands of the W. Indies stretching from Puerto Rico to S. Amer., including the Virgin Islands, Leeward Islands, Windward Islands, the islands of the Netherlands W. Indies, Barbados, Trinidad, and Tobago.

Les·sing (lĕs´ĭng), **Gotthold Ephraim** (1729–81). German dramatist and critic, whose influence was of importance in freeing German literature from conventions of French classical school.

les·son (lĕs´*o*n) *n.* 1. Portion of Scripture etc. read at divine service. 2. Thing to be learned by pupil; amount of teaching given at one time, time assigned to it; occurrence, example, rebuke, etc., serving as encouragement or warning; (pl.) systematic instruction in subject.

les·sor (lĕs´ōr, lĕsōr´) *n.* Person who lets on lease.

lest (lĕst) *conj.* In order that . . . not, for fear that; (after *fear* etc.) that.

let[1] (lĕt) *v.t.* (**let, let·ting**). Hinder, obstruct. ~ *n.* Stoppage; hindrance (archaic); (tennis) serve that must be repeated, esp. one that hits net and falls into proper part of opponent's court.

let[2] (lĕt) *v.t.* & *auxil.* (**let, let·ting**). 1. Allow (confined fluid,

__Leprosy__ is a disease of the nerves which, if not treated, results in loss of feeling and atrophy of the skin. In advanced cases, hands, feet and face may become deformed. Treatment is with sulphonic drugs.

e.g. blood) to escape. 2. Grant use of for rent or hire; **to ~**, offered for rent. 3. Allow to, suffer to; cause to (only in **~ person know**, inform him). 4. **~ alone**, not interfere with, not attend to or do; (colloq. use of the imper.) not to mention; **~ be**, let alone; **~ down** (*v.*), lower; fail (friend) at need; disappoint; **let′down** (*n.*); **let fall**, drop; (geom.) draw (perpendicular) from outside point *on* line; **let go**, release, set at liberty; lose hold of, lose or relinquish hold *of*; dismiss from thought; cease to restrain; **let in**, admit, open door to; insert into surface of something; **let in for**, involve in (difficulty etc.); **let into**, admit to; insert into surface of; make acquainted with (secret etc.); **let loose**, release, unchain; **let off**, discharge (gun etc.); not punish or compel; punish *with* light penalty; allow or cause (fluid etc.) to pass away; **let on**, (colloq.) reveal (secret); pretend; **let out**, open door for exit to; allow to escape; make (garment) looser; put out to hire, esp. to several tenants; emit; divulge; **let slip**, loose from leash; say inadvertently; miss (opportunity); **~ up** (*v.*), cease, relax one's efforts; **let′up** (*n.*). 5. *v. auxil.* (followed by inf.) Supplying first and third person of imperative in exhortations, commands, assumptions, and permissions. **let** *n.* Letting for hire or rent.

le·thal (lē′th*a*l) *adj.* Causing, sufficient or designed to cause, death. **le·thal·i·ty** (lĭthăl′ĭtē) *n.*

leth·ar·gy (lĕth′*er*jē) *n.* (pl. **-gies**). Morbid drowsiness, prolonged and unnatural sleep; torpid, inert, or apathetic state, want of interest and energy. **le·thar·gic** (l*e*thâr′jĭk) *adj.* **le·thar′gi·cal·ly** *adv.*

Le·the (lē′thē). (Gk. myth.) One of the rivers of the underworld, whose water when drunk had the power of making the souls of the dead forget their life on earth. **Le·the·an** (lĭthē′*a*n, lē′thē-) *adj.* (Gk. *lēthē* oblivion]

Le·to (lē′tō). (Gk. myth.) Daughter of a Titan; mother, by Zeus, of Artemis and Apollo; identified as Roman *Latona*.

Lett (lĕt) *n.* A Latvian.

let·ter (lĕt′*er*) *n.* 1. Character representing one or more of the elementary sounds used in speech, one of the alphabetic symbols; (print.) type, font of type. 2. Written or printed message addressed to person(s); (freq. pl.) legal or formal statement indicating credentials, authority, etc.; **~s patent**: see PATENT. 3. Precise terms of statement etc., strict verbal interpretation. 4. (pl.) Literature; acquaintance with books, erudition; **man of ~s**, scholar, (now usu.) author; **profession of ~s**, authorship. 5. **letter case**, pocketbook for holding letters; **let′terhead**, printed heading on stationery; **let′terpress**, matter printed from letters or types, as distinguished from what is printed from plates

__Lesotho__ is a small mountainous state — the Maluti Mts are shown here — enclosed by South Africa. Some 25% of its labor force works in the South African gold mines and on farms.

Levee banks along the Mississippi River are there to control and prevent flooding. Many of the bigger rivers have naturally formed levees as a result of the deposit of silt and sediment.

or blocks. **letter** *v.t.* Impress title etc. on (book cover); inscribe in letters, *with* name etc. **let'tered** *adj.* (esp.) Literate, educated. **let'ter·ing** *n.*

Let·tish (lĕt'ĭsh) *adj.* & *n.* (Of) the language of the Letts, one of the Baltic group of Indo-European languages, closely related to Lithuanian.

let·tre de ca·chet (*Fr.* lĕtre de kăshĕ') (pl. ***let·tres de ca·chet*** *Fr.* pr. lĕ'tre de kăshĕ'). (Fr. hist.) Letter signed by king of France containing order emanating directly from the king himself, esp. one containing arbitrary order of imprisonment, exile, etc. [Fr., = "sealed letter"]

let·tuce (lĕt'ĭs) *n.* Garden herb of genus *Lactuca* with crisp leaves much used as salad.

Leu·cip·pus (lo͞osĭp'*u*s) (5th c. B.C.). Greek philosopher; regarded, with Democritus, as founder of ATOMISM.

leu·co·cyte (lo͞o'kosīt) *n.* Colorless or white corpuscle in blood, lymph, etc.

leu·cor·rhe·a, leu·cor·rhoe·a (lo͞okerē'*a*) *ns.* (path.) Whitish purulent mucous discharge from vagina and uterine canal.

Leuc·tra (lo͝ok'tr*a*). Village of Boeotia, scene of a battle (371 B.C.) in which Thebans under Epaminondas defeated Spartans.

leu·ke·mi·a (lo͞okē'mē*a*) *n.* Blood disease affecting the white corpuscles, freq. characterized by excess of these.

Lev. *abbrev.* Leviticus.

Le·vant (l*e*vănt'). Eastern part of the Mediterranean with its islands and neighboring countries. **le·vant'er** *n.* Strong Mediterranean easterly wind. [Fr. *levant* sunrise, east]

Le·van·tine (lĕv'*a*ntīn, -tēn, lĭvăn'tĭn, -tīn) *n.* Native, inhabitant, of the Levant, esp. one descended from European settlers. ~ *adj.* Of, trading to, the Levant.

lev·ee[1] (lĕv'ē, lĕvē') *n.* Reception of visitors on rising from bed (hist.); assembly held (in afternoon) by sovereign or his (or her) representative at which men only are received; reception.

lev·ee[2] (lĕv'ē) *n.* Natural embankment of alluvium built up by rivers on either side of their channels; artificial embankment raised to prevent inundations.

lev·el (lĕv'*e*l) *n.* 1. Instrument for testing whether things are horizontal; SPIRIT level; surveyor's instrument for observing levels. 2. Horizontal line or plane; plane or standard in social, moral, or intellectual matters; plane of rank or authority, e.g., *consultation at cabinet level*; **on a ~ with,** in same horizontal plane as; **on the ~,** (colloq.) straightforward(ly), honest(ly). 3. More or less flat surface; flat country. **level** *adj.* 1. Horizontal, perpendicular to the plumb line; on a level or equality (*with*). 2. Even, equable, uniform, well balanced, in quality, style, judgment, etc.; **one's ~ best,** (colloq.) one's very best; **~-headed,** mentally well balanced. **lev'el·ly** *adv.* **lev'el·ness** *n.* **level** *v.t.* (**-eled, -el·ing**; Brit. **-elled, -el·ling**). 1. Make level, even, or uniform; place on same level, bring *up* or *down* to a standard. 2. Raze, lay low; abolish (distinctions). 3. Aim (missile), lay (gun), direct (satire, accusation, etc.) *at, against.*

lev·el·er (lĕv'*e*l*e*r) *n.* (esp.) Person who would abolish social distinctions, advocate of equality, esp. **L~** (Engl. hist.), one of a party of extreme radical dissenters arising in army of Long Parliament (*c*1647) and advocating leveling of all ranks and completely democratic form of republican government.

lev·er (lĕv'*e*r, lē'v*e*r) *n.* Bar used to pry up heavy or fixed object; (mech.) straight bar or other rigid structure of which one point (*fulcrum*) is fixed, another is connected with the force (*weight*) to be resisted or acted upon, and a third is connected with the force (*power*) applied; **~ escapement,** escapement where connection between balance and escape wheel is made by a pivoted lever bearing the pallets; **~ watch,** watch with lever escapement. **lever** *v.* Use lever; lift, move, act on, with lever.

lev·er·age (lĕv'*e*rĭj, lĕv'rĭj, lē'v*e*rĭj, lē'vrĭj) *n.* Action of, way of applying, lever; set or system of levers; power, mechanical advantage gained by use, of lever; means of accomplishing a purpose, power, influence.

Le·vi (lē'vī). Hebrew patriarch, third son of Jacob and Leah (Gen. 29); tribe of Israel, traditionally descended from him.

le·vi·a·than (lĭvī'*a*th*a*n) *n.* Sea monster (bibl.); huge ship; anything very large of its kind.

lev·i·rate (lĕv'*e*rĭt, -āt, lē'v*e*rĭt, -āt) *n.* Ancient Jewish custom by which dead man's brother or next of kin had to marry his widow. **lev·i·rat·i·cal** (lĕv*e*răt'ĭk*a*l) *adj.*

lev·i·tate (lĕv'ĭtāt) *v.* (**-tat·ed, -tat·ing**). (Make) rise and float in air (esp. in spiritualist language). **lev·i·ta'tion** *n.*

Le·vite (lē'vīt) *n.* One of the tribe of Levi, whose members were priests of the sanctuary in ancient Israel (to 586 B.C.) and later (when priesthood was restricted to descendants of Aaron's family) assisted priests in caring for the Temple.

Le·vit·i·cal (lĭvĭt'ĭk*a*l) *adj.* 1. Of the Levites. 2. Of the book of Leviticus.

Le·vit·i·cus (lĭvĭt'ĭk*u*s). Third book of the Pentateuch, containing details of the law and ritual of the Levites.

lev·i·ty (lĕv´ĭtē) *n.* (pl. **-ties**). Want of thought, frivolity, unreasonable jocularity, inconstancy; light behavior.

lev·u·lose (lĕv´y*u*lōs) *n.* Fructose.

lev·y (lĕv´ē) *n.* (pl. **lev·ies**). Collecting of assessment, tax, etc.; enrolling of men for war etc.; amount or number levied, body of men enrolled; **capital ~**, appropriation by government of fixed proportion of all the wealth in the country. **levy** *v.t.* (**lev·ied, lev·y·ing**). Raise (contribution, taxes), impose (rate, toll); raise (sum) by legal execution or process *on* person's goods; extort; enlist, enroll (soldiers, army); collect men and munitions for, proceed to make (war; usu. *on, against*).

lewd (lōōd) *adj.* Base, worthless (bibl.); lascivious, indecent. **lewd´ly** *adv.* **lewd´ness** *n.*

lew·is (lōō´ĭs) *n.* Contrivance for gripping heavy blocks of stone for lifting, consisting of a tenon fitting into a shaped hole cut in the stone.

Lewis[1] (lōō´ĭs), **C(live) S(taples)** (1898–1963). British religious novelist and essayist, author of *The Screwtape Letters.*

Lewis[2] (lōō´ĭs), **John L(lewellyn)** (1880–1969). American labor leader, long president of the United Mine Workers; organizer and president of the C.I.O., 1935–40.

Lew·is[3] (lōō´ĭs), **Meriwether** (1774–1809). Explorer; governor of the Louisiana Territory, 1807–9; led **Lewis and Clark Expedition**, 1801–3, with William Clark; they followed the Missouri River to its source, crossed the Great Divide, and descended the Columbia River to the Pacific Ocean, bringing back information on geographical features, flora, fauna, etc.

Lew·is[4] (lōō´ĭs), **(Harry) Sinclair** (1885–1951). American novelist, author of *Babbitt, Main Street,* etc.; first American to win Nobel Prize for literature, 1930.

Lew·is[5] (lōō´ĭs) **gun.** Light magazine-fed, gas-operated, air-cooled machine gun. [Col. I. N. *Lewis* (1858–1931) of U.S. Army, inventor]

lew·is·ite (lōō´ĭsīt) *n.* Highly irritant and vesicant persistent poison gas (βchloro-vinyl-dichloroarsine), a heavy oily liquid. [W. L. *Lewis* (1878–1943), Amer. chemist]

lex·i·cal (lĕk´sĭk*a*l) *adj.* Of the vocabulary of a language; (as) of a lexicon. **lex´i·cal·ly** *adv.*

lex·i·cog·ra·phy (lĕksĭkŏg´r*a*fē) *n.* Dictionary making. **lex·i·cog´ra·pher** *n.* **lex·i·co·graph·i·cal** (lĕksĭk*o*grăf´ĭk*a*l) *adj.*

lex·i·con (lĕk´sĭkŏn) *n.* Dictionary, esp. of ancient Greek, Hebrew, Syriac, or Arabic.

Lex·ing·ton (lĕk´sĭngt*o*n). Name of several towns and cities of U.S., esp.: (1) in Massachusetts, a town and suburb of Boston; scene of the battle (1775) between British soldiers and Minutemen that began the Amer. Revolution; (2) city in the Bluegrass region of Kentucky; center of thoroughbred horse farms and tobacco growing.

lex ta·li·o·nis (lĕks´tălēō´nĭs). Law of retaliation, an eye for an eye. [L.]

Ley·den, Lei·den (lī´d*e*n). City of the SW. Netherlands; university, 1575; **~ jar**, device (invented 1745 at that university) for storing electric charge, consisting of a glass jar coated inside and outside with tinfoil, the electric energy being stored in the glass dielectric between the tinfoil electrodes.

Ley·te (lā´tē). One of the Philippine Islands, 2,785 sq. miles (7,213 sq. km), N. of Mindanao;

The Battle of ***Lexington*** *and Concord in 1775 marked the beginning of the American War of Independence although it was really more of a skirmish. The colonists were warned by Paul Revere.*

The British Museum **library** is the second-largest in the world and receives a free copy of every book published in the U.K. Its splendid Reading Room was constructed from designs by Sir Anthony Panizzi and was opened in 1857.

L ~ Gulf, inlet between Leyte and Samar Islands; site of a naval battle, 1944, during World War II, in which the Americans defeated the Japanese.

L.F., LF, l.f., l-f *abbrevs.* Low FREQUENCY.

Lha·sa (lah′sa, lăs′*a*). Capital city of Tibet, in the SE. at an altitude of 12,000 feet (3,658 m).

li·a·bil·i·ty (līabĭl′ĭtē) *n.* (pl. **-ties**). Being liable; what one is liable for; (pl.) debts, pecuniary obligations.

li·a·ble (lī′*a*bel) *adj.* 1. Legally bound; answerable *for*; subject *to* tax or penalty; under obligation *to* do. 2. Exposed or open *to*, apt *to* do or suffer, something undesirable; (colloq.) likely.

li·ai·son (lēāzawn′, lē′*a*zŏn, -zon, lēā′zŏn, -zon; *Fr.* lyĕzawṅ′) *n.* (pl. **-sons** pr. -zawnz′, -zŏnz, -zonz; *Fr.* -zawṅ′). 1. Illicit intimacy between a man and a woman. 2. Sounding of ordinarily silent final consonant before vowel or mute *h* in French. 3. (orig. mil.) Connection, communication (*between, with*).

li·a·na (lēah′n*a*, -ăn′*a*), **li·ane** (lēahn′) *ns.* Woody climbing and twining plant that uses another as support in reaching light, esp. in tropical forest.

Liao·ning (lyow′nĭng′). Province of China, in S. Manchuria.

li·ar (lī′*er*) *n.* Teller (esp. habitual) of lie(s).

Lib. *abbrev.* Liberal.

li·ba·tion (lībā′sh*o*n) *n.* Pouring of wine, wine poured, in honor of a god; (joc.) alcoholic beverage.

Lib·by (lĭb′ē), **Willard Frank** (1908–1980). American chemist; developed carbon 14 method of dating objects; received Nobel Prize for chemistry, 1960.

li·bel (lī′bel) *n.* 1. (civil and eccles. law) Plaintiff's written declaration. 2. (law) Published statement damaging to person's reputation, act of publishing it; (pop.) false and defamatory statement; (transf.) thing that brings discredit *on*. ~ *v.t.* (**-beled, -bel·ing**, Brit. **-belled, -bel·ling**). Defame by libelous statements, accuse falsely and maliciously; (law) publish libel against; (eccles. etc. law) bring suit against. **li′bel·ous** *adj.* **li′bel·ous·ly** *adv.*

Li·ber (lī′b*er*). (Rom. myth.) Ancient Roman god of wine and fruitfulness, identified with Dionysus or Bacchus. **Lib·er·a** (lĭb′*era*). Female counterpart of Liber.

lib·er·al (lĭb′*era*l, lĭb′*ra*l) *adj.* 1. Fit for a gentleman (now rare exc. in **education**, education directed to general enlargement of mind, not professional or technical); ~ **arts**: see ART[1]. 2. Generous, open-handed, not sparing *of*; abundant. 3. Not rigorous or literal, open-minded, unprejudiced. 4. (Pol.) (Moderately) progressive, favoring individual liberty and democratic reform; **L ~ Party**, any political party favoring liberal principles, esp. one of the two great parties of Great Britain (opp. Tory or Conservative Party) in later part of 19th and early 20th c. **lib′er·al·ly** *adv.* **liberal** *n.* Holder of liberal views; **L ~** (member of) Liberal Party. **lib′er·al·ism** *n.*

lib·er·al·i·ty (lĭberăl′ĭtē) *n.* (pl. **-ties**). Free giving, munificence; freedom from prejudice, breadth of mind.

lib·er·ate (lĭb′*e*rāt) *v.t.* (**-at·ed, -at·ing**). Set at liberty; release *from*; (chem.) set free from combination. **lib·er·a′tion, lib′er·a·tor** *ns.*

Li·ber·i·a (lībēr′ē*a*). Republic on coast of W. Africa between Ivory Coast and Sierra Leone; founded (1847) and settled by freed U.S. slaves; capital, Monrovia. **Li·ber′i·an** *adj.* & *n.*

lib·er·tar·i·an (lĭb*er*târ′ē*a*n) *n.* & *adj.* (Person) believing in free will; (person) advocating extreme liberty, esp. of thought and action.

lib·er·tine (lĭb′ertēn, -tĭn) *n.* 1. Freethinker on religion; antinomian; (transf.) one who follows his own inclinations. 2. Licentious or dissolute person. ~ *adj.* Freethinking; licentious, dissolute. **lib′er·tin·age, lib′er·tin·ism** *ns.*

lib·er·ty (lĭb′ertē) *n.* (pl. **-ties**). 1. Being free from captivity, imprisonment, slavery, or despotic control; right or power to do as one pleases or *to* do something; freedom from despotic rule personified; (pl.) privileges, immunities, or rights, enjoyed by prescription or grant; **at** ~, free; having the right *to* do; unemployed, out of work. 2. Setting aside of rules, license; **take the** ~, presume or venture; **take liberties**, be unduly familiar *with*; deal freely *with*. 3. **Liberty Ship**, prefabricated cargo ship built in great numbers by U.S. in World War II; **Statue of Liberty**, colossal bronze figure of a woman holding up a torch ("Liberty Enlightening the World"), gift of French people to U.S. to commemorate centenary of Amer. independence, erected on high granite pedestal on Liberty Island, New York harbor, 1885.

li·bid·i·nous (lĭbĭd′*in*us, -bē′d*i*-) *adj.* Lustful. **li·bid′i·nous·ly** *adv.*

li·bi·do (lĭbē′dō, -bī′-) *n.* (psychol.) Sexual drive; in Freudian theory the motive force of all human activity. **li·bid′i·nal** *adj.*

Li·bra (lē′br*a*, lī′-). The Scales, a constellation; 7th sign (♎) of the zodiac, into which the sun enters at the autumnal equinox.

li·brar·i·an (lībrār′ē*a*n) *n.* Custodian of library; member of library staff. **li·brar′i·an·ship** *n.*

li·brar·y (lī′brĕrē, -br*e*rē, -brē) *n.* (pl. **-brar·ies**). Room or building containing books for reading or reference; such a collection of books, series of books issued by publisher; **L~ of Congress**, U.S. national library, in Washington, D.C., which receives a copy of every book copyrighted in the U.S.; **circulating** ~, library lending books for a fee; **free** ~, library used by public without payment, esp. one maintained by municipality out of taxes.

li·brate (lī′brāt) *v.i.* (**-brat·ed, -brat·ing**). Oscillate like beam of balance. **li·bra·tion** (lībrā′sh*o*n) *n.* Librating; (astron.) real or apparent motion of oscillating kind; ~ **of moon**, apparent irregularity of moon's motion making part near edge of disk alternately visible and invisible.

li·bret·to (lĭbrĕt′ō) *n.* (pl. **-bret·tos, -bret·ti** pr. -brĕt′ē). Text of opera or other long vocal composition. **li·bret′tist** *n.*

Li·bre·ville (lēbr*e*vēl′). Capital and a port of Gabon, in the NW., on the Gulf of Guinea.

Lib·y·a (lĭb′ē*a*). 1. Ancient Greek name for the N. part of Africa W. of Egypt. 2. Republic in N. Africa between Egypt and Tunisia; formerly an Italian colony; independent 1951; capital, Tripoli.

Lib·y·an (lĭb′ē*a*n) *adj.* Of Libya or its people; ~ **Desert**, E. part of Sahara, bounded eastward by River Nile and extending from Mediterranean to Sudan. **Libyan** *n.*

lice: see LOUSE.

li·cense (lī′s*e*ns) *n.* 1. Leave, permission; formal, usu. printed or written, authority to marry, drive vehicle, carry on some profession or trade. 2. Liberty of action, esp. when excessive; abuse of freedom, disregard of law or propriety; licentiousness; writer's or artist's deviation from conventions of meter, perspective, etc. (usu. **poetic** ~). **license** *v.t.* (**-censed, -cens·ing**). Grant license to, authorize by license. **li′censed** *adj.* (esp.) Allowed complete freedom. **li′cen·sor, li·cen·see** (līs*e*nsē′) *ns.*

li·cen·ti·ate (līsĕn′shēĭt, -āt) *n.* (European practice) Holder of university license or attestation of competence from collegiate or examining body.

li·cen·tious (līsĕn′sh*u*s) *adj.* Lascivious, lewd. **li·cen′tious·ly** *adv.* **li·cen′tious·ness** *n.*

li·chee, li·chi = LITCHI.

li·chen (lī′k*e*n) *n.* Plant organism of the group Lichenes, composed of fungus and an alga in association, freq. gray or yellow and growing on rocks, trees, etc., some species of which are edible, others used in manufacture of dyes, perfumes and cosmetics.

lic·it (lĭs′ĭt) *adj.* Lawful, not forbidden. **lic′it·ly** *adv.*

*The Arab republic of **Libya** in North Africa was formerly an Italian colony. Under its head of state, Muammar Gaddafi, it became a strict Muslim country. Below: Map and flag of Libya. Below left: The **Statue of Liberty**.*

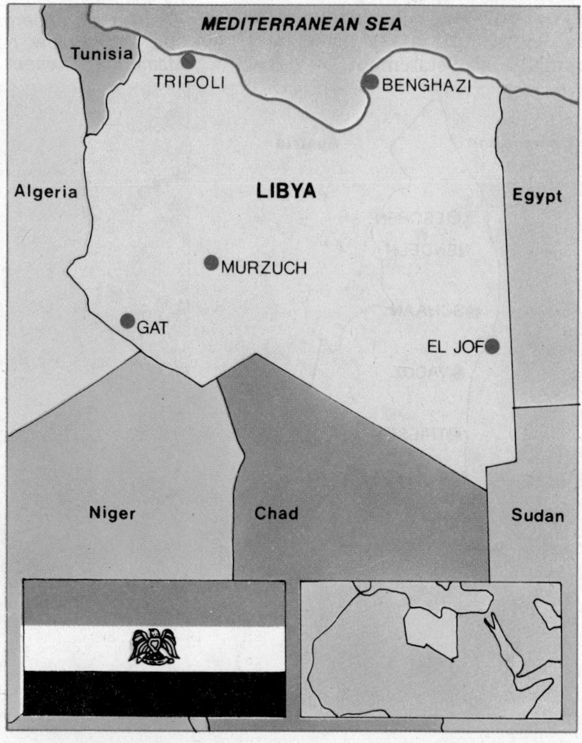

lick (lĭk) *v.* Pass tongue over to taste, moisten, clean, etc.; take *up* or *off*, make *clean*, by licking; (of waves, flame, etc.) play lightly over; (of flame) swallow *up* in passing; (slang) thrash, defeat; ~ **into shape**, mold, make presentable or efficient; ~ **one's wounds**, remain quiet after a defeat; ~ **person's boots** or **shoes**, show servility to him; **lick'spittle**, fawning flatterer, toady. **lick** *n.* Act of licking with tongue; place to which animals resort for salt (also **salt** ~); (slang) rapid pace; a blow; (pl.) (baseball) turn at bat; ~ **and a promise**, hasty performance of a task.

lic·o·rice, li·quo·rice (lĭk'*e*rĭs, -ərĭsh, lĭk'rĭsh) *ns.* (Flavoring for medicines, candy, liquor, etc., made from) root of leguminous plant *Glycyrrhiza glabra*.

lic·tor (lĭk'*ter*) *n.* (Rom. hist.) Officer attending magistrate, bearing fasces as emblem of office and executing sentence on offenders.

lid (lĭd) *n.* Hinged or detached cover for aperture, esp. for opening at top of container; eyelid; (bot., conch.) operculum. **lid'ded, lid'-less** *adjs.*

Li·di·ce (lē'dēchā, lĭd'ĭsē; *Czech.* lĭ'dyĭtsĕ). Czechoslovakian village completely destroyed by the occupying Nazis, 1942, in reprisal for civilian resistance; rebuilt as a national monument after World War II.

Li·do (lē'dō). Chain of sandy islands separating lagoon of Venice from Adriatic Sea, a fashionable bathing resort.

lie[1] (lī) *n.* Intentional false statement; imposture, false belief; **give the** ~ **to**, belie, serve to show falsity of; **tell a** ~, make intentionally false statement; ~ **detector**, instrument indicating physiological changes that occur under stress of emotion. **lie** *v.i.* (**lied, ly·ing**). Speak falsely, tell lie(s); take *away*, get *into*, *out of*, by lying; (of things) deceive.

lie[2] (lī) *v.i.* (**lay, lain** pr. lān, **ly·ing**). 1. (of persons or animals) Have one's body in more or less horizontal position along ground or surface; assume lying position (esp. ~ **down**); be kept, remain, in specified state; (archaic) have sexual intercourse *with*; (of the dead) be in the grave *at*, *in*. 2. (of things) Be at rest, usu. more or less horizontally, on surface; be stored up in specified place; remain in specified state; be situated; be spread out to view; exist, be found, reside, be arranged or related, in some position or manner; (of road) lead *through*, *by*, etc.; (of ship) float in berth or at anchor; (law) be admissible or sustainable; ~ **heavy**, be a weight *on* one's stomach or conscience. 3. **lie by**, be unused; keep quiet or retired; **lie down under**, accept without protest; **lie in** (*v.*), be brought to bed in childbirth; **lie off**, (naut.) stand some distance from shore or other ship; **lie over**, be deferred; **lie to**, (naut.) come almost to a stop with head near wind by backing or shortening sail. **lie** *n.* Way, direction, or position in which thing lies; place where beast, bird, or fish, is accustomed to lie; (golf) location of a ball after it has come to a stop.

Lie (lē), **Trygve Halvdan** (1896–1968). Norwegian statesman; first secretary-general of the U.N., 1946–53.

Liech·ten·stein (lĭk'*t*enstīn; *Ger.* lĭχ'tenshtīn). Small (62-square-mile, 161 sq. km) independent principality in Rhine valley between Austria and Switzerland; capital, Vaduz.

lied (lēd; *Ger.* lēt) *n.* (pl. **lied·er** pr. lē'*d*er; *Ger.* lē'*d*er). German song or poem of ballad kind. [Ger.]

lief (lēf) *adv.* (archaic) Gladly, willingly.

Li·ège (lēāzh'; *Fr.* lyĕzh). Port city in Belgium on the Meuse River; first mentioned in historic records in 558 A.D.; noted center of learning in the Middle Ages.

liege (lēj, lēzh) *adj.* (of superior) Entitled to receive, (of vassal) bound to give, feudal service or allegiance; ~ **lord**, feudal superior, sovereign. **liege** *n.* Liege lord; vassal, subject.

lien (lēn, lē'*e*n) *n.* (law) Right to keep possession of property till debt due in respect of it is discharged.

lieu (lo͞o) *n.* **in** ~, in place, instead, (*of*).

Lieut. *abbrev.* Lieutenant.

lieu·ten·ant (lo͞otĕn'*a*nt, lū-; *Brit.*, except in the navy, lĕftĕn'*a*nt) *n.* 1. Deputy, substitute, vicegerent, acting for a superior; ~ **governor**, deputy governor. 2. (mil.) Officer next in rank below captain; (navy) junior officer; officer of police force below captain; ~ **colonel**, army officer of rank next below colonel's, having actual command of a regiment; ~ **commander**, officer in navy of rank next below commander's and above lieutenant's; ~ **general**, officer in army of rank next below general's and above major general's. **lieu·ten'an·cy**

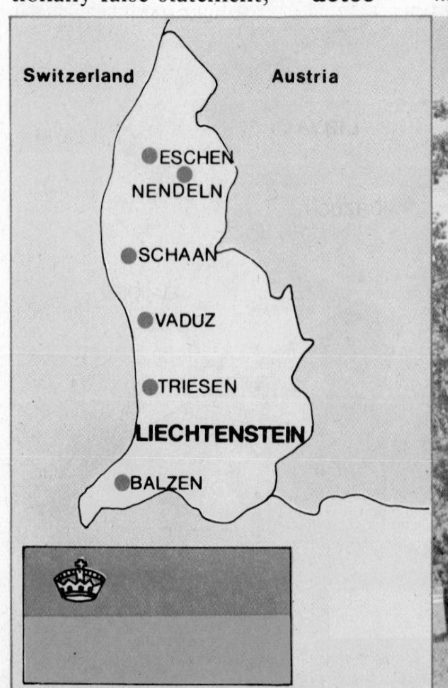

The miniature alpine principality of ***Liechtenstein*** *is bordered on the west by the Rhine and on the east by the Austrian Vorarlberg. Below left: Map and flag. Below right: Chapel of St. Mamertus, Triesen.*

2

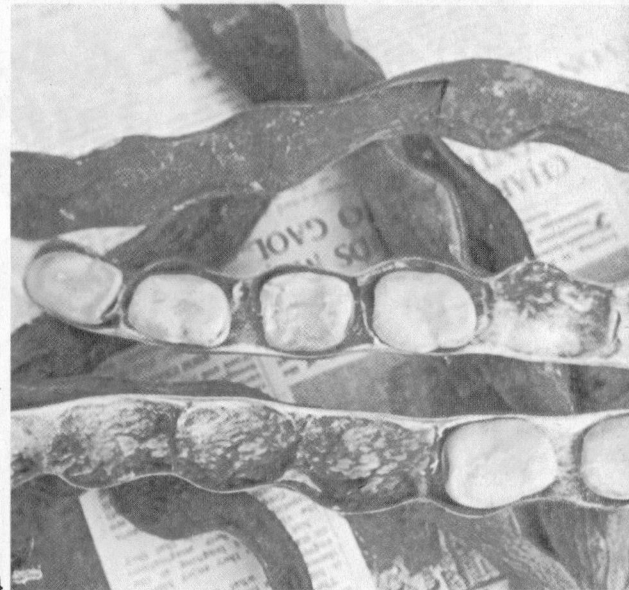

4

The ***life cycle*** *of the broad bean is shown here in its successive stages. 1. Straightening of the plumule. 2. Closeup of one flower. 3. Ripening pod. 4. Ripe pod open to show ripe seed. Bean plants tend to increase soil reserves of nitrogen and are often used in a farming rotation system. They are, like peas, an important vegetable for human consumption.*

n. (pl. **-cies**).

life (līf) *n.* (pl. **lives** pr. līvz). 1. Condition or fact of being living; that state of ceaseless change and functional activity which constitutes the essential difference between living organisms and dead or nonliving matter; continuance of animate existence (opp. death); energy, vivacity, animation; vivifying influence; living things; living form or model, life-size figure, etc.; (**a matter** etc.) **of ~ and death**, (something) on which it depends whether a person shall live or die, of vital importance; **for one's, for dear ~**, (as if) to escape death; **as large as ~**, life-size. 2. Period from birth to death, birth to present time, or present time to death; person considered with respect to expectation of life; **~ expectancy**, average period that person at specified age may expect to live; **have the time of one's ~**, enjoy oneself as never before; **~ annuity, sentence**, annuity, sentence, to continue for the rest of person's life. 3. Individual actions and fortunes, manner of existence; written story of these, biography; active part of existence, business and pleasures of the world; **eternal, everlasting, future, the other ~**, state of existence after death; **high, low ~**, social customs of upper, lower, classes; **see ~**, enjoy affairs of the world, esp. social activities; **this ~**, life on earth. 4. Time that an object etc. may last. 5. **~ belt**, belt of buoyant material to support human body in water; **life'blood**, blood necessary to life; vitalizing influence; **life'boat**, boat maintained at **lifeboat station** on shore, equipped to go to aid of ships in distress; boat carried by ship for use in emergency; **life buoy**: see BUOY; **life cycle**, (biol.) series of changes undergone by an organism from the union of gametes that produced it until its death (but in some animals and plants the life cycle includes the life and death of successive individuals); **life estate**, property that one holds for life but cannot

dispose of further; **life force**, vital energy, force conceived as striving for survival of individual and race; **life′guard**, person guarding safety of swimmers; **life insurance** (provision for) payment to a beneficiary on the death of insured person, or to the person, if he or she lives to a specified age; **life interest**, right to life estate; **life jacket**, life preserver shaped like sleeveless jacket; **life line**, rope used for life saving, e.g., that attached to life buoy; diver's signaling line; **life′long**, lasting one's life; **life preserver**, buoyant ring, jacket, belt, etc., to support human body in water; **Life Saver**, (trademark) hard candy shaped like a ring life preserver; **life-size(d)**, of same size as object represented; **life′time**, duration of person's life; **life′work**, task pursued through one's whole life. **life′less** *adj.* Dead; lacking animation, energy, etc. **life′less·ly** *adv.* **life′less·ness** *n.* **life′like** *adj.* Resembling life; exactly like real person or thing.

lif·er (lī′*fer*) *n.* (slang) One sentenced to penal servitude for life.

Lif·fey (lĭf′ē). River in the Republic of Ireland flowing 50 miles (81 km) from County Wicklow in Dublin Bay.

LIFO *abbrev.* Last-in, first-out.

lift (lĭft) *v.* 1. Raise to higher position, take up, hoist; rise from ground; elevate to higher plane of thought or feeling; give upward direction to; hold or have on high; hit (golf ball etc.) into air; (of ship etc. afloat) rise on wave; (of cloud, fog, etc.) rise, disperse; **~-off**, vertical take-off of spacecraft or rocket; **~ one's hand against**, strike. 2. (slang) Steal (esp. a wallet). 3. **have one's face lifted**, undergo operation to remove wrinkles etc. on face. **lift** *n.* 1. Lifting. 2. Help (esp. given to walker by taking him some distance in vehicle). 3. One layer of leather in boot heel. 4. (Brit.) Elevator. 5. Lifting power. 6. (slang) Air transport of cargo or passengers.

lig·a·ment (lĭg′*a*ment) *n.* (anat.) Short band of tough flexible fibrous tissue binding the two bones at a joint; (loosely) any membranous fold keeping organ in position; similar part in lower organisms. **lig·a·men·tal** (lĭg*a*mĕn′t*a*l), **lig·a·men′ta·ry, lig·a·men′tous** *adjs.*

lig·a·ture (lĭg′*a*cher, -choor) *n.* 1. Thing used in tying, esp. (surg.) cord or band used to tie off blood vessels to stop hemorrhage or

Specially designed to negotiate the surf, the ***lifeboat*** *(above) is used by Australian* ***lifeguards.*** *Other equipment used by them includes the surf reel and harness, surfboards and surf skis.*

Aerodynamic ***lift*** *is the upward force acting on the aircraft, equal and opposite to the pull of gravity on the craft and its load. Drag is the resistance the aircraft meets in moving forward through the air. The Bell 205 Helicopter here (RAAF) is lifting a car, increasing the degree of aerodynamic lift needed to fly.*

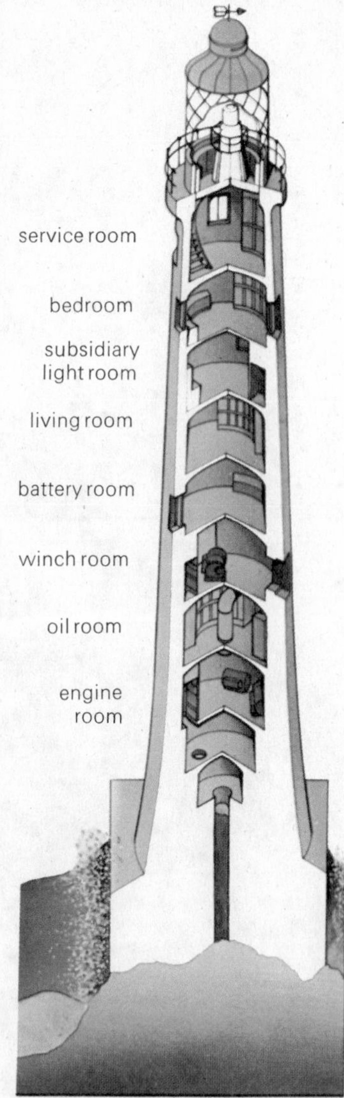

Above: Beachy Head ***lighthouse,*** *U.K. Right: Cross-section of an offshore lighthouse built of interlocking stone blocks. The detailed section of the service room and lantern gallery (below) shows the way the stones are fitted together. This type of construction can withstand strong winds and high seas.*

obstruct blood flow. 2. Thing that unites, bond; (mus.) group of two or more notes sung to one syllable, slur, tie; (print etc.) two or more letters joined together in one character, as *œ*. ~ *v.t.* (**-tured, -tur·ing**). Bind with ligature.

light[1] (līt) *n.* 1. Visible form of electromagnetic radiation produced by energy changes within the atoms of a substance, esp. when excited by intense heat; that which evokes functional activity of organ of sight; natural agent emanating from sun; medium or condition of space in which vision is possible; appearance of brightness; amount of illumination in a place, one's fair or ordinary share of this; daylight; vivacity in person's eyes; favoring aspect; **come, bring, to ~**, be revealed, reveal; **see the ~**, be born, (also fig., see below). 2. Object from which brightness emanates; sun or other heavenly body; illuminating agent, as lamp etc., (collect.) lamps etc. illuminating place; beacon lamp, esp. of ship or lighthouse; traffic light; lighthouse; (fig.) eminent person or luminary; **Feast, Festival, of L~s**: see HANUKKAH; **~s out**, (mil.) last bugle call of the day, signal for all lights be be put out. 3. Mental illumination, illumination of soul by divine truth or love etc.; elucidation, enlightenment; fact or discovery serving to explain subject; (pl.) natural or acquired mental powers; (sing.) aspect in which thing is viewed; **in a good or bad ~**, favorably, unfavorably; **see the ~**, become enlightened or convinced. 4. Window or opening in wall for admission of light; perpendicular division of mullioned window; glazed compartment of side or roof in greenhouse. 5. (paint, etc.) Illuminated surface, part of picture represented as lighted up. 6. Flame or spark serving to ignite; thing used for igniting, spill, taper, match. 7. **light'house**, tower or other structure containing beacon light(s) for warning or guiding ships at sea; **light'ship**, ship, moored or anchored, containing similar lights; **light-year**, (astron.) distance that light travels in one year (approx. 9.46×10^{12} km or 6 trillion miles), as unit in measuring interstellar distances. **light'less** *adj.*

light[2] (līt) *adj.* Well provided with light, not dark; pale-colored, pale.

light[3] (līt) *v.* (**light·ed, lit, light·ing**). Set (lamp, fire, etc.) burning; (of fuel etc.) take fire, begin to burn; give light to; brighten with animation; show (person his) way or surroundings with a light; **~ up**, begin to smoke pipe etc.; kindle or turn on lights in street, room, etc., at dusk; light brightly, make conspicuous by light.

light[4] (līt) *adj.* 1. Of little weight, not heavy; deficient in weight; of small specific gravity; having or intended for small load; (of ship, cart, etc.) made lightly for small loads and quick movement; (of building) not looking heavy, graceful, elegant. 2. Acting gently, applied delicately, not violent; not dense, tenacious, or cohesive; easy to digest; not grave or important; trivial; nimble; inconstant; (of wine etc.) not strong; (of syllable) unemphatic. 3. Easily borne or done; aimed or aiming at entertainment merely; (of sleep) easily disturbed, not profound. 4. **~-fingered**, given to stealing; **~-footed**, springy, nimble; **~-handed**, having a light hand, managing tactfully; **light'headed**, slightly disoriented, e.g. from drink or joy; **light heart**, heart free from sorrow; **light'hearted**, gay, untroubled; **light horse**, lightly armed cavalry; **light marching order**, that in which only arms and ammunition are taken; **light-minded**, frivolous, thoughtless; **light'weight**, person etc. of less than average weight; person of no influence; boxer of weight between featherweight and welterweight. **light'ly** *adv.* **light'ness** *n.* **light** *adv.* In light manner.

light[5] (līt) *v.* 1. (naut.) Lift (rope etc.) along, lend a hand in hauling ropes etc. 2. Alight, descend, come down (archaic); chance, come by chance *on*.

light·en[1] (lī'ten) *v.* Shed light upon, make bright; grow bright, shine, flash; emit lightning. **light'en·er** *n.*

light·en[2] (lī'ten) *v.* Reduce load of (ship etc.), (of ship) have load reduced; relieve (heart etc.), be relieved, of weight; reduce weight of; mitigate; grow lighter.

light·er[1] (lī'ter) *n.* (esp.) Instrument for producing flame or spark for igniting cigarette, gas jet, etc.

light·er[2] (lī'ter) *n.* Boat, usu. flat-bottomed, for unloading and loading ships not brought to wharf and for transporting goods in harbor. **light'er·age** *n.* Transport of goods by lighter. **light'er·man** *n.* **lighter** *v.t.* Remove (goods) in lighter.

light·ning (līt'nĭng) *n.* Visible electric discharge between clouds or cloud and ground; **forked, chain(ed), ~**, lightning flash in form of zigzag or divided line; **sheet ~**, lightning flash of diffused brightness; **summer, heat ~**, sheet lightning without audible thunder, result of distant storm; **like ~**, with greatest conceivable speed; **~ bug**, firefly; **~ conductor, rod**, metal rod or wire fixed to exposed part of building or to mast to divert lightning into earth or sea. **lightning** *adj.* Very swift; **~ strike**, sudden strike taking place without warning.

lights (līts) *n.pl.* Lungs of sheep, pigs, etc., used as food esp. for cats and dogs.

light·some (līt'som) *adj.* Gracefully light; merry; agile. **light'some·ly** *adv.* **light'some·ness** *n.*

light·wood (līt'wo͝od) *n.* 1. Any of various trees with light wood, in Australia chiefly *Acacia melanoxylon*. 2. Wood used in lighting fire, esp. resinous pinewood.

lign·al·oes (līnăl'ōz, lĭg-) *n.* (usu. considered sing.). The drug aloes; aloeswood, an aromatic Mexican wood. [L., = "wood of the aloe"]

lig·ne·ous (lĭg'nēus) *adj.* Woody (esp. of plants).

lig·ni·fy (lĭg'nifī) *v.* (**-fied, -fy·ing**). Make, become woody. **lig·ni·fi·ca·tion** (lĭgnĭfikā'shon) *n.*

lig·nin (lĭg'nĭn) *n.* (bot.) Hardening material impregnating cell walls of woody tissues.

lig·nite (lĭg'nīt) *n.* Brown coal, a deposit formed usu. after the Carboniferous age, showing visible traces of its plant structure and containing much carbon, the oldest approximating to bituminous coal, the newest to peat.

__Lightning__ is a visible discharge of electricity at very high voltage. It usually occurs in cumulonimbus clouds and such discharges may be between two clouds, or between the cloud and the earth.

lig·num vi·tae (lĭg'num vī'tē). Either of two tropical evergreen Amer. trees, *Guiacum officinale* or *G. sanctum*, with extremely heavy and hard wood. [L., = "wood of life"]

lig·u·late (lĭg'yulĭt, -lāt) *adj.* Strap-shaped; (bot.) with strap-shaped florets.

lig·ule (lĭg'ūl) *n.* (bot.) Thin appendage at base of leaf blade, esp. in grasses; ligulate corolla in composites.

Li·gu·ri·a (lĭgūr'ēa). Region of N. Italy, once forming the republic of Genoa or **Ligurian Republic**, formed 1797 after Napoleon's Italian campaign, annexed to France 1805, and subsequently merged into Italy.

Li·gu·ri·an (lĭgūr'ēan) *adj.* Of Liguria or its people or language; of an ancient race (**Ligures**) inhabiting NW. Italy, Switzerland, and SE. Gaul and speaking a pre-Italic Indo-European language; **~ Republic**: see LIGURIA; **~ Sea**, part of Mediterranean between Corsica and NW. coast of Italy around Genoa. **Ligurian** *n.* Native, inhabitant, language, of Liguria.

like[1] (līk) *adj.* Similar, resembling something, each other, or the original; resembling, such as; characteristic of; in promising state or right mood for *doing*; (archaic) likely (*to*); **what is he ~?**, what sort of person is he?; **look ~**, have the appearance of being; give promise, indicate the presence, of;

~ **that**, of the kind just seen or referred to; ~**-minded**, having same tastes, views, etc. **like** *prep.* In the manner of, to the same degree as; ~ **a shot**, without demur, willingly, regardless of consequences; rapidly. **like** *adv.* In the same manner *as* (archaic); (illit.) so to speak. ~ *conj.* (illit. and colloq.) As. ~ *n.* Counterpart, equal, like thing or person; thing(s) of the same kind; **the** ~**(s) of**, (colloq.) such a person or thing as; **and the** ~, etcetera.

like[2] (līk) *v.* (**liked, lik·ing**). 1. Be pleasing to (archaic, chiefly impers.). 2. Find agreeable, congenial, or satisfactory; feel attracted by; wish for; ~ **to**, ~**d to**, (slang) almost, came close to. **like** *n.* (usu. pl.) Liking, predilection. **lik'a·ble, like'a·ble** *adjs.* **lik'a·ble·ness, like'a·bil'i·ty** *ns.*

like·li·hood (līk'lēho͝od) *n.* Being likely, probability.

like·ly (līk'lē) *adj.* (**-li·er, li·est**). Probably; such as might well happen, or be or prove true, or turn out to be the thing specified; to be expected *to*; promising, apparently suitable *for*, *to*, capable looking. ~ *adv.* **most** or **very** ~, probably.

lik·en (lī'ken) *v.t.* Find or point out resemblance in (thing) *to*.

like·ness (līk'nĭs) *n.* 1. Being like, resemblance. 2. Representation, copy, portrait; person or thing having exact appearance of another.

like·wise (līk'wīz) *adv.* & *conj.* Similarly (bibl.); also, moreover.

lik·ing (lī'kĭng) *n.* What one likes, one's taste; regard, taste, *for*.

li·lac (lī'l*a*k) *n.* Oleaceous shrub or small tree of genus *Syringa*, esp. *S. vulgaris* which has fragrant, usu. pale pinkish-violet, blossoms; color of these. ~ *adj.* Of lilac color.

lil·i·a·ceous (lĭlēā'sh*u*s) *adj.* Of lilies or the order Liliaceae; lilylike.

Lil·ith (lĭl'ĭth). In the Talmud, the first wife of Adam, dispossessed by Eve; in Jewish folklore, female demon who tries to kill newborn children; in cabalistic literature, symbol of sexual lust.

Li·li·u·o·ka·la·ni (lēlēo͞o͞okahlah'nē), **Lydia Kamekeha** (1838–1917). Last native ruler and queen of the Hawaiian Islands, 1891–3; deposed.

Lil·li·put (lĭl'ĭpŭt, -p*u*t). In Swift's *Gulliver's Travels*, a country inhabited by people 6 inches high. **Lil·li·pu·tian** (lĭlĭpū'sh*a*n) *adj.* Of Lilliput; of diminutive size; petty.

Li·long·we (lēlawng'wā). Capital of Malawi, replacing Zomba.

lilt (lĭlt) *v.t.* Sing melodiously or rhythmically. ~ *n.* (Song with) marked rhythmical cadence.

lil·y (lĭl'ē) *n.* (pl. **lil·ies**). 1. Flower of genus *Lilium* of bulbous herbs bearing large showy white, reddish, or purplish flowers, freq. spotted, on tall slender stem, esp. *L. candidum*, the white or madonna lily; any of various plants of allied genera; **tiger** ~: see TIGER; **water** ~: see WATER; ~ **of the valley**, spring flower, *Convallaria majalis*, with (usu.) two longish leaves and racemes of fragrant white bell-shaped flowers. 2. Heraldic fleur-de-lis; **the (golden) lilies**, arms of French monarchy, the Bourbon dynasty. 3. (attrib.) Delicately white; pallid; ~**-livered**, cowardly; ~ **pad**, broad flat leaf of water lily lying on water; ~**-white**, white as a lily; containing no black people; pertaining to groups or organizations that discriminate against blacks.

Li·ma (lē'm*a*). Capital city of Peru; **l**~ (lī'm*a*) **bean**, kind of bean (*Phaseolus limensis*) native to tropical America, with flat usu. white seeds.

limb[1] (lĭm) *n.* Leg, arm, or wing; main branch of tree; branch of cross; spur of mountain; (colloq., also ~ **of the devil, of Satan**), mischievous child; **out on a** ~, (colloq.) in a vulnerable position; isolated. **limb'less** *adj.* **limb** *v.t.* Cut off the limbs of.

limb[2] (lĭm) *n.* Edge of surface; graduated edge of quadrant etc.; edge of sun, moon, etc.; expanded part of petal, sepal, or leaf.

lim·bate (lĭm'bāt) *adj.* (biol.) Having distinct or different colored border.

lim·ber[1] (lĭm'b*e*r) *n.* Detachable front of gun carriage (two wheels, axle, pole, and ammunition box). ~ *v.t.* Attach limber to (gun), fasten together two parts of gun carriage (usu. *up*).

lim·ber[2] (lĭm'b*e*r) *adj.* Flexible; lithe, nimble. ~ *v.* Make limber or supple; ~ **up**, exercise in preparation for athletic etc. exertion. **lim'ber·ly** *adv.* **lim'ber·ness** *n.*

lim·bo[1] (lĭm'bō) *n.* Region on border of hell, supposed abode of just men who died before Christ's

Lilac includes among its 30 species some of the most fragrant and beautiful of northern spring-flowering garden shrubs and small trees. The common lilac is widely cultivated.

***Lima,** the capital of Peru, was founded by Pizarro in 1535. It is eight miles from its port, Callao, on the central coast. Peru's Government Palace is shown here.*

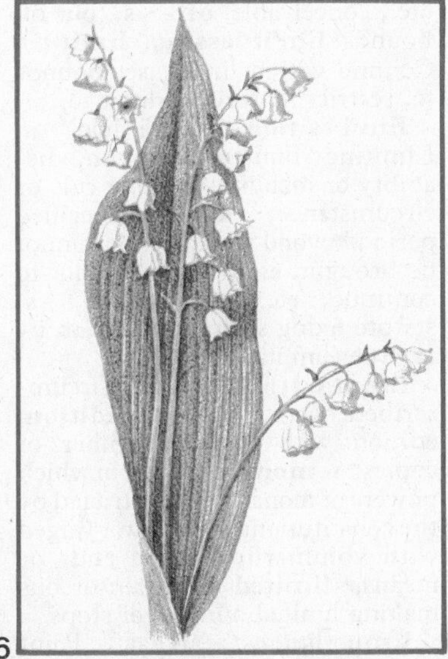

coming and of unbaptized infants; prison; condition of neglect or oblivion. [L. *in limbo* at the edge]

lim·bo[2] (lĭm′bō) *n.* W. Indian dance in which dancer bends back and passes repeatedly under gradually lowered horizontal bar just above ground. [Caribbean name]

Lim·burg, Lim·bourg (lĭm′-bĕrg). 1. Ancient duchy of the Low Countries. 2. (**Limbourg**) Province of NE. Belgium, part of the old duchy. 3. (**Limburg**) Province of extreme SE. of the Netherlands, including another part of the old duchy. **Lim·burg·er** (lĭm′bĕrg*er*) *n.* (also ~ **cheese**) Soft white compressed cheese orig. from Limbourg, Belgium, with characteristic smell.

lime[1] (līm) *n.* 1. White caustic alkaline substance, quicklime (calcium oxide, CaO), made by heating

There are about 80 species of ***lily*** *belonging to the genus Lilium, most of which are cultivated as ornamental plants. Shown here are: 1. Tiger lily. 2. Candlestick lily. 3. Spider lily. 4. 'Prosperity lily' (lilium oregon hybrid). 5. African lily. 6. Lily of the Valley, which is not of the genus Lilium but belongs to the lily family. Its scented flowers are distilled for perfume.*

chalk or limestone and used for making mortar; (pop., in **carbonate, chloride**, etc., *of* ~) calcium; (theatr.) limelight. 2. **bird′lime**: see BIRD; ~ **burner**, maker of lime; **lime′kiln**, kiln for burning limestone; **lime′light**, intense white light got by heating lime in oxyhydrogen flame, formerly used in theaters to light up important figures etc.; (fig.) glare of publicity; **lime pit**, limestone quarry; pit for steeping hides

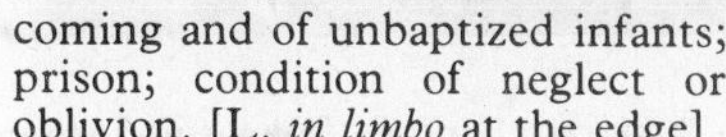

*The flowers of the **lime** or linden tree are fragrant and rich in nectar. Linden honey, light in color, is highly regarded for its food value. The tree is widely planted for shade.*

to remove hair; **lime'stone**, rock consisting chiefly of calcium carbonate; **lime twig**, twig smeared with birdlime; **lime'water**, solution of calcium hydroxide ($Ca(OH)_2$) used medicinally as an antacid. **lime** *v.t.* (**limed, lim·ing**). Smear (twigs), catch (bird), with birdlime; treat with lime.

lime[2] (līm) *n.* Round fruit of tree *Citrus aurantifolia*, smaller and more acid than lemon; ~ **juice**, juice of this used as beverage and as antiscorbutic.

lime[3] (līm) *n.* (also ~ **tree**) Ornamental tree (*Tilia*, esp. *T. glabra*) with heart-shaped leaves and small fragrant yellowish blossom; linden tree.

lime·ade (līmād', lī'mād) *n.* Beverage of sweetened lime juice and water.

li·men (lī'm*e*n) *n.* (pl. **li·mens, lim·i·na** pr. lĭm'*i*n*a*). (psych.) = THRESHOLD. **lim·i·nal** (lĭm'*i*n*a*l) *adj.* [L., = "threshold"]

Lim·er·ick (lĭm'*e*rĭk). County in the Republic of Ireland; a town and port at head of estuary of River Shannon.

lim·er·ick (lĭm'*e*rĭk) *n.* Verse, now usu. epigrammatic and freq. indecent, consisting of five lines (two of 3 ft., two of 2 ft., and one of 3 ft.) with rhymes *aabba*; first found c1820, and popularized by Edward LEAR[2]. [said to be f. chorus "Will you come up to Limerick?" sung after extempore verses contributed by each member of party]

lim·ey (lī'mē) *n.* (pl. **-eys**). (slang) English sailor; Englishman.

lim·it (lĭm'ĭt) *n.* Bounding line, terminal point, bound that may not or cannot be passed; **the** ~, (slang) the last straw, the worst, etc., conceivable; **off-~s**, (out of) bounds; **lim'it·less** *adj.* **limit** *v.t.* Confine within limits, set bounds to, restrict *to*; serve as limit to.

lim·i·ta·tion (lĭmĭtā'sh*o*n) *n.* Limiting; limited condition, disability or inability; limiting rule or circumstance; legally specified period beyond which action cannot be brought, estate or law is not to continue, etc.; **statute of ~s**, statute fixing such period. **lim·i·ta·tive** (lĭm'ĭtātĭv) *adj.*

lim·it·ed (lĭm'ĭtĭd) *adj.* Circumscribed, narrow; scanty; ~ **edition**, edition with limited number of copies; ~ **monarchy**, one in which powers of monarch are restricted by the constitution; ~ **war**, war waged with voluntarily limited ends or means. **limited** *n.* Train or bus making limited number of stops.

limn (lĭm) *v.t.* (archaic) Paint (picture); portray (in words). **limn'er** *n.*

***Limestone** rocks represent 20% of all sedimentary rocks and occur on all continents among strata of every age. This crinoidal limestone is from the Carboniferous period.*

lim·nol·o·gy (lĭmnŏl'*o*jē) *n.* Study of fresh waters and their inhabitants.

Li·moges (lĭmōzh'). City of W. central France, famous in 16th and 17th centuries for enamel work and later for porcelain.

lim·ou·sine (lĭm'*o*zēn, lĭm*o*zēn') *n.* Automobile with closed body and partition behind driver; luxurious automobile; large automobile or small bus used to transport passengers to and from airports. [Fr., f. *Limousin*, former province of W. central France]

limp[1] (lĭmp) *v.i.* Walk lamely; (of verse) halt; (of ship) proceed slowly and with difficulty because of damage. **limp'ing·ly** *adv.* **limp** *n.* Lame walk.

limp[2] (lĭmp) *adj.* Not stiff, flexible; wanting in energy; (of bookbindings) not stiffened with board. **limp'ly** *adv.* **limp'ness** *n.*

lim·pet (lĭm'pĭt) *n.* Gastropod mollusk, as of the families Acmaeidae or Patellidae, with low conical shell found adhering tightly to rocks; (fig.) person who clings persistently.

lim·pid (lĭm'pĭd) *adj.* Pellucid, clear, not turbid. **lim'pid·ly** *adv.* **lim'pid·ness, lim·pid·i·ty** (lĭmpĭd'ĭtē) *ns.*

Lim·po·po (lĭmpō´pō). River of SE. Africa, rising near Johannesburg and flowing 1,000 miles (1,610 km) to the Indian Ocean.

lin·age (lī´nĭj) *n.* Number of lines in printed matter; payment according to this.

linch·pin (lĭnch´pĭn) *n.* Pin passed through axle end to keep wheel on; (fig.) element or person vital to an organization etc.

Lin·coln[1] (lĭng´kon). Capital and commercial center of Nebraska, in the SE.

Lin·coln[2] (lĭng´kon), **Abraham** (1809–65). American statesman and 16th president of the U.S., 1861–5, during the Civil War; prominent lawyer, congressman from Illinois, 1847–9; took stand against slavery during famous debates against Stephen A. Douglas; issued Emancipation Proclamation declaring freedom of slaves in all rebellious states; famous for address dedicating national cemetery at Gettysburg, 1863; assassinated in Ford's Theater by John Wilkes Booth, 1865.

Lind (lĭnd), **Johanna Maria ("Jenny")**, afterward Madame Jenny Lind-Goldschmidt (1820–1887). Swedish-born Brit. coloratura soprano.

Lind·bergh (lĭnd´bẽrg, lĭn´-), **Charles A(ugustus)** (1902–74). American aviator; made first nonstop flight of the Atlantic, 1927.

lin·den (lĭn´den) *n.* Any of several trees of the genus *Tilia* with large heart-shaped leaves and fragrant yellowish-white flowers, including *T. americana*, basswood.

Lind·say (lĭn´zē), **(Nicholas) Vachel** (1879–1931). American poet who tried to follow the troubadour tradition; wrote "The Congo" etc.

line[1] (līn) *n.* 1. Piece of rope (esp. naut.); wire or cable for telegraph or telephone, route traversed by this; cord bearing fishhook(s); cord for measuring, leveling, etc.; ~ **of credit**, maximum amount of credit made available by a bank, store, credit card agency, etc., to a customer. 2. Long narrow mark traced on surface; mark limiting games court or ground or special parts of them; thing resembling traced mark, band of color, seam, furrow, wrinkle, fold in palm of hand supposed to indicate fate, character, etc.; equator; straight line; contour, outline; limit, boundary; (as measure) $\frac{1}{12}$ in.; one of the very narrow sections in which televised scenes are photographed and reproduced; (math.) continuous extent (straight or curved) of length without breadth or thickness, curve connecting all points having a common property; (pl.) plan or draft (esp. of ship) in horizontal, vertical, and oblique sections; (pl.) manner of procedure; ~ **drawing**, drawing done with pen or similar instrument; ~ **engraving**, incising of lines on metal plate, print taken from such plate. 3. Row of persons or things; direction indicated by them; row of words in page or newspaper column; short letter; single verse of poetry, (pl.) piece of poetry; (mil.) double row (front and rear ranks) of men ranged side by side; trench, (pl.) connected series of fieldworks; regular fighting force of all arms; (pl.) words of actor's part; **all along the** ~, at every point; **down the** ~; thoroughly, completely; **draw the** ~, restrict, impose a limit; **get a** ~ **on**, gain a clue to; **hold the** ~, remain unyielding; **in** ~ **for**, likely to get; **into** ~, into a straight row or (fig.) agreement; ~ **of battle**: see BATTLE; ~ **of scrimmage**: see SCRIMMAGE; **~-up, ~ up**, (specific order of) persons or things arranged in a line, esp. listing of players in a game and their positions on the team; **on the** ~, (slang) at great risk; with money, as opposed to credit; **out of** ~, (slang) discordant; **read between the ~s**, discover meaning or purpose not expressed or not obvious; **scrimmage** ~: see SCRIMMAGE. 4. Series or regular succession of steamers, buses, aircraft, etc., traveling between certain places; connected series of persons or things following one another in time, esp. several generations of family; family, lineage, stock. 5. Direction, course, track; course followed in riding to hounds; course of procedure, conduct, thought, etc.; department of activity, province, branch of business; (rail.) single track of rails, one branch of system, whole system under one management; (commerc.) class of goods, order for stock of this. **line** *v.* (**lined, lin·ing**). Mark *in*, *off*, *out*, with lines on paper etc.; cover with lines; draw *up* in line; come *up*, spread *out*, in lines; post troops etc. along (road etc.), (of troops) form line along; (of things) stand at intervals along (wall etc.).

*The Lincoln Memorial in Washington D.C. commemorates the 16th U.S. President **Abraham Lincoln,** who was assassinated days after the end of the Civil War by John Wilkes Booth.*

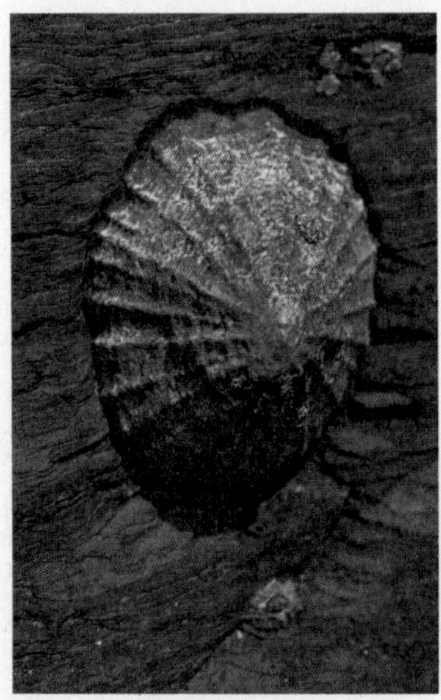

*The **limpet,** a mollusk with a conical shell, clings mostly to rocks near the shore. This Patella vulgata is a species commonly found in Britain and northern Europe.*

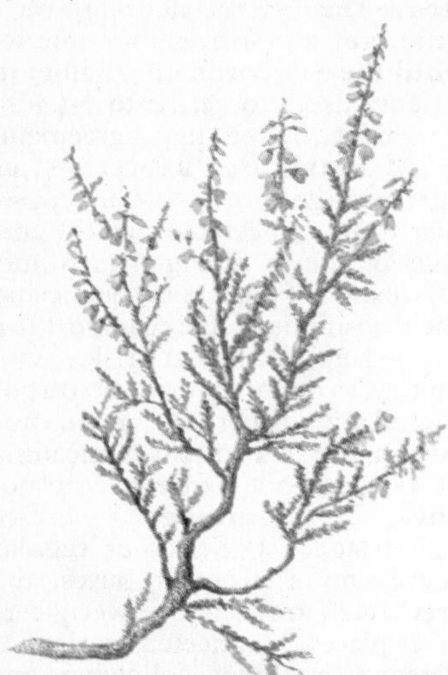

Ling is another name for the common heather. This low evergreen shrub is found in the open woods of western Europe and the British Isles, and in eastern North America.

line[2] (līn) *v.t.* (**lined, lin·ing**). Apply layer of (usu. different) material to inside of (garment, box, etc.); fill (purse, pocket, stomach, etc.); serve as lining for; ~ **one's pockets**, make money, esp. at the expense of other people. **lin'ing** *n.*

lin·e·age (lĭn'ēĭj) *n.* Lineal descent, ancestry, pedigree.

lin·e·al (lĭn'ēal) *adj.* In the direct line of descent or ancestry; (rare) of, in, line(s), linear. **lin'e·al·ly** *adv.*

lin·e·a·ment (lĭn'ēament) *n.* (usu. pl.) Distinctive feature(s) or characteristic(s), esp. of face.

lin·e·ar (lĭn'ēer) *adj.* 1. Of, in, line(s); (of work of art) conceived or expressed in lines rather than masses. 2. Long, narrow, and of uniform breadth. 3. (math., phys.) Involving measurement in one dimension only. **lin'e·ar·ly** *adv.*

lin·e·a·tion (lĭnēā'shon) *n.* Drawing of, marking with, arrangement of, lines.

line·back·er (līn'băker) *n.* (football) Defensive player, usu. just behind the ends and tackles.

lin·en (lĭn'en) *adj.* Made of flax. ~ *n.* Cloth woven from flax; particular kind of this; (collect.) garments etc. orig. of linen, now of other materials; undergarments, bed linen, table linen.

lin·er[1] (lī'ner) *n.* Ship belonging to line of passenger ships; aircraft belonging to a regular line, esp. for passenger transport.

lin·er[2] (lī'ner) *n.* Removable metal lining to prevent wear and tear in guns or other machinery; removable substance for lining.

lines·man (līnz'man) *n.* (pl. **-men** pr. -mĕn). Official assisting umpire or referee by deciding whether or where ball touches or crosses line.

Flax is the plant which produces the fiber to make ***linen.*** *Here it is seen drying in racks, just one of the processes involved in extracting the fiber. Linen has been used extensively since the time of the pharaohs.*

ling (lĭng) *n.* (collect. **ling**, pl. **lings**). Long slender N. European sea fish (*Molva molva*) used (often salted or split and dried) for food.

lin·ger (lĭng'ger) *v.i.* Put off departure, esp. from reluctance to go; stay about, not depart or arrive at expected or right time; dally *around* place, *over*, *on*, subject; drag *on* a feeble existence; be protracted; be tardy, delay. ~ *v.t.* Throw (time) *away* in delays. **lin'ger·er** *n.* **lin'ger·ing·ly** *adv.*

lin·ge·rie (lahnzherā', lăn'zherē, -je-) *n.* Women's underclothes.

lin·go (lĭng'gō) *n.* (pl. **-goes**). (slang) Foreign language; language belonging to special subject or class of people. [corrupt. of LINGUA (FRANCA)]

lin·gua fran·ca (lĭng'gwa frăng'ka) (pl. **lin·gua fran·cas, lin·guae fran·cae** pr. lĭng'gwē frăn'sē). 1. Mixture of Italian, French, Greek, and Spanish, used in Levant. 2. Any language spoken or understood by various peoples over a wide area. [It., = "Frankish tongue"]

lin·gual (lĭng'gwal) *adj.* Of the tongue; of speech or languages. **lin'gual·ly** *adv.*

lin·gui·form (lĭng'gwifōrm) *adj.* (bot., anat., zool.) Tongue-shaped.

lin·guist (lĭng'gwĭst) *n.* Person skilled in (foreign) languages. **lin·guis·tic** (lĭnggwĭs'tĭk) *adj.* Of the study of languages; of language. **lin·guis'ti·cal·ly** *adv.* **lin·guis'tics** *n.* Study of language.

lin·i·ment (lĭn'iment) *n.* Liquid preparation, usu. made with oil, for application to the skin as treatment for sprains.

link[1] (lĭngk) *n.* One ring or loop of chain; as measure, $\frac{1}{100}$ of surveying chain, 7.92 in.; CUFF[1]-link; connecting part, thing or person that unites others, filler of gap, member of series; **missing** ~: see MISSING. **link** *v.* Connect, join *together*, *to*, or *up*; clasp (hands);

hook (arms, arm *in* or *through* another's); attach oneself *on*, *in*, to system, company, etc.

link[2] (lĭngk) *n.* Torch of pitch and tow formerly used for lighting people along streets and carried by **link'man** or **link'boy**.

link·age (lĭng'kĭj) *n.* 1. Act, state, or condition of being linked. 2. (esp. biol.) Relative inseparability of two or more heritable characteristics owing to their factors being in the same chromosome.

links (lĭngks) *n.pl.* Level or undulating sandy ground near seashore, with turf and coarse grass (Sc.); golf course.

Lin·nae·us (lĭnē'*us*), **Carolus** (1707–78). Latinized name of Carl von Linné, Swedish botanist; originator of system of taxonomy. **Lin·nae'an, Lin·ne'an** *adjs.* Of Linnaeus; (esp.) of his system of botanical binomial classification, dividing all plants into 24 classes, most of which were based on the number or arrangement of stamens.

lin·net (lĭn'ĭt) *n.* Common brown or warm-gray Old World songbird, *Carduelis cannabina*. [Fr. *lin* flax, seeds of which are its food]

li·no·le·um (lĭnō'lē*u*m) *n.* Floor covering of canvas coated with oxidized linseed oil and usu. pigments.

Lin·o·type (lī'notīp) *n.* (trademark) Machine that casts a slug or line of type from a line of assembled and justified matrices at a single operation of casting. **lin'o·typ·er** *n.* [= *line o' type*]

lin·sang (lĭn'săng) *n.* 1. Member of an oriental genus (**L**~) of civet cats resembling the true cats in several features. 2. African civet cat of genus *Poiana*.

lin·seed (lĭn'sēd) *n.* Seed of flax; ~ **cake**, linseed pressed into cake in process of extracting oil and used as cattle food; ~ **oil**, oil obtained by pressure from linseed.

lin·sey-wool·sey (lĭn'zē wo͝ol'-zē) *n.* (pl. **-seys**). Dress material of cotton (orig. linen) warp and wool weft; (fig.) any incongruous mixture.

lin·stock (lĭn'stŏk) *n.* (hist.) Staff with forked end to hold lighted match, used for applying fire to touchhole of a cannon.

lint (lĭnt) *n.* Soft material for dressing wounds, obtained by raveling or scraping linen cloth; fluff of any material; raw cotton fiber. **lint'er** *n.* Machine for stripping off short-staple cotton fiber from cottonseed after ginning; (pl.) these fibers. **lint'y** *adj.* (**lint·i·er, lint·i·est**).

lin·tel (lĭn'tel) *n.* Horizontal timber or stone over door or window.

Li·nus (lī'n*u*s). (Gk. myth.) Hero whose untimely death was celebrated in a dirge sung annually at harvest time; perhaps orig. a corn spirit.

li·on (lī'*o*n) *n.* (pl. **lions**, collect. **lion**). 1. Large member of cat family, a powerful tawny carnivore (*Felis leo*), with tufted tail and (in the male) a mane, now native only in Africa and S. Asia. 2. Courageous person. 3. Person of literary or other celebrity much sought after for social gatherings. 4. Lion as national emblem of Great Britain. 5. **the L**~: see LEO[1]. 6. **(American) mountain** ~, puma; ~ **and unicorn**, supporters of English royal arms; **li'on-hearted**, courageous; **lion hunter**, person who makes much of celebrities; **Lion of Lucerne**, lion carved in rock at Lucerne, Switzerland, as monument to Swiss Guards who fell defending Louis XVI of France in attack on Tuileries, 1792; **Lion of St. Mark**, winged lion as emblem of St. Mark (from traditional interpretation of Ezek. 1), esp. that in Piazzetta of Venice, of which city he is patron saint; **Lion of the North**, Gustavus Adolphus, king of Sweden; **lion's mouth**, perilous position; **lion's share**, largest or best part. **li·on·ess** (lī'*o*nĭs) *n.* Female lion.

li·on·ize (lī'*o*nīz) *v.t.* (**-ized, -iz·ing**). Treat (person) as celebrity.

*The **linnet** is native to Europe, north Africa and central Asia. It is seed-eating and is brownish-grey and white. About 5 inches long, it is found in hedgerows. Flocks of linnets forage for seed in open country.*

*The **lion**, the 'king of beasts', has been, since earliest times, one of the best known of wild animals. It inhabits open country and is found mainly in Africa south of the Sahara, living often in groups or prides. Above: Lion feeding on a wildebeest carcass. Below: Lion family.*

lip (lĭp) *n.* 1. One of the fleshy edges of the opening of the mouth; edge of cup, vessel, cavity, wound, etc.; (slang) insolent talk; **bite one's ~**, show vexation; repress emotion; **hang on the ~s of**, listen with rapt attention to; **keep a stiff upper ~**, (slang) face adversity courageously; **smack one's ~s**, express relish for food; (fig.) express delight. 2. (attrib., phon.) Formed or produced by lips; **~ reading**, understanding (esp. by deaf person) of what another says by watching movements of lips; **~ salve**, ointment for sore lips; (fig.) flattery; **~ service**, devotion expressed in words only, superficial respect; **lip′stick**, stick of cosmetic for coloring lips; **lip sync, lip synch**, synchronization of filmed or live lip movements with previously recorded sound. **lip** *v.t.* (**lipped, lip·ping**). Touch with lips, apply lips to; (of water) lap.

li·pid (lī′pĭd, lĭp′ĭd) *n.* (chem.) Substance that has the general properties of fats but is not necessarily a glyceride.

Li Po (lē′pō′; *Chin.* lē′baw′) = LI TAI PO.

Lip·pi (lĭp′ē; *It.* lē′pē). Name of two Florentine painters of the early Renaissance: **Fra Filippo** or **Lippo ~** (1406–69), and **Filippo** or **Filippino ~** (1457–1504), his natural son.

Fra Filippo Lippi, the 15th-century Florentine painter, was the father of Filippino Lippi. His best known works are brilliant frescoes in the Prato Cathedral, such as the 'Virgin and Child' below.

li·quate (lī′kwāt) *v.t.* (**-quat·ed, -quat·ing**). Separate or purify (metals) by liquefying. **li·qua·tion** (lĭkwā′shon) *n.*

liq·ue·fy (lĭk′wefī) *v.* (**-fied, -fy·ing**). Reduce to liquid condition; become liquid. **liq·ue·fa·cient** (lĭkwefā′shent), **liq·ue·fac·tion** (lĭkwefăk′shon) *ns.*

li·ques·cent (lĭkwĕs′ent) *adj.* Becoming, apt to become, liquid.

li·queur (lĭkẽr′; *Brit.* lĭkūr′) *n.* Strong sweet drink with base of brandy or other spirit and flavoring of aromatic substances, taken in small quantities usu. after meals; mixture of sugar and certain wines, or sugar and alcohol, used to flavor champagne; **~ glass**, very small glass for liqueurs.

liq·uid (lĭk′wĭd) *adj.* In that condition (the normal condition of water, oil, etc.) in which particles move freely over each other but do not tend to separate like those of gases, fluid; watery; having the transparency, translucence, or brightness, of water or wine; (of sounds) flowing clear, fluent, pure, not grating or discordant, not guttural, vowel-like; not fixed, unstable; (of assets, securities, etc.) easily convertible into cash; **~ air**, air reduced to the liquid state under high pressure and low temperature, used as a refrigerant. **liq′uid·ly** *adv.* **liq′uid·ness, li·quid·i·ty** (lĭkwĭd′ĭtē) *ns.* **liq·uid·ize** (lĭk′widīz) *v.t.* (**-ized, -iz·ing**). **liquid** *n.* 1. Liquid substance. 2. (phon.) Sound of one of the letters *l*, *r* (and sometimes *m*, *n*).

liq·ui·date (lĭk′widāt) *v.* (**-dat·ed, -dat·ing**). Pay, clear off, (debt); wind up, ascertain liabilities and apportion assets of, (company, firm); go into liquidation; put an end to, stamp out, wipe out. **liq·ui·da·tion** (lĭkwidā′shon) *n.* **go into ~**, (of company) have its affairs wound up, become bankrupt.

liq·uor (defs. 1 and 2 lĭk′er; def. 3 lĭk′wōr) *n.* 1. Liquid part of secretion or product of chemical operation; liquid used as wash etc.; water used in brewing; liquid contained in oysters. 2. Liquid (usu. fermented or distilled) for drinking. 3. (pharm. etc.) Solution of specified drug in water.

li·quo·rice = LICORICE.

li·ra (lēr′a; *It.* lē′rah) *n.* (pl. **li·re** pr. lēr′ā; *It.* lē′rĕ, **li·ras**). Principal monetary unit of Italy and Turkey.

Lis·bon (lĭz′bon). Capital city and port of Portugal.

*The **mountain lion** or puma is found in the New World from British Columbia to Patagonia in habitats as varied as mountains, deserts and jungles. In some regions, however, it is extinct.*

Lisbon is the capital of Portugal and a great port at the mouth of the Tagus. In 1755 an earthquake destroyed half the city which was afterwards rebuilt. Shown here is the National Pantheon.

lisle (līl) *n.* (also ~ **thread**) Fine smooth thread (orig. linen, now cotton) used in manufacture of stockings etc. [former spelling of *Lille* in France]

lisp (lĭsp) *v.* Substitute sound approaching that of English *th* for sibilants in speaking; (of child) speak with imperfect pronunciation. ~ *n.* Lisping pronunciation; (poet.) sound resembling this. **lisp'er** *n.* **lisp'ing·ly** *adv.*

lis·some, lis·som (lĭs'*o*m) *adjs.* Lithe, supple, agile. **lis'some·ly, lis'som·ly** *advs.* **lis'some·ness, lis'som·ness** *ns.*

list[1] (lĭst) *n.* 1. Selvage or edge of cloth, usu. of different material; such edges used for slippers, cushions, etc. 2. (pl.) Palisades enclosing tilting ground (see TILT[2] *n.* def. 2); this ground; (fig.) scene of contest.

list[2] (lĭst) *n.* Roll or catalog of names, of persons or things belonging to a class, of articles with prices, of things to be done etc. ~ *v.* Enter in list.

list[3] (lĭst) *n.* Inclination of ship etc. to one side (owing to leak, shifting cargo, etc.). ~ *v.i.* Lean over to one side.

list[4] (lĭst) *v.* (archaic) Listen, listen to.

lis·ten (lĭs'*e*n) *v.* Make effort to hear something, hear with attention, give ear *to*; yield *to* temptation or request; ~ **in**, tap telephonic communication; listen to radio transmission. **lis'ten·er** *n.*

Lis·ter (lĭs'*t*er), **Joseph, 1st Baron Lister** (1827–1912). English surgeon; founder of antiseptic surgery.

list·less (lĭst'lĭs) *adj.* Languid; without interest. **list'less·ly** *adv.* **list'less·ness** *n.*

Liszt (lĭst), **Franz** (1811–86). Hungarian pianist and composer, whose best-known compositions are his "Hungarian Rhapsodies."

lit (lĭt): see LIGHT[3].

Li Tai Po (lē'tī'pō'; *Chin.* lē'tī'baw') (*c*701–62). One of the greatest Chinese poets.

lit·a·ny (lĭt'*a*nē) *n.* (pl. **-nies**). Series of petitions for use in church services or processions, recited by clergy and responded to usu. in recurring formula(s) by people.

li·tchi, li·chee, li·chi (lē'chē) *ns.* (pl. **-tchis, -chees, -chis**). Sweetish pulpy fruit with shell and single seed; tree bearing this (*Litchi chinensis*) orig. from China, now grown in Bengal and S. Africa.

li·ter, Brit. **li·tre** (lē*t*er) *ns.* Unit of capacity in the metric system, one cubic decimeter (approx. 0.22 gal.).

lit·er·a·cy (lĭt'*e*rasē) *n.* Ability to read and write.

lit·er·al (lĭt'*e*ral) *adj.* Of, in, expressed by, letter(s) of alphabet; following the letter, text, or exact or original words; taking words in their usual or primary sense without mysticism, allegory, or metaphor; so called, so described without exaggeration; (of persons) prosaic, matter-of-fact. **lit'er·al·ly** *adv.* **lit'er·al·ness, lit'er·al·ism, lit·er·al·i·ty** (lĭterăl'ĭtē) *ns.*

lit·er·ar·y (lĭt'*e*rĕrē) *adj.* Of, constituting, occupied with, literature, polite learning, or books and written records esp. of the kind valued for form; (of word etc.) uncolloquial, affected by writers; ~ **property**, property consisting of written or printed compositions; exclusive right of publication as recognized and limited by law. **lit'er·ar·i·ly** *adv.* **lit'er·ar·i·ness** *n.*

lit·er·ate (lĭt'*e*rĭt) *adj.* Having some acquaintance with literature; (now usu.) able to read and write. ~ *n.* Literate person.

lit·e·ra·ti (lĭterah'tē, -rā'tī) *n.pl.* Men or women of letters; literate or learned class.

lit·er·a·ture (lĭt'*e*racher, -choor, lĭt'*r*a-) *n.* Literary culture (archaic); literary production, the literary profession; realm of letters; writings of a country or period; writings whose value lies in beauty of form or emotional effect; books etc. treating *of* a subject; (colloq.) printed matter.

lith·arge (lĭth'ārj, lĭthārj') *n.* Lead monoxide (PbO), a hard yellowish-red crystalline substance, prepared by prolonged heating of lead in air, used in the paint and varnish industry and in the manufacture of lead glazes.

lithe (līdh) *adj.* (**lith·er, lith·est**). Flexible, supple. **lithe'ness** *n.* **lithe'some** *adj.*

lith·i·a (lĭth'ēa, -ya) *n.* Lithium monoxide (Li_2O); ~ **water**, mineral water containing lithium salts.

lith·ic[1] (lĭth'ĭk) *adj.* Of the stone or calculus; of stone.

lith·ic[2] (lĭth'ĭk) *adj.* (chem.) Of lithium.

lith·i·um (lĭth'ēum) *n.* (chem.) Soft, silver-white metallic element, the lightest of the alkali metals, occurring in small quantities in various minerals; symbol Li, at. no.

3, at. wt. 6.941.

lith·o·graph (lĭth'ŏgrăf, -grahf) *n.* Print taken from stone block which, after design is traced on it with greasy chalk, is so treated with acid, gum, and water that the unchalked parts reject ink and make no impression; print produced (from stone or metal) by variants of this process. **li·thog·ra·phy** (lĭthŏg'rafē) *n.* 1. Art or process of producing a lithograph. 2. Printing process based on this method but using flexible metal plates instead of stones. See also PHOTOLITHOGRAPHY. **lith·o·graph·ic** (lĭthográf'ĭk) *adj.* **lith'o·graph** *v.i.* Produce, copy, by lithographic process.

li·thol·o·gy (lĭthŏl'ojē) *n.* Science of the nature and composition of stones and rocks. **lith·o·log·i·cal** (lĭtholŏj'ĭkal) *adj.*

lith·o·phyte (lĭth'ofīt) *n.* 1. (zool.) Polyp whose skeletal substance is calcareous, as some corals. 2. (bot.) Plant that grows on stone.

lith·o·sphere (lĭth'osfēr) *n.* (geol.) Outer crust of Earth, consisting of soil and rock, dist. from the BARYSPHERE, which it encloses and the HYDROSPHERE, through which it projects to form the continents.

li·thot·o·my (lĭthŏt'omē) *n.* (pl. **-mies**). Operation of cutting into the bladder and removing stone.

Lith·u·a·ni·a (lĭth o͞oā'nēa). Area between Latvia and Poland, on the Baltic Sea; formerly a Baltic province of the Russian Empire; declared an independent republic in 1918; incorporated in 1940 in the U.S.S.R., of which it is a constituent republic (properly *Lithuanian Soviet Socialist Republic*); capital, Vilnius (Vilna). **Lith·u·a'ni·an** *adj.* & *n.* 1. (native, inhabitant) of Lithuania. 2. (Of) the language of the Lithuanians, one of the highly inflected Baltic group of Indo-European languages.

lit·i·gate (lĭt'igāt) *v.* (**-gat·ed, -gat·ing**). Go to law, be party to lawsuit; contest (point) at law. **lit'i·gant** *adj.* & *n.* **lit·i·ga·tion** (lĭtigā'shon) *n.*

li·ti·gious (lĭtĭj'us) *adj.* Given to litigation, fond of going to law; disputable at law, offering matter for lawsuit; of lawsuits. **li·ti'gious·ly** *adv.* **li·ti'gious·ness** *n.*

lit·mus (lĭt'mus) *n.* Blue coloring matter from lichens that is turned red by acids and restored to blue by alkalis; ~ **paper**, unsized paper stained with litmus, as test for acids etc.

lit·o·ral = LITTORAL.

li·to·tes (lī'totēz, -tō-, lĭt'o-, lītō'tēz) *n.* (pl. **-tes**). Ironically moderate form of speech, esp. expression of affirmative by negative of its contrary, as *not bad* for *good.*

li·tre = LITER.

Litt.D. *abbrev. Litterarum doctor* (L., = Doctor of Letters).

*The main stages of **lithographic** printing. Left to right: The drawing is done on the lithographic stone with a stylus. A thin film of nitric acid is spread over the stone. The stone is inked and only the inscribed portions become impregnated with ink. The print is taken by placing the sheet of paper on the lithographic stone and applying pressure. Below: Lithograph of the Crystal Palace, London, by Vincent Brooks.*

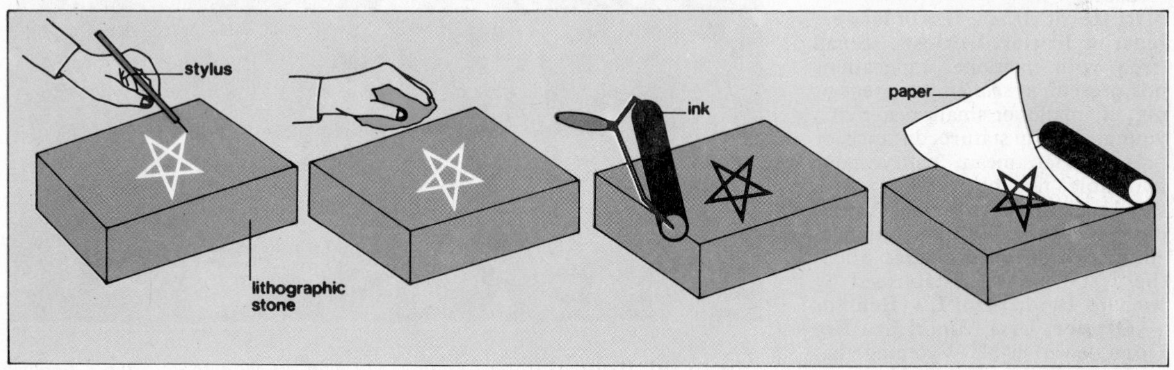

Lithuania, a constituent republic of the U.S.S.R. on the Baltic Sea, is a low-lying region with many lakes. Its chief industries are heavy engineering and shipbuilding.

lit·ter (lĭt′*er*) *n.* 1. Vehicle containing bed shut in by curtains and carried on men's shoulders or by beasts; framework with couch for transporting sick and wounded. 2. Straw, rushes, etc., as bedding esp. for animals; straw and dung of farmyard. 3. Odds and ends, leavings; state of untidiness; disorderly accumulation of papers etc. 4. Young (of sow, bitch, etc.) brought forth at one birth. ~ *v.* 1. provide (horse etc.) with litter as bed; spread litter or straw on stable floor etc. 2. Make (place) untidy; scatter and leave lying. 3. (of animals) Bring forth (young).

lit·té·ra·teur, lit·te·ra·teur (lĭterat*ẽr*′; *Fr.* lētĕrahtör′) *ns.* (pl. **-teurs** pr. -t*ẽr*z′; *Fr.* -tör′). Literary man. [Fr.]

lit·ter·bug (lĭt′*er*bŭg) *n.* One who carelessly litters streets, buildings, etc., with papers and other refuse.

lit·tle (lĭt′*el*) *adj.* (**less** or **less·er, least** or **lit·tler, lit·tlest**). Small (freq. with emotional implications not present in *small*); not great or big; of smaller or smallest size etc.; young; short in stature, distance, or time; trivial; mean, paltry, contemptible; not much; **in ~**, on a small scale; **L~ America**, American bases for polar exploration in Antarctica on the Ross Ice Shelf; the first base was established by Richard Byrd, 1929; **L~ Bear** or **~ Dipper**, Ursa Minor; **L~ Big Horn**, river in N. Wyoming that joins the Bighorn in S. Montana; along its banks Gen. Custer and his troops were defeated and wiped out by the Indians, 1876; **L~ League**, baseball league for children of ages 8 to 12; **~ magazine**, literary magazine, usu. with experimental writing and in small format; **littleneck**, small young quahog clam suitable for eating raw; **Little Missouri**, river flowing from NE. Wyoming 560 miles (902 km) to the Missouri in North Dakota; **Little Rock**, capital of Arkansas, in the center of the state, on the Arkansas River; **little theater**, small theater, esp. an amateur repertory theater; drama suited to this. **little** *n.* Not much, only a small amount, a mere trifle; a certain but no great amount; (for a) short time or distance; **a ~**, rather, somewhat; **~ by ~**, by degrees; **~ or nothing**, hardly anything; **make ~ of**, look upon or dismiss as unimportant; disparage; **not a ~**, to a great degree; **think ~ of**, consider insignificant or trivial. **little** *adv.* (**less, least**). To a small extent only; not at all.

David Livingstone, the Scottish missionary and explorer in Central Africa, discovered the Victoria Falls (1855) and explored the upper reaches of the Congo River.

lit·to·ral, lit·o·ral (lĭt′*er*al) *adjs.* Of, on, near, the shore. ~ *n.* Region lying along the shore, esp. land lying between high and low tide levels.

lit·ur·gy (lĭt′*er*jē) *n.* (pl. **-gies**). 1. Communion office of Eastern Church. 2. Form of public worship, set of formularies for this. **li·tur·gi·cal** (lĭt*ẽr*′jĭk*a*l) *adj.* **li·tur′gi·cal·ly** *adv.*

live[1] (līv) *adj.* (**liv·er, liv·est**). That is alive, living; full of power, energy, or importance, not obsolete or exhausted; (of combustibles) glowing; (of shell, bomb, etc.) unexploded, unkindled; (of wire) charged with electricity; (of parts of machinery etc.) moving or imparting motion; (of broadcast) heard, viewed, during its occurrence, not recorded; **~ bait**, living fish or worm as fishing bait; **~ oak**, American evergreen oak (*Quercus virginiana*), of southern Atlantic states; **live′stock**, domestic animals kept or dealt in for use or profit; **live wire**, (fig.) person full of energy.

live[2] (lĭv) *v.* (**lived, liv·ing**). 1. Be alive, have animal or vegetable life; subsist *on*; depend *on* for subsistence; get livelihood *by* (one's wits etc.); (fig.) sustain one's position or repute (*on*). 2. Conduct oneself, arrange one's habits, expenditure, feeding, etc., in specified way; spend, pass, experience (life, day, etc.); wear *down* (scandal, prejudice, etc.) by blameless course of life; express in one's life; **~ a double life**, sustain two different characters, act two different parts, in life; **~ together**, (esp. of unmarried couples) share living quarters; **~ up to**, (principles, faith, etc.) put (them) into practice; **~ with**, tolerate, find congenial; share living quarters with. 3. Enjoy life intensely; **~ it up**, (colloq.) live gaily and extravagantly. 4. Continue alive, have one's life prolonged; (of things) survive; (of ship) escape destruction. 5. Dwell; spend daytime *in* room; **~ in, out,**

Little Rock, Arkansas takes its name from two rock formations named by explorer La Harpe in 1722, La Petite Roche and La Grande Roche.

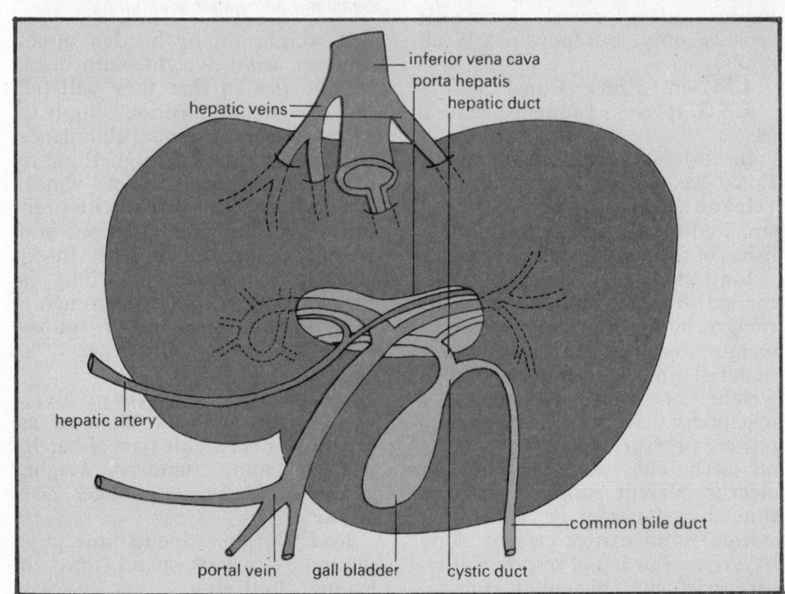

*The functions of the **liver** include: the regulation of blood volume; the manufacture of certain blood-clotting factors; the metabolism of proteins, carbohydrates and fats; and the formation of bile.*

(of servant or employee), reside on, off, premises where one works. **liv'a·ble, live'a·ble** *adjs.* Fit to live in; that can be lived, bearable; easy to live with, companionable.

live·li·hood (līv'lēhŏŏd) *n.* Means of living, sustenance.

live·long (lĭv'lawng, -lŏng) *adj.* (poet., rhet., of time) Whole length of (with implication of weariness or delight).

live·ly (līv'lē) *adj.* (**-li·er, -li·est**). Lifelike, realistic; full of life, energetic, brisk, interesting; (of color) bright, gay; (of boat etc.) rising lightly to waves; (joc.) exciting, dangerous, difficult. **live'ly** *adv.* **live'li·ness** *n.*

liv·en (lī'ven) *v.* Brighten (*up*).

liv·er[1] (lĭv'*er*) *n.* Large dark-red organ in abdomen of vertebrates, the chief site of metabolic reactions, also functioning as a gland, secreting bile; organ of similar function in other animals; flesh of animals' liver used as food; color of liver, dark reddish brown; diseased state of liver; (archaic) liver as set of emotion; **lily ~**, cowardice; **~ fluke**, flatworm parasitic in the liver, esp. (*Fasciola hepatica*) in liver of sheep; **liv'er-wort**, primitive seedless plant allied to mosses. **liv'er·ish** *adj.* Having symptoms of disordered liver; feeling out of sorts, irritable.

liv·er[2] (lĭv'*er*) *n.* One who lives in specified way, esp. **high ~**, who lives extravagantly.

liv·er·ied (lĭv'*er*ēd, lĭv'rēd) *adj.* Wearing livery.

Liv·er·pool (lĭv'*er*pōōl). City and seaport on the Mersey estuary in SW. Lancashire, England. **Liv·er·pud·li·an** (lĭv*er*pŭd'lē*an*) *n.* Person who is born in or lives in Liverpool.

liv·er·wurst (lĭv'*er*wērst, -woorst) *n.* Sausage made with a large amount of chopped pork liver.

liv·er·y (lĭv'*er*ē, lĭv'rē) *n.* (pl. **-er·ies**). 1. Allowance of food or clothing provided esp. for retainers etc. (hist.); allowance of provender for horses; **at ~**, (of horse) kept for owner and fed and groomed for fixed charge. 2. Distinctive clothes worn by a male servant. 3. (law) Legal delivery of property, writ allowing this; **liv'er·y·man**, keeper of or attendant in livery stable; **livery stable**, stable where horses are kept at livery or let out for hire.

Liv·i·a (lĭv'ē*a*) (58 B.C.–29 A.D.). Roman empress; wife of Tiberius Claudius Nero and mother by him of the Emperor Tiberius; married Octavian (Augustus) after her divorce from her first husband.

liv·id (lĭv'ĭd) *adj.* Of bluish leaden color; discolored as by bruise; (colloq.) furiously angry. **liv'id·ly** *adv.* **li·vid·i·ty** (lĭvĭd'ĭtē), **liv'id·ness** *ns.*

liv·ing (lĭv'ĭng) *n.* (esp.) 1. Livelihood, maintenance; **~ room**, room for general day use; **~ wage**, one on which it is possible to live. 2. (eccles.) Benefice. **living** *adj.* (esp.) 1. Contemporary, now existent; **the ~**, those now alive; **in the land of the ~**, alive; **within ~ memory**, within memory of persons still living. 2. (of likeness) Exact. 3. (of rock) Native, in native condition and site, as part of Earth's crust.

Liv·ing·stone (lĭv'ĭngst*o*n), **David** (1813–73). Scottish medical missionary in central Africa; explored the course of the Zambesi and the sources of the Nile; was thought to be missing in Africa and was searched for and found by HENRY STANLEY, 1871, whose first words to him were, "Dr. Livingstone, I presume?"

Liv·ing·stone (lĭv'ĭngst*o*n) **Mountains.** Range of high land in Tanzania.

Liv·y (lĭv´ē). **Titus Livius** (59 B.C.–17 A.D.), Roman historian; author of a history of Rome (*Annales*) from the foundation of the city to the death of Drusus (9 B.C.).

lix·iv·i·ate (lĭksĭv´ēāt) *v.t.* (**-at·ed, -at·ing**). Separate (substance) into soluble and insoluble constituents by percolation of water. **lix·iv·i·a·tion** (lĭksĭvēā´sh*o*n) *n.*

liz·ard (lĭz´*e*rd) *n.* Reptile of suborder Lacertilia, related to snakes but distinguished by having (usu.) four legs, movable eyelids, eardrums, and fleshy tongue.

ll. *abbrev.* Lines.

lla·ma (lah´m*a*) *n.* S. Amer. mammal (*Lama glama*) related to the camel but smaller, humpless, and woolly-haired, used as beast of burden; (material made of) its wool; **the ~s**, (zool.) group of camellike S. Amer. mammals including, besides the llama, the alpaca, huanaco, and vicuna.

lla·no (lah´nō; *Sp.* yah´nō) *n.* (pl. **-nos** pr. -nōz; *Sp.* -nōs). Treeless grassland of Orinoco basin and Guiana highlands in S. America.

LL.B., LL.D. *abbrevs. Legum baccalaureus, doctor* (L., = Bachelor, Doctor, of Laws).

Llew·el·lyn (lo͞oĕl´lĭn). Name of two Welsh princes; **~ ab Iorwerth** (d. 1240) and **~ ab Gruffydd** (d. 1282), his nephew, last Welsh prince of Wales.

Lloyd George (loid jōrj´), **David, 1st Earl Loyd George of Dwyfor** (1863–1945). British Liberal politician; coalition prime minister 1916–22.

Lloyd's (loidz). (also **~ of London**) London association of underwriters (orig. meeting in coffeehouse opened by Edward Lloyd 1688) and agency for arranging insurance (formerly marine insurance only, but now nearly all kinds).

The **llama,** a domesticated animal related to the camel, is a native of South America. Used primarily as a beast of burden, its wool is woven and it is also killed for meat.

Lloyd George at his home in Surrey. As Britain's chancellor of the exchequer (1908–15) he introduced many social reforms in the U.K. including old age pensions and national insurance.

LM (lĕm) *abbrev.* Lunar module.

LNG *abbrev.* Liquefied natural gas.

lo (lō) *int.* (archaic and poet.) Look! see!

loach (lōch) *n.* Any of several small edible European fresh-water fishes of the subfamily Cobitidinae.

load (lōd) *n.* What is (to be) carried, burden; amount usu. carried, recognized unit in measure or weight of certain substances; material object or force acting as weight or clog, resistance of machinery worked to motive power, pressure of superstructure on arch etc., total amount of electric current supplied at given time by dynamo or generating station; solid matter carried along by a river; burden of responsibility, care, grief, etc.; (pl., colloq.) plenty, superabundance, heaps, lots, *of*; **take a ~ off someone's mind**, relieve him of anxiety; **~-shedding**, cutting off of the electricity supply to an area as a means of avoiding excessive loading of generating plant; **load´star**: see LODE; **load´stone, lode´stone**, variety of magnetite; piece of it used as magnet; thing that attracts. **load** *v.* 1. Put load on or aboard, take load aboard, etc.; place (load, cargo) aboard ship, on vehicle, etc.; add weight to, be burden upon, oppress *with*; weight with lead; weight *dice* so that they will fall into a particular position; supply in excess or overwhelming abundance *with*; adulterate with something to increase weight or (of wines) strength; charge (words) with prejudicial meaning or emotion; add weight to (arguments). 2. Insert charge or ammunition into (a firearm); insert film into (camera). **load´ed** *adj.* (esp. slang) 1. Intoxicated by alcohol or drugs. 2. Wealthy.

loaf[1] (lōf) *n.* (pl. **loaves** pr. lōvz). Piece of bread baked alone or as separate or separable part of batch, usu. of some standard weight; conical molded mass of sugar (also **sugar ~**).

loaf[2] (lōf) *v.* Spend time idly; saunter; **~ away**, spend (time) in loafing. **loaf´er** *n.*

loam (lōm) *n.* 1. Fertile soil chiefly of clay and sand with admixture of decayed vegetable matter; (geog.) deposit of mixed sand, silt, and clay. 2. Paste of clay and water; composition of moistened clay and sand with chopped straw etc., used in making bricks. **loam´y** *adj.* (**loam·i·er, loam·i·est**).

There are some 3,000 species of **lizard** which are grouped in the reptile order Lacertilia. Except for legless varieties, all have four legs and differ from snakes by having movable eyelids and openings to the ears. They are found in most parts of the world but are most numerous in warmer regions.

Nile monitor
plumed basilisk lizard
flying (draco) lizard
frilled lizard
blue-tongued skink
common lizard
slow-worm
horned lizard

loan (lōn) *n.* Thing, esp. sum of money, lent to be returned with or without interest; word, custom, etc., adopted by one people from another; lending or being lent; ~ **shark**, (colloq.) person who lends money at excessive interest rates; usurer; ~ **word**, word adopted from another language. **loan** *v.t.* Lend.

loath, loth (lōth, lōdh) *adjs.* Disinclined, reluctant, unwilling; **nothing** ~, very willing(ly).

loathe (lōdh) *v.t.* (**loathed, loath·ing**). Regard with disgust, abominate, detest. **loath'ing** *n.* **loath'ing·ly** *adv.*

loath·some (lōdh'som, lōth'-) *adj.* Exciting nausea or disgust, offensive to the senses, odious. **loath'some·ly** *adv.* **loath'some·ness** *n.*

lob (lŏb) *v.* (**lobbed, lob·bing**). Walk, run, or move, heavily, clumsily, or slowly; toss, bowl, strike, (ball) slowly or with high arc motion. ~ *n.* Ball sent high in air in tennis or other sport.

lo·bate (lō'bāt) *adj.* (biol.) Having lobe(s). **lo'bate·ly** *adv.* **lo·ba·tion** (lōbā'shon) *n.*

lob·by (lŏb'ē) *n.* (pl. **-bies**). Porch, anteroom, entrance hall, corridor. ~ *v.* (**-bied, -by·ing**). Influence (member of legislature), get (bill etc.) *through* by personal solicitation; frequent a legislature to solicit members' votes. **lob'by·ism, lob'by·ist** *ns.*

lobe (lōb) *n.* Roundish and flattish projecting or pendulous part of an organ, often one of two or more such parts divided by fissure, esp. of cerebrum or lung; lower soft pendulous external part of ear. **lobed** (lōbd) *adj.*

lo·bel·ia (lōbēl'ya) *n.* Herbaceous (rarely shrubby) plant of genus *L*~, with blue, scarlet, purple, or white flowers having deeply cleft corolla without spur. [M. de *Lobel* (1538–1616), Flemish botanist and physician to James I]

lob·lol·ly (lŏb'lŏlē) *n.* (pl. **-lies**). (also ~ **pine**) Tree (*Pinus taeda*) growing in swamps in southern U.S.

lo·bot·o·my (lōbŏt'omē) *n.* (pl. **-mies**). (surg.) Cutting a lobe of the brain, esp. in treatment of mental disorders.

lob·scouse (lŏb'skows) *n.* (naut.) Dish of meat stewed with vegetables and ship's biscuit.

lob·ster (lŏb'ster) *n.* (pl. **-sters**, collect. **-ster**). Large marine crustacean of family Homaridae, a decapod having a pair of heavy pincerlike claws and stalked eyes, which is eaten as a delicacy and turns from bluish black to bright red when boiled; its flesh as food; ~**-eyed**, with protruding eyes; ~ **pot**, basket in which lobsters are trapped.

The 200–300 species of ***lobelia*** *are native to tropical and sub-tropical areas. Many have been grown for their flowers including the trailing variety (above).*

lob·ule (lŏb'ūl) *n.* Small lobe. **lob·u·lar** (lŏb'ūler) *adj.*

lob·worm (lŏb'wērm) *n.* Large earthworm used as fishing bait; lugworm.

lo·cal (lō'kal) *adj.* 1. Of, concerned with, place; in regard to place. 2. Belonging to, existing in, or peculiar to, certain place(s); ~ **authority**, body charged with administration of local government; ~ **color**, details characteristic of the scene or time represented in novel or other literary work, inserted to give actuality; the peculiar nature or flavor of a place; ~ **government**, system of administration of local affairs by local authorities; ~ **option**, system by which inhabitants of district may prohibit sale of liquor in it. 3. Affecting, of, a part and not the whole (~ **anesthetic, pain, remedy**); ~ **color**, (in picture) that natural to particular objects as distinct from that seen by painter or chosen for sake of color scheme (see also sense 2 above). 4. (math.) Of a locus. 5. ~ **call**, telephone call to nearby place, charged at local rate. **lo'cal·ly** *adv.* **local** *n.* 1. Person living or working in a particular district. 2. Local train or bus. 3. Local or regional branch of trade union etc.

lo·cale (lōkăl', -kahl') *n.* Scene or locality of operations or events.

lo·cal·ism (lō'kalĭzem) *n.* Attachment to a place; limitation of ideas etc., resulting; favoring of what is local; local idiom, custom, etc.

lo·cal·i·ty (lōkăl'ĭtē) *n.* (pl. **-ties**). Position of something, place where it is, site or scene of something.

lo·cal·ize (lō'kalīz) *v.t.* (**-ized, -iz·ing**). Invest with characteristics or particular place; restrict to particular place; attach to districts, decentralize; concentrate (attention) *upon*. **lo'cal·iz·a·ble** *adj.* **lo·cal·i·za·tion** (lōkalīzā'shon) *n.*

Lo·car·no (lōkar'nō). Town at N. end of Lake Maggiore, Switzerland; **Pact (Treaty) of** ~, series of agreements drawn up at Locarno, 1925, for peace and arbitration and signed by representatives of Germany, France, Belgium, Great Britain, Italy, Poland, and Czechoslovakia.

lo·cate (lō'kāt, lōkāt') *v.* (**-cat·ed, -cat·ing**). Establish in a place; (pass.) be situated; state locality of; discover exact place of; take up residence, settle. **lo·ca'tion** *n.* (esp. cinemat.) Place, other than studio, chosen for photographing scene of film.

loc. cit. (lŏk'sĭt') *abbrev. Loco citato* (L., = in the passage already quoted).

loch (lŏk, lŏχ) *n.* Scottish lake or narrow or landlocked arm of the sea.

Loch (lŏk, lŏχ) **Ness monster.** Large underwater creature (nicknamed Nessie) alleged to exist in Loch NESS.

lock[1] (lŏk) *n.* Single hair; group of hairs, of head or beard; tuft of wool or cotton; (pl.) hair of head.

lock[2] (lŏk) *n.* 1. Appliance for fastening door, lid, etc., with bolt that requires key of particular shape to work it; appliance to keep wheel from revolving or slewing; mechanism for exploding charge of gun; **under ~ and key**, locked up; ~**, stock, and barrel**, whole of thing; completely. 2. Portion of canal or river shut off by folding gates provided with sluices to let the water in and out and thus raise or lower boats from one level to another; (also **air** ~) antechamber to chamber in which engineering work is done in compressed air; similar intermediate chamber. 3. ~ **keeper**, keeper of lock on canal or river; ~ **nut**, extra nut screwed over another to prevent its becoming slack; **lock'smith**, maker and mender of locks; **lock stitch**, sewing or knitting machine stitch by which two threads or stitches are firmly locked together. **lock** *v.* 1. Fasten with lock, shut *up* by fastening doors etc. with lock and key; admit of being so fastened; shut *up, in, into*; (of land, hills, etc.) hem in (usu. pass.); (fig.) store *up, away*, inaccessibly; imprison; keep *out* by locking door (esp. of employer coercing workmen by refusing them work). 2. Come or bring into rigidly fixed position; engage, (make) catch, fasten by interlacing

__Lobsters__ are found in all but polar seas and the greater depths and are valued for their delicate flesh. The spiny lobster (above), unlike true lobsters, does not have large claws.

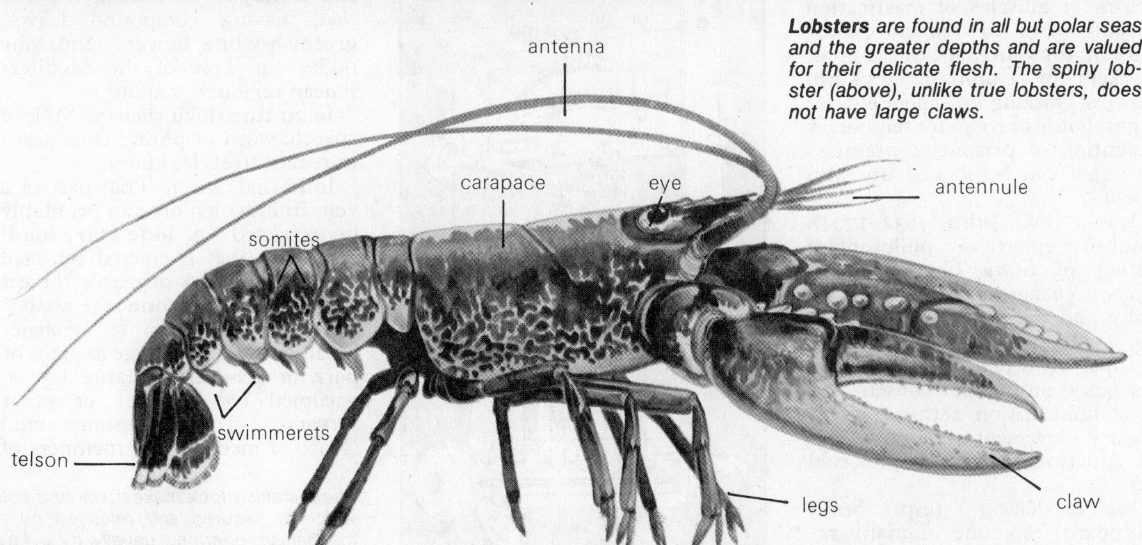

This canal ***lock,*** *by controlling the level of the water, provides access from one level reach of navigable water to another. The mitred canal gate, angled into the downward force of the stream, may be Leonardo's invention.*

or fitting of corresponding parts; entangle, (past part.) joined in hostile or other embrace; (mil., of rear rank) march so close to front rank that feet overlap. 3. Provide canal with locks; convey (boat) *up, down,* through lock; go through lock. 4. **lock'jaw** (pop. name for) trismus, a variety of tetanus, tonic spasm of muscles of mastication causing jaws to remain rigidly closed; **lock'out**, locking out of workers by employer; **lock'up,** (time of) locking up school etc. for night; house or room for temporary detention of prisoners; premises etc. that can be locked up (also attrib.).

Locke (lŏk), **John** (1632–1704). English empirical philosopher; author of *Essay Concerning the Human Understanding*; his philosophy and political thinking, esp. his contention that rebellion is permissible when government is not based on popular consent had great influence on 18th-c. revolutionary movements in France and N. America. **Lock·e·an** (lŏk'ēan) *adj.*

lock·er (lŏk'*er*) *n.* (esp.) Small cupboard, esp. one of many reserved each for individual's use in public room; (naut.) chest or compartment for clothes, stores, ammunition, etc.

lock·et (lŏk'ĭt) *n.* Metal plate or band on scabbard; small esp. gold or silver case holding portrait, lock of hair, etc., and usu. hung from neck.

lo·co (lō'kō) *n.* (pl. **-cos**). Locoweed. ~ *adj.* (slang) Insane. [Span., = "insane"]

lo·co·mo·tion (lōk*o*mō'sh*o*n) *n.* (Power of) motion from place to place; travel, means (esp. artificial) of traveling.

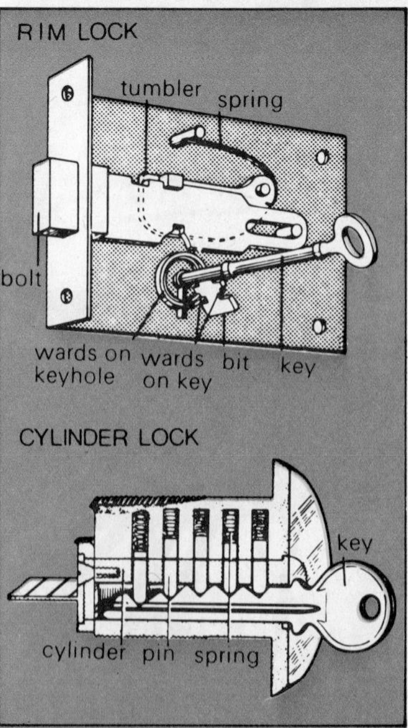

The fastening ***lock*** *makes use of a bolt which is secured and released by a mechanism operated usually by a key acting on moving components. The rim and cylinder locks are examples.*

This steam ***locomotive*** *is typical of those that played a large part in the unification of the U.S. in the mid- to late-19th century. The U.S.A. has more railway track laid than any country in the world.*

lo·co·mo·tive (lōk*o*mō'tĭv) *adj.* Of locomotion, (joc.) of travel; having power of or given to locomotion, not stationary; effecting locomotion. ~ *n.* Self-propelled vehicle; (esp.) railroad engine.

lo·co·weed (lō'kōwēd) *n.* Leguminous plant of western and southwestern U.S., causing brain-affecting disease in cattle.

loc·ule (lŏk'ūl) = LOCULUS.

loc·u·lus (lŏk'y*u*l*u*s) *n.* (pl. **-li** pr. -lī). (anat., bot., zool.) One of a number of small separate cavities.

lo·cum (lō'k*u*m) *n.* (colloq.) Locum tenens.

lo·cum te·nens (lō'k*u*m tē'nĕnz, tĕn'ĭnz) (pl. **lo·cum te·nen·tes** pr. t*e*nĕn'tēz). Deputy acting esp. for clergyman or doctor. **lo·cum-te·-nen·cy** (lōk*u*m tē'n*e*nsē, tĕn'*e*n-) *n.* [L., "holding place"]

lo·cus (lō'k*u*s) *n.* (pl. **-ci** pr. -sī, **-ca** pr. -k*a*). Locality or exact place of something; (math.) curve etc. made by all points satisfying particular equation of relation between coordinates, or by point, line, or surface, moving according to mathematically defined conditions; ~ **classicus**, best-known or most authoritative passage on a subject.

lo·cust (lō'k*u*st) *n.* 1. Any of various kinds of short-horned grasshoppers that migrate in swarms and consume vegetation of whole areas. 2. **17-year** ~: see SEVENTEEN. 3. Any of various trees, esp. the eastern N. Amer. **black** ~ (*Robinia pseudoacacia*), having compound leaves, clusters of white flowers, and hard, durable wood, and **honey** ~ (*Gleditsia triacanthos*) having compound leaves, greenish-white flowers, and long pods. 4. Tree of the Mediterranean region = CAROB.

lo·cu·tion (lōkū'sh*o*n) *n.* Style of speech; word or phrase considered in regard to style, idiom.

lode (lōd) *n.* 1. That part of a vein from which ore can profitably be extracted. 2. **lode'star, load'star**, star that is steered by, esp. polestar; guiding principle, object of pursuit; **lode'stone**: see LOAD.

lodge[1] (lŏj) *n.* 1. (archaic) Small house. 2. Cottage at gates of park or grounds of large house, occupied by gardener or other servant. 3. (freemasonry etc.) (Place of meeting for) members of

1246
1246

__Locusts__ (above and right) are short-horned grasshoppers that often increase greatly in number and migrate long distances in destructive swarms. Once developed, a locust plague is almost impossible to control although destroying egg masses and dusting and spraying are carried out.

branch. 4. Beaver's or otter's lair. 5. N. Amer. Indian's tent or wigwam.

lodge[2] (lŏj) *v.* (**lodged, lodging**). 1. Provide with sleeping quarters; receive as guest or inmate; establish as resident *in* house or room(s), (pass.) be *well*, *ill*, etc., accommodated in regard to housing. 2. Serve as habitation for, contain, (pass.) be contained *in*. 3. Leave *in* place or *with* person for security. 4. Deposit in court or with official a formal statement of (complaint, information); (pop.) allege (objection etc.). 5. Place (power etc.) *in*, *with*, etc. 6. (Make, let) stick or remain in place without falling or going farther. 7. Reside, be situated; be inmate paying for accommodation, in another's house, hence **lodg'er** *n.*

lodg·ing (lŏj'ĭng) *n.* (esp.) Accommodation in hired rooms; dwelling place, abode, (pl.) room(s) hired elsewhere than in hotel for residing in; ~ **house**, house in which lodgings are let.

lodg·ment (lŏj'ment) *n.* Firm position gained, foothold; accumulation of matter intercepted in fall or transit; (mil.) temporary defensive work on captured part of enemy's works; (law) deposit(ing) of money.

lo·ess (lō'ĕs, lĕs, lŭs) *n.* Light-colored fine-grained deposit formed by windblown dust, very fertile when irrigated, found esp. in Mississippi basin, Rhine valley, and N. China.

loft (lawft, lŏft) *n.* Attic; room over stable; pigeon house, flock of pigeons; gallery in church or hall; upper floor; lofting stroke; backward slope on face of golf club. ~ *v.t.* Hit, throw, etc., (ball) into air over obstacle, etc.; keep (pigeons) in loft.

loft·y (lawf'tē, lŏf'-) *adj.* (**loft·i·er, loft·i·est**). Of imposing height; haughty, exalted, sublime. **loft'i·ly** *adv.* **loft'i·ness** *n.*

log[1] (lawg, lŏg) *n.* 1. Unhewn piece of felled tree or similar rough mass of wood. 2. Apparatus for gauging speed of ship; also **log'book**) book in which all particulars of a ship's or aircraft's voyages are entered. 3. ~ **cabin**, cabin built of logs; **log'jam**, crowded mass of logs in river, (fig.) deadlock; **log'rolling**, (f. phrase **roll my log and I'll roll yours**) mutual help, esp. unprincipled combination in politics; **log'wood**, wood of Amer. tree (*Haemotoxylon campechianum*) used in dyeing. **log** *v.t.* (**logged, log·ging**). Cut into logs; enter in logbook, (of ship or aircraft) make, travel for, (distance or time); enter (seaman's name, with offense committed) in logbook, fine (offender).

log² (lawg, lŏg) *n.* = LOGARITHM (prefixed to number or algebraic symbol).

lo·gan·ber·ry (lō'ganbĕrē) *n.* (pl. **-ries**). Hybrid of raspberry and American blackberry. [raised by Judge *Logan* in California, 1883]

log·a·rithm (law'gerĭdhem, lŏg'e-) *n.* One of a class of arithmetical functions tabulated for simplifying computation; the sum of the logarithms of any numbers is the logarithm of their product; thus, a table of logarithms enables one to substitute addition and subtraction for multiplication and division. **log·a·rith'mic, log·a·rith'mi·cal** *adjs.* **log·a·rith'mi·cal·ly** *adv.*

loge (lōzh) *n.* Box in a theater etc.; front section of balcony in some theaters.

log·ger·head (law'gerhĕd, lŏg'er-) *n.* 1. (archaic) Blockhead. 2. Iron instrument with ball at end heated for melting pitch etc.; post built into boat for catching turn of rope to. 3. Large-headed species of turtle (*Caretta caretta*). 4. **at ~s** (*with*), disagreeing or disputing (*with*).

log·gia (lŏj'a, law'ja; *It.* lawd'jah) *n.* (pl. **-gias**; *It.* **-gie** pr. -jĕ). Gallery or arcade having one or more of its sides open to the air; open-sided extension to house etc.

log·ic (lŏj'ĭk) *n.* Science of reasoning; scheme of or treatise on this; chain of reasoning, arguments. **lo·gi·cian** (lōjĭsh'an) *n.*

log·i·cal (lŏj'ĭkal) *adj.* Of logic or formal argument; not contravening the principles of logic, correctly reasoned; following as reasonable inference or natural consequence; capable of correct reasoning; ~ **positivism**, (philos.) form of positivism rejecting transcendental metaphysics and emphasizing the linguistic nature of philosophical problems. **log·i·cal'i·ty** (lŏjĭkăl'ĭtē), **log'i·cal·ness** *ns.* **log'i·cal·ly** *adv.*

lo·gi·on (lō'gēŏn, -jē-, lŏg'ē-) *n.* (pl. **lo·gi·a** pr. lō'gēa, -jēa, lŏg'ēa, **lo·gi·ons**). Saying of Christ not recorded in Gospels but preserved elsewhere.

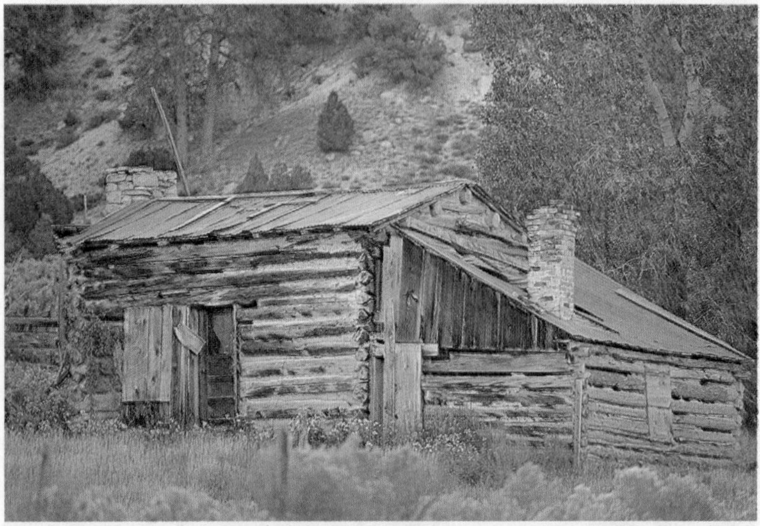

***Log** cabins have been built and lived in since medieval times. In the U.S.A. they provided shelter for lumberjacks who built them very simply and used local soil and vegetation to seal the joins.*

lo·gis·tics (lōjĭs'tĭks, lo-) *n.* (considered sing. or pl.) Science and practice of moving, lodging, and supplying troops. **lo·gis'tic, lo·gis'ti·cal** *adjs.*

log·jam (lawg'jăm, lŏg') *n.* Immovable mass of floating logs jammed together; (fig.) any similar stoppage, esp. in negotiations or legislation.

log·o·gram (law'gogrăm, lŏg'o-) *n.* Sign or character representing word in shorthand.

lo·gog·ra·pher (lōgŏg'rafer) *n.* (Gk. antiq.) Writer of traditional history in prose.

log·o·griph (law'gogrĭf, lŏg'o-) *n.* Kind of anagrammatic word puzzle.

lo·gom·a·chy (lōgŏm'akē) *n.* (pl. **-chies**). Dispute about words, controversy turning on merely verbal points.

Lo·gos (lō'gŏs, -gōs, lŏg'ŏs) *n.* (theol.) Word of God, second person of the Trinity.

log·o·type (law'gotīp, lŏg'o-) *n.* (print.) Type containing word, or two or more letters, cast in one piece but not as ligature.

*These **logs**, which have been floated down river to Lake Oyeren in Norway, are sorted for different timber mills. In Norway, where about 25% of the land is forested, pulp and paper are important exports.*

*The **Loire Valley** in France is famous for its chateaux, built during the 15th and 16th centuries. Chenonceaux has a Long Gallery astride the river, in a formal Renaissance style.*

*The plain of **Lombardy** in northern Italy is one of Europe's most densely populated areas. Intensive farming (maize, rice and cattle) is carried out on farms like this one.*

-logue, -log *suffixes.* Forming nouns denoting talk (*dialogue*) or compilation (*catalog*).

lo·gy (lō′gē) *adj.* (**-gi·er, -gi·est**). Lethargic, sluggish; dull, inert. **lo′gi·ness** *n.*

-logy *suffix.* Forming nouns denoting character of speech or language (*analogy*) or subject of study (*sociology*, *theology*).

Lo·hen·grin (lō′engrĭn). (Ger. legend) Son of Parsifal; he was summoned from the temple of the Grail and borne in a swan boat to Antwerp to defend Elsa of Brabant against Frederick of Telramund, who claimed her in marriage; Lohengrin himself married Elsa but was carried away again in the swan boat when she asked his name.

loid (loid) *v.t.* (slang) Open (door) by inserting piece of celluloid, plastic, etc. between the jamb and the edge of the door so as to open a spring lock.

loin (loin) *n.* (pl.) Part of body on both sides of spine between false ribs and hipbones; (sing.) cut of meat including vertebrae of loins; (pl., bibl.) this part of body regarded as part that should be covered by clothing, or as seat of physical strength and generative power; **loin′cloth**, cloth worn about loins.

Loire (lwahr). River rising in S. central France and flowing N. and then W. to the Atlantic.

loi·ter (loi′t*er*) *v.* Linger on the way, hang about; travel indolently and with frequent pauses; pass (time etc.) *away* in loitering. **loi′ter·er** *n.* **loi′ter·ing·ly** *adv.*

loll (lŏl) *v.* Hang (tongue) *out*, (of tongue) hang (*out*); stand, sit, recline, in lazy attitude; let (head, limbs) rest lazily on something.

Lol·lard (lŏl′*erd*) *n.* One of the English 14th-c. heretics who were followers of Wycliffe or held opinions similar to his on the necessity for the church to aid men to live a life of evangelical poverty and imitate Christ. **Lol′lard·ism, Lol′lard·y, Lol′lard·ry** *ns.*

lol·li·pop, lol·ly·pop (lŏl′ēpŏp) *ns.* Piece of hard candy on a small stick.

Lom·bard (lŏm′b*er*d, -bard, lŭm′-) *adj.* & *n.* (Member) of a Germanic people from the lower Elbe who invaded Italy in 568 A.D. and founded a kingdom (overthrown by Charlemagne, 774) in the valley of the Po. **Lom·bar′dic** *adj.*

Lom·bar·dy (lŏm′b*er*dē, lŭm′-). Region of N. Italy, lying roughly between the Alps and the river Po; ~ **poplar**, tall columnar variety of the black poplar (*Populus nigra italica*).

Lo·mé (lōmā′). Capital and a port of Togo, on the Gulf of Guinea.

lo·ment (lō′mĕnt) *n.* (bot.) Legume that is contracted in spaces between seeds, breaking up when mature into one-seeded joints. **lo·men·ta·ceous** (lōm*e*ntā′sh*u*s) *adj.*

Lo·mond (lō′m*o*nd), **Loch.** Largest lake in Scotland (about 20 miles long and 5 miles wide), N. of the Clyde.

Lon·don (lŭn′d*o*n). Capital of England and of the United Kingdom, a port on the Thames River, comprising the ancient CITY of London, the city of WESTMINSTER, the royal borough of Kensington and Chelsea, and numerous other boroughs; ~ **Bridge**, bridge across Thames about ½ mile above the **Tower of** ~, ancient fortress and prison. **Lon′don·er** *n.* Native, inhabitant, of London.

Lon·don (lŭn′d*o*n, **Jack** (1876–1916). American writer and adventurer; wrote *The Call of the Wild*, *The Sea Wolf*, etc.

lone (lōn) *adj.* Solitary, companionless, single (poet. or rhet.); ~ **wolf**, person who chooses to act or live etc. alone.

lone·ly (lōn′lē) *adj.* (**-li·er, -li·est**). Solitary, companionless, isolated; unfrequented. **lone′li·ness** *n.*

lone·some (lōn′s*o*m) *adj.* Lonely. **lone′some·ly** *adv.* **lone′-**

some·ness *n.*

long[1] (lawng, lŏng) *adj.* Measuring much from end to end in space or time; (colloq.) tall; far-reaching, acting at a distance, involving great interval or difference; in length; of elongated shape; remarkable for, distinguished by, concerned with, length or duration; prolix, tedious; lasting, going far back or forward; (phonet., pros., of vowel or syllable) having the greater of the two recognized durations; **long'boat,** (hist.) sailing ship's largest boat; **long'bow,** (esp. medieval) bow drawn by hand (as dist. from *crossbow*) and discharging long feathered arrow; **long chance,** one involving much risk; **long distance,** telephone service between distant places; **long-distance** (*adj.* & *adv.*); **long face,** dismal countenance; **long'hair,** (colloq.) (sometimes **long-haired**) person with intellectual tastes, esp. in art, music, literature; **long'hand,** ordinary writing (opp. SHORThand); **long-headed,** (esp.) sagacious; **long horn,** long-horned ox or cow; **long-horned grasshopper,** orthopterous jumping insect with very long antennae; **long johns,** (slang) winter underwear covering entire body except for head, hands, and feet; **long jump,** jump (as athletic competition) measured along ground; **long-lived** (pr. -līvd), having a long life, durable; **long measure,** lineal measure, measure of length; **long on,** (colloq.) well supplied with (attribute, money, etc.); **Long Parliament,** English Parliament that sat from Nov. 1640 to March 1653, was restored in 1659, and finally dissolved in 1660; **long pig,** sailors' translation of cannibals' name for human flesh; **long-playing,** (of microgroove phonograph record) playing for about 10 to 30 minutes a side, esp. one turning at 33⅓ revolutions per minute; **long-range,** (of gun or projectile) firing a long distance; (of forecast, plan, etc.) applying to the more distant future; **in the long run,** in the end, ultimately; **long'shore,** found or employed on the shore; **long'shoreman** (pl. **-men**), man employed in loading ships, shore fishing, etc.; **long shot,** bet at long odds; (cinemat.) shot that includes figures or scenery at a distance; **long suit,** (cards) suit in which more than three cards are held; (fig.) one's strong point; **long-term,** (of plan, policy, etc.) designed to meet the circumstances of a long time ahead; **long wave,** radio wave of more than 800 meters; **long-winded,** talking or writing at tedious length. **long'ish** *adj.* **long'ways, long'wise** *advs.* **long** *n.* (usu. colloq.) Long interval or period; long syllable; **the ~ and the short of it,** all that need be said.

long[2] (lawng, lŏng) *adv.* For a long time; by a long time; throughout specified time; **as** or **so ~ as,** provided that, if only; (comp. **longer,** with **no, any,** etc.) after implied point of time; **~ ago,** (belonging to) the distant past; **~-drawn (-out),** unduly prolonged; **long'standing,** that has long existed; **long-suffering,** (state of) bearing provocation patiently.

long[3] (lawng, lŏng) *v.i.* Yearn, wish vehemently (*for, to*). **long'ing** *n.* & *adj.* **long'ing·ly** *adv.*

long. *abbrev.* Longitude.

Long (lawng), **Huey (Pierce)** (1893–1935). American politician, called "Kingfish," noted for his

This aerial view of ***London*** *shows the City, one of the world's leading banking and financial centers, surrounding the great dome of St. Paul's Cathedral, built by Sir Christopher Wren from 1675 to 1710.*

*The **loom** is among the most ancient of devices and was in use in 5400 B.C. according to evidence found in tombs. Handlooms are still used for weaving in many countries, and modern high-speed industrial looms work on the same basic principles.*

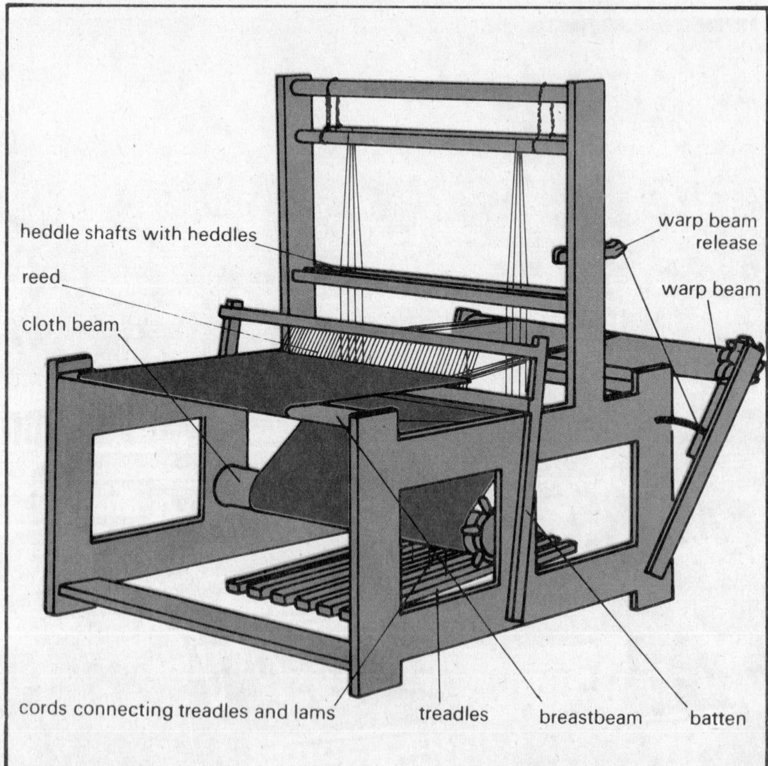

folksy manner while the flamboyant, demagogic, domineering governor of Louisiana, 1928–31, and U.S. senator, 1931–5; known for his "share-the-wealth" public works and public welfare programs and his "every man a king" slogan; assassinated, 1935.

longe: see LUNGE.[1]

lon·ge·ron (lŏn′jeron) *n.* (usu. in pl.) Longitudinal member of airplane fuselage.

Long·fel·low (lawng′fĕlō, lŏng′-), **Henry Wadsworth** (1807–82). American poet, author of "Hyperion," "Hiawatha," "The Wreck of the Hesperus," "Evangeline," "The Village Blacksmith," "The Children's Hour," etc.

lon·gi·corn (lŏn′jĭkōrn) *n.* Beetle of the family Cerambycidae with very long antennae.

Lon·gi·nus (lŏnjī′n*u*s). Traditional name of the Roman soldier who pierced with his spear the side of Jesus Christ at the Crucifixion.

Long (lawng, lŏng) **Island.** Island of New York State, adjacent to and including sections of New York City on its W. end; separated from mainland of Connecticut by **Long Island Sound**, an arm of the Atlantic Ocean.

lon·gi·tude (lŏn′jĭto͞od, -tūd) *n.* (geog.) Angular distance along equator E. or W. from standard meridian, as that of Greenwich, to meridian of any place; (astron.) angular distance eastward on ecliptic from vernal equinoctial point to great circle through body or point perpendicular to ecliptic.

lon·gi·tu·di·nal (lŏnjĭto͞o′d*i*nal, -tū′-) *adj.* Of or in length; running lengthwise; of longitude. **lon·gi·tu′di·nal·ly** *adv.*

loo[1] (lo͞o) *n.* (pl. **loos**). (archaic) Round card game, played with three or five cards, with penalties paid to the pool; (having to pay) such penalty.

loo[2] (lo͞o) *n.* (Brit. colloq.) Lavatory.

loo·fa, loo·fah (lo͞o′fa) *ns.* Fibrous pod of plant (*Luffa aegyptiaca*) used as flesh brush. [Arab. *lufah* (name of the plant)]

look (lo͝ok) *v.* 1. Use one's sight; turn eyes in some direction, direct eyes *at*; stare, show surprise; contemplate, examine; express, threaten, show, by one's looks; ascertain or observe by sight; (fig.) make mental search, inquire, aim one's attention *at* and consider; take care or make sure *that*, expect *to* do; **to ~ at**, judging by the looks of; **will not ~ at,** refuses to take, rejects, scorns; **~ here!**, (imper.) formula for demanding attention or expostulating; **~ sharp**, orig., keep strict watch; now, lose no time, bestir oneself. 2. (of things) Face, be turned, have or afford outlook, in some direction; tend, point; have certain appearance, seem; seem to be; **~ alive**, make haste; **~ as if**, suggest by appearance the belief that; **~ like**, seem to be, threaten or promise. 3. (with preps.) **~ about one**, examine one's surroundings, take time to

*The **looper** caterpillar, so called for its movement — arching into loops as it proceeds, is the geometrid moth before its transformation to the chrysalis stage.*

form plans; ~ **after**, follow with the eye; seek for; attend to, take care of; ~ **for**, expect, hope or be on the watch for; search for; ~ **into**, examine the inside of; dip into (book); investigate; ~ **on**, regard *as*, regard *with* some feeling; ~ **over**, inspect; ~ **through**, penetrate with a look; glance through (book etc.); ~ **to**, consider, take care of, be careful about; keep watch over; rely on *for*; expect, count upon; aim at. 4. (with advs.) ~ **down on**, consider oneself superior to; ~ **forward to**, anticipate (usu. with pleasure); ~ **in**, make short visit or call; ~ **on**, be (mere) spectator; ~ **out**, direct eyes or put head out of window etc.; be vigilant; keep one's eyes open *for*, be prepared *for*; have or afford outlook *on*, *over*, etc.; ~ **over**, inspect; ~ **through**, survey with searching glance; inspect exhaustively or successively; ~ **up**, search for (esp. word in dictionary, fact in book of reference); call on (person); ~ **up to**, respect, venerate. 5. ~-**alike**, person or thing closely resembling another; **look'ing glass**, mirror made of glass backed with a film of silver etc.; **look'out**, watch, looking out; post of observation; man, party, etc., stationed to look out; view over landscape; prospect of luck; person's own concern; **look-see**, (slang) look. **look** *n.* Act of looking, direction of eyes, glance; appearance (of things etc.); (sing. or pl.) appearance of face, expression, personal aspect.

look·er (lo͝ok'*er*) *n.* (slang) Good-looking person; ~-**on**, (colloq.) onlooker, one who looks on without taking part.

Look·out (lo͝ok'owt) **Mountain.** Mountain ridge in SE. Tennessee; site of a victory by Union troops over the Confederates, 1863, during the Civil War.

loom[1] (lo͞om) *n.* 1. Apparatus for weaving threads into fabric by crossing warp with weft, by means of a device that parts the warp threads so that the shuttle carrying the weft can pass between them. 2. (Inboard part of) shaft or oar.

loom[2] (lo͞om) *v.i.* Appear indistinctly, be seen in vague and often magnified or threatening shape. ~ *n.* Indistinct and exaggerated appearance of object first coming into view, esp. at sea.

loon[1] (lo͞on) *n.* (Sc. and archaic) Scamp; fellow.

loon[2] (lo͞on) *n.* Any of several large fish-eating diving birds of the genus *Gavia* of northern waters; the common loon (*G. immer*) is noted for its weird, laugh-like cry.

loon·y (lo͞o'nē) *adj.* (**loon·i·er, loon·i·est**) & *n.* (pl. **loon·ies**). (slang) Lunatic; ~ **bin**, (slang) mental hospital.

loop (lo͞op) *n.* Doubling or return into itself of string, thong, etc., so as to leave an aperture between the parts, portion so doubled; stitch in knitting; ring or curved piece of metal as handle etc.; intrauterine contraceptive device; railroad or telegraph line that diverges from main line and joins it again; circuit in roller coaster etc. along top of which passenger travels head downward, similar path described by airplane; (skating) curve crossing itself made on single edge; **the L**~, the downtown business district of Chicago. **loop** *v.* Form into loop(s); enclose (as) with loop; fasten (*up*, *back*) or join (*together*) with loops; ~-**the**-~, (of aircraft) describe loop in air.

loop·er (lo͞o'p*er*) *n.* 1. Caterpillar of geometrid moth, progressing by arching itself into loops. 2. Contrivance in sewing machine etc. for making loops.

loop·hole (lo͞op'hōl) *n.* Narrow vertical slit in wall for shooting or looking through, or to admit light or air; outlet, means of evading rule, etc.

loose (lo͞os) *adj.* (**loos·er, loos·est**). 1. Released from bonds or restraint; detached or detachable

__Long Island,__ which is 118 miles long and 12–20 miles wide, serves the city of New York as a dormitory suburb, market garden and beach resort. The boroughs of Brooklyn and Queens are on its western end.

from its place; uncombined, as a chemical element; hanging partly free; not rigidly fixed, apt to shift; slack, relaxed, not tense or tight; not compact, dense, or serried; (of bowels) relaxed; **at ~ ends**, without definite occupation; **with a ~ rein**, (fig.) indulgently; **~ change**, money kept or left unsecured for casual use; **~-leaf**, (of ledger etc.) with each leaf separate and detachable; **~ tongue**, one given to blabbing. 2. (of statements, ideas, etc.) Not exact; (of translation) not close or faithful; (of style) ungrammatical. 3. Morally lax; sexually promiscuous. **loose′ly** *adv.* **loose′ness** *n.* **loose** *v.t.* (**loosed, loos·ing**). Release, set free, free from constraint; untie, undo; detach from moorings; relax (hold).

loos·en (lo͞o′s*e*n) *v.* Make or become less tight or compact or firm; loose (person's tongue); relieve (bowels) from constipation or (cough) from dryness; relax (discipline etc.).

loose·strife (lo͞o′strīf) *n.* 1. Marsh plant of genus *Lysimachia*, esp. *L. vulgaris*, with golden-yellow flowers. 2. Marsh plant of genus *Lythrum*, esp. *L. salicaria* with purple-red flowers.

loot (lo͞ot) *n.* Goods taken from enemy, spoil, booty; illicit gains. ~ *v.* Plunder, sack; carry off as booty. **loot′er** *n.*

lop[1] (lŏp) *n.* Small branches and twigs of trees. ~ *v.* (**lopped, lop·ping**). Cut off branches and twigs of (tree); strip tree of (branches etc.); cut off (person's limb or head); make cutting strokes *at*.

lop[2] (lŏp) *v.* (**lopped, lop·ping**). Hang limply; **~ ear**, kind of rabbit with lop ears; **~ ears**, drooping ears; **lop′sided(ly)**, with one side lower or smaller than the other; unevenly balanced; **lop′sidedness** (*n.*).

lope (lōp) *v.i.* (**loped, lop·ing**) & *n.* (Run with) long bounding stride (esp. of animals).

Lo·pe de Ve·ga (lō′pā d*e* vā′g*a*; *Sp.* law′pĕ dhē vĕ′gah) = VEGA[2].

loq. *abbrev.* *Loquitur* (L., = "speaks," with speaker's name added as stage direction or notice to reader).

lo·qua·cious (lōkwā′sh*u*s) *adj.* Talkative; chattering, babbling. **lo·qua′cious·ly** *adv.* **lo·qua′cious·ness** *n.* **lo·quac·i·ty** (lōkwăs′ĭtē) *n.* (pl. **-ties**).

lo·quat (lō′kwŏt, -kwăt) *n.* (Small reddish fruit of) Chinese and Japanese tree, *Eriobotrya japonica*, introduced into S. Europe, California, Australia, etc. [Chin. *luh kwat* rush orange]

lor·an (lōr′*a*n, lōr′-) *n.* Long-range navigational system enabling a navigator to determine his position by analyzing time intervals between radio signals from two known positions. [*lo*(ng) *ra*(nge) *n*(avigation)]

Lor·ca (lōr′k*a*; *Sp.* lōr′kah). **Federico Garcia**: see GARCIA LORCA.

lord (lōrd) *n.* 1. Master, ruler, chief, feudal superior (hist.); magnate in some trade; (poet.) owner; (poet. or joc.) husband; (astrol.) dominant planet; **~s of creation**, mankind. 2. **L~**, God; (usu. **the or our L~**) Christ; **in the year of our L~**, Anno Domini; **L~'s Day**, Sunday; **L~'s Prayer**, prayer taught by Christ to his disciples (Matt. 6); **L~'s Supper**, (Brit.) Holy Communion. 3. Nobleman, peer of the realm or person entitled by courtesy to prefix **Lord** as part of his ordinary style; member (whether peer or not) of board performing duties of high state office put in commission; forming part of many official titles, as **L~ Chamberlain, L~ Chan-**

The richly decorated chamber of the ***House of Lords*** *in the Houses of Parliament, U.K. The Palace of Westminster was completely burnt down in 1834 and the new building begun in the Gothic style in 1840.*

Yellow Loosestrife *grows in England and eastern North America and is a member of the Lythraceae family. It is usually found growing on riverbanks.*

cellor, etc.; **House of Lords**, (also **the Lords**) temporal and spiritual peers of Parliament, forming upper legislative chamber of United Kingdom; building where these meet; committee of specially qualified members of this appointed as ultimate judicial court of appeal; **Sea L~**, naval member of Admiralty Board; **~-in-waiting**, lord attending sovereign; **L~ Mayor**, mayor of London, York, and other cities. 4. **L~**, prefixed title, part of customary appellation of marquis, earl, viscount, or baron; followed by Christian (and family) name of younger son of duke or marquis. **lord** *v.* Play the lord *over*.

lord·ly (lōrd′lē) *adj.* (**-li·er, -li·est**). Haughty, imperious, lofty, disdainful; grand, magnificent, fit for or belonging to a lord; **lord′-li·ness** *n.*

lor·do·sis (lōrdō′sĭs) *n.* (path.) Anterior curvature of spine, producing convexity in front.

lord·ship (lōrd′shĭp) *n.* Dominion, rule, ownership *of* or *over*, domain, estate, manor; personality of lord.

lore[1] (lōr, lōr) *n.* Doctrine (archaic); erudition, scholarship (archaic); body of traditions or knowledge relating to some subject.

lore[2] (lōr, lōr) *n.* (zool.) Space between bird's eye and upper mandible, or between reptile's eye and nostril.

lo·re·al (lōr′ēal, lōr′-) *adj.* (zool.) Of the LORE[2].

Lor·e·lei (lōr′elī; *Ger.* lō′relī). Rock or cliff on Rhine River; in German legend, the home of a siren whose song lured sailors to destruction.

lor·gnette (lōrnyĕt′) *n.* Pair of eyeglasses or opera glasses held in hand, usu. by long handle.

lor·i·cate (lōr′ĭkāt, lăr′-, -kĭt) *adj.* & *n.* (zool.) (Animal) having defensive armor of bone, plates, scales, etc.

lor·i·keet (lōr′ĭkēt, lăr′-, lōrĭkēt′, lăr-) *n.* Any of various small brightly-colored parrots (**rainbow ~, musk ~**, etc.) of Australia etc. [LORY + ending of *parakeet*]

lo·ris (lōr′ĭs, lōr′-) *n.* (pl. **-ris**). Any of several tailless or stump-tailed nocturnal arboreal primates found in Africa and tropical Asia, related to the lemurs, and including **slender ~** (*Loris tardigradus*), **slow ~** (*Nycticebus coucang*), and potto.

lorn (lōrn) *adj.* (poet. and joc.) Desolate, forlorn.

Lor·raine (lorān′; *Fr.* lawrĕn′). Medieval kingdom on W. bank of Rhine, extending from North Sea to Italy, and divided into two duchies; Upper Lorraine passed to France in 1766; part of Lorraine was acquired with Alsace by Germany in 1871 but was restored to France after World War I; **Cross of ~**, cross having two transoms.

*There are about 60 species of **lorikeet**. These small, brightly colored parrots are found mostly in New Guinea, Indonesia and Australia.*

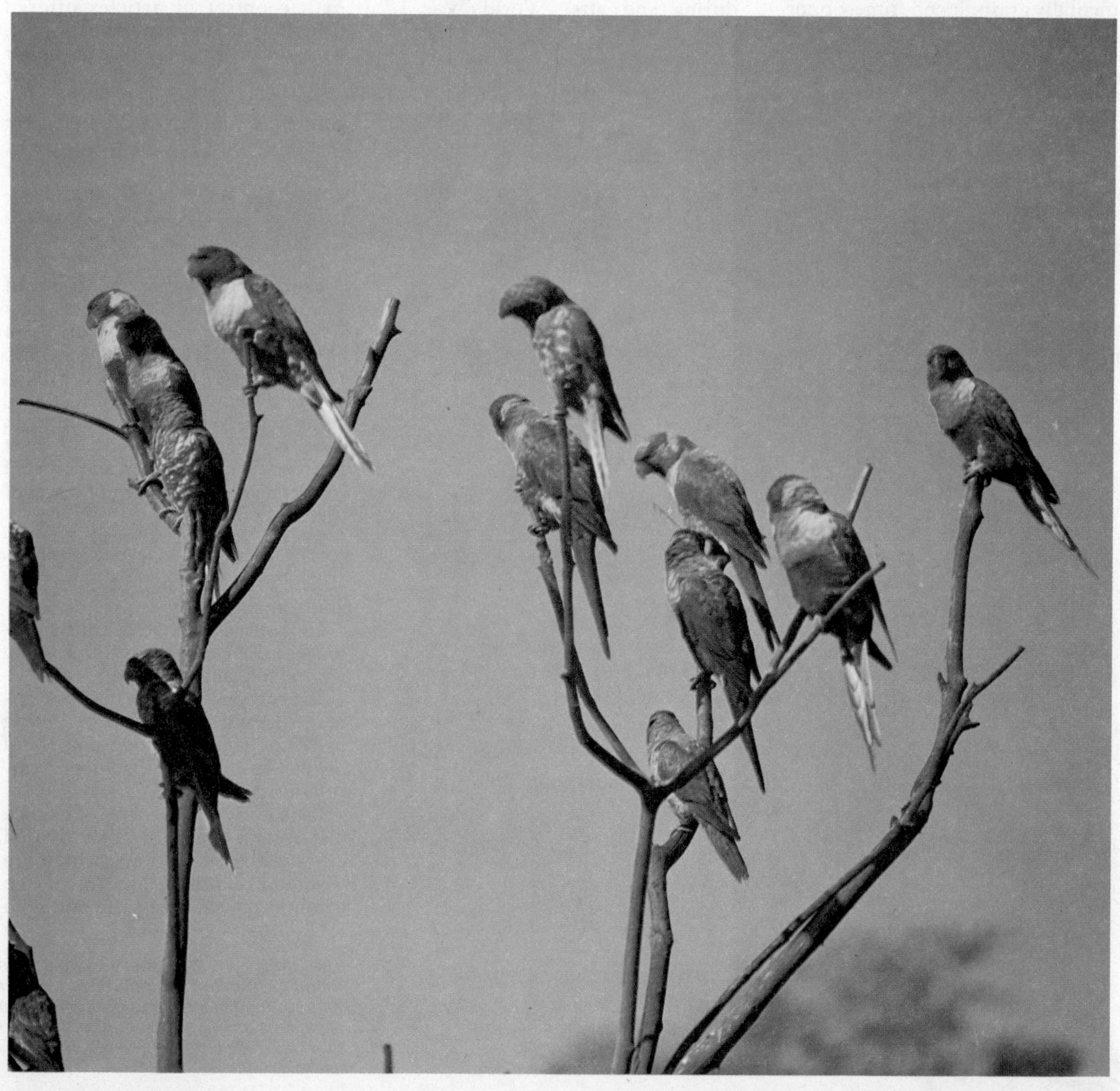

[med. *L. Lotharingia*, f. *Lothair*, name of king]

lor·ry (lŏr′ē, lăr′ē) *n.* (pl. **-ries**). Long low flat sideless wagon; (Brit.) motor truck; truck running on rails.

lo·ry (lōr′ē, lŏr′ē) *n.* Any of various bright-plumaged parrots of SE. Asia and New Guinea.

Los Al·a·mos (laws ăl′amōs, lŏs). Town in N. New Mexico; site of the research center that produced the first atomic bomb.

Los An·ge·les (laws ăn′jeles, -lēz, lŏs; sometimes ăng′geles, -lēz). City on coast of S. California with a suburb, Hollywood, which is the center of the American motion-picture industry.

lose (lōōz) *v.* (**lost** pr. lawst, lŏst, **los·ing**). 1. Be deprived of, cease, by negligence, misadventure, separation, death, etc., to possess or have; suffer loss or detriment, incur disadvantage, be the worse off in money or otherwise *by* transaction etc.; become unable to find, fail to keep in sight or follow or mentally grasp; spend (time, opportunities, pains) to no purpose, waste; fail to obtain, catch, see, or hear; forfeit (stake), be defeated in (game, battle, lawsuit, etc.); fail to carry (motion); cause person the loss of, cost; ~ **interest**, cease to be interested; cease to interest; ~ **one's life**, be killed; ~ **patience, one's temper**, become impatient, angry; **losing game**, one in which defeat seems inevitable. 2. (pass.) Disappear, perish, die or be dead; (refl. and pass.) go astray; become merged or engrossed (*in*); be obscured in. **los′a·ble** *adj.* **los′er** *n.*

loss (laws, lŏs) *n.* Losing or being lost; person, thing, or amount lost; detriment, disadvantage, resulting from loss; **at a** ~, at less than cost; puzzled; ~ **leader**, (commerc.) article of trade sold at low price to attract customers to buy other things.

lost (lawst, lŏst) *adj.* see LOSE; (esp.) ~ **cause**, one with no hope of success; **L~ Generation**, generation reaching maturity during and after World War I, lacking cultural and emotional stability; ~ **soul**, damned soul; **L~ Tribes**, ten tribes of Israel taken away *c*722 B.C. by Sargon II to captivity in Assyria (2 Kings 17), from which they are believed never to have returned.

Lot (lŏt). Son of Abraham's brother Haran and legendary ancestor of the Ammonites and Moabites; his wife, fleeing with him from the destruction of Sodom and Gomorrah, looked back, and was turned into a pillar of salt (Gen. 19).

lot (lŏt) *n.* 1. One of set of objects used to secure a chance decision in dividing goods, selecting officials, etc. (now only in **draw, cast, ~s**, and **throw in one's ~ with**, share fortunes with); this method of deciding, choice resulting from it; what falls to a person by lot, share; person's destiny, fortune, condition. 2. Plot or portion of land belonging to particular owner, piece of land set apart for particular purpose; plot or portion of land offered for sale. 3. Article or set of articles offered separately at sale; item at auction. 4. Number or quantity of persons or things of same kind or somehow associated; (colloq.) considerable number or amount, a good or great deal (also in pl., as **~s of money**); **the** ~, the whole number or quantity. **lot** *v.t.* (**lot·ted, lot·ting**). Divide (land *out*, or goods for sale) into lots.

loth = LOATH.

Lo·thar·i·o (lōthăr′ēō). Name of a seducer in Nicholas Rowe's play *The Fair Penitent*; hence, a libertine, deceiver, rake.

Lo·thi·ans (lō′dhēanz, -thē-), **The.** Region of E. Scotland, comprising the city of Edinburgh and the former counties of East Lothian, West Lothian, and most of Midlothian; (hist.) all the E. part of the Scottish Lowlands.

Lo·ti (lawtē′), **Pierre** (1850–1923). Pen name of Louis Marie Julien Viaud, French naval officier and romantic novelist.

lo·tion (lō′shon) *n.* Liquid preparation used externally for healing wounds, beautifying skin, etc.

lot·ter·y (lŏt′erē) *n.* (pl. **-ter·ies**). Arrangement for distributing prizes by chance among holders of tickets; (fig.) thing that defies calculation.

lot·to (lŏt′ō) *n.* Game of chance played with boards or cards divided into numbered sections, which are covered as numbers are drawn, the winning player being the one who

slow loris

slender loris

*The **loris**, an Indo-Malay primate, is found in forested regions. The slender loris is found in India and Sri Lanka. The slow loris is more robust but slower-moving. Both feed on insects and small animals.*

***Lothian** in east Scotland, U.K. includes the city of Edinburgh and the former counties of East and West Lothian and most of Midlothian. Shown here is Bass Rock in the Firth of Forth.*

first covers a row of numbers. Cf. BINGO.

lo·tus, lo·tos (lō′t*u*s) *ns.* (pl. **-tus·es, -tos·es**). 1. Plant represented in ancient Greek legend as inducing luxurious dreaminess and distaste for active life; **~-eater**, person given to indolent enjoyment, sybarite. 2. Water lily of Egypt and Asia, species of *Nymphaea* and *Nelumbium*; (archit.) ornament representing Egyptian water lily; **~ position**, cross-legged position of meditation.

loud (lowd) *adj.* Strongly audible, sonorous; clamorous, noisy; (of color etc.) obtrusive, flashy; **loud′mouthed**, given to loud, bragging or indiscreet talk; **loud′speaker**, instrument (esp. as part of radio receiving apparatus) for converting electrical impulses into sounds loud enough to be heard at a distance. **loud′ly** *adv.* **loud′ness** *n.* **loud** *adv.*

Lou·is (lo͞o′ē, lo͞o′ĭs; *Fr.* lwē). Name of many French kings: **Louis I** (778–840), "the Pious"; third son of Charlemagne; emperor with his father, 813; sole emperor, 814; **Louis II** (846–79), "the Stammerer"; son of Charles the Bald; king of the West Franks 877–9; **Louis III** (*c*863–82), joint king of France with his brother Carloman, 879–82; **Louis IV** (921–54), king of France 936–54; fled to England when his father, Charles III, was imprisoned; **Louis V** (967–87), last Carolingian king of France 986–7; **Louis VI** (1081–1137), "the Fat"; king 1108–37; soldier and popular hero who opposed the English in Normandy; **Louis VII** (*c*1121–1180), king of France 1137–80; proclaimed and led the disastrous second CRUSADE, 1146–9; **Louis VIII** (1187–1226), king of France 1223–6; leader of crusade against the Albigenses; **Louis IX** (1214–1270), St. Louis, king of France 1226–70; went on crusade 1248, was captured 1250 and passed 4 years in Syria; returned to France 1254; sailed for Tunis 1270 on a second crusade, and died there of the plague; canonized 1297; **Louis X** (1287–1316), "the Quarrelsome"; king of France 1314–16; **Louis XI** (1423–83), king of France 1461–1483); ruled as absolute monarch and greatly increased the royal domain; **Louis XII** (1462–1515), king of France 1499–1515; **Louis**

*Hollywood lies 8 miles northwest of **Los Angeles,** a suburb originally formed in 1887. L.A., the second largest city in the U.S., is a place of great contrasts, dominated by its freeway system.*

Louis XVI of France, husband of Marie Antoinette, reigned for 18 years. Despite his attempts to accede to the wishes of the Republicans, he and his wife were tried for treason and guillotined in January 1793.

XIII (1601–43), king of France 1610–43; **Louis XIV** (1638–1715), "the Sun King"; king of France 1643–1715; during his minority, power was in the hands of his mother, Anne of Austria, and her minister Mazarin; his own rule was a time of absolute monarchy, wars, and great extravagance at court; **Louis XV** (1710–74), great-grandson and successor of Louis XIV; king of France 1715–74; his reign saw the Seven Years War and the loss to France of India and Canada; **Louis XVI** (1754–93), grandson and successor of Louis XV; king of France from 1774 to 1792, when the Convention of the French Revolution declared royalty abolished; he was guillotined; **Louis XVII** (1785–1795?), titular king of France; second son of Louis XVI; he was reported to have died in prison, but there are many legends of his escape; **Louis XVIII** (1755–1824), younger brother of Louis XVI; fled from France 1791; proclaimed himself king after death of Louis XVII (1795); was restored to the throne after defeat of Napoleon I in 1814.

lou·is d'or (lo͞oē dôr′; *Fr.* lwē dôr′) (pl. **lou·is d'or** pr. lo͞oēz dôr′; *Fr.* lwē dôr′). French gold coin, first issued by Louis XIII in 1640 and superseded in 1795; gold 20-france piece, napoleon.

Lou·ise (lo͞oēz′), **Lake.** Lake in Banff National Park, SW. Alberta, Canada, known for its scenic beauty.

Lou·i·si·an·a (l*u*wēzēăn′*a*, lo͞oizē-lo͞oē-). State in southern U.S. with a 397-mile (639 km) coastline on the Gulf of Mexico; capital, Baton Rouge; ~ **Territory**, vast territory extending from the Mississippi River to the Rocky Mountains between the Mexican and Canadian borders; was claimed by France in 1682 and named in honor of Louis XIV, transferred to Spain 1762 and back to France 1800, and finally sold by the French to the U.S. in 1803 for $15,000,000; ~ **Purchase**, territory sold by France to the U.S. in 1803.

Lou·is Phil·ippe (lo͞o′ē; *Fr.* lwē, fēlēp′) (1773–1850). Duke of Orleans, son of Philippe Egalité; spent many years in exile in England and America; was appointed king (called "the Citizen King") of France by the French Chamber after the July revolution of 1830; forced to abdicate in 1848.

Lou·is Qua·torze, Quinze, Seize, (lo͞o′ē; *Fr.* lwē, kătôrz′; kănz; sĕz) (of style of furniture, architecture, etc.) Of the reign of Louis, XIV, XV, XVI, of France.

lounge (lownj) *v.* (**lounged, loung·ing**). Go lazily; loll, recline; idle. ~ *n.* Spell of, place for, lounging; sitting room, esp. in hotel etc.; sofa or deep chair. **loung′er** *n.*

loupe (lo͞op) *n.* Magnifying instrument, esp. for watchmakers, consisting of a system of lenses mounted on a frame.

loup·ing (low′pĭng, lō′-, lo͞o′-) **ill.** Disease of sheep, a form of encephalitis, caused by a virus which occas. attacks other mammals including man.

lour = LOWER².

Lourdes (loord, loordz; *Fr.* lo͞ord). Town of SW. France at foot of Pyrenees, site of a shrine and center of pilgrimage where many miraculous cures have been reported (see BERNADETTE).

louse (lows) *n.* (pl. **lice** pr. līs). 1. (zool.) One of various wingless bloodsucking insects of orders Anoplura, parasitic on mammals, and Mallophaga, with biting mouthparts, parasitic on birds; esp. the best-known species of these (*Pediculus humanus*), which infests man and is agent in transmission of many diseases, e.g., typhus. 2. (slang, pl. **lous·es**) Low contemptible person. **lous·y** (low′zē) *adj.* (**lous·i·er, lous·i·est**). Infested with lice; (slang) disgusting; (slang) swarming *with*, abundantly supplied *with* money etc. **lous′i·ness** *n.*

lout (lowt) *n.* Hulking or rough-mannered fellow. **lout′ish** *adj.* **lout′ish·ly** *adv.* **lout′ish·ness** *n.*

lou·ver (lo͞o′v*e*r) *n.* Domed turretlike erection on medieval hall roof etc., with side openings to let smoke out or air in; (pl.) arrangement of overlapping boards or strips of glass etc. to admit air but exclude light or rain. **lou′vered** *adj.*

Lou·vre (lo͞ov; *Fr.* lo͞o′vre). Ancient palace of the kings of France, on N. bank of Seine in Paris; rebuilt in the reign of Philip II and enlarged by François I and his successors down to Napoleon III; now the principal art museum of France.

lov·a·ble, love·a·ble (lŭv′abel) *adjs.* Deserving love. **lov′a·ble·ness, love′a·ble·ness** *ns.* **lov′a·bly, love′a·bly** *advs.*

lov·age (lŭv′ĭj) *n.* Any of various plants, esp. the S. European umbelliferous herb (*Levisticum officinale*), grown for use in flavoring etc.

love (lŭv) *n.* 1. Warm affection, attachment, liking, or fondness; paternal benevolence; affectionate devotion. 2. Sexual affection, passion, or desire; affection between sweethearts, this feeling as literary subject, personified influence, or a god; (**L ~**) representation of Cupid or of naked winged child symbolizing love; **labor of ~**, task one delights in or does for love of someone; **in ~ (with)**, feeling love (for); **fall in ~ (with)**, experience (esp. sudden) feelings of love (toward); feel strong liking for (object); **make ~**, behave as a lover; engage in sexual intercourse. 3. Beloved one, sweetheart; (colloq.) delightful person, pretty young woman. 4. (tennis) No score, nothing, nil; **~ all**, state of game when neither side has yet scored; **~ game**, one in which loser has not scored. 5. **~ affair**, temporary relationship between two people who have fallen in love; **~ apple** (old name for) tomato; **love′bird**, one of several species of parakeet, esp. the W. Afr. *Agapornis pullarius*, remarkable for the affection it shows its mate; **love child**, illegitimate child; **love feast**, meal in token of brotherly love among early Christians; religious service among modern Christian sects; celebration, such as a banquet, held to create good feeling, to honor a special guest, etc.; **love-in-a-mist**, garden plant (*Nigella damascena*), with blue flowers surrounded by green threadlike bracts; S. Amer. passionflower, *Passiflora foetida*, with similar bracts; **love-in-idleness**, wild pansy; **love knot**, intricate knot of ribbon etc. with double bow; **love letter**, letter between sweethearts expressing love; **love-lies-bleeding**, garden plant (*Amaranthus caudatus*), with long drooping spikes of purplish-red bloom; **love′lock**, tress or curl worn on temple or forehead; **love′lorn**, pining with love, deserted by one's love; **love match**, marriage for the sake of love, not for money or convenience; **love seat**, armchair or sofa for two persons; **love′sick**, languishing with love; **love song**, song about or expressing love; **love story**, novel etc. of which main theme is love; story of a wooing etc.; **love token**, thing given in sign of love. **love** *v.* (**loved, lov·ing**). Hold dear, bear love for; be in love (with); be fond of; cling to, delight in, enjoy having, be addicted to, admire or be glad

***Lake Louise,** situated in the Banff National Park, Alberta, Canada, is renowned for its scenic beauty and draws many visitors each year who also come to explore the mountains.*

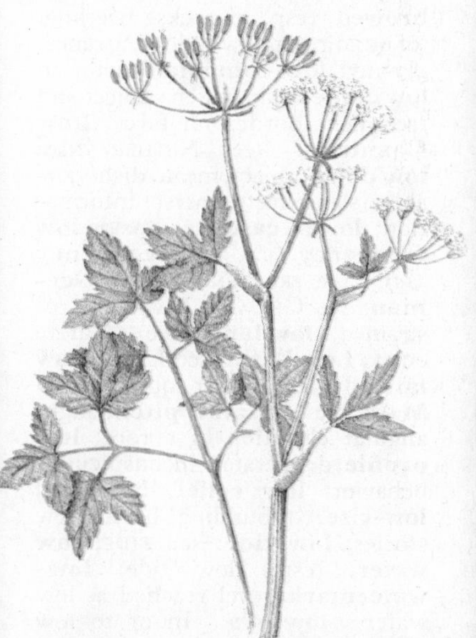

***Lovage** is cultivated for its stalks and foliage which are used for tea, as a vegetable and to flavor foods, particularly meats. Its flavor is similar to that of celery.*

*After the Vatican upheld claims that an apparition of the Virgin Mary had been seen, and that a nearby spring had healing powers, the town of **Lourdes** in the Hautes-Pyrénées has become a shrine for Roman Catholic pilgrims.*

of the existence of; be (habitually) inclined *to*; (colloq.) like, be delighted.

Love·lace (lŭv′lās), **Richard** (1618–58). English lyric poet.

love·less (lŭv′lĭs) *adj.* Unloving; unloved. **love′less·ly** *adv.* **love′less·ness** *n.*

love·ly (lŭv′lē) *adj.* (**-li·er, -li·est**). Attractively or admirably beautiful; (colloq.) delightful, very pleasing, intensely amusing. **love′li·ness** *n.* **lovely** *n.* (pl. **-lies**). Glamorously beautiful (young) woman.

lov·er (lŭv′*er*) *n.* 1. Man in love with a woman, (formerly) suitor; man having extramarital sexual relations with a woman; (pl.) two people in love or having a love affair; **~'s knot**, love knot. 2. Admirer, devotee, *of* thing etc. **lov′er·less, lov′er·like** *adjs.*

love·some (lŭv′s*o*m) *adj.* (archaic) Lovable; loving.

lov·ing (lŭv′ĭng) *adj.* That loves, affectionate; manifesting or proceeding from love; **~ cup**, large drinking vessel, usu. of silver with two or more handles passed around at banquet; **~-kindness**, tender regard.

low[1] (lō) *v.i.* Utter cry (as) of cow, moo. **~** *n.* Cow's cry.

low[2] (lō) *adj.* 1. Not reaching far up, not high or tall (not used of persons); not elevated in geographical etc. position. 2. Of small amount as measured by a scale or degrees; (of liquid, receptacle, supply of anything) nearly exhausted or empty; **at low′est**, to mention the least possible amount etc. 3. Of or in humble rank or position; not exalted or sublime, commonplace, undignified, little civilized, not highly organized; abject, mean, degraded, coarse, vulgar. 4. Weak, dejected; (of diet) not nourishing. 5. (of sound) Not shrill or high, produced by slow vibrations; not loud. 6. (of church etc.) Giving low place to authority of bishops and priests, inherent grace of sacraments, ecclesiastical organization, and ritual; not sacerdotal; approximating to Protestant nonconformity; **L~ Church, Churchman**, (member of) party in Church of England thus minded. 7. **bring ~**, depress, reduce, in health, wealth, or position; **lay ~**, overthrow; **lie ~**, crouch; be prostrate, dead, or abased; (slang) keep quiet or out of the way, say nothing; bide one's time. 8. **low′boy**, low chest of drawers on legs like the lower part of a highboy; **low′brow** (*n.*), **lowbrow** (*adj.*), (colloq.) (of person) not highly or not pretentiously intellectual; **low-browed**, (esp. of rocks) beetling, (of building etc.) with low entrance, gloomy; **low comedian**, actor in **low comedy**, in which subject and treatment border on farce; **Low Countries**: see NETHERLANDS; **low′down**, abject, mean, dishonorable; (slang) facts, correct information; **lower case**: see CASE[2]; **low frequency** (*n.*), **low-frequency** (*adj.*): see FREQUENCY; **Low German**: see GERMAN; **low-key**, restrained; **low′land**: see separate entry; **Low Latin**: see LATIN; **low latitudes**, those near equator; **Low Mass**: see MASS; **low pitch**, slight angular elevation of a roof; **low profile**, deliberately inconspicuous behavior; **low relief**, bas-relief; **low-rise**, (of building) having few stories; **low tide**: see TIDE; **low water**, (esp.) low tide; **low-watermark**, level reached at low water. **low** *adv.* In or to low or mean position; on poor diet; for small stakes; in low tone, on or to low note; **low′born**, of humble birth; **low′bred**, of vulgar manners; **low′er·most, low′ish** *adjs.* **low′ness** *n.* **low** *n.* What is

***Love** between people has been celebrated in myth, legend, art and song since the beginning of history. The god of Love (Cupid or Eros) in Greek and Roman mythology was depicted as a winged youth. Left: 'Psyche Crowning Love' a painting by Greuze. Right: 'The Kiss', by Rodin.*

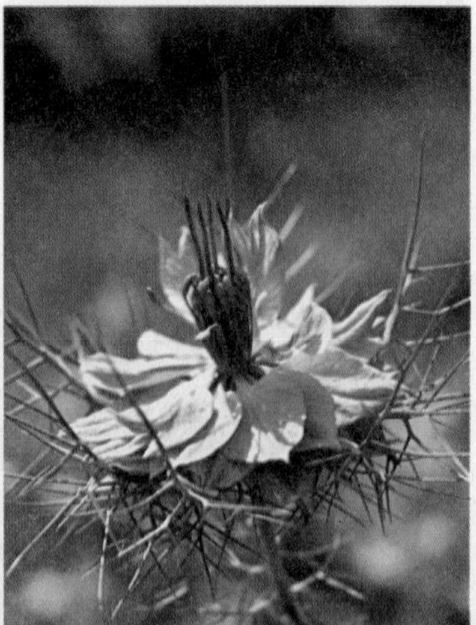

***Love-in-a-mist** is a herbaceous plant of the buttercup family and is grown in gardens in temperate regions of the world. It is 18 to 24 ins. tall and has blue flowers.*

low; low level or figure; area of low atmospheric pressure, center of a depression.

Low·ell[1] (lō´el), **Amy (Lawrence)** (1874–1925). American poet; leader of the imagist movement in the U.S.; used much free verse and "polyphonic prose."

Low·ell[2] (lō´el), **James Russell** (1819–91). American poet, essayist, and editor; now best remembered as a distinguished popular poet of his day and as author of *The Biglow Papers*; he was also a leading linguist, first editor of *The Atlantic Monthly* magazine (1857), co-editor of *The North American Review*, and U.S. minister to Spain and England.

Low·ell[3] (lō´el), **Percival** (1855–1916). American astronomer; founder of the ~ **Observatory** at Flagstaff, Arizona.

Low·ell[4] (lō´el), **Robert** (1917–1977). American poet; author of *Lord Weary's Castle, Imitations*, etc.

low·er[1] (lō´*er*) *v.* Let or haul down; (naut.) let down boat, haul down sail etc.; diminish height of; sink, descend, slope downward; diminish (price etc.); (of price etc.) come down; diminish in intensity or pitch; degrade, disgrace; reduce bodily condition of.

low·er[2], **lour** (low´*er*) *vbs.i.* Frown, scowl, look sullen; (of clouds etc.) look dark and threatening. ~ *n.* Scowl; gloominess of sky etc. **low´er·ing·ly** *adv.* **low´er·y** *adj.*

low·land (lō´l*a*nd) *n.* (usu. pl.) Less mountainous part of a country, esp. (Lowlands) that part of Scotland S. and E. of Highlands. ~ *adj.* **low´land·er** *n.* Inhabitant of lowlands, esp. (**L** ~) those of Scotland.

low·ly (lō´lē) *adj.* (**-li·er, -li·est**). Humble in feeling, behavior, or condition; modest. ~ *adv.* In lowly manner. **low´li·ness** *n.*

lox[1] (lŏks) *n.* Smoked salmon.

lox[2] (lŏks) *n.* Liquid oxygen. [*l*(iquid) *ox*(ygen)]

loy·al (loi´*a*l) *adj.* True, faithful, to duty, love, or obligation (*to*); faithful in allegiance to sovereign, government, or mother country; enthusiastically devoted to sovereign's person and family; exhibiting loyalty. **loy´al·ly** *adv.* **loy´al·ism, loy´al·ist** *ns.*

loy·al·ty (loi´*a*ltē) *n.* (pl. **-ties**). Loyal temper or conduct.

Loy·o·la (loiō´l*a*) = IGNATIUS LOYOLA.

loz·enge (lŏz´ĭnj) *n.* 1. Rhomb, diamond figure, esp. as bearing in heraldry; lozenge-shaped shield for spinster's or widow's arms; lozenge-shaped facet of cut gem; lozenge-shaped pane in casement etc. 2. Small tablet, orig. lozenge-shaped, usu. of flavored or medicated sugar, to be dissolved in mouth.

LP (pl. **LPs, LP's**). (trademark) Microgroove phonograph record making 33⅓ revolutions a minute.

L.P., l.p. *abbrevs.* Low pressure.

LPG *abbrev.* Liquefied petroleum gas.

LPN *abbrev.* Licensed practical nurse.

L.S., l.s. *abbrevs.* *Locus sigilli* (L., = the place of the seal, on documents).

LSD *abbrev.* Lysergic acid diethylamide ($C_{20}H_{25}N_3O$), derivative of lysergic acid, powerful hallucinogenic drug, occas. used in psychiatric treatment.

£.s.d. *abbrev.* Pounds, shillings, and pence. [L. *librae, solidi, denarii*]

Lt. *abbrev.* Lieutenant.

Ltd., ltd. *abbrevs.* (Brit.) Limited (liability company).

Lu *symbol.* Lutetium.

Lu·an·da (lo͞oăn´d*a*). Capital and a seaport of Angola, on the Atlantic Ocean.

lu·au (lo͞o´ow) *n.* (pl. **lu·aus**). Hawaiian-style party.

lub·ber (lŭb´*er*) *n.* Big clumsy stupid fellow, lout; clumsy seaman, unseamanlike fellow; **~'s line** (or ~ **line**), **mark**, vertical line inside a compass case, indicating the direction of the ship's head. **lub´ber·ly** *adj.* & *adv.*

Lü·beck (lü´bĕk). City of N. Germany, a Baltic seaport, formerly head of the HANSEatic League.

lu·bri·cate (lo͞o´br*i*kāt) *v.t.* (**-cat·ed, -cat·ing**). Make slippery or smooth by applying fluid or lubricant; minimize friction of (machinery) with grease etc. **lu´bri·cant** *adj.* & *n.* **lu·bri·ca·tion** (lo͞obr*i*kā´sh*o*n), **lu´bri·ca·tor** *ns.*

lu·bric·i·ty (lo͞obrĭs´ĭtē) *n.* Slipperiness, smoothness, oiliness; lewdness, wantonness.

lu·cent (lo͞o´s*e*nt) *adj.* Shining, luminous, translucent. **lu´cen·cy** *n.* **lu´cent·ly** *adv.*

Lu·cerne (lo͞osern´). (Ger. *Luzern*) Canton and city of central Switzerland; **Lake of** ~, the principal lake of central Switzerland, the city is on its NW. shore.

lu·cid (lo͞o´sĭd) *adj.* Bright (poet.); clear, pellucid; (entom., bot.) with smooth shining surface; ~ **interval**, period of sanity between attacks of madness. **lu´cid·ly** *adv.* **lu·cid´i·ty, lu´cid·ness** *ns.*

Lu·ci·fer (lo͞o´s*i*f*er*) 1. The planet Venus when it appears in the sky before sunrise; the morning star. 2. By misunderstanding of Isa. 14 (where the Hebrew epithet "shining one," translated as *Lucifer* in the Vulgate, is applied to the king of Babylon), Satan, the rebel archangel, before his fall; now chiefly in phr. **as proud as Lucifer.** [L., = "light bringer"]

Lu·ci·na (lo͞osī´n*a*). (Rom. myth.) Goddess who presided over birth; chiefly as epithet of Juno or occas. of Diana.

Lubeck, a seaport in Schleswig-Holstein, West Germany, is linked by canal with the Elbe. This medieval gate and adjoining churches survived air raids in the 1939–45 war.

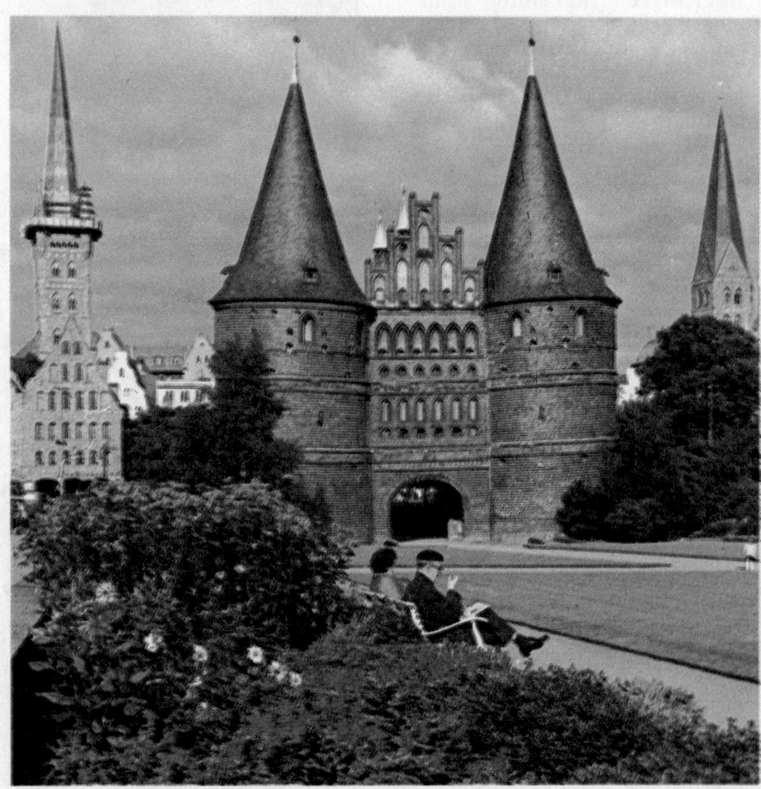

***Lucknow,** the capital of Uttar Pradesh, India, in the Ganges valley, is a commercial center with textile, chemical and engineering industries. Shown here is the Old Turkish Gateway near the great Inambara Mosque.*

Lu·cite (lo͞o′sīt) *n.* (trademark) Tough unsplinterable transparent acrylic thermoplastic, much lighter than glass, for which it is widely used as a substitute.

luck (lŭk) *n.* (Chance as bestower of) good or ill fortune; fortuitous event affecting one's interests; person's apparent tendency to be (un)fortunate; supposed tendency of chance to bring a succession of (un)favorable events; good fortune, success due to chance; **as ~ would have it**, fortunately or unfortunately; **down on one's ~**, dispirited by misfortune, temporarily unfortunate; **for ~**, to bring good luck; **~ out**, have good luck; **try one's ~**, venture at gambling table etc.; **worse ~**, more's the pity. **luck′less** *adj.* **luck′less·ness** *n.*

luck·i·ly (lŭk′*i*lē) *adv.* Fortunately.

Luck·now (lŭk′now). Capital city of Uttar Pradesh, India, formerly capital of Oudh.

luck·y (lŭk′ē) *adj.* (**luck·i·er, luck·i·est**). Constantly attended by good luck, enjoying it on a particular occasion; (of guess etc.) right by luck, of the nature of a fluke; occurring by chance and bringing happy results; presaging, bringing, worn, etc. for, good luck, well-omened. **luck′i·ness** *n.*

lu·cra·tive (lo͞o′kratĭv) *adj.* Yielding gain, profitable. **lu′cra·tive·ly** *adv.* **lu′cra·tive·ness** *n.*

lu·cre (lo͞o′k*e*r) *n.* (derog.) Gain, pecuniary profit as motive; **filthy ~**: see FILTHY.

Lu·cre·tia (lo͝okrē′sh*a*). (Rom. legend) Wife of Lucius Tarquinius Collatinus; she was raped by Sextus, son of Tarquinius Superbus, and took her own life; this led to the expulsion of the Tarquins from Rome and the establishment of the republic.

Lu·cre·tius (lo͝okrē′sh*u*s). Titus Lucretius Carus (*c*94–55 B.C.), Latin poet; author of a philosophical poem "De Rerum Natura," in which he tried to show that the course of the world can be explained without postulating divine intervention.

lu·cu·brate (lo͞o′kyo͝obrāt) *v.i.* (**-brat·ed, -brat·ing**). Express one's meditations in writing; produce lucubrations. **lu·cu·bra·tion** (lo͝okyo͝obrā′sh*o*n) *n.* Nocturnal study or meditation; literary work

***Ludwig II** of Bavaria, a patron of Wagner, built this fantastic Gothic castle, Neuschwanstein, in 1869 on a dramatic mountain site. He was declared insane in 1886.*

Lake Lugano has an area of 19½ sq. miles, 18 of which are in Ticino canton, Switzerland, and the remainder in Lombardy, Italy. Its wooded shores are mostly precipitous and desolate.

esp. of pedantic or elaborate character. [L. *lucubrare*, work by lamplight (*lux*, light)]

Lu·cul·lus (lo͞okŭl'*us*), **Lucius Licinius** (*c*110–50 B.C.). Roman general; consul 74 B.C.; famous for magnificence and luxury esp. in his banquets. **Lu·cul'lan, Lu·cul·le·an** (lo͞o*k*ulē'*an*), **Lu·cul'li·an** *adjs.*

Lu·cy (lo͞o'sē), **St.** (3rd c. A.D.). Sicilian virgin and martyr, commemorated Dec. 13; patron saint of the blind.

Lud·dite (lŭdīt) *adj.* & *n.* (Member) of organized bands of English artisans who in the period 1811–16 destroyed newly introduced machinery in the Midlands and N. of England on the ground that it took away their livelihood. [said to be f. Ned *Ludd*, a feeble-minded person who broke up some machinery in a fit of insane rage]

Lu·den·dorff (lo͞o'd*e*ndôrf), **Erich von** (1865–1937). German general in World War I; was associated with Hitler in the "Beer-Hall Putsch" at Munich, 1923.

lu·di·crous (lo͞o'd*i*kr*us*) *adj.* Absurd, ridiculous; exciting or deserving derision. **lu'di·crous·ly** *adv.* **lu'di·crous·ness** *n.*

Lud·wig (lo͝od'vĭg). Name of three kings of Bavaria: **Ludwig I** (1786–1868), king 1825–48; was most popular until he allowed most of the power of government to fall into the hands of his mistress, Lola Montez; abdicated 1848 in favor of his son Maximilian II; **Ludwig II** (1845–86), son of Maximilian II, king 1864–86; patron of the arts, esp. music, and friend of Wagner; built fantastic Gothic castles; was declared insane and committed suicide 1886; **Ludwig III** (1845–1921), crowned king of Bavaria 1913, abdicated 1918.

Luft·waf·fe (lo͞oft'vahf*e*) *n.* German Air Force. [Ger.]

lug[1] (lŭg) *n.* (also **lug·worm** pr. lŭg'wěrm). Large marine worm (*Arenicola marina*) burrowing in sand, and used for bait.

lug[2] (lŭg) = LUGSAIL.

lug[3] (lŭg) *v.* (**lugged, lug·ging**). Drag or tug (heavy object) with effort or violence; pull hard *at*; force (person) along. ~ *n.* Hard or rough pull.

lug[4] (lŭg) *n.* Ear (Sc.); projection or handle on vase etc.; projection from a casting etc. by which it may be fixed in place.

Lu·ga·no (lo͞ogah'nō), **Lake of.** Lake of N. Italy and S. Switzerland, in foothills of the Alps; center of resort area.

lug·gage (lŭg'ĭj) *n.* Suitcases, bags, etc., (for) containing traveler's belongings

lug·sail (lŭg'sāl; *naut.* lŭg's*a*l) *n.* Four-cornered sail bent on yard slung at a third or quarter of its length from one end.

lu·gu·bri·ous (lo͞ogo͞o'brē*us*, -gū'-) *adj.* Doleful, dismal, mournful. **lu·gu'bri·ous·ly** *adv.* **lu·gu'bri·ous·ness** *n.*

lug·worm = LUG.[1]

Luke (lo͝ok), **St.** Apostle, a physician, possibly the son of a Greek freedman of Rome, closely associated with St. Paul, and author of the third Gospel and the Acts of the Apostles; commemorated Oct. 18; third Gospel.

luke·warm (lo͞ok'wôrm') *adj.* Moderately warm, tepid; not zealous, indifferent. **luke'warm'ly** *adv.* **luke'warm'ness** *n.*

lull (lŭl) *v.* Soothe or send to sleep by sounds or caresses; quiet (suspicion etc.); (usu. pass.) quiet (sea, storm); (of storm etc.) lessen, fall quiet. ~ *n.* Intermission in storm, interval of quiet.

lull·a·by (lŭl'*a*bī) *n.* (pl. **-bies**). Soothing refrain or song to put child to sleep. ~ *v.t.* (**-bied, -by·ing**). Sing to sleep.

Lul·ly (lo͞o'lē, *Fr.* lülē), **Jean-Baptiste** (1639–87). Italian-born French violinist, court composer, and composer of operas; founder of French grand opera; wrote the song "Au Clair de la Lune" etc.

lum·ba·go (lŭmbā'gō) *n.* Painful affection, usu. inflammatory, of the muscles of the loins.

lum·bar (lŭm'b*er*, -bar) *adj.* Of the loin(s).

lum·ber[1] (lŭm'b*er*) *v.i.* Move in clumsy, blundering, often noisy way. **lum'ber·ing** *adj.* & *n.* **lum'ber·ing·ly** *adv.*

lum·ber[2] (lŭm'b*er*) *n.* Roughly prepared timber; **lum'ber·jack,** lumberman; **lum'ber·man** (lŭm'b*er*m*a*n), feller, dresser, or conveyer of lumber; **lum'ber·mill,** sawmill for cutting up lumber. **lumber** *v.* Cut and prepare forest timber. **lum'ber·er** *n.*

lum·bri·cal (lŭm'brĭk*a*l) *adj.* ~ **muscle,** one of the muscles flexing fingers or toes. **lumbrical** *n.* Lumbrical muscle.

lu·men[1] (lo͞o'm*e*n) *n.* (pl. **-mi·na** pr. -m*i*n*a*). Unit of light energy or luminous flux, the light energy emitted in a unit solid angle by a uniform point source of one candle; **~-hour,** unit of luminous energy, equal to the emission of 1 lumen for 1 hour.

lu·men[2] (lo͞o'men) *n.* (pl. **-mi·na** pr. -m*i*n*a*). (physiol.) Canal, duct, or bore of a tubular organ.

Lu·mière (lo͞omyar'; *Fr.* lümyěr'), **Auguste Marie Louis Nicholas** (1862–1954); his brother, **Louis Jean** (1864–1948). French chemists, inventors, and pioneers in photography and color photography; invented an early motion-picture camera.

Lu·mi·nal (lo͞o'm*i*n*a*l) *n.* (trademark) Phenobarbital, a preparation of phenobarbitone ($C_{12}H_{12}O_3N_2$), used medicinally as a sedative.

lu·mi·nance (lo͞o'm*i*n*a*ns) *n.* Luminosity; (measure of) brightness.

lu·mi·nar·y (lo͞o'm*i*nĕrē) *n.* (pl. **-nar·ies**). Natural light-giving body, esp. sun or moon; person of intellectual, moral, or spiritual eminence.

lu·mi·nes·cent (lo͞omĭnĕs′ent) *adj.* Emitting light from some cause other than high temperature. **lu·mi·nes′cence** *n.*

lu·mi·nif·er·ous (lo͞omĭnĭf′erus) *adj.* Producing or transmitting light.

lu·mi·nous (lo͞o′minus) *adj.* Emitting or full of light, bright, shining; ~ **paint**, phosphorescent paint making thing conspicuous at night. **lu′mi·nous·ly** *adv.* **lu′mi·nous·ness, lu·mi·nos·i·ty** (lo͞ominŏs′ĭtē) *ns.*

lump[1] (lŭmp) *n.* Compact shapeless or unshapely mass; great quantity, lot, heap; mass of clay or dough ready for molding or baking; protuberance, excrescence, swelling, bruise; heavy dull person; ~ **in throat**, feeling of pressure caused by emotion; ~ **sugar**, loaf sugar broken or cut into lumps or cubes; ~ **sum**, sum covering or including a number of items; sum paid down at once (opp. INSTALLMENTS). **lump** *v.* Put together in one lump; mass *together*, treat as all alike, disregard differences between or among; rise or collect into lumps; go heavily *along*, sit heavily *down*.

lump[2] (lŭmp) *v.t.* Put up with, endure (unpleasant necessity), as **if you don't like it, ~ it**.

lump·fish (lŭmp′fĭsh) *n.* (pl. **-fish·es**, collect. **-fish**). Sluggish spiny-finned leaden-blue fish (*Cyclopterus lumpus*) of the N. Atlantic with sucking disk on belly.

lump·ish (lŭm′pĭsh) *adj.* Heavy and clumsy; stupid, lethargic. **lump′ish·ly** *adv.* **lump′ish·ness** *n.*

lump·y (lŭm′pē) *adj.* (**lump·i·er, lump·i·est**). Full of or covered with lumps; (of water) cut up by wind into small waves. **lump′i·ly** *adv.* **lump′i·ness** *n.*

lu·na·cy (lo͞o′nasē) *n.* (pl. **-cies**). Being a lunatic, insanity (formerly of the intermittent kind attributed to moon's changes); great folly.

lu·nar (lo͞o′ner) *adj.* Of, in, as of, the moon; (of light, glory, etc.) pale, feeble; crescent-shaped; of or containing silver (from alchemists' use of *luna* (L., = moon) for silver); ~ **bone** = LUNATE bone; ~ **caustic**, silver nitrate, esp. in stick form for surgical use; ~ **distance**, distance of moon from sun, planet, or star, used in finding longitude at sea; ~ **module**: see MODULE; ~ **month**: see MONTH; ~ **rainbow**, one made by moon's rays.

lu·nate (lo͞o′nāt), **lu·nat·ed** (lo͞o′nātĭd) *adj.* Crescent-shaped; ~ **bone**, crescent-shaped bone in carpal bones. **lunate** *n.* Lunate bone; lunate prehistoric implement, etc.

lu·na·tic (lo͞o′natĭk) *adj.* Insane; (of action etc.) outrageously foolish. ~ *n.* Insane person; ~ **asylum**, (formerly) mental institution; ~ **fringe**, fanatical or eccentric or visionary minority of political party etc. [L. *luna* moon, because insanity was thought to be caused by the moon's changes]

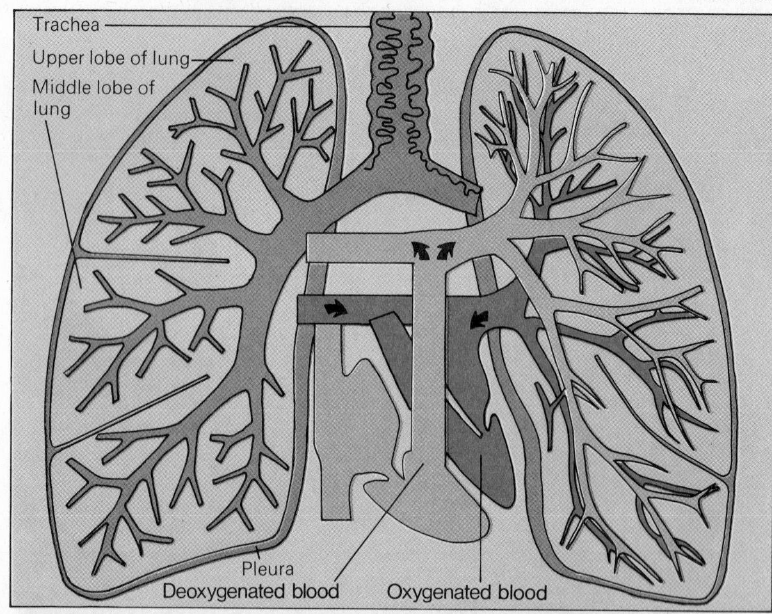

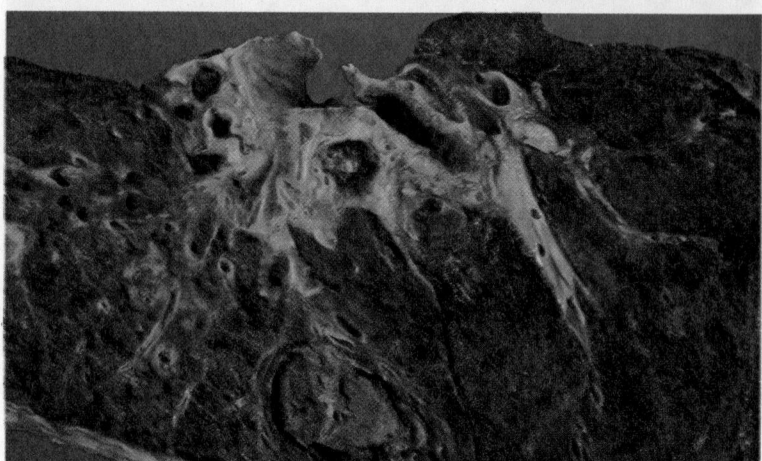

*The human **lungs** (top) are soft, spongy, elastic organs that are responsible for providing the body with air and for discharging certain waste products. Diseases of the lungs can cause serious illness and their incidence has increased. Above: A lung inflamed by exposure to irradiation.*

lu·na·tion (lo͞onā′shon) *n.* Time from one new moon to next.

lunch (lŭnch) *n.* (now the more usual word, exc. in formal use, for) Luncheon. ~ *v.* Take lunch; (colloq.) provide lunch for.

lunch·eon (lŭn′chon) *n.* (orig.) Slight repast between two ordinary mealtimes, esp. breakfast and midday dinner; now the midday meal, usu. less substantial and less ceremonious than dinner; ~ **meat**, cooked meat in loaf form ready to cut and eat.

lune (lo͞on) *n.* (geom.) Figure formed on sphere or plane by two arcs of circles enclosing a space.

lu·nette (lo͞onĕt′) *n.* Arched aperture in concave ceiling to admit light; crescent-shaped or semicircular space in dome or ceiling decorated with painting etc.; watch glass of flattened shape; hole for neck in guillotine.

lung (lŭng) *n.* Either of the pair of saccular respiratory organs in man and other vertebrates, placed within cavity of thorax on either side of heart and communicating with trachea or windpipe; (pl.) open space(s) in or near a city; **lung′fish**, fish having lungs as well as gills; **lung power**, power of voice; **lung′wort**, European plant (*Pulmonaria officinalis*, order Boraginaceae) having leaves with white spots supposed to resemble those of diseased lung; plant of allied Amer. genus *Mertensia*.

lunge[1], **longe** (lŭnj) *ns.* Long rope with which horse trainer holds horse while he makes it canter in circle; circular exercise ground for training horses. ~ *v.t.* (**lunged, lung·ing**). Exercise (horse) with or in lunge.

*The **lupin,** of which there are about 200 species, occurs in the western hemisphere and in the Mediterranean region. The attractive flowers grow in long terminal clusters.*

lunge[2] (lŭnj) *n.* Thrust with sword etc., esp. in fencing; sudden forward movement, plunge, rush; (gymnastics) forward movement, in which one foot is advanced, the knee being bent and directly over the instep, while the other foot remains stationary. ~ *v.* (**lunged, lung·ing, longed, long·ing**). Make lunge in fencing or gymnastics, deliver blow from shoulder in boxing; drive (weapon etc.) violently in some direction; rush, make sudden start in some direction.

lu·ni·so·lar (lo͞onĭsō′ler) *adj.* Of mutual relations or combined action of sun and moon; ~ **period,** cycle of 532 years between agreement of solar and lunar cycles (which are of 28 and 19 years); ~ **year,** year with divisions regulated by changes of moon and average total length made to agree with revolution of sun.

lunk·head (lŭngk′hĕd) *n.* (slang) Stupid, dull person. **lunk′head·ed** *adj.*

Lu·per·cal (lo͞o′perkăl). Cave on Palatine hill in ancient Rome, sacred to **Lu·per·cus** (lo͞opẽr′kus), or Faunus in the guise of a wolf-deity, connected with the story of Romulus and Remus. **Lu·per·ca·li·an** (lo͞operkā′lēan) *adj.*

lu·pine[1], **lu·pin** (lo͞o′pĭn) *ns.* Plant of genus *Lupinus*, esp. *L. albus*, cultivated in warmer districts of Europe for fodder, and the Amer. species cultivated in gardens, with long tapering spikes of flowers; (usu. pl.) seed of any of these.

lu·pine[2] (lo͞o′pĭn) *adj.* Of wolf or wolves, wolflike.

lu·pus (lo͞o′pus) *n.* Ulcerous disease of skin; ~ **vulgaris,** tuberculosis of the skin.

lurch[1] (lẽrch) *n.* **leave in the** ~, desert (friend, ally) in difficulties. [formerly = state of score in some games in which one player was far ahead of the other, f. Fr. *lourche* game like backgammon, also bad defeat in this]

lurch[2] (lẽrch) *n.* Sudden lean to one side, stagger. ~ *v.i.* Make lurch(es), stagger.

lure (loor) *n.* 1. Falconer's apparatus for recalling hawk, usu. a bunch of feathers (within which hawk finds food during training) attached to cord. 2. Something used to entice; enticing quality *of*. ~ *v.t.* (**lured, lur·ing**). Recall (hawk) with lure; entice (*away, into*, etc.).

lu·rid (loor′ĭd) *adj.* Wan and sallow, ghastly; shining with a red glare or glow amid darkness; terrible, ominous, sensational; (bot. etc.) dingy yellowish brown. **lu′rid·ly** *adv.* **lu′rid·ness** *n.*

lurk (lẽrk) *v.i.* Be hidden *in, under*, etc., prowl; escape notice, exist unobserved, be latent. **lurk′ing·ly** *adv.*

Lu·sa·ka (lo͞osah′ka). Capital of Gambia in the S. central part.

lus·cious (lŭsh′us) *adj.* Richly sweet in taste or smell; sickly sweet, cloying; (of style etc.) overly rich in sound, imagery, or voluptuous suggestion. **lus′cious·ly** *adv.* **lus′cious·ness** *n.*

lush[1] (lŭsh) *adj.* 1. (of vegetation, esp. grass) Luxuriant and succulent. 2. Characterized by or having luxuriant vegetation or growth. 3. Opulent; luxurious; abundant. **lush′ness** *n.*

lush[2] (lŭsh) *n.* (slang) Person who habitually drinks too much whiskey; alcoholic; drunkard.

lust (lŭst) *n.* Sensuous appetite regarded as sinful (esp. bibl., theol.); animal desire for sexual indulgence; passionate enjoyment or desire *of*. ~ *v.i.* Have strong or excessive desire (*after, for*).

*The **lungwort,** which is widespread in the open woods and thickets of Europe, is grown as a garden flower. It has drooping pink flowers that turn blue, and white spotted leaves.*

lust′ful *adj.* **lust′ful·ly** *adv.* **lust′ful·ness** *n.*

lus·ter, Brit. **lus·tre** (lŭs′ter) *ns.* 1. Quality of shining by reflected light, often with effect of changing color; sheen, gloss; luminous splendor, radiant beauty; splendor, glory, distinction. 2. (Prismatic glass pendant of) chandelier. 3. Fabric with lustrous surface. 4. Iridescent glaze applied to pottery and porcelain; ware glazed with this. ~ *v.t.* Put luster on. **lus′ter·less, lus·trous** (lŭs′trus) *adjs.* **lus′trous·ly** *adv.*

lus·tral (lŭs′tral) *adj.* Of, used in, ceremonial purification.

lus·trate (lŭs′trāt) *v.t.* (**-trat·ed, -trat·ing**). Purify by expiatory sacrifice, ceremonial washing, or other rite. **lus·tra′tion** *n.* [see LUSTRUM]

lus·trum (lŭs′trum) *n.* (pl. **-trums, -tra** pr. -tra). Period of five years. [L. orig. purificatory sacrifice made every five years after census had been taken]

lust·y (lŭs′tē) *adj.* (**lust·i·er, lust·i·est**). Healthy and strong; vigorous, lively. **lust′i·ly** *adv.* **lust′i·ness** *n.*

*This Australian **lungfish** is found in Queensland. It uses gills when swimming in well oxygenated waters, but when necessary it can breathe gaseous oxygen (air). Similar fish are found in Africa and South America.*

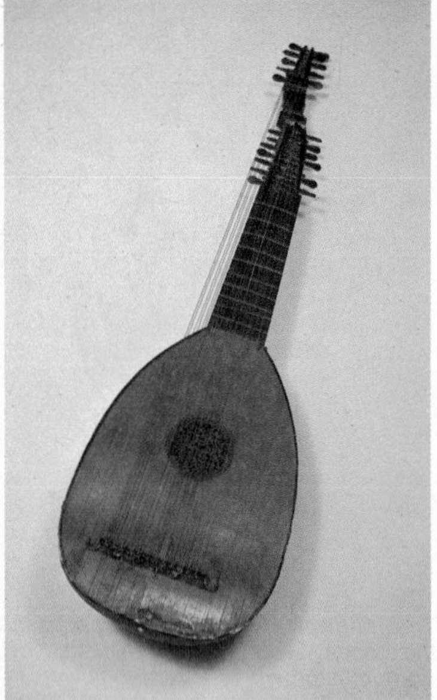

*This **theorbo lute** or bass lute is a modification of the stringed instrument which was so popular in Europe in the Renaissance and Baroque periods. The lute was brought from Arab countries to Europe.*

*The Grand Duchy of **Luxemburg** in west Europe has an area of 999 sq. miles. Its most important industry is steel, 90% of which is exported. Above: Beaufort Castle in Luxemburg. Above right: Map and flag of Luxemburg.*

lu·tan·ist, lu·te·nist (lōō′t*a*nĭst) *ns.* Lute player.

lute[1] (lōōt) *n.* Musical instrument much used in 14th–17th centuries, with pear-shaped body, with strings struck with fingers of right hand and stopped on frets with those of left. [Arab. *al'ud* the lute (*'ud* orig. wood)]

lute[2] (lōōt) *n.* Tenacious clay or cement used to stop hole, make joint airtight, coat crucible, protect graft, etc. ~ *v.t.* (**lut·ed, lut·ing**). Apply lute to.

lu·te·ous (lōō′tē*u*s) *adj.* Greenish or brownish yellow.

lu·te·ti·um (lōōtē′shē*u*m) *n.* (chem.) Metallic element of rare-earth group, resembling ytterbium in properties; symbol Lu, at. no. 71, at. wt. 174.97. [f. *Lutetia*, Latin name of Paris]

Lu·ther (lōō′th*e*r), **Martin** (1483–1546). Leader of the Protestant Reformation in Germany; translator (1522–34) of the Bible into German and author of many hymns. **Lu·ther·an** (lōō′th*e*r*a*n, -thrĭn) *adj.* Of Luther, his opinions and followers, or the Lutheran Church; ~ **Church**, those churches, esp. in Germany and Scandinavia, that accept the doctrines of the Augsburg Confession (1530) and whose cardinal doctrine is that of justification by faith alone.

lux (lŭks) *n.* (pl. **lu·ces** pr. lōō′sēz). International unit of illumination, the illumination of a surface at a uniform distance of 1 meter from a symmetrical point source of 1 candle, equal to 1 LUMEN[1] per square meter.

lux·ate (lŭk′sāt) *v.t.* (**-at·ed, -at·ing**). Dislocate (joint etc.). **lux·a′tion** *n.*

Lux·em·bourg[1], **Lux·em·burg** (lŭk′s*e*mbẽrg; *Fr.* lüksahṅboor′). Small (999 sq. mile, 2,588 sq. km) constitutional monarchy and grand duchy in W. Europe, S. of Belgium and between France and W. Germany; (also ~ **City**) its capital.

Lux·em·bourg[2] (lŭk′s*e*mbẽrg; *Fr.* lüksahṅboor′), **Palais du.** Palace S. of the Seine in Paris, built 1615–20 for Marie de Médicis and now the meeting place of the French Senate, with gardens open to the public.

Lux·or (lŭk′sōr). Town of Upper Egypt on E. bank of the Nile, 415 miles (668 km) S. of Cairo; contains Karnak and the ruins of ancient THEBES.

lux·u·ri·ant (lŭgzhoor′ē*a*nt, lŭkshoor′-) *adj.* Prolific, profuse of growth, exuberant, rank; florid, richly ornamented. **lux·u′ri·ant·ly** *adv.* **lux·u′ri·ance** *n.*

lux·u·ri·ate (lŭgzhoor′ēāt, lŭkshoor′-) *v.i.* (**-at·ed, -at·ing**). Revel, enjoy oneself; take one's ease, be luxurious.

lux·u·ri·ous (lŭgzhoor′ē*u*s, lŭkshŏŏr′-) *adj.* Given, contributing, to luxury, self-indulgent, voluptuous, very comfortable. **lux·u′ri·ous·ly** *adv.* **lux·u′ri·ous·ness** *n.*

lux·u·ry (lŭk′sh*e*rē, lŭg′zh*e*rē) *n.* (pl. **-ries**). (Habitual use of) choice or costly food, dress, furniture, etc.; refined and intense enjoyment; thing conducive to comfort or enjoyment in addition to what are considered necessaries, thing desirable but not essential.

Lu·zon (lōōzŏn′). Largest island, 40,420 square miles (104,688 sq. km), in the N. part of the Republic of the Philippines.

ly·can·thro·py (līkăn′thr*o*pē) *n.* 1. Witchcraft consisting in assumption by human beings of form and nature of wolves. 2. Form of insanity in which the sufferer imagines himself a beast and exhibits depraved appetites etc. **ly·can·thrope** (lī′k*a*nthrōp, līkăn′-thrōp) *n.* 1. Werewolf. 2. Person afflicted by lycanthropy.

Ly·ca·on (līkā′ŏn, -on). (Gk. legend) King of Arcadia who, as the host of Zeus, offered him human flesh to eat, in order to try his divinity; he was killed by lightning or turned into a wolf.

ly·cée (lēsā′) *n.* (pl. **-cées** pr. -sāz′; *Fr.* -sā′). State secondary school in France (dist. from *collège*, municipal secondary school). [Fr. f. LYCEUM]

ly·ce·um (līsē′*u*m) *n.* 1. (**L~**) Grove and gymnasium near Athens, sacred to Apollo Lyceus, where Aristotle taught; hence, Aristotle's philosophy or followers. 2. Institution providing literary or scientific lectures, concerts, etc.

lych·nis (lĭk′nĭs): see CAMPION.

ly·co·pod (lī′k*o*pŏd) *n.* (bot.) Club moss.

ly·co·po·di·um (līk*o*pō′dē*u*m) *n.* Cryptogamous plant of genus *L*~, club moss; highly inflammable powder from spores of species of this, used in fireworks etc.

lydd·ite (lĭd′īt) *n.* High explosive chiefly of picric acid, formerly used in shells. [*Lydd* in Kent, where first tested in England]

Lyd·gate (lĭd′gāt, -gĭt), **John** (*c*1370–*c*1451). English poet; author of devotional, philosophical, and historical poems and of allegories and moral romances.

Lyd·i·a (lĭd′ea). Ancient kingdom and (7th to 6th c. B.C.) empire of W. Asia Minor.

Lyd·i·an (lĭd′ēan) *adj.* 1. Of ancient Lydia, its people, or their language. 2. ~ **mode**, (mus.) ancient Greek mode, reputedly effeminate in character; fifth of ecclesiastical modes with F as final and C as dominant. 3. Soft or effeminate; voluptuous. **Lydian** *n.* Lydian person or language.

lye (lī) *n.* Water made alkaline by lixiviation of vegetable ashes; any strong alkaline solution esp. for washing, any detergent.

ly·ing[1] (lī′ĭng) *adj.*: see LIE[1]; (esp.) deceitful, false. **ly′ing·ly** *adv.*

ly·ing[2] (lī′ĭng) *adj.*: see LIE[2]; (esp.) ~ **down**, (fig.) without protest (of insult etc.). **lying** *n.* (esp.) ~ **-in**, being confined in childbirth.

Lyl·y (lĭl′ē), **John** (*c*1554–1606). English author of plays, pamphlets, and a prose romance, *Euphues, or the Anatomy of Wit*.

lymph (lĭmf) *n.* 1. (poet.) Pure water. 2. (physiol.) Colorless slightly alkaline fluid derived from the blood by permeation through the walls of the capillaries, and drains into the lymphatic vessels; exudation from sore etc.; (also **calf, vaccine,** ~) preparation derived from cowpox vesicles, used in vaccination against smallpox; ~ **glands (nodes)**, small masses of specialized tissue at intervals in lymphatic system, filtering off foreign particles from lymph and producting lymphocytes. **lymph·oid** (lĭm′foid) *adj.*

lym·phat·ic (lĭmfăt′ĭk) *adj.* 1. Of, secreting, conveying, lymph; ~ **duct, gland**, one in the system of fine vessels in which lymph circulates and which communicates with the venous system. 2. Flabby-muscled, pale-skinned, sluggish (qualities formerly attributed to excess of lymph). **lymphatic** *n.* Veinlike vessel conveying lymph.

lym·pho·cyte (lĭm′fosīt) *n.* Form of white blood cell.

lyn·ce·an (lĭnsē′an) *adj.* Lynx-eyed, keen-sighted.

lynch (lĭnch) *v.t.* Condemn and punish by ~ **law,** (1) infliction of summary punishment on offender by self-constituted court with no legal authority, (2) summary execution of one charged with some offense. **lynch′er, lynch′ing** *ns.* [After Capt. W. *Lynch* (1742–1820) of Pittsylvania, Virginia]

lynx (lĭngks) *n.* (pl. **lynx·es,** collect. **lynx**). Any of various members of the cat family found only in N. hemisphere, with tufted ear tips, short tail, spotted fur, esp. **Canada** ~ (*L. canadensis*), having soft gray-brown fur with white

*A street scene in **Luxor**. This city is a centre for tourists wishing to visit the many ruins and monuments of ancient Egypt that are in or near to the city. Its population of about 150 000 is supported by tourism and agriculture.*

*The **lynx** is found in the forests of Europe, Asia and North America. It is nocturnal and climbs and swims well. It feeds on birds and small mammals. Below: Desert or Persian lynx. Bottom: European lynx.*

markings; and **bay** ~ (= BOBCAT); lynx fur; **~-eyed**, sharp-sighted.

Ly·ons (lēawṅ'). (Fr. **Lyon**) City of E. central France at confluence of Saône and Rhone, famous esp. for manufacture of silk.

Ly·ra (lī'ra). (astron.) The Harp, a northern constellation containing Vega, the 4th brightest star in the heavens.

ly·rate (lī'rāt, -rĭt) *adj.* (biol.) Lyre-shaped.

lyre (līr) *n.* (Gk. antiq.) Instrument of harp kind, chiefly used for accompanying voice, with strings supported by two symmetrically curved horns, stopped with the left hand and struck with a plectrum in the right; **lyre'bird**, Australian passerine bird (*Menura superba*), with lyre-shaped tail. **lyr·ist** (līr'ĭst) *n.* Lyre player.

Ly·san·der (līsăn'der) (d. 395 B.C.). Spartan naval commander in latter part of Peloponnesian War.

ly·ser·gic (līsėr'jĭk, lī-) *adj.* ~ **acid**, crystalline solid ($C_{15}H_{15}N_2$ COOH), obtained from ergot or produced synthetically; ~ **acid diethylamide**: see LSD.

Ly·sim·a·chus (līsĭm'akus) (*c*355–281 B.C.). Macedonian general who served under Alexander the Great and became king of Thrace.

Ly·sip·pus (līsĭp'us) (4th c. B.C.). Greek sculptor of Sicyon who was famous for his statues of Zeus and portraits of Alexander the Great.

ly·sis (lī'sĭs) *n.* (physiol.) Disintegration of bacterial or other cells.

Ly·sol (lī'sōl, -sawl, -sŏl) *n.* (trademark) Mixture of cresols and soft soap, used as an antiseptic and disinfectant.

Lyt·ton (lĭt'on), **Edward George Earle Lytton Bulwer-, first Baron Lytton** (1803–73). English novelist and politician; author of *Eugene Aram*, *Rienzi*, *The Last Days of Pompeii*, etc.

*The **lyre-bird** found only in Australia, is so called because of the shape of its tail when spread in courtship display. Menura superba (left and below) is the most splendid of the two species found. It sings with far-carrying melodious notes and is an excellent mimic.*

lyr·ic (lĭr'ĭk) *adj.* Of or for the lyre, meant to be sung; of the nature of, expressed or fit to be expressed in, song; (of poem) short, usu. divided into stanzas or strophes, and directly expressing poet's own thoughts and sentiments rather than a description of events; (of poet) writing in this manner. ~ *n.* Lyric poem; (esp. pl., theatr.) words of song.

lyr·i·cal (lĭr'ĭkal) *adj.* Resembling, couched in, or using language appropriate to, lyric poetry. **lyr'i·cal·ly** *adv.* **lyr'i·cal·ness** *n.*

lyr·i·cism (lĭr'isĭzem) *n.* Lyric character or expression; high-flown sentiments.

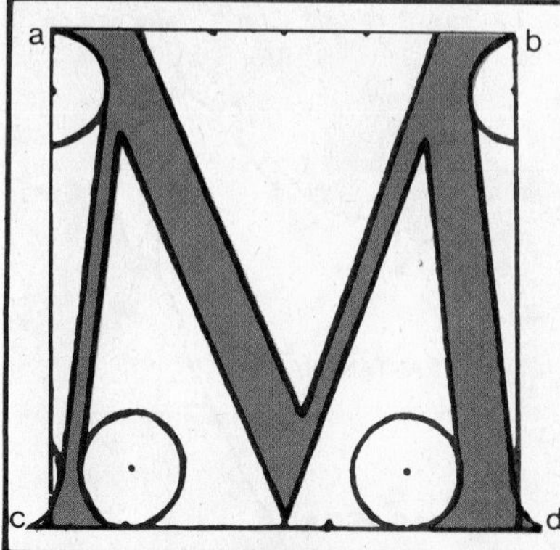

M m is the 13th letter in the English and other west European alphabets. It was the 12th letter in the Greek alphabet and the 14th in early Slavonic alphabets. As a symbol in Roman numeration M stood for 1,000.

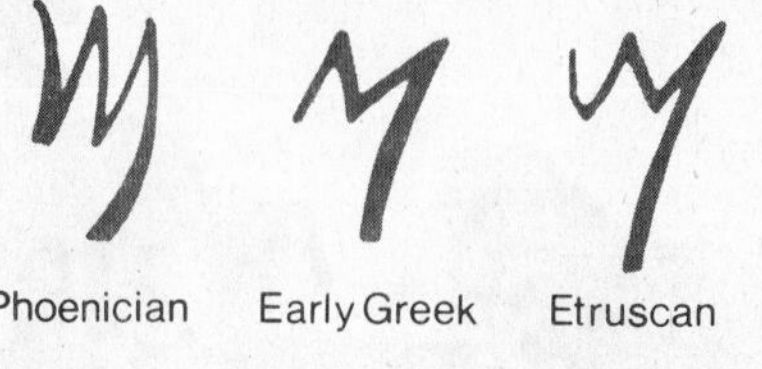

Early Latin Classical Latin Italian

The ***macaw*** *has the brightest plumage of all parrots and the 15 species are found only in Central and South America. The scarlet macaw is about 40 ins. long and is the largest of these birds.*

M, m (ĕm) (pl. **M's, m's** or **Ms, ms**). 1. Thirteenth letter of modern English and 12th of ancient Roman alphabet, representing a bilabial nasal (usu. voiced) consonant; the form of the letter is derived from Phoenician ɱ (early Gk. and L. ɱ, ɱ, M). 2. Roman numeral symbol for 1,000. 3. (print.) = EM.

M. *abbrev.* Mega-; monsieur.

m. *abbrev.* Male; mark(s) (coin); married; masculine; meter(s); mile(s); milli-; million(s); minim; minute(s); month; moon; noon.

MA *abbrev.* Massachusetts.

M.A. *abbrev.* Master of Arts.

ma (mah) = MAMA.

ma'am (măm, mahm) *n.* Madam.

Mac (măk) *n.* (slang) Word of address to someone whose name is unknown to speaker.

ma·ca·bre (m*a*kahb′r*e*, -kăb′-) *adj.* Grim, gruesome; **danse ~**, (Fr.) Dance of Death.

ma·ca·co (m*a*kah′kō, -kā′-) *n.* (pl. **-cos** pr. -kōz). Any of several lemurs, esp. the black lemur (*Lemur macaco*).

mac·ad·am (m*a*kăd′*a*m) *n.* (Material for) road surface made with successive layers of small broken stones rolled in with some binding material. **mac·ad·am·ize** (m*a*kăd′*a*mīz) *v.t.* (**-ized, -iz·ing**). **mac·ad·am·i·za·tion** (m*a*kăd*a*mĭzā′sh*o*n) *n.* [John Loudon *McAdam*, Scottish engineer (1756–1836)]

Ma·cao (m*a*kow′). Island in the South China Sea 40 mi. (64 km) W. of Hong Kong; ~, Portuguese colony on the peninsula of this island and name of chief town.

ma·caque (m*a*kahk′) *n.* Monkey of genus *Macaca*, of Asia and N. Africa.

mac·a·ro·ni (măk*a*rō′nē) *n.* (pl. **-nis, -nies**). Pasta formed into long tubes; (hist.) 18th-c. dandy affecting continental manners and fashions.

mac·a·ron·ic (măk*a*rŏn′ĭk) *adj.* (of verse) Of burlesque form containing Latin or other foreign words and vernacular words with Latin etc. terminations. **mac·a·ron′ics** *n.pl.* Macaronic verse.

mac·a·roon (măk*a*r o͞on′) *n.* Small cookie of ground almonds, white of egg, sugar, etc.

Mac·Ar·thur (m*a*kār′th*e*r), **Douglas** (1880–1964). American general; commanded "Rainbow" Division in World War I; superintendent of West Point, 1919–22; department commander in Philippines, 1928–30; Army chief of staff, 1930–5; routed "Bonus Army" from Washington, D.C., 1932; organized Philippine defense forces and appointed field marshal of the Philippines; supreme commander of Allied Forces in the SW. Pacific in World War II; commander of Allied occupation of Japan, 1945–1951; commander of United Nations forces in Korea, 1950–1, until relieved of command by President Harry S. Truman for disagreeing openly with U.S. policy on war aims.

Ma·cas·sar (m*a*kăs′*e*r) *n.* Oil said to consist of ingredients obtained from Macassar, a port of Celebes, formerly used as a hairdressing; similar oil or preparation. Also **~ oil.**

Ma·cau·lay (m*a*kaw′lē), **Thomas Babington, 1st Baron Macaulay** (1800–59). English historian and essayist.

ma·caw (m*a*kaw′) *n.* Any of several large long-tailed brightly colored parrots, mostly native to S. and Central America.

Macc. *abbrev.* Maccabees (Apocr.).

Mac·ca·bees (măk′*a*bēz) *n.pl.* Family of Jews, consisting of Mattathias and his five sons, Jochanan, Simon, Judas, Eleazar, and Jonathan, who led a revolt against the oppression of the Syrian king Antiochus Epiphanes (175–165 B.C.), and established a dynasty of priest-kings that ruled until the time of Herod (40 B.C.); **(Books of) ~**, four books of Jewish history and theology, of which the first two are

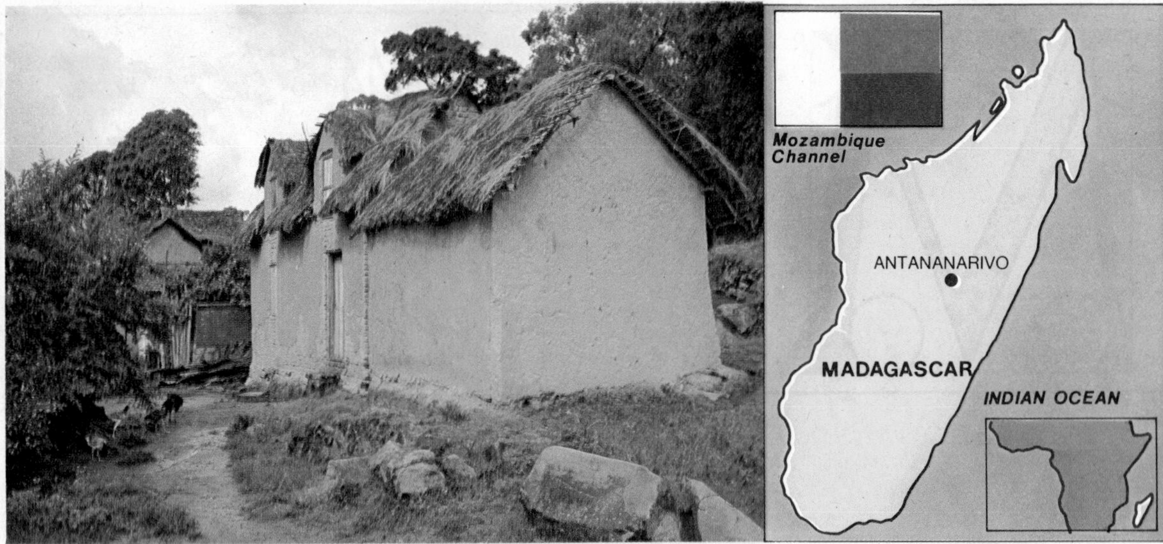

Madagascar is an island republic about 250 miles off the east coast of Africa, which was known as the Malagasy Republic from 1958 to 1976. Above: Primitive housing on the island. Above right: Map and flag.

included in the Apocrypha. **Mac·ca·be·an** (măk*a*bē′*a*n) *adj.*

Mac·Dow·ell (m*a*kdow′*e*l), **Edward Alexander** (1861–1908). Amer. composer of piano sonatas, orchestral suites, and symphonic poems.

Mace (mās) *n.* (trademark) Chemical used to incapacitate rioters by causing temporary eye or skin irritation.

mace[1] (mās) *n.* 1. (hist.) Heavy usu. metal-headed and spiked club. 2. Staff of office resembling this; **the M~**, the symbol of the Speaker's authority in the British House of Commons, placed on the table when he is in the chair.

mace[2] (mās) *n.* Dried outer covering of nutmeg, as spice.

mac·é·doine (măs*e*dwahn′; *Fr.* mahsādwahn′) *n.* (pl. **-doines** pr. -dwahnz′; *Fr.* -dwahn′). Mixed fruit or vegetables, esp. cut up small. [Fr. *Macedoine* Macedonia]

Mac·e·do·ni·a (măs*e*dō′nē*a*, -dōn′y*a*). Mountainous Balkan country, N. of ancient Greece, now divided between Greece and Yugoslavia; under Philip II and his son Alexander III (the Great) it dominated Greece in the 4th c. B.C.: in 146 B.C. it became a Roman province, and when the Roman Empire was divided it was assigned to the eastern half; in the 5th c. A.D. Slavs began to invade and colonize it and it became in turn an independent kingdom, a part of the Bulgarian and then of the Serbian Empire; from the end of the 14th c. until the Balkan war of 1912 it was under Turkish rule. **Mac·e·do′ni·an** *adj.* & *n.*

mac·er·ate (măs′*e*rāt) *v.* (**-at·ed, -at·ing**). Make or become soft by soaking; become emaciated by fasting. **mac·er·a·tion** (măs*e*rā′sh*o*n) *n.*

mach (mahk, măk) *n.* (also ~ **number**) Ratio of the velocity of a body passing through a fluid medium to the velocity of sound in that medium; **~meter**. [E. *Mach* (1838–1916), Austrian physicist]

Ernst Mach, the Austrian physicist, did much of the pioneer work on projectiles traveling through air at supersonic speeds. Aircraft speeds exceeding that of sound are expressed as 'Mach numbers'.

ma·chet·e (m*a*shĕt′ē, -chĕt′ē) *n.* (pl. **-es**). Broad heavy knife used in Central America and W. Indies as implement and weapon.

Mach·i·a·vel·li (măkē*a*vĕl′ē, mahky*a*-), **Niccolo di Bernardo dei** (1469–1527). Florentine political philosopher, author of a famous and influential treatise on statecraft, *The Prince* (*Il Principe*, 1513), advocating the principle that any political means, however unscrupulous, are justifiable if they strengthen the power of a government; hence, an unscrupulous schemer, one who practices duplicity in statecraft. **Mach·i·a·vel′li·an** *adj.* & *n.* **Mach·i·a·vel′li·an·ism, Mach·i·a·vel′lism** *ns.*

mach·i·nate (măk′*i*nāt) *v.i.* (**-nat·ed, -nat·ing**). Lay plots, intrigue. **mach·i·na·tion** (măk*i*nā′sh*o*n), **mach′i·na·tor** *ns.*

ma·chine (m*a*shēn′) *n.* Apparatus for applying mechanical power, having several parts each with definite function (the kind often being specified as **sewing,**

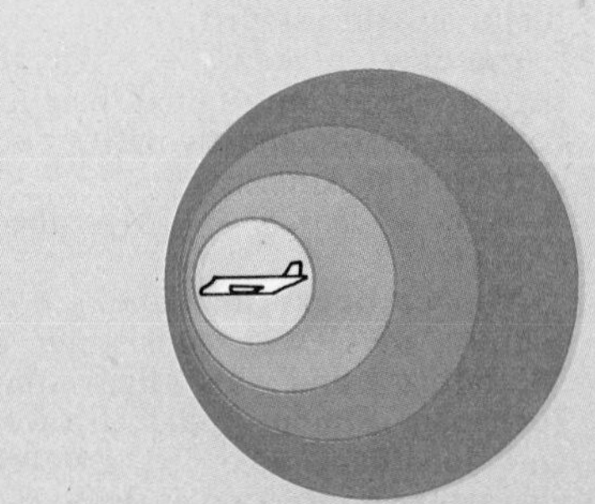

MACH less than 1 - Subsonic
Aircraft moving at less than speed of sound, pressure waves in front of aircraft.

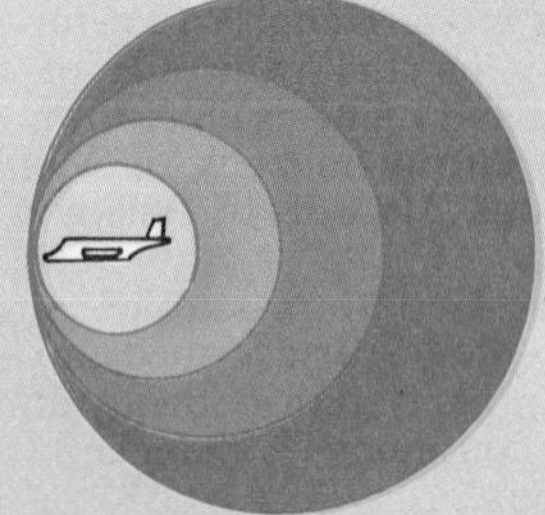

MACH number 1 - Sonic
Pressure waves and aircraft equal in velocity 'Sonic boom' caused by sudden discontinuity of pressure and air temperature in front of aircraft.

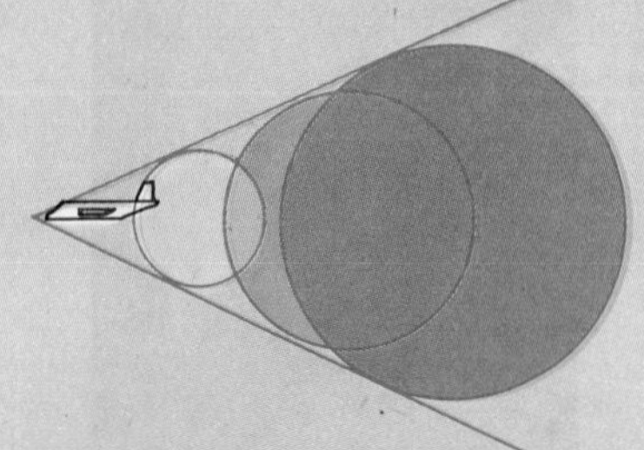

Above MACH 1 - Supersonic
Shock waves behind aircraft – Mach cone formed.

printing ~); bicycle, motorcycle, etc.; aircraft; person who acts mechanically and without intelligence or with unfailing regularity; instrument directing application of, or transmitting, force; organized system for carrying out specific functions, as the **political, party** ~; ~ **gun**, belt-fed, water-cooled, single-barreled gun, firing solid bullets from a fixed mounting, designed to utilize part of the energy of one explosion to extract the spent cartridge and load and fire the next round and capable of very high rates of continuous firing; hence ~ **gunner;** ~ **tool**, cutting or shaping tool, worked by machinery, not by hand. **machine** *v.t.* (**-chined, -chin·ing**). Make, operate on, print, sew, etc., with a machine.

ma·chin·er·y (m*a*shē′nerē) *n.* (pl. **-er·ies**). Machines; mechanism; organization.

ma·chin·ist (m*a*shē′nĭst) *n.* Maker of machinery; worker who operates a machine.

ma·chis·mo (m*a*chĭz′mō, -chēz′-) *n.* Need to prove virility or courage by daring action; also **ma·cho** (mah′chō) *n.* Strong, virile male. **macho** *adj.* Strong, manly. [Sp. *macho*, male, f. L. *masculus*]

Ma·chu Pic·chu (mah′cho͞o pēk′cho͞o). Site of ruins of an ancient Incan city in the Andes, altitude about 7,000 ft. (2,100 m), in S. central Peru.

Mac·ken·zie (m*a*kĕn′zē), **Sir Alexander** (1764–1820). Scottish explorer of NW. Canada; **MacKenzie River**, second-longest river in N. America, flowing 2,500 mi. (4,025 km) from the Canadian Northwest Territories to Mackenzie Bay.

mack·er·el (măk′*e*rel, măk′rel) *n.* Edible sea fish (*Scomber scombrus*) of N. Atlantic, having a silvery belly and greenish back with dark blue stripes; ~ **sky**, sky covered with clouds resembling the patterns on a mackerel's back (cirrocumulus).

Mack·i·nac (măk′*i*naw), **Straits of.** Strait separating Upper and Lower Michigan peninsula connecting lakes Huron and Michigan; **Mackinac Island**, island and resort in Lake Huron, at the mouth of the strait.

Mac·Leish (m*a*klēsh′), **Archibald** (1892–1982). Amer. poet and dramatist; librarian of Congress, 1939–44; assistant secretary of state, 1944–5; awarded Pulitzer Prize, 1933, 1953.

Mac·Mil·lan (m*a*kmĭl′*a*n), **Harold** (**Maurice**) (1894–). British Conservative statesman; prime minister, 1957–63.

Mâ·con (mahkawn′) *n.* Wine made near Mâcon, a city on the river Saône in central France.

mac·ra·mé (măk′r*a*mā) *n.* Fringe or trimming of knotted thread or cord.

macro- *prefix.* Large (opp. *micro-*).

mac·ro·bi·ot·ic (măkrōbīŏt′ĭk) *adj.* Relating to a diet of grains, vegetables, etc., believed to prolong life. ~**s**, *n.*

mac·ro·ce·phal·ic (măkrōs*e*făl′ĭk) *adj.* Long- or large-headed.

mac·ro·cosm (măk′r*o*kŏzem) *n.* Great world, universe (contrasted with *microcosm*); any great whole.

mac·ro·e·co·nom·ics (măkrōēk*o*nŏm′ĭks, ĕk*o*-) *n.* (usu. considered sing.). Study of general economics of large units.

mac·ro·mol·e·cule (măkr*o*mŏl′ekūl) *n.* Very large molecule like those in proteins, synthetic plastics, etc.

mac·ro·pho·tog·ra·phy (măkr*o*fotŏg′r*a*fē) *n.* Photography of macroscopic objects.

mac·ro·scop·ic (măkr*o*skŏp′ĭk) *adj.* Visible to the naked eye (opp. *microscopic*). **mac·ro·scop′i·cal·ly** *adv.*

mac·u·la (măk′y*u*l*a*) *n.* (pl. **-lae** pr. -lē). Dark spot on sun or moon; spot in mineral due to presence of particles of another mineral; spot, blemish, on the skin; (anat.; also ~ **lu′tea**) region of greatest visual acuity in the retina. **mac′u·lar** *adj.* **mac·u·la·tion** (măky*u*lā′sh*o*n) *n.*

mad (măd) *adj.* Of disordered mind, insane; (of animals) rabid; wildly foolish; (colloq.) annoyed; ~ **about**, (colloq.) infatuated with; **mad′cap**, wildly impulsive person; **mad′house**, lunatic asylum; **mad′man** (pl. **-men**), **mad′woman** (pl. **-women**). **mad′ly** *adv.* **mad′ness** *n.*

Mad·a·gas·car (măd*a*găs′k*e*r). Fourth largest island in the world, off the SE. coast of Africa; Democratic Republic of **M**~, also Malagasy Republic, co-extensive with Madagascar Island; former French colony; capital, Antananarivo.

mad·am (măd′*a*m) *n.* Polite formal address to woman; woman in charge of a brothel. [OF. *ma dame* my lady]

Mad·ame (măd′*a*m, m*a*dahm′) *n.* (pl. **Mes·dames**, pr. mādahm′). Title of (corresp. to *Mrs.*) or form of address to French married woman. [Fr.]

mad·den (măd′*e*n) *v.* Make, become, mad; irritate.

mad·der (măd′*e*r) *n.* Herbaceous climbing plant (*Rubia tinctorum*) with yellowish flowers; red dye obtained from its root.

made (mād) *adj.*: see MAKE[1]; ~ **man**, one who has attained success in life; ~**-to-order**, made to particular specifications; custom-made; appropriate.

Ma·dei·ra[1] (m*a*dēr′*a*, -dār′*a*). Island in Atlantic Ocean, off W.

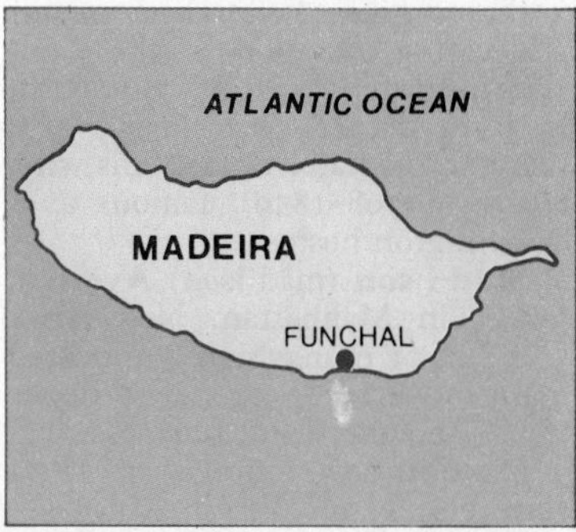

Madeira, a mountainous sub-tropical island, is in the Atlantic Ocean about 360 miles west of Morocco. Its most famous product is a fortified wine, but fishing (below) is important. Right: Map of the island.

*The city of **Madras** on the east coast of India is a port and commercial center. Its main industries are textiles, tanning, pottery and dye-making. Shown: the Church of St. Thomas, Madras.*

coast of Africa, in Portuguese possession; ~, river in NW. Brazil, 2,000 mi. (3,220 km), flowing from the Bolivian border to the Amazon.

Ma·dei·ra[2] (m*a*dēr′*a*, -dār′*a*) *n.* 1. Fortified wine produced in Madeira, amber-colored or brownish, varying in sweetness, and resembling sherry. 2. (also ~ **cake**) Kind of rich sweet cake without fruit.

Mad·e·moi·selle (mădem*o*zĕl′, mădmw*o*-) *n.* (pl. **Mes·de·moi·selles** pr. mādm*o*zĕl′, mādmw*o*-). Title of (corresp. to *Miss*) or form of address to French unmarried woman; **m** ~, French governess in U.S. [Fr.]

Ma·di·nat al Shaab (mahdĭnaht′ ahl shahb′). Administrative capital of the People's Democratic Republic of Yemen, formerly Southern Yemen, in the SE. part.

Mad·i·son[1] (măd′ĭs*o*n). Capital of Wisconsin in the S. part.

Mad·i·son[2] (măd′ĭs*o*n), **James** (1751–1836). Amer. statesman and fourth president of the U.S., 1809–1817, during War of 1812; co-authored "The Federalist" papers advocating adoption of the Constitution; member of House of Representatives, 1789–97; secretary of state, 1801–9; his wife, **Dolley** (1768–1849), famous as a Washington hostess.

Mad·i·son (măd′ĭs*o*n) **Avenue.** Street in Manhattan, New York City, on or near which are located many advertising agencies; hence (fig.) the advertising business.

Ma·don·na (m*a*dŏn′*a*) *n.* (Picture, statue, of) Virgin Mary; ~ **lily**, tall white lily (*Lilium candidum*), as often depicted in pictures of the Annunciation.

Ma·dras (m*a*drăs′, -drahs′). Seaport on E. coast of India, capital of Tamil Nadu; **madras**, cotton cloth usu. striped or corded.

mad·re·pore (măd′r*o*pōr) *n.* Perforate coral of genus *Madrepora*; animal producing this. [It. *madre* mother + *poro* corallike but porous substance]

Ma·drid (m*a*drĭd′). Capital city of Spain.

mad·ri·gal (măd′r*i*g*a*l) *n.* Short amatory poem; part song for several voices in elaborate contrapuntal style, usu. without accompaniment.

Mae·an·der (mēăn′d*er*). Ancient name of a river of Phrygia, (now R. *Menderes*) remarkable for its winding course.

Mae·ce·nas (mēsē′n*a*s, mī-), **Gaius Cilnius** (*c*70–8 B.C.). Roman knight; patron of Virgil and Horace and friend and adviser of Augustus; celebrated for his patronage of learning and letters; hence, generous patron of literature or art.

mael·strom (māl′str*o*m) *n.* Great whirlpool (also fig.). [f. *Maelström*, the whirlpool S. of the Lofoten Is. off W. coast of Norway]

mae·nad (mē′năd) *n.* Bacchante. **mae·nad′ic** *adj.*

maes·tro (mīs′trō) *n.* (pl. **-tros** pr. -trōz, **-tri** pr. -trē). Eminent musical composer, teacher, or conductor.

Mae·ter·linck (mā′t*er*lĭngk), **Maurice** (1862–1949). Belgian poet and dramatist; received Nobel Prize for literature 1911.

Mae West (mā′ wĕst′). Inflatable life jacket. [professional name of Amer. film actress (1892–1980)]

Maf·e·king (mah′f*e*kĭng). Town in Cape Province, S. Africa; during the second Boer War a small British force under Baden-Powell withstood a siege there for seven months; its relief, in May 1900, caused riotous rejoicing (**mafficking**) in London.

***Mafeking,** a small town in Cape Province, South Africa, is remembered for the siege that took place there during the Boer War. The British force, under Baden-Powell, was relieved after seven months in May 1900.*

maf·fick·ing (măf′*i*kĭng) *n.*: see MAFEKING.

ma·fi·a (mah′fē*a*) *n.* 1. (in Sicily) Spirit of hostility to the law and its ministers prevailing among a part of the population; also, those who share in this spirit. 2. (**M** ~) Secret international criminal organization.

ma·fi·o·so (mahfēō′sō) *n.* (pl. **-si** pr. -sē). Member of the Mafia.

Ma·ga·lla·nes (mahgahyah′nĕs). Formerly Punta Arenas, world's southernmost city, in Chile on Strait of Magellan.

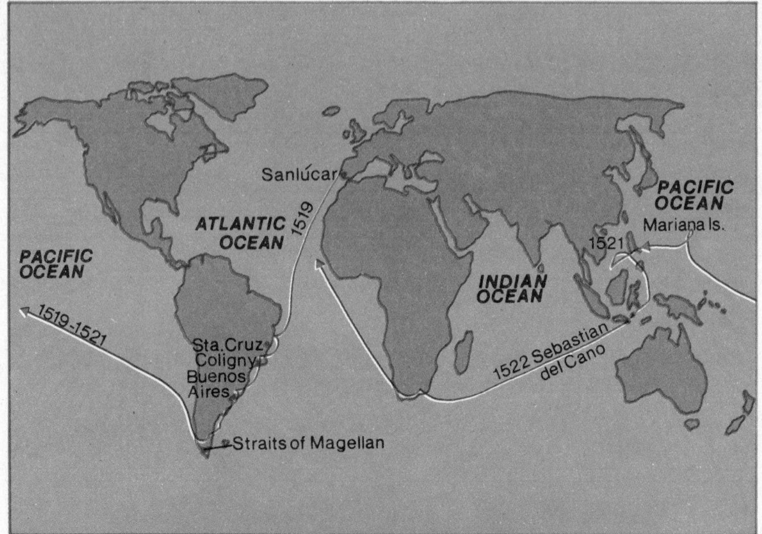

Ferdinand ***Magellan,*** *a Portuguese navigator, was commander of the first expedition to circumnavigate the world. As he was killed in the Philippines, the honor went to Juan Sebastian de Cano, a fellow officer.*

The ***maggot*** *of the hoverfly feeds on other insects including the black citrus aphid, which it sucks dry. Maggots of other species of insect feed on plants, decaying organic matter, dung and mud.*

mag·a·zine (măg′azēn, măgazēn′) *n.* 1. Store for explosives, arms, or military provisions; receptacle for number of rounds loaded at one time in rifle and various types of automatic gun; reservoir or supply chamber in a machine, store, battery, etc. 2. Periodical publication containing articles on various subjects by different writers. [Arab. *makhasin* storehouses]

Mag·da·lene (măg′dalēn), **Mag·da·len** (măg′dalĭn). Appellation of Mary of Magdala (Luke 8), a disciple of Christ, commonly identified with the "sinner" of Luke 7 and traditionally represented as a prostitute restored to purity and sanctified by repentance and faith; hence, a reformed prostitute.

Mag·da·le·ni·an (măgdalē′nēan) *adj.* Of the paleolithic culture that followed the Aurignacian and Solutrean and is characterized by weapons and tools of horn and bone. [f. rock shelter of La *Madeleine*, Dordogne, France]

Mag·de·burg (măg′debêrg). City in E. Germany; ~ **hemispheres**, pair of copper hemispheres joined to form a hollow globe from which the air could be extracted, after which they were practically inseparable, devised by a German physicist, Otto von Guericke (1602–86), to demonstrate the effect of air pressure.

Ma·gel·lan (majĕl′an). **Fernão de Magalhães** (*c*1470–1521), Portuguese navigator; the first European to pass through the strait that bears his name, between Tierra del Fuego and the S. Amer. mainland; he undertook the first expedition around the world, but perished in the Philippines (only one of his ships completed the voyage).

ma·gen·ta (majĕn′ta) *n.* Brilliant crimson aniline dye (fuchsin), discovered in the year of the battle of Magenta; color of this.

Mag·gio·re (mahjō′rĕ), **Lake.** Alpine lake and resort area between N. Italy and S. Switzerland.

mag·got (măg′ot) *n.* Grub or larva, esp. of bluebottle or cheesefly; (rare) fad, whim. **mag′got·y** *adj.* 1. Full of maggots. 2. (rare) Full of strange whims.

Ma·ghreb, Ma·ghrib (mahgrēb′). Arabic name for the region of NW. Africa usu. including Morocco, Tunisia, Algeria, and sometimes Libya.

Ma·gi (mā′jī): see MAGUS.

mag·ic (măj′ĭk) *n.* Pretended art of influencing events by occult control of nature or of spirits, witchcraft; mysterious agency or power; **black, white,** ~, magic performed by aid of demons, of benevolent spirits. **magic** *adj.* Of, producing, produced by, magic; ~ **latern**: see LANTERN; ~ **square**, square divided into smaller squares each containing a number, so arranged that the sums of the rows, vertical, horizontal, or diagonal, are the same. **mag′i·cal** *adj.* **mag′i·cal·ly** *adv.*

ma·gi·cian (majĭsh′an) *n.* One skilled in magic, wizard.

Ma·gi·not (măzh′inō) **line.** Line of fortifications built in the years preceding World War II along the eastern borders of France from Montmédy to Belfort; crossed by German forces in 1940. [André *Maginot* (1877–1932), French war minister]

mag·is·te·ri·al (măjĭstēr′ēal) *adj.* Of a magistrate; dictatorial. **mag·is·te′ri·al·ly** *adv.*

mag·is·tra·cy (măj′ĭstrasē) *n.* (pl. **-cies**). Magistrates; magisterial office.

mag·is·trate (măj′ĭstrāt, -strĭt) *n.* Civil officer administering law; person appointed to try minor offenses and small civil cases and conduct preliminary hearing of serious offenses. **mag′is·trate·ship, mag·is·tra·ture** (măj′ĭstrăcher) *ns.*

mag·ma (măg′ma) *n.* (pl. **-mas, -ma·ta** pr. -mata). (geol.) Mixture of molten and crystalline materials that, on cooling, forms igneous rocks.

Mag·na Char·ta, Car·ta (măg′na kâr′ta). Great charter of the liberties of England, granted by

Right: ***Magnetic** lines of force radiate from the poles of a magnet, where the magnet field is strongest. Below right: Magnetic north and south poles lie close to but not exactly at the geographical poles. Magnetic north pole is near Prince of Wales Island, North Canada. Magnetic south pole is in Wilkes Land, Antarctica.*

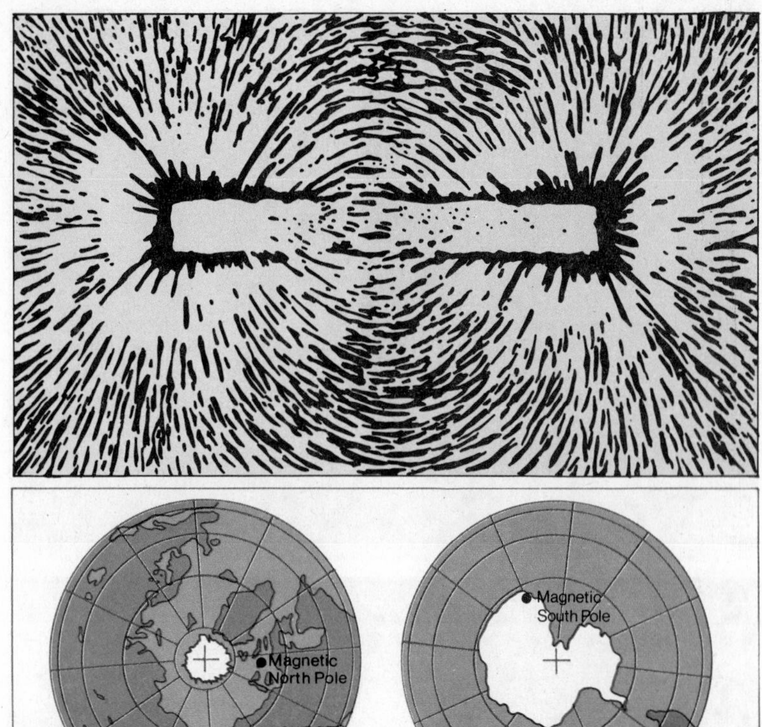

King John, under pressure from his barons, at Runnymede in 1215; among its chief provisions was that no freeman should be imprisoned or banished except by the law of the land and that supplies should not be exacted without the consent of the Common Council of the realm. [L. *magna carta* great charter]

mag·na cum lau·de (măg′na ko͝om low′de). College or university degree granted with high honors; the winner of such honors. [L., = "with great praise"]

mag·nan·i·mous (măgnăn′imus) *adj.* Forgiving, free from petty resentment. **mag·nan′i·mous·ly** *adv.* **mag·na·nim·i·ty** (măgnanĭm′ĭtē) *n.*

mag·nate (măg′nāt, -nĭt) *n.* Man of high position, wealth, authority, power, etc., often with reference to class or occupation, as **financial ~**.

mag·ne·sia (măgnē′zha, -sha, -zēa) *n.* (chem.) Magnesium oxide (MgO); **milk of ~**, suspension of magnesium hydroxide in water, used medicinally. **mag·ne′sian** *adj.*

mag·ne·si·um (măgnē′zēum, -zhum, -shum) *n.* (chem.) Silvery-white metallic element, symbol Mg, at. no. 12, at. wt. 24.305, burning with a bright white light.

mag·net (măg′nĭt) *n.* 1. Piece of iron, steel, cobalt, nickel, or one of their alloys to which has been imparted by contact, induction, or electric current the property of attracting iron and of pointing north. 2. (fig.) Thing that attracts.

mag·net·ic (măgnĕt′ĭk) *adj.* Of or like or acting as magnet; (fig.) very attractive; ~ **declination, deviation**, angular difference between true and magnetic meridians; ~ **dip**, magnetic inclination; ~ **equator**, imaginary line around Earth, at all points along which the magnetic inclination is zero; ~ **field**: see FIELD; ~ **inclination**, vertical angle between the horizontal and the direction of Earth's magnetic field at any point; ~ **mine**, sea mine designed to be detonated by the magnetic field of a steel ship passing near it; ~ **moment**, torque exerted by a magnetic field on any magnetized object within it; ~ **needle**: see NEEDLE def. 2; ~ **north**, magnetic pole some 6 degrees W. of true north; ~ **pole**, either of the poles of a magnet; either of the two points on Earth's surface toward which the compass needle points and at which it dips vertically; ~ **storm**, erratic disturbance of Earth's magnetism, probably due to solar electric activity; ~ **tape**, strip of usu. plastic material coated with magnetic oxide to make it sensitive to electromagnetism. **mag·net′i·cal·ly** *adv.* **mag·net′ics** *n.* Branch of physics that deals with magnetic phenomena.

mag·net·ism (măg′netĭzem) *n.* 1. Magnetic phenomena; science of these; **terrestrial ~**, magnetic properties of Earth as a whole. 2. (fig.) Attraction, personal charm.

mag·net·ite (măg′netīt) *n.* Magnetic iron oxide (Fe_3O_4).

mag·net·ize (măg′netīz) *v.t.* (**-ized, -iz·ing**). Make into a magnet; attract as a magnet does. **mag·net·i·za·tion** (măgnetīzā′shon) *n.*

mag·ne·to (măgnē′tō) *n.* (pl. **-tos**). Magnetoelectric machine, esp. an alternating current generator with permanent magnets used to generate the electric ignition spark in an internal combustion engine.

mag·ne·to·chem·is·try (măgnētōkĕm′ĭstrē) *n.* That branch of science which treats of the relation of magnetic to chemical phenomena. **mag·ne·to·chem′i·cal** *adj.*

mag·ne·to·e·lec·tric·i·ty (măgnētōĭlĕktrĭs′ĭtē) *n.* Electricity generated by relative movement of electric conductors and magnets. **mag·ne·to·e·lec′tric** *adj.*

mag·ne·tom·e·ter (măgnetŏm′eter) *n.* Instrument for the measurement of magnetic forces, esp. terrestrial magnetism.

mag·ne·to·mo·tive (măgnētōmō′tĭv) *adj.* ~ **force**, (abbrev. mmf or m.m.f.) sum of the magnetizing forces in a magnetic circuit (the magnetic analogy of electromotive force).

mag·ne·ton (măg′netŏn) *n.* Unit of magnetic moment, used in measuring the magnetic moment of electrons and protons.

mag·ne·tron (măg′netrŏn) *n.* 1. Kind of thermionic vacuum tube in which the motion of the electrons is controlled by an externally applied magnetic field. 2. Electronic device utilizing an axial magnetic field for generating electromagnetic radiations of very short wavelength. [f. *magnet* and *electron*]

mag·nif·i·cent (măgnĭf′isent) *adj.* Splendid, sumptuous; imposing, stately; fine, excellent. **mag·nif′i·cent·ly** *adv.* **mag·nif′i·cence** *n.*

mag·ni·fy (măg′nifī) *v.t.* (**-fied, -fy·ing**). Increase apparent size of, as with lens, microscope, or concave mirror; exaggerate; (archaic) extol. **mag·ni·fi·ca·tion** (măgnifikā′shon) *n.* **angular ~**, (optics) ratio of the angle subtended by the object.

mag·nil·o·quent (măgnĭl′-

*o*kwent) *adj.* Lofty in expression; boastful. **mag·nil′o·quence** *n.* **mag·nil′o·quent·ly** *adv.*

mag·ni·tude (măg′nĭtōōd, -tūd) *n.* Largeness; size; importance; one of the classes into which the fixed stars have been arranged acc. to their brilliancy; **of the first ~**, (fig.) of great importance.

mag·no·lia (măgnōl′y*a*, -nō′lē*a*) *n.* (pl. **-lias**, collect. **-lia**). Tree of genus *M~*, with conspicuous wax-like flowers and dark green foliage, native in America and Asia. [Pierre *Magnol*, Fr. botanist (1638–1715)]

mag·num (măg′n*u*m) *n.* (Bottle containing) two quarts (of wine etc.).

mag·num o·pus (măg′n*u*m ō′p*u*s). Chief production of a writer or other artist; great literary undertaking. [L., = great work]

Magog: see GOG AND MAGOG.

mag·pie (măg′pī) *n.* Any of various birds of the family Corvidae with long pointed tail and black and white plumage, noted for their chattering; the species *Pica pica* is common in N. Europe and Western N. America; (fig.) idle chatterer.

ma·gus (mā′g*u*s) *n.* (pl. **-gi** pr. -jī). 1. Member of ancient Persian priestly caste; one skilled in Oriental magic and astrology. 2. **the Magi**, the (traditionally three) "wise men" who came from the East bearing gifts to the infant Jesus Christ (Matt. 2). **ma·gi·an** (mā′jē*a*n) *adj.* & *n.* **ma′gi·an·ism** *n.* Doctrines, philosophy, of the Persian magi.

Mag·yar (măg′yār; *Hung.* mŭd′-yŭr) *n.* Member, language, of a Mongoloid people predominant in Hungary; Hungarian. ~ *adj.* Of the Magyars.

Ma·ha·bha·ra·ta (m*a*hahbah′-r*a*t*a*). One of the two great epics

*The **magnolia** is native to Asia and North America and has about 80 species. It is valued for its large and fragrant white, yellow, pink or purple flowers which have a waxy quality.*

(the other being the Ramayana) of the Hindus, supposed to have been composed *c*500 B.C.

ma·ha·ra·jah ma·ha·ra·ja (mahh*a*rah′j*a*) *ns.* Title of some Indian princes. **ma·ha·ra·nee, ma·ha·ra·ni** (mahh*a*rah′nē) *ns.* Maharajah's wife. [Hind. *mahā* great, *rāja* king, *rānī* queen]

ma·hat·ma (m*a*haht′m*a*, -hăt′-) *n.* In Buddhism, one of a class of persons with preternatural powers supposed to exist in India and Tibet; person regarded with reverence. [Sansk. *mahātman* great souled]

Ma·ha·ya·na (mahh*a*yah′n*a*) *n.* One of the two great schools of BUDDHISM, developed in China, Japan, and Tibet. [Sansk. *mahâ* great, *yâna* vehicle]

__Maidenhair__ fern, one of 200 species, has delicate and often drooping fronds. It is widely cultivated as an ornamental plant but is susceptible to frost and heat.

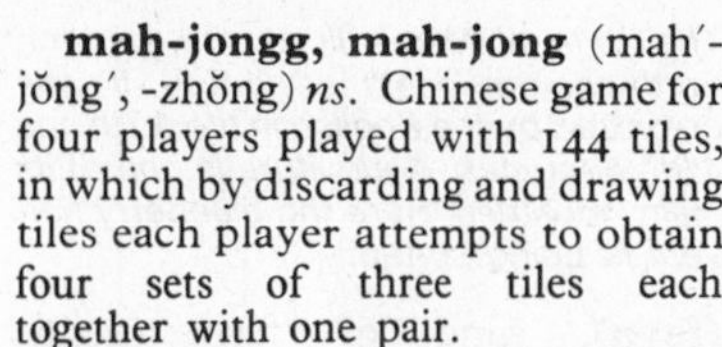

mah-jongg, mah-jong (mah′-jŏng′, -zhŏng) *ns.* Chinese game for four players played with 144 tiles, in which by discarding and drawing tiles each player attempts to obtain four sets of three tiles each together with one pair.

Mah·ler (mah′l*er*), **Gustav** (1860–1911). Austrian conductor and composer, esp. of symphonies.

ma·hog·a·ny (m*a*hŏg′*a*nē) *n.* Reddish-brown wood esp. of a tropical Amer. tree (*Swietenia mahogani*), used for furniture etc. and taking high polish; tree producing this; color of this wood.

Ma·hom·et (m*a*hŏm′ĭt). Var. of MUHAMMAD.

ma·hout (m*a*howt′) *n.* Elephant driver.

Ma·ia (mī′*a*). 1. (Gk. myth.) Daughter of Atlas and mother of Hermes. 2. (Rom. myth.) Goddess associated with Vulcan, and also (by confusion with 1 above) with Mercury. [Gk., = "mother," "nurse"]

maid (mād) *n.* 1. (archaic and poet.) maiden; **the M~ (of Orleans)**, Joan of Arc; **old ~**, elderly spinster; game of cards; ~ **of honor**, unmarried woman attending bride. 2. Female servant.

maid·en (mā′d*e*n) *n.* 1. (archaic and poet.) Girl; spinster; virgin. 2. (hist.) One of two supports for bobbin in spinning wheel. 3. (hist.) Kind of guillotine formerly used in Edinburgh. 4. Maiden horse. ~ *adj.* Unmarried (usu. in ~ **aunt, lady**); (obs.) virgin; untried; with blank record; (of horse) that has never won a race; **maidenhair**

*The Australian **magpie** has a loud, metallic call and black and white plumage. It is aggressive, especially during the breeding season, and attacks larger birds and even man.*

The state of ***Maine*** *is on the extreme north-eastern coast of U.S.A. It was colonized by the English in the 17th and 18th centuries. Agriculture is one of its main industries. Here the blueberry harvest is being sorted.*

(**fern**), kind of fern (genus *Adiantum*), with hairlike stalks and delicate fronds; **maidenhair tree**, GINKGO; **maid'enhead**, virginity; hymen; **maiden name**, woman's surname before marriage; **maiden speech**, one made in legislature by a member speaking for the first time. **maid'en·hood** *n.* **maid'en·ly** *adv.*

mail[1] (māl) *n.* (hist.) Armor of rings or chainwork, or of metal plates; **mailed fist**, (fig.) armed power.

mail[2] (māl) *n.* (Letter etc. conveyed by) post; train or other vehicle carrying post; **mail'box**, public box for depositing outgoing mail; private box for incoming mail; **mail'man**, postman, man who carries and delivers mail; **mail order**, order for goods to be sent by mail; **mail order** (attrib.). **mail** *v.t.* Send by post.

Mail·lol (mahyawl'), **A·ris·tide** (ahrĭstēd') (1861–1944). French painter and sculptor; known for statues sculpted in the Greek tradition of the 5th c. B.C.

maim (mām) *v.t.* Cripple, mutilate.

Mai·mon·i·des (mīmŏn'*i*dēz). Moses ben Maimon (1135–1204), Spanish-Jewish philosopher and Rabbinic scholar, much influenced by Greek, esp. Aristotelian, philosophy.

Main (mīn). River in West Germany flowing W. from N. Bavaria into the Rhine at Mainz.

main[1] (mān) *adj.* Chief, principal; exerted to the full; ~ **chance**, opportunity for greatest (personal) advantage; **main'land**, country or continent without its adjacent islands; so **main'lander**; **Main Line**, fashionable suburbs W. of Philadelphia along the railroad line; **main line**, principal railroad line or highway; (slang) principal vein esp. as site of drug injection; **main'line** (*v.*) (**-lined, -lin·ing**), (slang) take drugs thus; **main'lin·er** *n.* **main'mast**, principal mast of a ship; **main'sail** (*naut.* pr. măn'*s*al), (in square-rigged vessel) lowest sail of mainmast; (in fore-and-aft rig) sail set on after part of mainmast; **main'spring**, chief spring of watch or clock (also fig.); **main'stay**, stay running from top of mainmast to foot of foremast; (fig.) chief support; **main'stream**, (fig.) principal course or trend. **main'ly** *adv.*

main[2] (mān) *n.* Physical force (only in **with might and** ~); (poet.) high sea; principal channel, duct, conductor, etc., for water, sewage, electricity, etc.; *Spanish M*~: see SPANISH.

Maize *(corn) is used as food for both livestock and humans and as a raw material in industry. It is the most important crop in the U.S.A. which produces almost half the world's total supply.*

Maine (mān). Northeastern state of U.S., on the Atlantic coast; admitted to the Union in 1820; capital, Augusta.

main·tain (māntān') *v.t.* Carry on, keep up; support; assert as true.

main·te·nance (măn'te*n*ans) *n.* Maintaining; (provision of) means of subsistence.

mai·tre d'hô·tel (māt*er* dōtĕl', māt*r*e; *Fr.* mĕtr dōtĕl') *n.* (pl. **mai·tres d'hô·tel** pr. māt*erz* dōtĕl', mātr*ez*; *Fr.* mĕtr dōtĕl'). Major-domo; HEADwaiter; (colloq.) **maître d'.** [Fr., = master of hotel]

maize (māz) *n.* 1. corn. 2. Corncolor, pale yellow.

Maj. *abbrev.* Major.

ma·jes·tic (m*a*jĕs'tĭk) *adj.* Characterized by majesty, imposing, stately. **ma·jes'ti·cal·ly**

Majolica was produced in Italy in the 14th century at such centers as Faenza, Orvieto, Florence and Savona. This majolica dish depicting the 'Judgement of Paris' shows the typical metallic colors.

Majorca is the largest of the Balearic Islands in the western Mediterranean. It is a Spanish province and has a mild sunny climate which makes it a popular tourist center. Shown here is La Cartuja Monastery on the island.

adv.

maj·es·ty (măj'ĭstē) *n.* (pl. **-ties**). 1. Impressive stateliness; sovereign power; **Your, His, Her, M~**, title used in speaking to or of sovereign. 2. Representation of God or Christ (or occas. Virgin Mary) enthroned within an aureole; so **Christ in M~**.

ma·jol·i·ca (majŏl'ĭka, -yŏl'-) *n.* Italian earthenware coated with an opaque white enamel ornamented with metallic colors; modern imitation of this. [It., f. former name of *Majorca*, ships of which brought Spanish wares to Italy]

ma·jor¹ (mā'jer) *n.* Army officer next in rank below lieutenant colonel and above captain.

ma·jor² (mā'jer) *adj.* Greater of two things, classes, etc.; senior; (mus.) of intervals, greater by a chromatic semitone than those called minor; normal or perfect; (of keys) in which the scale has a major third; ~ **premise**, (logic) first of a syllogism, containing a statement of the general rule; ~ **suit**, (bridge) spades or hearts; ~ **term**, (logic) predicate of the conclusion of a syllogism. **major** *n.* Person of full legal age; major premise; (in colleges) subject to which special attention is given in a course of study, whence ~ (*v.i.*) take, or qualify *in*, such subject; **~-do·mo** (-dō'mō), steward or butler; ~ **general**, Army officer ranking next above a brigadier general and below a lieutenant general.

Ma·jor·ca (majŏr'ka, -yŏr'-). (*Sp.* **Mallorca** pr. mahlyŏrkah) Largest of the Balearic Islands.

ma·jor·i·ty (majŏr'ĭtē, -jăr'-) *n.* (pl. **-ties**). 1. Greater number or part (*of*); **absolute ~**, more than half number of electors or actual voters. 2. Number by which votes cast on one side exceed those on the other. 3. Full legal age. 4. Office of major in military. 5. ~ **leader**, leader of majority party in a legislature, as in U.S. Senate or House.

ma·jus·cule (majŭs'kūl, măj'-us-) *adj.* (paleog.; of a letter) Large (whether capital or uncial); written in majuscule. ~ *n.* Majuscule letter; formal script, orig. based on Roman monumental lettering, used in manuscripts until the development of the MINUSCULE from cursive writing. **ma·jus'cu·lar** *adj.*

Ma·ka·lu (mŭk'aloo). Mountain, 27,790 ft. (8,337 m), in the Himalayas on the Nepal-Tibet border near Mt. Everest.

make¹ (māk) *v.* (**made, mak·ing**). Create, manufacture; cause to exist, bring about; amount to, constitute; bring total up to; represent as being or doing; acquire by effort, earn; win (trick at cards); score (touchdown, goal, etc.); produce by cookery; perform, execute; utter or record (remark etc.); (slang) seduce, persuade to have sexual intercourse; ~ **believe**, pretend; **~-believe** (*n.*) pretense; ~ **do**, manage *with* what is available or inferior substitute; ~ **for**, take direction of; ~ **good**, fulfill (promise etc.), prove (statement); pay for, repair (damage etc.); succeed in an undertaking; ~ **off**, depart hastily; ~ **off with**, carry away, steal; ~ **out**, draw up or write out (list etc.); prove; represent as; understand; (colloq.) succeed; (slang) neck, pet; **make'shift** (*n.* & *adj.*) temporary (expedient); **make up**, supply deficiency, complete; arrange; concoct usu. as

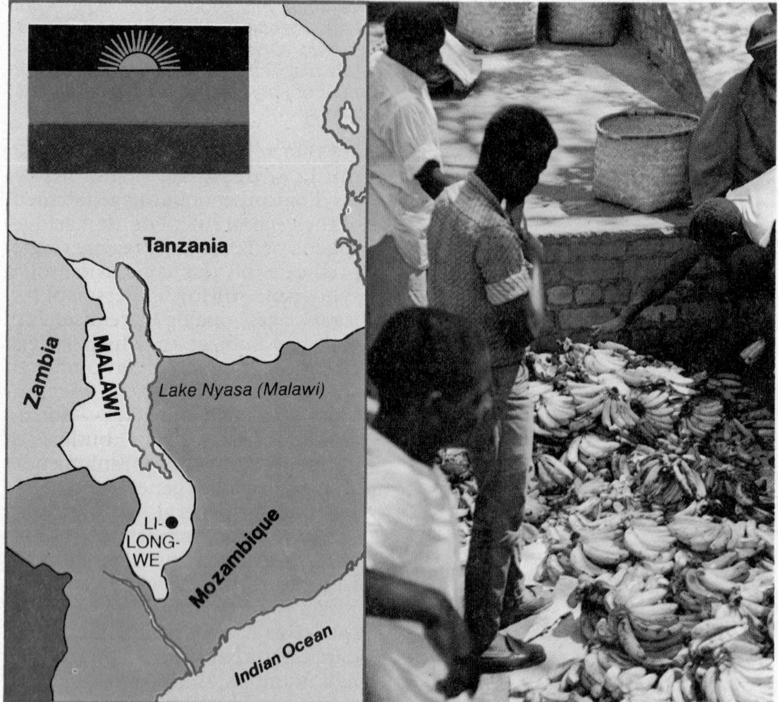

The central African republic of ***Malawi*** *is separated from Mozambique and Tanzania by Lake Nyasa (Malawi), the third largest lake in Africa. Blantyre is one of the main industrial centers, and a market town for crops.*

fiction; put an end to (a quarrel); adapt (face etc. of actor) for his part; apply cosmetics (to); **make-up** (*n.*) way actor etc. is made up; way type is made up into pages; fundamental qualities of person's nature; ~ **up to**, curry favor with; **make'-weight**, small quantity added to make up required weight; unimportant argument etc. to supply deficiency.

make[2] (māk) *n.* Way thing is made; figure, shape; brand, sort; **on the** ~, (slang) intent on gain; (slang) or seeking sexual partners.

mak·er (mā'ker) *n.* One who makes; esp. **M** ~, the Creator.

mak·ing (mā'king) *n.* Creating, manufacturing, etc.; (pl.) what one earns; essential qualities, as *he has the* ~*s of a general.*

mal- *prefix.* 1. Bad(ly), as *maltreat.* 2. Un-, as *maladroit.*

Mal·a·bar (măl'*a*bar̄). Coastal district of SW. India.

Ma·la·bo (mah'lahbō). Formerly Santa Isabel; capital, Equatorial Guinea.

Ma·lac·ca (m*a*lăk'*a*). State of Malaysia, on W. coast Malay Peninsula; its capital; **Strait of** ~, strait *c*500 miles (805 km) long between SW. end of Malay Peninsula and Sumatra; ~ **cane**, rich brown walking cane made of the stem of a palm tree (*Calamus scipionum*).

Mal·a·chi (măl'*a*kī). Prophetic book of the Old Testament, belonging to a period immediately before Ezra and Nehemiah; Malachi is prob. not a personal name. [Heb., = "my messenger"]

mal·a·chite (măl'*a*kīt) *n.* Hydrated copper carbonate, a bright green mineral taking a high polish and used as decorative stone.

mal·ad·just·ment (măl*a*jŭst'-m*e*nt) *n.* Faulty adjustment; person's psychological inability to adjust himself, his wishes, etc., to his environment. **mal·ad·just'ed** *adj.*

mal·ad·min·is·tra·tion (măl-*a*dmĭnĭstrā'sh*o*n) *n.* Faulty administration.

mal·a·droit (măl*a*droit') *adj.* Bungling; tactless. **mal·a·droit'ly** *adv.* **mal·a·droit'ness** *n.*

mal·a·dy (măl'*a*dē) *n.* (pl. **-dies**). Ailment, disease.

Mal·a·ga[1] (măl'*a*g*a*; *Sp.* mah'-lahgah). Province of S. Spain, part of the ancient kingdom of Granada; its capital, a Mediterranean seaport.

Mal·a·ga[2] (măl'*a*g*a*) *n.* Dark sweet fortified wine produced near the city of Malaga.

Mal·a·gas·y (măl*a*găs'ē) *adj.* & *n.* (Native, language) of Madagascar; ~ **Republic**: see MADAGASCAR.

ma·laise (mălāz'; *Fr.* mălĕz') *n.* Feeling of uneasiness or discomfort.

Mal·a·prop (măl'*a*prŏp), **Mrs.** In Sheridan's play *The Rivals* (1775), a lady who ludicrously misuses long words, as *illiterate him from your memory.* **mal'a·prop·-ism** *n.* Misapplication of a (long) word.

mal·ap·ro·pos (mălăpr*o*pō') *adv.* & *adj.* (Done, said, etc.) inopportunely. ~ *n.* Inopportune remark etc.

ma·lar·i·a (m*a*lār̄'ē*a*) *n.* Intermittent and remittent fever, caused by a microorganism (*Plasmodium*) which is transmitted by the bite of certain mosquitoes of the genus *Anopheles.* **ma·lar'i·al, ma·lar'-i·ous** *adjs.* [It. *mal'aria* bad air (because formerly attributed to unwholesome exhalations of marshes)]

Ma·la·wi (mahlah'wē). Republic of central Africa; member nation of the Brit. Commonwealth; formerly the British protectorate of Nyasaland, independent 1964; capital, Lilongwe.

Ma·lay (mā'lā, m*a*lā') *n.* Member of a light brown people of mixed Caucasian and Mongolian stock, predominating in the Malay Peninsula and Archipelago; language of this people. ~ *adj.* Of Malays or their country or language; ~ **Archipelago**, very large group of islands, including Sumatra, Java, Borneo, the Philippines, and New Guinea, lying SE.

The federation of ***Malaysia*** *was established in 1963. It is the world's leading producer of tin, and palm oil, rubber, rice and copra are important products. Shown here: Malaysia's map and flag. Facing page: Women planting rice in Sabah.*

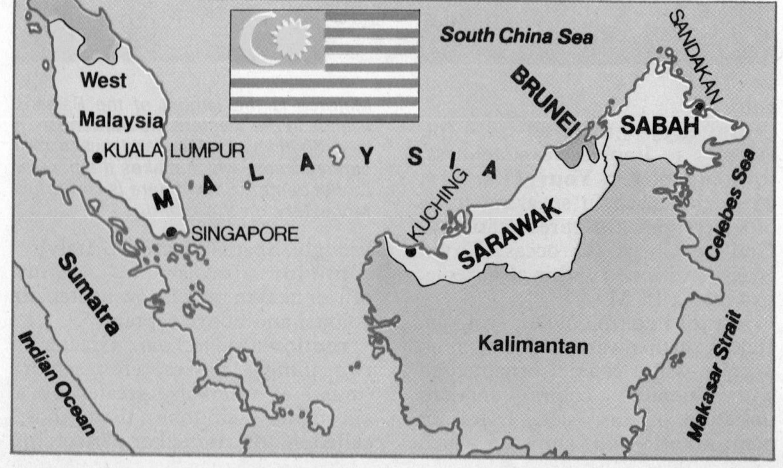

of Asia and N. and NE. of Australia; ~ **Peninsula**, most southerly projection of the mainland of Asia, running southward from Thailand.

Ma·lay·a (m*a*lā′*a*). Known as West Malaysia since 1966; a former federation of 11 Malay States, 1957–63, now part of the Federation of Malaysia.

Ma·lay·sia (m*a*lā′zh*a*, -sh*a*). Federation of States within the British Commonwealth, formed in 1963, comprising West Malaysia, Sabah, and Sarawak; capital, Kuala Lumpur. **Ma·lay′sian** *adj.* & *n.*

mal·con·tent (măl′k*o*ntĕnt) *n.* Discontented person, one inclined to rebellion.

mal de mer (măl d*e* mār′). Seasickness. [Fr.]

Mal·dives (măl′dīvz). Formerly called Maldive Islands; a republic consisting of a group of islands in the Indian Ocean SW. of Sri Lanka; formerly a British protectorate, independent since 1965; capital, Malé; **Mal·div·i·an** (măldĭv′ē*a*n) *adj.* & *n.*

male (māl) *adj.* 1. Of the sex in human beings, other animals, and plants, that begets young by fecundating the female; ~ **chauvinist** (*n.*), (derog.) man showing excessive loyalty to other men and prejudice against women; also ~ **chauvinist(ic) pig**; ~ **chauvinism** (*n.*). 2. (of part of machinery etc.) designed to enter or fill the corresponding female (hollow) part; ~ **screw**: see SCREW[1]; ~ **fern**, fern (*Dryopteris filixmas*), producing an oleoresin used for expelling tapeworms. **male** *n.* Male person, animal, or plant.

Ma·lé (mahlē′). Principal island and capital of the Maldives.

mal·e·dic·tion (măl*e*dĭk′sh*o*n) *n.* Curse. **mal·e·dic′to·ry** *adj.*

mal·e·fac·tor (măl′*e*făkt*e*r) *n.* Criminal, evildoer. **mal·e·fac·tion** (măl*e*făk′sh*o*n) *n.*

ma·lef·ic (m*a*lĕf′ĭk) *adj.* Harmful, baneful. **ma·lef′i·cent** *adj.* Hurtful; criminal. **ma·lef′i·cence** *n.*

ma·lev·o·lent (m*a*lĕv′*o*lent) *adj.* Wishing ill to others. **ma·lev′o·lence** *n.* **ma·lev′o·lent·ly** *adv.*

mal·fea·sance (mălfē′z*a*ns) *n.* Official misconduct.

mal·for·ma·tion (mălfōrmā′sh*o*n) *n.* Faulty formation. **mal·formed** (mălfōrmd′) *adj.*

Ma·li (mah′lē). Republic in W. Africa; formerly the French colony of Sudan; capital, Bamako.

mal·ice (măl′ĭs) *n.* Ill will; desire to do harm. **ma·li·cious** (m*a*lĭsh′*u*s) *adj.* **ma·li′cious·ly** *adv.*

ma·lign (m*a*līn′) *adj.* Maleficent; (of disease) malignant. **ma·lign′ly** *adv.* **malign** *v.t.* Speak ill of, slander.

ma·lig·nant (m*a*lĭg′n*a*nt) *adj.* 1. Feeling or showing intense ill will. 2. (path., of disease) Of the form that kills, as dist. from milder forms; (of tumor) cancerous, growing into surrounding tissue and destroying it and giving rise to secondary growths in other parts (opp. BENIGN). **ma·lig′nan·cy** *n.* **ma·lig′nant·ly** *adv.*

The republic of ***Mali*** *in West Africa is largely desert and arid grazing land. Timbuktu, the old center of the caravan trade, is located in Mali. These cone-shaped houses are typical village dwellings in Mali.*

ma·lig·ni·ty (m*a*lĭg′nĭtē) *n.* (pl. **-ties**). Malignant character or feeling.

ma·lin·ger (m*a*lĭng′g*e*r) *v.i.* Pretend illness to escape duty. **ma·lin′ger·er** *n.*

mall (mawl, mahl) *n.* Sheltered walk as promenade; shopping area.

mal·lard (măl′*e*rd) *n.* (pl. **-lards**, collect. **-lard**). Wild duck (*Anas platyrhynchos*), from which most domestic ducks are descended, the male being distinguished by a green or dark-blue head and a white ring around the neck.

Mal·lar·me′ (măl ārmā′), **Stéphane** (1842–98). French symbolist poet; author of "L'Après-midi d'un Faune."

mal·le·a·ble (măl′ē*a*bel) *adj.* (of metal etc.) That can be hammered, beaten, or rolled into a different form without a tendency to return to its original form or to fracture; adaptable, pliable. **mal·le·a·bil′i·ty** *n.*

mal·let (măl′ĭt) *n.* Hammer (usu. wooden); implement for striking croquet or polo ball.

mal·le·us (măl′ē*u*s) *n.* (pl. **-le·i** pr. -lēī). Small bone of middle ear transmitting vibrations of tympanum to incus. [L., = "hammer"]

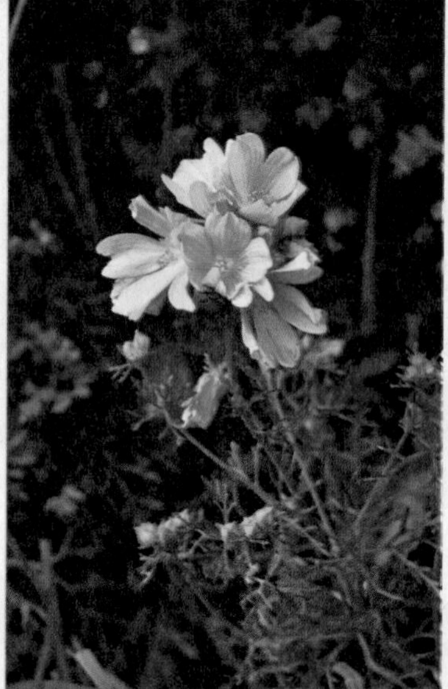

The ***mallow*** *occurs in all except the coldest parts of the world, but is most numerous in the tropics. This musk mallow, which is one of about 1,000 species, is cultivated as a garden plant.*

Mal·lor·ca (mahyōr′k*a*; *Span.* mahlyōr′kah): see MAJORCA.

mal·low (măl′ō) *n.* Plant of genus *Malva*, usu. with purple, pink, or white flowers; any of various related plants, such as **rose** ~ or ~ **rose** (*Hibiscus moscheutos*).

mal·nu·tri·tion (mălnōōtrĭsh′*o*n, -nū-) *n.* Underfeeding; diet that does not include what is needed for health.

mal·o·dor·ous (mălō′d*e*r*u*s) *adj.*

Malta, *an independent state in the Mediterranean, comprises the islands of Malta, Gozo and Comino. It was a British naval base during the 1939-45 war. Its capital is Valletta, whose Grand Harbor is shown here.*

The ***mamba,*** *a large dangerous and poisonous snake, is found in Africa south of the Sahara where it hunts small animals. This green mamba is about 9ft. long.*

Evil-smelling.

Mal·o·ry (măl′*e*rē), **Sir Thomas** (d. 1471). English author; his *Le Morte d'Arthur*, a collection of Arthurian stories, was one of the first books printed by Caxton (1485).

Mal·pi·ghi (mahlpē′gē), **Marcello** (1628–94). Italian physician and anatomist, first to observe the movement of blood through the capillaries. **Mal·pigh·i·an** (mălpĭg′ēan) *adj.* (anat.) Of certain structures (esp. in the substance of the kidneys) discovered by Malpighi.

mal·prac·tice (mălprăk′tĭs) *n.* Wrongdoing; (law) improper treatment of patient by medical attendant; illegal action for one's own benefit while in position of trust.

malt (mawlt) *n.* Barley or other grain for brewing, steeped in water, allowed to germinate and then dried slowly in a kiln; ~ **liquor**, liquor made from fermented malt (e.g. beer), not by distillation. **malt** *v.t.* Convert grain into malt.

Mal·ta (mawl′t*a*). Principal island of a group of three forming a nation in the Mediterranean, south of Sicily; member state of the British Commonwealth, independent 1964; capital, Valletta; occupied successively by Arabs (870), Sicily (1090), the Order of St. John (1530), France (1788), and Britain (1814).

Mal·tese (mawltēz′, -tēs′) *adj.* Of Malta; ~ **cross**, cross of the Knights of Malta, (a military religious order founded in 1099) with four equal limbs broadened at the ends and indented. ~ *n.* (pl. and collect. **-tese**). Native, inhabitant, of Malta; its language, a dialect of Arabic, written in Roman characters.

Mal·thus (măl′th*u*s), **Thomas Robert** (1766–1835). English clergyman and economist, author of an essay (1798) arguing that population increases faster than the means of subsistence and urging that its increase should be checked, mainly by sexual restraint. **Mal·thu·si·an** (mălthōō′zēan) *adj.* & *n.* **Mal·thu′si·an·ism** *n.*

malt·ose (mawl′tōs) *n.* (chem.) Sugar obtained by hydrolysis of starch by enzymes present in malt.

mal·treat (măltrēt′) *v.t.* Ill-treat. **mal·treat′ment** *n.*

ma·ma (mah′m*a*, m*a*mah′) *n.* (Child's name for) mother.

mam·ba (mahm′bah) *n.* Venomous African snake of genus *Dendraspis.*

mam·bo (mahm′bō) *n.* (pl. **-bos**). Latin-Amer. dance like rumba; music for it. [Amer. Sp. prob. f. Haitian]

mam·ma[1] (mah′m*a*, m*a*mah′) = MAMA.

mam·ma[2] (măm′*a*) *n.* (pl. **-mae** pr. -mē). (anat.) Milk-secreting organ of female in mammals; corresponding rudimentary structure in males. **mam·mif·er·ous** (mămĭf′*e*r*u*s) *adj.*

mam·mal (măm′*a*l) *n.* Member of the Mammalia, class of animals having mammae. **mam·ma·li·an** (m*a*mā′lē*a*n, -māl′y*a*n) *adj.* & *n.*

mam·mal·o·gist (m*a*măl′*o*jĭst), **mam·mal·o·gy** (m*a*măl′*o*jē) *ns.* Student, study, of mammals.

mam·ma·ry (măm′*a*rē) *adj.* Of the mammae.

mammato- *prefix.* (meteor.) Descriptive of clouds resembling rounded festoons, as *~-cirrus, ~-cumulus.*

mam·mil·la (m*a*mĭl′*a*) *n.* (pl. **-lae** pr. -lē). Nipple of female breast; nipple-shaped organ. **mam·mil·lar·y** (măm′*i*lĕr′ē), **mam·mil·late** (măm′*i*lāt) *adjs.*

Mam·mon (măm′*o*n). Aramaic word for "riches" used in Matt. 6 and Luke 16, taken by medieval writers as the proper name of the devil of covetousness; this use was revived by Milton in *Paradise Lost*; hence, as personification, term of opprobrium for wealth regarded as an idol or evil influence. [Aram. *māmôn*]

mam·moth (măm′*o*th) *n.* Large extinct elephant with long hairy coat and curved tusks whose fossilized remains are found in N. America, northern Europe, and Asia. ~ *adj.* Huge.

Mam·moth (măm′*o*th) **Cave National Park.** National park in central Kentucky known for its limestone caverns.

mam·my (măm′ē) *n.* (pl. **-mies**). (Child's word for) mother; (chiefly U.S. Southern) black nurse of white children (usu. considered offensive).

man (măn) *n.* (pl. **men** pr. mĕn). 1. Human being, individual of the genus *Homo*, distinguished from other animals by superior mental development, power of articulate speech, and upright posture, etc.; person; human race. 2. Adult human male; husband; manservant; workman; (pl.) soldiers, the rank and file, as dist. from officers. 3. Piece in chess, checkers, etc. 4. **As one ~**, in unison; **to a ~**, without exception; **~ about town**, man leading fashionable social life; **~ and boy** (*adv.*) from boyhood on; **~-eater**, cannibal; man-eating shark or tiger; **~ Friday**, male assistant with various duties; **man′han′dle** (*v.t.*) (**-dled, -dling**), handle roughly; **man′-hole**, opening in floor, pavement, usu. with cover, giving access to a sewer etc.; **man-hour**, one hour's work by one man, as measure of output in industry etc.; **man′hunt**, organized search for person, esp. criminal; **man in the street**, average citizen, ordinary person; **man-of-war**, warship; **man′-power**, amount of men available for military or other service; **The Man**, (black slang) all white men, a white man (derog.). **man** *v.t.* (**manned, man·ning**). Furnish with men for service or defense; place men at (part of ship); fill (post).

Man. *abbrev.* Manitoba.

ma·na (mah′n*a*) *n.* Power, authority; magical or supernatural power. [Polynesian]

man·a·cle (măn′*a*k*e*l) *n.* (usu. pl.) & *v.t.* (**-cled, -cling**). Fetter, handcuff.

man·age (măn′ĭj) *v.* (**-aged, -ag·ing**). Handle, wield (tool etc.); conduct working of (business etc.); have effective control of (household, institution, etc.); subject (animal, person, etc.) to one's control; gain one's ends with (person etc.) by flattery etc.; contrive (*to* do), succeed in one's aim; cope with. **man·age·a·bil·i·ty** (mănĭj*a*bĭl′ĭtē) *n.* **man′age·a·ble** *adj.* **man′age·a·ble·ness** *n.* **man′age·a·bly** *adv.*

man·age·ment (măn′ĭjm*e*nt) *n.* Act of managing; state of being managed; body of persons managing a business etc.; administration of business concern or public undertaking.

man·ag·er (măn′ĭj*e*r) *n.* Person conducting a business, institution, etc. **man·a·ge·ri·al** (mănĭjēr′ē*a*l) *adj.*

Ma·na·gua (mahnah′gwah). Lake in W. Nicaragua; capital of Nicaragua on the S. shore of the lake.

man·a·kin (măn′*a*kĭn) *n.* One of the small gaily-colored birds of the passerine family Pipridae, inhabiting Central and S. America.

Ma·na·ma (mănăm′*a*). Capital and principal port of Bahrein.

Ma·nas·sas (m*a*năs′*a*s). Town in NE. Virginia where Civil War battles of BULL RUN were fought, 1861 and 1862, called Battles of Manassas by Confederates.

man·a·tee (măn′*a*tē, măn*a*tē′) *n.*

*The **mammoth** was about the same size or slightly smaller than the modern elephant. The woolly mammoth which was found preserved in ice in Siberia was covered in long, reddish-brown hair. Mammoths figure significantly in the art of primitive man.*

Large aquatic herbivorous mammal of genus *Trichechus*, living off W. African and Amer. tropical coasts.

Man·chu (mănchōō′) *adj.* & *n.* (pl. **-chus**, collect. **-chu**). (Member) of a Tartar people who conquered China and founded the Ch'ing dynasty (1644–1912); (of) their language, written in a modified Mongolian script, at one time an official language of China, but now spoken only in parts of N. Manchuria.

Man·chu·kuo (măn′chōō′kwō′): see MANCHURIA.

Man·chu·ri·a (mănchoor′ē*a*). Region forming the NE. portion of China; in 1932 declared an independent nation by Japan and renamed **Manchukuo**; restored to China in 1945.

The Toucan has an enormous ***mandible*** *(beak). The reason for its size is not known. There are 37 species of the bird, which live in the tropical forests of America.*

Man·dae·an (măndē′*a*n) *adj.* & *n.* (Member) of a Gnostic sect, of which a small community survives in Iraq, very hostile to Christianity since Byzantine times.

Man·da·lay (măn′d*a*lā, măn-d*a*lā′). City of central Burma, on the Irrawaddy River.

man·da·mus (măndā′m*u*s) *n.* (pl. **-mus·es**). Judicial writ issued as command to inferior court. [L., = "we command"]

man·da·rin (măn′d*e*rĭn) *n.* 1. Former Chinese official in any of the nine grades; (transf.) pedantic official bureaucrat; form of the Chinese language spoken by officials and educated persons and used in official documents. [Sansk. *mantrin* counselor] 2. Citrus fruit.

man·da·tar·y (măn′d*a*tĕrē) *n.* (pl. **-tar·ies**). One to whom a MANDATE is given.

man·date (măn′dāt, -dĭt) *n.* Authoritative command from superior; commission to act for another, esp. one given by League of Nations to a nation (the **mandatary**) to administer certain colonies of the defeated enemy powers in the war of 1914–18 for the benefit of the inhabitants; political instructions inferred from votes of electorate. ~ (măn′dāt) *v.t.* (**-dat·ed, -dat·ing**). Commit (nation etc.) *to* mandatary.

man·da·to·ry (măn′d*a*tōrē) *adj.* Of, conveying, a command. ~ *n.* = MANDATARY.

man·di·ble (măn′d*i*b*e*l) *n.* Lower jawbone; either part of bird's beak; either half of crushing organ in mouth parts of many arthropods. **man·dib·u·lar** (măndĭb′y*u*l*er*), **man·dib′u·lar·y** *adjs.*

man·do·lin (măn′d*o*lĭn, măn-d*o*lĭn′) *n.* Musical instrument of lute kind with paired metal strings stretched on deeply rounded body, played tremolo with a plectrum.

man·drake (măn′drāk, -drĭk), **man·drag·o·ra** (măndrăg′*era*, -dr*a*gōr′*a*) *ns.* Poisonous plant with emetic and narcotic properties, with root formerly thought to resemble human form and to shriek when plucked up from the ground.

man·drel, man·dril (măn′dr*e*l) *ns.* Axis on which material revolves in lathe; rod around which metal etc. is forged or shaped.

man·drill (măn′drĭl) *n.* Large and ferocious baboon (*Mandrillus sphinx*) of W. Africa with highly colored patches and callosities on face and hindquarters.

mane (mān) *n.* Long hair on neck of horse, lion, etc. (also fig. of person's hair).

The ***manatee*** *is a slow-moving inoffensive creature that feeds on aquatic vegetation. It has no natural enemies but in some areas is hunted for its meat, hide and oil.*

The **mango** is one of the most important and widely cultivated fruits of the tropical world. Its juicy fruit is a rich source of vitamins A, C and D.

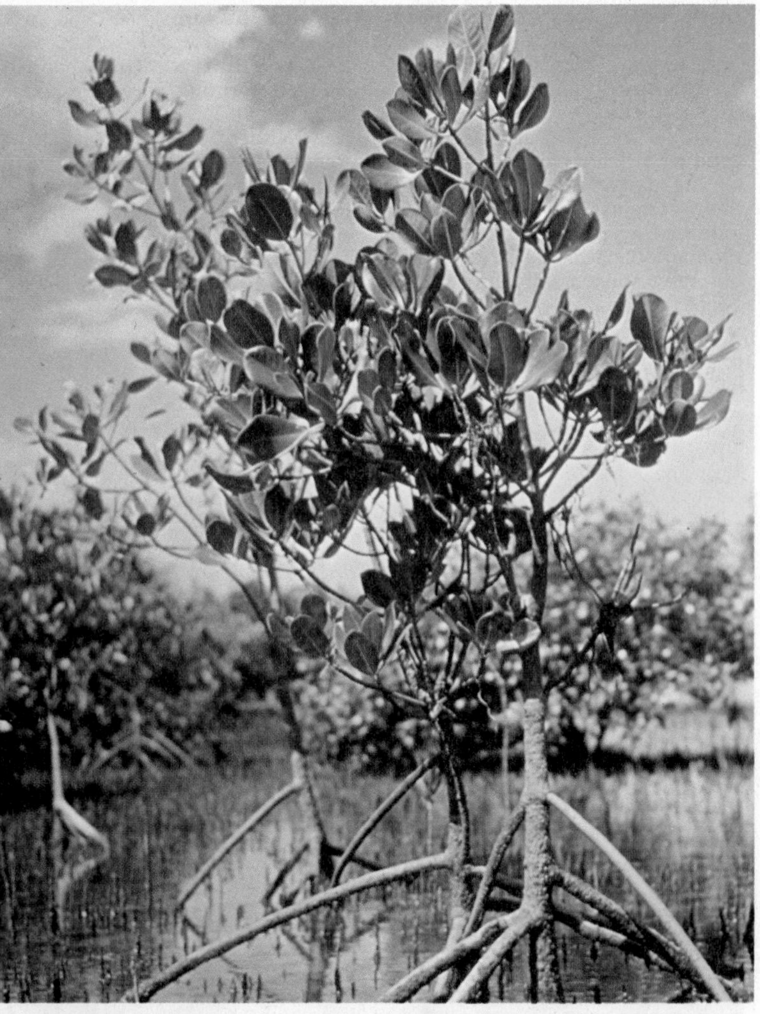

These Australian coastal **mangroves** have exposed supporting roots. These project above the mud, and have small openings through which air enters, passing through soft, spongy tissue to the roots beneath the mud.

Ma·nes (mā'nēz) (*c*215–75). (also **Manichaeus**) Founder of MANICHEISM.

ma·nes (mā'nēz; *Lat.* mah'nĕs) *n.* 1. (usu. considered pl.; Rom. myth.) Deified souls of departed ancestors. 2. (usu. considered sing.) Shade of dead person as object of reverence.

Ma·net (mănā'), **Edouard** (1832–83). French Impressionist painter.

ma·neu·ver (manōō'v*er*) *n.* Planned movement, (in pl.) large-scale exercise, of troops, warships, etc.; deceptive or elusive movement; skillful plan. ~ *v.* Perform, cause (troops etc.) to perform, maneuvers; employ artifice; force, manipulate, (person, thing *into*, *out*, etc.) by scheming or adroitness. **ma·neu'ver·a·ble** *adj.* **ma·neu·ver·a·bil'i·ty** *n.* (pl. **-ties**).

man·ful (măn'f*u*l) *adj.* Brave, resolute. **man'ful·ly** *adv.* **man'ful·ness** *n.*

man·ga·bey (măng'g*a*bā) *n.* (pl. **-beys**). Small long-tailed W. African monkey of genus *Cercocebus.* [name of a region in Madagascar]

man·ga·nese (măng'g*a*nēs, -nēz) *n.* (chem.) Gray brittle metallic element, used in making alloys of steel, symbol Mn, at. no. 25, at. wt. 54.9380; ~ **dioxide**, black mineral (MnO_2) used as an oxidizing agent, esp. in glass-making, electric batteries, etc. [Fr. *manganèse*, corrupt. of MAGNESIA]

mange (mānj) *n.* Skin disease caused by a parasite that destroys hairy coat of animals, occas. communicated to man.

man·ger (mān'j*er*) *n.* Box or trough in stable etc. for horses or cattle to eat from.

man·gle[1] (măng'g*e*l) *n.* Machine of two or more cylinders between which washed clothes are rolled to press out the water. ~ *v.t.* (**-gled, -gling**). Press (clothes) in mangle.

man·gle[2] (măng'g*e*l) *v.t.* (**-gled, -gling**). Hack, cut about, mutilate; spoil, garble (text, pronunciation, etc.).

man·go (măng'gō) *n.* (pl. **-goes, -gos**). Fleshy fruit, eaten ripe or used green for pickles etc., of the Indian tree *Mangifera indica*; this tree.

man·grove (măng'grōv, măn'-) *n.* Tropical tree or shrub growing in mud at seashore with aerating roots above ground, esp. the **red** ~ (*Rhizophora mangle*) from coastal Florida to S. America.

man·gy (mān'jē) *adj.* (**-gi·er, -gi·est**). Having the mange; squalid, shabby. **man'gi·ly** *adv.* **man'gi·ness** *n.*

Man·hat·tan (mănhăt'*a*n, m*a*n-). Island and borough of New York City at the mouth of the Hudson River.

man·hat·tan (mănhăt'*a*n, m*a*n-) *n.* Cocktail made of sweet vermouth and whiskey with a dash of bitters.

man·hood (măn'hŏŏd) *n.* State of being a man; manliness, courage; men of a country etc.

ma·ni·a (mā'nē*a*) *n.* 1. Mental derangement marked by excitement, hallucination, and violence. 2. Excessive enthusiasm.

ma·ni·ac (mā'nēăk) *n.* Person afflicted with mania. **ma·ni·a·cal** (m*a*nī'*a*k*a*l) *adj.* **ma·ni'a·cal·ly** *adv.*

man·ic (măn'ĭk, mā'nĭk) *adj.* Of, affected with, mania; ~**-depressive**, (person) affected with mental disorder characterized by alternating mania and depression.

Man·i·che·ism, Man·i·chae·ism (măn'ĭkēĭz*e*m) *ns.* Dualistic ascetic religious system, regarding existence as a conflict between the powers of light and the demons of darkness, which was widely accepted from the 3rd to the 5th c., founded by MANES. **Man·i·che'an, Man·i·chae'an** *adjs.* & *ns.*

Manhattan, a borough of New York City consisting of Manhattan Island (12 ½ miles long and 2 ½ miles wide), is the financial, commercial and cultural center of the city.

Man·i·che′an·ism, Man·i·chae′-an·ism *ns.* **Man′i·chee** *n.* Manichean.

man·i·cure (măn′*i*kūr) *n.* Cosmetic care and treatment of hands and (esp.) fingernails. ~ *v.t.* (**-cured, -cur·ing**). Apply manicure treatment to. **man′i·cur·ist** *n.*

man·i·fest[1] (măn′*i*fĕst) *n.* List of ship's cargo for use of customs officials.

man·i·fest[2] (măn′*i*fĕst) *adj.* Clear to sight or mind. **man′i·fest·ly** *adv.* **manifest** *v.* Show plainly to eye or mind; be evidence of, prove; display, evince (quality, feeling) by one's acts; (of thing) reveal *itself*; (of ghost) appear. **man·i·fes·ta·tion** (măn*i*fĕstā′-sh*o*n) *n.* **man·i·fes·ta·tive** (măn*i*-fĕs′t*a*tĭv) *adj.*

man·i·fes·to (măn*i*fĕs′tō) *n.* (pl. **-toes**). Public declaration by sovereign, nation, or body of individuals, of principles and future policy.

man·i·fold (măn′*i*fōld) *adj.* Having various forms, applications, functions, etc.; many and various. ~ *v.t.* Multiply copies of (letter etc.). ~ *n.* (mech.) Pipe or chamber with several openings. **man′i·fold·ly** *adv.* **man′i·fold·ness** *n.*

man·i·kin, man·a·kin, man·ni·kin (măn′*i*kĭn) *ns.* Little man, dwarf; artist's lay figure; anatomical model of the body; mannequin.

Ma·nil·a[1] (m*a*nĭl′*a*). City on island of Luzon, principal city and administrative capital of the Philippine Islands; ~ (or **Manilla**) **hemp**, a fibrous material, obtained from the leaves of *Musa textilis*, a tree native to the Philippines, and used for ropes, matting, textiles, etc.; ~ **paper**, brown wrapping paper orig. made from Manila hemp.

Ma·nil·a[2], **Ma·nil·la** (m*a*nĭl′*a*) *ns.* Manila hemp; Manila paper; cigar or cheroot made of Philippine tobacco.

man·i·oc (măn′ēŏk, mā′nē-) = CASSAVA. [native Brazilian *mandioca*]

man·i·ple (măn′*i*p*e*l) *n.* 1. (Rom. antiq.) Subdivision of a legion, containing 120 or 60 men. 2. One of the Eucharistic vestments, orig. a napkin, consisting now of a strip of cloth 2–4 ft. in length, worn hanging from left arm.

ma·nip·u·late (m*a*nĭp′y*u*lāt) *v.t.* (**-lat·ed, -lat·ing**). Handle; deal skillfully with; manage craftily. **ma·nip·u·la·tion** (m*a*nĭpy*u*lā′-sh*o*n), **ma·nip′u·la·tor** *ns.*

Man·i·to·ba (măn*ĭ*tō′b*a*). Province of central Canada, with coastline on Hudson Bay; capital, Winnipeg; **Lake** ~, lake, 1,817 sq. mi. (2,925 km), in S. part of this province.

man·i·tou (măn′ĭto͞o) *n.* (pl. **-tous**, collect. **-tou**). (Algonquian Ind.) Good or evil spirit, thing having supernatural power.

man·kind (mănkīnd′, măn′kīnd) *n.* 1. Human species. 2. Male sex, males.

man·like (măn′līk) *adj.* Like a man; (of woman) mannish.

man·ly (măn′lē) *adj.* (**-li·er, -li·est**). Having the qualities or bearing of a man; befitting a man. **man′li·ness** *n.*

Mann[1] (măn), **Horace** (1796–1859). Amer. educator and lawyer; revolutionized public school system; member of U.S. House of Representatives, 1848–53; president of Antioch College, 1852–1859.

Mann[2] (mahn), **Thomas** (1875–1955). German novelist; U.S. citizen from 1944; awarded Nobel Prize for literature, 1929; author of *Buddenbrooks*, *Death In Venice*, *The Magic Mountain*, etc.

man·na (măn′*a*) *n.* Substance miraculously supplied as food to Israelites in wilderness (Exod. 16).

man·ne·quin, man·i·kin (măn′ĭkĭn) *ns.* Woman who models clothing; dummy figure for shop windows etc.

man·ner (măn′*er*) *n.* Way a thing is done or happens; outward bearing; (pl.) behavior in social intercourse; habits indicating good breeding. **man′nered** *adj.* Showing mannerisms, affected; **ill-, well-** ~, having bad, good, manners. **man′ner·less** *adj.* Ill-mannered.

man·ner·ism (măn′*er*ĭzem) *n.* 1. Trick of speech, gesture, or style; excessive addiction to a distinctive manner in art or literature. 2. Style of art which originated in Italy *c*1530 and preceded the Baroque, characterized by contorted figures, startling light effects, etc. **man′-**

ner·ist *adj.* & *n.* (Exponent) of mannerism in art, etc.

man·ner·ly (măn'*er*lē) *adj.* Well-mannered, polite. **man'ner·li·ness** *n.*

man·nish (măn'ĭsh) *adj.* Characteristic of a man as opp. to a woman; (of woman) masculine. **man'nish·ness** *n.*

Ma·no·le·te (mahnawlĕ'tĕ) (1917–47). Original name, Manuel Laureamo Rodriguez y Sanchez; Spanish matador.

ma·nom·e·ter (m*a*nŏm'*e*t*er*) *n.* Instrument for measuring the pressure of gases and vapors by the difference in level which they produce in a liquid in a U-tube, one side of which may be open to the atmosphere or evacuated and sealed off.

man·or (măn'*er*) *n.* English territorial unit, orig. feudal, the lord's demesne and lands from whose holders he could exact certain fees etc.; ~ **house**, house of lord of the manor. **ma·no·ri·al** (m*a*nōr'ēal, -nōr'-) *adj.*

man·sard (măn'sard) *n.* Form of roof (usu. ~ **roof**) in which each face has two slopes, the lower one steeper than the upper, usu. broken by projecting windows. [François *Mansart* (1598–1666), Fr. architect]

manse (māns) *n.* Ecclesiastical residence, esp. that of Scottish Presbyterian minister.

man·sion (măn'sh*o*n) *n.* Large residence.

man·slaugh·ter (măn'slawt*er*) *n.* Slaughter of human beings; (law) unlawful killing of a human being without malice aforethought.

man·sue·tude (măn'swĕtōōd, -tūd) *n.* Gentleness, meekness.

man·ta (măn't*a*) *n.* Very large ray of the family Mobubidae, living in tropical seas, with winglike fins; also called ~ **ray**.

man·tel (măn't*e*l) *n.* Structure of wood, marble, etc., above and around fireplace; **man'telpiece**, mantel; shelf above fireplace.

man·tel·et, mant·let (măn'-t*e*lĕt, -tlĭt) *ns.* Short mantle or cape; bulletproof screen for gunners.

man·tic (măn'tĭk) *adj.* Of divination.

man·til·la (măntĭl'*a*, -tē'*a*) *n.* Lace veil worn by Spanish women over head and shoulders.

man·tis (măn'tĭs) *n.* Orthopterous insect, esp. the **praying** ~ (*Mantis religiosa*), which holds its forelegs in a position suggesting hands folded in prayer. [Gk., = "prophet"]

man·tis·sa (măntĭs'*a*) *n.* Decimal part of a logarithm. [L., = "makeweight"]

man·tle (măn't*e*l) *n.* Loose sleeveless cloak; fragile hood consisting usu. of oxides of thorium and cerium, fixed around gas jet to give incandescent light (also **gas** ~); (zool.) covering or envelope, as that enclosing body of mollusk; (ornith.) back, scapulars, and wing coverts of bird, esp. when of distinguishing color; (geol.) region lying between

*The **mantis** feeds exclusively on living insects. There are about 1,800 species found mainly in tropical or sub-tropical regions. It may be disguised to resemble foliage, a lichen, a brightly colored flower or an ant.*

*Welding in a steel plant in Chicago. Steel **manufacture** is a primary industry in Chicago, and the volume produced is the highest of any city in the U.S.A. Allied metal industries are also widespread.*

crust and core of Earth; (fig.) covering. ~ *v.* (**-tled, -tling**). Envelop, cover (as) with mantle; (of liquids) form a scum; (of blood) suffuse cheeks; blush.

man·u·al (măn'ūal) *adj.* Of or done with the hands. **man'u·al·ly** *adv.* **manual** *n.* 1. Handbook, textbook, primer. 2. Keyboard of organ.

man·u·fac·ture (mănу*u*făk'-ch*er*) *n.* Making of articles by physical labor or machinery, esp. on large scale; branch of such an industry; anything manufactured from raw products. ~ *v.t.* (**-tured, -tur·ing**). Produce by labor, esp. on large scale; invent, fabricate. **man·u·fac'tur·er** *n.*

man·u·mit (mănу*u*mĭt') *v.t.* (**-mit·ted, -mit·ting**). Give freedom to (slave). **man·u·mis·sion** (mănу*u*mĭsh'*o*n) *n.*

ma·nure (manoor', -nūr') *n.* Substance, esp. dung, used for fertilizing soil. ~ *v.t.* (**-nured, -nur·ing**). Apply manure to.

ma·nus (mā'n*u*s) *n.* (pl. **-nus**). (zool.) That part of the forelimb of any tetrapod which corresponds to the human hand, esp. the bones within it.

man·u·script (măn'у*u*skrĭpt) *adj.* & *n.* (Book, document) written by hand, not printed; (of) author's written or typed copy for printer (abbrev. MS., pl. MSS.).

For long the effective ruler of China and the chairman of China's Communist Party, **Mao Tse-Tung,** a poet as well as a political theorist, was responsible for China's development as a major power.

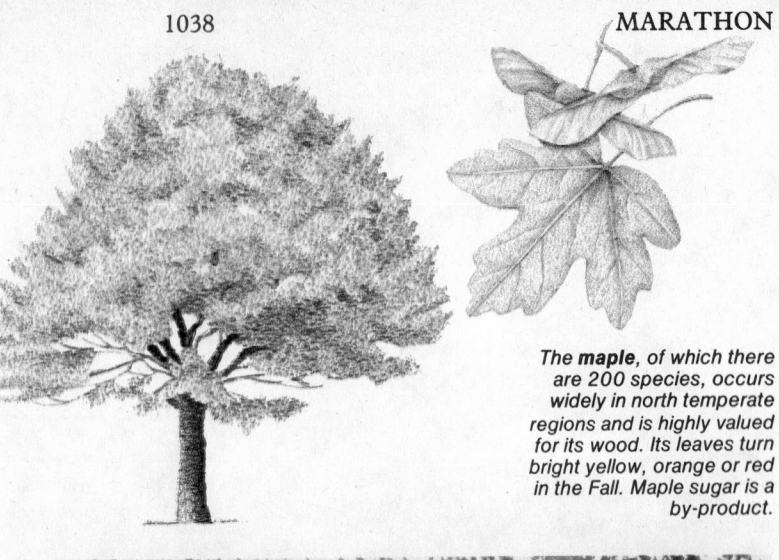

*The **maple**, of which there are 200 species, occurs widely in north temperate regions and is highly valued for its wood. Its leaves turn bright yellow, orange or red in the Fall. Maple sugar is a by-product.*

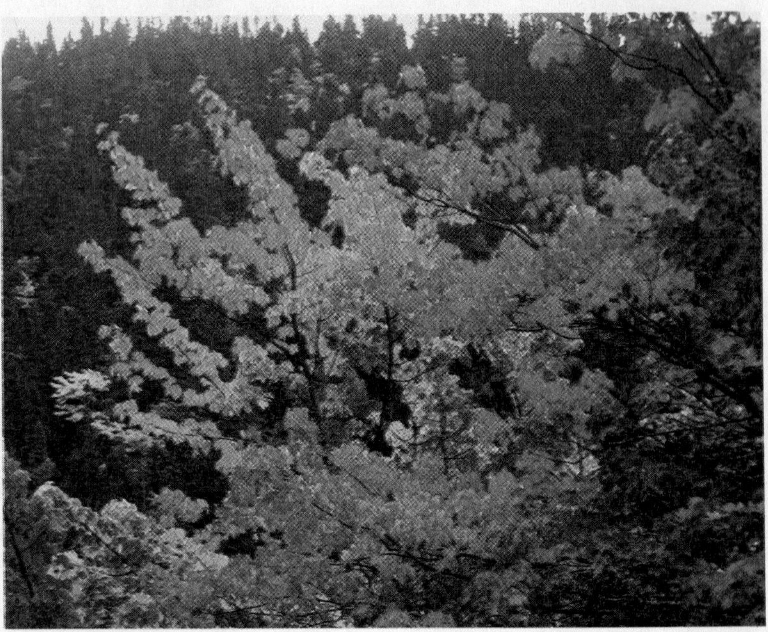

Manx (măngks) *adj.* Of the Isle of Man; of the Celtic language there; ~ **cat**, cat of tailless breed originating there. **Manx** *n.* Manx language.

man·y (mĕn′ē) *adj.* (**more, most**) & *n.* (Consisting of) a large number; **the** ~, the multitude; ~**-sided**, having many sides; having a variety of interests, capabilities, etc.; ~**-sidedness** (*n*).

Ma·o·ri (mahōr′ē, mow′rē) *n.* (pl. **-ris**, collect. **-ri**). (Member, language, of) aboriginal people of New Zealand, of Polynesian stock.

Mao Tse-tung (mow′dze-do͞ong′, tse to͞ong′) (1893–1976). Chinese revolutionary leader; became head of the Communist republic in Kiangsi province (SE. China), 1931; after defeat by Kuomintang forces, led his followers on the "long march" of 1934–5 to Shensi province (N. China) where they established a new government; chairman of central committee of Chinese Communist party from 1936 to death; chairman of the People's Republic of China 1949–58.

Mao Ze·dong (mow′dze do͞ong′) = MAO TSE-TUNG.

map[1] (măp) *n.* Representation on paper etc. of Earth's surface or part of it, showing physical and political features etc.; similar representation of heavens showing position of stars etc.; **put on the** ~, establish position or vogue of.

map[2] *v.t.* (**mapped, map·ping**). Make map of; ~ **out**, plan out, arrange in detail.

ma·ple (mā′pel) *n.* Tree or shrub of genus *Acer* grown for shade, ornament, wood, or sugar; ~ **leaf**, leaf of maple, emblem of Canada; ~ **sugar**, sugar from SUGAR maple.

ma·quis (mahkē′) *n.* (pl. **-quis** pr. -kē′). Dense scrubby forest of various dwarf trees and shrubs in Corsica etc.; **M**~, secret army of patriots in France during the German occupation (1940–5), so named as if from hiding in the undergrowth. **ma·quis·ard** (mahkēzār′) *n.* Member of the Maquis. [Fr., f. Corsican It. *macchia* thicket]

mar (mār) *v.t.* (**marred, mar·ring**). Spoil, impair the perfection of.

Mar. *abbrev.* March.

mar·a·bou (măr′abo͞o, măr-abo͞o′) *n.* (pl. **-bous**, collect. **-bou**). Large W. African stork (*Leptoptilus crumeniferus*) (also ~ **stork**); tuft of down from its wings or tail as trimming for hat etc.

Ma·ra·cai·bo (mărakī′bō), **Lake.** Lake in NW. Venezuela, 5,000 sq. mi. (8,050 km), the largest in South America; seaport of Venezuela; one of world's leading oil export centers.

mar·a·schi·no (măraskē′nō, -shē′-) *n.* Strong sweet liqueur made from the *marasca*, a small black cherry grown in Dalmatia.

ma·ras·mus (maraz′mus) *n.* (path.) Wasting away of the body. **ma·ras′mic** *adj.*

Ma·rat (mără′), **Jean Paul** (1743–93). French revolutionary leader, philosopher, and scientist; stabbed to death by Charlotte Corday.

Mar·a·thon (măr′athŏn). Plain on E. coast of Attica, Greece, where the invading Persian army was defeated by the Athenians and Plataeans under Miltiades (490 B.C.); the Athenian courier Pheidippides ran to Sparta to bring the news of the Persian landing and ask for help, and is said to have completed the distance (150 miles, 241.5 km) in two days.

mar·a·thon (măr′athŏn) *n.* Long-distance road race, esp. the race (26 miles 385 yards 41.86 km)

*The **marabou stork** is a large African bird of the stork family. It is mainly grey and white and has an inflatable throat pouch. It swallows great chunks of carrion whole.*

that is a principal event of the modern Olympic Games (also attrib. of any lengthy feat of great endurance). [f. MARATHON]

ma·raud (m*a*rawd′) *v.i.* Make raid, pillage. **ma·raud′er** *n.*

mar·ble[1] (mâr′b*e*l) *n.* Limestone in crystalline or granular state and capable of taking polish, used in sculpture etc.; (pl.) collection of sculptures; small ball of marble, glass, clay, etc., used as toy; **M~ Arch**, arch with three gateways erected (1827) in front of Buckingham Palace, London, and moved (1851) to present site in NE. corner of Hyde Park.

mar·ble[2] (mâr′b*e*l) *v.t.* (**-bled, -bling**). Stain, color, to look like variegated marble. Also **mar′ble·-ize** (**-ized, -iz·ing**).

mar·ca·site (mâr′k*a*sīt) *n.* Crystalline iron pyrites; piece of this used as ornament.

mar·cel (mârsĕl′) *n.* (also **~ wave**) Kind of deep-grooved artificial wave in hair. ~ *v.t.* (**-celled, -cel·ling**). Wave (hair) in marcel fashion. [f. name of Paris hairdresser]

March (mârch). Third month of Gregorian (first of Julian) calendar, with 31 days. [L. *Martius (mensis)* month of Mars]

march (mârch) *v.* (Cause to) walk in military manner or with regular paces; progress steadily. ~ *n.* (pl. **march·es**). Marching of troops; progress; distance covered in marching or walking; uniform step of troops etc.; piece of music meant to accompany march, usu. in $\frac{4}{4}$, $\frac{2}{4}$, or $\frac{6}{8}$ time; musical composition, or part of one, of similar character; **steal a ~ on**, gain advantage over, esp. surreptitiously.

mar·chion·ess (mâr′sh*o*nĭs, mârsh*o*nĕs′) *n.* (pl. **-ess·es**). Wife, widow, of a marquis; lady holding in her own right rank equal to that of marquis.

march·pane (mârch′pān) = MARZIPAN.

Mar·co·ni (mârkō′nē), **Guglielmo** (1874–1937). Italian electrical engineer; inventor of wireless telegraphy; awarded the Nobel Prize for physics in 1909.

Marco Polo: see POLO.

Mar·di gras (mâr′dē grah). (Merrymaking on) Shrove Tuesday, the day before Lent; last day of carnival. [F., = "fat Tuesday"]

***Marble** is capable of taking a high polish and is often veined or mottled. The cutting of these marble blocks at Carrara, Italy, is done by means of a continuous twisted wire driven electrically.*

__Marie Antoinette,__ in this painting taking part in a court ballet, was the wife of Louis XVI and queen of France at the outbreak of the French Revolution. She was imprisoned with her husband and guillotined in 1793.

mare (mār) *n.* Female of horse or other equine animal; **~'s-nest,** illusory discovery; **~'s-tail,** tall slender plant (*Hippuris vulgaris*) growing in marshy ground; long straight streaks of cirrus cloud.

Mar·ga·ret (mār'gerĭt, -grĭt), **Queen** (d. 1093). Scottish saint and queen of Scotland.

mar·ga·rine (mār'jerĭn, -jerēn, mārj'rĭn) *n.* Edible fat made by the catalytic reduction of unsaturated acids in animal and vegetable oils and fats and freq. colored to resemble butter.

mar·gay (mār'gā) *n.* (pl. **-gays,** collect. **-gay**). Small S. Amer. tiger cat (*Felis tigrina*) related to the ocelot.

mar·gin (mār'jĭn) *n.* Border; strip near edge of anything; plain space around printed page, picture, etc.; extra amount over what is necessary; difference between cost and selling price; sum deposited with stockbroker to cover risk of loss on transaction.

mar·gin·al (mār'jinal) *adj.* Of, written in, the margin; of, at, the edge; close to the limit (freq. fig.). **mar'gin·al·ly** *adv.*

mar·gi·na·li·a (mārjinā'lēa, -nāl'ya) *n.pl.* Marginal notes.

mar·grave (mār'grāv) *n.* (hist.) German title, orig. of ruler of a border province; later, hereditary title of some princes of the Holy Roman Empire. **mar·gra·vine** (mār'gravēn) *n.* Margrave's wife.

Mar·gre·the II (mārgrā'te) (1940–). Queen of Denmark since 1972.

mar·gue·rite (mārgerēt') *n.* Plant (*Chrysanthemum frutescens*), having white or pale yellow flowers resembling those of the daisy. [Gk. *margaritēs* pearl]

ma·ri·a·chi (mārēah'chē) *n.* (pl. **-chi**). 1. (Member of) small band of Mexican strolling musicians dressed in native costume. 2. Music of such bands.

Mar·i·an (mār'ēan) *adj.* Of the Virgin Mary.

Mar·i·a·na Is·lands, Mar·i·a·nas (mārēah'na, mārēah'naz). Group of islands in the NW. Pacific administered (except for GUAM) by U.S. under trusteeship of U.N.

Ma·rie An·toi·nette (marē' ăntwonĕt') (1755–93). Daughter of Maria Theresa and queen of Louis XVI of France; guillotined on Oct. 16, 1793.

Ma·rie-Lou·ise (marē'lōōēz') (1791–1847). Second wife of Napoleon I, 1810, and mother of Napoleon II.

These __Royal Marine Commandos__ are on arctic warfare exercises in Norway. Marine troops are specially recruited, trained and organized for service at sea and in land operations related to naval campaigns.

mar·i·gold (măr'igōld) *n.* 1. Any of several plants of genera *Calendula* and *Tagetes*, with bright yellow or golden composite flowers. 2. = MARSH marigold. [f. *Mary* (prob. the Virgin) + *gold*]

ma·ri·jua·na, ma·ri·hua·na (măriwah'na, -hwah'-, mār-) *ns.* Dried leaves of Indian hemp, used to make narcotic cigarettes (reefers); the plant itself.

ma·rim·ba (marĭm'ba) *n.* Primitive African xylophone; modern orchestral instrument evolved from this.

ma·ri·na (marē'na) *n.* Pleasure boat harbor.

mar·i·nade (mărinād', -nahd') *n.* Mixture of wine or vinegar with herbs and spices, in which fish or meat is steeped before cooking. ~ (măr'inād) *v.t.* (**-nad·ed, -nad·ing**). Steep in marinade.

mar·i·nate (măr'ināt) *v.t.* (**-nat·ed, -nat·ing**). Marinade.

ma·rine (marēn') *adj.* Of, from, beside, the sea; for use at sea; of shipping; ~ **stores,** old ships' materials as merchandise; shop selling them. **marine** *n.* Country's fleet of ships, naval or mercantile; member of body of troops trained to fight on land or sea; (pl.) this branch of armed forces (in U.S., Marine Corps).

mar·i·ner (măr'iner) *n.* Sailor; **master ~,** captain of a merchant ship.

mar·i·o·nette (mărēonĕt') *n.* Puppet worked with strings.

mar·i·tal (măr'ĭtal) *adj.* Of a husband; of or between husband

*The **marigold,** of which there are about 80 species, is an annual plant grown as a garden ornamental. Most species have strongly scented leaves and yellow, orange or red flowers.*

*The **market,** as a center where sellers display and sell their goods, has existed since earliest times. This pottery market is in Tepotzotlan, Mexico.*

and wife. **mar'i·tal·ly** *adv.*

mar·i·time (măr'ĭtīm) *adj.* Of or connected with the sea or seafaring; situated near the sea; **M ~ Provinces,** common name of three provinces in E. Canada: Nova Scotia, Prince Edward Island, and New Brunswick.

mar·jo·ram (mar̄'j*e*ram) *n.* Any of several aromatic herbs of genus *Origanum* or esp. O. majorana, used for flavoring.

mark[1] (mar̄k) *n.* 1. = DEUTSCHE MARK. 2. (abbrev. M.) Monetary unit of the German Democratic Republic.

mark[2] (mar̄k) *n.* 1. Target, thing aimed at; **beside, wide of, the ~,** not hitting it, (fig.) not to the point; (slang) person easily duped. 2. Trace left by something; stain, scar, spot, dent. 3. Sign, indication, (*of* quality, character, etc.). 4. Affixed or impressed sign, seal, etc.; written symbol; cross etc. made by person who cannot write his name. 5. Unit in appraising merit of schoolchild's work in class, candidate's in examination, etc. 6. Line serving to indicate position, e.g. starting point in race. 7. **M ~ I, M ~ II,** etc., designation of weapon or piece of equipment indicating first, second, etc., design. **mark ~** *v.* Make a mark on; distinguish with a mark; characterize or serve as a mark of; assign marks of merit to; notice, observe, watch; **~ down,** note and remember (place etc.); (also) reduce price of; **~ off,** separate by boundary; **~ out,** trace out (boundary etc.); **~ time,** move feet as in marching, but without advancing (often fig.); **~ up,** raise price of.

Mark (mar̄k), **St.** Apostle, companion of Peter and Paul; traditional author of the 2nd Gospel (the earliest in date); commemorated April 25; 2nd Gospel.

marked (mar̄kt) *adj.* (esp.) Noticeable, conspicuous. **mark·ed·ly** (mar̄'kĭdlē) *adv.*

mark·er (mar̄'k*e*r) *n.* 1. Thing used to mark place (in book etc.). 2. Anything used to indicate position on ground to aircraft, course at sea to boats, etc. 3. (slang) I.O.U.

mar·ket (mar̄'kĭt) *n.* Gathering of people for sale of provisions, livestock, etc.; time of this, space or building used for it; demand *for*; seat of trade; **buyer's ~,** state of purchasing favorable to buyer; so **seller's ~; ~ day,** day on which market is held; **mar'ketplace,** square, open place, where market is held; **market price,** prevailing price in ordinary conditions; **market town,** town where market is held on fixed days; **market value,** salable value. **market** *v.* Buy, offer for sale, in market. **mar'ket·a·ble** *adj.* Fit for sale; sellable.

mark·ing (mar̄'kĭng) *n.* (esp.) Coloring of feathers, skin, etc.; **~ ink,** indelible ink for marking linen.

marks·man (mar̄ks'm*a*n) *n.* (pl. **-men** pr. -m*e*n). One skilled at aiming at mark, esp. rifleman of certain standard of proficiency. **marks'man·ship** *n.*

mar·lin (mar̄'lĭn) *n.* (pl. **-lins,** collect. **-lin**). Large sea fish of genus *Makaira.*

mar·line (mar̄'lĭn) *n.* (naut.) Small line of two strands used for binding shrouds etc.; **mar'line·spike,** pointed tool for separating strands of rope in splicing.

Mar·lowe (mar̄'lō), **Christopher** (1564–93). English poet and playwright; author of *Tamburlaine*, *The Jew of Malta*, *Edward II*, and *The Tragedy of Dr. Faustus.*

mar·ma·lade (mar̄'m*a*lād) *n.* Preserve of oranges or other citrus fruit, cut up and boiled with the peel and sugar; orange-yellow color, esp. of cats. [Port. *marmelada* f. *marmelo* quince]

Mar·ma·ra (mar̄'m*e*ra), **Sea of.** Small inland sea lying between the Black Sea and the Aegean.

mar·mo·re·al (mar̄mōr'ē*a*l, -mōr'-) *adj.* Of or like marble.

mar·mo·set (mar̄'m*o*zĕt) *n.* Small tropical Amer. monkey with bushy tail, of several genera in family Callithricidae.

mar·mot (mar̄'m*o*t) *n.* Any burrowing rodent of the genus *Marmota,* with bushy tail and short legs, found throughout N. hemisphere; WOODCHUCK; WHISTLER.

Marne (mar̄n). River in NE. France; center of battles in World War I, 1914 and 1918, and during World War II, 1944.

Mar·o·nite (măr'*o*nīt) *n.* One of a sect of Syrian Christians living in Lebanon, named after their founder, Maron, who lived probably in the 4th c.

ma·roon[1] (m*a*rōōn') *n.* 1. Brownish-crimson color. 2. Explosive device producing loud report. **~** *adj.* Maroon-colored. [Fr. *marron* chestnut]

ma·roon[2] (m*a*rōōn') *n.* One of a group of blacks, orig. fugitive slaves, living in mountains of W. Indies; marooned person. **~** *v.t.* Put (person) ashore and leave on desolate island or coast as punishment; leave without means of getting away. [Fr. *marron*, perh. f. Span. *cimarron* wild]

marque (mar̄k) *n.* (hist.) **letters of ~,** license given to private person to fit out armed vessel and employ it in capture of enemy's merchant shipping.

mar·quee (mar̄kē') *n.* Large tent, esp. one used at fêtes, shows, etc.

This picture of the surface of ***Mars,*** *taken by Viking 1, shows an orange-red surface covering a darker bedrock. The reddish material is thought to be limonite. The picture was taken at approximately 12 noon Mars time.*

Mar·que·sas (mar̄kā′zaz, -saz, -sas) **Islands.** Group of islands in the Pacific; part of French Polynesia.

mar·que·try, mar·que·te·rie (mar̄′kĭtrē) *ns.* (pl. **-tries**). Decoration of flat surface, as of furniture, by gluing together shaped pieces of wood, ivory, or other substance(s) so as to cover the whole surface; also, inlay; furniture etc. so decorated.

Mar·quette (mar̄kĕt′), **Jacques** (**Père**) (1637–75). French Jesuit missionary and explorer in America; accompanied Joliet on voyage down Wisconsin and Mississippi rivers and up Illinois River.

mar·quis (mar̄′kwĭs, mar̄kē′) *n.* (pl. **-quis·es, -quis** pr. -kwĭsez, -kēz′). (esp. Brit.) **mar·quess** (mar̄′kwĭs) Noble ranking below duke and above earl or count; **Marquis of Queensbury Rules**, set of rules for boxing in Gt. Britain and the basis for boxing worldwide, based on those drawn up in 1867 under supervision of 8th Marquis of Queensbury. **mar·quis·ate** (mar̄′kwĭzĭt) *n.*

mar·quise (mar̄kēz′) *n.* (pl. **-quis·es** pr. -kē′zĭz). (also ~ **ring**) Ring with head shaped like ~ **cut,** a boat-shaped brilliant cut.

Mar·ra·kesh (mărakĕsh′). City in W. central Morocco, and the former capital; in medieval period, one of the great Islamic cities.

mar·riage (măr′ĭj) *n.* Act, ceremony, or procedure by which a man and a woman are legally united for the purpose of living together; (fig.) intimate union; **communal** ~, (anthrop.) system by which within a small community all the men are regarded as married to all the women; **companionate** ~, probationary union of man and woman; ~ **articles**, agreement concerning rights of property, succession, etc., made before marriage; ~ **license**, official permit for two persons to marry. **mar′riage·a·ble** *adj.*

mar·ron gla·cé (Fr. mărawn′ glăsā′). Chestnut preserved in sugar as sweet.

mar·row (măr′ō) *n.* 1. Soft fatty substance in cavities of bones; essential or best part of anything, essence; **mar′rowbone**, bone containing edible marrow; (pl., facet.) knees; **mar′rowfat** (**pea**), kind of large rich pea. 2. (Brit.) (also **vegetable** ~) Kind of edible gourd, the fruit of *Cucurbita pepo.* **mar′row·y** *adj.*

The ***marmot*** *inhabits open country in mountains or plains and lives in burrows or among boulders. It has strong feet and claws adapted for digging, and feeds on green plants.*

mar·ry (măr′ē) *v.* (**-ried, -ry·ing**). Unite, give, or take in marriage; take a wife or husband; (fig.) unite intimately.

Mars (mar̄z). 1. (Rom. myth.) God of war, identified with the Greek ARES. 2. (astron.) Fourth planet in the order of distance from the sun, with an orbit lying between that of Earth and Jupiter. **Mar·tian** (mar̄′shan) *adj.* & *n.* (Supposed inhabitant) of the planet Mars.

Mar·sa·la (mar̄sah′la) *n.* Fortified wine produced at Marsala, a town on the W. coast of Sicily, orig. as imitation of sherry for English consumption.

Mar·seil·laise (mar̄selāz′, -sāĕz′; *Fr.* mărsĕyĕz′), **The.** The French national anthem, composed by a young engineer officer, Rouget de Lisle, at Strasbourg in 1792, on the declaration of war against Austria, and first sung in Paris by Marseilles patriots.

Mar·seilles (mar̄sā′). Second-largest city and principal seaport of France in the SE. on the Mediterranean; a military and naval

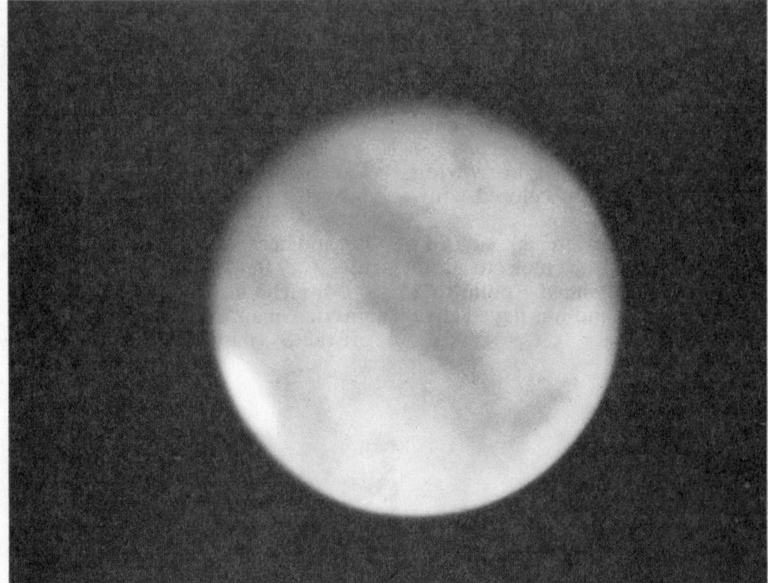

*The planet **Mars** is the fourth most distant from the sun and has a diameter about half that of earth. In 1976, the American Viking 1 space laboratory landed on this planet.*

station; site of ancient Greek colony of Massilia, settled *c*600 B.C.

marsh (mārsh) *n.* (pl. **marsh·es**). Low-lying land, more or less permanently waterlogged; bog, morass; ~ **gas**, methane; ~ **hawk**, American hawk **Circus cyaneus hudsonius**, nesting in meadows and marshes; ~ **mallow**, shrubby herb with pink flowers (*Althaea officinalis*) growing near salt marshes; **marsh·mal·low** (mārsh′mĕlō, -mălō), soft sweet containing albumen and gum arabic or gelatin; ~ **marigold**, plant (*Caltha palustris*) of family Ranunculus with bright golden flowers, growing in moist meadows, also called cowslip. **marsh′i·ness** *n.* **marsh′y** *adj.* (**marsh·i·er, marsh·i·est**).

mar·shal (mār′shal) *n.* 1. Official of a royal household or court directing ceremonies, in England the **Earl M~**. 2. Military officer of highest rank in some foreign armies, in the British Army, a **Field M~**. 3. Part of title of officers of high rank in the RAF, as **Air (Chief, Vice) M~**. **marshal** *v.t.* (**-shaled, -shal·ing**). Arrange in due order (soldiers, facts, etc.); lead, conduct, with ceremony; **marshaling yard**, railroad yard in which trains are assembled and distributed.

Mar·shall[1] (mār′sh*a*l), **George C(atlett)** (1880–1959). Amer. general and statesman; with A.E.F. in World War I, 1917–19; aide-de-camp to Gen. Pershing, 1919–24; served in China, 1924–7; chief of staff, U.S. Army, 1939–45; U.S. ambassador to China, 1945–7; secretary of state, 1947–9; secretary of defense, 1950–1; awarded Nobel Peace Prize, 1953; **M~ Aid,** financial aid given to certain European countries under the **M~ Plan,** 1948, initiated by Gen. Marshall under the European Recovery Program after World War II.

Mar·shall[2] (mār′sh*a*l), **John** (1755–1835). Amer. jurist and statesman; secretary of state, 1800–1801; chief justice of Supreme Court, 1801–35; established the fundamental principles for interpreting Constitutional law.

Mar·shall[3] (mār′sh*a*l), **Thomas Riley** (1854–1925). Vice president of the U.S. under Woodrow Wilson, 1913–21.

***Mars,** the ancient Roman god of war, was the most prominent of the military gods worshipped by Roman legions and was second only to Jupiter in prominence. Ares was his Greek equivalent. This painting of Mars is by Velazquez.*

Mar·shall[4] (mar̄′shal), **Thurgood** (1908–). Amer. jurist; first black associate justice of the U.S. Supreme Court, 1967.

Mar·shall (mar̄′shal) **Islands.** Group of islands in the NW. Pacific administered by U.S. under trusteeship of U.N.

***Marsupials** are found only in Australia, New Guinea and the Americas. The best-known are the Australian kangaroos and koalas and the American opossums. The Tasmanian 'wolf' is possibly extinct and was the largest flesh-eating marsupial. Bandicoots eat insects while kangaroos and wallabies feed only on herbage. Some Australian phalangers feed only on plants but others also eat insects.*

mar·su·pi·al (mar̄soo͞′pēal) *adj.* & *n.* (Animal) of the class of mammals that are born in a very immature condition, as e.g. the kangaroo and opossum, and are carried in a pouch (*marsupium*) until able to fend for themselves; ~ **mole**, small pouched burrowing animal with light-colored fur, native of Australia.

Mar·sy·as (mar̄′sēas). (Gk. myth.) Satyr, who took to flute playing; he challenged Apollo to a musical contest and was flayed alive when he lost.

mart (mar̄t) *n.* Marketplace; auction room; trade center.

mar·ten (mar̄′ten) *n.* Any of various carnivorous mammals of the genus *Martes*, resembling large weasels, with valuable fur.

Mar·tha (mar̄′tha). Sister of Lazarus and Mary and friend of Jesus Christ (Luke 10); in Christian allegory she symbolizes the active life and her sister the comtemplative life.

Mar·tha's (mar̄′thaz) **Vineyard.** Small island and resort area off the S. coast of Massachusetts.

Mar·tí (mär̄tē′), **José Julian** (1853–95). Cuban lawyer and patriot; inspired Cuban revolution; killed in skirmish with Spanish.

mar·tial (mär̄′shal) *adj.* Of, suitable for, appropriate to, warfare; militant, ready, eager, to fight; ~ **law**, military government, during which ordinary law is suspended. **mar′tial·ly** *adv.* **mar′tial·ize** *v.t.* (**-ized, -iz·ing**). Make suitable, prepare, for war; impart martial spirit to.

mar·tin (mär̄′tĭn) *n.* Name given to several birds of swallow family, esp. the Amer. purple martin (*Progne subis*), with a glossy blue-black plumage, and the European house martin (*Delichon urbica*).

mar·ti·net (mär̄tinĕt′, mär̄′tinĕt) *n.* Strict (esp. military) disciplinarian. [name of French drillmaster in reign of Louis XIV]

mar·tin·gale (mär̄′tingāl) *n.* 1. Strap fastened to bridle and girth of horse to prevent rearing etc. 2. Gambling system of doubling stakes at each venture.

mar·ti·ni (mär̄tē′nē) *n.* (pl. **-nis**). Cocktail of gin or vodka and vermouth. [perh. f. name of inventor]

Mar·ti·nique (märtinēk′). French W. Indian island, one of the Lesser Antilles; capital, Fort de France; the former capital, St. Pierre, was completely destroyed by an eruption of Mont Pelée in 1902.

mart·let (mär̄t′lĭt) *n.* Swift; martin.

mar·tyr (mär̄′ter) *n.* Person who undergoes death or suffering for any great cause, specif. one who suffers death on account of his adherence to the Christian faith; ~ **to**, constant sufferer from (ailment etc.) **martyr** *v.t.* Put to death as martyr; torment. [Gk. *martus* witness]

mar·tyr·dom (mär̄′terdom) *n.* Sufferings and death of martyr; torment.

mar·tyr·ize (mär̄′terīz) *v.t.* (**-ized, -iz·ing**). Make martyr of.

mar·vel (mär̄′vel) *n.* Wonderful thing; wonderful example *of* (quality). ~ *v.i.* (**-veled, -vel·ing**, Brit. **-velled, -vel·ling**). Be surprised (*at, that*); wonder (*how, why*, etc).

Mar·vell (mär̄′vel), **Andrew** (1621–78). English poet and political writer of Parliamentarian sympathies.

mar·vel·ous, Brit. **mar·vel·lous** (mär̄′velus) *adjs.* Astonishing; extravagantly improbable. **mar′vel·ous·ly** *adv.* **mar′vel·ous·ness** *n.*

Marx (mär̄ks), **Karl** (1818–83). German revolutionary writer; settled in England after 1849; wrote *Das Kapital* (1867), criticizing the capitalistic system as permitting a diminishing number of capitalists to appropriate the benefits of improved industrial methods, while the laboring class were left in increasing dependency and misery; held the remedy to be total abolition of private property, to be effected by class war; when the community owned all means of production and all property, it would provide every individual with work and the means of subsistence. **Marx′i·an, Marx′ist** *adjs.* & *ns.* **Marx′ism** *n.*

Mar·y[1] (mär̄′ē). (**Blessed**) **Virgin** ~, ~ **the Virgin**, mother of Jesus Christ; daughter of Joachim and Anne; was betrothed to Joseph of Nazareth at the time of the Annunciation.

Mar·y[2] (mär̄′ē). Name of two reigning queens of England: **Mary I** or Mary Tudor (1516–58), daughter of Henry VIII and Catherine of Aragon; reigned 1553–1558; married Philip II of Spain, 1554; fervently Catholic; known as "Bloody Mary" because of the religious persecutions of her reign; **Mary II** (1662–94), eldest child of James II; married William of Orange, 1677; was invited, with him, to take the throne of England

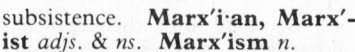

*The house **martin** is a common European swallow which feeds on insects it catches on the wing. It builds a cup-shaped nest of mud which it fastens on the wall of a building under the eaves or in the shelter of a beam.*

*Statue of Joan of Arc, saint and visionary, who led the French revolt against the English and Burgundians in the early 15th century. Burned at the stake as a heretic, she became a national heroine and **martyr** to the French.*

*The weasel-like **martens** are widely distributed in northern lands. They are forest-dwelling and usually solitary. They climb easily and feed rapaciously on animals, fruit and carrion. They are valued for their fur.*

and Scotland after the deposition of her father, and reigned 1689–94.

Mar·y Jane (mār′ē jān′) *n.* (slang) Marijuana.

Mar·y·land (mĕr′*i*land). State of U.S., on Atlantic coast, one of the original thirteen states of the Union (1788); capital, Annapolis. [named after Henrietta *Maria*, queen of Charles I]

Mar·y (mār′ē) **Magdalene**: see MAGDALENE.

Mar·y (mār′ē), **Queen of Scots** (1542–87). Mary Stuart, daughter of James V of Scotland and great-granddaughter of Henry VII; married the dauphin (François II) of France; claimed English throne on Mary I's death, and returned to Scotland, 1560; married, 1565, her cousin the Earl of Darnley, by whom she had a son (James I); soon after Darnley's mysterious death she married the Earl of Bothwell, 1567; was imprisoned by Elizabeth I, 1567, and was forced to abdicate; was tried for conspiracy, 1586, and beheaded.

mar·zi·pan (mar′zipăn) *n.* Paste of ground almonds, sugar, and white of egg, eaten as sweet and in cakes.

Ma·sac·cio (mahsah′chō), **Tommaso di Giovanni** (1401–1428). Italian painter of the early Renaissance.

Ma·sai (m*a*sī′) *n.* (pl. **-sais**, collect. **-sai**). (Member of) pastoral people of mixed Hamitic stock, inhabiting S. Kenya and Tanzania.

Ma·sa·ryk (măs′erĭk), **Thomas Garrigue** (1850–1937). Czech statesman and philosopher; first president of Czechoslovakia, 1918–1935.

mas·car·a (măskăr′*a*) *n.* Preparation for darkening eyelashes, eyebrows, etc., in make-up. [name of a town in Oran, Algiers]

mas·con (măs′kŏn) *n.* Massive concentration of dense matter with strong gravitational pull beneath surface of moon.

mas·cot (măs′kŏt) *n.* Person, animal, thing, supposed to bring luck; talisman.

mas·cu·line (măs′ky*u*lĭn) *adj.* 1. (gram.) Of the gender to which appellations of males belong; (of ending) proper to this gender. 2. Of men; manly; mannish. 3. (pros.) ~ **ending**, ending of line of verse with stress on final syllable; ~ **rhyme**, (in French verse) rhyme between words ending in stressed syllables, not *e* mute; hence, rhyme of stressed syllables. **masculine** *n.* (gram.) (Word having) masculine gender. **mas′cu·line·ness, mas·cu·lin′i·ty** *ns.*

The ***Masai*** *are nomadic pastoralists of East Africa. They number about 115,000 and inhabit parts of Kenya and Tanzania. Masai is essentially a linguistic term, referring to speakers of this Sudanic language.*

The ***Virgin Mary*** *was the mother of Jesus and according to the Gospel his only human parent. The Virgin Mary is venerated above all the saints in the Roman Catholic Church. This painting of the Nativity is by Piero della Francesca.*

ma·ser (mā′z*e*r) *n.* Device for amplifying microwaves; **optical** ~, laser. [*m*icrowave *a*mplification by *s*timulated *e*mission of *r*adiation]

Mas·er·u (măz′*e*roo). Capital and largest city of Lesotho in the W. part.

mash[1] (măsh) *n.* Malt mixed with water for brewing; boiled grain, bran, etc., given warm to horses etc.; soft pulp made by crushing, mixing with water, etc. ~ *v.t.* Make into mash; crush, pound, to pulp.

mash[2] (măsh) *v.* (obs. slang) Flirt with; force sexual attentions on (a woman). **mash′er** *n.*

mash·ie, mash·y (măsh′ē) *ns.* (pl. **mash·ies**). Metal-headed golf club with lofted face (no. 5 iron).

mask (măsk, mahsk) *n.* 1. Covering for concealing the face. 2. Covering of wire, gauze, etc., worn to protect (part of) face to

1. **Mary I** of England (Mary Tudor), half sister to Elizabeth I, restored Catholicism to England (1554). Her reign was marked by religious persecution, earning her the title 'Bloody Mary'. 2. **Mary, Queen of Scots** was forced to abdicate (1567) in favor of her son James VI of Scotland. A claimant to the English throne, she was imprisoned by Elizabeth I, and executed after 19 years in prison. 3. **Mary II** married William of Orange and became joint sovereign of England in 1689. 4. **Queen Mary** was the wife of George V and mother of George VI.

*Boston, capital of **Massachusetts** and one of the principal cultural centers of the U.S.A., is noted for its contribution to medicine and the sciences.*

filter air inhaled or exhaled; respirator. 3. Reproduction of face on cloth etc. worn by actor to symbolize character; grotesque representation of a face worn on festive and other occasions to produce a humorous or terrifying effect; hollow figure of human head esp. as worn by Greek and Roman actors. 4. Likeness of person's face, esp. one made by taking mold from face during life or after death (**life ~, death ~**). 5. (photog.) Screen used to cover or shield part of an image. 6. Face, head, of fox. 7. (fig.) Disguise. ~ *v.t.* Cover with mask; disguise or hide as with mask; **masked ball**, one at which masks are worn. **mask'er** *n.* One who takes part in masque or masquerade.

mas·och·ism (măs'*o*kĭz*e*m, măz'-) *n.* Deriving of pleasure from one's pain or humiliation, esp. as a method of sexual gratification (opp. SADISM). **mas'och·ist** *n.* **mas·och·is'tic** *adj.* [L. von Sacher-*Masoch* (1835–95), Austrian novelist who described it]

ma·son (mā'*s*on) *n.* 1. Worker in stone. 2. Freemason (see FREE). **ma·son·ic** (m*a*sŏn'ĭk) *adj.* Of Freemasons. **ma'son·ry** *n.* 1. Stonework. 2. Freemasonry.

Ma·son-Dix·on (mā'*s*on dĭk'*s*on) **line** (also **Mason and Dixon line**). Boundary between Maryland and Pennsylvania, partly surveyed (1763–7) by Charles Mason and Jeremiah Dixon, English astronomers; before the abolition of slavery popularly regarded as demarcation between free and slave states.

masque (măsk, mahsk) *n.* Amateur histrionic and musical performance, orig. in dumb show, later with metrical dialogue etc.; dramatic composition for this. **mas'quer** *n.* Masker.

mas·quer·ade (măsk*e*rād') *n.* Masked ball; false show, pretense. ~ *v.i.* (**-ad·ed, -ad·ing**). Appear in disguise; ~ **as**, pretend to be.

Mass (măs) *n.* Celebration (esp. R.C.) of the Eucharist; liturgy, musical setting of liturgy, used in this; **High ~**, with incense, music and assistance of deacon and subdeacon; **Low ~**, without music and with minimum of ceremony. [Low L. *messa*, possibly f. words of dismissal at end of service: *ite, missa est*]

mass (măs) *n.* Coherent body of matter of indefinite shape; dense aggregation, large number, *of*; unbroken expanse *of* (light etc.); majority or main part (*of*); (phys.) quantity of matter a body contains, as determined by comparing the changes in the velocities that result when the body and a standard body impinge; **the masses**, the lower classes of society; **mass-energy**: see ENERGY; **mass hysteria**, uncontrolled panic, enthusiasm, etc., affecting many persons at once; **mass media**, means of communication, as television, radio, newspapers, etc., directed to or reaching the majority of people; **mass meeting**, large assembly of people; **mass production**, production in large quantities of standardized article(s) by standardized mechanical means; hence, **mass-produce(d)**. **mass** *v.* Gather into mass; (mil.) concentrate (troops). **mass'y** *adj.* (**mass·i·er, mass·i·est**). Solid, bulky.

Mass. *abbrev.* Massachusetts.

Mas·sa·chu·setts (măs*a*chōō'*s*ets). New England state, one of the original thirteen states of the Union (1788); capital, Boston; ~ **Bay**, inlet of the Atlantic Ocean along the coast of Massachusetts between Cape Ann and Cape Cod; ~ **Bay Colony**, established 1630, along coast north of Plymouth, under leadership of Governor John Winthrop under auspices of ~ **Bay Company**.

mas·sa·cre (măs'*a*k*e*r) *n.* Indiscriminate killing, esp. of unresisting persons. ~ *v.t.* (**-cred, -cring**). Make a massacre of.

mas·sage (m*a*sahzh', -sahj'; *Brit.* măs'ahzh) *n.* Kneading and rubbing of muscles, joints, etc., with hands, to stimulate their action. ~ *v.t.* (**-saged, -sag·ing**). Apply massage to. [Fr., f. L. *massa* lump]

Mas·sa·soit (măs'*a*soit) (1580?–1661). Wampanoag Indian chief who befriended Mayflower Pilgrims and negotiated peace treaty with them, 1621.

mas·sé (măsā'; *Brit.* măs'ē) *n.* (billiards) Stroke made with cue held perpendicularly.

mas·seur (m*a*sēr'; *Fr.* măsör') *n.* (pl. **-seurs** pr. -sērz'; *Fr.* -sör'); (fem. **mas·seuse** pr. m*a*sōōs', -sōōz'; pl. **-seus·es** pr. -sōō'sĭz, -sōō'zĭz). One whose profession is providing massage.

mas·sif (măs'ĭf; *Fr.* măsēf') *n.* Mountain heights forming compact group; **M~ Central**, plateau in central France occupying about a fifth of the country and including the Cévennes, Auvergne, and Limousin mountains.

mas·sive (măs'ĭv) *adj.* Large and heavy or solid; (fig.) solid, substantial; (psychol., of sensation etc.) having large volume or magnitude. **mas'sive·ly** *adv.* **mas'sive·ness** *n.*

mast[1] (măst, mahst) *n.* Fruit of beech and other forest trees, esp. as food for swine.

mast[2] (măst, mahst) *n.* Long pole of timber etc. set upright in ship to support sails etc.; long pole supporting flag, radio aerial, etc.; **before the ~**, (hist.) as an ordinary seaman, so described because sailors were quartered in the forecastle; **half-~**: see HALF; **mast'-head**, highest part of mast, esp. lower mast, as place of observation or punishment.

mas·tec·to·my (măstĕk't*o*mē) *n.* (pl. **-mies**). Excision or amputation of a breast. [f. Gk. *mastos* + -ECTOMY]

mas·ter (măs't*e*r, mah'st*e*r) *n.*

***Masks** have been used throughout the world for social, religious or festive purposes in all periods since the Stone Age. The mask of the African Yaka tribe (above) is worn by boys during initiation ceremonies. The projection under the chin holds the mask in place. Above right: These masked New Guinea 'mudmen' represent evil spirits.*

1. Person having control; captain of merchant vessel; employer; owner of dog etc.; male head of household; one with thorough knowledge of subject or facility in technique; one who has or gets the upper hand. 2. Teacher in private secondary school. 3. Skilled workman or one in business on his own account. 4. Person eminently skilled in an art etc. 5. **M~**, title given to heads of certain colleges at Oxford and Cambridge (as ~ *of Balliol*). 6. One holding degree of Master of Arts or Science. 7. (in titles etc.) ~ **at arms**, police officer on warship or liner; **M~ of Arts** (M.A.), **Science** (M.S.), etc., holder of university degree ranking above bachelor, and orig. qualifying to teach in university; ~ **of ceremonies**, person presiding over arrangements at entertainment, social gathering, etc. 8. (attrib.) Commanding, superior (as *mas'termind*); principal (as ~ *bedroom*); ~ **key**, one made to open many locks, each also opened by separate key; **mas'terpiece**, consummate piece of workmanship, best work; **mas'tersinger**: see MEISTERSINGER; **master stroke**, masterly action. **master** *v.t.* Overcome; reduce to subjection; acquire complete knowledge of or facility in.

mas·ter·ful (măs'ter*ful*, mah'ster-) *adj.* Self-willed, imperious. **mas'ter·ful·ly** *adv.* **mas'ter·ful·ness** *n.*

mas·ter·ly (măs'terlē, mah'ster-) *adj.* Worthy of a master, very skillful.

Mas·ters (măs'terz, mah'sterz), **Edgar Lee** (1869–1950). Amer. poet and biographer; author of *Spoon River Anthology*, 1915, depicting realistically the life of a fictitious village in the Middle West.

mas·ter·y (măs'terē, mah'sterē) *n.* (pl. **-ter·ies**). Sway; masterly skill, use or knowledge; upper hand.

mas·tic (măs'tĭk) *n.* Gum or resin, exuding from certain trees growing esp. in the Levant, used in making varnish; trees yielding this; mastic color, pale yellow; kind of cement made of mastic.

mas·ti·cate (măs'tĭkāt) *v.t.*

***Masonry** is the craft of building in stone, with overlapping or bonded stones generally set in mortar but sometimes laid dry. Shown here are the different methods used by masons.*

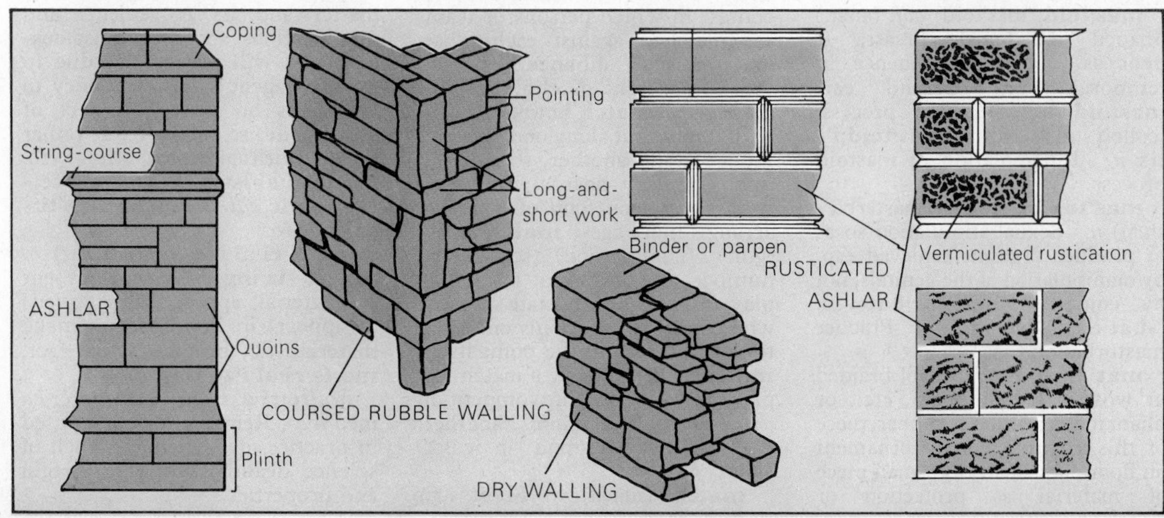

*In bullfighting, the **matador** is the man who works the cape and who must kill the bull with a sword thrust between the animal's shoulder blades. If the thrust is accurately placed the bull dies instantly.*

(**-cat·ed, -cat·ing**). Grind (food) with teeth, chew. **mas·ti·ca'tion, mas'ti·ca·tor** *ns.* **mas·ti·ca·to·ry** (măstĭkatōr'ē) *adj.* ~ *n.* (pl. **-ries**). Substance chewed to increase saliva.

mas·tiff (măs'tĭf, mah'stĭf) *n.* Large strong dog with drooping ears and pendulous lips, valuable as a watchdog.

mas·ti·tis (măstī'tĭs) *n.* Inflammation of the breast.

mas·to·don (măs'todŏn) *n.* Any of several large extinct mammals esp. of genus *Mammut*, resembling elephants but having nipple-shaped tubercles on crowns of molar teeth.

mas·toid (măs'toid) *adj.* (anat.) Shaped like female breast; ~ **process**, conical prominence in temporal bone behind ear. **mastoid** *n.* Mastoid process; (colloq.) mastoiditis. **mas·toid·i'·tis** *n.* Inflammation of mastoid process.

mas·tur·ba·tion (măsterbā'shon) *n.* Sexual stimulation so as to produce orgasm, achieved esp. by manipulation of the genitals, not by coition. **mas'tur·bate** *v.* (**-bat·ed, -bat·ing**). Practice masturbation (on).

mat[1] (măt) *n.* Fabric of braided or woven rushes, hemp, etc., or pliant material such as rubber; piece of this as protection or ornament on floor etc.; small rug; small piece of material as protection or ornament on surface of table etc.; thick pad on floor to cushion falls in gymnastics; sheet of cardboard used to make a border around a picture. ~ *v.* (**mat·ted, mat·ting**). Entangle, become entangled, in thick mass.

mat[2] (măt): see MATTE.

Ma·ta·di (matah'dē). Major port of Zaire, 100 mi. (161 km) from the mouth of the Congo River, in the W.

mat·a·dor (măt'adōr) *n.* Man appointed to kill bull in bullfight.

Ma·ta Ha·ri (mah'ta hăr'ē, măt'a hăr'ē) (1876–1917). Original name, Gertrud Margarete Zelle; French dancer who acted as spy for Germans in World War I and was executed.

match[1] (măch) *n.* Person equal in some particular, person or thing exactly corresponding, to another; contest in which persons or teams are matched against each other; matrimonial alliance; person viewed in light of eligibility for marriage; **match'board**, board with tongue cut along one edge and groove along another, so as to fit into similar boards; **match'·mak·er**, person fond of trying to arrange marriages; **match play**, (golf) (competition) scored by number of holes won; cf. MEDAL play; **match point**, state of game when one side needs only one point to win the match; the point itself. **match** *v.* Find or be a match for; place (person etc.) in competition *with*, in conflict *against*, another; be equal, correspond in color, shape, etc.

match[2] (măch) *n.* Short strip of paper or wood (**match'stick**) with tip (**match head**) covered with some combustible substance which ignites when rubbed on rough or (**safety match**) specially prepared surface; fuse for firing cannon etc.; **match'book**, small cardboard folder of cardboard safety matches; **match'box**, box for holding matches; **match'lock**, (hist.) (gun with) lock in which match was placed for igniting powder; **match'wood**, wood of suitable size for making matches; (wood reduced to) minute splinters.

match·less (măch'lĭs) *adj.* Without an equal, peerless. **match'less·ly** *adv.*

mate[1] (māt) *n.* (chess) = CHECKMATE; **fool's** ~, in which first player is mated at opponent's second move. **mate** *v.t.* (**mat·ed, mat·ing**). Checkmate.

mate[2] (māt) *n.* 1. Companion, fellow worker; (colloq.) friend (also used as form of address among equals). 2. Fitting partner in marriage; one of a pair, esp. of birds. 3. (naut.) Officer on merchant ship who sees to execution of master's commands and deputizes for him. 4. Assistant to some specialist, as *gunner's* ~. **mate** *v.* (**mat·ed, mat·ing**). Associate as mate; copulate (*with*); cause (animals) to copulate for breeding. **mate'y** *adj.* (colloq.) Companionable, sociable. **mate'·y·ness, ma'ti·ness** *ns.*

ma·té (mahtā', mă-) *n.* Paraguay tea (also **yerba** ~), brew of leaves of S. Amer. shrub *Ilex paraguayensis*; vessel for this.

ma·te·ri·al (matēr'ēal) *adj.* Concerned with or composed of matter; unspiritual; concerned with bodily comfort, riches, etc.; important, essential. **ma·te'ri·al·ly** *adv.* **material** *n.* Matter from which thing is made; elements; stuff, fabric; **writing** ~**s**, requisites for writing.

ma·te·ri·al·ism (matēr'ēalĭzem) *n.* Opinion that nothing exists but matter and its movements and modifications and that consciousness and will are wholly due to material agency; (art) tendency to lay stress on material aspect of objects; desire for material rather than spiritual prosperity etc. **ma·te'ri·al·ist** *n.* & *adj.* **ma·te·ri·al·is'tic** *adj.* **ma·te·ri·al·is'ti·cal·ly** *adv.*

ma·te·ri·al·ize (matēr'ēalīz) *v.* (**-ized, -iz·ing**). Make, represent as, material; appear, cause (spirit) to appear, in bodily form; make materialistic; become actual fact. **ma·te·ri·al·i·za'tion** *n.*

ma·te·ri·a med·i·ca (matēr'ēa mĕd'ĭka). Remedial substance used in practice of medicine; branch of science dealing with their origin and properties.

ma·té·ri·el, ma·te·ri·el (matērēĕl′) *ns.* Stock of materials, equipment, etc., used in any complex operation (PERSONNEL). [Fr.]

ma·ter·nal (matẽr′nal) *adj.* Of mothers; motherly; related on mother's side, as ~ **uncle,** mother's brother. **ma·ter′nal·ly** *adv.* **ma·ter′ni·ty** *n.* Motherhood; motherliness; ~ **home, hospital,** institution for care of women during (or immediately after) childbirth.

math (măth) *n.* (colloq.) Mathematics.

math·e·mat·ics (măthemăt′ĭks) *n.pl.* (usu. considered sing.) Abstract science of space and number (also **pure** ~); this applied to branches of physics etc. (also **applied** ~). **math·e·mat′i·cal** *adj.* Of mathematics; (of proof etc.) rigorously precise. **math·e·mat′i·cal·ly** *adv.* **math·e·ma·ti·cian** (măthematĭsh′an) *n.*

Math·er (mădh′er, măth′-), **Cotton** (1663–1728). Amer. Congregational minister and author of many religious books; leader in educational and charitable fields; his father, **Increase Mather,** (1639–1723), Amer. Congregational minister and colonial leader; president of Harvard, 1685–1701; influential in ending witchcraft trials.

mat·i·nee (mătinā′; *Brit.* măt′inā) *n.* Afternoon theatrical or musical performance, afternoon cinema show; ~ **idol,** handsome actor.

mat·ins, Mat·ins (măt′ĭnz) *ns.pl.* (usu. considered sing.) 1. (R.C. Ch.) Canonical HOUR; service for this, a midnight office, but also recited at daybreak. 2. Morning prayer in Church of England.

Ma·tisse (mătēs′), **Henri** (1869–1954). French Post-Impressionist painter.

ma·tri·arch (mā′trēărk) *n.* Woman corresponding in status to patriarch. **ma·tri·ar′chal** *adj.*

ma·tri·ar·chy (mā′trēărkē) *n.* (pl. **-chies**). Social organization in which the mother is head of the family and descent and relationship are reckoned through mothers.

mat·ri·cide (mat′rĭsīd, mā′trĭ-) *n.* Killing of one's own mother; person guilty of this. **mat·ri·cid′al** *adj.*

ma·tric·u·late (matrĭk′yulāt) *v.* (**-lat·ed, -lat·ing**). Admit, be admitted, to privileges of university. **ma·tric·u·la′tion** *n.* Matriculating; examination qualifying for this.

mat·ri·mo·ny (măt′rimōnē) *n.* (pl. **-nies**). Rite of marriage, state of being married. **mat·ri·mo′ni·al** *adj.* **mat·ri·mo′ni·al·ly** *adv.*

ma·trix (mā′trĭks) *n.* (pl. **-tri·ces** pr. -trisēz; **-trix·es**). Womb; place in which thing is developed; mass of rock etc. enclosing gems etc.; mold in which type etc. is cast or shaped; something to be mechanically reproduced; (physiol.) formative part of animal organ; (biol.) substance between cells; (math.) rectangular arrangement of quantities or symbols.

ma·tron (mā′tron) *n.* Married woman; woman managing domestic affairs of schools etc.; woman in charge of nursing in hospital. **ma′tron·age** *n.* **ma′tron·al** *adj.* **ma′tron·hood** *n.* **ma′tron·ly** *adj.* Resembling a married woman in appearance and bearing; staid; portly. **ma′tron·ship** *n.*

Matt. *abbrev.* Matthew (New Testament).

matte, matt (măt) *adjs.* Without luster ~ *v.t.* (**mat·ted, mat·ting**). Make (surface etc.) matte, frost (glass). ~ *n.* Dull gold border around framed picture; lusterless surface or appearance; roughened or frosted groundwork.

mat·ter (măt′er) *n.* 1. Substance(s) of which a physical thing is made; **gray** ~, parts of central nervous system that appear gray owing to presence of massed groups of nerve cells (also, joc., brain, intellectual power), as dist. from **white** ~, parts consisting mainly of nerve fiber tracts. 2. Physical substance in general as dist. from spirit, mind, etc. 3. Content as dist. from form; material for thought or expression; substance of book, speech, etc. 4. Thing(s); material, as *printed* ~. 5. Affair, concern; **no** ~, it is unimportant; ~ **of fact,** what pertains to the sphere of fact (opp. to opinion etc.); **as a** ~ **of fact,** (law) part of a judicial inquiry concerned with truth of alleged facts (opp. to ~ *of law*); **~-of-fact** (*adj.*) unimaginative, prosaic. **matter** *v.i.* Be of importance, signify.

Mat·ter·horn (măt′erhōrn).

*The **Matterhorn,** the famous mountain in the Pennine Alps, is 14,690 ft. high and is on the Swiss-Italian frontier. It was first climbed by the English mountaineer, Edward Whymper, in 1865.*

Alpine peak (14,701 ft. 4478 m) on Italian-Swiss frontier, first climbed in 1865.

Mat·thew (măth´ū), **St.** Apostle, a tax gatherer from Capernaum; traditionally but erroneously supposed to be the author of the first Gospel, which was written after 70 A.D., and based largely on St. Mark; commemorated Sept. 21; first Gospel.

mat·ting (măt´ĭng) *n.* Material for mats.

mat·tock (măt´*o*k) *n.* Tool shaped like pick, with adze and chisel edge as ends of head.

mat·tress (măt´rĭs) *n.* Case of canvas or other strong material stuffed with hair, straw, foam rubber, etc., as bed; series of wire springs stretched in frame as support for bed (also **spring ~**); series of wires (**wire ~**) stretched on frame to support mattress of hair etc. [It. *materasso* prob. f. Arab. *almatrah* place, cushion (*taraha* throw)]

mat·u·rate (măch´o͞orāt, măt´-yo͞o-) *v.i.* (**-rat·ed, -rat·ing**). (med.) Attain full development, ripen. **mat·u·ra´tion** *n.* Final series of changes in the growth and formation of germ cells. **ma·tur·-a·tive** (m*a*choor´*a*tĭv, măch´o͞orā-, măt´yo͞orā-) *adj.* Causing maturation.

ma·ture (m*a*toor´, -tūr´, -choor´) *adj.* Fully developed; ripe; adult; (in finance, of bonds etc.) due for payment. **ma·ture´ly** *adv.* **ma·-ture´ness, ma·tur´i·ty** *ns.* **mature** *v.* (**-tured, -tur·ing**). Bring to or reach mature state.

ma·tu·ti·nal (m*a*to͞o´t*i*n*a*l, -tū´-) *adj.* Of, in, the morning, early.

mat·zo (maht´s*o*, -sō) *n.* (pl. **-zos, -zoth** pr. -sōt). Unleavened bread for Passover. [Yiddish, f. Heb. *massāh*]

maud·lin (mawd´lĭn) *adj.* Mawkishly sentimental, esp. of tearful and effusively affectionate stage of drunkenness. ~ *n.* Mawkish sentiment. [f. MAGDALEN]

maul (mawl) *n.* Heavy hammer, usu. of wood. ~ *v.t.* Beat and bruise; handle or paw roughly; lacerate; damage by criticism.

maul·stick (mawl´stĭk) *n.* Light stick used by painters to support the hand with the brush. [Du. *maalstok* (*malen* paint, *stok* stick)]

Mau Mau (mow´mow) (pl. **Mau Maus**, collect. **Mau Mau**). (Member of) secret terrorist organization of Kikuyu tribesmen in Kenya rebelling against British rule in the 1950s.

Mau·na Lo·a (mow´n*a* lō´*a*). Active volcanic mountain, 13,680 ft. (4,104 m), on the island of Hawaii.

maun·der (mawn´d*er*) *v.i.* Talk ramblingly; wander about vaguely and listlessly.

***Mauritania** is composed mainly of desert. Rich deposits of iron ore and copper have transformed the country's economy, athough social organization is still largely tribal. These nomadic herdsmen tend sheep, goats and camels.*

maun·dy (mawn´dē) *n.* (hist.) Ceremony of washing the feet of the poor, performed by royal or other eminent persons on the Thursday before Easter (**M ~ Thursday**) in commemoration of Christ's washing of the Apostles' feet, and commonly followed by almsgiving. [L. *mandatum* commandment]

Mau·pas·sant (mōpăsahṅ´), **Guy de** (1850–93). French novelist, famous as a writer of short stories; author of "The Necklace," "Une Vie," "Bel Ami," etc.

Mau·re·ta·ni·a (mōret*a*tā´nē*a*). Ancient country and Roman province in N. Africa, corresponding roughly to N. Morocco and Algeria. [L., = "country of the Moors" (*Mauri*)]

Mau·ri·ta·ni·a (mōr*i*tā´nē*a*). Republic in NW. Africa; independent since 1960; capital, Nouakchott. **Mau·ri·ta´ni·an** *adj.* & *n.*

Mau·ri·tius (mawrĭsh´*u*s). Island in Indian Ocean E. of Madagascar; member nation of the British Commonwealth; formerly (1810–1968) a British colony; capital, Port Louis. **Mau·ri´tian** *adj.* & *n.*

Mau·rois (mawrwah´), **André** (1885–1967). Pen name of Emile Herzog, French biographer, historian, and novelist; known for his biographies of Shelley, Disraeli, Byron, Proust, and others.

mau·so·le·um (mawsolē´*u*m, -zo-) *n.* (pl. **-le·ums, -le·a** pr. -lē´*a*). Large, magnificent tomb, orig. that at Halicarnassus in Caria (formerly one of the Seven Wonders of the World) ordered for himself by Mausolus, king of Caria (d. 353 B.C.), and erected by his queen Artemisia (d. 351 B.C.).

mauve (mōv) *n.* Pale purple; delicate purple dye from coal tar aniline. ~ *adj.* [L. *malva* mallow]

mav·er·ick (măv´*e*rĭk, măv´rĭk) *n.* Unbranded calf etc.; unorthodox or undisciplined person.

ma·vin, ma·ven (mā´vĭn) *ns.* Expert. [Yiddish f. Heb., = connoisseur]

maw (maw) *n.* Stomach (of animal); abomasum.

mawk·ish (maw´kĭsh) *adj.* Of faint sickly flavor; feebly sentimental. **mawk´ish·ly** *adv.* **mawk´ish·ness** *n.* [obs. *mawk* maggot]

max·il·la (măksĭl´*a*) *n.* (pl. **max·il·lae** pr. măksĭl´ē). Upper jaw in most vertebrates; component of mouth parts of many arthropods. **max·il·lar·y** (măk′sılĕrē, măksĭl′-erē) *adj*. & *n*. (pl. **-lar·ies**).

max·im (măk′sĭm) *n*. General truth drawn from science or experience; principle, rule of conduct.

max·i·mal (măk′simal) *adj*. Greatest possible in size, duration, etc.

Max·i·mil·ian (măksimĭl′yan) (1832–67). Emperor of Mexico; brother of Austrian Emperor Francis Joseph; was offered throne of Mexico 1863; French troops supported him, but after their withdrawal he was defeated by republican forces, captured, and shot.

max·i·mize (măk′simīz) *v.t.* (**-mized, -miz·ing**). Increase, magnify, to the utmost; interpret (doctrine etc.) vigorously. **max·i·mi·za·tion** (măksimizā′shon) *n*.

max·i·mum (măk′simum) *n*. (pl. **-mums, -ma** pr. -ma). Highest possible or highest recorded magnitude or quantity (freq. attrib.).

max·well (măks′wel, -wĕl) *n*. Unit of magnetic flux in cgs system, equal to the flux of magnetic induction per square centimeter in a magnetic field whose intensity is one gauss (abbrev. Mx). [f. MAXWELL]

Max·well (măks′wel, -wĕl), **James Clerk** (1831–79). Professor of experimental physics at Cambridge University; contributed to the theory of the conservation of energy and of electricity and magnetism.

May (mā). Fifth month of Gregorian (third of Julian) calendar, with 31 days; ~ **apple**, plant (*Podophyllum peltatum*) of eastern N. Amer. woodlands, having large leaves, which with roots and seeds are poisonous, one cuplike white flower, and small fruit with edible pulp; ~ **Day**, May 1, traditionally celebrated with dancing around a Maypole, gathering garlands of flowers, and the choice of a May queen; since 1889, the international labor holiday; **may′flower**, flower that blooms in May, used locally for cowslip, lady's smock, etc.; **Mayflower**: see separate entry. **may′fly**, insect of the order Ephemeroptera; imitation of this used by anglers; **May′pole**, also **maypole**, gaily colored pole decorated with flowers and ribbons, which is danced around on May Day. [L. *Maius*, perh. f. the Roman goddess *Maia*]

may (mā) *v. auxil.* (past t. **might** pr. mīt). Expressing possibility, permission, request, wish.

Ma·ya (mah′ya) *n*. (pl. **-yas**, collect. **-ya**). Member, language, of an Amer. Indian people, remarkable for their art and knowledge of astronomy, who lived from *c*300 in Guatemala (the "Old Empire")

Mayflower is any of several plants blooming in May or in early spring. In the U.K. it refers particularly to the hawthorn, shown here, and in America to the trailing arbutus.

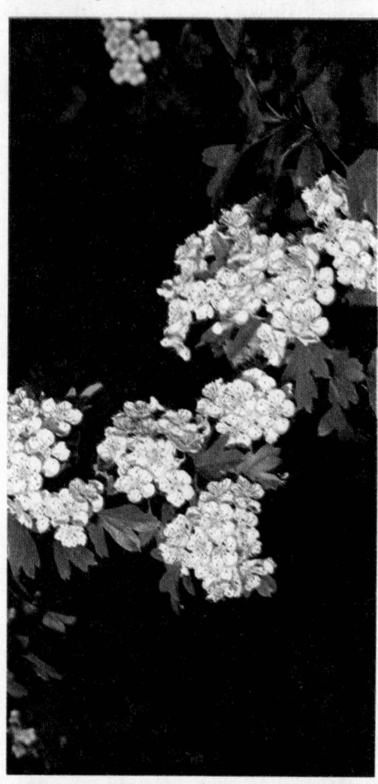

Mauritius is an island nation in the S.W. Indian Ocean. To date its economy has relied only on sugar exports but tea (below) and tobacco are also being grown. Tourism is also expanding.

The great *Mayan* civilization collapsed in about 900 A.D. Little remains for us to construct a clear picture of the time, although ruins such as these in Guatamala offer some clues.

in city states, and migrated in 9th c. to Yucatan in E. Mexico ("New Empire"), where their culture partially merged with that of the Toltecs, but disintegrated in mid-15th c. owing to civil wars, and was found in decay by the invading Spaniards in 1511. **Ma'yan** *adj.* & *n.*

may·be (mā'bē) *adv.* Perhaps.

May·day (mā'dā) *n.* International vocal radio-telephonic distress signal from aircraft or ship. [pron. of Fr. *m'aider* imp. infin. "help me!"]

May·flow·er (mā'flow*er*) *n.* Ship that carried Pilgrim Fathers from Southampton, England, to the New World; ~ **compact**, agreement to form government in the New World, entered into on November 11, 1620, aboard the *Mayflower*.

may·hem (mā'hĕm, mā'*e*m) *n.* Crime of causing malicious personal injury; also fig.

May·o (mā'ō), **Charles Horace** (1865–1939). Amer. surgeon; his brother, **William James** (1861–1939), Amer. surgeon; co-founders of the Mayo Clinic, 1889, in Rochester, Minnesota, and of the Mayo Foundation for Medical Education and Research, 1915, affiliated with the Univ. of Minnesota.

may·on·naise (mā*o*nāz', mā'*o*nāz) *n.* Sauce of yolk of eggs, oil, and vinegar used as dressing for salads, fish, etc.

may·or (mā'*er*, mār) *n.* Head of city, town, village. **may'or·al** *adj.* **may'or·al·ty** *n.* Mayor's (period of) office. **may·or·ess** (mā'erĭs) *n.* (rare) Woman mayor.

Maz·a·rin (măz'*er*ĭn, *Fr.* măzărăṅ'), **Jules** (1606–61). Italian papal legate in Paris, 1634; became cardinal, 1641, and succeeded Richelieu, 1642, as prime minister of France.

Maz·da·ism (măz'd*a*ĭz*e*m) *n.* Zoroastrianism. [Avestan *mazda* good principle in Persian theology (see ORMAZD)]

maze (māz) *n.* Confusing and baffling network of winding and intercommunicating paths with hedges on either side, designed as a puzzle for those who try to find their way in it; labyrinth; (fig.) confusion, bewilderment. ~ *v.t.* (**mazed, maz·ing**). (archaic) Confuse, bewilder. **ma'zy** *adj.* (**-zi·er, -zi·est**). **ma'zi·ly** *adv.* **ma'zi·ness** *n.*

ma·zel tov (mah'z*e*l tawv, tawf, tōv) *int.* Jewish expression of congratulation. [Yiddish f. Heb., = "good luck"]

ma·zur·ka (m*a*zēr'k*a*, -zoor'-) *n.* Lively Polish dance; music for this, in triple time. [Polish, = "woman of province of Mazovia"]

M.B.A. *abbrev.* Master of Business Administration.

*A replica of the original ship, **Mayflower II** was built in England, and sailed to Massachusetts in 53 days in 1957.*

Mc·Car·thy (m*a*kārthē), **Joseph R(aymond)** (1908–57). U.S. politician; senator from Wisconsin, 1946–57; chairman of Senate Permanent Investigating Subcommittee; conducted controversial investigation of Communists using allegedly irresponsible and sensational methods for which he was formally condemned by Senate; hence **Mc·Car'thy·ism** *n.* unfairness in investigative tactics by any government agency, newspaper, etc.

Mc·Clel·lan (m*a*klĕl'*a*n), **George Brinton** (1826–85). U.S. Army officer; Civil War general; commanded and reorganized the Dept. of the Potomac, 1861; general in chief of Union armies, 1861; commander of Army of the Potomac, 1862; removed from command for not fully pursuing Confederate forces to complete victory; Democratic presidential candidate, 1864, defeated by Lincoln; governor of New Jersey, 1878–81.

Mc·Cor·mick (m*a*kōr'mĭk), **Cyrus Hall** (1809–84). Amer. manufacturer; invented reaping machine, 1834.

Mc·Cul·lers (m*a*kŭl'*e*rz), **Carson Smith** (1917–67). Amer. novelist and playwright; wrote *The Heart Is a Lonely Hunter*, *Reflections in a Golden Eye*, *A Member of the Wedding*, etc.

Mc·Gill (m*a*gĭl'), **James** (1744–1813). Scottish-born Canadian philanthropist; founded a college at Montreal which became ~ **University** (1821).

Mc·Guf·fey (m*a*gŭf'ē), **William Holmes** (1800–73). Amer. educator and compiler of textbooks; best known as author of *Eclectic Series*, popularly called the McGuffey Readers for children.

Mc·Kin·ley (m*a*kĭn'lē), **William** (1843–1901). Twenty-fifth president of U.S., 1897–1901; assassinated by an anarchist; **Mount McKinley**, highest mountain, 20,320 ft. (6,096 m) in N. Amer., in S. central Alaska; also known by its Indian name, Denali.

MD, Md. *abbrevs.* Maryland.

Md *symbol.* Mendelevium.

M.D. *abbrev.* *Medicinae doctor* (L., = Doctor of Medicine).

ME, Me. *abbrevs.* Maine.

me (mē) *pron.* Objective (accus., dat.) case of I.

mead[1] (mēd) *n.* Alcoholic liquor of fermented honey and water.

mead[2] (mēd) (poet.) = MEADOW.

Mead (mēd), **Lake.** Artificial lake formed by Hoover Dam in the Colorado River, in NW. Arizona and SE. Nevada; a resort area.

Mead (mēd), **Margaret** (1901–1978). Amer. anthropologist and psychologist; best known for her books *Coming of Age in Samoa*, and

Auto **mechanics** repair and service road vehicles, keeping them roadworthy. Many specialize in one or two makes of car. Above, a mechanic is working on the engine of a Mercedes Benz.

Growing Up in New Guinea.

Meade (mēd), **George Gordon** (1815–72). General of the U.S. Army of the Potomac during the Civil War; repulsed Confederates under Gen. Lee at Gettysburg, 1863, but was criticized for not following through to obtain total victory.

mead·ow (mĕd′ō) *n.* Piece of grassland, esp. one used for hay; low-lying ground, esp. near river; ~ **beauty**, any plant of genus *Rhexia* of eastern and southeastern U.S., 1 to 3 feet high, with pink, purple, or crimson flowers. ~ **grass**, poa (esp. *Poa pratensis*); **mead′owlark**, Amer. songbird of genus *Sturnella*, related to bobolinks and orioles. **meadow saffron**, autumn crocus; **mead′owsweet**, rosaceous plant (esp. *Filipendula ulmaria*) common in meadows, growing to a height of about 2 feet, with dense heads of creamy white and very fragrant flowers.

mea·ger (mē′g*er*) *adj.* Lean, scanty. **mea′ger·ly** *adv.* **mea′ger·ness** *n.*

meal[1] (mēl) *n.* Edible part of any grain or pulse (usu. exc. wheat) rather coarsely ground. **meal′y** *adj.* (**meal·i·er, meal·i·est**). Of, like, meal; (of boiled potatoes) dry and powdery; **meal′ybug**, any insect of the genus *Pseudococcus*, with body covered with white powder some species of which infest vines, citrus trees, etc.; **mealy-mouthed**, apt to mince matters, soft-spoken. **meal′i·ness** *n.*

meal[2] (mēl) *n.* Customary, or any, occasion of taking food; food so taken; **meal′time**, usual time of eating.

mean[1] (mēn) *n.* 1. Condition, quality, amount, equally removed from two opposite extremes. 2. (pl.) That by which a result is brought about; pecuniary resources; wealth; **by all** (**manner of**) ~**s**, certainly, at any cost; **by no** (**manner of**) ~**s**, certainly not; **by** ~**s of**, using; (math.) intermediate in value, position, etc., between two other quantities, points, etc.; average. **mean′time, mean′while** *advs.* (also **in** or **for the meantime**) In the intervening time.

mean[2] (mēn) *adj.* Inferior, poor; shabby; ignoble, small-minded; stingy. **mean′ly** *adv.* **mean·ness** (mēn′nĭs) *n.*

mean[3] (mēn) *v.* (**meant** pr. mĕnt, **mean·ing**). Purpose; design, destine; intend to convey or indicate; signify, import. **mean′ing** *n.* What is meant. **mean′ing·ful** *adj.* Significant. **mean′ing·less** *adj.* **mean′ing·less·ness** *n.* **mean′ing** *adj.* Expressive, significant. **mean′ing·ly** *adv.*

me·an·der (mēăn′d*er*) *v.i.* Wind about; wander at random. ~ *n.* 1. (pl.) Sinuous windings, circuitous journey, winding paths, etc. 2. (geog.) Twisting course of river in its flood plain. 3. Fret pattern (see FRET[1]). [f. MAEANDER]

mea·sles (mē′z*e*lz) *n.* 1. (usu. considered sing. or pl.) Acute infectious disease (*Rubeola*) of man, usu. in childhood caused by a virus, and characterized by fever, skin rash, and inflammation of the conjunctival membranes and air passages; **German** ~: see GERMAN. 2. Disease in swine, caused by tapeworm. **mea′sly** *adj.* (**-sli·er, -sli·est**). Of, affected with, measles; (slang) contemptible, worthless.

meas·ure (mĕzh′*er*) *n.* 1. Size

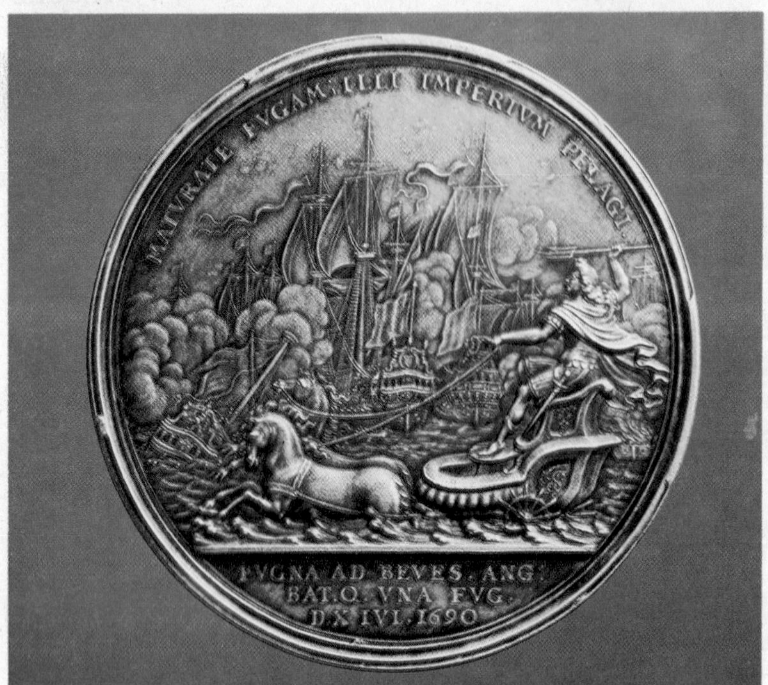

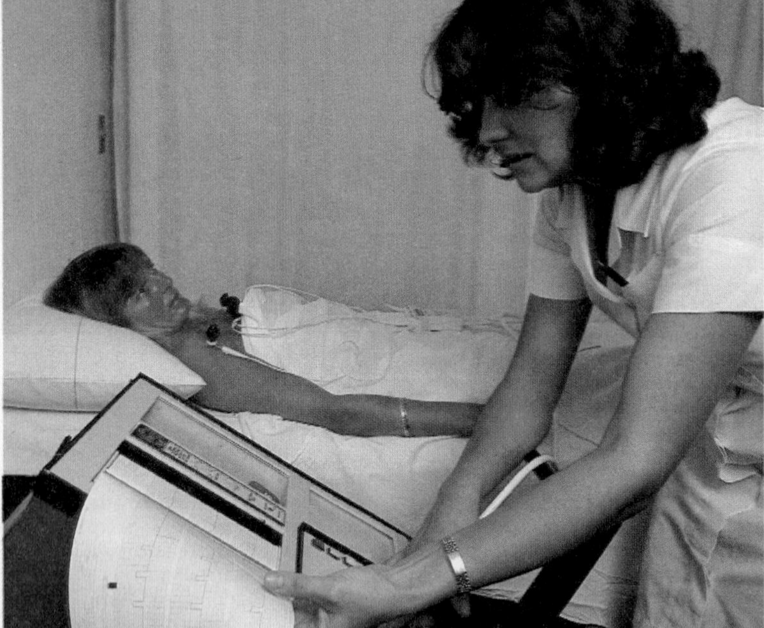

Top: ***Medals*** *commemorate an event, or are awarded in recognition of distinguished service, or for achievement. Bottom:* ***Medicine*** *has many branches, all of them dedicated to the alleviation of suffering.*

or quantity found by measuring; vessel of standard capacity for measuring liquids; rod, tape, etc., for measuring; system of measuring; degree, extent, amount; stratum or bed of mineral; (math.) quantity contained in another an exact number of times; **greatest common** ~, largest quantity exactly dividing each of two or more given quantities. 2. Prescribed extent or quantity. 3. Meter; time of piece of music; (archaic) dance. 4. Suitable action; legislative enactment. **measure** *v.* (**-ured, -ur·ing**). Ascertain extent or quantity of by comparison with fixed standard or thing of known size; mark off; be of specified length etc.; deal *out*; bring into competition *with*; ~ **up to**, meet the requirements of; **measuring worm**, larva of geometrid moth, which advances approximately one inch at a time (also called *inchworm*); **meas'ur·a·ble** *adj.* **meas'ur·a·bly** *adv.* **meas'ure·ment** *n.* **meas'ured** *adj.* Rhythmical, regular in movement; carefully weighed.

meat (mēt) *n.* Animal flesh as food, usu. excluding fish and poultry; **meat'ball**, chopped meat cooked in shape of a ball; **meat'head**, (slang) stupid or foolish person. **meat'y** *adj.* Full of meat; (fig.) full of substance; of or like meat.

me·a·tus (mēā'*tus*) *n.* (pl. **-tus·es, -tus**). (anat.) External opening of channel, duct, passage, in the body, as **auditory** ~, channel of the ear.

Mec·ca (mĕk'*a*). City now in Saudi Arabia, the birthplace of Muhammad and the chief place of Muslim pilgrimage.

me·chan·ic (m*e*kăn'ĭk) *n.* Skilled workman, esp. one who makes or uses machinery. **me·chan'ics** *n.* Branch of applied science treating of motion; mechanism, functioning; science of machinery.

me·chan·i·cal (m*e*kăn'*i*k*a*l) *adj.* Of machines or mechanism; like machines, automatic; working, produced, by machines; belonging to the science of mechanics; ~ **advantage**, ratio of load to effort; ~ **drawing**, drawing, as of machinery or construction, done with compasses, rulers, etc. ~ **engineer**(**ing**): see ENGINEER. **me·chan'i·cal·ly** *adv.* **me·chan'i·cal·ness** *n.*

mech·an·ism (mĕk'*a*nĭz*e*m) *n.* 1. Way a machine works; structure, parts, of a machine; (fig.) framework, structure, technique; (physiol.) system of mutually adapted parts working together. 2. (philos.) Theory that the origin of life can be ascribed to chemical and physical forces (opp. VITALISM). **mech'a·nist** *n.* 1. Expert in mechanics. 2. (philos.) Adherent of mechanism. **mech·a·nis'tic** *adj.*

mech·a·nize (mĕk'anīz) *v.t.* (**-nized, -niz·ing**). Make mechanical; replace manual labor with machinery; (mil.) equip with tanks etc. **mech·a·ni·za·tion** (mĕkanīzā'shon) *n.*

med. *abbrev.* Medical; medicine; medieval; medium.

med·al (mĕd'al) *n.* Piece of metal, usu. in form of coin, struck or cast with inscription and device to commemorate event etc., or awarded as distinction to soldier, scholar, etc., for services rendered; ~ **play**, (golf) scored by strokes, not by holes as in MATCH[1] play.

med·al·ist (mĕd'alĭst) *n.* 1. Winner of medal for golf etc. 2. Engraver, designer, of medals.

me·dal·lion (medăl'yon) *n.* Large medal; medal-shaped picture, panel, etc.

med·dle (mĕd'el) *v.i.* (**-dled, -dling**). Busy oneself unduly *with*; interfere *in*. **med'dle·some** *adj.* Given to meddling. **med'dle·some·ness** *n.*

Mede (mēd) *n.* One of the earliest Iranian inhabitants of Persia; **the law of the ~s and Persians**, an immutable law (Dan. 6). **Me'di·an, Me'dish** *adjs.*

Me·de·a (medē'a). (Gk. legend) Sorceress, daughter of Aeëtes, king of Colchis; helped JASON to obtain the Golden Fleece; married him but was deserted by him in Corinth and avenged herself by killing their two children.

me·di·a[1] (mē'dēa) *n.* (pl. **-di·ae** pr. -dēē). 1. (phonet.) Voiced stop consonant (*b, d, g*). 2. (anat.) Middle membrane of artery or vessel.

me·di·a[2] (mē'dēa) *n.* Pl. of MEDIUM (esp. sense 2).

me·di·ae·val (mēdēē'val, mĕdē-, mĭdē-, mĭdē'-) = MEDIEVAL.

me·di·al (mē'dēal) *adj.* Situated in the middle; of average size. **me'di·al·ly.** *adv.*

Me·di·an (mē'dēan): see MEDE.

me·di·an (mē'dēan) *adj.* Situated in the middle; relating to an arithmetic median; ~ **strip**, dividing strip between opposing lanes of automobile traffic. **median** *n.* 1. (anat.) Median artery, vein, nerve, etc. 2. (math.) Each of three lines drawn from the angles of a triangle to the middle points of the opposite sides and meeting in a point within it; middle value or number in a distribution or series of numbers.

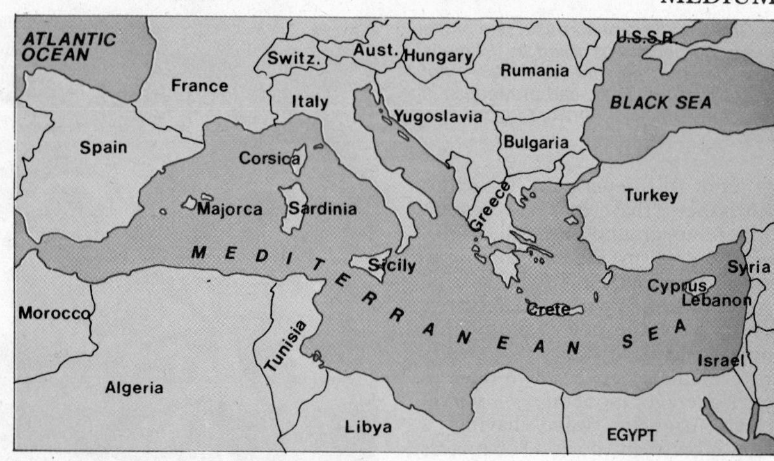

The ***Mediterranean Sea*** *has been an important trading area since ancient times, and was an invaluable trade route to the East after the opening of the Suez Canal in 1869.*

me·di·ate (mē'dēĭt) *adj.* Involving an intermediary. **me'di·ate·ly** *adv.* **mediate** (mē'dēāt) *v.* (**-at·ed, -at·ing**). Form connecting link; intervene (between two persons etc.) for purpose of reconciling them; be the medium for bringing about (result). **me·di·a'tion, me'di·a·tor** *ns.* **me·di·a·tor'i·al, me'di·a·to·ry** *adjs.*

med·ic (mĕd'ĭk) *n.* (slang) Doctor.

med·i·ca·ble (mĕd'ikabel) *adj.* Admitting of remedial treatment.

Med·i·caid (mĕd'ikād) *n.* Federal and state insurance for medical and hospital care for people of limited means.

med·i·cal (mĕd'ĭkal) *adj.* Of medicine; requiring, supplying, medical not surgical treatment. ~ *n.* (colloq.) Medical examination for fitness.

me·dic·a·ment (medĭk'ament, mĕd'ika-) *n.* Substance used in curative or palliative treatment.

Med·i·care (mĕd'ikār) *n.* Federal insurance for medical and hospital care for the aged.

med·i·cate (mĕd'ĭkāt) *v.t.* (**-cat·ed, -cat·ing**). Treat medically; impregnate with medicinal substance. **med·i·ca'tion** *n.*

Med·i·ci (mĕd'ĭchē; *It.* mĕ'dēchē). Name of the ruling family of Florence from 1434; orig. merchants and bankers; grand dukes of Tuscany 1569–1737; patrons of art and letters, esp. **Cosimo dei** (or **de'**) ~ (1389–1464), his son **Piero** (1416–69), Piero's son **Lorenzo "the Magnificent"** (1449–92), and Lorenzo's son **Giovanni** (1475–1521), who became Pope Leo X; **Giulio** (1478–1534) became Pope Clement VII; **Catarina** (CATHERINE[3] DE MÉDICIS) married Henri II; **Maria** (Marie de Médicis) married Henri IV. **Med·i·ce·an** (mĕdĭsē'an, -chē-) *adj.*

me·dic·i·nal (medĭs'ĭnal) *adj.* Of medicine; curative.

med·i·cine (mĕd'ĭsĭn; *Brit.* mĕd'sĭn) *n.* Art of restoring and preserving health, esp. by means other than surgery; substance taken internally for this purpose; ~ **ball**, large, heavy, stuffed ball to be thrown and caught for exercise; ~ **man**, tribal magician of primitive peoples.

med·i·co (mĕd'ikō) = MEDIC.

me·di·e·val, me·di·ae·val (mēdēē'val, mĕdē-, mĭdē-, mĭdē'-val) *adjs.* Of the Middle Ages. **me·di·e'val·ism, me·di·ae'val·ism, me·di·e'val·ist, me·di·ae'val·ist** *ns.*

Me·di·na (medē'na). City now in Saudi Arabia, to which Muhammad fled from Mecca and where he died and was buried.

me·di·o·cre (mēdēō'ker, mē'dēōker) *adj.* Of middling quality, indifferent. **me·di·oc·ri·ty** (mēdēŏk'rĭtē) *n.* (pl. **-ties**). Mediocre quality; mediocre person.

med·i·tate (mĕd'ĭtāt) *v.* (**-tat·ed, -tat·ing**). Plan mentally; exercise the mind in contemplation *on*. **med·i·ta'tion** *n.* **transcendental** ~: see TRANSCENDENTAL. **med'i·ta·tive** *adj.* **med'i·ta·tive·ly** *adv.*

med·i·ter·ran·e·an (mĕdĭterā'nēan) *adj.* (of land) Remote from coast; (of water surfaces) landlocked; **M~**, of the Mediterranean Sea, the region around it, or the peoples of this region; **M~ Sea**, inland sea lying between S. Europe and N. Africa, communicating with the Atlantic by the Strait of Gibraltar and with the Persian Gulf by the Suez Canal. **M~** *n.* Mediterranean Sea.

me·di·um (mē'dēum) *n.* (pl. **-di·a** pr. -dēa for senses 1–3, **-di·ums** for sense 4). 1. Middle quality, degree, etc. 2. Means, agency, esp. of communication. 3. (art) Method by which work of art is produced, branch of art (e.g. painting, sculpture); (also) liquid substance in which pigments are

*In Greek mythology **Medusa,** one of the three Gorgons, was killed by Perseus who looked on her reflection, not directly at her. This head of Medusa is from the Temple of Apollo, Didyma, Turkey.*

ground in preparation of paint; substance that makes pigment adhere to ground (e.g. oil, gum). 4. (spiritualism) Person claiming to be the vehicle for spirits' communication with human beings or to have the power of moving objects at a distance. ~ *adj.* Intermediate between two degrees etc.; average, moderate; ~ **wave,** electromagnetic wave having a length between 100 and 800 meters (in broadcasting, between 200 and 550 meters).

med·lar (mĕd'*ler*) *n.* (Tree, *Mespilus germanica,* with) fruit like small brown apple, eaten when decayed.

med·ley (mĕd'lē) *n.* (pl. **-leys**). Heterogeneous mixture; ~ **relay,** relay race in which each team member runs a different distance or uses a different swimming stroke.

Mé·doc (mādŏk'; *Fr.* mĕdawk') *n.* Wine produced in Médoc, a district in the Bordeaux region of France.

me·dul·la (m*e*dŭl'*a*) *n.* (pl. **-dul·las, -dul·lae** pr. -dŭl'ē). 1. Marrow of bones; spinal marrow. 2. Central parts of some organs, esp. kidney. 3. Cellular inner part of animal hair. 4. Soft internal tissue of plants. 5. (also ~ **oblongata**) Brainstem, prolonged hindmost segment of brain. **med·ul·lar·y** (mĕd'*u*lĕrē, mĕj'*u*-, m*e*dŭl'*e*rē) *adj.*

Me·du·sa (m*e*dōō's*a*, -z*a*, -dū'-). (Gk. myth.) One of the Gorgons, the only mortal one; slain by Perseus, who cut off her head.

me·du·sa (m*e*dōō's*a*, -z*a*, -dū'-) *n.* (pl. **-sas, -sae** pr. -sē, -zē). (zool.) Sexually reproductive form of hydrozoan or scyphozoan coelenterates, with jellylike body and stinging tentacles (pop. *jellyfish*).

meek (mēk) *adj.* Piously humble and submissive; tamely submissive. **meek'ly** *adv.* **meek'ness** *n.*

meer·schaum (mēr'sh*u*m, -shawm, -showm) *n.* Hydrated magnesium silicate, occurring in soft white masses, used for tobacco pipe bowls; pipe with bowl made of this. [Ger., = "sea foam"]

meet[1] (mēt) *adj.* (archaic) Suitable, fit. **meet'ly** *adv.* **meet'ness** *n.*

meet[2] (mēt) *v.* (**met** pr. mĕt, **meet·ing**). Come into contact or company (with); assemble; become perceptible to; satisfy (demand); experience. ~ *n.* Assembly for hunting, track-and-field, etc.

meet·ing (mē'tĭng) *n.* (esp.) Assembly of people for entertainment, worship, etc.; duel; race meeting; ~ **house,** Quakers' place of worship.

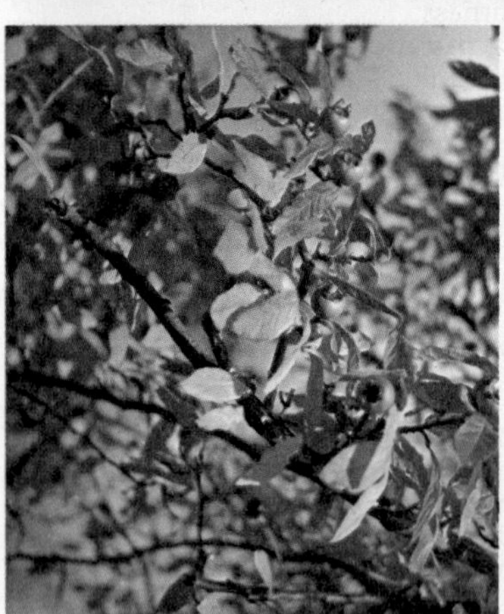

*The **medlar,** a small tree native to southern Europe and south-west Asia, is cultivated for its brownish fruit which is made into preserves or eaten when partly decayed.*

mega-, meg- *prefixes.* Great; (phys., prefixed to names of units of measurement, force, etc.) one million times (abbrev. M), as in *megacycle, megawatt,* etc.

***Megalith** building spread through the world during the Neolithic Period. Monuments take the forms of tombs, single and multiple stone circles and rows, and single stones.*

meg·a·cy·cle (mĕg'*a*sīk*e*l) *n.* One million cycles, as unit in measuring frequency of electromagnetic waves (abbrev. mc, Mc).

Me·gae·ra (m*e*jēr'*a*). (Gk. myth.) One of the Furies (see FURY).

meg·a·lith (mĕg'*a*lĭth) *n.* (archaeol.) Large stone used in construction or as a monument. **meg·a·lith'ic** *adj*.

meg·a·lo·ma·ni·a (mĕg*a*lomā'nē*a*) *n*. 1. (psychiatry) Form of insanity marked by delusions of grandeur. 2. Passion for doing things on an extravagant scale. **meg·a·lo·ma'ni·ac** *n*.

meg·a·phone (mĕg'*a*fōn) *n*. Large funnel-shaped speaking trumpet, used for making the voice travel to a distance.

meg·a·pod (mĕg'*a*pŏd), **meg·a·pode** (mĕg'*a*pōd) *ns*. Member of family of birds, almost all in Australasian region, whose eggs are left to hatch without incubation.

meg·a·ton (mĕg'*a*tŭn) *n*. Explosive force equal to 1,000,000 tons of TNT.

meg·a·watt (mĕg'*a*wŏt) *n*. One million watts (abbrev. mW, MW).

Me·gid·do (meg*ĭ*d'ō). Ancient city in NW. Palestine from about 2500–300 B.C.; probably the Armageddon mentioned in the Bible.

me·gil·lah (megĭl'*a*; *Heb*. mĕgēlah') *n*. (pl. **-gil·lahs** for 1, **-gil·loth** pr. -gēlōt' for 2). 1. (slang) Lengthy story or explanation. 2. Scroll of the Book of Esther, traditionally read in synagogues at the festival of Purim. [Heb., = scroll]

me·grim (mē'grĭm) *n*. Migraine; whim; (pl.) low spirits. [Fr. *migraine* (f. Gk. *hemi*- half, *kranion* skull)]

mei·o·sis (mīō'sĭs) *n*. (pl. **-ses** pr. -sēz). 1. Understatement, freq. ironical or jocular. 2. (biol.) Splitting of cell or nucleus without increase in number of chromosomes, so that each of the resulting two cells or nuclei has only half the chromosomes of the original one (cf. MITOSIS). **mei·ot·ic** (mīŏt'ĭk) *adj*.

Me·ir (māēr', mī-), **Golda** (1898–1978). Russian-born American woman who became an Israeli political leader; premier of Israel, 1969–74.

Meis·sen (mī's*e*n). City on the Elbe near Dresden in East Germany where the earliest European porcelain factory was founded, 1710, and still exists; ~ **china**, porcelain made there (freq. called *Dresden china*).

meis·ter·sing·er (mī'st*e*rsĭng*e*r, -zĭng-) *n.pl*. (pl. also **-sing·ers**). German lyric poets and musicians of 14th–17th centuries, organized in guilds and using elaborate technique; (sing.) member of such guild. [Ger., = "mastersingers"]

Meit·ner (mīt'n*e*r), **Lise** (1878–1968). Austrian-born Swedish physicist; worked in field of nuclear fission; together with Otto Hahn discovered protoactinium.

Me·kong (mā'kŏng', mē'-, -kawng'). River in SE. Asia flowing 2,600 mi. (4,186 km), from Tibet to the South China Sea; forms the borders between Laos and Burma and Laos and Thailand.

mel·an·cho·li·a (mĕl*a*nkō'lē*a*, -kōl'y*a*) *n*. Mental illness characterized by depression (obsolesc. as psychol. term). [Gk. *melas* black, *khole* bile]

mel·an·chol·ic (mĕl*a*nkŏl'ĭk) *adj*. (of person) Melancholy; liable to melancholy.

mel·an·chol·y (mĕl'*a*nkŏlē) *n*. (pl. **-chol·ies**). 1. (Habitual tendency to) sadness and

*This **Meissen** clock is decorated with figures of a maiden and cupids, and is surmounted by a cockerel. Its white porcelain case is painted with figures and flowers, and it has an enamel dial with gilt hands.*

__Megapods__ or mound-building birds lay eggs in huge mounds built by them from soil and vegetation. The rotting humus provides heat for this incubator. Below: The Mallee Fowl from S.E. Australia.

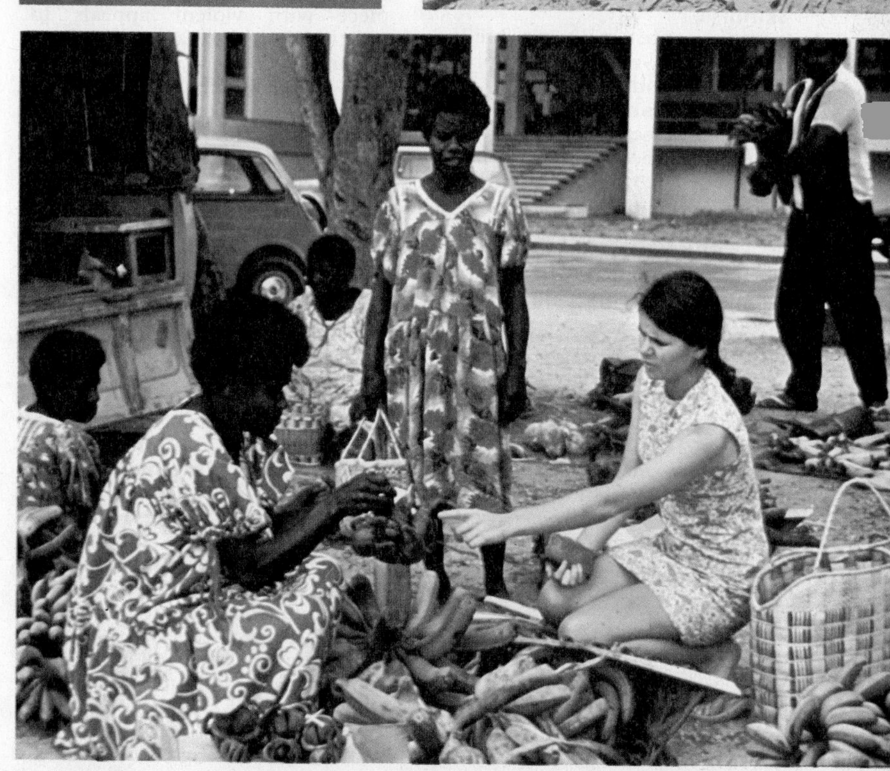

__Melanesia,__ the south-western division of Oceania, includes New Caledonia and the Bismarck, Solomon, New Hebrides, Fiji and smaller archipelagos. This market is in Vila the capital of the New Hebrides.

depression; pensive sadness. 2. (hist.) One of the four humors. ~ *adj.* Sad, saddening.

Mel·a·ne·sia (mĕlanē′zha,-sha). General term for islands of W. Pacific including New Hebrides, New Caledonia, Fiji, etc. **Mel·a·ne′sian** *adj.* & *n.* [Gk. *melas* black (from the color of the predominant native race, the Papuans), *nēsos* island]

mé·lange (*Fr.* mĕlahñzh′) *n.* (pl. **-langes** pr. *Fr.* -lahñzh′). Mixture, medley.

mel·a·nin (mĕl′anĭn) *n.* Dark brown or black pigment found in hair, skin, or tissues.

mel·a·nism (mĕl′anĭzem) *n.* Darkness of color resulting from abnormal development of black pigment in epidermis, hair, etc. **mel·a·nis′tic** *adj.*

mel·a·no·ma (mĕlanō′ma) *n.* (pl. **-mas, -ma·ta** pr. -mata). (path.) Dark-colored tumor.

mel·a·no·sis (mĕlanō′sĭs) *n.* Morbid deposit, abnormal development, of black pigment in tissue. **mel·a·not·ic** (mĕlanŏt′ĭk) *adj.*

Mel·ba (mĕl′ba) **toast.** Thin crisp toast. [f. Dame Nellie *Melba*, Australian prima donna d. 1931]

Mel·bourne (mĕl′bern). Capital of Victoria and second largest city in Australia (after Sydney).

Mel·chior (mĕl′kyōr). Traditional name of one of the Magi, a king of Nubia.

meld (mĕld) *v.* (cards) Declare [card(s)] for score; make meld. ~ *n.* Melding; card(s) melded.

me·lee, mê·lée (mā′lā, mālā′, mĕl′ā) *ns.* General fight, brawl, skirmish.

mel·io·rate (mēl′yerāt, mē′lē-) *v.* (**-rat·ed, -rat·ing**). Improve. **mel·io·ra′tion** *n.*

mel·io·rism (mēl′yerĭzem, mē′lē-) *n.* Doctrine that the world may be made better by human effort (opp. PESSIMISM). **mel′io·rist** *n.*

mel·lif·er·ous (melĭf′erus) *adj.* Yielding, producing, honey.

mel·lif·lu·ous (melĭf′lōōus) *adj.* (of voice, words, music) Sweet-sounding. **mel·lif′lu·ence** *n.* **mel·lif′lu·ent** *adj.*

Mel·lon (mĕl′on), **Andrew William** (1855–1937). Amer. financier, industrialist, and philanthropist; secretary of the treasury, 1921–32.

mel·low (mĕl′ō) *adj.* Soft and rich in flavor, color, or sound; softened by age or experience; genial, jovial; partly intoxicated. **mel′low·ly** *adv.* **mel′low·ness** *n.* **mellow** *v.* Make or become mellow; ripen.

me·lod·ic (melŏd′ĭk) *adj.* Of melody; ~ **minor,** (mus.) minor scale with major 6th and 7th when ascending and minor 6th and 7th when descending (so called as more suitable for melody than HARMONIC minor).

Melbourne, *a seaport and trading center, is the second largest city in Australia and the capital of the State of Victoria. These high rise office buildings line the banks of the River Yarra.*

me·lo·di·ous (melō′dēus) *adj.* Of, producing, melody; sweet-sounding. **me·lo′di·ous·ly** *adv.* **me·lo′di·ous·ness** *n.* **mel·o·dist** (mĕl′odĭst) *n.* Singer; composer of melodies.

mel·o·dra·ma (mĕl′odrahma, -drăma) *n.* Sensational dramatic piece with violent appeals to emotions and happy ending; language, behavior, suggestive of this; (formerly) play, or passage in play, using spoken voice against musical background. **mel·o·dra·mat·ic** (mĕlodramăt′ĭk) *adj.* **mel·o·dra·mat′i·cal·ly** *adv.* **mel·o·dram·a·tist** (mĕlodrăm′atĭst, -drah′ma-) *n.* **mel·o·dram′a·tize** *v.t.* (**-tized, -tiz·ing**).

mel·o·dy (mĕl′odē) *n.* (pl. **-dies**). Sweet music; arrangement of single notes in musically expressive succession; principal part in harmonized music.

mel·on (mĕl′on) *n.* (Any of several gourds bearing) sweet fruit, esp. the **musk′melon** (*Cucumis melo*) and **wa′termelon** (*Citrullus vulgaris*).

Me·los (mē′lŏs) (also **Mi·los, Mi·lo** pr. mē′lŏs, mē′law). Greek island in the Cyclades; **Venus de Milo,** Hellenistic marble statue of Aphrodite (now in the Louvre) found here in 1820.

Mel·pom·e·ne (mĕlpŏm′enē). (Gk. and Rom. myth.) Muse of tragedy.

melt (mĕlt) *v.* (**melt·ed** or **mol·ten, melt·ing**). (Cause to) become liquefied by heat; soften, be softened; dissolve; pass imperceptibly *into*; ~ **away,** dissolve, disappear; ~ **down,** reduce (metal articles etc.) to molten metal for use as raw material; **melt′down** *n.* melting of uranium fuel rods in nuclear reactor, possibly leading to catastrophic accident with attendant massive radioactive contamination. ~ *n.* Molten metal.

Dame Nellie Melba, *the Australian opera singer, was famed for her performances of coloratura roles and until her retirement in 1926 sang in the principal opera houses of Europe and the U.S.A.*

mel·ton (mĕl′ton) *n.* Kind of cloth with very close-cut nap, used for overcoats etc. [*Melton Mowbray*, town in Leicestershire, England]

Mel·ville[1] (mĕl′vĭl), **Herman** (1819–91). Amer. novelist; wrote stories based on his experiences at sea; author of *Omoo*, *Typee*, *Moby-Dick*, etc.

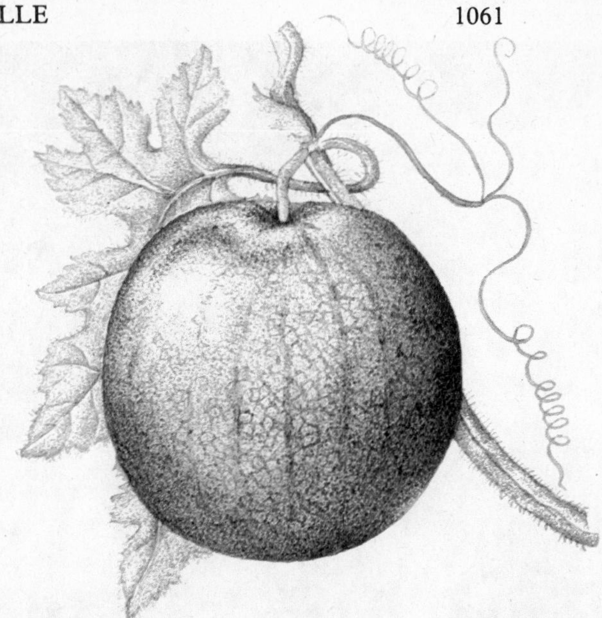

The **watermelon** belongs to the gourd family of flowering plants and is now under cultivation on every continent. Its fruit was depicted by early Egyptian artists.

Jefferson Memorial, viewed from the Washington Monument column, was designed by Pope, Eggers and Higgins and built in the classical style favoured by Jefferson, who is sculptured onto the pediment above the portico.

Mel·ville[2] (mĕl′vĭl) **Island.** Island, 16,500 sq. mi. (26,565 sq. km), in the Canadian Northwest Territories; **Melville Peninsula,** a northward-projecting peninsula, 24,156 sq. mi. (38,891 sq. km), in the E. part of the Canadian Northwest Territories.

mem·ber (mĕm′b*er*) *n.* 1. Limb or other bodily organ, constituent portion of complex structure. 2. Person belonging to a society etc.; **M~ of Parliament,** (abbrev. M.P.) person formally elected to the British House of Commons. **mem′ber·ship** *n.*

mem·brane (mĕm′brān) *n.* Fine layer of connective tissue enveloping an organ, lining a cavity, or separating adjacent parts in a living organism; (palaeog.) parchment skin. **mem·bra·nous** (mĕm′br*a*n*u*s) *adj.*

me·men·to (m*e*mĕn′tō) *n.* (pl. **-tos, -toes**). Object serving as reminder or warning, or kept as memorial; ~ **mori** (mōr′ī, -ē) (L., = remember you must die), warning or reminder of death, e.g. skull.

Mem·non (mĕm′nŏn). (Gk. legend) Ethiopian prince slain at Troy; a colossal statue at Thebes (in reality that of Amenhotep III), which gave forth a musical note when struck by the rays of the rising sun, was supposed to represent him.

mem·o (mĕm′ō) *n.* (pl. **mem·os**). (colloq.) Memorandum.

mem·oir (mĕm′wār, -wōr) *n.* Record, history, written from personal knowledge or special sources of information; (auto)-biography; essay on learned subject by expert.

mem·o·ra·bil·i·a (mĕm*e*rab*ĭ*l′ēa, -bĭl′y*a*) *n.pl.* (sing. **-o·rab·i·le** pr. -ĕrăb′*i*lē). Memorable things. [L.]

mem·o·ra·ble (mĕm′*e*rab*e*l) *adj.* Likely or worthy to be remembered. **mem·o·ra·bil′i·ty** *n.* **mem′o·ra·bly** *adv.*

mem·o·ran·dum (mĕm*e*răn′d*u*m) *n.* (pl. **-dums, -da** pr. -d*a*). Note to help the memory, record for future use; informal letter without signature etc.

me·mo·ri·al (m*e*mōr′ē*a*l, -mōr′-) *adj.* Commemorative, of memory. ~ *n.* Memorial object, monument, custom, etc.; **M~ Day,** formerly May 30, now usu. last Monday in May, a day commemorating dead servicemen of all wars. **me·mo′ri·al·ize** *v.t.* (**-ized, -iz·ing**). Commemorate; address memorial to.

mem·o·rize (mĕm′*e*rīz) *v.t.* (**-rized, -riz·ing**). Commit to memory.

mem·o·ry (mĕm′*e*rē, mĕm′rē) *n.* (pl. **-ries**). 1. Faculty by which things are recalled to or kept in the mind; recollection; posthumous repute; length of time over which memory extends. 2. Part of computer in which information is stored.

mem·sa·hib (mĕm′sahĭb, -ēb, -sahhĭb, -sahhēb): see SAHIB.

men·ace (mĕn′ĭs) *n.* Threat. ~ *v.t.* (**-aced, -ac·ing**). Threaten. **men′ac·ing·ly** *adv.*

mé·nage (mānahzh′, *Fr.* mĕnahzh′) *n.* (pl. **-nages** pr. -nah′zhĭz, *Fr.* -nahzh′). Household.

me·nag·er·ie (m*e*năj′*e*rē, -năzh′-) *n.* Collection of wild animals kept in captivity for exhibition etc.

Me·nan·der (m*e*năn′d*er*) (342–291 B.C.). Greek poet and writer of comedies.

Menck·en (mĕng′k*e*n), **H(enry) L(ouis)** (1880–1956). Amer. editor, critic, and satirist; author of books on American language; known especially for *The American Language*.

mend (mĕnd) *v.* Restore to sound condition, repair; improve; rectify; regain health. ~ *n.* Repaired place; **on the ~,** improving.

men·da·cious (mĕndā′sh*u*s) *adj.* Lying. **men·da′cious·ly** *adv.* **men·dac·i·ty** (mĕndăs′ĭtē) *n.* (pl. **-ties**).

Men·del (mĕn′d*e*l), **Gregor Johann** (1822–84). Abbot of Brünn, Moravia; his experiments in the cross-fertilization of garden peas led to the formulation of **~'s laws** of heredity, showing that certain

The study and treatment of **mental** *illness has developed into an important science in the 20th century. Mad houses, their inmates treated like animals, like this one depicted by Goya, were once common.*

characteristics, as height, color, etc., depend on the presence of hereditary determining factors (later called *genes*), which may be either dominant or recessive. **Men·de·li·an** (mĕndē′lēan, -dēl′yan) *adj.* **Men′del·ism** *n.*

Men·de·le·ev (mĕndelā′ef), **Dmitri Ivanovich** (1834–1907). Russian chemist; discovered the PERIODIC law.

men·de·le·vi·um (mĕndelē′vēum) *n.* (chem.) Transuranic element, symbol Md, at. no. 101. [f. MENDELEEV]

Men·dels·sohn (mĕn′delson; *Ger.* mĕn′delzawn), **Jacob Ludwig Felix** (1809–47). German musical composer of oratorios, symphonies, overtures, etc.

men·di·cant (mĕn′dikant) *adj.* Begging; living on alms. ~ *n.* Beggar; mendicant friar. **men′di·can·cy, men·dic·i·ty** (mĕndĭs′ĭtē) *ns.*

Men·e·la·us (mĕnelā′us). (Gk. legend) King of Sparta; brother of Agamemnon, and husband of Helen, who was stolen from him by Paris and restored after the fall of Troy.

men·folk (mĕn′fōk) *n.pl.* Men collectively, esp. of family or community.

men·ha·den (mĕnhā′den) *n.* (pl. **-den**). Kind of large herring (*Brevoortia tyrannus*) found on E. coast of N. America, used for fertilizer and yielding a valuable oil. [Amer. Ind.]

men·hir (mĕn′hēr) *n.* (archaeol.) Tall upright monumental stone. [Breton, = "long stone"]

me·ni·al (mē′nēal, mēn′yal) *adj.* Servile, degrading. ~ *n.* Household servant; servile person. **me′ni·al·ly** *adv.*

me·nin·ges: see MENINX.

men·in·gi·tis (mĕnĭnjī′tĭs) *n.* Inflammation of the meninges.

me·ninx (mē′nĭngks) *n.* (pl. **me·nin·ges** pr. menĭn′jēz). Any of three membranes (*dura mater, arachnoid, pia mater*) enveloping brain and spinal cord. **me·nin·ge·al** (menĭn′jēal) *adj.*

me·nis·cus (menĭs′kus) *n.* (pl. **-nis·ci** pr. -nĭs′ī, **-nis·cus·es**). Lens convex on one side and concave on the other; convex or concave upper surface of a column of liquid; (math.) figure of crescent form.

Men·nin·ger (mĕn′ĭnjer), **Charles F.** (1862–1933). Amer. psychiatrist; with his two sons, **Karl Augustus**, (1893–) and **William Claire** (1899–1966), founded the Menninger Neuropsychiatric Clinic in Topeka, Kansas.

Men·non·ite (mĕn′onīt) *n.* Member of a Christian sect that arose in Friesland in the 16th c., maintaining principles similar to those of the Anabaptists; they baptize only after confession of faith and will not take oaths or undertake military or state service; German Mennonites settled in Russia under Catherine the Great, but when rendered liable to conscription in the 19th c. many emigrated to U.S. and Brazil; most are farmers. [f. *Menno* Simons (1492–1559), their early leader]

men·o·pause (mĕn′opawz) *n.* Period of life, generally between 40 and 50, in women, at which menstruation ceases. **men·o·pau′sal** *adj.*

me·nor·ah (menōr′a, -nōr′a) *n.* Candelabrum used in Jewish worship.

men·or·rha·gi·a (mĕnerā′jēa, -ja) *n.* Excessive menstruation.

Me·not·ti (menŏt′ē), **Gian Carlo** (1911–). Italian-born Amer. operatic composer and

*The **merchant** fleet consists of those ships of a nation used in commerce. Shown here are some examples of the most famous 20th-century funnel markings and colors.*

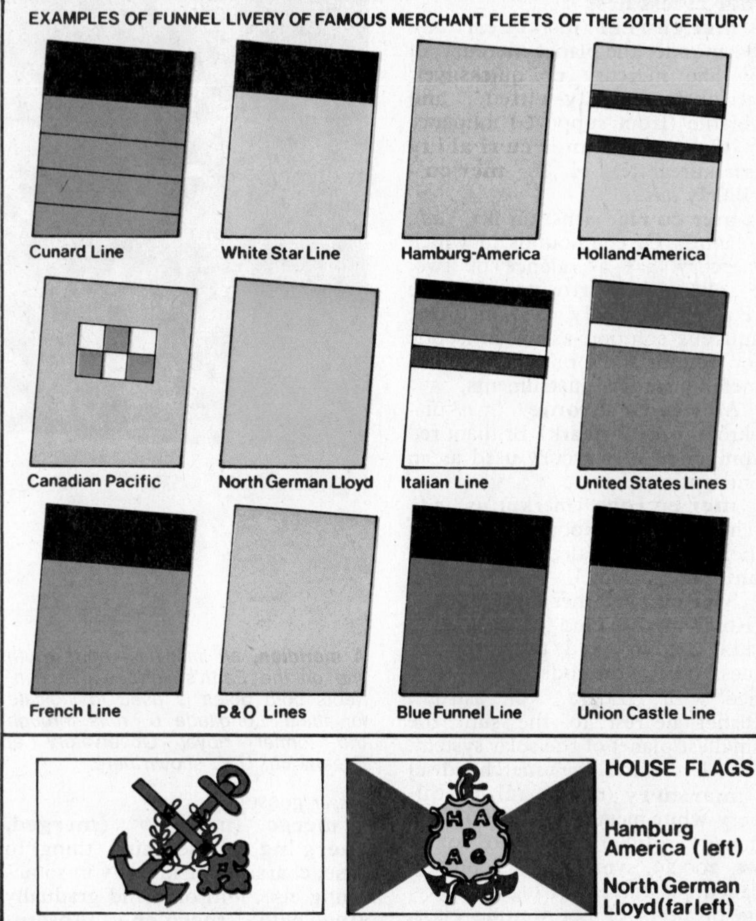

librettist; among his works are the operas *Amahl and the Night Visitors* and *The Consul.*

men·ses (mĕn′sēz) *n.pl.* (also considered sing.). Discharge of blood and tissue debris from uterus of primates, normally at monthly intervals. [L., = "months"]

Men·she·vik (mĕn′shevĭk; *Russ.* mĕnshĕvēk′) *n.* (pl. **-viks, -vi·ki** pr. -vĭkē, -vēkē; *Russ.* -vēkē′). Member of the moderate Socialist party in Russia, which was in the minority at the Socialist conference in 1903 and was overthrown by Lenin and the Bolsheviks at the Revolution of 1917, after being in power for a brief period. [Russ. *menshe* smaller]

-stral) *adj.* 1. Monthly. 2. (physiol.) Of the menses.

men·stru·ate (mĕn′stroōōāt) *v.i.* (**-at·ed, -at·ing**). Discharge the menses. **men·stru·a′tion** *n.*

men·stru·um (mĕn′stroōum) *n.* (pl. **-stru·ums, -stru·a** pr. -stroōa). (pharm.) Solvent.

men·sur·a·ble (mĕn′sherabel) *adj.* Measurable; (mus.) having fixed time or rhythm.

men·sur·al (mĕn′sheral) *adj.* Of measure; (mus.) measurable.

men·sur·a·tion (mĕnsherā′shon) *n.* Measuring; (math.) branch of mathematics concerned with measurement of lengths, areas, and volumes.

men·tal (mĕn′tal) *adj.* Of, relating to, the mind; ~ **age**, age at which normal children reach a certain stage of mental development, used as standard for assessing intelligence (e.g. a boy of 17 who has the mental development of a normal 10-year-old has a mental age of 10); ~ **arithmetic**, calculations performed without the use of written figures; ~ **deficiency**, congenital feeble-mindedness, condition of person who is unequal to the conduct of ordinary affairs; ~ **hospital**, institution for care of persons suffering from mental disorder or defect; ~ **patient**, one under care for disordered mind. **men′tal·ly** *adv.*

men·tal·i·ty (mĕntăl′ite) *n.* (pl. **-ties**). Mental quality; mode of thinking; (degree of) intellectual power; (loosely) mind, disposition, character.

men·thol (mĕn′thōl, -thawl, -thŏl) *n.* Crystalline camphorlike substance obtained from mint oils.

men·tion (mĕn′shon) *v.t.* Refer to; state incidentally; cite formally for meritorious achievement; **not to** ~, in addition to. **mention** *n.* Mentioning.

Men·tor (mĕn′ter, -tōr). (Gk. legend) Friend of Odysseus and guide and adviser of the young Telemachus.

men·tor (mĕn′ter, -tōr) *n.* Experienced and trusted counselor. [f. MENTOR]

men·u (mĕn′ū, mā′nū) *n.* Bill of fare. [Fr., = "detailed list", f. *adj.* = "small"]

me·ow (mēow′) *n.* & *v.i.* (Make) cat's cry, mew.

Meph·i·stoph·e·les (mĕfĭstŏf′elēz). In the legend of FAUST, the demon to whom Faust sold his soul. **Meph·is·to·phe·li·an, Meph·is·to·phe·le·an** (mĕfĭstōfē′lēan) *adjs.*

Mer·can·tile (mer′kantēl, -tīl, -tĭl) *adj.* Trading; of merchants or trade; mercenary, fond of bargaining; ~ **system**, that based on the old economic theory that money is the only form of wealth and that the object of trade is to export goods at the highest prices. **mer′can·til·ism, mer′can·til·ist** *ns.*

Mer·ca·tor (merkā′ter), **Gerardus.** Latinized name of *Gerhard Kremer* (1512–94), Flemish geographer; inventor of a system of projecting maps (~ **projection**) in which the globe is projected on to a cylinder and the meridians of longitude are at right angles to the parallels of latitude.

mer·ce·nar·y (mer′senĕrē) *adj.* Working merely for money or other reward; having love of money as motive; hired (now only of soldiers serving in a foreign army). ~ *n.* (pl. **-nar·ies**). Hired soldier. **mer′ce·nar·i·ness** *n.*

mer·cer·ize (mer′serīz) *v.t.* (**-ized, -iz·ing**). Prepare (cotton) for dyeing by treating with solution of caustic potash etc. that produces a silky luster. [John *Mercer* (1791–1866), inventor]

mer·chan·dise (mer′chandīz, -dīs) *n.* Mercantile commodities; goods for sale. ~ (mer′chandīz) *v.* (**-ised, -is·ing**). Trade (in); buy and sell; prepare for sale, by display, design, advertising, etc.

mer·chant (mer′chant) *n.* Wholesale trader, esp. one trading with foreign countries; retail trader; **mer′chantman**, merchant ship; **merchant marine, shipping,** commercial shipping; **merchant ship,** ship of merchant marine. **mer′chant·a·ble** *adj.* Salable, marketable.

mer·ci·ful (mer′sĭful) *adj.* Disposed to mercy; compassionate. **mer′ci·ful·ly** *adv.* **mer′ci·ful·ness** *n.*

mer·ci·less (mer′sĭlĭs) *adj.* Showing no mercy; pitiless, unrelenting. **mer′ci·less·ly** *adv.*

mer′ci·less·ness *n.*

mer·cu·ri·al (m*e*rkūr′ēal) *adj.* Born under the planet Mercury; of or like mercury or quicksilver; sprightly, ready-witted, and volatile (from supposed influence of the planet). **mer·cu·ri·al·i·ty** (m*e*rkūrēăl′*i*tē) *n.* **mer·cu′ri·al·ly** *adv.*

mer·cu·ric (m*e*rkūr′ĭk) *adj.* (chem.) Of compounds in which mercury has a valence of two; ~ **chloride**, corrosive sublimate ($HgCl_2$), formerly used in dilute aqueous solution as an antiseptic for wounds and for sterilizing non-metallic surgical instruments.

Mer·cu·ro·chrome (m*e*rkūr′-*o*krōm) *n.* (trademark) Brilliant red compound of mercury used as an antiseptic.

mer·cu·rous (m*e*rkūr′*u*s) *adj.* (chem.) Of compounds in which mercury has a valence of one; ~ **chloride**, calomel.

Mer·cu·ry (mẽr′kyerē). 1. (Rom. myth.) God of eloquence, skill, trading, and thieving, and messenger of the gods, early identified with HERMES. 2. (astron.) Planet nearest to the sun, the smallest planet of the solar system. [L. *Mercurius*, f. *merx* merchandise]

mer·cu·ry (mẽr′kyerē) *n.* Silvery-white metallic element of high density, symbol Hg, at. no. 80, at. wt. 200.29, symbol Hg, popularly called *quicksilver*; its high density, its property of not wetting glass, and the wide range of temperature at which it is liquid make it valuable for scientific instruments, esp. thermometers and barometers; it dissolves many metals, forming amalgams, and its compounds are used in medicine as laxatives and stimulants.

mer·cy (mẽr′sē) *n.* (pl. **-cies**). Forbearance and compassion toward an offender, enemy, or person in one's power; disposition to forgive; act of mercy, gift of God, blessing; **at the ~ of**, wholly in the power of or subject to; ~ **killing**, killing with the intention of preventing needless suffering; ~ **seat**, golden covering of Ark of Covenant; hence, throne of God.

mere[1] (mẽr) *n.* (poet.) Lake.

mere[2] (mẽr) *adj.* (*superl.* **mer·est**). Pure, unmixed; barely or only what it is said to be, nothing more than. **mere′ly** *adv.*

mer·e·tri·cious (mĕr*e*trĭsh′*u*s) *adj.* Showily attractive, flashy. **mer·e·tri′cious·ly** *adv.* **mer·e·tri′cious·ness** *n.* [L. *meretrix* prostitute]

mer·gan·ser (mergăn′s*e*r) *n.* (pl. **-sers**, collect. **-ser**). Any of various fish-eating ducks of great diving powers, with long narrow serrated bill hooked at the tip, inhabiting northern parts of Old World and N. America. [L. *mergus* diver, *anser* goose]

*A **meridian,** an imaginary north-south line on the Earth's surface that connects both poles is used to indicate longitude. Longitude 0° runs through the former Royal Observatory at Greenwich, U.K. shown here.*

merge (mẽrj) *v.* (**merged, merg·ing**). Lose, cause (thing) to lose, character or identity in something else; join or blend gradually (*into, with*). **merg′er** *n.* Absorption of estate etc. in another; consolidation of one company or corporation with another.

me·rid·i·an (merĭd′ēan) *n.* Great circle passing through celestial poles and zenith of any place on Earth's surface or passing through the poles and any place on Earth; point at which star or sun attains its highest altitude; prime, full splendor. ~ *adj.* Of noon; (fig.) of the period of greatest splendor, vigor, etc.

me·ringue (merăng′) *n.* Confection made of sugar and beaten white of egg, baked until crisp; shell of meringue filled with whipped cream.

me·ri·no (merē′nō) *n.* (pl. **-nos**). Variety of sheep with fine silky wool, orig. bred in Spain; fine yarn or soft fabric of this wool; fine woolen yarn; (also ~ **sheep**) the chief and best known wool-bearing breed of Australia and N.Z.

mer·i·stem (mĕr′ĭstĕm) *n.* (bot.) Cell or region where growth is initiated.

mer·it (mĕr′ĭt) *n.* Quality of deserving well or being entitled to reward or gratitude; goodness; (pl.) good works, deserts; intrinsic rights and wrongs (of case etc., esp. law); **Legion of M~**, U.S. military decoration for outstanding service. **merit** *v.t.* Deserve (reward, punishment).

***Merino** sheep are being inspected for the quality of their fleece at Sydney's Royal Easter Show, Australia. Originally a Spanish breed, they have been improved by cross-breeding.*

mer·i·to·ri·ous (mĕrĭtōr′ē*u*s, -tōr′-) *adj.* Deserving praise, reward, etc. (often as term of limited praise, = well-meant, well-meaning). **mer·i·to′ri·ous·ly** *adv.* **mer·i·to′ri·ous·ness** *n.*

Mer·lin (mẽr′lĭn). In Arthurian legend, a magician and bard who aided and supported King Arthur and made the Round Table.

mer·lin (mẽr′lĭn) *n.* Small European falcon (*Falco columbarius aesalon*); N. Amer. pigeon hawk (*F. columbarius columbarius*).

mer·maid (mẽr′mād) *n.* (masc. **mer·man** pr. mẽr′măn, pl. **-men** pr. -mĕn). Fabled being inhabiting the sea, with human head and trunk and tail of a fish. [f. *mere*[1]]

mer·o·blast (mĕr′*o*blăst) *n.* (physiol.) Ovum of two parts, one of which is germinal and the other nutritive.

Mer·o·vin·gi·an (mĕr*o*vĭn′jēan) *adj.* & *n.* (Member) of the line of Frankish kings founded by Clovis (481–511) and reigning in Gaul and Germany until 752.

Mer·ri·mack (mĕr′ĭmăk). Frigate fitted with iron plating used by the Confederates against the Union ship, Monitor, during the Civil War, in an inconclusive battle at Hampton Roads, 1862.

mer·ry (mĕr′ē) *adj.* (**-ri·er, -ri·est**). Mirthful, hilarious; full of animated enjoyment; slightly tipsy; **make ~**, be festive; **~-go-round**, revolving machine carrying wooden horses, cars, etc., for riding on or in; busy social life;

mer'rymaking, festivity. **mer'ri·ly** *adv.* **mer'ri·ment, mer'ri·ness** *ns.*

me·sa (mā'sa) *n.* High rocky tableland with precipitous sides; **M ~ Verde National Park**, area in SW. Colorado known for ruins of prehistoric cliff dwellings.

Me·sa·bi (mesah'bē) **Range.** Low narrow range of hills in Minnesota containing vast iron ore and taconite deposits.

mes·cal (mĕs'kăl, mĕskăl') *n.* 1. Strong spirit distilled from fermented sap of wild agave. 2. PEYOTE.

mes·ca·line (mĕs'kalēn, -lĭn), **mes·ca·lin** (mĕs'kalĭn) *ns.* Active ingredient in peyote.

mes·en·ter·y (mĕs'entĕrē, mĕz'-) *n.* (pl. **-ter·ies**). Fold of peritoneum attaching intestinal canal to posterior wall of abdomen. **mes·en·ter·ic** (mĕsentĕr'ĭk, mĕz-) *adj.* **mes·en·ter·i·tis** (mĕsĕnterī'tĭs, mĕz-) *n.* Inflammation of the mesentery.

mesh (mĕsh) *n.* One of the spaces between the threads of a net; (pl.) net. ~ *v.* Catch in a net; (of gearwheels etc.) engage, interlock.

Me·shach (mē'shăk). One of three Jewish youths who came unharmed from a furnace into which they were thrown by Nebuchadnezzar (Dan. 3).

mes·mer·ism (mĕz'merĭzem, mĕs'-) *n.* (archaic) Hypnotism. **mes·mer·ic** (mĕzmĕr'ĭk, mĕs-) *adj.* **mes'mer·ist** *n.* **mes'mer·ize** *v.t.* (**-ized, -iz·ing**). Hypnotize; fascinate, compel by fascination. [f. F. A. *Mesmer* (1734–1815), Austrian physician]

mes·o·carp (mĕz'okārp, mĕs'-, mē'zo-, -so-) *n.* (physiol.) Middle of three layers of cells formed by embryo at early stage, layer from which skeletal muscles, heart muscle, and blood are developed.

Mes·o·lith·ic (mĕzolĭth'ĭk, mĕs-, mē'zo, -so-) *adj.* (archaeol.) Of the Stone Age between Paleolithic and Neolithic.

me·son (mē'zŏn, -sŏn, mĕz'ŏn, mĕs'-) *n.* Elementary particle intermediate in mass between proton and electron; **mu** ~ = MUON.

mes·o·phyll (mĕz'ofĭl, mĕs'-, mē'zo-, -so-) *n.* (bot.) Inner tissue of leaf.

mes·o·phyte (mĕz'ofīt, mĕs'-, mē'zo-, -so-) *n.* Plant needing a moderate amount of moisture.

Mes·o·po·ta·mi·a (mĕsopotā'mēa). Region of SW. Asia, the larger part of modern Iraq, between the rivers Tigris and Euphrates;

*This Stone Age village in the Orkneys is a relic of the **Mesolithic** Age — in N.W. Europe from about 8,000 B.C. to about 3,400 B.C. — which was technologically intermediate between the cultures using only chipped stone and those using polished stone tools.*

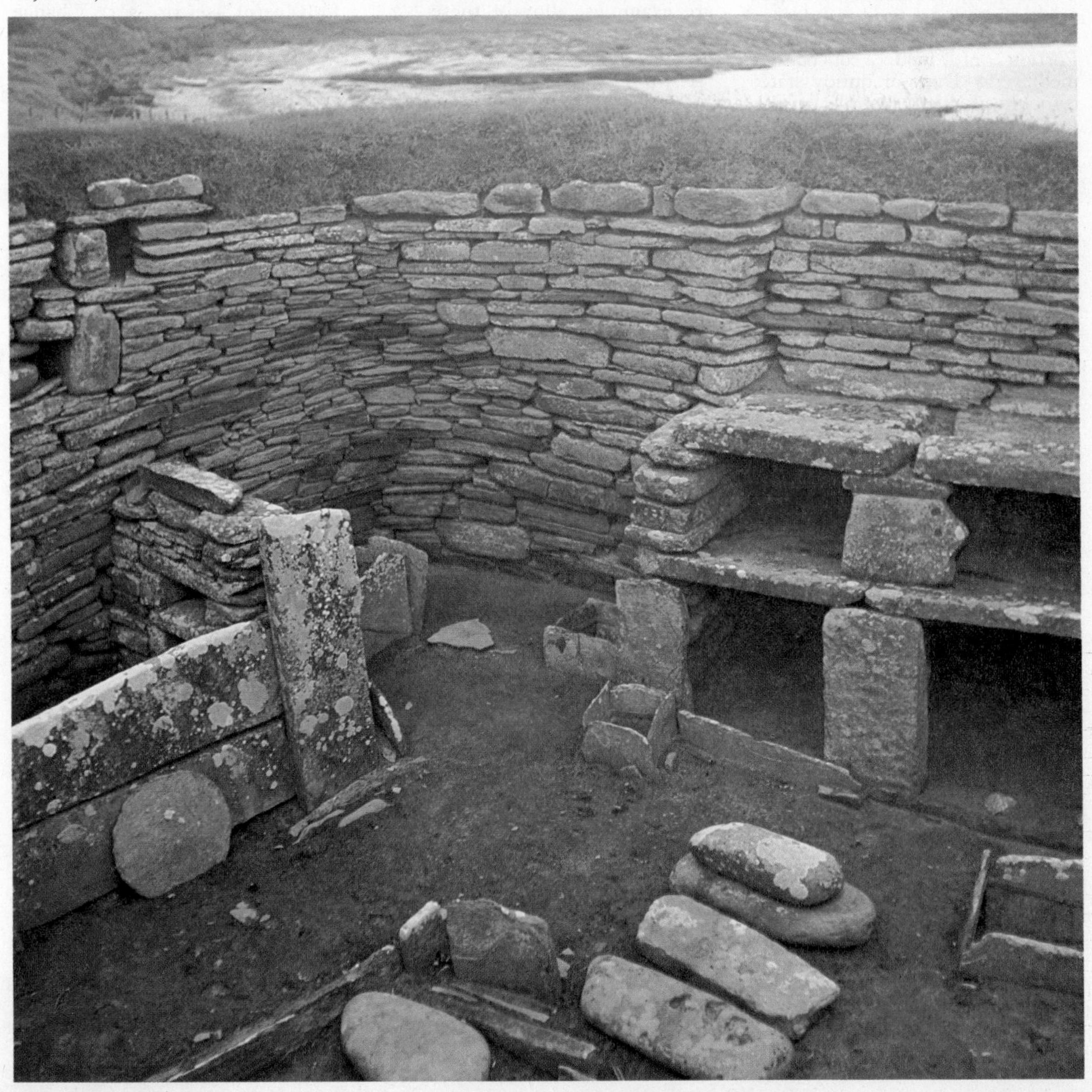

center of the ancient civilizations of SUMER, ASSYRIA, and BABYLON; scene (1915–16) of a disastrous British campaign against the Turks. **Mes·o·po·ta′mi·an** *adj.* [Gk., = "(country) between the rivers" (*mesos* middle, *potamos* river)]

mes·o·sphere (mĕz′*o*sfēr, mĕs′-, mē′zo-, -s*o*) *n.* Part of atmosphere above stratosphere, in which temperature generally falls with increasing height.

mes·o·tron (mĕz′*o*trŏn, mĕs′-, mē′zo-, -so-) = MESON.

Mes·o·zo·ic (mĕz*o*zō′ĭk, mĕs-, mēz*o*-, -so-) *adj.* & *n.* (geol.) (Of) the era or group of systems between Caenozoic and Paleozoic, characterized by the appearance of flowering plants and the emergence and extinction of dinosaurs.

mes·quite, mes·quit (mĕskēt′, mĕs′kēt) *ns.* Any of several deciduous trees or shrubs (genus *Prosopis*) of southwestern U.S. and Mexico, esp. *P. juliflora*, whose seed and pods are used as forage.

mess (mĕs) *n.* 1. (archaic) Portion of food; concoction, medley. 2. Dirty or untidy state; difficult situation, trouble; **make a ~ of**, bungle. 3. Spilled liquid etc. 4. Company of persons who take meals together, esp. in armed forces; taking of such a meal, place where it is eaten; **~ kit**, soldier's metal utensils, used for cooking. **mess** *v.* 1. Make dirty or untidy; putter *about*. 2. Take meals, esp. as member of a mess. **mess′y** *adj.* Untidy, dirty. **mess′i·ly** *adv.* **mess′i·ness** *n.*

mes·sage (mĕs′ĭj) *n.* Communication sent from one person to another; inspired utterance of a prophet or sage; teaching or moral of book, play, etc.; mission, errand.

mes·sen·ger (mĕs′*e*nj*e*r) *n.* Bearer of message.

Mes·si·ah (mesī′*a*) *n.* In Old Testament prophetic writings, the promised deliverer of the Jews; in Christian doctrine, Jesus Christ, regarded as this deliverer; name of an oratorio by Handel, based on Old Testament prophecies. **Mes·si·an·ic** (mĕsēăn′ĭk) *adj.* Of or relating to the or a Messiah. [Heb. *māšīah* anointed]

mes·sieurs (mĕs′*e*rz; *Fr.* mĕsyö′): see MONSIEUR.

Mes·si·na (mĕsē′n*a*). City and harbor of NE. Sicily; **Strait of ~**, that separating Sicily from Italy.

Messrs. (mĕs′*e*rz) *abbrev.* *Messieurs*; pl. of Mr., prefixed as title to name of firm etc. or introducing list of men.

mes·ti·zo (mĕstē′zō) *n.* (pl. **-zos, -zoes**). Person of Spanish and Amer. Indian ancestry; person of other combinations of ancestry. [Span., f. L. *miscere* mix]

met: see MEET[2].

met·a·bol·ic (mĕt*a*bŏl′ĭk) *adj.* Of metabolism.

me·tab·o·lism (m*e*tăb′*o*lĭz*e*m) *n.* Process in a cell or organism by which nutritive material is built up into living matter (*anabolism*) or by which protoplasm is broken down to perform special functions (*catabolism*); see BASAL. **me·tab′o·lize** *v.t.* (**-lized, -liz·ing**).

me·tab·o·lite (m*e*tăb′*o*līt) *n.* Substance undergoing change during metabolism.

met·a·car·pus (mĕt*a*kar′p*u*s) *n.* (pl. **-pi** pr. -pī). (anat.) Set of bones (5 in man) connecting carpus to phalanges; part of hand in which these are situated. **met·a·car′pal** *adj.* & *n.* (Bone) of the metacarpus.

met·a·gen·e·sis (mĕt*a*jĕn′ĭsĭs) *n.* (biol.) Reproduction of new generations by processes alternately sexual and asexual. **met·a·ge·net·ic** (mĕt*a*j*e*nĕt′ĭk) *adj.*

met·al (mĕt′*a*l) *n.* 1. One of a class of elements of which gold, silver, copper, iron, lead, and tin are examples; alloy of these. 2. Material for making glass, in molten state. ~ *v.t.* (**-aled, -al·ing**, Brit. **-alled, -al·ling**). Cover or supply with metal.

met·al·ize, met·al·lize (mĕt′*a*līz) *vbs.t.* (**-ized, -iz·ing; -lized, -liz·ing**). Render metallic. **met·al·i·za′tion** *n.*

me·tal·lic (m*e*tăl′ĭk) *adj.* Of or like metal; yielding metal.

met·al·log·ra·phy (mĕt*a*lŏg′r*a*fē) *n.* Study, description, of metals and alloys, their structure and properties.

met·al·loid (mĕt′*a*loid) *adj.* Having form or appearance of metal. ~ *n.* Element having physical properties of a metal and chemical properties of a nonmetal, e.g. tellurium.

met·al·lur·gy (mĕt′*a*lērjē) *n.* Science of the extraction, working, and properties of metals and their alloys. **met·al·lur′gic, met·al·lur′gi·cal** *adjs.* **met′al·lur·gist** *n.*

met·a·mere (mĕt′*a*mēr) *n.* (zool.) One of a series of more or less similar segments of an animal body, as of a worm. **met·a·mer·ic** (mĕt*a*mĕr′ĭk) *adj.* (zool.) Of metameres; (chem.) having same percentage composition and molecular weight, but different chemical properties. **me·tam·er·ism** (m*e*tăm′*e*rĭz*e*m) *n.*

met·a·mor·phic (mĕt*a*mōr′fĭk) *adj.* (geol., of rocks) Altered after formation by heat or pressure or both. **met·a·mor′phism** *n.* Metamorphic process.

met·a·mor·pho·sis (mĕt*a*mōr′f*o*sĭs) *n.* (pl. **-ses** pr. -sēz). Change of form, esp. magic transformation as of person into beast or plant etc.; changed form; change of character, circumstance, etc.; (zool.) change, usually rapid, between immature form and adult. **met·a·mor·phose** (mĕt*a*mōr′fōz, -fōs) *v.t.* (**-phosed, -phos·ing**). Change in form, change nature of.

met·a·phor (mĕt′*a*fōr, -f*e*r) *n.* Figure of speech in which name or descriptive term is transferred to an object to which it is not literally applicable (e.g. *a glaring error*); instance of this; **mixed ~**, combination of inconsistent metaphors. **met·a·phor·ic** (mĕt*a*fōr′ĭk, -far′-), **met·a·phor′i·cal** *adjs.* **met·a·phor′i·cal·ly** *adv.*

met·a·phys·ics (mĕt*a*fĭz′ĭks) *n.* (considered sing.) Branch of philosophy dealing with first principles of things, including such concepts as being, substance, space, time, identity, etc. **met·a·phys′i·cal** *adj.* Of metaphysics; **~ poets**, term used to designate certain 17th-c. English poets, including Donne, Cowley, Herbert, and Vaughan, addicted to "witty conceits" and far-fetched imagery. **met·a·phys′i·cal·ly** *adv.* **met·a·phy·si·cian** (mĕt*a*fĭzĭsh′*a*n) *n.* [Gk. *ta meta ta phusika* the works (of Aristotle) placed after the "Physics"]

me·tas·ta·sis (m*e*tăs′t*a*sĭs) *n.* (pl.

*The city of **Messina** in Sicily was almost totally destoyed by an earthquake in 1908. This cathedral of Annunciata dei Catalani, however, survived. Probably of Byzantine origin, it was rebuilt by the Normans in the 12th Century.*

*Man worked **metals** occurring in a naturally pure state before the Bronze Age. 1. The tradition of stylized bronze-casting in Benin, Africa, exemplified by this head, flourished until the 1650s. 2. Metal gates in St. Paul's Cathedral, London, U.K. designed in 1698 by Tijou. 3. Steel furnace. 4 Foundry workers in protective clothing.*

1

2

3

4

-ses pr. -sēz). (path.) Transference of disease or malignant cells from a primary focus to one in another part of the body by way of natural passages or of blood or lymph vessels. **met·a·stat·ic** (mĕtastăt′ĭk) *adj.* **me·tas′ta·size** *v.i.* (**-sized, -siz·ing**).

met·a·tar·sus (mĕtatār′sus) *n.* (pl. **-si** pr. -sī). Set of bones (5 in man) connecting tarsus to phalanges; part of foot or hind limb in which these are situated. **met·a·tar′sal** *adj.* & *n.* (Bone) of the metatarsus.

me·tath·e·sis (metăth′esĭs) *n.* (pl. **-ses** pr. -sēz). 1. (gram.) Transposition of letters or sounds. 2. (chem.) Substitution of one radical or atom for another in a molecule. **met·a·thet·i·cal** (mĕtathĕt′ĭkal) *adj.*

met·a·zo·an (mĕtazō′an) *adj.* & *n.* (zool.) (Member) of the order Metazoa, comprising multicellular animals with differentiated tissues, a nervous system, and coordination between the various cells.

mete (mēt) *v.t.* (**met·ed, met·ing**). (literary) Measure; portion *out*, allot (punishment, reward).

me·tem·psy·cho·sis (metĕmsĭkō′sĭs, mĕtemsī) *n.* (pl. **-sis** pr. -sēz). Supposed migration of soul at death into another body.

me·te·or (mē′tēer, -ōr) *n.* One of the small solid bodies in the solar system that become luminous when passing into Earth's atmosphere; (fig.) any bright, dazzling, but transient object. **me·te·or·ic** (mētēōr′ĭk, -ār′-) *adj.* Of the atmosphere; dependent on atmospheric conditions; of meteors; (fig.) dazzling, rapid.

me·te·or·ite (mē′tēerīt) *n.* Fallen meteor, fragment of rock or nickel iron that has fallen from space on to Earth's surface.

me·te·or·oid (mē′tēeroid) *n.* Body moving through space, of same nature as those which by passing into Earth's atmosphere become visible as meteors. **me·te·or·oid′al** *adj.*

me·te·or·ol·o·gy (mētēerŏl′ojē) *n.* Study of, science treating of, atmospheric phenomena, esp. for forecasting weather. **me·te·or·o·log·i·cal** (mētēerolŏj′ĭkal) *adj.* **me·te·or·o·log′i·cal·ly** *adv.* **me·te·or·ol′o·gist** *n.*

me·ter[1] (mē′ter) *n.* Apparatus for measuring, esp. automatically, and recording quantity of gas, water, electricity, etc., passing through, or time elapsed, etc. ~ *v.t.* Measure with meter.

me·ter[2] (mē′ter) *n.* Any regularly recurring poetic rhythm, determined by character and number of feet; group of metrical feet.

me·ter[3] (mē′ter) *n.* (abbrev. m) Basic unit of length in the metric system (approx. 39.37 in.), orig. representing one ten-millionth (10^{-7}) of a quadrant of the meridian passing through Paris; since 1960 defined as 1,650,763.73 wavelengths in a vacuum of the orange-red radiation of krypton 86; **~-kilogram-second** (*adj.*) (abbrev. mks) applied to a system of units of measurement based on the meter, kilogram, and second as units of length, mass, and time.

meth·ane (mĕth′ān) *n.* (chem.) Colorless inflammable gas (CH_4) formed by decay of vegetable matter in marshy places and coal seams.

meth·a·qua·lone (mĕthăk′walōn) *n.* Sedative drug usu. taken to induce sleep.

meth·od (mĕth′od) *n.* Procedure; way of doing anything, esp. according to a regular plan; systematic or orderly arrangement; orderliness and regularity. **me·thod·ic** (methŏd′ĭk), **me·thod′i·cal** *adjs.* **me·thod′i-**

*This vast **meteor** crater in Arizona is 4,000 ft. wide and 600 ft. deep. Its age has been disputed since it was discovered in 1891. Estimates range between 5,000 and 50,000 years.*

The very existence of meteors was questioned by 18th-century rationalists because of the veneration given these stones. A meteor shower in France in 1803 convinced them.

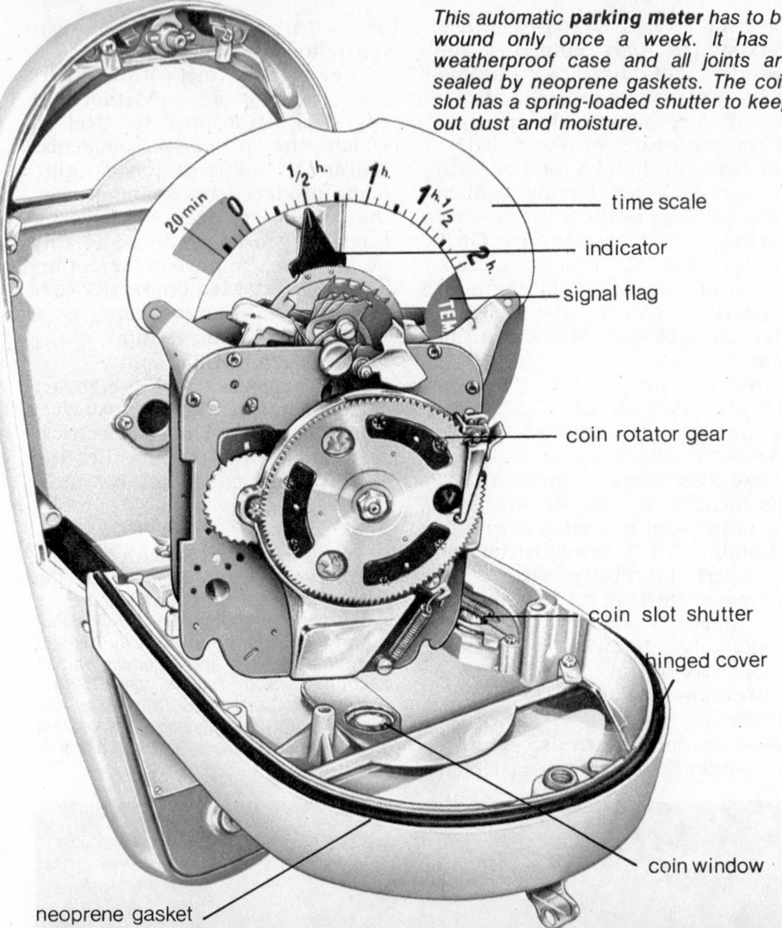

*This automatic **parking meter** has to be wound only once a week. It has a weatherproof case and all joints are sealed by neoprene gaskets. The coin slot has a spring-loaded shutter to keep out dust and moisture.*

cal·ly *adv.*

Meth·od·ism (mĕth′odĭzem) *n.* Religious movement, founded by John Wesley, his brother Charles, and George Whitefield, in reaction against apathy in the Church of England, and developed by missionary tours in U.S. and Gt. Britain; the meetings, often in the open air, were characterized (as now) by lay preaching and hymn singing; the movement later gave rise to various sects, but the principal groups (United Methodist Church, Primitive Methodists, and Wesleyan Methodists) united in 1932. **Meth′od·ist** *adj.* & *n.* [*Methodists*, applied to associates of the Wesleys at Oxford forming a religious society (nicknamed the "Holy Club"), prob. as following a specified "method" of devotional study]

Me·thu·se·lah (methōō′zela). Patriarch, grandfather of Noah, said (Gen. 5) to have lived 969 years, hence regarded as type of longevity.

meth·yl (mĕth′el) *n.* (chem.) Univalent organic radical (CH_3); ~ **alcohol,** colorless volatile liquid distilled from wood and also made synthetically; wood spirit. **meth·yl·ate** (mĕth′elāt) *v.t.* (**-at·ed, -at·ing**). Mix (alcohol) with wood spirit, usu. to render it unfit for drinking and therefore exempt from duty, as *methylated spirit*.

me·tic·u·lous (metĭk′yulus) *adj.* Extremely attentive to minute details. **me·tic′u·lous·ly** *adv.*

mé·tier (mā′tyā, mātyā′) *n.* Trade or profession; line.

Me·ton·ic (mĭtŏn′ĭk) **cycle.** Period of 19 solar years, after the lapse of which the new and full moons return to the same day of the year; it was the basis of the Greek calendar and is still used for calculating movable feast days, such as Easter. [f. *Meton*, Athenian astronomer (5th c. B.C.)]

me·ton·y·my (mĭtŏn′imē) *n.* Substitution of name of an attribute or adjunct for that of the thing meant (e.g. *the turf* for *horse racing*). **met·o·nym·i·cal·ly** (mĕtonĭm′-ĭklē) *adv.*

me·tre (mē′ter) (Brit.) = METER[2], METER[3].

met·ric (mĕt′rĭk) *adj.* Of the meter or metric system; using the metric system; ~ **system,** decimal measuring system based on the meter, orig. devised in 1791 by the French Academy of Sciences, with the meter, liter, and kilogram (orig. the gram) as units of length,

***Metazoa** includes all animal organisms of more than one cell, except usually sponges. This growing plant-like coral, from Australia's Great Barrier Reef, is a multi-cellular organism.*

capacity, and mass; ~ **ton**, 1,000 kilograms. **met·ri·ca·tion** (mĕtrĭkā'shon) *n.* Conversion to the metric system. **met·ri·cate** (mĕt'rĭkāt) *v.* (**-cat·ed, -cat·ing**).

met·ri·cal (mĕt'rĭkal) *adj.* Of, composed in, meter; of, involving, measurement, as ~ **geometry**. **met'ri·cal·ly** *adv.*

met·ro (mĕt'rō) *n.* (pl. **-ros**). Subway, esp. (**M**~) in Paris.

me·trol·o·gy (mĭtrŏl'ojē) *n.* (pl. **-gies**). Science, system, of weights and measures. **met·ro·log·i·cal** (mĕtrolŏj'ĭkal) *adj.*

met·ro·nome (mĕt'ronōm) *n.* (mus.) Instrument marking time by means of a graduated inverted pendulum with a sliding weight. **met·ro·nom·ic** (mĕtronŏm'ĭk) *adj.*

me·trop·o·lis (metrŏp'olĭs) *n.* Chief city, capital; see of metropolitan bishop. [Gk. *mētropolis* parent state (*mētēr* mother, *polis* city)]

met·ro·pol·i·tan (mĕtropŏl'ĭtan) *adj.* Of a metropolis; of, forming (part of) nation as dist. from its colonies or dependencies; ~ **bishop, archbishop**, one who has authority over the bishops of a province. **metropolitan** *n.* Metropolitan bishop or archbishop; inhabitant of a metropolis. **met·ro·pol·i·tan·ate** (mĕtropŏl'ĭtanĭt) *n.* Office, jurisdiction, of a metropolitan bishop.

Met·ter·nich (mĕt'ernĭk; *Ger.* mĕt'ernĭx). Prince Clemens Wenzel Lothar Metternich-Winneburg (1773–1859), Austrian statesman; led the Congress of VIENNA in devising the settlement of Europe after the Napoleonic Wars.

met·tle (mĕt'el) *n.* Quality of disposition; natural vigor and ardor, spirit, esp. of a horse. **met'tle·some** *adj.* High-spirited.

Meuse (mūz; *Fr.* möz). (*Dutch* **Maas** pr. mahz) River of NE. France, Belgium, and Netherlands.

mew[1] (mū) *n.* Gull, esp. the common gull (*Larus canus*); sea mew.

mew[2] (mū) *v.* (of hawk) Molt; shut up (hawk) in mew; shut *up*, confine. ~ *n.* Cage for hawks.

mew[3] (mū) *n.* & *v.i.* Meow.

mewl (mūl) *v.i.* Cry feebly, whimper; mew like a cat.

mews (mūz) *n.* Series of private stables built around a yard or on both sides of a lane (now freq. converted into dwellings etc.); area containing these. [f. MEW², orig. of royal stables on site of hawks' mews]

Mex·i·co (mĕk'sĭkō; *Sp.* mĕ'hēkaw). Federal republic of southern N. Amer.; orig. inhabited by various Amer. Ind. peoples, esp. Maya, Aztecs; was a Spanish colony ("New Spain"), *c*1519–1821; since then it has been a republic except for the years 1864–7 when MAXIMILIAN was emperor; the presidency of Diaz (1877–80 and 1884–1911) was followed by a period of revolution; the question of the possession of Texas led to war between the U.S. and Mexico in 1846–8, Texas having applied for admission to the U.S. as early as 1836; capital, Mexico City; **Gulf of** ~, area of Atlantic Ocean, almost surrounded by the southern coast of N. Amer., the coast of Mexico, and Cuba. **Mex'i·can** *adj.* & *n.*

me·ze·re·on (mĭzēr'ēŏn) *n.* Deciduous shrub (*Daphne mezereum*) with fragrant purple flowers.

mez·za·nine (mĕz'anēn, mĕzanēn') 1. *adj.* & *n.* (Low story) between two main stories of a building. 2. Lowest balcony or front part of a theater balcony.

mez·zo (mĕt'sō, mĕd'zō, mĕz'ō) *adv.* (mus.) Moderately; ~ **forte**, moderately loud; ~ **piano**, moderately soft.

mez·zo-so·pran·o (mĕt'sō soprăn'ō, -prah'nō, mĕd'zō, mĕz'ō) *n.* (pl. **-pran·os, -pran·i** pr. -prăn'ē, -prah'nē). (Person with, part for) voice between contralto and soprano.

mez·zo·tint (mĕt'sōtĭnt, mĕd'zō-, mĕz'ō-) *n.* Method of engraving on copper or steel in which the plate is roughened uniformly, lights and half-lights being produced by scraping away the roughness, deep shadows by leaving it; print produced in this way. ~ *v.t.* Engrave in mezzotint.

MF *abbrev.* Medium FREQUENCY.

mf *abbrev.* Mezzo forte.

Mg *symbol.* Magnesium.

mg *abbrev.* Milligram(s).

Mgr. *abbrev.* Monseigneur; Monsignor (pl. **Mgri.**); manager.

mho (mō) *n.* Unit of electrical conductance, the reciprocal of the ohm; thus, a conductor having a

***Mexico** is the largest Spanish speaking nation in the world. Almost half the population are peasants on a subsistence economy. Below: The Palace of Fine Arts in Mexico City is used for operas, plays and exhibits and is decorated with murals by Rivera, Orozco and Tamayo. Bottom: Map and flag of Mexico. Facing page: Harvesting the agave plant from which mescal is made.*

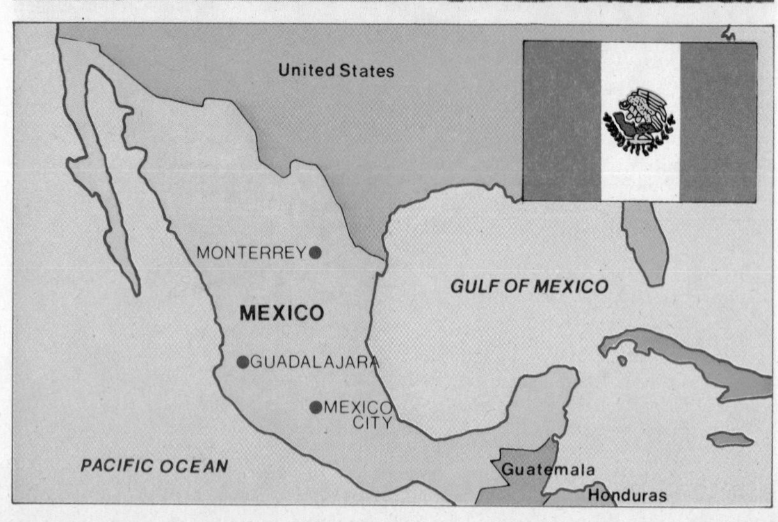

resistance of 4 ohms has a conductance of 0.25 mho.

MI *abbrev.* Michigan.

Mi·am·i (mīăm′ē, -ăm′*i*). City in SE. Florida; **M ~ Beach**, resort city on an island opposite Miami, across Biscayne Bay.

mi·as·ma (mīăz′m*a*, mē-) *n.* (pl. **-ma·ta** pr. -m*ata*, **-mas**). Noxious exhalation from marshes, putrid matter, etc. **mi·as′mic** *adj.*

Mic. *abbrev.* Micah (Old Testament).

mi·ca (mī′k*a*) *n.* One of a group of minerals composed of aluminum silicate combined with other silicates, occurring as small glittering scales in granite etc., or as larger crystals separable into thin transparent plates, used as a dielectric and insulator in electrical equipment etc. **mi·ca·ceous** (mīkā′sh*us*) *adj.* [L., = "crumb"]

Mi·cah (mī′k*a*). Hebrew minor prophet, a contemporary of Isaiah; book of Old Testament containing his prophecies.

Mi·caw·ber (mĭkaw′b*er*), **Mr.** In Dickens' *David Copperfield*, a sanguine idler trusting that something good will turn up.

mice: see MOUSE.

mi·celle (mĭsĕl′) *n.* (chem.) Minute particle formed by an aggregate of molecules, found in certain colloidal solutions.

Mich. *abbrev.* Michigan.

Mi·chael (mī′k*e*l), **St.** One of the archangels, usu. represented slaying a dragon (Rev. 12); commemorated Sept. 29.

Mi·chael·mas (mĭk′*e*lm*a*s). Feast of St. Michael, Sept. 29; **~ daisy**, herbaceous perennial of genus *Aster*, native in N. America, flowering at Michaelmas.

Mi·chel·an·ge·lo Buon·ar·ro·ti (mēkĕlahn′jĕlō bwawnahraw′tē) (1475–1564). Italian sculptor, painter, and poet; one of the greatest artists of the Renaissance; famous esp. for his frescoes in the Sistine Chapel at Rome.

***Michelangelo Buonarroti**, Italian sculptor, painter, poet and architect of the Renaissance, carved his Pietà (below) in about 1498. He later carved his famous statue of David, painted the frescos on the ceiling of the Sistine Chapel and rebuilt St. Peter's Basilica, Rome.*

Mi·chel·son (mī′k*e*ls*o*n), **Albert Abraham** (1852–1931). Amer. physicist; devised with E. W. Morley the **~-Morley experiment**, which attempted to discover the effect of the velocity of Earth on the velocity of light, as a means of measuring the velocity of Earth through the ether; the failure to discover any such effect was the starting point for the theory of RELATIVITY.

Mich·i·gan (mĭsh′*i*g*a*n). State in midwestern U.S., with its northern boundary formed by Lakes Huron and Superior; admitted to the Union in 1837; capital, Lansing; **Lake ~**, one of the chain of great lakes in N. America.

Mick·ey Finn (mĭk′ē fĭn′). (also **Mickey**) Surreptitiously drugged alcoholic drink; drink with knockout drops.

micro- *prefix.* Small, minute (contrasted with MACRO-); also used in names of units, = one millionth of (symbol μ).

mi·crobe (mī′krōb) *n.* (pop.) Microorganism, esp. one of the bacteria causing diseases and fermentation. **mi·cro·bi·al** (mīkrō′bē*a*l), **mi·cro′bic** *adjs.*

mi·cro·bi·ol·o·gy (mīkrōbīŏl′*o*jē) *n.* Study of microorganisms. **mi·cro·bi·ol′o·gist** *n.*

mi·cro·ce·phal·ic (mīkrōs*e*făl′ĭk) *adj.* Small-headed.

mi·cro·chip (mī′krōchĭp) *n.* Small thin chip of silicon holding a complex electronic circuit.

mi·cro·cosm (mī′kr*o*kŏz*e*m) *n.* Little world, world in miniature; miniature representation *of*; man, society, as an epitome of the world or universe. **mi·cro·cos·mic** (mīkr*o*kŏz′mĭk) *adj.*

mi·cro-dot (mī′kr*o*dŏt) *n.*

*The **Michaelmas Daisy**, a native of North America but also found in temperate regions of Europe, flowers from July to November. Its roots were often used as a wound-herb.*

Photograph reduced to the size of a dot.

mi·cro·e·lec·tron·ics (mīkrōĭlĕktrŏn′ĭks, -ēlĕk-) *n.* (usu. considered sing.). Branch of electronics dealing with miniaturized components.

mi·cro·fiche (mī′krofēsh) *n.* (pl. **-fiche**). Sheet of microfilm usu. 4 × 6 in., usu. showing many 8½ × 11 in. pages in reduced size.

mi·cro·film (mī′krofĭlm) *n.* Very small film; photographic reproduction on this, projected on screen for reading etc. ~ *v.t.* Photograph on microfilm.

mi·cro·lith (mī′krolĭth) *n.* (archaeol.) Minute worked flint, usu. for mounting as part of a composite tool, found esp. in mesolithic cultures.

mi·crom·e·ter (mīkrŏm′*eter*) *n.* Precision instrument, variously designed, for measuring minute distances.

mi·cro·min·i·a·tur·i·za·tion (mīkrōmĭnē*a*cherīzā′sh*on*) *n.* Making of electronic devices with greatly reduced size. **mi·cro·min·i·a·tur·ize** (mīkrōmĭn′ē*a*cherīz) *v.t.* (**-ized, -iz·ing**).

mi·cron (mī′krŏn) *n.* (pl. **-crons, -cra** pr. -kr*a*). One millionth of a meter (symbol μm).

Mi·cro·ne·sia (mīkronē′zh*a*, -sh*a*). Division of Oceania comprising the small SW. Pacific islands including the Mariana, Caroline, Marshall, and Gilbert Islands. **Mi·cro·ne′sian** *adj.* & *n.*

mi·cro·or·gan·ism (mī′kroōrgănĭzem, mīkroōr′-) *n.* Any of the organisms not visible to the unaided eye, as bacteria, protozoa, unicellular algae and fungi, and viruses.

mi·cro·phone (mī′krofōn) *n.* Instrument producing electrical impulses corresponding to the vibrations of sound waves falling on it and thus performing an essential part in telephonic and radio transmission. **mi·cro·phon·ic** (mīkrofŏn′ĭk) *adj.*

mi·cro·pho·to·graph (mī′krofōtogrăf, -grahf, mīkrofō′-) *n.* Photograph reduced to very small size.

mi·cro·scope (mī′kroskōp) *n.* Lens or combination of lenses magnifying near objects so that details invisible to the naked eye are revealed. **mi·cro·scop·ic** (mīkroskŏp′ĭk) *adj.* Of a microscope; with the functions of a microscope; so minute as only to be seen clearly with a microscope. **mi·cro·scop′i·cal** *adj.* Pertaining to a microscope. **mi·cro·scop′i·cal·ly** *adv.* **mi·cros·co·py** (mĭkrŏs′k*o*pē, mī′kroskōpē), **mi·cros′co·pist** *ns.*

mi·cro·some (mī′krosōm) *n.* (biol.) Small particle in a cell, not visible with an ordinary microscope.

mi·cro·struc·ture (mī′krōstrŭkch*er*) *n.* (metallurgy) Arrangement of crystals observable under a microscope. **mi·cro·struc·tur·al** (mīkrōstrŭk′cher*al*) *adj.*

mi·cro·tome (mī′krotōm) *n.* Instrument for cutting very thin sections of organic tissue for examination under the microscope.

mi·crot·o·my (mīkrŏt′*o*mē) *n.* (pl. **-mies**).

mi·cro·wave (mī′krōwāv) *n.* Electromagnetic wave having a wavelength between about 1 mm and 30 cm.

mi·crur·gy (mī′krerjē) *n.* Art or science of dissection and injection under a microscope. **mi·crur·gi·cal** (mīkrer′jĭk*al*) *adj.*

mic·tu·ri·tion (mĭkcherĭsh′*on*) *n.* Urination. **mic·tu·rate** (mĭk′cherāt) *v.i.* (**-rat·ed, -rat·ing**). Urinate.

mid (mĭd) *adj.* Middle of; intermediate; (phon.) pronounced with the tongue or part of it in a middle position between high and low; **mid′brain**: see BRAIN;

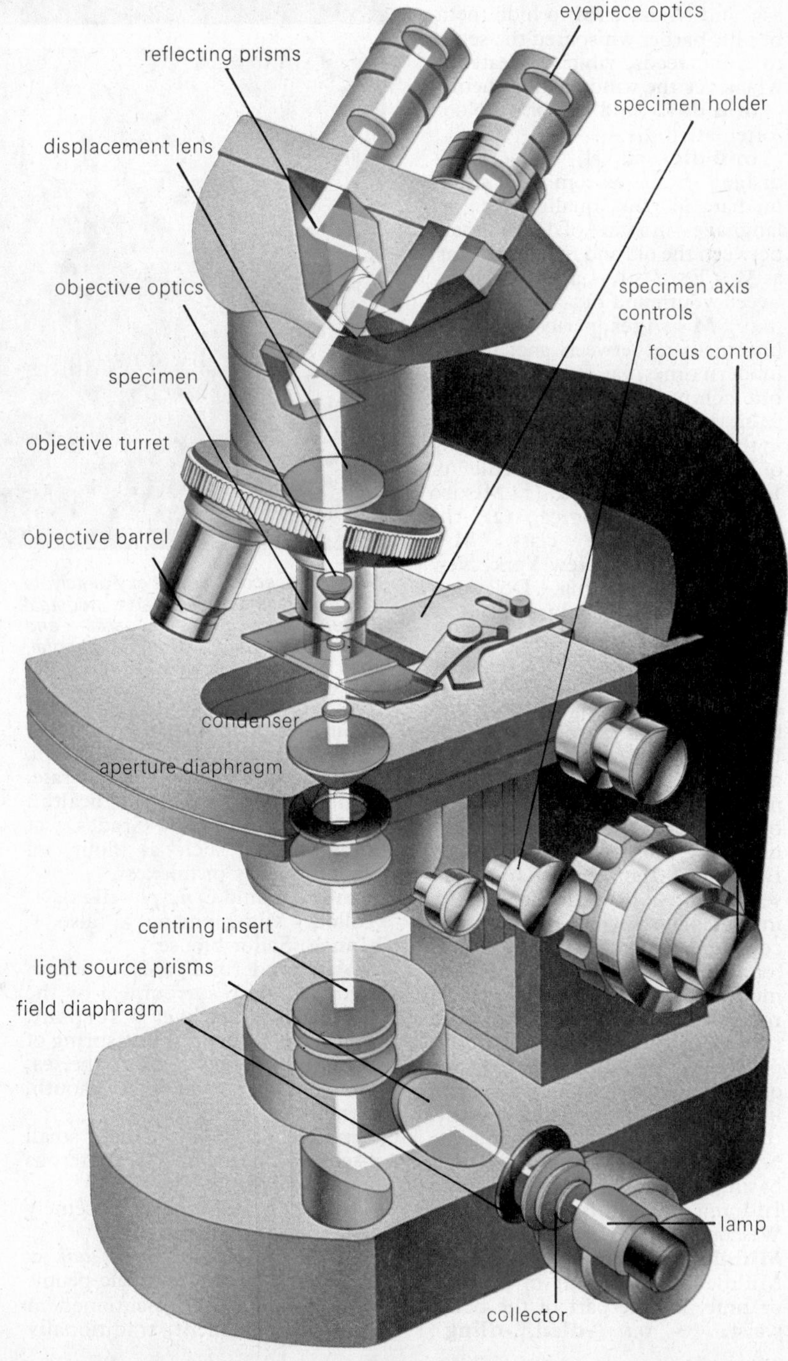

This Wild M20 laboratory ***microscope*** *has built-in illumination and sub-stage condensers. The binocular head does not give a stereoscopic image, but as both eyes are used equally it makes viewing less tiring.*

*These **midshipmen** are marching in formation at the U.S. Naval Academy in Annapolis, Maryland. They are the lowest grade of officer in the U.S. Navy.*

mid'rib, main vein of a leaf etc.

Mi·das (mī'das). (Gk. legend) King of Phrygia; was given by Dionysus the power of turning everything he touched into gold; unable to eat or drink, he prayed to be relieved of the gift, and was instructed to wash in the river Pactolus, whose sands turned to gold at his touch; another time, when Midas declared Pan a better flute player than Apollo, Apollo turned his ears into the ears of an ass, and Midas tried to hide them, but his barber whispered the secret to some reeds, which repeated it whenever the wind rustled them.

mid·day (mid'dā) *n.* Noon (often attrib.).

mid·dle (mĭd'el) *adj.* Equidistant from extremities; intermediate in rank, quality, etc.; (of languages) in a stage of development between the old and modern forms, as **M ~** ENGLISH; **~ age**, period between youth and old age; **~-aged** (*adj.*); **M ~ Ages**, period of history intermediate between ancient and modern times, variously calculated, but commonly applied to period from the fall of the Roman Empire in the West (5th c.) to the beginning of the Renaissance (middle of 15th c.); **~ America**, (1) Mexico and Central America; (2) the American middle class; **M ~ Atlantic States**, New York, New Jersey, Pennsylvania, Delaware, and Maryland; **~ class**, class of society between upper and lower, including professional and business classes (often attrib.); **~ distance**, that part of a picture that lies between the foreground and the background; (footracing) races of approximately 1 mile or 1500 meters; **M ~ East**, nations lying between the Near and Far East, including those countries between Egypt and Iran; **M ~ Kingdom**: see KINGDOM; **mid'dleman**, trader intermediate between producer and consumer; **middle-of-the-road**, (of person or course of action) moderate, avoiding extremes; **middle term**, (logic) term in a syllogism common to both premises; **mid'dleweight**, boxer of weight between welterweight and light heavyweight; **Middle West**, that part of the U.S. occupying the N. half of the Mississippi River basin, including the states of Ohio, Indiana, Illinois, Michigan, Wisconsin, Iowa, and Minnesota; **Middle Western(er)**. **middle** *n.* Middle part or point in position or time; middle part of the body, waist. **~** *v.t.* (**-dled, -dling**). (naut.) Fold, double, in the middle.

***Milan,** the second largest city of Italy, is a great communication and industrial center, especially for silks and manmade fibers. Its Gothic cathedral, seen here was begun in 1386.*

mid·dling (mĭd'lĭng) *adj.* & *adv.* Moderately good; second-rate; (colloq.) fairly well (in health). **mid'dlings** *n.pl.* Grades of commodities, such as flour, of second quality or fineness.

mid·dy (mĭd'ē) *n.* (pl. **-dies**). 1. (colloq.) Midshipman. 2. (also **~ blouse**) Sailor blouse.

Mid·gard (mid'gărd). (Scand. myth.) Region, surrounded by the sea, in which men live; **~ Serpent**, monstrous serpent, the offspring of Loki, thrown by Odin into the sea, where, with its tail in its mouth, it encircled Earth.

midge (mĭj) *n.* Gnat, small insect; (zool.) member of dipterous family Chironomidae.

midg·et (mĭj'ĭt) *n.* Extremely small person; (also attrib.).

Mid·i·an·ite (mĭd'ēanīt) *adj.* & *n.* (Member) of a nomadic people of N. Arabia often mentioned in the Old Testament, traditionally descended from Midian, son of Abraham (Gen. 25), proverbial for leading Israel astray.

mid·land (mĭd'land) *n.* Part of a country remote from the sea or borders; **the Midlands**, the counties of England S. of the Humber and Mersey Rivers and N. of the Thames, except Norfolk, Suffolk, Essex, Hertfordshire, Gloucestershire, and the counties bordering on Wales. **midland** *adj.* Of, in, the midland or (**M ~**) Midlands.

Mid·lo·thi·an (mĭdlō'dhēan). Former Scottish county on S. coast of Firth of Forth.

mid·night (mĭd'nīt) *n.* Middle of the night, 12 o'clock at night (often attrib.)

Mid·rash (mĭd'rahsh; *Heb.* mēdrahsh') *n.* (pl. **Mid·ra·shim** pr. mĭdrah'shĭm; *Heb.* mēdrahshēm'; **Mid·ra·shoth** mĭdrah'shōt; *Heb.* mēdrahshawt'). Ancient Jewish commentary on part of the Hebrew scriptures.

mid·riff (mĭd'rĭf) *n.* Diaphragm between thorax and abdomen; region of front of body over this; (part of) garment fitted to this region.

Milfoil or yarrow is a common wayside plant of the daisy family. Its leaves were smoked as tobacco and are still used in herbal medicine.

mid·ship (mĭd′shĭp) *n.* Middle part of ship or boat; **mid′shipman**, cadet or student training for commission in U.S. Navy or Coast Guard. **mid′ships** *adv.* Amidships.

midst (mĭdst) *n.* Middle. ~ *adv.* Amidst.

mid·sum·mer (mĭd′sŭm*er*, mĭdsŭm′-) *n.* Period of summer solstice, about June 21.

mid·term (mĭd′tẽrm) *n.* (colloq.) Examination given halfway through the school term. ~ *adj.* Occurring at or near the middle of a term.

Mid·way (mĭd′wā) **Islands.** Small coral atoll, 1,200 miles (1,932 km) NW. of Hawaii; scene of decisive battle in which U.S. naval forces repulsed Japanese, 1942.

mid·wife (mĭd′wīf) *n.* (pl. **-wives** pr. -wīvz). Woman who assists others in childbirth. **mid·wife·ry** (mĭd′wīferē, -wĭfrē) *n.*

*Wild **mignonette,** which has green flowers, grows wild in Europe and is common on dry wastes, especially in chalk and limestone districts.*

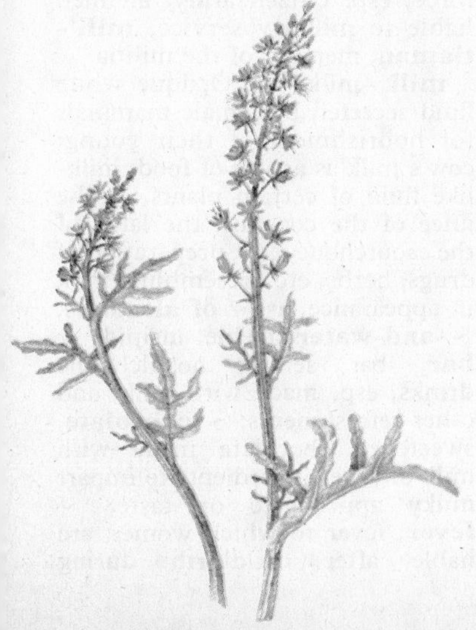

*Many animals, fish and birds (such as the ducks shown above) **migrate** from one place to another either to breed or to find food or warmth or both.*

mien (mēn) *n.* (literary) Bearing or look.

Mies van der Rohe (mēz′văn d*er* rō′; *Ger.* mēs′fahn d*er* rō′*e*), **Ludwig** (1886–1969). German-born American architect.

might[1] (mīt): see MAY; **~-have-been**, past possibility.

might[2] (mīt) *n.* Great (bodily or mental) strength; power to enforce one's will.

might·y (mī′tē) *adj.* (**might·i·er, might·i·est**). Powerful, strong in body or mind. ~ *adv.* (colloq.) Very, extremely. **might·i·ly** (mī′tĭlē) *adv.* **might′i·ness** *n.*

mi·gnon·ette (mĭnyonĕt′) *n.* Plant with fragrant grayish-green blossoms (*Reseda odorata*).

mi·graine (mī′grān) *n.* Recurrent paroxysmal headache, often accompanied by nausea, visual disturbances, and other severe symptoms. [Fr., f. Gk. *hemi* half, *kranion* skull]

mi·grant (mī′grant) *adj.* That migrates. ~ *n.* Migrant bird etc.; ~ **worker**, farm laborer who moves from one area to another to do seasonal work.

mi·grate (mī′grāt) *v.i.* (**-grat·ed, -grat·ing**). Move from one place of abode, or esp. one country, to another; (of birds, fishes, and animals) go from one habitat to another, esp. come and go regularly with the seasons. **mi·gra·tion** (mīgrā′shon) *n.* **mi·gra·to·ry** (mī′gratōrē, -tōrē) *adj.*

Mi·ka·do (mĭkah′dō) *n.* (pl. **-dos**). Popular title, as used by foreigners, of the Emperor of Japan. [Jap. *mi* august, *kado* door]

mike (mīk) *n.* (slang) Microphone.

mil (mĭl) *n.* $\frac{1}{1000}$ of an inch, 0.0254 mm.

Mi·lan (mĭlăn′, -lahn′). Second-largest city of Italy and an important commercial and manufacturing center in the N. central part.

Milkwort, *a small European perennial found in meadows, was formerly believed to increase lactation. Herbalists accordingly prescribed it for nursing mothers.*

Milk bottling *in factories like this one in Australia is carried out under strict hygienic conditions. The milk is processed before bottling to become pasteurized or homogenized.*

Millipedes *of which there are about 8,000 species live among and eat decaying plant matter. Most are slow-moving and inoffensive. This giant species is found in Africa.*

Mil·an·ese (mĭlanēz′, -nēs′; *It.* mēlahnĕ′zĕ) *adj.* Of Milan. ~ *n.* (pl. **-ese**). Native, inhabitant, of Milan.

milch (mĭlch) *adj.* Giving, kept for, milk; ~ **cow**, cow kept for milk.

mild (mīld) *adj.* Gentle; not severe or harsh or drastic; not bitter. **mild′ly** *adv.* **mild′ness** *n.* **mild** *n.* (Brit.) Mild beer.

mil·dew (mĭl′do͞o, -dū) *n.* Growth of minute fungi on plants or on leather etc. exposed to damp. **mil′dew·y** *adj.* **mildew** *v.* Taint, be tainted, with mildew.

mile (mīl) *n.* Unit of linear measure of 1,760 yards (1,584 m) (also **statute** ~); race extending over 1 mile; **geographical** ~, 1 minute of longitude (1/60°) measured on the equator, 6,087.2 ft. (1,826.16 m); **nautical, sea,** ~, length of 1 minute of latitude, standardized at 6,080 ft. (1,824 m) but actually varying with latitude (6,046–6,108 ft. 1,813.8–1,832.4 m); **mile′post, mile′-stone**, post, stone set up on road to indicate the miles to and from a given place; (fig.) stage, event, in life, progress, etc. [L. *mille* thousand (the Roman mile being 1,000 paces)]

mile·age, milage (mī′lĭj) *ns.* Distance in miles; traveling allowance at fixed rate per mile; number of miles in which a vehicle uses a given amount of fuel.

mil·er (mī′ler) *n.* (colloq.) Man, horse, trained specially to run a mile; also in comb. as *two-*~.

mil·foil (mĭl′foil) *n.* Common yarrow (*Achillea millefolium*), which has many finely divided leaves.

mil·i·ar·y (mĭl′ēēre, mĭl′yerē) *adj.* (path.) Marked by eruption of small red pustules resembling millet seeds; ~ **tuberculosis**, form of tuberculosis, usu. acute, in which small tubercular nodules are distributed throughout the body.

mi·lieu (mĭlyo͞o′, mēl-; *Fr.* mēlyö′) *n.* (pl. **mi·lieus**, *Fr.* **mi·lieux** pr. mēlyö′). Environment, state of life, social surroundings.

mil·i·tant (mĭl′ĭtant) *adj.* Engaged in warfare; warlike, combative; **church** ~, Christian church considered at war on earth with the powers of evil, contrasted with the heavenly *church triumphant*. **mil′i·tan·cy** *n.* **mil′i·tant·ly** *adv.* **militant** *n.* Militant person.

mil·i·ta·rism (mĭl′ĭterĭzem) *n.* Spirit, tendencies, of the professional soldier; undue reliance on, and exaltation of, military force and methods. **mil′i·ta·rist** *n.*

mil·i·ta·rize (mĭl′ĭterīz) *v.t.* (**-rized, -riz·ing**). Make military or warlike; instill principles of militarism into. **mil·i·ta·ri·za·tion** (mĭlĭterīzā′shon) *n.*

mil·i·tary (mĭl′ĭtĕrē) *adj.* Of, done by, befitting, soldiers, or the army (opp. *civil*); ~ **age**, age of eligibility for admission to the armed forces; ~ **band**, combination of woodwind, brass, and percussion instruments; ~ **police**, body of soldiers doing police duty in the army. **mil·i·tar·i·ly** (mĭlĭtĕr′ilē, mĭl′ĭtĕr-) *adv.* **military** *n.* (pl. **-tar·ies**, collect. **-tar·y**). Soldiery; esp. **the** ~, the defense establishment of a nation.

mil·i·tate (mĭl′ĭtāt) *v.i.* (**-tat·ed, -tat·ing**). (of facts, evidence, etc.) Have force, tell (*against* conclusion or result).

mi·li·tia (mĭlĭsh′*a*) *n.* Military force, esp. citizen army; all men liable to military service; **mili′-tiaman**, member of the militia.

milk (mĭlk) *n.* Opaque white fluid secreted by female mammals for nourishment of their young; cow's milk as article of food; milk-like fluid of certain plants, as the juice of the coconut, the latex of the caoutchouc, etc.; preparation of drugs, herbs, etc., resembling milk in appearance, as ~ **of almonds**; ~**-and-water**, feeble, insipid; ~ **bar**, bar selling nonalcoholic drinks, esp. made with milk, and other refreshments; ~ **chocolate**, sweetened chocolate made with milk or other ingredients to impart milky appearance or taste; ~ **fever**, fever to which women are liable after childbirth during lactation; ~ **glass**, opaque white glass; ~ **leg**, inflammatory condition of leg, in women after childbirth, accompanied by white swellings; **milk'maid**, woman who milks cows, etc. or is employed in dairy; **milk'man**, man who sells or delivers milk; **milk punch**, drink made of spirits and milk; **milk shake**, glass of milk or milk and egg, flavored and shaken up; ~ **snake**, nonvenomous snake (*Lampropeltis triangulum*) 30 to 50 in. long, having black-rimmed reddish-brown splotches, and feeding on rodents; also known as house snake, milk adder, red king snake; **milk'sop**, effeminate or spiritless fellow; **milk sugar**, lactose; **milk tooth**, one of the first, temporary set of teeth in young mammals; **milk'weed**, any plant of the genus *Asclepias*, esp. the common milkweed (*A. syriaca*), with clusters of purple flowers and pods that release seeds which float through the air on tufts of down or silk; **milk'wort**, any plant of genus *Polygala*, growing in meadows, formerly supposed to increase milk in nursing mothers. **milk** *v.t.* Draw milk from (cow, ewe, goat, etc.); get money out of, exploit (person); extract juice, venom, etc., from (snake etc.).

milk·y (mĭl'kē) *adj.* (**milk·i·er, milk·i·est**). Of, like, mixed with, milk; (of liquid) cloudy, not clear; effeminate, weakly amiable; **M ~ Way**, galaxy as seen from Earth, forming a faintly luminous band of innumerable stars too distant to be seen as separate by the naked eye.

mill[1] (mĭl) *n.* Building or apparatus for grinding corn; machine for grinding any solid substance to powder; any machine, or building fitted with machinery, for manufacturing processes etc., as **saw'mill, cotton mill; put through, go through, the mill**, subject to, undergo, training or experience; be severely disciplined; **mill'board**, stout pasteboard for bookbinding; **mill'dam**, dam across a stream to make water available for mill; **mill'pond**, pond formed by a milldam; **like a millpond**, said of very calm sea; **mill'race**, current of water that drives mill wheel; **mill'run**, millrace; output of a sawmill; **mill'-stone**, one of pair of circular stones used in grinding corn; (fig.) heavy burden, crushing weight; **mill'-wright**, one who repairs or constructs mills. **mill** *v.* Grind or treat in mill; produce grooves etc. in (metal) by rotary cutter; produce regular markings on edge of (coin, esp. in past part.); thicken (cloth) by fulling; beat (chocolate) to a froth; (slang) beat, strike, fight (person) (orig. of cattle etc.) move

*A wood pulp factory in Novia Scotia utilizes the offcuts from timber **mills**, and also timber of a low grade quality which is processed and used to make fiberboard.*

around and around in a mass; **milling machine**, rotary cutter for metal.

mill[2] (mĭl) *n.* One-thousandth part of a dollar, as a money of account.

Mill (mĭl), **John Stuart** (1806–1873). English political economist; author of *On Liberty* (1859) and *Utilitarianism* (1861).

Mil·lay (mĭlā'), **Edna St. Vincent** (1892–1950). Amer. poet and playwright; awarded Pulitzer Prize, 1923.

mil·le·nar·i·an (mĭlenār'ēan) *adj.* Of, expecting, the millennium. ~ *n.* Believer in the millennium.

mil·le·nar·y (mĭl'enĕrē) *adj.* Consisting of 1,000 (esp. years).

mil·len·ni·um (mĭlĕn'ēum) *n.* (pl. **-len·ni·ums, -len·ni·a** pr. -lĕn'ēa). Period of 1,000 years; period of 1,000 years foretold in Rev. 20 in which Christ will reign on Earth; period of happiness and prosperity. **mil·len'ni·al** *adj.*

mil·le·pede = MILLIPEDE.

mill·er (mĭl'er) *n.* One who works or owns a grain mill; (entom.) popular name for some varieties of white or white-powdered insects; ~**'s-thumb**, pop. name of a small fresh-water fish (*Cottus gobio*), also called the bullhead.

Mil·ler[1] (mĭl'er), **Arthur** (1915–). Amer. playwright; awarded Pulitzer Prize, 1949; author of *All My Sons, Death of a Salesman, A View From the Bridge, The Crucible.*

Mill·er[2] (mĭl'er), **Henry** (1891–1980). Amer. author whose novels include *Tropic of Cancer* (1931) and *Tropic of Capricorn* (1938).

mil·les·i·mal (mĭlĕs'imal) *adj.* Thousandth.

mil·let (mĭl'ĭt) *n.* Any of several cereal grasses of the family Gramineae, growing 3 or 4 ft. high and bearing a large crop of minute nutritious seeds, esp. *Panicum miliaceum*; ~ **grass**, tall N. Amer. woodland grass (*Milium effusum*).

Mil·let (mĭlā'), **Jean François** (1814–75). French landscape and genre painter of the Barbizon school.

milli- *prefix.* One thousandth of (abbrev. m).

mil·li·bar (mĭl'ibar̄) *n.* (meteor.) One thousandth of a BAR[2] (abbrev. mbar).

mil·li·gram (mĭl'igrăm) *n.* One thousandth of a gram (abbrev. mg).

Mil·li·kan (mĭl'ikan), **Robert Andrews** (1868–1953). Amer. nuclear physicist; first to isolate electron; awarded Nobel Prize in physics, 1923.

mil·li·li·ter (mĭl'ilēter) *n.* One thousandth of a liter.

mil·li·me·ter (mĭl'imēter) *n.* One thousandth of a meter. (abbrev. mm).

mil·li·ner (mĭl'iner) *n.* Maker or seller of women's hats. **mil·li·ner·y** (mĭl'inĕrē, -nerē) *n.* [f. MILAN; orig., = vendor of Milan goods]

mil·lion (mĭl'yon) *n.* (pl. **-lions,** following a numeral **-lion**). Cardinal number equal to one thousand thousand, 1,000,000 (abbrev. m.); also as ordinal when followed by other numbers; one million pounds, dollars, etc.; enormous number. ~ *adj.* Amounting to one million.

mil·lion·aire (mĭlyonār') *n.* Person who possesses a million dollars; person of great wealth.

mil·li·pede, mil·le·pede (mĭl'-ipēd) *ns.* Myriapod with numerous legs placed on each of the segments in double pairs.

mil·li·sec·ond (mĭl'isĕkond) *n.* One thousandth of a second (abbrev. msec.).

Mi·los, Mi·lo: see MELOS.

milt (mĭlt) *n.* Spleen of mammals; sperm of male fish. **milt'er** *n.* Male fish in the breeding season.

Mil·ti·a·des (mĭltī'adēz) (d. *c*488 B.C.). Athenian statesman and general, victor at MARATHON.

Mil·ton (mĭl'ton), **John** (1608–1674). English Puritan poet; author of the epics *Paradise Lost* and *Paradise Regained* and many other poems. **Mil·to·ni·an** (mĭltō'nēan), **Mil·ton·ic** (mĭltŏn'ĭk) *adjs.*

Mil·wau·kee (mĭlwaw'kē). Largest city and a commercial and industrial center in Wisconsin, in the SE. on Lake Michigan.

mime (mīm) *n.* 1. (Gk. and Rom. antiq.) Kind of simple farcical drama, characterized by mimicry and dialogue for this. 2. Similar modern performance, play with mimic gestures and action usu. without words. 3. Actor in a mime; buffoon, jester. ~ *v.* Act in mime.

mim·e·o·graph (mĭm'ēograf, -grahf) *n.* Apparatus in which stencils are placed for making copies of written pages. ~ *v.t.* Reproduce by mimeograph.

mi·me·sis (mĭmē′sĭs, mī-) *n.* Representation or imitation of nature in literature and art; (biol.) MIMICRY.

mi·met·ic (mĭmĕt′ĭk, mī-) *adj.* Of, addicted to, imitation, mimicry, or mimesis.

mim·ic (mĭm′ĭk) *adj.* Feigned, esp. to amuse; sham; imitative. ~ *n.* Person who mimics. ~ *v.t.* (**-icked, -ick·ing**). Copy speech or gestures of, esp. to amuse others, imitate closely. **mim′ic·ry** *n.* (pl. **-ries**). Mimicking; thing that mimics another; (biol.) protective similarity of one animal species to another, the second being distasteful or poisonous to predators, or to an object in the environment for disguise or concealment.

mi·mo·sa (mĭmō′sa, -za) *n.* (pl. **-sas**, collect. **-sa**). Leguminous plant of genus *M*~, including the sensitive plant.

mi·na = MYNA.

mi·na·ceous (mĭnā′shus) *adj.* Threatening. **mi·na′ceous·ly** *adv.*

min·a·ret (mĭnerĕt′, mĭn′erĕt) *n.* Tall slender tower or turret of mosque, with projecting balcony, from which muezzin proclaims the hour of prayer. [Arab. *manāra*]

min·a·to·ry (mĭn′atōrē, -tōrē) *adj.* Threatening.

mince (mĭns) *v.* (**minced, minc·ing**). Cut (meat etc.) very small; walk, speak, with affected delicacy; **not ~ words**, be outspoken esp. in condemnation. **mince** *n.* Minced meat; **mince′-meat**, mixture of raisins, currants, apples, suet, spices, etc.; **make mincemeat of**, (fig.) destroy, demolish utterly; **mince pie**, pie filled with mincemeat.

*The **minaret**, the tower from which faithful Muslims are called to prayer, is always connected with a mosque and has one or more balconies or open galleries. Below left: Madresseh minaret, Isfahan, Iran. Below right: The oldest minaret in Baghdad, Iraq.*

*In biology, **mimicry** takes several forms. Some creatures survive because they look like dangerous or unpalatable ones; others have protective shape or color like their surroundings, such as this stick insect (facing page).*

mind (mīnd) *n.* Seat of consciousness, thought, volition, and emotion; intellectual powers; memory; opinion; **have a good ~ to**, feel tempted or inclined to (*do* something). **mind** *v.* Bear in mind; heed; take charge of; be vexed; have an objection (to).

Min·da·na·o (mĭndanow′). Second-largest island, 36,530 sq. mi. (58,813 sq. km), in the S. part of the Republic of the Philippines; **~ Deep**, deepest point, 35,400 ft. (10,620 m), of any of the world's oceans, in the W. Pacific Ocean off NE. Mindanao.

mind·ed (mīn′dĭd) *adj.* Disposed, inclined; (colloq.) alive to importance of, keenly interested in, as *air-*, *politically ~*.

mind·ful (mīnd′ful) *adj.* Taking

thought or care (of). **mind′ful·ly** *adv.* **mind′ful·ness** *n.*

mine[1] (mīn) *poss. pron.* Absolute and predicate form of MY; (archaic and poet., used before initial vowel or silent "h," or following a noun) = MY.

mine[2] (mīn) *n.* 1. Excavation from which minerals are extracted; (fig.) abundant source (*of* information etc.). 2. (mil.) Subterranean gallery in which explosive is placed to destroy enemy's fortifications etc. 3. (mil., nav.) Case containing charge of high explosive, detonated acoustically, electrically, or on contact; **mine′field**, sea or land area sown with mines; **mine′layer**, vessel for laying sea mines; **mine′-sweeper**, vessel for sweeping and destroying sea mines. **mine** *v.* (**mined, min·ing**). Dig for minerals; burrow or make subterranean passage in; lay, sow, mines under or in.

min·er[1] (mī′ner) *n.* Worker in mine.

min·er[2] (mī′ner) *n.*: see LEAF-miner.

min·er·al (mĭn′eral, mĭn′ral) *n.* 1. Substance (e.g. metal, coal, salt) obtained by mining. 2. (chem.) Element or compound occurring naturally as a product of inorganic processes. 3. (pop.) Substance that is neither animal nor vegetable. ~ *adj.* Of, belonging to, minerals; belonging to any of the species into which inorganic substances are divided; ~ **water**, water naturally impregnated with mineral(s), esp. those of a medicinal character.

min·er·al·o·gy (mĭnerŏl′ojē, -răl′-) *n.* Scientific study of minerals. **min·er·al·og·i·cal** (mĭneralŏj′ĭkal) *adj.* **min·er·al·og′i·cal·ly** *adv.* **min·er·al·o′gist** *n.*

Mi·ner·va (mĭnẽr′va). (Rom. myth.) Goddess of wisdom, identified with Greek Athene (which led to her being regarded also as the goddess of war).

min·e·stro·ne (mĭnĭstrō′nē; *It.* mēnĕstraw′nĕ) *n.* Soup containing vegetables and pasta. [It.]

Ming (mĭng). Name of dynasty that ruled in China 1368–1644; hence, porcelain etc. of this period.

min·gle (mĭng′gel) *v.* (**-gled, -gling**). (Cause to) mix; blend; unite *with*.

Miniature *painting was a direct descendant of manuscript illumination. Nicholas Hilliard was perhaps the finest of English 16th-century miniaturists and this 'Youth' is one of his most famous works.*

mini- *prefix.* Miniature, (very) small, as **min′ibus**, small bus, **min′iskirt**, very short skirt.

min·i·a·ture (mĭn′ēacher, mĭn′acher) *n.* 1. Picture in illuminated manuscript. 2. Painted portrait on small scale and with minute finish; reduced image or representation. ~ *adj.* Represented, designed, on a small scale; ~ **camera**, camera producing negatives less than 6 sq. in. in area, (esp.) one using 35-mm film.

min′i·a·tur·ist *n.* Painter of miniatures. **min′i·a·tur·ize** *v.* (**-ized, -iz·ing**). [L. as prec.]

min·i·mal (mĭn′ĭmal) *adj.* Very minute, the least possible.

min·i·mize (mĭn′ĭmīz) *v.t.* (**-mized, -miz·ing**). Reduce to, estimate at, smallest possible amount or degree. **min·i·mi·za·tion** (mĭnĭmĭzā′shon) *n.*

min·i·mum (mĭn′ĭmum) *n.* (pl. **-mums, -ma** pr. -ma). Least amount attainable, usual, etc. (opp. MAXIMUM); ~ **wage**, lowest wage that may legally be offered.

min·ion (mĭn′yon) *n.* Spoiled darling, favorite; (contempt.) servile agent; (print.) size of type (7 point).

*The weasel-like **mink** is found in the forests of North America and Eurasia. It is trapped or reared commercially for its prized pelt.*

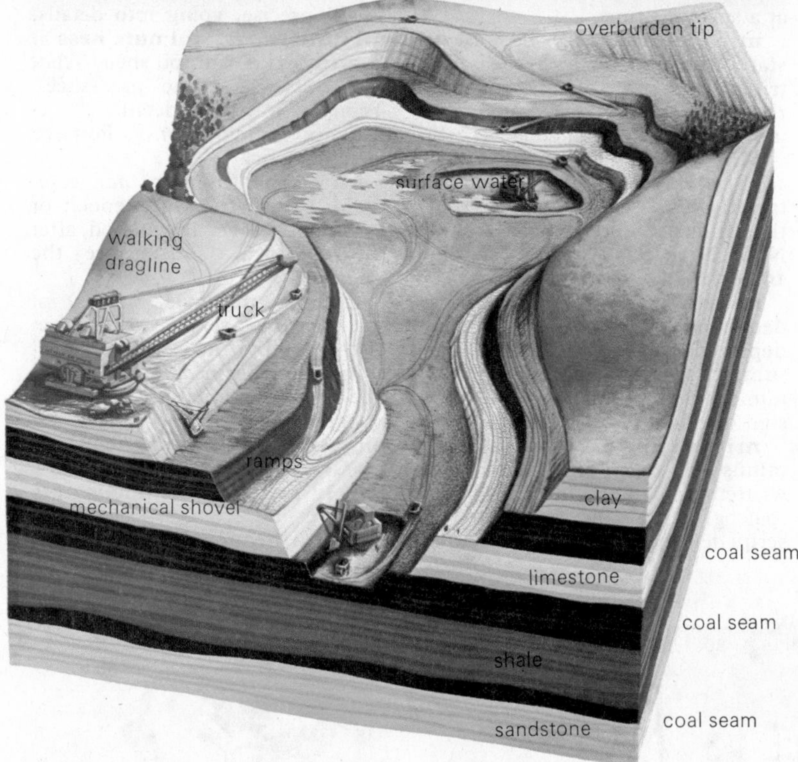

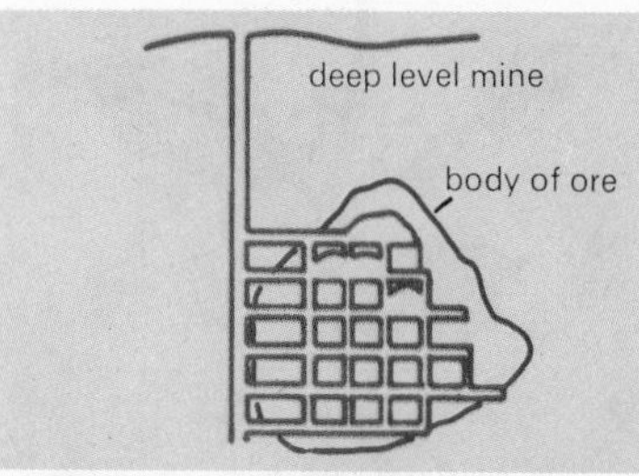

***Mining** can be broadly classified under two main headings — surface mining and underground mining. Top: Gold mining in South Africa, an example of underground mining. Center: Open-cut mining involves removal of waste material under which ores are situated. Left and below: Different mining systems.*

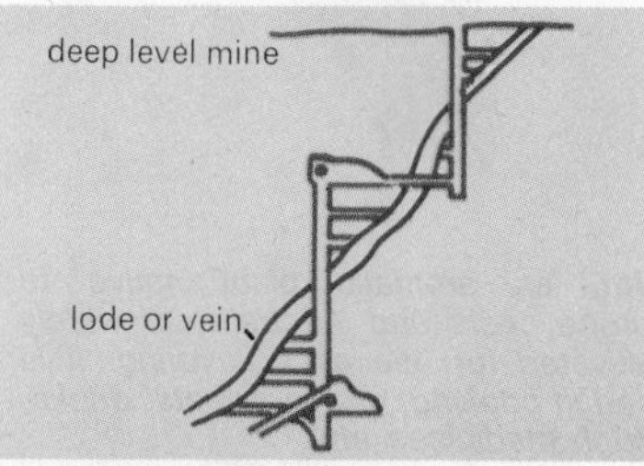

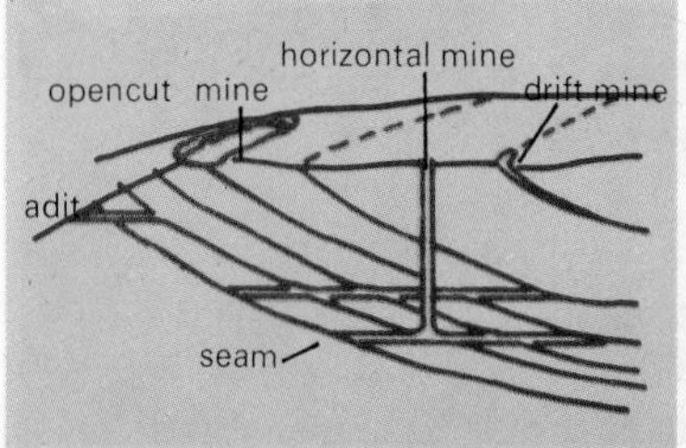

min·is·ter (mĭn´ĭster) *n.* 1. (Brit.) Executive agent; person in charge of a government department. 2. (Brit.) Diplomatic representative ranking below ambassador. 3. Clergyman. ~ *v.i.* Be serviceable or contributory; officiate as minister of religion.

min·is·te·ri·al (mĭnĭstēr´ēal) *adj.* Of a minister or his office; of the government.

min·is·tra·tion (mĭnĭstrā´shon) *n.* Ministering, esp. in religious matters. **min·is·trant** (mĭn´-ĭstrant) *adj.* & *n.*

min·is·try (mĭn´ĭstrē) *n.* (pl. **-tries**). 1. Priestly office; ministers of a church. 2. (Brit.) Office of minister of state; ministerial department of government, the building belonging to it; ministers forming a government.

mink (mĭngk) *n.* (pl. **minks**, collect. **mink**). Small semiaquatic weasellike animal of the family Mustelidae, esp. *Mustela vison* of N. Amer., valued for its thick brown fur; this fur.

Minn. *abbrev.* Minnesota.

Min·ne·ap·o·lis (mĭnēăp´olĭs). Largest city in Minnesota in the SE. on the Mississippi River.

min·ne·sing·er (mĭn´ĭsĭnger, -zĭng-) *n.* German lyrical poet and songwriter of the 12th to 14th centuries. [OHG. *minna* love]

Min·ne·so·ta (mĭnĭsō´ta). State in north-central U.S. on Canadian border; admitted to the Union in 1858; capital, St. Paul.

min·now (mĭn´ō) *n.* (pl. **-nows, -now**). Small fresh-water fish common in streams, ponds, etc.

Mi·no·an (mĭnō´an) *adj.* & *n.* (Person) of the Bronze Age civilization (lasting from *c*3000 to 1100 B.C.) revealed by excavations made in the Palace of Minos at Knossos in Crete.

mi·nor (mī´ner) *adj.* 1. Lesser (not followed by *than*); comparatively unimportant, as ~ **poet, prophet;** ~ **suit,** (bridge) diamonds or clubs; ~ **term,** (logic) subject of conclusion of categorical syllogism, contained in the ~ **premise**. 2. (mus.) Of intervals less by a semitone than the corresponding major intervals; ~ **key, mode,** one having a scale containing a minor 3rd (and a minor 6th and 7th); **in a** ~ **key,** (fig.) played down, doleful. **minor** *n.* 1. (law) Person below full age. 2. Minor interval, key, chord, etc. 3. Minor term or premise. 4. MINORITE.

Mi·nor·ca (mĭnōr´ka). Second largest of the Balearic Islands, in W. Mediterranean; hence, (also ~ **fowl**) black domestic fowl introduced from Spain.

Mi·nor·ite (mī´nerīt) *n.* Franciscan friar, so called because the Franciscans regarded themselves as of humbler rank than members of the other orders.

mi·nor·i·ty (mĭnŏr'ĭtē, -năr'-, mī-) *n.* (pl. **-ties**). 1. (law) State, period, of being under legal age (see MINOR). 2. Smaller number or part, esp. smaller party voting against majority; number of votes cast for this. 3. Group of persons smaller in number than majority group and differing from the majority in race, religion, language, opinion on an issue, etc. ~ *adj.* Of, relating to or done by a minority, as ~ *rights*; ~ **leader**, head of smaller party in a legislative body.

Mi·nos (mī'nos, -nŏs). Legendary king of Crete; in Attic tradition a cruel tyrant who every year exacted a tribute of Athenian youths and maidens, to be devoured by the Minotaur; **Palace of ~**, name given to the remains of the Bronze Age palace at Knossos.

Min·o·taur (mĭn'otŏr). (Gk. myth.) Monster half-man, half-bull, offspring of Pasiphaë and a bull, confined in Crete in a labyrinth made by Daedalus; eventually slain by Theseus.

Minsk (mĭnsk). Important commercial and industrial city in Russia near the Polish border.

min·strel (mĭn'strel) *n.* Medieval singer or musician; poet; one of a band of entertainers with blackened faces, dancing, telling jokes, and singing; ~ **show**, stage show with minstrels. **min·strel·sy** (mĭn'strelsē) *n.* Minstrels' art, poetry; body of minstrels.

mint[1] (mĭnt) *n.* Aromatic culinary herb of genus *Mentha*, esp. *M. viridis*, garden mint or spearmint; peppermint; ~ **sauce**, sauce made of finely chopped mint, vinegar, and sugar, used esp. with roast lamb; ~ **julep**: see JULEP.

mint[2] (mĭnt) *n.* Place, usu. under government control, where money is coined; (fig.) source of invention; vast sum *of money*; **in ~ condition**, (as if) newly issued from a mint, perfect. **mint** *v.t.* Coin (money); invent. **mint·age** (mĭn'tĭj) *n.* Coinage, money, esp. that issued from a particular mint at a specified time.

min·u·et (mĭnūĕt') *n.* Slow stately dance; music for this, in triple time; piece of music in this rhythm and style, often as movement of suite or sonata.

Min·u·it (mĭn'ūĭt), **Peter** (1580–1638). Dutch colonial administrator; purchased Manhattan from the Indians; director-general of New Netherlands (New York), 1626–31.

mi·nus (mī'nus) *prep.* With the deduction of (symbol −); (colloq.) deprived of. ~ *adj.* (indicating subtraction) Less; negative; (after number etc.) less than. ~ *n.* Minus sign or quantity.

mi·nus·cule (mĭn'uskūl, mĭnŭs'kūl) *adj.* Small; (paleog.) written in minuscule. ~ *n.* (paleog.) (Letter in) small cursive script developed in the early Middle Ages, dist. from MAJUSCULE or uncial; (mod. typ.) lower-case letter.

min·ute[1] (mĭn'ĭt) *n.* 1. Sixtieth part of an hour or of a degree (symbol '); short time. 2. Memorandum, brief summary, (pl.) official record of proceedings at a meeting. 3. ~ **hand**, hand indicating minutes on watch or clock; **min'uteman** (sometimes **M~**), Revolutionary War militiaman or citizen ready to march at a minute's notice; **minute steak**, thin slice of steak that can be cooked quickly. **minute** *v.t.* (**-ut·ed, -ut·ing**). 1. Draft; make minutes of. 2. Time exactly.

mi·nute[2] (mīnōōt', -nūt', mĭ-) *adj.* (**-nut·er, -nut·est**). Very small; precise, going into details. **mi·nute'ly** *adv.* **mi·nute'ness** *n.*

mi·nu·ti·a (mĭnōō'shēa, -sha, -nū'-) *n.* (pl. **-ti·ae** pr. -shēē). Trivial point; small detail.

minx (mĭngks) *n.* Pert or flirtatious girl.

Mi·o·cene (mī'osēn) *adj.* & *n.* (geol.) (Of) the third epoch or system of the Tertiary period, after the Oligocene and before the Pliocene.

mi·o·sis, my·o·sis (mīō'sĭs) *ns.* (pl. **-ses** pr. -sēz). Constriction of the pupil of the eye.

mir·a·cle (mĭr'akel) *n.* Event due to supernatural agency; remarkable event or object; ~ **play**, mystery play. **mi·rac·u·lous** (mĭrăk'yulus) *adj.* **mi·rac'u·lous·ly** *adv.* **mi·rac'u·lous·ness** *n.*

Mir·a·flo·res (mĭraflŏr'es,

*One of the original coin-stamping presses used by the **Mint** in Melbourne before 1965. Coins are now made in Australia at the Royal Australian Mint, Canberra.*

***Mint,** an aromatic plant native to Europe, Asia and Australia, is widely cultivated for use as a flavoring. It is used in cooking, and in sweets, drinks, cough medicines etc.*

-flōr′-). Village, artificial lake, and double locks on the W. side of the Panama Canal Zone.

mi·rage (mĭrahzh′) *n.* Optical illusion, common in sandy deserts, caused by refraction of nearly horizontal light rays by the hotter and therefore less dense layers of air near the surface, by which a distant object, directly invisible, appears to be near at hand, as though reflected in a sheet of water (also fig.).

mire (mīr) *n.* Swampy ground, boggy place; mud. ~ *v.* (**mired, mir·ing**). Sink in, bespatter with, mud. **mir·y** (mīr′ē) *adj.* (**mir·i·er, mir·i·est**).

mir·ror (mĭr′*er*) *n.* Polished or very smooth surface that reflects images; looking glass; (fig.) pattern, example; ~ **image**, image etc. with similar parts reversed as if reflected in a mirror. **mirror** *v.t.* Reflect as in a mirror (lit. and fig.).

mirth (mĕrth) *n.* Rejoicing, merriment. **mirth′ful** *adj.* **mirth′ful·ly** *adv.* **mirth′ful·ness** *n.* **mirth′less** *adj.*

MIRV (mĕrv) *n.* Guided missile that carries several warheads, each independently directed. [*m*(ultiple) *i*(ndependently) targeted *r*(eentry) *v*(ehicle)]

mis- *prefix.* Amiss, bad(ly), wrong(ly), unfavorably.

mis·ad·ven·ture (mĭs*a*dvĕn′ch*er*) *n.* Ill luck, bad fortune.

mis·al·li·ance (mĭs*a*lī′*a*ns) *n.* Unsuitable marriage.

mis·an·thrope (mĭs′*a*nthrōp, mĭz′-) *n.* Hater of mankind; one who avoids human society. **mis·an·throp·ic** (mĭs*a*nthrŏp′ĭk, mĭz-), **mis·an·throp′i·cal** *adjs.* **mis·an·thro·pist** (mĭsăn′thr*o*pĭst, mĭz-), **mis·an′thro·py** *ns.*

mis·ap·ply (mĭs*a*plī′) *v.t.* (**-plied, -ply·ing**). Apply wrongly. **mis·ap·pli·ca·tion** (mĭsăpl*ĭ*kā′sh*o*n) *n.*

mis·ap·pre·hend (mĭsăpr*e*hĕnd′) *v.t.* Misunderstand. **mis·ap·pre·hen·sion** (mĭsăpr*e*hĕn′sh*o*n) *n.*

mis·ap·pro·pri·ate (mĭs*a*prō′prēāt) *v.t.* (**-at·ed, -at·ing**). Apply dishonestly to one's own use. **mis·ap·pro·pri·a·tion** (mĭs*a*prōprēā′sh*o*n) *n.*

mis·be·got·ten (mĭsbĭgŏt′*e*n) *adj.* Illegitimate (often as vague term of opprobrium).

mis·be·have (mĭsbĭhāv′) *v. refl.* & *i.* (**-haved, -hav·ing**). Behave improperly. **mis·be·ha·vior** (mĭsbĭhāv′y*er*) *n.*

misc. *abbrev.* Miscellaneous; miscellany.

mis·cal·cu·late (mĭskăl′ky*u*lāt) *v.* (**-lat·ed, -lat·ing**). Calculate wrongly. **mis·cal·cu·la·tion** (mĭskălky*u*lā′sh*o*n) *n.*

mis·call (mĭskawl′) *v.t.* Call by wrong name; (sports) make incorrect call.

***Mirrors** using glass with a metallic backing were first produced in Venice in the late 12th century. This mirror with its ornate frame is in the Rococo style and is dated c.1740.*

mis·car·riage (mĭskăr′ĭj, mĭs′kăr-) *n.* Spontaneous abortion; failure of letter etc. to reach destination; ~ **of justice**, failure of court to do justice. **mis·car·ry** (mĭskăr′ē) *v.i.* (**-ried, -ry·ing**). 1. Fail; go astray. 2. Suffer a miscarriage.

mis·ce·ge·na·tion (mĭs*ĭ*j*e*nā′sh*o*n, mĭsĕj-) *n.* Interbreeding between races, esp. sexual union of whites with nonwhites.

mis·cel·la·ne·a (mĭs*e*lā′nē*a*) *n.pl.* Miscellany; odds and ends.

mis·cel·la·ne·ous (mĭs*e*lā′nē*u*s) *adj.* Of mixed character, of various kinds.

mis·cel·la·ny (mĭs′*e*lānē; *Brit.* mĭsĕl′*a*nē) *n.* (pl. **-nies**). Medley; miscellaneous writings etc. collected together.

mis·chance (mĭschăns′, -chahns′) *n.* (Piece of) ill luck, ill success.

mis·chief (mĭs′chĭf) *n.* Harm, evil, wrought by person or particular cause; worker of mischief; vexatious or annoying conduct, esp. of children; playful malice. **mis·chie·vous** (mĭs′ch*e*v*u*s) *adj.* **mis′chie·vous·ly** *adv.* **mis′chie·vous·ness** *n.*

mis·ci·ble (mĭs′*ĭ*b*e*l) *adj.* Capable of being mixed, esp. (of liquids) to form a homogeneous substance. **mis·ci·bil·i·ty** (mĭs*ĭ*bĭl′ĭtē) *n.*

mis·con·ceive (mĭsk*o*nsēv′) *v.* (**-ceived, -ceiv·ing**). Have wrong idea of, misunderstand. **mis·con·cep·tion** (mĭsk*o*nsĕp′sh*o*n) *n.*

mis·con·duct (mĭskŏn′dŭkt) *n.* Bad management; improper conduct, esp. adultery. ~ (mĭsk*o*ndŭkt′) *v.t.* & *refl.*

mis·con·strue (mĭsk*o*nstrōō′) *v.t.* (**-strued, -stru·ing**). Put wrong construction on (word, action). **mis·con·struc·tion** (mĭsk*o*nstrŭk′sh*o*n) *n.*

mis·count (mĭskownt′) *v.t.* Count wrongly. ~ (mĭs′kownt) *n.* Wrong count, esp. of votes.

mis·cre·ant (mĭs′krē*a*nt) *n.* Vile wretch, villain.

mis·cue (mĭskū′) *v.i.* (**-cued, -cu·ing**). (billiards) Fail to strike the ball properly. ~ *n.* Such a stroke.

mis·date (mĭsdāt′) *v.t.* (**-dat·ed, -dat·ing**). Put wrong date on.

mis·deal (mĭsdēl′) *v.* (**-dealt** pr. -dĕlt, **-deal·ing**). Make mistake in dealing (cards). ~ *n.* Wrong deal.

mis·deed (mĭsdēd′) *n.* Evil deed.

mis·de·mean·ant (mĭsdĭmē′n*a*nt) *n.* Person convicted of misdemeanor.

mis·de·mean·or (mĭsdĭmē′n*er*) *n.* Misdeed; (law) any indictable offense.

mis·di·rect (mĭsdĭrĕkt′) *v.t.* Direct wrongly; put wrong name, address, etc., on letter etc.; give wrong instructions to, specif. (of a judge) give wrong instructions to a jury; aim badly or without precision. **mis·di·rec′tion** *n.*

mis·do·ing (mĭsdōō′ĭng) *n.* Misdeed.

mise en scène (mēz ahṅ sĕn′). Scenery and properties of an acted play; (fig.) setting of an event or action. [Fr.]

mi·ser (mī′z*er*) *n.* One who lives miserably in order to hoard wealth. **mi′ser·ly** *adj.* **mi′ser·li·ness** *n.*

mis·er·a·ble (mĭz′*e*r*a*b*e*l) *adj.* Wretchedly unhappy, uncomfortable, or poor; causing wretchedness; pitiable, mean. **mis′er·a·bly** *adv.*

mis·er·i·cord (mĭz*e*rĭkōrd′, mĭzĕr′*ĭ*kōrd) *n.* 1. Room set apart in a monastery, where monks might take special food as an indulgence. 2. Projection on underside of hinged seat in choir stall, serving when seat is turned up to support person standing. 3. (hist.) Thin pointed dagger used in medieval warfare for giving coup de grâce to a fallen knight.

mis·er·y (mĭz′*e*rē) *n.* (pl. **-er·ies**). Wretched state of mind or circumstances.

mis·fea·sance (mĭsfē′z*a*ns) *n.* Wrongful exercise of lawful authority, as dist. from MALFEASANCE.

mis·fire (mĭsfīr′) *v.i.* (**-fired, -fir·ing**). (of gun) Fail to go off; (of internal combustion engine) fail to ignite (also transf.) ~ *n.* Failure to explode or ignite.

mis·fit (mĭs′fĭt) *n.* Garment etc.

*These Russian **missiles** were paraded in Moscow's Red Square in November 1971. A guided missile which is unmanned, may be remotely guided or direct itself to a preselected target.*

that does not fit; (fig.) person badly adjusted to his work or surroundings.

mis·for·tune (mĭsfôr′chun) *n.* Calamity, bad luck.

mis·give (mĭsgĭv′) *v.t.* (**-gave, -giv·en, -giv·ing**). (of heart, mind, etc.) Suggest misgivings to. **mis·giv′ing** *n.* Apprehension, uneasy doubt.

mis·han·dle (mĭshăn′del) *v.t.* (**-dled, -dling**). Handle (person, thing) roughly, rudely, or improperly.

mis·hap (mĭs′hăp, mĭshăp′) *n.* Unlucky accident.

mis·hear (mĭshēr′) *v.t.* (**-heard** pr. -hērd′, **-hear·ing**). Hear amiss or imperfectly.

mish·mash (mĭsh′măsh, -mŏsh) *n.* Confused mixture. [ME., redupl. of MASH[1]]

Mish·nah (mĭsh′na; *Heb.* mĭshnah′) *n.* (pl. **Mish·na·yoth** pr. mĭshnayōt′; *Heb.* mĭshnahyawt′). Collection of precepts forming basis of Talmud and embodying Jewish oral law. **Mish·na·ik** (mĭshnā′ĭk), **Mish′nic, Mish′-ni·cal** *adjs.*

mis·in·ter·pret (mĭsĭntēr′pret) *v.t.* Give wrong interpretation to; make wrong inference from.

mis·lay (mĭslā′) *v.t.* (**-laid, -lay·ing**). Put (thing) by accident where it cannot readily be found; hence, (euphemism for) lose.

mis·lead (mĭslēd′) *v.t.* (**-led** pr. -lĕd′, **-lead·ing**). Lead astray, give wrong impression to.

mis·man·age (mĭsmăn′ĭj) *v.t.* (**-aged, -ag·ing**). Manage badly or wrongly. **mis·man′age·ment** *n.*

mis·name (mĭsnām′) *v.t.* (**-named, -nam·ing**). Call by wrong name.

mis·no·mer (mĭsnō′mer) *n.* Wrongly applied name.

mi·sog·y·ny (mĭsŏj′inē, mī-) *n.* Hatred of women. **mi·sog′y·nist** *n.*

mis·place (mĭsplās′) *v.t.* (**-placed, -plac·ing**). Put in wrong place; bestow (affection etc.) on ill-chosen object. **mis·place′-ment** *n.*

mis·play (mĭs′plā) *n.* (sports) Wrong or faulty play.

mis·print (mĭs′prĭnt) *n.* Error in printing. ~ (mĭsprĭnt′) *v.t.*

mis·pri·sion (mĭsprĭzh′on) *n.* (law) Wrong action or omission, esp. on part of public official; concealment of knowledge of a felony by person not actively involved.

mis·pro·nounce (mĭspronowns′) *v.t.* (**-nounced, -nounc·ing**). Pronounce wrongly. **mis·pro·nun·ci·a·tion** (mĭspronŭnsēā′shon) *n.*

mis·quote (mĭskwōt′) *v.t.* (**-quot·ed, -quot·ing**). Quote wrongly. **mis·quo·ta·tion** (mĭskwōtā′shon) *n.*

mis·read (mĭsrēd′) *v.t.* (**-read** pr. -rĕd′, **-read·ing**). Read or interpret wrongly.

mis·rep·re·sent (mĭsrĕprĭzĕnt′) *v.t.* Represent wrongly, give false account of. **mis·rep·re·sen·ta·tion** (mĭsrĕprĭzĕntā′shon) *n.*

mis·rule (mĭsrōōl′) *v.t.* (**-ruled, -rul·ing**). Rule badly. ~ *n.* Bad government.

miss[1] (mĭs) *v.* Fail to hit, reach, meet, find, catch, or perceive; pass over; regret absence of; fail. ~ *n.* Failure.

miss[2] (mĭs) *n.* Title of (**M**~) or form of address to girl or unmarried woman with no superior title; girl (usu. contempt.); **misses,** applied to a range of garment sizes for women; so **junior miss,** (attrib.) for adolescent girls. [abbrev. of MISTRESS]

Miss. *abbrev.* Mississippi.

mis·sal (mĭs′al) *n.* (R.C. Ch.) Book containing the service of the Mass for whole year.

mis·sel (mĭs′el) **thrush** = MISTLE THRUSH.

mis·shap·en (mĭs shā′pen) *adj.* Deformed.

mis·sile (mĭs′il; *Brit.* mĭs′īl) *n.* Object or weapon capable of being thrown or shot.

miss·ing (mĭs′ĭng) *adj.* Not

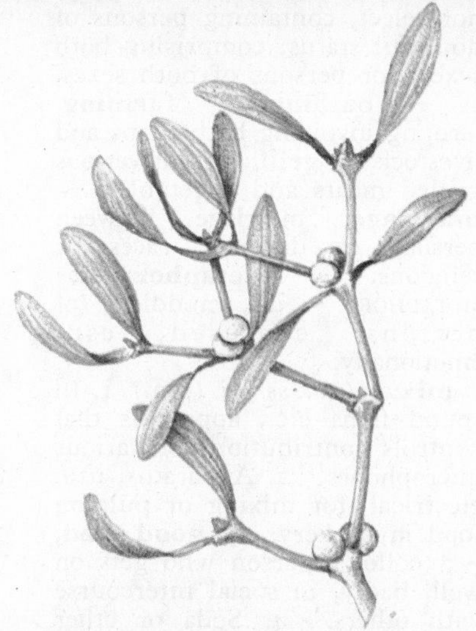

Commonly called ***mistletoe****, the Loranthaceae family of semi-parasitic plants is found in all tropical and many temperate zones of the world.*

present, not found; ~ **link**, pop. name of hypothetical intermediate type of animal between anthropoid apes and man.

mis·sion (mĭsh′*o*n) *n.* 1. Body of persons sent to foreign country to conduct negotiations etc. 2. Body sent by religious community to convert heathen; field of missionary activity; missionary post; organization in a district for conversion of the people; course of religious services etc. for this purpose. 3. Errand of political or other mission. 4. Operational sortie. 5. Person's vocation or divinely appointed work in life.

mis·sion·ar·y (mĭsh′*o*nĕrē) *adj.* Of religious missions. ~ *n.* (pl. **-ar·ies**). Person doing missionary work.

Mis·sis·sip·pi (mĭsĭsĭp′ē). State in southern U.S. on Gulf of Mexico; admitted to Union in 1817; capital, Jackson; ~ **River**, major river in N. Amer., 2,350 mi. (3,783.5 km), flowing from NW. Minnesota to the Gulf of Mexico, and forming borders of several states along its course.

mis·sive (mĭs′ĭv) *n.* Written message, letter.

Mis·sou·ri (mĭzoor′ē, *-i*). State in central part of the U.S.; admitted to Union, 1821; capital, Jefferson City; ~ **River**, longest river in U.S. flowing from W. Montana, 2,700 mi. (4,347 km), joining Mississippi River 10 mi. (16.1 km) N. of St. Louis, Missouri, and forming borders of several states along its course.

miss·y (mĭs′ē) *n.* (pl. **miss·ies**). Affectionate, playful form of address to girl or young woman, = MISS² (not followed by name).

mist (mĭst) *n.* 1. Water vapor precipitated in droplets smaller and more densely aggregated than those of rain; (meteor.) state of atmospheric obscurity (less dense than fog) produced by this, in which visibility exceeds 1 km (.621 mi.). 2. Dimness or blurred effect caused by tears in the eyes etc. **mist′y** *adj.* **mist′i·ly** *adv.* **mist′i·ness** *n.* **mist** *v.* Cover, be covered, (as) with a mist.

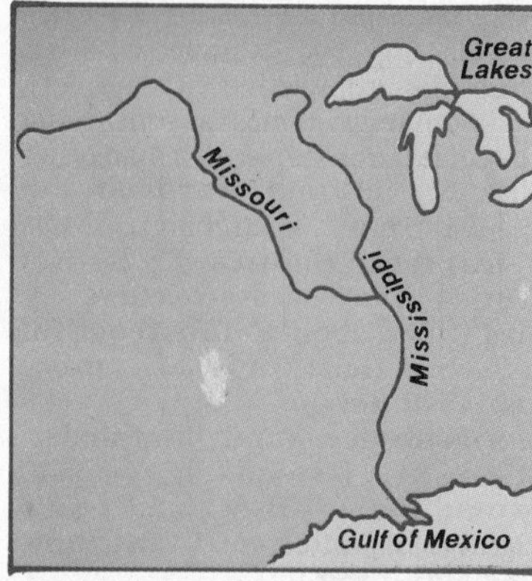

The ***Mississippi*** *(above) together with its main headstream, the Missouri, is the longest river in North America. Its combined length is 3,741 miles and there is a large delta where it enters the Gulf of Mexico.*

mis·take (mĭstāk′) *v.* (**-took** pr. -to͝ok′, **-tak·en, -tak·ing**). Misunderstand, take in wrong sense; be in error; take (one thing) erroneously *for* another; err in choice of. ~ *n.* Misunderstanding; something incorrectly done through ignorance or inadvertence. **mis·tak′a·ble** *adj.* **mis·tak′en·ly** *adv.* **mis·tak′en·ness** *n.*

mis·ter (mĭs′t*e*r) *n.* 1. (colloq.) Form of address to man, without any name following. 2. (colloq.) = MR.

mis·time (mĭstīm′) *v.t.* (**-timed, -tim·ing**). Time wrongly, do or perform at wrong time.

mis·tle (mĭs′*e*l) **thrush.** Large thrush (*Turdus viscivorous*) that feeds partly on mistletoe berries.

mis·tle·toe (mĭs′*e*ltō) *n.* Any of several evergreen plants of the Loranthaceae family, esp. *Phoradendron flavescens* of eastern N. Amer., parasitic on deciduous or evergreen trees, having thick yellowish-green leaves, small yellowish flowers, and white poisonous berries edible by birds; sprig of the plant often hung as Christmas decoration.

mis·tral (mĭs′tr*a*l, mĭstrahl′) *n.* Violent cold northerly or north-westerly wind in Mediterranean provinces of France etc., blowing esp. down Rhône valley. [L. *magistralis* masterful]

mis·tress (mĭs′trĭs) *n.* (pl. **-tress·es**). 1. Woman in authority over servants; female head of household. 2. Woman who has power to control or dispose *of*, as *you are*

~ *of the situation, you are your own* ~ (also fig.). 3. Woman who has thorough knowledge (*of* subject). 4. Woman who has a continuing sexual relationship with a man other than her husband; **wardrobe ~**: see WARDROBE. 5. (archaic) = MRS.

mis·trust (mĭstrŭst′) *v.t.* Not trust; have uneasy doubts or suspicions about. **mis·trust′ful** *adj.* **mis·trust′ful·ly** *adv.* **mis·trust′ful·ness** *n.*

mis·un·der·stand (mĭsŭnd*er*stănd′) *v.* (**-stood** pr. -sto͝od′, **-stand·ing**). Not understand rightly, misinterpret. **mis·un·der·stand′ing** *n.*

mis·use (mĭsūz′) *v.t.* (**-used, -us·ing**). Use wrongly, ill-use. ~ (mĭsūs′) *n.*

mite[1] (mīt) *n.* (orig.) Flemish copper coin of small value; hence (pop.) coin of very small value, esp. (also **widow's ~**) small money contribution (Mark 12); small object, esp. a child.

mite[2] (mīt) *n.* Any of several small arachnids of the order Acari, found as parasites.

mi·ter[1], Brit. **mi·tre** (mī′t*er*) *ns.* Bishop's tall pointed headdress, deeply cleft at the top; episcopal office or dignity. **mi′tered** *adj.* Wearing a miter.

mi·ter[2], Brit. **mi·tre** (mī′t*er*) *ns.* (carpentry) Joint in which line of junction bisects the angle between the two pieces, as in picture frame; ~ **box**, guide for saw in cutting miter joints. **miter** *v.* (**-tered, -ter·ing**). Join in miter; shape to a miter.

Mith·ras (mith′r*a*s). (Pers. myth.) God of light, often identified with the sun. **Mith·ra·ic** (mĭthrā′ĭk) *adj.* **Mith·ra·ism** (mĭth′r*a*ĭz*e*m) *n.* Religion involving worship of Mithras, introduced among the Romans under the Empire and spread over most of N. and W. Europe during the first three centuries A.D., becoming the principal rival at that time of Christianity.

Mith·ri·da·tes (mĭthrĭdā′tēz). Name of three kings of Parthia and of several kings of Pontus; **Mithridates VI Eupator** (131–63 B.C.), of Pontus, called "the Great," tried to drive the Romans out of Asia Minor, but was defeated by Sulla, and finally in 66 B.C. by Pompey; he was said to have rendered himself immune to poisons by taking them constantly in small quantities. **Mith·ri·dat·ic** (mĭthrĭdăt′ĭk) *adj.*

mit·i·gate (mĭt′*i*gāt) *v.t.* (**-gat·ed, -gat·ing**). Appease; alleviate, reduce severity of. **mit·i·ga·tion** (mĭt*i*gā′sh*o*n) *n.* **mit·i·ga·to·ry** (mĭt′*i*g*a*tōrē, -tōrē) *adj.*

mi·to·chon·dri·on (mīt*o*kŏn′drē*o*n, mīt*o*-) *n.* (pl. **-dri·a** pr. -drē*a*). Threadlike or granular organelle with outer and inner membrane, concerned in release of metabolic energy.

Moats *around a town or fortification were usually filled with water and designed to prevent invasion. This moat surrounds the medieval town of Aigues-Mortes in the Camargue, France.*

mi·to·sis (mītō′sĭs, mĭ-) *n.* (pl. **-ses** pr. -sēz). (biol.) Splitting of cell or nucleus accompanied by doubling of number of chromosomes, so that both the resulting two cells or nuclei have the same number as the original one (cf. MEIOSIS). **mi·tot·ic** (mītŏt′ĭk, mĭ-) *adj.*

mi·tral (mī′tr*a*l) *adj.* (anat.) Of the mitral valve; ~ **valve**, two-cusped valve (so called from fancied resemblance to bishop's miter) between left atrium and ventricle of human heart, preventing reflux of blood into atrium when ventricle contracts.

mi·tre (Brit.) = MITER[1, 2].

mitt (mĭt) *n.* Mitten; (slang, pl.) boxing gloves; baseball glove.

mit·ten (mĭt′*e*n) *n.* Glove leaving fingers and thumb tip bare; glove having no separate partitions for fingers, but only for thumb.

mix (mĭks) *v.* (**mixed, mixt, mix·ing**). Mingle, blend, into one mass; compound; ~ **it**, (colloq.) join in fighting; ~ **up**, confuse; **~-up** (*n.*), confusion; confused fight, mêlée. **mix** *n.* Mixture of materials (e.g. concrete, plastics) ready for a process.

mixed (mĭkst) *adj.* Of diverse qualities or elements; (of company) not select, containing persons of doubtful status; comprising both sexes; for persons of both sexes, as ~ **bathing;** ~ **farming**, farming involving both crops and livestock; ~ **grill**, dish of various grilled meats and vegetables; ~ **marriage**, marriage between persons of different races or religions; ~ **metaphor**: see METAPHOR; ~ **up**, muddled; (of persons) confused, esp. emotionally.

mix·er (mĭk′s*er*) *n.* (esp.) 1. In sound films etc., apparatus that controls contributions of various microphones. 2. Apparatus, usu. electrical, for mixing or pulping food in cookery. 3. **good, bad,** ~, (colloq.) person who gets on well, badly, in social intercourse with others. 4. Soda or other beverage used in mixed alcoholic drinks. 5. A party designed to help those who attend to meet others.

mix·ture (mĭks′ch*er*) *n.* Mixing; what is mixed, esp. medicinal preparation; mechanical mixing of two or more substances, involving no change in their character, opp. to *chemical combination*; (in internal combustion engine) gas or vaporized fuel mixed with air to form the explosive charges.

miz·zen (mĭz′*e*n) *n.* (naut.) Fore-and-aft sail on after side of **miz′zenmast**, the aftermost mast of a three-masted ship.

mk *abbrev.* Mark (coin).

mks *abbrev.* Meter-kilogram-second.

ml *abbrev.* Milliliter(s).

M.L.A. *abbrev.* Modern Language Association.

Mlle. *abbrev.* Mademoiselle (pl. **Mlles.**).

M.L.S. *abbrev.* Master of Library Science.

mm *abbrev.* Millimeter(s).

MM. *abbrev.* Messieurs.

Mme. *abbrev.* Madame (pl. **Mmes.**).

mmf, m.m.f. *abbrevs.* Magnetomotive force.

MN *abbrev.* Minnesota.

Mn *symbol.* Manganese.

mne·mon·ic (nĭmŏn′ĭk) *adj.* Of, intended to aid, the memory. ~ *n.* Mnemonic rhyme etc.; (pl.) mnemonic art or system.

Mne·mos·y·ne (nĭmŏs′*i*nē, -mŏz′-). Mother of the Muses. [Gk., = "memory"].

MO, Mo. *abbrevs.* Missouri.

Mo *symbol.* Molybdenum.

M.O. *abbrev.* Money order.

mo·a (mō′*a*) *n.* Any of various large extinct flightless birds of New Zealand, resembling ostrich (many species in family Dinornithidae). [Maori]

Mo·ab (mō′ăb). Ancient country of the Dead Sea.

Mo·ab·ite (mō′*a*bīt) *n.* (fem. **Mo·a·bit·ess** pr. mō*a*bī′tĭs). Member of a Semitic people traditionally descended from Lot (Gen. 19), living in Moab. ~ *adj.* Of Moab or the Moabites; ~ **Stone**, a monument erected by Mesha, king of Moab, *c*850 B.C., which describes the campaign between Moab and Israel of 2 Kings 3 and furnishes the earliest known inscription in the Phoenician alphabet; now in the Louvre, Paris.

moan (mōn) *n.* Low inarticulate sound expressing pain or grief. ~ *v.* Utter moan; lament.

moat (mōt) *n.* Deep, wide, usu. water-filled, ditch around castle, town, etc. **moat′ed** *adj.* Surrounded by a moat.

mob (mŏb) *n.* Riotous or tumultuous crowd; rabble; promiscuous gathering. **mob′bish** *adj.* **mob** *v.t.* (**mobbed, mob·bing**). Attack in a mob; crowd around and molest.

Mo·bile (mōbēl′, mō′bēl). Commercial city and seaport in SW. Alabama; ~ **Bay**, inlet of the Gulf of Mexico in SW. Alabama; scene of Civil War naval battle, 1864, in which the Union under Admiral Farragut routed the Confederate fleet.

mo·bile (mō′b*i*l) *adj.* Movable; characterized by freedom of movement; (of troops etc.) that may be easily moved from place to place; of changing expression, volatile. **mo·bil·i·ty** (mōbĭl′ĭtē) *n.* **mobile** (mōbēl) *n.* Piece of sculpture with parts free to move in currents of air; similar object of cardboard etc.

mo·bi·lize (mō′b*i*līz) *v.* (**-lized, -liz·ing**). Render movable, bring into circulation; call up, assemble, prepare, for war etc. **mo′bi·liz·a·ble** *adj.* **mo·bi·li·za·tion** (mōb*i*līzā′sh*o*n) *n.*

Mo·bu·tu (mōbo͞o′to͞o) **Se·se Se·ko** (sĕsĕ sĕ′kō) (1930–). Original name, Joseph Désiré Mobutu; president of Zaire since 1965; Lake **M ~ S ~ S ~**, formerly Lake Albert (see ALBERT).

moc·ca·sin (mŏk′*a*sĭn, -zĭn) *n.* 1. Amer. Inidan soft shoe of deerskin etc. 2. Amer. viper of genus *Ancistrodon.*

mo·cha (mō′k*a*) *n.* Coffee of fine quality orig. coming from Mocha, seaport of S. Yemen; flavoring of (chocolate and) coffee.

mock (mŏk) *v.* Hold up to ridicule; ridicule by imitation, counterfeit; jeer, scoff; befool, tantalize; **mock′ingbird**, Amer. passerine songbird (*Mimus polyglottos*) that imitates other birds' notes. **mock** *n.* Mockery; object of derision. ~ *adj.* Sham, counterfeit, pretended; **~-heroic**, burlesque imitation of, burlesquely imitating, the heroic style; ~ **olive**, Australian olive with succulent fruit and hard wood; ~ **orange**, shrub of genus *Philadelphus* (esp. *P. coronarius*), with creamy-white very fragrant flowers; sometimes called syringa; Australian native laurel (*Pittosporum undulatum*) with citrus-like leaves and heavily scented (usu. white) flowers; ~ **turtle soup**, soup made of calf's head to imitate real turtle soup; ~ **-up**, scale model.

mock·er·y (mŏk′*e*rē) *n.* (pl. **-er·ies**). Derision; laughingstock; impudent simulation; ludicrously or insultingly futile action.

mod (mŏd) *n.* 1. Style of dress that developed in England in the 1960s, characterized by bright colors, stripes, and designs. 2. British teenager of the 1960s who tried to appear worldly and detached and dressed cleanly and neatly in contrast to ROCKERS. ~ *adj.* 1. Pertaining to or characteristic of the mod style in dress and the people who adopted it. 2. Fashionable, esp. in dress.

mod·al (mō′d*a*l) *adj.* Of mode or form as opp. to substance; (mus.) of mode; (logic) involving affirmation of possibility, necessity, or contingency; (gram.) of the mood of a verb, (of particle) denoting manner. **mo·dal·i·ty** (mōdăl′ĭtē) *n.* (pl. **-ties**). **mo′dal·ly** *adv.*

mode (mōd) *n.* 1. Way, manner, in which thing is done; prevailing fashion or conventional usage. 2. (mus.) Ancient Greek scale system; any of the scale systems in medieval ecclesiastical music; in more modern music, the two (MAJOR[2] and MINOR) chief scale systems. 3. (statistics) That value of a character or graded quality at which the instances are most numerous.

***Model** making, as either a hobby or a craft, means producing replicas to scale of various structures such as buildings, automobiles, and human or animal figures. This example is of a model railway engine.*

mod·el (mŏd'*e*l) *n.* Representation in three dimensions of projected or existing structure or material object; design, pattern; object of imitation; (copy of) garment etc. by recognized designer; person employed to pose for artist etc. or to display clothes by wearing them; dummy for shop windows etc. ~ *adj.* That is a model; exemplary, excellent of its kind. ~ *v.* (**-eled, el·ing,** Brit. **-elled, -el·ling**). 1. Mold, fashion; produce in clay, wax, etc. 2. Wear for display; act as artist's model. **mod'el·ing** *n.* Making models, manipulating clay etc.; representation of form in sculpture or of material relief and solidity in painting.

mod·er·ate (mŏd'*e*rĭt) *adj.* Avoiding extremes, temperate; tolerable, mediocre; not excessive. **mod'er·ate·ly** *adv.* **mod'er·ate·ness** *n.* **moderate** *n.* Person, esp. politician, of moderate views. ~ (mŏd'*e*rāt) *v.* (**-at·ed, -at·ing**). Make or become less violent or excessive; act as moderator.

mod·er·a·tion (mŏd*e*rā'sh*o*n) *n.* 1. Moderating, moderateness. 2. Retardation of neutrons by MODERATOR.

mod·er·a·tor (mŏd'*e*rāt*e*r) *n.* 1. Mediator; Presbyterian minister presiding over presbytery, synod, or general assembly. 2. (nuclear phys.) Material used to dilute fissionable material so as to control nuclear reaction.

mod·ern (mŏd'*e*rn) *adj.* Of the present and recent times; new-fashioned, not antiquated; of school subjects, not concerned with the classics; ~ **face,** style of printing type. **mo·der·ni·ty** (m*o*dĕr'nĭtē, mō-) (pl. **-ties**), **mod'ern·ness** *ns.*

mod·ern·ism (mŏd'*e*rnĭz*e*m) *n.* Modern usage, expression, etc.; modern fashion in art; mode of theological inquiry in which the traditions and doctrines of Christianity are examined in the light of modern thought. **mod'ern·ist** *n.* Person favoring modernism. **mod·ern·is'tic** *adj.* (esp., of style) Following new fashions and innovations, advanced.

mod·ern·ize (mŏd'*e*rnīz) *v.t.* (**-ized, -iz·ing**). Make modern. **mod·ern·i·za·tion** (mŏd*e*rnīzā'sh*o*n) *n.*

mod·est (mŏd'ĭst) *adj.* Not overestimating one's own merits; not excessive; unpretentious; retiring, bashful; decorous, avoiding indecency. **mod'est·ly** *adv.* **mod'es·ty** *n.* (pl. **-ties**).

mod·i·cum (mŏd'*i*k*u*m) *n.* Small quantity or portion.

mod·i·fy (mŏd'*i*fī) *v.t.* (**-fied, -fy·ing**). Tone down; alter without radical transformation; (gram.) qualify sense of (word etc.); change vowel by mutation. **mod'i·fi·a·ble** *adj.* **mod·i·fi·ca·tion** (mŏd*i*f*i*kā'sh*o*n) *n.* Act of modifying, state of being modified.

Modular buildings make use of units which are completely prefabricated before assembly at the site. This method of construction is widely used for low-cost housing, school construction and other purposes.

*The **mole,** of which there are 22 species, is found throughout temperate Eurasia and North America. It is active day and night in rapid cycles of work and rest, and feeds on grubs and worms.*

mod·ish (mō'dĭsh) *adj.* Fashionable. **mod'ish·ly** *adv.* **mod'ish·ness** *n.*

mo·diste (mōdēst'; *Fr.* mawdēst') *n.* (pl. **-distes** pr. -dēsts'; *Fr.* -dēst'). Milliner, dressmaker.

Mo·dred (mō'drĭd) (also **Mordred**). In Arthurian legend, Arthur's nephew, who treacherously seized the kingdom during Arthur's absence and was killed by him in the last battle in Cornwall.

mod·u·lar (mŏj'*u*l*e*r, mŏd'y*u*-) *adj.* ~ **design,** (archit.) design based on a module or unit that is repeated throughout the building.

mod·u·late (mŏj'*u*lāt, mŏd'y*u*-) *v.* (**-lat·ed, -lat·ing**). 1. Adjust, tone down; attune to a certain pitch or key, vary in tone. 2. (mus.) Pass from one key to another. 3. (radio) Vary the frequency, amplitude, etc., of (a wave) by the effect of another. **mod·u·la·tion** (mŏj*u*lā'sh*o*n, mŏdy*u*-) *n.* Modulating, effect produced by this; **amplitude** ~, (abbrev. A.M.) transmission of signals by modulating the amplitude of the transmitted radio wave but keeping its frequency constant; **frequency** ~, (abbrev. F.M.) transmission of signals by modulating the frequency of the radio wave but keeping its amplitude constant.

mod·u·la·tor (mŏj'*u*lāt*e*r, mŏd'y*u*-) *n.* (radio) Apparatus used for modulating a carrier wave.

mod·ule (mŏj'o͞ol, mŏd'ūl) *n.* Unit of standard of measurement, as for flow of water; (archit.) unit of measurement for determining the proportions of a building, in classical architecture usu. half the diameter of a column at the base; independent unit forming section of spacecraft; **lunar** ~, self-contained segment of a spacecraft, designed to approach and land on moon independently.

mod·u·lus (mŏj'*u*l*u*s, mŏd'y*u*-) *n.* (math.) 1. Constant multiplier or coefficient, esp. for converting

Napierian into common logarithms. 2. Number by which two others are divided.

mo·dus (mō′d*u*s) *n.* Method, manner, mode; ~ **operandi**, method, system, of working; plan of operations; ~ **vivendi**, mode of living, esp. arrangement between disputants pending settlement.

Mo·ga·dish·u (mōg*a*dĭsh′o͞o). Capital and port city of Somalia, on the Indian Ocean.

Mo·gul (mō′g*u*l, mōgŭl′) *n.* 1. Mongolian, esp. one of the Muslim followers of Babur, who established an empire in India in 1526 that reached its zenith under Akbar and Aurangzeb, but declined after this, the last emperor being deposed by the British in 1857; **Great** ~, Mogul emperor. 2. **m**~, important or influential person. [Pers. *mugal, -ul*, pr. of *Mongol*]

mo·gul (mō′g*u*l) *n.* Small bump on a ski run.

mo·hair (mō′hār) *n.* (Yarn or fabric made from) hair of Angora goat; imitation of this made of a mixture of wool and cotton. [Arab. *mukayyar* cloth of goat's hair (lit. "select, choice," f. *kayyara* choose)]

Mo·ham·med[1] (mōhăm′ĭd, -hah′mĭd) = MUHAMMAD.

Mo·ham·med[2] **II** (mōhăm′ĭd, -hah′mĭd) (1430–81). Called "The Great" or "The Conqueror"; sultan of Turkey, 1451–81; captured Constantinople, 1453, effectively ending the Byzantine Empire.

Mo·hawk (mō′hawk) *n.* (pl. **-hawks**, collect. **-hawk**). (Member of) a tribe of N. Amer. Indians belonging to the Iroquois; language of this tribe.

Mo·hi·can (mōhē′k*a*n) *n.* (pl. **-cans**, collect. **-can**). (Member of) a warlike tribe of N. Amer. Indians, of Algonquin stock, formerly occupying W. parts of Connecticut and Massachusetts.

mo·ho (mō′hō) *n.* Discontinuity between Earth's crust and mantle; Mohorovicic discontinuity. **mo·hole** (mō′hōl) *n.* Hole drilled through seabed to mantle. [f. *A. Mohorovičić* (1857–1936), Yugoslav seismologist]

Mohs (mōz), **Friedrich** (1773–1839). German mineralogist, inventor of **Mohs' scale**: see HARDNESS def. 2.

moi·e·ty (moi′ĭtē) *n.* (pl. **-ties**). Half, esp. in legal use; (loosely) either of two parts into which thing is divided.

moire (mwār, mōr, mōr) *n.* Watered silk fabric. [Fr., perh. f. Engl. *mohair*]

moiré (mwahrā′, mōrā′, mawrā′) *adj.* (of silk) Watered; (of metals) having clouded appearance like watered silk. ~ *n.* (Fabric with) appearance like that of watered silk. [Fr., f. *moirer* water (silk)]

moist (moist) *adj.* Slightly wet, damp; rainy. **moist′ness** *n.*

mois·ten (moi′s*e*n) *v.* Make or become moist.

mois·ture (mois′ch*e*r, moish′-) *n.* Liquid diffused through air or solid, or condensed on a surface. **mois′tur·ize** *v.* (**-ized, -iz·ing**). Make moist; add moisture to.

Mo·ja·ve (mōhah′vē) **Desert.** Desert region in S. California.

mol *abbrev.* MOLE[4](S).

mo·lar[1] (mō′l*e*r) *adj.* & *n.* Grinding (tooth), back tooth of mammals. [L. *mola* millstone]

mo·lar[2] (mō′l*e*r) *adj.* (phys.) Of, acting on or by, masses (freq. opp. MOLECULAR); ~ **solution**, (chem.) solution containing one gram molecule of a specified substance per liter.

mo·las·ses (m*o*lăs′ĭz) *n.* Thick viscid syrup, drained from raw sugar during manufacture. [Port. *melaço* f. LL. *mellaceus* like honey]

mold,[1] Brit. **mould** (mōld) *ns.* Loose or broken earth, surface soil; earth of the grave; soil rich in organic matter; **mold′board**, curved iron plate at back of plowshare that turns over earth from the furrow.

mold[2] (mōld) *n.* Woolly or furry fungus growth forming on surfaces in moist warm air.

mold[3] (mōld) *n.* Matrix, vessel, in which fluid or plastic material is cast or shaped; pudding etc. shaped in mold; form, shape, distinctive nature. ~ *v.t.* Shape in or as in a mold; shape (bread) into loaves; model. **mold′er**[1] *n.* (esp.) Person employed in making molds for casting.

Mol·da·vi·a (mŏldā′vē*a*, -vy*a*). 1. (hist.) Danubian principality, from which, together with Wallachia, the kingdom of Rumania was formed in 1859. 2. Constituent republic (properly *Moldavian Soviet Socialist Republic*) of the U.S.S.R., formed from territory ceded by Rumania in 1940; capital, Kishinev.

mold·er[2] (mōl′d*e*r) *v.i.* Turn to dust by natural decay; crumble away.

mold·ing (mōl′dĭng) *n.* Molded object; ornamental contour given to stone, wood, or metalwork; material, esp. long piece of wood prepared for this.

mold·y (mōl′dē) *adj.* (**mold·i·er, mold·i·est**). Covered with MOLD[2]; moldering; stale, musty.

mole[1] (mōl) *n.* Abnormal pigmented prominence on skin.

mole[2] (mōl) *n.* Any of various small, insect-eating, burrowing mammals of the family Talpidae, having rudimentary eyes and very short strong forelimbs for burrowing; **mole′hill**, mound of earth thrown up by mole; **mole′skin**, mole's fur; strong, soft, fine-piled cotton twill, used for trousers etc.

mole[3] (mōl) *n.* Massive structure, esp. stone, serving as pier or breakwater.

mole[4] (mōl) *n.* Amount of a particular substance containing as many elementary entities (atoms, molecules, etc.) as there are atoms in 0.012 kg of carbon-12 (abbrev. mol).

mol·e·cule (mŏl′ekūl) *n.* 1. (chem., phys.) One of the minute groups of atoms of which material substances consist; smallest particle to which a compound can be reduced by subdivision without losing its chemical identity. 2. (loosely) Small particle. **mo·lec·u·lar** (mōlĕk′y*u*l*e*r, m*o*-) *adj.* Of molecules; ~ **weight**, weight of a molecule of a substance relative to weight of hydrogen atom.

mo·lest (m*o*lĕst′) *v.t.* Meddle with injuriously or with hostile intent. **mo·les·ta·tion** (mōlĕstā′sh*o*n) *n.*

Mo·lière (mōly ār′; *Fr.* mawlyĕr′). Pen name of Jean Baptiste Poquelin (1622–73), French author of comedies satirizing contemporary manners, including *The Misanthrope* and *The Imaginary Invalid*.

moll (mŏl) *n.* (slang) Gangster's female companion.

mol·li·fy (mŏl′ĭfī) *v.t.* (**-fied, -fy·ing**). Soften, appease. **mol·li·fi·ca·tion** (mŏl*ĭ*fĭkā′sh*o*n) *n.*

mol·lusk, mol·lusc (mŏl′*u*sk) *ns.* Any animal of the phylum Mollusca, which comprises soft-bodied unsegmented invertebrates (usu. having a hard protective shell) and includes limpets, snails, cuttlefish, oysters, etc. **mol·lus·cous** (m*o*lŭs′k*u*s) *adj.*

mol·ly·cod·dle (mŏl′ēkŏd*e*l) *n.* Person accustomed to coddling. ~ *v.t.* (**-dled, -dling**). Coddle.

Mo·loch (mō′lŏk, mŏl′*o*k). Canaanite god to whose image children were sacrificed as burnt offerings (Lev. 18, 2 Kings 23); hence, power or influence to which everything is sacrificed.

Mo·lo·kai (mō′l*o*kī). One of the Hawaiian Islands, 259 sq. mi. (417 sq. km); originally settled as a leper colony.

Mo·lo·tov (mŏl′*o*tawf, -tŏf, mawl′-; *Russ.* mawl′awtawf), **Vyacheslav Mikhailovich** (1890–1986). Russian statesman, minister for foreign affairs in U.S.S.R., 1939–49, 1953–6; ~ **cocktail**, crude incendiary hand grenade, consisting of a bottle of inflammable liquid and a wick, orig. used as antitank missile in World War II.

molt, Brit. **moult** (mōlt), *vbs.* (of birds or animals) Shed feathers, fur, skin, etc., which are later replaced by new growth; shed (feathers etc.) thus. ~ *n.* Molting.

mol·ten (mōl′ten) *adj.*: see MELT; (esp.) liquefied by heat.

mol·to (mōl′tō; *It.* mawl′taw) *adv.* (mus.) Very (preceding mus. direction, as ~ *allegro*).

Mo·luc·ca (mōlŭk′*a*) **Islands** (formerly Spice Islands). Group of islands forming part of the Republic of Indonesia.

mo·ly (mō′lē) *n.* (pl. **-lies**). (Gk. myth.) Fabulous plant with white flower and black root, given by Hermes to Odysseus as a charm against the sorceries of Circe.

mo·lyb·de·nite (molĭb′denīt, mŏlĭbdē′nīt) *n.* Molybdenum disulphide (MoS_2), a soft flaky black mineral resembling graphite.

mo·lyb·de·num (molib′den*u*m, mŏlĭbdē′n*u*m) *n.* (chem.) Grayish-white metallic element resembling tungsten and having a very high melting point, a constituent of special steel alloys; symbol Mo, at. no. 42, at. wt. 95.94. [Gk. *molubdos* lead]

Mom·ba·sa (mŏmbah′s*a*, -băs′*a*). Seaport of Kenya in the SE. part on the Indian Ocean.

mo·ment (mō′ment) *n.* Point of time, instant; importance, weight; (mech.) measure of power of a force to cause rotation around an axis.

mo·men·tar·y (mō′m*e*ntĕrē) *adj.* Lasting but for a moment. **mo·men·tar·i·ly** (mōm*e*ntĕr′*i*lē, -tār′-, mō′m*e*ntĕr-) *adv.* **mo′·men·tar·i·ness** *n.*

mo·men·tous (mōmĕn′t*u*s) *adj.* Important; weighty. **mo·men′·tous·ly** *adv.* **mo·men′tous·ness** *n.*

mo·men·tum (mōmĕn′t*u*m) *n.* (pl. **-ta** pr. -t*a*, **-tums**). (mech.) Quantity of motion of a moving body, product of mass multiplied by velocity; (pop.) impetus gained by movement.

Mo·mus (mō′m*u*s). (Gk. myth.) God of mockery; expelled from heaven for his criticisms and ridicule of the gods; hence, a fault-finder.

Mon. *abbrev.* Monday.

Mon·a·co (mŏn′*a*kō; *Fr.* mawnăkaw′). Independent principality, under French protection since 1861, on French Riviera, including Monte Carlo within its borders; capital, Monaco.

mon·ad (mŏn′ăd, mō′năd) *n.* 1. (hist.) Number one, unit. 2. (philos.) Ultimate unit of being (e.g. a soul, an atom, a person, God), esp. in philosophy of LEIBNITZ. 3. (biol.) Primary individual organism assumed as first term in a genealogy. **mo·nad·ic** (monăd′ĭk) *adj.* **mon·ad·ism** (mŏn′*a*dĭzem) *n.* Theory of monadic nature of matter or of substance generally, applied esp. to philosophy of Leibnitz.

Mo·na Li·sa (mō′n*a* lē′z*a*). Portrait, now in the Louvre, of a lady traditionally identified as the wife of Francesco del Gioconda, painted by Leonardo da Vinci and famous for its strange smile.

mon·arch (mŏn′*e*rk) *n.* 1. Sovereign with title of king, queen, emperor, or equivalent; supreme ruler (often fig.) 2. Large orange-and-black butterfly (*Danaus plexippus*). **mo·nar·chal** (monār′-k*a*l), **mo·nar′chic, mo·nar′chi·cal** *adjs.*

mon·ar·chism (mŏn′*e*rkĭzem) *n.* Principles of, attachment to, monarchy. **mon′ar·chist** *n.*

mon·ar·chy (mŏn′*e*rkē) *n.* (pl.

*These ruins are of the **monastery** of St. Honorat, Iles des Lerins, France. Monastic communities usually separate themselves from general society and are often self-sufficient.*

*This species of **monarch** butterfly (Danaus chrysippus) is found in Africa. It is often called the Plain Tiger butterfly. The best-known of the species is Danaus plexippus.*

*The **Mona Lisa** or 'La Gioconda' is Leonardo da Vinci's most famous painting. It was painted between 1503 and 1506 and portrays the wife of a Florentine official.*

-chies). (Nation under) monarchical government.

mon·as·ter·y (mŏn′astĕrē) *n.* (pl. **-ter·ies**). Residence of community of monks.

mo·nas·tic (monăs′tĭk) *adj.* Of monks or monasteries; secluded, austere. **mo·nas′ti·cal·ly** *adv.* **mo·nas·ti·cism** (monăs′tisĭzem) *n.*

mon·a·zite (mŏn′azīt) *n.* Phosphate mineral, containing thorium and rare-earth elements, found in alluvial sands in India and Brazil.

Mon·day (mŭn′dā, -dē) *n.* Second day of the week. [OE. *Monan daeg* (= moon's day), rendering of LL. *lunae dies*]

Mon·dri·an (mŏn′drēahn), **Piet Cornelis** (1872–1944). Dutch painter.

Mo·net (mōnā′; *Fr.* mawnĕ′), **Claude** (1840–1926). French Impressionist painter.

mon·e·tar·y (mŏn′ĭtĕrē, mŭn′-) *adj.* Of coinage or money. **mon′e·ta·rist** *n.* One who advocates control of money as chief method of stabilizing the economy.

mon·ey (mŭn′ē) *n.* (pl. **mon·eys, mon·ies**). 1. Current coin; coin and promissory documents representing it, esp. (**paper ~**) government and bank notes; (econ.) anything generally accepted in settlement of debts. 2. (with pl.) Particular coin. 3. (pl., archaic or legal) Sums of money. 4. **~ bill**, a bill, originating in the House of Representatives, involving expenditure or raising of money for public purposes; **mon′eychanger**, one whose business it is to change money at a fixed rate; **mon′ey-grubber**, one bent on accumulating money; avaricious person; **mon′eylender**, one who lends money at interest; **money market**, sphere of operations of dealers in loans, stocks, and shares; **money order**, order for payment of money, issued by a post office or bank; **money supply**, (econ.) amount of currency plus demand or checking account deposits in public hands; **money's worth**, anything recognized as good value for one's money; **mon′eywort**, creeping herb (*Lysimachia nummularia*) with round leaves and single yellow flower; creeping Jenny. **mon·eyed** (mŭn′ēd) *adj.* Wealthy.

Monet, *one of the founders of Impressionism, painted directly from nature. This painting, entitled 'Tempete, Rochers de Belle-Isle', was executed in 1886 when Monet visited this rugged island off Brittany.*

Moneywort, *a perennial trailing plant of European origin, has round glossy leaves and small yellow flowers in the axils of the leaves. It is also called Creeping Jenny.*

mon·ger (mŭng′ger, mŏng-′) *n.* Dealer, trader (chiefly in combination, as **fish′monger, i′ronmonger**, and fig. **scan′dal-monger**).

Mon·gol (mŏng′gol, -gōl, mŏn-′) *adj.* & *n.* 1. (Member, language) of a pastoral people of Mongolia.

2. (Person) with Mongoloid characteristics.

Mon·go·li·a (mŏnggō´lēa, mŏngō´-). Region in Asia including **Inner** and **Outer** ~: see MONGOLIAN.

Mon·go·li·an (mŏnggō´lēan, mŏngō´-) *adj.* Of the Mongols or their language; Mongoloid; **Inner ~ Autonomous Region**, autonomous region of China (formerly Inner Mongolia), capital, Huhehot; ~ **People's Republic**, republic N. of China (formerly Outer Mongolia); capital, Ulan Bator. **Mongolian** *n.* Mongolian person.

mon·go·lism (mŏng´golĭzem, mŏn´-) *n.* Type of congenital mental deficiency characterized by a supposedly Mongoloid appearance.

Mon·go·loid (mŏng´goloid, mŏn´-) *adj.* & *n.* 1. (Person) resembling the Mongolians, esp. (member) of the yellow-skinned division of mankind with high cheekbones, small nose, and broad face, found esp. in Mongolia and adjacent countries and including most of the Asian peoples. 2. **m** ~, (person) suffering from mongolism.

mon·goose (mŏng´go͞os, mŏn´-) *n.* (pl. **-goos·es**). 1. Small carnivorous mammal of Old World tropics esp. of genus *Herpestes*, esp. the Indian gray mongoose (*H. edwardsi*), known for its ability to kill snakes and rodents.

mon·grel (mŏng´grel, mŭng´-) *adj.* & *n.* (Animal, esp. dog) of no definable breed or type, resulting from various crossings; hybrid. **mon'grel·ism** *n.* **mon'grel·ize** *v.t.* (**-ized, -iz·ing**).

mon·ism (mŏn´ĭzem) *n.* (philos.)

The ***mongoose*** *is found in Africa, Asia and south Europe. It is an active, bold predator that lives in burrows and feeds on small animals, birds, reptiles and eggs. Shown here are the grey mongoose and the banded species.*

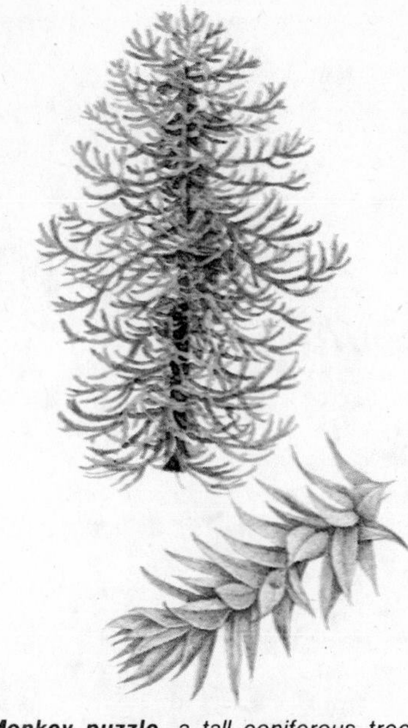

Monkey puzzle, *a tall coniferous tree native to Chile, has stiff, spirally-arranged leaves that discourage animals from attempting to climb the tree. It has edible seeds.*

Any theory denying the duality of matter and mind, as dist. from DUALISM and PLURALISM. **mon'ist** *n.* **mo·nis·tic** (monĭs´tĭk, mō-) *adj.*

mon·i·tor (mŏn´ĭter) *n.* 1. (archaic) One who admonishes. 2. (fem. **mon·i·tress** pr. mŏn´ĭtrĭs) Senior pupil in school with disciplinary functions. 3. One who is appointed to listen to and report on foreign broadcasts, telephone conversations, etc. 4. Receiving apparatus used in monitoring; detector for induced radioactivity, esp. among atomic plant workers. 5. Kind of Old World tropical lizard of genus *Varanus*, supposed to give warning of the vicinity of crocodiles. 6. (hist.) Ironclad vessel with low freeboard and revolving gun turrets, for coast defense, so called from name of first vessel of this type, designed by Capt. Ericsson, in the Civil War, 1862. ~ *v.t.* Act as monitor of (broadcast etc.). **mon·i·to·ry** (mŏn´ĭtōrē, -tōrē) *adj.* Admonishing; connected with, pertaining to, school monitors.

monk (mŭngk) *n.* Member of community of men living apart from the world under religious vows and according to a rule; **monks'hood**, aconite. **monk'-dom** *n.* **monk'ish** *adj.*

mon·key (mŭng´kē) *n.* (pl. **-keys**). 1. One of a group of mammals allied to and resembling man and ranging from anthropoid apes to marmosets; any animal of order Primates except man, the tarsiers, and the lemurs, usu. restricted to the small, long-tailed members, as dist. from the large, short-tailed apes. 2. Mischievous, playful young person. 3. Machine hammer for pile driving. 4. **have a ~ on one's back**, (slang) be a drug addict; ~ **bread**, fruit of the baobab tree; ~ **business**, (slang) mischief; ~ **engine**, engine that lifts the head of a pile driver; ~ **jacket**, sailor's short close-fitting jacket; ~ **puzzle**, S. Amer. coniferous tree (*Araucaria imbricata*) with broad prickly spines growing at intervals down the branches; **mon'keyshines**, (slang) mischief; **monkey wrench**, wrench or spanner with adjustable jaws. **monkey** *v.i.* (**-keyed, -key·ing**). Fool *about*, play mischievous tricks (*with*).

mono-, mon- *prefixes.* Alone, sole, single.

mon·o·ba·sic (mŏnobā´sĭk) *adj.* (chem., of an acid) Having only one acidic hydrogen atom in its molecule.

mon·o·car·pic (mŏnokar´pĭk), **mon·o·car·pous** (mŏnokar´pus) *adjs.* (bot.) Bearing fruit once and then dying.

mon·o·chrome (mŏn´okrōm) *n.* & *adj.* (Picture etc.) having only one color, or executed in different shades of one color. **mon·o·chro·mat·ic** (mŏnokrōmăt´ĭk, -ōkro-) *adj.*

mon·o·cle (mŏn´okel) *n.* Single eyeglass.

mon·o·cot·y·le·don (mŏno-kŏtĭlē´don) *n.* Plant having a single cotyledon or seed leaf. **mon·o·cot·y·le'don·ous** *adj.*

mo·noc·u·lar (monŏk´yuler) *adj.* Of, adapted for, one eye, as ~ **microscope**.

Some common ***monkeys*** *of the Old and New Worlds are shown here. Most monkeys are tree-dwellers and active by day; and many live in groups. They are popular zoo exhibits and are widely used in experimental studies because their physiology is similar to that of man.*

Humboldt's woolly monkey
Vervet monkey
Geoffreys spider monkey
Red howler monkey
colobus monkey
squirrel monkey
mona monkey
sooty mangabey
De Brazza's monkey
Diana monkey
Patas monkey

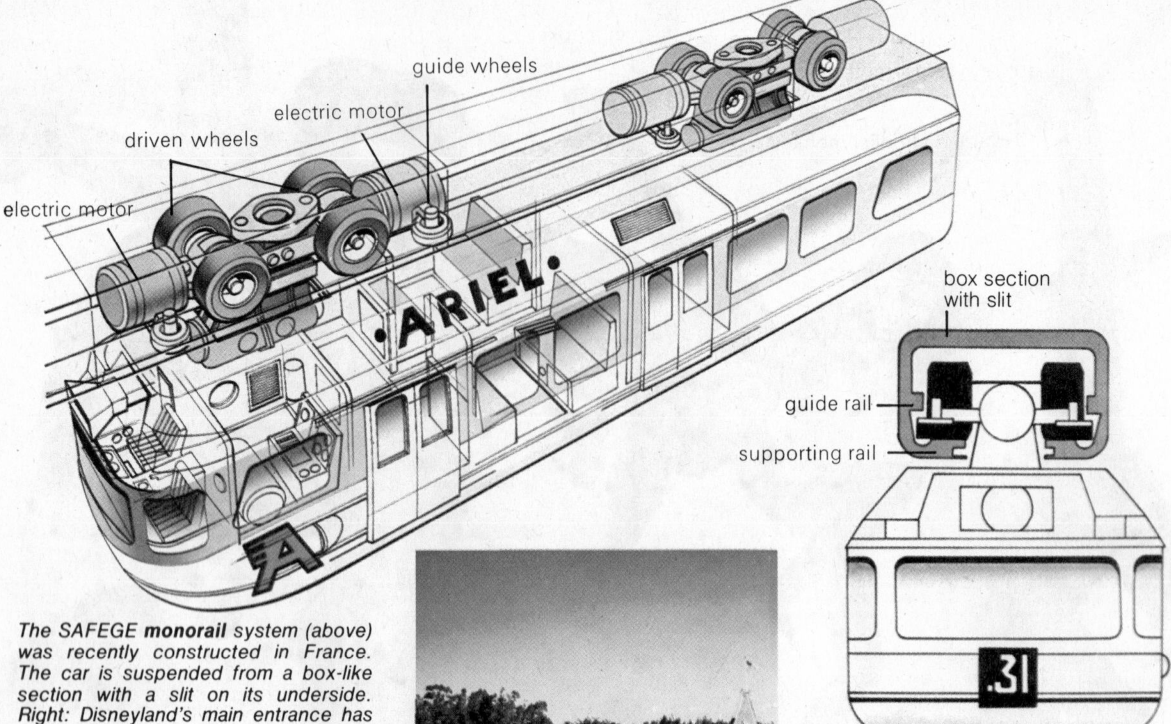

*The SAFEGE **monorail** system (above) was recently constructed in France. The car is suspended from a box-like section with a slit on its underside. Right: Disneyland's main entrance has this monorail train to carry visitors around the fair.*

mon·o·dy (mŏn′odē) *n.* (pl. **-dies**). 1. (Gk. antiq.) Lyric ode sung by a single voice. 2. Dirge, elegy. **mo·nod·ic** (monŏd′ĭk) *adj.* **mon′o·dist** *n.*

mo·noe·cious (monē′shus) *adj.* (bot.) Having reproductive organs of both sexes on same plant (but, if a flowering plant, in different flowers).

mo·nog·a·my (monŏg′amē) *n.* Condition, rule, or custom of being married to only one person at a time, as dist. from *polygamy*. **mo·nog′a·mist** *n.* **mo·nog′a·mous** *adj.*

mon·o·gram (mŏn′ogrăm) *n.* Character composed of two or more interwoven letters. **mon·o·gram·mat·ic** (mŏnogramăt′ĭk) *adj.*

mon·o·graph (mŏn′ogrăf, -grahf) *n.* Treatise on single object or class of objects. **mo·nog·ra·pher** (monŏg′rafer) *n.* **mon·o·graph·ic** (mŏnogrăf′ĭk, -grah′fĭk) *adj.* **mon·o·graph′i·cal·ly** *adv.*

mon·o·lith (mŏn′olĭth) *n.* 1. Single block of stone as pillar or monument. 2. (building) Mass of concrete, masonry, etc., forming a solid element in a structure. 3. Political or social structure presenting an indivisible or unbroken unity. **mon·o·lith·ic** (mŏnolĭth′ĭk) *adj.* Of, like, a monolith; unified and homogeneous; not exhibiting deviation or minority interests.

mon·o·logue (mŏn′olŏg, -lawg) *n.* Soliloquy; dramatic composition for a single performer. **mon·o·log·i·cal** (mŏnolŏj′ĭkal) *adj.*

mon·o·log·ist (mŏn′olŏgĭst, -lawg-, monŏl′ojĭst) *n.* **mo·nol·o·gize** (monŏl′ojīz) *v.i.* (**-gized, -giz·ing**).

mon·o·ma·ni·a (mŏnomā′nēa, -mān′ya) *n.* Form of insanity, obsession of the mind by a single idea or interest. **mon·o·ma·ni·ac** (mŏnomā′nēăk) *n.*

mon·o·mer (mŏn′omer) *n.* (chem.) 1. One of the units forming a polymer molecule (see POLYMER). 2. Compound that can undergo polymerization.

mon·o·met·al·ism (mŏnomĕt′alĭzem) *n.* Use of standard currency based on one metal.

mo·no·mi·al (mōnō′mēal, mo-) *adj.* & *n.* (alg.) (Expression) consisting of a single term.

Mo·non·ga·he·la (monŏnggahē′la). River flowing from N. West Virginia joining the Allegheny to form the Ohio River at Pittsburgh, Pennsylvania.

mon·o·nu·cle·o·sis (mŏnōnōōklēō′sĭs, -nū-, mōno-) *n.* Acute infectious disease with symptoms of sudden fever, benign swelling of lymph nodes, and presence of an abnormally large number of leucocytes with single nuclei in the bloodstream.

mon·o·phon·ic (mŏnofŏn′ĭk) *adj.* (of recording) Sounding as from a single source (opp. STEREOPHONIC).

mon·o·plane (mŏn′oplān) *n.* Airplane with one plane, as distinct from *biplane*.

mo·nop·o·list (monŏp′olĭst) *n.* Holder or supporter of monopoly.

mo·nop·o·lize (monŏp′olīz) *v.t.* (**-ized, -iz·ing**). Secure monopoly of. **mo·nop·o·li·za·tion** (monŏpolĭzā′shon) *n.*

mo·nop·o·ly (monŏp′olē) *n.* (pl. **-lies**). Exclusive possession or control; exclusive trading privilege; company or group having such control.

mon·o·rail (mŏn′orāl) *n.* Railroad in which the track consists of a single rail.

mon·o·so·di·um glu·ta·mate (mŏnosō′dēum glōō′tamāt), **sodium glutamate.** Crystalline, water-soluble salt, used to intensify food flavors (abbrev. MSG).

mon·o·syl·la·ble (mŏn′osĭlabel) *n.* Word of one syllable. **mon·o·syl·lab·ic** (mŏnosĭlăb′ĭk) *adj.*

mon·o·the·ism (mŏn′othēĭzem) *n.* Doctrine that there is only one God. **mon′o·the·ist** *n.* **mon·o·the·ist·ic** (mŏnothēĭs′tĭk) *adj.*

mon·o·tone (mŏn′otōn) *n.* Sound continuing or repeated on one note, or without change of tone. **mon·o·ton·ic** (mŏnotŏn′ĭk) *adj.* 1. (mus.) In monotone. 2. (math.) With all members of a sequence

either increasing or decreasing.

mo·not·o·nous (m*o*nŏt′*o*n*u*s) *adj.* Having no variation in tone or cadence; lacking in variety, always the same. **mo·not′o·nous·ly** *adv.* **mo·not′o·nous·ness, mo·not′o·ny** *ns.*

mon·o·treme (mŏn′*o*trēm) *n.* (zool.) Mammal of subclass Monotremata, primitive egg-laying forms of Australasia including duck-billed platypus and spiny anteaters.

mon·o·type (mŏn′*o*tīp) *n.* 1. Print taken from a freshly painted card, plate, or block. 2. **M～**, (trademark) printing apparatus that casts and sets up type in single letters by means of a perforated roll that has been previously produced on another part of the apparatus.

mon·o·va·lent (mŏn*o*vā′lent) *adj.* (chem.) Having a VALENCE of 1. **mon·o·va′lence, mon·o·va′len·cy** *ns.*

mon·ox·ide (m*o*nŏk′sīd, mŏn-) *n.* (chem.) Oxide with one oxygen atom in the molecule.

Mon·roe (m*o*nrō′), **James** (1758–1831). Fifth president of U.S., 1817–25; formulator (1823) of the **Monroe Doctrine** that interference by any European nation in the Spanish-American republics would be regarded as an act unfriendly to the U.S., and that the American continents were no longer open to European colonial settlement.

Mon·ro·vi·a (mŏnrō′vē*a*). Capital and principal seaport of Liberia in the NW. on the Atlantic.

Mon·sei·gneur (mawṅsĕnyör′) *n.* (pl. **Mes·sei·gneurs,** pr. mĕsĕnyör′). Title or form of address to French dignitaries, esp. princes, cardinals, and bishops (abbrev. Mgr). [Fr.]

mon·sieur (m*o*syö′) *n.* (pl. **mes·sieurs,** pr. mes′*erz*; *Fr.* mĕsyör′). Title (corresp. to *Mr.*) or form of address (corresp. to *Sir*) used of or to Frenchman.

Mon·si·gnor (mŏnsē′ny*er*; *It.* mawnsēnyōr′) *n.* (pl. **-si·gnors,** *It.* **-si·gno·ri** pr. -sēnyōr′e). (R.C. Ch.) Ecclesiastical title attached to office or distinction usu. bestowed by pope; in some countries (e.g. France) = MONSEIGNEUR. [It.]

mon·soon (mŏnsōōn′) *n.* Seasonal wind prevailing in southern Asia, from southwest (**wet**

Monotremes *are egg-laying mammals present today only in Australia and New Guinea. The aquatic platypus (above) lives in burrows at the water's edge. Echidnas are insectivorous and covered with sharp spines.*

Monsoons, *which are periodical winds, change direction between land and sea according to season. When they are reversing direction these winds give rise to disturbances such as tornadoes and hurricanes, but the heavy rains they bring are essential.*

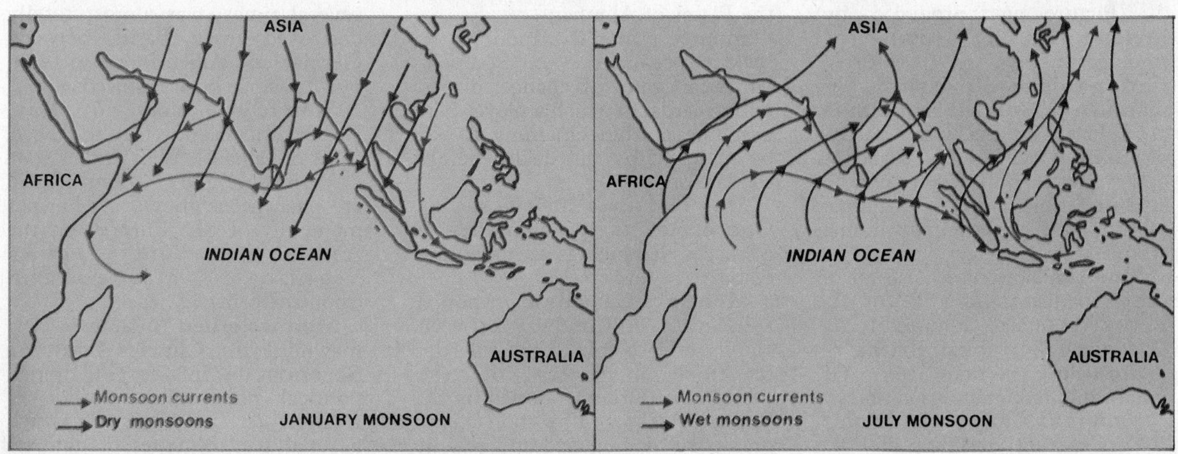

Montbretia, *although a native of South Africa, has become established in cooler climates as a garden ornamental. It belongs to the iris family and has reddish-orange flowers.*

~) in summer and northeast (**dry** ~) in winter; rainy season accompanying SW. monsoon. [prob. f. Arab. *mausim*, lit. season]

mon·ster (mŏn′st*er*) *n.* 1. Imaginary animal compounded of elements from various creatures. 2. Person or thing of portentous appearance or size. 3. Inhumanly cruel or wicked person. 4. (path.) Grossly malformed product of human conception.

mon·stros·i·ty (mŏnstrŏs′ĭtē) *n.* (pl. **-ties**). Monstrousness; misshapen or outrageous thing.

mon·strous (mŏn′str*us*) *adj.* Like a monster; huge; outrageous. **mon′strous·ly** *adv.* **mon′strous·ness** *n.*

Mont. *abbrev.* Montana.

mon·tage (mŏntahzh′; *Fr.* mawṅtahzh′) *n.* 1. (cinemat.) Selection, cutting, and arrangement of shots; presentation of a series of shots as a connected sequence. 2. (Picture etc. produced by) juxtaposition of (parts of) photographs etc.

Mon·taigne (mŏntān′; *Fr.* mawṅtĕn′y*e*), **Michel Eyquem de** (1533–92). French writer; author of *Essais*, which reveal a sagacious and tolerant philosophy of life, stressing the fallibility of the human reason and the relativity of human science.

Mon·tan·a (mŏntăn′*a*). State on the Canadian border E. of the Rocky Mountains; admitted to the Union in 1889; capital, Helena.

mon·tane (mŏntān′) *adj.* Of, inhabiting, mountainous country.

Mon·tauk (mŏn′tawk) **Point.** Resort area on the E. tip of Long

Montreal *is the largest city and chief port of Canada. French is spoken by two-thirds of the population, and the old French town (1642) is now the financial district. This view of the city is from Mont Royal Park.*

Island, New York State.

Mont Blanc (mawṅ blahṅ′). Mountain in France on Italian border; highest in Europe (15,782 ft., 4,810 m).

mont·bre·tia (mŏnbrē′sh*a*) *n.* English name of a commonly cultivated and extensively naturalized hybrid plant of two species of the genus *Crocosmia.* [A. F. E. Coquebert de *Montbret* (1780–1801), French botanist]

Mont·calm (mŏntkahm′; *Fr.* mawṅkăm′), **Louis-Joseph de Montcalm-Gozon, Marquis de** (1712–59). French commander of troops in New France; defended Quebec against Wolfe and was mortally wounded in the battle of the Plains of Abraham.

mon·te (mŏn′tē, mŏntā′) *n.* (also **three-card** ~). Spanish-American game of chance, played with 3 cards, in which a player bets that one of the remaining 2 will be matched by the dealer before the last one.

Mon·te Car·lo (mŏn′tĭ kar̄′lō). One of the three communes of Monaco; famous as a gambling resort.

Mon·te Cas·si·no (mŏn′tĭ kahsē′nō). Hill midway between Rome and Naples, site of the principal monastery of the Benedictine Order, founded by St. Benedict *c*529. The monastery, previously demolished and rebuilt

Bernard Law, ***1st Viscount Montgomery*** *of Alamein, defeated the German army under Rommel at Alamein in 1942, and was military commander of the Allied invasion of Normandy (1944).*

several times, was almost totally destroyed in a battle between German and Allied forces in 1944, but has since been restored.

Mon·te·go (mŏntē′gō) **Bay.** Resort and seaport on the NW. coast of Jamaica, West Indies.

Mon·te·ne·gro (mŏnt*e*nē′grō; *It.* mawntĕnĕ′graw). Former monarchy of SE. Europe, on the Adriatic; since 1919 a part of Yugoslavia. **Mon·te·ne·grin** (mŏnt*e*nē′grĭn) *adj.* & *n.*

Mon·tes·quieu (mŏn′teskū; *Fr.* mawnteskyö′), **Charles Louis de Secondat de** (1689–1755). French political philosopher; author of *L'Esprit des Lois* (1748), in which he analyzed the types of political

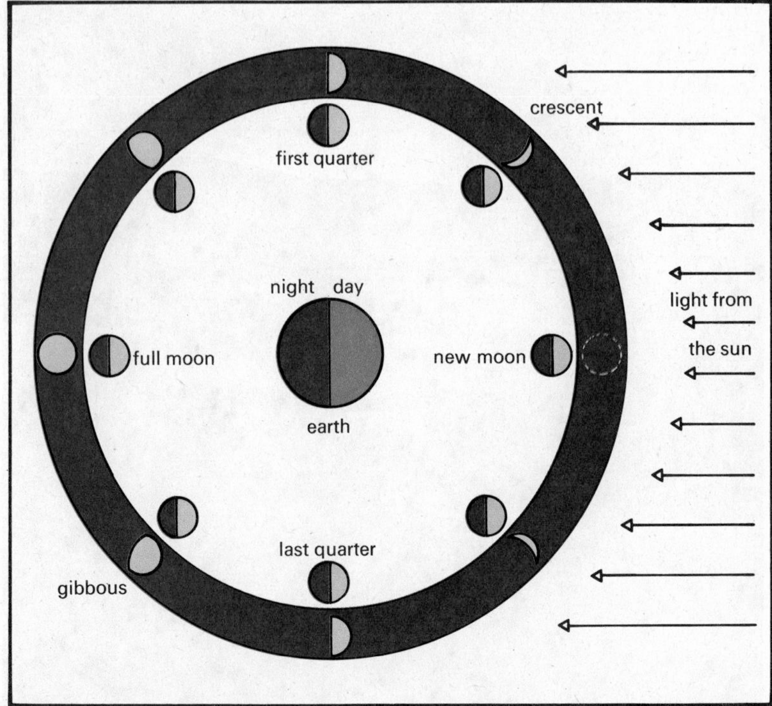

constitution and denounced the abuses of the French monarchy.

Mon·tes·so·ri (mŏnt*e*sōr´ē, -sōr´ē), **Maria** (1870–1952). Italian educator and physician; originator of a system of training small children by the use of apparatus teaching manual dexterity, the matching of colors or shapes, etc., under less rigid discipline than was formerly common.

Mon·te·vi·de·o (mŏnt*e*vĭdā´ō, -vĭd´ēō). Capital and seaport of Uruguay, in the S. part at the mouth of the Rio de la Plata.

Mon·te·zu·ma II (mŏnt*e*-zōō´m*a*) (1466–1520). Aztec emperor of Mexico at the time of the Spanish conquest; was seized and held as a hostage by Cortez, and mortally wounded when his people attempted to rescue him.

Mont·gom·er·y[1] (mŏntgŭm´*e*rē, -gŭm´rē). Capital of Alabama in the central part on the Alabama River; first capital of the Confederate States, Feb.–May, 1861.

Mont·gom·er·y[2] (mŏntgŭm´*e*rē, -gŭm´rē), **Bernard Law, Viscount Montgomery of Alamein** (1887–1976). British field marshal; commander of 8th Army from 1942 during the N. African campaign; commander-in-chief of British group of armies in France and Germany, 1944–6.

month (mŭnth) *n.* Period in which moon makes a complete revolution (**lunar** ~); one of 12 portions into which conventional year is divided (**calendar** ~); (loosely) period of four weeks.

month·ly (mŭnth´lē) *adj.* Done, recurring, payable, etc., once a

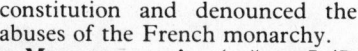

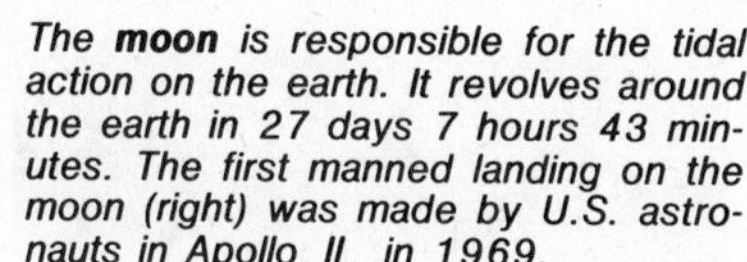
*The **moon** is responsible for the tidal action on the earth. It revolves around the earth in 27 days 7 hours 43 minutes. The first manned landing on the moon (right) was made by U.S. astronauts in Apollo II in 1969.*

month. ~ *adv.* Once a month; every month. ~ *n.* (pl. **-lies**). Magazine etc. published each month; (pl.) menses.

Mon·ti·cel·lo (mŏntĭsĕl´ō). Estate of Thomas Jefferson near Charlottesville, Virginia, including the mansion, which he designed, incorporating many innovations.

Mont·mar·tre (mawṅmar´tr*e*). District in the N. of Paris; during the 19th c. the artistic quarter and the site of many famous cafés and cabarets.

Mont·par·nasse (mawṅpar-nahs´). District in the S. of Paris on the left bank of the Seine known for the intellectuals and artists who gather there.

Mont·pe·lier (mŏntpēl´y*er*). Capital of Vermont in the central part.

Mon·tre·al (mŏntrēawl´, mŭn-). Largest city and a port in Canada, on the St. Lawrence River, in Quebec.

Mont Saint Mi·chel (mawṅ săṅ mēshĕl´). Islet off the coast of Normandy, a rocky peak crowned by a medieval Benedictine abbey fortress.

Mont·ser·rat (mŏnts*e*răt´, -raht´, mŏnt´s*e*răt, -raht). Island in the Lesser Antilles and a British dependency; capital, Plymouth.

mon·u·ment (mŏn´y*u*m*e*nt) *n.* Anything that by its survival commemorates person, action, or event, esp. erection intended to do this; a natural feature or area of special interest set aside by government as public property; work of enduring value.

mon·u·men·tal (mŏny*u*mĕn´-t*a*l) *adj.* Like, of, serving as, a monument; colossal, stupendous. **mon·u·men´tal·ly** *adv.* **mon·u·men·tal·i·ty** (mŏny*u*mĕntăl´ĭtē) *n.*

moo (mōō) *v.i.* (**mooed, moo·ing**) & *n.* (pl. **moos**). (Make) lowing sound.

mooch (mōōch) *v.i.* (slang) 1. Loaf *about*; slouch *along*. 2. Get food, money, etc. by begging.

mood[1] (mōōd) *n.* Frame of mind or state of feelings. **mood´y** *adj.* (**mood·i·er, mood·i·est**). Subject to changes of mood; depressed, sullen. **mood´i·ly** *adv.* **mood´i·ness** *n.*

mood[2] (mōōd) *n.* 1. (gram.) Group of forms in conjugation of verb serving to indicate function in which it is used, as INDICATIVE, IMPERATIVE, SUBJUNCTIVE ~. 2. (logic) Any of the classes into which each of the figures of a valid categorical syllogism is divided.

moon (mōōn) *n.* 1. Earth's satellite, a secondary planet reflecting light from sun to Earth during night, and revolving around Earth in one lunar month; first manned landing on moon was made on July 21, 1969, by U.S. astronauts Edwin Aldrin (1930–) and Neil Armstrong (1930–). 2. Aspect of moon at any one time as *full* ~, *new* ~, etc. 3. Any planetary satellite. 4. (poet.) Month. 5. **moon´beam**, ray of moonlight; **moon´calf**, born fool; **moon´light**, light of moon (often attrib.);

*The open **moor**, Exmoor in the U.K., has rich grazing land and its heathland is the home of red deer, grouse, ponies and sheep.*

moon'lighting, working at a second job after one's regular working hours; **moon'lit**, lit up by moon; **moon'scape**, general appearance of the moon's surface or a pictorial representation of it; **moon'shine**, moonlight; (fig.) visionary talk or ideas; illicitly distilled or smuggled spirits, esp. whiskey; hence, **moon'shiner**, illicit distiller, smuggler of spirits; **moon'shot**, (launching of) rocket or spacecraft traveling to moon; **moon'stone**, variety of feldspar having a pearly luster, used as a gem; **moon'struck** (*adj.*), lunatic, distracted or dazed, a condition formerly supposed to be due to the moon's influence; **moon'walk**, astronaut's walk on moon's surface. **moon'y** *adj.* (**moon·i·er, moon·i·est**). Of, like, the moon; listless, stupidly dreamy. **moon** *v.i.* Go *about* dreamily or listlessly.

Moon·ie (mo͞o'nē) *n.* (pl. **Moon·ies**). (slang) Youthful follower of Rev. Sun Myung Moon (1920?–), Korean anticommunist evangelist proselytizing in the U.S. beginning in the 1970s.

Moor (moor) *n.* One of a Muslim people of mixed Berber and Arab race, inhabiting NW. Africa, who in the 8th c. conquered Spain (see also MOROCCO). **Moor'ish** *adj.*

moor[1] (moor) *n.* (Brit.) Tract of unenclosed, often heather-covered wasteland, or of similar land preserved for shooting (also **moor'land**); **moor'hen**, water hen. **moor'ish, moor'y** (**moor·i·er, moor·i·est**) *adjs.*

moor[2] (moor) *v.t.* Attach (boat etc.) by rope to shore or something fixed. **moor'age** *n.* Place, charge, for mooring. **moor'ings** *n.pl.* Place where vessel can be moored.

Moore[1] (moor), **Henry** (1898–1986). English semi-abstract sculptor.

Moore[2] (moor), **Marianne Craig** (1887–1972). American poet.

moose (mo͞os) *n.* (pl. **moose**). Largest living species of deer (*Alces alces*) of Europe, Asia, and N. Amer.

moot (mo͞ot) *n.* (hist.) (Legislative or judicial) meeting. ~ *adj.* That can be argued, debatable; hence ~ **court**, in legal training, one in which students try hypothetical cases. **moot** *v.t.* Raise (question etc.) for discussion.

mop (mŏp) *n.* 1. Bundle of yarn etc. fixed to stick for use in cleaning, polishing, etc. 2. (slang) Head of hair, esp. of child. ~ *v.t.* (**mopped, mop·ping**). Clean or wipe with or as with mop; wipe tears, sweat, etc., from (brow etc.); ~ **up**, wipe up (as) with mop; (slang) absorb (profits etc.), dispatch, finish off, make an end of; (mil.) complete occupation of (place) by capturing or killing remaining enemy troops; ~ **up the floor with**, (slang) inflict humiliating defeat on.

mope (mōp) *v.i.* (**moped, mop·ing**). Be dull, dejected, and spiritless. ~ *n.* Person who mopes; (chiefly pl.) gloomy state of mind. **mop'ish** *adj.* **mop'ish·ness** *n.*

mo·ped (mō'pĕd) *n.* Motorized bicycle.

mo·raine (morān') *n.* Debris of sand, clay, and boulders deposited by melting glacier.

mor·al (mŏr'al, mär'-) *adj.* Concerned with character or disposition, or with the distinction between right and wrong; morally good, virtuous, righteous; ~ **certainty**, probability so great as to admit of no reasonable doubt; ~ **courage**, courage to encounter odium, contempt, etc., rather than abandon right course; ~ **philosophy**, ethics; **M~ Rearmament**, name of the ideological campaign launched by Dr. Buchman in 1938 as an extension of the Oxford Group, founded by him to foster morality in public and private life; ~ **support**, psychological support, encouragement; ~ **victory**, defeat, indecisive result, that eventually produces the moral effects of

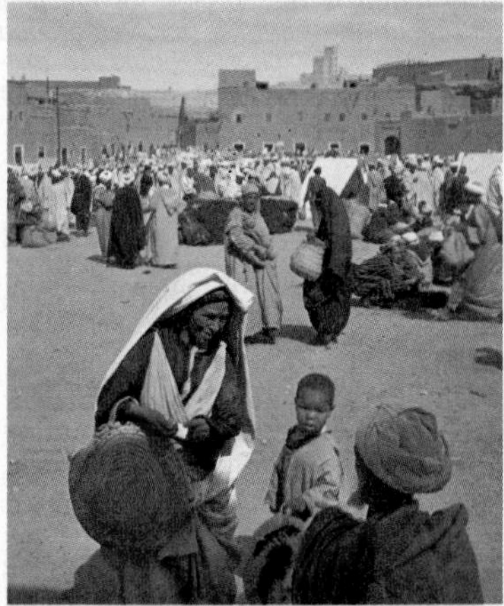

*The **Moors** of north-west Africa were originally called the Mauri and the name was modified when the area was occupied by the Romans. Those (above) are from south of the Atlas Mountains.*

*One of the U.K.'s most eminent sculptors, **Henry Moore,** carved monumental forms of a semi-abstract nature. This photograph shows the sculptor with one of his works.*

victory. **mor′al·ly** *adv.* **moral** *n.* Moral teaching (of fable, story, etc.); (pl.) habits or conduct from point of view of morality.

mo·rale (morăl′) *n.* Mental state or condition, esp. (of troops) as regards discipline and confidence.

mor·al·ist (mŏr′*a*lĭst, măr′-) *n.* One who practices or teaches morality. **mor·al·is·tic** (mŏr*a*lĭs′tĭk, măr-) *adj.*

mo·ral·i·ty (morăl′ĭtē, maw-) *n.* (pl. **-ties**). 1. Moral principles or rules; moral conduct. 2. Kind of drama (popular in 16th c.) inculcating moral or spiritual lesson.

mor·al·ize (mŏr′*a*līz, măr′-) *v.* (**-ized, -iz·ing**). Indulge in moral reflection; interpret morally or symbolically. **mor·al·i·za·tion** (mŏr*a*līzā′sh*o*n, măr-) *n.*

mo·rass (morăs′) *n.* Wet swampy tract, bog.

mor·a·to·ri·um (mŏr*a*tōr′ē*u*m, -tŏr′-, măr-) *n.* (pl. **-to·ri·a** pr. -tōr′ē*a*, -tŏr′ē*a*, **-to·ri·ums**). Legal authorization to debtor to postpone payment.

Mo·ra·vi·a (morā′vē*a*, -rah′-). Historic region and former province of Czechoslovakia.

mo·ray (mōr′ā, mŏr′ā, morā′, mawrā′) *n.* (pl. **-rays**). Any of

Sir Thomas More, *the English statesman, humanist scholar and canonized saint, was a friend of Colet, Erasmus and other Renaissance figures. His famous work 'Utopia' (1516) contains his views of the ideal state.*

several dangerous marine eels of the family Muraenidae, found chiefly in tropical coastal waters.

mor·bid (mŏr′bĭd) *adj.* (of mind, ideas, etc.) Unwholesome, sickly; (med.) of the nature, or indicative, of disease. **mor′bid·ly** *adv.* **mor′bid·ness** *n.* **mor·bid·i·ty** (mŏrbĭd′ĭtē) *n.* Morbidness; prevalence of disease (in a district).

mor·dant (mŏr′d*a*nt) *adj.* (of sarcasm etc.) Caustic, biting; pungent, smarting; (of acids) corrosive. ~ *n.* Substance used for fixing textile dyes; acid used in etching. **mor·da·cious** (mŏrdā′sh*u*s) *adj.* **mor·dac·i·ty** (mŏrdăs′ĭtē), **mor·dan·cy** (mŏr′d*a*nsē) *ns.*

Mor·dred (mŏr′drĭd) = MODRED.

more (mōr, mŏr) *adj.* (superl. **most**) & *n.* Greater number, quantity, or degree (of). ~ *adv.* To a greater extent, in a greater degree, additionally.

More (mōr, mŏr), **Sir Thomas** (1478–1535). English statesman, author of *Utopia* (1516), a description, in Latin, of an imaginary perfect nation; he succeeded Wolsey as Lord Chancellor, 1529, but resigned in 1532, refusing to take any oath that would impugn the pope's authority or assume the justice of Henry VIII's divorce from Catherine of Aragon; he was therefore indicted of high treason, found guilty, and beheaded; canonized (as **St. Thomas** ~), 1935.

Mo·re·a (mōrē′*a*, maw-). Peloponnese.

mo·rel (morĕl′) *n.* Edible mushroom of genus *Morchella.*

more·o·ver (mōrō′v*e*r, mŏr-, mōr′ō, mŏr′ō-) *adv.* In addition.

mo·res (mōr′āz, -ēz, mŏr′-) *n.pl.* Customs or conventions regarded as essential to or characteristic of a community. [L. pl. of *mos* custom]

Mor·gan[1] (mŏr′g*a*n) *n.* (One of) breed of American trotting and saddle horses. [f. Justin *Morgan* (1747–98), who owned the stallion from which the breed descended]

Mor·gan[2] (mŏr′g*a*n), **J(ohn) P(ierpont)** (1837–1913). Amer. financier, industrialist, and philanthropist; reorganized the railroads and formed U.S. Steel Corp.; art and rare book collector.

mor·ga·nat·ic (mŏrg*a*năt′ĭk) *adj.* (of a marriage) Between man of exalted rank and woman of lower rank in which it is provided that the wife and her children shall not share the rank or inherit the possessions of the husband. [OHG. *morgangeba* gift from husband to wife the morning after consummation of marriage]

Mor·gan le Fay (mŏr′g*a*n l*e* fā′). "Morgan the Fairy," a magician, sister of King Arthur.

morgue (mŏrg) *n.* Building (esp. one formerly in Paris) in which bodies of persons found dead are held for identification; (journalism) repository of material for obituary notices and other articles.

mor·i·bund (mŏr′*i*bŭnd, măr′-) *adj.* In a dying state.

Mor·mon (mŏr′m*o*n) *n.* Member of the Church of Jesus Christ of Latterday Saints, founded in New York State, 1830, by Joseph Smith of Vermont; he claimed that a parallel volume to the Bible, the "Book of Mormon," had been revealed to him, and that its author, the prophet Mormon, had been one of a race that had colonized America from Palestine in ancient times; the sect grew rapidly but met with hostility esp. for advocating polygamy (which they did until 1890); eventually, led by Brigham YOUNG[1], they migrated to Utah and there founded Salt Lake City in

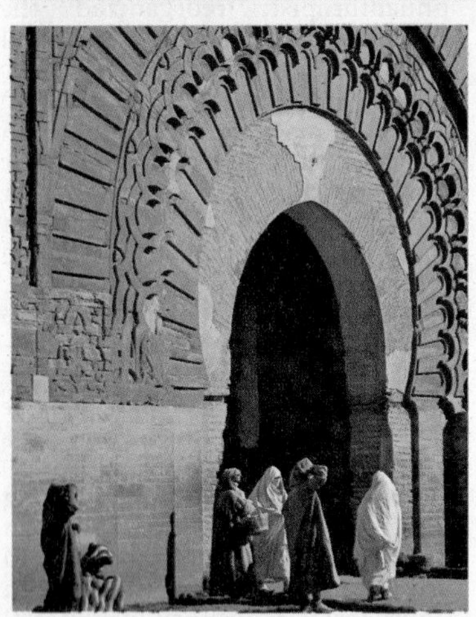

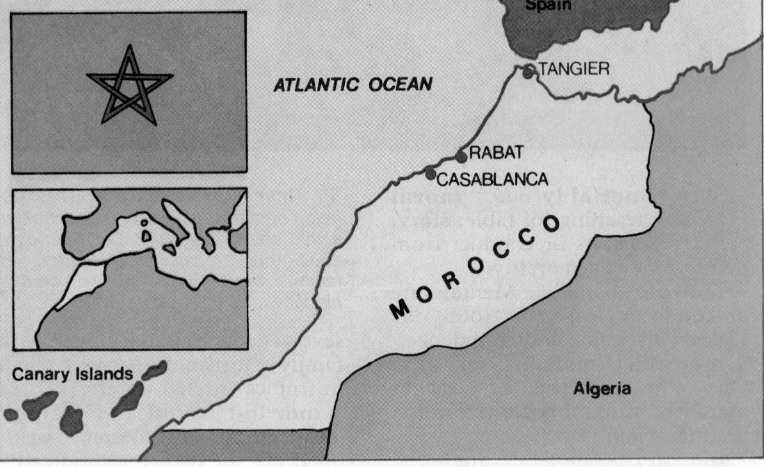

Morocco in North Africa is populated by Arabs and Berbers. Rabat is the capital, although the largest city is Casablanca. Phosphates are the country's major export. Top: Tan-Tan mosque. Above left: Bab Arguenaou, Marrakesh. Above: Map and flag.

1847. **Mor'mon·ism** *n.*

morn (mōrn) *n.* (poet.) Morning; dawn.

morn·ing (mōr'nĭng) *n.* Early part of daytime, ending at noon or at time of midday meal; **good ~**, form of greeting; **~ coat**, man's tail coat with front sloped away; **~ dress**, men's formal daytime wear; **~-glory**, Amer. plant of genus *Ipomoae*, with showy flowers; **~ room**, sitting room, other than dining or drawing room; **~ sickness**, nausea commonly experienced in morning in early months of pregnancy; **~ star**, Venus (or other planet or bright star) seen to the east before sunrise.

Mo·roc·co (morŏk'ō). Country of NW. Africa, bounded on N. and W. by the Mediterranean Sea and Atlantic Ocean and on S. and E. by Algeria; inhabited by people descended from Berbers, Arabs, and Moors; formerly a French protectorate, with a Spanish sphere of influence; since 1956 an independent kingdom; capital, Rabat; summer capital, Tangier. **Mo·roc·can** (morŏk'an) *adj.* & *n.*

mo·roc·co (morŏk'ō) *n.* Fine flexible leather made orig. in Morocco, now also elsewhere, from goatskins tanned with sumac; imitation of this made from calf- or sheepskins, grained to resemble true morocco; **Levant ~**, high-grade, large-grained morocco, used for bookbinding.

mo·ron (mōr'ŏn, mōr'-) *n.* Adult whose mental development corresponds to that of a normal average child between the ages of 8 and 12; (colloq.) very stupid person. **mo·ron·ic** (morŏn'ĭk) *adj.*

mo·rose (morōs') *adj.* Sour tempered, sullen, and unsocial. **mo·rose'ly** *adv.* **mo·rose'ness** *n.*

mor·pheme (mōr'fēm) *n.* (philol.) Morphological element considered in respect of its functional relations to a linguistic system.

William Morris, *the Pre-Raphaelite painter and designer, produced wallpapers, furniture, stained glass and textiles. This 'Daffodil Chintz' is an example.*

The ***Morse code*** *which was invented by Samuel F. B. Morse of the U.S.A. in 1837 is still used in radio telegraphy. This Morse code operator is from Interpol in Paris.*

Morning glory *is a widely cultivated twining vine from temperate North America. It has broad, heart-shaped leaves and blue or purplish flowers.*

Mor·phe·us (mōr′fē*us*, -fūs). (Rom. myth.) Son of Somnus, god of sleep, and himself the god of dreams.

mor·phi·a (mōr′fē*a*) *n.* Morphine.

mor·phine (mōr′fēn) *n.* Alkaloid narcotic principle of opium, used to alleviate pain. **mor·phin·ism** (mōr′fĭnĭzem) *n.* Effect of morphine; excessive use of morphine.

mor·phol·o·gy (mōrfŏl′*o*jē) *n.* 1. Study of the form of animals and plants. 2. Study of the form of words, branch of philology dealing with inflection and word formation. 3. **social** ~, study of the structure of society, i.e. of social groups and institutions. **mor·pho·log·i·cal** (mōrf*o*lŏj′ĭk*a*l) *adj.* **mor·pho·log′i·cal·ly** *adv.* **mor·phol′o·gist** *n.*

Mor·ris[1] **Jes·up** (mōr′ĭs jĕs′*u*p, mar′ĭs), **Cape.** Northernmost point of land in the world in N. Greenland on the Arctic Ocean.

Mor·ris[2] (mōr′ĭs, mar′-), **William** (1834–96). English designer, printer, poet, and prose writer.

Mor·ris (mōr′ĭs, mar′-) **chair.** Type of plain easy chair with adjustable back. [f. William MORRIS]

mor·ris (mōr′ĭs, mar′-) **dance.** English traditional dance in fancy costume, usu. representing characters from Robin Hood legend. [*morys*, var. of MOORISH]

mor·row (mōr′ō, mar′ō) *n.* (literary) Next day.

Morse (mōrs), **Samuel Finley Breese** (1791–1872). Amer. inventor of recording telegraph, deviser of the ~ **code**, a telegraphic alphabet in which letters are represented by combinations of short and long electrical contacts, sounds, flashes, etc. ("dots and dashes").

A	·—	S	···
B	—···	T	—
C	—·—·	U	··—
D	—··	V	···—
E	·	W	·——
F	··—·	X	—··—
G	——·	Y	—·——
H	····	Z	——··
I	··	1	·————
J	·———	2	··———
K	—·—	3	···——
L	·—··	4	····—
M	——	5	·····
N	—·	6	—····
O	———	7	——···
P	·——·	8	———··
Q	——·—	9	————·
R	·—·	0	—————

MORSE CODE

mor·sel (mōr′s*e*l) *n.* Mouthful; small piece, fragment.

mor·tal (mōr′t*a*l) *adj.* Subject to or causing death, fatal; (of enemy) implacable; (of sin) deadly, entailing spiritual death (opp. VENIAL); accompanying death, as ~ **agony**; ~ **enemy**, implacable enemy; ~ **fear**, dire fear. **mor′tal·ly** *adv.* **mortal** *n.* One who is subject to death; person.

mor·tal·i·ty (mōrtăl′ĭtē) *n.* (pl. **-ties**). Mortal nature; loss of life on large scale; death rate.

mor·tar (mōr′t*e*r) *n.* 1. Hard vessel in which ingredients are pounded with a pestle. 2. Short gun with large bore for throwing shells at high angles. 3. Mixture of lime, sand, and water used to make joints between stones and bricks in building; **mor′tarboard**, board for holding builders' mortar; cap with stiff flat square top, resembling this, worn as part of academic dress. **mortar** *v.t.* Bind, join (bricks or stones) together with mortar; fire upon with mortars.

mort·gage (mōr′gĭj) *n.* Conveyance of property as security for debt, with provision for reconveyance on repayment of the sum secured; deed effecting this. ~ *v.t.* (**-gaged, -gag·ing**). Make over by mortgage; pledge in

Moscow, capital of the U.S.S.R. and the country's chief communications center, has some magnificent examples of Byzantine architecture like the Cathedral of the Assumption pictured.

*For Muslims, the **mosque** is the center of community worship. The early mosques were modelled on the first built at Medina by Muhammad. Seen here is the interior of the Blue Mosque, Istanbul.*

advance. **mort·ga·gee** (mŏrgajē′) *n.* Holder of mortgage. **mort·ga·gor** (mŏr′gajer) *n.* Person who pledges property etc. in mortgage. [OF. *mort gage* dead pledge]

mor·tice = MORTISE.

mor·ti·cian (mŏrtĭsh′an) *n.* Undertaker.

mor·ti·fy (mŏr′tĭfī) *v.* (**-fied, -fy·ing**). 1. Chasten (the body, passions, etc.) by self-denial. 2. Cause (person) to feel humiliated, wound (feelings). 3. (of flesh) Become gangrenous. **mor·ti·fi·ca·tion** (mŏrtĭfĭkā′shon) *n.*

mor·tise, mor·tice (mŏr′tĭs) *ns.* Hole or cavity into which end of some other part of framework or structure is fitted; ~ **lock**, lock housed with a mortise. **mortise** *v.t.* (**-tised, -tis·ing**). Cut mortise in, fasten with mortise.

Mor·ton (mŏr′ton), **Levi Parsons** (1824–1920). Vice president of the U.S. under Benjamin Harrison, 1889–93.

mor·tu·ar·y (mŏr′choōĕrē) *adj.* Of or for burial or death. ~ *n.* (pl. **-ar·ies**). Place for temporary reception of corpses.

Mo·sa·ic (mōzā′ĭk) *adj.* Of MOSES; ~ **law**, ancient Hebrew law contained in the Pentateuch.

mo·sa·ic (mōzā′ĭk) *n.* (Production of) picture or pattern of small cubes of colored stone, glass, etc., cemented together (also fig. of any diversified whole); (also ~ **disease**) plant virus disease causing mottled patches on leaves. **mosaic** *adj.* Of or like such work. ~ *v.t.* (**-icked, -ick·ing**). Decorate with mosaics; combine (as) into mosaic. **mo·sa·i·cist** (mōzā′ĭsĭst) *n.* [med. L. *mosaicus*, f. Gk. *mousaikos* of the Muses]

mos·cha·tel (mŏskatĕl′, mŏs′-katĕl) *n.* Small plant (*Adoxa moschatellina*), having pale green flowers with a musky smell.

Mos·cow (mŏs′kow, -kō) (Russ. **Moskva**). Capital city of U.S.S.R. and Russian Soviet Federated Socialist Republic; capital of Russia from 1240 to 1703 (when the capital was transferred to St. Petersburg) and from 1918.

Mo·selle (mōzĕl′) *n.* Dry white wine produced in valley of the Moselle River, which rises in Vosges Mountains and flows into the Rhine at Coblenz.

Mo·ses[1] (mō′zĭz, -zĭs). Hebrew patriarch, the great lawgiver of the Jews; led them from Egypt after the captivity there; was inspired by God on Mount Sinai to write down the Ten Commandments on tablets of stone (Exod. 20); died before the Promised Land was reached (Joshua 1).

Moses,[2] **Anna Mary Robertson**: see GRANDMA MOSES.

mo·sey (mō′zē) *v.i.* (**-seyed, -sey·ing**). (colloq.) Walk (along) in leisurely or aimless manner.

Mos·lem (mŏz′lem, mŏs′-) (pl. **-lems**, collect. **-lem**) = MUSLIM.

mosque (mŏsk, mawsk) *n.* Muslim place of worship. [Fr. *mosquée*, f. Arab. *masjid*]

mos·qui·to (moskē′tō) *n.* (pl. **-toes**). Two-winged fly of the family Culicidae, gnat; (esp.) species of *Culex*, *Anopheles*, and *Aëdes*, females of which have a long bloodsucking proboscis; ~ **net**, fine-meshed net for keeping mosquitoes from room, bed, etc.

moss (maws, mŏs) *n.* (pl. **moss·es**). 1. Any of a variety of small green plants of the class Musci within the division Bryophyta, growing in soft clusters on trees, rocks, or damp ground. 2. Any of a number of similar plants, such as club moss, Spanish moss, algae, and lichens. 3. **moss′-back**, old shellfish or turtle with algae growing on its back; (colloq.) very old-fashioned or conservative person; **moss pink**, low-growing plant (*Phlox subulata*) forming mats of brilliant flowers ranging from pink to purple; **moss rose**, cabbage rose (*Rosa centifolia*), with mosslike growth on calyx and stalk. **moss'y** *adj.* (**moss·i·er, moss·i·est**). Of or like moss; overgrown with moss. **moss'i·ness** *n.*

most (mōst) *adj.* & *n.* Greatest number, quantity, or degree (of). ~ *adv.* In a great or the greatest degree. **most'ly** *adv.* For the most part.

mot (mō) *n.* (pl. **mots** pr. mōz). Witty saying; ~**juste** (pr. zhüst), expression that conveys a desired shade of meaning with more precision than any other. [Fr.]

mote (mōt) *n.* Particle of dust, esp. speck seen floating in sunbeam.

mo·tel (mōtĕl′) *n.* Roadside hotel or group of separate small buildings for accommodation of motorists. [blend of *motor* + *hotel*]

mo·tet (mōtet′) *n.* (mus.) Sacred musical composition, generally for unaccompanied voices; non-ecclesiastical work on similar lines. [Fr., dim. of *mot* word]

moth (mawth, mŏth) *n.* (pl. **moths** pr. mawdhz, mŏdhz, mawths, mŏths). Popular name for the majority of insects belonging to the order Lepidoptera, those not *butterflies*, distinguished from them by not having clubbed antennae and by being mostly nocturnal in habit; clothes moth or any other insect whose larvae feed on fabrics; (fig.) person hovering around temptation, as a moth flutters about light; **moth'ball**, small ball of naphthalene etc. used to keep moths away from fabrics etc.; (also) air-tight plastic cover sprayed on and enclosing working parts of gun mountings, machinery, etc. of ship; **moth-eaten**, injured by moths; (fig.) antiquated, time-worn. **moth'y** *adj.* (**moth·i·er, moth·i·est**). Infested by moths.

moth·er (mŭdh′*er*) *n.* Female parent (also transf.); head of female religious community (often ~ **superior**); (familiar) title of or form of address to elderly woman; incubator, artificial apparatus for rearing chickens; ~ **country**, country in relation to its colonies; native land; ~ **earth**, Earth as mother of its inhabitants; **M~ Goose**, legendary author of nursery rhyme collection published in England in 1760; **M~ Hubbard**, person in nursery rhyme; full loose dress, esp. that imposed by missionaries on native women in the Pacific; ~**-in-law**, wife's or husband's mother; ~**-of-pearl**, pearly iridescent lining of certain shells, as of oysters, mussels, etc., used in making buttons etc.; ~ **of vinegar**, mucilaginous substance produced in vinegar during fermentation by bacteria (usually of the Acetobacter family); **Mother's Day**, day for honoring one's mother, in U.S. a Sunday in May; **mother ship**, ship acting as base for submarines, aircraft, etc.; **mother tongue**, one's native language. **moth'er·hood** *n.* **moth'er·less** *adj.* **mother** *v.* Take care of as a mother; **moth'ering** *n.*

moth·er·ly (mŭdh′*er*lē) *adj.* Befitting or resembling a mother. **moth'er·li·ness** *n.*

mo·tif (mōtēf′) *n.* Distinctive feature or dominant idea of a design or composition; (mus.) FIGURE.

mo·tile (mō′t*i*l) *adj.* (zool., bot.). Capable of motion.

mo·tion (mō′sh*o*n) *n.* 1. Moving, movement; gait; gesture. 2. Proposition formally made in deliberative assembly; (law) application to judge or court for some rule or order of court. 3. ~ **picture**, continuous picture showing objects in motion, produced by projecting on to a screen a series of photographs of the scene with successive positions slightly changed. **mo'tion·less** *adj.* **motion** *v.* Make motion to direct or guide (person).

mo·ti·vate (mō′t*i*vāt) *v.t.* (**-vat·ed, -vat·ing**). Supply a motive to, be the motive of. **mo·ti-**

*The **mosquito,** of which there are 2,500 species, is important in public health because of the blood-sucking habits of the females. They are known to transmit such diseases as yellow fever, malaria and dengue.*

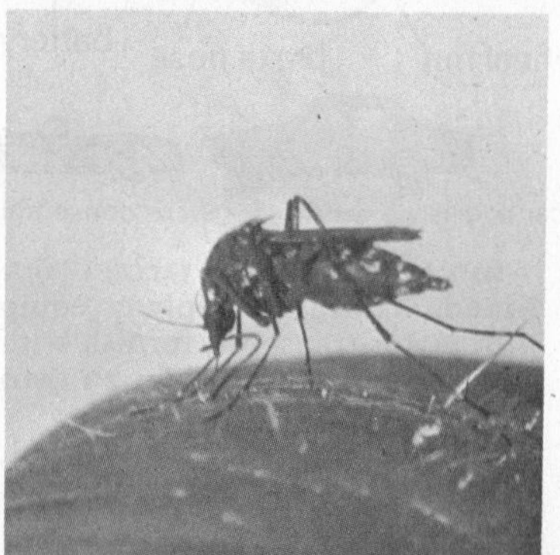

*The **club moss** is widely distributed but tropical forms predominate. It is a low, spreading evergreen plant with stems covered with many small leaves. These sometimes resemble normal leaves but can be in clusters.*

***Moths** form with butterflies the insect order Lepidoptera. Generally, moths are active by night, butterflies by day.*

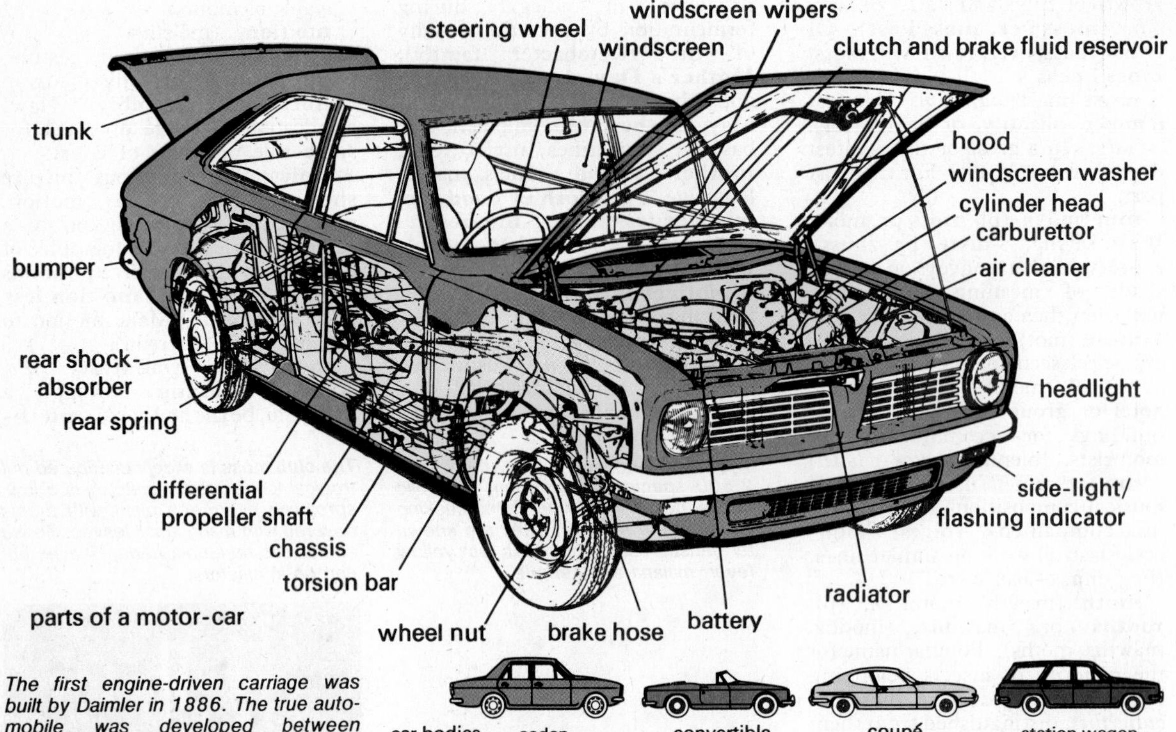

parts of a motor-car

The first engine-driven carriage was built by Daimler in 1886. The true automobile was developed between 1881–94. But it was not until the 1900s that ***motorcars*** *were being mass-produced. Their design and production are a major industry throughout the world.*

va·tion (mōtivā´shon) *n.*

mo·tive (mō´tĭv) *adj.* Tending to initiate motion; ~ **power**, esp. form of mechanical energy used to drive machinery. **motive** *n.* 1. That which induces a person to act, e.g. desire, fear, circumstance. 2. = MOTIF. **motive** *v.t.* (**-tived, -tiv·ing**). Motivate.

mot·ley (mŏt´lē) *adj.* Multicolored; heterogeneous. ~ *n.* Jester's motley garb.

mo·tor (mō´ter) *n.* Motive agent or force; motor muscle or nerve; apparatus or engine supplying motive power for vehicle or machinery, esp. internal combustion engine; automobile. ~ *adj.* 1. Giving, imparting, or producing motion; ~ **area**, that part of frontal lobe of mammal's brain from which muscular activity of opposite side of body is most easily evoked; ~ **nerve**, any nerve consisting of fibers that carry impulses from spinal cord or brain to induce contractions of muscle. 2. Driven by motor, as **mo´torbike** (colloq.), **mo´torboat, mo´torcycle; mo´torcar**, automobile. 3. Of, for, involving, motor vehicles; **mo´torcade**, procession of automobiles; **motor court**, motel; **mo´torman** (pl. **-men**), operator of subway train or streetcar. **motor** *v.* Go, convey, by automobile. **mo´tor·ist** *n.* Driver of automobile.

mo·tor·ize (mō´terīz) *v.t.* (**-ized, -iz·ing**). Supply or equip with motor transport; furnish with motor engine. **mo·tor·i·za·tion** (mōterīzā´shon) *n.*

mot·tle (mŏt´el) *v.t.* (**-tled, -tling**). Mark or cover with spots or blotches.

mot·to (mŏt´ō) *n.* (pl. **-toes, -tos**). Inscription on some object, expressing appropriate sentiment or aspiration; maxim adopted as rule of conduct; short quotation prefixed to book or chapter, suggestive of the contents.

The ***Mountain goat*** *is a native of the Rockies in the U.S.A. They are closely related to antelopes, living above the timberline, in small bands.*

mou·jik (mōōzhĭk´, mōō´zhĭk) = MUZHIK.

mould (Brit.) = MOLD.

moult (Brit.) = MOLT.

mound (mownd) *n.* Embankment; heap, bank, hillock, of earth etc.; **M~ Builder**, one of prehistoric N. Amer. Ind. people who erected burial mounds and other earthworks chiefly in the Mississippi valley and southeastern U.S.; **pitcher's ~**, elevated area from which baseball pitcher delivers ball to batter.

mount[1] (mownt) *n.* Mountain, hill (abbrev. Mt. preceding name, as **Mt. Everest**).

shoulder
col
peak
saddle
pass
cirque
arête
névé
medial moraine
couloir
lateral moraine
chimney
crevasses
séracs
terminal moraine

As the plates of the earth's crust shift, ***mountains*** *are formed. Then the forces of erosion — wind, water, heat, cold — attack the upthrust rocks and carve them into widely differing forms. Above: Effects of glacial erosion on a mountainous terrain.*

mount[2] (mownt) *v.* Ascend; climb on to; increase in amount; amount *to*; set on horseback, furnish (person) with saddle horse; put in position for use or exhibition; put (picture) in a MOUNT[3]; fit (gems etc.) in gold etc.; fix (object) on microscope slide; display specimen (e.g. butterfly); put (play) on stage; (mil.) organize (an offensive).

mount[3] (mownt) *n.* Margin surrounding picture, card on which drawing is mounted; ornamental metal parts of thing; horse for person to ride.

moun·tain (mown′tĭn) *n.* Natural elevation of Earth's surface of impressive height, esp. over 1,000 ft. (300 m); large heap or pile; ~ **ash**, tree of genus *Sorbus* with delicate pinnate leaves and scarlet berries; ~ **dew**, whiskey, esp. illegally distilled; ~ **goat** (also **Rocky M~ goat**), long-haired hoofed mammal (*Oreamnos americanus*) of Rocky Mountains with yellowish-white hair and short curving black horns; ~ **laurel**, N. Amer. shrub (*Kalmia latifolia*) with glossy, evergreen, poisonous leaves and umbels of white or pink flowers; ~ **lion**, tawny long-tailed cat (*Felis concolor*), larger than lynx and smaller than jaguar once common throughout N. and S. America, now rare in U.S. and Canada; also called cougar, catamount, panther, puma, etc.

moun·tain·eer (mowntinēr′) *n.* 1. One who lives in the mountains. 2. One who is skilled in climbing mountains. ~ *v.i.* Climb mountains.

moun·tain·ous (mown′tin*u*s) *adj.* Abounding in mountains; huge.

moun·te·bank (mown′tebăngk) *n.* Itinerant quack (archaic); impudent charlatan. [It. *montambanco* = *monta in banco* mount on bench]

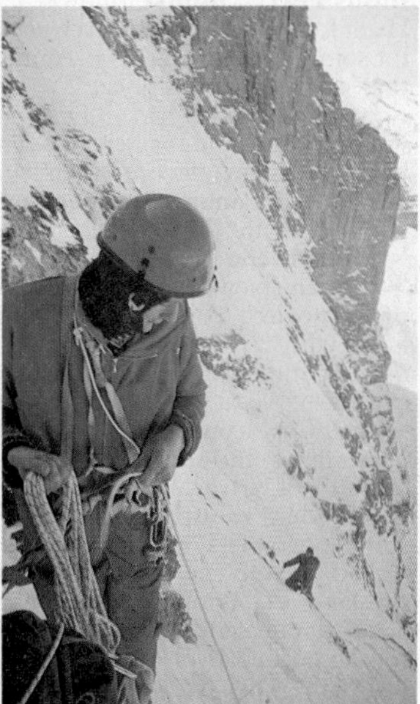

Mountaineering *as a sport was first begun in mid-19th century Switzerland by British tourists and local guides. Today nearly all the world's major peaks have been scaled.*

*When a public figure dies, thousands — even tens of thousands — of people unite in their grief and take to the streets in **mourning.***

Moun·tie (mown′tē) *n.* (colloq.) Member of the Royal Canadian Mounted Police.

Mount Rush·more (rŭsh′mōr, -mōr) **National Monument.** Portraits 60 ft. (18 m) high of presidents Washington, Jefferson, Lincoln, and T. Roosevelt carved in stone by John Gutzon Borglum on side of Mount Rushmore, in the Black Hills of South Dakota.

Mount Ver·non (vēr′non). Estate and burial place of George and Martha Washington on the Potomac River near Washington, D.C.

mourn (mōrn, mōrn) *v.* Sorrow, grieve, lament, esp. lament death of; put on mourning. **mourn′er** *n.* One who mourns; person attending funeral.

mourn·ful (mōrn′ful, mōrn′-) *adj.* Exhibiting, expressing, or feeling mourning or deep sorrow. **mourn′ful·ly** *adv.* **mourn′ful·ness** *n.*

mourn·ing (mōr′nĭng, mōr′-) *n.* (esp.) Feeling or expression of sorrow; (wearing of) black clothes as sign of bereavement; ~ **dove,** wild dove (*Zenaidura macroura*) of N. Amer., grayish brown with delicate pink on breast and having a distinctly sad call; also called turtledove.

mouse (mows) *n.* (pl. **mice** pr. mīs). Small rodent esp. of genus *Mus;* timid or shy person; **~-ear,** hawkweed; **mouse′trap,** trap for catching mice. **mous·y, mous·ey** (mow′sē, -zē) *adjs.* (**mous·i·er, mous·i·est**). **mouse** (mowz) *v.i.* Hunt for or catch mice; search *about* for something. **mous′er** *n.* Animal that catches mice, esp. cat.

mousse (mōōs) *n.* Dish of whipped cream, or cream and beaten eggs etc., flavored with fruit etc. or containing meat or fish. [Fr., = "froth"]

mous·tache = MUSTACHE.

mouth (mowth) *n.* (pl. **mouths** pr. mowdhz). External orifice in head, with cavity behind it containing apparatus for mastication and organs of vocal utterance; person viewed as consumer of food; opening or entrance of anything; outfall of river; ~ **organ** = HARMONICA; **mouth′piece,** part of some portable wind instruments placed before or between lips; similar part of tobacco pipe; part of telephone spoken into; one who speaks on behalf of others; (slang) lawyer; **mouth-to-mouth,** applied to a method of resuscitation in which a person places his mouth on the patient's and breathes expired air into his lungs; **down in the mouth,** (colloq.) having an unhappy face; depressed, woebegone; **mouth′wash,** liquid antiseptic and breath sweetener for use in cleaning the mouth; **mouth-watering** (*adj.*), highly appetizing; also fig. **mouth** (mowdh) *v.* Utter or speak pompously, declaim; take (food) in, touch with, mouth; train (horse) to answer to bit and reins; grimace. **mouth′ful** *n.* (pl. **-fuls**). Quantity that fills the mouth; small quantity (of food etc.); something difficult to say; (slang) something important said.

mouth·y (mow′dhē, -thē) *adj.* (**mouth·i·er, mouth·i·est**). Ranting, bombastic; prolix.

mou·ton (mōō′tŏn) *n.* (Coat of) sheepskin, sheared and treated to resemble seal or beaver.

mov·a·ble, move·a·ble (mōō′-vabel) *adjs.* That can be moved; (of property) that can be removed, personal as opp. to *real.* **mov·a·bil·i·ty** (mōōvabĭl′itē), **mov′a·ble·ness** *ns.*

move (mōōv) *v.* (**moved, mov·ing**). Change position (of); change residence; stir; rouse; cause (bowels) to act; affect with emotion; propose as resolution; **moving picture** (see MOTION); **moving staircase,** escalator. **move** *n.* Moving of piece at chess etc.; way in which piece is allowed to move; act of moving from rest; change of abode or premises; device, trick, action to some end.

move·ment (mōōv′ment) *n.* Moving; moving mechanism of watch etc.; principal division of (usu. instrumental) musical work; combined action or endeavor of body of persons for some special end, e.g. *the women's rights* ~.

mov·er (mōō′ver) *n.* Individual or company whose business it is to move contents of a house, office, etc. from one location to another; **prime** ~, initial source (natural or mechanical) of motive power; author of fruitful idea.

mov·ie (mōō′vē) *n.* (colloq.) Moving picture.

mow[1] (mō) *n.* Stack of hay, corn, etc.

mow[2] (mō) *v.* (**mowed, mown, mow·ing**). Cut down grass, corn, etc., with scythe or machine; (fig.) cut, sweep down, like grass; **mowing machine**, machine for cutting grass etc. **mow'er** *n.* Person who mows grass etc.; mowing machine, lawn mower.

Mo·zam·bique (mōzambēk'). Former Portuguese colony in E. Africa; independent 1975; capital, Maputo.

Mo·zart (mō tsärt), **Wolfgang Amadeus** (1756–91). Austrian composer of symphonies, chamber music, and such operas, as *The Marriage of Figaro, Don Giovanni, The Magic Flute.*

moz·za·rel·la (mŏtserĕl'*a*, mō-) *n.* Soft, white Italian cheese, often used melted in cooking.

M.P. *abbrev.* Member of Parliament; military police.

m.p. *abbrev.* Melting point.

mpg, m.p.g., mph, m.p.h. *abbrevs.* Miles per gallon, per hour.

Mr. (mĭs'ter) *n.* (pl. **Messrs.**). Title prefixed to surname of man with no superior title. [abbrev. of MISTER]

Mrs. (mĭ'sĭz) *n.* (pl. **Mesdames, Mmes.**) Title prefixed to name of married woman with no superior title. [abbrev. of MISTRESS]

MS *abbrev.* 1. Mississippi. 2. Multiple sclerosis.

MS. *abbrev.* (pl. **MSS.**). Manuscript.

Ms., Ms (mĭz) *ns.* Title prefixed to a woman's name, used to avoid distinguishing between married and unmarried women. [comb. of MRS., MISS[2]]

ms. *abbrev.* (pl. **mss.**). Manuscript; milliseconds.

MS. *abbrev.* 1. Master of Science. 2. Multiple sclerosis.

msec *abbrev.* Millisecond(s).

MSG *abbrev.* Monosodium glutamate.

Msgr. *abbrev.* Monseigneur; Monsignor.

M.Sgt. *abbrev.* Master Sergeant.

M.S.L. *abbrev.* Mean sea level.

MST, M.S.T. *abbrevs.* Mountain Standard Time.

M.S.W. *abbrev.* Master of Social Work.

MT *abbrev.* Montana.

Mt. *abbrev.* Mount.

M.T. *abbrev.* 1. Metric ton. 2. Mountain Time.

mu (mū, mōō) *n.* Thirteenth (later 12th) letter of Greek alphabet (M, μ), corresponding to *m*; μ, (phys. etc.) symbol for one millionth; μ, *mu*, (radio) symbol

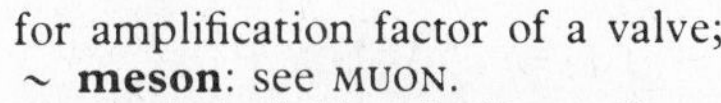

for amplification factor of a valve; ~ **meson**: see MUON.

much (mŭch) *adj.* & *n.* Great number, quantity, or degree (of); **make ~ of**, gain much advantage from; give much attention to; attach much importance to. ~ *adv.* In a great degree; pretty nearly; for a large part of one's time. **much'ness** *n.*

mu·ci·lage (mū'sĭlĭj) *n.* Viscous substance obtained from plants by maceration; adhesive substance. **mu·ci·lag·i·nous** (mūsĭlăj'inus) *adj.*

muck (mŭk) *n.* Farmyard manure; (colloq.) dirt, filth. ~ *v.* Manure; ~ **about**, (Brit. slang) loaf; go about aimlessly; ~ **out**, clean out (stable etc.); ~ **up**, (slang) bungle. **muck'y** *adj.* (**muck·i·er, muck·i·est**).

muck·a·muck (mŭk'amŭk), **muck·e·ty·muck** (mŭk'etēmŭk) *ns.* (slang, often derog.) Important person.

muck·rake (mŭk'rāk) *v.i.* (**-raked, -rak·ing**). Seek out and expose, particularly through the media, corruption in government or business. **muck'rak·er** *n.*

mu·cous (mū'kus) *adj.* Secreting or covered by mucus; ~ **membrane**, inner surface lining of hollow organs of the body. **mu·cos·i·ty** (mūkŏs'itē) *n.*

mu·cus (mū'kus) *n.* Sticky secretion of mucous glands usu. forming a protective covering for mucous membrane.

mud (mŭd) *n.* Wet soft soil or earthy matter, mire; ~ **bath**, bath in mud impregnated with salts, as a remedy for rheumatism etc.; ~ **flat**(**s**): see FLAT[2] *n.*; **mud'guard**, guard over wheel of cycle or other vehicle as protection against mud; **mud pie**, mud formed by children in the shape of a pie; **mud'slinging**, (fig.) personal abuse, invective.

mud·dle (mŭd'el) *v.* (**-dled, -dling**). Bewilder, confuse; bungle; act in confused, unmethodical, and ineffective manner; ~ **through**, finish successfully despite lack of method. **mud'dleheaded** *adj.* Mixed up in one's thinking; bungling. **muddle** *n.* Muddled condition.

mud·dy (mŭd'ē) *adj.* (**-di·er, -di·est**). Like mud; covered with, abounding in, mud; thick, turbid; not clear, mentally confused. **mud'di·ly** *adv.* **mud'di·ness** *n.* **muddy** *v.* (**-died, -dy·ing**). Make or become muddy.

mu·ez·zin (mūĕz'ĭn, mōō-) *n.* Official of Muslim mosque who proclaims hour of prayer from

The ***Mounties*** *claim that they always get their man. Founded in 1873, they are today responsible for the enforcement of Federal laws in all Canada except Quebec and Ontario.*

Almost every part of the world has at least one kind of ***mouse,*** *native or introduced. Mice can be solitary or social, and vary widely in their preferred diets.*

*One of the U.K.'s most spectacular wild plants, common **mullein** can grow to 7ft. tall with long spikes of yellow flowers rising above large oval leaves clothed with dense, silvery down.*

minaret. [Arab. *mu'addin* (*'addana* proclaim)]

muff[1] (mŭf) *n.* Tubular covering esp. of fur into which hands are thrust to keep them warm.

muff[2] (mŭf) *v.t.* Bungle, make muddle of; miss (catch at baseball).

muf·fin (mŭf'ĭn) *n.* Bread made with eggs, usu. baked in cup-shaped mold, often with berries in mix; **English** ~, light, flat, round spongy cake, eaten toasted and buttered.

muf·fle (mŭf'*e*l) *n.* Chamber or covering in furnace or kiln that protects contents from direct contact with fire. ~ *v.t.* (**-fled, -fling**). Wrap, cover *up* for warmth; wrap up (oars, bell, drum, etc.) to deaden sound; wrap up (head of person) to prevent his speaking; repress, deaden, sound of (curse etc., usu. in past part.).

muf·fler (mŭf'l*e*r) *n.* Wrap or scarf worn around neck for warmth; silencer in engine.

muf·ti (mŭf'tē) *n.* (pl. **-tis**). 1. Muslim priest or expounder of law. 2. Plain clothes worn by anyone who has the right to wear a uniform. [Arab. *al-muftī* official expounder of Islamic law]

mug (mŭg) *n.* 1. Drinking vessel, usu. cylindrical and with handle. 2. (slang) Face, mouth. 3. (slang) Stupid person, dupe. 4. (slang) Hoodlum, thug, ruffian. ~ *v.t.* (**mugged, mug·ging**). (slang) 1. Photograph (a person) for police records, official identification, etc. 2. Rob (a person in street), esp. with violence. ~ *v.i.* (slang) Make faces, esp. before an audience, camera, etc. **mug'shot** *n.* (slang) Photograph of face for official identification.

mug·ger (mŭg'*e*r) *n.* 1. Broad-snouted Indian crocodile (*Crocodylus palustris*) venerated by many Hindus. 2. (slang) One who assaults others on the street and robs them. 3. (slang) Person who makes faces, esp. before an audience, camera, etc.

mug·gy (mŭg'ē) *adj.* (**-gi·er, -gi·est**). (of weather etc.) Damp, warm, and oppressive. **mug'gi·ness** *n.*

mug·wump (mŭg'wŭmp) *n.* Great man, chief; political independent, (esp.) Republican who refused to support his party's nominee in presidential election of 1884. [N. Amer. Ind.]

Mu·ham·mad (mo͝ohăm'*a*d, -hah'm*a*d) (*c*570–632). Prophet of Islam, whose utterances are preserved in the KORAN; born at Mecca and buried at Medina; declared himself the Prophet, *c*611, and sought to turn his fellow Arabs from the local gods whom they then worshipped to the ancient religion of Abraham and other Old Testament patriarchs and prophets; meeting opposition in Mecca, he fled to Medina in 622; this flight (the HEGIRA) is regarded as beginning the Muslim era. **Mu·ham'mad·an** *adj.* & *n.* Muslim.

Mu·ham·mad A·li (mo͝ohăm'*a*d ah'lē, -hah'm*a*d) (1943–). Name assumed by Cassius Clay, U.S. prizefighter, three times world heavyweight champion.

Muir (mūr), **John** (1838–1914). Scottish-born Amer. naturalist, conservationist, and explorer; influential in establishing national park system and forest reserves; **Muir Woods**, national monument of giant redwood trees in California, N. of San Francisco.

mu·lat·to (m*u*lăt'ō, mū-, -lah'tō) *n.* (pl. **-toes**). Offspring of a white and a black parent. ~ *adj.* Of brownish-yellow color, as mulattoes. [Span. *mulato* young mule]

mul·ber·ry (mŭl'bĕrē, -b*e*rē) *n.* (pl. **-ries**). Tree of genus *Morus*, with dark purple or white edible berries, and leaves that are used for feeding silkworms; fruit of this; dark purple color.

mulch (mŭlch) *n.* Half-rotten straw, grass mowings, leaves, etc., spread on the ground to protect roots of plants or trees or conserve moisture etc. ~ *v.t.* Cover or spread with mulch.

mulct (mŭlkt) *v.t.* 1. Punish (person) by a fine; deprive (person *of*). 2. Swindle (person); obtain by swindling. ~ *n.* Fine imposed for offense.

mule[1] (mūl) *n.* 1. Offspring of male ass and mare; hence, stupid or obstinate person. 2. Kind of spinning jenny.

*The **mulberry** is grown all over the world both for its red, white, or black fruit — according to species — and for the leaves of the Oriental species on which silkworms feed.*

mule[2] (mūl) *n.* Kind of usu. backless slipper.

mu·le·teer (mūl*e*tēr') *n.* Mule driver.

mul·ish (mū'lĭsh) *adj.* Obstinate as a mule, intractable. **mul'ish·ly** *adv.* **mul'ish·ness** *n.*

mull[1] (mŭl) *v.t.* Make a mess or muddle of; ruminate, ponder *over*. ~ *n.* Mess, muddle.

mull[2] (mŭl) *v.t.* Make (wine, beer) into hot drink with sugar, spices, yolk of egg, etc.

mul·lah (mŭl'*a*, mo͝ol'*a*, mo͞o'l*a*) *n.* Muslim learned in theology and sacred law; expounder of the Koran. [Hind. *mulla*, ult. adapted f. Arab. *mawlā*]

mul·lein (mŭl'ĭn) *n.* Herbaceous plant of genus *Verbascum*, with woolly leaves and erect woolly spike of yellow flowers.

Mul·ler (mŭl'*e*r), **Johann**: see REGIOMONTANUS.

mul·let (mŭl'ĭt) *n.* (pl. **-lets**, collect. **-let**). Any of several spiny-rayed edible fishes of the family Muglidae, distributed worldwide in tropical and temperate waters, esp. the **striped** ~ (*Mugil cephalus*) of the Amer. gulf coast and Florida Keys.

mul·li·ga·taw·ny (mŭl*i*gataw'nē) *n.* Highly flavored E. Indian soup, made with curry powder and hot seasonings; ~ **paste**, curry paste used for this. [Tamil *milagutannir* pepper water]

mul·lion (mŭl'y*o*n) *n.* Vertical shaft dividing lights in a window. **mul'lioned** *adj.* Furnished with mullions.

multi- *prefix*. Much, many.

mul·ti·far·i·ous (mŭltĭfār′ēus) *adj*. Having great variety. **mul·ti·far′i·ous·ly** *adv*. **mul·ti·far′i·ous·ness** *n*.

mul·ti·form (mŭl′tĭfōrm) *adj*. Having many forms; manifold. **mul·ti·for·mi·ty** (mŭltĭfōr′mĭtē) *n*. Variety, diversity (opp. *uniformity*).

mul·ti·lat·er·al (mŭltĭlăt′*e*ral) *adj*. Having many sides; (of agreement, treaty, etc.) in which more than two sides or nations participate; ~ **trade**, trade carried on among several countries without the necessity of balancing trade or payments between them.

mul·ti·mil·lion·aire (mŭltĭmĭly*o*nār′, mŭltī-) *n*. Person with a fortune of several millions (of dollars, pounds, etc.).

mul·tip·a·ra (mŭltĭp′*e*ra) *n*. (pl. **-a·rae** pr. -*e*rē). (med.) Pregnant woman who has borne one child or more.

mul·tip·a·rous (mŭltĭp′*e*rus) *adj*. Producing more than one at birth.

mul·ti·par·tite (mŭltĭpăr′tīt) *adj*. Divided into many parts.

mul·ti·ple (mŭl′t*i*pel) *adj*. Of many parts, elements or individual components; (math.) repeated, occurring more than once; (elect.) of a circuit with a number of parallel conductors; ~ **choice**, (of question in examination) accompanied by several possible answers from which correct answer is to be selected. ~ **sclerosis**, chronic progressive sclerosis of brain and spinal cord. **multiple** *n*. (math.) Number or quantity containing another an exact number of times; **lowest (least) common** ~, (abbrev. L.C.M.) least quantity that contains two or more given quantities exactly, as 12 is the L.C.M. of 3 and 4.

mul·ti·plex (mŭl′t*i*plĕks) *adj*. Manifold, of many elements; involving simultaneous transmission of several messages along a channel of communication.

mul·ti·pli·a·ble (mŭl′t*i*plīabel), **mul·ti·plic·a·ble** (mŭlt*i*plĭk′*a*bel) *adjs*. Capable of being multiplied.

mul·ti·pli·cand (mŭlt*i*plĭkănd′) *n*. (math.) Number that is to be multiplied by another.

mul·ti·pli·ca·tion (mŭlt*i*plĭkā′sh*o*n) *n*. Multiplying; (math.) finding the quantity produced by taking a given quantity (MULTIPLICAND) as many times as there are units in another given quantity (MULTIPLIER); ~ **table**, set of numbers, usu. 1 to 12, with the products of multiplication by the same numbers successively. **mul·ti·pli·ca·tive** (mŭl′t*i*plĭkātĭv, mŭlt*i*plĭk′*a*-) *adj*.

mul·ti·plic·i·ty (mŭlt*i*plĭs′ĭtē) *n*. (pl. **-ties**). Manifold variety; great number *of*.

mul·ti·pli·er (mŭl′t*i*plīer) *n*. That which multiplies; (math.) number by which another number is multiplied; (elect.) device for multiplying intensity of force, current, etc., to bring it to a desired strength; (econ.) proportion of an increment of a consumer's income to the consequent increment of saving.

mul·ti·ply (mŭl′t*i*plī) *v*. (**-plied, -ply·ing**). Produce large number of (instances etc.); breed (animals), propagate (plants); (math.) perform process of multiplication (symbol ×).

mul·ti·tude (mŭl′tĭtōōd, -tūd) *n*. Great number; throng; **the** ~, the many, the common people. **mul·ti·tu·di·nous** (mŭltĭtōō′d*i*nus, -tū′-) *adj*. **mul·ti·tu′di·nous·ly** *adv*. **mul·ti·tu′di·nous·ness** *n*.

mum (mŭm) *adj*. Strictly silent.

mum·ble (mŭm′b*e*l) *v*. (**-bled, -bling**). Speak or utter indistinctly or with lips partly closed. ~ *n*.

mum·bo jum·bo (mŭm′bō jŭm′bō) *n*. (pl. **mum·bo jum·bos**). Meaningless ritual; mystifying or obscure language etc., intended to confuse. [f. name of grotesque idol said to have been worshipped by certain black tribes]

mum·mer (mŭm′*e*r) *n*. Actor in traditional popular performance in dumb show. **mum′mer·y** *n*. (pl. **-mer·ies**). Mummer's performance; buffoonery.

mum·mi·fy (mŭm′ĭfī) *v.t.* (**-fied, -fy·ing**). Make into a mummy. **mum·mi·fi·ca·tion** (mŭmĭfĭkā′sh*o*n) *n*.

mum·my[1] (mŭm′ē) *n*. (pl. **-mies**). Dead body preserved from decay by embalming, esp. one so preserved by the ancient Egyptians; dried-up body; rich brown pigment obtained from bitumen; ~ **case**, case of wood, modeled to shape of human body, in which Egyptian mummies were placed for burial. [Arab. *mūmīyā′*, med. L. *mumia* (Pers. *mūm* wax)]

mum·my[2] (mŭm′ē) *n*. (pl. **-mies**). (Child's word for) mother.

mumps (mŭmps) *n*. Virus infection that causes acute inflammation of parotid gland and consequent swelling of neck and face.

munch (mŭnch) *v*. Eat with noticeable action of the jaws.

mun·dane (mŭndān′, mŭn′dān) *adj*. Worldly; dull, routine. **mun·dane′ly** *adv*. **mun·dane′ness** *n*.

Mu·nich (mū′nĭk) (*Ger.* **München**). City of West Germany; ~ **Pact**, agreement among England, France, Germany, and Italy, signed at Munich on Sept. 29, 1938, under which part of Czechoslovakia was ceded to Germany.

mu·nic·i·pal (mūnĭs′*i*pal) *adj*. Of the local self-government or corporate government of city or town. **mu·nic′i·pal·ly** *adv*.

In ancient Egypt the bodies of the nobility were preserved as ***mummies****. The soft parts were removed and the rest soaked in various resins, which were later injected into the body, before bandaging.*

A **mural** by Mexican-Americans on a barbershop at San Fernando, California. The Spanish (left) reads 'My race is my pride.' Murals have been a popular artform for centuries.

The beautiful **murex** — related to the whelk — is today valued for its shell. However, 2,000 years ago its flesh was processed to yield a famous, highly prized dye, 'Tyrian purple'.

mu·nic'i·pal·ism, mu·nic'i·pal·ist *ns.*

mu·nic·i·pal·i·ty (mūnĭsĭpăl'ĭtē) *n.* (pl. **-ties**). Town, district, having local self-government; governing body of this.

mu·nif·i·cent (mūnĭf'ĭsent) *adj.* Splendidly generous. **mu·nif'i·cent·ly** *adv.* **mu·nif'i·cence** *n.*

mu·ni·tion (mūnĭsh'*on*) *n.* (pl. exc. in comb.). Military weapons, ammunition, equipment, and stores. ~ *v.* Provide, furnish with munitions.

mu·on (mū'ŏn) *n.* (phys.) Mu meson, meson having a mass of 206.7 times that of the electron.

mu·ral (mūr'*al*) *adj.* Of, on a wall; ~ **crown**, (Rom. antiq.) garland given to soldiers who first scaled walls of a besieged town. **mural** *n.* A picture painted on a wall.

Mur·chi·son (mẽr'chĭs*on*) **Falls.** Waterfall in the Victoria Nile, dropping to Lake Albert in Uganda; **Murchison River**, river in W. Australia flowing into Indian Ocean.

mur·der (mẽr'd*er*) *n.* Unlawful killing of person with malice aforethought, dist. from (*accidental* or *justifiable*) *homicide* and *manslaughter*. ~ *v.t.* Kill unlawfully and with malice aforethought; massacre, butcher; (fig.) spoil by bad execution, representation, etc. **mur'der·er** *n.* (fem. **mur'der·ess**). **mur'der·ous** *adj.* **mur'der·ous·ly** *adv.*

mu·rex (mūr'ĕks) *n.* (pl. **mu·ri·ces** pr. mūr'ĭsēz, **mu·rex·es**). Mollusk of genus *M*~, allied to whelks, yielding purple dye.

murk (mẽrk) *n.* Darkness, gloom. ~ *adj.* (archaic, poet.) Dark, gloomy; **murk'y** *adj.* (**murk·i·er, murk·i·est**). Dark, gloomy; (of darkness) thick. **murk'i·ly** *adv.* **murk'i·ness** *n.*

mur·mur (mẽr'm*er*) *n.* Subdued continuous sound; (med.) sound of this kind heard in auscultation; muttered grumbling or repining; subdued or nearly inarticulate speech. **mur'mur·ous** *adj.* **mur'mur·ous·ly** *adv.* **murmur** *v.* Produce murmur; speak or say in murmur.

Mur·phy's (mẽr'fēz) **Law.** (facetious) Engineers' observation that anything that can go wrong will go wrong.

Mur·ray (mẽr'ē, mŭr'ē), **Sir James** (1837–1915). Scottish philologist, editor of *A New* (later known as *The*) *Oxford English Dictionary*.

mur·rhine (mẽr'ĭn, -īn) *adj.* ~ **glass**, Modern delicate glassware from the East, with small particles of colored metal embedded in it. [L. *murra* substance of which precious vases were made]

mus·ca·dine (mŭs'k*a*dĭn, -dīn) = MUSCAT.

mus·ca·rine (mŭs'k*er*ĭn, -*e*rēn) *n.* Poisonous alkaloid obtained from fungus *Amanita muscaria*. **mus·ca·rin·ic** (mŭsk*er*ĭn'ĭk) *adj.*

Mus·cat (mŭskăt'). Capital and a seaport of Oman on the Gulf of Oman.

mus·cat (mŭs'kăt) *n.* Kind of grape with flavor or odor of musk.

mus·ca·tel (mŭsk*a*tĕl', mŭs'k*a*tĕl) *n.* Muscat; strong sweet white wine prepared from muscats; muscat raisin.

mus·cle (mŭs'*el*) *n.* Contractile fibrous band or bundle producing motion in animal body, muscular strength; **mus'clebound**, having the muscles stiff and enlarged owing to excessive exercise. **muscle** *v.i.* (**-cled, -cling**). (slang) Force one's way *in*. [L. *musculus* little mouse, f. fancied resemblance to a mouse]

Mus·co·vy (mŭs'k*o*vē). (hist.) Principality of Moscow; Russia in the period (16th and 17th centuries) when that principality was dominant; ~ **duck**, tropical Amer. duck (*Cairina moschata*) with slightly musky smell. **Mus·co·vite** (mŭs'k*o*vīt) *adj.* & *n.* (Native, inhabitant) of Muscovy or of Moscow. [*Muscovia*, Latinized form of Russ. *Moskva* Moscow]

mus·cu·lar (mŭs'ky*u*l*er*) *adj.* Of, in, the muscles; having well-developed muscles; ~ **atrophy,** ~ **dystrophy**, wasting disorders of the muscles. **mus·cu·lar·i·ty** (mŭsky*u*lăr'ĭtē) *n.*

mus·cu·la·ture (mŭs'ky*u*l*a*ch*er*)

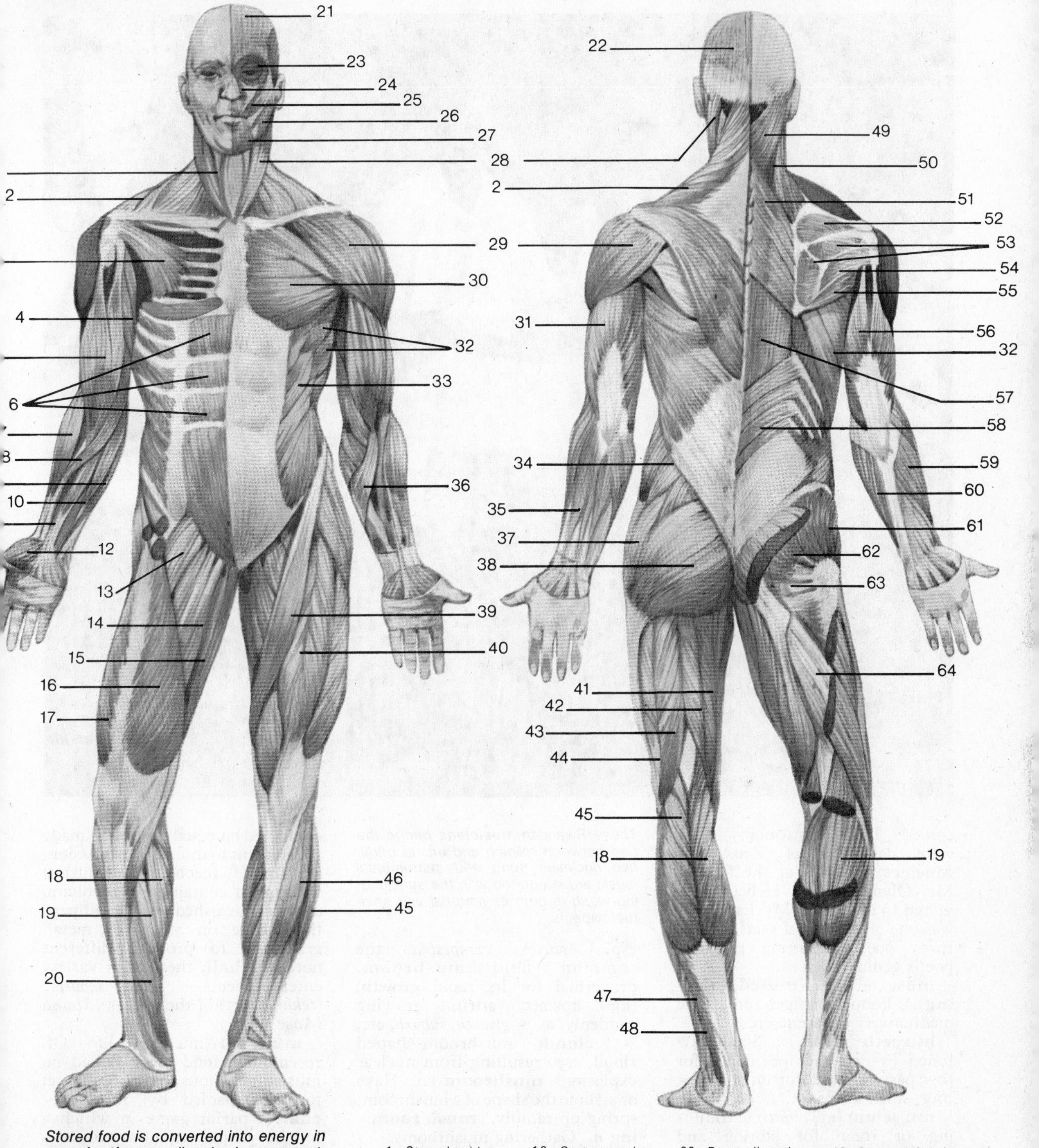

Stored food is converted into energy in ***muscle tissue:*** *all animal movement, except in unicellular creatures, depends on this process. In higher animals, some muscles directly obey the will while others maintain the body's functions.*

1. Sternohyoid
2. Trapezius
3. Pectoralis minor
4. Triceps
5. Biceps
6. Rectus abdominus
7. Brachioradialis
8. Pronator teres
9. Flexor carpi ulnaris
10. Flexor digitorum superficialis
11. Flexor carpi radialis
12. Flexor pollicis brevis
13. Iliacus
14. Adductor longus
15. Gracilis
16. Vastus medialis
17. Vastus lateralis
18. Gastrocnemius
19. Soleus
20. Flexor digitorum longus
21. Occipitofrontalis frontal
22. Occipitofrontalis rear
23. Orbicularis oculi
24. Levator labii superioris alaeque nasi
25. Levator anguli oris
26. Risorius
27. Depressor labii inferioris
28. Sternocleido-mastoid
29. Deltoid
30. Pectoralis major
31. Triceps
32. Serratus anterior
33. External oblique
34. Internal oblique
35. Extensor digitorum
36. Bicipital aponeurosis
37. Gluteus medius
38. Gluteus maximus
39. Sartorius
40. Rectus femoris
41. Gracilis
42. Semitendinosus
43. Biceps femoris
44. Vastus lateralis
45. Gastrocnemius
46. Tibialis anterior
47. Soleus
48. Peroneus brevis
49. Splenius capitis
50. Levator scapulae
51. Rhombodeus major
52. Supraspinatus
53. Infraspinatus
54. Teres minor
55. Teres major
56. Triceps
57. Longissimus thoracis
58. Serratus posterior
59. Brachioradialis
60. Flexor carpi ulnaris
61. Gluteus minimus
62. Piriformis
63. Gemellus
64. Biceps femoris

n. System, arrangement of muscles.

Muse (mūz) *n.* (Gk. and Rom. myth.) One of the nine goddesses who presided over the arts and sciences (Calliope, epic poetry; Clio, history; Erato, erotic poetry; Euterpe, lyric poetry; Melpomene, tragedy; Polyhymnia, sacred song; Terpsichore, dancing; Thalia,

comedy; Urania, astronomy); they were daughters of Zeus and Mnemosyne, born at the foot of Mt. Olympus; Mt. Helicon was sacred to them, and Mt. Parnassus was one of their chief seats; hence, **m ~**, poet's inspiring goddess, poet's genius.

muse (mūz) *v.i.* (**mused, mus·ing**). Ponder, reflect (*on*); gaze meditatively (*on* scene etc.).

mu·sette (mūzĕt′) *n.* Small soft-toned French bagpipe; dance for this; pastoral; reed stop on organ; **~ bag**, small knapsack.

mu·se·um (mūzē′*u*m) *n.* Building or room for storing and exhibiting objects illustrative of antiquities, natural history, the arts, etc.; **~ piece**, object of quality fit for a museum; person or thing regarded merely as a survival or curiosity. [Gk. *mouseion* seat of the Muses]

mush (mŭsh, *dial.* mo͞osh) *n.* Soft pulp; porridge made from corn meal; any soft, thick mass. **mush'y** *adj.* (**mush·i·er, mush·i·est**). Soft, pulpy; (fig.) weakly sentimental, rubbishy. **mush'i·ness** *n.*

mush·room (mŭsh′ro͞om) *n.* Popular name of any edible fungus, esp. *Agaricus campestris*, the common field mushroom, proverbial for its rapid growth; (fig.) upstart; (attrib.) growing suddenly, as ~ *growth, suburb*, etc; **~ cloud**, mushroom-shaped cloud, esp. resulting from nuclear explosion. **mushroom** *v.i.* Have or assume the shape of a mushroom; spring up rapidly. **mush'room·ing** *n.* Gathering mushrooms.

These Rwandan ***musicians*** *bridge the gap between religion and art. In primitive societies song and instrumental music are integrated with the surrounding world in both its material and spiritual aspects.*

mu·sic (mū′zĭk) *n.* Art of combining sounds for reproduction by the voice or various kinds of musical instruments in rhythmic, melodic, and harmonic form so as to express thought or feeling and affect the emotions; sounds so produced; pleasant sound, e.g. song of a bird, murmur of a stream, etc.; written or printed score of musical composition; **face the ~**, face the consequences of actions etc. without shirking; **~ drama**, Wagnerian form of opera in which music and the other elements are combined on equal terms and made subservient to dramatic expression; **~ box**, mechanical musical instrument containing a revolving cylinder furnished with small pegs that strike on strips of metal, graduated to produce different notes; **~ hall**, theater for variety entertainments. [Gk. *mousikē* (*tekhnē*) (art) of the Muses (*Mousa* Muse)]

mu·si·cal (mū′zĭk*a*l) *adj.* Of, resembling, fond of or skilled in, music; melodious, harmonious; set to, accompanied by, music; **~ chairs**, parlor game in which a number of players move around a row of chairs, less by one in number than the players, until music ceases, when the one who finds no seat is eliminated, and a chair is removed before the next round; **~ comedy**, (also **musical**) light dramatic entertainment of songs, dialogue, and dancing connected by a plot; **~ glasses**, set of glasses, graduated in tone, struck by small sticks; similar instrument with glass bowls or tubes; **~ instrument**, any of a variety of instruments with which music is produced, usu. classified as *string*, *wind*, and *percussion*.

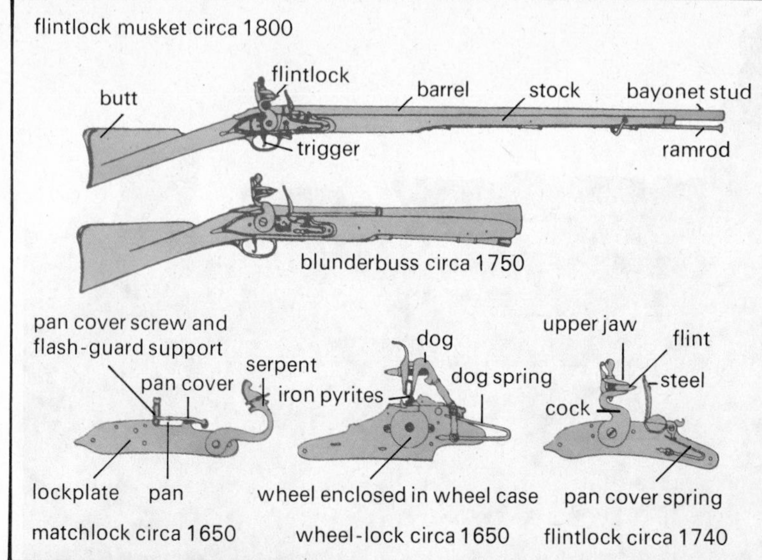

The ***musket*** *was the infantryman's long-range weapon for nearly 300 years. The design of the lock changed (match–wheel–flint–percussion) but the basic principle remained.*

Many types of ***mussel*** *are present in both sea and fresh waters throughout the world. Particular species are collected for culinary use, but others may also be eaten.*

mu'si·cal·ly *adv.* **mu'si·cal·ness** *n.* **musical** *n.* Film or theatrical piece (not opera or operetta) of which music is essential element; musical comedy.

mu·si·cian (mūzĭsh'*a*n) *n.* Person skilled in art or practice of music. **mu·si'cian·ship** *n.* Skill, insight, in interpreting and performing music.

mu·si·col·o·gy (mūzĭkŏl'*o*jē) *n.* All study of music except that directed to proficiency in performance or composition. **mu·si·co·log·i·cal** (mūzĭk*o*lŏj'ĭk*a*l) *adj.* **mu·si·col'o·gist** *n.*

musk (mŭsk) *n.* Odoriferous reddish-brown substance secreted in a gland or sac by male musk deer, used as a basis of perfumes; any of various plants with musky smell; ~ **deer**, small hornless deer (*Moschus*) of Central Asia; ~ **duck**, Muscovy duck; also, an Australian duck (*Biziura lobata*) so called from the musky smell of the male; **musk'melon**, any of several varieties of oblong or round fruits of the melon (*Cucumis melon*), a vine of the gourd family, as the canteloupe; **musk ox**, ruminant (*Ovibos moschatus*) allied to sheep and bovines, with curved horns and shaggy pelt, now found only in Arctic America; **musk'rat**, large aquatic rodent (*Ondatra zibethica*) common throughout N. America; **musk rose**, variety of climbing rose with fragrant white flowers; **musk tree, wood**, any of a variety of trees having a musky smell. **mus'ky** *adj.* (**mus·ki·er, mus·ki·est**).

mus·keg (mŭs'kĕg) *n.* Level swampy or boggy area in some regions of Canada.

mus·kel·lunge (mŭs'k*e*lŭnj) *n.* (pl. **-lunge**). Large N. Amer. pike (*Esox masquinongy*), found esp. in Great Lakes.

mus·ket (mŭs'kĭt) *n.* (hist.) Heavy handgun, esp. unrifled, carried by infantry soldier. [It. *moschetto* sparrow hawk]

mus·ket·eer (mŭskĭtēr') *n.* (hist.) Soldier armed with musket.

mus·ket·ry (mŭs'kĭtrē) *n.* (mil.) Instruction, practice, in rifle shooting.

Mus·lim (mŭz'lĭm, mo͝oz'-, mo͞os'-) *n.* (pl. **-lims, -lim**). One who professes Islam. ~ *adj.* Of Muslims.

mus·lin (mŭz'lĭn) *n.* Fine delicately woven cotton fabric. [*Mosul*, town in Iraq where muslin was orig. made]

mus·sel (mŭs'*e*l) *n.* Any of several genera of marine or fresh-water bivalve mollusks, esp. *Mytilus*, the common edible sea mussel, and *Unio*, the fresh-water pearl-forming mussel.

Mus·so·li·ni (mo͞osolē'nē, mo͞o-; *It.* mo͞osawlē'nē), **Benito** (1883–1945). Italian Fascist politician; dictator 1922–43.

Mus·sul·man (mŭs'*u*lm*a*n) *adj.* & *n.* (pl. **-mans**). Muslim.

must[1] (mŭst) *n.* New wine; unfermented or incompletely fermented grape juice.

must[2] (mŭst) *aux.v.* (followed by inf. without *to*) Be obliged to; be certain to. ~ *n.* (colloq.) Something that should not be missed.

mus·tache, mous·tache (mŭs'-tăsh, m*u*stăsh') *ns.* Hair growing on upper lip, esp. of a man; similar hair around mouths of some animals, as cats etc.; ~ **cup**, drinking cup with partial cover to prevent the mustache from becoming wet.

Mus·ta·fa Ke·mal (mo͞os'tahfah k*e*mahl') = ATATÜRK.

mus·tang (mŭs'tăng) *n.* 1. Wild or half-wild horse of Mexico, California, etc. 2. Small red Texas grape.

mus·tard (mŭs't*e*rd) *n.* Any of various annual plants (genus *Brassica*), having yellow flowers and slender pods; hot pungent powder made from the crushed

The Lion Gate (right) was the main entrance to the ancient acropolis or fortified section of the city of ***Mycenae,*** *the principal center of Aegean civilization in about 1,400 B.C.*

seeds of this plant, esp. *B. nigra* and *B. alba*, mixed to a paste with water (**English** ~) or with vinegar, spices, etc. (**French** ~) and used as a condiment with meat; ~ **gas**, dichlorodiethyl sulphide, a colorless oily liquid with faint garlic odor, the vapor of which is one of the vesicant gases used in chemical warfare; ~ **plaster**, plaster containing mustard, applied to the skin; ~ **pot**, vessel for holding mustard at table; **cut the** ~, (slang) reach requisite standard.

mus·ter (mŭs′t*er*) *n.* Assembling of men for inspection, instruction, etc.; **pass** ~, undergo muster without censure; bear examination or inspection; come up to standard; ~ **roll**, official list of officers and men in army or ship's company (also fig.). **muster** *v.* Collect or assemble for inspection etc.; collect, bring or come together; summon (courage, strength, etc., *up*).

mus·ty (mŭs′tē) *adj.* (**-ti·er, -ti·est**). Spoiled with damp; moist and fetid; moldy; (fig.) stale, antiquated. **mus′ti·ness** *n.*

mu·ta·ble (mū′t*a*b*e*l) *adj.* Liable to change, fickle. **mu·ta·bil·i·ty** (mūt*a*bĭl′ĭtē) *n.*

mu·tant (mū′t*a*nt) *adj.* & *n.* (biol.) (Individual) differing from its parents as a result of mutation.

mu·ta·tion (mūtā′sh*o*n) *n.* 1. Change, alteration. 2. (biol.) Occurrence of a new form differing from its parents as a result of change in the gene structure of a reproductive cell; mutant. 3. (gram.) Change in vowel sound through influence of another vowel in following syllable.

mu·ta·tis mu·tan·dis (mūtā′tĭs mūtăn′dĭs; *Lat.* mo͞otah′tēs mo͞otahn′dēs). With the necessary alterations or changes. [L.]

mute (mūt) *adj.* 1. Silent; not capable of speech, dumb; (of hounds) not giving tongue. 2. Not expressed in speech. 3. (of consonants) Stopped; produced with a closing at some point in throat or mouth, as *b*, *p*, *t*, etc.; (of letters) not pronounced, although written, as *e* in *mute*. **mute′ly** *adv.* **mute′ness** *n.* **mute** *n.* 1. Dumb person. 2. (mus.) Clip for deadening resonance of strings of violin etc.; pad for deadening sound of wind instrument. 3. Mute consonant. ~ *v.t.* (**mut·ed, mut·ing**). Deaden, soften, sound of a musical instrument with a mute; tone down.

mu·ti·late (mū′t*i*lāt) *v.t.* (**-lat·ed, -lat·ing**). Injure, make imperfect, by depriving of part. **mu·ti·la·tion** (mūt*i*lā′sh*o*n) *n.*

mu·ti·neer (mūt*i*nēr′) *n.* One who mutinies.

mu·ti·nous (mū′t*i*n*u*s) *adj.* Guilty of mutiny or rebellion. **mu′ti·nous·ly** *adv.*

mu·ti·ny (mū′t*i*nē) *n.* (pl. **-nies**). Open revolt against constituted authority, esp. refusal of five or more members of armed forces to obey orders of a superior officer. ~ *v.i.* (**-nied, -ny·ing**). Take part in mutiny.

mu·tism (mū′tĭz*e*m) *n.* Muteness, silence; dumbness.

mut·ter (mŭt′*er*) *v.* Speak, utter, in low and barely audible tones, with mouth nearly closed. ~ *n.* Muttering.

mut·ton (mŭt′*o*n) *n.* Flesh of sheep as food; **mut′tonchop**, piece of rib or loin of mutton, usu. served fried or grilled; **mut′tonchops**, short bushy whiskers shaped like a muttonchop.

mu·tu·al (mū′cho͞o*a*l) *adj.* (of feelings, actions, etc.) Felt, done, by each to(ward) the other, as ~ *affection*, *benefit*; performed by joint action, done in common; (colloq.) common to two or more persons, as *our* ~ *friend*; (insurance) of a system by which insured persons are shareholders of a company and share in its profits; ~ **fund**, investment company that invests shareholders' funds in securities (of various types). **mu′tu·al·ly** *adv.* **mu·tu·al·i·ty** (mūcho͞oăl′ĭtē) *n.* Reciprocity, interdependence.

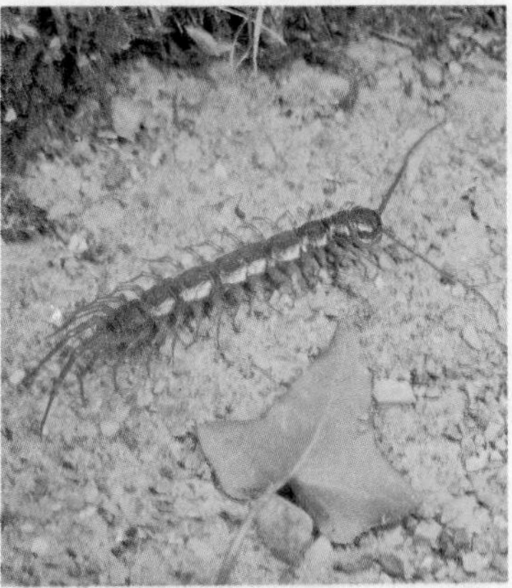

The familiar millipedes and centipedes (above) are both ***myriapods,*** *although very different in their habits. Carnivorous centipedes are fast-running creatures — one species can even catch flies — while millipedes are slower moving.*

muu·muu (mo͞o′mo͞o) *n.* Woman's loose, brightly colored dress. [Hawaiian]

Mu·zak (mū′zăk) *n.* (trademark) Recorded background music transmitted through telephone or radio to receivers in factories, restaurants, offices, etc.

mu·zhik, mou·jik (mo͞ozhĭk′, mo͞o′zhĭk) *ns.* Russian peasant.

muz·zle (mŭz′*e*l) *n.* 1. Projecting part of animal's head including nose and mouth; snout. 2. Arrangement of straps or wires over animal's mouth to prevent its biting, eating, etc. 3. End of firearm from which the projectile is discharged; **muz'zleloader,** firearm loaded at muzzle, dist. f. *breechloader*; **muzzle velocity,** velocity of projectile at its discharge from muzzle of a gun. **muzzle** *v.t.* (**-zled, -zling**). Put muzzle on (animal, and fig. a person); impose silence on, restrict freedom of speech of.

mV, mv *abbrevs.* Millivolt(s).

MVD *abbrev.* Secret police of U.S.S.R., 1946–60. [initials of Russ. *M*inistérstvo *V*nútrennikh *D*el, ministry of internal affairs]

mW, MW *abbrevs.* Megawatt(s).

Mx *abbrev.* Maxwell(s).

my (mī) *poss. pron.* Possessive case of *I* used as attrib. adjective, belonging to, affecting, me; prefixed to some terms of address, as ~ **lord.**

my·ce·li·um (mīsē'lēum) *n.* (pl. **-li·a** pr. -lēa). (bot.) Vegetative part of a fungus, consisting of microscopic threads.

My·ce·nae (mīsē'nē). City of ancient Greece in the plain of Argos; first inhabited *c*3000 B.C. by peoples akin to the Minoans of Crete; in the Bronze Age (*c*2100–1150 B.C.) occupied by a people whose language was probably an early form of Greek, who built the Lion Gate and beehive tombs, which still survive. **My·ce·nae·an** (mīsinē'an) *adj.* & *n.*

my·col·o·gy (mīkŏl'ojē) *n.* Study of fungi. **my·col'o·gist** *n.*

my·cor·rhi·za (mīkorī'za) *n.* (pl. **-zae** pr. -zē, **-zas**). (bot.) Association of a fungus with the roots of certain plants, in which the fungus forms a layer around or within the outer tissue of the roots.

my·e·li·tis (mīelī'tis) *n.* Inflammation of the spinal cord.

My·lar (mīlăr) *n.* (trademark) Tough polyester film used in electrical insulation etc.

my·na, mi·na, my·nah (mī'na) *ns.* One of a number of birds of starling family of India, esp. *Acridotheres tristis*, which has been introduced and has proliferated in other regions (e.g., Hawaii); and *Gracula religiosa*, or hill myna, an excellent mimic that can be trained to talk realistically.

my·o·car·di·um (mīokăr'dēum) *n.* Muscular substance of the heart. **my·o·car'di·al** *adj.*

my·ol·o·gy (mīŏl'ojē) *n.* Study of muscles. **my·o·log·i·cal** (mīolŏj'ĭkal) *adj.* **my·ol'o·gist** *n.*

my·op·a·thy (mīŏp'athē) *n.* Any disease of the muscles.

my·ope (mī'ōp) *n.* Near-sighted person.

my·o·pi·a (mīō'pēa) *n.* Near-sightedness, a condition of the eye in which the rays from distant objects are brought to a focus before they reach the retina and so form a blurred image.

The forget-me-not is the member of the genus ***Myosotis*** *most familiar to gardeners. Its delicate flowers and pale green leaves have made it a popular border perennial.*

my·op·ic (mīŏp'ĭk) *adj.* Near-sighted.

my·o·so·tis (mīosō'tĭs) *n.* (bot.) Small plant of genus *M*~, of which the forget-me-not is a species, with pink, blue, or white flowers.

myr·i·ad (mĭr'ēad) *adj.* & *n.* Ten thousand; (of) indefinitely great number.

myr·i·a·pod (mĭr'ēapŏd) *adj.* & *n.* (zool.) (Animal) with many legs, of the class of arthropods which includes the centipedes and millipedes.

Myr·mi·don (mĕr'mĭdŏn, -don) *n.* (pl. **-dons, Myr·mid·o·nes** pr. mĕrmĭd'onēz). (Gk. legend) One of a warlike people on the S. borders of Thessaly who followed Achilles to the siege of Troy.

myr·mi·don (mĕr'mĭdŏn, -don) *n.* Faithful follower; unscrupulously faithful attendant.

my·rob·a·lan (mīrŏb'alan, mĭ-) *n.* Dried astringent plumlike fruit of certain E. Indian trees, containing tannin and used in dyeing, tanning, etc.

myrrh (mĕr) *n.* Gum resin, obtained from certain plants of genus *Commiphora*, used in perfumes and incense, and in medicine as astringent and antiseptic mouthwash.

myr·tle (mĕr'tel) *n.* (bot.) Shrub of genus *Myrtus*, esp. *M. communis*, the European myrtle with dark glossy evergreen leaves and white fragrant flowers.

my·self (mīsĕlf') *pron.* (pl. **our·selves** pr. owrsĕlvz'). Emphatic and reflexive form corresponding to *I*, *me*.

mys·te·ri·ous (mĭstēr'ēus) *adj.* Full of, wrapped in, mystery; (of persons) delighting in, affecting, mystery. **mys·te'ri·ous·ly** *adv.* **mys·te'ri·ous·ness** *n.*

mys·ter·y (mĭs'terē, -trē) *n.* (pl. **-ter·ies**). 1. Hidden or inexplicable matter; secrecy, obscurity. 2. Religious truth known only by divine revelation; religious rite, esp. (pl.) Eucharist; (pl.) secret religious rites of Greeks, Romans, etc. 3. (also ~ **play**) Medieval drama based on Bible story or legend of saint.

mys·tic (mĭs'tĭk) *adj.* Spiritually symbolic; occult, esoteric; enigmatical. ~ *n.* One who seeks by contemplation and self-surrender to attain union with the Deity, or who believes in the spiritual apprehension of truths beyond the understanding. **mys'ti·cal** *adj.* Of mystics or mysticism; spiritually significant, connected with God in some way transcending understanding. **mys'ti·cal·ly** *adv.* **mys·ti·cism** (mĭs'tĭsĭzem) *n.*

mys·ti·fy (mĭs'tĭfī) *v.t.* (**-fied, -fy·ing**). Bewilder; hoax, humbug. **mys·ti·fi·ca·tion** (mĭstĭfĭkā'shon) *n.*

mys·tique (mĭstēk') *n.* Atmosphere of mystery and veneration investing some doctrines, arts, professions, etc., or personages; any professional skill or technique that mystifies and impresses the layman.

myth (mĭth) *n.* Fictitious (primitive) tale, usu. involving supernatural persons, embodying some popular idea concerning natural or historical phenomena; fictitious person or thing; fictitious idea or belief etc., esp. one that has been accepted uncritically. **myth'ic, myth'i·cal** *adjs.* **myth'i·cal·ly** *adv.*

myth·i·cize (mĭth'ĭsīz) *v.t.* (**-cized, -ciz·ing**). Treat (story etc.) as myth, interpret mythically. **myth·i·cism** (mĭth'ĭsĭzem) *n.*

my·thol·o·gy (mĭthŏl'ojē) *n.* (pl. **-gies**). Body of myths, esp. as relating to particular person or subject or current in a particular country; study of myths; picture etc. illustrating a myth. **my·thol'o·ger, my·thol'o·gist** *ns.* Student of myths. **myth·o·log·i·cal** (mĭtholŏj'ĭkal) *adj.* **myth·o·log'i·cal·ly** *adv.* **my·thol'o·gize** *v.t.* (**-gized, -giz·ing**). Treat of myths and mythology; invent myths.

myx·e·de·ma (mĭksĭdē'ma) *n.* Disorder due to deficient secretion of the thyroid gland.

myx·o·ma·to·sis (mĭksomatō'sĭs) *n.* Contagious usu. fatal disease of rabbits, caused by a virus.

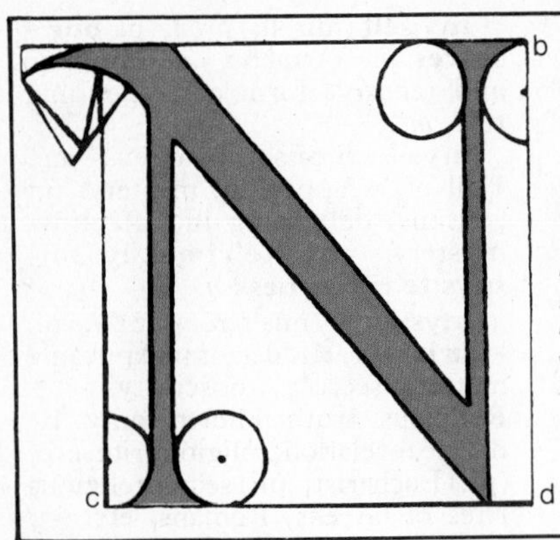

'Nun', the Semitic name for ***N n,*** *is thought to have meant 'fish', and the early form of the letter may derive from an ideogram. Over the millennia the letter shape has changed with alterations in writing methods.*

Phoenician Cretan Early Greek

Etruscan Roman Classical Latin

N, n (ĕn) (pl. **N's, n's** or **Ns, ns**). 1. Fourteenth letter of modern English and 13th of ancient Roman alphabet, representing historically Gk. *nu* and Semitic *nun*; earlier Greek forms were N and И, corresponding to Phoenician y; usu. denoting a voiced nasal consonant with front closure (point of tongue touching teeth or teeth-ridge), but sometimes also sonant or vowel, and before *g*, *k*, a nasal with back tongue closure. 2. (print.) = EN. 3. (math.) Indefinite number; **to the nth (power)**, to any required power; (fig.) to any extent, to the utmost.

N *abbrev.* Newton; north(ern).

N *symbol.* Nitrogen.

N. *abbrev.* Navy; new; noon; Norse; north(ern); November.

n. *abbrev.* Name; neuter; new; nominative; noon; north(ern); note; noun; number.

N.A. *abbrev.* North America; not applicable.

NAACP *abbrev.* National Association for the Advancement of Colored People.

nab (năb) *v.t.* (**nabbed, nab·bing**). (slang) Apprehend, arrest; catch in wrongdoing.

na·bob (nā´bŏb) *n.* 1. = NAWAB. 2. (hist.) Retired servant of East India Company, esp. between battle of Plassey, 1757, and appointment of Warren Hastings, 1772, returning to England with large fortune and orientalized ways. 3. Any ostentatiously wealthy person. **na'bob·ish** *adj.* **na'bob·ism** *n.*

Na·bo·kov (nah´bokawf), **Vladímir** (1899–1977). Russian-born author whose novels include *Lolita* (1959).

Na·both (nā´bŏth). Israelite who was stoned to death because he would not give up his vineyard to Ahab (1 Kings 21); **~'s vineyard**, possession that one will stop at nothing to secure.

na·celle (nasĕl´) *n.* Outer casing of aircraft's engine.

na·cre (nā´ker) *n.* (Shellfish yielding) mother-of-pearl. **na·cre·ous** (nā´krēus) *adj.*

na·dir (nā´dēr, -der) *n.* Point of heavens diametrically opposite zenith or directly under observer; (transf.) lowest point, place or time of great depression. [Arab. *nazīr as-samt* opposite to (zenith)]

nag[1] (năg) *n.* Small riding horse or pony; (colloq.) horse.

nag[2] (năg) *v.* (**nagged, nag·ging**). Find fault or scold persistently (*at* person); annoy thus. **nag'ging** *adj.* (esp. of pain) Gnawing, persistent.

Na·ga (nah´ga) *n.* 1. (Hindu myth.) One of a race of semihuman serpents, genii of rain, rivers, etc. 2. Member of one of a group of tribes inhabiting parts of Assam and Burma.

na·ga·na (nagah´na) *n.* Disease carried by certain species of tsetse fly affecting domestic animals and some wild ones. [Zulu *nakane*]

Na·ga·sa·ki (nahgasah´kē, năgasăk´ē). Seaport on W. Kyushu Island, Japan; almost half the city was destroyed by U.S. atomic bomb dropped Aug. 9, 1945, during World War II.

Na·hua·tl (nah´wahtel) (pl. **-hua·tls**, collect. **-hua·tl**) *adj.* & *n.* (Member, language) of a group of peoples of S. Mexico and Central America.

Na·hum (nā´hum). Hebrew minor prophet; book of Old Testament containing his prophecy against Nineveh (beginning of 7th c. B.C.).

nai·ad (nī´ăd, nā´-, -ad) *n.* (pl. **-ads, -a·des** pr. -adēz). Water nymph (esp. in Gk. myth.).

nail (nāl) *n.* 1. Horny oval-shaped protective covering of modified epidermis on upper surface of tip of finger or toe; claw, talon. 2. Hard excrescence on upper mandible of some softbilled birds. 3. Small metal spike, usu. with point and broadened head, driven in with hammer to hold things together or as peg or ornament; **hit the ~ on the head**, give true explanation, propose or do right thing, hit the mark. 4. **nail'brush**, small brush for cleaning fingernails; **nail'head**, architectural ornament shaped like head of nail; **nail file, nail scissors**, instruments for paring fingernails. **nail** *v.t.* Fasten with nail(s); fix or keep fixed (person, attention, etc.); secure, catch, engage, succeed in getting hold of; **~ down**, (colloq.) establish, settle once and for all; **~ to the floor**, (colloq.) follow shady merchant's practice of refusing to sell (advertised merchandise). **nail'er** *n.* Nailmaker.

Nai·ro·bi (nīrō´bē). Capital of Kenya.

Nai·smith (nā´smĭth), **James** (1861–1939). Canadian-born Amer. physical education professor; originator of basketball.

na·ive, na·ïve (nahēv´), **na·if, na·ïf** (nahēf´) *adjs.* Artless, innocent, unsophisticated; amusingly simple. **na·ive'ly, na·ïve'ly** *advs.* **na·ive·té, na·ïve·te** (nahēvtā´), **na·ive·ty** (nahēv´tē) *ns.*

na·ked (nā´kĭd) *adj.* 1. Unclothed; not covered by clothing; defenseless. 2. Unsheathed; plain, undisguised, exposed for examination. 3. Devoid *of*; treeless, leafless, barren; without ornament; (of rock) exposed; (of light, flame, etc.) not placed within case or receptacle; (bot., zool.) without pericarp, leaves, hairs, scales, etc. 4. Without addition, comment, support, etc. 5. **~ eye**, eye unassisted by telescope, microscope, etc.; **~ truth**, strict truth, without concealment or addition. **na'ked·ly** *adv.* **na'ked·ness** *n.*

N.A.M. *abbrev.* National Association of Manufacturers.

nam·by-pam·by (năm´bēpăm´-bē) *adj.* & *n.* (pl. **-bies**). Sentimental, pretty, trifling (work of art); (person) lacking in vigor. [formed on name of *Ambrose* Philips (d. 1749), pastoral poet]

name (nām) *n.* Word by which individual person, animal, place, or thing is spoken of or to; person as known, famed, or spoken of; family, clan; reputation; merely nominal existence, practically nonexistent thing; **by the ~ of**, named; **call names**, described by uncomplimentary names; **in the name of**, invoking; acting as deputy for or in the interest of; **keep one's name on, take one's name off, the**

books, remain, cease to be, member of organization; **put one's name down for**, apply as candidate etc.; **name day**, day of saint after whom person is named; **name-dropping**, familiar mention of well-known names as form of boasting; **name of the game**, (colloq.) central purpose, essence of action; **name′plate**, plate affixed with name of occupant etc.; **name′sake**, person or thing with same name as another. **name** *v.t.* (**named, nam·ing**). Give name to, call by right name, appoint (to office etc.); specify.

name·less (nām′lĭs) *adj.* Obscure, left unnamed; unknown; bearing no name or inscription; indefinable; too bad to be named.

name·ly (nām′lē) *adv.* That is to say; specifically.

Na·mi·bia (n*a*mĭb′ē*a*). Formerly South West Africa, now a mandate there under South African administration; transfer of power to Namibians under negotiation; capital, Windhoek.

Na·nak (nah′n*a*k) (1469–1538). Called "Guru"; Indian religious leader and founder of Sikhism.

Nan·jing (nănzhēng′) = NANKING.

nan·keen (nănkēn′), **nan·kin** (năn′kĭn) *ns.* Chinese cloth of natural buff-yellow cotton; cloth of dyed cotton resembling this; pale buff-yellow color. 2. Chinese blue-and-white porcelain. [f. NANKING]

Although there have been considerable technological advances in China since 1948, many traditional methods survive. Peasants near ***Nanking*** *(above) use pedal-driven scoops to raise water.*

Nan·king (nănkĭng′). City of China, on Yangtze, capital of China early in Ming dynasty, and from 1929 until the Japanese invasion of China in 1937. [Chin., = "southern capital"]

nan·ny (năn′ē) *n.* (pl. **-nies**). Child's nurse; **~ goat**, she-goat. [pet form of female name *Ann*]

nano- *prefix.* (abbrev. n) One billionth of, as *nanosecond.*

Nantes (nănts; *Fr.* nahn̄t). City of W. France, on Loire River; **Edict of ~**, edict of Henry IV of France (1598) granting toleration to Protestants, revoked by Louis XIV (1685).

Nan·tuck·et (năntŭk′ĭt). Island and resort area of Massachusetts, S. of Cape Cod, in the Atlantic.

Na·o·mi (nāō′mē, -mī). Mother-in-law of RUTH[1] (Ruth I).

nap[1] (năp) *v.i.* (**napped, nap·ping**). Sleep lightly or briefly;

The town of Aus, situated at the edge of the ***Namibia*** *Desert. The status of Namibia has been disputed since 1966, when the U.N. declared the South African mandate terminated and assumed responsibility until independence. South Africa has since contested this.*

The settlement which gave rise to ***Naples*** *is very old. Later settlers from Chalcis and Athens built a new 'city' named Neapolis. It is now the third largest Italian city.*

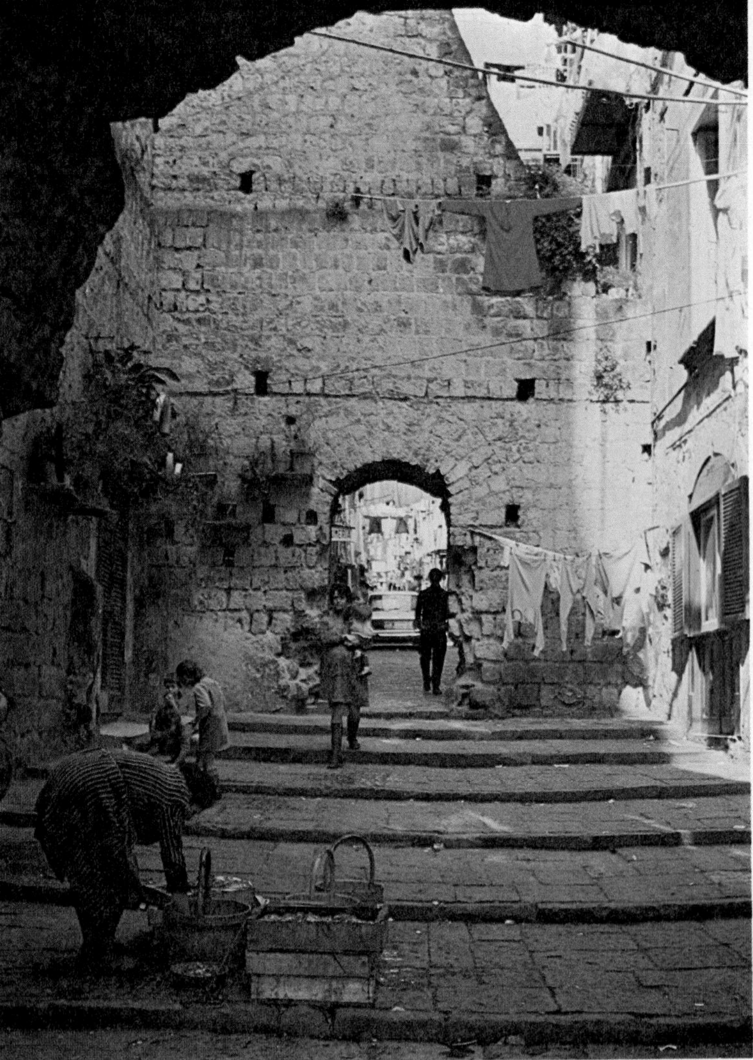

catch napping, find asleep; take unawares or off guard. **nap** *n.* Short sleep, doze, esp. by day.

nap[2] (năp) *n.* Surface given to cloth by raising the fibers; soft or downy surface. ~ *v.t.* (**napped, nap·ping**). Raise nap on (cloth). **nap'less** *adj.*

na·palm (nā'pahm) *n.* Mixture of aluminum salts of naphthenic acid from crude petroleum with palmitic and stearic acids obtained from coconut oil, for jellying gasoline for incendiary use in war (hence ~ **bomb**). [*na*(phthenic) + *palm*(itic)]

nape (nāp) *n.* Back of neck.

na·per·y (nā'perē) *n.* Household, esp. table, linen.

Naph·ta·li (năf'talī). Son of Jacob and Bilhah (Gen. 30); tribe of Israel traditionally descended from him.

naph·tha (năf'tha, năp'-) *n.* Orig. inflammable volatile liquid (a constituent of asphalt and bitumen) issuing from earth in some places; now, kinds of inflammable oil got by dry distillation of organic substances, esp. coal, shale, and petroleum.

naph·tha·lene (năf'thalēn, năp'-), **naph·tha·line, naph·tha·lin** (năf'thalĭn, năp'-) *ns.* White crystalline aromatic hydrocarbon, $C_{10}H_8$, with peculiar smell and pungent taste, obtained from coal tar etc. and used in the manufacture of dyes and chemicals and for soil fumigation.

naph·thene (năf'thēn, năp'-) *n.* One of a series of hydrocarbons occurring in petroleum, shale tar, etc.

naph·thol (năf'thōl, -thawl, -thŏl, năp'-) *n.* Either of two white crystalline hydroxyl derivatives of naphthalene, distinguished as **α-naphthol** and **β-naphthol**, used as disinfectants, in manufacture of dyes, etc.

Na·pi·er (nā'pēer, napēr'), **Ne·per** (nā'per), **John** (1550–1617). Scottish mathematician; inventor of logarithms and of the modern notation of decimal numbers. **Na·pier·i·an, Na·per·i·an** (napēr'ēan) *adjs.*

nap·kin (năp'kĭn) *n.* Square of material used for wiping lips or fingers at meals, or in serving certain dishes (**table** ~); ~ **ring**, ring for holding rolled up table napkin.

Na·ples (nā'pelz). (It. **Napoli**) City and seaport of SW. Italy. [L. *Neapolis* f. Gk. *nea polis* new city]

Na·po·le·on (napō'lēon). Name of several French rulers: **Napoleon I**, Napoleon Bonaparte (1769–1821), French soldier of Corsican family; became first consul of France, 1799, and emperor of the French, 1804; conquered large parts of Europe; after various defeats, abdicated and withdrew to Elba, 1814; returned to Paris, 1815; was defeated at Waterloo three months later and again abdicated; was exiled to St. Helena, where he died; **Napoleon II**, Napoleon Francois Joseph Charles, Duke of Reichstadt (1811–32), son of Napoleon I and Marie Louise; king of Rome; known as Napoleon II (although he never ruled France) because Napoleon I abdicated in his favor in 1814; **Napoleon III**, Charles Louis Napoleon Bonaparte (1808–73), nephew of Napoleon I; elected president of the French Republic 1848; proclaimed emperor 1852; captured by the Germans 1870, and deposed.

na·po·le·on (napō'lēon, -pōl'yon) *n.* 1. French gold coin of value 20 francs, issued by Napoleon I. 2. Kind of long boot. 3. Rich confection of puff pastry split and filled with cream.

Na·po·le·on·ic (napōlēŏn'ĭk) *adj.* Of Napoleon I; ~ **Wars**, series of campaigns (1799–1815), of French armies under Napoleon against Austria, Russia, Gt. Britain, Portugal, Prussia, and other powers.

narc, nark (nark) *ns.* (slang) Narcotics agent for the government.

nar·ce·ine (nar'sēēn, -ĭn) *n.* Bitter crystalline narcotic alkaloid present in opium.

nar·cis·sism (nar'sĭzĭzem) *n.* (psychol.) Excessive or erotic interest in one's own body or personality. **nar·cis·sis·tic** (narsĭsĭs'tĭk) *adj.* [f. NARCISSUS]

Nar·cis·sus (narsĭs'us). (Gk. myth.) Beautiful youth who, falling in love with his reflection in a

Resistance to ***Napoleonic*** *imperialism encouraged the development of new ideas of national identity, springing from language and culture, not dynastic factors. After Napoleon's fall these ideas helped to reshape Europe.*

spring, pined away, and was changed into the flower that bears his name.

nar·cis·sus (nārsĭs′*us*) *n.* Bulbous plant of genus *N~*, including the daffodil, esp. *N. poeticus*, bearing in spring heavily scented single white flower with undivided corona with a red crisped edge.

nar·co·lep·sy (nār′k*o*lĕpsē) *n.* Disease characterized by irresistible attacks of true sleep, usually of brief duration. **nar·co·lep·tic** (nārk*o*lĕp′tĭk) *adj.*

nar·co·sis (nārkō′sĭs) *n.* Operation or effects of narcotics; state of insensibility.

nar·cot·ic (nārkŏt′ĭk) *adj.* & *n.* (Substance) inducing drowsiness, sleep, stupor or insensibility (also fig.).

nard (nārd) *n.* (Plant, prob. *Nardostachys jatamansi*, yielding) aromatic balsam of ancients, usu. called *spikenard*.

na·res (nār′ēz) *n.pl.* (sing. **na·ris** pr. nār′ĭs). (anat.) Nostrils.

nar·ghi·le (nār′g*i*lē, -lā) *n.* Hookah. [Pers. *nārgīl* coconut]

nark = NARC.

Nar·ra·gan·sett (năr*a*găn′sĭt) *n.* (pl. **-setts**, collect. **-sett**). Member, Algonquian language, of an Amer. Indian tribe, formerly inhabiting parts of Rhode Island; ~ **Bay**, inlet of Atlantic in SE. Rhode Island.

nar·rate (năr′āt, nărāt′) *v.t.* (**-rat·ed, -rat·ing**). Relate, recount, give continuous account of. **nar·ra·tion** (nărā′sh*o*n), **nar′ra·tor, nar′rat·er** *ns.*

nar·ra·tive (năr′*a*tĭv) *n.* Tale, story, recital of facts; kind of composition or talk that confines itself to these. ~ *adj.* In the form of, concerned with, narration.

nar·row (năr′ō) *adj.* Of small, width in proportion to length, confining; restricted; with little margin; illiberal, prejudiced, exclusive, hence **~-minded(ly), ~-mindedness**; searching, precise; (phonet.) tense; **narrow gauge**, (on railroad) gauge of less than 4 ft. 8½ in. **nar′row·ly** *adv.* **nar′row·ness** *n.* **narrow** *n.* (usu. pl.) Narrow part of sound, strait, river, pass, etc. **narrow** *v.* Make or become narrower, diminish, lessen, contract.

nar·thex (nār′thĕks) *n.* Porch or vestibule in early Christian church, extending across width of nave at opposite end from main altar, and used by those not in full communion.

nar·whal, nar·wal (nār′w*a*l), **nar·whale** (nār′hwāl, -wāl) *ns.* Arctic cetacean (*Monodon monoceros*), the male having a very long spirally twisted straight tusk developed from one, or sometimes both, of its two teeth.

nar·y (nār′ē) *adj.* (dial.) Not a, no. [var. of *ne'er a*]

NAS *abbrev.* National Academy of Sciences; Naval Air Station.

NASA (năs′*a*, nah′s*a*) *n.* U.S. agency responsible for civilian programs of government in aeronautics and space research. [N(ational) A(eronautics and) S(pace) A(dministration)]

na·sal (nā′z*a*l) *adj.* Of the nose; (of sounds) produced with nose passages open (as *n*, *m*, *ng*); (of voice etc.) characterized by unusual or disagreeable number of sounds produced by means of nose. **na′sal·ly** *adv.* **na·sal·i·ty** (nāzăl′ĭtē) *n.* **na′sal·ize** *v.* (**-ized, -iz·ing**). **na·sal·i·za·tion** (nāz*a*lĭzā′sh*o*n) *n.* **nasal** *n.* Nasal letter or sound.

nas·cent (năs′*e*nt, nā′s*e*nt) *adj.* In the act of being born; just beginning to be, not yet mature; ~ **state**, (chem.) highly active condition of certain elements, esp. hydrogen, at the moment of liberation from a compound. **nas′cen·cy, nas′cence** *ns.*

Nash (năsh), **Ogden** (1902–71). Amer. poet and humorous writer.

The original Grand Ole Opry building in ***Nashville,*** *Tennessee, home of the famous folk music program which began in 1925. Nashville is also the center for country and western music and has a large recording industry.*

The vivid flowers of the ***nasturtium*** *have made it a popular garden plant. Climbing or trailing, its round leaves and orange, red, or yellow blooms provide an attractive splash of color.*

A typical ***Natchez*** *antebellum home, for which it is famous. This city in southwest Mississippi takes its name from the Natchez Indians, who were forced to move to Oklahoma after the French-Natchez wars in the 18th century.*

Once the haunt of pirates, the Bahamas are better known today as a resort where scenes such as this on the wharf in ***Nassau,*** *the capital, can be found.*

Nash·ville (năsh′vĭl). Capital and commercial city of Tennessee, on the Cumberland River in the N. central part; center of the U.S. country music recording industry.

naso- *prefix.* Of the nose, as in ~**frontal**, of nose and forehead.

Nas·sau (năs′aw). Capital city of Bahama Islands, on N. shore of New Providence.

Nas·ser (năs′*er*, nah′s*er*), **Gamel Abdel** (1918–70). Egyptian army officer and politician; premier of Egypt 1954–6, president 1956–8; president of United Arab Republic 1958–70; **Lake Nasser**, reservoir formed by the Aswan High Dam on the Nile between S. Egypt and N. Sudan.

Nast (năst), **Thomas** (1840–1902). German-born Amer. political cartoonist; his cartoons were held greatly responsible for reducing political corruption in New York.

na·stur·tium (năstēr′sh*u*m, n*a*-) *n.* Any of various plants of the genus *Tropaeolum* having bright flowers in shades of red, yellow, and orange.

nas·ty (năs′tē) *adj.* (**-ti·er, -ti·est**). Unpleasant to taste or smell; disgusting; obscene; spiteful; extremely disagreeable. **nas′ti·ly** *adv.* **nas′ti·ness** *n.*

Na·tal (n*a*tăl′, -tahl′). Eastern coastal province of Republic of South Africa; first settled by a few British traders in 1823, then by Boers in 1838, becoming a Boer Republic; annexed by British, 1845; representative government, 1856; responsible government, 1893; province of the Union of South Africa, 1910; capital, Pietermaritzburg. [named *Terra Natalis* by Vasco da Gama because he sighted the entrance to what is now Durban harbor on Christmas Day, 1497].

na·tal (nā′t*a*l) *adj.* Of, from, birth.

na·ta·tion (nātā′sh*o*n, nă-) *n.* Swimming.

na·ta·to·ri·al (nāt*a*tōr′ē*a*l, -tōr′-năt*a*-), **na·ta·to·ry** (nā′t*a*tōrē, -tōrē) *adjs.* Swimming, of swimming.

Natch·ez (năch′ĭz) *n.* (pl. **-ez**). Member of former Amer. Indian tribe, of lower Mississippi River, conquered and scattered by French in 1730; city and river port in SW. Mississippi.

na·tes (nā′tēz) *n.pl.* (anat.) Buttocks.

Na·than (nā′th*a*n). Hebrew prophet of time of David and Solomon (2 Sam.).

na·tion (nā′sh*o*n) *n.* Society united under one government in a country; considerable group of people having common descent or history.

Na·tion (nā'shon), **Carry Amelia Moore** (1846–1911). Amer. leader of temperance movement; notorious for the hatchet she used in wrecking saloons in Kansas.

na·tion·al (năsh'onal) *adj.* Of a (or the) nation; common to the whole nation, concerned with its interests as dist. from those of a faction or region; ~ **anthem**, song adopted by a nation as an expression of patriotism, and played or sung on formal and ceremonial occasions; **N~ Assembly**, (esp., hist.) first revolutionary assembly of France 1789–91; ~ **bank**, any of numerous banks chartered under the federal government; ~ **convention**, convention of major political party to nominate candidate for presidency etc.; ~ **debt**: see DEBT; **N~ Gallery**, gallery for permanent exhibition of pictures belonging to a nation, esp. those in Washington and London; **N~ Guard**, military reserve maintained by each state, subject to call into Federal service; ~ **income**, total money earned within a nation; ~ **park**, extensive area set aside by government for the preservation of historic or prehistoric sites and of flora and fauna, and for the benefit of the public; **N~ Socialist German Workers' Party**, party with extremely nationalistic, anti-Semitic, and totalitarian program, which acquired dictatorial power in Germany under HITLER in 1933; hence **N~ Socialism, N~ Socialist.** **na'tion·al·ly** *adv.* **national** *n.* Person legally considered a citizen of a specified country.

na·tion·al·ism (năsh'onalĭzem) *n.* Patriotic feeling, principle, or efforts; policy of national independence. **na'tion·al·ist** *adj.* & *n.* **na·tion·al·is·tic** (năshonalĭs'tĭk) *adj.*

Na·tion·al·ist (năsh'onalĭst) **China.** Unofficial name for the Republic of China (TAIWAN).

na·tion·al·i·ty (năshonăl'ĭtē) *n.* (pl. **-ties**). National quality; nation, existence as a nation; ethnic group; fact of belonging to a particular nation or ethnic group; cohesion due to common history etc.; person's status as member of a nation, alterable by legal process.

na·tion·al·ize (năsh'onalīz) *v.t.* (**-ized, -iz·ing**). Make national; make into a nation; transfer (land, mines, railroads, etc.) from private ownership and control to that of the government. **na·tion·al·i·za·tion** (năshonalĭzā'shon) *n.*

na·tive (nā'tĭv) *n.* One born in a particular place or country; original or usual inhabitant of country as dist. from strangers or foreigners. ~ *adj.* 1. Belonging to a person or thing by nature, innate, natural *to*; of one's birth; where one was born; belonging to one by right of birth. 2. (of metals etc.) Occurring naturally in pure state; occurring in nature, not produced artificially. 3. Born in a place, indigenous, not exotic; of the natives of a place. **na'tive·ly** *adv.* **na'tive·ness** *n.*

na·tiv·i·ty (natĭv'ĭtē, nā-) *n.* (pl. **-ties**). 1. Birth. 2. (**N~**) Birth of Christ; representation in art, esp. painting, of Christ newborn usu. with Virgin Mary, angels, etc.; festival of birth of Christ (Christmas); (astrol.) horoscope.

NATO (nā'tō) *n.* Alliance for collective defense against aggression established in 1949 by the U.S., Canada, and ten Western European nations. [N(orth) A(tlantic) T(reaty) O(rganization)]

nat·ty (năt'ē) *adj.* (**-ti·er, -ti·est**). Spruce, trim. **nat'ti·ly** *adv.* **nat'ti·ness** *n.*

nat·u·ral (năch'eral, năch'ral) *adj.* 1. Based on the innate moral sense, instinctive, as ~ *law*, ~ *justice.* 2. Constituted by nature; ~ **selection**: see DARWIN[1]. 3. Normal, conformable to the ordinary course of nature, not exceptional or miraculous; ~ **childbirth**, at which mother has been taught to relax so as not to need anesthesia etc.; ~ **death**, death by age or disease, not by violence. 4. Not enlightened, unregenerate, as ~ *man*; not communicated by revelation, as ~ *religion*, ~ *theology.* 5. Physically existing, not spiritual or intellectual or fictitious, as *the ~ world*; ~ **life**, duration of person's life on Earth. 6. Existing in or by nature, not artificial; innate, inherent; self-sown, uncultivated; ~ **gas**, inflammable gas occurring underground, consisting chiefly of methane and other simple paraffins and often found associated with petroleum. 7. Lifelike; unaffected, easy mannered; not disfigured or disguised. 8. Not surprising; to be expected. 9. Consonant or easy *to* (person etc.). 10. Destined to be such by nature, as ~ *enemies.* 11. So related by nature only, illegitimate, as ~ *child, son.* 12. Dealing with nature as a study; ~ **classification**, classification of species into natural orders, esp. Jussieu's arrangement of plant species acc. to

*Most visitors to London, U.K. include the **National Gallery** in their list of places to visit. Founded in 1824, the gallery contains examples of all older schools of European painting.*

*In some countries **nationalism** has more or less taken the place of religion. These young Chinese are marching in solemn yet triumphant procession to the Martyrs' Memorial Park, Canton.*

*The idea of preserving areas of a country as a **national park** for the whole people originated in 1872, in America, Yosemite, (facing page) was one of the earliest to be established.*

likeness as opp. to Linnaeus's system which was based on the number and characteristics of reproductive organs; ~ **history**, formerly, systematic study of all natural objects, animal, vegetable, and mineral; now usu., study of animal life, freq. implying popular rather than scientific treatment; aggregate of facts about the natural objects or characteristics of a place or class; so ~ **historian**; ~ **order**, (esp.) order resulting from natural classification; ~ **philosophy**, (hist.) natural science; physics; so ~ **philosopher;** ~ **science**: see SCIENCE. 13. (mus.) Not sharp or flat; (of scale or key) having no sharps or flats; ~ **scale**, scale of C major. **nat′u·ral·ness** *n.* **natural** *n.* 1. (mus.) Note in natural scale; white key on piano; sign ♮ used to cancel preceding sharp or flat. 2. (colloq.) Person etc. naturally endowed (*for*); easy or obvious choice (*for*). 3. Throw of 7 or 11 at craps.

nat·u·ral·ism (năch′*er*alĭz*e*m, năch′r*a*-) *n.* 1. Moral or religious system on purely natural basis; philosophy excluding supernatural or spiritual. 2. Faithful representation of nature or reality in literature, art, etc. **nat′u·ral·ist** *n.* 1. One who believes in or studies naturalism. 2. Student of animals or plants. **nat·u·ral·is·tic** (năch*er*alĭs′tĭk, năchr*a*-) *adj.* Of, according

Revenue for the mountainous province of ***Navarre*** *is from forestry and grazing. Sheep (above) are moved to higher pastures in summer, but feed in the valleys in winter, a procedure established long ago.*

to, naturalism in philosophy, literature, etc.; of natural history. **nat·u·ral·is′ti·cal·ly** *adv.*

nat·u·ral·ize (năch′*er*alīz, năch′r*a*-) *v.* (**-ized, -iz·ing**). Admit (alien) to citizenship; adopt (foreign word, custom, etc.); introduce (animal, plant) into new environment. **nat·u·ral·i·za·tion** (năch*er*alĭzā′sh*o*n, năchr*a*-) *n.*

nat·u·ral·ly (năch′*er*alē, năch′r*a*-) *adv.* (esp.) As might be expected, of course.

na·ture (nā′ch*er*) *n.* 1. Thing's essential qualities, person's innate character; general characteristics and feelings of mankind; specified element of human character; person of specified character; kind, sort, class; **by** ~, innately. 2. Inherent impulses determining character or action; vital force, functions, or needs; **against** ~, unnatural, immoral. 3. Creative and regulative physical power conceived of as immediate cause of phenomena of material world; these phenomena as a whole; these personified; naturalness in art etc.; **in the course of** ~, in the ordinary course; **in** ~, in real fact; **state of** ~, unregenerate condition (opp. *state of grace*); condition of man before society is organized; uncultivated or undomesticated state of plants or animals.

naught, nought (nawt) *ns.* Nothing, (arith.), cipher, zero; (fig.) ruin, failure, thing of no importance.

naugh·ty (naw′tē) *adj.* (**-ti·er, -ti·est**). (now used almost exclusively of, to, or by children) Wayward, disobedient, badly behaved; (archaic) wicked, blameworthy, indecent. **naught′i·ly** *adv.* **naught′i·ness** *n.*

nau·se·a (naw′zē*a*, -zh*a*, -sē*a*, -sh*a*) *n.* Feeling of sickness; seasickness; loathing. **nau·se·ate** (naw′zēāt, -zhē-, -sē-, -shē-) *v.i.* & *v.t.* (**-at·ed, -at·ing**). 1. Reject (food; usu. fig.) with loathing; affect with nausea, hence ~**ing** *adj.* 2. Feel sick (*at*), loathe, food, occupation, etc. **nau·se·a·tion** (nawzēā′sh*o*n, -zhē-, -sē-, -shē-) *n.*

nau·seous (naw′sh*u*s, -zē*u*s) *adj.* Causing nausea; offensive to taste or smell, nasty; disgusting, loathsome. **nau′seous·ly** *adv.* **nau′seous·ness** *n.*

Nau·sic·a·ä (nawsĭk′ē*a*, -ā*a*). (Gk. legend) Daughter of Alcinous; she found the shipwrecked Odysseus on the shore and took him to her father's palace.

nau·ti·cal (naw′tĭk*a*l) *adj.* Of sailors or navigation, naval, maritime; ~ **mile**: see MILE. **nau′ti·**-

*This early 19th-century patriotic print shows the fierce hand-to-hand fighting common in **naval** battles of the time, with officers and men side by side in attack or defense.*

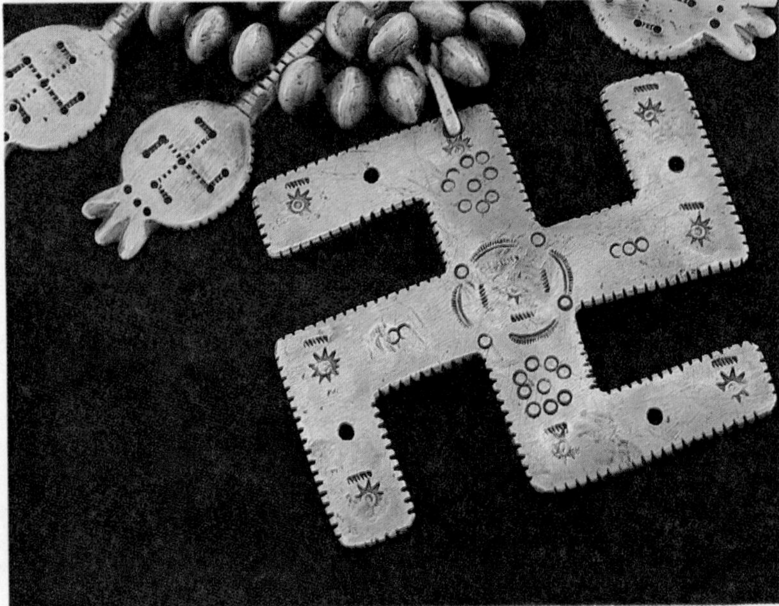

*This beautiful **Navajo** silver necklace utilizes the ancient swastika design, which comes from Sanskrit and means 'conducive to well-being'. It is a recurring theme in Navajo art.*

cal·ly *adv.*

nau·ti·lus (naw′t*i*l*u*s) *n.* (pl. **-lus·es, -li** pr. -lī). 1. (also **paper** ~) Small two-gilled cephalopod mollusk of warm seas (genus *Argonauta*), related to octopus, the female of which secretes in two of its arms a translucent single-chambered false shell. 2. (also **chambered** or **pearly** ~) Four-gilled cephalopod of Indian and Pacific Oceans (genus *N.*), having, in both sexes, a many-chambered true shell.

Nav·a·ho, Nav·a·jo (năv′*a*hō, nah′v*a*-) *ns.* (pl. **-hos, -hoes, -jos, -joes,** collect. **-ho, -jo**). (Member of) an Amer. Indian people of N. Arizona and New Mexico; ~ **blanket**, bright-colored woolen blanket with geometrical pattern, made by Navaho women.

na·val (nā′v*a*l) *adj.* Of ships, esp. ships of war; of the (or a) navy; ~ **officer**, officer in navy; customs official; ~ **stores**, supplies for warships. **na′val·ly** *adv.*

Na·varre (n*a*vār′). (Span. **Navarra**) Province of N. Spain; (hist.) medieval kingdom that also included parts of SW. France.

nave (nāv) *n.* Body of church from inner door to chancel or choir, usu. separated by pillars from aisles.

na·vel (nā′v*e*l) *n.* Depression in front of belly left by severance of umbilical cord; central point of anything; ~ **orange**, large orange with navel-like formation at top.

na·vic·u·lar (n*a*vĭk′y*u*l*e*r) *adj.* Boat-shaped; ~ **bone**, tarsal bone. **navicular** *n.* also **na·vic·u·lar·e** (n*a*vĭky*u*lār′ē, -lār′ē). Navicular bone.

nav·i·ga·ble (năv′ĭg*a*b*e*l) *adj.* Affording passage for ships; seaworthy. **nav·i·ga·bil·i·ty** (năvĭg*a*bĭl′ĭtē), **nav′i·ga·ble·ness** *ns.* **nav′i·ga·bly** *adv.*

nav·i·gate (năv′ĭgāt) *v.* (**-gat·ed, -gat·ing**). Voyage, sail ship; sail over, up, down (sea, river); manage,

1

2

3

4

direct course of (ship, aircraft, etc.) with the aid of instruments.

nav·i·ga·tion (năvĭgā′shon) *n.* Navigating; methods of determining position and course of ship, airplane, etc., by geometry and nautical astronomy; voyage; **inland** ~, communication by canals and rivers. **nav·i·ga′tion·al** *adj.*

nav·i·ga·tor (năv′ĭgāter) *n.* One charged with or skilled in navigation; sea explorer.

na·vy (nā′vē) *n.* (pl. **-vies**). 1. Branch of armed forces using ships; ~ **bean**, any of several varieties of the kidney bean, grown for their nutritious white seeds, which are stored dry and prepared for cooking and eating by soaking; ~ **blue**, (of) the dark blue used in naval uniform; **N**~ **Cross**, bronze cross decoration awarded by the U.S. Navy for great heroism in action against the enemy; ~ **cut**, cake tobacco finely sliced; ~ **yard**, government dockyard. 2. Navy blue.

na·wab (nawawb′) *n.* 1. Distinguished Muslim in Pakistan. 2. (hist.) Muslim noble in the Mogul Empire. [Arab. *nā'ib* deputy]

nay (nā) *n.* Negative vote; **nay′sayer**, person who habitually expresses opposition to proposed courses of action.

Naz·a·rene (năzarēn′, năz′arēn) *n.* 1. Native, inhabitant, of Nazareth; **the** ~, Jesus Christ. 2. (obs., in Muslim and Jewish use) Christian. 3. Member of an obscure early Jewish-Christian sect. ~ *adj.* Of Nazareth or Nazarenes.

Naz·a·reth (năz′arĭth). Town of Lower Galilee, now in Israel; home of Joseph and Mary, parents of Jesus, who spent his youth there.

Naz·a·rite[1] (năz′arīt) (rare) = NAZARENE 1.

Naz·a·rite[2] (năz′arīt) *n.* One of a Hebrew sect who abstained from all products of the vine, from cutting the hair, etc. (Num. 6). [Heb. *nāzîr* one consecrated, devoted]

Na·zi (nah′tsē, năt′sē) *n.* & *adj.* (pl. **-zis**). (Member, adherent) of the NATIONAL Socialist German Workers' party. **Na·zism** (nah′tsĭzem, năt′sĭz-, nah′tsēĭzem, năt′sē-) *n.* **na·zi·fy** (nah′tsĭfī, năt′sĭ-) *v.t.* (**-fied, -fy·ing**). **na·zi·fi·ca·tion** (nahtsĭfĭkā′shon, năt-) *n.* [repr. pron. of *Nati-* in Ger. *Nationalsozialist* National Socialist]

*Naval vessels have become more sophisticated with the development of radar and electronic technology. Most nations have a **navy** which participates in exercises designed to test potential combat situations.*
Facing Page: 1. A frigate. 2. A submarine. 3. An aircraft carrier. 4. U.S.S. John McCain depth charging.

NB *abbrev.* Nebraska.

Nb *symbol.* Niobium.

N.B. *abbrev.* New Brunswick; *nota bene* (L., = note well).

NC, N.C. *abbrevs.* North Carolina.

N.C.O., NCO *abbrevs.* Noncommissioned officer.

ND, N.D., N.Dak. *abbrevs.* North Dakota.

Nd *symbol.* Neodymium.

n.d. *abbrev.* No date; not dated.

NE, N.E., n.e. *abbrevs.* Northeast(ern).

Ne *symbol.* Neon.

NEA, N.E.A. *abbrevs.* National Education Association.

Ne·an·der·thal (nēăn′derthawl, -tawl, -tahl). Valley in Rhineland, Germany; ~ **man**, type of man widely distributed in paleolithic Europe in the early stages of the last glaciation, with long low wide skull, retreating forehead, and massive brow ridges (so called because parts of skeleton were discovered in a cave in this valley, 1857).

*For many thousands of years, **navigation** at sea depended on the visibility of the stars. Only after the 12th century were inventions such as the sextant (1) and the compass (2) available.*

1

2

neap (nēp) *adj.* Of those tides occurring soon after moon's first and third quarters in which high-water level is at lowest. ~ *n.* Neap tide.

Ne·a·pol·i·tan (nēapŏl′ĭtan) *adj.* Of Naples; ~**ice**, ice cream in layers of various colors and flavors. **Neapolitan** *n.* Native, inhabitant, of Naples. [see NAPLES]

near (nēr) *adv.* To, at, a short distance, in(to) proximity in space or time; nearly; closely; parsimoniously; ~ **at hand**, within easy reach; not far in the future; **near′-**

by, not far off; hence, **nearby** (*adj.*); **come near** (*to do, doing*), nearly do. **near** *prep.* Near in space, time, condition, or resemblance, to. **near** *adj.* 1. Closely related, intimate. 2. (of horse, part of vehicle etc.) Left (i.e. on the side where one mounts; opp. OFF; so ~ **side**). 3. Close at hand, close to, in place or time; (of road or way) direct. 4. (of guess, translation, escape, etc.) Close, narrow. 5. (of persons) Niggardly. 6. ~ **distance**, part of scene between background and foreground; **N~ East**, SE. parts of Europe; Balkan nations together with Asia Minor; ~ **miss**, (of shell, bomb, etc.) not a hit, but falling close enough to damage the target; something that narrowly misses its objective; **~-sighted**, myopic. **near** *v.* Draw near (to), approach. **near'ness** *n.*

near·ly (nēr'lē) *adv.* Closely, almost; **not** ~, nothing like.

neat[1] (nēt) *n.* Any animal of ox kind; (collect.) cattle; **neat'herd**, cowherd; **neat's-foot, -tongue**, foot, tongue, of ox as food; **neat's-foot oil**, light oil obtained from feet and shinbones of cattle, used to dress leather; **neat's leather**, ox hide.

neat[2] (nēt) *adj.* 1. (of liquor, esp. alcoholic) Undiluted. 2. Nicely made or proportioned; pleasantly simple or compact; deft, dextrous, cleverly done; tidy, methodical; (of language, style, etc.) brief, clear, and pointed, cleverly phrased, epigrammatic. **neat'ly** *adv.* **neat'ness** *n.*

'neath, neath (nēth) *preps.* (poet.) Beneath.

Neb., NE *abbrevs.* Nebraska.

neb·bish (něb'ĭsh) *n.* & *adj.* (slang) Submissive, timid (person). [f. Yiddish *nebach* poor thing!]

Ne·bras·ka (nebrăs'ka). State in northwestern U.S., admitted to the Union in 1867; capital, Lincoln.

Neb·u·chad·nez·zar (něb*u*kadněz'*er*, něby*u*-), **Neb·u·chad·rez·zar** (něb*u*kadrěz'*er*, něby*u*-). King of Babylon 605–562 B.C.; built the great walls of the city; after the rebellion of Jehoiakim of Judah he besieged and took Jerusalem 597; when ZEDEKIAH revolted, he took it again and destroyed it, 588.

neb·u·la (něb'y*u*la) *n.* (pl. **-las, -lae** pr. -lī, -lē). 1. Clouded speck on cornea causing defective sight. 2. (astron.) Cloud of dust or gas within the galactic system illuminated by neighboring stars. 3. (astron.) Luminous mass believed to consist of an enormous number of stars, usu. not separately discernible, situated outside the galactic system. **neb'u·lar** *adj.* Of nebula(e); ~ **hypothesis**, theory that solar and stellar systems developed from nebulae.

neb·u·lous (něb'y*u*l*u*s) *adj.* 1. Of, like, nebula(e). 2. Cloudlike; hazy, vague, indistinct, formless; clouded, turbid. **neb·u·los·i·ty** (něby*u*lŏs'ĭtē) *n.*

nec·es·sar·i·ly (nĕs*e*sĕr'ĭlē, nĕs-*e*sĕr-) *adv.* As a necessary result, inevitably.

nec·es·sar·y (nĕs'*e*sĕrē) *adj.* Indispensable, requisite; requiring to, that must, be done; determined by predestination or natural laws, not by free will; happening or existing by necessity; (of concept etc.) inevitably resulting from nature of things or the mind, inevitably produced by previous state of things; (of agent) having no independent volition. ~ *n.* (pl. **-sar·ies**). Thing without which life cannot be maintained; (loosely) desirable thing not generally regarded as a luxury.

ne·ces·si·tate (n*e*sĕs'ĭtāt) *v.t.* (**-tat·ed, -tat·ing**). Force, compel, *to* do (now rare); render necessary; involve as condition, accompaniment, or result. **ne·ces·si·ta·tion** (n*e*sĕsĭtā'sh*o*n) *n.*

ne·ces·si·tous (n*e*cĕs'ĭt*u*s) *adj.* Poor, needy.

ne·ces·si·ty (n*e*sĕs'ĭtē) *n.* (pl. **-ties**). 1. Constraint or compulsion regarded as a law prevailing through the material universe and governing all human action; constraining power of circumstances, state of things compelling to certain courses; **of** ~, unavoidably. 2. Imperative need (*for*); indispensability; indispensable thing, necessary. 3. Want, poverty, hardship, pressing need.

neck (nĕk) *n.* 1. Part of body that connects head with shoulders; flesh of animal's neck as food, this as cut of meat; part of garment covering or lying next to neck; **break one's** ~, dislocate cervical vertebrae, be killed so; (colloq.) make great effort; **get it in the** ~, (slang) suffer fatal or severe blow; **save one's** ~, escape being hanged (also transf.); **stick one's ~ out**, (colloq.) expose oneself to danger; ~ **and** ~, running even in race. 2. Narrow part *of* vessel, esp. of bottle near mouth, or *of* passage, pass, or channel; pass, narrow channel, isthmus; narrow connecting part between two parts of thing; (archit.)

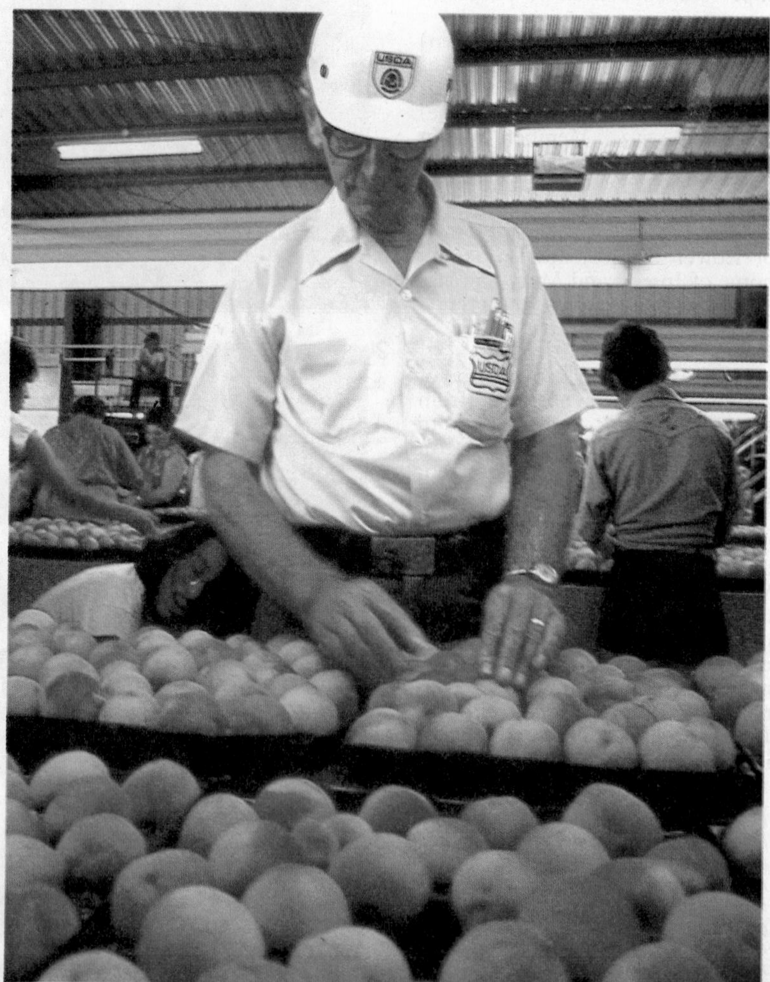

***Nectarine** and peach trees are indistinguishable, but the nectarine fruit is smooth skinned like a plum. Nectarines are known to have existed for 2,000 years.*

lower part of capital. 3. (geol.) Conical hill consisting of igneous rock that has accumulated in throat of volcano and been exposed later when the mountain itself weathered away; ~ **of the woods**, (slang) locality. 4. **neck'band**, part of garment around neck; **neck'cloth**, cravat; **neck'erchief**, kerchief worn around neck; **neck'lace**, ornament of precious stones, beads, etc., worn around neck; **neck'tie**, (esp.) narrow band of woven or knitted material placed around neck and tied in front. **neck** *v.i.* (slang) Hug, exchange kisses and caresses.

nec·ro·man·cy (nĕk'rəmănsē) *n.* Act of predicting by means of communication with the dead; magic, enchantment. **nec'ro·man·cer** *n.* **nec·ro·man·tic** (nĕkrəmăn'tĭk) *adj.*

ne·cro·phi·ly (nekrŏf'ilē) *n.* Morbid preoccupation with corpses, death, etc.

ne·crop·o·lis (nekrŏp'əlĭs) *n.* Cemetery.

nec·rop·sy (nĕkrŏp'sē) (pl. **-sies**), **ne·cros·co·py** (nekrŏs'kəpē) *ns.* (pl. **-pies**). Postmortem examination, autopsy.

ne·cro·sis (nekrō'sĭs) *n.* (path.) Death of circumscribed piece of tissue, esp. mortification of bones. **ne·crot·ic** (nekrŏt'ĭk) *adj.* **nec·ro·tize** (nĕk'rətīz) *v.i.* (**-tized, -tiz·ing**).

nec·tar (nĕk'tər) *n.* 1. (Gk. myth.) Drink of the gods; any delicious drink. 2. Sweet fluid or honey produced by plants. **nec·tar·e·an** (nĕktār'ēən), **nec·tar'e·ous, nec·tar·if·er·ous** (nĕktərĭf'ərus) *adjs.*

nec·tar·ine (nĕktərēn', nĕk'tərēn) *n.* Kind of peach with thin downless skin and firm flesh.

nec·ta·ry (nĕk'tərē) *n.* (pl. **-ries**). (bot.) Glandular organ or tissue secreting nectar, occurring mainly in flowers, occasionally in leaves and stems.

nee, née (nā) *adjs.* (before married woman's maiden name) Born, as *Mrs. Smith, née Jones.*

need (nēd) *n.* 1. Necessity arising from circumstances of case; imperative demand for presence or possession *of*; **have ~ of**, require, want. 2. Emergency, crisis, time of difficulty; destitution, lack of necessaries, poverty. 3. Thing wanted, respect in which want is felt, requirement. **need** *v.* (archaic) Be necessary; stand in need of, require; be needy; be under necessity or obligation to or *to* do. **need'ful** *adj.* Requisite, necessary, indispensable. **need'ful·ness** *n.*

nee·dle (nē'dəl) *n.* 1. Instrument used in sewing, usu. small slender piece of polished steel with fine point at one end and hole or eye for thread at other; knitting needle. 2. Piece of magnetized steel used as indicator compass or in magnetic or electrical apparatus (also **magnetic ~**); strip of gold or silver of standard fineness used with touchstone in testing purity of these metals. 3. Pointed etching or engraving instrument; long slender pointed instrument used in surgery; pointed end of hypodermic or other syringe; steel pin exploding cartridge or breechloader; (in

Since prehistoric times, people of all cultures have ornamented themselves with ***necklaces****. Here a Masai woman from Southern Africa shows the local custom of wearing multiple strings of small beads.*

Needlework *and embroidery have been used to fulfil a variety of needs. Persian armor in 490 B.C. consisted of embroidered quilting. More recently needlework has become a popular pastime led by an arts and crafts revival.*

*The genus **Nemesia** — part of the foxglove family — is native to South Africa. Its beautiful, fragrant flowers, however, have made many species popular garden plants.*

*One of England's distinguished heroes, **Nelson** entered the navy at the age of 12, and at 20 became a post captain. Despite repeated illnesses and severe injuries he was renowned for his bravery in battle.*

phonographs etc.) small pointed instrument transmitting vibrations from record to soundbox; stylus used in recording. 4. Obelisk (**Cleopatra's N~**); sharp rock, peak; beam of wood, esp. used as temporary support in underpinning; sharp slender leaf of fir or pine; (chem. etc.) needle-shaped crystal. 5. ~ **bath**, shower bath with fine strong spray; ~ **fish**, any of various fishes with very fine teeth, esp. garfish; ~ **point**, fine sharp point; **nee'dlepoint**: see LACE; **nee'dlewoman**, woman who sews, seamstress; **nee'dlework**, sewing, embroidery, etc. **needle** *v.* (**-dled, -dling**). Sew, pierce, operate on, with needle; (colloq.) goad, irritate; thread (one's way) between or through things; underpin with needle beams; form needle-shaped crystals.

need·less (nēd'lĭs) *adj.* Unnecessary, uncalled for. **need'less·ly** *adv.* **need'less·ness** *n.*

needs (nēdz) *adv.* Of necessity (now only after or before *must*).

need·y (nē'dē) *adj.* (**need·i·er, need·i·est**). Poor, indigent, necessitous. **need'i·ly** *adv.* **need'i·ness** *n.*

ne'er (nār) *adv.* (poet.) Never; **~-do-well**, good-for-nothing (person).

ne·far·i·ous (nefār'ēus, -făr'-) *adj.* Wicked, iniquitous. **ne·far'i·ous·ly** *adv.* **ne·far'i·ous·ness** *n.*

Nef·er·ti·ti (nĕfertē'tē). Egyptian queen of early 14th c. B.C.; noted for her beauty; wife of AKHNATON.

ne·gate (nĭgāt', nĕg'āt) *v.t.* (**-gat·ed, -gat·ing**). Nullify; deny existence of, imply or involve non-existence of; be the negation of.

ne·ga·tion (nĭgā'shon) *n.* 1. Denying; negative statement or doctrine; refusal, contradiction, denial *of*. 2. (logic) Affirmation of difference or exclusion. 3. Absence or opposite of something actual or positive; negative or unreal thing, nonentity. **neg·a·to·ry** (nĕg'atōrē, -tōrē) *adj.*

neg·a·tive (nĕg'atĭv) *adj.* 1. Expressing or implying denial, prohibition, or refusal; wanting, consisting in the want of, positive attributes; of opposite nature to thing regarded as possible. 2. (math., phys., etc.) Denoting quantities to be subtracted from others; less than zero; in the opposite direction to that which (arbitrarily or by convention) is regarded as positive; (elect.) having a negative charge; ~ **charge**, one of the 2 kinds of electric charge, the charge of an electron (cf. POSITIVE def. 6); ~ **pole**, region of excess of electrons, cathode; also (magnetism) applied to the south-seeking pole of a magnet and the corresponding (north) pole of Earth; ~ **sign**, minus sign. 3. (phot.) Applied to image in which lights appear dark and shadows light (see *n.* 3 below.) **neg'a·tive·ly** *adv.* **neg'a·tive·ness, neg·a·tiv·i·ty** (nĕgatĭv'ĭtē) *ns.* **negative** *n.* 1. Negative statement, reply, or word; right of veto; **in the ~**, negative(ly), no. 2. Negative quality, want of something; (math.) negative or minus quantity. 3. (phot.) Print in which lights and shadows of nature are reversed, made by direct action of light on an emulsion deposited on glass or other transparent substance, and used for producing a positive print. **negative** *v.t.* (**-tived, -tiv·ing**). Veto, reject, refuse to accept or countenance; disprove (inference, hypothesis); contradict (statement); neutralize (effect).

neg·a·tiv·ism (nĕg'atĭvĭzem) *n.* Doctrine characterized by denial of accepted beliefs etc. **neg'a·tiv·ist** *adj.* & *n.* **neg·a·tiv·is·tic** (nĕgatĭvĭs'tĭk) *adj.*

Ne·gev (nĕ'gĕv), **Ne·geb** (nĕ'gĕb). Semidesert region of Israel between Beersheba and the Gulf of Aqaba.

ne·glect (neglĕkt') *v.t.* Disregard, slight; leave uncared-for; omit *to* do. ~ *n.* Neglecting, being neglected; negligence. **ne·glect'ful** *adj.* **ne·glect'ful·ly** *adv.* **ne·glect'ful·ness** *n.*

neg·li·gee, né·gli·gé (nĕglĭzhā',

nĕg′lĭzhā) *ns.* Free-and-easy or unceremonious attire, esp. woman's loose garment worn on informal occasions or in dishabille.

neg·li·gence (nĕg′lĭjens) *n.* Want of proper care or attention, (piece of) carelessness; **contributory ~**, negligence on a person's part that has helped to bring about the injury that he has suffered. **neg′li·gent** *adj.* **neg′li·gent·ly** *adv.*

neg·li·gi·ble (nĕg′lĭjibel) *adj.* That need not be regarded, that may be neglected. **neg·li·gi·bil·i·ty** (nĕglĭjibĭl′ĭtē), **neg′li·gi·ble·ness** *ns.* **neg′li·gi·bly** *adv.*

ne·go·ti·ate (nĭgō′shēāt) *v.* (**-at·ed, -at·ing**). 1. Confer (*with* another) with view to compromise or agreement; arrange (affair), bring about (desired object) by negotiating. 2. Transfer (bill) to another for a consideration; convert into cash or notes, get or give value for (bill, check) in money. 3. Clear, get over, dispose of (fence, obstacle, difficulty). **ne·go·ti·a·ble** (nĭgō′shēabel, -sha-) *adj.* **ne·go·ti·ant** (nĭgō′shēant), **ne·go·ti·a·tion** (nĭgōshēā′shon), **ne·go′ti·a·tor** *ns.*

Ne·gress (nē′grĭs) *n.* (now considered offensive) Black woman.

Ne·gril·lo (nĭgrĭl′ō) *n.* (pl. **-los**, collect. **-lo**). Small black person; one of dwarf black people of Central and S. Africa.

Ne·gri·to (nĭgrē′tō) *n.* (pl. **-tos, -toes**). One of a small black people in Malaya–Polynesian region.

Ne·gro (nē′grō) *n.* (pl. **-groes**). (now considered offensive) Member, esp. male, of black-skinned race of mankind. ~ *adj.* Of black people.

Ne·groid (nē′groid) *adj.* & *n.* (Member) of the division of mankind with physical characteristics of black races.

Ne·gus (nē′gus) *n.* Supreme ruler of Ethiopia.

Ne·he·mi·ah (nēamī′a) (4th c. B.C.). Jewish governor of Judea under Artaxerxes; rebuilder of walls of Jerusalem; **Book of ~**, historical book of Old Testament, giving account of rebuilding of walls of Jerusalem and of various reforms.

Neh·ru (nār′ōō), **Pandit Jawaharlal** (1889–1964). Indian Congress leader; 1st prime minister of India 1947–64.

neigh (nā) *v.i.* & *n.* (Utter) cry (as) of horse.

neigh·bor (nā′ber) *n.* Dweller next door, near, in same street, village, or district, or in adjacent country, esp. regarded as one who should be friendly or as having claim on others' friendliness; person or thing next to or near another; (*attrib.*) neighboring. ~ *v.* Adjoin, border upon, border *on.* **neigh′bor·less** *adj.*

neigh·bor·hood (nā′berhŏŏd) *n.* Neighborly feeling or conduct; nearness, vicinity *of*; neighbors, people of a district, district (freq. *attrib.*, as in ~ *school* etc.).

neigh·bor·ly (nā′berlē) *adj.* Like a good neighbor, friendly, helpful. **neigh′bor·li·ness** *n.*

nei·ther (nē′dher, nī′-) *adv.* (introducing mention of alternatives or different things, about each of which a negative statement is made) Not either; not, nor yet; (strengthening preceding negative) either. ~ *adj.* & *pron.* Not the one or the other.

nek·ton (nĕk′ton, -tŏn) *n.* Group of forms of free-swimming organic life found at various depths in the ocean and in lakes, taken collectively.

nel·son (nĕl′son) *n.* (wrestling) Class of holds (**double, full, half, quarter ~**) in which arm is passed under opponent's from behind and the hand applied to his neck.

Nel·son (nĕl′son), **Horatio, Viscount Nelson, Duke of Bronté** (1758–1805). British admiral and naval hero, killed in battle against French and Spanish off Trafalgar, 1805.

nem·a·to·cyst (nĕm′atosĭst, nĭmăt′-) *n.* Cell in jellyfish, sea anemones, etc., containing coiled thread that can be projected as sting.

nem·a·tode (nĕm′atōd) *adj.* & *n.* (Worm) of slender unsegmented cylindrical shape, of the phylum Nematoda.

Nem·bu·tal (nĕm′byutawl) *n.* (trademark) Sodium salt of pentobarbitone, used as sedative and anticonvulsant.

Nem·e·sis (nĕm′ĭsĭs) *n.* (Gk. myth.) Goddess of vengeance; regarded as personification of the gods' resentment at, and punishment of, insolence toward them; hence **n ~**, retributive justice.

neo- *prefix.* New; modern, later or lately found or invented etc.

ne·o·dym·i·um (nēōdĭm′ēum) *n.* (chem.) Metallic element of rare-earth group; symbol Nd, at. no. 60, at. wt. 144.24. [NEO- + DIDYMIUM]

Ne·o·gene (nē′ojēn) *adj.* & *n.* (geol.) (Of) the later period of the Tertiary era including the Miocene and Pliocene epochs.

ne·o·lith·ic (nēolĭth′ĭk) *adj.* Of the later Stone Age (as contrasted with PALEOLITHIC), characterized by ground or polished stone implements and by great advances in food production and simple skills.

ne·ol·o·gism (nēŏl′ojĭzem) (pl. **-gisms**), **ne·ol·o·gy** (nēŏl′ojē) (pl. **-gies**) *ns.* 1. Coining or using of new words, newly coined word.

*Peoples such as the pygmies, Hottentots and Bantu all possess **negroid** characteristics. These Rwandan children show how much variation may occur between the peoples of a particular country.*

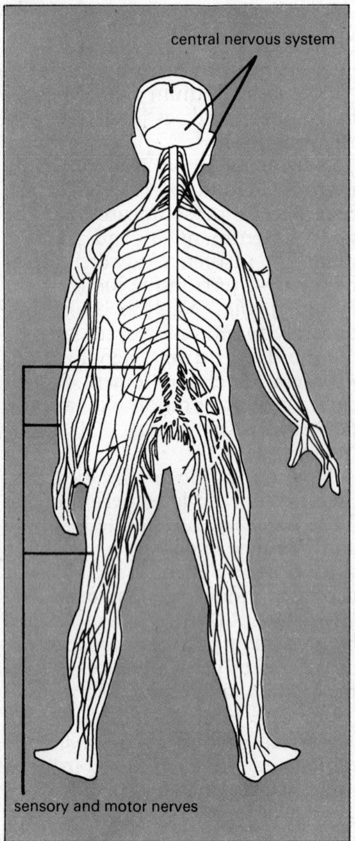

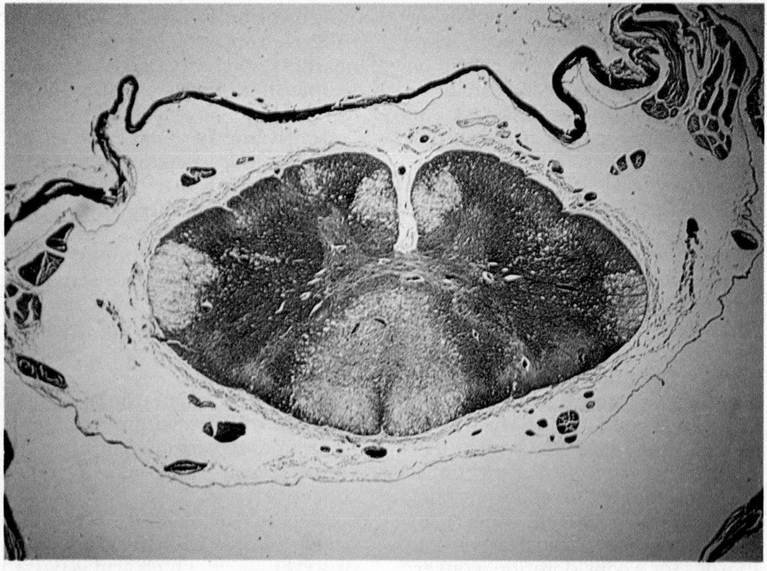

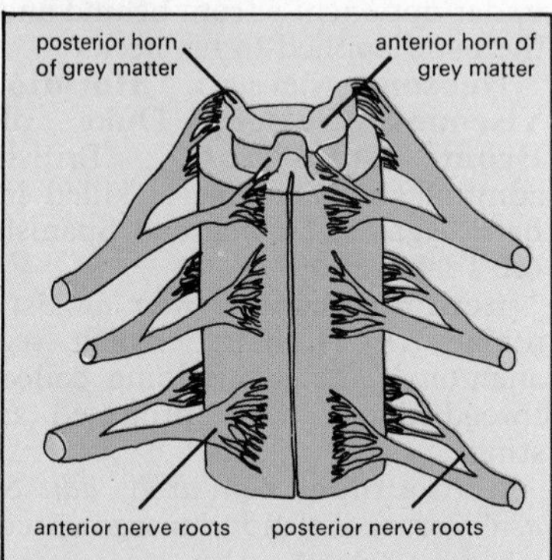

*Our **nerves** carry information to our brains and orders to our muscles. An elaborate network of specialized cells enables us — with a few tragic exceptions — to perceive, and respond appropriately to our environment.*

2. Tendency to, adoption of, novel or rationalistic religious views. **ne·ol′o·gist** *n.* **ne·ol·o·gis·tic** (nēŏlojĭs′tĭk), **ne·ol·o·gis′ti·cal** *adjs.*

ne·on (nē′ŏn) *n.* 1. (chem.) Colorless, odorless, inert, gaseous element present in minute quantities in the atmosphere; symbol Ne, at. no. 10, at. wt. 20.179; ~ **light,** bright orange-red light obtained by passing an electrical discharge through a tube or bulb containing neon at low pressure, extensively used for illuminated signs in advertising, etc.; also light of blue, green, etc. obtained by mixing other inert gases with neon; ~ **tetra,** small tropical American freshwater fish.

ne·o·phyte (nē′ofīt) *n.* New convert, esp. among primitive Christians or Roman Catholics; newly ordained R. C. priest, novice of religious order; beginner, novice, tyro.

Ne·o·pla·to·nism (nēŏplā′tonĭzem) *n.* Philosophical and religious system, chiefly consisting of a mixture of Platonic ideas with Oriental mysticism, which originated at Alexandria in the 3rd c. and is represented in the works of Plotinus, Porphyry, and Proclus. **Ne·o·pla·ton·ic** (nēŏplatŏn′ĭk) *adj.* **Ne·o·pla′to·nist** *n.*

Ne·op·tol·e·mus (nēŏptŏl′emus). (Gk. legend) Son of ACHILLES; in the Trojan War he killed PRIAM, and ANDROMACHE fell to his lot when the TROJAN captives were distributed.

Ne·pal (nāpawl′, -pahl′, -păl′, ne-). Independent kingdom between India and Tibet; capital, Katmandu. **Nep·a·lese** (nĕpalēz′, -lēs′) *adj.* & *n.*

ne·pen·the (nĭpĕn′thē) *n.* (pl. **-thes** pr. -thēz). Egyptian drug mentioned in the *Odyssey* as banishing grief; (poet.) any drug having this power.

Ne·per (nā′per) = NAPIER.

neph·ew (nĕf′ū; *Brit.* also nĕv′ū) *n.* Brother's or sister's son.

ne·phol·o·gy (nĕfŏl′ojē) *n.* Study of clouds.

neph·rite (nef′rīt) *n.* = JADE,[2] def. 1. [Gk. *nephros* kidney, from its supposed value in kidney disease]

ne·phrit·ic (nefrĭt′ĭk) *adj.* Of or in the kidneys, renal.

ne·phri·tis (nefrī′tĭs) *n.* Inflammation of the kidneys.

ne·phro·sis (nefrō′sĭs) *n.* Degenerative disease of kidneys. **ne·phrot·ic** (nefrŏt′ĭk) *adj.*

ne plus ul·tra (nē plŭs ŭl′tra; *Lat.* nĕ plōōs ōōl′trah). Farthest or highest point attained or attainable. [L., = "not more beyond" (supposed inscription on Pillars of Hercules)]

nep·o·tism (nĕp′otĭzem) *n.* Favoritism shown to relatives esp. in offering employment; (hist.) practice on the part of some medieval and renaissance popes of showing special favor to their natural children, who were known euphemistically as their nephews. **nep′o·tist** *n.*

Nep·tune (nĕp′tōōn, -tūn). 1. (Rom. myth.) God of the sea, identified with POSEIDON. 2. (astron.) Third largest of the planets, with two known satellites, discovered 1846 as a result of mathematical computations of J. C. Adams in England and Leverrier in France; symbol ♆. **Nep·tu·ni·an** (nĕptōō′nēan, -tū′-) *adj.*

nep·tu·ni·um (nĕptōō′nēum, -tū′-) *n.* (chem.) Transuranic element, not found in nature, occurring as a temporary stage in the formation of plutonium from uranium 238; symbol Np, at. no. 93, at. wt. 237.0482.

Ne·re·id (nēr′ēĭd) *n.* 1. (Gk. myth.) One of the sea nymphs, daughters of Nereus. 2. **n** ~, (zool.) marine polychaete worm.

Ne·re·us (nēr′ēus, -ōōs). (Gk. myth.) Sea deity having the power, like Proteus, of assuming various forms.

Ne·ro (nēr′ō). Nero Claudius Caesar Augustus Germanicus (A.D. 37–68), Roman emperor 54–68; proverbial for tyranny and brutality.

ner·o·li (nĕr′olē, nēr′-) **oil.** Essential oil from flowers of bitter orange, used in perfumery. [f. name

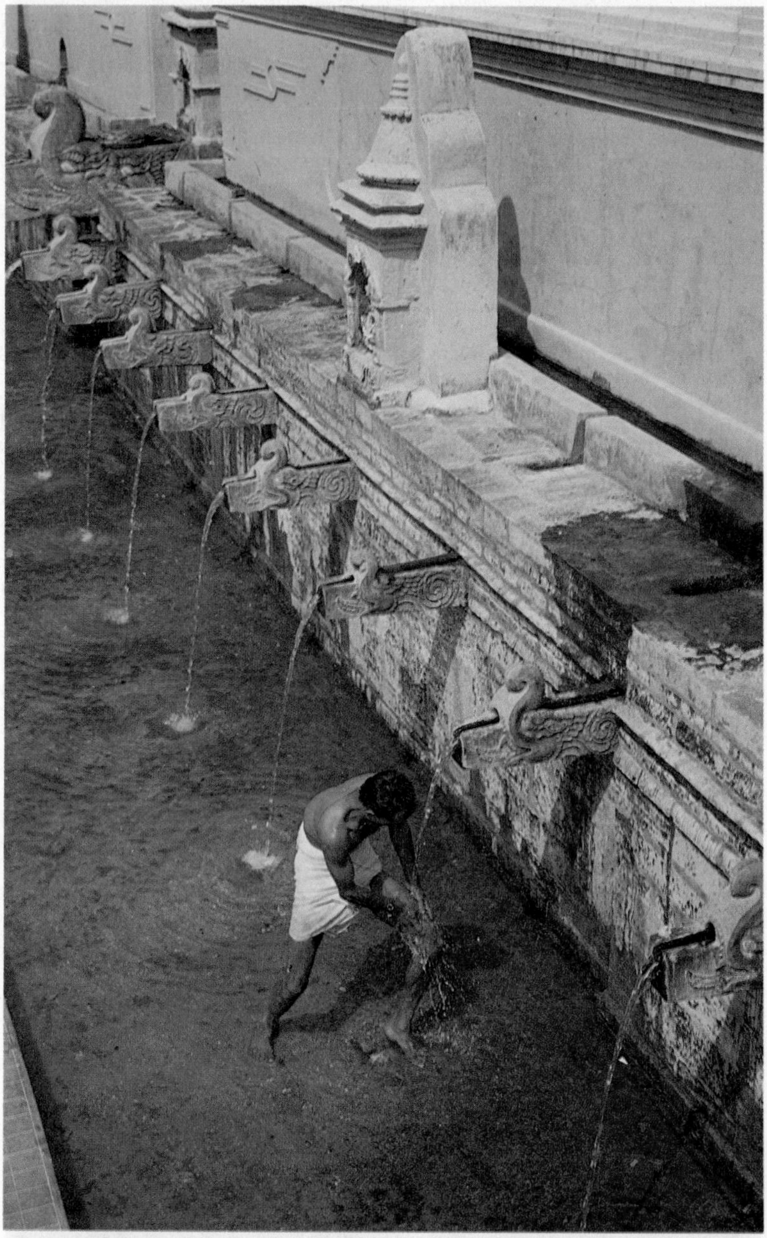

*Both industry and agriculture are being developed in **Nepal** but many of the traditional ways remain unchanged. This ancient fountain still provides water for people living near Katmandu.*

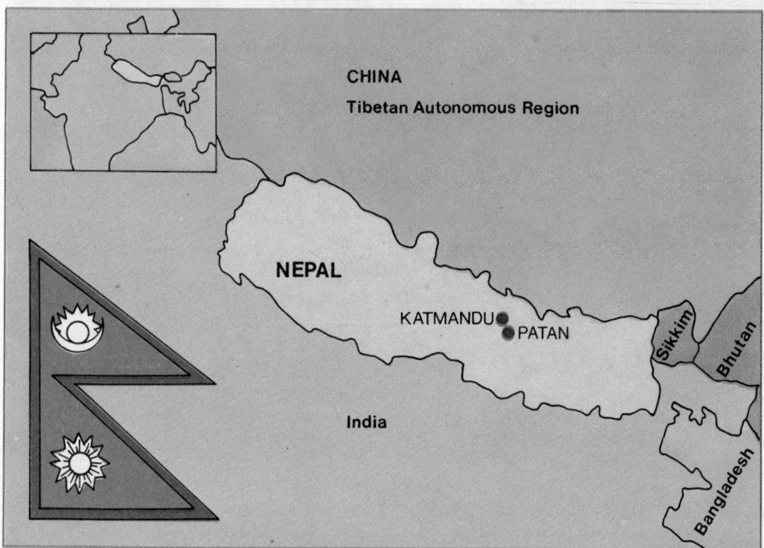

of Italian princess supposed to have invented it]

nerv·ate (nẽr′vāt) *adj.* (bot.) (of leaves) Having ribs. **ner·va·tion** (nẽrvā′shon) *n.*

nerve (nẽrv) *n.* 1. Sinew, tendon (now only poet. exc. in **strain every ~**, make all possible effort); vigor, energy, well-strung state. 2. (bot.) Rib, esp. midrib, of leaf. 3. (anat.) Fiber or bundle of fibers connecting and conveying impulses of sensation and motion between brain or spinal cord or ganglionic organ and some part of body; nervous fiber; (pl.) bodily state in regard to physical sensitiveness and interaction between brain and other parts, disordered state in these respects, exaggerated sensitiveness, nervousness; **get on one's nerves**, affect one with irritation, impatience, fear, etc.; **nerve center**, ganglion, group of closely connected nerve cells associated in performing some function; **nerve gas**, poison gas that attacks the nervous system, esp. affecting respiration. 4. Coolness in danger; boldness; assurance; (slang) audacity, impertinence; **lose one's nerve**, become timid or irresolute. **nerve** *v.t.* (**nerved, nerv·ing**). Give strength, vigor, or courage to; **~ oneself**, brace oneself (to face something unpleasant).

nerve·less (nẽrv′lĭs) *adj.* Inert, wanting in vigor or spirit, listless; undisturbed by danger, cool under attack; (bot., entom.) without nervures; (anat., zool.) without nerves. **nerve′less·ly** *adv.* **nerve′less·ness** *n.*

nerv·ous (nẽr′vus) *adj.* 1. Of the nerves; **~ breakdown**, (colloq.) loss of emotional and mental stability; **~ system**, system of specialized conducting tissue that enables an organism to coordinate its activity in relation to its environment. 2. Sinewy, muscular. 3. Having disordered or delicate nerves; excitable, highly strung, easily agitated, timid. **nerv′ous·ly** *adv.* **nerv′ous·ness** *n.*

ner·vure (nẽrv′yer) *n.* 1. One of the tubes strengthening an insect's wing. 2. Principal vein of leaf.

nerv·y (nẽr′vē) *adj.* (**nerv·i·er, nerv·i·est**). 1. Nervous; trying to the nerves; irritable, apprehensive. 2. (colloq.) Insolent; courageous.

nes·cience (nĕsh′ens, -ēens) *n.* Not knowing, absence of knowledge *of*. **nes′cient** *adj.* Ignorant (*of*); agnostic.

ness (nĕs) *n.* Promontory, headland, cape.

Ness (nĕs), **Loch.** Lake in

Inverness-shire, Scotland, forming part of Caledonian Canal.

-ness *suffix.* Having a specified state or condition.

Nes·sus (nĕs′*us*). (Gk. myth.) Centaur shot by Hercules for trying to carry off his wife Deianira; Nessus' blood-stained tunic, given to Deianira as a charm to reclaim an unfaithful husband, eventually caused Hercules' death.

nest (nĕst) *n.* Structure or place made or chosen by bird for laying eggs and sheltering young; animal's or insect's abode or spawning or breeding place; snug or secluded retreat, lodging, shelter, bed, receptacle; haunt *of* robbers etc.; fostering place *of* vice etc.; brood, swarm; collection, series of similar objects; set *of boxes, tables,* etc. fitting one inside another; ~ **egg**, real or imitation egg left in nest to induce hen to go on laying there; sum of money kept as reserve or nucleus. **nest** *v.* Make or have nest in specified place; take to nest building; take birds' nests.

nes·tle (nĕs′*el*) *v.* (**-tled, -tling**). Make nest (now rare); settle oneself, be settled, comfortably *down, in, among,* etc., leaves, wraps, chair, etc.; press oneself affectionately (*close*) *to* person; lie half-hidden or embedded; push (head, shoulder, etc.) affectionately or snugly *in*; hold embraced (usu. in past. part.). **nes′tler** *n.*

Nes·tor (nĕs′t*er*, -tŏr). (Gk. legend) King of Pylos; in old age led his subjects to the Trojan War, where his wisdom, justice, and eloquence were proverbial; hence, wise old man.

Nes·to·ri·us (nĕstŏr′ē*us*, -tŏr′-) (d. *c*451). Syrian ecclesiastic; disciple of St. John Chrysostom and patriarch of Constantinople (428–31); held that Christ had distinct human and divine persons and hence that the Virgin Mary should not be called "Mother of God"; was condemned by the Councils of Ephesus (431) and Chalcedon (451). **Nes′to·ri·an, Nes·to′ri·an·isn** *ns.*

net[1] (nĕt) *n.* Meshed fabric of twine, cord, hair, etc.; piece of this used for catching fish etc. or for covering, confining, protecting, carrying, etc.; moral or mental snare; reticulation, network; net stroke; ~ **stroke**, stroke in which ball hits this; **net′work**, arrangement with intersecting lines and interstices resembling those of net; complex system *of* railroads, rivers, canals, etc., ramification; broadcasting system of several stations linked together. **net** *v.* (**net·ted, net·ting**). Cover, confine, catch, with net(s); fish (river etc.) with nets, set nets in (river); make netting; make (purse, hammock, etc.) by netting.

net[2] (nĕt) *adj.* Free from deduction, remaining after necessary deductions; ~ **price**, real price off which discount is not allowed; ~ **profit**, true profit, actual gain after working expenses have been paid; ~ **weight**, weight excluding wrappings. **net** *v.t.* (**net·ted, net·ting**). Gain or yield (sum) as net profit.

neth·er (nĕdh′*er*) *adj.* (archaic or joc.) Lower. **neth′er·most** *adj.*

Neth·er·lands (nĕdh′*erlandz*). (Du. **Nederland**) 1. Small kingdom in N. Europe, in English freq. called Holland; capital, Amsterdam, seat of government, The Hague; principal language, Dutch. 2. (hist.) Low Countries, the whole area of the Rhine, Meuse, and Scheldt deltas, now occupied by Holland, Belgium, Luxembourg, and small parts of France and Germany. During the Middle Ages it was divided among numerous countships and dukedoms; by the mid-16th c. these were united under the Hapsburg emperor Charles V, but in the wars of religion the N. (Dutch) part revolted (1555–88) and became an independent Protestant Republic (**United Provinces of the** ~, or

*The practice of **nest building** is found in all groups of animals, from mammals to insects. Some nests are so ingeniously made as to remind us of human architecture, such as the martin's nest of dried mud (1) and the wasp's elegant paper structure (2).*

1

2

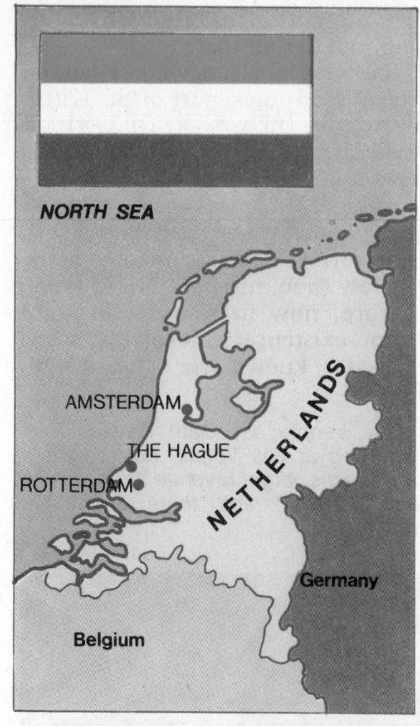

States General); meanwhile the S. part passed to the Spanish Hapsburgs (**Spanish ~**) and later, in 1713, to the Austrian Hapsburgs (**Austrian ~**). In 1815 both N. and S. were united under a monarchy (**Kingdom of the ~**), but the S. revolted in 1830 and became an independent kingdom, BELGIUM. **~ Antilles**, formerly Dutch West Indies; autonomous territory of the Netherlands in the Caribbean consisting of the islands of Curaçao, Aruba, Bonaire, St. Martin, St. Eustatius, and Saba; capital, Willemstad on Curaçao. **Neth′er·land·er** *n.*

ne·tsu·ke (nĕt′skē, -skā; *Jap.* nĕ′tsōōkĕ′) *n.* Carved or otherwise ornamented piece of ivory etc. once worn by Japanese as bob or button on cord by which articles were suspended from girdle.

Gaining their independence from Spain in the 80 Years' War, the United Provinces of the ***Netherlands*** *have, since the 17th century, grown into a modern industrial State.*

net·ting (nĕt′ĭng) *n.* (esp.) Netted string, wire, or thread; piece of this.

net·tle (nĕt′*e*l) *n.* Plant of genus *Urtica*, with two common species (*U. dioica* and *U. urens*) growing profusely on wasteland and noted for stinging properties of leaf hairs; plant resembling this, esp. stinging nettle; **~ rash**, skin eruption in patches like those produced by nettle stings, URTICARIA. **nettle** *v.t.* (**-tled, -tling**). 1. Beat or sting with nettles; get *oneself* stung with nettles. 2. Irritate, provoke.

neu·ral (noor′*a*l, nūr′-) *adj.* Of the nerves; of the nervous system.

neu·ral·gia (nōōrăl′j*a*, nyōō-) *n.* Condition of nerves (usu. of head or face) causing intense intermittent pain. **neu·ral′gic** *adj.*

neu·ras·the·ni·a (noor*a*sthē′nē*a*, nūr-) *n.* Functional nervous weakness, nervous debility. **neu·ras·then·ic** (noor*a*sthĕn′ĭk, nūr-) *adj.* & *n.*

neu·ri·tis (nōōrītĭs, nyōō-) *n.* Inflammation of nerve(s). **neu·rit·ic** (nōōrĭt′ĭk, nyōō-) *adj.*

neuro- *prefix.* Of nerves.

neu·rol·o·gy (nōōrŏl′*o*jē, nyōō-) *n.* Scientific study of the anatomy, functions, and diseases of the nervous system. **neu·ro·log·i·cal** (noor*o*lŏj′ĭk*a*l, nūr-) *adj.* **neu·rol′o·gist** *n.*

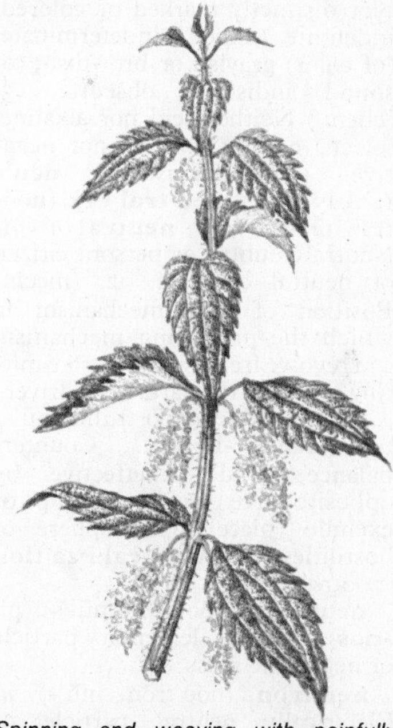

Spinning and weaving with painfully obtained ***nettle fibers*** *was often the lot of the heroine of old European folktales. The plant is, however, the food of many kinds of butterfly larvae.*

Probably ***nets*** *were among the first of man's inventions, both as an aid to hunting and for carrying provisions. Fishing nets can be fixed, moved by hand (like that of these Portuguese tunny fishers), or towed behind a boat.*

neu·ron (noor′ŏn, nūr′-), **neu·rone** (noor′ŏn, nūr′-) *ns.* Nerve cell with its appendages, the basic structural unit of the nervous system. **neu·ron·ic** (noorŏn′ĭk, nyōō-) *adj.*

neu·rop·ter·ous (nōōrŏp′ter*us*, nyōō-) *adj.* Of the Neuroptera, an order of insects having four naked membranous transparent wings with netlike vein patterns.

neu·ro·sis (nōōrō′sĭs, nyōō-) *n.* (pl. **-ses** pr. -sēz). (path., psychol.) Derangement of normal function due to disorders of nervous system, esp. such as are unaccompanied by demonstrable organic change. **neu·rot·ic** (nōōrŏt′ĭk, nyōō-) *adj.* & *n.* (Person) affected with neurosis. **neu·rot′i·cal·ly** *adv.*

neu·ter (nōō′ter, nū′-) *adj.* 1. (gram.) Neither masculine nor feminine. 2. Neither male nor female; (bot.) having neither pistils nor stamens; (entom.) sexually undeveloped, sterile. ~ *n.* 1. Word of neuter gender. 2. Sexually undeveloped female insect, esp. bee or ant; castrated animal. ~ *v.t.* Castrate.

neu·tral (nōō′tr*a*l, nū′-) *adj.* 1. Not assisting either of two belligerent nations, belonging to a nation remaining inactive during hostilities, exempted or excluded from warlike operations; taking neither side in dispute or difference of opinion, indifferent, impartial. 2. Not distinctly marked or colored, indefinite, vague, indeterminate; (of color) grayish or brownish; (of sound) indistinct, obscure. 3. (chem.) Neither acid nor alkaline; (elect.) neither positive nor negative. 4. Neuter, asexual. **neu′tral·ly** *adv.* **neu·tral·i·ty** (nōō-trăl′ĭtē, nū-) *n.* **neutral** *n.* 1. Neutral country or person; citizen of neutral country. 2. (mech.) Position of gear mechanism in which the propelling mechanism can revolve freely without transmitting power to the parts to be driven.

neu·tral·ize (nōō′tr*a*līz, nū′-) *v.t.* (**-ized, -iz·ing**). Counterbalance, render ineffective by opposite force or effect; exempt or exclude (place) from sphere of hostilities. **neu·tral·i·za·tion** (nōōtr*a*līzā′sh*o*n, nū-) *n.*

neu·tri·no (nōōtrē′nō, nū-) *n.* (pl. **-nos**). Neutral elementary particle of negligible mass.

neu·tron (nōō′trŏn, nū′-) *n.* Electrically neutral particle of almost the same mass as a proton, present in all atomic nuclei except those of hydrogen.

Nev., NV *abbrevs.* Nevada.

Ne·vad·a (nevăd*a*, -vah′d*a*). State of western U.S., admitted to the Union in 1864; capital, Carson City. **Ne·vad′an** *adj.* & *n.* (esp. geol.) Of an episode of mountain formation during the Mesozoic era.

né·vé (nāvā′, nā′vā) *n.* Expanse of granular snow not yet compressed into ice at head of glacier.

nev·er (nĕv′*er*) *adv.* At no time, on no occasion, not ever; not at all; (colloq., expressing surprise or incredulity) surely not; ~ **a**, not a, no — at all; ~ **a one**, none; ~ **mind, nev′ermind** (*v.*) do not be troubled (about); **nevermore′**, at no future time; **never-never land**, unreal, imaginary place or state of mind; **never so**, (in conditional clauses) to unlimited extent, ever so; **nevertheless′**, notwithstanding, but for all that.

Ne·vis (nē′vĭs, nĕv′ĭs). Island in the West Indies, part of St. Kitts.

ne·vus (nē′v*us*) *n.* (pl. **-vi** pr. -vī). (path.) Birthmark, congenital lesion of skin, a network of hypertrophied blood vessels causing sharply defined red patch level with skin surface; (also) pigmented mole.

new (nōō, nū) *adj.* Not existing before, now first made, brought into existence, invented, introduced, known or heard of,

*Many people associate **Nevada** with gambling at Las Vegas, but the State also earns large revenue from mining and industry; and there are cattle ranches.*

*The Port of St. John in the Bay of Fundy is the principal seaport for the province of **New Brunswick** in Canada. The fishing catch is mainly lobster and sardines.*

experienced, or discovered; unfamiliar *to*; renewed, fresh, further, additional; later, modern, newfangled; of recent growth, origin, arrival, or manufacture, now first used, not worn or exhausted; not yet accustomed *to*, fresh *from*; (of family or person) lately risen in position; **new'comer**, person lately arrived; **New Deal**: see DEAL³; **new'fan'gled**, different from the good old fashion, having no merit but novelty; **new-laid**, (of eggs) recently laid; **new learning**, study of the Bible and the Greek classics in their original language at the time of the Reformation and Renaissance in England; **new moon**, moon when first visible as a crescent after conjunction with sun, time of such appearance; **new'speak**, (joc. in derogatory sense) reformed version of a language [f. George Orwell's novel *1984*]; **New Style:** see STYLE; **New Testament:** see TESTAMENT; **New World**, the Americas, discovered at a comparatively late period; **New Year**, coming or lately begun year, first few days of year; **New Year's Day** (freq. **New Year's**), Jan. 1. **new'ish** *adj.* **new'ness** *n.* **new** *adv.* Newly, recently, just; anew.

New Britain. Island of Bismarck Archipelago.

New Brunswick. SE. maritime province of Canada; capital, Fredericton.

New Cal·e·do·ni·a (kălĕdō'nēa, -dōn'ya). Overseas territory of France in SW. Pacific 1,000 mi. (1,600 km) E. of Australia, consisting of this island and several smaller ones; capital, Nouméa.

*The capitol building in **New Hampshire,** New England. The State is one of the most industrialized in the U.S.A. With its beautiful scenery, tourists also contribute a large proportion to the State's economy.*

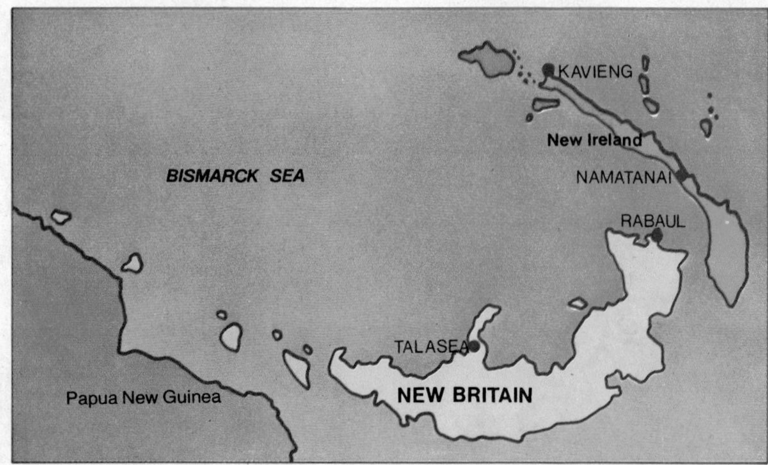

*The principal export of **New Britain** is copra, largely produced in the north of the island, but native cooperatives grow considerable amounts of other crops such as cocoa.*

New Del·hi (dĕl'ē). Capital of India in the N. part on the Jumna River, S. of Delhi.

new·el (nōō'el, nū'-) *n.* (archit.) Center pillar or (**open** or **hollow** ~) well of winding stair; post supporting stair handrail at top or bottom.

New England. Part of U.S. comprising NE. states of Maine, New Hampshire, Vermont, Massachusetts, Rhode Island, and Connecticut. **New Englander** *n.* Native, inhabitant, of New England.

New·found·land (nōō'fund-lănd, -land, -fun-, nū'-, nōōfownd'-land, nū-). Large island, with famous fisheries, at mouth of St. Lawrence River; discovered and claimed for England 1497 by John Cabot; formerly a Dominion of the British Empire; united with Canada as one of its provinces, 1949; capital, St. John's; ~ **dog**, large dog of a breed native to N. Amer., with thick coarse coat, noted for sagacity, good temper, strength, and swimming powers. **New·found·land·er** (nōōfownd'lander, nū-) *n.*

New Guinea. Pacific island N. of Australia, divided into (1) the Indonesian province of West Irian, and (2) Papua New Guinea.

New Hampshire. NE. state of U.S., one of the original 13 states of the Union (1788); capital, Concord.

New Ha·ven (hā'ven). City and port in Connecticut on Long Island Sound; site of Yale University.

New Hebrides. Now Vanuatu. Group of islands in W. Pacific; capital, Vila.

New Jersey. Middle Atlantic state of U.S., one of the original 13 states of the Union (1787); capital, Trenton.

new·ly (nōō'lē, nū'-) *adv.* Recently, just; in new manner;

***Newfoundland's** economy was at first based solely on cod fisheries. More recently, there has been expansion of mining and forestry.*

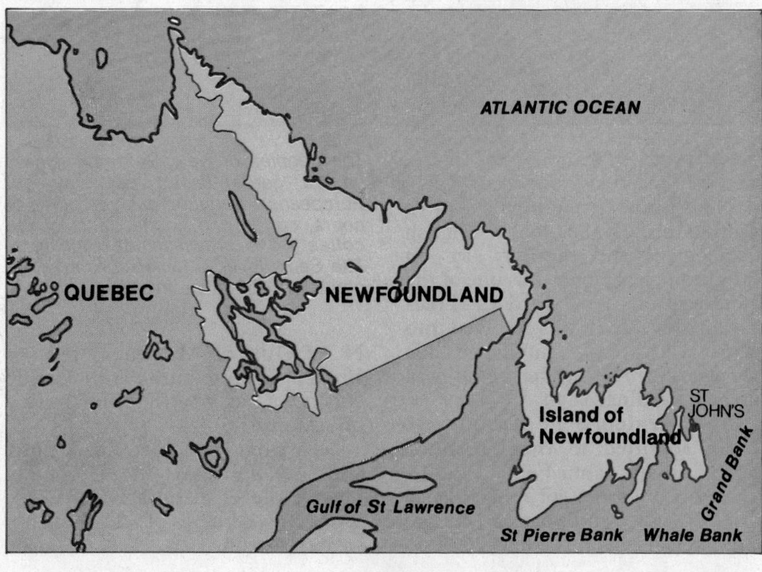

1

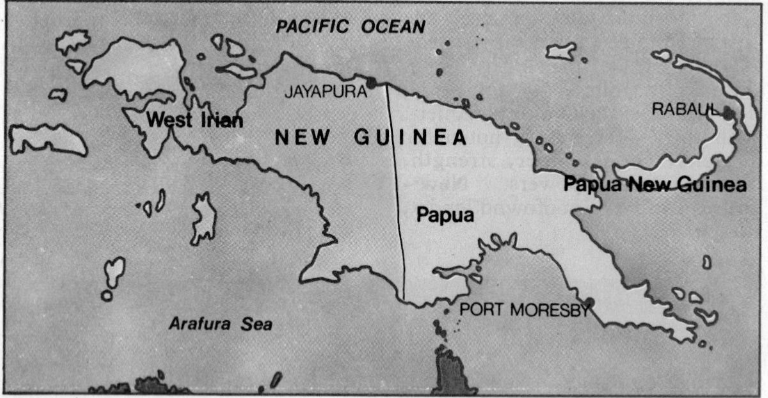

2

new′lywed(s) (*adj.* & *n.pl.*), recently married (couple).

New·man (no͞o′man, nū′-), **John Henry** (1801–90). English theologian and author; as an Anglican clergyman, was one of the founders of the Oxford or Tractarian movement; was received into R.C. Ch. 1845; published his *Apologia pro Vita sua* 1864; was created cardinal 1879.

New Mexico. State of southwest U.S.; admitted to the Union in 1912; capital, Santa Fe.

New Or·le·ans (ōr′lēenz, -lenz, ōrlēnz′). City and port on Mississippi in Louisiana, 100 mi. (160 km) N. of Gulf of Mexico; noted for French architecture and Creole cuisine of early settlers; birthplace of jazz music.

New·port (no͞o′pōrt, nū′-). Port and summer resort in SE. Rhode Island; site of elaborate mansions; formerly center of fashionable society season.

*The peoples of **New Guinea** originally had a garden-based economy but Europeans introduced cash cropping of copra, coffee and cocoa. Most of the coffee (1) is grown in the Highlands. The Sepik River is famed for the wood carving (2) of its people.*

Above: As an Anglican and later a Roman Catholic, ***John Henry Newman*** *was a significant leader in the development of religious philosophy in 19th century England.*

Above left: ***New York City,*** *largest city in the western hemisphere, with five counties in its boundaries. Left: Renovated tenements and housing in the Bronx, one of New York's boroughs.*

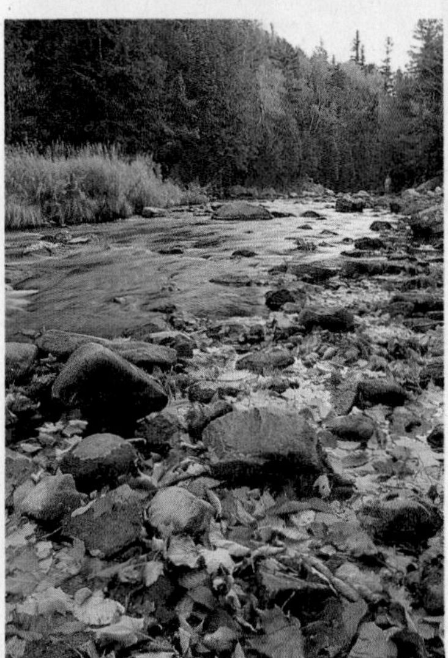

New York State *noted for its diverse scenery as well as its industrial and business centres has in the north the beautiful Adirondack Upland, seen here in the Fall.*

news (no͞oz, nūz) *n.* Tidings, new information, fresh event reported; radio or television report of this; **news'cast**, radio or television broadcast of news; **news'caster**, broadcaster of news on radio or television; **news'letter**, (orig.) letter containing news, sent out periodically to country towns etc.; now, periodical sent by mail to subscribers; **news'paper**, printed, now usu. daily or weekly, publication containing news, advertisements, and literary matter; **news'print**, paper for printing newspapers on; **news'reel**, motion picture giving items of recent news; **news'stand**, booth for sale of newspapers; **news'vendor**, newspaper seller.

news·y (no͞o'zē, nū'-) *adj.* (**news·i·er, news·i·est**). (colloq.) Full of (sensational) news.

newt (no͞ot, nūt) *n.* Small-tailed amphibian of the order Urodela.

new·ton (no͞o'tən, nū'-) *n.* (abbrev. N) Unit of force in meter-kilogram-second system, equal to the force producing an acceleration of 1 meter per second per second on a mass of 1 kilogram.

New·ton (no͞o'tən, nū'-), **Sir Isaac** (1642–1727). English natural philosopher; formulator of laws of motion and law of gravitation. **New·to·ni·an** (no͞otō'nēən, nū-) *adj.* & *n.* (Follower) of Newton or his theory of the universe.

New York. 1. Middle Atlantic state of U.S., one of the original 13 states of the Union (1788); capital, Albany. 2. Largest city of U.S., in New York State at mouth of Hudson River; **New York Bay**, inlet of Atlantic in SE. part of state; divided into Upper and Lower New York Bays, connected by the Narrows; **New York State Barge Canal**, system of waterways including the Erie, Oswego, and Champlain canals, connecting the Hudson River with Lake Erie at Buffalo and with the St. Lawrence through Lake Champlain. **New York'er** *n.* Native, inhabitant, of New York City.

New Zea·land (zē'lənd). Member nation of the Brit. Commonwealth, occupying 2 large and many

***Sir Isaac Newton,** a mathematician and scientist, possessed one of the most original and inquiring minds of his day. His findings in optics, astronomy, and mathematics matched his work on the nature of gravity.*

smaller islands in S. Pacific *c*1,000 miles (1,610 km) SE. of Australia; the islands were discovered by Tasman, 1642, and visited by Cook, 1769; became an English colony; acquired self-government 1852 and dominion status 1907; capital, Wellington. **New Zea'land·er** *n.* Native, inhabitant, of New Zealand. [f. *Zeeland*]

next (nĕkst) *adj.* Lying, living, being, nearest or nearest *to*; nearest in relationship or kinship; soonest come to, first ensuing, immediately following, coming nearest in order etc., *to*, immediately *before*; ~ **door**, (door of the) nearest or adjoining house (also fig.); **next-door to**, almost. **next** *prep.* In or into the next place, on the next occasion, in the next degree, to. ~ *n.* Next person or thing; ~ **of kin**, person most closely related (*to*).

nex·us (nĕk'sus) *n.* (pl. **nex·us, nex·us·es** pr. nĕk'susĭz). Bond, connection.

Nez Per·cé (nĕz'pẽrs') (pl. **Nez Per·cés** pr. nĕz'pẽr'sĭz, collect, for def. 1 **Nez Per·cé**). 1. (Member of) a N. Amer. Indian people, formerly in the Pacific Northwest. 2. Sahaptin language of the Nez Percé.

N.F., Nfld., Nfd. *abbrevs.* Newfoundland.

NFL *abbrev.* National Football League.

NH, N.H. *abbrevs.* New Hampshire.

NHL *abbrev.* National Hockey League.

Ni *symbol.* Nickel.

Ni·ag·a·ra (nīăg'ra, -era). N. Amer. river flowing from Lake Erie into Lake Ontario and forming part of boundary between Canada and U.S.; ~ **Falls**, waterfalls in this river comprising Horseshoe or

*Horseshoe Falls, on the Canadian side of **Niagara Falls.** Erosion of the soft top layer of rock is causing the 160 ft. high falls to recede 3 ft. each year upstream.*

Canadian Falls, 160 ft. (49 m) high, 2,500 ft. (763 m) wide, and American Falls, 167 ft. (51 m) high, 1,000 ft. (305 m) wide.

Nia·mey (nyahmā'). Capital of Niger in SW. part on ~ **River**.

nib (nĭb) *n.* Penpoint; point of tool etc.; (pl.) fragments of crushed cocoa beans.

nib·ble (nĭb'el) *v.* (**-bled, -bling**). Take small bites at; bite gently or cautiously or playfully. ~ *n.* Act of nibbling, esp. of fish at bait.

Ni·be·lungs (nē'belo͝ongz) *n.pl.* (sing. **-lung** pr. lo͝ong). (Germanic legend) Race of dwarfs in Norway. **Ni·be·lung·en·lied** (nē'belo͝ongenlēt) *n.* Thirteenth-c. German poem (embodying a story found in the EDDA) telling of the life and death of SIEGFRIED and of KRIEMHILD's revenge.

*Rugged mountains, snow covered in winter, extend like a backbone through the South Island of **New Zealand.** The country also has much thermal activity, epitomized by active volcanos and geysers. Its major exports are agricultural products.*

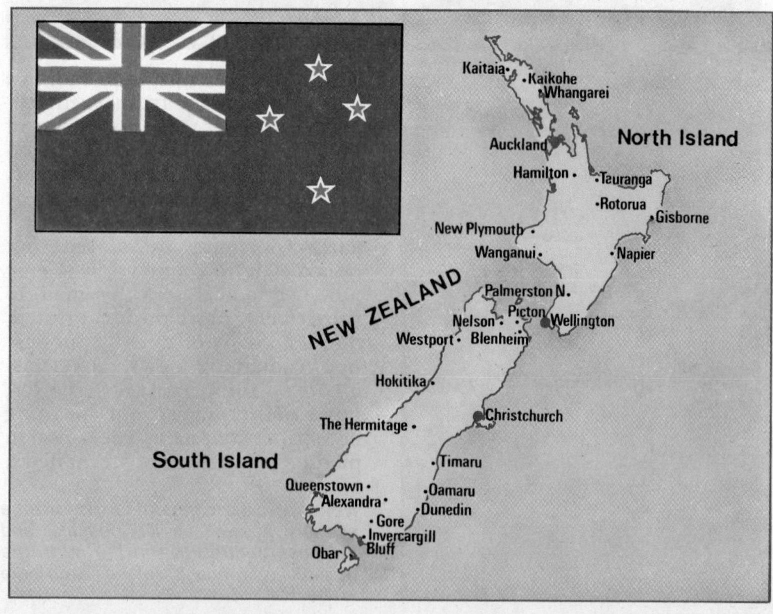

nib·lick (nĭb'lĭk) *n.* Golf club (no. 9 iron) with heavy lofted head, used esp. for playing out of bunkers.

Ni·cae·a (nīsē'*a*). (Turk. *Iznik*) Ancient city of Bithynia, scene of two ecumenical councils, the first (325) dealing with the Arian controversy and the second (787) the question of images.

Nic·a·ra·gua (nĭk*a*rah'gw*a*). Central American republic, between Honduras and Costa Rica; independent since 1821; capital, Managua; **Lake ~**, largest lake, 3,089 sq. mi. (8,001 sq. km) in Central America in S. Nicaragua. **Nic·a·ra'guan** *adj.* & *n.*

Nice (nēs). Port and resort city of SE. France on the Riviera near Italian border.

nice (nīs) *adj.* (**nic·er, nic·est**). 1. Fastidious; punctilious; requiring precision or discrimination; minute, subtle. 2. (colloq.) Agreeable, delightful; satisfactory; kind, friendly, considerate; generally commendable. **nice'ly** *adv.* **nice'ness** *n.*

Ni·cene (nīsēn', nī'sēn) *adj.* Of Nicaea; **~ Creed**, formal statement of Christian belief based on decisions of first Council of Nicaea, official creed of Orthodox, Roman Catholic, and some Protestant Churches.

ni·ce·ty (nī'sĭtē) *n.* (pl. **-ties**). Punctiliousness; precision, accuracy; minute distinction, subtle or unimportant detail, (pl.) minutiae; **to a ~**, as closely or precisely as possible.

niche (nĭch) *n.* Shallow recess in wall to contain statue, vase, etc.; (fig.) place or position adapted to the character, or suited to the merits, of a person or thing. **~** *v.t.* (**niched, nich·ing**). Place (as if) in a niche.

Nich·o·las[1] (nĭk'*o*l*a*s). (Russ. *Nikolai*) Name of two emperors of Russia: **Nicholas I** (1796–1855), emperor 1825–55; his accession, after the death of his brother Alexander I and the abdication of his brother Constantine, was marked by the DECEMBRIST revolution, which he subdued and punished mercilessly; **Nicholas II** (1868–1918), emperor of Russia 1894–1917; forced to abdicate, March 1917; killed with his family, 1918.

Nich·o·las[2] (nĭk'*o*l*a*s), **St.** (d. 326). Bishop of Myra in Asia Minor; patron of sailors and of children (cf. SANTA CLAUS), and patron saint of Russia; commemorated Dec. 6.

Birds and some reptiles have a 'third eyelid' or ***nictating membrane.*** *Usually this semi-transparent tissue is used to clean the eye without total loss of vision.*

Nick (nĭk). **Old ~**, the Devil.

nick (nĭk) *n.* Notch, groove, serving as catch, guide, mark, etc.; **in the ~ of time**, just at the right moment, only just in time. **nick** *v.* Make nick(s) in, indent; make incision at root of (horse's tail) to make him carry it higher.

nick·el (nĭk'*e*l) *n.* 1. (chem.) Hard silvery-white lustrous malleable ductile metallic element much used esp. in alloys; symbol Ni, at. no. 28, at. wt. 58.71. 2. Five-cent piece. 3. **~ silver**, alloy of nickel,

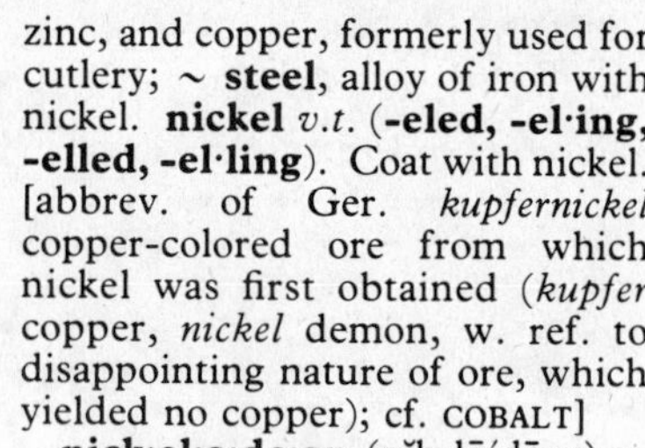

zinc, and copper, formerly used for cutlery; **~ steel**, alloy of iron with nickel. **nickel** *v.t.* (**-eled, -el·ing, -elled, -el·ling**). Coat with nickel. [abbrev. of Ger. *kupfernickel* copper-colored ore from which nickel was first obtained (*kupfer* copper, *nickel* demon, w. ref. to disappointing nature of ore, which yielded no copper); cf. COBALT]

nick·el·o·de·on (nĭk*e*lō'dē*o*n) *n.* 1. In early days of motion pictures, theater where admission price was 5 cents. 2. Early kind of jukebox.

A wide range of raw materials is exported by ***Nicaragua,*** *incuding cotton, sugar, and coffee, together with a number of minerals including those used in the manufacture of cement.*

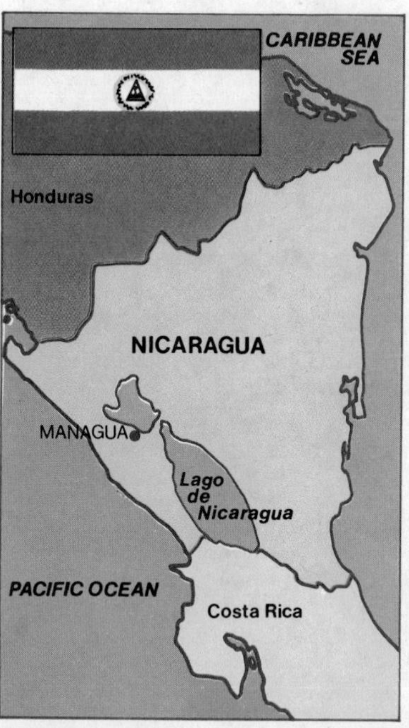

Tsar Nicholas I *(1796-1855) succeeded his brother Alexander in 1825. His reign was one in which the corrupt Russian administration was given a facade of efficiency without any real improvements being made.*

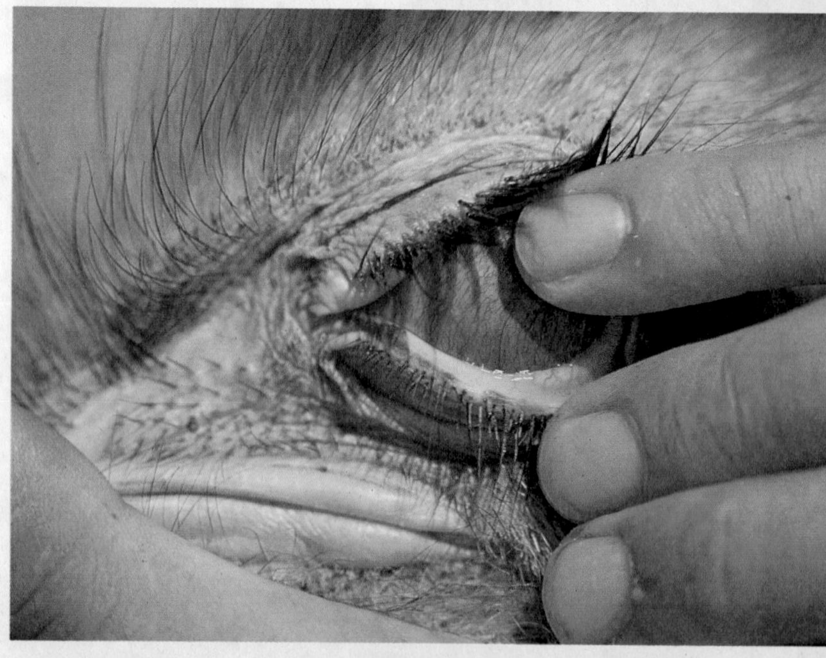

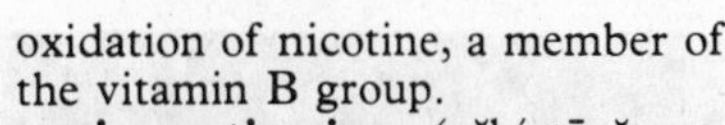

nick·nack = KNICK-KNACK.

nick·name (nĭk'nām) *n.* Name added to or substituted for proper name of person, place, or thing. ~ *v.t.* (**-named, -nam·ing**). Call (person etc. by a nickname), give nickname to.

Nic · o · de · mus (nĭkodē'm*u*s). Member of the Sanhedrin who helped Joseph of Arimathea to bury Jesus Christ (John 3, 7, 19).

Nic·o·si·a (nĭkosē'*a*). Capital of Cyprus in the N. central part.

ni · co · ti · a · na (nĭkōshēā'n*a*, -ăn'*a*, -ah'n*a*) *n.* Tobacco plant; any of several plants of genus *N*~, esp. *N. alata*, a garden variety with greenish-white flowers, grown for its sweet scent. [f. Jacques *Nicot*, who introduced tobacco into France in 1560]

nic·o·tine (nĭk'*o*tēn, -tĭn, nĭk*o*tēn') *n.* Poisonous alkaloid contained in tobacco, from which it is obtained as a pungent oily liquid soluble in water. **nic·o·tin·ic** (nĭk*o*tĭn'ĭk) *adj.* ~ **acid**, crystalline acid ($C_6H_5NO_2$), produced by oxidation of nicotine, a member of the vitamin B group.

nic · o · tin · ism (nĭk'*o*tēnĭz*e*m, -tĭn-, nĭk*o*tē'nĭz*e*m) *n.* Morbid state produced by excessive use of tobacco.

nic·tate (nĭk'tāt), **nic·ti·tate** (nĭk'tĭtāt) *vbs.i.* (**-tat·ed, -tat·ing**). Close and open the eyes, wink; chiefly in **nict(it)ating membrane**, 3rd or inner eyelid of many animals, vestigial in man. **nic·ta·tion** (nĭktā'sh*o*n), **nic·ti·ta·tion** (nĭktĭtā'sh*o*n) *ns.*

ni·dus (nī'd*u*s) *n.* (pl. **-di** pr. -dī). Place in which insects etc. deposit eggs; place in which spores or seeds develop; place of origin or development of disease etc.; place in which something is deposited or lodged.

Nie·buhr (nē'boor), **Reinhold** (1892–1971). Amer. Protestant theologian and educator.

niece (nēs) *n.* Brother's or sister's daughter.

ni·el·lo (nēĕl'ō) *n.* (pl. **-el·li** pr. -ĕl'ē). Black metallic amalgam of sulfur added to copper, silver, lead, etc., for filling engraved lines in silver or other metal, as decoration; (specimen of) such ornamental work; ~ **print**, print taken from engraved plate that is to be filled with niello.

Nie·tzsche (nē'ch*e*, -chē), **Friedrich Wilhelm** (1844–1900). German philosopher; originator of idea of "superman" and of doctrine of perfectibility of man through forcible self-assertion and superiority to ordinary morality. **Nie'tzsche·an** *adj.* & *n.*

nif·ty (nĭf'tē) *adj.* (**-ti·er, -ti·est**). (colloq.) Neat, smart, clever.

Ni·ger (nī'*j*er). 1. River of W. Africa, flowing in a curve from NE. frontier of Sierra Leone to Gulf of Guinea. 2. Republic in W. central Africa; capital, Niamey.

Ni·ge·ri·a (nījēr'ē*a*). Republic in W. Africa, member of the Brit. Commonwealth, occupying basin of lower Niger, with coastline on Gulf of Guinea; formerly a British protectorate; independent 1960; capital, Lagos.

*The **River Niger** rises in the Loma Mountains of Guinea, flowing north and east through Mali and Niger before reaching the Nigerian coast and forming a delta.*

*The former French colony of **Niger** is now an independent republic. The main exports are cotton and peanuts. Many of the people live by subsistence farming.*

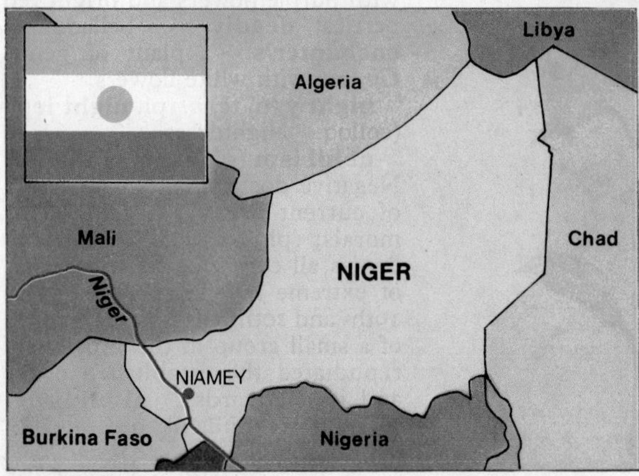

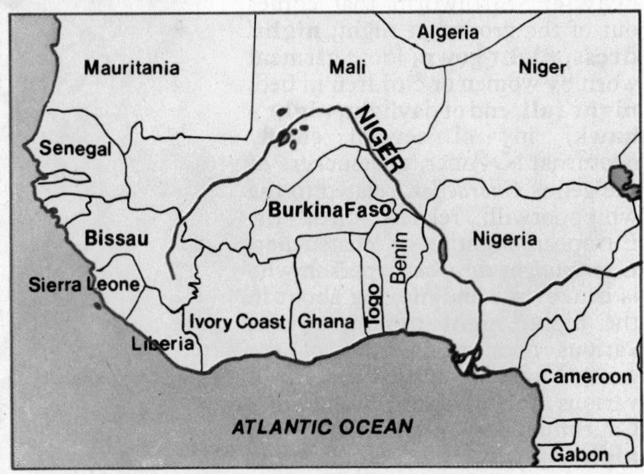

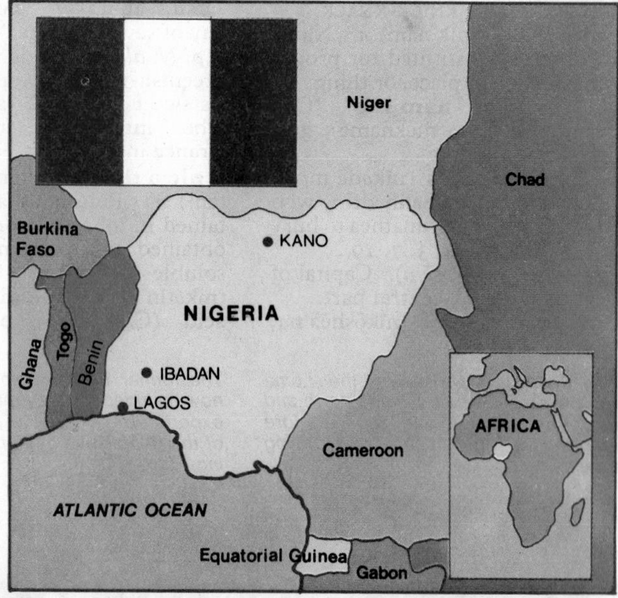

Above left: Pottery, using local clay, is made by the people of ***Nigeria,*** *a former British colony. There are up to 250 languages spoken by the many tribes.*

nig·gard (nĭg′erd) *n.* Stingy person, grudging giver *of.* ~ *adj.* (rhet. and poet.) Niggardly.

nig·gard·ly (nĭg′erdlē) *adj.* Parsimonious, stingy, sparing, scanty; giving or given grudgingly or in small amounts. **nig′gard·li·ness** *n.*

nig·gle (nĭg′el) *v.i.* (**-gled, -gling**). Spend time, be overly elaborate, on petty details. **nig′-gling** *adj.* & *n.* Trifling, petty; lacking in breadth, largeness, or boldness of effect; (of handwriting) cramped.

nigh (nī) *adv., prep.,* & *adj.* (archaic, poet., or dial.) Near.

night (nīt) *n.* Dark period between twilight and dawn, time from sunset to sunrise, darkness then prevailing, the dark; end of daylight; weather, experiences, or occupation of a night; **make a ~ of it**, spend night in festivity; **~ out**, festive evening; evening on which servant is allowed out; **~ blindness**: see NYCTALOPIA; **night′cap**, covering for the head, worn in bed; drink taken before going to bed; **night clothes**, clothes worn in bed; **night club**, club open at night for dancing, supper, etc.; **night crawler**, earthworm that comes out of the ground at night; **night′dress, night′gown**, loose garment worn by women or children in bed; **night′fall**, end of daylight; **night′hawk**, any of several chiefly nocturnal N. Amer. goatsuckers of the genus *Chordeiles*, related to the whippoorwill; related bird, the European nightjar or goatsucker, *Caprimulgus europaeus*; person who is usu. awake and moving about in the night; **night heron**, any of various nocturnal herons of the genus *Nycticorax*; **night′jar**, any of various nocturnal birds of family Caprimulgidae, with harsh cry; **night′life**, entertainments open at night; **night light**, lamp of low wattage for use at night, esp. in bedrooms; **night′mare**, female monster sitting upon and seeming to suffocate sleeper, incubus; oppressive, terrifying, or fantastically horrible dream; haunting fear, thing vaguely dreaded; **night owl**, (colloq.) person who goes about by night; **night′rider**, in the southern U.S., member of a band of mounted men who engaged in acts of terrorism for intimidation or revenge; **night school**, school, class, held in evening for those at work during day; **night soil**, (archaic) contents of cesspools etc., removed at night; **night stick**, stick carried by police, orig. at night; **night watch, night watchman**, (person or party keeping) watch by night.

Although tobacco can be grown in gardens, it is usually the related ornamental species of ***nicotiana*** *which are cultivated in temperate zones.*

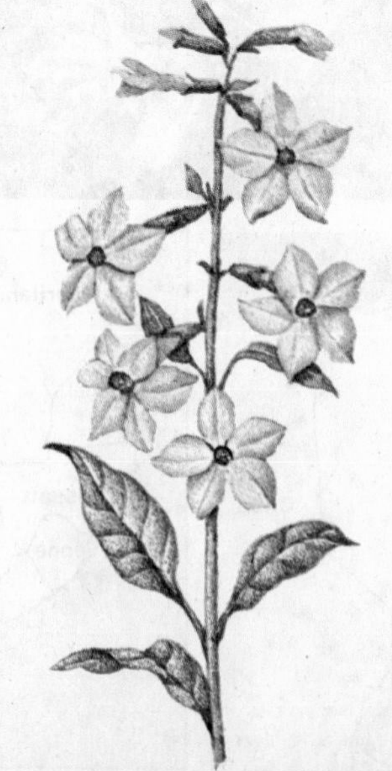

night·in·gale (nī′tĭn gāl, nī′tĭng-gāl) *n.* Small reddish-brown migratory bird of genus *Luscinia* (in Gt. Britain *L. megarhynchos*) celebrated for the melodious song of the male, often heard at night during the breeding season.

Night·in·gale (nī′tĭn gāl, nī′-tĭnggāl), **Florence** (1820–1910). English reformer; founder of modern nursing profession; organized hospital unit for Crimean War and established new type of war hospital in Crimea.

night·ly (nīt′lē) *adj.* Happening, done, existing, etc., in the night; happening every night. ~ *adv.* Every night.

night·shade (nīt′shād) *n.* Any of various plants of genus *Solanum*, esp. **black ~** (*S. nigrum*), with white flowers and black poisonous berries, **woody ~** (*S. dulcamara*), with purple flowers and bright red berries; **deadly ~**, belladonna; **enchanter's ~**, plant of genus *Circaea* with white flowers.

night·y (nī′tē) *n.* (pl. **night·ies**). (colloq.) Nightdress.

ni·hil·ism (nī′ĭlĭzem, nē′-) *n.* 1. Negative doctrines, total rejection of current beliefs, in religion or morals; (philos.) skepticism that denies all existence. 2. Doctrines of extreme revolutionary party in 19th- and 20th-c. Russia (orig. used of a small group in the 1860s who repudiated the established order and its standards). **ni′hil·ist** *n.* **ni·hil·is·tic** (nīĭlĭs′tĭk, nē-) *adj.* [L. *nihil* nothing]

Flying silently and often spending the day resting along instead of across a branch, the ***nightjar*** *is rarely observed even though it may live close to human habitation.*

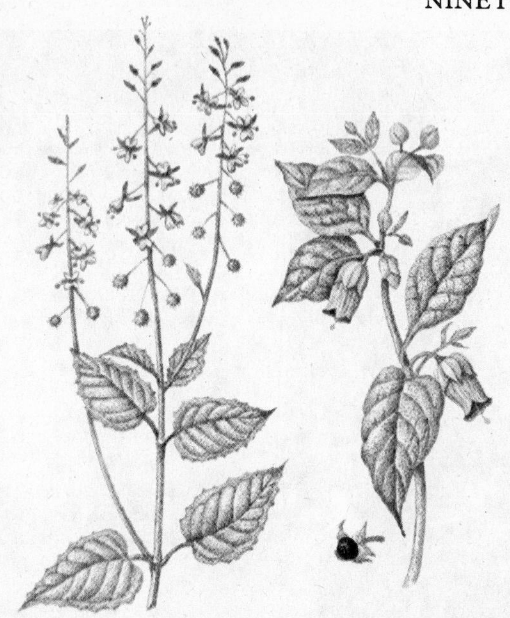

Many plants are given the name of ***nightshade,*** *including the poisonous members of the genus Solanum and other noxious or harmless herbs which resemble them.*

Ni·jin·sky (nĭzhĭn′skē, -jĭn′-), **Vas·lav** (vahtslahf′) (1890–1950). Russian ballet dancer and choreographer; most famous and greatest of his time; appeared in "L'Après-Midi d'un Faun," "Le Spectre de la Rose," etc.; in later life he became insane and was confined in an asylum.

-nik *suffix.* Forming nouns denoting person associated with specified thing or quality (*beatnik, nogoodnik*). [f. Russ. (as *sputnik*) and Yiddish]

Ni·ke (nī′kē). (Gk. myth.) 1. Goddess of victory, freq. identified with Athene; ~ **of Samothrace**: see WINGED Victory. 2. (mil.) One of a series of U.S. Army surface-to-air guided missiles for defense against enemy aircraft and missiles.

nil (nĭl) *n.* Nothing.

Nile (nīl). Longest river of Africa, flowing from E. Central Africa 4,000 miles (6,440 km) northward to Mediterranean; **Blue** ~, tributary joining the Nile at Khartoum; **White** ~, part of Nile above Khartoum; ~ **green** = EAU de Nil.

Ni·lot·ic (nīlŏt′ĭk) *adj.* Of the river Nile, the Nile region, or its inhabitants.

nim·ble (nĭm′b*e*l) *adj.* (**-bler, -blest**). Quick in movement, agile, swift; (of mind etc.) versatile, clever, quick to apprehend. **nim′ble·ness** *n.* **nim′bly** *adv.*

nim·bo-stra·tus (nĭmbō strā′t*u*s, -străt′*u*s) *n.* (meteor.) Type of low cloud, dark gray and sometimes trailing.

nim·bus (nĭm′b*u*s) *n.* Bright cloud or halo investing deity, person, or thing; bright disk, aureole, around or over head of saint etc. in picture.

Nîmes (nēm). City in S. France; site of famous Roman ruins, including amphitheater.

Nim·rod (nĭm′rŏd). Great-grandson of Noah, traditional founder of the Babylonian dynasty, noted as a great hunter (Gen. 10).

nin·com·poop (nĭn′k*o*mpōōp, nĭng′-) *n.* Simpleton.

nine (nīn) *adj.* Amounting to 9; **the N**~, the Muses; ~ **days' wonder**, novelty that attracts much attention but is soon forgotten; **nine′pin**, pin used in **nine′pins**, game of knocking down nine wooden pins by bowling a ball at them. **nine** *n.* One more than eight; symbol for this (9, ix, or IX); card with nine pips; nine o'clock; size etc. indicated by 9; set of nine things or persons; baseball team; **to the** ~**s**, to perfection (esp. in **dressed up to the** ~**s**). **nine′fold** *adj.* & *n.*

nine·teen (nīn′tēn′) *adj.* & *n.* One more than 18 (19, xix, or XIX). **nine′teenth′** *adj.* ~ **hole**, (colloq.) barroom in golf clubhouse.

nine·ty (nīn′tē) *adj.* Amounting to 90. ~ *n.* (pl. **-ties**). Cardinal number, 9 times 10 (90, xc, or XC); set of 90 things or persons; **nine-**

Florence Nightingale, *during a career lasting from 1851 to 1872, not only radically improved army medical care but raised the standard of general nursing in the U.K. as well.*

ties, (pl.) numbers etc. from 90 to 99; these years of century or life.

Nin·e·veh (nĭn'*eve*). Ancient capital of Assyrian Empire, on right bank of Tigris.

nin·ny (nĭn'ē) *n.* (pl. **-nies**). Simpleton.

ninth (nīnth) *adj.* Next after 8th. ~ *n.* Ninth part (see PART[1] def. 1); 9th thing etc.; (mus.) interval of octave and second. **ninth'ly** *adv.*

Ni·o·be (nī'ōbē). (Gk. legend) Daughter of Tantalus; Apollo and Artemis, enraged because she boasted herself superior to their mother Latona, slew her six sons and five of her six daughters; Niobe herself was turned into a rock, and her tears into streams that trickled from it. **Ni·o·bids** (nī'ōbĭdz) *n.pl.* Children of Niobe.

ni·o·bi·um (nīō'bē*um*) *n.* (chem.) Rare metallic element very similar to tantalum and usu. found associated with it; symbol Nb, at. no. 41, at. wt. 92.9064. [named after NIOBE]

nip[1] (nĭp) *v.* (**nipped, nip·ping**). Pinch, squeeze sharply, bite; pinch *off*; check growth of; (of cold) affect injuriously, pain; (slang) move rapidly or nimbly. ~ *n.* Pinch, sharp squeeze, bite; (check to vegetation caused by) coldness of air; ~ **and tuck**, neck and neck.

nip[2] (nĭp) *n.* Small quantity of liquor etc. ~ *v.* (**nipped, nip·ping**). Take nips (of).

nip·per (nĭp'*er*) *n.* 1. (Brit. slang) Young boy. 2. (pl.) Implement with jaws for gripping or cutting; forceps, pincers, pliers; (usu. pl.) crustacean's great claw.

nip·ple (nĭp'*el*) *n.* 1. Small projection in which mammary ducts terminate in mammal of either sex; teat, esp. on woman's breast; teat of nursing bottle. 2. Nipple-like protuberance on skin, glass, metal, etc.; small rounded elevation on mountain; short section of pipe with threading at each end for coupling.

Nip·pon·ese (nĭp*o*nēz', -nēs') *adj.* & *n.* Japanese. [f. *Nippon*, Jap. name for Japan, f. *ni-pun* sunrise (*ni* sun, *pon* origin)]

nip·py (nĭp'ē) *adj.* (**-pi·er, -pi·est**). (colloq.) Cold.

nir·va·na (nĭrvah'n*a*, -văn'*a*, n*er*-) *n.* In Buddhist theology, extinction of individual existence and absorption into supreme spirit, or extinction of all passions and desires and attainment of perfect beatitude. [Sansk. *nirvāna* blowing out, extinction]

Ni·sei (nē'sā') *n.* (pl. **-sei**). Person born in U.S. whose parents were immigrants from Japan. [Jap., lit. "2nd generation"]

ni·si (nī'sī) *conj.* (legal) Unless; **decree, order**, etc., ~, decree etc. valid unless cause is shown for rescinding it before appointed time at which it is made absolute.

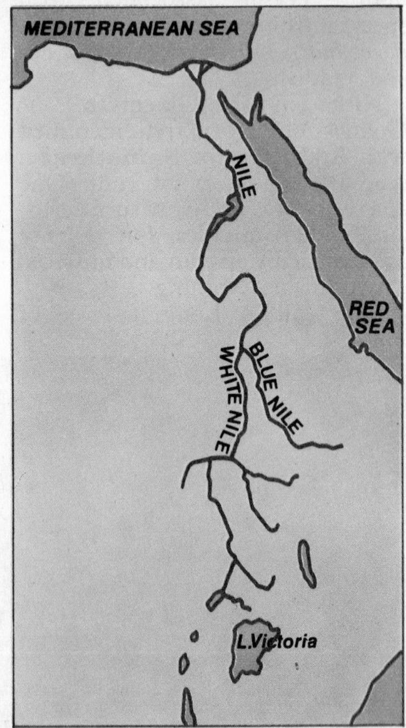

*The **Nile** is the longest river in Africa. It is fed by two main tributaries: the White Nile and the Blue Nile. Although used for irrigation since the ancient Egyptian civilizations, recent dams have also allowed its water to produce hydroelectricity.*

nit (nĭt) *n.* Egg of louse or other parasitic insect.

ni·ter, Brit. **ni·tre** (nī't*er*) *ns.* Saltpeter, potassium nitrate (KNO_3).

nit·pick (nĭt'pĭk) *v.i.* (colloq.)

Richard Nixon 37th President of the U.S.A. and the only one to resign. After a successful first term he was re-elected with a landslide victory. His popularity soured with the emergence of the Watergate scandal.

Find fault in petty manner. **nit′pick·er** *n.* **nit′pick·ing** *adj.* & *n.*

ni·trate (nī′trāt) *n.* Salt of nitric acid; potassium or sodium nitrate used as fertilizer. ~ *v.t.* (**-trat·ed, -trat·ing**). Treat, impregnate, or cause to interact, with nitric acid. **ni·tra·tion** (nītrā′sh*o*n) *n.*

ni·tric (nī′trĭk) *adj.* Of niter; ~ **acid**, clear, colorless, pungent, highly corrosive liquid (HNO_3); ~ **oxide**, colorless gas (NO), obtained by the action of nitric acid on copper turnings or by the combination of nitrogen and oxygen at high temperatures.

ni·tro·cel·lu·lose (nītrosĕl′y*u*-lōs) *n.* = CELLULOSE nitrate.

ni·tro·gen (nī′tr*o*j*e*n) *n.* Colorless, tasteless, odorless, gaseous element forming about 4/5 of the atmosphere and occurring also in nature as nitrates, and as proteins in animal and vegetable tissues, used commercially in the large-scale synthesis of ammonia; symbol N, at. no. 7, at. wt. 14.0067; ~ **cycle**, continuous series of processes by which nitrogen and nitrogenous compounds are converted into substances that can be utilized by plants, thence transferred to animals, and finally reconverted by decay of plant and animal tissue; ~ **fixation**, process by which atmospheric nitrogen is combined with other elements (1) in the manufacture of commercially important nitrogen compounds, as nitric acid, fertilizers, etc., (2) in nature by soil bacteria, and thereby made available to plants as food. **ni·trog·e·nous** (nītrŏj′*e*n*u*s) *adj.* Of, belonging to, containing, nitrogen. **ni·trog·e·nize** (nītrŏj′*e*nīz) *v.t.* (**-ized, -iz·ing**). Combine with nitrogen or nitrogenous compounds.

ni·tro·glyc·er·in (nītr*o*glĭs′*e*-rĭn), **ni·tro·glyc·er·ine** (nītr*o*glĭs′-*e*rĭn, -*e*rēn) *ns.* Glyceryl trinitrate, a yellowish, oily, violently explosive liquid formed by action of a mixture of nitric and sulfuric acid on glycerine; a constituent of dynamite, gelignite, and cordite.

ni·trous (nī′tr*u*s) *adj.* Of, like, impregnated with, niter; (chem.) of, containing, nitrogen, esp. of compounds in which nitrogen has a lower valence than nitric compounds; ~ **acid**, acid (HNO_2) containing less oxygen than nitric acid; ~ **oxide**, colorless sweet-smelling gas (N_2O), used as a mild anesthetic, laughing gas.

nit·wit (nĭt′wĭt) *n.* (slang) Person of little intelligence.

nix[1] (nĭks) *n.* (slang) Nothing.

nix[2] (nĭks) *n.* (pl. **nix·es**). Water elf.

Nix·on (nĭk′s*o*n), **Richard Milhous** (1913–). Thirty-seventh president of U.S., 1969–74 (resigned).

NJ, N.J. *abbrevs.* New Jersey.

NKVD, N.K.V.D. *abbrevs.* Secret police of U.S.S.R., 1939–45. [initials of *N*aródnyi *K*omissariát *V*nutrennikh *D*el, people's commissariat of internal affairs]

NLRB, N.L.R.B. *abbrevs.* National Labor Relations Board.

NM, n.m. *abbrevs.* Nautical mile.

NM, N.M., N.Mex. *abbrevs.* New Mexico.

NNE, N.N.E., n.n.e. *abbrevs.* North-northeast.

NNW, N.N.W., n.n.w. *abbrevs.* North-northwest.

no (nō) *adj.* Not any; not a, quite other than a; hardly any; **no′body** (pl. **-bodies**), no person; person of no importance; **no man**, no person; **no man's land**, piece of waste, unowned or debatable ground, esp. (mil.) the space between opposed lines; **no one**, no person; (as *adj.*) no single; **no-trumps**, (cards), (bid calling for) hand played without trump suit; **no′ways** (archaic), **no′wise**, in no manner, not at all. **no** *adv.* 1. (as alternative after *or*) Not. 2. (with comparatives) By no amount, not at all; ~ **more**, nothing further; not any more; no longer, never again, to no greater extent; just as little, neither. 3. Particle expressing negative reply to request, question, etc. ~ *n.* (pl. **noes, nos**). Word, answer, "no"; (pl.) voters against a motion.

No[1], **Noh** (nō) *ns.* Traditional Japanese drama evolved from the rites of Shinto worship and practically unchanged since 15th c.

No[2] (nō), **Lake.** Lake in S. central Sudan; source of White Nile.

No[3] *symbol.* Nobelium.

No., no. *abbrevs.* (pl. **Nos.**). Number.

No·a·chi·an (nōā'kēan) *adj.* Of Noah or his times.

No·ah (nō'*a*). Patriarch, represented as tenth in descent from Adam; at God's command he made the ark that saved his family and specimens of every animal from the flood sent by God to destroy the world; his sons, Shem, Ham, and Japheth were regarded as ancestors of all the races of mankind (Gen. 5–10).

nob (nŏb) *n.* (slang) Head.

No·bel (nōbĕl'), **Alfred Bernhard** (1833–96). Swedish chemist and engineer; inventor of dynamite and other high explosives; founder, by his will, of the five ~ **Prizes,** which are awarded annually to the persons adjudged by Swedish learned societies to have done the most significant work during the year in physics, chemistry, medicine, and literature, and to the person who is adjudged by the Norwegian parliament to have rendered the greatest service to the cause of peace; a ~ **Prize** for economic sciences was added in 1969.

no·bel·i·um (nōbē'lēum) *n.* (chem.) Transuranic element, symbol No, at. no. 102.

no·bil·i·ar·y (nōbĭl'ēērē) *adj.* Of (the) nobility; ~ **particle,** preposition (as French *de,* German *von*) prefixed to title.

no·bil·i·ty (nōbĭl'ĭtē) *n.* (pl. **-ties**). 1. Noble character, mind, birth, or rank. 2. Persons of noble rank as a class; (in England) the peerage.

no·ble (nō'bel) *adj.* (**-bler, -blest**). 1. Illustrious by rank, title, or birth, belonging to the nobility. 2. Of lofty character or ideals; showing greatness of character, magnanimous; splendid, magnificent, stately; impressive in appearance; excellent, admirable; (of metals such as gold, silver, sometimes platinum) resisting chemical action; **no'bleman, no'blewoman,** person of noble rank, peer(ess). **no'ble·ness** *n.* **no'bly** *adv.* **noble** *n.* Nobleman.

no·blesse o·blige (nōblĕs'-ōblēzh'). Privilege entails responsibility. [Fr.]

noc·tule (nŏk'chōōl) *n.* Great bat (*Nyctalus noctula*), largest British species of brown bat.

Alfred Nobel *obtained a large fortune from the development of dynamite and exploitation of oil fields at Baku. He left the money to endow the Nobel Prizes for peace, sciences and the arts.*

noc·tur·nal (nŏktẽr'n*a*l) *adj.* Of, in, done by, active in, the night. **noc·tur'nal·ly** *adv.*

noc·turne (nŏk'tẽrn) *n.* Soft, dreamy musical composition.

nod (nŏd) *v.* (**nod·ded, nod·ding**). Incline head slightly and quickly in salutation, assent, or command; let head fall forward in drowsiness, be drowsy, make mistake from inattention; **nodding acquaintance,** slight acquaintance. **nod** *n.* Nodding of the head; this as sign of absolute power; **land of N~,** (with pun on Gen. 4:16) sleep.

no·dal (nō'd*a*l) *adj.* Of a node.

node (nōd) *n.* 1. (bot.) Point at which leaves spring. 2. (path.) Hard tumor esp. on gouty or rheumatic joint. 3. (astron.) Intersecting point of planet's orbit and ecliptic or of 2 great circles of celestial sphere. 4. (phys.) Point or line of rest in vibrating body. 5. Central point in system. 6. (math.) Point at which curve crosses itself.

nod·ule (nŏj'ōōl) *n.* Small rounded lump of anything, small node in plant; small knotty tumor, ganglion. **nod·u·lar** (nŏj'*u*ler), **nod·u·lose** (nŏj'*u*lōs), **nod·u·lous** (nŏj'*u*lus) *adjs.*

No·el, no·el (nōĕl') *ns.* Christmas. [OF. f. L. *natalis* natal]

no·et·ic (nōĕt'ĭk) *adj.* Of the intellect; purely intellectual or abstract; given to intellectual speculation. **no·et'ics** *n.* Science of the intellect.

no-fault (nō'fawlt) *adj.* & *n.* (Of, pertaining to, requiring) type of automobile insurance that compensates policyholder in case of an accident regardless of liability; divorce granted when neither party is held to blame.

nog[1] (nŏg) *n.* Pin, peg, small block, of wood; wood block built into wall in place of a brick so that interior woodwork can be nailed to it; snag or stump on tree. ~ *v.t.* (**nogged, nog·ging**). Secure with nogs; build in form of nogging. **nog'ging** *n.* Brickwork between wooden quarters of framing.

nog[2] (nŏg) = EGGnog.

nog·gin (nŏg'ĭn) *n.* Small mug; small measure, usu. 1/4 pint, of liquor. 2. (slang) Head.

Noh (nō) = No[1].

noise (noiz) *n.* Sound, esp. loud or harsh one; din, clamor; ~ **pollution,** contamination of environment by too much loud sound, as of heavy traffic in city streets, airport traffic, etc. **noise'less** *adj.* **noise'less·ly** *adv.* **noise'less·ness** *n.* **noise** *v.t.* (**noised, nois·ing**). Make public, spread *abroad.*

noise·mak·er (noiz'māk*e*r) *n.* (esp.) Toy (of paper, metal, etc.) that makes noise.

noi·some (noi's*o*m) *adj.* Harmful, noxious; ill-smelling; objectionable, offensive. **noi'some·ly** *adv.* **noi'some·ness** *n.*

nois·y (noi'zē) *adj.* (**nois·i·er, nois·i·est**). Clamorous, turbulent; full of, making much, noise; loud. **nois'i·ly** *adv.* **nois'i·ness** *n.*

no·lens vo·lens (nō'lĕnz vō'-lĕnz) *adv.* Willy-nilly. [L., = "unwilling, willing"]

no·li me tan·ge·re (nō'lī mē tăn'jerē; *Lat.* nō'lē mĕ tahng'gĕrĕ). 1. Warning against interference etc.; person, thing, that must not be touched or interfered with. 2. Painting representing appearance of Jesus Christ to Mary Magdalen at the sepulcher (John 20:17). [L., = "touch me not" (Vulgate, John 20:17)]

nom. *abbrev.* Nominal; nominative.

no·mad (nō'măd) *n.* & *adj.* (Member of tribe) roaming from place to place for pasture; wanderer, wandering. **no·mad·ic** (nōmăd'ĭk) *adj.* **no·mad'i·cal·ly** *adv.* **no'mad·ism** *n.*

nom de guerre (nŏm d*e* gār'; *Fr.* nawṅ d*e* gĕr') (pl. ***noms de guerre*** pr. nŏmz d*e* gār'; *Fr.* nawṅ d*e* gĕr'). Pseudonym, sobriquet, assumed name under which person fights, plays, etc. [Fr., = "war name"]

nom de plume (nŏm d*e* plōōm'; *Fr.* nawṅ d*e* plüm') (pl. **noms de plume** pr. nŏmz d*e* plōōm; *Fr.* nawṅ d*e* plüm'). Writer's pseudonym, pen name. [Eng. formation on Fr. words *nom* name, *de* of, *plume* pen]

Nome (nōm). Westernmost city of continental U.S., in Alaska on Seward Peninsula; scene of great gold rush after discovery of gold, 1896.

no·men·cla·ture (nō′menklācher, nōmĕn′kla-) *n.* System of names for things; terminology of a science etc.; systematic naming. **no·men·cla·tive** (nō′menklātĭv) *adj.*

nom·i·nal (nŏm′inal) *adj.* Of, as, like, a noun; of, in, names; existing in name only, (of price etc.) very small, trifling; not real or substantial; consisting of, giving, the names. **nom′i·nal·ly** *adv.*

nom·i·nal·ism (nŏm′inalĭzem) *n.* (philos.) Doctrine of the scholastics that universal or abstract concepts are mere names, without any corresponding reality (opp. REALISM). **nom′i·nal·ist** *n.* **nom·i·nal·is·tic** (nŏminalĭs′tĭk) *adj.*

nom·i·nate (nŏm′ināt) *v.t.* (**-nat·ed, -nat·ing**). Name or appoint (date, place); appoint, propose for election, to office. **nom′i·na·tion** (nŏminā′shon) *n.* (esp.) Right of nominating for appointment. **nom′i·na·tor, nom·i·nee** (nŏminē′) *ns.*

nom·i·na·tive (nŏm′inatĭv, -nātĭv) *adj.* 1. (gram.) Of the case of the subject of a verb. 2. Of, appointed by, nomination. ~ *n.* (Word in) nominative case; ~ **absolute**, construction like Latin ablative absolute, as in *this being so, I did nothing.*

non- *prefix.* Not (now freely prefixed to nouns, adjectives, etc.)

non·age (nŏn′ĭj, nō′nĭj) *n.* Being under age, minority; immaturity, early stage.

non·a·ge·nar·i·an (nŏnajenār′ēan, nōna-) *adj.* & *n.* (Person) aged 90 years or more but less than 100.

non·a·gon (nŏn′agŏn) *n.* Plane figure with nine angles and nine sides. **non·ag·o·nal** (nŏnăg′onal) *adj.*

non·ap·pear·ance (nŏnapēr′ans) *n.* Failure to appear, esp. in court of law.

no·na·ry (nō′nerē) *adj.* (arith., of scale of notation) Having nine as basis.

non·bel·lig·er·ent (nŏnbelĭj′erent) *adj.* & *n.* (Nation) not taking active or open part in war. **non-bel·lig′er·en·cy** *n.*

nonce (nŏns) *n.* Time being, present occasion (only in **for the** ~); ~ **word**, word coined for a special occasion and used only for a short time.

non·cha·lant (nŏnshalahnt′, nŏn′shalant) *adj.* Unexcited, unmoved, cool, indifferent. **non-cha·lant′ly** *adv.* **non·cha·lance′** *n.*

non·com (nŏn′kŏm) *n.* (colloq.) Non-commissioned officer.

non·com·bat·ant (nŏnkŏm′batant, nŏnkombăt′ant) *adj.* Not fighting. ~ *n.* Civilian in time of war; member of army etc. whose duties do not include fighting.

non·com·mis·sioned (nŏnkomĭsh′ond) *adj.* Not holding commission (esp. of subordinate army ranks such as *sergeant, corporal*).

non·com·mit·tal (nŏnkomĭt′al) *adj.* Refusing to commit oneself to particular view or course of action.

non com·pos men·tis (nŏn kŏm′pos mĕn′tĭs; *Lat.* nōn kōm′pōs mĕn′tĭs). Not in one's right mind. [L.]

non·con·duc·ting (nŏnkondŭk′tĭng) *adj.* That does not conduct heat or electricity. **non·con·duc′tor** *n.*

non·con·form·ist (nŏnkonfōr′mĭst) *n.* One who does not conform to established doctrine or discipline, esp. dissenting member of church. **non·con·form′i·ty, non·con·form′ance** *ns.* Principles, practice, the body, of nonconformists; failure to conform (*to*); want of correspondence between things.

non·co·op·er·a·tion (nŏnkōŏperā′shon) *n.* Refusal or failure to cooperate with authority, esp. as policy of GANDHI and his followers in India from *c*1919.

non·de·script (nŏndĭskrĭpt′) *adj.* & *n.* (Person, thing) not easily classified, neither one thing nor another, hybrid.

none (nŭn) *pron.* Not any *of*; no person, no one (now rare); no persons. ~ *adj.* (usu. ellipt.) No, not any; not to be counted in specified class. ~ *adv.* By no amount, not at all. **none′the·less′** *adv.* Nevertheless.

non·en·ti·ty (nŏnĕn′tĭtē) *n.* (pl. **-ties**). Nonexistence, nonexistent thing, figment; person or thing of no importance, cipher.

nones (nōnz) *n.pl.* (sing. for def. 2 **None** pr. nōn). 1. (Rom. antiq.) Ninth day (by inclusive reckoning) before IDES; 7th of March, May, July, Oct., and 5th of other months. 2. **N**~, (R.C. Ch.) canonical HOUR, (orig. said at) 9th hour of day (3 p.m.).

non·es·sen·tial (nŏnĭsĕn′shal) *adj.* & *n.* (Thing) that is not essential.

none·such, non·such (nŭn′sŭch′) *ns.* Person or thing that is unrivaled, paragon.

non·ex·is·tent (nŏnĭgzĭs′tent) *adj.* Not existing. **non·ex·ist′ence** *n.*

non·fic·tion (nŏnfĭk′shon) *adj.* & *n.* (Of) prose writings that are not fiction, poetry, or drama.

non·flam·ma·ble (nŏnflăm′abel) *adj.* Noninflammable.

non·in·flam·ma·ble (nŏnĭnflăm′abel) *adj.* That cannot be set on fire.

non·in·ter·ven·tion (nŏnĭntervĕn′shon) *n.* Absence of intervention; esp., in international politics, systematic refusal to interfere in affairs of another nation.

non·pa·reil (nŏnparĕl′) *adj.* Unequaled, peerless. ~ *n.* 1. Person or thing without equal, something unique. 2. (print.) Size of type (6 point) intermediate between emerald and ruby. 3. Kind of finch. 4. Kind of moth. 5. Chocolate candy lozenge decorated with sugar pellets.

non·plus (nŏnplŭs′, nŏn′plŭs) *n.* State of perplexity, standstill. ~ *v.t.* (**-plused, -plus·ing**, Brit.

These Algerian Berbers following their laden beasts typify the restless life of all ***nomads,*** *possessions reduced to little beyond necessities.*

The harbor at Honfleur in ***Normandy,*** *a region of north-western France which has a rich and ancient history. Normandy was the scene of the Allied invasion in the 1939–45 war, which began the liberation of Europe.*

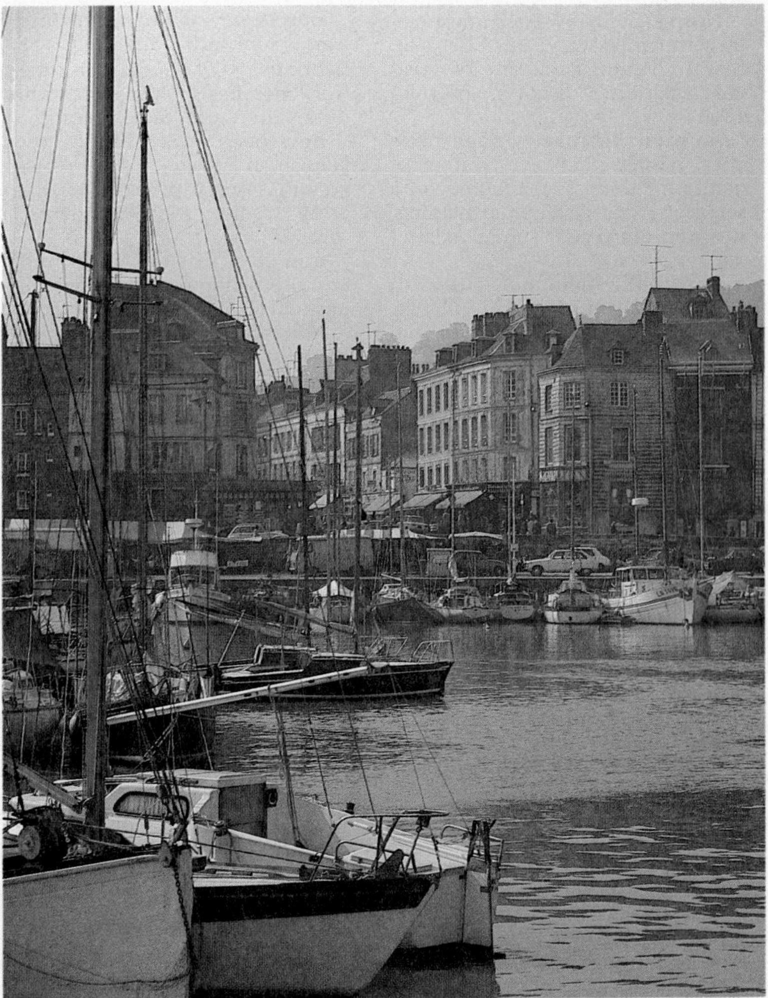

-plussed, -plus·sing). Reduce to hopeless perplexity. [L. *non plus* not more]

non·res·i·dent (nŏnrĕz'ĭdent) *adj.* Sojourning in place only for short time or residing elsewhere; not residing at one's place of work. ~ *n.* Nonresident person.

non·re·sis·tance (nŏnrĭzĭs'tans) *n.* (Principle of) not resisting authority even when it is unjustly exercised.

non·sense (nŏn'sĕns, -sens) *n.* Absurd or meaningless words or ideas, foolish or extravagant conduct, worthless things, rubbish (freq. as exclamation of contempt); **no** ~, no foolish or extravagant conduct, no foolery or humbug; ~ **verse(s)**, verse(s) having no sense or an absurd one. **non·sen·si·cal** (nŏnsĕn'sĭkal) *adj.* **non·sen'si·cal·ness** *n.*

non se·qui·tur (nŏn sĕk'wĭter). Illogical inference, paradoxical result. [L., = "it does not follow"]

non·skid (nŏn'skĭd') *adj.* (of tires or road surface) Designed to prevent or limit skidding.

non·smoker (nŏnsmō'ker) *n.* Person who does not smoke.

non·stop (nŏn'stŏp') *adj.* & *adv.* Traveling, performing, etc. without stopping at intermediate points. ~ *n.* Nonstop train etc.

non·such = NONESUCH.

non trop·po (nŏn trŏp'ō; *It.* nawn traw'pō). (mus.) Not too much. [It.]

non·un·ion (nŏnūn'yon) *adj.* Not belonging to a labor union; not made by union labor.

noo·dle[1] (nōō'del) *n.* 1. Simpleton. 2. (slang) Head.

noo·dle[2] (nōō'del) *n.* Strip or ball of pasta, used esp. in soup. [Ger. *Nudel*]

nook (nŏŏk) *n.* Secluded corner or place; recess.

noon (nōōn) *n.* Twelve o'clock in the day; **noon'day,** (poet.) noon. [L. *nona* (*hora*) 9th hour; orig., 3 p.m.]

noose (nōōs) *n.* Loop with running knot, tightening as string is pulled, halter; snare or bond. ~ *v.t.* (**noosed, noos·ing**). Capture with noose, ensnare; make noose on (cord); arrange (cord) in noose *around* neck etc.

no·pal (nō'pal) *n.* Amer. cactus (*Nopalea cochinellifera*) cultivated for breeding cochineal.

nor (nŏr) *conj.* Neither (archaic); and not, and no more, neither, and not either.

Nor. *abbrev.* North; Norway; Norwegian.

The Cornish font (above, left) and detail from the Bayeux Tapestry (above) show clearly many of the features associated with the art of the ***Norman*** *period.*

NOR·AD (nŏr'ăd) *n.* North American Air Defense Command.

Nor·dic (nŏr'dĭk) *adj.* & *n.* (Person) of the physical type of the Germanic peoples of N. Europe, esp. the Scandinavians, with tall stature, long narrow head, bony frame, and light coloring of hair, eyes, and skin.

norm (nŏrm) *n.* 1. Typical or standard pattern. 2. General level or average.

nor·mal (nŏr'mal) *adj.* 1. Rectangular (rare); standing at right angles, perpendicular. 2. Conforming to standard, regular, usual, typical; of average intelligence; mentally or emotionally sound; ~ **school,** (formerly) a school for training teachers. **nor'mal·ly** *adv.* **nor·mal·i·ty** (nŏrmăl'ĭtē), **nor'-**

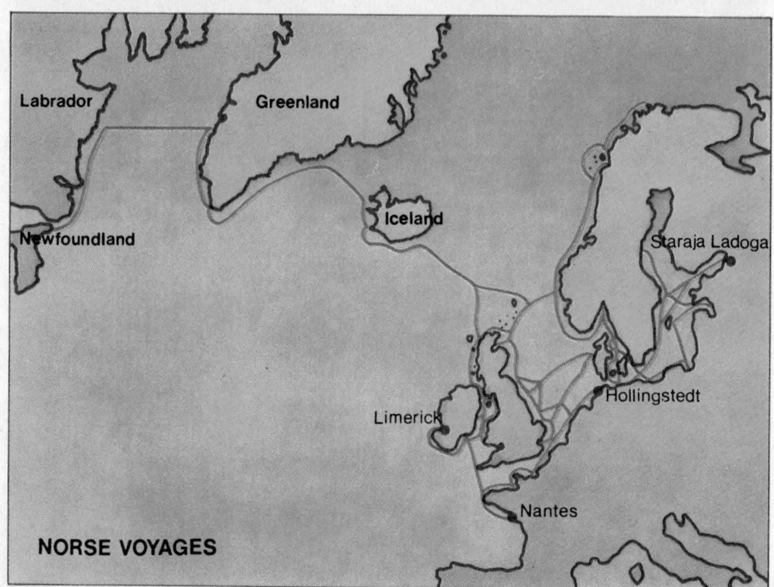

Raiders and settlers, the men who voyaged in **Norse** galleys like the Oseberg ship (top) had a lasting impact on the rest of Europe. Voyaging south to Nantes and across to Newfoundland, they played a part in the spread of cultural and other ideas.

*Children in traditional Lapp dress. The **Nordic** people are physically tall, and fair. Although Nordic also means people of northern Europe, among whom there are a number of different racial characteristics.*

mal·cy *ns.* **normal** *n.* (geom.) Normal line; usual state, level, temperature, etc.

nor·mal·ize (nōr′malīz) *v.t.* (**-ized, -iz·ing**). Make normal. **nor·mal·i·za·tion** (nōrmalīzā′-shon), **nor′mal·iz·er** *ns.*

Nor·man (nōr′man) *n.* Native or inhabitant of NORMANDY belonging to or descended from mixed Scandinavian and Frankish people inhabiting that part of France; orig. one of the Northmen or Scandinavians who conquered Normandy in 10th c. ~ *adj.* Of the Normans or Normandy; (archit.) of the style of round-arched Romanesque architecture developed by Normans and employed in England after Norman Conquest, with characteristic geometrical ornament; ~ **Conquest**, conquest of England by Normans under William of Normandy, 1066; ~ **French**, form of medieval French spoken by Normans; later form of this in English legal use.

Nor·man·dy (nōr′mandē). 1. Region and former province of NW. France with coastline on English Channel; given by Charles the Simple to Rollo, 1st duke of Normandy, 912; united to England intermittently from Norman Conquest until 1204; site of Allied landings in German-occupied France in World War II. 2. Name of English royal house, including William I and II, Henry I, and Stephen.

nor·ma·tive (nōr′mativ) *adj.* Of, establishing, a norm.

Norse (nōrs) *adj.* Of ancient Scandinavia, esp. Norway; of the language of its inhabitants. ~ *n.* **Old** ~, Germanic language of medieval Scandinavia.

north (nōrth) *adv.* Toward, in, the north. ~ *n.* 1. Point of horizon to the left of an observer who faces the rising sun at the equinox; this direction. 2. Cardinal point of the compass 90° to the left of east and 90° to the right of west. 3. (usu. **the N**~) That part of a country, district, etc., that lies to the north; in U.S., states lying north of the Mason-Dixon line. 4. **N**~, bridge player sitting opposite South and to the right of East. **north** *adj.* Lying toward, in, the north; (of wind) blowing from the north; **N~ Atlantic Treaty Organization**: see NATO; **N~ Pole**, point on Earth that is farthest north; **N~ Sea**, part of Atlantic between mainland of

The linen industry is still among the most important in ***Northern Ireland.*** *However, agricultural products also include large numbers of livestock for dairying and meat (right).*

Europe and E. coast of Gt. Britain; **north star**, polestar. **north'ward** *adv., adj., & n.* **north'ward·ly** *adv. & adj.* **north'wards** *adv.*

North America. Northern part of the continent of Amer., including Central Amer., Mexico, U.S., and Canada.

North Cape. Point on island in Arctic Sea off N. Norway; northernmost part of Europe.

North Carolina. South Atlantic state of U.S.; one of the original 13 states of the Union (1789); capital, Raleigh.

North Dakota. State in northwestern U.S.; admitted to the Union in 1889; capital, Bismarck.

north·east (nōrthēst'; naut. nōrēst') *adv. & n.* (Direction or compass point) between north and east. ~ *adj.* Of, in, to, from, the northeast; ~ **passage**, passage for ships along northern coasts of Europe and Asia, formerly thought of as possible route to Far East. **north·east'er** *n.* Northeast wind. **north·east'er·ly** *adj. & adv.* **north·east'ern** *adj.* **north·east'ward** *adv., adj., & n.* **north·east'ward·ly** *adv.* **north·east'wards** *adv. & n.*

north·er·ly (nōr'dherlē) *adj.* In the north; (of wind) blowing from the north. ~ *adv.* Toward the north. ~ *n.* North wind.

north·ern (nōr'dhern) *adj.* Of the north; lying or directed toward the north; (poet.) coming from the north; **N~ hemisphere**: see HEMISPHERE; ~ **lights**, aurora borealis. **north'ern·er** *n.* (also **N~**) Native, inhabitant, of the north. **north'ern·most** *adj.*

Northern Ireland. Autonomous unit of United Kingdom, constituted in 1920 (see IRELAND); capital, Belfast.

North Korea. Unofficial name of Democratic People's Republic of Korea.

North Platte River. River flowing from Colorado, 680 mi. (1,088 km) to South Platte River in SW. Nebraska; the two form the Platte.

North·um·bri·a (nōrthŭm'brēa). Ancient Anglo-Saxon kingdom, extending from Humber to Forth. **North·um'bri·an** *adj. & n.*

north·west (nōrthwĕst'; naut. nōrwĕst') *adv. & n.* (Direction or compass point) between north and west. ~ *adj.* Of, in, to, from, the northwest; ~ **passage**, presumed route along N. coast of Amer. from Atlantic to Pacific; **Northwest Territories**, part of Canada lying N. of 60th parallel; **Northwest Territory**, region of U.S. N. of the Ohio river. **north·west'er** *n.* Northwest wind. **north·west'er·ly** *adj. & adv.* **north·west'ern** *adj.* **north·west'ward** *adv., adj.,*

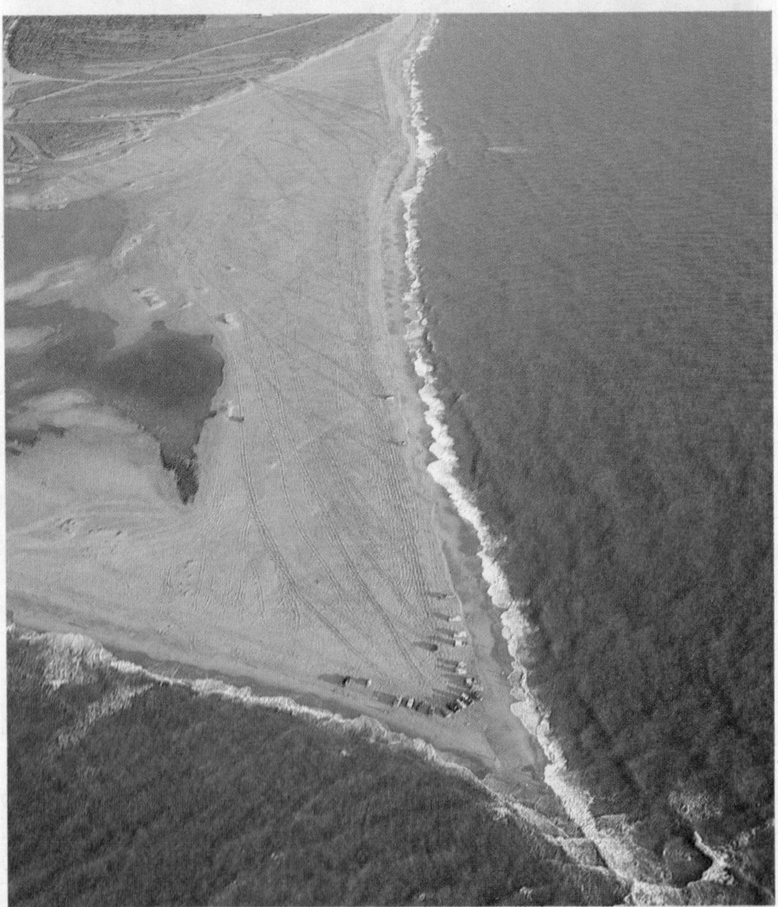

Cape Hatteras, a wild and unspoilt beach and dune area of ***North Carolina,*** *one of the original 13 colonies. Initially an agricultural based economy it has been industrialized since the 1939–45 war.*

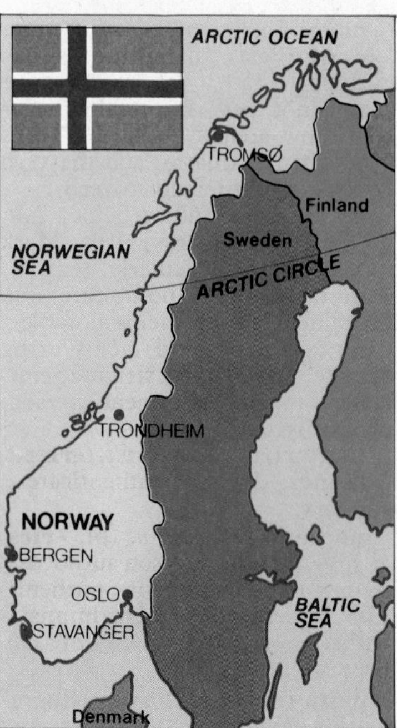

During the summer, the church and houses of Tromso in ***Norway*** *(left) are bathed by the light of the midnight sun. As in all regions very close to the poles the sun does not fully sink below the horizon in midsummer and never rises in midwinter.*

& *n.* **north·west′ward·ly** *adj.* & *adv.* **north·west′wards** *adv.* & *n.*

Nor·way (nŏr′wā). Kingdom of N. Europe occupying W. part of Scandinavian peninsula, founded 872; united with Denmark 1397–1814, and thereafter with Sweden under a personal union of the crowns which was dissolved in 1905; capital, Oslo.

Nor·we·gian (nŏrwē′jan) *adj.* Of Norway or its people or language. ~ *n.* 1. Norwegian person. 2. Language of Norway, in its literary form almost identical with Danish.

nor′west·er (nŏrwĕs′ter) = NORTHWESTER.

nose (nōz) *n.* 1. Member of face or head above mouth, containing nostrils and serving as organ of smell; sense of smell; **as plain as the ~ on your face**, easily seen; **lead by the ~**, make (person) submissively do one's bidding; **pay through the ~**, be charged exorbitant price; **poke, thrust, one's ~**, pry or intrude *into*; **put person's ~ out of joint**, supplant, disconcert, or frustrate him; **speak through the ~**, speak with nasal twang; **turn up one's ~ at**, show disdain for; **under person's ~**, right in front of him. 2. Open end or nozzle of pipe, tube, bellows, etc.; prow; projecting part. 3. **~ bag**, bag of fodder fastened around horse's head; **nose′band**, lower band of bridle passing over nose and attached to cheek straps; **nose cone**, cone-shaped forward section of a rocket or guided missile; **nose dive**, aircraft's downward plunge, with nose first; **nose-dive**, (*v.i.*) perform nose dive; **nose flute**, musical instrument blown with nose, among Siamese, Fijians, etc.; **nose′gay**, bunch of (esp. sweet-scented) flowers; **nose ring**, ring fixed in nose of bull etc. for leading, or worn in person's nose as ornament. **nose** *v.* (**nosed, nos·ing**). Perceive smell of, discover by smell; detect, smell *out* (fig.); rub with the nose, thrust nose against or into; sniff (*at* etc.), pry or search (*after, for*); push one's way, push (one's *way*), with the nose (esp. of ship); **~ over**, (of aircraft) fall nose forward.

nos·ey = NOSY.

nosh (nŏsh) *v.* (slang) Eat or drink, esp. between meals. ~ *n.* (slang) Food or drink, esp. snack. [Yiddish]

no-show (nō′shō′) *n.* Traveler who makes a reservation, esp. on an airplane, but neither uses nor cancels it.

nos·ing (nō′zĭng) *n.* Rounded edge of step, molding, etc., or metal or rubber shield for it.

no·sol·o·gy (nōsŏl′ojē) *n.* (Branch of medical science dealing with) classification of diseases.

nos·tal·gia (nŏstăl′ja, no-) *n.* 1. Severe homesickness. 2. Sorrowful longing *for* conditions of a past age; regretful or wistful memory of earlier time. **nos·tal′gic** *adj.* **nos·tal′gi·cal·ly** *adv.*

nos·toc (nŏs′tŏk) *n.* Unicellular alga of genus *N*~ with cells arranged in intertwining rows which form gelatinous mass. [name invented by Paracelsus]

Nos·tra·da·mus (nŏstradā′mus, -dah′-). Latinized name of Michel de Notredame (1503–66), Provençal astrologer; favorite of Catherine de Médicis and physician to Charles IX of France.

nos·tril (nŏs′tril) *n.* Either opening in nose admitting air to lungs and smells to olfactory nerves.

nos·trum (nŏs′trum) *n.* Medicine prepared by person recommending it, quack remedy, patent medicine; pet scheme for political or social reform etc. [L. neut. of *noster* our]

nos·y, nos·ey (nō´zē) *adjs.* (**nos·i·er, nos·i·est**). (slang) Inquisitive, curious.

not (nŏt) *adv.* Expressing negation; now archaic following verbs other than auxiliaries and the verb *be* (freq. as *n't* joined to verb).

no·ta be·ne (nō´ta bē´nē; *Lat.* nō´tah bĕ´nĕ). (abbrev. N.B.) Mark well, observe particularly. [L.]

no·ta·bil·i·ty (nōtabĭl´ĭtē) *n.* Prominent person; being notable.

no·ta·ble (nō´tabel) *adj.* Worthy of note, remarkable, striking, eminent. ~ *n.* Eminent person. **no'ta·bly** *adv.*

no·ta·rize (nō´terīz) *v.t.* (**-rized, -riz·ing**). Attest or authenticate as a notary.

no·ta·ry (nō´terē) *n.* (pl. **-ries**) (also ~ **public**). Person authorized by law to take affidavits, authenticate documents, and administer oaths. **no·tar·i·al** (nōtār´ēal) *adj.* **no·tar'i·al·ly** *adv.*

no·ta·tion (nōtā´shon) *n.* Representing of numbers, quantities, etc., by symbols; any set of symbols used for this, esp. in arithmetic, algebra, and music.

notch (nŏch) *n.* V-shaped indentation or incision on edge or across surface; nick on stick etc., by way of keeping count; deep narrow pass. ~ *v.t.* Make notches in; score, mark, record, by notches. **notched** *adj.*

note (nōt) *n.* 1. Written sign representing pitch and duration of a musical sound; key of piano etc.; single tone of definite pitch made by musical instrument, voice, etc.; (single tone in) bird's song or call. 2. Sign, token, characteristic, distinguishing feature; mark *of exclamation* or *interrogation*; **compare ~s**, exchange ideas or opinions: **strike a false, the right note**, act inappropriately, suitably. 3. Brief record of facts etc. to assist memory or serve as basis for fuller statement or as help in speaking (usu. pl.); annotation appended to passage in book etc. 4. Short or informal letter; formal diplomatic communication; banknote. 5. Distinction, eminence; notice, attention. 6. **note'book**, book for taking notes or containing notes and memoranda; **note'paper**, paper of size or quality used for correspondence. **note** *v.t.* (**not·ed, not·ing**). Observe, notice, give attention to; set down, set *down*, as thing to be remembered or observed; annotate; **not'ed**, celebrated, well-known *for*. **note·wor·thy** (nōt´wĕrdhē) *adj.* Worthy of note or attention, remarkable.

noth·ing (nŭth´ĭng) *n.* No thing; not anything, naught; trifle, very inferior thing; (arith.) no amount, naught; nonexistence, what does not exist; (with pl.) trifling thing, event, remark, person; **come to** ~, turn out useless, fail, not amount to anything; **have ~ on**, (1) possess no advantage over, know of nothing discreditable about; (iron.) be much inferior to; (2) be naked; (3) be free of engagements; **know from ~**, be completely ignorant (of item of information); **make ~ of**, do without hesitation; not understand. **nothing** *adv.* Not at all, in no way.

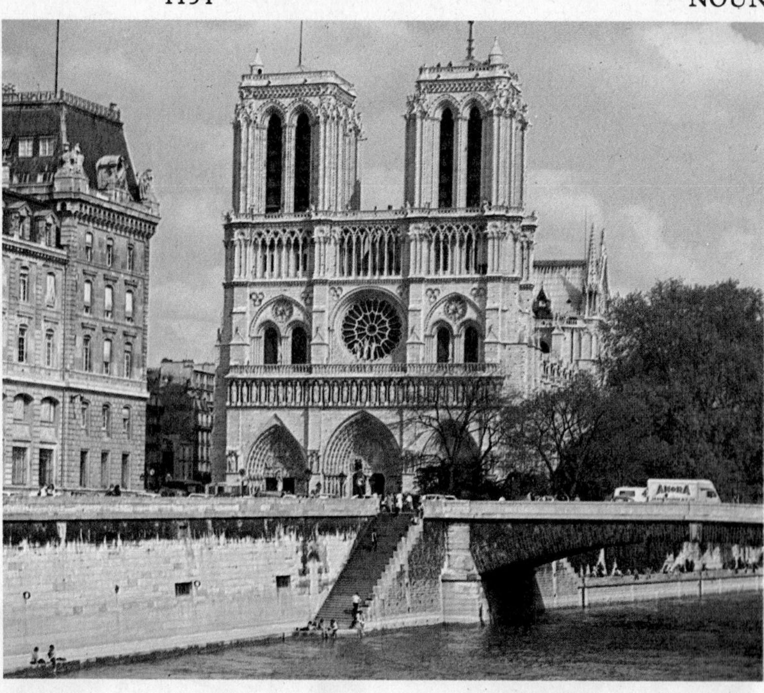

Building of the ***Notre Dame*** *cathedral in Paris, the most famous of churches dedicated to the Virgin Mary, began in 1163. It was also the setting for Victor Hugo's novel, 'The Hunchback of Notre Dame'.*

noth·ing·ness (nŭth´ĭngnĭs) *n.* Nonexistence, the nonexistent; worthlessness, triviality, unimportance.

no·tice (nō´tĭs) *n.* 1. Intimation, warning; placard etc. conveying information or directions; formal intimation of something or instructions *to* do something, announcement by party to agreement that it is to terminate at specified time (esp. between landlord and tenant or employer and employee). 2. Heed, attention, cognizance, observation; **take ~**, give heed. 3. Short comment, review, etc., in newspaper or journal etc. **notice** *v.t.* (**-ticed, -tic·ing**). Remark upon, speak of; perceive, take notice of; treat with attention, favor, or politeness. **no'tice·a·ble** *adj.* **no'tice·a·bly** *adv.*

no·ti·fy (nō´tifī) *v.t.* (**-fied, -fy·ing**). Make known, announce, report; inform, give notice to. **no·ti·fi·ca·tion** (nōtifĭkā´shon) *n.*

no·tion (nō´shon) *n.* General concept under which particular thing may be classed; idea, conception; view, opinion, theory; inclination, disposition, desire; (pl.) haberdashery, small wares, esp. cheap useful articles of some ingenuity.

no·tion·al (nō´shonal) *adj.* (of knowledge etc.) Speculative, not based on experiment or demonstration; (of things etc.) existing only in thought, imaginary; (of persons) fanciful. **no'tion·al·ly** *adv.*

no·to·chord (nō´tokōrd) *n.* In CHORDATE animals, rudimentary spinal cord, rod of tissue lying along back below nerve cord; in vertebrates, elongated cord of embryonic tissue from which vertebral column develops.

no·to·ri·ous (nōtōr´ēus, -tōr´-) *adj.* Well or commonly known; undisguised, talked of, generally known to deserve the name; unfavorably known (*for*). **no·to'ri·ous·ly** *adv.* **no·to·ri·e·ty** (nōtorī´etē) *n.* (pl. **-ties**).

No·tre Dame (nōtre dām´, dahm´, nōter; *Fr.* nawtre dahm´). Church dedicated to the Virgin Mary, esp. cathedral church of Paris. [Fr., = "Our Lady"]

not·with·stand·ing (nŏtwĭdhstăn´dĭng, -wĭth-) *prep.* In spite of, not the less for. ~ *adv.* Nevertheless, all the same. ~ *conj.* Although, in spite of the fact *that*.

Nouak·chott (nwahkshŏt´). Capital of Mauritania in SW. part about 3 mi. (4.8 km) from coast.

nou·gat (nōō´gat; *Brit.* nōō´gah) *n.* Confection of sugar, honey, almonds or other nuts, and egg white.

nought (nawt) = NAUGHT.

Nou·mé·a (nōōmā´a). Capital of New Caledonia on the SW. coast.

noun (nown) *n.* (gram.) Word used as name of person, place, thing, state, or quality.

nour·ish (nĕr′ĭsh, nŭr′-) *v.t.* Sustain with food; foster, cherish, nurse, (feeling, hope, etc.) in one's heart. **nour′ish·ing** *adj.* **nour′ish·ment** *n.* Sustenance, food; nourishing.

nou·veau riche (no͞o′vō rēsh′) (pl. **nou·veaux riches** pr. no͞o′vō rēsh′). Newly enriched person, parvenu. [Fr.]

Nov. *abbrev.* November.

no·va (nō′v*a*) *n.* (pl. **-vas, -vae** pr. -vē). Star showing sudden great increase in light and energy and then subsiding, formerly mistaken for new star.

No·va Sco·tia (nō′v*a* skō′sh*a*). Province of SE. Canada, comprising peninsula projecting into Atlantic and the adjoining Cape Breton Island; capital, Halifax. **No′va Sco′tian** *adj.* & *n.*

nov·el[1] (nŏv′*e*l) *n.* Fictitious prose narrative of sufficient length to fill one or more volumes; **the ~**, this type of literature.

nov·el[2] (nŏv′*e*l) *adj.* Of new kind or nature, strange, hitherto unknown.

nov·el·ette (nŏv*e*lĕt′) *n.* Short novel, story of moderate length, romantic novel without literary merit.

nov·el·ist (nŏv′*e*lĭst) *n.* Writer of novels. **nov·el·is·tic** (nŏv*e*lĭs′tĭk) *adj.* **nov·el·is′ti·cal·ly** *adv.*

nov·el·ize (nŏv′*e*līz) *v.t.* (**-ized, -iz·ing**). Convert into a novel. **nov·el·i·za·tion** (nŏv*e*līzā′sh*o*n) *n.*

no·vel·la (nōvĕl′*a*) *n.* (pl. **-vel·las, -vel·lae** pr. -vĕl′ē). Short novel. [It.]

nov·el·ty (nŏv′*e*ltē) *n.* (pl. **-ties**). New or unusual thing or occurrence; inexpensive trinket; novel character *of* something.

No·vem·ber (nōvĕm′b*e*r). Eleventh month of Gregorian (ninth of Julian) calendar, with 30 days. [L. *novem* nine]

no·ve·na (nōvē′n*a*) *n.* (pl. **-nas, -nae** pr. -nē). (R.C. Ch.) Special prayers or services on nine successive days.

nov·ice (nŏv′ĭs) *n.* Person received in religious house on probation before taking the vows; new convert; inexperienced person, beginner, tyro.

no·vi·ti·ate, no·vi·ci·ate (nōvĭsh′ēĭt, -āt) *ns.* Novice's probationary period, initiation, or apprenticeship; novice; quarters assigned to novices.

No·vo·caine, No·vo·cain (nō′v*o*kān) *ns.* (trademark) Synthetic drug used as a local anesthetic.

now (now) *adv.* 1. At the present time; by this time; immediately; in the immediate past; then, next, by that time; (**every**) **~ and then, ~ and again**, from time to time, intermittently. 2. In sentences expressing command, request, reproof, etc., with purely temporal sense weakened or effaced. **now** *conj.* Consequently upon or simultaneously with the fact that. **~** *n.* This time, the present (chiefly after prepositions). **now′a·days** *adv.* (At) the present day.

no·where (nō′hwār, -wār) *adv.* In, at, to, no place.

nox·ious (nŏk′sh*u*s) *adj.* Harmful, unwholesome. **nox′ious·ly** *adv.* **nox′ious·ness** *n.*

Noyes (noiz), **John Humphrey** (1811–86). Amer. social reformer; founder of Utopian communities, including Oneida, 1848, in New York State.

noz·zle (nŏz′*e*l) *n.* Projecting vent; small spout of hose pipe etc.

Np *symbol.* Neptunium.

N.P., n.p. *abbrevs.* Notary public.

n.p. *abbrev.* No pagination.

nr. *abbrev.* Near.

NRA, N.R.A. *abbrevs.* National Rifle Association of America; National Recovery Administration.

N.S. *abbrev.* New style; Nova Scotia.

n.s. *abbrev.* Not specified.

NSC *abbrev.* National Security Council.

NT, N.T. *abbrevs.* New Testament.

nu (no͞o, nū) *n.* Fourteenth (later 13th) letter of Greek alphabet (Ν, ν), corresponding to *n*.

nu·ance (no͞o′ahns, nū′-, no͞o-ahns′, nū-) *n.* Delicate difference in or shade of meaning, feeling, opinion, color, etc.

nub (nŭb) *n.* 1. Small knob or lump, esp. of coal. 2. Point or gist (*of* matter or story). **nub′ble** *n.* = NUB def. 1. **nub′bly** *adv.*

Nu·bi·a (no͞o′bē*a*, nū′-). Region of NE. Africa in Nile valley between Aswan and Khartoum. **Nu′bi·an** *adj.* & *n.* (Native, inhabitant, monosyllabic language) of Nubia.

Nu·bi·an (no͞o′bē*a*n, nū′-) **Desert.** Desert in NE. Sudan from Nile to Red Sea.

nu·bile (no͞o′bĭl, -bīl, nū′-) *adj.* Marriageable (esp. of women); of age or physical development appropriate to marriage. **nu·bil·i·ty** (no͞obĭl′ĭtē, nū-) *n.*

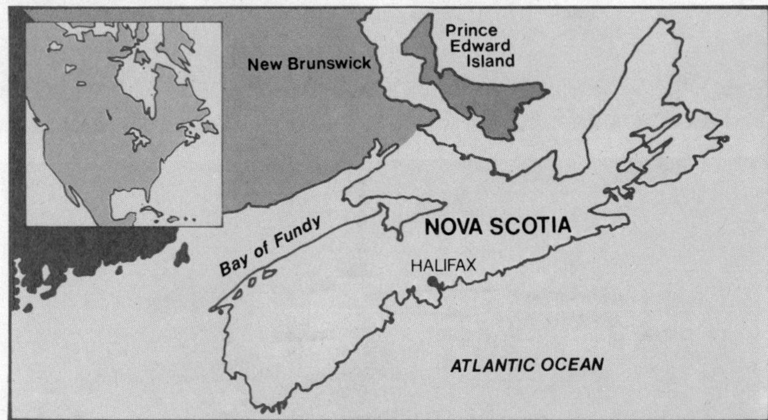

*Despite the recent growth of industry in **Nova Scotia,** many of the people still earn their living from fishing. Bottom: A typical port at Peggy's Bay.*

Interior (above) and exterior (right) of a prototype fast-breeder ***nuclear*** *reactor at Dounreay, Scotland. This is only one of many similar atomic power stations now contributing to electrical supplies. However, public concern with possible hazards has prevented others from being built.*

nu·cle·ar (nōō′klēer, nū′-) *adj.* 1. Of or constituting a nucleus. 2. Of, using, concerned with, nuclear energy or weapons; ~ **energy,** ATOMIC energy; ~ **fission,** splitting of a heavy nucleus into (usu. 2) parts with resulting release of large amounts of energy; ~ **fuel,** any substance from which atomic energy can be readily obtained; ~ **fusion,** union of atomic nuclei to form heavier nucleus, usu. with release of energy; the utilization of this process as source of energy.

nu·cle·ase (nōō′klēās, nū′-) *n.* (chem.) Enzyme that induces hydrolysis of nucleic acid.

nu·cle·ate (nōō′klēāt, nū′-) *v.* (**-at·ed, -at·ing**). Form (into) a nucleus. **nu·cle·a·tion** (nōōklēā′shon, nū-) *n.* **nu·cle·ate** (nōō′klēĭt, -āt, nū′-) *adj.*

nu·cle·ic (nŏŏklē′ĭk, nū-) **acid.** One of a group of acids found in all living cells, combined with proteins to form nucleoproteins.

nu·cle·o·lus (nŏŏklē′olus, nū-) *n.* (pl. **-li** pr. -lī). Spherical body observable in nucleus of living resting cells but disappearing during mitosis.

nu·cle·on (nōō′klēŏn, nū′-) *n.* (phys.) Proton or neutron of an atomic nucleus. **nu·cle·on·ics** (nŏŏklēŏn′ĭks, nū-) *n.* Branch of physics that treats of atomic nuclei esp. in practical applications, as in engineering.

nu·cle·us (nōō′klēus, nū′-) *n.* (pl. **-cle·i** pr. -klēī, **-cle·us·es**). Central part or thing around which others are collected; kernel of aggregate or mass; central part of ovule or seed; body, present in nearly all living cells, containing chromosomes; group of nerve cells in the central nervous system concerned with a particular function; (phys., chem.) internal core of an atom, surrounded by electrons and containing the positive charge of the electrically neutral atom.

nu·clide (nōō′klīd, nū′-) *n.* (phys.) Particular kind of atom defined by composition of its nucleus; hence **nu·clid·ic** (nŏŏklĭd′ĭk, nū-) *adj.*

nude (nōōd, nūd) *adj.* Naked, unclothed, undraped; ~ **contract,** (law) one lacking a consideration and therefore void unless under seal. **nude** *n.* Nude figure, in painting, etc.; **the** ~, the undraped human figure; the condition of being naked. **nu·di·ty** (nōō′-dĭtē, nū′-) *n.*

nudge (nŭj) *v.t.* (**nudged, nudg·ing**). Push slightly with elbow to draw attention privately; draw attention of. ~ *n.* Such a push.

nud·ist (nōō′dĭst, nū′-) *n.* One who advocates or practices going unclothed. ~ *adj.* Of nudists. **nud′ism** *n.*

nu·ga·to·ry (nōō′gatōrē, -tōrē, nū′-) *adj.* Trifling, worthless, futile; inoperative, not valid.

nug·get (nŭg′ĭt) *n.* Rough lump of native gold or platinum.

nui·sance (nōō′sans, nū′-) *n.* Anything injurious or obnoxious to the community or a member of it; obnoxious person, offensive object, annoying action; anything disagreeable.

nuke (nōōk, nūk) *n.* (slang) Nuclear or thermonuclear weapon.

Nu·ku·a·lo·fa (nōōkōōalaw′fa). Capital of Tonga on Tongatabu Island.

null (nŭl) *adj.* Not binding, invalid; without character or expression; (rare) nonexistent, amounting to nothing.

nul·li·fy (nŭl′ifī) *v.t.* (**-fied, -fy·ing**). Cancel, neutralize. **nul·li·fi·ca·tion** (nŭlifĭkā′shon) *n.*

nul·li·ty (nŭl′ĭtē) *n.* (pl. **-ties**). Being null, invalidity; act, document, etc., that is null; nothingness; a mere nothing.

numb (nŭm) *adj.* Deprived of feeling or power of motion. **numb′ly** *adv.* **numb′ness** *n.* **numb** *v.t.* Make numb; stupefy, paralyze.

num·ber (nŭm′ber) *n.* Count, sum, company, or aggregate, of persons, things, or abstract units; symbol or figure representing such aggregate; person or thing (esp. single issue of periodical) whose place in series is indicated by such figure; numerical reckoning; (sing. or pl.) large (or *large*, *small*, etc.) collection or company (*of*), (pl.) numerical preponderance; (gram.) property in words of denoting that one, two or more persons or things are spoken of, form of word expressing this; item (as song, dance) esp. on a program; (pl.) groups of musical notes, metrical feet, verses; **Numbers**, fourth book of Old Testament, earlier part of which contains census of Israelites; **his number is up**, he is doomed, his hour is come; **numbers game**, lottery based on occurrence of unpredictable numbers in results of races etc.; (slang) manipulation of statistical data with intention to befuddle (readers); (**times**) **out of number, without number,** innumerable (times); **number one**, oneself, esp. as object of selfish care; **Number 10**, (used for) 10 Downing Street, London, British prime minister's official residence. **num′ber·less** *adj.* **num′ber** *v.t.* Count, ascertain number of; include, regard as, *among, in,* or *with* some class; assign a number to, distinguish with a number; have lived, live (so many years); have, comprise (so many); equal, amount to; (pass.) be restricted or few in number.

*The cooling tower of a **nuclear** power station, similar to the one which formed a fault at Three Mile Island, threatening the surrounding population.*

*Throughout the history of art, the **nude** human figure has provided a challenge to artists and sculptors. Velazquez is still renowned for the 'Rokeby Venus' (below).*

nu·mer·a·ble (nōō′merabel, nū′-) *adj.* That can be numbered.

nu·mer·al (nōō′meral, nū′-) *adj.* & *n.* (Word, figure, group of figures) denoting a number; of number.

nu·mer·a·tion (nōōmerā′shon, nū-) *n.* Method or process of numbering or computing; calculation; assigning of numbers; (arith.) expression in words of number written in figures.

nu·mer·a·tor (nōō′merāter, nū′-) *n.* Number above line in common fraction, showing how many of the parts indicated by the denominator are taken; person who numbers.

__Nuremberg,__ possibly best remembered as the location of the trials of War Criminals after the 1939–45 war. A medieval town built around a castle and later walled now forms the town center.

nu·mer·i·cal (nōomĕr′ĭk*a*l, nū-) *adj.* Of, in, denoting, etc., number. **nu·mer′i·cal·ly** *adv.*

nu·mer·ol·o·gy (nōomer*ŏ*l′*o*jē, nū-) *n.* Study of (esp. occult) significance of numbers. **nu·mer·o·log·i·cal** (nōomer*o*lŏj′ĭk*a*l, nū-) *adj.* **nu·mer·ol′o·gist** *n.*

nu·mer·ous (nōō′mer*u*s, nū′-) *adj.* Comprising many units; coming from many individuals. **nu′mer·ous·ly** *adv.*

nu·mi·nous (nōō′min*u*s, nū′-) *adj.* Divine; suggesting or revealing the presence or influence of a god; awe-inspiring, mysterious. [L. *numen* divine will, divinity]

nu·mis·mat·ic (nōomĭzmăt′ĭk, -mĭs-, nū-) *adj.* Of coins or coinage. **nu·mis·mat′i·cal·ly** *adv.* **nu·mis·mat′ics, nu·mis·ma·tist** (nōomĭz′m*a*tĭst, -mĭs′-, nū-), **nu·mis·ma·tol·o·gy** (nōomĭzm*a*tŏl′*o*jē, -mĭs-, nū-) *ns.*

num·skull, numb·skull (nŭm′skŭl) *ns.* Blockhead.

nun (nŭn) *n.* Woman living in convent under religious vow. **nun′-like** *adj.*

nun·ci·o (nŭn′shēō, nōōn′-) *n.* (pl. **-ci·os**). Diplomatic representative of the pope at foreign court. **nun·ci·a·ture** (nŭn′shē*a*ch*e*r) *n.* (Tenure of) office of nuncio.

nun·ner·y (nŭn′*e*rē) *n.* (pl. **-ner·ies**). House, community, of nuns.

nup·tial (nŭp′sh*a*l) *adj.* Of marriage or wedding. ~ *n.* (usu. pl.) Wedding.

Nu·rem·berg (noor′*e*mbẽrg, nūr′-). (Ger. *Nürnberg*) City of Bavaria; ~ **laws**, series of laws, enacted under the Nazi regime, depriving Jews in Germany of certain civil rights and prohibiting intermarriage between Germans and Jews; ~ **trials**, trials of war criminals conducted at Nuremberg after World War II.

nurse (nẽrs) *n.* 1. Woman employed to look after young child (so **nurse′maid**, maidservant employed thus); wet nurse. 2. (fig.) Something that nourishes or fosters some quality etc. 3. Person, usu. woman, charged with or trained for care of the sick or infirm; **practical** ~, one trained in routine nursing but not registered; one with state board certification. 4. (entom.) Sexually imperfect bee, ant, etc., caring for the young brood, worker; (zool.) individual in asexual stage or metagenesis. **nurse** *v.* (**nursed, nurs·ing**). 1. Suckle (child), give suck, act as wet nurse; act as nursemaid to, have charge of; foster, tend, promote development of; manage (plants, estate) with solicitude; cherish (grievance etc.); (pass.) be brought up. 2. Wait upon, attend to, (sick person); try to cure (sickness); **nursing home**, house (freq. under private management) receiving surgical cases, invalids, etc. 3. Clasp or hold carefully or caressingly; conserve (a drink etc.).

The __nyala__ is a variety of antelope found only in parts of south-east Africa. The mountain nyala of Ethiopia lives only at altitudes above 4,000 ft. where it grazes on alpine herbs.

nurs·er·y (nẽr′s*e*rē) *n.* (pl. **-er·ies**). 1. Room assigned to children and their nurses; **day** ~, institution taking charge of young children during day. 2. Plot of ground in which young plants are reared for transplantation, esp. one in which trees or plants are reared for sale; fish-rearing pond; place where animal life is developed. 3. **nurs′eryman**, owner of nursery garden; **nursery rhyme**, simple short traditional verse for young children; **nursery school**, school for young children, esp. those under five years of age.

nur·ture (nẽr′ch*e*r) *n.* Bringing up, training, fostering care; nourishment. ~ *v.t.* (**-tured, -tur·ing**). Nourish, rear, foster, train, educate.

nut (nŭt) *n.* 1. Fruit consisting of hard or leathery indehiscent shell enclosing edible kernel; kernel of this; (slang) head; ~**s about, over**, (slang) devoted to, fond of; **off one's** ~, (slang) out of one's mind. 2. Small toothed projection on spindle engaging with cogwheel, small spur wheel; small block of metal etc. pierced with female screw for adjusting or tightening bolt; holder for tightening or relaxing horsehair of violin bow. 3. Very small lump of coal etc. 4. (slang) Eccentric or insane person. 5. **nut-brown**, colored like ripe hazelnut; **nut'cracker**, instrument for cracking nuts; corvine bird (*Nucifraga caryocatactes*) of mountain regions in Western U.S., having gray body with white patches on wings and tail; also called Clark's ~; **nut'gall**, gall found on oak; **nut'hatch**, any of several small nut-eating birds (family Sittidae), esp. *Sitta carolinensis* common throughout the U.S. and Canada, predominantly gray but having black on the head and a white throat; **nut'shell**, hard exterior covering of nut; something extremely small; **in a nutshell**, briefest possible way of expressing something; **nut tree**, tree bearing nuts, esp. hazel. **nut'ting** *n.* Gathering nuts.

nu·tant (nōō'tant, nū'-) *adj.* (bot.) Drooping.

nu·ta·tion (nōōtā'shon, nū-) *n.* Nodding; (astron.) oscillation of Earth's axis making motion of pole of equator around pole of ecliptic wavy; oscillation of spinning top in its precession around an axis.

nut·meg (nŭt'mĕg) *n.* Hard aromatic spheroidal seed from fruit of evergreen E. Ind. tree (*Myristica fragrans*), used as spice.

nu·tri·a (nōō'trēa, nū'-) *n.* (Fur of the) coypu.

nu·tri·ent (nōō'trēent, nū'-) *adj.* & *n.* (Substance etc.) serving as or providing nourishment.

nu·tri·ment (nōō'triment, nū'-) *n.* Nourishing food.

nu·tri·tion (nōōtrĭsh'on, nū-) *n.* (Supplying or receiving of) nourishment, food. **nu·tri'tion·al** *adj.* Of, relating to, nutrition. **nu·tri'tion·al·ly** *adv.* **nu·tri'tion·ist** *n.*

nu·tri·tious (nōōtrĭsh'us, nū-) *adj.* Nourishing, efficient as food. **nu·tri'tious·ly** *adv.* **nu·tri'tious·ness** *n.*

*Two species of **nutcrackers,** birds related to crows, are present in northern Europe and America. They collect food in summer which is stored for use in the winter.*

nu·tri·tive (nōō'trĭtĭv, nū'-) *adj.* Serving as food; concerned in nutrition.

nuts (nŭts) *adj.* (slang) Crazy.

nut·ty (nŭt'ē) *adj.* (**-ti·er, -ti·est**). 1. Abounding in nuts; tasting like nuts, of rich mellow flavor. 2. (slang) Silly.

nux vom·i·ca (nŭks vŏm'ĭka). Seed of pulpy fruit of E. Ind. tree (*Strychnos nux-vomica*), yielding strychnine.

nuz·zle (nŭz'el) *v.* (**-zled, -zling**). Nose; burrow, press, rub, sniff, with the nose; press nose or press (nose) *into, against*; nestle, lie snug.

*A popular food, these **nuts** are produced by the almond tree, Prunus dulcis, which grows in warm temperate climates. Oil extracted from almonds is used in cosmetics and as a lubricant.*

*The **nuthatch,** a tree-climbing bird found in most parts of the world except the Australian region, may also be aptly described as a tree-runner. The largest is 9 ins. long.*

NV *abbrev.* Nevada.

NW, N.W., n.w. *abbrevs.* Northwest(ern).

N.W.T. *abbrev.* Northwest Territories (Canada).

NY, N.Y. *abbrevs.* New York.

ny·a·la (nēah'la, nī-) *n.* (pl. **-las**, collect. **-la**). Large S. African antelope (*Tragelaphus angasi*), one of the bush bucks.

N.Y.C. *abbrev.* New York City.

nyc·ta·lo·pi·a (nĭktalō'pēa) *n.* Night blindness, inability to see in a dim light.

ny·lon (nī'lŏn) *n.* Any of a group of long-chain synthetic polymeric amines of which the structural units or molecules can be oriented in one direction, and which are thus capable of being formed into filaments of great tensile strength; textile fiber of this structure and character; (pl.) garments, esp. women's stockings, made of this.

nymph (nĭmf) *n.* 1. (myth.) One of class of semidivine maidens inhabiting sea, rivers, fountains, woods, or trees; (poet.) young and beautiful woman. 2. (zool.) Immature insect that from time of hatching has a general resemblance to the adult. 3. Edible frog.

nym·pho·ma·ni·a (nĭmfomā'nēa) *n.* (path.) Morbid and uncontrollable sexual desire in women. **nym·pho·ma'ni·ac** *adj.* & *n.*

NYSE *abbrev.* New York Stock Exchange.

nys·tag·mus (nĭstăg'mus) *n.* Rapid involuntary oscillation of eyeball. **nys·tag'mic** *adj.*

N.Z., N. Zeal. *abbrevs.* New Zealand.

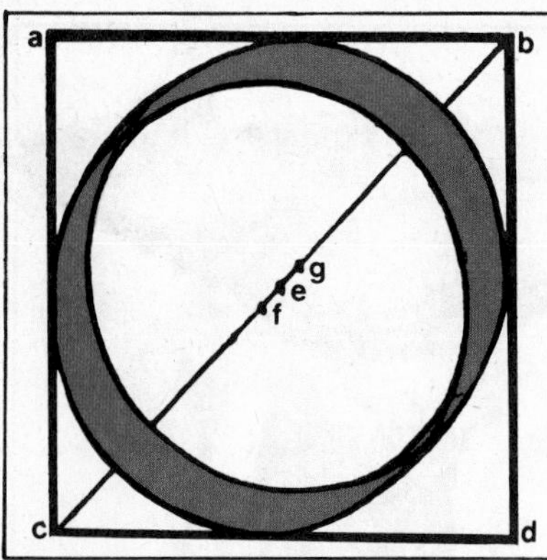

With a few exceptions, there has been little change in the form of the letter **O, o** throughout its development. Although similar to the symbol for zero, this letter has no connection with the numeral.

Phoenician Early Greek Etruscan

Early Latin Classical Latin Italian

O[1], **o** (ō) (pl. **O's, o's** or **Os, os**). 1. Fifteenth letter of modern English and 14th of ancient Roman alphabet, representing a variety of mid-back-round vowels, and corresponding in form to ancient Greek *O*, derived from Phoenician and ancient Semitic ○, ◊, ▽ (Heb. ע), which represent not a vowel but a glottal stop. 2. *O*, O-shaped mark, circle; cipher or naught.

O[2], **oh** (ō) *ints.* Exclamation expressing various emotions or prefixed to vocative name.

O[3] *symbol.* Oxygen.

O. *abbrev.* Ohio.

o' (*o*, ō) *prep.* Short for *of, on,* in some phrases as (= *of*) *o'clock, will-o'-the-wisp, man-o'-war.*

oaf (ōf) *n.* Awkward lout. **oaf'ish** *adj.* **oaf'ish·ly** *adv.* **oaf'ish·ness** *n.* [ON. *álfr* elf]

O·a·hu (ōah'hoo). One of the Hawaiian Islands, 589 square miles (1,526 sq. km), on which Honolulu, the state capital, is located.

oak (ōk) *n.* 1. Forest tree of genus *Quercus* with hard timber, bearing acorn as fruit; any of various trees or plants resembling this; ~**-leaf cluster**, U.S. military decoration granted to the holder of a medal for a second action meriting the same medal; **poison** ~: see POISON. 2. Wood of the oak; this as material for ships. **oak·en** (ō'ken) *adj.* (chiefly poet.) Made of oak.

Oak·land (ōk'land). City in N. California, opposite San Francisco, on San Francisco Bay.

Oak·ley (ōk'lē): see ANNIE OAKLEY.

Oak (ōk) **Ridge.** City in E. Tennessee; site of the original Oak Ridge National Laboratory for development and research of atomic energy and materials.

oa·kum (ō'kum) *n.* Loose fiber gotten by untwisting and picking old hemp ropes and used esp. in caulking.

oar (ōr, ōr) *n.* Long stout wooden shaft widened and flattened at one end into a blade, used to propel (row) a boat by leverage against a rowlock, which serves as a fulcrum, esp. pulled by one rower with both hands, as dist. from a scull (one hand) and a sweep (two rowers); oarsman; **put in one's** ~, interfere; **rest on one's** ~**s**, lean on handles of oars, raising blades out of water; (fig.) suspend one's efforts, take things easy; **oar'lock**, device, usu. U-shaped, set in swivel in gunwale of boat to hold oar. **oars'man**, rower; **oars'man·ship**.

OAS *abbrev.* Organization of American States.

o·a·sis (ōā'sĭs) *n.* (pl. **-ses** pr. -sēz). Depression in desert where cultivation is possible owing to presence of water (also fig.).

oat (ōt) *n.* (pl.) (Grain yielded by) hardy cereal (*Avena sativa*), grown in cool climates as food for man and horses; **wild** ~**s**: see WILD;

Oak trees of various types are native to the Americas, Europe, Africa and Asia. English oaks (left) were once essential to shipbuilding. Bark of the American red oak (below) was processed to extract the tannin.

1

2

Waikiki Beach on ***Oahu,*** *one of the Hawaiian Islands. Waikiki is a major tourist resort, renowned throughout the world. Honolulu, Hawaii's capital, is on the island. Its name means 'sheltered harbor'.*

In desert regions, an ***oasis*** *forms in a depression where underground water accumulates close to the surface. Above: A Tunisian oasis first recorded in Roman times.*

Principally a fodder crop, ***oats*** *are also used in breakfast cereals and their stalks used as hay, or processed in silage tanks. Oats are a very hardy plant and can survive in poor soil.*

oat'cake, thin unleavened cake of oatmeal; **oat'meal**, meal made from oats; oatmeal porridge; grayish fawn (color).

oath (ōth) *n.* (pl. **oaths** pr. ōdhz, ōths). 1. Solemn appeal to God (or to something scared), in witness of truth of statement or binding character of promise. 2. Name of God, or of something sacred, used as expletive to give emphasis or express anger etc.; piece of profanity in speech.

Ob (ŏb). River of Asiatic U.S.S.R., flowing north into **Gulf of Ob**, an arm of the Arctic Ocean.

ob. *abbrev. Obiit*, obstetrics.

O·ba·di·ah (ōbadī'*a*). Hebrew minor prophet; shortest book of Old Testament, bearing his name.

ob·bli·ga·to (ŏbl*i*gah'tō) *adj.* & *n.* (pl. **-tos,** *It.* **-ti** pr. -tē). (mus.) (Part, accompaniment) forming integral part of composition. [It.]

ob·du·rate (ŏb'do͝orĭt, -dyo͝o-) *adj.* Hardened, impenitent, stubborn. **ob'du·rate·ly** *adv.* **ob'du·ra·cy, ob'du·rate·ness** *ns.*

o·be·ah (ō'bē*a*), **o·bi**[2] (ō'bē) *ns.* Sorcery or witch doctoring associated with the snake god Obi whose worship was introduced by W. African slaves into W. Indies and U.S. **o'be·ah·ism** *n.*

o·be·di·ence (ōbē'd*e*ens) *n.* 1. Obeying as act, practice, or quality; submission to another's rule; compliance with law or command. 2. (eccles., esp. R.C.) (Sphere of) authority; district or body of persons subject to some rule.

o·be·di·ent (ōbē'dēent) *adj.* Submissive to, complying with, superior's will; dutiful. **o·be'di·ent·ly** *adv.*

o·bei·sance (ōbā'sans, ōbē'-) *n.* Gesture, esp. bow or curtsy, expressing submission, respect, or salutation. **o·bei'sant** *adj.* **o·bei'sant·ly** *adv.*

ob·e·lisk (ŏb'*e*lĭsk) *n.* Tapering shaft of stone, square or rectangular in section, with pyramidal apex; mountain, tree, etc., of similar shape.

O·ber·am·mer·gau (ōberah'm*e*rgow). Village in Upper Bavaria; in 1633 the inhabitants vowed that they would perform a Passion Play as an act of thanksgiving for deliverance from the plague; since 1680 the play has been performed every ten years exc. for 1810, 1920, and 1940.

O·ber·on (ō'berŏn). In W. European folklore, king of the fairies.

o·bese (ōbēs') *adj.* Corpulent. **o·bese'ly** *adv.* **o·bese'ness, o·be·si·ty** (ōbē'sĭtē) *ns.*

o·bey (ōbā´) *v.* Perform bidding of, be obedient (to); execute (command). **o·bey´a·ble** *adj.* **o·bey´er** *n.* **o·bey´ing·ly** *adv.*

ob·fus·cate (ŏb´fuskāt, ŏbfŭs´-) *v.t.* (**-cat·ed, -cat·ing**). Darken, obscure; stupefy, bewilder. **ob·-fus·ca·tion** (ŏbfŭskā´shon) *n.*

o·bi[1] (ō´bē) *n.* Japanese woman's bright-colored sash.

o·bi[2] = OBEAH.

o·bi·it (ō´bēĭt). Died (with date of death). [L.]

o·bit (ō´bĭt, ŏb´ĭt) *n.* Obituary; date of person's death.

ob·i·ter dic·tum (ŏb´ĭter dĭk´-tum) (pl. **dic·ta** pr. dĭk´ta). Judge's expression of opinion on matters of law, given in course of argument or judgment but not essential to decision and therefore without binding authority; incidental remark(s). [L.]

o·bit·u·ar·y (ōbĭch´ōōĕrē) *n.* (pl. **-ar·ies**). Notice of death, esp. in newspaper, brief biography of deceased person. ~ *adj.* Recording a death; concerning deceased person.

ob·ject[1] (ŏb´jĭkt, -jĕkt) *n.* 1. Thing placed before eyes or presented to sense; material thing; thing observed with optical instrument or represented in picture. 2. Person or thing of pitiable or ridiculous aspect. 3. Person or thing to which action or feeling is directed, subject *of* or *for*; thing aimed at, end, purpose; **no** ~, not to be taken into account; forming no obstacle. 4. (philos.) Thing thought of or apprehended as correlative to the thinking mind or subject; external thing. 5. (gram.) Substantive word, phrase, or clause governed by active transitive verb or by preposition; **direct, indirect,** ~, that primarily, secondarily, affected by action of verb. 6. ~ **glass, lens,** lens in telescope etc. nearest the object; ~ **lesson,** instruction about material object that is present for inspection; (fig.) striking practical application of some principle.

ob·ject[2] (objĕkt´) *v.* Bring forward or state in opposition, urge as objection; state objection; express or feel disapproval. **ob·jec´tor** *n.*

ob·jec·ti·fy (objĕk´tifī) *v.t.* (**-fied, -fy·ing**). Present as object of sense; make objective; express in concrete form, embody. **ob·jec·ti·fi·ca·tion** (objĕktifikā´shon) *n.*

ob·jec·tion (objĕk´shon) *n.* Objecting, thing objected; adverse reason or statement; expression or feeling of disapproval or dislike. **ob·jec´tion·a·ble** *adj.* Open to objection; undesirable, unpleasant, offensive. **ob·jec·tion·a·bil·i·ty** (objĕkshonabĭl´ĭtē), **ob·jec´tion·a·ble·ness** *ns.* **ob·jec´tion·a·bly** *adv.*

***Obelisks,** such as the one from Egypt in the square of Santa Maria Maggiore in Rome, were originally built as central cult objects for worship of the sun.*

ob·jec·tive (objĕk´tĭv) *adj.* 1. Belonging to what is presented to consciousness; that is the object of perception or thought, as dist. from perceiving or thinking subject; external to the mind, real. 2. Dealing with outward things and not with thoughts or feelings, exhibiting facts uncolored by exhibitor's feelings or opinions. 3. (gram.) Constructed as, appropriate to, the object. **ob·jec´tive·ly** *adv.* **ob·jec´tive·ness, ob·jec·tiv·i·ty** (ŏbjĕktĭv´ĭtē) *ns.* **ob·jec´tive** *n.* 1. Object glass. 2. (gram.) Objective case. 3. Object or purpose of an action; (mil.) position to the attainment or capture of which an operation is directed, objective point.

ob·jec·tiv·ism (objĕk´tivĭzem) *n.* Tendency to lay stress on the objective; doctrine that knowledge of observable phenomena is prior in sequence and importance to that of knowledge of self. **ob·jec´tiv·ist** *n.*

ob·jet d'art (ŏbzhā dār´) (pl. **ob·jets d'art** pr. ŏbzhā dār´). Object (esp. small) of artistic interest, curio. [Fr.]

ob·jur·gate (ŏb´jergāt) *v.t.* (**-gat·ed, -gat·ing**). Chide, scold. **ob·jur·ga´tion, ob´jur·ga·tor** *ns.* **ob·jur·ga·to·ry** (objẽr´gatōrē, -tōrē) *adj.*

ob·late[1] (ŏb´lāt) *n.* Person dedicated to monastic or religious life or work. **ob´late·ly** *adv.*

ob·late[2] (ŏb´lāt, ŏblāt´) *adj.* (geom., of spheroid) Flattened at the poles.

ob·la·tion (ŏblā´shon) *n.* (Presenting bread and wine to God in) Eucharist; thing offered to God, sacrifice, victim; donation for pious uses. **ob·la·to·ry** (ŏb´latōrē, -tōrē), **ob·la´tion·al** *adjs.*

ob·li·gate (ŏb´ligāt) *v.t.* (**-gat·ed, -gat·ing**). Bind (person, esp. legally) *to* do; oblige. **ob´li·ga·tor** *n.*

ob·li·ga·tion (ŏbligā´shon) *n.* 1. Binding agreement, esp. one enforceable under legal penalty, written contract, or bond; constraining power of a law, precept, duty, contract, etc.; one's bounden duty, a duty, burdensome task. 2. (Indebtedness for) service or benefit.

ob·lig·a·to·ry (oblĭg´atōrē, -tōrē, ŏb´lĭga-) *adj.* Legally or morally binding; imperative, not merely permissive; constituting an obligation.

o·blige (oblīj´) *v.t.* (**o·bliged, o·blig·ing**). 1. Bind by oath, promise, contract, etc., *to* (archaic, legal); be binding on. 2. Make indebted by conferring favor, gratify *by, with*; (colloq.) make contribution to entertainment (*with*); (pass.) be bound (*to*) by gratitude. 3. Constrain, compel, *to* do.

ob·li·gee (ŏblijē´) *n.* (law) Person to whom another is bound by contract or to whom bond is given.

o·blig·ing (oblī´jĭng) *adj.* Courteous, accommodating, ready to do kindness, complaisant. **o·blig´ing·ly** *adv.* **o·blig´ing·ness** *n.*

ob·li·gor (ŏbligōr´, ŏb´ligōr) *n.* (law) One who binds himself to another or gives bond.

ob·lique (ŏblēk´, oblīk´) *adj.* 1. Slanting; declining from vertical or horizontal; diverging from straight line or course; (geom.) (of line etc.) inclined at other than right angle, (of angle) acute or obtuse, (of cone etc.) with axis not perpendicular to plane of base; (anat.) neither parallel nor perpendicular to body's or limb's long axis; (bot., of leaf) with unequal sides. 2. Not going straight to the point, roundabout, indirect; ~ **speech,** indirect speech. **ob·lique´ly** *adv.* **ob·liq·ui·ty** (oblĭk´wĭtē) *n.*

ob·lit·er·ate (oblĭt´erāt) *v.t.* (**-at·ed, -at·ing**). Blot out, efface, erase, destroy. **ob·lit·er·a·tion** (oblĭterā´shon) *n.*

ob·liv·i·on (oblĭv´ēon) *n.* Having or being forgotten; disregard, unregarded state.

ob·liv·i·ous (oblĭv´ēus) *adj.* Forgetful, unmindful, (*of*); (poet.) of, inducing, oblivion. **ob·liv´i·ous·ly** *adv.* **ob·liv´i·ous·ness** *n.*

First recorded in the 13th century, ***Oberon*** *has been attributed with many forms. To the Germans he was an ugly dwarf. Shakespeare portrayed him as king of the fairies (opposite).*

ob·long (ŏb′lawng) *adj.* Elongated in one direction (usu. as deviation from exact square or circular form); (geom.) rectangular with adjacent sides unequal. ~ *n.* Oblong figure or object.

ob·lo·quy (ŏb′lokwē) *n.* (pl. **-quies**). Abuse, detraction; being generally ill spoken of.

ob·nox·ious (obnŏk′shus) *adj.* Offensive, objectionable, disliked. **ob·nox′ious·ly** *adv.* **ob·nox′ious·ness** *n.*

o·boe (ō′bō) *n.* Musical instrument of woodwind family, played vertically, with a double reed, having a range of nearly three octaves upward from the B flat below middle C, and a plaintive incisive tone; organ reed stop imitating this. **o′bo·ist** *n.*

ob·scene (obsēn′) *adj.* 1. (archaic) Repulsive. 2. Indecent, esp. grossly or repulsively so; lewd; (law, of publications) tending to deprave and corrupt. **ob·scene′ly** *adv.* **ob·scene′ness** *n.* **ob·scen·i·ty** (obsĕn′ĭtē) *n.* (pl. **-ties**).

ob·scu·rant (obskūr′ant) *n.* Opponent of inquiry, enlightenment, and reform. **ob·scu′rant·ism** *n.* **ob·scu′rant·ist** *n.* & *adj.*

ob·scure (obskūr′) *adj.* (**-scur·er, -scur·est**). 1. Dark, dim; (of color) dingy, dull, indefinite. 2. Indistinct, not clear; (of vowel) not clearly enunciated. 3. Hidden, remote from observation; unnoticed; unknown to fame, humble. 4. Unexplained, doubtful; not perspicuous or clearly expressed. **ob·scure′ly** *adv.* **ob·scure′ness, ob·scu·ri·ty** (obskūr′ĭtē) *ns.* **ob′scure** *v.t.* (**-scured, -scur·ing**). Make obscure, dark, indistinct, or unintelligible; dim glory of, outshine; conceal from sight. **ob·scu·ra·tion** (ŏbskūrā′shon) *n.*

ob·se·cra·tion (ŏbsekrā′shon) *n.* Earnest entreaty. **ob·se·crate** (ŏb′sekrāt) *v.t.* (**-crat·ed, -crat·ing**).

ob·se·quies (ŏb′sekwēz) *n. pl.* Funeral rites, funeral.

ob·se·qui·ous (obsē′kwēus) *adj.* Servile, fawning. **ob·se′qui·ous·ly** *adv.* **ob·se′qui·ous·ness** *n.*

ob·serv·ance (obzĕr′vans) *n.* Keeping or performance of law, duty, ritual, etc.; act of religious or ceremonial character, customary rite; rule of a religious order.

ob·serv·ant (obzĕr′vant) *adj.* 1. Attentive in observance. 2. Acute or diligent in taking notice. **ob·serv′ant·ly** *adv.*

ob·ser·va·tion (ŏbzĕrvā′shon) *n.* 1. Noticing or being noticed; perception, faculty of taking notice; (mil.) watching of fortress or hostile position or movements. 2. Observing scientifically, accurate watching and noting of phenomena as they occur in nature; taking of altitude of sun or other heavenly body to find latitude or longitude; reading or value of any observed quantity, esp. when noted down. 3. Remark, statement, esp. one of the nature of comment. **ob·ser·va′tion·al** *adj.* **ob·ser·va′tion·al·ly** *adv.*

ob·serv·a·to·ry (obzĕr′vatōrē, -tōrē) *n.* (pl. **-ries**). Building etc. whence natural, esp. astronomical, phenomena can be observed.

ob·serve (obzĕrv′) *v.* (**-served, -serv·ing**). 1. Keep, follow, adhere to, perform duly. 2. Perceive, watch, mark, take notice of, become conscious of; examine and note (phenomena) without aid of experiment. 3. Say, esp. by way of comment; make remark(s) *on.* **ob·serv′er** *n.* (esp.) Interested spectator; person carried in aircraft to note enemy's position etc.; person trained to watch and identify aircraft.

ob·sess (ŏbsĕs′) *v.t.* Dominate or preoccupy the thoughts of (a person). **ob·ses·sion** (obsĕsh′on) *n.* **ob·ses′sive, ob·ses′sion·al** *adjs.*

ob·sid·i·an (obsĭd′ēan) *n.* Dark vitreous volcanic rock with appear-

*The giant telescope at the **observatory** at Mount Palomar in the U.S.A. This is one of many forms of equipment now used by astronomers to gain better knowledge of the universe.*

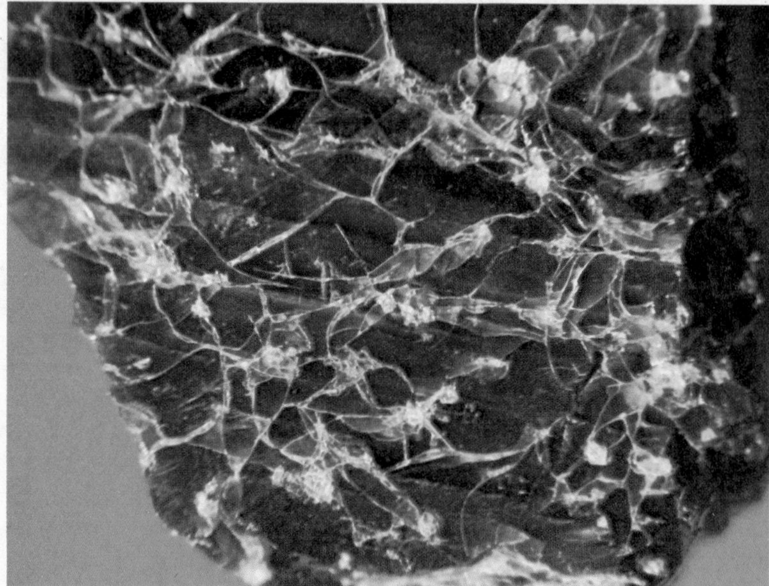

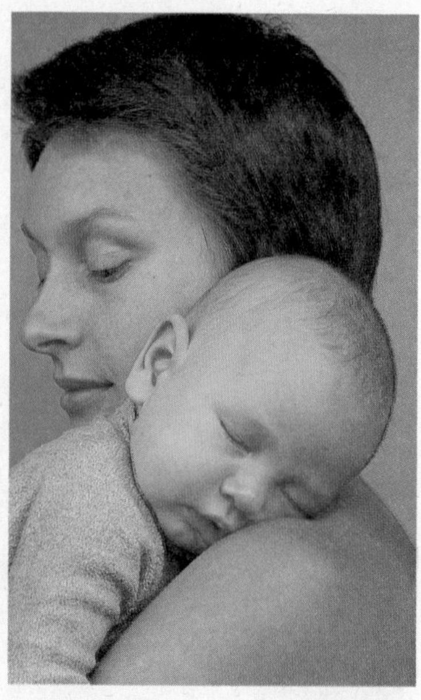

ance like glass, used by primitive societies for knives etc. [f. personal name *Obsius*]

ob·so·les·cent (ŏbsolĕs′ent) *adj.* Becoming obsolete; gradually disappearing. **ob·so·les′cence** *n.*

ob·so·lete (ŏbsolēt′, ŏb′solēt) *adj.* Disused, discarded, antiquated. **ob·so·lete′ly** *adv.* **ob·so·lete′ness** *n.*

ob·sta·cle (ŏb′stakel) *n.* Hindrance, impediment; ~ **race,** one in which artificial or natural obstacles have to be passed.

ob·stet·ric (obstĕt′rĭk), **ob·stet′ri·cal** *adjs.* Of midwifery; of, relating to, obstetrics. **ob·stet′rics** *n.* (usu. considered sing.) Branch of medicine and surgery concerned with the care of women before, during, and immediately after childbirth. **ob·ste·tri·cian** (ŏbstĭtrĭsh′an) *n.*

ob·sti·nate (ŏb′stinĭt) *adj.* Firmly adhering to one's own course, not yielding to argument or persuasion; inflexible, self-willed; (of disease etc.) not yielding readily to treatment. **ob′sti·nate·ly** *adv.* **ob′sti·nate·ness, ob·sti·na·cy** (ŏb′stinasē) *ns.*

ob·strep·er·ous (obstrĕp′erus) *adj.* Noisy, vociferous; turbulent, unruly, noisily resisting control. **ob·strep′er·ous·ly** *adv.* **ob·strep′er·ous·ness** *n.*

ob·struct (obstrŭkt′) *v.* Block up, fill with impediments, make impassable or difficult of passage; prevent or retard progress of, impede; practice obstruction. **ob·struc·tion** (obstrŭk′shon) *n.* Blocking or being blocked, making or becoming more or less impassable; hindering business by talking against time; obstacle. **ob·struc′tion·ist, ob·struc′tion·ism** *ns.*

ob·struc·tive (obstrŭk′tĭv) *adj.* Causing, intended to produce, obstruction. **ob·struc′tive·ly** *adv.* **ob·struc′tive·ness** *n.*

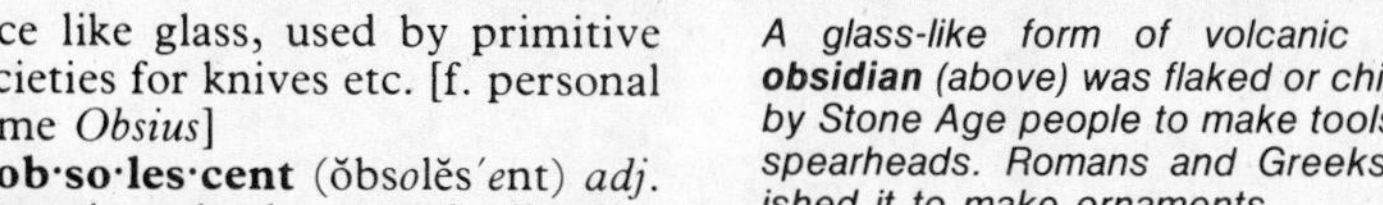

A glass-like form of volcanic rock, ***obsidian*** *(above) was flaked or chipped by Stone Age people to make tools and spearheads. Romans and Greeks polished it to make ornaments.*

ob·tain (obtān′) *v.* 1. Acquire, have granted one, get. 2. Be prevalent, established, or in vogue. **ob·tain′·a·ble** *adj.* **ob·tain′er, ob·tain′ment** *ns.*

ob·trude (obtrōōd′) *v.t.* (**-trud·ed, -trud·ing**). Thrust forward (*on, upon*) importunately. **ob·tru·sion** (obtrōō′zhon) *n.* **ob·tru·sive** (obtrōō′sĭv) *adj.* **ob·tru′sive·ly** *adv.* **ob·tru′sive·ness** *n.*

ob·tuse (ŏbtōōs′, -tūs′) *adj.* 1. Of blunt form, not sharp or pointed; (geom., of plane angle) greater than right angle. 2. Dull, not acute; stupid, slow of perception. **ob·tuse′ly** *adv.* **ob·tuse′ness** *n.*

ob·verse (ŏbvĕrs′, ŏb′vĕrs) *adj.* 1. Narrower at base or point of attachment than at apex. 2. Answering as counterpart to something else. **obverse** (ŏb′vĕrs) *n.* Side of coin or medal bearing head or principal design (opp. REVERSE); face of anything meant to be presented, front; counterpart of a fact or truth.

ob·vi·ate (ŏb′vēāt) *v.t.* (**-at·ed, -at·ing**). Clear away, get rid of, get around, neutralize (danger, inconvenience, etc.).

ob·vi·ous (ŏb′vēus) *adj.* Open to eye or mind, clearly perceptible, palpable, indubitable. **ob′vi·ous·ly** *adv.* **ob′vi·ous·ness** *n.*

oc·a·ri·na (ŏkarē′na) *n.* Small egg-shaped metal or porcelain musical wind instrument with whistle-like mouthpiece and finger holes, also called "sweet potato." [It. *oca* goose]

The ***obstetric*** *branch of medicine deals specifically with the care of women throughout the pregnancy and during and after the birth. This care has dramatically reduced infant mortality.*

O'Ca·sey (ōkā′sē), **Sean** (1884–1964). Irish playwright, author of *Juno and the Paycock, The Plough and the Stars,* etc.

Oc·cam = OCKHAM.

oc·ca·sion (okā′zhon) *n.* Juncture suitable for doing something, opportunity; reason, ground, justification, need; subsidiary, incidental, or immediate cause; (particular time marked by) special occurrence; (pl.) affairs, business. ~ *v.t.* Be the occasion or cause of; bring about, esp. incidentally; cause.

oc·ca·sion·al (okā′zhonal) *adj.* Arising out of, made or meant for, acting on, special occasion(s), as ~ *verse*; happening irregularly as occasion presents itself; coming now and then, not regular or frequent; ~ **table,** small table for use as required. **oc·ca′sion·al·ly** *adv.*

Oc·ci·dent (ŏk′sident) *n.* (chiefly poet.) The West; western Europe; Europe; Europe and America; America; European as opp. to Oriental civilization. **oc·ci·den′tal** *adj.* **oc·ci·den′tal·ly** *adv.* **Oc·ci·den′tal·ism** *n.* **Oc·ci·den′tal·ist** *n.* & *adj.*

oc·ci·put (ŏk′siput) *n.* (pl. **oc·ci·puts, oc·cip·i·ta** pr. ŏksĭp′ĭta). Back of head. **oc·cip′i·tal** *adj.* Of the occiput.

oc·clude (oklōōd′) *v.t.* (**-cluded, -clud·ing**). Stop up, close, obstruct; (chem.) absorb and retain (gases); **occluded front,** (meteor.) warm front forced upward by cold front when the cold air overtakes the warm and flows in underneath it.

oc·clu·sion (*o*klōō′zh*o*n) *n.* Act or process of occluding; position of teeth when jaws are brought together, bite; (phonet.) momentary closure of vocal passage as in formation of stop consonants; (chem.) absorption of gases by certain substances.

oc·clu·sive (*o*klōō′sĭv) *adj.* Tending to occlude; (phonet., of a consonant) produced with occlusion. **oc·clu′sive·ness** *n.*

oc·cult[1] (*o*kŭlt′, ŏk′ŭlt) *adj.* Kept secret, esoteric; recondite, mysterious, beyond the range of ordinary knowledge; involving the supernatural, mystical, magical; **the ~**, the supernatural. **oc·cult′ly** *adv.* **oc·cult′ness** *n.*

*Originally considered as a river encircling the land of the known world, the name **ocean** was retained when its immensity was later assessed. The name was also applied to certain areas such as the Atlantic (1), Pacific (2) and Antarctic (3) which separate the continents.*

oc·cult[2] (*o*kŭlt′) *v.* Conceal, cut off from view by passing in front (usu. astron.); **occult′ing light**, in lighthouse etc., light that is cut off at regular intervals.

oc·cul·ta·tion (ŏkŭltā′sh*o*n) *n.* (astron.) Eclipse of one heavenly body by another, usu. larger, passing between it and the Earth.

oc·cult·ism (*o*kŭl′tĭzem) *n.* Theory of, belief in, occult forces and powers. **oc·cult′ist** *n.* & *adj.*

oc·cu·pant (ŏk′y*u*p*a*nt) *n.* Person holding property, esp. land, in actual possession; one who occupies, resides in, or is in, a place; one who establishes title to ownerless thing by taking possession. **oc·cu·pan·cy** (ŏk′y*u*p*a*nsē) *n.*

oc·cu·pa·tion (ŏky*u*pā′sh*o*n) *n.* 1. Occupying or being occupied; taking or holding possession, esp. of country or district by military force; tenure, occupancy. 2. What occupies one, means of filling one's time; temporary or regular employment, business, calling, pursuit. **oc·cu·pa′tion·al** *adj.* (esp. of disease etc.) Incidental to, caused by, one's occupation; **~ therapy**,

therapy employing purposeful occupation, as handicrafts, cultural activities, etc.

oc·cu·py (ŏk′yupī) *v.t.* (**-pied, -py·ing**). Take possession of (country etc.) by military force or settlement; hold (office); reside in, tenant; take up or fill (space, time); be in (place, position); keep engaged. **oc′cu·pi·a·ble** *adj.* **oc′cu·pi·er** *n.* Person in (esp. temporary or subordinate) possession, esp. of land or house; holder, occupant.

oc·cur (*o*kẽr′) *v.i.* (**oc·curred, oc·cur·ring**). Be met with, be found, exist, in some place or conditions; come into one's mind; come into being at a point or period of time.

oc·cur·rence (*o*kẽr′*e*ns, *o*kŭr′-) *n.* Happening; incident, event. **oc·cur′rent** *adj.*

o·cean (ō′sh*a*n) *n.* Great body of water surrounding the land of the globe; one of the main areas into which this is geographically divided (usu. reckoned as five, the **Atlantic, Pacific, Indian, Arctic** and **Antarctic**); the sea; immense expanse or quantity of anything.

O·ce·an·i·a (ōshēăn′ē*a*, -ah′nē*a*). Islands of the central, western, and southern Pacific Ocean, usually including Australasia, New Zealand, and Malaysia. **O·ce·an′i·an** *adj.* & *n.*

o·ce·an·ic (ōshēăn′ĭk) *adj.* Of the ocean; **O~**, of Oceania.

O·ce·a·nid (ōsē′*a*nĭd) *n.* (pl. **O·ce·an·i·des** pr. ōsēăn′ĭdēz). (Gk. myth.) One of the ocean nymphs, daughters of Oceanus and Tethys.

o·cea·nog·ra·phy (ōsh*a*nŏg′-r*a*fē) *n.* Branch of science concerned with the study of the ocean, the composition and characteristics of the water, plant, and animal life, and the ocean floor. **o·cea·nog′ra·pher** *n.*

O·ce·a·nus (ōsē′*a*n*u*s). (Gk. myth.) Son of Uranus and Ge, and father of the Oceanids and river gods; personification of the river encircling the whole world.

o·ce·lot (ŏs′*e*lŏt, ō′s*e*-) *n.* One of the larger cats (*Felis pardalis*) of Central and S. America, with gray body marked with elongated fawn spots edged with black, and white or whitish underparts marked with black.

o·cher, o·chre (ō′k*e*r) *ns.* Mineral or class of minerals consisting of hydrated ferric oxide mixed with varying proportions of clay, used as pigment, ranging in color from light yellow to deep orange or brown. **o′cher·ous, o·chre·ous** (ō′k*e*r*u*s, ō′krē*u*s) *adjs.*

Ocelot

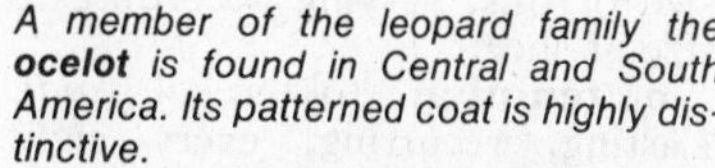

A member of the leopard family the ***ocelot*** *is found in Central and South America. Its patterned coat is highly distinctive.*

Ock·ham or **Oc·cam** (ŏk′*a*m), **William of** (*c*1300–*c*1349). English scholastic philosopher; founded a speculative sect reviving the doctrines of Nominalism; **Ockham's razor**, principle that assumptions introduced to explain something must not be unnecessarily multiplied.

o'clock (*o*klŏk′) *adv.* (of time) By the clock.

O'Con·nell (ōkŏn′*e*l), **Daniel** (1775–1847). Irish political leader who championed liberation of the Irish catholics and separation of Ireland from Gt. Britain.

OCS *abbrev.* Officer Candidate School.

Oct. *abbrev.* October.

oct. *abbrev.* Octavo.

octa-, oct- *prefixes.* Eight.

oc·tad (ŏk′tăd) *n.* Group of eight. **oc·tad′ic** *adj.*

oc·ta·gon (ŏk′t*a*gŏn) *n.* Plane figure of eight angles and sides; object or building of such section. **oc·tag·o·nal** (ŏktăg′*o*n*a*l) *adj.* **oc·tag′o·nal·ly** *adv.*

oc·ta·he·dron (ŏkt*a*hē′dr*o*n) *n.* (pl. **-drons, -dra** pr. -dr*a*). Solid figure of eight faces, usu. eight triangles; body, esp. crystal, of regular octahedral form; **regular ~**, figure contained by eight equal and equilateral triangles. **oc·ta·he′dral** *adj.*

oc·tane (ŏk′tān) *n.* (chem.) Hydrocarbon of the paraffin series (C_8H_{18}); **~ number**, measure of the knock prevention properties of gasoline; **high ~**, (of gasoline) having good antiknock properties.

oc·tave (ŏk′tĭv, -tāv) *n.* 1. (eccles.) Eighth day after a festival (both days being counted); period of eight days beginning with a festival. 2. Group or stanza of eight lines, octet. 3. (mus.) Note eight diatonic degrees above or below given note (both notes being counted), and produced by vibrations of twice or half the rate,

Oceania *includes many groups of small islands. At left, Pago Pago in American Samoa, Polynesia.*

interval between any note and its octave; series of notes etc. extending through this interval; two notes an octave apart played or sung together; organ stop sounding an octave higher than ordinary pitch.

Oc·ta·vi·a (ŏktā′vē*a*) (d. 11 B.C.). Sister of Augustus and wife of Mark Antony.

oc·ta·vo (ŏktā′vō, -tah′-) *n.* (pl. **-vos**). (abbrevs. 8vo, oct.). Book or page given by folding sheets three times or into eight leaves; size of this, varying according to size of sheet.

oc·ten·ni·al (ŏktĕn′ē*a*l) *adj.* Lasting, recurring, every eight years.

oc·tet, oc·tette (ŏktĕt′) *ns.* (Composition for) eight voices or instruments in combination; set of eight; group of eight lines, esp. the first eight of a sonnet.

octo-, oct- *prefixes.* Eight.

Oc·to·ber (ŏktō′ber). Tenth month of Gregorian (eighth of Julian) calendar, with 31 days; ~ **Revolution**: see Russian REVOLUTION. [L. *octo* eight]

Oc·to·brist (ŏktō′brĭst) *n.* Member of Russian moderate liberal political party, whose principles of constitutional government were proclaimed in the imperial Manifesto of Oct. 1905.

oc·to·dec·i·mo (ŏkt*o*dĕs′*i*mō) *n.* (pl. **-mos**). (abbrev. 18mo) (Size of) book or page given by folding sheets into 18 leaves.

oc·to·ge·nar·i·an (ŏkt*o*jenār′-ē*a*n) *adj.* & *n.* (Person) aged 80 years or more but less than 90.

oc·to·pod (ŏk′t*o*pŏd) *n.* Cephalopod of the order Octopoda with eight arms.

oc·to·pus (ŏk′t*o*p*u*s) *n.* (pl. **-puses, -pi** pr. pī). Cephalopod mollusk with eight arms, provided with suckers, surrounding mouth.

oc·to·roon (ŏkt*o*rōōn′) *n.* Person of one-eighth black parentage.

oc·to·syl·lab·ic (ŏktōsĭlăb′ĭk) *adj.* & *n.* Eight-syllable (verse).

oc·to·syl·la·ble (ŏk′t*o*sĭl*a*bel) *n.* (Verse, word) of eight syllables.

oc·tu·ple (ŏk′t*u*pel) *adj.* Eightfold. ~ *n.* Product (*of*) after multiplication by 8. ~ *v.t.* (**-pled, -pling**). Multiply by 8.

oc·u·lar (ŏk′y*u*ler) *adj.* Of, for, by, with, etc., the eye(s) or sight, visual. ~ *n.* Eyepiece of optical instrument.

Ranging in size from an inch or two across the longest arms, to a span of several feet, only the blue-ringed **octopus** *of Australia is dangerous to man. Most can adapt their color to their surroundings.*

oc·u·list (ŏk′y*u*lĭst) *n.* 1. Medical practitioner who specializes in diseases of the eye; ophthalmologist. 2. Optometrist.

OD (ōdē′) *n.* (slang) Overdose, esp. of a narcotic. ~ *v.i.* (**OD'd, OD'ing**) (ōdēd′, ōdē′ing). Take an overdose of a narcotic sufficient to cause death.

O.D. *abbrev.* Doctor of optometry; officer of the day.

o.d. *abbrev.* Olive drab; outside diameter.

o·da·lisque, o·da·lisk (ō′d*a*lĭsk) *ns.* (hist.) Eastern female slave or concubine, esp. in Turkish sultan's seraglio. [Fr., f. Turk. *odalik*]

odd (ŏd) *adj.* 1. Remaining over after division or distribution into pairs; (of number) not exactly divisible by 2; numbered or known by such a number; (appended to number, sum, weight, etc.) with something over of lower denomination etc. by which round number, given sum, etc., is exceeded. 2. Additional, casual, beside the reckoning, unconnected, unoccupied, incalculable; forming part of incomplete pair or set. 3. Extraordinary, strange, queer, remarkable, eccentric. 4. **O ~ Fellow**, member of Independent Order of Odd Fellows (founded prob. in early part of 18th c.) with rites imitative of freemasonry; **odd job,** casual disconnected piece of work. **odd'ly** *adv.* **odd'ness** *n.* **odd** *n.* Anything odd.

odd·i·ty (ŏd′ĭtē) *n.* (pl. **-ties**). Strangeness; peculiar trait; queer person; fantastic object, strange event.

odds (ŏdz) *n.pl.* Inequalities; difference; variance, strife; balance of advantage; equalizing allowance to weaken competitor; ratio between amounts staked by parties to bet, advantage conceded by one of the parties in proportion to assumed chances in his favor; chances or balance of probability in favor of some result; ~ **and ends**, remnants, stray articles; ~**-on** (*adj.*), (of chance or probability) in favor of some result etc.

ode (ōd) *n.* 1. (orig.) Poem meant to be sung; **choral** ~, song of chorus in Greek play etc. 2. Rhymed (or, rarely, unrhymed) lyric, often in form of address, usu. of exalted style and enthusiastic tone, often in varied or irregular meter, and usu. between 50 and 200 lines in length.

O·der (ō′der). River rising in N. central Czechoslovakia and flowing 560 miles (901 km) NW. through Poland and E. Germany to the Baltic Sea.

O·din (ō′dĭn). (Scand. myth.) Supreme god and creator, god of

victory and the dead; represented as an old one-eyed man of great wisdom.

o·di·ous (ō′dēus) *adj.* Hateful, repulsive. **o′di·ous·ly** *adv.* **o′di·ous·ness** *n.*

o·di·um (ō′dēum) *n.* General or widespread dislike or reprobation incurred by person or attaching to action.

o·dom·e·ter (ōdŏm′ĭter) *n.* Instrument for measuring distance traveled.

o·dor, Brit. **o·dour** (ō′der) *ns.* Pleasant or unpleasant smell; fragrance; (fig.) savor, trace; ~ **of sanctity**, sweet or balsamic odor supposed to be exhaled by dying or exhumed saint; reputation for holiness. **o′dor·ful, o′dor·less** *adjs.*

o·dor·if·er·ous (ōderĭf′erus) *adj.* Diffusing scent, fragrant. **o·dor·if′er·ous·ly** *adv.* **o·dor·if′er·ous·ness** *n.*

o·dor·ous (ō′derus) *adj.* Odoriferous. **o′dor·ous·ly** *adv.*

O·dys·se·us (ōdĭs′ēus, ōdĭs′ūs). (Gk. legend) King of Ithaca, called Ulysses by the Romans; renowned for cunning; he was a leader of the Greeks in the Trojan War, and after it Poseidon kept him from home a further ten years while his wife PENELOPE waited in Ithaca. **Od·ys·sey** (ŏd′ĭsē) *n.* Greek epic poem attributed to Homer, in 24 books, describing the wanderings and return of Odysseus.

od·ys·sey (ŏd′ĭsē) *n.* (pl. **-seys**). Long adventurous journey.

OECD *abbrev.* Organization for

*During a war, an **offensive** is an attempt by one side to gain advantage over the other. In Vietnam in 1968, (left) the civilians suffered more than the armies.*

Economic Cooperation and Development.

O.E.D. *abbrev.* Oxford English Dictionary.

Oed·i·pus (ĕd′ipus, ē′di-). (Gk. legend) Son of Laius king of Thebes, and Jocasta; he unwittingly killed his father and married his mother, and when the facts were discovered, went mad and put out his eyes, while Jocasta hanged herself; ~ **complex**, (psychol.) manifestation of infantile sexuality in relations of (esp. male) child to parents, with attraction towards parent of opposite sex and jealousy of other parent.

oe·no·phile (ē′nofīl) *n.* Connoisseur of wines.

o'er (ōr, ōr) *adv.* & *prep.* (poet.) = OVER.

oer·sted (ĕr′stĕd) *n.* Unit of magnetic intensity in cgs electromagnetic system. [Hans Christian *Oersted* (1777–1851), Danish physicist]

oeu·vre (ö′vre) *n.* (pl. ***oeu·vres*** pr. ö′vre). (Totality of) works of an author, painter, composer, etc. [F., = work, f. L. *opera*]

of (ŭv, ŏv, ov) *prep.* From; concerning; out of; among; relating to.

off (awf, ŏf) *adv.* Away, at or to a distance; (so as to be) out of position, not on or touching or dependent or attached; loose, separate, gone; so as to break continuity or continuance, discontinued, stopped, not obtainable, abstaining from, averse to; to the end, entirely, so as to be clear; (of food) deteriorated, unfit for consumption; **well, badly, comfortably,** etc., ~, so circumstanced or supplied with money; ~ **and on**, intermittently, waveringly, now and again. **off** *prep.* From; away, down or up from; disengaged or distant from; (so as to be) no longer on; **offcol′or**, offensive, risqué; (of person) slightly unwell; **off′-hand** (*adj.*), extempore, without premeditation, curt, casual, unceremonious; **off′hand′edly** (*adv.*); **off′hand′edness** (*n.*); **off′load**: see own entry; **off-peak**, outside peak hours; **off′print, off′shoot**: see own entries; **off′shore′** (*adv.* & *adj.*), a short way out to sea; **offshore wind**, one blowing out to sea; **off′side′** (*adj.* & *adv.*), (soccer, hockey) of a player in a position on the field where he may not kick, handle, or hit the ball or puck; (football) beyond the line of scrimmage before a play begins; **off-the-record** (*adj.*), not for publication or quotation; **off-the-shelf** (*adj.*), readily available, easily adaptable; **off′spring**: see own entry; **off′track′** (*adj.*), pertaining to legalized horse race gambling away from a track; **off** *adj.* 1. Farther, far; (of horse or vehicle) right (opp. NEAR; so **offside**). 2. Subordinate, divergent; disengaged. 3. ~ **chance**, slight or remote chance; ~**-season**, season when business is less active than usual. **off** *v.* (slang) Kill.

of·fal (aw′fal, ŏf′al) *n.* Refuse, waste stuff, scraps, garbage; parts cut off in dressing carcass of animal killed for food, orig. entrails, now a trade term for edible organs such as liver, kidneys, etc.; carrion, putrid flesh.

of·fend (ofĕnd′) *v.* 1. Commit an offense (*against*). 2. Wound feelings of, anger, cause resentment or disgust in, outrage. **of·fend′ed·ness, of·fend′er** *ns.*

of·fense (ofĕns′, ŏf′ĕns) *n.* 1. Attacking, aggressive action. 2. Wounding of the feelings; wounded feeling, annoyance, umbrage. 3. Transgression, misdemeanor, illegal act. **of·fense′less** *adj.*

of·fen·sive (ofĕn′sĭv, aw′fĕn-, ŏf′ĕn-) *adj.* 1. Aggressive, intended for or used in attack. 2. Meant to give offense, insulting. 3. Disgusting, repulsive. **of·fen′sive·ly** *adv.* **of·fen′sive·ness** *n.* **offensive** *n.* Attitude of assailant, aggressive action; attack, offensive campaign or stroke.

of·fer (aw′fer, ŏf′er) *v.* 1. Present to deity, revered person, etc., by way of sacrifice; give in worship or devotion. 2. Hold out in hand, or tender in words or otherwise, for acceptance or refusal; make proposal of marriage; show for sale; give opportunity to enemy for (battle); express readiness *to* to; essay, try to show (violence etc.); show an intention *to* do. 3. Present to sight or notice; present itself, occur. ~ *n.* Expression of readiness to give or do if desired, or to sell on terms; proposal, esp. of marriage; bid. **of′fer·ing** *n.* Thing offered.

of·fer·to·ry (aw′fertōrē, -tōrē, ŏf′er-) *n.* (pl. **-ries**). Part of Mass or Communion service at which offerings are made, offering of these, gifts offered; collection of money at religious service.

of·fice (aw′fĭs, ŏf′ĭs) *n.* 1. Act of kindness, attention, service. 2. Duty attaching to one's position, task, function. 3. Position with duties attached to it; place of authority, trust, or service, esp. of public kind; tenure of official position, esp. that of minister of state. 4. Ceremonial duty; (eccles.) authorized form of worship; (chants at beginning of) Mass or Communion service, any occasional service. 5. Place for transacting business; room etc. in which clerks and others work; consulting room of doctor etc. 6. Quarters, staff,

1

2

3

*In an attempt to discover fresh reserves of **oil,** there is increasing exploration for submarine oil-fields. When suitable sites have been located, an oil rig, built ashore, is towed to the site (1). It is then dropped on to the sea bed (2) and levelled so that drilling machinery aboard the rig (3) can be used to penetrate the sea bed.*

or collective authority of a business department etc.

of·fic·er (aw′fĭs*er*, ŏf′ĭ-) *n.* 1. Holder of public, civil, or ecclesiastical office; appointed or elected functionary; president, treasurer, secretary, etc., of company; policeman. 2. Person holding authority in armed forces or merchant marine, esp. one with a commission in the armed forces.

of·fi·cial (ofĭsh′*a*l) *adj.* Of an office, the discharge of duties, or the tenure of an office; holding office, employed in public capacity; derived from or vouched for by person(s) in office, properly authorized; usual with persons in office. **of·fi′cial·ly** *adv.* **of·fi·cial·dom** (ofĭsh′*a*ld*o*m), **of·fi′cial·ism** *ns.* **of·fi′cial·ize** *v.t.* (**-ized, -iz·ing**). **official** *n.* Person holding public office or engaged in official duties.

of·fi·ci·ate (ofĭsh′ēāt) *v.i.* (**-at·ed, -at·ing**). Discharge priestly office, perform divine service; act in some official capacity, esp. on particular occasion. **of·fi·ci·ant** (*o*fĭsh′ē*a*nt) *n.*

of·fi·cious (ofĭsh′*u*s) *adj.* (Given to) offering service that is not wanted, doing or undertaking more than is required, intrusive, meddlesome. **of·fi′cious·ly** *adv.* **of·fi′cious·ness** *n.*

off·ing (aw′fĭng, ŏf′ĭng) *n.* Part of visible sea distant from shore or beyond anchoring ground; position at distance from shore; **in the ~**, (fig.) nearby; ready or likely to appear.

off·ish (aw′fĭsh, ŏf′ĭsh) *adj.* (colloq.) Inclined to aloofness. **off′ish·ly** *adv.* **off′ish·ness** *n.*

off·load (awf′lōd′, ŏf′-) *v.* (colloq.) Unload (vehicle, airplane, or ship).

off·print (awf′prĭnt, ŏf′-) *n.* Separate copy of article etc. that was originally part of larger publication.

off·set (awf′sĕt, ŏf′-) *n.* 1. Short side shoot from stem or root serving for propagation; offshoot, scion. 2. Compensation, setoff, consideration or amount diminishing or neutralizing effect of contrary one. 3. (surv.) Short distance measured perpendicularly from main line of measurement. 4. (archit.) Sloping ledge in wall etc. where thickness of part above is diminished. 5. Bend made in pipe to carry it past obstacle. 6. (printing, engraving) Transfer of ink from a newly printed surface to another surface so that the final impression is in the same sense as the plate or type (**~ proof**, engraver's trial proof made thus as aid to working); **~ lithography**, method of printing in which ink is transferred from a lithographic stone or plate to a rubber roller and thence, while still wet, to paper. **offset** (awfsĕt′, ŏf-) *v.t.* (**-set, -set·ting**). Counterbalance, compensate for; print by

1 

2 

To cope with increasing demands for crude oil, tanker sizes have increased and many more ***oil-tankers*** *(1) have been built. If these ships are wrecked (2) there is grave risk of pollution from the spillage.*

offset.

off·shoot (awf′sho͞ot, ŏf′-) *n.* Side shoot or branch; derivative.

off·spring (awf′sprĭng, ŏf′-) *n.* (pl. **-spring, -springs**). Descendant.

oft (awft, ŏft) *adv.* Often (archaic exc. in comb.); **oft′times**, (archaic) often.

of·ten (aw′f*e*n, ŏf′*e*n sometimes awf′ten, ŏf′-) *adv.* Many times, at short intervals; in many instances; **of′tentimes**, (archaic) often.

o·gee (ō′jē) *n.* S-shaped curve; ~ **arch**, arch with two ogee curves meeting at apex.

og·ham, og·am (ŏg′*a*m, aw′-g*a*m) *ns.* Ancient British and Irish alphabet of characters formed by parallel strokes arranged along either side of, or crossing, continuous medial line, e.g. edge of stone; inscription in this; one of the characters.

B H M A
L D G O
V or F T NG U
S C ST or Z E
N Q R I
X as vowel, E; as consonant, C.
OGHAM

o·give (ō′jīv, ōjīv′) *n.* Diagonal groin or rib of vault; pointed or Gothic arch. **o·gi′val** *adj.*

o·gle (ō′g*e*l) *v.* (**o·gled, o·gling**). Cast amorous glances, eye amorously. ~ *n.* Amorous glance.

O·gle·thorpe (ō′g*e*lthōrp), **James Edward** (1696–1785). English army officer, member of Parliament, and humanitarian; founder of the American colony of Georgia, 1733.

OGPU = G.P.U.

o·gre (ō′g*e*r) *n.* (fem. **o·gress** pr. ō′grĭs). (in legend etc.) Man-eating giant; hence, terrifying person. **o′gre·ish** (o′g*e*rĭsh), **o′grish** *adjs.*

OH *abbrev.* Ohio.

oh (ō) = O[2].

O'Har·a (ōhăr′*a*, ōhār′*a*), **John (Henry)** (1905–70). American novelist and short-story writer; author of "Pal Joey" and the novels *Appointment in Samarra, Butterfield 8*, etc.

O·hi·o (ōhī′ō). State in mid-western U.S. between Ohio River in the S. and Lake Erie in the N.; admitted to the Union in 1803; capital, Columbus; ~ **River**, river formed by the Allegheny and Monongahela Rivers at Pittsburgh, Pennsylvania, and flowing 900 miles (1,449 km) SW. to the Mississippi at Cairo, Illinois; chief eastern tributary of the Mississippi.

ohm (ōm) *n.* Unit of electrical resistance, resistance of a circuit in which potential difference of one volt produces current of one ampere. **ohm·ic** (ō′mĭk) *adj.* [f. OHM]

Ohm (ōm), **Georg Simon** (1787–1854). German physicist who determined mathematically the law of the flow of electricity.

oil (oil) *n.* 1. One of a large group of liquid viscid substances with characteristic smooth and sticky feel, lighter than water and insoluble in it, inflammable, and chemically neutral, used as lubricants, in perfumery etc. (**essential** or **volatile** ~), and as fuel etc. (**mineral** ~); **drying** ~, any of those oils which by exposure to air harden into varnishes; **nondrying** ~, one that decomposes by exposure, used as lubricant, in making soap, etc. 2. Oil color (freq. pl.). 3. (pl.) Oilskins. 4. **oil′can**, can for holding oil, esp. with long nozzle for oiling machinery; **oil′cloth**, fabric waterproofed with oil, oilskin; canvas coated with preparation containing drying oil, used to cover tables etc.; **oil color**, paint made by grinding pigment in a drying oil; **oil field**, tract of petroleum-bearing strata; **oil paint**, oil color; **oil painting**, art of painting, picture painted, in oil colors; **oil′paper**, paper made transparent or waterproof by soaking in oil; **oil shale**, rock from which petroleum can be produced by distillation; **oil′skin**, cloth waterproofed with a drying oil; garment or (pl.) coat and trousers of this; **oil′stone**, fine-grained stone used with oil as whetstone; **oil well**, well yielding petroleum. **oil** *v.* 1. Apply oil to, lubricate. 2. Turn into oily liquid. 3. Impregnate or treat with oil. **oiled** (oild) *adj.* (slang) Slightly drunk.

oil·er (oi′l*e*r) *n.* Oilcan for oiling machinery; ship built for carrying oil.

oil·y (oi′lē) *adj.* (**oil·i·er, oil·i·est**). 1. Of, like, covered or soaked with, containing much, oil. 2. (of manner etc.) Fawning, too smooth. **oil′i·ness** *n.*

oint·ment (oint′m*e*nt) *n.* Emollient preparation applied to skin to heal or beautify, unguent.

O·jib·wa (ōjĭb′wā, -wa) *n.* (pl. **-was**, collect. **-wa**). (Member of a) tribe of N. Amer. Indians of Algonquian linguistic stock, inhabiting region around the Great Lakes.

O·jib·way (ōjĭb′wā) *n.* (pl. **-ways**, collect. **-way**) = OJIBWA.

OK *abbrev.* Oklahoma.

O.K., o·kay (ō′kā′, ōkā′) *adjs.* (orig. slang) All right. ~ *n.* (pl. **O.K.'s**) & *v.t.* (**O.K.'d, O.K.'ing**). (Mark with) the letters "O.K.," esp. as denoting approval of contents of document etc.; sanction. [possibly initials of *Old Kinderhook* (Kinderhook, near Albany, New York, birthplace of Democratic candidate, Martin van Buren) used *c*1840 as a slogan and passing into a term of approval, being interpreted as abbreviation of *oll korrect*, misspelling of *all correct*]

o·ka·pi (ōkah′pē) *n.* (pl. **-pis**, collect. **-pi**). Rare ungulate mammal, *Okapia johnstoni*, related to giraffes, found in dense forests of W. Africa.

o·kay (ō′kā′, ōkā′) *adj.* & *v.t.* = O.K.

O·kee·cho·bee (ōkēchō′bē), **Lake.** Lake, over 700 square miles (1,813 sq. km), in S. central Florida, 40 miles (65 km) NW. of Palm Beach; second largest lake wholly within the U.S.; part of cross-Florida waterway.

O' Keeffe (ō kēf′), **Georgia** (1887–1986). American landscape painter, especially of desert scenes.

O·ki·na·wa (ōkĭnah′wa). Largest of the Ryuku Islands, 794 square miles (2,057 sq. km) S. of Japan; scene of heavy fighting in World War II.

Okla. *abbrev.* Oklahoma.

O·kla·ho·ma (ōklahō′ma). State in southwestern U.S. between Texas on the S. and Kansas on the N.; admitted to the Union in 1907; capital, Oklahoma City.

o·kra (ō′kra) *n.* Tall malvaceous African plant (*Hibiscus esculentus*, called also *gumbo*) cultivated in W. Indies, southern U.S., etc., the young fruits of which are used as a vegetable and for thickening soups, and the stem fibers for ropes.

O·laf (ō′lahf). Name of two kings of Norway; **Olaf I Tryggvason** (*c*969–1000), king 995–1000; raided coast of France and British Isles but ceased when he became a Christian; hero of many legends; **Olaf II** (995–1030), "St. Olaf," patron saint of Norway; king of Norway 1015–28.

old (ōld) *adj.* (**old·er, old·est** or **eld·er, eld·est**). 1. Advanced in age, far on in natural period of existence, not young or near its beginning; having characteristics, experience, feebleness, etc., of age; worn, dilapidated, shabby. 2. (appended to period of time) Of age (as **ten years** ~); (ellipt.) person or animal, esp. race horse, of specified age (as **three-year-**~). 3. Practiced or inverterate *in* action or quality, or as agent etc. 4. Dating from far back; made long ago; long established, known, familiar, or dear; ancient, not new or recent, primeval; (of language) belonging to the earliest known period or stage; **of** ~ **standing**, long established. 5. Belonging only or chiefly to the past; obsolete, obsolescent, out of date, antiquated, antique; concerned with antiquity; not modern, bygone, former. 6. ~ **age pension(er)**, (person receiving) retirement pension; **O**~ **Believers**, Russian sect originating in 17th c. in protest against liturgical reforms; ~**-clothes man**, dealer in discarded clothes; **O**~ **Colony**, part of Massachusetts within original limits of Plymouth colony; ~ **countries**, countries long inhabited or civilized; **the** ~ **country, home**, etc., (used by emigrants etc. of) mother country; **O**~ **Dominion**, Virginia; ~ **English sheepdog**, medium-sized breed of dog with very long, shaggy whitish coat and short or no tail; **O**~ **Faithful**, geyser in Yellowstone National Park, Wyoming, erupting regulary at intervals of a little over an hour; ~**-fashioned**, belonging to a fashion that has gone or is going out; **O**~ **Fashioned**, cocktail of whiskey, bitters, etc.; **O**~ **Glory**, the Stars and Stripes; ~ **gold**, color of tarnished gold; ~ **guard**, established influential conservative group; ~ **hand**, practiced workman; person of experience in (*at*) something; **O**~ **Ironsides**, popular name of Amer. frigate, Constitution, active in War of 1812 and subject of poem by Oliver Wendell Holmes; **O**~ **Hickory**, nickname of Andrew JACKSON[2], from his toughness of character; ~ **lady**, (colloq.) mother or wife; ~ **maid**, (derog.) elderly spinster; person who is overly precise; (cards) game in which object is to avoid holding of unpaired card; ~**-maidish** (*adj*); ~ **man** (naut. slang) ship's captain; (colloq.) father or husband; ~ **man of the sea**, (from character in Arabian Nights tale of Sindbad the Sailor) person who cannot be shaken off; ~ **master**, (painting by) great painter of former times, esp. 13th–17th centuries in Europe; ~ **school tie**, necktie of characteristic pattern as worn by former members of a particular British school; used symbolically to denote extreme loyalty to a traditional mode of thought or behavior; **O**~ **Stone Age**, PALEOLITHIC age; **O**~ **Testament**: see TESTAMENT; ~-

*Related to the giraffe and living only in dense rainforests in central Africa, the **okapi** was first found by zoologists in 1901. Females are larger than males and have a shoulder height of 5 ft.*

time, of former times; **~-timer**, one whose experience goes back to old times; one of long standing; old-fashioned person or thing; **O~ Vic** (vĭk), theater in London; **~ wives' tale**: see WIFE; **~ woman**, (colloq.) wife; fussy or timid man; **O~ World**, eastern hemisphere; **O~-world**, of the Old World, not American; **~ year**, year just ended or about to end. **old'ish** *adj.* **old** *n.* Old time (only in **of old** (*adj.* & *adv.*) as *men of old, of old there were giants*). **old'ness** *n.*

old·en (ōl'd*e*n) *adj.* (archaic and literary) Old-time, of a former age.

old·ster (ōld'st*e*r) *n.* Old person.

Ol·du·vai (awl'do͞ovī) **Gorge.** Gorge along line of fault in N. Tanzania, 150 miles (242 km) W. of Mt. Kilimanjaro; archaeological site containing many fossil beds and remains of early man.

o·le·a·ceous (ōlēā'sh*u*s) *adj.* Of the Oleaceae or olive family of plants, including jasmine etc.

o·le·ag·i·nous (ōlēăj'*i*n*u*s) *adj.* Having properties of or producing oil; oily, fatty, greasy.

o·le·an·der (ō'lēănd*e*r, ōlēăn'-) *n.* Evergreen poisonous Levantine shrub (*Nerium oleander*) with leathery lanceolate leaves and handsome red or white flowers.

o·le·fin (ō'l*e*fĭn) *n.* (chem.) Any member of the ethylene series of hydrocarbons.

o·le·o·mar·ga·rine (ōlēōmar'-j*a*rĭn, -rēn) *n.* Fatty substance extracted from clarified beef fat and made into margarine with addition of butyrin, milk, etc.; margarine.

o·le·o·res·in (ōlēōrĕz'ĭn) *n.* Natural product containing a volatile oil and a resin, e.g. exudation from coniferous tree.

ol·fac·tion (ŏlfăk'sh*o*n, ōl-) *n.* Smelling, sense of smell. **ol·fac'·tive** *adj.* **ol·fac·to·ry** (ŏlfăk't*e*rē, ōl-) *adj.* Concerned with smelling.

ol·i·garch (ŏl'*i*gark) *n.* Member of oligarchy.

ol·i·gar·chy (ŏl'*i*garkē) *n.* (pl. **-chies**). Government, state governed, by a few persons; members of such a government. **ol·i·gar·chic** (ŏl*i*gar'kĭk), **ol·i·gar'chi·cal** *adjs.* **ol·i·gar'chi·cal·ly** *adv.*

Ol·i·go·cene (ŏl'*i*gōsēn) *adj.* & *n.* (geol.) (Of) the third epoch or system of the Tertiary period.

ol·i·gop·o·ly (ŏl*i*gŏp'*o*lē) *n.* State of market allowing limited competition between few producers or sellers.

o·li·o (ō'lēō) *n.* (pl. **o·li·os**). Mixed dish, hotchpotch, stew of various meats and vegetables; medley, miscellany.

ol·i·va·ceous (ŏl*i*vā'sh*u*s) *adj.* Olive-green, of dusky yellowish

ol·i·va·ry (ŏl'*i*vĕrē) *adj.* (anat.) Olive-shaped, oval.

ol·ive (ŏl'ĭv) *n.* 1. Evergreen

*The **Old Faithful** geyser in Yellowstone National Park. Geysers are incorrectly supposed to erupt at regular intervals. Even Old Faithful erupts at varying intervals.*

tree (*Olea europaea*), esp. the cultivated variety, with narrow leaves green above and hoary below and axillary clusters of small whitish flowers, bearing small oval drupes, blackish when ripe, with bitter pulp abounding in oil, and hard stone, cultivated in Mediterranean countries etc. for its fruit and oil; fruit of this tree; any tree of the genus *Olea*, tree or shrub resembling this. 2. Leaf, branch, or wreath of olive as emblem of peace. 3. Olive-shaped gastropod mollusk (*Oliva*). 4. Olive color. 5. **~ branch**, branch of olive tree, esp. as emblem of peace (freq. fig.); **~ oil**, clear, pale-yellow, non-drying oil obtained from pulp of olives, used in cooking, salads, as a medicine, as a lubricant, and in the manufacture of toilet soap, etc., **~ drab**, grayish olive color of U.S. Army uniform; hence, (slang) **~ drabs**, such a uniform; **Mount of Olives**, ridge facing Temple mount at Jerusalem on the east, with Garden of Gethsemane on western slope. **olive** *adj.* Colored like unripe olive, dull yellowish green; (of complexion etc.) brownish yellow; of color of olive foliage, dull ashy green with silvery sheen.

__Olives__ have been eaten and pressed for their oil for centuries. Europe cultivates more than 75 per cent of the world's olive crop.

O·liv·i·er (ōlĭv'ēā), **Sir Laurence (Kerr)** (1907–). English actor and director.

Olm·sted (ōm'stĕd), **Frederick Law** (1822–1903). Amer. landscape architect; cooperated with Calvert Vaux on design of Central Park in New York City, designed Prospect Park in Brooklyn, etc.

O·lym·pi·a (ōlĭm'pē*a*). 1. Plain on N. bank of river Alpheus about 20 miles from W. coast of Peloponnese; in ancient Greece a great religious center second only to Delphi, and site of OLYMPIC Games. 2. Capital of state of Washington, on Puget Sound.

o·lym·pi·ad (ōlĭm'pēăd) *n.* (often cap.) 1. Period of four years between celebrations of OLYMPIC Games, used by ancient Greeks in dating events, 776 B.C. being first year of first Olympiad. 2. Meeting of modern Olympic Games.

O·lym·pi·an (ōlĭm'pē*a*n) *adj.* Of Olympus, celestial; (of manners) magnificent, condescending, superior; aloof. **~** *n.* Dweller in Olympus, one of the greater ancient

Greek gods; person of superhuman calm and detachment.

O·lym·pic (ōlĭm′pĭk) *adj.* Of Olympia in Greece; of the Olympic Games; ~ **Games**, (1) athletic contests held by the ancient Greeks every fourth year at Olympia and including foot races, boxing, wrestling, and chariot and horse races; (2) international amateur athletic contests begun in 1896 as revival of ancient Greek games and held every fourth year, organized by an international committee which decides where each festival is to be held, and including athletics, gymnastics, combative sports, swimming, equestrian sports, the pentathlon, and the decathlon. **O·lym′pics** *n.pl.* Olympic Games.

O·lym·pus (ōlĭm′pus), **Mount.** Highest mountain (9,750 feet, 2,972 m) in Greece, about ten miles inland from the Aegean Sea at E. end of range dividing Thessaly from Macedonia; in Greek mythology the court of Zeus and home of the gods.

Om (ŏm). In Hinduism etc., mystic and holy word regarded as summing up all truth.

O·ma·ha (ō′mahah). Industrial city on the Missouri River in E. Nebraska; known for its stockyards and meat-packing plants.

O·ma·ha (ō′mahah) **Beach.** Code name for beach in Normandy, France, as landing place of some units of Amer. troops during invasion of France in World War II, June 6–10, 1944.

O·man (ōmahn′). Sultanate in SE. Arabia; capital, Muscat; **Gulf of** ~, arm of the Arabian Sea, between Oman and Iran, extending toward the Persian Gulf.

O·mar (ō′mār) (*c*581–644). Second Muslim caliph, 634–44; reputed builder of **Mosque of** ~, on platform of Temple at Jerusalem, a much-altered Byzantine church, containing rock on which, acc. to Jewish legend, Abraham prepared to sacrifice Isaac, and from which, acc. to Muslims, Muhammad ascended to heaven.

O·mar Khay·yám (ō′mār kīyahm′, -yăm). ‘Umar Khayyām (*c*1100), Persian astronomer, mathematician and poet; author of the *Rubáiyát*.

o·ma·sum (ōmā′sum) *n.* (pl. **-sa** pr. -sa). Ruminant's third stomach.

OMB *abbrev.* Office of Management and Budget.

om·buds·man (ŏm′bo͝odzman) *n.* (pl. **-men** pr. -men). Official who investigates complaints of maladministration, esp. by government departments. [Swed. = "commissioner"]

o·me·ga (ōmē′ga, ōmā′-, ōmĕg′a) *n.* Last letter of Greek alphabet (Ω, ω), corresponding to *o* (pr. ō). [Gk. = "great o"]

om·e·let, om·e·lette (ŏm′lĭt, ŏm′elĭt) *ns.* Dish of eggs lightly beaten and cooked usu. in butter in a frying pan, often with filling; **Western** ~, omelet with filling of diced ham, green pepper, and onion.

o·men (ō′men) *n.* Event or object portending good or evil; prophetic signification.

om·i·cron (ŏm′ikrŏn, ō′mi-) *n.* Sixteenth (later 15th) letter of Greek alphabet (O, o) corresponding to *o* (pr. ŏ). [Gk., = "small o"]

om·i·nous (ŏm′inus) *adj.* Of evil omen, inauspicious, threatening. **om′i·nous·ly** *adv.* **om′i·nous·ness** *n.*

o·mis·sion (ōmĭsh′on) *n.* Omitting, noninclusion; nonperformance, neglect, duty not done.

o·mit (ōmĭt′) *v.t.* (**o·mit·ted, o·mit·ting**). Leave out, not insert or include; leave undone, neglect *doing*, fail *to* do.

om·ni·bus (ŏm′nibŭs, -bus) *n.* (pl. **-bus·es**). 1. = BUS. 2. Volume containing a number of stories, plays, etc. ~ *adj.* Serving several objects at once; comprising several items. [L., = "for all," i.e. everyone]

om·ni·di·rec·tion·al (ŏmnĭdirĕk′shonal) *adj.* (of antenna etc.) Receiving or transmitting in all directions.

om·nip·o·tence (ŏmnĭp′otens) *n.* Infinite power; God; great influence. **om·nip′o·tent** *adj.* **om·nip′o·tent·ly** *adv.*

om·ni·pres·ence (ŏmniprĕz′ens) *n.* Ubiquity; being widespread or constantly met with. **om·ni·pres′ent** *adj.*

om·nis·cience (ŏmnĭsh′ens) *n.* Infinite knowledge; God; wide information or the affectation of it. **om·nis′cient** *adj.* **om·nis′cient·ly** *adv.*

om·niv·o·rous (ŏmnĭv′erus) *adj.* (of animals) Feeding on both plants and flesh; (fig.) taking in everything, esp. in choice of reading. **om·niv′o·rous·ly** *adv.* **om·niv′o·rous·ness** *n.* **om·ni·vore** (ŏm′nivōr, -vōr) *n.*

om·pha·los (ŏm′falos) *n.* 1. (Gk. antiq.) Boss on shield; conical stone at Delphi supposed to be central point of earth. 2. Center, hub. 3. Navel.

on (ŏn, awn) *prep.* 1. (So as to be) supported by, attached to, covering, or enclosing; ~ **one**, about one's person. 2. With axis, pivot, basis, motive, standard, confirmation, or guarantee, consisting in. 3. (So as to be) close to, in the direction of, touching, arrived at, against, just at. 4. (of time) During, exactly at, contemporaneously with, immediately after, as a result of; ~ **time**, punctual(ly). 5. In manner specified by adjective, or state or action specified by noun; concerning, about, while engaged with, so as to affect; taking (a drug) regularly. 6. Added to. 7. Against (a person); (colloq., esp. of treat of any kind) to be paid for by; **have something** ~, have advantage

Since they were instituted in 1896, by Baron Pierre de Coubertin, the modern ***Olympic Games*** *have been held at four-yearly intervals. However, these games are held in different countries and have far more events than the ones in ancient Greece. Ceremonies open with a parade of competitors (below left), the lighting of the Olympic Flame (below) and impressive stadia are often built for athletic and other events (facing).*

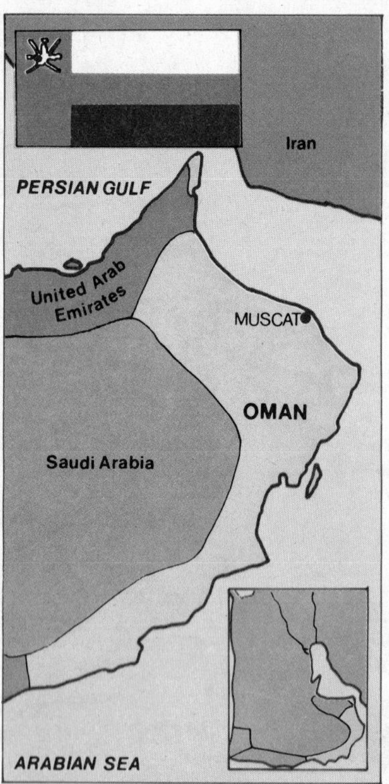

over. **on** *adv.* 1. (So as to be) supported by, attached to, covering, enclosing, or touching, something. 2. In some direction, toward something; farther forward, toward point of contact, in advanced position or state; with continued movement or action, in operation or activity; **broadside, end, head,** etc., ~, with that part forward; ~ **line**, (equipment) operating; ~-**line**, (computers) (carried out while) directly connected to the central processing unit, directly controlled by the computer; **send** ~, send in front of oneself, in advance; **gas, water**, etc., **is** ~, gas, water, etc., is turned on, running, or procurable by turning tap; **get, be,** ~, make, have made, bet. 3. ~ **to** (compound prep. corresponding to *on* as *into* to *in*, but often written as two words), to a position on. **on** *adj.*

on·a·ger (ŏn′*a*j*e*r) *n.* Wild ass, esp. the species *Equus onager* of Central Asia, with broad brown stripe along the back.

o·nan·ism (ō′n*a*nĭz*e*m) *n.* Interrupted coition; masturbation. [f. *Onan* (Gen. 38)]

once (wŭns) *adv.* 1. For one time or on one occasion only; multiplied by one, by one degree; ~ **or twice**, a few times; ~ **(and) for all**, in final manner, definitively; ~ **in a while**, very rarely. 2. (in negative or conditional etc. clause) Ever, at all, even for one or the first time. 3. On a certain but unspecified past occasion; at some period in the past, former(ly). 4. **at** ~, immediately, without

The ancient Muslim Fort Jalali, built on this crag at Muscat, is now the national prison for the Sultanate of **Oman** *in the south of the Arabian Peninsula.*

delay; at the same time; **for (this, that)** ~, on one occasion by way of exception; ~-**over**, (colloq.) single and rapid survey or examination. **once** *conj.* As soon as; if once; when once.

on·col·o·gy (ŏngkŏl′*o*jē) *n.* Science of tumors.

one (wŭn) *adj.* 1. Being, amounting to, the lowest cardinal number, number of a single thing without any more; a; ~ **or two**, a few. 2. Only, without others; forming a unity, united; identical, the same, unchanging; a particular but undefined, to be contrasted with another; **become** ~, coalesce; **made** ~, married. **one** *n.* The lowest cardinal number; its symbol (1, i, or I); one o'clock; size etc. indicated by I; die face or domino with one pip; single thing, person, or example; also, freq. used as substitute for repetition of noun previously expressed or implied; **at** ~, reconciled in agreement; **go** ~ **better**, bid, offer, risk, more by one point; **ten** etc. **to** ~, long odds, high probability; ~ **and all**, all jointly and severally; ~ **another**, formula of reciprocity with *one* orig. subjective and *another* objective or possessive; ~ **too many for**, too hard etc. for ... to deal with; ~ **up (on)**, having gained an advantage (over). **one** *pron.* A particular but unspecified person; person of specified kind; any person, esp. the speaker, spoken of as representing people in general.

one- (wŭn) in comb.: ~-**armed bandit**, (slang) slot machine operated by pulling down armlike handle; ~-**eyed**, having only, blind of, one eye; ~-**horse**, drawn or worked by single horse; (fig.) petty, poorly equipped; ~-**man**, requiring, consisting of, done or managed by, one man; ~-**night stand**, (colloq.) single performance of play, concert, etc., in a place; sexual liaison for a single night; ~-**sided**, having, occurring on, one side only; larger etc. on one side; partial, unfair, prejudiced; ~-**sidedly** (*adv.*), ~-**sidedness** (*n.*); ~-**step**, ballroom dance in quick time with steps resembling walk; **one′time**, former; ~-**track**, (of mind) that is fixed on one line of thought or action; ~-**up·man·ship** (-ŭp′m*a*nshĭp) (*n.*), art or practice of demonstrating superiority to gain advantage; ~-**way**, (of thoroughfares) along which traffic is permitted in one direction only.

O·nei·da (ōnī′d*a*) *n.* (pl. **-das**, collect. **-da**). Member of a N. Amer. Indian tribe of Iroquoian stock, formerly living near Lake Oneida in New York State; ~ **Community**, Christian communist society founded 1848 at Oneida Creek, New York State, by J. H. Noyes (1811–86), whose members held that true sinlessness could be realized through communion with Christ; dissolved (1881).

O'Neill (ōnēl′), **Eugene**

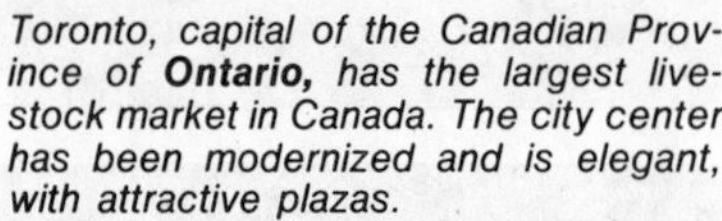

*Toronto, capital of the Canadian Province of **Ontario,** has the largest livestock market in Canada. The city center has been modernized and is elegant, with attractive plazas.*

*One of the first of the wild horse family to be tamed, the **onager** was used by Sumerians about 2,500 B.C. when the rein-ring (above) was made. These wild asses later drew chariots.*

(**Gladstone**) (1888–1953). American playwright, author of *The Emperor Jones, Mourning Becomes Electra, The Iceman Cometh, Ah, Wilderness!*, etc.

one·ness (wŭn′nĭs) *n.* Being one, singleness; singularity, uniqueness; wholeness, unity, union, agreement; identity, changelessness.

on·er·ous (ŏn′*erus*, ō′ner-) *adj.* Burdensome, causing or requiring trouble. **on′er·ous·ly** *adv.* **on′er·ous·ness** *n.*

one·self, one's·self (wŭnsĕlf′, wŭnzsĕlf′) *prons.* Emphatic and reflexive form corresp. to ONE.

on·ion (ŭn′yon) *n.* (Plant, *Allium cepa*, with) edible rounded bulb of close concentric leaves, with pungent smell and flavor, used as culinary vegetable; **on′ionskin,** outermost or any outer coat of onion; very thin smooth translucent kind of paper. **on′ion·y** *adj.*

on·look·er (ŏn′lo͝o*ker*, awn′-) *n.* One who looks on.

on·ly (ōn′lē) *adj.* That is (or are) the one (or all the) specimen(s) of the class, sole. ~ *adv.* Solely, merely, exclusively; and no one or nothing more, besides, or else; and that is all. ~ *conj.* Only thing to be added being; with this restriction, drawback, or exception only; but then.

on·o·mat·o·poe·ia (ŏn*o*măt*o*pē′*a*, -maht*o*-) *n.* Formation of names or words from sounds resembling those associated with the object or action to be named, or seemingly naturally suggestive of its qualities (e.g. *cuckoo, rustle*); word so formed. **on·o·mat·o·poe′ic, on·o·mat·o·po·et·ic** (ŏn*o*măt*o*pōĕt′ĭk, -maht*o*-) *adjs.* **on·o·mat·o·poe′i·cal·ly, on·o·mat·o·po·et′i·cal·ly** *advs.*

On·on·da·ga (ŏn*o*ndaw′g*a*, -dah′-) *n.* (pl. **-gas**, collect. **-ga**). (Member of) a N. Amer. Indian tribe of Iroquoian stock, formerly living in New York State and Ontario; one of the Six Nations, and guardians of the council fire of the Iroquois.

on·rush (ŏn′rŭsh, awn′-) *n.* Onset.

on·set (ŏn′sĕt, awn′-) *n.* Attack, assault, impetuous beginning.

on·slaught (ŏn′slawt, awn′-) *n.* Onset, fierce attack.

Ont. *abbrev.* Ontario.

On·tar·i·o (ŏntār′ēō). Province of SE. Canada, between Hudson Bay in the N. and the Great Lakes in the S.; capital, Toronto; **Lake** ~, smallest and most easterly of the Great Lakes, lying between the Canadian province and New York State.

on·to (ŏn′to͞o, awn′-) *prep.*: see ON def. 3.

on·to·gen·e·sis (ŏnt*o*jĕn′ĭsĭs) *n.* = ONTOGENY. **on·to·ge·net·ic** (ŏntōjenĕt′ĭk), **on·to·ge·net′i·cal, on·to·gen′ic** *adjs.* **on·to·ge·net′i·cal·ly** *adv.*

on·tog·e·ny (ŏntŏj′*e*nē) *n.* (biol.) History of the development of an individual organism (opp. PHYLOGENY).

on·tol·o·gy (ŏntŏl′*o*jē) *n.* Branch of metaphysics concerned with the essence of things or being in the abstract. **on·to·log·i·cal** (ŏnt*o*lŏj′ĭk*a*l) *adj.* **on·tol′o·gist** *n.*

o·nus (ō′n*u*s) *n.* (pl. **o·nus·es**). Burden, duty, responsibility.

on·ward (ŏn′*w*erd, awn′-) *adv.* & *adj.* (Directed) farther on, toward the front; with advancing motion. **on′wards** *adv.*

on·yx (ŏn′ĭks) *n.* Type of chalcedony with different colors in layers, a form of silica, regarded as semiprecious stone.

oo·dles (o͞o′delz) *n.pl.* (colloq.) Superabundance (*of money* etc.).

o·o·gen·e·sis (ōojĕn′ĭsĭs) *n.* (biol.) Process leading to production of ripe ovum from germ cell.

o·o·lite (ō′olīt) *n.* Rock, freq. a limestone, composed of minute spheres of carbonate, resembling fish roe in appearance, found esp. in the Jurassic strata. **o·o·lit·ic** (oolĭt′ĭk) *adj.*

oo·long (o͞o′lawng, -lŏng) *n.* Dark-colored kind of tea grown in China and Taiwan: see TEA. [Chin. *wu* black, *lung* dragon]

oom (o͞om) *n.* (S. Afr.) Uncle; **Oom Paul,** President KRUGER[1].

oo·mi·ak (o͞o′mēăk) *n.* Var. of UMIAK.

ooze (o͞oz) *n.* 1. Wet mud, slime,

Op art (right) is a form of abstract art whereby painters use contrasting colors to create an illusion, often of movement. Other optical illusions were used by earlier painters.

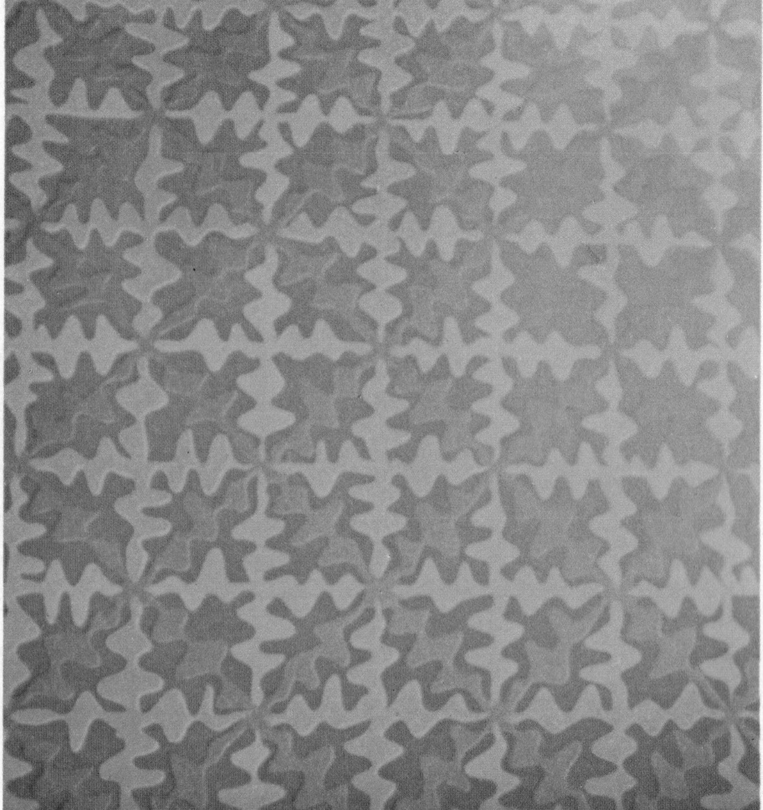

esp. in riverbed or estuary or on ocean bottom. 2. Tanning liquor, infusion of oak bark etc. 3. Exudation; sluggish flow; something that oozes. **ooz'y** *adj.* **ooz'i·ly** *adv.* **ooz'i·ness** *n.* **ooze** *v.* (**oozed, ooz·ing**). (of moisture) Pass slowly through the pores of a body, exude, percolate; exude moisture; emit (moisture, information, etc.); (fig.) leak *out* or *away*.

Op. *abbrev.* Opus.

O.P. *abbrev.* Observation post.

o.p. *abbrev.* Out of print.

o·pac·i·ty (ōpăs'ĭte) *n.* Being opaque.

o·pal (ō'pal) *n.* Amorphous quartzlike form of hydrated silica, some kinds of which are valued as gems and show changing colors (**common ~**, milk-white or bluish with green, yellow, and red reflections); (commerc.) semitranslucent white glass.

o·pal·es·cence (ōpalĕs'ens) *n.* Changing of color as in an opal. **o·pal·es'cent** *adj.* Showing opalescence, iridescent.

o·pal·ine (ō'palīn, -lēn) *adj.* Opal-like; opalescent. ~ *n.* Opal glass.

o·paque (ōpāk') *adj.* Not transmitting light, not transparent; obscure, not lucid; dull witted. **o·paque'ly** *adv.* **o·paque'ness** *n.*

op (ŏp) **art.** Style of abstract art using contrasting colors, often black and white, to create optical illusions, esp. of movement.

op. cit. *abbrev.* *Opere citato* (L., = in the work quoted).

OPEC (ō'pĕk) *n.* Organization of Petroleum Exporting Countries.

o·pen (ō'pen) *adj.* 1. Not closed or blocked up; allowing of entrance, passage, or access; having gate, door, lid, or part of boundary withdrawn; unenclosed, unconfined, uncovered, bare, exposed, undisguised; public, manifest; not exclusive or limited; (of account) not paid. 2. (of vowel) Produced with wider opening of oral cavity than close vowel; (mus., of organ pipe) not closed at top; (mus., of string) not stopped by finger; (of note) produced by such pipe or string, or without aid of slide, key, or piston. 3. Expanded, unfolded, outspread; spread out, not close, without intervals; porous; communicative, frank. 4. ~ **air**, outdoors; **~-and-shut**, (colloq.) immediately obvious; **with ~ arms**, heartily; ~ **boat**, undecked boat; ~ **country**, country unenclosed or affording wide views; **the ~ door**, principle of free

Obtained mainly from Australia and Mexico, ***opals*** *are distinctive gems because the multi-colored 'fire' is within the stone and can be seen when present in rock, or when cut and polished.*

commerce for all comers; **with ~ eyes**, not unconsciously or under misapprehension; in eager attention or surprise; so **~-eyed** (*adj.*); ~ **hand**, freedom in giving, generosity; **o'penhand'ed** (*adj.*) **o'penhand'edly** (*adv.*), **o'penhand'edness** (*n.*); **open-heart surgery**, surgery performed on the exposed heart with the bloodstream diverted around the heart, to a machine and back to the patient's circulatory system; **keep open house**, entertain all comers; **open letter**, letter addressing an individual but published in newspaper etc.; **open mind**, accessibility to new ideas; unprejudiced or undecided state; **open-minded** (*adj.*), **open-mindedly** (*adv.*), **open-mindedness** (*n.*); **open order**, formation with wide spaces between men or ships; **open question**, matter on which differences of opinion are legitimate; **open syllable**, syllable ending with a vowel; **Open University**, (Brit.) university (established 1969) with no formal requirement for entry to its first degree courses, and providing instruction by a combination of television, radio, and correspondence courses and by audio-visual centers; **o'penwork**, pattern with interstices in material. **o'pen·ness** *n.* **open** *n.* **the ~**, open space or country or air, public view. **open** *v.* 1. Make or become open or more open; start, establish, set going (business, campaign, etc.); **~ debate**, be first speaker; **~ the door to**, give opportunity for; **~ one's eyes**, show surprise; **~ the eyes of**, undeceive, enlighten. 2. Commence speaking; make a start; begin to be sold. 3. **~ out**, unfold, develop, expand; **~ up**, make accessible; bring to notice, reveal; become communicative; begin firing *on.* **o'pen·er** *n.* (esp.) Device for opening bottles, cans, etc.

o·pen·ing (ō'pening) *adj.* (esp.) Initial, first. **~** *n.* (esp.) Gap, passage, aperture; commencement, initial part; initial public performance (of a play etc.); opportunity, favorable conjuncture *for*; (chess) recognized sequence of moves for beginning game.

o·pen·ly (ō'penlē) *adv.* Without concealment, publicly, frankly.

op·er·a (ŏp'era, ŏp'ra) *n.* Dramatic performance or composition of which music is an essential part; branch of art concerned with this; **comic ~**, opera of humorous character; **grand ~**, opera, usu. on serious theme, without spoken dialogue; **light ~**, = OPERETTA def. 2; **o·pé·ra bouffe** (*Fr.* awpérah bōōf'), **o·pe·ra buf·fa** (*It.* aw'pĕrah bōō'fah) French, Italian, types of comic opera (Ital. *buffa* comic); **opera glass(es)**, small binoculars for use at opera or theater; **opera hat**: see HAT; **opera house**, theater for performance of opera.

op·er·a·ble (ŏp'erabel) *adj.* (med.) That admits of being operated upon. **op·er·a·bil·i·ty** (ŏperabĭl'ĭtē) *n.* **op'er·a·bly** *adv.*

op·er·ate (ŏp'erāt) *v.* (**-at·ed, -at·ing**). 1. Be in action, produce an effect, exercise influence; play *on*, try to act *on*; have desired effect. 2. Perform surgical or other operation; carry on warlike operations; deal or speculate in stocks and shares. 3. Bring about, accomplish; manage, work, conduct. 4. Conduct, be in charge of (machine, apparatus). **op'er·at·ing** *n.* (esp.) **~ table**, table for use in surgery; **~ theater**, room reserved in hospital etc. for the performance of surgery. **op'er·a·tor** *n.*

op·er·at·ic (ŏperăt'ĭk) *adj.* Of, like, opera. **op·er·at'i·cal·ly** *adv.*

op·er·a·tion (ŏperā'shon) *n.* 1. Working, action, way thing works; efficacy, validity, scope. 2. Active process, activity, performance; discharge of function; financial transaction. 3. Act or series of acts performed with hand or instrument on some part of body to remedy deformity, injury, disease, pain, etc.; (esp.) piece of surgery. 4. Strategic movement of troops, ships, etc. 5. (math.) Subjection of number or quantity to process affecting its value or form, e.g. multiplication. **op·er·a'tion·al** *adj.* (esp.) Engaged on, used for, warlike operations.

op·er·a·tive (ŏp'eratĭv, ŏp'erā-) *adj.* 1. Having effect, in operation, efficacious; practical, not theoretical or contemplative. 2. Of surgical operations. **op'er·a·tive·ly** *adv.* **op'er·a·tive·ness** *n.* **operative** *n.* A secret or trusted agent.

o·per·cu·lum (ōpẽr'kyulum) *n.* (pl. **-la** pr. -la, **-lums**). Gill cover of fish; lid or valve closing aperture of shell when tenant is retracted; similar lidlike structure in plants etc. **o·per'cu·lar, o·per·cu·late** (ōpẽr'kyulĭt), **o·per·cu·lat·ed** (ōpẽr'kyulātĭd) *adjs.*

op·er·et·ta (ŏperĕt'a) *n.* 1. Short opera. 2. Opera in simple popular style. **op·er·et'tist** *n.*

O·phel·ia (ōfēl'ya). In Shakespeare's *Hamlet*, daughter of Polonius, who went mad and drowned herself because of HAMLET's treatment of her and his killing of her father.

o·phid·i·an (ōfĭd'ēan) *adj.* & *n.* (Member) of the Ophidia, a suborder of reptiles including snakes.

oph·thal·mi·a (ŏfthăl'mēa, ŏp-) *n.* Inflammation of the eye, esp. affecting the conjunctiva.

oph·thal·mic (ŏfthăl'mĭk, ŏp-) *adj.* Of, relating to, or situated near, the eye.

oph·thal·mol·o·gy (ŏfthălmŏl'ojē, -tha-, ŏp-) *n.* Study of the eye and its diseases. **oph·thal·mol'o·gist** *n.*

oph·thal·mo·scope (ŏfthăl'-

***Ophthalmology** is the medical study of the eye and its diseases. A major advance has been the introduction of contact lenses, first conceived by Leonardo da Vinci. Below: an ophthalmologist at work.*

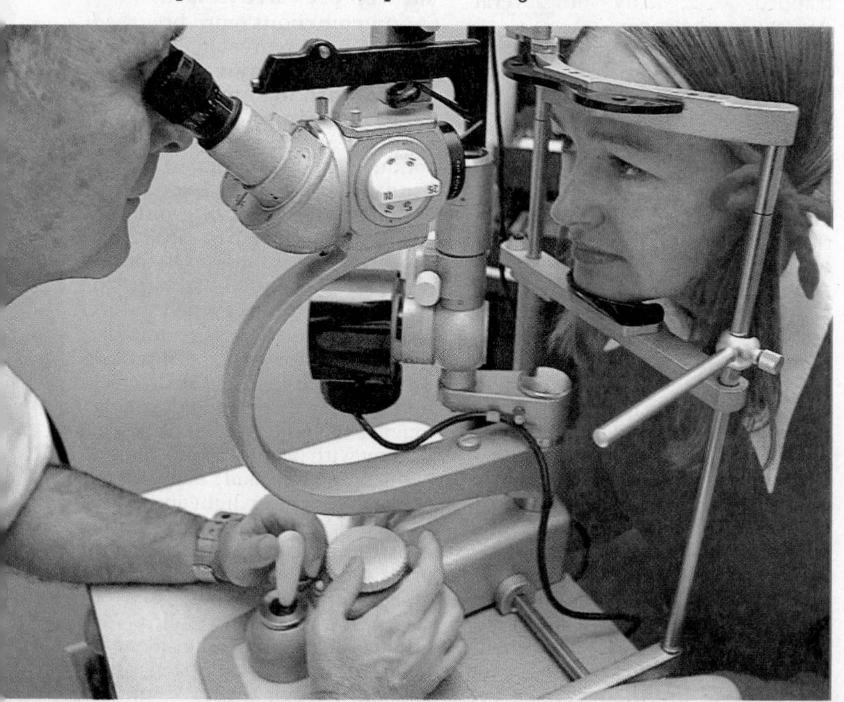

*The Australian Opera presented a magnificent spectacle on stage during its production of 'Turandot', a grand **opera** composed by Puccini and performed without any spoken words.*

moskōp, ŏp-) *n.* Instrument for inspecting the interior of the eye, esp. the retina.

o·pi·ate (ō′pēĭt, -āt) *adj.* Containing opium, narcotic, soporific. ~ *n.* Drug prepared from opium; sleep-inducing drug, narcotic.

o·pine (ōpīn′) *v.t.* (**o·pined, o·pin·ing**). Express or hold the opinion (*that*).

o·pin·ion (opĭn′yon) *n.* Judgment or belief based on grounds short of proof; views or sentiment, esp. on moral questions, prevalent among people in general; formal statement by expert consulted; professional advice.

o·pin·ion·at·ed (opĭn′yonātĭd), **o·pin·ion·a·tive** (opĭn′yonātĭv) *adjs.* Obstinate in opinion, dogmatic; self-willed. **o·pin′ion·at·ed·ness** *n.* **o·pin′ion·at·ed·ly** *adv.* **o·pin′ion·at·ive·ly** *adv.* **o·pin′ion·at·ive·ness** *n.*

o·pi·um (ō′pēum) *n.* Dried latex from unripe capsules of a poppy (*Papaver somniferum*), of reddish-brown color, with heavy smell and bitter taste, smoked or eaten as stimulant, intoxicant, or narcotic, and used in medicine as sedative; ~ **den**, haunt of opium smokers.

o·pos·sum (opŏs′um, pŏs′um) *n.* (pl. **-sums**, collect. **-sum**). 1. Any of various small, nocturnal, tree-dwelling Amer. marsupials (family Didelphidae), esp. *Didelphis marsupialis* or *D. virginiana*, of ratlike appearance

***Opossums** are the only marsupials surviving in America. The North-American variety (above) and the mouse opossum (below) are arboreal but the yapok of South America is aquatic and has webbed feet.*

and having the habit of collapsing as if dead when threatened or trapped. 2. Any of several Australian phalangers.

opp. *abbrev.* Opposite.

op·po·nent (opō′nent) *n.* Person opposed or on the opposing side in a contest etc.

op·por·tune (ŏpertōōn′, -tūn′) *adj.* (of time) Suitable, well-selected, favorable; (of action or event) well-timed, done or occurring at favorable conjuncture. **op·por·tune′ly** *adv.* **op·por·tune′ness** *n.*

op·por·tun·ism (ŏpertōō′nĭzem, -tū′-) *n.* Policy of doing what is opportune or at the time expedient, in politics, as opp. to rigid adherence to principles; method or course of action adapted to the circumstances of the moment. **op·por·tun′ist** *n.* **op·por·tun·is′tic** *adj.* **op·por·tun·is′ti·cal·ly** *adv.*

op·por·tu·ni·ty (ŏpertōō′nĭtē, -tū′-) *n.* (pl. **-ties**). Favorable juncture, good chance, opening.

op·pose (opōz′) *v.t.* (**-posed, -pos·ing**). 1. Place, produce, or cite as obstacle, antagonist, counterpoise, or contrast to; represent as antithetical. 2. Set oneself against, withstand, resist, obstruct; propose the rejection of; act as opponent or check. **op·posed′** *adj.* (esp.) Contrary, opposite, contrasted; hostile, adverse. **op·pos′a·ble** *adj.* (of digit, esp. thumb) Capable of being applied so as to meet another.

op·po·site (ŏp′ozĭt, -sĭt) *adj.* 1. Facing, front to front or back to back (with); ~ **number**, person or thing similarly placed in another set etc. to the given one. 2. Of contrary kind, diametrically different *to* or *from*; *the* other of a contrasted pair. **op′po·site·ly** *adv.* **op′po·sit·ness** *n.* **opposite** *n.* Opposite thing or term. ~ *adv.* In opposite place or direction; on opposite sides. ~ *prep.* In an opposite place or direction to; **play** ~, (of lead in play or film) have (specified actor or actress) as one's leading man or lady.

op·po·si·tion (ŏpozĭsh′on) *n.* 1. Placing opposite; diametrically opposite position (esp. astron., of two heavenly bodies when their longitude differs by 180°; opp. CONJUNCTION). 2. Contrast, antithesis; (logic) relation between two propositions with same subject and predicate but differing in quantity or quality or both. 3. Antagonism, resistance, being hostile; any party opposed to some proposal.

op·press (oprĕs′) *v.t.* Overwhelm with superior weight or numbers, or irresistible power; lie heavy on, weigh down (spirits etc.); govern tyrannically, keep under by coercion, subject to continual cruelty or injustice. **op·pres·sion** (oprĕsh′on), **op·pres′sor** *ns.* **op·pres′sive** *adj.* **op·pres′sive·ly** *adv.* **op·pres′sive·ness** *n.*

op·pro·bri·ous (oprō′brēus) *adj.* Conveying reproach, abusive, vituperative. **op·pro′bri·ous·ly** *adv.* **op·pro′bri·ous·ness** *n.*

op·pro·bri·um (oprō′brēum) *n.* Disgrace attaching to some act or conduct, infamy, crying of shame.

opt (ŏpt) *v.i.* Exercise an option, make a choice; ~ **out (of)**, choose not to take part (in).

op·tic (ŏp′tĭk) *adj.* Of the eye or sense of sight; ~ **nerve**, 2nd cranial nerve, from eyeball to forebrain, conducting the impulses responsible for visual sensations. **optic** *n.* Eye (now usu. joc.). **op′tics** *n.* (pl. considered as sing.) Science of sight, branch of physics dealing with properties etc. of light.

op·ti·cal (ŏp′tĭkal) *adj.* Visual, ocular; of sight or light in relation to each other; belonging to optics; constructed to assist sight or on the principles of optics; ~ **activity**, (chem.) property possessed by certain transparent solids and liquids of rotating the plane of polarization of polarized light passing through them; ~ **maser**:

Opiates stem from many obscure sources, such as the humble poppy flower. The effects of opiates on Western nations in the last decades have been devastating, despite the efforts of police forces.

Garden **orache** or mountain spinach is a herb native to temperate Europe and Asia which has been grown in England and North America as a substitute for green vegetables. It may also be used in soup.

see MASER. **op'ti·cal·ly** *adv.*

op·ti·cian (ŏptĭsh'*a*n) *n.* Maker or seller of optical instruments.

op·ti·mal (ŏp'tim*a*l) *adj.* Most satisfactory, best possible under the circumstances.

op·ti·mism (ŏp'timĭz*e*m) *n.* Doctrine, esp. as set forth by Leibniz, that the actual world is the best of all possible worlds; view that good must ultimately prevail over evil in the universe; sanguine disposition, inclination to take bright views. **op'ti·mist** *n.* **op·ti·mis'tic, op·tis·mis'ti·cal** *adjs.* **op·ti·mis'ti·cal·ly** *adv.*

op·ti·mum (ŏ'tim*u*m) *n.* (pl. **-ma** pr. -m*a*, **-mums**). (biol.) That degree or amount of heat, light, food, moisture, etc. most favorable for growth or other vital processes; (also attrib.) best. [L., = "best"]

op·tion (ŏp'sh*o*n) *n.* Choice, choosing, thing that is or may be chosen; liberty of choosing, freedom of choice; purchased right to call for or make delivery within specified time of specified stocks etc. at specified rate; **local ~**: see LOCAL. **op'tion·al** *adj.* Not obligatory. **op'tion·al·ly** *adv.*

op·tom·e·try (ŏptŏm'ĭtrē) *n.* Art or profession of measuring certain visual impairments and treating them by corrective lenses or other methods. **op·tom·e·trist** (ŏptŏm'ĭtrĭst) *n.* Practitioner (not usu. a licensed physician) of optometry.

op·u·lent (ŏp'y*u*l*e*nt) *adj.* Rich; abounding, abundant, well-stored. **op'u·lent·ly** *adv.* **op'u·lence** *n.*

o·pus (ō'p*u*s) *n.* (pl. **o·pus·es, o·per·a** pr. ō'p*e*r*a*, ŏp'*e*r*a*). Musical composition or set of compositions as numbered among works of composer in order of publication etc. (abbrev. op.); **magnum ~**, great literary undertaking, writer's or other artist's chief production. [L., = "work"]

OR, Or. *abbrevs.* Oregon.

or (ōr, *e*r) *conj.* Introducing alternatives.

or·ach, or·ache (ōr'*a*ch, ār'-) *ns.* Herb or small shrub, often mealy, of various species of genus *Atriplex*, commonest by the seashore.

or·a·cle (ōr'*a*k*e*l, ār'-) *n.* Place at which ancient Greeks etc. were accustomed to consult the gods for advice or prophecy; response, freq. ambiguous or obscure, given at such place; holy of holies or mercy seat in ancient Hebrew temple; (vehicle of) divine inspiration or revelation; infallible guide, test, or indicator; authoritative, profoundly wide, or mysterious judge, judgment, prophet, etc.

o·rac·u·lar (awrăk'y*u*l*e*r) *adj.* Of an oracle; obscure like an oracle. **o·rac'u·lar·ly** *adv.*

o·ral (ōr'*a*l, ōr'-) *adj.* Spoken, verbal, by word of mouth; of the mouth; done or taken by the mouth; **~ examination**, in which a candidate answers questions put by the examiner in a personal interview (opp. *written*); **~ stage**, (psychoanalytic theory) the first stage of psychosexual development in which the mouth and the activities associated with it are the source of sexual gratification. **o'ral·ly** *adv.* **oral** *n.* Oral examination.

O·ran (ōrăn', aw-). Mediterranean port city in NW. Algeria.

Oranges have been grown in Italy since the beginning of the Christian era. They were originally from China or Malaya and their cultivation was propagated by Arab traders.

The glazed and heated structure erected at Heidelberg in 1619 to allow oranges to be grown was known as an ***orangery.*** *The one illustrated is at Uppsala in Sweden.*

or·ange (ŏr´ĭnj, ăr´-) *n.* 1. Evergreen tree, *Citrus aurantium* and allied species, native of the East, widely cultivated in S. Europe and other warm, temperate, or subtropical regions, with fragrant white flowers and large globose many-celled berries with subacid juicy pulp and tough outer rind of bright reddish-yellow; fruit of this; **mock ~**: see MOCK; **~ blossom,** flowers of orange or mock orange, freq. worn or carried by bride at wedding; **~ flower water,** fragrant aqueous solution of orange flowers; **~ (wood) stick,** small stick of orangewood used for manicuring nails. 2. Color of orange rind, reddish yellow. **orange** *adj.* Orange-colored. [Arab. *nāranj*]

or·ange·ade (ŏrĭnjād´, ăr-) *n.* Drink of sweetened orange juice and water; synthetic substitute for this.

Or·ange (ŏr´ĭnj, ăr´-) **Free State.** Inland province of the Republic of S. Africa between the Orange and Vaal Rivers; first settled by Boers from Cape Colony (1836–8); annexed by Britain 1848, but restored in 1854 to Boers who established the Orange Free State Republic; annexed again by Britain during the Boer War (1899–1902) and renamed Orange River Colony; province of the Union of South Africa (1910) as Orange Free State; capital, Bloemfontein.

or·ange·ry (ŏr´ĭnjrē, ăr´-) *n.* (pl. **-ries**). Building, hothouse, for protection of orange trees; esp., in 17th c. mansions, (part of) building having solid N. wall and large freq. arched windows on S. side.

o·rang·u·tan, o·rang·ou·tang (orăng´*u*tăn, -tăng) *ns.* Large long-armed mainly arboreal anthropoid ape, *Pongo pygmaeus*, of Borneo, Sumatra, and formerly Java. [Malay *orang-uton* man of the woods]

o·rate (ōrāt´, aw- ŏr´āt, ŏr´-) *v.i.* (**o·rat·ed, o·rat·ing**). (joc.) Make an oration.

o·ra·tion (ōrā´shon aw-) *n.* Formal address, harangue, or discourse, esp. of ceremonial kind.

or·a·tor (ŏr´*a*ter, ăr´-) *n.* Maker of a speech; eloquent public speaker.

or·a·to·ri·o (ŏr*a*tōr´ēō, -tŏr´-, ăr-) *n.* (pl. **-ri·os**). Semidramatic musical composition usu. on sacred theme performed by soloists, chorus, and orchestra, without action, scenery, or costume. [It., orig. of musical services at Oratory of St. Philip Neri, Rome]

Found only in Indonesia, the ***orangutan*** *is one of the larger apes. The native name meant 'jungle-man' and these primates are considered to be the strongest of all apes, although only 4 ft. 6 ins. tall.*

Billy Graham, Christian evangelist whose ***oratory*** *has captured the imagination and attention of followers all over the world. Here he is speaking at Tampa Stadium in Florida.*

or·a·to·ry[1] (ŏr´*a*tōrē, -tōrē, ăr´-) *n.* (Art of making) speeches, rhetoric; highly colored presentment of facts, eloquent or exaggerating language. **or·a·tor·i·cal** (ŏr*a*tŏr´ĭk*a*l, or*a*tăr´-) *adj.* **or·a·tor´i·cal·ly** *adv.*

or·a·to·ry[2] (ŏr´*a*tōrē, -tōrē, ăr´-) *n.* (pl. **-ries**). Small chapel, place for private worship.

orb (ŏrb) *n.* Circle, disk, ring (now rare); sphere, globe; heavenly body; eyeball, eye (poet.); globe surmounted by cross as part of regalia, symbolizing domination of the world by Christ. **~** *v.* Enclose in, gather into, orb.

or·bit (ŏr´bĭt) *n.* 1. Eye socket; border around eye of bird or insect. 2. Curved course esp. of planet, comet, satellite, spacecraft, or binary star; complete circuit of this; (fig.) range, sphere, of action; **in ~**, traveling in an orbit. **or·bit** *v.* (Cause to) travel in an orbit.

The **orc**, or killer whale (Orcinus orca) is usually a very predatory creature. It attacks seals, walruses and, in packs, even large whales. It has a high dorsal fin and rounded flippers. It is found world-wide.

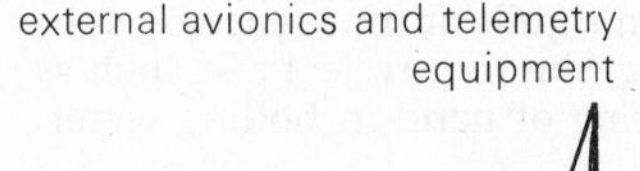

Vehicles launched into space are often placed in an **orbit** which circles the earth or other planets. More recently, orbital laboratories (below) have been launched where experiments can be conducted that are impossible on Earth.

or·bit·al (ōr′bĭtal) *adj.* Of an orbit. ~ *n.* (phys.) That part of the region surrounding an atomic nucleus in which an associated electron is most likely to be found; mathematical equation describing this.

orc (ōrk), **or·ca** (ōr′ka) *ns.* Cetacean, esp. the killer whale

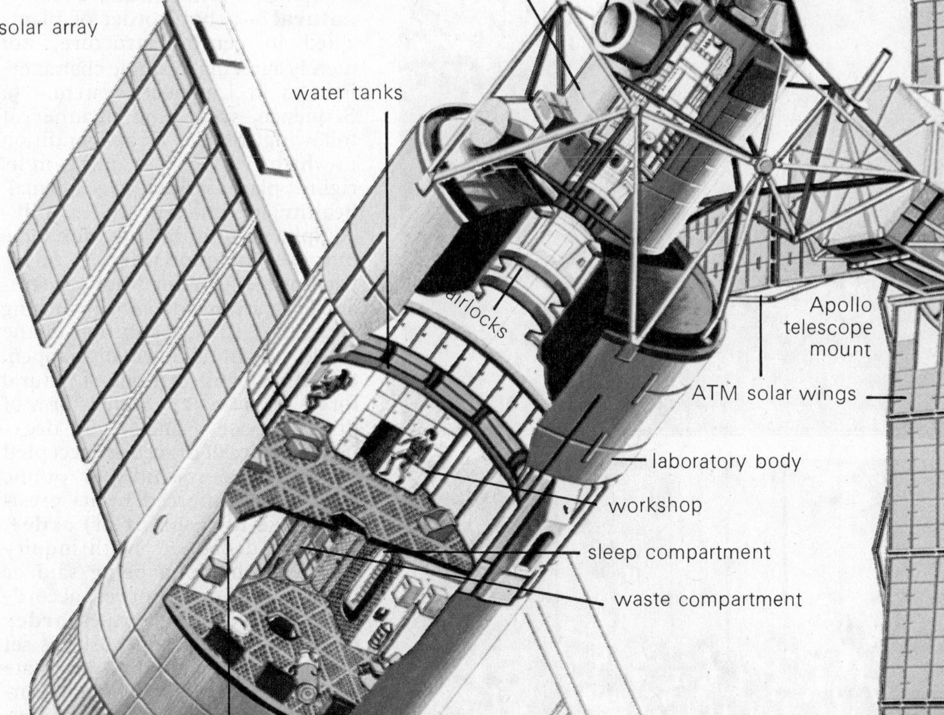

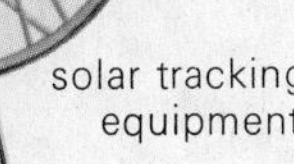

or·chard (ōr'cherd) *n.* Enclosure with fruit trees; ~ **grass**, weedy grass (*Dactylis glomerata*), often planted in pastures.

or·ches·tra (ōr'kĭstra) *n.* 1. Semicircular space in front of stage in ancient Greek theater, where chorus danced and sang. 2. Front section of seats in a theater closest to the orchestra pit; entire main floor of theater. 3. Body of instrumental performers, or combination of string, woodwind, brass, and percussion instruments, in theater or concert room; ~ **pit**, pit for orchestra below and in front of stage. **or·ches·tral** (ōrkĕs'tral) *adj.* **or·ches'tral·ly** *adv.*

or·ches·trate (ōr'kĭstrāt) *v.* (**-trat·ed, -trat·ing**). Arrange, or score, (music) for orchestral performance. **or·ches·tra·tion** (ōrkĭstrā'shon), **or'ches·tra·tor, or'ches·trat·er** *ns.*

or·chid (ōr'kĭd) *n.* Plant of the Orchidaceae, a large and widely distributed order of monocotyledons with three sepals and three petals, of which one (the lip or labellum) is usu. much larger than the others and of special color or shape; esp. one of the exotic cultivated species, freq. brilliantly colored or grotesquely shaped. **or·chi·da·ceous** (ōrkĭdā'shus) *adj.*

or·chil (ōr'kĭl, -chĭl) *n.* Red or violet dye from certain lichens, esp. *Roccella tinctoria*.

ord. *abbrev.* Ordained; order; ordinance; ordnance.

or·dain (ōrdān') *v.t.* 1. Appoint ceremonially to ministry; confer holy orders (esp. those of priest) on; authorize as a rabbi. 2. Destine, appoint; appoint authoritatively, decree, enact.

or·deal (ōrdēl', -dē'al, ōr'dēl) *n.* Experience that tests character or endurance, severe trial; (hist.) primitive (esp. ancient Teutonic) mode of deciding suspected person's guilt or innocence by subjecting him to physical test such as plunging of hand in boiling water, safe endurance of which was taken as divine acquittal.

*In an **orchard**, it is often necessary to spray at various times to kill insects or their larvae which would damage the fruit, and lower its value when offered for sale.*

or·der (ōr'der) *n.* 1. Rank of community, social division, grade or stratum; definite rank in state; separate and homogeneous set of persons. 2. Kind, sort. 3. ~**s of angels**: see ANGEL. 4. Grade of Christian ministry; (pl.) status of clergyman; **holy ~s**, orders of bishops, priests, and deacons; **minor ~s**, in R.C. Church (until 1973) orders of acolyte, exorcist, reader, and doorkeeper; **in ~s**, ordained; **take ~s**, be ordained. 5. (Brit.) Fraternity of monks or friars, or formerly of knights, bound by common rule of life; one of the companies (**Orders of Chivalry**), usu. instituted by sovereign, to which distinguished persons are admitted by way of honor or reward, insignia worn by member of such a company. 6. (archit.) Mode of treatment with established proportions between parts, esp. one of the **five (classical) orders** of column and entablature (Doric, Ionic, Corinthian, Tuscan, and Composite, the first three of Greek origin, the others Roman). 7. (math.) Degree of complexity. 8. (biol.) Classificatory group below *class* and above *family*; **natural ~**, (bot.) order of plants allied in general structure, not merely agreeing in single characteristic as in Linnaean system. 9. Sequence, succession, manner of following; regular array, condition in which every part or unit is in its right place; tidiness; normal, healthy, or efficient state; (mil.) equipment, uniform, etc., for some purpose; **in (good) order**, fit for use; **out of order**, not systematically arranged; not working correctly. 10. Constitution of the world, way things normally happen, collective manifestations of natural forces or laws. 11. Stated form of divine service; principles of decorum and rules of procedure accepted by legislative assembly or public meeting, or enforced by its president; **rise to (a point of) order**, interrupt debate etc. with inquiry whether something being said or done is in or out of order, according or not according to rules; **order of the day**, program, business set down for treatment; prevailing state of things. 12. Prevalence of constituted authority, law-abiding state. 13. Act or instance of ordering; authoritative direction or instruction (freq. pl.); (banking etc.) instruction to pay money or deliver property signed by owner

*Only during the 19th century did new instruments enable composers such as Berlioz to write music for an **orchestra** of more than 100 players. Left: Montreal Symphony.*

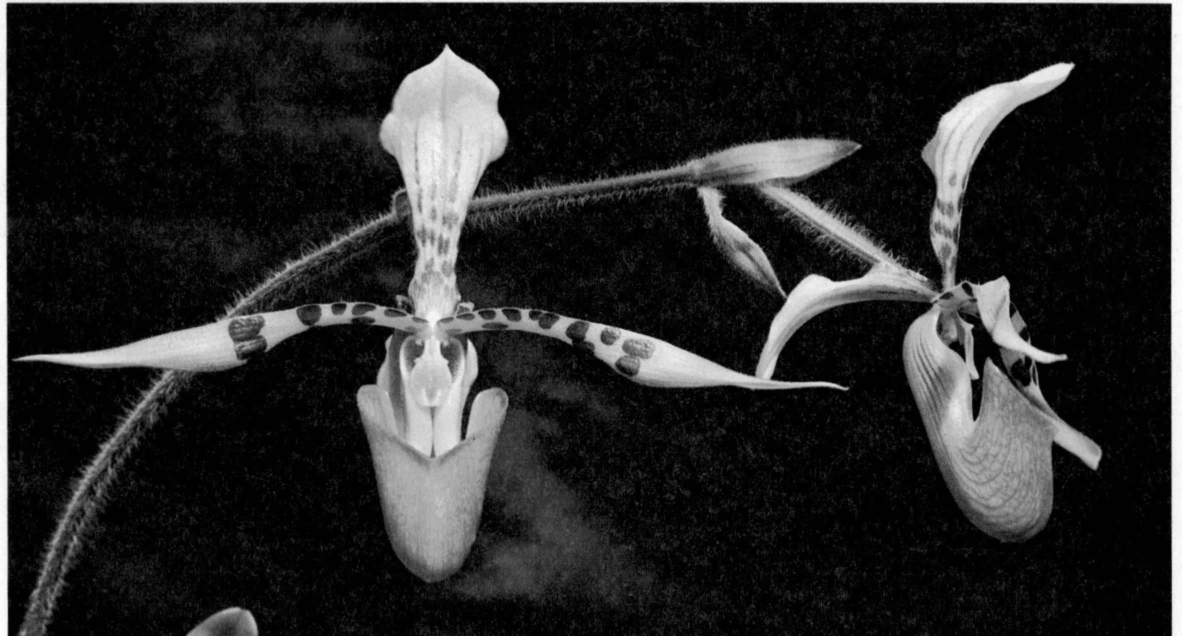

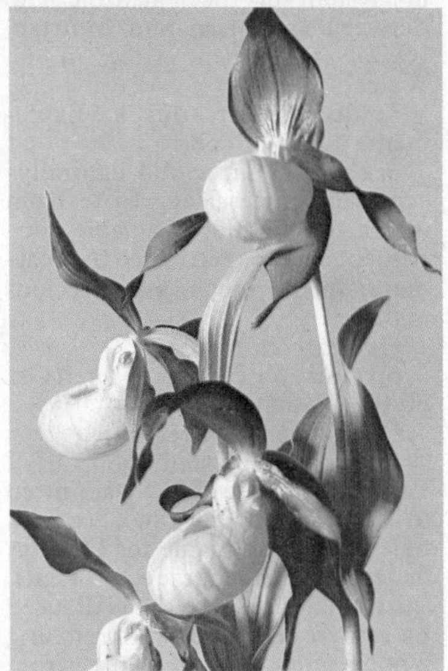

or responsible agent; direction to manufacturer, tradesman, etc., to supply something; **in order**, suitable, fitting, appropriate; **in short order**, without delay, immediately; **large** or **tall order**, (colloq.) difficult undertaking; **made to order**, made according to special directions, to suit individual measurements etc. (opp. *ready-made*); **money, postal order**, order issued by post office or bank for specific amount of money; **on order**, ordered but not yet supplied. 14. **in order to do**, with a view to, for the purpose of, doing; **in order that**, with the intention or to the end that. 15. **order of magnitude**, class in a system of classification determined by size, usu. by powers of 10. **order** *v.t.* 1. Put in order. 2. State with authority that (action must be performed, person must

*With 17,000 species described, the variety of **orchid** flowers exceeds the imagination. The Paphiopedilum (top) from the Solomon Islands, the lady's slipper from England (right), and the Australian species (above), are all orchids.*

perform action); prescribe; command or direct to go *to*, *away*, etc.; direct merchant etc. to supply (article).

or·der·ly (ōr′derlē) *adj.* Methodically arranged or inclined, regular, obedient to discipline, not unruly, well-behaved; (mil.) on duty, concerned with carrying out orders; ~ **room**, one set apart in barracks etc. for administrative business. **or′der·li·ness** *n.* **orderly** *n.* (pl. **-lies**). Soldier in attendance on officer to execute orders etc.; attendant in (esp. military) hospital.

or·di·nal (ōr′dinal) *adj.* Of or defining a thing's position in a series (~ **numbers** = *first*, *second*, etc.). **ordinal** *n.* 1. Ordinal number. 2. Prescribed form of ceremony to be observed at consecration of bishops and ordination of priests and deacons; book containing words and directions for this ceremony.

or·di·nance (ōr′dinans) *n.* Authoritative direction, decree; religious rite; statute.

or·di·nar·y (ōr′dinĕrē) *adj.* 1. Regular, normal, customary, usual; not exceptional, not above the usual, commonplace; ~ **seaman**, (abbrev. O.S.) lower rating than *able seaman*. 2. Having immediate or *ex officio* and not deputed jurisdiction. **ordinary** *n.* (pl. **-nar·ies**). 1. Ordinary authority; **the *O*~**, archbishop in province, bishop in diocese. 2. Rule or book laying down order of divine service. 3. Ordinary condition, course, etc.; what is ordinary. **or·di·nar·i·ly** (ōrd*i*năr′*i*lē, -nĕr′-) *adv.* **or′di·nar·i·ness** *n.*

or·di·nate (ōr′d*i*nĭt, -nāt) *n.* (geom.) Any of series of parallel chords of conic section in relation to bisecting diameter (esp. used of half the chord, from curve to diameter); straight line from any point drawn parallel to one co-ordinate axis and meeting the other (correlative to ABSCISSA).

or·di·na·tion (ōrd*i*nā′sh*o*n) *n.* 1. Arrangement in ranks, classification. 2. Conferring of holy orders, admission to church ministry. 3. Decreeing, ordainment.

ord·nance (ōrd′n*a*ns) *n.* Military weapons and ammunition; branch of public service dealing esp. with military stores and materials.

Or·do·vi·cian (ōrd*o*vĭsh′*a*n) *adj.* & *n.* (geol.) (Of) the second period or system of the Paleozoic era, between Cambrian and Silurian. [*Ordovices*, ancient tribe in N. Wales]

or·dure (ōr′j*e*r, -dūr) *n.* Excrement, dung.

ore (ōr, ōr) *n.* Solid naturally-occurring mineral aggregate from which one or more valuable constituents may be recovered by treatment; (poet.) metal, esp. precious metal.

Ore. *abbrev.* Oregon.

o·re·ad (ōr′ēăd, ōr′-) *n.* (Gk. myth.) Mountain nymph.

Oreg. *abbrev.* Oregon.

Or·e·gon (ōr′*e*g*o*n, -gŏn, ăr′-). Pacific NW. state of U.S.; admitted to the Union in 1859; capital, Salem; ~ **pine**, name for Douglas fir, esp. in timber trade; ~ **Trail,** (hist.) major route to the NW. used by settlers, esp. 1942–7, stretching 2,000 miles (3,219 km) from Independence, Missouri, over plains, desert, mountain passes, and rivers to Astoria, Oregon, at the mouth of the Columbia River.

O·res·tes (ōrĕs′tēz, aw-). (Gk. legend) Son of AGAMEMNON and Clytemnestra; killed his mother and her lover Aegisthus in revenge because they had murdered his father; was pursued by the Furies until he was pardoned by Artemis, having rescued her statue (and his sister Iphigenia) from the island of Tauris; became king of Argos, Sparta, and Mycenae, and married Hermione, daughter of Menelaus.

or·gan (ōr′g*a*n) *n.* 1. Part of animal or vegetable body adapted for special vital function, as ~*s of digestion, speech*, etc. 2. Person's voice with ref. to its power or quality. 3. Medium of communication, esp. newspaper or journal representing a party, cause,

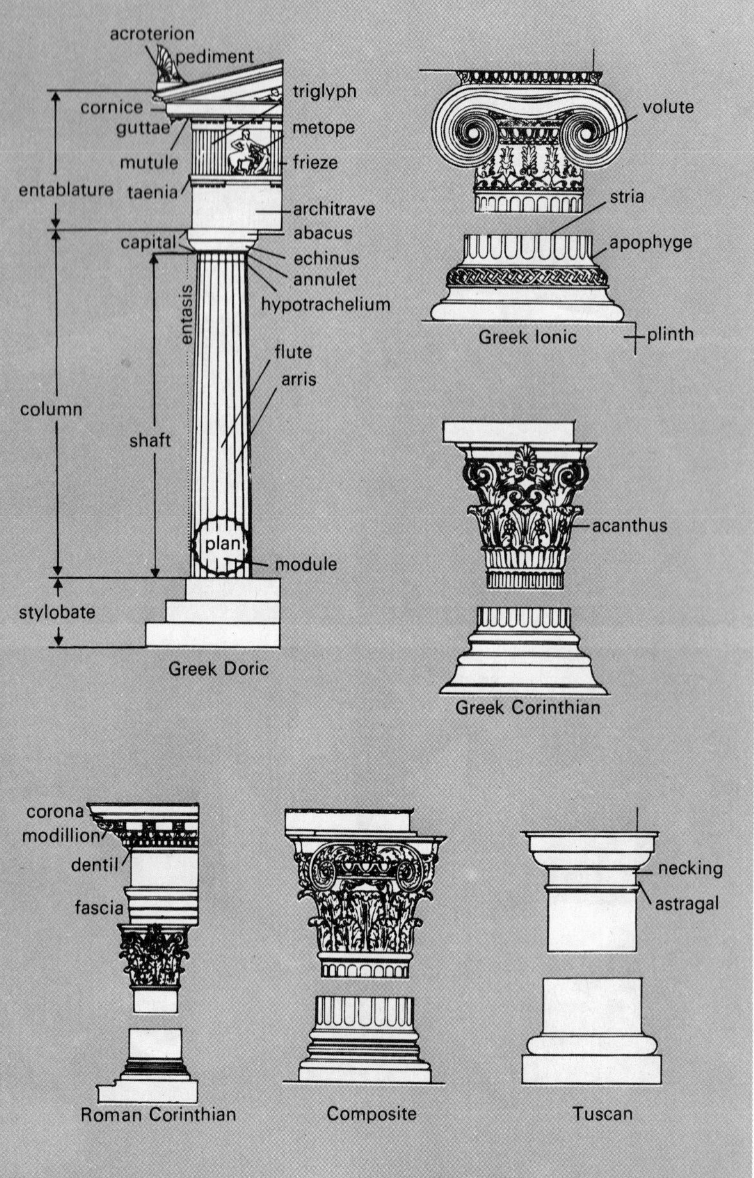

Architectural **orders** *originated in ancient Greece and Rome and were concerned with the proportions and styles of buildings using columns. Eventually later architects analysed these and added variations.*

etc. 4. Musical instrument consisting essentially of pipes arranged in ranks (*stops*) which are supplied with wind by a bellows or electric fan and sounded by means of keys arranged in rows and pedals, each key or pedal controlling the mechanism (usu. a valve) that admits air to a particular pipe. 5. Any of various keyboard instruments producing more or less similar effects by different means, as ELECTRONIC ~. 6. **mouth** ~: see HARMONICA; ~ **grinder**, player on BARREL organ; ~ **loft**, loft or gallery in which organ is placed, freq. above **organ screen**, ornamental screen between nave and choir in church; ~**-pipe cactus**, tall cactus (*Pachycereus marginatus*), of southwest U.S. and Mexico, resembling pipe organ; ~ **stop**, set of pipes of similar tone quality in organ; handle or knob of mechanism that brings such a set into action.

or·gan·dy, or·gan·die (ōr′g*a*ndē) *ns.* (pl. **-dies**). Thin stiff translucent cotton or silk fabric.

or·gan·elle (ōrg*a*nĕl′) *n.* (biol.) Part of a cell, having a particular function.

or·gan·ic (ōrgăn′ĭk) *adj.* 1. Of the bodily organs, vital; (path., of disease) affecting structure of an organ (opp. *functional*). 2. Having organs or organized physical structure; of animals or plants; (chem., of compound substances) occurring naturally as constituent of organized bodies formed from such

*The original musical **organs** were devised about 250 B.C. but the ancestor of present instruments was made in the 14th century with three keyboards. The organ at St James' Church, Piccadilly, London, was made in the 1600s.*

compounds (all of which contain or are derived from hydrocarbon radicals); ~ **chemistry**: see CHEMISTRY. 3. Constitutional, inherent, fundamental, structural; organized, systematic, coordinated. **or·gan′i·cal·ly** *adv.*

or·gan·ism (ōr′ganĭzem) *n.* Living animal or plant; anything capable of maintaining the processes characteristic of life, esp. reproduction; (material structure of) individual animal or plant; whole with interdependent parts compared to living being. **or·gan·is′mic, or·gan·is′mal** *adjs.*

or·gan·ist (ōr′ganĭst) *n.* Player of organ.

or·gan·i·za·tion (ōrganĭzā′shon) *n.* (esp.) Organized body, system, or society. **or·gan·i·za′tion·al** *adj.* **or·gan·i·za′tion·al·ly** *adv.*

or·gan·ize (ōr′ganīz) *v.* (**-ized, -iz·ing**). 1. Furnish with organs, make organic, make into living being or tissue (usu. in past part.); become organic. 2. Form into an organic whole; give orderly structure to, frame and put into working order; make arrangements for, get up (undertaking involving cooperation). **or′gan·iz·a·ble** *adj.* **or′gan·iz·er** *n.*

or·ga·non (ōr′ganŏn) *n.* (pl. **-nons, -na** pr. -na). Instrument of thought, system of or treatise on logic. [Gk. *organon* tool, work; *Organon* was the title of Aristotle's logical writings, and *Novum* (new) *Organum* that of Bacon's]

or·ga·num (ōr′ganum) *n.* (pl. **-na** pr. -na, **-nums**) = ORGANON.

or·gan·za (ōrgăn′za) *n.* Thin stiff transparent fabric of silk or synthetic fiber.

or·gan·zine (ōr′ganzēn) *n.* Strongest kind of silk thread, in which main twist is in contrary direction to that of strands.

or·gasm (ōr′găzem) *n.* Paroxysm of excitement or rage; climax of sexual excitement esp. in coition. **or·gas′mic, or·gas′tic** *adjs.*

or·gi·as·tic (ōrjēăs′tĭk) *adj.* Of the nature of an orgy.

or·gy (ōr′jē) *n.* (pl. **-gies**). 1. (Gk. and Rom. antiq., usu. pl.) Secret rites in worship of various gods, esp. festival in honor of Dionysus (Bacchus), celebrated with extravagant dancing, singing,

*Not all of **Oregon** is as rugged as Mount Hood (left). The state is the major timber production area for the U.S.A. and irrigation has enabled many other crops to be grown. Fishing also contributes to the economy.*

drinking, etc. 2. Drunken or licentious revel; (pl.) revelry, debauchery.

o·ri·el (ōr′ēel, ōr′-) *n.* Large windowed polygonal recess projecting usu. from upper story and supported from ground or on corbels; (also ~ **window**) window or oriel, projecting window of upper story.

O·ri·ent (ōr′ēent, ōr′-, -ĕnt) *n.* 1. The East of Asia, esp. the countries of E. Asia; (poet.) eastward part of sky or earth. 2. (o~) Orient pearl. **orient**[1] *adj.* 1. (of precious stones, esp. pearls, of finest kinds, as coming anciently from the East) Lustrous, sparkling, precious. 2. (archaic, of sun etc.) Rising, nascent.

o·ri·ent[2] (ōr′ēĕnt, ōr′-) *v.t.* 1. Place (building etc.) so as to face east; build (church) with chancel end due E.; bury with feet eastward. 2. Place or exactly determine position of with regard to points of compass, settle or find bearings of; (fig.) bring into clearly understood relations; ~ **oneself**, determine how one stands; get one's bearings.

o·ri·en·tal (ōrēĕn′tal, ōr-) *adj.* Of the Orient, esp. Asiatic; occurring in, coming from, the East, characteristic of its civilization etc.; (of pearls) orient. **o·ri·en′tal·ly** *adv.* **O·ri·en′tal** *n.* Native, inhabitant, of the Orient. **O·ri·en′tal·ism** *n.* **O·ri·en·tal·ize** (ōrēĕn′talīz, ōr-) *v.* (**-ized, -iz·ing**). Make, become, Oriental.

o·ri·en·tate (ōr′ēĕntāt, ōr′-) *v.t.* (**-tat·ed, -tat·ing**) = ORIENT. **o·ri·en·ta·tion** (ōrēĕntā′shon, ōr-) *n.*

O·ri·en·te (ōrēĕn′tā). Province of Cuba where Fidel Castro and his supporters organized the overthrow of Batista, 1959.

or·i·fice (ōr′ifīs, ăr′-) *n.* Aperture, mouth of cavity, perforation, vent.

o·ri·ga·mi (ōrĭgah′mē) *n.* (pl. **-mis**). Japanese art of folding paper into decorative forms; example of this.

or·i·gin (ōr′ĭjĭn, ăr′-) *n.* Derivation, beginning or rising from something; extraction; source, starting point.

o·rig·i·nal (orĭj′inal) *adj.* 1. Existent from the first; primitive, innate, initial, earliest; ~ **sin**, (Christian theol.) innate depravity common to all human beings in consequence of the fall of man. 2. That has served as pattern, of which copy or translation has been made; not derivative or dependent, firsthand, not imitative; novel in character or style, inventive, creative; thinking or acting for oneself. **o·rig′i·nal·ly** *adv.* **o·rig·i·nal·i·ty** (orĭjinăl′ĭtē) *n.* **original** *n.* Pattern, archetype; thing from which another is copied or imitated; eccentric person.

o·rig·i·nate (orĭj′ināt) *v.* (**-nat·ed, -nat·ing**). Give origin to, initiate, cause to begin; have origin, take rise. **o·rig·i·na·tion** (orĭjinā′shon), **o·rig′i·na·tor** *ns.*

O·ri·no·co (ōrinō′kō). River rising in SE. Venezuela and looping 1,500 miles (2,414 km) W., then N., and finally E. to the Atlantic Ocean.

o·ri·ole (ōr′ēōl, ōr′-) *n.* 1. Any of a family (Oriolidae) of characteristically bright yellow and black birds of the Old World. 2. Any of a family (Icteridae) of Amer. birds, including the BALTIMORE oriole, the orchard oriole (*Icterus spurius*) and Bullock's oriole (*I. bullockii*), of which the males have bright yellow or orange and black plumage.

O·ri·on (ōrī′on, aw). 1. (Gk. legend) Giant and hunter of Boeotia, changed at his death into a constellation. 2. (astron.) Conspicuous constellation containing many bright stars; ~**'s belt**, three bright stars in short line across Orion.

or·i·son (ōr′ĭzon, ăr′-) *n.* (archaic) Prayer.

Ork·ney (ōrk′nē). Group of islands off N. coast of Scotland.

Or·lan·do (ōrlăn′dō). City and resort area in central Florida; site of Disneyworld.

Or·le·ans (ōr′lēanz; *Fr.* ōrlāahṅ′). (Fr. *Orléans*) French city on River Loire; besieged by the English, 1428, and relieved by Joan of Arc.

Or·ly (ōr′lē; *Fr.* ōrlē′). Suburb SE. of Paris; site of major international airport.

Or·mazd (ōr′mazd). In the Zoroastrian system, the supreme deity, principle of goodness and light, in perpetual conflict with Ahriman.

or·mo·lu (ōr′molōō) *n.* Gilded bronze used for the mounts of furniture and other decorative metalwork, esp. in 18th c. France; imitation of this, esp. gold-colored alloy of copper, zinc, and tin; articles made of or decorated with this. [Fr. *or moulu* ground gold (for use in gilding)]

or·na·ment (ōr′nament) *n.* 1. (eccles., usu. pl.) Accessories of church or worship (e.g. altar, chalice, service books, vestments, organ, bells, etc.). 2. Thing used

*With widespread distribution, the golden **oriole** lives on fruit and insects. Similar birds, grouped into a different genus, are present in the Americas.*

or serving to adorn; quality or person whose existence or presence confers grace or honor. 3. Adorning, being adorned, embellishment; features or work added for decorative purposes. 4. (pl. mus.) Grace notes. **or·na·men'tal** *adj.* **or·na·men'tal·ly** *adv.* **ornament** (ōr'n*a*mĕnt) *v.t.* Adorn, beautify. **or·na·men·ta·tion** (ōrn*a*mĕntā'sh*o*n) *n.*

or·nate (ōrnāt') *adj.* Elaborately adorned; embellished. **or·nate'ly** *adv.* **or·nate'ness** *n.*

or·ni·thol·o·gy (ōrn*i*thŏl'*o*jē) *n.* Branch of zoology dealing with birds. **or·ni·tho·log·i·cal** (ōrn*i*th*o*lŏj'ĭk*a*l), **or·ni·tho·log'ic** *adjs.* **or·ni·tho·log'i·cal·ly** *adv.* **or·ni·thol'o·gist** *n.*

o·ro·tund (ōr'*o*tŭnd, ōr'-) *adj.* Magniloquent, pompous. **o·ro·tun·di·ty** (ōr*o*tŭn'dĭtē, ōr-) *n.* [L. *ore rotundo* with round mouth]

O·roz·co (awraws'kaw), **José Clemente** (1883–1949). Mexican artist and lithographer associated with modernist school; best known for patriotic murals.

or·phan (ōr'f*a*n) *n.* & *adj.* (Child) bereaved of parent(s). ~ *v.t.* Bereave of parent(s). **or·phan·age** (ōr'f*a*nĭj) *n.* (hist.) Institution for care of orphans.

Or·phe·us (ōr'fē*u*s, -fūs). (Gk. legend) Legendary Thracian pre-Homeric poet; son of Calliope or another Muse; played so marvelously on the lyre (given to him by Apollo) that wild beasts were spellbound by his music; visited Hades and charmed Pluto into releasing his wife Eurydice from the dead, but lost her because he failed to obey the condition that he must not look back at her until they had reached the world of the living.

Or·phic (ōr'fĭk) *adj.* Of Orpheus or Orphism. **Or·phism** (ōr'fĭz*e*m) *n.* Mystic religion of ancient Greece, originating in 7th or 6th c. B.C. and based in poems (now lost) attributed to Orpheus, emphasizing the mixture of good (or divine) and evil in human nature and the necessity that the individual should rid himself of the evil part by ritual and moral purification throughout a series of reincarnations.

or·pi·ment (ōr'pim*e*nt) *n.* Bright yellow mineral, arsenic trisulfide (As_2S_3), used as a pigment.

or·pine (ōr'pĭn) *n.* Succulent herbaceous plant (*Sedum telephium*) with smooth fleshy leaves and corymbs of purple flowers.

or·ris (ōr'ĭs, ăr'-) *n.* (also **or'risroot**) Powdered violet-

2

*People of many nations have long used **ornamentation** for both body and belongings. The Indian woman (1) is lavishly adorned with intricate silverwork. The beauty of the altar (2) symbolizes man's worship of God.*

scented root of three species of iris used in perfumery etc.

ort (ōrt) *n.* (dial. and archaic; usu. pl.) Refuse, scrap(s), leavings.

Or·te·ga y Gas·set (ōrtā'gah ē gahsĕt'), **José** (1883–1955). Spanish writer, philosopher, and statesman.

or·tho·chro·mat·ic (ōrthokrōmăt'ĭk) *adj.* (phot.) Reproducing colors in their correct relative intensities.

or·tho·don·tia (ōrthodŏn'sha), **or·tho·don·tics** (ōrthodŏn'tĭks) *ns.* Branch of dentistry concerned with the correction of malformations of the teeth. **or·tho·don'tic** *adj.* **or·tho·don'tist** *n.*

or·tho·dox (ōr'thodŏks) *adj.* Holding correct or currently accepted opinions esp. on religious doctrine; not heretical, original, or independent in mind; generally accepted as right or true, esp. in theology; in harmony with what is authoritatively established; approved, conventional; ***O~* Church**, (also **Eastern** or **Greek Church**) part of Christian Church separated from Catholic Church in 9th c., recognizing patriarch of Constantinople as head; any of the national Churches of Russia, Bulgaria, Rumania, etc., in communion with this. **or'tho·dox·y** *n.* Being orthodox.

or·tho·e·py (ōrthō'epē, ōr'-thōĕpē) *n.* Study of correct pronunciation. **or·tho·ep·ic** (ōr-thōĕp'ĭk) *adj.* **or·tho·e·pist** (ōrthō'epĭst) *n.*

or·tho·gen·e·sis (ōrthojĕn'ĭsĭs) *n.* View of evolution according to which variations follow a defined direction and are not merely sporadic and fortuitous.

or·thog·ra·phy (ōrthŏg'rafē) *n.* 1. Correct or conventional spelling; spelling with reference to its correctness. 2. Orthographic projection. **or·tho·graph·ic** (ōrthográf'ĭk) *adj.* (of perspective projection in maps, elevations, etc.) In which point of sight is supposed to be at infinite distance, so that rays are parallel. **or·tho·graph'i·cal** *adj.* Of orthography. **or·tho·graph'i·cal·ly** *adv.*

or·tho·pe·dic (ōrthopē'dĭk) *adj.* Of, relating to, orthopedics. **or·tho·pe'dics** *n.* Branch of surgery dealing with abnormalities and injuries of the bones and muscles, esp. in children. **or·tho·pe'dist** *n.*

or·thop·ter·ous (ōrthŏp'terus) *adj.* Of the order Orthoptera of insects, including grasshoppers, crickets, etc., with straight narrow forewings, broad longitudinally folded hind wings, and incomplete metamorphosis.

or·thop·tic (ōrthŏp'tĭk) *adj.* Of, concerning, the right or normal use of the eyes. **or·thop'tics** *n.* Correction of defective vision by means of exercises of the eye muscles. **or·thop'tist** *n.*

or·tho·rhom·bic (ōrthorŏm'-bĭk) *adj.* (cryst.) Having the three axes mutually at right angles and unequal.

or·tho·scop·ic (ōrthoskŏp'ĭk) *adj.* Having, producing, correct vision; free from, constructed to correct, optical distortion.

or·to·lan (ōr'tolan) *n.* One of the buntings (*Emberiza hortulana*), a small bird of Europe, N. Africa, and W. Asia, esteemed as table delicacy; the BOBOLINK.

Or·well (ōr'wĕl), **George** (1903–50). Pseudonym of Eric Arthur Blair, English novelist, essayist, and political satirist; born in India; author of *Animal Farm* (1945), *1984* (1949), etc.

Osaka, *the 2nd-largest city in Japan. No other country in the world has had a more rapid industrial and economic growth since the 1939–45 war. Pictured is the traditional Osaka Castle.*

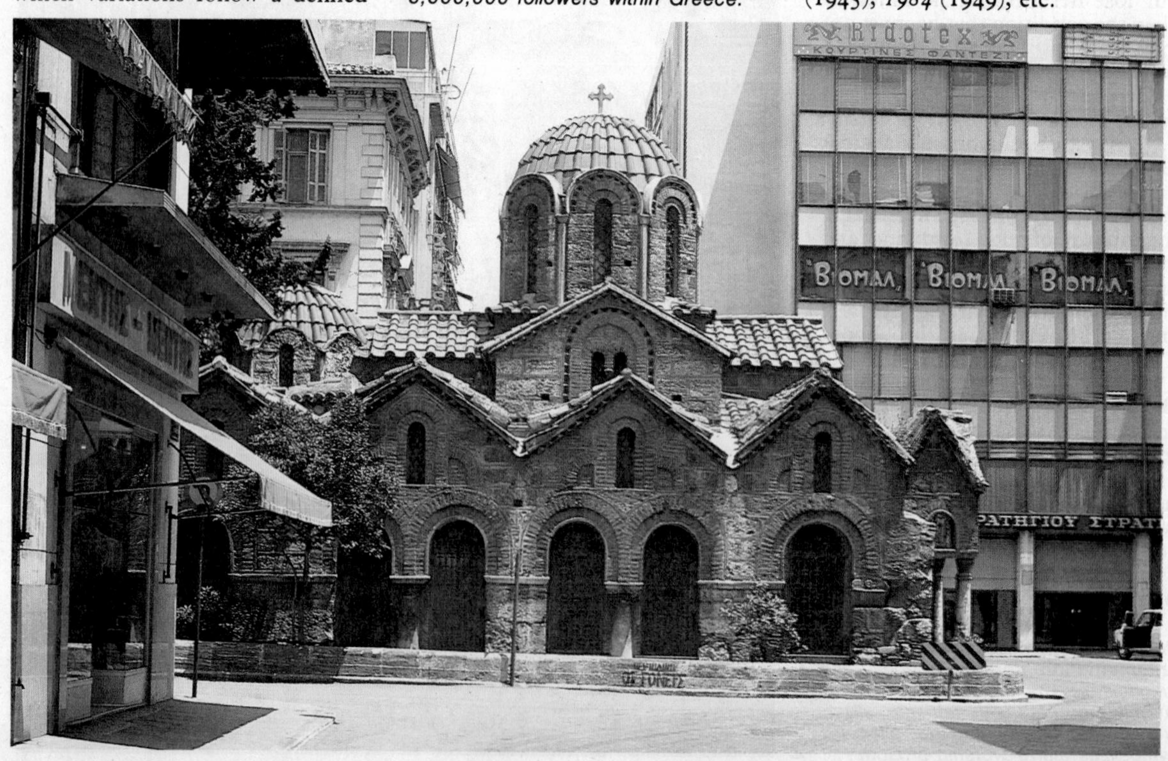

A Greek ***Orthodox*** *church in Athens, Greece. Declared ecclesiastically independent in 1833, the church has over 8,000,000 followers within Greece.*

Larger forms of antelope, the **oryx** of Africa and Arabia have had their populations reduced by excessive hunting and by agricultural intrusion on their grazing land. However, some species are now protected.

o·ryx (ōr'ĭks, ōr'-, ar'-) *n.* (pl. **o·ryx·es**, collect. **o·ryx**). Large antelope (genus **O** ~) of Africa and Arabia, with long straight pointed horns.

O.S. *abbrev.* Ordinary seaman; out of stock.

O·sage (ō'sāj, ōsāj') *n.* (pl. **O·sag·es**, collect. **O·sage**). (Member of) N. Amer. Indian tribe of Siouan linguistic stock, formerly occupying territory in Missouri and Arkansas; ~ **orange**, N. Amer. thorny tree of mulberry family with large yellow fruit and hard flexible yellow wood; ~ **River**, river flowing from E. Kansas to join the Missouri River in central Missouri.

O·sa·ka (ōsah'kah). Industrial city and seaport, second largest city in Japan, on SW. Honshu Island.

Os·can (ŏs'kan) *adj.* & *n.* (Of) the ancient Italic language spoken in Campania and farther S., and surviving only in inscriptions in an alphabet derived from Etruscan.

Os·car (ŏs'ker) *n.* Gold-plated statuette awarded annually by the Academy of Motion Picture Arts and Sciences, of Hollywood, California, for highest achievement in film acting production, etc. (loosely) similar award.

os·cil·late (ŏs'ĭlāt) *v.* (**-lat·ed, -lat·ing**). 1. Swing like pendulum, move to and fro; vacillate. 2. (of radio receiver) Radiate electromagnetic waves owing to faulty operation or construction. **os·cil·la·tion** (ŏsĭlā'shon) *n.* **os·cil·la·to·ry** (ŏs'ĭlatōrē, -tōrē) *adj.*

os·cil·lo·scope (osĭl'oskōp) *n.* Device in which variations in an electrical quantity produce a temporary trace on the fluorescent screen of a cathode ray tube.

Os·co-Um·bri·an (ŏs'kōŭm'-brēan) *adj.* & *n.* (Of) the group of Italic languages comprising Oscan, Umbrian, and Volscian.

os·cu·lar (ŏs'kyuler) *adj.* Of the mouth; of kissing; (math.) that osculates.

Jack Lemmon (left) with the **Oscar** he was awarded in 1973 by the Academy of Motion Picture Arts and Sciences. These highly-prized awards have been made since 1927–28.

os·cu·late (ŏs'kyulāt) *v.* (**-lat·ed, -lat·ing**). 1. Kiss (usu. joc.). 2. (biol., of species etc.) Have contact through intermediate species etc.; have common characters *with*. 3. (math., of curve or surface) Have contact of higher order with, coincide in three or more points. **os·cu·lant** (ŏs'kyulant), **os·cu·la·to·ry** (ŏs'kyulatōrē, -tōrē) *adjs.* **os·cu·la·tion** (ŏskyulā'shon) *n.*

os·cu·lum (ŏs'kyulum) *n.* (pl. **-la** pr. -la). Mouthlike aperture; mouth of sponge.

Osh·kosh (ŏsh'kŏsh). Resort city on Lake Winnebago in E. Wisconsin.

o·sier (ō'zher) *n.* (Shoot of) species of willow, esp. *Salix viminalis*, with tough pliant branches used in basketwork; attrib., of osiers.

O·si·ris (ōsī'rĭs). (Egyptian myth.) God of the underworld and husband of Isis; sometimes identified with the sun.

Os·ler (ŏs'ler, ŏz'-) **Sir William** (1849–1919). Canadian physician; founder member of (Brit.) Royal Society of Medicine; was a distinguished teacher and medical historian.

Os·lo (ŏz'lō, ŏs'-). Capital city of Norway, on SE. coast, founded c1050; (1624–1925) called Christiania in honor of King Christian IV, who refounded it after its destruction by fire in 1624.

os·mi·um (ŏz'mēum) *n.* (chem.) Metallic element of the platinum group, hard, brittle, bluish-white, and of high density; symbol Os, at no. 76, at. wt. 190.2. [Gk. *osmē* smell]

os·mo·sis (ŏzmō'sĭs, ŏs-) *n.* Tendency of a solvent, when separated from a solution by a suitable membrane (often animal or vegetable), to pass through the membrane so as to dilute the solution. **os·mot·ic** (ŏzmŏt'ĭk, ŏs-) *adj.* ~ **pressure**, pressure produced by the solvent in osmosis. **os·mot'i·cal·ly** *adv.*

os·prey (ŏs'prē, -prā) *n.* (pl. **-preys**). 1. Large diurnal bird of prey, *Pandion haliaetus*, found on inland waters and preying on fish; fish hawk. 2. Egret plume formerly worn as ornament on hat etc.

Os·sian (ŏsh'an, ŏs'ēan). Legendary Gaelic 3rd-c. warrior and bard. **Os·si·an·ic** (ŏshēăn'ĭk, ŏsē) *adj.* Of Ossian; of the style or character of the rhythmic prose of Macpherson's supposed translation of the poems of Ossian; hence, bombastic, grandiloquent.

os·si·cle (ŏs'ĭk*e*l) *n.* (anat.) Small bone, esp. one of three in the middle ear; small piece of bony, chitinous, or calcareous substance in animal framework. **os·sic·u·lar** (ŏsĭk'-*yu*ler), **os·sic·u·late** (ŏsĭk'*yu*lĭt) *adjs.*

os·si·fy (ŏs'*i*fī) *v.* (**-fied, -fy·ing**). Turn into bone; harden; make or become rigid, callous, or unprogressive. **os'si·fi·er, os·si·fi·ca·tion** (ŏs*i*f*i*kā'sh*o*n) *ns.*

os·su·ar·y (ŏsh'ōōĕrē, ŏs'-) *n.* (pl. **-ar·ies**). Place or receptacle for bones of the dead.

os·ten·si·ble (ŏstĕn's*i*b*e*l) *adj.* Professed, for show, put forward to conceal the real. **os·ten'si·bly** *adv.*

os·ten·sor·i·um (ŏstĕnsōr'*e*um, -sōr'-) *n.* (pl. **-sor·i·a** pr. -sōr'ēa, -sōr'ēa). Receptacle for displaying the Host to congregation. **os·ten·so·ry** (ŏstĕn's*o*rē) *n.* (pl. **-ries**).

os·ten·ta·tion (ŏstĕntā'sh*o*n) *n.* Pretentious display, esp. of wealth or luxury; showing off; attempt or intention to attract notice. **os·ten·ta·tious** (ŏstĕntā'sh*u*s) *adj.* **os·ten·ta'tious·ly** *adv.* **os·ten·ta'tious·ness** *n.*

osteo- *prefix.* Bone.

os·te·o·ar·thri·tis (ŏstēōârthrī'-tĭs) *n.* Degenerative arthritis, esp. in elderly persons.

os·te·ol·o·gy (ŏstēŏl'*o*jē) *n.* Branch of anatomy concerned with the study of the skeleton and the structure of bones. **os·te·o·log·i·cal** (ŏstē*o*lŏj'ĭk*a*l) *adj.* **os·te·o·log'i·cal·ly** *adv.* **os·te·ol'o·gist** *n.*

os·te·o·my·e·li·tis (ŏstēōmīelī'-tĭs) *n.* Inflammation of (esp. the marrow) a bone.

os·te·op·a·thy (ŏstēŏp'*a*thē) *n.* Theory of disease and method of cure based on assumption that deformation of part of skeleton, notably the spine, and consequent interference with nerves and blood vessels, are the cause of most diseases. **os·te·o·path·ic** (ŏstē*o*-păth'ĭk) *adj.* **os·te·o·path'i·cal·ly** *adv.* **os·te·o·path** (ŏs'tē*o*păth) *n.* Practitioner of osteopathy.

Ost·po·li·tik (awst'pawlĭtēk') *n.* Policies of a European country toward Communist countries. [Ger. *ost*, east]

os·tra·cize (ŏs'tr*a*sīz) *v.t.* (**-cized, -ciz·ing**). 1. (in ancient Athens) Banish (dangerously powerful or unpopular citizen) for 5 or 10 years by voting with potsherds or tiles (*ostraka*) on which name of person to be banished was written. 2. Exclude from society, refuse to associate with. **os·tra·cism** (ŏs'tr*a*sĭz*e*m) *n.*

os·trich (aw'strĭch, ŏs'trĭch) *n.* (pl. **-trich·es**, collect. **-trich**). Very large swift-running bird (*Struthio camelus*) of sandy plains of Africa and formerly Arabia, with small wings useless for flight, and habit of swallowing hard substances to assist working of gizzard; proverbial for self-delusion owing to the (unfounded) belief that when pursued the ostrich buries its head in the sand imagining that it cannot then be seen; **~ plume**, wing or tail feather of ostrich as ornament.

Os·tro·goth (ŏs'tr*o*gŏth) *n.* Member of eastern branch of GOTHS, who toward end of 5th c. conquered Italy, and under their leader THEODORIC established a kingdom in Italy, Sicily, and Dalmatia which lasted until 555. **Os·tro·goth'ic** *adj.*

Os·wald (ŏz'wawld), **Lee Harvey** (1939–1963). Alleged assassin of President John F. Kennedy, 1963; while being transferred from jail, he was himself shot and killed.

OT, O.T. *abbrevs.* Old Testament.

o·ta·ry (ō't*a*rē) *n.* Member of the Otariidae, a mainly Antarctic family of seals with small external ear, including fur seals and sea lions; eared seal.

oth·er (ŭdh'*e*r) *adj.* Not the same as one or more or some already mentioned or implied; separate in identity, distinct in kind; alternative, further, or additional; **every ~**, every alternate; **the ~**, the one remaining; **the ~ day**, a few days ago; **on the ~ hand**, in contrast (with fact or argument just mentioned); **~ than**, different from; **~ things being equal**, with conditions alike in everything but the point in question; **the ~ world**, life after death; **oth'er·world'ly** (*adj.*), concerned with or thinking of this or some imagined world to the neglect of the present one. **other** *n.* or *pron.* (orig. elliptic use of adj.) Other person, thing, specimen, etc.; **someone or ~**, a person unknown. **other** *adv.* Otherwise.

oth·er·wise (ŭdh'*e*rwīz) *adv.* In a different way; if circumstances are or were different, else, or; in other respects; in a different state.

o·tic (ō'tĭk, ŏt'ĭk) *adj.* Of the ear.

o·ti·ose (ō'shēōs, ō'tē-) *adj.* Not required, serving no practical

*The **osprey** or fish-hawk hunts by diving and seizing fish at the surface in its talons. It has wide distribution though populations have been depleted by pesticides which accumulate in fish and sterilize the birds' eggs.*

purpose. **o'ti·ose·ly** *adv.* **o·ti·os·i·ty** (ōshēŏs'ĭtē, ōtē-), **o'ti·ose·ness** *ns.*

o·ti·tis (ōtī'tĭs) *n.* Inflammation of the ear.

o·to·lar·yn·gol·o·gy (ōtōlărĭng-gŏl'ojē), **o·to·rhi·no·lar·yn·gol·o·gy** (ōtōrī'nōlărĭnggŏl'ojē) *ns.* Branch of medicine dealing with diseases of ear, nose, and throat. **o·to·lar·yn·gol'o·gist, o·to·rhi'-no·lar·yn·gol'o·gist** *ns.*

ot·ta·va ri·ma (awtah'văh rē'-mah). Italian stanza of eight 11-syllabled lines (ten-syllabled in English), the first six lines rhyming alternately, the last two forming a couplet.

Ot·ta·wa (ŏt'*awa*). City of Ontario and capital of Canada, situated on the ~ **River**, a tributary of the St. Lawrence.

ot·ter (ŏt'*er*) *n.* (pl. **-ters**, collect. **-ter**). 1. Aquatic fur-bearing carnivorous mammal of genus *Lutra* and related genera, feeding chiefly on fish, with webbed feet and pointed tail somewhat flattened horizontally; fur of this. 2. (minesweeping) Steel frame shaped like a box kite for holding sweep wires at required depth.

Ot·to·man (ŏt'*oman*) *adj.* Of the Ottoman Empire; ~ **Empire**, Turkish Empire in SW. Asia, NE. Africa, and SE. Europe, founded *c*1300 and lasting until 1919; capital, Constantinople. **Ottoman** *n.* (pl. **-mans**). Turk.

ot·to·man (ŏt'*oman*) *n.* (pl. **-mans**). Cushioned seat like sofa or chair without back or arms (freq. a box with cushioned top).

Oua·ga·dou·gou (wahg*a*dōō'-gōō). Capital of Burkina Faso, in the central region.

ou·bli·ette (ōōblēēt') *n.* Secret dungeon with entrance only by trapdoor above.

ouch (owch) *int.* Exclamation of pain or annoyance.

ought[1], **aught** (awt) *ns.* (colloq.) Figure denoting nothing, nought.

ought[2] (awt) *v. aux.* Expressing duty, rightness, shortcoming, advisability, or strong probability.

ought[3] (awt) = AUGHT.[1]

Oui·ja (wē'*ja*, -jē) **board.** (trademark) Board with letters, signs, etc., used with planchette for obtaining messages in spiritualist séances. [Fr. *oui* yes; Ger. *ja* yes]

ounce[1] (owns) *n.* (abbrev. oz.). Unit of weight, $\frac{1}{16}$ lb. in avoirdupois, $\frac{1}{12}$ lb. in troy weight; **fluid** ~, 8 (fluid) drachms, $\frac{1}{16}$ of pint, $\frac{1}{20}$ of imperial pint; (fig.) very small quantity. [L. *uncia* twelfth (of pound or foot)]

ounce[2] (owns) *n.* 1. (poet.) Lynx or other vaguely identified feline beast. 2. (zool.) Snow leopard (*Uncia uncia*) of highlands of central Asia, smaller and lighter in color than leopard but with similar markings.

The largest living bird, the flightless ***ostrich,*** *was once present in south-west Asia. Today it is confined to east Africa although it is still farmed in South Africa. It can run at 40 m.p.h.*

our (owr, ow'*er*, ār) *poss. pron.* Possessive case of WE used as attrib. adjective, with absolute and predicate form **ours** (pr. owrz, ow'*erz*, ārz), belonging to us.

our·self (owrsĕlf', ow*er*-, ār-) *pron.* (pl. **-selves** pr. -sĕlvz). Emphatic and reflexive form corresp. to WE, US.

ou·sel (ōō'zel) = OUZEL.

oust (owst) *v.t.* Put out of possession, eject, expel *from*, drive out; force oneself or be put into the place of.

out (owt) *adv.* 1. Away from or not in or at a place, the right or normal state, the fashion, etc.; not at home; (of calculation) inaccurate; (boxing) unable to put up a defense,

The giant **otter** *from Brazil (left) can be up to 8 ft. long and may weigh 75 lb. The European variety (right) is only a third or less of the other's weight. Both are aquatic carnivores.*

e.g. ~ **for the count** (i.e. the counting of seconds from one to ten); not at work, on strike; (of fire etc.) no longer burning. 2. In(to) the open, publicity, hearing, sight, notice, etc.; ~ **for,** ~ **to do,** (colloq.) engaged in seeking; ~ **and about,** able to leave bed or house. 3. To or at an end, completely; (in oral communication by radio etc., as indication) transmission ends; **all** ~, with greatest effort; ~ **and away,** by far; ~ **and** ~, thorough(ly), surpassing(ly). 4. ~ **of,** from within; not within; from among; beyond range of; (so as to be) without; from, owing to, by use of (material); at specified distance from; beyond; transgressing rules of; (of animals) having as dam; ~ **of doors,** in, into the open air; ~ **of it,** not included, forlorn, at a loss; ~**-of-the-way,** remote; uncommon, remarkable; ~ **of this world,** (esp.) superlatively good. **out** *prep.* Out of (now only in **from** ~). **out** *adj.* 1. External, living etc. outside. 2. (baseball) Not successful in reaching base safely. ~ *n.* 1. Way of escape. 2. (baseball) Any play that retires a batter or base runner; player thus retired. 3. (tennis) Return or serve hit out of bounds. 4. (pl.) **ins and** ~**s**: see IN; **on the** or **at** ~**s**, at variance or enmity.

out- *prefix.* External; detached; out of; to excess; so as to surpass.

out·back (*adj.* owt′băk′; *n.* owt′-băk) *adj.* & *n.* (Austral.) (Of) the more remote settlements. **out′-back·er** *n.* Dweller in outback.

out·bid (owtbĭd′) *v.t.* (**-bid, -bid·den** or **-bid, -bid·ding**). Outdo in bidding, offer more than.

out·board (owt′bōrd, -bŏrd) *adj.* On, toward, nearer to, outside of ship or aircraft; (of motorboat) with engine and propeller attached outside boat at stern. ~ *adv.* To, toward, outside of ship or aircraft.

out·break (owt′brāk) *n.* Breaking out of emotion (esp. anger), hostilities, disease, fire, volcanic energy, etc.; outcrop; insurrection.

out·build·ing (owt′bĭldĭng) *n.* House, building, shed belonging to and near or built against main house.

out·burst (owt′bĕrst) *n.* Explosion of feeling, esp. expressed by vehement words; volcanic eruption.

out·cast (owt′kăst, -kahst) *adj.* & *n.* 1. (Person) cast out from home and friends; homeless and friendless (vagabond). 2. (Person) who has lost or been expelled from his caste, or who does not belong to a caste.

out·class (owtklăs′, -klahs′) *v.t.* Belong to higher class than, completely beat or surpass.

out·come (owt′kŭm) *n.* Issue, result.

out·crop (owt′krŏp) *n.* Emergence of stratum, vein, or rock at surface.

out·cry (owt′krī) *n.* (pl. **-cries**). Clamor, uproar.

out·dis·tance (owtdĭs′tans) *v.t.* (**-tanced, -tanc·ing**). Get far ahead of.

out·do (owtdōō′) *v.t.* (**-did, -done, -do·ing**). Surpass, excel.

out·door (owt′dōr, -dŏr) *adj.* Done, existing, or used outdoors. **out·doors** (owtdōrz′, -dŏrz′) *adv.* Out of doors.

out·er (ow′ter) *adj.* Farther from center or inside, relatively far out; external, of the outside; objective, physical, not subjective or psychical. **out·er·most** (ow′termōst) *adj.*

out·face (owtfās′) *v.t.* (**-faced, -fac·ing**). Look out of countenance, stare down; confront fearlessly or impudently, brave, defy.

out·field (owt′fēld) *n.* Outer part of baseball field, beyond the baseball DIAMOND; hence **out′-field·er** *n.*

out·fit (owt′fĭt) *n.* Complete equipment; party traveling or in charge of herds of cattle etc.; (colloq.) organized group of persons (esp. military unit). ~ *v.t.* (**-fit·ted, -fit·ting**). Provide with outfit; supply *with.* **out′fit·ter** *n.* Supplier of equipment; retailer of men's ready-made clothes.

out·flank (owtflăngk′) *v.t.* Get beyond flank of (opposing army), outmaneuver by flanking movement. **out·flank′er** *n.*

out·flow (owt′flō) *n.* What flows out, amount flowing out.

out·fox (owtfŏks′) *v.t.* Outwit.

out·gen·er·al (owtjĕn′eral) *v.t.* (**-aled** or **-alled, -al·ing** or **-al·ling**). Defeat by superior generalship.

out·go (owt′gō) *n.* (pl. **-goes**). Expenditure, outlay.

out·go·ing (owt′gōing) *adj.* 1. Friendly. 2. Retiring from a position. 3. (of, ebbing tide) Going out.

out·grow (owtgrō′) *v.t.* (**-grew, -grown, -grow·ing**). Grow faster, get taller, than; get too big for (clothes); get rid of (childish habit, ailment, taste) with advancing age.

out·growth (owt′grōth) *n.* Offshoot; consequence.

out-Her·od (owt-hĕr′od) *v.t.* Be more violent or hectoring than Herod (represented in old mystery plays as a blustering tyrant); outdo, surpass.

out·house (owt′hows) *n.* (pl.

-hous·es pr. -howzĭz). Privy.

out·ing (ow'tĭng) *n.* Pleasure trip, holiday away from home.

out·land·er (owt'lănd*er*) *n.* 1. (esp. poet.) Alien. 2. = UITLANDER.

out·land·ish (owtlăn'dĭsh) *adj.* Foreign looking or sounding; unfamiliar, bizarre, uncouth. **out·land'ish·ly** *adv.* **out·land'ish·ness** *n.*

out·last (owtlăst') *v.t.* Last longer than.

out·law (owt'law) *n.* Person deprived of protection of the law, banished or exiled person. ~ *v.t.* Proscribe, declare outlaw. **out·law·ry** (owt'lawrē) *n.* Condition of, condemnation as, outlaw.

out·lay (owt'lā) *n.* What one spends, expenses.

out·let (owt'lĕt, -lĭt) *n.* Means of exit or escape, vent, way out; market for goods.

out·line (owt'līn) *n.* Line(s) enclosing the apparently plane figure presented by any object to sight, contour, external boundary; sketch containing only contour lines and no shading; rough draft, verbal description of essential parts only, summary; (pl.) main features, general principles. ~ *v.t.* (**-lined, -lin·ing**). Draw or describe in outline; mark outline of. **out·lin'er** *n.*

out·live (owtlĭv') *v.t.* (**-lived, -liv·ing**). Live beyond; come safely through, get over effect of; live longer than.

out·look (owt'lo͝ok) *n.* What one sees on looking out, view, prospect; person's general view of life; what seems likely to happen.

out·ly·ing (owt'līĭng) *adj.* Situated far from a center, remote.

out·ma·neu·ver (owtm*a*no͞o'v*er*) *v.t.* Get the better of by superior strategy.

out·match (owtmăch') *v.t.* Be more than a match for.

out·mod·ed (owtmō'dĭd) *adj.* Out of date, old-fashioned.

out·most (owt'mōst) *adj.* Outermost.

out·num·ber (owtnŭm'b*er*) *v.t.* Exceed in number.

out·pa·tient (owt'pāsh*e*nt) *n.* One receiving treatment at hospital etc. without being lodged in it.

out·play (owtplā') *v.t.* Surpass in playing; play better than.

out·point (owtpoint') *v.t.* 1. Score more points than. 2. (nautical) Sail closer to the wind than. 3. (boxing) Win through superior skill rather than through knockout.

out·post (owt'pōst) *n.* Detachment on guard at some distance from army to prevent surprise.

out·pour·ing (owt'pōrĭng, -pŏr-) *n.* Effusion; verbal or literary expression of emotion.

out·put (owt'po͝ot) *n.* 1. Amount produced by manufacture, mining, labor, etc.; product; current etc. produced by electrical device. 2. Information, results, etc. produced by a computer. ~ *v.t.* (**-put·ted, -put·ting**). (of a computer) To produce such information.

out·rage (owt'rāj) *n.* Forcible violation of others' rights, sentiments, etc.; deed of violence, gross or wanton offense or indignity. ~ *v.t.* (**-raged, -rag·ing**). Do violence to, subject to outrage, injure, insult, violate; infringe (law, morality, etc.) flagrantly. **out·ra·geous** (owtrā'j*u*s) *adj.* Immoderate, extravagant, extraordinary; violent, furious; grossly cruel, immoral, offensive, or abusive. **out·ra'geous·ly** *adv.* **out·ra'geous·ness** *n.*

out·rank (owtrăngk') *v.t.* Be superior in rank to.

*In Australia, the **outback** was a term derived from 'back blocks' — land made available for grazing after the 1850s and distant from any centres of population.*

***Outrigger** canoes on Sanur beach in Bali. These speedy lightweight canoes have a small sail which adds to their range. The two struts on either side give it an additional stability.*

*Stone **ovens** are still used in the open in Bergama, Turkey (above right) and elsewhere. Compared with them, modern kitchen stoves seem to be as advanced mechanically as industrial kilns used by potteries in Northern Ireland (right).*

ou·tré (ōōtrā′) *adj.* Outside the bounds of propriety, eccentric. [Fr.]

out·reach (owtrēch′) *v.t.* Reach farther than; surpass; (poet.) stretch out (arm etc.).

out·rid·er (owt′rīd*er*) *n.* Mounted attendant riding before, behind, or with carriage.

out·rig·ger (owt′rĭg*er*) *n.* Beam, spar, framework, rigged out and projecting from or over ship's side for various purposes; bracket supporting rowlock beyond boat's side to enable a long oar to be conveniently used in a narrow boat; boat with such outriggers; ~ **canoe**, canoe having a long float parallel to its side, attached by beams.

out·right (owt′rīt′) *adv.* Altogether, entirely, once for all, not by degrees or installments or half-and-half; without reservation, openly. **outright** (owt′rīt) *adj.* Downright, direct, thorough. **out′right·ness** *n.*

out·run (owtrŭn′) *v.t.* (**-ran, -run, -run·ning**). Outstrip in running; pass the limit of.

out·set (owt′sĕt) *n.* Start, commencement.

out·shine (owtshīn′) *v.t.* (**-shone, -shin·ing**). Surpass in brightness, splendor, or excellence.

out·side (owt′sīd′, owt′sīd, outsīd′) *n.* 1. Outer side or surface; (of path) side away from wall or next to road. 2. Outer part, exterior; outward aspect. 3. Highest computation. **outside** (owtsīd′, owt′sīd) *adj.* Situated on, derived from, the outside; not belonging to some circle or institution; greatest existent or possible; ~ **chance**, remote, very unlikely chance. **outside′** *adv.* On or to the outside, the open air, open sea, etc.; not within. **outside** (owtsid′, owt′sīd) *prep.* External to; beyond the limits of; at or to the outside of.

out·sid·er (owtsī′d*er*) *n.* Nonmember of some circle, party, profession, etc., uninitiated person, layman; person without special knowledge, breeding, etc., or not fit to mix with good society; horse or person not thought to have a chance in race or competition.

out·size (owt′sīz) *n.* Person or thing larger than the normal, esp. ready-made article of dress larger than the standard size (also attrib.).

out·skirts (owt′skērts) *n.pl.* Outer border, fringe, of city, district, etc.

out·smart (owtsmart′) *v.t.* Outwit, be smarter than.

out·spo·ken (owtspō′k*en*) *adj.* Frank, unreserved. **out·spo′ken·ly** *adv.* **out·spo′ken·ness** *n.*

out·spread (owt′sprĕd′) *adj.* Spread out.

out·stand·ing (owtstăn′dĭng) *adj.* Prominent; still unsettled. **out·stand′ing·ly** *adv.* **out·stand′ing·ness** *n.*

out·stay (owtstā′) *v.t.* Stay

*This suburb on the **outskirts** of Phoenix, Arizona is a clear indication of that city's encroachment on the agricultural surrounds. As the population increases the urban spread continues.*

*When the sky is **overcast,** masses of clouds cover it so that no direct sunlight reaches the earth. Common in temperate zones, this also occurs during the wet season in the tropics.*

beyond limits of, exhaust by staying; stay longer than.

out·strip (owtstrĭp′) *v.t.* (**-stripped, -strip·ping**). Pass in running etc.; surpass in competition or relative progress or ability.

out·vote (owtvōt′) *v.t.* (**-vot·ed, -vot·ing**). Outnumber in voting.

out·ward (owt′werd) *adj.* Outer (archaic); directed toward the outside; bodily, external, material, visible, apparent, superficial; ~ **form**, appearance. **outward** *adv.* (*also* **out′wards**) In an outward direction; ~**-bound**, (of ship or passenger) going away from home. **out′ward·ly** *adv.* **out′ward·ness** *n.*

out·weigh (owtwā′) *v.t.* Exceed in weight, value, importance, or influence.

out·wit (owtwĭt′) *v.t.* (**-wit·ted, -wit·ting**). Prove too clever for, overreach, take in.

out·work (owt′wẽrk) *n.* Part of fortifications lying outside parapet; detached or advanced part of fortification. **out·work′** *v.t.* (**-worked** or **-wrought, -work·ing**). Surpass in work.

out·worn (owtwōrn′, -wōrn′) *adj.* Worn out; exhausted, spent.

ou·zel, ou·sel (o͞o′zel) *ns.* 1. Any of several black European thrushes. 2. see DIPPER.

ou·zo (o͞o′zō) *n.* (pl. **-zos**). Greek liqueur flavored with anise.

o·val (ō′val) *adj.* Egg-shaped, ellipsoidal; having the outline of an egg, elliptical; **the O~ Office**, White House office of the U.S. President; hence, the Presidency. **oval** *n.* Closed curve with one axis longer than the other, like ellipse or outline of egg; thing with oval outline.

o·va·ry (ō′varē) *n.* (pl. **-ries**). Organ of female reproductive system, that in which ova or eggs are produced; in plants, lowest part of pistil, ultimately becoming fruit or seed vessel. **o·var·i·an** (ōvār′ēan) *adj.*

o·vate (ō′vāt) *adj.* (biol.) Egg-shaped, oval.

o·va·tion (ōvā′shon) *n.* Enthusiastic reception, spontaneous applause. **o·va′tion·al** *adj.*

ov·en (ŭv′en) *n.* Enclosed chamber or compartment for baking, heating, drying, etc.; **Dutch ~**: see DUTCH; **ov′enware**, dishes that can be used for cooking food in an oven.

o·ver (ō′ver) *adv.* 1. Outward and downward from brink (as *push ~ the edge*) or from erect position (*lean ~*). 2. So as to cover or touch whole surface (*paint it ~*). 3. With motion above something so as to pass across something (*climb ~*). 4. So as to produce fold or reverse position (*bend it ~*; *turn ~*, turn other side of leaf up). 5. Across street or other space or distance; ~ **against**, in opposite situation to, in contrast with. 6. With transference or change from one hand, party, etc., to another; (in radio communication etc., as indication) changing from transmission to reception. 7. Too, in excess; in addition, besides; more; apart; ~ **and above**, moreover, into the bargain. 8. From beginning to end, with repetition, with detailed consideration (*read ~, talk (matter) ~*). 9. At an end, done with (*the war is ~*). **over** *prep.* 1. Above, on, at all or various points upon; to and fro upon, all through, round about; concerning, engaged with. 2. With or so as to get or give superiority to; beyond, more than; ~ **and above**, besides, not to mention. 3. Out and down from, down from edge of; so as to clear; across, on or to the other side of; throughout, through duration of, till end of; **stumble ~**, be tripped up by.

over- *prefix.* Over; upper, outer; superior; excessive.

o·ver·act (ōverăkt′) *v.* Act (part, emotion, etc.), act part, with exaggeration.

o·ver·all (ō′verawl) *n.* Garment worn over others as protection against wet, dirt, etc.; (pl.) trousers with chest piece for dirty work. **o·ver·all′** *adj.* Taking into account all features or aspects; inclusive. ~ *adv.* In all parts; taken as a whole.

o·ver·arm (ō′verārm) *adv.* & *adj.* = OVERHAND.

o·ver·awe (ōveraw′) *v.t.* (**-awed, -aw·ing**). Restrain, control, or repress by awe.

o·ver·bear (ōverbār′) *v.t.* (**-bore, -borne, -bear·ing**). Bear down or upset by weight or force; put down, repress, by power or authority; surpass in importance etc., outweigh. **o·ver·bear′ing** *adj.* Domineering, masterful **o·ver·bear′ing·ly** *adv.* **o·ver·bear′ing·ness** *n.*

o·ver·blown (ōverblōn′) *adj.* (of flower) Too fully open, past its prime.

o·ver·board (ō′verbōrd, -bōrd) *adv.* From within ship into water; **throw ~**, (fig.) abandon, discard.

o·ver·bur·den (ōverbẽr′den *v.*; ōv′erbẽr′den *n.*) *v.t.* Burden too much, overload, overcharge. ~ *n.* (geol.) Soil etc. overlying a mineral deposit.

o·ver·call (ōverkawl′) *v.t.* (bridge) Bid more on (hand) than it is worth; bid higher than (opponent, previous bid, one's partner when opponent has not done so). **o′vercall** *n.* Bid made over partner's bid.

o·ver·cap·i·tal·ize (ōverkăp′ĭ-

talīz) *v.t.* (**-ized, -iz·ing**). Fix or estimate capital of (company etc.) too high. **o·ver·cap·i·tal·i·za·tion** (ō´verkăpĭtalīzā´shon) *n.*

o·ver·cast (ōverkăst´, ō´verkăst) *v.t.* (**-cast, -cast·ing**). 1. Cover (sky etc.) with clouds or darkness (usu. in past part. **overcast**). 2. Sew over raw edges of (material, esp. with blanket or buttonhole stitch) to prevent unraveling.

o·ver·charge (ōverchärj´) *v.t.* (**-charged, -charg·ing**). 1. Charge too highly with explosive, electricity, etc. 2. Put exaggerated details or too much detail into (description etc.). 3. Charge too high a price for (thing) or to (person); charge (specified sum) beyond right price. **o´ver·charge** *n.* Excessive charge. **o·ver·charg´er** *n.*

o·ver·coat (ō´verkōt) *n.* Large coat worn over ordinary clothing, esp. in cold weather.

o·ver·come (ōverkŭm´) *v.* (**-came, -come, -com·ing**). Prevail over, master, get the better of; be victorious. ~ *adj.* (esp.) Exhausted, made helpless, deprived

*An **overpass** in Massachusetts (above) is typical of methods adopted by modern traffic engineers to allow faster traffic flow and to reduce the incidence of accidents by eliminating cross-roads.*

of self-possession.

o·ver·crowd (ōverkrowd´) *v.* Crowd to excess; esp., crowd more people into a space than there is proper accommodation for.

o·ver·do (ōverdōō´) *v.t.* (**-did, -done, -do·ing**). Carry to excess, go too far in; cook too long (esp. in past part.); overtax strength of (esp. in past part.). **o·ver·do´er** *n.*

o·ver·dose (ō´verdōs) *n.* Excessive dose.

o·ver·draft (ō´verdrăft) *n.* Overdrawing of bank account; amount by which check exceeds balance.

o·ver·draw (ōverdraw´) *v.* (**-drew, -drawn, -draw·ing**). 1. Draw check in excess of (one's account). 2. Exaggerate in describing.

o·ver·dress (ōverdrĕs´) *v.* Dress with too much display and ornament.

o·ver·drive (ō´verdrīv) *n.* (mech.) System by which a speed higher than that maintained by the engine is passed to the propeller shaft.

o·ver·due (ōverdōō´, -dū´) *adj.* More than due; late, in arrear.

o·ver·eat (ōverēt´) *v.* (**-ate, -eat·en, -eat·ing**). Eat to excess.

o·ver·es·ti·mate (ōverĕs´timāt) *v.t.* (**-mat·ed, -mat·ing**). Estimate too highly. ~ (ō´verĕs´-timĭt) *n.* Too high an estimate. **o´ver·es·ti·ma´tion** *n.*

o·ver·flow (ō´verflō) *n.* What overflows or is superfluous; outlet for excess liquid; ~ **meeting**, meeting elsewhere of those who have not found room at demonstration etc. **overflow´** *v.* (**-flowed, -flown, -flow·ing**). Flow over (brim etc.), flood (surface); extend beyond limits of; (of receptacle) be so full that contents overflow; (of kindness, harvest, etc.) be very abundant. **o·ver·flow´ing** *n.* & *adj.* **o·ver·flow´ing·ly** *adv.*

o·ver·fly (ōverflī´) *v.t.* (**-flew, -flown, -fly·ing**). (of aircraft) Fly over (territory); fly beyond.

o·ver·glaze (ō´verglāz) *n.*

Special mountaineering techniques are needed to negotiate an ***overhang*** *when a cliff is being scaled. The overhang illustrated above is in the Swiss Alps.*

Second glaze applied to pottery over first glaze. ~ *adj.* (of painting etc.) Done on glazed surface.

o·ver·grow (ōvergrō′) *v.* (**-grew, -grown, -grow·ing**). Grow over, cover with growth; grow too large; grow too big etc. for.

o·ver·hand (ōverhănd) *adv.* & *adj.* (sports) With hand above object held; with hand above shoulder in baseball etc.; with hand or arm out of water in swimming. **o′ver·hand·ed** *adv.*

o·ver·hang (ōverhăng′) *v.* (**-hung, -hang·ing**). Jut out over, jut; (fig.) impend (over). **o′ver·hang** *n.* Thing that overhangs; fact or amount of overhanging.

o·ver·haul (ōverhawl′) *v.t.* Take apart for purpose of examining, examine condition of and repair; (esp. naut.) catch up, come up with. **o·ver·haul′er** *n.*

o·ver·head (ō′verhĕd′) *adv.* On high; in the sky; in the story above. **o′verhead** *adj.* Placed overhead. ~ *n.* 1. The general expenses of running a business. 2. A stroke in a racket game made with a downward motion from above head height.

o·ver·hear (ōverhēr′) *v.t.* (**-heard, -hear·ing**). Hear as eavesdropper or unperceived or unintended listener.

o·ver·joyed (ōverjoid′) *adj.* Transported with joy (*at*).

o·ver·kill (ō′verkĭl) *n.* Amount by which (capacity for) destruction (lit. or fig.) exceeds what is necessary for victory over or annihilation of enemy.

o·ver·lad·en (ōverlā′den) *adj.* Overloaded, overburdened.

o·ver·land (ō′verlănd, -land) *adv.* By land and not sea. ~ *adj.* Entirely or partly by land.

o·ver·lap (ōverlăp′) *v.* (**-lapped, -lap·ping**). Partly cover; cover and extend beyond; partly coincide. **o′verlap** *n.* Thing that overlaps; fact or amount of overlapping.

o·ver·lay (ōverlā′) *v.t.* (**-laid, -lay·ing**). Cover surface of *with* coating etc. **o′verlay** *n.* Thing laid over something, coverlet, small tablecloth, etc.

o·ver·leaf (ō′verlēf) *adv.* On other side of leaf (of book etc.).

o·ver·leap (ōverlēp′) *v.t.* (**-leaped** or **-leapt, -leap·ing**). Leap over, surmount; omit, ignore.

o·ver·load (ōverlōd′) *v.t.* Load to excess. **o′verload** *n.* Excessive load or charge, as of electric current.

o·ver·look (ōverlo͝ok′) *v.t.* 1. Have prospect of or over from above; be higher than. 2. Fail to observe, take no notice of, condone. 3. Superintend, oversee. 4. Bewitch with evil eye.

o·ver·lord (ō′verlôrd) *n.* Supreme lord, suzerain. **o′ver·lord·ship** *n.*

o·ver·ly (ō′verlē) *adv.* Over, excessively.

o·ver·much (ō′vermŭch′) *adj.*, *n.*, & *adv.* Too much.

o·ver·night (ō′vernīt′) *adv.* On the preceding evening (in relation to following day); through the night (till the following morning). **o′ver·night** *adj.* Done etc. overnight.

o·ver·pass (ō′verpăs) *n.* Road bridge over another road, esp. over a motorway.

o·ver·play (ōverplā′) *v.t.* Play part to excess; give undue importance to; ~ **one's hand** (cards or fig.) be unduly optimistic as to one's capabilities.

o·ver·pow·er (ōverpow′er) *v.t.* Reduce to submission, subdue, master; be too intense or violent for, overwhelm. **o·ver·pow′er·ing** *adj.* **o·ver·pow′er·ing·ly** *adv.* **o·ver·pow′er·ing·ness** *n.*

o·ver·print (ōverprĭnt′) *v.t.* Print (photographic print) darker than intended; print (additional matter or another color) on already printed surface, esp. of postage stamp. **o′ver·print** *n.*

o·ver·rate (ōverrāt′) *v.t.* (**-rat·ed, -rat·ing**). Have too high an opinion of; assess too high for rating purposes.

o·ver·reach (ōverrēch′) *v.* 1. (refl.) Strain *oneself* by reaching too far; (of horse) injure forefoot by striking it with hind hoof. 2. Circumvent, outwit, get the better of by cunning or artifice.

o·ver·ride (ōverrīd′) *v.t.* (**-rode, -rid·den, -rid·ing**). 1. Exhaust (horse) by riding. 2. Ride over (enemy's country) with armed force; trample (person) under one's horse's hoofs; (fig.) trample under foot, set aside, refuse to comply with, have or claim superior authority to. **o′verride** *n.* Sales commission paid to executive in addition to that paid to salesperson.

o·ver·rule (ōverro͞ol′) *v.t.* (**-ruled, -rul·ing**). Set aside (decision, argument, etc.) by superior authority; annul decision

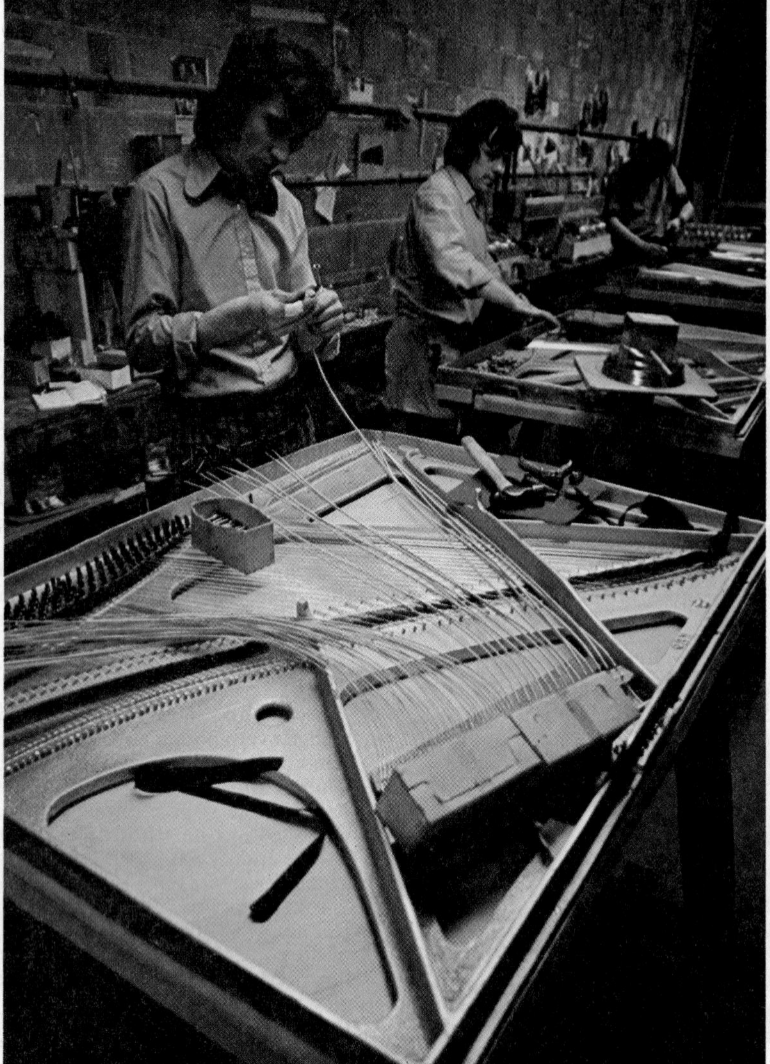

Making ***overstrung*** *pianos (above) demands painstaking craftsmanship. By placing the bass strings so that they partly overlap the tenor ones, but on a different plane, space is saved and the finished instruments produce greater resonance.*

or reject proposal of (person).

o·ver·run (ōverrŭn′) *v.t.* (**-ran, -run, -run·ning**). Flood, harry and spoil (enemy's country); swarm or spread over; exceed (limit). **o′verrun** *n.* Amount by which (cost, production, etc.) exceeds forecast or estimate, as in *cost* ~.

o·ver·seas (ōversēz′) *adv.* Across or beyond sea. **o′ver·seas′** *adj.*

o·ver·see (ōversē′) *v.t.* (**-saw, -seen, -see·ing**). Superintend, look after (workmen, execution of work, etc.). **o′ver·se·er** *n.*

o·ver·sexed (ōversĕkst′) *adj.* Having unusually great sexual desires.

o·ver·shad·ow (ōvershăd′ō) *v.t.* Cast a shadow over; (fig.) be more conspicuous than, outshine.

o·ver·shoe (ō′vershōō) *n.* Shoe of rubber, felt, etc., worn outside another.

o·ver·shoot (ōvershōōt′) *v.t.* (**-shot, -shoot·ing**). Send missile, go, beyond (mark etc.); ~ **the mark**, go too far, exaggerate, overdo something.

o·ver·shot (ō′vershŏt) *adj.* (of wheel) Turned by water flowing above it.

o·ver·sight (ō′versīt) *n.* 1. Supervision. 2. Omission to notice, mistake of inadvertence.

o·ver·sleep (ōverslēp′) *v.refl.* & *i.* (**-slept, -sleep·ing**). Miss intended hour of rising by sleeping too long.

o·ver·state (ōverstāt′) *v.t.* (**-stat·ed, -stat·ing**). State too strongly, exaggerate. **o′ver·state′-ment** *n.*

o·ver·steer (ōverstēr′) *v.i.* (of vehicle) Have tendency to steer toward the inner side on a curve. **o′versteer** *n.* Oversteering.

o·ver·step (ōverstĕp′) *v.t.* (**-stepped, -step·ping**). Pass over (boundary).

o·ver·strain (ōverstrān′) *v.t.* Damage by exertion; make too much of (argument etc.).

o·ver·strung (ō′verstrŭng′) *adj.* 1. (of piano) With strings arranged in sets crossing each other obliquely. 2. (of person, nerves, etc.) Intensely strained.

o·ver·stuff (ōverstŭf′) *v.t.* Stuff more than is necessary; ~**ed** (of furniture) made soft and comfortable by thick upholstery. **o·ver·stuffed′** *adj.*

o·ver·sub·scribe (ōversubskrīb′) *v.t.* (**-scribed, -scrib·ing**). (usu. in past part.) Subscribe more than amount of (loan etc.). **o·ver·-sub·scrib′er, o·ver·sub·scrip′-tion** *ns.*

o·vert (ōvẽrt′, ō′vẽrt) *adj.* Openly done, unconcealed, patent. **o·vert′ly** *adv.*

o·ver·take (ōvertāk′) *v.t.* (**-took, -tak·en, -tak·ing**). Come up with, catch up; (of storm, misfortune, etc.) come suddenly upon; (of vehicle) pass (vehicle) traveling in same direction.

o·ver·tax (ōvertăks′) *v.t.* Make excessive demand on (person's strength etc.); burden with excessive taxes.

o·ver·throw (ōverthrō′) *v.t.* (**-threw, -thrown, -throw·ing**). Upset, knock down; cast out from power; vanquish, subvert; put an end to. **o′verthrow** *n.* Defeat, subversion.

o·ver·time (ō′vertīm) *adv.* Beyond regular hours of work. ~ *n.* Time during which workman etc. works beyond regular hours; payment for this.

o·ver·tone (ō′vertōn) *n.* (mus.) Harmonic; (subtle or elusive) secondary quality, color, etc.; implication.

o·ver·ture (ō′vercher, -choor) *n.* 1. Opening of negotiations with another (usu. pl.); formal proposal or offer. 2. (mus.) Orchestral piece beginning opera, oratorio, etc.

o·ver·turn (ōvertẽrn′) *v.* Upset; (cause to) fall down or over; overthrow, subvert; abolish. **o′ver·-turn** *n.*

o·ver·ween·ing (ō′verwē′nĭng) *adj.* Arrogant, presumptuous. **o·ver·ween′ing·ly** *adv.* **o·ver·-ween′ing·ness** *n.*

o·ver·weight (ō′verwāt) *n.* Preponderance; excessive weight. ~ *adj.* Beyond weight allowed or desirable. **o·ver·weight′** *v.t.* Impose too great weight or burden on.

o·ver·whelm (ōverhwĕlm′, ōverwĕlm′) *v.t.* Bury beneath overlying mass, submerge utterly; crush, bring to sudden ruin; overpower with emotion etc.; deluge *with*. **o·ver·whelm′ing** *adj.* Irresistible by reason of numbers, amount, etc. **o·ver·whelm′ing·ly** *adv.* **o·ver·whelm′ing·ness** *n.*

o·ver·wind (ōverwīnd′) *v.t.*

(**-wound, -wind·ing**). Wind too far.

o·ver·work (overwĕrk′) *v.* (**-worked** or **-wrought, -work·ing**). (Cause to) work too hard; weary or exhaust with work. **o′ver-work** *n.* Excessive work.

o·ver·wrought (ōverrawt′) *adj.* 1. Overexcited; suffering reaction from excitement. 2. Too elaborate.

Ov·id (ŏv′ĭd). Publius Ovidius Naso (43 B.C.–*c*18 A.D.), Roman poet; author of *Ars Amatoria, Metamorphoses*, etc. **O·vid·i·an** (ŏvĭd′ēan) *adj.* **o·vi·duct** (ō′vĭdŭkt) *n.* (anat., zool.) One of pair of ducts carrying eggs from ovary.

o·vi·form (ō′vĭfŏrm) *adj.* Egg-shaped.

o·vine (ō′vīn) *adj.* Of, like, sheep.

o·vip·a·rous (ōvĭp′arus) *adj.* (zool.) Producing young by means of eggs expelled from body before being hatched. **o·vip′ar·ous·ly** *adv.*

o·vi·pos·i·tor (ōvĭpŏz′ĭter) *n.* (zool.) Organ with which female animal, insect, etc., deposits eggs.

o·void (ō′void) *adj.* Solidly or superficially egg-shaped, oval with one end more pointed. ~ *n.* Ovoid body.

o·vo·tes·tis (ōvōtĕs′tĭs) *n.* (pl. **-tes** pr. -tēz). (zool.) Organ in certain animals that produces both ova and spermatozoa; hermaphrodite gland.

o·vo·vi·vip·a·rous (ōvōvīvĭp′-*arus*) *adj.* (zool.) Producing young by means of eggs which hatch before reaching exterior (cf. OVIPAROUS). **o·vo·vi·vip′ar·ous·ly** *adv.*

o·vu·la·tion (ŏvyulā′shon, ŏv-yu-) *n.* Development of ova; discharge of ova from ovary in mammals. **o·vu·late** (ō′vyulāt, ŏv′yu-) *v.i.* (**-lat·ed, -lat·ing**).

o·vule (ō′vūl) *n.* (bot.) Female germ cell of seed plant. **o·vu·lar** (ō′vyuler) *adj.*

o·vum (ō′vum) *n.* (pl. **o·va** pr. ō′va). (biol.) Female germ cell capable of developing into new individual when fertilized by male sperm; egg esp. of mammals, fish, or insects. [L., = "egg"]

owe (ō) *v.* (**owed, ow·ing**). Be under obligation to pay, repay, or render; be in debt (*for*); be indebted for *to*.

Ow·en (ō′ĭn), **Robert** (1771–1858). Brit. industrialist and socialist reformer; with his son, **Robert Dale** (1801–77), he established the

As nocturnal hunters, all owls have eyes about 35 to 100 times more sensitive than those of man. Those of the snowy **owl** *are the same size as a man's and enable it to hunt at night for the rodents and other small fauna which are its prey.*

A member of the chrysanthemum genus, the ***ox-eye daisy*** *has flowers with a yellow central disk surrounded by long white petals. It is common in England.*

Utopian community of New Harmony, Indiana (1825–28).

Ow·ens (ō´ĭnz), **Jesse** (1913–80). Amer. track and field athlete; hero of the Olympic Games in Berlin, 1936.

ow·ing (ō´ĭng) *pred. adj.* Yet to be paid, owed, due; ~ **to** (also used adverbially), attributed to, caused by.

owl (owl) *n.* 1. Bird of prey, esp. nocturnal, of the order Strigiformes, with large head, raptorial beak, large eyes directed forward and soft plumage enabling it to fly noiselessly, feeding on mice, small birds, etc. 2. Solemn person. **owl′ish** *adj.* **owl′ish·ly** *adv.* **owl′ish·ness** *n.*

owl·et (ow´lĭt) *n.* Owl, young owl.

own[1] (ōn) *adj.* (appended to poss. adjective or case) In full ownership, proper, peculiar, individual, and not another's; (abs.) private property, kindred, etc.; **of one's** ~, belonging to one; **hold one's** ~, maintain position, not be defeated; **on one's** ~, (colloq.) independently, on one's own account, responsibility, or resources; **get one's** ~ **back**, be revenged (*on*).

own[2] (ōn) *v.* 1. Have as property, possess. 2. Acknowledge authorship, paternity, or possession, of; admit as existent, valid, true, etc; ~ **up**, (colloq.) make frank confession. **own′er, own′er·ship** *ns.* **own′er·less** *adj.*

ox (ŏks) *n.* (pl. **ox·en**). Large domestic bovine animal, esp. male castrated and used as draft animal or reared for food; any bovine animal; **ox′eye daisy**, common meadow plant (*Chrysanthemum leucanthemum*) with flowers having a yellow disk and long white rays; **ox′herd**, cowherd; **ox·lip** (ŏks´lĭp), kind of primula; (pop.) hybrid of primrose and cowslip; **ox′tail**, tail of ox, much used for making soup.

ox·al·ic (ŏksăl´ĭk) *adj.* ~ **acid**, highly poisonous and intensely sour acid $(COOH)_2$ found in wood sorrel etc., used in bleaching etc. [Gk. *oxalis* wood sorrel]

Wild cattle were domesticated as early as 4,500 B.C. and ***oxen,*** *males castrated to make them more docile, were used to draw sledges. Below: Modern farmers in Sri Lanka still use oxen.*

Ox·ford (ŏks´ferd). City on Thames River in Oxfordshire, seat of university organized as a *studium generale* soon after 1167, the first of its colleges, University College, being founded in 1249; ~ **accent**, style of pronouncing English popularly supposed to be characteristic of members of Oxford University; ~ **blue**, dark blue; ~ **gray**, dark gray; ~ **Group**, religious movement founded by Dr. Frank N.D. Buchman in Oxford in 1921; ~ **movement**: see TRACTARIANISM; ~ **shoe**, kind of low walking shoe laced over instep. **ox′fords** *n.pl.* Oxford shoes. [*ox*(*en*) + *ford*]

ox·i·dase (ŏk´sĭdās, -dāz) *n.* (physiol., bot.) One of a group of enzymes concerned with the uptake of oxygen by living cells (respiration).

ox·ide (ŏk´sīd) *n.* Compound of oxygen with another element or with a radical.

ox·i·dize (ŏk´sĭdīz) *v.* (**-dized, -diz·ing**). Cause to combine with oxygen; cover (metal) with coating of oxide, make rusty; take up or enter into combination with oxygen, rust; **oxidized silver**, silver with dark coating of silver sulphide. **ox·i·da·tion** (ŏksĭdā´shon) *n.* **ox′i·diz·er** *n.*

Oxon. *abbrev. Oxoniensis* (L., = of Oxford); Oxford University.

ox·y·a·cet·y·lene (ŏksēasĕt´ilēn, -ilĭn) *adj.* Using mixture of oxygen and acetylene (esp. of flame produced in this way for cutting and welding metals).

ox·y·gen (ŏk´sĭjen) *n.* (chem.) Colorless, tasteless, odorless, gaseous element, essential to life and to combustion, comprising about one-fifth of the air, and present in combination in water and most minerals and organic substances; symbol O, at no. 8, at. wt. 15.9994; ~ **tent**: see TENT[1].

ox·y·gen·ate (ŏk´sĭjenāt) *v.t.* (**-at·ed, -at·ing**). Supply, treat, or mix with oxygen, oxidize; charge (blood) with oxygen by respiration. **ox·y·gen·a·tion** (ŏksĭjenā´shon) *n.*

ox·y·gen·ize (ŏk´sĭjenīz) *v.t.* (**-ized, -iz·ing**). Oxygenate.

ox·y·mo·ron (ŏksĭmōr´ŏn, -mōr´-) *n.* (pl. **-mo·ra** pr. -mōr´a, -mōr´a). (rhet.) Figure of speech with pointed conjunction of seeming contradictions (e.g. *faith unfaithful kept him falsely true*).

ox·y·te·tra·cy·cline (ŏksĭtĕtrasī´klĭn, -klēn, -klīn) *n.* Dull yellow,

Oxford *is the oldest university in Britain. The town began beside a ford which crossed the Thames and was mentioned about 1,000 years ago. Teaching by monks began in the 12th century. Today, the Bodleian Library has 2 million books.*

*The **oyster-catcher** (above) has a world-wide distribution and feeds on small mollusks and worms in tidal areas. **Oysters** (right) are the mollusks most valued by man not only as food, but also for pearl-shell and pearls.*

crystalline antibiotic powder used in treatment of infections.

oys·ter (oi′ster) *n.* Edible bivalve mollusk of family Ostreidae, usu. eaten alive, esp. the common European *Ostrea edulis* and the Amer. *O. virginica* and *O. lurida* (**Californian ~**); oyster-shaped morsel of meat in fowl's back; **~ bank, bed**, part of sea bottom where oysters breed or are bred; **~ bar**, counter where oysters are served; **oys′tercatcher**, maritime wading bird (*Haematopus*) with black-and-white or black plumage and brilliant red feet and beak; **oyster farm**, sea bottom used for breeding oysters; **oyster knife**, knife of shape adapted for opening oysters.

oz. *abbrev.* Ounce(s).

O·zark (ō′zärk) **Mountains.** (also **Ozarks**) Range of low mountains spreading over a 60,000 sq. mile (155,400 sq. km) area between Arkansas and Missouri rivers, mainly in SW. Missouri, NW. Arkansas, and E. Oklahoma.

o·zone (ō′zōn) *n.* 1. Allotropic form of oxygen with three atoms to the molecule (O_3), a pale-blue gas with a peculiarly pungent smell, formed by action of electric discharge or ultraviolet light, used for sterilizing water and purifying air. 2. (pop.) Invigorating, bracing air, esp. that of the seaside. **o·zon·ic** (ōzŏn′ĭk, ōzō′nĭk) *adj.*

***Oyster farm** at Wallis Lake in N.S.W., Australia. Edible oysters are ready for harvesting within 3 to 5 years. Pearls from edible oysters are valueless.*

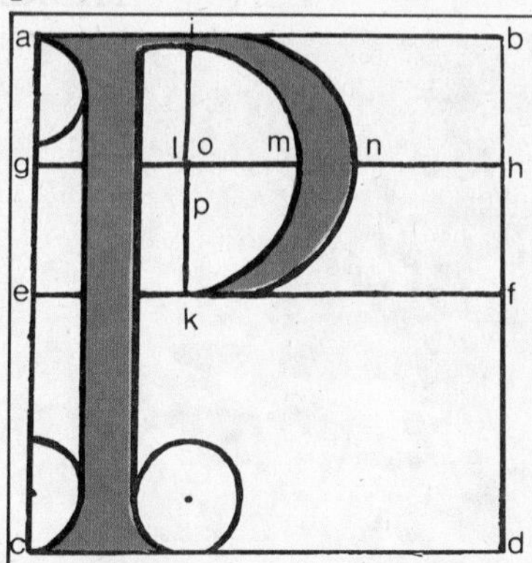

Phoenician Early Greek Etruscan

Early Latin Classical Latin Italian

Shaped like a shepherd's crook, and turning both to right and left during its development, the symbol ***P, p*** *has usually represented the same sound. If combined with 'h' or 's' it results in sounds 'f' and 's' today.*

P, p (pē) (pl. **P's, p's** or **Ps, ps**) Sixteenth letter of modern English and 15th of ancient Roman alphabet, corresponding to Gk. *pi* (*Π*, *π*) and Semitic ך, ר, and representing a voiceless labial stop; **mind one's P's and Q's**, be careful not to do or say the wrong thing.

P *symbol*. Phosphorus.

P. *abbrev*. President.

p. *abbrev*. Page; participle; past; penny, pence, pressure; *piano*[1].

Pa *symbol*. Protactinium.

pa (pah) *n*. (colloq.) Papa.

Pa., PA *abbrevs*. Pennsylvania.

P.A. *abbrev*. Press agent, power of attorney, purchasing agent.

p.a. *abbrev*. Per annum.

pab·u·lum (păb'yulum) *n*. 1. Food, sustenance. 2. Weak intellectual nourishment.

pa·ca (pah'ka, păk'a) *n*. Spotted cavy (*Cuniculus paca*), a nocturnal rodent of Central and S. Amer.

pace (pās) *n*. 1. Single step in walking or running; space traversed in this, as vague measure of distance (about 30 in.); space between successive stationary positions of same foot in walking (about 5 ft.). 2. Mode of walking or running, gait; any or various gaits of (esp. trained) horse, etc.; amble; **put (person) through his ~s**, test his qualities in action, etc. 3. Speed in walking or running; rate or progression; **keep ~**, advance at equal rate *with*; **pace'maker**, rider, runner, etc., who sets pace for another in race etc.; electrical device for stimulating the heart muscle. **pace** *v*. (**paced, pac·ing**). Walk with slow or regular pace; traverse thus; measure (distance) by pacing; (of horse) amble; set pace for (rider, runner, etc.). **pac'er** *n*. (esp.) Horse that paces.

pa·cha = PASHA.

pa·chin·ko (pachĭng'kō) *n*. Japanese form of pinball. [Jap.]

pach·y·derm (păk'iderm) *n*. Large thick-skinned mammal esp. elephant or rhinoceros. **pach·y·der'mal, pach·y·der'mous, pach·y·der·ma·tous** (păkĭder'matus) *adjs*.

pach·y·san·dra (păkĭsăn'dra) *n*. Any plant of the genus *Pachysandra*, often used as a ground cover.

Pa·cif·ic (pasĭf'ĭk) *adj*. Of, adjoining, the Pacific Ocean; ~ **Islands, Trust Territory of the**, approximately 2,000 islands including the Caroline, Marshall, and Mariana Islands under the trusteeship of the U.S., approved by the United Nations in 1947; the 17 islands of the Northern Marianas became a commonwealth under U.S. sovereignty in 1976; ~ **Ocean**, largest body of water on Earth's surface, bounded by N. and S. Amer. and Asia and Australia. **Pacific** *n*. Pacific Ocean. [so named by Magellan, its first European navigator, because he experienced calm weather there]

Considered to be the largest expanse of water in the world, the ***Pacific Ocean*** *is broadly bounded by America, Asia and Australia. Large distances separate many of the groups of islands and this isolation has resulted in the development of many diverse cultures.*

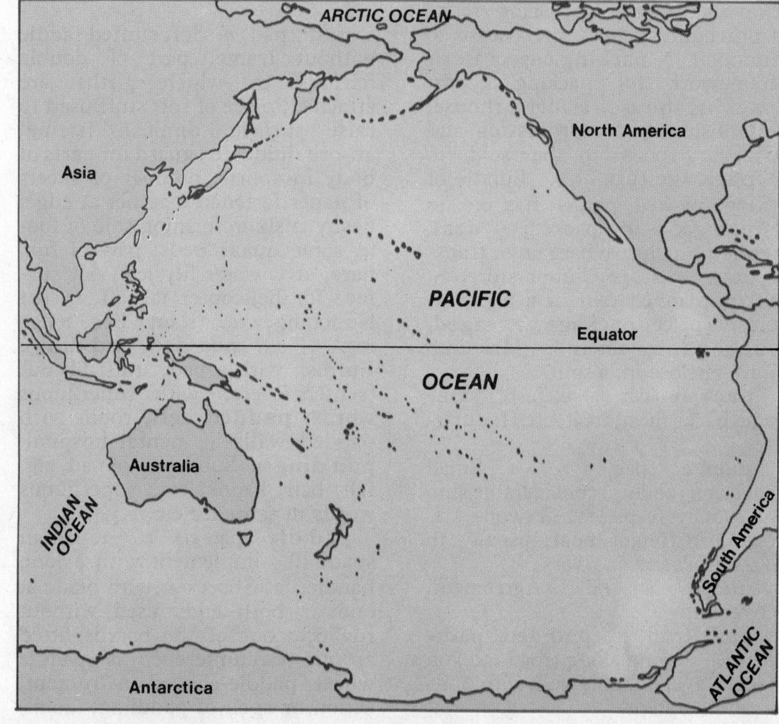

pa·cif·ic (pasĭf'ĭk) *adj*. Tending to peace, of peaceful disposition. **pa·cif'i·cal·ly** *adv*.

pac·i·fi·ca·tion (păsifikā'shon) *n*. Pacifying; being pacified. **pa·cif·i·ca·to·ry** (pasĭf'ikatōrē, -tōrē) *adj*.

pac·i·fism (păs'ifĭzem) *n*. (Support of) policy of avoiding or abolishing war by means of arbitration in settling international disputes. **pac'i·fist** *n*.

pac·i·fy (păs'ifī) *v.t.* (**-fied, -fy·ing**). Make calm or quiet; reduce (country etc.) to state of peace. **pac'i·fi·a·ble** *adj*. **pac'i·fi·er** *n*. (esp.) Infant's teething ring or rubber nipple.

pack (păk) *n*. 1. Bundle of things wrapped up or tied together for carrying esp. on shoulders or back; (commerc.) method of packing for the market. 2. Set, lot (usu. derog., as ~ of fools, lies, etc.); large quantity. 3. Number of animals or birds kept together or naturally

*The U.S.S. 'Glacier' with its helicopter unloads on **pack-ice** during the Antarctic winter. This compressed ice forms a stable platform where scientists can make observations of many aspects of the life in such frigid areas.*

congregating; group; set of playing cards. 4. Large area of large pieces of floating ice (~ **ice**) driven or packed together into nearly continuous mass. 5. Quantity of fish, fruit, etc., packed in a season etc. 6. (med.) Swathing of body or part of it in wet sheet, blanket, etc.; sheet etc. so used; wad of gauze etc. for packing an orifice; **ice** ~, compress of crushed ice. 7. Substance (esp. paste) applied to skin or hair as cosmetic treatment; treatment using this. 8. **pack'horse,** horse for carrying packs; **pack rat,** large, hoarding rodent; (fig.) person who saves useless small items; **pack'-saddle,** one adapted for supporting packs; **pack'thread,** strong thread for sewing or typing up packs; **pack train,** line of loaded animals, esp. horses or mules. **pack** *v.* 1. Put (things) together into bundle, box, bag, etc., for transport or storing (freq. ~ **up,** esp. abs.). 2. Prepare and put up (meat, fruit, etc.) in jars, cans, etc. for preservation. 3. Put closely together; crowd together; form into pack. 4. Cover (thing) with something pressed or wedged tightly around; (med.) wrap (body etc.) tightly in wet cloth. 5. Fill (bag, box, etc.) with clothes etc.; cram (space etc. *with*); load (beast) with pack. 6. Take oneself off with one's belongings; **send** (person) **packing,** dismiss him summarily; **pack** (person) **off,** send him away; **pack up,** (slang) retire from fight, contest, etc.; cease to function. 7. **packing case,** case or framework for packing goods; **packing house,** slaughterhouse; establishment for processing and packing foods to be sold to

pack·age (păk'ĭj) *n.* Bundle of things packed, parcel; box etc. in which goods are packed; ~ **deal,** (colloq.) inclusive bargain or transaction; ~ **store,** liquor store; ~ **tour,** planned tour at a fixed inclusive price. **package** *v.t.* (**-aged, -ag·ing**). (commerc.) Make up into, enclose in, a unit.

pack·er (păk'*er*) *n.* (esp.) One who packs meat, fruit, etc., for market.

pack·et (păk'ĭt) *n.* 1. Small package; (colloq.) considerable sum of money (esp. lost or won). 2. Mail or freight boat, usually in coastal waters or rivers.

pact (păkt) *n.* Agreement, covenant.

pad[1] (păd) *v.* (**pad·ded, pad·ding**). Tramp along (road etc.) on foot; travel on foot; walk with dull-sounding steps.

*Above: **Paddle-wheel** boats are still used on lakes at Fairbanks, Alaska, and on other waterways where there is shallow water, or where there can be considerable seasonal variations in the water level.*

pad[2] (păd) *n.* Soft stuffed saddle without frame; part of double harness to which girths are attached; piece of soft stuff used to raise surface, diminsh jarring, absorb fluid, etc.; guard for parts of body in sports; number of sheets of paper fastened together at edge; fleshy cushion forming sole of foot in some quadrupeds; paw of fox, hare, etc.; water lily leaf; flat surface for helicopter takeoff, rocket launching, etc.; (slang) bed, lodging. ~ *v.t.* (**pad·ded, pad·ding**). Furnish with a pad, stuff; fill out (sentence etc.) with superfluous words; **padded cell,** room with padded walls in mental hospital. **pad'ding** *n.* Substance of pad, e.g. felt, hair, kapok, etc.; superfluous words in sentence etc.

pad·dle (păd'*el*) *n.* 1. Small spade-like implement with a long handle. 2. Short oar with blade at one or both ends used without rowlock; one of the boards fitted around circumference of paddle wheel; paddle-shaped instrument; action or spell of paddling; (zool.) fin or flipper; ~ **wheel,** wheel for propelling ship, with boards around and at right angles to the circumference so as to press backward against the water. ~ *v.* (**-dled, -dling**). Move on water, propel canoe, by means of paddles; row gently; walk with bare feet in shallow water; dabble; spank, thrash.

pad·dock (păd'*ok*) *n.* Small field, esp. as part of stud farm; enclosure near racecourse, where horses are assembled before race. ~ *v.t.* Enclose or fence in (a sheep run etc.); shut up in a paddock.

Pad·dy (păd'ē) (pl. **-dies**). (Nickname for) Irishman; **paddy wagon,** patrol wagon. [pet form of *Padraig* Patrick]

pad·dy (păd'ē) *n.* (pl. **-dies**). Rice in the straw or in the husk; rice field. [Malay *padi*]

Pa·de·rew·ski (păd*e*rĕf'skē), **Ignacy Jan** (1860–1941). Polish pianist, composer and statesman; prime minister of Poland 1919–21 and 1940–1.

pad·lock (păd'lŏk) *n.* Detachable lock hanging by hinged or pivoted hoop on object fastened. ~ *v.t.* Secure with padlock.

pa·dre (pah'drā, -drē) *n.* (mil. slang). Chaplain. [Port. etc., = "father," "priest"]

*Racehorses being led around the **paddock** at Newmarket, England. This word also means a small field for grazing horses, or (in Australia) any large field.*

pa·dro·ne (p*a*drō´nē) *n.* Master of Mediterranean trading vessel; Italian employer of street musicians, begging children, etc.; proprietor of Italian inn.

pae·an (pē´*a*n) *n.* Song of praise or thanksgiving; shout or song of triumph, joy, or exultation. [Gk. *paian* hymn to Apollo under name of Paian]

pa·el·la (pah-ĕl´*a*, -ā´l*a*, -y*a*; *Sp.* pah-ĕl´yah, -ĕ´yah) *n.* Spanish dish of rice with chicken, vegetables, etc., seasoned with saffron.

pa·gan (pā´g*a*n) *n.* & *adj.* Heathen, esp. in antiquity. **pa´gan·ism** *n.* **pa´gan·ize** *v.* (**-ized, -iz·ing**).

page[1] (pāj) *n.* Boy employed (esp. in hotels) to attend to door, go on errands, etc. (also ~ **boy**); boy employed as personal attendant of person of rank; small boy attending bride at wedding; (hist.) boy in training for knighthood and attached to knight's service. **page** *v.t.* (**paged, pag·ing**). Communicate with by means of page; call name of (person sought) in public rooms of hotel etc.

page[2] (pāj) *n.* One side of leaf of book etc. ~ *v.t* (**paged, pag·ing**). Put consecutive numbers on pages of (book etc.).

pag·eant (păj´*e*nt) *n.* Brilliant spectacle, esp. procession, arranged for effect; spectacular representation of past history of place etc.; (hist.) tableau, allegorical device, etc., on fixed stage or moving car; (fig.) empty or specious show. **pag·eant·ry** (păj´*e*ntrē) *n.* (pl. **-tries**). Slendid display; empty show.

pag·i·nal (păj´*i*n*a*l). Of pages; page for page.

pag·i·nate (păj´*i*nāt) *v.t.* (**-nat·ed, -nat·ing**). Page (book etc.). **pag·i·na·tion** (păj*i*nā´sh*o*n) *n.*

pa·go·da (p*a*gō´d*a*) *n.* Temple or sacred building in India, China, etc., esp. tower, usu. of pyramidal form, built over relics of Buddha or a saint; ornamental imitation of this; ~ **tree**, one of several kinds of Chinese, Japanese, and Indian trees, growing in pagoda form.

Pa·go Pa·go (pahn´gō pahn´go). Capital of Amer. Samoa on the S. coast of Tutuila Island.

Pah·la·vi (pah´l*a*vē), **Peh·le·vi** (pā´l*e*vē) *ns.* Iranian language, the ancestor of modern Persian, used in Persia from *c*3rd c. onward, distinguished from other dialects of

*Left: The Ban Fu Poh **pagoda** at Penang in Malaysia is one of several forms of temple erected in Asia to exemplify the range and wisdom of the teaching of the founder of Buddhism.*

Middle Persian chiefly by its script, which has some Aramaic characters; **Mohammed Riza ~** (1919–80), shah of Iran from 1941; forced to leave country, 1979. [Pers. *Pahlav* Parthia]

paid (pād) *adj.*: see PAY[1]; (esp.) **mark ~**, (colloq.) settle the affairs of, finish off; **~-in capital**, that part of the subscribed capital of an undertaking that has actually been paid.

pail (pāl) *n.* 1. Bucket. 2. (also **dinner ~**) Vessel in which workman's midday meal etc. is carried.

pail·lasse, pal·liasse (păl′yăs, pălyăs′) *ns.* Straw mattress.

pain (pān) *n.* 1. Sensation experienced when the body is injured, or afflicted by certain diseases; suffering, distress, of body or mind; (pl.) labor pains of childbirth. 2. (pl.) Trouble taken; **pains′taking**, careful, industrious. 3. Punishment (now only in **on pain of**). **pain** *v.t.* Inflict pain upon. **pain′ful** *adj.* **pain′ful·ly** *adv.* **pain′ful·ness** *n.* **pain′less** *adj.* **pain′less·ly** *adv.* **pain′less·ness** *n.*

Paine (pān), **Thomas** (1737–1809). Brit.-born pamphleteer and political radical in Amer. and France; in Amer. wrote influential *Common Sense* (1776) urging Amer. Revolution and independence; published the *Crisis* periodical supporting Amer. cause during war of Independence; in Europe, 1787, associated himself with the French Revolution; wrote *The Rights of Man* (1791–2) defending revolutionary France; member of French National Convention 1792–3; wrote *The Age of Reason* (1794, 1796).

paint (pānt) *n.* Solid coloring matter, suspended in a liquid vehicle used to impart color to a surface; something, esp. medicament, put on like paint with brush; cosmetic coloring matter applied to face etc.; **~ brush**, house painter's or artist's brush. **paint** *v.t.* 1. Portray, represent, in colors; adorn (wall etc.) with painting; (fig.) represent in words vividly as by painting. 2. Cover surface of with paint, apply paint of specified color to; **~ the town red**, cause commotion by riotous spree etc. 3. Apply liquid or cosmetic to (skin, face, etc.). 4. **painted lady**, orange-red butterfly (*Vanessa cardui*) with black and white spots; **Painted Desert**, plateau area in E. central Arizona known for its colorful eroded rock formations.

paint·er[1] (pān′ter) *n.* 1. One who paints pictures. 2. Workman who coats woodwork etc. with paint. **paint′er·ly** *adj.* (transl. of Ger. *malerisch*) (of work of art) Executed with attention to light and shade, mass, tone, etc., rather than line (opp. LINEAR).

paint·er[2] (pān′ter) *n.* Rope attached to bow of boat for making it fast to ship, stake, etc.

Thomas Paine, *a revolutionary whose controversial ideas of civic and political freedom were famous, served the revolutionary forces in France and America but died in jail.*

paint·ing (pān′ting) *n.* A painted picture; the art of doing this.

pair (pār) *n.* (pl. **pairs, pair**). 1. Set of two, couple (esp. of things that usu. exist or are used in couples); article consisting of two corresponding parts not used separately; second member of a pair; two playing cards of same denomination. 2. Engaged or married couple; mated couple of animals; two horses harnessed together. 3. Two voters on opposite sides absenting themselves from voting by mutual agreement. **~** *v.* Arrange, be arranged, in couples; unite in love or marriage; mate; unite (*with* one of opposite sex); **~ off**, put two by two; go off in pairs; make a pair; (colloq.) marry (*with*).

Pais·ley (pāz′lē). Town of Strathclyde near Glasgow; **paisley shawl**, shawl in soft bright colors, orig. made at Paisley; **paisley (pattern)**, characteristic pattern of such shawl.

Pai·ute (pīoot′) *n.* (pl. **-utes**, collect. **-ute**). (Member of) either of two distinct Indian tribes of the Shoshonean subfamily, formerly living in southwestern U.S., comprising the **Northern ~** and **Southern ~**.

pa·ja·mas, py·ja·mas (pajah′maz, -jăm′az) *ns. pl.* Loose silk or cotton trousers tied around waist, worn by both sexes in the East and adapted esp. for night wear by Europeans; sleeping suit of loose trousers and jacket. [Hind. *pāē jāma, pā jāma* loose drawers]

Pa·ki·stan (pahkĭstahn′, păk′ĭstăn). Islamic republic in SE. Asia, formed in 1947 from regions where Muslims predominated; member of the Brit. Commonwealth until 1972; capital, Islamabad. **Pa·ki·sta·ni** (pahkĭstah′nē, păkĭstăn′ē) *adj.* & *n.* [earlier *Pakstan*, f. initials of *P*unjab, *A*fghan Frontier, *K*ashmir, *S*ind, and last 3 letters of Baluchis*tan*]

pal (păl) *n.* (slang) Comrade, friend. **~** *v.i.* (**palled, pal·ling**). (usu. **~ up**) Associate, make friends (*with*). [Engl. Gypsy *pal* brother, mate]

pal·ace (păl′ĭs) *n.* Official residence of sovereign, archbishop, or bishop; stately mansion; spacious building for entertainment, refreshment, etc. [L. *Palatium* PALATINE HILL, Augustus' house built on it]

pal·a·din (păl′adĭn) *n.* 1. Any of the 12 Peers of Charlemagne's court, of whom the Count Palatine was the chief; knight errant. 2. Heroic champion.

pal·an·quin, pal·an·keen (pălankēn′) *ns.* Covered litter for one, in India etc., carried usu. by four or six men. **pal·an·quin′er, pal·an·keen′er** *ns.* [Malya *palangki*]

pal·at·a·ble (păl′atabel) *adj.* Pleasant to the taste; (fig.) agreeable to the mind. **pal′at·a·bly** *adv.*

pal·a·tal (păl′atal) *adj.* Of the palate; (of sound) produced by placing tongue against or near the palate, usu. hard palate. **~** *n.* Palatal sound. **pal′a·tal·ize** *v.t.* (**-ized, -iz·ing**). Make palatal, modify into palatal sound. **pal′a·tal·ly** *adv.*

pal·ate (păl′ĭt) *n.* 1. Roof of the mouth in vertebrates, partly bony and partly fleshy structure separating cavity of mouth from that of nose; **bony or hard ~**, front part of this; **soft ~**, back part of this, pendulous fold of musculo-membranous tissue separating mouth cavity from pharynx. 2. Sense of taste; mental taste, liking.

pa·la·tial (palā′shal) *adj.* Like a palace; splendid. **pa·la′tial·ly** *adv.* **pa·la′tial·ness** *n.*

pa·lat·i·nate (palăt′ĭnāt, -nĭt) *n.* Territory under a palatine; **P~** (hist., Ger. *Pfalz*), state of the Rhine, constituting with **Upper P~** an electorate of the Holy Roman Empire, now part of West Germany.

pal·a·tine[1] (păl′atĭn) *adj.* 1. Of a palace; palatial. 2. Possessing royal privileges, having jurisdiction (within the territory) such as elsewhere belongs to the sovereign alone. 3. Of or belonging to a count palatine; **count ~**, orig. in the later Roman Empire a count (*comes*) attached to the imperial palace and having supreme judicial authority in certain causes. **palatine** *n.*

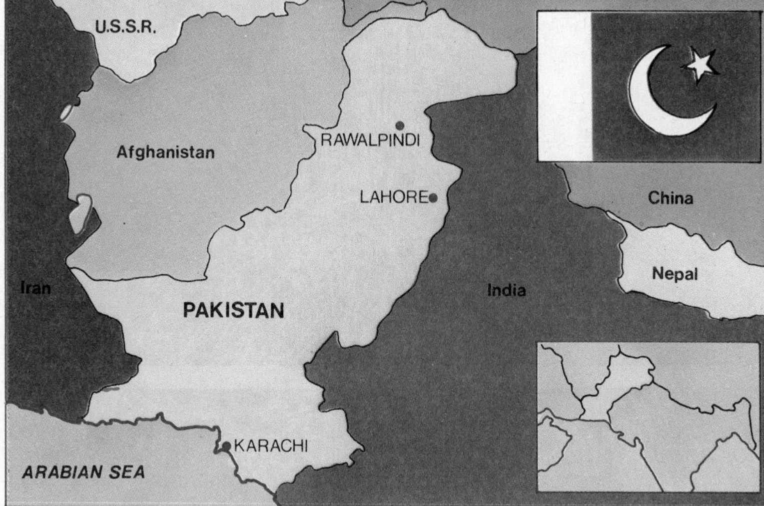

Top: Wandering musicians entertaining at a Bugti tribal wedding in ***Pakistan.*** *This Muslim state (see map above) was formed in 1947 but the eastern half seceded to become Bangladesh in 1971 after a very bitter and savage war.*

Office of imperial palace; lord having sovereign power over province or dependency of empire or realm; **P ~**, PALATINE HILL.

pal·a·tine[2] (păl′atīn, -tĭn) *adj.* Of the palate. ~ *n.* Either of two bones forming hard palate.

Pal·a·tine (păl′atīn, -tĭn) **Hill.** One of the seven Hills of Rome, that on which the first Roman settlement was made; later, site of imperial palaces.

Pa·lau (pahlow′). Group of approximately 100 small islands in the Caroline Islands.

pa·lav·er (palăv′er. -lah′ver) *n.* Conference, discussion, esp. in tribal custom; profuse or idle talk. ~ *v.i.* Engage in palaver.

pale[1] (pāl) *n.* 1. Pointed piece of wood for fence etc., stake. 2. Boundary; enclosed place; **the P ~**, (hist.) part of Ireland under English jurisdiction.

pale[2] (pāl) *adj.* (**pal·er, pal·est**). (of person or complexion) Of whitish or ashen appearance; (of colors) faint; faintly colored; of faint luster, dim; **pale′face**, supposed N. Amer. Ind. name for white man. **pale′ly** *adv.* **pale′ness** *n.* **pale** *v.* (**paled, pal·ing**). Grow or make pale; (fig.) become pale in comparison (usu. *before* or *beside*).

Pa·le·o·cene (pā′lēosēn, păl′ē-) *adj.* & *n.* (geol.) (Of) the earliest epoch of the Tertiary period.

pa·le·og·ra·phy (pālēŏg′rafē, pălē-) *n.* Study of ancient writing and inscriptions. **pa·le·og′ra·pher** *n.* **pa·le·o·graph·ic** (pālēográf′ĭk, pălē-) *adj.*

pa·le·o·lith·ic (pālēolĭth′ĭk, pălē-) *adj.* Of the earlier Stone Age (as contrasted with NEOLITHIC), characterized by chipped stone implements and weapons.

pa·le·on·tol·o·gy (pālēŏntŏl′ojē, pălē-) *n.* Study of extinct animals and plants. **pa·le·on·tol′o·gist** *n.*

Pa·le·o·zo·ic (pālēozō′ĭk, pălē-) *adj.* & *n.* (Of) the era or group or systems containing ancient forms of life, including the periods from Cambrian to Permian.

Pal·es·tine (păl′ĭstīn). Former name of country of Asia at E. end of Mediterranean, now divided between ISRAEL and JORDAN; ancient home of the Jews and the Holy Land of Christendom; it was conquered by the Romans, 65 B.C., and by Arabs, 634 A.D.; from then on, except when ruled by Crusaders (1098–1187), it remained under Muslim dominion until the defeat of Turkish and German forces by the British at Megiddo in World War I; under British mandate, 1923–48. **Pal·es·tin·i·an** (pălĭstĭn′ēan) *adj.* & *n.*

pa·les·tra (palĕs′tra) *n.* (pl. **-tras, -trae** pr. -trē). (Gk. antiq.) Wrestling school, gymnasium.

pal·ette (păl′ĭt) *n.* Artist's thin usu. oval or rectangular board or plate, with hole for thumb, for arranging and mixing colors on; range of colors used by particular artist or on particular occasion; ~ **knife,** flexible steel blade with handle for mixing colors, also used for applying them to canvas.

pal·frey (pawl′frē) *n.* (pl. **-freys**). (archaic, poet.) Saddle horse for ordinary riding, esp. for ladies.

Pa·li (pah′lē) *n.* Indo-Aryan language spoken in N. India in the 5th–2nd centuries B.C.; as the language of a large part of the Buddhist scriptures, it was brought to Sri Lanka and Burma, and, though not spoken there, became the vehicle of a large literature of commentaries and chronicles. [fr. Sansk. *pāli-bhāsā* (*pāli* canon, *bhāsā* language)]

pal·imp·sest (păl′ĭmpsĕst) *n.* Writing material or manuscript on which the original writing has been effaced to make room for a second writing.

pal·in·drome (păl′ĭndrōm) *n.* & *adj.* (Word, verse, etc.) that reads the same backward as forward (e.g. *madam*).

pal·ing (pā′lĭng) *n.* (Fence of) pales.

pal·i·sade (pălĭsād′) *n.* Fence of pales or of iron railings; (mil.) strong pointed wooden stake, of which a number are fixed deeply in ground in close row as defense; (pl.) line of cliffs. ~ *v.t.* (**-sad·ed, -sad·ing**). Furnish, enclose, with palisade.

pall[1] (pawl) *n.* 1. Cloth, usu. of black, purple, or white velvet, spread over coffin, hearse, or tomb; coffin; **pall′bearer**, one of several persons who carry a coffin, or serve as attendants, at a funeral. 2.

Pampas grass grows wild in parts of South America. There are about six species with similar characteristics. As a decorative addition to a garden, pampas grass is popular in warm countries where it can grow easily.

Woolen vestment (now a narrow band passing over shoulders, with short lappets) worn by pope and some metropolitans or archbishops; (fig.) mantle, cloak.

pall[2] (pawl) *v.* Become insipid (now only fig.); satiate, clog.

Pal·la·di·an (palā´dēan) *adj.* 1. Of Pallas ATHENA. 2. Of PALLADIO or his style (~ **window**). **Pal·la'di·an·ism** *n.* Style, opinions, of the followers of Palladio.

Pal·la·dio (pahlah´dyō). Andrea di Pietro (1508–80), Italian architect of Vicenza, who revived classical Roman styles and had great influence through his *Four Books of Architecture* (1570). [It., = "man of Pallas (Athena)"]

Pal·la·di·um (palā´dēum) *n.* Image of the goddess Pallas in the citadel of Troy, on which the safety of the city was held to depend, reputed to have been brought from there to Rome; (pl. **-di·a** pr. -dēa) (usu. l.c.) safeguard.

pal·la·di·um (palā´dēum) *n.* (chem.) Hard silvery-white metallic element of platinum group; symbol Pd, at. no. 46, wt. 106.4. [f. the asteroid *Pallas*]

Pal·las (păl´as). 1. (Gk. myth.) One of the names (of unknown meaning) of ATHENA. 2. (astron.) Second largest of the asteroids.

pal·let[1] (păl´ĭt) *n.* Straw bed; mattress.

pal·let[2] (păl´ĭt) *n.* 1. Flat wooden blade with handle, used by potters etc. 2. Projection on part of a machine, engaging with teeth of wheel and converting reciprocating into rotary movement, or vice versa. 3. Portable platform for transporting and storing loads.

pal·liasse = PAILLASSE.

pal·li·ate (păl´ēāt) *v.t.* (**-at·ed, -at·ing**). Alleviate (disease) without curing; extenuate, excuse. **pal·li·a·tion** (pălēā´shon), **pal'li·a·tor** *ns.*

pal·li·a·tive (păl´ēātĭv, -ēatĭv) *adj.* & *n.* (Thing) serving to palliate.

pal·lid (păl´ĭd) *adj.* Pale, sickly looking. **pal'lid·ly** *adv.* **pal'lid·ness** *n.*

pal·li·um (păl´ēum) *n.* (pl. **-li·a** pr. lēa, **-li·ums**). 1. Man's large rectangular cloak, esp. among Greeks. 2. Archbishop's or pope's PALL[1]. 3. Integumental fold or mantle of mollusk.

Pall Mall (pĕl´mel´, păl´măl´). Street in London on site of former pall-mall alley, noted for its clubs.

pall-mall (pĕl´mĕl´, păl´măl´) *n.* Sixteenth- and 17th-c. game in which a boxwood ball was driven with a mallet through an iron ring suspended at the end of a long alley. [It. *palla* ball, *maglio* mallet]

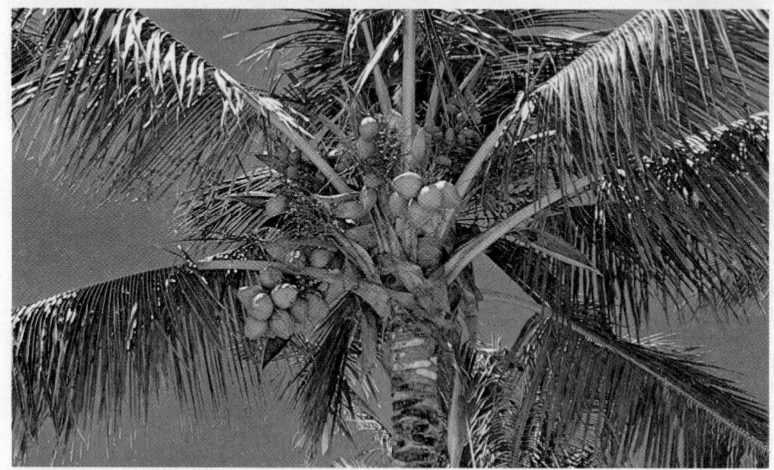

Depending on the species, ***palm*** *trees can provide food, oil, and timber. Foliage from some varieties has been used for thatching and weaving.*

pal·lor (păl´er) *n.* Paleness.

palm[1] (pahm) *n.* 1. Tree or shrub of an order of monocotyledons widely distributed in warm climates, with stem usu. upright and unbranched, head or crown of very large pinnate or fan-shaped leaves, and fruit of various forms; leaf of palm tree as symbol of excellence; supreme excellence, prize for this. 2. Branch of various trees substituted for palm in northern countries, esp. in celebrating Palm Sunday. 3. ~ **oil**, oil obtained from various palms; **P~ Sunday**, Sunday before Easter, on which Christ's entry into Jerusalem is celebrated, freq. with processions in which branches of palm are carried. **palm'like** *adj.* **pal·ma·ceous** (pălmā'shus, pahmā'-) *adj.*

palm[2] (pahm) *n.* Part of hand between wrist and fingers, esp. its inner surface; part of glove that covers this; **grease person's ~**, bribe him. **palm** *v.t.* Impose fradulently, pass *off* (thing *on* person); conceal (cards, dice, etc.) in hand in sleight of hand etc.; bribe.

Pal·ma (pahl'mah). 1. (*San Miguel de la Palma*) Spanish island, part of the Canary Islands in the Atlantic off NW. coast of Africa. 2. Capital of the Balearic Islands, on Majorca in the Mediterranean, E. of Spain.

pal·mate (păl'māt, pah'māt), **pal·mat·ed** (păl'mātĭd, pah'mā-) *adjs.* Shaped like open palm or hand.

palm·er (pah'mer, pahl'mer) *n.* 1. Pilgrim who returned from Holy Land with palm branch or leaf; itinerant monk under vow of poverty. 2. (also **palm'erworm**) One of various kinds of destructive hairy caterpillars of migratory or wandering habits; hairy artificial fly.

pal·met·to (pălmĕt'ō) *n.* (pl. **-tos, -toes**). Any of various small species of palms, esp. cabbage palmetto (*Sabal palmetto*) of southeastern U.S.

palm·is·try (pah'mĭstrē) *n.* Art or practice of telling character or fortunes from the lines etc. in palm of hand. **palm'ist** *n.*

palm·y (pah'mē) *adj.* (**palm·i·er, palm·i·est**). Of, like, abounding in, palms; triumphant, flourishing (esp. in ~ *days.*)

Pal·my·ra (pălmī'ra). (Aram. *Tadmor*) Ancient city at an oasis in the Syrian Desert on the caravan route from Damascus to the Euphrates.

pal·my·ra (pălmī'ra) *n.* Species of palm (*Borassus flabellifer*) grown in India and Sri Lanka with fan-shaped leaves used for matting etc.

pal·o·mi·no (pălomē'nō) *n.* (pl. **-nos**). Sand-colored horse with white mane and tail.

This non-flying grasshopper, the Horse lubber, is found in parts of Arizona, Texas and Mexico. The ***palpus*** *or feelers enable it to sense food.*

palp (pălp) = PALPUS.

pal·pa·ble (păl'pabel) *adj.* That can be touched or felt; readily perceived by senses or mind. **pal·pa·bil·i·ty** (pălpabĭl'ĭtē), **pal'pa·ble·ness** *ns.* **pal'pa·bly** *adv.*

pal·pate (păl'pāt) *v.t.* (**-pat·ed, -pat·ing**). Examine by touch, handle, esp. in medical examination. **pal·pa·tion** (pălpā'shon) *n.*

pal·pi·tate (păl'pĭtāt) *v.i.* (**-tat·ed, -tat·ing**). Pulsate, throb; tremble. **pal·pi·ta·tion** (pălpĭtā'shon) *n.* Throbbing; increased activity of heart due to exertion, agitation, or disease.

pal·pus (păl'pus) *n.* (pl. **-pi** pr. -pī). Jointed sense organ in insects etc., feeler.

pal·sy (pawl'zē) *n.* (pl. **-sies**). Paralysis (also fig.); **cerebral ~**, condition of weakness, imperfect control of movement, and spasticity, following damage to brain at birth. **palsy** *v.t.* (**-sied, -sy·ing**). Paralyze.

pal·try (pawl'trē) *adj.* (**-tri·er, -tri·est**). Worthless, petty, contemptible. **pal'tri·ly** *adv.* **pal'tri·ness** *n.*

pam·pas (păm'paz, pahm'pas) *n.pl.* Vast treeless grassy plains of S. Amer. S. of the Amazon, esp. great plain of Argentina stretching from Atlantic coast to Andes, and from Rio Colorado to Gran Chaco; **~ grass**, gigantic grass (*Cortaderia selloana*) with silvery-colored silky panicles on stalks sometimes 12 or 14 ft. high, introduced into Europe and N. Amer. from S. Amer. [Quechua *pampa* plain]

pam·per (păm'per) *v.t.* Over-indulge.

pam·phlet (păm'flĭt) *n.* Small unbound treatise, esp. on subject of current interest. **pam·phlet·eer** (pamflĭtēr') *n.* Writer of pamphlets. ~ *v.i.* Write pamphlets. [prob. f. *Pamphilet, Panflet*, familiar name of 12th-c. Latin amatory poem or comedy "Pamphilus, seu de Amore"]

Pam·plo·na (pahmplō'na). City in N. Spain, capital of Navarre Province; site of annual "running of the bulls" through streets to bull-fight arena.

Pan (păn). (Gk. myth.) God of flocks and shepherds; orig. and chiefly an Arcadian deity, represented with the horns, ears, and legs of a goat; he invented the musical pipe (PANPIPE) and was reputed to cause sudden groundless fear such as that felt by travelers in remote and desolate places.

pan[1] (păn) *n.* 1. Metal or earthenware vessel, usu. shallow

The distinctive colors of a ***palomino*** *can be obtained only by breeding parents of different colors. If palominos are mated, their offspring do not have the colors that breeders want.*

and freq. open, for domestic purposes; panlike vessel in which substances are heated etc.; contents of pan, panful. 2. Pan-shaped depression or concavity of any vessel or structure; part of lock that held priming in obsolete types of gun. 3. Hollow in ground, esp. salt pan; **hard ~**, substratum of soil, more or less impervious to moisture. **pan** *v*. (**panned, pan·ning**). Wash (gold-bearing gravel) in pan; **~ out**, yield gold, (fig.) succeed, work (*well* etc.).

pan[2] (pahn) *n*. Betel leaf; combination of this with areca nut etc. for chewing. [Hind. *pān*]

pan[3] (păn) *v*. (**panned, pan·ning**). (film) Pivot (camera) to obtain panoramic effect or follow moving object; (of camera) be pivoted thus.

pan- *prefix*. All.

pan·a·ce·a (pănasē′*a*) *n*. Universal remedy.

pa·nache (p*a*năsh′, -nahsh′) *n*. Tuft, plume, of feathers, esp. as headdress or on helmet; (fig.) display, swagger.

Pan·a·ma[1] (păn′*a*mah). Republic of Central America, lying between Costa Rica and Colombia; its capital city, at Pacific end of Panama Canal; **~ Canal**, 50-mile-long ship canal connecting the Atlantic and Pacific through narrow **Isthmus of ~**, completed by the U.S. in 1914. **Panama Canal Zone**, strip of land 50 mi. (80 km) long, and 10 mi. (16 km) wide, across the Isthmus of Panama along the Canal; in a 1903 treaty, the Republic of Panama gave the U.S. perpetual sovereign rights in the Canal Zone in exchange for U.S. building and operating of the canal; in 1978, the U.S. signed a new treaty promising to turn over control of the Canal and the Canal Zone to Panama by the year 2,000. **Pan·a·ma·ni·an** (păn*a*mā′nē*a*n) *adj*. & *n*.

Pan·a·ma[2] (păn′*a*mah) *n*. (also **~ hat**) Fine soft plaited hat made from undeveloped leaves of stemless screw pine (*Carludovica palmata*) of tropical S. Amer., or an imitation of this.

Pan-A·mer·i·can (păn*a*mĕr′ĭk*a*n) *adj*. Of all nations of N. and S. Amer.; of all Americans.

pan·cake (păn′kāk) *n*. Thin flat cake of batter fried in pan; **flat as a ~**, quite flat; **~ landing**, (slang) landing of aircraft without use of undercarriage; **~ make-up**, make-up in cake form.

pan·chro·mat·ic (pănkrōmăt′ĭk) *adj*. (phot.) Equally sensitive to all colors of spectrum, representing all colors in proper intensities. **pan·chro·ma·tism** (pănkrō′m*a*tĭz*e*m) *n*.

pan·cre·as (păn′krē*a*s, păng′-) *n*. Gland near stomach discharging a digestive secretion (**pancreatic juice**) through ducts into duodenum, and also producing INSULIN, which it passes directly into the bloodstream. **pan·cre·at·ic** (pănkrēăt′ĭk, păng-) *adj*.

pan·da (păn′d*a*) *n*. Raccoon-like animal (*Ailurus fulgens*) of SE. Himalayas, with reddish-brown fur and long bushy ring-marked tail; **giant ~**, large rare bearlike black-and-white mammal (*Ailuropoda melanoleuca*) of E. Tibet and Szechuan.

Pan·da·rus (păn′d*a*r*u*s). (Gk. legend) One of the Trojan leaders; in the medieval legend of Troilus and Cressida, Cressida's uncle, who acted as go-between for the lovers.

pan·dem·ic (păndĕm′ĭk) *adj*. & *n*. (Disease, usu. infectious) of world-wide distribution.

pan·de·mo·ni·um (pănd*e*mō′nē*u*m) *n*. Abode of all demons; place of lawless violence or uproar; utter confusion. [word coined by Milton]

pan·der (păn′d*e*r) *n*. (also **pan′der·er**) Go-between in amorous intrigues, procurer; one who ministers to evil designs. **~** *v*. Minister (*to* base passions, evil designs) (also fig.); act as pander to. [f. PANDARUS]

Pan·do·ra (păndōr′*a*, -dōr′*a*). (Gk. myth.) First woman, made by Hephaestus at the order of Zeus to punish the human race because PROMETHEUS had stolen fire from heaven for their use; she became wife of Epimetheus, brother of Prometheus, and from a box (**~'s box**) given her by Zeus let loose all the evils that afflict mankind, hope alone remaining in the bottom of the box.

pan·do·ra (păndōr′*a*, -dōr′*a*), **pan·dore** (păn′dōr, -dōr) *ns*. Wire-stringed musical instrument of guitar type.

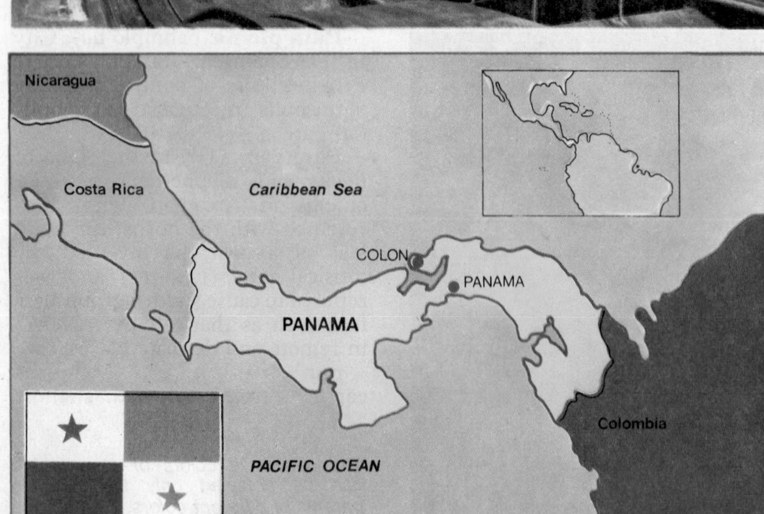

*The 28,575 sq. mile Republic of **Panama** is at the narrowest part of the isthmus linking North and South America. The canal (top left) is 40 miles long.*

*Found only in bamboo forests of Yunnan and Szechuan, the giant **panda** can weigh up to 400 lb. The 'fire fox' or lesser panda is cat-sized and is found also in Nepal.*

pane (pān) *n.* Single sheet of glass in compartment of window; rectangular division of checkered pattern etc. **pane'less** *adj.*

pan·e·gyr·ic (pănĭjēr'ĭk, -jī'rĭk) *n.* & *adj.* Laudatory (discourse). **pan·e·gyr'i·cal** *adj.* **pan·e·gyr'i·cal·ly** *adv.*

pan·e·gy·rize (păn'ĭjĭrīz) *v.t.* (**-rized, -riz·ing**). Speak, write, in praise of, eulogize. **pan·e·gyr·ist** (pănĭjĭr'ĭst, -jī'rĭst) *n.*

pan·el (păn'el) *n.* 1. List of jurors, jury. 2. Group of people gathered, esp. as experts, to hold discussion, make judgments, etc.; panelists. 3. Distinct section, esp. of surface, as of door, etc., often sunk below or raised above general level; strip of material in dress etc. ~ **truck**, small delivery truck having fully enclosed body. **panel** *v.t.* (**-eled** or **-elled, -el·ing** or **-el·ling**). Saddle (beast) with panel; fit (wall, door, etc.) with panels; ornament (dress etc.) with panels. **pan'el·ing, pan'el·ling, pan·el·ist** (păn'elĭst) *ns.*

pang (păng) *n.* Shooting pain; sudden sharp mental pain.

pan·go·lin (pănggō'lĭn) *n.* Scaly anteater, large mammal of genus *Manis* (order Pholidota), of tropical Asia and Africa. [Malay *penggoling* roller]

pan·han·dle (păn'hăndel) *n.* Handle of pan; narrow prolongation of country or territory extending between 2 others. ~ *v.* (**-dled, -dling**). (slang) Beg. **pan'han·dler** *n.* (slang) Beggar.

Pan·hel·len·ism (pănhĕl'enĭzem) *n.* Political union of all Greeks. **Pan·hel·len·ic** (pănhelĕn'ĭk) *adj.*

*The scale-covered insectivorous **pangolin** is native to Asia and Africa. When threatened, it rolls itself into a ball, but unlike hedgehogs or spiny anteaters, some pangolins are arboreal.*

pan·ic[1] (păn'ĭk) *n.* (also ~ **grass**) Grass of genus *Panicum* including Italian millet, freq. cultivated as cereal grain.

pan·ic[2] (păn'ĭk) *adj.* (of terror) Unreasoning, excessive. ~ *n.* Infectious fright; sudden general alarm leading to hasty measures. ~ *v.* (**-icked, -ick·ing**). Affect, be affected, with panic. **pan'ick·y** *adj.* [Gk. *panikos* of PAN, reputed to cause panic]

pan·i·cle (păn'ĭkel) *n.* (bot.) Compound inflorescence in which some pedicels branch again or repeatedly, forming loose irregular cluster, as in oats. **pan'i·cled** *adj.*

Pan·ja·bi = PUNJABI.

pan·jan·drum (pănjăn'drum) *n.* Mock title of exalted personage; pompous official or pretender. [app. invented by S. Foote, 1720–77, in a piece of nonsense verse]

Pank·hurst (păngk'hērst), **Mrs. Emmeline Goulden** (1858–1928). English leader of militant suffragism.

pan·nier, pan·ier (păn'yer, -ēer) *ns.* 1. Basket, esp. one of those carried, usu. in pairs, by beast of burden or on person's shoulders. 2. Frame distending woman's skirt at the hips, part of skirt looped up around hips.

pan·ni·kin (păn'ĭkĭn) *n.* Small metal drinking vessel; its contents.

pan·o·ply (păn'oplē) *n.* (pl. **-plies**). Complete suit of armor; (fig.) complete or splendid array. **pan'o·plied** *adj.*

pan·o·ram·a (pănorăm'a, -rah'ma) *n.* Picture of landscape etc. arranged on inside of cylindrical surface or successively rolled out before spectator; continuous passing scene; unbroken view of surrounding region. **pan·o·ramʹic** *adj.* **pan·o·ramʹi·cal·ly** *adv.*

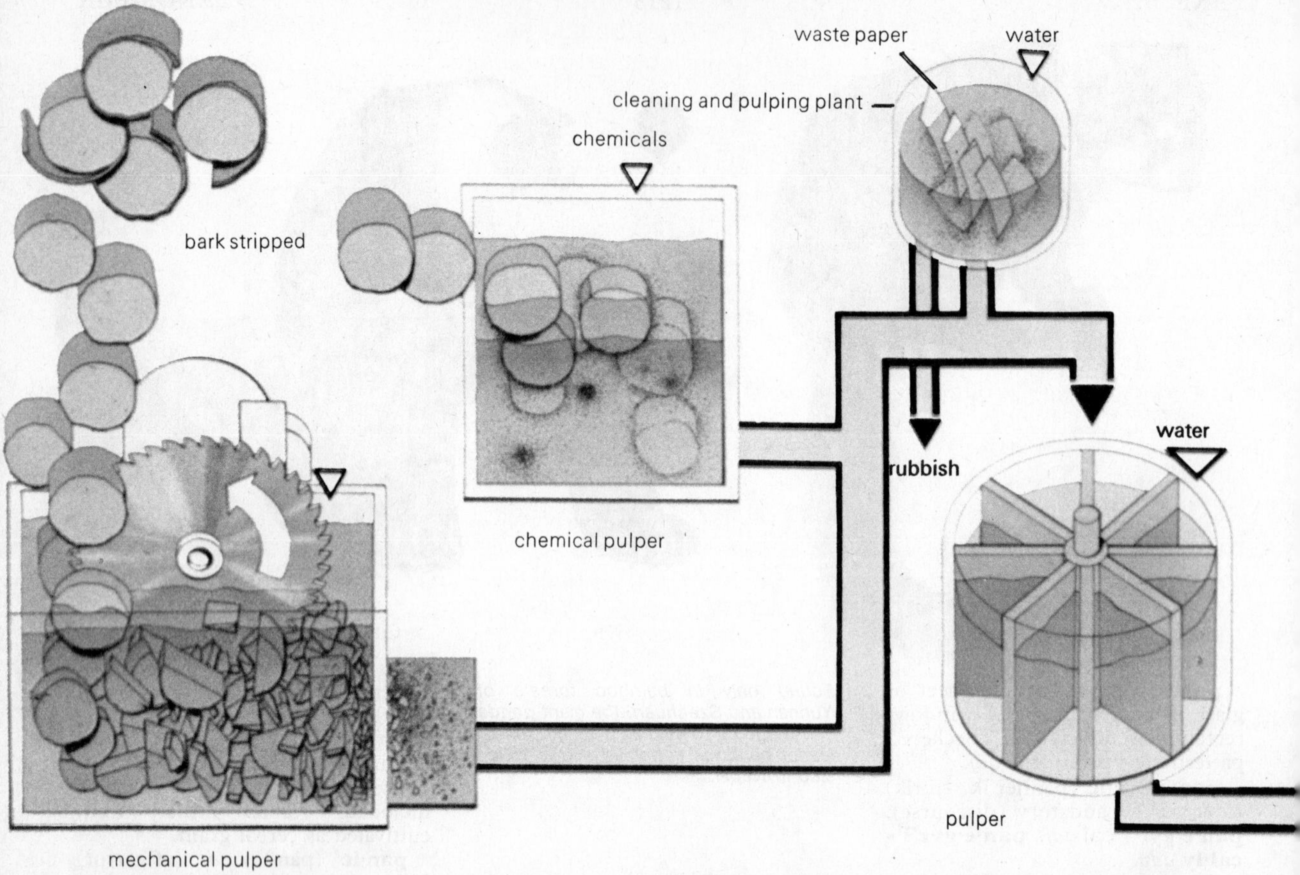

pan·pipe (pănʹpīp) *n.* (also **panʹpipes, Pan's' pipes'**) Musical instrument of graduated series of reeds forming scale, with open ends level. [f. PAN]

pan·sy (pănʹzē) *n.* (pl. **-sies**). 1. Wild or cultivated plant (*Viola tricolor*) with variously colored flowers; heartsease. 2. (colloq. offensive) Effeminate man; male homosexual.

pant (pănt) *v.* Gasp for breath; yearn (*for, after, to*); throb violently; utter gaspingly. ~ *n.* Gasp, throb.

Pan·tag·ru·el (păntăgʹro͞oĕl, păntagro͞oʹel). One of the characters of RABELAIS, giant son of Gargantua, represented as a great eater and drinker and an extravagant and satirical humorist. **Pan·ta·gru·el·i·an** (păntagro͞oĕlʹēan) *adj.*

Pan·ta·loon (pănʹtalo͞on). Venetian character in Italian comedy represented as foolish old man wearing spectacles, pantaloons, and slippers; clown's butt and abettor in harlequinade or pantomime. [It. *Pantalone*, perh. f. San Pantaleone, favorite Venetian saint]

pan·ta·loons (păntalo͞onzʹ) *n.pl.* Garment of breeches and stockings in one piece; tight-fitting trousers fastened with ribbons or buttons below calf, or strap passing under boots; (archaic) trousers.

pan·the·ism (pănʹthēĭzem) *n.* Doctrine that God is everything and everything is God; worship of all the gods. **panʹthe·ist** *n.* **pan·the·isʹtic, pan·the·isʹti·cal** *adjs.* **pan·the·isʹti·cal·ly** *adv.*

pan·the·on (pănʹthēŏn, -on) *n.* 1. Temple dedicated to all the gods, esp. the circular temple still standing in Rome, erected in early 2nd C. A.D. prob. on site of an earlier one built by Agrippa. 2. Building (esp. former church of St. Genevieve in Paris) in which illustrious dead are buried or have memorials. 3. Deities of a people collectively.

pan·ther (pănʹther) *n.* (pl. **-thers**, collect. **-ther**). 1. = LEOPARD, esp. male (now chiefly **black** ~, black form of leopard common in S. India). 2. = MOUNTAIN lion.

pant·ies (pănʹtēz) *n.pl.* Underpants worn by women and girls.

pan·to·graph (pănʹtograf) *n.* 1. Instrument of four rods jointed together in parallelogram form, with tracing points on one free end and one terminal joint, for copying plans etc. on any scale. 2. (elect.) Device on top of electrically operated vehicle that conveys current from overhead wires. **pan·to·graphʹic** *adj.*

pan·to·mime (pănʹtomīm) *n.* 1. (hist.) Roman actor performing in dumb show. 2. (Brit.) Dramatic entertainment now usu. produced at Christmas time and based on a traditional fairy tale, with singing, dancing, acrobatics, clowning, topical jokes, a transformation scene, and certain stock roles. 3. Dumb show. **pan·to·mim·ic** (păntomĭmʹĭk) *adj.*

pan·try (pănʹtrē) *n.* (pl. **-tries**). Room in which bread and other

*The **pansy** which now grows wild in some gardens, was bred from a wild flower common in England and the Pyrenees. The multitude of colors has been developed within 170 years.*

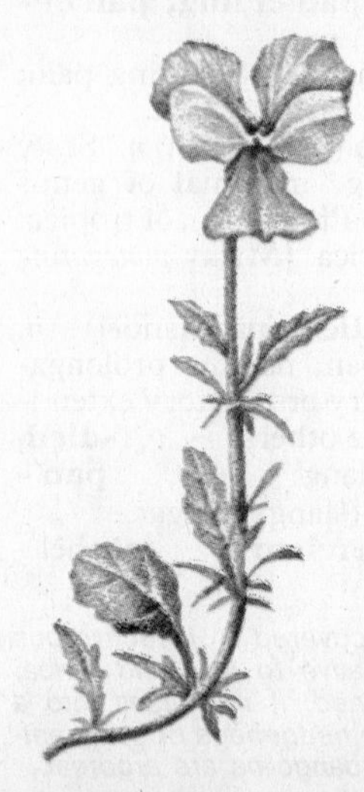

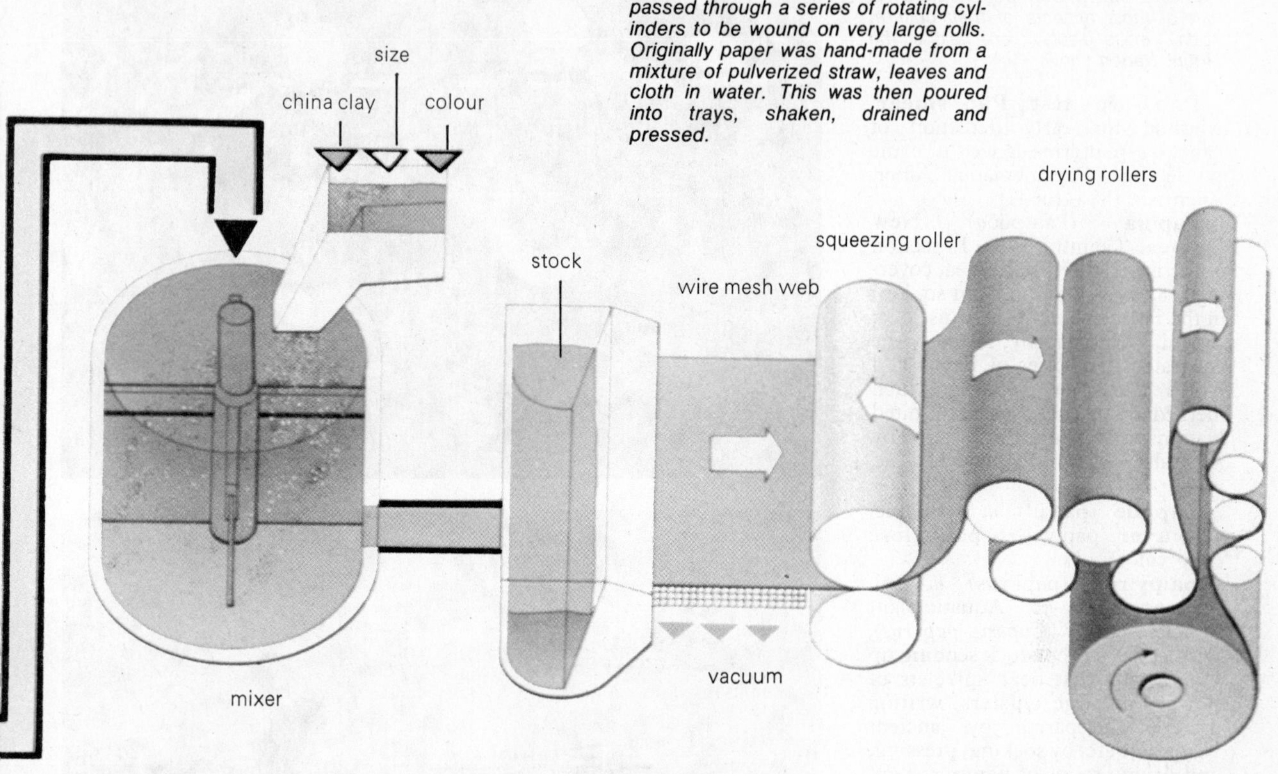

***Paper** is made from vegetable fibers which are formed into pulp. This is passed through a series of rotating cylinders to be wound on very large rolls. Originally paper was hand-made from a mixture of pulverized straw, leaves and cloth in water. This was then poured into trays, shaken, drained and pressed.*

provisions, or (**butler's ~**) plates, table linen, etc., are kept.

pants (pănts) *n.pl.* 1. Men's underpants; PANTIES. 2. Trousers.

pan·ty (păn′tē) **hose.** One-piece garment combining PANTIES and stockings.

pan·zer (păn′zer, pahn′tser) *n.* Armor; freq. attrib., as ~ *division.* [Ger.]

pap[1] (păp) *n.* (archaic) Nipple of woman's breast; corresponding part of man.

pap[2] (păp) *n.* Soft or semiliquid food for infants or invalids; mash, pulp.

pa·pa (pah′p*a*, p*a*pah′) *n.* (Child's name for) father.

pa·pa·cy (pā′p*a*sē) *n.* (pl. **-cies**). Pope's (tenure of) office; papal system.

pa·pal (pā′p*a*l) *adj.* Of the pope or his office; **P ~ States**, district of central Italy until 1870 subject to the Apostolic See. **pa′pal·ly** *adv.* **pa′pal·ism** *n.* **pa′pal·ist** *n.* & *adj.*

pa·paw (paw′paw, p*a*paw′), **paw·paw** (paw′paw) *ns.* 1. = PAPAYA. 2. Small N. Amer. tree (*Asimina triloba*) with purple flowers; oblong edible fruit of this, with beanlike seeds embedded in sweet pulp.

pa·pa·ya (p*a*pah′y*a*) *n.* Palmlike tree (*Carica papaya*) of S. Amer.; fruit of this, usu. oblong, of dull orange color, with thick fleshy rind and numerous black seeds embedded in pulp, used as food.

Pa·pe·e·te (pahpēā′tā). Capital of French Polynesia, on the NW. coast of Tahiti Island in the E. Pacific Ocean.

pa·per (pā′p*e*r) *n.* 1. Substance composed of fibers interlaced into a compact web, made from linen and cotton rags, straw, wood, certain grasses, etc., which are macerated into a pulp, dried and pressed into a thin flexible sheet, used for writing, printing, drawing, wrapping up parcels, covering the interior of walls, etc.; substance of similar texture, as that made by wasps for their nests; substance made from paper pulp, as papier-mâché etc. 2. Negotiable documents, e.g. bills of exchange; bank notes etc. used as currency (opp. COIN). 3. (slang) (Persons admitted by) free passes to theater etc. 4. (pl.) Documents proving person's or ship's identity, standing, etc.; **send in one's ~s**, resign. 5. Set of questions in examination; essay, dissertation, esp. one read to learned society. 6. Newspaper. 7. Paper used as wrapper or receptacle; small paper parcel; sheet of paper with pins or needles stuck in it. 8. **on ~**, hypothetically, to judge from statistics, etc.; **pa′per·back**, (book) bound in paper, freq. as cheap reprint; **pa′perboy**, boy who sells or delivers newspapers; **pa′perhang·er**, one who hangs wallpaper; **paper knife**, blunt knife for cutting open letters, leaves of book etc.; **paper mill**, mill in which paper is made; **paper profits**, profits not yet realized; **pa′perweight**, small heavy object laid on loose papers to prevent their being scattered; **paper work**, clerical work involving keeping of records etc. **pa′per·y** *adj.* **paper** *v.t.* Enclose in paper; decorate (wall etc.) with wallpaper; furnish with paper; (slang) fill (theater etc.) by means of free passes. **pa′per·er** *n.*

pa·pier-mâ·ché, pa·per-mâché (pāp*e*rm*a*shā′) *ns.* Molded paper pulp used for boxes, trays, etc. [Fr., = "chewed paper"]

pa·pil·la (p*a*pĭl′*a*) *n.* (pl. **-pil·lae** pr. -pĭl′ē). Small nipple-like protuberance in a part or organ of the body; (bot.) small fleshy projection on plant. **pap·il·lar·y** (păp′ĭlĕrē, p*a*pĭl′*a*rē), **pap·il·late** (păp′ĭlāt, p*a*pĭl′ĭt), **pap·il·lose** (păp′ĭlōs, p*a*pĭl′ōs) *adjs.*

pap·il·lon (păp′ĭlŏn) *n.* (Breed of) toy dog with ears suggesting form of butterfly.

pa·pist (pā′pĭst) *n.* Advocate of papal supremacy; (usu. derog.) Roman Catholic. **pa·pis′tic, pa·pis′ti·cal** *adjs.* **pa·pist·ry** (pā′pĭstrē) *n.*

pa·poose, pap·poose (păpōōs′, p*a*-) *ns.* N. Amer. Ind. young child.

pa·pri·ka (păprē′k*a*, păp′rĭk*a*) *n.* Ripe fruit of sweet pepper; red condiment made from this. [Hungarian]

*Among the peoples of **Papua New Guinea,** decoration, singing and dancing have always formed an essential part of most aspects of their culture. Today, mass displays are held at the Mount Hagen show.*

Pap (păp) **test, Pap smear.** Method for early detection of cancer, esp. uterine cancer. [f. name of George Papanicolaou, Amer. scientist (1883–1962)]

Pap·ua (Pah'pōōa) **New Guinea.** Country in the E. section of the island of New Guinea, covering 178,259 sq. mi. (461,691 sq. km) in the Pacific Ocean N. of Australia; capital, Port Moresby; formerly the Australian territories of Papua and North East New Guinea, which merged in 1945 and became a United Nations trusteeship administered by Australia until independence in 1975.

pap·ule (păp ūl) *n.* Pimple. **pap·u·lar** (păp'*yuler*), **pap·u·lose** (păp'*yulōs*) *adjs.*

pa·py·rus (papī'rus) *n.* (pl. **-rus·es, -ri** pr. -rī). Aquatic plant of sedge family (*Cyperus papyrus*), with creeping rootstock sending up long stems that bear spikelets of flowers in large clusters; writing material prepared by ancient Egyptians etc. by soaking, pressing, and drying strips of papyrus stem, laying them side by side, and placing similar layers over these at right angles; manuscript written on this. **pap·y·rol·o·gy** (păpirŏl'ojē) *n.* The scholarly study of papyrus manuscripts. **pap·y·rol'o·gist** *n.*

par (par) *n.* Equality, equal footing; average or normal amount, degree, or condition; (golf) number of strokes that scratch player should require for hole or course, allowing two putts for each green; **above ~**, at a premium; **at ~**, (of stocks etc.) at face value; **below ~**, at a discount; below the average degree, quality, etc.; not in one's usual health. [L., = "equal(ity)"]

par. *abbrev.* Paragraph; parallel; parenthesis.

para- *prefix.* Beside; beyond; wrong; irregular.

par·a·ble (păr'*abel*) *n.* Fictitious narrative used to point a moral or illustrate some spiritual relation or condition; short allegory.

pa·rab·o·la (parăb'*ola*) *n.* Plane curve formed by intersection of cone with plane parallel to its side.

par·a·bol·ic (părabŏl'ĭk), **par·a·bol'i·cal** *adjs.* 1. Of, expressed in, a parable. 2. Of, like, a parabola. **par·a·bol'i·cal·ly** *adv.*

pa·rab·o·loid (parăb'oloid) *n.* Solid some of whose plane sections are parabolas, esp. that generated by revolution of parabola about its axis (**~ of revolution**).

Par·a·cel·sus (părasĕl'sus), **Philippus Aureolus.** Name taken by Theophrastus Bombastus von Hohenheim (1493–1541), German–Swiss physician, alchemist, and astrologer.

*Bundles of **papyrus** near the pyramids. This aquatic reed was the main material used for paper making until the 4th century A.D. Although less is obtained from Egypt today, it is still profuse in east and north Africa.*

par·a·chute (păr'ashōōt) *n.* Umbrella-shaped apparatus of silk or other material attached by ropes to person or heavy object falling or being dropped from a height, esp. from aircraft, and designed to be expanded by the air it is falling through (or other means) and by its resulting drag to reduce the speed of falling to some desired limit, usu. one consistent with safety; **~ troops**, PARATROOPS. **parachute** *v.* (**-chut·ed, -chut·ing**). Convey, descend, by parachute. **par'a·chut·ist** *n.*

pa·rade (parăd') *n.* 1. Display, ostentaion. 2. Muster of troops etc. for inspection, esp. one held regularly at set hours; ground used for this. 3. Public square or promenade. **~** *v.* (**-rad·ed, -rad·ing**). 1. Assemble (troops etc.) for review or other purpose; march through (streets etc.) with display; march in procession with display. 2. Display ostentatiously. **pa·rad'er** *n.*

par·a·digm (păr'adīm, -dĭm) *n.* Example, pattern, esp. of inflection of noun, verb, etc. **par·a·dig·mat·ic** (păradĭgmăt'ĭk) *adj.*

par·a·dise (păr'adīs) *n.* Garden of Eden (also **earthly ~**); heaven; region, state, of supreme bliss; **bird of ~**: see BIRD; **~ duck**, brightly colored N.Z. duck (*Tadorna variegata*), species of sheldrake. **par·a·di·sa·i·cal** (păradĭsā'ĭkal, -zā'-), **par·a·di·sa'ic, par·a·dis·al** (păradī'sal, -dī'zal), **par·a·di·si·a·cal** (păradĭsī'akal, -zī-'), **par·a·dis·i·ac** (păradĭs'ēăk, -dĭz'-) *adjs.* [O. Pers, *pairidaeza* park]

*A **parade** at Disneyland, California, which was the first of the amusement parks to open in the U.S.A. in 1955. A second park was begun and remained unfinished until 1971, during which time Walt Disney died.*

par·a·dox (păr´*a*dŏks) *n.* Statement contrary to accepted opinion; seemingly absurd though perhaps really well-founded statement; self-contradictory, essentially absurd or false, statement; person, thing, conflicting with preconceived notions of what is reasonable or possible. **par·a·dox´i·cal** *adj.* **par·a·dox´i·cal·ly** *adv.* **par·a·dox·i·cal´i·ty** *n.*

par·af·fin (păr´*a*fĭn) *n.* 1. (also ~ **wax**) White tasteless odorless waxy substance, chemically a mixture of higher hydrocarbons, solid at ordinary temperatures and obtained by distillation of petroleum etc., used for making candles, rendering paper waterproof (*wax paper*), etc. 2. (chem.) Any of a series of saturated hydrocarbons of which methane is the simplest member. [L. *parum* little, *affinis* having affinity, referring to the relative unreactivity of the paraffins]

par·a·gon (păr´*a*gŏn, -g*o*n) *n.* 1. Model of excellence, supremely excellent person or thing, model (*of* virtue etc.). 2. Perfect diamond, 100 carats or more. 3. (print.) Large size of type, between great primer

*The bright plumage and long tail feathers of the **bird of paradise** contribute to its spectacular appearance.*

Prince Rudolph's Blue Bird of Paradise

Count Raggis Bird of Paradise

Magnificent Bird of Paradise

*Small to medium-sized parrots with long tails have been called **parakeets** though there is no scientific basis for this discrimination. Many, like the larger ones, have brilliant plumage.*

and double pica (two-line long primer, 20 point).

par·a·graph (păr′*a*grăf, -grahf) *n.* Distinct passage or section in book etc., usu. marked by indentation of first line; symbol (usu. ¶) formerly used to mark new paragraphs, now as a reference mark; detached short item of news etc. in newspaper. ~ *v.t.* Arrange (article etc.) in paragraphs. **par′a·graph·er** *n.* **par·a·graph′ic** *adj.*

Par·a·guay (păr′*a*gwā, -gwī). Inland republic of S. Amer.; capital, Asunción; ~ **River**, river in S. central S. Amer., flowing 1,584 mi. (2,549 km) from SW. Brazil to the Paraná in SW. Paraguay. **Par·a·guay′an** *adj.* & *n.*

par·a·keet, par·ra·keet (păr′*a*kēt) *ns.* Any of several small esp. long-tailed kinds of parrot; budgerigar. [OF., f. It. *parrochetto* dim. of *parroco* parson, or *parrucchetto* dim. of *parrucca* peruke]

par·al·de·hyde (p*a*răl′d*e*hīd) *n.* Polymer of aldehyde ($C_6H_{12}O_3$), used as a sedative.

par·al·lax (păr′*a*lăks) *n.* Apparent displacement of object, caused by actual change of point of observation; angular amount of this displacement. **par·al·lac·tic** (păr*a*lăk′tĭk) *adj.*

par·al·lel (păr′*a*lĕl) *adj.* (of lines) Continuously equidistant (*to*); precisely similar, analogous, or corresponding; ~ **bars**, pair of horizontal parallel bars supported on posts for gymnastic exercises; ~ **circuit**, (elect.) circuit connecting the same two points as are connected by another circuit; ~ **ruler**, two rulers connected by pivoted crosspieces or single ruler fitted with rollers, for drawing parallel lines. **parallel** *n.* 1. (also ~ **of latitude**) Each of the parallel circles marking degrees of latitude on Earth's surface on globe; line on map corresponding to one of these. 2. Person, thing, precisely analogous to another; comparison. 3. Parallel position. 4. Two parallel lines (‖) as reference mark. ~ *v.t.* (**-leled** or **-lelled, -lel·ing** or **-lel·ling**). Represent as similar, compare (*with, to*); find, mention, something parallel or corresponding to; be parallel, correspond, to.

par·al·lel·e·pi·ped (păr*a*lĕl*e*pī′pĭd, -pĭp′ĭd) *n.* Solid contained by parallelograms.

par·al·lel·ism (păr′*a*lĕlĭzem) *n.* Being parallel; comparison or correspondence of successive passages.

par·al·lel·o·gram (păr*a*lĕl′*o*grăm) *n.* Four-sided rectilineal figure whose opposite sides are parallel.

pa·ral·y·sis (p*a*răl′ĭsĭs) *n.* (pl. **-ses** pr. -sēz). Impairment or loss of motor or sensory function of nerves; (fig.) state of utter powerlessness.

par·a·lyt·ic (păr*a*lĭt′ĭk) *adj.* & *n.* (Person) afflicted with paralysis. **par·a·lyt′i·cal·ly** *adv.*

par·a·lyze (păr′*a*līz) *v.t.* (**-lyzed, -lyz·ing**). Afflict with paralysis; render powerless, cripple.

Par·a·mar·i·bo (păr*a*măr′*i*bō). Capital and chief seaport of Suriname on the Suriname River in northeastern S. Amer.

par·a·me·ci·um (păr*a*mē′shē*u*m, -sē*u*m) *n.* (pl. **-ci·a** pr. -shē*a*, -sē*a*). Ciliated freshwater protozoan of genus **P**~.

pa·ram·e·ter (p*a*răm′ĭt*e*r) *n.* (math.) Quantity constant in case considered, but varying in different cases. **par·a·met·ric** (păr*a*mĕt′rĭk), **par·a·met′ri·cal** *adjs.*

par·a·mil·i·tar·y (păr*a*mĭl′ĭtĕrē) *adj.* Ancillary to or as substitute for armed forces.

par·a·mo (păr′*a*mō) *n.* (pl. **-mos**). High treeless plateau in tropical S. Amer.

par·a·mount (păr′*a*mownt) *adj.* Supreme; preeminent; superior (*to*). **par′a·mount·cy** *n.* **par′a·mount·ly** *adv.*

par·a·mour (păr′*a*moor) *n.* Illicit lover of married person.

Pa·ra·ná (pār*a*nah′). River in central S. Amer. flowing 1,827 mi. (2,940 km) from S. Brazil along the S. border of Paraguay to the Rio de la Plata in E. Argentina.

par·a·noi·a (păr*a*noi′*a*) *n.* Form of mental illness characterized by systematic delusions, esp. of grandeur, persecution, etc. **par·a·noi·ac** (păr*a*noi′ăk, -ĭk) *adj.* & *n.*

par·a·noid (păr′*a*noid) *adj.* Resembling, characterized by, paranoia.

par·a·pet (păr′*a*pĭt, -pĕt) *n.* Low wall at edge of balcony, roof, etc., or along sides of bridge etc.; (mil.) defense of earth, stone, etc., to conceal and protect troops, esp. mound along front of trench. **par′a·pet·ed** *adj.* Having a parapet.

par·a·pher·nal·ia (păr*a*f*e*rnāl′y*a*, -fenāl′-) *n.pl.* Personal belongings; accessories, odds and ends of equipment; (formerly) articles of personal property that law allowed married woman to keep and treat as her own.

par·a·phrase (păr′afrāz) *n.* Free rendering or amplification of a passage, expression of its sense in other words. ~ *v.t.* (**-phrased, -phras·ing**). Express meaning of (passage) in other words. **par·a·phras·tic** (părafrăs′tĭk) *adj.* **par·a·phras′ti·cal·ly** *adv.*

par·a·ple·gi·a (păraplē′jēa, -ja) *n.* Paralysis confined to the lower limbs. **par·a·ple·gic** (păraplē′jĭk) *adj.* & *n.* (Person) affected with paraplegia.

pa·ra·pro·fes·sion·al (părapro-fĕsh onal) *n.* Trained assistant to teacher, doctor, or other professional.

par·a·psy·chol·o·gy (părasīkŏl′ojē) *n.* Study of mental phenomena lying outside the sphere of ordinary psychology; study of psychical phenomena. **par·a·psy·cho·log′i·cal** *adj.*

par·a·se·le·ne (părasĭlē′nē) *n.* (pl. **-nae** pr. -nē). Bright spot on lunar halo, mock moon; moondog.

par·a·site (păr′asīt) *n.* 1. Interested hanger-on, toady. 2. Animal, plant, living in or upon another and deriving nutriment from it to the detriment of the host; (loosely) plant that climbs about another plant, walls, etc. **par·a·sit·ic** (părasĭt′ĭk), **par·a·sit′i·cal** *adjs.* **par·a·sit′i·cal·ly** *adv.* **par′a·sit·ism** *n.* **par·a·si·tize** (păr′asĭtīz, -sī-) *v.t.* (**-tized, -tiz·ing**). Infest as a parasite.

par·a·sol (păr′asawl, -sŏl) *n.* Light umbrella used to give protection from the sun.

par·a·sym·pa·thet·ic (părasĭmpathĕt′ĭk) *adj.* Of that part of the nervous system which consists of fibers connecting with nerve cells grouped within or near the viscera, so called because its peripheral nerves often run alongside those of the sympathetic system.

par·a·thy·roid (părathī′roid) *adj.* (anat.) Situated near the thyroid; ~ **gland**, one of four small bodies adjacent to thyroid gland, producing a secretion that maintains the balance between the calcium in the blood and that in the bones. **parathyroid** *n.* Parathyroid gland.

par·a·troops (păr′atrōōps) *n.pl.* Assault troops transported by aircraft to combat area and then dropped by parachute. **par′a·troop·er** *n.*

par·a·ty·phoid (părati′foid) *n.* Form of enteric fever milder than true typhoid and bacteriologically distinguishable from it.

par·a·vane (păr′avān) *n.* Apparatus towed from bows of a ship at a depth regulated by its vanes, with saw-edged jaws for cutting the moorings of submerged mines.

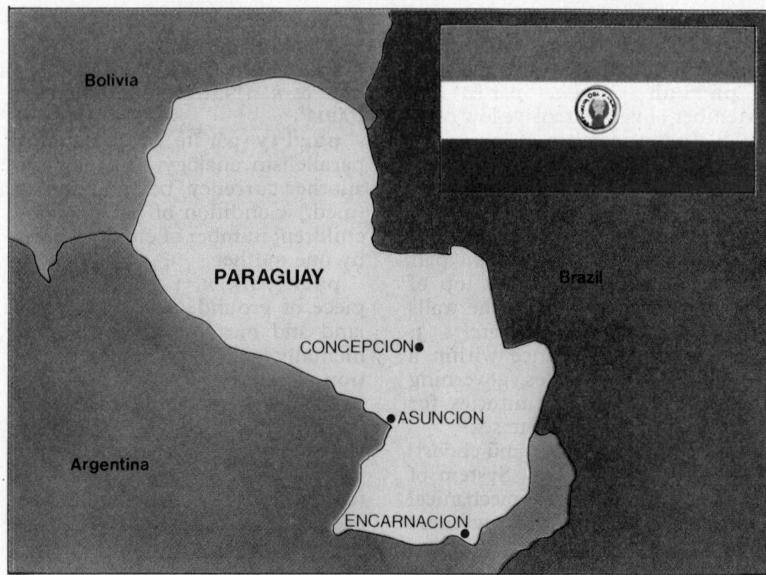

Meat and vegetable oils are the main exports of ***Paraguay,*** *a land-locked country in South America. The main industries are based on the processing of timber and agricultural products.*

par a·vi·on (pār ăvyawn′). By air mail. [Fr., by plane]

par·boil (pār′boil) *v.t.* Boil partially; (fig.) overheat.

par·cel (pār′sel) *n.* 1. Part (esp. in **part and parcel**); piece of land, esp. as part of estate. 2. Goods etc. wrapped up in single package; ~ **post**, branch of postal service concerned with parcels. **parcel** *v.t.* (**-celed** or **-celled, -cel·ing** or **-cel·ling**). 1. Divide (usu. *out*) into portions; make (*up*) into parcel(s). 2. (naut.) Cover (caulked seam) with canvas strips and pitch; wrap (rope) with canvas strips. **par′cel·ing, par′cel·ling** *ns.* (esp., naut.) Strip of canvas, usu. tarred, for binding around rope.

parch (pārch) *v.* Roast slightly; make or become hot and dry.

parch·ment (pārch′ment) *n.* Skin (strictly, inner part of split skin of sheep) dressed and prepared for writing, painting, etc.; parchmentlike skin, esp. husk of coffee bean; ~ **paper**, thick, strong, specially toughened paper.

par·don (pār′don) *n.* Forgiveness; (law) remission of legal consequences of crime; courteous forbearance (esp. in *I beg your* ~, formula of apology); (eccles.) indulgence. **pardon** *v.t.* Forgive; make allowance for, excuse. **par′don·a·ble** *adj.* **par′don·a·bly** *adv.*

par·don·er (par′doner) *n.* (hist.) Person licensed to sell pardons or indulgences.

pare (pār) *v.t.* (**pared, par·ing**). Trim (thing) by cutting away irregular parts etc.; cut away skin, rind, etc., of (fruit etc.); shave, cut *off, away* (edges etc.); (fig.) diminish little by little. **par′er, par′ing** *ns.*

par·e·gor·ic (păregōr′ĭk, -gār′-) *n.* Camphorated tincture of opium flavored with aniseed and benzoic acid, taken for relief of diarrhea and intestinal pain. ~ *adj.* Soothing.

pa·ren·chy·ma (parĕng′kima) *n.* 1. (anat.) Tissue of gland, organ, etc., as dist. from flesh and connective tissue. 2. (bot.) Tissue of cells of about equal length and breadth placed side by side, usu. soft and succulent, found esp. in softer parts of leaves, pulp of fruits, etc. **pa·ren′chy·mal, par·en·chym·a·tous** (părĕngkĭm′atus) *adjs.*

par·ent (pār′ent, păr′-) *n.* Father or mother; forefather; animal, plant, from which others are derived; (fig.) source, origin. **pa·ren·tal** (parĕn′tal) *adj.* **pa·ren′tal·ly** *adv.* **par′ent·hood** *n.*

par·ent·age (pār′entĭj, păr′-) *n.* Descent from parents, lineage.

pa·ren·the·sis (parĕn′thĭsĭs) *n.* (pl. **-ses** pr. -sēz). Word, clause, sentence, inserted into a passage to which it is not grammatically essential, and usu. marked off by brackets, dashes, or commas; (sing. or pl.) round brackets () used for this. **pa·ren·the·size** (parĕn′thĭsīz) *v.t.* (**-sized, -siz·ing**). Insert as parenthesis; put between marks of parenthesis; **par·en·thet·ic** (părenthĕt′ĭk), **par·en·thet′i·cal** *adjs.* Of, inserted as a, parenthesis; (fig.) interposed. **par·en·thet′i·cal·ly** *adv.*

pa·re·sis (parē′sĭs, păr′ĭsĭs) *n.* Partial paralysis or weakening of muscular power. **pa·ret·ic** (parĕt′ĭk, parē′tĭk) *n.* & *adj.* **pa·ret′i·cal·ly** *adv.*

par ex·cel·lence (pār ĕksel-lahṅs′). By virtue of special excellence, above all others that may be so called. [Fr.]

par·fait (pa̅rfa̅′) *n.* Dessert of layers of ice cream, fruit, etc., served in tall glass.

pa·ri·ah (parī′*a*, păr′ēa) *n.* Member of very extensive low caste in S. India; member of low or no caste; (fig.) social outcast. [Tamil *paṛaiyar* (hereditary) drummers]

pa·ri·e·tal (parī′it*a*l) *adj.* 1. Of the wall of the body or of any of its cavities; ~ **bones**, pair forming part of sides and top of skull. 2. (bot.) Of or on the walls of a hollow structure etc. 3. Pertaining to residence within a college, esp. to rules governing visiting hours in dormitories for members of the opposite sex.

par·i·mu·tu·el (păr′imū′chōō*e*l) *n.* (also ~ **machine**) System of betting, carried on by a mechanical apparatus, in which the winners divide the losers' stakes less a percentage for managerial expenses (see TOTALIZATOR).

Par·is[1] (păr′ĭs). Capital city of France, on Seine River; **plaster of** ~: see PLASTER; ~ **green**, vivid light green pigment prepared from arsenic trioxide and copper acetate. [*Parisii*, L. name of Gallic tribe that settled there]

Par·is[2] (păr′ĭs). (Gk. legend) Son of Priam and Hecuba; as a baby he was left to die because of a prophecy that he would bring destruction upon Troy, but shepherds found him and brought him up; he awarded apple of discord to Aphrodite, who offered him the fairest woman in the world; he chose and abducted HELEN, thus bringing about the Trojan War in which he was killed and Troy sacked.

par·ish (păr′ĭsh) *n.* 1. Subdivision of diocese, having its own church and clergyman; inhabitants of this. 2. County in Louisiana. 3. Members of a parish; all the parishioners of a particular parish.

pa·rish·ion·er (parĭsh′*o*ner) *n.* Member of parish.

Pa·ri·sian (parē′zh*a*n, -rĭzh′*a*n) *adj.* & *n.* (Native, inhabitant) of PARIS[1].

par·i·ty (păr′ĭtē) *n.* 1. Equality; parallelism, analogy; equivalence in another currency, being at par. 2. (med.) Condition of having borne children; number of children borne by one mother.

park (pa̅rk) *n.* 1. Large enclosed piece of ground, usu. with woodland and meadow, in town ornamentally laid out for public recreation; large tract of land kept in natural state for public benefit. 2. (Space occupied by) artillery, stores, etc., in encampment; area where vehicles may be left temporarily. 3. Area or stadium used for sports, as **ball** ~. **park** *v.* Enclose (ground) in or as park; arrange (artillery etc.) compactly in a park; place or leave (vehicle) in park etc. temporarily; (transf.) leave in suitable place until required; **park′ing meter**, coin-operated meter that registers time allowed for a vehicle to be parked.

par·ka (pa̅r′k*a*) *n.* Long fur jacket with attached hood worn in Arctic regions; garment resembling this.

Park·in·son's (pa̅r′kĭns*o*nz) **disease.** Chronic progressive disease of the nervous system (*Paralysis agitans*, "shaking palsy") characterized by tremor, muscular rigidity, defective gait, and emaciation. [James *Parkinson*, British physician (1755–1824)]

Park·in·son's (pa̅r′kĭns*o*nz) **Law.** (joc.) Fact that work expands to fill the time available for doing it. [C. N. *Parkinson*, 1909–]

Park·man (pa̅rk′m*a*n), **Francis** (1823–93). Amer. historian; famous for his account of his experiences with the Sioux Indians and his trip over the Oregon Trail, *The California and Oregon Trail.*

*The opening of the British Parliament with Monarch, Lords and MPs present (facing) reflects the development of **parliament** from the days when the King summoned his council of important men.*

park·way (pa̅rk′wa̅) *n.* Broad landscaped highway, sometimes with landscaped strips.

par·lance (pa̅r′l*a*ns) *n.* (Particular) way of speaking as regards choice of words (*in common*, *legal*, etc. ~).

par·lay (pa̅r′la̅, -lē) *v.t.* Use (money won on bet) as further stake; increase in value (as if) by parlaying. ~ *n.* Act of parlaying; bet so made.

par·ley (pa̅r′lē) *n.* (pl. **-leys**). Conference for debating of points in dispute, esp. (mil.) discussion of terms. ~ *v.* (**-leyed, -ley·ing**). Discuss terms (*with*); speak (esp. foreign languages).

par·lia·ment (pa̅r′l*a*m*e*nt) *n.* Council forming with the sovereign the supreme legislature of United Kingdom, consisting of the House of Lords (see LORD) and the House of Commons (see COMMONS); corresponding legislative assembly in other countries; **Long** ~, see LONG.

par·lia·men·tar·i·an (pa̅rl*a*mĕntār′ē*a*n) *n.* Skilled debater in parliament; adherent of parliament in English civil war of 17th c.

par·lia·men·ta·ry (pa̅rl*a*mĕn′terē, -trē) *adj.* Of a parliament; enacted, established, by parliament; (of language) admissible in parliament, (colloq.) civil; body of rules prescribing procedures to be followed in legislative or organizational debate.

par·lor, Brit. **par·lour** (pa̅r′ler) *ns.* Ordinary sitting room of family in private house; **beauty** ~, see BEAUTY; ~ **car**, railroad car fitted with individual reserved seats; ~ **game**, game (esp. word game or quiz) played indoors.

par·lous (pa̅r′l*u*s) *adj.* (archaic) Perilous; hard to deal with.

Par·men·i·des (pa̅rmĕn′ĭdēz). (6th c. B.C.) Greek philosopher of Elea (Italy); founder of the ELEATIC school, which believed in a single eternal god not resembling mortals.

Par·me·san (pa̅r′mezahn, -zăn, -z*a*n) *adj.* Of Parma; esp. applied to hard, easily grated kind of cheese made there and in other parts of N. Italy. **par·mi·gia·na** (pa̅rm*i*zhah′-*na*), **par·mi·gia·no** (pa̅rm*i*zhah′-nō) *adjs.* Cooked with Parmesan cheese.

Par·nas·sus (pa̅rnăs′*u*s). Lofty mountain of Greece, N. of Delphi; associated in classical Greece with worship of Apollo and the Muses.

*A **park** in Baton Rouge, Louisiana, capital of the state and seat of the Louisiana University-Baton Rouge campus.*

Par·nell (pārnĕl′, pār′nel), **Charles Stewart** (1846–91). Irish nationalist politician; leader of Irish home rule movement.

pa·ro·chi·al (parō′kēal) *adj.* Of a parish; (fig.) confined to narrow area; narrow, provincial. **pa·ro′chi·al·ism** *n.* **pa·ro′chi·al·ly** *adv.*

par·o·dy (păr′odē) *n.* (pl. **-dies**). Composition in which an author's characteristics are ridiculed by imitation; feeble imitation, travesty. ~ *v.t.* (**-died, -dy·ing**). Imitate (composition etc.) humorously. **par′o·dist** *n.*

pa·role (parōl′) *n.* Word of honor, esp. prisoner's promise that he will not attempt escape, or will return to custody if liberated, or will refrain from taking up arms against captors for stated period; **on** ~, (liberated) on parole. **parole** *v.t.* (**-roled, -rol·ing**). Put (prisoner) on parole.

pa·rot·id (parŏt′ĭd) *adj.* Situated near the ear, esp. ~ **gland,** (in man, largest of three salivary glands) situated in front of ear. ~ *n.* Parotid gland. **par·o·ti·tis** (părotī′tĭs) *n.* (path.) Inflammation of parotid gland, mumps.

par·ox·ysm (păr′oksĭzem) *n.* Fit of disease; fit (*of* rage, laughter, etc.). **par·ox·ys′mal** *adj.* [Gk. *oxunō* goad, render acute]

par·quet (pārkā′, -kĕt′) *n.* Wooden flooring of pieces of wood, freq. of different kinds, arranged in pattern. ~ *v.t.* (**-queted, -quet·ing** pr. -kād′, -kā′ing). Floor (room) thus. **par·quet·ry** (pār′kĭtrē) *n.*

parr (pār) *n.* (pl. **parrs,** collect. **parr**). Young salmon.

Parr (pār), **Catherine** (1512–1548). Sixth wife of Henry VIII, whom she outlived.

par·ra·keet = PARAKEET.

par·ri·cide (păr′ĭsīd) *n.* 1. One who murders his father. 2. Murder of father, parent, near relative, or one whose person is considered sacred. **par·ri·cid′al** *adj.*

par·rot (păr′ot) *n.* Bird of large mainly tropical group (order Psittaciformes) with short hooked bill, and freq. brilliant plumage, many species of which can be taught to repeat words and sentences; person who repeats another's words or imitates his actions unintelligently; ~ **fever,** PSITTACOSIS; ~ **fish,** any of various fishes with brilliant coloring or strong, hard mouth like parrot's bill. **parrot** *v.t.* Repeat (words etc.) mechanically.

par·ry (păr′ē) *v.t.* (**-ried, -ry·ing**). Ward off, avert (weapon, blow, etc.). ~ *n.* (pl. **-ries**). Warding off. [L. *parare* prepare]

parse (pārs) *v.t.* (**parsed, pars·ing**). Describe (word) grammatically, stating inflection, relation to sentence, etc.; resolve (sentence) into component parts of speech and describe them grammatically.

par·sec (pār′sĕk) *n.* (astron.) Unit in measuring stellar distances, distance at which a star would have an annual PARALLAX of 1 second of an arc, equivalent to 206,265 astronomical units (3.258 light-years). [*par*(*allaz*) + *sec*(*ond*)]

Par·see, Par·si (pār′sē, pārsē′) *adjs.* & *ns.* 1. (One) of the followers of ZOROASTER, descendants of those Persians who fled to India in 7th and 8th centuries to escape Muslim persecution. 2. (Of) the Iranian dialect of the Parsee religious literature.

par·si·mo·ny (pār′simōnē) *n.* Extreme or excessive carefulness in employment of money, etc.; reluctance to give or spend. **par·si·mo′ni·ous** *adj.* **par·si·mo′ni·ous·ly** *adv.* **par·si·mo′ni·ous·ness** *n.*

pars·ley (pārs′lē) *n.* Biennial umbelliferous plant (*Petroselinum crispum*) with white flowers and aromatic leaves, finely divided and curled in commonly cultivated variety, used for seasoning and garnishing dishes.

pars·nip (pār′snĭp) *n.* Biennial umbelliferous plant (*Pastinaca sativa*) with pinnate leaves, yellow flowers, and (in cultivated variety) large, pale yellow, sweet, fleshy, and nutritious root used as culinary vegetable; root of this.

par·son (pār′son) *n.* Rector; vicar or any beneficed clergyman; (colloq.) any clergyman; ~**'s nose,** (Brit.) rump of cooked fowl; pope's nose. **par·son·ic** (pārsŏn′ĭk), **par·son′i·cal** *adjs.*

par·son·age (pār′sonĭj) *n.* Parson's official home.

part[1] (pārt) *n.* 1. Some but not all of a thing or number of things; division or section; section of book etc., esp. as much as is issued at one time; each of several equal portions of a whole (as third, fourth, etc. ~, one of three, four, etc. equal parts); individual component of machine etc.; ~ **of,** a part of, some of. 2. Portion allotted, share; interest, concern; person's share in action, his function, business, duty. 3. Character assigned to actor on stage; words spoken by actor on stage; copy of these; (fig.) character sustained by anyone. 4. Melody assigned to particular voice or instrument in harmonic music. 5. (archaic, pl.) Abilities, capacities, (as in *man of* ~*s*). 6. (pl.) Region. 7. Side in dispute. 8. Dividing line along which something is parted. 9. **for my** ~, as far as I am concerned; **in** ~, partly; **the most** ~, the greatest part, most; **for the most** ~, in most cases, mostly; **take** ~, assist (*in*); **take the** ~ **of,** support, back up; ~ **and parcel,** (emphatic) constituent, element; essential portion; ~ **of speech,** each of the grammatical categories of words (noun, adjective, pronoun, verb, adverb, preposition, conjunction, article, interjection); ~ **song,** song for three or more voice parts, usu. without accompaniment and in simple harmony. **part** *adv.* In part, partly; ~ **owner** etc., owner etc. in common with another or others; ~**-time** (*adj.*) employed for, taking up, only part of the working day; ~**-timer** (*n.*).

part[2] (pārt) *v.* Divide into parts, suffer division; separate (hair), as with comb, on each side of dividing line or part; separate (combatants, friends, etc.); quit one another's company; ~ **company,** dissolve companionship (*with*); **part from, with,** say good-by to; **part with,** give up, surrender (property etc.); pay (money). **part′ing** *n.* (esp.) Leave-taking; ~ **of the ways,** point at which road divides into 2 or more; (fig.) moment for decision in choice between alternative courses.

par·take (pārtāk′) *v.* (**-took, -tak·en, -tak·ing**). Take a share in; take a share (*in, of, with*); take, esp. eat or drink some or (colloq.) all *of.* **par·tak′er** *n.*

par·terre (pārtār′) *n.* 1. Level space in garden occupied by flower beds. 2. Part of ground floor of theater under rear balcony.

par·the·no·gen·e·sis (pārthenōjĕn′ĭsĭs) *n.* (biol.) Reproduction from gametes without fertilization, esp. among invertebrates and lower plants. **par·the·no·ge·net·ic** (pārthenōjenĕt′ĭk) *adj.* **par·the·no·ge·net′i·cal·ly** *adv.*

Par·the·non (pār′thenŏn, -non). Temple of Athen Parthenos ("the maiden") on the Acropolis at Athens, erected 447–438 B.C. under Pericles' administration and decorated with sculptures by Phidias or his school.

par·tial (pār′shal) *adj.* 1. Biased, unfair; ~ **to,** having a liking for. 2. Forming only a part; not complete or total. **par′tial·ly** *adv.* **par·ti·al·i·ty** (pārsheăl′ĭtē, pārshăl′-) *n.* (pl. **-ties**). Bias, favoritism; fondness (*for*).

par·ti·ble (pār′tibel) *adj.* That can or must be divided (*among*; esp. of heritable property).

par·tic·i·pate (pārtĭs′ipāt) *v.* (**-pat·ed, -pat·ing**). Have share in; have share (*in*); have something *of.* **par·tic·i·pant** (pārtĭs′ipant) *n.* & *adj.* **par·tic·i·pa·tion** (pārtĭsipā′shon), **par·tic′i·pa·tor** *ns.*

par·ti·ci·ple (pār′tĭsĭpel) *n.* Verbal adjective ending in *ing* or *ed*, qualifying noun but retaining some

There are about 320 species of ***parrot*** *found in tropical parts of the world, ranging in size from tiny budgerigars to 2 ft.-long palm cockatoos of New Guinea, and the flightless kakapo of New Zealand. Most are distinguished by vivid plumage and raucous cries.*

Indian Ring-Necked Parakeet
Princess Alexandra's Parakeet
Plum-Headed Parakeet
African Grey Parrot
St. Vincent Parrot
Red-Winged Parakeet
Splendid Grass Parakeet
Bourke's Parakeet
Crimson Rosella
Turquoise Grass Parakeet
Blue-Fronted Parrot
Masked Lovebirds
Madagascar Lovebird

properties of verb, e.g., tense and government of object. **par·ti·cip·i·al** (pa͡rtĭsĭp'ēal) *adj.*

par·ti·cle (pa͡r'tĭkel) *n.* Minute portion of matter; smallest possible amount; minor part of speech, esp. short indeclinable one; prefix or suffix having distinct meaning.

par·ti-col·ored (pa͡r'tēkŭlerd) *adj.* Partly of one color, partly of another.

par·tic·u·lar (pertĭk'yuler) *adj.* 1. Relating to one as distinguished from others, special; one considered apart from others, individual. 2. Worth notice, special. 3. Detailed, minute; scrupulously exact; fastidious (*about*). **par·tic·u·lar·i·ty** (pertĭkyulăr'ĭtē) *n.* (pl. **-ties**). **par·tic'u·lar·ly** *adv.* **particular** *n.* Detail, item; (pl.) detailed account; **in ~**, especially.

par·tic·u·lar·ize (pertĭk'yulerīz) *v.t.* (**-ized, -iz·ing**). Name specially or one by one, specify. **par·tic·u·lar·i·za·tion** (pertĭkyulerīzā'shon) *n.*

par·tic·u·late (pertĭk'yulĭt) *adj.* Of the nature of a particle; composed of particles.

par·ti·san (pa͡r'tĭzan) *n.* Adherent of party, cause, etc., esp. unreasoning one; (hist.) member of light irregular troops employed in special enterprises; (in World War II) guerrilla (applied orig. to Russians resisting in parts of their country occupied by the enemy). ~ *adj.* **par'ti·san·ship** *n.*

par·tite (pa͡r'tīt) *adj.* (bot., entom.) Divided (nearly) to the base.

par·ti·tion (pa͡rtĭsh'on) *n.* Division into parts; such part; structure separating 2 such parts, esp. slight wall. ~ *v.t.* Divide into parts; ~ **off**, separate (part of room etc.) by a partition.

par·ti·tive (pa͡r'tĭtĭv) *adj.* Dividing into parts; (gram.) denoting part of a collective whole. **par'ti·tive·ly** *adv.* **partitive** *n.* Partitive word.

part·ly (pa͡rt'lē) *adv.* With respect to a part; in some degree.

part·ner (pa͡rt'ner) *n.* Sharer; person associated with others in business of which he shares risks and profits; wife, husband; companion in dance; player associated with another in bridge, tennis, etc. ~ *v.t.* Associate as partners; be partner of. **part'ner·ship** *n.*

par·tridge (pa͡r'trĭj) *n.* (pl. **-tridg·es**, collect. **-tridge**). Any

The purple blooms of the ***pasque-flower,*** *a wild anemone native to the chalky areas of England, usually flowers in spring and its name is adapted from a French word meaning 'Easter'. Similar spring-flowering anemones grow wild in Europe and North America.*

Found in Europe, Asia and Africa, the ***partridge*** *has long been nurtured in England where hunting it was considered a traditional sport. The grey or common partridge (Perdix perdix, below) is about 12 inches long and has distinctive chestnut breast-markings.*

of various game birds, esp. British and central European **common** or **gray** ~ (*Perdix perdix*); any of various birds of grouse or pheasant family; **partridgeberry,** N. Amer. trailing evergreen (*Mitchella repens*) with white flowers and scarlet berries.

par·tu·ri·ent (pār̄toor′ēent, -tūr̄′-) *adj.* About to bring forth young. **par·tu·ri·tion** (pār̄turĭsh′-on, pār̄chu-) *n.* Act of bringing forth young.

par·ty (pār̄′tē) *n.* (pl. **-ties**). 1. Those on one side in a contest etc., esp. considered collectively; persons united in maintaining cause, policy, etc., in opposition to others; system of taking sides on public questions, system of parties. 2. Body of persons traveling or engaged together. 3. Social gathering, esp. of invited guests at private house. 4. Each of the two or more persons making the two sides in legal action, contract, marriage, etc.; **third** ~, person or persons other than these, esp. in insurance matters. 5. Participator, accessory (*to* action). 6. (now vulg. or joc.) Person. 7. ~ **line**, telephone line shared by number of subscribers;

*The viaduct which winds through the **Great St. Bernard Pass** in Switzerland indicates the engineering ability needed to build roads even through the lower altitudes of such mountainous regions.*

(also) set policy of political party.

par·ve·nu (pār̄′venōō, -nū) *n.* Person of obscure origin who has gained wealth or position, upstart.

pas (pah) *n.* (pl. **pas** pr. pah, pahz). 1. Precedence. 2. Step in dancing (e.g. **pas de deux**, dance for two persons). [Fr.]

Pas·cal (păskăl′), **Blaise** (1623–1662). French mathematician and religious philosopher; author of *Pensées.*

pas·chal (păs′kal) *adj.* Of the Passover; of Easter; ~ **lamb,** (hist.) lamb slaughtered and eaten at Passover SEDER; **P~ Lamb,** Christ.

pa·sha, pa·cha (pah′sha, păsh′a, pashah′) *ns.* Title, placed after name, formerly used by senior officers in Turkish dominions. **pa·sha·lik, pa·sha·lic** (pashah′lĭk) *ns.* Jurisdiction of pasha.

Pash·to (pŭsh′tō), **Push·tu** (pŭsh′tōō) *adjs.* & *ns.* (Of) the language of the Afghans, belonging to the Eastern Iranian group of the Indo-European family.

pasque·flow·er (păsk′flower) *n.* Any of several plants of the genus *Anemone*, having large purple, blue, or white cup-shaped flowers; esp. *A. patens* of W. N. Amer. [Fr. *passefleur* surpassing flower, with assim. to *Pasque* Easter]

pass[1] (păs) *v.* 1. Move onward, proceed; circulate, be current; be transported from place to place; change; die; go by; come to an end. 2. Get through, effect a passage; go uncensured, be accepted as adequate; be known as a member of a group other than one's own; (of bill in legislature, proposal, etc.) be sanctioned; (of candidate) satisfy examiner. 3. (law) Adjudicate (*on, upon*); (of judgment) be given (*for* plaintiff etc.). 4. (cards etc.) Decline, declare inability, to play, bid, make trump, etc.; throw up one's hand. 5. Leave on one side or behind as one goes; go across (sea, frontier, mountain range). 6. (of bill) Be examined and approved by legislature; reach standard required by (examiner, examination); ~ **muster**: see MUSTER. 7. Outstrip, surpass; be beyond compass or range of, transcend (any faculty or expression). 8. Transport (usu. with preposition or adverb), move, cause to go; emit from the body as excrement; cause to go by; hand around, transfer; give currency to; (football etc.) transfer (ball) to another player on the same side. 9. Cause, allow, (bill in legislature, candidate for examination, etc.) to proceed after scrutiny. 10. Spend (*time* etc.); utter (criticism, judicial sentence, *upon*). 11. ~ **away**, die, come to an end; ~ **by**, omit, disregard; walk etc. past; ~ **for**, be accepted as; ~ **off**, palm off (thing *for* or *as* what it is not); distract attention from (awkward situation etc.); ~ **out**, (colloq.) distribute (papers, examinations); become unconscious (from drinking etc.); ~ **over**, omit; make no remark upon; ~ **the time**: see TIME; ~ **through**, experience; ~ **up**, (colloq.) reject, as an opportunity. **pass** *n.* 1. Passing, esp. of examination. 2. Critical position, juncture, predicament. 3. Written permission to pass into or out of a place, be absent from quarters etc.; ticket authorizing holder to travel free on railroad etc. 4. Thrust in fencing; juggling trick; passing of hands over anything, esp. in mesmerism; (football etc.) transference of ball to another player on same side; **make a** ~ **at**, (colloq.) try to attract sexually; try (to do anything). 5. **pass'book**, book

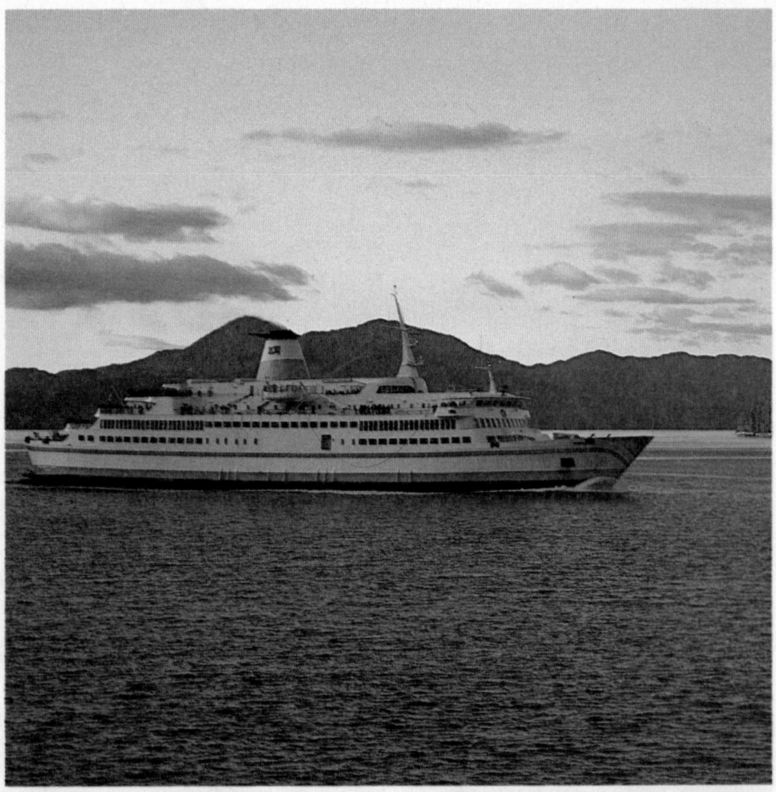

*A **Passion Play** has been performed every ten years by people at Oberammergau in West Germany, since it celebrated the end of a plague in 1634. Once these dramas were performed widely throughout Europe.*

*This ship is on a **passenger** cruise in Alaskan waters. The largest peninsula in the Western Hemisphere, with spectacular coastal scenery, Alaska has been building a successful tourist industry.*

supplied by bank to person having current or deposit account, showing all sums deposited and drawn; **pass'key**, private key to gate etc. for special purposes; master key; **pass'word**, selected word or phrase distinguishing friend from enemy.

pass[2] (pās) *n.* Narrow passage through mountains; navigable channel, esp. at river's mouth.

pass·a·ble (pās'*a*bel) *adj.* (esp.) That can pass muster, fairly good. **pass'a·ble·ness** *n.* **pass'a·bly** *adv.*

pas·sa·ca·glia (pahs*a*kahl'y*a*, pās*a*-) *n.* (mus.) Instrumental composition in $\frac{3}{4}$ time, based on an unvarying ground; (orig.) Spanish or Italian dance tune. [It., perh. f. Span. *pasar* pass, *calle* street, because freq. played in street]

pas·sage (pās'ĭj) *n.* 1. Passing, transit; transition from one state to another; liberty, right, to pass through; voyage, crossing from port to port; right of conveyance as passenger by sea; **bird of ~**, see BIRD. 2. Passing of a measure into law. 3. Way by which person or thing passes; corridor etc. giving communication between different rooms in house. 4. What passes between two persons mutually, interchange of confidences, etc. 5. (also **~ at arms**) Fight (freq. fig.). 6. Part of speech or literary work taken for quotation etc.

pas·sé (pāsā') *adj.* Past the prime; behind the times.

passe·men·terie (pāsmĕn'trē) *n.* Trimming of gold or silver lace, braid, beads, etc. [Fr.]

pas·sen·ger (pās'*e*nj*e*r) *n.* Traveler in (public) conveyance by land, air, or water; traveler in automobile who is not driving; **~ pigeon**, N. Amer. wild pigeon (*Ectopistes migratorius*) capable of long sustained flight (now extinct).

passe-par·tout (pāspartōō') *n.* 1. Master key. 2. Adhesive tape fastening edges of glass to mount of photograph or small picture as substitute for frame. [Fr., = "pass everywhere"]

pass·er (pās'*e*r) *n.* One who passes; **~-by**, one who passes, esp. casually.

pas·ser·ine (pās'*e*rīn) *adj.* & *n.* (Bird) of the order Passeriformes (perchers).

pas·si·ble (pās'*i*bel) *adj.* (theol.) Capable of feeling or suffering. **pas·si·bil'i·ty** *n.*

pass·ing (pās'ĭng) *n.* **~ bell**, bell rung at moment of person's death; **in ~**, incidentally, by the way; **~ note**, (mus.) note not belonging to harmony, interposed for purpose of passing smoothly from one to the other of two notes essential to it. **passing** *adj.* (esp.) Transient, fleeting, cursory, incidental. **~** *adv.* (archaic) Very.

pas·sion (păsh'*o*n) *n.* 1. Strong emotion; outburst of anger; sexual love; strong enthusiasm (*for*). 2. **P~**, sufferings of Christ during Christ's last days and (esp.) on the cross; (musical setting of) narrative of this from Gospels; **pas'sion-flower**, flower of genus *Passiflora* of (chiefly climbing) plants with parts supposed to suggest instruments of Christ's Passion, the corona representing the crown of thorns, etc.; **pas'sionfruit**, granadilla; **Passion Play**, mystery play representing Christ's Passion; **Passion Sunday**, second Sunday before Easter; **Pas'siontide**, period of 2 weeks before Easter; **Passion Week**, week following Passion Sunday (but in Anglican usage freq. = week before Easter, Holy Week). **passion** *v.i.* (poet.) Feel or express passion. **pas'sion·less** *adj.* **pas'sion·less·ly** *adv.* **pas'sion·less·ness** *n.*

Of about 500 varieties of ***passion-flower,*** *those most cultivated produce passion-fruit or granadillas. The juice and pulp of the fruits are extracted and are often canned for export. Below: Passiflora caerulea.*

pas·sion·al (păsh'*o*n*a*l) *adj.* Of, marked by, passion. **~** *n.* Book of the sufferings of saints and martyrs.

pas·sion·ate (păsh'*o*nĭt) *adj.* Easily moved to anger; dominated by, easily moved to, strong feeling; due to, showing, passion. **pas'sion·ate·ly** *adv.* **pas'sion·ate·ness** *n.*

pas·sive (pās'ĭv) *adj.* 1. Suffering action, acted upon; (gram.) applied to a voice of the verb comprising those forms in which action of verb is treated as attribute of thing toward which action is directed; (loosely, of verb) in which the subject is acted on by something or suffers the action. 2. Offering no opposition, submissive; **~ resistance**: see RESISTANCE. 3. Not active, inert. **pas'sive·ly** *adv.* **pas'sive·ness, pas·siv'i·ty** *ns.* **passive** *n.* Passive voice or form of verb.

Pass·o·ver (pās'ōv*e*r). Jewish festival beginning with the Seder in the evening of the 14th of Nisan and lasting eight days (Nisan approx. = April), commemorating the escape of the Jews from Egypt after the "passing over" (i.e. sparing) of their houses whose doorposts were marked with the blood of the lamb, when the Egyptians were smitten with the death of their first-born (Exod. 12).

pass·port (păs´pōrt, -pōrt) *n.* Document issued by competent authority serving as identification of person and his nationality, esp. when traveling abroad; (fig.) thing that ensures admission.

past[1] (păst, pahst) *adj.* (also rare *past part.* of PASS). (esp.) Gone by in time; just gone by; (gram.) expressing past action or state; ~ **master**, thorough master (*in*, *of*, subject); ~ **perfect** = PLUPERFECT. **past** *n.* Past time; what has happened in past time; person's past life or career, esp. one that will not bear inquiry.

past[2] (păst, pahst) *prep.* Beyond in time or place; beyond the range or compass of. ~ *adv.* So as to pass by, as *hastens* ~.

pas·ta (pah´sta) *n.* Dried flour paste used in Italian cooking, in various shapes such as macaroni, spaghetti, vermicelli.

paste (pāst) *n.* Flour moistened and kneaded, with lard, butter, suet, etc., as cooking material; any of various sweet doughy confections; relish of pounded fish, meat, etc.; adhesive; any soft plastic mixture; mixture of clay, water, etc., used in making pottery; hard vitreous composition used in making imitation gems; **paste´-board**, stiff substance made by pasting together sheets of paper; (attrib., fig.) unsubstantial, flimsy. **paste** *v.t.* (**past·ed, past·ing**). Fasten with paste; stick *up* on wall etc. with paste; cover (as) by pasting on or over; (slang) beat, thrash; bomb heavily.

pas·tel (păstĕl´) *n.* Drawing instrument consisting of a stick of powdered pigment bound with gum, usu. covered with paper; drawing made with pastels (usu. in several colors); (attrib., of light color) soft, subdued. **pas·tel´ist, pas·tel´list** *ns.*

Pas·ter·nak (păs´ternăk), **Boris Leonidovich** (1890–1960). Russian translator, novelist, and poet best known for his novel *Doctor Zhivago* (1957); awarded the 1958 Nobel Prize for literature but declined.

Pas·teur (păstẽr´), **Louis** (1822–1895). French chemist and biologist; founder of bacteriology and inventor of method of inoculation for hydrophobia.

Trail-riding on horseback is a popular ***pastime*** *in the U.S.A. The increase in national parks and monuments, plus a growing desire among people to explore their natural environment, has led to a revival of this hobby.*

pas·teur·ize (păs´cherīz, păs´te-) *v.t.* (**-ized, -iz·ing**). Partially sterilize by Pasteur's method, prevent or arrest fermentation in (milk etc.) by keeping for some time at a temperature (55°–60 C.) that does not greatly affect chemical composition. **pas·teur·i·za´tion** *n.*

pas·tiche (păstēsh´, pah-) *n.* 1. Medley, esp. musical composition, picture, made up from various sources. 2. Literary or other work of art composed in the style of a known author.

pas·tille (păstēl´), **pas·til** (păs´tĭl) *ns.* 1. Small roll of aromatic paste burned as deodorant etc. 2. Small sweet, freq. medicated, lozenge.

pas·time (păs´tīm) *n.* Recreation; game, sport.

pas·tor (păs´ter) *n.* Minister in charge of church or congregation; person exercising spiritual guidance. [Anglo-Fr., f. L. *pastor* shepherd]

pas·to·ral (păs´teral) *adj.* 1. Of shepherds; (of land) used for pasture; (of poems etc.) portraying country life. 2. Of a pastor; **P~ Epistles**, those of Paul to Timothy and Titus, dealing with pastor's work. **pas´to·ral·ly** *adv.* **pas´-to·ral** *n.* 1. Pastoral play, poem, etc. or picture. 2. (mus.) = PASTORALE. 3. Letter from pastor,

*A **pasteurizing** plant in New Zealand. Pasteurizing is a method of preventing the fermentation of various liquids, e.g. milk, by retaining the liquid at a certain temperature.*

*Left: An early 19th-century **pastil** burner. The scented smoke emerged through the chimney of the porcelain cottage. Today, the oriental types of incense burners are used and aromatic sticks are more popular than pastil.*

*Cattle grazing in a **pasture.** Where there is low rainfall and no irrigation, stock must feed on natural grasses, but they put on more weight more quickly on specially planted pastures.*

esp. bishop, to clergy or people. **pas′to·ral·ism** *n.* Convention of pastoral poetry etc.

pas·to·rale (păst*o*rahl′, -răl′) *n.* (pl. **-rales, -ra·li** pr. -rah′lē). 1. Simple opera etc. with rural subject. 2. Slow, quiet instrumental composition.

pas·tor·ate (păs′t*e*rĭt) *n.* Pastor's (tenure of) office; body of pastors.

pas·tra·mi (p*a*strah′mē) *n.* Seasoned smoked beef. [Yiddish]

pas·try (pā′strē) *n.* (pl. **-tries**). Paste of flour, fat, water, etc., rolled and baked; articles of food (pies, tarts, etc.) made wholly or partly of this; ~ **chef**, one who makes pastry, esp. for public sale.

pas·tur·age (păs′ch*e*rĭj) *n.* Pasturing; grass for cattle etc.; pasture land.

pas·ture (păs′ch*er*) *n.* (Piece of) land covered with grass. ~ *v.* (**-tured, -tur·ing**). Lead, put, (cattle etc.) to pasture. **pas′tur·a·ble** *adj.* **pas′tur·er** *n.*

past·y[1] (păs′tē) *n.* (pl. **past·ies**). Pie of meat or other food seasoned and enclosed in crust of pastry and baked.

past·y[2] (pā′stē) *adj.* (**past·i·er, past·i·est**). Of, like, paste; of pale complexion. **past′i·ness** *n.*

pat[1] (păt) *n.* Stroke, tap, esp. with hand as caress etc.; small mass (esp. of butter) formed (as) by patting; sound made by striking lightly with something flat, such as hand. ~ *v.* (**pat·ted, pat·ting**). Strike (thing) gently with flat surface; flatten thus; strike gently with inner surface of fingers, esp. to mark sympathy, approbation, etc.; beat lightly *on*; ~ **on the back**, express approbation of.

pat[2] (păt) *adv.* & *adj.* Apposite(ly), opportune(ly); ready for any occasion; **stand** ~, hold firm to a decision; in poker, make decision not to try to improve one's hand.

Pat·a·go·ni·a (păt*a*gō′nē*a*, -gōn′y*a*). Southern region of S. Amer., in Argentina between Andes and Atlantic. **Pat·a·go′ni·an** *adj.* & *n.* [f. obs. *Patagon*, one of the S. Amer. Indians inhabiting this region]

patch (păch) *n.* 1. Piece of cloth, metal, etc., put on to mend hole or rent or strengthen weak place; piece of plaster etc. put over wound; pad worn to protect injured eye. 2. Large or irregular spot on surface; piece of ground; number of plants growing on this: small area, as a ~ **of ice**; ~ **pocket**, pocket sewn on like patch; ~ **test**, test for allergy by applying to the skin patches containing allergenic substances. **patch** *v.t.* Put patch(es) on; serve as patch to; piece (things) together; appear as patches on (surface); ~ **up**, repair with patches; put to-

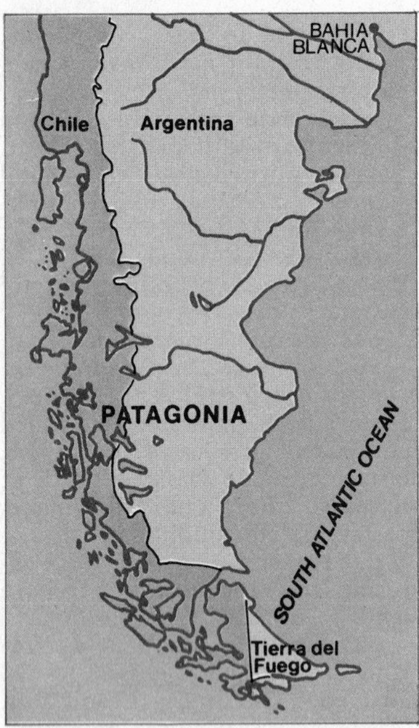

Despite the inhospitable appearance of the wind-swept plains of ***Patagonia,*** *the far south of Argentina, very large numbers of Merino, Corriedale and Romney Marsh sheep are bred at altitudes exceeding 2,000 ft.*

gether hastily; (fig.) repair; set right (matter, quarrel, etc.); **patch′-work**, work made up of fragments of different colors sewn together (freq. fig.). **patch′y** *adj.* (**patch·i·er, patch·i·est**). **patch′i·ly** *adv.* **patch′i·ness** *n.*

patch·ou·li (păch′o͞olē, pacho͞o′lē) *n.* Odoriferous plant (*Pogostemon patchouly*) having leaves that yield axomatic oil used in perfume manufacture; penetrating and lasting perfume prepared from this.

pate (pāt) *n.* (colloq.) Head, often as seat of intellect; top of the head.

pa·té (pahtā′) *n.* Paste of meat etc. often baked in pastry; ~ **de foie gras** (de fwah grah′), paste of liver of fatted geese. [Fr.]

pa·tel·la (patĕl′*a*) *n.* (pl. **-tel·lae** pr. -tĕl′ē, **-tel·las**). Kneecap. **pa·tel′lar, pa·tel·late** (patĕl′ĭt) *adjs.*

pat·en (păt′*en*) *n.* Shallow dish used for bread at Eucharist; thin circular plate of metal.

pat·ent (păt′ent) *adj.* 1. (of rights etc.) Conferred, protected, by **letters** ~, open document under seal of government, granting right, title, etc., esp. sole right for a term to make, use, or sell some invention. 2. Obvious to everyone; plain. 3. ~ **leather**: see LEATHER; ~ **medicine**, proprietary medicine, esp. one of which formula is not disclosed on container and which is obtainable without a prescription. **pa·ten·cy** (pā′tensē) *n.* **pat′ent·a·ble** *adj.* **pat′ent·ly** *adv.* **patent** *n.* Letters patent; government grant of exclusive privilege of making or selling new invention; invention, process, so protected. ~ *v.t.* Obtain patent for (invention).

pat·ent·ee (pătentē′) *n.* Holder of a patent, person for the time being entitled to the benefit of a patent.

pa·ter·nal (patẽr′nal) *adj.* Of a father; fatherly; related through the father, on the father's side. **pa·ter′nal·ly** *adv.*

pa·ter·ni·ty (patẽr′nĭtē) *n.* Fatherhood; one's paternal origin; (fig.) authorship, source.

pa·ter·nos·ter (pā′ternŏs′ter, păt′*er*-) *n.* (also **Pater Noster**) Lord's Prayer, esp. in Latin; bead in rosary indicating that paternoster is to be said. [L. *pater noster* our father]

path (păth, pahth) *n.* (pl. **paths** pr. pădhz, pahdhz, păths, pahths). Footway, esp. one merely beaten by feet, not specially constructed; track laid for foot or cycle racing; line along which person or thing moves; **path′finder**, person who makes a path for those who follow, esp. in wilderness. **path′less** *adj.*

Pa·than (patahn′) *adj.* & *n.* (Member) of a Pashto-speaking people inhabiting E. Afghanistan, NW. Pakistan, and other parts of the Indian peninsula.

pa·thet·ic (pathĕt′ĭk) *adj.* Exciting pity or sadness; of the emotions; ~ **fallacy**, ascription of human emotion to inanimate nature. **pa·thet′i·cal·ly** *adv.*

path·o·gen·ic (păthojĕn′ĭk) *adj.* Capable of producing disease. **path·o·gen** (păth′*o*jen) *n.*

pa·thol·o·gy (pathŏl′ojē) *n.* (pl. **-gies**). Systematic study of physical diseases, their causes, symptoms, and treatment. **path·o·log·i·cal** (păthŏlŏj′ĭkal), **path·o·log′ic** *adjs.* **path·o·log′i·cal·ly** *adv.* **pa·thol′o·gist** *n.*

pa·thos (pā′thŏs) *n.* Quality in speech, events, etc., that excites pity or sadness. [Gk., = "suffering"]

pa·tience (pā′shens) *n.* 1. Calm endurance of pain or any provocation; forbearance; quiet and self-possessed waiting for something; perseverance; **have no ~ with**, (colloq.) be unable to bear patiently;

out of ~, provoked so as no longer to have patience. 2. (cards) Game in which object is to arrange cards in some systematic order.

pa·tient (pā′shent) *adj.* Having, showing, patience. **pa′tient·ly** *adv.* **patient** *n.* Person under medical treatment, esp. with reference to his doctor.

pat·i·na (păt′ina) *n.* Incrustation, usu. green, on surface of old bronze, esteemed as ornament; (by extension) gloss on woodwork etc., produced by long use.

pa·ti·o (păt′ēō, pah′tēō) *n.* (pl. **-ti·os**). Inner court open to sky; paved usu. roofless area adjoining a house. [Span.]

pat·ois (păt′wah) *n.* (pl. **pat·ois** pr. păt′wahz). Regional dialect of rural people; jargon; mixture of two or more languages.

pa·tri·arch (pā′trēa͡rk) *n.* 1. Father and ruler of family or tribe; one of the forefathers of Abraham, as ancestors of the human race; Abraham, Isaac, Jacob, or any of Jacob's 12 sons, as progenitors of the Hebrew peoples. 2. (in early and Orthodox Churches) Bishop, esp. of Antioch, Alexandria, Constantinople, Jerusalem, or Rome; (in R.C. Ch.) pope, or a bishop ranking next above primates and metropolitans and immediately below the pope. 3. Founder of an order, science, etc.; venerable old man; oldest living representative (*of*). **pa·tri·ar′chal** *adj.* **pa·tri·ar′chal·ly** *adv.*

pa·tri·ar·chate (pā′trēa͡rkĭt) *n.* Office, see, residence, of ecclesiastical patriarch; rank of tribal patriarch.

pa·tri·ar·chy (pā′trēa͡rkē) *n.* (pl. **-chies**). Government by father or eldest male of tribe or family; community so organized.

pa·tri·cian (patrĭsh′an) *n.* 1. Ancient Roman noble (contrasted with PLEBEIAN), one belonging to one of the original citizen families from whom, in early years of Republic, senators, consuls and pontifices were exclusively chosen; member of noble order in later Roman Empire; officer representing Roman emperor in provinces of Italy and Africa. 2. Nobleman, esp. (hist.) in some medieval Italian republics. ~ *adj.* Noble, aristocratic; of the ancient Roman nobility.

pat·ri·cide (păt′rĭsīd) *n.* Parricide. **pat·ri·cid′al** *adj.*

Pat·rick (păt′rĭk), **St.** (c389–c461). Patron saint and apostle of Ireland; prob. of mixed Roman and British parentage; missionary to Ireland, from which, according to legend, he drove all snakes; commemorated Mar. 17, **St. Patrick's Day**; **St. ~'s cross**, red saltire on white ground, the national cross of Ireland.

pat·ri·mo·ny (păt′rimōnē) *n.* (pl. **-nies**). Property inherited from one's father or ancestors, heritage; endowment of church etc. **pat·ri·mo′ni·al** *adj.*

pa·tri·ot (pā′trēot, -ŏt) *n.* One who defends or is zealous for his country's freedom or rights. **pa·tri·ot·ic** (pātrēŏt′ĭk) *adj.* **pa·tri·ot′i·cal·ly** *adv.* **pa·tri·ot·ism** (pā′trēotĭzem) *n.*

pa·tris·tic (patrĭs′tĭk) *adj.* Of (the study of the writings of) the fathers of the church.

Pa·tro·clus (patrō′klus). (Gk. legend) Grecian warrior at siege of Troy, friend of Achilles; slain by Hector.

pa·trol (patrōl′) *n.* Going the rounds of garrison, camp, etc.; tour of town etc. by police; detachment of guard, police officers, assigned to

A ***patient*** *has his blood pressure checked. With ever-advancing medical technology, people are living longer, and surviving once-incurable diseases.*

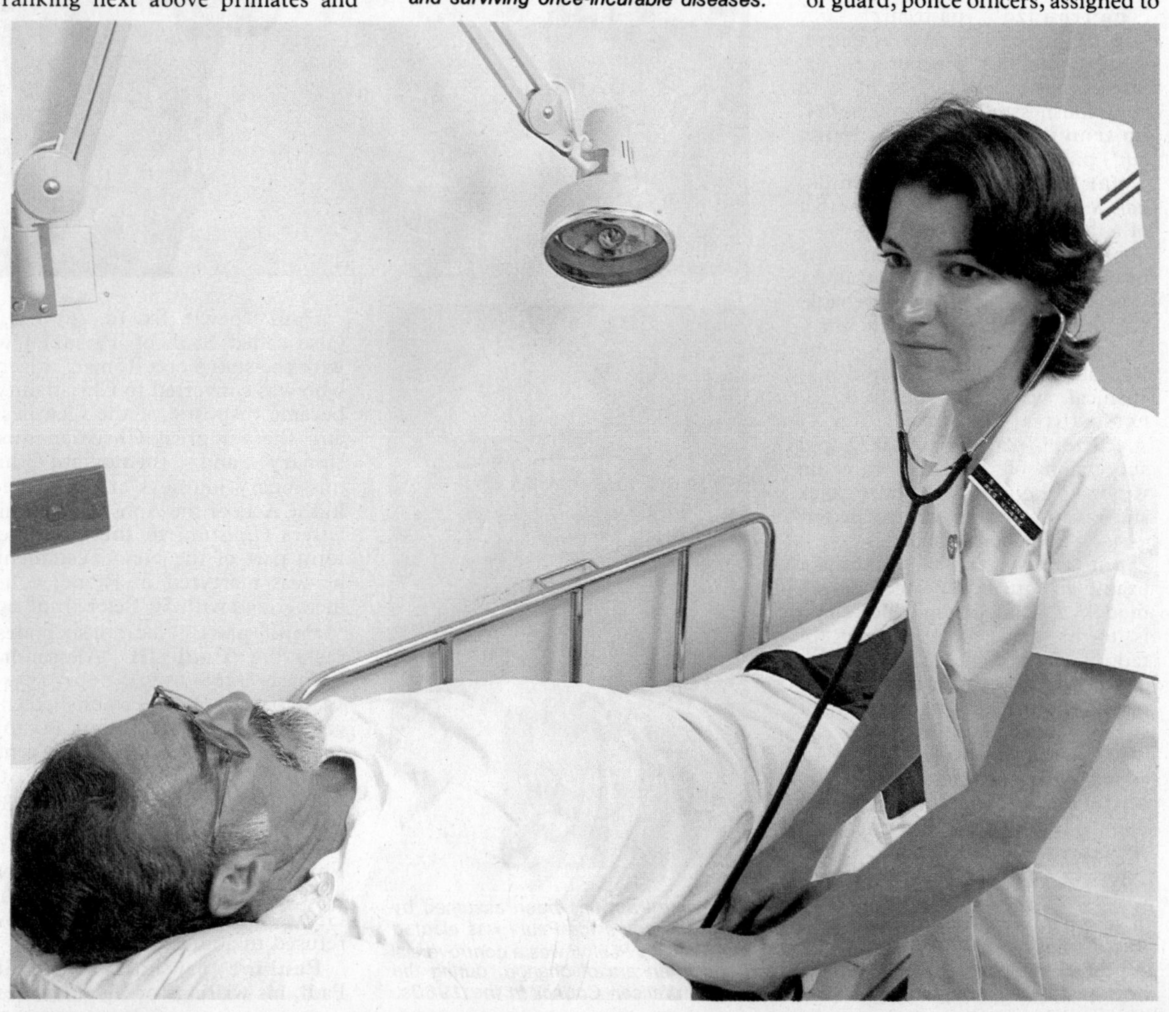

*Soldiers from the British Army on **patrol** in Belfast during a recent period of civil unrest. Such surveillance has probably been practiced by soldiers, police and other law-enforcement agents since the first armies were formed.*

this; ships, aircraft, guarding sea route, etc.; routine operational flight of aircraft; detachment of troops sent out to reconnoiter; unit of Scouts (6 under ~ **leader**); **patrol'man** (pl. **-men**), police officer attached to particular beat or district; **patrol wagon**, police van for prisoners. **patrol** *v.* (**-trolled, -trol·ling**). Act as patrol; go around (camp, town, etc.) as patrol. **pa·trol'ler** *n.* [Fr. *patrouiller*, orig. = "paddle in mud"]

pa·tron (pā'trən) *n.* (fem. **pa·tron·ess** pr. pā'trənĭs). One who countenances, protects, or gives influential support to; customer, esp. regular one, of shop, restaurant, etc.; (usu. ~ **saint**) tutelary saint of person, place, craft, etc.

pa·tron·age (pā'trənĭj) *n.* 1. Support, encouragement, given by patron; customer's support. 2. Right of presentation to benefice or office. 3. Patronizing airs.

pa·tron·ize (pā'trənīz) *v.t.* (**-ized, -iz·ing**). 1. Act as patron toward, support, encourage. 2. Treat (person, thing) as if with consciousness of one's superiority. **pa'tron·iz·er** *n.* **pa'tron·iz·ing** *adj.* **pa'tron·iz·ing·ly** *adv.*

pat·ro·nym·ic (pătrənĭm'ĭk) *adj.* & *n.* (Name) derived from that of a father or ancestor.

pat·ter[1] (păt'er) *n.* Jargon of any profession or class; oratory, speechifying, of mountebank, conjurer, etc.; rapid speech introduced into (comic) song. ~ *v.* Repeat (prayers etc.) in rapid mechanical way; talk glibly. [f. PATERNOSTER]

pat·ter[2] (păt'er) *v.* Make rapid succession of taps, as rain on windowpane; run with short quick steps; cause (water etc.) to patter. ~ *n.* Succession of taps.

pat·tern (păt'ern) *n.* 1. Excellent example; (attrib.) perfect, ideal, model. 2. Model from which thing is to be made. 3. Sample (of tailor's cloth, etc.). 4. Decorative design as executed on carpet, wallpaper, cloth, etc.; distribution of shots, bombs, etc., on target. 5. (fig.) Arrangement of things or actions, as ~ *of behavior, life*, etc. **pattern** *v.t.* Model (thing *after*, upon design, etc.); decorate with pattern. **pat'ternmaker** *n.*

pat·ty (păt'ē) *n.* (pl. **-ties**). Little pie or pasty; flat, round piece of chopped or ground meat, esp. **hamburger** ~.

pau·ci·ty (paw'sĭtē) *n.* Smallness of number or quantity.

*The name **Paul** has been assumed by various Popes since Paul I was elected in A.D. 757. Paul VI was a controversial Pope in an era of change, during the second Vatican Council in the 1960s.*

Paul[1] (pawl), **St.** (d. *c*67 A.D.). (also called Saul, of Tarsus) Jew, with the status of a Roman citizen, who was converted to Christianity, became "Apostle of the Gentiles" and the 1st great Christian missionary and theologian; his missionary journeys are described in the Acts of the Apostles, and his letters (*Epistles*) to the Churches form part of the New Testament; he was martyred in Rome; commemorated with St. Peter, June 29.

Paul[2] (pawl). Name of six popes, including **Paul III** (Alessandro Farnese, 1468–1549), pope 1534–1549, patron of art, established the constitution of the Jesuits (1540), convened the Council of Trent; **Paul VI** (Giovanni Battista Montini, 1897–1978), pope 1963–1978.

Paul[3] (pawl). (1754–1801) Emperor of Russia 1796–1801; son of Peter III and Catherine the Great; was murdered when he refused to abdicate.

Paul·ine (paw'līn) *adj.* Of St. Paul, his writings or his doctrines;

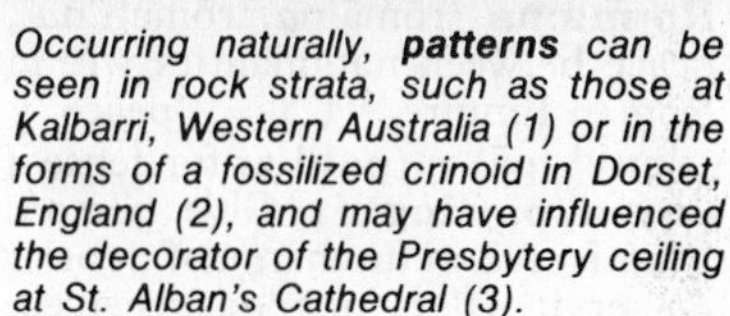
*Occurring naturally, **patterns** can be seen in rock strata, such as those at Kalbarri, Western Australia (1) or in the forms of a fossilized crinoid in Dorset, England (2), and may have influenced the decorator of the Presbytery ceiling at St. Alban's Cathedral (3).*

~ **epistles**, those in New Testament attributed to St. Paul. **Pauline** *n.* Member of one of many orders dedicated to St. Paul.

Paul·ing (paw´lĭng), **Linus Carl** (1901–). Amer. chemist noted for work on molecular structure and on chemical bond; received Nobel Prize for chemistry, 1954, and for peace, 1962.

paunch (pawnch) *n.* Belly, abdomen; protruding belly. **paunch'y** *adj.*

pau·per (paw´p*e*r) *n.* Person without means of livelihood, beggar; (hist.) recipient of charity; (law) person allowed to sue or defend *in forma pauperis*. **pau'per·ism, pau·per·i·za·tion** (pawperīzā´sh*o*n) *ns.* **pau'per·ize** *v.t.* (**-ized, -iz·ing**).

pause (pawz) *n.* Interval of inaction or silence, esp. from hesitation; break made in speaking or reading; (mus.) mark (𝄐 or 𝄑)

***Pattern-making** is a skilled part of a shoemaker's trade. In some traditional companies a model of the customer's foot is taken and kept as a reference for future orders.*

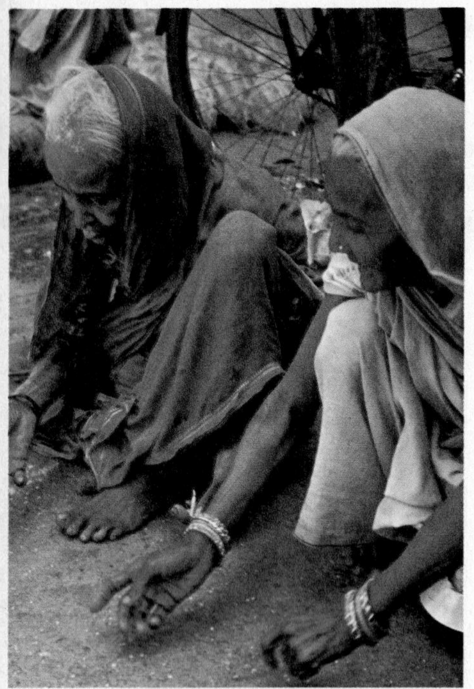

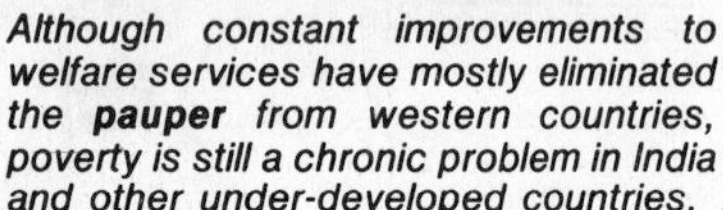

Although constant improvements to welfare services have mostly eliminated the ***pauper*** *from western countries, poverty is still a chronic problem in India and other under-developed countries.*

The Russian ballerina, ***Anna Pavlova,*** *is best remembered for her creation of the role of 'Le Cygne' choreographed for her by Fokine in 1905. It was one among her large repertoire of ballets.*

A ***pawnbroker*** *is a money-lender or small-scale banker and the three balls which identify a pawnshop are said to be derived from the arms of the Medici family, who were bankers in Florence.*

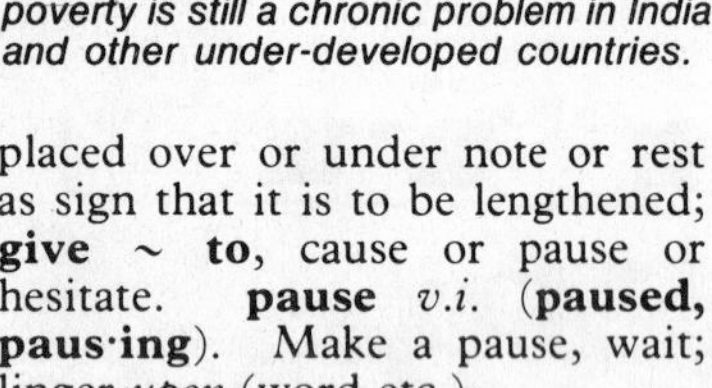

placed over or under note or rest as sign that it is to be lengthened; **give ~ to,** cause or pause or hesitate. **pause** *v.i.* (**paused, paus·ing**). Make a pause, wait; linger *upon* (word etc.).

pa·vane (p*a*vahn′, -văn′), **pav·an** (păv′*a*n) *ns.* Stately dance of 16th and 17th centuries in which dancers were elaborately dressed; music for this, in slow time.

pave (pāv) *v.t.* (**paved, pav·ing**). Cover (street, floor, etc.) with or as with pavement; (fig.) prepare (*the way for*). **pav·ior** (pāv′y*e*r) *n.*

pave·ment (pāv′m*e*nt) *n.* Covering of street, floor, etc., made of stones, tiles, wooden blocks, asphalt, etc.; (zool.) pavementlike formation of close-set teeth etc.

pa·vil·ion (p*a*vĭl′y*o*n) *n.* 1. Tent, esp. large peaked one; light ornamental building, esp. one attached to baseball field etc. for spectators and players; projecting (usu. highly decorated) subdivision of building. 2. Part of brilliant-cut gemstone below girdle. ~ *v.t.* Enclose (as) in, furnish with, pavilion. [L. *papilionem*, butterfly, in LL., tent]

Pav·lov (păv′lŏv; *Russ.* pahv′lŏf), **Ivan Petrovich** (1849–1916). Russian physiologist; awarded Nobel Prize for medicine, 1904; noted for research on conditioned reflexes.

Pav·lo·va (păvlō′v*a*; *Russ.* pahv′lōvah), **Anna Matveevna** (1885–1931). Russian ballerina.

paw (paw) *n.* Foot of beast having claws or nails; fur from lower part of animal's leg; (colloq.) hand. ~ *v.* Strike with paw; (of horse) strike (ground), strike ground, with hoofs; (colloq.) handle awkwardly or rudely.

pawl (pawl) *n.* Short pivoted catch engaging with toothed wheel to prevent recoil, (naut.) short bar used to prevent capstan, windlass, etc., from recoiling. ~ *v.t.* Secure (capstan etc.) with pawl.

pawn[1] (pawn) *n.* One of the pieces of smallest size and value in chess; (fig.) unimportant person used by another as a mere tool. [AF. *poun*, f. med. L. *pedonem* foot soldier]

pawn[2] (pawn) *n.* Thing, person, left in another's keeping as security, pledge; state of being pledged; **pawn′broker,** one who lends money at interest on security of personal property pawned; **pawn′-broking,** his occupation; **pawn′-shop,** pawnbroker's place of business; **pawn ticket,** receipt for thing pledged with pawnbroker. **pawn** *v.t.* Deposit (thing) as security for payment of money or performance of action; (fig.) pledge.

Paw·nee (pawnē′) *n.* (pl. **-nees,** collect. **-nee**). Indian of a N. Amer. confederacy, formerly living in Nebraska, now in Oklahoma.

paw·paw = PAPAW.

pax (păks) *n.* 1. Kiss of peace as liturgical form at High Mass. 2. ~ **vo·bis·cum** (vōbĭs′k*u*m), (as salutation) peace be with you. 3. **Pax Bri·tan·ni·ca** (brĭtăn′ĭk*a*), peace imposed by British rule; **Pax Ro·ma·na** (rōmā′n*a*, rōmah′n*a*), peace between nationalities within Roman Empire. [L., = "peace"]

pay[1] (pā) *v.* (**paid** or for sense 4 **payed, pay·ing**). 1. Give (person) what is due in discharge of debt or *for* services done or goods received; recompense (work); hand over (money owed); hand over amount of (debt, wages, etc.); (fig.) reward, recompense; ~ **for,** hand over the price of, bear the cost of; (fig.) be punished for; ~ **in,** pay to account; ~ **off,** pay in full and discharge or be quit of (ship's crew, creditor, etc.); (colloq.) bring success; ~ (person) **out,** punish or have revenge on him; disburse; ~ **up,** pay full amount of (arrears; or abs.); ~ **one's way,** not get into debt. 2. Render, bestow (attention, court, compliment, etc., *to*). 3. (of business etc.) Yield adequate return to (person); yield adequate return. 4. (naut.) ~ **off,** (of ship) fall off to leeward when helm is put up; ~ **out, away,** let out (rope) by slackening it. 5. **~-as-you-go,** policy of managing finances by meeting obligations from current income instead of by borrowing; **pay′off,** time of reckoning; dénouement; (colloq.) bribe. 6. **paying guest,** resident in boardinghouse etc. **pay** *n.* Amount paid; wages, hire, salary; **in the ~ of,** employed by; **pay′check,** bank

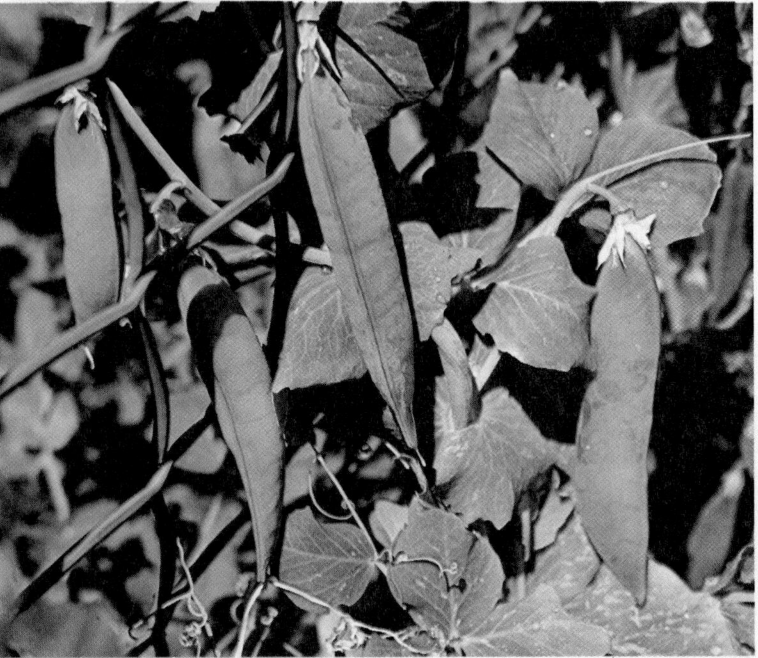

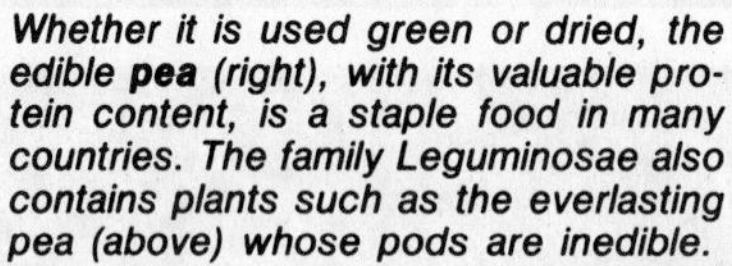

Whether it is used green or dried, the edible* pea *(right), with its valuable protein content, is a staple food in many countries. The family Leguminosae also contains plants such as the everlasting pea (above) whose pods are inedible.

check given as salary or wages; **pay′day**, day on which payment (esp. of wages) is (to be) made; ~ **dirt**, (mining) earth or ore containing precious metal or other mineral in sufficient quantity to be profitably worked; (fig.) any source of wealth or income; **pay envelope**, envelope containing employee's wages; **pay′load**, weight of goods, passengers, etc., carried by aircraft etc.; **pay′master**, officer, official, who pays troops, workmen, etc.; **pay′roll**, list of employees receiving regular pay; **pay phone, pay station**, public, coin-operated telephone; **pay toilet**, public toilet with coin-operated door. **paying** *adj.* Profitable (enterprise, mine, etc.).

pay[2] (pā) *v.t.* (**payed** or **paid, pay·ing**). (naut.) Smear with tar, pitch, etc., to render waterproof.

pay·a·ble (pā′*a*bel) *adj.* That must be paid, due; that may be paid.

pay·ee (pāē′) *n.* Person to whom payment is made.

pay·ment (pā′m*e*nt) *n.* Paying; amount paid; (fig.) recompense.

Pb *symbol.* Lead.

PBB *abbrev.* Toxic chemical used in industry, now considered to be contaminating farm products. [*p*(oly) *b*(rominated) *b*(iphenyl)]

PBS *abbrev.* Public Broadcasting Service.

PBX *abbrev.* Private branch exchange (private telephone switchboard).

p.c. *abbrev.* Percent; petty cash; post card.

PCB *abbrev.* Toxic chemical used in industry, now considered to be contaminating river fish. [*p*(oly) *c*(hlorinated) *b*(iphenyl)]

Pd *symbol.* Palladium.

P.D.Q. (pēdēkū′) *abbrev.* (slang) Pretty damn quick.

P.E. *abbrev.* Physical education; Professional Engineer; Protestant Episcopal.

pea (pē) *n.* (pl. **peas**; archaic or Brit. dial. **pease**). Hardy climbing leguminous plant (*Pisum sativum*), with large flowers and long pods each containing a row of round seeds; any of various related leguminous plants; seed of this as food; **green ~s**, peas gathered for food while still young and tender; **everlasting ~**, plant (*Lathyrus latifolius*) cultivated for its variously colored flowers; **sweet ~**: see SWEET; **pea′nut**, (fruit of) *Arachis hypogaea*, with pod ripening underground, containing seeds like peas, valued as food and for their oil; **peanut butter**, paste of ground peanuts; **pea′shooter**, toy weapon, tube from which dried peas are shot by blowing; **pea soup**, soup made from (esp. dried) peas; (attrib., esp. of fog) suggestive of this in its dull-yellow color or thick consistency.

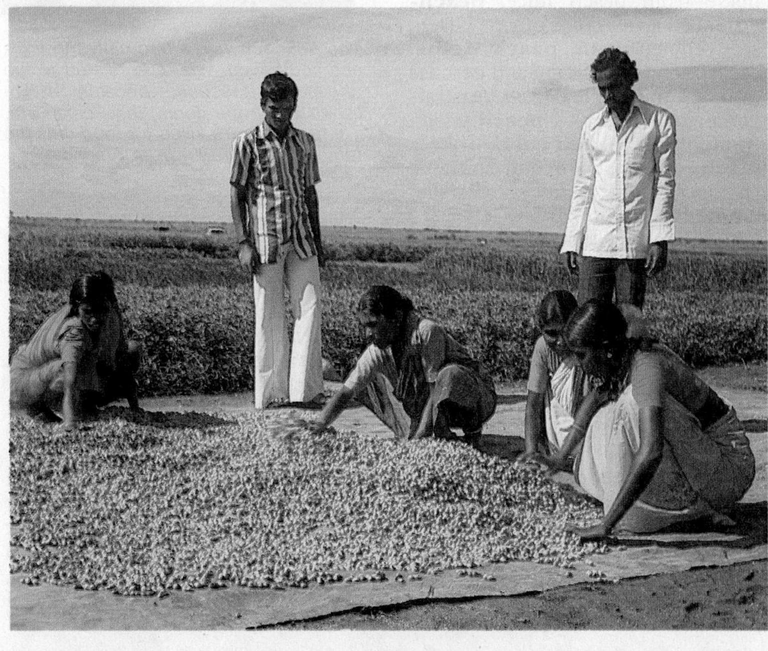

Sorting groundnuts, or* peanuts, *after the harvest in India, where they are grown extensively. Where the rainfall is insufficient to sustain the crop irrigation is used. In the U.S.A. half the crop is used to make peanut-butter.

Related to the almond and nectarine, the sweet, juicy ***peach*** *(right) has become a popular fruit in warmer regions, far from China where it originated.*

peace (pēs) *n.* 1. Freedom from, cessation of, war; ratification or treaty of peace between powers previously at war. 2. Freedom from civil disorder; general peace of a country as secured by law. 3. Quiet, tranquility; mental calm. 4. **at ~**, in state of friendliness, not at strife (*with*); **hold one's ~**, keep silence; **keep the ~**, prevent, refrain from, strife; **make one's ~** (*with*), become reconciled (*with*); **make ~**, bring hostilities to an end. 5. **peace'keeping**, (committed to) maintaining peace between nations, esp. in *U.N. peacekeeping forces*; **peace'maker**, one who brings about peace; **peace offering**, propitiatory gift; (bibl.) offering presented as thanksgiving to God; **peace officer**, policeman, sheriff; **peace pipe**, calumet; **Peace Corps**, organization of volunteers working in developing countries.

peace·a·ble (pē'sabel) *adj.* Disposed, tending, to peace; free from disturbance, peaceful. **peace'a·ble·ness** *n.* **peac'a·bly** *adv.*

peace·ful (pēs'ful) *adj.* Characterized by, belonging to a state of, peace; not violating or infringing peace. **peace'ful·ly** *adv.* **peace'ful·ness** *n.*

peach (pēch) *n.* Large roundish fruit with downy white or yellow skin flushed with red, highly flavored sweet pulp, and rough furrowed stone; tree (*Prunus persica*) bearing this, a native of Asia very early introduced into Europe; peach color; (slang) person or thing of superlative merit, attractive young woman; **~ brandy**, liquor made from peach juice; **peach-color(ed)**, (of) color of ripe peach, soft yellowish pink; **peach Melba**, confection of ice cream and peaches (after Dame Nellie *Melba*, Australian prima donna). **peach'y** *adj.* (**peach·i·er, peach·i·est**). Like a peach, esp. in color and softness. [L. *persicum* (*malum*) Persian (apple)]

pea·cock (pē'kŏk) *n.* (pl. **-cocks,** collect. **-cock**). 1. Male bird of any species of *Pavo*, esp. of *P. cristatus*, native of India, with striking plumage and upper tail coverts marked with iridescent ocelli, able to expand its tail erect like fan (freq. as type of ostentatious display). 2. European butterfly (*Nymphalis io*) with ocellated wings. 3. **peacock blue**, lustrous blue of peacock's neck feathers; **peacock throne**, former throne of kings of Delhi, adorned with representation of fully expanded tail coverts of peacock composed of precious stones. **peacock** *v.i.* Make display; strut about ostentatiously. **pea'cock·er·y** *n.* **pea'cock·ish, pea'cock·y** *adjs.*

The ***peacock*** *was a bird native to India and south-east Asia, and related to the pheasant. Peacocks became established in Europe during the Roman era. There they were killed for food until the turkey was brought from America.*

pea·fowl (pē'fowl) *n.* (pl. **-fowls**, collect. **-fowl**). Peacock or peahen.

pea·hen (pē'hĕn) *n.* Female of the peacock.

pea (pē) **jacket.** Sailor's short double-breasted overcoat of coarse woolen cloth.

peak[1] (pēk) *n.* 1. Projecting part of brim of cap; (naut.) narrow part of ship's hold, esp. (**forepeak**) at bow; upper outer corner of sail extended by gaff. 2. Pointed top, esp. of mountain; point, e.g. of beard; highest point in curve or record of fluctuations (hence **peak load,** greatest frequency or maximum of electric power, traffic, etc.; **peak hour**, time of day when this occurs).

peak[2] (pēk) *v.i.* Waste away. **peak·ed** (pē'kĭd) *adj.* Sharp-featured, pinched. **peak'y** *adj.* Sickly, puny.

peak[3] (pēk) *v.* 1. (naut.) Tilt (yard) vertically; raise (oar blades) almost vertically. 2. Reach highest point.

peal (pēl) *n.* Loud ringing of bell(s), esp. series of changes on set of bells; set of bells; loud volley of sound, esp. of thunder or laughter. **~** *v.* Sound forth in a peal; ring (bells) in peals; utter sonorously.

pear (pār) *n.* (Fleshy fruit, tapering toward stalk, of) the tree *Pyrus communis*, or other species with similar fruit; **alligator ~** = AVOCADO. **prickly ~**: see PRICKLY. **pear'-shaped** *adj.*

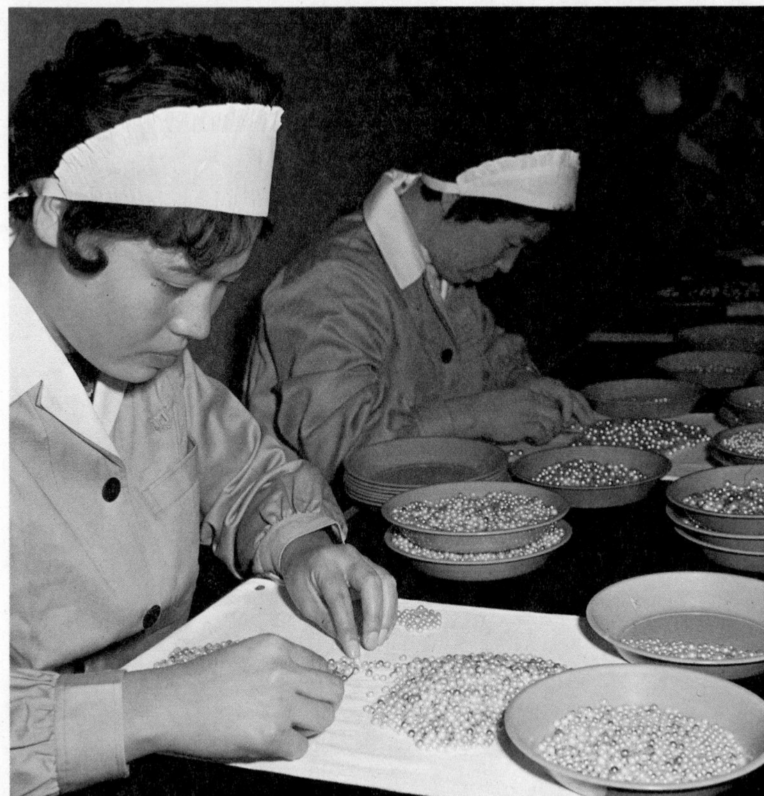

*A **pearl** is formed by an oyster or other bivalve to prevent a grain of sand from irritating it. When the Japanese learnt how to induce this artificially and to keep oysters in enclosures until harvesting, the need for divers was greatly reduced. Left: Sorting pearls at Toba.*

*Mentioned by Homer, the **pear** (above) has been used as a dessert fruit for thousands of years. Today it is grown in many temperate areas and is also canned and dried.*

pearl (pẽrl) *n.* 1. Concentration, usu. white or bluish-gray, formed around foreign body within shell of certain bivalve mollusks, having beautiful luster and highly prized as gem; precious thing, finest example (*of* its kind); pearllike thing, e.g. dewdrop, tear, tooth; **mother-of-~**: see MOTHER. 2. Small fragment of various substances. 3. **pearl ash**, commercial potassium carbonate; **pearl barley**, barley reduced by attrition to small rounded grains; **pearl button**, button made of mother-of-pearl or imitation of it; **pearl diver**, one who dives for pearl oysters; **pearl fisher**, one who fishes for pearls; **pearl oyster**, oyster of family Pteriidae, which often produce pearls; **pearl shell**, mother-of-pearl as naturally found. **pearl** *v.* Sprinkle with pearly drops; make pearly in color etc.; reduce (barley, etc.) to small pearls;

*Kinder Scout (left) in the **Peak** District of Derbyshire, England, now attracts campers, people on hiking tours, and pot-holers who explore the water-worn caverns in the area.*

__Peat__ (right) is dug by hand in Ireland where it is used as fuel. Its origin is evident from the roots and branches which have not decayed. Archaeologists have also found textiles and other relics in it.

The __pecan__ nut is a member of the walnut family and is an important economic crop in south-eastern U.S.A. It is also grown to a lesser extent in Australia and South Africa.

form pearllike drops; fish for pearls. **pearl'y** *adj.* (**pearl·i·er, pearl·i·est**). **pearl'i·ness** *n.* **pearl** *adj.* Of the color of pearl.

Pearl (pērl) **Harbor.** Harbor on island of Oahu, near Honolulu, Hawaii, site of U.S. naval base, bombed in surprise attack by Japan, Dec. 7, 1941.

pearl·ite (pēr'līt) *n.* Microstructural constituent of iron, a conglomerate of cementite and ferrite.

Pea·ry (pēr'ē), **Robert Edwin** (1856–1920). Amer. naval officer and Arctic explorer; reached N. Pole on Apr. 6, 1909; **Peary Land**, mountainous peninsula in N. Greenland on the Arctic Ocean.

peas·ant (pĕz'ant) *n.* Countryman, rustic, esp. one working on land as small farmer or laborer. **peas·ant·ry** (pĕz'antrē) *n.* (Body of) peasants.

pease (pēz) *n.* (pl. **pease**). (Brit. or archaic) Peas, esp. in ~ **porridge**.

peat (pēt) *n.* Accumulation of partially decayed vegetable matter found in damp or marshy regions; cut piece of this, used as fuel; ~ **bog**, broken ground from which peats have been cut. **peat'y** *adj.*

peb·ble (pĕb'el) *n.* 1. Small stone worn and rounded by natural action. 2. Colorless transparent rock crystal used for spectacles, lens of this. **peb'bly** *adj.*

pe·can (pĭkahn', -kăn', pē'kăn) *n.* Species of hickory (*Carya illinoensis*) common in Ohio and Mississippi valleys; olive-shaped finely flavored nut of this.

Found only in America from the south-west U.S.A. to the Rio Platte in Argentina, the two species of __peccary__ travel in groups, usually in isolated areas. They have been tamed and reared like pigs.

pec·ca·ble (pĕk'abel) *adj.* Liable to sin. **pec·ca·bil'i·ty** *n.*

pec·ca·dil·lo (pĕkadĭl'ō) *n.* (pl. **-loes, -los**). Trifling offense.

pec·ca·ry (pĕk'arē) *n.* (pl. **-ries**, collect. **-ry**). Either of two piglike mammals, the collared ~ (*Taxassu tajacu*) or the white-lipped ~, ranging from SW. U.S. to S. Amer. and having a musk gland, sharp tusks, and gray to brown bristles.

pêche mel·ba (pēch' mĕl'ba, pĕsh') = PEACH Melba.

peck[1] (pĕk) *n.* Measure of capacity for dry goods, 2 gallons, ¼ bushel; vessel used as peck measure.

peck[2] (pĕk) *v.* 1. Strike (thing) with beak; pluck *out* thus; make (hole) thus; aim *at* with beak; (colloq.) eat in nibbling fashion. 2. Strike with pick or other pointed tool. 3. **peck'ing order**, hierarchy apparently recognized among domestic birds (also transf.). **peck**

n. Stroke with beak; mark made with this; (joc.) kiss like bird's peck; ~ **order**, pecking order.

peck·er (pĕk´er) *n.* Bird that pecks; (slang) courage, resolution; (vulg.) penis.

pec·tin (pĕk´tĭn) *n.* (chem.) White gelatinous substance soluble in water, closely related to the carbohydrates, formed in the ripening of fruits, and constituting the gelatinizing agent in vegetable juices. **pec´tic** *adj.*

pec·to·ral (pĕk´toral) *adj.* Of the breast or chest; remedying diseases of the chest; worn on the breast; ~ **cross**, cross of precious metal worn on the breast by bishops, cardinals, and abbots. **pectoral** *n.* Ornamental breastplate, esp. that of Jewish high priest.

pec·tose (pĕk´tōs) *n.* (chem.) Insoluble substance related to cellulose and occurring with it in vegetable tissues, esp. in unripe fruits and fleshy roots, converted by the action of acids into PECTIN.

pec·u·late (pĕk´yulāt) *v.* (**-lat·ed, -lat·ing**). Embezzle. **pec·u·la·tion** (pĕkyulā´shon), **pec´u·la·tor** *ns.*

pe·cu·liar (pĭkūl´yer) *adj.* Belonging exclusively *to*; belonging to the individual; particular, special; singular, strange, odd; ~ **institution**, (U.S. hist., archaic) institution of slavery peculiar to southern states before the Civil War. **peculiar** *n.* 1. Peculiar property, privilege, etc. 2. (Brit. hist.) Parish, church, exempt from jurisdiction of diocese in which it lies.

*A **pedestal** was an architectural term used to describe the foot or base which supported a column. Later it was used to refer to both the base and a short column on which a vase or statue was placed.*

pe·cu·li·ar·i·ty (pĭkūlēăr´ĭtē, -kūlyăr´-) *n.* (pl. **-ties**). Being peculiar; characteristic; oddity.

pe·cul·iar·ly (pĭkūl´yerlē) *adv.* As regards oneself alone, individually; especially, more than usually; oddly.

pe·cu·ni·ar·y (pĭkū´nēĕrē) *adj.* (Consisting) of money. **pe·cu·ni·ar·i·ly** (pĭkūnēār´ĭlē) *adv.*

ped·a·gogue, ped·a·gog (pĕd´agŏg, -gawg) *ns.* Schoolmaster, teacher (usu. contempt.). **ped·a·gog·ic** (pĕdagŏj´ĭk, -gō´jĭk), **ped·a·gog´i·cal** *adjs.* **ped·a·gog´i·cal·ly** *adv.*

ped·a·go·gy (pĕd´agōjē, -gŏjē), **ped·a·gog·ics** (pĕdagŏj´ĭks, -gō´jĭks) *ns.* Science of teaching.

ped·al[1] (pĕd´al) *n.* 1. Lever worked by the foot to transmit power in machine, e.g. bicycle. 2. Foot lever in various musical instruments; in harp, for altering pitch of strings; in organ, each of keys played upon by feet, (also) foot lever for drawing out several stops at once, opening swell box, etc.; in piano, foot lever for raising dampers from strings, thus sustaining tone and making it fuller (**loud** ~), or for softening tone (**soft** ~) by shifting hammers so as to strike only one or two strings instead of three, by diminishing length of blow, or by interposing strip of cloth between hammers and stings. 3. (mus.) Note sustained or reiterated in one part (usu. bass) through a series of harmonies. 4. ~ **board**, row of pedals in an organ or pedal piano; ~ **note**, note sounded by the pedals of an organ; (also) in brass instruments, one of the fundamental notes which are below their normal compass; ~ **organ**, that part of an organ controlled by the pedals; ~ **pushers**, woman's slacks reaching to calf. **ped´al** *v.* (**-aled** or **-alled, -al·ing** or **-al·ling**). Work pedals of bicycle etc.; work (bicycle etc.) thus; play on organ pedals.

ped·al[2] (pē´dal) *adj.* (zool.) Of the feet or foot, esp. of mollusk.

ped·ant (pĕd´ant) *n.* One who overrates or parades book learning or technical knowledge, or insists on strict adherence to formal rules. **pe·dan·tic** (pedăn´tĭk) *adj.* **pe·dan´ti·cal·ly** *adv.* **ped·ant·ry** (pĕd´antrē) *n.*

ped·ate (pĕd´āt) *adj.* (zool.) Footed.

ped·dle (pĕd´el) *v.* (**-dled, -dling**). Follow occupation of peddler; trade or deal in as peddler.

ped·dler, ped·lar, ped·ler (pĕd´ler) *ns.* Traveling vendor of small wares, usu. carried in pack; (fig.) retailer (*of* gossip etc.).

ped·er·as·ty (pĕd´erăstē) *n.* Sodomy with a boy. **ped´er·ast** *n.*

ped·es·tal (pĕd´ĭstal) *n.* Base supporting column in construction; base of statue etc.; each of 2 supports of kneehole writing table; foundation; ~ **table**, one with massive central support. **pedestal** *v.t.* (**-taled** or **-talled, -tal·ing** or **-tal·ling**). Set, support, on pedestal.

pe·des·tri·an (pedĕs´trēan) *adj.* Going, performed, on foot; of walking; for those who walk; prosaic, dull, uninspired; ~ **crossing**, crossing place for pedestrians over highway. **pedestrian** *n.* One who walks or goes on foot. **pe·des´tri·an·ism** *n.*

pe·di·at·ric (pēdēăt´rĭk) *adj.* Of diseases of children.

pe·di·a·tri·cian (pēdēatrĭsh´an) *n.* Specialist in pediatrics.

pe·di·at·rics (pēdēăt´rĭks) *n.* (usu. considered sing.) Study of children's diseases.

*In Greek architecture, the **pediment** was a triangular or semi-circular form of gable, usually built to crown the front of a temple or other building. Various designs were used.*

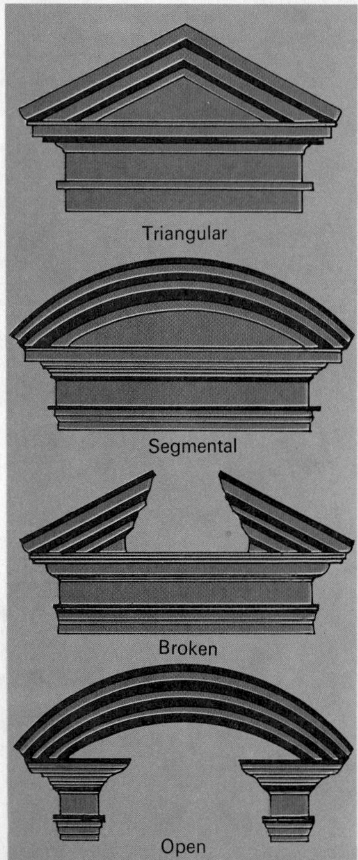

*The Temple of Manly Fortune in Rome exhibits the classical triangular **pediment.** Originally developed by the Greeks, the Romans took up this feature of Greek architecture and used it widely.*

ped·i·cel (pĕd′ĭsel, -sĕl) *n.* (bot. zool.) Small, esp. subordinate, stalk-like structure in plant or animal. **pe·dic·u·late** (pedĭk′yulĭt, -lāt) *adj.*

pe·dic·u·lar (pedĭk′yuler), **pe·dic·u·lous** (pedĭkyulus) *adjs.* Lousy. **pe·dic·u·lo·sis** (pedĭkyulō′sĭs) *n.* Infestation with lice.

ped·i·cure (pĕd′ĭkūr) *n.* 1. Chiropody. 2. Chiropodist. ~ *v.t.* (**-cured, -cur·ing**). Cure or treat (feet) by removing corns etc. **ped′i·cur·ist** *n.*

ped·i·gree (pĕd′igrē) *n.* Genealogical table; ancestral line (of man or animal); derivation (of word); ancient descent; (attrib.) having a known line of descent. **ped′i·greed** *adj.* [OF. *pie de grue* crane's foot, mark ⅄ denoting succession in pedigrees]

ped·i·ment (pĕd′iment) *n.* Triangular low-pitched gable crowning front of building in Greek style, esp. over portico; similarly placed member of same or other form in Roman and Renaissance styles; **broken** ~, one without an apex. **ped·i·men·tal** (pĕdimĕn′tal), **ped′i·ment·ed** *adjs.*

ped·lar, ped·ler = PEDDLER.

pe·dol·o·gy (pĭdŏl′ojē) *n.* Science of soils.

pe·dom·e·ter (pĭdŏm′ĭter) *n.* Instrument for estimating distance traveled on foot by recording number of steps taken.

pe·dun·cle (pĭdŭng′kel) *n.* (bot.) Stalk of flower, fruit, or cluster, esp. main stalk bearing solitary flower or subordinate stalks; (zool.) stalk-like process in animal body. **pe·dun·cu·lar** (pĭdŭng′kyuler), **pe·dun·cu·late** (pĭdŭng′kyulĭt, -lāt), **pe·dun′cu·lat·ed** *adjs.*

peek (pēk) *v.i.* Peep, peer; **peek·a·boo** (pēk′aboo͞), game of hiding and suddenly appearing to child. **peek** *n.* Peep, glance (*take a* ~ *at*).

peel (pēl) *v.* Strip peel, rind, bark, etc., from (fruit, vegetable, tree, etc.); take *off* (skin, peel, etc.); become bare of bark, skin, etc.; (of bark, surface, etc.) come off like peel; (slang, of person) strip for exercise etc.; (colloq.) **keep one's eyes peeled**, keep a sharp lookout. **peel** *n.* Rind, outer coating, of fruit; **candied** ~, candied rind of various species of citrus fruit, used

*The outer coating, called **peel**, of these oranges and mandarins is being cut into strips and is often used in this way in cookery and confectionary.*

in cookery and confectionery. **peel'a·ble** *adj.* **peel'er** *n.* **peel'ings** *n.pl.* What is peeled off.

peen (pēn) *n.* Pointed, edged, or ball-shaped end of hammer opposite face.

peep[1] (pēp) *v.i.* & *n.* (Make) feeble shrill sound of young birds, mice, etc.; chirp, squeak.

peep[2] (pēp) *v.i.* Look through narrow aperture; look furtively; come cautiously or partly into view, emerge; (fig.) show itself unconsciously; **peeping Tom**, voyeur (f. name of tailor in story of Lady GODIVA). **peep** *n.* Furtive or peering glance; 1st appearance, esp. *of dawn, of day*; **peep'hole**, small hole to peep through; **peep show**, small exhibition of pictures etc. viewed through lens in small orifice.

peep·er[1] (pē'p*er*) *n.* Any of various frogs making a shrill call, esp. the spring peeper (*Hyla crucifer*).

peep·er[2] (pē'p*er*) *n.* One who peeps; (slang) eye.

pee·pul = PIPAL.

peer[1] (pēr) *n.* (fem. **peer·ess** pr. pēr'ĭs). 1. Equal in civil standing or rank; equal in any respect. 2. Member of one of the degrees (duke, marquis, earl, viscount, baron) of nobility in United Kingdom; noble (of any country); **life ~**, (since 1958) one whose title is not hereditary; **~ of the realm**, one of the peers of the United Kingdom, all of whom when of age may sit in the House of Lords.

peer[2] (pēr) *v.i.* Look narrowly; appear, peep out; come in sight.

peer·age (pēr'ĭj) *n.* Peers; nobility, aristocracy; rank of peer; book containing list of peers with genealogy etc.

peer·less (pēr'lĭs) *adj.* Having no equal, unrivaled. **peer'less·ly** *adv.* **peer'less·ness** *n.* [f. PEER[1]]

peeved (pēvd) *adj.* (slang) Irritated.

pee·vish (pē'vĭsh) *adj.* Querulous, irritable. **pee'vish·ly** *adv.* **pee'vish·ness** *n.*

pee·wit (pē'wĭt, pū'ĭt): see LAPWING.

peg (pĕg) *n.* 1. Pin, bolt, of wood, metal, etc., usu. round and slightly tapering, for holding together parts of framework etc., stopping up vent of cask, hanging hats etc. on, holding ropes of tent, tightening or loosening strings of violin etc., marking cribbage score etc.; (fig.) occasion, pretext, theme (*to hang* discourse etc. *on*); **peg'board**, board with holes and pegs, esp. for game, commercial displays, or home use; **take** (person) **down a peg or two**, humble him; **peg leg**, wooden leg; **peg-top trousers**, trousers wide at hips, narrow at ankles. 2. (Brit.) Drink, esp. of whiskey and soda or brandy and soda. **peg** *v.* (**pegged, peg·ging**). Fix with peg; (stock exch.) prevent price of (stock etc.) from falling or rising by freely buying or selling at given price; mark score with pegs on cribbage board; mark out boundaries of (mining claim etc.); strike, pierce, aim *at*, with peg; (slang) throw (stone or baseball), throw stones etc. (*at*); work (*away*) persistently (*at*); **~ down**, restrict (*to* rules etc.).

Both an ancient and modern capital of China, ***Peking*** *shows evidence of its past in (top) the gateway to the old summer palace. Above: Modern city streets are dominated by huge colored hoardings.*

Peg·a·sus (pĕg'*asus*). 1. (Gk. myth.) Winged horse, favorite of the Muses, sprung from blood of MEDUSA. 2. (astron.) Northern constellation, figured as a winged horse, containing three stars of the second magnitude forming with one star of Andromeda a large square (**square of ~**).

Peh·le·vi = PAHLAVI.

peign·oir (pānwär', pĕn-) *n.* Woman's loose dressing gown.

Peirce (pērs), **Charles Sanders** (1839–1914). Amer. philosopher, mathematician and physicist; founder of pragmatism.

pe·jo·ra·tive (pĭjōr'*a*tĭv, -jär'-, pĕj'*o*rā-, pē'*jo*-) *adj.* & *n.* Depreciatory (word).

Pe·kin·ese (pēk*i*nēz', -nēs') = PEKINGESE def. 2.

Pe·king (pē'kĭng'), now known as Beijing. Capital city of China; **~ man**, hominid (*Pithecanthropus pekinensis*) represented by at least a dozen skulls and other remains found near Peking. [Chin. = "northern capital"]

Pe·king·ese (pekĭngēz', -ēs', pēk*i*nēz', -nēs') *adj.* Of Peking. **~** *n.* (pl. **-ese**). 1. Native, inhabitant, of Peking. 2. (Breed of) small dog of the pug type, with long silky coat, flat face, and prominent eyes, orig. brought to Europe from Summer Palace in Peking in 1860.

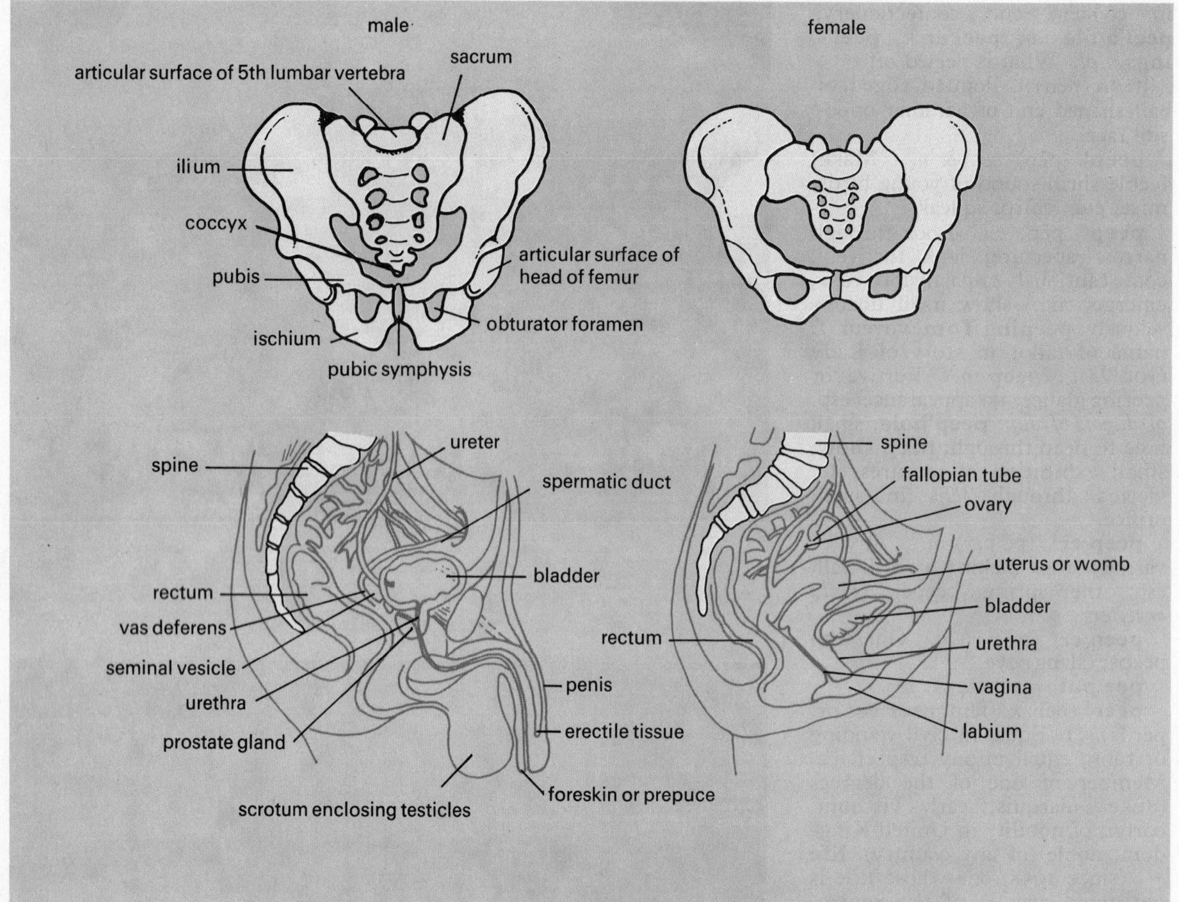

*The bones of the **pelvis** act both as a support for the human body and its internal organs, and as pivots for the legs whose uppermost sockets fit into ball-joints on the ends of the pelvis. The shape differs between male and female.*

pe·koe (pē´kō) *n.* Superior kind of black tea. [Chin. *pek-ho* white down (leaves being picked young with down on them)]

pe·lag·ic (pelăj´ĭk) *adj.* Of, inhabiting, the open sea.

pel·ar·go·ni·um (pĕlar̄gō´nē*u*m) *n.* Plant of genus *P*~ with showy flowers and fragrant leaves (pop. called *geranium*). [Gk. *pelargos* stork]

pelf (pĕlf) *n.* Money, wealth (usu. contempt.).

pel·i·can (pĕl´ĭk*a*n) *n.* Any of various large aquatic birds (genus *Pelecanus*) of warm regions, including the brown ~ (*P. occidentalis*) of Amer. coastal waters and the white ~ (*P. erythrorhynchos*) ranging from the Pacific Coast to the gulf of Mexico, both being webfooted and having large membranous pouch beneath lower bill.

Pe·li·on (pē´lē*o*n). Wooded mountain near coast of SE. Thessaly, Greece; in Gk. myth., home of centaurs.

pel·la·gra (pelăg´r*a*, -lā´gr*a*) *n.* Deficiency disease, endemic in countries whose populations live chiefly on cereals with low protein content, characterized by disorders of the skin, digestion, and nervous system. [It., perh. orig. *pelle agra* rough skin]

pel·let (pĕl´ĭt) *n.* Small ball of paper, bread, etc.; pill; small shot. **pel´let·ed** *adj.* Formed into a pellet.

pel·li·cle (pĕl´ĭk*e*l) *n.* Thin skin; membrane; film. **pel·lic·u·lar** (pelĭk´y*u*l*e*r) *adj.*

pel·li·to·ry (pĕl´ĭtōrē, -tor̄ē) *n.* (pl. **-ries**). (also ~ **of Spain**) Composite plant (*Anacyclus pyrethrum*), native of Barbary, with pungent root used as local irritant etc.

pell-mell, pell·mell (pĕl´mĕl´) *advs.* In disorder, promiscuously; headlong, recklessly. ~ *adj.* Confused; tumultuous. ~ *n.* Confusion, medley, mêlée.

pel·lu·cid (pel o͞o´sĭd) *adj.* Transparent, clear; clear in style or expression; mentally clear. **pel·lu·cid·i·ty** (pĕly o͞osĭd´ĭtē) *n.* **pel·lu´cid·ly** *adv.*

Pel·o·pon·ne·sus (pĕl*o*ponē´s*u*s), **Pel·o·pon·nese** (pĕl*o*ponēz´, -nēs´). That part of Greece S. of Isthmus of Corinth. **Pel·o·pon·ne·sian** (pĕl*o*ponē´zh*a*n, -sh*a*n) *adj.* ~ **War,** war (431–404 B.C.) waged by Sparta and her allies upon Athens and Athenian Empire resulting in the surrender of Athens and transfer, for a brief period, of leadership of Greece to Sparta.

pe·lo·ta (pelō´t*a*) *n.* Jai alai ball used in jai alai. [Span., = "ball" (f. L. *pila*)]

pelt[1] (pĕlt) *n.* Skin of sheep or goat with short wool on; skin of furbearing animal, esp. undressed; raw skin of sheep etc. stripped of wool or fur. **pelt·ry** (pĕl´trē) *n.* (pl. **-ries**). Pelts collectively.

pelt[2] (pĕlt) *v.* Assail with missiles; (of rain etc.) beat with violence; strike *at* repeatedly with missiles; go on throwing (missiles). ~ *n.* Pelting.

pel·vis (pĕl´vĭs) *n.* (pl. **-vis·es, -ves** pr. -vēz). 1. Basin-shaped cavity at lower end of trunk in most vertebrates, formed in man by innominate bones with sacrum and coccyx. 2. Funnel-shaped origin of ureter, having a wide end that lies within the kidney. **pel·vic** (pĕl´vĭk) *adj.*

pem·mi·can, pem·i·can (pĕm´ĭk*a*n) *ns.* N. Amer. Ind. food of lean meat dried, pounded, mixed into paste with melted fat and pressed into cakes; beef similarly treated and freq. flavored with currants etc. for Arctic and other travelers.

pen[1] (pĕn) *n.* Small enclosure for cows, sheep, poultry, etc.; enclosure resembling this, as *sub-*

*Very large and highly adapted to swimming and fishing, the **pelican** is famous for the deep pouch beneath its bill, its large webbed feet and its powerful wings.*

marine ~; (W. Ind.) farm, plantation. **pen** *v.t.* (**penned** or **pent, pen·ning**). Enclose, shut *up*, shut *in*; shut up (cattle etc.) in pen.

pen[2] (pĕn) *n.* Quill feather with quill pointed and split into two sections, for writing with ink; small instrument of gold, steel, etc., similarly pointed and split, fitted into rod of wood etc. (**pen′holder**); pen and penholder together; any contrivance for writing with fluid ink; writing, style of this; **ballpoint ~, fountain ~**: see BALL[1] and FOUNTAIN; **~-and-ink**, (attrib., of drawing etc.) done, made, with pen and ink; **pen′knife**, small knife usu. carried in pocket, orig. for making or mending quill pens; **pen′man**, one who writes a (*good, bad*, etc.) hand; author; **pen′manship**, style of handwriting; **pen name**, literary pseudonym; **pen pal**, friend with whom one corresponds without meeting; **pen wiper**, appliance usu. of small pieces of cloth for wiping pen after use. **pen** *v.t.* (**penned, pen·ning**). Write, compose and write (letter etc.).

pen[3] (pĕn) *n.* Female mute swan.

pen[4] (pĕn) *n.* (slang) Prison. [abbrev. of *penitentiary*]

Pen., pen. *abbrevs.* Peninsula.

P.E.N. *abbrev.* (International Association of) Poets, Playwrights, Editors, Essayists, and Novelists.

pe·nal (pē′n*a*l) *adj.* Of punishment, concerned with inflicting this; (of offense) punishable, esp. by law; inflicted as punishment; used as place of punishment, as in ~ *colony*. **pe′nal·ly** *adv.*

pe·nal·ize (pē′n*a*līz, pĕn′*a*-) *v.t.* (**-ized, -iz·ing**). Make, declare, penal; subject to handicap or comparative disadvantage (also freq. fig.).

pen·al·ty (pĕn′*a*ltē) *n.* (pl. **-ties**). Punishment, esp. (exaction of) sum of money, for breach of law, rule, or contract; money thus paid; (sport etc.) disadvantage imposed on competitor for breaking rule or winning previous contest; (bridge) points added to opponents' score when declarer fails to make a contract; ~ **box**, (ice hockey) place adjacent to rink for penalized players; ~ **kick**, (soccer) free kick allowed for certain infringements of rules.

pen·ance (pĕn′*a*ns) *n.* (R.C. and Orthodox Churches) Sacrament including contrition, confession, satisfaction, and absolution for sin; act of self-mortification as expression of penitence, esp. one imposed by priest; **do ~**, perform such act.

Pe·nang (pĭnăng′, -nahng′). State of Malaysia consisting of island in SE. Asia off the W. coast of the Malay Peninsula, covering 110 sq. mi. (285 sq. km); and strip of territory on the Malay Peninsula; capital, ~, formerly George Town.

***Penang**, an island off the west coast of Malaysia, is about 15 miles long and no more than 8 miles wide. Many of its inhabitants are fishermen (above) and others follow the ancient tradition of making joss sticks, seen drying (right).*

pe·na·tes (pe*n*ā′tēz, -nah′-) *n.pl.* (Rom. myth.) Gods of the storeroom, worshipped, together with the lares, by households.

pence (pĕns) *n.* (Brit.) Alternative plural of PENNY, esp. in combination, as *sixpence*.

pen·chant (pĕn′ch*a*nt) *n.* Inclination, liking, (*for*).

pen·cil (pĕn′s*i*l) *n.* 1. (archaic) Artist's paintbrush; (fig.) painter's art or style. 2. Instrument for drawing or writing, esp. (**lead ~**) of graphite enclosed in wooden cylinder or in metal case with tapering end; pencil-shaped object; **~ case**, case for holding pencils etc. 3. (optics) Set of rays meeting at a point. 4. (geom.) Figure formed by set of straight lines meeting at a point. **pencil** *v.t.* (**-ciled** or **-cilled, -cil·ing** or **-cil·ling**). Tint or mark (as) with lead pencil; jot down with pencil; (esp. in past part.) mark delicately with thin concentric lines of color or shading.

pen·dant (pĕn′d*a*nt) *n.* 1. Hanging ornament, esp. one attached to necklace, bracelet, etc. 2. (naut.) Short rope hanging from head of mast etc. with eye at lower end for receiving hooks of tackles; tapering flag, esp. that flown at masthead of vessel in commission. 3. Shank and

ring of watch by which it is suspended. 4. Match, parallel, companion, complement (*to*).

pen·dent (pĕn′d*e*nt) *adj.* Hanging; overhanging; undecided, pending. **pen′den·cy** *n.* **pen′dent·ly** *adv.*

pend·ing (pĕn′dĭng) *adj.* Undecided, awaiting decision or settlement. **~** *prep.* During; until.

pen·du·late (pĕn′julāt, pĕn′dy*u*-) *v.i.* (**-lat·ed, -lat·ing**). Swing like a pendulum.

pen·du·lous (pĕn′j*u*l*u*s, pĕn′dy*u*-) *adj.* Suspended, hanging down; oscillating. **pen′du·lous·ly** *adv.* **pen′du·lous·ness** *n.*

pen·du·lum (pĕn′j*u*l*u*m, -dy*u*-) *n.* Body suspended so as to be free to swing, esp. rod with weighted end regulating movement of clock's works; person, thing, that oscillates.

Pe·nel·o·pe (penĕl′opē). (Gk. legend) Wife of Odysseus; when her husband did not return after fall of Troy, she told her importunate suitors that she would marry one of them when she had finished the piece of weaving on which she was engaged, but every night she undid the work that she had done during the day.

pen·e·trate (pĕn′ĭtrāt) *v.* (**-trat·ed, -trat·ing**). Find access into or through, pass through; make a way (*with, through, to*); (of sight) pierce through; permeate; imbue (*with*); (fig.) see into, find out, discern (design, the truth, etc.). **pen′e·trat·ing** *adj.* (esp.) Gifted with or suggestive of insight; (of voice etc.) easily heard through or above other sounds. **pen·e·tra·bil·i·ty** (pĕnĭtr*a*bĭl′ĭtē), **pen·e·tra′tion** *ns.* **pen·e·tra·ble** (pĕn′ĭtr*a*bel), **pen·e·tra·tive** (pĕn′ĭtrātĭv) *adjs.*

pen·guin (pĕn′gwĭn, pĕng′-) *n.* Any bird of the family Spheniscidae, including several genera of seabirds of the southern hemisphere, with wings reduced to scaly flippers with which they swim under water.

pen·i·cil·late (pĕnĭsĭl′ĭt, -āt) *adj.*

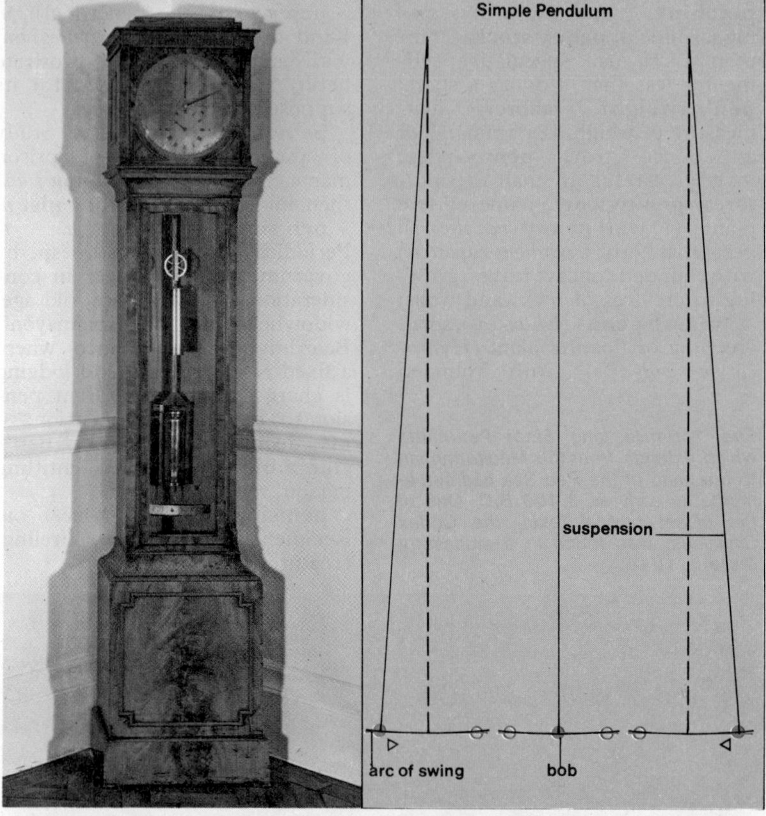

Although Galileo was probably the first man to recognize the properties of the ***pendulum,*** *it was Christian Huyghens in 1657 who first adapted it to regulate a clock, as had been proposed, but not done, by Galileo.*

(biol.) Furnished with, forming, small tuft(s); marked with streaks as of pencil or brush.

pen·i·cil·lin (pĕnĭsĭl′ĭn) *n.* Substance obtained from the mold *Penicillium notatum,* effective against many microorganisms of disease (the first ANTIBIOTIC to be used therapeutically, during World War II). [L. *penicillus* painter's brush, f. brushlike sporangia of the mold]

pen·in·su·la (penĭn′s*u*la, -sy*u*la) *n.* Piece of land almost surrounded by water, or projecting far into the sea.

pen·in·su·lar (penĭn′s*u*ler, -sy*u*ler) *adj.* Of (the nature of) a peninsula; **P~ War,** that carried on in Spain and Portugal (1808–1814) between French under Napoleon and English, Spanish and Portuguese under Wellington. **peninsular** *n.* Inhabitant of a peninsula.

pe·nis (pē′nĭs) *n.* (pl. **-nis·es, -nes** pr. -nēz). Organ of urination and copulation in male animals.

pen·i·tent (pĕn′ĭtent) *adj.* That repents, contrite. ~ *n.* Repentant sinner; person doing penance under direction of confessor; (pl.) any of various R.C. congregations or orders associated for mutual discipline, giving religious aid to criminals etc. **pen′i·tent·ly** *adv.* **pen′i·tence** *n.*

pen·i·ten·tial (pĕnĭtĕn′sh*a*l) *adj.* Of penitence or penance; ~ **Psalms,** those expressing penitence (Pss. 6, 32, 38, 51, 102, 130, 143). **pen·i·ten′tial·ly** *adv.*

pen·i·ten·tia·ry (pĕnĭtĕn′sh*a*rē) *n.* (pl. **-ries**). 1. Office in papal court deciding questions of penance, dispensations, etc.; **grand p~,** cardinal presiding over this. 2. Reformatory prison; state prison. **penitentiary** *adj.* Of penance; of reformatory treatment of criminals.

Penn (pĕn), **William** (1644–1718). English Quaker, founder of Pennsylvania, 1681; framed government to meet popular demands of colonists and granted a liberal charter to the colony.

Penn., Penna. *abbrevs.* Pennsylvania.

pen·nant (pĕn′*a*nt) *n.* = PENNON; flag awarded as distinction, esp. in baseball.

pen·ni·less (pĕn′ēlĭs) *adj.* Having no money; poor, destitute.

Rock-hopper ***penguins*** *(left), like other species, are unable to fly but use their wings as paddles when swimming. Most live in the cooler latitudes of the southern hemisphere, but one species nests in the Galapagos Islands.*

pen·non (pĕn′on) *n.* Long narrow flag, triangular or swallow-tailed; long pointed streamer of ship; flag.

Penn·syl·va·ni·a (pĕnsilvā′nēa, -vān′ya). Middle Atlantic state of U.S.; one of the original 13 states (1787); capital, Harrisburg. [named 1681 in honor of Admiral Sir William *Penn*, father of William PENN, founder of the colony]

pen·ny (pĕn′ē) *n.* (pl. **pen·nies**, collect. **pence**). $\frac{1}{100}$ of a U.S. dollar; $\frac{1}{100}$ of a British POUND[1]; until 1971, $\frac{1}{12}$ of a shilling; (bibl.) denarius; **a bad** ~, someone or something repeatedly present when not desired; ~ **ante**, poker game in which the stakes are a penny or other small amount; **a pretty** ~, a large sum of money; **turn an honest** ~, earn money by an odd job; ~ **candy**, (archaic), candy sold for a penny; ~ **dreadful**: see DREADFUL; **pennies from heaven**, unexpected benefits; **penny-pinching** (*adj.*) niggardly; (*n.*) niggardliness; **penny stocks**, common stocks, usu. speculative, selling for less than a dollar a share; **pen′nyweight**, (abbrev. dwt) measure of weight, 24 grams, $\frac{1}{20}$ of an ounce troy; **penny-wise**, (overly) careful in small expenditures; **pen′nywort**, name of two plants: (1) **wall penny** (*navelwort*), perennial herb (*Umbilicus rupestris*) with rounded concave leaves, growing in crevices of rocks and walls; (2) **marsh penny** (*white-rot*), small creeping or floating plant (*Hydrocotyle vulgaris*), with rounded leaves, growing in marshy places.

pen·ny·roy·al (pĕnēroi′al) *n.* Kind of mint (*Mentha pulegium*) with small leaves and prostrate habit, formerly cultivated for its supposed medicinal virtues.

pe·nol·o·gy (pēnŏl′ojē) *n.* Study of punishment and of prison management. **pe·no·log·i·cal** (pēnolŏj′ĭkal) *adj.* **pe·nol′o·gist** *n.*

pen·sion (pĕn′shon) *n.* 1. Periodical payment made esp. by government or employer in consideration of past service, old age, widowhood, etc. 2. (pr. pahṅsyōṅ′) Boardinghouse (in France) where a fixed rate for board and lodging is charged. ~ *v.t.* Grant pension to; buy over with pension; ~ **off**, dismiss with pension. **pen′sion·a·ble** *adj.* Entitled, entitling person, to pension.

pen·sion·er (pĕn′shoner) *n.* Recipient of pension; hireling, creature.

*The 140-mile long **Sinai Peninsula** which extends from the Mediterranean to the head of the Red Sea had settlements as early as 3,400 B.C. One of the oldest biblical texts, the Codex Sinaiticus, was found in a monastery there in 1844.*

*The **Pennsylvania** Canal, built in the mid-1800's to transport freight, is an example of the ingenuity which has characterized the economic development of the state which continues to prosper.*

*The full-dress uniform of the Chelsea **pensioner.** About 600 invalid soldiers now live at the Royal Hospital, Chelsea, which was founded by Charles II and built by Christopher Wren. Each year Founders Day is celebrated.*

pen·sive (pĕn′sĭv) *adj.* Plunged in thought; melancholy. **pen′sive·ly** *adv.* **pen′sive·ness** *n.*

pen·ste·mon (pĕnstē′mon) = PENTSTEMON.

pent (pĕnt) *adj.* Closely confined, shut *in* or *up.* ~ *v.* Past t. and past part. of PEN[1].

penta-, pent- *prefixes.* Five.

pen·ta·chord (pĕn′takōrd) *n.* Musical instrument with five strings; system or series of five notes.

pen·ta·cle (pĕn′takel) *n.* Figure used as symbol, esp. in magic; prop. = pentagram.

pen·tad (pĕn′tăd) *n.* Set, group, of five.

pen·ta·gon (pĕn′tagŏn) *n.* Plane figure of five angles and sides; **P**~, U.S. Department of Defense headquarters, Arlington, Va. (from shape of its building). **pen·tag·o·nal** (pĕntăg′onal) *adj.*

pen·ta·he·dron (pĕntahē′dron) *n.* Solid figure of five faces. **pen·ta·he′dral** *adj.*

pen·tam·e·ter (pĕntăm′ĭter) *n.* (Engl. pros.) Line of verse of 5 ft., e.g. heroic or iambic verse of 10 syllables, thus: ˘/|˘/|˘/|˘/|˘/|

pen·tane (pĕn′tān) *n.* Any of a group of paraffin hydrocarbons containing five carbon atoms, including several colorless volatile liquids occurring in petroleum.

Pen·ta·teuch (pĕn′tatōōk, -tūk) *n.* First five books of Old Testament (Genesis, Exodus, Leviticus, Numbers, Deuteronomy) traditionally ascribed to Moses. **Pen′ta·teuch·al** *adj.*

pen·tath·lon (pĕntăth′lon) *n.* 1. In ancient Greece, athletic contest of five events in each of which the same competitors took part (foot race, long jump, javelin-throwing, discus-throwing, wrestling). 2. Similar contest in modern times, comprising five different events.

pen·ta·tom·ic (pĕntatŏm′ĭk) *adj.* (chem.) Containing five atoms in the molecule.

pen·ta·ton·ic (pĕntatŏn′ĭk) *adj.* (mus.) Consisting of five notes or sounds; ~ **scale**, scale without semitones.

pen·ta·va·lent (pĕntavā′lent) *adj.* (chem.) Having a valency of five; quinquivalent.

Pen·te·cost (pĕn′tĭkawst, -kŏst). 1. Christian festival on seventh Sunday after Easter commemorating the descent of the Holy Spirit on the Apostles. 2. Jewish harvest festival (Shabuoth) observed on 50th day after the second day of Passover (Lev. 23). **Pen·te·cos′tal** *adj.* [Gk. *pentēkostē (hēmera)* fiftieth (day)]

Pen·the·si·le·a (pĕnthesĭlē′a). (Gk. legend) Queen of Amazons; came to help of Troy after death of Hector and was slain by Achilles.

pent·house (pĕnt′hows) *n.* Sloping roof, esp. as subsidiary structure attached to wall of main building; awning, canopy, or the like; separate apartment or home atop roof of apartment house.

pen·ti·men·to (pĕntĭmĕn′tō) *n.* (pl. **-ti** pr. -tē). Reappearance of earlier underlying painting when layer added later becomes transparent, revealing artist's change of mind etc.

pen·to·bar·bi·tal (pĕntōbar′bitawl) *n.* Narcotic and sedative barbiturate drug.

pen·tode (pĕn′tōd) *n.* Vacuum tube with five main electrodes.

pen·tom·ic (pĕntŏm′ĭk) *adj.* Organized into five battle groups, each with supporting units ready to maneuver in accordance with the needs of atomic warfare.

pen·tose (pĕn′tōs) *n.* (chem.) Sugar with five carbon atoms in the molecule.

Pen·to·thal (pĕn′tothawl) *n.* (trademark) Thiopental.

pent·ste·mon (pĕntstē′mon) *n.* N. Amer. herbaceous plant of genus *P*~, allied to foxglove with showy flowers, usu. tubular and two-lipped.

pe·nult (pē′nŭlt, pĭnŭlt′), **pe·nul·ti·mate** (pĭnŭl′timĭt) *ns.* Last

*Found throughout the northern hemisphere, the **peony** is now a popular flower in gardens. In ancient times, the strong-smelling roots of the common variety were considered to have medicinal properties.*

syllable but one. ~ *adjs.* Last but one.

pe·num·bra (pĭnŭm′bra) *n.* (pl. **-brae** pr. -brē, **-bras**). Partly shaded region around shadow of opaque body, esp. round total shadow of moon or Earth in eclipse; lighter outer part of sunspot; partial shadow. **pe·num′bral** *adj.*

pe·nu·ri·ous (penoor′ēus, -nūr′-) *adj.* Poor, scanty; stingy, grudging. **pe·nu′ri·ous·ly** *adv.* **pe·nu′ri·ous·ness** *n.*

pen·u·ry (pĕn′yurē) *n.* Destitution, poverty; lack, scarcity, (*of*).

pe·on (pē′on, -ŏn) *n.* 1. In India, office messenger, attendant, orderly. 2. In Spanish Amer., day laborer; in Mexico etc., debtor held in servitude by creditor until debts are worked off. **pe′on·age** *n.* Employment, service, of peons.

pe·o·ny (pē′onē) *n.* (pl. **-nies**). Plant of genus *Paeonia* with large handsome crimson, pink, or white, globular flowers, in cultivation freq. double.

peo·ple (pē′pel) *n.* (pl. **peo·ple**). 1. (pl. **people** or **peoples**) Persons composing community, tribe, race, or nation; persons belonging to a place or forming a company or class etc.; subjects of king etc.; congregation of parish priest etc. 2. Parents or other relatives; commonalty; persons in general. 3. (sing. or pl.) Body of enfranchised or qualified citizens; **People's Charter**: see CHARTIST. **people** *v.t.* (**peo·pled, peo·pling**). Fill with people, populate, fill (place *with*); inhabit, occupy, fill (esp. in past part.).

pep (pĕp) *n.* (colloq.) Vigor, go, spirit; ~ **pill**, pill containing stimulant drug; ~ **rally**, meeting, esp. of students, prior to an athletic contest, to inspire enthusiasm by singing, cheering, speeches, etc.; ~ **talk**, exhortation to exceptional effort etc. **pep** *v.t.* (**pepped, pep·ping**). Fill *up* or inspire with energy and vigor. [abbrev. of *pepper*]

pep·er·o·ni, pep·per·o·ni (pĕperō′nē) *ns.* Sausage of highly seasoned beef and pork. [It., = cayenne peppers]

Pep·in (pĕp′ĭn). Name of several members of the Carolingian family: **Pepin I** (of Landen) (d. 639), Frankish mayor of the palace; **Pepin II** (of Héristal) (d. 714), Frankish ruler, father of Charles Martel; **Pepin III** "the Short" (714–68), Frankish king, younger son of Charles Martel and father of Charlemagne.

pep·per (pĕp′er) *n.* 1. Pungent aromatic condiment harvested from dried berries of plants of genus *Piper*, used whole (**peppercorns**) or ground into powder; climbing shrub of East Indies, cultivated also in West Indies, from which this is chiefly obtained; **black** ~, shrub (*P. nigrum*); most usual form of the condiment, prepared from slightly unripe berries; **white** ~, milder form prepared from ripe berries, or from black by removing outer husk. 2. Capsicum; **red** ~, (large red or yellow edible fruit of) plant *Capsicum frutescens*; cayenne pepper; often eaten when green, **green** ~; also called **sweet** ~. 3. **pepper-and-salt**, (cloth) of dark and light threads woven together, showing small dots of dark and light intermingled; **pep′perbox**, small usu. round box with perforated lid for sprinkling pepper; **pep′percorn**, dried berry of black pepper; **pepper mill**, utensil for grinding peppercorns by hand; **pepper pot**, W. Indian stew of meat with cayenne pepper etc.; **pepper tree**, any of various S. Amer. evergreen trees of the genus *Schinus*. **pepper** *v.t.* Sprinkle, treat, with pepper; sprinkle as with pepper; pelt with missiles.

pep·per·mint (pĕp′ermĭnt) *n.* Kind of mint (*Mentha piperita*), cultivated for its essential oil; this oil, with characteristic pungent aromatic flavor leaving aftersensation of coolness; candy flavored with this.

pep·per·o·ni = PEPERONI.

pep·per·y (pĕp′erē) *adj.* Of, like, abounding in, pepper; (fig.) pungent, stinging, hot-tempered.

pep·sin (pĕp′sĭn) *n.* Enzyme contained in gastric juice, converting proteins into peptones in presence of dilute acid.

pep·tic (pĕp′tĭk) *adj.* Digestive; ~ **gland**, gland secreting gastric juice; ~ **ulcer**, any ulcer of the digestive system.

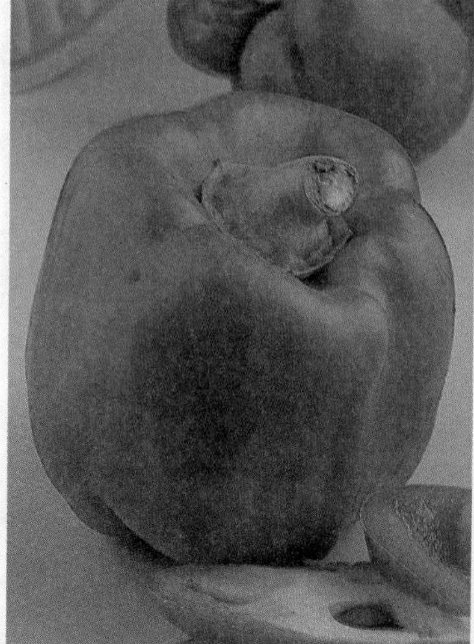

*The **green pepper** is a member of the capsicum family and a native of tropical America. If allowed to ripen properly it becomes a red or yellow color and softens slightly. Usually peppers are eaten crisp and green.*

***Pepper** is made from the dried seeds of a tree which grows in India and South-east Asia. White pepper has the skin removed. Cayenne is from the skin of a capsicum, originally from South America.*

pep·ti·dase (pĕp′tĭdās) *n.* Enzyme that hydrolyzes peptides or peptones and releases amino acids.

pep·tide (pĕp′tīd) *n.* Compound with two or more amino acids linked in linear sequence with elimination of water molecules.

pep·tone (pĕp′tōn) *n.* Any of a class of easily soluble albuminoid substances into which proteins are converted by action of pepsin etc. **pep·to·nize** (pĕp′tonīz) *v.t.* (**-nized, -niz·ing**). (esp.) Subject (food) to artificial process of partial digestion, as aid to weak digestion. **pep·ton·ic** (pĕptŏn′ĭk) *adj.*

Pepys (pēps), **Samuel** (1633–1703). English diarist; secretary of Admiralty 1673–9, 1684–8.

per (pẽr) *prep.* 1. Through, by means of (esp. in L. phrases, for which see entries); **as ~ usual**, (joc.) as usual. 2. For each; **per annum, per capita:** see own entries; **per·cent** (persĕnt′), **per cent′**, (symbol %) in every hundred; **per diem**: see own entry; **per head**, for each person; **per hour**, in each hour (of speed); **per se**: see own entry; **per second per second**, (abbrev. per sec./sec.) per second every second (of rate of acceleration).

per- *prefix.* Completely, very; to destruction, to the bad; (in chem. compounds) denoting maximum of some element in combination.

per·ad·ven·ture (pẽradvĕn′cher, pĕr-) *adv.* (archaic) Perhaps. ~ *n.* Uncertainty, chance, conjecture; **beyond, without, (all) ~**, without doubt.

per·am·bu·late (perăm′byulāt) *v.t.* (**-lat·ed, -lat·ing**). Walk through, over, or about; travel through and inspect (territory). **per·am·bu·la′tion** *n.* **per·am·bu·la·to·ry** (perăm′byulatōrē, -tōrē) *adj.*

per·am·bu·la·tor (perăm′byulāter) *n.* (esp. Brit.) = BABY carriage.

per an·num (pẽr ăn′um). (So much) by the year. [L.]

per·cale (perkăl′) *n.* Plain-woven cotton fabric resembling calico, but finer and wider.

per cap·i·ta (pẽr kăp′ita). For each person.

per·ceive (persēv′) *v.t.* (**-ceived, -ceiv·ing**). Apprehend with the mind, observe, understand; apprehend through one of the senses, esp. sight. **per·ceiv′a·ble** *adj.* **per·ceiv′a·bly** *adv.*

per·cent·age (persĕn′tĭj) *n.* Rate, proportion, percent; (loosely) proportion.

per·cept (pẽr′sĕpt) *n.* (philos.) Object of perception; mental product, as opp. to action, of perceiving. **per·cep·tu·al** (persĕp′chooal) *adj.*

per·cep·ti·ble (persĕp′tibel) *adj.* That can be perceived by senses or intellect. **per·cep·ti·bil′i·ty** *n.* **per·cep′ti·bly** *adv.*

per·cep·tion (persĕp′shon) *n.* Act, faculty, of perceiving; intuitive recognition (*of*); (philos.) action by which the mind refers its sensations to external object as cause. **per·cep′tion·al** *adj.* **per·cep·tive** *adj.* **per·cep′tive·ly** *adv.* **per·cep′tive·ness, per·cep·tiv·i·ty** (pẽrsĕptĭv′ĭtē) *ns.*

perch[1] (pẽrch) *n.* (pl. **perch·es**, collect. **perch**). Common N. Amer. spiny-finned freshwater fish (*Perca flavescens*) used as food; related European species (*P. fluviatilis*).

perch[2] (pẽrch) *n.* 1. Horizontal bar for bird to rest upon; anything serving for this; (fig.) elevated or secure position; **knock** (person) **off his ~**, vanquish, destroy, make less confident or condescending. 2. (also POLE[1], ROD) (Brit.) Measure of length, esp. for land, 5½ yds.; measure of area (also **square ~**), 30¼ sq. yds. **perch** *v.* Alight, rest, as bird (*on* bough etc.); settle, alight (*on*); place (as) on perch. **perch′er** *n.* Passerine bird with feet adapted for perching.

per·chance (perchăns′, -chahns) *adv.* (archaic) By chance; possibly, maybe.

Per·che·ron (pẽr′cherŏn, -she-) *n.* Strong Swift horse of breed originating in le Perche, district in department of Orne, N. France.

per·chlo·ric (pẽrklōr′ĭk) *adj.* Containing chlorine in maximum valence.

per·cip·i·ent (persĭp′ēent) *adj.* Perceiving, conscious. ~ *n.* One who perceives, esp. (telepathy etc.) something outside range of senses. **per·cip′i·ence, per·cip′i·en·cy** *ns.*

per·co·late (pẽr′kolāt) *v.* (**-lat·ed, -lat·ing**). Filter, ooze, through (freq. fig.); permeate;

*This young **peregrine** falcon is tearing at the carcass used to lure it back to its handler. A predator of small and medium-sized birds, the peregrine has been known to nest in cities.*

strain (liquid etc.) through pores etc. **per·co·la'tion** *n.*

per·co·la·tor (pẽr'kol*ā*t*er*) *n.* (esp.) Apparatus for making coffee by allowing water to filter repeatedly through ground coffee.

per·cuss (p*er*kŭs') *v.t.* (med.) Tap gently with finger or instrument for purposes of diagnosis etc.

per·cus·sion (p*er*kŭsh'*o*n) *n.* Forcible striking of one (usu. solid) body against another; (med.) percussing; ~ **instrument**, (mus.) instrument played by percussion, esp. struck with a stick or the hand (drum, triangle, tambourine) or struck together in pairs (cymbals); ~ **cap**, small copper cap or cylinder in firearm, containing explosive powder and exploded by percussion of a hammer. **per·cus·sive** (p*er*kŭs'ĭv) *adj.*

per di·em (p*er* dē'em, dīem). (So much) by the day. [L]

per·di·tion (p*er*dĭsh'*o*n) *n.* Eternal death, damnation.

per·dur·a·ble (p*er*door'*a*bel, -dūr'-) *adj.* Permanent; eternal; durable. **per·dur·a·bil'i·ty** *n.* **per·dur'a·bly** *adv.*

per·e·gri·nate (pĕr'*e*grin*ā*t) *v.i.* (**-nat·ed, -nat·ing**). (joc.) Travel, journey. **per·e·gri·na'tion, per'e·gri·na·tor** *ns.*

per·e·grine (pĕr'*e*grĭn, -grēn, -grīn) *n.* (also ~ **falcon**) Species of falcon (*Falco peregrinus*) esteemed for hawking (so called because the young were not taken from the nests but caught on their passages from their breeding places).

per·emp·to·ry (p*e*rĕmp't*o*rē) *adj.* 1. Decisive, final; esp. (law) ~ **edict**, one in which the command is absolute; ~ **writ**, enforcing defendant's appearance without option. 2. (of statement or command) Admitting no denial or refusal; absolutely fixed, essential; (of person etc.) dogmatic, imperious, dictatorial. **per·emp'to·ri·ly** *adv.* **per·emp'to·ri·ness** *n.*

per·en·ni·al (p*e*rĕn'ē*a*l) *adj.* Lasting through the year; (of stream) flowing through all seasons of the year; lasting long or forever; (of plant) living several years (cf. ANNUAL). **per·en'ni·al·ly** *adv.* **perennial** *n.* Perennial plant.

per·fect (pẽr'fĭkt) *adj.* 1. Complete, not deficient; faultless; (of lesson) thoroughly learned; thoroughly trained or skilled (*in*); exact, precise; entire, unqualified. 2. (gram., of tense) Denoting completed event or action viewed in relation to the present; **future** ~, expressing action completed at the time indicated. 3. (bot.) Having all 4 whorls of the flower; (mus., of interval) not augmented or diminished, in normal form; ~ **cadence**, one consisting of direct chord of tonic preceded by dominant or subdominant chord. **per'fect·ly** *adv.* **per'fect·ness** *n.* **perfect** *n.* Perfect tense. ~ (p*er*fĕkt') *v.t.* Complete, carry through; make perfect; improve. **per·fect·i·bil·i·ty** (p*er*fĕkt*i*bĭl'ĭtē) *n.*

per·fec·tion (p*er*fĕk'sh*o*n) *n.* Completion; making perfect; full development; faultlessness; perfect person or thing; highest pitch, extreme, perfect specimen or manifestation (*of*).

per·fec·tion·ist (p*er*fĕk'sh*o*nĭst) *n.* One who holds that perfection may be attained in religion, morals, politics, etc.; one who insists upon perfection; **P**~, member of the ONEIDA Community. **per·fec'-**

tion·ism *n.*

per·fec·to (pe*r*fĕk′tō) *n.* (pl. **-tos**). Large thick cigar tapering to point at both ends.

per·fi·dy (pe͞r′fĭdē) *n.* (pl. **-dies**). Breach of faith, treachery. **per·fid·i·ous** (pe*r*fĭd′ēus) *adj.* **per·fid′i·ous·ly** *adv.* **per·fid′i·ous·ness** *n.*

per·fo·rate (pe͞r′forāt) *v.* (**-rat·ed, -rat·ing**). Make hole(s) through, pierce; esp. make rows of holes in (sheet) to separate stamps, coupons, etc.; make an opening into; pass, extend, through; penetrate (*into, through*, etc.). **per·fo·ra′tion** *n.*

per·force (pe*r*fōrs′, -fōrs′) *adv.* Of necessity.

per·form (pe*r*fōrm′) *v.* Carry into effect (command, promise, task, etc.); be agent of; go through, execute (public function, play, piece of music, etc.); act in play, sing, etc.; (of trained animals) execute feats or tricks, esp. at public show. **per·form′er** *n.* **per·form′ing** *adj.*

per·for·mance (pe*r*fōr′mans) *n.* Execution (*of* command etc.); carrying out, doing; notable feat; performing of play, public exhibition.

per·fume (pe͞r′fūm, pe*r*fūm′) *n.* Sweet smell; smell; fluid containing essence of flowers etc., scent. **per′fume·less** *adj.* **perfume** (pe*r*fūm′, pe͞r′fūm) *v.t.* (**-fumed, -fum·ing**). Impart sweet scent to, impregnate with sweet smell (esp. in past part.).

per·fum·er (pe*r*fū′me*r*) *n.* Maker, seller, of purfumes. **per·fum′er·y** *n.* (pl. **-er·ies**).

per·func·to·ry (pe*r*fŭngk′torē) *adj.* Done merely for sake of getting through a duty, acting thus, superficial, mechanical. **per·func′to·ri·ly** *adv.* **per·func′to·ri·ness** *n.*

per·go·la (pe͞r′gol*a*) *n.* Arbor, covered walk, formed of growing plants trained over trellis.

per·haps (pe*r*hăps′) *adv.* It may be, possibly.

peri- *prefix.* Around, about.

per·i·anth (pĕr′ēănth) *n.* Outer part or envelope of flower, enclosing stamens and pistils; corolla and calyx, or either of these.

per·i·car·di·um (pĕr*i*kär′dē*u*m) *n.* (pl. **-di·a** pr. -dē*a*). Membranous sac enclosing heart. **per·i·car′di·al, per·i·car′di·ac** *adjs.*

per·i·carp (pĕr′*i*kärp) *n.* Wall of ripened ovary of plant.

per·i·chon·dri·um (pĕr*i*kŏn′drē*u*m) *n.* (pl. **-dri·a** pr. -drē*a*). Membrane enveloping cartilages (except at joints).

Per·i·cles (pĕr′*i*klēz) (*c*495–429 B.C.). Athenian statesman and military commander, under whose administration (460–429 B.C.) Athens reached the summit of her power. **Per·i·cle′an** *adj.*

per·i·cli·nal (pĕr*i*klī′n*a*l) *adj.* (geol.) Domelike.

per·i·cra·ni·um (pĕr*i*krā′nē*u*m) *n.* (pl. **-ni·a** pr. -nē*a*). Membrane enveloping skull; (joc.) skull, brain; intellect.

per·i·gee (pĕr′*i*jē) *n.* That point in planet's (esp. moon's) orbit at which it is nearest to Earth (opp. *apogee*). **per·i·ge′an, per·i·ge′al** *adjs.*

per·i·he·li·on (pĕr*i*hē′lē*o*n, -hēl′y*o*n) *n.* (pl. **-he·li·a** pr. -hē′lē*a*, -hēl′y*a*). That point in planet's orbit at which it is nearest sun (opp. *aphelion*).

per·il (pĕr′*i*l) *n.* Danger, risk. **per′il·ous** *adj.* **per′il·ous·ly** *adv.* **per′il·ous·ness** *n.*

pe·rim·e·ter (pe*r*ĭm′ĭte*r*) *n.* 1. Circumference, outline, of closed figure; length of this. **per·i·met·ric** (pĕr*i*mĕt′rĭk), **per·i·met′ri·cal** *adjs.*

per·i·ne·um (pĕr*i*nē′*u*m) *n.* (pl. **-ne·a** pr. -nē′*a*). (anat.) Lower end of trunk with its contents, extending from coccyx or tail bone to pubic symphysis. **per·i·ne′al** *adj.*

pe·ri·od (pe͞r′ē*o*d) *n.* 1. Length of time marked by recurrence of astronomical coincidences; time of planet's revolution; time during which disease runs its course; menses. 2. Indefinite portion of history, life, etc.; any portion of time; (attrib., esp. of furniture, architecture, etc.) of, characteristic of, a particular (past) period. 3. Full

***Performances** of plays, such as this performance of Shakespeare's* Othello, *have been seen by millions of people over more than 400 years, testimony to the love mankind has for being on the stage and seeing others there.*

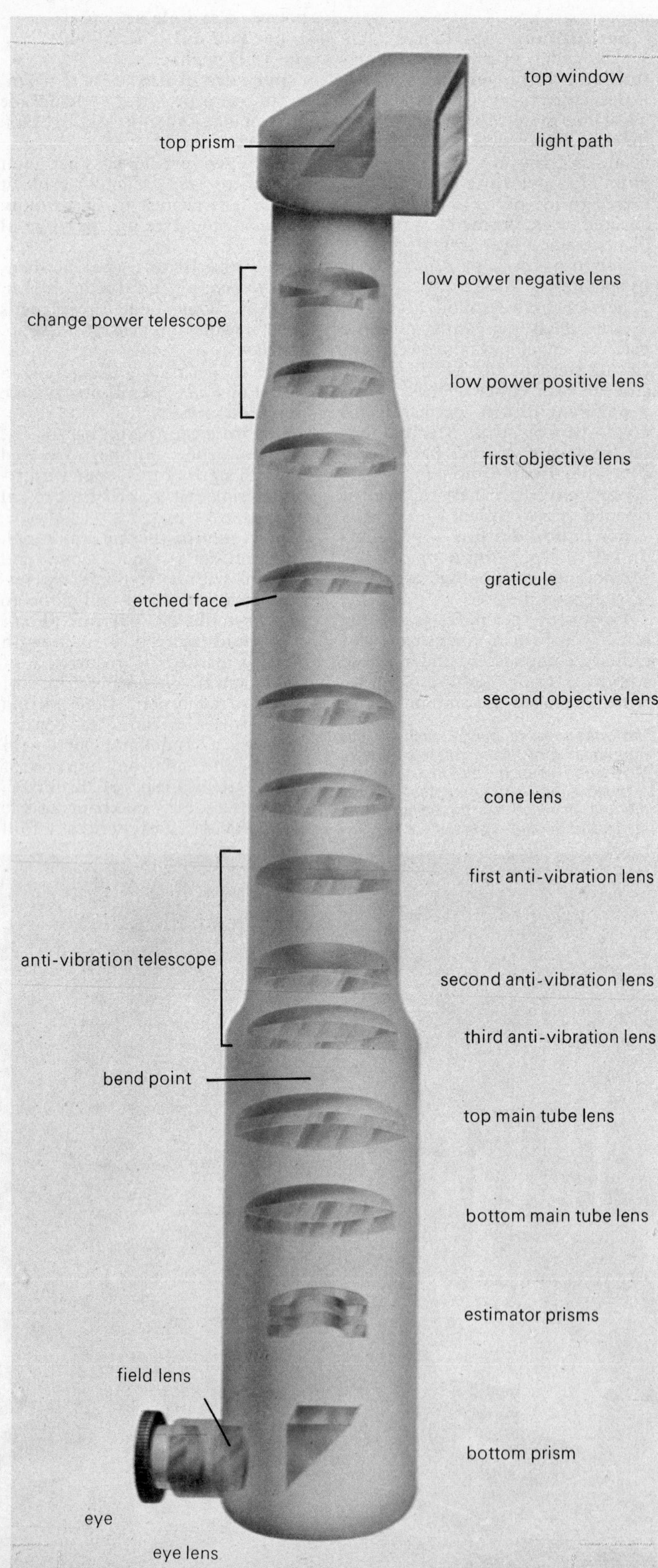

*Known since at least the 17th century, the **periscope** has proved much more than a simple optical device for looking round corners. Since the 19th century it has helped artillerymen and submariners find their targets.*

pause at end of sentence, point or character (.) marking this; **put a ~ to**, bring to an end.

pe·ri·od·ic (pērēŏd′ĭk) *adj.* 1. Of revolution of heavenly body (~ **motion**); recurring at (regular) intervals. 2. Expressed in (rhetorical) periods. 3. (chem.) ~ **law**, statement of fact that properties of chemical elements are periodic functions of their atomic weights, i.e. that when they are arranged in order of those weights, elements having similar chemical and physical properties occur at regular intervals; ~ **table**, table of chemical elements illustrating this law. **pe·ri·o·dic·i·ty** (pērē*o*dĭs′ĭtē) *n.*

pe·ri·od·i·cal (pērēŏd′ĭk*a*l) *adj.* = PERIODIC, 1; (of magazine, miscellany, etc.) published at regular intervals, e.g. monthly. **pe·ri·od′i·cal·ly** *adv.* **periodical** *n.* Periodical magazine etc.

per·i·o·don·tal (pĕrēōdŏn′t*a*l) *adj.* Of the tissues surrounding the teeth.

per·i·os·te·um (pĕrēŏs′tē*u*m) *n.* (pl. **-te·a** pr. -tē*a*). Dense fibrovascular membrane enveloping bones (except where they are covered by cartilage), from inner layer of which bone substance is produced. **per·i·os′te·al** *adj.*

per·i·pa·tet·ic (pĕrĭp*a*tĕt′ĭk) *adj.* 1. P~, of the school of Aristotle, Aristotelian (from Aristotle's custom of teaching while walking in the Lyceum at Athens). 2. Walking from place to place on one's business, itinerant. **per·i·pa·tet′i·cal·ly** *adv.* **peripatetic** *n.*

pe·riph·er·y (p*e*rĭf′*e*rē) *n.* (pl. **-er·ies**). Bounding line esp. of closed curvilinear figure; external boundary or surface. **pe·riph·er·al** (p*e*rĭf′*e*r*a*l) *adj.* (esp.) Of the periphery, of minor importance; applied to equipment used in conjunction with a computer without being an integral part of it, and to operations involving such equipment. **pe·riph′er·al·ly** *adv.* **peripheral** *n.* Peripheral device.

pe·riph·ra·sis (p*e*rĭf′r*a*sĭs) *n.* (pl. **-ses** pr. -sēz). Roundabout way of speaking, circumlocution; roundabout phrase. **per·i·phras·tic** (pĕrĭfrăs′tĭk) *adj.* **per·i·phras′ti·cal·ly** *adv.*

pe·rique (p*e*rēk′) *n.* Kind of dark strong-flavored Louisiana tobacco.

per·i·scope (pĕr′ĭskōp) *n.* Apparatus of tube and mirrors giving view of things above surface to observer in submarine or trench, or enabling person to see over the heads of others in a crowd. **per·i-**

scop·ic (pĕrĭskŏp´ĭk), **per·i·scop´-i·cal** *adjs.* Enabling one to see distinctly for some distance around axis of vision.

per·ish (pĕr´ĭsh) *v.* Suffer destruction, lose life, come to untimely end; (of cold or exposure) reduce to distress or inefficiency (usu. in pass.). **per´ish·ing** *adj.* **per´ish·ing·ly** *adv.*

per·ish·a·ble (pĕr´ĭsh*a*bel) *adj.* Liable to perish; subject to speedy decay. **per´ish·a·bles** *n.pl.* Things, esp. foodstuffs in transit, of this nature.

per·i·stal·sis (pĕrĭstawl´sĭs, -stăl´-) *n.* (pl. **-ses** pr. -sēz). (physiol.) Automatic muscular movement consisting of successive waves of contraction and relaxation, by which contents of alimentary canal etc. are propelled along it. **per·i·stal´tic** *adj.* **per·i·stal´ti·cal·ly** *adv.*

per·i·stome (pĕr´ĭstōm) *n.* 1. (bot.) Fringe of small teeth around mouth of capsule in mosses. 2. (zool.) Part around mouth in various invertebrates.

per·i·style (pĕr´ĭstīl) *n.* Row of columns surrounding temple, court, cloister, etc.; space so surrounded.

per·i·to·ne·um (pĕrĭt*o*nē´um) *n.* (pl. **-to·ne·ums, -to·ne·a** pr. -t*o*nē´*a*). (anat.) Double serous membrane lining cavity of abdomen, of complex form, with numerous folds investing and supporting abdominal viscera. **per·i·to·ne´al** *adj.* **per·i·to·ni·tis** (pĕrĭtonī´tĭs) *n.* Inflammation of (part of) peritoneum.

per·i·wig (pĕr´ĭwĭg) *n.* (archaic) Wig. [Fr. *perruque* peruke]

per·i·win·kle[1] (pĕr´ĭwĭngkel) *n.* Plant of genus *Vinca*, esp. the European **lesser** and **greater** ~ (*V. Minor, V. Major*), evergreen trailing shrubs with light blue starry flowers; (also ~ **blue**) color of these flowers.

per·i·win·kle[2] (pĕr´ĭwĭngkel) *n.* Gastropod mollusk (*Littorina*), esp. common European and N. Amer. coast species (*L. littorea*), with dark-colored turbinate shell, much used for food.

per·jure (pẽr´j*e*r) *v. refl.* (**-jured, -jur·ing**). Give false testimony under oath (~ **oneself**); **perjured**, guilty of perjury; involving perjury. **per´jur·er** *n.*

per·ju·ry (pẽr´j*e*rē) *n.* (pl. **-ries**). Swearing to statement known to be false; willful utterance of false evidence while under oath; breach of oath.

perk[1] (pẽrk) *n.* (Brit. slang) Perquisite.

perk[2] (pẽrk) *v.* Lift (*up*) one's head, carry oneself smartly or briskly; smarten *up*; hold *up* (head, tail) self-assertively. **perk´y** *adj.* (**perk·i·er, perk·i·est**). Self-assertive, saucy, pert. **perk´i·ly** *adv.* **perk´i·ness** *n.*

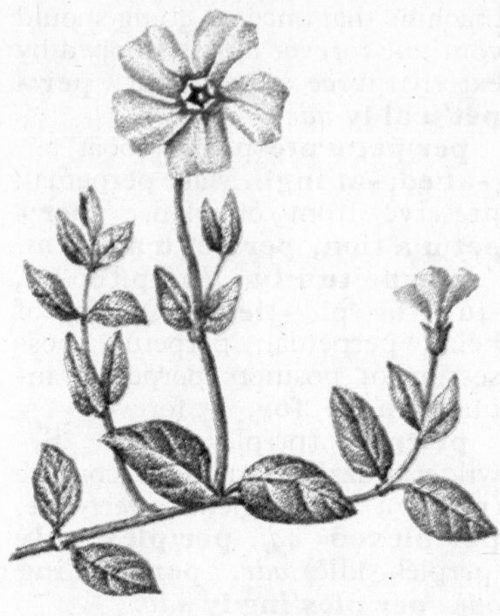

*The **periwinkle,** a wild flower native to Europe, North Africa and western Asia, is an evergreen whose pale-blue star-shaped flowers appear in spring. There are five species.*

perk[3] (pẽrk) *v.* (colloq.) Percolate (coffee).

per·lite (pẽr´līt) *n.* Obsidian or other vitreous rock with concentric structure, expansible by heating.

per·ma·frost (pẽr´m*a*frawst, -frŏst) *n.* Permanently frozen subsoil etc. in Arctic regions. [f. *perma(nent) frost*]

perm·al·loy (pẽrmăl´oi, pẽr´-m*a*loi) *n.* Nickel steel alloy, containing about 78% nickel, characterized by a very high permeability in low magnetic fields. [f. *perm(eable) alloy*]

per·ma·nent (pẽr´m*a*n*e*nt) *adj.* Lasting, intended to last, indefinitely; ~ **magnet**, one whose property continues after the magnetizing agent has been removed; ~ **press**, (of fabric) requiring little or no ironing after being washed; ~ **wave**, artificial wave in hair that lasts until hair grows out. **per´ma·nent·ly** *adv.*

*The **periwinkle** is common in Europe and North America, inhabiting rocky shores and feeding on algae. It has been used as a food source for many centuries.*

per·ma·nence (pẽr´m*a*nens) *n.* Being permanent. **per´ma·nen·cy** *n.* Being permanent; permanent thing or arrangement.

per·man·ga·nate (permăng´-g*a*nāt) *n.* (chem.) Salt of permanganic acid; (also **potassium** ~, ~ **of potash**) crystalline substance ($KMnO_4$), dark purple when dissolved, used as a disinfectant, stain, etc. **per·man·gan·ic** (pẽr-măngăn´ĭk) *adj.* ~ **acid**, acid ($HMnO_4$) known only in solution and from its salts.

per·me·ate (pẽr´mēāt) *v.* (**-at·ed, -at·ing**). Penetrate, pervade, saturate; diffuse itself *through, among*, etc. **per·me·a·ble** (pẽr´mē*a*bel) *adj.* **per·me·a·bil´i·ty** *n.*

Per·mi·an (pẽr´mē*a*n) *adj.* & *n.* (geol.) (Of) the latest period or system of the Paleozoic. [f. *Perm*, former province of E. Russia]

per·mis·si·ble (permĭs´*i*bel) *adj.* Allowable. **per·mis·si·bil´i·ty** *n.*

per·mis·sion (permĭsh´on) *n.* Consent or liberty (*to* do).

per·mis·sive (permĭs´ĭv) *adj.* Giving permission; tolerant of behavior that some might condemn. **per·mis´sive·ly** *adv.* **per·mis´-sive·ness** *n.*

per·mit (permĭt´) *v.* (**-mit·ted, -mit·ting**). Give consent or opportunity; admit *of*. ~ (pẽr´mĭt, permĭt´) *n.* Written order giving permission esp. for landing or removal of dutiable goods, entry into a place, etc.

per·mu·ta·tion (pẽrmy*u*tā´-shon) *n.* (math.) Variation of order of a set of things lineally arranged; each of different arrangement of which such a set is capable. **per·mu·tate** (pe͞r'myutāt) *v.t.* (**-tat·ed, -tat·ing**). Arrange in different order or combination.

per·mute (permūt') *v.t.* (**-mut·ed, -mut·ing**). Put in different order, change sequence of (things etc.).

Per·nam·bu·co (pĕrnahmbōō'-kō) = RECIFE.

per·ni·cious (pernĭsh'us) *adj.* Destructive, ruinous, fatal; ~ **anemia**, progressive and, unless checked, fatal form of anemia. **per·ni'cious·ly** *adv.* **per·ni'cious·ness** *n.*

per·nick·e·ty (pernĭk'ĭtē), **per·snick·et·y** (persnĭk'ĭtē) *adjs.* (colloq.) Fastidious; ticklish, requiring careful handling.

Pe·rón (pĕrōn'), **Juan Domingo** (1895–1974). Argentinean general; seized government and became dictator 1943; was elected president 1946, 1951; exiled, after a revolution, 1955; returned to Argentina in 1972; was elected president 1973. **Pe·ro·nis·ta** (pĕronĭs'ta) *n.* Supporter of Perón.

per·o·rate (pĕr'orāt) *v.i.* (**-rat·ed, -rat·ing**). Sum up and conclude speech; speak at length. **per·o·ra'tion** *n.*

per·ox·ide (perŏk'sīd) *n.* (chem.) Compound of oxygen and another element containing greatest possible proportion of oxygen; (also ~ **of hydrogen**) colorless liquid (H_2O_2) used in aqueous solution as oxidizing and bleaching agent and antiseptic, in pure state a concentrated source of oxygen. ~ *v.t.* (**-id·ed, -id·ing**). Bleach (esp. hair) with peroxide.

per·pen·dic·u·lar (pe͞rpendĭk'-yuler) *adj.* 1. At right angles to plane of horizon; (loosely) very steep; erect, upright; (joc.) in standing position. 2. (geom.) At right angles (*to* given line, plane, or surface). 3. **P** ~, (archit.) of the style of English Gothic architecture prevailing from the middle of the 14th c. to the middle of the 16th c., characterized by the vertical lines of its tracery. **per·pen·dic·u·lar·i·ty** (pe͞rpendĭkyulăr'ĭtē) *n.* **per·pen·dic'u·lar·ly** *adv.* **perpendicular** *n.* Plumb rule or other instrument for showing perpendicular line; perpendicular line; **the** ~, perpendicular line or direction.

per·pe·trate (pe͞r'pĭtrāt) *v.t.* (**-trat·ed, -trat·ing**). Perform, commit (crime, blunder, etc.). **per·pe·tra'tion, per'pe·tra·tor** *ns.*

per·pet·u·al (perpĕch'ōōal) *adj.* Eternal; permanent during life; applicable, valid, forever or for indefinite time; continuous; (colloq.) frequent, repeated; ~ **calendar**, that can be used for any year or over a long period of time; ~ **motion**, motion of hypothetical machine that once set going should continue forever unless stopped by external force or worn out. **per·pet'u·al·ly** *adv.*

per·pet·u·ate (perpĕch'ōōāt) *v.t.* (**-at·ed, -at·ing**). Make perpetual; preserve from oblivion. **per·pet·u·a'tion, per·pet'u·a·tor** *ns.*

per·pe·tu·i·ty (pe͞rpĭtōō'ĭtē, -tū'-) *n.* (pl. **-ties**). Quality of being perpetual; perpetual possession or position; perpetual annuity; **in, to, for,** ~, forever.

per·plex (perplĕks') *v.t.* Bewilder, puzzle; complicate, confuse (matter); entangle, intertwine. **per·plexed'** *adj.* **per·plex·ed·ly** (perplĕk'sĭdlē) *adv.* **per·plex'ing** *adj.* **per·plex'ing·ly** *adv.*

per·plex·i·ty (perplĕk'sĭtē) *n.* (pl. **-ties**). Bewilderment; cause of this; entangled state.

per·qui·site (pe͞r'kwĭzĭt) *n.* Customary gratuity; incidental income or privilege beyond customary salary.

Per·ry (pĕr'ē), **Matthew Calbraith** (1794–1858). Amer. naval officer; negotiated treaty opening commerce with Japan, 1853–4; his brother, **Oliver Hazard** ~ (1785–1819), an Amer. naval officer, commanded fleet on Lake Erie during the War of 1812, and announced the British defeat in the famous dispatch: "We have met the enemy and they are ours."

per se (per sā', sē'). By or in itself, intrinsically. [L.]

per·se·cute (pe͞r'sekūt) *v.t.* (**-cut·ed, -cut·ing**). Pursue with enmity and injury (esp. holder of opinion held to be heretical); harass, worry; importune (*with* questions etc.). **per·se·cu'tion** *n.* **delusions of** ~, insane delusions that one is persecuted. **per'se·cu·tive** *adj.* **per'se·cu·tor** *n.*

Juan Domingo Perón made economic and diplomatic reforms but his rule was marred by graft and civil oppression. His wife, Eva, supported him with her vast popular following.

Per·se·id (pe͞r'sēĭd) *n.* (astron.) One of a group of shooting stars appearing yearly near beginning of August and radiating from a point near the constellation Perseus.

Per·seph·o·ne (persĕf'onē). (Gk. myth.) Daughter of Zeus and DEMETER; called by the Romans Proserpina; goddess of spring; while gathering flowers she was carried off by Pluto and made queen of Hell; Demeter persuaded Zeus to let her return to earth for some months of each year.

Per·sep·o·lis (persĕp'olĭs). Ancient capital of Persian Empire, now in S. Iran.

Per·se·us (pe͞r'seus, -sōōs). 1. (Gk. myth.) Hero, son of Zeus and DANAË; cut off the head of the gorgon MEDUSA, and gave it to Athena; saved ANDROMEDA from a sea monster, married her, and founded the city of Mycenae. 2. (astron.) Northern constellation between Cassiopeia and Taurus.

per·se·ver·ance (pe͞rseve͞r'ans) *n.* Steadfast pursuit of an aim, constant persistence; (theol.) continuance in state of grace. **per·se·ver'ant** *adj.*

per·se·vere (pe͞rseve͞r') *v.i.* (**-vered, -ver·ing**). Continue steadfastly, persist (*in, with*). **per·se·ver'ing** *adj.* **per·se·ver'ing·ly** *adv.*

Per·sia (pe͞r'zha, -sha). Ancient and (now) alternative name of IRAN.

Per·sian (pe͞r'zhan, -shan) *adj.* Of Persia or its language or people; ~ **blinds**, PERSIENNES; ~ **cat**, cat of domesticated breed, with long silky hair, bushy tail, and round head; ~ **carpet, rug**, carpet or rug made in Persia, usu. oblong, of very fine skillful weave, of silk or wool pile and traditional, freq. geometrical, patterns; ~ **Empire**, empire formed (6th c. B.C.) by conquest of Media, Lydia, and Babylonia under Cyrus, including at its greatest all western Asia, Egypt, and parts of eastern Europe, and overthrown by Alexander the Great, 331 B.C.; ~ **Gulf**, landlocked sea extending in southeasterly direction from confluence of Euphrates and Tigris and communicating with Arabian Sea through Strait of Hormuz and Gulf of Oman; ~ **knot**, kind of knot used in carpet making; ~ **lamb**, caracul; ~ **Wars**, wars in which Darius and Xerxes vainly attempted to conquer Greece (499–449 B.C., but the defeat of Xerxes at SALAMIS, 479, decided the issue). **Persian** *n.* 1. Native, inhabitant, of Persia. 2. Indo-European Iranian language; **Middle** ~, Pahlavi; **Old** ~, ancient W. Iranian language,

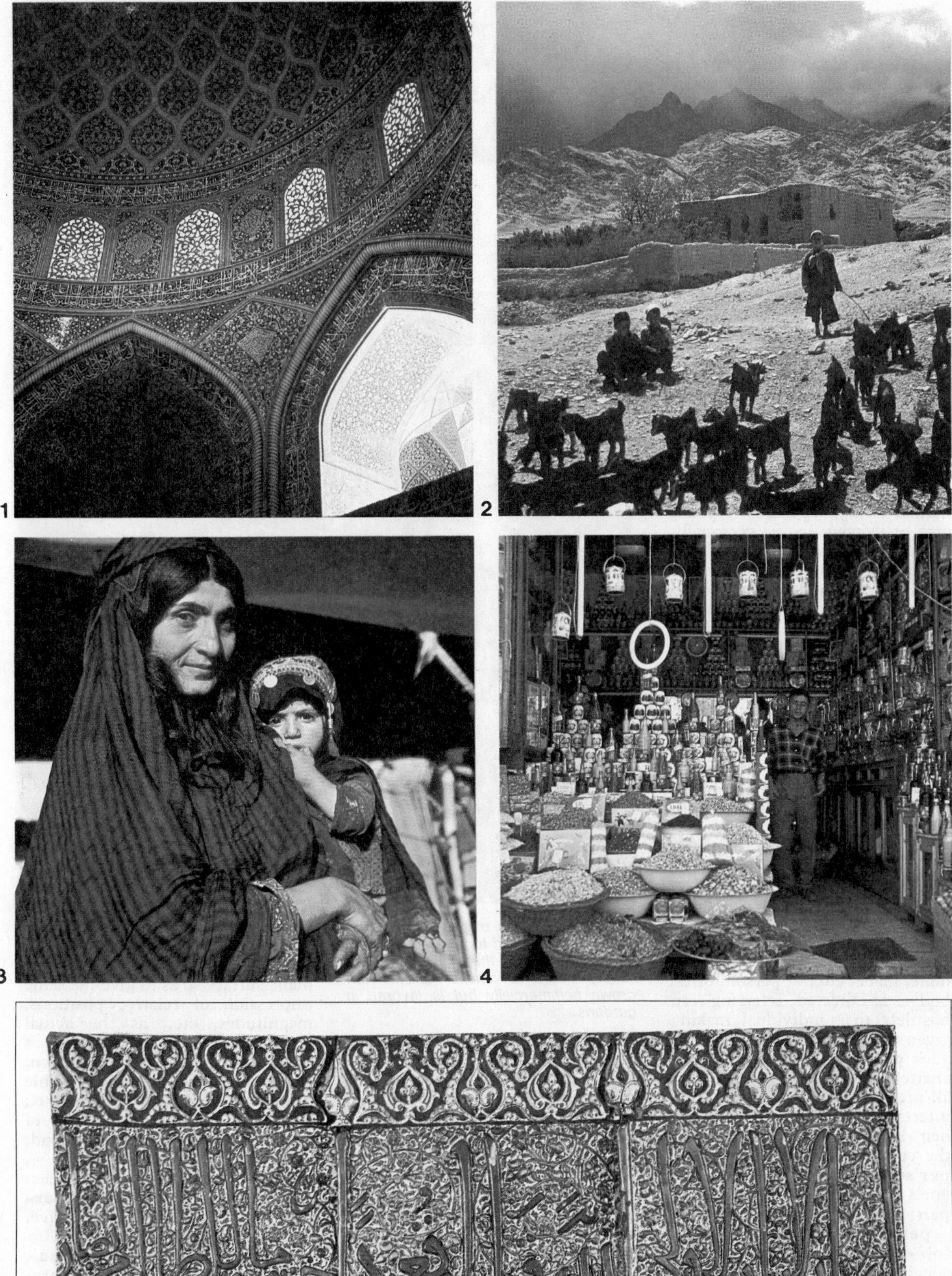

In Iran, despite the country's recent moves towards modernization, there is still a wealth of traditional **Persian** art and activities. 1. Intricate mosaics completely cover the inside of the dome of Sheikh Lutfullah's mosque built in 1617. 2. In the arid mountains, children tend flocks of goats. 3. In the same area women continue to dress in garments similar to those worn for hundreds of years. 4. Even the open-fronted shops, with their fluorescent lights, contain a mixture of new and traditional foods. 5. Early 13th-century wall-tiles from a mosque at Meshhed.

known from cuneiform inscriptions. 3. Persian cat.

per·si·ennes (pĕrzēĕnz′) *n.pl.* Outside window blinds of light horizontal laths; Persian blinds.

per·si·flage (pĕr′*si*flahzh) *n.* Light raillery, banter.

per·sim·mon (*per*sĭm′*on*) *n.* Yellowish-orange plumlike astringent fruit, becoming sweet when softened by frost, of the Amer. tree *Diospyros virginiana*; large red fruit of Chinese and Japanese species (*D. kaki*).

per·sist (*per*sĭst′, -zĭst′) *v.i.* Continue firmly or obstinately (*in* opinion, course, etc.) esp. against remonstrance etc. **per·sist′ence, per·sist′en·cy** *ns.* **per·sist′ent** *adj.* (esp., of horns, hair, leaves, etc.) Remaining after such parts normally wither or fall off. **per·sist′ent·ly** *adv.*

per·snick·et·y = PERNICKETY.

per·son (pĕr′*son*) *n.* 1. Individual human being; living body of human being; **young** ~, young man or woman; **in** ~, personally, oneself. 2. (gram.) Each of 3 classes of personal pronouns, and corresponding distinctions in verbs, indicating the person(s) speaking (**first** ~), spoken to (**second** ~), and spoken of (**third** ~).

per·so·na (*per*sō′*na*) *n.* (pl. **-nae** pr. -nē). (Jungian psychol.) Outer aspect of personality as revealed to other persons.

per·son·a·ble (pĕr′*sonabel*) *adj.* Handsome, comely.

per·son·age (pĕr′*son*ĭj) *n.* Person of rank or importance; person; character in play etc.

per·so·na (non) gra·ta (*per*sō′*na* nōn grah′*ta*, -grăt′*a*, grā′*ta*) (pl. ***per·so·nae (non) gra·tae*** pr. *per*sō′nē nōn grah′tē, grăt′ē, grā′tē). (Un)acceptable person. [L.]

per·son·al (pĕr′*sonal*) *adj.* 1. One's own, individual, private; done, made, etc., in person; of the body. 2. Directed, referring (esp. hostilely) to an individual; making, given to making, personal remarks. 3. ~ **property**, **estate**, etc., (law) chattels or chattel interests in land, all property except land and those interests in land that pass to one's heir. 4. (gram.) Of, denoting, one of the 3 persons (esp. in ~ **pronoun**). **per′son·al·ly** *adv.* In person, in one's own person; for one's own part.

per·son·al·i·ty (pĕr*s*onal′ĭtē) *n.* (pl. **-ties**). 1. Being a person; personal existence or identity; distinctive personal character; person; ~ **cult**, extreme adulation of an individual person; **multiple** ~, (psych.) apparent existence of two or more distinct and alternating personalities in a single individual. 2. (of remarks) Fact of being personal; (usu. pl.) personal remarks.

per·son·al·ize (pĕr′*sonal*īz) *v.t.* (**-ized, -iz·ing**). Personify; mark with one's name etc. **per·son·al·i·za·tion** (pĕr*sonal*īzā′sh*on*) *n.*

*There are 2 types of **persimmon,** the Oriental, introduced to the U.S.A. in the 19th century, and the native American variety which is smaller and is not grown commercially but is favored in gardens.*

per·son·al·ty (pĕr′*sonal*tē) *n.* (pl. **-ties**). Personal property.

per·son·i·fi·ca·tion (*per*sŏn*ifi*kā′sh*on*) *n.* Personifying; person, thing, viewed as striking example or embodiment *of*.

per·son·i·fy (*per*sŏn′*if*ī) *v.t.* (**-fied, -fy·ing**). Attribute personal nature to (abstraction); symbolize (quality) by figure in human form; embody (quality) in one's own person, exemplify typically (esp. in past part.)

per·son·nel (pĕr*son*ĕl′) *n.* Body of persons employed in an organization, as distinct from the equipment; ~ **department, manager,** those concerned with appointment, advising, training, etc., of employees.

per·spec·tive (*per*spĕk′tĭv) *n.* Art of delineating solid objects on a plane surface so as to give the same impression of relative positions, magnitudes, etc., as the actual objects do when viewed from a particular point; picture so drawn; apparent relation between visible objects as to position, distance, etc.; (fig.) relation in which parts of subject are viewed by the mind; view, prospect (lit. and fig.); **in** ~, drawn according to rules of perspective; foreshortened. **perspective** *adj.* Of, in perspective. **per·spec′tive·ly** *adv.*

per·spi·ca·cious (pĕrsp*i*kā′sh*us*) *adj.* Having mental penetration or discernment. **per·spi·ca′cious·ly** *adv.* **per·spi·cac·i·ty** (pĕrsp*i*kăs′ĭtē) *n.*

per·spic·u·ous (*per*spĭk′ūus) *adj.* Easily understood, clearly expressed; (of person) clear in expression. **per·spic′u·ous·ly** *adv.* **per·spi·cu·i·ty** (pĕrsp*i*kū′ĭtē), **per·spic′u·ous·ness** *ns.*

1

2

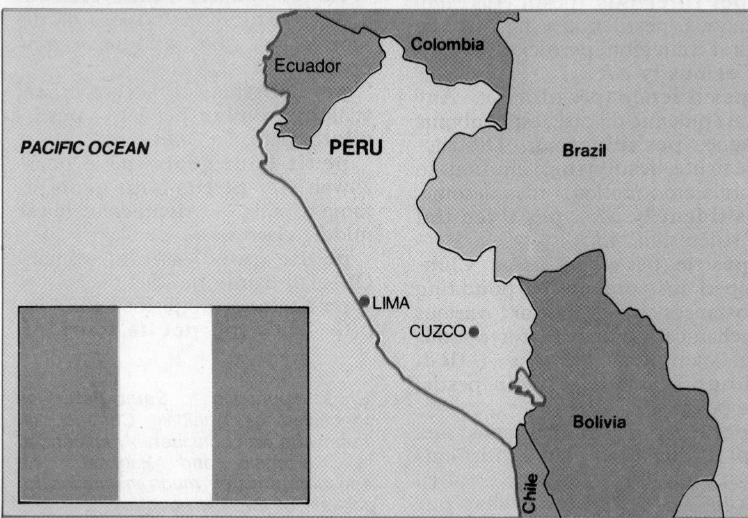

*The Incas of **Peru** were capable of incredible feats of engineering, such as these roads (1) snaking over the mountains to cities like Macchu Picchu (2), near Cuzco.*

per·spi·ra·tion (pẽrspirā′shon) *n.* Sweating; sweat. **per·spir·a·to·ry** (perspī′ratōrē, -tōrē) *adj.*

per·spire (perspīr′) *v.* (**-spired, -spir·ing**) Sweat.

per·suade (perswād′) *v.t.* (**-suad·ed, -suad·ing**). Cause (person, oneself) to have belief (*of, that*); induce (*to* do, *into* action); **persuaded**, convinced (*of, that*). **per·suad′a·ble, per·sua·si·ble** (perswā′sibel) *adjs.* **per·sua·si·bil′i·ty** *n.*

per·sua·sion (perswā′zhon) *n.* Persuading; persuasiveness; conviction; religious belief, sect holding this.

per·sua·sive (perswā′sĭv) *adj.* Able to persuade, winning. **per·sua′sive·ly** *adv.* **per·sua′sive·ness** *n.*

pert (pẽrt) *adj.* Forward, saucy, in speech or conduct; lively, sprightly, cheerful. **pert′ly** *adv.* **pert′ness** *n.*

per·tain (pertān′) *v.i.* Belong as part, appendage, or accessory, *to*; be appropriate *to*; have reference, relate, *to*.

per·ti·na·cious (pẽrtinā′shus) *adj.* Stubborn, persistent, obstinate. **per·ti·na′cious·ly** *adv.* **per·ti·nac·i·ty** (pẽrtinăs′ĭtē), **per·ti·na′cious·ness** *ns.*

per·ti·nent (pẽr′tinent) *adj.* Pertaining, relevant, apposite, (*to* matter in hand etc.); to the point. **per′ti·nent·ly** *adv.* **per′ti·nence, per′ti·nen·cy** *ns.*

per·turb (pertẽrb′) *v.t.* Upset, disquiet, throw into agitation. **per·tur·ba·tion** (pẽrterbā′shon) *n.*

Pe·ru (peroo′). Republic of Pacific coast of S. Amer.; inhabited during the Middle Ages by the Incas (see INCA); won independence from Spain 1821; capital, Lima; ~ **Current**: see HUMBOLDT CURRENT.

pe·ruke (perook′) *n.* Wig, esp. kind worn in 17th–18th c.

pe·ruse (perooz′) *v.* (**-rused, -rus·ing**). Read thoroughly or carefully; read; examine carefully. **pe·rus·al** (peroo′zal) *n.*

Pe·ru·vi·an (peroo′vēan) *adj.* Of Peru or its people; ~ **bark**, cinchona bark. **Peruvian** *n.* Native, inhabitant, of Peru. [*Peruvia*, Latinized name of PERU]

per·vade (pervād′) *v.t.* (**-vad·ed, -vad·ing**). Spread through, permeate, saturate. **per·va·sion** (pervā′zhon) *n.* **per·va·sive** (pervā′sĭv) *adj.* **per·va′sive·ly** *adv.* **per·va′sive·ness** *n.*

per·verse (pervẽrs′) *adj.* Persistent in error; different from what is reasonable or required; wayward; peevish; perverted, wicked; (of ver-

*Spraying vineyards in France with **pesticide.** Excessive use of such chemicals has also killed natural predators of pest species and results in the need for still more spraying.*

dict) against weight of evidence or judge's direction. **per·verse′ly** *adv.* **per·verse′ness, per·ver·si·ty** (pervēr′sĭtē) *ns.*

per·vert (pervērt′) *v.t.* Turn aside (thing) from its proper use; misconstrue, misapply (words etc.); lead astray (person, mind) from right opinion or conduct, or esp. religious belief. **per·ver·sion** (pervēr′zhon, -shon) *n.* **per·ver·sive** (pervēr′sĭv) *adj.* **pervert** (pēr′vert) *n.* Perverted person; person showing perversion of sexual instincts.

per·vi·ous (pēr′vēus) *adj.* Affording passage (*to*); permeable; (fig.) accessible (*to* reason etc.). **per′vi·ous·ly** *adv.* **per′vi·ous·ness** *n.*

Pe·sach (pā′sahx) = PASSOVER.

Pes·ca·do·res (pĕskadōr′ĭs, -ēz). Group of islands of China in Formosa Strait between China to the W. and Taiwan to the E.

pes·ky (pĕs′kē) *adj.* (**pes·ki·er, pes·ki·est**). (colloq.) Troublesome, confounded, annoying.

pe·so (pā′sō) *n.* (pl. **-sos**). Principal monetary unit in Argentina, Bolivia, Colombia, Cuba, Dominican Republic, Mexico, Philippines, and Uruguay.

pes·sa·ry (pĕs′arē) *n.* (pl. **-ries**). Instrument, medicated plug, inserted into or worn in vagina to prevent uterine displacements or as contraceptive.

pes·si·mism (pĕs′imĭzem) *n.* Tendency to look at the worst aspect of things; doctrine that this world is the worst possible, or that all things tend to evil. **pes′si·mist** *n.* **pes·si·mis′tic** *adj.* **pes·si·mis′ti·cal·ly** *adv.*

pest (pĕst) *n.* Troublesome or destructive person, animal, or thing; (obs.) pestilence.

Pes·ta·loz·zi (pĕstalŏt′sē), **Johann Heinrich** (1746–1827). Swiss educator; influenced methods of teaching in elementary schools in Amer. and Europe, with an emphasis on primacy of child's sensory experience and use of objects.

pes·ter (pĕs′ter) *v.t.* Trouble, plague. **pes′ter·er** *n.*

pes·ti·cide (pĕs′tĭsīd) *n.* Substance for destroying pests, esp. insects.

pes·tif·er·ous (pĕstĭf′erus) *adj.* Noxious, pestilential; (fig.) having moral contagion, pernicious. **pes·tif′er·ous·ly** *adv.*

pes·ti·lence (pĕs′tilens) *n.* Any fatal epidemic disease, esp. bubonic plague. **pes′ti·lent** *adj.* Destructive to life, deadly; (fig.) injurious to morals etc.; (colloq.) troublesome. **pes′ti·lent·ly** *adv.* **pes·ti·len·tial** (pĕstilĕn′shal) *adj.*

pes·tle (pĕs′el, pĕs′tel) *n.* Club-shaped instrument for pounding substances in a mortar; various mechanical appliances for pounding, stamping, etc. ~ *v.* (**-tled, -tling**). Pound (as) with pestle; use pestle.

pet[1] (pĕt) *n.* Animal tamed and kept as favorite or treated with fondness; darling, favorite (often attrib.); ~ **aversion**, what one specially dislikes; ~ **name**, one expressing fondness or familiarity. **pet** *v.* (**pet·ted, pet·ting**). Treat as a pet, fondle, caress; indulge in hugging, kissing, and fondling.

pet[2] (pĕt) *n.* Offense at being slighted, ill humor.

Pet. *abbrev.* Peter (New Testament).

pet·al (pĕt′al) *n.* Each of the divisions of the corolla of a flower, esp. when separate. **pet·a·loid** (pĕt′aloid) *adj.*

pe·tard (pĭtārd′) *n.* Small engine of war, orig. of metal, later wooden box charged with powder, formerly used to blow in door etc.; kind of firework; **hoist with one's own** ~: see HOIST[2].

pet·cock (pĕt′kŏk) *n.* (also **pet′ cock**) Small valve for draining, letting out steam, etc.

pe·ter (pē′ter) *v.i.* (orig. mining colloq.) ~ **out**, give out, come to an end.

Pe·ter[1] (pē′ter). Name of three tsars of Russia: **Peter I** (1672–1725), "the Great," reigned 1682–1725; founded St. Petersburg (Leningrad); introduced many elements of Western civilization into Russia; **Peter II** (1715–30), grandson of Peter I, reigned 1727–30; **Peter III** (1728–62), maternal grandson of Peter I, reigned 1761–1762; murdered prob. by orders of his wife, CATHERINE[1] the Great.

Pe·ter[2] (pē′ter), **St.** (d. *c*67). Apostle, orig. called Simon; most prominent of the disciples during the ministry of Jesus and in the early Church; martyred, probably in Rome; in R.C. tradition, founder and 1st bishop of Church of Rome: in popular belief, keeper of the door of heaven; commemorated with St. Paul, June 29; (**Epistle of St.**) ~, either of the 2 epistles of New Testament ascribed to him; **rob** ~ **to pay Paul**, take away from one person, cause, etc., to pay, give, etc., to another. [Gk. *petros* rock]

Pe·ter (pē′ter) **Pan.** Hero of J. M. Barrie's play (1904) of the same name, a boy who never grew up.

pet·i·ole (pĕt′ēōl) *n.* (bot.) Leaf stalk. **pet·i·o·lar** (pĕt′ēoler), **pet·i·o·late** (pĕt′ēolāt) *adjs.*

pe·tit bour·geois (pĕt′ē boorzhwah′) (pl. **pe·tits bour·geois** pr. same as sing.). Member of lower middle classes.

pe·tite (petēt′) *adj.* (of woman) Of small dainty build.

pe·tit four (pĕt′ē fōr′, fōr′; *Fr.* petē′ foor′) (pl. **pet·its fours** pr.

*'Christ Appearing to **Saint Peter**' as conceived by Annibale Carracci, an Italian who was considerably influenced by Correggio and Raphael. The Apostles provided much inspiration for painters of the 16th century.*

***Petrified** trees in Petrified Forest National Park in Arizona. The wood has gradually been replaced by minerals and become fossilized. In some cases it is still possible to detect the original cell structure which has been preserved in the minerals.*

*Wherever there is salt water, one or more members of the extensive **petrel** family will be found like the Giant Petrel of Antarctica (above).*

pĕt'ē fōrz', fōrz; Fr. petē foor'). Very small fancy cake. [Fr.]

pe·ti·tion (petĭsh'on) *n.* Asking, supplication, request; formal written supplication, request; (law) kind of formal written application to a court. ~ *v.* Make petition to (sovereign etc. *for, to*); ask humbly (*for, to*). **pe·ti'tion·ar·y** *adj.* **pe·ti'tion·er** *n.* (esp.) Plaintiff in divorce suit.

pe·tit lar·ce·ny (pĕ'tē lar'senē) = PETTY larceny.

pe·tit mal (petē' măl', pĕt'ē). Mild form of epilepsy (opp. GRAND MAL). [Fr.]

pe·tit (pĕt'ē) **point.** Embroidery on canvas using small stitches.

Pe·trarch (pē'trark, pĕt'rark). Francesco Petrarca (1304–74), Italian poet and humanist; famous for his odes and sonnets to "Laura." **Pe·trar·chan** (pĭtrar'-kan) *adj.* ~ **sonnet**: see SONNET.

pet·rel (pĕt'rel) *n.* Any of various seabirds of the order Procellariiformes (which also includes the shearwaters and albatrosses); **stormy** ~, small bird (*Hydrobates pelagicus*) with black and white plumage.

pe·tri (pē'trē) **dish.** Shallow covered dish used for culture of microorganisms etc. [J. R. *Petri* (d. 1921), German bacteriologist]

pet·ri·fac·tion (pĕtrifăk'shon), **pet·ri·fi·ca·tion** (pĕtrifikā'shon) *ns.* Petrifying; petrified substance or mass.

Petrified (pĕt'rifīd) **Forest National Park.** Area in E. Arizona covering 93,493 acres (37,837 hectares) and containing many petrified trees.

pet·ri·fy (pĕt'rifī) *v.* (**-fied, -fy·ing**). Convert into stone or stony substance, be so converted (esp. of dead organism becoming fossilized); (fig.) paralyze, stupefy, with astonishment, terror, etc.; deprive (mind etc.) of vitality, stiffen.

Pe·trine (pē'trīn) *adj.* Of St. PETER².

petro- *prefix.* Rock.

pet·ro·chem·i·cal (pĕtrōkĕm'-ĭkal) *n.* Substance obtained from petroleum or natural gas. ~ *adj.* Of petrochemicals or petrochemistry.

pe·tro·chem·is·try (pĕtrōkĕm'-ĭstrē) *n.* Chemistry of rocks or of petroleum.

pet·ro·glyph (pĕt'roglĭf) *n.* Rock carving (usu. prehistoric). **pet·ro·glyph'ic** *adj.*

Pet·ro·grad (pĕt'rogrăd). Name of St. Petersburg from 1917 to 1924, when it was renamed LENINGRAD.

pe·trog·ra·phy (pĭtrŏg'rafē) *n.* Scientific description of formation and composition of rocks. **pe·trog'ra·pher** *n.* **pe·tro·graph·ic** (pĕtrografĭk), **pe·tro·graph'i·cal** *adjs.*

pe·tro·le·um (petrō'lēum) *n.* Crude oil; inflammable mineral oil, varying from light yellow to dark brown or black, found in many places in the upper strata of Earth, containing large numbers of different hydrocarbons and refined for use as fuel for heating and in internal combustion engines, as illuminant, as dry-cleaning agent, etc.; ~ **jelly,** translucent gelatinous hydrocarbon mixture derived from petroleum and used in ointments etc. [L. and Gk. *petra* rock, L. *oleum* oil]

pe·trol·o·gy (pĭtrŏl'ojē) *n.* Study of origin, structure, etc., of rocks. **pet·ro·log·ic** (pĕtrolŏj'ĭk), **pet·ro·log'i·cal** *adjs.* **pet·ro·log'i·cal·ly** *adv.* **pe·trol'o·gist** *n.*

Pe·tro·ni·us Ar·bi·ter (pĭtrō'-nēus ar'bĭter), **Gaius** (d. 66 A.D.). Roman satirist, author of the *Satyricon*; arbiter of taste (*elegentiae arbiter*) at Nero's court; committed suicide to avoid being killed by Nero.

pet·rous (pĕt'rus) *adj.* Of, like, rock; esp. (anat.) applied to dense hard part of temporal bone forming protective case for internal ear.

pet·ti·coat (pĕt'ēkōt) *n.*

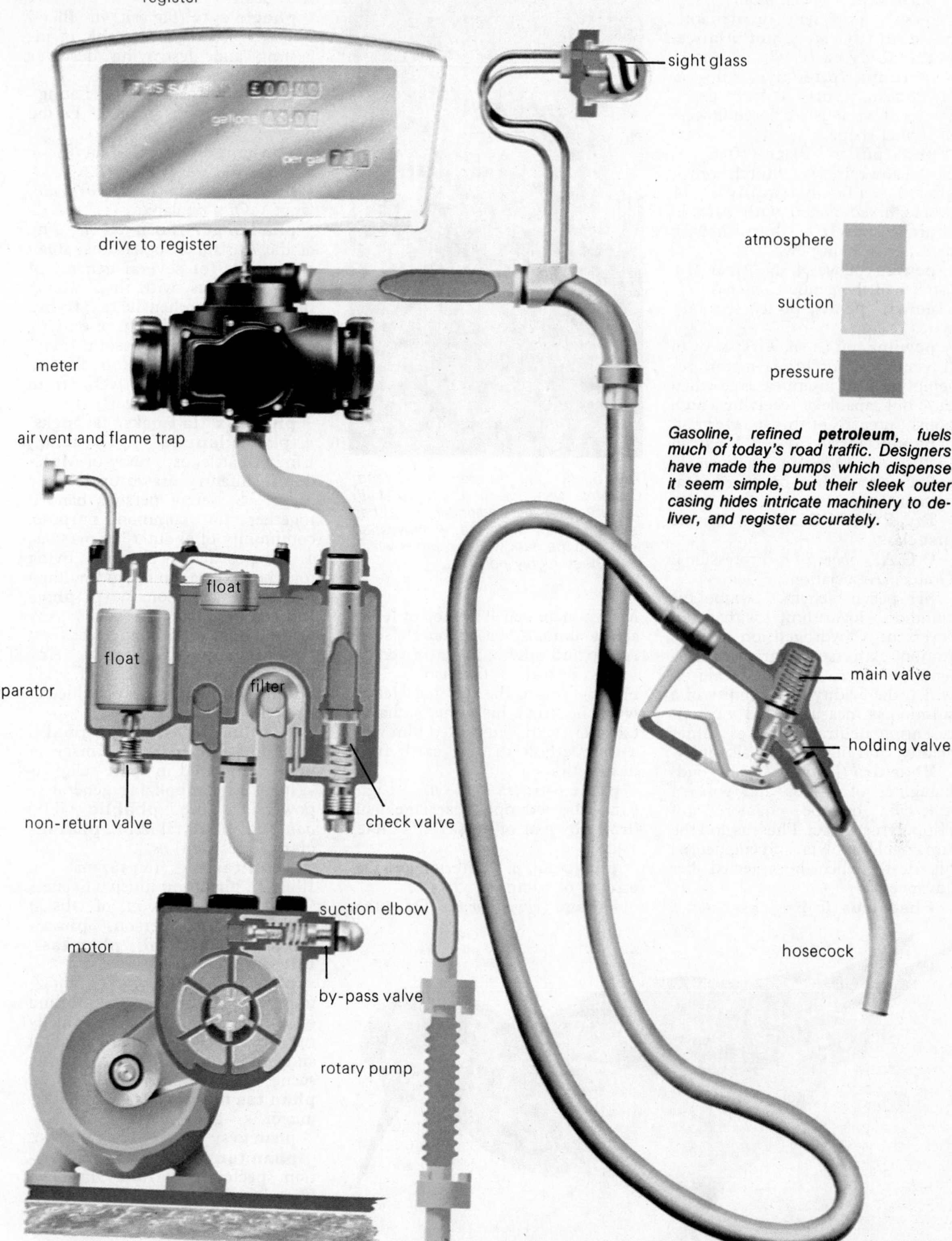

*Gasoline, refined **petroleum**, fuels much of today's road traffic. Designers have made the pumps which dispense it seem simple, but their sleek outer casing hides intricate machinery to deliver, and register accurately.*

Woman's undergarment hanging from waist or shoulders; ~ **government**, predominance of women in politics or organizational life.

pet·ti·fog (pĕt′ēfŏg, -fawg) *v.i.* (**-fogged, -fog·ging**). Practice legal chicanery; quibble, wrangle, about petty points. **pet′ti·fog·ger** *n.* Inferior legal practitioner; rascally attorney; petty practitioner in any department. **pet′ti·fog·ger·y** *n.* **pet′ti·fog·ging** *adj.*

pet·tish (pĕt′ĭsh) *adj.* Peevish, petulant, easily put out. **pet′tish·ly** *adv.* **pet′tish·ness** *n.*

pet·ty (pĕt′ē) *adj.* (**-ti·er, -ti·est**). Unimportant, trivial; small-minded; minor, inferior, on a small scale; ~ **cash**, small cash items of receipt or expenditure; ~ **larceny**, larceny involving goods whose value is below a certain amount (see GRAND larceny); ~ **officer**, officer in navy corresponding in rank to army N.C.O. **pet′ti·ly** *adv.* **pet′ti·ness** *n.*

pet·u·lant (pĕch′*u*l*a*nt) *adj.* Peevishly impatient or irritable. **pet′u·lant·ly** *adv.* **pet′u·lance, pet′u·lan·cy** *ns.*

pe·tu·nia (pet*ōō*′ny*a*, -tū′-) *n.* Herbaceous plant of S. Amer. genus *P*~, with variously colored flowers of funnel shape.

pew (pū) *n.* Place (often enclosed and raised) in church appropriated to a family (**family** ~) or others; fixed bench with back in church. **pew** *v.t.* Furnish with pews, enclose in pew.

pe·wee (pē′wē) *n.* N. Amer. flycatcher of the genus *Contopus.*

pe·wit (pē′wĭt, pū′ĭt): see LAPWING.

pew·ter (pū′t*er*) *n.* Gray alloy of tin and lead or other metal, resembling lead in appearance when dull, but capable of receiving a high polish; utensils of this; pewter pot.

pe·yo·te (pāō′tē) *n.* Mexican cactus (*Lophophora williamsii*); hallucinogenic drug produced from tops of this.

Pfc, Pfc., PFC. *abbrevs.* Private first class.

P.G.A. *abbrev.* Professional Golfers' Association.

pH (pēăch′) (chem.) Symbol for common logarithm, with sign reversed, of hydrogen ion concentration, expressed in gram equivalents per liter; ~ **scale**, scale on which the acidity or alkalinity of a solution is measured, pH 7.0 representing neutrality, lower values acidity, and higher ones alkalinity.

Phae·dra (fē′dr*a*). (Gr. legend) Daughter of Minos and wife of Theseus; became enamored of Hippolytus, son of Theseus and the Amazon Hippolyta, and engineered his death when he rejected her advances.

Phae·drus (fē′dr*u*s) (1st c. A.D.). Macedonian slave; author of fables about animals, based on those of Aesop and others, in Latin verse.

The Santa Ines Mission in Solvang, California was built in the early 19th century and its traditional style has been retained with the whitewashed walls and the dark wooden ***pews*** *which have been highly polished.*

Pha·ë·thon (fā′*e*th*o*n). (Gk. myth.) Son of the sun god Helios; when he drove his father's chariot too near earth Zeus killed him with a thunderbolt to save earth from destruction.

pha·e·ton (fā′ĭt*o*n) *n.* Light four-wheeled open carriage usu. drawn by pair of horses. [f. PHAETHON]

phage (fāj) *n.* (bacteriology) Destroyer of bacteria.

-phage (*comb. form*) (One) that eats, destroys.

phag·o·cyte (făg′*o*sīt) *n.* Blood cell, esp. leucocyte, capable of ingesting and destroying dead or foreign material.

-phagous (*comb. form*) Eating.

-phagy (*comb. form*) Eating of.

phal·ange (făl′*a*nj, f*a*lănj′) = PHALANX def. 3.

pha·lan·ge·al (f*a*lăn′jē*a*l) *adj.* (anat.) Of a phalanx.

pha·lan·ger (f*a*lăn′j*er*) *n.* Any of the Australian opossums, small marsupials (of several genera) of arboreal habits, with thick woolly fur and freq. prehensile tail; **flying** ~, one of those that have a flying membrane, flying opossum. [mod. L. invented by Buffon f. Gk. *phalanggion* spider's web, from webbed toes of hind feet]

pha·lanx (fā′lăngks, făl′ăngks) *n.* (pl. **pha·lanx·es**). 1. (Gk. antiq.) Line of battle, esp. body of Macedonian infantry drawn up in close order. 2. Set of persons banded together for common purpose; community of about 1800 persons, as proposed by Fourier, living together as one family and holding property in common. 3. (pl. **pha·lan·ges** pr. f*a*lăn′jēz) (anat.) Any of the bones of the fingers or toes.

phal·a·rope (făl′*a*rōp) *n.* Any of several related species of small wading and swimming bird allied to snipe.

phal·lus (făl′*u*s) *n.* (pl. **phal·li** pr. făl′ī, **phal·lus·es**). Image of penis, venerated in some religious systems as symbolizing generative power in nature. **phal·lic** (făl′ĭk) *adj.* **phal·lism** (făl′ĭz*e*m), **phal·li·cism** (făl′ĭsĭz*e*m) *ns.*

phan·tasm (făn′tăz*e*m) *n.* Illusion, phantom; illusive likeness (*of*); supposed vision of absent (living or dead) person. **phan·tas·mal** (făntăz′m*a*l), **phan·tas′·mic** *adjs.*

phan·tas·ma·go·ri·a (făntăzm*a*gōr′ē*a*, -gōr′-) *n.* Exhibition of optical illusions produced chiefly by means of magic lantern, first shown in London in 1802; shifting scene of real or imagined figures. **phan·tas·ma·gor·ic** (făntăzm*a*gōr′ĭk, -gŏr′-) *adj.*

phan·ta·sy (făn′t*a*sē, -zē): = FANTASY.

phan·tom (făn′t*o*m) *n.* Apparition, specter; image (*of*); vain show, form without substance or reality; mental illusion; (attrib.) apparent, illusive, imaginary.

Phar·aoh (fār′ō). Title of ruler of ancient Egypt. [Hebraized version of Egyptian title meaning "great house"]

The female red-necked ***Phalarope*** *(left) is much brighter than the male. The birds breed in Scandinavia and on the Baltic Coast, then fly south to warmer waters.*

*Left: Golden funeral mask of Tutankhamen, probably the best-known **Pharaoh** or king of Egypt. Pharaohs ruled from about 3,000 B.C. to 1,050 B.C. and were responsible for the building of the pyramids.*

Phar·i·see (făr´ĭsē) *n.* Member of Jewish sect of 1st c. B.C. to 1st c. A.D. distinguished by their strict observance of the traditional and written law, represented in New Testament as having pretensions to superior sanctity; hence, self-righteous person; formalist; hypocrite. **Phar·i·sa·ic** (fărĭsā´ĭk), **Phar·i·sa´i·cal** *adjs.* **Phar·i·sa·ism** (făr´ĭsāĭzem), **Phar·i·see·ism** (făr´ĭsēĭzem) *ns.*

phar·ma·ceu·ti·cal (fārmasōō´tĭkal) *adj.* Of, engaged in, pharmacy; of the use or sale of medicinal drugs. **phar·ma·ceu´ti·cal·ly** *adv.* **phar·ma·ceu´tics** *n.*

*The **pharmaceutical** industry has become a major worldwide commercial enterprise involving highly competitive marketing. Below: Interior of a typical Australian **pharmacy.** The pharmacist is responsible for dispensing prescribed drugs.*

phar·ma·cist (fār´masĭst) *n.* Pharmaceutical chemist; qualified person engaged in pharmacy.

phar·ma·col·o·gy (fārmakŏl´ojē) *n.* Science concerned with the nature and action of drugs. **phar·ma·co·log·i·cal** (fārmakolŏj´ĭkal) *adj.* **phar·ma·col´o·gist** *n.*

phar·ma·co·poe·ia (fārmakopē´a) *n.* Book (esp. one officially published) containing list of drugs with directions for use; stock of drugs. **phar·ma·co·poe´ial** *adj.*

phar·ma·cy (fār´masē) *n.* (pl. **-cies**). Preparation and (esp. medicinal) dispensing of drugs; pharmacist's shop.

pha·ryn·ge·al (farĭn´jēal, -jal, fărĭnjē´al), **pha·ryn·gal** (farĭng´gal) *adjs.* Of the pharynx.

phar·yn·gi·tis (fărĭnjī´tis) *n.* Inflammation of the membranes of the pharynx.

pharyngo- *prefix.* Pharyngeal.

pha·ryn·go·scope (farĭng´goskōp) *n.* Instrument for examining pharynx.

phar·ynx (făr´ĭngks) *n.* (pl. **pha·ryn·ges** pr. farĭn´jēz, **phar·ynx·es**). Cavity, with enclosing muscles and mucous membrane, connecting mouth and nasal passages with esophagus; corresponding part in invertebrates.

phase (fāz) *n.* 1. State of change or development. 2. (astron.) Aspect of moon or planet acc. to amount of illumination (esp. applied to new moon, 1st quarter, full moon, last quarter). 3. (phys.) Particular state or point in a recurring sequence of movements or changes, e.g. a vibration or undulation; time (measured from an arbitrary zero) at which a vibration attains a

particular state; **three-~** (of alternating currents), supplied in three parts differing in phase by $\frac{1}{3}$ of a period, or 120°; also of electric apparatus, producing or using such currents. 4. (physical chem.) Each of three different physical states, usu. solid, liquid, and gas, in which a substance can exist. **pha'sic** *adj.* **phase** *v.t.* (**phased, phas·ing**). Schedule, order; **~ in, out,** bring into or out of use gradually.

Ph.D. *abbrev.* *Philosophiae doctor* (L., = Doctor of Philosophy).

pheas·ant (fĕz'ant) *n.* (pl. **-ants,** collect. **-ant**). Long-tailed bright-plumaged gallinaceous game bird, esp. *Phasianus colchicus,* long naturalized in Europe; any of various unrelated birds resembling this; **~-eyed,** (of flowers) with rings of color like pheasant's eye; **pheasant's eye,** any of various flowers with dark center, esp. *Adonis annua* and common narcissus. [Gk. *Phasiános* (bird) of the river Phasis]

Phei·dip·pi·des (fīdĭp'ĭdēz). (Gk. hist.) Athenian runner dispatched to solicit help from Sparta upon the news of the Persian landing at MARATHON, 490 B.C.

phe·nac·e·tin (fenăs'ĭtĭn) *n.* White crystalline substance (ethyl

*The many members of the **pheasant** family are widely distributed over Europe and Asia, with one — the Congo peafowl — in Africa: this collared pheasant is European.*

ether of acetanilide), used in medicine as antipyretic.

pheno-, phen- *prefixes.* (chem.) Denoting certain substances derived from coal tar (orig. in manufacture of illuminating gas).

phe·no·bar·bi·tal (fēnōbar'-bĭtawl) *n.* Hypnotic and sedative drug ($C_{12}H_{12}N_2O_3$).

phe·nol (fē'nōl) *n.* 1. Hydroxybenzene (C_6H_5OH), commonly called *carbolic acid,* obtained from coal tar and used esp. as an antiseptic. 2. Any of the hydroxy compounds of benzene and its homologues with the hydroxyl groups attached to the nucleus, e.g. cresol, thymol, pyrogallol.

phe·nom·e·nal (fĭnŏm'enal) *adj.* Of the nature of a phenomenon; cognizable by, evidenced only by, the senses; concerned with phenomena; remarkable, prodigious. **phe·nom'e·nal·ly** *adv.*

phe·nom·e·nal·ism (fĭnŏm'-enalĭzem) *n.* Doctrine that phenomena are the only objects of knowledge. **phe·nom'e·nal·ist** *n.* **phe·nom·e·nal·is'tic** *adj.*

phe·nom·e·non (fĭnŏm'enŏn) *n.* (pl. **-na** pr. -na). Thing that appears or is perceived, esp. thing the cause of which is in question; (philos.) that of which a sense or the mind directly takes note, immediate object of perception; (pl. **-nons**) remarkable person, thing, occurence, etc.

phe·no·type (fē'notīp) *n.* (biol.) Organism as it appears, as dist. from its genetic constitution (*genotype*). **phe·no·typ·ic** (fēnotĭp'ik), **phe·no·typ'i·cal** *adjs.* Appearing in an organism as a result of its genetic potentialities in a given environment.

phen·yl (fĕn'il, fē'nil) *n.* Monovalent organic radical C_6H_5.

phew (fū, fōō, hwū) *int.* Exclamation of impatience, disgust, exhaustion, relief, etc.

phi (fī) *n.* Letter of Greek alphabet (Φ, ϕ) = ph.

phi·al (fī'al) *n.* Small glass bottle, esp. for medicine.

Phi Be·ta Kap·pa (fī' bā'ta kăp'a, bē'ta). Honor society in some U.S. universities and colleges; election for membership is based on high academic qualifications in one of three groups: undergraduates studying the liberal arts, graduates, and distinguished alumni and faculty members;

founded in 1776 at the College of William and Mary, Williamsburg, Virginia. [f. the initial letters Φ, β, K, of Gk. *philosophia biou kubernētes* philosophy the guide to life]

Phid·i·as (fĭd′ēas) (5th c. B.C.). Greek sculptor; famous in antiquity for colossal statues of gold and ivory, which have not survived; the sculptures of the Parthenon were prob. made under his supervision.

Phil·a·del·phi·a (fĭladĕl′fēa). Largest city in Pennsylvania, in the SE. part at the junction of the Delaware and Schuykill rivers; founded by Quaker William Penn, 1681; site of 1st Continental Congress, 1774, which called for colonial boycott of Brit. trade, and Second Continental Congress, 1775–6, which adopted the Declaration of Independence; site of meeting that formulated the Federal Constitution, effective March, 1789. **Phil·a·del′phi·an** *adj.* & *n.*

phi·lan·der (fĭlăn′der) *v.i.* Make love, esp. insincerely. **phi·lan′der·er** *n.*

phil·an·throp·ic (fĭlanthrŏp′ĭk) *adj.* Loving one's fellow men, benevolent, humane. **phil·an·throp′i·cal·ly** *adv.*

phi·lan·thro·pist (fĭlăn′thropĭst) *n.* Lover of mankind; one who exerts himself for the well-being of his fellow men. **phi·lan′thro·pism** *n.*

phi·lan·thro·py (fĭlăn′thropē) *n.* Love, practical benevolence, toward mankind.

phi·lat·e·ly (fĭlăt′elē) *n.* Study and collection of stamps and other postal material. **phil·a·tel·ic** (fĭlatĕl′ĭk), **phil·a·tel′i·cal** *adjs.* **phi·lat′e·list** *n.* [Gk. *philos* lover of, *ateleia* exemption from payment]

phil·har·mon·ic (fĭlhārmŏn′ik) *adj.* & *n.* (Person) fond of music (freq. used in names of musical societies, orchestras, etc.).

Phil·ip[1] (fĭl′ĭp). Name of several kings of France: **Philip I** (1052–1108), reigned 1060–1108; **Philip II** (1165–1223), "Philip Augustus," reigned 1180–1223; reconquered Normandy from English; **Philip III** (1245–85), "the Bold," reigned 1270–85; **Philip IV** (1268–1314), "le Bel," reigned 1285–1314; in his reign the papacy was established at Avignon; **Philip V** (*c*1294–1322), reigned 1316–22; **Philip VI** (1293–1350), reigned 1328–50; his reign saw beginning of Hundred Years War.

Phil·ip[2] (fĭl′ĭp). Name of several kings of Spain: **Philip II** (1527–98), reigned 1556–98; married Mary I of England; launched the Spanish Armada against England, 1588; **Philip III** (1578–1621), reigned 1598–1621; **Philip IV** (1605–65), reigned 1621–65; **Philip V** (1683–1746), reigned 1700–46; founder of Bourbon dynasty in Spain.

Phil·ip[3] (fĭl′ĭp). (382–336 B.C.) King of Macedonia 359–336; reorganized Macedonian army and conquered Greece; father of Alexander the Great.

Phil·ip[4] (fĭl′ĭp), **King** (d. 1676). Indian name, Metacomet. N. Amer. Ind. chief, son of Massasoit; sachem of Wampanoag tribe, 1662–1676; led Indians against the New England colonists in King Philip's War, 1675–6.

Phi·lip·pi (fĭlĭp′ī). Ancient city of Macedonia, fortified by Philip of Macedon and named after him; scene of battle (42 B.C.) in which Octavian and Mark Antony defeated Brutus and Cassius.

Phi·lip·pi·an (fĭlĭp′ēan) *adj.* Of Philippi. ~ *n.* Native, inhabitant, of Philippi; (**Epistle to the**) **~s**, book of New Testament, epistle of St. Paul to the church at Philippi.

Phi·lip·pic (fĭlĭp′ĭk) *n.* Any of the three speeches of Demosthenes against Philip of Macedon; (also) Cicero's speeches against Antony; hence (**p~**) bitter invective.

Phil·ip·pines (fĭl′ipēnz, fĭlipēnz′). Republic in the Pacific Ocean, about 500 mi. (805 km) SE. of Asia, consisting of about 7,000 islands, the largest being Luzon and

The Liberty Bell Pavilion in ***Philadelphia.*** *Last rung for George Washington's birthday in 1846, it hung in the Independence Hall until 1976 when it was moved to the new pavilion.*

After a long colonial history the ***Philippines,*** *with their varying cultural and linguistic population-groups, are fast becoming a prosperous modern state with many industries as well as the tourism encouraged by landscapes like this.*

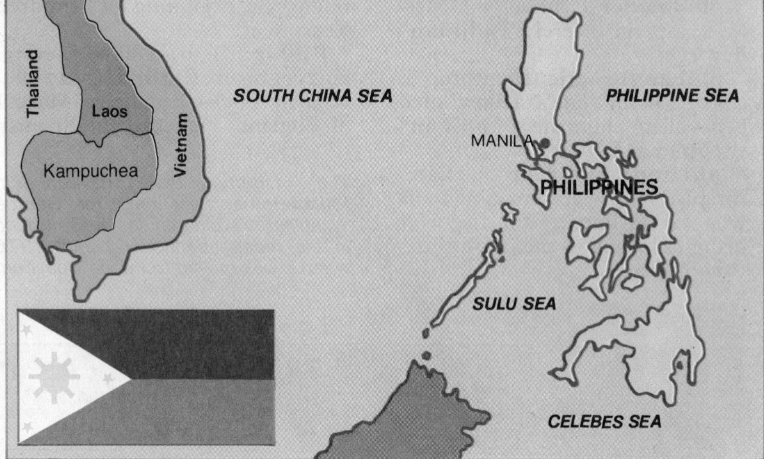

Mindanao; capital, Quezon City; discovered by Magellan, 1521, and under Spanish control until 1899 when it was ceded to the U.S. following the Spanish–American War; Commonwealth established, 1935; captured during World War II by Japanese and held until Oct., 1944, when Gen. Douglas MacArthur led U.S. forces into the country; granted independence on July 4, 1946.

Phil·is·tine (fĭl′ĭstēn, -stīn, fĭlĭs′tĭn, -tēn) *n.* 1. One of the warlike inhabitants of ancient Philistia, a district comprising the fertile Mediterranean coastal plain from Jaffa to Egypt, who in early times constantly harassed the Israelites. 2. Illiberal person, one whose interests are material and commonplace. ~ *adj.* Uncultured, commonplace, materialistic. **Phil·is·tin·ism** (fĭl′ĭstēnĭzem, fĭlĭs′tinĭzem) *n.* [Vulgate *Philistīnī*; sense 2 taken f. Ger. *philister*, used by univ. students of townsmen, allegedly since 1693 when a student was killed at Jena in a "town-and-gown" brawl and the sermon at his funeral was based on the text "The Philistines be upon thee!"]

phil·o·den·dron (fĭlodĕn′dron) *n.* (pl. **-drons, -dra** pr. -dra). Tropical Amer. climbing plant (family Araceae) with large shiny leaves, used as house plant.

phi·lol·o·gy (fĭlŏl′ojē) *n.* Science of language. **phi·lol′o·gist** *n.* **phil·o·log·i·cal** (fĭlolŏj′ĭkal) *adj.* **phil·o·log′i·cal·ly** *adv.*

Phil·o·me·la (fĭlomē′la). (Gk. myth.) Daughter of Pandion, a legendary king of Athens; was turned into a swallow and her sister Procne into a nightingale (or, in Latin versions, into a nightingale, and Procne into a swallow).

phi·los·o·pher (fĭlŏs′ofer) *n.* Lover of wisdom; student of philosophy; one who shows philosophic calmness in trying circumstances; **~'s stone**, supreme object of alchemy, substance supposed to change other metals into gold or silver.

phil·o·soph·ic (fĭlosŏf′ĭk), **phil·o·soph·i·cal** (fĭlosŏf′ĭkal) *adjs.* Of, consonant with, philosophy; skilled in, devoted to, philosophy (freq. in titles of societies); wise; calm; temperate. **phil·o·soph′i·cal·ly** *adv.*

phi·los·o·phize (fĭlŏs′ofīz) *v.* (**-phized, -phiz·ing**). Play the philosopher; speculate, theorize; moralize; render philosophic.

phi·los·o·phy (fĭlŏs′ofē) *n.* (pl. **-phies**). 1. Love, study, or pursuit, of wisdom or knowledge, esp. that which deals with ultimate reality, or with the most general causes and principles of things; philosophical system; system for conduct of life; **moral ~, natural ~**: see these words. 2. Serenity, resignation.

phil·ter (fĭl′ter) *n.* Love potion.

phle·bi·tis (flebī′tĭs) *n.* Inflammation of walls of a vein. **phle·bit·ic** (flebĭt′ĭk) *adj.*

phle·bot·o·my (flebŏt′omē) *n.* (pl. **-mies**). Cutting into a vein, bloodletting, an early and now obsolete form of medical treatment.

Phleg·e·thon (flĕg′ethŏn). (Gk. and Rom. myth.) River of fire, one of the 5 rivers of Hades.

phlegm (flĕm) *n.* 1. Thick slimy substance secreted by mucous membrane of respiratory passages; (hist.) one of the 4 humors. 2. Coolness, sluggishness, apathy (supposed to result from predominance of phlegm in constitution). **phleg·mat·ic** (flĕgmăt´ĭk) *adj.* **phleg·mat′i·cal·ly** *adv.*

phlo·em (flō´ĕm) *n.* (bot.) Softer portion of the fibrovascular tissue, as dist. from the xylem or woody portion; soft bast.

phlo·gis·tic (flōjĭs´tĭk) *adj.* Of phlogiston; (med.) inflammatory.

phlo·gis·ton (flōjĭs´t*o*n) *n.* Hypothetical substance formerly supposed to exist in combustible bodies.

phlox (flŏks) *n.* Plant of N. Amer. genus *P*~ of chiefly herbaceous plants with clusters of usu. showy flowers. [Gk. = "flame"]

Phnom Penh (nŏm´ pĕn´, p*e*nawm´ pĕn´). Capital and largest city of Kampuchea (Cambodia), in the S. part on the Mekong River.

pho·bi·a (fō´bē*a*) *n.* Fear, horror, or aversion, esp. morbid. **pho·bic** (fō´bĭk) *adj.*

phoe·be (fē´bē) *n.* Amer. flycatcher of genus *Sayornis*, with gray or brown back and a short crest.

Phoe·be (fē´bē), **Phoe·bus** (fē´b*u*s). (Gk. myth.) Artemis and Apollo as goddess of moon and god of sun; moon and sun personified. [Gk., = "bright," "radiant"]

Phoe·ni·cia (fĭnĭsh´*a*, -nē´sh*a*). Ancient country of E. Mediterranean, a narrow strip along the coast of modern Lebanon, including Tyre and Sidon. **Phoe·ni·cian** (fĭnĭsh´*a*n, -nē´sh*a*n) *adj.* & *n.* (Member) of the Semitic people who inhabited this area from at least 2000 B.C., famous as pioneers of navigation and trade (Carthage was their colony) and as craftsmen, regarded by the Greeks as inventors of letters, since the Greek alphabet was based on the Phoenician.

Phoe·nix (fē´nĭks). Capital and largest city of Arizona, in the SW. central part.

phoe·nix (fē´niks) *n.* Mythical bird, the only one of its kind, that after living 5 or 6 centuries in the Arabian desert burned itself on a funeral pile and rose from the ashes with renewed youth to live through another cycle; paragon.

phon (fŏn) *n.* (phys.) Unit used in measuring sound.

phone[1] (fōn) *n.* Elementary sound of spoken language.

phone[2] (fōn) *n.* & *v.* (**phoned, phon·ing**). (colloq.) Telephone.

pho·neme (fō´nēm) *n.* (phonet). Group of variants regarded as essentially the same vocal sound. **pho·ne·mic** (f*o*nē´mĭk, fō-) *adj.*

pho·net·ic (f*o*nĕt´ĭk) *adj.* Representing vocal sounds, esp. (of systems of spelling) using always same symbol for same sound; of the sounds of spoken language. **pho·net′i·cal·ly** *adv.* **pho·ne·ti·cian** (fōnĭtĭsh´*a*n) *n.* **pho·net′ics** *n.* Study of phonetic phenomena; (as pl.) phonetic phenomena.

pho·ne·tist (fō´nĭtĭst) *n.* One versed in phonetics, advocate of phonetic spelling.

pho·ney = PHONY.

phon·ic (fŏn´ĭk) *adj.* Of sound, acoustic; of vocal sounds.

pho·no·gram (fō´n*o*grăm) *n.* Symbol representing sound, syllable, or word, without reference to meaning. **pho·no·gram′ic, pho·no·gram′mic** *adjs.*

pho·no·graph (fō´n*o*grăf) *n.* Machine for reproducing recorded speech, music, etc. **pho·no·graph′ic** *adj.* **pho·no·graph′i·cal·ly** *adv.* **pho·nog·ra·phy** (fōnŏg´r*a*fē) *n.*

pho·nol·o·gy (fōnŏl´*o*jē) *n.* Science of vocal sounds; system of sounds in a language. **pho·no·log·ic** (fōn*o*lŏj´ĭk), **pho·no·log′i·cal** *adjs.* **pho·no·log′i·cal·ly** *adv.* **pho·nol′o·gist** *n.*

pho·ny, pho·ney (fō´nē) *adjs.* (**pho·ni·er, pho·ni·est**). (slang) Sham, false, counterfeit. ~ *n.* (pl. **-nies, -neys**). Phony person or thing.

phos·gene (fŏz´jēn) *n.* Carbonyl chloride ($COCL_2$), a poisonous colorless gas with a characteristic suffocating smell.

phos·phate (fŏs´fāt) *n.* (chem.) Salt or ester of phosphoric acid; substance containing this, used as a fertilizer. **phos·phat·ic** (fŏsfătĭk) *adj.*

phos·phide (fŏs´fīd) *n.* (chem.) Compound of phosphorus with other element or radical.

phos·phor (fŏs´f*e*r) *n.* 1. Phosphorus; esp. in ~ **bronze, copper**, etc., alloys of phosphorus with metals named. 2. Fluorescent material, esp. that used to form screen of cathode ray tube.

phos·pho·res·cence (fŏsf*e*rĕs´-*e*ns) *n.* Radiation similar to fluorescence but detectable after excitation ceases; emission of light without combustion or perceptible heat. **phos·pho·resce** (fŏsf*e*rĕs´) *v.i.* (**-resced, -resc·ing**). Emit phos-

***Phoenix,** capital city of the state of Arizona. Developed by irrigation from various dams, the semi-arid region began to burgeon in the late 19th century. After the 1939–45 war the city expanded rapidly. Various manufacturing industries have developed, increasing the state's prosperity.*

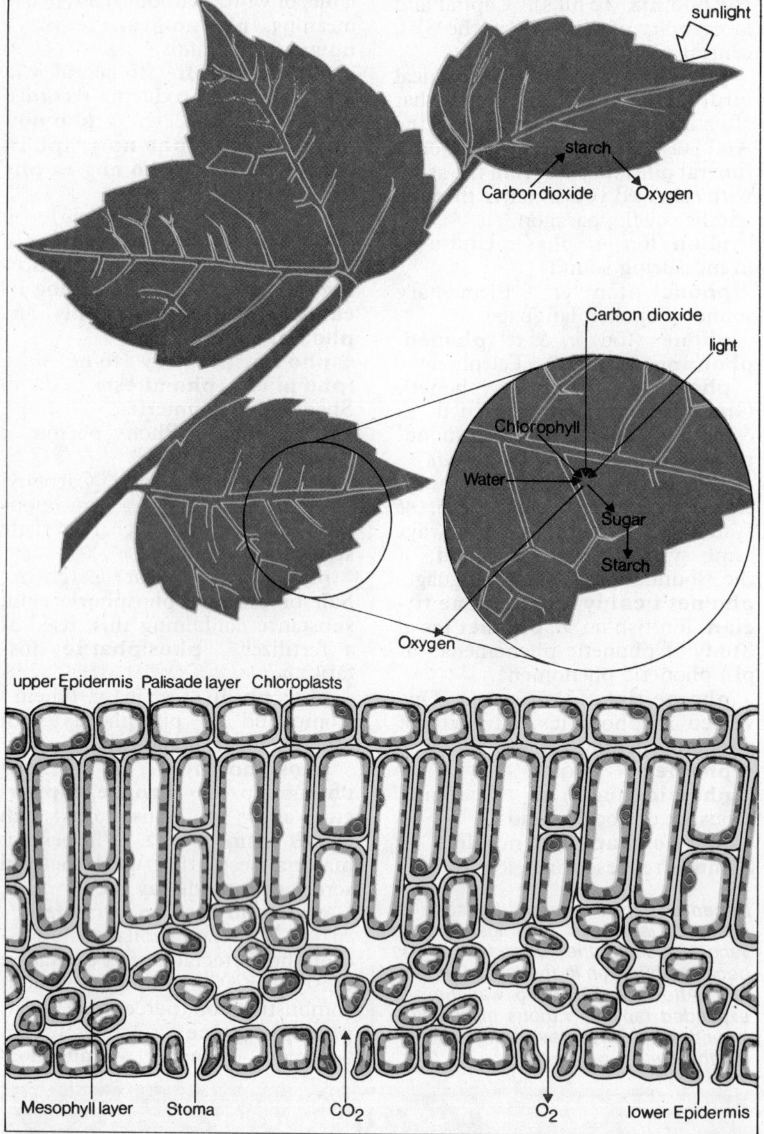

Photosynthesis is essential to all life on earth, not merely to plants. The complex process, involving light-sensitive pigments, maintains the supply of atmospheric oxygen on which animals and man depend. It also provides a continuous supply of food, directly for herbivores, indirectly for predators.

phorescence. **phos·pho·res′cent** *adj.*

phos·phor·ic (fŏsfŏr′ĭk, -făr′-) *adj.* Containing phosphorus in its higher valence.

phos·pho·rous (fŏs′ferus, fŏsfŏr′us, fōr′-) *adj.* Containing phosphorus in its lower (trivalent) valence.

phos·pho·rus (fŏs′ferus) *n.* (pl. **-ri** pr. -rī). (chem.) Nonmetallic element found in all animal and vegetable organisms and in some minerals (symbol P, at. no. 15, at. wt. 30.97376) and occurring in several allotropic forms: **yellow ~**, white or cream-colored waxlike highly inflammable solid, not found in free state, oxidizing rapidly in air, appearing luminous, and transformed esp. in sunlight into **red ~**, a stable dark red microcrystalline powder, nonpoisonous and less readily inflammable, used in safety matches. [L. *phosphorus* morning star (Gk. *phōs* light, *phorus* bringing)]

phot (fŏt) *n.* (phys.) Unit of illumination equal to 1 LUMEN per sq. cm.

pho·to (fō′tō) *n.* (pl. **-tos**). (colloq.) Photograph; **~ finish**, close finish of race in which winner is identified by photography.

pho·to·chem·is·try (fōtōkĕm′ĭstrē) *n.* Branch of chemistry dealing with the chemical action of light. **pho·to·chem·i·cal** (fōtōkĕm′ĭkal) *adj.*

pho·to·cop·y (fō′tokŏpē) *n.* (pl. **-cop·ies**) & *v.t.* (**-cop·ied, -cop·y·ing**). (Make) photographic copy (of).

pho·to·e·lec·tric (fōtōĭlĕk′trĭk) *adj.* Marked by or utilizing emission of electrons from solid, liquid, or gaseous bodies when exposed to light of suitable wavelengths; **~ cell**, cell or vacuum tube that uses the photoelectric effect to produce an electric current; also called ELECTRIC EYE. **pho·to·e·lec·tric·i·ty** (fōtōĭlĕktrĭs′ĭtē) *n.*

pho·to·gen·ic (fōtojĕn′ĭk) *adj.* 1. Producing or emitting light. 2. Suitable for photography; photographing well (of person as good subject for photography). **pho·to·gen′i·cal·ly** *adv.*

pho·to·gram·me·try (fōtogrăm′ĭtrē) *n.* Process of making surveys or geodetic measurements by photography.

pho·to·graph (fō′tograf) *n.* Picture, likeness, taken by means of chemical action of light on sensitive film. **~** *v.* Take photograph of; **~ well, badly**, be a good, bad subject for photography. **pho·tog·ra·pher** (fotŏg′rafer), **pho·tog·ra·phy** (fotŏg′rafē) *ns.* **pho·to·graph·ic** (fōtogrăf′ĭk), **pho·to·graph′i·cal** *adjs.* **pho·to·graph′i·cal·ly** *adv.*

pho·to·gra·vure (fōtogravūr′) *n.* Printing process in which the subject matter is photographically etched into a polished copper cylinder; this process. **~** *v.t.* (**-vured, -vur·ing**). Reproduce by photogravure.

pho·to·li·thog·ra·phy (fōtōlĭthŏg′rafē) *n.* Lithographic process in which printing plates are made photographically. **pho·to·lith·o·graph** (fōtolĭth′ograf) *n.* **pho·to·lith·o·graph′ic** *adj.*

pho·to·me·chan·i·cal (fōtōmekăn′ĭkal) *adj.* Pertaining to the production of pictures by mechanical printing from a photographic plate. **pho·to·me·chan′i·cal·ly** *adv.*

pho·tom·e·ter (fōtŏm′ĭter) *n.* Instrument for measuring intensity of light. **pho·to·met·ric** (fōtomĕt′rĭk), **pho·to·met′ri·cal** *adjs.* **pho·tom·e·try** (fōtŏm′ĭtrē) *n.*

pho·ton (fō′tŏn) *n.* Quantum unit of light or other radiant energy equal to the product of Planck's constant *h* and the frequency *v*.

pho·to-off·set (fōtōawf′sĕt) *n.* Offset printing with plates made photographically.

pho·to·sphere (fō′tosfēr) *n.* Luminous envelope of sun or star from which its light and heat radiate.

Pho·to·stat (fō′tostăt) *n.* (trademark) Apparatus for making photographic copies of documents etc.; (usu. l.c.) copy made by this. **pho·to·stat′ic** *adj.*

pho·to·syn·the·sis (fōtosĭn′thĭsĭs) *n.* (bot.) Process by which carbon dioxide is converted into carbohydrates by chlorophyll under influence of light. **pho·to·syn·thet·ic** (fōtosĭnthĕt′ĭk) *adj.*

pho·to·syn·thet′i·cal·ly *adv.*

pho·to·trop·ic (fōtotrŏp′ĭk) *adj.* (of plant leaves etc.) Bending or turning toward or away from a source of light. **pho·to·trop′i·cal·ly** *adv.* **pho·tot·ro·pism** (fōtŏt′ropĭzem) *n.*

phrase (frāz) *n.* 1. Mode of expression, diction; idiomatic expression; small group of words, usu. without predicate, esp. preposition with the word(s) it governs, equivalent to adjective, adverb, or noun; short pithy expression; (pl.) mere words. 2. (mus.) Short and more or less independent passage forming part of longer passage or of whole piece. **phras·al** (frā′zal) *adj.* **phrase** *v.t.* (**phrased, phras·ing**). Express in words; divide (music) into phrases; group (notes) in phrase.

phra·se·ol·o·gy (frāzēŏl′ojē) *n.* Choice or arrangement of words; mode of expression. **phra·se·o·log·i·cal** (frāzēolŏj′ĭkal) *adj.* **phra·se·o·log′i·cal·ly** *adv.*

phre·net·ic (frenĕt′ĭk), **phre·net·i·cal** (frenĕt′ĭkal) = FRENETIC.

phren·ic (frĕnĭk) *adj.* (anat.) Of the diaphragm.

phre·nol·o·gy (frĭnŏl′ojē) *n.* Study of external contours of cranium as index to development and position of organs supposedly belonging to the different mental faculties. **phren·o·log·ic** (frĕnolŏj′ĭk), **phren·o·log′i·cal** *adjs.* **phren·o·log′i·cal·ly** *adv.* **phre·nol′o·gist** *n.*

Phryg·i·a (frĭj′ēa). Ancient region of central and N. Asia Minor.

Phryg·i·an (frĭj′ēan) *adj.* Of Phrygia or its people or language; ~ **mode**, ancient Greek MODE, reputedly warlike in character; 3rd of ecclesiastical modes, with E as final and C as dominant. **Phrygian** *n.* Native, inhabitant, language, of Phrygia.

phthal·ic (thăl′ĭk, fthăl′-) *adj.* ~ **acid**, any of three isomeric acids, $C_6H_4(COOH)_2$.

phthi·sis (thī′sĭs, fthī′-) *n.* Pulmonary tuberculosis; (formerly) any progressive wasting disease. **phthis·ic** (tĭz′ĭk), **phthis′i·cal, phthis′ick·y** *adjs.* Of, having, phthisis.

phy·lac·ter·y (fĭlăk′terē) *n.* (pl. **-ter·ies**). 1. Small leather box containing portions of Hebrew texts (Deut. 6:4–9, 11:13–21; Exod. 13:1–10, 11–16) on vellum, worn by Jews during morning prayer as reminder of obligation to keep the law. 2. Amulet, charm.

phy·le (fī′lē) *n.* (pl. **-lae** pr. -lē). Ancient Greek clan or tribe; in Attica, political, administrative, and military unit, based on geographical division.

phy·let·ic (fīlĕt′ĭk) *adj.* (biol.) Of a phylum or line of descent.

phyl·lox·e·ra (fĭloksēr′a, fĭlŏk′sera) *n.* Any of several plant lice of genus *P*~, esp. species very destructive to grapevine.

phy·lo·gen·e·sis (fīlojĕn′esĭs) = PHYLOGENY.

phy·log·e·ny (fīlŏj′enē) *n.* (biol.) History of the evolution of a kind or type of organism (opp. ONTOGENY). **phy·lo·ge·net·ic** (fīlojenĕt′ĭk), **phy·lo·gen·ic** (fīlojĕn′ĭk) *adjs.* **phy·lo·ge·net′i·cal·ly** *adv.*

phy·lum (fī′lum) *n.* (pl. **-la** pr. -la). (biol.) Major division of animals or plants, above CLASS, comprising those of the same general form.

phys·ic (fĭz′ĭk) *n.* (archaic) Art of healing; medical profession; (colloq.) medicine; cathartic. ~ *v.t.* (**-icked, ick·ing**). Treat with physic.

phys·i·cal (fĭz′ĭkal) *adj.* 1. Of matter, material; of the body; of, according to the laws of, natural philosophy; ~ **chemistry**: see CHEMISTRY; ~ **geography**, that dealing with natural features. 2. Of the science of physics. **phys′i·cal·ly** *adv.*

phy·si·cian (fĭzĭsh′an) *n.* Medical practitioner, esp. one specializing in medical (opp. surgical) diagnosis and treatment; (fig.) healer.

phys·ics (fĭz′ĭks) *n.* Science of the properties and nature of matter in general (excluding chemistry), the various forms of energy, and the mutual interaction of energy and matter. **phys·i·cist** (fĭz′ĭsĭst) *n.*

phys·i·og·no·my (fĭzēŏg′nomē, -ŏn′omē) *n.* (pl. **-mies**). Art of judging character from features of face or form of body; cast of features, type of face; face; external features of country etc.; characteristic (moral or other) aspect. **phys·i·og·nom·ic** (fĭzēŏgnŏm′ĭk, -ēonŏm′-), **phys·i·og·nom′i·cal** *adjs.* **phys·i·og·nom′i·cal·ly** *adv.* **phys·i·og′no·mist** *n.*

phys·i·og·ra·phy (fĭzēŏg′rafē) *n.* Description of nature, of natural phenomena, or of a class of objects; physical geography. **phys·i·og′ra·pher** *n.* **phys·i·o·graph·ic** (fĭzēogrăf′ĭk), **phys·i·o·graph′i·cal** *adjs.*

phys·i·ol·o·gy (fĭzēŏl′ojē) *n.* Science dealing with the functions of living organisms or their parts; these functions. **phys·i·o·log·i·cal** (fĭzēolŏj′ĭkal), **phys·i·o·log′ic** *adjs.* **phys·i·o·log′i·cal·ly** *adv.* **phys·i·ol′o·gist** *n.*

phys·i·o·ther·a·py (fĭzēōthĕr′apē) *n.* Treatment of disease by exercise, massage, heat, light, electricity, or other physical agencies, not by drugs. **phys·i·o·ther′a·pist** *n.*

phy·sique (fĭzēk′) *n.* Bodily structure, organization, and development.

pi[1] (pī) *n.* (pl. **pis**). Seventeenth (later 16th) letter of Greek alphabet (Π, π) corresponding to *p*; esp. (math.) as symbol of ratio of circumference of circle to diameter (3.14159).

pi[2], **pie**[2] (pī) *ns.* (pl. **pies**). Confused mass of printers' type; (fig.) chaos. ~ *v.t.* (**pied, pi·ing**). Mix (type).

pi·a ma·ter (pī′a mā′ter). (anat.) Delicate fibrous innermost meninx, consisting of a network of blood vessels, covering the brain and spinal cord. [med. L. transl. of Arab. anatomical term, = "tender mother"]

pi·a·nis·si·mo (pēanĭs′imō) *adv.*, *n.* (pl. **-mos**), & *adj.* (mus.) (Passage performed) very soft(ly).

pi·an·ist (pēăn′ĭst, pē′anĭst) *n.* Player of piano.

pi·a·nis·tic (pēanĭs′tĭk) *adj.* Of, adapted for playing on a piano.

pi·a·no[1] (pēah′nō, pyah′nō) *adv.*, *n.* (pl. **-nos**), & *adj.* (mus.) (Passage performed) soft(ly). [It.]

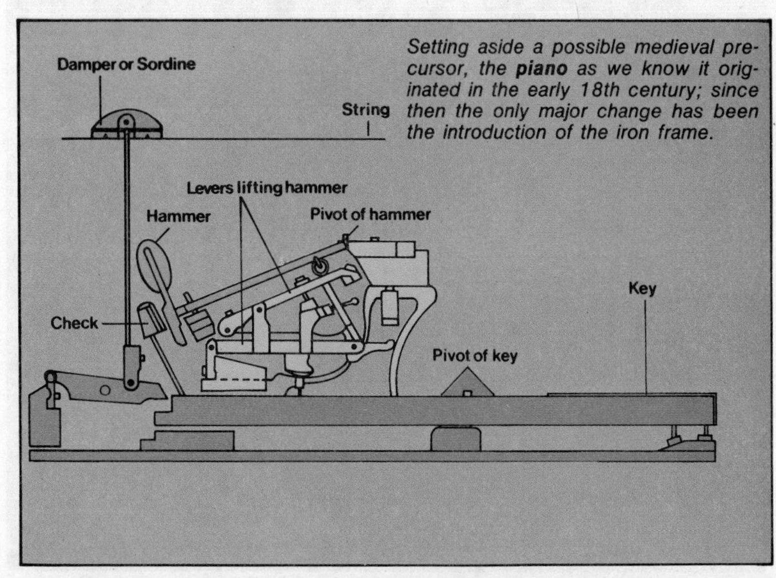

*Setting aside a possible medieval precursor, the **piano** as we know it originated in the early 18th century; since then the only major change has been the introduction of the iron frame.*

pi·an·o[2] (pēăn'ō, pyăn'ō) *n.* (pl. **-an·os**). Large musical instrument played by means of keys that cause hammers to strike on metal strings (the vibrations being stopped by dampers); **baby grand** ~, the smallest size grand piano; **grand** ~, large wing-shaped piano of full tone with strings arranged horizontally; **player** ~, mechanical piano; **spinet** ~, (also **spinet**) small upright piano (see also SPINET); **upright** ~, piano with strings in vertical position; ~ **roll**, in player piano, the paper roll that regulates performance of the instrument. [It., earlier *piano e forte* soft and strong, i.e. loud]

pi·an·o·for·te (pēăn*o*fōr'tē, -tā, -fōr'-, -fōrt', -fōrt') = PIANO[2].

pi·as·ter, pi·as·tre (pēăs'*ter*) *ns.* Small coin of Middle Eastern countries.

pi·az·za (pēăz'*a*, -ah'*za*, -ăt'*sa*, -ah'ts*a*) *n.* (pl. **pi·az·zas, pi·az·ze** pr. pēăt'sā, -ah'tsā). Public square or marketplace, esp. in Italian town; verandah of house. [It., ult. f. Gk. *plateia* (*hodos*) broad (street)]

pi·ca (pī'k*a*) *n.* (print.) Size of type (12 point), of about six lines to the inch.

pic·a·dor (pĭk'*a*dōr, pĭk*a*dōr') *n.* Mounted man with lance in bullfight.

pic·a·resque (pĭk*a*rĕsk') *adj.* (of a style of fiction) Dealing with adventures of rogues.

Pi·cas·so (pĭkah'sō), **Pablo** (1881–1973). Spanish painter in France, a founder of CUBISM., famous esp. for *Guernica* and *The Three Musicians*.

pic·a·yune (pĭkēūn') *n.* (formerly) Small coin; (colloq.) small, mean, or insignificant thing. ~ *adj.* Mean, contemptible, paltry.

pic·ca·lil·li (pĭk'*a*lĭlē) *n.* (pl. **-lis**). Relish of chopped vegetables, mustard, and hot spices.

pic·co·lo (pĭk'*o*lō) *n.* (pl. **-los**). Small flute, an octave higher than the ordinary flute. **pic'co·lo·ist** *n.* [It., = "small"]

*An intrinsic part of the corrida is the skill with which the **picador** does his share of weakening the bull's neck muscles with lance-thrusts.*

pich·i·ci·a·go (pĭchĭsēah'gō, -ā'gō) *n.* (pl. **-gos**). Small pink burrowing armadillo (genus *Chlamyphorus*) of Argentina. [perh. f. native *pichey* little armadillo, Span. *ciego* blind]

pick[1] (pĭk) *n.* Tool consisting of an iron bar, usu. curved with a point at one end and a point or chisel edge at the other, with a wooden handle passing through the middle perpendicularly, used for breaking up hard ground etc.; instrument for picking, toothpick.

pick[2] (pĭk) *v.* 1. Break surface of (ground etc.) with or as with pick; make (hole etc.) thus. 2. Probe (teeth etc.) with pointed instrument to remove extraneous matter; clear (bone, carcass) of adherent flesh. 3. Detach (flowers, fruit, etc.) from place of growth. 4. (of birds) Take up (grains etc.) in bill; (of persons) eat in small bits; ~ **at** (food), eat in a fussy way; eat lightly. 5. Select carefully; ~ **and choose**, select fastidiously. 6. Pull apart; ~ **to pieces**, pull apart; (fig.) criticize hostilely. 7. ~ **a lock**, open a lock (esp. with intent to rob) with pointed instrument etc.; ~ **a pocket**, steal its contents; ~ **a quarrel**, contrive to quarrel *with*; ~ **off**, pluck off; shoot deliberately one by one; (of baseball pitcher) throw to first base to put base runner out; ~ **on**, select; single out for criticism etc.; ~ **out**, take or choose from a number of others, distinguish from surrounding objects; relieve (ground color *with* another); make out (meaning of passages etc.), play (tune) by ear; ~ **up**, break up (ground etc.) with pick; lay hold of and take up; raise from a fall etc.; gain, acquire (livelihood, profit, tricks, information); take (person, or thing) along with one; regain; recover health; (colloq.) make acquaintance casually with (person of opposite sex); succeed in receiving by radio, see with searchlight etc.; (games) select (sides) by alternate choosing; (of motor etc.) recover speed, accelerate. 8. ~**-me-up**, stimulating drink; **pick'pocket**, one who steals from pockets; **pick'up**, picking up (of ball in baseball etc.); game between sides chosen casually; (colloq.) casual, esp. unintroduced, acquaintance; power (of motor, etc.) to accelerate; mechanism (replacing soundbox of phonograph) that converts impulses imparted to needle by record into electrical impulses that can then be amplified; small motor truck with open body. **pick'er** *n.*

*Reminiscent of Van Gogh, 'Child with a Dove' painted by **Picasso** in 1901 predates his better known Blue Period. Later, Picasso experimented in so many ways that he was possibly the leading innovator in 20th-century art.*

*Fertile sub-alpine valleys (right) are only part of **Piedmont's** agricultural resources. The wide plain of the Po and the southern hills are highly, and diversely, productive (Italy).*

pick *n.* 1. Picking; selection; best part *of.* 2. (weaving) Thread, group of threads, of weft.

pick·a·back (pĭk′*a*băk) = PIGGYBACK.

pick·a·nin·ny (pĭk′*a*nĭne) *n.* (pl. **-nies**). (offensive) Small black child.

pick·ax, pick·axe (pĭk′ăks) *ns.* (pl. **-ax·es**) = PICK[1]. ~ *v.* (**-axed, -ax·ing**). Break (ground etc.) with pickax; work with pickax.

pick·er·el (pĭk′*e*rel) *n.* (pl. **-els**, collect. **-el**). Any of several small N. Amer. freshwater fishes (genus *Esox*), including the Eastern ~ (*E. niger*) and the grass ~ (*E. americanus*).

pick·et (pĭk′ĭt) *n.* 1. Pointed stake or peg driven into ground to form palisade, tether horse, etc.; (hist.) (stake with pointed top on which person stood as) form of military punishment. 2. (mil.) Small body of troops sent out to watch for enemy or held ready in quarters; party of sentinels, outpost; (now, chiefly) camp guard doing police duty in garrison town etc. 3. Person stationed by labor union outside a business that is on strike to dissuade others from work during strike. ~ *v.* Secure (place) with stakes; tether; post (people) as pickets; beset with pickets during strike etc.; act as picket. **pick′et·er, pick′et·ing** *ns.*

pick·ing (pĭk′ĭng) *n.* Act of selecting; (pl.) gleanings, remaining scraps; pilferings.

pick·le (pĭk′*e*l) *n.* Brine, vinegar, or similar liquid in which flesh, vegetables, etc., are preserved; food, esp. (usu. pl.) vegetables preserved in pickle and eaten as relish; acid solution for cleaning purposes etc.; (fig.) plight, predicament. ~ *v.t.* (**-led, -ling**). Preserve in pickle; treat (wood etc.) with acid solution. **pick′led** *adj.* (slang) Drunk.

pick·y (pĭk′ē) *adj.* (**pick·i·er, pick·i·est**). Excessively fastidious.

pic·nic (pĭk′nĭk) *n.* Pleasure party including meal out of doors; ~ **ham, shoulder**, shoulder cut of pork cured like a ham. **picnic** *v.i.* (**-nicked, -nick·ing**). Take part in picnic. **pic′nick·er** *n.*

pic·ric (pĭk′rĭk) *adj.* ~ **acid**, trinitrophenol, intensely bitter yellow crystalline substance used, in aqueous solution, as a treatment for burns etc., and formerly as a high explosive (lyddite).

Pict (pĭkt) *n.* One of an ancient, prob. pre-Celtic, people formerly inhabiting parts of N. Britain and Ireland, later (9th c.) united with Scots. **Pict′ish** *adj.* & *n.*

*A restored **Pictish** settlement at Jarlshof in the Shetland Islands. These 'painted people' are known from A.D. 297 until their conquest by Kenneth MacAlpine, about A.D. 850.*

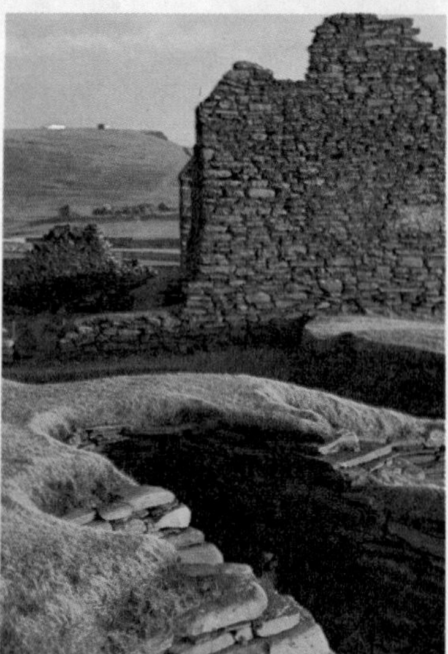

pic·to·graph (pĭk′t*o*grăf, -grahf) *n.* Pictorial symbol that stands for the thing depicted, e.g. representation of an eye standing for "eye"; primitive writing or record consisting of these. **pic·to·graph′ic** *adj.* **pic·to·graph′i·cal·ly** *adv.* **pic·tog·ra·phy** (pĭk-tŏg′r*a*fē) *n.*

pic·to·ri·al (pĭktōr′ē*a*l, -tōr′-) *adj.* Of, expressed in, pictures; illustrated; picturesque. **pic·to′ri·al·ly** *adv.* **pictorial** *n.* Periodical of which pictures are main feature.

pic·ture (pĭk′ch*e*r) *n.* 1. Painting, drawing, of objects esp. as work of art; portrait; beautiful object; (fig.) symbol, type, figure. 2. Scene, total visual impression produced; mental image; **be out of the** ~, not have all the relevant information. 3. Visible reproduction of film; image on television screen; (pl.) exhibition of motion-picture film(s), place where these are exhibited. 4. ~ **card**, one above a 10 in bridge deck; ~ **gallery**, (hall etc. containing) collection of pictures; ~ **hat**, woman's wide-brimmed hat resembling those in pictures by Reynolds and Gainsborough: ~ **postcard**, postcard with picture on back; ~ **tube**, vacuum tube used in television sets etc. to produce visible images; ~ **writing**, mode of recording events etc. by pictures, as in hieroglyphs etc.; ~ **window**, large window facing attractive view. **picture** *v.t.* (**-tured, -tur·ing**). Represent in picture; describe graphically; imagine.

pic·tur·esque (pĭkch*e*rĕsk′) *adj.* Like, fit to be the subject of, a striking picture; (of language etc.) strikingly graphic, vivid. **pic·tur·esque′ly** *adv.* **pic·tur·esque′ness** *n.*

pid·dle (pĭd′*e*l) *v.i.* (**-dled, -dling**). Work, act, in trifling way; (colloq. or childish) urinate. **pid′dling** *adj.* (colloq.) Trivial.

pidg·in (pĭj′ĭn) *n.* Jargon chiefly of English words used esp. between Melanesian or Chinese and European (also ~ **English**); mixed simplified form of English used elsewhere. [Chin. corrup. of *business*]

pie[1] (pī) *n.* Dish of meat, fruit, etc., encased in or covered with or surrounded by crust and baked; any of various other baked dishes of meat, fish, etc.; **easy as ~**, very easy; **have a finger in the ~**, be (esp. officiously) concerned in the matter; **~ chart**, one representing relative quantities by areas of sectors of a circle; **pie′crust**, baked dough of pie; **pie-eyed**, (slang) drunk; **pie in the sky**, (slang) prospect of future happiness after present suffering.

pie[2] (pī) *n.* & *v.* (**pied, pie·ing**) = PI[2].

pie·bald (pī′bawld) *adj.* Of 2 colors irregularly arranged, esp. black and white; (of horse) with black and white patches on body and legs; (fig.) motley, mongrel.

piece (pēs) *n.* 1. One of the distinct portions of which thing is composed; **in ~s**, broken; **break to ~s**, break into fragments; **pull** or **tear to ~s**, (fig.) criticize severely. 2. Enclosed portion *of* (land); detached portion (*of* a substance); definite quantity in which thing is made up; **a ~ of one's mind**, one's candid opinion, rebuke. 3. Example, specimen. 4. Cannon, gun, pistol; man at chess, checkers, etc.; coin; **~ of eight**, (hist.) Spanish dollar (that was marked with figure 8), of value of eight reals; **say one's ~**, (fig.) give one's opinion; make prepared statement. 5. Picture; literary or musical composition, usu. short; drama. 6. **by the ~**, (bought or

*Originally built as a breakwater or jetty, the **pier** later became an extension of the promenade with amusement arcades and even a theater to entertain holiday-makers, particularly at English seaside resorts.*

sold) individually; (payment etc.) according to amount done (not time taken); **of a ~**, uniform, consistent, in keeping (*with*); **~ goods**, textile fabrics (esp. cotton goods) woven in recognized lengths; **piece′work**, work paid for by the piece. **piece** *v.t.* (**pieced, piec·ing**). Put together, form into a whole; join thread in spinning; fit *on* (thing *to* another); eke *out*; make *out* (story, theory, etc.) by combination of parts; join *together*; patch *up*.

pièce de ré·sis·tance (pyĕs d*e* rāzēstahṅs′). Principal dish of a meal; most important or remarkable event, picture, etc. [Fr.]

piece·meal (pēs′mēl) *adv.* Piece by piece, part at a time. **~** *adj.* Done etc. piecemeal.

pied (pīd) *adj.* Parti-colored.

Pied·mont (pēd′mŏnt). (It. *Piemonte*) District of NW. Italy, united with Italy 1859. **Pied·mon·tese** (pēdmŏntēz′, -tēs′) *adj.* & *n.* (pl. **-tese**).

pier(pēr) *n.* Solid structure of stone etc., extending into sea or tidal river, to protect or enclose a harbor; structure of iron or wood, open below, running out into sea, lake, etc. and used as walk and loading area; support of spans of bridge; pillar; solid masonry between windows etc.

***Franklin Pierce,** 14th president of the U.S.A., unexpectedly won the election in 1852 having resigned from politics some years before. His single term was notable for the opening up of the northwest, railroad development and dissent over slavery.*

pierce (pērs) *v.* (**pierced, pierc·ing**). Penetrate; prick (*with* pin etc.); make hole in; force one's way through or into; penetrate *through*, *into*, etc. **pierc′er** *n.* **pierc′ing** *adj.* **pierc′ing·ly** *adv.*

Pierce (pērs), **Franklin** (1804–1869). Fourteenth president of U.S., 1853–7.

Pie·ro del·la Fran·ce·sca (pyār′ō dĕl*a* frănchĕs′k*a*) (1420?–1492). Italian painter and mathematician; famous for frescoes in the

There is much diversity in size and color among various members of the ***pigeon*** *family, and they are present in most parts of the world. All can produce 'pigeon's milk', a secretion of curd-like material which adults regurgitate from the crop to feed the young. The largest pigeons come from New Guinea.*

church of St. Francis at Arezzo, *The Legend of the Holy Cross.*

Pierre (pēr). Capital of South Dakota, in the central part on the Missouri River.

pie·tà (pyātah′) *n.* (often cap.) Picture, sculpture, of Virgin Mary holding dead body of Christ on her lap. [L. *pietas* piety.]

pi·e·tism (pī′etĭzem) *n.* Movement for revival of piety in the Lutheran Church begun by P. J. Spener about 1670; pious sentiment, exaggeration or affectation of this. **pi′e·tist** *n.* **pi·e·tis′tic, pi·e·tis′ti·cal** *adjs.*

pi·e·ty (pī′etē) *n.* Quality of being pious.

pi·e·zo·e·lec·tric·i·ty (pīēzōĭlĕktrĭs′ĭtē) *n.* Electricity or electric polarity produced by pressure on a nonconducting crystal. **pi·e·zo·e·lec·tric** (pīēzōĭlĕk′trĭk) *adj.* (also ~ **effect**) Property of certain crystals of generating electricity when subjected to pressure and (conversely) undergoing mechanical stress when subjected to voltage. **pi·e·zo·e·lec′tri·cal·ly** *adv.*

pif·fle (pĭf′el) *v.i.* (**-fled, -fling**). Talk or act feebly, trifle. ~ *n.* Twaddle. **pif′fling** *adj.* Trivial, worthless.

pig (pĭg) *n.* 1. Domesticated hog (*Sus scrofa*); flesh of (usu. young or suckling) pig as meat; (colloq.) greedy, dirty, sulky, obstinate, or annoying person; **buy a ~ in a poke**, buy something without seeing it or knowing its value; **in a ~'s eye**, (slang) certainly not. 2. Oblong mass of metal (usu. cast iron) cooled in a mold into which it is run from smelting furnace. 3. **pig′headed**, obstinate, stupid; **pig iron**; see def. 2 above, and IRON; **pig Latin**, made-up jargon of schoolchildren; **pig′nut**, bitter nut, esp. that of the brown hickory (*Carya glabra*) and the tuber of *Conopodium denudatum*; **pig′skin**, (leather made of) pig's skin, a football; **pig′sticking**, hunting of wild boar with spear; **pig′sty**, = STY[1];

pig'tail, braid of hair hanging from back of head, esp. as worn by Chinese under the Manchus, by young girls, and formerly by soldiers and sailors; **pig'weed**, herb (esp. of genus *Amaranthus*) eaten by pigs; wild edible plant (*Chenopodium album*), cooked like spinach, also called *lamb's quarters*. **pig** *v.* (**pigged, pig·ging**). Bring forth (pigs), bring forth pigs; herd together like pigs, live in disorderly or untidy fashion.

pi·geon (pĭj'on) *n.* 1. Bird of the family Columbidae; dove, esp. *Columba livia*, which haunts rocks and large buildings and is also domesticated in many varieties produced by fancy breeding; **carrier** ~, homing pigeon for carrying message attached to its neck or leg; **clay** ~: see CLAY; **homing** ~, pigeon trained to fly home over long distances; **wood** ~, ringdove (*Columba palumbus*), a wild bird eaten as game; ~ **breast**, deformed human breast laterally constricted; **pi'geonhole**, small recess for pigeon to nest in; one of a set of compartments in cabinet etc. for papers, etc.; ~ (*v.t.*) (**-holed, -hol·ing**) deposit (document) in this, put aside (matter) for future consideration; assign (thing) to definite place in memory; **pigeon's milk**, partly digested food with which pigeons feed their young; **pigeon-toed**, (of persons) turning toes or feet inward. 2. (colloq.) Simpleton, person easily swindled.

*It is now believed that the domestic **pig** of Europe originated from two wild species. One was distributed by migrating tribes from the Danube area.*

*The Berkshire (black), and Gloucester Old Spot are only two of the scores of breeds of **pig** which have been produced by centuries of breeding for different desired qualities.*

pig·ger·y (pĭg'erē) *n.* (pl. **-ger·ies**). Pig breeding establishment; pigsty; dirty place; piggishness.

pig·gish (pĭg'ĭsh) *adj.* Like a pig, esp. greedy or dirty. **pig'gish·ly** *adv.* **pig'gish·ness** *n.*

pig·gy (pĭg'ē) *n.* (pl. **-gies**). (nursery, colloq.) Little pig; ~ **bank**, money box, esp. of china, made in the shape of a pig. **piggy** *adj.* Piggish.

pig·gy·back (pĭg'ēbăk) *adv.* On the shoulders or back like a bundle; on the back or top of a larger object.

pig·let (pĭg'lĭt) *n.* Young pig.

pig·ment (pĭg'ment) *n.* Coloring matter in a paint or dye; (biol.) natural coloring matter of a tissue. **pig·men·tal** (pĭgmĕn'tal), **pig'·men·tar·y** (pĭg'mentĕrē), **pig'·ment·ed** *adjs.* **pig·men·ta·tion** (pĭgmentā'shon) *n.* Coloring (esp. of tissue) by pigment.

Pig·my: see PYGMY.

pi·ka (pē'ka, pī'ka) *n.* Any of several small mammals of family Ochotonidae, akin to rabbit but small-eared.

pike[1] (pīk) *n.* 1. Long wooden shaft with steel or iron head, infantry weapon superseded by bayonet; (dial.) pickax, spike. 2. Peaked top of hill. 3. (pl. **pikes**, collect. **pike**) Large voracious freshwater fish (*Esox lucuis*) of northern temperate zone, with long slender snout (prob. abbrev. of *pike fish*, from its pointed snout). ~ *v.t.* (**piked, pik·ing**). Thrust through, kill with pike.

pike[2] (pīk) *n.* Turnpike road.

Pike (pīk), **Zeb·u·lon** (zĕb'yulon) **Montgomery** (1779–1813). Amer. Army officer and explorer of the Mississippi, Arkansas, and Red rivers; **Pike's Peak**, mountain in E. central Colorado in the Rocky Mountains, 14,110 ft. (4,300 m) high discovered by him, 1806.

pik·er (pī'ker) *n.* (colloq.) Cautious gambler; petty or very cautious person.

pi·laf, pi·laff (pĭlahf', pē'lahf) *ns.* Oriental dish of rice usu. with meat, spices, etc.

pi·las·ter (pĭlăs'ter) *n.* Column of rectangular section projecting from a wall.

Pi·late (pī'lat), **Pontuis.** Roman governor of Judea 26–36 A.D.; presided at trial of Jesus Christ.

pil·chard (pĭl'cherd) *n.* Small sea fish (*Sardina pilchardus*) allied to herring but smaller and rounder.

*When the 'New York Weekly Journal' in the U.S.A. was declared to be libelous in 1734, copies were burned and the printer, John Peter Zenger, was lucky not to be placed in the **pillory.** Instead, he was acquitted.*

pile[1] (pīl) *n.* Pointed stake or post; heavy beam or column of wood, concrete, steel, etc., driven or bored into the ground as support for heavy structure; ~ **driver**, machine for driving piles into the ground. **pile** *v.t.* (**piled, pil·ing**). Furnish with piles; drive piles into.

pile[2] (pīl) *n.* 1. Heap of things laid more or less regularly upon one another. 2. (also **voltaic** ~) Series of plates of dissimilar metals, such as copper and zinc, laid one upon another alternately, with cloth or paper moistened with an acid solution placed between each pair, for producing electric current; any similar arrangement for producing electric current. 3. (also **atomic** ~) Nuclear REACTOR. 4. (colloq.) Heap of money, fortune. 5. Heap of combustibles on which corpse is burned. **pile** *v.t.* (**piled, pil·ing**). Heap up (freq. with *up, on*); load (table, etc., *with*); **pile up**, (naut.) run (ship) on rocks or aground; **pile'up**, (colloq.) collision involving several vehicles.

pile[3] (pīl) *n.* 1. Soft hair, down, wool of sheep. 2. Soft surface of some woven fabrics, produced by weaving in extra yarns and cutting them short (as in ~ **velvet**) or by knotting them on to warp threads (as in ~ **carpet**).

pile[4] (pīl) *n.* (Popular name for) hemorrhoid (usu. pl.).

pil·fer (pĭl´fer) *v.* Steal, esp. in small quantities. **pil·fer·age** (pĭl´ferĭj), **pil'fer·er** *ns.*

pil·grim (pĭl´grĭm, -grim) *n.* One who journeys to sacred place as act of religious devotion; person regarded as journeying to a future life; traveler; **P ~ Fathers**, earliest English Puritan settlers of colony of Plymouth, Massachusetts, and esp. those who left Delft Haven and Plymouth, England, in the *Mayflower* in 1620.

pil·grim·age (pĭl´grimĭj) *n.* Pilgrim's journey; (fig.) mortal life viewed as a journey.

pi·lif·er·ous (pīlĭf´erus) *adj.* (chiefly bot.) Having hair.

Pil·i·pi·no (pĭlipē´nō) *n.* Language of Filipinos, based on Tagalog.

pill (pĭl) *n.* 1. Small ball or disk of medicine to be swallowed whole; **the** ~, (colloq.) oral contraceptive. 2. (fig.) Something unpleasant that has to be accepted. 3. (baseball slang) Ball. 4. **pill'box**, shallow cylindrical box for holding pills; hat shaped like this; (mil.) small round concrete emplacement; **pill'wort**, plant of genus *Pilularia*, with small globular involucres.

*The **pilot** of a modern military aircraft has to be highly skilled as his cockpit is increasingly filled with technical instruments which he must be able to note and use.*

pil·lage (pĭl´ĭj) *n.* Plunder, esp. as practiced in war. ~ *v.t.* (**-laged, -lag·ing**). Sack, plunder. **pil'lag·er** *n.*

pil·lar (pĭl´er) *n.* Vertical structure of stone, wood, metal, etc., slender in proportion to height, used as support or ornament; post, pedestal; upright mass of air, water, etc.; (mining) solid mass of coal etc. left to support roof of the working; (fig.) person who is a main supporter (*of*); **from ~ to post**, to and fro, from one resource to another; **Pil'lars of Hercules**, two promontories, Calpe (Gibraltar) in

*Sometimes called the Poor Man's Weatherglass, from its habit of closing when the sky is overcast, the **pimpernel** is a common weed of grassland all over Europe.*

Europe and Abyla (Ceuta) in Africa, at E. end of Strait of Gibraltar, anciently supposed to have been parted by the arm of Hercules and regarded as the western limits of the inhabited world. **pillar** *v.t.* Support (as) with pillars. **pil'lared** *adj.*

pil·lo·ry (pĭl'orē) *n.* (pl. **-ries**). Wooden framework with holes for head and hands of offender exposed to public ridicule etc. ~ *v.t.* (**-ried, -ry·ing**). Put in the pillory; (fig.) expose to ridicule.

pil·low (pĭl'ō) *n.* Cushion as support for head, esp. in bed; (techn.) pillow-shaped block or support; **pil'lowcase, pil'lowslip**, washable cover for pillow; **pillow fight**, mock fight with pillows in bedroom. **pillow** *v.* Rest, prop up, (as) on pillow.

pi·lose (pī'lōs), **pi·lous** (pī'l*u*s) *adjs.* Covered with hair. **pi·los·i·ty** (pīlŏs'ĭtē) *n.*

pi·lot (pī'l*o*t) *n.* 1. Person qualified to take charge of ships entering or leaving a harbor, or wherever navigation requires local knowledge. 2. One who operates flying controls of an aircraft, one

*Pieces of skull found in 1912 and named **'Piltdown man'** were only exposed as a forgery in 1953–54 when it was shown that the jaw was an orangutan's and the skull had been stained.*

duly qualified to do so; automatic device for maintaining an airplane in flight. 3. (fig.) Guide, esp. in hunting field; (attrib.) small-scale, experimental. 4. ~ **balloon**, small balloon whose movements are observed as it rises in the air, used to ascertain direction and velocity of currents at various altitudes; ~ **bird**, rare dark brown Australian bird (*Pycnoptilus floccosus*) with loud and distinctive note; ~ **chute**, small parachute serving to bring main one into operation; ~ **engine**, locomotive engine going on ahead of a train to make sure that the way is clear; **pi'lotfish** (pl. **-fish·es**, collect. **-fish**), small silvery-blue dark-barred fish of warm seas (*Naucrates ductor*), said to act for shark as pilot or guide to food; ~ **lamp**, electric indicator light or control light; ~ **light**, small gas burner kept lighted to kindle large burner as required. **pilot** *v.t.* Conduct as pilot; act as pilot on. **pi·lot·age** (pī'l*o*tĭj) *n.* **pi'lot·less** *adj.* (of aircraft) Without human pilot aboard, guided by remote control.

pi·lous = PILOSE.

Pil·sen (pĭl'z*e*n). German name of Plzen, town of Czechoslovakia, famous for lager beer (**Pil·sen·er** pr. pĭlz'n*e*r, pĭls'-).

Pil·sud·ski (pĭlsōōt'skē), **Joseph** (1867–1935). Polish soldier and statesman; 1st marshal of Poland; chief of state 1918–23; prime minister and virtual dictator 1926–1928, 1930–5.

Pilt·down (pĭlt'down). Down near Lewes, England, where prehistoric remains of a human skull and apelike lower jaw, and of worked flints and bone implements, were discovered (1912); they were claimed as belonging to the early Pleistocene period but proved by scientific tests (1953) to have been assembled as a hoax.

pi·men·to (pĭmĕn'tō) *n.* (pl. **-tos**). 1. (Dried aromatic berry of) West Indian evergreen tree (*Pimenta officinalis*); allspice. 2. (also **pi·mien·to** pr. pĭmyĕn'tō, -mĕn'- pl. **-tos**). Any of various peppers.

pimp (pĭmp) *n.* Man who solicits clients for a prostitute or brothel. ~ *v.i.* Act as pimp.

pim·per·nel (pĭm'p*e*rnĕl, -n*e*l) *n.* Small annual (*Anagallis arvensis*) found in cornfields and waste ground, with scarlet (also blue or white) flowers closing in cloudy or rainy weather.

pim·ple (pĭm'p*e*l) *n.* Small solid round swelling of the skin, usu. inflammatory. **pim'pled, pim'ply** *adjs.*

pin (pĭn) *n.* Thin piece of metal with sharp point and round flattened head for fastening together parts of dress, papers, etc.; peg of wood or metal for various purposes; peg on musical instrument; (pl. colloq.), legs; **cotter pin**, metal pin to be passed through hole and held there by gaping of its split end; **pins and needles**, tingling sensation in limb recovering from numbness; **on pins and needles**, in state of mental agitation due to suspense; **pin'cushion**, small cushion for sticking pins in to keep them ready for use; **pin'feather**, ungrown feather; **pin'head**, stupid or silly person; (fig.) minute thing; **pin'hole**, hole made by pin or into which peg fits; **pin money**, (orig.) allowance to women for dress expenses etc.; hence, very small sum; **pin'point**, point of a pin; (attrib. of targets) small and requiring very accurate and precise bombing and shelling; (*v.t.*) locate or bomb (such target) with the accuracy and precision required (also fig.); **pin'prick**, (fig.) trifling irritation; **pin stripe**, very narrow stripe in textile fabric; **pin'tail** (pl. **-tails**, collect. **-tail**), duck or grouse with pointed tail, esp. N. Amer. duck (*Anas acuta*), having long neck, gray, brown, and white plumage, and white underparts; **pin'tuck**, narrow ornamental tuck; **pin'wheel**, small wheel with paper vanes pinned to a stick so as to rotate in the wind; **pin'worm**, threadworm (*Enterobius vermicularis*) parasitic in human rectum. **pin** *v.t.* (**pinned, pin·ning**). Fasten (*to, together, up*) with pin(s); transfix with pin, lance, etc.; seize and hold fast; bind (person *down*) *to* (promise, arrangement); ~ **up**, (archit.) underpin; fasten (on wall etc.) by means of a pin; **pin'up** (*n.*) (picture pinned up on wall etc. portraying) sexually attractive woman or man; such a person. **pin'like** *adj.* **pin'ner** *n.*

pin·a·fore (pĭn'afōr, -fōr) *n.* Washable sleeveless covering worn over dress etc. to protect from dirt.

pince-nez (păns'nā, pĭns') *n.* (pl. **pince-nez** pr. păns'nāz, pĭns'). Pair of eyeglasses with spring to clip on to nose. [Fr., = "pinch-nose"]

pin·cers (pĭn'serz) *n.pl.* (also **pair of** ~) Gripping tool made of two limbs pivoted together forming pair of jaws with manipulating handles; similar organ in crustaceans, etc.; ~ (also **pincer**) **movement**, (mil.) operation involving the convergence of two forces on enemy position like the jaws of a pair of pincers. **pin'cer·like** *adj.*

pinch (pĭnch) *n.* Nip, squeeze; as much as can be taken up with tips of finger and thumb; (fig.) stress (of poverty etc.); **in a** ~, in a strait or exigency. **pinch** *v.* Nip with finger and thumb, pain or injure by squeezing; (of cold, hunger, etc.) nip, shrivel; stint; be niggardly; sail (vessel) close hauled; (slang) steal; arrest.

Pin·dar (pĭn'der) (518–438 B.C.). Greek lyric poet. **Pin·dar·ic** (pĭndăr'ĭk) *adj.* Of Pindar; resembling the style, diction, etc., of Pindar; ~ **ode**, (English pros.) ode with irregular number of feet in lines and arbitrary disposition of rhymes.

pine[1] (pīn) *n.* Tree of genus *Pinus* with evergreen needle-shaped leaves growing in sheathed clusters of 2 or more, many species of which afford timber, tar, and turpentine; ~ **cone**, charactertistic organ of the pine, containing its

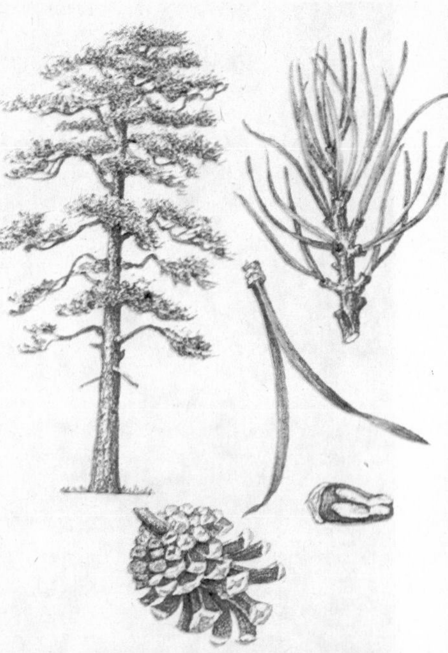

*The Scots **pine** is one of the most beautiful as well as one of the most useful conifers. Its durable hardwood has long been used in building and cabinet-making.*

***Pindar** (shown here in a painting by the 19th-century painter Ingres) was one of Greece's greatest and most distinctive poets, writing in many verse-forms for various clients.*

*The garden **pink** and the carnation are both derived from the wild Dianthus which grows in the Mediterranean region. Others grow in Asia and Africa.*

*The most important use of **pinnacles** in Gothic architecture was to give strong vertical emphasis, as here: they were also used to strengthen flying buttresses by adding weight.*

seeds; ~ **nut**, edible seed of some pine trees.

pine² (pīn) *v.i.* (**pined, pin·ing**). Languish, waste away, from grief, disease, etc.; long eagerly (*for, after, to*).

pin·e·al (pĭn′ēal) *adj.* (anat.) Shaped like a pine cone; ~ **body**, small conical body of unknown function behind third ventricle of brain.

pine·ap·ple (pīn′ăpel) *n.* Juicy edible collective fruit of *Ananas*, surmounted by crown of small leaves (so called from resemblance to pine cone); (slang) hand grenade, bomb.

ping (pĭng) *n.* Abrupt ringing sound as of rifle bullet flying through air. ~ *v.i.* 1. Produce abrupt ringing sound; fly with this. 2. (of internal combustion engine) Knock, emit dull metallic sound from explosion of (part of) charge, due usu. to poor quality of fuel.

Ping-Pong (pĭng′pŏng) *n.* (trademark) Table tennis.

pin·ion¹ (pĭn′yon) *n.* Terminal segment of bird's wing; any flight feather of wing; (in carving) part of wing corresponding to forearm; (poet.) wing. ~ *v.t.* Cut off pinion of (wing, bird) to prevent flight; bind the arms of (person), bind (arms); bind (person etc.) fast *to*.

pin·ion² (pĭn′yon) *n.* Small cogwheel engaging with larger one; cogged spindle engaging with wheel.

pink¹ (pĭngk) *n.* 1. Garden plant, species of *Dianthus* (esp. *D. plumarius*), native to E. Europe, with white, crimson, pink, or variegated sweet smelling flowers; allied or similar plant. 2. Finest example of excellence, flower; **in the** ~, (slang) healthy. 3. Pale red slightly inclining to purple. 4. Fox hunter's red coat; cloth of this; fox hunter. **pink** *adj.* Of pale red color of various kinds, as *rose, salmon, pink*; (joc.) mildly communist; **pink′eye**, contagious ophthalmia in man, marked by redness of the eyeball. **pink′ish** *adj.*

pink² (pĭngk) *v.t.* Pierce with sword etc.; ornament (leather etc.) with perforations; cut scalloped or zigzag edge on; adorn, deck (freq. ~ **out**); **pink′ing shears**, dressmaker's serrated shears for cutting zigzag edge.

Pink·er·ton (pĭng′kerton), **Allan** (1819–84). Scottish-born Amer. detective; founded (1850) a detective agency; Union intelligence agent in Civil War; forestalled an attempt on life of Abraham Lincoln, 1861.

pin·nace (pĭn′ĭs) *n.* Man-of-war's double-banked (usu. eight-oared) boat; also applied to other ships' boats, now usu. driven by motor; (hist.) small, usu. two-masted, vessel.

pin·na·cle (pĭn′akel) *n.* Small ornamental turret usu. ending in pyramid or cone, crowning a buttress, roof, etc.; natural peak; (fig.) culmination, climax. ~ *v.t.* (**-cled, -cling**). Set (as) on pinnacle; form the pinnacle of; furnish with pinnacles.

pin·nate (pĭn′āt, -ĭt) *adj.* 1. (bot., of compound leaf) With series of leaflets on each side of common stalk. 2. (zool.) With branches, tentacles, etc., on each side of an axis. **pin′nate·ly** *adv.*

pin·no·there (pĭn′othēr) *n.* Small crab of genus *Pinnotheres*, inhabiting shells of oysters, mussels, etc., and sharing their food.

pin·nule (pĭn′ūl) *n.* 1. (bot.) Secondary division of pinnate leaf. 2. (zool.) Part, organ, like small wing or fin. 3. Sight at end of index of astrolabe etc. **pin·nu·lar** (pĭn′yuler) *adj.*

pi·noch·le, pi·noc·le (pē′nŭkel, -nŏk-) *ns.* Card game using 48 cards, with two of every card above

*Rock **pipits** are found only on the rocky coasts and offshore islands of western Europe from France to northern Sweden; they nest in crevices on cliffs.*

the 8; occurrence of queen of spades and jack of diamonds together in this game.

pi·ñon (pin´yon, pēn´yōn; *Sp.* pēnyawn´) *n.* (pl. **pi·ñons,** *Sp.* **pi·ño·nes** pr. pēnyaw´nēs). Nut pine tree *Pinus edulis monophylla quadrifolia* of western N. Amer.; its edible fruit.

pint (pīnt) *n.* Measure of capacity, liquid or dry, equal to ½ quart.

pin·tle (pĭn´tel) *n.* Bolt or pin, esp. one on which some other part turns.

pin·to (pĭn´tō) *adj.* & *n.* (pl. **-tos**). Piebald (horse); ~ **bean,** mottled kidney bean used for food in Southwest. [Span., = "painted"]

pin·y (pī´nē) *adj.* (**pin·i·er, pin·i·est**). Of, like, abounding in, pines.

pin·yin (pĭn´yĭn´) *n.* System of romanized spelling for Chinese language.

pi·o·neer (pīonēr´) *n.* 1. Member of military unit equipped to prepare road for troops. 2. Initiator of enterprise; original explorer. ~ *v.* Act as pioneer (to); conduct; open up (road etc.) as pioneer.

pi·ous (pī´us) *adj.* Devout, religious; (archaic) dutiful. **pi´ous·ly** *adv.* **pi´ous·ness** *n.*

pip[1] (pĭp) *n.* Disease of poultry, hawks, etc., marked by thick mucus in throat and often by white scale on tip of tongue; **the** ~, (slang) a feeling of disgust, depression, or bad temper.

pip[2] (pĭp) *n.* Each spot on playing cards, dice, or dominoes, or star on army officer's shoulder; single blossom of clustered inflorescence; rhomboidal segment of surface of pineapple; image that an object produces on a radar screen.

pip[3] (pĭp) *n.* Seed of apple, pear, orange, etc.

pi·pal, pee·pul (pē´pal) *ns.* Indian species of fig tree (*Ficus religiosa*) regarded as sacred.

pipe (pīp) *n.* 1. Tube of wood, metal, etc., esp. for conveying water, gas, etc. 2. Musical wind instrument consisting of single tube blown by mouth; each of tubes by which sounds are produced in organ; boatswain's whistle, sounding of this; (pl.) bagpipes. 3. Voice, esp. in singing; song, note, of bird. 4. Tubular organ, vessel, etc., in animal body; cylindrical vein of ore; channel of decoy for wild fowl.

*A re-enactment of a **pioneer** Oregon trail wagon-train in Nebraska. The pioneers suffered the most appalling hardships to reach and open up new territories in the U.S.A.*

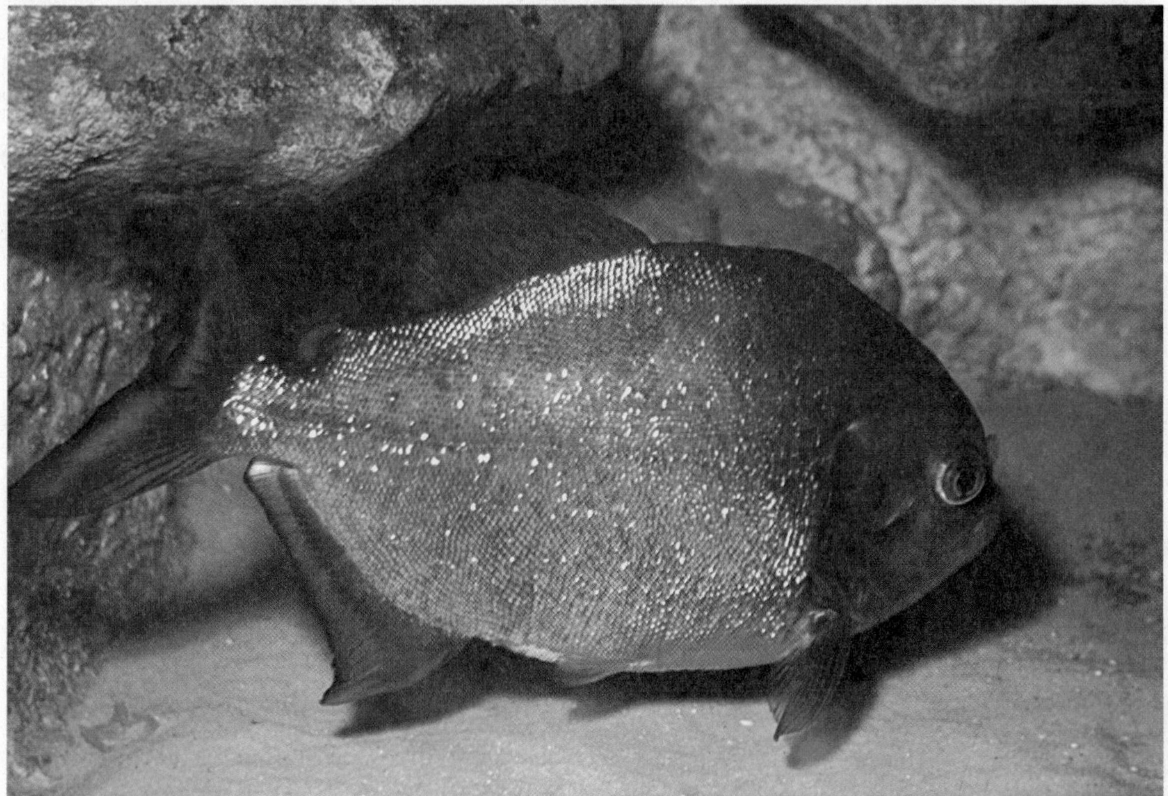

Red ***piranha*** *(Rooseveltia natteri) grow up to 12 inches long and, like all other piranhas, are vicious fish. Some piranhas work in packs, devouring quite large animals with their dreadful teeth.*

5. Narrow tube of clay, wood, etc., with bowl at one end, for drawing in smoke of tobacco; quantity of tobacco held by this; ~ **of peace, peace** ~, calumet; **put that in your** ~ **and smoke it**, digest that fact etc. if you can. 6. Cask for wine, esp. as measure usu. = about 126 gallons. 7. ~ **clay**, fine white clay used for tobacco pipes and (esp. by soldiers) for cleaning white breeches, belts, etc.; (*v.t.*) whiten with pipe clay; ~ **dream**, (colloq.) kind of extravagant fancy induced by smoking opium; hence, notion unlikely to be realized; ~ **fitter**, mechanic who installs and maintains plumbing pipes, steampipes, etc.; **pipe′line**, line of pipes for conveying petroleum, gas, or water across country; channel of supply, communication, etc.; **pipe rack**, rack for tobacco pipes; **pipe′stone**, hard red clay used by Amer. Indians for tobacco pipes. **pipe** *v.* (**piped, pip·ing**). 1. Play (tune etc.) on pipe; lead, bring, (person etc.) by sound of pipe; summon (crew) by sounding whistle; utter in shrill voice; ~ **down**, (slang) become quiet; ~ **up**, speak up; sing. 2. Trim (garment), ornament (cake etc.) with piping. 3. Furnish with pipes.

pip·er (pī′p*e*r) *n.* One who plays on pipe, esp. strolling musician; bagpiper; **pay the** ~, defray cost, bear expense or loss, of proceeding etc.; pay the cost of doing as one pleases.

pi·pette, pi·pet (pīpĕt′) *ns.* Slender tube filled usu. by suction, used in laboratories for measuring and transferring small quantities of liquid. ~ *v.* (**-pet·ted, -pet·ting**).

pip·ing (pī′pĭng) *n.* (esp.) Ornamental pipelike fold of cloth, often enclosing cord, for trimming edge of seam of garment, upholstery, etc.; ornamental cord-like line of icing on cake etc. ~ *adj.* Shrill; playing on a pipe. ~ *adv.* ~ **hot**, so hot as to make piping or hissing sound; very hot.

pip·i·strelle (pĭpĭstrĕl′, pĭp′-ĭstrĕl) *n.* Small bat of genus *Pipistrellus.*

pip·it (pĭp′ĭt) *n.* Bird of a group superficially resembling larks but allied to the wagtails, of *Anthus* and related genera, including **water** ~ (*A. spinoletta*). [prob. imit.]

pip·kin (pĭp′kĭn) *n.* Small earthenware pot or pan.

pip·pin (pĭp′ĭn) *n.* Any of several kinds of apple raised from seed.

pip-squeak (pĭp′skwēk) *n.* (slang) Insignificant person, petty object.

pi·quant (pē′k*a*nt, -kahnt, pēkahnt′) *adj.* Agreeably pungent, sharp, appetizing; (fig.) pleasantly stimulating or disturbing to the mind. **pi′quant·ly** *adv.* **pi′quan·cy, pi′quant·ness** *ns.*

pique (pēk) *v.t.* (**piqued, piqu·ing**). Irritate, wound the pride of; arouse (interest, curiosity); plume (oneself). ~ *n.* Ill feeling, resentment.

pi·qué (pĭkā′, pē-) *n.* Stiff fabric, usu. cotton, with lengthwise ribs.

pi·quet (pĭkĕt′, -kā′) *n.* Card game for two players with pack of 32 cards, points being scored on various groups or combinations of cards.

pi·ra·cy (pī′r*a*sē) *n.* (pl. **-cies**). Action of a pirate; **air** ~, hijacking of aircraft.

pi·ra·nha (pĭrahn′y*a*, -răn′-) *n.* Tropical Amer. voracious freshwater fish (*Serrasalmo piraya*) with serrated belly and strong lancet-shaped teeth.

pi·rate (pī′r*a*t) *n.* (Ship used by) sea robber; marauder; one who infringes another's copyright. ~ *v.* (**-rat·ed, -rat·ing**). Plunder; reproduce (book etc.) without authorization of copyright owner; play the pirate. **pi·rat·i·cal** (pīrăt′ĭk*a*l), **pi·rat′ic** *adjs.* **pi·rat′i·cal·ly** *adv.*

pir·ou·ette (pĭrōōĕt′) *n.* & *v.i.* (**-et·ted, -et·ting**). (ballet) Spin around on one foot or on point of toe. [Fr., = "top"]

Pi·sa (pē′z*a*). City of Tuscany, N. Italy; **Leaning Tower of** ~, campanile of cathedral, built 1174–1350, about 180 ft. (54.9 m) high and leaning some 16 ft. (4.8 m) from the perpendicular.

pis·ca·to·ry (pĭs′k*a*tōrē, -tōrē)

*Possibly the most popular form of **pistol** is the revolver. Its relatively simple mechanism, developed perhaps 300 years ago, has stood the tests both of time and of operating conditions such as sandy deserts. Its greatest practical advantage, apart from this, is its better 'stopping power' as compared with an automatic pistol.*

adj. Of fishermen or fishing; addicted to fishing. **pis·ca·to·ri·al** (pĭskatōr′ēal, -tōr′-) *adj.*

Pis·ces (pī′sēz, pĭs′ēz). The Fishes, a constellation; 12th sign (♓) of the zodiac, which sun enters about Feb.

Pis·gah (pĭz′ga). Mountain of Transjordan, NE. of Dead Sea, from which Moses viewed the Promised Land (Deut. 3) before his death.

pis·mire (pĭs′mīr) *n.* Ant. [f. *piss* (from smell of ant hill), and obs. *mire* ant, f. Du. *mier.*]

piss (pĭs) *v.* (**pissed, piss·ing**). (vulg.) Urinate; discharge with the urine; wet with urine. ~ *n.* Urine.

pis·ta·chi·o (pĭstăsh′ēō, -stah′-shēō) *n.* (pl. **-chi·os**). Tree (*Pistacia vera*) of W. Asia, cultivated in S. Europe; nut of this, with greenish edible kernel; color of the kernel.

pis·til (pĭs′tĭl) *n.* Organ of flower bearing ovules, comprising ovary, style, and stigma. **pis·til·late** (pĭs′tĭlĭt, -lāt) *adj.*

pis·tol (pĭs′tol) *n.* Small firearm, usu. with curved butt, held and fired by one hand; ~ **grip, handle**, handle shaped like butt of pistol; **pistol-whip**, beat with pistol.

pis·tole (pĭstōl′) *n.* (hist.) Foreign gold coin, esp. Spanish.

pis·ton (pĭs′ton) *n.* Disk or short cylinder fitting closely within cylindrical vessel in which it moves to and fro, used in steam engine, pump, etc., to impart or receive motion by means of ~ **rod**; sliding valve in cornet etc.; ~ **ring**, metallic expansible packing ring fitted on piston.

pit (pĭt) *n.* 1. Natural hole in ground; hole made in digging for mineral etc. or for industrial purposes; (shaft of) coal mine; depression in floor of workshop enabling persons to reach underside of motor vehicles for inspection or repair; covered hole as trap. 2. **the** ~, hell. 3. (hist.) Enclosure for cockfights etc. 4. Hollow in animal or plant body or on any surface; depressed scar, as after smallpox; (bot.) hollow between plant cells on either side of lamella (~ **membrane**); ~ **of the stomach**, depression between cartilages of false ribs. 5. Hard stone of a fruit. 6. (Brit.) That part of auditorium of theater etc. which is on floor of house; now usu. the part of this behind stalls; section of theater in front of stage, used for members of the orchestra. 7. Part of floor of commodities exchange appropriated for special branch of business, e.g. *wheat* ~. 8. (usu. pl.) Place at side of racing track for refueling etc. 9. **pit′fall**, covered pit as trap; (fig.) unsuspected snare or danger. **pit** *v.* (**pit·ted, pit·ting**). Put into a pit; remove pits from (fruit); set (cocks etc.) to fight in pit (*against* each other), (fig.) match (*against*); make pits, esp. scars, in (esp. in past part.); (of flesh etc.) retain impression of finger etc. when touched. **pit′ted** *adj.*

pit·a·pat (pĭt′apăt) *adv.* & *n.* (With) sound as of light quick steps.

Pit·cairn (pĭt′kārn) **Island.** Small island in S. Pacific (British since 1839) between Tahiti and Easter Island; settled in 1790 by mutineers from the BOUNTY and inhabited by their descendants.

pitch[1] (pĭch) *n.* Black or dark brown tenacious resinous substance, the residue from distillation of tar or turpentine, hard when cold but becoming viscid and semiliquid when heated, used for caulking seams of ships, protecting wood from moisture, road-making, etc.;

*Buildings like the leaning tower show the prosperity of medieval **Pisa**. Important even before Roman times, Pisa has remained a flourishing city to the present day.*

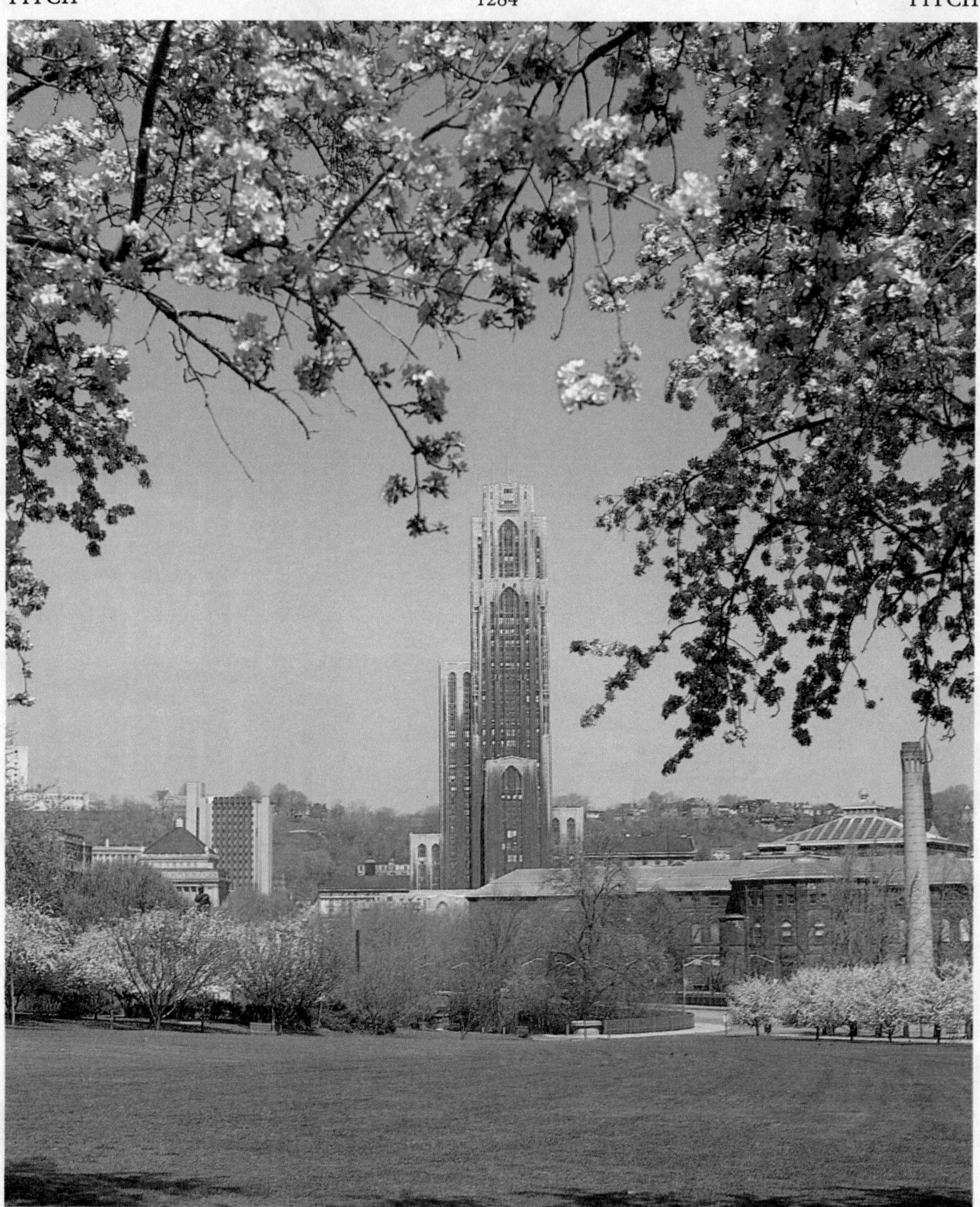

The Cathedral of Learning at the University of ***Pittsburgh,*** *Pennsylvania. The city of Pittsburgh is one of the U.S.A.'s major steel manufacturers, with a diversity of satellite industries.*

~**-black**, with no light at all; so ~**-dark(ness); pitch'blende**, mineral containing uranium oxide, one of the chief sources of radium and uranium; **pitch pine**, especially resinous kinds of pine. **pitch'y** *adj.* (**pitch·i·er, pitch·i·est**). Of, like, dark as, pitch. **pitch'i·ness** *n.* **pitch** *v.t.* Smear, cover, coat, with pitch.

pitch[2] (pĭch) *v.* Fix and erect (tent, camp); encamp; fix, plant, (thing) indefinite position; pave (road) with set stones; **pitched' battle**, battle of set kind; battle with forces intensely committed, not casual. 2. (mus.) Set at particular pitch; (fig.) express in particular style. 3. Throw, fling; (in games) throw (flat object) toward a mark; throw (ball) to batter in baseball etc.; (of ball etc.) land, fall (in specified manner or position); fall heavily. 4. (slang) Tell (tale, yarn); deliver high-pressure sales talk. 5. (of ship) Plunge in longitudinal direction. 6. Incline, dip (of stratum, roof, etc.). 7. **pitch in**, (colloq.) set to work vigorously; **pitch into**, (colloq..) assail forcibly with blows, words, etc.; make vigorous attack on. **pitch** *n.* 1. Pitching; mode of delivering ball in cricket, baseball, etc. 2. (chiefly Brit.) Place at which street performer is stationed; (cricket) place between and about wickets. 3. Height to which falcon etc. soars before swooping on prey; height, degree, intensity (*of* quality etc.); (mus.) quality of musical sound depending on comparative rapidity of vibrations producing it, degree of acuteness (international standard pitch is set by fixing the A above middle C at 440 vibrations per second); ~ **pipe**, small pipe blown by mouth to set pitch for singing or tuning. 4. Degree of slope; steepness of roof's slope. 5. (mech.) Distance between successive points or lines, e.g. between successive teeth of cogwheel; ~ **wheel**, toothed wheel engaging with another. 6. (slang) Sales talk.

pitch·er[1] (pĭch'*er*) *n.* (esp.) Player who delivers ball, esp. in baseball.

pitch·er[2] (pĭch'*er*) *n.* Vessel, usu. of earthenware, with handle or two ears and usu. a lip, for holding liquids; (bot.) modified leaf in pitcher form; ~ **plant**, any of various plants with such leaves, freq. containing liquid secretion by which insects are caught and digested. **pitch·er·ful** (pĭch'*er*fo͝ol) *n.* (pl. **-fuls**).

Pitch·er (pĭch'*er*), **Molly** (1754–1832). (original name, Mary Ludwig Hays McCauley) Amer. Revolutionary War heroine who carried water to weary and wounded soldiers during the battle of Monmouth, June, 1778, and took her husband's place at his cannon when he was overcome by heat.

pitch·fork (pĭch'fŏrk) *n.* Long-handled fork with 2 or more sharp prongs for pitching hay etc.; tuning fork. ~ *v.t.* Cast (as) with pitchfork.

pitch·man (pĭch'm*a*n) *n.* (pl. **-men** pr. -m*e*n). 1. Itinerant vendor of small merchandise. 2. (slang) High-pressure salesman.

pit·e·ous (pĭt'ē*u*s) *adj.* Such as to cause pity, deplorable. **pit'e·ous·ly** *adv.* **pit'e·ous·ness** *n.*

pith (pĭth) *n.* 1. Spongy cellular tissue in stem and branches of dicotyledonous plants; similar tissue lining rind of orange etc.; spinal cord; (fig.) essential part, quintessence. 2. Physical strength, vigor; force, energy. **pith'less** *adj.* **pith** *v.t.* Slaughter (animal) by severing spinal cord.

pith·y (pĭth'ē) *adj.* (**pith·i·er, pith·i·est**). Of, like, full of, pith; condensed and forcible, terse. **pith'i·ly** *adv.* **pith'i·ness** *n.*

pit·i·a·ble (pĭt'ē*a*bel) *adj.* Deserving of pity or contempt. **pit'i·a·ble·ness** *n.* **pit'i·a·bly** *adv.*

pit·i·ful (pĭt'ĭf*u*l) *adj.* Arousing pity; contemptible. **pit'i·ful·ly** *adv.* **pit'i·ful·ness** *n.*

pit·i·less (pĭt'ĭlĭs) *adj.* Showing no pity. **pit'i·less·ly** *adv.* **pit'i·less·ness** *n.*

pi·ton (pē't*o*n) *n.* Metal spike or peg used in mountaineering as support or belaying pin.

Pi·tot (pētō'), **Henri** (1695–1771). French physicist; **Pitot tube**, right-angled tube open at both ends, used in anemometers and for determining velocity of fluids; similar device used for measuring velocity of aircraft.

pit·tance (pĭt'*a*ns) *n.* 1. (hist.) Pious bequest to religious house for extra food etc. 2. Allowance, remuneration, esp. scanty one; small number or amount.

Pitts·burgh (pĭts'b ĕrg). Industrial city and major river port in SW. Pennsylvania, where the confluence of the Allegheny and Monongahela rivers forms the Ohio River.

pi·tu·i·tar·y (pĭto͞o'ĭtĕrē, -tū'-) *adj.* (archaic) Of or secreting phlegm; ~ **gland**, small bilobed ductless gland at base of brain producing hormones that regulate many important bodily functions and coordinate the working of other endocrine organs. **pituitary** *n.* (pl. **-tar·ies**). Pituitary gland. **pi·tu·i·tous** (pĭto͞o'ĭt*u*s, -tū'-) *adj.* **pi·tu·i·trin** (pĭto͞o'ĭtrĭn, -tū'-) *n.* Hormone produced by pituitary gland; solution of this used medicinally.

pit·y (pĭt'ē) *n.* (pl. **pit·ies**). 1. Feeling of tenderness aroused by distress or suffering; **take ~ on**, feel or act compassionately toward. 2. Regrettable fact, ground for regret; **more's the ~**, so much the worse. **pity** *v.t.* (**pit·ied, pit·y·ing**). Feel pity for. **pit'y·ing·ly** *adv.*

Pi·us (pī'*u*s). Name of 12 popes, including **Pius II** (Enea Silvio de Piccolomini, 1405–64); pope 1458–1464; author and patron of letters; **Pius IV** (Giovanni Angelo Medici, 1499–1565); pope 1559–65; reconvened Council of TRENT in 1562; **Pius IX** (Giovanni Maria Mastai-Jenetti, 1792–1878); pope 1846–78; during this pontificate the temporal power of the papacy was lost and the doctrine of papal infallibility proclaimed; **Pius XI** (Achille Ratti, 1857–1939); pope 1922–39; the breach between church and state was healed in this pontificate and the Vatican City State was founded; **Pius XII** (Eugenio Pacelli, 1876–1958); pope 1939–58.

piv·ot (pĭv'*o*t) *n.* Short shaft or pin on which something turns or oscillates; (mil.) soldier on whom body of troops on parade wheels; (fig.) cardinal or central point. **piv'ot·al** *adj.* **pivot** *v.i.* Turn as on pivot, hinge (*on*).

pix·ie, pix·y (pĭk'sē) *ns.* (pl. **pix·ies**). Supernatural being akin to fairy. **pix·i·lat·ed** (pĭk's*i*lātĭd) *adj.* Enchanted, slightly crazy.

Pi·zar·ro (pĭzăr'ō), **Francisco** (*c*1471–1541). Spanish conquistador; discoverer and conqueror of Peru.

pizz. *abbrev.* Pizzicato.

piz·za (pēt's*a*) *n.* Italian dish of flat open crust containing cheese etc., therefore, **piz·ze·ri·a** (pēts*e*rē'*a*), place where pizzas are made and sold.

piz·zi·ca·to (pĭts*i*kah'tō) *adv., n.* (pl. **-tos, -ti** pr. -tē) & *adj.* (mus.) (Passage, note, played) by plucking string of violin etc. with finger instead of using bow. [It.]

pk. *abbrev.* (pl. **pks.**). Pack; park; peak; peck.

pkg. *abbrev.* Package, packages.

pkwy. *abbrev.* Parkway.

pl. *abbrev.* Place; plate; plural.

*The best-known result of **pituitary** malfunction is abnormal growth. However the gland is also very important as a controller of other glands, such as the thyroid. Location of the pituitary in the human brain is shown below.*

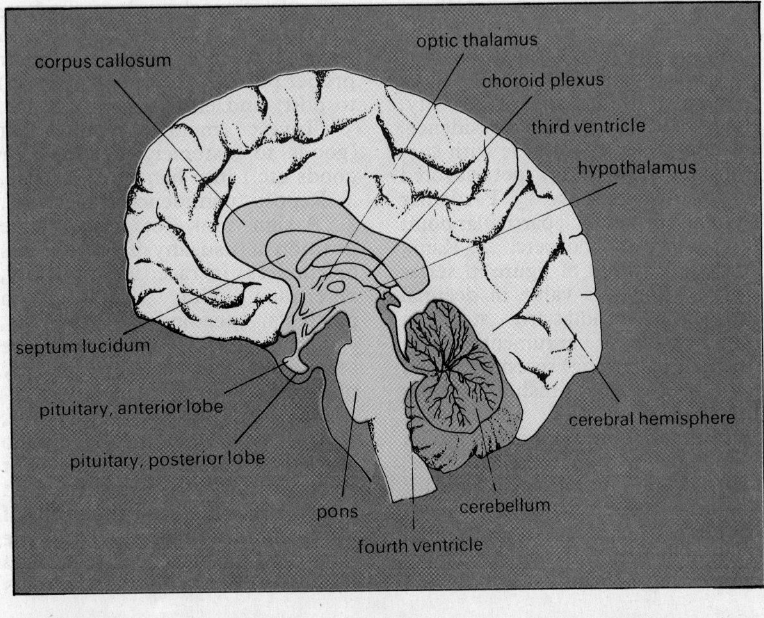

Piux XII, the first Pope to make extensive use of radio as a means of reaching wide audiences, did much to pave the way for the full ecumenical movement.

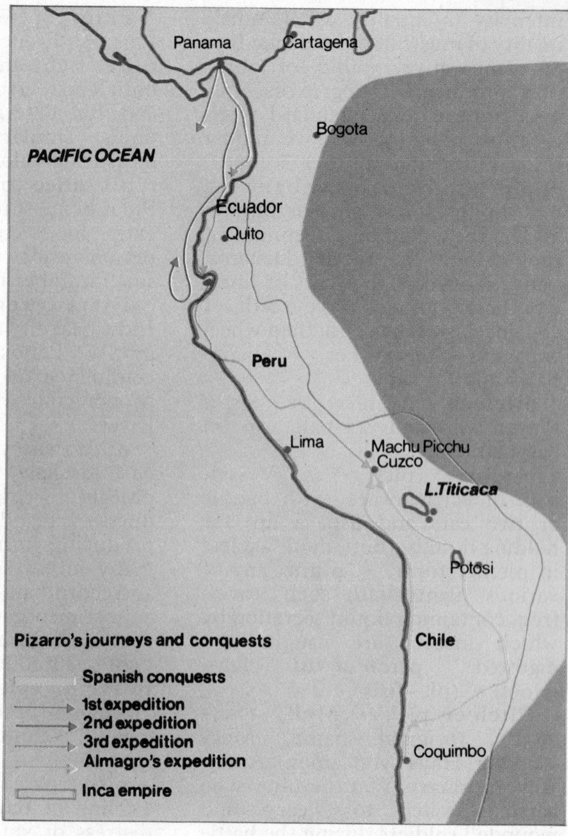

Pizarro conquered the empire of the Incas in 1531 with about 180 men and a few horses. His success was due to his capture of Atahualpa which resulted in a huge ransom being paid.

plac·a·ble (plăk'*a*bel, plā'k*a*-) *adj.* Easily appeased, mild, forgiving. **plac·a·bil'i·ty** *n.* **plac'a·bly** *adv.*

plac·ard (plăk'ârd, -*e*rd) *n.* Document printed on 1 side of single sheet for posting in a public place, poster. ~ *v.t.* Set up placards on (wall etc.); advertise (wares etc.) by placards; display (poster etc.) as placard.

pla·cate (plā'kāt, plăk'āt) *v.t.* (**-cat·ed, -cat·ing**). Pacify, conciliate. **pla'cat·er, pla·ca·tion** (plākā'sh*o*n) *ns.* **pla'ca·tive, pla·ca·to·ry** (plā'k*a*tōrē, -tōrē, plăk'*a*-) *adjs.*

place (plās) *n.* 1. Particular part of space; part of space occupied by person or thing; street. 2. City, town, village, etc.; residence, dwelling; vacation house with surroundings; building, spot, devoted to specified purpose. 3. Particular spot on surface etc.; particular point or passage in book etc. 4. Rank, station; position of figure in series as indicating its value in decimal or similar notation; step in progression of argument, statement, etc.; (racing) second position among those that finish. 5. Proper or natural position; space, seat, accommodation, for person etc. at table, in conveyance, etc.; **in ~ of,** instead of; **~ card,** small card for name of a guest at table; **~ mat,** small mat used at an individual setting at table; **~ setting,** dishes and eating utensils set at a diner's place at table; **take the ~ of,** substitute for. 6. Office, employment, esp. government appointment; duties of office etc. 7. **give ~ to,** make room for; be succeeded by; **out of, in, ~,** (un)suitable, (in)appropriate; **take ~,** happen. 8. **~ kick,** (football) kick made when ball is held on ground by another player. **place** *v.t.* (**placed, plac·ing**). 1. Put in particular place; arrange in their proper places. 2. Appoint (person) to post; find employment etc. for. 3. Invest (money); dispose of (goods) to customer; put (order for goods etc.) into hands of firm etc. 4. Repose (confidence etc. *in, on*). 5. Assign rank to; locate; state position of (usu. any of first 3 horses or runners) in race; identify fully, determine who (or what) a particular person (or thing) is, assign to a class; **be placed,** be second in race. 6. Get (goal) by place kick.

pla·ce·bo (pl*a*sē'bō) *n.* (pl. **-bos, -boes**). 1. Medicine having no intrinsic therapeutic value but given to humor patient (also used in experiments to test the effect of drugs, the drug being given to one group and the placebo to those who act as controls). 2. (eccles.) Vespers for the dead, opening chant of the vespers. [L., = "I shall be acceptable," 1st word of Ps. 114:9 in Vulgate]

pla·cen·ta (pl*a*sĕnt*a*) *n.* (pl. **-tas, -tae** pr. -tē). 1. Spongy vascular structure (in some mammals and some other vertebrates) formed by the interlocking of fetal and maternal tissue, through which the fetus is supplied with nutriment and rid of waste products. 2. (bot.) Part of carpel to which ovules are attached. **pla·cen'tal** *adj.*

plac·er (plăs'*e*r) *n.* Deposit of sand, gravel, etc., in bed of stream etc., containing valuable minerals in particles.

plac·id (plăs'ĭd) *adj.* Mild; peaceful; serene. **plac'id·ly** *adv.* **pla·cid·i·ty** (pl*a*sĭd'ĭtē), **plac'id·ness** *ns.*

pla·gia·rize (plā'j*a*rīz) *v.t.* (**-rized, -riz·ing**). Take and use another person's (thoughts, writings, inventions) as one's own. **pla'gia·rism, pla'gia·rist** *ns.* **pla'gia·ry** *n.* (pl. **-ries**). Plagiarist; plagiarism. **pla·gia·ris'tic** *adj.* **pla·gia·ris'ti·cal·ly** *adv.*

plague (plāg) *n.* 1. Affliction, esp. as divine punishment; (colloq.) nuisance, trouble. 2. Pestilence, esp. oriental or bubonic plague;

Great P ~, bubonic plague that afflicted London in 1665; (fig.) source or symptom of moral corruption. **plague** *v.t.* (**plagued, pla·guing**). Afflict with plague; (colloq.) annoy, bother.

plaice (plās) *n.* (pl. **plaice, plaic·es**). European marine flatfish, *Pleuronectes platessa*, much used as food; allied Amer. species of flatfishes and flounders, esp. *Hippoglossoides platessoides.*

plaid (plăd) *n.* Long piece of twilled woolen cloth, usu. with checkered or tartan pattern, outer article of Highland costume; cloth used for this, other fabric with tartan pattern.

plain (plān) *adj.* 1. Clear, evident; simple, readily understood; not elaborate or intricate. 2. Unembellished, (of drawings etc.) not colored; (of food) not rich or highly seasoned; not luxurious; so ~ **cook**, person able to do ~ **cooking**, simple cooking. 3. Outspoken, straightforward. 4. Unsophisticated, ordinary, simple; of homely manners, dress, or appearance; not beautiful, ill-favored. 5. ~ **clothes**, ordinary civil dress, not uniform or fancy dress, therefore, **plain·clothes·man** (plān′-klōz′m*a*n) (pl. **-men** pr. -m*e*n), policeman wearing civilian clothing while on duty; **plain dealing**, candor, straightforwardness; **plain′-song**, traditional church music sung in unison in medieval modes and in free rhythm depending on accentuation of the words; **plain-spoken**, outspoken. **plain** *adv.* Clearly; plainly. **plain′ly** *adv.* **plain′ness** *n.* **plain** *n.* Level tract of country. **plains·man** (plānz′m*a*n) (pl. **-men**). Inhabitant of a plain.

Plains (plānz) **of Abraham.** Plateau W. of Quebec, Canada; battle site during the French and Indian War, where the French under General Montcalm were defeated by the Brit. under General Wolfe, Sept., 1759.

plaint (plānt) *n.* 1. (law) Accusation, charge. 2. (poet.) Lamentation, complaint.

plain·tiff (plān′tĭf) *n.* Party who brings suit into court of law, prosecutor.

plain·tive (plān′tĭv) *adj.* Expressive of sorrow; mournful. **plain′tive·ly** *adv.* **plain′tive·ness** *n.*

plait (plāt, plăt) *n.* 1. Interlacing of three or more strands of hair, ribbon, straw, etc. 2. Fold, crease (now usu. PLEAT). ~ *v.t.* Form (hair, straw, etc.) into plait.

plan (plăn) *n.* Drawing, diagram, made by projection on flat surface, esp. one showing relative position of parts of (floor of) a building; large-scale detailed map of town or district; table indicating times, places, etc., of intended proceedings, etc.; scheme of arrangement; project, design; way of proceeding; (perspective) any of the imaginary planes, perpendicular to line of vision, passing through objects shown in picture; ~ **position indicator**, (airborne) radar display used as navigational aid in which position of the detector appears as a spot on a map of the area around the detector. **plan′less** *adj.* **plan** *v.t.* (**planned, plan·-ning**). Make a plan of (ground, existing building); design (building to be constructed etc.); scheme, arrange beforehand.

*Its resistance to most forms of atmospheric pollution has made the **plane** a popular tree for city planting.*

planch·et (plăn′chĭt) *n.* Plain disk of metal of which coin is made.

plan·chette (plănshĕt′) *n.* Small usu. heart-shaped board (esp. a OUIJA board) supported by two castors and a pencil, which, when one or more persons rest their fingers lightly on the board, is supposed to write without conscious direction.

Planck (plahngk), **Max** (1858–1947). German physicist; received Nobel Prize for physics, 1918; originator of the QUANTUM theory; **~'s constant**, (phys.) constant in the expression for the quantum of energy, symbol h, numerical value 6.61×10^{-27}.

plane[1] (plān) *n.* (also ~ **tree**) Tall spreading tree of genus *Platanus*, esp. *P. orientalis* and *P. occidentalis* (sycamore or buttonwood) with broad angular palmately lobed leaves, and bark that scales off in irregular patches.

plane[2] (plān) *n.* Tool for smoothing surface of woodwork by paring shavings from it, consisting of wooden or metal stock from smooth bottom of which projects a steel blade; similar tool for smoothing metal; **molding ~**, one for making moldings; **smoothing ~**, one used to finish surface. **plane** *v.t.* (**planed, plan·ing**). Smooth (wood, metal) with plane; pare *away* or *down* (irregularities) with plane. **plan′er** *n.*

plane[3] (plān) *n.* 1. Surface such that the straight line joining any two points in it lies wholly in it; imaginary surface of this kind in which points or lines in material bodies lie; level surface. 2. Flat thin object, esp. one used in aeronautical experiments; (one of) the principal supporting surface(s) in an airplane; airplane; each of natural faces of a crystal. 3. (fig.) Level (*of* thought, knowledge, etc.). 4. ~ **sailing**, art of determining ship's place on the theory that the ship is moving on a plane; (fig., now usu. **plain sailing**) simple course. **plane** *v.i.* (**planed, plan·-ing**). Travel, glide (*down* etc.) in airplane; (of speedboat, automobile, etc.) skim over water. ~ *adj.* Perfectly level, forming a plane; (of angle, figure, etc.) lying in a plane; ~ **chart**, one on which meridians and parallels of latitude are represented by equidistant straight lines, used in plane sailing; ~ **table**, surveying instrument used for measuring angles in mapping, consisting of a circular drawing table mounted on a tripod and a ruler for pointing

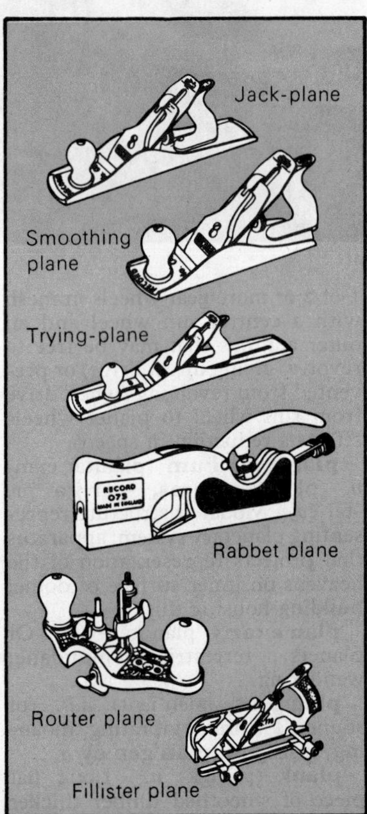

*Although a simple wooden smoothing **plane** has been used by carpenters for many centuries, the metal plane, with its many variations was only invented by Leonard Bailey in the 19th century.*

1

2

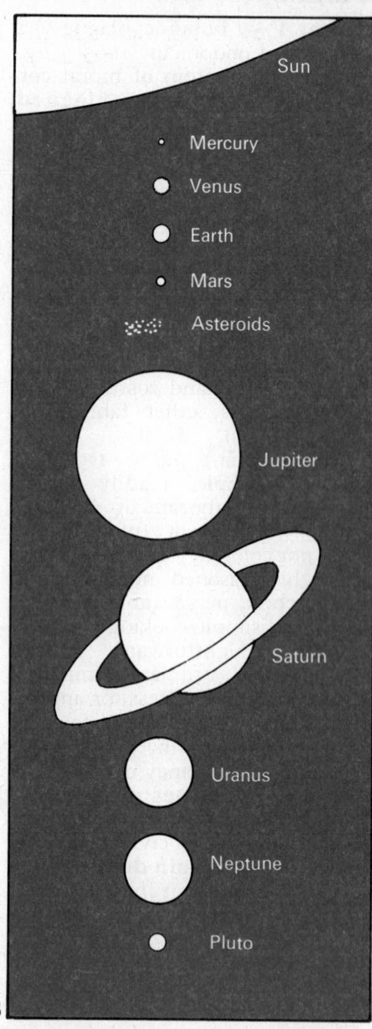

3

*The ancient Greeks called the **planets** 'wandering stars', since they seemed to stray irregularly across the sky. Five can be seen with the naked eye: advances in telescope design made the discovery of the rest possible. As far as is known there is no life on any of them except the earth. (1. Jupiter; 2. Saturn; 3. sizes and positions in relation to the sun.)*

at the object observed; **plane-table** (*v.t.*) (**-tabled, -tabling**), survey (area) with this.

plan·et (plăn′ĭt) *n.* 1. (hist.) Heavenly body distinguished from fixed stars by having apparent motion of its own, esp. (astrol.) with reference to its supposed influence on persons and events. 2. Each of the heavenly bodies revolving in approximately circular orbits around sun (**primary ~s**), or of those revolving around these (**secondary ~s** or *satellites*); **major ~s**, (in order of increasing distance from sun) Mercury, Venus, Earth, Mars, Jupiter, Saturn, Uranus, Neptune, Pluto; **minor ~s**, asteroids (with orbits between those of Mars and Jupiter); **~ gear(ing)**, gearing in which planet wheels are used; **~ wheel**, 1 of 2 or more gear wheels in mesh with a central sun wheel and an outer annulus that may be free to revolve (giving direct drive) or prevented from revolving (when drive from sun wheel to planet wheels effects a reduction in speed).

plan·e·tar·i·um (plănĭtār′ēum) *n.* (pl. **-tar·i·ums, -tar·i·a** pr. -tār′ēa). Model or structure representing planetary system; apparatus that projects representation of the heavens on inner surface of dome; building housing this.

plan·e·tar·y (plăn′ĭtĕrē) *adj.* Of planets; terrestrial, mundane; wandering.

plan·gent (plăn′jent) *adj.* (of sound) Thrilling, vibrating, moaning, insistent. **plan′gen·cy** *n.*

plank (plăngk) *n.* Long flat piece of smoothed timber thicker than a board; (fig.) item of political or other platform or program; **walk the ~**, walk blindfolded into sea along plank laid over side of ship, esp. as pirates' method of disposing of victims; **~ bed**, bed of boards, without mattress. **plank** *v.t.* Furnish, cover, floor, with planks; cook (fish) by splitting open and fixing to board; (slang) put *down* (esp. money on the spot).

plank·ton (plănk′ton) *n.* (biol.) Collective name for all the forms of drifting or floating organic life found at various depths in the ocean or in fresh water.

plano- *prefix.* Flatly, in a flattened manner; comb. of plane with another surface.

pla·no-con·cave (plānōkŏn′-kāv) *adj.* With one surface plane and the other concave.

pla·no-con·vex (plānōkŏn′vĕks) *adj.* With one surface plane and the the other convex.

plant (plănt) *n.* 1. Living organism generally capable of living wholly on inorganic substances and having neither power of locomotion nor special organs of sensation or digestion, member of the vegetable kingdom (freq. restricted to the smaller plants, excluding trees and shrubs); ~ **louse**, any of various insects infesting plants, esp. aphid. 2. Mode of planting oneself, pose. 3. Fixtures, implements, machinery, etc., used in industrial process. 4. (slang) Planned swindle or burglary; hoax. **plant** *v.t.* 1. Place (tree, shoot, seed, etc.) in ground that it may take root and grow; naturalize (animals, fish, etc.); cause (idea etc.) to take root *in* (mind); ~ **out**, transfer (plant) from pot or frame to open ground; set out (seedlings) at intervals. 2. Fix firmly (*in*, *on*, ground, etc.); station (person), esp. as spy; ~ **oneself**, take up a position. 3. Establish, found (community, city, church); settle (person) in place as colonist etc. 4. Furnish (land *with* plants, district *with* settlers, etc.). 5. Deliver (blow, thrust) with definite aim. 6. (slang) Conceal (stolen goods etc. on innocent person's premises to incriminate him); bury, place (gold dust, ore) in mining claim to encourage prospective buyer; devise (fraudulent scheme).

Plan·tag·e·net (plăntăj′enĭt). Orig., nickname of Geoffrey, Count of Anjou, father of Henry II of England; adopted as surname (*c*1460) by Richard, Duke of York; applied to the whole royal house that occupied English throne 1154–1399 (Henry II to Richard II). [L. *planta* sprig, *genista* broom, with ref. to Geoffrey's habit of wearing on his helmet a sprig of the common broom of Anjou]

plan·tain[1] (plăn′tĭn) *n.* Plant of genus *Plantago*, esp. **greater** ~ (*P. major*), low herb with broad flat leaves spread out close to ground and dense cylindrical spikes of seeds.

plan·tain[2] (plăn′tĭn) *n.* Treelike tropical herbaceous plant (*Musa paradisiaca*) allied to banana, with immense undivided oblong leaves, cultivated for its fruit borne in long densely clustered spikes; long pod-shaped somewhat fleshy fruit of this.

plan·tar (plăn′ter) *adj.* (anat.) Of the sole of the foot.

plan·ta·tion (plăntā′shon) *n.* 1. Assemblage of planted growing plants, esp. trees. 2. Estate on which cotton, tobacco, etc., are cultivated (formerly by servile labor). 3. (hist.) Colonization; colony.

plant·er (plăn′ter) *n.* 1. Cultivator of soil. 2. Occupier of plantation, esp. in tropical and subtropical countries. 3. Machine for planting.

plaque (plăk) *n.* 1. Ornamental tablet of metal, porcelain, etc., plain or decorated; small tablet as badge of rank in honorary order. 2. Film on teeth where bacteria proliferate (also **dental** ~).

plasm (plăz′em) = PLASMA def. 2.

plas·ma (plăz′ma) *n.* 1. Green variety of quartz. 2. (also **plasm**) (physiol.) Coagulable solution of salts and protein in which corpuscles are suspended. 3. (phys.) Ionized gas in which numbers of electrons and positive ions are approximately equal. **plas·mat·ic** (plăzmăt′ĭk), **plas′mic** *adjs.*

plas·mo·di·um (plăzmō′dēum) *n.* (pl. **-di·a** pr. -dēa). 1. (biol.) Mass of naked protoplasm formed by fusion or aggregation of amoeboid bodies. 2. Protozoan of genus *P*~, causing malaria in man.

plas·mol·y·sis (plăzmŏl′ĭsĭs) *n.* Contraction of protoplasm of vegetable cell due to loss of water to solution with which it is in contact.

plas·ter (plăs′ter) *n.* 1. Curative application consisting of some sub-

*The surname **Plantagenet** is given to the descendants of Henry II of England, though he was the only one who actually used it. Geoffrey Plantagenet's tomb, Le Mans (below).*

*The **plantain,** indistinguishable from a banana (below right) except for its larger fruit, has a high starch content. It is slightly bitter and is baked or boiled before eating.*

stance spread upon muslin etc. and capable of adhering at temperature of the body. 2. Soft plastic mixture, esp. of lime, sand, and hair, spread on walls etc. to form smooth surface; **plas'terboard**, board containing plaster core, used for walling, ceilings, etc. 3. Sulfate of lime, gypsum; ~ **of Paris**, fine white plaster of calcined gypsum used to make molds or casts, as cement etc. (orig. prepared from gypsums of Montmartre, Paris). **plas'ter·y** *adj.* **plaster** *v.t.* Cover with or like plaster; apply, stick, etc., like plaster to; coat, bedaub; (slang) bomb or shell heavily; **plas'tered**, (slang) drunk. **plas'-ter·er** *n.*

plas·tic (plăs'tĭk) *adj.* 1. Molding, giving form to clay, wax etc.; produced by molding; capable of being (easily) molded; (fig.) pliant, supple; ~ **arts**, those concerned with modeling, e.g. sculpture, ceramics; ~ **bomb**, bomb of soft pliable explosive substance; ~ **clay**, (geol.) middle group of Eocene beds; ~ **surgery**, repair or replacement of lost, damaged, or deformed tissue etc. 2. Causing growth of natural forms, formative; (biol.) capable of forming living tissue, accompanied by this process. **plas'ti·cal·ly** *adv.* **plastic** *n.* Any of a group of substances, natural or synthetic, chiefly polymers of high molecular weight, that can be molded into any form by heat or pressure or both. **plas·-tic·i·ty** (plăstĭs'ĭtē) *n.*

plas·ti·cize (plăs'tĭsīz) *v.* (**-cized, -ciz·ing**). Make, become, plastic. **plas'ti·ciz·er** *n.*

plat (plăt) *n.* Patch, plot, of ground.

Pla·ta (plah'tah), **Rio de la.** Plate River, long funnel-shaped estuary on E. side of S. Amer., between Argentina and Uruguay; scene (1939) of naval battle between German "pocket battleship" *Admiral Graf Spee*, subsequently scuttled, and three British cruisers, *Ajax*, *Achilles*, and *Exeter*. [Span., = "river of silver," with ref. to export of silver from the region]

plate[1] (plāt) *n.* 1. Flat thin usu. rigid sheet of metal etc. of even surface and more or less uniform thickness; this as part of mechanism etc., esp. one of the sheets of which a ship's armor and steam boilers are composed; (anat., zool., and bot.) thin flat organic structure or formation. 2. The portion of a denture that fits to the mouth and holds the teeth. 3. Smooth piece of metal etc. for engraving; impression from this, esp. as illustration of book; full-page illustration of book; bookplate. 4. Piece of metal with name or inscription for affixing to something; (baseball) home plate. 5. Stereotype or electrotype

Picking tea on a ***plantation*** *near Hangchow in China. The use of plantations (large organized areas of tree or shrub-borne crops) was essential for economic development in agriculture.*

Armor-plating reinforces the hull and deck of the U.S.S. Missouri. Armor ***plate*** *seems to have been used first in the 12th century and gradually became more sophisticated.*

In tropical countries such as Peru (left) the height of a ***plateau*** *above sea level may provide an area where temperate-zone agriculture is possible, despite the latitude.*

cast of page of composed movable types, from which sheets are printed. 6. Thin sheet of metal, glass, etc., coated with sensitive emulsion, for taking photographs. 7. Horizontal timber laid along top of wall to support ends of joists or rafters, or at top or bottom of a framing. 8. (collect. sing.) Table and domestic utensils of silver, gold, or other metals; silver or gold cup as prize for (orig. horse) race, such race. 9. Shallow usu. circular vessel, now usu. of earthenware or china, from which food is eaten; contents of this; similar vessel used for collection in churches etc. 10. ~ **glass**, flat glass of fine quality cast, ground, and polished in a continuous ribbon; ~ **mark** = HALLMARK; (also) impression left on margin of engraving by edge of plate; imitation of this on mount of photograph; hence **~-marked** (*adj.*); ~ **rack**, rack in which dining plates are kept or placed to drain after washing. **plate·ful** (plāt′fo͞ol) *n.* (pl. **-fuls**). **plate** *v.t.* (**plat·ed, plat·ing**). Cover (esp. ship) with plates of metal for protection, ornament, etc.; cover (other metal) with thin coat of silver, gold, tin, etc.; make a plate of (type) for printing.

pla·teau (plătō′) *n.* (pl. **-teaus, -teaux** pr. -tōz′). Elevated tract of comparatively flat or level land, tableland.

plate·let (plāt′lĭt) *n.* (also **blood** ~) Ovoid or circular body suspended in the plasma, important in blood clotting.

plat·en (plăt′en) *n.* Iron plate in printing press by which paper is pressed against inked type; corresponding part in typewriter etc.

plat·er (plā′ter) *n.* One who plates with silver etc.; one who makes or applies plates in shipbuilding; inferior race horse, competing chiefly for plates.

plat·form (plăt′fôrm) *n.* 1. Raised level surface, natural or artificial terrace; raised surface along side of line at railroad station, from which passengers enter the carriages, and upon which they alight on leaving the train. 2. Raised flooring in hall or open air from which speaker addresses audience; (fig.) political basis of party etc. program, esp. declaration of principles, long-range and immediate aims, etc. issued by repre-

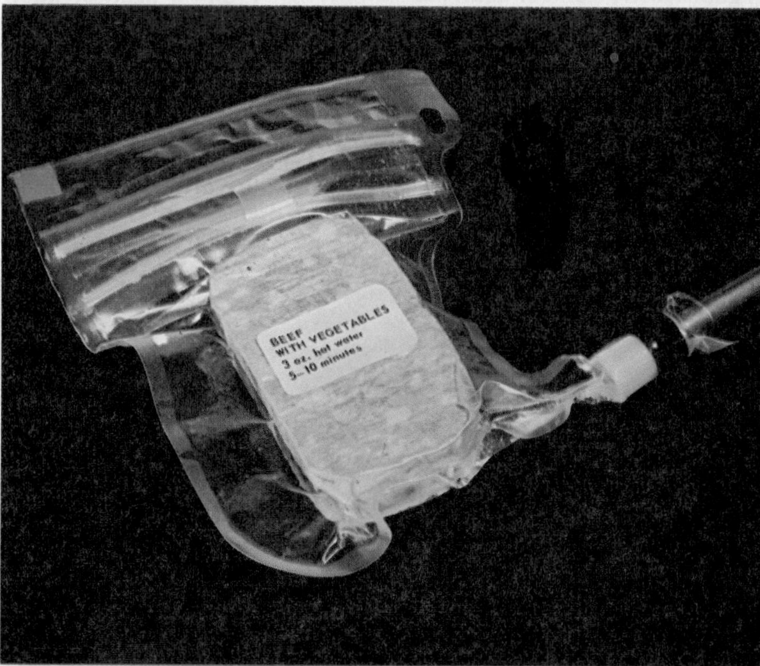

The different artificial substances all called ***'plastics'*** *have between them made possible a whole range of new processes, among them the vacuum-sealing of food for astronauts.*

sentatives of party assembled to nominate candidates for election.

plat·ing (plā´tĭng) *n.* (esp.) Coating of gold, silver, etc.

plat·i·num (plăt´*n*um, plăt´*i*-*n*um) *n.* (chem.) Somewhat rare metallic element, white, of high density, ductile and malleable, unaffected by simple acids and fusible only at very high temperatures; symbol Pt, at. no. 78, at. wt. 195.09; ~ **black**, platinum in form of finely divided black powder; ~ **blonde**, (woman with) very light, silvery blonde hair.

plat·i·tude (plăt´ĭtōōd, -tūd) *n.* Commonplaceness; commonplace remark, esp. one solemnly delivered. **plat·i·tu·di·nous** (plătĭtōō´d*i*n*u*s, -tū´-) *adj.* **plat·i·tu´di·nous·ly** *adv.*

Pla·to (plā´tō) (*c*429–347 B.C.). Greek philosopher, pupil of SOCRATES and author of dialogues (based on his teaching and on the doctrines of Pythagoras), including *Protagoras, Phaedo, Symposium*, and *Republic*.

Pla·ton·ic (pl*a*tŏn´ĭk, plā-) *adj.* Of Plato or his doctrines; esp. applied to love or affection for one of the opposite sex entirely free from sensual desire (orig. used without reference to women).

Pla·to·nism (plā´t*o*nĭz*e*m) *n.* Philosophical system of Plato, of which central conception is that there exists a world of ideas, divine types, or forms of material objects, and that the ideas alone are real and permanent, while individual material things are but their ephemeral and imperfect imitations. **Pla´to·nist** *adj.* & *n.* (Follower) of Plato. **Pla·to·nis´tic** *adj.*

pla·toon (pl*a*tōōn´) *n.* 1. (hist.) Small infantry detachment, esp. a unit for volley firing etc.; volley fired by it; (now) subdivision of a company, a tactical unit commanded by a lieutenant and divided into three squads. 2. Group of players within a football team trained as a unit for offense or defense and sent into or taken out of the game as a single unit.

plat·ter (plăt´*er*) *n.* 1. Flat dish or plate from which food is served. 2. (slang) Phonograph record.

platy- (*comb. form*) Broad, flat.

plat·y·hel·minth (plătĭhĕl´mĭnth) *n.* One of the phylum Platyhelminthes, including tapeworms and flukes; flatworm.

plat·y·pus (plăt´ĭp*u*s, -pōōs) *n.* (pl. **-pus·es**). (also **duckbill** ~) Primitive aquatic and burrowing mammal (*Ornithorhynchus anatinus*) of Tasmania and SE. Australia, which has a bony ducklike beak and flattened tail, and lays eggs encased in shells. [Gk. *platas* broad, *pous* foot]

plat·yr·rhine (plăt´ĭrīn, -rĭn), **plat·yr·rhin·i·an** (plătĭrĭn´ē*a*n) *adjs.* 1. (anthrop.) Having a broad nose with flat bridge. 2. (zool.) Of the Platyrrhini, a group of New World monkeys with broad flat nose. ~ *n.* Platyrrhine monkey.

plau·dit (plaw´dĭt) *n.* (usu. pl.) Round of applause; emphatic expression of approval. [shortened f. L. *plaudite* applaud, imper. of *plaudere*, customary appeal for applause by Roman actors at end of play]

plau·si·ble (plaw´zĭb*e*l) *adj.* (of arguments etc.) Seeming reasonable or probable; (of persons) fair-spoken (usu. implying deceit). **plau·si·bil´i·ty, plau´si·ble·ness** *ns.* **plau´si·bly** *adv.*

Plau·tus (plaw´t*u*s), **Titus Maccius** (d. *c*184 B.C.). Roman comic dramatist.

play (plā) *v.* 1. Move about in lively or capricious manner, frisk, flit, flutter, pass gently; strike lightly; alternate rapidly; (of part of mechanism etc.) have free movement. 2. Allow (fish) to exhaust itself by pulling against line; direct (light *on, over*, etc.); (of light) pass (*over, along*, etc.). 3. Perform, execute (trick, prank, etc.). 4. Amuse oneself, sport, frolic; employ oneself in the game of; pretend for fun; (of ground etc.) be in good etc. condition for play; contend against (person) in game; employ (person) to play in game, include in team; ~ **at**, engage in (game); (fig.) engage in (work etc.) in trivial or half-hearted way; ~ **ball**, (fig.) cooperate (with); ~ **fair, foul**, play or (fig.) act (un)fairly; ~ **false**, deceive, betray; ~ **the game**, observe the rules of the game, play fair (freq. fig.); ~ **into the hands of**, act so as to give advantage to (opponent or partner); ~ **the market**, speculate in the stock market; ~ **on words**, pun; ~ **safe**, act with caution; ~ **up**, emphasize; ~ **with**, amuse oneself with, trifle with, treat lightly; **played out**, exhausted of energy, vitality, or usefulness. 5. Move (piece in chess etc.); take (playing card) from one's hand and lay it face upward on table in one's turn; strike (ball) in specified, esp. defensive, manner; **play one's cards well**, (fig.) make good use of opportunities; **play off**, oppose (person *against* another) esp. for one's own advantage; cause (person) to exhibit himself disadvantageously; play extra game or match to decide draw or tie; pass off as something else. 6. Perform on (musical instrument), perform (*on* instrument); perform (music *on* instrument); **play back**, reproduce (newly recorded music etc.); **play** (congregation etc.) **in, out**, play on organ etc., as they come in, go out; **play on**, make use of (person's fears, credulity, etc.). 7. Perform (drama) on stage; act (*in* drama); act (part) in drama; (fig.) act in real life the part of (*the man, truant*, etc.); **play up to**, flatter, toady.

play *n.* 1. Brisk, light, or fitful movement; activity, operation, freedom of movement, space for this, scope for activity. 2. Amusement; playing of game; manner, style, of this; **at** ~, engaged in playing; **in** ~, not seriously; (of ball) being used in ordinary course of play; **play-off**, extra match or game to decide tie; **play on words**,

*When the **platypus** feeds on the bottom of streams, its eyes and ears are closed and it locates the crustacea and insects, which are its food, by means of its sensitive muzzle.*

pun. 3. Dramatic piece, drama. 4. Gaming, gambling. 5. **play'-acting**, playing a part, posing; **play'actor**, actor (usu. contempt.); **play'back**, reproduction of previously recorded sound; **play'bill**, placard, announcing theatrical play; program for this; **play'boy**, man fond of pleasure and gaiety; **play'fellow**, companion in (usu. children's) play; **play'goer**, frequenter of theater; **play'ground**, area used for play, esp. at school; **play group**, group of children below school age, organized for playing etc. under supervision; **play'house**, theater (obs. exc. in title); **play'mate**, playfellow; **play'pen**, portable enclosure for keeping young child out of harm's way; **play'thing**, toy; (fig.) person, etc., treated as mere toy; **play'-wright**, dramatist.

play·er (plā'*er*) *n.* (esp.) Person engaged at the time, person skillful, in a game; professional baseball player etc.; actor, performer on musical instrument; ~ **piano**: see PIANO².

play·ful (plā'*f*ul) *adj.* Frolicsome, sportive; humorous, jocular. **play'ful·ly** *adv.* **play'ful·ness** *n.*

play·ing (plā'ĭng) *n.* (esp.) ~ **card**: see CARD² def. 2.

plea (plē) *n.* Pleading, argument, excuse; (law) formal statement by or on behalf of defendant; (hist.) action at law; **special** ~, defendant's plea alleging new fact; (slang) **cop a** ~, plead guilty to a lesser offense than the one alleged; hence, ~ **bargain**, seek to settle for such a plea.

*Pewter **platters** like these were essential household equipment in the days of massive joints and puddings. Today they find a place, however, which is just decorative.*

plead (plēd) *v.* (**plead·ed** or **pled, plead·ing**). 1. Address court as advocate on behalf of either party; maintain (cause) in court; allege formally as plea; (fig.) allege as excuse etc.; ~ **guilty**, admit liability or guilt, ~ **not guilty**, deny it. 2. Ask earnestly *for* help etc.; ~ **with**, make earnest appeal to (person). **plead'ing** *adj.* **plead'ing·ly** *adv.* **plead'er** *n.*

plead·ing (plē'dĭng) *n.* (esp.) Formal (now usu. written) statement of cause of action or defense.

pleas·ant (plĕz'*a*nt) *adj.* Agreeable to mind, feelings, or senses. **pleas'ant·ly** *adv.* **pleas'ant·ness** *n.*

pleas·ant·ry (plĕz'*a*ntrē) *n.* (pl. **-ries**). Jocularity; humorous speech, jest.

please (plēz) *v.* (**pleased, pleas·ing**). 1. Be agreeable (to); ~ **oneself**, do as one likes, take one's own way; **be pleased with**, derive pleasure from. 2. Be pleased, like; have the will or desire, think proper; (also **if you** ~) if you like (as courteous qualification to request etc.). **pleased, pleas'ing** *adjs.* **pleas'ing·ly** *adv.*

pleas·ur·a·ble (plĕzh'*er*ab*e*l) *adj.* Affording pleasure. **pleas'-ur·a·ble·ness** *n.* **pleas'ur·a·bly** *adv.*

pleas·ure (plĕzh'*er*) *n.* 1. Feeling of satisfaction; sensuous gratification. 2. Will, desire.

pleat (plēt) *n.* Fold, crease; esp., flattened fold in cloth; **accordion** ~**s**, narrow pleats resembling accordion bellows; **box** ~, double pleat; **inverted** ~, reverse form of box pleat; **knife** ~**s**, narrow overlapping pleats. **pleat** *v.t.* Fold (cloth etc.) in pleats. **pleat'er** *n.*

ple·be·ian (plebē'*a*n) *n.* Commoner in ancient Rome; commoner. ~ *adj.* Of low birth; of the common people; coarse, base, ignoble. **ple·be'ian·ism, ple·be'-ian·ness** *ns.*

pleb·i·scite (plĕb'ĭsĭt, -sīt) *n.* 1. (Rom. hist.) Law enacted by the commons (plebeians) voting by tribes. 2. Direct vote of all electors of community on important public question; public expression of community's opinion, with or without binding force.

plec·trum (plĕk'tr*u*m) *n.* (pl. **-tra** pr. -tr*a*, **-trums**). Small spike of ivory, quill, metal, etc., sometimes attached to a ring fitting on the finger, for plucking strings of guitar, zither, etc.; part of keyboard instrument with same function.

pled (plĕd) *v.* Past t. and past part. of PLEAD.

pledge (plĕj) *n.* 1. Thing handed

*The Seven Sisters, or **Pleiades** — most people can only see six; the seventh is just visible to the keen-sighted — are grouped in fact as well as myth, unlike many constellations.*

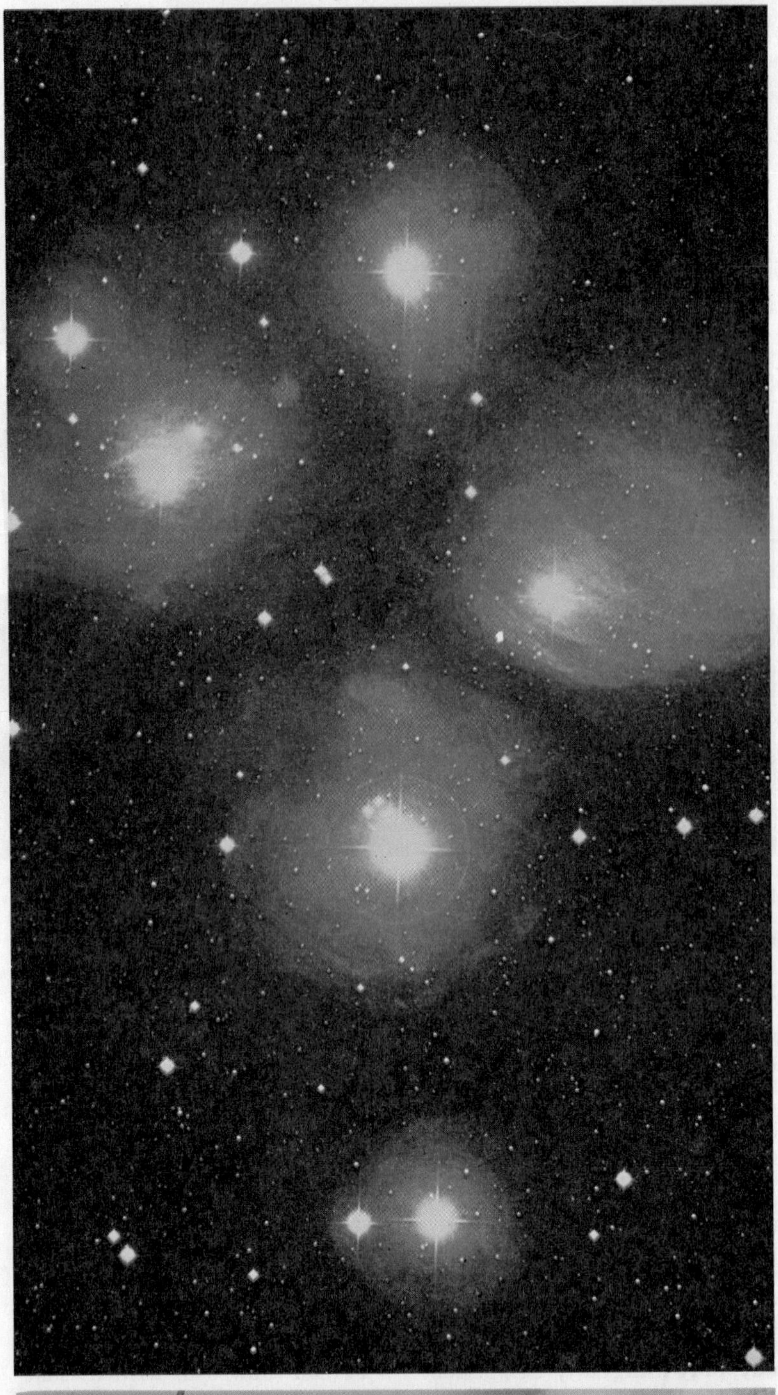

over to person as security for fulfillment of contract, payment of debt, etc., and liable to forfeiture in case of failure; thing put in pawn. 2. Thing given as token of favor etc. or of something to come; drinking of a health, toast. 3. Vow, promise; **the ~**, solemn engagement to abstain from intoxicants. 4. State of being pledged. **pledge** *v.t.* (**pledged, pledg·ing**). 1. Deposit as security, pawn. 2. Promise solemnly; bind (oneself) by pledge. 3. Drink to the health of.

Ple·ia·des (plē´*a*dēz, plī´-). 1. (Gk. myth.) Seven daughters of Atlas, turned, when they died, into a constellation. 2. (astron.) Conspicuous constellation or cluster of stars in Taurus.

Pleis·to·cene (plī´stosēn) *adj.* & *n.* (geol.) (Of) the earlier part or system of the Quaternary period, characterized by the formation of glaciers and in which man first appeared. [Gk. *pleistos* most, *kainos* new]

ple·na·ry (plē´n*e*re, plĕn´*a*-) *adj.* Entire, absolute, unqualified; (of assembly) attended by all members. **ple´na·ri·ly** *adv.*

plen·i·po·ten·ti·ar·y (plĕnĭpotĕn´shēĕrē, -sh*e*rē) *adj.* Invested with full power, esp. as ambassador deputed to act at discretion; (of power) absolute. ~ *n.* (pl. **-ar·ies**). Person invested with full power.

plen·i·tude (plĕn´ĭtōōd, -tūd) *n.* Fullness, completeness; abundance.

plen·te·ous (plĕn´tē*u*s) *adj.* (chiefly poet.) Plentiful. **plen´te·ous·ly** *adv.* **plen´te·ous·ness** *n.*

plen·ti·ful (plĕn´tĭf*u*l) *adj.* Abundant, copious. **plen´ti·ful·ly** *adv.* **plen´ti·ful·ness** *n.*

plen·ty (plĕn´tē) *n.* Abundance, as much as one could desire. ~ *adv.* (colloq.; with adjective followed by *enough*) Quite.

ple·num (plē´n*u*m, plĕn´*u*m) *n.* (pl. **ple·nums, ple·na** pr. plē´n*a*, plĕn´*a*). Space filled with matter; full assembly.

ple·o·nasm (plē´onăzem) *n.* (gram.) Redundancy of expression. **ple·o·nas´tic** *adj.* **ple·o·nas´ti·cal·ly** *adv.*

ple·si·o·sau·rus (plēsē*o*sōr´*u*s) *n.* (pl. **-sau·rus·es, -sau·ri** pr. -sōr´ī). Member of a genus (*P~*) of extinct marine reptiles with long neck, small head, short

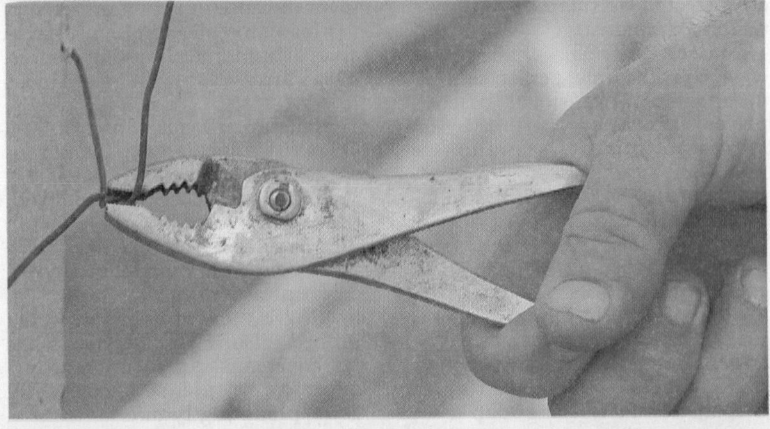

*Crude versions of **pliers** have been used for many centuries. Remains have been found indicating the use of pliers by Roman carpenters, and blacksmiths who used them to remove old nails from hoofs.*

tail, and four large paddlelike limbs. [Gk. *plesios* near, *sauros* lizard]

pleth·o·ra (plĕth'*era*) *n.* Overabundance, glut. **ple·thor·ic** (plethŏr'ĭk, -thăr'-, plĕth'erĭk) *adj.* **ple·thor'i·cal·ly** *adv.*

pleu·ra (ploor'*a*) *n.* (pl. **pleu·rae** pr. ploor'ē, **pleu·ras**). Either of two serous membranes lining thorax in mammals and enveloping lungs. **pleu'ral** *adj.*

pleu·ri·sy (ploor'ĭsē) *n.* Inflammation of the pleura, marked by pain in chest or side, fever, etc. **pleu·rit·ic** (ploorĭt'ĭk) *adj.*

pleu·ron (ploor'ŏn) *n.* (pl. **pleu·ra** pr. ploor'*a*). Either of the two side plates of the exoskeleton in arthropods.

Plex·i·glas (plĕk'*s*iglăs) *n.* (trademark) Transparent acrylic plastic.

plex·us (plĕk'*sus*) *n.* (pl. **-us·es, -us**). Network of nerve fibers or minute blood vessels in animal body; network, complication.

pli·a·ble (plī'*a*bel), **pli·ant** (plī'*a*nt) *adjs.* Bending, supple; (fig.) yielding, compliant. **pli·a·bil'i·ty, pli'a·ble·ness, pli'an·cy** *ns.* **pli'a·bly, pli'ant·ly** *advs.*

pli·cate (plī'kāt, -kĭt), **pli·cat·ed** (plī'kātĭd) *adjs.* (bot., zool., geol.) Folded. **pli·ca·tion** (plĭkā'sh*o*n), **plic·a·ture** (plĭk'*a*cher) *ns.* Folding; fold; folded condition.

At the headquarters of Coastal Command of the R.A.F., the modern war officer receives information from many sources. He must ***plot*** *this on huge charts to enable him to make tactical decisions.*

pli·é (plēā') *n.* (pl. **-és**). (ballet) Bending of knees while holding back straight.

pli·ers (plī'*erz*) *n.pl.* (also **pair of ~**) Pincers having long jaws, usu. with parallel surfaces, sometimes toothed, for bending wire, holding small objects, etc.

plight[1] (plīt) *v.t.* (literary) Pledge (troth, faith, etc., esp. in past part.); engage *oneself* (*to* person).

plight[2] (plīt) *n.* Condition, state (usu. unhappy).

plinth (plĭnth) *n.* Lower square member of base of column; projecting part of wall (or piece of furniture) immediately above ground.

Plin·y (plĭn'ē). **~ the Elder** (Gaius Plinius Secundus, *c*23–79 A.D.), Roman author of *Natural History*, who perished in the eruption of Vesuvius; **~ the Younger**, his nephew (Gaius Plinius Caecilius Secundus, *c*61–*c*112 A.D.), famous for his published *Letters*.

Pli·o·cene (plī'*o*sēn) *adj.* & *n.* (geol.) (Of) the latest epoch or system of the Tertiary period. [Gk. *pleion* more, *kainos* new]

P.L.O. *abbrev.* Palestine Liberation Organization.

plod (plŏd) *v.* (**plod·ded, plod·ding**). Walk laboriously, trudge; drudge, slave (*at*); make (one's way) laboriously. **~** *n.* Laborious walk or work. **plod'der** *n.* **plod'ding** *adj.* **plod'ding·ly** *adv.*

plo·sive (plō'sĭv) *adj.* & *n.* (phonet.) Explosive (consonant).

plot (plŏt) *n.* 1. Piece of ground, usu. small. 2. Plan, story, of play, poem, novel, etc. 3. Conspiracy; sly plan. **~** *v.t.* (**plot·ted, plot·ting**). Make plan or map of (existing object, place or thing to be laid out, constructed, etc.); mark the position of values of a variable on a graph or the like; plan, contrive (evil object, or abs.). **plot'less** *adj.* **plot'less·ness, plot'ter** *ns.*

Plo·ti·nus (plōtī'*n*us) (*c*205–69 A.D.). Egyptian-born Roman founder of NEOPLATONISM. His philosophical teachings (*Enneads*, in Greek) were published posthumously.

plov·er (pluv'*er*, plō'*ver*) *n.* (pl. **plov·ers**, collect. **plov·er**). Any of several gregarious birds of family Charadriidae, found in open country, esp. by seashores, and nesting on the ground; **green ~**, lapwing.

plow, Brit. **plough** (plow) *ns.* Implement for cutting furrows in soil and turning it up, consisting

*Two types of **plow**, one an antique version drawn by a cable-attachment to a steam-engine (right) and the other by a modern tractor (lower right), demonstrate the progressive mechanization of farming.*

essentially of a vertical blade that cuts the furrow from the unplowed ground, a **plow'share** that cuts the furrow horizontally underneath, and a board that turns it over, drawn by horses etc. (or now, by tractor), and guided by **plow'man**; plowed land; instrument resembling plow, for cutting up blocks of ice, clearing away snow, etc.; **plow'boy**, boy who leads plow horses etc.; **plow'land**, (hist.) as much land as could be plowed by a team of 8 oxen in a year, unit of assessment in N. and E. counties of England after Norman Conquest; arable land; **plowman** and **plowshare**: see above; ~ **tail**, rear of plow. **plow** *v.* 1. Turn up (earth, or abs.) with plow, esp. before sowing; rout *out*, cast *up*, thrust *down* (roots, weeds) with plow; furrow, scratch (surface) as with plow; produce (furrow, line) thus; ~ **back**, plow (grass, clover, etc.) into soil to enrich it; (fig.) reinvest (profits) in business etc. 2. Advance laboriously (*through* snow, book, etc.); (of ship etc.) cleave (surface of water, its way, etc.). **plow'a·ble** *adj.*

ploy (ploi) *n.* Stratagem, maneuver to gain advantage.

pluck (plŭk) *n.* 1. Plucking, twitch. 2. Heart, liver, and lungs, of beast as food. 3. Courage, spirit. ~ *v.* 1. Pull off, pick (flower, feather, hair); pull at, twitch; tug, snatch, *at*; strip (bird) of feathers; (archaic) pull, drag, snatch (*away*, *off*, etc.). 2. (slang) Plunder, swindle. 3. ~ **up spirits**, take courage. **pluck'y** *adj.* (**pluck·i·er, pluck·i·est**). Brave, spirited. **pluck'i·ly** *adv.* **pluck'i·ness** *n.*

plug (plŭg) *n.* 1. Piece of wood etc. fitting tightly into hole, used to fill gap or act as wedge etc.; freq. in technical use, e.g. pin etc. for making electrical contacts, spark plug (see SPARK[1]); natural or morbid concretion acting thus; kind of stopper for vessel or pipe; fireplug, hydrant. 2. Tobacco pressed into cake or stick; piece of this cut off for chewing. 3. (slang) Worn-out horse. ~ *v.* (**plugged, plug·ging**). Stop (*up*) with plug; (slang) shoot; (slang) strike with fist; (colloq.) plod (*away at* work etc.); (colloq.) popularize (song etc.) by frequent repetition or through publicity.

*The golden **plover** mostly breeds near the Arctic circle but migrates to lower latitudes at the end of summer, to spend winter as far south as the Mediterranean or on the shores of the Atlantic.*

plum (plŭm) *n.* 1. Any of several small trees (genus *Prunus*) bearing roundish fleshy fruit with sweet pulp and flattish pointed stone. 2. Dried grape or raisin as used for puddings, cakes, etc. 3. (fig.) Good thing; best of a collection; prize in life. 4. ~ **cake**, cake containing raisins, currants, etc.; ~ **pudding**, boiled or steamed pudding containing raisins, currants, eggs, spices, etc., eaten esp. at Christmas.

plum·age (plo͞o'mĭj) *n.* Bird's feathers.

plumb (plŭm) *n.* Ball of lead, esp. that attached to plumb line; ~ **line**, string with weight attached for testing perpendicularity of wall, etc.; sounding lead, plummet; **out**

Wild species of **plum** are native to Europe, Asia, and North America. Long domestication and selection have resulted in a large range of varieties.

The date when **plums** were introduced to the U.S.A. is uncertain, but it is thought they were introduced by the earliest colonists. There are now myriad varieties grown.

of ~, not vertical; ~ **rule**, mason's plumb line attached to board. **plumb** *adj.* Vertical; level, true; (fig.) downright, sheer. ~ *adv.* Vertically; (fig.) exactly; (colloq.) quite, utterly. ~ *v.* 1. Sound (sea), measure (depth), with plummet; make vertical. 2. Work as plumber. 3. Examine in order to understand fully.

plumb·er (plŭm′*er*) *n.* Mechanic who fits and repairs pipes, cisterns, tanks, etc.; ~**'s friend** = PLUNGER def. 3.

plumb·ing (plŭm′ĭng) *n.* System of water and drainage pipes in a building etc.

plum·bism (plŭm′bĭzem) *n.* Poisoning caused by absorption of lead into the system.

plume (plo͞om) *n.* Feather, esp. large one used for ornament; feathery ornament in hat, hair, etc.; (zool.) featherlike part or formation. ~ *v.t.* (**plumed, plum·ing**). Furnish with plume(s); (of bird) preen (feathers). **plume′like** *adj.*

plum·met (plŭm′ĭt) *n.* (Weight attached to) plumb line; sounding lead; weight attached to fishing line to keep float upright. ~ *v.i.* Plunge.

plu·mose (plo͞o′mōs) *adj.* Feathered; featherlike.

plump[1] (plŭmp) *adj.* (esp. of persons or parts of body) Full, rounded, fleshy, filled out. ~ *v.* Make or become plump, fatten *up*, swell *out*. **plump′ly** *adv.* **plump′-ness** *n.*

plump[2] (plŭmp) *v.* Drop or plunge with abrupt descent; vote *for* (1 candidate alone, when one might vote for 2); ~ **for**, vote for, choose (something). **plump** *n.* Abrupt plunge, heavy fall. ~ *adv.* With sudden or heavy fall; flatly, bluntly. ~ *adj.* Direct, unqualified.

plu·mule (plo͞om′ūl) *n.* Rudimentary stem of embryo plant; little feather of down. **plu·mu·lar** (plo͞om′y*uler*), **plu·mu·la·ceous** (plo͞omy*u*lā′sh*us*) *adjs.*

plun·der (plŭn′d*er*) *v.t.* Rob (place, person) forcibly of goods, esp. as in war; rob systematically; steal, embezzle. ~ *n.* Violent or dishonest acquisition of property; property so acquired; profit, gain. **plun′der·er** *n.*

plun·der·age (plŭn′d*er*ĭj) *n.* Plundering, esp. embezzling of goods on shipboard; spoil thus obtained.

plunge (plŭnj) *v.* (**plunged, plung·ing**). Thrust violently (*into* liquid, cavity, etc.); throw oneself, dive, (*into*); enter impetuously; descend abruptly and steeply; (of horse) throw itself violently forward; (of ship) pitch; (slang) gamble deeply, run into debt. ~ *n.* Plunging, dive; place for plunging; (fig.) critical step.

plung·er (plŭn′j*er*) *n.* (esp.) 1. Part of mechanism that works with plunging motion. 2. (slang) Gambler, speculator. 3. Rubber cup on handle for removal of pipe blockages by suction.

plu·per·fect (plo͞opėr′fĭkt) *adj.* & *n.* (gram.) (Tense now *past perfect*) expressing action completed prior to some past point of time specified or implied (as *I had seen*). [L. *plus quam perfectum* more than perfect]

plu·ral (ploor′*a*l) *adj.* (gram.) Denoting more than one (or, in languages with dual form, more than two); more than one in number. **plu′ral·ly** *adv.* **plural** *n.* Plural form.

plu·ral·ism (ploor′*a*lĭzem) *n.* 1. (hist.) Holding of more than one office, esp. benefice, at a time. 2. (philos.) System that recognizes more than one ultimate principle. 3. Form of society in which members of minority groups maintain independent traditions. **plu′-ral·ist** *n.* **plu·ral·is′tic** *adj.*

plu·ral·i·ty (plo͞orăl′ĭtē) *n.* (pl. **-ties**). State of being plural; large number, multitude; greater number of votes cast for one candidate than for any other but less than a majority.

plu·ral·ize (ploor′alīz) *v.* (**-ized, -iz·ing**). Make plural, express in the plural.

plus (plŭs) *prep.* With the addition of (symbol +); (colloq.) with, and also. ~ *adj.* Extra (indicating addition); positive; (after number etc.) more than; ~ **fours**, long wide knickers, suit with these, freq. associated with golf, so named because, to produce the overhang, the length was orig. increased by 4 in. ~ *n.* Plus sign or quantity; (colloq.) advantage. [L., = "more"]

plush (plŭsh) *n.* Cloth of silk, cotton, etc., resembling velvet but with longer and softer pile. ~ *adj.* Made of plush; luxurious. **plush′ly** *adv.* **plush′ness** *n.* **plush′y** *adj.* (**plush·i·er, plush·i·est**). **plush′i·ness** *n.*

Plu·tarch (ploo͞′tark) (*c*46–120 A.D.). Greek biographer and moral philosopher, author of *The Parallel Lives* of eminent Greeks and Romans.

plu·tar·chy (ploo͞′tarkē) *n.* Plutocracy.

Plu·to (ploo͞′tō). 1. (Gk. and Rom. myth.) God of the infernal regions, brother of ZEUS and Poseidon. 2. (astron.) Planet, remoter than Neptune, discovered in 1930.

plu·toc·ra·cy (ploo͞tŏk′rasē) *n.* (pl. **-cies**). Rule of the wealthy; ruling class of wealthy persons. **plu·to·crat** (ploo͞′tokrăt) *n.* **plu·to·crat′ic, plu·to·crat′i·cal** *adjs.*

Plu·to·ni·an (ploo͞tō′nēan), **Plu·ton·ic** (ploo͞tŏn′ĭk) *adjs.* Of PLUTO or his kingdom; infernal.

plu·to·ni·um (ploo͞tō′nēum) *n.* (chem.) Transuranic element, not found in nature, formed from uramium in a nuclear reactor, used as a nuclear explosive; symbol Pu, at. no. 94, principal isotope at. wt. 239. [named after planet PLUTO]

plu·vi·al (ploo͞′vēal) *adj.* Of rain, rainy; (geol.) caused by rain. ~ *n.* (eccles. hist.) Long cloak as ceremonial vestment.

plu·vi·om·e·ter (ploo͞vēŏm′ĭter) *n.* Rain gauge. **plu·vi·o·met·ric** (ploo͞vēomĕt′rĭk), **plu·vi·o·met′ri·cal** *adjs.*

ply[1] (plī) *n.* Fold, thickness, layer, of cloth, etc.; strand of rope, etc.; **two-, three-**, etc. ~, having two etc. thicknesses or strands; **ply′wood**, strong thin board made by gluing or cementing layers of wood together with grains crosswise.

ply[2] (plī) *v.* (**plied, ply·ing**). 1. Use, wield vigorously (tool, weapon); work at (business, task); supply (person etc.) persistently *with* (food etc.); assail vigorously (*with* questions, arguments). 2. Work to windward (naut.); (of vessel, its master, etc.) go to and fro *between* (places); (of porter, cab driver, etc.) attend regularly for custom (*at* place).

__Plymouth Rock,__ traditionally regarded as the landing site of the Pilgrims on the Mayflower. The original rock has been covered by the granite portico. Plymouth's historical past makes it popular with tourists.

Monument to the Pilgrim Fathers at __Plymouth,__ Massachusetts. The town was founded in 1620 and named by the original settlers after the port of departure in England.

Plym·outh (plĭm′uth). Town in SE. Massachusetts on ~ **Bay**, landing place of Pilgrims from the *Mayflower* (1620); ~ **Colony**, site of settlement in SE. Massachusetts; founded by the Pilgrims, 1620; became part of the Massachusetts Bay Colony, 1691; ~ **Rock**, (1) granite boulder at Plymouth on which Pilgrims are supposed to have stepped from *Mayflower*; (2) domestic fowl of medium size and usu. with gray plumage barred with blackish stripes and yellow beak, legs, and feet.

Pm *symbol.* Promethium.

P.M. *abbrev.* Prime Minister; Provost Marshal; Police Magistrate; *post meridiem.*

p.m. *abbrev. Post meridiem*; (L., = after noon).

pneu·mat·ic (noo͞măt′ĭk, nyoo͞-) *adj.* Of, acting by means of, wind or (compressed) air; containing, connected with, air cavities, esp. in bones of birds; ~ **tire**, one inflated with air; ~ **tube**, one for pneumatic delivery (of mail etc.). **pneu·mat′i·cal·ly** *adv.* **pneu·mat′ics** *n.* (usu. considered sing.) Science of mechanical properties of air or other gases.

pneu·mo·coc·cus (noo͞mokŏk′us, nū-) *n.* (pl. **-coc·ci** pr. -kŏk′sī). Infective microorganism (*Diplococcus pneumoniae*) in pneumonia.

pneu·mo·co·ni·o·sis (noo͞mokō-nēō′sĭs, nū-) *n.* Any of a group of chronic lung diseases (e.g. silicosis) caused by inhaling abrasive dust.

pneu·mo·gas·tric (noo͞mogăs′trĭk, nū-) *adj.* Of lungs and stomach; ~ **nerve**, vagus nerve.

pneu·mo·nia (noo͞mōn′ya, nyoo͞-) *n.* Acute inflammation of the lungs, converting their normally spongy tissue into a solid mass, caused esp. by infection with pneumococcus. **pneu·mon·ic**

Pochards and their relatives are diving ducks, preferring open water. The red-crested Pochard in particular lives on large lakes or brackish lagoons.

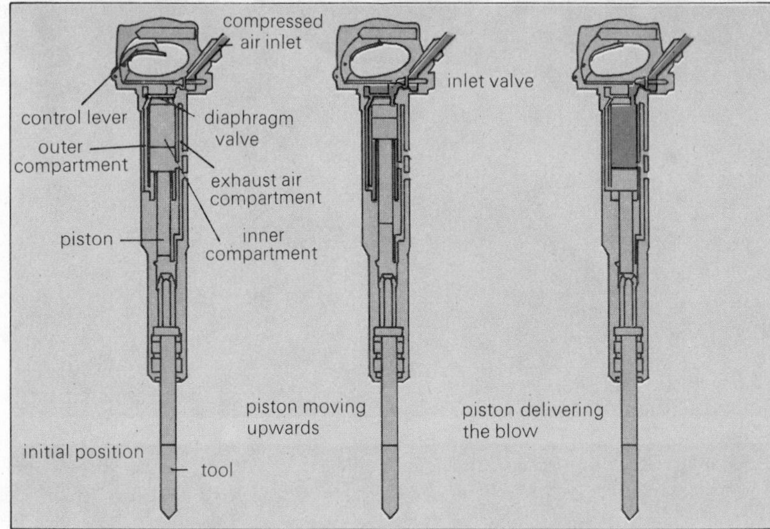

*Compressed air has been used in many ways to replace human effort. One of these is the **pneumatic hammer,** by which powerful blows can be delivered in very quick succession, so that the work can be done better and faster than by hand.*

(nōōmŏn´ĭk, nyōō-) *adj.*

Po *symbol.* Polonium.

P.O. *abbrev.* Petty Officer; postal (money) order; post office.

poach[1] (pōch) *v.t.* Cook (egg) without its shell by boiling in water or steaming; cook (fish, fruit, etc.) by simmering.

poach[2] (pōch) *v.* 1. Trample, cut *up* (turf etc.) with hoofs; (of land) become sodden by being trampled. 2. Encroach, trespass (*on* person's *preserves* (freq. fig.), lands, etc.), esp. in order to steal fish or game; trespass on (land etc.); capture (game, fish) by illicit or unsportsmanlike methods; (in various games) enter on partner's portion of field or court, depriving him of some of his share in the game. **poach'er** *n.*

Po·ca·hon·tas (pōk*a*hŏn´t*a*s) (1594–1617). Daughter of Powhatan, an Indian chief in Virginia; acc. to the story of Capt. John Smith, she rescued him from death at the hands of her father, who had imprisoned him; she was seized as a hostage, 1612, and married John Rolfe; was taken to England, 1616, and died there.

po·chard (pō´ch*e*rd, -k*e*rd) *n.* (pl. **-chards**, collect. **-chard**). Diving duck, esp. *Aythya ferina*, of Europe, N. Asia, and N. Amer., male of which has bright reddish-brown head and neck.

pock (pŏk) *n.* Eruptive spot esp. in smallpox; pockmark.

pock·et (pŏk´ĭt) *n.* 1. Small bag inserted in garment for carrying small articles, as money, etc.; (fig.) pecuniary resources; **put one's pride in one's ~**, humble oneself; **in ~**, having money available; having (so much) as profit; **out of ~**, losing money (by some transaction); **out-of-~ expenses**, actual outlay incurred. 2. Pouch at each corner and on each side of billiard table into which balls are driven; pouch-like compartment in bag, suitcase, etc.; cavity in earth filled with gold or other ore; cavity in rock esp. (geol.) filled with foreign matter; AIR pocket; isolated area occupied by the enemy, forces occupying this. 3. (attrib.) Of suitable size or shape for carrying in pocket; small, diminutive; **~ battleship**, (esp. German) ship armored and equipped like, but smaller than, a battleship; **pock'etbook**, notebook, booklike case for papers, currency, etc., carried in pocket; handbag; **pocket borough**: see BOROUGH; **pocket handkerchief**, one carried in pocket; **pock'etknife**, knife with folding blade(s) to be carried in pocket; **pocket money**, money for occasional expenses, esp. that allowed to children; **pocket veto**, indirect veto of bill by retention in hands of executive without signature until adjournment of legislature. **pock·et·ful** (pŏk´ĭtfŏŏl) *n.* (pl. **-fuls**). **pocket** *v.t.* Put into one's pocket; confine as in pocket; hem in (competitor) in race; appropriate, usu. dishonestly; (billiards) drive (ball) into pocket. **pock'et·ed** *adj.* Fitted with, enclosed in, pocket(s).

pod[1] (pŏd) *n.* Socket of brace and bit.

pod[2] (pŏd) *n.* Long seed vessel, esp. of leguminous plants; cocoon of silkworm; case of locust's eggs; narrow-necked eel net. **~** *v.* (**pod·ded, pod·ding**). Form pods; shell (peas etc.). **pod'like** *adj.*

pod[3] (pŏd) *n.* Small herd of seals or whales. **~** *v.t.* (**pod·ded, pod·ding**). Drive (seals etc.) into pod or bunch for purpose of clubbing them.

po·di·um (pō´dē*u*m) *n.* (pl. **-di·ums, -di·a** pr. -dē*a*). Continuous projecting base or pedestal; raised platform around arena of amphitheater; continuous bench around room.

pod·zol (pŏd´zŏl), **pod·sol** (pŏd´sŏl) *ns.* Stratified soil in which various materials have been leached from the upper layers and redeposited in a well-defined lower stratum. **pod·zol·ize** (pŏd′zolīz) *v.* (**-ized, -iz·ing**). Make into, become, podzol. **pod·zol·i·za·tion** (pŏdzolīzā′sh*o*n) *n.*

POE *abbrev.* Port of embarkation; port of entry.

Poe (pō), **Edgar Allan** (1809–1849). Amer. short-story writer, poet, and journalist; best known for the poems "The Raven," "Annabel Lee," and "The Bells" and the tales "The Fall of the House of Usher," "The Gold Bug," and "The Murders in the Rue Morgue."

po·em (pō′*e*m) *n.* Metrical composition, esp. of elevated character; elevated composition in prose or verse; (fig.) something (other than a composition of words) akin or compared to a poem.

po·e·sy (pō′ĭsē, -zē) *n.* (pl. **-sies**). (archaic) Art, composition, of poetry; poems collectively.

po·et (pō′ĭt) *n.* (fem. **po·et·ess** pr. pō′ĭtĭs). Writer of poems; writer in verse, esp. one possessing high powers of imagination, expression, etc.; ~ **laureate**: see LAUREATE; **Poets' Corner**, part of south transept of Westminster Abbey, London, containing graves or monuments of several great poets. **po·et·as·ter** (pō′ĭtăst*e*r) *n.* Inferior poet.

po·et·ic (pōĕt′ĭk) *adj.* Of, proper to, poets or poetry; having the good qualities of poetry; ~ **justice, license**: see JUSTICE, LICENSE. **po·et′i·cal** *adj.* Of, proper to, poets or poetry; written in verse. **po·et′i·cal·ly** *adv.* **po·et′ics** *n.* Part of literary criticism dealing with poetry; treatise on poetry, esp. (**P**~) that of Aristotle.

po·et·ry (pō′ĭtrē) *n.* Art, work, of the poet; expression of beautiful or elevated thought, imagination, or feeling in appropriate language and usu. in metrical form; poems; quality (in anything) that calls for poetical expression; **prose** ~, prose having all the qualities of poetry except meter.

po·go (pō′gō) **stick.** Toy consisting of a stick with handles and a pair of pedals attached to a spring, used for jumping about.

po·grom (p*o*grŏm′, -grŭm′, pō-) *n.* Organized massacre, orig. that of Jews in Russia (1905–6). [Russ. = "destruction" (*grom* thunder)]

poign·ant (poin′y*a*nt, poin′*a*nt) *adj.* Sharp, pungent, in taste or smell; painfully sharp; pleasantly piquant. **poign′an·cy** *n.* **poign′ant·ly** *adv.*

poin·ci·an·a (poinsēă′n*a*) *n.* Tropical tree (Poinciana pulcherrima) with bright red flowers.

poin·set·ti·a (poinsĕt′ē*a*, -sĕt′*a*) *n.* Plant of Mexican species of *Euphorbia, E. pulcherrima*, with large scarlet bracts surrounding small yellowish flowers. [f. J.R. *Poinsett*, Amer. minister to Mexico, who discovered it]

point (point) *n.* 1. Small dot on a surface. 2. Stop or punctuation mark; dot, small stroke, used in Semitic script to indicate vowels or distinguish consonants; dot separating integral from fractional parts in decimals, as *two* ~ *five* (2.5). 3. Single item, detail, particular; thing under discussion; **beside the** ~, irrelevant(ly); **make a** ~, establish proposition, prove contention; **make a** ~ **of**, treat as essential, insist on; **to the** ~, relevant(ly). 4. Distinctive trait, characteristic, as **good, bad,** ~**; strong** ~, thing one is good at. 5. Salient feature of story, joke, etc.; pungency, effectiveness. 6. Unit in appraising qualities of exhibit in show or achievements of competitor in contest; unit (of varying value) in quoting price of stocks etc.; unit of value in rationing; **give** ~**s to,** allow (opponent) to count so many points at starting, (fig.) be superior to; **win on** ~**s**, (boxing) win by securing more points in a bout, not by knockout. 7. (print.) Unit of measurement for type bodies, in U.S. and Britain 0.0138 in. ($\frac{1}{72}$ in., $\frac{1}{12}$ of a pica). 8. (geom.) That which has position but not magni-

Intensive selection has developed the ***pointer*** *from its primitive ancestor into a highly specialized hunting dog, bred to indicate the position of the quarry in silence.*

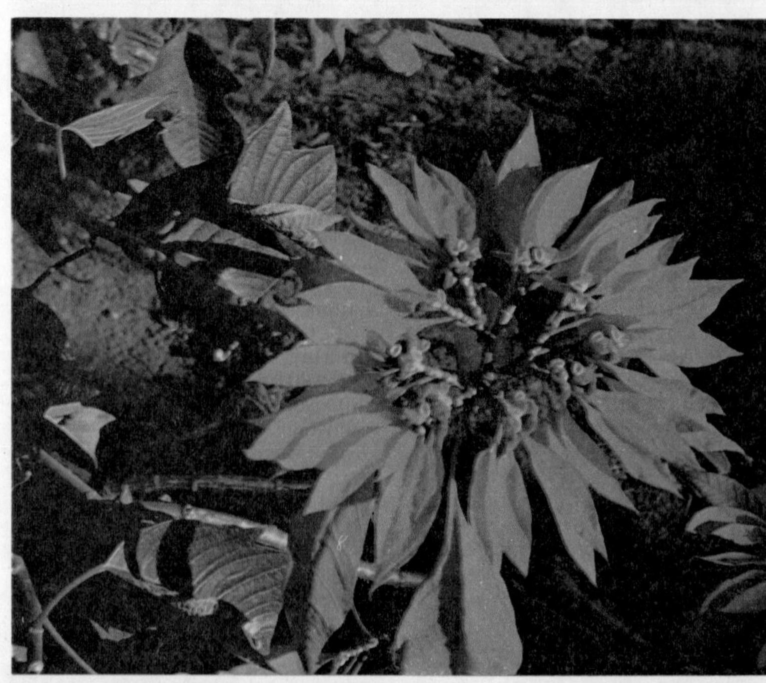

The vivid ***poinsettia*** *is a tropical and sub-tropical plant which flowers at the end of summer. Although hardy in those regions, it needs particular care when grown in cooler climates.*

tude, as the intersection of two lines. 9. Precise place or spot, as ~ *of contact*. 10. (hunting) Spot to which straight run is made, such run. 11. Stage, degree, in progress or increase, esp. of temperature, as **boiling ~, freezing ~**. 12. Precise moment for action etc.; exact moment (of death etc.). 13. (mus.) Important phrase or subject, esp. in contrapuntal music. 14. Sharp end of tool, weapon, pin, pen, etc.; sharp-pointed tool, e.g. etching needle; (elect.) contact, terminal; socket; (also ~ **lace**) lace made wholly with needle. 15. Tip; promontory, esp. in names, as *Montauk P~*; (pl.) extremities of a horse or dog; (pl., of Siamese cat) colored ears, feet, tail, and face; (ballet, usu. pl.) tips of toes; (mil.) small leading party of advance guard. 16. Tine of deer's horn. 17. Tapering movable rail by which train is directed from one line to another. 18. Tapered division on backgammon board. 19. (hist.) Tagged lace for lacing bodice, attaching hose to doublet, etc. 20. (naut.) Short piece of cord at lower edge of sail for tying up a reef. 21. Horizontal direction on compass; corresponding point of horizon, direction. 22. (of dog) Act of pointing. 23. **at all ~s**, in every part; **in ~ of fact**, as a matter of fact; **on the point of**, on the verge of (action, *doing*); ~ **of honor**, matter regarded as vitally affecting one's honor. **point** *v.* 1. Sharpen (pencil etc.); furnish with point; give point to (words, actions). 2. Insert points in Semitic script; mark ((Psalms etc.) for chanting, by means of points. 3. Fill in joints of (masonry etc.) with mortar etc.; prick *in* (manure), turn *over* (soil), with point of spade. 4. Direct attention *to, at*, by or as by extending finger; (of dog) indicate presence of (game) by standing rigidly, looking toward it; direct (finger, weapon, etc., *at*); direct attention of (person *to*); aim *at*, tend toward; ~ **out**, indicate, show.

point-blank (point'blăngk') *adj.* & *adv.* With aim or weapon level; at short range; (fig.) direct(ly). [prob. f. *blank* white spot in center of target]

point·ed (poin'tĭd) *adj.* Having, sharpened to, a point; (of remark, etc.) having point, penetrating, cutting; emphasized, made evident; (of Semitic script) having the vowels marked. **point'ed·ly** *adv.* **point'-ed·ness** *n.*

point·er (poin'ter) *n.* (esp.) 1. Index hand of clock, balance, etc. 2. Rod used for pointing to words etc. on blackboard, map, etc. 3. Dog that on scenting game stands rigidly, with muzzle stretched toward it and usu. one foot raised. 4. (pl.) Two stars in Great Bear, straight line through which points nearly to polestar.

poin·til·lé (pwăñtēyā') *adj.* 1. (of bookbinding) Decorated with gilt dots. 2. (of picture) Painted with numerous small spots of two or more pure colors that at a distance produce the effect of a mixed color, hence **Poin·til·lism** (pwăn'tĭlĭzem) *n.* **poin'til·list** *n.* Painter using technique of Pointillism.

point·ing (poin'tĭng) *n.* (esp.) 1. (Insertion of) points in Semitic script, Psalms, etc. 2. (Insertion of) facing in joints of masonry etc.

point·less (point'lĭs) *adj.* Without a point, blunt; without point, meaningless; not having scored a point. **point'less·ly** *adv.* **point'-less·ness** *n.*

poise (poiz) *v.* (**poised, pois·-ing**). Balance; hold suspended or supported; carry (one's head etc.) in specified way; be balanced; hover in air etc. ~ *n.* Balance, equilibrium; state of indecision, suspense; carriage (of head etc.); ease of manner, grace, assurance.

poi·son (poi'zon) *n.* Substance that when introduced into or absorbed by a living organism destroys life or injures health, esp. (pop.) one that rapidly destroys life when taken even in small quantity; (slang) any alcoholic drink; (fig.) baneful principle, doctrine, etc.; ~ **gas**: see GAS; ~ **ivy**, N. Amer. trailing or climbing vine or shrub (*Rhus radicans*), having trifoliate leaves and causing skin rash when touched; ~ **oak**, shrub (*Rhus Toxicodendron*) of SE. U.S., similar in appearance and effects to poision ivy; ~ **pen**, anonymous writer of libelous or scurrilous letters; ~ **sumac**, shrub (*Rhus vernix*) of E. U.S. swampy areas, having compound leaves and greenish-white berries and causing severe skin rash on contact. **poi·-son·ous** (poi'zonus) *adj.* **poi'son·-**

*The shrub **poison ivy** is native to North America. The normal reaction to contact with poison ivy is the development of a skin rash, or severe dermatitis.*

*'Sunday Afternoon on the Island of Grande Jatte', a typical work by the **pointillist** Georges Seurat. He tried to develop impressionism into a scientific art according to color analysis.*

Right: The Tatra Mountains in Poland are part of the Carpathians. While much of this country is still in a natural state, ***Poland*** *has many large cities and is a major industrial producer among the nations of eastern Europe.*

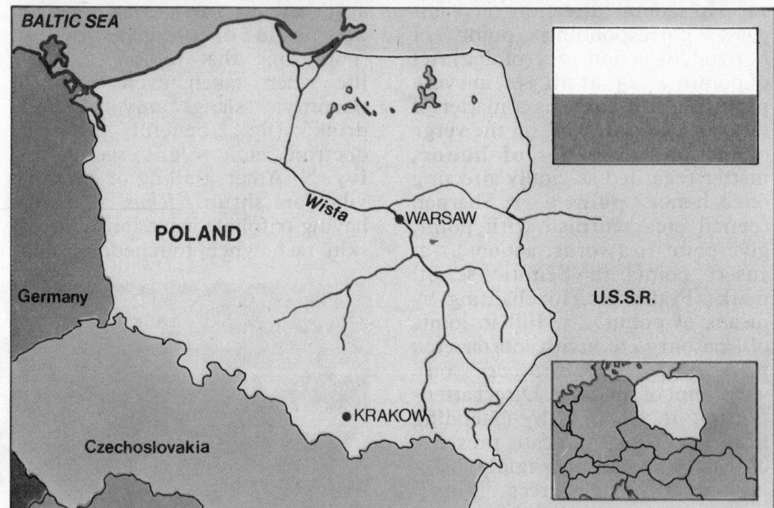

ous·ly *adv.* **poison** *v.t.* Administer poison to; kill, injure, thus; produce morbid effects in (blood etc.); infect (air, water, etc.), smear (weapon) with poison; corrupt, pervert (person, mind); destroy, spoil (pleasure etc.); render (land etc.) foul and unfit for its purpose by noxious applications, etc. **poi'son·er, poi'son·ing** *ns.*

Poi·tou (pwahtōō'). Former province of W. central France and scene of many battles; Visigoths defeated by Franks, 507; Saracens defeated by Charles Martel, 732; it was occupied by England and France alternately 12th–14th c.; scene of peasant insurrections against French Revolutionary government, 18th c.

poke[1] (pōk) *n.* Bag, sack (now dial. exc. in **buy a pig in a ~**: see PIG).

poke[2] (pōk) *v.* (**poked, pok·ing**). Thrust, push (thing *in*, *up*, *down*, etc.) with hand, arm, point of stick, etc.; stir (fire) with poker; produce (hole etc. *in*) by poking; make thrusts with stick, etc. (*at* etc.); thrust forward, esp. obtrusively; pry (*into*); **~ about**, look here and there; busy oneself in a desultory way; **~ along**, proceed in a desultory manner; **~ fun at**, ridicule. **poke** *n.* 1. Poking; thrust, nudge. 2. Device fastened on cattle etc., to prevent their breaking through fences.

pok·er[1] (pō'ker) *n.* Stiff metal rod with handle, for poking fire.

pok·er[2] (pō'ker) *n.* Card game for two or more players, each of whom receives five or more cards, who bet on the value of their hands, the winner being the one who holds the strongest hand or who succeeds in bluffing the others into throwing in their hands; **~ face**, (person with) face that does not reveal thoughts or feelings.

poke·weed (pōk'wēd) *n.* Tall herb (*Phylotacca americana*) of N. Amer., having purple berries yielding emetic and cathartic.

pok·y, pok·ey (pō'kē) *adjs.* (**pok·i·er, pok·i·est**). 1. (of place, room etc.) Confined, mean, shabby. 2. (of persons) Annoyingly slow.

Po·land (pō'land). Country of NE. Europe, formerly a kingdom, that was divided by partitions of 1772, 1793, and 1795 among Prussia, Russia, and Austria; reconstituted by Napoleon, but repartitioned at the Congress of Vienna (1815); recognized as an independent republic by treaties of Versailles (1919) and Riga (1921); invaded and overrun by German and later by Russian armies, 1939, and again recognized as an independent republic in 1945; capital, Warsaw.

Po·land Chi·na (pōl'and chī'na). (One of) an American breed of large black-and-white pigs.

po·lar (pō'ler) *adj.* 1. Of, near, either pole of the Earth or of the celestial sphere; **~ bear**, white bear (*Thalarctos maritimus*); **~ circle**, Arctic or Antarctic Circle, at distance of 23° 28′ from the poles; **~ distance**, angular distance of point on sphere from nearer pole. 2. Having polarity, having associated positive and negative poles (either electrical or magnetic); (of forces) acting in 2 opposite directions; (of molecules) symmetrically arranged in definite directions. 3. (geom.) Relating to a pole. 4. (zool.) Of poles of nerve cell, ovum, etc. 5. (fig.) Analogous to pole of Earth or to polestar; directly opposite in character. **polar** *n.* (geom.) Curve related in particular way to given curve and fixed point called pole; in conic sections, straight line joining points at which tangents from fixed point touch curve.

po·lar·im·e·ter (pōlerĭm'ĭter) *n.* Instrument for measuring polarized light or degree of polarization. **po·lar·im·e·try** (pōlarĭm'ĭtrē) *n.* Measurement of polarization.

Po·lar·is (pōlār'ĭs, -ăr'ĭs) *n.* 1. (astron.) Polestar of North Star; see POLE[2]. 2. A two-stage, solid-propellant intermediate range ballistic missile developed by the

U.S. navy, that can be fired from submerged submarines as well as surface vessels.

po·lar·i·ty (pōlăr′ĭtē, po-) *n.* Tendency of magnetized bar etc. to point with its extremities to magnetic poles of Earth; tendency of a body to place its mathematical axis in particular direction; possession of two poles having contrary qualities; electrical condition of body as positive or negative; (fig.) direction (of thought, feeling, etc.) toward a single point.

po·lar·ize (pō′lerīz) *v.* (**-ized, -iz·ing**). 1. Restrict vibrations of (transverse waves, esp. light) so that they have different amplitudes in different directions. 2. Give polarity to. 3. Divide into two groups at opposite extremes of opinion etc. **po·lar·i·za·tion** (pōlerīzā′shon), **po′lar·iz·er** *ns.*

Po·lar·oid (pō′leroid) *n.* (trademark) Thin, transparent, filmlike plastic capable of polarizing light, thereby reducing glare; used in photography, optical devices, etc.

pol·der (pōl′der) *n.* Piece of low-lying land reclaimed from sea or river in Netherlands.

Pole (pōl) *n.* Native or inhabitant of Poland.

pole[1] (pōl) *n.* 1. Long slender rounded piece of wood or metal, esp. as support for tent, telegraph wires, etc., to propel punt etc.; wooden shaft fitted to carriage of vehicle and attached to yokes or collars of horses etc.; ~ **position**, inside track at start of race; ~ **vault**, jump etc. with help of pole held in hands. 2. (as measure) Rod,

The intelligent and playful ***polecat*** *is found in varying forms all over Europe and western and northern Asia, living either alone or in temporary family groups of mother and young. Its greatest enemy is man.*

perch, $5\frac{1}{2}$ yds.; (also **square** ~) $30\frac{1}{4}$ sq. yds. **pole** *v.t.* (**poled, pol·ing**). Furnish with poles; push, move, with pole.

pole[2] (pōl) *n.* 1. Either of the 2 points (**north** and **south** ~) in celestial sphere about which the stars appear to revolve; N. and S. extremities of Earth's axis; **pole′-star**, star of Ursa Minor, now about $1\frac{1}{4}°$ distant from north pole of the heavens; Polaris or North Star. 2. (geom.) Each of two points of a circle of the sphere in which axis of that circle cuts surface of sphere; fixed point to which others are referred. 3. Each of two opposite points on surface of magnet at which magnetic forces are manifested; each of two terminal points (POSITIVE and NEGATIVE) of electric cell, battery, etc. 4. (biol.) Extremity of main axis of any spherical or oval organ. 5. (fig.) Each of two opposed principles etc., hence **~s apart**, as far apart or different as it is possible to be.

pole·ax, pole·axe (pōl′ăks) *ns.* (pl. **-ax·es**). Battle ax; ax formerly used in naval warfare as weapon and for cutting ropes etc.; halbert; butcher's ax with hammer at back. ~ *v.t.* (**-axed, -ax·ing**). Slaughter (beast etc.) with poleax.

pole·cat (pōl′kăt) *n.* (pl. **-cats**, collect. **-cat**). Small dark brown fetid carnivorous European mammal of weasel family, esp. *Mustela putorius*; skunk.

po·lem·ic (polĕm′ĭk) *adj.* Controversial, disputatious. ~ *n.* Controversial discussion; (pl.) practice of this, esp. in theology; (sing.) controversialist. **po·lem′i·cal** *adj.* & *n.* **po·lem′i·cal·ly** *adv.*

po·len·ta (pōlĕn′ta) *n.* Italian dish of milk thickened with corn, barley, etc.

pole·star (pōl′stār′): see POLE[2].

po·lice (polēs′) *n.* Civil administration, public order; department of government concerned with this; civil force responsible for maintain-

The north ***pole*** *lies in a waste of water: it is only possible for its site to be marked because the upper layers of the Arctic Ocean are frozen solid, forming a false 'land'.*

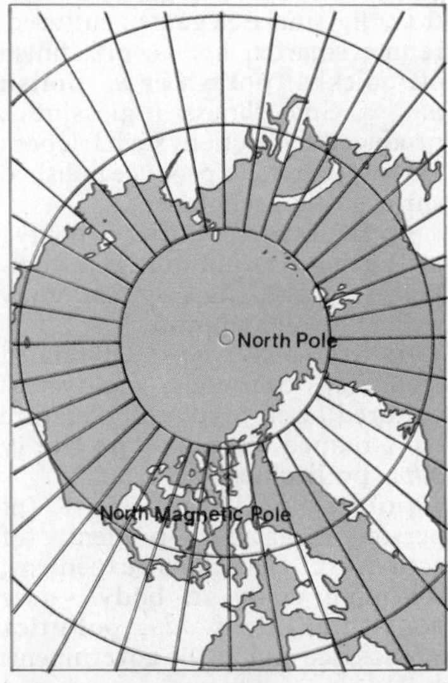

*The role of **police** is to maintain law and order and they may be called to help where there has been an accident, even if there are no suspicious factors (1). Some like those in Samoa (2), are armed and have conspicuous uniforms, while men who control traffic in places like Hong Kong (3) must have shelter.*

1

2

3

ing public order; (collect.) members of this; any body officially employed to keep order, enforce regulations, etc.; ~ **dog**, dog employed by police to track criminals, etc.; **police′man** (pl. **-men**), **police′woman** (pl. **-women**), member of police force; **police officer**, policeman, policewoman; **police state**, state regulated by means of a national police having secret supervision and control of the citizens' activities; **police station**, office of local police force. **police** *v.t.* (**-liced, -lic·ing**). Control (country etc.) by means of police; furnish with police; (fig.) administer, control; ~ (**up**), clean (military barracks, camp, etc.).

pol·i·cy[1] (pŏl′ĭsē) *n.* (pl. **-cies**). Political sagacity; statecraft; prudent conduct, sagacity; craftiness; course of action adopted by government, party, etc.

pol·i·cy[2] (pŏl′ĭsē) *n.* (pl. **-cies**). (also **insurance** ~) Document containing contract of insurance.

po·li·o (pō′lēō) *n.* (colloq.) Poliomyelitis; hence, ~ **vaccine**, one used in immunization against poliomyelitis.

po·li·o·my·e·li·tis (pōlēōmīelī′tĭs) *n.* (in full **acute anterior** ~) Infectious disease of the central nervous system, with temporary or permanent paralysis. [Gk. *polios* gray, *muelos* marrow]

Po·lish (pō′lĭsh) *adj.* Of Poland or the Poles; ~ **Corridor**: see CORRIDOR. **Polish** *n.* Language of Poland, belonging to Western branch of Slavonic languages.

pol·ish (pŏl′ĭsh) *v.* Make, become, smooth and glossy by friction; (fig.) make elegant or cultured, refine; smarten *up*; ~ **off**, finish off quickly. **pol′ish·er** *n.* **polish** *n.* Smoothness, glossiness, produced by friction; such friction; substance used to produce polished surface; (fig.) refinement.

po·lit·bu·ro (pŏl′ĭtbūr′ō, polĭt′-) *n.* Principal committee of a communist party; (fig.) similar body with controlling power.

po·lite (polīt′) *adj.* Of refined manners, courteous; cultivated, cultured; well-bred; (of literature etc.) refined, elegant. **po·lite′ly** *adv.* **po·lite′ness** *n.*

pol·i·tic (pŏl′ĭtĭk) *adj.* 1. (of person) Sagacious, prudent; (of action etc.) judicious, expedient; scheming, crafty. 2. **body** ~: see BODY. **pol′i·tic·ly** *adv.* **pol′i·tics** *n.* Science and art of government; political affairs or life; (as pl.) political principles.

po·lit·i·cal (polĭt′ĭkal) *adj.* 1. Of the state or its government; of public affairs; of politics; (of person) engaged in civil administration. 2. Having an organized polity. 3. Belonging to, taking, a side in politics. 4. ~ **economy**: see ECONOMY; ~ **geography**, that dealing with boundaries, divisions, and possessions of nations; ~ **prisoner**, one imprisoned for a political offense. **po·lit′i·cal·ly** *adv.*

pol·i·ti·cian (pŏlĭtĭsh′an) *n.* One skilled in politics, statesman; one interested or engaged in politics, esp. as profession; one who makes a trade of politics. **pol·i·tick** (pŏl′ĭtĭk) *v.i.* Engage in politics.

po·lit·i·co (polĭt′ĭkō) *n.* (pl. **-cos**). Political agent, officer, or resident.

pol·i·ty (pŏl′ĭtē) *n.* (pl. **-ties**). Condition of civil order; form, process, of civil government; organized society, state.

Polk (pōk), **James Knox** (1795–1849). Eleventh president of U.S.,

Modern industrial advances have given the world the problem of ***pollution.*** *Both human health (threatened by fumes, above) and wildlife are at risk from poisoning of the environment.*

Bees transfer ***pollen*** *from male to female flowers but fruit-growers cannot always rely on insects. The earliest records show that date-growers in the Middle East had to pollinate by hand.*

1845–9; under his administration the U.S. obtained the Oregon territory boundary to the 49th parallel, the Texas boundary to the Rio Grande, and California and New Mexico territories from Mexico after the Mexican War.

pol·ka (pōl′k*a*, pō′k*a*) *n.* Lively dance of Czech origin, with music in double time; music for this; ~ **dot,** one of a pattern of dots of uniform size and arrangement.

poll (pōl) *n.* 1. Human head (now dial. or joc.); part of head on which hair grows; ~ **tax,** tax levied on every adult, sometimes as a requirement for voting. 2. Counting of voters; voting at election; number of votes recorded. 3. Questioning of a sample of the population in order to estimate trend of public opinion. **poll·ster** (pōl′st*e*r) *n.* One who takes public-opinion polls. **poll** *v.* 1. Crop the hair of (archaic), cut off top of (tree, plant), esp. make a pollard of; cut off horns of (cattle, esp. in past part.). 2. Take the votes of; (of candidate) receive (so many votes); give (vote); give one's vote. ~ *adj.* Polled or cut even at edge.

pol·lack, pol·lock (pŏl′*a*k) *ns.* (pl. **-lacks, -locks,** collect. **-lack, -lock**). Sea fish (*Pollachius virens*) allied to cod but with lower jaw protruding, used as food.

pol·lard (pŏl′*e*rd) *n.* 1. Animal that has cast or lost its horns; ox, sheep, goat, of hornless variety. 2. Tree polled so as to produce close rounded head of young branches. 3. Bran sifted from flour; fine bran containing some flour. ~ *v.t.* Make a pollard of (tree).

pol·len (pŏl′*e*n) *n.* Fine powdery substance discharged from anther of flower, male element that fertilizes ovules; ~ **count,** index of amount of pollen in air, published as warning to sufferers from respiratory ailments. **pol·lin·ic** (pol*ĭ*n′ĭk), **pol·li·nif·er·ous** (pŏl*i*nĭf′*e*r*u*s) *adjs.*

pol·lex (pŏl′ĕks) *n.* (pl. **pol·li·ces** pr. pŏl′ĭsēz). Innermost digit of forelimb; in man, thumb.

pol·li·nate (pŏl′*i*nāt) *v.t.* (**-nat·ed, -nat·ing**). Sprinkle with pollen, shed pollen upon. **pol·li·na′tion** *n.*

Pol·lock (pŏl′*o*k), **Jackson** (1912–56). Amer. abstract expressionist painter famous for his "action paintings" made by dripping paint onto the canvas.

pol·lute (p*o*lo͞ot′) *v.t.* (**-lut·ed, -lut·ing**). Destroy the purity or sanctity of; make (water etc.) foul or filthy. **pol·lu′tion** *n.* (esp.) Contamination or defilement of man's environment.

Pol·lux (pŏl′*u*ks). 1. (Gk. myth.) Twin brother of CASTOR. 2. (astron.) Bright star in the constellation Gemini.

Pol·ly·an·na (pŏlēăn′*a*). Irrepressibly optimistic person (based on a character in Eleanor

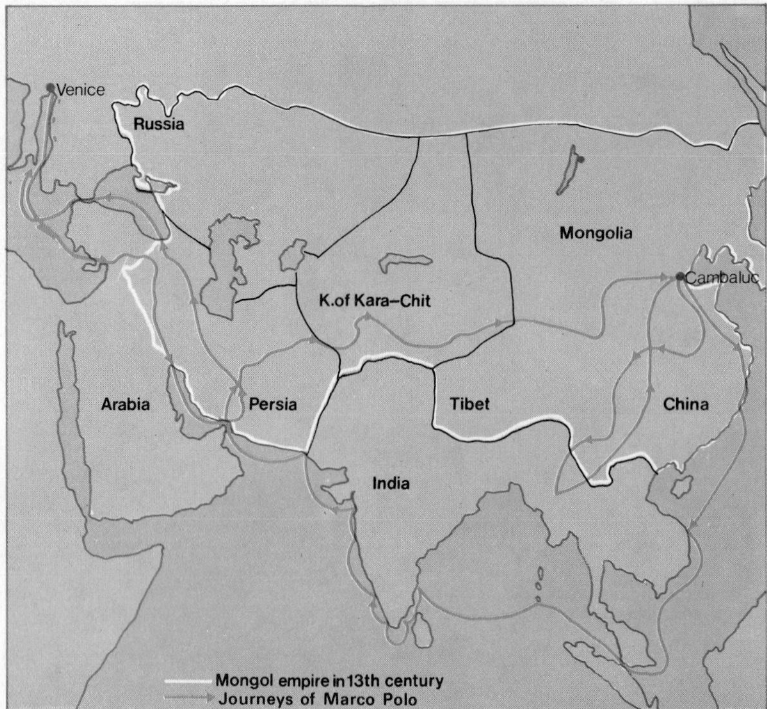

Taken to the East by his father and uncle, ***Marco Polo*** *remained for 17 years in the service of Kublai Khan. During this time he made notes about everything he saw: some years after their return he had these made into a book.*

Although the word ***polo*** *is derived from the Tibetan for ball — pulu — the game seems to have started in Persia, at least as far back as the time of Darius the Great.*

Porter's book of the same name, 1913).

po·lo (pō'lō) *n.* Game of Eastern origin resembling hockey, played on horseback by teams of usu. four players, with long-handled mallets (~ **sticks**) and wooden ball; ~ **shirt**, knitted pullover sport shirt; **water** ~, game resembling basketball played by swimmers with ball like soccer ball.

Po·lo (pō'lō), **Marco** (1254–1324). Venetian traveler; reached the court of Kublai Khan in China; spent 17 years in China and wrote an account of his experiences.

pol·o·naise (pŏlonāz', pōlo-) *n.* 1. (hist.) Woman's dress consisting of bodice with skirt open from waist downward. 2. (Music for) slow dance in triple rhythm of Polish origin, with intricate march or procession of dancers in couples. [Fr., fem. of *polonais* Polish]

po·lo·ni·um (polō'nēum) *n.* (chem.) Radioactive metallic element discovered by Pierre and Marie Curie in pitchblende; symbol Po, at. no. 84, principal isotope at. wt. 210. [med. L. *Polonia* Poland]

pol·ter·geist (pōl'tergīst) *n.* Noisy spirit manifesting its presence by mischievous behavior, such as the overturning of furniture, breaking of crockery, etc. [Ger.]

pol·troon (pŏltrōōn') *n.* Spiritless coward. **pol·troon'er·y** *n.*

poly- *prefix.* Many.

pol·y·am·ide (pŏlēăm'ĭd) *n.* (chem.) Polymer containing more than 1 amide group.

pol·y·an·drous (pŏlēăn'drus) *adj.* 1. Of, practicing, polyandry. 2. (bot.) With numerous stamens.

pol·y·an·dry (pŏl'ēăndrē, pŏlēăn'-) *n.* Plurality of husbands.

pol·y·an·thus (pŏlēăn'thus) *n.* (pl. **-thus·es**). Cultivated primula with flowers of various colors.

pol·y·chaete (pŏl'ikēt) *adj.* & *n.* (Animal) of the Polychaeta, a class of the Annelida comprising worms, mostly marine, with many bristles on the foot stumps.

pol·y·chro·mat·ic (pŏlēkrōmăt'ĭk), **pol·y·chro·mic** (pŏlēkrō'mĭk), **pol·y·chro'mous** *adjs.* Many-colored.

pol·y·chrome (pŏl'ēkrōm) *adj.* Painted, printed, decorated, in many colors. ~ *n.* Work of art in several colors, esp. colored statue. **pol·y·chro·my** (pŏlēkrō'mē) *n.* Art of painting in several colors, esp. as applied to ancient pottery or sculpture.

pol·y·clin·ic (pŏlēklĭn'ĭk) *n.* Clinic or hospital devoted to treatment of various diseases.

pol·y·es·ter (pŏl'ēĕster, pŏlēĕs'-) *n.* (chem.) Any of several synthetic resins, used esp. in making plastics, fibers, adhesives etc.

pol·y·eth·yl·ene (pŏlēĕth'ilēn) *n.* Tough light thermoplastic polymer of ethylene, used for packaging etc.

po·lyg·a·mous (polĭg'amus) *adj.* 1. Having more than one wife or (less usu.) husband at once. 2. (zool.) Having more than one mate at one time. 3. (bot.) Bearing some flowers with stamens only, some with pistils only, some with both, on same or different plants. **po·lyg·a·mist** (polĭg'amĭst), **po·lyg·a·my** (polĭg'amē) *ns.*

pol·y·glot (pŏl'ēglŏt) *adj.* Of many languages; speaking or writing several languages; (of book, esp. Bible) written in several languages. ~ *n.* Polyglot person or book.

pol·y·gon (pŏl'ēgŏn) *n.* Figure (usu. plane rectilinear) with many (usu. more than four) angles or sides; ~ **of forces**, polygon

*Generally man is either monogamous or polygamous. Rarely, however, a people develops **polyandry,** living in groups like this: the reason is probably that it keeps family property together.*

illustrating theorem relating to number of forces acting at a point, each represented in magnitude and direction by one side of the figure. **po·lyg·o·nal** (polĭg′onal) *adj.* **po·lyg′o·nal·ly** *adv.*

po·lyg·o·num (polĭg′onum) *n.* Plant of large and widely distributed genus *P*~ (including knot grass, etc.) with swollen stem joints sheathed by stipules, and small flowers.

pol·y·graph (pŏl′ēgrăf, -grahf) *n.* 1. Lie detector. 2. Writer of many or various works. **pol·y·graph′ic** *adj.*

po·lyg·y·nous (polĭj′inus) *adj.* 1. Of, practicing, polygyny. 2. (bot.) With many pistils, styles, or stigmas. **po·lyg·y·ny** (polĭj′inē) *n.* Plurality of wives.

pol·y·he·dron (pŏlēhē′dron) *n.* (pl. **-drons, -dra** pr. -dra). Many- (usu. more than six-) sided solid. **pol·y·he′dral** *adj.*

Pol·y·hym·ni·a (pŏlihĭm′nēa). (Gk. and Rom. myth.) Muse of the mimic art.

pol·y·mer (pŏl′imer) *n.* (chem.) Compound formed by the combination of a (usu. very large) number of identical molecules of a simpler substance. **pol·y·mer·ic** (pŏlimĕr′ĭk) *adj.* (of compounds) Composed of the same elements in the same proportions but differing in molecular weight.

po·lym·er·ize (polĭm′erīz, pŏl′imerīz) *v.* (**-ized, -iz·ing**). (chem., of a number of identical molecules) Combine together to form a polymer. **po·lym·er·i·za·tion** (polĭmezā′shon, pŏlimer-) *n.*

pol·y·mor·phism (pŏlēmōr′fĭzem) *n.* Diversity occurring within biological populations, determined genetically or by environment.

pol·y·mor·phous (pŏlēmōr′fus), **pol·y·mor·phic** (pŏlēmōr′fĭk) *adjs.* Multiform; esp. (biol., of a species) of which more than one form exists in a population.

Pol·y·ne·sia (pŏlinē′zha, -sha). One of the three divisions of Oceania; a scattered group of islands in the central and W. Pacific Ocean lying E. of Melanesia and Micronesia, extending from New Zealand N. to the Hawaii Islands and E. to Easter Island. **Pol·y·ne′sian** *adj.* & *n.*

pol·y·no·mi·al (pŏlēnō′mēal) *adj.* & *n.* (Expression) of more than two terms, esp. (sum) of terms containing different powers of the same variable(s).

pol·yp (pŏl′ĭp) *n.* 1. (zool.) Single individual of a coelenterate or other colony; similar individual of a noncolonial form, e.g. sea anemone (ill. HYDRA). 2. (path.) Small tumor with a stalk, formed by overgrowth of tissue. **pol·yp·oid** (pŏl′ipoid), **pol′yp·ous** *adjs.*

*The **polychaete** worm, Torrea candida, is well adapted to free-swimming, carnivorous life, with prominent, efficient eyes, bristly paddles along each side, and large jaws which it shoots out at its prey, the smaller creatures of the Mediterranean and similar seas.*

pol·y·pep·tide (pŏlēpĕp′tīd) *n.* Substance formed by union of three or more amino acids.

Pol·y·phe·mus (pŏlifē′mus). (Gk. legend) CYCLOPS from whom Odysseus and some of his companions escaped by putting out his one eye while he slept.

pol·y·phon·ic (pŏlēfŏn′ĭk), **po·lyph·o·nous** (polĭf′onus) *adjs.* 1. (mus.) Of polyphony, contrapuntal. 2. Producing many sounds.

po·lyph·o·ny (polĭf′onē) *n.* (mus.) Simultaneous combination

Above: Long clean beaches and lush vegetation have enabled islands in ***Polynesia*** *to develop a tourist industry. This has proved more reliable than the cultivation of the coconut palm as a cash crop (right) to satisfy demands for copra.*

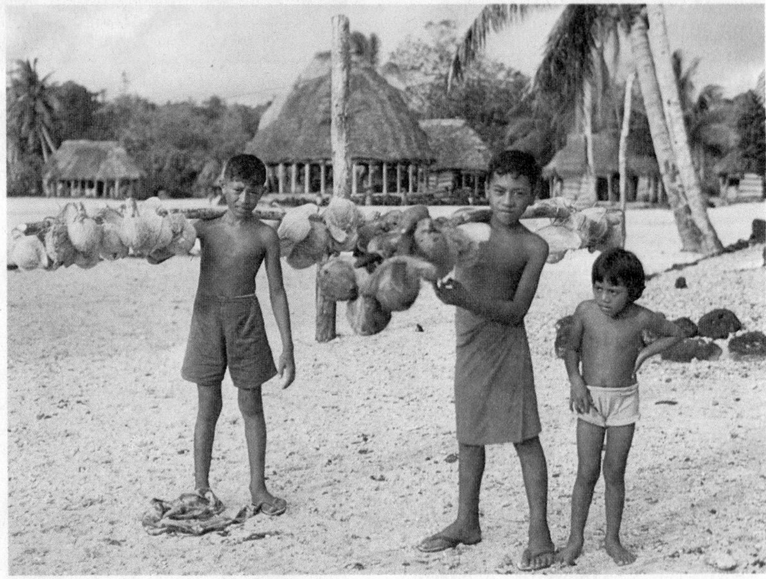

of number of parts, each forming an individual melody; style of composition in which parts are so combined; counterpoint.

pol·y·ploid (pŏl′ĕploid) *adj.* & *n.* (biol.) (Organism) having a chromosome number that is a multiple greater than two of the basic group number. **pol·y·ploi′dic** *adj.* **pol′y·ploi·dy** *n.*

pol·y·pod (pŏl′ĕpŏd) *adj.* & *n.* (Animal) with many feet.

pol·y·po·dy (pŏl′ĕpōdē) *n.* (pl. **-dies**). Fern of large and widely distributed genus *Polypodium*, esp. *P. vulgare*, growing on moist rocks, old walls, and trees.

pol·y·pore (pŏl′ĕpōr, -pōr) *n.* Fungus of the family Polyporaceae whose members have large fruiting bodies in which the spores are produced in tubes.

pol·y·pro·pyl·ene (pŏlĕprō′pĭlēn) *n.* (chem.) Plastic polymer of propylene, used esp. for packaging, containers, and electrical insulation.

pol·y·sty·rene (pŏlĕstī′rēn) *n.* Transparent thermoplastic material, a polymer of styrene.

pol·y·syl·lab·ic (pŏlĕsĭlăb′ĭk) *adj.* (of word) Having many syllables; marked by polysyllables. **pol·y·syl·lab′i·cal·ly** *adv.* **pol·y·syl·la·ble** (pŏl′ĕsĭlabel, pŏlĕsĭl′-) *n.* Polysyllabic word.

pol·y·tech·nic (pŏlĕtĕk′nĭk) *adj.* Dealing with, devoted to, various arts. ~ *n.* College of higher education providing courses in various subjects.

pol·y·the·ism (pŏl′ĕthēĭzem, pŏlĕthē′-) *n.* Belief in, worship of, many gods or more than one god. **pol′y·the·ist** *n.* **pol·y·the·is′tic** *adj.*

pol·y·un·sat·u·rat·ed (pŏlĕūnsăch′ĕrātĭd) *adj.* Of fats that have many double bonds in the molecule; in diet they give rise to less cholesterol in blood than other fats.

pol·y·vi·nyl (pŏlĕvī′nĭl) *adj.* ~ **chloride**, (abbrev. PVC) vinyl plastic used for insulation, as fabric for clothing and furnishings, etc.

pol·y·zo·an (pŏlĕzō′an) = BRYOZOAN.

pom·ace (pŭm′ĭs) *n.* Mass of crushed apples in cider-making before or after juice is pressed out; any pulp; refuse of fish, etc., after oil has been extracted, used as fertilizer.

po·made (pomād′, -mahd′, pō-) *n.* Scented ointment (perh. orig. from apples) for hair and skin of head. ~ *v.t.* (**-mad·ed, -mad·ing**). Anoint with pomade.

po·ma·tum (pōmā′tum, -mah′-, po-) *n.* & *v.t.* Pomade.

pome (pōm) *n.* (bot.) Succulent fruit with firm fleshy body enclosing carpels forming core, e.g. apple, pear, quince; (poet.) apple. **po·mif·er·ous** (pōmĭf′erus) *adj.* Bearing pomes.

pome·gran·ate (pŏm′grănĭt, pŏm′e-, pŭm′-) *n.* Large roundish many-celled berry about size of orange with tough golden or orange rind and acid reddish pulp enveloping the many seeds; tree (*Punica granatum*) bearing this, native to N. Africa and W. Asia.

Pom·er·a·ni·a (pŏmerā′nēa, -rān′ya). (Ger. *Pommern*) Province of Poland with seacoast on Baltic, formerly part of Prussia. **Pom·er·a′ni·an** *adj.* & *n.* (Native, inhabitant) of Pomerania; (also ~

*Known also as bracket or shelf fungus, some types of **polypore** grow on the trunks of elms and other deciduous trees between spring and fall in the northern hemisphere. Their smell has been likened by some observers to that of uncooked tripe.*

***Polypody,** the common name for Polypodium vulgare (above), a fern common in Britain, is only one of 75 species at present grouped together by botanists. Another variety is highly specialized and has developed special pouches which collect rain and store it for use in a drought.*

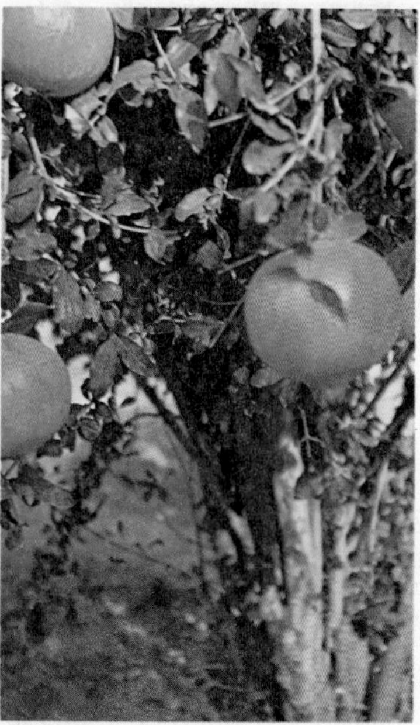

*The refreshing fruit of the **pomegranate** has made it popular around the Mediterranean since Biblical times: it was one of the things missed by the Israelites as they wandered in the desert after their departure from Egypt.*

dog) dog of small breed with long thick silky hair, usu. black or white, pointed muzzle, pricked ears, and prominent eyes.

po·mi·cul·ture (pō´mĭkŭlch*er*) *n.* Fruit-growing.

Pom·mard (pŏmar̄d´, -mar̄´) *n.* Dry red wine produced near Pommard in Burgundy.

pom·mel (pŭm´*e*l, pŏm´-) *n.* 1. Rounded knob esp. at end of sword hilt. 2. Upward projecting front part of saddle. ~ *v.t.* (**-meled** or **-melled, -mel·ing** or **-mel·ling**). Pummel.

po·mol·o·gy (pōmŏl´*o*jē) *n.* Science of fruit-growing. **po·mo·log·i·cal** (pōm*o*lŏj´ĭk*a*l) *adj.* **po·mol´o·gist** *n.*

Po·mo·na (p*o*mō´n*a*). (Rom. myth.) Goddess of fruit trees.

pomp (pŏmp) *n.* Splendid display, splendor.

pom·pa·dour (pŏm´p*a*dōr, -dōr, -door) *n.* Style of women's hairdressing with hair turned back from forehead in high roll. [f. POMPADOUR]

Pom·pa·dour (pŏm´p*a*door, pŏmp*a*door´), **Marquise de** (1721–1764). Jeanne Antoinette Poisson le Normant d'Étoiles, mistress of Louis XV of France.

Pom·peii (pŏmpā´). Ancient town of Campania, Italy, buried by eruption of Mt. Vesuvius in 79 A.D. and since 1755 gradually laid bare by excavation.

Pom·pey (pŏm´pē). Gnaeus Pompeius Magnus (106–48 B.C.), Roman general and consul; member, with Julius Caesar and Crassus, of the 1st triumvirate; later he opposed Caesar and was defeated by him at Pharsalia, 48 B.C.

pom-pom (pŏm´pŏm) *n.* 1. Automatic quick-firing gun. 2. Pompon.

pom·pon (pŏm´pŏn) *n.* Ornamental tuft or bunch of silk threads, ribbon, etc., on hat, shoe, dress, etc.; variety of chrysanthemum or dahlia with small globular flowers.

pomp·ous (pŏm´p*u*s) *n.* Magnificent, splendid; self-important, consequential; (of language) inflated. **pomp´ous·ly** *adv.* **pom·pos·i·ty** (pŏmpŏs´ĭtē), **pomp´ous·ness** *ns.*

Pon·ce de Le·ón (pŏns´ d*e* lē´*o*n; *Sp.* pawn´thĕ dhĕ lĕawn´), **Juan** (*c*1460–1521). Spanish explorer, conqueror and governor (1510–12) of Puerto Rico, and discoverer of Florida (1513).

pon·cho (pŏn´chō) *n.* (pl. **-chos**). S. Amer. cloak, oblong piece of cloth with slit in middle for head.

pond (pŏnd) *n.* Small body of still water artificially formed by hollowing or embanking; natural pool or small lake; (joc.) sea, esp. Atlantic Ocean; ~ **lily**, water lily; **pond´weed**, aquatic herb (esp. of genus *Potamogeton*) growing in still waters.

pon·der (pŏn´d*er*) *v.* Weigh mentally, think over; think *on*, muse *over*. **pon´der·er** *n.*

pon·der·a·ble (pŏn´d*e*r*a*bel) *adj.* Having appreciable weight. **pon·der·a·bil´i·ty** *n.*

pon·der·ous (pŏn´d*e*r*u*s) *adj.* Heavy; unwieldy; laborious; labored. **pon´der·ous·ly** *adv.* **pon´der·ous·ness, pon·der·os·i·ty** (pŏnd*e*rŏs´ĭtē) *ns.*

pone (pōn) *n.* Orig., N. Amer.

*The destruction of **Pompeii** was a tragedy for the citizens, but it has given historians a remarkable insight into everyday Roman life, since so much was preserved under the lava.*

The Connemara (1) and Shetland (2) are only two of the many breeds of ***pony*** *which exist as a result of natural and planned selection, from the heavy types such as the Fell and Dale to yard-high miniatures. Most have become popular as children's mounts because of their intelligence and small size.*

Ind. bread, thin cakes of corn flour cooked in hot ashes; now, in southern U.S., any corn bread; also, very fine light bread made with eggs, milk, etc., and baked in flat cakes.

pon·gee (pŏnjē´, pŏn´jē) *n.* Soft, freq. unbleached fabric of Chinese or Japanese silk, made from cocoons of a wild silkworm feeding on oak leaves; imitation of this in cotton etc. [perh. f. Chin. *pun-chi* own loom]

pon·iard (pŏn´y*e*rd) *n.* Dagger. ~ *v.t.* Stab with poniard.

pons (pŏnz) *n.* (pl. **pon·tes** pr. pŏn´tēz). (anat.) Band of nerve fibers in brain connecting 2 hemispheres of cerebellum, and medulla with cerebrum; also called ~ **Va·ro·li·i** (var*ō*´lēī) ("bridge of Varoli," after an Italian 16th-c. anatomist). [L., = "bridge"]

Pon·ta Del·ga·da (pawn´t*a* dĕlgah´d*a*). Capital of the Azores, on the SW. coast of São Miguel Island in the N. Atlantic Ocean.

Pont·char·train (pŏn´-ch*e*rtrăn), **Lake.** Lake in SE. Louisiana near New Orleans covering about 600 sq. mi. (1,554 sq. km), and connected with the Gulf of Mexico and the Mississippi River.

Pon·ti·ac (pŏn´tēăk) (d. 1769). Amer. Ind. chief from Ottawa; led Indians in **~'s War** or **Conspiracy** against British at Detroit, 1763.

pon·ti·fex (pŏn´tĭfĕks) *n.* (pl. **pon·tif·i·ces** pr. pŏntĭf´ĭsēz). (Rom. antiq.) Member of principal college of priests in Rome; ~ **maximus**, head of this; pope.

pon·tiff (pŏn´tĭf) *n.* Pope; bishop; chief priest.

pon·tif·i·cal (pŏntĭf´ĭk*a*l) *adj.* Of, befitting, a pontiff; solemnly dogmatic; **P~ Mass**, Mass celebrated by bishop wearing full vestments. **pon·tif´i·cal·ly** *adv.* **pontifical** *n.* Book of Western Church containing forms for rites to be performed by bishops; (pl.) vestments and insignia of bishop.

pon·tif·i·cate (pŏntĭf´*i*kĭt, -kāt) *n.* Office of pontifex, bishop, or pope; period of this. ~ (pŏntĭf´-ĭkāt) *v.i.* (**-cat·ed, -cat·ing**). Officiate as bishop, esp. at Mass; assume airs of pontiff, act pompously or dogmatically.

pon·tine (pŏn´tĭn, -tēn) *adj.* Of the PONS.

pon·toon (pŏnto͞on´) *n.* Flat-bottomed boat used as ferryboat etc.; one of several boats, also called ~ **boats**, or hollow metal cylinders, etc., used to support temporary bridge; caisson.

po·ny (pō´nē) *n.* (pl. **-nies**). 1. Horse of any small breed, esp. not more than 13 or (pop.) 14 hands high. 2. (slang) School crib. 3. ~ **express**, formerly in the Amer. West, a rapid postal system using ponies and relays of riders. 4. **po´nytail**, hair worn drawn back, gathered at crown of head, and hanging loose behind.

pooch (po͞och) *n.* (colloq.) Dog.

poo·dle (po͞o´d*e*l) *n.* Dog of breed with long curling hair, usu. black or white, often elaborately clipped and shaved. [Ger. *pundel(hund)*, f. *pudeln* splash]

pooh (po͞o) *int.* Exclamation of impatience or contempt. **pooh´-pooh´** *v.t.* Express contempt for, make light of.

Pooh-Bah (po͞o´bah´) *n.* Holder of many offices at once. [name of character in Gilbert and Sullivan's *The Mikado*]

pool[1] (po͞ol) *n.* Small body of still water, usu. of natural formation; puddle of any liquid; deep still place in river; **swimming ~**: see SWIM.

pool[2] (po͞ol) *n.* 1. (in some card games) Collective amount of players' stakes and fines; receptacle for these. 2. Game on billiard table with balls numbered from 1 to 15, number of ball pocketed being added to player's score. 3. Collective stakes in betting etc.; arrangement between competing parties by which prices are fixed and business is divided to do away with competition; common fund, e.g. of profit of separate firms; common supply of commodities, persons, etc. 4. **football ~**, system of betting on results of football games. **pool** *v.t.* Place in common fund; merge (supplies from several sources); (of competing companies etc.) share (traffic, profits).

poop (po͞op) *n.* 1. Stern of ship; aftermost and highest deck (also ~ **deck**). 2. (slang) Information; news; hence ~ **sheet**, fact sheet or press release distributed to inform. 3. (slang) Feces, esp. of dog; hence, **pooper-scooper**, device for picking up dog feces from street for sanitary disposal. **poop** *v.t.* (of wave) Break over stern of (ship); (of ship) receive (wave) over stern. ~ *v.i.* Exhaust; tire out; (slang) excrete feces.

poor (poor) *adj.* 1. Lacking means to procure comforts or necessities of life; ill supplied, deficient (*in* possession or quality); (of soil) unproductive; **the ~**, poor people as a class. 2. Scanty, inadequate, less than is expected; paltry, sorry; spiritless, despicable; humble, insignificant. 3. (expr. pity or sympathy) Unfortunate, hapless. 4. ~ **box**, money box esp. in church for relief of the poor; **poor´-house**, (hist.) institution where paupers were maintained; **poor white** (**trash**), (contempt.)

***Pop Art** and Pop Music are often interlinked: artists may use images of those who have become known as musicians to create dreamlike visions like this of the Beatles (above). Groups like the Rolling Stones (left) have visual elements in their performance.*

Southern white people of no substance; **poor-mouth** (*v.i.*) complain about one's financial status.

poor·ly (poor′lē) *adv.* Scantily, defectively; with no great success.

poor·ness (poor′nĭs) *n.* Defectiveness; lack of some good quality or constituent.

pop[1] (pŏp) *v.* (**popped, pop·ing**). 1. Make small quick explosive sound as of cork when drawn; let off (firearm etc.); fire gun (*at*); **pop′gun**, child's toy gun shooting pellets by compression of air with piston; **pop off**, (slang) die suddenly; speak or write emotionally. 2. Put (*in, out, down,*

***Pope's** translations made him a wealthy man, but he is best remembered today as the author of such works as 'The Rape of the Lock', a humorous mock-epic.*

etc.) quickly or suddenly; move, come, go (*in* etc.) thus; put (question) abruptly; **pop the question**, (colloq.) propose marriage. 3. Parch (corn) till it bursts open; **pop'corn**, corn so parched. **pop** *n.* Abrupt, not very loud, explosive sound; (colloq.) effervescing drink. ~ *adv.* With (the action or sound of) a pop.

pop[2] (pŏp) = PAPA.

pop[3] (pŏp) *adj.* (of music, art, etc.) Popular.

pop. *abbrev.* Population; popular; popularity.

pope[1] (pōp) *n.* 1. Bishop of Rome as head of the R.C. Ch.; **P ~ Joan**, fabulous female pope placed by some chroniclers *c*855, under name of John; **~'s nose**, rump of (cooked) fowl. 2. (fig.) Person assuming or credited with infallibility. **pope'dom** *n.*

pope[2] (pōp) *n.* Parish priest of Greek Church in U.S.S.R. etc. [Russ. *pop*]

Pope (pōp), **Alexander** (1688–1744). English poet, satirist, and translator of Homer; best known for his mock-heroic poem "The Rape of the Lock" and his "Essay on Man."

pop·er·y (pō'perē) *n.* (in hostile use) Papal system, Roman Catholicism.

pop·in·jay (pŏp'ĭnjā) *n.* 1. (archaic) Parrot; (hist.) figure of parrot on pole as mark to shoot at. 2. Fop, coxcomb, conceited person.

pop·ish (pō'pĭsh) *adj.* Of popery, papistical; **P ~ Plot**, supposed plot to murder Charles II and suppress Protestantism (1678). **pop'ish·ly** *adv.* **pop'ish·ness** *n.*

pop·lar (pŏp'ler) *n.* Large tree of rapid growth (genus *Populus*), freq. with tremulous leaves; soft light loose-textured wood of this.

pop·lin (pŏp'lĭn) *n.* Closely woven fabric with corded surface, orig. of silk warp and worsted woof, now freq. of cotton. [It. *papalina* papal (because made in the papal town of Avignon)]

Po·po·ca·té·petl (pōpokăt'epĕtel, pawpawkahtĕ'petel). Volcanic mountain, dormant since 1802, in Mexico.

pop·o·ver (pŏp'ōver) *n.* Biscuit made from thin egg-rich batter that expands during baking into a hollow shell.

pop·per (pŏp'er) *n.* Covered basket or other device for popping corn.

pop·py (pŏp'ē) *n.* (pl. **-pies**). Plant or flower of genus *Papaver* of temperate and subtropical regions, having milky juice with narcotic properties, showy flowers of scarlet or other color, and roundish capsules containing numerous small seeds; artificial poppy (also **Flanders ~**) worn on Veteran's Day; **California ~**, ESCHSCHOLTZIA; **horn(ed) ~**, any plant of genus *Glaucium*, distinguished by its long hornlike capsules; **opium ~**: see OPIUM; **prickly ~**, any plant of genus *Argemone*, esp. *A. mexicana*, with yellow or white flowers and prickly leaves and capsules; **P ~ Day**, formerly Armistice Day, now Veteran's Day, on which artificial poppies are worn (because poppies were very conspicuous on the Flanders battlefields); **pop'py-head**, capsule of poppy; (archit.) carved finial crowning end of seat in church.

*Despite its name, the Lombardy **poplar** was originally native to the temperate regions of Asia. Its elegant form resulted in its cultivation in Italy, and later in many other parts of the world.*

pop·py·cock (pŏp'ēkŏk) *n.* (colloq.) Nonsense, rubbish.

pop·u·lace (pŏp′yulas) *n.* Common people.

pop·u·lar (pŏp′yuler) *adj.* 1. Of, carried on by, the people; adapted to the understanding, taste, or means of the people; prevalent among the people; ~ **front**, political group representing leftish elements. 2. Liked, admired, by the people or by people generally or a specified class. **pop′u·lar·ly** *adv.* **pop·u·lar·i·ty** (pŏpyulăr′ĭtē) *n.*

pop·u·lar·ize (pŏp′yulerīz) *v.t.* (**-ized, -iz·ing**). Make popular, cause to be generally known or liked; extend to the common people; present in popular form. **pop·u·lar·i·za·tion** (pŏpyulerīzā′shon), **pop′u·lar·iz·er** *ns.*

pop·u·late (pŏp′yulāt) *v.t.* (**-lat·ed, -lat·ing**). Inhabit, form the population of (country, town, etc.); supply with inhabitants. **pop·u·la′tion** *n.* Degree in which place is populated; total number of inhabitants; people of a country etc.

Pop·u·list (pŏp′yulĭst) *n.* 1. Adherent of a Russian political movement (*c*1870–80) advocating collectivism. 2. Adherent of a U.S. political party (1892–1904) aiming at public control of railroads, graduated income tax, etc. **pop′u·list** *n.* & *adj.* (Adherent) of political policy claiming to represent the whole of the people.

pop·u·lous (pŏp′yulus) *adj.* Thickly inhabited. **pop′u·lous·ly** *adv.* **pop′u·lous·ness** *n.*

por·ce·lain (pōr′selĭn, pōr′-; pōrs′lĭn, pōrs′-) *n.* Finest and hardest kind of earthenware, consisting largely of kaolin or feldspathic clay, baked at a high temperature and usu. covered with a colored or transparent glaze; article or vessel of this; (attrib.) of porcelain, (fig.) delicate, fragile; ~ **shell**, cowrie. **por·ce·la·ne·ous, por·cel·la·ne·ous** (pōrselā′nēus, pōr-) *adjs.* [It. *porcellana* (*porcella* dim. of *porca* sow, f. resemblance of the shell to hog's back)]

porch (pōrch, pōrch) *n.* 1. Covered approach to entrance of building. 2. Veranda. 3. **the P** ~, public ambulatory in marketplace of ancient Athens to which Zeno and his disciples resorted; Stoic school or philosophy.

por·cine (pōr′sīn, pōr′-) *adj.* Of or like swine.

por·cu·pine (pōr′kyupīn) *n.* (pl. **-pines**, collect. **-pine**). Rodent, esp. *Erethizon dorsatum*, with body and tail covered with long erectile spines.

pore[1] (pōr, pōr) *n.* Minute opening in skin of animal body or membrane of plant, for transpiration, absorption, etc.

*Many kinds of **poppy** are grown as garden flowers all over the world. One of the best-known is the brilliantly colored oriental poppy shown here.*

*This charming group was made in biscuit or unglazed **porcelain** and is typical of the figures made in the late 18th century at the Sèvres factory.*

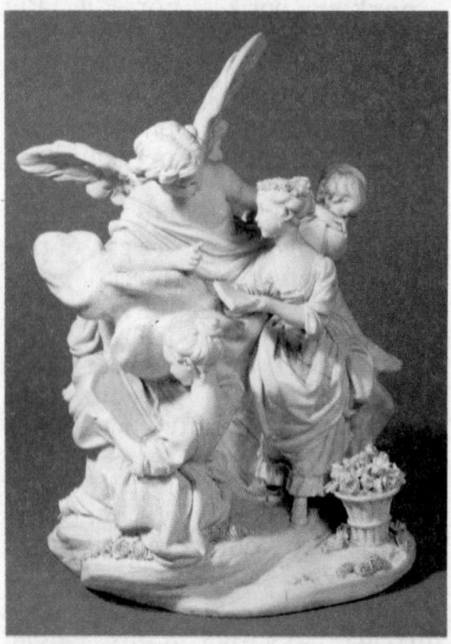

*Various species of **porcupine** are native to the Americas, Africa and Asia. All are herbivorous but only the North American porcupine (far right) consistently climbs trees to seek food.*

African Crested Porcupine

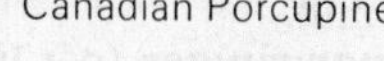

Canadian Porcupine

*The **porringer** has inspired many designers and craftsmen since the form originated. This delicate porcelain one was made at a Derby factory sometime about 1785.*

pore[2] (pōr, pōr) *v.* (**pored, por·ing**). **~ over**, be absorbed in studying (book etc.); (fig.) meditate, think intently upon (subject).

por·gy (pōr′gē) *n.* (pl. **-gies, -gy**). Sea fish of family Sparidae related to the bass, of wide distribution.

pork (pōrk, pōrk) *n.* Flesh of swine as food; **~ barrel**, (fig.) public treasury viewed as source of grants for local purposes; **pork′-pie**, cylindrical pie of chopped pork; (attrib., of hat) with flat crown and no brim, or brim turned up all around. **pork′like** *adj.*

pork·er (pōr′ker, pōr′-) *n.* Pig raised for food; young fattened hog.

porn (pōrn), **por·no** (pōr′nō) *ns.* (colloq.) Pornography.

por·nog·ra·phy (pōrnŏg′rafē) *n.* Explicit description or exhibition of sexual activity in literature, films, etc., intended to stimulate erotic feelings; literature etc. of this kind. **por·nog′ra·pher** *n.* **por·no·graph·ic** (pōrnogrăf′ĭk) *adj.*

po·rous (pōr′us, pōr′-) *adj.* Full of pores; not watertight. **po′rous·ly** *adv.* **po′rous·ness, po·ros·i·ty** (pōrŏs′ĭtē, paw-, po-) *ns.*

por·phy·rite (pōr′ferīt) *n.* Rock resembling porphyry but with slightly different composition of crystals.

Por·phy·ry (pōr′ferē). Porphyrius (233–*c*305 A.D.), scholar and philosopher; orig. called Malchus; by birth prob. a Syrian; became a disciple of Plotinus at Rome; author of numerous works in Greek.

por·phy·ry (pōr′ferē) *n.* (pl. **-ries**). Volcanic purplish-red rock composed of large crystals set in a fine-grained ground mass, anciently quarried in Egypt as material for statues etc. **por·phy·rit·ic** (pōrferĭt′ĭk) *adj.*

por·poise (pōr′pos) *n.* (pl. **-poises**, collect. **-poise**). Small whale of genus *Phocaena*, esp. *P. phocaena*, about 6 ft. (1.8 m) long, blackish above and paler beneath, with blunt rounded snout.

por·ridge (pōr′ĭj, păr′-) *n.* Soft food made by stirring oatmeal or other meal or cereal in boiling water or milk.

por·rin·ger (pōr′ĭnjer, păr′-) *n.* Small basin from which soup etc. is eaten.

***Porpoises** and dolphins are often confused, they are in fact different species of the whale family. Right: Camden Harbour in Maine, an attractive fishing **port** in an area noted for its wide variety of marine life.*

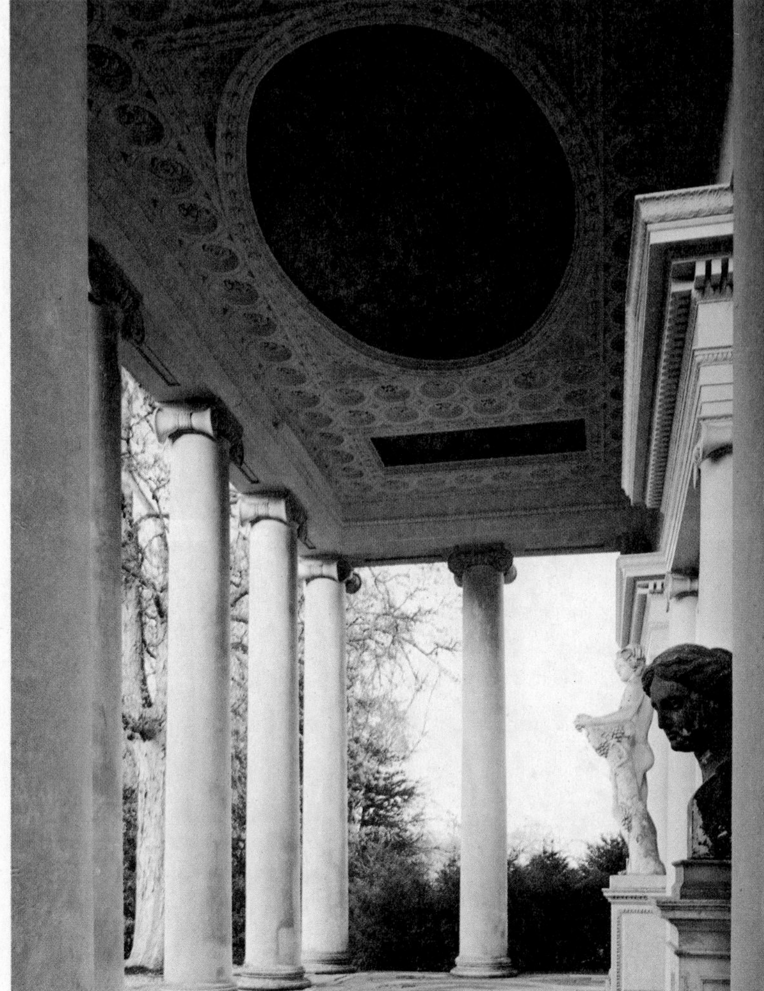

The ***portico*** *is an architectural feature suited to countries where the midday sun is too hot and bright for comfort. Transferred to northern lands, it can appear incongruous, if elegant, like this one at West Wycombe, U.K.*

Por·se·na (pōr′sena), **Lars.** (Rom. hist.) King of Clusium in Etruria, who vainly laid siege to Rome (508 B.C.) in an attempt to restore the exiled Tarquinius Superbus (see TARQUIN) or (acc. to another tradition) conquered and ruled Rome.

port[1] (pōrt, pōrt) *n.* Harbor; town, place, possessing harbor, esp. one where customs officers are stationed; ~ **of call**, one visited by a ship to take on or discharge cargo or passengers; ~ **of embarkation**, one from which passengers leave a country, also ~ **of origin;** ~ **of entry**, one at which customs officials are stationed to supervise entry of passengers and cargo.

port[2] (pōrt, pōrt) *n.* 1. (chiefly Sc.) Gate, gateway, esp. of walled town. 2. Opening in side of ship for entrance, loading, etc.; aperture in cylinder for passage of steam, water, etc.; curved mouthpiece of some bridlebits; (also **port′hole**) aperture in ship's or aircraft's side for admission of light and air; aperture in wall etc. for firing through.

port[3] (pōrt, pōrt) *v.t.* (mil.) Carry (rifle, sword) diagonally across and close to the body, with barrel or blade opposite middle of left shoulder.

port[4] (pōrt, pōrt) *n.* Left side of ship looking forward (formerly called larboard); corresponding side of aircraft. ~ *v.* Turn (helm) to left side of ship; (of ship or aircraft) turn to port side.

port[5] (pōrt, pōrt) *n.* Heavy sweet fortified wine, dark red or (less freq.) white, made in the Douro valley of Portugal; wine of similar type made in other countries. [*Oporto*, seaport where the wine is shipped]

port·a·ble (pōr′tabel, pōr′-) *adj.* Movable, convenient for carrying. **port·a·bil′i·ty** *n.*

por·tage (pōr′tĭj, pōr′-) *n.* Carrying, carriage; cost of this; carrying of boats or goods across land between 2 navigable waters, place at which this is necessary. ~ *v.t.* (**-taged, -tag·ing**). Convey (boat, goods) over a portage.

por·tal[1] (pōr′tal, pōr′-) *n.* Door(way), gate(way), esp. elaborate one.

por·tal[2] (pōr′tal, pōr′-) *adj.* Of the *porta* or transverse fissure of the liver; ~ **vein**, great vein (*vena portae*) formed by union of veins from stomach, intestine, and spleen, conveying blood to the liver.

Port (pōrt, pōrt) **Arthur.** (now Lüshun) Harbor in S. Manchuria, leased to Russia 1898; besieged and taken by Japanese, 1904, in Russo-Japanese war; restored to U.S.S.R. in 1945.

Port-au-Prince (pōrtōprĭns′, pōrt-; *Fr.* pōrtōprăṅs′). Capital and chief port of Haiti, in the SE. part on the Gulf of Gonave.

port·cul·lis (pōrtkŭl′ĭs, pōrt-) *n.* Strong heavy grating blocking gateway of fortress, made to slide up and down in vertical grooves.

porte-co·chere, porte-co·chère (pōrtkōshār′, pōrt-) *ns.* Gateway and passage for vehicles through house into courtyard. [Fr.]

por·tend (pōrtĕnd′, pōr-) *v.t.* Foretell, foreshadow, as an omen; give warning of.

por·tent (pōr′tĕnt, pōr′-) *n.* Omen, significant sign; prodigy, marvelous thing. **por·ten·tous** (pōrtĕn′tus, pōr-) *adj.* **por·ten′tous·ly** *adv.* **por·ten′tous·ness** *n.*

por·ter[1] (pōr′ter, pōr′-) *n.* Gatekeeper, doorkeeper, esp. of large building, public institution, etc.

por·ter[2] (pōr′ter, pōr′-) *n.* Person employed to carry burdens, esp. employee of railroad company who handles luggage; attendant in Pullman coaches etc.; ~**'s knot**, pad resting on shoulders and secured to forehead used by porters in carrying loads. **por·ter·age** (pōr′terĭj, pōr′-) *n.* Work of porters; charge for this.

por·ter[3] (pōr′ter, pōr′-) *n.* Dark brown bitter beer, like stout but weaker, brewed from charred or browned malt (now chiefly in Ireland); **por′terhouse**, house at which porter etc., was retailed; place where steaks, chops, etc., were served, chophouse; **por′terhouse steak**, choice cut of beef between sirloin and tenderloin, orig. as served at a porterhouse. [short for *porter's ale* etc., app. because orig. brewed for porters and other laborers]

port·fo·li·o (pōrtfō′lēō, pōrt-) *n.* (pl. **-li·os**). Case, usu. like large book cover, for keeping loose sheets of paper, drawings, etc.; (fig.) office of high government official; **minister without** ~., one not in charge of any department of government.

por·ti·co (pōr′tĭkō, pōr′-) *n.* (pl. **-coes, -cos**). Colonnade, roof supported by columns at regular intervals, usu. attached as porch to

*The **Portuguese man-of-war** is not one animal but a community of three highly specialized polyps, concerned respectively with feeding, reproduction and killing prey. The stinging tentacles may be up to 40 ft. long.*

a building.

por·tiere, por·tière (pōrtyār̄′, pōr̄-) *ns.* Curtain hung over doorway.

por·tion (pōr′sh*o*n, pōr̄′-) *n.* Part, share; dowry; one's destiny, one's lot; amount of a dish served to a person in a restaurant etc.; some (*of*) anything. ~ *v.t.* Divide (thing) into shares, distribute *out*; assign (*to* person) as share; give inheritance or dowry to.

Port·land[1] (pōrt′l*a*nd, pōr̄t′-). Seaport city in SW. Maine.

Port·land[2] (pōrt′l*a*nd, pōr̄t′-). City in NW. Oregon, on the Willamette River near its confluence with the Columbia River.

Port·land[3] (pōrt′l*a*nd, pōr̄t′-) **cement.** Kind of cement hardening in water and resembling stone when set.

Port (pōrt, pōr̄t) **Louis.** Capital and principal port of Mauritius, in the Indian Ocean.

port·ly (pōrt′lē, pōr̄t′-) *adj.* (**-li·er, -li·est**). Bulky, corpulent; of stately appearance. **port′li·ness** *n.*

port·man·teau (pōrtmăn′tō, pōr̄t-, -măntō′) *n.* (pl. **-teaus, -teaux** pr. -tōz). Oblong case for carrying clothing etc., opening like book with hinges in middle of back; ~ **word,** word like those invented by Lewis Carroll, blending the sounds and combining the meanings of 2 others (e.g. *slithy* = lithe and slimy).

Port Mores·by (pōrt mōrz′bē, pōr̄t mōr̄z′-). Capital and administrative center of Papua New Guinea of SE. coast of New Guinea.

Port-of-Spain (pōrt′*o*v spān′, pōr̄t′-). Capital and chief port of Trinidad and Tobago, in the NW. part of Trinidad in the SE. West Indies.

Por·to·lá (pōr̄tawlah′), **Gaspar de** (1723?–84?). Spanish soldier and explorer; founded San Diego and Monterey after a 1,000 mi. (1,600 km), march from lower to upper California; governor of California, 1767–70.

Por·to-No·vo (pōr′tō nō′vō, pōr̄′-). Capital and port of the People's Republic of BENIN, in the SE. part.

por·trait (pōr′trĭt, -trāt, pōr̄′-) *n.* Likeness of person or animal made by drawing, painting, photography, etc.; verbal picture,

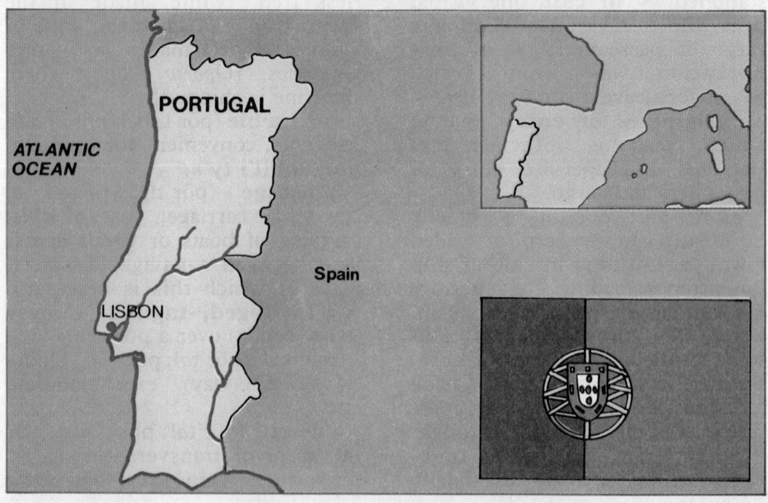

***Portugal** is mainly thought of as a producer of wine, from vineyards like these. Olive oil, cork, and sardines are also exported in quantity, together with fruit, and different kinds of manufactured goods.*

graphic description; (fig.) type, similitude. **por′trait·ist** *n.* Maker of portraits.

por·trai·ture (pōr′trĭch*er*, pōr′-) *n.* Portraying; portrait; graphic description.

por·tray (pōrtrā′, pōr-) *v.t.* Make likeness of; describe graphically. **por·tray′al, por·tray′er** *ns.*

Port Sa·id (pōrt, pōrt sah ēd′). Egyptian seaport at Mediterranean end of Suez Canal.

Por·tu·gal (pōr′ch*u*g*a*l, pōr′-). Republic (kingdom until 1910) occupying W. part of Iberian peninsula; capital, Lisbon.

Por·tu·guese (pōrch*u*gēz′, -gēs′, pōr-) *adj.* Of Portugal or its people or language; ~ **man-of-war**, marine hydrozoan of genus *Physalia*. **Portuguese** *n.* (pl.

The mouse-sized ***honey possum*** *has a tongue especially adapted to obtaining nectar but it also eats insects. The rare Leadbeater's variety of south-east Australia is wholly insectivorous. Some pygmy possums store fat in their tails.*

-guese). Portuguese person; Romance language of Portugal, spoken also in Brazil.

pose[1] (pōz) *n.* Attitude of body or mind, esp. one assumed for effect. ~ *v.* (**posed, pos·ing**). Lay down (assertion, claim, etc.); propound (question); place (artist's model etc.) in certain attitude; assume an attitude, esp. for artistic purposes; set up, give oneself out, *as.*

pose[2] (pōz) *v.t.* (**posed, pos·ing**). Puzzle (person) with question or problem. **pos′er** *n.* (esp.) Puzzling question or problem.

Po·sei·don (pōsī′d*o*n, p*o*-). (Gk. myth.) God of the sea, brother of ZEUS and Pluto; identified by the Romans with Neptune.

po·seur (pōzer̄′) *n.* Affected person.

posh (pŏsh) *adj.* (slang) Smart, stylish; first-rate, high-class.

pos·it (pŏz′ĭt) *v.t.* Assume as fact, postulate; put in position, place.

po·si·tion (p*o*zĭsh′*o*n) *n.* 1. (chiefly logic and philos.) Proposition; laying down of this. 2. Bodily posture, attitude. 3. Mental attitude, way of looking at question. 4. Place occupied by a thing, site, situation; **in (out of)** ~, in (out of) its proper place; (mil.) place where troops are posted esp. for strategical reasons. 5. Situation in regard to other persons or things; condition. 6. Rank, social status; official employment. **position** *v.t.* Place in position; determine position of. **po·si′tion·al** *adj.*

pos·i·tive (pŏz′ĭtĭv) *adj.* 1. Explicitly laid down; definite; unquestionable. 2. Absolute, not relative; (gram., of degree of adjective or adverb) expressing simple quality, without qualification or comparison; (colloq.) downright, out-and-out. 3. (of person) Confident, assured; opinionated; (also) given to constructive action. 4. (philos.) Dealing only with matters of fact, practical. 5. Marked by presence, not absence, of qualities; tending in the direction regarded as that of increase or progress. 6. (math., phys., etc.) Greater than zero; in the direction which for purposes of calculation is to be regarded as upward from zero; (elect.) having a positive charge; ~ **charge**, one of the 2 kinds of electric charge, that of the atomic nucleus as dist. from the negative charge of the electrons (the terms *positive* and *negative* were applied to electricity before the discovery of electrons, and their meaning is now purely conventional); ~ **pole**, region of deficiency of electrons, anode; also (magnetism) applied to the north-seeking pole of a magnet and the corresponding (south) pole of Earth; ~ **sign**, the sign +, plus sign. 7. (photog.) Showing lights and shadows as seen in nature. **pos′i·tive·ly** *adv.* **pos′i·tive·ness** *n.* **positive** *n.* Positive degree, adjective, quantity, photograph, etc.

pos·i·tiv·ism (pŏz′ĭtĭvĭz*e*m) *n.* Philosophical system of Auguste Comte, recognizing only positive facts and observable phenomena and abandoning all inquiry into causes or ultimate origins; religious system founded upon this. **pos′i·tiv·ist** *n.* & *adj.* **pos·i·tiv·is′tic** *adj.*

Mail boxes are the starting point of the **post office's** work of delivering mail. From here, mail enters the U.S. Mail's complex system of sorting and transport so that it arrives promptly at destinations all over the world.

The **poster** has been used as a form of advertising since ancient times but pictorial versions only became possible with new printing methods in the 19th century (above right). Designs have since reflected changes in art.

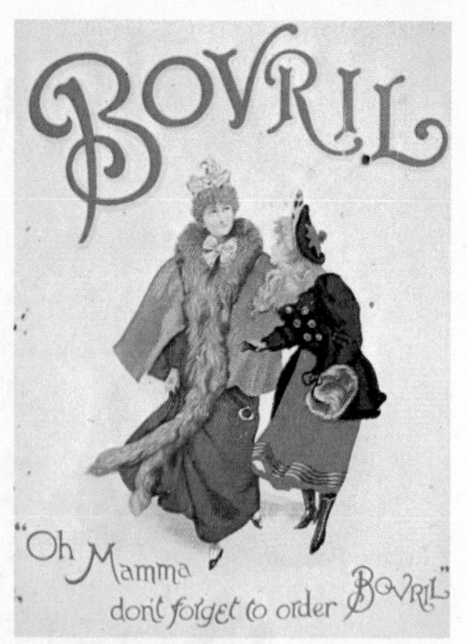

pos·i·tron (pŏz′ĭtrŏn) *n.* (phys.) Positive particle with mass equal to that of the electron and electrically its counterpart. [*posit*(*ive elect*)*ron*]

pos·se (pŏs′ē) *n.* Body of police (also ~ **co·mi·ta·tus** (kŏmĭtah′t*u*s, -tā′-) or of men summoned to aid sheriff in an emergency.

pos·sess (p*o*zĕs′) *v.t.* Hold as property, own; have (faculty, quality, etc.); maintain (*in* patience etc.); (of demon or spirit) occupy, dominate (person etc.); ~ **oneself of**, take, get for one's own; **be possessed of**, own, have. **pos·ses′sor** *n.*

pos·ses·sion (p*o*zĕsh′*o*n) *n.* 1. Possessing; actual holding or occupancy; (law) visible power of exercising such control as attaches to (but may exist apart from) lawful ownership; **in** ~, (of thing) possessed; (of person) possessing; **in ~ of**, having in one's possession; **in the ~ of**, possessed or held by; **~ is nine points (or tenths) of the law**, possession or occupancy gives every advantage short of actual lawful ownership. 2. Thing possessed; subject territory, esp. foreign dominion(s); (pl.) property, wealth.

pos·ses·sive (p*o*zĕs′ĭv) *adj.* Of possession; indicating possession; desirous of keeping as one's own. **pos·ses′sive·ly** *adv.* **pos·ses′sive·ness** *n.* **possessive** *n.* (Word in) possessive case.

pos·si·bil·i·ty (pŏs*i*bĭl′ĭtē) *n.* (pl. **-ties**). State, fact, of being possible; thing that may exist or happen; capability of being used, improved, etc.

pos·si·ble (pŏs′*i*b*e*l) *adj.* That can exist, be done, or happen; that may be or become; tolerable to deal with, reasonable, intelligible. **pos′si·bly** *adv.* In accordance with possibility; perhaps, maybe, for all one knows to the contrary. **possible** *n.* Highest possible score, esp. in rifle practice; possible candidate, member, etc.

pos·sum (pŏs′*u*m) *n.* (colloq.) Opossum; **play** ~, feign illness, death, etc.

post[1] (pōst) *n.* 1. Stout piece of timber usu. cylindrical or square and of considerable length placed vertically as support in building; stake, stout pole, for various purposes; post marking point in a race; winning post. 2. Vertical mass of coal left as support in mine; thick compact stratum of sandstone etc. 3. ~ **and rail**(**s**), open fence made of posts and rails. **post** *v.t.* Stick (paper etc., usu. *up*) to post or in prominent place; advertise (fact, thing, person) by placard; enter the name of in a public list; publish name of (ship) as overdue or missing; placard (wall etc.) with bills.

post[2] (pōst) *n.* 1. (hist.) One of series of men stationed with horses along roads at intervals, the duty of each being to ride forward with letters to next stage; (hist.) courier, letter carrier. 2. (chiefly Brit.) Single dispatch of letters, letters so dispatched; letters taken from post office or mailbox on one occasion; letters delivered at one house on one occasion. 3. (chiefly Brit.) Official conveyance of letters, parcels, etc.; post office or postal letter box; **by return** ~, (hist.) by same courier who brought the dispatch; (now) by next mail in opposite direction. 4. **post′card**, card, usu. with a picture on one side (**picture postcard**), the reverse being left blank for a short message, address, and postage stamp; **post chaise**, (hist.) traveling carriage hired from stage to stage or drawn by horses so hired; **post′-haste′**, with great speed; **post horse**, one of those formerly kept at inns etc. for use of posts or travelers; **post′man** (pl. **-men**), one who delivers or collects letters; **post′mark**, official mark stamped on letters etc., formerly giving place, date, and hour of dispatch or arrival, and serving to cancel stamp; **post′mark** (*v.t.*); **post′master** (fem. **post′mistress**), official in charge of a post office; **post office**, room or building in which postal business is carried on; **post-office box**, numbered box in post office for receiving letters addressed to particular firm or person; **post′paid′**, on which postage has been paid. **post** *adv.* (archaic) With post horses; express, with haste. ~ *v.* 1. (hist.) Travel with relays of horses; travel with haste, hurry. 2. Put (letter etc.) into post office or mailbox for transmission. 3. (bookkeeping) Carry (entry) from auxiliary book to more formal one, esp. from daybook or journal to ledger; (fig.) supply (person) with full information.

post[3] (pōst) *n.* 1. Place where soldier is stationed, (fig.) place of duty; position taken by body of soldiers, force occupying this; fort; (also **trading** ~) place occupied for purposes of trade esp. in undeveloped region. 2. ~ **exchange**, (mil.) camp store. 3. Situation, employment. **post** *v.t.* Direct (soldiers etc.) to go to a specified station etc.

post- *prefix.* After, behind.

post·age (pō′stĭj) *n.* Amount charged for carriage of letters etc. by mail, now usu. prepaid by ~ **stamp**, adhesive label to be affixed (or stamp embossed or impressed) on envelope etc., having specified value, or by franking.

post·al (pōs′t*a*l) *adj.* Of the

Post-Impressionist painters such as Cézanne (self-portrait right), while continuing to follow many of the trails blazed by the Impressionists, re-emphasized the importance of form as well as color.

POST[2] *n.*; ~ **order**: see ORDER def. 13; (**Universal**) **P ~ Union**, union of governments of various countries for regulation of international postage.

post-clas·si·cal (pōstklăs´ĭk*a*l) *adj.* Occurring later than the classical period of (esp. Greek and Latin) language, literature, or art.

post·date (pōstdāt´) *v.t.* (**-dat·ed, -dat·ing**). Affix, assign, to (document, event, etc.) a date later than the actual one.

post·er (pō´st*e*r) *n.* 1. One who posts bills. 2. Placard displayed in public place.

pos·te·ri·or (pŏstēr´ē*e*r) *adj.* 1. Later, coming after in series, order, or time. 2. Hinder; as viewed from behind. ~ *n.* Buttocks. **pos·te·ri·or·i·ty** (pŏstērēōr´ĭtē, -ār´-) *n.* **pos·te´ri·or·ly** *adv.*

pos·ter·i·ty (pŏstĕr´ĭtē) *n.* Descendants; all succeeding generations.

post·gla·cial (pōstglā´sh*a*l) *adj.* (geol.) Occurring or formed after a glacial period. ~ *n.* Postglacial period.

post·grad·u·ate (pōstgrăj´ōōĭt, -āt) *adj.* (of course of study) Carried on after graduation. ~ *n.* Student taking postgraduate course.

post hoc, er·go prop·ter hoc (pōst hŏk´ ēr´gō prŏp t*e*r hŏk; *Lat.* pōst hōk´ ĕr´gō prōp´tĕr hōk). "After this, therefore on account of this," used to ridicule the tendency to confuse sequence with consequence. [L.]

post·hu·mous (pŏs´ch*u*m*u*s) *adj.* Occurring after death; (of child) born after death of its father; (of book etc.) published after author's death.

pos·til·ion, pos·til·lion (pōstĭl´-y*o*n, pŏ-) *ns.* One who rides the near horse of the leaders when four or more are used in a carriage, or the near horse when only one pair is used and there is no driver on box.

Post-Im·pres·sion·ism (pōst ĭmprĕsh´*o*nĭz*e*m) *n.* Comprehensive term for various developments in painting (Neo-Impressionism, Expressionism, Cubism, etc.) which followed IMPRESSIONISM in late 19th and early 20th centuries. **Post-Im·pres´sion·ist** *n.* One of the painters responsible for Post-Impressionism (as Cézanne, Gauguin, Van Gogh, Picasso). **post-im·pres·sion·is·tic** *adj.*

post·lude (pōst´lōōd) *n.* (mus.) Concluding piece or movement played at end of oratorio.

post·mas·ter (pōst´măst*e*r): see POST[2] *n.*

post me·ri·di·em (pōst m*e*rĭd´-ē*e*m). (abbrev. p.m.) Between noon and midnight. **post·me·rid´i·an** *adj.* [L.]

post·mor·tem (pōstmōr´t*e*m) *adj.* After death. ~ *n.* Examination made after death to determine its cause; analysis of event after its occurrence, esp. of game of bridge.

post·na·sal (pōst´nā´zal) **drip.** Trickling of mucus from behind the nose onto the pharynx.

post·na·tal (pōstnā´t*a*l) *adj.* Occurring after childbirth.

post·nup·tial (pōstnŭp´sh*a*l, -ch*a*l) *adj.* Subsequent to marriage.

post·op·er·a·tive (pōstŏp´-*e*ratĭv, -erātĭv) *adj.* Occurring after surgery.

post·pone (pōstpōn´, pōspōn´) *v.* (**-poned, -pon·ing**). Cause to take place at later time than the present or the one arranged. **post·pon´-a·ble** *adj.* **post·pone´ment, post·pon´er** *ns.*

post·pran·di·al (pōstprăn´dē*a*l) *adj.* (chiefly joc.). Done etc. after dinner.

post·script (pōst´skrĭpt, pōs´-skrĭpt) *n.* (abbrev. P.S.) Additional paragraph esp. at end of letter after signature.

pos·tu·lant (pŏs′ch*u*lant) *n.* Candidate, esp. for admission into religious order.

pos·tu·late (pŏs′ch*u*lĭt, -lāt) *n.* Thing claimed or assumed as basis of reasoning, fundamental condition; prerequisite; (geom.) claim to take for granted possibility of simple operation, e.g. of drawing straight line between any two points; simple problem of a self-evident nature (dist. from AXIOM). ~ (pŏs′ch*u*lāt) *v.* (**-lat·ed, -lat·ing**). Demand, require, claim, take for granted; stipulate *for*; (eccles. law) nominate or elect to ecclesiastical dignity, subject to sanction of superior authority. **pos·tu·la′tion, pos′tu·la·tor** *ns.*

pos·ture (pŏs′ch*er*) *n.* Carriage, attitude of body or mind; condition, state (*of* affairs, etc.). ~ *v.* (**-tured, -tur·ing**). Dispose the limbs of (person) in particular way; assume posture.

post·war (pōst′wŏr′) *adj.* Of the period after a war, esp. World War I or II.

po·sy (pō′zē) *n.* (pl. **-sies**). Bunch of flowers; flower; (archaic) short motto, line of verse, etc., inscribed within ring.

pot[1] (pŏt) *n.* 1. Rounded vessel of earthenware, metal, glass etc., for holding liquids or solids; chamber pot; flowerpot, teapot, coffeepot, etc.; such vessel for cooking; drinking vessel of pewter etc.; contents of pot; **go to** ~, (colloq.) be ruined or destroyed. 2. Fish pot, lobster pot; chimney pot. 3. Large sum; (racing slang) large sum staked or betted. 4. **pot′belly** (pl. **-bellies**), protuberant belly; **pot′-boiler**, work of literature etc. done merely to make a living; writer or artist who produces this; **pot cheese**, cheese of coagulated milk from which water is separated by heating in a pot; **pot′herb**, herb grown in kitchen garden; **pot′-hook**, hook over fireplace for hanging pot etc. on, or for lifting hot pot; curved stroke in handwriting, esp. as made in learning to write; **pot′luck**, whatever is to be had for a meal; **pot metal**, glass melted with stained glass in melting pot so that the color pervades the whole; cast iron suitable for manufacturing pots; **pot roast**, meat cooked slowly in covered dish; **pot′ shot**, shot taken at random; an easy shot; casual criticism; **pot still**, kind of still in which heat is applied directly and not by steam jacket. **pot·ful** (pŏt′fo͞ol) *n.* (pl. **-fuls**). **pot** *v.* (**pot·ted, pot·ting**). Place (butter, fish, meat, etc.) in pot or other vessel to cook or preserve it; plant (plant) in pot; kill (animal) by pot shot; shoot (*at*); seize, secure.

pot[2] (pŏt) *n.* (slang) Marijuana.

*The poisonous fruits of the **potato** present no threat to the gardener or farmer, since the tubers are usually harvested, as here, before the fruits are formed.*

*Making **pots** is one of man's earliest crafts, and one in which form and decoration — as in the jars on this Goanese stall — often seem to have come down unchanged through the millennia.*

*Investigation of a **pot-hole,** while viewed by some people as a new form of adventure, has enabled scientists to discover fossils and other data which give an indication of life in former times in a particular area.*

po·ta·ble (pō′tabel) *adj.* Drinkable. **po·ta·bil′i·ty** *n.* **po′ta·bles** *n.pl.* (usu. joc.) Drinkables.

po·tage (pōtahzh′) *n.* Thick soup.

pot·ash (pŏt′ăsh) *n.* Alkaline substance, crude potassium carbonate; (also **caustic** ~) potassium hydroxide (KOH), white brittle substance, soluble in water and deliquescent in air, with powerful caustic and alkaline properties. [Du. *potasschen*, because orig. gotten by leaching vegetable ashes and evaporating the solution]

po·tas·si·um (potăs′ēum) *n.* (chem.) Light metallic element, one of the alkali metals, which is soft at ordinary temperatures, oxidizes immediately on exposure to air, and instantly decomposes water on contact with it, liberating and igniting hydrogen, which burns with a characteristic violet flame; symbol K (f. *kalium*), at. no. 19, at. wt. 39.102. [Latinized form of POTASH]

po·ta·tion (pōtā′shon) *n.* Drinking; (usu. pl.) tippling; draft. **po·ta·to·ry** (pō′tatōrē, -tōrē) *adj.*

po·ta·to (potā′tō) *n.* (pl. **-toes**). Plant (*Solanum tuberosum*), native of Pacific slopes of S. Amer., introduced into Europe late in 16th c., with roundish or oval starch-containing tubers used for food; tuber of this; ~ **beetle,** ~ **bug,** (also called **Colorado beetle**), small beetle native to Rocky Mountains but also introduced into Europe, *Leptinotarsa decemlineata*, whose larva is very destructive to potato plants; **potato chip**, thin, crisp slice of fried (and usu. salted) potato [Haitian *batata*]

po·tent (pō′tent) *adj.* Powerful, mighty (chiefly poet. or rhet.); having sexual power; (of reasons etc.) cogent; (of drugs etc.) strong. **po′ten·cy** *n.* **po′tent·ly** *adv.*

po·ten·tate (pō′tentāt) *n.* Monarch, ruler.

po·ten·tial (potĕn′shal) *adj.* Capable of coming into being or action, latent; ~ **energy**, (phys.) energy existing in potential form, not as motion. **po·ten′tial·ly** *adv.* **potential** *n.* (Amount of energy or quantity of work denoted by) potential function; possibility, potentiality; resources that can be employed for an undertaking. **po·ten·ti·al·i·ty** (potĕnshēăl′ĭtē) *n.* (pl. **-ties**). Inherent, latent, capacity to exert power; possibility, promise, of development.

po·ten·ti·ate (potĕn′shēāt) *v.t.* (**-at·ed, -at·ing**). Endow with power; make possible.

po·ten·ti·om·e·ter (potĕnshēŏm′ĭter) *n.* Instrument for measuring differences of electrical potential.

poth·er (pŏdh′er) *n.* Choking smoke or cloud of dust; noise, din; verbal commotion or fuss.

pot·hole (pŏt′hōl) *n.* (geol.) Deep hole of more or less cylindrical shape; esp. one formed by wearing away of rock by rotation of a stone, or gravel, in an eddy of running water, or in glacier bed; depression or hollow in road surface caused by traffic etc. **pot′hol·er, pot′hol·ing** *ns.* (Brit.) Explorer, exploring of potholes.

po·tion (pō′shon) *n.* Dose, draft, of liquid medicine or of poison.

Pot·i·phar (pŏt′ifer). Egyptian officer whose wife tried to seduce

*Loading crayfish **pots** at Port Fairy, south-eastern Australia. Closely related to the lobster, they are fished in a similar way with baited pots as a lure, and are a lucrative catch.*

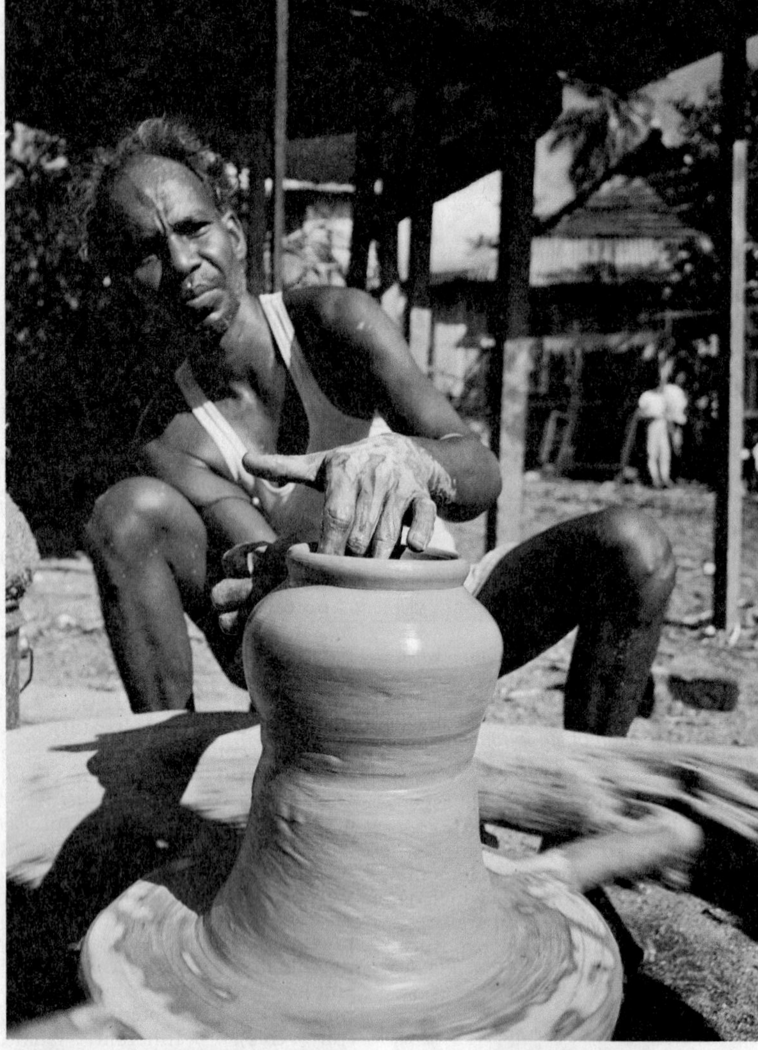

The earliest craftsmen formed urns from ropes of clay. These ***potters*** *in Singapore (left and below) are using the potter's wheel, invented in Mesopotamia about 3,500 B.C. It makes more symmetrical earthenware.*

Joseph and then falsely accused him of an attempt on her virtue (Gen. 39).

Po·to·mac (potō′mak). River flowing 287 mi. (462 km), from the Allegheny Mountains in West Virginia, along the Virginia and Maryland boundary, to Chesapeake Bay; navigable to Washington, D.C.

pot·pour·ri (pōpo͞orē′, pō′po͞orē) *n.* (pl. **-ris**). Mixture of dried petals and spices kept in jar for its perfume; musical or literary medley. [Fr., lit. rotten pot]

Pots·dam (pŏts′dăm; *Ger.* pawts′dahm). City in central East Germany, on the Havel River SW. of West Berlin; site of World War II meeting of Brit., Amer., and Soviet leaders to arrange post-war partition and government of Germany.

pot·sherd (pŏt′shẽrd) *n.* (archaeol.) Broken piece of earthenware.

pot·tage (pŏt′ĭj) *n.* (archaic) Soup, stew (esp. with ref. to Gen. 25).

pot·ter (pŏt′*er*) *n.* Maker of earthenware vessels; **~'s field,** burial place for paupers and unidentified bodies; (after Matt. 27); **~'s wheel,** wheel on which, as it spins rapidly around, the potter molds the clay. **pot·ter·y** (pŏt′*er*ē) *n.* (pl. **-ter·ies**). Earthenware (sometimes distinguished from PORCELAIN); potter's work or workshop.

Pot·ter (pŏt′*er*), **Helen Beatrix** (1866–1943). English author and illustrator of books for children.

pot·to (pŏt′ō) *n.* (pl. **-tos**). Reddish gray loris (*Perodicticus potto*) a slow-moving arboreal mammal of Africa.

pot·ty[1] (pŏt′ē) *adj.* (**-ti·er, -ti·est**). (chiefly Brit. slang) 1. Insignificant, trivial. 2. Foolish, crazy.

pot·ty[2] (pŏt′ē) *n.* (pl. **-ties**). Child's chamber pot.

pouch (powch) *n.* Small bag or detachable outside pocket for carrying e.g. tobacco; mailbag; baglike receptacle in which marsupials carry their undeveloped young; cheek pouch or other baglike natural receptacle; (bot.) baglike cavity in plant, esp. purselike seed vessel. ~ *v.* Put into pouch; take possession of, pocket.

poult (pōlt) *n.* Young of domestic fowl, turkey, pheasant, etc.

poul·tice (pōl′tĭs) *n.* Paste of bread, linseed, etc., usu. made with boiling water and spread on muslin

Bosman's ***potto*** *lives in the lower branches of high trees, sometimes coming down to the ground. It has a mixed animal and vegetable diet: when asleep, it rolls up so that the spikes growing from its spine project.*

etc., applied to sore or inflamed part. ~ *v.t.* (**-ticed, -tic·ing**). Apply poultice to.

poul·try (pōl′trē) *n.* Domestic fowls, ducks, geese, turkeys, etc., reared for food.

pounce[1] (powns) *n.* Claw, talon, of bird of prey; pouncing, sudden swoop. ~ *v.* (**pounced, pounc·ing**). Swoop down upon and seize; make sudden attack *on*, seize eagerly *on*.

pounce[2] (powns) *n.* Fine powder, formerly used to prevent ink from spreading on unsized paper etc.; powdered charcoal etc. dusted over perforated pattern to transfer design to object beneath. ~ *v.t.* (**pounced, pounc·ing**). Smooth (paper etc.) with pumice or pounce; transfer (design) by use of pounce, dust (pattern with pounce).

pound[1] (pownd) *n.* (pl. **pounds**, collect. **pound**). 1. (abbrev. lb.) Measure of weight, 16 oz. avoirdupois, 12 oz. troy. 2. (also ~ **sterling**; written £ before figure) Principal monetary unit of the United Kingdom = 100 pence. 3. Principal monetary unit of various Commonwealth countries and of Egypt (£E), Israel, Lebanon, Sudan (£S), and Syria. 4. ~ **cake**, rich cake containing 1 lb. (or equal weight) of each of chief ingredients; ~ **note**, bank or treasury note for £1; ~ **of flesh**, (fig.) any legal but unconscionable demand (from Shakespeare's *Merchant of Venice*, Shylock's demand for retribution).

pound[2] (pownd) *n.* Enclosure for animals; (fig.) place of confinement.

pound[3] (pownd) *v.* Crush, bruise, as with pestle; thump, pummel, with fists etc.; knock, beat (*to pieces, into a jelly*, etc.); deliver heavy blows, fire heavy shot (*at* etc.); walk, run, ride, make one's way, heavily; ~ **one's ear**, (slang) sleep; ~ **out**, produce (typewritten text, music) with a heavy touch; ~ **the pavement**, (slang) walk the streets, esp. when looking for work. **pound′er** *n.*

Pound (pownd), **Ezra Loomis** (1885–1972). Amer. poet, editor, and critic, esp. of early works of T. S. Eliot, James Joyce, William Carlos Williams, etc.; a founder of IMAGISM; best known for his series of volumes of *Cantos* (1925–40).

pound·al (pown′d*a*l) *n.* (phys.) Unit of force which, when acting on a mass of 1 lb., will impart to it an acceleration of 1 ft. per sec. per sec., corresponding to the DYNE except that pound and foot replace gram and centimeter.

pour (pōr, pōr) *v.* Cause (liquid, granular substance, light, etc.) to flow, discharge copiously; discharge (missiles etc.) copiously or in rapid succession; send *forth, out* (words, music, etc.); flow (*forth, out, down*) in stream (also fig. of crowd etc.); (of rain) descend heavily; (fig.) come (*in, out*) abundantly. ~ *n.* Heavy fall of rain, downpour; (founding) amount of molten metal etc. poured at a time. **pour′er** *n.* **pour′ing** *adj.*

pout[1] (powt) *v.* Protrude (lips), protrude lips, (of lips) protrude, esp. as sign of displeasure. ~ *n.* Protrusion of the lips. **pout′ing·ly** *adv.* **pout′y** *adj.* (**pout·i·er, pout·i·est**).

pout[2] (powt) *n.* (pl. **pouts** collect. **pout**). Any of several fishes, including the eelpout (family Zoarcidae).

pout·er (pow′t*e*r) *n.* Person, animal, that pouts; (esp.) domestic variety of pigeon with great power of inflating crop.

pov·er·ty (pŏv′*e*rtē) *n.* Indigence, want; deficiency (*in, of*); inferiority, poorness; ~**-stricken,** poor.

POW, P.O.W. *abbrevs.* Prisoner of war.

pow·der (pow′d*e*r) *n.* Mass of dry particles or granules, dust; medicine in the form of powder; cosmetic powder applied to face, skin, or hair; gunpowder; (of) pale blue color; ~ **flask**, case for carrying gunpowder; ~ **horn**, powder flask orig. and esp. of horn; ~

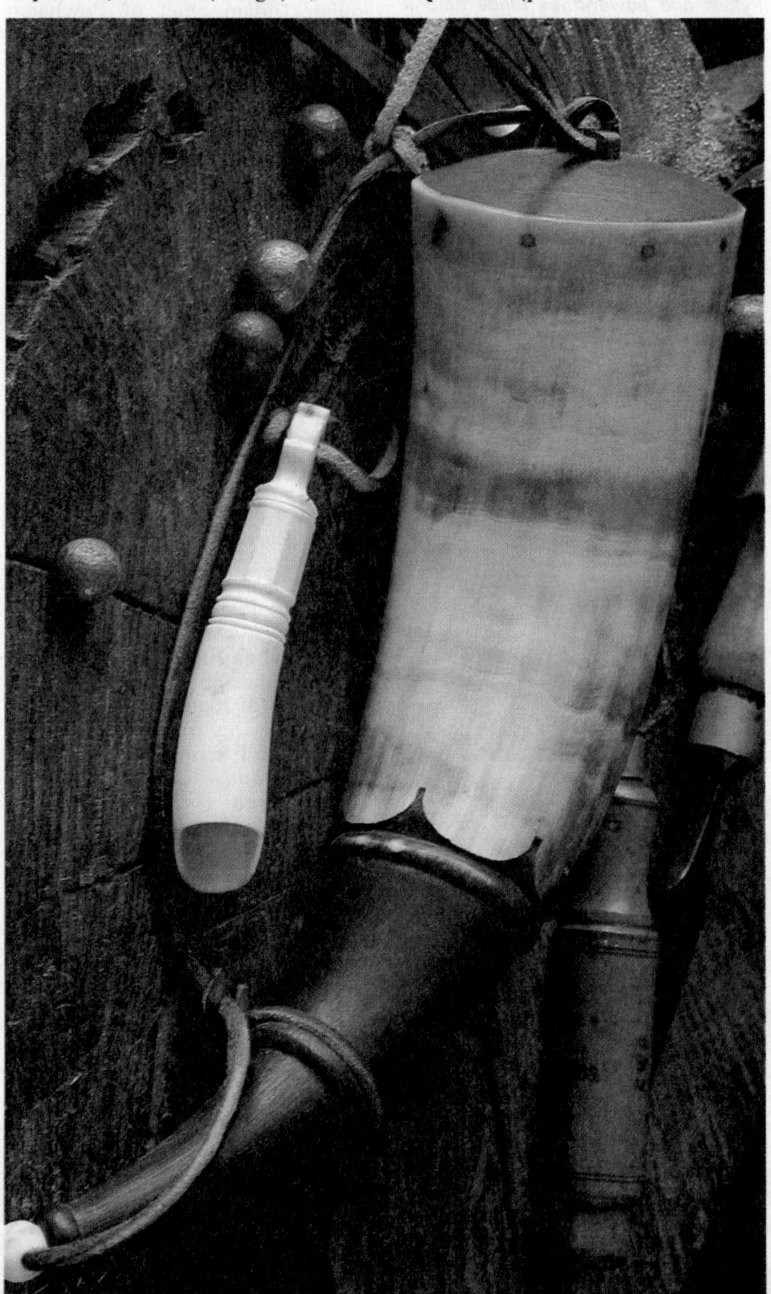

Powder horns *were used to keep gunpowder clean and dry when muzzle-loading pistols and rifles were still in use. The shape of the horn meant that powder could be transferred straight from the horn into the muzzle of the gun.*

magazine, place where gunpowder is stored; ~ **metallurgy**, molding of finely ground (esp. metal) powders into intricate shapes to which solidity is restored afterward by special treatment; ~ **puff**, soft pad for applying powder to skin; ~ **room**, (euphem.) women's lavatory, esp. in restaurant; ~ **snow**, loose dry snow on a ski run, etc.; **take a** ~, (slang) run away, leave without due notice. **powder** *v.t.* Sprinkle powder upon, cover (with powder etc.); apply powder to (hair, face, etc.); decorate (surface) with spots or small figures; reduce to powder; ~ **one's nose**, (slang, of woman) retire to lavatory. **pow'der·y** *adj.* **pow'der·er** *n.*

pow·er (pow'*er*) *n.* 1. Ability to do or act; vigor, energy; particular faculty of body or mind. 2. Active property, as *heating* ~. 3. Government, influence, authority (*over*); personal ascendancy (*over*); political ascendancy. 4. Authorization, delegated authority; ~ **of attorney**: see ATTORNEY. 5. Influential person, body, or thing; nation having international influence; **the ~s that be**, (w. ref. to Rom. 13) constituted authorities. 6. Deity; (pl.) order of angels (see ANGEL). 7. Mechanical energy as opp. to hand labor (freq. attrib., as ~ *lathe*, ~ *loom*); capacity for exerting mechanical force, esp. horsepower; electrical power distributed to consumer; ~ **factor**, ratio between actual power delivered and apparent power suggested by voltage and current; **pow'erhouse**, power station; (fig.) source of drive or influence. 8. (math., of a number or algebraic quantity) Product of a specified number of factors, each of which is the number or quantity itself, the specified number of factors being the *index*. 9. Magnifying power of lens. 10. **power dive**, (of aircraft), dive made without shutting off the motor power; **power politics**, diplomacy backed by (threat of) force; **power station**, station in which electric power is generated for distribution. **power** *v.t.* Supply with mechanical power. **pow'ered** *adj.*

Pylons and ***power-lines*** *stride across the countryside in Arizona, bringing electricity to isolated areas which before their installation would have been inaccessible. Appropriately the word pylon comes from the Greek 'gateway'.*

pow·er·ful (pow'*er*ful) *adj.* Having great power or influence. **pow'er·ful·ly** *adv.* **pow'er·ful·ness** *n.*

pow·er·less (pow'*er*lĭs) *adj.* Without power; wholly unable (*to* help etc.). **pow'er·less·ly** *adv.* **pow'er·less·ness** *n.*

Pow·ha·tan (powh*a*tăn', -hăt'*e*n) (1550?–1618). Amer. Algonquian Indian chief of Powhatan confederacy and father of Pocahontas.

pow·wow (pow'wow) *n.* 1. N. Amer. Ind. medicine man or sorcerer. 2. Magic ceremonial, conference, of N. Amer. Indians. 3. (colloq.) Conference or meeting. ~ *v.i.* Hold powwow; (colloq.) confer.

pox (pŏks) *n.* Disease characterized by pocks, esp. syphilis.

pp. *abbrev.* Pages; past participle; *pianissimo*.

P.P., p.p. *abbrevs.* Past participle; parcel post; prepaid; postpaid.

PPI *abbrev.* Plan position indicator.

PPM, ppm, p.p.m. *abbrevs.* Parts per million.

Pr *symbol.* Praseodymium.

pr. *abbrev.* Pair; present; price; pronoun.

P.R. *abbrev.* Proportional representation; Puerto Rico; public relations.

prac·ti·ca·ble (prăk'tĭk*a*bel) *adj.* That can be done, feasible; that can be used, (of road etc.) that can be traversed. **prac·ti·ca·bil'i·ty, prac'ti·ca·ble·ness** *ns.* **prac'ti·ca·bly** *adv.*

prac·ti·cal (prăk'tĭk*a*l) *adj.* 1. Of, concerned with, shown in, practice; available, useful, in practice; engaged in practice, practicing; ~ **joke**: see JOKE. 2. Inclined to action rather than speculation. 3. That is such in effect though not nominally, virtual. **prac'ti·cal·ness, prac·ti·cal·i·ty** (prăktĭkăl'ĭtē) *ns.* **prac'ti·cal·ly** *adv.* In a practical manner; virtually, almost.

prac·tice[1] (prăk'tĭs) *n.* 1. Habitual action or carrying on; method of legal procedure; habit, custom; repeated exercise in an art,

Power *comes in many forms, including solar power as seen on this experimental house in Arizona. Solar power has many advantages over conventional fossil-fuel plants, including its cost and minimal disruption to the environment.*

***Power stations** of many types have been developed all over the world since the first steam-driven ones were built in the late 19th century. Fueled by coal, oil, natural gas, or nuclear energy, or driven by the power of tides or falling water, they provide the electrical power required for modern life.*

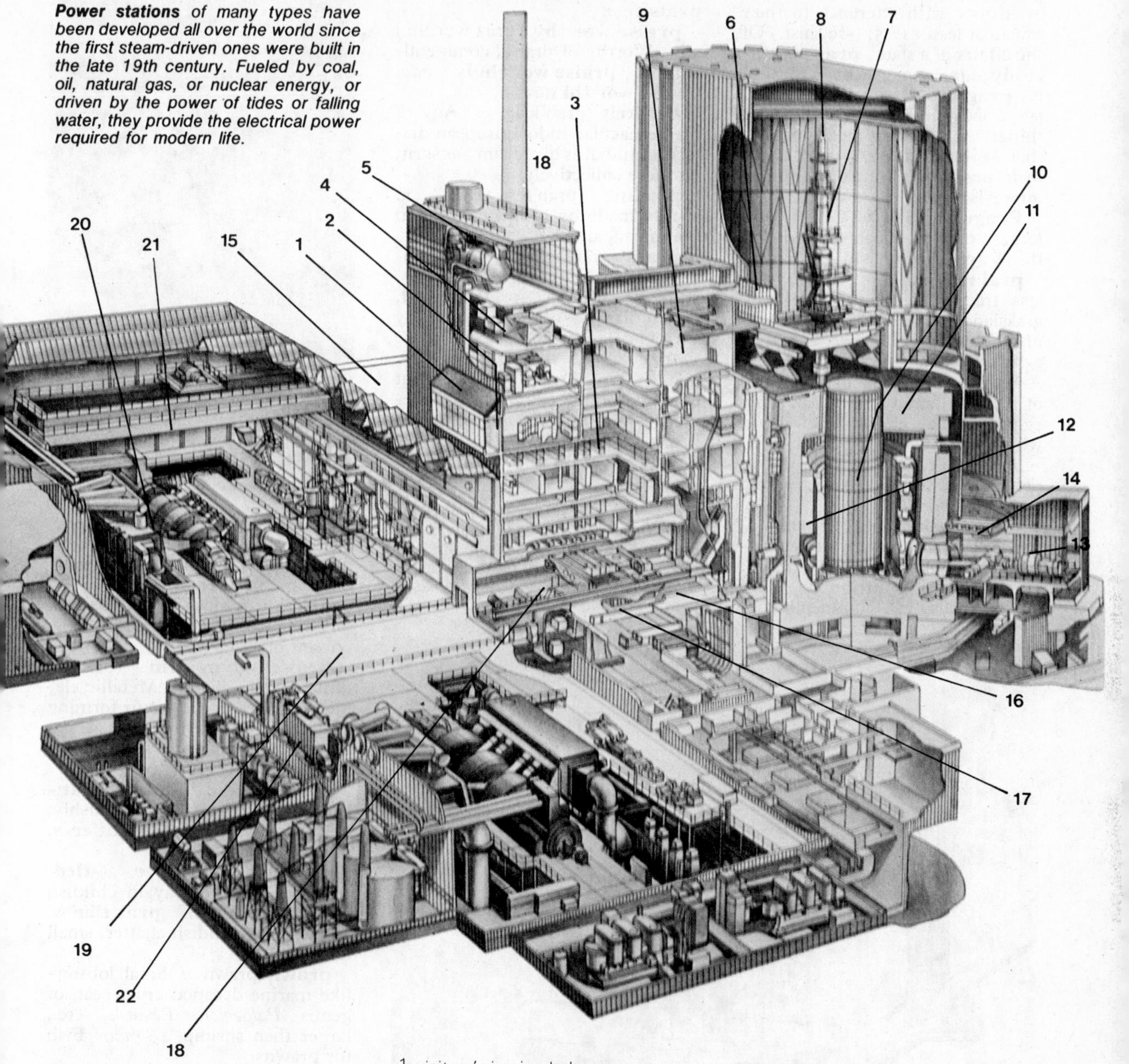

1 visitors' viewing balcony
2 main control room
3 data processing room
4 tank floor and heating plant
5 deaerator
6 visitors' charge face viewing room
7 fuelling machine
8 fuelling machine maintenance crane
9 maintenance area
10 fuelling standpipes
11 pre-stressed concrete reactor vessel
12 boiler
13 gas circulator
14 gas circulator maintenance crane
15 essential supplies room
16 irradiated fuel disposal chute
17 cooling pond
18 flask handling area
19 loading bay
20 turbo generator
21 turbine unit maintenance crane
22 evaporator plant

handicraft, etc.; spell of this. 2. Professional work, business, or connection, of lawyer or doctor. 3. (archaic) Scheming, (usu. underhand) contrivance, artifice (esp. pl.); **sharp** ~: see SHARP. 4. **in** ~, in the realm of action; actually; skilled through having recently had practice; **put in(to)** ~, carry out.

prac·tice[2] (prăk′tĭs) *v.* (**-ticed, -tic·ing**). Perform habitually, carry out in action; exercise, pursue (profession); exercise oneself in or on (art, instrument, or abs.); exercise (*in* action or subject); (archaic) scheme, contrive; ~ **on**, impose upon, take advantage of. **prac′-ticed** *adj.* Experienced, expert. **prac·tise (-tised, -tis·ing)** (Brit.).

prac·ti·tion·er (prăktĭsh′*o*ner) *n.* Professional or practical worker, esp. in medicine; **general** ~: see GENERAL.

Pra·do (prah′dō). Spanish national museum of painting and sculpture, in Madrid, containing part of the royal collections. [Span., = "meadow," f. the adjoining park]

prae·tor, pre·tor (prē′ter) *ns.* (Rom. hist.; orig.) Consul as leader of army; (later) annually elected magistrate performing some duties of consul. **prae·to·ri·al** (prētōr′ēal, -tōr′-) *adj.*

prae·to·ri·an (prētōr′ē*a*n, -tōr′-) *adj.* Of a praetor; **P**~ **Guard**, bodyguard of a Roman general or emperor. **praetorian** *n.* Man of praetorian rank, soldier of praetorian guard.

prag·mat·ic (prăgmăt′ĭk), **prag·mat·i·cal** (prăgmăt′ĭkal) *adjs.* 1. Meddlesome; dogmatic. 2. Practical, in action or thought, opp. theoretical. 3. Of philosophical pragmatism. 4. (**-ic**) Treating facts of history with reference to their practical lessons. 5. (**-ic**, hist.) Of the affairs of a state. **prag·mat'i·cal·ly** *adv.* **prag·mat'i·cal·ness** *n.* **prag·ma·tism** (prăg'matĭzem) *n.* 1. Matter-of-fact treatment of things. 2. Philosophical doctrine that evaluates any assertion solely by its practical bearing upon human interests. **prag'ma·tist** *n.*

Prague (prahg). Capital and largest city of Czechoslovakia, in the W. part on the Moldau River.

prai·rie (prār'ē) *n.* Large treeless tract of level or undulating grassland, esp. in N. Amer.; ~ **chicken, hen,** N. Amer. grouse of genus *Tympanuchus*; ~ **dog,** N. Amer. burrowing rodent (*Cynomys*) of squirrel family; ~ **oyster,** raw egg seasoned and swallowed in whiskey; testis of a calf as food; ~ **schooner,** large covered wagon of kind used by pioneers in crossing N. Amer. plains.

praise (prāz) *v.t.* (**praised, prais·ing**). Express warm approbation of, commend the merits of; glorify, extol the attributes of. ~ *n.* Praising, commendation. **prais'er** *n.*

praise·wor·thy (prāz'wẽrdhē) *adj.* Worthy of praise, commendable. **praise'wor·thi·ly** *adv.* **praise'wor·thi·ness** *n.*

Pra·krit (prah'krĭt) *n.* Any of the vernacular Indo-European dialects of India, as dist. from Sanskrit; all these collectively.

pra·line (prah'lēn, prā'-) *n.* Candy made by browning nuts in boiling sugar.

pram (prăm) *n.* (Brit.) Perambulator.

prance (prăns) *v.* (**pranced, pranc·ing**). (of horse) Rise by springing from hind legs; cause (horse) to do this; (fig.) walk, behave, in elated or arrogant manner. ~ *n.* Prancing (movement). **pranc'er** *n.* **pranc'ing·ly** *adv.*

pran·di·al (prăn'dēal) *adj.* (joc.) Of dinner.

*The site of **Prague** has been inhabited since the Palaeolithic age, though perhaps not continuously until the 9th century A.D. It became of major European importance in the 14th century as a center of trade and culture.*

__Prairie dogs__ are actually rodents belonging to the squirrel family. They live in burrows and are named for the barking sound they make when alarmed.

prank[1] (prăngk) *n.* Mad frolic, practical joke. **prank'ish** *adj.* **prank'ish·ly** *adv.* **prank'ish·ness, prank'ster** *ns.*

prank[2] (prăngk) *v.* Dress, deck (*out*); adorn, spangle (*with*); show oneself off.

pra·se·o·dym·i·um (prāzēōdĭm'ēum) *n.* (chem.) Metallic element of rare-earth group forming leek-green salts; symbol Pr, at. no. 59, at. wt. 140.9077. [Gk. *prasios* leek-green, (DI) DYMIUM]

prate (prāt) *v.* (**prat·ed, prat·ing**). Chatter; discourse foolishly; talk solemn nonsense. **prat'er** *n.* **prat'ing·ly** *adv.*

prat·tle (prăt'el) *v.* (**-tled, -tling**). Talk or say in childish or artless fashion. **prat'tler** *n.* **prattle** *n.* Childish chatter, small talk.

prawn (prawn) *n.* Small lobster-like marine decapod crustacean of genus *Palaemon, Penaeus,* etc., larger than shrimp. ~ *v.i.* Fish for prawns.

Prax·it·e·les (prăksĭt'elēz) (4th c. B.C.). Greek sculptor, creator of "Apollo Slaying a Lizard" and "Hermes with the Infant Dionysus."

pray (prā) *v.* Make devout supplication to (God, object of worship); beseech earnestly (*for, to, that*); ask earnestly for; engage in prayer, make entreaty; ~ (contr. of *I pray you*), used parenthetically for emphasis, e.g. *what,* ~, *is the use of that?*

prayer[1] (prār) *n.* Solemn

__Prayer__ is thought by many theologians to be the most important aspect of a religion. Through the ages it has taken many forms, private as in (2), the expression of mass feeling as shown by the packed mosque of (1), or even — strange though it may seem — regulated by devices like the prayer wheels used in Buddhist lands (3).

3

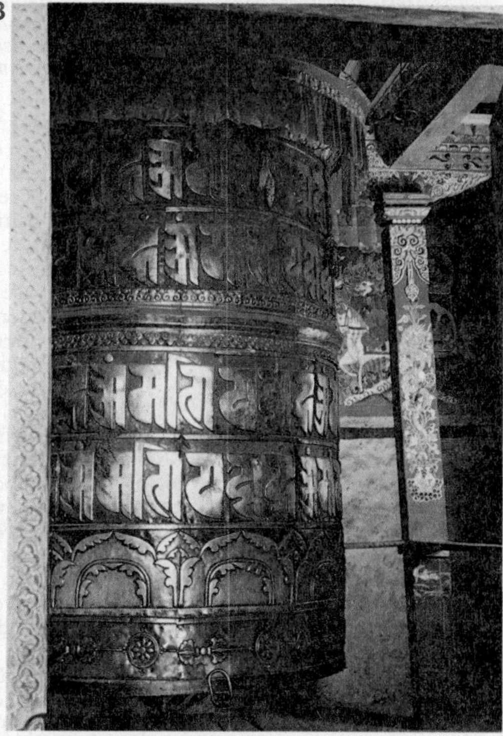

request to God or object of worship; formula used in praying; form of divine service consisting largely of prayers; action, practice, of praying; entreaty to a person; thing prayed for; ~ **book,** book of prayers, esp. **Book of Common P~**: see COMMON; ~ **meeting,** religious meeting at which several persons offer prayer; ~ **wheel,** revolving cylindrical box inscribed with or containing prayers, used esp. by Buddhists of Tibet. **prayer·ful** (prār'ful) *adj.* **prayer'ful·ly** *adv.* **prayer'ful·ness** *n.*

pray·er² (prā'er) *n.* Person who prays.

pre- *prefix.* Before.

preach (prēch) *v.* Deliver sermon or religious address, deliver (sermon); give moral advice in obtrusive way; proclaim, expound (the Gospel, Christ, etc.) in public discourses; advocate, inculcate (quality, conduct, etc.) thus. **preach'ing** *n.* **preach'ing·ly** *adv.* **preach'er** *n.* **preach'ment** *n.* (usu. contempt.).

preach·i·fy (prē'chifī) *v.i.* (**-fied, -fy·ing**). (colloq.) Preach, moralize, hold forth, tediously.

preach·y (prē'chē) *adj.* (**preach·i·er, preach·i·est**). (colloq.) Fond of preaching or holding forth.

pre·ad·am·ite (prēăd'amīt) *adj.* & *n.* (One of supposed race) existing before time of Adam. **pre·a·dam·ic** (prēadăm'ĭk) *adj.*

pre·am·ble (prē'ămbel, prēăm'-) *n.* Preliminary statement in speech or writing; introductory part of statute, deed, etc. ~ *v.i.* (**-bled, -bling**). Make preamble.

pre·ar·range (prēarānj') *v.t.* (**-ranged, -rang·ing**). Arrange beforehand. **pre·ar·range'ment** *n.*

Pre·cam·bri·an (prēkăm'brēan) *adj.* & *n.* (geol.) (Of) the earliest period or system, occurring before the Cambrian.

pre·can·cer·ous (prēkăn'serus) *adj.* Likely to become cancerous.

pre·car·i·ous (prĭkār'ēus) *adj.* Held during the pleasure of another; doubtful, uncertain; dependent on chance; perilous. **pre·car'i·ous·ly** *adv.* **pre·car'i·ous·ness** *n.*

pre·cast (prē'kăst') *adj.* (of concrete) Cast in blocks, slabs, etc. before use in construction.

pre·cau·tion (prĭkaw'shon) *n.* Prudent foresight; measure taken beforehand to ward off evil or ensure good result. **pre·cau·tion·ar·y** (prĭkaw'shonĕrē), **pre·cau·tious** (prĭkaw'shus) *adj.*

pre·cede (prĭsēd') *v.* (**-ced·ed, -ced·ing**). Go before in rank or importance; come before in order; walk or proceed in advance of; come before in time; cause to be preceded by.

Many aspects of the various ***Pre-Columbian*** *cultures are still not fully understood, but the skill of their craftsmen, as shown in this Mexican pyramid, needs no interpretation.*

prec·e·dence (prĕs'ĭdens, prĭsē'dens) *n.* Priority in time or succession; superiority, higher position; right of preceding others in ceremonies and social formalities. **prec·e·den·cy** (prĕs'ĭdensē, prĭsē'densē) *n.* (pl. **-cies**). Precedence.

prec·e·dent¹ (prĕs'ĭdent) *n.* Previous case taken as example for subsequent cases or as justification; (law) decision, procedure, etc., serving as rule or pattern. **prec'e·dent·ed** *adj.* Having a precedent; supported by precedent. **prec·e·den·tial** (prĕsĭdĕn'shal) *adj.*

pre·ced·ent² (prĭsē'dent, prĕs'ĭdent) *adj.* Preceding in time, order, rank, etc.

pre·cept (prē'sĕpt) *n.* Command, maxim; moral instruction; writ, warrant. **pre·cep·tive** (prĭsĕp'tĭv) *adj.*

pre·cep·tor (prĭsĕp'ter, prē'sĕp-) *n.* (fem. **pre·cep·tress** prĭsĕp'trĭs). Teacher, instructor. **pre·cep·to·ri·al** (prēsĕptōr'ēal, -tōr'-), **pre·cep'tor·al** *adjs.* **pre·cep'tor·ship** *n.*

pre·cess (prēsĕs') *v.i.* (of rapidly revolving globe, spinning top, etc.) Sway in such a way that its axis describes a circle.

pre·ces·sion (prēsĕsh'on) *n.* ~ **of the equinoxes,** earlier occurrence of the equinoxes in each successive sidereal year through a slow change in the direction of the Earth's axis, which moves (like the axis of a spinning top) so that the pole of the equator describes an approximate circle around the pole of the ecliptic once in about 25,800 years.

pre-Chris·tian (prēkrĭs'chan) *adj.* Before Christ, before Christianity.

pre·cinct (prē'sĭngkt) *n.* 1. Space enclosed by walls or other boundaries of a place or building, esp. of place of worship; boundary; (pl.) environs. 2. Subdivision of county or city or ward for election and police purposes.

pre·ci·os·i·ty (prĕshēŏs'ĭtē) *n.* (pl. **-ties**). Affectation of refinement or distinction.

pre·cious (prĕsh′*us*) *adj.* 1. Of great price, costly; of great non-material worth; ~ **metals**, gold, silver, (sometimes) platinum; ~ **stone**, stone of great value, used in jewel. 2. Affectedly refined in language, workmanship, etc. 3. Beloved; (abs. as noun) beloved person. ~ *adv.* (colloq.) Extremely, very. **pre′cious·ly** *adv.* **pre′cious·ness** *n.*

prec·i·pice (prĕs′*i*pĭs) *n.* Vertical or steep face of rock, cliff, mountain, etc.

pre·cip·i·tate[1] (prĭsĭp′ĭtāt) *v.t.* (**-tat·ed, -tat·ing**). 1. Throw down headlong, hurl, fling; hurry, urge on; hasten the occurrence of. 2. (chem.) Cause (a solid substance) to be deposited from a solution by the addition of another solution; condense (vapor) into drops and so deposit. **pre·cip′i·ta·tor** *n.* **pre·cip·i·ta′tion** *n.* (esp., meteor.) Fall of rain, sleet, snow, or hail. **precipitate** (prĭsĭp′ĭtĭt, -tāt) *n.* (chem.) Substance precipitated from solution; moisture condensed from vapor by cooling and deposited.

pre·cip·i·tate[2] (prĭsĭp′ĭtĭt -tāt)

Attractiveness as well as rarity have made gold a ***precious*** *metal: even in a photograph (U.S.A. foreign gold reserves, above) its beauty is apparent. It is not, though, the only precious metal — others are platinum and silver.*

adj. Headlong, violently hurried; hasty, rash, inconsiderate. **pre·cip′i·tate·ly** *adv.* **pre·cip′i·tate·ness, pre·cip′i·tan·cy, pre·cip′i·tance** *ns.*

pre·cip·i·tous (prĭsĭp′ĭt*us*) *adj.* Of, like, a precipice; steep. **pre·cip′i·tous·ly** *adv.* **pre·cip′i·tous·ness** *n.*

pré·cis (prāsē′, prā′sē) *n.* (pl. **-cis** pr.- -sēz′, -sēz). Summary, abstract.

pre·cise (prĭsīs′) *adj.* Accurately expressed, definite, exact; punctilious, scrupulous in observance of rules etc. **pre·cise′ly** *adv.* In precise manner; (in emphatic or formal assent) quite so. **pre·cise′ness** *n.*

pre·ci·sion (prĭsĭzh′*o*n) *n.* Accuracy; (attrib., of apparatus) designed for exact or precise work. **pre·ci′sion·ist** *n.*

pre·clas·si·cal (prēklăs′ĭk*a*l) *adj.* Before the classical age (usu. of Greek and Roman literature or civilization).

pre·clude (prĭklo͞od′) *v.t.* (**-clud·ed, -clud·ing**). Exclude, prevent, make impracticable. **pre·clu·sive** (prĭklo͞o′sĭv) *adj.* **pre·clu′sive·ly** *adv.* **pre·clu·sion** (prĭklo͞o′zh*o*n) *n.*

pre·co·cious (prĭkō′sh*us*) *adj.* (of plant) Flowering or fruiting early; (of person) prematurely developed in some faculty; (of actions etc.) indicating such development. **pre·co′cious·ly** *adv.* **pre·co′cious·ness, pre·coc·i·ty** (prĭkŏs′ĭtē) *ns.*

pre·cog·ni·tion (prēkŏgnĭsh′*o*n) *n.* 1. Antecedent knowledge. 2. Extrasensory perception of an event before it occurs. **pre·cog·ni·tive** (prēkŏg′nĭtĭv) *adj.*

pre-Co·lum·bi·an (prēk*o*lŭm′bē*a*n) *adj.* Before the discovery of Amer. by Columbus.

pre·con·ceive (prēk*o*nsēv′) *v.t.* (**-ceived, -ceiv·ing**). Conceive beforehand, anticipate in thought. **pre·con·cep·tion** (prēk*o*nsĕp′sh*o*n) *n.* (esp.) Prejudice.

pre·con·di·tion (prēk*o*ndĭsh′*o*n) *n.* Prior condition, one that must be fulfilled beforehand.

pre·con·scious (prēkŏn'sh*u*s) *adj.* Antecedent to consciousness; (psychol.) of the foreconscious.

pre·cur·sor (prĭkẽr'*s*er, prē'-kẽr-) *n.* Forerunner, harbinger; one who precedes in office etc. **pre·cur·so·ry** (prĭkẽr'serē) *adj.* Preliminary, introductory, serving as harbinger (*of*). **pre·cur·sive** (prĭkẽr'sĭv) *adj.*

pre·da·cious, pre·da·ceous (prĭdā'sh*u*s) *adjs.* (of animals) Predatory. **pre·dac·i·ty** (prĭdăs'-ĭtē), **pre·da'cious·ness, pre·da'-ceous·ness** *ns.*

pred·a·tor (prĕd'*a*ter) *n.* Animal that preys upon others.

pred·a·to·ry (prĕd'*a*tōrē, -tôrē) *adj.* Of, addicted to, plunder or robbery; (of animals) preying upon others.

pre·de·cease (prēdĭsēs') *v.t.* (**-ceased, -ceas·ing**). Die before (another).

pred·e·ces·sor (prĕd'ĭsĕs*e*r, prē'dĭ-) *n.* Former holder of any office or position; thing to which another thing has succeeded; fore-father.

pre·des·ti·nate (prēdĕs'tĭnāt) *v.t.* (**-nat·ed, -nat·ing**). (of God) Foreordain (person) to salvation or *to* (any fate), *to* (do); determine beforehand. ~ (prēdĕs'tĭnĭt, -nāt) *adj.*

pre·des·ti·na·tion (prēdĕst*i*nā'-sh*o*n) *n.* God's appointment from eternity of some of mankind to salvation and eternal life; God's foreordaining of all that comes to pass; fate, destiny.

pre·des·tine (prēdĕs'tĭn) *v.t.* (**-tined, -tin·ing**). Determine beforehand; appoint as if by fate; (theol.) predestinate.

pre·de·ter·mine (prēdĭtẽr'mĭn) *v.t.* (**-mined, -min·ing**). Decree beforehand; predestine; (of motive, etc.) impel (person) beforehand. **pre·de·ter·mi·nate** (prēdĭtẽr'-mĭnĭt, -nāt) *adj.* **pre·de·ter·-mi·na'tion** *n.*

pred·i·ca·ble (prĕd'ĭk*a*bel) *adj.* That may be predicated or affirmed. **pred·i·ca·bil'i·ty, pred'i·ca·ble·ness** *ns.* **pred'i·ca·-bly** *adv.* **predicable** *n.* Predicable thing, esp. (pl.) Aristotle's classes of predicates viewed relatively to their subjects (viz. genus, definition, property, accident).

pre·dic·a·ment (prĭdĭk'*a*ment) *n.* 1. (also pr. prĕd'ĭk*a*ment) Thing predicated, esp. (pl.) ten categories of predications formed by Aristotle. 2. Unpleasant, trying, or dangerous situation.

pred·i·cant (prĕd'ĭk*a*nt) *adj.* (of religious order, esp. Dominicans) Engaged in preaching.

pred·i·cate (prĕd'ĭkĭt) *n.* (logic) What is predicated; what is affirmed or denied of the subject by means of the copula (e.g. *a fool* in *he is a fool*); (gram.) what is said of the subject, including the copula (e.g. *is a fool* in preceding example); quality, attribute. ~ (prĕd'ĭkāt) *v.t.* (**-cat·ed, -cat·ing**). Assert, affirm, as true or existent; (logic) assert (thing) about subject. **pred·i·ca'tion** *n.*

pred·i·ca·tive (prĕd'ĭk*a*tĭv, -kātĭv) *adj.* Making a predication; (gram., of adjective or noun, opp. attributive) forming part or the whole of the predicate. **pred'i·ca·-tive·ly** *adv.*

pre·dict (prĭdĭkt') *v.t.* Forecast, prophesy. **pre·dict'a·ble, pre·-dic'tive** *adjs.* **pre·dic·tion** (prĭdĭk'sh*o*n), **pre·dic'tor** *ns.*

pre·di·gest (prēdĭjĕst', -dĭ-) *v.t.* Render (food) easily digestible before introduction into stomach. **pre·di·ges'tion** *n.*

pre·di·lec·tion (prĕd*i*lĕk'sh*o*n, prē-) *n.* Special liking, partiality (*for*).

pre·dis·pose (prēdĭspōz') *v.t.* (**-posed, -pos·ing**). Render liable, subject, or inclined (*to*). **pre·dis·-po·si·tion** (prēdĭsp*o*zĭsh'*o*n) *n.* State of mind or body favorable *to*.

pre·dom·i·nate (prĭdŏm'*i*nāt) *v.i.* (**-nat·ed, -nat·ing**). Have or exert control (*over*), be superior; be the stronger or main element, preponderate. **pre·dom·i·nance** (prĭdŏm'*i*n*a*ns), **pre·dom'i·-nan·cy** *ns.* **pre·dom'i·nant** *adj.* **pre·dom'i·nant·ly** *adv.*

pre·dy·nas·tic (prēdīnăs'tĭk) *adj.* Of the period before the 1st dynasty, esp. in Egypt.

pre·em·i·nent, pre-em·i·nent (prēĕm'*i*nent) *adjs.* Excelling others; distinguished beyond others in some quality. **pre·em'i·nence, pre-em'i·nence** *ns.* **pre·em'i·-nent·ly, pre-em'i·nent·ly** *advs.*

pre·empt, pre-empt (prē-ĕmpt') *vbs.t.* Obtain by preemption; occupy (public land) so as to have right of preemption; appropriate beforehand. **pre·emp'tor, pre-emp'tor** *ns.*

pre·emp·tion, pre-emp·tion (prēĕmp'sh*o*n) *ns.* Purchase by one person etc. before opportunity is offered to others; right of actual occupant to purchase public land thus at nominal price, on condition of his improving it. **pre·emp·tive, pre-emp·tive** (prēĕmp'tĭv) *adjs.* (esp., in bridge, of bid) Higher than necessary, so as to prevent opponents from exchanging information by bidding. **pre·emp'-tive·ly, pre-emp'tive·ly** *advs.*

preen (prēn) *v.t.* (of bird) Trim (feathers) with beak and oil secreted by gland; trim *oneself*, smooth and adorn *oneself* (also fig., show satisfaction). **preen'er** *n.*

pref. *abbrev.* Preface; preference; preferred; prefix.

pre·fab (prē'făb) *n.* (colloq.) Prefabricated building.

pre·fab·ri·cate (prēfăb'r*i*kāt) *v.t.* (**-cat·ed, -cat·ing**). Make (building etc.) in sections for assembly on a site. **pre·fab·ri·-ca'tion** *n.*

pref·ace (prĕf'ĭs) *n.* Introduction to book stating subject, scope, etc.; preliminary part of a speech; introduction to central part of the Mass. ~ *v.* Furnish (book etc.) with preface, introduce (*with*); lead up to (event etc.); make preliminary remarks. **pref·a·to·ry** (prĕf'*a*tōrē, -tôrē), **pref·a·to'ri·al** *adjs.* **pref'a·to·ri·ly** *adv.*

pre·fect (prē'fĕkt) *n.* 1. (Rom. hist.) Any of various civil and military officers e.g. civil governor of province, colony, etc. 2. Chief administrative officer of French department; **P ~ of Police**, head of police administration of Paris and the department of the Seine. 3. (in some Brit. schools) Senior pupil

Mere size is not essential for a ***predator.*** *The tree spider (1) can seize prey larger than itself, although this is not usually the case with birds of prey such as (2): among mammals, a pack may join in bringing down the quarry.*

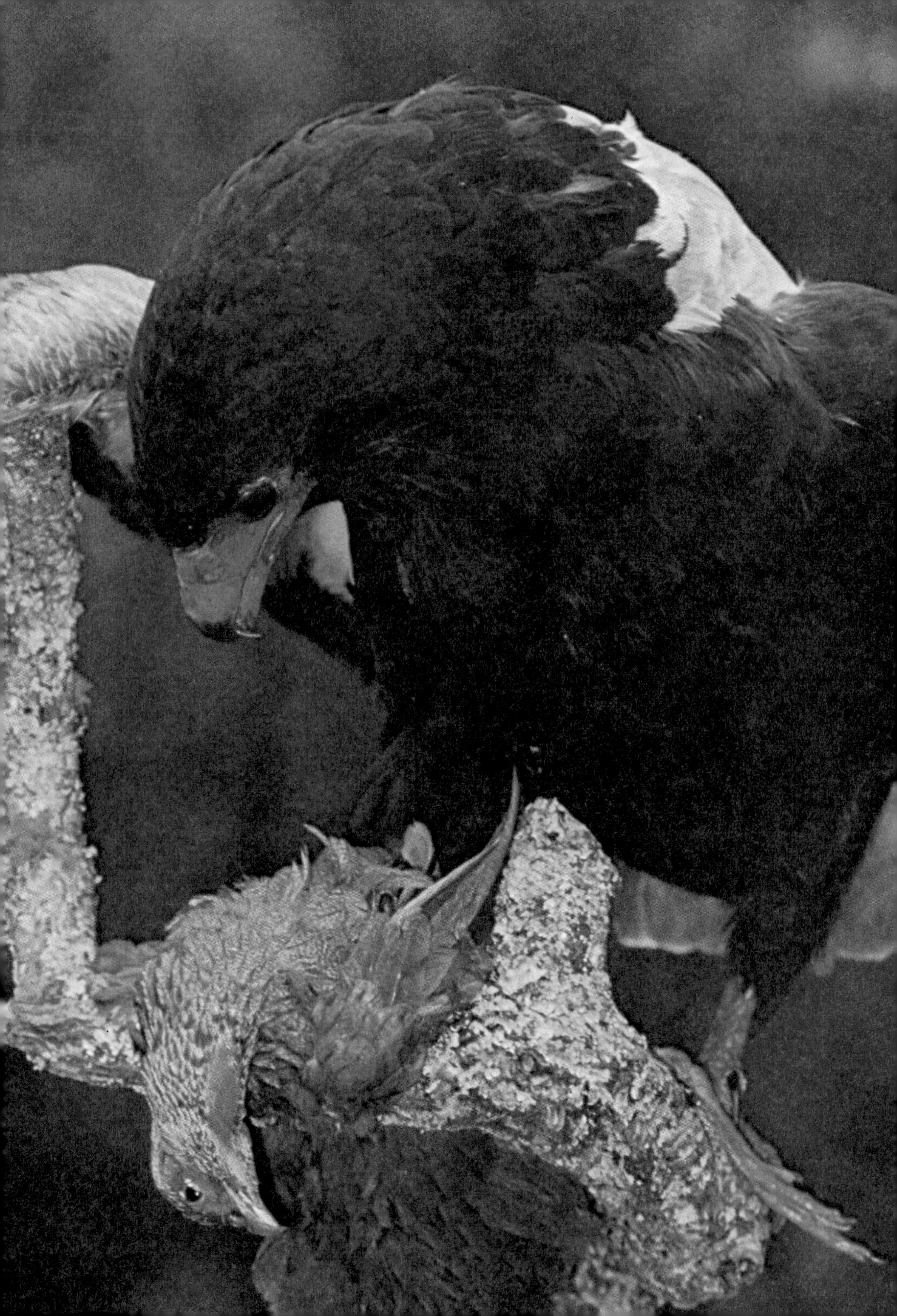

authorized to maintain discipline. **pre·fec·to·ri·al** (prēfĕktōr´ēal, -tōr´-) *adj.*

pre·fec·ture (prē´fĕkcher) *n.* (Period of) office, official residence, district under government, of a prefect. **pre·fec·tur·al** (prĭfĕk´cheral) *adj.*

pre·fer (prĭfẽr´) *v.t.* (**-ferred, -fer·ring**). 1. Promote (person *to* office). 2. Bring forward, submit (statement, information, etc., *to* person in authority etc. *against* offender etc.). 3. Choose, like better, (than someone or something else); **preferred stock**, one on which dividend is paid before any is paid on common stock. **pref·er·a·ble** (prĕf´erabel, prĕf´ra-) *adj.* **pref´er·a·bly** *adv.*

pref·er·ence (prĕf´erens, prĕf´rens) *n.* Liking of one thing better than another; thing one prefers; prior right esp. to payment of debts; favoring of one person or country before others in business relations, esp. favoring of country by admitting its products at lower import duty.

pref·er·en·tial (prĕferĕn´shal) *adj.* Of, giving, receiving, preference; (of duties etc.) favoring particular countries. **pref·er·en´tial·ly** *adv.*

pre·fer·ment (prĭfẽr´ment) *n.* Advancement, promotion; appointment, esp. ecclesiastical, giving social or financial advancement.

pre·fig·ure (prēfĭg´yer) *v.t.* (**-ured, -ur·ing**). Represent beforehand by figure or type; picture to oneself beforehand. **pre·fig·u·ra·tion** (prēfĭgyerā´shon) *n.* **pre·fig·ur·a·tive** (prēfĭg´yeratĭv) *adj.* **pre·fig´ure·ment** *n.*

pre·fix (prē´fĭks) *n.* Verbal element placed at beginning of word to qualify meaning or (in some languages) as inflectional formative; combining form; word (esp. preposition or adverb) used in combination; title placed before name. ~ (prēfĭks´, prē´fĭks) *v.t.* Add (*to* book etc.) as introduction; join as prefix (*to* word).

pre·form (prē´fōrm´) *v.t.* Form beforehand. **pre·for·ma·tion** (prēfōrmā´shon) *n.* Previous formation.

pre·form·a·tive (prēfōr´matĭv) *adj.* Forming beforehand; prefixed as formative element, esp. in Semitic languages. ~ *n.* Preformative letter or syllable.

preg·na·ble (prĕg´nabel) *adj.* Capable of being captured.

preg·nant (prĕg´nant) *adj.* 1. (of woman or female animal) With child(ren) or young in the womb. 2. Teeming with ideas, imaginative, inventive; fruitful in results; (of words or acts) having a hidden meaning, significant, suggestive. **preg´nan·cy** *n.* (pl. **-cies**). **preg´nant·ly** *adv.*

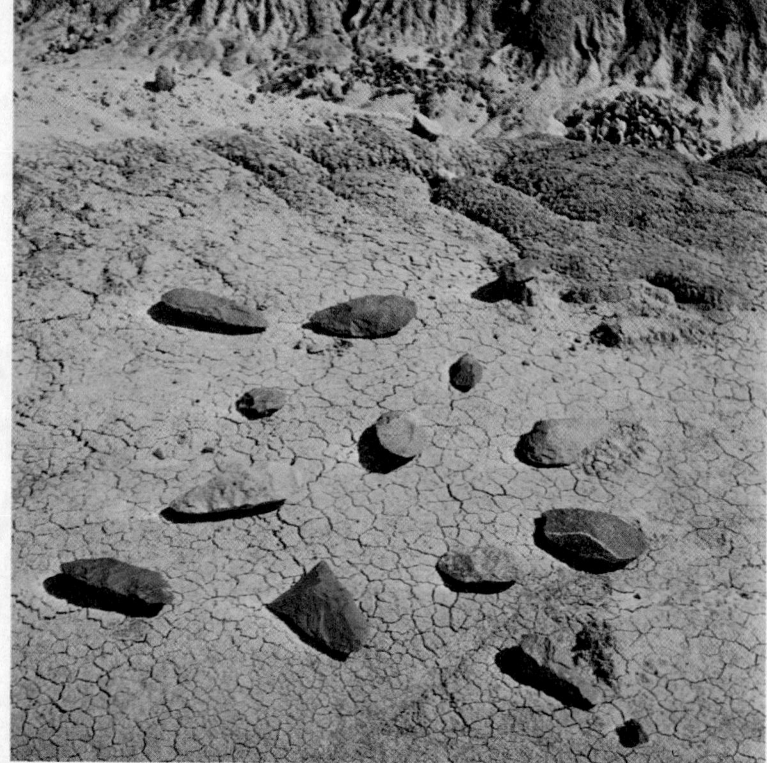

1

All we know of ***prehistoric*** *man comes from the material remains he left. Sometimes, as in the case of these stone tools from Africa (1), their use is clear: but are these Breton monoliths (3) purely ritual or a calendar, these animals from Lascaux (2) magic or art?*

pre·hen·sile (prēhĕn´sĭl, -sīl) *adj.* (zool., of tail or limb) Capable of grasping.

pre·his·tor·ic (prēhĭstōr´ĭk, -stăr´-), **pre·his·tor´i·cal** *adjs.* Of the period antecedent to history. **pre·his·tor´i·cal·ly** *adv.*

pre·his·to·ry (prēhĭs´terē) *n.* Prehistoric matters or times. **pre·his·to·ri·an** (prēhĭstōr´ēan, -stōr´, -stăr´-) *n.*

pre·ig·ni·tion (prēĭgnĭsh´on) *n.* Early ignition in internal combustion engine.

pre·judge (prējŭj´) *v.t.* (**-judged, -judg·ing**). Pass judgment on before trial or proper inquiry; form premature judgment upon. **pre·judg´ment**, esp. Brit. **pre·judge´ment** *ns.*

prej·u·dice (prĕj´udĭs) *n.* Preconceived opinion, bias; injury that results or may result from some action or judgment; **without** ~, without detriment to existing right or claim. **prejudice** *v.t.* (**-diced, -dic·ing**). Impair the validity of (right, claim, etc.); cause (person) to have a prejudice (*against, in favor of*).

prej·u·di·cial (prĕjudĭsh´al) *adj.* Causing prejudice, detrimental (*to*). **prej·u·di´cial·ly** *adv.*

prel·a·cy (prĕl´asē) *n.* (pl. **-cies**). Office, rank, see, of a prelate; prelates collectively; church, government by prelates.

prel·ate (prĕl´ĭt) *n.* High ecclesiastical dignitary, e.g. (arch)bishop, metropolitan, patriarch; (hist.) abbot or prior. **pre·lat·ic** (prĭlăt´ĭk) *adj.*

prel·a·ture (prĕl´acher) *n.* Prelacy.

pre·lim·i·nar·y (prĭlĭm´inĕrē) *adj.* Introductory, preparatory. ~ *n.* (pl. **-nar·ies**). Preliminary arrangement. **pre·lim´i·nar·i·ly** *adv.*

prel·ude (prĕl´ūd, prāl´-, prē´lo͞od, prā´-) *n.* Performance, action, event, condition, serving as introduction (*to* another); (mus.) introductory movement or piece of music, esp. one preceding fugue or forming 1st part of suite; short piece of music of similar type and on 1 theme. ~ *v.* (**-ud·ed, -ud·ing**). Serve as prelude to, introduce, foreshadow; introduce with a prelude; be, give, a prelude *to*; (mus.) play a prelude. **pre·lu·sion** (prĭlo͞o´zhon) *n.* **pre·lu·sive** (prĭlo͞o´sĭv) *adj.*

pre·ma·ture (prēmatoor´, -tūr´, -choor´) *adj.* Occurring, done, before the usual or proper time, too early, hasty; ~ **baby**, baby born before expected date or weighing under $5\frac{1}{2}$ lbs. (2,500 g). **pre·ma·ture´ly** *adv.* **pre·ma·ture´ness, pre·ma·tu´ri·ty** *ns.*

pre·max·il·la (prēmăksĭl´a) *n.* (pl. **-max·il·lae** pr. -măksĭl´ē). Bone forming front of upper jaw in

2

3

vertebrates, bearing the incisors. **pre·max·il·lar·y** (prēmăk′s*i*lĕrē) *adj.*

pre·med·i·ca·tion (prēmĕdĭkā′-sh*o*n) *n.* Administration of sedative or hypnotic drug to patient before giving general anesthetic.

pre·med·i·tate (prĭmĕd′ĭtāt) *v.t.* (**-tat·ed, -tat·ing**). Think out, design, beforehand. **pre·med′i·tat·ed, pre·med′i·ta·tive** *adjs.* **pre·med′i·tat·ed·ly** *adv.* **pre·med′i·ta·tor, pre·med·i·ta′tion** *ns.*

pre·mier (prĭmēr′, prēmyēr′) *adj.* (now chiefly slang and journalese) First in position, importance, order, or time. ~ *n.* Prime minister. **pre·mier′ship** *n.*

pre·miere, pre·mière (prĭmēr′, -myār′) *ns.* First performance of play etc.

prem·ise (prĕm′ĭs) *n.* 1. Previous statement from which another is inferred; **major** and **minor ~s**, two propositions from which the conclusion is derived in a SYLLOGISM. 2. (pl.) Aforesaid, foregoing, esp. (law) aforesaid houses, lands, or tenements. 3. (pl.) House, building, with grounds and appurtenances. ~ *v.t.* (**-ised, -is·ing**). Say, write, by way of introduction.

pre·mi·um (prē′mē*u*m) *n.* 1. Reward, prize (now chiefly in **put a ~ on**, provide or act as incentive to). 2. Amount to be paid in consideration of contract of insurance. 3. Sum additional to interest, wages, etc., a bonus; fee for instruction in profession etc.; charge for changing one currency into another of greater value; **at a ~**, at more than nominal value; (fig.) in high esteem.

*The **Pre-Raphaelite** movement had its roots in a reaction against what its members saw as the falseness of 19th-century art. They drew their inspiration from literature, as in this 'Legend of the Briar Rose'.*

pre·mo·lar (prēmō′l*er*) *adj.* & *n.* (Tooth) developed between canines and molars; (in man) bicuspid.

pre·mo·ni·tion (prēm*o*nĭsh′*o*n, prĕm*o*-) *n.* Forewarning; presentiment. **pre·mon·i·to·ry** (prĭmŏn′-ĭtōrē, -tōrē) *adj.* **pre·mon′i·to·ri·ly** *adv.*

pre·na·tal (prēnā′t*a*l) *adj.* Existing, occurring, before birth or childbirth. **pre·na′tal·ly** *adv.*

pre·nup·tial (prēnŭp′sh*a*l, -ch*a*l) *adj.* Before a marriage.

pre·oc·cu·pa·tion (prēŏky*u*pā′-sh*o*n) *n.* Prepossession, prejudice; occupation of a place beforehand; occupation, business, that takes precedence over all others; mental absorption.

pre·oc·cu·py (prēŏk′y*u*pī) *v.t.* (**-pied, -py·ing**). Engage beforehand, engross (mind etc.); appropriate beforehand. **pre·oc′cu·pied** *adj.* Distracted, with thoughts elsewhere.

pre·or·dain (prēōrdān′) *v.t.* Appoint beforehand; foreordain. **pre·or·di·na′tion** *n.*

prep (prĕp) *adj.* Preparatory (as ~ *school*).

prep. *abbrev.* Preposition.

pre·pack·age (prēpăk′ĭj) *v.t.* (**-aged, -ag·ing**). (also **pre·pack′**) Pack (goods) ready for sale before distributing them.

prep·a·ra·tion (prĕp*e*rā′sh*o*n) *n.* 1. Preparing; (usu. pl.) thing(s) done to make ready (*for*). 2. Substance, e.g. food or medicine, specially prepared.

pre·par·a·to·ry (prĭpăr′*a*tōrē, -tōrē, prĕp′*era*-) *adj.* Serving to prepare, introductory (*to*); ~ **school**, school where pupils are prepared for college. **pre·par′a·to·ri·ly** *adv.*

pre·pare (prĭpār′) *v.* (**-pared, -par·ing**). Make ready (*for*); make (food, meal) ready for eating; make mentally ready or fit (*for* news, *to* hear, etc.); get (lesson, speech, etc.) ready by previous study, get (person) ready by teaching (*for* college, examination, etc.); make preparations (*for, to* do, etc.); make (chemical product etc.) by regular process; **be prepared**, be ready or willing (*to* do).

pre·pay (prēpā′) *v.t.* (**-paid, -pay·ing**). Pay (charge) beforehand; pay (postage), pay postage of (parcel etc.) beforehand, e.g. by affixing stamp. **pre·pay′ment** *n.*

pre·pon·der·ate (prĭpŏn′d*e*rāt) *v.i.* (**-at·ed, -at·ing**). Weigh more, be heavier; be of greater moral or intellectual weight; be the chief element, predominate; ~ **over**,

*Before the Reformation, church design drew the worshipper's eyes and thoughts to the **presbytery,** and the sacramental part of the service.*

exceed in number, quantity, etc. **pre·pon·der·ance** (prĭpŏn′der*ans*), **pre·pon′der·an·cy** *ns.* **pre·pon′der·ant** *adj.* **pre·pon′der·ant·ly** *adv.*

prep·o·si·tion (prĕp*o*zĭsh′*on*) *n.* Indeclinable word serving to indicate relation between the noun or pronoun it governs and another word (as shown by the italicized prepositions in the following examples: found him *at* home, wait *in* the hall, what did you do it *for?*, the bed he slept *in*, won *by* waiting, came *through* the roof, that is what I was thinking *of*). **prep·o·si′tion·al** *adj.* **prep·o·si′tion·al·ly** *adv.*

pre·pos·sess (prēp*o*zĕs′) *v.t.* Imbue, inspire (*with*); (of idea etc.) take possession of (person); prejudice, usu. favorably. **pre·pos·sess′ing** *adj.* (esp.) Making a favorable impression. **pre·pos·sess′ing·ly** *adv.* **pre·pos·ses′sion** *n.*

pre·pos·ter·ous (prĭpŏs′ter*us*, -tr*us*) *adj.* Contrary to nature, reason, or common sense; perverse, foolish; absurd. **pre·pos′ter·ous·ly** *adv.* **pre·pos′ter·ous·ness** *n.*

pre·puce (prē′pūs) *n.* Loose integument covering end of penis. **pre·pu·tial** (prĭpū′sh*al*) *adj.*

Pre-Raph·a·el·ite (prērăf′ēelīt, -rā′fē-) *adj.* & *n.* (Member, follower) of the ~ **Brotherhood,** a group of young English artists and men of letters including Holman Hunt, Millais, D. G. and W. M. Rossetti, formed *c*1848 to resist existing conventions in art and literature by a return to standards they supposed to have existed in European art before the time of Raphael. **Pre-Raph′a·el·it·ism** *n.*

pre·req·ui·site (prĭrĕk′wĭzĭt) *adj.* & *n.* (Thing) required as prior condition.

pre·rog·a·tive (prĭrŏg′*a*tĭv) *n.* 1. **royal** ~, right of the sovereign, theoretically subject to no restriction. 2. Peculiar right or privilege; natural, or divinely given advantage, privilege, faculty. **prerogative** *adj.* Privileged, enjoyed by privilege; (Rom. hist.) having the right to vote first.

Pres. *abbrev.* President.

pres·age (prĕs′ĭj) *n.* Omen, portent; presentiment, foreboding. **pres′age·ful** *adj.* **pres′age·ful·ly** *adv.* **presage** (prĕs′ĭj, prĭsāj′) *v.t.* (**-aged, -ag·ing**). Portend, foreshadow; give warning of (event etc.) by natural means; (of person) predict; have presentiment of.

pres·by·o·pi·a (prĕzbēō′pē*a*, prĕs-) *n.* Form of farsightedness occurring in old age, caused by loss of power of accommodation. **pres·by·op·ic** (prĕzbēŏp′ĭk, prĕs-) *adj.*

pres·by·ter (prĕz′bĭt*er*, prĕs′-) *n.* (in early Christian church) One of several officers managing affairs of local church; (in Episcopal Church) minister of second order, priest; (in Presbyterian Church) elder. **pres·byt·er·al** (prĕzbĭt′*eral*, prĕs-), **pres·by·te·ri·al** (prĕzbĭtēr′ē*al*, prĕs-) *adjs.* **pres·byt·er·ate** (prĕzbĭt′*er*ĭt, -*er*āt, prĕs-) *n.*

Pres·by·te·ri·an (prĕzbĭtēr′ē*an*, prĕs-) *adj.* Of the ~ **Church,** church recognizing no higher office than that of presbyter or elder and holding doctrines that are Protestant with a strong element of Calvinism; the national Church of Scotland. **Presbyterian** *n.* Member of the Presbyterian Church. **Pres·by·te′ri·an·ism** *n.*

pres·by·ter·y (prĕz′bĭtĕrē, prĕs′-) *n.* (pl. **-ter·ies**). 1. Eastern part of chancel beyond choir, sanctuary. 2. Body of presbyters; district represented by this.

pre·sci·ent (prē′shēent, -shent, prĕsh′ēent, prĕsh′*e*nt) *adj.* Having foreknowledge or foresight. **pre′sci·ent·ly** *adv.* **pre′sci·ence** *n.*

pre·scind (prĭsĭnd′) *v.* Cut off (part *from* whole), esp. prematurely or abruptly; ~ **from,** leave out of consideration.

Pres·cott (prĕs′k*o*t), **William Hickling** (1796–1859). Amer. historian, author of *History and Conquest of Mexico* and *The Conquest of Peru.*

pre·scribe (prĭskrīb′) *v.* (**-scribed, -scrib·ing**). 1. Lay down or impose authoritatively; (med.) advise use of (medicine etc.). 2. Assert prescriptive right or claim (*to, for*).

pre·script (prē′skrĭpt) *n.* Ordinance, law, command.

pre·scrip·tion (prĭskrĭp′sh*o*n) *n.* 1. Prescribing; physician's (usu. written) direction for composition and use of medicine. 2. (law, also **positive** ~) Uninterrupted use or possession from time immemorial, or for period fixed by law as giving title or right; such title or right; **negative** ~, limitation of the time within which action or claim can be raised; (fig.) ancient custom viewed as authoritative, claim founded on long use.

pre·scrip·tive (prĭskrĭp′tĭv) *adj.* Prescribing; based on prescription, as ~ **right** (see PRESCRIPTION def. 2); prescribed by custom. **pre·scrip′tive·ly** *adv.*

pres·ence (prĕz′*e*ns) *n.* 1. Being present; place where person is; **the** ~, ceremonial attendance on person of high esp. royal rank. 2. Carriage, bearing. 3. ~ **of mind,** calmness and self-command in emergencies.

pres·ent[1] (prĕz′*e*nt) *adj.* 1. Being in the place in question (chiefly pred.); being dealt with, discussed, etc. 2. (archaic) Ready at hand; ready with assistance. 3. Existing, occurring, being such, now; (gram., of tense) denoting

John Quincy Adams (1), 6th ***president*** *of the U.S.A. and one of the great diplomats who supported, the anti-slavery cause. (2). Dwight D. Eisenhower, 34th president of the U.S.A. and commander of the allied forces during the 1939–45 war. He served 2 full terms in office, retiring in 1961.*

action etc. now going on; true for all time, or future time; ~ **participle**, one used with auxiliary verbs to express continuing or present actions or states of being, e.g. She is *listening*; ~ **perfect**, tense indicating an action or state of being completed at the time of writing or speaking without specifying a past time, e.g. They *have disappeared*. **present** *n.* Present time; present tense; **at** ~, now; **for the** ~, just now, as far as the present is concerned; **by these** ~**s**, by this document (now legal or joc.).

pres·ent[2] (prĕz′ent) *n.* Gift.

pre·sent[3] (prĭzĕnt′) *v.* 1. Introduce (*to*); introduce (person) to another formally; (of theatr. manager) cause (actor) to take part in play, produce (play); ~ **oneself**, appear esp. as candidate for examination etc. 2. Exhibit (*to*); show (quality etc.); (of idea etc.) offer, suggest *itself*; (physiol., of part of unborn child) be foremost at outlet of womb; (law) bring formally under notice, submit (complaint, offense, *to* authority); (mil. etc.) aim (weapon *at*), hold out (weapon) in position for aiming; hold (firearm) in position for taking aim; (also ~ **arms**) hold firearm etc. in deferential position in saluting. 3. Offer, give, as present; offer (compliments, regards, *to*); deliver (bill, etc.) for acceptance etc.; ~ (person) **with** (thing), present it to him. **pre·sent′er** *n.* **present** (prĕz′ent) *n.* Act of aiming weapon, esp. firearm; position of weapon when aimed; position of *present arms* in salute.

pre·sent·a·ble (prĭzĕn′t*a*b*e*l) *adj.* Of decent appearance, fit to be introduced or go into company; suitable for presentation as a gift etc. **pre·sent·a·bil′i·ty, pre·sent′a·ble·ness** *ns.* **pre·sent′a·bly** *adv.*

pres·en·ta·tion (prĕz*e*ntā′sh*o*n, prēz*e*n-) *n.* Presenting, esp. formal; gift, present; exhibition, theatrical representation, etc.; formal introduction, esp. at court. **pres·en·ta′tion·al** *adj.*

pre·sen·tient (prēsĕn′sh*e*nt, -shēent) *adj.* Having a presentiment (*of*).

pre·sen·ti·ment (prĭzĕn′t*i*m*e*nt) *n.* Vague expectation, foreboding.

pres·ent·ly (prĕz′*e*ntlē) *adv.* Soon; at present.

pre·sent·ment (prĭzĕnt′m*e*nt) *n.* 1. Theatrical representation. 2. Description (*of*); act, mode, of presenting to the mind. 3. (law) Statement on oath by jury of fact within their knowledge.

pres·er·va·tion (prĕz*e*rvā′sh*o*n) *n.* Preserving, being preserved; or keeping from injury or destruction; state of being well or ill preserved.

pre·serv·a·tive (prĭzẽr′v*a*tĭv) *adj.* & *n.* (Drug, measure, etc.) tending to preserve; (substance, esp. chemical) for preserving perishable foodstuffs etc.

pre·serve (prĭzẽrv′) *v.t.* (**-served, -serv·ing**). Keep safe (from harm etc.); keep alive; maintain (state of things); retain (quality, condition); prepare (fruit, meat, etc.) by boiling with sugar, pickling, etc., to prevent decomposition or fermentation; keep from decomposition, by chemical treatment etc.; keep (game, river, etc.) undisturbed for private use; **well-preserved**, (of elderly person) showing little sign of age. **preserve** *n.* 1. (also pl.) Preserved fruit; jam. 2. Ground or water set apart for protection of game or fish. **pre·serv′a·ble** *adj.* **pre·serv′er** *n.*

pre·side (prĭzīd′) *v.i.* (**-sid·ed, -sid·ing**). Occupy chair of authority at meeting of society or company; sit at head of table; exercise control, sit or reign supreme; **presiding officer**, person in charge of meeting, organization, etc. **pre·sid′er** *n.*

pres·i·den·cy (prĕz′ĭd*e*nsē) *n.* (pl. **-cies**). Office of president; period of tenure of this.

pres·i·dent (prĕz′ĭd*e*nt) *n.* (often **P**~) Head of temporary or permanent body of persons, presiding over their meetings and proceedings; head of some colleges; person presiding over meetings of academy, literary or scientific society, etc.; person presiding over proceedings of bank or company;

head of advisory council, board, etc.; elected head of government in modern republics. **pres·i·den·tial** (prĕzĭdĕn′sh*a*l) *adj*. **pres·i·den′-tial·ly** *adv*.

pre·sid·i·um (prĭsĭd′ē*u*m) *n*. Presiding body or standing committee (esp. in communist organization).

press[1] (prĕs) *v*. 1. Exert steady force against (thing in contact); move by pressing; exert pressure, bear with weight or force; squeeze (juice etc. *from* etc.); compress, squeeze, (thing) to flatten or shape or smooth it, or to extract juice etc.; iron (clothes etc.). 2. Bear heavily on in attack etc.; weigh down, oppress; produce strong mental or moral impression, esp. weigh heavily *on* (mind, person); **be pressed for**, have barely enough (time etc.); **press the button**, set electrical machinery in motion (freq. fig.). 3. Be urgent, demand immediate action; urge, entreat; urge (course etc. *upon* person). 4. Force (offer, gift, etc. *upon*). 5. (sports) Attempt to perform better than can be done with accuracy; (football and basketball) push hard on opposing players. 6. Crowd, throng; hasten, urge one's way, *on*, *forward*, etc. **press** *n*. 1. Crowding; crowd (*of* people etc.); throng, crush, in battle. 2. Pressure, hurry, of affairs; pressing; (naut.) ~ **of sail, canvas**, as much sail as wind etc. will allow. 3. Instrument for compressing, flattening, or shaping, or for extracting juice, etc. 4. Machine for printing; printing house or publisher; art, practice, of printing; newspapers generally; **in the** ~, being printed; **freedom of the** ~, right to print and publish anything without censorship; ~ **agent**, person employed by theater, actor, etc., to attend to advertising and other publicity; ~ **box**, reporters' enclosure, esp. at sports events; ~ **conference**, interview given to journalists by celebrity, official, etc.; ~ **clipping**: see CLIPPING; ~ **gallery**, gallery for reporters esp. in Congress; **press·-man** (prĕs′m*a*n) (pl. **-men**), operator of printing press.

press[2] (prĕs) *v.t.* Force to serve in army or navy, impress[2]. (hist.); ~ **into service**, take for use in an emergency. **press** *n*. (hist.) Compulsory enlistment in navy or (less usu.) army; ~ **gang**, (hist.) body of men employed to press men.

Popular captains who ran their ships well and won prizes in time of war could attract volunteers. Otherwise the Royal Navy depended on the ***press-gang*** *to drag able-bodied men off the streets as in this painting.*

press·ing[1] (prĕs′ĭng) *adj*. (esp.) Urgent; importunate; persistent. **press′ing·ly** *adv*.

pres·sing[2] (prĕs′ĭng) *n*. 1. Phonograph record; series of records made at one time from one mold. 2. Act of occupation of ironing clothing.

pres·sure (prĕsh′*er*) *n*. 1. Exertion of continuous force, force so exerted upon or against a body by another body, or by a liquid or gas, in contact with it; amount of this, expressed by the force upon a unit area; **blood** ~: see BLOOD; **high, low, (atmospheric)** ~: see ATMOSPHERE; **high-**~, (of engines or turbines) used esp. of those in which steam is used at different pressures in different parts of the machine; ~ **casting**, metal casting obtained by injecting fluid metal under pressure into a rigid mold; ~ **cooker**, strong sealed metal vessel for cooking in steam at high pressure; (fig.) place of employment or situation in which people perform under great pressure; ~ **mine**, mine detonated by pressure. 2. Affliction, oppression; trouble, embarrassment; constraining influence; ~ **group**, body of people exerting pressure upon legislature etc. by concerted agitation. **pres-sure** *v.t.* (**-sured, -sur·ing**). (fig.) Pressurize.

pres·sur·ize (prĕsh′erīz) *v.t.* (**-ized, -iz·ing**). Maintain normal air pressure artificially, esp. in aircraft at high altitudes; (fig.) exert pressure on, force by pressure.

pres·ti·dig·i·ta·tor (prĕstĭdĭj′-ĭtāter) *n.* Conjurer. **pres·ti·dig·i·ta′tion** *n.*

pres·tige (prĕstēzh′, -stēj′) *n.* Influence, reputation, derived from past achievements, associations, etc. **pres·ti·gious** (prĕstĭj′us, -stē′jus) *adj.*

pres·to[1] (prĕs′tō) *adv., n.* (pl. **-tos**) & *adj.* (mus.) (Passage performed) quick(ly). [It.]

pres·to[2] (prĕs′tō) *adv.* (in magician's formula, esp. ~ **change-o!**) Quickly. ~ *adj.* Rapid.

pre·stressed (prēstrĕst′) *adj.* (of concrete) Strengthened by compression with steel rods under tension, to counteract stress.

pre·sume (prĭzo͞om′) *v.* (**-sumed, -sum·ing**). Take the liberty, venture (*to* do); assume, take for granted; be presumptuous, take liberties; ~ **upon**, take advantage of, make unscrupulous use of. **pre·sum′a·ble** *adj.* **pre·sum′a·bly, pre·sum′ing·ly** *advs.* **pre·sum′er** *n.*

pre·sump·tion (prĭzŭmp′shon) *n.* Arrogance, assurance; taking for granted, thing taken for granted; ground for presuming; (law) ~ **of fact**, inference of fact from known facts; ~ **of law**, assumption of truth of thing until contrary is proved; inference established by law as universally applicable to certain circumstances.

pre·sump·tive (prĭzŭmp′tĭv) *adj.* Giving ground for presumption; **heir** ~, one whose right of inheritance is liable to be defeated by birth of nearer heir. **pre·sump′tive·ly** *adv.*

pre·sump·tu·ous (prĭzŭmp′cho͞ous) *adj.* Unduly confident, arrogant, forward. **pre·sump′tu·ous·ly** *adv.* **pre·sump′tu·ous·ness** *n.*

pre·sup·pose (prēsupōz′) *v.t.* (**-posed, -pos·ing**). Assume beforehand; involve, imply. **pre·sup·po·si·tion** (prēsŭpozĭsh′on) *n.* Presupposing; thing assumed beforehand as basis of argument etc.

pre·tend (prĭtĕnd′) *v.* 1. Feign, give oneself out (*to* be or do); make believe in play; profess falsely to have; allege falsely. 2. Venture, aspire, presume (*to* do); lay claim *to* (right, title, etc.); ~ **to**, try to win (person, person's hand) in marriage; profess to have (quality etc.). **pre·tend′ed** *adj.* **pre·tend′ing·ly** *adv.*

*Although **Pretoria** is mainly an administrative and cultural center, focused on Church Square (right), it also has an important iron and steel industry.*

pre·tend·er (prĭtĕn′der) *n.* One who makes baseless pretensions (*to* title etc.); **Old P~**, James Francis Edward Stuart (1688–1766), James II's son, called by Jacobites James III; took part in the unsuccessful Scottish rising of 1715; **Young P~**, Charles Edward Stuart (1720–1788), son of the Old Pretender; led the rebellion of 1745.

pre·tense, Brit. **pre·tence** (prĭtĕns′, prē′tĕns) *ns.* 1. Claim (*to* merit etc.). 2. Ostentation, display; false profession of purpose, pretext; pretending, make-believe.

pre·ten·sion (prĭtĕn′shon) *n.* Assertion of a claim; justifiable claim; pretentiousness.

pre·ten·tious (prĭtĕn′shus) *adj.* Making claim to great merit or importance, esp. when unwarranted; ostentatious. **pre·ten′tious·ly** *adv.* **pre·ten′tious·ness** *n.*

*The **prickly pear** grows throughout southern U.S.A. Introduced to Australia it became a widespread pest until a Mexican insect was found whose larvae killed the plant, controlling its growth.*

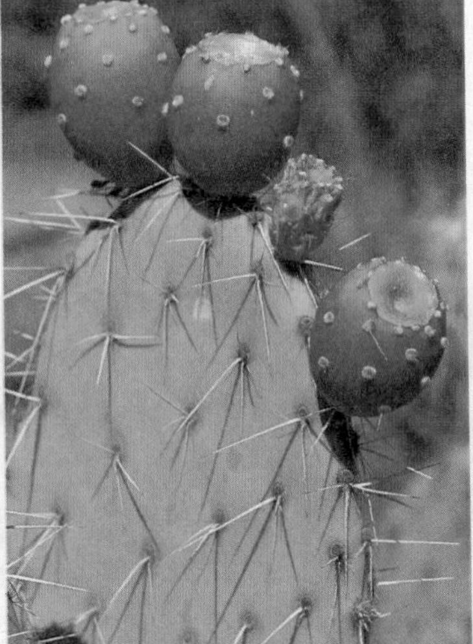

preter- *prefix.* Past, beyond.

pre·ter·hu·man (prēterhū′man) *adj.* Beyond what is human, superhuman.

pret·er·it, pret·er·ite (prĕt′erĭt) *adjs.* (gram.) Expressing past action or state. ~ *n.* Preterit tense or verb.

pret·er·i·tion (prĕterĭsh′on) *n.* Omission, disregard (*of*); (theol.) passing over of the nonelect.

pre·ter·nat·u·ral (prēternăch′-eral, -năch′ral) *adj.* Outside the ordinary course of nature; supernatural. **pre·ter·nat′u·ral·ly** *adv.*

pre·text (prē′tĕkst) *n.* Ostensible reason, excuse.

pre·ton·ic (prētŏn′ĭk) *adj.* Coming immediately before stressed syllable.

pre·tor = PRAETOR.

Pre·to·ri·a (prĭtōr′ēa, -tōr′-). Administrative capital of Republic of South Africa, 35 miles (56 km) NE. of Johannesburg. [Andries Wilhelmus Jacobus *Pretorius* (1799–1853), South African Boer leader, one of founders of Transvaal]

pre·to·ri·an (prĭtōr′ēan, -tōr′-) = PRAETORIAN.

pret·ti·fy (prĭt′ifī) *v.t.* (**-fied, -fy·ing**). Make pretty; represent with finicking prettiness.

pret·ty (prĭt′ē) *adj.* (**-ti·er, -ti·est**). 1. Beautiful in diminutive or trivial way; attractive to eye, ear, or aesthetic sense. 2. Good, fine (also iron.); **a ~ penny**, a good deal of money. 3. (abs. as noun) Pretty one, pretty thing. **pret′ti·ly** *adv.* **pret′ti·ness** *n.* **pret′ty·ish** *adj.* **pretty** *adv.* Fairly, moderately, as ~ *good*, ~ *well.*

pret·zel (prĕt′sel) *n.* Crisp salted biscuit, freq. baked in form of a

knot.

pre·vail (prĭvāl′) *v.i.* Gain the mastery, be victorious (*against*, *over*); be the more usual or prominent, predominate; exist, occur, in general use or experience, be current; ~ **upon**, persuade. **pre·vail′ing, prev·a·lent** (prĕv′*a*-lent) *adjs.* **prev′a·lence** *n.* **prev′a·lent·ly** *adv.*

pre·var·i·cate (prĭvăr′*i*kāt) *v.i.* (**-cat·ed, -cat·ing**). Speak, act, evasively; quibble, equivocate; lie. **pre·var·i·ca′tion, pre·var′i·ca·tor** *ns.*

pre·vent (prĭvĕnt′) *v.t.* 1. Hinder, stop. 2. (archaic) Meet, deal with (wish, question, etc.) before it is expressed; (theol., of God) go before, guide. **pre·vent′a·ble, pre·vent′i·ble** *adjs.* **pre·ven·tion** (prĭvĕn′sh*o*n) *n.*

pre·ven·ta·tive (prĭvĕn′*t*atĭv) *adj.* & *n.* Preventive.

pre·ven·tive (prĭvĕn′tĭv) *adj.* Serving to prevent, esp. (med.) to keep off disease; ~ **detention,** (law) incarceration of criminal to prevent crime; (Brit.) imprisonment of habitual criminal for period of corrective training etc. **pre·ven′tive·ly** *adv.* **pre·ven′tive·ness** *n.* **preventive** *n.* Preventive agent, measure, drug, etc.

pre·view (prē′vū) *n.* Viewing of a picture, film, etc., arranged before it is open to public.

pre·vi·ous (prē′vē*u*s) *adj.* Coming before in time or order; prior *to*; (slang) done or acting hastily; ~ **question,** (parl.) question whether vote shall be taken on main question (put to avoid putting of main question). **pre′vi·ous·ly** *adv.* **pre′vi·ous·ness** *n.* **previous** *adv.*

pre·vise (prēvīz′) *v.t.* (**-vised, -vis·ing**). Foresee, forecast. **pre·vi·sion** (prēvĭzh′*o*n) *n.* **pre·vi′sion·al** *adj.*

pre·war (prē′wŏr′) *adj.* Before the war (esp. of World War I or II).

prey (prā) *n.* Animal hunted or killed by carnivorous animal for food; person, thing, that falls a victim (*to* sickness, fear, etc.); **beast of** ~, animal that kills and devours other animals; **bird of** ~: see BIRD. **prey** *v.i.* ~ **on**, seek, take, as prey, plunder; exert baneful or wasteful influence upon.

Pri·am (prī′*a*m). (Gk. legend) Last king of Troy, father of 50 sons and many daughters; slain by Neoptolemus after the fall of Troy.

pri·a·pism (prī′*a*pĭz*e*m) *n.* Licentiousness; (path.) persistent erection of penis. [f. PRIAPUS]

Pri·a·pus (prīā′p*u*s). (Gk. myth.) God of fertility whose cult spread from Asia Minor to Greece and Italy; he became the god of gardens and herds and is represented as small, grotesque, and misshapen.

Prib·i·lof (prĭb′*i*lawf) **Islands.** Group of islands belonging to the U.S. in the Bering Sea, SW. of Alaska and N. of the Aleutian Islands; breeding grounds for most of world's fur-bearing seals.

price (prīs) *n.* Money for which thing is bought or sold; (betting) odds; (fig.) what must be given, done, sacrificed, etc., to obtain a thing; **above, beyond, without,** ~, so valuable that no price can be stated; **at any** ~, whatever it may cost; (with neg.) on any terms, for any consideration; **at a** ~, at a relatively high cost; **what** ~ **...?**, (slang) taunting allusion to worthlessness or failure of something; ~ **on person's head**, reward offered for his death or capture. **price** *v.t.* (**priced, pric·ing**). Fix, inquire, the price of (thing for sale); estimate the value of. **priced** *adj.* To which a price is assigned.

Lions eating their ***prey*** *in Uganda. Carnivorous animals can only survive by hunting and killing other animals, which is an essential biological instinct.*

price·less (prīs′lĭs) *adj.* Invaluable; (slang) incredibly or extremely amusing, absurd, etc. **price′less·ness** *n.*

prick (prĭk) *n.* Pricking, puncture; mark made by pricking; (archaic) goad for oxen, esp. in **kick against the** ~**s**, (fig.) hurt oneself by useless resistance (Acts 9); ~ **ears**, erect pointed ears of some dogs etc.; conspicuous ears of person. **prick** *v.* Pierce slightly, make minute hole in; cause sharp pain to; feel pricking sensation; make a thrust (*at, into*, etc.); mark off (name etc. in list) with a prick; mark (pattern *off, out*) with dots; (archaic) spur, urge on (horse); advance on horseback; ~ *in, out, off*, plant (seedlings etc.) in small holes pricked in earth; ~ **up**, (of animal) erect (ears) when on the alert; (of animal's ears) rise or stand erect; ~ **up one's ears**, (fig.) become suddenly attentive. **prick′ing** *n.*

prick·er (prĭk′*e*r) *n.* (esp.) Pricking instrument, e.g. awl.

prick·et (prĭk′ĭt) *n.* 1. Male of fallow deer in 2nd year, with straight unbranched horns. 2. Spike to stick candle on.

prick·le (prĭk′*e*l) *n.* Thornlike process developed from epidermis of plant and capable of being peeled off with it; (pop.) small thorn; hard-pointed spine of porcupine etc. ~ *v.* (**-led, -ling**). Affect, be affected, with sensation as of prick.

prick·ly (prĭk′lē) *adj.* (**-li·er, -li·est**). Armed with prickles; tingling; ~ **heat**, inflammatory disease of the skin (miliaria) accompanying profuse sweating, caused by blocking of the sweat glands; ~ **pear**, species of cactus of genus *Opuntia*, with pear-shaped fleshy edible fruit; this fruit. **prick′li·ness** *n.*

pride (prīd) *n.* 1. Unduly high opinion of one's own qualities, merits, etc., considered the first of the 7 deadly sins; arrogant bearing or conduct; ~ **of place**, exalted position, consciousness of this, arrogance. 2. (also **proper** ~) Sense of what befits one's position, preventing one from doing unworthy thing; **false** ~, mistaken feeling of this kind. 3. Feeling of elation and pleasure; object of this feeling, e.g., one's child (in *my ~ and joy*); **take ~ in**, be proud of. 4. Company (of lions). **pride** *v.refl.* (**prid·ed, prid·ing**). **~ oneself on**, be proud of. **pride'ful** *adj.* **pride'ful·ly** *adv.* **pride'less** *adj.* **pride'ful·ness** *n.*

prie-dieu (prē dyōō') *n.* (pl. **-dieus, -dieux** pr. -dyōōz'). Kneeling desk; chair with tall sloping back for use in praying.

priest (prēst) *n.* Clergyman, esp. one with authority to administer sacraments and pronounce absolution; Episcopalian minister of the altar; official minister of non-Christian religion (fem. **priest'ess**); **high ~**: see HIGH; **priest'craft**, ambitious or worldly policy of priests; **~-ridden**, held in subjection by priest(s). **priest'hood** (prēst'hŏŏd) *n.* **priest'like** *adj.*

Priest·ley (prēst'lē), **Joseph** (1733–1804). English chemist and clergyman; discoverer of oxygen.

priest·ly (prēst'lē) *adj.* (**-li·er, -li·est**). Of, like, befitting, a priest; **P~ Code** (Old Testament criticism) one of the constituent elements of the Hexateuch, constituting framework of whole in its existing form.

prig (prĭg) *n.* Person exhibiting excessive precision in speech or manners; conceited or didactic

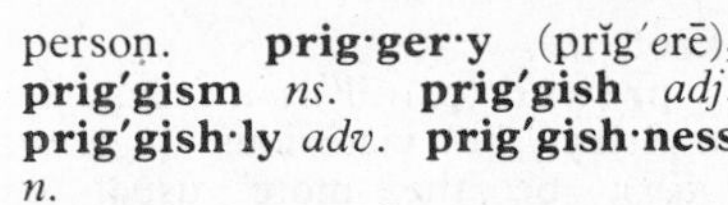

person. **prig·ger·y** (prĭg'ərē), **prig'gism** *ns.* **prig'gish** *adj.* **prig'gish·ly** *adv.* **prig'gish·ness** *n.*

prim (prĭm) *adj.* (**prim·mer, prim·mest**). Consciously or affectedly precise; formal, demure. **~** *v.* (**primmed, prim·ming**). Assume prim air; form (face, lips, etc.) into prim expression. **prim'ly** *adv.* **prim'ness** *n.*

pri·ma·cy (prī'məsē) *n.* (pl. **-cies**). Office of a primate; preeminence.

pri·ma don·na (prē'mə dŏn'ə, prĭm'ə). Principal female singer in opera; (fig.) temperamental person. [It., = "first lady"]

pri·ma fa·ci·e (prī'mə fā'shēē, fā'shē, fā'shə) *adv.* & *adj.* (Arising) at first sight, (based) on the first impression. [L.]

pri·mal (prī'məl) *adj.* Primitive, primeval; chief, fundamental. **pri'mal·ly** *adv.*

pri·ma·ry (prī'mĕrē, -mərē) *adj.* Earliest, original; of the first rank in a series, not derived; of the first importance, chief; (geol., **P~**) of the lowest series of strata, Paleozoic; (biol.) belonging to 1st stage of development; **~ color**: see COLOR; **~ coolant system**, system of pipes, pumps, etc., cooling core of nuclear reactor; **~ education**, that which begins with the rudiments of knowledge, esp. that provided for children under 11 years; **~ feather**, one of large flight feathers of bird's wing, growing directly from manus; **~ planets**, those revolving directly around sun as center; **~ school**, school for primary education. **primary** *n.* (pl. **-ries**). 1. Primary planet, meeting, feather, etc.; **P~**, (geol.) primary period. 2. Election held among members of a political party

*Although **Joseph Priestley** is best remembered as one of the discoverers of oxygen, his scientific work was only a hobby. He was a Presbyterian minister and a writer.*

*The **primates** are an order which at first sight seems to contain animals too different to be grouped together: a gorilla appears to have little in common with a lemur. But anatomy, ancestry, and habits unite them despite dissimilarities.*

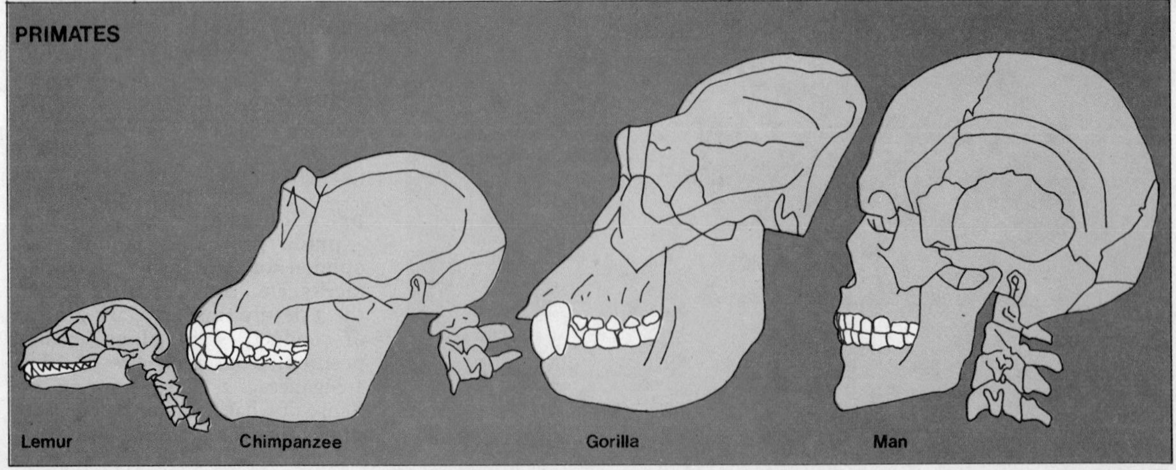

to choose candidates for elective office. **pri·ma·ri·ly** (prīmĕr′ĭlē, prī′mĕr-) *adv.*

pri·mate (prī′māt) *n.* 1. (also pr. prī′mĭt) Archbishop; **P ~ of all England**, archbishop of Canterbury; **P ~ of England**, archbishop of York. 2. (zool.) Member of order of mammals including man, apes, monkeys, tarsiers, and lemurs.

prime[1] (prīm) *n.* 1. State of highest perfection; best part (*of* thing). 2. Beginning, first age, of anything. 3. Prime number. 4. (mus.) Fundamental note or tone; lower of any 2 notes forming an interval. 5. Position in fencing, first of the 8 parries or guards in swordplay, used to protect the head; thrust in such position. ~ *adj.* 1. Chief, most important; ~ **minister**, principal minister of any sovereign or nation (now official title of head minister of state in Gt. Britain). 2. First-rate (esp. of beef), excellent. 3. Primary, fundamental; (arith., of number) having no integral factors except itself and unity (e.g. 2, 3, 5, 7, 11). 4. ~ **mover**: see MOVER; ~ **vertical** (**circle**), great circle of the heavens passing through E. and W. points of horizon and through zenith, where it cuts meridian at right angles. **prime′ness** *n.*

prime[2] (prīm) *v.* (**primed, prim·ing**). Supply (firearm, or abs.) with gunpowder for firing charge (hist.); wet (pump) to make it start working; equip (person *with* information etc.); inject gasoline into (carburetor or cylinder of

internal combustion engine); fill (person *with* liquor); cover (wood, canvas, etc.) with glue, gesso, oil, etc. to prevent paint from being absorbed; (of engine boiler) let water pass with steam into cylinder in form of spray.

prim·er[1] (prī′mer) *n.* 1. Cap, cylinder, etc., used to ignite powder of cartridge etc. 2. Priming coat of paint.

prim·er[2] (prĭm′er) *n.* 1. Elementary schoolbook for teaching

*It is almost unbelievable that these seemingly **primitive** arrangements of lines illustrate complex myths, but the art of Central Australian aborigines is highly stylized.*

*The **primrose** of England, with its pale yellow flowers and delicate perfume, is for many people the epitome of spring. It is in the Primula family.*

children to read; small introductory book; (hist.) prayer book for use of laity esp. before Reformation. 2. **great** ~, (print.) size of type (about 18 points); **long** ~, size of type (about 10 points).

pri·me·val (prīmē′val) *adj.* Of the 1st age of the world; ancient, primitive. **pri·me′val·ly** *adv.*

prim·ing (prī′mĭng) *n.* (esp.) 1. Gunpowder placed in pan of firearm. 2. Train of powder used to ignite charge in blasting etc. 3. Mixture used by painters for preparatory coat. 4. Preparation of sugar added to beer. 5. Hasty imparting of knowledge, cramming.

pri·mip·a·rous (prīmĭp′erus) *adj.* Bearing child for the first time. **pri·mip·a·ra** (prīmĭp′era) *n.* (pl. **-a·ras, -a·rae** pr. -erē). Primiparous woman.

prim·i·tive (prĭm′ĭtĭv) *adj.* Ancient; of early, simple, or old-fashioned kind; (anthro.) (of peoples) at an early stage of cultural development; (geol.) Paleozoic; (biol.) appearing in early stage of evolution; only slightly evolved from ancestral types; **P ~ Methodism, Methodist**, principles, member, of **P ~ Methodist Connection**, society of Methodists founded 1810 by Hugh Bourne by secession from main body. **prim′i·tive·ly** *adv.* **prim′i·tive·ness, prim·i·tiv′i·ty** *ns.* **primitive** *n.* (Picture by) painter of period before Renaissance; (picture by) untutored painter who ignores rules of perspective etc.; primitive word, line, etc.; (**P ~**) Primitive Methodist.

pri·mo·gen·i·tor (prīmojĕn′ĭter) *n.* Earliest ancestor; (loosely) ancestor.

pri·mo·gen·i·ture (prīmojĕn′ĭcher) *n.* Fact of being the first-born of the children of the same parents; (also **right of ~**) right of succession belonging to first-born, esp. feudal rule by which the whole real estate of an intestate passes to the eldest son.

pri·mor·di·al (prīmōr′dēal) *adj.* Existing at or from the beginning, primeval. **pri·mor′di·al·ly** *adv.* **pri·mor·di·al·i·ty** (prīmōrdēăl′ĭtē) *n.*

primp (prĭmp) *v.* Smarten, dress up, esp. in front of a mirror.

prim·rose (prĭm′rōz) *n.* Plant, esp. the **English** ~ (*Primula vulgaris*), bearing pale yellowish flowers in early spring, growing wild in woods and hedges and on banks, and with many cultivated varieties; color of flower of this; **evening** ~, plant of genus *Oenothera*, with large pale yellow flowers opening in evening; ~

Primula scotica, one plant included in a large genus of herbs which also includes the primrose and the cowslip. More than 500 species are native to the northern hemisphere.

The Prince of Wales derives his title from the formerly independent rulers of Wales who were reduced in status — from kings to princes — after the Anglo-Saxon and Norman wars of the 11th century.

path, pursuit of pleasure (w. ref. to *Hamlet*, I. iii. 50).

prim·u·la (prĭm'yula) *n.* Herbaceous perennial of genus *P*~, of low growing habit with yellow, white, pink, or purple flowers mostly borne in umbels. **prim·u·la·ceous** (prĭmyulā'shus) *adj.*

pri·mus in·ter pa·res (prī'mus ĭn'ter pār'ēz; *Lat.* prē'mōōs ĭn'tĕr pah'rĕs). First among equals (in a group). [L., = "first among equals"]

Pri·mus (prī'mus) **stove.** (trademark) Portable stove burning vaporized kerosene.

prince (prĭns) *n.* 1. Sovereign ruler (now rhet.); ruler of small state, actually or nominally feudatory to king or emperor; **P~ of Peace**, Christ; ~ **of darkness**, Satan. 2. (Title of) male member of royal family, esp. (in U.K.) son or grandson of king or queen; **P~ of Wales**, title (since 1301) conferred upon eldest son and heir apparent of British sovereign. 3. (as English rendering of foreign titles) Noble usu. ranking next below duke; (as courtesy title in some connections) duke, marquis, earl; (fig.) chief, greatest (*of*); ~ **of the (Holy Roman) Church**, title of cardinal. 4. ~ **consort**, husband of reigning female sovereign being himself a prince; esp., Albert, Prince of Saxe-Coburg, as husband of Queen Victoria; **P~ Imperial**, Napoléon Eugène Louis Jean Joseph (1856–79), only son of Napoleon III, killed with British forces in Zulu war of 1879; **Princes in the Tower**, Edward V and his brother Richard, Duke of York, sons of Edward IV, alleged to have been lodged in the Tower of London and there murdered in 1483. **prince·dom** (prĭns'dom), **prince·ling** (prĭns'lĭng) *ns.*

Prince (prĭns) **Edward Island.** Smallest province of Canada, a large island in the Gulf of St. Lawrence; capital, Charlottetown.

prince·ly (prĭns'lē) *adj.* (**-li·er, -li·est**). (Worthy) of a prince; sumptuous, splendid. **prince'li·ness** *n.*

Prince (prĭns) **of Wales Island.** Island in SE. Alaska, largest in the Alexander Archipelago, covering 1,500 sq. miles (3,885 sq. km); island of the Northwest Territories, Canada, in the Arctic Ocean between Victoria and Somerset Islands.

prin·cess (prĭn'sĭs, -sĕs) *n.* 1. (Title of) queen (archaic); wife of prince, daughter or granddaughter of sovereign; ~ **royal**, (title conferrable on) sovereign's eldest daughter. 2. (also **prin'cesse**) attrib. (of dress etc.) Made in panels with flared skirt and without a seam at the waist. **prin'cess·ly** *adj.*

Prince·ton (prĭns'ton). City in W. central New Jersey; site of Princeton University.

prin·ci·pal (prĭn'sipal) *adj.* First in rank or importance, chief; main, leading; (of money) constituting the original sum invested or lent; ~ **clause** (gram.) one to which another is subordinate; ~ **parts**, parts of verb from which the others can be derived. **principal** *n.* 1. Head, ruler, superior; head of some schools. 2. Person for whom another acts as agent etc.; person for whom another is surety; combatant in duel. 3. Capital sum as distinguished from interest, sum lent or invested on which interest is paid. 4. Organ stop of same quality as open diapason, but an octave higher in pitch. **prin'ci·pal·ship** *n.*

prin·ci·pal·i·ty (prĭnsipăl'ĭtē) *n.* (pl. **-ties**). Government of a prince; state ruled by a prince; (pl.) order of angels (see ANGEL).

prin·ci·pal·ly (prĭn'sipalē, -sĭplē) *adv.* For the most part, chiefly.

prin·ci·pate (prin'sipāt) *n.* 1. (Rom. hist.) Rule of early emperors while some republican forms were retained. 2. State ruled by a prince.

prin·ci·ple (prĭn'sipel) *n.* 1. Fundamental source, primary element; fundamental truth as basis of reasoning etc.; law of nature seen in working of machine etc.; (phys. etc.) general or inclusive law exemplified in numerous cases; general law as guide to action. 2. (pl. and collect. sing.) Personal code of moral conduct; **on** ~, from settled moral motive. 3. (chem.) Constituent of a naturally occurring substance, esp. one giving rise to some quality etc.

print (prĭnt) *n.* 1. Indentation in surface preserving the form left

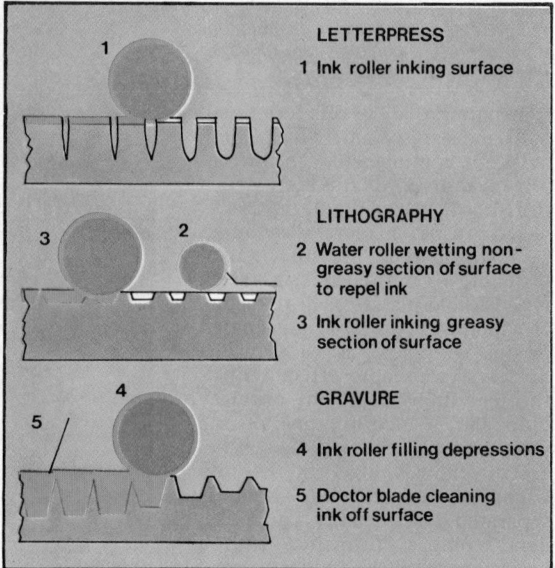

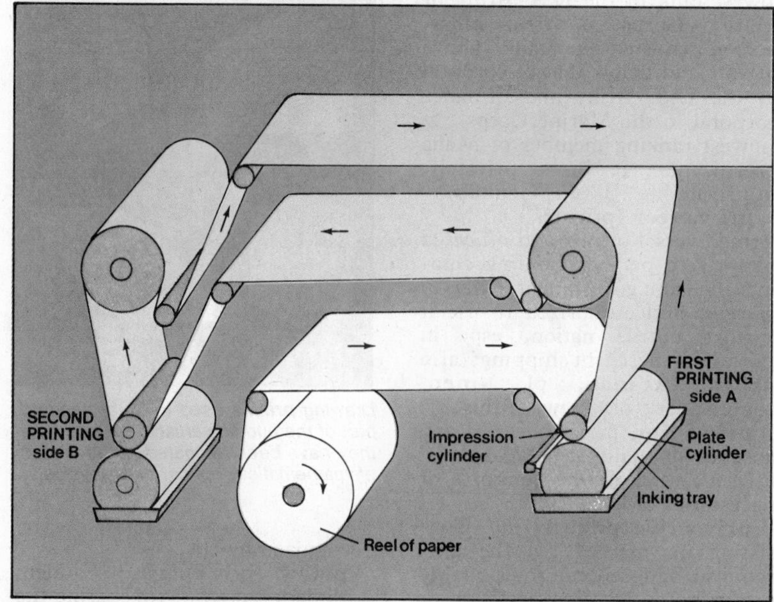

The craft of printing began with the use of wood blocks to ***print*** *repeated patterns on pottery, more than 5,000 years ago. The technique was adopted in the 15th century to reproduce the text of manuscripts which were cut on a single slab. Modern printing resulted from Gutenberg's movable type and the development of presses to produce hundreds of newspapers.*

by pressure of some body; mark, spot, stain. 2. Language embodied in printed form, printed lettering; handwritten letters imitating this. 3. State of being printed; **book is in** ~, (i) in printed form, (ii) on sale, not **out of** ~ (sold out). 4. Printed publication, esp. newspaper. 5. Printed cotton fabric. 6. Picture, design, printed from block or plate; (photog.) picture produced from negative; **print′out**, computer output in printed form. **print** *v.t.* 1. Impress, stamp, (surface *with* seal, die, etc.; mark or figure *on, in,* surface); (fig.) impress (*on* mind, memory). 2. Produce (book, picture, etc., or abs.) by applying inked types, blocks, or plates to paper, vellum, etc.; cause (book, MS.) to be so printed; express, publish, in print; write (words etc.) in imitation of typography; ~ **out**, produce computer output in printed form. 3. Mark (textile fabric) with decorative design in colors; transfer (colored design) from paper etc. to unglazed surface of pottery; (photog.) produce (picture) by transmission of light through negative. 4. **print′ed circuit**, (elect.) circuit of conductive strips on a nonconducting material. **print′a·ble** *adj.*

print·er (prĭn′t*er*) *n.* (esp.) One who prints books; owner of printing business; printing instrument; ~**'s devil**: see DEVIL def. 4.

pri·or[1] (prī′*er*) *n.* (fem. **pri·or·ess** pr. prī′*er*ĭs). Superior officer of religious house or order; (in abbey) officer next under abbot; (hist.) chief magistrate in some Italian republics. **pri′or·ship** *n.*

pri·or[2] (prī′*er*) *adj.* Earlier; antecedent in time, order, or importance. ~ *adv.* ~ **to**, before. **pri·or·i·ty** (prīŏr′ĭtē, -ăr′-) *n.* (pl. **-ties**). Condition or quality of being earlier in time, or *of* preceding something else; precedence in order, rank, or dignity; interest having prior claim to consideration, often with qualification, as *first, top* ~.

pri·o·ry (prī′*er*ē) *n.* (pl. **-ries**). Monastery, nunnery, governed by prior or prioress.

prise: see PRIZE[3].

prism (prĭz′*em*) *n.* Solid figure whose two ends are similar, equal, and parallel rectilineal figures and whose sides are parallelograms;

*These **prisoners** in Bangladesh are being treated in accord with emotion, not reason, the common fate of those who lose a bitter civil war.*

transparent body of this form, usu. of triangular section, which splits light into a rainbowlike spectrum.

pris·mat·ic (prĭzmăt´ĭk), **pris·mat·i·cal** (prĭzmăt´ĭkal) *adjs.* Of, like, a prism; (of colors) distributed by transparent prism, (also) brilliant; ~ **binoculars, glasses,** type of field glasses each telescope of which contains two right-angled prisms so placed as to secure a better stereoscopic effect with a shorter tube than an ordinary binocular; ~ **color**, one of the seven colors (violet, indigo, blue, green, yellow, orange, and red) into which a ray of white light is separated by a prism; ~ **compass,** hand compass furnished with a prism enabling the holder to read the compass while taking a bearing or sight. **pris·mat´i·cal·ly** *adv.*

pris·moid (prĭz´moid) *n.* Body, figure, resembling a prism, with similar but unequal parallel polygonal ends. **pris·moi´dal** *adj.*

pris·on (prĭz´*on*) *n.* Place in which person is kept in captivity, esp. building to which person is legally committed while awaiting trial or for punishment; custody, confinement.

pris·on·er (priz´*oner*, prĭz´n*er*) *n.* Person kept in prison; (also ~ **of war**), member of armed forces captured in war and imprisoned; ~ **of state, state** ~, one confined for political reasons; **take** (person) ~, seize and hold as prisoner; ~**s' base**, game played by two parties of boys etc., each occupying distinct base or home, aim of each side being to make prisoner by touching any player who leaves his base.

pris·sy (prĭs´ē) *adj.* (**-si·er, -si·est**). Prim, overly decorous. **pris´si·ly** *adv.* **pris´si·ness** *n.*

pris·tine (prĭs´tēn, prĭstēn´) *adj.* Ancient, primitive, unspoiled.

prith·ee (prĭdh´ē) *int.* (archaic) Pray, please. [= (I) pray thee]

pri·va·cy (prī´*v*asē) *n.* Being withdrawn from society or public interest; avoidance of publicity.

pri·vate (prī´vĭt) *adj.* 1. Not holding public office or official position. 2. Kept, removed, from public knowledge; not open to the public; ~ detective, person undertaking special inquiries for pay; ~ **eye,** (slang) private detective; ~ **means,** income not derived from employment; ~ **parts,** genitals; ~ **school,** elementary or secondary school owned and managed by private individual(s). 3. One's own; individual, person, not affecting the community; confidential. 4. (of place) Retired, secluded; (of person, archaic) given to retirement. **pri´vate·ly** *adv.* **pri´vate·ness** *n.*

private *n.* 1. Person enlisted in lowest rank in the U.S. Army or Marine Corps; ~ **first class,** person enlisted in rank above private and below that of corporal in the U.S. Army and of lance corporal in the Marine Corps. 2. Lowest ranking member of Mafia organization. 3. **in** ~, privately; in private life. 4. (pl.) Genitals.

pri·va·teer (prīv*a*tēr´) *n.* (hist.) Armed vessel owned and officered by private persons holding commission from government (*letters of marque*) and authorized to use it against hostile nation, esp. in capture of merchant shipping; (also **pri·va·teers´man,** pl. **-men**) commander, (pl.) crew, of this.

pri·va·tion (prīvā´sh*o*n) *n.* Loss, absence (*of* quality), as *cold is the ~ of heat*; want of the comforts or necessaries of life.

priv·a·tive (prĭv´*a*tĭv) *adj.* Consisting in, marked by, the loss, removal, or absence of some quality or attribute; denoting privation or absence of quality etc.; (gram.) expressing privation. **priv´a·tive·ly** *adv.*

priv·et (prĭv´ĭt) *n.* Bushy evergreen shrub (*Ligustrum vulgare*) with smooth dark green leaves, clusters of small white flowers, and small shining black berries, much used for hedges; other species of *Ligustrum* or similar (usu. evergreen) shrub.

priv·i·lege (prĭv´*i*lĭj, prĭv´lĭj) *n.* Right, advantage, immunity, belonging to person, class, or office; special advantage or benefit; special immunity granted to officials and others, esp. members of Congress, to free them from obligations or liabilities. ~ *v.t.* (**-leged, -leg·ing**). Invest with privilege; allow (*to* do) as privilege; exempt (*from* burden etc.). **priv´i·leged** *adj.*

priv·i·ty (prĭv´ĭtē) *n.* (pl. **-ties**). 1. Being privy (*to*). 2. (law) Any relation between 2 parties that is recognized by law.

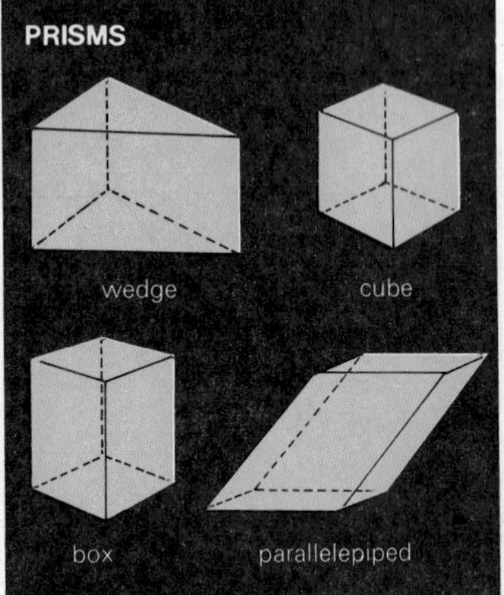

*Drawing **prisms** used to be a standard part of the budding artist's training. Now they have been relegated to the worlds of mathematics, optics, and physics.*

priv·y (prĭv´ē) *adj.* Hidden, secluded; secret; ~ **to,** sharing the secret of (person's designs, etc.); **P~ Council,** sovereign's private counselors; (in Gt. Britain) body of advisers chosen by sovereign (now chiefly as personal dignity), together with princes of the blood, archbishops, etc.; ~ **purse,** allowance from public revenue for monarch's private expenses; keeper of this; ~ **seal,** (hist.) seal affixed to documents that are afterward to pass. **priv·i·ly** (prĭv´*i*lē) *adv.* **privy** *n.* (pl. **priv·ies**). 1. Outhouse. 2. (law) Person having a part or interest in any action, matter, or thing.

prize[1] (prīz) *n.* Reward given as symbol of victory or superiority, to student in school or college who excels in attainments, to competitor in athletic contest, to exhibitor of best specimen of manufactured products, works of art, etc., in exhibition; (fig.) anything striven for or worth striving for; (~) money (also **money** ~) or other reward offered for competition by chance, in lottery, etc.; **prize'fight**, boxing match for money; **prize'fighter**; **prize ring**, enclosed area (now usu. square), for prizefighting. **prize** *v.t.* (**prized, priz·ing**). Value highly.

prize[2] (prīz) *n.* Ship, property, captured at sea in virtue of rights of war; (fig.) find or windfall; ~ **court**, one concerned with prizes; ~ **money**, money realized by sale of prize. ~ *v.t.* (**prized, priz·ing**). Make prize of.

prize[3], **prise** (prīz) *v.t.* (**prized, priz·ing, prised, pris·ing**). (esp. Brit.) Force (lid etc. *up, out*, box etc. *open*) by leverage. ~ *n.* Leverage, purchase.

PRO *abbrev.* (mil.) Public Relations Officer.

pro[1] (prō) *n.* (pl. **pros**). (colloq.) Professional.

pro[2] (prō) *adv.* & *n.* (pl. **pros**). (Argument) in favor of a proposition etc. (usu. pl., in ~**s and cons**, (arguments for and against)). [L.]

pro- *prefix.* 1. In front of, for, on behalf of, on account of. 2. Favoring or siding with.

prob·a·bi·lism (prŏb'*abĭlĭzem*) *n.* Doctrine that where authorities differ any course may be followed for which a recognized doctor of the church can be cited; theory that there is no certain knowledge, but there may be grounds of belief sufficient for practical life. **prob'a·bi·list** *n.* & *adj.*

prob·a·bil·i·ty (prŏb*a*bĭl'ĭtē) *n.* (pl. **-ties**). Quality of being probable; (most) probable event; (math.) likelihood of an event, measured by the ratio of the favorable cases to the whole number of cases possible; **in all** ~, most likely.

prob·a·ble (prŏb'*abel*) *adj.* That may be expected to happen or prove true, likely. **prob'a·bly** *adv.*

pro·bate (prō'bāt) *n.* Official proving of will; verified copy of will with certificate as handed to executors; ~ **court**, one that administers wills and estates of dead persons.

pro·ba·tion (prōbā'sh*o*n) *n.* Testing of conduct or character of person, esp. of candidate for membership in religious body, profession, etc.; moral trial or discipline; (law) method of dealing with offenders by releasing them from custody and placing them under supervision; ~ **officer**, person appointed to supervise such offenders. **pro·ba'tion·al, pro·ba'tion·ar·y** *adjs.* Of, serving for, done in the way of, probation; undergoing probation.

pro·ba·tion·er (prōbā'sh*oner*) *n.* Person on probation, esp. novice in religious house, nurse in training, offender on probation.

pro·ba·tive (prō'b*a*tĭv), **pro·ba·to·ry** (prō'b*a*tōrē, -tōrē) *adjs.* Affording proof, evidential. **pro'ba·tive·ly** *adv.*

probe (prōb) *n.* Blunt-ended surgical instrument for exploring wound etc.; act of probing; unmanned exploratory spacecraft transmitting information about its environment. ~ *v.t.* (**probed, prob·ing**). Explore (wound, part of body) with probe; penetrate (thing) with sharp instrument; (fig.) examine closely, sound. **prob'er** *n.* **prob'ing** *adj.* & *n.* **prob'ing·ly** *adv.*

pro·bi·ty (prō'bĭtē, prŏb'ĭ-) *n.* Uprightness, honesty.

prob·lem (prŏb'l*e*m) *n.* Doubtful or difficult question; thing hard to understand; (geom.) proposition in which something has to be done; (logic) question (usu. only implied) involved in a syllogism; (phys., math.) inquiry starting from given conditions to investigate a fact, result, or law; (chess, bridge, etc.) arrangement of pieces on board, or of cards dealt, etc., in which player is challenged to accomplish specified result, often under prescribed conditions; (attrib.; of child) difficult to train; (of literature etc.) treating subject of social or other problem.

prob·lem·at·ic (prŏbl*e*măt'ĭk) *adj.* Doubtful, questionable; (logic)

Topiary Gardens at Levens Hall in Cumbria, U.K. ***Privet*** *is one of several shrubs used for hedges and which can be trimmed into various shapes.*

enunciating or supporting what is possible but not necessarily true. **prob·lem·at'i·cal** *adj.* **prob·lem·at'i·cal·ly** *adv.*

pro·bos·cis (prōbŏs'ĭs) *n.* (pl. **-bos·cis·es, -bos·ci·des** pr. -bŏs'ĭdēz). Elephant's trunk; long flexible snout of tapir etc.; elongated part of mouth in some insects; sucking organ in some worms; (joc.) human nose; ~ **monkey**, large, long-tailed Bornean ape (*Nasalis larvatus*) the male of which has nose projecting far beyond mouth.

pro·ce·dure (prosē'jer) *n.* Proceeding; mode of conducting business or legal action. **pro·ce'dur·al** *adj.*

pro·ceed (prosēd') *v.i.* Go on, make one's way, (*to*); go on (*with, in,* action etc., *to* do, *to* another course etc.); adopt course of action; go on to say; come forth, issue, originate; take legal proceedings *against;* (of action) be carried on, take place. **pro·ceed'ing** *n.* (esp.) Action, piece of conduct; (pl.) record of account of doings of a society; **legal ~s,** (steps taken in) legal action.

pro·ceeds (prō'sēdz) *n.pl.* Results, profit.

proc·ess (prŏs'ĕs, prō'sĕs) *n.* (pl. **proc·ess·es** pr. prŏs'ĕsĭz, -esēz, prō'sĕsĭz, -sesēz). 1. Progress, course; **in ~ of time,** as time goes on; natural or involuntary operation, series of changes; course of action, proceeding, esp. method of operation in manufacture, printing, photography, etc. 2. (Print from block produced by) method (e.g. chemical or photographic) other than simple engraving by hand; ~ **block**, block for printing from, produced by such method. 3. Action at law; formal commencement of this; summons or writ; ~ **server**, officer of court who serves processes or summonses. 4. (anat., zool., bot.) Outgrowth, protuberance. **process** *v.t.* 1. Institute legal process against (person). 2. Treat (material), preserve (food), reproduce (drawing etc.) by a process. 3. Subject to administrative process, examine, attend to, and dispose of (papers).

pro·ces·sion (prosĕsh'on) *n.* 1. Proceeding of body of persons (or of boats etc.) in orderly succession, esp. as religious ceremony or on festive occasion; body of persons doing this. 2. (theol.) Emanation of the Holy Ghost. ~ *v.* Go in procession; walk along (street) in procession.

pro·ces·sion·al (prosĕsh'onal) *adj.* Of processions; used, carried, sung, in processions. ~ *n.* Processional hymn, (eccles.) office book of processional hymns etc. **pro·ces'sion·al·ly** *adv.*

pro·claim (prōklām', pro-) *v.t.* Announce publicly and officially; declare (war, peace); announce officially the accession of (sovereign); declare (person, thing) officially to be (traitor etc.); declare publicly or openly (thing, *that*); place (district etc.) under legal restrictions, prohibit (meeting etc.), by declaration. **proc·la·ma·tion** (prŏklamā'shon) *n.* **pro·clam·a·to·ry** (prōklăm'atōrē, -tōrē) *adj.*

Elephants are the only living ***proboscideans,*** *descended through 50,000,000 years of change from a tapir-like creature about 2 ft. tall.*

pro·cliv·i·ty (prōklĭv'ĭtē) *n.* (pl. **-ties**). Tendency (*to, toward,* action or habit, esp. bad one).

Proc·ne (prŏk'nē). (Gk. myth.) Sister of PHILOMELA; for feeding the flesh of her son to her husband, Tereus, she was turned into a swallow.

pro·con·sul (prōkŏn'sul) *n.* 1. (Rom. hist.) Governor of Roman province, in later republic usu. an ex-consul; (under empire) governor of senatorial province. 2. (rhet.) Governor of modern colony etc.; deputy consul. **pro·con'su·lar** *adj.* **pro·con'su·late, pro·con'sul·ship** *ns.*

pro·cras·ti·nate (prōkrăs'tinăt, pro-) *v.i.* (**-nat·ed, -nat·ing**). Defer action, be dilatory. **pro·cras·ti·na'tion** *n.* **pro·cras'ti·na·tive, pro·cras·ti·na·to·ry** (prōkrăs'tinatōrē, -tōrē, pro-) *adjs.* **pro·cras'ti·na·tor** *n.*

pro·cre·ate (prō'krēāt) *v.t.* (**-at·ed, -at·ing**). Generate (offspring). **pro·cre·ant** (prō'krēant) *adj.* **pro·cre·a'tion** *n.* **pro'cre·a·tive** *adj.* **pro'cre·a·tor** *n.*

Pro·crus·tes (prōkrŭs'tēz). (Gk. legend) Robber who laid travelers on a bed and made them fit it by cutting off their limbs or stretching them; he was killed by Theseus. **Pro·crus'te·an** *adj.* Compelling conformity by violent means.

proc·tor (prŏk'ter) *n.* 1. Person appointed to administer school examinations and guard against cheating. 2. (law) Person managing causes in court (now chiefly eccles.) that administers civil or canon law. **proc·to·ri·al** (prŏktōr'ēal, -tōr'-) *adj.* **proc'tor·ship** *n.*

proc·to·scope (prŏk'toskōp) *n.* Surgical instrument for inspecting the interior of the rectum.

pro·cum·bent (prōkŭm'bent) *adj.* Lying on the face, prostrate; (bot.) growing along the ground.

proc·u·ra·tion (prŏkyurā'shon) *n.* 1. Procuring, obtaining; bringing about. 2. Function, authorized

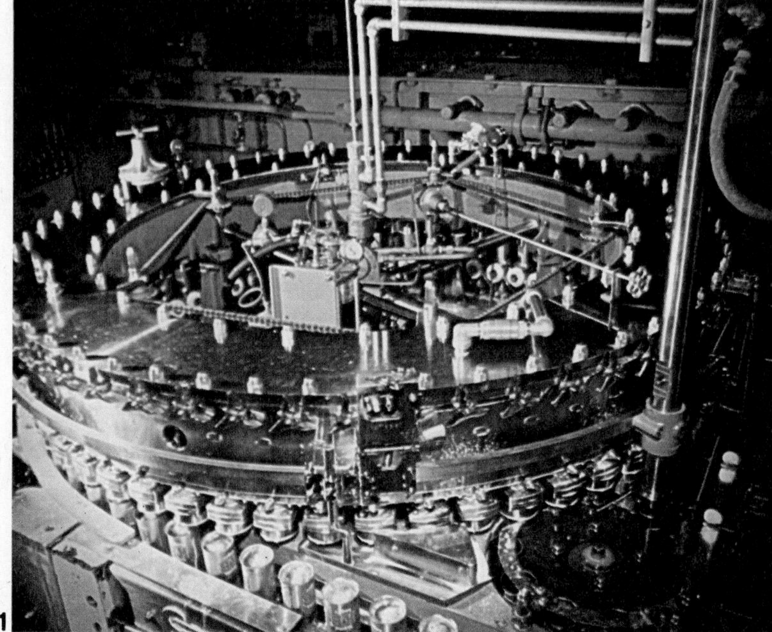

1

2

*Food **production** techniques have been mechanized to allow a greater output to be obtained from a smaller workforce. Both beer (1) and cheese (2) were once made by hand but increasing demand is satisfied by use of machinery.*

action, of attorney or agent. 3. Procurer's trade or offense.

proc·u·ra·tor (prŏk′yurāter) *n.* 1. (Rom. hist.) Treasury officer in imperial province. 2. Agent, proxy, esp. one who has power of attorney. 3. Magistrate in some Italian cities. **proc·u·ra·to·ri·al** (prŏkyuratŏr′-ēal, -tōr′-) *adj.* **proc′u·ra·tor·ship** *n.*

proc·u·ra·to·ry (prŏk′yuratōrē, -tōrē) *n.* Authorization to act for another.

pro·cure (prōkūr′) *v.* (**-cured, -cur·ing**). Obtain by care or effort, acquire; act as procurer or procuress; (archaic) bring about. **pro·cur′a·ble** *adj.* **pro·cur′ance, pro·cure′ment** *ns.*

pro·cur·er (prōkūr′er) *n.* (fem. **pro·cur·ess** pr. prōkūr′ĭs). Pimp.

prod (prŏd) *v.t.* (**prod·ded, prod·ding**). Poke with pointed instrument, end of stick, etc.; goad, irritate. ~ *n.* Poke, thrust; pointed instrument; **cattle ~**, one equipped with an electrical charger for moving cattle and, sometimes, people in crowd control.

prod·i·gal (prŏd′igal) *adj.* Recklessly wasteful; lavish *of*; **P~ Son**, repentant wastrel in parable (Luke 15). **prod′i·gal·ly** *adv.* **prod·i·gal·i·ty** (prŏdigăl′ĭtē) *n.* **prodigal** *n.* Prodigal person.

pro·di·gious (prodĭj′us) *adj.* Marvelous, amazing; enormous; abnormal. **pro·di′gious·ly** *adv.* **pro·di′gious·ness** *n.*

prod·i·gy (prŏd′ijē) *n.* (pl. **-gies**). Marvelous thing, esp. one out of the course of nature; wonderful example *of* (some quality); person endowed with surprising qualities or abilities, esp. precocious child.

pro·duce (prodōōs′, -dūs′) *v.t.* (**-duced, -duc·ing**). 1. Bring forward for inspection or consideration; bring (play, performer, book, etc.) before the public. 2. (geom.) Extend, continue (line *to* a point). 3. Manufacture (goods) from raw materials etc. 4. Bring about, cause (sensation etc.). 5. Yield (produce); bear, yield (offspring, fruit). **pro·duc′i·ble** *adj.* **produce** (prŏd′ōōs, -ūs, prō′dōōs, -dūs) *n.* Amount produced, yield, esp. in assay of ore; agricultural and natural products collectively; result (*of* labor, efforts, etc.).

pro·duc·er (prodōō′ser, -dū′-) *n.* 1. (econ.) One who produces articles for consumption (opp. *consumer*); person financing a film, play, etc. and controlling its production. 2. (also **gas ~**) Special form of furnace for making **~ gas**, an inflammable gas containing carbon monoxide together with nitrogen, made by passing air through red-hot coke.

prod·uct (prŏd′ukt) *n.* Thing produced by natural process or manufacture; result; (math.) quantity obtained by multiplying quantities together; (chem.) compound formed during chemical reaction.

pro·duc·tion (produk′shon) *n.* Producing; thing(s) produced; literary or artistic work.

pro·duc·tive (produk′tĭv) *adj.* Producing, tending to produce; producing abundantly; (econ.) producing salable commodities. **pro·duc′tive·ly** *adv.* **pro·duc′tive·ness** *n.* **pro·duc·tiv·i·ty** (prōdŭktĭv′ĭtē, prŏdŭk-) *n.* (esp.) Efficiency in industrial production.

pro·em (prō′ĕm) *n.* Preface, preamble; beginning, prelude. **pro·e·mi·al** (prōē′mēal) *adj.*

Prof., prof. *abbrevs.* Professor.

pro·fane[1] (prōfān′, pro-) *adj.* Not belonging to what is sacred or biblical; not initiated into religious rites or any esoteric knowledge; (of rites etc.) heathen; irreverent, blasphemous. **pro·fane′ly** *adv.* **pro·fane′ness, pro·fan′er** *ns.* **pro·fan·i·ty** (prōfăn′ĭtē, pro-) *n.* (pl. **-ties**). (esp.) Profane words or acts.

pro·fane[2] (prōfān′, pro-) *v.t.* (**-faned, -fan·ing**). Treat (sacred thing) with irreverence or disregard; violate, pollute (what is entitled to respect). **prof·a·na·-**

tion (prŏf*a*nā´sh*o*n) *n.*

pro·fess (pr*o*fĕs´, prō-) *v.* 1. Lay claim to (quality, feeling); pretend (*to* be or do); openly declare; take vows of religious order; receive into religious order. 2. Make (law, medicine, etc.) one's profession or business.

pro·fessed (pr*o*fĕst´, prō-) *adj.* Self-acknowledged; alleged, ostensible; claiming to be duly qualified; that has taken the vows of a religious order. **pro·fess·ed·ly** (pr*o*fĕs´ĭdlē) *adv.*

pro·fes·sion (pr*o*fĕsh´*o*n) *n.* 1. Declaration, avowal; declaration of belief in a religion; vow made on entering, fact of being in, a religious order. 2. Vocation, calling, esp. one that involves some branch of higher learning or science; body of persons engaged in this, esp. (theatr. slang) actors.

pro·fes·sion·al (pr*o*fĕsh´*o*n*a*l) *adj.* Of, belonging to, connected with, a profession; following occupation (esp. one usu. engaged in as pastime or by amateurs) as means of livelihood; making a trade of something usu. or properly pursued from higher motives; maintaining a proper standard, businesslike, not amateurish. ~ *n.* Professional man or woman, esp. (abbrev. pro) athlete playing for

Roscoe Tanner, U.S. tennis player. The life of a ***professional*** *player on the international circuit may seem an enviable one, but it can be arduous.*

money (opp. amateur). **pro·fes´sion·al·ly** *adv.*

pro·fes·sion·al·ism (pr*o*fĕsh´-*o*n*a*lĭz*e*m) *n.* Qualities, stamp, of a profession; practice of employing professionals in sport etc. **pro·fes´sion·al·ize** *v.t.* (**-ized, -iz·ing**).

pro·fes·sor (pr*o*fĕs´*er*) *n.* 1. One who makes profession (*of* a religion). 2. Teacher or scholar of high rank, sometimes holder of a chair, in a college or university (prefixed as title, abbrev. Prof.). **pro·fes´sor·ate, pro·fes´sor·ship** *ns.* Position, period of activity, of college or university professor. **pro·fes·so·ri·al** (prōf*e*sōr´ē*a*l, -sŏr´-, prŏf*e*-) *adj.* **pro·fes·so´ri·al·ly** *adv.*

prof·fer (prŏf´*er*) *v.t.* & *n.* (literary) Offer.

pro·fi·cient (pr*o*fĭsh´*e*nt) *adj.* & *n.* Adept, expert (*in, at*). **pro·fi´cient·ly** *adv.* **pro·fi´cien·cy** *n.*

pro·file (prō´fīl) *n.* Drawing, silhouette, or other representation, of side view esp. of human face; side outline esp. of human face; flat outline piece of scenery on stage; (fort.) transverse vertical section of fort; comparative thickness of earthwork etc.; (journalism) biographical sketch of a subject, sometimes accompanied by a portrait. ~ *v.t.* (**-filed, -fil·ing**). Represent in profile; give a profile to.

prof·it (prŏf´ĭt) *n.* Advantage, benefit; financial gain, excess of returns over outlay (usu. pl.); ~ **and loss account**, (bookkeeping) account in which gains are credited and losses debited so as to show net profit or loss at any time; ~ **sharing**, sharing of profits esp. between employer and employed. **prof´it·less** *adj.* **prof´it·less·ly** *adv.* **prof´it·less·ness** *n.* **profit** *v.* Be of advantage to; be of advantage; be benefited or assisted.

prof·it·a·ble (prŏf´ĭt*a*b*e*l) *adj.* Beneficial, useful; yielding profit, lucrative. **prof·it·a·bil´i·ty, prof´it·a·ble·ness** *n.* **prof´it·a·bly** *adv.*

prof·it·eer (prŏfĭtēr´) *v.t.* Make inordinate profits on sale of necessary supplies or goods, esp. in time of war or supply shortage. **prof·it·eer´ing** *n.* **profiteer** *n.* Profiteering person.

prof·li·gate (prŏf´lĭgĭt, -gāt) *adj.* & *n.* Licentious, dissolute, or recklessly extravagant (person). **prof´li·gate·ly** *adv.* **prof´li·gate·ness, prof·li·ga·cy** (prŏf´lĭg*a*sē) *ns.*

Silhouettes, normally of the subject's ***profile,*** *were most popular during the 18th and 19th century. They have also been used in animated cartoons and, as pictured, are continued at Disneyland.*

pro for·ma (prō fŏr′ma). Done for form's sake, as a matter of form. [L.]

pro·found (profownd′) *adj.* 1. Having, showing, great knowledge or insight; demanding deep study or thought. 2. (of state or quality) Deep, intense, unqualified. 3. Having, coming from, extending to, a great depth. **pro·found′ly** *adv.* **pro·found′ness, pro·fun·di·ty** (profŭn′dĭtē) *ns.* **profound** *n.* (poet.) Vast depth.

pro·fuse (profūs′) *adj.* Lavish, extravagant (*in, of*); exuberantly plentiful. **pro·fuse′ly** *adv.* **pro·fuse′ness, pro·fu·sion** (profū′zhon) *ns.*

pro·gen·i·tor (prōjĕn′ĭter) *n.* Ancestor; (fig.) political or intellectual predecessor, original of a copy. **pro·gen·i·to·ri·al** (prōjĕnĭtōr′ēal, -tōr′-) *adj.*

prog·e·ny (prŏj′enē) *n.* (pl. **-nies**). Offspring; descendants; (fig.) issue, outcome.

pro·ges·ter·one (prōjĕs′terōn) *n.* Hormone produced by the ovaries (or prepared synthetically) that prepares the uterus for pregnancy.

prog·na·thous (prŏg′nathus, prŏgnā′-) *adj.* With projecting jaws; (of jaws) projecting. **prog·nath·ic** (prŏgnăth′ĭk) *adj.* **prog·na·thism** (prŏg′nathĭzem) *n.*

prog·no·sis (prŏgnō′sĭs) *n.* (pl. **-ses** pr. -sēz). Prognostication, esp. (med.) forecast of course of disease.

prog·nos·tic (prŏgnŏs′tĭk) *n.* Preindication, omen (*of*); prediction, forecast. ~ *adj.* Foretelling, predictive (*of*).

prog·nos·ti·cate (prŏgnŏs′tĭkāt) *v.t.* (**-cat·ed, -cat·ing**). Foretell; presage. **prog·nos·ti·ca′tion** *n.* **prog·nos′ti·ca·tive, prog·nos′ti·ca·to·ry** *adjs.*

pro·gram, Brit. **pro·gramme** (prō′grăm, -gram) *ns.* 1. Descriptive notice of series of events, e.g. of course of study, concert, etc.; definite plan of intended proceedings. 2. Entertainment etc., esp. consisting of several items; a broadcast production. 3. Series of coded instructions for a computer. 4. ~ **music**, music intended to suggest scenes or events. **program** *v.t.* (**-gramed** or **-grammed, -gram·ing** or **-gram·ming**). Express (problem) as a program; instruct (computer) by means of a program. **pro′gram·mer** *n.* **pro·gram·mat·ic** (prōgramăt′ĭk) *adj.*

prog·ress (prŏg′rĕs; *Brit.* prō′grĕs) *n.* Forward or onward movement in space; advance, development. ~ (progrĕs′) *v.i.* Move forward or onward; be carried on; advance, develop.

pro·gres·sion (progrĕsh′on) *n.* 1. Progress. 2. (mus.) Passing from one note or chord to another. 3. (math.) Succession of series of quantities, between every 2 successive terms of which there is some constant relation; **arithmetical** ~, series in which each number increases or decreases by the same quantity, as 2, 4, 6, etc.; **geometrical** ~, series in which the increase or decrease is by a common ratio, as 3, 9, 27. 4. (astron.) Movement of planet in order of signs of zodiac, i.e. from west to east. **pro·gres′sion·al** *adj.*

pro·gres·sive (progrĕs′ĭv) *adj.* 1. Moving forward; proceeding step by step, successive; ~ **bridge** etc., bridge etc. played by several sets of players at different tables, certain players passing after each round to next table; ~ **jazz**, jazz combined with classical elements in dissonant arrangements. 2. Advancing in social conditions, character, efficiency, etc.; favoring progress or reform; (of disease) continuously increasing. **pro·gres′sive·ly** *adv.* **pro·gres′sive·ness** *n.* **progressive** *n.* Advocate of progressive policy.

pro·hib·it (prōhĭb′ĭt) *v.t.* Forbid, debar. **pro·hib′it·ed** *adj.*

pro·hi·bi·tion (prōĭbĭsh′on, prōhi-) *n.* 1. Forbidding; edict, order, that forbids. 2. (also **P**~) Forbidding by law of sale of intoxicants for common consumption; **P~ Amendment**, 18th Amendment to U.S. Constitution, ratified

1919, which, together with the enabling Volstead Act of Congress, imposed on the nation prohibition of alcoholic drinks in spite of widespread opposition and violation; it was repealed in 1933 by ratification of the 21st Amendment. **pro·hi·bi'tion·ist** *n.* Advocate of prohibition (esp. of sale etc. of intoxicants).

pro·hib·i·tive (prōhĭb'ĭtĭv) *adj.* Prohibiting; (of tax etc.) serving to prevent the use or abuse of something; (of price) so high that it precludes purchase. **pro·hib'i·tive·ly** *adv.* **pro·hib'i·tive·ness** *n.* **pro·hib·i·to·ry** (prōhĭb'ĭtōrē, -tōrē) *adj.*

pro·ject (project') *v.* 1. Plan, contrive; form a project of. 2. Cast, throw, impel; cause (light, shadow) to fall on surface; (fig.) cause (idea etc.) to take shape. 3. Jut out, protrude. 4. (geom.) Draw straight lines from a center through every point of (given figure) to produce corresponding figure on a surface by intersecting it; draw (such lines), produce (such corresponding figure); make projection of (Earth, sky, etc.). ~ (prŏj'ĕkt) *n.* Plan, scheme; (in schools) scheme of study lasting for a limited period (e.g. 1 term) during which the pupils make their own inquiries and record their findings. **pro·ject'ed, pro·ject'ing** *adjs.*

pro·jec·tile (projĕk'tĭl, -tīl) *adj.* 1. Impelling, as ~ *force.* 2. Capable of being projected by force, esp. from gun. ~ *n.* Projectile missile, shell, bullet.

pro·jec·tion (projĕk'shon) *n.* 1. Throwing, casting. 2. Protruding; protruding thing; thrusting forward. 3. Planning; mental image viewed as objective reality; (psych.) unconscious transfer of one's own impressions or feelings to external objects or persons. 4. (geom.) Projecting of a figure (see PROJECT *v.* def. 4); ~ **of a point**, point in derived figure corresponding to point in original figure. 5. (geog.) Any orderly system of representing the meridians and parallels of Earth (or celestial sphere) by lines on a plane surface, e.g. by first projecting the meridians on to a cone (**conical** ~) or a cylinder (**cylindrical** ~). 6. Display of film in theater by throwing image on screen (and producing corresponding sound). 7. (alchemy) Transmutation of metals by casting **powder of** ~ (powder of philosophers' stone) into crucible containing them.

One of the map-maker's problems is transferring an accurate image of a curved surface — the earth's — on to a flat one, particularly when the map is of a large area. To solve this, various ***projections*** *have been worked out which limit distortion as much as possible.*

pro·jec·tion·ist (projĕk'shonĭst) *n.* Person who projects slides or film.

pro·jec·tive (projĕk'tĭv) *adj.* Mentally projecting or projected; (geom.) of, derived by, projection; ~ **property** (of a figure), property unchanged after projection. **pro·jec'tive·ly** *adv.*

pro·jec·tor (projĕk'ter) *n.* 1. One who forms a project or scheme. 2. Apparatus for projecting rays of light, as from a lighthouse lantern; apparatus for throwing a picture onto a screen; (**sound** ~, one for sound film, producing corresponding sound at same time).

Pro·kof·iev (prokawf'yef, -yĕf), **Sergei Sergeevich** (1891–1953). Russian composer and pianist, best known for his opera *Love for Three Oranges* and a fairy tale for orchestra and narrator, *Peter and the Wolf.*

pro·lapse (prōlăps') *v.i.* (**-lapsed, -laps·ing**). (path.) Slip forward or down out of place. ~ (prō'lăps, prōlăps'), **pro·lap·sus** (prōlăp'sus) *ns.* (path.) Slipping forward or down of part or organ, esp. of uterus or rectum.

pro·le·gom·e·non (prōlegŏm'enŏn, -non) *n.* (usu. in pl. **-na** pr. -na). Preliminary discourse or matter prefixed to book etc. **pro·le·gom'e·nous** *adj.*

pro·lep·sis (prōlĕp'sĭs) *n.* (pl. **-ses** pr. -sēz). Anticipation; representation of thing as existing

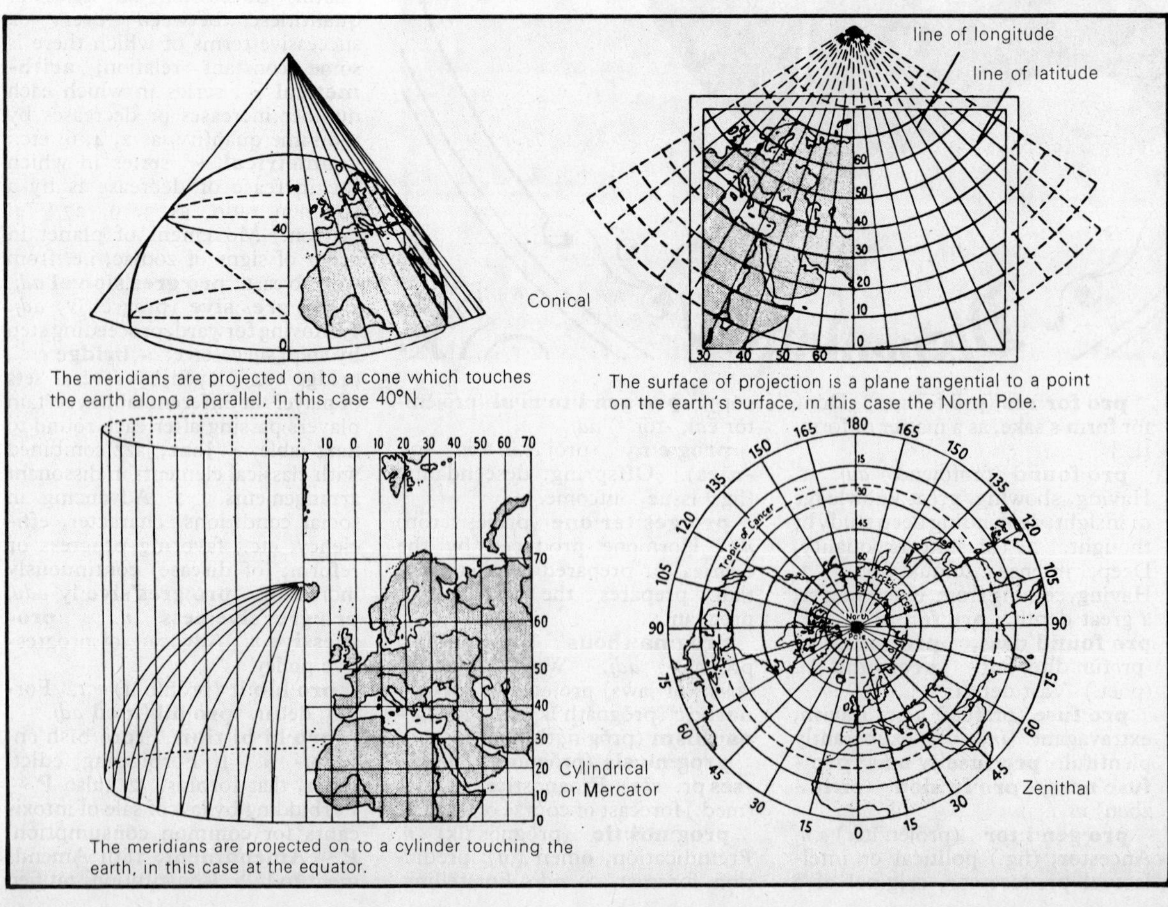

The meridians are projected on to a cone which touches the earth along a parallel, in this case 40°N.

The surface of projection is a plane tangential to a point on the earth's surface, in this case the North Pole.

The meridians are projected on to a cylinder touching the earth, in this case at the equator.

Epidiascope
projector lens
mirror
reflecting mirror
lamp
glass top
manuscript
backing plate

Slide projector
reflector mirror
lamp
heat filter
projection lens
slide
fan
condenser lenses

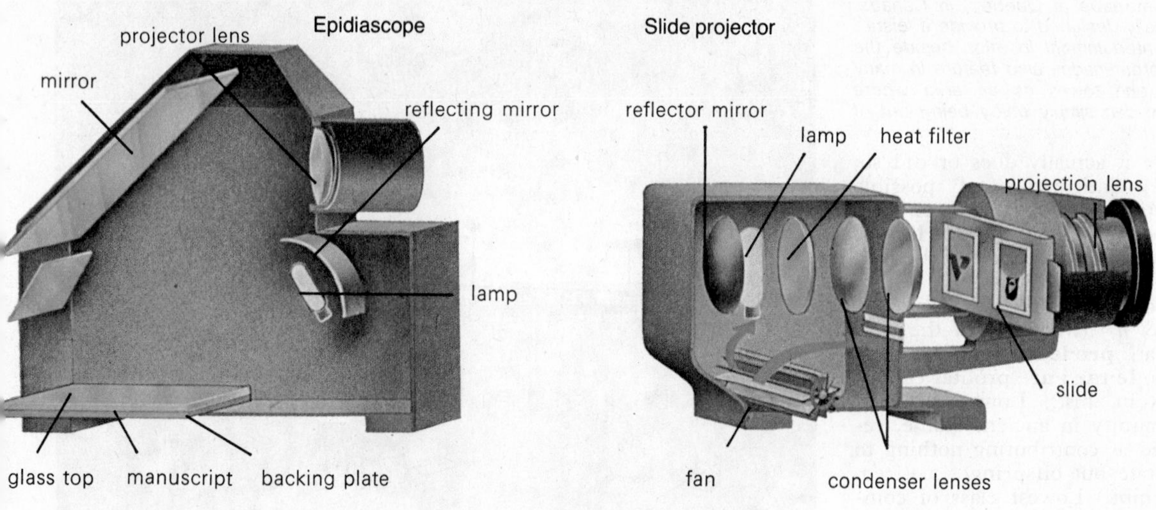

*The development of the **projector** has been rapid. The projection of a still picture became possible in the 1850s with the magic lantern, a forerunner of the slide projector (above). Moving pictures, in 1895, needed advances in photography and in light transmission and mechanics. They enabled a much larger audience to watch performances and led to a new form of entertainment.*

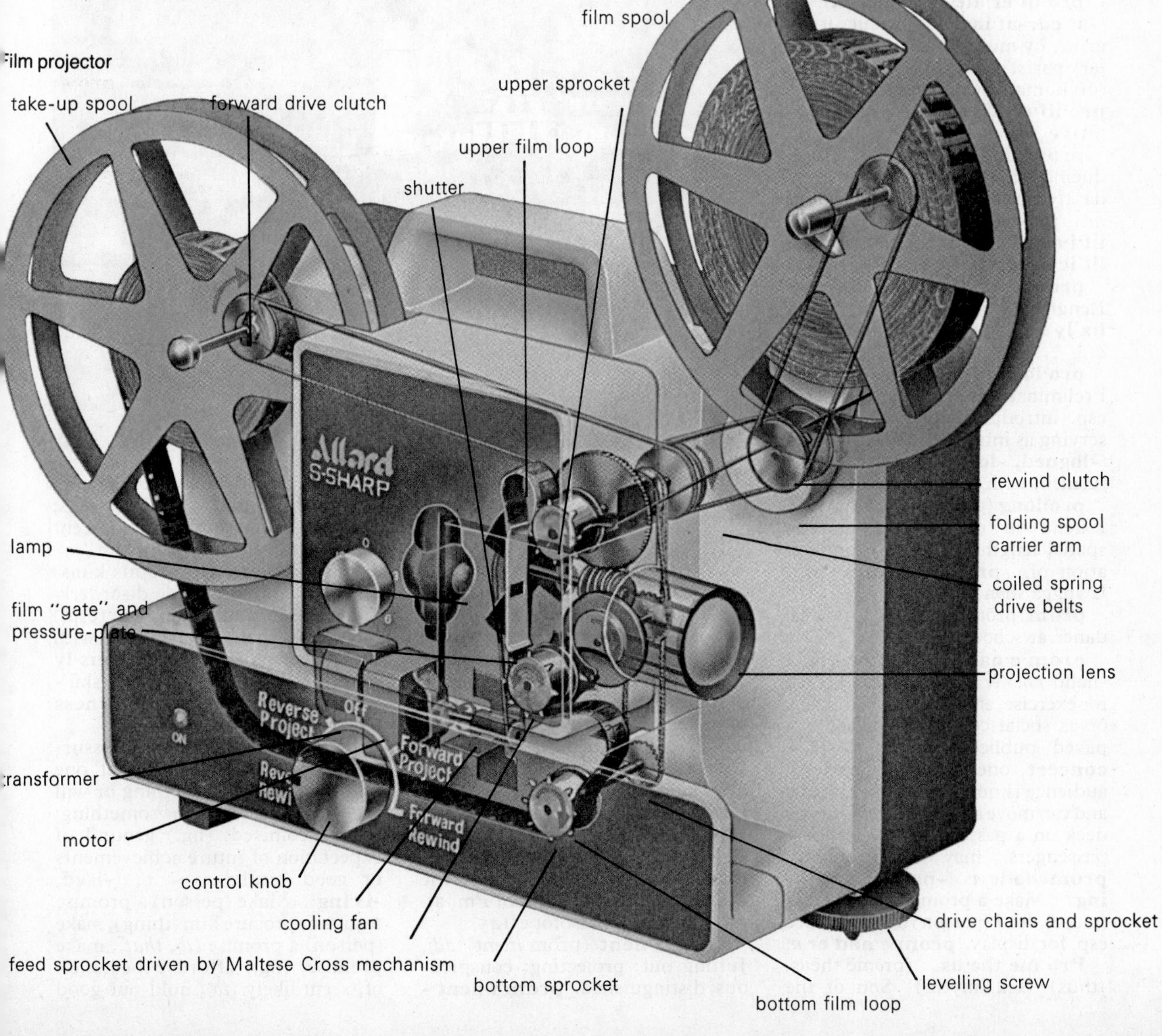

Film projector
film spool
take-up spool
forward drive clutch
upper sprocket
upper film loop
shutter
Allard
S-SHARP
rewind clutch
folding spool
carrier arm
lamp
coiled spring
drive belts
film "gate" and
pressure-plate
projection lens
Reverse Project
Off
Forward Project
Reverse Rewind
Forward Rewind
ON
transformer
motor
control knob
cooling fan
feed sprocket driven by Maltese Cross mechanism
bottom sprocket
drive chains and sprocket
levelling screw
bottom film loop

*A **promenade** at Quebec, in Canada. Originally designed to provide a leisure and entertainment location beside the sea, promenades also feature in many cities and towns as an area where people can simply enjoy being out of doors.*

before it actually does or did so; (rhet.) anticipation of possible objections in order to answer them before they are raised. **pro·lep·tic** (prōlĕp´tĭk) *adj.* **pro·lep´ti·cal·ly** *adv.*

pro·le·tar·i·an (prōlĭtār´ēan) *adj.* & *n.* (Member) of the proletariat. **pro·le·tar´i·an·ism** *n.*

pro·le·tar·i·at (prōlĭtār´ēat) *n.* 1. (Rom. hist.) Lowest class of community in ancient Rome, regarded as contributing nothing to the state but offspring. 2. (freq. contempt.) Lowest class of community; (econ.) class that is dependent on daily labor for subsistence, and has no reserve of capital; sometimes, all wage earners; **dictatorship of the ~**, communist ideal of domination by the proletariat after the suppression of capitalism and the bourgeoisie.

pro·lif·er·ate (prōlĭf´erāt) *v.* (**-at·ed, -at·ing**). Reproduce itself, grow, by multiplication of elementary parts; produce (cells etc.) thus; (of human beings etc.) multiply. **pro·lif·er·a´tion** *n.* **pro·lif´er·a·tive** *adj.*

pro·lif·ic (prōlĭf´ĭk) *adj.* Producing (much) offspring; abundantly productive (*of*), abounding *in*. **pro·lif´i·cal·ly** *adv.* **pro·lif·i·ca·cy** (prōlĭf´ĭkasē), **pro·lif´ic·ness** *ns.*

pro·lix (prōlĭks´, prō´lĭks) *adj.* Lengthy, wordy, tedious. **pro·lix´ly** *adv.* **pro·lix·i·ty** (prōlĭk´sĭtē) *n.*

pro·logue (prō´lawg, -lŏg) *n.* Preliminary discourse, poem, etc., esp. introducing play; act, event, serving as introduction (*to*). ~ *v.t.* (**-logued, -logu·ing**). Introduce, furnish, with a prologue.

pro·long (prolawng´, -lŏng´) *v.t.* Extend in duration; extend in spatial length; lengthen pronunciation of. **pro·lon·ga·tion** (prōlawnggā´shon, -lŏng-) *n.*

prom (prŏm) *n.* (colloq.) Formal dance at school or college.

prom·e·nade (prŏmenād´, -nahd´) *n.* Walk, ride, drive, taken for exercise, amusement, or display, or as social ceremony; place, esp. paved public walk for this; ~ **concert**, one at which (part of) audience is not provided with seats and can move about; ~ **deck**, upper deck on a passenger vessel, where passengers may walk about. **promenade** *v.* (**-nad·ed, -nad·ing**). Make a promenade through (place); lead (person) about a place esp. for display. **prom·e·nad´er** *n.*

Pro·me·the·us (promē´thēus, -thūs). (Gk. myth.) Son of the Titan Iapetus; he made mankind out of clay, taught them many arts, and stole fire for them from heaven; to punish him, Zeus chained him to a rock in the Caucasus, where a vulture fed each day on his liver, which grew again in the night. **Pro·me·the·an** (promē´thēan) *adj.* Of, like, Prometheus in his skill or punishment.

pro·me·thi·um (promē´thēum) *n.* (chem.) Radioactive element of the rare-earth group, formed by the fission of uranium; symbol Pm, at. no. 61, principal isotope 145.

prom·i·nent (prŏm´inent) *adj.* Jutting out, projecting; conspicuous; distinguished. **prom´i·nent·ly** *adv.* **prom´i·nence** *n.* Being prominent; thing that projects; **solar ~**, cloud of incandescent hydrogen projecting from sun.

*The **promontory** at Portland Head in Maine. Because of the way the waves are formed on the headland, the surrounding coastline may become selectively eroded.*

pro·mis·cu·ous (promĭs´kūus) *adj.* Of mixed and disorderly composition; indiscriminate; (esp.) having sexual intercourse with many persons. **pro·mis´cu·ous·ly** *adv.* **prom·is·cu·i·ty** (prŏmĭskū´ĭtē, prōmĭ-), **pro·mis´cu·ous·ness** *ns.*

prom·ise (prŏm´ĭs) *n.* Assurance given to a person that one will do or not do something or will give or procure him something; thing promised; (fig.) ground of expectation of future achievements or good results. ~ *v.* (**-ised, -is·ing**). Make (person) a promise to give or procure him (thing); make (person) a promise (*to, that*); make promise; (fig.) afford expectation of, seem likely (*to*); hold out good etc. prospect; ~ **oneself**, look forward to; **Prom'ised Land**, Canaan, as promised to Abraham and his posterity (Gen. 12, 13, etc.); heaven, any place of expected felicity.

prom·is·ee (prŏmĭsē') *n.* (law) Person to whom promise is made.

prom·is·ing (prŏm'ĭsĭng) *adj.* Likely to turn out well, hopeful, full of promise. **prom'is·ing·ly** *adv.*

prom·is·so·ry (prŏm'ĭsōrē, -sōrē) *adj.* Conveying or implying a promise; ~ **note**, signed document containing written promise to pay stated sum to specified person or to bearer at specified date or on demand.

prom·on·to·ry (prŏm'ontōrē, -tōrē) *n.* (pl. **-ries**). Point of high land jutting out into sea etc., headland; (anat.) any of various protuberances in body.

pro·mote (promōt') *v.t.* (**-mot·ed, -mot·ing**). 1. Advance, prefer (person *to* position, higher office). 2. Help forward, encourage (process, result); support actively the passing of (law). 3. Advance (child) to next grade (in school). 4. (slang) Obtain by trickery or sharp practice. 5. (slang) Organize (boxing match etc.) **pro·mot'er** *n.* 1. One who promotes formation of business company (freq. with implication of fraud or sharp practice). 2. One who promotes (sales, boxing matches, etc.). **pro·mo·tion** (promō'shon) *n.* Promoting; **sales** ~, (commerc.) information or instruction given to dealer by manufacturer or agent to facilitate sale of a product. **pro·mot'a·ble, pro·mo'tive** *adjs.*

Pro·mo·tor Fi·de·i (promō'ter fī'dēī). (R.C. Ch.) Officer of Sacred Congregation of Rites at Rome who advances all possible arguments against candidate for beatification or canonization (pop. called devil's advocate). [L., = "promoter of the faith"]

prompt[1] (prŏmpt) *adj.* Ready in action, acting with alacrity; made, done, etc., readily or at once. **prompt'ly** *adv.* **promp·ti·tude** (prŏmp'tĭtood, -tūd), **prompt'ness** *ns.*

prompt[2] (prŏmpt) *v.t.* 1. Incite, move (person etc. *to*); inspire, give rise to (feeling, thought, action). 2. Supply (actor, reciter) with the words that come next; assist (hestitating speaker) with suggestion. ~ *n.* Thing said to help memory, esp. of actor; **prompt'-book**, copy of play for prompter's use. **prompt'er** *n.* One who prompts, esp. (theatr.) person stationed out of sight of audience to prompt actors.

prom·ul·gate (prŏm'ulgāt, prōmŭl'-) *v.t.* (**-gat·ed, -gat·ing**). Make known to the public, disseminate, proclaim. **prom·ul·ga·tion** (prŏmulgā'shon, prōmul-), **prom'ul·ga·tor** *ns.*

pro·na·os (prōnā'ŏs) *n.* (pl. **-na·oi** pr. -nā'oi). (Gk. antiq.) Space in front of body of temple, enclosed by portico and projecting side walls.

pro·nate (prō'nāt) *v.t.* (**-nat·ed, -nat·ing**). (physiol.) Put (hand, forelimb) into prone position. **pro·na'tion** *n.*

pro·na·tor (prōnā'ter, prō'nā-) *n.* (anat.) Muscle that effects or helps pronation.

prone (prōn) *adj.* 1. Having the front or ventral part downward, lying face downward; (loosely) lying flat, prostrate. 2. (of ground) Having downward aspect or direction; (loosely) steep, headlong. 3. Disposed, liable (*to*). **prone'ly** *adv.* **prone'ness** *n.*

prong (prawng, prŏng) *n.* Forked instrument, e.g. hayfork; each pointed member of fork; **prong'horn (antelope)**, N. Amer. deerlike ruminant (*Antilocapra americana*), both sexes of which have deciduous horns with short prong in front. **prong** *v.t.* Pierce, stab, turn up (soil etc.) with prong. **prong'like** *adj.*

pro·nom·i·nal (prōnŏm'inal) *adj.* Of (the nature of) a pronoun. **pro·nom'i·nal·ly** *adv.*

pro·noun (prō'nown) *n.* Word used instead of (proper or other) noun to designate person or thing already mentioned, known from context, or forming subject of inquiry; **demonstrative** ~**s**, this, that, these, those; **distributive** ~**s**, each, either; **indefinite** ~**s**, any, some, etc.; **interrogative** ~**s**, who? what? which?; **personal** ~**s**, I, we, thou, you, he, she, it, they; **possessive** ~**s**, (also *possessive adjectives*), representing possessive case of personal pronouns (my, our, etc.) with absolute forms (mine, ours, etc.); **reflexive** ~**s**, myself, ourselves, etc.; **relative** ~**s**, who, which, that, what.

pro·nounce (pronowns') *v.* (**-nounced, -nounc·ing**). 1. Utter, deliver (judgment, curse, etc.) formally or solemnly; state, declare, as one's opinion; pass judgment, give one's opinion. 2. Utter, articulate, esp. with reference to different modes of pronunciation; **pronounc'ing dictionary**, one in which pronunciation is indicated. **pro·nounce'a·ble** *adj.* **pro·nounc'er** *n.*

pro·nounced (pronownst') *adj.* (esp.) Strongly marked, decided. **pro·nounc·ed·ly** (pronown'sĭdlē) *adv.*

pro·nun·ci·a·men·to (pronŭnsēamĕn'tō) *n.* (pl. **-tos**). Proclamation, manifesto, esp. (in Spanish-speaking countries) one issued by insurrectionists.

pro·nun·ci·a·tion (pronŭnsēā'shon) *n.* Mode in which a word is pronounced; a person's way of pronouncing words.

proof (proof) *n.* 1. Evidence sufficing or helping to establish a fact; spoken or written legal evidence; proving, demonstration. 2. Test, trial; (place for) testing of firearms or explosives; ~ **stress**, (eng.) load slightly greater than that which a mechanism etc. will normally have to bear. 3. Standard of strength of distilled alcoholic liquors; ~ **spirit**, standard mixture of pure alcohol and water (containing one-half alcohol by volume) in terms of which the alcoholic strengths of liquors are computed. 4. Trial impression taken from type, in which corrections etc. may be made; each of limited number of careful impressions made before printing; **artist's, engraver's** ~,

*The **prong-horned antelope** became nearly extinct as a result of excessive hunting in the 19th century. Now, however, it is protected and has greatly increased in numbers.*

one taken for examination or alteration by him; **signed ~**, early proof signed by artist; **proof'reader**, person employed in reading and correcting printers' proofs; so **proof'read** (*v.*) (**-read, -read·-ing**). 5. Rough uncut edges of shorter or narrower leaves of book, left to show it has not been cut down in binding. **proof** *adj.* (of armor) Of tried strength; impenetrable esp. as second element of compound, as *bomb'proof, wind'-proof*. **proof** *v.t.* Make (thing) proof; make (fabric etc.) waterproof; submit (mechanism etc.) to proof stress.

prop[1] (prŏp) *n.* Rigid support, esp. one not forming structural part of thing supported; (fig.) person etc. who upholds institution etc. ~ *v.t.* (**propped, prop·ping**). Support (as) by prop, hold *up* thus.

prop[2] (prŏp) *n.* (colloq.) Stage property; (pl.) property man etc.

prop[3] (prŏp) *n.* (colloq.) Aircraft propeller.

prop. *abbrev.* Proposition; proper; properly.

prop·a·gan·da (prŏpagăn'da) *n.* 1. (**Congregation, College, of**) **the P ~**, committee of cardinals of R.C. Ch. in charge of foreign missions. 2. Association, organized scheme, for propagation of a doctrine or practice; doctrines, information, etc., thus propagated (freq. with implication of bias or falsity, esp. in politics); efforts, schemes, principles, of propagation. **prop·a·gan·dism** (prŏpagăn'dĭzem) *n.* **prop·a·gan'dist** *n.* & *adj.* **prop·a·gan·dize** (prŏpagăn'dīz) *v.* (**-dized, -diz·ing**).

The same principle is used to pull a small crop-spraying aircraft (1) and an ocean liner (2). However, the ***propeller*** *of an aircraft rotates at high speed and is narrow, while that of a ship has wider blades and moves more slowly in the denser water.*

prop·a·gate (prŏp'agāt) *v.* (**-gat·ed, -gat·ing**). 1. Multiply specimens of (plant, animal, disease, etc.) by natural process from parent stock; (of plant etc.) reproduce (*itself*). 2. Hand down (quality etc.) from one generation to another. 3. Disseminate (statement, belief, practice). 4. Extend the action or operation of, transmit, convey in some direction or through some medium. **prop·a·ga'tion** *n.* **prop'a·ga·tive** *adj.* **prop'a·ga·tor** *n.*

pro·pane (prō'pān) *n.* (chem.) Colorless inflammable hydrocarbon gas (C_3H_8), one of the paraffin series, occurring in natural gases.

pro·pel (propĕl') *v.t.* (**-pelled, -pel·ling**). Drive forward, give onward motion to. **pro·pel'lent** *adj.* Propelling.

pro·pel·lant (propĕl'ant) *n.*

1

2
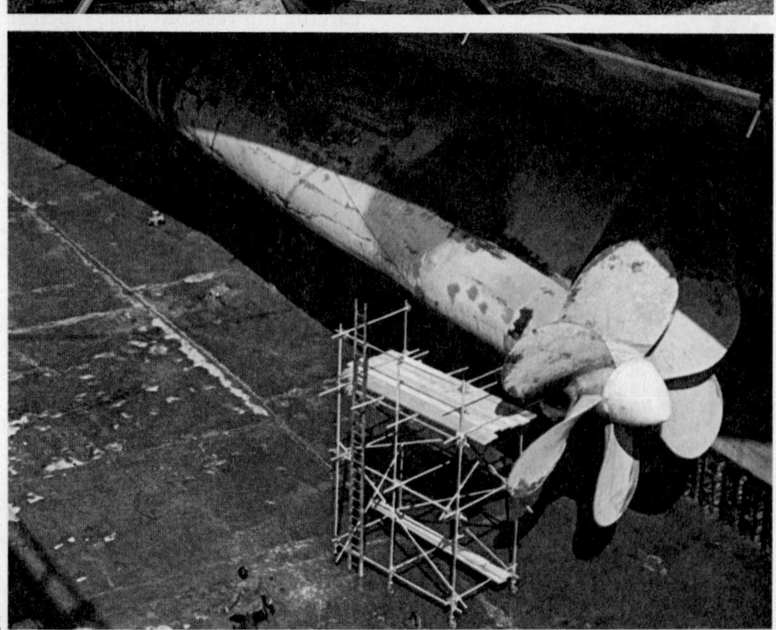

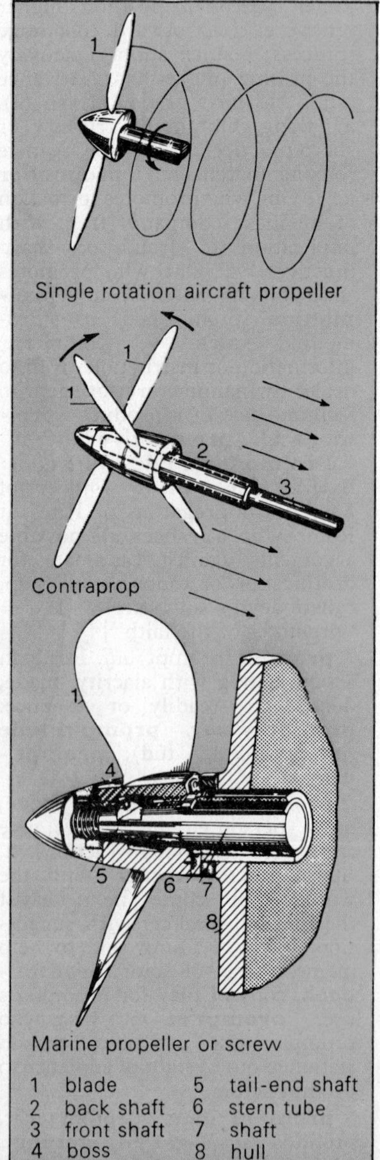

*Construction of the **Propylaea** of the Acropolis at Athens began during the 5th century B.C. But Pericles' concept was never completed, probably because of the costly Peloponnesian War.*

Propelling agent; explosive that propels projectile from firearm; fuel or oxidizer for propelling a rocket.

pro·pel·ler (propĕl′*er*) *n.* (esp.) Revolving shaft with blades usu. set at an angle and twisted like thread of screw, for propelling ship; similar device on an aircraft producing the thrust that drives it forward.

pro·pen·si·ty (propĕn′sĭtē) *n.* (pl. **-ties**). Inclination, tendency (*to, for*).

prop·er (prŏp′*er*) *adj.* 1. (archaic) Own; (astron.) ~ **motion**, that part of apparent motion of fixed star etc. supposed to be due to its actual movement in space. 2. Belonging, relating, exclusively or distinctively (*to*); ~ **name, noun**, name, part of speech, used to designate an individual person, animal, town, ship, etc. 3. Accurate, correct; (usu. following its noun) strictly so called, real, genuine; thorough, complete (colloq.); handsome (archaic); ~ **fraction**, one whose value is less than unity. 4. Suitable, right; in conformity with demands of society, decent, respectable. **prop′er·ly** *adv.* Fittingly, suitably; rightly, duly; with good manners; (colloq.) thoroughly. **prop′er·ness** *n.*

prop·er·ty (prŏp′*er*tē) *n.* (pl. **-ties**). 1. Owning, being owned; thing owned; landed estate; ~ **tax**, one levied directly on property. 2. (theatr.) Portable thing, as article of costume, furniture, etc., used on stage; ~ **man**, person in charge of stage properties. 3. Attribute, quality; (logic) quality common to a whole class but not necessary to distinguish it from others.

proph·e·cy (prŏf′ĭsē) *n.* (pl. **-cies**). Faculty of a prophet; prophetic utterance; foretelling of future events.

proph·e·sy (prŏf′ĭsī) *v.* (**-sied, -sy·ing**). Speak as a prophet, foretell (future events); (archaic) expound the Scriptures. **proph′e·si·er** *n.*

proph·et (prŏf′ĭt) *n.* (fem. **proph·et·ess**, pr. prŏf′ĭtĭs, tĕs). Inspired teacher, revealer or interpreter of God's will; spokesman, advocate (*of*); one who foretells events; (pl.) prophetic writers of the Old Testament, the first four (Isaiah, Jeremiah, Ezekiel, Daniel) being called the **major** ~**s** since more of their writings have survived, and the last 12 (from Hosea to Malachi), the **minor** ~**s** whose extant writings are relatively short; **the P** ~, Muhammad; (also) Joseph Smith, founder of Mormonism.

pro·phet·ic (pr*o*fĕt′ĭk) *adj.* Of a prophet; predicting, containing a prediction *of*. **pro·phet′i·cal** *adj.* **pro·phet′i·cal·ly** *adv.*

pro·phy·lac·tic (prōf*i*lăk′tĭk, prŏf*i*-) *adj.* & *n.* (Medicine, measure) tending to prevent disease. ~ *n.* CONDOM. **pro·phy·lac′ti·cal·ly** *adv.* **pro·phy·lax·is** (prōf*i*lăk′sĭs, prŏf*i*-) *n.* (pl. **-lax·es** pr. -lăk′sēz). Preventive treatment of disease.

pro·pin·qui·ty (prōpĭng′kwĭtē) *n.* Nearness in place; close kinship; similarity.

pro·pi·on·ic (prōpēŏn′ĭk) *adj.* ~ **acid**, colorless liquid with odor resembling that of acetic acid, present in products of the distillation of wood.

pro·pi·ti·ate (prōpĭsh′ēāt, pr*o*-) *v.t.* (**-at·ed, -at·ing**). Appease (offended person etc.); make propitious. **pro·pi·ti·a·ble** (prōpĭsh′ē*a*b*e*l, pr*o*-) *adj.* **pro·pi·ti·a′tion** *n.* Appeasement; atonement; (archaic) gift etc. meant to propitiate. **pro·pi′ti·a·tive** *adj.* **pro·pi′ti·a·tor** *n.*

pro·pi·ti·a·to·ry (prōpĭsh′ē*a*tōrē, -tōrē, pr*o*-) *adj.* Serving, meant, to propitiate.

pro·pi·tious (pr*o*pĭsh′*u*s) *adj.* Well-disposed, favorable; suitable *for*, favorable *to*. **pro·pi′tious·ly** *adv.* **pro·pi′tious·ness** *n.*

pro·por·tion (pr*o*pōr′sh*o*n, -pōr′-) *n.* Comparative part, share; comparative relation, ratio; due relation of one thing to another or between parts of a thing; (pl.) dimensions; (math.) equality of ratios between two pairs of quantities, set of such quantities; (arith.) method by which, three quantities being given, a fourth is found, having same ratio to third as second has to first. ~ *v.t.* Make proportionate *to*. **pro·por′tioned** *adj.* **pro·por′tion·er, pro·por′tion·ment** *ns.*

pro·por·tion·al (pr*o*pōr′sh*o*n*a*l, -pōr′-) *adj.* In due proportion, corresponding in degree or amount; ~ **representation**, method of legislative representation designed to permit the various political parties to be represented in proportion to their voters and characterized by the use of the transferable vote, i.e. the filling up of seats, where a quota is not secured by 1st choices, by the transference of votes from second choices, and so on. **pro·por·tion·al·i·ty** (pr*o*pōrsh*o*năl′ĭtē, -pōr-) *n.* **pro·por′tion·al·ly** *adv.* **pro·por·tion·ate** (pr*o*pōr′sh*o*nĭt, -pōr′-) *adj.* **pro·por′tion·ate·ly** *adv.*

pro·pos·al (pr*o*pō′z*a*l) *n.* Act of proposing something; offer of marriage; scheme of action etc. proposed; formal business offer to perform work.

pro·pose (pr*o*pōz′) *v.* (**-posed, -pos·ing**). Put forward for consideration, propound; set up as an aim; nominate (person) as member of society etc.; offer (person, person's health, etc.) as toast; make offer of marriage (*to*); put forward as a plan; intend, purpose. **pro·pos′a·ble** *adj.* **pro·pos′er** *n.*

prop·o·si·tion (prŏp*o*zĭsh′*o*n) *n.* 1. Statement, assertion, esp. (logic) form of words consisting of predicate and subject connected by copula; (math., abbrev. prop.) formal statement of theorem or problem, freq. including the demonstration. 2. Proposal; task, project, problem for solution. **prop·o·si′tion·al** *adj.* **proposi-**

tion *v.t.* Make a proposition to, esp. in regard to illicit sexual relations.

pro·pound (pr*o*pownd′) *v.t.* Offer for consideration, propose (question, problem, scheme, etc.). **pro·pound′er** *n.*

pro·pri·e·tar·y (pr*o*prī′ĭtĕrē) *adj.* Of a proprietor; holding property; held in private ownership (esp. of medicines etc. of which manufacture or sale is restricted by patent or otherwise). ~ *n.* (pl. **-tar·ies**). Proprietorship; body of proprietors.

pro·pri·e·tor (pr*o*prī′ĭter) *n.* (fem. **pro·pri·e·tress**, pr. pr*o*prī′ĭtrĭs). Owner. **pro·pri·e·to·ri·al** (pr*o*prīĭtōr′ēal, -tōr′-) *adj.* **pro·pri·e·to′ri·al·ly** *adv.* **pro·pri′e·tor·ship** *n.*

pro·pri·e·ty (pr*o*prī′ĭtē) *n.* (pl. **-ties**). Fitness, rightness; correctness of behavior or morals; (pl.) details of correct conduct.

pro·pul·sion (pr*o*pŭl′sh*o*n) *n.* Driving or pushing forward; means of this; (fig.) impelling influence. **pro·pul·sive** (pr*o*pŭl′sĭv) *adj.*

pro·pyl (prō′pĭl) *n.* (chem.) Hydrocarbon radical C_3H_7; ~ **alcohol**, colorless liquid (C_3H_7OH), occurring in fusel oil and separated by distillation, used as a solvent. **pro·pyl·ene** (prō′p*i*lēn) *n.* Colorless hydrocarbon gas (C_3H_6), occurring esp. in the gases from the cracking of petroleum.

prop·y·lae·um (prŏp*i*lē′*u*m) *n.* (pl. **-lae·a** pr. -lē′*a*). Entrance to temple; **Propylaea**, entrance to the Acropolis at Athens.

pro ra·ta (prō rā′t*a*, rah′t*a*). Proportional(ly). **pro-ra′ta** *adj.*

pro·sa·ic (prōzā′ĭk) *adj.* Like prose, lacking poetic beauty; unromantic, commonplace, dull. **pro·sa′i·cal·ly** *adv.* **pro·sa′ic·ness** *n.*

After the execution of Charles I of England various attempts were made at Parliamentary rule. These failed, and Oliver Cromwell (1) became ***Lord Protector,*** *ruling mainly through the army. On his death his son Richard (2) tried unsuccessfully to assume power.*

pro·sce·ni·um (prōsē′nē*u*m) *n.* (pl. **-ni·a** pr. -nē*a*). 1. (Gk. and Rom. antiq.) Stage. 2. (in theater) Space between curtain and orchestra, esp. with the enclosing arch.

Although geological surveys using all the resources of modern technology are made before new mines are sunk, there is still room for the old-style ***prospector*** *to pan for gold.*

pro·scribe (prōskrīb′) *v.t.* (**-scribed, -scrib·ing**). Put (person) out of protection of law; banish, exile; reject, denounce (practice etc.) as dangerous etc. **pro·scrib′er, pro·scrip·tion** (prōskrĭp′sh*o*n) *n.* **pro·scrip·tive** (prōskrĭp′tĭv) *adj.* **pro·scrip′tive·ly** *adv.*

prose (prōz) *n.* Ordinary nonmetrical form of written or spoken language; plain matter-of-fact quality; tedious discourse. ~ *v.* (**prosed, pros·ing**). Talk prosily.

pros·e·cute (prŏs′*e*kūt) *v.t.* (**-cut·ed, -cut·ing**). 1. Follow up, pursue (inquiry, studies); carry on (trade, pursuit). 2. Institute legal proceedings against or with reference to. **pros′e·cut·a·ble** *adj.*

pros·e·cu·tion (prŏs*e*kū′sh*o*n) *n.* Prosecuting; carrying on of legal proceedings against person; prosecuting party; (law) institution and pursuit of criminal charge before court.

pros·e·cu·tor (prŏs′*e*kūt*er*) *n.* One who prosecutes, esp. in criminal court; **public** ~, law officer conducting criminal proceedings in public interest.

pros·e·lyte (prŏs′*e*līt) *n.* Convert from one opinion, creed, or party, to another; convert to another faith. ~ *v.t.* (**-lyt·ed, -lyt·ing**). Make proselyte of. **pros·e·lyt·ism** (prŏs′*e*lĭtĭz*e*m, -lī-) *n.* **pros·e·lyt·ize** (prŏs′*e*lĭtīz, -lī-) *v.t.* (**-ized, -iz·ing**). **pros′e·lyt·iz·er** *n.*

Pro·ser·pi·na (prōsẽr′p*i*n*a*), **Pro·ser·pi·ne** (prōsẽr′p*i*nē, prŏs′*e*rpīn) = PERSEPHONE.

pros·o·dy (prŏs′*o*dē) *n.* Science or study of versification. **pro-**

sod·ic (pr*o*sŏd´ĭk, -zŏd´-), **pro·sod´i·cal** *adjs.* **pro·sod´i·cal·ly** *adv.* **pros´o·dist** *n.*

pros·pect (prŏs´pĕkt) *n.* 1. Extensive view of landscape etc.; mental scene. 2. Expectation; what one expects. 3. (colloq.) Possible or likely purchaser, subscriber, etc. 4. (mining) Spot giving prospects of mineral deposit; sample of ore for testing, resulting yield. ~ *v.* Explore region (*for* gold etc.); explore (region) for gold etc., work (mine) experimentally; (of mine) promise (well, ill; specified yield). **pros·pec·tor** (prŏs´pĕkt*er*, pr*o*s-pĕk´-) *n.*

pro·spec·tive (pr*o*spĕk´tĭv) *adj.* Concerned with, applying to, the future; expected, future, some day to be. **pro·spec´tive·ly** *adv.*

pro·spec·tus (pr*o*spĕk´t*u*s) *n.* (pl. **-tus·es**). Circular describing chief features of school, commercial enterprise, forthcoming book, etc.

pros·per (prŏs´p*er*) *v.* Succeed, thrive; make successful. **pros´per·ing** *adj.* **pros·per·i·ty** (prŏs-pĕr´ĭtē) *n.*

pros·per·ous (prŏs´p*er*us) *adj.* Flourishing, successful, thriving; auspicious. **pros´per·ous·ly** *adv.* **pros´per·ous·ness** *n.*

pros·tate (prŏs´tāt) *n.* (also ~ **gland**) Large gland, accessory to male generative organs and surrounding neck of bladder and commencement of urethra. **pros·tat·ic** (prŏstăt´ĭk) *adj.*

pros·the·sis (prŏs´thĭsĭs; also for def. 1 prŏsthē´sĭs) *n.* (pl. **-ses** pr. -sēz). 1. (surg.) Making up of deficiencies (with artificial teeth, limb, etc.); this as branch of surgery. 2. (gram.) Addition of letter or syllable at beginning of word. **pros·thet·ic** (prŏsthĕt´ĭk) *adj.* Of prosthesis; (biochem.) of a group or radical of a different kind added or substituted in a compound.

pros·ti·tute (prŏs´tĭtoot, -tūt) *n.* One who engages in indiscriminate sexual intercourse for payment. ~ *v.t.* (**-tut·ed, -tut·ing**). Make a prostitute of; (fig.) sell for base gain, put (abilities etc.) to ignoble use. **pros·ti·tu·tion** (prŏstĭtoo´sh*o*n, -tū´-) *n.*

pros·trate (prŏs´trāt) *adj.* Lying with face to ground, esp. as token of submission or humility; lying in horizontal position; overcome, overthrown; physically exhausted; (bot.) lying flat on ground. ~ *v.t.* (**-trat·ed, -trat·ing**). Lay flat on ground; cast *oneself* down prostrate; (fig.) overcome, make submissive; (of fatigue etc.) reduce to extreme physical weakness. **pros·tra·tion** (prŏstrā´sh*o*n) *n.*

pro·style (prō´stīl) *adj.* & *n.*

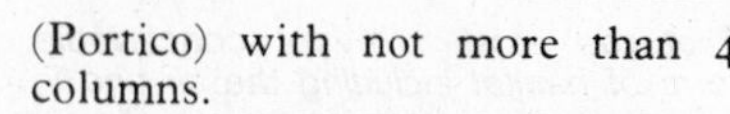

(Portico) with not more than 4 columns.

pros·y (prō´zē) *adj.* (**pros·i·er, pros·i·est**). Commonplace, tedious, dull. **pros´i·ly** *adv.* **pros´i·ness** *n.*

pro·tac·tin·i·um (prōtăktĭn´-ē*u*m) *n.* (chem.) Radioactive element of the actinium series, which by disintegration yields actinium; symbol Pa, at. no. 91, at. wt. 231.0359.

pro·tag·o·nist (prōtăg´*o*nĭst) *n.* Chief person in drama or plot of story; leading person in contest, champion of cause, etc.

Pro·tag·o·ras (prōtăg´*er*as) (5th c. B.C.). Greek sophist philosopher; portrayed in Plato's dialogue of that name.

pro·ta·mine (prō´t*a*mēn, -mĭn) *n.* (chem.) One of the simple basic proteins, present only in sperm, containing a higher percentage of nitrogen than most proteins.

pro·te·an (prō´tē*a*n, prōtē´-) *adj.* Variable, versatile; of or like Proteus.

pro·tect (pr*o*tĕkt´) *v.t.* Keep safe, defend, guard (*from, against*); provide (machinery etc.) with appliances to prevent injury from it; (econ.) guard (home, industry) against competition by imposing tariffs on foreign goods. **pro·tect´ing** *adj.* **pro·tect´ing·ly** *adv.*

pro·tec·tion (pr*o*tĕk´sh*o*n) *n.* Protecting, defense; patronage; protecting person or thing; safe conduct; system or policy of protecting home industries by tariffs etc.; security from threatened violence, obtained by payment to racketeers; such payment. **pro·tec´tion·ism, pro·tec´tion·ist** *ns.*

pro·tec·tive (pr*o*tĕk´tĭv) *adj.* Serving to protect; ~ **custody**, detention of person by government ostensibly for his own protection. **pro·tec´tive·ly** *adv.* **pro·tec´tive·ness** *n.*

pro·tec·tor (pr*o*tĕk´t*er*) *n.* (fem. **pro·tec·tress** pr. pr*o*tĕk´trĭs). Person who protects; thing, device, that protects; regent in charge of kingdom during minority, absence, etc., of sovereign; **Lord P ~ of the Commonwealth**, title of Oliver Cromwell 1653–8 and Richard Cromwell 1658–9. **pro·tec´tor·al** *adj.* **pro·tec´tor·ship** *n.*

pro·tec·tor·ate (pr*o*tĕk´t*er*ĭt) *n.* 1. Office of protector of kingdom or nation; period of this. 2. Authority assumed by a strong nation over a weak or underdeveloped one that it protects and partially controls; period of such authority; state so protected.

pro·té·gé, fem. **pro·té·gée** (prō´-t*e*zhā, prōt*e*zhā´) *ns.* Person under protection or patronage of another.

pro·te·i·form (prōtē´ĭfôrm) *adj.* Multiform, extremely changeable.

pro·tein (prō´tēn, -tēĭn) *n.* Any

__Proteins__ are essential parts of animal diet: many of their constituent amino acids cannot be made in the human body and so have to be taken in as food, often in the form of meat, to maintain tissue growth.

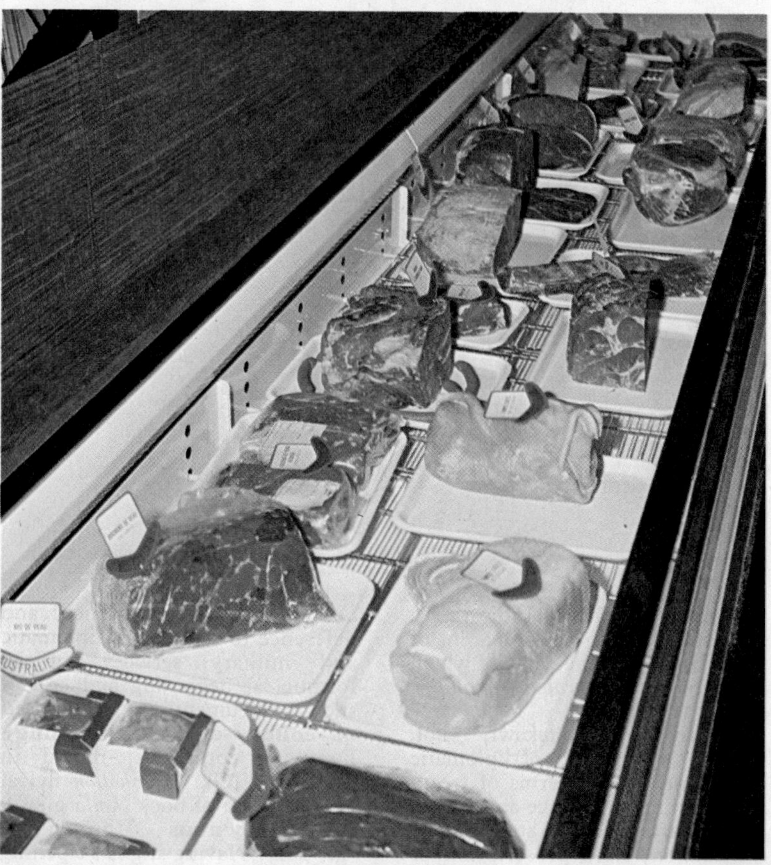

***Protozoa** exist in every conceivable form of habitat including the air and in animal bodies. While some are harmless, others cause malaria, amoebic dysentery and other major diseases.*

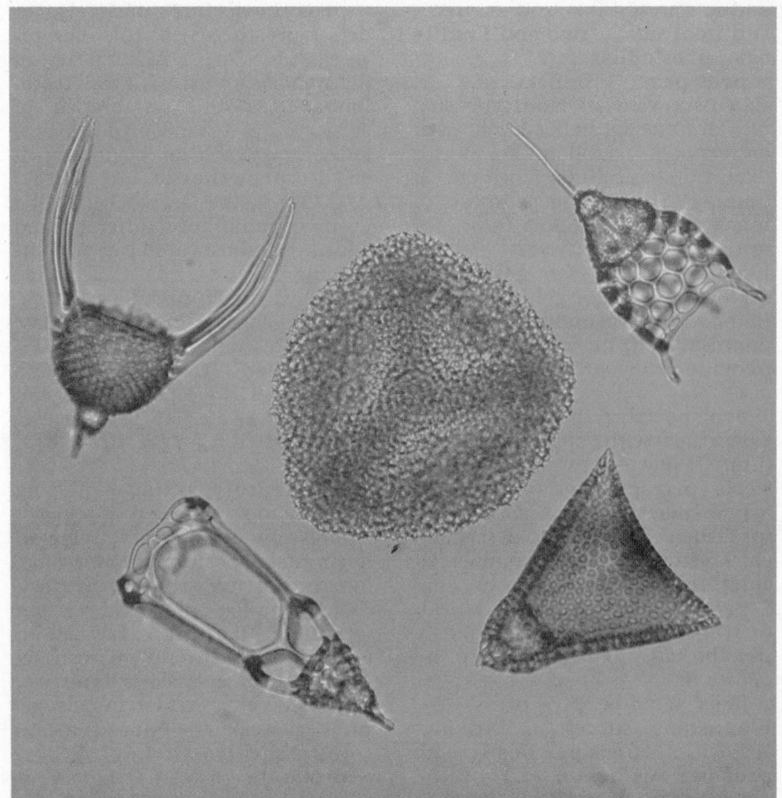

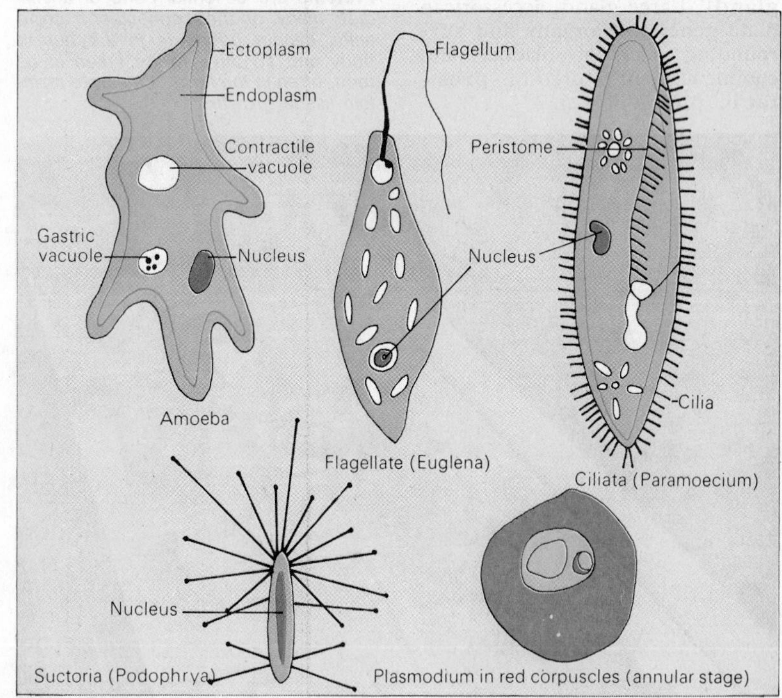

of a class of organic compounds (of carbon, hydrogen, oxygen, nitrogen, and often sulfur) forming an important part of all living organisms and the essential nitrogenous constituents of the food of animals.

pro tem·po·re (prō tĕm′perē). (abbrev. pro tem) For the time, temporary, temporarily. [L.]

pro·test (prō′tĕst) *n.* Formal statement of dissent or disapproval, remonstrance; (sports) formal objection to (umpire's etc.) decision. ~ *v.* (protĕst′, prō-, prō′tĕst). Affirm solemnly; make (freq. written) protest *against* (action, proposal). **pro·test′er** *n.* **pro·test′ing·ly** *adv.*

prot·es·tant (prŏt′ĭstant) *n.* 1. **P**~, member, adherent, of any of the Christian churches or bodies that repudiated papal authority and were separated from R.C. communion in the Reformation (16th c.), or of any church or body descended from them; (hist., usu. pl.) those German princes and free cities that dissented from the decision of the Diet of Speyer (1529), which reaffirmed the edict of the Diet of Worms against the Reformation. 2. (also pr. protĕs′tant) One who protests. **Prot′es·tant·ism** *n.* **Prot′es·tant** *adj.* Of Protestants or Protestantism; ~ **Episcopal Church**: see EPISCOPAL.

prot·es·ta·tion (prŏtĭstā′shon, prōtĭ-) *n.* Solemn affirmation; protest.

Pro·te·us (prō′tēus, -tūs). (Gk. myth.) Sea god, son of Oceanus and Tethys, with power of assuming different shapes.

pro·tha·la·mi·on (prōthalā′mēon) *n.* (pl. **-mi·a** pr. -mēa). Song or poem celebrating a marriage.

proth·e·sis (prŏth′ĭsĭs) *n.* (pl. **-ses** pr. -sēz). 1. (eccles.) Placing of the elements etc. in readiness for use in the Mass; table on which elements are placed, part of the church where this stands. 2. (gram.) = PROSTHESIS. **pro·thet·ic** (prothĕt′ĭk) *adj.* **pro·thet′i·cal·ly** *adv.*

pro·thon·o·tar·y (prōthŏn′otĕrē, prōthonō′terē) *n.* (pl. **-tar·ies**). Chief clerk in some law courts; **P~ Apostolic(al)**, (R.C. Ch.) member of the chief college of prelates in the Curia; ~ **warbler**, brilliant yellow songbird, *Protonotaria citrea*, of eastern U.S.

pro·ti·um (prō′tēum, -shēum) *n.* Common isotope of hydrogen, as dist. from the heavy isotopes deuterium and tritium.

proto- *prefix.* 1. First, primary, primitive. 2. (chem.) Indicating a substance held to be the parent of the substance to the name of which it is prefixed, as *protoactinium* (= PROTACTINIUM).

pro·to·col (prō′tokawl, -kŏl, -kōl) *n.* Original draft of diplomatic document, esp. of terms of treaty agreed to in conference and signed by the parties; formal statement of transaction; rigid prescription or observance of precedence and deference to rank as in diplomatic and military services; official formula at beginning and end of such a document. ~ *v.* (**-coled** or **-colled, -col·ing** or **-col·ling**). Draw up protocols; record in protocol. [Gk. *protokollon* flyleaf glued to case of book (*kolla* glue)]

pro·to·gy·nous (prōtojī′nus, -gī′-) *adj.* Having stigmas ripening

The ancient towns of ***Provence*** *such as Les Baux (left), seem almost to have grown out of the rocks, their square, flat-topped houses echoing nature's forms.*

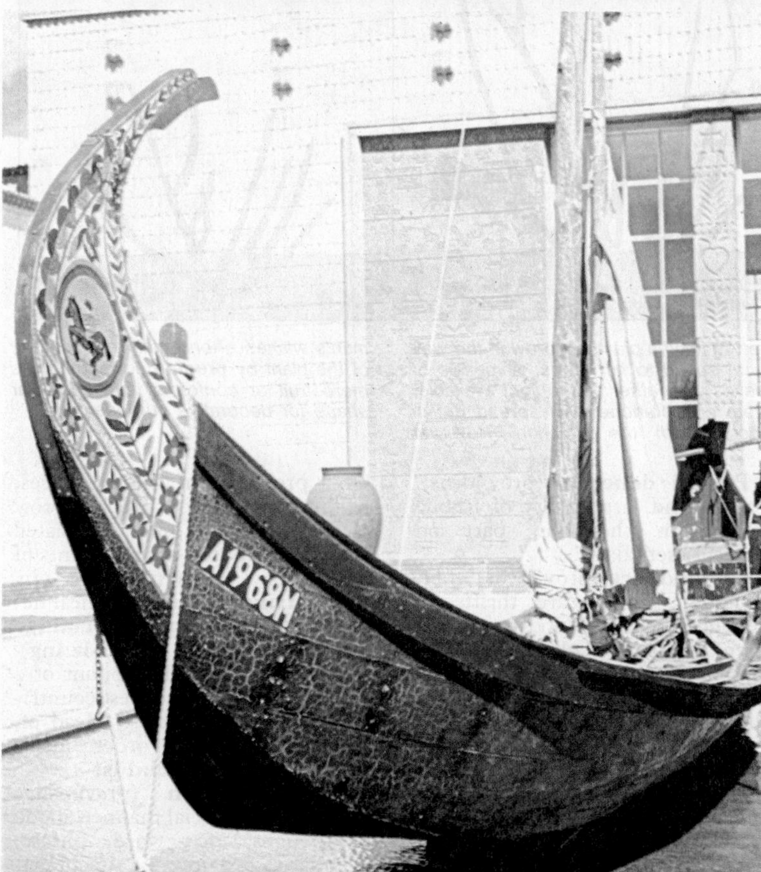

The ***prow*** *of a Portuguese fishing boat is similar to that of a Venetian gondola, and may also be a relic of earlier times when prows carried spikes to ram other vessels.*

before the stamens.

pro·ton (prō′tŏn) *n.* (phys. chem.) Fundamental atomic particle forming part (or in hydrogen the whole) of the nucleus, having a single positive electric charge equal and opposite to that of the electron.

pro·ton·o·tar·y (prōtŏn′*o*tĕrē, prōt*o*nō′*te*rē) (pl. **-tar·ies**) = PROTHONOTARY.

pro·to·phyte (prō′t*o*fīt) *n.* Unicellular plant.

pro·to·plasm (prō′t*o*plăz*e*m) *n.* Viscous translucent substance, the essential matter of living organisms, the substance of which cells principally consist, capable of being irritated, of moving spontaneously, contracting itself, assimilating other matter, and reproducing itself, differentiated (in most organisms) into the *nucleus*, or reproductive part, and the *cytoplasm*, a viscous fluid forming the general body of the cell. **pro·to·plas·mic** (prōt*o*plăz′mĭk) *adj.*

pro·to·plast (prō′t*o*plăst) *n.* Mass of cytoplasm that is visibly distinct from the rest. **pro·to·plas′tic** *adj.*

pro·to·type (prō′t*o*tīp) *n.* Original thing or person in relation to any copy, imitation, representation, later specimen, improved form, etc. **pro·to·typ·al** (prōt*o*tī′p*a*l), **pro·to·typ·ic** (prōt*o*tĭp′ĭk), **pro·to·typ′i·cal** *adjs.*

pro·to·zo·an (prōt*o*zō′*a*n) *n.* Member of the Protozoa, a division of the animal kingdom comprising animals of the simplest type, each essentially consisting of a simple cell, usu. of microscopic size.

pro·to·zo·ic (prōt*o*zō′ĭk) *adj.* (geol., of strata) Containing earliest traces of living beings.

pro·to·zo·on (prōt*o*zō′ŏn, -*o*n) (pl. **-zo·a** pr. -zō′*a*) = PROTOZOAN.

pro·tract (prōtrăkt′) *v.t.* 1. Prolong, lengthen out; extend. 2. Draw (plan of ground etc.) to scale. **pro·tract′ed** *adj.* **pro·tract′ed·ly** *adv.* **pro·tract′ed·ness** *n.* **pro·tract′i·ble** *adj.* **pro·trac′tive** *adj.*

pro·trac·tile (prōtrăk′tĭl, -tīl) *adj.* (zool.) (of organ etc.) That can be extended.

pro·trac·tion (prōtrăk′sh*o*n) *n.* 1. Protracting; action of protractor muscle. 2. Drawing to scale.

pro·trac·tor (prōtrăk′t*er*) *n.* 1. Instrument for setting off and measuring angles, usu. in form of graduated semicircle. 2. (physiol.) Muscle serving to extend limb etc.

pro·trude (prōtrōōd′) *v.* (**-trud·ed, -trud·ing**). Thrust forth, cause to project; stick out, project; obtrude. **pro·tru′dent** *adj.* **pro·tru·sion** (prōtrōō′zh*o*n) *n.* **pro·tru·si·ble** (prōtrōō′s*i*b*e*l), **pro·tru′sive** *adjs.*

pro·tu·ber·ant (prōtōō′b*e*r*a*nt, -tū′-) *adj.* Bulging out, prominent. **pro·tu′ber·ance** *n.* **pro·tu′ber·ant·ly** *adv.*

proud (prowd) *adj.* 1. Valuing oneself highly or too highly, esp. on the ground *of* (qualities, rank, etc.); haughty, arrogant; feeling oneself greatly honored; feeling or showing a proper pride; (of actions etc.) showing pride; of which one is or may be justly proud. 2. (of things) Imposing, splendid; slightly projecting; (of flesh) overgrown, around healing wound; (of waters) swollen, in flood. ~ *adv.* **do someone** ~, treat someone generously or lavishly. **proud'ly** *adv.* **proud'ness** *n.*

Proust (proo͞st), **Marcel** (1871–1922). French novelist; author of the series of volumes grouped under the title *Remembrance of Things Past.*

Prov. *abbrev.* Proverbs (Old Testament); Provence; Provençal; provost; province.

prove (proo͞v) *v.* (**proved, proved** or **prov·en, prov·ing**). 1. Test qualities of, try (archaic exc. in technical uses); subject (manufactured article etc.) to testing process; (arith.) test correctness of (calculation); take proof impression of (composed type, stereotype plate, etc.). 2. Establish as true, demonstrate truth of by evidence or argument; establish genuineness and validity of, obtain probate of (will). 3. Show itself, turn out, to be (or *to* be or do); ~ **oneself**, prove one's ability, character, etc. **prov·en** (proo͞'ven) *adj.* **not** ~, not proved (verdict used in certain courts outside the U.S. when evidence is legally insufficient to justify conviction). **prov'a·ble** *adj.* **prov'a·ble·ness** *n.* **prov'a·bly** *adv.* **prov'er** *n.*

prov·e·nance (prŏv'enans) *n.* (Place of) origin.

Pro·ven·çal (prōvensahl', prŏven-; *Fr.* prawvahnsăl') *adj.* & *n.* Native, inhabitant of Provence; (of) the Romance language spoken in S. France, esp. in the old province of Provence.

Pro·vence (prawvahns'). District, former province, of SE. France; orig. a Roman province, the 1st to be established outside Italy. [L. *provincia* (*romana*) (the Roman) province]

prov·en·der (prŏv'ender) *n.* Food, provisions, esp. for horses.

prov·erb (prŏv'erb) *n.* Short pithy saying in general use, adage, saw; byword, thing that is proverbial or matter of common talk; (**Book of**) **Proverbs**, didactic poetical book of Old Testament consisting of maxims ascribed to Solomon and others.

pro·ver·bi·al (provĕr'bēal) *adj.* Of, expressed in, proverbs; that has become a proverb or byword, notorious. **pro·ver'bi·al·ly** *adv.*

pro·vide (provīd') *v.* (**-vid·ed, -vid·ing**). 1. Make due preparation (*for, against*); stipulate (*that*); (freq. ~ **with**) give or lend (what is needed); make provision, esp. secure maintenance (*for*). 2. (hist.) Appoint (incumbent *to* benefice); (of pope) appoint (successor *to* benefice not yet vacant). **pro·vid'a·ble** *adj.* **pro·vid'er** *n.*

pro·vid·ed (provī'dĭd), **pro·vid·ing** (provī'dĭng) *conjs.* On the condition or understanding (*that*).

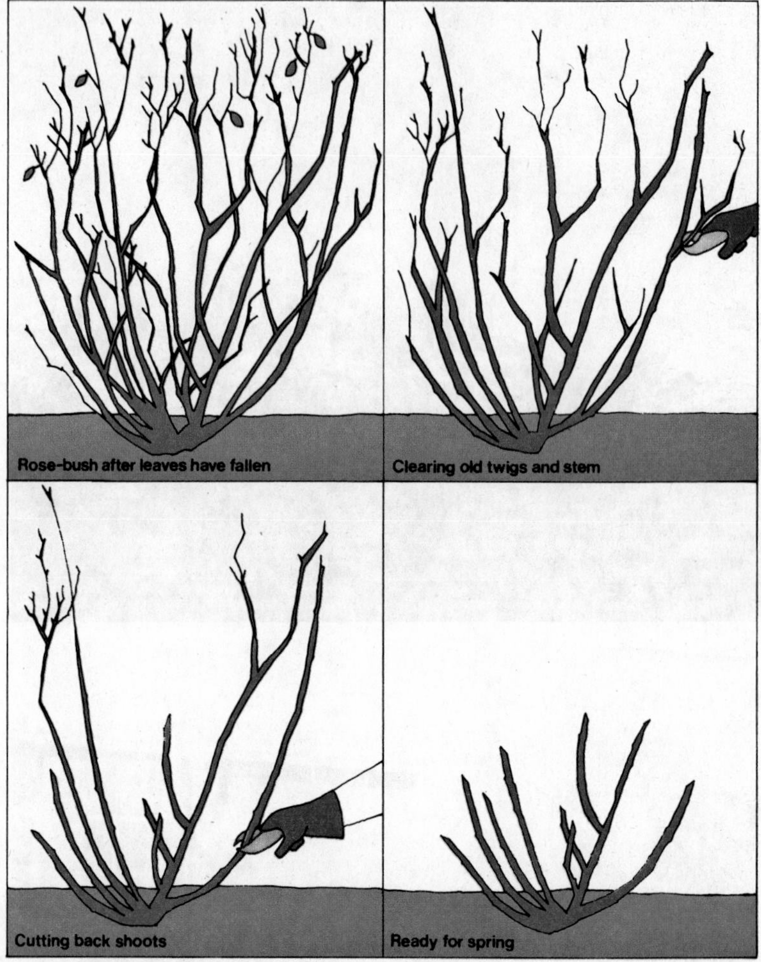

Left to itself a plant will grow in the way most suited to its needs. A mosaic of leaves will gather all the light available, stem and branches will spread out in accord with the situation. However man's wishes often entail restructuring of the plant by ***pruning*** *so that it gives more fruit or conforms to a particular shape for decorative purposes.*

Prov·i·dence (prŏv'ĭdens). Capital and largest city of Rhode Island, in the NE. part on Narragansett Bay.

prov·i·dence (prŏv'ĭdens) *n.* 1. Foresight, timely care; thrift. 2. Beneficent care of God or nature; **special** ~, particular instance of this. 3. **P**~, God.

prov·i·dent (prŏv'ĭdent) *adj.* Having or showing foresight, thrifty. **prov'i·dent·ly** *adv.*

prov·i·den·tial (prŏvĭdĕn'shal) *adj.* Of, by, divine foresight or interposition; opportune, lucky. **prov·i·den'tial·ly** *adv.*

prov·ince (prŏv'ĭns) *n.* 1. (Rom. hist.) Territory outside Italy under Roman governor. 2. Administrative (esp. principal) division of country or government, esp. one that has been historically, linguistically, etc., distinct; (eccles.) district under archbishop or metropolitan; (usu. joc.) **the** ~**s,** all parts of country outside the principal city. 3. Sphere of action, business; branch of learning etc.

pro·vin·cial (provĭn'shal) *adj.* Of a province; of the provinces; having the manners, speech, narrow views or interests, etc., associated with or attributed to inhabitants of provinces. **pro·vin'cial·ly** *adv.* **pro·vin·ci·al·i·ty** (provĭnshēăl'ĭtē) *n.* (pl. **-ties**). **pro·vin·cial·ize** (provĭn'shalīz) *v.t.* (**-ized, -iz·ing**). **provincial** *n.* 1. Inhabitant of a province or the provinces; countrified person. 2. (eccles.) Head of, chief of religious order in, a province. **pro·vin'cial·ist** *n.*

pro·vin·cial·ism (provĭn'shalĭzem) *n.* Provincial manner, mode of thought, etc.; word, phrase, peculiar to province(s); attachment to one's local area, esp. its customs and standards.

pro·vi·sion (provĭzh'on) *n.* 1. Providing (*for, against*); provided amount *of* something; (pl.) supply of food and drink. 2. Legal or formal statement providing for something; clause of this; (English hist., pl.) certain statutes or ordinances. ~ *v.t.* Supply with provisions. **pro·vi'sion·er** *n.*

pro·vi·sion·al (provĭzh'onal),

pro·vi·sion·ar·y (provĭzh'onĕrē) *adjs.* For the time being, temporary, subject to revision. **pro·vi'sion·al·ly** *adv.*

pro·vi·so (provī'zō) *n.* (pl. **-sos, -soes**). Stipulation; clause of stipulation or limitation in document.

prov·o·ca·tion (prŏvokā'shon) *n.* Incitement, instigation, irritation.

pro·voc·a·tive (provŏk'atĭv) *adj.* Tending to provocation (*of* curiosity etc.); intentionally irritating. **pro·voc'a·tive·ly** *adv.* **pro·voc'a·tive·ness** *n.*

pro·voke (provōk') *v.t.* (**-voked, -vok·ing**). Rouse, incite (*to*); irritate; instigate, tempt, allure; call forth (anger, inquiry, etc.); cause. **pro·vok'er** *n.* **pro·vok'ing** *adj.* **pro·vok'ing·ly** *adv.*

pro·vost (prō'vōst, prŏv'ost, prō'vost) *n.* 1. Administrative officer in some universities; (hist.) head of chapter or religious community; Protestant clergyman in charge of principal church of town etc. in Germany etc. 2. (mil., usu. prō'vō) Officer of military police in garrison, camp, etc.; ~ **marshal**, head of military police in camp or on active service; naval officer in charge of prisoner to be tried in court martial. **prov'ost·ship** *n.*

prow (prow) *n.* Forepart of boat or ship, bow.

prow·ess (prow'ĭs) *n.* Valor, gallantry; exceptional ability.

prowl (prowl) *v.* Go about in search of plunder or prey; traverse (streets, place) thus. **prowl'er** *n.* **prowl'ing·ly** *adv.* **prowl** *n.* Prowling; **on the** ~, searching stealthily; ~ **car**, (slang) police car.

prox·i·mal (prŏk'simal) *adj.* (anat.) Situated toward center of body or point of attachment. **prox'i·mal·ly** *adv.*

prox·i·mate (prŏk'simĭt) *adj.* Nearest, next before or after; approximate; nearly accurate. **prox'i·mate·ly** *adv.*

prox·im·i·ty (prŏksĭm'ĭtē) *n.* Nearness in space, time, etc.; ~ **of blood**, kinship.

prox·y (prŏk'sē) *n.* (pl. **prox·ies**). Agency of substitute or deputy; person authorized to act for another; writing authorizing person to vote on behalf of another, vote so given; (attrib.) done, given, made, by proxy.

prude (pro͞od) *n.* Person of extreme (esp. affected) propriety in conduct or speech. **prud·er·y** (pro͞o'derē) *n.* **prud'ish** *adj.* **prud'ish·ly** *adv.* **prud'ish·ness** *n.*

pru·dent (pro͞o'dent) *adj.* Sagacious, discreet, worldly wise. **pru'dent·ly** *adv.* **pru'dence** *n.*

pru·den·tial (pro͞odĕn'shal) *adj.* Of, involving, marked by prudence. **pru·den'tial·ly** *adv.*

prune[1] (pro͞on) *n.* Dried plum; color of its juice, dark reddish purple.

prune[2] (pro͞on) *v.t.* (**pruned, prun·ing**). Trim (tree etc.) by cutting away superfluous branches etc.; lop *off*, *away* (branches etc.); (fig.) remove (superfluities), clear *of* what is superfluous; **prun'ing hook**, curved knife used for pruning.

pru·ri·ent (proor'ēent) *adj.* Given to the indulgence of lewd ideas. **pru'ri·ence, pru'ri·en·cy** *ns.* **pru'ri·ent·ly** *adv.*

pru·ri·tus (pro͞orī'tus) *n.* (med.) Itching of skin. **pru·rit·ic** (pro͞orĭt'ĭk) *adj.*

Prus·sia (prŭsh'a). (Ger. *Preussen*) Former state of N. Europe; a kingdom 1701–1871; the dominant federal state of Germany 1871–1918; a republic until 1946, when Germany as a political unit was formally dissolved by the Allied Control Council, and the land divided among East and West Germany, Poland, and the U.S.S.R.

Prus·sian (prŭsh'an) *adj.* Of Prussia, its people or language; ~ **blue** (so-called from its discovery in Berlin, 1704), deep greenish-blue pigment of great covering power, formerly regarded as ferric ferrocyanide. ~ *n.* Prussian person or language; **Old** ~, language that became extinct in 17th c., belonging to the Baltic group of languages.

prus·sic (prŭs'ĭk) *adj.* Of, got from, Prussian blue; ~ **acid**, solution in water of hydrocyanic acid.

pry[1] (prī) *v.i.* (**pried, pry·ing**). Look, peer, inquisitively; inquire impertinently *into*. **pry'ing** *adj.* **pry'ing·ly** *adv.*

pry[2] (prī) *v.t.* (**pried, pry·ing**). Raise or move with a lever, crowbar or other tool. ~ *n.* (pl. **pries**). Lever or crowbar for prying.

PS, P.S. *abbrevs.* Postscript; public school.

P.S., Ps., Psa. *abbrevs.* Psalm(s) (Old Testament).

psalm (sahm) *n.* Sacred song, hymn; (**Book of**) **Psalms**, book of Old Testament consisting of psalms (pop. **Psalms of David**). **psalm'ist** *n.* Author of a psalm; **the P**~, David.

psal·mo·dy (sah'modē, săl'mo-) *n.* (pl. **-dies**). Practice, art, of singing psalms, hymns, anthems, etc., esp. in public worship; arrangement of psalms for singing, psalms so arranged. **psal·mo·dic** (sahmŏd'ĭk, săl-) *adj.* **psal'mo·dist** *n.*

Psal·ter (sawl'ter) *n.* 1. Book of Psalms; version of this. 2. (also **p** ~) Copy of the Psalms esp. for liturgical use.

psal·te·ri·um (sawltēr'ēum) *n.* (pl. **-te·ri·a** pr. -tēr'ēa). Omasum.

psal·ter·y (sawl'terē) *n.* (pl. **-ter·ies**). Ancient and medieval triangular stringed instrument, like dulcimer, but played by plucking with fingers or plectrum.

pseudo-, pseud- *prefixes.* False(ly), seeming(ly), professed(ly) but not real(ly).

pseu·do·graph (so͞o'dōgrăf, -grahf) *n.* Literary work purporting to be by a person other than the real author.

pseu·do·morph (so͞o'domōrf) *n.* False form, esp. (min.) crystal etc. consisting of one compound but having the form proper to another. **pseu·do·mor'phic, pseu·do·mor'phous** *adjs.* **pseu·do·mor'phism** *n.*

pseu·do·nym (so͞o'donĭm) *n.* Fictitious name, esp. one assumed by author. **pseu·don·y·mous** (so͞odŏn'imus) *adj.* Writing, written, under a false name. **pseu·do·nym'i·ty** *n.*

pseu·do·pod (so͞o'dopŏd) = PSEUDOPODIUM.

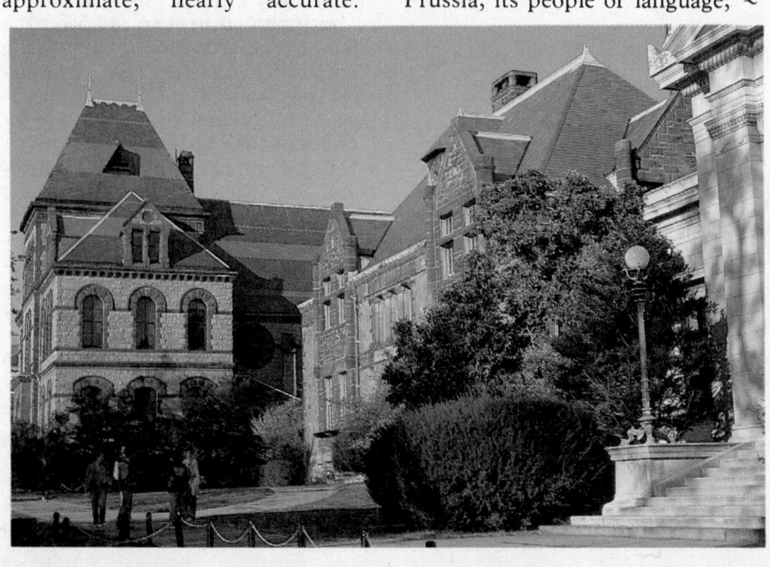

*Brown University at **Providence,** Rhode Island, one of the oldest cities in the U.S.A. with a rich history of trading and religious tolerance.*

pseu·do·po·di·um (sōōdopō′dēum) *n.* (pl. **-di·a** pr. -dēa). Temporary protrusion of protoplasm in a protozoan, for movement or feeding.

pshaw (shaw) *int.* & *n.* Exclamation of contempt or impatience. ~ *v.* Say "pshaw!" (*at*).

psi (sī, psē) *n.* (pl. **psis**). Twenty-third letter of Greek alphabet (Ψ, ψ) = ps.

psi, p.s.i. *abbrevs.* Pounds per square inch.

psil·o·cy·bin (sĭlosī′bĭn, sīlo-) *n.* Hallucinogen found in Mexican mushrooms of genus *Psilocybe.*

psit·ta·cine (sĭt′asīn) *adj.* Of parrots, parrot-like.

psit·ta·coid (sĭt′akoid) *adj.* Like, akin, to the Psittacidae or parrots.

psit·ta·co·sis (sĭtakō′sĭs) *n.* Contagious disease of birds, esp. parrots, characterized by diarrhea and wasting, and causing bronchial pneumonia when communicated to human beings.

pso·ri·a·sis (sorī′asĭs) *n.* Noncontagious skin disease marked by red scaly patches. **pso·ri·at·ic** (sōrēăt′ĭk, sōr-) *adj.*

Psy·che (sī′kē). (Gk. myth.) Soul personified as beloved of Eros and represented in art with butterfly wings, or as butterfly.

psy·che (sī′kē) *n.* Soul, spirit, mind.

psy·che·del·ic (sīkĭdĕl′ĭk) *adj.* (of drug) Hallucinatory, giving illusion of freedom from limitations of reality; suggesting experience or effect of such drugs.

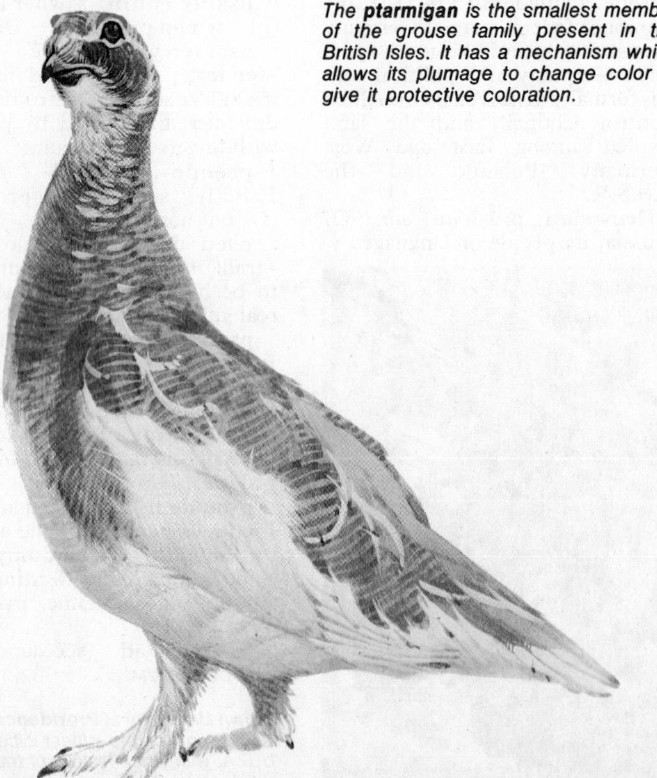

psy·chi·a·try (sīkī′atrē, sī-) *n.* Study and treatment of mental illness. **psy·chi·at·ric** (sīkēăt′rĭk), **psy·chi·at′ri·cal** *adjs.* **psy·chi·at′ri·cal·ly** *adv.* **psy·chi·a·trist** (sīkī′atrĭst, sī-) *n.*

psy·chic (sī′kĭk) *adj.* Psychical; susceptible to psychic or occult influences. ~ *n.* Psychic person.

psy·chi·cal (sī′kĭkal) *adj.* 1. Of the soul or mind. 2. Of phenomena and conditions apparently outside domain of physical law and therefore attributed by some to spiritual or hyperphysical agency. **psy′chi·cal·ly** *adv.*

psy·cho·a·nal·y·sis (sīkōanăl′ĭsĭs) *n.* Therapeutic method, devised by FREUD, of dealing with certain mental disorders by bringing to light complexes or repressed affects persisting in the unconscious mind; branch of psychology dealing with unconscious mind. **psy·cho·an·a·lyze** (sīkōăn′alīz) *v.t.* (**-lyzed, -lyz·ing**). **psy·cho·an·a·lyt·ic** (sīkōănalĭt′ĭk), **psy·cho·an·a·lyt′i·cal** *adjs.* **psy·cho·an·a·lyt′i·cal·ly** *adv.* **psy·cho·an·a·lyst** (sīkōăn′alĭst) *n.*

psy·cho·ki·ne·sis (sīkōkĭnē′sĭs, -kī-) *n.* Supposed interference with physical causation by mental influence.

psy·cho·log·i·cal (sīkolŏj′ĭkal), **psy·cho·log·ic** (sīkolŏj′ĭk) *adjs.* Of psychology; of, relating to, the mind; ~ **moment**, (f. Fr. mistranslation of Ger. *moment* (neuter) potent element, momentum, as *moment* (masc.) moment of time), psychologically appropriate moment; (esp. joc.) nick of time; ~ **warfare**, (achieving aims by) acting on minds of enemy troops or population. **psy·cho·log′i·cal·ly** *adv.*

*The **ptarmigan** is the smallest member of the grouse family present in the British Isles. It has a mechanism which allows its plumage to change color to give it protective coloration.*

psy·chol·o·gy (sīkŏl′ojē) *n.* (pl. **-gies**). Science of the nature, functions, and phenomena of human mind and conduct; treatise on, system of, this; mental characteristics; **analytical** ~, introspective analysis of mental processes; (also) method of psychological inquiry akin to psychoanalysis, system elaborated by C. G. JUNG. **psy·chol·o·gist** (sīkŏl′ojĭst) *n.*

psy·chom·e·try (sīkŏm′ĭtrē) *n.* 1. Alleged faculty of divining from physical contact or proximity the qualities of an object or of persons etc. that have been in contact with it. 2. Measurement of mental abilities etc. **psy·cho·met·ric** (sīkōmĕ′trĭk) *adj.*

psy·cho·mo·tor (sīkōmō′ter) *adj.* Of motion resulting from mental activity.

psy·cho·neu·ro·sis (sīkōnōōrō′sĭs, -nyōō-) *n.* (pl. **-ses** pr. -sēz). Functional disorder of the nervous system characterized by anxiety, depression, or obsessional states, without any ascertainable organic disease. **psy·cho·neu·rot·ic** (sīkōnōōrŏt′ĭk, -nyōō-) *adj.* & *n.*

psy·cho·path (sī′kopăth) *n.* Mentally deranged person; emotionally unstable person. **psy·cho·path′ic** *adj.* **psy·cho·path′i·cal·ly** *adv.*

psy·cho·pa·thol·o·gy (sīkōpathŏl′ojē) *n.* Pathology of the mind.

psy·chop·a·thy (sīkŏp′athē) *n.* Mental disease or disorder, esp. one affecting character or moral sense.

psy·cho·sex·u·al (sīkōsĕk′shōōal) *adj.* Pertaining to the relation between sexual and psychological phenomena.

psy·cho·sis (sīkō′sĭs) *n.* (pl. **-ses** pr. -sēz). Severe form of mental illness involving the entire personality. **psy·chot·ic** (sīkŏt′ĭk) *adj.*

psy·cho·so·mat·ic (sīkōsōmăt′ĭk, -so-) *adj.* (of illness) Involving both mind and body; (esp.) exhibiting physical symptoms but instigated by mental processes. **psy·cho·so·mat′i·cal·ly** *adv.*

psy·cho·ther·a·py (sīkōthĕr′apē) *n.* Treatment of disease by action on the mind only, by hypnotism, suggestion, psychoanalysis, etc. **psy·cho·ther·a·peu·tic** (sīkōthĕrapū′tĭk) *adj.* **psy·cho·ther·a·pist** (sīkōthĕr′apĭst) *n.*

psy·chrom·e·ter (sīkrŏm′ĭter) *n.* Wet-and-dry-bulb thermometer, used for measuring the relative humidity of the atmosphere.

Pt *symbol.* Platinum.

pt. *abbrev.* Part; pint; point.

P.T. *abbrev.* Physical training.

p.t. *abbrev.* Past tense; pro

*The John Steinbeck Room at the John Steinbeck Public Library, Salinas, California, a **public utility** which performs an educational function providing information of interest.*

tempore.

P.T.A. *abbrev.* Parent-Teacher Association.

ptar·mi·gan (tar′m*i*gan) *n.* (pl. **-gans**, collect. **-gan**). Any of several grouses (genus *Lagopus*) with black, gray, or brown plumage in summer and white in winter, inhabiting high altitudes in Scotland and N. Europe, the Alps and Pyrenees, and western N. Amer.; [Gaelic *tarmachan*] esp. the willow ptarmigan (*L. lagopus*), the rock ptarmigan (*L. mutus*), and the white-tailed ptarmigan (*L. leucurus*).

pter·o·dac·tyl (tĕr*o*dăk′tĭl) *n.* Extinct winged reptile, one of the pterosaurs.

pter·o·pod (tĕr′*o*pŏd) *n.* Mollusk of the group Pteropoda with middle part of foot expanded into winglike lobes for swimming.

pter·o·pus (tĕr′*o*pus) *n.* Member of genus *P*~ of large tropical and subtropical bats, flying fox.

pter·o·saur (tĕr′*o*sōr) *n.* One of the Pterosauria, an extinct order of mesozoic flying reptiles, with one digit of each forefoot prolonged to great length and supporting flying membrane.

Ptol·e·ma·ic (tŏlemā′ĭk) *adj.* 1. Of the PTOLEMIES. 2. Of the astronomer PTOLEMY; ~ **system**, astronomical system elaborated by Ptolemy, in which the relative motions of the sun, moon, and planets are explained as taking place around a stationary Earth.

Ptol·e·mies (tŏl′*e*mēz). Dynasty of kings named Ptolemy, of Macedonian origin, that ruled over Egypt from death of Alexander the Great until Roman conquest in the reign of Cleopatra.

Ptol·e·my[1] (tŏl′*e*mē). Claudius Ptolemaeus (2nd c. A.D.), Greek astronomer, mathematician, and geographer of Alexandria.

Ptol·e·my[2] **I** (tŏl′*e*mē) (367?–283 B.C.). (also called **Ptolemy Soter**) King of Egypt, 303–285 B.C.; founder of Ptolemaic dynasty.

pto·maine (tō′mān, tōmān′) *n.* One of a group of organic amine compounds, some of which cause toxic symptoms when injected or taken by mouth; ~ **poisoning**, (formerly, erron.) food poisoning. [Gk. *ptoma* corpse]

pto·sis (tō′sĭs) *n.* (pl. **-ses** pr. -sēz). (path.) Drooping of one or both upper eyelids; downward displacement of any organ.

Pu *symbol.* Plutonium.

pub (pŭb) *n.* (esp. Brit. colloq.) Public house; ~ **crawl**, calling at several pubs and drinking at each.

pu·ber·ty (pū′b*e*rtē) *n.* Being functionally capable of procreation; **age of** ~, age at which puberty begins (in common law, 14 in boys, 12 in girls).

pu·bes (pū′bēz) *n.* (pl. **pu·bes**). Hypogastric region, covered with hair in the adult.

pu·bes·cence (pūbĕs′*e*ns) *n.* 1. Arrival at puberty. 2. (bot.) Soft down on leaves and stems of plants; downiness; (zool.) soft down on parts of animals, esp. insects. **pu·bes′cent** *adj.*

pu·bic (pū′bĭk) *adj.* Of pubes or pubis.

pu·bis (pū′bĭs) *n.* (pl. **-bes** pr. -bēz). Part of innominate bone forming anterior wall of pelvis.

pub·lic (pŭb′lĭk) *adj.* 1. Of, concerning, the people as a whole. 2. Done by or for, representing, the people. 3. Open to, shared by, the people; provided by, managed or controlled by, the community as a whole; ~ **accountant**, accountant whose services are available to the general public as opposed to one who is in full-time service with a company; ~ **address system**, equipment of loudspeakers etc. to enable speaker, musician, etc. to be heard by audience; ~ **enemy**, criminal whose activities are considered by police to menace the public; ~ **health**, protection of the public from disease and epidemics by provision of adequate sanitation, standards of hygiene, etc.; ~ **house**, (Brit.) establishment providing alcoholic liquors to be consumed on the premises; ~ **law**, law of relations between persons and state; ~ **nuisance**, (law) illegal act harming community rather than an individual; ~ **relations**, (esp. good) relations between organization etc. and the general public; ~ **relations officer**, (abbrev. PRO) person who gives out information to the public in connection with some office of government, corporation, etc.; ~ **school**, (Brit.) endowed grammar (usu. boarding) school administered by board of governors, and of which the head is a member of the Headmasters' Conference; (U.S.) primary or secondary school provided at public expense and managed by public authority as part of system of public (and usu. free) education; ~ **servant**, government official, elected or appointed; ~ **utilities**, services or supplies commonly available in large towns, as buses, drainage, water, gas, electricity, etc. 4. Open to general observation, done or existing in public; of, engaged in, the affairs or service of the people; ~**-spirited**, animated or prompted by zeal for the common good. **pub′lic·ly** *adv.* **public** *n.* 1. (Members of) the community in general; section of the community; **in** ~, publicly, openly. 2. (Brit. colloq.) Public house, hence **publican**, keeper of the public house.

pub·li·ca·tion (pŭbl*i*kā′sh*o*n) *n.* Making publicly known; issuing of book, engraving, music, etc., to the public; book etc. so issued.

pub·li·cist (pŭb′lĭsĭst) *n.* 1. Writer on, person skilled in, international law. 2. Writer on current public topics, esp. journalist. 3. Publicity agent.

pub·lic·i·ty (pŭblĭs′ĭtē) *n.* Being or making public; esp. (business of) advertising or making events or persons publicly known; ~ **agent**, person employed for this purpose.

pub·li·cize (pŭb′lĭsīz) *v.t.* (**-cized, -ciz·ing**). Bring to public notice, advertise.

pub·lish (pŭb′lĭsh) *v.t.* Make generally known; announce formally, promulgate (edict etc.);

(Brit.) ask, read (banns of marriage); issue copies of (book etc.) for sale to the public. **pub'lish·a·ble** *adj.* **pub'lish·er** *n.* (esp.) One whose business is producing copies of books etc., and distributing them to booksellers etc. or to the public.

Puc·ci·ni (po͞ochē'nē), **Giacomo** (1858–1924). Italian operatic composer, famous for his *La Bohème*, *Tosca*, and *Madame Butterfly*.

puce (pūs) *adj.* & *n.* Purplish brown.

Puck (pŭk). Merry mischievous sprite or goblin (as in Shakespeare's *A Midsummer Night's Dream*) believed, esp. in 16th and 17th centuries, to haunt the English countryside; in earlier superstition, an evil demon. **puck'ish** *adj.* **puck'ish·ly** *adv.* **puck'ish·ness** *n.*

puck (pŭk) *n.* Rubber disk used in ice hockey.

puck·er (pŭk'*er*) *v.* Contract, gather (*up*), into wrinkles, folds, or bulges, intentionally or as fault e.g. in sewing; ~ **up**, contract the lips, as before kissing. **pucker** *n.* Such wrinkle etc.

pud·ding (po͝od'ĭng) *n.* Dish made of a mixture of ingredients, usu. including flour, eggs, and milk as well as seasoning and flavoring.

pud·dle (pŭd'*el*) *n.* 1. Small dirty pool, esp. of rain on road etc. 2. Clay (and sand) mixed with water as watertight covering for embankments etc. ~ *v.* (**-dled, -dling**). 1. Dabble, wallow (*about*) in mud or shallow water; make (water) muddy. 2. Knead (clay and sand) into, make, line (canal etc.) with, puddle. 3. Stir (a mixture of molten cast iron and iron ore) in a furnace so as to expel the carbon and convert it into malleable iron. **pud'dler** *n.* **pud'dly** *adj.*

pu·den·dum (pūdĕn'd*u*m) *n.* (usu. in pl. **-da** pr. -d*a*). External genital organs. **pu·den'dal** *adj.* [L. *pudere* be ashamed]

pudg·y (pŭj'ē) *adj.* (**pudg·i·er, pudg·i·est**). Short and fat. **pudg'i·ness** *n.*

pueb·lo (pwĕb'lō) *n.* (pl. **-los**). 1. Town or village, esp. communal village or settlement of Indians in Arizona, New Mexico, and adjacent parts of Mexico and Texas. 2. **P** ~, member of a group of Indian peoples of several linguistic stocks, dwelling in pueblos in areas in SW. of N. Amer.

pu·er·ile (pūr'ĭl, -īl pū'*er*ĭl, -īl) *adj.* Boyish, childish; trivial. **pu'er·ile·ly** *adv.* **pu·er·il·i·ty** (pū*er*ĭl'ĭtē), **pu'er·ile·ness** *ns.*

pu·er·per·al (pūĕr'p*e*ral) *adj.* Of, due to, childbirth; ~ **fever**, fever following childbirth and caused by uterine infection.

Puer·to Ri·co (pwĕr'*to* rē'kō, pōr'-, pŏr'-). Island of the central

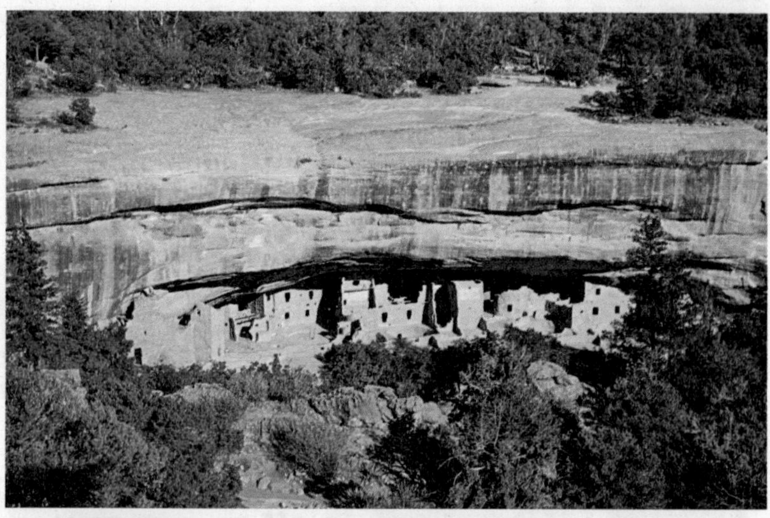

These communal dwellings were built on shelves in the rock walls of the Mesa Verde, Colorado, by the **Pueblo** Indians between 1,200 and 1,500 A.D., as protection against nomadic tribes.

Related to the auk, the **puffin** breeds on oceanic coasts, the nesting female laying only one egg in a burrow of a rabbit or shearwater. Young are fed on fish, caught by either parent.

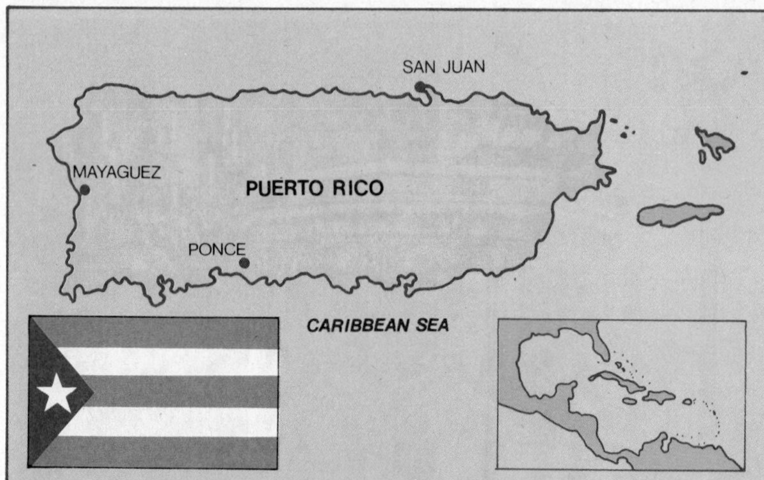

Puerto Rico is the summit of a long-drowned mountain, one of a range forming the Greater Antilles. Thus while the coastal plains are fertile, much of the island is rugged.

West Indies 100 mi. (160 km) long, 35 mi. (56 km) wide, in the NE. Caribbean Sea; discovered by Columbus, 1493; became U.S. territory after Spanish-American War, 1898; self-governing Commonwealth since 1952; capital, San Juan. **Puer'to Ri'can** *adj.* & *n.*

puff (pŭf) *n.* 1. Short quick blast of breath or wind; sound (as) of this; small quantity of vapor, smoke, etc., emitted at one puff. 2. Round soft protuberant mass of material in dress, of hair of head, etc.; POWDER puff. 3. Piece, cake, etc., of light pastry, esp. of ~ **paste, pastry**, light flaky pastry. 4. Unduly or extravagantly laudatory review of book, advertisement of product etc. for sale, esp. in newspaper. 5. ~ **adder**, large venomous African viper (esp. *Bitis arietans*) that inflates upper part of body when excited; **puff'ball**, fungus (*Lycoperdon*) with ballshaped spore case, emitting spores in cloud of fine powder when broken; **puff sleeve**, puffed sleeve. **puff** *v.* 1. Emit puff of air or breath; come *out*, *up*, in puffs; breathe hard, pant; put out of breath; utter pantingly; emit puffs, move with puffs; blow (dust, smoke, light object, *away*, *out*, etc.) with puff; smoke (pipe) in puffs. 2. Blow *out*, *up*, inflate; become inflated, swell *up*, *out*; ~ **up**, elate, make proud (esp. in past part.); **puffed sleeve**, short very full sleeve gathered at shoulder and lower edge. 3. Advertise (goods etc.) with exaggerated or false praise.

puf·fin (pŭf'ĭn) *n.* Seabird of *Fratercula* and related genera, esp. *F. arctica* of N. Atlantic with very large furrowed particolored bill.

puff·y (pŭf'ē) *adj.* (**puff·i·er, puff·i·est**). Gusty; short-winded; puffed out; corpulent. **puff'i·ness** *n.*

pug[1] (pŭg) *n.* Dwarf squat-faced breed of dog like miniature bulldog; ~**-nose(d)**, (having) short squat or snub nose.

pug[2] (pŭg) *n.* Loam or clay mixed and prepared for brickmaking etc. ~ *v.t.* (**pugged, pug·ging**). Prepare (clay) for brickmaking by kneading and working it into soft and plastic condition; pack (space, esp. that under floor, to deaden sound) with pug, cement, etc.

pug[3] (pŭg) *n.* (slang) Pugilist.

Pu·get (pū'jĭt) **Sound.** Pacific Ocean inlet in NW. Washington, extending S. 80 mi. (129 km) from Juan de Fuca Strait to Olympia.

pug·ga·ree, pug·a·ree (pŭg'-*a*rē), **pug·gree** (pŭg'rē) *ns.* Indian's light turban; thin scarf of muslin etc. worn around hat and sometimes hanging down behind to keep off sun.

pu·gil·ist (pū'j*i*lĭst) *n.* Boxer, fighter. **pu'gil·ism** *n.* **pu·gil·is'tic** *adj.* **pu·gil·is'ti·cal·ly** *adv.*

pug·na·cious (pŭgnā'sh*u*s) *adj.* Disposed to fight, quarrelsome. **pug·na'cious·ly** *adv.* **pug·nac·i·ty** (pŭgnăs'ĭtē), **pug·na'cious·ness** *ns.*

puke (pūk) *v.* (**puked, puk·ing**). Vomit.

puk·ka (pŭk'*a*) *adj.* (Ind.) Real, genuine, true; permanent, solidly built; ~ **sahib**, (freq. derisive) real gentleman. [Hindi *pakkā* cooked, ripe; thorough, permanent]

Pu·las·ki (po͝olăs'kē), **Casimir** (1748?–79). Polish-born patriot; general in Amer. Revolutionary War.

pul·chri·tude (pŭl'krĭto͞od, -tūd) *n.* Beauty. **pul·chri·tu·di·nous** (pŭlkrĭto͞o'd*i*n*u*s, -tū'-) *adj.*

pule (pūl) *v.i.* (**puled, pul·ing**). Cry querulously or weakly, whine. **pul'er** *n.* **pul'ing** *adj.* **pul'ing·ly** *adv.*

pu·li (po͞ol'ē, pū'lē) *n.* (pl. **-lis, -lik** pr. po͞ol'ĕk, pū'lĕk). One of a breed of Hungarian sheepdogs whose long hair often mats, making the coat appear corded.

Pul·it·zer (po͝ol'ĭts*e*r, pū'lĭt-), **Joseph** (1847–1911). Amer. newspaper owner and editor, one of the founders of American sensational journalism; ~ **Prize**, one of a group of money prizes established under his will and offered annually to U.S. citizens for work in music, journalism, American history and biography, poetry, drama, and fiction.

pull (po͝ol) *v.* 1. Exert upon (thing) force tending to draw it to oneself; draw (thing etc.) toward oneself or in direction so regarded; exert pulling force; pluck (plant, freq. *up*) by root; proceed with effort (*up* hill etc.); (of horse) strain against bit; draw or fire (gun etc.); ~ **person's leg**: see LEG. 2. Draw, suck, *at* (pipe, beverage glass, etc.); tear, pluck, *at*. 3. Print upon (sheet), print (copy, proof), orig. in old hand press by pulling bar toward one. 4. Move (boat), move boat, by pulling oar; (of boat) be rowed, be rowed by (so many oars); ~ **one's weight**, row with effect in proportion to one's weight; perform one's due share of work etc. 5. Check (horse), esp. so as to make him lose race. 6. (golf, baseball) Hit (ball) widely to the left, or (of left-handed player) to the right. 7. ~ **down**, demolish (building etc.); lower in health, spirits, price, etc.; ~ **in**, (of train) arrive at station; (of vehicle) move in (nearer) to roadside; (colloq.) arrest (person); ~ **off**, (slang) complete (scheme etc.) successfully; remove (garment); steer (vehicle) to side of road; ~ **out**, row out; draw out of (a position); (colloq.) abandon project etc.; (of train) move out of station; (of vehicle) move out from roadside or line of traffic; **pull'out** (*n.*) page or plate in book that folds out from front edge of leaves to facilitate reference; **pull'over**, garment for upper part of body, pulled on over head; **pull through**, get (person), get oneself, safely through (danger, illness, etc.); **pull together**, work in harmony; **pull oneself together**, rally, recover oneself; **pull up**, cause (person, horse, vehicle) to stop; reprimand; check oneself; advance one's relative position in race etc. **pull** *n.* 1. Act of pulling, wrench, tug; force thus exerted; (fig.) means of exerting influence, interest with the powerful. 2. (print.) Rough proof. 3. Pulling at bridle to check horse; (baseball, golf) pulled stroke; deep drink of liquor; draw at pipe. 4. Handle etc. by which pull is applied. **pull'er** *n.*

pul·let (po͝ol'ĭt) *n.* Young fowl, esp. hen from time it begins to lay till 1st molt.

*A pre-Reformation 'wine-glass' **pulpit** at Cirencester parish church U.K., is remarkable for its open-tracery stonework which has been enriched with gilding and paintwork.*

pul·ley (po͞ol'ē) *n.* (pl. **-leys**). One of the simple mechanical powers, consisting of grooved wheel(s) for cord etc. to pass over, mounted in block and used for lifting a weight or changing direction of power; wheel, drum, fixed on shaft and turned by belt, used esp. to increase speed or power. ~ *v.t.* (**-leyed, -ley·ing**). Hoist, furnish, work, with pulley.

Pull·man (po͞ol'm*a*n) *n.* (trademark) Type of comfortable railroad car (PARLOR CAR) with fitted tables on which refreshments can be placed; sleeping car. [George M. *Pullman* (1831–97), Amer. designer]

pul·lu·late (pŭl'y*u*lāt) *v.i.* (**-lat·ed, -lat·ing**). (of shoot, bud) Sprout out, bud; (of seed) sprout; (fig.) develop, spring up. **pul·lu·la'tion** *n.*

pul·mo·nar·y (pŭl'm*o*nĕrē, po͞ol'-) *adj.* Of, in, connected with, the lungs; having lungs or lunglike organs; affected with, subject to, lung disease. **pul·mo·nate** (pŭl'm*o*nāt, -nĭt), **pul·mon·ic** (pŭlmŏn'ĭk) *adjs.*

Pul·mo·tor (pŭl'mōt*e*r, po͞ol'-) *n.* (trademark) Apparatus for forcing oxygen into lungs to give artificial respiration.

pulp (pŭlp) *n.* Fleshy part of fruit; any fleshy or soft part of animal body, e.g. nervous substance in interior cavity of tooth; soft formless mass, esp. that of linen, wood, etc., from which paper is made; ore pulverized and mixed with water; ~ **magazine**, trashy magazine; ~ **wood**, timber suitable for making pulp. **pulp** *v.* Reduce to pulp; remove pulp from; become pulpy. **pulp'er, pulp'i·ness** *ns.* **pulp'y** *adj.* (**pulp·i·er, pulp·i·est**).

pul·pit (po͞ol'pĭt, pŭl'-) *n.* Raised enclosed platform from which preacher in church, chapel, or synagogue delivers sermon; profession of preaching, preachers; (in small sailing vessel) guardrail, usu. waist-high, fixed at bow or stern.

pul·que (po͞ol'kē, po͞ol'kā) *n.* Mexican fermented drink from sap of agave etc.

pul·sar (pŭl'sär) *n.* Cosmic source of rapidly pulsating radio signal.

pul·sate (pŭl'sāt) *v.* (**-sat·ed, -sat·ing**). Expand and contract rhythmically, beat, throb; vibrate, quiver, thrill; agitate (diamonds,

*Although only a by-product of a volcanic eruption, **pumice** is of value to man. It can be used as a grinding and polishing medium and replaces gravel in lightweight concrete.*

*Despite the many technological advances made by man, not all are adopted in all places. In Spain, animal power is still used to raise water (left) although many types of mechanical **pump** have been designed for continuous operation by wind or engine.*

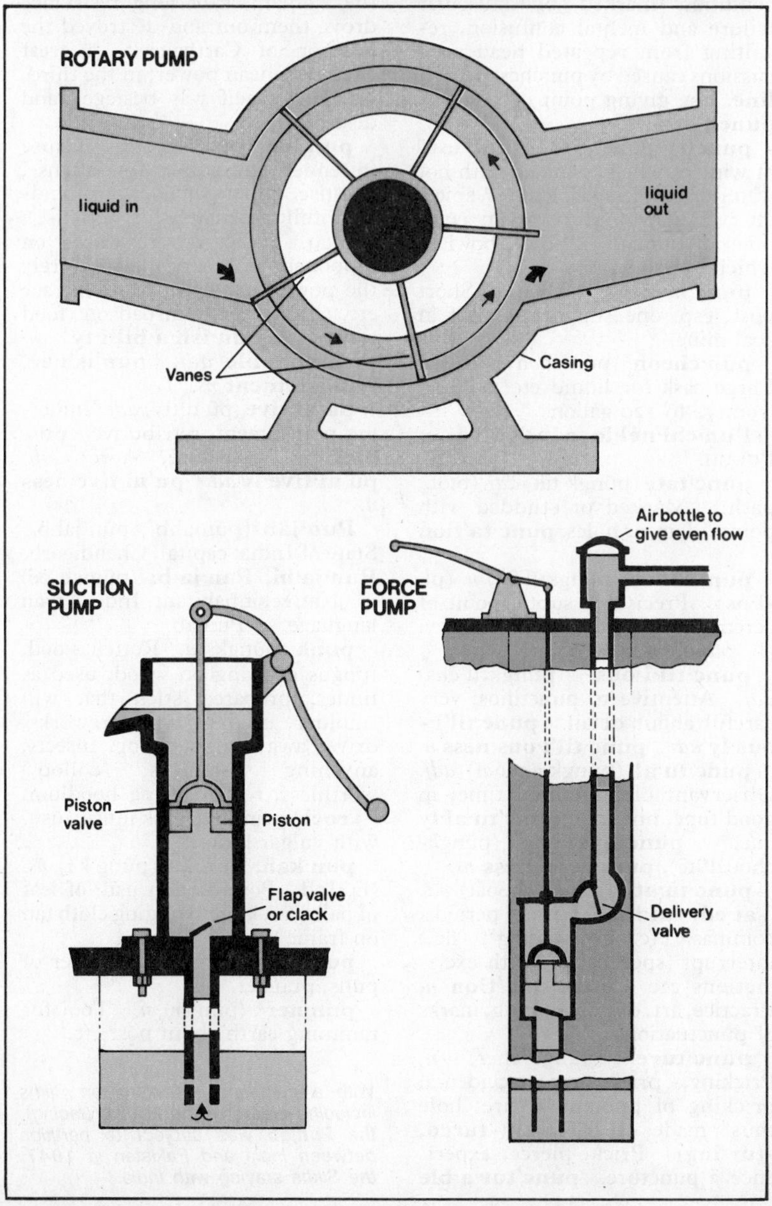

ROTARY PUMP
liquid in
liquid out
Vanes
Casing

SUCTION PUMP
Piston valve
Piston
Flap valve or clack

FORCE PUMP
Air bottle to give even flow
Delivery valve

stones, etc.) with pulsator. **pul·sa'tion** *n.* **pul·sa·tive** (pŭl'satĭv), **pul·sa·to·ry** (pŭl'satōrē, -tōrē) *adjs.* **pul·sa·tor** (pŭl'sāter, pŭlsā'-) *n.* Machine operating with throbbing movement.

pulse[1] (pŭls) *n.* Rhythmical throbbing of arteries as blood is pumped into them from the heart, used, as felt in wrists, temples, etc., to measure the heart rate; each successive beat of arteries or heart; (fig.) throb, thrill, of life or emotion; rhythmical recurrence of strokes, e.g. of oars; single beat or vibration of sound, light, etc.; (mus.) beat. **pulse'less** *adj.* **pulse'less·ly** *adv.* **pulse'less·ness** *n.* **pulse** *v.* (**pulsed, puls·ing**). Pulsate; send *out, in,* etc., by rhythmic beats.

pulse[2] (pŭls) *n.* Edible seeds of leguminous plants, e.g. peas, beans, lentils; (with pl.) any kind of these.

pul·ver·ize (pŭl'verīz) *v.* (**-ized, -iz·ing**). Reduce to powder or dust, crumble into dust; (fig.) demolish, crush, smash. **pul'ver·iz·a·ble, pul'ver·a·ble** *adjs.* **pul·ver·i·za·tion** (pŭlverīzā'shon), **pul'ver·iz·er** *ns.*

pul·ver·u·lent (pŭlvĕr'yulent) *adj.* Powdery, of dust; covered with powder; (of rock etc.) of slight cohesion, apt to crumble. **pul·ver'u·lence** *n.* **pul·ver'u·lent·ly** *adv.*

pu·ma (pū'ma, pōō'-) (pl. **-mas**, collect. **-ma**) = MOUNTAIN lion.

pum·ice (pŭm'ĭs) *n.* (also ~ **stone**) Very light porous stone formed by the solidified froth on the surface of glassy lava, used, freq. powdered, for polishing and abrading; piece of this for removing stains etc. from the skin.

pum·mel (pŭm'el) *v.t.* (**-meled, -melled, -mel·ing, -mel·ling**). Strike repeatedly, esp. with fist.

pump[1] (pŭmp) *n.* Machine for moving fluid from one place to another, e.g. raising water, for compressing gas, or for similar purpose, e.g. inflating tires, formerly always with rod and piston, now freq. rotary in action; action of working a pump; stroke of pump; ~ **room**, room where pump is worked. **pump** *v.* 1. Work a pump; remove, raise, (water etc.) thus; make *dry* by pumping; inflate (pneumatic tire), inflate tires of (bicycle etc.). 2. Bring out, pour forth (*on*) as by pumping; elicit information from (person) by artful or persistent questions; ~ **priming**, (fig.) stimulation of national economy, business, etc. by investment, tax cuts, etc. **pump'er** *n.*

pump[2] (pŭmp) *n.* Light shoe, usu. without fastening, for dancing etc.

pum·per·nick·el (pŭm'pernĭkel) *n.* German wholemeal rye bread, dark brown, coarse, and sour.

pump·kin (pŭmp'kĭn, pŭm'-) *n.* Trailing plant (*Cucurbita pepo*) with heart-shaped five-lobed leaves; large egg-shaped or globular fruit of this, with edible layer next to rind.

pun (pŭn) *n.* Humorous use of word to suggest different meanings, or of words of same sound with different meanings, play on words. ~ *v.i.* (**punned, pun·ning**). Make puns (*on*). **pun'ning·ly** *adv.*

Punch (pŭnch). Hook-nosed humpbacked buffoon, a stock character derived from Italian popular comedy who appeared in Italy as Pulcinella, in France as Polichinelle, in England and the U.S. as Punchinello or Punch; ~ **and Judy**, open-air puppet show performed at fairs etc. [Neapolitan dial. *policenella*, dim. of *policena* turkey cock, prob. with ref. to its hooked beak]

punch[1] (pŭnch) *n.* Instrument or machine for cutting holes in leather, metal, paper, etc., or for driving a bolt etc. out of a hole (**starting** ~) or forcing a nail beneath a surface (**driving** ~); tool or machine for impressing design or stamping die on material.

*An African monarch butterfly on the point of emerging from its **pupal** casing. Many insects pass through a pupal stage during their metamorphosis from egg to adult.*

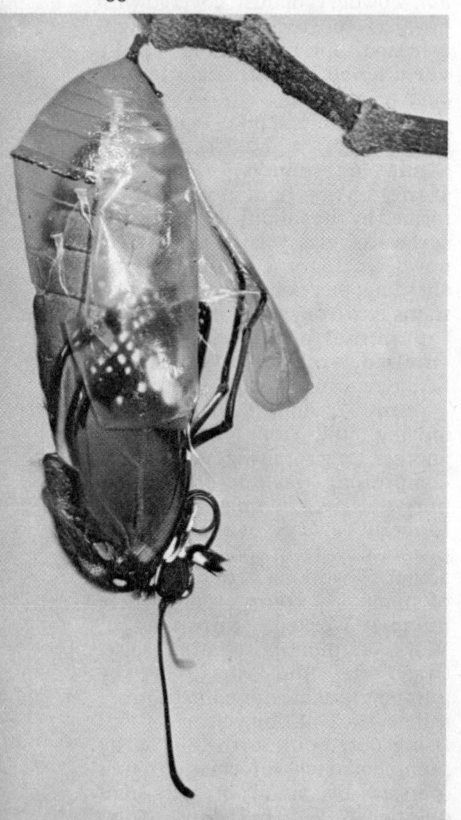

punch[2] (pŭnch) *v.* 1. Strike, esp. with closed fist; prod with stick etc., esp. drive (cattle) thus; **punch'ing bag**, stuffed or inflated ball held by chain etc., and punched as form of exercise; ~**-up** (*n.*, Brit. slang) fight with fists, brawl. 2. Pierce (metal, leather, railroad ticket, etc.) as or with punch; pierce (hole) thus; drive (nail etc. *in, out*) with punch; ~**(ed) card, tape**, magnetic tape, perforated according to specified code, for conveying instructions to computer etc. **punch** *n.* Blow with fist; **pull one's punches**, refrain from using one's full force; **punch-drunk** (*adj.*) stupefied through being severely and repeatedly punched; (of pugilists), morbid condition marked by muscular failure and mental confusion, resulting from repeated head concussions caused by punches; **punch line**, line giving point of joke etc. **punch'er** *n.*

punch[3] (pŭnch) *n.* Drink usu. of wine of whiskey mixed with hot water or milk, sugar, lemons, spice, etc.; similar mixture taken cold; bowl of punch; ~ **bowl**, bowl in which punch is mixed.

pun·cheon[1] (pŭn'chon) *n.* Short post, esp. one supporting roof in coal mine.

pun·cheon[2] (pŭn'chon) *n.* (hist.) Large cask for liquid etc. holding from 72 to 120 gallons.

Pun·chi·nel·lo (pŭnchinĕl'ō) = PUNCH.

punc·tate (pŭngk'tāt) *adj.* (biol., path.) Marked or studded with points, dots, or holes. **punc·ta'tion** *n.*

punc·til·i·o (pŭngktĭl'ēō) *n.* (pl. **-i·os**). Precise or subtle point of ceremony or honor; petty formality. [It. *puntiglio* little point]

punc·til·i·ous (pŭngktĭl'ēus) *adj.* Attentive to punctilios; very careful about detail. **punc·til'i·ous·ly** *adv.* **punc·til'i·ous·ness** *n.*

punc·tu·al (pŭngk'chōōal) *adj.* Observant of appointed time; in good time, not late. **punc'tu·al·ly** *adv.* **punc·tu·al·i·ty** (pŭngkchōōăl'ĭtē), **punc'tu·al·ness** *ns.*

punc·tu·ate (pŭngk'chōōāt) *v.t.* (**-at·ed, -at·ing**). Insert periods, commas, etc. in (writing); (fig.) interrupt (speech etc.) with exclamations etc. **punc·tu·a'tion** *n.* Practice, art, of punctuating; marks of punctuation.

punc·ture (pŭngk'cher) *n.* Pricking, prick, esp. accidental pricking of pneumatic tire; hole thus made. ~ *v.* (**-tured, -tur·ing**). Prick, pierce; experience a puncture. **punc'tur·a·ble** *adj.*

pun·dit (pŭn'dĭt) *n.* Hindu learned in Sanskrit and in philosophy, religion, and jurisprudence of India; (joc.) learned expert or teacher.

pun·gent (pŭn'jent) *adj.* 1. Sharp-pointed (bot.); (of reproof, etc.) biting, caustic; mentally stimulating, piquant. 2. Affecting organs of smell or taste, or skin etc., with pricking sensation. **pun'gent·ly** *adv.* **pun'gen·cy** *n.*

Pu·nic (pū'nĭk) *adj.* Of Carthage, Carthaginian; of the character attributed by the Romans to the Carthaginians, treacherous, perfidious; ~ **Wars**, three wars between Romans and Carthaginians (264–241, 218–201, 149–146 B.C.); in the first, Rome captured Sicily, her 1st province, from the Carthaginians under Hamilcar; in the second, the Carthaginians under Hannibal invaded Italy and the Romans after long resistance drove them out and destroyed the position of Carthage as a great Mediterranean power; in the third, Carthage itself was besieged and destroyed.

pun·ish (pŭn'ĭsh) *v.t.* Cause (offender) to suffer for offense, chastise, inflict penalty on (offender), inflict penalty for (offense); (colloq.) inflict severe blows on (opponent in boxing), tax severely the powers of (competitor in race etc.); make heavy inroad on (food etc.). **pun·ish·a·bil'i·ty** *n.* **pun'ish·a·ble** *adj.* **pun'ish·er, pun'ish·ment** *ns.*

pu·ni·tive (pū'nĭtĭv) *adj.* Inflicting punishment, retributive. **pu·ni·to·ry** (pū'nĭtōrē, -tōrē) *adj.* **pu'ni·tive·ly** *adv.* **pu'ni·tive·ness** *n.*

Pun·jab (pŭnjahb', pŭn'jahb). State of India; capital, Chandigarh. **Pun·ja·bi, Pan·ja·bi** (pŭnjah'bē) *ns.* Native, inhabitant, Indo-Aryan language, of Punjab.

punk (pŭngk) *n.* Rotten wood, fungus growing on wood, used as tinder; prepared stick that will smolder, used to light fireworks, drive away night-flying insects; anything worthless; (colloq.) worthless, rotten young hoodlum; ~ **rock**, primitive rock music, usu. with vulgar lyrics.

pun·kah, pun·ka (pŭng'ka) *ns.* (E. Ind.) Portable fan usu. of leaf of palmyra; large swinging cloth fan on frame worked by cord.

pun·ner[1] (pŭn'er) *n.* Maker of puns, punster.

pun·ner[2] (pŭn'er) *n.* Tool for ramming earth about post etc.

*With a population of 4 million Sikhs including elders of the Nihang (facing), the **Punjab** was subject to partition between India and Pakistan in 1947, the Sikhs staying with India.*

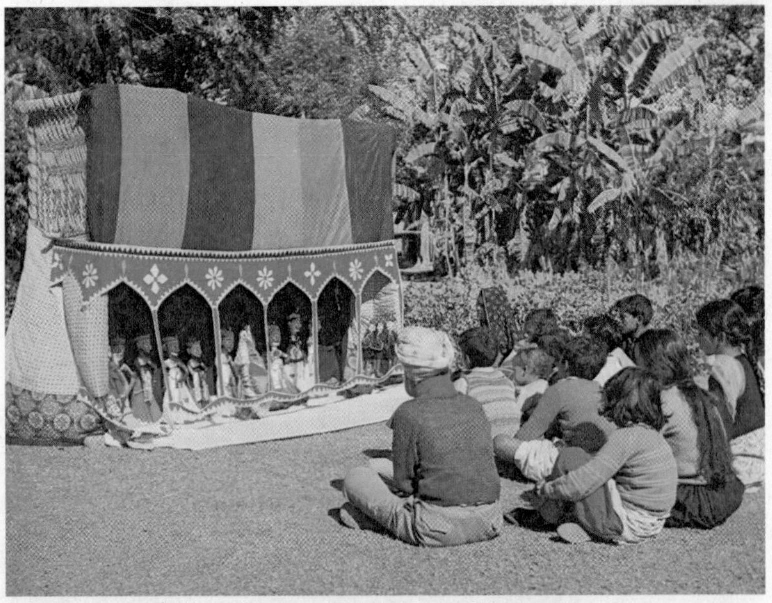

*Village children in India await the start of a **puppet** theatre. This traditional form of entertainment was practiced in ancient Egypt and Greece.*

pun·ster (pŭn′ster) *n.* Habitual maker of puns.

punt[1] (pŭnt) *n.* Flat-bottomed shallow boat, broad and square at both ends, propelled by long pole thrust against bottom of river etc. ~ *v.* Propel (punt, boat, or abs.) thus; convey in a punt. **punt′er**[1] *n.*

punt[2] (pŭnt) *v.t.* (football) Kick ball after it has dropped from the hands and before it reaches ground. ~ *n.* Punting kick; player who punts. **punt′er**[2] *n.*

punt[3] (pŭnt) *v.i.* (at faro and other card games) Lay stake against bank; (colloq.) bet on race horse etc. **punt′er**[3] *n.*

pu·ny (pū′nē) *adj.* (**-ni·er, -ni·est**). Undersized; weak, feeble; petty. **pu′ni·ness** *n.*

pup (pŭp) *n.* Puppy; ~ **tent**, small tent of simple design. **pup** *v.i.* (**pupped, pup·ping**). Give birth to puppies.

pu·pa (pū′pa) *n.* (pl. **-pae** pr. -pē, **-pas**). Insect in its inactive preadult form, after larva but before imago, chrysalis of butterfly or moth. **pu′pal** *adj.* **pu·pate** (pū′pāt) *v.i.* (**-pat·ed, -pat·ing**). Become a pupa. **pu·pa′tion** *n.*

pu·pil (pū′pil) *n.* 1. One who is taught by another, scholar. 2. Opening (circular, in man) in center of iris of eye regulating passage of light to the retina. **pu·pil·age** (pū′pilĭj) *n.* Nonage, minority; being a pupil.

pup·pet (pŭp′ĭt) *n.* Figure, usu. small, representing human being etc., esp. one with jointed limbs moved by strings etc. (MARIONETTE) or one made to fit over the operator's hand so that its head and arms can be manipulated by his fingers; person whose acts are controlled by another; ~ **show**, one with puppets as characters; ~ **state**, one professing to be independent but actually under the control of some greater power. **pup·pet·ry** (pŭp′ĭtrē) *n.* [Fr. *poupette* doll]

pup·py (pŭp′ē) *n.* (pl. **-pies**). Young dog; conceited young man. **pup′py·dom, pup′py·hood** *ns.* **pup′py·ish** *adj.*

pur·blind (pẽr′blīnd) *adj.* Partly blind, dim-sighted; (fig.) obtuse, dull. ~ *v.t.* Make purblind. **pur′blind·ly** *adv.* **pur′blind·ness** *n.*

pur·chase (pẽr′chas) *n.* 1. Buying; (law) acquisition of

*'The **Purification** of the Temple' by Jacopo da Bassano, a 16th-century Venetian painter, showing people, who had used the temple for commercial purposes, being driven out.*

property by one's personal action, not by inheritance; thing bought; (hist.) practice of buying commissions in army; ~ **money**, price (to be) paid for purchased property etc. 2. Mechanical advantage, leverage, fulcrum; appliance for gaining this, esp. (naut.) rope, windlass, pulley. **purchase** *v.t.* (**-chased, -chas·ing**). Buy; acquire (*with* toil, blood, etc.); (naut.) haul up (anchor etc.) by means of pulley, lever, etc. **pur'chas·a·ble** *adj.* **pur'chas·er** *n.*

pur·dah (per'da) *n.* (in India, Pakistan, etc.) Curtain, esp. one serving to screen women from sight of strangers; striped material for curtains; (fig.) Indian system of secluding women of rank.

pure (pūr) *adj.* (**pur·er, pur·est**). Not mixed or adulterated; (of sounds) not discordant, esp. (mus.) perfectly in tune; of unmixed descent, purebred; mere, simple, nothing but, sheer; not corrupt; morally undefiled, guiltless, sincere; sexually chaste; **pure mathematics**, theoretical mathematics, not including practical applications. **pure'bred** *adj.* Of unmixed descent. **pure'ly** *adv.* **pure'ness** *n.*

pu·rée (pyŏŏrā', -rē', pūr'ā, -ē) *n.* Pulp of cooked vegetables or fruit passed through sieve.

pur·ga·tion (pergā'shon) *n.* Purification, purging; purging of bowels; spiritual cleansing, esp. (R.C. Ch.) of soul in purgatory; (hist.) clearing of oneself from accusation or suspicion by oath or ordeal.

pur·ga·tive (per'gativ) *adj.* Cathartic; serving to purify. ~ *n.* Purgative medicine. **pur'ga·tive·ly** *adv.* **pur'ga·tive·ness** *n.*

pur·ga·to·ry (per'gatōrē, -tōrē) *n.* (pl. **-ries**). Condition, place of spiritual purging, esp. (R.C. Ch.) of souls departing this life in grace of God but requiring to be cleansed from venial sins etc.; place of temporary suffering or expiation. ~ *adj.* Purifying. **pur·ga·to'ri·al** *adj.*

purge (perj) *v.t.* (**purged, purg·ing**). Make physically or spiritually clean; rid (political party, army, etc.) of objectionable, alien, or extraneous elements or members; remove by cleansing process; (of medicine) clear (bowels) by evacuation; clear (*of* charge, suspicion); (law) atone for, wipe out, (offense, sentence) by expiation and submission. ~ *n.* 1. Purgative medicine. 2. Purging; ridding of objectionable or hostile elements.

pu·ri·fi·ca·tion (pūrifikā'shon) *n.* Purifying; ritual cleansing, esp. that of women after childbirth enjoined by Jewish law; **P ~ (of the Blessed Virgin Mary)**, festival (in Western Church, Feb. 2) of presentation of Christ in the temple on completion of days of Virgin Mary's purification (Luke 2). **pu·rif·i·ca·to·ry** (pyŏŏrif'ikatōrē, -tōrē) *adj.*

pu·ri·fi·ca·tor (pūr'ifikāter) *n.* (eccles.) Cloth used at communion for wiping chalice, and fingers and lips of celebrant.

pu·ri·fy (pūr'ifī) *v.t.* (**-fied, -fy·ing**). Make pure, cleanse (*of, from*, impurities, sin, etc.); make ceremonially clean; clear of foreign elements. **pu'ri·fi·er** *n.*

Pu·rim (poor'im; *Heb.* pŏŏrēm'). Jewish festival on 14 and 15 of month Adar (Feb.–March), commemorating defeat of Haman's plot against the Jews (Esther 9).

pur·ist (pūr'ist) *n.* Stickler for, affecter of, scrupulous purity esp. in language. **pur'ism** *n.* **pu·ris·tic** (pyŏŏris'tik), **pu·ris'ti·cal** *adjs.*

Pu·ri·tan (pūr'itan) *n.* 1. (hist.) Member of that party of English Protestants who regarded the Reformation under Elizabeth I as incomplete and demanded further purification of the church from forms and ceremonies still retained; any of those who later separated from the established church on points of ritual, policy, or doctrine, held by them to be at variance with pure New Testament principles. 2. One who is, or is thought or affects to be, extremely strict, precise, or scrupulous in religion or morals. **pu·ri·tan·ic** (pūrităn'ik), **pu·ri·tan'i·cal** *adjs.* **pu·ri·tan'i·cal·ly** *adv.* **pu·ri·tan'i·cal·ness** *n.* **Pu'ri·tan·ism, pu'ri·tan·ism** *ns.*

pu·ri·ty (pūr'itē) *n.* Pureness, cleanness, freedom from physical or moral pollution.

***Purslane** is the name given to a genus of plants which grow in a wide range of conditions and climates, and whose young shoots are edible.*

purl[1] (perl) *n.* 1. Cord of twisted gold or silver wire for bordering; chain of minute loops, each loop of this, ornamenting edges of lace, ribbon, etc. 2. (knitting) Stitch in which second needle is inserted through loop on 1st from right to left, and yarn is looped over second needle from the front. ~ *v.* Border with purl; make purl stitches in knitting.

purl[2] (perl) *v.i.* (of brook etc.) Flow with whirling motion and babbling sound. ~ *n.* Purling motion or sound.

pur·loin (perloin', per'loin) *v.t.* Steal, pilfer. **pur·loin'er** *n.*

pur·ple (per'pel) *n.* 1. Color mixed of red and blue in varying proportions. 2. (also **Tyrian ~**) Color got from the mollusks *Purpura, Thais*, and *Murex*, and associated with the dress and rank or office of emperors, consuls, kings, etc.; crimson; **the ~**, imperial, royal, or consular rank, power, or office; scarlet official dress of cardinal's rank or office. **purple** *adj.* Of the color purple; **P ~ Heart**, U.S. decoration awarded to person wounded in action; ~ **martin**, large N. Amer. swallow (*Progne subis*) with bluish-black plumage; ~ **passage, prose**, literary passage marked by exaggerated style. **pur·plish** (per'plish), **pur·ply** (per'plē) *adjs.* **pur'ple** *v.* (**-pled, -pling**). Make, become, purple.

pur·port (per'pōrt, -pōrt) *n.* Meaning, sense, tenor, of document or speech. ~ (perpōrt', -pōrt') *v.t.* (of document or speech) Have as its meaning, convey, state; profess, be intended to seem (*to* do).

pur·pose (per'pos) *n.* Object, thing intended; fact, faculty, of resolving on something; **on ~**, in order (*to, that*); designedly, not by accident; **to the ~**, relevant, useful for one's purpose; **to good, little, no**, etc., **~**, with good, little, etc., effect or result. **purpose** *v.t.* (**-posed, -pos·ing**). Design, intend. **pur'pose·ly** *adv.* **pur'pose·ful** *adj.* **pur'pose·ful·ly** *adv.* **pur'pose·ful·ness** *n.* **pur'pose·less** *adj.* **pur'pose·less·ly** *adv.* **pur'pose·less·ness** *n.*

pur·pos·ive (per'posiv) *adj.* Having, serving, done with, a purpose; having purpose and resolution.

purr (per) *v.* (of cat or other feline animal, fig. of person) Make low continuous vibratory sound expressing pleasure; utter, express (words, contentment) thus. ~ *n.* Purring sound. [imit.]

purse (pers) *n.* Small pouch of leather etc. for carrying money on the person, orig. closed by drawing strings together; (fig.) money, funds; sum collected, subscribed, or given, as present or as prize for

***Putting** on the greens at the Australian Golf Club. The game developed in Scotland and was played as early as the 15th century, James I and Mary Stuart were both avid players of the game.*

contest; baglike natural or other receptacle, pouch, cyst, etc.; **public ~**, national treasury; **~ strings**, strings for closing mouth of purse; **hold the ~ strings**, have control of expenditure. **purse** *v.* (**pursed, purs·ing**). Contract (lips etc., freq. *up*) in wrinkles; become wrinkled.

purs·er (pẽr′*ser*) *n.* Officer on ship who keeps accounts and usu. has charge of provisions; in passenger ship, head of stewards' department, superintending comfort and requirements of passengers.

purs·lane (pẽrs′lăn, -lĭn) *n.* Low succulent herb (*Portulaca oleracea* var. *sativa*) formerly used in salads and pickled.

pur·su·ance (*per*sōō′*ans*) *n.* Carrying out, pursuing, esp. in **in ~ of** (plan etc.).

pur·su·ant (*per*sōō′*ant*) *adj.* Pursuing. **~** *adv.* Conformably *to.* **pur·su′ant·ly** *adv.*

pur·sue (*per*sōō′) *v.* (**-sued, -su·ing**). Follow with intent to capture or kill; (fig.) persistently attend, stick to; seek after, aim at; proceed in compliance with (plan etc.); proceed along, continue, follow (road, inquiry, studies, etc.); go in pursuit. **pur·su′a·ble** *adj.* **pur·su′er** *n.*

pur·suit (*per*sōōt′) *n.* Pursuing; profession, employment, recreation, that one follows.

pu·ru·lent (pūr′*ulent*, pūr′*yu-*) *adj.* Of, full of, discharging, pus. **pu′ru·lent·ly** *adv.* **pu′ru·lence, pu′ru·len·cy** *ns.*

pur·vey (*per*vā′) *v.* Provide, supply (articles of food) as one's business; make provision, act as purveyor. **pur·vey′a·ble** *adj.*

pur·vey·or (*per*vā′*er*) *n.* One whose business it is to supply (esp.) articles of food, dinners etc., on large scale.

pur·view (pẽr′vū) *n.* Enacting clauses of statute; scope, intention, range (*of* act, document, etc.); range of physical or mental vision.

pus (pŭs) *n.* (path.) Yellowish viscid fluid formed by the liquefaction of dead tissues, usu. containing leucocytes, cell debris, and bacteria.

push (pōōsh) *v.* 1. Exert upon (body) force tending to move it away; move thus; exert such pressure; (cause to) project, thrust *out, forward*, etc.; make one's way forcibly or persistently, force (*one's way*) thus; **~ off**, (of person in boat) push against bank etc. with oar to get boat out into stream etc.; (slang) leave, go away. 2. Exert oneself, esp. to surpass others or succeed in one's business etc.; urge, impel; follow up (claim etc.); carry (action, matter, etc.) to further point, or to furthest limit; press the adoption, use, sale, etc., of (goods, etc.) esp. by advertisement; (slang) sell (illicit drugs); press (person) hard, esp. in passive. **push′er** *n.* (esp., slang) Illegal seller of drugs. **push′ing** *adj.* **push′ing·ly** *adv.* **push′y** *adj.* (**push·i·er, push·i·est**). **push** *n.* 1. Act of pushing, shove, thrust; thrust of weapon, beast's horn, etc. 2. Vigorous effort, (mil.) attack in force; exertion of influence; pressure of affairs, crisis, pinch. 3. Enterprise, determination to get on, self-assertion. 4. **push′ball**, game in which very large pall is pushed, not kicked, toward opponents' goal; **~ button**, knob or button pressed to operate mechanism; **push-button**, (*adj.*) operated by pressing a button (also transf.); **push′cart**, handcart; **push′over**, (slang) easy mark, esp. girl or woman easily seduced; **push′up**, (usu. pl.) exercise in which one raises one's prone body by pressing down on hands to straighten arms.

*Open buds of the **pussy willow**, bear little resemblance to the furry or silky catkins which inspired the common name of this tree.*

Push·kin (po͝osh′kĭn), **Alexander Sergeevich** (1799–1837). Russian poet and prose writer, the first national poet of Russia.

Push·tu = PASHTO.

pu·sil·lan·i·mous (pŭsĭlăn′-imus) *adj.* Faint-hearted, mean-spirited. **pu·sil·lan′i·mous·ly** *adv.* **pu·sil·la·nim·i·ty** (pŭsĭl-anĭm′ĭtē) *n.*

puss (po͝os) *n.* Cat (esp. as conventional proper name); (colloq.) girl; ~ **in the corner**, children's game in which player standing in center tries to capture one of the bases as the others change places.

puss·y[1] (po͝os′ē) *n.* (pl. **puss·ies**). Cat (esp. in nursery use); ~ **willow**, Amer. willow (*Salix discolor*) and allied species, with silky catkins.

pus·sy[2] (pŭs′ē) *adj.* (**-si·er, -si·est**). Containing or resembling pus.

puss·y·foot (po͝os′ēfo͝ot) *v.i.* (colloq.) Tread softly or lightly; proceed warily; avoid committing oneself. [nickname of Amer. prohibition lecturer, W. E. Johnson (1862–1945), given because of his stealthy methods when a magistrate]

pus·tu·late (pŭs′chulāt) *v.* (**-lat·ed, -lat·ing**). Form into pustules.

pus·tule (pŭs′cho͞ol) *n.* Pimple. **pus·tu·lar** (pŭs′chuler), **pus′tu·lous** *adjs.*

put (po͝ot) *v.* (**put, put·ting**). 1. Propel, hurl (**the shot**) from hand placed close to shoulder, as athletic exercise; (naut.) proceed, take one's course (*about, back, in, off, out,* etc.). 2. Move (thing etc.) so as to place it in some situation; convey (person) across river etc.; harness (horse etc.) *to* vehicle. 3. Bring into some relation, state, or condition; translate *into* another language, turn (*into* speech or writing, words); apply *to* use or purpose; submit *to* vote etc.; subject *to* (suffering); ~ **an end, stop, to,** bring to an end, stop; ~ **upon,** oppress, victimize; ~ (horse) **at,** urge him toward (obstacle etc.). 4. ~ **about** = TACK[1] *v.* def. 2; ~ **away,** lay by (money etc.) for future use; (slang) consume (food, drink); ~ **back,** check the advance of, retard; move back the hands of (clock); restore to former place; ~ **by,** lay aside esp. for future use; ~ **down,** suppress by force or authority; take down, snub, put to silence; put (animal) to death; cease to maintain (expensive thing); account, reckon; write on paper; ~ **forth,** exert (strength, effort, etc.); (of plant) send out (buds, leaves, etc.); ~ **forward,** thrust into prominence; advance, set forth (theory etc.); ~ **in,** install in office etc.; present formally (evidence, plea, etc.) as in law court; interpose; throw in (additional thing); (colloq.) pass, spend (time); make (an appearance); ~ **off,** postpone; postpone engagement with (person); evade (person, demand, freq. *with* excuse, etc.); hinder, dissuade *from;* foist (thing *upon* person); remove, take off (clothes); (of boat etc.) leave shore; ~ **on,** clothe oneself or another with; assume, take on (character, appearance); develop additional (flesh, weight); add (*to*); stake (*on* horse etc.); bring into action, exert (force, speed, steam, etc.); appoint, arrange for; ~ **out,** (baseball) retire (batter or base runner); extinguish; disconcert, confuse; annoy, irritate; put to inconvenience; exert (strength etc.); lend (money) at interest, invest; give (work) to be done off the premises; ~ **through,** carry out (task); place (person) in telephonic connection with another through exchange(s); ~ **together,** form (whole) by combination of parts; ~ **up,** raise (price); present (petition); propose for election; offer for sale by auction or for competition; place (in jar or can) for preservation; sheathe (knife); lodge and entertain; construct, build; ~ **person's back up,** enrage him; ~ **(person) up to,** incite him; ~ **up with,** submit to, tolerate; ~**-up** (*adj.*) fraudulently concocted (scheme etc.). **put** *n.* Throw, cast, of the shot; **put′down,** (slang) belittling remark; ~**-on,** (slang) trickery (of someone) by taking advantage of his credulity; **put′out,** (baseball) play by which batter or runner is retired.

pu·ta·tive (pū′tatĭv) *adj.* Reputed, supposed. **pu′ta·tive·ly** *adv.*

pu·tre·fy (pū′trefī) *v.i.* (**-fied, -fy·ing**). Become putrid, rot, go bad; fester, suppurate. **pu·tre·fac·tion** (pūtrefăk′shon) *n.* **pu·tre·fac′tive** *adj.*

pu·tres·cent (pūtrĕs′ent) *adj.* In process of rotting; of, accompanying, this process. **pu·tres′cence** *n.*

pu·trid (pū′trĭd) *adj.* Decomposed, rotten; foul, noxious; (fig.) corrupt; (slang) of poor or bad quality, unpleasant. **pu′trid·ly** *adv.* **pu′trid·ness, pu·trid′i·ty** *ns.*

putsch (po͝och) *n.* Attempt at revolution, *coup d'état.* [Swiss Ger., = "thrust," "blow"]

putt (pŭt) *v.* Strike golf ball, strike (golf ball) gently and carefully with the putter so as to make it roll along the putting green with the object of getting it into the hole; **putt′ing green,** smooth piece of turf around each hole on golf course on which the ball is putted. **putt** *n.* Putting stroke.

put·tee (pŭt′ē) *n.* Long strip of cloth wound spirally around leg from ankle to knee for protection and support. [Hind. *patti* bandage]

putt·er[1] (pŭt′er) *n.* Straight-faced golf club used in putting.

***Pylon** at the temple of Edfu in Egypt. Like similar structures of the period, the walls were decorated with figures and hieroglyphics which usually stated why it was erected and in whose honor, and gave other relevant information.*

put·ter[2] (pŭt′*er*) *v.* Work in feeble or desultory manner (*at, in*); dawdle, loiter (*about* etc.); trifle *away* (time etc.).

put·ty (pŭt′ē) *n.* (pl **-ties**). 1. (**jewelers' ~**) Powder of calcined tin (and lead) for polishing glass or metal. 2. (**plasterers' ~**) Fine mortar of lime and water without sand. 3. (**glaziers' ~**) Cement of whiting, raw linseed oil, etc., for securing panes of glass, filling up holes in woodwork, etc. **putty** *v.t.* (**-tied, -ty·ing**). Cover, fix, join, fill *up*, with putty.

puz·zle (pŭz′*e*l) *n.* Bewilderment, perplexity; perplexing question, enigma; problem, toy, contrived to exercise ingenuity and patience. ~ *v.* (**-zled, -zling**). Perplex; be perplexed; make *out* by exercising ingenuity and patience. **puz′zle·ment** *n.* **puz′zling·ly** *adv.*

PVC *abbrev.* Polyvinyl chloride.

Pvt. *abbrev.* Private (soldier or marine).

PW *abbrev.* Prisoner of war.

PX *abbrev.* Post Exchange.

py·e·mi·a (pīē′mē*a*) *n.* Severe infection of the blood by virulent bacteria accompanied by acute fever and formation of abscesses in liver, lungs, kidneys, etc. **py·e·mic** (pīē′mĭk) *adj.*

Pyg·ma·li·on (pĭgmā′lē*o*n, -māl′y*o*n). (Gk. legend) King of Cyprus who made a statue of a woman and fell in love with it; he prayed to Aphrodite for a wife like it, and she endowed the statue with life.

Pyg·my, Pig·my (pĭg′mē) *ns.* (pl. **-mies**). 1. One of a diminutive race of people stated in ancient history and tradition to have inhabited parts of Ethiopia or India. 2. Member of a Negrillo people of very small stature. 3. (**p~**) Very small person or thing. **p~** *adj.* Of pygmies; dwarf; stunted. [Gk. *pugmé* length from elbow to knuckle]

py·ja·mas = PAJAMAS.

py·lon (pī′lŏn) *n.* 1. Gateway, esp. of Egyptian temple, with two truncated pyramidal towers connected by lower architectural member containing the gate. 2. Structure used to mark out airplane course; tall (metal) structure for supporting power cables.

py·lo·rus (pīlōr′*u*s, -lōr′-, pĭ-) *n.* (pl. **-lo·ri** pr. -lōr′ī, -lōr′ī). (anat.)

*Pygmies of the Ituri Forest in Zaire. Similar **pygmy** groups are found in New Guinea and the Andaman Islands, but there is no evidence of any link between these groups.*

*Although the **pyramid** is an architectural feature of several early civilizations, there is no known cultural connection. Those at Giza in Egypt (above) were tombs of the pharaohs, while Chichen Itza in Mexico and others in Peru and Central America were temples to the Sun and have flat tops.*

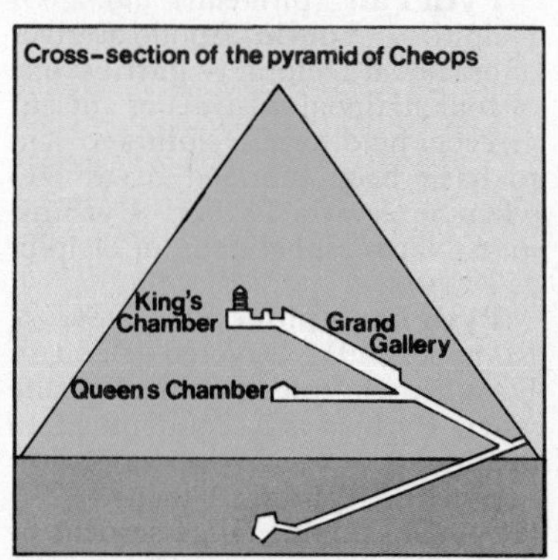

Opening from stomach into duodenum; part of stomach where this is. **py·lor·ic** (pīlōr′ĭk, -lŏr′-, pī-) *adj.* [Gk. *pulōros* gatekeeping]

Pyong·yang (pyŭng′yahng′). Capital of Democratic Peoples' Republic of Korea, in the SW. part on the Taedong River.

py·or·rhe·a, py·or·rhoe·a (pīorē′*a*) *ns.* Disease of the tooth sockets, accompanied by a discharge of pus and slight local hemorrhage. **py·or·rhe′al, py·or·rhoe′al** *adjs.*

pyr·a·can·tha (pĭr*a*kăn′th*a*, pīr*a*-) *n.* Evergreen thorny shrub of genus *Pyracantha* with white flowers and scarlet berries.

pyr·a·mid (pĭr′*a*mĭd) *n.* Monumental structure of stone etc. with polygonal or (usu.) square base and sloping sides meeting at apex, constructed by ancient Egyptians over a royal burial chamber and by Aztecs and Mayas as stepped platform for a temple; solid of this shape with base of three or more sides; pyramid-shaped thing or pile of things; fruit tree trained in pyramid shape. **py·ram·i·dal** (pĭrăm′ĭd*a*l) *adj.* **py·ram′i·dal·ly** *adv.*

Pyr·a·mus (pĭr′*a*m*u*s). (Rom. legend) Youth of Babylon, lover of Thisbe; forbidden to marry by their parents, who were neighbors, they conversed through a chink in the wall and agreed to meet at a tomb outside the city; here Thisbe was frightened away by a lioness, and Pyramus, finding her bloodstained cloak and supposing her dead, stabbed himself; Thisbe finding his body, threw herself upon his sword.

pyre (pīr) *n.* Heap of combustible material, esp. funeral pile for burning corpse.

py·rene (pīrēn′) *n.* (chem.) Solid aromatic hydrocarbon obtained from dry distillation of coal etc.

Pyr·e·nees (pĭr′*e*nēz). Range of mountains in SW. Europe separating Spain from France. **Pyr·e·ne′an** *adj.*

py·re·thrum (pīrē′thr*u*m) *n.* Any of several chrysanthemums, esp. *Chrysanthemum coccineum* and *C. cinerariaefolium*; insecticide made from powdered heads of this.

Py·rex (pī′rĕks) *n.* (trademark) Heat-resistant glass used for manufacturing esp. ovenware.

py·rex·i·a (pīrĕk′sē*a*) *n.* (med.) Fever.

pyr·i·dine (pĭr′ĭdēn) *n.* (chem.) Colorless volatile liquid base with offensive odor, present in bone oil and coal tar, from which it is obtained by distillation.

py·ri·tes (pīrī′tēz, p*i*-, pī′rīts) *n.* (pl. **-tes**). (**iron** ~) Iron sulfide (FeS_2) occurring as a mineral; (**copper** ~) double sulfide of copper and iron ($Cu_2S.Fe_2S_3$). **py·ri·tic** (pīrĭt′ĭk, p*i*-) *adj.*

pyro- *prefix.* Fire or heat.

py·ro·gal·lol (pīr*o*găl′awl, -ōl, -ŏl) *n.* (also **py·ro·gal·lic** pr. pīr*o*găl′ĭk **acid**) White crystalline substance, trihydroxybenzene, very soluble in water, used as a developer in photography etc.

py·ro·gen·ic (pīr*o*jĕn′ĭk) *adj.* Fever-producing.

py·rol·at·ry (pīrŏl′*a*trē) *n.* Fire worship.

py·ro·man·cy (pī′r*o*mănsē) *n.* Divination by fire. **py′ro·man·cer** *n.*

py·ro·ma·ni·a (pīr*o*mā′nē*a*) *n.* Incendiary mania. **py·ro·ma′ni·ac** *n.*

py·rom·e·ter (pīrŏm′ĭt*e*r) *n.* Instrument for measuring high temperatures. **py·ro·met·ric** (pīr*o*mĕt′rĭk), **py·ro·met′ri·cal** *adjs.* **py·rom′e·try** *n.*

py·ro·tech·nic (pīr*o*tĕk′nĭk), **py·ro·tech·ni·cal** (pīr*o*tĕk′nĭk*a*l) *adjs.* Of (the nature of) fireworks; (fig., of wit etc.) brilliant, sensational. **py·ro·tech′ni·cal·ly** *adv.*

The Persians are credited with the discovery of the insecticidal properties of ***Pyrethrum.*** *These chrysanthemums were grown in Dalmatia in the 19th century and in Japan, East Africa and, since 1945, Ecuador and Papua New Guinea.*

py·ro·tech′nics *n.* Art of making, display of, fireworks. **py·ro·tech′-nist, py′ro·tech·ny** *ns.*

py·rox·ene (pīrŏk′sēn) *n.* Black crystalline mineral common in igneous rocks. **py·rox·en·ic** (pīrŏksĕn′ĭk) *adj.*

py·rox·y·lin (pīrŏk′s*i*lĭn), **py·rox·y·line** (pīrŏk′s*i*lēn, -lĭn) *ns.* Any of a class of highly inflammable compounds (nitrates of cellulose), produced by treating vegetable fibers with a mixture of nitric and sulfuric acids.

Pyr·rhic (pĭr′ĭk) *adj.* Of PYRRHUS; ~ **victory**, victory achieved at too great a cost (from saying attributed to Pyrrhus after battle of Asculum, where he routed the Romans but lost the flower of his army: "One more such victory and we are lost").

Unlike the related boas which give birth to live young, the ***python*** *lays eggs. Like all constrictors, this snake lives on small mammals, reptiles and birds which it crushes to death before swallowing whole.*

pyr·rhic[1] (pĭr′ĭk) *adj.* & *n.* (Of) a war dance of the ancient Greeks, performed in armor, with mimicry of actual warfare.

pyr·rhic[2] (pĭr′ĭk) *adj.* & *n.* (Metrical foot) of two short or unstressed syllables, ˘˘.

Pyr·rhus (pĭr′*u*s) (319–272 B.C.). King of Epirus, military adventurer who fought a series of campaigns against Rome in Italy and Sicily (280–275); see also PYRRHIC.

Py·thag·o·ras (pĭthăg′*e*r*a*s) (6th c. B.C.). Greek philosopher and mathematician of Samos; his philosophical teaching included the doctrine of the immortality and transmigration of the soul; he evolved the idea that the explanation of the universe is to be sought in numbers and their relations. **Py·thag·o·re·an** (pĭthăg*e*rē′*a*n) *adj.* & *n.* ~ **theorem**, geometrical proposition, of which Pythagoras is credited with discovering the proof, that the square on the hypotenuse of a right-angled triangle is equal to the sum of the squares on the other two sides.

Pyth·i·a (pĭth′ē*a*). (Gk. Hist.) Priestess of Apollo at Delphi, who delivered the oracles.

Pyth·i·an (pĭth′ē*a*n) *adj.* Of Delphi; ~ **Apollo**, Apollo as giver of oracles at Delphi; ~ **games**, one of four national festivals of ancient Greece, held near Delphi and said to have been founded by Apollo when he slew the Python. **Pythian** *n.* 1. Native, inhabitant, of Delphi. 2. PYTHIA.

Pyth·i·as (pĭth′ē*a*s). (Gk. & Rom. legend) Devoted friend of DAMON, who pledged his own life when Pythias was condemned to death.

py·thon (pī′thŏn, -th*o*n) *n.* 1. (**P** ~, Gk. myth.) Huge serpent or monster slain near Delphi by Apollo. 2. Member of genus *P* ~ of large nonpoisonous snakes inhabiting the tropical regions of the Old World, or of related genera, which kill their prey by constriction; other related snakes. **py·thon·ic** (pīthŏn′ĭk) *adj.*

py·tho·ness (pī′th*o*nĭs, pĭth′*o*-) *n.* Woman soothsayer; see PYTHIA.

pyx (pĭks) *n.* (eccles.) Vessel, often of precious metal, in which host is reserved.

Many religions through the ages have required the dead to be burned on ***pyres.*** *Facing: Balinese mourners near an elaborate structure and decorated coffin, already blazing fiercely.*

*The letter **Q, q** derives its form from the Semitic sign koph, probably meaning 'a needle's eye'. It was dropped from the Greek alphabet after the 5th century B.C., only surviving as the sign for 90, but was kept by the Romans.*

Phoenician Early Greek Early Etruscan

Early Latin Classical Latin Italian

Q, q (kū) (pl. **Q's, q's** or **Qs, qs**). Seventeenth letter of modern English and 16th of ancient Roman alphabet, derived from Phoenician Ϙ, Φ, ϙ (representing guttural *k* sound).

q. *abbrev.* Quart, quarto, queen, question, query.

Qa·tar (kah'tar̄). Independent sheikdom on peninsula on W. coast of Persian Gulf; capital, Doha.

Q.E.D. *abbrev. Quod erat demonstrandum.* [L., = which was to be demonstrated]

Q-fe·ver (kū'fēv*er*). Disease allied to typhus but milder, caused by a different variety of rickettsia. [f. Queensland, Australia, where first observed]

Qi·a·na (kēăn'*a*, -ah'*na*) *n.* (trademark) Light nylonlike synthetic fiber.

QM, Q.M. *abbrevs.* Quartermaster.

QMG, Q.M.G. *abbrevs.* Quartermaster General.

qr. *abbrev.* (pl. **qrs.**) Quarter.

qt. *abbrev.* (pl. **qts.**) Quart(s).

q.t. *abbrev.* (slang) Quiet; **on the ~**, silently, stealthily.

qu. *abbrev.* Quart, queen, query, question.

qua (kwā, kwah) *adv.* As, in the capacity of.

Quaa·lude (kwā'lo͞od, -lūd, kwah-) *n.* (trademark) Methaqualone.

quack[1] (kwăk) *v.i.* & *n.* (Utter) harsh cry characteristic of duck.

quack[2] (kwăk) *n.* Ignorant pretender to skill esp. in medicine; charlatan. **quack'er·y** *n.* (pl. **-er·ies**). **quack** *adj.* Fraudulent, (esp.) alleged to cure disease.

quad (kwŏd) *n.* (colloq.) Quadrangle; quadraphonic sound system; QUADRAT; quadruplet.

quad·ran·gle (kwŏd'rănggel) *n.* Four-sided figure, esp. square or rectangle; four-sided court (partly) enclosed by parts of large building; such court with buildings around it. **quad·ran·gu·lar** (kwŏdrăng'gy*u*ler) *adj.* **quad·ran'gu·lar·ly** *adv.*

quad·rant (kwŏd'r*a*nt) *n.* 1. Quarter of circumference of circle; plane figure enclosed by two radii of circle at right angles and arc cut off by them; quarter of sphere. 2. Object, esp. graduated strip or plate of metal, shaped like quarter circle. 3. Instrument, usu. with calibrated arc of 90°, used for measuring angles and formerly (now superseded by SEXTANT) altitudes. **quad·ran·tal** (kwŏdrăn't*a*l) *adj.*

quand·ra·phon·ic (kwŏdr*a*fŏn'ĭk) *adj.* Of, pertaining to, or designating method of reproducing recorded sound using four individual transmission channels.

quad·rat (kwŏd'răt, rĭt) *n.* Metal block smaller than metal type, used by printers to create a blank space within printed matter.

quad·rate (kwŏd'rĭt, -rāt) *adj.* Square, rectangular (rare exc. anat. in names of squarish parts of body); **~ bone**, bone in heads of birds, amphibians, reptiles, and fish, by which lower jaw is articulated to skull. **quadrate** *n.* Quadrate bone, muscle, etc.

*Like many people in the 18th century, Hogarth's Rake (below) visited a **quack**. With his mixture of ancient magic and modern science the quack, then as now, inhabited a medical shadow-world.*

quad·rat·ic (kwŏdrăt'ĭk) *adj.* (math.) Involving the second and no higher power of an unknown quantity or variable (esp. **~ equation**). **quadratic** *n.* Quadratic equation. **quad·rat'ics** *n.* Branch of algebra dealing with quadratic equations.

quad·ren·ni·al (kwŏdrĕn'ē*a*l) *adj.* Occurring every, lasting, four years.

quadri-, quadru-, quadr- (before vowel) *prefixes.* Four.

quad·ric (kwŏd'rĭk) *adj.* (math.) Of the second degree. **~** *n.* Quadric function; surface whose equation is in the second degree.

quad·ri·ceps (kwŏd'rĭsĕps) *n.* (pl. **-cep·ses** pr. -sĕpsĭz, **-ceps**). Large muscle at front of thigh with four heads or attachments.

quad·ri·lat·er·al (kwŏdrĭlăt'*e*r*a*l) *adj.* & *n.* (Figure) bounded by four straight lines; (space, area)

1

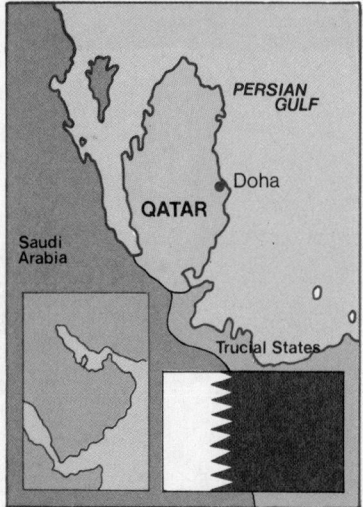

2

PERSIAN GULF

Doha

QATAR

Saudi Arabia

Trucial States

having four sides.

qua·drille[1] (kwŏdrĭl′) *n.* Card game fashionable in 18th c., played by four persons with 40 cards (i.e. an ordinary pack without the 8s, 9s, and 10s).

qua·drille[2] (kwŏdrĭl′) *n.* Square dance for four couples, containing five figures; music for this. [Fr. f. Span. *cuadrilla* squadron (*cuadra* square)]

quad·ril·lion (kwŏdrĭl′yon) *n.* Fifth power of a thousand (1 followed by 15 zeros). **quad·ril′-lionth** *adj.* & *n.*

quad·ri·par·tite (kwŏdrĭpar̄′tīt) *adj.* Consisting of four parts; shared by or involving four parties.

With a large revenue from oil, ***Qatar*** *has introduced television (1) which provides entertainment for many of its 90,000 people. However, most of the income is spent on welfare. Old customs continue, including regular attendance at the huge mosques (2).*

quad·ri·ple·gi·a (kwŏdrĭplē′jēa) *n.* Complete paralysis of the body beginning at the neck. **quad·ri·-ple′gic** *adj.* & *n.*

quad·ri·va·lent (kwŏdrĭvā′lent, -drĭv′*a*-) *adj.* (chem.) Having four valences.

quad·riv·i·um (kwŏdrĭv′ēum) *n.* (pl. **quad·riv·i·a** pr. kwŏdrĭv′-ēa). In Middle Ages, the higher division of the seven liberal arts, comprising arithmetic, geometry, astronomy, and music.

quad·roon (kwŏdrōōn′) *n.* Offspring of white and mulatto, person having one-quarter black ancestry.

quad·ru·ped (kwŏd′rupĕd) *n.* Four-footed animal, esp. four-footed mammal. ~ *adj.* Four-footed. **quad·ru·pe·dal** (kwŏd-rōō′pedal, kwŏd′rupĕdal) *adj.*

quad·ru·ple (kwŏdrōō′pel, kwŏd′rōō-) *adj.* Fourfold, consisting of four parts or involving four parties; amounting to four times the number or amount *of*, equivalent to fourfold the amount of, superior by four times in amount or number *to*; ~ **rhythm** or **time**, (mus.) with four beats to a measure. **quad-ru'ple** *n.* Number or amount four times greater than another. ~ *v.* (**-pled, -pling**). Multiply by 4.

quad·ru·plet (kwŏdrŭp'lĭt, -drōō'plĭt, kwŏd'ruplĭt) *n.* One of four children born at a single birth.

quad·ru·pli·cate (kwŏdrōō'pl*i*-kĭt) *adj.* Fourfold, four times repeated or copied. ~ *n.* **in** ~, in four exactly similar examples or copies; (pl.) four such copies. ~ (kwŏdrōō'pl*i*kāt) *v.t.* (**-cat·ed, -cat·ing**). Multiply by 4; make in quadruplicate. **quad·ru·pli·ca·tion** (kwŏdrōōpl*i*kā'sh*o*n) *n.*

quaes·tor, ques·tor (kwĕs't*e*r, kwē'st*e*r) *ns.* (Rom. hist.) Magistrate in charge of public funds, as treasury officer etc. **quaes·to·ri·al** (kwĕstōr'ē*a*l, -stōr'-, kwē-) *adj.* **quaes'tor·ship** *n.*

quaff (kwahf, kwăf, kwawf) *v.* Drink, drain (cup etc.), in long or copious drafts. **quaff'er** *n.*

quag (kwăg, kwŏg) *n.* Quagmire.

quag·ga (kwăg'*a*) *n.* Species of zebra (*Equus quagga*) of South Africa, now extinct.

quag·mire (kwăg'mīr) *n.* Quaking bog, fen, marsh, slough; (fig.) difficult situation or problem.

qua·hog, qua·haug (kwaw'hŏg, -hawg, kw*a*hawg', -hŏg') *ns.* Large, thick-shelled edible clam species of U.S. Atlantic Coast.

quail[1] (kwāl) *n.* (pl. **quails**, collect. **quail**). Migratory bird of Old World allied to partridge, esp. *Coturnix coturnix*, esteemed as food; any of various Amer. birds (genus *Colinus*) resembling this, esp. the BOBWHITE.

quail[2] (kwāl) *v.* Flinch, be cowed, give way *before*.

quaint (kwānt) *adj.* Attractive or piquant by virtue of unfamiliar, esp. old-fashioned, appearance, ornamentation, manners, etc.; daintily odd. **quaint'ly** *adv.* **quaint'ness** *n.*

quake (kwāk) *v.i.* (**quaked, quak·ing**). Shake, tremble. **quak'y** *adj.* (**quak·i·er, quak·i·est**). **quake** *n.* Act of quaking; earthquake.

Quak·er (kwā'k*e*r) *n.* (fem. **Quak·er·ess** pr. kwā'k*e*rĭs). Member of the religious Society of Friends founded by George Fox in 1648–50, distinguished by peaceful principles and plainness of dress and manners; **~(s') meeting**, religious meeting of the Friends, silent except when some member feels stirred to speak; hence, silent meeting, company in which conversation flags. **Quak'er·ism** *n.* **Quak'er·ly** *adv.* & *adj.* [nickname of early members of the society, who were said to "tremble at the Word of the Lord"]

qual·i·fi·ca·tion (kwŏl*i*f*i*kā'sh*o*n) *n.* 1. Modification, restriction, limitation; restricting or limiting circumstance. 2. Quality, accomplishment, etc., fitting person or thing (*for* a position etc.). 3. Condition that must be fulfilled before right can be acquired or office held.

qual·i·fy (kwŏl'*i*fī) *v.* (**-fied, -fy·ing**). 1. Attribute quality to, describe *as*; (gram., of adjective) express some quality of noun. 2. Invest or provide with the necessary qualities, make competent, fit, or legally entitled (*for, to*); make oneself competent (*for*) or capable of holding some office, exercising some function, etc. 3. Modify (statement etc.), make less absolute or sweeping, subject to reservation or limitation; moderate, mitigate, esp. make less violent, severe, or

***Quagmires** are often thought of as useless wasteland, fit only to be drained and reclaimed. But to naturalists they are the homes, feeding areas, or breeding grounds of many fascinating creatures.*

*The European **quail** (above) feeds on insects when young, but later eats seeds and shoots too. It is a nocturnal migrant, and spends the summer months in Britain. Gambell's variety (left) is found only in desert areas of the southern States of the U.S.A.*

unpleasant. **qual'i·fied** *adj.* **qual'i·fi·er** *n.*

qual·i·ta·tive (kwŏl'ĭtātĭv) *adj.* Concerned with, depending on, quality.

qual·i·ty (kwŏl'ĭtē) *n.* (pl. **-ties**). 1. Degree of excellence, relative nature or kind or character (opp. QUANTITY); class or grade of thing as determined by this; general excellence. 2. Characteristic trait, mental or moral attribute. 3. (archaic) High rank or social standing; **the ~**, people of high rank or social standing. 4. (logic, of proposition) Being affirmative or negative. 5. (of sound, voice, etc.) Distinctive character apart from pitch or loudness, timbre.

qualm (kwahm, kwawm) *n.* Momentary faint or sick feeling, queasiness; misgiving, sinking of heart; scruple of conscience. **qualm'ish·ly** *adv.* **qualm'ish·ness** *n.*

quan·da·ry (kwŏn'derē) *n.* (pl. **-ries**). State of perplexity, difficult situation, practical dilemma.

quan·ta (kwŏn'ta): see QUANTUM.

quan·ti·fy (kwŏn'tifī) *v.t.* (**-fied, -fy·ing**). 1. (logic) Determine application of (term, proposition) by use of *all, some,* etc. 2. Determine quantity of, measure, express as quantity. **quan'ti·fi·a·ble** *adj.* **quan·ti·fi·ca·tion** (kwŏntĭfĭkā'shon) *n.*

quan·ti·ta·tive (kwŏn'tĭtātĭv) *adj.* Measured or measurable by, concerned with, quantity; of, based on, the quantity of vowels. **quan'ti·ta·tive·ly** *adv.*

quan·ti·ty (kwŏn'tĭtē) *n.* (pl. **-ties**). 1. Property of things that is regarded as determinable by measurement of some kind; amount, sum; (mus.) length or duration of notes. 2. Specified or considerable portion, number, or amount of something; (pl.) large amounts or numbers, abundance. 3. (math.) Thing having quantity, figure or symbol representing this; **unknown ~**, (fig.) person or thing whose action cannot be foreseen.

quan·tum (kwŏn'tum) *n.* (pl. **-ta** pr. -ta). Sum, amount; share, portion; (phys.) discrete unit quantity of energy, proportional to frequency of radiation, emitted from or absorbed by atom; **~ electrodynamics, mechanics,** etc., dynamics, etc., taking account of quanta; **~ number**, one of a set of intergers or half intergers describing the energy level of a particle or system of particles; **~ jump**, abrupt change in energy level of molecule or atom accompanied by absorption or emission of radiant energy equalling the difference between the two levels; (fig.) any abrupt and wide-ranging shift or change; **~ theory**, theory originated by M. Planck (1910) and extended by N. Bohr, which accounts for certain atomic phenomena by assuming that radiant energy (heat, light, etc.) is emitted from atoms only in discrete amounts or quanta and not continuously.

quar·an·tine (kwŏr'antēn, kwăr'-) *n.* (Period, orig. 40 days, of) isolation imposed on infected ship, or on persons (esp. travelers) who might spread contagious or infectious diseases; (period of) isolation for animals (esp. dogs and cats) after landing from abroad. **~** *v.t.* (**-tined, -tin·ing**). Impose such isolation on, put in quarantine. [prob. f. It. *quarantina* 40 days]

quark (kwărk, kwŏrk) *n.* (One of three kinds of) hypothetical component of subatomic particles.

quar·rel[1] (kwŏr'el, kwăr'-) *n.* Short heavy arrow or bolt formerly used in crossbow.

quar·rel[2] (kwŏr'el, kwăr'-) *n.* Occasion of complaint against person or his actions; violent contention or altercation *between* persons, rupture of friendly relations.

*Michelangelo obtained his marble for sculpting from a **quarry** at Carrara (1) which has been worked for 2,000 years, mostly for building materials. In Kent, England (2), chalk is quarried to make lime, used in cement and as a fertilizer.*

~ *v.i.* (**-reled, -rel·ing, -relled, -rel·ling**). Take exception, find fault *with*; contend violently (*with* person), fall out, have dispute, break off friendly relations. **quar'rel·some** *adj.* **quar'rel·some·ly** *adv.* **quar'rel·some·ness** *n.*

quar·rel³ (kwŏr'el, kwăr'-) *n.* (also **quarry**) Square or diamond shape; object with this shape, as diamond-shaped pane of glass. [f. It. *quadrello*, dim. of *quadro* square]

quar·ry¹ (kwŏr'ē, kwăr'ē) *n.* (pl. **-ries**). Object of pursuit by bird of prey, hounds, hunters, etc.; intended victim or prey. [OF. *curée* (*cuir* skin); orig. sense, parts of deer placed on hide and given to hounds]

quar·ry² (kwŏr'ē, kwăr'ē) *n.* (pl. **-ries**). Excavation made by taking stone for building etc. from its bed; place from which stone etc., can be extracted. ~ *v.* (**-ried, -ry·ing**). Extract (stone) from quarry; form quarry in (hill etc.); cut or dig (as) in quarry.

quart¹ (kwŏrt) *n.* Measure of capacity, quarter of gallon, two pints; pot or bottle containing this amount.

quart² (kărt) *n.* (in piquet) Sequence of four playing cards in one suit.

quar·ter (kwŏr'ter) *n.* 1. Fourth part; one of four equal or corresponding parts; fourth part of. 2. Quarter of dollar, 25 cents, as amount or coin. 3. One of four parts, each including a limb, into which beast's or bird's carcass is divided; (pl.) similar parts of traitor quartered after execution; (freq. pl.) haunch(es) of living animal or man. 4. Either side of stern of ship to the rear of the beam. 5. Fourth part of cwt., 25 lb. (in Brit. 28 lb.). 6. Quarter-mile race or running distance. 7. Fourth part of year, three months. 8. Fourth part of lunar period, moon's position between first and second or third and fourth of these. 9. Point of time 15 minutes before or after any hour. 10. (Region lying about) point of compass; direction; district, locality; (colloq.) portion or member of community, some thing or things, without reference to actual locality. 11. Division of town, esp. one appropriated to or occupied by special group. 12. (pl.) Lodgings, abode, esp. place where troops are lodged or stationed; assigned or appropriate places, station; **winter ~s**, place occupied, esp. by troops, for winter. 13. Exemption from death offered or granted to enemy in battle who will surrender. 14. **quar'terback** (*n.* & *v.*), (in football) (player) direct(ing) attacking play (also fig.); **quarter binding**, (of book) with narrow strip of leather at back and none elsewhere; **quar'terdeck**, part of upper deck between stern and after mast, usu. reserved for officers; **quarter horse**, breed of saddle horse in western U.S. (orig. trained for races of ¼ mi.); **quar'termaster**, (naut.) petty officer in charge of steering, signals, hold stowing, etc.; (mil., abbrev. Q.M.) officer with duties of obtaining and looking after food, clothing, equipment, etc.; **quar'termaster general** (pl. **quar'termasters general**) (abbrev. Q.M.G.) (in U.S. Army) major general commanding the **Quartermaster Corps**, the supply branch of the U.S. Army; **quarter note**, (music) note having ¼ the time value of a whole note; **quarter section**, ¼ of sq. mi. of land, 160 acres; **quar'terstaff**, stout iron-tipped pole 6–8 ft. long formerly used as weapon; **quarter tone**, (mus.) half a semitone. **quarter** *v.t.* 1. Divide into four equal parts; (hist.) divide (traitor's body) into quarters. 2. Put (esp. soldiers) into quarters; station or lodge in specified place. 3. (of searchers or search dogs) Traverse (ground) in orderly pattern to ensure thorough coverage.

quar·ter·age (kwŏr'terĭj) *n.* Quarterly payment; a quarter's wages, allowance, pension, etc.

quar·ter·ly (kwŏr'terlē) *adj.* 1. Occurring every three months. 2.

Divided quarterly or by lines at right angles. ~ *n.* (pl. **-lies**). Quarterly review or magazine. ~ *adv.* 1. Once every three months. 2. In, by quarters.

quar·tet, Brit. **quar·tette** (kwôrtĕt′) *ns.* 1. (mus.) (Composition for) four voices or instruments in combination; players or singers rendering this; **piano** ~, three stringed instruments with piano; **string** ~, two violins, viola, and cello. 2. Set of four persons or things.

quar·tile (kwôr′tīl, -tĭl) *n.* (statistics) One of values of a variable dividing a population into four equal groups having equal frequencies as regards the value of that variable.

quar·to (kwôr′tō) *n.* (pl. **-tos**). Size given by folding sheet of paper twice (into four leaves); book consisting of sheets so folded.

quartz (kwôrts) *n.* Any of several varieties of silica occurring in masses or crystals.

quartz·ite (kwôrt′sīt) *n.* Hard sandstone containing quartz grains.

qua·sar (kwā′zâr, -*zer*, -sâr, -*ser*) *n.* Any of a number of celestial objects emitting strong radio waves and varying between 4 and 10 billion light-years in distance from Earth. [*quas*(i-stell)*ar* (radio source)]

quash (kwŏsh) *v.t.* Put an end to; suppress.

qua·si (kwā′zī, -sī, kwah′zē, -sē) *adj.* & *adv.* Resembling, seeming to be, as it were, almost, not exactly.

quasi- *prefix.* Seeming(ly), not real(ly); practical(ly); half-, almost.

quas·sia (kwŏsh′*a*, -ē*a*) *n.* Tropical Amer. tree (*Quassia amara*), found esp. in Surinam; wood, bark, or root of this and other trees (now esp. *Picraena excelsa*, bitter wood tree, of W. Indies etc., yielding bitter medicinal tonic and also much used horticulturally for destroying aphids). [S. Amer. tree named by Linnaeus after *Graman Quassi*, Surinam black slave who discovered its medicinal properties in 1730]

qua·ter·cen·te·na·ry (kwaht*er*-sĕn′*t*enĕrē, -sĕntĕn′*er*ē; *Brit.* kwaht*er*sĕntē′*n*erē) *n.* Four hundredth anniversary.

qua·ter·na·ry (kwah′t*er*nĕrē, kwahtêr′*n*erē) *adj.* 1. Having four parts; (chem.) compounded of four elements or radicals. 2. **Q**~, (geol.) of the period or system subsequent to the Tertiary, of recent and present-day formations, yielding fossils of shells, bones, and plants, all of which represent species still living. ~ *n.* (pl. **-ries**). 1. Set of four things; number 4. 2. **Q**~, (geol.) Quarternary period or system.

qua·ter·ni·on (kw*a*têr′nē*o*n) *n.* Set of four; (math.) quotient of two vectors or operator that changes one vector into another (so named as depending on four geometrical elements); (pl.) form of calculus of vectors in which this operator is used.

quat·rain (kwŏt′rān; *Brit.* kwŏt′rĭn) *n.* Stanza, poem of four lines, usu. with alternate rhymes.

quat·re·foil (kăt′*er*foil, kăt′r*e*-) *n.* Four-cusped figure, esp. as opening in architectural tracery, resembling symmetrical four-lobed leaf or flower.

quat·tro·cen·to (kwŏtrōchĕn′-tō) *n.* Fifteenth century as period of Italian art and literature. [It., = "four hundred," short for *mil quattrocento* 1400]

qua·ver (kwā′v*er*) *v.* Vibrate, shake, tremble (esp. of voice or musical sound); use trills in singing; sing with trills; say in trembling tones. ~ *n.* 1. Trill in singing; tremulousness in speech. 2. (music, chiefly Brit.) Note having ⅛ the time value of a whole note. **qua′ver·-ing·ly** *adv.* **qua′ver·y** *adj.*

quay (kē, kā, kwā) *n.* Solid stationary artificial landing place usu. of stone or iron, lying alongside or projecting into water, for (un)loading ships. **quay′age** *n.*

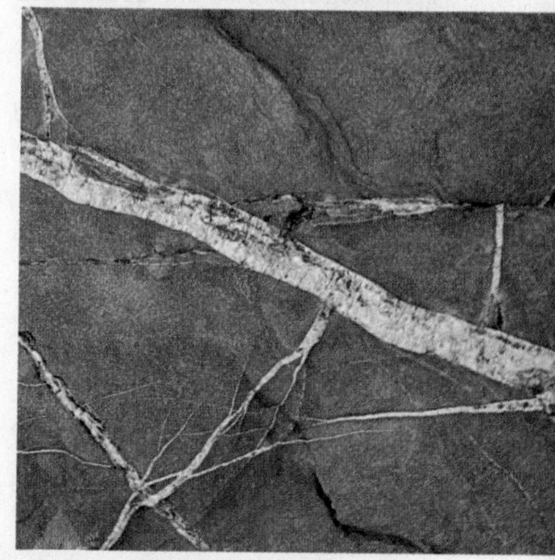

*Top: A beautifully-crafted **quartz** egg on display at the Smithsonian Institution. Quartz is formed in volcanic rocks, but during geological history may be dissolved by waters passing through the rocks, which then deposit it in cracks.*

*The four-lobed decoration repeated on the frontage of Little Moreton Hall in Cheshire, England, is a **quatrefoil** and was first used in heraldry.*

*The **Quechua** culture, which flourished in the Inca empire in Peru, Ecuador and Bolivia until the Spanish conquest, consequently declined, though the language is still widely spoken.*

Quays collectively; space occupied by quays and their activities; duty levied on ships using quay.

Que. *abbrev.* Quebec.

quea·sy (kwē´zē) *adj.* (**-si·er, -si·est**). (of person, stomach) Easily upset, inclined to sickness or nausea; (of conscience etc.) tender, scrupulous. **quea′si·ly** *adv.* **quea′si·ness** *n.*

Que·bec (kwĭbĕk´, kĭ-). Province of E. Canada; its capital, on the St. Lawrence River, orig. settled by the French, and captured from them by a British force under Wolfe, 1759.

Quech·ua (kĕch´wah, -w*a*) *n.* (pl. **-uas,** collect. **-ua**). Member of a group of tribes that formed the ruling class of the Incas; language of these tribes, still spoken among Peruvian Indians. **Quech′uan** *adj.* & *n.*

queen (kwēn) *n.* 1. King's wife (also ~ **consort** for distinction from sense 2; ~ **dowager,** wife of late king; ~ **mother,** queen dowager who is mother of sovereign); also prefixed to personal name as title. 2. Female sovereign ruler, usu. hereditary. 3. Adored woman, goddess, etc. (**Q~ of Heaven,** the Virgin Mary; **queen of love,** Venus); majestic woman; belle, mock sovereign, on some occasion (as **Q~ of the May** at May festival); personified best example of anything regarded as feminine. 4. Woman, country, etc. regarded as ruling over some sphere. 5. Fertile female of bee, wasp, ant, or termite. 6. (slang) Male homosexual, esp. one having effeminate traits. 7. (chess) Piece with greatest freedom of movement, placed next to king at beginning of game. 8. One of face cards in each suit of deck of playing cards, bearing figure of a queen. 9. ~ **bee,** fully developed fertile female bee; ~ **post,** one of two upright timbers between tie beam and principal rafters of roof truss; **~-size** (**bed**), bigger than double bed, but less than king-size, usu. 5 by 6 ft. **queen′like** *adj.* **queen** *v.* 1. Make (woman) queen. 2. (chess) Advance (pawn) to opponent's end of board, where it is replaced by a queen or other piece; (of pawn) reach this position.

Queen (kwēn) **Charlotte Islands.** Group of islands in the Pacific off the coast of British Columbia, N. of Vancouver Island.

Queen (kwēn) **Elizabeth Islands.** Group of islands in the Arctic Ocean, N. of the Northwest Territories, N. Canada, and including Ellesmere and Devon Islands, and the Sverdrup and Parry island groups.

queen·ly (kwēn´lē) *adj.* (**-li·er, -li·est**). Fit for, appropriate to, a queen; majestic, queenlike. **queen′li·ness** *n.*

Queen (kwēn) **Maud Gulf.** Gulf between SE. Victoria Island and the Northwest Territories in N. Canada; **Queen Maud Land,** section of land in Antarctica, bounded by Coats Land in the W. and Enderby Land in the E.; a Norwegian dependency since 1949.

Queens·ber·ry (kwēnz´bĕrē, -b*e*rē) **Rules**: see MARQUIS of Queensberry Rules.

Queens·land (kwēnz´lănd, -l*a*nd). State of NE. Australia; capital, Brisbane.

queer (kwēr) *adj.* Strange, odd, eccentric; of questionable character, shady, suspect; out of sorts, giddy, faint. **queer′ly** *adv.* **queer′ness** *n.* **queer** *n.* (slang) Homosexual. ~ *v.t.* (slang) Spoil, put out of order.

quell (kwĕl) *v.t.* Suppress, forcibly put an end to; quiet, pacify. **quell′er** *n.*

Que·moy (kĭmoi´). Island in the Formosa Strait off the SE. coast of China, governed by Taiwan.

quench (kwĕnch) *v.t.* Extinguish; cool, esp. with water (heat, heated thing); stifle, suppress (desire etc.); slake (thirst). **quench′a·ble** *adj.*

que·nelle (k*e*nĕl´) *n.* (cooking) Seasoned ball of fish or meat pounded to paste and poached.

quern (kwērn) *n.* Hand mill for grinding grain; small hand mill for pepper etc.

quer·u·lous (kwĕr´*u*l*u*s, -y*u*l*u*s) *adj.* Complaining, peevish. **quer′u·lous·ly** *adv.* **quer′u·lous·ness** *n.*

que·ry (kwēr´ē) *n.* (pl. **-ries**). Question; question mark (?) or word *query* or *qu.*, used to indicate doubt of correctness of statement in writing. ~ *v.* (**-ried, -ry·ing**). Ask, inquire; put a question; call in question, question accuracy of.

quest (kwĕst) *n.* Seeking, search; thing sought, esp. object of medieval knight's pursuit; **in ~ of,** seeking. **quest** *v.* Search *for* something; go on a quest.

ques·tion (kwĕs´ch*o*n, kwĕsh´-) *n.* 1. Interrogative statement of

The cores of former volcanoes in the coastal plain of south-east ***Queensland,*** *Australia, the Glasshouse Mountains, can be seen at sea and were named by James Cook.*

some point to be investigated or discussed; problem; subject for discussion in meeting etc.; subject of discussion, debate, or strife; **the ~**, the precise matter receiving or requiring discussion or deliberation; **beg the ~**: see BEG; **in ~**, under consideration; **it is a ~ of**, what is required or involved is; **out of the ~**, not to be considered or thought of; **without ~**, certainly, undoubtedly. 2. Sentence in interrogative form, meant to elicit information, interrogation, inquiry; **~ mark**, punctuation mark (?) placed at end of sentence, phrase, or word to denote a direct question; interrogation mark. 3. Action of questioning. **question** *v.t.* Ask questions of, interrogate, subject (person) to examination; seek information from study of (phenomena, facts); call in question, throw doubt upon, raise objections to. **ques'tion·er** *n.* **ques'tion·ing·ly** *adv.*

ques·tion·a·ble (kwĕs'ch*o*n*a*bel, kwĕsh'-) *adj.* (esp.) Doubtfully true; not clearly consistent with honesty, honor, or wisdom. **ques'tion·a·bly** *adv.* **ques'tion·a·ble·ness, ques·tion·a·bil·i·ty** (kwĕsch*o*n*a*bĭl'ĭtē, kwĕsh-) *ns.*

ques·tion·naire (kwĕsch*o*nār', kwĕsh-) *n.* Series of printed questions usu. for obtaining information on special points esp. in statistical investigations.

quet·zal (kĕtsahl', -săl; *Brit.* kĕt's*a*l) *n.* (pl. **quet·zals, quet·za·les** pr. kĕtsah'lās). Beautiful Central Amer. bird (*Pharomachrus mocino*), cock of which has very long golden-green tail feathers. [Aztec *quetzalli* tail feather of this bird]

Quet·zal·co·a·tl (kĕtsahlkōah'-t*e*l). Aztec and Toltec god worshipped as bestower of arts of civilization on mankind, having as symbol a plumed serpent (snake with quetzal feathers instead of scales).

queue (kū) *n.* 1. Pigtail, or long braid of real or artificial hair worn hanging down the back of the neck. 2. Line of persons, vehicles, etc., awaiting their turn to be attended to or proceed. **~** *v.i.* (**queued, queu·ing**). Form *up* in, take one's place in, queue.

Que·zon[1] (kā'zŏn) **City.** Designated capital of the Republic of the Philippines, on S. Luzon Island, NE. of MANILA,[1] which remains the administrative capital.

The largest park in ***Quebec,*** *the Plains of Abraham, site of the battle that routed the French defenders of Quebec, who had been under seige for two months in 1759, harrassed constantly by British troops.*

Que·zon[2] (kā´zŏn), **Manuel Luis** (1878–1944). (also called **Quezon y Molina**) Philippine statesman; 1st president of the Commonwealth of the Philippines, 1935–44.

quib·ble (kwĭb´*e*l) *n.* 1. (archaic) Play on words, pun. 2. Equivocation, evasion; unsubstantial or purely verbal argument etc., esp. one depending on ambiguity of word. ~ *v.i.* (**-bled, -bling**). Use quibbles. **quib'bler** *n.* **quib'bling** *adj.*

quiche (kēsh) *n.* Open pastry shell containing baked custardlike dish, often with cheese.

quick (kwĭk) *adj.* 1. (archaic) Living, alive. 2. Vigorous, lively, active; prompt to act, perceive, be affected, etc. 3. Moving rapidly, rapid, swift; done in short time or with little interval. 4. **~-freeze** (*v.t.*), subject (food) to rapid freezing, permitting retention of flavor and juices and indefinite storage at low temperatures; **quick'lime** = LIME[1] def. 1; ~ **one**, (colloq.) quick drink; **quick'sand**, (bed of) loose wet sand readily swallowing up any heavy object resting on it or person or animal walking on it; **quick'silver**, mercury; (*v.t.*) coat back of (mirror glass) with amalgam of tin; **quick'-step**, (mus.) march in military quick time; ~ **time**, fast military marching pace of 120 steps per minute; ~ **trick**, (bridge) sure trick that can be taken in 1st or 2nd round of play. **quick'ly** *adv.* **quick** *n.* Tender or sensitive flesh below skin or esp. nails; tender part of wound or sore where healthy tissue begins; seat of feeling or emotion; (also fig.). ~ *adv.* Quickly, at rapid rate, in comparatively short time; ~ *v.* (imper.) make haste.

quick·en (kwĭk´*e*n) *v.* 1. Give or restore natural or spiritual life or vigor to; animate, stimulate, rouse, inspire; receive, come to, life; (of woman) reach stage of pregnancy at which fetus makes clearly perceptible movements. 2. Accelerate; make or become quicker.

quick·ie (kwĭk´ē) *n.* (colloq.) Thing done, made, or consumed hastily; film so produced.

quick·ness (kwĭk´nĭs) *n.* Readiness or acuteness of perception or apprehension; speed, suddenness.

quid[1] (kwĭd) *n.* (pl. **quid**). (Brit.) Sum of £1; one-pound bank note.

quid[2] (kwĭd) *n.* Lump of tobacco etc. for chewing.

quid·di·ty (kwĭd´ĭtē) *n.* (pl. **-ties**). 1. Essence of a thing, what makes a thing what it is. 2. Quibble, captious subtlety.

quid pro quo (kwĭd prō kwō´) (pl. **quid pro quos**). Compensation, return made, consideration. [L., = "something for something"]

qui·es·cent (kwēēs´*e*nt, kwī-)

*The **quetzal** is found only in the dense mountainous forests of Central America. The 2ft.-long metallic green plumes of the male were worn by native chiefs as a sign of prestige.*

adj. Motionless, inert, silent, dormant. **qui·es'cent·ly** *adv.* **qui·es'cence, qui·es'cen·cy** *ns.*

qui·et (kwī´ĭt) *n.* Peaceful condition of affairs in social or political life; silence, stillness; freedom from disturbance, agitation, etc.; rest, repose, peace of mind; unruffled deportment, calm. ~ *adj.* 1. Making no stir, commotion, or noise; not active; free from excess, not going to extremes; avoiding or escaping notice, secret, private. 2. Free from disturbance, interference, or annoyance; calm, unruffled, silent, still. **qui'et·ly** *adv.* **qui'et·ness, qui·e·tude** (kwī´*e*to͞od, -tūd) *ns.* **quiet** *v.* Reduce to quietness, soothe, calm; become quiet.

qui·e·tus (kwīē´t*u*s) *n.* (pl. **-tus·es**). Acquittance, receipt, given on payment of account etc. (now rare); release from life, extinction, final riddance; anything that kills or eliminates; finishing blow, final stroke. [med. L. *quietus* (*est*) (he is) quit, used as receipt form]

quill (kwĭl) *n.* Hollow stem of feather; whole large feather of wing or tail; pen, plectrum, or toothpick, made of this; spine of porcupine; bobbin of hollow reed, any bobbin; musical pipe made of hollow stem (archaic); curled up piece of cinnamon or cinchona bark.

quilt (kwĭlt) *n.* Coverlet, esp. made of padding enclosed between 2 layers of fabric and kept in place by lines of stitching. ~ *v.t.* Cover, line, etc., with padded material; make or join together after the manner of a quilt. **quilt'er, quilt'ing** *ns.*

quin·a·crine (kwĭn´*a*krēn) **hydrochloride.** Antimalarial drug derived from acridine.

quince (kwĭns) *n.* Hard acid fruit like a large yellow apple used as preserve or as flavoring; small tree (*Cydonia oblonga*) bearing this. [ult. f. L. *Cydonium* of Cydonia in Crete]

quin·cen·te·nar·y (kwĭnsĕn´-t*e*nĕrē, -sĕntĕn´*e*rē; *Brit.* kwĭnsĕn-tē´n*e*rē) *n.* Five hundredth anniversary.

quin · cunx (kwĭng´kŭngks, kwĭn´-) *n.* (Arrangement of) five objects set so that four are at corners of square or rectangle and the other at its center, esp. as basis of arrangement in planting trees.

qui·nine (kwī´nīn; *Brit.* kwĭnēn´) *n.* Alkaloid found in cinchona bark and used in treatment of malaria and as febrifuge and tonic; (pop.) quinine sulfate, usual form in which it is taken. [Peruv. *kina* bark]

qui·none (kwĭnōn´, kwĭn´ōn) *n.* 1. Crystalline compound ($C_6H_4O_2$) obtained by oxidizing aniline. 2. General name for a benzene derivative in which two oxygen atoms replace two hydrogen.

quin·qua·ge·nar·i·an (kwĭng-kw*a*j*e*nār´ē*a*n, kwĭnkw*a*-) *adj.* & *n.* (Person) aged 50 or more but less than 60.

quinque- *prefix.* Five.

quin·quen·ni·um (kwĭnkwĕn´-ē*u*m, kwĭng-) *n.* (pl. **-quen·ni·ums, -quen·ni·a** pr. -kwĕn´ē*a*). Five-year period; also **quinquenniad. quin·quen'ni·al** *adj.* Happening every five years; lasting five years.

quin·que·va·lent (kwĭngkw*a*-vā´l*e*nt, kwĭn-, -kwĕv´*a*-) *adj.* (chem.) Having a valence of 5.

quin·sy (kwĭn´zē) *n.* Abscess forming around the tonsil usu. as a complication of tonsillitis. [Gk. *kunaghkē*(*kuōn kun-* dog, *aghkōm* throttle)]

The Dionne **quintuplets** were born in Callander, Ontario, in 1934. Their survival through childhood was the first case recorded by science. However, one girl died at 20 and another in 1970.

quint (kwĭnt) *n.* (colloq.) Quintuplet.

quin·tal (kwĭn′tal) *n.* Weight of 100 lbs., hundredweight; 100 kilograms. [Arab. *kintār*]

quin·tes·sence (kwĭntĕs′ens) *n.* 1. (ancient and medieval philos.) Fifth substance, apart from the four elements of earth, air, fire, and water, composing the heavenly bodies entirely and latent in all things, extraction of which was one of the aims of alchemy. 2. Most essential part of any substance, refined extract; purest and most perfect form, manifestation, or embodiment, *of* some quality or class. **quin·tes·sen·tial** (kwĭntesĕn′shal) *adj.* [*quinta essentia* fifth essence]

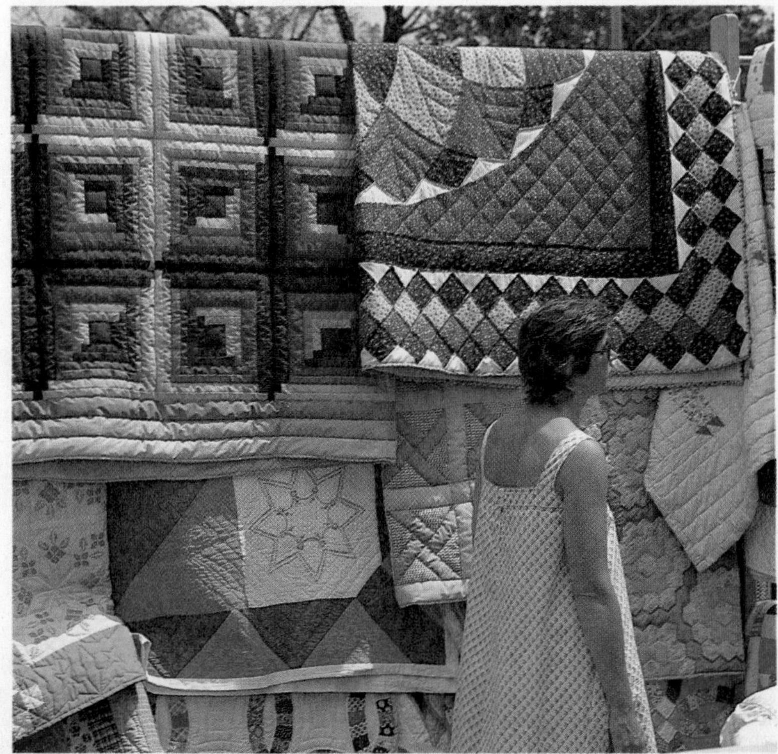

quin·tet, (Brit.) **quin·tette** (kwĭntĕt′) *ns.* 1. (mus.) (Composition for) five voices or instruments in combination; players or singers rendering this; **clarinet, piano,** etc., ~, four stringed instruments plus instrument named. 2. Set of five persons or things.

Quin·til·ian (kwĭntĭl′yan, -ēan). Marcus Fabius Quintilianus (1st c. A.D.), Roman rhetorician, author of *De Institutione Oratoria*, the tenth book of which contains judgments on Greek and Roman writers.

quin·til·lion (kwĭntĭl′yon) *n.* (pl. **-lions**, following a numeral **-lion**). Cube of a million (1 with 18 zeros).

quin·tu·ple (kwĭntōō′pel, -tū′-, -tŭp′el, kwĭn′tupel, -tyu-) *adj.* Fivefold; consisting of five things or parts. ~ *v.* (**-pled, -pling**). Multiply, increase, fivefold.

quin·tu·plet (kwĭntŭp′lĭt, -tōō′-plĭt, -tū′-, kwĭn′tuplĭt, -tyu-) *n.* 1. Set of five things. 2. One of five children born at a birth.

quin·tu·pli·cate (kwĭntōō′plikĭt, -tū′-) *adj.* Quintuple. ~ (kwĭntōō′plikāt, -tū′-) *v.t.* (**-cat·ed, -cat·ing**).

quip (kwĭp) *n.* Cleverly sarcastic remark, brief offhand witty remark or reply; gibe; quibble. ~ *v.* (**quipped, quip·ping**).

qui·pu (kē′pōō, kwĭp′ōō) *n.* Ancient Peruvian device for sending messages, keeping accounts, etc., by variously knotting threads of various colors. [Quechua, = "knot"]

quire (kwīr) *n.* Set of four sheets of paper etc. folded to form eight leaves as in medieval manuscripts; any collection of leaves within one another in manuscript or book; 24 sheets (now sometimes 25) of writing paper; **in ~s**, (of book) in folded sheets, unbound.

Quir·i·nal (kwĭr′ĭnal). One of the Hills on which ancient Rome was built; site of Italian royal residence 1870–1947, now of official residence of president of the republic.

quirk (kwẽrk) *n.* 1. Quibble, quip; trick of action or behavior; twist or flourish in drawing or writing. 2. (archit.) Acute hollow between convex part of molding and soffit or fillet. **quirk′y** *adj.* (**quirk·i·er, quirk·i·est**). **quirk′-i·ness** *n.*

quirt (kwẽrt) *n.* Short-handled riding whip with braided leather lash used in western U.S. and Latin America.

quis·ling (kwĭz′lĭng) *n.* Person cooperating with an enemy who has occupied his country. [Major

Quilting *exhibition in Texas. Although practiced worldwide, the art of quilting has been perfected in the U.S.A. Many unique designs were created during the 18th and 19th centuries.*

Vidkun *Quisling*, a Norwegian who collaborated with the Germans when they invaded Norway 1940]

quit[1] (kwĭt) *pred. adj.* Free, clear, absolved (archaic); rid *of*; **quit'claim**, renunciation of legal right; (*v.t.*) renounce claim to, give up (thing) *to*; **quit'rent**, (usu. small) rent paid by freeholder or copyholder in lieu of service.

quit[2] (kwĭt) *v.* (**quit** or **quit·ted, quit·ting**). 1. (archaic) Rid oneself *of*; behave, acquit, conduct (oneself) *well* etc. 2. Give up, let go, abandon; depart from, leave; (abs., of tenant) leave occupied premises. **quit'ter** *n.* One who abandons project, gives up, etc. easily.

quitch (kwĭch) **grass** = COUCH[2] grass.

quite (kwīt) *adv.* 1. Completely, wholly, entirely, altogether, to the utmost extent, in the fullest sense, positively, absolutely. 2. Rather, to some extent, as ~ *a long time*; ~ **a few**, a fair number.

Qui·to (kē'tō). Capital of Ecuador, on the equator, at an altitude of 9,300 ft. (2,835 m).

quits (kwĭts) *pred. adj.* On even terms by retaliation or repayment.

quit·tance (kwĭt'ens) *n.* Release *from*; acknowledgment of payment, receipt.

quiv·er[1] (kwĭv'*er*) *n.* Case for holding arrows.

quiv·er[2] (kwĭv'*er*) *v.* Tremble or vibrate with slight rapid motion; make (something) quiver. ~ *n.* Quivering motion or sound. **quiv'-er·er** *n.* **quiv'er·ing·ly** *adv.* **quiv'er·y** *adj.*

qui vive (kē vēv'). **on the** ~, on the alert. [Fr., = "(long) live who?" i.e. "on whose side are you?" as sentinel's challenge]

Qui·xo·te (kēhō'tā), **Don.** Hero of romance (1605–15) by CERVANTES, written to ridicule the books of chivalry; hence, enthusiastic visionary, pursuer of lofty but impracticable ideals.

quix·ot·ic (kwĭksŏt'ĭk) *adj.* Extremely idealistic, chivalrous, and romantic to the point of impracticality. **quix·ot'i·cal·ly** *adv.*

quiz (kwĭz) *n.* (pl. **quiz·zes**). Odd or eccentric person (now rare); informal oral examination of class or pupil; test of knowledge, esp. one organized as an entertainment or competition. ~ *v.t.* (**quizzed, quiz·zing**). Put series of questions to (person). **quiz'zi·cal** *adj.* Questioning; with an air of puzzlement. **quiz'zi·cal·ly** *adv.*

quod e·rat de·mon·stran·dum (kwŏd ĕr'ăt dĕm*o*nstrăn'd*u*m). (abbrev. Q.E.D.) Which was to be proved (formula concluding geometrical demonstration etc.). [L.]

quod vi·de (kwŏd vī'dē). (abbrev. q.v.) Which see (in cross references etc.). [L.]

quoin (kwoin, kwoin) *n.* 1. External angle of building; stone or brick forming angle, cornerstone. 2. Wedge for locking type in chase, raising level of gun, keeping barrel from rolling, etc. ~ *v.t.* Raise or secure with quoins.

quoit (kwoit, koit) *n.* Heavy, flattish ring of wood, rope, etc., thrown to encircle iron peg or to stick in ground near it; (pl. with sing. verb) game in which quoits are thrown thus.

quon·dam (kwŏn'd*a*m) *adj.* Former. [L., = "formerly"]

Quon·set (kwŏn'sĭt) **hut.** (trademark) Prefabricated, portable, semicylindrical building made of corrugated metal.

quo·rum (kwōr'*u*m, kwōr'-) *n.* Fixed minimum number of members that must be present to make proceedings of assembly, society, board, etc., valid. [L., = "of whom"]

quot. *abbrev.* Quotation.

quo·ta (kwō't*a*) *n.* Part or share that is, or ought to be, contributed by one to a total sum or amount; part or share of a total that belongs, is given, or is due, to one; maximum number that is one's share; (colloq.) limit (of number, amount, etc.). [L. *quota* (*pars*) how great (a part), f. *quot* how many]

quo·ta·tion (kwōtā'sh*o*n) *n.* Quoting, passage quoted; amount stated as current price of stocks or commodities; ~ **marks,** (' ' or " ") punctuation marks raised above line at beginning and end of quotation.

quote (kwōt) *v.t.* (**quot·ed, quot·ing**). Cite or appeal to (author, book, etc.) in confirmation of some view, repeat or copy out passage(s) from; repeat or copy out (borrowed passage) usu. with indication that it is borrowed; (abs.) make quotations (*from*); adduce or cite *as*; state price of (usu. *at* figure). ~ *n.* (colloq.) Passage quoted; (usu. pl.) quotation mark(s). **quot'a·ble, quo·ta'tion·al** *adjs.* **quo·ta'tion·al·ly** *adv.* **quot'er** *n.*

quo·tid·i·an (kwōtĭd'ē*a*n) *adj.* Daily, of every day; commonplace, trivial.

quo·tient (kwō'sh*e*nt) *n.* Result given by dividing one quantity by another.

Qu·ran (ko͝orahn', -răn') = KORAN.

q.v. *abbrev.* Which see. [L. *quod vide*, which see]

Qy., qy. *abbrevs.* Query.

Don Quixote, absurd and yet basically good, typified for his creator the Spain which was passing away. The Don attacked imaginary foes, as in this Daumier picture, but for chivalrous if confused reasons.

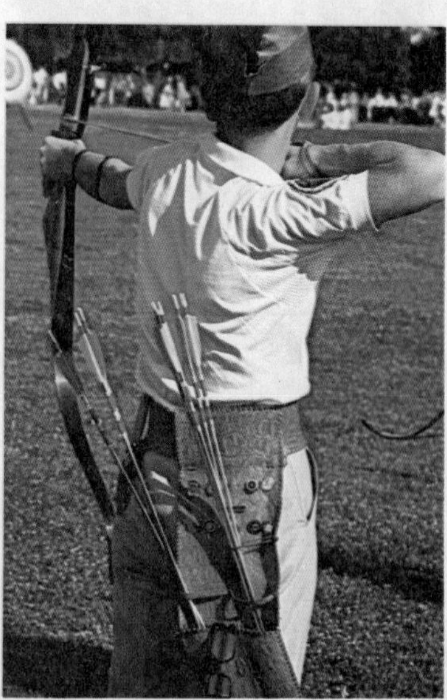

*Arrows projecting from the **quiver** of an archer in Australia (right). Although the bow and arrow have been used for centuries, the quiver was not. Even today, hunters in New Guinea carry a variety of arrows in their hands but use no equivalent of the quiver, which allows both hands to remain free.*

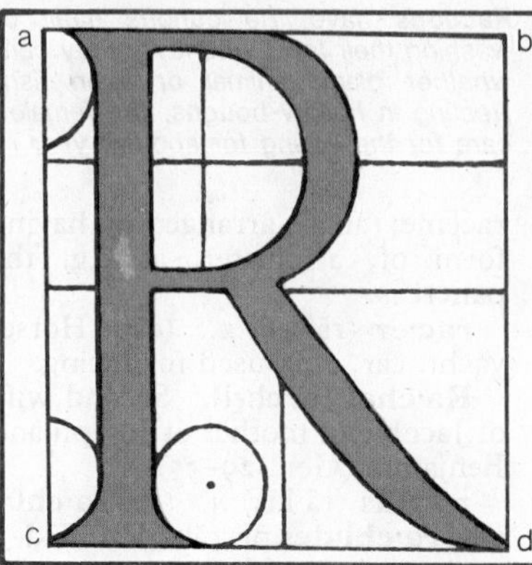

*The original symbol which has been transformed into the modern **R, r** was probably a pictograph for a head (the Semitic 'resh'). During its history, its direction was reversed, possibly because of changes in writing.*

Phoenician Early Greek Early Etruscan

Archaic Latin Ionic Classical Latin

R, r (ār) (pl. **R's, r's** or **Rs, rs**). Eighteenth letter of modern English and 17th of ancient Roman alphabet, derived through early Greek Ρ, Ρ from Phoenician 𐤓; in modern standard English representing, before a vowel, an open voiced consonant, with almost no trill.

R *abbrev.* (chem.) Radical; (elect.) resistance; restricted (rating of motion picture to which children less than 17 years old are admitted only with an adult); (chess) rook; rupee; **the three ~'s**, reading, (w)riting, and (a)rithmetic, as basis of elementary education.

r *abbrev.* (math.) Radius; (physics) roentgen(s).

R. *abbrev.* Radius; railroad; Réaumur; Regina; Republican; Rex; right; river; road.

r. *abbrev.* (elect.) Resistance; right; rod(s); roentgen(s); (baseball) run(s).

Ra[1] *symbol.* Radium

Ra[2] (rah). (Egyptian myth.) Sun god, freq. represented with head of falcon.

R.A. *abbrev.* Rear admiral; regular army; (astron.) right ascension; Royal Academy.

Ra·bat (rahbaht'). Capital and port of Morocco, on the Atlantic Ocean NE. of Casablanca.

rab·bet (răb'ĭt) *n.* Step-shaped reduction cut along edge, face, or projecting angle of wood, etc., usu. to receive edge or tongue of another piece. ~ *v.t.* (**-bet·ed, -bet·ing**). Join, fix, with rabbet; make rabbet in.

rab·bi (răb'ī) *n.* (pl. **-bis**). 1. Title of Jewish scholar or teacher of civil and religious law from New Testament times on. 2. Ordained spiritual leader of a Jewish congregation. **rab·bin·ate** (răb'*i*nĭt) *n.* 1. Office of rabbi; term of this. 2. Rabbis collectively. **rab'bin·ism** *n.* **rab·bin·i·cal** (r*a*bĭn'ĭk*a*l), **rab·bin'ic** *adjs.* **rab·bin'i·cal·ly** *adv.*

rab·bit (răb'ĭt) *n.* (pl. **-bits**, collect. **-bit**). Burrowing herbivorous gregarious mammal, esp. *Sylvilagus*, the cottontail, allied to the hare but with shorter legs and smaller ears, brownish-gray in the wild, also black, white, or pied in domestication; ~ **ears**, (colloq.) television antenna; ~ **fever**, TULAREMIA; ~ **punch**, (boxing) short (illegal) chop with edge of hand to opponent's nape; ~**('s) foot clover**, clover (*Trifolium arvense*) with flowers resembling rabbits' paws. **rabbit** *v.i.* Hunt rabbits.

rab·ble[1] (răb'*e*l) *n.* Disorderly crowd, mob; contemptible or inferior set of people; lowest classes of the populace; ~**-rouser**, one who stirs up the rabble in agitation for social or political change.

rab·ble[2] (răb'*e*l) *n.* Iron bar with bent end for stirring molten metal in puddling.

***Rabbits** are often leading characters in children's books. However, to farmers and gardeners they can be a real pest, causing great damage to crops, and weakening banks by burrowing.*

Rab·e·lais (răb'*e*lā; *Fr.* răblĕ'), **François** (*c*1495–1553). French humanist and satirical writer; author of *Pantagruel* and *Gargantua.* **Rab·e·lai·si·an** (răb*e*lā'-zēan, -zh*a*n) *adj.* & *n.* Of or like Rabelais; having the exuberance and coarse humor characteristic of Rabelais.

rab·id (răb'ĭd) *adj.* Furious, violent, raging, unreasoning; (esp. of dog) affected with rabies; of rabies. **rab'id·ly** *adv.* **rab'id·ness, ra·bid·i·ty** (răbĭd'ĭtē) *ns.*

ra·bies (rā'bēz) *n.* Viral, usu. fatal disease, esp. of dogs, foxes, bats, squirrels, etc., but affecting most warm-blooded animals, including man, and transmitted by the bite of an infected animal; also called hydrophobia, esp. in human beings.

rac·coon, ra·coon (răkōōn') *ns.* (pl. **-coons**, collect. **-coon**). Nocturnal N. Amer. carnivore (*Procyon*

Racoons *have the curious habit of washing their food whenever they can, whether plant, animal or even fish. Nesting in hollow boughs, the females care for the young for about a year.*

lotor), having grayish-brown fur, markings around eyes, sharp snout, and bushy blackringed tail.

race[1] (rās) *n.* 1. Onward sweep or movement, esp. strong current in sea or river. 2. Channel of stream; track or channel in which something moves or slides. 3. Contest of speed between runners, ships, horses, etc., or persons doing anything; (pl.) series of these for horses at fixed time on regular course; **race'horse**, horse bred or kept for racing; **race'track**, (usu. oval) track for horse or vehicle races; **race'way**, channel for water; track for trotting or pacing races; track for racing stock cars, hot rods, etc. **race** *v.* (**raced, rac·ing**). Compete in speed *with*; have race with, try to surpass in speed; cause (horse etc.) to race; indulge in horse racing; make (person, thing) move at full speed; go at full speed; (of machinery) move, revolve with uncontrolled speed, when resistance is diminished, as when the propeller of a ship is raised out of the water.

race[2] (rās) *n.* Group of persons, animals, or plants connected by common descent; posterity *of* (person); house, family, tribe, or nation regarded as of common stock; (pop.) distinct ethnic stock; any great division of living creatures; descent, kindred; class of persons etc. with some common feature; (biol.) subdivision of a species; variety.

ra·ceme (rāsēm', r*a*-) *n.* (bot.) Inflorescence opening successively from base to apex, with flowers on short lateral stalks springing from a central stem, as in hyacinth, lily of the valley, etc.

ra·ce·mic (rāsē'mĭk, -sĕm'ĭk, r*a*-) *adj.* (chem.) ~ **acid**, colorless crystalline acid, an optically inactive variety of tartaric acid, found in the juice of grapes.

rac·e·mose (răs'*e*mōs) *adj.* (bot.) Arranged in, having form of, a raceme; (anat.) arranged in, having form of, a cluster, as e.g. the pancreas.

Modern **racing cars** *keep to the circuits, which are designed to take them in relative safety: they are now so far removed from ordinary cars that they cannot be driven on the roads.*

rac·er (rā'*ser*) *n.* (esp. Horse, yacht, car, etc., used for racing.

Ra·chel (rā'ch*e*l). Second wife of Jacob and mother of Joseph and Benjamin (Gen. 29–35).

ra·chis (rā'kĭs) *n.* (pl. **ra·chi·ses, ra·chi·des** pr. răk'ĭdēz, rā'kĭ-). 1. (bot.) Axis of inflorescence with flower stalks at short intervals, as in grasses; axis of pinnately compound leaf or frond. 2. (anat.) Vertebral column or cord from which it develops.

ra·chi·tis (r*a*kī'tĭs) *n.* Rickets. **ra·chit·ic** (r*a*kĭt'ĭk) *adj.*

Rach·ma·ni·noff, Rach·ma·ni·nov (rahkmah'nĭnawf; *Russ.* rah*x*mah'nĭnawf), **Sergei Vasilyevich** (1873–1943). Russian composer and pianist.

ra·cial (rā'sh*a*l) *adj.* Of, belonging to, characteristic of, race. **ra'cial·ly** *adv.*

Ra·cine (răsēn'), **Jean** (1639–1699). French tragic poet and dramatist; author of *Phèdre, Andromaque*, etc.

rac·ism (rā'sĭz*e*m) *n.* 1. Theory that distinctive characteristics, abilities, etc., are determined by race. 2. Belief that one human race, esp. one's own, is superior; social or political system based on this; (encouragement of) antagonism between races. **rac'ist** *n.* & *adj.*

rack[1] (răk) *n.* 1. Driving clouds. 2. Destruction (only in ~ **and ruin**). **rack** *v.i.* (of clouds) Drive before wind.

rack[2] (răk) *n.* 1. Fixed or mov-

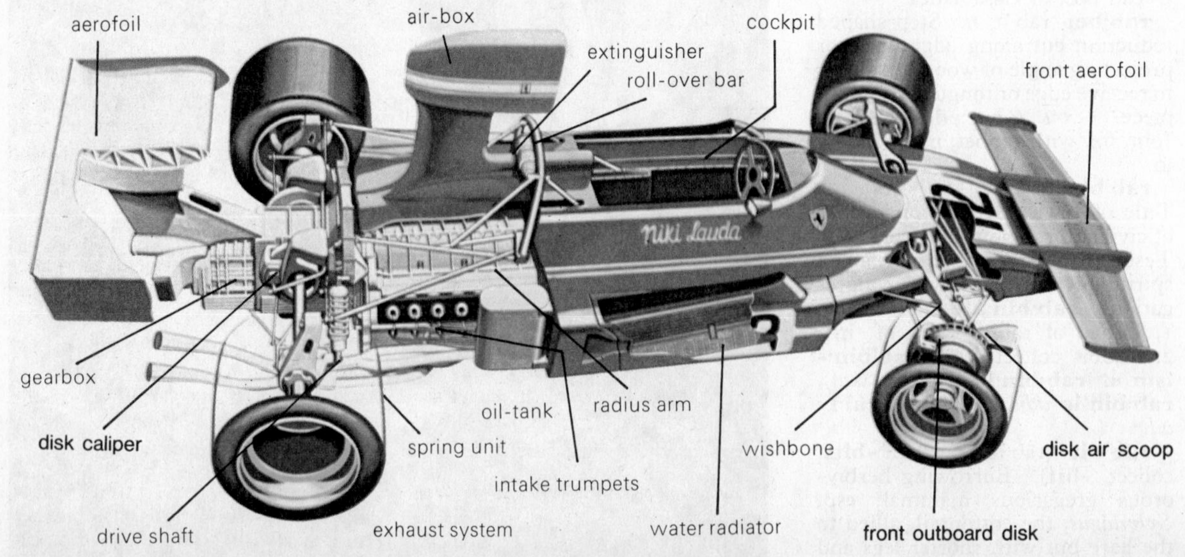

1

2

First developed as a means of plotting movements of enemy aircraft, ***radar*** *is now used for various purposes on ships as the different aerials demonstrate (1). In Australia, a form has been developed which will help aircraft to make more accurate instrument landings (2).*

able frame of wooden or metal bars for holding fodder; framework with rails, bars, pegs, or shelves, for keeping articles on or in. 2. Cogged or indented bar or rail gearing with wheel, pinion, or worm, or serving with pegs etc. to adjust position of something; ~ **railway**: see COG railway. **rack** *v.* Place in or on rack.

rack[3] (răk) *v.t.* Stretch joints of (person) by pulling esp. with instruments of torture made for the purpose; (of disease etc.) inflict tortures on; shake violently, strain, task severely. ~ *n.* Instrument of torture, frame with roller at each end to which victim's wrists and ankles were tied so that his joints were stretched when rollers were turned; also fig.

rack[4] (răk) *n.* Horse's gait between trot and canter, both legs of one side being lifted almost at once, and all four feet being off ground together at moments. ~ *v.i.* Progress thus.

rack[5] (răk) *v.t.* Draw off (wine etc.) from the dregs.

rack·et[1], **rac·quet** (răk′ĭt) *ns.* 1. Bat used in tennis, badminton, etc.; network of cord, catgut, nylon, etc., stretched across elliptical frame with handle attached. 2. (**racquets**) see RACQUET sense 2. 3. Snowshoe resembling racket.

rack·et[2] (răk′ĭt) *n.* 1. Disturbance, uproar. 2. (slang) Line of business; scheme, procedure, for obtaining money etc. by dubious or illegal means, esp. as form of organized crime. **rack′e·ty** *adj.* Noisy; dissipated.

rack·et·eer (răkĭtēr′) *n.* Member of criminal gang practicing extortion, intimidation, violence, etc., esp. on large scale. **rack·et·eer′ing** *n.* Systematic extortion of money by threats, violence, or other illegal methods.

rac·on·teur (răkŏntēr′), fem. **ra·con·teuse** (răkŏntōōz′) *ns.* Teller of anecdotes.

ra·coon = RACCOON.

rac·quet (răk′ĭt) *n.* 1. RACKET[1]. 2. (pl. with sing. verb) Ball game similar to tennis played by two or four players in a closed four-walled court.

rac·y (rā′sē) *adj.* (**rac·i·er, rac·i·est**). Of distinctive quality or vigor, not smoothed into sameness or commonness; lively, spirited, piquant; ribald, risqué. **rac′i·ly** *adv.* **rac′i·ness** *n.*

rad[1] (răd) *n.* (phys.) Unit of absorbed dose of ionizing radiation, corresponding to 100 ergs per gram of absorbing material.

rad[2] *abbrev.* Radian(s).

ra·dar (rā′dār) *n.* System for ascertaining direction and range of aircraft, ships, coasts, and other objects by sending out electromagnetic radiations of short wavelength and interpreting the reflections of these produced by certain types of surface; apparatus used for this. [f. *ra*dio *d*etection *a*nd *r*anging]

ra·di·al (rā′dēal) *adj.* 1. Arranged like rays or radii, having position or direction of a radius; having spokes or radiating lines; acting or moving along lines that diverge from a center; ~ **engine**, internal combustion engine, as formerly used in some propeller-driven airplanes, with cylinders arranged like spokes of wheel; ~ **(ply) tire**, motor vehicle tire in which ply cords extend straight across at right angles to travel direction. 2. Of the radius of the forearm. **ra′di·al·ly** *adv.* **radial** *n.* Radial part, radius, ray; radial nerve or artery.

ra·di·an (rā′dēan) *n.* (abbrev. rad) Angle at center of circle (approx. 57.296°) subtending arc whose length is equal to the radius.

ra·di·ant (rā′dēant) *adj.* Emitting rays of light; beaming with joy, hope, etc.; issuing in rays, bright, shining, splendid; extending or operating radially; ~ **energy**, energy transmitted as electromagnetic waves; ~ **heat**, electromagnetic radiation emitted by hot bodies, having a wavelength greater than that of visible light and capable of crossing a vacuum. **ra′di·ant·ly** *adv.* **ra′di·ance, ra′di·an·cy** *ns.* **radiant** *n.* Point or object from which light or heat radiates; (astron.) apparent origin or focal point of meteoric shower.

ra·di·ate[1] (rā′dēĭt, -āt) *adj.* Having divergent rays or parts radially arranged. **ra′di·ate·ly** *adv.*

ra·di·ate[2] (rā′dēāt) *v.* (**-at·ed, -at·ing**). Emit rays of light, heat, etc.; issue in rays; diverge or spread from central point; emit (light, heat, etc.) from center.

ra·di·a·tion (rādēā′shon) *n.* Manner in which the energy of a vibrating body is transmitted in all directions by a surrounding medium; emission and diffusion of heat rays; emission of Roentgen or x-rays, or the rays and particles characteristic of radioactive substances; ~ **sickness**, sickness caused by exposure to ionizing radiation, as from x-rays or radioactive materials, with symptoms ranging from nausea, headache, vomiting, and diarrhea to hemorrhaging, loss of teeth and hair, reduction in blood cell count, sterility, and death.

ra·di·a·tor (rā´dēāt*er*) *n.* (esp.) Metal case containing arrangement of pipes heated with hot air, steam, etc., and radiating warmth into room; that part of the engine cooling system of most motor vehicles etc. in which the circulating fluid is cooled.

rad·i·cal (răd´ĭk*a*l) *adj.* 1. Of the root(s); naturally inherent, essential, fundamental; forming the basis, primary. 2. Affecting the foundation, going to the root; sweeping, extreme, (pol.) desiring or advocating fundamental or revolutionary changes. 3. (philol.) Of the roots of words. 4. (bot.) Of, springing directly from, the root, or the main stem close to it. 5. (math.) Of the root of a number or quantity; ~ **sign**, sign $\sqrt{}$ ($\sqrt[3]{}$ $\sqrt[4]{}$ etc.) used to indicate that the square (cube, fourth, etc.) root of the number to which it is prefixed is to be extracted. **rad´i·cal·ize** *v.t.* (**-ized, -iz·ing**). **rad´i·cal·ly** *adv.* **radical** *n.* 1. Fundamental thing or principle. 2. (pol.) Person holding radical opinions. 3. (philol.) Root. 4. (math.) Quantity forming or expressed as root of another; radical sign. 5. (chem.) Element or atom, or group of these, forming base of compound and remaining unchanged during ordinary chemical reactions to which this is liable.

rad·i·cle (răd´ĭk*e*l) *n.* 1. Part of plant embryo that develops into primary root; small root. 2. (anat.) Rootlike subdivision of nerve or vein.

ra·di·i: see RADIUS.

ra·di·o (rā´dēō) *n.* (pl. **-os**). 1. Transmission and reception of messages etc. by means of electromagnetic waves of frequency between 10^4 Hz and 3×10^{12} Hz approx. (see FREQUENCY), either as acoustic signals or as Morse code signals; wireless, broadcasting. 2. Radio receiver. 3. (attrib.) Of radio; concerned with phenomena occurring at radio frequency. 4. ~ **astronomy**, branch of astronomy dealing with investigation of celestial bodies by radar, and with electromagnetic radiations from outside Earth's atmosphere; ~ **receiver**, apparatus that detects signals transmitted by radio frequency waves and reproduces them as audible sounds; ~ **telescope**: see TELESCOPE.

radio- *comb. form.* Connected with: (1) radio (*radiosonde*); (2) radioactivity (*radiocarbon*); (3) rays or radiation (*radioscopy*).

ra·di·o·ac·tive (rādēōăk´tĭv) *adj.* Of, exhibiting, radioactivity. **ra·di·o·ac·tiv·i·ty** (rādēōăktĭv´ĭtē) *n.* (phys.) Property possessed by certain elements of high atomic weight (radium, thorium, uranium, etc.) of spontaneously emitting alpha, beta, or gamma rays (which are capable of penetrating opaque

Each year, the versatility of ***radio*** *increases. At Parkes, Australia (1), huge dish antennae receive radio signals from outer space. To give better reception in long-distance transmissions, log-period aerials (2) have become increasingly complex.*

1 

2 

bodies and affecting a photographic plate even when separated from it by thin sheets of metal), by the disintegration of the nuclei of the atoms, or induced in certain non-radioactive elements by exposure to the action of bombarding particles. **ra·di·o·ac′tive·ly** *adv.*

ra·di·o·bi·ol·o·gy (rādēōbīŏl′-*o*jē) *n.* Branch of biology concerned with effects of radiation on living organisms and with use of radioactive tracers for biological studies. **ra·di·o·bi·o·log·i·cal** (rādēōbī*o*-lŏj′ĭk*a*l) *adj.* **ra·di·o·bi·ol′o·gist** *n.*

ra·di·o·car·bon (rādēōkar′b*o*n) *n.* Radioactive isotope of carbon existing in organic matter and having its origin in the radioactive carbon dioxide produced by the interaction of carbon ray neutrons and atmospheric nitrogen at high altitudes; ~ **dating**, method of dating organic materials from ancient deposits, esp. archaeological remains, made possible by the discovery that after the death of plants and animals the radiocarbon content decays at a regular rate (by half in every period of *c*5600 years); also called *carbon-14 dating.*

ra·di·o·gram (rā′dēōgrăm) *n.* 1. Image produced on photographic plate by x-rays. 2. Message sent by radiotelegraphy.

ra·di·o·graph (rā′dēōgrăf, -grahf) = RADIOGRAM def. 1. **ra·di·o·graph·ic** (rādēōgrăf′ĭk) *adj.*

ra·di·og·ra·phy (rādēŏg′r*a*fē) *n.* Photography by means of x-rays. **ra·di·og′ra·pher** *n.*

ra·di·o·i·so·tope (rādēōī′s*o*tōp) *n.* Radioactive isotope.

ra·di·o·lar·i·an (rādēōlar′ē*a*n) *n.* Protozoan of the order Radiolaria, with siliceous skeleton and radiating pseudopodia.

ra·di·o·lo·ca·tion (rādēōlōkā′-sh*o*n) *n.* Determination of the position of course of ships, aircraft, etc., by means of RADAR.

ra·di·ol·o·gy (rādēŏl′*o*jē) *n.* Scientific study of x-rays, radioactivity, and other radiations, and (esp.) the use of these in medicine. **ra·di·o·log·i·cal** (rādēōlŏj′ĭk*a*l) *adj.* **ra·di·ol′o·gist** *n.*

ra·di·om·e·ter (rādēŏm′*e*t*e*r) *n.* Instrument showing conversion of radiant energy into mechanical force.

ra·di·os·co·py (rādēŏs′k*o*pē) *n.* Examination of the internal structure etc. of opaque bodies by means of x- or other rays.

ra·di·o·sonde (rā′dēōsŏnd) *n.* Miniature radio transmitter, carried aloft in a balloon and descending by parachute, broadcasting to observers on the ground information about atmospheric conditions at various levels.

ra·di·o·tel·e·gra·phy (rādēō-tel*ĕ*g′r*a*fē) *n.* Transmission and reception of Morse code signals by electromagnetic waves of radio frequency.

ra·di·o·te·leph·o·ny (rādēō-telĕf′*o*nē) *n.* Transmission and reception of acoustic signals by electromagnetic waves of radio frequency. **ra·di·o·tel·e·phone** (rādēōtĕl′*e*fōn), **ra·di·o·phone** (rā′dēōfōn) *ns.* Apparatus used in radiotelephony.

ra·di·o·ther·a·py (rādēōthĕr′-*a*pē) *n.* Treatment of disease by x-rays or other forms of radiation. **ra·di·o·ther′a·pist** *n.*

rad·ish (răd′ĭsh) *n.* Cruciferous plant, *Raphanus sativus*; fleshy slightly pungent root of this, eaten raw.

ra·di·um (rā′dē*u*m) *n.* (chem.) Rare radioactive metallic element isolated from pitchblende in 1898 by P. and M. Curie; symbol Ra, at. no. 88, at. wt. 226.0254; (pop.) any of various salts of this element, used in radiotherapy etc.

ra·di·us (rā′dē*u*s) *n.* (pl. **-di·i** pr. -dēī, **-us·es**). 1. Thicker and shorter bone of forearm in man; corresponding bone in beast's foreleg or bird's wing. 2. (math.) Straight line from center to circumference of circle or sphere; radial line from focus to any point of curve; ~ **vector** (pl. **ra·di·i vec·to·res**, pr. rā′dēī vĕktōr′ēz, -tōr′ēz, ~ **vectors**), variable line drawn to curve from fixed point, esp. (astron.) from sun or planet to path of satellite. 3. Any of set of lines diverging from a point like radii of circle, object of this kind (e.g. spoke). 4. Circular area as measured by its radius.

ra·dix (rā′dĭks) *n.* (pl. **rad·i·ces** pr. răd′ĭsēz, rā′dĭ-, **ra·dix·es**). Number or symbol used as base of a system of numbers; source or origin *of.* [L., = "root"]

ra·dome (rā′dōm) *n.* Dome or covering protecting radar equip-

Radiosondes *give essential information about the upper air as the balloons to which they are attached rise through the atmospheric layers. More than 1,000 of these balloons are used each day throughout the world.*

*White-water rafting has become a popular sport for those with a taste for adventure. Originally **rafts** were of very simple design and were built to drift with the current, but they can also be navigable and seaworthy.*

ment, esp. on outer surface of aircraft.

ra·don (rā'dŏn) *n.* (chem.) Chemically inert heavy gaseous radioactive element, the first disintegration product of radium; symbol Rn, at. no. 86, principal isotope at. wt. 222. [f. *radium* and the termination of *argon*, *neon*, etc.]

rad·u·la (răj'o͞ol*a*) *n.* (pl. **-lae** pr. -lē). File-like structure in mollusks used to scrape off particles of food and draw them into the mouth.

RAF, R.A.F. *abbrevs.* Royal Air Force.

raf·fi·a (răf'ē*a*) *n.* Palm of genus *Raphia*; soft fiber from leaves of *R. ruffia* and *R. pedunculata*, used for making hats, baskets, mats, etc.

raff·ish (răf'ĭsh) *adj.* Disreputable, dissipated, esp. in appearance. **raff'ish·ly** *adv.* **raff'ish·ness** *n.*

raf·fle[1] (răf'*e*l) *n.* Lottery in which prize is assigned by lot to 1 person of a number who have each bought one or more chances or have paid a certain part of its value. ~ *v.* (**-fled, -fling**). Take part in raffle *for* (thing); sell (thing) by raffle.

raf·fle[2] (răf'*e*l) *n.* Rubbish.

raft (răft, rahft) *n.* Collection of logs, casks, etc., fastened together in the water for transportation; flat floating structure of timber etc., for conveying persons or things, esp. as substitute for boat in emergencies; floating accumulation of trees, ice, etc.; (slang) large collection of things. ~ *v.* Transport (as) on raft; form into a raft; cross (water) on raft(s); work raft.

raft·er (răf't*e*r, rahf'-) *n.* One of the sloping supporting beams forming framework of pitched roof.

rag[1] (răg) *n.* Torn or frayed piece of woven material; one of the irregular scraps to which cloth etc. is reduced by wear and tear; piece of music in ragtime; (contempt.) flag, handkerchief, newspaper, etc.; (pl.) tattered clothes; (collect.) rags used as material for making paper, stuffing, etc.; **rag'bag**, bag in which scraps of linen etc. are kept for use; **rag doll**, stuffed doll made of cloth; **rag paper**, good quality paper made from rags; **rag'tag (and bobtail)**, riffraff; **rag'time**, elaborately syncopated jazz with steadily accented base accompaniment; **rag'weed**, any of various mainly N. Amer. composite plants (genus *Ambrosia*) having greenish flowers, whose abundant pollen is a major cause of hay fever; **rag'wort**, any of several common yellow-flowered ragged-leaved plants, incl. *Senecio aureus*, the golden ragwort of N. Amer.

*English Electric's Lightning fighter with its considerable range of weaponry is among the precursors of today's **R.A.F.** aircraft — supersonic, heavily armed and equipped with sophisticated instruments.*

rag[2] (răg) *n.* Large coarse roofing slate.

rag[3] (răg) *n.* (chiefly Brit.) Act of ragging, noisy disorderly conduct. ~ *v.* (**ragged, rag·ging**). Annoy, tease, torment; (Brit. university slang) play rough jokes upon, throw into wild disorder (person's room etc.) by way of practical joke; act in this way.

rag·a·muf·fin (răg'*a*mŭfĭn) *n.* Child in ragged dirty clothes.

rage (rāj) *n.* (Fit of) violent anger; violent operation of some natural force or some sentiment; vehement desire or passion (for); object of widespread temporary enthusiasm or fashion. ~ *v.i.* (**raged, rag·ing**). Rave, storm, speak madly or furiously, be full

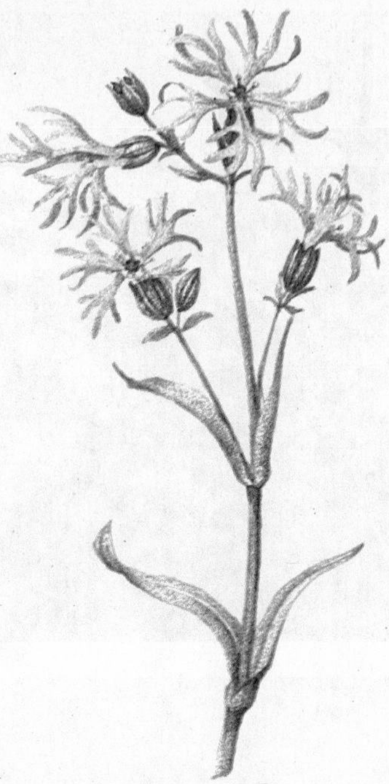

The immediately recognizable flowers of ***ragged robin*** *are a common sight during the summer in marshes, fens, and wet woodlands, giving place after fertilization to narrow fruits.*

Ragweed *is native to North America and is also known by the name American wormwood. It has a very high pollen yield and is a major contributor to the discomfort of hayfever sufferers.*

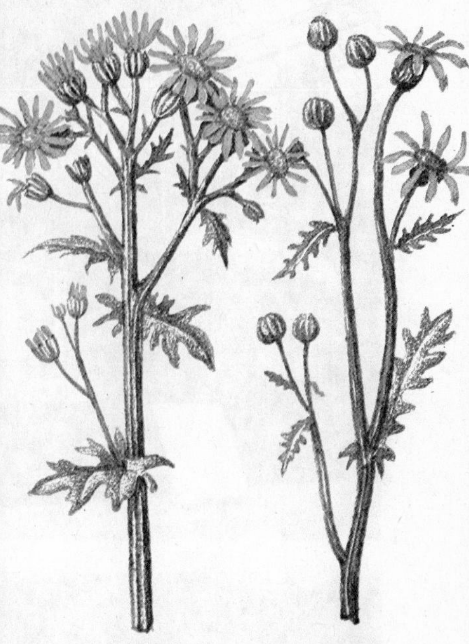

Common (left) and marsh ***ragworts*** *have a strong family resemblance. However, the marsh species has glossier leaves and the plants are shorter and more widely branched.*

of anger; (of wind, sea, passion, battle, etc.) be violent, be at the height, operate unchecked, prevail. **rag'ing·ly** *adv.*

rag·ged (răg'ĭd) *adj.* Rough, shaggy, hanging in tufts; of broken jagged outline or surface, full of rough or sharp projections; faulty, wanting finish, smoothness, or uniformity; rent, torn, frayed, in ragged clothes; ~ **robin**, reddish or white wild flower (*Lychnis floscuculi*) with deeply lobed petals. **rag'ged·ly** *adv.* **rag'ged·ness** *n.*

rag·lan (răg'lan) *n.* Coat, jacket, or sweater without shoulder seams, top of sleeve being carried up to neck; ~ **sleeve**, sleeve of this kind. [f. Lord *Raglan*, British commander in Crimean War]

ra·gout (răgōō') *n.* Meat in small pieces stewed with vegetables and highly seasoned.

rah (rah) *int.* Hurrah.

raid (rād) *n.* Sudden incursion of military force into or upon a country for the purposes of plunder or attack; sudden descent of police etc. upon suspected premises or illicit goods. ~ *v.* Make raid *into* etc.; make raid on. **raid'er** *n.*

rail[1] (rāl) *n.* 1. Horizontal or inclined bar or continuous series of bars of wood or metal used to hang things on, as top of banisters, as part of fence, as protection against contact or falling over, or for similar purpose; any horizontal piece in frame of wooden paneling. 2. Iron bar or continuous line of bars laid on ground as one side or half of railroad track; railroad (esp. by ~); **rail'head**, farthest point reached by railroad under construction; (mil.) point on railroad where supplies can be unloaded; **rail'road**, (*n.*) track or set of tracks of iron or steel rails for passage of trains of cars drawn by locomotive and conveying passengers and freight; tracks of this kind worked by a single company; (hist.) road laid with rails for heavy horsecarts; (*v.*) transport, travel, by rail; (colloq.) accomplish (action) with great speed; (slang) convict unfairly; rush *into*, through, etc.; **rail'way**, railroad esp. in local area service, as street railway;

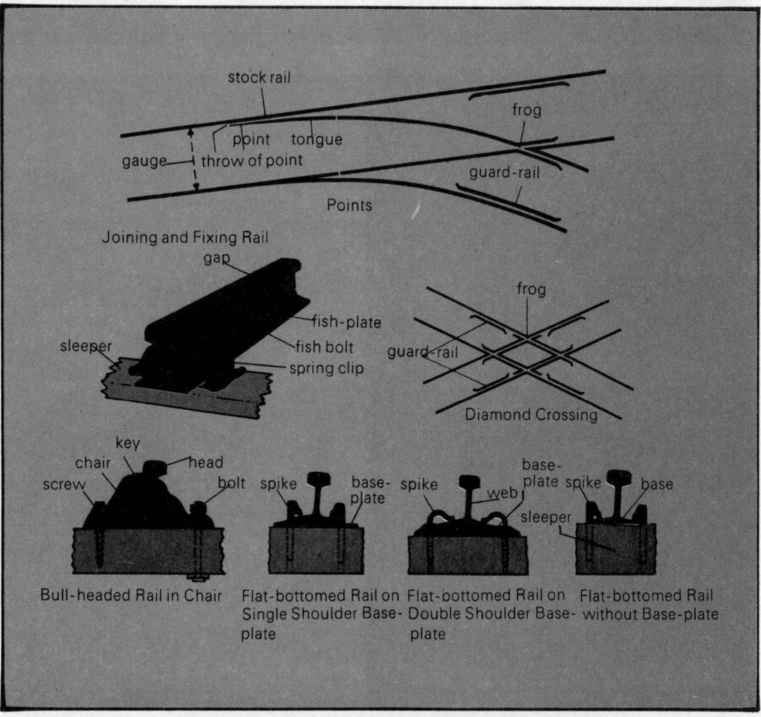

The first railways were wooden tramways laid down in quarries and collieries, with wagons pulled by horses. With the development of the iron industry, cast-iron ***rails*** *came into use and proved more durable as well as easier to install.*

1

2

3

5

4

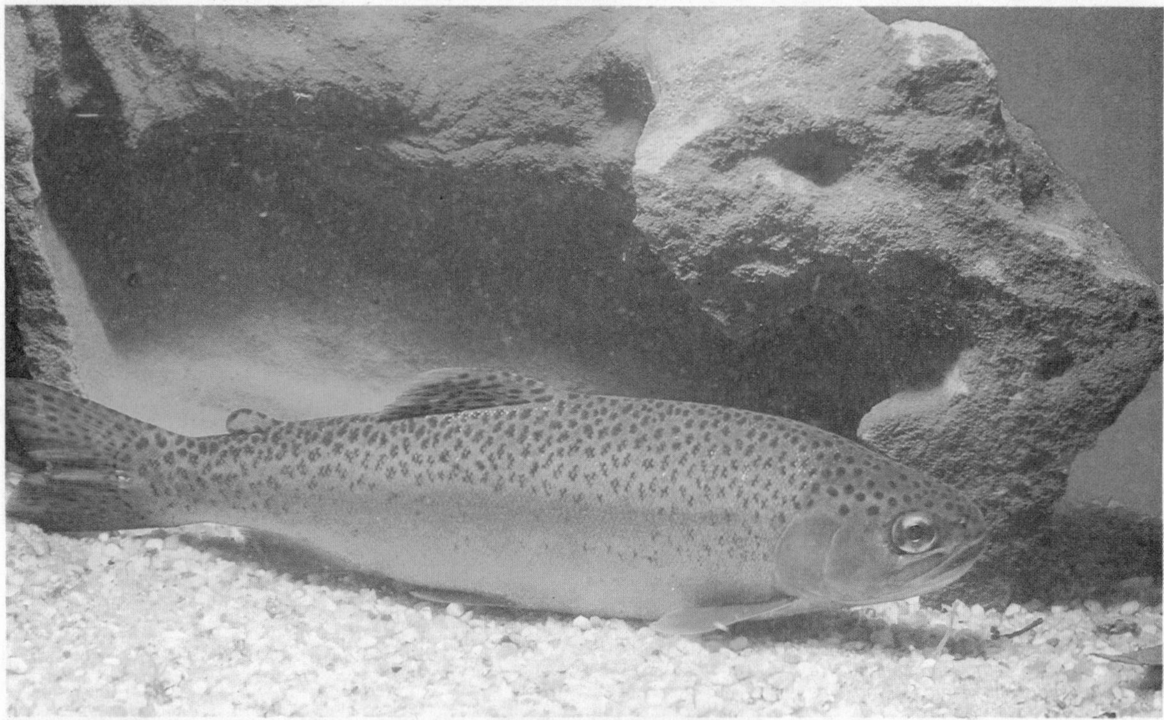

(chiefly Brit.) railroad. **rail** *v.* Furnish or enclose with rail (often ~ **in, off**); provide with rail; lay (railroad route) with rails.

rail[2] (rāl) *n.* (pl. **rails**, collect. **rail**). Any of various small marsh birds of the family Rallidae, characterized by their short wings used only for short flights.

rail[3] (rāl) *v.i.* Use abusive language (*at, against*).

rail·ing (rā′lĭng) *n.* (esp.) Fence or barrier of rails etc.

rail·ler·y (rā′lerē) *n.* (pl. **-ler·ies**). (Piece of) good-humored ridicule, banter.

rai·ment (rā′ment) *n.* (poet., rhet.) Clothing, dress.

rain (rān) *n.* Condensed moisture of atmosphere falling visibly in separate drops; fall of such drops; (rain-like descent of) falling liquid or solid particles or bodies; (pl.) showers of rain; **the ~s,** rainy season in tropical countries; ~ **check**, ticket given for later use when baseball game etc. is interrupted by bad weather; (fig.) promise that a postponed offer will still stand; **rain′coat,** (waterproof) coat worn as protection against rain; ~ **day, date**, alternative day on which an outdoor fair, game, etc., is to be held if rain causes it to be canceled on original date; **rain′drop**, single drop of rain; **rain′fall**, shower; quantity of rain falling within given area in given time; ~ **forest**, forest characteristic of rainy tropical regions; ~ **gauge**, instrument measuring rainfall; **rain′making**, act or process of making or increasing rainfall or trying to do so, esp. by artificial means (**rain′maker** *n.*); **rain′water**, water that has fallen from clouds as rain (not got from wells, a city water supply, etc.). **rain′less** *adj.* **rain** *v.* 1. **it ~s, it is raining**, rain falls; there is a shower of (something falling etc.); **it ~s cats and dogs**, it rains violently. 2. Send down rain; fall or send down in showers or like rain.

*Stephenson's **railway** engines are now museum pieces (1), but some steam trains (2, in Wales) are still run by enthusiasts. Mountain railways (3, in Austria) use rack-and-pinion tracks. Modern, high speed trains (4) run on rails like these being laid by machine in Western Australia (5).*

*The **rainbow trout** is identified by a spotted body and rainbow-colored band which extends from gills to tail. A native of the U.S., it has been introduced all over the world. Some species migrate to the sea and return to the river of their birth to spawn.*

rain·bow (rān′bō) *n.* Arch showing PRISMATIC colors in their order formed in sky (or across waterfall etc.) opposite sun by reflection, double refraction, and dispersion, of sun's rays in falling drops of rain, spray, etc.; (attrib.) many-colored; ~ **trout**, N. Amer. species of trout (*Salmo gairdneri*) with a reddish band on sides and dark spots.

Rai·nier (rānēr′, rā′nēr), **Mount.** Highest peak in Washington, 14,410 ft. (4,392 m), in the Cascade Range in the W. central part.

rain·y (rā′nē) *adj.* (**rain·i·er, rain·i·est**). In or on which rain is falling or much rain usu. falls; (of clouds, wind, etc.) laden with, bringing, rain; ~ **day**, (fig.) time of need. **rain′i·ness** *n.*

raise (rāz) *v.t.* (**raised, rais·ing**). 1. Set upright, make stand up, restore to or toward vertical position; rouse; ~ **from the dead**, restore to life. 2. Build up, construct; propagate; rear, bring up (a child); utter, make audible; start; give occasion for, elicit; set up, advance; ~ **one's voice**, speak; speak louder. 3. Elevate, put or take into higher position; direct upward; promote to higher rank; make higher or nobler; cause to ascend; make (voice) louder or

__Rails__ can be found almost all over the world, wherever the environment is suitable. Many species, like the American clapper rail (below) are hunted as game birds.

Probably best known as the man who introduced the potato and tobacco to England, ***Walter Raleigh*** *was also renowned as an author and courtier. He fell from favor with James I and was beheaded.*

shriller; increase amount of, heighten level of; (naut.) come in sight of (land, ship); ~ **bread** etc., cause it to rise with yeast etc.; ~ **Cain, hell**, etc., (colloq.) make a disturbance; become violently angry; ~ **one's eyebrows**, look supercilious or shocked; also fig. 4. Collect, bring together, procure, manage to get. 5. Relinquish, cause enemy to relinquish (siege, blockade). **raise** *n.* Increase in amount, esp. of stakes at poker, bid at bridge, etc.; rise (in salary etc.).

rai·sin (rā´zĭn) *n.* Partially dried grape.

rai·son d'ê·tre (rā´zōn dĕt´r*e*; *Fr.* rĕzawṅ´ dĕ´tr*e*) (pl. **rai·sons d'ê·tre** pr. rā´zōnz dĕt´re; *Fr.* rĕzawṅ´ dĕ´tr*e*). Reason or justification for existing.

raj (rahj) *n.* (Ind.) Sovereignty, rule.

ra·jah, ra·ja (rah´j*a*) *ns.* (hist.) Indian king or prince (also as title of petty dignitary or noble in India, or of Malay or Javanese chief). [Hind. *rājā*]

Raj·put (rahj´pōōt). Member of Hindu landowning warrior caste of NW. India.

rake[1] (rāk) *n.* Implement consisting of pole with crossbar toothed like comb at end for drawing together hay etc., or smoothing loose soil or gravel; implement resembling rake used for other purposes, e.g. by croupier drawing in money at gaming table. ~ *v.* (**raked, rak·ing**). Collect, gather *up*, pull *out*, clear *off*, (as) with rake; clean or smooth with rake; search (as) with rake; make *level*, *clean*, etc., with rake; use rake, search as with rake; sweep with shot, enfilade, send shot along (ship) from stem to stern; sweep with the eyes; **rake-off**, (slang) profit or commission made, often illegitimately, by one or more persons concerned in a transaction; **rake over, up**, revive memory of (past quarrels, grievances, etc.).

rake[2] (rāk) *n.* Dissipated or immoral man of fashion.

rake[3] (rāk) *v.* (**raked, rak·ing**). (of ship, its bow or stern) Project at upper part of bow or stern beyond keel; (of masts or funnels) incline from perpendicular toward stern; give backward inclination to. ~ *n.* Amount to which thing rakes; raking position or build.

Why ***rainbows*** *occur was first scientifically explained in the 17th century. Before that, various religious or magical reasons were given for their appearance.*

rak·ish[1] (rā´kĭsh) *adj.* (As) of, like, a RAKE[2].

rak·ish[2] (rā´kĭsh) *adj.* (of ship) Smart and fast looking; jaunty. [perh. same word as preceding, with extra association of raking masts]

rale (răl, rahl) *n.* (path.) Sound additional to that of respiration heard in auscultation of unhealthy lungs.

Ra·leigh[1] (raw´lē, rah´-). Capital of North Carolina, in the E. central part.

Ra·leigh[2], **Ral·egh** (raw´lē, rah´-), **Sir Walter** (*c*1552–1618). English military and naval commander, explorer, courtier, and poet; expored the eastern seaboard of Amer. and wrote accounts of his adventures; fell out of favor with Elizabeth I; was convicted of conspiring against James I, 1603, reprieved, but eventually executed.

ral·ly[1] (răl´ē) *v.* (**-lied, -ly·ing**). Reassemble, get together again,

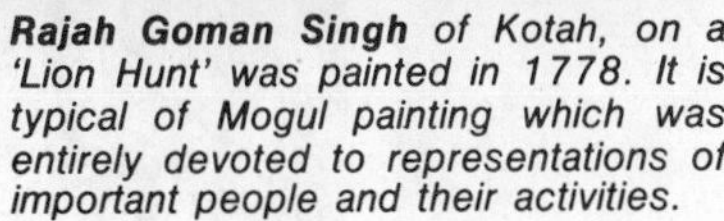

***Rajah Goman Singh** of Kotah, on a 'Lion Hunt' was painted in 1778. It is typical of Mogul painting which was entirely devoted to representations of important people and their activities.*

***Rajput** warriors have traditionally provided guards for the palace at Jaipur, and some are still recruited for service despite the modernization of the present Indian army.*

after rout or dispersion, (cause to) renew conflict; bring, come, together as support or for concentrated action; revive (faculty etc.) by effort of will, pull oneself together, assume or rouse to fresh energy. ~ *n.* (pl. **-lies**). 1. Act of rallying, reunion for fresh effort; recovery of energy; mass meeting; competitive automobile race over a fixed course of public roads under specified rules. 2. (tennis etc.) Series of strokes made between service and failure to return the ball.

ral·ly[2] (răl′ē) *v.t.* (**-lied, -ly·ing**). Banter.

ram (răm) *n.* 1. Uncastrated male sheep. 2. **the R ~**: see ARIES. 3. (hist.) Swinging beam for breaching walls, battering ram; (warship with) projecting beak at bow for charging side of other ships. 4. Falling weight of pile driver; rammer; hydraulic water-raising or lifting machine; piston of hydrostatic press; plunger of force pump; **ram′jet**, jet engine for aircraft in which the motion through the air provides compression. **ram** *v.t.* (**rammed, ram·ming**). 1. Beat down (soil etc.) into solidity with wooden block etc.; make (post, plant, etc.) firm by ramming soil around it; drive (pile etc.) *down, in,* etc., by heavy blows; force (charge) home, pack (gun) tight, with ramrod; squeeze or force into place by pressure; (abs.) use rammer; **ram′rod,** (hist.) rod for ramming home charge of muzzleloader. 2. (of ship) Strike with ram; dash or violently impel *against, at,* etc. **ram′mer** *n.*

Ra·ma (rah′m*a*). Any of three incarnations of Vishnu: Balarama, Parashurama, or Ramachandra.

Ram·a·dan (răm*a*dahn′, -dăn′). Ninth month of Muslim year, rigidly observed as 30 days of fasting during daylight hours.

Ra·ma·krish·na (rahm*a*-krĭsh′n*a*) (1834–86). Hindu mystic.

Ra·man (rah′m*a*n), **Sir Chandrasekhara Venkata** (1888–1970). Indian physicist; awarded Nobel Prize for physics, 1930; ~ **effect**, appearance of additional lines (~ **lines**) in the spectrum of light when scattered by the molecules of a substance; ~ **spectrum**, spectrum so obtained.

Ra·ma·ya·na (rahmah′y*a*n*a*). Ancient Sanskrit epic poem (500–300 B.C.), regarded as sacred text by Hindus, relating the adventures of Ramachandra, the seventh of Vishnu's incarnations.

ram·ble (răm′b*e*l) *v.i.* (**-bled, -bling**). Walk for pleasure and without definite route; wander in discourse, talk or write disconnectedly. ~ *n.* Rambling walk.

ram·bler (răm′bl*e*r) *n.* (esp.) Any of several kinds of freely climbing rose.

ram·bling (răm′blĭng) *adj.* Peripatetic, wandering; disconnected, desultory, incoherent; (of plants) straggling, climbing; (of house, street, etc.) irregularly planned. **ram′bling·ly** *adv.*

ram·bunc·tious (rămbŭngk′-sh*u*s) *adj.* Unruly; uncontrollably exuberant. **ram·bunc′-tious·ness** *n.*

Ra·meau (rămō′), **Jean Philippe** (1683–1764). French composer of operas and harpsichord music.

ram·e·kin, ram·e·quin (răm′-*e*kĭn) *ns.* Small quantity of cheese baked with bread crumbs, eggs, etc.; small dish in which this is baked and served.

Ram·e·ses: see RAMSES.

ram·i·fi·ca·tion (răm*i*f*i*kā′sh*o*n) *n.* Ramifying, (arrangement of) tree's branches; subdivision of complex structure comparable to tree's branches.

ram·i·fy (răm′*i*fī) *v.* (**-fied, -fy·ing**). Form branches, subdivisions, or offshoots; branch out; (usu. pass.) cause to branch out, arrange in branching manner.

ra·mose (rā′mōs, r*a*mōs′) *adj.* Branched, branching.

ramp (rămp) *n.* Slope, inclined plane joining two levels of ground, esp. in fortification, or of wall coping; inclined plane serving instead of steps at entrance of building, connecting different floors or levels etc.; mobile staircase for boarding and leaving airplane; upward bend in stair rail. ~ *v.* (chiefly of lion or other beast) Stand on hind legs with forepaws in air, assume or be in threatening posture.

ram·page (rămpāj′) *v.i.* (**-paged, -pag·ing**). Behave violently, storm, rage, rush about. ~ (răm′pāj) *n.* Violent behavior. **ram·pa·geous** (rămpā′j*u*s) *adj.* **ram·pa′geous·ness, ram·pag′er** *ns.*

ramp·ant (răm′p*a*nt) *adj.* Ramping (chiefly of lion in her.); violent or extravagant in action or opinion, arrant, aggressive, unchecked, prevailing; rank, luxuriant; (of arch etc.) having one abutment higher than the other, climbing. **ramp′ant·ly** *adv.* **ramp′an·cy** *n.*

ram·part (răm′pārt) *n.* Broad-topped and usu. stone-parapetted defensive mound of earth; (fig.), defense, protection. ~ *v.t.* Fortify or protect (as) with rampart.

ram·pi·on (răm′pē*o*n) *n.* Flower, esp. European campanula (*Campanula rapunculus*), with white tuberous, edible roots; any plant of genus *Phyteuma*, with heads or spikes of blue flowers.

Ram·say (răm′zē), **Sir William** (1852–1916). Brit. chemist; discoverer of helium, argon (with Rayleigh), and neon in the atmosphere; Nobel Prize for chemistry, 1904.

Ram·ses (răm′sēz), **Ram·e·ses** (răm′*e*sēz). Name of several Egyptian kings of 19th and 20th dynasties; **Rameses II** (? 1292–1225 B.C.) is sometimes supposed to have been the Pharaoh who oppressed the Jews.

ram·shack·le (răm′shăk*e*l) *adj.* Tumbledown, rickety.

ram·son (răm′s*o*n) *n.* Broad-leaved garlic (*Allium ursinum*); bulbous root of this, used in salads and relishes.

ran: see RUN[1].

ranch (rănch, rahnch) *n.* 1. Large farm, esp. in western U.S. and Canada, including buildings, grazing lands, etc., where cattle, sheep, or horses are raised. 2. Any large farm specializing in a crop or particular kind of animal; ~ **house**, suburban house with all rooms on one floor, usu. with attached garage. **ranch** *v.* Operate or work on ranch. **ranch′er** *n.* **ranch′man** *n.* (pl. **-men**). [Span. *rancho* mess, persons feeding together]

ran·cid (răn′sĭd) *adj.* Smelling or tasting like rank stale fat. **ran′cid·ness, ran·cid·i·ty** (rănsĭd′ĭtē) *ns.*

ran·cor (răng′k*e*r) *n.* Inveterate bitterness, malignant hate, spitefulness. **ran′cor·ous** *adj.* **ran′cor·ous·ly** *adv.*

R & D, R. & D. *abbrevs.* Research and development.

Ran·dolph (răn′dŏlf), **Edmund Jennings** (1753–1813). Amer. statesman; governor of Virginia, 1786–8; delegate to the Constitutional Convention, 1787, where

*In many international and some domestic air terminals roll-up **ramps** have been replaced by permanently installed walkways which protect passengers from any inclement weather and make boarding speedier.*

*Of the twelve Egyptian kings in the 19th Dynasty, Rameses, who used the name **Rameses III** (1198–69 B.C.) is acknowledged to have been one of the greatest. He conquered Ethiopia and fought the Greeks and Philistines.*

To protect flora and fauna on proclaimed reserves, and other species which may occur outside those areas, governments employ **rangers.** This ranger in N.S.W., Australia is talking to a local property owner.

he presented the Virginia Plan, which provided for two legislative houses and legislatively selected judicial and executive branches; first U.S. attorney general, 1789–1794; U.S. secretary of State, 1794–1795.

ran·dom (răn′dom) *n.* **at ~,** unsystematically; without aim, purpose, or principle. **~** *adj.* Made, done, etc., at random. **ran′dom·ize** *v.t.* (**-ized, -iz·ing**). **ran′dom·ly** *adv.* **ran′dom·ness** *n.* [OF. *random* great speed (*randir* gallop)]

R & R, R and R *abbrevs.* Rest and recreation; rest and recuperation.

ran·dy (răn′dē) *adj.* (**-di·er, -di·est**). Lustful, eager for sexual gratification.

ra·nee: RANI.

rang: see RING[2].

range (rānj) *n.* 1. Row, line, tier, or series, of things, esp. of mountains; horizontal direction, lie. 2. Liberty to range; area over which ranging takes place or is possible; stretch of grazing or hunting ground; piece of ground with targets for shooting; area over which plant etc. is distributed, area included in or concerned with something, scope, compass, register; limits of variation, limited scale or series; distance attainable by gun or projectile, distance between gun, camera, etc., and objective; **~ finder,** instrument for estimating this distance. 3. Large cooking stove, usu. with oven(s), broiler(s), and top plate for boiling, frying, etc. **range** *v.* (**ranged, rang·ing**). 1. Place or arrange in a row or ranks or in specified situation, order, or company; run in a line, reach, lie spread out, extend; be found or occur over specified district; vary between limits; be level (*with*), rank or find right place *with* or *among.* 2. Rove, wander; go all about (place), sail along or about (coast, sea). 3. (of gun) Throw projectile over, (of projectile) traverse, (distance).

rang·er (rān′jer) *n.* (esp.) 1. Warden of forest, national park, etc. 2. Member of commando unit.

Ran·goon (rănggōōn′). Capital city and seaport of Burma, on Rangoon River, one of the mouths of the Irrawaddy.

rang·y (rān′jē) *adj.* (**rang·i·er, rang·i·est**). Having long slender form.

ra·ni, ra·nee (rah′nē) *ns.* (pl. **-nis, -nees**). (hist.) Hindu queen or princess. [Hind. *rāṇī, rānī* fem. of RAJAH]

rank[1] (răngk) *n.* 1. Row, line; (mil.) number of soldiers drawn up in single line abreast; **the ~s, ~ and file,** common soldiers; (transf.) ordinary people, as dist. from their leaders. 2. Distinct social class, grade of dignity, station; high station; **persons of ~,** members of nobility. 3. Place in a scale. **rank** *v.* Arrange (esp. soldiers) in rank; classify, give certain grade to; have rank or place; have senior position among members of hierarchy etc.

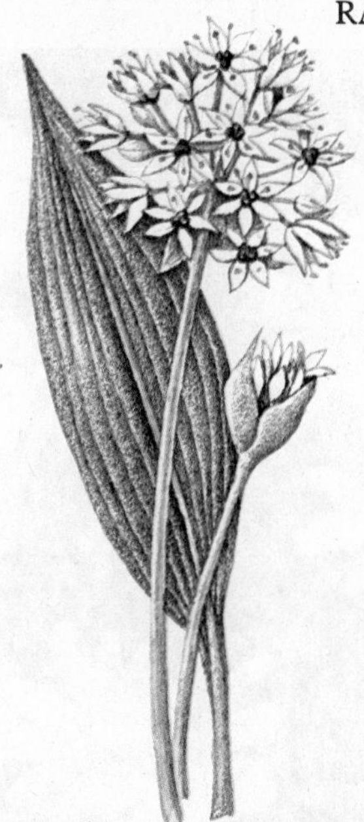

The **ramson** or broad-leaved garlic, which was native to western Asia and eastern Europe, has long been considered both a medicinal and a culinary herb. However, ordinary garlic is preferred.

rank[2] (răngk) *adj.* Too luxuriant, coarse, choked with or apt to produce weeds; foul-smelling, offensive; loathsome, corrupt; flagrant, virulent. **rank′ly** *adv.* **rank′ness** *n.*

Ran·kin (răng′kĭn), **Jeanette** (1880–1973). Amer. feminist leader and legislator; 1st woman member of U.S. House of Representatives, 1917–19, 1941–3.

ran·kle (răng′kel) *v.i.* (**-kled, -kling**). (of wound etc.) Fester (archaic); (of unpleasant experience, insult, etc.) remain as painful memory, cause continued bitterness or resentment. [OF. (*d*)*rancle* festering sore, f. LL. *dracunculus,* dim. of *draco* serpent]

ran·sack (răn′săk) *v.t.* Thoroughly search; pillage, plunder. **ran′sack·er** *n.*

ran·som (răn′som) *n.* (Liberation of prisoner of war or other captive in consideration of) sum of money or value paid for release; **king's ~,** large sum. **ransom** *v.t.* Buy freedom or restoration of; set free on payment of ransom.

rant (rănt) *v.* Speak, declaim,

Known both as the lesser celandine and the pilewort, this plant is grouped in the genus ***ranunculus.*** *This contains both annuals and perennials, which are found in temperate and cold areas, and in mountains in the tropics.*

A martial eagle with a freshly caught rabbit. The eagle is a ***raptorial,*** *or predatory, creature. The term can be used to describe birds or animals which prey on others, such as lions, leopards, hawks and bustards.*

recite in a vehement or loud manner. ~ *n.* Piece of ranting, tirade; empty turgid talk. **rant'er** *n.*

ra·nun·cu·lus (r*a*nŭng'kyul*u*s) *n.* (pl. **-lus·es, -li** pr. -lī). Plant of genus *R*~, including buttercups.

rap[1] (răp) *n.* Smart slight blow; sound made by knocker on door etc.; sound as of striking wooden surface supposed to be produced by spirit at seance; (slang) chat, discussion; (slang) blame, punishment (esp. in **take the** ~); **beat the** ~, (slang) evade punishment. **rap** *v.* (**rapped, rap·ping**). Strike (esp. person's knuckles) smartly; make the sound called a rap; (slang) talk, discuss.

rap[2] (răp) *n.* Counterfeit coin passed for halfpenny in Ireland in 18th c.; the least bit (esp. in *not care a* ~).

ra·pa·cious (r*a*pā'sh*u*s) *adj.* Grasping, avaricious; predatory. **ra·pa'cious·ly** *adv.* **ra·pac·i·ty** (r*a*păs'ĭtē), **ra·pa'cious·ness** *ns.*

rape[1] (rāp) *v.t.* (**raped, rap·ing**). Take by force (poet.); violate chastity of, force to submit to sexual intercourse. ~ *n.* Carrying off by force (poet.); ravishing or violation of a person; (law) unlawful sexual intercourse with a woman without her consent. **rap'er, rap'ist** *ns.*

rape[2] (rāp) *n.* Plant (*Brassica napus*) grown as fodder and for its seed, **rape'seed**, which yields oil; coleseed.

rape[3] (rāp) *n.* Refuse of grapes after wine-making, used in making vinegar.

Raph·a·el[1] (răf'ēel, rā'fē-; *It.* rahfahyĕl'). One of the archangels; commemorated Oct. 24.

Raph·a·el[2] (răf'ēel, rā'fē-; *It.* rahfahyĕl') (1483–1520). Full name Raffaello Sanzio or Santi; Italian Renaissance painter; famous for "La Belle Jardinière," "Coronation of the Virgin," the Vatican frescoes; chief architect of St. Peter's in Rome. **Raph·a·el·esque** (răf-ēelĕsk', rahfīlĕsk') *adj.* In the style of Raphael.

rap·id (răp'ĭd) *adj.* Characterized by, moving or acting with, great speed. **ra·pid·i·ty** (r*a*pĭd'ĭtē), **rap'id·ness** *ns.* **rap'id·ly** *adv.* **rapid** *n.* Steep descent in riverbed, with swift current.

ra·pi·er (rā'pē*e*r) *n.* Light slender sword for thrusting only.

rap·ine (răp'ĭn, -īn) *n.* (rhet.) Plundering, robbery.

Rap·pa·han·nock (răp*a*hăn'*o*k). River in NE. Virginia, flowing SE. 185 mi., (298 km), from the Blue Ridge Mountains to Chesapeake Bay.

rap·pel (răpĕl', r*a*-) *n.* & *v.* (**-pelled, -pel·ling**). (Make) descent of steep rock face by using doubled rope fixed at higher point.

rap·port (răpōr', -pŏr') *n.* (Esp. useful) communication, (harmonious) relationship, or connection (*in rapport with*).

rap·proche·ment (rahprawshmahṅ') *n.* Reestablishment or recommencement of harmonious relations, esp. between nations. [Fr.]

rap·scal·lion (răpskăl'y*o*n) *n.* Rogue.

rapt (răpt) *adj.* (orig. past part. of RAPE[1]) Carried away in spirit from consciousness or ordinary thoughts and perceptions; absorbed, enraptured, intent.

rap·to·ri·al (răptōr'ēal, -tŏr'-) *adj.* Predatory, (as) of predatory birds or animals; (zool.) of the Raptores, an order of birds of prey, including eagles, hawks, buzzards, etc.

rap·ture (răp'ch*e*r) *n.* (Expression of) ecstatic delight. **rap·tur·ous** *adj.* **rap'tur·ous·ly** *adv.*

ra·ra a·vis (rār'*a* ā'vĭs; *Lat.* rah'rah ah'wĭs) (pl. **ra·rae a·ves** pr. rār'ē ā'vēz; *Lat.* rah'rī ah'wēs). Rarity, kind of person or thing rarely encountered. [L., = "rare bird"]

rare[1] (rār) *adj.* (**rar·er, rar·est**). 1. (of gases) Not dense; with constitutent particles not closely packed together. 2. Uncommon, unusual, seldom found or occurring; highly valued owing to uncommonness or scarcity; very amusing. 3. ~ **earth**, (basic oxide of) a ~**-earth element**, any of

Related to the cabbage and similar vegetables, ***rape*** *has long been cultivated for its seeds which are crushed to produce colza oil. It is used as a lubricant, and in soap; and, after processing, for cooking in India.*

the elements from lanthanum to lutetium inclusive in the PERIODIC table, together with those of scandium and yttrium. **rare'ly** *adv.* **rare'ness** *n.*

rare[2] (rār) *adj.* (**rar·er, rar·est**). (of meat) Cooked only a short time, still red or pink inside.

rare·bit (rār'bĭt): see WELSH rabbit.

rar·e·fy (rār'efī) *v.* (**-fied, -fy·ing**). Lessen density or solidity of (esp. air); purify, refine.

rar·ing (rār'ĭng) *adj.* (colloq.) Enthusiastic, eager, (*to go* etc.).

rar·i·ty (rār'ĭtē, răr'-) *n.* (pl. **-ties**). Rareness; uncommon thing, thing valued as being rare.

Ra·ro·ton·ga (rărotŏng'ga). Island in the Cook Islands in the S. Pacific Ocean; site of Avarua, capital of the Cook Islands.

ras·cal (răs'kal, rahs'-) *n.* Rogue (freq. used playfully to child etc.). **ras·cal·i·ty** (răskăl'ĭtē, rahs-) *n.* **ras'cal·ly** *adj.* & *adv.*

rase: RAZE.

rash[1] (răsh) *n.* Eruption of the skin in spots or patches.

rash[2] (răsh) *adj.* Hasty, impetuous, overbold, reckless; acting or done without due consideration. **rash'ly** *adv.* **rash'ness** *n.*

rash·er (răsh'er) *n.* Thin slice of bacon; a serving of bacon, usu. three or four slices.

rasp (răsp, rahsp) *n.* Coarse kind of file with separate teeth raised by means of pointed punch; harsh, grating sound. ~ *v.* Scrape with rasp; scrape roughly; grate upon, irritate; make grating sound. **rasp'er** *n.* **rasp'ing·ly** *adv.* **rasp'y** *adj.* (**rasp·i·er, rasp·i·est**).

rasp·ber·ry (răz'bĕrē, -berē, rahz'-) *n.* (pl. **-ries**). 1. (Plant, *Rubus strigosus* of eastern N. Amer. and *R. idaeus* of Europe bearing) usu. red subacid fruit of many small juicy drupelets arranged on conical receptacle. 2. (slang) Sound or gesture expressing derision or dislike.

Ras·pu·tin (răspū'tĭn; *Russ.* rahspōō'tĭn), **Grigori Efimovich** (1871–1916). Russian monk and mystic who acquired great influence over the household of Nicholas II; he was assassinated as result of a conspiracy among a group of nobles.

Ras·ta·fa·ri·an (rŭstafār'ēan) *adj.* & *n.* (Member of) Jamaican

This serene painting by ***Raphael*** *of St. Catherine of Alexandria against a placid Italian landscape, is typical of the Renaissance with its expressive pose and subtle coloring.*

sect regarding blacks as a chosen people. [f. *Ras Tafari*, title and orig. name of Emperor Haile Selassie of Ethiopia (1891–1975), venerated by sect as a god]

rat (răt) *n.* 1. Rodent of genus *Rattus*, esp. the **black** ~ (*R. rattus*), found esp. on shipboard, and the larger **brown** ~ (*R. norvegicus*) which is now the commoner, both regarded as pests, infesting sewers, warehouses, docks, etc., and acting as carriers of several diseases; any rodent resembling this. 2. (slang) Despicable person; betrayer; informer; sneak. 3. **smell a** ~, have suspicions; ~**s**! (slang) expression of disappointment or disbelief; **rat'catcher**, person whose business is to catch rats; **rat race**, (colloq.) fiercely competitive struggle, struggle to maintain one's position in work or life; **rats'bane**, rat poison; **rat-tail**(**ed**), (of file etc.) shaped like rat's tail. 4. **rat'trap**, trap for rats. **rat** *v.i.* (**rat·ted, rat·ting**). Hunt or kill rats; betray or inform on one's friends. **rat'ter** *n.*

rat-a-tat (răt'*a*tăt), **rat-a-tat-tat** (răt'*a*tăttăt') *ns.* Series of short sharp sounds, as rapid knocks, machine gun fire, etc.

ratch·et (răch'ĭt) *n.* Set of angular or sawlike teeth on edge of bar or wheel, into which a cog, click, or pawl may catch, usu. for the purpose of preventing reversed motion; (also ~ **wheel**) wheel with rim so toothed.

rate[1] (rāt) *n.* 1. Estimated value or worth; price, sum paid or asked

The Australian black-footed tree ***rat*** *is one of the true rats found in Australia. Some of these are introduced pest species. The kangaroo rat is more correctly a hopping mouse but in behavior and adaptation it is similar to the jerboa of North Africa.*

stick rat
fat sand rat
African giant rat
wood rat
black rat
brown rat
kangaroo rat

for single thing. 2. Amount or number of one thing corresponding or having some relation to certain amount or number of another thing; value as applicable to each piece or equal quantity of something; basis of exchange; amount (*of* charge or payment), esp. in relation to some other amount or basis of calculation; degree of speed, relative speed; relative amount of variation, increase, etc. 3. Degree of action, feeling, etc. 4. **at any** ~, at all events, at least; **at this (that) rate**, things being so, under these circumstances. **rate** *v.* (**rat·ed, rat·ing**). Estimate worth or value of; assign fixed value to in relation to monetary standard; consider, regard as; rank or be rated *as*.

rate[2] (rāt) *v.* (**rat·ed, rat·ing**). Scold angrily.

rath·er (rădh´*er*, rah´dh*er*) *adv.* 1. More truly or correctly, more properly speaking; more readily, all the more. 2. More (so) than not; to some extent, somewhat, slightly. 3. By preference, for choice, sooner (*than*); more properly. 4. (chiefly Brit. colloq., pr. rah´dhēr´, in answer to question) Most emphatically, yes without doubt.

raths·kel·ler (răt´skĕl*er*, raht´-, răth´-) *n.* Restaurant in style of basement of a German town hall (*Rathaus*) where beer is sold.

rat·i·fy (răt´*ifī*) *v.t.* (**-fied, -fy·ing**). Confirm or make valid (esp. what has been done or arranged for by another) by giving consent, approval, or formal sanction. **rat·i·fi·ca·tion** (răt-*ifi*kā´sh*on*) *n.*

ra·ti·né (răt*i*nā´) *n.* Dress fabric of rough open texture.

rat·ing[1] (rā´tĭng) *n.* (esp.) 1. Classification according to class, grade, or rank. 2. Limit of performance, as of range, operational capability, etc. 3. Estimated standing of person, esp. *credit* rating. 4. Estimated number of audience as index of popularity of a broadcast.

rat·ing[2] (rā´tĭng) *n.* Angry reprimand.

ra·tio (rā´shō, -shēō) *n.* (pl. **-tios**). Quantitative relation between two similar magnitudes determined by number of times one contains the other integrally or fractionally (*27 and 18 are in the ~ of 3 to 2 or 3 : 2; the ~s 1 : 5 and 20 : 100 are the same*).

ra·ti·o·ci·nate (răshēōs´*i*nāt) *v.i.* (**-nat·ed, -nat·ing**). Reason, carry on process of reasoning. **ra·ti·o·ci·na·tion** (răshēōs*i*nā´sh*on*) *n.* **ra·ti·o´ci·na·tive** *adj.* **ra·ti·o´ci·na·tor** *n.*

ra·tion (răsh´*on*, rā´sh*on*) *n.* Fixed allowance or individual share of provisions, esp. daily allowance for person in armed forces; (pl.) provisions. ~ *v.t.* Put on fixed allowance of provisions etc.; share (food etc.) in fixed quantities; limit to specific allotment, as during wartime or a time of scarcity.

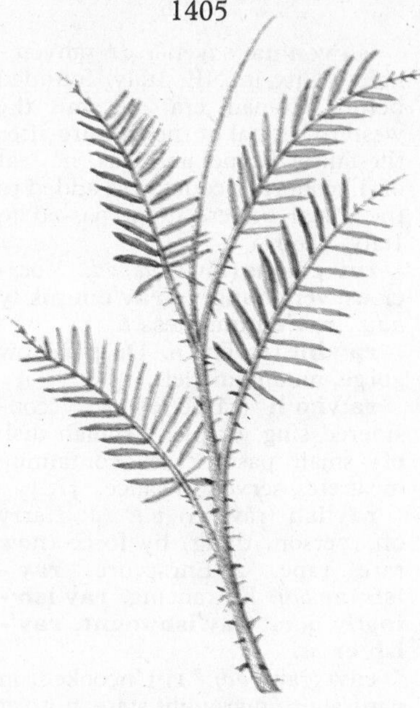

Although ***rattan*** *is now grown widely in Asia, this climbing palm was originally native to Assam and India where its shoots and seeds are eaten, and its vines used for basketwork.*

ra·tion·al (răsh´*on*al) *adj.* Endowed with reason, reasoning; sensible, sane; based on, derived from, reason or reasoning; not foolish, absurd, or extravagant; (math., of ratio or quantity) expressible without radical signs; ~ **number**, number that can be expressed exactly as an integer or quotient of the integers. **ra´tion·al·ly** *adv.* **ra·tion·al·i·ty** (răsh*o*năl´ĭtē) *n.* (pl. **-ties**).

ra·tion·ale (răsh*o*năl´) *n.* Reasoned exposition of principles; logical or rational basis *of* or *for*.

ra·tion·al·ism (răsh´*o*nalĭzem) *n.* Practice of explaining the supernatural in religion in a way consonant with reason, or of treating reason as the ultimate authority in religion as elsewhere; theory that reason is foundation of certainty in knowledge. **ra´tion·al·ist** *n.* & *adj.* **ra·tion·al·is·tic** (răsh*o*nalĭs´tĭk) *adj.* **ra·tion·al·is´ti·cal·ly** *adv.*

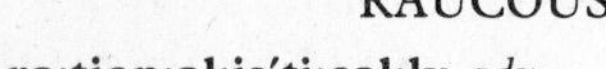

ra·tion·al·ize (răsh´*o*nalīz) *v.* (**-ized, -iz·ing**). 1. Explain, explain *away*, by rationalism; bring into conformity with reason; be or act as a rationalist. 2. (math.) Clear from irrational quantities. **ra·tion·al·i·za·tion** (răsh*o*nalĭzā´sh*o*n), **ra´tion·al·iz·er** *ns.*

rat·ite (răt´īt) *adj.* & *n.* (Flightless bird) having a flat unkeeled breastbone, as the ostrich and emu.

rat·line, rat·lin (răt´lĭn) *ns.* (One of) small lines fastened across ship's shrouds like ladder rungs.

ra·toon (rătōōn´) *n.* New shoot springing from foot of plant, esp. sugar cane, after cropping ~ *v.* Send up ratoons; cut down (plant) to induce ratooning.

rat·tan (rătăn´) *n.* Climbing palm of genus *Calamus* with long thin pliable jointed stems, growing chiefly in E. Indies; piece of rattan stem used as cane or for other purposes; rattans used as material in building etc.

rat·tle (răt´*el*) *v.* (**-tled, -tling**). 1. Give out rapid succession of short sharp hard sounds, cause such sounds by shaking something; move or fall with rattling noise; make rattle. 2. Say or recite rapidly; talk in lively thoughtless way. 3. (slang) Shake nerves of, fluster, frighten. ~ *n.* 1. Instrument or plaything made to rattle, esp. in order to make music or to amuse babies; end of rattlesnake's tail (see below). 2. Rattling sound; rattling sound in throat caused by partial obstruction; noisy flow of words; empty or trivial talk. 3. **rat´tle-snake**, any of several venomous Amer. snakes of genus *Crotalus* or *Sistrurus*, with horny rings at end of tail making rattling noise when vibrated; **rat´tletrap**, rickety, shaky vehicle.

rat·tler (răt´l*er*) *n.* (esp.) Rattlesnake.

rat·tling (răt´lĭng) *adj.* (slang) Remarkably good.

rat·ty (răt´ē) *adj.* (**-ti·er, -ti·est**). Ratlike, esp. (slang) shabby, dilapidated.

rau·cous (raw´kus) *adj.* Hoarse, harshsounding. **rau´cous·ly** *adv.* **rau´cous·ness** *n.*

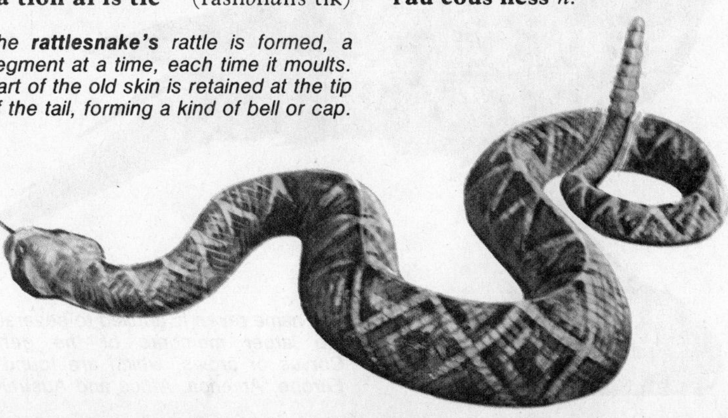

The ***rattlesnake's*** *rattle is formed, a segment at a time, each time it moults. Part of the old skin is retained at the tip of the tail, forming a kind of bell or cap.*

raun·chy (rawn′chē, rahn′-) *adj.* (**-chi·er, -chi·est**). (slang) 1. Slovenly and dirty. 2. Smutty, obscene. **raun′chi·ness** *adj.*

rau·wol·fi·a (rawŏŏl′fēa) *n.* Any of several tropical trees and shrubs of the genus *R*∼ many of which are poisonous and some of which yield medicinal substances, esp. *R. serpentina*, from whose roots the alkaloid reserpine is extracted.

rav·age (răv′ĭj) *v.* (**-aged, -ag·ing**). Devastate, plunder; make havoc. ∼ *n.* Devastation, damage, (esp., pl.) destructive effects *of*. **rav′a·ger** *n.*

rave (rāv) *v.* (**raved, rav·ing**). Talk wildly or furiously (as) in delirium; (of sea, wind, etc.) howl, roar; utter with ravings; speak or write with rapturous admiration *about* or *of*, go into raptures. ∼ *n.* Act, instance, of raving. ∼ *adj.* (of review of play, book, etc.) Extravagantly enthusiastic.

rav·el (răv′el) *v.* (**-eled, -el·ing**, Brit. **-elled, -el·ling**). 1. Entangle or become entangled, confuse, complicate. 2. Disentangle, unravel. ∼ *n.* Entanglement, knot, complication; frayed or loose end.

Ra·vel (ravĕl′; *Fr.* rahvĕl′), **Maurice** (1875–1937). French impressionistic musical composer.

ra·ven[1] (rā′ven) *n.* Large black hoarse-voiced bird (*Corvus corax*), both Amer. and European, feeding chiefly on carrion or other flesh; related species. ∼ *adj.* Of glossy black.

rav·en[2] (răv′en) *v.* Plunder, go plundering *about*, seek *after* prey or booty; prowl for prey; eat voraciously.

Ra·ven·na (ravĕn′a; *It.* rahvĕn′-nah). City in NE. Italy, founded before Roman era; became the western capital of the Empire after the fall of Rome, and was the seat of Theodoric's court; was added to the Papal States, 1509; passed to Italy, 1860.

rav·e·nous (răv′enus) *adj.* Voracious; very hungry. **rav′e·nous·ly** *adv.* **rav′e·nous·ness** *n.*

ra·vine (ravēn′) *n.* Deep narrow gorge, mountain cleft.

ra·vi·o·li (răveō′lē) *n.* (considered sing. or pl.) (Italian dish of) small pasta cases containing meat etc., served in sauce. [It.]

rav·ish (răv′ĭsh) *v.t.* 1. Carry off (person, thing) by force (now rare); rape. 2. Enrapture. **rav′ish·ing** *adj.* Entrancing. **rav′ish·ing·ly** *adv.* **rav′ish·ment, rav′ish·er** *ns.*

raw (raw) *adj.* 1. Uncooked; in natural or unwrought state, not yet dressed or manufactured; **raw′hide**, untanned leather; rope or whip of this; **raw material**, that out of which any process of manufacture makes the articles it produces; **raw silk**, silk as reeled from cocoons. 2. Crude, not brought to perfect composition or finish; uncivilized, brutal; **raw deal**, (colloq.) harsh or unfair treatment. 3. Inexperienced, untrained; unskilled. 4. Stripped of skin, excoriated; sensitive to touch from being so exposed; **raw′boned**, with projecting bones hardly covered with flesh, gaunt. 5. (of weather etc.) Damp and chilly, bleak. **raw′ness** *n.*

ray[1] (rā) *n.* 1. Single line or narrow beam of light; straight line in which radiant energy capable of producing sensation of light is propagated to or from given point; analogous propagation line of heat or other nonluminous physical energy; (fig.) remnant or beginning of enlightening or cheering influence; ROENTGEN ∼, X-RAY: see these words. 2. Any of the lines forming a set of straight lines passing through one point; any of a set of radiating lines, parts, or things; (bot.) marginal part of composite flower, as daisy; (zool.) radial division of starfish or other echinoderm. **ray** *v.* Issue, come *forth, off, out*, in rays; radiate (poet.).

*The name **raven** is applied to several of the larger members of the genus Corvus or crows, which are found in Europe, America, Africa and Australia.*

ray[2] (rā) *n.* Any of several cartilaginous fishes (order Rajiformes), as the electric ray, stingray, skate, etc., having broad, flat bodies, expanded fins, whiplike tails.

Ray·burn (rā′bern), **Sam**(**uel Taliaferro**) (1882–1961). Amer. lawyer and politician; member of U.S. House of Representatives, 1913–61, and speaker of the House, 1940–6, 1949–53, 1955–61.

Ray·leigh (rā′lē), **John William Strutt, 3rd Baron** (1842–1919). English mathematician and physicist; discoverer (with Ramsay) of argon; received Nobel Prize for Physics, 1904.

ray·on (rā′ŏn) *n.* Textile fiber made from cellulose; any of various textiles made from such fiber.

raze, Brit. **rase** (rāz) *v.t.* (**razed, raz·ing**, Brit. **rased, ras·ing**). Completely destroy; level with the ground.

ra·zor (rā′zer) *n.* Sharp-edged instrument used in shaving hair from skin; **ra′zorback**, kind of whale, rorqual; ∼**-billed auk**, N. Atlantic seabird (*Alca torda*) with black and white plumage; ∼ **edge**, keen edge. [f. OF. *rasor*, f. *raser*]

razz (răz) *v.* (slang) Tease, ridicule. ∼ *n.* = RASPBERRY sense 2.

raz·zle-daz·zle (răz′eldăz′el) *n.* (slang) Excitement, bustle, stir, etc., often intended to confuse or bewilder.

razz·ma·tazz (răz′matăz) *n.* (slang) 1. Liveliness; excitement. 2. Flashy behavior meant to deceive or mislead.

Rb *symbol.* Rubidium.

r.b.i., rbi *abbrevs.* (baseball) Runs batted in.

R.C. *abbrev.* Red Cross; Roman Catholic.

R.C.A.F., RCAF *abbrevs.* Royal Canadian Air Force.

R.C.M.P. *abbrev.* Royal Canadian Mounted Police.

Rd., rd. *abbrevs.* Road.

R.D. *abbrev.* Rural delivery.

Re *symbol.* Rhenium.

re *prep.* In the matter of, concerning (chiefly in legal and business use as first word of heading stating matter to be dealt with). [L., ablative of *res* thing]

re- *prefix.* 1. Once more; afresh; repeated. 2. Back, with return to previous state.

REA, R.E.A. *abbrevs.* Rural Electrification Administration.

reach (rēch) *v.* Stretch out, extend; stretch out the hand etc.,

Similar to sharks in that they have cartilage but no true bones, most of the fish called **rays** are adapted to bottom dwelling. Like sharks, most give birth to live young.

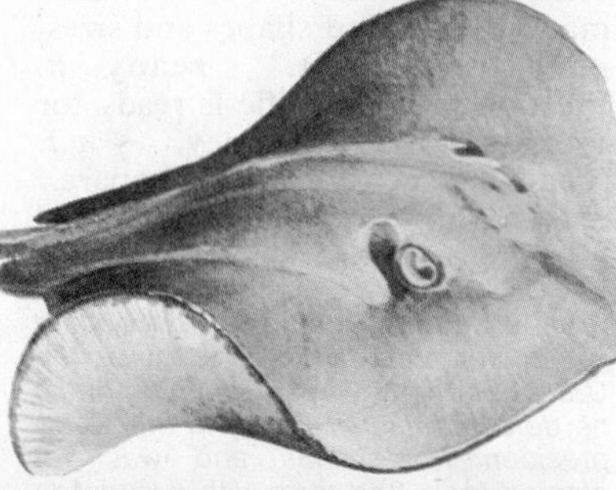

make reaching motion or effort (lit. and fig.); succeed in touching or grasping with hand or anything held in it, etc., extend to; come to, arrive at; hand, pass or take with outstretched hand; (naut.) sail with the wind abeam. ~ *n.* 1. Act of reaching out; extent to which hand etc. can be reached out; scope, range, compass. 2. Continuous extent, esp. part of river etc. lying between 2 bends.

re·act (rēăkt′) *v.i.* Act in return (*against* agent or influence); act, display energy, in response to stimulus; act in opposition to some force; move or tend in reverse direction; undergo change (esp. chemical change) under some influence.

re·act·ance (rēăk′t*a*ns) *n.* (elect.) That part of the impedance of an alternating current circuit which is due to capacitance or induction or both.

re·ac·tion (rēăk′sh*o*n) *n.* 1. Responsive or reciprocal action; return of previous condition after interval of opposite (e.g. depression after excitement); (loosely) opinion, impression; (physiol.) response of organ etc. to external stimulus; (chem.) interaction of 2 or more substances resulting in chemical change. 2. (pol.) (Movement toward) extreme conservatism. **re·ac·tion·ar·y** (rēăk′sh*o*nĕrē) *adj.* & *n.* (pl. **-ar·ies**). (Person) inclined or favorable to reaction.

re·ac·tive (rēăk′tĭv) *adj.* Tending to react.

re·ac·tor (rēăk′t*er*) *n.* 1. Person or thing that reacts. 2. (elect.) Element, as a coil, put into a circuit to introduce reactance. 3. Apparatus in which nuclear fission chain reactions are started and controlled for generation of energy and production of medical and experimental materials; atomic pile (reactor), nuclear reactor.

read (rēd) *v.* (**read** pr. rĕd, **read·ing**). 1. Discover or expound significance of (dream, riddle, etc.); foresee, foretell (esp. *the future, one's fortune*). 2. (Be able to) convert into the intended words of meaning (written, printed, or other symbols, or things, expressed by their means); reproduce mentally or vocally, while following their symbols with eyes or fingers, the words of (author, book, letter, etc.); study by reading; find (thing) stated, find statement, in print, etc.; convey when read, run; (of recording instrument) present (figure, etc.) to one reading it; (of computer) copy or transfer (data) from (~ **in**) or to (~ **out**) magnetic

***Razorbills** spend the bulk of their time in coastal or offshore waters, rather than far out at sea. They are sociable, often associating with guillemots at cliff breeding sites.*

tape etc., hence **read'in**, input of data to a computer; **read'out**, retrieval of information from digital computer; such information. 3. Interpret (statement, action) in certain sense; assume as intended in or deducible from writer's words, find implications; (of manuscript, editor, etc.) give as the word(s) probably used or intended by author; **read well, badly**, etc., (of written matter) sound or affect reader thus. 4. Bring into specified state by reading; **read out**, expel (from political party etc.) (as if) by reading form of dismissal. **read** (rĕd) *adj.* (esp., in active sense) **well** ~, versed *in* subject by reading; with good knowledge of literature.

Read (rēd), **Sir Herbert** (**Edward**) (1893–1968). English poet and critic; author of *The Philosophy of Modern Art, Poetry and Anarchism*, etc.

read·a·ble (rē'dabel) *adj.* Interestingly written; legible. **read'-a·ble·ness, read·a·bil'i·ty** *ns.* **read'a·bly** *adv.*

read·er (rē'der) *n.* (esp.) 1. Person employed by publisher to read and report on proffered manuscripts; proofreader. 2. Person appointed to read aloud, esp. (**lay** ~) parts of service in church. 3. Book containing passages for exercise in reading, instruction in foreign language, etc. **read'er·ship** *n.* Readers of, subscribers to, a publication.

read·i·ly (rĕd'ĭlē) *adv.* Without showing reluctance, willingly; without difficulty.

read·i·ness (rĕd'ēnĭs) *n.* Prompt compliance, willingness; facility, prompt resourcefulness, quickness in argument or action; ready or prepared state.

read·ing (rē'dĭng) *n.* (esp.) 1. Entertainment at which something is read to audience. 2. Word(s) read or given by an editor etc. or found in manuscript in text of a passage; interpretation, view taken, rendering. 3. Figure etc. shown by graduated instrument. 4. (Specified quality of) matter to be read. 5. ~ **desk**, desk for supporting book, etc., lectern; ~ **room**, room in library, club, etc., for persons wishing to read.

read·y (rĕd'ē) *adj.* (**read·i·er, read·i·est**). With preparations complete; in fit state; with resolution nerved, willing; apt, inclined; about *to*; prompt, quick, facile; provided beforehand; within reach, easily secured; unreluctant; easy; fit for immediate use; **make** ~, prepare; ~ **money**, cash, actual coin; money available for spending. **ready** *adv.* Beforehand, so as not to require doing when the time comes; ~**-made**, (of clothes etc.) made in standard shapes and sizes, not custom-made. **ready** *n.* Position in which rifle is ready for use; (slang) ready money. ~ *v.t.* (**read·ied, read·y·ing**). Prepare.

Rea·gan (rā'gan), **Ronald** (1911–). Fortieth president of the U.S., 1981–1988; governor of California, 1966–74. Reagan defeated President Carter in a landslide victory, capturing 43 states and a total of 483 electoral votes, 270 more than needed for election.

***Ronald Reagan,** retired Hollywood and T.V. actor and 40th president of the U.S.A. Formerly Governor of California, he defeated Jimmy Carter in the 1980 presidential elections and was re-elected for a 2nd term with a landslide victory in 1984.*

re·agent (rēā'jent) *n.* Chemical substance used to produce a chemical reaction.

re·al[1] (rē'al, rēl; *Sp.* rĕahl') *n.* (pl. **re·als**; Sp. **re·a·les** pr. rĕah'lĕs). Former silver coin and money of account used in Spain and some Spanish-speaking countries. [Spain, f. L. *regalis* regal]

re·al[2] (rē'al, rēl) *adj.* 1. Actually existing as a thing or occurring in fact, objective; genuine, rightly so called; natural, not artificial or depicted; actually present or involved, not merely apparent; **the** ~ **thing**, the thing itself, not an imitation or inferior article. 2. (law) Relating to things, esp. stationary or fixed property; ~ **estate**: see ESTATE; (philos. etc.) relating to, concerned with, things. **real** *adv.* (colloq. usu. with adjectives) Really; very, extremely. ~ *n.* Real thing; what actually exists, esp. opp. the ideal.

re·al·gar (rēăl'ger) *n.* Arsenic disulfide (As_2S_2), red arsenic occurring as ore, used as pigment and in fireworks. [Arab. *rahj al-gār* dust of the cave]

re·al·ism (rē'alĭzem) *n.* 1. Scholastic doctrine that universal or general ideas have objective existence; belief that matter as object of perception has real existence. 2. Practice of regarding things in their true nature and dealing with them as they are; fidelity of representation, rendering precise details of real thing or scene. **re'al·ist** *n.* **re·al·is·tic** (rēalĭs'tĭk) *adj.* **re·al·is'ti·cal·ly** *adv.*

re·al·i·ty (rēăl'ĭtē) *n.* (pl. **-ties**). Property of being real; resemblance to original; real existence, what is real, what underlies appearances; existent thing; real nature *of*; ~ **principle**, (psychoanal.) understanding of and adjustment to environment resulting in satisfaction of needs and achieving of long-range goals.

re·al·ize (rē'alīz) *v.t.* (**-ized, -iz·ing**). 1. Convert (hope, plan, etc.) into fact; give apparent reality to, make realistic, present as reality. 2. Conceive as real; apprehend clearly or in detail. 3. Make a gain or profit of; amass (fortune, specified profit), fetch as price. **re'al·iz·a·ble** *adj.* **re·al·i·za·tion** (rēalīzā'shon), **re'al·iz·er** *ns.*

re·al·ly (rē'alē, rē'lē) *adv.* In fact, in reality; positively, indeed; (interrog.) is that so?

realm (rĕlm) *n.* Kingdom; sphere, province, domain.

re·al·po·li·tik (rāahlpōlĭtēk') *n.*

Politics based on realities and material needs, not on ideology or ethics. [Ger., = "real politics"]

Re·al·tor (rē′*alter*, rēl′-) *n.* (trademark) Real-estate agent who is a member or affiliated member of the National Association of Real Estate Boards.

re·al·ty (rē′*altē*, rēl′-) *n.* Real estate.

ream[1] (rēm) *n.* Five hundred sheets of paper; (freq. pl.) large quantity; **printers'** ~, 516 sheets. [Arab. *rizmah* bundle]

ream[2] (rēm) *v.t.* Widen (hole in metal or smoker's pipe) with reamer. **ream′er** *n.* Device, usu. metal, used in reaming.

reap (rēp) *v.* Cut (grain or similar crop), cut grain, etc., with sickle etc. in harvest; gather in thus, or fig. as harvest; harvest crop of (field etc.).

reap·er (rē′p*er*) *n.* 1. One who reaps; **grim** ~, death. 2. Mechanical device for reaping crops (and binding sheaves) without manual labor.

rear[1] (rēr) *n.* 1. Hindmost part of army or fleet; back of, space behind, position at back, of, army or camp or person; back part of anything; **bring up the** ~, come last. 2. (attrib.) Hinder, back; ~ **admiral**, officer in navy, next

*The 19th-century term **realism** was adopted by writers such as de Maupassant and Flaubert and painters including Courbet, whose 'La Fileuse Endormie' confirms the view that everything should be portrayed objectively.*

below vice admiral; ~ **guard**, body of troops detached to protect rear, esp. in retreats. **rear′most** *adj.* Farthest back. **rear′ward, rear′wards** *adjs.* & *advs.* **rear′ward** *n.*

rear[2] (rēr) *v.* 1. Raise, set upright, build. 2. Bring up, raise (children); breed; cultivate. 3. (of horse etc.) Rise on hind feet.

re·arm (rēärm′) *v.* Arm again, esp. with more modern weapons or after disarming. **re·ar′ma·ment** *n.*

rea·son (rē′z*on*) *n.* 1. (Fact adduced or serving as) argument, motive, cause, or justification; (logic) one of premises of syllogism, esp. minor premise when given after conclusion. 2. Intellectual faculty characteristic esp. of human beings by which conclusions are drawn from premises; intellect personified; (tr. Kant's *Vernunft*) faculty transcending the understanding and providing a priori principles, intuition. 3. Sanity; sense; sensible conduct; what is right, practical, or practicable; moderation; **listen to** ~, allow oneself to be persuaded; **it stands to** ~, it cannot reasonably be denied. **rea′son·er** *n.* **reason** *v.* 1. Use argument *with* person by way of persuasion; persuade by argument *out of, into*. 2. Form or try to reach conclusions by connected thought; discuss *what, whether*, etc.; conclude, assume as step in argument, say by way of argument, (*that*); express in logical or argumentative form; think *out*. **rea′son·ing** *adj.* & *n.*

rea·son·a·ble (rē′z*onabel*) *adj.* 1. Endowed with reason, reasoning (rare). 2. Of sound judgment, sensible, moderate, not expecting too much, ready to listen to reason. 3. Agreeable to reason, not absurd, within the limits of reason; not greatly less or more than might be expected; inexpensive, not extortionate; tolerable, fair. **rea′son·a·ble·ness** *n.* **rea′son·a·bly** *adv.*

re·as·sure (rē*ashoor*′) *v.* (**-sured, -sur·ing**). Restore (person etc.) to confidence; confirm again in opinion or impression; reinsure. **re·as·sur′ance** *n.* **re·as·sur′ing·ly** *adv.*

re·a·ta: RIATA.

Ré·au·mur (rā′*u*mūr; *Fr.* rĕō-mür′), **René Antoine Ferchault**

de (1683–1757). French scientist; ~ **scale**, scale in which the freezing point of water is 0° and the boiling point 80°.

reave, reive (rēv) *vbs.* (**reaved** or **reft** pr. rĕft, **reav·ing, reived, reiv·ing**). (archaic, poet.) Commit ravages; forcibly deprive *of* (usu. in past part.); bereave; take by force, carry off. **reiv'er** *n.* Marauder, raider.

re·bate (rē'bāt) *n.* Deduction from sum to be paid, discount, return of part of payment. ~ (rĭbāt', rē'bāt) *v.t.* (**-bat·ed, -bat·ing**). Deduct or return from payment.

re·bec, re·beck (rē'bĕk) *ns.* Medieval three-stringed instrument, early form of fiddle. [Arab. *rabāb*]

Re·bec·ca (rĭbĕk'*a*). Wife of Isaac and mother of Jacob and Esau (Gen. 25 ff.).

reb·el (rĕb'el) *n.* Person who rises in arms against, resists, or refuses allegiance to, the established government; person or thing that resists authority or control; (attrib.) rebellious, of rebels, in rebellion. ~ (rĭbĕl') *v.i.* (**-elled, -el·ling**). Act as rebel (*against*); feel or manifest repugnance to some custom etc. (*against*).

re·bel·lion (rĭbĕl'yon) *n.* Organized armed resistance to established government; open resistance to any authority.

re·bel·lious (rĭbĕl'yus) *adj.* In rebellion; disposed to rebel, insubordinate, defying lawful authority; unmanageable, refractory. **re·bel'lious·ly** *adv.* **re·bel'lious·ness** *n.*

A law that miners had to pay for licences to prospect at the Ballarat gold rush in Australia in 1854, resulted in a ***rebellion*** *known as the Eureka Stockade. It was the beginning of colonial Australia's move towards self-government.*

re·birth (rēbĕrth', rē'bĕrth) *n.* New or second birth (fig.); fresh incarnation; spiritual enlightenment; revival. (John 3).

re·born (rēbōrn') *adj.* Having undergone rebirth.

re·bound (rĭbownd') *v.i.* Spring back after impact; have reactive effect, recoil upon agent. ~ (rē'bownd, rĭbownd') *n.* Act of rebounding, recoil; reaction after emotion.

re·buff (rĭbŭf') *n.* Check given to one who makes advances, proffers help or sympathy, shows interest or curiosity, makes request, etc.; snub. ~ *v.t.* Give rebuff to.

re·buke (rĭbūk') *v.t.* (**-buked, -buk·ing**). Convey stern disapproval or censure to (person) *for* fault etc. ~ *n.* Rebuking, being rebuked; reproof. **re·buk'ing·ly** *adv.*

re·bus (rē'bus) *n.* (pl. **-bus·es**). Enigmatic representation of name, word, etc., by pictures etc. suggesting its syllables.

re·but (rĭbŭt') *v.t.* (**-but·ted, -but·ting**). Force or turn back, give check to (archaic); refute, disprove (evidence, charge). **re·but'tal, re·but'ter** *ns.*

re·cal·ci·trant (rĭkăl'sĭtrant) *adj.* & *n.* Obstinately disobedient or refractory (person). **re·cal'ci·trance, re·cal'ci·tran·cy** *ns.*

re·call (rĭkawl') *v.t.* Summon back from or to a place, from different occupation, inattention, digression, etc.; bring back *to* memory, cause to remember; recollect, remember; restore; take back, withdraw; call back (dangerous or defective manufactured item) for modification or replacement. ~ (rĭkawl', rē'kawl) *n.* Summons to return to or from a place; signal to return; possibility of recalling, revoking, or annulling; recollection, remembrance; act of removing, or right of removal of, an official from public office by popular vote after petition; process of calling back (esp. automobile) for replacement or repair. **re·call'a·ble** *adj.*

re·cant (rĭkănt') *v.* Withdraw and renounce (opinion, statement, etc.) as erroneous or heretical; disavow former opinion, esp. with public confession of error. **re·can·ta·tion** (rēkăntā'shon), **re·cant'er** *ns.*

re·cap[1] (rē'kăp) *v.* (**-capped, -cap·ping**). (colloq.) Recapitulate. ~ *n.* Recapitulation.

re·cap[2] (rē'kăp, rēkăp') *v.* (**-capped, -cap·ping**). Put cap back on (bottle etc.); RETREAD.

re·ca·pit·u·late (rēkapĭch'*u*lāt) *v.t.* (**-lat·ed, -lat·ing**). Give gist or substance of (what has already been said); summarize, restate briefly. **re·ca·pit·u·la·tion** (rēkapĭchulā'shon) *n.* **re·ca·pit'u·la·tive** *adj.*

re·cast (rēkăst', -kahst') *v.t.* (**-cast, -cast·ing**). (esp.) Refashion, remodel, reconstruct; give new form or character to.

recd., rec'd. *abbrevs.* Received.

re·cede (rĭsēd′) *v.i.* (**-ced·ed, -ced·ing**). Go back or farther off; become more distant; slope backward; withdraw (*from* opinion etc.).

re·ceipt (rĭsēt′) *n.* 1. (archaic) Recipe. 2. Amount of money received; fact or action of receiving or being received into person's hands or possession; written acknowledgment of such receipt, esp. of payment of sum due. ~ *v.t.* Write or print receipt on (bill).

re·ceive (rĭsēv′) *v.t.* (**-ceived, -ceiv·ing**). 1. Take into one's hands or possession; accept (something proffered); accept or buy (stolen goods) from thief; take (bread and wine of Eucharist); admit, consent or prove able to hold, provide accommodation for; submit to, endure; admit (impression etc.) by yielding or adaptation of surface. 2. Entertain as guest; greet, welcome; give specified reception to; admit *into* membership of society etc.; (abs.) receive company, hold reception. 3. Acquire, get, come by; be given or provided with; have sent to or conferred or inflicted on one. 4. (radio etc.) Transform incoming electromagnetic waves into the original signal, as sound or as light on screen. **re·ceiv′a·ble** *adj.* (esp.) Awaiting or demanding payment. **re·ceiv′a·bles** *n.pl.* Business assets representing amounts due.

re·ceiv·er (rĭsē′v*er*) *n.* (esp.) 1. Person appointed by court to administer property of bankrupt or property under litigation. 2. Person who receives stolen goods. 3. Receptacle etc. for receiving something in machine or instrument; part of telephone containing ear piece; radio or television receiving set.

re·cen·sion (rĭsĕn′sh*o*n) *n.* Revision of, revised, text.

re·cent (rē′s*e*nt) *adj.* Not long past, that happened or existed lately, late; not long established, lately begun, modern; **R**~, (geol.) of the latter part of the Quaternary period or system, including the present time. **re′cent·ly** *adv.* **re′cent·ness, re′cen·cy** *ns.* **Re′cent** *n.* (geol.) Recent epoch.

re·cep·ta·cle (rĭsĕp′t*a*k*e*l) *n.* 1. Vessel, place, or space that contains. 2. (bot.) Common base of floral organs, axis of cluster.

re·cep·tion (rĭsĕp′sh*o*n) *n.* 1. Receiving, being received; receiving esp. of person, being received, into a place or company; formal or ceremonious welcome; occasion of receiving guests, assembly held for this purpose; ~ **room**, waiting room, room for receiving guests or customers. 2. Receiving of ideas or impressions into the mind. 3. Welcome or greeting of specified kind; demonstration of feeling toward person or project; **warm** ~, enthusiastic welcome; (satirically) vigorous resistance. 4. (radio etc.) Receiving signals, efficiency with which they are received.

Spiro Agnew, former Vice-President of the U.S. at a ***reception*** *in Canberra, Australia, with the then-Australian Prime Minister, Sir John Gorton, who objected to President Johnson's bombing of North Vietnam.*

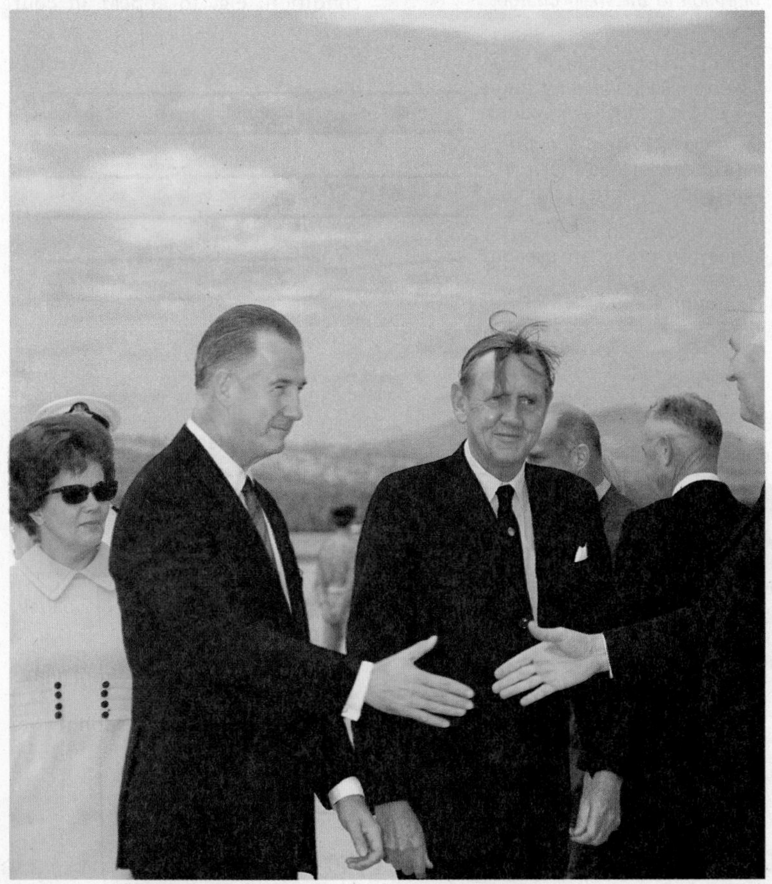

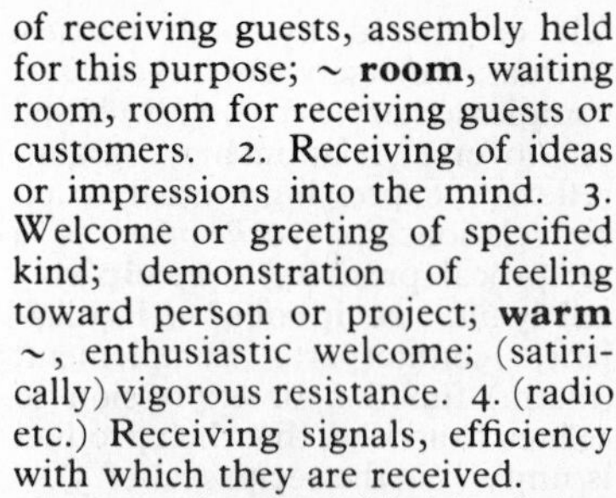

re·cep·tion·ist (rĭsĕp′sh*o*nĭst) *n.* Person employed to receive clients, patients, etc.

re·cep·tive (rĭsĕp′tĭv) *adj.* Able or quick to receive impressions or ideas. **re·cep′tive·ly** *adv.* **re·cep′tive·ness, re·cep·tiv·i·ty** (rēsĕptĭv′ĭtē) *ns.*

re·cep·tor (rĭsĕp′t*e*r) *n.* (physiol.) Minute organ at peripheral end of sensory nerve, capable of specially sensitive response to a particular form of energy, as light or heat.

re·cess (rĭsĕs′, rē′sĕs) *n.* 1. Temporary cessation from work, short school vacation. 2. Secret or secluded place; niche or alcove of wall; (anat.) fold or indentation in organ. ~ *v.t.* Place in a recess; set back; provide with recess(es).

re·ces·sion (rĭsĕsh′*o*n) *n.* 1. Receding, withdrawal, from a place or point. 2. Temporary decline or setback in industrial or economic activity or prosperity. **re·ces′sion·ar·y** *adj.*

re·ces·sion·al (rĭsĕsh′*o*n*a*l) *adj.* Of recession. ~ *n.* Hymn sung while clergy and choir withdraw after church service.

re·ces·sive (rĭsĕs′ĭv) *adj.* 1. Tending to recede. 2. (biol., of an inherited character) Not manifest in the organism that inherits it, though liable to be manifest in the next generation; having its effect obscured by a DOMINANT character.

re·cher·ché (r*e*shăr′shā; *Fr.* r*e*shĕrshā′) *adj.* Devised or got with care or difficulty; choice, farfetched, overrefined.

re·cid·i·vist (rĭsĭd′ĭvĭst) *n.* One who relapses into crime. **re·cid′i·vism** *n.* **re·cid·i·vis·tic** (rĭsĭdĭvĭs′tĭk), **re·cid′i·vous** *adjs.*

rec·i·pe (rĕs′*i*pē) *n.* 1. Statement of ingredients and procedure for preparing dish etc. 2. (archaic) Medical prescription or remedy prepared from it. 3. Expedient, device, etc., for effecting something. [2nd pers. sing. imp. of L. *recipere* receive (i.e. take) as used in prescriptions]

re·cip·i·ent (rĭsĭp′ē*e*nt) *adj.* Receptive. **re·cip′i·ence, re·cip′i·en·cy** *ns.* **recipient** *n.* Person who receives something.

re·cip·ro·cal (rĭsĭp′r*o*k*a*l) *adj.* Given, felt, shown, etc., in return;

felt or shared by both parties, mutual; inversely correspondent, complementary, esp. (math.) based on inverse relationship; (gram.) reflexive, expressing mutual action or relationship (*each other* is a reciprocal pronoun). **re·cip'ro·cal·ly** *adv.* **reciprocal** *n.* Equivalent, counterpart, complement; (math.) function or expression so related to another that their product is unity ($\frac{1}{5}$ is the reciprocal of 5).

re·cip·ro·cate (rĭsĭp'rokāt) *v.* (**-cat·ed, -cat·ing**). 1. (mech.) Go with alternate backward and forward motion; give such motion to. 2. Give and receive mutually, interchange; return, requite (affection etc.); make a return (*with*). **re·cip·ro·ca·tion** (rĭsĭprokā'shon) *n.* **re·cip'ro·ca·tive, re·cip·ro·ca·to·ry** (rĭsĭp'rokatōrē, -tōrē) *adjs.*

rec·i·proc·i·ty (rĕsĭprŏs'ĭtē) *n.* (pl. **-ties**). Reciprocal condition, mutual action; principle or practice of give-and-take, esp. interchange of privileges between nations as basis of commercial relations.

re·cit·al (rĭsī'tal) *n.* 1. Detailed account *of* a number of connected things or facts, relation *of* the facts of an incident etc. 2. Act of reciting; performance of music or dance, esp. by one person or a small group. **re·cit'al·ist** *n.*

rec·i·ta·tion (rĕsĭtā'shon) *n.* (esp.) Reciting as entertainment, poem or passage recited; oral repetition of prepared lesson or exercise.

rec·i·ta·tive (rĕsĭtatēv') *n.* Musical declamation, between song and ordinary speech, of kind usual in narrative and dialogue parts of opera and oratorio; words, part given in recitative.

re·cite (rĭsīt') *v.* (**-cit·ed, -cit·ing**). 1. Repeat aloud or declaim (poem, passage) from memory, esp. before audience; give recitation. 2. Rehearse (facts) in document; mention in order, enumerate. **re·cit'er** *n.*

reck·less (rĕk'lĭs) *adj.* Devoid of caution, regardless of consequences, rash; heedless *of* danger etc. **reck'less·ly** *adv.* **reck'less·ness** *n.*

reck·on (rĕk'on) *v.* 1. Ascertain (number, amount), ascertain number or amount of, by counting or usu. by calculation, compute; count, sum up character of; arrive at as total; include *in* computation; make calculations, cast up account or sum; settle accounts *with*. 2. Consider (*to be*); conclude after calculation; be of the confident opinion (*that*); rely, base plans, *on*. **reck'on·er** *n.*

reck·on·ing (rĕk'onĭng) *n.* (esp.) Statement of amount due, bill; **day of ~**, time when something must be atoned for or avenged; **dead ~**: see DEAD.

re·claim (rĭklām') *v.* Win back, recall, from wrong course, error, etc.; reform, tame, civilize; bring back (land) into cultivation from a waste state or from the sea. ~ *n.* Reclaiming, reclamation.

rec·la·ma·tion (rĕklamā'shon) *n.* Reclaiming, being reclaimed.

ré·clame (rāklahm') *n.* Art or practice by which publicity is secured; public acclaim. [Fr.]

rec·li·nate (rĕk'lĭnāt, -nĭt) *adj.* (biol.) Bending downward.

re·cline (rĭklīn') *v.* (**-clined, -clin·ing**). Lay (esp. one's head, body, limbs) in more or less horizontal or leaning position; assume or be in recumbent position, lie, lean, sit with back or side supported at considerable inclination. **re·clin'er** *n.* (esp.) Easy chair with back and footrest that automatically adjust to reclining position of occupant.

rec·luse (*adj.* rĭklōōs'; *n.* rĕk'lōōs, rĭklōōs') *adj.* & *n.* (Person) given to or living in seclusion, retirement, or isolation. **re·clu·sive** (rĭklōō'sĭv) *adj.*

rec·og·ni·tion (rĕkognĭsh'on) *n.* Recognizing, being recognized.

re·cog·ni·zance (rĭkŏg'nĭzans, -kŏn'ĭ-) *n.* 1. Recorded obligation by which person engages before court or magistrate to observe some condition, e.g. to appear in court

The problem of **recoil** *has concerned engineers since guns were invented, but the first practical solution was not devised until the early 1900s. At first lead shot was fired in the opposite direction to the main charge.*

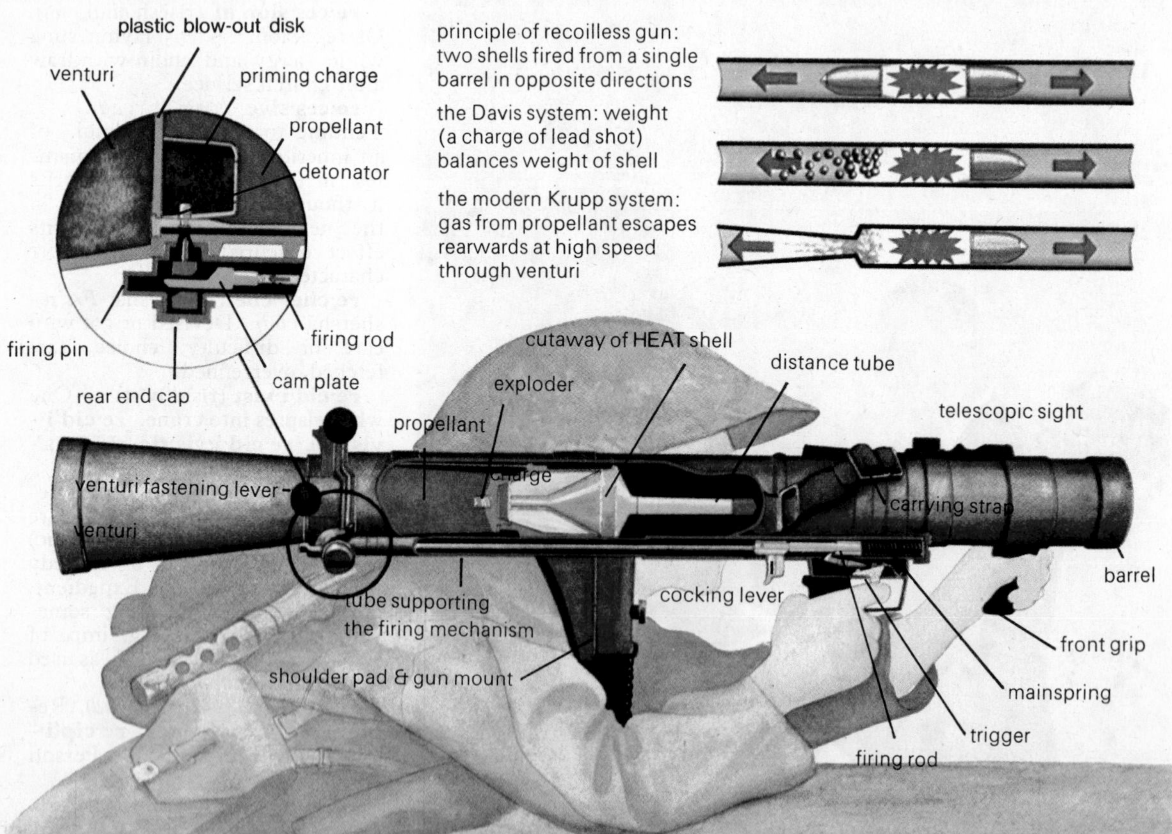

when summoned; sum pledged as surety for such observance. 2. Recognition. **re·cog'ni·zant** *adj.*

rec·og·nize (rĕk'ognīz) *v.t.* (**-nized, -niz·ing**). 1. Acknowledge validity, genuineness, character, claims, or existence of; accord notice or consideration to; discover or realize nature of; treat *as*, acknowledge *for*; realize or admit *that*. 2. Know again, identify as known before. **rec'og·niz·a·ble** *adj.* **rec'og·niz·a·bly** *adv.*

re·coil (rĭkoil') *v.i.* Retreat before enemy etc.; start or spring back, shrink mentally, in fear, horror, or disgust; rebound after impact; spring back to original position or starting point; (of firearms) be driven backward by discharge kick. ~ (rē'koil, rĭkoil') *n.* Act, fact, sensation, of recoiling. **re·coil'less** *adj.* (chiefly of guns).

rec·ol·lect (rĕkolĕkt') *v.t.* Succeed in remembering, recall to mind, remember. **rec·ol·lec·tion** (rĕkolĕk'shon) *n.* Act, power, of recollecting; thing recollected; person's memory, time over which it extends.

rec·om·mend (rĕkomĕnd') *v.t.* 1. Give (oneself or another, one's spirit, etc.) in charge *to* God, a person, his care, etc. 2. Speak or write of, suggest, as fit for employment or favor or trial; make acceptable, serve as recommendation of. 3. Counsel, advise. **rec·om·mend'a·ble, rec·om·mend·a·to·ry** (rĕkomĕn'datōrē, -tōrē) *adjs.* **rec·om·men·da·tion** (rĕkomĕndā'shon), **rec·om·mend'er** *ns.*

rec·om·pense (rĕk'ompĕns) *v.t.* (**-pensed, -pens·ing**). Requite, reward; make amends to (person) or for (another's loss, injury, etc.). ~ *n.* Reward, requital; atonement or satisfaction for injury; retribution.

rec·on·cile (rĕk'onsīl) *v.t.* (**-ciled, -cil·ing**). 1. Make friendly after estrangement. 2. Bring into state of acquiescence or submission (*to*). 3. Adjust, settle (quarrel etc.); make (facts, statements, etc.) consistent or accordant; make compatible or consistent, regard or show as consistent (*with*). **rec'on·cil·a·ble** *adj.* **rec'on·cile·ment, rec·on·cil·i·a·tion** (rĕkonsĭlēā'shon) *ns.*

rec·on·dite (rĕk'ondīt, rĭkŏn'-) *adj.* Abstruse, out of the way, little known; dealing in recondite knowledge or allusion, obscure. **rec'on·dite·ly** *adv.* **rec'on·dite·ness** *n.*

re·con·di·tion (rēkondĭsh'on) *v.t.* Restore to proper, habitable, or usable condition, overhaul, repair.

re·con·nais·sance (rĭkŏn'asans) *n.* Reconnoitering.

rec·on·noi·ter (rēkonoi'ter, rĕko-) *v.* Approach and try to learn position and condition or strategic features of (enemy, area), make reconnaissance.

*The first sound **recordings** were made in 1877 by Edison, and developed in the 1880s. The first records were cylinders; in the 1890s Berliner invented the disk, and a way of taking copies from a master negative. From then continual progress was made, and today stereo and quadraphonic reproduction are available.*

re·con·struct (rēkonstrŭkt') *v.* Build again; restore (past event) mentally; reorganize.

re·con·struc·tion (rēkonstrŭk'shon) *n.* 1. Process of reconstructing; thing reconstructed. 2. (**R**~), reincorporation of seceded states into U.S. after Civil War; period during which this occurred (1865–77).

re·cord (rĭkōrd') *v.t.* Register, set down for remembrance or reference, put in writing or other legible shape; represent in some permanent form, esp. on phonograph record, magnetic tape, video disk, film, etc. for reproduction. ~ (rĕk'erd) *n.* 1. State of being recorded or preserved in writing, esp. as authentic legal evidence; official report of proceedings and judgment in cause before a court, copy of pleading etc. constituting case to be decided by a court; piece of recorded evidence or information, account of fact preserved in permanent form, document or monument preserving it; object serving as memorial of something; **matter of** ~, something recorded and thereby established as fact; **off the** ~, unofficial(ly). 2. Track made by marker in groove of revolving disk or cylinder, from which sounds can afterward be reproduced by means of a phonograph or other device; similar track made on tape or wire by mechanical, magnetic, photographic, or other means; grooved

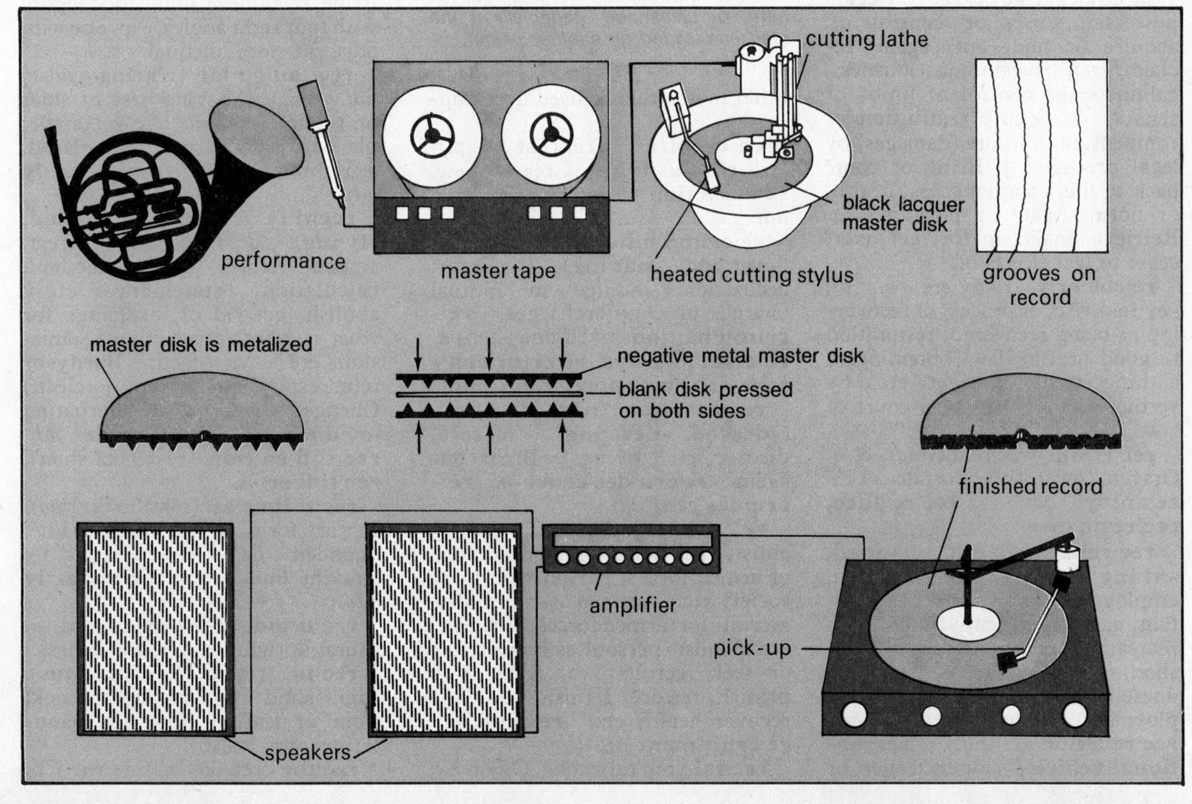

disk, cylinder, etc., bearing such track; ~ **player**, apparatus for reproducing sound of phonograph record. 3. Facts known about person's past. 4. Best performance or most remarkable event of its kind on record; (*attrib.*) best hitherto recorded; **break, beat, the** ~, outdo all predecessors.

re·cord·er (rĭkōr′d*er*) *n.* (esp.) 1. One whose official duty is to record. 2. Recording apparatus or instrument. 3. Woodwind flute, played vertically, and varying in range.

re·cord·ing (rĭkōr′dĭng) *n.* (esp.) Process of registering wave form by mechanical, photographic, electrical, or magnetic means for subsequent reproduction by record player, movie projector, radio, television, etc.; disk, film, or tape on which the wave form has been registered; program so reproduced.

re·count[1] (rĭkownt′) *v.t.* Narrate, tell in detail.

re·count[2] (rēkownt′) *v.t.* Count afresh. **re-count, re·count** (rē′kownt) *ns.* Recounting, esp. of election votes.

re·coup (rĭkōōp′) *v.* Compensate for (loss), compensate (*for*); (law) deduct, keep back (part of sum due), make such deduction; (refl.) recover what one has expended or lost. **re·coup′ment** *n.*

re·course (rē′kōrs, -kōrs, rĭkōrs′, -kōrs′) *n.* Resorting or betaking of oneself *to* possible source of help; thing resorted to; **have ~ to**, adopt as adviser, helper, or expedient.

re·cov·er (rĭkŭv′*er*) *v.* 1. Regain possession, use, or control of; acquire or find (out) again; reclaim; (refl.) regain consciousness, calmness, or control of limbs or senses. 2. Secure restitution or compensation, secure (damages) by legal process. 3. Bring or come back to life, consciousness, health, or normal state or position. 4. Retrieve, make up for; get over, cease to feel effects of.

re·cov·er·y (rĭkŭv′*er*ē) *n.* (pl. **-er·ies**). Act or process of recovering or being recovered; restoration to good health; (law) obtaining of a thing, right, damages, etc., by verdict or judgment of a court of law.

rec·re·ant (rĕk′rēant) *adj.* & *n.* Craven, coward(ly), apostate. **rec′re·ant·ly** *adv.* **rec′re·ance, rec′re·an·cy** *ns.*

rec·re·ate[1] (rĕk′rēāt) *v.* (**-at·ed, -at·ing**). (of pastime, vacation, employment, etc.) Refresh, entertain, agreeably occupy; indulge in recreation. **rec·re·a·tion** (rĕkrēā′sh*o*n) *n.* (esp.) Means of recreating oneself, pleasurable exercise or employment. **rec′re·a·tive** *adj.* **rec·re·a′tion·al** *adj.* **recreational vehicle**, camper, trailer, or other motor vehicle used for camping.

*The **recovery** of a spacecraft is an essential part of the entire mission, whether the capsule is manned, as here, or unmanned, especially if the craft has landed on another planet.*

re·cre·ate[2] (rēkrēāt′) *v.t.* (**-at·ed, -at·ing**). Create anew. **re·cre·a′tion** *n.* **re·cre·a′tive** *adj.*

re·crim·i·nate (rĭkrĭm′ĭnāt) *v.i.* (**-nat·ed, -nat·ing**). Retort accusation, indulge in mutual charges or countercharges. **re·crim·i·na·tion** (rĭkrĭmĭnā′sh*o*n) *n.* **re·crim′i·na·tive, re·crim·i·na·to·ry** (rĭkrĭm′ĭnatōrē, -tōrē) *adjs.*

re·cru·desce (rēkrōōdĕs′) *v.i.* (**-desced, -desc·ing**). (of sore, disease, etc., or fig.) Break out again. **re·cru·des′cence** *n.* **re·cru·des′cent** *adj.*

re·cruit (rĭkrōōt′) *n.* Newly enlisted and not yet trained member of armed forces; person who joins society etc.; tyro. ~ *v.* 1. Enlist recruits for (armed forces, business, etc.); enlist (person) as recruit; get or seek recruits. 2. (rare) Replenish, restore, refresh; (seek to) recover health etc. **re·cruit′er, re·cruit′ment** *ns.*

rec·tal (rĕk′tal) *adj.* Of or by the rectum. **rec′tal·ly** *adv.*

rec·tan·gle (rĕk′tănggel) *n.* Plane rectilinear four-sided figure with four right angles, esp. one with adjacent sides unequal.

rec·tan·gu·lar (rĕktăng′gy*uler*) *adj.* Shaped, having base or sides or section shaped, like rectangle; placed, having parts or lines placed, at right angles. **rec·tan′gu·lar·ly** *adv.*

rec·ti·fy (rĕk′tĭfī) *v.t.* (**-fied, -fy·ing**). 1. Put right, correct, amend, reform, adjust (method, calculation, statement, etc.); abolish, get rid of, exchange for what is right (error, abuse, omission, etc.). 2. (chem.) Purify or refine esp. by distillation. 3. (elect.) Change (current) from alternating to direct. **rec′ti·fi·a·ble** *adj.* **rec·ti·fi·ca·tion** (rĕktĭfĭkā′sh*o*n), **rec′ti·fi·er** *ns.*

rec·ti·lin·e·ar (rĕkt*i*lĭn′ē*er*) *adj.* In or forming a straight line; bounded or characterized by straight lines. **rec·ti·lin′e·ar·ly** *adv.*

rec·ti·tude (rĕk′tĭtōōd, -tūd) *n.* Moral uprightness, righteousness.

rec·to (rĕk′tō) *n.* (pl. **-tos**). Right-hand page of open book; front of leaf of book or manuscript (opp. VERSO).

rec·tor (rĕk′t*er*) *n.* 1. (in Ch.

of England) Parish incumbent, (hist.) one entitled to receive all tithes of parish; (in Protestant and Episcopal Ch.) minister in charge of parish; (R.C. Ch.) head parish priest. 2. Head of certain universities, colleges, schools, or religious institutions. **rec·to·rate** (rĕk′terĭt) *n.* **rec·to·ri·al** (rĕktōr′ēal, -tōr′-) *adj.*

rec·to·ry (rĕk′terē) *n.* (pl. **-ries**). Rector's benefice; rector's house.

rec·tum (rĕk′tum) *n.* (pl. **-tums, -ta** pr. -ta). Final section of the large intestine terminating at the anus. [L. *rectum* (*intestinum*) straight (intestine)]

re·cum·bent (rĭkŭm′bent) *adj.* Lying down, reclining. **re·cum′bent·ly** *adv.* **re·cum′ben·cy** *n.*

re·cu·per·ate (rĭkōō′perāt) *v.* (**-at·ed, -at·ing**). Restore, be restored or recover, from exhaustion, illness, loss, etc. **re·cu·per·a·tion** (rĭkōōperā′shon) *n.* **re·cu·per·a·tive** (rĭkōō′perātĭv, -pera-) *adj.*

re·cur (rĭkėr′) *v.i.* (**-curred, -cur·ring**). Go back in thought or speech *to*; (of idea etc.) come back *to* one's mind etc., return to mind; (of problem etc.) come up again; occur again, be repeated; **recurring decimal**, see REPEATING DECIMAL. **re·cur′rence** *n.*

re·cur·rent (rĭkėr′ent) *adj.* Occurring again, often, or periodically; (of nerve, vein, etc.) turning back so as to reverse direction. **re·cur′rent·ly** *adv.*

re·curve (rĭkėrv′) *v.* (**-curved, -curv·ing**). Bend backward. **re·cur·vate** (rĭkėr′vĭt, -vāt) *adj.*

rec·u·sant (rĕk′yuzant, rĭkū′-) *n.* & *adj.* (Person) who refused to attend Church of England services (hist.); (person) refusing submission to authority or compliance with regulation. **rec′u·san·cy** *n.*

re·cy·cle (rēsī′kel) *v.* (**-cled, -cling**). Return to previous stage of cyclic process, esp. convert (waste) to reusable material.

red (rĕd) *adj.* (**red·der, red·dest**). 1. Of or approaching the color seen at lower or least refracted end of visible spectrum, of shades varying from crimson to bright brown and orange, esp. those seen in blood, sunset clouds, rubies, glowing coals, and human lips; stained or covered with blood; (of eyes) bloodshot, or with lids sore from weeping; (of persons or animals) having red or tawny hair; (of certain peoples, esp. N. Amer. Indians) having reddish skin. 2. Anarchistic or communistic; Russian, Soviet. 3. **red′bird**: see CARDINAL *n.* 3 and TANAGER; **red-blooded**, full of vigor and zest; virile; **red′breast**: see ROBIN; **red′brick** (**university**), applied attrib. to 19th c. English universities built of red brick, to distinguish them from Oxford and Cambridge; **red′bud**, any shrub or small tree of genus *Cercis*, esp. *C. canadensis* of Mexico and E. U.S., also called Judas tree, having clusters of pinkish to lavender flowers, and *C. occidentalis* of SW. U.S., having lavender flowers, both species blooming before leaves appear; **red′cap**, railroad station porter; **red carpet**, (fig.) elaborate form of reception for dignitaries etc.; **red cent**, (colloq.) copper penny (in *not worth, not have a red cent* etc.); **red′coat**, British soldier during the Revolutionary War and the War of 1812, so called from the scarlet uniform coat formerly worn by most regiments of the army; **Red Cross**, emblem of red cross on white ground (Swiss flag with colors reversed) adopted at the Geneva Convention of 1864 for the international societies organized for

1 

2 

3 

An English private or ***redcoat*** *in the uniform of the mid-18th century (1). This distinctive color was first used in Cromwell's New Model Army and its danger to the wearer was not appreciated until the 19th century when less conspicuous uniforms were worn.*

The emblem of the ***Red Cross*** *(2) as worn by these Australian girls, is adopted from the Swiss flag. Sioux Indians at Wounded Knee when there was trouble between themselves and the authorities (3). Use of the term* ***redskin*** *has largely been discontinued.*

*The **redstart** (right) and the **redwing** (below right) are both grouped in the subfamily Turdinae which includes the thrushes and chats. Both are songbirds but the redstart (a chat) is less melodious and breeds in central Africa though it spends the summer in northern Europe. The redwing has a similar range.*

the treatment of sick and wounded in war and borne by ambulances, hospitals, etc., attached to such service; **red deer**, reddish-brown species of deer (*Cervus elaphus*) of Europe, W. Asia, and N. Africa; **red'eye** (pl. **-eyes**, collect. **-eye**), any of various Amer. fishes with red eyes; (slang) whiskey of poor quality; **red'fish** (pl. **-fishes**, collect. **-fish**), any of various Amer. red or reddish fishes; **red flag**, symbol of revolution or socialism; (also) danger signal; **red fox**, any of several foxes of the genus *Vulpes*, typically having reddish fur, including *V. vulpes* of Europe and *V. fulva* of N. Amer.; **red giant**, (astron.) star in intermediate stage of evolution, with reddish hue; **red gum**, (eucalyptus tree yielding) reddish resin; **red-handed**, in the act of crime; **red herring**, herring reddened by being cured in smoke; something introduced to turn attention from the real issue (as *draw a red herring across the track*, with ref. to use of herring in exercising hounds); **red-hot**, heated to redness; highly excited, enthusiastic, furious; **red lead**, red oxide of lead, much used as pigment; **red-letter**, (of day) marked with red letter(s) in calendar as saint's day or festival; memorable as date of joyful occurrence; **red light**, red traffic or danger signal; **red-light district**, district containing many prostitutes, brothels, etc.; **red'lining**, refusal by banks

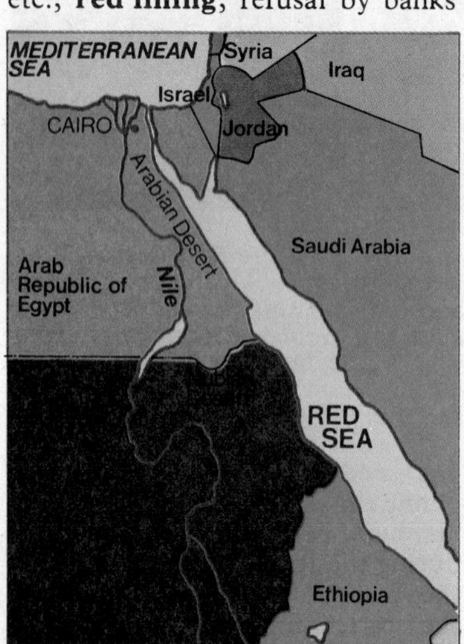

*The **Red Sea** is part of a great system of rifts, stretching south to the great African lakes. Its nearly landlocked nature has made its waters much saltier than those of the oceans.*

__Redpoll cattle__ are found in America, northern Europe and Asia. The distinctive red crown on their heads has given them their name.

to lend mortgage money on property in deteriorating urban areas, designated by red lines on map (**red'line** *v.*); **red man,** N. Amer. Ind.; **red meat,** beef, venison, etc., as dist. from veal, pork, or chicken; **red'neck,** (derog.) poor, white, uneducated rural farm worker in southern U.S.; **red pepper**: see PEPPER def. 2; **red'poll,** one of two small N. Amer. and Eurasian finches of the genus *Acanthis*, having bright red cap; **Red Poll,** one of a breed of red-haired polled cattle; **Red River,** (1) river in southwestern U.S. flowing 1,018 mi. (1,638 km) from E. New Mexico along the Texas-Oklahoma boundary through Arkansas to the Mississippi River in Louisiana; (2) river in N. central and S. Canada flowing N. 533 mi. (858 km) from the Minnesota-North Dakota boundary to Lake Winnipeg in S. Canada; **Red Sea,** long narrow strip of water between Asia and Africa, connected with Mediterranean by Suez Canal and with Arabian Sea by Gulf of Aden; **red shift**: see SHIFT def. 1; **red'skin,** (offensive) N. Amer. Ind.; **red snapper,** any of several reddish food fishes of the genus *Lutjanus*, esp. *L. blackfordi* found in the Gulf of Mexico; **red'start,** one of two brightly colored N. Amer. warblers of the genus *Setophaga*; any of several Old World thrushes of genus *Phoenicurus*; **red tape,** excessive use of or adherence to formalities esp. in public business (from pink tape used to tie English government and legal documents); **red tide,** brownish-red discoloration of ocean waters, caused by overabundance of one-celled animals, and fatal to fish; **red'wing,** N. Amer. red-winged blackbird (*Agelaius phoeniceus*); **red'wood**: see SEQUOIA. **red'den** *v.* **red'dish** *adj.* **red'ly** *adv.* **red'ness** *n.* **red** *n.* Red color; shade of red; red color in roulette etc.; red cloth or clothes; radical, anarchist, or (esp.) communist; **in the ~,** (bookkeeping) showing a deficit; **see ~,** become so angry as to lose self-control.

re·dact (rĭdăkt') *v.t.* Put into literary form, edit. **re·dac'tion, re·dac'tor** *ns.*

redd (rĕd) *v.t.* (**redd** or **redd·ed, redd·ing**). (regional) Put in order, tidy.

re·deem (rĭdēm') *v.t.* 1. Buy back, recover by expenditure of effort or by stipulated payment. 2. Compound for, buy off, (charge or obligation) by payment; perform (promise); purchase the freedom of, save (one's life), by ransom; save, rescue, reclaim; (of God or Christ) deliver from sin and damnation. 3. Make amends for, counter-

The giant ***redwood*** *or sequoia is a type of cypress which grows on the Pacific slopes of the Sierra Nevada at altitudes from 5,000–8,000 ft. The largest trees may be 3,000 years old.*

balance (fault, defect); save *from* a defect. **re·deem'a·ble** *adj.* **re·deem'er** *n.* (esp., **R~,** of Christ).

re·demp·tion (rĭdĕmp'shon) *n.* Redeeming or being redeemed, esp. the deliverance from sin and damnation wrought by Christ's atonement; thing that redeems; purchase. **re·demp'tive, re·demp'to·ry** *adjs.*

red·in·gote (rĕd'ĭnggōt) *n.* Woman's long double-breasted outer coat with skirt sometimes cut away in front. [Fr., f. English *riding coat*]

red·o·lent (rĕd'olent) *adj.* Fragrant; having a strong smell; strongly suggestive or reminiscent *of.* **red'o·lence, red'o·len·cy** *ns.* **red'o·lent·ly** *adv.*

re·dou·ble[1] (rĭdŭb'el) *v.* (**-bled, -bling**). Intensify, increase; make or grow greater or more intense or numerous.

re·dou·ble[2] (rēdŭb'el) *v.t.* (**-bled, -bling**). (bridge) Double again (bid already doubled by opponent). **~** *n.* Instance of redoubling.

re·doubt (rĭdowt') *n.* (fort.) Outwork or fieldwork, usu. square or polygonal and without flanking defenses.

re·doubt·a·ble (rĭdow'tabel) *adj.* Formidable.

re·dound (rĭdownd') *v.i.* Result in, have effect of, contributing or turning *to* some advantage or disadvantage; turn *to* credit etc.; (of advantage, honor, disgrace, etc.) result, attach, *to* (person), recoil or come back *upon.*

re·dress (rĭdrĕs') *v.t.* Adjust, set straight again; set right, remedy, make up for, rectify (distress, wrong, damage, etc.). **~** (re'drĕs, rĭdrĕs') *n.* Reparation for wrong, redressing of grievances, etc.

re·duce (rĭdōōs', -dūs') *v.* (**-duced, -duc·ing**). 1. Bring *to* certain order or arrangement, *to* a certain form or character; convert (*in*)*to* different physical state or form, esp. crush *to* powder etc. 2. Bring by force or necessity *to* some state or action, subdue. 3. Bring down, lower; weaken, impoverish; diminish, contract; degrade (noncommissioned officer) to lower rank; **reduced circumstances,** poverty after prosperity. 4. (surg.) Restore (dislocated, fractured, or ruptured part) to proper position. 5. (chem.) Remove from (a compound) oxygen or other electronegative atom or group; add to (compound) hydrogen or other electropositive atom or group. 6. (arith.) Change (number, quantity) (*in*)*to* another denomination or different form. 7. (logic) Bring syllogism into different form. 8. (intrans.) Lessen one's weight. **re·duc'er** *n.* **re·duc'i·ble** *adj.* **re·duc'i·bly** *adv.*

re·duc·tion (rĭdŭk'shon) *n.* Reducing or being reduced; reduced copy of picture, map, etc. **re·duc'tive** *adj.* **re·duc'tion·al** *adj.*

re·dun·dant (rĭdŭn'dant) *adj.* Superfluous; repetitive; (of employee or his post) liable to be dispensed with because no longer necessary. **re·dun'dant·ly** *adv.* **re·dun'dan·cy** *n.* (pl. **-cies**).

re·du·pli·cate (rĭdōō'plĭkāt, -dū-') *v.t.* (**-cat·ed, -cat·ing**). Make double, repeat; (gram.) repeat (letter, syllable); form (tense) by repetition of letter or syllable. **re·du·pli·ca·tion** (rĭdōōplĭkā'shon, -dū-) *n.*

re·ech·o, re-ech·o, re·ëch·o (rēĕk'ō) *vbs.* (**-ech·oed, -ech·o·ing**). Echo; echo again and again, resound.

reed (rēd) *n.* 1. (Tall straight stalk of) firm-stemmed plant of genus *Phragmites* or *Arundo*; (collect.) reeds, growth or bed of reeds. 2. Musical pipe of reed or straw; one of two vibrating concave wedge-shaped pieces of reed or cane fixed face to face on metal tube as part of mouthpiece of oboe or bassoon; small metal tube with opening closed by vibrating metal tongue in lower end of organ pipe; metal tongue, slip of cane, producing sound by vibration, in organ pipe, clarinet, etc.; (pl.) reed instrument(s). 3. Weaver's instrument of metal wires (formerly thin strips of reed or cane) fixed into parallel bars of wood, for separating threads of warp and beating up weft. 4. (archit.) One of a set of small semicylindrical moldings. 5. **reed'bird**, bobolink; **reed mace**, cattail; **reed pipe**, reeded organ pipe; **reed stop**, organ stop consisting of reed pipes.

Reed (rēd), **Walter** (1851–1902). U.S. Army surgeon; headed commission to study yellow fever in Cuba, 1900, and identified the mosquito that was the source of transmission of the disease.

reed·y (rē'dē) *adj.* (**reed·i·er, reed·i·est**). 1. Abounding with reeds; made of reed (chiefly poet.). 2. (of voice) Like reed instrument in tone, scratchy, not round and clear. **reed'i·ness** *n.*

reef[1] (rēf) *n.* One of three or four strips across top of square or bottom of fore-and-aft sail that can be taken in or rolled up to reduce sail's surface; ~ **knot**, square knot. **reef** *v.* Take in reef(s) of sail; shorten (topmast etc.).

reef[2] (rēf) *n.* Ridge of rock, shingle, or sand, at or just above or below surface of water; (gold etc. mining) vein, bedrock.

reef·er[1] (rē'fer) *n.* 1. One who reefs. 2. Close-fitting double-breasted stout jacket.

reef·er[2] (rē'fer) *n.* (slang) Marijuana cigarette.

reek (rēk) *n.* 1. Smoke; vapor. 2. Foul or stale odor; fetid atmosphere. ~ *v.i.* Emit smoke; emit vapor; smell unpleasantly (usu. *of*). **reek'y** *adj.* (**reek·i·er, reek·i·est**). **reek'er** *n.*

reel[1] (rēl) *n.* Rotatory apparatus on which thread, silk, yarn, paper, wire, etc., is wound at some stage of manufacture; apparatus capable of easy revolution for winding and unwinding cord, line, etc.; small cylinder, with rim at each end, on which sewing cotton etc. is wound for convenience; cylinder on which length of film, esp. motion-picture film, is wound; quantity wound on a reel. ~ *v.* Wind on reel; take (thread, silk, etc.) *off*, draw (fish etc.) *in* or *up*, by use of reel; rattle (story, list, etc.) *off* without pause or apparent effort.

reel[2] (rēl) *v.i.* Be in a whirl, be dizzy; sway, stagger; stand, walk, or run unsteadily; be shaken physically or mentally; seem to shake.

reel[3] (rē) *n.* Lively Scottish dance; Virginia reel; music for either of these.

re·en·try (rēĕn'trē) *n.* (pl. **-tries**). (esp.) 1. (law) Act of reentering upon possession of lands, tenements, etc., previously granted or let to another. 2. Return of rocket etc. into Earth's atmosphere from outer space.

reeve[1] (rēv) *n.* (hist.) Chief magistrate of town or district; (Canada) president of village or town council.

reeve[2] (rēv) *v.t.* (**reeved** or **rove** pr. rōv, **reev·ing**). (naut.) Thread (rope etc.) *through* ring or other aperture; thread (aperture, block, etc.) with rope; fasten (rope, block, etc.) *in, on, to,* something by reeving.

ref (rĕf) *n.* (colloq.) Referee. ~ *v.* (**reffed, ref·fing**).

ref. *abbrev.* Referee; reference; referred; refining; reformation; reformed; refund(ing).

re·fec·tion (rĭfĕk'shon) *n.* Refreshment by food or drink; light meal, repast.

re·fec·to·ry (rĭfĕk'terē) *n.* (pl. **-ries**). Room used for meal in monasteries etc.; ~ **table**, long narrow table.

re·fer (rĭfer') *v.* (**-ferred, -fer·ring**). 1. Trace or ascribe *to* person or thing as cause or source; assign *to* certain date, place, or class. 2. Send on or direct (person), make appeal or have recourse, *to* some authority or source of information; cite authority or passage. 3. (of statement etc.) Have relation, be directed; make allusion, direct attention, *to*. **ref·er·a·ble** (rĕf'erabel) *adj.* **re·fer'rer** *n.*

ref·er·ee (rĕferē') *n.* Arbitrator, person to whom dispute is to be or is referred for decision; umpire, esp. in football; ring official supervising boxing match. ~ *v.* (**-eed, -ee·ing**). Act as referee (for), esp. in boxing.

ref·er·ence (rĕf'erens) *n.* 1. Referring of matter for decision, settlement, or consideration, to some authority; scope given to such authority. 2. Relation, respect, correspondence, *to*; **in, with ~ to**, regarding, as regards, about; **without ~ to**, irrespective of. 3. Allusion *to*. 4. Direction *to* book, passage etc. where information may be found; mark used to refer reader of text to note etc.; act of looking up passage etc. or of referring another or applying to person, for information; ~ **book**, book designed for occasional consultation rather than for continuous reading; ~ **library**, library where books may be consulted without being taken away. 5. Person named by one applying for post or offering goods etc. as willing to vouch for him or them; (loosely) testimonial. **ref·er·en·tial** (rĕferĕn'shal) *adj.*

ref·er·en·dum (rĕferĕn'dum) *n.* (pl. **-dums, -da** pr. -da). Referring of question at issue to electorate for direct decision by a general vote; such a vote.

ref·er·ent (rĕf'erent) *n.* What is symbolized by word etc.

re·fill (rēfĭl') *v.t.* Fill again. ~ (rē'fĭl) *n.* Supply of material to refill container when contents are used up.

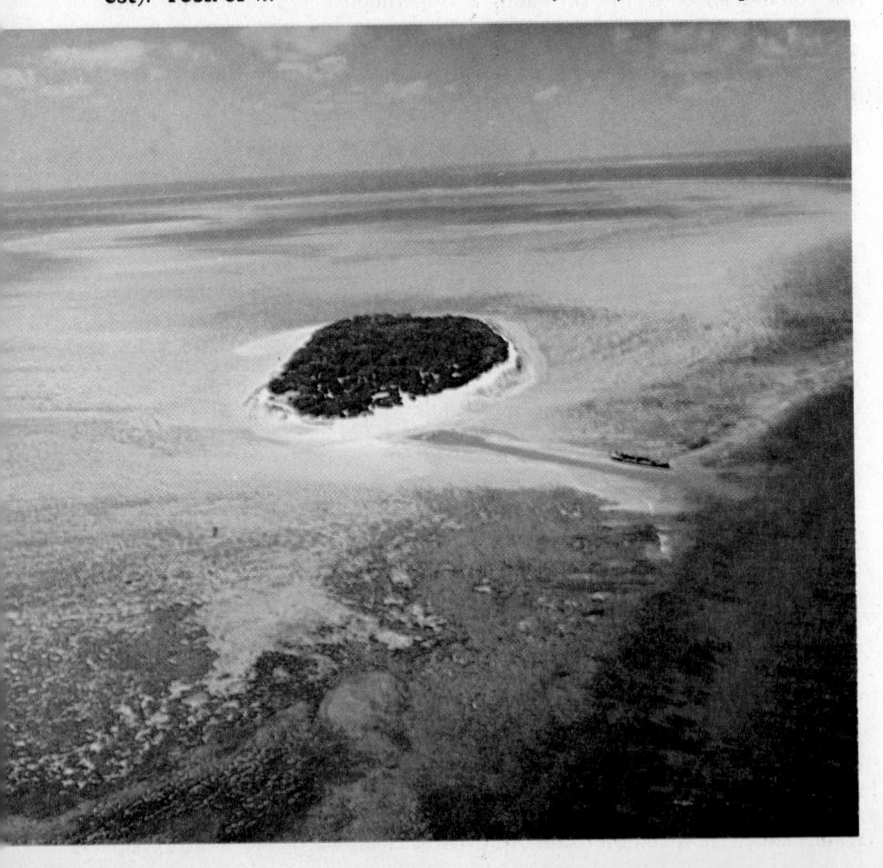

Heron Island on the Great Barrier Reef off eastern Australia is a coral cay. Formation of ***reef*** *coral is a long and complex process, governed by water temperatures and many other factors.*

re·fine (rĭfīn′) *v.* (**-fined, -fin·ing**). 1. Free from dross, impurities, or defects; purify, clarify; become pure. 2. Polish, improve, make or become more elegant or cultured; use or affect subtlety of thought or language.

re·fine·ment (rĭfīn′ment) *n.* Refining or being refined; fineness of feeling or taste, polished manners, etc.; subtle or ingenious manifestation *of* (luxury etc.), piece of elaborate arrangement; piece of subtle reasoning, fine distinction.

re·fin·er (rĭfī′ner) *n.* (esp.) Person whose business is to refine metal, sugar, etc. **re·fin′er·y** *n.* (pl. **-er·ies**). Place where raw material (e.g. sugar, petroleum) is refined.

re·fit (rēfĭt′) *v.* (**-fit·ted, -fit·ting**). Restore (ship) to serviceable condition; equip and prepare for new or additional use.

re·flect (rĭflĕkt′) *v.* 1. (of surface or body) Throw (heat, light, sound, etc.) back, cause to rebound; (of mirror etc.) show image of, reproduce to eye or mind, exactly correspond in appearance or effect to; (of action etc.) bring back or cause to rebound (credit, discredit, etc.), bring discredit, *on* person etc. 2. Go back in thought, meditate, or consult with oneself (*on*).

re·flec·tion, Brit. **re·flex·ion** (rĭflĕk′shon) *ns.* 1. Reflecting or being reflected; reflected light, heat, color, or image; **angle of ~**, acute angle made by path of a reflected body or reflected light ray with a line at right angles to the surface at the point of reflection. 2. Thing bringing discredit *on*. 3. Reconsideration, meditation; mental faculty dealing with products of sensation and perception; idea arising in the mind.

re·flec·tive (rĭflĕk′tĭv) *adj.* 1. Giving back reflection or image. 2. Concerned in reflection or thought; thoughtful, given to meditation. **re·flec′tive·ly** *adv.*

re·flec·tor (rĭflĕk′ter) *n.* Body or surface reflecting rays, esp. piece of glass, metal, etc., usu. concave, for reflecting in required direction; (telescope etc. provided with) concave mirror for bringing parallel light to a focus.

re·flex (rē′flĕks) *n.* 1. Reflected light, color, or glory; reflection, image. 2. Reflex action; **conditioned ~**: see CONDITION *v.t.* **reflex** *adj.* Turned backward; reflected; coming by way of return or reflection; **~ action**, involuntary action of muscle, nerve, etc., excited as automatic response to stimulus of sensory nerve (e.g. sneezing); **~ angle**: see ANGLE[1]; **~ camera**, hand camera in which, by means of a pivoted mirror, the reflected image can be seen and focused up to the point of exposure.

reflex (rĭflĕks′) *v.t.* Bend back, recurve (only in past part.; chiefly bot.).

re·flex·ive (rĭflĕk′sĭv) *adj.* & *n.* (gram.) (Word, form) implying agent's action upon himself; (verb) of which subject and object are the same person or thing; (personal pronoun or possessive adjective) referring to subject. **re·flex′ive·ly** *adv.* **re·flex′ive·ness** *n.*

*The discovery and exploitation of large deposits of crude oil in Iraq resulted in the construction of this **refinery** at Baghdad. Similar plants have been built in many places.*

*The **referee** has the crucial role of maintaining fair play by warning players, as in this picture of the 1974 Holland v Sweden World Cup match, or sending them off.*

*The **reflex** camera lets the photographer focus correctly by altering his depth of focus until the reflected image is correct. Reflex reflectors make it easier to see vehicles at night.*

ref·lu·ent (rĕf'lo͞oent) *adj.* Flowing back. **ref'lu·ence** *n.*

re·flux (rē'flŭks) *n.* Flowing back; ebb.

re·form (rĭfôrm') *v.* Make or become better by removal or abandonment of imperfections, faults, or errors; abolish, cure (abuse, malpractice); **reformed churches**, Protestant denominations that have accepted the principles of the Reformation; esp. (**Reformed**) applied to Calvinist bodies, esp. contrasted with Lutherans. **reform** *n.* Removal of abuse(s) esp. in politics; improvement made or suggested. **re·form'a·ble, re·form'a·tive, re·formed'** *adjs.* **re·form'er** *n.*

ref·or·ma·tion (rĕfermā'shon) *n.* Reforming or being reformed, esp. radical change for the better in political, social, etc. affairs; **R**~, 16th-c. religious movement to reform doctrines and practices of R.C. Ch., and ending in establishment of reformed or Protestant churches of central and NW. Europe.

re·form·a·to·ry (rĭfôr'matōrē, -tōrē) *adj.* Tending or intended to produce reform. ~ *n.* (pl. **-ries**). Institution to which juvenile offenders are sent for reform purposes.

re·form·ism (rĭfôr'mĭzem) *n.* Policy of reforming existing institutions rather than abolishing or revolutionizing them.

re·fract (rĭfrăkt') *v.t.* Deflect (ray of light, energy, etc.) at certain angle at point of passage from one medium into another of different density; **refract'ing telescope**: see TELESCOPE. **re·frac'tion, re·frac'tive·ness, re·frac·tiv·i·ty** (rēfrăktĭv'ĭtē) *ns.* **re·frac'tive** *adj.*

re·frac·tor (rĭfrăk'ter) *n.* Refracting medium, lens, or telescope.

re·frac·to·ry (rĭfrăk'terē) *adj.* Stubborn, unmanageable, rebellious; (of wounds etc.) not yielding *to* treatment; (of substances) hard to fuse or work. **re·frac'to·ri·ly** *adv.* **re·frac'to·ri·ness** *n.* **refractory** *n.* (pl. **-ries**). Substance, as graphite, silica, especially resistant to the action of heat and suitable for lining furnaces etc. where high temperatures must be withstood.

re·frain[1] (rĭfrān') *n.* Recurring phrase or line, esp. at end of stanzas.

re·frain[2] (rĭfrān') *v.* 1. (archaic) Curb. 2. Abstain (*from*). **re·frain'ment** *n.*

re·fran·gi·ble (rĭfrăn'jibel) *adj.* That can be refracted. **re·fran·gi·bil·i·ty** (rĭfrănjibĭl'ĭtē), **re·fran'gi·ble·ness** *ns.*

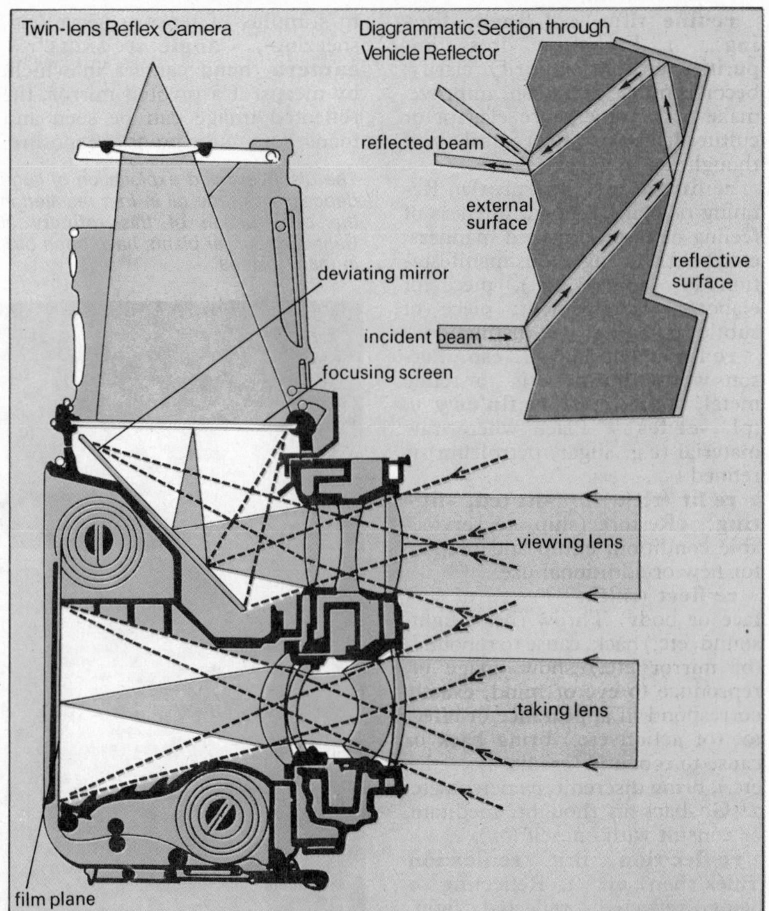

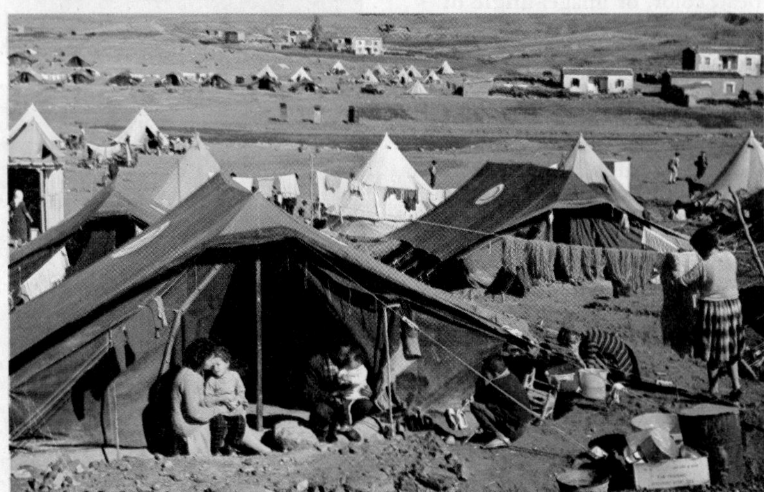

*In times of war, many members of the civilian population may have to leave their homes. They are often accommodated in **refugee** camps like that near Nicosia, Cyprus (above).*

re·fresh (rĭfrĕsh') *v.* Impart fresh vigor to, by food, rest, etc., reanimate, reinvigorate; freshen up (memory); restore (fire etc.) with fresh supply of fuel etc.; refresh oneself, take refreshment. **re·fresh'ing** *adj.* **re·fresh'ing·ly** *adv.*

re·fresh·er (rĭfrĕsh'er) *n.* 1. That which refreshes. 2. (attrib., of course of instruction etc.) Serving to refresh memory or make up to date.

re·fresh·ment (rĭfrĕsh'ment) *n.* Refreshing or being refreshed in mind or body; thing, esp. (usu. in pl.) food or drink, that refreshes.

re·frig·er·ate (rĭfrĭj'erāt) *v.* (**-at·ed, -at·ing**). Make, become, cool or cold; expose (food) to low temperature in order to preserve it. **re·frig'er·ant** *adj.* & *n.* (Medium etc.) that refrigerates. **re·frig·er·a·tion** (rĭfrĭjerā'shon) *n.* **re·frig·er·a·tor** (rĭfrĭj'erāter) *n.*

The ***regalia*** *used in the coronation of a British monarch all have ancient symbolic significance. The swords denote justice, and mercy; the sceptre — authority; the orb — Christianity.*

(esp.) Apparatus in which ice can be made and food etc. kept cold by the mechanical production of low temperature.

reft: see REAVE.

re·fu·el (rēfū′*e*l, -fūl) *v.* (**-eled, -el·ing**). Replenish with, take on, fresh supply of fuel.

ref·uge (rĕf′ūj) *n.* (Place of) shelter from pursuit, danger, or trouble; person, thing, course, that gives shelter or is resorted to in difficulties; **city of ~**, in ancient Israel, sanctuary for those guilty of manslaughter; **City of R~**, national historical part on the island of Hawaii, until 1819 sanctuary for those vanquished in battle or condemned to death for breaking taboo.

ref·u·gee (rĕfy*u*jē′, rĕf′y*u*jē) *n.* Person escaped, esp. to foreign country, from religious or political persecution, war, etc.

re·ful·gent (rĭfŭl′jent) *adj.* Shining, gloriously bright. **re·ful′gent·ly** *adv.* **re·ful′gence, re·ful′gen·cy** *ns.*

re·fund (rĭfŭnd′) *v.* Pay back (money received or taken, expenses incurred by another); reimburse; make repayment. **~** (rē′fŭnd) *n.* Repayment. **re·fund′a·ble** *adj.* **re·fund′er** *n.*

re·fus·al (rĭfū′z*a*l) *n.* 1. Act or instance of refusing. 2. Right or privilege of deciding to take or leave a thing before it is offered to others.

re·fuse[1] (rĭfūz′) *v.* (**-fused, -fus·ing**). Say or convey by action that one will not accept, submit to, give, grant, gratify, consent; deny (*to* person etc.), refuse request of; make refusal; (of horse) stop short at (fence etc.), fail to take jump.

ref·use[2] (rĕf′ūs) *n.* & *adj.* (What is) rejected as worthless or left over after use; rubbish, trash.

re·fute (rĭfūt′) *v.t.* (**-fut·ed, -fut·ing**). Prove falsity or error of (statement, argument, etc.), rebut or repel by argument. **re·fut·a·ble** (rĭfū′t*a*bel, rĕf′y*u*-) *adj.* **ref·u·ta·tion** (rĕfy*u*tā′sh*o*n), **re·fut′er** *ns.*

reg. *abbrev.* Regiment; register(ed); region.

re·gain (rĭgān′) *v.t.* Recover possession of; reach (place) again; recover (*feet, footing*, etc.).

re·gal (rē′g*a*l) *adj.* Of or by kings; fit for a king, magnificent. **re′gal·ly** *adv.*

re·gale (rĭgāl′) *v.* (**-galed, -gal·ing**). Entertain sumptuously with food and drink; give delight to; feast (*on*). **re·gale′ment** *n.*

re·ga·li·a (rĭgā′lē*a*, -gāl′y*a*) *n.pl.* Insignia of royalty used at coronations; decorations or insignia of an order.

re·gal·i·ty (rĭgăl′ĭtē) *n.* (pl. **-ties**). Attribute of kingly power, being king; royal privilege.

re·gard (rĭgârd′) *v.* 1. Gaze upon; bestow attention or notice on, show interest in. 2. Give heed to; take into account in regulating actions or conduct; show consideration for; pay attention, give heed. 3. Look on *as* being something; look on *with* some feeling; consider. 4. Concern, have relation to; **as ~s**, so far as relates to. **re·gard′ing** *prep.* In or with regard to. **regard** *n.* 1. Look, gaze; observant attention or heed; consideration; care or concern *for*. 2. Thing or circumstance looked to or taken into account, respect;

A ***refrigerated*** *road-train travels through the Pilbara in Western Australia taking frozen food and vegetables to remote areas that are not accessible by rail or air. Many isolated communities are dependent on these trucks.*

in ~ to, with ~ to, in respect of, with respect or reference to. 3. Esteem, kindly feeling or respectful opinion (*for*); (pl.) as expression of friendliness in letter etc. **re·gard′less** *adj.* Without paying attention; without regard or consideration (*of*). **re·gard′less·ly** *adv.* (colloq.) Anyway; in spite of everything. **re·gard′less·ness** *n.*

re·gat·ta (rĭgăt′*a*, -gah′t*a*) *n.* Meeting for boat or yacht races; series of races.

re·gen·cy (rē′jensē) *n.* (pl. **-cies**). (Period of) office of regent or regents; **R ~**, (Engl. hist.) period (1810–20) in which George, Prince of Wales, acted as regent; (attrib.) of the style of architecture, dress, etc., of this period.

re·gen·er·ate (rĭjĕn′*e*rāt) *v.* (**-ated, -at·ing**). 1. Invest with new and higher spiritual nature; improve moral condition of; breathe new, more vigorous, and higher life into. 2. Generate again; bring or come into renewed existence. **re·gen·er·ate** (rĭjĕn′*e*rĭt), **re·gen′er·a·tive** *adjs.* **re·gen·er·a·tion** (rĭjĕn*e*rā′sh*o*n), **re·gen′er·a·cy, re·gen′er·a·tor** *ns.*

re·gent (rē′jent) *n.* 1. Person appointed to administer kingdom during minority, absence, or incapacity of monarch. 2. Member of governing board of some universities etc. ~ *adj.* (placed after noun) Acting as, having position of, regent; **Prince R ~**, (Brit. hist.), George, Prince of Wales (later George IV), who was regent 1810–20 during incapacity of George III.

reg·i·cide (rĕj′ĭsīd) *n.* 1. Killer or participator in killing of a king. 2. Killing of a king. **reg·i·cid·al** (rĕjĭsī′d*a*l) *adj.*

re·gime, ré·gime (r*e*zhēm′, rā-) *ns.* Method of government; prevailing system of things; **ancien ~**: see ANCIEN RÉGIME.

reg·i·men (rĕj′*i*m*e*n) *n.* (med.) Prescribed course of exercise, way of life, and esp. diet.

reg·i·ment (rĕj′*i*m*e*nt) *n.* Army unit consisting of at least two battalions and usually with a permanent depot and headquarters; large array or number, legion. ~ (rĕj′*i*mĕnt) *v.t.* Form (men) into regiment or regiments; organize (workers etc.) into groups or according to a system; impose uniformity or order upon.

reg·i·men·tal (rĕj*i*mĕn′t*a*l) *adj.* Of a regiment; military, maintaining or demanding strict discipline. **reg·i·men′tals** *n.pl.* Dress worn by regiment; military uniform.

reg·i·men·ta·tion (rĕj*i*mĕntā′sh*o*n) *n.* Regimenting, organizing.

re·gi·na (r*e*jī′n*a*) *n.* Reigning queen; **R ~**, (abbrev. R.) reigning queen (esp. following name in signature to certain official documents, as *Elizabeth R.*). [L.]

re·gion (rē′j*o*n) *n.* Tract of country, place, space, of more or less definitely marked boundaries or characteristics; separate part of world or universe; sphere or realm *of*; part of the body around or near some organ etc. **re′gion·al** *adj.* **re′gion·al·ly** *adv.* **re′gion·al·ism** *n.* 1. Quality or trait distinctive in particular region or area. 2. Word, speech, custom, etc. distinctive in certain region.

reg·is·ter (rĕj′ĭst*e*r) *n.* 1. Book in which entries are made of details to be recorded for reference; official or authoritative list kept e.g. of births, marriages, and burials or deaths, shipping, medical practitioners, qualified voters in constituency, etc. 2. (Set of pipes controlled by) slides in an organ; compass of voice or instrument (**upper, lower**, etc., ~, part of this). 3. Adjustable plate for widening or narrowing an opening that admits heated or cooled air into a room. 4. Recording indicator of speed, force, etc. 5. (print.) Exact correspondence or placement of the colors or plates used in printing for clear images. **register** *v.* 1. Set down (name etc.) formally, record in writing; enter or cause to be entered in particular register; write name in register of hotel on arrival; (fig.) make mental note of; send (letter, package, etc.) by registered mail; **registered mail**, mail that is registered at the post office and a receipt given to the sender; **registered nurse**, completely trained nurse who has passed state examination on nursing

The Venetian painter Canaletto is famous for his pictures of spectacles on the water in and around the city. This glittering ***regatta*** *scene shows the splendor with which such events were surrounded in the 18th century.*

1

2

3

4

The ***Regency*** *period in England was accompanied by extravagance, especially in men's dress as epitomized by 'dandies' (1), in ornate furniture (2) and even in the hair style favored by the future George IV (3) and architecture dominated by ornate curved facades and balconies (4).*

services. 2. (of instrument) Record automatically, indicate; (of person) express or show (emotion etc.) in face, or in any manner. 3. (print. etc.) Correspond, make correspond, exactly. **reg·is·tra·tion** (rĕjĭstrā′shon) *n.*

reg·is·trar (rĕj′ĭstrar̄, rĕjĭstrar̄′) *n.* Official recorder, person charged with keeping register; college or university official who keeps records of the enrollment and academic standing of students; corporate official who keeps records of ownership of corporation's stocks etc.

reg·is·try (rĕj′ĭstrē) *n.* (pl. **-tries**). 1. Registration. 2. Place, office, where registers are kept. 3. Ship's registered nationality (often for financial or insurance purposes).

reg·nant (rĕg′nant) *adj.* Reigning; predominant, prevalent.

__Reinforced__ concrete is extensively used in all sorts of building today. This block under construction in Ottawa shows how work proceeds storey by storey, with pre-formed elements swung into place by crane.

re·gorge (rēgōrj′) *v.* (**-gorged, -gorg·ing**). Disgorge.

re·gress (rē′grĕs) *n.* Going back. ~ (rĭgrĕs′) *v.t.* Move backward; return to a previous or less advanced state or condition.

re·gres·sion (rĭgrĕsh′*o*n) *n.* Backward movement, retreat; relapse, reversion. **re·gres′sive** *adj.* **re·gres′sive·ly** *adv.* **re·gres′sive·ness** *n.*

re·gret (rĭgrĕt′) *v.* (**-gret·ted, -gret·ting**). Remember (something lost) with distress or longing, feel sorrow for loss of; grieve at, feel mental distress because of; feel regret. ~ *n.* Sorrow for loss; repentance or sorrow for something done or left undone; (intimation of) sorrow or disappointment at inability to do something, esp. accept invitation. **re·gret′ful** *adj.* **re·gret′ful·ly** *adv.* **re·gret′ta·ble** *adj.* **re·gret′ta·bly** *adv.*

regt. *abbrev.* Regiment.

reg·u·lar (rĕg′y*u*ler) *adj.* 1. (eccles.) Bound by religious rule; belonging to religious or monastic order. 2. Following or exhibiting a principle; harmonious, consistent, systematic; symmetrical; (geom.) having equal sides and angles. 3. Acting, done, recurring, uniformly or calculably in time or manner; habitual, constant, not capricious or casual; orderly; **keep ~ hours**, do same thing at same time daily. 4. Conforming to a standard, in order; properly constituted or qualified, not defective or amateur, devoted exclusively or primarily to its nominal function. 5. (gram., of verbs, nouns, etc.) Following a normal type of inflection. 6. (colloq.) Real; complete, thorough. 7. **R~ Army**, army of professional soldiers as opp. to militia, or temporary soldiers; permanent part of U.S. Army. **reg′u·lar·ly** *adv.* **regular** *n.* One of the regular clergy; regular soldier; (colloq.) regular customer, contributor, etc. **reg·u·lar·i·ty** (rĕgy*u*lăr′ĭtē) *n.* (pl. **-ties**). **reg′u·lar·ize** *v.t.* (**-ized, -iz·ing**). **reg·u·lar·i·za·tion** (rĕgy*u*lerīzā′sh*o*n) *n.*

reg·u·late (rĕg′y*u*lāt) *v.t.* (**-lat·ed, -lat·ing**). Control by rule, subject to restrictions; moderate, adapt to requirements; adjust (machine, clock) to work accurately. **reg·u·la·tive** (rĕg′-y*u*lātĭv, -l*a*tĭv), **reg·u·la·to·ry** (rĕg′y*u*l*a*tōrē, -tōrē) *adjs.*

reg·u·la·tion (rĕgy*u*lā′sh*o*n) *n.* 1. Regulating, being regulated. 2. Prescribed rule, authoritative direction; (attrib.) fulfilling what is laid down by regulations, ordinary, usual, formal.

__Rehearsal__ is essential for a successful dramatic performance. These actors in New Zealand have reached the dress rehearsal stage, traditionally the last rehearsal before the opening night.

reg·u·la·tor (rĕg′y*u*lāt*er*) *n.* (esp.) Device for regulating passage of gases, liquids, electric current, etc.; device for regulating speed of watch etc. by adjusting balance.

reg·u·lus (rĕg′y*u*l*u*s) *n.* (pl. **-lus·es, -li** pr. -lī). (chem.) Metallic content of mineral, liberated by reduction and sinking to bottom in crucible; impure metallic product of smelting various ores.

re·gur·gi·tate (rĭgẽr′jĭtāt) *v.* (**-tat·ed, -tat·ing**). Gush back; (of stomach or receptacle) pour or cast out again; vomit. **re·gur·gi·ta·tion** (rĭgẽrjĭtā′sh*o*n) *n.*

re·ha·bil·i·tate (rēh*a*bĭl′ĭtāt) *v.t.* (**-tat·ed, -tat·ing**). Restore to rights, privileges, reputation, etc., reinstate; restore to previous condition; enable (disabled person, convict, etc.) to earn his living or resume normal life through therapy, training, etc. **re·ha·bil·i·ta·tion** (rēh*a*bĭlĭtā′sh*o*n) *n.* **re·ha·bil·i·ta·tive** (rēh*a*bĭl′ĭtātĭv) *adj.*

re·hash (rēhăsh′) *v.t.* Put (material) into new form without real change or improvement; repeat, discuss again. ~ (rē′hăsh) *n.* Presentation of same material in new form or words.

re·hears·al (rĭhẽr′s*a*l) *n.* Rehearsing; practicing of play, concert, etc. before performing it in public; **in ~**, in process of being rehearsed.

re·hearse (rĭhẽrs′) *v.t.* (**-hearsed, -hears·ing**). Recite, say over, repeat from beginning to end; give list of, recount, enumerate; have rehearsal of (play, part, concert, etc.); practice for later public performance.

Re·ho·bo·am (rēobō′am), **Ro·bo·am** (rōbō′am). Son of Solomon; succeeded him as king of Israel; the northern tribes broke away from his rule and set up a new kingdom under Jeroboam, after which he continued as 1st king of JUDAH.

Reich (rīx) *n.* Government or territory of a German empire or republic; **First ~**, the Holy Roman Empire, 962–1806 A.D.; **Second ~**, 1871–1918; **Third ~**, Nazi regime, 1933–45.

Reichs·tag (rīxs′tahx). Supreme legislature of the former German Empire and of the Republic; building in Berlin in which this met, burned down on Nazi accession to power (1933).

reign (rān) *n.* Sovereignty, rule, sway; period during which sovereign reigns; **~ of terror**, time in which community lives in dread of death or outrage, esp. the **R ~ of Terror** (1793–4) during the French Revolution. **reign** *v.i.* Hold royal office, be king or queen; exercise authority, hold sway, rule; be acknowledged as supreme.

re·im·burse (rēimbers′) *v.t.* (**-bursed, -burs·ing**). Repay (person who has expended money, out-of-pocket expenses). **re·im·burs′a·ble** *adj.* **re·im·burse′ment** *n.*

Reims, Rheims (rēmz; *Fr.* răns). Industrial city and important champagne-producing center in NE. France; site of 13th-c. Gothic cathedral; Germany signed World War II unconditional surrender here, May 7, 1945.

*The common names **reindeer** and caribou are only the European and American terms for the same deer (Rangifer tarandus) which has several subspecies.*

rein (rān) *n.* Long narrow strap with each end attached to bit, used to guide or check horse etc. in riding or driving (freq. pl. in same sense); (fig.) means of control; **give ~ to**, let have free scope. **rein** *v.t.* Check or manage with reins; pull *up* or *back*, hold *in* with reins; guide, control.

re·in·car·nate (rēinkar′nāt) *v.t.* (**-nat·ed, -nat·ing**). Incarnate again. ~ (rēinkar′nit) *adj.*

re·in·car·na·tion (rēinkarnā′shon) *n.* Belief in the return to earth in a new form of the soul after death.

rein·deer (rān′dēr) *n.* (pl. **-deer**). Caribou; subarctic deer of genus *Rangifer* with large branching or palmated antlers in both sexes, used for drawing sleds and kept in herds for its milk, flesh, and hide.

re·in·force (rēinfōrs′, -fors′) *v.t.* (**-forced, -forc·ing**). Strengthen or support by additional men or material or by increase of numbers, quantity, size, thickness, etc.; **reinforced concrete**, concrete with steel bars or wire netting embedded in it to increase its tensile strength.

re·in·force·ment (rēinfōrs′ment, -fors′-) *n.* Reinforcing, being reinforced; anything that reinforces; (freq. pl.) additional men, ships, aircraft, etc., for military, naval, or air force.

re·in·state (rēinstāt′) *v.t.* (**-stat·ed, -stat·ing**). Restore to, replace *in*, lost position, privileges, etc.; restore to health or proper order. **re·in·state′ment** *n.*

re·in·sure (rēinshoor′) *v.t.* (**-sured, -sur·ing**). Insure again, esp. (of insurer or underwriter) against risk one has undertaken. **re·in·sur′ance, re·in·sur′er** *ns.*

re·it·er·ate (rēit′erāt) *v.t.* (**-at·ed, -at·ing**). Repeat, say over again or several times. **re·it·er·a·tive** (rēit′erātiv, -erativ) *adj.*

reive, reiv·er: see REAVE.

re·ject (rijĕkt′) *v.t.* 1. Put aside as not to be accepted, practiced, believed, chosen, used, etc. 2. Cast up again, vomit, evacuate. ~ (rē′jĕkt) *n.* Thing rejected. **re·jec·tion** (rijĕk′shon) *n.* **~ slip**, formal notice from editor or publisher accompanying rejected manuscript. **re·ject′er** *n.*

re·joice (rijois′) *v.* (**-joiced, -joic·ing**). Cause joy to, make glad; feel great joy; be glad (*that, in, at*); make merry, celebrate some event. **re·joic′ing, re·joic′er** *ns.*

re·join (def. 1. rijoin′; def. 2 rējoin′) *v.* 1. Reply to charge or pleading, esp. to plaintiff's reply to defendant's plea (law); say in answer, retort. 2. Join again.

re·join·der (rijoin′der) *n.* What is rejoined or said in reply, retort.

re·ju·ve·nate (rĭjo͞o′venāt) *v.* (**-nat·ed, -nat·ing**). Make or become young again. **re·ju·ve·na·tion** (rĭjo͞ovenā′shon) *n.*

re·lapse (rĭlăps′) *v.i.* (**-lapsed, -laps·ing**). Fall back, sink again, into wrongdoing, error, heresy, weakness, illness, etc. ~ (rĭlăps′, rē′lăps) *n.* Act or fact of relapsing, esp. deterioration in patient's condition after partial recovery.

re·late (rĭlāt′) *v.* (**-lat·ed, -lat·ing**). 1. Narrate, recount. 2. Bring into relation, establish relation between; have reference *to*, stand in some relation *to*. **re·lat′er** *n.* **re·lat′ed** *adj.* (esp.) Connected, allied, akin by blood or marriage.

re·la·tion (rĭlā′shon) *n.* 1. Narration; a narrative; (law) referring of an act to an earlier date as the time of its taking effect. 2. Way in which one thing is thought of in connection with another; any connection, correspondence, or association between things or persons; (pl.) dealings or connections with others, sexual intercourse. 3. Kinsman, kinswoman, relative. **re·la′tions** *n.* **re·la′tion·ship** *n.* Being related; kinship. **re·la′tion·al** *adj.*

rel·a·tive (rĕl′atĭv) *adj.* 1. (gram.) Referring, and attaching a subordinate clause, to an expressed or implied antecedent; (of clause) attached to antecedent by relative word. 2. Comparative; in relation to something else; proportioned to something else; involving or implying comparison or relation; having application or reference *to*, with reference *to*; ~ **humidity**: see HUMIDITY. **rel′a·tive·ly** *adv.* **relative** *n.* 1. (gram.) Relative word, esp. pronoun, as *who, which, that, what*. 2. (philos.) Relative thing or term. 3. Kinsman, kinswoman; one related by blood or marriage. **rel′a·tive·ness** *n.*

rel·a·tiv·ism (rĕl′atĭvĭzem) *n.* Doctrine that knowledge is of relations only; theory that ethical truth is relative to the individual, time, and place.

rel·a·tiv·i·ty (rĕlatĭv′ĭtē) *n.* 1. Relativeness. 2. Branch of physics concerned with correlation of descriptions of phenomena by observers using frames of reference in relative motion with respect to each other; (**special**) **theory of** ~, theory, propounded mainly by Einstein, based on principle of constant velocity of light and showing that all motion is relative, treating space and time as 4 related dimensions, and invalidating previous conceptions of geometry; (**general**) **theory of** ~, that developed by Einstein in 1915, extending the special theory to include cases of acceleration and the phenomena of gravity.

re·lax (rĭlăks′) *v.* Cause or allow to become loose, slack, or limp; enfeeble, mitigate, abate; grow less tense, rigid, stern, etc. **re·lax′er, re·lax′ant** *ns.* **re·lax·a·tion** (rēlăksā′shon) *n.* Partial remission *of* penalty, duty, etc.; cessation from work; recreation, amusement; diminution of tension, severity, precision, etc.

These idealized portraits of bygone writers and thinkers are a section of one of the ***reliefs*** *on the Albert Memorial, Queen Victoria's monument commemorating the Prince Consort's support for the arts.*

re·lay (rē′lā; for sense 1 also rĭlā′) *n.* 1. Set of fresh horses substituted for tired ones; work crew, shift, that relieves another. 2. Switch or other device by which one electric current is made to control another; instrument used in long-distance telegraphy to reinforce weak current with local battery etc. 3. ~ **race**, one between teams of which each person does part of the distance, the 2nd etc. members starting when the 1st etc. end. **relay** (rĭlā′) *v.* (**-layed, -lay·ing**). Arrange in, provide with, replace by, get, relays; pass on or rebroadcast (radio signal, program, etc., originating at, and received from, another station).

re·lease (rĭlēs′) *v.t.* (**-leased, -leas·ing**). 1. (law) Remit (debt), surrender (right), make over (property) to another. 2. Set free, liberate, deliver, unfasten (*from*). 3. Exhibit (motion picture etc.) for 1st time, or generally. 4. Make (information) public. ~ *n.* 1. Deliverance, liberation, from trouble, life, duty, confinement, etc. 2. Written discharge, receipt; legal conveyance of right or estate to another, document effecting this. 3. Handle, catch, etc., that releases part of machine etc. 4. Public exhibition of motion picture etc. for 1st time, or generally; film etc. so shown. 5. Statement etc. containing information, issued for publication.

rel·e·gate (rĕl′egāt) *v.t.* (**-gat·ed, -gat·ing**). Banish *to* some place of exile (rare); consign or dismiss *to* some usu. inferior position, sphere, etc.; transfer (matter) for decision or execution. **rel·e·ga·tion** (rĕlegā′shon) *n.*

re·lent (rĭlĕnt′) *v.i.* Relax severity, become less stern; abandon harsh intention, yield to compassion. **re·lent′less** *adj.* **re·lent′less·ly** *adv.* **re·lent′less·ness** *n.*

rel·e·vant (rĕl′evant) *adj.* Bearing upon, pertinent *to*, the matter in hand. **rel′e·vant·ly** *adv.* **rel′e·vance, rel′e·van·cy** *ns.*

re·li·a·ble (rĭlī′abel) *adj.* That may be relied upon; of sound and consistent character or quality. **re·li·a·bil·i·ty** (rĭlīabĭl′ĭtē), **re·li′a·ble·ness** *ns.* **re·li′a·bly** *adv.*

re·li·ance (rĭlī′ans) *n.* Trust, confidence; thing depended upon. **re·li′ant** *adj.*

rel·ic (rĕl′ĭk) *n.* 1. Part of holy person's body or belongings kept after his death as object of reverence; memento, souvenir; (pl.) dead body, remains, of person. 2. (pl.) What has survived destruction or wasting, remnant, residue, scraps; (sing.) surviving trace or memorial *of* custom, period, people, etc.; object interesting for its age or associations.

1

2

3

*Each **religion** has its own means of propagating its beliefs. Although dealing with Australian Aboriginals (1) the Roman Catholics adopt a formal approach, far different from the informality of a Salvation Army man in Papua New Guinea (2). Buddhist monks in Bangkok pray in formal splendor (3).*

re·lief[1] (rĭlēf′) *n.* 1. Alleviation of or deliverance from pain, distress, anxiety, etc.; redress of hardship or grievance. 2. Feature etc. that affords a welcome diversion or relaxes tension. 3. Assistance given to the poor or needy; ~ **work**, organized effort to help the poor or victims of earthquake or other calamity. 4. Reinforcement and esp. raising of siege *of* besieged town. 5. (Replacing of person or persons on duty by) persons(s) appointed to take turn of duty; ~ **pitcher**, (baseball) pitcher who replaces another pitcher during game.

re·lief[2] (rĭlēf′) *n.* Method of molding, carving, or stamping in which design stands out from plane or curved surface with projections proportioned and more or less closely approximating to those of objects imitated (HIGH, LOW[2], ~: see the adjectives); piece of sculpture etc. in relief; distinctness of outline, vividness; ~ **map**, map in which the conformation of an area of Earth's surface is shown by (exaggerated) elevations and depressions or by contour lines or colors.

re·lieve (rĭlēv′) *v.t.* (**-lieved, -liev·ing**). 1. Bring, give, be, relief to; ease, free, from pain, discomfort, etc.; make less burdensome, monotonous, etc.; release from watch or other duty by becoming or providing a substitute; raise siege of. 2. Bring into relief, make stand out.

re·li·gion (rĭlĭj′*o*n) *n.* 1. Belief in superhuman controlling power and esp. of a personal God or gods entitled to obedience and worship; effect of such recognition on conduct or mental attitude; expression of such belief; particular system of faith and worship, as *Christian, Muslim, Hindu*, ~. 2. **make a ~ of**, make a point of (esp. doing some habitual action).

re·li·gi·ose (rĭlĭj′ēōs, -lĭjēōs′) *adj.* Conspicuously or excessively religious. **re·li·gi·os·i·ty** (rĭlĭjēŏs′ĭtē) *n.* Being religious or religiose.

re·li·gious (rĭlĭj′*u*s) *adj.* 1. Imbued with religion, god-fearing, devout. 2. Of, concerned with, religion; scrupulous, conscientious. 3. Of, belonging to, an order of monks or nuns. **re·li′gious·ly** *adv.* **re·li′gious·ness** *n.* **religious** *n.* (pl. **-gious**). Member of a religious order.

re·lin·quish (rĭlĭng′kwĭsh) *v.t.* Give up, abandon, resign, surrender; let go (something held). **re·lin'quish·ment** *n.*

rel·i·quar·y (rĕl'ĭkwĕrē) *n.* (pl. **-quar·ies**). Receptacle for religious relic(s).

rel·ish (rĕl'ĭsh) *n.* 1. Flavor, distinctive taste *of*; appetizing flavor, attractive quality; thing eaten with plainer food to add flavor. 2. Enjoyment of food or other things; zest; liking *for*. ~ *v.* Give flavor to; make piquant etc.; get pleasure out of, like, be pleased with. **rel'ish·a·ble** *adj.*

re·luc·tant (rĭlŭk'tant) *adj.* Unwilling, disinclined (*to*). **re·luc'tant·ly** *adv.* **re·luc'tance** *n.*

re·ly (rĭlī') *v.i.* (**-lied, -ly·ing**). Put one's trust, depend with confidence, *on*.

REM (rĕm) *n.* Intermittent, quick, jerky movements of closed eyes during sleep, esp. while dreaming. [*r*(apid) *e*(ye) *m*(ovement)]

rem (rĕm) *n.* Unit of effective absorbed dose of ionizing radiation in human tissue, equivalent to 1 roentgen of x-rays. [*r*(oentgen) *e*(quivalent) *m*(an)]

re·main (rĭmān') *v.i.* 1. Be left over after removal of some part or quantity, or after part has been done or dealt with in some way. 2. Be in same place or condition during further time; continue to exist, be extant; be left behind; continue to be (something specified). ~ *n.* (usu. pl.) What remains over, surviving members, parts, or amount; (usu. pl.) relic(s) of obsolete custom or of antiquity; (pl.) dead body.

re·main·der (rĭmān'der) *n.* 1. (law) Residual interest in estate devised to another simultaneously with creation of estate; right of succession to title or position on holder's decease. 2. Residue, remaining persons or things; (arith.) number left after subtraction; number left over after preliminary division; copies of book etc. left unsold when demand has ceased and often offered at reduced price. ~ *v.t.* Treat or dispose of (books) as remainders.

re·mand (rĭmănd', -mahnd') *v.t.* Send back (person in custody) to prison, another court, etc., for further proceedings. ~ *n.* Recommittal to custody. **re·mand'ment** *n.*

re·mark (rĭmark') *v.* Take notice of, observe; say by way of comment; make comment *on*. ~ *n.* Observing, commenting; written or spoken comment, anything said.

re·mark·a·ble (rĭmarkabel) *adj.* Worth notice, exceptional, striking, conspicuous. **re·mark'a·ble·ness** *n.* **re·mark'a·bly** *adv.*

Rem·brandt (rĕm'brănt, -brahnt), (**Harmensz**) **van Rijn** (1606–69). Dutch painter and etcher; called the "King of Shadows," from his practice of painting pictures illuminated by a clear but limited light, emerging in the midst of masses of shadow.

re·me·di·al (rĭmē'dēal) *adj.* Affording a remedy; intended to remedy disease, deficiency, etc. (~ *reading*, *English*, etc.). **re·me'di·al·ly** *adv.*

rem·e·dy (rĕm'edē) *n.* (pl. **-dies**). Cure for disease, healing medicine or treatment; means of removing, counteracting, or relieving any evil; redress, legal or other reparation; the small margin within which coins as minted are allowed to vary from the standard fineness and weight (also called the *tolerance*). ~ *v.t.* (**-died, -dy·ing**). Rectify, make good. **re·me·di·a·ble** (rĭmē'dēabel) *adj.*

re·mem·ber (rĭmĕm'ber) *v.t.* 1. Retain in, recall to, the memory, recollect, not forget (freq. abs.). 2. Fee, reward, tip; convey greetings from (person) *to* another. **re·mem'ber·a·ble** *adj.* **re·mem'ber·er** *n.*

re·mem·brance (rĭmĕm'brans) *n.* Remembering, being remembered, memory, recollection; keepsake, souvenir, memorial.

re·mind (rĭmīnd') *v.t.* Put (person) in mind *of*, *to* do, etc.

re·mind·er (rĭmīn'der) *n.* Thing that reminds or is meant to remind.

Rem·ing·ton[1] (rĕm'ĭngton), **Eliphalet** (1793–1861). Amer. firearms manufacturer. After his death his firm also manufactured typewriters and sewing machines.

Rem·ing·ton[2] (rĕm'ĭngton), **Frederic** (1861–1909). Amer. painter and sculptor; noted for portrayals of the Amer. West.

rem·i·nisce (rĕminĭs') *v.i.* (**-nisced, -nisc·ing**). Indulge in reminiscence(s).

rem·i·nis·cence (rĕminĭs'ens) *n.* Remembering; act of recovering knowledge by mental effort; expression, fact, etc., recalling something else; remembered fact or incident; (pl.) collection in literary form of person's memories etc.

*Strongly influenced by Caravaggio, the paintings of **Rembrandt** attained the ultimate effect from chiaroscuro (bright light, contrasting with deep shadows). His 'Adoration of the Shepherds' (left), shows this at its best. His self-portrait (facing) was painted about a year before he died.*

rem·i·nis·cent (rĕmĭnĭs′ent) *adj.* Recalling past things; given to or concerned with retrospection, mindful or having memories *of*; reminding or suggestive *of*. **rem·i·nis′cent·ly** *adv.*

re·mise (rĭmīz′) *v.t.* (**-mised, -mis·ing**). (law) Surrender, make over (right, property).

re·miss (rĭmĭs′) *adj.* Careless of duty, lax, negligent; lacking force or energy. **re·miss′ly** *adv.* **re·miss′ness** *n.*

re·mis·si·ble (rĭmĭs′ĭbel) *adj.* That may be remitted or forgiven.

re·mis·sion (rĭmĭsh′on) *n.* Forgiveness *of* sins etc., forgiveness of sins; remittance of debt, penalty, etc.; diminution of force, effect, degree, violence, etc. (esp. of disease or pain). **re·mis′sive** *adj.*

re·mit (rĭmĭt′) *v.* (**-mit·ted, -mit·ting**). 1. Pardon (sins etc.); refrain from exacting, inflicting, or executing (debt, punishment, sentence). 2. Abate, slacken, mitigate. 3. Refer (matter for decision etc.) *to* some authority; send back (case) to lower court; send or put back *(in)to* previous state; postpone, defer, *to* or *until*. 4. Transmit, get conveyed by post etc. (money etc.).

re·mit·tance (rĭmĭt′ans) *n.* Money sent to person; sending of money; ~ **man**, person living abroad on remittances; person paid to stay away from home.

re·mit·tent (rĭmĭt′ent) *adj.* Abating at intervals.

rem·nant (rĕm′nant) *n.* Small remaining part, quantity, or number; small remaining quantity, part, or piece, esp. end of piece of cloth etc. left over after rest has been used or sold.

re·mon·strance (rĭmŏn′strans) *n.* 1. (hist.) Formal statement of public grievances. 2. Remonstrating, expostulation; protest. **re·mon′strant** *adj.* & *n.* **re·mon′strant·ly** *adv.*

re·mon·strate (rĭmŏn′strāt, rĕm′on-) *v.* (**-strat·ed, -strat·ing**). Make protest, expostulate; urge in remonstrance. **re·mon·stra·tive** (rĭmŏn′strativ) *adj.* **re·mon·stra·tion** (rēmŏnstrā′shon, rĕmon-), **re·mon′stra·tor** *ns.*

rem·o·ra (rĕm′era) *n.* Fish (of family Echenaedidae) that attaches itself to sharks, turtles, ships, etc., by means of adhesive organ on top of head.

re·morse (rĭmōrs′) *n.* Bitter repentance of wrong committed; compunction, compassionate reluctance to inflict pain or be cruel. **re·morse′ful** *adj.* **re·morse′ful·ly** *adv.* **re·morse′less** *adj.* **re·morse′less·ly** *adv.* **re·morse′less·ness** *n.*

re·mote (rĭmōt′) *adj.* (**-mot·er, -mot·est**). Far apart; far away or off in place or time; not closely related; distant, widely different, *from*; out of the way, secluded; (chiefly superl., of idea etc.) slight(est), faint(est); ~ **control**, control of apparatus etc. from a distance by means of electrically operated device, radio, etc. **re·mote′ly** *adv.* **re·mote′ness** *n.*

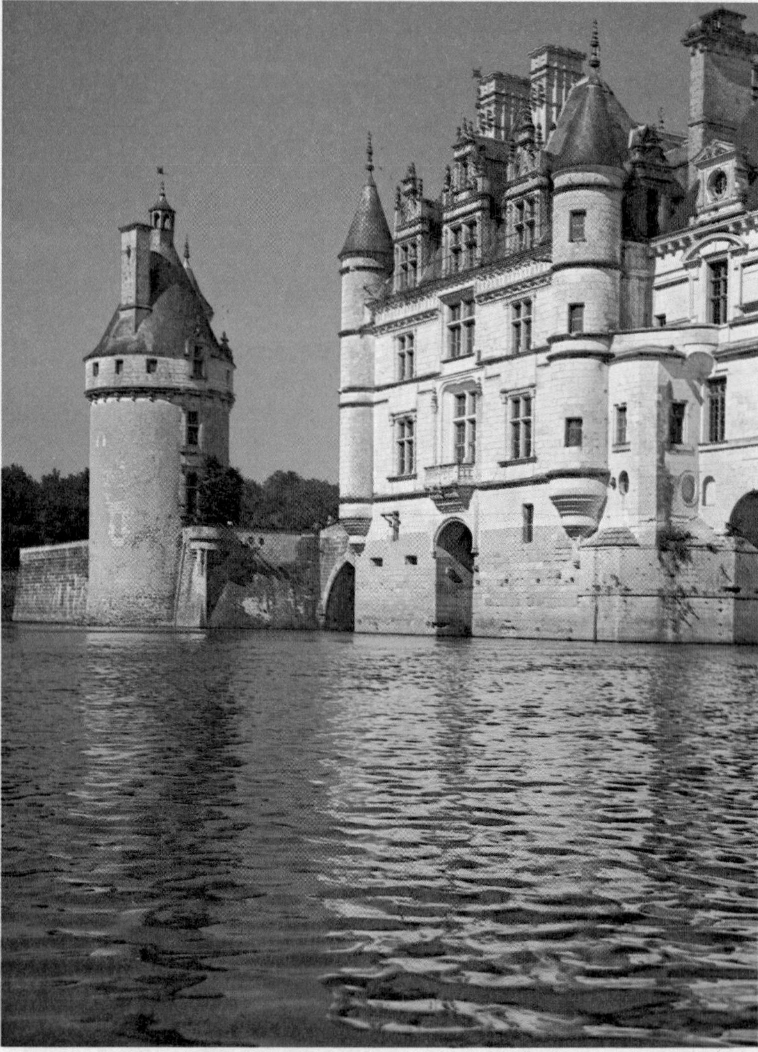

Design of the chateau at Chenonceaux in France was influenced by Diane de Poitiers and Catherine de Medici. It is typical of a new form of architecture used during the ***renaissance*** *in France.*

re·mount (rēmownt′) *v.* Mount (horse etc.) again; go up again, get on horseback again; provide (cavalry) with fresh horses. ~ (rē′mownt) *n.* (mil.) Horse to replace another which is worn out or killed.

re·mov·al (rĭmōō′val) *n.* Removing; being removed.

re·move (rĭmōōv′) *v.* (**-moved, -mov·ing**). Take off or away from place occupied, convey to another place; change situation of; get rid of, dismiss. **re·moved′** *adj.* (esp.) Distant or remote *from*; (of cousins) **once, twice**, etc., ~, with difference of one, two, etc., generations. **re·mov·a·ble** (rĭmōō′vabel) *adj.* **re·mov·a·bil·i·ty** (rĭmōōvabĭl′ĭtē) *n.* **remove** *n.* 1. Act of removing, removal. 2. Distance; stage in gradation, degree, esp. in consanguinity.

re·mu·ner·ate (rĭmū′nerāt) *v.t.* (**-at·ed, -at·ing**). Reward, pay for services rendered; serve as or provide recompense for (toil etc.) or to (person). **re·mu·ner·a·tion** (rĭmūnerā′shon) *n.* **re·mu·ner·a·tive** (rĭmū′nerātĭv, -eratĭv) *adj.* **re·mu′ner·a·tive·ly** *adv.* **re·mu′ner·a·tive·ness, re·mu′ner·a·tor** *ns.*

Re·mus (rē′mus). (Rom. legend) Twin brother of ROMULUS.

Ren·ais·sance (rĕnĭsahns′, -zahns′, rĕn′ĭsahns, -zahns; *Brit.* rĭnā′sans) *n.* Great revival in 14th–16th centuries of art and letters, under influence of classical models, beginning in Italy; style of art or architecture characteristic of this period (freq. attrib.); **r**~, any similar revival.

re·nal (rē′nal) *adj.* Of the kidneys.

Re·nan (renahn′), **Ernest**

Now remembered mainly for his sensual nudes, **Renoir** only began painting them after he was 40. He adopted the colors of the impressionists but retained his own style.

(1823–92). French scholar, philosopher, and historian; author of *Origines du Christianisme*, in which he applied the method of the historian to the biblical narrative.

re·nas·cence (rĭnăs′ens) *n.* (also **R**~) Rebirth, renewal; RENAISSANCE. **re·nas′cent** *adj.* Springing up anew, being reborn.

rend (rĕnd) *v.* (**rent** pr. rĕnt, **rend·ing**). Tear, wrench (*off*, *away*, *apart*, etc.); split or divide in 2, in pieces, or (usu.) into factions.

ren·der (rĕn′d*er*) *v.t.* 1. Give in return; give back, restore (archaic); hand over, deliver, give *up*, surrender (chiefly archaic); pay (tribute etc.), show (obedience etc.), do (service etc.); submit produce for inspection or payment. 2. Reproduce, portray; give representation or performance of, execute; translate. 3. Make, cause to be, convert into. 4. Melt (fat) *down*, extract by melting; cover (stone, brick) with first coat of plaster. **ren′der·ing** *n.* (esp.) Depiction, interpretation of building, dramatic part, musical composition, etc. **ren′der·er** *n.*

ren·dez·vous (rahn′d*e*voo, -dā-; *Fr.* rahndĕvoo′) *n.* (pl. **-vous** pr. -vooz; *Fr.* -voo′). Place appointed for assembling of troops, ships, or aircraft; place of common resort; meeting place agreed on, meeting by agreement. ~ *v.i.* (**-voused**, -vood, **-vous·ing**, -vooing). Meet at rendezvous.

ren·di·tion (rĕndĭsh′*o*n) *n.* Rendering, performance, of dramatic role, musical piece, etc.; translation.

ren·e·gade (rĕn′*e*gād) *n.* Apostate; deserter of party or principles, turncoat; outlaw.

re·nege (rĭnĭg′, -nĕg′, -năg′, -nēg′) *v.* (**-neged, -neg·ing**). 1. Fail to keep one's word. 2. (bridge) Revoke. **re·neg′er** *n.*

re·new (rĭnoo′, -nū′) *v.* 1. Restore to original state, make (as good as) new; regenerate; patch, fill up, reinforce, replace. 2. Get, begin, make, say, or give, anew; grant or be granted continuation of lease, loan, etc. **re·new′a·ble** *adj.* **re·new′al, re·new′er** *ns.*

ren·net (rĕn′ĭt) *n.* Curdled milk found in stomach of unweaned calf, used in curdling milk for making cheese, junket, etc.; preparation of inner membrane of calf's stomach, or of kinds of plant, used for this and other purposes.

Re·no (rē′nō). City in NW. Nevada, N. of Lake Tahoe; tourist center famous for gambling casinos.

Re·noir (rĕn′wār, rĕnwār′), **Pierre Auguste** (1841–1919). French Impressionist painter; his son, **Jean Renoir**, (1894–1979), French motion picture director.

re·nounce (rĭnowns′) *v.* (**-nounced, -nounc·ing**). Resign, surrender, esp. completely and formally; cast off, repudiate; discontinue, give up, esp. openly; (law) refuse or resign right or position, esp. as heir etc. **re·nounce′ment** *n.*

ren·o·vate (rĕn′*o*vāt) *v.t.* (**-vat·ed, -vat·ing**). Make new again, repair, (house, garment, etc.); restore to good condition. **ren·o·va·tion** (rĕn*o*vā′sh*o*n), **ren′o·va·tor** *ns.*

re·nown (rĭnown′) *n.* Celebrity, fame, high distinction. **re·nowned′** *adj.* Famous, celebrated.

rent[1] (rĕnt) *n.* Tear in garment, etc.; opening in clouds etc. resembling tear; cleft, fissure, gorge.

rent[2] (rĕnt) *n.* Tenant's periodical payment to owner or landlord for use of land or occupancy of building, house, room, etc.; payment for hire of machinery etc.; **~-free**, exempt from rent. **rent** *v.* Take, occupy, use, at a rent; let or hire for rent; be occupied or hired *at* specified rent.

rent[3]: see REND.

rent·al (rĕn′t*a*l) *n.* Income from rents; amount paid or received as rent; property, building, apartment, etc. for renting.

rent·er (rĕn′t*er*) *n.* One who holds land etc. by payment of rent.

re·nun·ci·a·tion (rĭnŭnseā′sh*o*n, -shē-) *n.* Renouncing, document expressing this; self-denial, giving up of things. **re·nun·ci·a·tive** (rĭnŭn′sē*a*tĭv, -shē*a*-), **re·nun·ci·a·to·ry** (rĭnŭn′sē*a*tōrē, -tōrē, -shē*a*-) *adjs.*

rep[1], **repp** (rĕp) *ns.* Textile fabric with corded surface, resembling poplin but heavier, used for curtains, upholstery, etc.

rep[2] (rĕp) *n.* (colloq.) Repertory (theater); representative; reputation.

re·pair[1] (rĭpār′) *v.i.* Resort, have recourse, go often or in numbers, *to*.

re·pair[2] (rĭpār′) *v.t.* Restore to good condition, mend, by replacing or fixing parts or compensating loss or exhaustion; remedy, set right again, make amends for (loss, wrong, error); **repair'man,** person whose work is repairing things. **repair** *n.* Restoring to sound condition; **in good ~,** in good (working) condition. **re·pair'er** *n.*

rep·a·ra·ble (rĕp'*e*rab*e*l) *adj.* (of loss etc.) That can be repaired.

rep·a·ra·tion (rĕp*e*rā'sh*o*n) *n.* Repairing or being repaired, repair; making of amends, compensation (esp., pl., that paid to victorious country by defeated one for damage done in war). **re·par·a·to·ry** (rĭpăr'*a*tōrē, -tōrē), **re·par'a·tive** *adjs.*

rep·ar·tee (rĕpärtē', -tā') *n.* Witty retort; (making of) witty retorts.

re·past (rĭpăst', -pahst') *n.* (Food supplied for or eaten at) meal.

re·pa·tri·ate (rēpā'trēāt) *v.t.* (**-at·ed, -at·ing**). Restore or return to native land. **~** *n.* Person who has been repatriated. **re·pa·tri·a·tion** (rēpātrēā'sh*o*n) *n.*

re·pay (rĭpā') *v.* (**-paid, -pay·ing**). Pay back (money); return, retaliate (blow, service, visit, etc.); give in recompense *for;* make repayment to (person); make return for, requite (action); make repayment. **re·pay'a·ble** *adj.* **re·pay'ment** *n.*

re·peal (rĭpēl') *v.t.* Revoke, rescind, annul (law etc.). **~** *n.* Abrogation, repealing; **R~,** repeal of PROHIBITION. **re·peal'er** *n.*

re·peat (rĭpēt') *v.* Say or do over again; recite, report, reproduce; recur, appear again or repeatedly; (of firearm) fire several shots without needing to be reloaded; (refl.) recur in same form, say or do same thing over again; **repeating decimal,** decimal fraction in which same figures are repeated indefinitely. **repeat** *n.* Repeating; something repeated, shown, or broadcast again; (mus.) passage intended to be repeated, mark indicating this. **re·peat'a·ble** *adj.* **re·peat'ed·ly** *adv.*

re·peat·er (rĭpē't*e*r) *n.* (esp.) Watch or clock that strikes the hour and will strike it again if required; firearm etc. that repeats.

re·pel (rĭpĕl') *v.t.* (**-pelled, -pel·ling**). 1. Drive back, repulse, ward off; refuse admission, acceptance, or approach to. 2. Be repulsive or distasteful to. **re·pel'lent** *adj.*

re·pent[1] (rĭpĕnt') *adj.* (chiefly bot.) Creeping, esp. growing along or just under surface of ground.

re·pent[2] (rĭpĕnt') *v.* Feel contrition, compunction, sorrow, or regret for what one has done or left undone; think with contrition or regret *of.* **re·pent'ance** *n.* **re·pent'ant** *adj.* **re·pent'ant·ly** *adv.*

re·per·cus·sion (rēp*e*rkŭsh'*o*n) *n.* Repulse or recoil after impact; return or reverberation of sound, echo; indirect effect or reaction *of* event or act. **re·per·cus·sive** (rēp*e*rkŭs'ĭv) *adj.*

rep·er·toire (rĕp'*e*rtwār, -twōr) *n.* Stock of dramatic or musical pieces etc. that company or player is accustomed or prepared to perform.

rep·er·to·ry (rĕp'*e*rtōrē, -tōrē) *n.* (pl. **-ries**). 1. Storehouse or repository, where something may be found. 2. Repertoire; **~ company,** theatrical company that keeps a stock of plays ready for performance.

rep·e·ti·tion (rĕpetĭsh'*o*n) *n.* Repeating or being repeated; recitation of something learned by heart, piece set to be learned and recited; copy, replica. **rep·e·ti·tious** (rĕpetĭsh'*u*s), **re·pet·i·tive** (r*e*pĕt'ĭtĭv) *adjs.* **re·pet'i·tive·ly** *adv.* **re·pet'i·tive·ness** *n.*

re·pine (rĭpīn') *v.i.* (**-pined, -pin·ing**). Fret, be discontented (*at*).

re·place (rĭplās') *v.t.* (**-placed, -plac·ing**). Put back in place; take place of, succeed, be substituted for; fill up place of (*with, by*), find or provide substitute for; (pass.) be succeeded, have one's or its place filled *by.* **re·place'a·ble** *adj.* **re·place'ment** *n.*

re·play (rēplā') *v.t.* Play (recording, tape) over again. **~** (rē'plā) *n.* Act of replaying; thing that is replayed; **instant ~**: see INSTANT.[1]

re·plen·ish (rĭplĕn'ĭsh) *v.t.* Fill up again (*with*). **re·plen'ish·ment** *n.*

re·plete (rĭplēt') *adj.* Filled, stuffed, fully imbued, well stocked, *with;* gorged, sated (*with*). **re·ple·tion** (rĭplē'sh*o*n) *n.*

re·plev·in (rĭplĕv'ĭn) *n.* Restoration or recovery of personal property unlawfully taken; legal action arising out of, replevin. **~** *v.t.* (**-plev·ined, -plev·in·ing**), **re·plev·y** (rĭplĕv'ē) *v.t.* (**-plev·ied, -plev·y·ing**). Recover by replevin.

rep·li·ca (rĕp'lĭk*a*) *n.* Duplicate made by original artist of his picture etc.; facsimile, exact copy.

re·ply (rĭplī') *v.* (**-plied, -ply·ing**). Make answer, respond, in word or action (*to, that*). **~** *n.* (pl. **-plies**). Act of replying; what is replied, response; (law) pleading by plaintiff after delivery of defendant's plea. **re·pli'er** *n.*

re·port (rĭpōrt', -pōrt') *v.* Relate, give an account of; convey, repeat (something said or heard); take down (speech etc.) in writing, esp. with view to publication in newspaper etc.; give formal account or statement of; make report; relate or state as result of observation or investigation; name (person) to superior authority as having offended in some way; (refl. and intrans.) make known to some authority that one has arrived or is present. **~** *n.* 1. Common talk, rumor; way person or thing is spoken of, repute. 2. Account given or opinion formally expressed after investigation or consideration; account of conduct and progress of a matter, business, etc. (**progress ~**). 3. Sound of explosion; resounding noise. **re·port'a·ble** *adj.*

re·port·age (rĭpōr'tĭj, -pōr', rĕpōrtahzh', -pōr-) *n.* (Style of) reporting events for the press.

re·port·er (rĭpōr't*e*r, -pōr') *n.* (esp.) One employed to report events for newspaper or radio or television newscast.

re·pose[1] (rĭpōz') *v.t.* (**-posed, -pos·ing**). Place (trust etc.) *in.*

re·pose[2] (rĭpōz') *v.* (**-posed, -pos·ing**). Rest; lay (oneself down) to rest; lie, be lying, esp. in sleep or death. **~** *n.* Rest, cessation of activity or excitement; sleep; peaceful or quiescent state, stillness, tranquillity; restful effect; composure or ease of manner. **re·pose'ful** *adj.* **re·pose'ful·ly** *adv.* **re·pos'er** *n.*

re·pos·i·to·ry (rĭpŏz'ĭtōrē, -tōrē) *n.* (pl. **-ries**). Place where things are stored or may be found, museum, warehouse, etc.; burial place; recipient of confidences or secrets.

re·pous·se (rĕpōōsā') *adj.* & *n.* (Ornamental metal work) hammered into relief from reverse side.

repp: REP[1].

rep·re·hend (rĕprĭhĕnd') *v.t.* Rebuke, blame, find fault with. **rep·re·hen·si·ble** (rĕprĭhĕn'sĭb*e*l) *adj.* **rep·re·hen'si·bly** *adv.* **rep·re·hen·sion** (rĕprĭhĕn'sh*o*n) *n.*

rep·re·sent (rĕprĭzĕnt') *v.t.* 1. Bring clearly before the mind, esp. by description or imagination; point out explicitly or seriously, freq. in expostulation etc.; describe as having specific character or quality. 2. Display to the eye, make visible; (esp.) exhibit by means of painting, sculpture, etc.; reproduce in action or show, play, perform, act the part of. 3. Symbolize, serve as embodiment of; serve as specimen or example of; stand for or in place of, denote *by* a substitute; take or fill the place of, be substitute for in some capacity; (esp.) be accredited deputy for (number of persons) in deliberative or legislative assembly. **rep·re·sen·ta·tion** (rĕprĭzĕntā'sh*o*n) *n.* **proportional ~**: see PROPORTIONAL. **rep·re·sent'a·ble** *adj.*

*This **replica** of the 'Golden Hind' was built in Appledore, U.K., to be sailed approximately along Drake's course to San Francisco where it now is an historical exhibit.*

1

3

As the first animals with backbones to become completely adapted to life on land, ***reptiles*** *are an important source of study for zoologists. Those surviving include the crocodiles (1), tortoises, terrapins and turtles (2), a wide range of lizards including the Australian frilled variety (3), and tree snakes (4). There is also the tuatara of New Zealand.*

rep·re·sen·ta·tive (rěprĭzěn′t*a*-tĭv) *adj.* Serving to represent; esp. typical of a class; holding place of, acting for, larger body of persons (esp. the whole people) in government or legislation; of, based upon, system by which people are thus represented. **rep·re·sent′a·tive·ly** *adv.* **rep·re·sent′a·tive·ness** *n.* **representative** *n.* 1 Sample, specimen; typical embodiment *of.* 2. Agent, delegate, substitute; person appointed to represent sovereign or nation in foreign court or country; one representing section of community as member of legislative body; **R~**, member of the U.S. House of Representatives or of lower house of a state legislature.

re·press (rĭprěs′) *v.t.* Check, restrain, put down, keep under; reduce to subjection, subdue, suppress, quell; (psychol.) actively exclude (distressing idea or memory) from the field of conscious awareness. **re·pres·sion** (rĭp-rěsh′*o*n) *n.* **re·pres·sive** *adj.* **re·pres′sive·ly** *adv.*

re·prieve (rĭprēv′) *v.t.* (**-prieved, -priev·ing**). Suspend or delay execution of (condemned person); give respite to. ~ *n.* Reprieving, being reprieved; (warrant for) remission, commutation, or postponement of capital sentence; respite.

rep·ri·mand (rěp′r*i*mănd, -mahnd) *n.* Official rebuke; rebuke, censure. ~ (rěp′r*i*mănd, -mahnd, rěpr*i*mănd′, -mahnd′) *v.t.* Rebuke officially; rebuke, censure severely.

re·print (rēprĭnt′) *v.t.* Print again, esp. in new edition. ~ (rē′prĭnt) *n.* Reproduction in print of matter previously printed; new impression.

re·pris·al (rĭprī′z*a*l) *n.* Act of retaliation; (hist.) forcible seizure of foreign subjects' persons or property in retaliation.

re·prise (rĭprēz′) *n.* Repeated passage in music; repeated song etc. in musical program.

re·proach (rĭprōch′) *v.t.* Express, convey, disapproval to (person) for fault etc. ~ *n.* Reproaching; thing that brings disgrace or discredit (*to*); opprobrium, disgraced or discredited state. **re·proach′a·ble, re·proach′ful** *adjs.* **re·proach′ful·ly** *adv.* **re·proach′ful·ness** *n.* **re·proach′ing·ly** *adv.*

re·pro·bate (rĕp′r*o*bāt) *v.t.* (**-bat·ed, -bat·ing**). Express or feel disapproval of, censure; (of God) cast off, exclude from salvation. **rep·ro·ba·tion** (rĕpro-bā′sh*o*n) *n.* **reprobate** *adj.* & *n.* (Person) cast off by God, hardened in sin, of abandoned character, immoral.

re·pro·duce (rēpr*o*dōōs′, -dūs′) *v.* (**-duced, -duc·ing**). (esp.) Produce copy or representation of; multiply by generation. **re·pro·duc·tion** (rēpr*o*dŭk′sh*o*n) *n.* **re·pro·duc·tive** (rēpr*o*dŭk′tĭv) *adj.* **re·pro·duc′tive·ness** *n.* **re·pro·duc′i·ble** *adj.*

re·proof (rĭprōōf′) *n.* Blame; rebuke, expression of blame.

re·prove (rĭprōōv′) *v.t.* (**-proved, -prov·ing**). Rebuke. **re·prov′er** *n.* **re·prov′ing·ly** *adv.*

rep·tant (rĕp′t*a*nt) *adj.* (biol.) Creeping, crawling.

rep·tile (rĕp′tĭl, -tīl) *n.* Crawling animal; (biol.) member of the Reptilia, a class of cold-blooded, lung-breathing vertebrates, usu. with scales or horny plates, which includes snakes, lizards, crocodiles, turtles, dinosaurs, etc.; also (fig.) a mean, treacherous person. ~ *adj.* Of reptiles; creeping. **rep·til·i·an** (rĕptĭl′y*a*n) *adj.*

re·pub·lic (rĭpŭb′lĭk) *n.* State in which supreme power rests in the people and their elected representatives and officers, as opp. to one governed by king etc.; any community or society with equality between members; **First, Second, Third, Fourth, Fifth R~**: see FRANCE[1].

re·pub·li·can (rĭpŭb′lĭk*a*n) *adj.* 1. Of, constituted as, characterizing, republic(s); advocating or supporting republican government. 2. **R~ Party**, the political party that opposes the DEMOCRATIC Party in U.S.; it was formed in 1854 and its 1st leader to achieve the presidency was Abraham Lincoln; (also, hist.) first party that supported Jefferson. **republican** *n.* Person supporting or advocating republican government; **R~**, member, supporter, of Republican Party. **re·pub′li·can·ism** *n.*

re·pu·di·ate (rĭpū′dēāt) *v.t.* (**-at·ed, -at·ing**). Cast off, disown (person, thing); refuse to accept or entertain, or to have dealings with; refuse to recognize or obey (authority) or discharge (obligation, debt). **re·pu·di·a·tion** (rĭpūdēā′-sh*o*n), **re·pu′di·a·tor** *ns.*

re·pug·nance (rĭpŭg′n*a*ns), **re·pug·nan·cy** (rĭpŭg′n*a*nsē) *ns.* (logic) Contradiction, incompatibility, of ideas; antipathy, aversion (*to*).

re·pug·nant (rĭpŭg′n*a*nt) *adj.* (logic) Contradictory (*to*), incompatible (*with*); distasteful, objectionable, *to*. **re·pug′nant·ly** *adv.*

re·pulse (rĭpŭls′) *v.t.* (**-pulsed, -puls·ing**). Drive back (attack, attacking enemy) by force of arms; rebuff (friendly advances etc.); refuse (request, offer, etc.) ~ *n.* Repulsing or being repulsed; rebuff.

re·pul·sion (rĭpŭl′sh*o*n) *n.* 1. (phys.) Tendency of bodies to repel each other or increase their mutual distance; **capillary ~**: see CAPILLARY. 2. Aversion, disgust.

re·pul·sive (rĭpŭl′sĭv) *adj.* 1. (phys.) Exercising repulsion. 2. Exciting aversion or loathing, disgusting. **re·pul′sive·ly** *adv.* **re·pul′sive·ness** *n.*

rep·u·ta·ble (rĕp′y*u*t*a*bel) *adj.* Of good repute. **rep′u·ta·bly** *adv.* **rep·u·ta·bil·i·ty** (rĕpy*u*t*a*bĭl′ĭtē) *n.*

rep·u·ta·tion (rĕpy*u*tā′sh*o*n) *n.* What is generally said or believed about the character of a person or thing; state of being well reported of, credit, respectability, good fame; *the* credit or distinction *of*.

re·pute (rĭpūt′) *v.t.* (**-put·ed, -put·ing**). (usu. pass.) Be generally considered, reckoned, spoken, or reported of. **re·put′ed** *adj.* (esp.) Supposed, accounted. **re·put′ed·ly** *adv.* **repute** *n.*

re·quest (rĭkwĕst′) *n.* Act of asking for something, petition; thing asked for; **by ~**, in response to expressed wish. ~ *v.t.* Seek permission *to* do; ask to be given, allowed, or favored with; ask (person) *to* do; ask *that*.

Re·qui·em (rĕk′wēem, rē′kwē-) *n.* (also **r~**) Mass for repose of souls of the dead; musical setting for this; dirge. [L. (accus.), = "rest," first word of Introit in Mass for the Dead]

re·qui·es·cat (rĕkwēĕs′kăt) *n.* Prayer for repose of soul of the dead. [L. *requiescat in pace* "may he rest in peace"]

re·quire (rĭkwīr′) *v.t.* (**-quired, -quir·ing**). 1. Demand of (person) *to* do; demand or ask in words, esp. as of right; lay down as imperative. 2. Need, call for, depend for success, etc., on. **re·quire′ment** *n.*

The first ***Republican*** *President was Abraham Lincoln and the sentiments of the Republican Party are embodied in the Lincoln Memorial in Washington.*

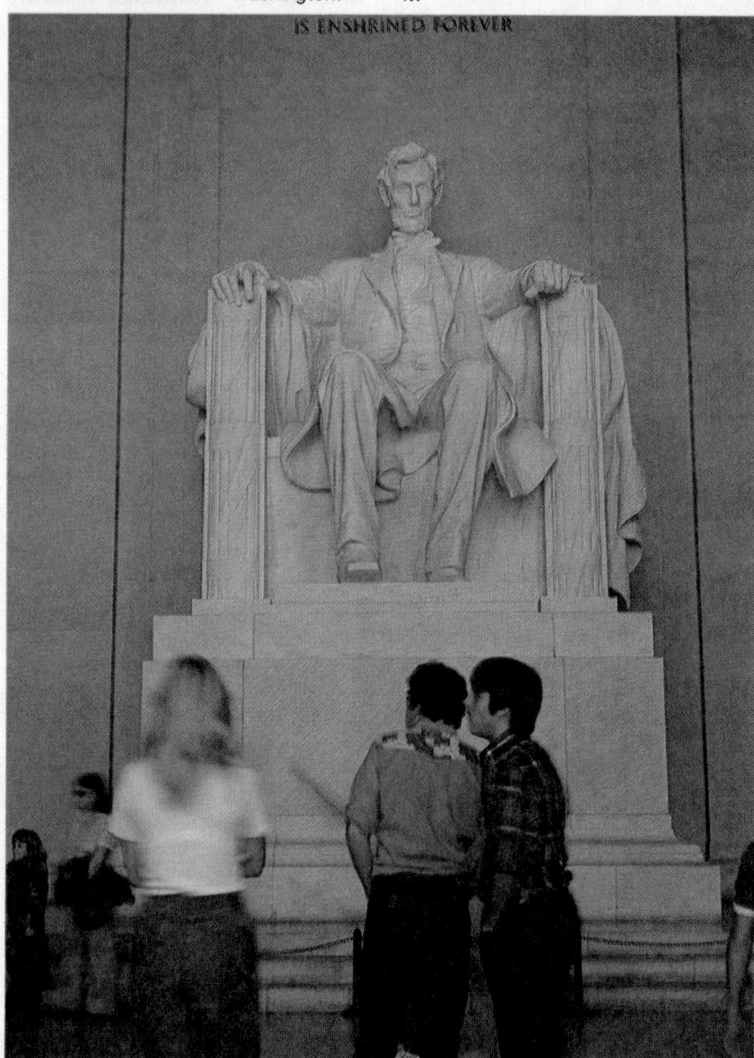

req·ui·site (rĕk′wĭzĭt) *adj.* Required by circumstances, necessary. ~ *n.* Requirement; what is required or necessary. **req′ui·site·ly** *adv.*

req·ui·si·tion (rĕkwĭzĭsh′*o*n) *n.* Requiring, demand made, esp. formal and usu. written demand that some duty be performed, some supplies be furnished, etc. ~ *v.t.* Demand use or supply of for military purposes or public services; demand such supplies etc. from (town, individual, etc.); press into service, call in for some purpose.

re·quite (rĭkwīt′) *v.t.* (**-quit·ed, -quit·ing**). Make return for, reward or revenge (*with*); make return to, repay with good or evil; give in return. **re·quit′al, re·quit′er** *ns.*

re·run (rērŭn′) *v.* (**-ran, -run·ning**). Run (race, film, etc.) again. ~ (rē′rŭn) *n.* Act of rerunning, esp. of film, tape of television program, etc.; film, tape, etc. thus shown.

re·scind (rĭsĭnd′) *v.t.* Abrogate, revoke, annul, cancel. **re·scind′a·ble** *adj.* **re·scis·sion** (rĭsĭzh′*o*n) *n.*

res·cue (rĕs′kū) *v.t.* (**-cued, -cu·ing**). Deliver from or *from* attack, custody, danger, or harm; (law) unlawfully liberate (person), forcibly recover (property). **res′cu·er** *n.* **rescue** *n.* Rescuing, being rescued; deliverance; illegal liberation, forcible recovery.

re·search (rĭsẽrch′, rē′sẽrch) *n.* Careful search or inquiry; (freq. pl.) endeavor to discover facts by scientific study of a subject, course of critical investigation. ~ *v.* Make researches (into). **re·search′er** *n.*

re·sect (rĭsĕkt′) *v.t.* (surg.) Cut out or pare down (bone, cartilage, nerve, etc.). **re·sec·tion** (rĭsĕk′sh*o*n) *n.*

re·se·da (rĭsē′d*a*) *n.* 1. Herbaceous plant of genus **R**~ that includes mignonette. 2. Pale grayish-green color, as of mignonette.

re·sem·ble (rĭzĕm′b*e*l) *v.t.* (**-bled, -bling**). Be like, have similarity to or some feature or property in common with. **re·sem′blance** *n.*

re·sent (rĭzĕnt′) *v.t.* Show or feel indignation at, feel injured or insulted by. **re·sent′ful** *adj.* **re·sent′ful·ly** *adv.* **re·sent′ment** *n.*

re·ser·pine (r*e*sẽr′pĭn, -pēn, rĕs′*e*rpĭn, -pēn) *n.* Alkaloid from plants of genus *Rauwolfia* used as tranquilizer and in treatment of hypertension.

res·er·va·tion (rĕz*e*rvā′sh*o*n) *n.* (esp.) 1. Tract of land reserved for special purpose, esp. for exclusive occupation by Indian tribe. 2. Express or tacit limitation or exception made about something; **mental** ~, qualification tacitly added in making statement, taking oath, etc. 3. Securing of seat, hotel room, etc., in advance; seat etc. so engaged.

re·serve (rĭzẽrv′) *v.t.* (**-served, -serv·ing**). 1. Keep for future use, enjoyment, or treatment, keep back for later occasion, hold over; keep *oneself* in reserve *for.* 2. Retain possession or control of, esp. by legal or formal stipulation; set apart, destine, *for* some use or fate; engage (seat, room, etc.) beforehand; (pass.) be left by fate *for*, fall first or only *to.* **re·served′** *adj.* (esp., of person) Reticent, slow to reveal emotions or opinions, uncommunicative. **re·serv′ed·ly** *adv.* **re·serv′ed·ness** *n.* **reserve** *n.* 1. Something reserved for future use, extra stock or amount; **in** ~, unused but available. 2. (banking) That part of the assets held in the form of cash; (in central banks) that part of the assets held in the form of gold or foreign exchange. 3. (in corporations) That part of the profit not distributed to shareholders but added to capital. 4. Troops withheld from action to reinforce or to cover retreat; forces not in regular service, liable to be called out in emergencies; (in games) extra player chosen in case substitute should be needed. 5. Tract of land reserved for some special purpose = RESERVATION. 6. Limitation, exception, restriction, or qualification, attached to something; **without** ~, fully. 7. Reticence; want of cordiality or friendliness.

re·serv·ist (rĭzẽr′vĭst) *n.* Member of reserve military forces.

res·er·voir (rĕz′*e*rvwâr, -vwôr) *n.* Receptacle constructed of earthwork, masonry, etc., in which large quantity of water is stored; any natural or artificial receptacle esp. for or of fluid; place where fluid etc. collects; part of machine, organ of body, holding fluid; reserve supply or collection *of* knowledge, facts, etc.

re·set (rēsĕt′) *v.t.* (**-set, -set·ting**). Set again (gem, book or its type, etc.).

re·shuf·fle (rēshŭf′*e*l) *v.t.* (**-fled, -fling**). Shuffle again; interchange (appointments, responsibilities, etc.) within a group. ~ *n.*

re·side (rĭzīd′) *v.i.* (**-sided, -sid·ing**). Have one's home, dwell permanently; (of power, rights, etc.) rest or be vested *in* person etc.; (of qualities) be present or inherent *in.* **re·sid′er** *n.*

res·i·dence (rĕz′ĭdens) *n.* Residing; place where one resides, abode *of*; house esp. of considerable pretension, mansion; **in** ~, living or staying regularly at or in some place for the discharge of special duties, or to comply with some regulation.

res·i·den·cy (rĕz′ĭdensē) *n.* (pl. **-cies**). (hist.) Area in a protected state under authority of a resident governor; official residence of such a governor; period of specialized medical training.

res·i·dent (rĕz′ĭd*e*nt) *adj.* Residing; (of birds etc.) staying all year,

The Tennessee Valley Authority ***reservoir*** *on the Tennessee River. Created in 1933, the authority has been responsible for bringing civilized changes to the lives of many Tennesseans.*

***Resin** oozing from a pine trunk damaged by deer, acts in a manner similar to the red corpuscles of the blood. It congeals and forms a protective layer against infection and loss of sap.*

*A ruler whose authority is no longer accepted has the options, either of clinging to office until removed, or of **resignation:** the Watergate scandal forced Richard Nixon to choose the latter.*

not migrating; staying at or in some place in fulfillment of duty or compliance with regulation. ~ *n.* 1. Permanent inhabitant (opp. VISITOR). 2. (hist.) Resident governor or political representative. 3. Physician or other professional person living in, employed in, hospital during specialized medical training, intern.

res·i·den·tial (rĕzĭdĕn'shal) *adj.* Suitable for or occupied by private houses; connected with residence. **res·i·den'tial·ly** *adv.*

re·sid·u·al (rĭzĭj'ōōal) *adj.* Remaining, left over, left as residue. ~ *n.* Residual quantity; remainder; residue. **re·sid'u·al·ly** *adv.*

re·sid·u·ar·y (rĭzĭj'ōōĕrē) *adj.* (law) Of the residue of an estate; of a residue.

res·i·due (rĕz'ĭdōō, -dū) *n.* Remainder, rest, what is left or remains over; what remains of estate after payment of charges, debts, and bequests; (chem. etc.) substance left after combustion or evaporation.

re·sid·u·um (rĭzĭj'ōōum) *n.* (pl. **-sid·u·a** pr. -zĭj'ōōa). What remains, esp. (chem. etc.) residue.

re·sign (rĭzīn') *v.* Relinquish, surrender, give up, hand over (office, right, charge, hope, etc.); reconcile *oneself*, one's *mind*, etc. (*to*); give up office, retire; (chess) discontinue play and admit defeat. **re·signed'** *adj.* Submissive, acquiescent, having resigned oneself to sorrow etc. **re·sign'ed·ly** *adv.*

res·ig·na·tion (rĕzĭgnā'shon) *n.* (esp.) 1. Resigning of an office, document conveying this. 2. Being resigned, uncomplaining endurance of sorrow, misfortune, etc.

re·sil·ience (rĭzĭl'yens) *n.* Rebound, recoil; elasticity, power of resuming original shape or position after compression, bending, etc. **re·sil'ien·cy** *n.* Resilience; buoyancy, power of recovery. **re·sil'ient** *adj.* **re·sil'ient·ly** *adv.*

res·in (rĕz'ĭn) *n.* Adhesive, highly inflammable substance, hardening on exposure to air, formed by secretion in trees and plants and exuding naturally from many of them (as fir and pine) or obtained by incision, and used in varnishes, medicines, etc. **resin** *v.t.* **res·in·ate** (rĕz'ināt) *v.t.* (**-at·ed, -at·ing**). Rub or treat with resin. **res·in·if·er·ous** (rĕzinĭf'erus) *adj.* Yielding, containing, resin.

res·in·ous (rĕz'inus) *adj.* Of, containing, resin.

re·sist (rĭzĭst') *v.* Stop course of, withstand action or effect of; strive against, oppose; offer resistance. **re·sist'ant, re·sist'i·ble, re·sis'tive** *adjs.* **re·sis·tiv·i·ty** (rēzĭstĭv'ĭtē) *n.* **resist** *n.* Composition applied to surfaces for protection. **re·sist'er** *n.*

re·sist·ance (rĭzĭs'tans) *n.* 1. Power of resisting; (also ~ **movement**), any (esp. underground) organization resisting authority, esp. the **R~**, resisting German authority in occupied countries during World War II; **passive ~**, resistance without resort to violence or active opposition; noncooperation. 2. Hindrance, impeding or stopping effect, exercised by material thing upon another; (elect., magn., heat) nonconductivity; (elect.) measure of capacity in a conducting body to resist flow of a current (the resistance of a circuit is given by OHM'S law as the ratio of the applied voltage (electromotive force) to the current that flows); part of apparatus used to offer definite resistance to current; **line of ~**, direction in which resistance acts; **line of least ~**, (fig.) easiest method or course.

re·sist·less (rĭzĭst'lĭs) *adj.* 1. That cannot be resisted. 2. Unresisting. **re·sist'less·ly** *adv.*

re·sis·tor (rĭzĭs'ter) *n.* Device used to introduce resistance into an electrical circuit.

re·sol·u·ble (rĭsŏl'yubel, -zŏl'-) *adj.* That can be dissolved again.

res·o·lute (rĕz'olōōt; *Brit.* rĕz'olūt) *adj.* Determined, decided, bold, not vacillating, unshrinking, firm of purpose. **res'o·lute·ly** *adv.* **res'o·lute·ness** *n.*

res·o·lu·tion (rĕzolōō'shon; *Brit.* rĕzolū'shon) *n.* 1. Separation into components, analysis; (med.) disappearance of inflammation, return of diseased tissue to normal state; (mus.) process by which discord is made to pass into concord; (optics) quality of optical instruments whereby definition of fine detail is obtained. 2. Solving *of* doubt, problem, question, etc. 3. Formal expression of opinion by legislative body or public meeting; form proposed for this. 4. Resolve, thing resolved on; determined temper or character, boldness and firmness of purpose.

re·solve (rĭzŏlv') *v.* (**-solved, -solv·ing**). 1. Break up into parts, convert or be converted *into*; reduce by mental analysis *into*; (of telescope, microscope) render visible,

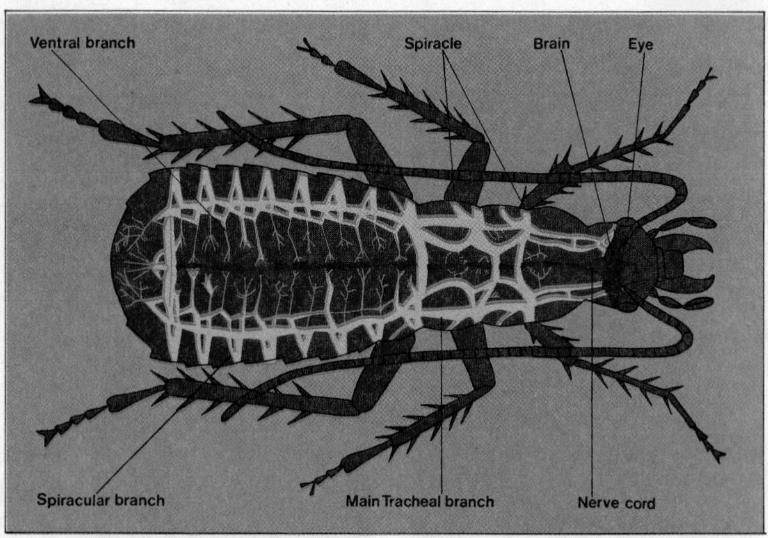

*In most insects **respiration** is not carried out by organs separate from the rest of the body. A network of tubes, the tracheae, carries air through the body, oxygenating the blood.*

distinguish (objects, parts of image); (mus.) convert (discord), be converted, into concord. 2. Solve, explain, clear up, settle. 3. Decide upon, make up one's mind *upon* action or *to* do; form mentally or (of legislative body or public meeting) pass by vote the resolution *that*; (of circumstances etc.) bring (person) to resolution *to* do, *upon* action. **re·solved'** *adj.* **resolve** *n.* Determination or resolution come to in the mind; (poet.) resolution, steadfastness. **re·solv'a·ble** *adj.* **re·solv'er** *n.*

re·sol·vent (rĭzŏl'vent) *adj.* & *n.* (chiefly med. and chem.) (Drug, application, substance) effecting resolution of tumor etc. or division into component parts.

res·o·nant (rĕz'onant) *adj.* (of sound) Reechoing, resounding; (of body) causing reinforcement or prolongation of sound, esp. by vibration; (of place) echoing, resounding, *with*; (phys.) responding to vibrations of a particular frequency. **res'o·nant·ly** *adv.* **res'o·nance** *n.*

res·o·nate (rĕz'onāt) *v.i.* (**-nat·ed, -nat·ing**). Produce or show resonance. **res'o·na·tor** *n.* (esp.) Appliance for increasing sound by resonance.

res·or·cin·ol (rĭzōr'sĭnōl, -nawl, -nŏl) *n.* Synthetic substance ($C_6H_4(OH)_2$), used in the production of various dyestuffs and drugs.

re·sort (rĭzōrt') *v.i.* 1. Turn for aid *to*. 2. Go in numbers or often *to*. ~ *n.* 1. Thing to which recourse is had, what is turned to for aid, expedient; recourse; **the last ~**, a last expedient. 2. Place frequented, usu. for specified purpose or quality (as *health, vacation, seaside,* ~); also attrib., as *resort city*.

re·sound (rĭzownd') *v.* 1. (of place) Ring or echo (*with*); (of voice, sound, etc.) produce echoes, go on sounding, fill place with sound. 2. Repeat loudly (praises etc.); reecho. **re·sound'ing** *adj.* **re·sound'ing·ly** *adv.*

re·source (rē'sōrs, -sōrs, -zōrs, -zōrs, rĭsōrs', -sōrs', -zōrs', -zōrs') *n.* 1. (usu. pl.) Means of supplying a want, supply that can be drawn on. 2. Expedient, device; skill in devising expedients, ingenuity. **re·source'ful** *adj.* **re·source'ful·ly** *adv.* **re·source'ful·ness** *n.*

re·spect (rĭspĕkt') *n.* 1. Reference, relation. 2. Heed or regard *to, of,* attention *to*. 3. Particular detail, point, aspect. 4. Deferential esteem felt or shown toward person or quality; state of being esteemed or honored; (pl.) polite messages or attentions. ~ *v.t.* 1. Refer or relate, to. 2. Treat or regard with deference, esteem, or honor; treat with consideration, spare. **re·spect'er** *n.* **re·spect'ing** *prep.* Having reference to; about, concerning.

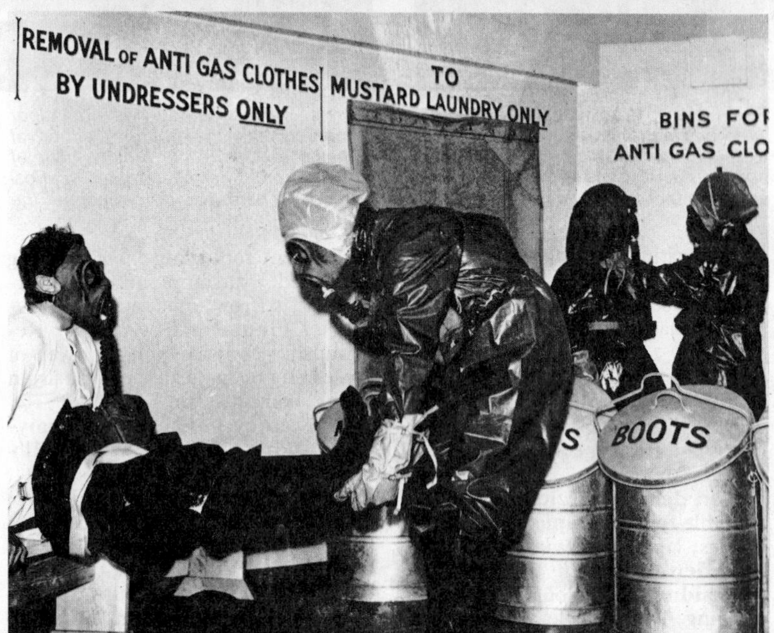

***Respirators** were first developed during the 1914–18 war, when poison gases such as phosgene were used. Since then developments in the field of chemical warfare have been matched by improvements in respirator design.*

re·spect·a·ble (rĭspĕk'tabel) *adj.* 1. Deserving respect. 2. Considerable in number, size, quantity, etc.; fairly good, tolerable. 3. Of good or fair social standing, worthy; befitting respectable persons. **re·spect·a·bil·i·ty** (rĭspĕktabĭl'ĭtē) *n.* **re·spect'a·bly** *adv.*

re·spect·ful (rĭspĕkt'ful) *adj.* Showing deferential esteem. **re·spect'ful·ly** *adv.* **re·spect'ful·ness** *n.*

re·spec·tive (rĭspĕk'tĭv) *adj.* Pertaining to, connected with, each individual, group, etc., of those in question; separate, several, particular. **re·spec'tive·ly** *adv.*

res·pi·ra·tion (rĕsperā'shon) *n.* Breathing; single inspiration and expiration; (biol.) process by which an organism uses oxygen from its environment and gives out carbon dioxide; **artificial ~**, any of various methods of restoring the natural function of breathing when this has been suspended.

res·pi·ra·tor (rĕs'perāter) *n.* 1. Apparatus worn over mouth and nose to filter inhaled air or prevent inhalation of noxious materials. 2. Device for maintaining respiration artificially.

re·spire (rĭspīr') *v.* (**-spired, -spir·ing**). Inhale and exhale air; breathe; breathe again, take breath, recover hope or spirit, get rest or respite. **res·pi·ra·to·ry** (rĕs′p*e*ra-tōrē, -tōrē, rĭspīr′*a*-), **res·pir·a·ble** (rĕs′p*e*r*a*bel, rĭspīr′*a*-) *adjs*.

res·pite (rĕs′pĭt) *n.* Delay permitted in the discharge of an obligation or suffering of a penalty; interval of rest or relief. ~ *v.t.* (**-pit·ed, -pit·ing**). Grant respite to; postpone execution or exaction of (sentence, obligation).

re·splend·ent (rĭsplĕn′d*e*nt) *adj.* Brilliant, dazzlingly or gloriously bright. **re·splend′ent·ly** *adv.* **re·splend′ence, re·splend′en·cy** *ns.*

re·spond (rĭspŏnd′) *v.i.* Make answer; act in response (*to*). **re·spond′er** *n.*

re·spond·ent (rĭspŏn′d*e*nt) *adj.* Making answer; responsive *to*; in position of defendant. ~ *n.* One who answers; defendant in divorce case.

re·sponse (rĭspŏns′) *n.* Answer; (eccles.) responsory; any part of liturgy said or sung by congregation in answer to priest; (mus.) repetition by one part of a theme given by another part.

re·spon·si·bil·i·ty (rĭspŏnsĭbĭl′-ĭtē) *n.* (pl. **-ties**). Being responsible; charge for which one is responsible.

re·spon·si·ble (rĭspŏn′sĭb*e*l) *adj.* Liable to be called to account, answerable; morally accountable for actions, capable of rational conduct; of good credit and repute, reliable, trustworthy; involving responsibility. **re·spon′si·ble·ness** *n.* **re·spon′si·bly** *adv.*

re·spon·sive (rĭspŏn′sĭv) *adj.* Answering; by way of answer; responding readily to or *to* some influence, impressionable, sympathetic; (of liturgy etc.) using responses. **re·spon′sive·ly** *adv.* **re·spon′sive·ness** *n.*

re·spon·so·ry (rĭspŏn′s*e*rē) *n.* (pl. **-ries**). (eccles.) Anthem said or sung by soloist and choir after lesson.

rest[1] (rĕst) *v.* 1. Take repose by lying down, esp. in sleep; lie in death or the grave; cease, abstain or be relieved from exertion, action, movement, or employment; be at ease or in peace, stay, remain; give rest or repose to, lay to rest; allow to rest or remain inactive or quiescent. 2. Have place or position, place, set, lay, (*on*); (of eyes) be directed (*on*); lie or lean, lay, *on* for repose or support; rely, depend, be based, base, found, allow to depend *on*. 3. **resting place**, place provided or used for resting; **last resting place**, the grave; **rest up**, rest thoroughly. **rest** *n.* 1. Repose or sleep, esp. in bed at night; intermission of, freedom from, labor, exertion, or activity; freedom from distress, trouble, etc.; quiet or tranquillity of mind; repose of the grave; **at** ~, tranquil, inert; settled; **set at** ~, satisfy, assure; settle; **day of** ~, sabbath; **lay to** ~, bury; dispense with. 2. Place of resting or abiding; lodging place or shelter. 3. Prop, support; what something rests on. 4. (mus.) Interval of silence, pause, indicated by various signs according to duration; pause in elocution, caesura in verse. 5. ~ **cure**, rest in bed as medical treatment; ~ **room**, (euphem.) public lavatory.

The ***restoration*** *of this house in Williamsburg, Virginia is an example of the care taken by modern-day enthusiasts who want to keep their heritage.*

rest[2] (rĕst) *v.i.* Remain over (now rare); remain in specified state; ~ **with**, be left in the hands or charge of. **rest** *n.* Remainder or remaining parts or individuals (*of*) (with sing. or pl. verb); **for the** ~, as regards anything beyond what has been specially mentioned.

res·tau·rant (rĕs′t*e*r*a*nt, -t*e*-rahnt, -tr*a*nt) *n.* Place where meals or refreshments may be had.

res·tau·ra·teur (rĕst*e*r*a*tēr′) *n.* Restaurant owner.

rest·ful (rĕst′f*u*l) *adj.* Favorable to repose, free from disturbing influences, soothing. **rest′ful·ly** *adv.* **rest′ful·ness** *n.*

res·ti·tu·tion (rĕstĭtōō′sh*o*n, -tū′-) *n.* Restoring of or *of* thing to proper owner; reparation for injury; restoring or return of a previous state or position.

res·tive (rĕs′tĭv) *adj.* (of horse) Refusing to go forward, obstinately moving backward or sideways when being driven or ridden, intractable, resisting control; (of person) unmanageable, rejecting control, fidgety. **res′tive·ly** *adv.* **res′tive·ness** *n.*

rest·less (rĕst′lĭs) *adj.* Finding or affording no rest; uneasy, agitated, unpausing, fidgeting. **rest′less·ly** *adv.* **rest′less·ness** *n.*

res·to·ra·tion (rĕst*e*rā′sh*o*n) *n.* (esp.) 1. **R** ~, reestablishment of monarchy in England with return of Charles II to the throne in 1660; period between this and the revolution of 1688. 2. Action or process of restoring to original form or perfect condition.

re·stor·a·tive (rĭstōr′*a*tĭv, -stōr′-) *adj.* Tending to restore health or strength. ~ *n.* Restorative food, medicine, or agency.

re·store (rĭstōr′, -stōr′) *v.t.*

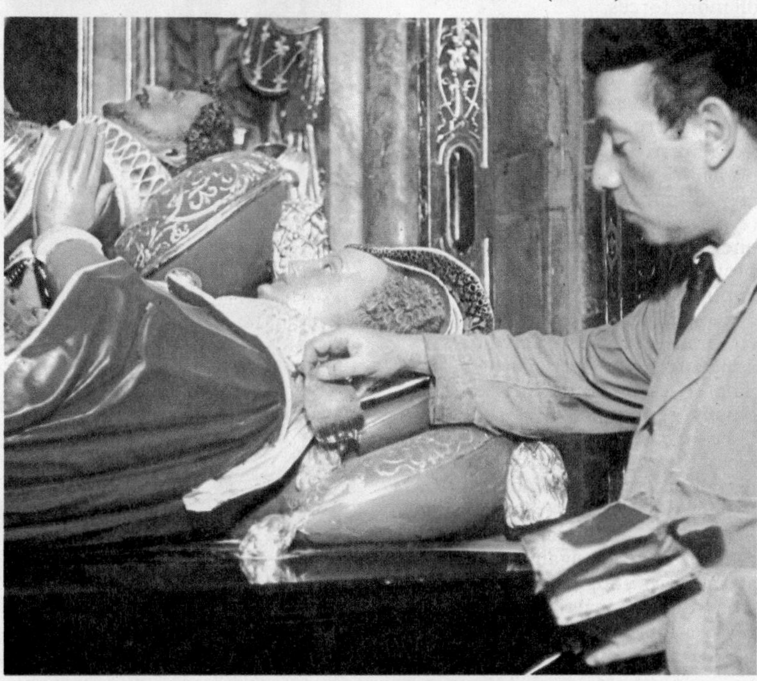

When paintings or other ancient monuments need ***restoration,*** *including the tombs in Westminster Abbey, U.K., all efforts are devoted to reproducing the original impression, often by scientific analysis of the original paint.*

(**-stored, -stor·ing**). 1. Give back, make restitution of. 2. Repair, alter, (building, painting, etc.) so as to bring back as nearly as possible to original form, state, etc.; reinstate, bring back *to* dignity or right; bring back *to* health, cure. 3. Reestablish, renew, bring back into use; replace or insert (words etc. in text, missing parts of thing etc.); replace, bring *to* former place or condition. **re·stor'er** *n.*

re·strain (rĭstrān') *v.t.* Check or hold in *from*, keep in check or under control or within bounds, repress, keep down; confine, imprison. **re·strained', re·strain'a·ble** *adjs.* **re·strain'er** *n.*

re·straint (rĭstrānt') *n.* 1. Restraining, being restrained; check; controlling agency or influence; confinement; **without** ~, freely, copiously. 2. Constraint, reserve.

re·strict (rĭstrĭkt') *v.t.* Confine, bound, limit (*to, within*). **re·strict'ed·ly** *adv.* **re·stric·tion** (rĭstrĭk'shon) *n.* **re·stric'tive** *adj.* ~ **covenant**, real-estate agreement barring free use of property for particular purposes or (usu. clandestine or illegal) for occupancy by or sale to members of specified ethnic group(s). **re·strict'ed** *adj.* **re·stric'tive·ly** *adv.* **re·stric'tive·ness** *n.*

re·sult (rĭzŭlt') *v.i.* Arise as consequence, effect, or conclusion *from*; end *in* specified way. ~ *n.* Consequence, issue, outcome; quantity, formula, etc., obtained by calculation.

re·sult·ant (rĭzŭl'tant) *adj.* Resulting. ~ *n.* Product, outcome; force that is equivalent of two or more forces acting from different directions at one point; composite or final effect of any two or more forces.

re·sume (rĭzōōm'; *Brit.* rĭzūm') *v.* (**-sumed, -sum·ing**). 1. Get or take again or back; recover; reoccupy. 2. Begin again; go on (with) after interruption; recommence.

ré·su·mé, re·su·me (rĕz'ōōmā, rā'sōō-, rĕzōōma', rāzōō-) *ns.* Summary, epitome, abstract; (esp.) written summary or list of one's education, qualifications, and previous jobs submitted with job application.

re·sump·tion (rĭzŭmp'shon) *n.* Resuming. **re·sump'tive** *adj.*

re·sur·gent (rĭsẽr'jent) *adj.* That rises or tends to rise again. **re·sur'gence** *n.*

res·ur·rect (rĕzurĕkt') *v.t.* Raise from the dead; bring back to life; revive practice or memory of.

res·ur·rec·tion (rĕzurĕk'shon) *n.* 1. **R**~, rising of Christ from the grave; rising again of the dead at the Last Judgment. 2. Revival from disuse, inactivity, or decay; restoration to vogue or memory. **res·ur·rec'tion·al** *adj.*

re·sus·ci·tate (rĭsŭs'ĭtāt) *v.* (**-tat·ed, -tat·ing**). Revive, return or restore to life, consciousness, vogue, vigor, etc. **re·sus·ci·ta·tion** (rĭsŭsĭtā'shon), **re·sus'ci·ta·tor** *ns.* **re·sus'ci·ta·tive** *adj.*

ret (rĕt) *v.t.* (**ret·ted, ret·ting**). Soften (flax, hemp) by soaking in water or exposing to moisture.

ret. *abbrev.* Retired.

re·tail (rē'tāl) *n.* Sale of goods in small quantities to the consumer (freq. attrib. and in adverbial expressions; opp. WHOLESALE). ~ (rē'tāl for def. 1; rētāl' for sense 2) *v.* 1. Sell (goods) by retail; (of goods) be retailed. 2. Recount, relate details of. **re'tail·er** *n.*

re·tain (rĭtān') *v.t.* 1. Keep in place, hold fixed; **retaining wall**, one supporting and confining mass of earth or water. 2. Secure services of (esp. lawyer or consultant) by engagement and preliminary payment. 3. Keep possession of, continue to have; continue to practice or recognize, allow to remain or prevail, keep unchanged; bear in mind, remember. **re·tain'ment** *n.*

re·tain·er (rĭtā'ner) *n.* 1. Fee paid to engage the services of a lawyer, consultant, etc.; sum paid to secure special services. 2. One who retains. 3. (hist.) Dependent or follower of person of rank or position; domestic servant. 4. Orthodontic device used to hold teeth in desired position.

re·tal·i·ate (rĭtăl'ēāt) *v.* (**-at·ed, -at·ing**). Repay (esp. injury, insult, etc.) in kind; make return or requital (esp. of injury). **re·tal·i·a·tion** (rĭtălēā'shon) *n.* **re·tal·i·a·to·ry** (rĭtăl'ēatōrē, -tōrē) *adj.*

re·tard (rĭtārd') *v.* Make slow

*The **Resurrection** of Jesus Christ is one of the cornerstones of Christianity and has been portrayed frequently in religious art. Below is a 14th-century altar piece from an Italian church, painted in Orcagna's style.*

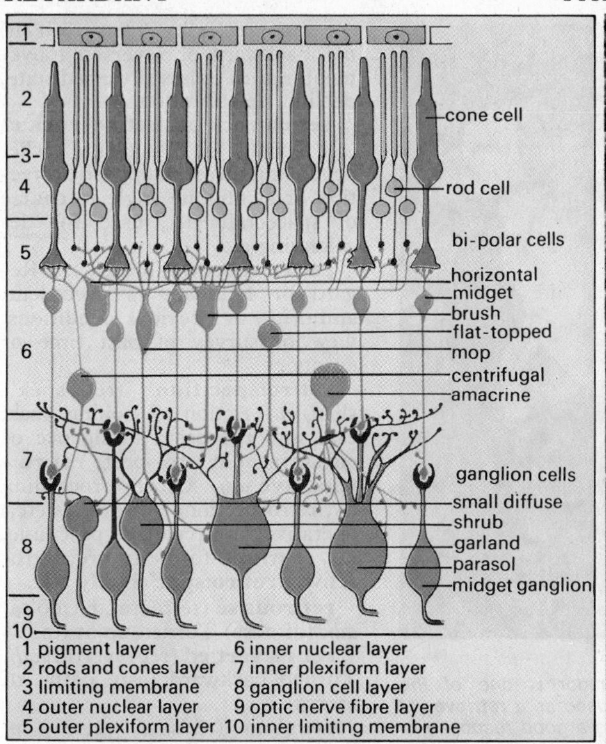

*The **retina** is the area at the back of the eye which is linked by a complicated structure (shown diagrammatically above), which transforms images received through the lens into impulses which are transmitted to the brain.*

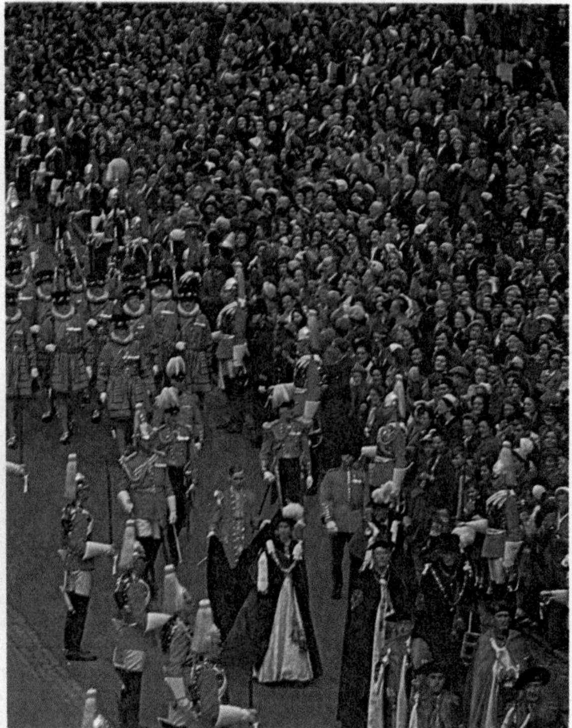

*Queen Elizabeth II, on her way to the presentations of the Order of the Garter, is accompanied by a **retinue,** formerly a group of people dependent on the goodwill of the monarch, but whose present-day obligation is to the Crown.*

or late, delay progress, arrival, accomplishment, or happening of. **re·tard·ate** (rĭtar̄′dāt) *adj.* & *n.* Mentally retarded (person). **re·tard′ed** *adj.* With mental or physical development behind what is normal. **re·tar·da·tion** (rētar̄dā′sh*o*n) *n.* **retard** *n.* Delay; (mus.) slackening of tempo.

re·tard·ant (rĭtar̄′d*a*nt) *n.* (chem.) Substance capable of delaying chemical reaction. ~ *adj.* Able to retard.

retch (rĕch) *v.i.* Make motion of vomiting, esp. ineffectually and involuntarily. ~ *n.* Retching motion or sound.

re·ten·tion (rĭtĕn′sh*o*n) *n.* Retaining; esp. (med.) retaining in body of secretion usually evacuated.

re·ten·tive (rĭtĕn′tĭv) *adj.* 1. (of memory) Tenacious, not forgetful. 2. Tending, inclined, apt, to retain. **re·ten′tive·ness, re·ten·tiv·i·ty** (rētĕntĭv′ĭtē) *ns.*

ret·i·cence (rĕt′ĭs*e*ns), **ret·i·cen·cy** (rĕt′ĭs*e*nsē) *ns.* Reserve in speech, avoidance of saying too much or of speaking freely. **ret′i·cent** *adj.* **ret′i·cent·ly** *adv.*

ret·i·cle (rĕt′ĭk*e*l) *n.* Network of fine threads or lines in object glass of optical instrument to help accurate observation.

re·tic·u·lar (rĭtĭk′y*u*ler) *adj.* Netlike.

re·tic·u·late (rĭtĭk′y*u*lāt) *v.* (**-lat·ed, -lat·ing**). Divide, be divided or marked, into a network; arrange, be arranged, in small squares or with intersecting lines. **re·tic·u·late** (rĭtĭk′y*u*lĭt, -lāt), **re·tic′u·lat·ed** *adjs.* **re·tic′u·late·ly** *adv.* **re·tic·u·la·tion** (rĭtĭky*u*lā′sh*o*n) *n.*

ret·i·cule (rĕt′ĭkūl) *n.* 1. Reticle. 2. (archaic) Lady's bag of woven or netlike material carried or worn to serve purpose of pocket.

re·tic·u·lum (rĭtĭk′y*u*l*u*m) *n.* (pl. **-la** pr. -l*a*). 1. Second stomach of ruminant. 2. Netlike structure, reticulated membrane, etc.

ret·i·na (rĕt′*i*n*a*) *n.* (pl. **-nas, -nae** pr. -nē). Innermost layer or coating, sensitive to light, at back of eyeball, in which optic nerve terminates. **ret′i·nal** *adj.*

ret·i·nue (rĕt′*i*no͞o, -nū) *n.* Suite or train of persons in attendance upon great personage. **ret′i·nued** *adj.*

re·tire (rĭtīr′) *v.* (**-tired, -tir·ing**). 1. Withdraw, go away, seek seclusion or shelter; withdraw *to* usual place or occupation, to bed, etc.; retreat, move back or away, recede. 2. Cease *from* or give up office, profession, employment, or business, esp. to live on savings, income, or pension; compel (officer, employee) to retire; (baseball) cause (batter or side) to conclude an inning. 3. (mil.) Move back. **re·tired′** *adj.* **re·tir′ing** *adj.* (esp.) Shy; fond of seclusion. **re·tir·ee** (rĭtīrē′, -tīr′ē) *n.* One who has retired from a career or occupation.

re·tire·ment (rĭtīr′m*e*nt) *n.* (esp.) Seclusion; secluded place; condition of having retired from work.

re·tort[1] (rĭtōrt′) *v.* 1. Repay (esp. injury) in kind. 2. Reply quickly and sharply; present a counterargument; make, say by way of, repartee. ~ *n.* Incisive reply, repartee; turning of argument or charge against its author; piece of retaliation. **re·tort′er** *n.*

re·tort[2] (rĭtōrt′) *n.* Vessel usu. of glass with long downward-bent neck used in distilling liquids; clay or iron cylinder in which coal is heated to produce gas; furnace in which iron is heated with carbon to produce steel.

re·touch (rētŭch′) *v.t.* Amend or improve by fresh touches, touch up (esp. photographic negative or print). **re·touch′a·ble** *adj.* **re·touch′er** *n.*

re·trace (rĭtrās′) *v.t.* (**-traced, -trac·ing**). Trace back to source or beginning; go back over (one's steps, way, etc.). **re·trace′a·ble** *adj.*

re·tract (rĭtrăkt′) *v.* 1. Draw (esp. part of one's body or of machine) back or in; (of such part etc.) shrink back or in, be capable of being retracted; (phonet.) pronounce with tongue retracted. 2. Withdraw, revoke, cancel opinion or statement as erroneous or unjustified. **re·tract′a·ble** *adj.* **re-**

The golden labrador is one of the breeds of dogs used as a ***retriever*** *of game and, having a good response to training, is most favored as a guide dog for the blind.*

trac′tion *n.*

re·trac·tile (rĭtrăk′tĭl) *adj.* Capable of being retracted, as cats' claws.

re·tread (rētrĕd′) *v.t.* (**-tread·ed, -tread·ing**). Furnish (tire) with fresh tread. ~ (rē′-trĕd) *n.* Tire renovated thus.

re·treat (rĭtrēt′) *v.* Go back, retire, relinquish a position (esp. of army etc.); recede; (chiefly in chess) move (piece) back from forward or threatened position. ~ *n.* 1. Act of, (mil.) signal for, retreating; (mil.) bugle call signifying lowering of flag at sunset; **beat a ~**, retreat, abandon undertaking. 2. Withdrawing into privacy or security; (place of) seclusion; place of shelter; (place of) temporary retirement for religious exercises.

re·trench (rĭtrĕnch′) *v.* 1. Reduce amount of (esp. expenses etc.); economize; remove, delete, omit. 2. (fort.) Furnish with inner line of defense, usu. consisting of trench and parapet. **re·trench′ment** *n.*

re·trial (rētrī′*a*l) *n.* Retrying of a case in a court of law.

ret·ri·bu·tion (rĕtrĭbū′sh*o*n) *n.* Recompense, usu. for evil, vengeance, requital. **re·trib·u·tive** (rĭtrĭb′y*u*tĭv), **re·trib·u·to·ry** (rĭtrĭb′y*u*tōrē, -tōrē) *adjs.*

re·trieve (rĭtrēv′) *v.* (**-trieved, -triev·ing**). 1. (of dogs) Find and bring in (killed or wounded game); find and bring back; get back, regain. 2. Recall to mind, remember. 3. Rescue *from* bad state etc.; restore to flourishing state, revive (esp. fortunes etc.); repair, set right (loss, disaster, error). ~ *n.* (Possibility of) recovery. **re·triev′a·ble** *adj.* **re·triev′al** *n.* Information retrieval: see INFORMATION.

re·triev·er (rĭtrē′v*e*r) *n.* Dog of breed specially adapted for retrieving game.

retro- *prefix.* Backward, back.

ret·ro·act (rĕtrōăkt′) *v.i.* React; operate in backward direction; (law) have retrospective effect, be effective as of past date. **ret·ro·ac′tion** *n.* **ret·ro·ac′tive** *adj.* **ret·ro·ac′tive·ly** *adv.*

ret·ro·cede[1] (rĕtr*o*sēd′) *v.i.* (**-ced·ed, -ced·ing**). Move back, recede.

ret·ro·cede[2] (rĕtr*o*sēd′) *v.t.* (**-ced·ed, -ced·ing**). Cede (territory) back again.

ret·ro·fire (rĕt′r*o*fīr) *v.* (**-fired, -fir·ing**). Ignite (retrorocket).

ret·ro·fit (rĕtr*o*fĭt′) *v.* (**-fit·ted, -fit·ting**). Alter or improve machine, building, etc. already in use by adding more modern features.

ret·ro·gra·da·tion (rĕtrōgrādā′-sh*o*n) *n.* 1. (astron.) Apparent backward motion of planet in zodiac; apparent motion of heavenly body from east to west among the stars; backward movement of lunar nodes on ecliptic. 2. Retrogression.

ret·ro·grade (rĕt′r*o*grād) *adj.* 1. (astron.) In or showing retrogradation. 2. Directed backward, retreating; reverting, esp. to inferior state, declining; inverse, reversed. ~ *v.i.* (**-grad·ed, -grad·ing**). Show retrogradation, move backward, recede, retire, decline, revert.

ret·ro·gress (rĕtr*o*grĕs′, rĕt′r*o*-grĕs) *v.i.* Go back, move backward; deteriorate. **ret·ro·gres′sive** *adj.* **ret·ro·gres′sive·ly** *adv.*

ret·ro·gres·sion (rĕtr*o*grĕsh′*o*n) *n.* Backward or reversed movement; return to less advanced state, decline, deterioration.

ret·ro·rock·et, ret·ro-rock·et (rĕt′rōrŏkĭt) *ns.* Auxiliary rocket producing thrust in opposite direction or at oblique angle to course of spacecraft etc., used for decelerating etc.

ret·ro·spect (rĕt′r*o*spĕkt) *n.* Regard or reference *to* precedent, authority, or previous conditions; view or survey of past time or events.

ret·ro·spec·tion (rĕtr*o*spĕk′-sh*o*n) *n.* Action of looking back, esp. into the past, indulgence or engagement in retrospect. **ret·ro·spec′tive** *adj.* Of, in, proceeding by, retrospection; (of statutes etc.) operative with regard to past time, not restricted to the future, retroactive. **ret·ro·spec′tive·ly** *adv.*

ret·rous·sé (rĕtrōōsā′, r*e*trōō′sā) *adj.* (of nose) Turned up at tip.

ret·ro·vert·ed (rĕt′r*o*vẽrtĭd) *adj.* Turned backward (esp. path., of uterus).

ret·si·na (rĕt′sin*a*, rĕtsē′-) *n.* Resin-flavored Greek wine.

re·turn (rĭtẽrn′) *v.* 1. Come or go back; revert. 2. Bring, convey, give, send, put, or pay, back or in return or requital; give, render (thanks). 3. Say in reply, retort. 4. Report in answer to official demand for information, state by way of report or verdict; reelect, reappoint (esp. a legislator, public official) to office. ~ *n.* 1. Coming back; coming around again; return ticket; (**many**) **happy ~s** (**of the day**), birthday or festival greeting; **return ticket**, ticket for journey to place and back again to point of departure. 2. Side or part receding, usu. at right angles, from front or direct line of any work or structure. 3. (Coming in of) proceeds or profit of undertaking. 4. Giving, sending, putting, or paying back; thing so given, sent, etc., esp. report in answer to writ or official demand for information, esp. (*income*) *tax return.* **re·turn′a·ble** *adj.* **re·turn′er, re·turn·ee** (rĭtẽrnē′, -tẽr′nē) *ns.*

re·tuse (rĭtōōs′, -tūs′) *adj.* (of leaf, part of insect, etc.) Having a broad or rounded end with depression in center.

Reu·ben (rōō′bĭn). Hebrew patriarch, eldest son of Jacob and Leah (Gen. 29); tribe of Israel traditionally descended from him.

re·un·ion (rēūn′y*o*n) *n.* Reuniting, being reunited; social gathering of intimates or persons with common interests; esp. of the members of a family once a year (**family ~**) or of a school's graduating class of a particular year (**class ~**).

Ré·un·ion (rēūn′y*o*n). (formerly

Bourbon) Island and French overseas department, in the Indian Ocean E. of Madagascar, 70 sq. mi. (181 sq. km); capital, Saint-Denis.

re·u·nite (rēūnīt′) *v.* (**-nit·ed, -nit·ing**). Bring or come together again, join after separation.

rev (rĕv) *n.* (colloq.) (mech.) Revolution. ~ *v.* (**revved, rev·ving**). Cause (internal combustion engine) to run quickly, esp. before bringing it into use, speed *up*; (of engine) revolve, be speeded *up*.

Rev. *abbrev.* Revelation (New Testament); Reverend.

re·vamp (rēvămp′) *v.* Vamp or patch up again; renovate, revise, improve.

re·vanch·ism (rĭvahn′chĭzem) *n.* (pol.) Policy of seeking to recover lost territory etc.

re·veal (rĭvēl′) *v.t.* Disclose, make known, divulge; display, show, let appear. **re·veal′ing·ly** *adv.* **re·veal′ment** *n.*

re·veil·le (rĕv′elē) *n.* Military waking signal sounded in morning on bugle or drums. [Fr. *réveillez*, imper. pl. of *réveiller* awaken, f. L. *vigilare* keep watch]

rev·el (rĕv′el) *v.i.* (**-eled, -el·ing**, Brit. **-elled, -el·ling**). Make merry, be riotously festive; take keen delight *in*. **rev′el·er,** Brit. **rev′el·ler** *ns.* **revel** *n.* Reveling; (occasion of indulgence in) merrymaking (freq. pl.). **rev′el·ry** *n.* (pl. **-ries**).

rev·e·la·tion (rĕvelā′shon) *n.* 1. Disclosing of knowledge, knowledge disclosed, esp. to man by divine or supernatural agency; **R~** (**of St. John the Divine**), (pop. **Revelations**), last book of New Testament, the Apocalypse. 2. Striking disclosure; revealing of some fact. **re·vel·a·to·ry** (revĕl′atōrē, -tōrē, rĕv′ela-) *adj*

re·venge (rĭvĕnj′) *v.* (**-venged, -veng·ing**). Avenge *oneself* (*on* a person); inflict punishment, exact retribution, for (injury, harm, etc.); avenge (person). ~ *n.* Revenging, act done in revenging; desire to revenge, vindictive feeling; (in games) opportunity given for reversing former result by return game. **re·venge′ful** *adj.* **re·venge′ful·ly** *adv.* **re·venge′ful·ness** *n.*

Paul Revere, master silversmith, earned his legendary status by riding to warn the colonial patriots that the British troops were moving on Lexington. The ensuing conflict was the beginning of the War of Independence.

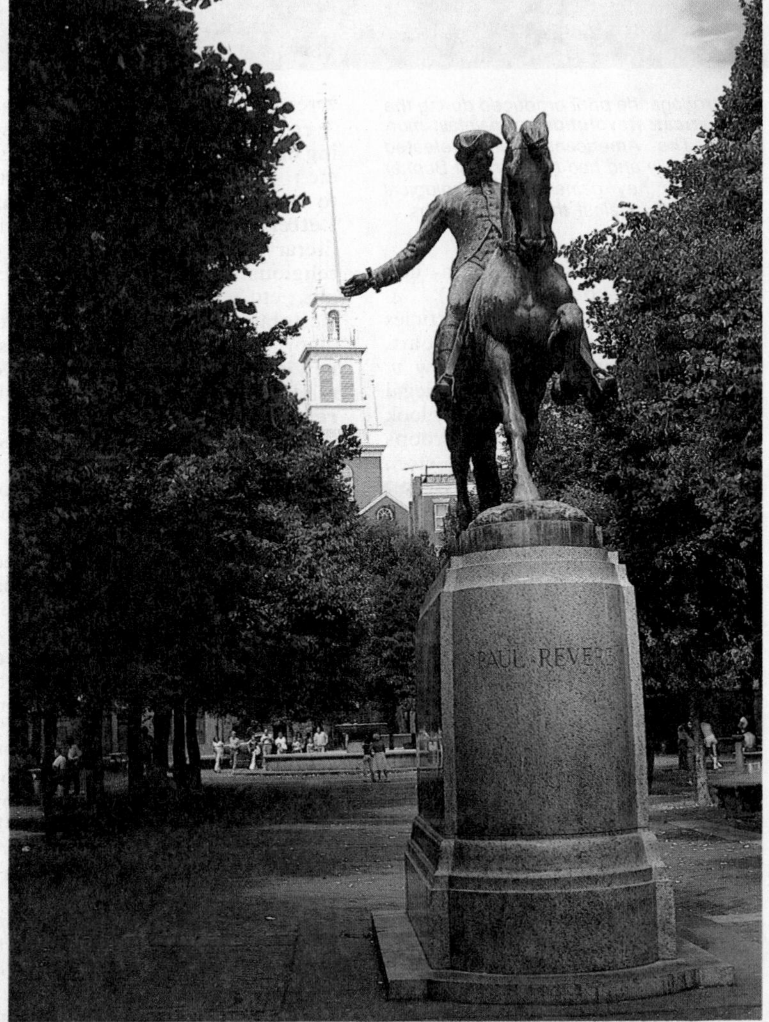

rev·e·nue (rĕv′enū, -nōō) *n.* Income, esp. of large amount, from any source; (pl.) collective items or amounts constituting this; (sing.) annual income of government or state, from which public expenses are met.

re·ver·ber·ate (rĭvẽr′berāt) *v.* (**-at·ed, -at·ing**). Return, reflect, reecho (sound, light, etc.); be reflected or reechoed; (of flame, heat, etc.) be forced back *into, over, on* (furnace, substance, etc.); subject to action of reverberatory furnace. **re·ver·ber·a·tion** (rĭvẽrberā′shon) *n.* **re·ver′ber·ant, re·ver′ber·a·to·ry, re·ver·ber·a·tive** (rĭvẽr′berativ) *adjs.*

re·vere (rĭvēr′) *v.t.* (**-vered, -ver·ing**). Regard as sacred or exalted, hold in deep and usu. affectionate or religious respect, venerate.

Re·vere (rĭvēr′), **Paul** (1735–1818). Amer. silversmith, engraver, patriot, famous for his midnight ride from Charlestown to Lexington (1775) to give warning that Brit. troops were advancing from Boston.

rev·er·ence (rĕv′erens) *n.* Revering; capacity for this; gesture indicating respect; **your, his, R~**, titles used to, of, clergyman. **rev·er·en·tial** (rĕverĕn′shal) *adj.* **rev·er·en′tial·ly** *adv.* **reverence** *v.t.* (**-enced, -enc·ing**). Regard with reverence, venerate.

rev·er·end (rĕv′erend) *adj.* Deserving reverence by age, character, or associations; esp. as respectful epithet applied to members of the clergy, freq. (abbrev. Rev.) prefixed to name and designation of clergyman; of, connected with, the clergy, e.g., *Right R~*, title of Episcopal, Anglican, bishop; *Most Reverend*, of R.C. bishop.

rev·er·ent (rĕv′erent) *adj.* Feeling or showing reverence. **rev′er·ent·ly** *adv.*

rev·er·ie (rĕv′erē) *n.* (Mood of) musing, daydream(ing).

re·verse (rĭvẽrs′) *adj.* Opposite (*of*) or contrary to in character or order; back or backward, upside down. **re·verse′ly** *adv.* **reverse** *n.* 1. Contrary, opposite; gear permitting vehicle to be driven backward; **in ~**, with the position reversed, the other way around; (of vehicle) in reverse gear, moving backward. 2. (Device on) side of coin, medal, etc., that does not bear main device or inscription; verso (of leaf in book etc.); back. 3. Misfortune, disaster, esp. defeat in battle; (pl.) financial setback. **re·verse** *v.* (**-versed, -vers·ing**). Turn the other way around or up, or inside out; invert; transpose; ~

A propaganda print produced during the ***American Revolution*** *to maintain morale. The Americans were defeated technically and had to reform at Bunker Hill, but they gained a psychological advantage against the British troops.*

the charges, make recipient of telephone call responsible for payment; convert to opposite character or effect; cause (engine etc.) to work in contrary direction; revoke, annul (decree, act, etc.). **re·vers'er, re·ver'sal** *ns.* **re·vers'i·ble** *adj.* **re·vers·i·bil·i·ty** (rĭvĕrsĭbĭl'ĭtē), **re·vers'i·ble·ness** *ns.*

re·ver·sion (rĭvĕr'zhon, -shon) *n.* 1. (Return to grantor or his estate right of ultimate succession to) estate granted till specified date or event, esp. death of original grantee. 2. Return to a previous state, habit, etc., esp. (biol.) to ancestral type. **re·ver'sion·ar·y** *adj.*

re·ver·sion·er (rĭvĕr'zhoner, -sho-) *n.* One who has the reversion of an estate.

re·vert (rĭvĕrt') *v.* 1. (of property or money) Return to original owner or his heirs. 2. Return *to* former condition, primitive state, etc.; fall back into wild state. **re·vert'i·ble** *adj.* (of property) Subject to reversion.

re·vet (rĭvĕt') *v.t.* (**-vet·ted, -vet·ting**). Face (rampart, wall, etc.) with masonry etc., esp. in fortification. **re·vet'ment** *n.* Retaining wall or facing.

re·view (rĭvū') *n.* 1. Display and formal inspection of troops, fleet, etc.; **pass in ~**, (fig.) examine, be examined. 2. General survey or reconsideration of subject or thing. 3. Published account or criticism of literary work, play, film, etc. (esp. a new or recent one). 4. Periodical publication with articles on current events, new books, art, etc. 5. Second view. **review** *v.* View again; subject to esp. legal revision; survey, glance over, look back on; hold review of (troops etc.); write review of (book etc.), write reviews. **re·view'er** *n.* (esp.) Writer of review(s).

re·vile (rĭvīl') *v.* (**-viled, -vil·ing**). Call by derogatory names, abuse; talk abusively. **re·vile'·ment, re·vil'er** *ns.* **re·vil'ing·ly** *adv.*

re·vise (rĭvīz') *v.t.* (**-vised, -vis·ing**). Read carefully over, examine, go over again, in order to correct, improve, or amend (literary matter, printer's proofs, law, etc.); **Revised Version**, (abbrev. R.V.) Brit. revision (1870–1884) of 1611 Authorized Version of Bible; **Revised Standard Version**, Amer. revision (1946–57) of the 1901 American Standard Version. **re·vis'al, re·vi·sion** (rĭvĭzh'on) *ns.* **re·vi'sion·ism** *n.* Departure from authoritative (esp. Marxist) doctrine. **re·vi'sion·ist** *n.* **re·vi'sion·al, re·vi·so·ry** (rĭvī'zerē) *adjs.* **re·vis'er, re·vi'sor** *ns.*

re·viv·al (rĭvī'val) *n.* 1. Bringing or coming back into vogue, use, etc.; restoring of old play etc. to stage etc.; **R~ of Learning, Letters**, the Renaissance in its literary aspect. 2. Reawakening of religious fervor; campaign, meeting, etc., to promote this. 3. Restoration to bodily or mental vigor or to life or consciousness. **re·viv'a·lism** *n.* State or kind of religion characterized by revivals. **re·viv'al·ist** *n.*

re·vive (rĭvīv') *v.* (**-vived, -viv·ing**). Come or bring back to life, consciousness, existence, vigor, notice, activity, validity, or vogue. **re·viv'er** *n.*

re·viv·i·fy (rĭvĭv'ĭfī) *v.t.* (**-fied, -fy·ing**). Restore to animation, activity, vigor, or life. **re·viv·i·fi·ca·tion** (rĭvĭvĭfĭkā'shon) *n.*

re·voke (rĭvōk') *v.* (**-voked, -vok·ing**). 1. Repeal, annul, withdraw, rescind, cancel (decree, consent, promise, permission). 2. (bridge etc.) Make a revoke. ~ *n.* (bridge, etc.) Failure to follow suit when able to do so. **rev·o·ca·ble** (rĕv'okabel), **re·vok·a·ble** (rĭvō'kabel), **rev·o·ca·to·ry** (rĕv'okatōrē, -tōrē) *adjs.* **rev·o·ca·tion** (rĕvokā'shon) *n.*

re·volt (rĭvōlt') *v.* 1. Cast off allegiance; make, take part in rebellion; fall away *from* or rise *against* ruler. 2. Feel revulsion or disgust *at*, rise in repugnance against, turn in loathing *from*; affect with strong disgust, nauseate. **re·volt′ing** *adj.* **re·volt′ing·ly** *adv.* **revolt** *n.* 1. Act of revolting, state of having revolted; uprising, insurrection. 2. Sense of loathing; rebellious or protesting mood.

rev·o·lu·tion (rĕvolōō′sh*o*n) *n.* 1. Revolving; motion in orbit or circular course, or around axis or center; rotation; single completion of orbit or rotation, time it takes. 2. Complete change, turning upside down, great reversal of conditions, fundamental reconstruction; esp. forcible substitution by subjects of new ruler or polity for the old; **American R~**: see AMERICAN; **English Revolution**, expulsion (1688) of Stuart dynasty under James II and transfer of sovereignty to William and Mary; **French Revolution**: see FRENCH; **Russian Revolution**, series of revolutionary movements in Russia in 1917, beginning with a revolt of workers, peasants, and soldiers in March (February Old Style, hence **February Revolution**) and formation of a provisional government, and culminating in the **Bolshevik Revolution** in November (October Old Style, hence **October Revolution**), which led to the establishment of the U.S.S.R. **rev·o·lu′tion·ize** *v.t.* (**-ized, -iz·ing**).

rev·o·lu·tion·ar·y (rĕvolōō′sh*o*nĕrē) *adj.* Of revolution; involving great and usu. violent changes; **R~**, of or pertaining to the period of the American Revolution. **revolutionary** *n.* (pl. **-ar·ies**). One who instigates or favors political revolution; one who takes part in a revolution.

rev·o·lu·tion·ist (rĕvolōō′sh*o*nĭst) *n.* Revolutionary.

re·volve (rĭvŏlv′) *v.* (**-volved, -volv·ing**). Turn around (and around); rotate; go in circular orbit; roll along. **re·volv′a·ble** *adj.*

re·volv·er (rĭvŏl′v*er*) *n.* (esp.) Handgun with mechanism by which set of cartridge chambers is revolved and presented in succession before hammer, so that several shots may be fired without reloading.

re·vue (rĭvū′) *n.* Theatrical entertainment reviewing (often satirically) current fashions, events, etc.; (freq.) entertainment consisting of numerous unrelated scenes or episodes.

re·vul·sion (rĭvŭl′sh*o*n) *n.* 1. Sudden violent change of feeling, esp. to disgust or loathing; sudden reaction in taste, fortune, etc. 2. (rare) Drawing or being drawn away. **re·vul′sive** *adj.*

re·ward (rĭwōrd′) *n.* Return or recompense for service or merit, requital for good or evil; sum offered for detection of criminal, restoration of lost property, etc. ~ *v.t.* Repay, requite, recompense; give a reward; give pleasure or satisfaction.

re·word (rēwĕrd′) *v.* Change wording of.

re·write (rērīt′) *v.* (**-wrote, -writ·ten**). Write again or differently. ~ (rē′rīt) *n.* Rewriting; thing rewritten; ~ **man**, journalist whose job is to put material submitted by reporter into publishable form.

rex (rĕks) *n.* (also **R~**) (abbrev. R.) Reigning king (cf. REGINA).

Rey·kja·vik (rā′ky*a*vēk). Capital city of Iceland, in the SW. on Faxa Bay.

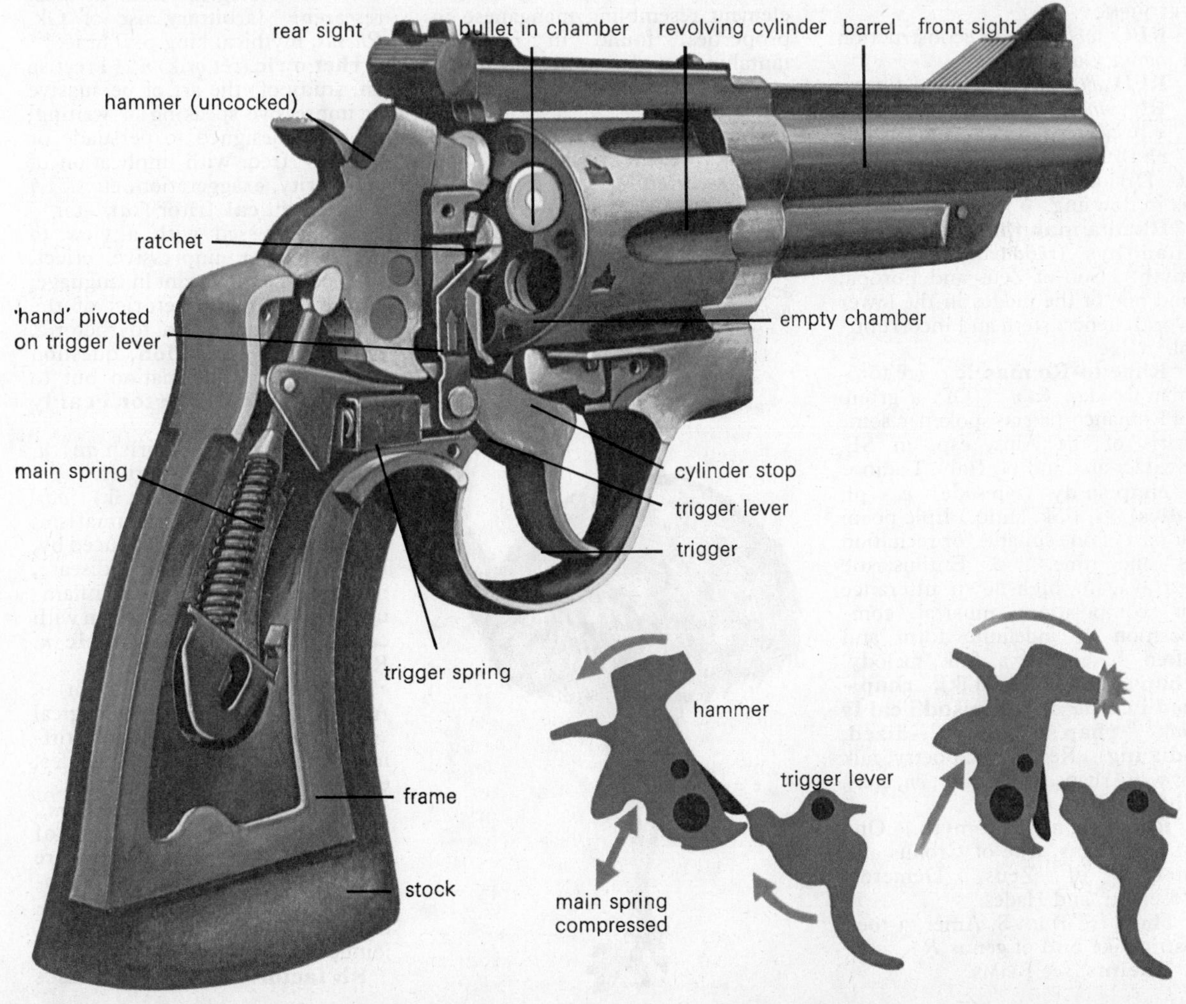

When the trigger of a double-action ***revolver*** *is squeezed, it performs several functions. It cocks the hammer, rotates and locks the cylinder, and releases the hammer to fire the cartridge. The prototype was invented in 1855: only effective at short range.*

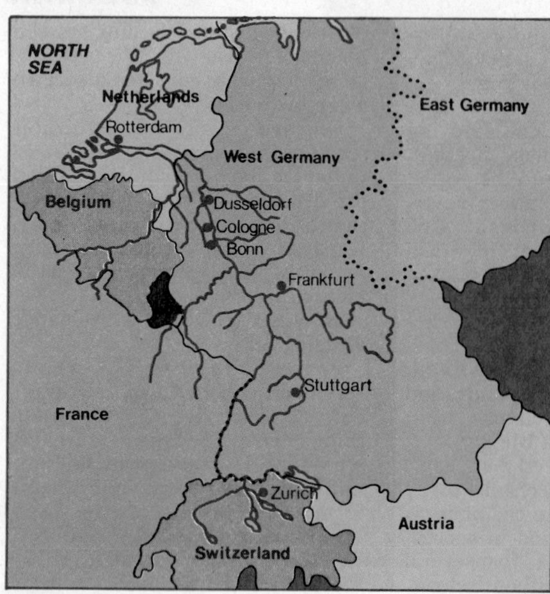

*The river **Rhine** has been a major north European trade route for many centuries. It still provides vital access for fleets of cargo ships which bring raw materials and leave with export goods.*

*Above right: The nave of the cathedral at **Rheims,** a Gothic building which was begun in A.D. 1211. From the fifth century, French rulers were crowned in this city.*

*'The Countess of Pembroke and her son' as portrayed by English painter **Sir Joshua Reynolds** (facing). In 1768 he was made President of the newly-formed Royal Academy.*

Reyn·olds (rĕn′oldz), **Sir Joshua** (1723–92). English portrait painter.

r.f., R.F. *abbrevs.* Radio FREQUENCY.

RFC *abbrev.* Reconstruction Finance Corporation.

RFD *abbrev.* Rural free delivery.

Rh *symbol.* Rhodium.

r.h. *abbrev.* Right hand.

rhab·do·man·cy (răb′domănsē) *n.* Divination by means of a rod, as in dowsing.

Rhad·a·man·thus, Rhad·a·man·thys (rădamăn′thus). (Gk. myth.) Son of Zeus and Europa, and one of the judges in the lower world; hence, stern and incorruptible judge.

Rhae·to-Ro·man·ic (rē′tōrōmăn′ĭk) *adj.* & *n.* (Of) a group of Romance dialects spoken in some parts of the Alps, esp. in SE. Switzerland and N. Italy; Ladino.

rhap·so·dy (răp′sodē) *n.* (pl. **-dies**). 1. (Gk. antiq.) Epic poem or part of one suitable for recitation at one time. 2. Enthusiastic extravagant high-flown utterance or composition; musical composition of indefinite form and often based on a folk melody. **rhap·sod·ic** (răpsŏd′ĭk), **rhap·sod′i·cal** *adjs.* **rhap·sod′i·cal·ly** *adv.* **rhap′so·dize** *v.* (**-dized, -diz·ing**). Recite epic poetry; talk or write rhapsodies (*about, on,* etc.). **rhap′so·dist** *n.*

Rhe·a (rē′*a*). (Gk. myth.) One of the Titans, wife of Cronus and mother of Zeus, Demeter, Poseidon, and Hades.

rhe·a (rē′*a*) *n.* S. Amer. 3-toed ostrichlike bird of genus *R*∼.

Rheims: see REIMS.

Rhen·ish (rĕn′ĭsh) *adj.* Of the Rhine or neighboring regions.

rhe·ni·um (rē′nēum) *n.* (chem.) Rare, very hard, very heavy metallic element resembling manganese in properties, found in ores of tantalum and platinum; symbol Re, at. no. 75, at. wt. 186.2. [L. *Rhenus* Rhine]

rhe·o·stat (rē′ostăt) *n.* Device for varying the resistance to an electric current.

*Related to the ostrich but found only in South America, the **rhea** lives on plants and insects. One male is usually accompanied by 6–8 females, and he helps them make their nests.*

rhe·sus (rē′*sus*) *n.* Small catarrhine monkey (*Macaca mulatta*) common in N. India and widely used in biological and medical research. [arbitrary use of Gk. *Rhesus*, mythical king of Thrace]

rhet·o·ric (rĕt′orĭk) *n.* (Treatise on, study of) the art of persuasive or impressive speaking or writing; language designed to persuade or impress (freq. with implication of insincerity, exaggeration, etc.).

rhe·tor·i·cal (rĭtŏr′ĭkal, -tăr′-) *adj.* Expressed with a view to persuasive or impressive effect; artificial or extravagant in language; of the nature of rhetoric; of the art of rhetoric; given to rhetoric, oratorical; ∼ **question**, question asked not for information but to produce effect. **rhe·tor′i·cal·ly** *adv.*

rhet·o·ri·cian (rĕtorĭsh′an) *n.* Rhetorical speaker or writer.

rheu·mat·ic (ro͞omăt′ĭk) *adj.* Of, suffering from, rheumatism; subject to, producing, produced by, this; ∼ **fever**, acute febrile disease, mainly in children, with inflammation and pain of joints, often with cardiac damage. **rheumatic** *n.* Rheumatic patient.

rheu·ma·tism (ro͞o′matĭzem) *n.* Any of several pathological conditions involving pain and stiffness in joints, tendons, muscles, etc.; (pop.) rheumatoid arthritis.

rheu·ma·toid (ro͞o′matoid) *adj.* Having the character of rheumatism; ∼ **arthritis**, severe chronic progressive disease of uncertain origin, leading to inflammatory changes in the tissues, esp. joints.

Rh factor. (referring to RHESUS

monkey in whose blood the antigen was first discovered) ~ **factor**, inheritable antigen usu. present in human red blood cells, capable of causing a serious reaction in person who lacks them; **Rh positive, Rh negative**, having, not having, the Rh factor; **Rh baby**, infant with hemolytic disorder from its blood being Rh positive and its mother's being Rh negative.

rhi·nal (rī′n*a*l) *adj.* (anat. etc.) Of nostril or nose.

Rhine (rīn). (Ger. *Rhein*) Great European river, rising in Switzerland and flowing northward through West Germany and the Netherlands to North Sea; ~ **wine**, wine produced in valley of Rhine, usu. white, light, and dry. **Rhine·land** (rīn′lănd, -l*a*nd), valley of the Rhine.

rhine·stone (rīn′stōn) *n.* Artificial gem of paste or glass cut like diamond. [f. RHINE]

rhi·ni·tis (rīnī′tĭs) *n.* Inflammation of (mucous membrane of) nose.

rhi·no (rī′nō) *n.* (pl. **-nos**, collect. **-no**). (colloq.) Rhinoceros.

rhi·noc·er·os (rīnŏs′*e*r*o*s) *n.* (pl. **-os·es**, collect. **-os**). Large mammal of Africa and S. Asia, usu. with a horn on nose (or, in some species, two) and very thick freq. folded skin.

rhi·nol·o·gy (rīnŏl′*o*jē) *n.* Branch of medicine dealing with diseases of the nose.

rhi·no·scope (rī′n*o*skōp) *n.* Instrument for inspecting nasal cavity. **rhi·nos·co·py** (rīnŏs′k*o*pē) *n.* Examination of nasal cavity with rhinoscope.

rhi·zoid (rī′zoid) *adj.* (bot.) Resembling a root. ~ *n.* Root hair or filament.

rhi·zome (rī′zōm) *n.* Horizontal rootlike stem growing along or under the ground and emitting roots from the lower side and sending up leafy shoots from the upper surface. **rhi·zom·a·tous** (rīzŏm′*a*t*u*s) *adj.*

rho (rō) *n.* (pl. **rhos**). Twentieth (later 17th) letter of Greek alphabet (*P*, *ρ*), corresponding to *r*.

Although the ***black rhinoceros*** *of Africa is still plentiful, the other species of rhinoceros are all endangered. Estimates of numbers are 25 in Java, 100 in Sumatra and 400 in India.*

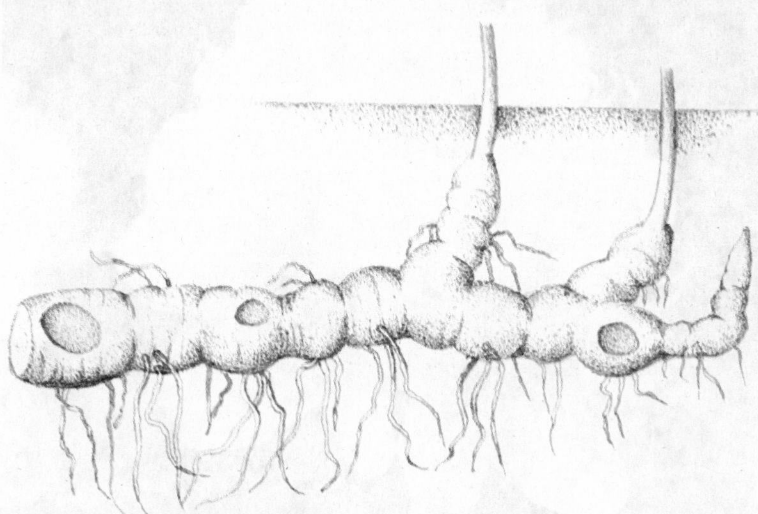

A *rhizome* is an underground stem and serves as food storage to allow leaves to grow to a stage where they can obtain nourishment from the sun. It also has rootlets to obtain food from the soil.

Rhode (rōd) **Island.** S. New England state, smallest of the U.S., one of the original 13 (1790); capital, Providence; ~ ~ **Red**, (one of) an Amer. breed of domestic fowls with brownish-red plumage.

Rhodes[1] (rōdz). (Gk. *Rhodos*) Most easterly island of Aegean Sea, SW. of Turkey, largest of the Dodecanese, acquired by Italy 1912 and restored to Greece 1946; its principal city and harbor.

Rhodes[2] (rōdz), **Cecil John** (1853–1902). English imperialist, largely instrumental in extending Brit. territory in S. Africa and in development of Rhodesia; **Rhodes scholarship**, one of the scholarships endowed at Oxford University under will of Cecil Rhodes, for students from the principal Brit. colonies and dominions and from every state and territory of the U.S.; hence **Rhodes scholar**.

Rho·de·sia (rōdē'zh*a*, -zē*a*, -sh*a*). Former name of ZIMBABWE. **Rho·de'sian** *adj.* & *n.* [named after Cecil RHODES[2]]

rho·di·um (rō'dē*u*m) *n.* (chem.)

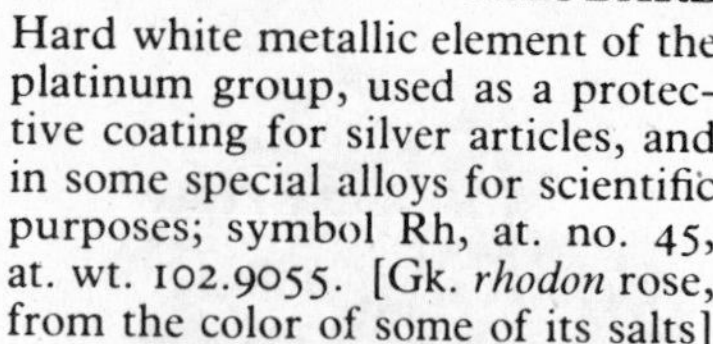

Hard white metallic element of the platinum group, used as a protective coating for silver articles, and in some special alloys for scientific purposes; symbol Rh, at. no. 45, at. wt. 102.9055. [Gk. *rhodon* rose, from the color of some of its salts]

rho·do·den·dron (rōd*o*děn'dr*o*n) *n.* Evergreen shrub or low tree with large flowers of genus *R*~, which includes azaleas. [Gk. *rhodon* rose, *dendron* tree]

rhomb (rŏm, rŏmb) = RHOMBUS.

rhom·bic (rŏm'bĭk) *adj.* Rhombus-shaped.

rhom·bo·he·dron (rŏmb*o*hē'dr*o*n) *n.* (pl. **-drons, -dra** pr. -dr*a*). (Crystal in shape of) solid bounded by 6 equal rhombuses. **rhom·bo·he'dral** *adj.*

rhom·boid (rŏm'boid) *adj.* Of or near the shape of a rhombus. ~ *n.* Quadrilateral figure having its opposite sides and angles equal. **rhom·boi·dal** (rŏmboi'd*a*l) *adj.*

rhom·bus (rŏm'b*u*s) *n.* (pl. **-bus·es, -bi** pr. -bī). Plane equilateral figure with opposite angles equal, two being acute and two obtuse.

Rhône, Rhone (rōn). River rising in Switzerland and flowing 505 mi. (808 km) W. through Lake of Geneva into France and then southward to Mediterranean.

rhu·barb (ro͞o'bārb) *n.* 1. (Purgative made from) root of Chinese and Tibetan species of the herb *Rheum*, orig. imported into

Cecil Rhodes made a fortune from diamond mining and his ambition was that all of southern Africa should be united as a single British federation. He left money for Rhodes scholarships.

Victoria Falls, on the Zambesi River, probably represents the best-known geographical attraction in Zimbabwe, formerly **Rhodesia**. The Falls were discovered in 1855 by David Livingstone.

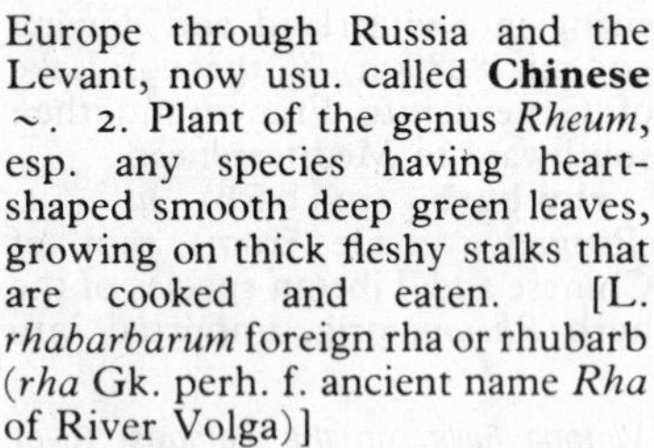

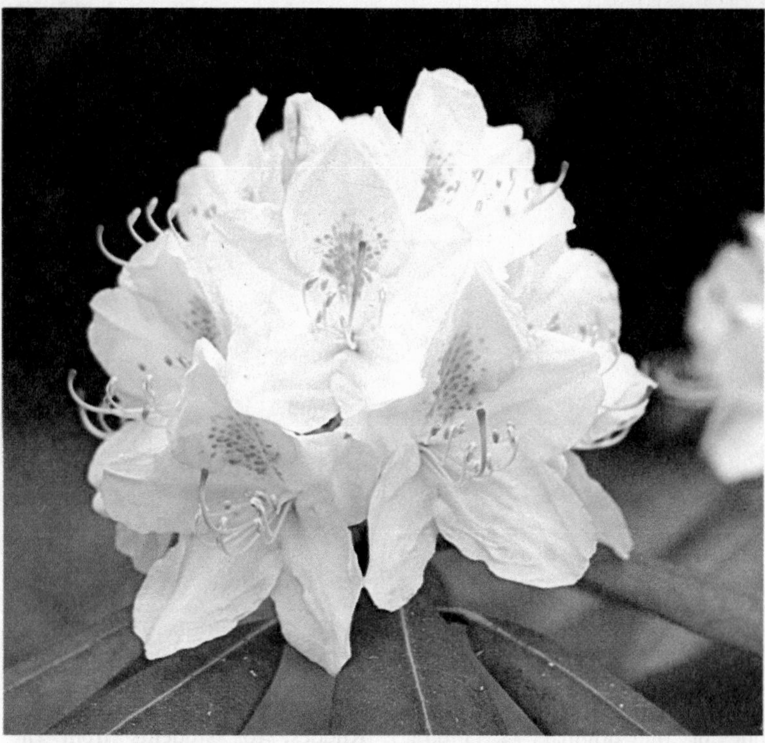

*The **rhododendron** probably originated in Asia although the first plants were taken to England in 1629. While some grow into small trees, others remain as shrubs.*

Europe through Russia and the Levant, now usu. called **Chinese** ~. 2. Plant of the genus *Rheum*, esp. any species having heart-shaped smooth deep green leaves, growing on thick fleshy stalks that are cooked and eaten. [L. *rhabarbarum* foreign rha or rhubarb (*rha* Gk. perh. f. ancient name *Rha* of River Volga)]

rhumb (rŭm) *n.* Any of the 32 points of the compass; (also ~ **line**) line on the surface of a sphere that makes equal oblique angles with all meridians, indicating the course of an object moving always in the same compass direction.

rhyme (rīm) *n.* Agreement in terminal sounds of two or more words or metrical lines, such that (in English prosody) the last stressed vowel and any sounds following it are the same, while the preceding sounds are different (examples: *which, rich*; *peace, increase*; *decended, extended*); verse marked by rhymes; poem with rhymes; employment of rhyme; word providing a rhyme (*with* another); **feminine, masculine** ~: see FEMININE, MASCULINE; **rhyme royal**, stanzas of seven ten-syllable lines, rhyming *a b a b b c c*; **nursery rhyme**: see NURSERY; **neither rhyme nor reason**, nothing reasonable. **rhyme** *v.* (**rhymed, rhym·ing**). Write rhymes, versify; put or make (story etc.) into rhyme; (of words or lines) terminate in sounds that form a rhyme, form a rhyme *with*; use (words) as rhymes; **rhyming dictionary**, book in which words are arranged in groups according to the sound of their last syllable or syllables; **rhyming slang**, vocabulary (esp. in Cockney use) dating from early 19th c., of rhyming substitutions for certain words, e.g. *apples and pears* = *stairs*.

rhy·o·lite (rī′olīt) *n.* Fine-grained volcanic rock.

rhythm (rĭdh′em) *n.* Metrical movement determined by relation of long and short, or stressed and unstressed, syllables in foot or line; measured flow of words and phrases in verse or prose; (mus.) systematic grouping of notes, beats, measures, and phrases, giving an effect of forward movement; (art etc.) harmonious correlation of parts, movement with regulated succession of strong and weak elements or of opposite or different conditions; ~ **method**, method of contraception by avoidance of sexual intercourse as time of ovulation recurs. **rhyth·mic** (rĭdh′mĭk), **rhyth′mi·cal** *adjs.* **rhyth′mi·cal·ly** *adv.*

rhythm-and-blues (rĭdh′em-an-bloōz′) *n.* Form of black music marked by blues themes and strong rhythm.

RI, R.I. *abbrevs.* Rhode Island.

ri·a·ta, re·a·ta (rēah′ta) *ns.* LARIAT.

rib (rĭb) *n.* 1. One of the curved bones articulated in pairs to spine and enclosing and protecting thoracic cavity and its organs; one of these bones from animal carcass, with the meat adhering to it, as food. 2. Denser, firmer, or stronger part extending along or through organ or structure; any shaping or supporting part similar to a rib; central vein of leaf, shaft or quill of feather; one of ship's curved timbers to which planks are nailed, or corresponding ironwork; arch supporting vault, groin, raised molding on groin or across ceiling etc.; hinged rod of umbrella frame; combination of plain and purl stitches in knitting, producing a riblike fabric with a certain elasticity. ~ *v.* (**ribbed, rib·bing**). Provide with ribs, act as ribs of; mark with ridges; knit in rib stitch; (colloq.) make fun of, tease.

rib·ald (rĭb′ald) *adj.* Scurrilous, irreverent; vulgar, lewd (esp. of humor). ~ *n.* Ribald person. **rib′ald·ry** *n.*

rib·bon (rĭb′on) *n.* (Piece or length of) silk, satin, or other fine material woven into narrow band, esp. for adorning costume; ribbon of special color etc. worn to indicate membership in knightly order, possession of medal, order, or other distinction or membership; long narrow strip of anything, ribbonlike object or mark; **blue** ~: see BLUE; **rib′bonfish** (pl. **-fishes**, collect. **-fish**), any of several marine fishes, mainly of the genus *Trachipterus*, having long, slender, flattened bodies.

ri·bo·fla·vin (rībofla′vĭn, rī′-boflā-) *n.* Factor of vitamin B complex required for growth, found in milk, egg yolks, fresh meat, leafy vegetables, etc., or made synthetically.

Although its stems are edible, the leaves of **rhubarb** contain oxalic acid which is poisonous. The best stalks for eating are grown by 'forcing' beneath an opaque cover.

Bo Sang umbrella village in Thailand. The **ribs** of the umbrellas are covered with durable material. Below: The nave of Exeter Cathedral in Devon, England. Note the **rib-like** fan vaulting.

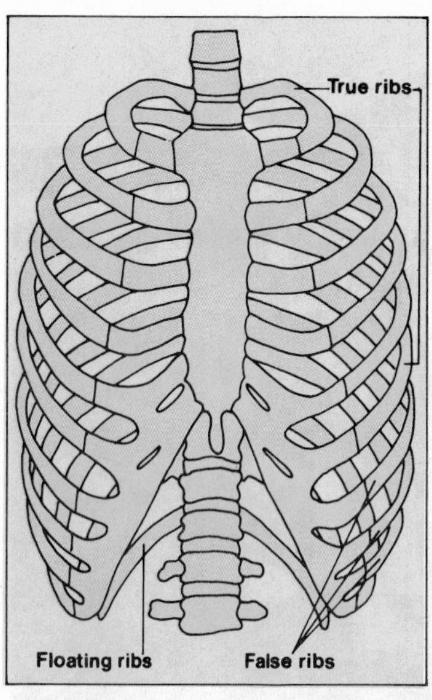

The human **rib cage** consists of 24 rounded bones which form a wall for the thorax. They protect the lungs and are capable of providing substantial resistance to pressure.

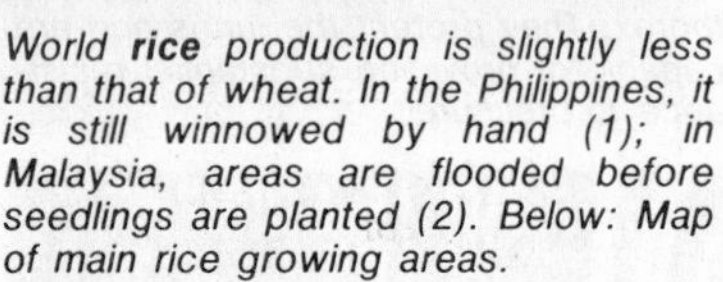
*World **rice** production is slightly less than that of wheat. In the Philippines, it is still winnowed by hand (1); in Malaysia, areas are flooded before seedlings are planted (2). Below: Map of main rice growing areas.*

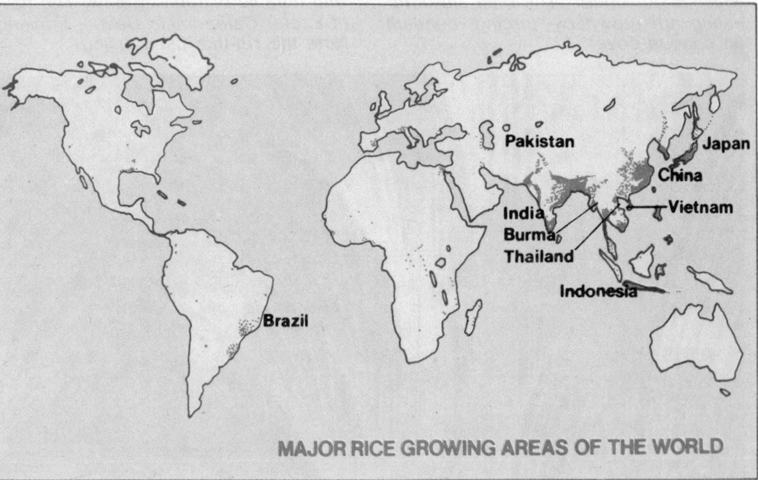

ri·bo·nu·cle·ic (rībōnōōklē´ĭk, -nū-) **acid**: see RNA.

Ri·car·do (rĭkar´dō), **David** (1772–1823). English political economist of the free trade school, author of *Principles of Political Economy and Taxation*. **Ri·car·di·an** (rĭkar´dēan) *adj.*

rice (rīs) *n.* Seeds (usu. pearl white), used as staple food and in puddings etc., of an annual cereal grass (*Oryza sativa*) cultivated in marshy or easily flooded ground in warm climates; this plant; **rice´-bird**, (esp.) bobolink; **rice paper**, thin paper made from rice straw; Chinese painting paper (so named in error) made from pith of tree *Tetrapanax papyriferum*; edible paper used in baking; **rice pudding**, baked pudding of sweetened milk and rice. **rice** *v.* (**riced, ric·ing**). Pass (cooked potatoes etc.) through device to form thin strings. **ric´er** *n.*

rich (rĭch) *adj.* 1. Wealthy, having riches; abounding in or *in* natural resources or some valuable possession or production, fertile; abundant, ample. 2. Valuable; splendid, costly, elaborate. 3. (of food) Containing a large proportion of fat; (of cake etc.) containing a large proportion of fat, eggs, fruit, etc. 4. (of colors, sounds, etc.) Mellow, deep, full, not thin. 5. (colloq.) Highly amusing. **rich´ness** *n.*

Rich·ard (rĭch´*e*rd). Name of three kings of England: **Richard I** (1157–99), "Coeur de Lion" or "the Lion-Heart," reigned 1189–1199, third son of Henry II; a leader in the third Crusade, on his return from which he was captured and held for ransom by Leopold of Austria; **Richard II** (1367–1400), reigned 1377–99, son of the Black Prince, deposed and imprisoned by Henry IV; **Richard III** (1452–85), reigned 1483–5, last king of House of York; younger brother of Edward IV; defeated and killed at Bosworth Field in the final battle of the Wars of the Roses.

Rich·ard·son (rĭch´*e*rds*o*n), **Samuel** (1689–1761). English novelist, author of *Pamela*, *Clarissa Harlowe*, etc.

Ri·che·lieu (rĭsh´*e*lōō; *Fr.* rēshelyö´), **Armand Jean du Plessis, Duc de** (1585–1642). French cardinal and statesman; chief minister of Louis XIII, under whom he had virtually dictatorial powers, 1624–42.

rich·es (rĭch´ĭz) *n.pl.* Wealth; valuable possessions.

rich·ly (rĭch´lē) *adv.* In rich manner; amply, fully, thoroughly.

Rich·mond (rĭch´m*o*nd). Capital and largest city of Virginia, on the James River in the E. central part; capital of the Confederacy during the Civil War.

Rich·ter (rĭk´t*e*r) **scale.** Logarithmic scale, having steps graded from 1 to 10, for measuring earthquake intensity.

rick (rĭk) *n.* Stack of hay, straw, etc., esp. one regularly built and thatched or covered for protection from the weather. ~ *v.t.* Form into rick(s).

rick·ets (rĭk´ĭts) *n.* Disease, chiefly of children, marked by softening of the bones and consequent distortion (bowlegs, curvature of spine, etc.), resulting from a deficiency of vitamin D or lack of exposure to sunlight.

rick·ett·si·a (rĭkĕt´sē*a*) *n.* (pl. **-si·ae** pr. -sēē, **-si·as**). One of a group of microorganisms of genus *R*~, apparently intermediate

Left: ***Richard II*** *ascended the British throne at the age of 10 and was probably murdered in 1400. In contrast* ***Richard III*** *(right) only attained the crown after other claimants had been killed.*

between bacteria and viruses, carried as parasites by fleas, lice, and ticks and causing typhus, Rocky Mountain spotted fever, etc. in man. **rick·ett'si·al** *adj.* [Howard T. *Ricketts*, Amer. pathologist]

rick·et·y (rĭk'ĭtē) *adj.* Of (the nature of), suffering from, rickets; shaky, insecure. **rick'et·i·ness** *n.*

rick·ey (rĭk'ē) *n.* Drink of carbonated water, lime juice, and usu. gin.

rick·rack (rĭk'răk) *n.* Zigzag braid trimming for garments.

rick·shaw, rick·sha (rĭk'shaw) = JINRICKSHA.

ric·o·chet (rĭkoshā', rĭk'oshā) *n.* Rebounding of projectile or other object from an object that it strikes, hit made after this. ~ *v.t.* (**-cheted, -chet·ing**). (of projectile) Glance or skip with rebound(s).

ri·cot·ta (rĭkŏt'*a*, -kaw'ta) *n.* Italian cottage cheese.

ric·tus (rĭk'tus) *n.* (pl. **-tus, -tus·es**). (anat., zool.) Gape of mouth or beak.

rid (rĭd) *v.t.* (**rid** or **rid·ded, rid·ding**). Make free, disencumber, *of* (often in past part. with *be* or *get*, as *get* ~ *of him*). **rid·dance** (rĭd'*a*ns) *n.* (esp. in **good ~!** as exclamation of joy). **rid'der** *n.*

rid·den: see RIDE.

rid·dle[1] (rĭd'*e*l) *n.* Question, statement, etc. designed or serving to test ingenuity of hearers in divining its answer, meaning, or reference; conundrum, enigma; puzzling or mysterious fact, thing, or person. ~ *v.* (**-dled, -dling**). Speak in, propound, riddles; solve (riddle).

rid·dle[2] (rĭd'*e*l) *n.* Coarse sieve for gravel etc. ~ *v.t.* (**-dled, -dling**). 1. Pass (gravel etc.) through riddle, sift. 2. Fill, pierce (ship, person, etc.) with holes esp. of gunshot; (fig.) refute (person, theory) with facts.

ride (rīd) *v.* (**rode** pr. rōd, **rid·den** pr. rĭd'*e*n, **rid·ing**). 1. Sit on and be carried by horse etc.; go on horseback etc. or on bicycle etc. or in automobile, train, or other vehicle; sit, go, be *on* something as on horse; sit on and manage horse; (of boat etc.) lie at anchor; float buoyantly; ~ **for a fall**, ride, (fig.) act, recklessly; ~ **down**, overtake on horseback in automobile, etc., allow one's mount to trample on (person); ~ **high**, (fig.) be successful; ~ **out the storm**, (of ship, and fig.) come safely through it; ~ **roughshod**: see ROUGH; ~ **to hounds**, go fox hunting; ~ **up**, (of garment) work upward during wear. 2. Traverse on horseback etc., ride over or through. 3. Dominate, tyrannize over; (colloq.) ridicule, annoy. 4. Give ride to, cause to ride. **ride** *n.* Journey in vehicle; spell of riding on horse, bicycle, person's back, etc.; **take for a** ~, (slang) kidnap and murder; make a fool of.

rid·er (rī'd*e*r) *n.* (esp.) 1. Additional clause amending or supplementing document. 2. One,

As minister of State to Louis XIII, ***Cardinal Richelieu*** *became one of the most powerful men in Europe. With almost dictatorial power, he suppressed Spanish influence and made France the dominant nation.*

*The mechanism of a Browning automatic **rifle** is operated by gases remaining after a bullet is fired. This system developed from such guns as the Spencer carbine. By depressing the lever, the spent cartridge was ejected and another was thrust into the breech.*

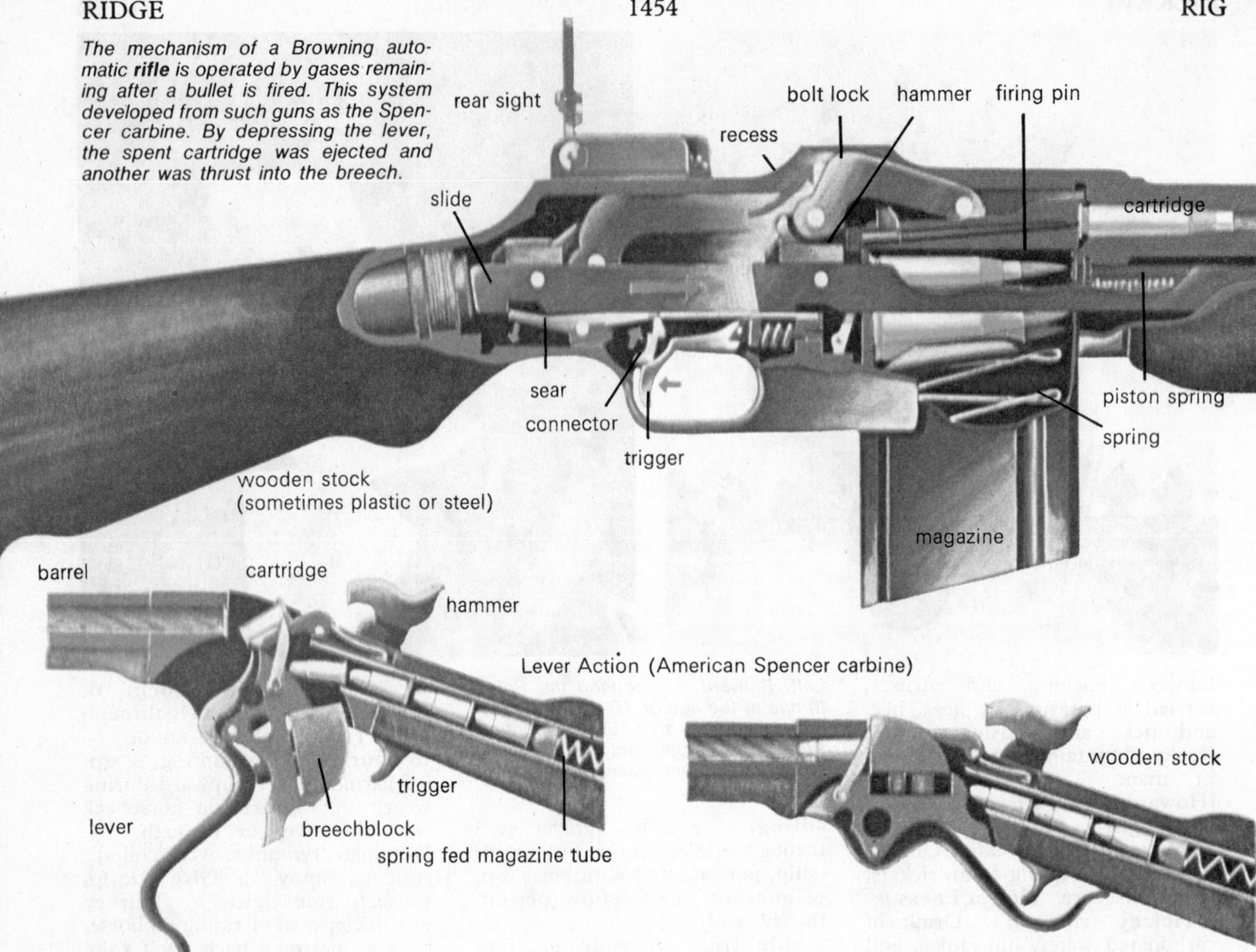

who rides. **rid'er·less** *adj.*

ridge (rĭj) *n.* Line of junction of two upward sloping surfaces; any narrow elevation across surface; long narrow hilltop, mountain range, watershed; (agriculture) one of a set of raised strips separated by furrows; (meteor.) elongated region of higher barometric pressure between two of lower; **ridge'-pole**, horizontal pole of long tent; horizontal beam at ridge of a roof. **ridge** *v.* (**ridged, ridg·ing**). Mark with, form (into) ridges. **ridg'y** *adj.* (**ridg·i·er, ridg·i·est**).

rid·i·cule (rĭd'ĭkūl) *n.* Holding or being held up as object of contemptuous laughter. ~ *v.t.* (**-culed, -cul·ing**). Treat with ridicule.

ri·dic·u·lous (rĭdĭk'yulus) *adj.* Deserving to be laughed at, absurd, unreasonable. **ri·dic'u·lous·ly** *adv.* **ri·dic'u·lous·ness** *n.*

Rie·mann (rē'man; *Ger.* rē'mahn), **Georg Friedrich Bernhard** (1826–66). German mathematician, originator of a non-Euclidean system of geometry, **Riemann geometry**, based on the postulate that there are no completely parallel lines.

Ri·en·zi (rēĕn'zē), **Ri·en·zo** (rēĕn'zō), **Co·la di** (kaw'lah dē) (*c*1313–54). Tribune of the people at Rome; led rebellion against nobles and established a republic (1347), but was excommunicated, exiled, and, after returning to Rome, assassinated.

Ries·ling (rēz'lĭng, rēs'-) *n.* (Dry white wine made from) European variety of grape.

Rif[1], **Riff**[1] (rĭf), **Er** (ĕr). Mountain system of Mediterranean coast of Morocco.

rife (rīf) *pred. adj.* Of common occurrence, met with in numbers or quantities, prevailing, current, numerous; well provided *with.* **rife'ness** *n.*

Riff[2], **Rif**[2] (rĭf) *ns.* (pl. **Riffs, Riff·i** pr. rĭf'ē, collect. **Riff**). Member of a Berber people living in Rif area of N. Morocco.

riff (rĭf) *n.* Short repeated phrase in jazz and similar music.

rif·fle (rĭf'el) *n.* 1. Shallow part of stream where water flows brokenly; patch of waves or ripples on water. 2. Process or method of riffling cards. ~ *v.* (**-fled, -fling**). Shuffle (playing cards) rapidly, esp. by flexing and combining 2 halves of pack.

riff·raff (rĭf'răf) *n.* Rabble, disreputable persons.

ri·fle (rī'fel) *v.* (**-fled, -fling**). 1. Search and rob, esp. all that can be found in various pockets or storing places; ransack; pillage. 2. Make spiral grooves in (gun barrel) to produce rotatory motion in projectile; **rifled**, having such grooves. **rifle** *n.* Firearm with rifled bore and designed to be fired from the shoulder; (pl.) troops armed with rifles; **ri'fleman** (pl. **-men**), soldier or other man armed with rifle; shooter of a rifle; **rifle range**, distance coverable by shot from rifle; place for rifle practice. **ri'fling** *n.*

rift (rĭft) *n.* Cleft, fissure, chasm, in earth or rock (freq. fig.); rent, crack, split, in an object, opening in cloud, etc.

rig[1] (rĭg) *v.* (**rigged, rig·ging**). Provide (ship), (of ship) be provided, with necessary spars, ropes, etc.; prepare for sea in this respect; fit (*out, up*) with or *with* clothes or other equipment; set *up* (structure) hastily or as makeshift or by using odd materials. ~ *n.* Way ship's masts, sails, etc., are arranged; special equipment, apparatus, etc. for a particular purpose; wagon or buggy with its horse or horses; (colloq.) outfit, costume.

rig[2] (rĭg) *v.t.* (**rigged, rig·ging**).

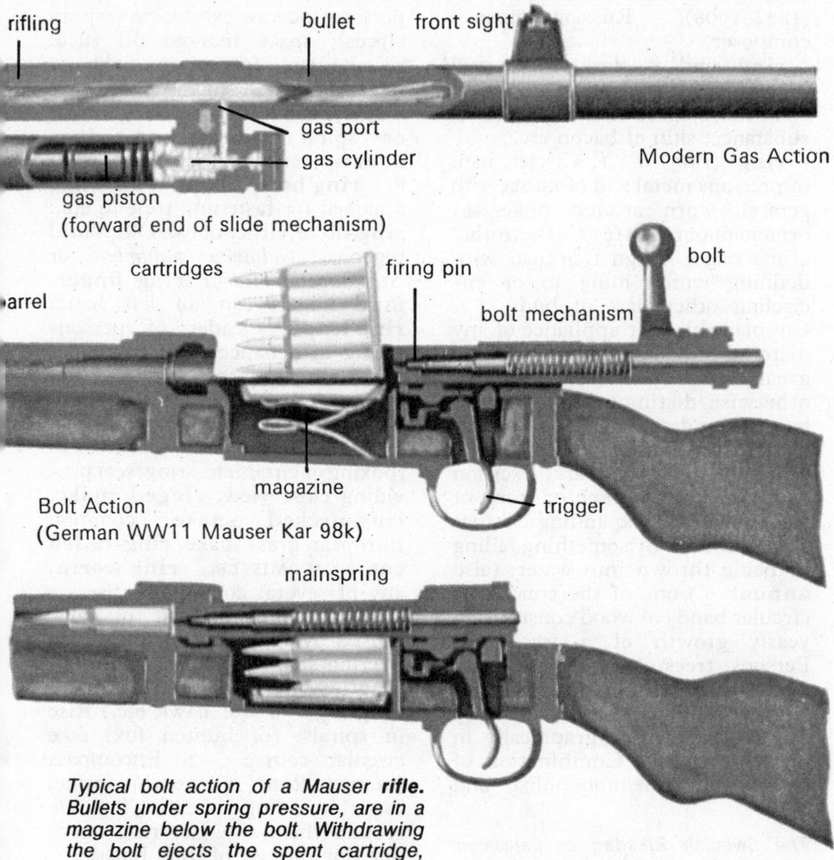

Typical bolt action of a Mauser ***rifle.*** *Bullets under spring pressure, are in a magazine below the bolt. Withdrawing the bolt ejects the spent cartridge, another rises and is thrust home by the bolt.*

Manage or conduct fraudulently.

Ri·ga (rē′ga). Seaport and capital city of the Latvian Republic of the U.S.S.R., on the Baltic Sea; **Gulf of ~**, inlet of Baltic Sea between the Latvian Republic and Estonia.

Ri·gel (rī′jel, -gel). (astron.) Very bright star of first magnitude in foot of constellation Orion.

rig·ger (rĭg′er) *n.* (esp.) Person who assembles parachutes, aircraft parts, etc.

rig·ging (rĭg′ĭng) *n.* (esp.) Ropes etc. used to support masts and work or set yards, sails, etc.

right (rīt) *adj.* 1. Straight (archaic; now only in **~ line, ~-lined**); **~ angle**: see ANGLE[1]; involving right angles, not oblique; **at ~ angles**, turning or placed with right angle; **~ ascension**, (astron.) celestial longitude; **~ cone, cylinder, prism**, etc., cone, etc., with ends or base perpendicular to axis. 2. Just, morally good, required by equity or duty, proper; (freq. in comb., as **~-minded, ~-principled**). 3. Correct, true; preferable or most suitable; in good or normal condition, sound, sane, satisfactory, well-advised, not mistaken; **get ~**, bring or come into right state; **put, set, ~**, restore to order, health, etc.; correct mistaken ideas of; **in one's ~ mind**, sane, not mad; **~ side**, side (of fabric etc.) meant for use or show; **on the ~ side of**, younger than (specified age); in person's good favor. 4. (archaic) Rightful, real, veritable, properly so called; **~ whale**: see WHALE[1]. 5. (of position) On or toward side of body toward the east when facing north; having corresponding relation to front of any object; (of bank of river etc.) on right hand of person looking downstream; **~-about**, (turn) so far to right as to face opposite way; **~ and left**, to or on both sides or all sides; **~ arm**, (fig.) most reliable helper; **~ hand**, hand on right side; region or direction on this side of person; chief or indispensable assistant; **~-hand**, placed on the right hand; **~-hand man**, chief or indispensable assistant; **~-handed**, using right hand more than left; **~ turn**, turn right into a position at right angles with original one; **~ wing**, (esp.) extreme right in politics (see **right** *n.*, sense 5). **right′ness** *n.* **right** *v.* 1. Restore to proper, straight, or vertical position; (refl.) recover one's balance, (of ship) recover vertical position. 2. Make reparation for or to, avenge (wrong, wronged person); correct (mistakes etc.), correct mistakes in, set in order. **~** *n.* 1. What is just; fair treatment; **the ~**, what is right, the cause of truth or justice; **by right**(**s**), if right were done; **in the right**, with truth or justice on one's side. 2. Justification; fair claim; being entitled to privilege or immunity; thing one is entitled to; **assert, stand on, one's rights,** refuse to relinquish them; **Declaration** or **Bill of Rights**: see BILL[3]; **divine right**: see DIVINE[2]; **right of way**, right of using path etc. over another's ground; path etc. so used; right of one traveling vehicle to take precedence over another. 3. (pl.) Right condition, true state; **set** or **put to rights**, arrange properly. 4. Right-hand part, region, or direction; (boxing) right-handed blow. 5. (sometimes **Right**) Conservative or reactionary members of legislature, those who sit on right of chamber; hence, conservative political party, group, etc. (**right′ist** *adj.* & *n.*). **right** *adv.* 1. Straight; all the way *to* etc.; completely *off*, *out*, etc.; straight away, immediately. 2. Exactly, quite. 3. Justly, properly, correctly, aright, truly, satisfactorily; **it serves him ~**, it is no worse than he deserves; **R~ Honorable, R~ Reverend**: see these words. 4. To right hand. **right** *int.* Exclamation of agreement or consent; **~ on!** (slang) exclamation of approval. **right′er** *n.*

right·eous (rī′chus) *adj.* Morally good; acting in a moral way, virtuous; morally justifiable. **right′eous·ly** *adv.* **right′eous·ness** *n.*

right·ful (rīt′ful) *adj.* Equitable, fair; legitimately entitled to position etc.; that one is entitled to. **right′ful·ly** *adv.* **right′ful·ness** *n.*

right·ly (rīt′lē) *adv.* Justly, fairly; properly, correctly, accurately; justifiably.

rig·id (rĭj′ĭd) *adj.* Not flexible, stiff, unyielding; inflexible, harsh, strict, precise. **rig′id·ly** *adv.* **ri·gid·i·ty** (rĭjĭd′ĭtē), **rig′id·ness** *ns.*

rig·ma·role (rĭg′marōl) *n.* Rambling or meaningless talk or tale; complicated procedure. [app. f. obs. *ragman roll* list, catalog]

rig·or (rĭg′er) *n.* 1. (path.) Sudden chill with shivering; **~ mortis**, stiffening of body after death. 2. Severity, strictness, harshness; (pl.) harsh measures; (sing.) strict enforcement *of* rules etc.; extremity or excess *of* weather, hardship, famine, etc., great distress; austerity of life, Puritanic strictness of observance or doctrine; logical accuracy, exactitude. **rig′-**

or·ous *adj.* **rig′or·ous·ly** *adv.*

Rig-Ve·da (rĭgvā′da, -vē′-) *n.* Oldest and most important of the Vedas (see VEDA). [Sansk.]

Riks·dag (rĭks′dahg) *n.* Parliament of Sweden.

rile (rīl) *v.t.* (**riled, ril·ing**). Raise anger in, irritate.

Ri·ley (rī′lē), **James Whitcomb** (1849–1916). Amer. poet; noted for simple, dialect poems, as "Little Orphant Annie," "When the Frost is on the Punkin," etc.

Ril·ke (rĭl′kē), **Rainer Maria** (1875–1926). Austrian lyric poet and writer of lyrical prose.

rill, rille (rĭl) *ns.* 1. Small stream, rivulet. 2. (astron.) Long narrow trench or valley on moon's surface.

rim (rĭm) *n.* Outer ring of wheel (not including tire), connected with hub by spokes etc.; edge, margin, border, esp. a raised one, etc., of more or less circular object; **rim′-rock**, outcrop with steep face. **rim** *v.t.* (**rimmed, rim·ming**). Furnish with rim, serve as rim to, edge, border. **rim′less** *adj.*

Rim·baud (rămbō′; *Fr.* rănbō′), **(Jean Nicolas) Arthur** (1854–91). French symbolist poet.

rime[1] = RHYME.

rime[2] (rīm) *n.* 1. (meteor.) Water droplets from cloud or fog that freeze on hilltops, high branches, etc., esp. in windy weather. 2. (chiefly poet.) Hoar frost. ~ *v.t.* (**rimed, rim·ing**). Cover with rime. **rim′y** *adj.* (**rim·i·er, rim·i·est**).

Rim·i·ni (rĭm′ĭnē). Port and tourist center in NE. Italy, on the Adriatic Sea.

Rim·sky-Kor·sa·kov, Rim·ski-Kor·sa·koff (rĭm′skē kōr′-sakawf), **Nikolay Andreevich** (1844–1908). Russian musical composer.

rind (rīnd) *n.* Bark of tree; peel of fruit or vegetable; harder enclosing surface of cheese or other substance; skin of bacon etc.

ring[1] (rĭng) *n.* 1. Circlet, usu. of precious metal and often set with gem(s), worn around finger as ornament or token (esp. of betrothal or marriage) or signet, or (usu. with defining word) hung to or encircling other part of body. 2. Circular object or appliance of any material and any (but esp. of no great) size. 3. Raised, sunk, or otherwise distinguishable line or band around cylindrical or circular object, rim; circular fold, coil, bend, structure, part, or mark; excision of bark around branch or trunk of tree; one of the expanding circular ripples caused by something falling or being thrown into water; (also **annual** ~) one of the concentric circular bands of wood constituting yearly growth of a tree. 4. Persons, trees, etc., disposed in a circle, such disposition; (chem.) number of atoms so united that they can be represented graphically in cyclic form. 5. Combination of traders etc. to monopolize and control a particular trade, market, or policy, or to stabilize or keep up price of goods. 6. Circular enclosure for some sport, performance, or exhibition (esp. in circus); space marked off (usu. rectangular) for prize fight or wrestling match, enclosed space for displaying livestock etc. 7. Circular or spiral course; **run rings around**, excel or surpass easily. 8. **ring′bolt**, bolt with ring attached for fastening rope to etc.; **ring′dove**, either of two Old World pigeons, *Columba palumbus* or *Streptopelia risoria*; **ring finger**, third finger, esp. of left hand; **ring′leader**, leader of persons acting in defiance of law or rules etc.; **ring′master**, manager of circus performance; **ring-necked**, with band(s) of color around neck; **ring′side (seat)**, area, seat close to (boxing or circus etc.) ring; seat providing close view; **ringed snake, ring-necked snake**, common European grass snake; **ring-tailed cat** = CACOMISTLE; **ring′worm**, any of several contagious diseases (*tinea*) of the skin, hair, or nails, caused by fungi and characterized by ring-shaped patches. **ringed, ring′less** *adjs.* **ring** *v.* (**ringed, ring·ing**). 1. (of hawk etc.) Rise in spirals; (of hunted fox) take circular course. 2. Encompass (*around, about, in*); hem in (game, cattle) by riding or beating in circle around them. 3. Put ring upon; put ring in nose of (pig, bull).

*The Swedish **Riksdag** or parliament meets in this late 19th-century building on Helgeandsholmen, in the northern district of old Stockholm, a city containing buildings of many periods.*

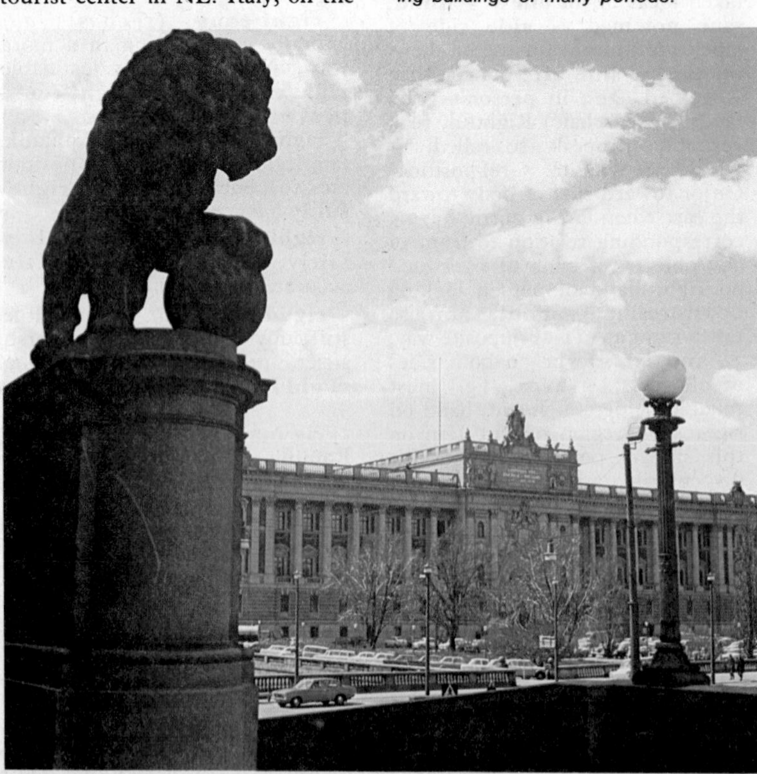

ring[2] (rĭng) *v.* (**rang** pr. răng, **rung** pr. rŭng, **ring·ing**). 1. Give out clear resonant sound (as) of vibrating metal; (of bell) convey summons by ringing; (of place) resound, reecho (*with*); (of utterance or other sound) linger *in* one's ears, memory, etc.; (of ears) be filled with sensation as of bell ringing; ~ **true, false** (of coin tested by throwing on counter, and fig. of sentiments, etc.) sound, genuine, counterfeit. 2. Make (bell) ring; ring bell as summons; sound (peal, knell, etc.) on bell(s); announce (hour etc.) by sound of bell(s); usher *in, out*, with bell ringing; **ring back**, (chiefly Brit.) call back; **ring off**, (chiefly Brit.) terminate telephone call; **ring up**, register sale on cash register; (chiefly Brit.) make telephone call to; **ring the bell**, (colloq.) achieve complete success; strike a sympathetic or responsive note; **ring the changes**: see CHANGE; **ring the curtain up** or **down**, (in theater) direct it by bell to be raised or lowered; (fig.) begin, end. **ring** *n.* Set *of* (church) bells; ringing sound; ringing tone in voice etc.; resonance of coin or vessel; act of ringing bell, sound so produced; (colloq.) call on the telephone.

ring·er (rĭng′*er*) *n.* 1. Horseshoe

Left: *Open air ice-skating* ***rink*** *in Central Park, New York. A form of skates was made about 1,500 years ago. Others were used by Dutch soldiers during a battle in 1572.*

Rising in Colorado and flowing south to Mexico, the ***Rio Grande*** *has been dammed in various places to provide water for irrigation. This gorge (above) is near Taos in New Mexico.*

or quoit thrown so it encircles the peg. 2. Bell ringer; device for ringing bell. 3. (slang) Substituted racehorse etc.; person's double.

ring·let (rĭng´lĭt) *n.* Curly lock of hair, curl; (rare) small ring, fairy ring on grass, ring-shaped mark, etc. **ring′let·ed** *adj.*

Ring·ling (rĭng´lĭng). Name of 5 brothers who were Amer. circus owners; bought the Barnum and Bailey circus, 1907.

rink (rĭngk) *n.* Expanse of ice used for game of curling; sheet of natural or artificial ice for skating, building containing this; floor for roller-skating.

rinse (rĭns) *v.t.* (**rinsed, rins·ing**). Wash out or *out* (vessel, mouth) by filling with water etc. and shaking and emptying; pour liquid over or wash lightly; put (clothes etc.) through clean water to remove soap; clear (soap, impurities) *out* or *away* by rinsing. ~ *n.* Rinsing or being rinsed; preparation used for rinsing the hair, esp. for tinting it.

Ri·o de Ja·nei·ro (rē´ō dā zhanār´ō, *ja-*, dē, d*e*). Seaport and former capital of Brazil.

Rí·o de la Pla·ta (rē´ō dĕ lah plah´tah). Atlantic Ocean estuary on the SE. coast of S. Amer., formed by the Paraná and Uruguay rivers; extends inland 171 mi. (275 km) between Argentina and Uruguay.

Ri·o Grande (rē´ō grănd´, grăn´dē, grahn´dā). River rising in S. Colorado and flowing 1,885 mi. (3,034 km) S. and E. to Gulf of Mexico, forming much of the U.S.–Mexican border.

ri·ot (rī´*o*t) *n.* 1. Loud revelry, revel; unrestrained indulgence in or display or enjoyment of something. 2. **run ~**, (orig. of hunting hounds, now usu. fig.) act without restraint or control, disregard all limitations. 3. Disorder, tumult, disturbance of the peace, outbreak of lawlessness, on part of a crowd; **Riot Act**, Brit. act (1715) providing that if 12 or more persons unlawfully or riotously assembled refuse to disperse within an hour after specified law has been read aloud by a competent authority, they shall be considered as felons; hence, (fig.) **read the riot act**, announce that some course of action or conduct must cease; chastise severely. **ri′ot·ous** *adj.* **ri′ot·ous·ly** *adv.* **ri′ot·ous·ness** *n.* **riot** *v.* Make or engage in riot; revel. **ri′ot·er** *n.*

rip[1] (rĭp) *n.* (colloq.) Worthless horse; dissolute person, rake.

rip[2] (rĭp) *v.* (**ripped, rip·ping**). 1. Cut or tear (thing) quickly or forcibly away from something; make long cut or tear in, cut or tear vigorously apart; ~ **off**, (slang) defraud; steal, rob, hence **rip′off** (*n.*); split, saw (wood) with the grain; come violently asunder, split; **rip cord**, cord for releasing parachute, opening balloon gasbag, etc.; **rip-roaring**, (slang) wildly noisy; **rip′saw**, saw for ripping wood; **ripsnort′er**, (slang) person or thing that is very energetic, forceful, wild, etc. 2. Rush along; **let her rip**, (slang) do not check speed or interfere; **rip into**, (colloq.) attack verbally; **rip out**, (colloq.) exclaim violently or suddenly. **rip** *n.* Rent made by ripping. **rip′per** *n.*

rip[3] (rĭp) *n.* Stretch of broken water in river.

R.I.P. *abbrev.* *Requiesca(n)t in pace* [L., = may he or she, they, rest in peace].

ri·par·i·an (rĭpār´ēan) *adj.* Of, on, riverbank.

ripe (rīp) *adj.* (**rip·er, rip·est**). Ready to be reaped, gathered, eaten, used, or dealt with; fully developed, mellow, mature; prepared or able *to* undergo something, in fit state *for*. **ripe′ly** *adv.* **ripe′ness** *n.* **rip·en** (rī´pen) *v.*

ri·poste, ri·post (rĭpōst´) *ns.* Quick return thrust in fencing; counterstroke; retort. ~ *v.i.* (**-post·ed, -post·ing**). Deliver riposte.

rip·ple[1] (rĭp´el) *n.* Toothed implement used to clear seeds from flax. ~ *v.t.* (**-pled, -pling**). Treat with ripple.

rip·ple[2] (rĭp´el) *n.* Ruffling of water's surface, small wave(s); wavy or crinkled appearance in hair, ribbons, etc.; gentle lively sound that rises and falls. **rip′ply** *adj.* (**-pli·er, -pli·est**). **ripple** *v.* Form, flow in, show, agitate or mark with, sound like, ripples.

rip·rap (rĭp′răp) *n.* Loose stone as foundation for structure.

Rip·u·ar·i·an (rĭpūār′ēan) *adj.* Of the ancient Franks living on Rhine between Moselle and Meuse; ~ **law**, code observed by them.

Rip van Win·kle (rĭp′văn wĭng′-kel). Hero of a story (1820) by Washington Irving; he fell asleep in the Catskill Mountains and awoke after 20 years to find the world completely changed.

rise (rīz) *v.* (**rose** pr. rōz, **ris·en** pr. rĭz′en, **ris·ing**). 1. Get up from lying, sitting, or kneeling position; get out of bed; (of meeting etc.) cease to sit for business, adjourn; recover standing or upright position, become erect; leave ground; come to life again (freq. *from the dead*). 2. Cease to be quiet; abandon submission, revolt; **make one's gorge** ~, disguise, make indignant. 3. Come or go up; grow upward; ascend, soar; project or swell upward; become higher, reach higher position, level, price, pitch, or amount; incline upward; come to surface; (of fish) come to surface of water to take fly, bait, etc.; become or be visible above or *above* surroundings; (of sun, moon, etc.) appear above horizon; develop greater energy or intensity; be progressive; (of dough etc.) swell with yeast or other agent; (of spirits) become more cheerful; **rise in the world**, attain higher social position. 4. Develop powers equal *to* (an *occasion* etc.). 5. Have origin, begin to be, flow, *from, in, at*, etc. **rise** *n.* 1. Ascent, upward slope; knoll, hill. 2. Social advancement; upward progress; increase in power, rank, value, price, amount, height, pitch, etc. 3. Movement of fish to surface; **get a ~ out of**, (fig. colloq.) draw (person) into display of temper or other foible. 4. Vertical height of step, arch, incline, etc.; riser of staircase. 5. Origin, start; **give rise to**, induce.

ris·er (rī′zer) *n.* (esp.) 1. Vertical piece between treads of staircase. 2. Vertical pipe for flow of liquid or gas.

ris·i·ble (rĭz′ĭbel) *adj.* Inclined to laugh; of laughter; laughable, ludicrous. **ris·i·bil·i·ty** (rĭzĭbĭl′ĭtē) *n.* (pl. **-ties**).

ris·ing (rī′zĭng) *n.* (esp.) Uprising, insurrection, revolt. ~ *adj.* That rises; advancing toward maturity (*the ~ generation*) or toward a specified age; (of ground) sloping upward.

risk (rĭsk) *n.* Hazard; chance of or *of* bad consequences, loss, etc.; exposure to mischance; **run ~s, run a** or **the risk**, expose oneself, be exposed, to loss etc. **risk** *v.t.* Expose to chance of injury or loss; venture on, take the chance of. **risk′y** *adj.* (**risk·i·er, risk·i·est**). **risk′i·ly** *adv.* **risk′i·ness** *n.*

Ri·sor·gi·men·to (rēsōrjē-mĕn′tō) *n.* Movement of middle 19th c. for union and liberation of Italy associated with names of Cavour, Mazzini, and Garibaldi. [It., = "resurrection"]

ris·qué (rĭskā′) *adj.* Suggestive; bordering on indecency.

ris·sole (rĭsōl′, rĭs′ōl; *Fr.* rēsawl′) *n.* (pl. **ris·soles** pr. rĭsōlz′, rĭs′olz; *Fr.* rēsawl′). Fried ball or cake of minced meat or fish coated with bread crumbs etc.

ris·so·lé (rĭs′olē, rĭsolā′; *Fr.* rēsawlā′) *adj.* Sautéed.

rite (rīt) *n.* Religious or solemn ceremony or observance; form of procedure, action required or usual, in this.

rit·u·al (rĭch′ōōal) *adj.* Of, with, consisting in, involving, religious rites. **rit′u·al·ly** *adv.* **ritual** *n.* Prescribed order of performing religious service; performance of ritual acts.

rit·u·al·ism (rĭch′ōōalĭzem) *n.* (Excessive) practice of ritual. **rit′u·al·ist** *n.* **rit·u·al·is·tic** (rĭchōō-alĭs′tĭk) *adj.*

ritz·y (rĭt′sē) *adj.* (**ritz·i·er, ritz·i·est**). (colloq.) High-class, luxurious; ostentatiously smart. **ritz′i·ness** *n.*

The ***Salt River*** *in Arizona forms part of the Colorado River drainage basin. An irrigation project using various dams in the area is underway to make fertile this arid region.*

ri·val (rī′val) *n.* Person's competitor for some prize (esp. woman's or man's love) or in some pursuit or quality (also of things). ~ *adj.* That is a rival or are rivals. ~ *v.t.* (**-valed, -val·ing**). Vie with, be comparable to, seem or claim to be as good etc. as. **ri′val·ry** *n.* (pl. **-ries**). [L. *rivalis*, orig. = "on same stream," f. *rivus* stream]

rive (rīv) *v.* (**rived, riv·en** pr. rĭv′en or **rived, riv·ing**). Tear

Tribesmen in Zaire pay homage in a ***rite*** *to their god of fire. Smoke emitted by their pipes symbolizes the vapor which issues from the vents of a volcano, the god's home.*

Ruins beside the Appian Way, Italy, (top) testify to the antiquity of what became the prototype of the finest **road** system of ancient times. Above: Modern traffic needs freeways like those in Houston, Texas.

apart, rend, lacerate, tear; split (esp. wood, stone); rend (heart etc.), be rent, with painful thoughts or feelings; cleave, split, crack; admit of splitting. **riv·en** (rĭv′*en*) *adj.*

riv·er[1] (rī′v*er*) *n.* One who rives or splits.

riv·er[2] (rĭv′*er*) *n.* Copious stream of water flowing in channel to sea, lake, marsh, or another river; copious flow or stream *of*; (freq. attrib., prefixed to many names of animals, plants, and things living in, situated or used on, rivers); ~ **bottom**, low-lying alluvial land along banks of river; **sell down the** ~, (colloq.) defraud, betray; **up the** ~, (colloq.) into or in prison.

Ri·ve·ra (rĭvār′*a*; *Sp.* rēvĕ′rah), **Diego** (1886–1957). Mexican painter noted for large, vivid murals of historical subjects.

riv·er·ine (rĭv′*er*īn, -rĭn) *adj.* Of, on, river or its banks.

riv·et (rĭv′ĭt) *n.* Nail or bolt for holding together metal plates etc., its headless end being beaten out or pressed down after insertion. ~ *v.t.* (**-et·ed, -et·ing**). Clinch (bolt); join or fasten with rivets; fix, make immovable; concentrate, direct intently (eyes etc. *upon*); engross (attention), engross attention of. **riv′et·er** *n.*

Riv·i·er·a (rĭvēār′*a*). Strip of coast and resort area of N. Italy and S. France, between mountains and Mediterranean, famous for its beauty and mild climate.

riv·u·let (rĭv′y*u*lĭt) *n.* Small stream.

Ri·yadh (rēyahd′). Capital of Saudi Arabia, in the E. central part; site of royal palace.

rm. *abbrev.* Room.

rms *abbrev.* Root mean square.

Rn *symbol.* Radon.

R.N. *abbrev.* Registered Nurse; Royal Navy.

RNA *abbrev.* Ribonucleic acid, any of the class of nucleic acids containing ribose, present in the nucleoli and cytoplasm of living cells and concerned in the synthesis of proteins.

roach[1] (rōch) *n.* Cockroach; (slang) butt of marijuana cigarette.

roach[2] (rōch) *n.* (pl. **roach·es**, collect. **roach**). Small freshwater fish (*Rutilus rutilus*) of the carp family of N. European rivers; small fish resembling this, including some N. Amer. sunfishes.

road (rōd) *n.* 1. (usu. pl.; also **road′stead**) Sheltered area of water near shore in which ships can ride at anchor. 2. Open way, course, or path between places for use of vehicles, people, and animals; way of getting *to*; one's way or route; **the** ~, the highway; **on the** ~, traveling; **royal road**, smooth or easy way (*to* success etc.); **rule of the** ~, custom regulating side to be taken by vehicles, riders, or ships meeting or passing each other; **take to the** ~, start traveling. 3. Railroad. 4. **road′bed**, foundation that supports railroad tracks; foundation and traveling surface of highway; **road′block**, obstruction on road for stopping or slowing traffic; (fig.) anything that impedes; **road company**, theatrical group that visits cities and towns, usu. presenting one play; **road hog**, reckless, dangerous, or bad-mannered driver of motor vehicle etc.; **road′house**, inn, restaurant, bar, or nightclub on road outside a city; **road′-runner**, large, crested, terrestrial bird of SW. Amer. (*Geococcyx californianus*) feeding on snakes and lizards; **road′side**, border of road (esp. attrib.); **road′stead**: see sense 1; **road′way**, road; central part of road, esp. part used by vehicular traffic; **road′work**, long-distance running or jogging as exercise, conditioning for prizefighters, etc.

road·a·bil·i·ty (rōd*a*bĭl′ĭtē) *n.* Qualities that make a vehicle comfortable to travel in and easy to drive under various road conditions.

road·ster (rōd′st*er*) *n.* (archaic) Horse for use on the road; small two- or three-seat open automobile.

roam (rōm) *v.* Ramble, wander; walk or travel unsystematically over, through, or about (country, seas, etc.). **roam′er** *n.* **roam** *n.* Ramble, rambling walk.

roan[1] (rōn) *adj.* (of animal) With

*Yugoslavian farmers **roast** pigs on spits over an open fire. This method of spit roasting adds a distinctive flavour to food.*

coat in which the prevailing color is thickly interspersed with another, esp. bay, sorrel, or chestnut mixed with white or gray. ~ *n.* Roan horse.

roan[2] (rōn) *n.* Soft sheepskin leather used in bookbinding as substitute for morocco. [perh. f. *Rouen*]

Ro·a·noke (rō′*a*nōk) **Island.** Island off the coast of North Carolina; site of first attempted English settlement in N. Amer., established by Sir Walter Raleigh, 1585; second attempted colony, called "the lost colony," established 1587; all settlers disappeared.

roar (rōr, rōr) *n.* Loud deep hoarse sound (as) of lion, person or company in pain or rage or loud laughter, the sea, cannon, thunder, furnace, etc. ~ *v.* Utter, send forth, roar; (of place) be full of din, reecho; say, sing, utter (words etc.) in loud tone. **roar′er** *n.*

roar·ing (rōr′ĭng, rōr′-) *adj.* (esp.) Riotous, noisy, boisterous, brisk.

roast (rōst) *v.* Cook (esp. meat) by exposure to open fire or dry heat in oven; heat or calcine (ore) in furnace; heat (coffee beans) in preparation for grinding; expose to fire or great heat; ridicule, banter, chaff; undergo roasting. ~ *n.* Cut of meat for roasting; roasted meat; operation of roasting.

roast·er (rō′st*er*) *n.* (esp.) Kind of oven for roasting; large pan for roasting meat in; ore roasting furnace; coffee roasting apparatus; fowl etc. fit for roasting or baking.

roast·ing (rō′stĭng) *adj.* (esp.) Very hot.

rob (rŏb) *v.t.* (**robbed, rob·-bing**). Despoil (person etc.) of or *of* property by violence; feloniously plunder; deprive *of* what is due; (abs.) commit robbery. **rob′ber·y** *n.* (pl. **-ber·ies**). Stealing with (threat of) force.

Rob·bia (rŏb′ē*a*), **del·la** (dĕl′*a*). Name of Florentine family of sculptors in glazed terracotta: **Luca** ~ (1400–82); **Andrea** ~, his nephew (1435–1525); **Giovanni** ~, son of Andrea (1469–1529).

robe (rōb) *n.* 1. Long loose outer garment, esp. one worn as indication of wearer's rank, office, profession, etc., gown, vestment; dressing gown, bathrobe. 2. Dressed skin of animal used as garment or rug. ~ *v.* (**robed, rob·ing**). Invest (person) in robe; dress; assume one's robes or vestments.

Rob·ert (rŏb′*ert*). Name of 3 kings of Scotland: **Robert I**: see BRUCE; **Robert II**, "the Steward" (1316–90), son-in-law of Robert I, reigned 1371–90; **Robert III** (*c*1340–1406), illegitimate son of Robert II, reigned 1390–1406.

Robe·son (rōb′s*o*n), **Paul** (1898–1976). Amer. singer and actor; appeared in the musical, *Showboat*, and the plays *All God's Chillun Got Wings, Emperor Jones, Othello*, etc.

Robes·pierre (rōbz′pēr, -pēar; *Fr.* rawbĕspyĕr′), **Maximilien François Marie Isidore de** (1758–94). French revolutionist; leader of extreme party and chief promoter of the Reign of Terror; overthrown and guillotined, 1794.

*Roman Catholic priests in Lourdes, France. The **robes** worn by the clergy often denote rank. The purple biretta (hat) indicates that the man is a bishop, as do the purple clothes. The man in black is a priest.*

rob·in (rŏb′ĭn) *n.* Red-breasted N. Amer. thrush (*Turdus migratorius*); small brown red-breasted European bird (*Erithacus rubecula*); any of various birds of Australia, New Zealand, India, etc., some having red breasts. [OF. dim. of *Robert*]

Rob·in (rŏb′ĭn) **Hood.** Legendary English outlaw, hero of many ballads and plays, who robbed the rich to aid the poor; said to have lived in 12th–13th centuries.

Rob·in·son[1] (rŏb′ĭns*o*n), **Edwin Arlington** (1869–1935). Amer. poet; author of "The Man Who Died Twice" (1925), and "Tristram" (1927), for which he won Pulitzer Prizes.

A hen **robin** has to feed a cuckoo baby (above) hatched from an egg laid by an interloper. Insects provide the bulk of the diet of both birds. The robin was voted as Britain's national bird in a poll of newspaper readers.

Rob·in·son[2] (rŏb´ĭnson), **Jack Roosevelt ("Jackie")** (1919–72). Amer. baseball player; first black major league player, signed with the Brooklyn Dodgers, 1947.

Rob·in·son Cru·soe (rŏb´ĭnson kroo͞´sō). Hero of a novel (1719) by DEFOE, based on adventure of Alexander Selkirk, who lived alone on the uninhabited Pacific island of Juan Fernandez for five years (1704–9).

Ro·bo·am = REHOBOAM.

ro·bot (rō´bŏt, -bot) *n.* Apparently human automaton; machinelike person, soulless automaton. [term for mechanical man in play *R.U.R.* by Karel Čapek; f. Czech *robota* compulsory labor, *robotnik* serf]

Rob Roy (rŏb´roi´). Robert Macgregor or Campbell (1671–1734), Scottish Highland freebooter, leader of the clan Macgregor, and Jacobite hero.

rob roy (rŏb´roi´). Cocktail of Scotch, sweet vermouth, and bitters. [f. ROB ROY]

Robt. *abbrev.* Robert.

ro·bust (rōbŭst´, rō´bŭst) *adj.* Of strong health and physique; vigorous; (of exercise etc.) tending to or requiring strength, invigorating. **ro·bust´ly** *adv.* **ro·bust´ness** *n.*

roc (rŏk) *n.* Gigantic bird of Eastern legend.

Roch·es·ter (rŏch´ĕster, -ĭs-). 1. Industrial port in W. New York, on the New York State Barge Canal and Genesee River, near Lake Ontario. 2. City in SE. Minnesota, 70 mi. (113 km) SE. of St. Paul; site of Mayo Clinic, established in 1889.

roch·et (rŏch´ĭt) *n.* Surplice-

Fall foliage in **Rochester,** New York. The city was originally laid out in 1811 by Colonel Nathaniel Rochester. Within 20 years it became an industrial and commercial success.

Legends telling of **Robin Hood** can be dated to 1377, but no evidence has been found to prove he ever existed. The statue at Nottingham Castle, U.K. (below) is inspired by imagination.

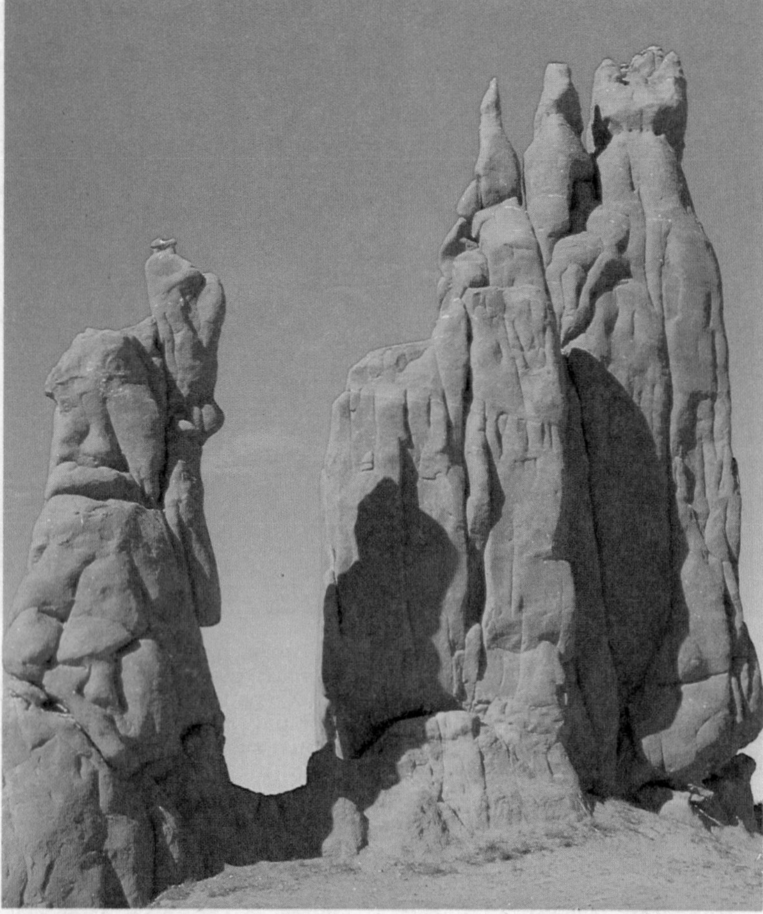

***Rock** can be sculpted into remarkable shapes by erosion. Left: Witch Rock in Arizona has been eroded into strange figures. Wave Rock in Western Australia (facing) was smoothed for millions of years by flowing water.*

like vestment used chiefly by bishops and abbots.

rock[1] (rŏk) *n.* 1. Large rugged mass of stone forming cliff, crag, or prominence; boulder; stone of any size; sure foundation or support, shelter or protection; **on the ~s,** (colloq.) in financial straits; (of drink) served over ice cubes without water or soda. 2. Hard and massive stone; (geol.) any formation of natural origin in the earth's crust, whether composed of a single mineral or an aggregate of many. 3. ~ **barnacle**: see BARNACLE; ~ **bottom**, (slang, of prices etc.) very lowest; ~**-bound**, bordered or enclosed by rocks; ~ **candy**, hard candy; large, hard crystals of sugar; ~ **crystal**, crystallized quartz; **rock'fish** (pl. **-fishes**, collect. **-fish**), fish (esp. of family Scorpaenidae) frequenting rocks or rocky bottoms; **rock garden**, artificial mound or bank of stones with plants; **rock hound,** (colloq.) person whose hobby is searching for and making collection of rocks; **rock-ribbed**, having rocky out-crop or ridges; (fig.) stern, unyielding, rigid; **rock'rose**, plant of genus *Cistus* or *Helianthemum* with yellow, pink, or salmon flowers; **rock salt**: see SALT *n.* sense 1; **rock wool**, material resembling spun glass, made from molten slag subjected to steam blast and used for building insulation.

rock[2] (rŏk) *v.* Move gently to and fro (as) in cradle; set or keep (cradle etc.), be, in such motion; sway, cause to sway, from side to side; shake, oscillate, reel; ~ **the boat**, (colloq.) upset the balance of a situation; **rocking chair**, one mounted on rockers or with seat arranged to rock; **rocking horse**, wooden horse on rockers for child. **rock** *n.* 1. Act of rocking. 2. Rocking motion; ~ **and** (or **'n'**) **roll**, (popular dance to) music with heavy beat, simple melody and elements of blues, jazz, and country and western.

Rock·e·fel·ler (rŏk'efĕler). Name of prominent wealthy Amer. family, including **John D(avison)** ~ (1839–1937), Amer. financier and philanthropist who made a fortune from petroleum and established and endowed four charitable foundations, including the Rockefeller Foundation,

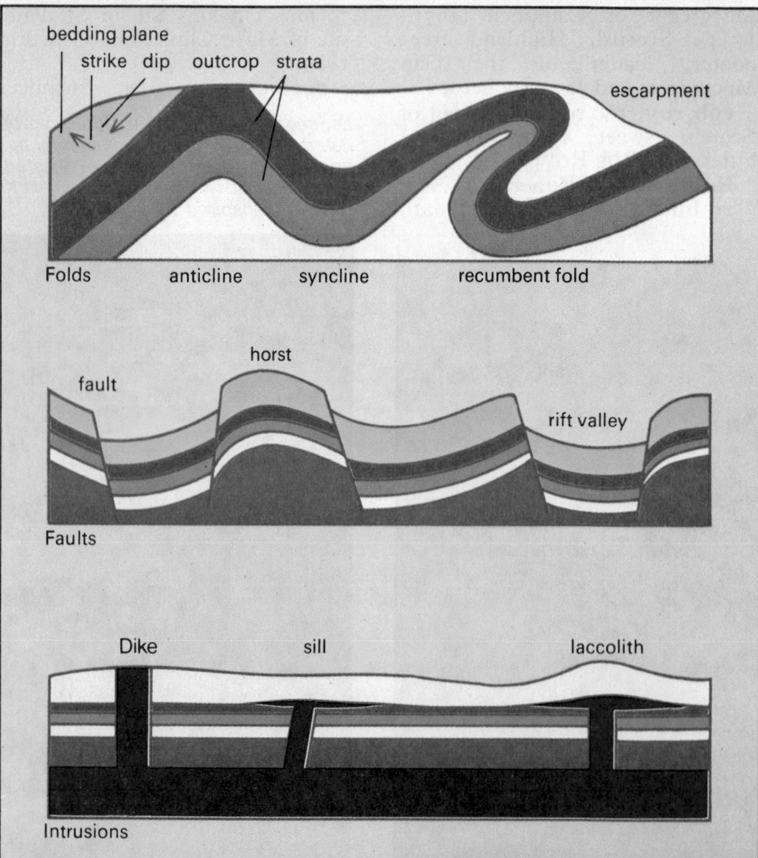

*Various earth movements are responsible for **rock** formation. Above left: The effects of surface folding. Center: Upthrust or collapse. The lower diagram shows the effects of volcanic action, and lava penetration.*

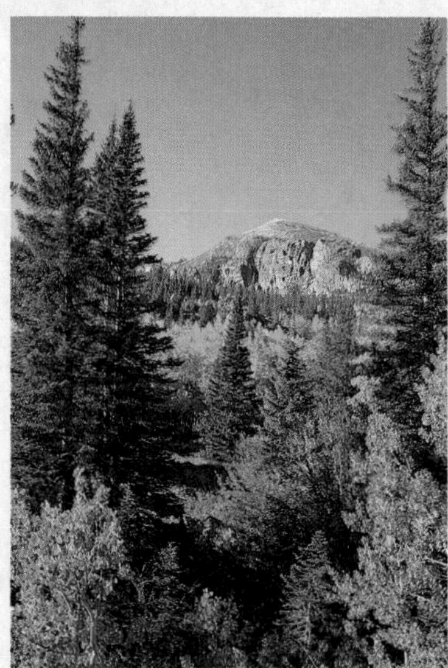

*The **Rocky Mountains** extend for more than 3,000 miles, from Alaska to New Mexico. One of the world's youngest mountain ranges, it was formed about 70 million years ago.*

established 1913; his son, **John D(avison)** ~ (1874–1960), continued with his father's business and philanthropic interests and planned and built Rockefeller Center in New York City; **Nelson Aldrich** ~ (1908–79), grandson of John D., Sr.; Amer. politician; governor of New York, 1959–73, and U.S. vice president, 1974–7, under Gerald Ford; **Winthrop** ~ (1912–73), grandson of John D., Sr.; Amer. businessman and politician; governor of Arkansas, 1967–70.

rock·er (rŏk'*er*) *n.* (esp.) One of the curved bars upon which cradle, chair, etc., rocks; **off one's** ~, (slang) crazy; rocking chair; goldminer's cradle; engraver's cradle for roughening surface of plate; skate with highly curved blade.

rock·er·y (rŏk'*er*ē) *n.* (pl. **-er·ies**). Artificial heap of rough stones and rock for growing (usu. small) plants adapted to such terrain.

rock·et[1] (rŏk'ĭt) *n.* Cruciferous plant of genus *Hesperis*, esp. *H. matronalis*, sweet-scented after dark. [It. *ruchetta* f. L. *eruca* because formerly applied to the salad plant *Eruca sativa*]

rock·et[2] (rŏk'ĭt) *n.* 1. Cylindrical case that can be projected to a height or distance by the reaction of the gases discharged from the rear when its (highly combustible) contents are ignited, used as fireworks, for signaling, to carry life line, propel military warhead, put spacecraft into orbit, etc. 2. Shell or bomb propelled by rocket. ~ *v.t.* Bound upward like rocket; fly straight upward, fly fast and high; (of prices) rise rapidly. **rock'et·ry** *n.* Science, practice, of rocket propulsion.

Rock·ies (rŏk'ēz) = ROCKY[1] Mountains.

Rock·ne (rŏk'nē), **Knute Kenneth** (1888–1931). Norwegian-born Amer. football player; head coach at the University of Notre Dame, 1918–31.

Rock·well (rŏk'wĕl), **Norman** (1894–1978). Amer. painter; famous for illustrations of typical Amer. family life, many appearing on *Saturday Evening Post* covers.

rock·y[1] (rŏk'ē) *adj.* (**rock·i·er, rock·i·est**). Of rock, full of or abounding in rocks; like rock in ruggedness, firmness, solidity, etc.; **R**~ **Mountains**, (also **Rockies**) the major mountain range of western N. Amer., extending 3,000 mi. (4,800 km) from N. Mexico to Alaska; **Rocky Mountain National Park**, area in N. central Colorado NW. of Denver, covering 262,324 acres (106,162 hectares); **Rocky Mountain sheep**: see BIGhorn; **Rocky Mountain (spotted) fever**: see RICKETTSIA. **rock'i·ness** *n.*

rock·y[2] (rŏk'ē) *adj.* (**rock·i·er, rock·i·est**). Unsteady, tottering.

ro·co·co (r*o*kō'kō) *adj.* Of the style of decoration, originating in France and Italy in the late 17th c. and prevalent in Europe until *c*1770, characterized esp. by scrollwork, shell motifs, asymmetrical effects, and lightness of coloring; (loosely) frivolous, sophisticated, overly ornamental. ~ *n.* Rococo style. [Fr., f. *rocaille* rock work (in ref. to encrusting grottoes with shells)]

*Scrolls and shells were used extravagantly in designs for decoration during the **rococo** period. It flourished, especially in France and Italy, for the first 70 years of the 18th century.*

rod (rŏd) *n.* 1. Slender straight round stick growing as shoot on tree or cut from it or made from wood; switch, wand (freq. as symbol of office etc.). 2. Such stick, or bundle of twigs, for use in caning or flogging. 3. Fishing rod. 4. Linear measure equal to 5.5 yards or 5.03 meters. 5. Slender metal bar, connecting bar, shaft; rod-

*Testing a Saturn V **rocket** for the Apollo 16 space mission. These rehearsals are designed to simulate all possible equipment failures which astronauts may have to cope with in space.*

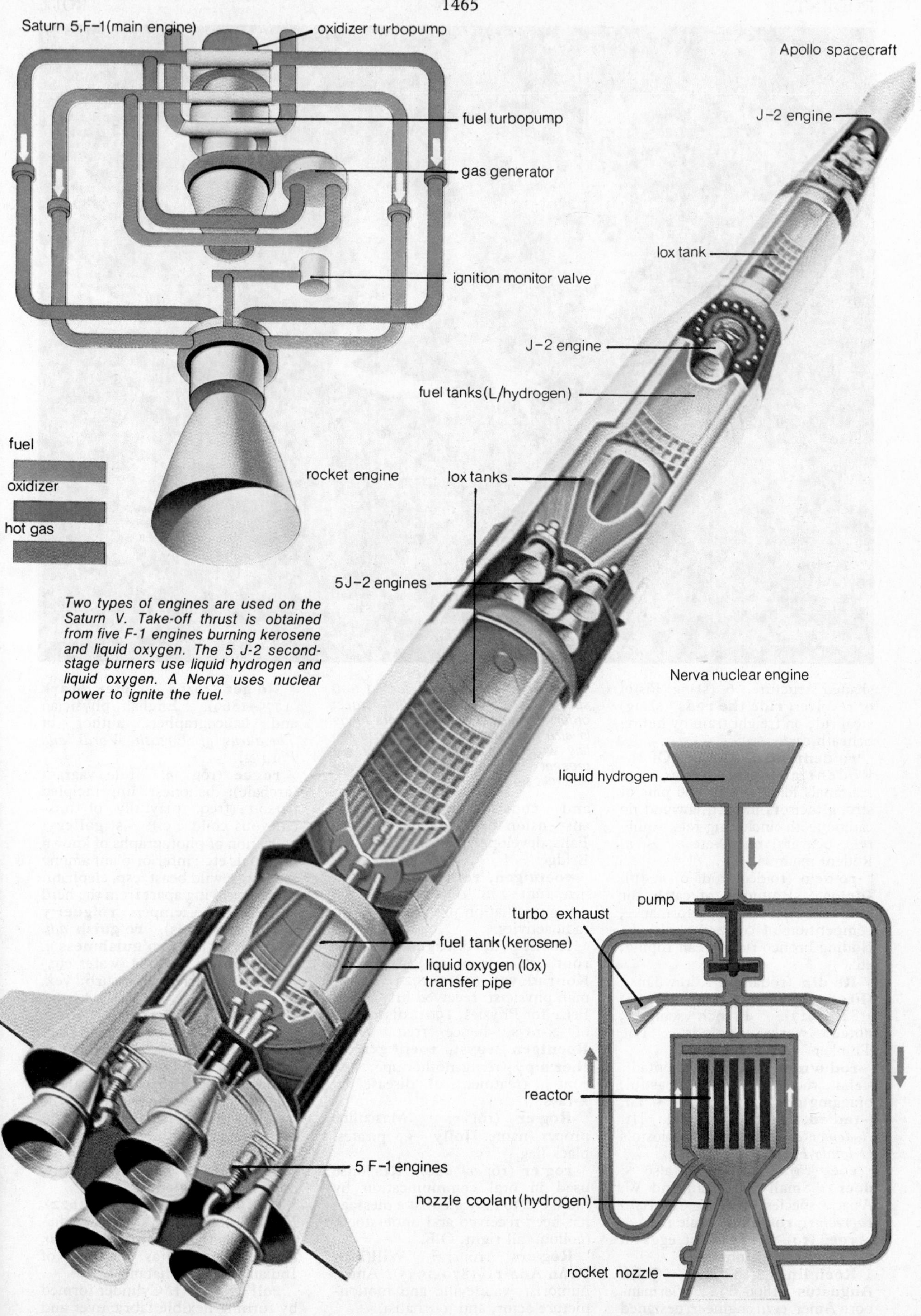

Two types of engines are used on the Saturn V. Take-off thrust is obtained from five F-1 engines burning kerosene and liquid oxygen. The 5 J-2 second-stage burners use liquid hydrogen and liquid oxygen. A Nerva uses nuclear power to ignite the fuel.

shaped structure. 6. (slang) Pistol or revolver; **ride the rods,** (slang) steal ride on freight train by hiding beneath car.

ro·dent (rō′dent) *adj.* Of the Rodentia, an order of mammals having only one pair of strong incisors in each jaw and no canine teeth (including rats, squirrels, beavers, mice, etc.). ~ *n.* Rodent mammal.

ro·de·o (rō′dēō, rōdā′ō) *n.* (pl. **-de·os**). Roundup of cattle for branding etc.; public performance, competition of cowboy skills, including bronco riding, calf roping, etc.

Ro·din (rōdăn′; *Fr.* rawdăn′), **(François) Auguste (René)** (1840–1917). French sculptor; noted works include "The Thinker" and "The Kiss."

rod·o·mon·tade (rŏdomŏntād′, -tahd′, rōdo-) *n.* & *adj.* Boastful, bragging (saying or talk). ~ *v.i.* (**-tad·ed, -tad·ing**). Brag. [It. *Rodomonte,* character in Ariosto's *Orlando Furioso*]

roe[1] (rō) *n.* (pl. **-roe**). (also ~ **deer**) Small European and W. Asiatic species of deer (*Capreolus capreolus*); **roe′buck,** male roe.

roe[2] (rō) *n.* Mass of eggs in fish's ovarian membrane.

Roeb·ling (rō′blĭng), **John Augustus** (1806–69). German-born Amer. civil engineer; designed

*The term **rodent** includes 1,500 species which comprise the largest order of mammals. Its members range in size from the 4-ft. capybara to the tiny wood mouse (above). They are present on all continents except Antarctica.*

and constructed first U.S. suspension bridge, over Niagara Falls; developed plans for Brooklyn Bridge.

roent·gen, rönt·gen (rĕnt′gen, -jen, rŭnt′-) *ns.* Quantity of x or gamma radiation used as a unit of radioactivity.

Roent·gen, Rönt·gen (rĕnt′gen, rŭnt′-; *Ger.* rönt′gen), **Wilhelm Konrad von** (1845–1923). German physicist: received first Nobel Prize for Physics, 1901; discoverer of x-rays, hence freq. called **Roentgen rays; roent·gen·o·ther·a·py** (rĕntgenōthĕr′apē, -je-; rŭnt-), treatment of disease by x-rays.

Rog·er (rŏj′er). Masculine proper name: **Jolly** ~, pirates' black flag.

rog·er (rŏj′er) *adv.* Response used in oral communication by radio etc. to indicate that a message has been received and understood; (colloq.) all right, O.K.

Rog·ers (rŏj′erz), **Will(iam Penn Adair)** (1879–1935). Amer. humorist, vaudeville and motion-picture actor, and journalist.

Ro·get (rōzhā′), **Peter Mark** (1779–1869). English physician and lexicographer; author of *Thesaurus of English Words and Phrases.*

rogue (rōg) *n.* Idle vagrant (archaic); dishonest, unprincipled person (freq. playfully of mischievous child etc.); ~**s' gallery,** collection of photographs of known criminals etc.; inferior plant among seedlings; wild beast, esp. elephant, driven or living apart from the herd and of savage temper. **ro′guer·y** *n.* (pl. **-guer·ies**). **ro′guish** *adj.* **ro′guish·ly** *adv.* **ro′guish·ness** *n.*

roil (roil) *v.* Make (water etc.) turbid by stirring; perturb; vex, annoy.

roist·er (roi′ster) *v.i.* Revel noisily, be uproarious (esp. in part. **roistering** as adj.). **roist′er·er** *n.*

Ro·land (rō′land). Hero of medieval (esp. French and Italian) legend, nephew and one of the paladins of Charlemagne; killed in battle against the Saracens at Roncevaux in the Pyrenees.

role, rôle (rōl) *ns.* Actor's part; one's task or function.

Rolfe (rŏlf), **John** (1585–1622). English colonist in Virginia; discovered method of curing tobacco; married Pocahontas, daughter of Indian chief Powhatan.

roll[1] (rōl) *n.* 1. Cylinder formed by turning flexible fabric over and over upon itself without folding; quantity of textile fabric rolled thus (esp. as definite measure of cloth); (slang) quantity of bills rolled together, person's money. 2. Document, esp. official record, in this form. 3. List of names (freq. fig.); ~ **call**, calling over of list (as in school or army) so that each person present answers to his name and absentees are detected; **honor** ~, (esp.) list of those who have died for their country in war; list of outstanding students. 4. More or less (semi-) cylindrical straight or curved mass of anything, however formed; small loaf of bread for one person. 5. Cylinder, roller; in steel mill, grooved cylinder, usu. one of a set revolving simultaneously, beneath which or between which white-hot ingots are passed to shape them. 6. Bookbinder's revolving patterned tool for marking cover.

roll[2] (rōl) *v.* 1. Move, send, go, in some direction by turning over and over on axis; (cause to) go, convey, with smooth rolling or sweeping motion (freq. fig.); undulate; make revolve between two surfaces; wrap (*up in*) by rolling motion; (of eyes) change direction (of) with rotatory motion. 2. Wallow, turn about in fluid or loose medium; (of animal) lie on back and kick about; sway or rock, walk with swaying gait as of sailor, reel. 3. (of sound) Utter, be uttered, sound, with vibratory, undulating, or trilling effect. 4. Flatten by passing roller over or by passing between rollers; shape (metal) by passing between or beneath rolls. 5. Turn over and over upon itself into more or less cylindrical shape. 6. Form into cylindrical or spherical shape or accumulate into mass, by rolling. 7. ~ **back**, reduce (wages, prices, etc.) to earlier level, usu. by order of government (**roll'back** *n.*); **roll bar**, strong metal bar built into automobile roof to protect passenger(s) in case of accidental overturn; **roll on**, (*adj.*) applying (liquid) by means of a rotating ball in the neck of a container; **roll-top desk**, desk with flexible cover sliding in curved grooves. **roll'ing** *adj.* & *n.* (esp.) ~ **mill**, mill that rolls steel into sheets or bars; ~ **pin**, cylindrical roller for rolling out dough; ~ **stock**, railroad's locomotives and cars; ~ **stone**, (fig.) person who has not settled down. **roll** *n.* 1. Rolling motion; rolling gait; turn of aircraft about its longitudinal axis through 360°. 2. Quick continuous beating of drum; long peal of thunder or shout; rhythmic flow of words.

*The **roe** or eggs of the Australian lungfish. From these emerge young in a tadpole-like form. Unlike their parents, they need to remain in very shallow water.*

roll·er (rō'ler) *n.* (esp.) 1. Cylinder of wood, stone, metal, etc., used alone or as rotating part of machine for lessening friction, pressing, stamping, crushing, flattening, spreading printer's ink, rolling up cloth on, etc.; hollow cylinder of plastic, wire, etc., for rolling hair for setting. 2. ~ **skate**, skate with 4 (occas. 2) small wheels instead of blade, for skating on sidewalks, smooth flooring, etc.; ~ **towel**, towel with ends joined, running on roller.

rol·lick (rŏl'ĭk) *v.i.* Be jovial, indulge in high spirits, enjoy life boisterously, revel (chiefly in part. **rollicking** as adjective).

ro·ly-po·ly (rō'lēpō'lē) *adj.* & *n.* (pl. **-lies**). (Person who is) pudgy, short and plump.

rom, rom. *abbrevs.* Roman (type).

Rom. *abbrev.* Romans (New Testament).

Ro·ma·ic (rōmā'ĭk) *adj.* & *n.* (Of) the vernacular language of modern Greece.

ro·maine (rōmān') *n.* Variety of lettuce (*Lactuca sativa longifolia*) having long leaves that form a cylindrical head.

Ro·mains (rawmăṅ'), **Jules.** Pen name of Louis Farigoule (1885–1972), French novelist, poet, and playwright.

Ro·man (rō'man) *adj.* 1. Of

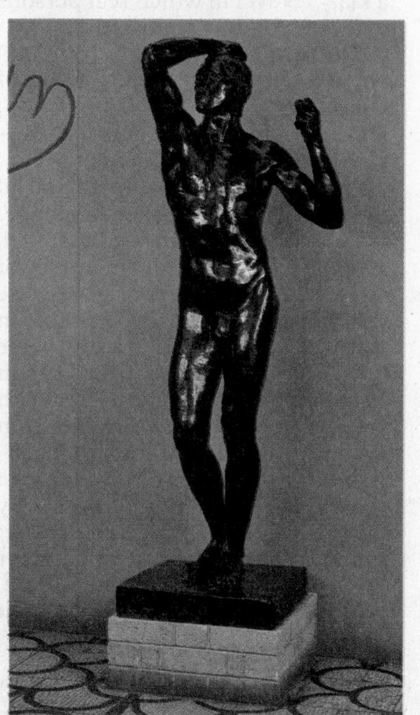

*Of all the sculptors in the 19th century, **Rodin** was one of the most prodigious. His modeling of the human figure was outstanding, as shown by 'The Age of Bronze', Tate Gallery, London, U.K.*

*Originating in the U.S.A., the **rodeo** is now a familiar form of entertainment in outback towns of Australia. The buckjumping contest (below) is at Katherine in the Northern Territory.*

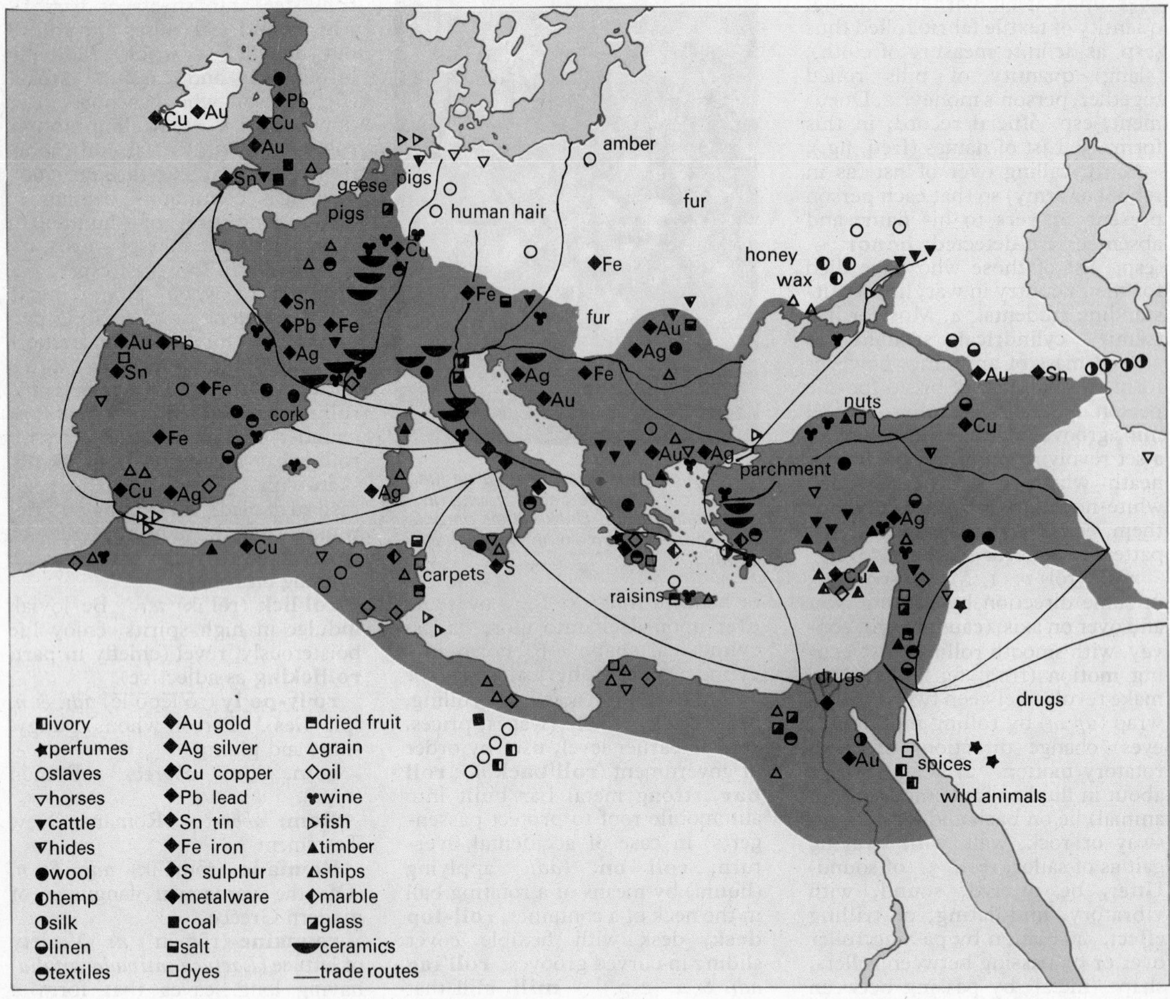

*When the **Roman Empire** was at its zenith in the 3rd century A.D., the Caesars and other nobles were able to enjoy the finest produce available. This came not only from territories they had conquered, but also from traders who arrived from Asia to barter their wares in the Middle East. In this diagram, purple marks the extent of the Empire in 3 A.D.*

ancient or modern Rome or the Roman republic or Empire. 2. Of the R.C. Ch. 3. (of nose) Having prominent upper part or bridge like those seen in portraits of ancient Romans. 4. **r ~**, of the modern kind of lettering or type that most directly represents that used in ancient Roman inscriptions, of the kind now in ordinary use in Amer. and W. Europe; upright, as dist. from *italic*. 5. (of numerals) Expressed in letters of the Roman alphabet, thus: I = 1, V = 5, X = 10, L = 50, C = 100, D = 500, M = 1,000; the letters composing a number are arranged in order of value and the number meant is found by addition, e.g. MDCLXVI = 1,666; if a letter or set of letters is placed before a letter of higher value, it is to be subtracted from it before the addition is done, e.g. XIV = 14; XLIV = 44; MCM = 1,900. 6. **~ candle**, tube discharging colored balls in fireworks; **~ Catholic**, (member) of that part of the Western or Latin Christian Church that owes its allegiance to the Bishop of Rome (the Pope); so **~ Catholicism; ~ Empire**, that established by Augustus 27 B.C. and divided by Theodosius 395 A.D. into the Western Empire with Rome as its capital and the Eastern Empire with Byzantium as its capital (see BYZANTINE); **Holy ~ Empire**, confederation of Germanic states regarded as the revival of the Western Empire, formed in 962 when Otto I was crowned emperor (or sometimes regarded as originating with Charlemagne in 800); so **Holy ~ Emperor; ~ law**, system of law of ancient Rome, esp. as codified under the Emperor JUSTINIAN; code, modified or derived from the Justinian code, in force in many parts of Europe in modern times; **~ road**, road surviving from the period of Roman rule. **Roman** *n.* 1. Native, inhabitant, of ancient or modern Rome, the Roman republic or Empire; (**Epistle to the**) **~s**, Book of New Testament, an Epistle written by St Paul to the Christians of Rome. 2. **r ~**, roman lettering or type.

ro·man à clef (rawmahn´ ă klā´) (pl. **ro·mans à clef** pr. rawmahnz´ ă klā´). Novel in which real persons or events appear in disguise.

Ro·mance (rōmăns´, rō´măns) *adj.* & *n.* (Of) the group of languages descended from Latin, including French, Spanish, Portuguese, Italian, Rumanian, etc.; derived or descended from Latin; composed in a Romance language.

ro·mance (rōmăns´, rō´măns) *n.* 1. Medieval tale, usu. in verse, of some hero of chivalry (orig. because written in Romance, i.e. not in Latin). 2. Prose or rarely verse tale (esp. of the class prevalent in 16th and 17th centuries) with settings and incidents remote from everyday life; class of literature consisting of such tales; episode, love affair, etc., suggesting such tale by its strangeness or moving nature; romantic or imaginative character or quality. **~** (rōmăns´) *v.i.* (**-manced, -manc·ing**). Invent romances; exaggerate fantastically. **ro·manc´er** *n.*

Ro·man·esque (rōmanĕsk´) *adj.* Of the style of art and architecture prevalent in W. Europe between the end of the classical period and the rise of Gothic style, (esp.) of the style prevalent from mid-11th c. until end of 12th c., characterized by the use of massive stone vaulting and the round arch, often with richly carved columns and capitals, and sculptured figures. ~ *n.* Romanesque style.

Ro·ma·nia, Ro·mâ·nia: RUMANIA.

Ro·man·ize (rō′manīz) *v.t.* (**-ized, -iz·ing**). Render Roman in character; bring under the influence or rule of Rome; put into Roman alphabet or roman type; convert to Roman Catholicism.

Ro·ma·nov (rō′manawf, -nŏf; *Russ.* rawmah′nawf). Surname of the imperial dynasty ruling in Russia from the accession of Michael Romanov (elected tsar 1613) to 1917.

ro·mansh (rōmănsh′, -mahnsh′) *adj.* & *n.* (Of) the Rhaeto-Romaic dialect spoken in the Grisons, E. Switzerland.

ro·man·tic (rōmăn′tĭk) *adj.* Characterized by, suggestive of, given to, romance; imaginative, remote from experience, visionary; (of projects etc.) fantastic, impractical, quixotic, dreamy; (of music, literary or artistic method, etc., opp. CLASSIC) preferring grandeur, picturesqueness, passion, or irregular beauty to finish and proportion, subordinating whole to parts or form to matter; **R~ Movement, Revival,** movement of European literature and art of late 18th and early 19th centuries. **ro·man′ti·cal·ly** *adv.* **ro·man·ti·cism** (rōmăn′tĭsĭzem), **ro·man′ti·cist** *ns.* **ro·man′ti·cize** *v.* (**-cized, -ciz·ing**). **romantic** *n.* Romantic person; **R~**, participant in the Romantic Movement.

A rival of Reynolds as a portraitist, ***George Romney*** *was especially able to express character, in subjects as diverse as 'The Parson's Daughter', or those with Lady Hamilton as his model.*

Rom·a·ny (rŏm′anē, rō′ma-) *n.* (pl. **-nies**). (Of) the gypsies; (of) the language of the gypsies, an Indo-European language related to Hindi.

Rome (rōm). (It. *Roma*) 1. City on Tiber River, about 20 mi. (32 km) from sea near center of W. coast of Italy, founded 753 B.C.; a republic from *c*500 B.C. until the reign of Augustus (31 B.C.), and conqueror and chief city of most of the known world; in modern times, capital city of Italy. 2. See of the pope and original capital of

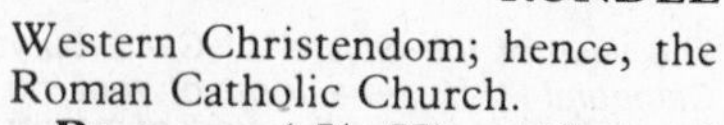

Western Christendom; hence, the Roman Catholic Church.

Ro·me·o (rō′mēō). Hero of Shakespeare's romantic tragedy *Romeo and Juliet*; hence, romantic young lover.

Rom·ney (rŏm′nē), **George** (1734–1802). English portrait painter.

romp (rŏmp) *v.i.* (of children etc.) Play about together, chase each other, wrestle, etc.; (esp. sports slang) get *along, past,* etc., without effort, win easily. ~ *n.* **romp′ers** *n.pl.* Garment, usu. covering trunk only, for young child to play in.

Rom·u·lus (rŏm′yulus). (Rom. legend) Founder of Rome, son of Mars by the vestal Rhea Silvia; with his twin brother Remus was abandoned at birth and found and suckled by a she-wolf; founded Rome 753 B.C., and became its first king.

Ron·ces·valles (rŏn′sevălz; *Sp.* rŏnthĕsvahl′yĕs), **Ronce·vaux,** (*Fr.* rawṅsvō′). Village in Navarre, N. Spain, in W. Pyrenees, site of legendary defeat of rear guard of Charlemagne's army and death of ROLAND.

ron·deau (rŏn′dō) *n.* (pl. **-deaux**). Poem of 10 or 13 lines having only two rhymes throughout and with opening words used twice as refrain.

ron·del (rŏn′del) *n.* Poem of 13 or 14 lines, with two rhymes only, and with the first two lines recurring after the sixth, and the first two or the first only at the end.

Rome, *capital of Italy, as seen from the dome of St. Peter's. The basilica is actually located in the Vatican which is a separate State situated within the city of Rome.*

The ***romantic*** *movement in literature had its origins in Germany but soon spread to France. One of its exponents was Anne de Stael, portrayed here as 'Corinne', one of her heroines.*

The vault of the cloister at Canterbury Cathedral, U.K. — a form of ***roof*** *no longer built — shows the work of master craftsmen. Below are illustrated various types of roof and their construction.*

ron·do (rŏn′dō) *n.* (pl. **-dos** pr. -dōz). Piece of music (freq. as last movement of sonata) in which principal theme recurs twice or oftener in same key, after introduction of contrasting themes.

Ron·sard (rawn̄sar̄′), **Pierre de** (1524–85). Chief lyric poet of French renaissance.

Rönt·gen: ROENTGEN.

rönt·gen: ROENTGEN.

rood (ro͞od) *n.* 1. (esp. **holy ~**) Cross of Christ (archaic); crucifix, esp. one raised on middle of **rood screen**, wooden or stone carved screen separating nave and choir. 2. (Brit.) Measure of land, ¼ acre or 40 sq. rods, but varying locally; esp. as loose term for small piece of land.

roof (ro͞of, ro͝of) *n.* (pl. **roofs**). Upper covering of house or building, usu. supported by its walls; top of covered vehicle; **~ of the mouth**, palate; **roof′tree**, ridgepole of roof. **roof′ing, roof′er** *ns.* **roof** *v.t.* Cover with roof; be roof of.

rook[1] (ro͝ok) *n.* Common black raucous-voiced European and Asiatic bird (*Corvus frugilegus*) of crow family, nesting in colonies. ~ *v.t.* (slang) Cheat, swindle; charge (customer) extortionately.

rook[2] (ro͝ok) *n.* (chess) One of 4 pieces that, at beginning of game, are set in corner squares and have power of moving in a straight line forward, backward, or laterally over any number of unoccupied squares. [f. (ult.) Arab. *rukk*]

rook·er·y (ro͝ok′erē) *n.* (pl. **-er·ies**). Breeding and nesting place of colony of rooks; breeding ground of certain other birds and animals, as penguins, seals, etc.

rook·ie (ro͝okē) *n.* Untrained recruit; novice or first-year player on baseball team etc.

room (ro͞om) *n.* 1. Space that is or might be occupied by something; capaciousness, ability to accommodate contents; **make ~ for**, clear a space for person or thing by removal of others. 2. Opportunity, scope, *to* do or *for*. 3. Part of house or other building enclosed by walls or partitions; (pl.) set of these occupied by person or family, apartments or lodgings; **~ and board**, meals and lodging; **~ clerk**, clerk at motel or hotel in charge of guest registration, room assignments, etc; **~ divider**, piece of furniture used to divide room into separate parts; **room·ette′**, private single compartment in railroad sleeping car; **rooming house**, house where furnished rooms are rented; **room′mate**, person

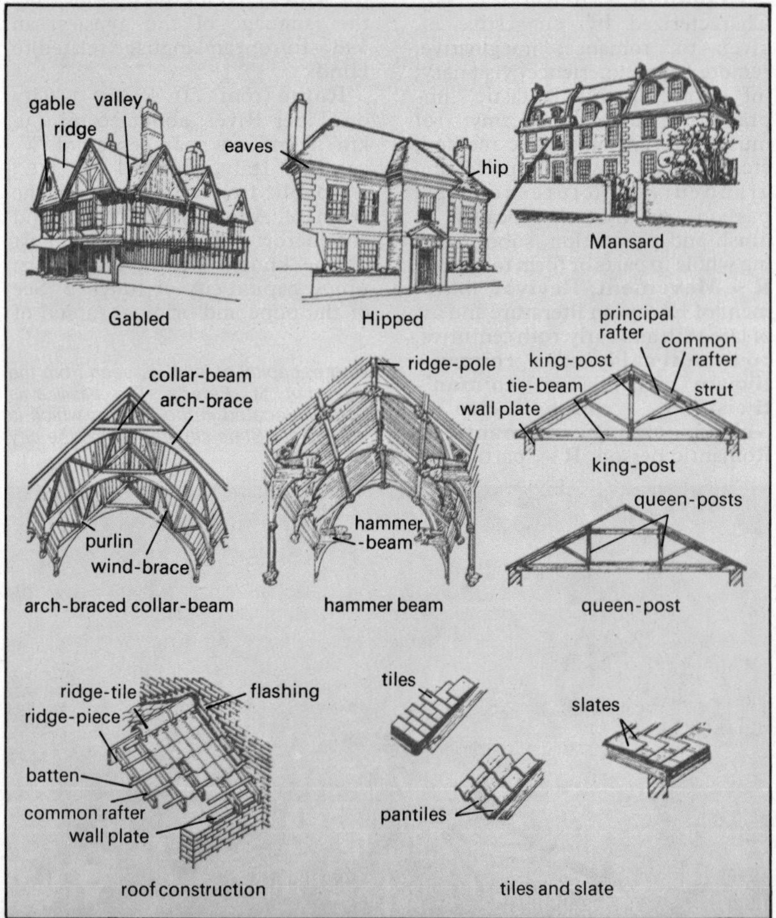

occupying same room as another; **room service**, (department of hotel responsible for) serving food and drinks to guests in their rooms; **room temperature**, normal temperature of room, about 68 Farenheit (20 Celsius). **room′ful** *n.* (pl. **-fuls**). **room** *v.i.* Have room(s), share room(s), lodge, board. **room′er** *n.* Lodger.

room·y (ro͞o′me) *adj.* (**room·i·er, room·i·est**). Capacious, large, of ample dimensions.

Roo·se·velt[1] (rō′zevĕlt), **Franklin Delano** (1882–1945). Amer. politician; assistant secretary of the

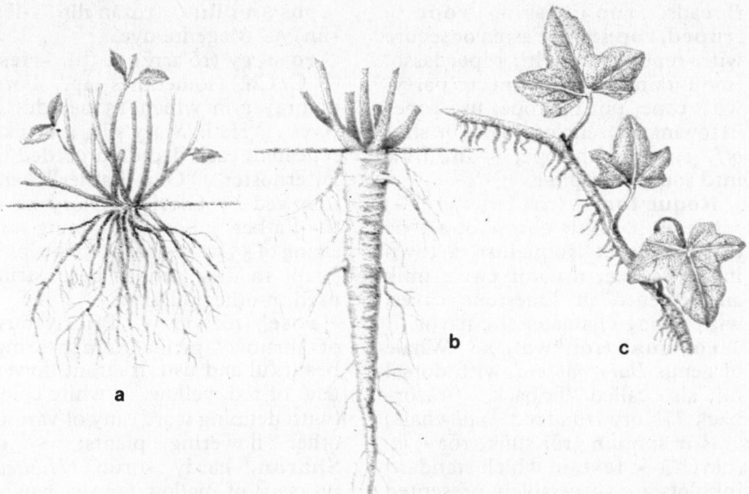

Annual plants usually have a fibrous ***root*** *structure (a), but those with a longer life may store food in a tap-root (b). Roots which grow from a stem (c) are known as adventitious.*

Navy 1913–20; governor of New York, 1929–33; 32nd U.S. president, 1933–45, first president to be reelected to a third and fourth term; pledged a "New Deal" to counter the problems of the Depression; established many government programs and agencies; with Winston Churchill drew up the Atlantic Charter formulating Anglo-Amer. international policy, 1941; distant cousin of Theodore Roosevelt.

Roo·se·velt[2] (rō′zevĕlt), **Theodore** (1858–1919). Amer. politician; governor of New York, 1899, 1900; organized and led the "Rough Riders," a volunteer cavalry unit famous for its charge up San Juan Hill during Spanish-Amer. War; U.S. vice president, 1901, becoming 26th U.S. president, 1901–1909, upon William McKinley's death; promised a "Square Deal" to all; his administration was noted for "trust busting," conservation of national resources, passage of the Pure Food and Drug Act, and the establishment of the Department of Commerce and Labor; received the Nobel Peace Prize, 1906, the first Amer. to receive any Nobel Prize.

roost (ro͞ost) *n.* Bird's perching or resting place, esp. henhouse or part of it in which fowl sleep; **come home to ~**, come back upon originator; **rule the ~**, be the leader or master. **roost** *v.* (of birds etc.) Settle for sleep, be perched or lodged for night. **roos′ter** *n.* Male of the common domestic fowl.

root[1] (ro͞ot, ro͝ot) *n.* 1. Part of plant normally below earth's surface and serving to attach it to earth and convey nourishment to it from soil; (pl.) such part divided into branches or fibers; (sing.) corresponding organ of epiphyte, tendril attaching ivy to its support; permanent underground stock of plant; (hort.) small plant with root for transplanting; **pull up by the ~s**, uproot; **take ~**, begin to draw nourishment from soil; get established; **root′stock**, rootlike stem; source, origin. 2. (Plant, such as turnip, carrot, etc. with) root used for food or in medicine. 3. Imbedded part of some bodily organ or structure, as hair, tooth, nail; part of thing attaching it to greater or more fundamental whole. 4. Source or origin (*of*); basis, dependence, means of continuance, or growth; bottom, essential substance or nature. 5. (math.) Number, quantity, or dimension that, when multiplied by itself a requisite number of times, produces a given expression (symbol √); value(s) of an unknown quantity that will satisfy a given equation; **~ mean square,** (abbrev. rms) square root of the arithmetic mean of the squares of a set of numbers. 6. (philol.) Ultimate unanalyzable element of language, forming basis of vocabulary. 7. (mus.) Fundamental note of chord. **root′let** *n.* **root′like, root′less** *adjs.* **root** *v.* 1. (Cause to) take root; fix firmly to the spot; establish. 2. Dig up by the roots; **~ out,** exterminate.

root[2], **rout** (ro͞ot, ro͝ot) *vbs.* 1. (of swine etc.) Turn up ground with snout etc., in search of food; turn *up* (ground) thus. 2. Search *out*, hunt *up*, rummage *in*.

Franklin D. Roosevelt, *32nd President of the U.S.A. and arguably one of its greatest. He managed to steer America through 2 of its major crises, the Great Depression and the 1939–45 war, and was elected for 4 terms, although he died a few months into the 4th in 1945.*

Theodore Roosevelt, *the 26th U.S. President and the youngest ever to take office. Then 42, he was regarded by conservatives as a radical and lived up to his reputation in some respects, although his famous 'busting' of business trusts was fairly ineffectual.*

A member of the crow family, the ***rook*** *is present in Europe and parts of Asia. Some live in large colonies of hundreds of birds, which was the origin of the term 'rookery'.*

root[3] (rōōt, rŏŏt) *v.* Be active *for* another by giving encouraging applause or support. **root'er** *n.*

Root (rōōt), **Elihu** (1845–1937). Amer. lawyer and statesman; U.S. secretary of War, 1899–1904, secretary of State, 1905–09, senator from New York, 1909–15; received Noble Peace Prize, 1912.

rope (rōp) *n.* 1. (Length of) stout cord of twisted hemp or other fiber; **the ~**, cord with a noose for hanging person; **the ~s**, those enclosing boxing ring or other arena; **give one (enough) ~ (to hang himself), plenty of ~**, etc., not check him, trust to his bringing about his own downfall; **know the ~s**, be familiar with the conditions in some sphere of action; **~ of tobacco** etc., tobacco etc. strung together. 2. Viscid or gelatinous stringy formation in liquid. 3. **~ ladder**, 2 long ropes connected by cross-ropes as ladder. **rop'y** *adj.* (**rop·i·er, rop·i·est**). Rope-like; forming viscid glutinous or slimy threads. **rop'i·ness** *n.* **rope** *v.* (**roped, rop·ing**). Fasten or secure with rope; catch with rope; lasso; (mountaineering) connect (party) with rope, put on rope; use ropes in towing etc.; enclose, close *in*, shut *off*, (space) with rope; **~ in**, draw into some enterprise.

Roque·fort (rōk'fert, rŏk'-) (**cheese**) *n.* Blue cheese of a type orig. made at Roquefort, a town in S. France, usu. of ewe's milk and ripened in limestone caves, with strong characteristic flavor.

ror·qual (rōr'kwal) *n.* Whale of genus *Balaenoptera*, with dorsal fin; also called "finback," "razor-back." [Norw. *raud* red, *hval* whale]

Ror·schach (rōr'shŏk, rōr'-) *n.* (psych.) **~ test**, in which standard inkblots are successively presented to subject for statement of what they suggest.

ro·sa·ceous (rōzā'shus) *adj.* Of the order Rosaceae, of which the rose is the type.

ros·an·i·line (rōzăn'ilĭn, -lēn, -līn) *n.* Magenta dye.

ro·sa·ry (rō'zerē) *n.* (pl. **-ries**). (R.C. Ch.) (sometimes cap.) Form of prayer in which 15 decades of Aves ("Hail Mary's") are usu. repeated, each decade preceded by Paternoster ("Our Father") and followed by Gloria ("Glory be to the Father"); book containing this; string of 55 or 165 beads for keeping count in this; similar bead string used in other religions.

rose[1] (rōz) *n.* 1. (Prickly bush or shrub of genus *Rosa* bearing) beautiful and usu. fragrant flowers usu. of red, yellow, or white color; (with defining word) any of various other flowering plants; **~ of Sharon**, hardy shrub (*Hibiscus syriacus*) of mallow family, having large white, purple, pink, or reddish flowers; (also Brit.) shrublike plant (*Hypericum calycinum*) native of Eurasia, having big, yellow blossoms and evergreen leaves; **bed of ~**, perfect conditions, pleasant easy post or condition. 2. Representation of the flower in heraldry or decoration; rose-shaped design; rosette worn on shoe or clerical hat; rose window; **Wars of the Roses**, series of civil wars in England during the reigns of Henry VI, Edward IV, and Richard III (15th c.), between followers of house of York (with white rose as badge) and of house of Lancaster (red rose), ended by the accession in 1485 of the Lancastrian Henry Tudor (Henry VII), who united the 2 houses by marrying Elizabeth, daughter of Edward IV. 3. Light crimson color, pink; rosy com-

*The wild **rose** (Rosa villosa) (below), is one of 250 species from which cultivated varieties like the 'fragrant cloud rose' (top left) were bred. The term may also be used for unrelated plants with rose-like blooms. Bottom left: the rock rose (Cistacea).*

Hemp being hung to dry in Taiwan is later processed and the fibers drawn and twisted to make yarn, which is formed into various strands which, when combined, become **rope.**

Both as a poet and a painter, **Dante Gabriel Rossetti** was acclaimed in the mid-19th century. 'The Bride' or 'The Beloved' typifies his capability as a colorist.

plexion. 4. **rose'bud**, bud of rose; **rose'bush**, rose plant; **rose chafer**, beetle of genus *Macrodactylus* frequenting roses, very destructive in grub state; **rose-colored**, rosy; (fig.) optimistic, cheerful; **rose fever**, type of hay fever supposedly caused by rose pollen in spring or early summer; **rose water**, perfume distilled from roses; **rose window**, round window, usu. filled with tracery suggesting rose shape or divided by spoke-like mullions; **rose'-wood**, any of various kinds of valuable close-grained fragrant cabinet wood. **rose** *adj*. Colored like a pale red rose, of warm pink.

rose[2]: see RISE.

ro·sé (rōzā') *n*. Short for *vin rosé*, pink, light table wine, made from red grapes whose skins have been removed during fermentation. [Fr.]

ro·se·ate (rō'zēĭt, -āt) *adj*. Rose-colored, cheerful, optimistic. **ro'-se·ate·ly** *adv*.

rose·mar·y (rōz'mārē) *n*. (pl. **-mar·ies**). Evergreen fragrant shrub (*Rosmarinus officinalis*), native of S. Europe, with leaves used in perfumery and cooking. [L. *ros* dew, *marinus* marine]

ro·se·o·la (rōzēō'l*a*) *n*. (path.) Any reddish rash; measles, rubeola.

Ro·set·ta (rōzĕt'*a*) **stone.** Stone found near Rosetta on the W. mouth of the Nile by Napoleon's soldiers in 1799; its inscription, in Egyptian hieroglyphics, demotic characters, and Greek, made it possible to decipher hieroglyphics.

ro·sette (rōzĕt') *n*. Rose-shaped ornament or badge made of ribbons, silk, etc.; roselike object or arrangement of leaves, parts, etc.; (archit.) carved or molded conventional rose on wall etc.; rose window.

Rosh Ha·sha·nah (rawsh hahshaw'n*a*, -shah'-, rōsh, h*a*-). Jewish New Year, celebrated in late September or early October.

Ro·si·cru·cian (rōz*i*krōō'sh*a*n, rŏz*i*-) *n*. Member of secret mystical society in 17th and 18th centuries claiming magical knowledge of life, the elements, and elemental spirits; member of the ~ **Order**, or Ancient Mystic Order Rosae Crucis, an international fraternity of religious mysticism. [L. *rosa crux* rose cross, as transl. of Ger. *Rosenkreuz*]

ros·in (rŏz'ĭn) *n*. Resin (esp. of solid residue after distillation of oil of turpentine from crude turpentine). ~ *v.t.* Smear, seal up, rub (e.g. violin bow or string), with rosin.

Ross[1] (raws, rŏs), **Betsy (Griscom)** (1752–1836). Amer. patriot formerly credited with making the first U.S. flag; the design of stars and stripes was adopted by the Continental Congress, June 14th, 1777.

Ross[2] (raws, rŏs), **Sir James Clark** (1800–62). English admiral and explorer of the Arctic and Antarctic; **Ross Sea**, Pacific Ocean inlet in Antarctica, between Edward VII Peninsula and Victoria Land; **Ross Island**, island of Antarctica in the W. part of the Ross Sea, separated from Victoria Land by McMurdo Sound; highest point, Mount Erebus, 12,450 ft. (3,795 m); **Ross Shelf Ice**, also called **Ross Barrier**, ice wall in Antarctica in the S. part of the Ross Sea, extending 400 mi. (644 km), from Ross Island to Edward VII Peninsula.

Ros·set·ti (rōsĕt'ē, -zĕt'ē). Name of English family of Italian origin: **Dante Gabriel** ~ (1828–1882), poet and painter, and his brother **William Michael** ~ (1829–1919), critic, both members of the PRE-RAPHAELITE Brotherhood; **Christina Georgina** ~ (1830–94), their sister, lyric poet.

Ros·si·ni (rawsē'nē), **Gioacchino Antonio** (1792–1868). Italian composer of *The Barber of Seville*, *William Tell*, and other operas; also composed sacred music, opera bouffe, etc.

Ros·tand (rawstahṅ'), **Edmond** (1868–1918). French poet and dramatist, author of the play *Cyrano de Bergerac*.

ros·tel·lum (rŏstĕl'*u*m) *n*. (pl. **-tel·la** pr. -tĕl'*a*). 1. (bot.) Short beak-shaped process on stigma of many violets and orchids. 2. (zool.) Hooked projection on head of tapeworm.

ros·ter (rŏs't*e*r) *n*. (mil.) List of officers and men enrolled for active duty; list of names. [Du. *rooster* list, orig. gridiron (*rooster* roast) w. ref. to parallel lines]

ros·trum (rŏs'tr*u*m) *n*. (pl. **-trums, -tra** pr. -tr*a*). 1. Platform for public speaking (orig. that in Roman forum adorned with beaks of captured galleys); pulpit; office etc. that enables person to gain the public ear. 2. (Rom.

antiq.) Beak of war galley. 3. (zool., entom., bot.) Beak, stiff snout, beaklike part. **ros′tral** *adj.* Of a beak; adorned with beaks. **ros·trate** (rŏs′trāt), **ros′trat·ed** *adjs.* Beaked.

ros·y (rō′zē) *adj.* (**ros·i·er, ros·i·est**). Colored like a red rose (esp. of complexion as indicating health, of blush, sky, etc.); (fig.) rose-colored, promising, hopeful. **ros′i·ly** *adv.* **ros′i·ness** *n.*

rot (rŏt) *n.* 1. Decay, putrefaction, rottenness (esp. in timber). 2. (slang; freq. as int. of contempt or ridicule) Nonsense; absurd statement, argument, or proposal. ~ *v.* (**rot·ted, rot·ting**). Undergo natural decomposition, decay, putrefy; cause to rot, make rotten; (fig. also ~ **away**) gradually perish from want of vigor or use; **rot′-gut**, (slang) cheap liquor.

ro·ta (rō′t*a*) *n.* 1. (chiefly Brit.) List of persons acting, or duties to be done, in rotation; roster. 2. (R.C. Ch.) Supreme ecclesiastical and secular court. [L., = "wheel"]

Ro·tar·i·an (rōtār′ē*a*n) *adj.* & *n.* (Member) of a ROTARY Club.

Ro·ta·ry (rō′t*e*rē) *adj.* ~ **Club**, local organization of businessmen, founded 1905 by Paul Harris in Chicago; it aims at furthering business service and social relations and promoting international understanding and goodwill; **Rotary International**, international organization of Rotary Clubs.

ro·ta·ry (rō′t*e*rē) *adj.* Of, acting by, rotation; ~ **engine**, internal combustion engine that supplies power directly without reciprocating parts. **rotary** *n.* Part, machine, device, etc. that rotates; traffic circle.

ro·tate (rō′tāt, rōtāt′) *v.* (**-tat·ed, -tat·ing**). Move around axis or center, revolve; plant or grow (crops) in fixed order of succession to maintain soil fertility; do, take, schedule in rotation. **ro′tat·a·ble, ro·ta·to·ry** (rō′t*a*tōrē, -tōrē), **ro·ta·tive** (rō′tātĭv) *adjs.*

ro·ta·tion (rōtā′sh*o*n) *n.* Rotating; recurrence, recurrent series or period, regular succession in office etc. **ro·ta′tion·al** *adj.*

ro·ta·tor (rō′tāt*e*r, rōtā′-) *n.* Revolving apparatus or part.

ROTC *abbrev.* Reserve Officers' Training Corps.

rote (rōt) *n.* Mere habituation, knowledge got by repetition, unintelligent memory (usu. **by** ~).

Roth·schild (rŏth′chīld, rawth′-). Name of family of financiers, founders in Germany, toward end of 18th c., of famous banking house, with branches at Paris, Vienna, London, and Naples.

ro·ti·fer (rō′tĭf*e*r) *n.* Member of the phylum Rotifera of minute (usu. microscopic) metazoan animals with (usu.) ring(s) of beating cilia giving the impression of revolving wheels; wheel animalcule.

ro·tis·ser·ie (rōtĭs′*e*rē) *n.* Broiler with motor-driven spit.

ro·to·gra·vure (rōt*o*gr*a*vūr′, -grāv′y*e*r) *n.* Intaglio printing process that transfers images etched on copper cylinders to paper etc. on rotary press; material printed by this process.

ro·tor (rō′t*e*r) *n.* Rotary part of machine; rotating horizontal blades of a helicopter etc.

rot·ten (rŏt′*e*n) *adj.* 1. Affected with rot; perishing of decay; falling to pieces, friable, easily breakable or tearable, from age or use. 2. Morally, socially, or politically corrupt. 3. (slang) Disagreeable, regrettable, ill-advised; very bad, wretched. 4. ~ **borough**: see BOROUGH; **rot′tenstone**, decomposed siliceous limestone used as polishing powder. **rot′ten·ly** *adj.* **rot′ten·ness** *n.*

Rot·ter·dam (rŏt′*e*rdăm). City and principal port of the Netherlands, on the Rhine-Meuse delta.

ro·tund (rōtŭnd′) *adj.* Round, circular (rare); (of speech etc.) as uttered from a rounded mouth, sonorous, sounding, grandiloquent; (of persons) plump, pudgy. **ro·tund′ly** *adv.* **ro·tund′ness** *n.*

ro·tun·da (rōtŭn′d*a*) *n.* Circular building, hall, lobby, etc., esp. one with dome or high ceiling.

Rou·ault (rōōō′), **Georges** (1871–1958). French expressionist painter.

rou·ble: see RUBLE.

rou·é (rōōā′) *n.* Debauchee, rake. [Fr., past part. of *rouer* break on wheel, = one deserving this]

Rou·en (rōōahṅ′). City of N. France, on river Seine; ancient capital of Normandy; famous for its cathedral and as Joan of Arc's place of execution.

rouge (rōōzh) *n.* Fine red powder made (orig.) from safflower and used for coloring cheeks and lips; any cosmetic used thus; red powder of ferric oxide, used to polish metal, glass, etc.; red in ~ **et noir**, gambling card game played on table with two red and two black diamond-shaped marks upon which stakes are placed. **rouge** *adj.* Red. ~ *v.* (**rouged, roug·ing**). Color, adorn oneself, with rouge.

rough (rŭf) *adj.* 1. Of uneven or irregular surface; not smooth, level, or polished; diversified or broken by prominences; hairy, shaggy, coarse in texture, rugged. 2. Not mild, quiet, or gentle; unrestrained, violent, stormy, boisterous, disorderly, riotous; harsh, unfeeling; grating, astringent. 3. De-

The main ***rotor*** *of a helicopter consists of overhead blades. When rotated they produce vertical lift. The tail rotor acts as a rudder and a stabilizer against torque.*

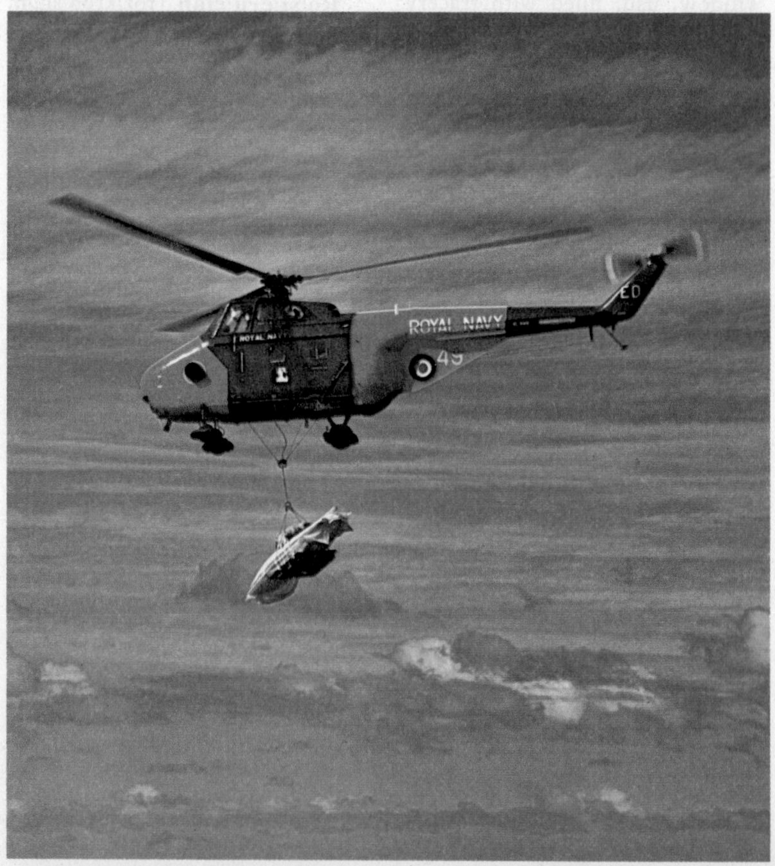

The term **roundup** is derived from a method of mustering cattle or sheep whereby they are made to move in a circle to stop any breaking away from the main group.

ficient in finish, elaboration, or delicacy; incomplete, rudimentary; entirely or partly unwrought; inexact, approximate, preliminary. 4. **~-and-ready**, not overparticular; roughly efficient or effective; **~-and-tumble**, disorderly, regardless of procedural rules; **rough'cast**, (coat, coated, with) plaster of lime and gravel for walls; (*v.*) (**-cast, -cast·ing**), coat with roughcast; **rough coat**, 1st coat of plaster laid on; **rough-hew**, (**-hewed, -hewed** or **-hewn, -hew'ing**) shape out roughly, give crude form to; (in past part.) uncouth, unrefined; **rough'house**, rowdy play; **rough'neck**, rowdy or pugnacious fellow; **rough on**, bearing, what bears, hard on (person); **rough'rider**, man who can ride unbroken horses; bronco buster; **Rough Riders**, in Spanish-Amer. war, Theodore Roosevelt's volunteer cavalry composed of many cowboys; **rough'shod**, (of horse) having shoes with the nailheads projecting to prevent slipping; **ride roughshod over**, treat arrogantly or inconsiderately. **rough'en** *v.* **rough'ish** *adj.* **rough'ly** *adv.* **rough'ness** *n.* **rough** *adv.* In rough manner. ~ *n.* 1. Rough ground; (golf) rough uncut ground bordering the fairway or between the tee and the green. 2. Rowdy, ruffian. 3. Unfinished or natural state. 4. Rough drawing etc. ~ *v.t.* 1. Turn *up* (feathers, hair, etc.) by rubbing against the grain. 2. Shape or plan *out*, sketch *in*, roughly; give first shaping to. 3. ~ **it**, do without ordinary conveniences of life.

rough·age (rŭf'ĭj) *n.* Indigestible fibrous matter or cellulose in foodstuffs.

rou·lade (ro͞olahd') *n.* 1. Florid passage of runs etc. in solo vocal music, usu. sung to 1 syllable; drum roll. 2. Slice of meat rolled up around a filling and cooked.

rou·lette (ro͞olĕt') *n.* 1. Gambling game played on table with rotating disk on which small ball is set in motion, and finally drops into one of set of numbered, alternately red and black, slots. 2. Revolving toothed wheel for making dotted lines in engraving, similar wheel for perforating postage stamps.

Rou·ma·nia = RUMANIA.

round[1] (rownd) *adj.* 1. Spherical, circular, or cylindrical, or approaching these forms; presenting convex outline or surface; done with or involving circular motion; (of cheeks) plump. 2. Entire, continuous, sound, smooth; complete (as ~ dozen); (of tones etc.) full and mellow. 3. ~ **arch**, semicircular arch characteristic of Romanesque architecture; ~ **dance**, one in which dancers form a ring; ~ **figure**(**s**), round number; figure given as an approximate estimation; **Round'head**, member or supporter of Parliamentary or Puritan party in English Civil War, 1642–9; **round'house**, circular building where locomotives are repaired; (baseball) widely curved pitch; (boxing) blow given with wide swing of arm; **round number**, number (as tens, hundreds, etc.) stated without odd units; **round robin**, tournament in which each competitor plays against every other; petition with signatures in circle to conceal order of signing; letter written by members of a group, each individual contributing short section; **round-shouldered**, having shoulders so bent forward that back is convex; **Round Table**, that around which King Arthur and his knights are supposed to have sat, so that none might have precedence; **round trip**, outward and return journey; **round'worm**, nematode worm, often parasitic, e.g. species infesting human intestines. **round'ish** *adj.* **round'ness** *n.*

Nematodes, which include the **round worm,** are mostly parasites. These worms have no segments and may live in the bodies of humans, horses and many domesticated animals.

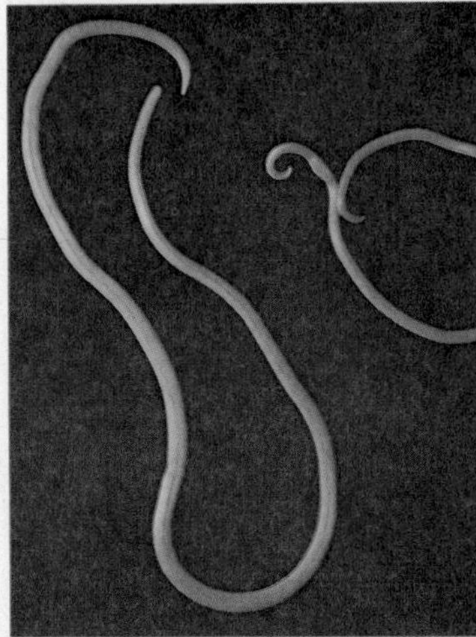

round[2] (rownd) *n.* 1. Round object; rung of ladder; large round piece *of* beef, cut from haunch; rounded or convex form. 2. Revolving motion; circular, circuitous, or recurring course; circuit, cycle, series; (often pl.) course of customary places, duties, or actions, as of inspection, deliveries, etc.; (golf) playing of all holes in course once. 3. (mus.) Kind of

Henri Rousseau had a flair for brilliant color and developed an original, if primitive, style. His impressions of tropical flora were gained from hothouse plants and he never left France.

canon for three or more voices singing the same melody, the first voice completing a phrase before the second enters, and so on. 4. Allowance of something distributed or measured out; one of set or series; one bout or spell; one stage in competition; single discharge of shot by firearm; ammunition for this; (archery) fixed number of arrows discharged at fixed distance; **in the ~**, with spectators, congregation, etc. sitting all around central stage, altar, etc.

round[3] (rownd) *adv.* 1. Around. 2. **~ about,** in a ring (about), all around; on all sides; circuitously; **round′a·bout** (*adj.*) circuitous; circumlocutory; (Brit.) (*n.*) traffic circle. **round** *prep.* Around; throughout; in circumference; **~-the-clock**, for 24 hours; unceasingly.

round[4] (rownd) *v.* 1. Invest with, assume round shape; round the lips in pronouncing (vowel); bring to complete, symmetrical, or well-ordered state; make round number (freq. **~ off**). 2. Gather *up* (cattle) by riding around (freq. transf.), hence, **round′up** (*n.*) this action. 3. (naut.) Sail around, double (headland etc.).

roun·del (rown′del) *n.* Small disk, esp. decorative medallion etc.

roun·de·lay (rown′delā) *n.* Short simple song with refrain.

round·ers (rown′derz) *n.* English bat-and-ball game, precursor of baseball.

round·ly (rownd′lē) *adv.* 1. In thoroughgoing manner; bluntly, with plain speech; without qualification, severely. 2. In circular way.

roup (ro͞op) *n.* Highly infectious poultry disease characterized by an acute fever generally ending in death.

rouse (rowz) *v.* (**roused, rous·ing**). 1. Startle (game) from lair or cover; bring out of a state of sleep, quiescence, etc.; provoke temper of, inflame with passion; evoke (feelings). 2. Cease to sleep; become active. **rous′ing** *adj.* (esp.) Exciting, stirring; brisk, lively. **rous′er** *n.*

Rous·seau[1] (ro͞osō′), **Henri** (1844–1910). French primitive painter; a customs officer, hence called "Le Douanier."

Rous·seau[2] (ro͞osō′), **Jean Jacques** (1712–78). French philosopher, advocate of return to natural state, in which man is both good and happy; the *Contrat Social* (1762), expounding the view that society is founded on a contract and that the head of a state is not the people's master but their mandatory, had profound influence on French thought and prepared the way for the Revolution.

roust·a·bout (rows′tabowt) *n.* Deck or dock worker; circus worker who helps put up and take down tents etc.; any unskilled or migrant worker, as in oil fields, on ranches, etc.

rout[1] (rowt) *n.* 1. Assemblage of company esp. of revelers or rioters; riot, tumult, disturbance, clamor, fuss. 2. Disorderly retreat of defeated army or troops; **put to ~**, utterly defeat. **rout** *v.t.* Put to rout.

rout[2] (rowt, ro͞ot) *v.* = ROOT[2]; (also) force out, eject. **rout′er** *n.* (esp.) Kind of plane used in molding.

route (ro͞ot, rowt) *n.* Way taken in getting from starting point to destination; customary line of travel; course or territory of a deliveryman, salesman, etc.; highway (**R~** when followed by a number and used as a highway name). **route** *v.t.* (**rout·ed, rout·ing**). Plan route of (goods, travelers, etc.); send along a specific route.

rou·tine (ro͞oten′) *n.* Regular course of procedure, unvarying performance of certain acts; set form, fixed arrangement (e.g. of steps in dancer's performance); (attrib.) performed by rule or habitually. **rou·tine'ly** *adv.* **rou·tin'-ism, rou·tin'ist** *ns.* **rou·tin·ize** (rōōtē'nīz, rōō'te-) *v.t.* (**-ized, -iz·ing**).

roux (rōō) *n.* (cookery) Flour cooked in melted fat, used to thicken sauces etc. [Fr., = "red," "browned"]

rove[1] (rōv) *v.* (**roved, rov·ing**). Wander without fixed destination, roam, ramble; (of eyes) look in various directions; wander over or through. ~ *n.* Act of roving. **rov'er**[1] *n.* (esp.) Pirate. [orig. term used in archery, = "shoot at casual mark with range not determined"]

rove[2] (rōv) *n.* Sliver of cotton, wool, etc., drawn out and slightly twisted. ~ *v.t.* (**roved, rov·ing**). Form into roves. **rov'er**[2] *n.*

row[1] (rō) *n.* Number of persons or things in a more or less straight line; street with continuous line of buildings on one or each side (freq. in street names); line of seats in theater etc.; row of plants in garden etc.; **a hard ~ to hoe**, difficult task; **~ house**, one of a line of identical houses, usu. with common walls along sides.

row[2] (rō) *v.* Propel boat, propel (boat), convey (passengers, goods) in boat, with oars or sweeps; pull (oar) as part of racing crew; race *against* by rowing; (of boat) be fitted with (so many *oars*); **row'boat**, boat propelled with oars. **row'er** *n.* **row** *n.* Period of rowing, boat excursion.

row[3] (row) *n.* (colloq.) Disturbance, commotion, noise, dispute; free fight; being reprimanded; **make a ~**, make a fuss or protest.

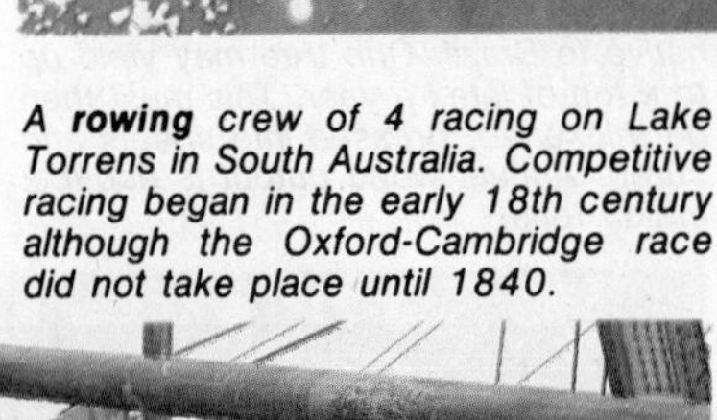

A **rowing** crew of 4 racing on Lake Torrens in South Australia. Competitive racing began in the early 18th century although the Oxford-Cambridge race did not take place until 1840.

Roustabouts working on an Indonesian drilling rig. Traditionally, roustabout means an unskilled laborer but rig work requires training for the long hours and hard work.

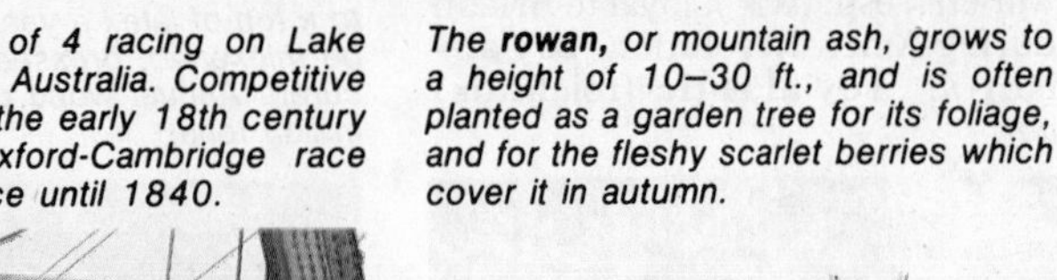

The **rowan,** or mountain ash, grows to a height of 10–30 ft., and is often planted as a garden tree for its foliage, and for the fleshy scarlet berries which cover it in autumn.

row·an (rō'*an*, row'-): see MOUNTAIN ash.

row·dy (row'dē) *adj.* (**-di·er, -di·est**) & *n.* (pl. **-dies**). Rough, disorderly, and noisy (person). **row'di·ness, row'dy·ism** *ns.*

roy·al (roi'*al*) *adj.* 1. Of, from, suited to, worthy of, belonging to family of, in service or under patronage of, a king or queen; **R ~ Academy of Arts**, institution, founded 1768 in London under patronage of George III, for annual exhibition of works of contemporary artists and establishment of school of art; **~ blue**, deep vivid blue. 2. Kingly, majestic, stately, (colloq.) splendid, first-rate; on grand scale; of exceptional size etc.; **battle ~**, free fight; heated dispute; **~ fern**, flowering fern (*Osmunda regalis*), with tall upright fronds; **~ flush**, (poker) highest hand in poker, straight flush headed by ace; **~ jelly**, substance secreted by worker bees, fed to all larvae in first few days of life and afterward only to those selected to develop into queens; **~ palm**, any of several fast-growing palm trees (genus *Roystonea*) of W. Indies and Florida, noted for adaptability, having long, bare trunk crowned with large cluster of pinnate leaves. **roy'al·ly** *adv.* **royal** *n.* Size of paper, 19 × 24 in. for writing and 20 × 25 in. for printing.

Roy·al (roi'*al*) **Gorge.** Canyon in S. central Colorado extending 4.5 mi. (7 km), along the Arkansas River, with walls rising 1,000 ft. (304 m).

roy·al·ist (roi'*al*ĭst) *n.* Monarchist, supporter of monarchy as institution or of the royal side in civil war etc.; esp. (**R ~**), loyal to Britain during Amer. Revolution. **roy'al·ism** *n.* **roy·al·is·tic** (roi*a*lĭs'tĭk) *adj.*

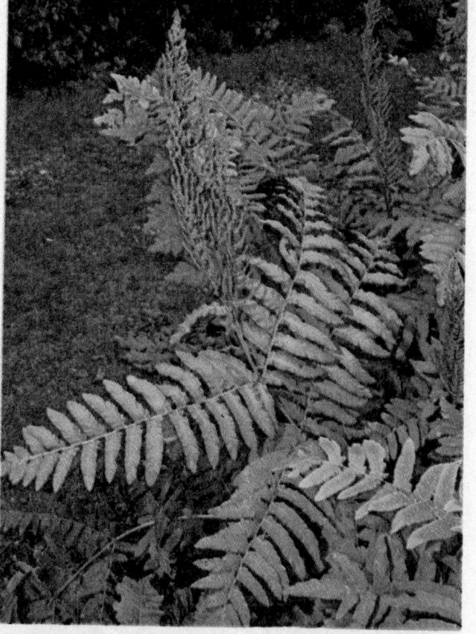

*With some ten species growing in temperate and tropical regions, the **royal fern** may attain a height of 6 ft. Its rootstock, similar to that on a tree fern, can be about a foot high.*

roy·al·ty (roi'*al*tē) *n.* (pl. **-ties**). 1. Office, dignity, or power of king or queen; sovereignty. 2. Royal persons; member of royal family. 3. Prerogative or privilege of sovereign (usu. pl.). 4. Sum paid to patentee for use of patent or to author, composer, etc., for each copy of book, piece of music, etc., sold, or for each public performance of work.

rpm, r.p.m. *abbrevs.* Revolutions per minute.

Rs., Rs, rs. *abbrevs.* Rupees.

RSFSR, R.S.F.S.R. *abbrevs.* Russian Soviet Federal Socialist Republic.

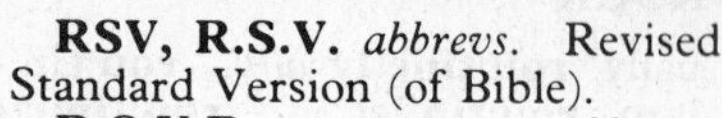

RSV, R.S.V. *abbrevs.* Revised Standard Version (of Bible).

R.S.V.P., r.s.v.p. *abbrevs.* Répondez s'il vous plaît (Fr., = "answer, if you please").

rte. *abbrev.* Route.

Rt. Hon. *abbrev.* Right Honorable.

Rt. Rev. *abbrev.* Right Reverend.

Ru *symbol.* Ruthenium.

rub (rŭb) *v.* (**rubbed, rub·bing**). 1. Subject to friction, slide one's hand or an object along, over, or up and down the surface of; polish, clean, abrade, chafe, make *bare, dry, sore*, etc., by rubbing; slide (hands, object) *against, on* or *over* something, (objects) *together*, with friction; bring *away, off*, or *out*, force *in, into, through*, reduce *to* powder, etc., bring size or level of *down*, spread *over*, groom *down*, freshen or brush *up*, by rubbing (lit. and fig.); **~ down**, smooth or polish by rubbing; massage; hence **rub'down** *n.* **~ in**, (fig., colloq.) emphasize; **~ noses**, rub nose against another's in greeting; **~ one's hands (together)**, rub each with the other, usu. in sign of keen satisfaction; **~ shoulders**, come into close contact *with* (other people); **~ the wrong way**, stroke against the grain, irritate or repel as by stroking cat upward. 2. Prepare RUBBING. 3. Come into or be in sliding contact, exercise friction, *against* or *on*; (of cloth, skin, etc.) get frayed, worn, sore, or bare with friction. **rub** *n.* Spell of rubbing; impediment, difficulty (*there's the rub*).

rub-a-dub (rŭb'*a*dŭb) *n.* Rolling sound of drum. [imit.]

Rub·al Kha·li (rōōb'*al* kah'lē). (also called Ar Rimal or Great Sandy Desert) Desert in the S. Arabian peninsula covering 250,000 sq. mi. (647,500 sq. km), extending from NE. Yemen to

__Rubber__ sap is 'milked' from a tree once native to Brazil. One tree may yield up to a ton of latex a year. This must then be thickened, pressed into sheets and cured. Annual world output is about 2 million tons.

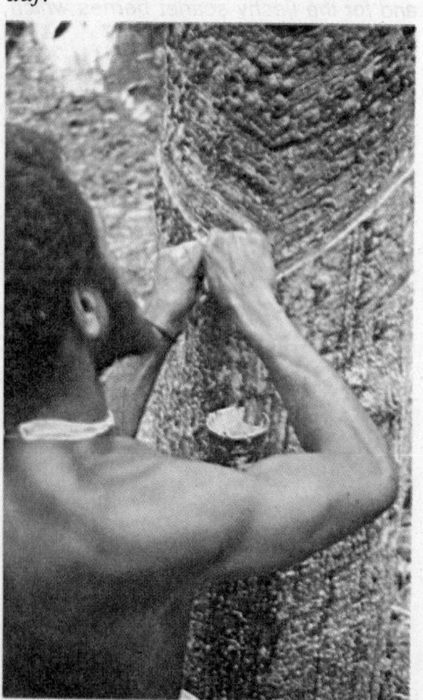

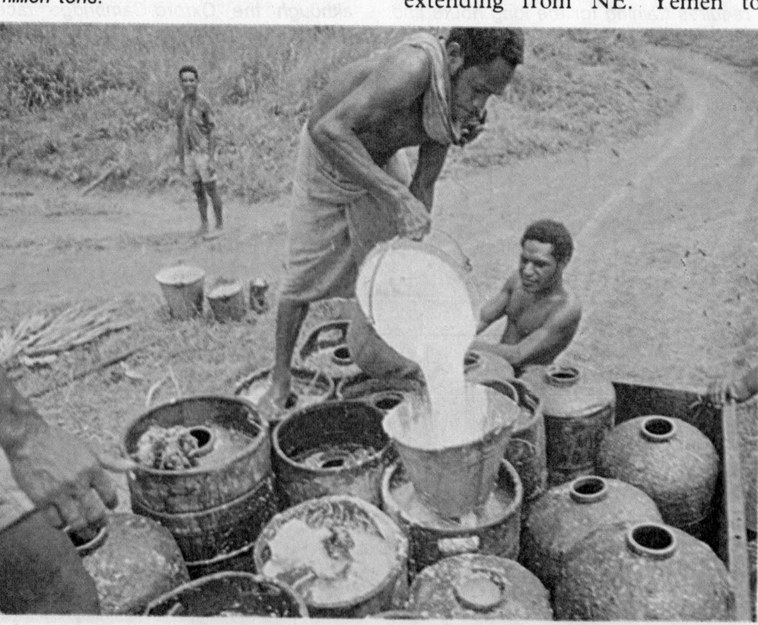

central Oman and including a large section of SE. Saudi Arabia.

rub·ber[1] (rŭb′*er*) *n.* 1. Person who rubs. 2. Implement used for rubbing. 3. (from its use in erasing pencil marks; also **india rubber**) Elastic solid made from milky juice (latex) of certain plants and trees (esp. *Hevea brasiliensis*) of S. Amer., Africa, the E. Indies, etc., and used for many purposes in industry, e.g. for making tires and waterproofing cloth; (chiefly Brit.) piece of this or other substance for erasing pencil marks; (pl.) galoshes, pair of low rubber overshoes; **rub′berneck,** (slang) sightseeing tourist, inquisitive person; (*v.*) act as rubberneck; **rubber stamp,** stamp for quickly endorsing papers with signature, date, etc., hence **rubber-stamp** (*v.*) give (unconsidered) endorsement to others' decision. **rub′ber·y** *adj.*

rub·ber[2] (rŭb′*er*) *n.* Three successive games (or two games won by same side) between sides or persons at bridge, whist, cribbage, backgammon, etc.

rub·bing (rŭb′ĭng) *n.* Reproduction of incised or raised surface of sepulchral stone or brass made by rubbing gently with charcoal, colored chalk, etc. on paper placed over surface.

rub·bish (rŭb′ĭsh) *n.* Waste material, debris, refuse, litter; worthless material or articles, trash; absurd ideas or suggestions, nonsense (freq. as excl. of contempt). **rub′bish·y** *adj.*

rub·ble (rŭb′*el*) *n.* Waste fragments of stone, brick, etc., esp. from old or demolished buildings; pieces of undressed stone used, esp. as filling, for walls; (geol.) loose angular stones etc. forming upper covering of some rocks; waterworn stones. **rub′bly** *adj.*

rube (ro͞ob) *n.* (slang) Country bumpkin.

ru·be·fa·cient (ro͞ob*e*fā′sh*e*nt) *n.* & *adj.* (med.) (Counterirritant etc.) producing redness or slight inflammation. **ru·be·fac·tion** (ro͞ob*e*făk′sh*o*n) *n.*

ru·bel·la (ro͞obĕl′*a*) = GERMAN measles.

ru·bel·lite (ro͞obĕl′īt, ro͞o′b*e*līt) *n.* Red variety of tourmaline.

Ru·bens (ro͞o′bĭnz), **Sir Peter Paul** (1577–1640). Flemish painter active at Antwerp and in Italy, France, Spain, and England.

ru·be·o·la (ro͞obē͞o′l*a*) = MEASLES.

Ru·bi·con (ro͞o′b*i*kŏn). Ancient name of a small stream flowing into Adriatic, forming part of boundary of Cisalpine Gaul; by taking his army across it, i.e. outside his own province, in 49 B.C., Julius Caesar committed himself to war against the Senate and Pompey; hence, **cross, pass, the ~,** take decisive

The paintings of ***Peter Paul Rubens*** *are renowned for their vivacity and power, well demonstrated in his 'Rape of the Sabine Women', a huge canvas housed in the National Gallery, London, U.K.*

The ***Royal*** *family in England are expected to maintain a public profile but to exercise no authority in political matters, although Queen Elizabeth II has weekly meetings with the Prime Minister and may register her opinion.*

step, begin undertaking from which one cannot turn back.

ru·bi·cund (ro͞o'bĭkŭnd) *adj.* (esp. of complexion) Ruddy. **ru·bi·cun'di·ty** *n.*

ru·bid·i·um (ro͞obĭd'ēum) *n.* (chem.) Rare soft silvery metallic element, one of the alkali metals; symbol Rb, at. no. 37, at. wt. 85.4678. [L. *rubidus* red, from 2 red lines in its spectrum]

Ru·bin·stein[1] (ro͞o'bĭnstīn), **Anton Grigorevich** (1829–94). Russian pianist and musical composer.

Ru·bin·stein[2] (ro͞o'bĭnstīn), **Artur** (1887–1982). Polish-born Amer. concert pianist.

ru·ble, rou·ble (ro͞o'bel) *ns.* Principal monetary unit of U.S.S.R. = 100 kopecks.

ru·bric (ro͞o'brĭk) *n.* Heading of chapter, section, etc., also special passage or sentence, written or printed in red or in special lettering; direction for conduct of divine service (prop. in red) inserted in liturgical book; (red-letter entry in) calendar of saints (now rare). **ru'bri·cal** *adj.* **ru'bri·cal·ly** *adv.* **ru·bri·cian** (ro͞obrĭsh'an) *n.*

ru·bri·cate (ro͞o'brĭkāt) *v.t.* (**-cat·ed, -cat·ing**). Mark with, print or write in, red; furnish with rubrics. **ru·bri·ca·tion** (ro͞obrĭkā'shon) *n.*

ru·by (ro͞o'bē) *n.* (pl. **-bies**). 1. Rare and valuable precious stone (**true** or **Oriental** ~), a species of corundum, of color varying from deep crimson to pale rose red. 2. Color of ruby, a rich glowing purple-tinged red. **ruby** *adj.* Of ruby color.

ruche (ro͞osh) *n.* Frill or gathering of lace etc. as trimming, esp. one with both edges sewn to garment; parallel rows of gathering.

ruck[1] (rŭk) *n.* Undistinguished crowd or general run of persons or things.

ruck[2] (rŭk) *n.* & *v.* Crease, wrinkle.

ruck·sack (rŭk'săk, ro͝ok'-) *n.* Hiker's knapsack slung by straps from both shoulders and resting on back.

ruck·us (rŭk'us) *n.* (colloq.) Ruction.

ruc·tion (rŭk'shon) *n.* (slang, usu. pl.) Disturbance, tumult.

rud·der (rŭd'er) *n.* Broad flat wooden or metal piece hinged to vessel's sternpost for steering with; similar device on an aircraft; (fig.) guiding principle, etc. **rud'der·less** *adj.*

rud·dy (rŭd'ē) *adj.* (**-di·er, -di·est**). 1. Freshly or healthily red; reddish; ~ **duck**, small Amer. duck (*Oxyura jamaicensis rubida*) having white head, uptilted tail, and (in the male) bright ruddy color. 2. (esp. Brit. slang) = BLOODY sense 3. **rud'di·ly** *adv.* **rud'di·ness** *n.*

***Ruin** of the temple of Aphaea on Aegina Island, about 17 miles south-west of Athens. In the 12th century the island was a pirates' haven until the Venetians drove them out.*

rude (ro͞od) *adj.* (**rud·er, rud·est**). 1. Primitive, simple; in natural state; uncivilized, uneducated; roughly made, contrived, or executed. 2. Violent, not gentle; unrestrained, startling, abrupt. 3. Insolent, impertinent, offensive. **rude'ly** *adv.* **rude'ness** *n.*

ru·di·ment (ro͞o'dĭment) *n.* 1. (pl.) Elements or first principles of or *of* knowledge or some subject. 2. (pl.) Imperfect beginning of something that will develop or might have developed. 3. Part or organ incompletely developed, as a vestigial one or one having no function. **ru·di·men·ta·ry** (ro͞odĭmĕn'terē) *adj.*

*Common **rue** is a perennial herb whose leaves are used to flavor meats and sauces. A bitter oil can be distilled from the young shoots and is used in perfumery and for flavorings.*

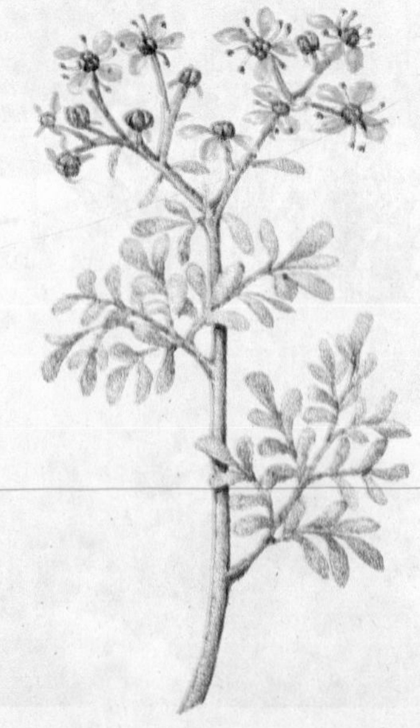

Ru·dolf[1] **I** (ro͞o'dŏlf). (1218–1291). Founder of Hapsburg dynasty; king of Germany and Holy Roman Emperor, 1273–91.

Ru·dolf[2] (ro͞o'dŏlf) **of Hapsburg** (1858–1889). Archduke and crown prince of Austria; only son of Emperor Franz Joseph; his death and that of Baroness Marie Vetsera were officially reported as suicides when their bodies were found together at his hunting lodge at Mayerling.

rue[1] (ro͞o) *v.t.* (**rued, ru·ing**). (pres. part. **rueing**). Repent of, bitterly feel the consequences of, wish undone or unbefallen. **rue** *n.* (archaic) Repentance, dejection at some occurrence. **rue'ful** *adj.* Doleful, dismal. **rue'ful·ly** *adv.* **rue'ful·ness** *n.*

rue[2] (ro͞o) *n.* Evergreen shrub (*Ruta graveolens*) with bitter strong-scented leaves.

ruff[1] (rŭf) *n.* Deep projecting starched frill of several separately ridged or pleated folds of linen or muslin worn around neck, esp. in 16th c.; projecting or conspicuously colored ring of feathers or hair around bird's or beast's neck. **ruffed** *adj.* ~ **grouse,** Amer. game bird (*Bonasa umbellus*) with strongly marked tail that the male spreads in display while drumming with his wings.

ruff[2] (rŭf) *n.* Small European freshwater fish of perch family (*Acerina cernua*), olive-brown with rough prickly scales and brown and black spots.

ruff[3] (rŭf) *n.* & *v.* Trump(ing) at bridge, etc.

ruf·fi·an (rŭf'ēan) *n.* Brutal bully, violent lawless person. **ruf'fi·an·ism** *n.* **ruf'fi·an·ly** *adj.*

ruf·fle (rŭf'el) *v.* (**-fled, -fling**). 1. Disturb smoothness or tranquillity of; (of bird) erect (feathers) in anger etc.; (fig.) irritate, perturb. 2. Suffer ruffling. 3. Gather (lace etc.) into a ruffle. ~ *n.* 1. Perturbation, bustle (rare); rippling effect on water. 2. Ornamental gathered or pleated frill of lace etc. worn at opening of garment, esp. about wrist, breast, or neck; ruff of bird etc.

ru·fous (ro͞o'fus) *adj.* (Chiefly biol.) Reddish brown.

rug (rŭg) *n.* 1. (chiefly hist.) Large wrap or coverlet of thick wool, animal skin, etc. 2. Piece of shaggy material or thick pile used to cover portion of floor; **pull the** ~ **(out) from under,** (fig.) remove support or concealment of (person).

Rug·by (rŭg'bē). Town in England, site of private school founded 1567; **rugby**, Brit. form of football played with 15 or 13 players on a side, with an elliptical football punted, dribbled, or passed

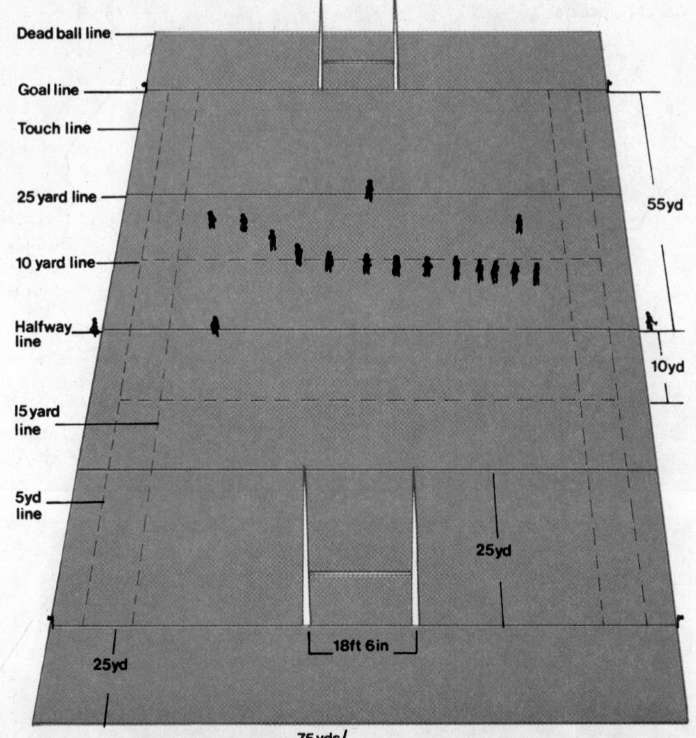

The original English game of ***rugby football*** *has never had the same support as soccer. However, large crowds are attracted to matches such as that between England and Ireland (below left). Several versions are played.*

from hand to hand, the object being to touch down behind the opponents' line and score a try, and to kick the ball over the crossbar of the H-shaped goal.

rug·ged (rŭg´ĭd) *adj.* Of rough uneven surface; lacking gentleness or refinement; harsh in sound; austere, unbending; involving hardship. **rug'ged·ly** *adv.* **rug'ged·ness** *n.*

ru·gose (rōō´gōs, rōōgōs´) *adj.* (chiefly biol.) Wrinkled, corrugated. **ru'gose·ly** *adv.* **ru·gos·i·ty** (rōōgŏs´ĭtē) *n.*

Ruhr (roor). River of West Germany, flowing into Rhine; coal mining district, with iron and steel and other heavy industries, along this river.

ru·in (rōō´ĭn) *n.* Downfall, fallen or wrecked state (lit. or fig.); (freq. pl.) what remains of building, town, structure, etc., that has suffered ruin; (sing.) what causes ruin, destroying agency, havoc. ~ *v.t.* Reduce (place) to ruins; bring to ruin. **ru·in·a·tion** (rōōĭnā´shon) *n.*

ru·in·ous (rōō´ĭn*u*s) *adj.* In ruins, dilapidated; bringing ruin, disastrous. **ru'in·ous·ly** *adv.* **ru'in·ous·ness** *n.*

rule (rōōl) *n.* 1. Principle to which action or procedure conforms or is bound or intended to conform; dominant custom, canon, standard, normal state of things; **as a ~**, usually, more often than not; **~ of thumb**, rough practical method based on experience or practice, not theory. 2. Sway, government, dominion. 3. (eccles.) Code of discipline observed by religious order; (law) order made by judge or court with reference to particular case only. 4. Graduated, freq. jointed, strip of metal or wood used for measuring, esp. by carpenters etc.; (print.) thin slip of metal for separating headings, columns, etc. **rule** *v.* (**ruled, rul·ing**). 1. Exercise sway or decisive influence over; keep under control, curb; (pass.) consent to follow advice, be guided *by*; **ruling passion**, motive that habitually directs one's actions. 2. Be the ruler(s), have the sovereign control of or *over*, bear rule. 3. Give judicial or authoritative decision; **rule out**, exclude, pronounce irrelevant or ineligible. 4. Make parallel lines across (paper); make (straight line) with ruler or mechanical help.

rul·er (rōō´l*e*r) *n.* 1. Person or thing bearing (esp. sovereign or dictatorial) rule. 2. Straight strip (usu. of wood) used in ruling paper or lines. **rul'er·ship** *n.*

rul·ing (rōō´lĭng) *n.* (esp.) Authoritative pronouncement, judicial decision.

rum (rŭm) *n.* 1. Alcoholic liquor distilled from products of sugar cane, chiefly in W. Indies and Guyana. 2. Any intoxicating liquor; **rum'runner**, (colloq.) smuggler of alcoholic liquor.

Ru·ma·ni·a, Rou·ma·ni·a (rōō-mā´nē*a* -mān´y*a*), **Ro·ma·ni·a** (rō-mā´nē*a*, -mān´y*a*). Country of SE. Europe, on the Black Sea, formed by union in 1861 of Moldavia and Wallachia; a monarchy from 1881 to 1947, when it was declared a republic; capital, Bucharest. **Ru·ma'ni·an** *adj.* & *n.* 1. (Native, inhabitant) of Rumania. 2. (Of) the language of Rumania, a Romance language much influenced by Slavonic.

rum·ba (rŭm´b*a*, rōōm´-) *n.* Cuban dance; ballroom dance imitative of this.

rum·ble (rŭm´b*e*l) *v.* (**-bled, -bling**). Make sound (as) of thunder, earthquake, heavy cart, etc.; go *along, by*, etc., making or in vehicle making such sound; utter, say, give *out, forth*, with such sound. ~ *n.* 1. Rumbling sound; (slang) street fight between teenage gangs. 2. Hind part of carriage; luggage compartment or servant's seat at rear of carriage; **~ seat**, uncovered folding seat at rear of 2-seater automobile. **rum'bler** *n.* **rum'bling·ly** *adv.* **rum'bly** *adj.*

*With substantial mineral reserves, including the largest oil fields in eastern Europe, **Rumania** has a thriving manufacturing industry with steelworks, and machinery and chemical plants.*

ru·men (ro͞o′m*e*n) *n.* (pl. **-mi·na** pr. -m*i*n*a*). Ruminant's first stomach.

ru·mi·nant (ro͞o′m*i*n*a*nt) *n.* Animal that chews the cud. ~ *adj.* 1. Belonging to the ruminants. 2. Given to, engaged in, rumination.

ru·mi·nate (ro͞o′m*i*nāt) *v.* (**-nat·ed, -nat·ing**). 1. Chew the cud. 2. Meditate, ponder. **ru·mi·na′tion** *n.* **ru′mi·na·tive** *adj.* **ru′mi·na·tive·ly** *adv.*

rum·mage (rŭm′ĭj) *v.* (**-maged, -mag·ing**). Ransack, make search in or *in*, make search; discover by thorough search; disarrange, throw *about*, in search. ~ *n.* Rummaging; miscellaneous accumulation; ~ **sale**, clearance sale of unclaimed articles at docks etc.; sale of miscellaneous used objects, esp. old clothes, contributed by donors to raise money for charity etc.

rum·my (rŭm′ē) *n.* Card game played by two or more players, the object being to get rid of cards by forming sequences or sets of three or more cards.

ru·mor, Brit. **ru·mour** (ro͞o′m*e*r) *ns.* General talk, report, or hearsay, of doubtful accuracy; current but unverified statement or assertion. ~ *v.t.* (chiefly pass.) Report by way of rumor.

rump (rŭmp) *n.* 1. Tail end, posterior, buttocks; ~ **roast, steak**, roast, steak cut from steer's rump. 2. Last remaining remnant, esp. of a legislative body considered unrepresentative and having no authority because of expulsion or departure of many original members.

rum·ple (rŭm′p*e*l) *v.t.* (**-pled, -pling**). Crease, ruffle, wrinkle; tousle, disorder.

rum·pus (rŭm′p*u*s) *n.* Disturbance, brawl, row, uproar; ~ **room**, room for games, parties, etc.

run (rŭn) *v.* (**ran** pr. răn, **run, run·ning**). 1. (of persons) Move legs quickly (one foot being lifted before the other is set down) so as to go at faster pace than walking; (of animals) go at quick pace, amble, trot, gallop, etc.; flee, abscond; go or travel hurriedly, precipitately, etc. 2. Compete in or *in* race; seek election etc. (*for* Congress, president, etc.). 3. Go straight and fast (of fish, ship, etc.); advance (as) by rolling or on wheels, spin around or along, revolve (as) on axle; go with sliding, smooth, continuous, or easy motion; be in action; work freely; be current or operative; (of play) be presented (for specified number of performances etc.) (of train, bus, etc.) go back and forth on route; (of news etc.) spread rapidly from point to point; ~ **in the family**, be found in members of it, as a genetic or other trait. 4. (of color in fabric, ink on paper, etc.) Spread from marked or dyed to other parts. 5. (of thought, eye, etc.) Pass in transitory or cursory way. 6. (of liquid etc., vessel, faucet, etc.) Flow, drip; (of nose, eyes, etc.) drop mucus or tears; (of sore) suppurate; **make person's blood ~ cold**, horrify, thoroughly frighten; **feeling ~s high**, excitement, partisanship, etc., is prevalent etc.; ~ **dry**, cease to flow, be exhausted; ~ **low, short**, become scanty. 7. Extend, be continuous; have a certain course or order, progress, proceed; have a tendency, common characteristic, or average price or level. 8. (with

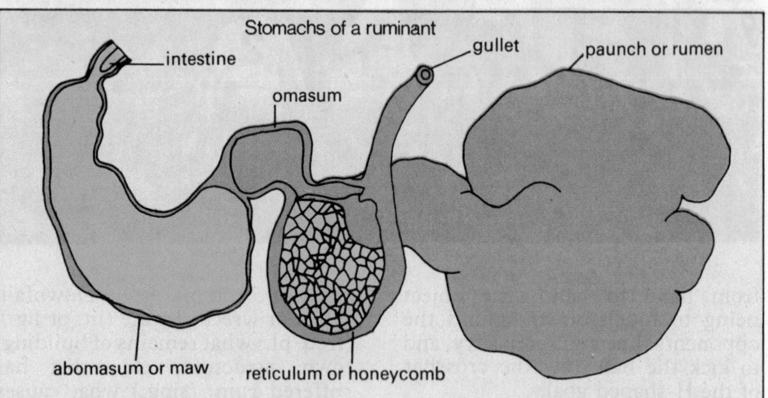

*The multiple stomach of a **ruminant** allows it to digest food at leisure, an advantage to wild animals such as antelopes, but of little value to domesticated cattle and sheep.*

cognate object) Pursue, follow, traverse, cover; make way swiftly through or over; perform; ~ **the blockade**: see BLOCKADE; ~ **errands**, perform errands; ~ **the gauntlet**: see GAUNTLET[2]; ~ **rapids**, shoot them; ~ **risk**, see RISK. 9. Chase, hunt; have running race with; ~ **to earth**, chase to its lair; (fig.) discover after long search. 10. Make run or go; smuggle (contraband goods) by evading coast guard etc.; keep (train, bus, ship, business, etc.) going, manage, conduct operations of; ~ **the show**, (slang) dominate in an undertaking etc. 11. **run'about**, small open car or motorboat; **run'away**, fugitive; unchecked, out of control; **run'way**, track or gangway; specially prepared surface on airfield for taking off and landing; groove in which thing slides; place for fowls to run in. 12. (with preps.) ~ **across**, fall in with; ~ **after**, pursue with attentions; seek society of; ~ **into**, incur difficulties, luck, etc.; be continuous or coalesce with; have collision with; meet unexpectedly; ~ **over**, review, glance over, repeat, recapitulate; (of vehicle) pass over (animal etc.); ~ **through**, examine cursorily; peruse; deal successively with; consume (estate etc.) by reckless or quick spending; pierce, stab; ~ **to**, reach (amount, number, etc.). 13. (with adverbs) ~ **about**, bustle, hurry from one person etc. to another; play or wander without restraint; ~ **away**, flee, abscond, elope; (of horse) bolt; get clear away *from* competitors in race; ~ **away with**, carry off; (slang) win easily; ~ **down**, (of clock etc.) stop for want of winding; (of health etc.) become enfeebled from overwork, lack of proper food, etc.; knock down or collide with; overtake in pursuit; discover after search; disparage; read through hastily; ~ **in**, (football) carry ball over opponents' goal line to score touchdown; (colloq.) arrest and take to prison; ~ **off**, flee; flow away; produce on machine; decide (race) after tie or trial heats; ~ **on**, continue in operation; elapse; speak volubly, talk incessantly; (print.) begin in same line as what precedes; ~ **out**, come to an end; exhaust one's stock of; ~ **out on**, (colloq.) take away support from, desert; ~ **over**, overflow; ~ **through**, pierce with sword etc.; ~ **up**, rise in price; accumulate (sum, debt) quickly; force up (price etc.); raise or construct (building, house, wall, etc.) rapidly; sew (garment) quickly. **run** *n*. 1. Act or period of running; **at a** ~, running; **on the** ~, fleeing or hiding from enemy, police, etc.; retreating; bustling about; **a** ~ **for one's money**, close or strong competition; (a chance for) enjoyment, profit, etc. in return for expenditure or effort. 2. (mus.) Rapid sequence of notes. 3. Continuous stretch, spell, or course; distance traveled by a ship in a specified time; long series or succession; general demand; **in the long** ~; see LONG[1]; **a** ~ **on the bank**, sudden demand from many customers for immediate repayment. 4. Common, general, average, or ordinary type or class; shoal of fish in motion. 5. Regular track of some animals; enclosure for fowls, dogs, etc.; range of pasture; trough for water to run in. 6. Small stream or watercourse. 7. Unraveled tear, ladder in stocking etc. 8. **run'around**, (colloq.) evasion etc. of person's need, request, etc.; **run'back**, (football) run by player after catching kick, pass, etc.; **run'down**, quick summary; **run-in**, (colloq.) quarrel, angry argument; **run-of-the-mill**, (*adj.*) ordinary, not outstanding; **run'off**, (pol.) election to decide tied vote; deciding race after dead heat; **run-on**, piece of added information or material, as a *run-on in a dictionary definition*.

*The great **rune** stone at Jelling near Jutland in Denmark. This early Germanic alphabet seems to have originated in the 2nd or 3rd century A.D. and was used until the Middle Ages.*

run·ci·ble (rŭn'sĭbel) *adj.* (Orig.) nonsense word used by Edward Lear; ~ **spoon**, (now) three-pronged pickle fork, curved like spoon, with one sharp edge.

rune (rōōn) *n*. Letter or character of earliest Teutonic alphabet (most extensively used by Scandinavians and Anglo-Saxons), dating from at least 2nd or 3rd c. A.D. and based on Roman or Greek letters modified to make them suitable for cutting on wood or stone; similar character of mysterious or magic significance. **ru'nic** *adj.*

F U Th O R C G W H N I J/A I/H P

[X] S T B E Ng D L M Œ A Æ Y Ea

RUNES WITH ROMAN EQUIVALENTS

rung[1]: see RING[2].

rung[2] (rŭng) *n*. Bar attached at each end as rail, spoke, or crossbar in chair etc., or esp. in ladder.

run·ner (rŭn'er) *n*. (esp.) 1. Messenger; competitor in a race; (baseball) player on base or going toward base. 2. Naked creeping stem thrown out from base of main stem of strawberry or other plant, and itself taking root; any of various kinds of cultivated bean (esp. SCARLET ~) that twine around stakes for support. 3. Ring etc. that slides on rod, strap, etc. 4. Long piece of wood or metal, curved at end(s), supporting body of sled etc.; blade of skate. 5. Groove or rod for thing to slide along; roller for moving heavy article. 6. Long narrow strip of (embroidered) cloth etc., placed along or across table etc., as ornament; long narrow rug or strip of carpet. **runner-up** (pl. **-ners-up**), competitor or team taking 2nd place.

run·ning (rŭn'ĭng) *n*. (esp.) Condition of ground to be run or raced on; **in, out of, the** ~, with good, no, chance of winning; ~ **board**, narrow footboard extending along either side of older kind of automobile etc. **running** *adj.* That runs; (placed after noun) in

Running the rapids at Lava Falls, Grand Canyon, Arizona — an exhilarating and sometimes dangerous sport which requires great skill and judgement.

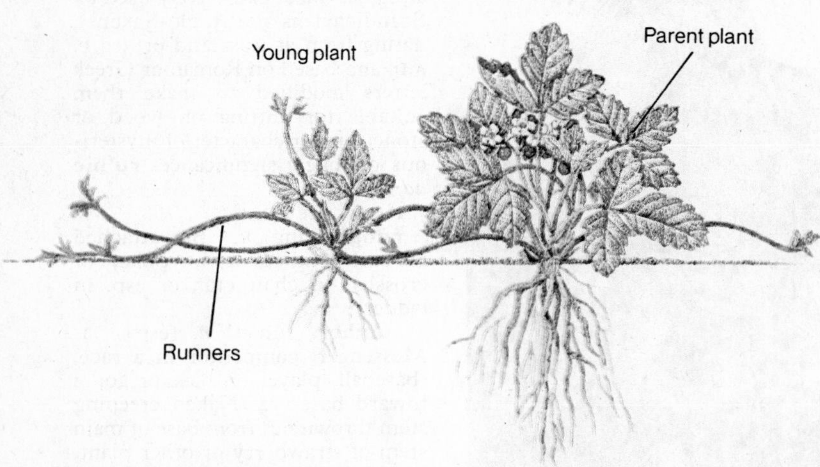

succession, following each other without interval; ~ **fight**, continuing fight or disagreement; ~ **head, title**, heading of page, repeated or varying according to content; ~ **jump**, one in which jumper runs to the takeoff; ~ **light**, any of several lights displayed by a ship or airplane at night; ~ **mate**, horse that sets pace for another horse during race; candidate for secondary position in election; ~ **stitch**, one of a line of small straight stitches made by passing needle in and out through material.

run·ny (rŭn′ē) *adj.* (**-ni·er, -ni·est**). Tending to run or flow; excessively fluid.

Run·ny·mede (rŭn′ĭmēd). Meadow at Egham on S. bank of Thames, 19 mi. (31 km) from London, famous for its association with the Magna Carta, which was signed by King John on the meadow or on the island nearby in 1215.

runt (rŭnt) *n.* Smallest animal of a litter; dwarfed or undersized animal or person. **runt′y** *adj.* (**runt·i·er, runt·i·est**). **runt′i·ness** *n.*

ru·pee (ro͞opē′, ro͞o′pē) *n.* Monetary unit of India, Nepal, Pakistan, Sri Lanka, Mauritius, Maldives, and Seychelles. [Hind. *rūpiyah*, f. Sansk. *rūpya* wrought silver]

Ru·pert's (ro͞o′pe*r*ts) **Land.** Region in N. and W. Canada owned by Hudson's Bay Company until 1869, then incorporated into the Northwest Territories.

rup·ture (rŭp′che*r*) *n.* 1. Breach of harmonious relations, disagreement and parting. 2. (path.) Abdominal HERNIA. 3. Breaking, breach. ~ *v.* (**-tured, -tur·ing**). Burst, break (cell, vessel, membrane); sever (connection etc.); affect with hernia; suffer rupture.

ru·ral (roor′*a*l) *adj.* In, of, suggesting, the country; pastoral or agricultural; **rural delivery, rural free delivery**, delivery of

Plants like the strawberry, which are able to propagate by a ***runner,*** *are likely to have a greater chance of survival than those which reproduce by other means.*

mail in rural areas. **ru′ral·ly** *adv.* **ru·ral·i·ty** (ro͞orăl′ĭtē) (pl. **-ties**), **ru·ral·i·za·tion** (roor*a*lĭzā′-sh*o*n) *ns.* **ru′ral·ize** *v.* (**-ized, -iz·ing**).

Ru·rik (roor′ĭk), **Ryu·rik** (rūr′ik) (d. 879). Reputed founder of Russian empire, Varangian chief who settled in Novgorod in 862; founder of dynasty that ruled Russia until 1598.

ruse (ro͞oz, ro͞os) *n.* Stratagem, feint, trick.

rush[1] (rŭsh) *n.* Marsh plant of order Juncaceae, with naked slender tapering pith-filled or hollow stems, used for making chair bottoms and plaiting baskets etc.;

Although considered only as marsh plants in England, the stems of ***rush*** *were once used to weave mats and chair seats. The pith was used to make candlewicks and rush lights.*

stem of this; (collect.) rushes as a material; **rush′light, rush candle**, candle made by dipping pith of a rush in tallow.

rush[2] (rŭsh) *v.* 1. Impel, drag, force, carry along, violently and rapidly; (colloq.) be very attentive to, woo intensively; give parties etc. for (prospective members of sorority or fraternity) prior to offering membership; make sudden vehement assault or attack. 2. Run precipitately, violently, or with great speed; go or resort without proper consideration; flow, fall, spread, roll, impetuously or fast; ~ **at**, charge. **rush** *n.* Act of rushing, violent or tumultuous advance, spurt, charge, onslaught; (football) attempt to move the ball by running with it; sudden migration of large numbers, esp. to new goldfield; strong run *on* or *for* some commodity; (pl., motion-picture industry) preliminary showings of film before cutting; (slang) feeling of sudden euphoria after use of narcotic, esp. after injecting narcotic drug into vein; ~ **hour**, time at which traffic is busiest.

Rush (rŭsh), **Benjamin** (1745–1813). Amer. physician and politician; member of the Continental Congress, 1776–7, and signer of the Declaration of Independence.

rusk (rŭsk) *n.* Piece of bread dried and rebaked.

Rus·kin (rŭs′kĭn), **John** (1819–1900). English writer, art critic, and social reformer; author of the 5-volume *Modern Painters, The Seven Lamps of Architecture*, etc.

Rus·sell[1] (rŭs′*e*l), **Bertrand Arthur William, 3rd Earl Russell** (1872–1970). English philosopher and mathematician; author of many works on philosophy, logic, education, economics, and politics; won Nobel Prize for literature, 1950.

Rus·sell[2] (rŭs′*e*l), **George William**: see A.E.

rus·set (rŭs′ĭt) *n.* 1. (hist.) Coarse homespun reddish-brown or gray cloth. 2. Reddish brown. 3. Rough-skinned russet-colored apple. ~ *adj.* 1. Reddish brown. 2. Of russet cloth.

Rus·sia (rŭsh′*a*). Vast territory of E. Europe and N. Asia, until 1917 an empire under the tzars; since 1917 a federation of socialist republics (see UNION OF SOVIET SOCIALIST REPUBLICS).

Rus·sian (rŭsh′*a*n) *adj.* Of Russia or the U.S.S.R., its people or language; ~ **ballet**, form of ballet developed at the beginning of the 20th c. at the Imperial

A scene of ***rural*** *tranquility in the Appalachian Mountains. Agricultural production in the U.S.A. increased considerably during the 1950s and 1960s.*

Located in Red Square, Moscow, the inspirational centre of ***Russia****, and near Lenin's tomb, the onion domes of the Cathedral of St. Basil reveal fairytale splendor (below).*

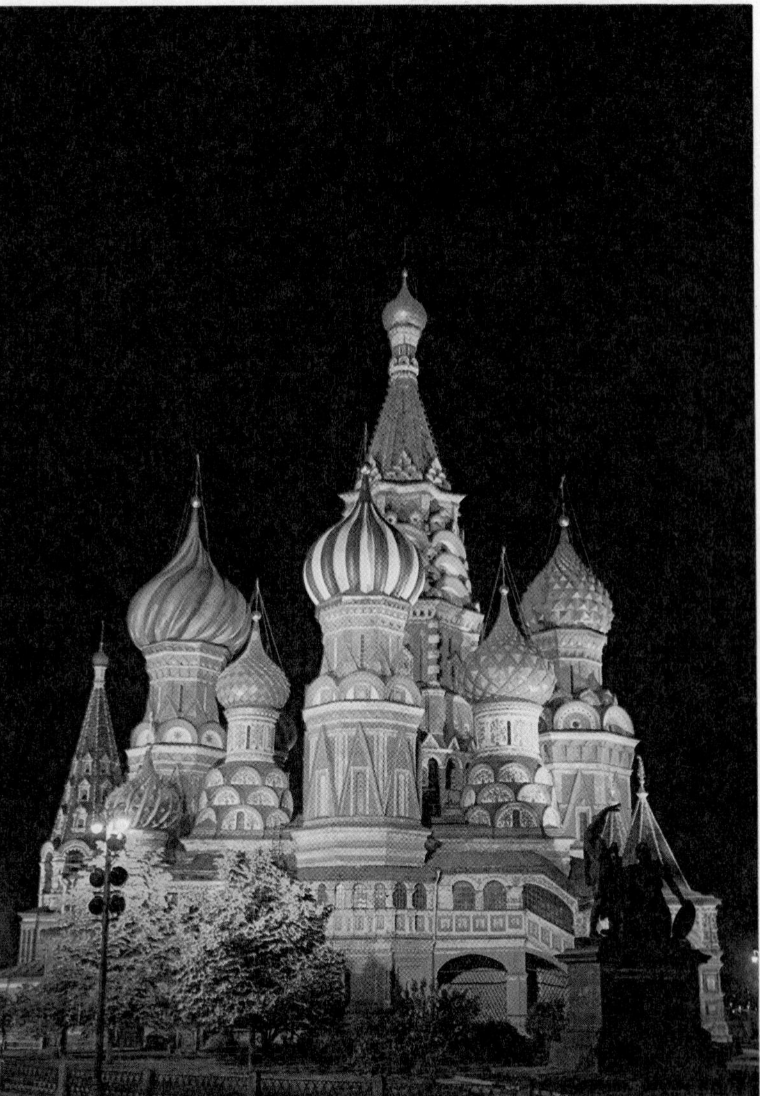

School of Ballet at St. Petersburg from older Italian ballet; ~ **roulette**, firing of revolver held to one's head with one chamber of revolver loaded; ~ **wolfhound** = BORZOI. **Russian** *n.* 1. Russian person. 2. Official language of the U.S.S.R., a Slavic language of the Russian people.

Russian Soviet Federated Socialist Republic. (abbrev. R.S.F.S.R.) Largest and most important of the constituent republics of the U.S.S.R.; occupies more than ¾ of the total area of the U.S.S.R., contains more than half its population, and consists of 12 autonomous republics and numerous provinces; capital, Moscow.

Russo- *prefix.* Russia; of Russia and —; ~**-Japanese War**, war between Russia and Japan, 1904–5, in which Russia was defeated.

rust (rŭst) *n.* 1. Yellowish-brown coating formed on iron or steel by oxidation, esp. as effect of moisture, and gradually corroding the metal; similar coating on other metals; color of this; (fig.) impaired state because of disuse or inactivity, inaction as deteriorating influence. 2. (Plant disease with rust-colored spots caused by) any of various fungi. ~ *v.* Contract rust, undergo oxidation or blight; lose quality or efficiency by disuse or inactivity; effect with rust, corrode.

rus·tic (rŭs'tĭk) *adj.* Rural; having the appearance or manners of country people, characteristic of peasants, unsophisticated, unpolished, clownish; of rude or country workmanship; of untrimmed branches or rough timber; (archit.) with rough-hewn or roughened surface or with chamfered joints. **rus'ti·cal·ly** *adv.* **rus·tic·i·ty** (rŭstĭs'ĭtē) *n.* **rustic** *n.* Countryman, peasant.

rus·ti·cate (rŭs'tĭkāt) *v.* (**-cat·ed, -cat·ing**). Retire to, sojourn in, the country, lead a rural life; countrify. **rus·ti·ca·tion** (rŭstĭkā'shon) *n.*

rus·tle (rŭs'*e*l) *v.* (**-tled, -tling**). 1. Make sound (as) of dry leaves blown, silk garments, etc. in motion; go with rustle; cause to rustle. 2. (colloq.) Forage, acquire (also ~ **up**); steal (cattle or horses). **rustle** *n.* Sound of rustling. **rus'tler** *n.* Cattle or horse thief. **rus'tling·ly** *adv.*

rust·y (rŭs'tē) *adj.* (**rust·i·er, rust·i·est**). Rusted, affected with rust; out of practice; antiquated, behind the times; impaired by neglect; rust-colored. **rust'i·ly** *adv.* **rust'i·ness** *n.*

rut[1] (rŭt) *n.* Track sunk by passage of wheels; established mode of procedure, beaten track, groove. **rut'ty** *adj.* (**-ti·er, -ti·est**). **rut** *v.t.* (**rut·ted, rut·ting**). Mark with ruts (usu. in past part.).

rut[2] (rut) *n.* Periodic sexual excitement of male deer (also of goat, ram, etc.). **rut'tish** *adj.* **rut** *v.i.* (**rut·ted, rut·ting**). Be affected with rut.

ru·ta·ba·ga (rōōt*a*bā'g*a*) *n.* Turnip (*Brassica napobrassica*) having large, edible, yellow root.

ruth (rōōth) *n.* (archaic) Pity, compassion.

Ruth[1] (rōōth). 1. Moabite woman; her widowed mother-in-law Naomi returned to her own country of Judah, and Ruth being also a widow went with her; in Bethlehem Ruth gleaned corn in the

Winter rye *growing in Georgia. This grain is grown extensively in Asia, Europe and North America. It is used to make flour for bread, as stock feed and also to produce alcoholic beverages.*

Modern tourist accommodation in ***Rwanda*** *is designed to simulate the traditional village styles. With much of the country above 5,000 ft., its climate is attractive to visitors and tourists.*

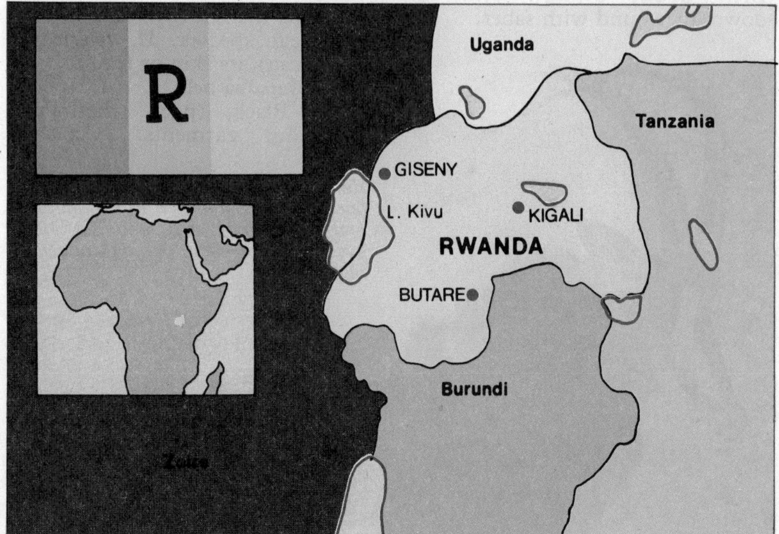

fields of Boaz, who proved to be her husband's kinsman and married her. 2. Book of Old Testament telling story of Ruth.

Ruth[2] (ro͞oth), **George Herman** ("Babe") (1895–1948). (also called "the Bambino," "The Babe," and "the Sultan of Swat") Amer. baseball player, 1914–35; pitcher for Baltimore and the Boston Red Sox, then outfielder for New York Yankees from 1920; held major league home run records, including hitting 60 home runs in 1927 and 714 in his professional career.

Ru·the·ni·a (ro͞othē'nē*a*). Former province of Czechoslovakia, since 1945 incorporated in the Ukraine. **Ru·the'ni·an** *adj.* & *n.*

ru·the·ni·um (ro͞othē'nē*u*m) *n.* (chem.) Rare metallic element of the platinum group, a hard, grayish-white metal; symbol Ru, at. no. 44, at. wt. 101.07. [med. L. *Ruthenia* Russia (from its discovery in the Urals)]

Ruth·er·ford[1] (rŭdh'*er*f*er*d), **Daniel** (1749–1819). Scottish physician who discovered nitrogen.

Ruth·er·ford[2] (rŭdh'*er*f*er*d), **Ernest, 1st Baron Rutherford of Nelson** (1871–1937). New Zealand-born physicist working in Canada and England; investigated the nature of radioactive transformations and the structure of the atom; received Nobel Prize for chemistry 1908.

ruth·less (ro͞oth'lĭs) *adj.* Without pity. **ruth'less·ly** *adv.* **ruth'less·ness** *n.*

RV *abbrev.* Recreational vehicle; Revised Version (of Bible).

R.V. *abbrev.* Revised Version (of Bible).

Rwan·da (ro͞owahn'd*a*). Republic of E. central Africa, between Zaire and Tanzania, a former Belgian trust territory; independent since 1962; capital, Kigali.

Rx *abbrev.* (in medical prescriptions) Recipe. [L., = take]

rye (rī) *n.* (Grain of) a cereal, *Secale cereale*, widely grown for use as livestock feed, in making flour, and in making whiskey; (also ~ **whiskey**) whiskey made from rye; **rye'grass**, fodder grass of genus *Lolium*, esp. *L. perenne*, common rye, and *L. italicum*.

ry·ot (rī'*o*t) *n.* Indian peasant.

Ryu·kyu (rēo͞o'kū; *Jap.* rū'kū) **Islands.** Pacific Ocean archipelago extending in a 600 mi. (966 km) arc from Japan S. to Taiwan.

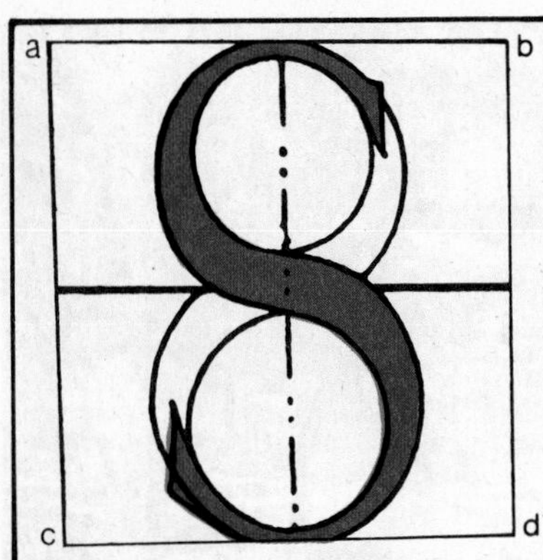

The letter **S, s** *is derived from one of 4 sibilants used in Hebrew, Greek and Etruscan. Similar forms were used throughout the Mediterranean but it was not until the 5th century B.C. that rounded forms began to replace jagged ones.*

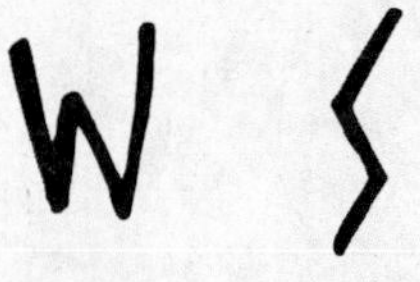

Phoenician Early Greek Corinthian

Roman Ionic Classical Latin

S, s (ĕs) (pl. **S's, s's** or **Ss, ss**). 1. Nineteenth letter of modern English and 18th of ancient Roman alphabet, derived in form (through early Latin and Greek ϟ, ϟ, ϟ) from Phoenician ᴡ (Hebrew ש), representing *s* or *sh* in Semitic languages, in modern English representing chiefly a voiceless sibilant (*s*), the corresponding voiced sound (*z*), and frequently the phonetic combinations (*sy*), (*zy*). 2. Thing shaped like S.

S *symbol*. Sulfur.

S. *abbrev.* (pl. **SS.**). Saint; Signor; South(ern).

s. *abbrev.* Second; shilling; sign; singular; son; south(ern); stere(s); substantive.

-s[1] *suffix*. Denoting pls. of nouns.

-s[2] *suffix*. Denoting third pers. sing. pres. ind. of verbs.

-s[3] *suffix*. Forming adverbs (*besides, afterwards*, etc.).

-'s[1] *suffix*. Denoting possessive case of sing. nouns (*child's, woman's*) and irregularly formed pl. nouns (*children's, women's*).

-'s[2] *suffix*. Used as a contraction of *is* (*she's there*), *has* (*he's walked*), *us* (*let's*), *does* (*what's he say?*).

S.A. *abbrev*. Salvation Army; South Africa; South America.

Saar (zār, sār). River in W. Europe, flowing 150 mi. (241 km), from NE. France to the Moselle River in the west of West Germany.

Sab·ba·tar·i·an (săbatār'ēan) *n*. 1. Person observing Saturday as the Sabbath, as in Judaism etc. 2. Person believing in strict observance of Sunday as the Sabbath. ~ *adj*. Of the Sabbath or Sabbatarian tenets. **Sab·ba·tar'·i·an·ism** *n.*

Sab·bath (săb'ath) *n*. 1. (also ~ **day**) Seventh day of week (Saturday) as day of religious rest enjoined on Israelites; also, the Christian Sunday, esp. as day of obligatory abstinence from work and play. 2. **Witches' Sabbath**: see WITCH[1]. [Heb. *šabbāt*, f. *šāḇaṯ* to rest]

sab·bat·i·cal (sabăt'ĭkal), **sab·bat·ic** (sabăt'ĭk) *adjs*. Of, appropriate to, the Sabbath; ~ **year**, seventh year in which Israelites were to cease tilling and release debtors and Israelite slaves; year of absence from duty, with pay, for purposes of study and travel, granted to teachers and others in universities etc. at certain intervals, traditionally every seven years. **sab·bat'i·cal·ly** *adv*.

sa·ber, Brit. **sa·bre** (sā'ber) *ns*. Cavalry sword having curved blade; light fencing sword with tapering blade; ~ **rattling**, display of military strength; ~ **saw**, small electric jigsaw; ~**-toothed tiger**, extinct mammal having long saber-shaped upper canines. **saber** *v*. (**-bered, -ber·ing**, Brit. **-bred, -bring**). Kill, cut down, or wound with saber.

Herds of the **sable** *antelope are not uncommon in southern Africa and several sub-species are recorded. However, only 500–700 of the giant variety remain.*

Sa·bin (sā'bĭn), **Albert Bruce** (1906–). Amer. physician and microbiologist; famous for development of **Sabin vaccine**, oral vaccine against polio, made from live virus strains. See SALK.

Sa·bine (sā'bīn) *adj*. & *n*. (Member) of a tribe in ancient Italy, whose lands were in the neighborhood of Rome, celebrated in legend as having taken up arms against the Romans to avenge the carrying off of their women by the Romans at a spectacle to which they had been invited.

sa·ble[1] (sā'bel) *n*. (pl. **-bles**, collect. **-ble**). Small dark-brown furred arctic and subarctic carnivorous marten (*Martes zibellina*, European species; *M. americana*, American); its skin or fur.

sa·ble[2] (sā'bel) *n*. 1. (poet., rhet.) Black; (poet., rhet.; pl.) mourning garments. 2. ~

antelope, large stout-horned antelope of S. and E. Africa (*Hippotragus niger*), male of which is dark glossy brown with white belly. **sable** *adj.* (poet., rhet.) Black, dusky; somber.

Sa·ble (sā'bel), **Cape.** Cape in SW. Florida, southernmost point in the continental United States.

sab·ot (săb'ō; *Fr.* săbō') *n.* (pl. **sab·ots** pr. săb'ōz; *Fr.* săbō'). Shoe hollowed out from one piece of wood, worn by French peasants etc.; wooden-soled shoe.

sab·o·tage (săb'*o*tahzh, săb*o*tahzh') *n.* Deliberate destruction of machinery, damaging of equipment, manufacture of faulty product, etc., by dissatisfied or disaffected workmen, or by hostile agents esp. in wartime. ~ *v.t.* (**-taged, -tag·ing**). Commit sabotage on; (fig.) destroy, render useless. **sab·o·teur** (săb*o*tẽr') *n.* One who commits sabotage.

sa·bra (sah'br*a*) *n.* Native-born Israeli.

sa·bre: SABER.

SAC *abbrev.* Strategic Air Command.

Sac = SAUK.

sac (săk) *n.* Baglike membrane enclosing cavity in animal or vegetable organism; membranous envelope of hernia, cyst, tumor, etc.

Sac·a·ja·we·a (săk*a*j*a*wē'*a*) (1788?–1812). Amer. Shoshone Indian woman who acted as guide for Lewis and Clark expedition.

sac·cha·rate (săk'*e*rāt) *n.* Salt of saccharic acid.

sac·char·ic (s*a*kăr'ĭk) *adj.* ~ **acid**, dibasic acid (HOOC(CHOH)$_4$COOH) formed by oxidation of dextrose.

sac·cha·rin (săk'*e*rĭn) *n.* White intensely sweet crystalline substance prepared from toluene and used as a substitute for sugar. **sac·cha·rine** (săk'*e*rĭn, -īn) *adj.* Sugary (also fig.); of, containing, like, sugar. **sac'cha·rine·ly** *adv.* **sac·cha·rin·i·ty** (săk*e*rĭn'ĭtē) *n.*

sac·cha·rose (săk'*e*rōs) = SUCROSE.

sac·cule (săk'ūl) *n.* Small sac or cyst. **sac·cu·late** (săk'y*u*lāt), **sac'cu·lat·ed** *adjs.* **sac·cu·la·tion** (săky*u*lā'shon) *n.*

sac·er·do·tal (săs*e*rdō't*a*l, săk-) *adj.* Of priest(s) or priesthood, priestly; (of doctrines etc.) ascribing sacrificial functions and supernatural power to ordained priests, claiming excessive authority for the priesthood. **sac·er·do'tal·ly** *adv.* **sac·er·do'tal·ism** *n.*

sa·chem (sā'chem, săch'em) *n.* 1. Supreme chief of some Amer. Ind. tribes. 2. (hist.) One of 12 high officials in Tammany Society.

sa·chet (săshā'; *Brit.* săsh'ā) *n.* Small perfumed bag; (packet of) dry perfume for laying among clothes etc.

For ***safety,*** *laws have been passed in some countries which make it obligatory for motor-cycle riders to wear crash helmets whenever they mount their machines. Frames are also stronger.*

sack[1] (săk) *n.* 1. Large, usu. oblong, bag of coarse flax, hemp, etc., usu. open at one end, and used for storing and conveying goods; sack with contents; amount (of wheat, coal, flour, etc.) usu. put in sack as unit of measure or weight. 2. Woman's short loose dress of sacklike shape; (also ~ **dress**). 3. **sack'cloth**, coarse fabric of flax or hemp, sacking; (fig.) mourning or penitential garb (esp. in **sackcloth and ashes**); **sack race**, race between runners with lower part of body in sacks. **sack'ful** *n.* (pl. **-fuls**). **sack** *v.t.* Put into sack(s); (football slang) overwhelm (quarterback) before he can throw the ball. **sack'ing** *n.* Closely woven material of hemp, jute, flax, etc., for sacks etc.

sack[2] (săk) *v.t.* Plunder (captured town etc.). ~ *n.* Act or instance of sacking.

sack[3] (săk) *n.* (hist.) Any of various white wines imported from Spain and the Canary Islands to England in the 16th and 17th centuries. [Fr. *vin sec* dry wine]

sac·ra·ment (săk'r*a*ment) *n.* Religious ceremony or act symbolizing or conferring grace (in the Eastern pre-Reformation Western, and R.C. Churches, one of the seven rites of baptism, confirmation, the Eucharist, penance, extreme unction, orders, and matrimony; restricted by many Protestants to baptism and the Eucharist); thing of mysterious and sacred significance, sacred influence, symbol, etc.; oath or solemn engagement taken; (often cap.) (also **blessed** or **holy** ~, ~ **of the altar**) Eucharist; consecrated elements, esp. the bread or Host.

sac·ra·men·tal (săkr*a*mĕn't*a*l) *adj.* Of (the nature of) a or the sacrament. ~ *n.* Observance analogous to but not reckoned among the sacraments, e.g. use of holy water or sign of the cross. **sac·ra·men'tal·ly** *adv.* **sac·ra·men'tal·ist** *n.*

Sac·ra·men·tar·i·an (săkr*a*mĕntār'ē*a*n) *n.* One who holds that the bread and wine of the Sacrament are only symbols of the body and blood of Christ. **s**~ *adj.* Pertaining to a sacrament or the sacraments; **S**~ pertaining to sacramentarians. **sac·ra·men·tar'i·an·ism** *n.*

Sac·ra·men·to (săkr*a*mĕn'tō). Captial of California, in the N. central part, on the **Sacramento River**, longest river in California, flowing 382 mi. (615 km) from NW. California S. to San Francisco Bay.

sa·crar·i·um (s*a*krār′ēum) *n.* (pl. **-crar·i·a** pr. -krār′ē*a*). Sanctuary, part of church within altar rails.

sa·cred (sā′krĭd) *adj.* Consecrated, esteemed dear, *to* a deity; dedicated, reserved, appropriated, *to* some person or purpose; made holy by religious association, hallowed; safeguarded or required by religion, reverence, or tradition; indefeasible, inviolable, sacrosanct; ~ **cow**, idea, institution, etc., unreasonably held to be immune from criticism; **S~ Heart**, (R.C. Ch.) heart of Jesus Christ or Mary, as object of devotion. **sa′cred·ly** *adv.* **sa′cred·ness** *n.*

sac·ri·fice (săk′r*i*fīs) *n.* 1. Slaughter of animal or person, surrender of possession, as offering to a deity; what is thus slaughtered, surrendered, or done, offering. 2. Give up of thing for the sake of another that is more important, worthy, or urgent; thing thus given up, loss thus entailed; **make the supreme ~**, die for one's country. **sacrifice** *v.* (**-ficed, -fic·ing**). Offer (as) sacrifice (*to*); give up, devote *to*. **sac·ri·fi·cial** (săkr*i*fĭsh′*a*l) *adj.* **sac·ri·fi′cial·ly** *adv.* **sac′ri·fic·er** *n.*

sac·ri·lege (săk′r*i*lĭj) *n.* Robbery or profanation of sacred building, outrage on consecrated person or thing, violation of what is sacred. **sac·ri·le·gious** (săkr*i*lĭj′*u*s, -lē′j*u*s) *adj.* **sac·ri·le′gious·ly** *adv.* **sac·ri·le′gious·ness** *n.* [L. *sacrilegus* one who steals sacred things (*sacer* holy *legere* gather)]

sac·ris·tan (săk′rĭst*a*n), **sa·crist** (săk′rĭst, sā′krĭst) *ns.* Sexton of parish church; official in charge of sacristy.

sa·cris·ty (săk′rĭstē) *n.* (pl. **-ties**). Repository for vestments, vessels, etc., of a church.

sac·ro·il·i·ac (săkrōĭl′ēăk, sā-krō-) *n.* Joint between sacrum and ilium. ~ *adj.* Of, pertaining to, or affecting this joint or its cartilage.

sac·ro·sanct (săk′rōsăngkt) *adj.* Secured by religious sanction against outrage, inviolable. **sac·ro·sanc·ti·ty** (săkrōsăngk′tĭtē) *n.*

sa·crum (sā′kr*u*m, săk′r*u*m) *n.* (pl. **sa·cra** pr. sā′kr*a*, săk′r*a*). Composite triangular bone of ankylosed vertebrae forming back of pelvis. **sa′cral** *adj.* [L. *os sacrum* sacred bone (from sacrificial use)]

sad (săd) *adj.* (**sad·der, sad·dest**). 1. Sorrowful, mournful; showing or causing sorrow. 2. Deplorably bad; sorry. 3. (of color) Dull, neutral-tinted. **sad′den** *v.* **sad′ly** *adv.* **sad′ness** *n.*

Sa·dat (sahdaht′), **Anwar el** (1918–1981). Egyptian politician; president of Egypt since 1970; co-recipient, with Prime Minister Begin of Israel, of Nobel Peace Prize, 1978.

sad·dle (săd′*e*l) *n.* 1. Rider's seat placed on back of horse etc. (usu. concave, of leather, with side flaps and girths and stirrups) or forming part of bicycle etc.; **in the ~**, mounted; (fig.) in office or control. 2. Saddle-shaped thing, e.g. ridge between 2 summits; part of back of various animals, as dog; cut *of* meat, esp. mutton or venison, consisting of the 2 loins. 3. **~-backed**, with upper outline concave; **sad′dle-bag**, one of pair of bags laid across horse, etc., behind saddle; **sad′dle-bow**, arched front of saddle; **sad′dlecloth**, cloth laid on horse's back under saddle; **saddle horse**, horse for riding; **saddle shoe**, Oxford shoe with contrasting band across upper part; **sad′dletree**, frame of saddle. **saddle** *v.t.* (**-dled, -dling**). Put saddle on (horse etc.); burden (person) *with* task, responsibility, etc.; put (burden) *on* person.

sad·dler (săd′l*e*r) *n.* Maker of or dealer in saddles and other equipment for horses. **sad′dler·y** *n.* (pl. **-dler·ies**).

Sad·du·cee (săj′*u*sē, săd′y*u*-) *n.* Member of a Jewish sect of 1st c. B.C.–1st c. A.D., opposed to the Pharisees, who repudiated oral tradition and accepted the written Law only, rejecting belief in the resurrection of the body and the existence of angels and spirits. **Sad·du·ce·an** (săj*u*sē′*a*n, sădy*u*-) *adj.* [Heb. *ṣᵉdûḳīy* prob. = descendant of Żadok]

Sade (sahd, săd), **Do·na·ti·en** (dawnahsyăń′) **Alphonse, Count** (generally known as Marquis) **de**

*Below left: With an Aboriginal guide, visitors go on **safari** in northern Australia. Below: An ancient **sacred** stone from Sarawak whose significance is no longer known.*

In Kurdistan, ceremonial saddles are covered with ornate embroidery. It is not widely appreciated that the **saddle** was not used until the 3rd or 4th century A.D.

The world's most expensive herb, **saffron,** is made from the dried stigmas of the saffron crocus. It has a strong exotic aroma and a bitter taste.

(1740–1814). French author and libertine, whose accounts of sexual perversions have given his name to SADISM.

sad·ism (săd′ĭzem, sā′dĭz-) *n.* Deriving of pleasure from the infliction of cruelty upon others, esp. as method of sexual gratification. **sad′ist** *n.* **sa·dis·tic** (s*a*dĭs′tĭk) *adj.* [f. Count D. A. de SADE]

sad·o·mas·o·chism (sădōmăs′-*o*kĭzem, sādō-) *n.* Combination of sadism and masochism in one person. **sad·o·mas′o·chist** *n.* **sad·o·mas·o·chis·tic** (săd*o*măso-kĭs′tĭk, sādō-) *adj.*

SAE, S.A.E. *abbrevs.* Society of Automotive Engineers.

sa·fa·ri (s*a*făr′ē) *n.* (pl. **-ris**). Journey or expedition in E. Africa esp. for hunting or observing wildlife. [Swahili, f. Arab. *safar* journey]

safe[1] (sāf) *n.* Strong locked repository for valuables; ~ **deposit**, strongroom or vault, usu. in a bank, containing safe with boxes or drawers for storing papers, jewelry, or other valuables.

safe[2] (sāf) *adj.* (**saf·er, saf·est**). 1. Uninjured (pred. after *bring, keep*, etc.); secure, out of or not exposed to danger. 2. Affording security or not involving danger; **on the ~ side**, with margin of security against risks. 3. Debarred from escaping or doing harm. 4. Cautious and unenterprising; consistently moderate; that can be reckoned on, unfailing, certain *to* do or be; sure to become. 5. **safe-conduct**, (document conveying) privilege granted by sovereign, commander, etc., of being protected from arrest or harm on particular occasion or in district; **safe period**, (colloq.) time during and near menstrual period, when conception is least likely; **safe′keep′ing**, custody. **safe′ly** *adv.* **safe′ness** *n.*

safe·guard (sāf′gărd) *n.* Safe-conduct; (usu.) proviso, stipulation, quality, or circumstance that tends to prevent some evil or protect. ~ *v.t.* Guard, protect (esp. rights, etc.) by precaution or stipulation.

safe·ty (sāf′tē) *n.* (pl. **-ties**). 1. Being safe, freedom from danger or risks; safeness, being sure or likely to bring no danger. 2. (football) Play in which offensive team grounds the ball behind its own goal line, scoring two points for opposing team (cf. TOUCHBACK); either of two defensive backs farther behind line of scrimmage; ~ **belt** = SEAT belt; ~ (**catch**), device for locking gun trigger; ~ **glass**, glass so made as to prevent splintering; ~ **lamp**, miner's lamp so constructed as to prevent the flame from coming into direct contact with firedamp and causing an explosion; ~ **match**, one igniting only on specially prepared surface; ~ **pin**, pin bent back on itself so as to form a spring, with guard or sheath to cover point; ~ **razor**, razor with blade fitted into holder having guard to prevent it from cutting deeply; ~ **valve**, valve in steam boiler etc. opening automatically to relieve excessive pressure; (fig.) means of giving harmless vent to excitement etc.

saf·flow·er (săf′low*er*) *n.* Thistlelike plant (*Carthamus tinctorius*) with flowers whose dried petals yield red dye, and with seeds that yield oil used in cooking, cosmetics, etc.

saf·fron (săf′r*o*n) *n.* Kind of crocus (*Crocus sativus*) cultivated for its flowers, the stigmas of which yield an orange-yellow substance used for coloring and flavoring food; this substance; color of this. ~ *adj.* Of saffron color.

sag (săg) *v.* (**sagged, sag·ging**). Sink or subside under weight or pressure; droop; be lopsided; have downward bulge or curve in middle, cause to curve thus; (commerc.) decline in price; (of ship) drift to leeward. ~ *n.* Sagging; amount that rope etc. sags. **sag′gy** *adj.* (**-gi·er, -gi·est**).

sa·ga (sah′g*a*) *n.* Medieval Icelandic or Norwegian prose narrative, esp. one embodying history of Icelandic family or Norwegian king; story of heroic achievement or adventure; long family chronicle. [ON., = "narrative"]

sa·ga·cious (s*a*gā′sh*u*s) *adj.* Mentally penetrating, gifted with discernment, practically wise, acute-minded, shrewd; (of speech etc.) showing wisdom. **sa·ga′cious·ly** *adv.* **sa·gac·i·ty** (s*a*găs′ĭtē) *n.* (pl. **-ties**).

sag·a·more (săg′*a*mōr, -mōr) *n.* Chief, or subordinate chief, of some Amer. Ind. tribes.

sage[1] (sāj) *n.* Aromatic herb (*Salvia officinalis*) with dull grayish-green leaves; its leaves used in cookery; any plant of the genus *Salvia*; **sage′brush**, any of various N. Amer. hoary-leaved shrubs of genus *Artemisia*, freq. covering large arid tracts in Western states; **sage grouse**, large N. Amer. grouse (*Centrocercus urophasianus*) in sagebrush country, the male's display being spectacular.

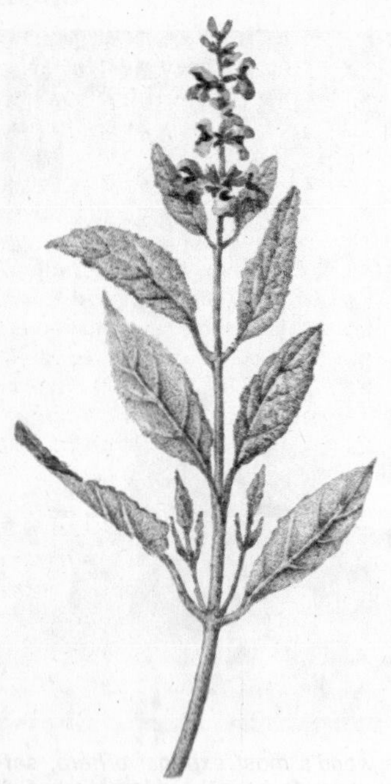

Garden ***sage,*** *an aromatic herb originally from the Mediterranean region, is now grown widely in temperate areas. It is a savory ingredient in meat dishes and soups.*

sage[2] (sāj) *adj.* (**sag·er, sag·est**). Wise, discreet, judicious, having the wisdom of experience; of or indicating profound wisdom. **sage'ly** *adv.* **sage'ness** *n.* **sage** *n.* Profoundly wise man, esp. any of the ancients traditionally reputed wisest of their time.

Sa·git·ta (s*a*jĭt'*a*). The Arrow, a northern constellation.

sag·it·tal (săj'ĭtal) *adj.* (anat.) In the same plane as the **sagittal suture** (suture between parietal bones of skull), i.e. longitudinal and from front to back. **sag'it·tal·ly** *adv.*

Sag·it·ta·ri·us (săjĭtār'ēus). The Archer, a southern constellation; 9th sign (♐) of the zodiac, which the sun enters about Nov. 22. **Sag·it·ta'ri·an** *adj.* & *n.*

sa·go (sā'gō) *n.* (pl. **-gos**). Palm or cycad esp. of genus *Metroxylon*; kind of starch used in cooking, obtained from pith of these plants.

sa·gua·ro (s*a*gwār'ō, s*a*wār'ō) *n.* Giant cactus (*Carnegiea gigantea*) of southwestern U.S. and northern Mexico, growing up to 60 ft. and having thick upward-curving branches, white flowers, and edible fruit.

Sa·hap·tin (s*a*hăp'tĭn) *adj.* & *n.* (pl. **-tins,** collect. **-tin**). (Member, language) of a N. Amer. Ind. tribe of Washington, Oregon, and Idaho.

Sa·har·a (s*a*hār'*a*, -hār'*a*). Vast desert in N. Africa, largest in the world, covering 3,500,000 sq. mi. (9,065,000 sq. km), extending from the Atlantic coast E. to the Red Sea and S. to the Sudan. **Sa·ha'ran, Sa·har'i·an** *adjs.*

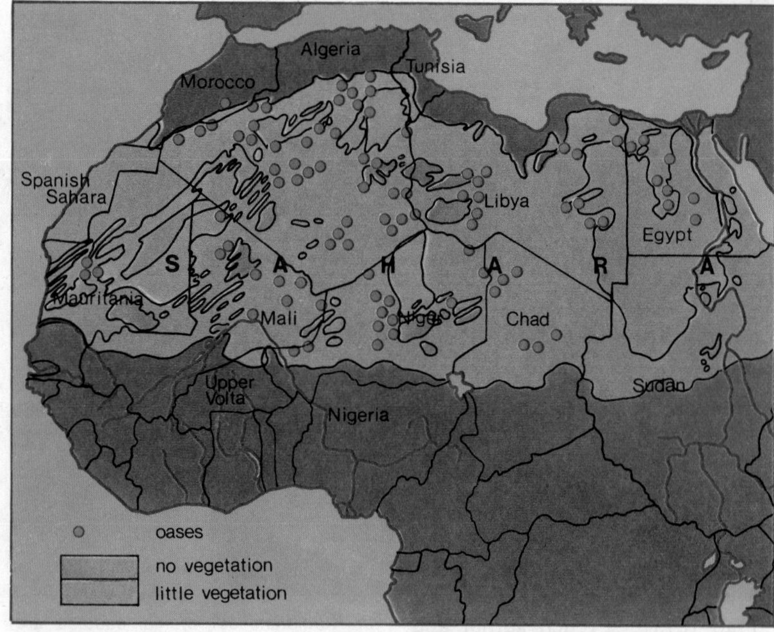

The largest desert in the world, the ***Sahara*** *has an area of 3.5 million square miles. Most of it is an elevated plateau and the area covered by sand dunes is relatively small.*

sa·hib (sah'ĭb, -ēb) *n.* (fem. **mem-sa·hib**) Former title or form of address used in colonial India to Europeans.

said (sĕd) *adj.*: see SAY; (esp.) aforesaid.

Sai·gon (sīgŏn'). Capital city and main port of Vietnam, on the ~ **River** in the S. part of the country; now called Ho Chi Minh City.

sail[1] (sāl) *n.* 1. Piece of canvas or other textile material extended on rigging to catch wind and propel vessel; (collect.) some or all of ship's sails; **under** ~, with sails set. 2. (collect.) Ships; ship. 3. Blade of windmill; sailfish's dorsal fin; **sail'cloth,** canvas for sails; kind of coarse linen; **sail'fish** (pl. **-fishes,** collect. **-fish**), any of various tropical, marine game and food fishes of the genus *Istiophorus*, related to swordfish and marlin, 6

The skill needed to handle a ***sailing*** *vessel is dependent on the captain's ability to assess the strength and direction of the wind and to relate this to the capability of his vessel. The techniques of sailing were evolved long ago, but new designs in boats have resulted in a need for new techniques or variations of earlier ones.*

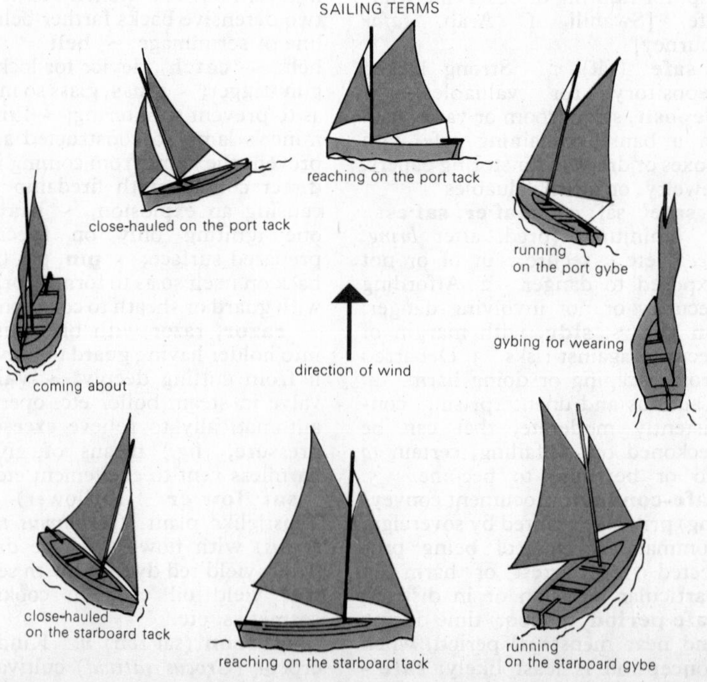

to 10 ft. long, weighing from 60 to 100 lbs., and having a high, wide, blue dorsal fin and sword-shaped upper jaw.

sail[2] (sāl) *v.* 1. (of vessel or person on board) Travel on water by use of sails or engine power; start on voyage. 2. Move in stately or smooth manner; travel over or along, navigate, glide through (sea, sky, etc.); (of bird etc.) glide in air. 3. Control navigation of (ship), set (toy boat) afloat. 4. ~ **close to** or **near the wind**, sail nearly against it; come near transgressing a law or moral principle; ~ **into**, (slang) attack physically or verbally. **sail** *n.* Voyage or excursion in sailing vessel; voyage of specified duration; **sail′boat**, boat or sails propelled by sail; **sail′plane**, soaring glider.

sail·ing (sā′lĭng) *n.* 1. Act of person or thing that sails. 2. Skill needed to navigate sailing vessel. 3. Sport of riding in or handling sailboat. 4. Departure time of ship or person on it; ~ **ship, vessel,** vessel propelled by sails, not engines.

sail·or (sā′ler) *n.* One who is employed in navigating a ship; member of ship's crew or company below rank of officer; **good, bad** ~, person not, very, liable to seasickness; **sailor hat**, straw hat with narrow brim and flat top. **sail′or·ly** *adj.*

sain·foin (săn′foin) *n.* Low-growing perennial herb (*Onobrychis viciifolia*) with pinnate leaves and pink flowers, cultivated as fodder. [Fr. *sain* wholesome, *foin*, hay]

saint (sānt) *adj.* Canonized or officially recognized by the R.C. Ch. or certain other Christian churches as having won by exceptional holiness a high place in heaven and veneration on earth, usu. abbrev. St. or S., pl. Sts., SS., as prefix to name(s) of person or archangel(s) as *St. Paul*, *St. Michael*; hence, in names of churches and of towns called after their churches, and in Christian and family names, taken from patron saint etc. ~ *n.* One of the blessed dead or other member of the company of heaven; canonized person; (bibl., archaic, and in some modern sects, esp. Mormon) one of God's chosen people, member of Christian church or of some branch of it (usu. cap.); person of great holiness; **patron** ~, saint selected as heavenly protector of person or place, esp. church, often named after him; **saint's day**, church festival in memory of a saint, freq. observed as holiday. **saint′like** *adj.* **saint′ly** *adj.* (**-li·er, -li·est**). **saint′dom, saint′li·ness, saint′hood** *ns.* **saint** *v.t.* Canonize, admit to the calendar of saints; call

1 jigger topsail
2 spanker
3 mizzen royal
4 mizzen topgallant
5 mizzen upper topsail
6 mizzen lower topsail
7 mizzen crojack
8 mizzen topmast staysail
9 mizzen topgallant staysail
10 mainsail
11 main lower topsail
12 main upper topsail
13 main topgallant
14 main royal
15 main skysail
16 main royal staysail
17 main topgallant staysail
18 main topmast staysail
19 main staysail
20 foresail
21 fore lower topsail
22 fore upper topsail
23 fore topgallant
24 fore royal
25 fore skysail
26 upper studding sail
27 upper topsail studding sail
28 lower topsail studding sail
29 lower studding sail
30 fore staysail
31 fore topmast staysail
32 jib
33 flying jib
34 jib martingale
35 jib stay
36 flying jib martingale
37 flying jib stay
38 flying jib stay
39 fore royal stay
40 fore skysail stay
41 fore skysail backstay
42 fore royal backstay
43 skysail stay
44 foot ropes
45 skysail braces
46 royal braces

Noted for its vivid red flowers, the ***sainfoin*** *(Onobrychis viciifolia), is a type of clover which is used both as green fodder and for hay.*

Completed in 1959, the ***St. Lawrence Sea-way*** *was a joint project between the U.S.A. and Canada, providing large shipping with access to North America.*

or regard as a saint; **saint'ed**, worthy to be so regarded, of saintly life; hallowed, sacred.

Saint (sānt) **Bernard.** Very large dog of breed orig. kept by monks of Hospice on Great St. Bernard Pass in Alps for rescue of travelers.

Sainte-Beuve (sănt böv′), **Charles Augustin** (1804–69). French literary critic, poet, and historian.

Saint-De·nis (săndenē′). 1. Industrial city and suburb of Paris; site of 12th-c. Gothic church containing tombs of many monarchs, including Louis XII and XIII, and Marie Antoinette. 2. Capital of Réunion Island in the Indian Ocean.

Saint-Gau·dens (sāntgaw′-denz), **Augustus** (1848–1907). Irish-born Amer. sculptor; noted for his public monuments, including statues of General Sherman, Lincoln, etc.

St. Hel·e·na (sānt helē′na). Island in S. Atlantic, a British possession, the place of Napoleon Bonaparte's exile (1815–21).

St. James's (sānt jāmz′). Old Tudor palace of English monarchs in London, built by Henry VIII; **Court of ~**, official title of British court, to which ambassadors from foreign countries are accredited.

Saint John (sānt jŏn′). Largest city and principal port of New Brunswick, Canada, at the mouth of the St. John River on the Bay of Fundy.

Saint Johns (sānt jŏnz′). Capital of Antigua, one of the Leeward Islands, West Indies.

St. Law·rence (sānt lŏr′ens, lăr′-) **River.** River in SE. Canada, flowing NE. 760 mi. (1,223 km), from Lake Ontario, along the New York-Ontario border, to the **Gulf of Saint Lawrence**, gulf of the N. Atlantic between SE. Canada and Newfoundland; **Saint Lawrence Seaway**, water between Montreal, Canada, and Lake Ontario, covering 182 mi. (293 km), along the Saint Lawrence River, enabling deep-draft vessels to travel between the Atlantic Ocean and the Great Lakes; jointly constructed by the U.S. and Canada, 1955–9.

Saint-Saëns (săn sahn′), **Charles Camille** (1835–1921). French musical composer, noted for his symphonic poems and the opera *Samson and Delilah*.

The lives of the saints have provided inspiration for painters throughout history. Adam Elsheimer followed the style of Tintoretto in this study of ***Saint John the Baptist.***

St. Thom·as (sānt tŏm′as). Second largest island of the U.S. Virgin Islands, covering 28 sq. mi., (73 sq. km), in the Caribbean; capital of the U.S. Virgin Islands, Charlotte Amalie, on S. coast.

St. Wenceslas: see WENCESLAS[1].

Sai·pan (sīpăn). Largest of the Mariana Islands, covering 70 sq. mi. (181 sq. km), in the W. Pacific Ocean; site of World War II Japanese air base captured by Americans, 1944, and then used as a U.S. air base.

Sa·is (sā′ĭs). Ancient capital of lower Egypt, in the Nile delta. **Sa·ite** (sā′īt) *n.* **Sa·it·ic** (sāĭt′ĭk) *adj.*

saith (sĕth) *v.* (archaic) Pres. ind. third pers. sing. of SAY.

sake[1] (sāk) *n.* **for the ~ of, for** (someone's or something's) **~**, out of consideration for, in the interest of (someone or something); **for goodness', heaven's, ~**, form of entreaty or exclamation; **for old time's ~**, in memory of old days.

sa·ke[2], **sa·ki** (sah′kē) *ns.* Japanese fermented liquor made from rice.

Sa·kha·lin (sahxahlēn′). (formerly *Saghalien*) Island of the U.S.S.R., off the SE. coast N. of Japan in the Sea of Okhotsk; divided in 1905, with the S. part being called Karafuto and belonging to Japan until it was returned to the U.S.S.R. in 1945.

Sa·kya·mu·ni (sahkyamōōn′ē): see BUDDHA.

sal (săl) *n.* Salt. [L.]

sa·laam (salahm′) *n.* Muslim salutation "Peace"; obeisance accompanying this, low bow of head and body with right palm on forehead. ~ *v.* Make salaam (to). [Arab. *salām*]

sal·a·ble, sale·a·ble (sā′label) *adjs.* Fit for sale; attractive to purchasers. **sal·a·bil·i·ty** (sālabĭl′ĭtē) *n.*

*There is a noticeable difference in aquatic dependence between different species of **salamander.** The fire variety only enters water to lay eggs, but the mud salamander (behind) spends all its life in water.*

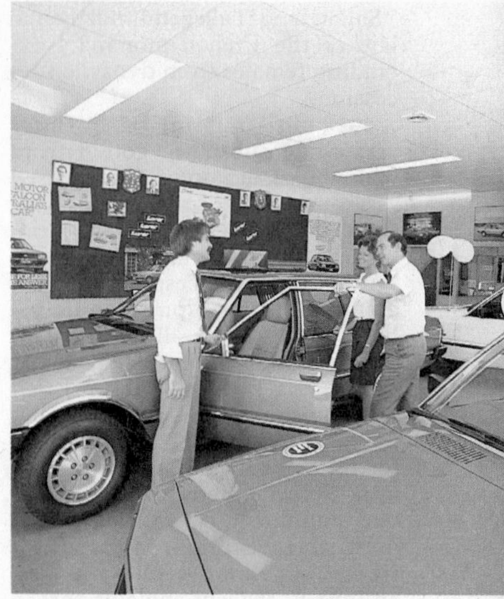

*Consistent with the upgrading and increase of road systems, vehicle **sales** are also escalating and creating pollution problems in major cities.*

sa·la·cious (s*a*lā′sh*u*s) *adj.* Lustful; (of literature) dealing with or suggestive of lewdness. **sa·la′cious·ly** *adv.* **sa·la′cious·ness, sa·lac·i·ty** (s*a*lăs′ĭtē) *ns.*

sal·ad (săl′*a*d) *n.* Cold dish of usu. uncooked vegetables; cold dish of meat, fish, etc., with salad (e.g. *chicken* ~); vegetable (e.g. lettuce, endive) suitable for eating raw in salads; ~ **days**, one's inexperienced youth; ~ **dressing**, mixture of oil and vinegar, or mayonnaise, or other sauce, used on salad; ~ **oil**, olive or other vegetable oil used for dressing salads.

Sal·a·din (săl′*a*dĭn) (1137–93). Sultan of Egypt, who invaded Palestine and captured Jerusalem.

Sal·a·man·ca (săl*a*măng′k*a*). Province of W. Spain; capital of this province, scene of a battle (1812) in which the French were defeated by Wellington; the Nationalist capital during the Spanish Civil War, 1937–38.

sal·a·man·der (săl′*a*mănd*e*r) *n.* 1. Lizardlike animal supposed to live in fire. 2. (zool.) Tailed urodele amphibian, related to newts, of family Salamandridae.

sa·la·mi (s*a*lah′mē) *n.* Highly seasoned sausage, freq. flavored with garlic.

Sal·a·mis (săl′*a*mĭs; *Gk.* sahlahmēs′). Island off SW. coast of Attica, near the Piraeus, scene of a naval battle in 480 B.C. in which the Persian fleet under Xerxes was defeated by the Greeks.

sal am·mo·ni·ac (săl*a*mō′nēăk): see AMMONIAC.

sal·a·ry (săl′*e*rē) *n.* (pl. **-ries**). Fixed periodical payment made to person for services. **sal′a·ried** *adj.* Receiving a salary. [L. *salarium*, orig. soldier's salt money, f. *sal* salt]

sale (sāl) *n.* Exchange of a commodity for money or other valuable consideration, selling; amount sold; rapid disposal at reduced prices of (part of) store's stock at end of season etc.; **for, on** ~, offered for purchase; **white** ~, sale of household linen etc.; **sales′man** (pl. **-men**), **sales′woman** (pl. **-women**), **sales′person**, person engaged in selling goods in store etc., or as middleman between producer and retailer; **sales′manship**, skill in selling; **sales resistance**, opposition or apathy of the prospective customer regarded as requiring to be overcome by salesmanship; **sales talk**, persuasive reasoning to prospective customer.

sale·a·ble: SALABLE.

Sa·lem[1] (sā′l*e*m). Place mentioned in Gen. 14 as the seat of the kingdom of Melchizedek, doubtfully identified with Jerusalem.

Sa·lem[2] (sā′l*e*m). 1. Massachusetts seaport, in the NE. part, on the Atlantic Ocean; during the 17th c. site of witchcraft trials and executions. 2. Capital of Oregon, in the NW. part, on the Willamette River.

Sa·li·an (sā′lē*a*n, sāl′y*a*n) *adj.* & *n.* (Member) of Frankish tribe on the lower Rhine from which the Merovingians were descended.

Sal·ic (săl′ĭk, sā′lĭk), **Sa·lique** (sălēk′, săl′ĭk, sā′lĭk) *adjs.* Of the Salian Franks; **Salic Law**, code of law of the Salian Franks that maintains that a woman can have no portion of the inheritance of the

*The John Turner House in **Salem,** Massachusetts which was the inspiration for Nathaniel Hawthorne's book, House of the Seven Gables. Today industry and tourism are the city's source of income.*

"Salian land"; alleged fundamental law of the French monarchy excluding females from dynastic succession.

sal·i·cin (săl'ĭsĭn) *n.* Bitter crystalline substance gotten from willow bark etc. and formerly used as an analgesic. **sal·i·cyl·ic** (sălĭsĭl'ĭk) *adj.* ~ **acid,** ($C_7H_6O_3$) orig. obtained from salicin but now made synthetically, used esp. in the form of its acetyl ester, aspirin. **sa·lic·y·late** (salĭs'ĭlāt, -lĭt, sălĭsĭl'āt, săl'ĭsĭlāt) *n.* Salt of salicylic acid.

sa·li·ent (sā'lēent, sāl'yent) *adj.* 1. Leaping or dancing (pedantic, joc.); (of water etc., poet.) jetting forth. 2. (of angle, esp. in fortification) Pointing outward. 3. Jutting out; prominent, conspicuous, most noticeable. **sa'lient·ly** *adv.* **sa'lience, sa'lien·cy** (pl. **-cies**) *ns.* **salient** *n.* Salient angle or part in fortification; projecting section of line of offense or defense.

sa·li·en·ti·an (sālēĕn'shēan) *adj.* & *n.* (Member) of the Salientia, an order of amphibians comprising frogs and toads, the adult forms of which have no tails or gills but have strong hind legs for leaping or swimming.

sa·lif·er·ous (salĭf'erus) *adj.* (geol.) (of stratum) Containing much salt.

sa·line (sā'lēn, -līn) *adj.* (of natural waters, springs, etc.) Impregnated with salt or salts; (of taste) salt; of chemical salts, of the nature of a salt; (of medicines) containing salt(s) of alkaline metals or magnesium. ~ *n.* Saline solution. **sa·lin·i·ty** (salĭn'ĭtē) *n.*

Sa·lique: SALIC.

Salis·bur·y[1] (sawlz'bĕrē, -berē). Now known as HARARE. Capital city of Zimbabwe, formerly Rhodesia.

*A **salientian,** which can be a frog or toad, is usually a ground dwelling animal. However, tree frogs, such as the one illustrated, are able to gain access to many places.*

Salis·bur·y[2] (sawlz'bĕrē, -berē) **Plain.** Plateau in S. England; site of Stonehenge.

Salis·bur·y (sawlz'bĕrē, -berē, sălz'-) **steak.** Ground beef, rolled into hamburger patty and fried or broiled.

sa·li·va (salī'va) *n.* Colorless, normally alkaline liquid, the mixed secretion of salivary glands and mucous glands of the mouth, which mixes with food in mastication; spittle. **sal·i·var·y** (săl'ĭvĕrē) *adj.* Secreting or conveying, of, existing in, saliva.

sal·i·vate (săl'ĭvāt) *v.* (**-vat·ed, -vat·ing**). Produce unusual secretion of saliva in (person), usu. with mercury; secrete or discharge saliva. **sal·i·va·tion** (sălĭvā'shon) *n.*

Salk (sawk, sawlk), **Jonas E**(**dward**) (1914–). U.S. physician and microbiologist, developed first successful poliomyelitis vaccine (**Salk vaccine**), made from killed virus strains. See SABIN.

sal·low[1] (săl'ō) *n.* European willow, esp. of low-growing or shrubby kinds; shoot or wood of this.

sal·low[2] (săl'ō) *adj.* (of skin or complexion) Sickly yellow or yellowish-brown color; having skin of this color. ~ *v.* Make, grow, sallow. **sal'low·ness** *n.*

sal·ly (săl'ē) *n.* (pl. **-lies**). 1. Rush (*forth*) from besieged place upon enemy, sortie; excursion; ~ **port,** opening in fortified place for making sallies from. 2. Sudden start into activity, outburst; outburst, flash (esp. *of* wit); witticism, piece of banter, lively remark. **sally** *v.i.* (**-lied, -ly·ing**). Make sally (usu. *forth*); go *forth* on journey, for a walk, etc.

*All **salmon** attempt to return to the stream where they were hatched when the time comes to breed. It has been proved that they locate the correct waterway by its smell.*

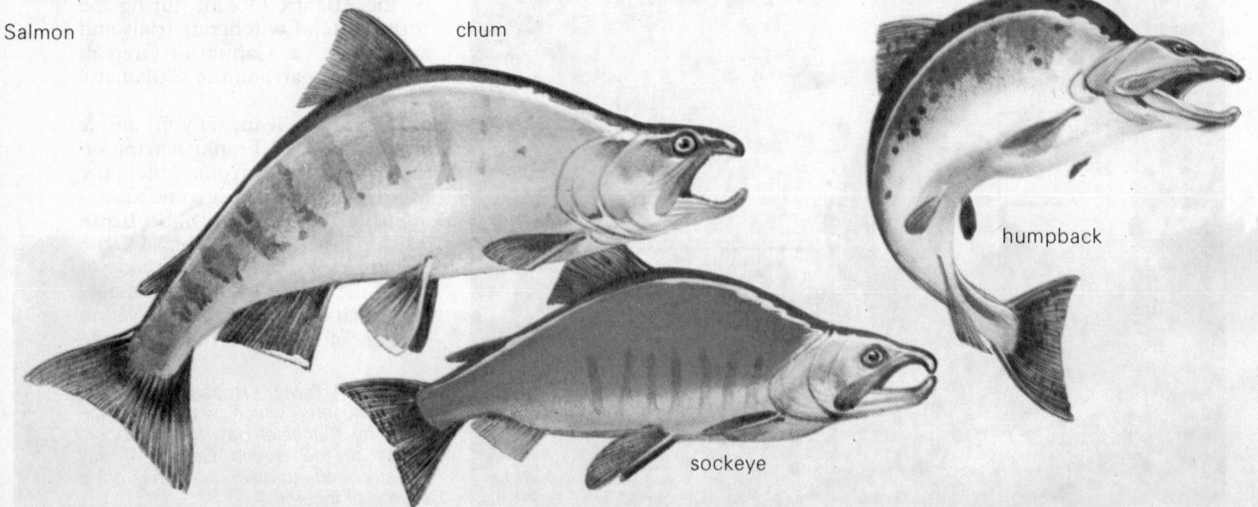

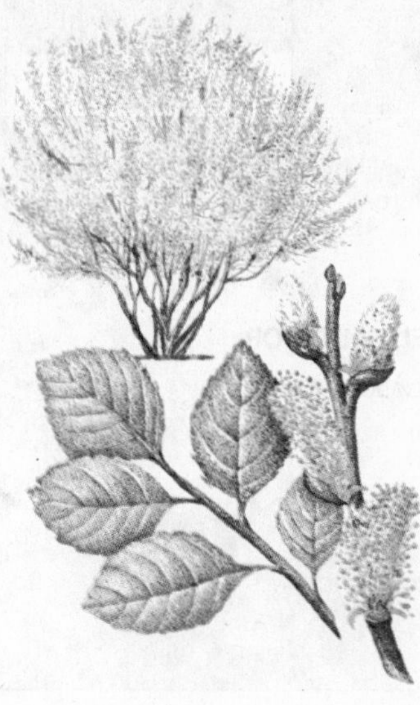

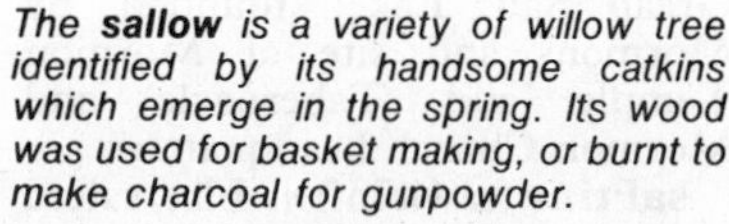

*The **sallow** is a variety of willow tree identified by its handsome catkins which emerge in the spring. Its wood was used for basket making, or burnt to make charcoal for gunpowder.*

*One of the most vivid flowers in any garden, the **salpiglossis** needs to be grown in sheltered sunny locations in a temperate climate. It thrives in warmer latitudes.*

sal·ma·gun·di (sălm*a*gŭn′dē) *n.* Dish of chopped meat, eggs, anchovies, onions, etc., with oil and condiments; general mixture, miscellaneous collection. [Fr. *salmigondis*]

sal·mi, sal·mis (săl′mē) *ns.* Ragout, esp. of game birds, partly roasted and then stewed with wine or sauce. [Fr., prob. short for *salmigondis*: see SALMAGUNDI]

salm·on (săm′*o*n) *n.* (pl. **-ons,** collect. **-on**). Large silver-scaled pink-fleshed fish of genus *Salmo*, esp. *S. salar*, which swims up rivers to spawn, much prized for food and sport; any of various other fishes (esp. *Oncorhynchus*) of same family, or resembling salmon; the orange-pink color of salmon flesh. ~ *adj.* Salmon pink.

sal·mo·nel·la (sălm*o*nĕl′*a*) *n.* (pl. **-nel·lae** pr. -nĕl′ē, **-nel·la, -nel·las**). Microorganism of the genus *S*~, members of which are responsible for many forms of enteritis, typhoid fever, etc. [D. E. *Salmon* (1850–1914), Amer. pathologist]

sal·mo·nid (săl′m*o*nĭd) *adj.* & *n.* (zool.) (Fish) of the family Salmonidae (salmon, trout, etc.).

Sa·lo·me (s*a*lō′mē). Stepdaughter of Herod Antipas; she pleased him with her dancing and at the bidding of her mother, Herodias, asked for the head of John the Baptist in a dish as a reward (see Matt. 14).

sa·lon (s*a*lŏn′, săl′ŏn) *n.* Reception room in continental, esp. French, great house; (assembly of prominent people in) reception room of (esp. Parisian) lady of fashion; (exhibition in) gallery etc. for showing works of art, photographs, etc., esp. (**the S**~) annual exhibition of living artists' pictures in Paris; room or establishment where hairdresser, dressmaker, etc., receives clients.

Sa·lo·ni·ka, Sa·lo·ni·ca (s*a*lŏn′ĭk*a*, sălonē′k*a*). (Gk. *Thessaloniki*, the ancient THESSALONICA) Seaport in NE. Greece, capital of Macedonia.

sa·loon (s*a*lo͞on′) *n.* 1. Hall or large room, esp. in hotel or place of public resort, fit for assemblies, exhibitions, etc. 2. Large cabin for first-class or for all passengers on ship etc., esp. serving as lounge. 3. Tavern, bar; ~ **keeper**, keeper of saloon or tavern.

sal·pi·glos·sis (sălpĭglŏs′ĭs, -glaw′sĭs) *n.* Showy-flowered herbaceous garden plant allied to petunia, orig. from Chile. [Gk. *salpigx* trumpet, *glōssa* tongue]

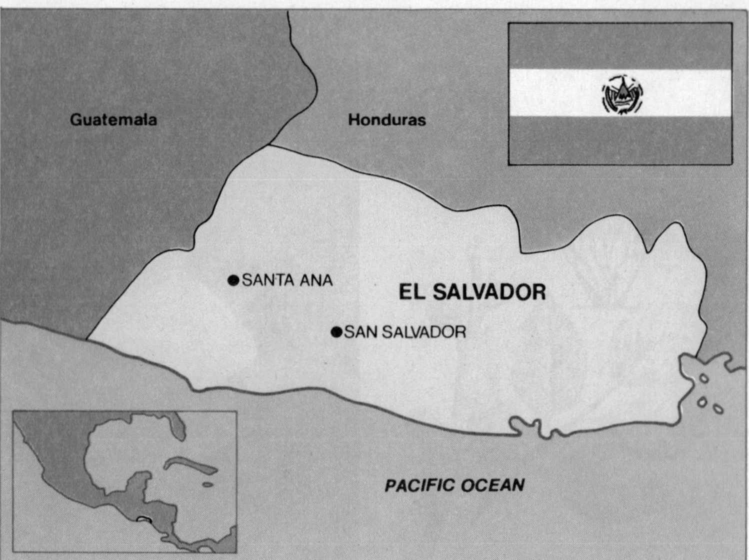

Church of Guadalupe, in San Salvador, capital of ***El Salvador.*** *With a population of 3.9 million (1974) and an area of 8,260 sq. miles, this country has the highest population density in Central America.*

sal·si·fy (săl'sĭfē) *n.* (pl. **-fies**). Biennial composite plant (*Tragopogon porrifolius*) with long cylindrical fleshy roots eaten as vegetable.

SALT (sawlt) *n.* & *adj.* Strategic Arms Limitation Talks.

salt (sawlt) *n.* 1. (also **common** ~) Sodium chloride, a substance with characteristic taste, very abundant in nature (in the sea, and in crystalline form), used as a condiment, as a preservative of food, and in many industrial processes; **rock** ~, common salt occurring in large solid masses; **table** ~, common salt for table use; **take with a grain of** ~, accept (statement etc.) with reserve; **worth one's** ~, efficient, useful; **the** ~ **of the earth**, people for whose existence the world is better, moral élite (see Matt. 5). 2. Vessel, usu. open, for table salt, saltcellar (now chiefly in trade use and hist. in **above the** ~, seated with family and their equals, and **below the** ~, among servants and dependents). 3. Sting, piquancy, pungency, wit. 4. (chem.) Substance formed from an acid when all or part of its hydrogen is replaced by a metal or metallic radical. 5. Experienced sailor (esp. **old** ~). 6. **salt'cellar**, vessel holding salt for table use; **salt dome**, mass of salt forced up into sedimentary rocks; **salt grass**, type of grass growing in salt marshes and alkaline regions; **salt lick**, place where animals come to lick earth impregnated with salt; **salt marsh**, marsh frequently overflowed by sea; **salt mine**, mine yielding rock salt; (fig., usu. pl.) place of unremitting toil; **salt'wort**, any of various maritime and salt marsh plants of the genus *Salsola*. **salt** *adj.* Impregnated with, containing, tasting of, cured or preserved or seasoned with, salt; (of plants) growing in sea or salt marshes; ~ **water**, water containing a large proportion of salt; sea water; **salt'water**, of, living in, the sea. **salt'ed** *adj.* **salt'y** *adj.* (**salt·i·er, salt·i·est**). 1. Containing or tasting of salt. 2. Lively, racy, witty. **salt'i·ness, salt'ness** *ns.* **salt** *v.t.* 1. Preserve, season, or treat with salt; ~ **away**, (colloq.) put by, store away (money etc.). 2. Render piquant, enliven. 3. Make (mine etc.) appear to be paying one by fraudulently introducing rich ore etc. **salt'er** *n.*

Salt (sawlt) **Lake City.** Capital and largest city of Utah, in the N. part on the Jordan River near the Great Salt Lake; founded by Mormons and site of Mormon Temple and Tabernacle and Mormon Church headquarters.

An ornate Vivyan ***salt cellar*** *made of silver and gilt in 1592–93, has painting on glass panels. Such luxurious salt containers demonstrated the wealth of their owners.*

sal·tine (sawltēn') *n.* Flat, salted cracker.

salt·pe·ter, Brit. **salt·pe·tre** (sawltpē'*ter*) *ns.* Niter, potassium nitrate (KNO_3), white crystalline salty substance used as constituent of gunpowder, in preserving meat etc.; sodium nitrate ($NaNO_3$). [prob. f. L. *sal petrae* salt of stone, because it occurs as an incrustation on stones]

sa·lu·bri·ous (s*a*loo'brē*u*s) *adj.* Healthy (chiefly of air, climate, etc.). **sa·lu'bri·ous·ly** *adv.* **sa·lu·bri·ty** (s*a*loo'brĭtē), **sa·lu'bri·ous·ness** *ns.*

sa·lu·ki (s*a*loo'kē) *n.* Tall, swift, slender silky-coated dog, developed in Arabia and Egypt.

sal·u·tar·y (săl'y*u*tĕrē) *adj.* Producing good effect, beneficial.

sal·u·ta·tion (sălyutā'sh*o*n) *n.* (Use of) words spoken or written to convey interest in another's health etc., pleasure at sight of or communication with person, or courteous recognition of person's arrival or departure; greeting.

sa·lute (s*a*loot') *v.* (**-lut·ed, -lut·ing**). Make salute or salutation (to). ~ *n.* Gesture expressing respect, homage, or courteous recognition; (mil., nav., etc.) prescribed movement (esp., of hand to forehead) or position of body or weapons, use of flag(s), discharge of gun(s), in sign of respect; (fencing) formal performance of certain guards, etc., by fencers before engaging. **sa·lut'er** *n.*

Sal·va·dor (săl'v*a*dōr): EL SALVADOR.

sal·vage (săl'vĭj) *n.* (Payment made or due for) saving of a ship or its cargo from loss by wreck or

1

2

Huge deposits of **salt** form naturally from evaporation at Lake Etosha in south-west Africa (1) and at Uyuni, in Bolivia, where it is cut into blocks (2). In the Canary Islands (3) and Australia (4) special areas are deliberately flooded and, when the water evaporates, salt is harvested by machinery.

Salt Lake City is largely influenced by the presence of the Mormon Church, the reason for this city's existence. It was founded in 1847 by Brigham Young and a dedicated group of Mormons escaping religious persecution.

3

4

capture; rescue of property from fire etc.; saving and use of waste material of all kinds; property salvaged. ~ *v.t.* (**-vaged, -vag·ing**). Make salvage of, save from wreck, fire, etc. **sal'vage·a·ble** *adj.*

sal·va·tion (sălvā'shon) *n.* 1. Saving of the soul; deliverance from sin and its consequences, and admission to heaven, brought about by the merits of Christ's death. 2. Preservation from loss, calamity, etc.; thing that preserves from these. **sal·va'tion·al** *adj.*

Sal·va·tion (sălvā'shon) **Army.** Organization founded by the Rev. William Booth in 1878 and established on a quasi-military basis and engaging in evangelical and charitable work among the destitute throughout the world. **Sal·va'tion·ist** *n.* Member of the Salvation Army; (**s** ~) person who preaches salvation.

salve[1] (săv, sahv) *n.* Healing ointment for sores or wounds; something that soothes wounded feelings or uneasy conscience. ~ *v.t.* (**salved, salv·ing**). Anoint (wound etc.); soothe (pride, conscience, etc.).

salve[2] (sălv) *v.t.* (**salved, salv·ing**). Save (ship, cargo) from loss at sea or (property) from fire etc.

sal·ver (săl'ver) *n.* Meat tray for handing refreshments or presenting letters etc. [f. Fr. *salve* tray for presenting certain things to king, f. Span. *salva* assaying of food (*salvo* safe)]

sal·vi·a (săl'vēa) *n.* Plant of genus *S*~, comprising the sages; flower of this cultivated for its bright blue or scarlet color.

sal·vo (săl'vō) *n.* (pl. **-vos, -voes**). Simultaneous discharge of artillery, rockets, etc.; burst of applause, cheers, etc.

sal·vor, sal·ver (săl'ver) *ns.* Person, ship, making or assisting in salvage.

Salz·burg (sawlz'bẽrg; *Ger.* zahlts'boorχ). City and resort in W. central Austria, birthplace of Mozart, where a summer festival of music and drama has been held annually, except in wartime, since 1920.

SAM (săm) *n.* Surface-to-air missile.

Sam. *abbrev.* Samuel (Old Testament).

sam·a·ra (săm'era, samăr'a, -mār'a) *n.* Winged one-seeded indehiscent fruit, single (as in ash) or double (as in sycamore).

Sa·mar·i·a (samār'ēa). Ancient capital of Israel; ancient northern kingdom of Israel (see ISRAEL[1], sense 3); region surrounding this, W. of the Jordan, bounded by Galilee and Judea.

Sa·mar·i·tan (samăr'ĭtan) *n.* 1. Native, inhabitant, language, of Samaria. 2. **good** ~, person always ready to help the unfortunate (with ref. to Luke 10 etc.). **Samaritan** *adj.* Of Samaria or Samaritans.

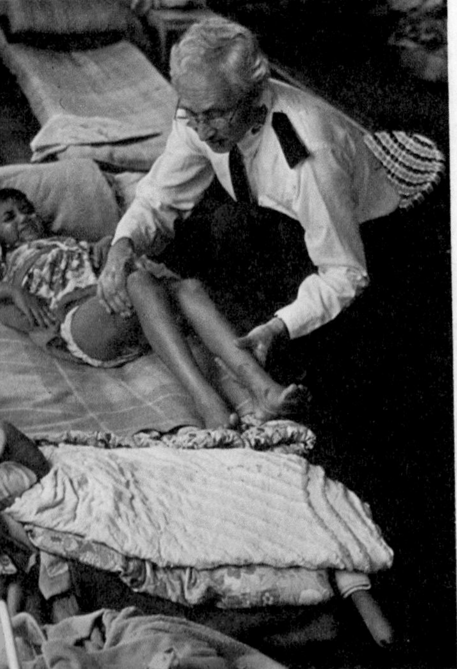

Always available in times of natural disaster, officers of the ***Salvation Army*** *are among the first to arrive and offer help, as during floods in Brisbane, Australia.*

Winged seeds of the sycamore are typical of ***samara,*** *single-seeded fruits whose membraneous extensions allow them to be carried by the wind. They also develop on ash and elm trees.*

Salzburg *in western-central Austria. Renowned for its scenic beauty and cultural heritage, it has become a major tourist center, particularly during festival time.*

sa·mar·i·um (samār'ēum) *n.* (chem.) Element of rare-earth group, symbol Sm, at. no. 62, at. wt. 150.4.

Sam·ar·kand (săm'erkănd). City in the SW. Soviet Union, SW. of Tashkent; important stop on the Silk Route from China to Europe during the 7th c.; became capital of Tamburlaine's empire, 1370.

sam·ba (sahm'ba, săm'-) *n.* Brazilian dance of African origin; ballroom dance imitative of this; music for this dance.

Sam Browne (săm' brown') **belt.** Leather belt with a supporting strap passing diagonally over the right shoulder, worn as part of some military and police uniforms. [f. name of Brit. Gen. Sir *Sam*uel J. *Browne*, 1824–1901]

same (sām) *adj.* 1. Not different; the very. 2. (pred.) Not changed; not varying; equally acceptable. 3. Aforesaid. 4. (*abs.* and as *pronoun*) **the** ~, the same person; the same thing. 5. **the** ~ (*adv.*) in the same manner; **all the** ~, nevertheless; **just the** ~, in spite of changed conditions. **same'ness** *n.*

sam·i·sen (săm'ĭsĕn) *n.* Long three-stringed Japanese guitar, played with plectrum.

sam·iz·dat (săm'ĭzdăt) *n.* System of clandestine publication of banned literature in U.S.S.R.

Sam·nite (săm'nīt) *adj.* & *n.* (Member) of an ancient tribe of S. central Italy, inhabiting the district of Samnium.

The tiled domes and towers at Shahi-Zendah are among a group of 12th-century mausoleums in ***Samarkand,*** *which is now in the Uzbek S.S.R., and is the oldest surviving city in central Asia.*

Sam·oa (Sah'mōa). Group of Polynesian islands, of which the eastern part (**American** ~) is a U.S. territory; **Western** ~, republic, independent since 1962; member nation of the Brit. Commonwealth; capital, Apia. **Sam'oan** *adj.* & *n.*

Sa·mos (sā'mŏs, săm'ōs). Greek island in the Aegean off the W. coast of Turkey.

Sam·o·thrace (săm'*o*thrās). Greek island in the NE. Aegean.

sam·o·var (săm'*o*var̄, săm*o*var̄') *n.* Russian tea urn. [Russ., = "self-boiler"]

Sam·o·yed (săm'*o*yĕd, săm*o*-yĕd') *n.* 1. (also **Sam·o·yede'**) Member, language, of a Mongolian people of Siberia. 2. Dog of white Arctic breed, used for pulling sleds. **Sam·o·yed·ic** (săm*o*yĕd'ĭk) *adj.*

sam·pan (săm'păn) *n.* Small boat used in river and coastal traffic of China, Japan, and neighboring islands, rowed with a scull from the stern and usu. having a sail of matting and an awning. [Chin. *san-pan* boat (*san* 3, *pan* board)]

sam·ple (săm'p*e*l, sahm'-) *n.* Small separated part of something illustrating qualities of the mass etc. it is taken from, specimen, pattern. ~ *v.t.* (**-pled, -pling**). Take or give samples, try the qualities, get representative experience, of. **sam'pler**[1] *n.*

sam·pler[2] (săm'pl*e*r, sahm'-) *n.* Piece of embroidery worked as specimen of proficiency, usu. containing alphabet and various decorative motifs.

Sam·son (săm's*o*n). Israelite judge famous for his strength (Judges 13–16); he confided to a woman, Delilah, that his strength lay in his hair, and she betrayed him to the Philistines, who cut off his hair while he slept and captured and blinded him; but when his hair grew again, his strength returned and he pulled down the pillars of the house of Gaza, destroying himself and a large concourse of Philistines; hence, man of phenomenal strength.

Sam·u·el (săm'ū*e*l). Hebrew prophet who rallied the Israelites after their defeat by the Philistines and became their ruler; (**First and Second Book of**) ~, two books of Old Testament covering the history of Israel from Samuel's birth to the end of the reign of David.

sam·u·rai (săm'o͞orī) *n.* (pl. **-rai**). In Japanese feudal system, military retainer of the chief territorial nobles; any member of military caste.

Sa·n'a (sahnah'). Capital and largest city of Yemen Arab Republic, in the central part of the country, in the SW. Arabian Peninsula.

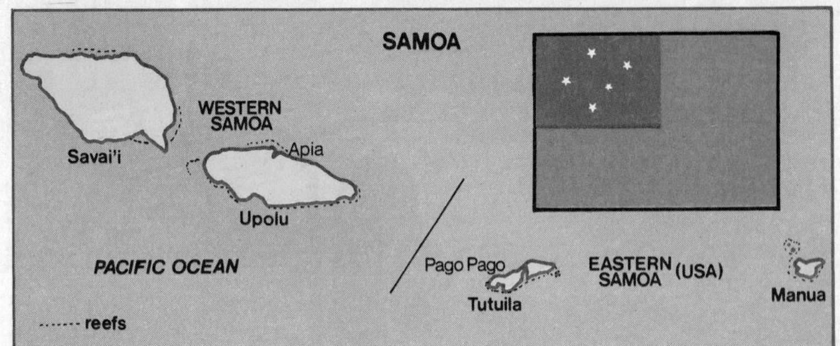

*Although **Western Samoa** became the first fully independent Polynesian state in 1962, the eastern islands where Pago Pago (above) is located, are still controlled by the U.S.A.*

*The **sand dollar** is usually found in warm waters, living and feeding under the sand. It is related to the starfish and sea urchin families. The shell is usually 3 to 4 ins. long.*

*Many of the boats which serve as homes to people in Hong Kong are known as a form of **sampan,** although their design may differ from the classical definition.*

*In times when girls stayed at home to learn the arts of housewifery, the **sampler** served as both an achievement and an example of proficiency in needlework. These were made in England in 1832.*

San An·to·ni·o (săn ăntō´nēō). Commercial city in S. central Texas, on the San Antonio River, SW. of Austin; site of the Alamo.

san·a·to·ri·um (sănatōr´ēum, -tōr´-) (pl. **-to·ri·ums, -to·ri·a** pr. -tōr´ēa, -tōr´ēa), **san·i·tar·i·um** (sănitār´ēum) (pl. **-tar·i·ums, -tar·i·a** pr. -tār´ēa) *ns.* 1. Establishment for treatment of chronic diseases (as tuberculosis, mental disorders, etc.) or for convalescents. 2. Health resort.

San·cho Pan·za (săn´chō păn´za, sahn´chō pahn´za). Squire of DON QUIXOTE, who accompanies him on his adventures; he is an ignorant and credulous peasant, but has a store of proverbial wisdom and is thus a foil to his master.

sanc·ti·fy (săngk´tĭfī) *v.t.* (**-fied, -fy·ing**). Consecrate, make holy; purify from sin; give authority to, justify. **sanc·ti·fi·ca·tion** (săngktĭfĭkā´shon), **sanc'ti·fi·er** *ns.*

sanc·ti·mo·ni·ous (săngktĭmō´nēus) *adj.* Make a show of sanctity or piety. **sanc·ti·mo'ni·ous·ly** *adv.* **sanc·ti·mo'ni·ous·ness** *n.*

sanc·tion (săngk´shon) *n.* 1. (hist.) Law or decree. 2. Penalty imposed for noncompliance with a law, custom, etc., or with an international agreement. 3. Confirmation or ratification of law etc. by supreme authority; express authoritative permission; countenance or encouragement given to action etc. by custom etc. **sanction** *v.t.* Authorize; countenance; permit. **sanc'tion·er** *n.*

sanc·ti·tude (săngk´tĭtōōd, -tūd) *n.* (now rare) Saintliness.

sanc·ti·ty (săngk´tĭtē) *n.* (pl. **-ties**). Saintliness; sacredness; inviolability; (pl.) sacred obligations, feelings, etc.

sanc·tu·ar·y (săngk´chōōĕrē) *n.* (pl. **-ar·ies**). 1. Place recognized as holy part of church within altar rails. 2. Sacred place by retiring to which fugitive from law, or debtor, was secured by medieval church law against arrest or violence; place in which similar immunity was established by custom or law; place of refuge; (right of affording) such immunity. 3. Reserved area where animals, birds, etc. are protected from hunting.

sanc·tum (săngk´tum) *n.* (pl. **-tums, -ta** pr. -ta). 1. Sacred or holy place; person's private room, study or den. 2. Place in Jewish tabernacle or temple where Ark of the Covenant was located; ~ **sanc·to·rum** (săngktōr´um, -tōr´-), holy of holies.

Sanc·tus (săngk´tus; *Lat.* sahngk´tōōs) *n.* Hymn (from Isa. 6) beginning *"Sanctus, sanctus, sanctus"* or *"Holy, holy, holy,"* forming conclusion of Eucharistic preface; music for this; ~ **bell**, bell rung at the Sanctus.

sand (sănd) *n.* Minute fragments resulting from wearing down of esp. siliceous rocks and found covering parts of the seashore, river beds, deserts, etc.; (pl.) expanse or tracts of sand; **sand'bag**, bag filled with sand, used to protect trenches, buildings, etc. against blast and splinters, to protect against floods, as ballast, as weapon leaving no mark on victim, etc.; (*v.t.*) (**-bagged, -bag·ging**) protect with sandbags; fell with blow from sandbag; **sand'bar**, shoal of sand in sea or river; **sand'blast**, jet of sand impelled by compressed air or steam for giving rough surface to glass, cleaning buildings, etc.; (*v.t.*) clean, polish, etc. with a sandblast; **sand'box**, large, low box of sand for children to play in; **sand casting**, metal casting obtained from sand mold; process of making such castings; **sand dollar**, round, flat sea urchin; **sand'fly** (pl. **-flies**), any of various biting flies of genus *Phlebotomus;* **sand'hog**, laborer who works under compressed air on underwater or underground construction projects; **sand hopper**, small jumping crustacean of family Talitridae, most species

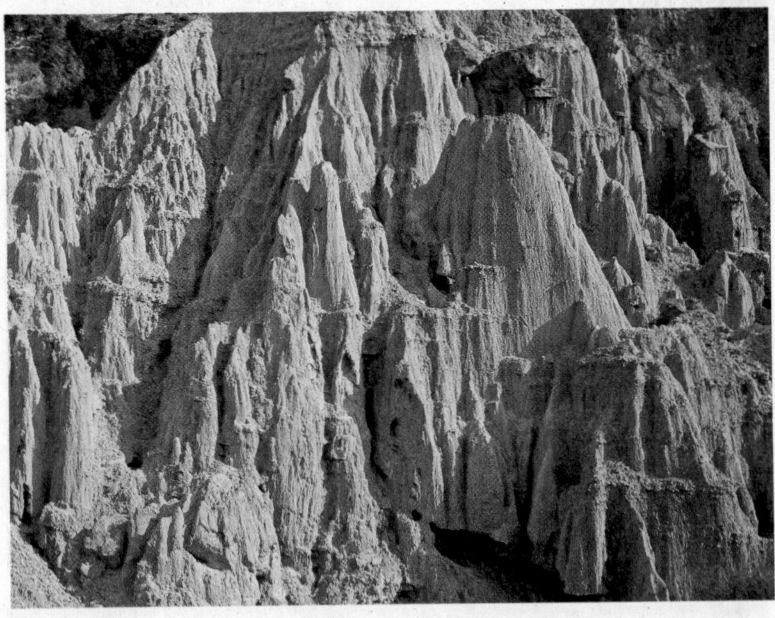

***Sandstone** is a sedimentary rock which can be susceptible to erosion. A result of wind-erosion can be seen (above) in grains of sand from the Kalahari Desert. Weathering from wind and rain can cause effects such as those seen in outcrops in Spain (right).*

of which burrow in sand of seashore; **sand'lot** (*adj.*), of or pertaining to games, esp. baseball, played by amateurs, orig. in a vacant lot; **sand'man**, (nursery name for) personification of sleep or sleepiness; **sand'paper**, paper with layer of sand or other abrasive stuck on for smoothing or polishing wood etc.; (*v.t.*) polish with sandpaper; **sand'piper**, any of various small wading birds of family Scolopacidae, haunting open wet sandy places; **sand'stone**, sedimentary rock composed of small grains usu. of quartz cemented together; **sand'storm**, desert storm of wind with clouds of sand. **sand** *v.t.* Sprinkle, cover, mix, or polish with sand. **sand'er** *n.*

Sand (sănd; *Fr.* sahṅ), **George.** Pen name of Amandine Lucie Aurore Dupin-Dudevant (1804–1876), French novelist, author of *Indiana*, *Lélia*, *Consuelo*, etc.

san·dal (săn'd*a*l) *n.* Sole without upper, attached to foot by thongs passing over instep and around ankle; modification of this, worn by ancient Greeks and Romans, by some Orientals, as modern revival, etc. ~ *v.t.* (**-daled, -dal·ing**). Put sandals on (foot, person; esp. in past part.).

san·dal·wood (săn'd*a*lwo͝od) *n.* Any of various scented woods, true sandalwood being obtained from species of Asian tree of genus *Santalum*.

san·da·rac (săn'd*a*răk) *n.* Resin exuding from NW. African tree (*Tetraclinis articulata*), used in making varnish.

Sand·burg (sănd'bẽrg, săn'-), **Carl** (1878–1967). Amer. poet and biographer; awarded Pulitzer Prize for history, 1939, for *Abraham Lincoln—The War Years*, and for poetry, 1951, for *Complete Poems*.

san·der·ling (săn'd*e*rlĭng) *n.* Common sandpiper (*Crocethia alba*).

sand·wich (sănd'wĭch, săn'-) *n.* Two or more slices of bread etc. with meat, cheese or other filling between; (also **open-face(d)** ~) slice of bread etc. with meat, cheese, etc. on top; two wafers, cookies, etc. with icing, filling, etc. between; ~ **board**, board carried by sandwich man; ~ **man**, man walking street with two advertising placards hung one before and one behind. **sandwich** *v.t.* Insert (thing, statement, etc.) between two of another character. [perh. f. name of 4th Earl of *Sandwich* (1718–92), said to have eaten slices of cold beef between slices of toast, while gaming for 24 hours]

sand·y (săn'dē) *adj.* (**sand·i·er, sand·i·est**). Covered with sand; sand-colored, (of hair) yellowish red; having such hair. **sand'i·ness** *n.*

sane (sān) *adj.* (**san·er, san·est**). Of sound mind, not mad; sensible, rational. **sane'ly** *adv.* **sane'ness** *n.*

San Fran·cis·co (săn frănsĭs'kō). Port and city in N. California, on the W. side of San Francisco Bay on the Pacific Ocean; severely damaged April 18, 1906 in earthquake caused by movement in the San Andreas Fault, which runs through the ~ peninsula; ~ **Bay**, inlet in N. California, about 60 mi. (97 km) long; connected with the Pacific Ocean by Golden Gate strait.

sang: see SING.

san·ga·ree = SANGRIA.

Sang·er (săng'*e*r) **Margaret** (**Higgins**) (1883–1966). Amer. nurse and social reformer; advocate of birth control.

sang-froid (sahṅfrwah') *n.* Composure, coolness, in danger or under agitating circumstances. [Fr., = "cold blood"]

san·grí·a (sănggrē'*a*), **san·ga·ree** (sănggerē') *ns.* Cold drink of wine, citrus juices or slices, sugar, and spices. [Span., "bleeding," a drink of red wine and citrus juices]

san·gui·nar·y (săng'gwinĕrē) *adj.* Attended by, delighting in, bloodshed or slaughter, bloody, bloodthirsty. **san'gui·nar·i·ly** *adv.* **san'gui·nar·i·ness** *n.*

san·guine (săng'gwĭn) *adj.* 1. Blood-red. 2. (hist.) Belonging to that one of the four HUMORS supposed to be characterized by predominance of blood over other humors, and indicated by ruddy face and courageous, hopeful, and amorous disposition; (mod., of complexion) ruddy, florid. 3. Habitually hopeful, confident; expecting things to go well. **san'guine·ly** *adv.* **san'guine·ness** *n.*

san·guin·e·ous (sănggwĭn'ēus) *adj.* Of blood; blood-colored.

San·hed·rin (sănhĕd'rĭn, -hē'drĭn, săn'hĭdrĭn), **San·he·drim** (săn'hĭdrĭm) *ns.* (Jewish hist.) Highest court of justice and supreme council, of 71 members, in ancient Jerusalem, esp. between 5th c. B.C. and 70 A.D. [late Heb., f. Gk. *sunedrion* (*sun* together, *hedra* seat)]

san·i·cle (săn'ĭk*e*l) *n.* Umbelliferous plant of genus *Sanicula* having small greenish flowers.

san·i·tar·i·um = SANATORIUM.

san·i·tar·y (săn'ĭtĕrē) *adj.* Free from or designed to obviate influences deleterious to health; clean; hygienic; ~ **napkin**, pad used in menstruation. **san'i·tar·i·ly** *adv.*

san·i·ta·tion (sănĭtā'sh*o*n) *n.*

Left: The ***sand-piper*** *is a wading bird which frequents tidal river flats in a wide range of northern latitudes, but some migrate to the southern hemisphere.*

San Francisco, *financial center of the U.S. west coast, was annexed by America after the Mexican War in 1846. Now a tourist center with a huge population and many industrial and trading interests.*

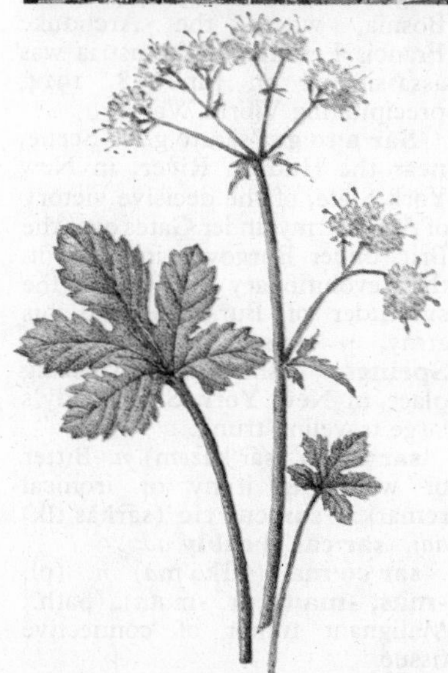

Sanicle *is a perennial plant whose umbels stand about a foot above the ground during the summer months. It has pink or white flowers which develop into spiny fruits.*

Measures designed to preserve public health, esp. efficient drainage and disposal of sewage, pure water supply, etc.; (specif.) drainage and disposal of sewage.

san·i·tize (săn'ĭtīz) *v.* (**-tized, -tiz·ing**). Make sanitary.

san·i·ty (săn'ĭtē) *n.* Being sane, mental health; tendency to avoid extreme views.

San Jo·sé (sahn hawsĕ'). Capital and largest city of Costa Rica, in the central part.

San Juan (săn wahn', hwahn'). Capital and seaport of Puerto Rico, on the N. coast; ~ **Hill**, hill in SE. Cuba near Santiago de Cuba; site of victory over Spanish by Cuban and Amer. forces, including Theodore Roosevelt and the "Rough Riders," in the Spanish-Amer. War, July, 1898.

sank: see SINK².

San Ma·ri·no (săn marē'nō). Small republic occupying 23 sq. mi. (59 sq. km) near Rimini, Italy, on the Adriatic; its capital.

sans (sănz, sahnz) *prep.* (archaic) Without.

San Sal·va·dor (săn săl'vadōr). Capital of El Salvador, in the central part of the country.

sans-cu·lotte (sănzkūlŏt'; *Fr.* sahṅkülawt') *n.* (pl. **sans-cu·lottes** pr. sănzkūlŏts'; *Fr.* sahṅkülawt'). Republican of Parisian lower classes in French Revolution; any extreme republican or revolutionary. [Fr., lit. "without breeches," the revolutionaries wore pantaloons and men of the upper classes wore knee breeches]

san·sei (sahn'sā') *n.* (pl. **-sei, -seis**). (also **S** ~) U.S.-born grandchild of Japanese who came to Amer. [cf. NISEI]

San·skrit, San·scrit (săn'skrĭt) *adjs.* & *ns.* (Of) the ancient, classical, and sacred language of the Hindus in India, in which the Vedic hymns were composed, the oldest known member of the Indo-European family of languages. **San·skrit·ic** (sănskrĭt'ĭk) *adj.*

sans ser·if (săn sĕr'ĭf, sahn) *n.* & *adj.* (Form of type) without serifs.

San·ta Claus (săn'ta klawz). (also *Saint Nicholas, Saint Nick*) Patron saint of children who dispenses gifts to them on Christmas Eve.

San·ta Cruz (săn'ta krōōz') **Islands.** Island group in the SW. Pacific Ocean covering 362 sq. mi. (937 sq. km).

San·ta Fe (săn'ta fā'). Capital of New Mexico, in the N. central part between the Pecos and Rio Grande Rivers; oldest U.S. capital; ~ **Trail**, 19th-c. trade route to the West covering 800 mi. (1,287 km) between Independence, Missouri, and Santa Fe, New Mexico.

San·ta·ya·na (săntēăn'a, sahntāah'na), **George** (1863–1952). Spanish-born Amer. poet and philosopher; author of *Persons and Places*, etc., and one novel, *The Last Puritan*.

San·ti·a·go (sahntēah'gō, -tyah'gō). Capital of Chile, in the central part on a plateau W. of the Andes.

San·to Do·min·go (săn'tō domĭng'gō). (formerly Ciudad Trujillo) Capital of the Dominican Republic, on the S. coast, on the Caribbean Sea.

São Mi·guel (sowṅ' mēgĕl'). Largest island of the Azores, covering 288 sq. mi. (746 sq. km).

São Pau·lo (sowṅ' pow'lōō).

The ancient citadel of 'La Rocca' in the republic of **San Marino.** It is located in eastern Italy, about 10 miles southwest of Rimini and was first granted independence in the 13th century.

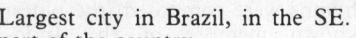

Portrait of Nancy, Lady Astor by **J. S. Sargent,** whose claim to fame relies on his perpetuation of naturalistic techniques when most painters had agreed that modern art needed innovation.

Largest city in Brazil, in the SE. part of the country.

São Tia·go (sowṅ′ tyah′gōō). Largest of the Cape Verde Islands, covering 383 sq. mi. (991 sq. km); location of the capital of the archipelago, Praia.

São To·mé (sowṅ′ tōōmĕ′). Island in the Gulf of Guinea, off the coast of W. Africa, covering 330 sq. mi. (855 sq. km); became independent from Portugal, 1975.

São To·mé e Prin·ci·pe (sowṅ′ tōōmĕ′ ĕ prēn′sēpĕ). Democratic Republic in the Gulf of Guinea off the coast of W. Africa, comprising the islands of São Tomé, Principe, Pedras Tinhosas, and Rolas; Portuguese overseas province until 1975.

sap[1] (săp) *n.* Juice in plants; **sap′wood,** soft layers of wood growing between the bark of trees and the heartwood, alburnum. **sap′py** *adj.* (**-pi·er, -pi·est**). **sap** *v.t.* (**sapped, sap·ping**). (fig.) Exhaust vigor of.

sap[2] (săp) *n.* Making of trenches or tunnels to cover assailant's approach to besieged place or enemy's trenches; covered siege trench. ~ *v.* (**sapped, sap·ping**). Dig sap, approach by sap; undermine, make insecure by removing foundations; (fig.) destroy insidiously.

sap[3] (săp) *n.* (slang) Simpleton, fool. **sap′py** *adj.*

sap·a·jou (săp′ajōō) *n.* CAPUCHIN monkey.

sa·pi·ent (sā′pēent) *adj.* Wise (now rare); would-be wise, of fancied sagacity, aping wisdom. **sa′pi·ent·ly** *adv.* **sa′pi·ence** *n.*

sap·ling (săp′lĭng) *n.* Young tree; (fig.) a youth.

sap·o·dil·la (săpodĭl′*a*) *n.* Large evergreen tropical Amer. tree (*Achras zapota*), with durable wood and edible fruit, and that yields chicle; fruit of this.

sap·o·na·ceous (săponā′sh*u*s) *adj.* Of, like, containing, soap; soapy.

sa·pon·i·fy (s*a*pŏn′ĭfī) *v.* (**-fied, -fy·ing**). (chem.) Convert (fat or oil) into soap by boiling with alkali; convert (an ester) into its constituent acid and alcohol; be converted thus. **sa·pon·i·fi·ca·tion** (s*a*pŏnĭfĭkā′sh*o*n) *n.*

sap·phire (săf′īr) *n.* Transparent blue precious stone, variety of corundum; (min.) any precious transparent crystalline corundum, including sapphire and ruby; bright blue of sapphire, azure. ~ *adj.* Of sapphire blue.

Sap·pho (săf′ō). Greek lyric poetess of Lesbos (flourished 610 B.C.); according to legend, she threw herself into the sea in despair at her unrequited love for Phaon.

sap·ro·phyte (săp′rofīt) *n.* Vegetable organism living on decayed organic matter. **sap·ro·phyt·ic** (săprofĭt′ĭk) *adj.*

sar·a·band (săr′*a*bănd) *n.* Stately Spanish dance in triple time; music for this or in rhythm of it (often with long note on second beat of bar).

Sar·a·cen (săr′*a*s*e*n) *n.* (hist.) Member of the nomadic peoples of the Syro-Arabian desert; hence, Arab; by extension, Muslim, esp. with reference to the crusades. **Sar·a·cen·ic** (săr*a*sĕn′ĭk), **Sar·a·cen′i·cal** *adjs.* Of, connected with, the Saracens.

Sar·ah (sār′*a*, săr′a). Wife of Abraham and mother of Isaac (Gen. 17:ff.).

Sa·ra·je·vo (săr*a*yā′vō). City of Yugoslavia, formerly capital of Bosnia, where the Archduke Francis Ferdinand of Austria was assassinated on June 28, 1914, precipitating World War I.

Sar·a·to·ga (săr*a*tō′g*a*). Scene, near the Hudson River, in New York State, of the decisive victory of Amer. army under Gates over the Brit. under Burgoyne in 1777, in the Revolutionary War, and of the surrender of Burgoyne and his army; ~ **trunk,** (19th c.; f. ~ **Springs,** fashionable watering place in New York State) lady's large traveling trunk.

sar·casm (sār′kăz*e*m) *n.* Bitter or wounding irony or ironical remark. **sar·cas·tic** (sārkăs′tĭk) *adj.* **sar·cas′ti·cal·ly** *adv.*

sar·co·ma (sārkō′m*a*) *n.* (pl. **-mas, -ma·ta** pr. -m*a*t*a*). (path.) Malignant tumor of connective tissue.

sar·coph·a·gus (sārkŏf′*a*g*u*s) *n.* (pl. **-gi** pr. -jī, -gī, -gē, **-gus·es**). Stone coffin, esp. one adorned with sculpture or bearing inscription etc. [L. f. Gk. *sarkophagos,* orig. = flesh-consuming (stone) (*sar* flesh,

Found in Europe but now resting in the gardens of Cliveden in England, this ***sarcophagus*** *shows people and animals known to the man originally interred within it.*

Sarsaparilla, *native to the southern and western coasts of Mexico and Peru, is used as a flavoring for various soft drinks and medical compounds, and used to be drunk as a general tonic.*

Sardinia, *second-largest island in the Mediterranean, is part of Italy. Sheep and goats are grazed in the hills and agriculture is centered around Cagliari.*

-*phagos* eating)]

sard (sar̄d), **sar·di·us** (sar̄′dēus) *ns.* Yellow or orange chalcedony. [f. *Sardis* in Lydia]

sar·dine (sar̄dēn′) *n.* (pl. **-dines**, collect. **-dine**). Young herring or related fishes, freq. cured and tightly canned in oil.

Sar·din·i·a (sar̄dĭn′ē*a*). Mountainous island in the Mediterranean Sea W. of Italy and S. of Corsica, covering 9,301 sq. mi. (24,090 sq. km); a department of Italy, capital, Cagliari. **Sar·din′i·an** *adj.* & *n.*

Sar·dis (sar̄′dĭs). Ancient city in W. Asia Minor, once capital of the kingdom of Lydia.

sar·di·us = SARD.

sar·don·ic (sar̄dŏn′ĭk) *adj.* (of laughter etc.) Bitter, scornful, mocking, sneering, cynical. **sar·don′i·cal·ly** *adv.* [Gk. *sardonios* Sardinian, substituted for Homeric *sardanios* (epithet of bitter or scornful laughter) because of belief that convulsive laughter ending in death resulted from eating a Sardinian plant]

sar·don·yx (sar̄dŏn′ĭks, sar̄′d*o*nĭks) *n.* Variety of onyx with white layers alternating with brownish-yellow or orange sard.

sar·gas·so (sar̄găs′ō) *n.* (pl. **-sos**). Seaweed of genus *Sargassum* with berrylike air vessels, found in islandlike masses in Gulf Stream.

Sar·gas·so (sar̄găs′ō) **Sea.** Region in N. Atlantic, between the West Indies and the Azores, with an abundance of floating sargasso.

sarge (sar̄j) *n.* (colloq.) Sergeant.

Sar·gent (sar̄′j*e*nt), **John Singer** (1856–1925). Amer. portrait and genre painter, chiefly active in England.

sa·ri (sar̄′ē) *n.* (pl. **-ris**). Length of material wrapped around the body, worn as main garment by Hindu women.

Sark (sar̄k). One of the Channel Islands, 1,274 acres.

sa·rong (s*a*rawng′, -rŏng′) *n.* Malay and Javanese garment, long piece of cloth worn as skirt, tucked around waist or under armpits.

sar·sa·pa·ril·la (sar̄sp*a*rĭl′*a*, -rĕl′*a*, săs-) *n.* Any of various tropical Amer. plants of the genus *Smilax*; dried roots of these, or extract of them, used to flavor soft drinks; soft drink with this flavoring.

Sar·to (sar̄′tō): see ANDREA DEL SARTO.

sar·to·ri·al (sar̄tōr′ē*a*l, -tōr′-) *adj.* Of tailors or tailoring; of men's clothes. **sar·to′ri·al·ly** *adv.*

sar·to·ri·us (sar̄tōr′ē*u*s, -tōr′-) *n.* (pl. **-to·ri·i** pr. -tōr′ēī, -tōr′ēī). Long narrow muscle crossing thigh obliquely in front. [mod. L., so called as being concerned in producing tailor's cross-legged working position]

Sar·tre (sar̄′tr*e*, sar̄t), **Jean Paul** (1905–1980). French writer and philosopher, leader in existentialist movement; author of *Being and Nothingness*, the play *No Exit*, etc.

sash[1] (săsh) *n.* Ornamental scarf worn over 1 shoulder or around

*Indian woman trying on lengths of material for use as a **sari**. Despite its apparent simplicity, skill is needed to adjust and wear it effectively.*

waist by man, usu. as part of uniform or insignia, or by woman or child around waist. [Arab. *shāsh* muslin, band twisted around head as turban]

sash[2] (săsh) *n.* Frame, usu. of wood, fitted with pane(s) of glass forming (part of) window, esp. sliding frame or one of pair of frames made to slide up and down. [corrupt. of CHASSIS]

sa·shay (săshā′) *v.i.* (colloq.) Walk or move ostentatiously, casually, or diagonally.

sa·shi·mi (sah′shĭmē) *n.* Japanese dish of garnished raw fish in thin slices.

Sas·katch·e·wan (săskăch′-*e*wahn, -w*a*n). 1. River of Canada, flowing from the Rocky Mountains to Lake Winnipeg. 2. Province of central Canada; capital, Regina.

sas·quatch (sahs′kwahch) *n.* (also **S~**) Supposed yeti-like animal of northwestern N. Amer.; also called Bigfoot.

sass (săs) *n.* (colloq.) Impertinence; back talk. ~ *v.t.* (**sassed, sass·ing**) Respond or talk rudely. **sass′y** *adj.* (**sass·i·er, sass·i·est**).

sas·sa·fras (săs′*a*frăs) *n.* Tree of genus *S~* of laurel family, esp. N. Amer. *S. albidum*, with green apetalous flowers and dimorphous leaves; dried bark of root of this used medicinally and for flavoring.

SAT *abbrev.* Scholastic Aptitude Test.

sat (săt): see SIT.

Sat. *abbrev.* Saturday.

Sa·tan (sā′t*a*n). The devil, Lucifer. **sa·ta·nic** (sătăn′ĭk, s*a*-), **sa·tan′i·cal** *adjs.* (also **S~**) Of, like, or befitting Satan, diabolical. **sa·tan′i·cal·ly** *adv.* [Heb. *šāṭān* enemy]

Sa·tan·ism (sā′t*a*nĭzem) *n.* Worship of the devil with a travesty of Christian ceremonial and with celebration of the Black Mass; diabolical wickedness. **Sa′tan·ist** *n.*

satch·el (săch′*e*l) *n.* Small bag, esp. for carrying schoolbooks etc., freq. with shoulder strap.

sate (sāt) *v.t.* (**sat·ed, sat·ing**). Gratify (desire, appetite, etc.) to the full; surfeit.

sa·teen (sătēn′) *n.* Cotton fabric, glossy on 1 side, woven like satin.

sat·el·lite (săt′*e*līt) *n.* 1. Follower, hanger-on; member of great man's retinue, underling. 2. Small or secondary planet revolving around larger one; (also) artificial body launched from Earth and encircling it or other celestial body; **fixed ~**: see FIXED. 3. Nation nominally independent but dominated by powerful neighbor. 4. **~ town**, small town built near larger one to house excess population.

sa·ti·ate (sā′shēĭt, -āt) *adj.* Sated, satiated. ~ (sā′shēāt) *v.t.* (**-at·ed, -at·ing**). Sate. **sa·ti·a·tion** (sāshēā′sh*o*n) *n.*

sa·ti·e·ty (s*a*tī′etē) *n.* State of being glutted or satiated; feeling of disgust or surfeit caused by excess.

sat·in (săt′ĭn) *n.* Fabric of silk or similar yarn with glossy surface on one side produced by twill weave in which weft threads are almost concealed by warp, or vice versa; **~ stitch**, in embroidery, long straight stitches laid close together, producing smooth surface; **sat′in-wood**, (hard light-colored wood with satiny surface, of) Indian tree (*Chloroxylon swietenia*) and various W. Indian, Australian, etc., trees. **satin, sat′in·y** *adjs.* Resembling satin; very smooth.

sat·ire (săt′īr) *n.* Poem or prose composition ridiculing vice or folly; lampoon; branch of literature containing such compositions; use of ridicule, sarcasm, or irony to expose folly. **sa·tir·ic** (s*a*tĭr′ĭk), **sa·tir′i·cal** *adj.* **sa·tir′i·cal·ly** *adv.* **sat·i·rist** (săt′erĭst) *n.* Writer of satires; satirical person. **sat·i·rize** (săt′erīz) *v.t.* (**-rized, -riz·ing**). Write satires on; describe satirically.

*The **sassafras** of North America is useful to man. Oil for perfumes is obtained from the flowers and roots; dried roots are used by chemists; and beer is made from young leaf shoots.*

sat·is·fac·tion (sătĭsfăk′sh*o*n) *n.* 1. Payment of debt, fulfillment of obligation, atonement *for*; thing accepted by way of satisfaction; penance; atonement. 2. Opportunity of satisfying one's honor by

A Syncon communications **satellite,** one of a series now in orbit over the earth, which have had a revolutionary impact on trans-continental telephone, radio and television contacts.

Two schoolchildren are seen here carrying their **satchels**, small bags used especially for carrying schoolbooks.

duel, acceptance of challenge to duel. 3. Satisfying, being satisfied, in regard to desire or want or doubt; thing that satisfies desire or gratifies feeling.

sat·is·fac·to·ry (sătĭsfăk'terē) *adj.* Sufficient, adequate, (of argument) convincing; such as one may be content or pleased with. **sat·is·fac'to·ri·ly** *adv.* **sat·is·fac'to·ri·ness** *n.*

sat·is·fy (săt'ĭsfī) *v.* (**-fied, -fy·ing**). 1. Pay (debt), fulfill (obligation), (now rare except in law); pay (creditor); make atonement or reparation. 2. Meet expectations or desires of, come up to (notion etc.), be accepted by (person etc.) as adequate, content; give satisfaction, leave nothing to be desired; fully supply needs of, put an end to (appetite etc.) by fully supplying it; furnish with adequate proof, convince; adequately meet (objection, doubt, etc.); (math.) be a solution e.g. of an equation; (pass.) be content or pleased (*with*); demand no more than, consider it enough *to* do. **sat'is·fi·er** *n.* **sat'is·fy·ing** *adj.* **sat'is·fy·ing·ly** *adv.*

sa·to·ri (satōr'ē, -tōr'ē) *n.* (Zen Buddhism) Sudden enlightenment.

sa·trap (sā'trăp, săt'răp) *n.* 1. Holder of provincial governorship in ancient Persian Empire. 2. Subordinate ruler, colonial governor, etc. (freq. with implication of luxury or tyranny). **sa·trap·y** (sā'trapē, săt'ra-) *n.* (pl. **-trap·ies**). Office, province, of satrap. [Pers. *khsatrapava* province guardian]

Sa·tsu·ma (sah'tsōōmah) *n.* (also ~ **ware**) Kind of Japanese glazed pottery with a yellow ground. [former province of Japan]

sat·u·rate (săch'erāt) *v.t.* (**-rat·ed, -rat·ing**). 1. Soak thoroughly, imbue *with.* 2. (phys. etc.) Cause to absorb or hold the maximum quantity of moisture, electrical charge, etc., that can be held under given conditions of temperature etc.; (chem.) cause (a substance) to combine with or dissolve the maximum quantity possible of another substance. 3. Bomb (target) from the air so thoroughly that antiaircraft defenses are powerless. **sat'u·ra·ble** *adj.* **sat'u·rat·ed** *adj.* (esp., of a solution) Containing the maximum quantity possible of the dissolved substance at a given temperature (cf. UNSATURATED, able to dissolve more than it contains); (also, of chemical compounds, esp. hydrocarbons) containing no double bonds and hence unable to undergo addition reactions (*unsaturated*, containing one or more double bonds and capable of such reactions). **sat·u·ra·tion** (săcherā'shon) *n.*

Sat·ur·day (săt'erdē) *n.* Seventh day of the week; **~-night special,** (slang) any cheap handgun. [OE., f. L. *Saturni dies* day of Saturn]

Sat·urn (săt'ern). 1. (Rom. myth.) Ancient Italian god of agriculture, ruler of the world in a golden age of innocence and plenty, later identified with the Greek CRONUS. 2. (astron.) Major planet, next in size to Jupiter, distinguished by its 10 satellites or moons and its engirdling system of rings. 3. (alchemy) The metal lead.

Sat·ur·na·li·a (săternā'lēa) *n.* (pl. **-li·a, -li·as**). (also as pl.) (Rom. antiq.) Yearly festival of Saturn, held in December, observed as a time of unrestrained merrymaking with temporary release of slaves; hence, **s~**, scene or time of wild revelry or tumult. **Sa·tur·na'li·an** *adj.*

Sa·tur·ni·an (satēr'nēan) *adj.* Of the god or the planet Saturn.

sat·ur·nine (săt'ernīn) *adj.* 1. Born under, influenced by, the planet Saturn (astrol.); sluggish, cold and gloomy in temperament, (of looks etc.) suggesting such temperament. 2. Of lead; of, affected by, lead poisoning. **sat·ur·nin·i·ty** (săternĭn'ĭtē), **sat'ur·nine·ness** *ns.*

sa·tyr (sā'ter, săt'er) *n.* (Gk. myth.) One of a class of woodland spirits, usu. represented as being young with ears, tail, and legs of goat, and budding horns; lecher; man afflicted with satyriasis. **sa·tyr·ic** (sātĭr´ĭk, sa-) *adj.*

sa·ty·ri·a·sis (sātĭrī´asĭs, săti-) *n.* Excessive sexual desire in males.

sauce (saws) *n.* 1. Preparation, usu. liquid or soft, taken as relish or dressing with some article of food; (fig.) something that adds piquancy; stewed or puréed sweetened fruit as part of meal, as *applesauce*; **hard** ~: see HARD; **tartar(e)** ~, sharp-flavored sauce consisting of mayonnaise with chopped pickles, capers, herbs, etc., served with fish. 2. (colloq.) Impudence. 3. **sauce´boat,** vessel in which sauce is served. **sauce** *v.t.* (**sauced, sauc·ing**). 1. Season with sauces or condiments (rare); (fig.) make piquant, add relish to. 2. (colloq.) Be impudent to.

sauce·pan (saws´păn) *n.* Kitchen utensil of metal with handle projecting from side, in which food is boiled, steamed, etc.

sau·cer (saw´ser) *n.* Shallow dish with slight circular depression in center for standing esp. coffee cup or teacup on, to catch liquid that may be spilled from it; any dish or small shallow object resembling this; **flying** ~: see FLYING.

sau·cy (saw´sē) *adj.* (**-ci·er, -ci·est**). Impudent, pert; (slang) smart-looking. **sau´ci·ly** *adv.* **sau´ci·ness** *n.* [orig., = savory, flavored with sauce]

Sau·di (sahōō´dē, sow´dē, saw´-) **Arabia.** Kingdom on the Arabian Peninsula, SW. Asia, with the Red Sea and the Gulf of Aqaba to the W. and the Persian Gulf to the E.; capital, Riyadh. **Sau´di A·ra´bi·an** *adj.* & *n.*

sau·er·kraut (sow´erkrowt, sowr´-) *n.* Cabbage cut fine and pickled in brine. [Ger.]

Sauk (sawk), **Sac** (sawk, sahk, săk) *ns.* (pl. **Sauks, Sacs,** collect. **Sauk, Sac**). Tribe of Algonquian-speaking N. Amer. Indians, orig. in Michigan, later in Wisconsin, and, after merging with the Fox, in Illinois; now in Iowa and Oklahoma; member of this tribe.

Saul (sawl). 1. First king of Israel (11th c. B.C.). 2. (also ~ **of Tarsus**) Original name of St. PAUL[1].

sau·na (saw´na, sow´-) *n.* Steam bath or bathhouse, of Finnish origin.

saun·ter (sawn´ter, sahn´-) *v.i.* Walk in leisurely way, stroll. ~ *n.* Leisurely ramble or gait. **saun´ter·er** *n.*

sau·ri·an (sōr´ēan) *adj.* & *n.* (Of or like) a lizard.

sau·sage (saw´sĭj) *n.* Meat minced, seasoned, and stuffed into long cylindrical case made from intestine, bladder, or other animal tissue, or synthetic material; short length of this made by twisting or

*In the Asir Province of **Saudi Arabia,** ancient, primitive abodes stand sentinel over the terraced slopes of Asir Mountain which has been sculptured and cultivated for growing crops.*

*The National Congress building in Brasilia, capital of the Republic of Brazil, features an unique **saucer**-shaped inverted dome which is the focal point of the building architecturally.*

*Much of **Saudi Arabia** is overlain with rocks of ancient volcanic origin. However, the oil, which provides the nation's wealth, is in sedimentary rocks.*

*The pampas of Argentina is typical of **savannah** country, and these vast expanses permit large-scale raising of cattle and sheep, as does similar country in Australia and the U.S.A.*

tying the containing case; ~ **meat,** meat minced and seasoned to be used in sausages or as stuffing etc.

sau·té (sōtā', saw-) *v.t.* (**-téed** or **-téd, -té·ing**). (cooking) Fry lightly in fat. ~ *n.* Sautéed food; sautéed dish.

sau·terne (sōtẽrn', saw-) *n.* Light sweet white wine from the Bordeaux region of France. [*Sauternes*, name of a district of Gironde, France]

sav·age (săv'ĭj) *adj.* Uncultivated, wild (archaic); uncivilized, in primitive state; fierce, cruel, furious; (colloq.) angry, out of temper. **sav'age·ly** *adv.* **sav'age·ness** *n.* **sav'age·ry** *n.* (pl. **-ries**). **savage** *n.* Member of savage tribe, esp. one living by hunting or fishing; brutally cruel or barbarous person. ~ *v.t.* (**-aged, -ag·ing**). (of animal, esp. horse) Attack and bite (person etc.).

sa·van·na, sa·van·nah (sa-văn'a) *ns.* Wide treeless grassland, esp. in tropical Amer.

Sa·van·nah (savăn'a). Seaport and city in Georgia, in the E. part.

sa·vant (săvahnt', savănt', săv'-ant; *Fr.* săvahṅ') *n.* (pl. **sa·vants** pr. săvahnts', savănts', săv'ants; *Fr.* săvahṅ'). Person of learning, scholar.

sa·vate (savăt', -vaht') *n.* Kind of French boxing in which blows are given with feet as well as hands. [Fr.]

save[1] (sāv) *v.* (**saved, sav·ing**). 1. Rescue, preserve, deliver from danger, misfortune, harm, or discredit; bring about spiritual salvation of, preserve from damnation; prevent loss of (game etc.), (soccer, hockey, etc.) prevent opponent from scoring; ~ **the day,** find or provide way out of difficulty. 2. Keep for future use, husband, reserve, put by; lay by money; live economically; ~ **up,** accumulate money by economy. 3. Relieve from need of expending (money, trouble, etc.) or from exposure to (annoyance etc.). **save** *n.* Act of preventing other side from scoring in soccer, hockey, etc. **sav'a·ble, save'a·ble** *adjs.* **sav'er** *n.*

save[2] (sāv) *prep.* Except, but. ~ *conj.* (archaic) Useless, but.

sav·in, sa·vine (săv'ĭn) *ns.* European and W. Asiatic small bushy evergreen shrub (*Juniperus sabina*) with dark green leaves and small bluish-purple berries; dried tops of this, used as drug; any of various similar shrubs, esp. red cedar (*J. virginiana* and *J. horizontalis*). [L. (*herba*) *Sabina* Sabine herb]

sav·ing (sā'vĭng) *n.* (esp., usu. pl.) Sum of money saved and put by; ~**s account,** bank deposit receiving interest but allowing withdrawals only with passbook or written authorization, distinct from CHECKING ACCOUNT; ~**s bank,** bank for savings accounts. **saving** *adj.* (esp.) Making a reservation, furnishing a proviso. ~ *prep.* & *conj.* = SAVE[2] *prep.* & *conj.*

sav·ior (sāv'yer) *n.* Deliverer, redeemer; **the, our, S**~, Christ.

sa·voir-faire (săv'wãrfãr'). Quickness to see and do the right thing, tact. [Fr.]

Sav·o·na·ro·la (săvonarō'la), **Gi·ro·la·mo** (jĭrōl'amō) (1452–98). Dominican monk whose sermons at Florence gave expression to the religious reaction against the artistic license and social corruption of the Renaissance; he became the leader of the democratic party in Florence after the expulsion of the

*A large **sawmill** at Kawerau in Auckland, New Zealand. The timber industry in that country is significant as a provider of wood, woodchips for export, and material used in paper-making.*

*Today, a **saw** has been devised for almost every application. However it is little known that saws were used in ancient Rome, though there was little development until the Middle Ages.*

Medici, but aroused the hostility of Pope Alexander VI and was excommunicated and burned at the stake as a heretic.

sa·vor (sā′v*er*) *n.* Characteristic taste, flavor; power of affecting sense of taste; essential virtue or property; tinge, hint, smack, *of.* **sa′vor·i·ness** *adj.* **savor** *v.* Appreciate flavor of, enjoy; smack or suggest presence *of.*

sa·vor·y[1] (sā′verē) *n.* (pl. **-vor·ies**). Herb of genus *Satureia* of mint family, used in cooking; esp. *S. hortensis* (**summer ~**), and *S. montana* (**winter ~**).

sa·vor·y[2] (sā′verē) *adj.* (**-vor·i·er, -vor·i·est**). With appetizing taste or smell; free from bad smells, fragrant (now only with negative); (of dishes etc.) of stimulating or piquant flavor and not sweet.

Sa·voy (s*a*voi′). Region in SE. France; formerly a duchy and part of the kingdom of Sardinia; ceded to France in 1860.

Sa·voy·ard (s*a*voi′*er*d, săv′oiârd, săvwahyârd′) *n.* 1. Native of SAVOY. 2. Professional performer or enthusiastic admirer of Gilbert and Sullivan operas, many of which were first presented at London's Savoy Theatre.

sav·vy (săv′ē) *v.* (**-vied, -vy·ing**). (slang) Know. **~** *n.* (slang) Knowingness, wits. [corrupt. of Span. *sabe usted* you know]

saw[1] (saw) *n.* Tool, worked by hand or power, for cutting wood, metal, stone, bone, etc., consisting essentially of plate, band, or tube of steel, one edge of which (except in some stonecutting saws) is formed into continuous series of teeth; **hand′saw**, saw managed by one hand; **saw′buck**, sawhorse, esp. with cross-shaped legs extending above crossbar; (slang) $10 bill; **saw′dust**, tiny fragments of wood produced in sawing, used for stuffing, packing, etc.; **saw′fish** (pl. **-fishes**, collect. **-fish**), sea fish (*Pristis*) with snout ending in long flat projection with teeth on each edge; **saw′fly** (pl. **-flies**), insect of family Tenthredinidae, usu. very destructive to vegetation, with saw-like ovipositor; **saw′horse**, frame or trestle for supporting wood being sawed; **saw′mill**, mill in which wood is sawed into planks or logs by machinery; **saw-whet owl**, (*Aegolius acadicus*), tiny brown and white, tuftless N. Amer. owl, whose note resembles sound of saw being filed. **saw** *v.* (**sawed**, esp. Brit. **sawn, saw·ing**). Cut (wood etc.) with, make (boards etc.) with, use, saw; move backward and forward, divide (the air etc.) with motion as of saw or person sawing; admit of being sawed *easily, badly*, etc.; **saw′bones**, (slang) surgeon; **sawed-off** (*adj.*), (of gun) with part of barrel removed by sawing; (of person, colloq.) undersized.

saw[2] (saw) *n.* Proverbial saying, old maxim.

saw·yer (saw′y*er*) *n.* Person employed in sawing timber.

sax (săks) *n.* (colloq.) Saxophone.

sax·a·tile (săk′s*a*tĭl) *adj.* Living or growing among rocks.

Saxe-Co·burg-Go·tha (săks′-kō′bergō′th*a*). Former German duchy; name of the British royal family from the accession of Edward VII in 1901 (dropped during World War I because of its

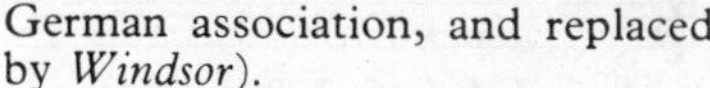

German association, and replaced by *Windsor*).

sax·i·frage (săk′sĭfrĭj) *n.* Alpine or rock plant of genus *Saxifraga*, with tufted foliage and panicles of white, yellow, or red flowers. [L. *saxifraga* spleenwort, f. *saxum* rock, *frangere* break (prob. because growing in rock clefts)]

Sax·on (săk′sŏn) *n.* Member, language, of a Germanic people that, in the early centuries of the Christian era, dwelled in a region near the mouth of the Elbe, and of which one portion, distinguished as the Anglo-Saxons, conquered and occupied part of Britain in the 5th and 6th centuries, while the other, the Old Saxons, remained in Germany; native of modern Saxony; Englishman as opp. to Irish and Welsh, Scottish Lowlander as opp. to Highlander; Germanic elements in the English language. ~ *adj.* Connected with, pertaining to, the Saxons, their language or country; (of English words) of Germanic origin.

Sax·on·ism (săk′sŏnĭzem) *n.* Word, idiom, surviving in English, derived from Anglo-Saxon (opp. LATINISM).

Sax·o·ny (săk′sonē). Former duchy of Germany in the E. central part; later became successively an electorate, kingdom, Prussian province, German free state, and republic; absorbed in East Germany, 1952; **Lower ~**, state of West Germany; capital, Hanover.

sax·o·phone (săk′sofōn) *n.* Keyed wind instrument with conical tube, made of brass but regarded as belonging to woodwind group, its mouthpiece being equipped with a reed like that of a clarinet. **sax′o·phon·ist** *n.* [invented *c*1840 by Adolphe *Sax*, Belgian instrument maker]

say (sā) *v.* (**said** pr. sĕd, **say·ing**). Utter, recite, rehearse, in ordinary speaking voice; put into words, express; adduce or allege in argument or excuse; form and give

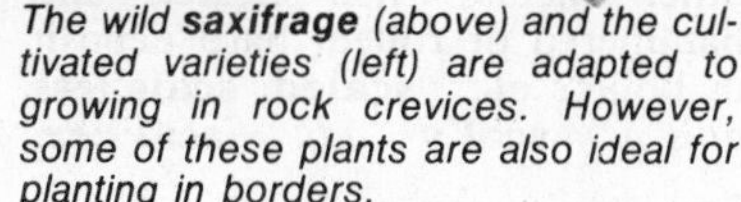

*The wild **saxifrage** (above) and the cultivated varieties (left) are adapted to growing in rock crevices. However, some of these plants are also ideal for planting in borders.*

opinion or decision; select as example, assume, take as near enough; **that is to ~**, in other words, more explicitly; or at least; **you can ~ that** (**again**), (colloq.) I agree emphatically. **say′ing** *n.* (esp.) Sententious remark, maxim. **say** *n.* (Opportunity of saying) what one has to say; share in decision; **~-so** (pl. **~-sos**), (colloq.) assertion; authority.

Sb *symbol.* Antimony.

sb. *abbrev.* Substantive.

S.B. *abbrev.* Bachelor of Science. [L. *Scientiae Baccalaureus*]

SBA *abbrev.* Small Business Administration.

SC, S.C. *abbrevs.* South Carolina.

Sc *symbol.* Scandium.

scab (skăb) *n.* 1. Dry rough incrustation formed over sore in healing, cicatrice. 2. Cutaneous disease in animals, resembling scabies. 3. Parasitic disease of plants causing scablike roughness. 4. (slang) Mean low fellow; worker

*Field **scabious** is one of a group of herbs, which include both annuals and perennial plants. Some have flowers up to 1½ ins. in diameter and are usually blue, though there are pink and white varieties.*

who refuses to join a union or a strike; strikebreaker. **scab′bi·ly** *adv.* **scab′bi·ness** *n.* **scab′by** *adj.* (**-bi·er, -bi·est**). **scab** *v.* (**scabbed, scab·bing**). Form scab, heal over.

scab·bard (skăb′erd) *n.* Sheath of sword, bayonet, etc.

sca·bies (skā′bēz) *n.sing.* Contagious skin disease due to a parasite, the mite *Sarcoptes scabiei*. **sca′bi·ous**[1] *adj.*

sca·bi·ous[2] (skā′bēus) *n.* Herbaceous plant of genus *Scabiosa*, with blue, pink, or white pincushion-shaped aggregate flowers. [med. L. *scabiosa* (*herba*), named as specific against itch, f. SCABIES]

scab·rous (skăb′rus, skā′brus) *adj.* 1. (zool., bot., etc.) With rough surface, scurfy. 2. Salacious; indecent. **scab′rous·ness** *n.*

*Once a German republic, **Saxony,** with its capital, Hanover, is now part of West Germany. The building (below) is the Neues Rathaus or New Town Hall in Hanover.*

scad (skăd) *n.* (pl. **scads,** collect. **scad**). Fish of family Carangidae, including the horse mackerel, with enlarged plates on side of body.

scads (skădz) *n.pl.* (colloq.) Large quantities *of.*

scaf·fold (skăf′old) *n.* 1. Temporary raised platform for execution of criminals. 2. SCAFFOLDING sense 1. ~ *v.t.* Attach scaffolding to.

scaf·fold·ing (skăf′olding) *n.* 1. Temporary structure of wooden poles (or metal tubes) and planks providing platform(s) for workmen to stand on while erecting or repairing building. 2. Materials for making such structure. 3. Temporary framework for other purposes (also fig.).

scal·a·wag, scal·la·wag, scal·ly·wag (skăl′*a*wăg) *ns.* (colloq.) Rogue or rascal; (hist.) native white of southern state accepting Republican principles after Civil War.

scald (skawld) *v.t.* Injure or pain with hot liquid or vapor; affect like boiling water; cleanse with boiling water; pour hot liquid over; heat (liquid, esp. milk) nearly to boiling point. ~ *n.* Injury to skin by scalding.

scale[1] (skāl) *n.* One of the small thin membranous horny or bony outgrowths or modifications of skin in many fishes, reptiles, etc., freq. overlapping, and forming covering for (part of) the body. 2. Flattened membranous plate of cellular tissue (usu. rudimentary or degenerate leaf) as covering of lead buds of deciduous trees etc. 3. Protective covering of many female insects (~ **insect**) of family Coccidae infesting and injuring various plants. 4. Thin plate, lamina, or film of any kind; (usu. collect.) film of oxide forming on iron or other metal when heated and hammered or rolled; hard deposit in boilers etc. **scaled, scale′less** *adjs.* **scal′y** *adj.* (**scal·i·er, scal·i·est**). Covered with, having, scales. **scale** *v.* (**scaled, scal·ing**). Take away scale(s) from; form, come off in, drop, scales; (of scales) come *off.*

*On a Zaire plantation, branches lashed together form **scaffolding.** For the type of building this is just as effective as the steel tubing and planks used by more sophisticated builders.*

scale[2] (skāl) *n.* 1. Pan of balance; weighing instrument, esp. (also **pair of ~s**) one consisting of beam pivoted at middle and with dish, pan, etc., suspended at either end; **turn the ~s,** exceed weight in other pan etc. of balance; (fig.) outweigh other considerations, motives, etc. 2. **the Scales**: see LIBRA. **scale** *v.* (**scaled, scal·ing**). Weigh (specified amount).

scale[3] (skāl) *n.* 1. (mus.) Definite series of sounds ascending or descending by fixed intervals; any of graduated series of sounds into which octave may be divided; any of these series as subject of instruction or practice. 2. Series of degrees, graduated arrangement, system, or classification; standard of measurement, calculation, etc.; (arith.) system of numeration or numerical notation, in which the value of a figure depends on its place in the order (the usual is that in which successive places from right to left represent units, tens, hundreds, etc.); relative dimensions, proportion that representation of an object bears to the object itself. 3. Set of marks at measured distances on line for use in

SCALES

1. Tonic. 2. Supertonic. 3. Mediant. 4. Subdominant. 5. Dominant. 6. Submediant. 7. Leading note. 8. Tonic (octave above 1). 1–2, 2–3, 4–5, 5–6, 6–7 are tones; 3–4, 7–8 are semitones

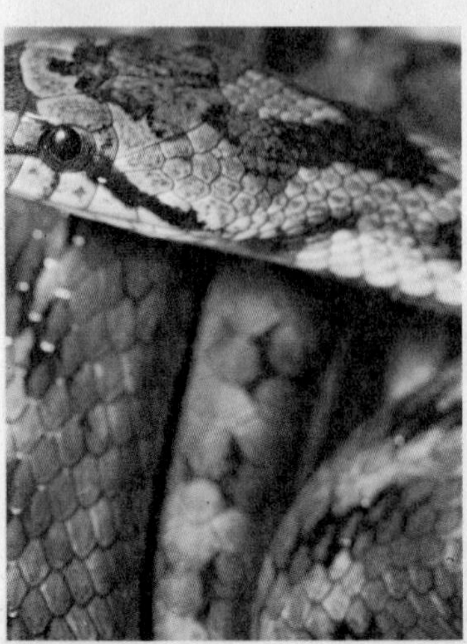

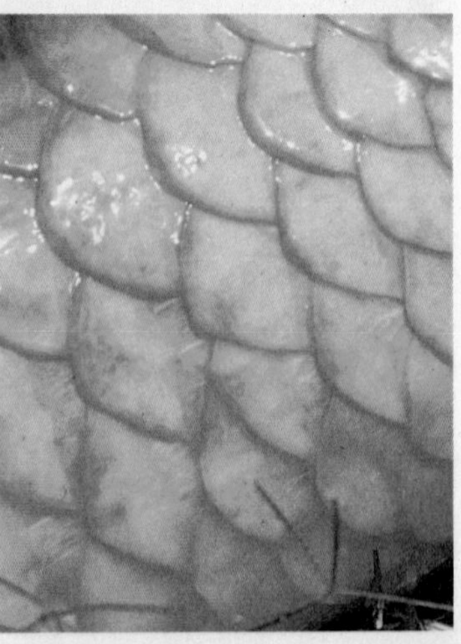

*Each **scale** on a lung-fish (left) is different from that on other fish, and similar only to those found on fossils. Those of a snake (far left) are extensions of the skin and the underneath ones help it to move.*

measuring or making proportional reductions or enlargements; rule determining intervals between these; piece of metal, wood, etc., apparatus, on which they are marked. **scale** *v.* (**scaled, scal·ing**). 1. Climb with ladder or by clambering; **scaling ladder**, one used for climbing high walls. 2. Represent in dimensions proportional to actual ones; reduce to common scale; **scale up, down**, make larger, smaller, in due proportion. 3. (of quantities etc.) Have common scale, be commensurable.

sca·lene (skā′lēn, skālēn′) *adj.* ~ **cone, cylinder**, one of which axis is not perpendicular to base; ~ **triangle**, triangle with no two sides equal.

scal·la·wag: SCALAWAG.

scal·lion (skăl′yon) *n.* Onion that fails to bulb but forms long neck and strong blade; young onion before bulb forms; shallot. [OF. *eschaloigne*, see SHALLOT]

scal·lop, scol·lop (skŏl′op, skăl′-) *ns.* 1. Bivalve mollusk of genus *Pecten*, with shell having ridges radiating from middle of hinge and edged with small rounded lobes; edible muscle of this; one valve of this as utensil in which various dishes (of fish, minced meat, etc., with bread crumbs or sauce) are cooked and served. 2. One of series of rounded projections at edge of garment etc. ~ *v.t.* 1. Bake in scallop shell or similar shallow pan or dish, usu. with milk and bread crumbs. 2. Ornament (edge, material) with scallops. **scal′lop·er** *n.*

scal·op·pi·ne, scal·op·pi·ni (skahlopē′nē, skălo-) *ns.* Very thin slices of meat, esp. veal, cooked slowly in sauce of wine or tomatoes and herbs.

scal·ly·wag: SCALAWAG.

scalp (skălp) *n.* Skin of upper part of head, with hair covering it; this cut or torn from person's head as battle trophy by Amer. Indians (freq. fig.). ~ *v.t.* Take scalp of; (fig.) criticize severely; defeat, humiliate; (colloq.) buy (tickets etc.) to resell for quick or high profit; hence **scalp′er** *n.*

scal·pel (skăl′pel) *n.* Small straight knife used in surgery and dissection.

scam (skăm) *n.* (slang) Confidence game; see CONFIDENCE.

scamp[1] (skămp) *n.* Rascal, knave (freq. joc.).

scamp[2] (skămp) *v.t.* Do (work etc.) in perfunctory or inadequate way.

scam·per (skăm′per) *v.i.* Run or caper about nimbly, rush hastily. ~ *n.* Scampering run.

scam·pi (skăm′pē, skahm′-) *n.pl.* Large shrimps; dish of these, esp. cooked with garlic. [It.]

The 300 or so species of ***scallop*** *show much difference in markings and size. They move by a form of water-jet propulsion and can attain remarkable acceleration when threatened.*

scan (skăn) *v.* (**scanned, scan·ning**). 1. Analyze, test meter of (verse) by examining number and quantity of feet and syllables; (of verse) be metrically correct. 2. Look intently at all parts successively of. 3. Resolve (a picture) into elements of light and shade in a prearranged number and pattern of lines as a stage in televising. 4. (radar) Traverse (region) with controlled beam. **scan′ner** *n.*

scan·dal (skăn′dal) *n.* (Thing that occasions) general feeling of outrage or indignation, esp. as expressed in common talk; malicious gossip. **scan′dal·ous** *adj.* **scan′dal·ous·ly** *adv.* **scan·dal·mon·ger** (skăn′dalmŭngger, -mŏng-) *n.* One who invents or spreads scandals.

scan·dal·ize (skăn′dalīz) *v.t.* (**-ized, -iz·ing**). Offend moral feelings, sense of propriety, etc.; shock.

Scan·di·na·vi·a (skăndinā′vēa). Geographical term for Sweden, Norway, and Denmark, together with the adjacent islands and sometimes Iceland. **Scan·di·na′vi·an** *adj.* & *n.* (Native, inhabitant, family of languages) of Scandinavia.

scan·di·um (skăn′dēum) *n.* (chem.) Rare metallic element (discovered 1879 in Scandinavian mineral euxenite) usu. included in rare-earth group; symbol Sc, at. no. 21, at. wt. 44.9559. [L. *Scandia* Scandinavia]

scan·ner (skăn′er) *n.* (esp.) 1. Instrument that scans television pictures. 2. (radar) Apparatus that directs beam in scanning (SCAN sense 4).

scan·sion (skăn′shon) *n.* Metrical scanning; way verse scans.

scant (skănt) *adj.* Barely sufficient, deficient, with scanty supply *of.*

scant·ling (skănt′lĭng) *n.* 1. Small timber or beam of wood; block or slice of stone of fixed size. 2. Size to which stone or timber is to be cut; set of standard dimensions for parts of structure, esp. in shipbuilding.

scant·y (skăn′tē) *adj.* (**scant·i·er, scant·i·est**). Of small extent or amount; barely sufficient. **scan′ties** *n.pl.* (colloq.) Women's short panties. **scant′i·ly** *adv.* **scant′i·ness** *n.*

scape (skāp) *n.* 1. (archit.) Shaft of column. 2. (bot.) Long flower stalk rising directly from root or rhizome of plant having only radical leaves. 3. (entom.) First segment of antenna. 4. (ornith.) Shaft of feather.

scape·goat (skāp′gōt) *n.* (in Mosaic ritual of Day of Atonement) Goat allowed to escape into wilderness, the sins of the people having been symbolically laid upon it (see Lev. 16); hence, person blamed or punished for sins of others.

scape·grace (skāp′grās) *n.* Reckless or careless person, esp. young man or boy constantly in scrapes. [= "one who escapes the grace of God"]

scaph·oid (skăf´oid) *adj.* (anat.) Shaped like a boat; ~ **bone**, navicular. **scaphoid** *n.* Scaphoid bone.

scap·u·la (skăp´yu*la*) *n.* (pl. **-lae** pr. -lē, **-las**). Shoulder blade.

scap·u·lar (skăp´yu*ler*) *adj.* Of the scapule; ~ **feather**, feather growing from scapular region. **scapular** *n.* 1. (eccles.) Monk's short cloak covering shoulders; badge of affiliation to religious order consisting of two strips of cloth hanging down breast and back and joined across shoulders, worn under clothing. 2. Scapular feather. **scap·u·lar·y** (skăp´yulĕrē) *n.* (pl. **-lar·ies**) = SCAPULAR *n.* def. 1.

scar (skār) *n.* Trace of healed wound, sore, or burn, cicatrice (freq. fig.); mark on plant left by fall of leaf etc.; hilum. ~ *v.* (**scared, scar·ring**). Mark with scar or scars; heal over, form scar.

scar·ab (skăr´*a*b) *n.* 1. Dung beetle (*Scarabaeus sacer*) revered by ancient Egyptians as symbol of resurrection and immortality. 2. Gem or stone in form of beetle, with intaglio design on flat underside, worn in ring or as pendant around neck, esp. by ancient Egyptians, Etruscans, etc.

scar·a·bae·id (skăr*a*bē´ĭd) *adj.* & *n.* (Beetle) of family Scarabaeidae, including June bugs, dung beetles, etc.

scarce (skārs) *adj.* (**scarc·er, scarc·est**). Insufficient, not plentiful, scanty; seldom met with, rare; **make oneself** ~, go away, keep away. **scarce** *adv.* (archaic, poet., rhet.) Scarcely. **scarce´ly** *adv.* Hardly, barely, only just. **scarce´ness, scar´ci·ty** *ns.* (pl. **-ties**).

scare (skār) *v.t.* (**scared, scar·ing**). Strike with sudden terror,

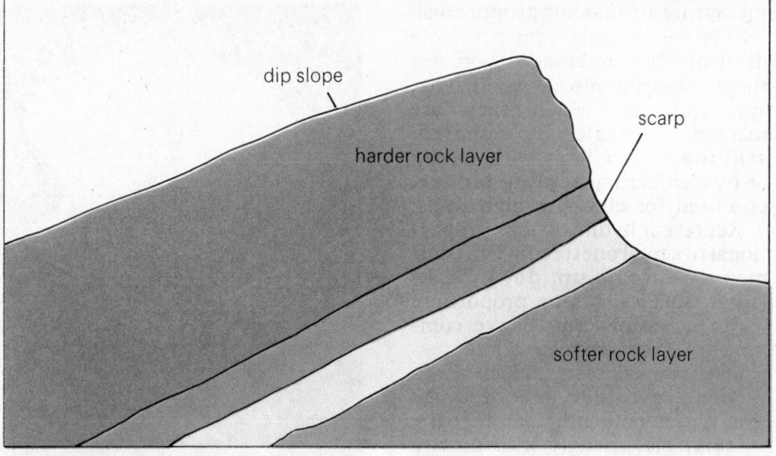

A ***scarp*** *may be formed naturally when a block of soft rock, capped with a harder substance, is tilted and subjected to erosion. This wears the softer rock more quickly, forming a steeper slope.*

frighten; frighten away, drive off; **scare´crow**, device for frightening birds away from crops, usu. figure of man in ragged clothes; bogy; badly dressed or esp. very thin person. **scare** *n.* Sudden fright or alarm; general public alarm caused by baseless or exaggerated rumors. **scare·mon·ger** (skār´-mŭngger, -mŏng-) *n.* Alarmist.

scarf[1] (skārf) *n.* (pl. **scarfs, scarves** pr. skārvz). Long narrow strip of material worn for ornament or warmth around neck over shoulders, from 1 shoulder to opposite hip, or around waist, with ends hanging; square of material worn at neck.

A ***scarab*** *made from blue glass-paste in Egypt about 600 B.C. The dung-beetle on which it was modelled, was thought to symbolize some celestial power which rotated the earth, and also the moon.*

scarf[2] (skārf) *v.t.* Join ends of (pieces of timber, metal, or leather) by beveling or notching so that they overlap without increase of thickness and then bolting, brazing, or sewing them together. ~ *n.* (pl. **scarfs**). Joint made by scarfing, notch, groove.

scar·i·fy (skăr´ĭfī, skār´-) *v.t.* (**-fied, -fy·ing**). Make superficial incisions in (surg.); make sore, wound (now fig.); break up ground. **scar·i·fi·ca·tion** (skărĭfĭkā´shon, skār-) *n.*

Scar·lat·ti (skārlah´tē). Name of two Italian composers: **Alessandro** ~ (1658–1725), founder of the Neapolitan school of opera; (**Giuseppe**) **Domenico** ~ (1685–1757), his son; composer of many sonatas.

scar·let (skār´lĭt) *adj.* Of brilliant red color inclining to orange; ~ **fever**, contagious fever,

The New Zealand ***scaup*** *or black teal is native to that country but early settlers greatly reduced its numbers. However, conservation measures have gradually enabled its population to grow.*

Dung-beetles are ***scatophagous*** *creatures, that is, they feed on dung. In doing this they aid in the breakdown of dung and help to reduce it to a form more easily utilised by plants.*

Vultures in Uganda feed on the carcass of a giraffe. A ***scavenger*** *is part of a natural system which ensures that the bodies of dead animals become a useful part of the ecosystem.*

due to hemolytic streptococcal infection, with scarlet eruptions of skin and mucous membrane of mouth and pharynx; ~ **hat**, cardinal's hat, esp. as symbol of the rank of cardinal; ~ **pimpernel**, red-flowered common pimpernel (*Anagallis arvensis*); ~ **runner**, red-flowered climbing bean (*Phaseolus coccineus*); ~ **tanager**, songbird of eastern U.S. (*Piranga olivacea*), the male in breeding season a brilliant scarlet with black wings and tail; ~ **woman**, prostitute. **scarlet** *n.* Scarlet color; scarlet cloth or clothes. [perh. f. Pers. *sagalat* scarlet cloth]

scarp (skārp) *n.* 1. Line of cliffs caused by geologic faulting or erosion; escarpment. 2. Inner wall or slope of ditch in fortification. ~ *v.t.* Give steep face to, slope steeply.

scar·y (skār'ē) *adj.* (**scar·i·er, scar·i·est**). (colloq.) 1. Causing terror, fright, etc. 2. Easily frightened. **scar'i·ness** *n.*

scat[1] (skăt) *v.i. imper.* (colloq.) Go away quickly: used imperatively.

scat[2] (skăt) *n.* & *v.* (**scat·ted, scat·ting**). (colloq.) (Sing) wordless jazz song using voice to imitate musical instrument.

scathe (skādh) *v.t.* (**scathed, scath·ing**). Injure, esp. by fire etc. (poet.); wither with fierce invective or satire. **scath'ing** *adj.* **scath'ing·ly** *adv.*

sca·tol·o·gy (skătŏl'*o*jē, sk*a*-) *n.* 1. (med.) Study of feces. 2. Preoccupation with excrement. 3. Preoccupation with obscenity in literature. **scat·o·log·i·cal** (skăt*o*lŏj'ĭk*a*l), **scat·o·log'ic** *adjs.*

sca·toph·a·gous (sk*a*tŏf'*a*g*u*s) *adj.* Feeding on, eating, dung (as some beetles, flies, etc.).

scat·ter (skăt'*er*) *v.* 1. Throw here and there, strew, sprinkle; (of gun, cartridge) distribute (shot); (phys.) diffuse by reflection from particles. 2. Separate and disperse in flight etc. 3. **scat'terbrain**, heedless person; **scat'terbrained**, heedless, desultory. **scat'tered** *adj.* (esp.) not situated together, wide apart; sporadic. **scatter** *n.* Act of scattering; extent of distribution, esp. of shot; ~ **rug**, small rug covering part of floor.

scaup (skawp) *n.* (pl. **scaups**, collect. **scaup**). Either of two wild ducks, *Aytha affinis* or *A. marila*, the male of the former having black head glossed with purple, and of the latter a green-glossed head.

scav·eng·er (skăv'ĭnj*er*) *n.* Person employed to keep streets etc. clean by carrying away refuse; person who collects discarded objects from garbage dumps etc.; animal feeding on carrion, garbage, or any decaying organic matter. **scav'enge** *v.* (**-enged, -eng·ing**). Be, act as, scavenger.

sce·nar·i·o (sĭnār'ēō, -nār'-) *n.* (pl. **-nar·i·os**). 1. Skeleton libretto or outline of play, opera, etc. 2. Complete plot of film play, with all necessary directions for actors, details of scenes, etc. **sce·nar·ist** (sĭnār'ĭst, -nār'-) *n.* Writer of scenario, sense 2. [It., f. *scena* scene]

scene (sēn) *n.* 1. (hist.) Stage. 2. Place where action of (part of) play, novel, etc., is supposed to take place; locality of event. 3. Portion of a play during which action is continuous; subdivision (rarely, the whole) of an act; episode, situation, as subject of narrative or description; action, episode, situation, in real life. 4. Stormy encounter or interview; agitated colloquy, esp. with display of temper. 5. Any of the pieces of painted canvas, woodwork, etc., used to represent scene of action on stage; picture presented by these to audience; (transf.) landscape or view spread before spectator like scene in theater; **behind the ~s**, amid actors and stage machinery; (fig.) in private among the principals of a business, group, etc.

sce·ner·y (sē'n*e*rē) *n.* (pl. **-ner·ies**). 1. Accessories used in theater to make stage resemble supposed scene of action. 2. General appearance of natural features etc. of place or district; picturesque features of landscape.

sce·nic (sē'nĭk) *adj.* Of, on, the stage; of the nature of a show; having fine natural scenery, giving landscape views; ~ **railway**, miniature railway running through artificial scenery. **sce'ni·cal·ly** *adv.*

scent (sĕnt) *v.* 1. Discern by smell; perceive as if by smell, detect. 2. Impregnate with odor, perfume. ~ *n.* 1. Distinctive odor, esp. of agreeable kind; odor of man or animal as means of pursuit by hound, trail; **throw off the ~**, deceive by false indications. 2. (of

A lavish ***scene*** *during a performance of the opera 'Aida' at the Royal Opera House, Covent Garden, U.K. Dramatic stage settings are needed to create the correct atmosphere for the production.*

animals, esp. dogs) Power of detecting or distinguishing smells.

scep·ter, Brit. **scep·tre** (sĕp´t*e*r) *ns.* Staff borne in hand as symbol of regal or imperial authority; (fig.) royal or imperial dignity, sovereignty.

sch. *abbrev.* School.

sched·ule (skĕj´o͞ol, -o͞o*u*l, -*u*l) *n.* Tabulated statement of details, inventory, list, prices, etc.; timetable; **on ~**, at time provided for in timetable etc. **schedule** *v.t.* (**-uled, -ul·ing**). Make schedule of; enter in schedule.

scheel·ite (shā´līt, shē´-) *n.* (min.) Calcium tungstate, an important ore of tungsten.

Sche·her·a·za·de (sh*e*hĕr*a*-zah´d*e*, -zahd´). (Arab. legend) Wife of the sultan of Samarkand who dissuaded him from killing her by narrating *The Arabian Nights' Entertainments.*

sche·ma (skē´m*a*) *n.* (pl. **-ma·ta** pr. -m*a*t*a*). Diagram, outline. **sche·mat·ic** (skēmăt´ĭk) *adj.* **sche·mat´i·cal·ly** *adv.* **sche·ma·tize** (skē´m*a*tīz) *v.t.* (**-tized, -tiz·ing**).

scheme (skēm) *n.* 1. Systematic arrangement; table of classification or of appointed times; plan for doing something. 2. Artful or underhand design. ~ *v.i.* (**schemed, schem·ing**). Make plans, plan esp. in secret or underhand way. **schem´er** *n.* **schem´ing** *adj.*

scher·zo (skĕr´tsō) *n.* (pl. **-zos, -zi** pr. -tsē). (mus.) Vigorous (properly light and playful) composition, independent or as movement in work of sonata type. [It., f. Teut. (Ger. *Scherz* merriment, prank, jest)]

Schick (shĭk), **Béla** (1877–1967). Hungarian-born Amer. pediatrician; invented **Schick test,** intracutaneous skin test for susceptibility to diphtheria.

Schil·ler (shĭl´*e*r), **Johann Christoph Friedrich von** (1759–1805). German dramatist, lyric poet, and historian; author of the dramas *Wallenstein, William Tell,* etc.

schism (sĭz´*e*m) *n.* Breach of unity of a church, separation into two churches or secession of part of church owing to difference of opinion on doctrine or discipline; offense of promoting schism; splitting of a group into mutually opposing parties.

schis·mat·ic (sĭzmăt´ĭk), **schiz·mat·i·cal** (sĭzmăt´ĭk*a*l) *adjs.* & *ns.* (Person) tending to, guilty of, schism; (member) of seceded branch of a church. **schis·mat´i·cal·ly** *adv.*

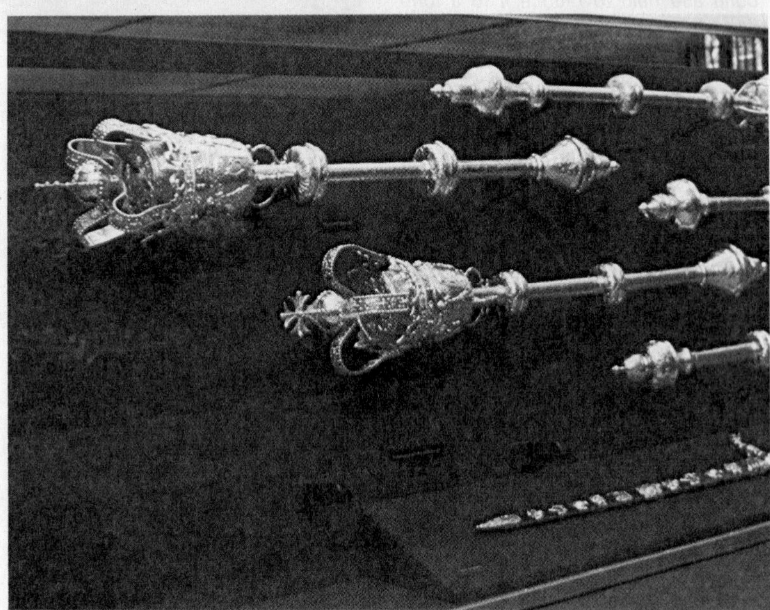

The ***sceptre,*** *a symbol of authority, is common in the regalia of most nations. Five are held in the British collection and of these, two are used in Coronation ceremonies.*

schist (shĭst) *n.* Fine-grained metamorphic rock with component minerals arranged in more or less parallel layers, splitting in thin irregular plates. **schist·ose** (shĭs´tōs), **schis·tous** (shĭs´t*u*s) *adjs.*

schiz·oid (skĭt´soid, skĭd´zoid) *adj.* Of, resembling, afflicted with, schizophrenia. ~ *n.* Schizophrenic person.

schiz·o·my·cete (skĭz*o*mīsēt´) *n.* Member of class Schizomycetae of minute, freq. single-celled, lowly organisms between algae and fungi, including bacilli, bacteria, etc. **schiz·o·my·ce´tous, schiz·o·my·ce´tic** *adjs.*

schiz·o·phre·ni·a (skĭts*o*frē´-nē*a*, -frēn´y*a*, skĭdz*o*-, skĭz*o*-) *n.* Mental disease characterized by dissociation,. delusions, and inability to distinguish reality. from imagination. **schiz·o·phren·ic** (skĭts*o*frĕn´ĭk, skĭdz*o*, skĭz*o*-, -frē´-nĭk) *adj.* & *n.*

schle·miel (shl*e*mēl´) *n.* (slang) Foolish or unlucky person. [Yiddish]

schlep, schlepp (shlĕp) *vbs.* (**schlepped, schlep·ping**). (slang) 1. Haul, drag, carry, etc., with effort or in clumsy manner. 2. Go or move about with difficulty or clumsily. ~ *n.* 1. Tiresome journey. 2. Stupid, ineffectual person.

__Schist__ is found in areas where there have been considerable movements of the earth. The various types are usually named after the dominant mineral but all consist of fine crystalline leaves.

Schlie·mann (shlē′mahn), **Heinrich** (1822–90). German archaeologist who excavated Troy, Tiryns, and Mycenae.

schlock (shlŏk) *adj.* & *n.* (slang) Poor quality or secondhand (material). [Yiddish]

schmaltz, schmalz (shmahlts, shmawlts) *ns.* Sickly sentimentality. **schmaltz′y** *adj.* (**schmaltz·i·er, schmaltz·i·est**). [Ger.]

schnapps, schnaps (shnahps) *ns.* (pl. **schnapps, schnaps**). Strong Holland gin. [Ger. *Schnaps* mouthful, dram of liquor]

schnau·zer (shnow′zer) *n.* Wire-coated black, black-and-brown, or pepper-and-salt terrier of German breed.

schnit·zel (shnĭt′sel) *n.* Veal cutlet, esp. (**Wiener ~**) one fried in bread crumbs in the Viennese style and garnished with lemon, anchovies, etc.

schnook (shnōōk) *n.* (slang) Person easily cheated or victimized; dupe. [Yiddish]

schnor·kel = SNORKEL.

schnoz·zle (shnŏz′el) *n.* (slang) Nose. [Yiddish]

schol·ar (skŏl′er) *n.* 1. (archaic) Pupil. 2. Holder of scholarship. 3. Learned person, person versed in literature. **schol′ar·li·ness** *n.* **schol′ar·ly** *adv.*

schol·ar·ship (skŏl′ership) *n.* 1. Attainments of a scholar; learning, erudition. 2. (Right to) emoluments paid, during a fixed period, from funds of charity, school, college, university, etc., or government, for defraying cost of education or studies, usu. granted after competitive examination.

scho·las·tic (skolăs′tĭk), **scho·las·ti·cal** (skolăs′tĭkal) *adjs.* 1. Of schools or other educational establishments; educational, academic; pedantic, formal. 2. (As) of the schoolmen (see SCHOOL[1]) dealing in logical subtleties. **scho·las′ti·cal·ly** *adv.* **scho·las·ti·cism** (skolăs′tĭsĭzem) *n.* **scholastic** *n.* 1. Schoolman; modern theologian of scholastic tendencies. 2. Jesuit between novitiate and priesthood.

school[1] (skōōl) *n.* 1. Institution for educating children or giving instruction, usu. of more elementary or more technical kind than that given at universities; time given to teaching; being educated in a school; (fig.) circumstances or occupation serving to discipline or instruct. 2. Organized body of teachers and scholars in any of higher branches of study in Middle Ages, esp. as constituent part of medieval university; special division (freq. graduate) of a university; buildings, pupils, of this. 3. Disciples, imitators, followers, of philosopher, artist, etc.; band or succession of persons devoted to some cause, principle, etc. 4. **~ board**, body of persons appointed or elected by taxpayers of a district etc. to provide and maintain public schools; board of education; **school′boy**, boy at school; **school days**, time of being at school; **school′girl**, girl at school; **school′ma′am, school′marm**, (colloq.) schoolmistress; **school′man** (pl. **-men**), teacher in medieval university; writer (9th–14th centuries) treating of logic, metaphysics, and theology as taught

The __Schnauzer__, first bred in 16th century Germany was a work dog before becoming a show dog. Careful breeding produced three varieties, the standard, miniature and great.

1

2

3

4

Whether housed in an old building in England (1) or a modern one in Norway (2), a ***school*** *serves the same purpose. In New Zealand (3), lessons may sometimes be held in the open air. Lessons may be made more pertinent, like this one in Peking (4), given near the Memorial to the Revolution.*

in medieval schools or universities of Europe; **school′master, school′mistress**, teacher in school; **school′room**, room used for lessons in school or private house; **school′teacher**, teacher esp. in elementary school. **school** *v.* Send to school, provide for education of (rare); discipline, bring under control, train or accustom *to.* **school′ing** *n.*

school[2] (skōōl) *n.* Great number of fish, whales, etc. swimming in company.

schoon·er[1] (skōō′n*e*r) *n.* Small seagoing fore-and-aft rigged sailing vessel, orig. with only two masts, later with three or four and usu. carrying one or more topsails.

schoon·er[2] (skōō′n*e*r) *n.* (colloq.) Large, tall beer glass.

Scho·pen·hau·er (shō′p*e*nhow*e*r), **Arthur** (1788–1860). German pessimistic philosopher who taught that the absolute reality is a blind and restless will, that all existence is essentially evil, and that release can be attained only by overcoming the will to live.

schot·tische (shŏt′ĭsh, shŏtēsh′) *n.* Kind of dance like polka but slower; music for this. [Ger. = "Scottish"]

Schu·bert (shōō′b*e*rt), **Franz Peter** (1797–1828). Austrian composer, esp. famous for his songs.

Schu·mann (shōō′mahn), **Robert Alexander** (1810–56). German Romantic composer, author of many songs and much piano and chamber music etc.

schuss (shōōs) *n.* & *v.* (Make) straight downhill run on skis.

Schuy·ler (skī′l*e*r), **Philip John** (1733–1804). Amer. statesman and general in Revolutionary War; delegate to Continental Congress, 1775; U.S. senator, 1789–91, 1797–8.

schwa (shwah) *n.* (phonet.) Indistinct vowel sound, as in second syllable of *common* or *comma*, represented as ə.

Schwei·tzer (shwīt′s*e*r, shvīt′-), **Albert** (1875–1965). French theologian, missionary, doctor, musicologist; founded Lambaréné Hospital in French Equatorial Africa, now called Gabon, 1913; edited organ music of J. S. Bach; received Nobel Peace Price, 1952.

sci·at·ic (sīăt′ĭk) *adj.* Of the hip; of, affecting, the sciatic nerve; suffering from, liable to, sciatica; ~ **nerve**, each of two divisions of the sacral plexus.

sci·at·i·ca (sīăt′ĭk*a*) *n.* Neuritis or neuralgia of sciatic nerve, with paroxysms of pain along course of nerve and its branches.

sci·ence (sī′*e*ns) *n.* 1. Systematic and formulated knowledge; pursuit of this, principles regulating such pursuit. 2. Branch of knowledge, organized body of the knowledge that has been accumulated on a subject; **abstract** ~, theoretical, not applied, science; **applied** ~, one studied for practical purposes (opp. *pure* ~); **exact** ~, one admitting of quantitative treatment; **natural** ~, science(s) concerned with the physical world (as chemistry, biology) (opp. *abstract* ~); **pure** ~, science studied without its applications to practical use (opp. *applied* ~); ~ **fiction**, form of fiction that assumes an imaginary technological advance or change in environment etc., freq. dealing with space travel and life on other planets. 3. Natural sciences collectively, the systematic study of the phenomena of the material universe and their laws. 4. (in sport, esp. boxing) Expert's skill as opp. to strength or natural ability.

sci·en·tif·ic (sīentĭf′ĭk) *adj.* Of science, esp. the natural sciences; devised according to the rules of science for testing soundness of conclusions etc.; systematic, accurate; assisted by expert knowledge. **sci·en·tif′i·cal·ly** *adv.*

sci·en·tist (sī′entĭst) *n.* One who studies or professes the natural sciences.

sci-fi (sī′fī) *adj.* & *n.* (slang) Science fiction.

scil·la (sĭl′*a*) *n.* Liliaceous bulbous plant of genus *S*~, esp. the frequently cultivated blue-flowered *S. sibirica*; squill.

Scil·ly (sĭl′ē), **Isles of.** (also **Scillies**) Group of small islands off W. extremity of Cornwall, England.

scim·i·tar, scim·i·ter (sĭm′ĭt*er*) *ns.* Oriental short curved single-edged sword, usu. broadening toward point.

scin·til·la (sĭntĭl′*a*) *n.* Spark, atom.

scin·til·late (sĭn′tĭlāt) *v.t.* (**-lat·ed, -lat·ing**). Sparkle, twinkle (freq. fig.); emit sparks. **scin′til·lat·ing·ly** *adv.* **scin′til·lant** *adj.* **scin·til·la·tion** (sĭntĭlā′sh*on*) *n.*

sci·o·list (sī′*o*lĭst) *n.* Superficial pretender to knowledge, smatterer. **sci′o·lism** *n.* **sci·o·lis·tic** (sī*o*lĭs′tĭk) *adj.*

sci·on (sī′*on*) *n.* Shoot of plant, esp. one cut for grafting or planting; descendant, young member of (esp. noble) family.

scir·rhus (skĭr′*u*s, sĭr′-) *n.* (pl. **scir·rhi** pr. skĭr′ī, sĭr′ī, **scir·rhus·es**). (path.) Hard carcinoma; organ that has hardened. **scir′rhoid, scir′rhous** *adjs.*

scis·sion (sĭzh′*on*, sĭsh′-) *n.* Cutting, being cut; division, split.

scis·sors (sĭz′*er*z) *n.pl.* 1. (also

The training ship 'Winston Churchill' is a three-masted ***schooner,*** *somewhat larger than the original two-masted vessels which carried the name. However, smaller sailing ships with the older sail arrangement are still numerous.*

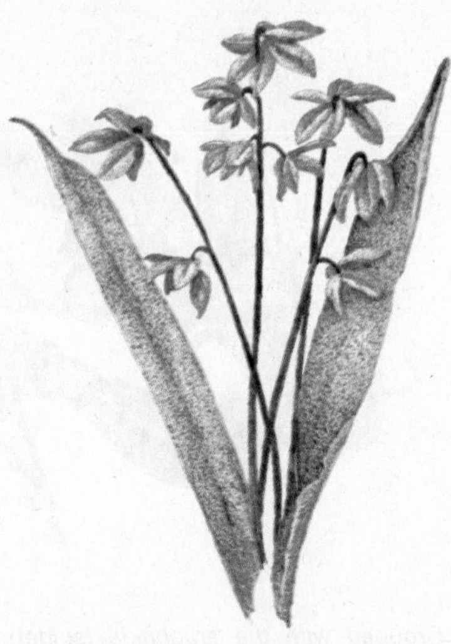

Lilies in the genus ***Scilla*** *may bear flowers which are blue, pink, or white. Several species are now grown in gardens in Britain. Once, gum from them was used to fix flights to arrows.*

pair of ~) Cutting instrument consisting of pair of handled blades so pivoted that the instrument can be opened to X-shape and then closed with the object to be cut between the edges of the blades. 2. (wrestling) Hold in which opponent's head or body is clasped between legs; ~ **kick**, (swimming) kick used esp. with sidestroke in which legs move like scissors; **scis′sortail flycatcher**, bird (*Muscivora forficata*) of Texas open country, having spectacularly long-forked tail. **scis′sor** *v.t.* Cut with scissors.

scle·ra (sklēr′*a*) = SCLEROTIC *n.*

scle·ren·chy·ma (sklĭrĕng′-k*i*m*a*) *n.* Hard tissue of coral; tissue of higher plants composed of cells with thickened and lignified walls, forming e.g. nutshell or seed coat.

scle·ro·sis (sklĭrō′sĭs) *n.* (pl. **-ses** pr. -sēz). 1. (path.) Replacement of normal tissue, esp. of nervous system or arteries, by overgrowth of fibrous or supporting tissue, resulting in hardening and and loss of function; **multiple** ~, chronic progressive sclerosis of brain and spinal cord. 2. (bot.) Hardening of cell wall by lignification.

scle·rot·ic (sklĭrŏt′ĭk) *adj.* Of, affected with, sclerosis; of the sclerotic. ~ *n.* Hard opaque white outer coat covering eyeball except over cornea and forming white of eye.

scoff (skŏf, skawf) *v.i.* Speak derisively, esp. of something deserving respect, mock, jeer (*at*);

scoff'law, (colloq.) person who disregards laws, esp. one who fails to pay traffic fines. **scoff'ing·ly** *adv.* **scoff** *n.* Derisive jest; object of derision or scoffing. **scoff'er** *n.*

scold (skōld) *v.* Castigate (person) verbally for fault etc. **scold'ing** *adj.* & *n.* **scold'-ing·ly** *adv.* **scold** *n.* Railing or nagging woman.

sconce[1] (skŏns) *n.* Flat candlestick with handle; bracket candlestick to hang on wall.

sconce[2] (skŏns) *n.* Small fort or earthwork, usu. covering a ford, pass, etc.

Scone (skōōn, skōn). Village in Perthshire, Scotland, ancient capital where Scottish kings were crowned; **Stone of ~**, stone on which Scottish kings sat at coronation ceremony, brought to England by Edward I and now preserved in coronation chair at Westminster Abbey.

scone (skōn, skŏn) *n.* Soft flat cake of flour, freq. with currants etc., usu. round or quadrant-shaped, orig. baked on a griddle.

scoop (skōōp) *n.* 1. Short-handled deep shovel for dipping up and carrying such materials as flour, grain, coal; long-handled ladle; instrument with spoon- or gouge-shaped blade for cutting out piece from soft material or removing embedded substance, core, etc.; coal scuttle. 2. Motion as of, act of, scooping; slurring of interval by singer or fiddler. 3. (colloq.) Obtaining of news etc. by newspaper before, or to exclusion of, competitors, news so obtained. ~ *v.t.* 1. Lift (*up*), hollow (*out*), (as) with scoop. 2. (colloq.) Get advantage over (rival) by obtaining newspaper scoop.

scoot (skōōt) *v.i.* Run, dart, make off.

scoot·er (skōō'tėr) *n.* 1. Child's toy vehicle, consisting of a narrow footboard mounted on 2 tandem wheels, the front one attached to a long steering handle, propelled by pushes of 1 foot on the ground, the other foot resting on the footboard; (also **motor ~**) similar heavier vehicle for adults, with seat and motor. 2. Sailboat with runners for use on either ice or water.

scope (skōp) *n.* End aimed at, purpose (now rare); outlook, purview, sweep or reach of observation or action, range; opportunity, outlet; (naut.) length of cable out when ship rides at anchor; (colloq.) telescope or other instrument whose name ends in -SCOPE.

-scope *suffix.* Forming nouns denoting: (1) thing looked at or through (*kaleidoscope, telescope*); (2) instrument for observing or showing (*gyroscope, oscilloscope*).

Scopes (skōps), **John Thomas** (1901–70). Amer. teacher; convicted for breaking a law prohibiting teaching theory of evolution in Tennessee schools, 1925.

Grouped with the arachnids (spiders) and represented in fossils that are 300 million years old, the largest ***scorpion*** *is an 8-in. long giant in West Africa. Some smaller ones have lethal stings.*

sco·pol·a·mine (skopŏl'amēn, -mĭn) *n.* Syrupy alkaloid obtained from certain plants of nightshade family (Solanaceae), esp. henbane (*Hyoscamus niger*) and belladonna (*Atropa belladonna*); used as sedative, antispasmodic, and, combined with morphine, as an anesthetic.

scor·bu·tic (skōrbū'tĭk) *adj.* & *n.* Of, like, (person) affected with, scurvy.

scorch (skōrch) *v.* Burn surface of with flame or heat so as to discolor, injure, or pain; affect with sensation of burning; become discolored, slightly burned, etc., with heat; **scorched earth**, policy of a country threatened by invasion of destroying all means of sustenance and supply that might be of use to the invading enemy.

score (skōr, skōr) *n.* 1. Notch cut, line cut, scratched, or drawn. 2. Account showing amount owed; reckoning, esp. for entertainment. 3. Wrong or grievance for which one seeks redress (**pay off old ~s**). 4. Reason, motive; **on that ~**, so far as that matter is concerned. 5. Number of points made by player or team in many games; **score'-board**, large board for publicly displaying score; **score'card**, card for keeping score of game, contest, etc., and identifying players by name, number, and position. 6. Grade given on test or examination. 7. (pl. **score** exc. in **scores** = large numbers) Twenty; set of 20. 8. (mus.) Copy of composition showing instrumental and vocal parts; music for theatrical presentation, motion picture, etc. 9. (colloq.) Piece of good luck; situation, facts; **know the score**, (fig.) be aware of essential facts. **score** *v.* (**scored, scor·ing**). 1. Mark with notches, incisions, or lines, slash, furrow; make (line, notch, incision). 2. Mark *up* amount owed; (fig.) mentally record (offense *against* offender). 3. Record (score in games), keep score; win and be credited with, make points in game, secure an advantage, have good luck. 4. Criticize (person) severely. 5. (mus.) Orchestrate; arrange *for* an instrument; write out in score. **score'less** *adj.* **scor'er** *n.*

sco·ri·a (skōr'ēa, skōr'-) *n.* (pl. **sco·ri·ae** pr. skōr'ēē, skōr'-). Cellular lava, fragments of this; slag. **sco·ri·a·ceous** (skōrēā'shus, skōr-) *adj.*

sco·ri·fy (skōr'ĭfī, skōr'-) *v.t.* (**-fied, -fy·ing**). Reduce to scoria or slag, esp. in assaying. **sco·ri·fi·ca·tion** (skōrĭfĭkā'shon, skōr-) *n.*

scorn (skōrn) *v.t.* Hold in contempt, despise; abstain from, refuse *to* do, as unworthy. ~ *n.* Contempt, derision; object of this. **scorn'ful** *adj.* **scorn'ful·ly** *adv.* **scorn'ful·ness, scorn'er** *ns.*

Scor·pi·o (skōr'pēō), **Scor·-pi·us** (skōr'pēus). The Scorpion, a constellation; eighth sign (♏) of the zodiac, which the sun enters about Oct. 23.

scor·pi·on (skōr'pēon) *n.* 1. Arachnid with lobsterlike claws and segmented tail that can be bent over to inflict poisoned sting on prey held in claws. 2. (Old Testament) Kind of whip, prob. armed with metal points. 3. **the S~**: see SCORPIO.

Scot (skŏt) *n.* 1. Native of Scotland. 2. (hist.) One of an ancient Gaelic-speaking people who migrated from Ireland to Scotland in 6th c.

scot (skŏt) *n.* (hist.) Payment corresponding to modern tax or other assessed contribution; **~-free**, unharmed, unpunished, safe, esp. in *get off, go, ~-free.*

Scotch (skŏch) *adj.* Of Scotland or its inhabitants (the modern in-

Rugged coastline at Caithness (above) typifies the severity of some of the landscape in ***Scotland.*** *Traditional activities include hammer-throwing at the Royal Braemar Gathering held annually in the Grampian region.*

habitants of Scotland usu. prefer the form **Scottish** except in such expressions as *Scotch whisky*); in the dialect(s) of English spoken in Scotland; ~ **broth**, mutton broth thickened with pearl barley and vegetables; **Scotch′man** (pl. **-men**), **Scotch′woman** (pl. **-women**), (Sc. **Scots-**), native of Scotland; **Scotch mist**, thick wet mist; **Scotch** (also **Scots**) **pine**, common pine (*Pinus sylvestris*) native to N. Europe and imported into N. Amer. as ornamental and timber tree; **Scotch tape**, (trademark) adhesive, usu. transparent, cellulose tape; **Scotch terrier**, short-legged terrier with a rough, wiry, grayish coat and short erect tail; **Scotch whisky**, whiskey, often having a smoky flavor of peat, as distilled in Scotland. **Scotch** *n.* 1. Scottish form of English. 2. (colloq.) Scotch whisky.

sco·ter (skō′t*er*) *n.* (pl. **-ters**, collect. **-ter**). Any of several large sea ducks (genus *Melanitta*) of northern parts of Northern Hemisphere.

sco·tia (skō′sh*a*) *n.* Concave molding esp. in base of column.

Scot·land (skŏt′l*a*nd). Northern part of Gt. Britain, formerly a separate kingdom; capital, Edinburgh; the crowns of England and Scotland were united by the accession of James VI of Scotland (James I of England) to the English throne in 1603; the two parliaments were united by the Act of Union in 1707, when Scotland became a part of the United Kingdom.

Scot·land (skŏt′l*a*nd) **Yard.** Headquarters of London metropolitan police, formerly in Great Scotland Yard, a short street off

Above left: ***Robert Falcon Scott,*** *the British Antarctic explorer who reached the South Pole in 1912, only to perish on his return. Above right:* ***Sir Walter Scott,*** *prolific writer of historical novels.*

Whitehall; in 1890 moved to New Scotland Yard on Thames Embankment and in 1967 to Broadway, Westminster; allusively, the Criminal Investigation Department (C.I.D.) of the Metropolitan Police Force.

Scoto- *prefix.* Scottish.

Scots (skŏts) *adj.* Scottish; **Scots'man** (pl. **-men**), **Scots'-woman** (pl. **-women**), native of Scotland. **Scots** *n.* Scottish (esp. Lowlands) form of English.

Scott[1] (skŏt), **Dred** (1795?–1858). Black slave who sued for freedom on grounds of having spent some time in a nonslave state, but failed, U.S. Supreme Court refusing to recognize his status as a citizen.

Scott[2] (skŏt), **Robert Falcon** (1868–1912). British explorer, leader of 2 Antarctic expeditions, in the 2nd of which the S. Pole was reached on Jan. 18, 1912, but Scott and the rest of the party perished in a blizzard on the return journey.

Scott[3] (skŏt), **Sir Walter** (1771–1832). Scottish writer of historical novels and verse romances, author of *The Lady of the Lake* (in verse), and the novels *Waverley, Ivanhoe,* etc.

Scott[4] (skŏt), **Winfield** (1786–1866). Amer. army officer; commander of U.S. forces in Mexican War.

Scot·ti·cism (skŏt'ĭsĭzem) *n.* Scots phrase, idiom, word, pronunciation, etc.

Scot·tie, Scot·ty (skŏt'ē) *ns.* (pl. **-ties**). (colloq.) Scotch terrier.

Scot·tish (skŏt'ĭsh) *adj.* Connected with, pertaining to, Scotland, its people, language, etc.

scoun·drel (skown'drel) *n.* Unscrupulous person, villain, rogue. **scoun'drel·ly** *adj.*

scour[1] (skowr, skow'*er*) *v.t.* Cleanse or brighten by friction; clean out by flushing with water, or (of water) by flowing through or over; purge drastically; clear (rust, stain) *away, off,* by rubbing etc. ~ *n.* Act, action, of scouring; artificial current or flow for clearing channel etc.; kind of diarrhea in cattle.

scour[2] (skowr, skow'*er*) *v.* Rove, range, go along hastily; hasten over or along, search rapidly.

scourge (skẽrj) *n.* Whip for punishing persons; person or thing regarded as instrument of divine or other vengeance or punishment. **scourg'er** *n.* **scourge** *v.t.* (**scourged, scourg·ing**). Use scourge on; chastise, afflict, oppress. [LL. *excoriare* strip off the hide]

scout[1] (skowt) *n.* 1. Soldier, plane, ship etc., sent out to reconnoiter position and movements of enemy. 2. Person whose job is to obtain information or locate new talent. 3. Member of the Boy Scouts of America, associated with an international scouting movement founded in 1908 in England by Lord Baden-Powell to develop boys' character by open-air activities; member of the Girl Scouts of the USA. 4. **scout master**, man in charge of group of scouts (sense 3). **scout** *v.i.* Act as scout.

scout[2] (skowt) *v.t.* Reject with scorn or ridicule.

scow (skow) *n.* Kind of large flat-bottomed square-ended boat used esp. as lighter.

scowl (skowl) *v.i.* Wear sullen look, frown ill-temperedly. ~ *n.* Scowling aspect, angry frown. **scowl'er** *n.* **scowl'ing·ly** *adv.*

Scrab·ble (skrăb'el) *n.* (trademark) Game in which players form words by placing lettered tiles on board similar to crossword puzzle diagram.

scrab·ble (skrăb'el) *v.i.* (**-bled, -bling**). Scratch or grope (*about*) to find or collect something. **scrab'bler** *n.*

scrag (skrăg) *n.* Lean skinny person, animal, etc.; bony part of animal's carcass, esp. of neck of mutton, as food; (slang) person's neck. **scrag'gy** *adj.* (**-gi·er, -gi·est**). **scrag'gi·ly** *adv.* **scrag'-gi·ness** *n.* **scrag** *v.t.* (**scragged, scrag·ging**). Hang (on gallows), wring neck of, garotte.

scrag·gly (skrăg'lē) *adj.* (**-gli·er, -gli·est**). Scrubby, ragged, uneven, irregular.

scram (skrăm) *v.i.* (**scrammed, scram·ming**). (slang) Go away quickly, get out (usu. as imper.).

scram·ble (skrăm'bel) *v.* (**-bled, -bling**). 1. Make way over steep or rough ground by clambering, crawling, etc.; struggle to secure as much as possible of something from competitors; deal with in a hasty manner. 2. Cook (eggs) by stirring slightly in pan with butter, milk, etc., and heating; mix together indiscriminately or confusedly; alter frequency of the voice in telephoning or radiotelephony by means of automatic mechanical or electrical devices fitted to the transmitter so as to make the message unintelligible except to a person using a receiver fitted with a similar device. 3. (of military aircraft or their pilots) (Hasten to aircraft and) take off in response to alert. ~ *n.* 1. Eager struggle or competition (*for*). 2. Climb or walk over rough ground; motorcycle race over rough ground.

scram·bler (skrăm′bler) *n.* (esp.) Telephone or wireless transmitter fitted with a device for scrambling speech.

scrap[1] (skrăp) *n.* Small detached piece; shred or fragment; short piece of writing etc.; (pl.) odds and ends, fragments of uneaten food; (collect.) waste material, clippings, etc., of metal collected for reworking; metal wasted in production; residuum of melted fat; **scrap′book**, book for collection of newspaper clippings etc.; **scrap iron, metal**, scrap. **scrap′per** *n.* **scrap′py** *adj.* (**-pi·er, -pi·est**). Fragmented, disconnected. **scrap** *v.t.* (**scrapped, scrap·ping**). Consign to scrap heap; condemn as past use; discard.

scrap[2] (skrăp) *n.* (colloq.) Fight, quarrel. ~ *v.i.* Engage in a scrap. **scrap′per, scrap′pi·ness** *ns.* **scrap′py** *adj.* (**-pi·er, -pi·est**).

scrape (skrāp) *v.* (**scraped, scrap·ing**). 1. Clean, clear of projections, abrade, smooth, polish, etc., by drawing sharp or angular edge breadthways over, or by causing to pass over such edge; take (projection, stain, etc.) *off, out, away*, by scraping. 2. Draw along with scraping sound, produce such sound from, emit such sound. 3. Pass along something so as to graze or be grazed by it or just avoid doing so; ~ **through**, get through with a squeeze or narrow shave (freq. fig.). 4. Amass by scraping, with difficulty, by parsimony, etc.; contrive to gain; practice economy. **scrape** *n.* 1. Act or sound of scraping; scraping of foot in bowing. 2. Awkward predicament, difficult position, esp. as result of escapade etc. **scrap′er** *n.* (esp.) Scraping instrument in various technical operations; appliance fixed outside door of house, with horizontal blade for scraping mud etc. from shoes; (archaeol.) primitive wedge-shaped flint implement.

Scratch (skrăch). **Old** ~, the devil.

scratch (skrăch) *v.* 1. Score surface of, make long narrow superficial wounds in, with nail, claw, or something pointed; get (part of body) scratched; form, excavate, by scratching; scrape without marking, esp. with fingernails to relieve itching; scratch oneself; make scratch; scrape *together* or *up*. 2. Score (something written) *out*, strike *off* with pencil etc.; erase name of, withdraw, from list of competitors etc. ~ *n.* 1. Mark or sound made by scratching; sound made by friction of needle in sound-recording apparatus and heard in playing of record etc.; spell of scratching oneself; slight wound. 2. Line from which competitors in race, or those receiving no start in handicap, start; zero, par, in games or contests in which handicaps are allowed; **come up to** ~, be ready to start race, match, etc., at the proper time; (fig.) be ready to embark on an enterprise, to fulfill one's obligations; **start from** ~, have no handicap (also fig.); ~ **pad**, pad of paper for jotting or scribbling on. **scratch** *adj.* Collected by haphazard, scratched together, heterogeneous.

scratch·y (skrăch′ē) *adj.* (**scratch·i·er, scratch·i·est**). (of drawing etc.) Done in scratches, careless, unskillful; (of pen) making scratching sound or liable to catch in paper; (of action etc.) uneven, ragged. **scratch′i·ly** *adv.* **scratch′i·ness** *n.*

scrawl (skrawl) *v.* Write, draw, in hurried, sprawling, untidy way; cover with scrawls. ~ *n.* Something scrawled; hasty or illegible writing. **scraw′ly** *adj.* (**scrawl·i·er, scrawl·i·est**).

scraw·ny (skraw′nē) *adj.* (**-ni·er, -ni·est**). Scraggy. **scraw′ni·ness** *n.*

scream (skrēm) *v.* Utter piercing cry, normally expressive of terror, pain, sudden or uncontrollable mirth, etc.; make noise like this; utter in screaming tone. **scream′ing** *adj.* **scream′ing·ly** *adv.* **scream** *n.* Screaming cry or sound; (slang) irresistibly comical affair, person, or object.

scream·er (skrē′mer) *n.* (esp.) Large S. Amer. bird of family Anhimidae, with harsh cry; (slang) something that raises screams of laughter; (slang) exclamation mark.

scree (skrē) *n.* (freq. pl.) (Mountain slope covered with) loose stones that slide when trodden on.

screech (skrēch) *n.* Loud shrill harsh cry; ~ **owl**, small Amer. tufted owl (*Otus asio*) having quavering wail; (occas. pop.) barn owl or other small owl. **screech** *v.* Make, utter with, screech. **screech′y** *adj.* (**screech·i·er, screech·i·est**).

screed (skrēd) *n.* 1. Long and tedious harangue, letter, etc. 2. (plastering etc.) Strip of accurately leveled plaster on wall, ceiling, etc., as guide in running cornice, laying coat of plaster, etc.; board, strip of wood, used for leveling concrete etc.

screen (skrēn) *n.* 1. Partition partly shutting off part of church or room, esp. that between nave and choir of church; ornamental wall masking front of building. 2. Movable piece of furniture designed to shelter from excess of heat, light, draft, etc., or from observation; any object utilized as shelter esp. from observation, measure adopted for concealment, protection afforded by these; SMOKE screen; wind screen; (window) frame holding wire etc. mesh to let in air but keep out insects; (baseball) high barrier to keep ball

*A Chinese lacquer **screen**, now housed in the Victoria and Albert Museum, U.K., gives some indication of the fine degree of craftsmanship achieved in China during the times of the Emperors.*

*The **screw-palm** or pandanus tree is represented throughout the tropics of Asia, Africa and Australia. The leaves were used for plaiting and the 'nuts' (right) were roasted for eating by Australian Aboriginals.*

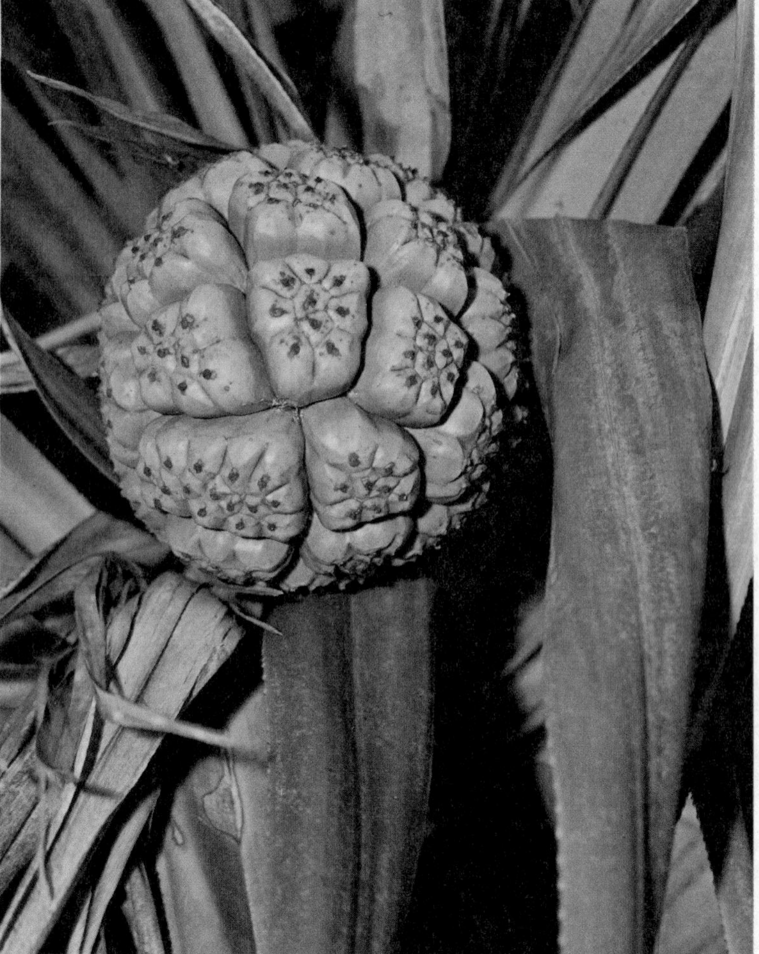

from striking spectators, going out of play, etc. 3. Upright surface on which images are projected or received, objects displayed, etc.; (also **silver ~**) moving pictures, films; **screen′play**, (script of) film; **screen′writer**, writer of this script. 4. Body, part of optical, electrical, or other instrument, serving to intercept light, heat, electricity, etc.; (photog.) transparent plate ruled with fine cross-lines, through which picture etc. is photographed for halftone reproduction. 5. Large sieve to separate coarser from finer parts of sand, grain, coal, etc. 6. **screen printing**, process like stenciling with ink forced through prepared sheet of fine material (orig. silk), serigraphy. **screen** *v.t.* 1. Afford shelter to; hide partly or completely; (mil.) employ a body of men to cover (troop movement); furnish (radio tube) with screen; prevent from causing electrical interference; **~ off**, shut off by means of, conceal behind, screen. 2. Show (esp. motion picture) on screen. 3. Clean, sift, grade (coal, gravel, etc.) by passing through a screen; scrutinize, subject (person) to tests to establish reliability etc.

screen·ings (skrē′nĭngz) *n.pl.* Material that has been screened; refuse separated by screening.

screw (skrōō) *n.* 1. Cylinder with spiral ridge (*thread*) running around it outside (**male ~**) or inside (**female ~**); metal male screw with slotted head and sharp point for fastening pieces of wood etc. together, or with blunt end to receive nut and bolt things together; wooden or metal etc. screw as part of appliance for exerting pressure; **have a ~ loose**, (colloq.) be slightly mad; **put the ~s on, apply the ~s to**, (fig.) put moral pressure on, coerce. 2. (also **~ propeller**) Propeller. 3. **screw′-driver**, tool with thin wedge-shaped end or blade for turning screws by slot in head; **screw eye**, screw having loop for head; **screw pine**, plant of tropical genus *Pandanus*, with slender palmlike stems and branches, with terminal crown of swordlike leaves; **screw′-worm**, parasitic larva of any of certain Amer. flies (genus *Callitroga*), which often infests wounds, nostrils, navel, etc. of animals, causing injuries, illness, or death. **screw** *v.* 1. Fasten, tighten, etc., by use of screw or screws; turn (screw), twist around like screw; make tauter or more efficient; revolve like screw. 2. Press hard on, oppress. 3. Be miserly; squeeze, extort *out* of. 4. Contort, distort, contract. 5. (vulg., of male) Copulate (with); **~ up**, (slang) make mess of, bungle.

screw·ball (skrōō′bawl) *n.* & *adj.* (slang) Mad, crazy (person); (baseball) pitch that curves in opposite direction to normal curve.

screw·y (skrōō′ē) *adj.* (**screw·i·er, screw·i·est**). (slang) Mad, crazy, suspicious.

scrib·ble (skrĭb′*el*) *v.* (**-bled, -bling**). Write hurriedly or carelessly. **scrib′bler** *n.* **scribble** *n.* Careless writing, thing carelessly written, scrawl.

scribe (skrīb) *n.* 1. Copyist, transcriber of manuscripts, calligrapher; (obs.) clerk, secretary. 2. Ancient Jewish maker and keeper of records etc.; member of class of professional interpreters of the Law after return from Captivity. 3. Tool for marking or scoring (wood, bricks, etc.) to indicate shape to be cut etc. **~** *v.t.* (**scribed, scrib·ing**). Mark with scribe.

scrim (skrĭm) *n.* Open-weave fabric used in bookbinding, upholstery, plastering, etc.

scrim·mage (skrĭm′ĭj) *n.* Tussle, confused struggle, brawl; (football) play in which center places it flat on ground with long axis at right angles to goal line, and puts it in play; **line of ~, ~ line**, imaginary line parallel to goal line passing through point of ball closer to defensive goal line when ball is resting on ground before being put in play. **scrimmage** *v.i.* (**-maged, -mag·ing**). Engage in scrimmage.

*Coastal **scrub** in Crete (left). Vegetation of this type is common in regions of poor soil, aridity and exposure to wind.*

*The **scrum** is a particular feature of Rugby football and it is a means of allowing the forwards of each team to work en masse to obtain possession of the ball.*

scrimp (skrĭmp) *v.* Be frugal or sparing; skimp. **scrimp'y** *adj.*

scrim·shaw (skrĭm'shaw) *n.* Shells, pieces of ivory, etc., adorned with carved or colored designs done by sailors for amusement at sea.

scrip (skrĭp) *n.* 1. Provisional document issued to holder of fractional share of stock. 2. (hist.) Paper money in denominations of less than $1, issued in U.S.; temporary document issued in lieu of and resembling paper currency. [abbrev. of (*sub*)*scrip*(*tion receipt*)]

script (skrĭpt) *n.* 1. (law) Original document. 2. Handwriting, written characters; printed cursive characters, imitation of handwriting in type; style of handwriting in which characters resemble those of print and are not joined together. 3. Manuscript, typescript, of play, film, etc.; text of broadcaster's announcement or talk. ~ *v.i.* (colloq.) Compose script of play etc.

Script. *abbrev.* Scriptural; Scripture.

scrip·ture (skrĭp'ch*er*) *n.* Sacred book or writings; (usu. **S**~ freq. pl.) Bible; (attrib.) taken from or relating to the Bible. **scrip'tur·al** *adj.* **scrip'tur·al·ly** *adv.*

scrive·ner (skrĭv'n*er*) *n.* (hist.) Writer, drafter of documents, notary, broker, moneylender.

scrod (skrŏd) *n.* Young codfish.

scrof·u·la (skrŏf'y*u*l*a*) *n.* Name formerly given to a prob. tubercular condition affecting the lymphatic glands and bones. **scrof'u·lous** *adj.*

scroll (skrōl) *n.* 1. Roll of parchment or paper, esp. written on; book or volume of ancient roll form. 2. Ornamental design, esp. in architecture, made to imitate scroll of parchment more or less exactly; volute of Ionic capital or of chair etc., head of violin etc., flourish in writing; any tracery of spiral or flowing lines. 3. ~ **saw**, fret saw, saw stretched in frame, for carving curved lines; **scroll'-work**, ornament of spiral or curving lines, esp. as cut by scroll saw. **scroll** *v.* Curl or roll up like paper; adorn with scrolls.

Scrooge (skrōōj), **Ebenezer.** Miserly curmudgeon in Charles Dickens' *Christmas Carol*; hence **scrooge**, miser.

scro·tum (skrō't*u*m) *n.* (pl. **-ta** pr. -ta, **-tums**). (anat.) Pouch or bag enclosing testicles. **scro'tal** *adj.*

scrounge (skrownj) *v.* (**scrounged, scroung·ing**). (colloq.) Appropriate without permission; cadge; search about. **scroung'er** *n.*

scrub[1] (skrŭb) *n.* (Ground covered with) plant community dominated by shrubs; stunted or insignificant person, animal, etc.; ~ **oak, pine**, stunted oak, pine, of several Amer. species; ~ **typhus,** acute febrile disease, caused by bites of certain larval mites, esp. prevalent in Japan; Japanese river fever. **scrub'by** *adj.* (**-bi·er, -bi·est**).

scrub[2] (skrŭb) *v.* (**scrubbed, scrub·bing**). 1. Rub hard to clean or brighten, esp. with soap and water applied with hard-bristled brush (**scrubbing brush**); use such brush; **scrub-up**, (esp., of surgeons etc.) scrub hands and arms thoroughly before performing surgical operation. 2. **scrub** (colloq.) Drop, cancel, postpone, (plan, event, etc.). 3. Pass (gas) through a scrubber to extract certain components. **scrub** *n.* Scrubbing, being scrubbed; (colloq.) second, usu. inferior, team.

scrub·ber (skrŭb'*er*) *n.* (esp.) Apparatus for removing impurities etc. from gas, smoke, etc., by passing it through a body or stream of water.

scruff (skrŭf) *n.* (also ~ **of the neck**) Back outer part of neck.

scruff·y (skrŭf'ē) *adj.* (**scruff·i·er, scruff·i·est**). Unkempt.

scrum (skrŭm) *n.* (Rugby footb.) Formation in which two sets of forwards pack themselves together with heads down and try to obtain ball placed on the ground between them by pushing their opponents away from it.

scrump·tious (skrŭmp'sh*u*s) *adj.* (slang) Delicious, delightful.

scrunch (skrŭnch) *n.* & *v.* = CRUNCH.

1 Rustic capitals, 4th-5th c.
2 Uncial, mid-5th c.
3 Half-uncial, 6th c.
4 Insular (Anglo-Saxon) majuscule, early 8th c.
5 Carolingian minuscule, early 9th c.
6 Gothic, circa 1250
7 Humanist script, late 15th c.
8 Italic, late 15th c.
9 Secretary hand, 1593
10 Court hand, 1611
11 Copperplate, 1673

*The various forms of handwriting or **script** have often been determined by the writing materials, the time available and the need for legibility. Aesthetic factors have also been influential.*

scru·ple (skrōō′p*e*l) *n.* 1. In apothecaries' weight, unit equivalent to 20 grains or $\frac{1}{3}$ drachm; symbol ℈. 2. Doubt, uncertainty, or hesitation in regard to right and wrong, duty, etc. ~ *v.i.* (**-pled, -pling**). Hesitate owing to scruples *to* do.

scru·pu·lous (skrōō′py*u*lus) *adj.* Conscientious even in small matters, not neglectful of details, punctilious; overattentive to details, esp. to small points of conscience. **scru′pu·lous·ly** *adv.* **scru′pu·lous·ness** *n.* **scru·pu·los·i·ty** (skrōōpy*u*lŏs′ĭtē) *n.* (pl. **-ties**).

scru·ti·nize (skrōō′tinīz) *v.t.* (**-nized, -niz·ing**). Look closely at, examine in detail. **scru′ti·niz·er** *n.*

scru·ti·ny (skrōō′tinē) *n.* (pl. **-nies**). Critical gaze; close investigation, examination into details.

scu·ba (skōō′b*a*) *n.* & *adj.* Self-contained underwater breathing apparatus.

scud (skŭd) *v.i.* (**scud·ded, scud·ding**). Run, fly, straight and fast, esp. with smooth or easy motion; (naut.) run before the wind. ~ *n.* Driving shower of rain, gust of wind.

scuff (skŭf) *v.* Walk with dragging feet, shuffle; shuffle, drag along (feet); wear, rub, esp. with feet. ~ *n.* Mark of scuffing; backless slipper.

scuf·fle (skŭf′*e*l) *v.i.* (**-fled, -fling**) & *n.* (Engage in) confused struggle or scrambling fight.

scull (skŭl) *n.* Each of pair of light oars used by single rower; oar used to propel boat by working it from side to side over stern, reversing blade at each turn; light, narrow boat for sculling, esp. for racing. ~ *v.* Propel (boat), propel boat, with scull(s). **scull′er** *n.* User of sculls; boat intended for sculling.

scul·ler·y (skŭl′*e*rē) *n.* (pl. **-ler·ies**). Back kitchen, small room attached to kitchen for washing dishes etc.

scul·lion (skŭl′y*o*n) *n.* (archaic and rhet.) Menial servant, washer of dishes and pots.

scul·pin (skŭl′pĭn) *n.* (pl. **-pins**, collect. **-pin**). Small Amer. sea fish of family Cottidae, with barbels on head.

sculpt (skŭlpt) *v.* Sculpture.

sculp·tor (skŭlp′t*e*r), fem.

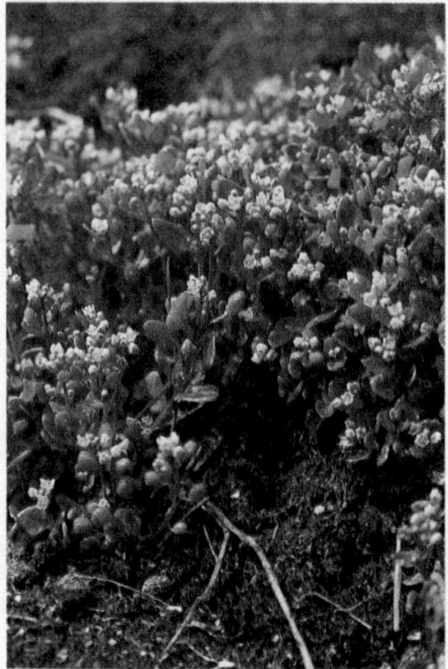

*Despite its name, **scurvy grass** is a form of cress, and not a grass. It grows in Europe and parts of Asia and was once used to prevent scurvy among sailors.*

*Reeds for thatching need to be as long as possible. In marshy areas of Norfolk, U.K., where the mechanical mower cannot be used, a **scythe** will cut them close to the ground.*

sculp·tress (skŭlp′trĭs) *ns.* One who practices sculpture.

sculp·ture (skŭlp′ch*er*) *n.* 1. Art of forming representations of objects etc. or abstract designs in the round or in relief by chiseling stone, carving wood, modeling clay, casting metal, or similar processes; work of sculpture. 2. (zool., bot.) Raised or sunk markings on shell etc. **sculp′tu·ral** *adj.* **sculp′tu·ral·ly** *adv.* **sculpture** *v.* (**-tured, -tur·ing**). Form by, represent in, sculpture; adorn with sculpture; be sculptor, practice sculpture. **sculp′tured** *adj.* (esp. biol.) With markings etc. like those produced by sculpture; (as though) chiselled.

scum (skŭm) *n.* Impurities that rise to surface of liquid; (fig.) worst part, refuse. **scum′my** *adj.* (**-mi·er, -mi·est**). **scum** *v.* (**scummed, scum·ming**). Take scum from, skim; be, form, scum on; (of liquid) develop scum.

scup·per (skŭp′*er*) *n.* Opening in ship's side level with deck to drain off water.

scurf (skẽrf) *n.* Flakes on surface of skin cast off as fresh skin develops below, esp. those of head; any scaly matter on a surface. **scurf′y** *adj.* (**scurf·i·er, scurf·i·est**).

scur·ril·ous (skẽr′*ilus*, skŭr′-) *adj.* Grossly or obscenely abusive; given to, expressed with, low buffoonery. **scur′ril·ous·ly** *adv.* **scur·ril·i·ty** (sk*u*rĭl′ĭtē) *n.* (pl. **-ties**).

scur·ry (skẽr′ē, skŭr′ē) *v.i.* (**-ried, -ry·ing**). Run hurriedly, scamper. ~ *n.* Act of scurrying, rush, bustle; flurry.

scur·vy (skẽr′vē) *n.* Disease resulting from deficiency of vitamin C, characterized by swollen gums, hemorrhage, esp. into skin and mucous membrane, and great debility, formerly common among sailors and others who lived for long periods without fresh vegetables; ~ **grass**, any of several cresses used against scurvy, esp. *Cochlearia officinalis*, found in Arctic regions. **scurvy** *adj.* (**-vi·er, -vi·est**). (archaic) Contemptible, low, mean. **scur′vi·ly** *adv.*

scutch (skŭch) *v.t.* Dress (fibrous material, esp. retted flax) by beating. **scutch′er** *n.* Hand tool for scutching flax; machine for scutching; part of threshing machine for striking off the grain. **scutch** *n.* 1. Scutcher. 2. Bricklayer's tool for cutting bricks etc. 3. Refuse of scutched flax.

scutch·eon (skŭch′*on*) *n.* ESCUTCHEON; pivoted cover of keyhole; plate for name or inscription.

scu·tel·lum (skūtĕl′*um*) *n.* (pl. **-tel·la** pr. -tĕl′*a*). Small shield, plate, or scale, in plants; shieldlike part of insect; one of the horny scales on bird's foot. **scu·tel·late** (skūtĕl′ĭt, -āt, skū′t*e*lāt), **scu·tel·lat·ed** (skū′t*e*lātĭd) *adjs.* **scu·tel·la·tion** (skūt*e*lā′sh*on*) *n.*

scut·tle[1] (skŭt′*el*) *n.* 1. Shallow open basket for carrying corn, earth, etc. 2. Metal or other receptacle for carrying and holding small supply of coal (**coal** ~) for a fire in a room.

scut·tle[2] (skŭt′*el*) *n.* Lidded opening smaller than hatchway in ship's deck; similar opening in ship's side for ventilation, lighting, etc.; lidded opening in floor or roof of house; **scut′tlebutt**, ship's cask of drinking water; (colloq.) gossip, rumor. **scuttle** *v.t.* (**-tled, -tling**). Cut hole(s) in (ship, boat, etc.), sink thus; (also fig.).

scut·tle[3] (skŭt′*el*) *v.i.* (**-tled, -tling**). Scurry, run away, make off. ~ *n.* Hurried gait, precipitate flight or departure.

scu·tum (skū′t*um*) *n.* (*pl.* **-ta** pr. -t*a*). (zool.) Bony, horny, etc., plate, esp. second of three parts forming upper surface of dorsal part of thorax in insects; shieldlike dermal plate in crocodile, turtle, etc.

Scyl·la (sĭl′*a*). (Gk. myth.) Female sea monster who devoured sailors when they tried to navigate the narrow channel between her cave and the whirlpool CHARYBDIS; later legend substituted a dangerous rock for the monster and located it on the Italian side of the Strait of Messina; hence, ~ **and Charybdis**, dangers such that to avoid the one is to court the other.

scy·pho·zo·an (sĭf*o*zō′*an*) *adj.* & *n.* (Member) of the Scyphozoa, a class of coelenterates comprising the true marine jellyfishes.

scythe (sīdh) *n.* Agricultural implement for mowing and reaping, with long thin slightly curved blade fastened at an angle with handle and wielded with long sweeping stroke. ~ *v.t.* (**scythed, scyth·-ing**). Cut with scythe.

SD *abbrev.* South Dakota.

S.D. *abbrev.* South Dakota; special delivery.

S. Dak. *abbrev.* South Dakota.

SE, S.E., s.e. *abbrevs.* South-east(ern).

Se *symbol.* Selenium.

sea (sē) *n.* 1. Continuous body of salt water covering most of Earth's surface; part of this having certain land limits or washing a particular coast and having a proper name; large lake or landlocked body of water; **at ~**, away from land, aboard ship; (fig.) perplexed, bewildered, at a loss; **the high ~s**: see HIGH; **the seven ~s**, the Arctic, Antarctic, N. and S. Pacific, N. and S. Atlantic, and Indian Oceans. 2. Local motion or state of the sea; swell, rough water. 3. Large quantity or level expanse *of*. 4. **~ anchor**, floating, expanding anchor, usu. of canvas, used to keep a boat's head into the wind in rough weather; drag anchor; **~anemone**, any of numerous usu. large and solitary polyps with bright colors and many petallike tentacles surrounding mouth: **sea'bed**, bottom of ocean; **Sea'bee**, member of naval construction battalion; **sea'-bird**, bird frequenting sea; **sea'-board**, coast bordering the sea; **sea'borne**, conveyed by sea; **sea breeze**, cool breeze blowing landward from sea, usu. in daytime; **sea calf**, common seal; **sea chest**, sailor's chest; **sea coal**, (archaic) coal (because formerly brought by sea from Newcastle to London etc.); coal mined from seacoast veins; **sea'coast**, land adjacent to the sea; **sea'cock**, valve by which seawater can be let into ship's interior; **sea'cow**, manatee or other sirenian; **sea cucumber**, one of the holothurians, esp. the bêche-de-mer; **sea dog**, old sailor, privateer or pirate, esp. of Elizabethan days; **sea eagle**, any of the various eagles feeding largely on fish, esp. the white-tailed eagle; **sea ear**, haliotis; **sea elephant**, elephant seal, large seal of S. hemisphere with proboscis; **sea fan**, coral with fanlike skeleton; **sea'farer**, traveler by sea, sailor; **sea'faring** (*adj.* & *n.*); **sea'food**, sea fish, shellfish, as food; **sea front**, part of town etc. facing sea; **sea'going**, (of ship) designed for open sea, not rivers, etc.; seafaring; **sea green** (*n.*) **sea-green** (*adj.*), (of) bluish green, as of sea; **sea gull**, gull; **sea hog**, porpoise; **sea horse**, hippocampus, small fish covered with rough bony plates, with prehensile tail and forepart of body resembling horse's head and neck; walrus; (Gk. and Rom. myth.) fabulous marine animal with foreparts of horse and tail of fish, drawing sea god's chariot; **sea-island cotton**, fine variety of long-stapled cotton, grown orig. and esp. on islands off coast of Georgia and South Carolina; **Sealab**, one of several U.S. Navy laboratories for deep-sea research in oceanography etc.; **sea lane**, course prescribed for ocean steamers; **sea lavender**, any maritime herb of genus *Limonium*, of plumbago family; **sea lawyer**, argumentative or captious sailor; **sea legs**, ability to walk on deck of rolling ship; **sea level**, mean level of sea, mean level between high and low tides, used as a standard for measurements of heights and depths; **sea lily**, crinoid; **sea lion**, any of several large-eared seals; **sea'man**, (pl. **-men**), sailor; sailor below rank of officer; navigator; **sea'manship**, skill of good seaman; **sea'mark**, conspicuous object serving to guide or warn sailors in navigation; **sea mew**, common gull; **sea mile**: see MILE; **sea'mount**, underwater mountain; **sea mouse**, pop. name of marine annelid worm, covered with minute iridescent setae, of the genus *Aphrodite*; **sea onion**, squill; **sea otter**, rare (once almost extinct) large otter (*Enhydra lutris*) of the N. Amer. Pacific coast, having lustrous, extremely valuable fur; **sea pink**, see THRIFT def. 2; **sea'plane**, airplane fitted with floats to enable it to alight or take off from water; **sea'port**, (town

*The southern **sea lion** is one of several varieties of eared-seals. They differ from the fur seals by having blunt snouts, a less luxuriant coat, and different hind-flippers.*

Sea-lions

male

female

young

*Because man has always been a land dweller, it is not surprising that some of the stranger marine organisms were given common names which are based more on their superficial resemblance to land objects, than to their true status. For example, a **sea cucumber** is not a plant but an animal; a **sea horse** is a fish; although a **sea slug** is a mollusk.*

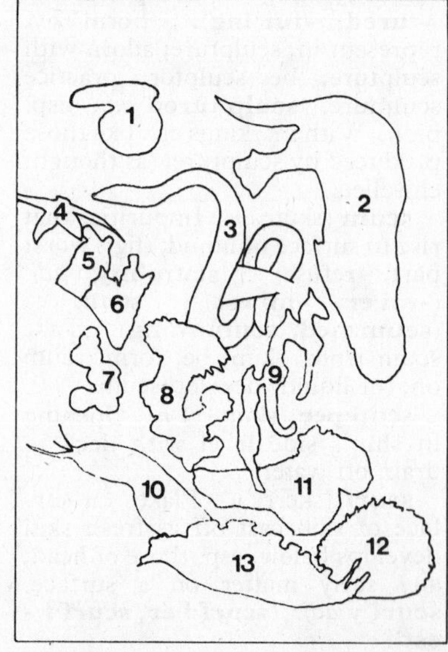

1 sea-snail. 2 sea-otter. 3 sea-snake. 4 purple starfish. 5 gooseberry sea-squirt. 6 sea-vases. 7 periwinkles. 8 sea-anemones. 9 sea-horses. 10 sea-mouse. 11 sea-cucumber. 12 sea-urchins. 13 sea-slug.

with) harbor or port on seacoast; **sea power**, naval strength, nation having this; **sea robin**, any of a family (Triglidae) of marine fishes having spiny fins, broad bony heads, and very long pectoral fins; **sea room**, unobstructed space at sea for ship to maneuver in; **sea rover**, pirate; **sea'scape**, picture of a scene at sea; **Sea Scout**, member of organization training SCOUTS (sense 3) in seamanship; **sea serpent**, sea monster of great length and more or less resembling a serpent, freq. alleged to have been seen at sea; **sea'shell**, shell of any saltwater mollusk; **sea'shore**, land close to sea, ground between high- and low-water marks; **sea'sick**, suffering from nausea and vomiting induced by motion of ship at sea; **sea'sickness** (*n.*); **sea'side**, edge of sea, seacoast as health or pleasure resort; **sea slug**, marine gastropod mollusk of which the shell is absent or internal; **sea snake**, any of several poisonous marine snakes (family Hydrophidae), living chiefly in the Pacific and Indian oceans; **sea squirt**, sessile marine animal of subphylum Urochordata, which squirts water when touched; **sea swallow**, tern; **sea trout**, salmon trout; any of various sea fishes; **sea urchin**, marine animal of order Echinoidea, esp. one of nearly globular form covered with (freq. very sharp) movable spines; **sea'wall**, wall or embankment made to check encroachment of sea or act as breakwater; **sea'ward**, with sea exposure; from the sea; (also **seawards**) in the direction of, or toward, the sea; **sea'weed**, plant growing in sea, esp. marine alga; **sea'worthy**, (of ship) in fit state to put to sea, **sea'worthiness** (*n.*)

*Depending on the weather, the **sea** has many moods. When backed by an ocean and often by storm winds, the effect of waves can have a strong erosive effect on rock.*

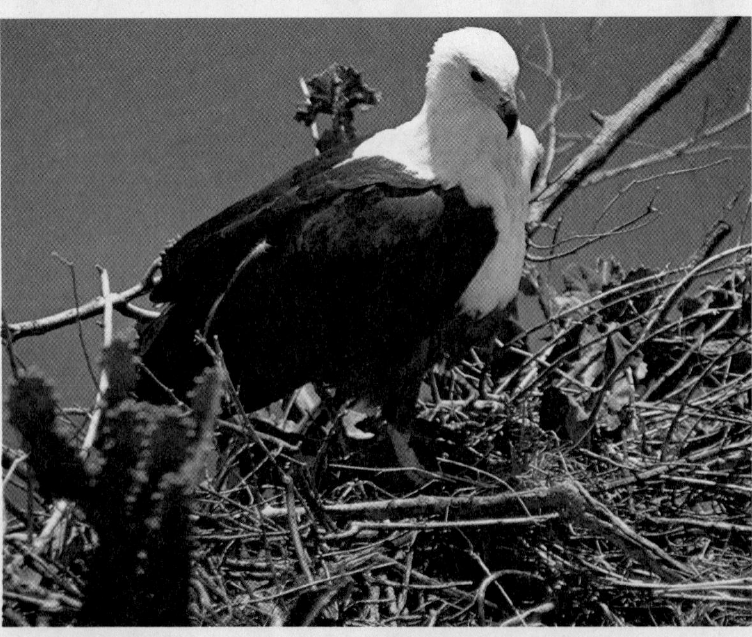

Sea (sē) **Islands.** Group of islands in the Atlantic Ocean, off the coasts of South Carolina, Georgia, and N. Florida.

seal[1] (sēl) *n.* (pl. **seals**, collect. **seal**). Marine amphibious fish-eating mammal, of family Phocidae, with limbs developed into flippers and adapted for swimming, elongated body covered with thick fur or bristles, and short tail, hunted for its hides and oil; (also **seal'skin**) skin or prepared fur of seals; coat, cape, etc. made of this. **seal** *v.i.* Hunt seals. **seal'er** *n.* (esp.) Ship or man engaged in seal hunting.

seal[2] (sēl) *n.* 1. (Impressed device on) piece of wax etc. attached to document as evidence of authenticity of signature etc., or on folded letter, envelope flap, door, lid of box, etc., so that it cannot be opened without breaking seal; impression stamped on a wafer etc. stuck to document as symbol equivalent to wax seal; decorative adhesive stamp other than postage stamp; (fig.) mark of ownership; obligation to silence or secrecy. 2. Engraved stamp of metal or other hard material used to make impression on wax etc., used as seal; this as mark of office; **Great S~**, seal used for authentication of important documents issued in name of highest executive authority of nation or state; **~ ring**, finger ring with seal. 3. Substance used to close aperture etc., esp. water standing in drainpipe to prevent ascent of foul air. **seal** *v.t.* Place seal on (document), fasten (letter etc.), esp. with seal or sealing wax; close tightly or hermetically; stop or shut *up*; (fig.) prove authenticity of (devotion etc.) *with* one's life etc.; set significant mark on; set apart, destine, devote; decide irrevocably; **~ off**, cut off (an area) so as to prevent entry or exit. **sealed** *adj.* **seal'ing** *n.* (esp.) **~ wax**, colored mixture of shellac, rosin, and turpentine, which becomes soft when heated and hardens as it cools, thus easily receiving and preserving the impression of a seal, used for sealing letters, documents, etc.

seal·ant (sē'lant) *n.* Sealing substance.

Seal·y·ham (sē'lēhăm, -lēam) *n.* Wiry-haired, long-bodied, short-legged terrier, usu. white with brown or gray markings on head, noted for spirit and gameness. [f. name of estate in Dyfed, Wales]

seam (sēm) *n.* Line of junction between two edges, esp. those of two pieces of cloth etc. sewn together, or of boards fitted edge

*The Madagascar fish or **sea eagle** is one of the smallest birds in a group of predators which include the bald eagle of the U.S.A. While some birds catch live fish, others eat carrion.*

***Seals** are aquatic mammals found in circumpolar waters of both hemispheres of the earth. The largest animal in the group is the elephant seal which may be up to 20 ft. long and an adult male can weigh up to 8,000 lb. In contrast, the ringed seal is only 5 ft. long and rarely exceeds a weight of 200 lb. Other varieties vary between these extremes.*

to edge; line, groove, furrow, formed by two abutting edges, mark resembling this; scar; line of purl stitches in knitting resembling sewn seam; thin layer or stratum, esp. of coal, between two wider strata. ~ *v.* Join *together*, *up*, etc., with seam(s); (knitting) make seam stitch; score or mark with seams, furrow, ridge. **seam'less** *adj.* **seam'er** *n.*

seam·stress (sēm'strĭs; *Brit.* sĕm'strĭs), **semp·stress** (sĕmp'-strĭs, sĕm'-) *ns.* Sewing woman.

seam·y (sē'mē) *adj.* (**seam·i·er, seam·i·est**). Showing seams; ~ **side**, wrong side of garment etc. where rough edges of seams are visible; (usu. fig.) of worst, roughest, or least presentable aspect, esp. of life.

Sean·ad Eir·eann (shăn'adh ār'an). Upper Chamber (Senate) of the Republic of Ireland, with 60 members. [Ir., = "Irish senate"]

sé·ance (sā'ahns) *n.* Sitting of society or deliberative body; meeting for exhibition or investigation of spiritualistic phenomena.

sear (sēr) *v.t.* Wither up, blast (rare); scorch, esp. with hot iron, cauterize, brand; (fig.) render (conscience etc.) incapable of feeling. ~ *adj.* SERE.

search (sẽrch) *v.* Examine thoroughly (place, person, etc.) for what may be found or to find something of which presence is known or suspected; make search or investigation (*for*); ~ **me!** (slang) exclamation implying that the speaker has no knowledge of some fact or no idea what course to take. **search'ing** *adj.* (of examination etc.) Thoroughgoing, leaving no loopholes. **search'ing·ly** *adv.* **search** *n.* Act of searching, investigation, quest; **right of** ~, belligerent's right to stop neutral vessel and search it for contraband; **search'light**, lamp designed to throw strong beam of light in any desired direction, used in warfare for discovering hostile aircraft, observing movements of troops, passing ships, etc.; light from this; **search party**, party of persons going out to look for lost or concealed person or thing; **search warrant**, legally issued warrant to enter premises to search for suspected persons, stolen property, or other things kept or concealed in violation of law.

sea·son (sē'zon) *n.* 1. Each of the periods into which year is divided by Earth's changing position in regard to sun, with particular conditions of weather etc., esp. one of the four equal periods (spring, summer, autumn, winter) marked by passage of sun from equinox to solstice and from solstice to equinox; or each of two periods, rainy and dry, into which year is divided in tropical climates; time of year when a plant flourishes, blooms, etc., or when an animal pairs, breeds, is hunted, etc., or which is regularly devoted to a particular occupation etc., or when a particular place is most frequented by fashionable society. 2. Proper time, favorable opportunity; period of indefinite or various length; ~ **ticket**, ticket issued, usu. at reduced rates, permitting any number of journeys to be taken, performances attended, etc., within specified length of time. **season** *v.* 1. Bring into efficient or sound condition by habituation, exposure, special preparation, use, or lapse of time; inure, mature; become fit for use by being seasoned. 2. Make palatable or piquant by introduction of salt, condiments, wit, jests, etc.; give zest to, flavor; temper, moderate.

sea·son·a·ble (sē'zonabel) *adj.* Suitable to, of the kind usual at, the season; opportune, meeting the needs of the occasion. **sea'son·a·bly** *adv.* **sea'son·a·ble·ness** *n.*

sea·son·al (sē'zonal) *adj.* Occurring at a particular season; (of trades, workers, etc.) dependent on the seasons, employed only during a particular season. **sea'son·al·ly** *adv.* **sea'son·er** *n.*

sea·son·ing (sē'zonĭng) *n.* (esp.) Substance for seasoning food (see SEASON *v.* sense 2).

seat (sēt) *n.* 1. Manner of sitting, esp. on horse. 2. Place on which person sits; (right to) use of seat; right to sit as member esp. of legislature, court, etc.; authority or dignity symbolized by sitting on particular seat or throne; something made for sitting upon; part of chair etc. on which occupant sits; sitting part of body, buttocks; part of garment covering this; ~ **belt**, strap securing occupant to seat in aircraft, automobile, etc. 3. Site, location, temporary or permanent scene; country mansion, esp. with park or large grounds. **seat** *v.t.* 1. Cause to sit, place *oneself* in sitting posture. 2. Fit or provide with seats; (of room etc.) have seats for (specified number). 3. Mend seat of (chair, trousers, etc.). 4. Establish in position; fix in particular place.

-seater *n.* (in comb.) **single-**~, **two-**~, etc., automobile, airplane, etc., with seat(s) for one, two, etc.

seat·ing (sē'tĭng) *n.* (esp.) Seats; arrangement, provision, of seats.

SEATO, S.E.A.T.O. *abbrevs.*

*A Gipsy **seamstress** sits on the shafts of a caravan as she sews colorful decorations on to a garment. Some women earn money by sewing at home for clothing manufacturers.*

Picking grapes in a South Australian vineyard. In Australia and the U.S.A., there are many **seasonal** workers, who move from district to district, harvesting different crops according to season.

South East Asia Treaty Organization.

se·ba·ceous (sĭbā′sh*u*s) *adj.* Of tallow or fat, fatty; ~ **duct, gland,** etc., organ secreting or conveying fatty matter that lubricates hair and skin.

Se·bas·tian (sĭbăs′ch*a*n), **St.** (3rd c.). Roman soldier and Christian martyr, usu. represented as youth pierced by many arrows.

Se·bas·to·pol (sĭbăs′t*o*pōl) = SEVASTOPOL.

seb·or·rhe·a (sĕbo̤rē′*a*) *n.* Excessive discharge from the sebaceous glands. **seb·or·rhe′ic, seb·or·rhe′al** *adjs.*

SEC *abbrev.* Securities and Exchange Commission.

sec[1] (sĕk) *n.* (colloq.) SECOND *n.*

sec[2] (sĕk) *adj.* (of wine) Dry.

sec[3] (sĕk) *abbrev.* SECANT *n.* sense 1.

sec. *abbrev.* Secretary.

se·cant (sē′kănt, -k*a*nt) *adj.* (math.) Cutting, intersecting. ~ *n.* 1. (trig., function of angle in right-angled triangle) Ratio of side adjacent given acute angle to the hypotenuse (reciprocal of COSINE). 2. (geom.) Line cutting another, esp. straight line cutting curve at two or more points.

se·cede (sĭsēd′) *v.i.* (**-ced·ed, -ced·ing**). Withdraw formally from membership esp. of church or federation of states. **se·ced′er** *n.*

se·ces·sion (sĭsĕsh′*o*n) *n.* Act of seceding, body of seceders; **War of S**~, CIVIL WAR (1861–5), which arose from an attempt by 11 of the southern states to secede from the U.S. **se·ces′sion·al** *adj.* **se·ces′-sion·ism, se·ces′sion·ist** *ns.*

se·clude (sĭklo͞od′) *v.t.* (**-clud·-ed, -clud·ing**). Keep retired or away from company.

se·clu·sion (sĭklo͞o′zh*o*n) *n.* Secluding, being secluded; retirement, privacy, avoidance of company; secluded place.

sec·ond (sĕk′*o*nd) *adj.* Next after first in order of time, position, quality, etc.; next in rank, quality, degree, etc., *to*; other, another; (mus., of part) next below highest in concerted music; that performs such a part; ~ **base,** (baseball) base opposite home plate on diamond, touched second by runner; ~ **best,** (what is) next in quality, inferior, to the first; **come off** ~ **best,** be beaten (in argument etc.); ~ **class,** class next to first; (of postal matter) consisting of periodicals sent from publishing office; ~**-class** (*adj.*) inferior in quality, second-rate; (*adv.*) by the second class; **S**~ **Coming,** return of Christ in glory, esp. as preliminary to Last Judgment; ~ **cousin**: see COUSIN; **S**~ **Empire,** (Ger. hist.) see GERMANY; (Fr. hist.) that of Napoleon III (1852–70); ~ **fiddle,** secondary role or person playing such role; ~ **growth,** tree growth in area stripped of virgin forest; ~**-guess** (*v.*), know only by hindsight; predict (event) or correctly guess what another intends; **sec′ondhand,** not new, not original, previously worn, used, etc., by another; **second lieutenant,** U.S. Army, Marine, or Air Force officer of lowest commissioned rank; **second nature,** acquired tendency or habit that has become instinctive; **second person,** (gram.) form of verb or pronoun referring to person(s) addressed; **second-rate,** of inferior quality, value, etc.; **second-rater,** one of inferior quality; **Second Republic,** French Republic of 1848–52; **second sight,** faculty, claimed by, or attributed to, some persons, of seeing, as in a vision, future events; **second-story man,** (colloq.) burglar who enters by climbing to upper story; **second-string,** (colloq.) substitute player for position on football etc. team; lower in rank, significance, etc.; **second thoughts,** reconsideration, decision or opinion after reconsidering matter; **second wind,** breathing with less effort after exhaustion that occurs during initial stages of great effort; renewed energy for continuing any task. **second** *n.* 1. Second thing etc.; second person in race etc.; (person who takes) second class in examination. 2. (mus.) Next to highest part; interval of which the span involves only two alphabetical names of notes; harmonic combination of the two notes thus separated. 3. (pl.) Goods of quality inferior to best. 4. Supporter, helper, esp. person representing and supporting principal in boxing or duel. 5. Sixtieth part of minute of time or angular measurement; vaguely, a short time; ~ **hand,** hand or pointer in some watches and clocks recording seconds. 6. (in motor vehicle) Second gear. **second** *adv.* Second-class. ~ *v.t.* Supplement, support, back up; esp. support (motion, mover) in debate etc. as necessary preliminary to further discussion or adoption of motion. **sec′ond·ly** *adv.* **sec′ond·-er** *n.*

sec·ond·ar·y (sĕk′*o*ndĕrē) *adj.* Not in the first class in dignity, importance, etc., of minor importance, subordinate; subsidiary, auxiliary; not original or primary, derivative, belonging to a second stage or period; ~ **accent** (**stress**), accent weaker than primary accent;

*Found only in Africa, south of the Sahara, the **secretary bird** is conspicuous for its long legs and tail. Its name is derived from its backward sloping crest which was said to resemble a writer in earlier times who had his pens stuck behind his ear. The birds are about 18 ins. tall.*

~ **color**: see COLOR; ~ **education**, education between primary or elementary and higher or university education; ~ **feather**, feather growing from second joint of bird's wing; ~ **school**, school giving secondary education; ~ **sex characteristic**, any physical characteristic distinctive of one sex but not directly related to reproduction. **sec′ond·ar·i·ly** *adv.* **sec′ond·ar·y** *n.* (pl. **-ar·ies**). Secondary feather; **S** ~, (geol.) Secondary period.

sec·ond·ly (sĕk′ondlē) *adv.* In the second place.

se·cre·cy (sē′kresē) *n.* (pl. **-cies**). Being secret.

se·cret (sē′krĭt) *adj.* Hidden, concealed, not (to be) made known; known only to the initiated; not given to revealing secrets; ~ **agent**, spy; ~ **ballot**, ballot in which voters' choices are not made public; ~ **police**, political police of a totalitarian state; ~ **service**, government department that secures information etc. without public disclosure; **S** ~ **Service**, arm of U.S. Treasury Department responsible for suppression of counterfeiters and guarding the President and his family. **se′cret·ly** *adv.* **secret** *n.* Thing (to be) kept secret; thing known only to initiated or to a limited number; mystery; **in** ~, secretly.

sec·re·tar·i·at (sĕkrĭtār′ēat) *n.* Office of secretary; members of government administrative office collectively; (premises of) administrative office or department headed by secretary-general.

sec·re·tar·y (sĕk′rĭtĕrē; *Brit.* sĕk′rĭtrē) *n.* (pl. **-tar·ies**). 1. Person employed by another to assist him in correspondence, literary work, and other confidential matters; official appointed by society, company, etc., to keep its records, conduct correspondence, etc. 2. Principal assistant of government minister or ambassador etc.; ~**-general**, (pl. **-tar·ies-general**), principal administrative officer of organization; ~ **of state**, U.S. Cabinet member who administers State Department and is responsible for conduct of nation's foreign policy. 3. Writing desk, escritoire. 4. ~ **bird**, long-legged long-tailed raptorial African bird (*Sagittarius serpentarius*), with crest of long feathers (thought to resemble pens stuck behind the ear). **sec·re·tar·i·al** (sĕkrĭtĕr′ēal) *adj.* **sec′re·tar·y·ship** *n.*

se·crete (sĭkrēt′) *v.t.* (**-cret·ed, -cret·ing**). 1. Put into place of concealment. 2. Produce by secretion. **se·cre′to·ry** *adj.*

se·cre·tion (sĭkrē′shon) *n.* 1. Concealing, concealment. 2. Action of gland etc. in extracting and elaborating certain substances from blood, sap, etc., to fulfill function within body or be excreted; any substance (as saliva, urine, resin) produced by such process.

se·cre·tive (sē′krĭtĭv, sĭkrē′-) *adj.* Given to making secrets, uncommunicative, needlessly reserved. **se′cre·tive·ly** *adv.* **se′cre·tive·ness** *n.*

sect (sĕkt) *n.* Body of persons agreed upon religious doctrines usu. different from those of an established or orthodox church; party or faction in a religious body; religious denomination; school of opinion in philosophy, politics, etc. **sec·tar·i·an** (sĕktār′ēan) *adj.* & *n.* **sec·tar′i·an·ism** *n.*

sect. *abbrev.* Section.

sec·tion (sĕk′shon) *n.* 1. Cutting (rare exc. in ref. to surgery etc.). 2. Part cut off from something; one of the parts into which something is divided; one of the minor subdivisions of a book etc. (usu. indicated by ~ **mark**, §, as § 15); (mil.) subdivision of platoon; part of community having separate interests or characteristics; thin slice of something cut off for microscopic examination; area of 1 sq. mi., $\frac{1}{36}$ of a township; part of sleeping car containing two berths. 3. Cutting of solid by plane, (area of) figure resulting from this; representation of internal structure of something supposed to be cut thus; **conic** ~**s**, (math.) study of curves of intersection produced by allowing plane to cut cone at various angles. 4. Section mark (see sense 2) used as mark of reference or to indicate beginning of section. **sec′tion·al** *adj.* **sec′tion·al·ly** *adv.* **section** *v.t.* Arrange in, divide into, sections.

sec·tor (sĕk′ter) *n.* 1. Plane figure contained by two radii and the arc of a circle, ellipse, etc.; anything having this shape; ~ **of a sphere**, solid generated by revolution of plane sector about one of its radii. 2. Mathematical instrument, now consisting of two flat rules inscribed with various scales and stiffly hinged together, for mechanical solution of various problems; astronomical instrument, telescope turning about center of graduated arc, for measuring angles. 3. (mil.) Subdivision of defensive position or system under one commander; territory for which one group, e.g. of air-raid wardens, is responsible.

sec·u·lar (sĕk′yuler) *adj.* 1. Occurring once in, lasting for, an age or a century; lasting or going on for ages or an indefinitely long time. 2. Concerned with the affairs of this world, worldly; not sacred;

not monastic or ecclesiastical, temporal, profane, lay; skeptical of religious truth or opposed to religious education; ~ **clergy, priests**, those not belonging to monastic orders (opp. *regular*). **sec'u·lar·ly** *adv.* **sec'u·lar·ism** *n.* **sec'u·lar·ist** *n.* & *adj.* **sec'u·lar·ize** *v.t.* (**-ized, -iz·ing**). **sec·u·lar·i·za·tion** (sĕkyulerīzā'shon) *n.* **sec·u·lar·i·ty** (sĕkyulăr'ĭtē) *n.* (pl. **-ties**). **secular** *n.* Secular priest. **sec'u·lar·i·zer** *n.*

se·cure (sĭkūr') *adj.* 1. Untroubled by danger or apprehension; safe against attack, impregnable. 2. Reliable, certain not to fail or give way; (usu. pred.) in safe keeping, firmly fastened. 3. Having sure prospect *of*; safe *against, from*. **se·cure'ly** *adv.* **secure** *v.t.* (**-cured, -cur·ing**). 1. Fortify. 2. Confine, enclose, fasten, close, securely. 3. Guarantee, make safe against loss. 4. Succeed in getting, obtain. **se·cure'ness, se·cur'er** *ns.*

se·cu·ri·ty (sĭkūr'ĭtē) *n.* (pl. **-ties**). (esp.) 1. Thing deposited or given as pledge for fulfillment of undertaking or payment of loan; document as evidence of loan; (usu. pl.) certificate of stock, bond, etc. 2. Precautions against theft, espionage, etc. 3. **S ~ Council**, council of the General Assembly of the United Nations, consisting of 15 members of which five (People's Republic of China, France, U.K., U.S., U.S.S.R.) are permanent and the remainder elected, charged with the duty of dealing with disputes between nations that threaten the peace of the world.

se·dan (sĭdăn') *n.* 1. (also ~ **chair**) 17th–18th c. portable covered chair for one person, usu. carried on poles by two men. 2. Automobile with enclosed body for four or more persons including driver.

se·date (sĭdāt') *adj.* Tranquil, equable, composed, settled; not impulsive or lively. **se·date'ly** *adv.* **se·date'ness** *n.* **sedate** *v.t.* (**-dat·ed, -dat·ing**). Put (person) under sedation.

se·da·tion (sĭdā'shon) *n.* (med.) Treatment by sedatives.

sed·a·tive (sĕd'atĭv) *adj.* & *n.* (Drug etc.) tending to soothe.

sed·en·tar·y (sĕd'entĕrē) *adj.* Sitting; (of occupation etc.) requiring continuance in sitting posture; (of persons) accustomed or addicted to sitting still, engaged in sedentary occupation; (zool.) permanently attached; (of spiders) lying in wait until prey is in web.

The spider maintains a ***sedentary*** *position in the web waiting for its prey to become entangled in the sticky substance that prevents escape. When the prey is secured, the spider will advance.*

sed'en·tar·i·ly *adv.* **sed'en·tar·i·ness** *n.*

Se·der (sā'der) *n.* (pl. **Se·ders**, Heb. **Si·dar·im** pr. sĭdār'ĭm). Ritual for the first night or first two nights of Passover.

sedge (sĕj) *n.* Grasslike plant of genus *Carex*, growing in marshes or by waterside; bed of such plants. **sedg'y** *adj.* (**sedg·i·er, sedg·i·est**).

sed·i·ment (sĕd'ĭment) *n.* Matter that settles to bottom of liquid, lees, dregs; (geol.) waterborne or windborne matter that settles and may become consolidated into rock. **sed·i·men·ta·ry** (sĕdimĕn'terē) *adj.* **sed·i·men·ta·tion** (sĕdimentā'shon) *n.*

se·di·tion (sĭdĭsh'on) *n.* Conduct or language directed unlawfully against state authority; public commotion, riot, not amounting to insurrection or rebellion and therefore not treason. **se·di·tious** (sĭdĭsh'us) *adj.* **se·di'tious·ly** *adv.* **se·di'tious·ness** *n.*

se·duce (sĭdo͞os', -dūs') *v.t.* (**-duced, -duc·ing**). Lead astray, tempt into sin or crime; persuade (esp. someone young or innocent) to have sexual intercourse with one. **se·duc'er**, fem. **se·duc·tress** (sĭdŭk'trĭs) *ns.*

se·duc·tion (sĭdŭk'shon) *n.* Seducing, being seduced; thing that seduces.

se·duc·tive (sĭdŭk'tĭv) *adj.* (esp.) Alluring, enticing, winning. **se·duc'tive·ly** *adv.* **se·duc'tive·ness** *n.*

sed·u·lous (sĕj'ulus) *adj.* Diligent, persevering, assiduous, painstaking. **sed'u·lous·ly** *adv.* **sed'u·lous·ness, se·du·li·ty** (sĭdo͞o'lĭtē, -dū'-) *ns.*

se·dum (sē'dum) *n.* Fleshy-leaved plant of genus *S* ~, cultivated for its foliage and pink, white, or yellow flowers.

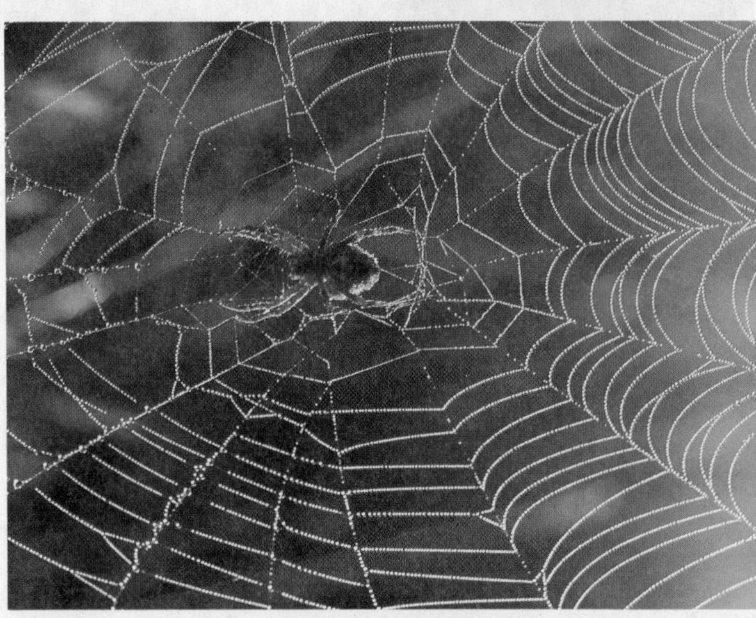

see[1] (sē) *v.* (**saw** pr. saw, **seen, see·ing**). Have the faculty of discerning objects with the eyes, exercise this faculty; perceive mentally; learn by reading; look at, visit; admit as visitor; ascertain by inspection, experiment, consideration, etc.; supervise; escort *home, to the door*, etc.; consider, judge; know by observation, experience; imagine; ~ **about**, attend to; take into consideration; ~ **after**, take care of; **Seeing Eye dog**, (named after Seeing Eye, Inc., of N.J.) guide dog; **see red**, (fig.) be enraged; **see stars**, have dancing lights before eyes from blow on head; **see the light**, (fig.) undergo conversion etc.; realize one's errors etc.; **see things**, suffer from hallucinations; **see through**, (esp.,

Despite its grass-like appearance, ***sedge*** *is a herb, widespread in Asia, Europe and North America. It was often cut for use as straw. Many species have both male and female flowers.*

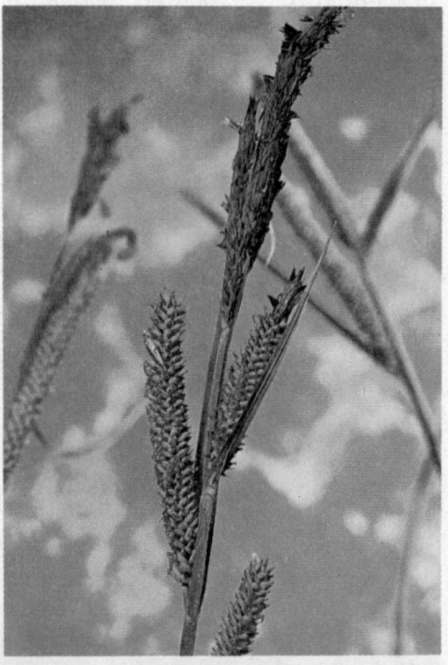

fig.) penetrate, see real character of through disguise or false appearance; continue to watch or take care of until the end, or until difficulties are overcome; **see'through** (*adj.*), (esp. of clothing) transparent; **see to**, attend to; take special care about. **see'a·ble** *adj.*

see[2] (sē) *n.* Office, position, jurisdiction, of a bishop; **Apostolic, Holy, Papal,** or **Roman S~**, office, jurisdiction, authority, of pope.

seed (sēd) *n.* (pl. **seeds**, collect. **seed**). 1. (One of) grains or ovules of plants, esp. as used for sowing; seedlike fruit, any other part of plant (as bulb) used for propagating new crop; **go, run, to ~**, cease flowering as seed develops; (fig.) become shabby, worn out, etc. 2. (bot.) Fertilized and ripened ovule of flowering plant, containing embryo capable of developing by germination. 3. Sperm, semen, milt; germ or latent beginning *of* (idea etc.). 4. (bibl.) Progeny, descendants. 5. Seeded player. 6. **seed'cake**, cake flavored with caraway seeds; **seed corn**, grain preserved to sow for new crop; **seed money**, money used to launch a project; **seed pearl**, very small pearl; **seeds'man** (pl. **-men**), sower, dealer, in seeds; **seed'time**, sowing season; **seed vessel**, pericarp. **seed'less** *adj.* Having no seeds. **seed** *v.* Go to seed, produce or let fall seed; sprinkle (as) with seed; remove seeds from; disperse chemical material in (cloud) to make rain; (sport, esp. tennis) sort (competitors in tournament) so that the best players do not meet in the early rounds; hence **seeded player**, one so selected.

seed·ling (sēd'lĭng) *n.* Young plant raised from seed.

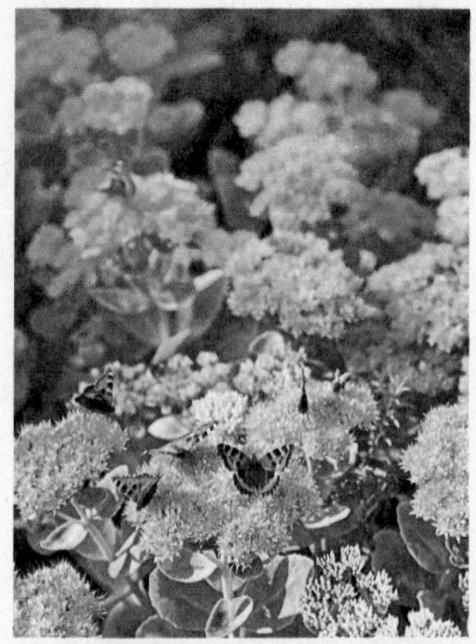

*A succulent plant native to arid areas in various parts of the world, **sedum** from various places has been acclimatized in the U.S.A. and other temperate zones so that its flowers may be grown.*

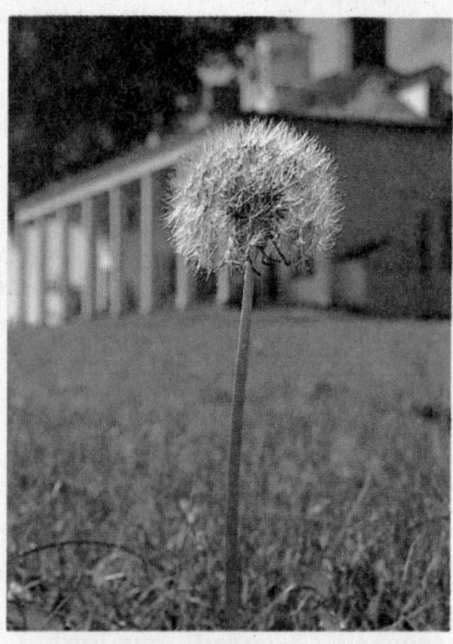

*Dandelion 'clock' on the lawn at Mt. Vernon, the estate of George Washington. The clock, which is made up of many **seeds**, is named for the children's game of blowing it to tell the time.*

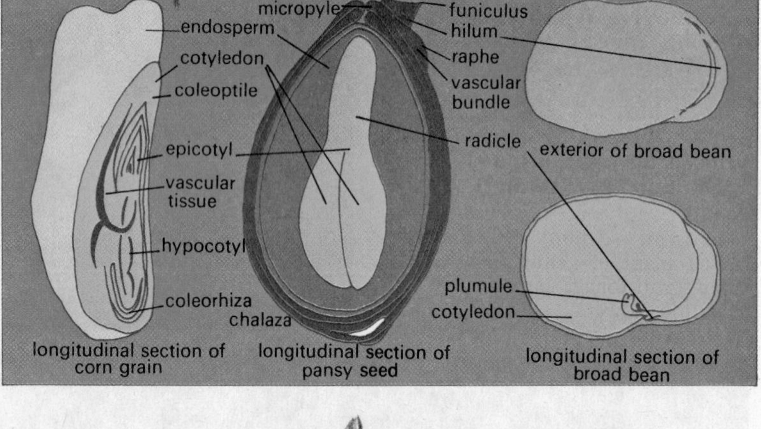

*Development of a **seed** into a **seedling** is a process which is similar in most plants, from microscopic spores to giant coconuts. The endosperm serves as a store of food for the embryo but on beans, for example, more food is obtained from the cotyledons.*

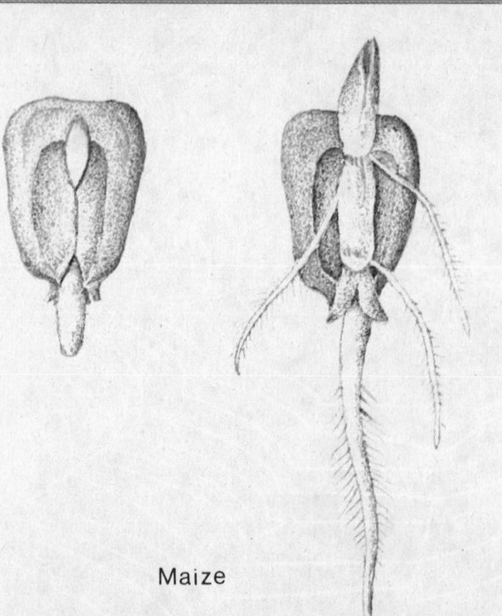

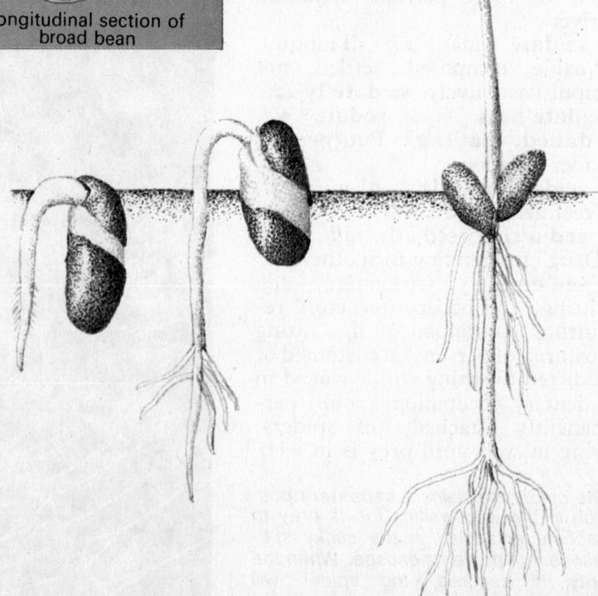

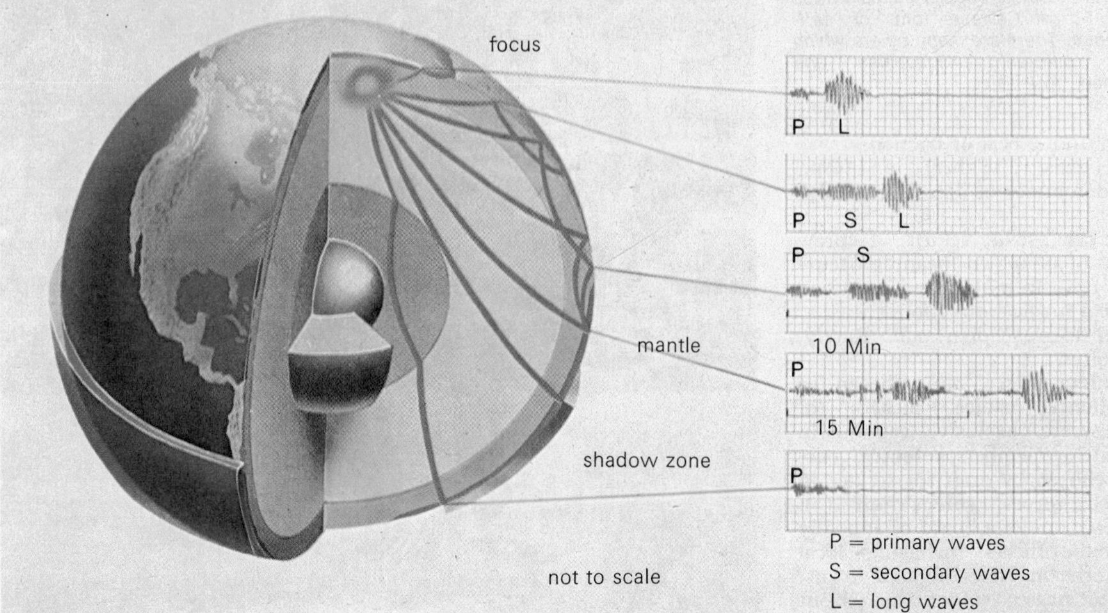

*To locate the position and assess the strength of an earthquake, a single **seismograph** is insufficient. Several are needed, each recording earth movements in horizontal and vertical directions, for triangular plotting.*

seed·y (sē′dē) *adj.* (**seed·i·er, seed·i·est**). 1. Full of seed. 2. Shabby, ill-looking; unwell, out of sorts. **seed′i·ly** *adv.* **seed′i·ness** *n.*

see·ing (sē′ĭng) *conj.* Considering the fact *that*; since, because.

seek (sēk) *v.* (**sought**, pr. sawt, **seek·ing**). Go in search of, look for; try to obtain or bring about, *to* do; ask for, request; make search. **seek′er** *n.*

seem (sēm) *v.i.* Have the appearance of, be apparently; appear *to be* or *do*; appear to exist; appear to be true or the fact. **seem′ing** *adj.* Apparent; apparent only. **seem′ing·ly** *adv.* **seem′ing·ness** *n.*

seem·ly (sēm′lē) *adj.* (**-li·er, -li·est**). Decent, decorous, becoming. **seem′li·ness** *n.*

seen (sēn): see SEE[1].

seep (sēp) *v.i.* Ooze, percolate. **seep′age** *n.*

seer (sēr, sē′*er*) *n.* Visionary, prophet, one gifted with second sight.

seer·suck·er (sēr′sŭk*er*) *n.* Thin linen, cotton, or other fabric with puckered surface, freq. striped, orig. of Indian manufacture. [Pers. *shīr o shakkar* milk and sugar]

see·saw (sē′saw) *adj.* & *adv.* With backward-and-forward or up-and-down motion. ~ *n.* Game in which two persons sit at each end of a long board balanced on a central support and move each other up and down alternately; board thus used (freq. fig.). ~ *v.i.* Play at seesaw; move up and down as in game of seesaw; vacillate.

seethe (sēdh) *v.* (**seethed, seeth·ing**). Cook by boiling (archaic); (fig.) boil, bubble, be agitated. **seeth′ing·ly** *adv.*

seg·ment (sĕg′ment) *n.* 1. (geom.) Plane figure contained by chord and arc of circle; finite part of line between two points; ~ **of a sphere**, part cut off by plane; (phys.) each of parts into which length of vibrating string etc. is divided by nodes. 2. Division, section, of something, esp. each of longitudinal divisions of body of some animals. 3. Segmental arch. **segment** (sĕgmĕnt′) *v.* Divide into segments; (of cell) undergo cleavage or divide into many cells. **seg·men·tal** (sĕgmĕn′t*al*) *adj.* (esp. of arch, pediment, etc.) Having form of segment of circle. **seg·men·tar·y** (sĕg′mentĕrē) *adj.* **seg·men·ta·tion** (sĕgmentā′sh*on*) *n.*

se·go (sē′gō) **lily.** N. Amer. plant (*Calochortus nuttallii*) with green and white trumpet-shaped flowers.

seg·re·gate (sĕg′r*e*gāt) *v.* (**-gat·ed, -gat·ing**). Set apart, isolate; subject (people) to racial segregation; enforce racial segregation in (community, institution, etc.); separate from general mass and collect together, as in crystallization or solidification; (biol., of Mendelian hybrids) separate into dominants, recessives, and hybrids, in conformity with numerical law. **seg·re·ga·tion** (sĕgr*e*gā′sh*on*) *n.* (esp.) Enforced separation of different racial groups in a country, community, or institution. **seg·re·ga′tion·ist** *n.* **seg′re·gat·ed** *adj.* Isolated, set apart (rare); (zool., bot., etc.) separated from the parent or from one another, not aggregated. ~ (sĕg′r*e*gĭt, -gāt) *n.* (zool., bot.) Species separated from aggregate species; (biol.) segregated individual.

sei·gneur (sānyēr′; *Fr.* sĕnyör′) *n.* (pl. **sei·gneurs** pr. sānyērz′; *Fr.* sĕnyör′). Feudal lord, lord of manor (formerly in France and Canada and still in Channel Islands). **sei·gneur·i·al** (sānyēr′ēal) *adj.*

Seine (sān; *Fr.* sĕn). River of N. France flowing 482 mi. (776 km) through Paris NW. to the English Channel near Le Havre.

seine (sān) *n.* (also ~ **net**) Fishing net hanging vertically in water, with ends being drawn together to enclose fish. **seine** *v.* (**seined, sein·ing**). Catch, catch fish, with seine; use seine in.

seis·mic (sīz′mĭk, sīs′-), **seis·mal** (sīz′m*al*, sīs′-), **seis·mi·cal** sīz′mĭk*al*, sīs′-) *adjs.* Of earthquakes. **seis′mi·cal·ly** *adv.* **seis·mic·i·ty** (sīzmĭs′ĭtē, sīs-) *n.* (pl. **-ties**).

seis·mo·graph (sīz′m*o*grăf, -grahf, sīs′-) *n.* Instrument for recording tremors of earthquakes. **seis·mog·ra·phy** (sīzmŏg′r*a*fē, sīs-), **seis·mol·o·gy** (sīzmŏl′*o*jē, sīs-) *ns.* Scientific study of earthquakes. **seis·mog′ra·pher** *n.* **seis·mo·graph·ic** (sīzm*o*grăf′ĭk, sīs-), **seis·mo·log·i·cal** (sīzm*o*lŏj′ĭk*al*, sīs-) *adjs.* **seis·mol′o·gist** *n.*

seize (sēz) *v.* (**seized, seiz·ing**). 1. (law) Put in possession *of*; take possession of, confiscate, by warrant or legal right, impound, attach. 2. Lay hold of forcibly or suddenly, snatch; grasp with hand or mind, comprehend quickly or clearly; lay hold eagerly *upon.* 3. (naut.) Lash, fasten with several turns of cord. 4. ~ (**up**), (of bearings or other moving part of machinery) become stuck, jam,

One of the most popular martial arts is Kung-Fu a Chinese form of ***self-defense.*** *There are many others which offer different philosophies and methods to initiates.*

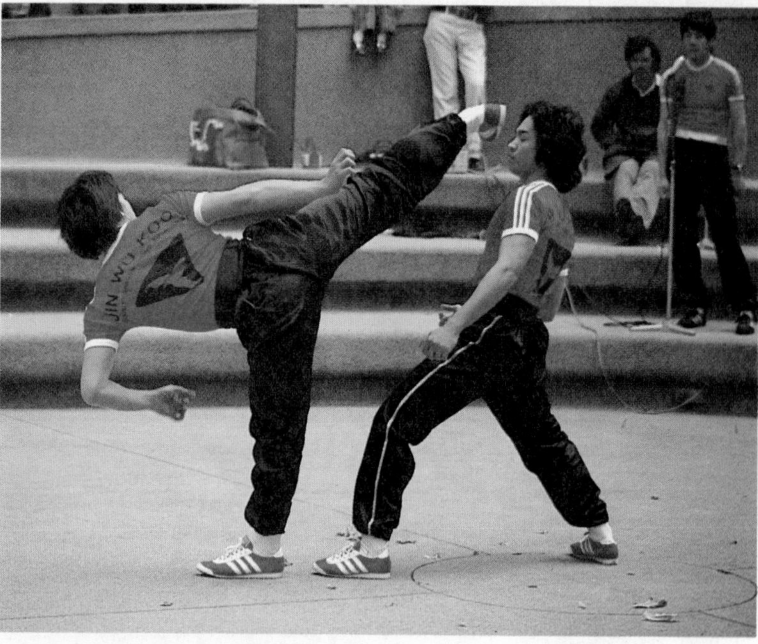

from undue heat or friction.

sei·zure (sē'zh*er*) *n.* (esp.) Sudden attack of illness or paralysis.

se·lah (sē'l*a*, sĕl'*a*). Hebrew word of unknown meaning occurring freq. in psalms and supposed to be a musical direction.

sel·dom (sĕl'd*o*m) *adv.* Rarely, not often.

se·lect (sĭlĕkt') *adj.* Chosen for excellence, choice, picked; (of society etc.) exclusive, cautious in admitting members; **selectee'**, person chosen by draft for service in armed forces; **select'man** (pl. **-men**), one of a board of annually elected officers managing local concerns in New England towns. **se·lect'ness** *n.* **select** *v.t.* Pick out as best or most suitable. **se·lec·tion** (sĭlĕk'sh*o*n) *n.* Selecting, choice; what is selected; (biol.) sorting out in various ways of the types of animal or plant better fitted to survive, regarded as a factor in evolution. **se·lec'tive** *adj.* Using selection; characterized by selecting; (electr.) able to receive a desired frequency to the exclusion of others; ~ **service**, service in armed forces under conscription. **se·lec'tive·ly** *adv.* **se·lec·tiv·i·ty** (sĭlĕktĭv'ĭtē) *n.*

Se·le·ne (sĭlē'nē). (Gk. myth.) Goddess of the moon, in later myths identified with Artemis.

se·le·nic (sĭlē'nĭk, -lĕn'ĭk) *adj.* ~ **acid**, acid (H_2SeO_4), crystalline when pure, resembling sulfuric acid in many of its characteristics.

se·le·ni·ous (sĭlē'nē*u*s) *adj.* ~ **acid**, colorless crystalline acid (H_2SeO_3).

sel·e·nite (sĕl'*e*nīt) *n.* 1. (min.) Calcium sulfate ($CaSO_42H_2O$), gypsum, in crystalline or foliated form; slip of this used to polarize light. 2. (chem.) Salt of selenious acid. **sel·e·nit·ic** (sĕl*e*nĭt'ĭk), **sel·e·nit'i·cal** *adjs.*

se·le·ni·um (sĭlē'nē*u*m) *n.* (chem.) Nonmetallic element, chemically resembling sulfur and tellurium, having the property that its conductivity of electricity increases with intensity of light falling on it and hence used in various photoelectric devices; symbol Se, at. no. 34, at. wt. 78.96; ~ **cell**, piece of selenium to which electrical connections are made, used as a photoelectric device etc. [Gk. *selēnē* moon; named f. its association in nature with *tellurium*]

sel·e·nog·ra·phy (sĕl*e*nŏg'r*a*fē) *n.* Science dealing with the physical geography of the moon, mapping the moon's surface.

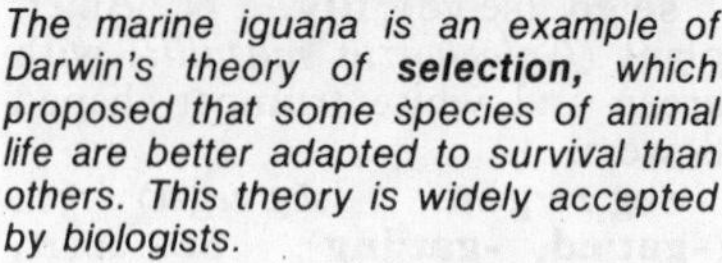

The marine iguana is an example of Darwin's theory of ***selection,*** *which proposed that some species of animal life are better adapted to survival than others. This theory is widely accepted by biologists.*

sel·e·nol·o·gy (sĕl*e*nŏl'*o*jē) *n.* Science of the moon.

self (sĕlf) *n.* (pl. **selves** pr. sĕlvz). Person's or thing's own individuality or essence, person or thing as object of introspection or reflexive action; one's own interests or pleasure, concentration on these. ~ *adj.* Uniform, the same throughout.

self- *prefix.* Combining form of SELF; **~-abuse**, blame or reproach of oneself; masturbation; **~-acting**, acting automatically; **~-addressed**, addressed for return to sender; **~-assertion**, insistence on one's own rights, claims, individu-

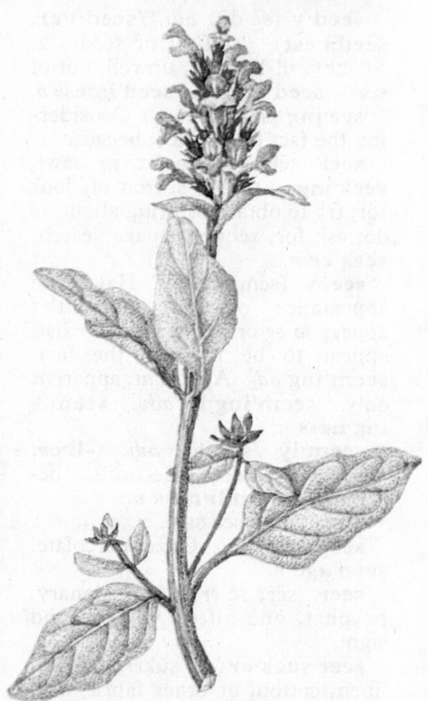

Widespread in Europe, Asia and North America, Prunella vulgaris became known as ***self-heal*** *because of the claims that tea made from its leaves would cure a multitude of sicknesses.*

ality, etc.; self-confidence; **~-centered**, centered in oneself, itself, engrossed in self, preoccupied with one's own personality or affairs; **~-command**, self-control; **~-complacency**, complacency; **~-complacent** (*adj.*); **~-confidence**, confidence in oneself; **~-confident** (*adj.*); **~-conscious**, having consciousness of one's identity, actions, sensations, etc.; unduly or morbidly preoccupied with oneself; **~-consciously** (*adv.*), **~-consciousness** (*n.*); **~-contained,** complete in itself; (of person) uncommunicative; **~-control,** control of oneself, one's desires, emotions, etc. **~-defense,** (esp.) in phr. **in ~-defense,** not by way of aggression; (**noble**) **art of ~-defense,** boxing; **~-denial** (*n.*), **~-denying** (*adj.*) sacrificing one's personal desires; **~-determination,** (esp.) a people's decision of its political status, as form of government, independence, etc.; **~-effacing,** keeping oneself inconspicuous; retiring; **~-employed,** running own business etc.; **~-esteem,** favorable opinion of oneself; **~-evident,** not needing demonstration, axiomatic; **~-governing,** (esp., of colony, territory, etc.) governing itself; **~-government** (*n.*); **self'heal,** any of various plants credited with great healing properties, esp. *Prunella vulgaris*, a blue-flowered mint of Europe and Asia; **self-help,** providing for oneself without assistance from others; **self-important,** having an exaggerated idea of one's own importance; **self-importantly** (*adv.*); **self-importance** (*n.*); **self-indulgence,** indulgence of one's own desires for ease, pleasure, etc.; **self-indulgent** (*adj.*), **self-indulgently** (*adv.*); **self-interest,** what one conceives to be for one's own interests; **self-interested** (*adj.*); **self-love,** selfishness, self-centeredness; **self-made,** made by one's own action or efforts; **self-made man,** one who has risen from obscurity or poverty by his own exertions; **self-opinionated,** obstinately adhering to one's own opinion; **self-portrait,** artist's portrait of himself; **self-possessed,** cool, composed, in command of one's faculties or feelings; **self-possession** (*n.*); **self-preservation** (*n.*), (esp.) natural instinct impelling living creatures to go on living and avoid injury; **self-reliance,** reliance on one's own powers etc.; **self-reliant** (*adj.*); **self-respect** (*n.*) proper regard for one's dignity, standard of conduct etc.; **self-righteous,** righteous in one's own esteem, smug; **self-rising,** (*adj.*), (of flour) not needing addition of baking powder etc.; **self-sacrifice,** subordinating private interest and desires to those of others; **self'same** (*adj.*), (the) very same; **self-satisfaction,** conceit; **self-sealing,** having a device for filling up a hole in a structure caused by shot etc.; **self-seeking** (*adj.* & *n.*), seeking one's own advantage only; **self-service,** arrangement of store, restaurant, etc., whereby customers help themselves and pay cashier afterward (also attrib. of store etc.); **self-sown,** grown from chance-dropped seed; **self-starter,** device for starting internal combustion engine without use of crank or auxiliary starting engine; person who needs no outside stimulus to work; **self-styled,** having taken name or description on one's own initiative; **self-sufficient,** requiring nothing from outside, independent; sufficient in one's own opinion; **self-sufficiency** (*n.*); **self-will,** obstinate pursuing of one's own desires or opinions; **self-willed** (*adj.*); **self-winding,** (of clock etc.) with automatic winding mechanism. **self'less** *adj.* Oblivious of self, incapable of selfishness. **self'less·ness** *n.*

self·ish (sĕl'fĭsh) *adj.* Deficient in consideration for others, regarding chiefly personal profit or pleasure; actuated by, appealing to, self-interest. **self'ish·ly** *adv.* **self'ish·ness** *n.*

Sel·kirk (sĕl'kĕrk), **Alexander** (1676–1721). Scottish sailor; at his own request he was put ashore on the uninhabited island of Juan Fernandez, where he remained 1704–9; the original of *Robinson Crusoe*.

sell (sĕl) *v.* (**sold** pr. sōld, **sell·ing**). 1. Make over, dispose of, in exchange for money; keep stock of for sale, deal in; betray for money or other reward; promote sales (of); gain acceptance of, advertise or publish merits of; (of goods) be sold at a specific price; find purchaser(s); **~ off,** sell remainder of (goods), clear out stock, at reduced prices; **~ one's life dear**(**ly**), (fig.) do great injury before being killed; **~ out,** (hist.) leave army by selling commission; sell (one's shares in company, whole stock in trade, etc.); (colloq.) turn traitor, betray. 2. (slang) Trick, take in. **sell'er** *n.* One who sells; **~'s market,** market in which supplies are short and prices high. **sell'ing** *n.* **sell** *n.* (slang) Hoax, swindle; disappoint-

In markets all over the world, there can be found people who specialize in ***selling.*** *This vendor of olives and other Mediterranean food is in Sydney, Australia.*

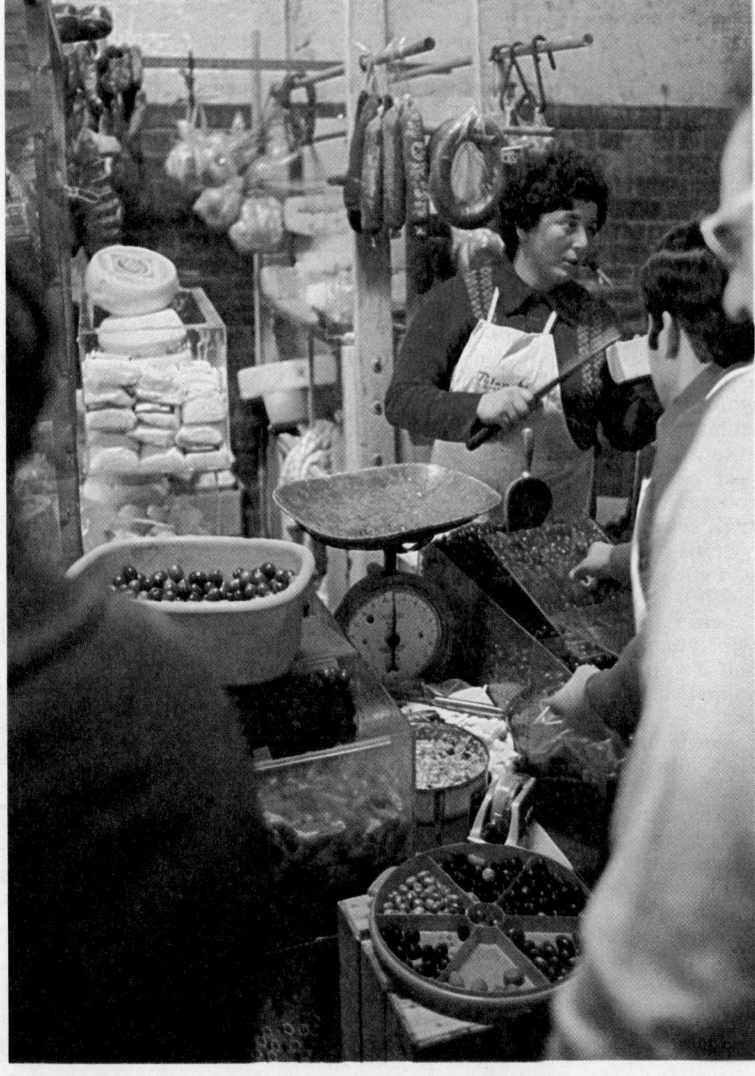

ment; **sell'out,** betrayal; selling of all copies, seats, etc., commercial success.

Selt·zer (sĕlt'ser) *n.* (also ~ **water**) Effervescent mineral water from Nieder-Selters, near Wiesbaden, Germany; (freq. **s** ~) similar artificial mineral water.

sel·vage, sel·vedge (sĕl'vĭj) *ns.* Edge of piece of material so woven that weft will not unravel; edge plate of lock with opening for bolt. **sel'vaged** *adj.*

selves: see SELF.

Sem (sem): SHEM.

se·man·tic (sĭmăn'tĭk) *adj.* Of meaning. **se·man'tics** *n.pl.* (usu. w. sing. verb) Branch of philology concerned with meanings. **se·man·ti·cist** (sĭmăn'tĭsĭst) *n.*

sem·a·phore (sĕm'afōr, -fōr) *n.* Signaling apparatus of post with one or more movable arms; signal(ing) by person holding flag in each hand. **sem·a·phor·ic** (sĕmafōr'ĭk, -făr'-) *adj.* **sem·a·phor'i·cal·ly** *adv.* **semaphore** *v.* (**-phored, -phor·ing**). Signal, send, by semaphore.

sem·blance (sĕm'blans) *n.* Outward appearance; likeness, image, *of*; resemblance.

se·mei·ol·o·gy, se·mi·ol·o·gy (sēmīŏl'ojē), **se·mei·ot·ics, se·mi·ot·ics** (sēmīŏt'ĭks) *ns.* Study of signs or sign language; (med.) study of symptoms of disease. **se·mei·ot'ic, se·mi·ot'ic, se·mei·ot'i·cal, se·mi·ot'i·cal** *adjs.*

Sem·e·le (sĕm'elē). (Gk. myth.) Daughter of Cadmus and Harmonia and mother, by Zeus, of Dionysus; she entreated Zeus to come to her in his full majesty and was destroyed by his lightning.

se·men (sē'men, -mĕn) *n.* Seed, esp. of flowering plants; viscous whitish fluid secreted by male animal, containing spermatozoa.

se·mes·ter (sĭmĕs'ter) *n.* Half-year course or term in schools, colleges, and universities. **se·mes'tral, se·mes'tri·al** *adjs.*

semi- *prefix.* Half-, partly-, to some extent; partial(ly), imperfect(ly).

sem·i·an·nu·al (sĕmēăn'ūal, sĕmī-) *adj.* Half-yearly; lasting half a year (only). ~ *n.* Semi-annual plant. **sem·i·an'nu·al·ly** *adv.*

sem·i·cir·cle (sĕm'ĭserkel) *n.* Half of circle divided by its diameter, or half its circumference; anything in this shape. **sem·i·cir·cu·lar** (sĕmĭser'kyuler) *adj.* ~ **canal,** any of the three curving fluid-filled channels in ear giving information to the brain to help maintain balance.

sem·i·co·lon (sĕm'ĭkōlon) *n.* Punctuation mark (;), indicating a more marked separation than the comma, and less than a period.

sem·i·con·duc·tor (sĕmēkondŭk'ter, sĕmī-) *n.* Electrical conductor with resistance less than that of insulator but greater than that of metal etc.

sem·i·cyl·in·der (sĕmēsĭl'ĭnder, sĕmī-) *n.* Half of cylinder cut longitudinally. **sem·i·cy·lin·dri·cal** (sĕmēsĭlĭn'drĭkal, sĕmī-), **sem·i·cy·lin'dric** *adjs.*

sem·i·de·tached (sĕmēdĭtăcht', sĕmī-) *adj.* (of house) Joined to another by common wall on one side only.

sem·i·fi·nal (sĕmēfī'nal, sĕmī-) *adj.* & *n.* (Match, round) preceding final.

sem·i·flu·id (sĕmēfloo'ĭd, sĕmī-) *adj.* & *n.* (Substance) of consistency halfway between fluid and solid.

sem·i·lu·nar (sĕmēloo'ner, sĕmī-) *adj.* Half-moon-shaped, crescent.

sem·i·nal (sĕm'inal) *adj.* Of seed, semen, or reproduction; germinal, reproductive, propagative; providing a source of future development; ~ **fluid,** semen. **sem'i·nal·ly** *adv.*

sem·i·nar (sĕm'inăr) *n.* (Meeting of) group of advanced students pursuing special study; meeting for discussion.

sem·i·nar·y (sĕm'inĕrē) *n.* (pl. **-nar·ies**). 1. Training college for ministers, priests, rabbis, etc. 2. (archaic) School, esp. institution for higher education of young women. **sem·i·nar·i·an** (sĕminăr'ēan) *n.*

Sem·i·nole (sĕm'inōl) *adj.* & *n.* (pl. **-noles,** collect. **-nole**). (Member) of tribe of N. Amer. Indians, allied to Creeks, formerly and still partly resident in Florida.

sem·i·of·fi·cial (sĕmēofĭsh'al, sĕmī-) *adj.* Having some degree of official authority. **sem·i·of·fi'cial·ly** *adv.*

Possibly derived from smoke signals ***semaphore*** *was first put to practical use, in France during the Napoleonic wars, to communicate accurate messages at distances.*

Botanically, the term ***semi-annual*** *is meaningless, but is usually applied to plants like the pansy which may be either annuals or biennials, depending on the variety, or where they are grown.*

se·mi·ol·o·gy (sēmīŏl'ojē), **se·mi·ot·ics** (sēmīŏt'ĭks): see SEMEIOLOGY.

sem·i·per·me·a·ble (sĕmēpĕr'mēabel, sĕmī-) *adj.* Permeable to small molecules but not large molecules.

sem·i·pre·cious (sĕmēprĕsh'us, sĕmī-) *adj.* (of gems) Of less value than those called *precious* (as amethyst, jade, garnet, etc.).

sem·i·pri·vate (sĕmēprī'vĭt, sĕmī-) *adj.* Partly but not entirely private, as hospital room occupied by several but not many patients.

sem·i·qua·ver (sĕm'ēkwāver) *n.* (mus. chiefly Brit.) Note having $\frac{1}{16}$ the time value of a whole note (♬).

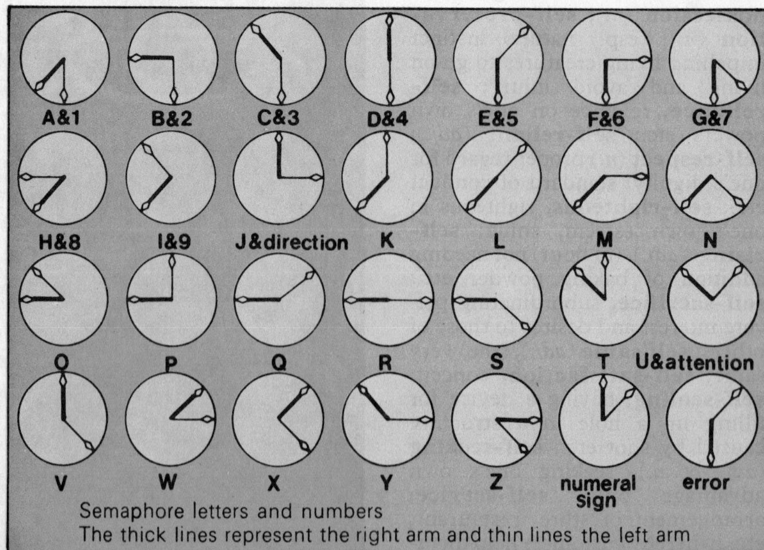

Semaphore letters and numbers
The thick lines represent the right arm and thin lines the left arm

Above: Student priests at a **seminary** at Kimmage Manor in Dublin. After ordination, they may serve their church in Ireland, or overseas, either as incumbents of a parish, or as missionaries.

Se·mir·a·mis (sĭmĭr′amĭs). Mythical queen of Assyria, of great beauty and wisdom, wife and successor of Ninus, reputed founder of Nineveh; she built many cities, including Babylon.

sem·i·skilled (sĕmēskĭld′, sĕmī-) *adj.* Having or requiring some training but less than skilled work(er).

Sem·ite (sĕm′īt) *n.* Member of any of the peoples supposed to be descended from SHEM (Gen. 10), including Jews, Arabs, Assyrians, Phoenicians, and other peoples of SW. Asia.

Se·mit·ic (sĭmĭt′ĭk) *adj.* 1. Of the group of languages now spoken chiefly in N. Africa and SW. Asia, including Hebrew, Aramaic, Arabic, ancient Assyrian, and Ethiopic. 2. Of the Semites. ~ *n.* 1. Semitic family of languages. 2. Semite.

Sem·i·tism (sĕm′ĭtĭzem; *Brit.* sĕ′mĭtĭzem) *n.* 1. Semitic characteristics; (esp.) Jewish ideas, influence, etc. 2. Semitic word or idiom.

sem·i·tone (sĕm′ētōn) *n.* (mus.) Interval of (approximately) half a tone.

sem·i·trail·er (sĕm′ētrāl*er*) *n.* Trailer having wheels at back but supported by towing vehicle in front.

sem·o·li·na (sĕmolē′*na*) *n.* Hard portions of durum wheat that resist action of millstones and are collected in form of rounded grains and used in puddings and in pasta.

sem·per fi·de·lis (sĕm′p*er* fĭdā′lĭs, -dē′-; *Lat.* sĕm′pĕr fĭdā′lĭs). Always faithful: U.S. Marine Corps motto. [L.]

sem·per pa·ra·tus (sĕm′p*er* parāt*us*; *Lat.* sĕm′pĕr pahrah′to͞os). Always prepared: U.S. Coast Guard motto. [L.]

Above: Agate and other **semi-precious** stones as they are found. Below center: A finely carved bowl of jade is typical of the objets d'art that these materials may be used for.

sem·pi·ter·nal (sĕmpĭtẽr′n*a*l) *adj.* (rhet.) Everlasting, eternal.

semp·stress: see SEAMSTRESS.

Sen., sen. *abbrevs.* Senate; senator; senior.

sen·ate (sĕn′ĭt) *n.* 1. (Rom. hist.) Roman legislative and administrative body, orig. of representatives elected by patricians, later of appointed members and actual and former holders of various high offices. 2. (cap.) Upper branch of the legislature in U.S. and various other countries. 3. Governing body of some universities; council in some Amer. colleges composed of members of faculty and elected students, and having control of discipline etc.

sen·a·tor (sĕn′*ater*) *n.* Member of senate. **sen·a·to·ri·al** (sĕn*a*tōr′-ēal, -tŏr′-) *adj.* **sen′a·tor·ship** *n.*

send (sĕnd) *v.* (**sent** pr. sĕnt, **send·ing**). Cause to go, dispatch, secure conveyance of, to some destination, *to, into, away*, etc.; propel; drive, cause to go, *into* some condition, *to sleep*, etc.; send message or letter; (of deity) grant, bestow, inflict, bring about, cause to be; (slang) excite, put into ecstasy; ~ **down**, (Brit.) suspend, expel, from university; ~ **for**, summon; esp., of head of state, summon politician in order to offer him premiership; ~ **off**, send away; witness departure of (person) as sign of respect, etc.; ~ **-off** (*n.*); ~ **up** (**the river**), (slang) send to prison. **send′er** *n.*

Sen·e·ca[1] (sĕn′*eka*) *n.* (pl. **-cas**, collect. **-ca**). Member, language, of a numerous and warlike tribe of Iroquoian Indians, formerly occupying W. part of New York State.

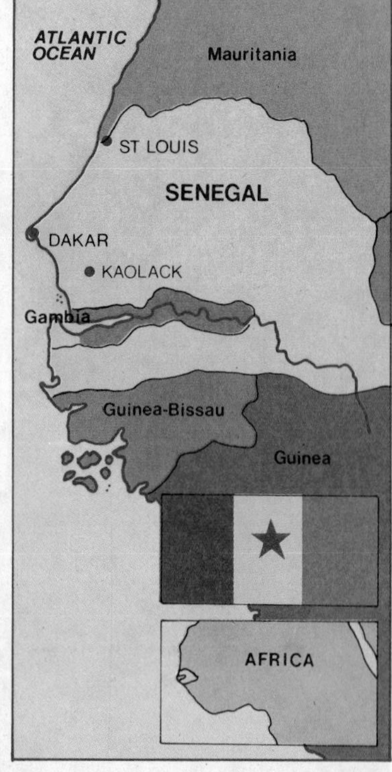

Mosque on Gorée, an island opposite Dakar, capital of ***Senegal.*** *This former French colony once relied on peanuts as its main cash crop, but today rice and sorghum are also grown.*

Sen·e·ca[2] (sĕn′eka), **Lucius Annaeus** (*c*4 B.C.–65 A.D.). Roman Stoic philosopher and author of tragedies; tutor and adviser to Nero; ordered to take his own life on charge of complicity against Nero conspiracy.

Sen·e·gal (sĕnegawl′). Republic in W. Africa, formerly part of French W. Africa; achieved independence, 1960; capital, Dakar, is westernmost point in Africa. **Sen·e·gal·ese** (sĕnegawlēz′, -lēs′, -ga-) *adj.* & *n.* (pl. **-lese**).

se·nes·cent (senĕs′ent) *adj.* Growing old. **se·nes′cence** *n.*

se·nile (sē′nīl, sĕn′īl) *adj.* Belonging, incident, peculiar, to old age; having weakness of old age. **se·nil·i·ty** (sĭnĭl′ĭtē) *n.*

sen·ior (sēn′yer) *adj.* More advanced in age, older in standing; superior in age or standing *to*; of higher or highest degree; senior to another of the same name; belonging to final year in university, school, etc.; ~ **citizen**, elderly person, esp. if retired; ~ **high school**, high school usu. including grades 10, 11, and 12; ~ **partner**, head of firm. **sen·ior·i·ty** (sēnyŏr′ĭtē, -yăr′-) *n.* (pl. **-ties**). **senior** *n.* One superior or worthy of deference etc. by reason of age; person of comparatively long service, standing, etc.; one's elder or superior in length of service, membership, etc.; senior student.

sen·na (sĕn′*a*) *n.* (Dried pods or leaflets, used as purgative, of) species of *Cassia.*

se·ñor (sĕnyōr′, -yōr′), **se·ño·ra** (sĕnyōr′*a*, -yōr′*a*), **se·ño·ri·ta** (sĕnyorē′t*a*) *ns.* (pl. **se·ñors**, Sp. **se·ño·res** pr. sĕnyōr′ĕs; **se·ño·ras** pr. *Sp.* sĕnyōr′ahs; **se·ño·ri·tas** pr. *Sp.* sĕnyawrē′tahs). (Title of or form of address to) Spanish man, woman, young or unmarried woman.

sen·sa·tion (sĕnsā′sh*o*n) *n.* 1. Consciousness of perceiving or seeming to perceive some state or affection of one's body, its parts or senses, or of one's mind or its emotions; contents of such consciousness. 2. Excited or violent feeling, strong impression, as of horror, surprise, esp. among community; event, person, etc. arousing this. **sen·sa′tion·al** *adj.* **sen·sa′tion·al·ly** *adv.*

sen·sa·tion·al·ism (sĕnsā′sh*o*nalĭzem) *n.* 1. (philos.) Theory that sensation is sole source of knowledge. 2. Pursuit of the sensational in literature, journalism, etc. **sen·sa′tion·al·ist** *n.*

sense (sĕns) *n.* 1. Any of those faculties, each dependent upon specialized groups of receptors connected with the brain, by which man and other animals are aware of their environment or recognize changes in their own bodily condition such as pain, movement of muscles and joints, or cold and warmth; **the five ~s**, those providing knowledge of the external world (sight, hearing, smell, taste, touch); ~ **datum**, element of experience due to stimulation of a sense organ; ~ **organ**, part of body concerned in producing sensation. 2. (pl.) The senses considered as channels for gratifying the desire for pleasure. 3. (pl.) Person's sanity regarded as attested by possession of the senses. 4. Ability to perceive or feel; consciousness *of*; quick or accurate appreciation *of*; instinct regarding, insight into, specified matter. 5. Practical wisdom, judgment, common sense, conformity to these. 6. Meaning, way in which word etc. is to be understood; intelligibility, coherence, possession of a meaning; **in a ~**, in a way, under limitations. 7. Prevailing sentiment among a number of people. **sense** *v.t.* (**sensed, sens·ing**). Perceive by sense; (esp.) be vaguely aware of.

sense·less (sĕns′lĭs) *adj.* 1. Deprived of sensation; unconscious; unfeeling. 2. Extremely foolish. 3. Meaningless, purposeless. **sense′less·ly** *adv.* **sense′less·ness** *n.*

sen·si·bil·i·ty (sĕnsibĭl′ĭtē) *n.* (pl. **-ties**). 1. Capacity to feel. 2. Susceptibility, sensitiveness (*to*); delicacy of feeling; oversensitiveness.

sen·si·ble (sĕn′sibel) *adj.* 1. Perceptible by the senses; great enough to be perceived, appreciable. 2. Aware, not unmindful, *of*. 3. Of good sense, reasonable, judicious; moderate; practical. **sen′si·ble·ness** *n.* **sen′si·bly** *adv.*

sen·si·tive (sĕn′sĭtĭv) *adj.* Having sensibility *to*; very open *to* or acutely affected by external impressions, esp. those made by the moods or opinions of others in relation to oneself; (of instrument etc.) readily responding to or recording slight changes of condition; (chem.) readily affected by or responsive *to* appropriate agent; (photog., of paper, etc.) susceptible to influence of light; ~ **plant**, tropical Amer. plant (*Mimosa pudica*) with leaflets that fold together at slightest touch; plant with similar quality. **sen'si·tive·ly** *adv.* **sen'si·tive·ness** *n.* **sen·si·tiv·i·ty** (sĕnsĭtĭv'ĭtē) *n.* ~ **training**, group discussion etc. often involving confrontation, designed to increase learning through feedback from others.

sen·si·tize (sĕn'sĭtīz) *v.t.* (**-tized, -tiz·ing**). Make sensitive; render (photographic paper etc.) sensitive to light; render (organism, tissue) sensitive to substance normally inert, or highly reactive to drug etc. **sen·si·ti·za·tion** (sĕnsĭtĭzā'shon) *n.*

sen·sor (sĕn'ser) *n.* Device giving signal for detection or measurement of a physical property to which it responds.

sen·so·ri·al (sĕnsōr'ēal, -sōr'-) *adj.* Of the sensorium, sensation or sensory impressions.

sen·so·ri·um (sĕnsōr'ēum, -sōr'-) *n.* (pl. **-so·ri·ums, -so·ri·a** pr. -sōr'ēa, -sōr'-). Brain as seat of sensation; whole sensory apparatus.

sen·so·ry (sĕn'serē) *adj.* Of sensation or the senses; ~ **nerve**, nerve consisting of fibers conducting impulses from the peripheral sense organs to the central nervous system.

sen·su·al (sĕn'shōōal) *adj.* Of or dependent on the senses only, voluptuous; given to the pursuit of sensual pleasures or gratification of the appetites; licentious. **sen'su·al·ly** *adv.* **sen'su·al·ism, sen'su·al·ist, sen·su·al·i·ty** (sĕnshōōăl'ĭtē) *ns.* **sen·su·al·is·tic** (sĕnshōōalĭs'tĭk) *adj.*

sen·su·ous (sĕn'shōōus) *adj.* Of, derived from, affecting, delighting in pleasures of, the senses. **sen'su·ous·ly** *adv.* **sen'su·ous·ness** *n.*

sent: see SEND.

sen·tence (sĕn'tens) *n.* 1. Judgment or decision of court esp. as to punishment allotted to person condemned in criminal trial (also transf.); the punishment itself. 2. Series of words in connected speech or writing, forming grammatically complete expression of single thought, and usu. containing subject and predicate, and conveying statement, question, command, or request; loosely, part of writing or speech between two periods; SIMPLE, COMPLEX, COMPOUND[1] ~: see these. **sentence** *v.t.* (**-tenced, -tenc·ing**). Pronounce judicial sentence on, condemn *to* a punishment.

sen·ten·tious (sĕntĕn'shus) *adj.* Aphoristic; full of, given to, pointed maxims; pompously moralizing. **sen·ten'tious·ly** *adv.* **sen·ten'tious·ness** *n.*

sen·tient (sĕn'shent) *adj.* Having the power of sense perception, that feels or is capable of feeling. **sen'tience** *n.* **sen'tient·ly** *adv.*

sen·ti·ment (sĕn'timent) *n.* 1. Mental attitude; opinion, view. 2. Mental feeling, emotion, thought, or reflection colored by or proceeding from emotion; emotional thought expressed in literature, art, etc.; feeling or meaning (intended to be) conveyed by passage etc. 3. Refined and tender feeling; emotional weakness, mawkish tenderness, nursing of the emotions. **sen·ti·men·tal** (sĕntimĕn'tal) *adj.* Swayed or dictated by shallow emotion; designed to excite or gratify the softer emotions (~ **value**, value of thing to particular person because of its associations). **sen·ti·men'tal·ly** *adv.* **sen·ti·men'tal·ism, sen·ti·men'tal·ist, sen·ti·men·tal·i·ty** (sĕntimĕntăl'ĭtē) *ns.* **sen·ti·men'tal·ize** *v.* (**-ized, -iz·ing**).

sen·ti·nel (sĕn'tinel) *n.* Sentry (lit. or fig.).

sen·try (sĕn'trē) *n.* (pl. **-tries**). Soldier etc. posted to keep guard; ~ **box**, hut for sentry to stand in.

se·pal (sē'pal, sĕp'al) *n.* (bot.) One of leaves or divisions of calyx.

sep·a·rate (sĕp'erĭt, sĕp'rĭt) *adj.* Divided or withdrawn from others, detached, shut off; forming a unit that is or may be regarded as apart or by itself, distinct, individual, of individuals; ~ **but equal**, of or relating to a policy of segregating the races but providing equal educational etc. opportunities for all. **sep'a·rate·ly** *adv.* **sep'a·rate·ness** *n.* **sep'a·rates** *n.pl.* Separate articles of dress suitable for wearing together in various combinations. **separate** (sĕp'erāt) *v.* (**-rat·ed, -rat·ing**). Make separate, sever, disunite; keep from union or contact; part, secede *from*, go different ways; remove (substance) *from* another with which it is combined or mixed, as cream from milk, esp. by some technical process. **sep·a·ra·ble** (sĕp'erabel, sĕp'ra-), **sep·a·ra·tive** (sĕp'eratĭv, -erā-) *adjs.*

sep·a·ra·tion (sĕperā'shon) *n.* (esp.) Cessation of conjugal cohabitation without dissolution of marriage tie, either by mutual consent or (**judicial** ~) imposed by judicial decree; ~ **center**, place where members of armed forces are released from military service to return to civilian life.

*Best known for their use as a purgative, pods of the **senna** plant were usually soaked in water, to extract the active ingredients.*

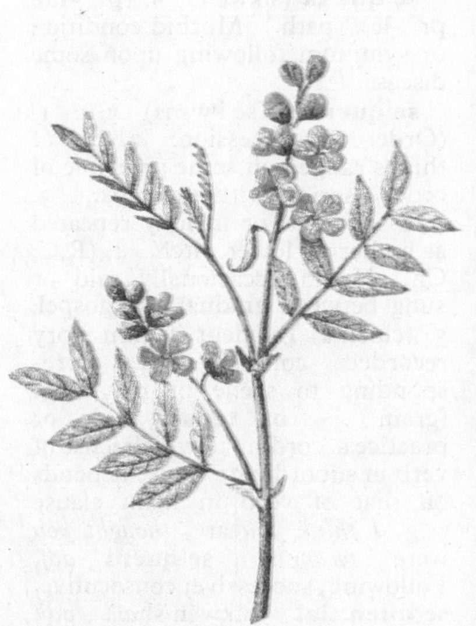

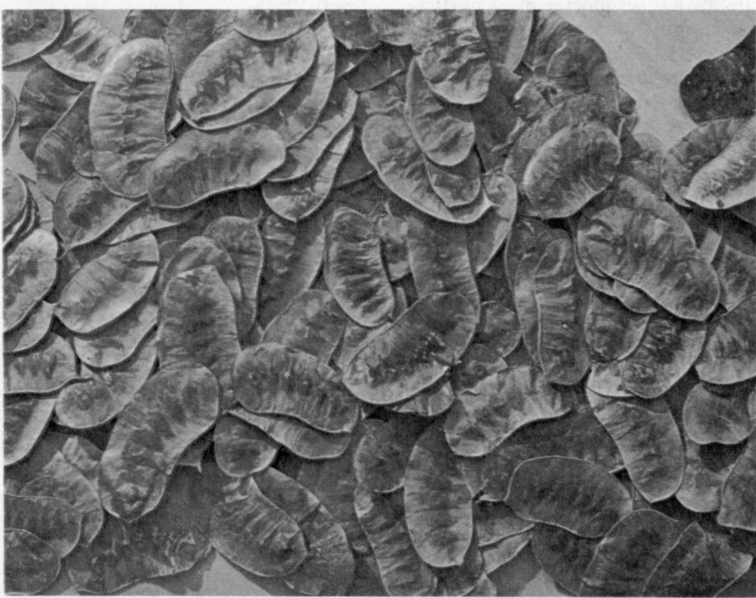

sep·a·ra·tist (sĕp′*e*ratĭst, sĕp′-r*a*-, -*e*rā-) *n.* One who favors separation, esp. for political or ecclesiastical independence. **sep′-a·ra·tism** *n.*

sep·a·ra·tor (sĕp′*e*rāt*er*) *n.* (esp.) Machine or appliance for separating, esp. cream from milk by centrifugal force.

Se·phar·di (s*e*fâr′dē) *n.* (pl. **Se·phar·dim** pr. s*e*fâr′dĭm, s*e*fâr-dēm′). Member of one of the two main divisions of Jews, Jews of Spanish or Portuguese descent; cf. ASHKENAZI. **Se·phar′dic** *adj.* [mod. Heb., f. *s^e^pārad*, a country mentioned once in Old Testament and held in late Jewish tradition to be Spain]

se·pi·a (sē′pē*a*) *n.* (Rich brown color of) pigment made from inky secretion of cuttlefish; a sepia drawing. ~ *adj.* Of color of sepia; drawn in sepia.

se·poy (sē′poi) *n.* (hist.) Native Indian soldier under European, esp. Brit. discipline; **S ~ Rebellion** (**Mutiny**), revolt of sepoy troops in Bengal army of Brit. East India Co. (1857–8), which led to abolition of the company and assumption of direct rule by Brit. crown; also called Indian Mutiny. [Hind., f. Pers. *sipāhī* soldier (*sipāh* army)]

sep·pu·ku (sĕpōō′kōō) *n.* Harakiri. [Jap.]

sep·sis (sĕp′sĭs) *n.* (pl. **-ses** pr. -sēz). State of poisoning of the tissues or bloodstream, caused by bacteria.

Sept. *abbrev.* September.

sept-, septi- *prefixes.* Seven.

sep·tal (sĕp′t*a*l) *adj.* Of a septum or septa. **sep·tate** (sĕp′tāt) *adj.* Having a septum or septa.

Sep·tem·ber (sĕptĕm′b*er*). Ninth month of Gregorian (seventh of Julian) calendar, with 30 days. [L. *septem* seven]

Sep·tem·brist (sĕptĕm′brĭst). (Fr. hist.) Supporter of or participator in massacre of political prisoners in Paris Sept. 2–6, 1792.

sep·ten·ni·al (sĕptĕn′ē*a*l) *adj.* Of, for, (recurring) every, seven years. **sep·ten′ni·al·ly** *adv.*

sep·tet, sep·tette (sĕptĕt′) *ns.* 1. (mus.) (Composition for) seven voices or instruments in combination. 2. Set of seven persons or things.

sep·tic (sĕp′tĭk) *adj.* Putrefying; caused by or in a state of sepsis; ~ **tank**, tank in which organic matter in sewage is rapidly decomposed through agency of anaerobic bacteria. **sep′ti·cal·ly** *adv.*

sep·ti·ce·mi·a, sep·ti·cae·mi·a (sĕptĭsē′mē*a*) *ns.* Disease caused by pathogenic bacteria in the blood, blood poisoning.

sep·tu·a·ge·nar·i·an (sĕpchōō*a*-jenâr′ē*a*n) *adj.* & *n.* (Person) aged 70 or more but less than 80.

Sep·tu·a·ges·i·ma (sĕptōō*a*-jĕs′*i*m*a*, -tū-, -chōō-). Third Sunday before Lent. [L., = "70th"]

Sep·tu·a·gint (sĕp′tōō*a*jĭnt, -tū-, -chōō-) *n.* (symbol LXX) Greek version of Old Testament, traditionally said to have been the work of 72 Jewish translators in 3rd c. B.C.; copy of this. **Sep·tu·a·gint·al** (sĕptōō*a*jĭn′t*a*l, -tū-, -chōō-) *adj.* [L. *septuaginta* 70]

sep·tum (sĕp′t*u*m) *n.* (pl. **-tums, -ta** pr. -t*a*). (anat., bot., zool.) Partition, dividing wall, membrane, layer, etc., e.g. that between the nostrils.

sep·ul·cher, Brit. **sep·ul·chre** (sĕp′*u*lk*er*) *ns.* Tomb, esp. cut in rock or built of stone or brick, burial vault or cave; **Holy S ~**, cave in which Jesus Christ was buried outside walls of Jerusalem; **whited ~**, hypocrite (see Matt. 23).

se·pul·chral (sepŭl′kr*a*l) *adj.* Of sepulcher(s) or sepulture; suggestive of the tomb, funereal, gloomy, dismal. **se·pul′chral·ly** *adv.*

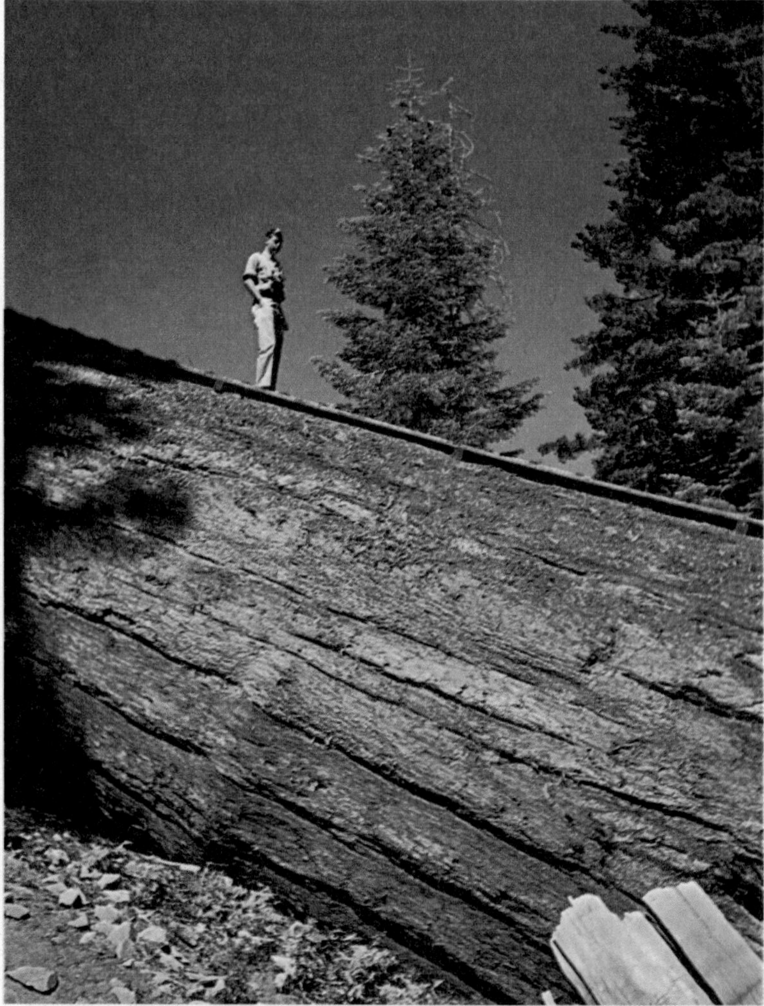

With trunks up to 25 ft. diameter, the ***sequoias*** *of California are claimed to be the largest trees in the world. Some specimens measured had a calculated age of 2,500–3,000 years.*

seq., seqq. *abbrevs. Sequens, sequentes, -ia.* [L., = "the following"]

se·quel (sē′kw*e*l) *n.* What follows after, continuation or resumption of a story, process, etc., after pause or provisional ending; aftereffects, upshot.

se·que·la (sĭkwē′l*a*) *n.* (pl. **-lae** pr. -lē). (path.) Morbid condition or symptom following upon some disease.

se·quence (sē′kw*e*ns) *n.* 1. (Order of) succession. 2. Set of things ranged on some principle of order, series without gaps. 3. (mus.) Phrase or melody repeated at higher or lower pitch. 4. (R.C. Ch.) Hymn occasionally said or sung between gradual and gospel. 5. (cinema) Incident in film story recorded consecutively, corresponding to scene of play. 6. (gram.) ~ **of tenses**, rule or practice according to which tense of verb in subordinate clause depends on that of verb in main clause (e.g. *I think you* are, *thought you* were, *wrong*). **se′quent** *adj.* Following; successive; consecutive. **se·quen·tial** (sĭkwĕn′sh*a*l) *adj.* **se·quen′tial·ly** *adv.*

se·ques·ter (sĭkwĕs'ter) *v.t.* 1. Seclude, isolate, set apart. 2. Confiscate, appropriate; seize temporary possession of (debtor's effects).

se·ques·trate (sĭkwĕs'trāt) *v.t.* (**-trat·ed, -trat·ing**) = SEQUESTER (sense 2); divert (income of estate) temporarily from owner until claims are satisfied. **se·ques·tra·tion** (sēkwĕstrā'shon) *n.*

se·quin (sē'kwĭn) *n.* 1. (hist.) Venetian gold coin. 2. Small circular spangle. **se'quined** *adj.*

se·quoi·a (sĭkwoi'a) *n.* One of 2 California evergreen trees of genus *S*~, the giant sequoia or giant redwood (*S. gigantea*), the largest known tree, or the coast(al) redwood (*S. sempervirens*), the tallest known tree, or a Chinese deciduous conifer, the dawn redwood (*Metasequoia glyptostroboides*) resembling these but much smaller; **S~ National Park**, area in S. central California in the Sierra Nevada Mountains, covering 386,862 acres, (156,590 hectares), noted for its many sequoia trees and mountains. [f. name (*Seqouiah*) of the Cherokee Indian who invented a syllabary for his language]

se·ra: see SERUM.

se·ra·glio (sĭrăl'yō, -rahl'-) (pl. **-glios**), **se·rail** (sĭrīl' -rāl') *ns.* Walled palace, esp. (hist.) that of sultan at Constantinople; harem.

se·ra·i (serah'ē, serī') *n.* (pl. **-ra·is**) = CARAVANSARY. [Pers., = "palace"]

se·ra·pe (serah'pē) *n.* Shawl or blanket worn as cloak in Latin America.

ser·aph (sĕr'af) *n.* (pl. **-aphs, -a·phim** pr. -afĭm). 1. (pl. also **-s**) One of the **seraphim**, in bibl. use, the living creatures with three pairs of wings, seen in Isaiah's vision as hovering above the throne of God. 2. (pl.) Order of angels (see ANGEL).

se·raph·ic (serăf'ĭk) *adj.* Of or like seraphim; angelic, sublime. **se·raph'i·cal·ly** *adv.*

Se·ra·pis (sĭrā'pĭs). (Egyptian myth.) God combining the Egyptian Osiris with attributes of Zeus, Hades, and Aesculapius invented and introduced into Egypt by Ptolemy I to unite Greeks and Egyptians in common worship.

Serb (sẽrb) *n.* 1. Member, language, of a Slav tribe settled at the invitation of the emperor Heraclius in the Roman province of Moesia, S. of the Danube and N. of Thrace; Serbian. 2. Serbian language.

Ser·bi·a (sẽr'bēa). Former Balkan kingdom, since 1919 part of Yugoslavia. **Ser'bi·an** *adj.* & *n.* (Native, inhabitant, language) of Serbia.

Ser·bo-Cro·a·tian (sẽrbōkrōā'shan) *adj.* & *n.* (Of, pertaining to) Slavonic language of Yugoslavia, written with Cyrillic letters in Serbia and Roman in Croatia; (of) its speaker(s).

Named because of the alleged similarity of its patterns to those on a snakeskin, ***serpentine*** *is a familiar rock in Cornwall, England, especially near the Lizard. It is made into ornaments.*

Ser·bo·nis (sẽrbō'nĭs). Boggy lake in the delta of the Nile, in which whole armies were said to have been swallowed up. **Ser·bo'ni·an** *adj.* ~ **bog**, Serbonis; (fig.) difficult position from which escape is impossible.

sere, sear (sēr) *adjs.* (now poet. or rhet.) Dry, withered.

ser·e·nade (sĕrenād') *n.* Performance of music at night in open, esp. by lover under lady's window; piece of music suitable for such performance; instrumental composition in several movements. ~ *v.* (**-nad·ed, -nad·ing**). Entertain with, perform, a serenade.

Ser·en·dip (sĕrendĭp'), **Ser·en·dib** (sĕrendēb'). Two variants of the ancient name of Sri Lanka.

ser·en·dip·i·ty (sĕrendĭp'ĭtē) *n.* Faculty of making happy discoveries by accident. [coined by Horace Walpole f. title of a tale, "The Three Princes of Serendip"]

se·rene (serēn') *adj.* Clear and calm; unruffled; placid, tranquil, unperturbed. **se·rene'ly** *adv.* **se·ren·i·ty** (serĕn'ĭtē), **se·rene'ness** *ns.*

serf (sẽrf) *n.* Villein, person whose service is attached to the soil and transferred with it (hist.); oppressed person, drudge. **serf'age, serf'dom, serf'hood** *ns.*

Serg., Sergt. *abbrevs.* Sergeant.

serge (sẽrj) *n.* Kind of durable twilled worsted cloth. [L. *serica* silk f. *Seres* the Chinese]

ser·geant (sar'jant) *n.* Noncommissioned officer above corporal; police officer ranking just below inspector or lieutenant; **~-at-arms** (pl. **~s-at-arms**), officer who keeps order in legislative chamber, courtroom, etc.; ~ **first class**, enlisted man of seventh grade in U.S. Army, ranking above staff sergeant and below first or master sergeant; ~ **major** (pl. **~s major**), noncommissioned officer functioning as chief administrative assistant at a U.S. Army, Marine Corps, or Air Force headquarters. **ser'gean·cy** (pl. **-cies**), **ser'geant·ship** *ns.*

se·ri·al (sẽr'ēal) *adj.* Of, in, forming, a series; (of story etc.) issued in installments; ~ **number**,

Chinese women sort cocoons from the moths especially farmed to produce them. ***Sericulture*** *or silk-farming has been practiced in China since prehistoric times.*

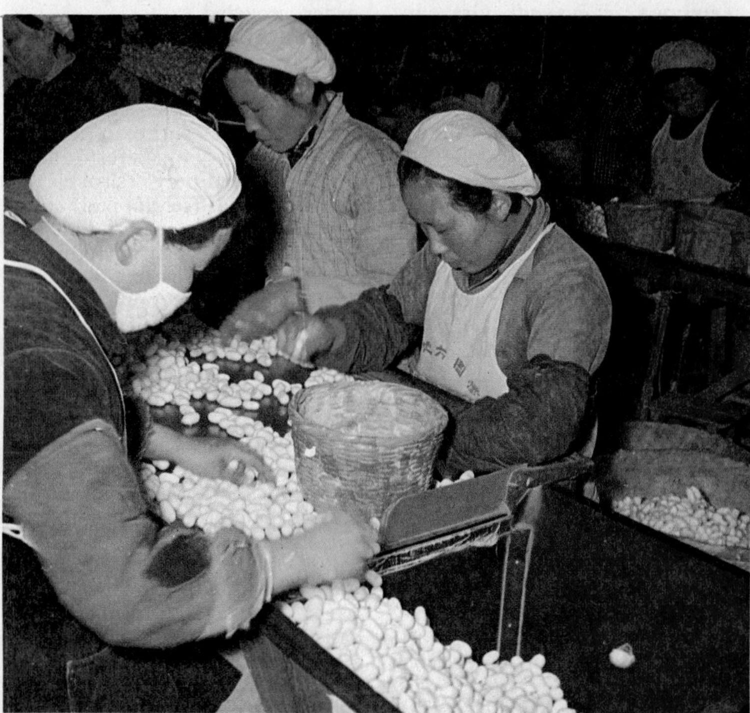

number in series, for identification. **se'ri·al·ly** *adv.* **serial** *n.* Serial story. **se'ri·al·ize** *v.t.* (**-ized, -iz·ing**).

se·ri·a·tim (sērēā'tĭm, sĕr-) *adv.* One after another, one by one in succession.

ser·i·cul·ture (sĕr'ĭkŭlcher) *n.* Silkworm breeding, production of raw silk.

se·ries (sēr'ēz) *n.* (pl. **-ries**). Succession, sequence, or set of similar or similarly related things etc.; repertoire of plays presented in successive weeks or on successive nights by same actors, lectures by same speaker, successive games between same teams, esp. (baseball) World Series; set of successive issues of periodical, of literary compositions, of books issued by one publisher in common form and with some similarity of subject or purpose etc.; (geol.) set of strata with common characteristic; (chem.) group of elements with common properties or of compounds related in composition and structure; (math.) set of terms constituting PROGRESSION or having common relation between successive terms; (elect.) set of circuits so arranged (**in ~**) that same current traverses all circuits; (zool.) number of connected genera, families, etc.

ser·if (sĕr'ĭf) *n.* Crossline finishing off a stroke of a letter.

ser·i·graph (sĕr'ĭgrăf, -grahf) *n.* Print made by serigraphy. **se·rig·ra·phy** (sĭrĭg'rafē) *n.* SCREEN printing, esp. by silkscreen. **se·rig'ra·pher** *n.*

se·ri·o·com·ic (sērēōkŏm'ĭk) *adj.* Partly serious and partly comic.

se·ri·ous (sēr'ēus) *adj.* Grave in appearance, manner, intention, purpose, etc., solemn, earnest, not frivolous, trifling, or playful; requiring earnest thought or application; important, not slight; earnest about things of religion, religious-minded. **se'ri·ous·ly** *adv.* **se'ri·ous·ness** *n.*

ser·mon (sēr'mon) *n.* Discourse delivered from pulpit and usu. based on text of Scripture, by way of religious exhortation or instruction; similar discourse on religious or moral subject delivered elsewhere or published; moral reflection(s), homily. **S~ on the Mount**, discourse of Christ recorded in Matt. 5–7. **ser'mon·ize** *v.* (**-ized, -iz·ing**).

se·rous (sēr'us) *adj.* Of, like, serum; wheylike; **~ membrane**, delicate membrane lining closed cavities of the body.

ser·pent (sēr'pent) *n.* 1. Snake, esp. large snake; treacherous person. 2. Kind of firework with serpentine motion in air or on ground.

ser·pen·tine (sēr'pentēn, -tīn)

Servants, *such as the postillion (above) and the carpenter (right) were employed at one time in the households of wealthy people in Europe and the U.S.A.*

adj. Of or like a serpent, winding; writhing, coiling, tortuous, sinuous; cunning, subtle, treacherous. ~ *n.* 1. (hist.) Kind of cannon. 2. Dull green (or occas. red or brown) soft rock or mineral, chiefly hydrated magnesium silicate, with markings resembling those of snake's skin.

ser·rate (sĕr'ĭt, -āt), **ser·rat·ed** (sĕr'ātĭd, sĭrā'-) *adjs.* Having, forming, row of small projections like teeth of saw; notched like saw. **ser·ra·tion** (sĕrā'shon, sĭ-), **ser·ra·ture** (sĕr'acher) *ns.*

ser·ried (sĕr'ēd) *adj.* (of ranks etc.) Pressed close together, in close order, crowded.

se·rum (sēr'um) *n.* (pl. **se·rums, se·ra** pr. sēr'a). 1. Amber-colored liquid that separates from clot when blood coagulates. 2. Blood serum as antitoxin or therapeutic agent. 3. Watery animal fluid. **se·rol·o·gy** (sĭrŏl'ojē) *n.* **se·ro·log·i·cal** (sērolŏj'ĭkal) *adj.*

serv·ant (sērv'ant) *n.* One who has undertaken, usu. in return for salary or wages, to carry out orders of individual or corporate employer, esp. one who waits on master or mistress or performs domestic duties in household; devoted follower, person willing to serve another; **civil ~**: see CIVIL; **public ~**, government official.

serve (sērv) *v.* (**served, serv·ing**). 1. Be servant (to), render service, be useful (to); be employed (*in* army, navy, etc.); be soldier, sailor, etc. (*in* war, *against* enemy, etc.); **~ at table**, act as waiter. 2. Meet needs (of), avail, suffice, satisfy; punish, requite (*serves him right*); perform function, be suitable, do what is required for; **~ one's apprenticeship**, go through training; **~ a (prison) sentence**, undergo it; **~ (one's) time**, undergo imprisonment, serve a sentence; serve apprenticeship. 3. Dish *up*, set (food) on table; set out ready; distribute; supply (person *with*); make legal delivery of (writ etc.), deliver writ etc. to (person); set ball, set (ball) in play; (tennis etc.) start play by striking ball toward opponent, into opposite court etc.; (of male animal) impregnate (the female). **serv'er** *n.* (Usu. lay) attendant on priest at Mass, who brings bread and wine to altar, makes responses, etc., acolyte. **serve** *n.* (tennis etc.) = SERVICE[1] def. 5. **serv'ing** *n.* Single portion of food or drink.

serv·ice[1] (sēr'vĭs) *n.* 1. Being servant, serving a master; work or duty of a servant; duty that feudal tenant was bound to render to lord; person's disposal or behalf; use, assistance. 2. Department or agency, usually governmental, in which work is done to meet some general need; persons engaged, employment, in this, esp. army, navy, or air force; (attrib.) belonging, issued, etc., to armed force. 3. Liturgical form or office appointed for use on some occasion; single meeting of congregation for worship; musical setting of (parts of) liturgical service. 4. Legal serving of or *of* writ etc. 5. Act of serving ball in tennis etc., way of doing this, ball served. 6. Set of dishes, plates, etc., required for serving meal. 7. Set of trains, steamers, buses, etc., plying at stated times; supply of gas, water, etc., through pipes to private houses etc.; provision of what is necessary, esp. maintenance and repair work carried out by vendor after sale. 8. **~ club**, any of various organizations that benefit their own members and promote community welfare; recreation center for armed forces enlisted personnel; **ser'viceman, service**

woman, person in armed forces; person providing maintenance for appliance etc.; **service module**, module containing main engine and power supplies of spacecraft; **service pipe**, one conveying water or gas from the main to a building; **service station**, place providing maintenance service, gasoline, oil, etc., for motor vehicles; service woman: see SERVICEMAN. **service** *v.t.* (**-iced, -ic·ing**). Provide service for, do routine maintenance work on (automobile, washing machine, etc.).

serv·ice[2] (sẽr'vĭs) *n.* (also ~ **tree**) European tree (*Sorbus domestica*), like mountain ash, with small round or pear-shaped fruit edible when overripe; (also **ser'viceberry** (pl. **-ries**): see SHADBUSH).

serv·ice·a·ble (sẽr'vĭsabel) *adj.* Profitable, useful, capable of rendering service; durable, hard-wearing, for rough or ordinary use rather than ornament. **serv'ice·a·ble·ness, serv·ice·a·bil·i·ty** (sẽrvĭsabĭl'ĭtē) *ns.* **serv'ice·a·bly** *adv.*

ser·vi·ette (sẽrvēĕt') *n.* Table napkin.

ser·vile (sẽr'vīl) *adj.* Of, being, suitable to, a slave or slaves; slavish, cringing, fawning. **ser'vile·ly** *adv.* **ser·vil·i·ty** (sẽrvĭl'ĭtē) *n.* (pl. **-ties**).

ser·vi·tude (sẽr'vĭtōōd, -tūd) *n.* Slavery, subjection, bondage.

ser·vo·mech·a·nism (sẽr'vō-mĕkanĭzem, sẽrvōmĕk'-) *n.* Power-assisted device, usu. for controlling movement (e.g. a brake), freq. deriving its power from the source of energy over which it exercises control.

ses·a·me (sĕs'amē) *n.* (Seeds of) E. Indian herbaceous plant (*Sesamum indicum*) yielding oil and used as food; **open** ~, password or charm at which doors or barriers fly open (see ALI BABA).

ses·a·moid (sĕs'amoid) *adj.* Shaped like a sesame seed, nodular (esp. of small independent bones developed in tendons passing over angular structure, as the kneecap or the navicular bone). ~ *n.* Sesamoid bone.

sesqui- *prefix.* One and a half, the ratio 3:2, etc.

ses·qui·cen·ten·ni·al (sĕskwĭ-sĕntĕn'ēal) *adj.* & *n.* (Of) 150th anniversary. **ses·qui·cen·ten'ni·al·ly** *adv.*

ses·qui·pe·da·li·an (sĕskwĭ-pĭdā'lēan, -dāl'yan), **ses·quip·e·dal** (sĕskwĭp'edal) *adjs.* (of word) Excessively (literally one and one-half feet) long; cumbrous, pedantic.

ses·sile (sĕs'ĭl, -īl) *adj.* (bot., zool.) Immediately attached; without footstalk, peduncle, etc.

ses·sion (sĕsh'on) *n.* Sitting, continuous series of sittings, term of such sittings, of court, legislative or administrative body, etc., for conference or transaction of business; (universities, etc.) part of year during which instruction is given. **ses'sion·al** *adj.*

ses·tet (sĕstĕt', sĕs'tĕt) *n.* Sextet; last six lines of sonnet.

Set (sĕt). (Egyptian myth.) God of evil, brother (or son) of Osiris and his constant enemy; represented with head of beast with long pointed snout.

A pair of miniature paintings ***set*** *into an elaborate locket which could be closed and worn as a piece of jewellery. The one below was made about 1590.*

set[1] (sĕt) *v.* (**set, set·ting**). 1. Put, lay, stand; apply (thing) *to*; station, place ready; place, turn, in right or specified position or direction; dispose suitably for use, action, or display; plant (seed etc.) in ground; give sharp edge to (razor), bend teeth of (saw) alternately; ~ **sail**, hoist sail; begin voyage; ~ **table**, lay table for meal; ~ **(up) type**, arrange it for printing. 2. Join, attach, fasten; fix; determine, decide, appoint, settle, establish; put parts of (broken bone etc.) into right relative position after fracture or dislocation; insert (precious stone etc.) in gold etc. 3. Bring by placing, arranging, etc., into specified state; make sit down *to* task, cause *to* work, apply oneself *to work*; exhibit or arrange as pattern or as material to be dealt with; draw up (questions, paper) to be answered by examinees; make insertions in (surface) *with*; ~ **to music**, provide (song, words) with music usu. composed for the purpose. 4. Put or come into a settled or rigid position or state; curdle, solidify, harden; take shape, develop into definiteness; fix (hair) when dampened so that it dries in desired style. 5. (of sun, moon, etc.) Appear to descend toward and below horizon. 6. (of tide, current, etc.) Have motion, gather force, sweep along; show or feel tendency. 7. (of sporting dog) Take rigid attitude indicating presence of game; (of dancers) take position facing partners; (of garment) adapt itself to figure, sit *well, badly*, etc. 8. ~ **about**, begin, take steps toward; (colloq.) set on, attack; ~ **against**, contrast or compare, weigh, balance; make hostile or unfriendly toward; ~ **aside**, reserve; reject, disregard; annul; ~ **back**, impede or reverse progress of; (slang) cost (person) specified amount; **set'back** (*n.*), reversal or arrest of progress; (archit.) recession of upper part of building; **set down**, put in writing; attribute *to*, explain or describe oneself *as*; allow (passenger) to alight; **set forth**, make known, declare, expound; begin journey or expedition; **set in**, arise, get vogue, become established; fit (part of garment) into the rest; **set off**, act as adornment or foil to, enhance, make more striking; start (person) laughing, talking, etc.; begin journey; **set'off** (*n.*), thing set off against another, thing of which the amount or effect may be deducted from another by opposite tendency; counterpoise, counterclaim; offset; embellishment, adornment *to* something; (archit.) sloping or horizontal member connecting lower and thicker part of wall etc. with upper receding part; **set on**, urge

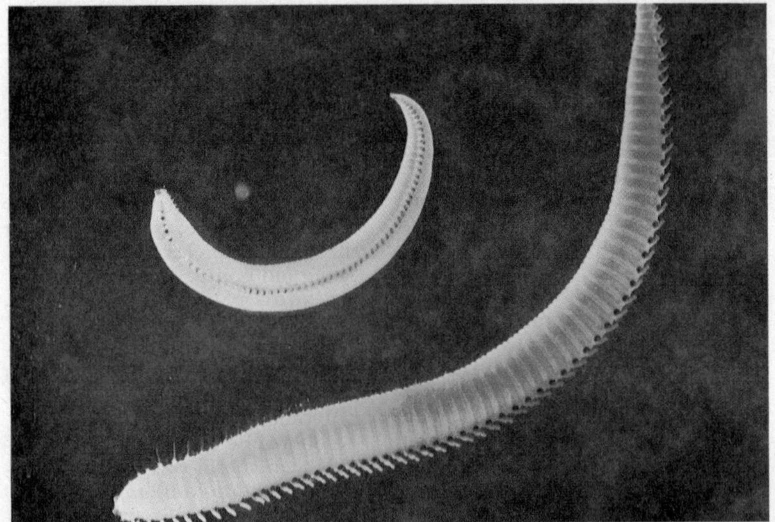

*Bristle worms (right) received their name from the rows of **setae.** They use these to help them move along the ocean bed in search of microscopic organisms which they eat.*

(dog etc.) to attack (person etc.); attack; **set out**, demonstrate; exhibit; declare; begin journey; **set to**, begin doing something, esp. fighting or arguing, vigorously; **set-to** (*n.*) (pl. **-tos**), combat, esp. with fists; **set up**, start; occasion, cause; establish (person, oneself) in some capacity; place in view; raise, begin to utter (cry, protest, etc.); propound (theory); prepare (machine) for operation; **set'up** (*n.*), manner or position in which a thing is set up; structure or arrangement of an organization, or the like; (colloq.) faked contest.

set[2] (sĕt) *adj.* (esp.) Unmoving; fixed; (of persons) determined or resolved *on*; (of speech) composed beforehand; (of phrases) customary; ~ **piece**, fireworks arranged on scaffolding etc.; formal or elaborate arrangement, esp. in art or literature; **of ~ purpose**, intentionally, deliberately; ~ **scene**, stage scene built up of more or less solid material; ~ **screw**, screw to hold 2 parts together or to regulate tension of a spring.

set[3] (sĕt) *n.* 1. Number of things or persons belonging together as essentially similar or complementary; group, clique, collection; (tennis etc.) group of games counting as unit of match; radio or television receiving apparatus. 2. Slip or shoot for planting; young fruit just set. 3. (poet.) Setting *of* sun or day. 4. Way current, wind, opinion, etc., sets; drift or tendency *of*; configuration, conformation, habitual posture; warp, bend, displacement, caused by continued pressure or position; (amount of) alternate deflection of sawteeth; fixing of dampened hair. 5. Last coat of plaster on wall; timber frame supporting gallery etc. in coal mine; width of body of type in printing; clutch of eggs; setter's pointing in presence of game; **dead ~**, pointed attack, determined onslaught *at* or *against* (also attrib.). 6. Theatrical or film setting, stage furniture, etc.

se·ta (sē'ta) *n.* (pl. **-tae** pr. -tē). (bot., zool.) Stiff hair, bristle. **se·ta·ceous** (sĭtā'shus), **se·tose** (sē'tōs, sĭtōs') *adjs.*

Seth (sĕth). Third son of Adam (Gen. 4).

Se·ton (sē'ton), **Elizabeth Ann** (nee Bayley) (1774–1821). Amer. widow who founded Sisters of Charity of St. Joseph, 1809, and Society for Relief of Poor Widows with Small Children, 1797; canonized on September 14, 1975.

set·tee (sĕtē') *n.* Long seat with back and usu. arms, for more than one person.

*The distinctive rich golden-chestnut coat of the **Irish setter** has long been admired by dog breeders. The original setters were recognized as a distinct breed as early as 1570.*

set·ter (sĕt'er) *n.* One of several varieties of sporting dogs, with long silky coat, trained to stand rigid on scenting game, as **English ~**, white with brownish and black markings, **Gordon ~**, black with tan markings, **Irish ~**, dark red or chestnut color.

set·ting (sĕt'ĭng) *n.* (esp.) 1. Music composed for particular words. 2. Frame in which jewel is set; surroundings or environment of anything; mounting of play, film, etc., scenery, stage furniture, etc.

set·tle[1] (sĕt'el) *n.* Bench with high back and arms, and freq. with box or chest under seat.

set·tle[2] (sĕt'el) *v.* (**-tled, -tling**). 1. Establish, become established, in more or less permanent abode, place, or way of life; (cause to) sit down (or *down*) to stay for some time; cease from wandering, motion, change, disturbance, or turbidity; bring to, attain, fixity, composure, certainty, decision, etc., determine, decide, appoint. 2. Colonize, establish colonists in, settle as colonists in (country). 3. Subside, sink to bottom of liquid or into lower position. 4. Deal effectually with, dispose or get rid of, do for; pay (bill), pay bill; ~ **up** (**accounts**). 5. Bestow legally for life *on*.

set·tle·ment (sĕt'elment) *n.* (esp.) 1. (law) Conveyance of, creation of estate(s) in, property, esp. on marriage. 2. Company of social workers established in poor or crowded district to give educational, medical, recreational, etc., services. 3. Newly settled tract of country, colony. 4. Arrangement, adjustment, of disagreement, strike, etc.; payment of debt etc.

set·tler (sĕt'ler) *n.* (esp.) One who settles in new colony or newly developed country, early colonist.

Se·vas·to·pol (sevăs'topōl). (formerly *Sebastopol*) City and port

A romantic impression of a **settler** with his family and bullock-drawn wagon train. 'Crossing the Rockies' during the mid-19th century. Such long treks occurred also in Australia and Africa.

Inspection of underground sewers in London, U.K. Until the 18th century, open drains and cesspools carried refuse. The first underground **sewer** was built in France in the mid-18th century.

of the Crimea, in U.S.S.R., on the Black Sea; besieged in Crimean War (1854–5) and World War II (1941–2).

sev·en (sĕv′*en*) *adj.* Amounting to 7; ~ **deadly sins**: see DEADLY; ~ **seas**: see SEA; **S~ Sisters**, the PLEIADES; **S~ Weeks' War**, that of 1866 between Austria and Prussia, as result of which Prussia became the predominant German power; **S~ Wonders of the World**, structures regarded as the most remarkable monuments of antiquity: the Pyramids, the Mausoleum at Harlicarnassus, the Hanging Gardens of Babylon, the temple of Artemis at Ephesus, Phidias's statue of Zeus at Olympia, the Colossus of Rhodes, and the Pharos or lighthouse at Alexandria; **S~ Years' War**, that waged 1756–63 by France, Austria, and Russia against Frederick the Great of Prussia and Gt. Britain, in which France lost to Britain her possessions in Amer. and India. **seven** *n.* One more than six; symbol for this (7, vii, or VII); card with seven pips; seven o'clock; size etc. indicated by 7; set of seven things or persons.

sev·en·teen (sĕv′*en*tēn′) *adj.* & *n.* One more than 16 (17, xvii, or XVII); ~**-year locust**, cicada (*Magicicada septendecim*) of eastern U.S. living in soil as larva for 13 to 17 years. **sev′en·teenth′** *adj.* & *n.*

sev·enth (sĕv′*enth*) *adj.* Next after sixth; ~**-day**, Saturday (in Quaker speech and among sects keeping Saturday as sabbath); **S~-Day Adventists,** sabbatarian Christian sect; ~ **heaven**, abode of supreme bliss, highest of seven heavens in Muslim and some Jewish systems. **sev′enth·ly** *adv.* In the seventh place. **seventh** *n.* Seventh part (see PART[1] def. 1); seventh thing etc.; (mus.) interval of which the span involves seven alphabetical names of notes; harmonic combination of notes thus separated.

sev·en·ty (sĕv′*entē*) *adj.* Amounting to 70; ~**-five** (*n.*) 75-mm gun. **seventy** *n.* (pl. **-ties**). Cardinal number, 7 times 10 (70, lxx, or LXX); set of 70 things or persons; **sev′enties,** (pl.) numbers etc. from 70 to 79; these years of century or life. **sev′en·ti·eth** *adj.* & *n.*

sev·er (sĕv′*er*) *v.* Separate, divide, part, disunite; cut or break off, take away, (part) from whole. **sev·er·ance** (sĕv′*erans*, sĕv′*rans*) *n.* ~ **pay**, amount paid to dismissed employee in good standing.

sev·er·al (sĕv′*eral*, sĕv′*ral*) *adj.* 1. Separate, distinct, individual, respective. 2. A few, more than two or three but not many. ~ *pron.* Moderate number of persons or things. **sev′er·al·ly** *adv.*

se·vere (sevēr′) *adj.* (**-ver·er, -ver·est**). Austere, strict, harsh; violent, vehement, extreme; trying, making great demands on endurance, energy, skill, etc.; unadorned, without redundance, restrained. **se·vere′ly** *adv.* **se·ver·i·ty** (sevĕr′ĭtē) (pl. **-ties**), **se·vere′ness** *ns.*

Sè·vres (sĕv′*re*, sĕv). Town near Paris, site of the French national porcelain factory since 1756; porcelain from this factory.

sew (sō) *v.* (**sewed, sewn**, pr. sōn or **sewed, sew·ing**). Fasten, join (pieces of material, leather, etc.) by passing thread through series of punctures made by needle carrying the thread or with an awl; make by sewing; fasten together sheets of (book) by passing thread or wire through back fold of each sheet; use needle and thread or sewing machine; ~ **up,** (colloq.) be sure of; control completely; **sewing machine**, machine for sewing or stitching. **sew′er** *n.*

sew·age (so͞o′ĭj) *n.* Spent water supply of a community, including wastes from domestic and trade premises etc. and ground water; ~ **treatment plant**, plant for purifying sewage by artificial methods, rendering it fit for discharge into river, lake, or tidal waters.

Sew·ard (so͞o′*erd*), **William Henry** (1801–72). Amer. statesman; senator, 1849–61, secretary of State, 1861–9; remembered for **Seward's Folly**, his purchase of Alaska from Russia in 1867 for $7,200,000; **Seward Peninsula**, peninsula in W. Alaska, extending 180 mi. (290 km) to Cape Prince of Wales on Bering Strait; westernmost point on the N. Amer. continent.

sew·er (so͞o′*er*) *n.* Pipe or

*Before the invention of the **sextant** from John Hadley's reflecting quadrant in 1731, navigators on ships had to use a crude cross-staff to measure the angle of sun or stars.*

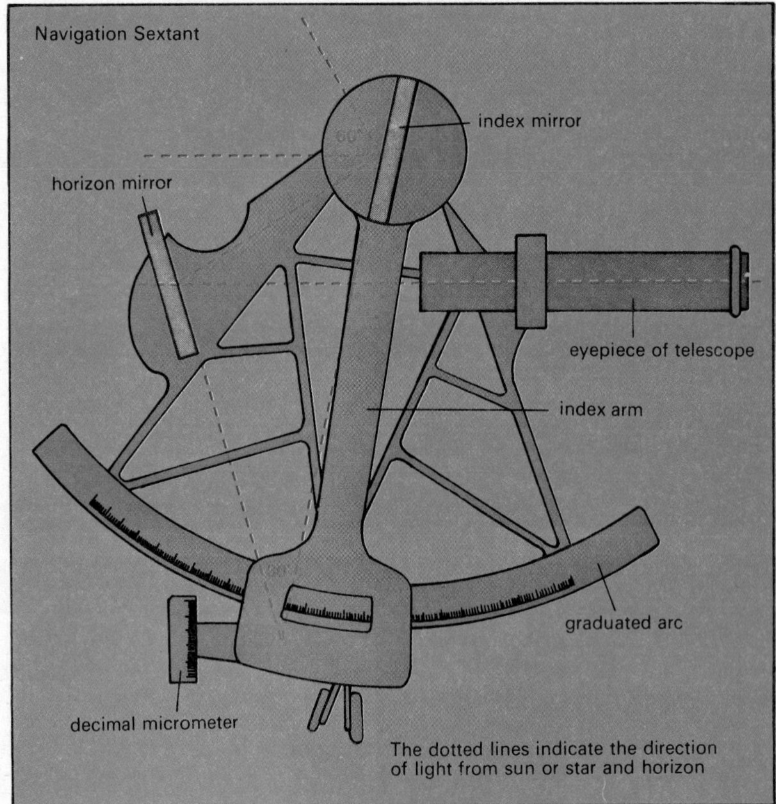

conduit for conveying sewage. **sew'er·age** *n.*

sewn: see SEW.

sex (sĕks) *n.* Sum of the physiological differences in structure and function that distinguish the male from the female in animals and plants; males or females collectively; (loosely) sexual instincts, desires, etc., or their manifestation; (colloq.) sexual intercourse; (attrib.) arising from sex; ~ **appeal**, qualities attracting members of the opposite sex; ~ **chromosome**, one affecting the determination of sex of an organism; **~-limited**, (of Mendelian character) expressed only in one sex, although the controlling gene is not on a sex chromosome; **~-linked**, (of Mendelian character) controlled by a gene that is carried on a sex chromosome. **sex** *v.t.* Examine in order to determine the sex of. **sex'ism** *n.* Discrimination or bias against women. **sex'ist** *n.* One so biased. **sex'less** *adj.* **sex'less·ly** *adv.* **sex'less·ness** *n.* **sex'pot** *n.* (slang) Girl or woman of overly obvious sexual attractiveness.

sex-, sexi- *prefixes.* Six.

sex·a·ge·nar·i·an (sĕks*a*j*e*nār'ĕan) *adj.* & *n.* (Person) aged 60 years or more but less than 70.

Sex·a·ges·i·ma (sĕks*a*jĕs'ĭm*a*). Second Sunday before Lent. [L., = "60th"]

sex·a·ges·i·mal (sĕks*a*jĕs'ĭm*a*l) *adj.* Proceeding by sixties; of, based on, involving, division into 60 equal parts.

sex·en·ni·al (sĕksĕn'ĕal) *adj.* Lasting, (occurring) once in, six years.

sext (sĕkst) *n.* (R.C. Ch.) Canonical HOUR, (orig. said at) sixth hour of day (noon).

sex·tant (sĕks't*a*nt) *n.* Instrument with mirrors and graduated arc of sixth part of circle, used by navigators for finding position by measuring altitudes of heavenly bodies or horizontal angles between terrestrial objects.

sex·tet, sex·tette (sĕkstĕt', sĕks'tĕt) *ns.* 1. (mus.) (Composition for) six voices or instruments in combination. 2. Set of six persons or things.

sex·ton (sĕks't*o*n) *n.* Church officer having care of building and contents of church, freq. with duties of bell ringer and gravedigger.

sex·tu·ple (sĕkstōō'p*e*l, -tū'-, -tŭp'*e*l, sĕks'tup*e*l) *adj.* & *n.* Sixfold (amount). ~ *v.* (**-pled, -pling**). Multiply by six.

sex·u·al (sĕk'shōō*a*l) *adj.* 1. Of sex; of, occurring between, members of the two sexes; ~ intercourse, copulation, esp. of man and woman. 2. (biol.) Having sex or sexual organs; reproducing by union of male and female gametes (opp. *asexual*). 3. (bot., of classification) Based on distinction of sexes in plants. **sex'u·al·ly** *adv.* **sex·u·al·i·ty** (sĕkshōōăl'ĭtē) *n.*

sex·u·al·ize (sĕk'shōō*a*līz) *v.t.* (**-ized, -iz·ing**). Make sexual, attribute sex to. **sex·u·al·i·za·tion** (sĕkshōō*a*lĭzā'sh*o*n) *n.*

sex·y (sĕk'sē) *adj.* (**sex·i·er, sex·i·est**). (colloq.) Sexually attractive or provocative; engrossed with sex. **sex'i·ly** *adv.* **sex'i·ness** *n.*

Sey·chelles (sāshĕlz', sāshĕl'). Republic in the Indian Ocean, NE. of Madagascar, consisting of a group of about 90 islands, including Mahé, Praslin, La Digue; capital, Victoria, on Mahé; member of Brit. Commonwealth.

Sey·mour (sē'mōr, -mōr), **Jane** (*c*1509–37). Third queen of Henry VIII of England and mother of Edward VI.

sf, SF *abbrevs.* Science fiction.

s.g. *abbrev.* Specific gravity.

*Crude dwellings of corrugated iron and stone on the Black River in Jamaica. Poverty in that country still compels many families to live in **shacks,** although better housing is being built.*

Sgt, Sgt. *abbrevs.* Sergeant.

sh *int.* = HUSH.

Shaan·xi (shĕn′shē′) = SHENSI.

shab·by (shăb′ē) *adj.* (**-bi·er, -bi·est**). Contemptible, paltry, dishonorable; dingy and faded from wear or exposure; worn, dilapidated; shabbily dressed; **~-genteel**, attempting to look genteel or keep up appearances in spite of shabbiness. **shab′bi·ly** *adv.* **shab′bi·ness** *n.*

shack (shăk) *n.* Roughly built hut or shanty. **~** *v.i.* **~ up (with)**, (slang) live (with) as husband or wife without marriage.

shack·le (shăk′*e*l) *n.* Metal loop or staple, bow of padlock, link closed by bolt for connecting chains etc., coupling link; (pl.) fetters, impediments, restraints. **~** *v.t.* (**-led, -ling**). Fetter, impede trammel. **shack′ler** *n.*

shad (shăd) *n.* (pl. **shads,** collect. **shad**). Any of various deep-bodied herringlike fishes of genus *Alosa*, esp. *A. sapidissima*, much used as food; **shad′bush**, any of several N. Amer. trees and shrubs (genus *Amelanchier*), having creamy white blossoms and small blue-black or purple fruit; also called Juneberry and shadblow.

shad·dock (shăd′*o*k) *n.* (Tree, *Citrus grandis*, bearing) largest citrus fruit, esp. large coarse pear-shaped varieties of this (the smaller and rounder being called grapefruit). [Captain *Shaddock*, who introduced the plants into Barbados (1696)]

shade (shād) *n.* 1. Comparative or partial darkness, esp. caused by more or less opaque object intercepting rays of sun or other source of light; comparative obscurity; darker part of picture; place sheltered from sun, cool or sequestered retreat; (pl.) darkness *of* night or evening; **the ~s**, the abode of the dead, Hades. 2. Color, esp. with regard to its depth or as distinguished from one nearly like it; gradation of color; (painting) color darkened by admixture of black; darker tone of a color as dist. from *tint*. 3. Slight difference, small amount; unsubstantial or unreal thing. 4. Soul after death, ghost, disembodied spirit. 5. Screen excluding or moderating light, heat, etc.; eye shield; cover for lamp etc.; **shades**, (slang) sunglasses. **shade′less** *adj.* **shade** *v.* (**shad·ed, shad·ing**). Screen from excessive light; cover, keep off, or moderate power of (luminous object, light) with or as intervening object; make dark or gloomy; darken (parts of drawing etc.), esp. with parallel pencil lines, to give effects of light and shade or gradations of color; (of color, opinion, etc.) pass *off* by degrees into another color or variety, make pass thus *into* another. **shad′ed** *adj.* **shad′ing** *n.*

*The **shackle** on this steam train is an example of those used before the advent of the modern train. Carriages and rolling stock are now secured without the use of retaining chains.*

shad·ow (shăd′ō) *n.* 1. Shade; dark part of picture, room, etc.; patch of shade, dark figure projected by body intercepting rays of light, this regarded as appendage of person or thing; (fig.) inseparable attendant or companion. 2. Reflected image; delusive semblance or image; type, foreshadowing, adumbration; slightest trace; phantom, ghost. 3. Protection, shelter. 4. **shad′owboxing**, boxing against imaginary opponent as form of training; **shadow cabinet**, (Brit. politics) members of opposition party who would be cabinet ministers if that party became the government. **shad′ow·less, shad′ow·y** *adjs.* **shadow** *v.t.* 1. Cast shadow over. 2. Indicate obscurely, set *forth* dimly or in slight outline, prefigure. 3. Follow closely; follow and watch secretly. **shad′ow·er** *n.*

Shad·rach (shăd′răk). One of three Jewish youths who came unharmed from a furnace into which they were thrown by Nebuchadnezzar (Dan. 3).

shad·y (shā′dē) *adj.* (**shad·i·er, shad·i·est**). 1. Affording shade; shaded; **on the ~ side of**, older than (specified age). 2. Not able to bear the light, disreputable, of doubtful honesty. **shad′i·ly** *adv.* **shad′i·ness** *n.*

shaft (shăft, shahft) *n.* 1. Long slender rod forming body of spear, lance, or arrow; spear (archaic); arrow; ray *of* light, streak *of* lightning; (fig.) barbed remark, sarcasm. 2. Stem; part of column between base and capital; upright part of cross; part of chimney above roof; rib of feather; more or less long, narrow, and straight part supporting or connecting part(s) of greater thickness etc.; part of golf club between handle and head; handle, haft, of tool, etc. 3. (mech.) Long cylindrical rotating rod upon which

*Still a British colony, the **Seychelles** consists of more than 80 islands and atolls. The people are mostly of African descent and grow coconuts, cinnamon and vanilla as cash crops.*

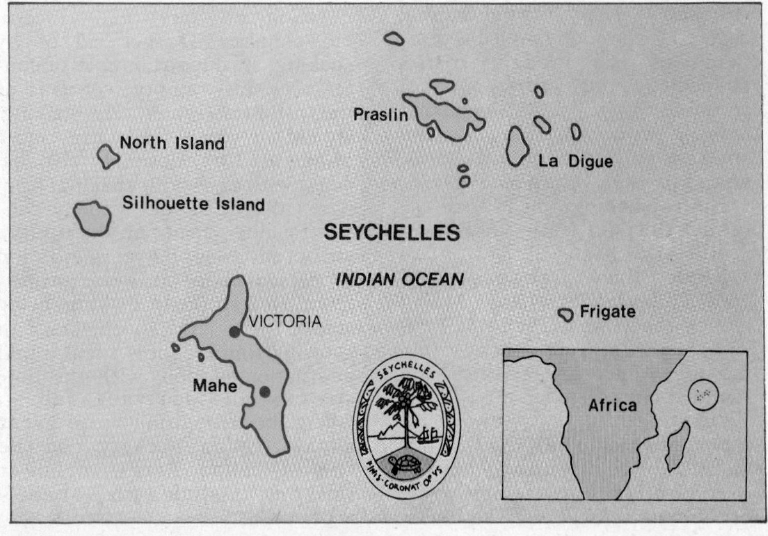

are fixed wheels, propeller, gears, etc. for transmission of motive power. 4. One of long bars between pair of which horse is harnessed to vehicle. 5. Vertical or inclined well-like excavation giving access to mine, tunnel, etc.; any similar well-like excavation or passage, as that in which elevator runs etc.

shag (shăg) *n.* 1. Rough growth or mass of hair etc. 2. (archaic) Long-napped rough cloth. 3. Strong, coarse kind of cut tobacco. 4. Cormorant.

shag·bark (shăg´bärk) *n.* (Wood, nut of) hickory tree (*Carya ovata*) having thick, gray, curling bark.

shag·gy (shăg´ē) *adj.* (**-gi·er, -gi·est**). Hairy, rough-haired; covered with rough tangled vegetation; (of hair) rough, coarse, tangled; ~ **dog story**, type of anecdote (orig. about a talking animal) with much detail, usu. amusing only in its pointlessness. **shag´gi·ly** *adv.* **shag´gi·ness** *n.*

shah (shah) *n.* Title of the former rulers of Iran. **shah´dom** *n.* [Pers., = "king"]

Shah (shah) **Ja·han** (1592?–1666). (also Shah Jehan) Mogul emperor in India, 1628–58; built Taj Mahal at Agra, 1632–45, a mausoleum for his favorite wife; founded city of Delhi.

shake (shāk) *v.* (**shook** pr. shōōk, **shak·en, shak·ing**). Move violently or quickly up and down or to and fro; (cause to) tremble, rock, or vibrate; jolt, jar; brandish;

Thomas Hare's impression of workers at the ***'Shaft Bottom'*** *of a coal-mine. Coal is no longer hand-winched to the surface in baskets, but brought up by continuous conveyor systems.*

weaken, make less firm or stable; agitate, shock, disturb; ~ **down**, cause to settle, descend, by shaking; test or try out, as ship or airplane; (slang) extort money from; **shake´-down** (*n.*), improvised bed; (slang) extortion of money by blackmail, violence, etc.; thorough search of person or place; **shake hand**(**s**), clasp right hands at meeting or parting, over concluded bargain, in congratulation, etc.; **shake head**, move it from side to side in refusal, negation, disapproval, concern, etc.; **shake off**, get rid of by shaking; **shake out**, empty of contents or dust, empty (contents or dust) from vessel, etc., by shaking; spread or open (sail, flag, etc.); **shake up**, mix, loosen, by shaking; rouse with or as with shaking; (esp. fig.) enliven, disturb (stodgy conventionality); hence **shake´up** (*n.*), abrupt and sweeping reorganization of personnel in business, government, etc.; **shake** *n.* shaking, being shaken; jolt, jerk, shock; crack in growing timber; (mus.) trill, rapid alternation of note with the note above; = MILK shake; **get a fair** ~, (slang) be treated fairly; **no great shakes**, (colloq.) not very good; **the shakes**, (colloq.) fit of trembling or shivering. **shak´a·ble, shake´-a·ble** *adjs.*

shak·er (shā´kẽr) *n.* (esp.) 1. Vessel in which ingredients of cocktails are shaken; vessel to sprinkle salt etc. on food. 2. **S** ~, member of Amer. religious celibate sect living in mixed communities, orig. founded (1747) in Manchester, England, by secession from the Quakers, and named from dancing movements that formed part of their worship.

Shake·speare, Shak·spere (shāks´pēr), **William** (1564–1616). England's greatest dramatist and poet; author of the comedies, *Twelfth Night, A Midsummer Night's Dream, The Tempest, The Merchant of Venice, Much Ado About Nothing*, etc.; the tragedies, *Romeo and Juliet, Julius Caesar, Hamlet, Othello, King Lear, Macbeth*, etc.; the histories, *Henry IV, Henry V, Henry VIII*, etc.; and the poems, "Venus and Adonis," "The Rape of Lucrece," etc., and many sonnets. **Shake·spear´e·an, Shake·spear´i·an, Shak·sper´i·an** *adjs.* & *ns.* ~ **sonnet**: see SONNET.

shak·o (shăk´ō, shā´kō) *n.* (pl. **shak·os, shak·oes**). Military cap, more or less cylindrical, with peak and upright plume or tuft. [Magyar csákó]

shak·y (shā´kē) *adj.* (**shak·i·er, shak·iest**). Unsteady, trembling, unsound, infirm; unreliable. **shak´i·ly** *adv.* **shak´i·ness** *n.*

shale (shāl) *n.* Very fine-grained laminated sedimentary rock consisting of consolidated mud or clay;

~ **oil**, oil obtained from bituminous shale. **shal'y** *adj*. (**shal·i·er, shal·i·est**).

shall (shăl) *v.aux*. (2nd pers. sing. archaic **shalt** pr. shălt, past and conditional **should** pr. shŏŏd). Forming compound tenses or moods expressing: (1) (in first pers.) simple future action; (2) (in other person) command; (3) (in all persons) obligation, intention, necessity, etc.

shal·lot (sha*l*ŏt', shăl'*o*t) *n*. Onionlike plant (*Allium ascalonicum*), native to Syria, with small clustered bulbs, resembling but milder than those of garlic, used for flavoring. [Fr. *eschalotte*, dim. of *eschaloigne* f. L. *ascalonia*, f. *Ascalon* in Palestine]

shal·low (shăl'ō) *adj*. Of little depth (lit. and fig.), superficial, trivial. **shal'low·ly** *adv*. **shal'low·ness** *n*. **shallow** *n*. Shallow place, shoal. ~ *v*. Become shallower; make shallow.

shalt: see SHALL.

sham (shăm) *n*. Imposture, pretense, humbug; person, thing, pretending or pretended to be something that he or it is not. ~ *adj*. Pretended, counterfeit, imitation. ~ *v*. (**shammed, sham·ming**). Feign, simulate; pretend to be. **sham'mer** *n*.

sha·man (shah'm*a*n, shā'-) *n*. (pl. **-mans**). Priest or witch doctor in shamanism. **sha'man·ism** *n*. Primitive religion of Ural-Altaic peoples of N. Asia in which gods, spirits, and demons influencing all human life are believed to be responsive to shamans; any similar religion, esp. among N. Amer. Indians.

sham·ble (shăm'b*e*l) *v.i*. (**-bled, -bling**). Walk, run, in shuffling, awkward, or decrepit way. ~ *n*. Shambling gait.

sham·bles (shăm'b*e*lz) *n.pl*. (usu. considered sing.). Butchers' slaughterhouse; scene of carnage or chaotic confusion.

shame (shām) *n*. Feeling of humiliation excited by consciousness of guilt or shortcoming, of appearing ridiculous, or of having offended against propriety etc.; fear of this as restraint on behavior; state of disgrace, ignominy, or discredit; person or thing that brings disgrace; (colloq.) regrettable or unlucky thing. **shame'ful, shame'less** *adjs*. **shame'ful·ly, shame'less·ly** *advs*. **shame'ful·ness, shame'less·ness** *ns*. **shame** *v.t*. (**shamed, sham·ing**). Bring shame on, be a shame to, make ashamed; put to shame by superior

This cliff face shows a layer of ***shale*** *compressed between two layers of sandstone, the result of changes in alluvial deposits over long periods of time.*

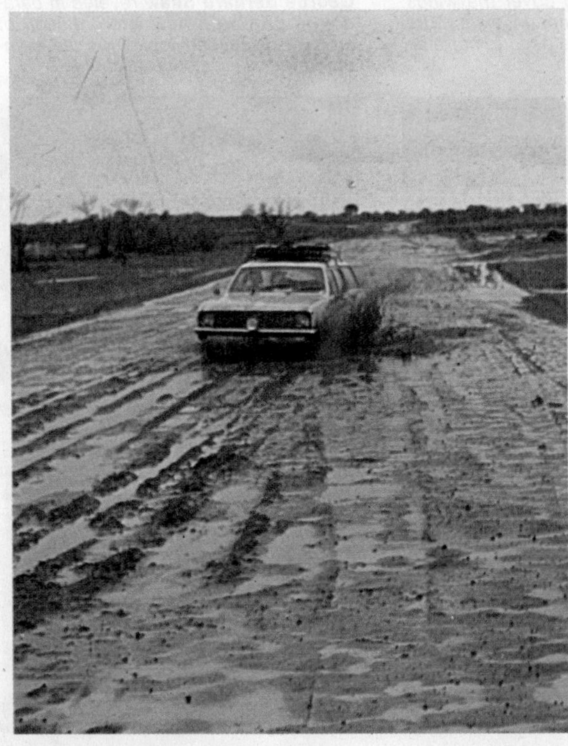

Even when ***shallow*** *water floods an unsurfaced road in the Northern Territory of Australia, cars can get bogged. If they drive too fast, drivers may find that they are in an uncontrollable skid.*

If the few proven facts of his life are assessed, it is astonishing that so many books could be written about ***William Shakespeare.*** *The first 'Life' by Nicholas Rowe was published in 1709.*

excellence; drive *into, out of*, through shame or fear of shame.

shame·faced (shām′fāst) *adj.* Ashamed; embarrassed. **shame·fac·ed·ly** (shāmfā′sĭdlē, shām′fāstlē) *adv.* **shame·fac′ed·ness** *n.*

sham·poo (shămpōō′) *v.t.* (**-pooed, -poo·ing**). Wash (hair) with cleansing preparation; use cleansing preparation on surface of (carpet, upholstery, etc.). ~ *n.* Shampooing (preparation). **sham·poo′er** *n.* [prob. f. Hind. *cā̃po*, imper. of *cā̃pnā* press, knead (dough or limbs)]

sham·rock (shăm′rŏk) *n.* Trifoliate plant, used, according to tradition, by St. Patrick to illustrate doctrine of Trinity, and hence adopted as national emblem of Ireland; (now usu.) lesser yellow trefoil (*Trifolium dubium*). [Ir. *seamróg*, dim. of *seamar* clover]

Shan (shahn, shăn) *n.* (pl. **Shans,** collect. **Shan**). Member, language, of a Thai people of Burma; ~ **State,** state of E. Burma.

Shan·dong (shahn′dawng′) = SHANTUNG.

Shang·hai (shănghī′; *Chin.* shahng′hī′). Principal seaport and commercial center of China, in the E., near the mouth of the Yangtze River.

shang·hai (shănghī′, shăng′hī) *v.t.* (**-haied, -hai·ing**). Drug or otherwise render insensible and ship as sailor while unconscious. [f. SHANGHAI]

Shan·gri·la (shănggrĭlah′, shăng′grĭlah) *n.* Imaginary hidden paradise on Earth. [f. place in James Hilton's novel *Lost Horizon* (1933)]

shank (shăngk) *n.* 1. Leg, lower part of leg from knee to ankle; shinbone, tibia; (part of) leg of bird (pop.); lower part of foreleg of horse; cut of meat. 2. Stem; straight part of nail, pin, fishhook, etc.; stem of key, spoon, anchor, etc.; shaft of tool between head etc. and handle; narrow part of shoe beneath instep; body of type.

Shan·si (shahn′sē′). Province of N. China.

shan't (shănt, shahnt) *v.* Contr. of *shall not.*

Shan·tung (shăn′tŭng′; *Chin.* shahn′dōōng′). Maritime province of NE. China.

shan·tung (shăntŭng′) *n.* Soft undressed Chinese silk, usu. undyed and sometimes mixed with cotton. [f. SHANTUNG]

shan·ty (shăn′tē) *n.* (pl. **-ties**). Hut, cabin; mean roughly constructed dwelling. [Canadian-Fr. *chantier* log hut, f. Fr., = "workshop"]

Shan·xi (shahn′shē′) = SHANSI.

SHAPE (shāp) *n.* Supreme Headquarters Allied Powers Europe.

shape (shāp) *n.* 1. External form, contour, configuration; visible appearance characteristic of person, thing, etc.; guise; concrete presentment, embodiment; phantom (now rare); dimly seen figure. 2. Kind, description, sort. 3. Definite or regular form, orderly arrangement. **shape′less** *adj.* **shape′less·ly** *adv.* **shape′less·ness** *n.* **shape** *v.* (**shaped, shap·ing**). Create, form, construct; model, mold, bring into desired or definite figure or form; frame mentally, imagine; assume form, develop into shape, give signs of future shape; ~ **up,** take (specified or favorable) form; behave better; exercise for health.

shape·ly (shāp′lē) *adj.* (**-li·er, -li·est**). Well-formed or proportioned, of pleasing shape. **shape′li·ness** *n.*

shard (shārd), **sherd** (shērd) *ns.* 1. = POTSHERD. 2. Hard wing case of beetle, elytron.

share[1] (shār) *n.* Portion detached for individual from common amount; part one is entitled to have or expected to contribute, equitable portion; part one gets or contributes; part proprietorship of property held by joint owners, esp. one of the equal parts into which company's capital is divided; **share′cropper,** tenant farmer paying rent with part of his crop; **share′holder,** owner of shares in corporation. **share** *v.* (**shared, shar·ing**). Apportion, give share of; give away part of; get or have share of; possess, use, endure, jointly with others; have share(s), be sharer(s); (in the language of some religious groups) communicate to others one's spiritual experiences.

share[2] (shār) *n.* PLOWshare; blade of cultivator or other agricultural tool for cutting soil.

shark (shārk) *n.* Any of various long-bodied cartilaginous fish, esp. large voracious kinds; rapacious person, swindler; (colloq.) expert in some particular activity; **shark′skin,** skin of shark used as leather etc.; worsted twill woven fabric; smooth fabric of rayon etc.

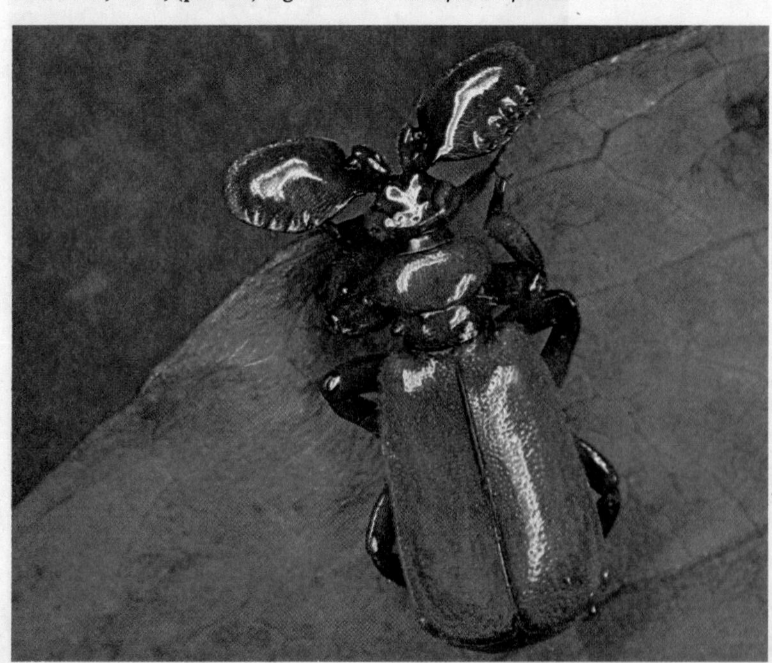

*A paussid beetle showing the shiny **shard** or elytra which cover the wings when the insect is not in flight. The space beneath may be used to store air in aquatic species.*

*As a dramatist, critic or propagandist, **George Bernard Shaw** reveled in paradox to provide a new interpretation of an over-discussed topic. His life demonstrated similar contradictions.*

sharp (shârp) *adj.* 1. Having keen edge or point, not blunt; peaked, pointed, edged; well-defined; abrupt, angular. 2. Keen, pungent, acid, tart; shrill, piercing; biting, harsh, severe, intense, painful. 3. Acute, sensitive, keen-witted, vigilant, clever; quick to take advantage, artful, unscrupulous, dishonest; **~ practice**, relentless pursuit of advantage; trickery. 4. Vigorous, speedy, impetuous. 5. (mus.) Above true pitch, too high; (following name of note, as *C sharp* etc.) a semitone higher than the note named; (of key) having sharps in the signature. 6. (slang) Very fashionably dressed; **~-shinned hawk, sharp'shin**, small N. Amer. hawk (*Accipiter striatus*) with long tail and rounded wings. **sharp'ly** *adv.* **sharp'ness** *n.* **sharp** *n.* 1. Sewing needle with sharp point. 2. (mus.) Note raised by a semitone above natural pitch; symbol (♯) indicating this raising. 3. (pl.) Finer parts of husk and coarser particles of flour of wheat and other cereals. **~** *adv.* Sharply; abruptly; punctually; (mus.) above true pitch; **sharp'shooter**, skilled marksman; businessman interested in quick profit with no regard for ethical practices. **sharp** *v.i.* Cheat, swindle, esp. at cards. **sharp'er** *n.* Cheat, swindler, esp. at cards. **sharp'en** *v.* Make, become sharp.

shash·lik (shahsh'lĭk, shahsh-lĭk') *n.* Marinated cubes of meat, esp. lamb, broiled on skewer; shish kebab.

Shas·ta (shăst'*a*), **Mount.** Extinct volcano in N. California, 14,162 ft. (4,317 m), in the Cascade Mountain Range.

shat·ter (shăt'*er*) *v.* Break suddenly and violently in pieces; utterly destroy, wreck; **shat'ter-proof**, able to resist or withstand shattering. **shat'ter·ing·ly** *adv.*

shave (shāv) *v.* (**shaved, shaved** or **shav·en, shav·ing**). 1. Remove (hair), free (chin etc.) of hair, relieve of hair on chin etc., with razor; shave oneself; **shaving brush**, brush for applying lather before shaving. 2. Cut or pare away surface of (wood etc.) with plane or other sharp tool. 3. Pass close to without touching; miss narrowly, nearly graze. **shave** *n.* 1. Shaving, being shaved. 2. Close approach without contact; narrow miss, escape, or failure. 3. Knife blade with handle at each end for shaving wood etc. **shav'a·ble, shave'a·ble** *adjs.*

shav·en (shā'ven) *adj.* Shaved, tonsured; closely clipped.

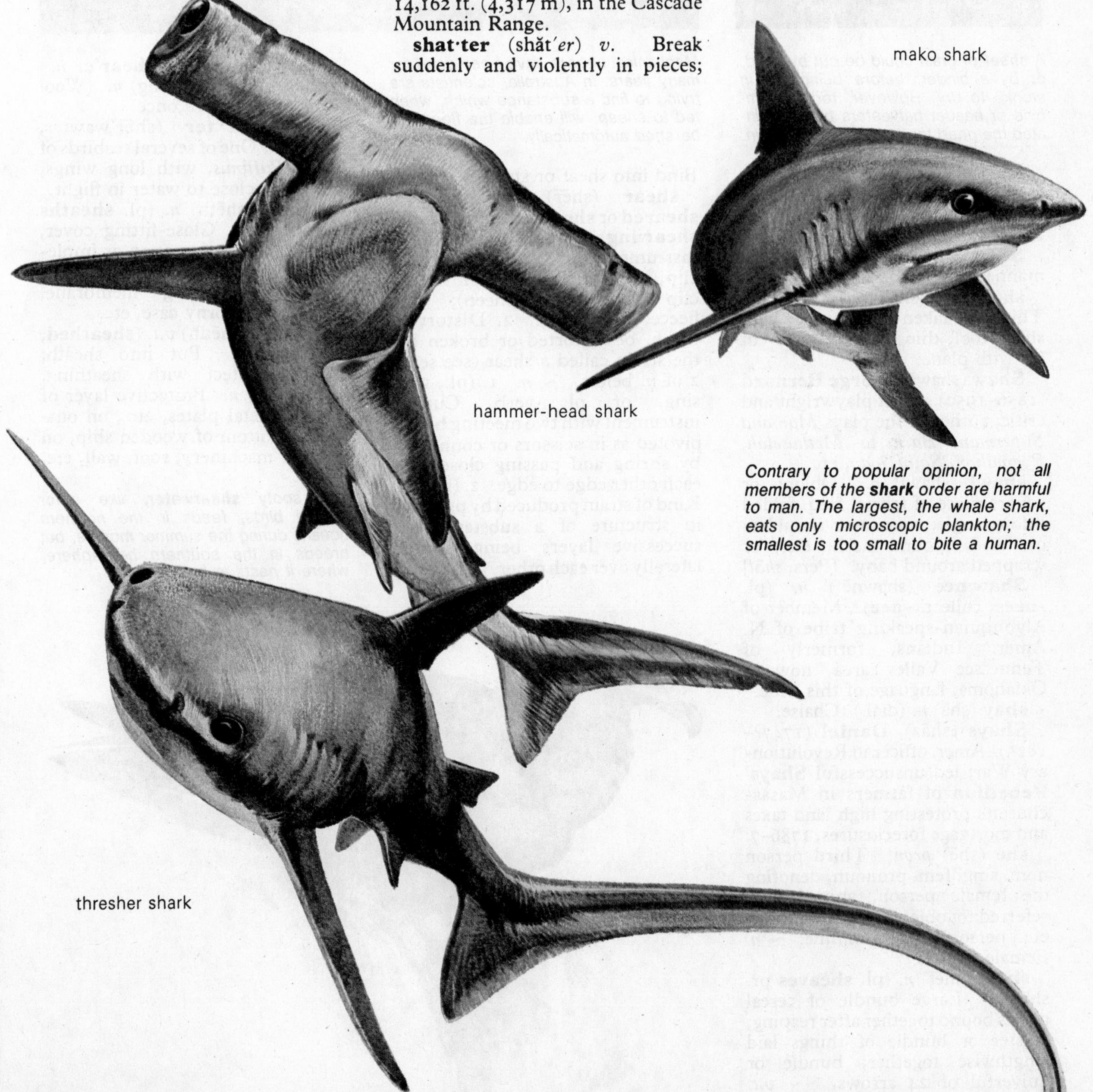

Contrary to popular opinion, not all members of the ***shark*** *order are harmful to man. The largest, the whale shark, eats only microscopic plankton; the smallest is too small to bite a human.*

*A **sheaf** of grain could be cut by hand, or by a binder, before being put in stooks to dry. However, today, combine or header harvesters have eliminated the need for early cutting of grain.*

*Mechanical **shears** have been used for many years. In Australia, scientists are trying to find a substance which, when fed to sheep, will enable the fleece to be shed automatically.*

shav·er (shā′v*er*) *n.* (esp.) 1. (colloq.) Lad, youngster. 2. Electrical appliance for shaving hair from face.

Sha·vi·an (shā′vēan) *adj.* (In the manner) of G. B. SHAW.

shav·ing (shā′vĭng) *n.* (esp.) Thin slice taken from surface with sharp tool; thin slice of wood cut off with plane.

Shaw (shaw), **George Bernard** (1856–1950). Irish playwright and critic; author of the plays *Man and Superman, Back to Methuselah, Pygmalion, Saint Joan*, etc.

shawl (shawl) *n.* Oblong or square piece of fabric, freq. folded into triangle, worn over shoulders or head, around neck, etc., or wrapped around baby. [Pers. *shāl*]

Shaw·nee (shawnē′) *n.* (pl. **-nees**, collect. **-nee**). Member of Algonquian-speaking tribe of N. Amer. Indians, formerly of Tennessee Valley area, now in Oklahoma; language of this tribe.

shay (shā) *n.* (dial.) Chaise.

Shays (shāz), **Daniel** (1747?–1825). Amer. officer in Revolutionary War; led unsuccessful **Shays' Rebellion** of farmers in Massachusetts protesting high land taxes and mortgage foreclosures, 1786–7.

she (shē) *pron.* Third person nom. sing. fem. pronoun, denoting the female person, animal, etc. referred to; object, device, country, etc., personified as feminine. ~ *n.* Female animal.

sheaf (shēf) *n.* (pl. **sheaves** pr. shēvz). Large bundle of cereal plants bound together after reaping; cluster or bundle of things laid lengthwise together; bundle or quiverful of 24 arrows. ~ *v.t.* Bind into sheaf or sheaves.

shear (shēr) *v.* (**sheared, sheared** or **shorn** pr. shōrn, shōrn, **shear·ing**). 1. Cut with sharp instrument (poet. and archaic); clip, cut with scissors or shears; clip wool from (sheep); (fig.) fleece, strip bare. 2. Distort or break, be distorted or broken by, the strain called a shear (see sense 2 of *n.* below). ~ *n.* 1. (pl., with sing. or pl. verb) Cutting instrument with two meeting blades pivoted as in scissors or connected by spring and passing close over each other edge to edge. 2. (mech.) Kind of strain produced by pressure in structure of a substance, its successive layers being shifted laterally over each other. 3. (pl., also ~ **legs**): see SHEERS. **shear′er** *n.*

shear·ling (shēr′lĭng) *n.* (Wool from) sheep shorn once.

shear·wa·ter (shēr′wawt*er*, -wŏt*er*) *n.* One of several seabirds of genus *Puffinus*, with long wings, skimming close to water in flight.

sheath (shēth) *n.* (pl. **sheaths** pr. shēdhz). Close-fitting cover, esp. for blade of weapon or implement; (bot., anat., etc.) sheathlike covering, investing membrane, tissue, skin, horny case, etc.

sheathe (shēdh) *v.t.* (**sheathed, sheath·ing**). Put into sheath; encase, protect with sheathing. **sheath′ing** *n.* Protective layer of boards, metal plates, etc., on outside of bottom of wooden ship, on piece of machinery, roof, wall, etc.

*The sooty **shearwater,** like other related birds, feeds in the northern oceans during the summer months, but breeds in the southern hemisphere, where it nests in burrows.*

Classing wool from exhibition class ***sheep*** *at an Australian show. Although some breeds are raised for wool, others provide meat, and some sheep serve both purposes.*

sheave[1] (shĭv, shēv) *n.* Grooved wheel or pulley of pulley block etc.

sheave[2] (shēv) *v.t.* (**sheaved, sheav·ing**). Gather (corn etc.) into sheaves.

sheaves: see SHEAF.

She·ba (shē′ba), **Queen of.** Balkis, who visited Solomon to test his wisdom (I Kings 10).

she·bang (shebăng′) *n.* (slang) House, hut; matter, business.

shed[1] (shĕd) *n.* Slight structure for shelter, storage, etc., freq. built as lean-to, and sometimes with open front or sides; similar but large and strongly built structure on pier, at airport, etc.

shed[2] (shĕd) *v.t.* (**shed, shed·ding**). Part with, let fall (off), drop; cause (blood) to flow; disperse, diffuse, spread abroad; **~ light on**, illuminate, esp. fig.

she'd (shēd). Contr. of *she had, she would.*

sheen (shēn) *n.* Splendor, radiance, luster. **sheen'y** *adj.* (**sheen·i·er, sheen·i·est**).

sheep (shēp) *n.* (pl. **sheep**). Wild or domesticated timid, gregarious, woolly, often horned, ruminant mammal of genus *Ovis*, closely allied to goat, bred for flesh and wool; (usu. pl.) member(s) of minister's flock, parishioners, etc.; person as stupid, poor-spirited, unoriginal, or timid as a sheep; **~-dip**, preparation for cleansing sheep of vermin or preserving their wool; place for such cleansing; **sheep'dog**, dog trained to herd sheep; **Old English sheep'dog**, shaggy-coated bobtailed dog used for guarding and herding sheep; **sheep's eyes**, amorous glances; **sheep laurel**, low-growing evergreen (*Kalmia angustifolia*) of eastern N. Amer., having pink flowers and poisonous leaves; **sheep'shank**, knot for temporarily shortening rope, made by doubling rope in three parts and taking hitch over bight at each end; **sheeps'head** (pl. **-head, -heads**), (dish of) head of sheep; large food fish of Atlantic coasts of U.S., with head supposed to resemble sheep's; **sheep'skin**, garment or rug of sheep's skin with wool on; leather of sheep's skin used in bookbinding, etc.; parchment of sheep's skin, diploma engrossed on this; diploma (colloq.).

sheep·ish (shē′pĭsh) *adj.* Embarrassed, shamefaced. **sheep'-ish·ly** *adv* **sheep'ish·ness** *n.*

The ability to train certain breeds of dog into efficient controllers of sheep has resulted in several types of ***sheepdog.*** *They will round up a flock with as much speed and skill as a horseman.*

sheer[1] (shēr) *adj.* Mere, unqualified, undiluted, absolute; (of textile fabric) thin, diaphanous; (of rock, fall, ascent, etc.) perpendicular, very steep and without a break. ~ *adv.* Plumb, perpendicularly, outright. **sheer'ly** *adv.* **sheer'ness** *n.*

sheer[2] (shēr) *v.i.* (naut.) Deviate from course; ~ **off**, swerve away; make off.

sheer[3] (shēr) *n.* Upward slope of ship's lines toward bow and stern; deviation of ship from course.

sheers, shears (shērz) *ns.* (pl.; also **shear legs** or **sheer legs**) Hoisting apparatus of two or more poles attached at or near top and separated at bottom for masting ships or putting in engines etc., used in dockyards. [var. of SHEAR; named from resemblance to pair of shears]

sheet (shēt) *n.* 1. Rectangular piece of linen, cotton, etc., used as one of a pair of inner bedclothes. 2. Broad, flat piece of some thin material, as paper; complete piece of paper of the size in which it was made; newspaper. 3. Wide expanse of water, snow, ice, flame, color, etc. 4. Rope or chain at lower corner of sail, used to extend it or alter its direction. 5. (pl.) Spaces of open boat forward of (**foresheets**) and abaft (**stern sheets**) thwarts. 6. **in sheets**, (of book) printed but not bound; **three sheets to the wind**, rather or very drunk. 7. **sheet bend**, kind of knot made to join two ropes; **sheet glass**, kind made first as hollow cylinder that is cut open and flattened in furnace; **sheet iron, metal**, etc., spread by rolling, hammering, etc., into thin sheets; **sheet lightning**, sheetlike illumination caused by reflection and diffusion of lightning on clouds; **sheet music**, music published in sheets, not in book form; **Sheet'rock**, (trademark) gypsum plasterboard covered with paper. **sheet** *v.t.* Furnish with sheets; cover with sheet; secure (sail) with sheet.

Shef·field (shĕf'ēld). City in south Yorkshire, England, famous for manufacture of cutlery and steel; ~ **plate**, copperware coated with silver by process now disused.

sheik, sheikh (shēk, shāk) *ns.* Chief, head, of Arab tribe, family, or village; title of eminent Muslim. **sheik'dom, sheikh'dom** *ns.* Office, territory, of sheik.

shek·el (shĕk'el) *n.* Ancient Babylonian, Phoenician, Hebrew, etc., weight; coin of this weight; monetary unit of Israel; (pl., colloq.) money, riches.

shel·drake (shĕl'drāk) *n.* (pl. **-drakes**, collect. **-drake**) (fem. **shel·duck** pr. shĕl'dŭk). Bright-plumaged wild duck of genus *Tadorna*, frequenting sandy coasts in Europe, N. Africa, and Asia.

*Made in the 1760s by a process now discarded, this **Sheffield plate** coffee pot is 11 ins. high and illustrates the workmanship needed to produce such decorative effects.*

shelf (shĕlf) *n.* (pl. **shelves** pr. shĕlvz). Projecting slab of stone or board let into or hung on wall to support things; one of boards in cabinet, bookcase, etc., on which contents stand; ledge, horizontal steplike projection in cliff face etc.; reef or sandbank under water; **on the** ~, (fig.) put aside, done with; ~ **life**, time for which packaged food etc. can be stored and remain usable; ~ **mark**, mark, number, on book indicating its place on library shelf.

shell (shĕl) *n.* 1. Hard outer case enclosing kernel of nut, some kinds of seed or fruit, egg, some mollusks or crustaceans, etc.; (fig.) reticent attitude concealing emotions. 2. Walls of unfinished or gutted building, ship, etc.; light narrow racing boat; conch-shaped structure for outdoor concerts etc.; domed arena etc. 3. Explosive artillery projectile; cartridge. 4. **shell'back**, (joc.) old sailor; **shell'-bark** (**hickory**): see SHAGBARK; **shell'fire**, shooting or firing of explosive shells; **shell'fish** (pl. **-fishes**, collect. **fish**), any aquatic animal with shell, esp. crustacean or mollusk; **shell game**, swindling sleight-of-hand trick with three thimble-shaped cups and pea, and bystanders betting which cup covers pea; any trick or game that takes unfair advantage of customers; **shell jacket**, semi-formal tight-fitting jacket reaching only to waist behind, worn esp. instead of tuxedo by officers; **shell shock**, BATTLE fatigue. **shelled, shell'-less, shell'y** *adjs.* (**shell·i·er, shell·i·est**). **shell** *v.t.* 1. Take out of shell, remove shell or pod from; ~ **out**, (slang) pay up, hand over (money). 2. Bombard, fire at, with shells. **shell'er** *n.*

*A cowry **shell** collected from the Great Barrier Reef off Queensland, Australia. Excessive collection of such decorative shells has resulted in parts of the reef being bereft of certain shellfish.*

she'll (shēl). Contr. of *she shall, she will.*

shel·lac, shel·lack (shelăk') *ns.* Purified lac, esp. in thin plates, used in varnishes, insulating materials, (formerly) phonograph records, because of its high gloss, adhesiveness, and toughness. ~ *v.t.* (**-lacked, -lack·ing**). Varnish, coat with shellac; (slang) thrash, defeat by wide margin. **shel·lack'-ing** *n.* Utter defeat.

Shel·ley (shĕl'ē), **Percy Bysshe** (1792–1822). English Romantic poet, author of "Ode to the West Wind," "To a Skylark," "Ado-

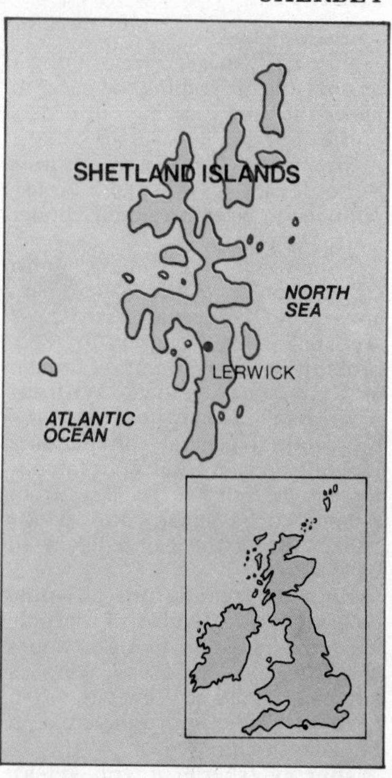

A village built in the Bronze Age at Jarlshof in the ***Shetland Islands.*** *Today these Scottish offshore islands are known for distinctive woolen garments made by the inhabitants.*

One of the greatest British lyric poets, ***Percy Bysshe Shelley*** *spent his last years in Italy after offending society by his support of atheism and his rejection of marital fidelity.*

nais," etc. and of the dramas *The Cenci, Prometheus Unbound,* etc.; **Mary Wollstonecraft Shelley** (1797–1851), his second wife, author of *Frankenstein.*

shel·ter (shĕl′t*er*) *n.* Object serving as shield or barrier against attack, danger, heat, wind, etc.; screen or cabin to keep off wind, rain, etc.; place of safety or immunity; sheltered or protected state (usu. **seek, take** ~); **tax** ~: see TAX. **shelter** *v.* Act or serve as shelter to; protect, conceal, harbor, defend *from* blame, screen, shield; take shelter.

shel·ty, shel·tie (shĕl′tē): see SHETLAND pony, SHETLAND sheepdog.

shelve[1] (shĕlv) *v.t.* (**shelved, shelv·ing**). Put on shelf; provide with shelves, esp. bookshelves; put aside (question etc.) from consideration; remove (person) from office, employment, etc. **shelv′ing** *n.* (esp.) Shelves, material for shelves.

shelve[2] (shĕlv) *v.i.* (**shelved, shelv·ing**). Slope gently.

Shem (shĕm), **Sem** (sĕm). Eldest son of Noah (Gen. 10).

Shen·an·do·ah (shĕnandō′*a*). River flowing NE. 55 mi. (88 km), from N. Virginia to Harpers Ferry, West Virginia, emptying into the Potomac River; ~ **National Park,** area in N. Virginia covering 302 sq. mi. (782 sq. km), including part of the Blue Ridge Mountains.

she·nan·i·gan (sh*e*năn′*i*g*a*n) *n.* (usu. pl.) (colloq.) Nonsense; trickery; high-spirited behavior.

Shen·si (shĕn′sē′). Province of N. China.

She·ol (shē′ōl). Hebrew underworld, abode of the dead, represented as subterranean region of thick darkness from which return is impossible.

shep·herd (shĕp′*erd*), fem. **shep·herd·ess** (shĕp′*erd*ĭs) *ns.* Person who guards, tends, and herds flock of sheep; pastor; **~'s pie,** pie of chopped or minced meat with crust of mashed potatoes; **shepherd's-purse,** common cruciferous white-flowered weed, *Capsella bursa-pastoris,* with pouchlike pods. **shepherd** *v.t.* Tend as shepherd; marshal, conduct, guide people etc., like sheep.

Sher·a·ton (shĕr′*a*t*o*n), **Thomas** (1751–1806). English furniture designer; light, graceful style of furniture designed by Sheraton.

sher·bet (shẽr′bĭt) *n.* Confection of flavored and frozen water and sugar with added gelatin, egg white, or milk. [f. Turk. Pers. *šerbet* f. Arab. *šarba* drink]

sherd: SHARD.

sher·iff (shĕr'ĭf) *n.* Officer responsible for keeping the peace in his county and carrying out orders of the court.

Sher·man[1] (shẽr'm*a*n), **James Schoolcraft** (1855–1912). Amer. politician; vice president under Taft, 1909–12.

Sher·man[2] (shẽr'm*a*n), **John** (1823–1900). Amer. statesman; sponsor of **Sherman Antitrust Act**, passed by Congress in 1890, prohibiting any restraints of foreign or interstate trade; **William Tecumseh Sherman** (1820–91), his brother, general commanding Union troops in Civil War; famous for his March to the Sea, from Atlanta to Savannah, Nov.–Dec., 1864, cutting the Confederacy in half.

Sher·pa (shẽr'p*a*) *n.* (pl. **-pas**, collect. **-pa**). Member of a people of Mongolian origin living on slopes of Himalayas and speaking a language allied to Tibetan, often used as guides, porters, etc., on Himalayan climbs.

sher·ry (shĕr'ē) *n.* (pl. **-ries**). Still wine made near Jerez de la Frontera in Andalusia, Spain, varying in color from pale gold to dark brown and usu. fortified; similar wine made elsewhere. [Span. (*vino de*) *Xeres* (wine of) Jerez]

Shet·land (shĕt'l*a*nd). ~ **Islands** (also **Shetlands**), group of islands NNE. of Scottish mainland; ~ **pony**, pony of small hardy rough-coated breed orig. from Shetland Islands, also called sheltie; ~ **sheepdog**, any of a breed of dogs developed in Shetland Islands and resembling small collie, also called sheltie; ~ **wool**, fine thin loosely twisted wool from Shetland sheep. **Shetland** *n.* Shetland pony. **Shet'land·er** *n.*

Shi·ah (shē'*a*). Muslim sect (chiefly represented by Persians) holding that Muhammad's cousin and son-in-law Ali was the prophet's true successor and that the three first Sunnite caliphs were usurpers. **Shi·ite** (shē'īt) *n.* & *adj.* [Arab. *al-šīʿa* party, sect (of Ali)]

shib·bo·leth (shĭb'*o*lĭth) *n.* Test word, principle, opinion, etc., the use of or inability to use which betrays one's party, nationality, etc. (Judges 12:6) catchword, (esp. outworn or empty) formula, etc., distinguishing a party or sect. [Heb. *šibbōleṯ*]

shield (shēld) *n.* Article of defensive armor carried in hand or on arm as protection from weapons of enemy; protective plate or screen in machinery etc.; mass of concrete or lead around nuclear reactor to prevent escape of radiation; person or thing serving as protection or defense; shieldlike part in animal or plant; (her.) escutcheon; policeman's shield-shaped badge. ~ *v.t.* Protect, screen, esp. from censure or punishment. **shield'er** *n.*

shift (shĭft) *n.* 1. Change of place or character; substitution of one thing for another; vicissitude; rotation; **red** ~, (astron.) apparent shift in spectra of light from distant galaxies toward the long wave or red end of the spectrum, indicating that the galaxies are receding; ~ **key**, key for adjusting typewriter when capitals etc. are to be used. 2. Expedient, device, stratagem, resource; dodge, trick, piece of evasion or equivocation. 3. Chemise. 4. Relay or change of workmen; length of time during which such relay works; **gear'-shift**: see GEAR. **shift** *v.* 1. Change or move from one position to another, change form or character. 2. Use expedients, contrive; manage, get along; ~ **for oneself**, depend on one's own efforts.

shift·less (shĭft'lĭs) *adj.* Lacking in resourcefulness; lazy, inefficient. **shift'less·ly** *adv.* **shift'less·ness** *n.*

shift·y (shĭf'tē) *adj.* (**shift·i·er, shift·i·est**). Not straightforward, evasive, deceitful. **shift'i·ly** *adv.* **shift'i·ness** *n.*

Shih Tzu (shĭ'dzōō') (pl. **Shih·-Tzus,** collect. **Shih·Tzu**). (Breed of) short-legged toy dog having long, silky hair of various colors. [Chin., "lion dog"]

Shi·ite: see SHIAH.

shik·sa (shĭk's*a*) *n.* (disparaging) Non-Jewish girl or woman; Jewish girl or woman with attitudes etc. felt to resemble those of gentiles. [Yiddish]

shill (shĭl) *n.* Person employed to decoy or entice others.

shil·le·lagh, shil·la·lah (sh*e*lā'-l*a*, -lē) *ns.* Irish cudgel of black-

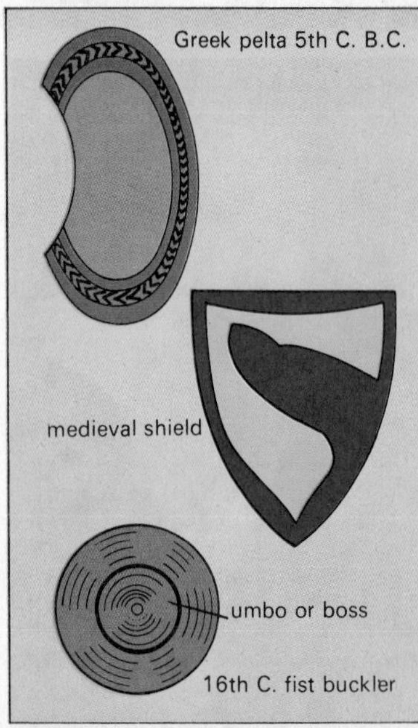

Left: A steel ***shield*** *made in the 16th century and ornamented with gold. Above: Various designs of shield used at different periods. Shape was determined by the weapons used.*

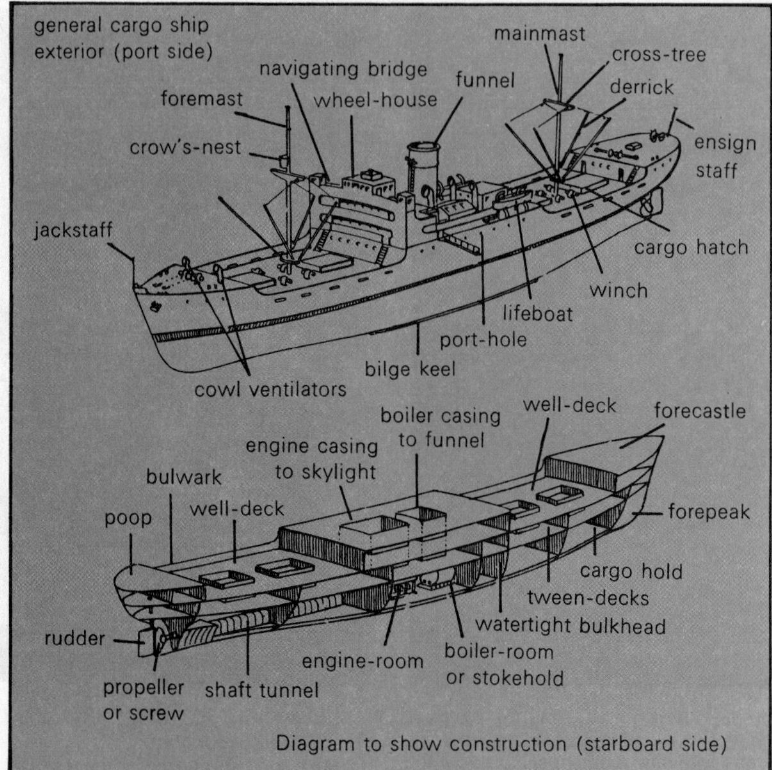

Design of a cargo ***ship*** *is constantly changing as new methods are devised for loading goods. The design shown left is now matched by bulk carriers and container ships.*

thorn or oak. [*Shillelagh* name of village in County Wicklow]

shil·ling (shĭl'ĭng) *n.* (abbrev. s.) Monetary unit of Kenya, Somalia, Tanzania, and Uganda; until 1971, monetary unit of U.K., = $\frac{1}{20}$ of a pound.

shil·ly-shal·ly (shĭl'ē shăl'ē) *n.* Vacillation, irresolution, indecision. ~ *v.i.* (**-lied, -ly·ing**). Vacillate, be irresolute or undecided. **shil'ly-shal'li·er** *n.* [orig. *shill I, shall I*]

shim (shĭm) *n.* Thin slip or wedge used in machinery etc. to make parts fit. ~ *v.* (**shimmed, shim·ming**). Fit or fill up thus.

shim·mer (shĭm'*er*) *v.i.* & *n.* (Shine with) tremulous or faint diffused light. **shim'mer·ing·ly** *adv.* **shim'mer·y** *adj.*

shim·my (shĭm'ē) *n.* (pl. **-mies**) *n.* 1. Kind of fox trot of 1920's accompanied by much shaking of body. 2. Abnormal vibration of (front) wheels of automobile. ~ *v.* (**-mied, -my·ing**). 1. Dance a shimmy; move in similar manner. 2. Vibrate abnormally.

shin (shĭn) *n.* Front of human leg below knee; lower part of leg of beef; **shin'bone**, tibia; **shin guard**, guard worn in soccer, hockey, etc. to protect the shins. **shin** *v.i.* (**shinned, shin·ning**). Climb up by using arms and legs, without help of ladder, irons, etc.

shin·dig (shĭn'dĭg) *n.* (colloq.) Festive gathering (esp. boisterous one).

shine (shīn) *v.* (**shone** pr. shōn, **shined, shin·ing**). Emit or reflect light, be bright, glow; be brilliant, excel, in some respect or sphere; (colloq.) make bright, polish (boots etc.); ~ **up to**, (slang) seek to ingratiate oneself with. **shine** *n.* Light, brightness; sunshine; luster, sheen; **take a** ~ **to**, (slang) take immediate liking to.

shin·er (shī'n*er*) *n.* (esp.) 1. (slang) Black eye. 2. Any of various small silvery fresh-water fishes of the genus *Notropis.*

shin·gle (shĭng'gel) *n.* 1. Thin rectangular piece of wood etc. thicker at one end, used overlapping for roof or siding; small signboard esp. of doctor, lawyer, etc. 2. Shingled hair. ~ *v.t.* (**-gled, -gling**). 1. Cover, roof, with shingles. 2. Cut (woman's hair) short so that it tapers from back of head to nape of neck. **shin'gler** *n.*

shin·gles (shĭng'g*e*lz) *n.* (pop., considered sing. or pl.) = HERPES zoster. [L. *cingulum* girdle, because eruptions freq. appear around trunk]

shin·ny (shĭn'ē) *v.i.* (**-nied, -ny·ing**). (colloq.) Shin *up* (tree etc.)

shin·splints (shĭn'splĭnts) *n.pl.* (colloq., used with sing. verb) Aching strain in lower leg extensor muscles.

Shin·to (shĭn'tō) *n.* Ancient religion of Japan, based on worship of ancestors and of nature, gradually absorbed and superseded by Buddhism from 6th c. onward, but reestablished as the state religion from 1868 to 1945, with the emperor considered the descendant of the sun; after World War II the emperor disavowed his divinity and governmental support of Shinto was forbidden. **Shin'to·ism** *n.* **Shin'to·ist** *n.* & *adj.* [Chin. *shin* god, *tao* doctrine, way]

shin·y (shī'nē) *adj.* (**shin·i·er, shin·i·est**). Glistening, shining, polished, rubbed bright. **shin'i·ness** *n.* **shin'i·ly** *adv.*

ship (shĭp) *n.* Any large seagoing vessel, propelled by sails, steam, or other mechanical means; (specif.) sailing vessel with bowsprit and three square-rigged masts, each divided into lower, top, and topgallant mast; aircraft; ~**('s) biscuit**, hard coarse kind of biscuit made for keeping, formerly much used on board ship; **ship'board** (*adj.*), used, occurring, done, etc. on ship; **on ship'board**, (adverbial phrase) on board ship; **ship'builder**, one whose business it is to build ships; **ship'building; ship canal**, canal large enough for seagoing vessels; **ship('s) chandler**, dealer supplying ships with stores; **ship'load**, quantity of something forming whole cargo; **ship'mate**, fellow sailor; **ship's company**, crew of a ship, not including the officers; **ship'shape**, in good order, trim and neat; **ship's papers**, documents carried on board ship establishing ownership, nationality, nature of cargo, etc.; **ship'way**, inclined track on which a ship is built and down which it is launched; **ship'worm**, worm-shaped mollusks of the genera *Teredo* and *Barkia* that bore into ship's timbers; **ship'wreck**, (cause, suffer) destruction of ship by storm, foundering, striking rock, etc.; (fig.) ruin; **ship'wright**, shipbuilder, ship's carpenter; **ship'yard**, shipbuilding establishment. **ship** *v.* (**shipped, ship·ping**). 1. Put, take, send away, on board ship; take ship, embark; take service on ship; deliver (goods) to forwarding agent for conveyance by land or water. 2. Fix (mast, rudder, etc.) in its place; remove (oars) from rowlocks and lay them inside boat; (of vessel) take in (water) over the side.

-ship *suffix.* Specified character, office, skill, etc. (*friendship, premiership, seamanship*).

ship·ment (shĭp'ment) *n.* Putting of goods etc. on ship; amount shipped, consignment.

ship·per (shĭp'*er*) *n.* Merchant etc. who sends or receives goods by ship.

ship·ping (shĭp'ĭng) *n.* (esp.) Ships, esp. the ships of a country, port, etc.; ~ **clerk**, employee who

attends to incoming and outgoing shipments of merchandise and keeps records of it.

shirk (shẽrk) *v.t.* Avoid meanly, evade, shrink selfishly from (duty, responsibility, etc.). **shirk'er** *n.*

shirr (shẽr) *v.t.* 1. Gather (material) with several parallel threads. 2. Bake (eggs removed from shells) in shallow dish(es). ~ *n.* Shirring, shirred trimming.

shirt (shẽrt) *n.* Man's loose sleeved garment for upper part of body; **in ~-sleeves**, without coat, or coat and vest; **keep one's ~ on**, (slang) keep one's temper; **lose one's ~**, (slang) lose all one's possessions; **~ front**, breast of shirt, freq. stiffened or starched; dicky; **shirt'tail**, back part of shirt below waist. **shirt'ing** *n.* Material for shirts.

Above: A large container terminal in Melbourne, Australia, is needed to cope with new forms of shipping cargo. Right: In Britain, the ***shipbuilding*** *yards still produce vessels which maintain an elegant line, despite their size.*

shish ke·bab (shĭsh'kebŏb) *n.* Pieces of marinated meat and vegetables cooked on skewers.

shit (shĭt) *v.i.* (**shit, shit·ting**). (vulg.) 1. Evacuate bowels. 2. Speak untruthfully with intent to deceive. ~ *n.* (vulg.) 1. Feces. 2. Act of evacuating bowels. 3. Useless junk. 4. Nonsense. 5. Contemptible person. 6. Narcotic, esp. heroin. ~ *int.* (vulg., used to express anger, contempt, disappointment, etc.).

shiv (shĭv) *n.* (slang) Razor or knife used as weapon.

Shi·va (shē'va), **Si·va** (sē'va, shē'va). (Hinduism) One of the supreme gods, third deity of the triad of which Brahma and Vishnu are the other members; he represents the principle of destruction and the regeneration that follows destruction. **Shi'va·ism, Si'va·ism** *ns.* Worship of Shiva.

shiv·er[1] (shĭv'er) *n.* Quivering or trembling, esp. of body under influence of cold, fear, etc. ~ *v.i.* Tremble, shake, quiver, esp. with cold or fear. **shiv'er·er** *n.* **shiv'er·y** *adj.* **shiv'er·ing·ly** *adv.*

shiv·er[2] (shĭv'er) *n.* One of many small pieces into which thing is shattered by blow or fall. ~ *v.* Break into shivers.

shoal[1] (shōl) *adj.* (of water) Shallow. ~ *n.* Shallow place in water, sandbank or bar. ~ *v.i.* Grow shallow(er). **shoal'y** *adj.* (**shoal·i·er, shoal·i·est**).

shoal[2] (shōl) *n.* Multitude, crowd, great number, esp. of fish swimming in company. ~ *v.i.* Form shoals.

shoat (shōt) *n.* Young (esp. weanling) pig.

shock[1] (shŏk) *n.* Violent collision, concussion, or impact; one of the violent shakes or tremors of part of Earth's surface constituting an earthquake; sudden and disturbing mental or physical impression; stimulation of nerve(s) with muscular contraction and

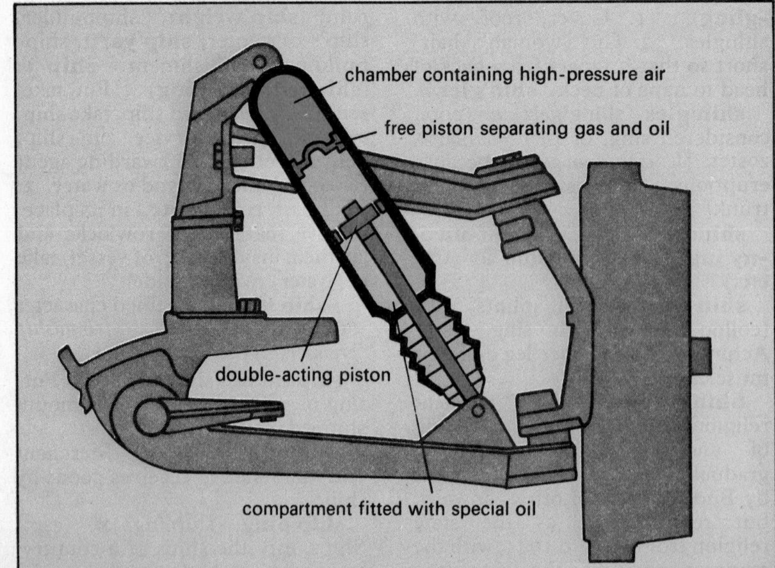

Left: Section showing the working parts of a hydraulic ***shock-absorber.*** *Best known for their use on automobiles, similar damping devices have many other applications in industry.*

feeling of concussion by passage of electric current through body; (path.) acute state of prostration accompanied by lowering of blood volume and pressure and weakening of pulse and respiration, commonly following accidents, wounds, or burns; ~ **absorber**, device for absorbing vibration in mechanically propelled vehicles; device on aircraft to lessen shock of landing; ~ **tactics**, sudden and violent action; ~ **therapy, treatment**, treatment of mental disorders by application of electric shock to central nervous system; ~ **troops**, picked troops for offensive action; ~ **wave**, disturbance produced when body travels through medium at speed greater than that at which medium transmits sound, or by explosion; (also fig.). **shock** *v.t.* Affect with intense aversion, disgust, or strong disapproval, scandalize; outrage sentiments, prejudices, etc., of; cause to suffer shock; administer electric shock to. **shock'proof, shock'ing** *adjs.* **shock'ing·ly** *adv.* **shock'ing·ness** *n.*

shock[2] (shŏk) *n.* Group of sheaves of corn etc. propped upright against each other in field to dry and ripen. ~ *v.t.* Arrange in shocks.

shock[3] (shŏk) *n.* Unkempt or shaggy mass of hair.

shock·er (shŏk'*er*) *n.* (esp. colloq.) Sensational novel, film, etc.

At the mouth of many rivers, a ***shoal*** *may form like that on Mondego in Portugal (below). It may be clearly visible at low tide, but is a navigational hazard in poor light at high water.*

shod (shŏd) *adj.*: see SHOE *v.t.;* (esp.) wearing shoes; tipped, edged, or sheathed with metal.

shod·dy (shŏd'ē) *n.* (pl. **shod·dies**). (Cloth of) woolen yarn made from shreds of knitted or loosely woven woolen fabrics; inferior cloth, anything of worse quality than it claims or seems to have. ~ *adj.* (**-di·er, -di·est**). Of poor material or quality. **shod'di·ly** *adv.* **shod'di·ness** *n.*

shoe (shōō) *n.* (pl. **shoes**). 1. Outer covering for foot, of leather or other material, with more or less stiff sole and lighter upper part, esp. not reaching above ankle; **fill someone's ~s**, take place of someone; **the ~ is on the other foot**, the situation is exactly opposite to what it was; **where the ~ pinches**, where one's difficulty or trouble is. 2. Plate of metal, usu. iron, nailed to underside of horse's hoof. 3. Thing like shoe in shape or use, e.g. ferrule or metal sheath for pole etc., wheel drag, socket; part of brake that presses lining against wheel to slow it down; casing of pneumatic tire; (elect.) cast iron block sliding over live rail to collect current therefrom; **shoe'horn**, curved piece of horn, metal, etc., for easing the heel into the back of a shoe; **shoe'lace**, lace for tying up shoe; **shoe'maker**, one who makes, mends shoes; **shoe'shine**, cleaning and polishing of shoes; one who does this for a fee; (also **shoeshine boy**); **shoe'string**, shoelace; (*adj.*) cut into long thin strips (**shoestring potatoes**); around the ankles (**shoestring tackle**); **on a shoestring**, (fig.) with minimal expenditure. **shoe** *v.t.* (**shod** pr. shŏd or **shoed** pr. shōōd, **shoe·ing**). Fit with shoe(s).

sho·far (shō'fer; *Heb.* shōfär') *n.* (pl. **-fars**; *Heb.* **-froth** pr. -frawt'). Ram's horn trumpet used by Jews in religious ceremonies and as ancient battle signal.

sho·gun (shō'gŭn, -gōōn) *n.* (hist.) Japanese hereditary commander in chief and virtual ruler for some centuries until the office was abolished in 1868. **sho·gun·ate** (shō'g*u*nĭt, -nāt) *n.* [Jap., short for *sei-i-tai shōgun* barbarian-subduing great general]

sho·ji (shō'jē) *n.* (pl. **-ji, -jis**). Translucent rice paper screen used in Japanese houses as sliding door or partition.

shone: see SHINE.

shoo (shōō) *int.* Exclamation used to frighten birds etc. away.

A ***shoal*** *of yellowtail, a common fish in some Australian waters. Certain species tend to congregate in large numbers when following food in a coastal current.*

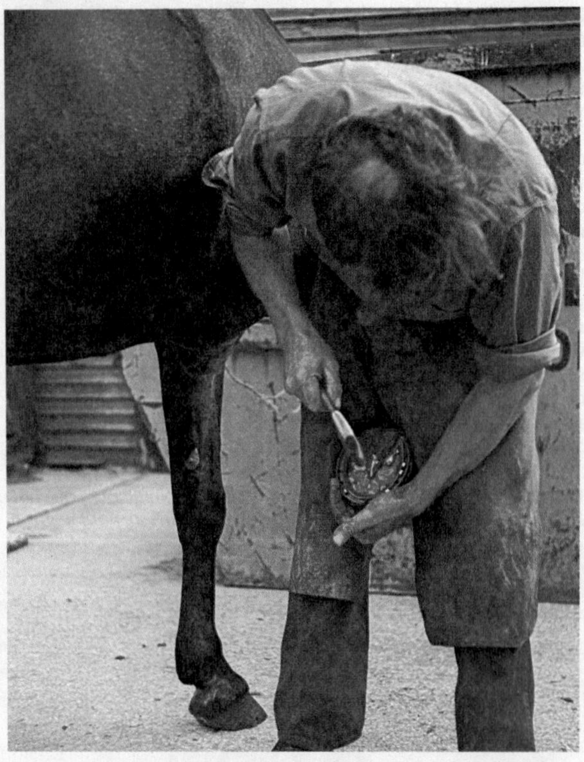

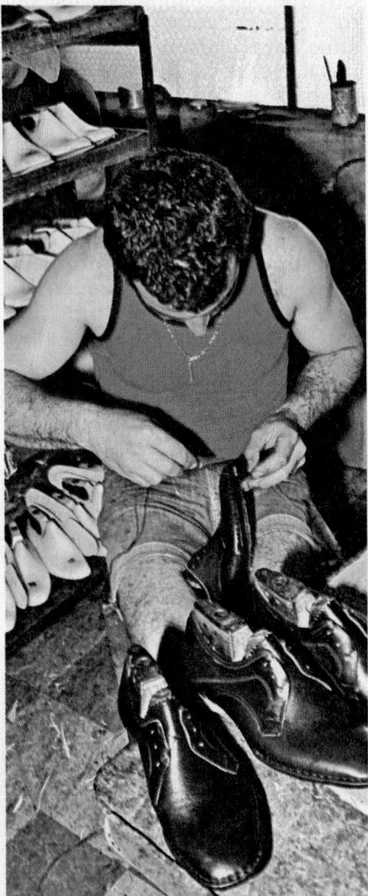

Although mechanization has been extensively applied to the manufacture of **shoes,** many details still have to be done by hand.

Although there are far fewer blacksmiths than in the past, many horses still need shoeing. When a new **shoe** *is to be fitted, the hoof must be trimmed (1) before the hot shoe is positioned, and nailed to the hoof (2).*

~ *v.* (**shooed, shoo·ing**). Utter shoo; drive *away* etc. thus; **shoo'fly pie**, open pie filled with molasses and brown sugar; **shoo-in**, (colloq.) something easy or certain to succeed.

shoot (shōōt) *v.* (**shot** pr. shŏt, **shoot·ing**). 1. Come or go vigorously or swiftly; pass quickly under (bridge), over (rapids), in boat; ~ **up**, (esp.) grow rapidly. 2. Discharge or propel quickly; discharge (bullet etc.) from gun etc., cause (bow, gun, etc.) to discharge missile, discharge gun etc.; kill or wound with missile from gun etc.; hunt game etc. with gun; (of gun etc.) go off, send missile; throw (dice); (soccer, basketball) take shot at goal, basket; (slang) inject (drug) intravenously; ~ **down**, bring down (aircraft) by gunfire; ~ **it out**, (slang) engage in decisive gun battle, or **shoot'out** (*n.*); ~ **up**: see sense 1; hit with many shots; (colloq.) terrorize (area) by indiscriminate shooting; (slang) inject (narcotic) into vein. 3. Photograph or (esp.) film. **shoot'er** *n.* **shoot'ing** *n.* (esp.) Right of shooting over particular land; ~ **box**, (Brit.) sportsman's lodge for use in shooting season; ~ **gallery**, place where shooting at targets with rifles is practiced; ~ **iron**, (slang) firearm; ~ **star**, meteor; any of a genus (*Dodecatheon*) of N. Amer. perennials of the primrose family, having clusters of bright flowers with turned back petals; ~ **war**, one in which there is shooting; ~ **stick**, walking stick that can be adapted to form a seat. **shoot** *n.* 1. Young branch or sucker. 2. Shooting party, expedition, practice, or land.

shop (shŏp) *n.* Building, room, etc., for retail sale of some commodity; small store; workshop of a carpenter, tinsmith, etc.; engineering works or yard; (slang) institution, establishment; one's profession, trade, or business (esp. in **talk** ~); **set up** ~, open or begin business, professional practice, etc.; **close up** ~, cease business for the day or permanently; **shop'keeper**, owner and manager of shop; **shop'lifter**, pretended customer who steals goods in shop; **shop steward**, union member elected by fellow workers in shop or department of factory etc. to act as their spokesman in dealings with employer; **shop'talk**, specialized vocabulary of an occupation; conversation of people about their work, esp. outside working hours, **shop'worn**, soiled or damaged through being displayed or handled in store; also fig. **shop** *v.* (**shopped, shop·ping**). Go to shop(s) to make purchases. **shop'per** *n.* Person who shops, esp. one who shops carefully. **shop'ping** *n.* ~ **center**, group of stores in one building or several closely related buildings with nearby parking area, usu. in suburbs.

shore[1] (shōr, shôr) *n.* Land that

borders sea or large body of water; (law) land between ordinary high- and low-water marks; **in** ~, on water near(er) to shore; **shore′bird**, any of various birds that live in seashore areas; **shore leave**, (naut.) permission to go ashore; **shore′line**, line where water and shore meet; **shore patrol**, members of U.S. Navy, Marine Corps, or Coast Guard assigned to police duties on shore. **shore′less** *adj.* **shore′ward** *adj.* & *adv.*

shore² (shōr, shôr) *n.* Prop, beam, set obliquely against ship, wall, tree, etc., as support. ~ *v.t.* (**shored, shor·ing**). Support, prop *up*, with shores.

shorn: see SHEAR.

short (shôrt) *adj.* 1. Measuring little from end to end in space or time, soon traversed or finished; of small stature, not tall; not far-reaching, acting near at hand. 2. Deficient, scanty, in want *of*, below the degree *of*; (of weight, change, etc.) less than it should be; concise, brief, curt; (phonet., pros., of vowel or syllable) having the lesser of 2 recognized durations; (of stocks, broker, crops, etc.) sold, selling, etc., when stocks etc. are not in hand, in reliance on getting them in time for delivery. 3. (of pastry, clay, etc.) Friable, crumbling. 4. **short′bread, short′cake**, crisp dry cake made with flour and butter and sugar without liquid; **short-change′** (*v.t.*), (colloq.) cheat by giving insufficient money as change; **short circuit**, electric circuit through much smaller resistance than in the normal circuit, thus allowing a large current to flow through and causing overheating, fusing, etc.; **short-circuit** (*v.t.*) cause short circuit in; shorten (process) by eliminating intermediate stages; **short′coming**, failure to come up to a standard, deficiency, defect; **short′cut**, shorter route to reach same location; (fig.) any means of saving time, work, money, etc.; **short′fall**, output less than expected; shortage; **short′hand**, stenography, system of graphic notation in which speech is recorded at great speed by using contractions, symbols, etc.; **short′-handed**, undermanned, understaffed; **short′horn**, one of a short-horned breed of cattle; **short-lived**, having a short life; brief, ephemeral; **short order**, food that can be quickly prepared and served, as at diner, lunch counter, etc.; hence **short-order**, *adj.*; **in short order**, immediately; **short-range**, (of gun, missile, etc.) firing or reaching a short distance, (of forecast, plan, etc.) relating to the near future; **short shrift**: see SHRIFT; **short′sighted**, lacking imagination, deficient in foresight; **short′sightedly, short′sightedness**; **short′stop**, (baseball) infielder between second and third bases; **short story**, story with a fully worked out motif but much shorter than a novel; **short-tempered**, having a temper easily roused; **short-term**, (of plan, policy, etc.) designed to meet the circumstances of a short time ahead; **short′wave**, radio wavelength of 60 meters or less; **short-winded**, short of breath, becoming out of breath after slight exertion; **short-windedly, short-windedness**. **short′ness** *n.* **short** *adv.* Abruptly; before the natural or expected time; in short manner. ~ *n.* Short syllable or vowel, mark indicating that a vowel is short; (colloq.) short circuit; short motion picture film; (pl.) short trousers reaching to any point between crotch and knee; (pl.) men's underpants. ~ *v.t.* (colloq.) Short-circuit.

short·age (shôr′tĭj) *n.* (Amount of) deficiency.

short·en (shôr′ten) *v.* Become, make, actually or apparently short(er), curtail; reduce amount of (*sail*) spread; make (pastry etc.) flaky or crumbly.

short · en · ing (shôr′tenĭng, shôrt′nĭng) *n.* Fat used for making pastry flaky or crisp.

short·ly (shôrt′lē) *adv.* Before long; a short time *before, after*; in few words, briefly; curtly.

Sho · sta · ko · vich (shŏstakō′-vĭch), **Dmitri** (1906–75). Russian composer of symphonies, operas, piano music, etc.

shot (shŏt) *n.* (pl. **shots**, for def. 1 **shot**). 1. Single missile for cannon or gun, nonexplosive projectile; (pl. same) small lead pellets of which a quantity is used for single charge or cartridge, esp. in

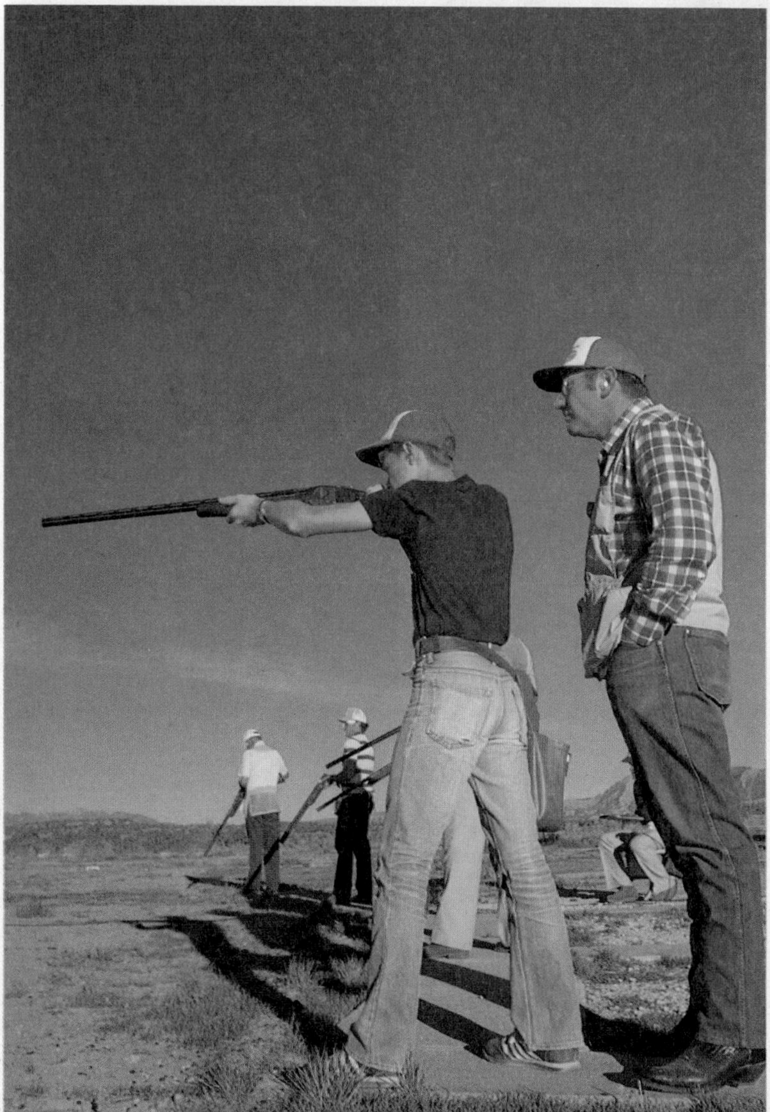

Clay pigeon shooting allows the participants to enjoy the excitement and expertise of the ***shoot*** *without having to kill. As a recognized sport it is growing in popularity and has been an Olympic event since 1900.*

*Above: The Memphis **showboat** anchored on the Mississippi between voyages. These floating theaters were introduced early in the 19th century and ranged from crude rafts to elaborate steamers.*

*Another obstacle cleared during the Munich Olympics in 1972. **Show jumping** began in Paris in 1886 and equestrian events were introduced to the Olympic Games in 1912.*

sporting guns. 2. (colloq.) Injection; (slang) drink of whiskey. 3. Discharge of cannon or gun; attempt to hit with projectile or missile; (fig.) attempt to guess or do something; aim or stroke, esp. in a game, as tennis, golf, billiards; (basketball, soccer, etc.) attempt to score by putting ball into basket, goal, etc. 4. Possessor of specified skill with rifle, gun, pistol, etc. 5. Range, reach, distance to or at which thing will carry or act, as *ear'shot, rifle shot*. 6. Photograph; (portion of) film scene photographed as a unit. 7. **shot'gun**, smoothbore gun for firing small shot; **shot'gun wedding**, forced wedding, esp. one necessitated by pregnancy; **shot put**, athletic event in which heavy metal ball is thrown as far as possible; **shot tower**, tower in which shot is made from molten lead poured through sieves at the top and falling into water at the bottom. **shot** *v.t.* (**shot·ted**, **shot·ting**). Load, weight, etc., with shot.

should: see SHALL.

shoul·der (shōl'd*er*) *n.* Part of body at which arm, foreleg, or wing is attached; either lateral projection below or behind neck; combination of end of upper arm with ends of collarbone and shoulder blade; cut of meat consisting of upper foreleg and adjoining parts; part of mountain, bottle, tool, etc., projecting like human shoulder; (pl.) upper part of back; body regarded as bearing burdens; strip on either side of roadway; **put one's ~ to the wheel**, make effort; **~ blade**, either of the pair of large flat bones of upper back, scapula; **~ patch**, military insigne indicating unit in which wearer serves, sewn onto uniform sleeve just below shoulder; **~ strap**, band over shoulder connecting front and back of (esp. woman's) garment; band at shoulder of uniform keeping shoulder belt in place and bearing name or number of regiment etc.; **straight from the ~**, (of blow or verbal attack) well delivered or frank. **shoulder** *v.* Push with shoulder, jostle, make one's *way* thus; take (burden) on one's shoulders (also fig.); **~ arms**, (mil.) hold rifle vertically in front of shoulder with butt resting in palm of hand, the arm being fully extended downward.

shout (showt) *n.* Loud cry expressing joy, grief, pain, defiance, etc., or to attract attention at a distance. **~** *v.* Utter shout; speak loudly; say loudly, call out. **shout′er** *n.*

shove (shŭv) *n.* (Strong) push. **~** *v.* (**shoved, shov·ing**). Push, esp. vigorously or roughly; jostle; (colloq.) put; **~ off**, start from shore in boat; (colloq.) depart.

shov·el (shŭv′*el*) *n.* Spadelike implement, freq. with slightly concave blade, for shifting coal, earth, grain, etc. **shovel** *v.t.* (**-eled, -el·ing,** Brit. **-elled, -el·ling**). Shift with shovel or spade.

shov·el·er, Brit. **shov·el·ler** (shŭv′*eler*) *ns.* Brightly colored river duck (*Anas* or *Spatula clypeata*) with large very broad bill.

show (shō) *v.* (**showed, shown** or **showed, show·ing**). 1. Allow or cause to be seen, expose to view, exhibit, reveal, point out; be visible or noticeable, come into sight; appear in public; have some appearance. 2. Demonstrate, prove, expound; point out. 3. **~ around**, take (person) to all points of interest; **~ off**, display to advantage; act or talk for show, make ostentatious display of abilities etc., hence **show′off** (*n.*), person who shows off; **show up**, make, be, conspicuous or clearly visible; arrive at place; expose (fraud, impostor). 4. **show′down**, final test. **show** *n.* 1. Showing; display; spectacle, exhibition, entertainment; exhibit; **~ bill**, advertising sheet or poster; **~ business**, profession of (esp. theatrical) entertainment (colloq. abbrev. **show-biz**); **show′boat**, passenger boat, esp. on Mississippi, used as theater; **show′case**, (1) glass-enclosed case for exhibiting goods, curiosities, etc.; (2) opportunity for exhibiting (esp. theatrical talent); **show girl**, chorus girl; **~ of hands**, voting by raising of hands; **show′man** (pl. **-men**), exhibitor or proprietor of show; **show′manship**, (esp.) capacity for exhibiting one's wares, capabilities, etc., to the best advantage; **show′piece**, excellent specimen used for show; **show′place**, place open to public to view its beauty, etc.; **show′room**, room in which goods are exhibited for sale; **show-stopper**, (colloq.) item in performance receiving prolonged applause; **show window**, (1) window of store where merchandise is on view; (2) outward appearance, semblance; parade, ostentation, pomp, display.

show·er (show′*er*) *n.* 1. Brief fall of rain, *of* rain, hail, arrows, dust, etc.; (also **~ bath**) bath in which water is sprayed from above. 2.

*The common **shoveller** is one of the dabbling group of ducks. Before the breeding season, the male has brilliant plumage. It is a surface feeder.*

*With more than 200 species, the **shrew** (family Soricidae) forms the largest group in the Insectivora order of mammals. All are aggressive and carnivorous and will attack prey larger than themselves. Some are semi-aquatic.*

web-footed water shrew
elephant shrew
mole shrew
pygmy shrew
piebald shrew

Party for giving presents, esp. to a prospective bride. **show'er·y** *adj.* **show'er·i·ness** *n.* **shower** *v.* 1. Discharge, descend, come, in a shower; bestow (gifts etc.) lavishly (*upon*). 2. Take shower bath.

show·y (shō'ē) *adj.* (**show·i·er, show·i·est**). Striking, making good display; brilliant, gaudy. **show'i·ly** *adv.* **show'i·ness** *n.*

shp *abbrev.* Shaft horsepower.

shrank: see SHRINK.

shrap·nel (shrăp'nel) *n.* Hollow projectile containing bullets scattered in shower by small bursting charge; fragments of any shell, bomb, etc., scattered by explosion. [General H. Shrapnel (1761–1842), inventor of the shell]

shred (shrĕd) *n.* Scrap, fragment; small torn, broken, or cut piece; small remains; least amount. ~ *v.t.* (**shred·ded** or **shred, shred·ding**). Tear or cut into shreds. **shred'der** *n.*

shrew (shrōō) *n.* 1. Small mouselike insectivore of *Sorex* and other genera, with long pointed snout. 2. Scolding woman. **shrew'ish** *adj.* Ill-tempered. **shrew'ish·ly** *adv.* **shrew'ish·ness** *n.*

shrewd (shrōōd) *adj.* Sagacious, sensible, discriminating, astute. **shrewd'ly** *adv.* **shrewd'ness** *n.*

shriek (shrēk) *n.* & *v.* (Utter) loud shrill cry or sound of terror, pain, mirth, etc.; (make) high-pitched piercing sound.

shrift (shrĭft) *n.* (archaic) Confession (and absolution); now only in **short** ~, little time between condemnation and execution or punishment; scant attention.

shrike (shrīk) *n.* Bird of family Laniidae, with strong hooked beak, preying usu. on insects, but also on mice and small birds, often impaling them on thorns or barbed wire; butcherbird.

shrill (shrĭl) *adj.* (of sound) Piercing and high-pitched; producing such sounds. ~ *v.* (poet. and rhet.) Sound, utter, shrilly. **shril'ly** *adv.* **shrill'ness** *n.*

shrimp (shrĭmp) *n.* (pl. **shrimps**, collect. **shrimp**). Any of the small marine decapod crustaceans of *Crangon* and allied genera, esp. the common shrimp, *C. vulgaris*, inhabiting sandy coasts, a common article of food; (slang) diminutive or puny person. ~ *v.i.* Go catching shrimps.

shrine (shrīn) *n.* Casket, esp. one holding sacred relics; tomb, usu. sculptured or highly ornamented, of saint etc.; place where worship is offered or devotions paid to saint or deity; place hallowed by

*The great grey **shrike** or butcherbird, like other birds in the Laniidae, impales its prey on a thorn after killing it. This species migrates to Britain in winter and is about 10 ins. long.*

*The inverted **shrimp** (Penedi abissal) is caught only in the ocean depths. Most commercial varieties swim closer to the surface and at times many tons may be netted.*

memory or associations.

Shrin·er (shrī′n*er*) *n.* Member of Ancient Arabic Order of Nobles of the Mystic Shrine, established in U.S. in 1872, and open only to Knights Templar and Freemasons of 32nd degree.

shrink (shrĭngk) *v.* (**shrank** pr. shrăngk or **shrunk** pr. shrŭngk, **shrunk** or rarely **shrunk·en, shrink·ing**). Become, make, smaller; (of textile fabric) contract when wetted, cause to do this; cower, huddle *together*, recoil, flinch *from*; be averse *from*. **shrink′a·ble** *adj.* **shrink′age** *n.*

shrive (shrīv) *v.t.* (**shrived** or **shrove** pr. shrōv., **shriv·en** pr. shrĭv′*e*n or **shrived, shriv·ing**). (archaic) Hear confession of, assign penance to, and absolve; ~ **one-self**, make one's confession.

shriv·el (shrĭv′*e*l) *v.* (**-eled, -el·ing**, Brit. **-elled, -el·ling**). Contract or wither into wrinkled, folded, contorted, or dried-up state.

shroud (shrowd) *n.* 1. Winding sheet, garment for the dead; (fig.) concealing agency. 2. (pl.) Set of ropes forming part of standing rigging and supporting mast or top-mast. ~ *v.t.* Clothe (corpse) for burial; cover or disguise.

Shrove·tide (shrōv′tīd) *n.* Three days before Ash Wednesday, period for confession before Lent; so **Shrove Tuesday**. [f. SHRIVE]

shrub[1] (shrŭb) *n.* Woody plant smaller than tree and usu. divided into separate stems from near the ground. **shrub′by** *adj.* (**-bi·er, -bi·est**).

shrub[2] (shrŭb) *n.* Cordial of juice of acid fruit, sugar, and spirit (usu. rum). [Arab. *sharāb*]

shrub·ber·y (shrŭb′*e*rē) *n.* (pl. **-ber·ies**). (Group of) shrubs.

shrug (shrŭg) *n.* Raising and contraction of shoulders to express dislike, disdain, indifference, etc.

Boxwood shrubs in a garden at Williamsburg, Virginia. Gardeners find that a ***shrub*** *needs far less maintenance than smaller plants, but can be very effective as decoration.*

~ *v.* (**shrugged, shrug·ging**). Raise (shoulders), raise shoulders, in shrug.

shrunk, shrunk·en: see SHRINK.

shtet·l (shtĕt′*e*l) *n.* (hist.) Jewish village or small community in E. Europe. [Yiddish, f. MHG. diminutive of *stat*, town]

shtick (shtĭk) *n.* (slang) Trait, talent, attribute, etc.; humorous routine or bit of stage business. [Yiddish]

shuck (shŭk) *n.* (colloq.) Husk, pod. **shucks** *int.* Exclamation of contempt or indifference. **shuck** *v.t.* Remove shucks of, shell.

shud·der (shŭd′*er*) *v.i.* & *n.* (Experience) sudden shivering due to fear, repugnance, or cold. **shud′der·ing·ly** *adv.*

shuf·fle (shŭf′*e*l) *n.* 1. Shuffling movement; shuffling of cards; general change of relative positions. 2. Piece of equivocation or sharp practice. 3. Quick scraping movement of feet in dancing. ~ *v.* (**-fled, -fling**). Move with scraping, sliding, dragging, or difficult motion; manipulate (cards in pack) so that their relative positions are changed; intermingle, confuse, push about or together in disorderly fashion; put *in, off, on*, etc., clumsily or fumblingly; put (responsibility etc.) *off, onto*, another etc., get *out of* shiftily or evasively; keep shifting position, fidget, vacillate; prevaricate, be evasive. **shuf′fler** *n.*

shuf·fle·board (shŭf′*e*lbōrd, -bōrd) *n.* (Shipboard) game in which wooden or iron disks are pushed along decks (or other flat surfaces) with shovel into divisions marked by chalk etc.

shun (shŭn) *v.t.* (**shunned, shun·ning**). Avoid, keep clear of. **shun′ner** *n.* **shun′pike** *v.i.* (**-piked, -pik·ing**). Travel on side roads avoiding turnpikes and expressways. **shun′piker, shun′pik·ing** *ns.*

shunt (shŭnt) *v.* Divert (train, part of an electric current, etc.), diverge, onto a side track. **shunt′er** *n.* Railroad worker shunting trains. **shunt** *n.* Turning, being turned, onto side track; conductor joining 2 points in an electric circuit so as to form a parallel circuit; such a circuit.

shut (shŭt) *v.* (**shut, shut·ting**). Close (door, aperture, window, etc.), close door etc. of (room, box, etc.); become, admit of being, closed; keep *in, out*, etc., by shutting door etc.; ~ **down**, close, terminate operation of (factory, nuclear reactor, etc.); (of factory etc.) cease working, hence **shut′down** (*n.*); **shut′eye** (*n.*), (slang) sleep; **shut one's eyes to**, (fig.) ignore; **shut in**, encircle, prevent free prospect or egress from or access to; **shut-in** (*adj.* & *n.*), (invalid) confined to home; **shut off**, stop flow of (water, gas, etc.) by shutting valve; separate *from*; **shut′out** (*n.*), game in which one side fails to score; **shut up**, close doors and windows of (house), close securely, decisively, or permanently, put away in box etc.; imprison; (colloq.) reduce to silence, shut one's mouth, stop talking; **shut up shop**, cease business.

shut·ter (shŭt′*er*) *n.* (esp.) Movable screen placed outside or inside window to shut off light or ensure privacy or safety; device for opening and closing aperture of photographic lens; **shut′terbug**, (slang) amateur photographer. **shutter** *v.t.* Provide with shutters, put up shutters of.

shut·tle (shŭt′*e*l) *n.* Weft carrier in a loom, a boat-shaped wooden implement with hollowed center to hold the weft thread, thrown from hand to hand by the weaver, or moved by mechanical means backward and forward across and through the warp; thread holder in sewing machine carrying lower thread through the loop of the upper one; (attrib.) denoting an out-and-back course, as in ~ **service, train**; **shut′tlecock**, small piece of weighted cork or other light material with feathers projecting in a ring from one side, struck to and fro with a racket in badminton.

shy[1] (shī) *adj.* (**shi·er** or **shy·er, shi·est** or **shy·est**). Easily startled, timid, avoiding observation, uneasy in company, bashful; avoiding company *of*, chary *of doing*; elusive; (as second element of compounds) frightened (*of*), averse (to), as gun-, work-~. **shy'ly** *adv.* **shi'er, shy'er, shy'ness** *ns.* **shy** *v.i.* (**shied, shy·ing**). Start suddenly aside in alarm (at object or noise, esp. of horse). ~ *n.* (pl. **shies**). Act of shying.

shy² (shī) *v.* (**shied, shy·ing**). (colloq.) Fling, throw. ~ *n.* (pl. **shies**). Act of shying.

Shy·lock (shī'lŏk). (freq. **s**~) Hardhearted moneylender. [character in Shakespeare's *Merchant of Venice*]

shy·ster (shīs'ter) *n.* (slang) Tricky, unscrupulous lawyer (or other professional man).

Si *symbol.* Silicon.

si·al (sī'ăl) *n.* (geol.) Lighter outer crust of Earth's surface, composed mainly of solid or molten rocks rich in silica and alumina. [f. *si*lica and *al*umina]

Si·am (sīăm', sī'ăm). Name until 1939 of THAIland.

si·a·mang (sē'amăng) *n.* Largest of the gibbons (*Symphalangus* or *Hylobates syndactylus*), found in Sumatra and the Malay peninsula.

Si·a·mese (sīamēz', -mēs') *adj.* Of Siam or its people or language; ~ **cat,** cat of domesticated breed notable for its raucous cry, having body of grayish or cream color with dark feet, face, and tail; ~ **twins,** two male Chinese born in Siam, Chang and Eng (1814–74), who were congenitally united by a thick fleshy ligament in the region of the waist; any pair of conjoined twins. **Siamese** *n.* (pl. **-mese**). Siamese person; Siamese language, one of the Thai group; Siamese cat.

sib (sĭb) *adj.* (archaic) Related, akin (*to*). ~ *n.* (genetics) Brother or sister (disregarding sex). **sib'-ling** *n.* One of two or more children having one or both parents in common.

Si·be·li·us (sĭbā'lēus, -bāl'yus), **Jean Julius Christian,** (1865–1957). Finnish musical composer of tone poems, symphonies, etc.

Si·be·ri·a (sībēr'ēa). Region of N. Asia between Ural Mountains and Pacific Ocean and from Arctic Ocean to borders of Mongolia and China, forming the larger part of the Russian Soviet Federal Socialist Republic; used under both tsarist and communist regimes as place of exile, concentration camps, etc.; hence (fig.) disgrace, disfavor. **Si·ber'i·an** *adj.* & *n.* Of Siberia; ~ **husky,** dog of breed resembling the Eskimo dog, used for drawing sleds.

sib·i·lant (sĭb'ilant) *adj.* Hissing, sounding like a hiss (of the consonants *s, z, sh*). **sib'i·lance** *n.* **sib'i·lan·cy** *n.* (pl. **-cies**). **sib'i·lant** *n.* (phon.) Sibilant speech sound. **sib'i·lant·ly** *adv.* **sib·i·late** (sĭb'ilāt) *v.* (**-lat·ed, -lat·ing**).

sib·yl (sĭb'ĭl) *n.* Any of the women who in ancient times acted in various places as mouthpiece of a god, uttering prophecies and oracles, the most famous of whom was the sibyl at Cumae in S. Italy

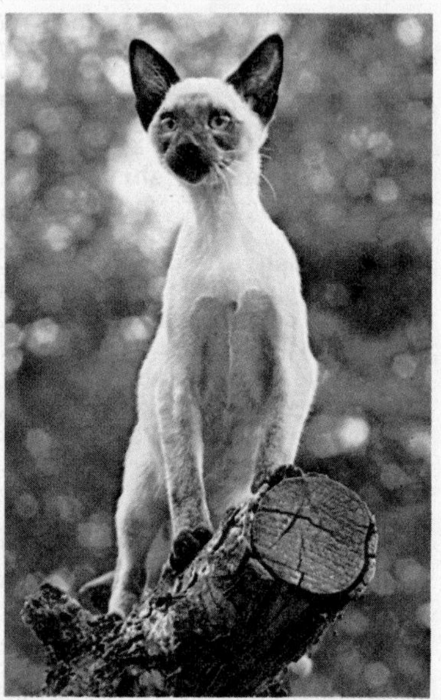

*With ears too large for its body, this half-grown seal-point **Siamese cat** may be a descendant of the wild golden cat of the Malay peninsula but there is little evidence to prove this.*

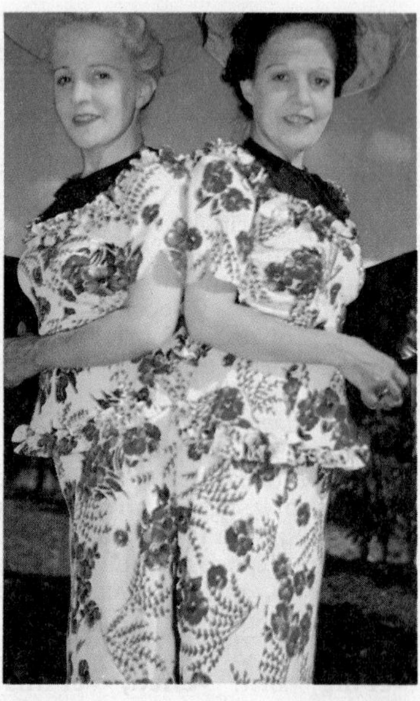

*Unless they share a vital organ, babies connected at birth are now separated surgically. The name **Siamese twins** comes from the Chang brothers, born in Siam (now Thailand) in 1811.*

*Work on the Trans-Siberian Railway, to link the Asian steppes with European Russia, began in 1891. **Siberia** has an area of more than 6 million sq. miles and has vast mineral deposits.*

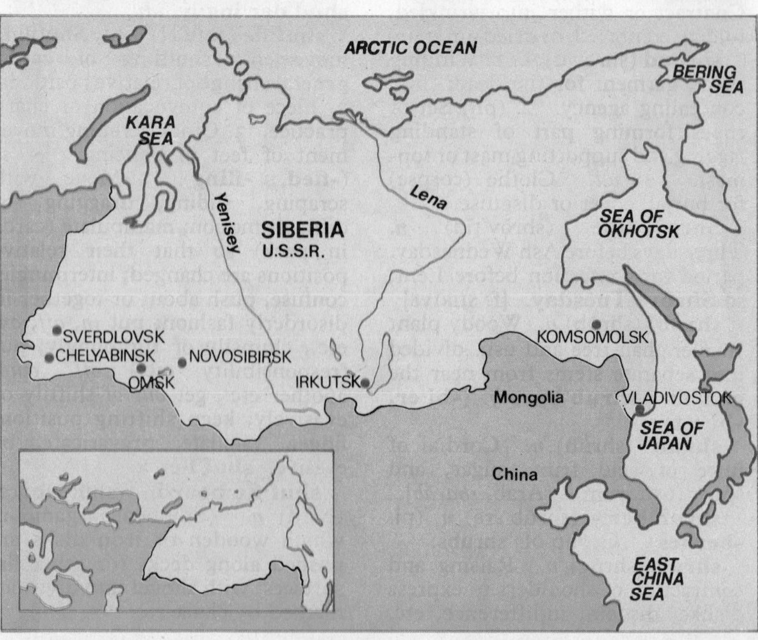

who (acc. to legend) guided Aeneas through the underworld; prophetess, fortuneteller, witch.

sib·yl·line (sĭb′ĭlīn, -lēn, -lĭn) *adj.* Of a sibyl, oracular, mysteriously prophetic; **S ~ Books,** collection of oracles kept in ancient Rome in temple of Jupiter Capitolinus and freq. consulted by magistrates for guidance; acc. to legend, nine of these books were offered to Tarquin by a sibyl, who burned three of them and then three more when they were refused because of their high price, and finally sold the last three at the same price as she had asked for them all.

sic[1] (sĭk) *v.t.* (**sicked, sick·ing**). Urge (dog) to attack or pursue.

sic[2] (sĭk) *adv.* (freq. parenth.) So, thus (used, spelled, etc.) with implication that this use is incorrect or absurd.

Si·chuan (sĭ′chwahn′) = SZECHUAN.

Si·cil·ian (sĭsĭl′yan) *adj.* Of Sicily; **~ Vespers,** riot that broke out at a church near Palermo while the vesper bell was ringing on Easter Monday 1282, and developed into a general massacre of the French in Sicily and the expulsion of the Angevins. **Sicilian** *n.* Native, inhabitant, of Sicily.

Sic·i·ly (sĭs′ĭlē). (It. *Sicilia*) Largest island in the Mediterranean Sea, 9,925 sq. mi. (25,706 sq. km); an autonomous Italian region separated from the SW. tip of Italy by the Strait of Messina; capital, Palermo.

sick (sĭk) *adj.* 1. Ill, unwell; disposed to vomit, vomiting. 2. Disordered, perturbed; suffering effects *of*; disgusted; pining *for*; surfeited and tired *of*; (of humor) morbid; suggesting callousness. 3. Of or for sick persons (~ *benefit, leave, pay*). 4. **~ bay**: see BAY[3]; **sick′bed,** invalid's bed; state of being invalid; **sick headache,** headache accompanied by nausea; migraine; **sick list,** list of sick esp. in military unit, aboard ship, etc.; **sick′out,** action against employers by group of employees who stay away from work, alleging illness as their excuse.

sick·en (sĭk′en) *v.* Begin to be ill, show symptoms of illness; feel nausea or disgust (*at* etc.); affect with inclination to vomit, loathing, disgust, weariness, or despair. **sick′en·ing** *adj.* **sick′en·ing·ly** *adv.*

sick·le (sĭk′el) *n.* Reaping hook, short-handled semicircular-bladed implement used for lopping, trimming, etc.; anything sickle-shaped, esp. crescent moon: **~ cell,** sickle-shaped erythrocyte, esp. as found in **~-cell anemia,** a severe hereditary anemia occurring chiefly among blacks.

sick·ly (sĭk′lē) *adj.* (**-li·er, -li·est**). Apt to be ill, chronically ailing; suggesting sickness, as of sick person, languid, pale; causing ill health or nausea; mawkish, weakly sentimental. **sick′li·ness** *n.* **sickly** *v.t.* (**-lied, -ly·ing**).

sick·ness (sĭk′nĭs) *n.* Being ill, disease; a disease; vomiting, inclination to vomit.

side (sīd) *n.* 1. One of the more or less flat surfaces bounding an object, esp. more or less vertical outer or inner surface; such surface as distinguished from top and bottom, front and back, or ends; either surface of thing regarded as

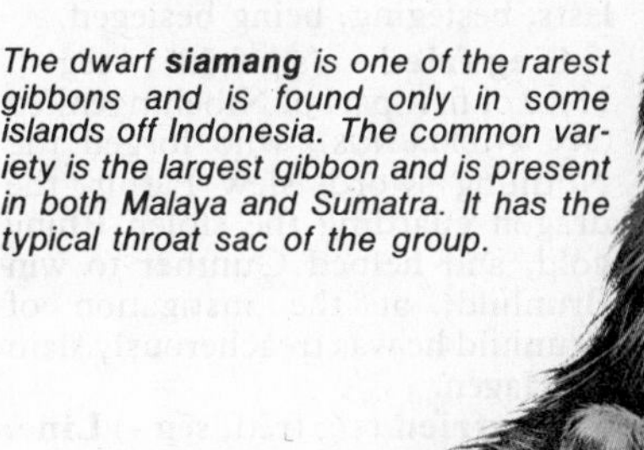

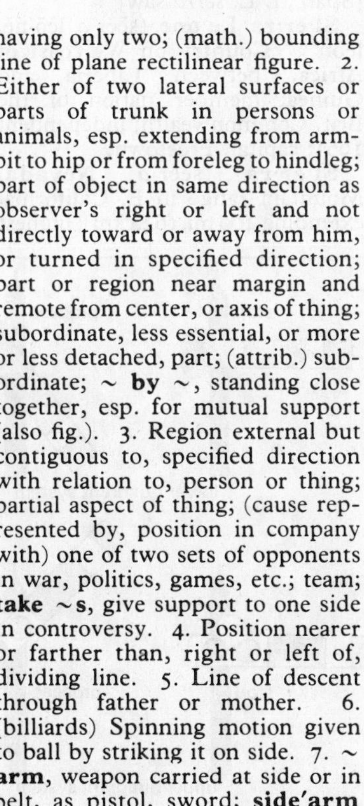

*The dwarf **siamang** is one of the rarest gibbons and is found only in some islands off Indonesia. The common variety is the largest gibbon and is present in both Malaya and Sumatra. It has the typical throat sac of the group.*

having only two; (math.) bounding line of plane rectilinear figure. 2. Either of two lateral surfaces or parts of trunk in persons or animals, esp. extending from armpit to hip or from foreleg to hindleg; part of object in same direction as observer's right or left and not directly toward or away from him, or turned in specified direction; part or region near margin and remote from center, or axis of thing; subordinate, less essential, or more or less detached, part; (attrib.) subordinate; **~ by ~,** standing close together, esp. for mutual support (also fig.). 3. Region external but contiguous to, specified direction with relation to, person or thing; partial aspect of thing; (cause represented by, position in company with) one of two sets of opponents in war, politics, games, etc.; team; **take ~s,** give support to one side in controversy. 4. Position nearer or farther than, right or left of, dividing line. 5. Line of descent through father or mother. 6. (billiards) Spinning motion given to ball by striking it on side. 7. **~ arm,** weapon carried at side or in belt, as pistol, sword; **side′arm** (*adj., adv.*), with sweeping forward motion of extended arm at or below shoulder level; **side′board,** piece of dining room furniture, freq. with drawers and cupboards, for holding dishes, wine, silver, etc.; **side′car,** car for passenger(s) attached to side of motorcycle; cocktail of brandy, orange liqueur, and lemon juice; **side dish,** extra dish, freq. of elaborate kind, at dinner, etc.; **side effect,** secondary, esp. undesirable, effect (as of drug) produced in addition to that intended; **side′kick,** (colloq.) close associate; **side′light,** port or starboard light on ship under way; light coming from the side, (fig.) incidental light *on* subject etc.; **side′line,** (esp.) boundary along side of field of play; subsidiary, secondary, or additional business, pursuit, etc.; **on the sidelines,** (transf.) looking on but not participating; **side road,** minor or subsidiary road; road joining or diverging from main road; **side′saddle,** saddle for rider, usu. woman, with both feet on 1 (usu. left) side of horse; **side′show,** minor show attached to principal one (freq. fig.); **side′slip,** skid; (of aircraft) move, motion, sideways;

side′splitting, causing violent laughter; **side step**, step taken sideways; **side′step** (*v.t.*) (**-stepped, -step·ping**), avoid, evade, (as) by stepping sideways; **side street**, street lying aside from main streets or roads; **side′stroke**, swimming stroke made lying on the side; **side′track**, siding; (*v.t.*) turn into siding, shunt, postpone or evade treatment or consideration of; **side view**, view obtained sideways; profile; **side′walk**, paved path for pedestrians at side of road or street; **side′wall**, side of tire between rim of wheel and tread; **side whiskers**, hair left unshaven on cheeks; **side′winder**, small rattlesnake (*Crotalus cerastes*) of SW. U.S. that moves forward by looping body sideways; (colloq.) powerful sideways blow of fist; (**Sidewinder**) short-range air-to-air missile. **side** *v.i.* (**sid·ed, sid·ing**). Take part, be on same side, *with*.

side·burns (sīd′bĕrnz) *n.pl.* Heavy side whiskers worn with mustache and with shaved chin. [f. A. E. *Burnside* (1824–81), Union general in Civil War]

side·long (sīd′lawng, -lŏng) *adv.* & *adj.* Inclining to one side, oblique(ly).

si·de·re·al (sīdēr′ēal) *adj.* Of the stars; (of time) measured by the stars; ~ **clock**, astronomical clock regulated to sidereal time; ~ **day, year**: see DAY, YEAR.

side·ward (sīd′werd), **sid·wards** (sīd′werdz) *advs.* & *adjs.* From, at, to, the side.

side·ways (sīd′wāz), **side·way** (sīd′wā), **side·wise** (sīd′wīz) *advs.* & *adjs.* Laterally, to or from a side.

sid·ing (sĭ′dĭng) *n.* 1. Short track by side of railroad line and connected with it by switches, for shunting etc. 2. (Material used for) outer wall of building.

si·dle (sī′del) *v.i.* (**-dled, -dling**). Walk obliquely, esp. in furtive or unobtrusive manner. **si′dling·ly** *adv.*

siege (sēj) *n.* Surrounding or hemming in of a fortified place by a military force to compel its surrender or to take it by direct attack, period during which this lasts; besieging, being besieged.

Sieg·fried (sĭg′frēd, sēg′-). Hero of first part of Nibelungenlied (see NIBELUNGS), who forged the Nothung sword, slew Fafnir, the dragon guarding the stolen Rhine gold, and helped Gunther to win Brunhild; at the instigation of Brunhild he was treacherously slain by Hagen.

Siegfried (sĭg′frēd, sēg′-) **Line.** German line of fortifications along the W. border of Germany from Cleves to Basel, constructed prior to World War II.

Sie·na (sēĕn′*a*). City of Tuscany, Italy. **Si·en·ese** (sēenēz′, -nēs′) *adj.* & *n.* (pl. **-ese**).

si·en·na (sēĕn′*a*) *n.* Ferruginous earth used as pigment, brownish yellow (**raw** ~) or reddish brown (**burnt** ~). [It. (*terra*) *di Siena* (earth of) SIENA]

si·er·ra (sēĕr′*a*) *n.* Range of mountains with serrated outline. [Span., f. L. *serra* saw]

Si·er·ra Le·one (sēĕr′*a* lēō′nē, lēōn′). Country on W. coast of Africa, between Liberia and Guinea; member nation of the Brit. Commonwealth; independent 1961; capital, Freetown.

Si·er·ra (sēĕr′*a*) **Nevada.** Mountain range in E. California, extending 400 mi. (644 km); highest peak, Mt. Whitney, 14,495 ft. (4,418 m).

si·es·ta (sīĕs′t*a*) *n.* Midday or afternoon rest in hot countries. [Span., f. L. *sexta* (*hora*) 6th (hour)]

sieve (sĭv) *n.* Utensil consisting of usu. circular frame with meshed or perforated bottom, for separating finer from coarser parts of loose material, or for straining liquids or pulping solids; coarsely woven basket for market produce, this as a measure. ~ *v.t.* (**sieved, siev·ing**). Put through, sift with, sieve.

sift (sĭft) *v.* Put through sieve; separate, get *out*, by use of sieve; use sieve; fall as from sieve; sprinkle (sugar etc.) with perforated spoon etc.; closely examine details of, analyze character of. **sift′er** *n.*

Sig. *abbrev.* Signor; signore; signori.

sig. *abbrev.* Signature; signal.

sigh (sī) *n.* Prolonged deep audible respiration expressive of dejection, weariness, longing, relief, etc. ~ *v.* Give sigh or (of wind etc.) sound resembling sigh; utter or express with sighs; yearn, long, *for*. **sigh′er** *n.*

sight (sīt) *n.* 1. Faculty of seeing. 2. Seeing, being seen; way of looking at or considering thing; view, point or position commanding view, of something; range or field of vision; **at, on,** ~, **at first** ~, as soon as person or thing has been seen; **know by** ~, recognize by appearance alone; ~**-reading, -singing**, reading music, singing, at sight. 3. Thing seen, visible, or worth seeing; display, show, spectacle; ridiculous, shocking, or repulsive sight; (colloq.) great quantity (*of*); **sight′seeing**, act of going to see places or objects of special interest, beauty, etc.; **sight′seer** (*n.*). 4. Device for assisting precise aim with gun,

*The first **signal** system for railways was adapted from semaphore in 1841. Later, signals were linked with movable points on the lines; and in 1893, the first automatic signals were used. Modern automatic systems make crewless trains the next step.*

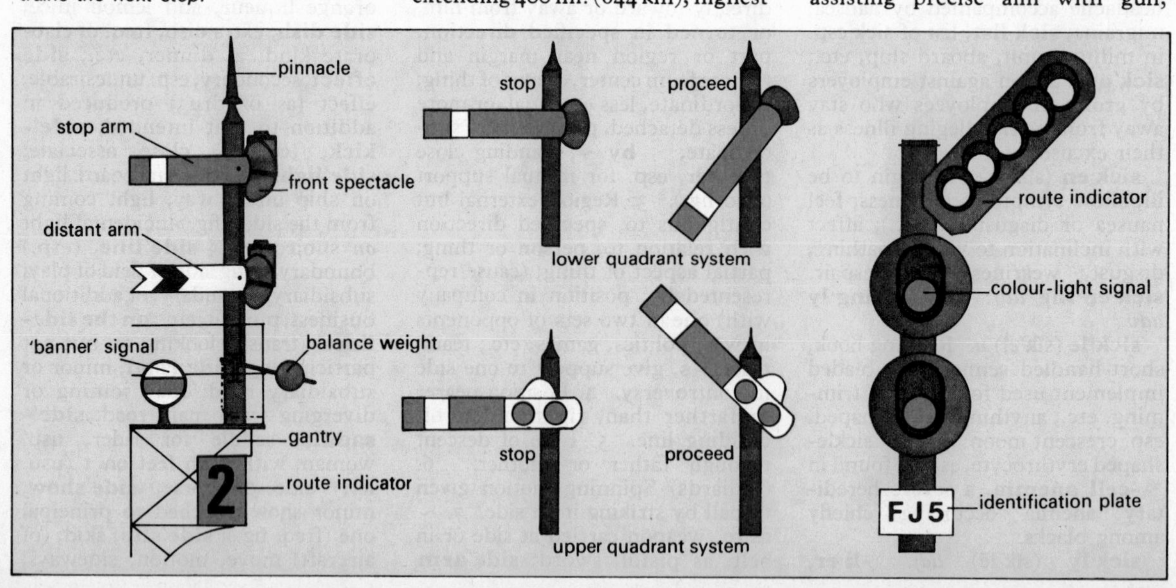

bomb, etc., or observation with optical instrument; **not by a long sight**, (colloq.) not nearly; emphatically not; **out of sight**, not in view; far away; (colloq.) out of or beyond reach; very high, as in quality, cost, etc.; **sight unseen**, without seeing (thing concerned) beforehand. **sight** *v.t.* Get sight of, esp. by coming near; take observation of (star etc.) with instrument; provide (gun etc.) with sights, adjust sights of; aim (gun etc.) with sights. **sight'ed** *adj.* Possessing vision; not blind. **sight'ing** *n.* Instance of seeing something, esp. aircraft etc.

sight·less (sīt'lĭs) *adj.* Blind.

sight·ly (sīt'lē) *adj.* (**-li·er, -li·est**). Pleasing to the sight, not unsightly. **sight'li·ness** *n.*

sig·ma (sĭg'm*a*) *n.* Letter of Greek alphabet (Σ, σ, or ς; uncial C) corresponding to *s*.

sig·moid (sĭg'moid), **sig·moi·dal** (sĭgmoi'd*a*l) *adjs.* Crescent-shaped, like the uncial sigma C; having double curve like letter *s*; of the ~ **flexure**, curving portion of intestine between colon and rectum.

sign (sīn) *n.* 1. Significant gesture; mark or device with special meaning or used to distinguish thing on which it is put; written mark conventionally used for word, phrase, etc., symbol; token, indication, trace (*of* something); omen, portent; miracle as demonstration of divine power or authority; (path.) objective evidence or indication of disease etc. (cf. SYMPTOM). 2. Board bearing name of business establishment and displayed in front of building housing it. 3. Any of 12 equal divisions of zodiac named from constellations formerly situated in them. 4. **sign'board**, = sense 2; **sign'post**, post at crossroads etc., with arm(s) indicating direction of place(s); **sign language**, communication by means of hand and finger gestures. **sign** *v.* 1. Mark *with* sign of the cross; mark with sign; make sign, intimate with sign; use sign language. 2. Attest or confirm by adding one's signature; write (name) as signature; affix one's signature; make *over*, give *away*, etc., by signing; ~ **in, out**, report, indicate, arrival, departure; ~ **off**, end broadcast by announcing one's name; ~ **on**, hire, be hired; ~ **up**, enlist for military duty. **sign'er** *n.*

Despite political upheavals since it attained independence in 1961, **Sierra Leone** is still an exporter of diamonds and iron ore, as well as palm kernels, coffee and cocoa.

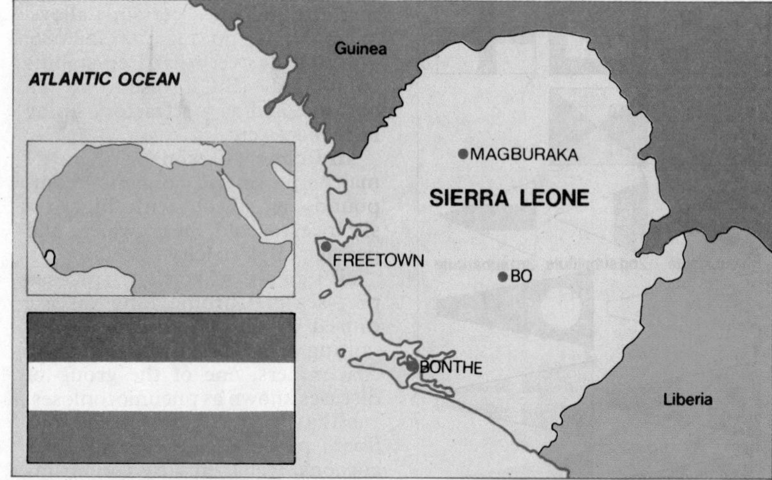

sig·nal[1] (sĭg'n*a*l) *n.* Prearranged or obvious sign conveying information or direction, esp. to person(s) at a distance; message made up of such signs; electrical impulse or radio wave transmitted or received; device, light, sound, gesture to warn, command, direct, as *traffic, railroad* ~; **S~ Corps**, branch of U.S. Army responsible for radio and other communications, weather studies, etc.; **signal tower**, railroad building with signaling apparatus; **sig'nalman** (pl. **-men**), signaler. **signal** *v.* (**-naled, -nal·ing**, Brit. **-nalled, -nal·ling**). Make signal(s) to; transmit, announce, by signal, direct (person) *to* do by signal.

sig·nal[2] (sĭg'n*a*l) *adj.* Remarkable, conspicuous, striking. **sig'nal·ly** *adv.*

sig·nal·ize (sĭg'n*a*līz) *v.t.* (**-ized, -iz·ing**). Distinguish, make conspicuous or remarkable.

sig·na·to·ry (sĭg'n*a*tōrē, -tôrē) *adj.* & *n.* (pl. **-ries**). (Party, esp. nation) whose signature is attached to document, esp. treaty.

sig·na·ture (sĭg'n*a*ch*e*r) *n.* 1. Name, initials, or mark written with person's own hand as authentication of document or other writing; distinguishing mark; stamp, impression. 2. Letter(s) or figure(s) placed by printer at foot of first page (and freq. other pages) of each sheet of book as guide in making up and binding; a sheet as distinguished by its signature; (mus.) sign(s) placed at beginning of piece of music, movement, etc., to indicate key and time.

sig·net (sĭg'nĭt) *n.* Small seal, esp. one fixed in finger ring; small seal for official documents etc.

sig·nif·i·cance (sĭgnĭf'ĭk*a*ns) *n.*, **sig·nif·i·can·cy** (sĭgnĭf'ĭk*a*nsē) *n.* (pl. **-cies**). Being significant, expressiveness; meaning, import; consequence, importance.

The magnificent cathedral built between 1288 and 1309 dominates the **Siena** skyline, just as the work of Sienese artists dominated Italian painting from the 13th to the 15th centuries.

sig·nif·i·cant (sĭgnĭf'ĭk*a*nt) *adj.* Having, conveying, a meaning; full of meaning, highly expressive or suggestive; important, notable. **sig·nif'i·cant·ly** *adv.*

sig·ni·fi·ca·tion (sĭgn*ĭ*fĭkā'sh*o*n) *n.* (esp.) Exact meaning or sense.

sig·nif·i·ca·tive (sĭgnĭf'*ĭ*kātĭv) *adj.* Signifying: having a meaning; serving as sign or indication *of*.

sig·ni·fy (sĭg'n*ĭ*fī) *v.* (**-fied, -fy·ing**). Be sign or symbol of; represent, mean, denote; communicate, make known; be of importance, matter.

si·gnor (sēnyŏr', -yōr'), **si·gno·ra** (sēnyŏr'*a*, -yōr'*a*), **si·gno·ri·na** (sēny*o*rē'n*a*) *ns.* (pl. **si·gnors**, It. **si·gno·ri** pr. sēnyōr'ē; **si·gno·ras**, It. **si·gno·re** pr. sēnyōr'ĕ; **si·gno·ri·nas**, It. **si·gno·ri·ne** pr. sēny*o*rē'nĕ). (Title of or form of address to) Italian man, woman, young or unmarried woman. [It.]

Sikh (sēk) *n.* Member of a monotheistic sect established in India (chiefly in Punjab) since 16th c.; esp., member of a martial community maintained by this sect; ~ **Wars**, wars between Sikhs and British, 1845 and 1848–9, culminating in the British annexation of the Punjab. **Sikh'ism** *n.*

si·lage (sī'lĭj) *n.* Preservation of green fodder in silo or pit without drying; fodder thus preserved.

si·lence (sī'l*e*ns) *n.* Abstinence from speech or noise, taciturnity, reticence; absence of sound, stillness, noiselessness; neglect or omission to mention, write, etc. ~ *v.t.* (**-lenced, -lenc·ing**). Make silent, reduce to silence; put down, repress (expression of opinion etc.); compel (gun, ship, etc.) to cease firing.

si·lenc·er (sī'l*e*ns*er*) *n.* (esp.) Device for rendering gun (comparatively) silent.

si·lent (sī'l*e*nt) *adj.* Not speaking; not uttering, making, or accompanied by, any sound; (of letter) not pronounced; taciturn, speaking little; not mentioning or referring to, passing over, something; ~ **partner**, partner who invests but does no actual work in business. **si'lent·ness** *n.* **si'lent·ly** *adv.*

Si·le·nus (sīlē'n*u*s). (Gk. myth.) 1. Foster father and teacher of Dionysus, freq. represented as a fat, jolly, drunken old man. 2. (**s**~) Bearded satyr with tail and legs of horse.

Si·le·sia (sīlē'zh*a*, -sh*a*). Ancient duchy and district of E. Europe, partitioned at various times among Prussia, Austria-Hungary, Poland, and Czechoslovakia; now largely under Polish administration.

sil·hou·ette (sĭlo͞oĕt', sĭl'o͞oĕt) *n.* Portrait of person in profile showing outline only, this being filled in with black, cut out in paper, etc.; dark outline, shadow in profile, thrown up against lighter background. ~ *v.t.* (**-et·ted, -et·ting**). Represent, exhibit, in silhouette. [named after Étienne de *Silhouette* (1709–67), French politician]

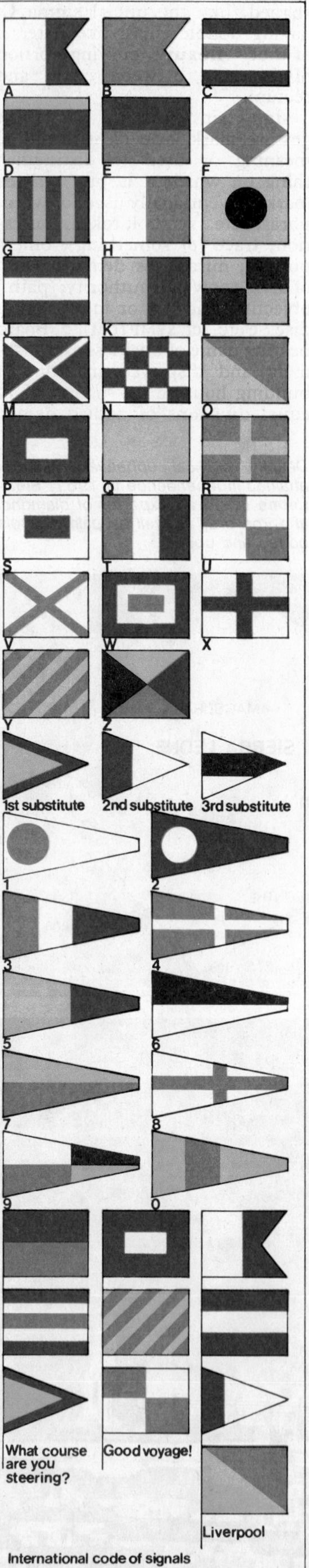

sil·i·ca (sĭl'ĭk*a*) *n.* Silicon dioxide (SiO_2), a hard, white or colorless, widely distributed mineral present in many precious and other stones, esp. quartz, and sand, used in the manufacture of glass, bricks, etc.

sil·i·cate (sĭl'ĭkĭt, -kāt) *n.* Salt of silicic acid; one of many insoluble compounds of metal(s), silicon, and oxygen, occurring widely in rocks of Earth's crust.

si·li·ceous, si·li·cious (sĭlĭsh'*u*s) *adjs.* Containing or consisting of silica.

sil·i·con (sĭl'*ĭ*k*o*n, -kŏn) *n.* (chem.) Nonmetallic element occurring only in combination, manufactured commercially by reduction of sand and used in the manufacture of certain alloys; symbol Si, at. no. 14, at. wt. 28.086; ~ **carbide**, very hard crystalline compound (SiC), used as an abrasive and as a refractory lining in furnaces etc.

sil·i·cone (sĭl'*ĭ*kōn) *n.* One of many polymeric organic compounds of silicon with high resistance to cold, heat, water, and passage of electricity.

sil·i·co·sis (sĭl*ĭ*kō'sĭs) *n.* (pl. **-ses** pr. -sēz). Chronic lung disease caused by inhalation of dust containing silica and freq. affecting coal miners, one of the group of diseases known as pneumoconioses.

silk (sĭlk) *n.* Strong soft lustrous fiber produced, to form their cocoons, webs, etc., by certain insect larvae, spiders, etc., esp. by silkworms (see below); thread or textile fabric made from this; similar lustrous filament or fiber made by chemical processes from cellulose; (in pl.) garments, uniform of such cloth, esp. jockey's cap and jacket in horse owner's colors; (attrib.) made of silk; ~ **cotton**, silky fiber, esp. kapok; ~**-cotton tree**, tree yielding this, esp. *Ceiba pentandra*, kapok tree; ~ **hat**, tall stiff cylindrical hat covered with silk plush; **Silk Route**, overland trade route that went from China through Central Asia and Persia to the Eastern Roman Empire; **silk'screen printing**: see SCREEN printing; **silk-stocking** (*n.* & *adj.*), (fig.) aristocratic, wealthy, luxurious (person); **silk'worm**, mulberry-feeding caterpillar of

The origin of **signal** *flags used by sailors is said to have been the raising of a red cloak in a ship's rigging to tell the Greek fleet to attack the Persians at Salamis in 480 B.C.*

The natural sheen of **silk** *enhances dyes and allows material for kimonos (above) to be brilliantly colored. Left: It may take many months to embroider a large wall-hanging by hand.*

moth (*Bombyx mori*), which spins cocoon of silk before changing into pupal state; caterpillar of other moths yielding silk cocoons of commerical value; **corn silk**: see CORN.

silk·en (sĭl′k*e*n) *adj.* Made of silk; clad in silk; soft or lustrous as silk.

silk·y (sĭl′kē) *adj.* (**silk·i·er, silk·i·est**). Like silk in smoothness, softness, fineness, or luster; **silky oak** (also **silk oak**), lofty Australian tree (*Grevillea robusta*) with fernlike foliage and attractive mottled wood. **silk′i·ness** *n.*

sill (sĭl) *n.* I. Horizontal piece or part at base of doorway or esp. window. 2. Horizontal timber, block, etc., serving as foundation for house wall. 3. Sheet of intrusive volcanic rock lying parallel to the bedding of other rocks.

sil·ly (sĭl′ē) *adj.* (**-li·er, -li·est**). Innocent, simple, helpless (archaic); foolish, weakminded, unwise, imbecile. **sil′ly, sil′li·ly** *advs.* **sil′li·ness** *n.*

si·lo (sī′lō) *n.* (pl. **-los**). I. Pit or airtight structure in which fodder is pressed to undergo fermentation for conversion into succulent winter feed. 2. Underground place where guided missile is kept ready for firing. ~ *v.t.* (**-loed, -lo·ing**). Put, store in silo.

silt (sĭlt) *n.* Sediment deposited by water in channel, harbor, etc. ~ *v.* Choke, be choked, (*up*) with silt. **sil·ta·tion** (sĭltā′sh*o*n) *n.* **silt′y** *adj.* (**silt·i·er, silt·i·est**).

Sil·u·res (sĭl′y*u*rēz, sĭlūr′-) *n.pl.* Members of a tribe in SE. Wales who resisted the Roman invasion (43 A.D.). **Si·lu·ri·an** (sĭloor′ē*a*n, sī-, -lūr′-) *adj.* & *n.* I. (One) of the Silures. 2. (geol.) (Of) the period or system of the Paleozoic between Ordovician and Devonian.

sil·van: SYLVAN.

Sil·va·nus (sĭlvā′n*u*s). (Rom. myth.) Spirit of woods, fields, flocks, etc.

sil·ver (sĭl′v*e*r) *n.* I. (chem.) White lustrous ductile malleable metallic element, one of the precious metals, used chiefly with alloy of harder metal for coin, jewelry, table utensils, etc., and in form of salts as the light-sensitive materials in photography; symbol Ag, at. no. 47, at. wt. 107.868. 2. Silver coins; cupronickel coins now substituted for these; silverware, silver plate; household cutlery. 3. (attrib.) **sil′versmith**, worker in silver, maker of silverware; **sil′verware**, articles made of silver. **silver** *adj.* Wholly or chiefly of, colored like, silver; having clear ringing sound; eloquent; (of lace etc.) containing silver threads; ~ **age**, (i) (Gk. and Rom. myth.) second age of the world, inferior to golden age; (ii) second phase of classical Latin (see Silver LATIN); ~ **bell** (**tree**), any of various trees or shrubs of the storax family (genus *Halesia*) of southeastern U.S. and China, esp. *H. carolina* having graceful bellshaped white flowers; ~ **birch**, any of several birches (genus *Betula*), from the light color of the bark; **sil′verfish** (pl. **-fishes**, collect. **-fish**), various silvery fishes, esp. white variety of goldfish; small silvery wingless insect (*Lepisma saccharine*) feeding on starch, books, wallpaper, etc.; **silver fox**, color form of Amer. red fox with highly prized black fur that appears silver-tipped because the long hairs are banded with white near tips; **silver gray**, lustrous gray; **silver iodide**, yellow powder that darkens when exposed to light, used in rainmaking, photography, medicine; **Silver Latin**, see LATIN; **silver lining**, sign of hope in gloom; **silver nitrate**, poisonous, colorless, corrosive, crystalline salt, used in photography, as an antiseptic, in silver-plating, mirror manufacturing etc.; **silver-plate** (*v.t.*) (**-plat·ed, -plat·ing**), plate with silver, electroplate; **sil'vertip**: see GRIZZLY; ~ **wedding**, 25th wedding anniversary; **sil'ver-weed**, any of several plants having leaves silvery white underneath esp. *Potentilla argentea* or *P. anserina*. **silver** *v*. Coat or plate with silver; give silvery appearance to; turn (hair etc.), become, white or gray; provide (mirror) with amalgam of tin.

sil·ver·y (sĭl'verē) *adj*. Resembling silver in luster, whiteness, ringing sound, etc. **sil'ver·i·ness** *n*.

si·ma (sī'ma) *n*. (geol.) Part of earth's crust immediately below SIAL. [f. *si*licon and *ma*gnesium]

Sim·e·on Sty·li·tes (sĭm'ēon stĭlī'tēz), **St.** (*c*390–459). First of the stylites; lived for 30 years on top of a pillar near Antioch in Syria.

sim·i·an (sĭm'ēan) *adj*. & *n*. (Of) one of the apes, esp. the anthropoid apes; ape(like), monkey(like).

sim·i·lar (sĭm'iler) *adj*. Like, alike, having mutual resemblance or resemblance *to*, of the same kind; (geom.) having same shape. **sim'i·lar·ly** *adv*. **sim·i·lar·i·ty** (sĭmilăr'ĭtē) *n*. (pl. **-ties**).

sim·i·le (sĭm'ilē) *n*. Figure of speech in which two unlike things are explicitly compared, usu. with introductory word *like* or *as* ("like a small gray coffeepot sits the squirrel"); passage effecting this.

si·mil·i·tude (sĭmĭl'ĭtōōd, -tūd) *n*. Guise, outward appearance; (obs.) simile.

sim·mer (sĭm'er) *v*. Be, keep, on the point of boiling, cook slowly in liquid at temperature just below boiling point (freq. fig.). ~ *n*. Simmering state.

Si·mon (sī'mon). 1. St. PETER². 2. Apostle, member of the Zealot party (~ **Zelotes** or **the Canaanite**); commemorated with St. Jude, Oct. 28. 3. Kinsman of Jesus Christ (Matt. 13, Mark 6). 4. (also ~ **Magus**) Sorcerer of Samaria who was converted by Philip; he offered money to the Apostles if they would confer upon him the power to impart the Holy Ghost, and was rebuked by Peter (Acts 8). 5. ~ **Le·gree** (legrē'), cruel, merciless master, from the character of the slave driver in Harriet Beecher Stowe's novel, *Uncle Tom's Cabin*.

simon-pure (sī'mon pūr') *adj*. Completely pure, genuine, real.

si·mo·ny (sī'monē, sĭm'o-) *n*. Buying or selling of ecclesiastical preferment. [f. SIMON Magus]

sim·pa·ti·co (sĭmpah'tĭkō, -păt'ĭ-) *adj*. Of similar disposition or outlook; congenial.

sim·per (sĭm'per) *n*. Affected and self-conscious smile, smirk. ~ *v*. Smile in silly affected manner, smirk; utter with simper. **sim'-per·ing·ly** *adv*. **sim'per·er** *n*.

sim·ple (sĭm'pel) *adj*. (**-pler, -plest**). 1. Not compound, complex, complicated, elaborate, involved, or composite; unmixed, consisting of one substance, ingredient, or element; presenting no difficulty; mere, pure, bare; ~ **equation**, one not involving second or any higher power of unknown quantity; ~ **interest**: see INTEREST; ~ **life**, life in more or less primitive conditions, without servants or luxuries; ~ **sentence**, one without subordinate clause. 2. Plain, unsophisticated, natural, artless; inexperienced; weak-minded; of low rank, ordinary; ~**-hearted**, free of guile, sincere, unsophisticated; ~**-minded**, ingenuous, mentally deficient, stupid; **S~ Simon**, foolish, silly person, from the nursery rhyme character. **sim'ply** *adv*. In simple manner; without exception, absolutely. **sim'ple·ness, sim·plic·i·ty** (sĭmplĭs'ĭtē) *ns*. (pl. **-ties**).

sim·ple·ton (sĭm'pelton) *n*. Foolish, gullible, or half-witted person.

sim·pli·fy (sĭm'plifī) *v.t*. (**-fied, -fy·ing**). Make simple, make easy to do or understand. **sim·pli·fi·ca·tion** (sĭmplifĭkā'shon) *n*.

sim·plism (sĭm'plĭzem) *n*. Affected simplicity; unjustifiable simplification of problem etc. **sim·plis·tic** (sĭmplĭs'tĭk) *adj*.

Sim·plon (sĭm'plŏn; *Fr*. săṅplawṅ'). Alpine pass in SW. Switzerland; ~ **tunnel**, railroad tunnel, about 12 mi. long, driven through Monte Leone, NE. of the pass.

sim·u·la·crum (sĭmyulā'krum) *n*. (pl. **-cra** pr. -kra). Image of something; shadowy likeness, deceptive substitute, mere pretense.

sim·u·late (sĭm'yulāt) *v.t*. (**-lat·ed, -lat·ing**). Feign, counterfeit; pretend to be, wear guise of, mimic. **sim'u·la·tive** *adj*. **sim·u·la·tion** (sĭmyulā'shon)

***Silverweed** (Potentilla anserina) which grows wild in many temperate areas of the northern hemisphere. Its roots once served as an emergency food and the leaves were used as a medicine.*

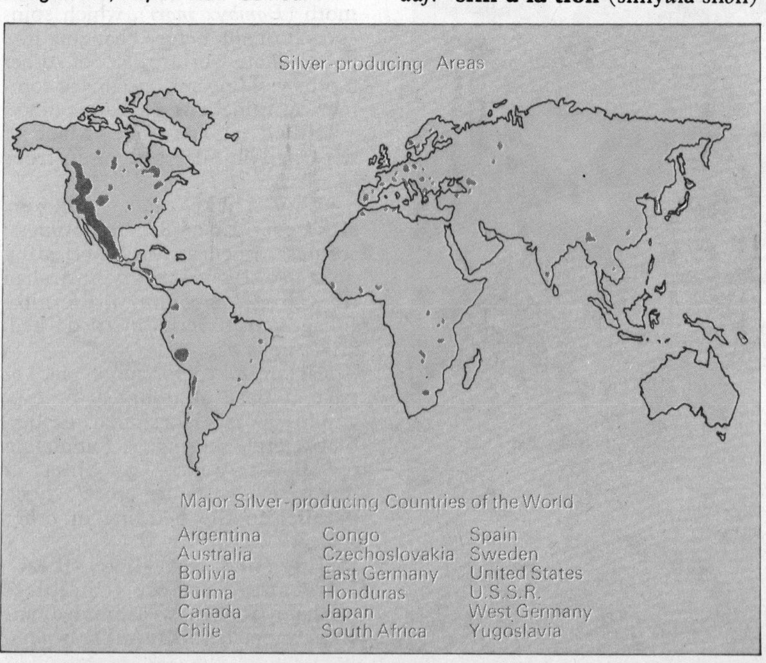

*Except in Peru and Norway, **silver** is mostly found in combination with other metals, particularly lead and zinc. It is present with gold, in copper deposits at Bougainville, Papua New Guinea.*

***Silversmith** Paul Harrison (below left) adopts the modern design concept of elegant simplicity. Others, anachronistically, attempt to ape the over-ornamentation of the 18th-century wine-cooler by Paul Storr, or the rococo of the Kaendler candelabrum (c. 1750).*

n. **sim′u·la·tor** *n.* (esp.) Machine simulating conditions experienced in flying aircraft, driving vehicle, etc., used esp. in training pilots etc.

si·mul·cast (sī′m*u*lkăst, -kahst, sĭm′*u*l-) *n.* Simultaneous transmission on radio and television.

si·mul·ta·ne·ous (sīm*u*ltā′nē*u*s, sĭm*u*l-) *adj.* Existing, occurring, operating, at the same time (*with*); ~ **equations**, equations involving the same values of the unknown quantity or quantities and solved in conjunction with each other. **si·mul·ta′ne·ous·ly** *adv.* **si·mul·ta′ne·ous·ness, si·mul·ta·ne·i·ty** (sīm*u*ltanē′ĭtē, sĭm*u*l-) *ns.*

sin[1] (sĭn) *n.* (A) transgression against divine law or principles of morality; offense *against* good taste, propriety, etc.; DEADLY, MORTAL, ORIGINAL, VENIAL ~: see these words; **live in** ~, (esp. colloq.) cohabit without marriage; **seven deadly sins**: see DEADLY. **sin′ful, sin′less** *adjs.* **sin′ful·ly, sin′less·ly** *advs.* **sin′ful·ness, sin′less·ness** *ns.* **sin** *v.i.* (**sinned, sin·ning**). Commit sin; offend *against*. **sin′ner** *n.*

sin[2] (sīn) *abbrev.* Sine.

Si·nai (sī′nī, -nīī). Peninsula of NE. Egypt, at the N. end of the Red Sea, extending 140 mi. (225 km), between the gulfs of Suez and Aqaba; occupied by Israeli forces June, 1967, during 6-Day War; returned to Egypt by Israeli-Egyptian peace treaty, 1979. **Mount Sinai**, mountain in S. part of this peninsula where the Ten Commandments and the Tables of the Law were given to Moses. **Si·na·it·ic** (sīnāĭt´ĭk), **Si·na·ic** (sīnā´ĭk, sī-) *adjs*.

Sin·bad: SINDBAD.

since (sĭns) *adv*. From that time till now; within the period between then and now, subsequently, later; ago, before now. ~ *prep*. From (specified time) till now; during the period between (specified past time) and now. ~ *conj*. 1. From the time that. 2. Seeing that, because, inasmuch as.

sin·cere (sĭnsēr´) *adj*. (**-cer·er, -cer·est**). Free from pretense or deceit, not assumed or put on, genuine, honest, frank. **sin·cere'ly** *adv*. In a sincere manner; **yours** ~, polite formula used before signature in letter (e.g. to acquaintance) that is neither formal nor intimate. **sin·cer·i·ty** (sĭnsĕr´ĭtē) *n*. (pl. **-ties**).

sin·ci·put (sĭn´sipŭt) *n*. (pl. **sin·ci·puts, sin·cip·i·ta** pr. sĭnsĭp´ĭta). Front part of head or skull.

Sind·bad, Sin·bad (sĭn´băd). (also ~ **the Sailor**) Hero of one of the tales in the *Arabian Nights*, who relates his fantastic adventures in a number of voyages.

si·ne (sīn) *n*. (trig., function of angle in right-angled triangle) Ratio of side opposite given acute angle to hypotenuse (abbrev. sin); ~ **curve**, graph in rectangular coordinates showing how this ratio varies with the angle.

si·ne·cure (sī´nekūr, sĭn´e-) *n*. Any office or post that involves little or no work, esp. one that brings profit.

si·ne di·e (sī´nē dī´ē; *Lat*. sĭ´nĕ dē´ĕ). (Adjourned) without any day for resumption of business etc. being specified; indefinitely. [L., = "without day"]

si·ne qua non (sī´nē kwā nŏn´; *Lat*. sĭ´nĕ kwah nōn´). Indispensable condition or qualification. [L., = "without which not"]

sin·ew (sĭn´ū) *n*. (Piece of) tough fibrous tissue uniting muscle to bone, tendon; (pl., loosely) muscles, bodily strength, wiriness (freq. fig., esp. in ~**s of war**, money). **sin'ew·y** *adj*.

sing (sĭng) *v*. (**sang** pr. săng or **sung** pr. sŭng, **sung, sing·ing**). Utter words or sounds, utter (words, sounds), in tuneful succession, esp. in accordance with a set tune; produce vocal melody, utter (song, tune); make inarticulate melodious, humming, buzzing, or whistling sounds; compose poetry, celebrate in verse; ~ **out**, (colloq.) call out loudly. **sing'er** *n*.

sing *abbrev*. Singular.

Sin·ga·pore (sĭng´gapōr, -pōr, sĭng´a-). Republic consisting of the island of Singapore and a number of smaller islands, S. of Malay peninsula; former Brit. colony; member nation of Brit. Commonwealth, independent 1965.

singe (sĭnj) *n*. Superficial burn. ~ *v.t.* (**singed, singe·ing**). Burn superficially or lightly, burn ends of edges of.

Sin·gha·lese (sĭnggalēz´, -lēs´) *n*. (pl. **-lese**). 1. (Member of) the majority community in Sri Lanka. 2. Indo-European language spoken in Sri Lanka, closely related to Pali, with many Dravidian words. ~ *adj*.

sin·gle (sĭng´gel) *adj*. One only, not double or multiple, undivided, individual, separate; of, for, one person only; solitary, lonely, unaided; unmarried; (of flower) not double, having only one whorl or set of petals; ~**-breasted**, (of garments) having buttons on one edge, not double-breasted; ~ **combat**, combat between two persons; ~ **entry**, simple method of bookkeeping in which transactions are entered in the ledger under one account only (opp. double ENTRY); ~ **file**, line of persons going one behind another, Indian file; ~**-handed**, (done etc.) without help from other persons; ~**-hearted**, sincere, honest; ~**-lens reflex**, type of reflex camera in which image is reflected through same lens onto film and ground glass viewing plate; ~**-minded**, single-hearted; also, keeping one purpose in view; **single-track**, one-track. **sin'gle·ness** *n*. **sin'gly** *adv*. **single** *n*. One person or thing; theater seat, hotel room, etc. for one person; (pl.) unmarried people collectively; (baseball) one-base hit; (pl., tennis) game for one person only on each side; (colloq.) dollar bill. ~ *v.t.* (**-gled, -gling**). Choose *out* as example, to serve some purpose etc.

sin·gle·ton (sĭng´gelton) *n*. 1. (bridge etc.) Card that is the only one of its suit in the hand. 2. Single thing; thing that exists by itself rather than as one of a pair or in a group.

sing·song (sĭng´sawng) *adj*. In, recited with, monotonous rhythm, rising and falling monotonously. ~ *n*. Monotonous rhythm or cadence; impromptu or informal vocal concert.

sin·gu·lar (sĭng´gyuler) *adj*. 1. (gram.) Denoting, expressing, 1 person or thing. 2. Unusual, uncommon, extraordinary, surprising; strange, odd, peculiar. **sin'gu·lar·ly** *adv*. **sin·gu·lar·i·ty** (sĭnggyulăr´ĭtē) *n*. (pl. **-ties**). (esp.) Eccentricity, oddness, strangeness. **singular** *n*. Singular number; word in singular form.

Sin·ha·lese (sĭnhalēz, -lēs´) = SINGHALESE.

sin·is·ter (sĭn´ĭster) *adj*. 1. Of evil omen; unfavorable, harmful; wicked, corrupt, evil; ill-looking, malignant, villainous. 2. (her.) On left side of shield etc. (from bearer's point of view); **bar, bend** ~: see BEND[1].

sin·is·tral (sĭn´ĭstral) *adj*. (of spiral shells) With whorls going to left; (of flat fishes) having left side of body turned uppermost.

sink[1] (sĭngk) *n*. 1. Place in which foul liquid collects (now usu. fig.). 2. Fixed basin with drain and faucets, in bathroom for washing face, hands, etc., in kitchen for washing dishes etc. 3. **heat** ~, device for dissipating heat in electrical circuit or steam engine. 4. Low-lying, poorly drained area.

sink[2] (sĭngk) *v*. (**sank** pr. săngk or **sunk** pr. sŭngk, **sunk** or rarely **sunk·en, sink·ing**). 1. Become wholly or partly submerged in water, quicksand, snow, etc. (freq. fig.); fall slowly downward, subside, descend, pass out of sight; pass, fall gently, lapse, degenerate, *into*; (of sun etc.) appear to move downward toward or pass below horizon; penetrate, make way *in(to)*. 2. Cause or allow to sink; send below surface of liquid or ground; lower level of; excavate, make by excavating; set aside, leave out of consideration; invest (money), lose by investment; (golf, basketball, etc.) get ball into hole, basket, etc.

sink·er (sĭng´ker) *n*. (esp.) Weight used to sink fishing or sounding line; (baseball) curve ball that drops as it crosses home plate.

Although 75 per cent of the ***Singaporean*** *people are of Chinese origin, some minority groups like the Hindu (facing) still practice their beliefs. Left: A typical Chinese street vendor who vies with huge supermarkets in the city.*

sink·ing (sĭng'kĭng) *n.* (esp.) Internal bodily sensation caused by hunger or apprehension; ~ **fund**, fund of money periodically set aside from revenue, usu. to reduce principal of national, municipal, or company's debt.

Sinn Fein (shĭn' fān'). Irish society, founded 1905 by Arthur Griffith, aiming at political independence and revival of Irish culture and language; policy of this; extreme Irish nationalist party. [Ir., = "we ourselves"]

Sino- *prefix.* Of China and —, as ~-*Soviet.*

Si·nol·o·gy (sīnŏl'*o*jē, sĭ-) *n.* Study of Chinese language, history, customs, etc. **Si·no·logue** (sī'nolawg, -lŏg), **Si·nol'o·gist** *ns.* Person versed in this.

Si·no·phile (sī'nofīl), **Si·no·phobe** (sī'nofōb) *ns.* One who loves, hates, the Chinese.

Si·no-Ti·bet·an (sīnōtĭbĕt'*a*n) *adj.* & *n.* (Of) the family of languages, mostly of the isolating type but orig. agglutinative, spoken over an area including N. India, Malay peninsula, China, and most of central and E. Asia (but not Japan).

sin·ter (sĭn'ter) *n.* Siliceous deposit often found around hot springs; substance produced by sintering. ~ *v.* (Cause to) coalesce from powder into solid by heating.

sin·u·ous (sĭn'ūus) *adj.* With many curves, tortuous, serpentine, undulating. **sin'u·ous·ly** *adv.* **sin'u·ous·ness** *n.* **sin·u·os·i·ty** (sĭnūŏs'ĭtē) *n.* (pl. **-ties**). Sinuousness; a curve or bend.

si·nus (sī'n*u*s) *n.* (pl. **-nus·es**). 1. (anat., zool.) Cavity of bone or tissue, esp. one of the cavities in the bone of the skull that communicate with the nostrils. 2. (path.) Passage communicating with deep-seated abscess, fistula. 3. (bot.) Curve between lobes of leaf.

si·nus·i·tis (sīn*u*sī'tĭs) *n.* Inflammation of sinus(es).

Sioux (sōō) *n.* (pl. **Sioux** pr. sōō, sōōz). (Member of) important group of N. Amer. Ind. tribes, orig. of district W. and S. of Lake Superior, later of plains of Minnesota, N. and S. Dakota, and Nebraska. **Siou·an** (sōō'*a*n) *adj.*

sip (sĭp) *n.* Small mouthful of liquid; act of sipping. ~ *v.* (**sipped, sip·ping**). Drink in sips, take sip of.

si·phon (sī'f*o*n) *n.* Pipe or tube bent so that one leg is longer than the other and used for drawing off liquids by atmospheric pressure, which forces liquid up the shorter leg and over the bend in the pipe; (also ~ **bottle**) aerated water bottle from which liquid is forced out by pressure of gas through tube inserted in bottle; (zool.) tubelike organ, esp. in mollusks, serving as canal for passage of fluid etc. **si'phon·al, si·phon·ic** (sīfŏn'ĭk) *adj.* **siphon** *v.* Conduct, flow, (as) through siphon.

sir (sẽr) *n.* 1. **S** ~, title of honor placed before Christian name of knight or baronet. 2. Used (without name) in formal or respectful address to a man; sometimes with scornful, indignant, contemptuous, etc., force; (**Dear**) **Sir**(**s**), opening of formal letter. **sir** *v.t.* Address as *sir.*

sire (sīr) *n.* 1. Father, forefather (poet.); male parent of beast, esp. stallion. 2. (archaic) = "your majesty." ~ *v.t.* (**sired, sir·ing**). Beget (esp. of stallions).

si·ren (sīr'*e*n) *n.* 1. (Gk. myth.) Any of several fabulous creatures, women or birds with women's heads, living on rocky isle to which they lured seafarers by their singing. 2. Sweet singer; dangerously fascinating woman, temptress; (attrib.) irresistibly tempting. 3. Apparatus producing loud sound by revolution of perforated disk over jet of compressed air or steam, used on fire engine, police car, as air raid warning, etc. 4. Eellike tailed amphibian of family Sirenidae, with short forelegs and no hindlegs.

si·re·ni·an (sīrē'nē*a*n) *adj.* & *n.* (Member) of order Sirenia of large aquatic herbivorous mammals, including manatee and dugong.

Sir·i·us (sĭr'ē*u*s). (astron.) Dog star, a brilliant white star in the constellation Canis Major, the brightest fixed star.

sir·loin (sẽr'loin) *n.* Upper and choicer part of loin of beef.

si·roc·co (sĭrŏk'ō) *n.* (pl. **-cos**). Hot and blighting oppressive wind blowing from N. coast of Africa over Mediterranean to parts of S. Europe. [It. *s(c)irocco*, f. Arab.

*A **Sioux** Indian dressed in full regalia. Also known as the Dakota, these people once dominated a large area of the country. Some were nomadic hunters, others grew crops.*

*The **sitar** is a traditional Indian instrument, resembling a guitar in form, but differing greatly in the sound it produces. The photograph shows one of the great exponents of the sitar, Professor Moni Lal Hazra.*

šarūḳ east wind]

sir·rah, sir·ra (sĭr′*a*) *ns.* (archaic) = SIR used in contempt, reproach, reprimand.

sir·up = SYRUP.

si·sal (sī′s*a*l, sĭs′*a*l) *n.* (also ~ **grass, hemp**) Strong durable white fiber of a Mexican agave (*Agave sisalana*) and similar plants, used for cordage etc. [*Sisal*, former seaport of Yucatan]

sis·kin (sĭs′kĭn) *n.* Small sharp-billed finch (*Spinus pinus*) of northern N. Amer., brown with yellow wing and tail patches.

sis·sy (sĭs′ē) *n.* (pl. **-sies**) & *adj.* Effeminate or cowardly boy or man; cowardly or timid person. **sis·si·fied** (sĭs′ĭfīd), **sis′sy·ish** *adjs.*

sis·ter (sĭs′t*er*) *n.* 1. Daughter of same parents as another person; one considered as or filling the place of a sister. 2. Member of a religious sisterhood, nun; **S**~, title of or form of address to nun; **~-in-law** (pl. **~s-in-law**), sister of one's husband or wife, wife of one's brother; **sister ship**, vessel built on same design as another.

sis·ter·hood (sĭs′t*er*ho͝od) *n.* 1. Being a sister, relation between sisters. 2. Society of women bound by monastic vows or devoting themselves to religious or charitable work.

Sis·tine (sĭs′tēn, -tīn, -tĭn) *adj.* 1. Of, pertaining to, built by, one of the popes named Sixtus; ~ **Chapel**, chapel in the Vatican, built by Sixtus IV, containing Michelangelo's painted ceiling and his fresco of the Last Judgment. 2. ~ **Madonna**, painting by Raphael formerly in the Church of San Sisto, Piacenza, and later in Dresden.

Sis·y·phus (sĭs′*i*f*u*s). (Gk. myth.) Legendary king of Corinth, condemned for his misdeeds to Hades; his eternal task was to roll a large stone to the top of a hill from which it rolled back again to the plain. **Sis·y·phe·an** (sĭs*i*fē′*a*n) *adj.* (As) of Sisyphus, everlastingly laborious.

sit (sĭt) *v.* (**sat** pr. săt, **sit·ting**). 1. Take, be in, position in which weight of body rests on buttocks; occupy seat as judge, with administrative function, as member of council or legislative assembly, etc.; (of assembly) hold a session, transact business; pose (*for* portrait etc. *to* painter etc.); (Brit.) take examination. 2. (of birds and some animals) Rest with legs bent and body close to ground or perch; remain on nest to hatch eggs. 3. (chiefly of inanimate things) Be in more or less permanent position. 4. Seat *oneself* (usu. *down*); cause to sit (usu. *down*); sit on (horse); (of bird) sit on, hatch (eggs). 5. ~ **down**, seat oneself; **~-down** (**strike**), one in which strikers refuse to leave the place where they are working; **~-in**, organized protest in which demonstrators occupy building etc.; ~ **in on**, be present as observer, participant; ~ **on**, hold session concerning; (slang) repress, squash, snub; ~ **out**, remain to end of; outstay; take no part in (dance etc.), sit out dance; ~ **up**, rise from lying to sitting posture; sit erect; (of animal) sit on hind legs with forelegs straight or lifted in begging posture; remain out of bed; (colloq.) be surprised, suddenly interested; **sit′up, sit-up** (*ns.*), exercise in which one raises the body from lying flat on back to sitting position without using arms or bending legs.

si·tar (sĭtär′) *n.* Long-necked seven-stringed Indian musical instrument resembling a lute.

sit·com (sĭt′kŏm) *n.* (colloq.) = SITUATION comedy.

site (sīt) *n.* Ground on which town, building, etc., stood, stands, or is to stand; ground set apart for some purpose. ~ *v.t.* (**sit·ed, sit·ing**). Locate, place, provide with site.

sit·ter (sĭt′*er*) *n.* (esp.) BABY sitter.

sit·ting (sĭt′ĭng) *n.* (esp.) 1. Time during which one sits or remains seated; single occasion of sitting for artist etc. 2. Clutch of eggs. 3. ~ **room**, space for sitting; room used expressly for sitting in. **sitting** *adj.* (of bird) Not flying;

Remains of a hypocaust or Roman form of central heating restored at an archaeological ***site*** *at Fishbourne, in Sussex, England. Such work can indicate what life was like in former times.*

(of animal) not running; (of hen) engaged in hatching; ~ **duck,** (colloq.) person or thing easily attacked.

Sit·ting (sĭt'ĭng) **Bull** (1834?–1890). Amer. Indian Sioux chief; leader during Sioux War, 1876–7, and at battle of the Little Big Horn, June 25, 1876, where the Amer. forces under Gen. George S. Custer were massacred.

sit·u·ate (sĭch' ōōāt) *v.t.* (**-at·ed, -at·ing**). Place or put in position, situation, etc. **sit'u·at·ed, situate** (sĭch'ōōĭt, -āt) *adjs.* In specified situation. **sit·u·a·tion** (sĭchōōā'sh*o*n) *n.* 1. Place, with its surroundings, occupied by something. 2. Set of circumstances, position in which one finds oneself; critical point or complication, position of affairs, in narrative, drama, etc.; ~ **comedy**, one in which humor derives from characters' misunderstandings and embarrassments. 3. Place or paid office, esp. of domestic servant. **sit·u·a'tion·al** *adj.*

sitz (sĭts, zĭtz) **bath.** Hip bath. [Ger. *Sitzbad*, f. *sitzen* sit]

Si·va = SHIVA.

six (sĭks) *adj.* Amounting to 6; **~-foot**, measuring six feet; **S~ Nations**, (hist.) confederation of N. Amer. Indians consisting of the FIVE Nations and the Tuscaroras; **~-pack**, six cans or bottles in one package, esp. when containing beer; **six'pence**, (Brit.) sum of six pence; coin formerly worth this; **six-shooter**, revolver capable of firing six shots without reloading. **six** *n.* One more than 5; symbol for this (6, vi, or VI); card, die face, or domino with six pips; six o'clock; size etc. indicated by 6; set of six things or persons. **six'fold** *adj.* & *adv.*

six·teen (sĭks'tēn') *adj.* One more than 15. ~ *n.* The number sixteen (16, xvi, or XVI). **six'-teenth'** *adj.* & *n.*

sixth (sĭksth) *adj.* Next after fifth; ~ **sense**, supposed faculty by which a person perceives facts and regulates action without the direct use of any of the five senses. **sixth** *n.* Sixth part (see PART[1] sense 1); sixth thing etc.; **sixth'ly** *adv.* In the sixth place.

Six·tus (sĭks't*u*s). Name of five popes, esp.: **Sixtus IV**, pope 1471–84, patron of art and letters, builder of the SISTINE Chapel, refounded the Vatican library; **Sixtus V**, pope 1585–90, reorganized the papal finances and issued (1590) an edition of the Vulgate known as the Sistine Vulgate.

six·ty (sĭks'tē) *adj.* Amounting to 60. ~ *n.* (pl. **-ties**). Cardinal number, 6 times 10 (60, lx, or LX); set of 60 things or persons; **six'ties**, numbers etc. from 60 to 69; these years of century or life. **six'ti·eth** *adj.* & *n.*

siz·a·ble, size·a·ble (sī'z*a*bel) *adjs.* Of fairly large size. **siz'-a·bly** *adv.*

size[1] (sīz) *n.* Dimensions, magnitude; one of usu. numbered classes into which things, esp. garments, are divided according to size. ~ *v.t.* (**sized, siz·ing**). Group or sort in sizes or according to size; ~ **up**, estimate size of; (colloq.) form judgment of.

size[2] (sīz) *n.* Glutinous substance, preparation of glue, shellac, etc., and water, used for glazing paper, stiffening textiles, mixing with colors, etc. ~ *v.t.* (**sized, siz·ing**). Treat with size.

size·a·ble: SIZABLE.

siz·zle (sĭz'el) *v.i.* (**-zled, -zling**). Make sputtering or hissing sound, esp. in frying, roasting, etc. ~ *n.* Sizzling noise.

S.J. *abbrev.* Society of Jesus.

Skag·er·rak (skăg'erăk). N. part of channel between S. Scandinavia and Denmark connecting North Sea with Baltic.

skate[1] (skāt) *n.* (pl. **skates,** collect. **skate**). Any of various ocean fish (family Rajidae), having a broad flat body and two wing-like dorsal fins.

skate[2] (skāt) *n.* One of a pair of steel blades, each attached beneath shoe sole, enabling wearer to glide over ice; ROLLER skate. ~ *v.i.* (**skat·ed, skat·ing**). Move, glide, (as) on skates. **skat'er** *n.*

As the representative of destruction, ***Siva*** *was always admired by Hindu ascetics. In other forms, he represents dance and free living, and is symbolized by a phallus.*

skate·board (skāt'bōrd, -bōrd) *n.* Short, oblong board or length of plastic having pair of roller skate wheels at each end, used for gliding, usu. on inclined surface. ~ *v.* Glide or coast on skateboard. **skate'board·er, skate'board·ing** *ns.*

ske·dad·dle (skĭdăd'el) *v.* (**-dled, -dling**). (colloq.) Run away, retreat hastily. ~ *n.* Precipitate retreat or flight, scurry.

skeet (skēt) *n.* Shooting sport in which clay target is thrown from trap to simulate flight of bird.

skein (skān) *n.* Quantity of yarn or thread coiled and usu. loosely twisted.

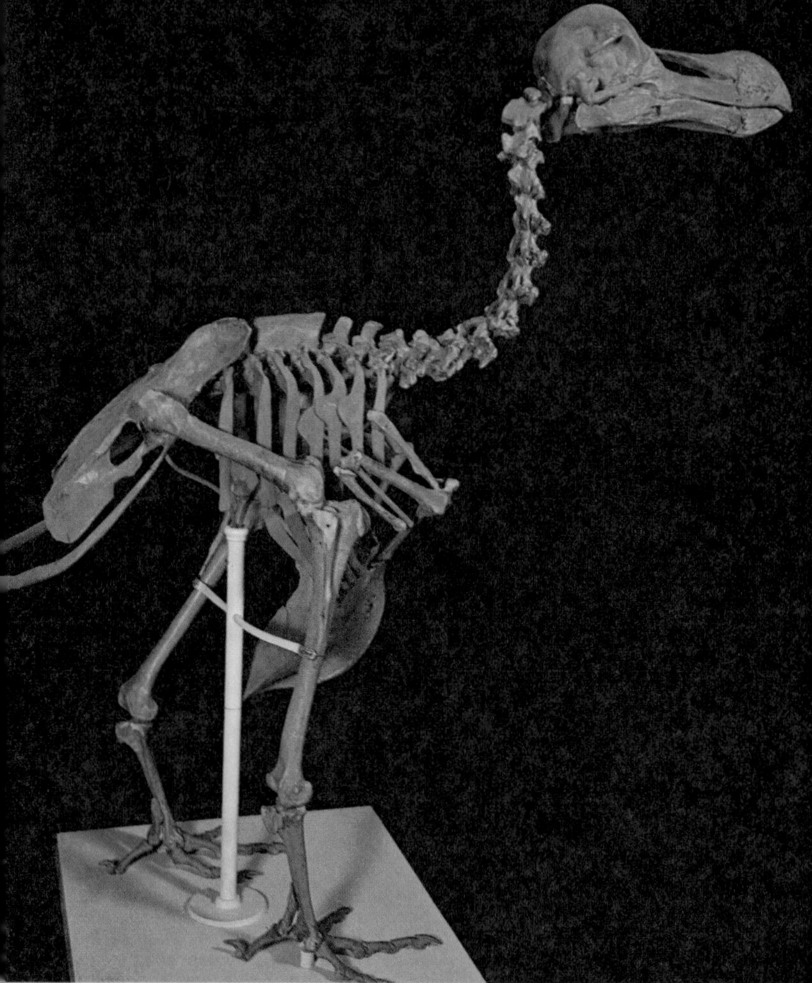

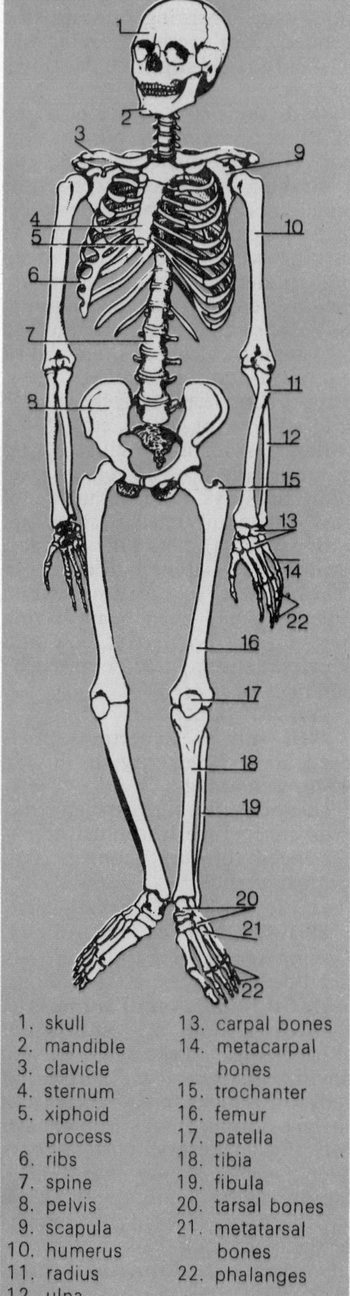

1. skull
2. mandible
3. clavicle
4. sternum
5. xiphoid process
6. ribs
7. spine
8. pelvis
9. scapula
10. humerus
11. radius
12. ulna
13. carpal bones
14. metacarpal bones
15. trochanter
16. femur
17. patella
18. tibia
19. fibula
20. tarsal bones
21. metatarsal bones
22. phalanges

*The **skeleton** of the dodo (above) and of man (right) show common features which indicate that despite the adaptation of each to different environments, it is probable that all vertebrates originally shared a single ancestor.*

skel·e·ton (skĕl′*e*t*o*n) *n.* 1. Hard internal or external framework of bones, cartilage, shell, woody fiber, etc., supporting or containing animal or vegetable body. 2. Dried bones of human being or other animal fastened together in same relative positions as in life; very thin or emaciated person, etc.; ~ **in the closet**, discreditable or humiliating fact concealed from strangers. 3. Mere outlines, supporting framework, main features or most necessary elements, *of* something; (attrib.) (of staff, company, etc.) of the minimum size, forming a nucleus that can be added to as occasion arises; ~ **key**, key fitting many locks by having large part of bit filed away. **skel′e·tal** *adj.* **skel′e·tal·ly** *adv.* **skel·e·ton·ize** (skĕl′*e*t*o*nīz) *v.t.* (**-ized, -iz·ing**). Reduce to a skeleton.

skep·tic, scep·tic (skĕp′tĭk) *ns.* One who doubts the possibility of real knowledge of any kind; one who doubts the truth of the Christian or of all religious doctrines; person of skeptical attitude, or unconvinced of the truth of a particular fact or theory. **skep′ti·cal** *adj.* Inclined to suspense of judgment, given to questioning of facts and soundness of inferences; incredulous, hard to convince. **skep′ti·cal·ly** *adv.* **skep·ti·cism** (skĕp′tĭsĭz*e*m) *n.*

sketch (skĕch) *n.* Preliminary, rough, slight, merely outlined, or unfinished drawing or painting; brief account or narrative without detail, rough draft, general outline; short slight play, freq. of single scene; **sketch′book, sketch book**, book of drawing paper for making sketches on. **sketch** *v.* Make or give sketch of; make sketches. **sketch′er** *n.*

sketch·y (skĕch′ē) *adj.* (**sketch·i·er, sketch·i·est**). Giving only a slight or rough outline; resembling a sketch; light, flimsy, hurried, rough. **sketch′i·ly** *adv.* **sketch′i·ness** *n.*

skew (skū) *v.t.* Make slanting; distort. ~ *v.i.* Move obliquely; twist. ~ *adj.* Oblique, slanting, squint, not symmetrical (now usu. archit., mech., etc.). ~ *n.* Sloping top of buttress; coping of gable; stone built into bottom of gable to support coping.

skew·er (skū′*er*) *n.* Pin for holding meat compactly together while cooking. ~ *v.t.* Fasten together, pierce, (as) with skewer.

ski (skē; *Norw.* shē) *n.* (pl. **skis, ski**). One of pair of long slender pieces of wood, plastic, etc., usu. pointed and curved upward at front, fastened to boot and enabling wearer to glide over snow-covered surface; ~ **boots, pants**, etc., garments for wear when skiing; ~ **jump**, steep slope leveling off before sharp drop, allowing skier to leap through air; ~ **lift**, device for transporting skiers up mountainside, usu. consisting of seats suspended from overhead cable. **ski** *v.i.* (**skied, ski·ing**). Slide, travel on skis.

skid (skĭd) *n.* 1. Piece of frame or timber serving as buffer, support, inclined plane, for logs, etc. 2. Braking device, esp. wooden or metal shoe, fixed under the wheel of a cart etc. and so preventing its turning when descending a steep hill; runner on aircraft to facilitate landing, etc. 3. Act of skidding; ~ **row,** section of city frequented by vagrants, alcoholics, etc. **skid** *v.* (**skid·ded, skid·ding**). 1. Support, move, protect, check, with skid(s). 2. (of wheel etc.) Slide without revolving, fail to grip ground, sideslip; (of vehicle etc.) slide sideways toward outside of curve when turning; slip, slide, esp. with (partial) loss of balance. **skid'dy** *adj.* (**-di·er, -di·est**).

skiff (skĭf) *n.* Any of several types of small open boats having flat bottom, pointed at bow and square at stern, sailed or rowed by one person.

skil·ful: SKILLFUL.

skill (skĭl) *n.* Expertness, practiced ability, dexterity, facility in doing something.

skilled (skĭld) *adj.* (esp., of workman etc.) Properly trained or experienced; (of work) requiring skill and experience.

skil·let (skĭl'ĭt) *n.* Frying pan.

skill·ful, skil·ful (skĭl'*f*ul) *adjs.* Having or showing skill (*at, in*); practiced, adept, expert, ingenious. **skill'ful·ly** *adv.* **skill'ful·ness** *n.*

skim (skĭm) *v.* (**skimmed, skim·ming**). Take scum, cream, floating matter, from surface of (liquid), remove (cream etc.) from surface of milk etc.; ~ **the cream off,** (fig.) take best part of; pass over (surface), pass *over, along,* rapidly and lightly with close approach or very slight contact; read superficially, look over cursorily. **skim** *adj.* **skim(med) milk,** milk with the cream removed. **skimming** *n.* (slang) Deliberate failure to report part of income, esp. from gambling, in order to evade tax.

skim·mer (skĭm'*er*) *n.* (esp.) 1. Ladle, usu. perforated, or other utensil for skimming liquids. 2. Long-winged marine bird of genus *Rynchops,* esp. **black** ~ (*R. nigra*), obtaining food by skimming along surface of water with knifelike lower mandible immersed.

skimp (skĭmp) *v.* Supply meagerly; be parsimonious. **skimp'y** *adv.* (**skimp·i·er, skimp·i·est**). Meager, inadequate. **skimp'i·ly** *adv.* **skimp'i·ness** *n.*

skin (skĭn) *n.* 1. Tough flexible continuous covering of human or other animal body, consisting of

Like most artists, Michelangelo, before he began a full-scale painting or sculpture, made a ***sketch*** *of various features that he wished to incorporate in the final work.*

The one class style of yacht racing has become increasingly popular particularly in the smaller classes such as the ***skiff.*** *There is often keen competition for sponsoring rights on successful boats.*

Determined skiers no longer need to confine their activities to the winter. This Australian competes in a **slalom** which is held on synthetic mats which are used to simulate snow.

The **ski lift** was designed to encourage people to become skiers, and prevents their wasting much time and energy in ascending those slopes that they wish to descend.

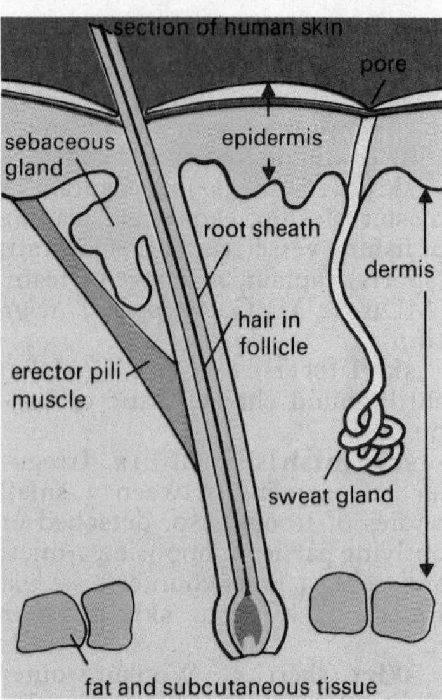

The **skin** of a human being consists of two layers and the outer one is constantly being replaced as dead scales are washed or worn away. The pores are remarkable non-return valves.

two layers, the *epidermis* or outer layer, and the *dermis* or inner layer, with (in mammals) its sebaceous glands, hair follicles, etc.; one of the separate layers of which skin is composed; hide of flayed animal, esp. of smaller animals, as sheep, goat, etc., with or without the hair or wool; vessel for wine or water made of animal's whole skin; **change one's ~**, undergo impossible change of character etc.; **get under one's ~**, take a strong hold on, irritate; **save one's ~**, avoid loss or injury; **thick (thin)** ~, imperviousness (sensitiveness) to affront, reproach, etc. 2. Outer coating, peel, rind, of fruit, vegetable, etc.; thin film or pellicle; outer covering of ribs or frame of ship, boat, or aircraft. 3. **~-deep**, superficial, not deep or lasting; **~-dive** (*v.i.* & *n.*), dive without diving suit (usu. in ref. to deep diving with respirator); so **~ diver**; **~ flick**, (slang) explicitly pornographic motion picture; **skin′flint**, miser; **skin game**, (slang) swindle; **skin graft**, skin cut from another part or person and surgically substituted for damaged part; **skin test**, test for allergy or disease made by observing skin reaction to application of test substance; **skin′tight**, (of garment) very closefitting. **skin** *v.* (**skinned, skin·ning**). 1. Cover (usu. *over*), as with skin; form, become covered (usu. *over*) with, new skin. 2. Strip skin from, flay; remove skin of. 3. (slang) Swindle, fleece.

skink (skĭngk) *n.* Any lizard of the family Scincidae, with smooth, overlapping scales.

skin·ny (skĭn′ē) *adj.* (**-ni·er, -ni·est**). (esp.) Lean, emaciated; **~-dip** (*v.*), (colloq.) Swim nude; so **~-dipper, -dipping** *ns.*

skip (skĭp) *v.* (**skipped, skip·ping**). Jump about lightly, frisk, gambol, caper, move lightly from one foot to the other; spring or leap lightly and easily, esp. over rope revolved over head and under feet; shift quickly from one subject or occupation to another; omit, make omissions, in reading, dealing with

Of the 19 families of lizard, none is better known than the **skink** group. In warmer regions, the smaller skinks are common in city gardens, although larger species survive in remote areas.

a series, etc.; cause (bomb) to ricochet from a surface toward a target; hence ~ **bombing**. **skip** *n.* Skipping movement, esp. quick shift from one foot to the other.

skip·per (skĭp′*er*) *n.* Captain or master of ship, esp. small trading or fishing vessel; captain of aircraft; (sports) captain, manager of team. [MDu. or MLG. *schipper*, f. *schip* ship]

skirl (skẽrl) *n.* & *v.i.* (Make) shrill sound characteristic of bagpipes.

skir·mish (skẽr′mĭsh) *n.* Irregular engagement between 2 small bodies of troops, esp. detached or outlying parties of opposing armies; any contest or encounter. ~ *v.i.* Engage in skirmish. **skir′mish·er** *n.*

skirt (skẽrt) *n.* Woman's outer garment hanging from waist, or this part of complete garment; underskirt, petticoat (archaic); flap of a saddle; border, rim, outskirts, boundary of anything; diaphragm or midriff of animal (esp. of beef) used for food. **skirt** *v.* Go along, around, or past the edge of; be situated along, go *along*, coast, wall, etc.

skit (skĭt) *n.* Light piece of satire, burlesque; short usu. humorous theatrical sketch.

skit·ter (skĭt′*er*) *v.i.* Skip or skim along surface, esp., of wildfowl, along water in rising or settling.

skit·tish (skĭt′ĭsh) *adj.* Frivolous, excessively lively; spirited; (of horse etc.) nervous, excitable, fidgety. **skit′tish·ly** *adv.* **skit′tish·ness** *n.*

skit·tle (skĭt′*el*) *n.* Pin used in ninepins or tenpins; (pl.) game of ninepins.

skiv·vy (skĭv′ē) *n.* (pl. **-vies**). (slang) 1. (also ~ **shirt**) Man's cotton undershirt; 2. (pl.) Man's undershirt and shorts.

*While resembling a gull, the **skua** is a type of semi-predator, attacking other sea-birds to make them disgorge their catch which the skua then obtains. This bird staunchly defends its territory and will attack man or animal approaching its nest.*

*The distinctive bone formation of the marine turtle's **skull** has led palaeontologists to believe that these reptiles separated from others at an early stage of evolution.*

sku·a (skū′*a*) *n.* Large rapacious predatory seabird (*Catharacta skua*), breeding in both Arctic and Antarctic.

skul·dug·ger·y, skull·dug·ger·y (skŭldŭg′*er*ē) *ns.* Rascally conduct, underhand plotting.

skulk (skŭlk) *v.i.* Lurk, conceal oneself, avoid observation, esp. with sinister motive or in cowardice.

skull (skŭl) *n.* Bony case of the brain, cranium; whole bony framework of head; ~ **and crossbones**, representation of human skull with two thighbones crossed below it, as emblem of death; **skull′cap**, close-fitting brimless cap for top of head; (anat.) cranial portion of skull.

skunk (skŭngk) *n.* (pl. **skunks**, collect. **skunk**). Small N. Amer. mammal of weasel family (genus *Mephitis* and related genera), with black coat striped with white, and bushy tail, able to emit, when attacked, powerful and offensive odor from two anal glands; fur of this; low contemptible person; ~ **bear**, (colloq.) wolverine; ~ **cabbage**, disagreeable-smelling perennial plant (*Symplocarpus foetidus*) of eastern N. Amer., thriving in swampy, wooded areas and having large leaves, small flowers enclosed in a purplish or greenish hooded spathe, and deep, tough root system; similar plant (*Lysichitum americanum*) growing in western N. Amer. **skunk** *v.t.* (slang) Defeat decisively in game. [Amer. Indian *segongw*]

sky (skī) *n.* (pl. **skies**). Apparent arch or vault of heaven; climate, clime; color of blue sky, sky blue; ~ **blue**, color of clear summer sky; **sky′cap**, porter at air terminal; **sky′diving**, sport of falling freely from aircraft and opening parachute only at last safe moment; **sky-high**, very high(ly); **sky′jack** (*v.t.*), (slang) hijack (aircraft); **Sky′lab**, U.S. space station launched in 1973, to house astronauts engaged in scientific work while they orbited Earth; it fell to Earth (1979); **sky lark**, common European lark, *Alauda arvensis*, which sings continuously while soaring; (*v.i.*) frolic, play tricks or practical jokes, indulge in horseplay; **sky′light**, window in roof; **sky′line**, silhouette of anything against sky; visible horizon; **sky marshal**, armed Federal guard who travels by commercial airlines

great skua

pomarine skua

*Although spectacular, the land available on **Skye** offers few opportunities for agriculture. Some people weave plaids at Portree while others work in a factory where diatomite is processed.*

to provide security against skyjacking; **sky'rocket**, rocket exploding high in air; (*v.i.*) ascend like skyrocket; **sky'scraper**, very high building; **sky'writing**, legible smoke trails made by aircraft, esp. for advertising purposes. **sky'ey** *adj.* **sky'ward** *adv.* & *adj.* **sky'wards** *adv.*

Skye (skī). Largest island of Inner Hebrides; ~ **terrier**, small, long-bodied, short-legged, long-haired variety of Scotch terrier, of slate or fawn color.

slab (slăb) *n.* Flat, broad, comparatively thick piece of solid material, as stone, timber, etc.; large flat piece of cake, chocolate, etc.; (logging) rough outside piece cut from log or tree trunk. ~ *v.t.* (**slabbed, slab·bing**). Cut slab(s) from (log, tree); cover, support, protect with slabs.

slack[1] (slăk) *adj.* Sluggish, remiss, relaxed, languid, loose, inactive, negligent; (of heat etc.) gentle, moderate. **slack'ly** *adv.* **slack'ness** *n.* **slack** *n.* Slack part of rope; slack time in business etc.; (pl.) trousers for informal or sports wear. ~ *v.* Slacken, make loose; take rest, be indolent, slow *up*; slake (lime); ~ **off**, abate vigor.

slack[2] (slăk) *n.* Very small or refuse coal, coal dust.

slack·en (slăk'*e*n) *v.* Make, become, loose or slack.

slack·er (slăk'*er*) *n.* Shirker, lazy person.

slag (slăg) *n.* Dross separated in fused vitreous state in smelting of ores; clinkers; volcanic scoria. **slag** *v.i.* (**slagged, slag·ging**). Form slag, cohere into slaglike mass.

slain: see SLAY.

slake (slāk) *v.t.* (**slaked, slak·ing**). Quench, allay (thirst), cause (lime) to heat and crumble by action of water or moisture.

sla·lom (slah'l*o*m) *n.* 1. Ski race downhill on zigzag course between artificial obstacles, usu. flags. 2. Canoe race in turbulent water through narrow passages (gates) marked by poles.

slam[1] (slăm) *v.* (**slammed, slam·ming**). Shut (door etc.) violently with loud bang; (of door etc.) shut thus; put *down* (object) with similar sound; (colloq.) criticize violently. ~ *n.* Sound (as) of slammed door; **~-bang** (*adj.* & *adv.*), (colloq.) with noise and violence; recklessly.

slam[2] (slăm) *n.* Winning of all tricks (**grand** ~) or of all tricks but one (**little** ~) in bridge etc.

slan·der (slăn'd*er*) *n.* False report maliciously uttered to person's injury; false oral defamation; defamation, calumny (cf. LIBEL). **slan'der·ous** *adj.* **slan'der·ous·ly** *adv.* **slan'der·er, slan'der·ous·ness** *ns.* **slander** *v.t.* Utter slander about, defame falsely.

slang (slăng) *n.* Language in common colloquial use but considered to be outside standard educated speech and consisting either of new words or phrases or of current words used in new sense; cant, special language of some class or profession. ~ *adj.* Of, expressed in, slang. ~ *v.t.* Use abusive language to.

slang·y (slăng'ē) *adj.* (**slang·i·er, slang·i·est**). Of the character of, given to the use of, slang. **slang'i·ly** *adv.* **slang'i·ness** *n.*

slant (slănt, slahnt) *n.* Slope, oblique position; point of view, way of regarding something; bias. ~ *adj.* Sloping, inclined, oblique. ~ *v.* Slope, diverge from a line, have or take oblique direction or position; present (news etc.) in biased way. **slant'ing·ly** *adv.* **slant'wise, slant'ways** *advs.* & *adjs.*

*All members of the weasel family have scent glands, but those of the **skunk** are most highly developed. The offensive fluid can be sprayed 10 ft. and will severely irritate a victim's skin.*

slap (slăp) *n.* Smart blow esp. with palm of hand or something flat; sharp rebuke; smack; ~ **in the face**, rebuff, insult. **slap** *v.t.* (**slapped, slap·ping**). Strike with such blow; **slap'dash**, hasty, careless, happy-go-lucky; (*adv.*) in slapdash manner; **slap'happy**, (colloq.) cheerfully casual; punch-drunk; **slap'stick**, (orig.) flexible lath used by harlequin in pantomime: (of) boisterous knockabout type of comedy. **slap** *adv.* Suddenly, noisily, headlong.

slash (slăsh) *v.* Cut, cut at, with sweep of sharp weapon or instrument; make gashes (in); slit (garment) to show contrasting lining etc.; lash with whip, crack (whip); make drastic economies in (budget etc.). ~ *n.* (Wound or slit made by) slashing cut. **slash'er** *n.*

slat (slăt) *n.* Long narrow strip of wood or metal, lath, esp. one of a series forming a Venetian blind, one of the crosspieces of a bedstead on which the mattress rests. ~ *v.* (**slat·ted, slat·ting**). Flap, strike, with noisy sound, esp. of sails, ropes, etc.

slate (slāt) *n.* 1. Very fine-

*A Lapp family with a **sleigh** drawn by a reindeer. The sleigh, drawn by dogs or horses, is still a commonplace form of winter transport in Canada, the U.S.S.R. and Scandinavia.*

grained gray metamorphic rock that cleaves perfectly in one direction, freq. at an angle to the bedding plane; thin usu. rectangular plate of this or other stone as roofing material; tablet of slate, usu. framed in wood, for writing on. 2. List of candidates supported by a political party. **slat'y** *adj.* (**slat·i·er, slat·i·est**). **slate** *v.t.* (**slat·ed, slat·ing**). 1. Cover, roof, with slates. 2. Designate for candidacy, appointment, etc. **slat'er** *n.*

slath·er (slădh′*er*) *v.t.* (colloq.) Spread thickly; squander.

slat·tern (slăt′*ern*) *n.* Sluttish woman. **slat'tern·ly** *adv.*

slaugh·ter (slaw′*ter*) *n.* Slaying, esp. of many persons or animals at once, carnage, massacre. **slaugh'terhouse**, place for killing cattle or sheep, shambles. **slaughter** *v.t.* Kill in ruthless manner or on great scale; butcher, kill for food. **slaugh'ter·er** *n.* **slaugh'ter·ous** *adj.*

Slav (slahv) *n.* Member of any of the peoples belonging to the Slavonic linguistic group, inhabiting large parts of E. and central Europe, and including Russians, Poles, Czechs, Bulgarians, Serbs, Croats, Slovenes, etc. ~ *adj.* Of the Slavs or their languages.

slave (slāv) *n.* Person who is the legal property of another, servant completely divested of freedom and personal rights; human chattel; helpless victim *to, of*, some influence; submissive or devoted servant; drudge; ~ **bracelet**, wide bracelet freq. worn above ankle; ~ **driver**, superintendent of slaves at work; hard taskmaster; ~ **ship**, ship employed in slave trade; ~ **states**, (hist.) those southern states of U.S. in which slaveholding was legal; ~ **trade**, traffic in slaves, esp. former transportation of African blacks to Amer. **slave** *v.i.* (**slaved, slav·ing**). Work like slave, drudge.

slav·er[1] (slā′*ver*) *n.* Ship or person engaged in slave trade.

slav·er[2] (slăv′*er*, slā′*ver*, slah′-) *n.* Saliva flowing or falling from mouth; nonsense. ~ *v.* Let saliva run from mouth; wet with saliva, slobber.

slav·er·y (slā′*verē*) *n.* Condition of a slave; slaveholding; drudgery.

Slav·ic (slah′vĭk) *adj.* Of, pertaining to, Slavs; ~ **languages**, group of Indo-European languages spoken in E. and central Europe, including Russian, Byelorussian, Ukrainian, Polish, Czech, Bulgarian, Serbo-Croatian, and Slovene.

slav·ish (slā′vĭsh) *adj.* Of, like a slave, servile; showing no originality or independence. **slav'ish·ness** *n.* **slav'ish·ly** *adv.*

*This railway **sleeper** yard in Alaska will soon be an unusual sight. Wooden sleepers are now being replaced by concrete ones which are more durable and not subject to termite attack.*

Sla·von·ic (sla*vŏn*′ĭk) *adj.* Slavic. ~ *n.* Slavonic languages; **Church ~, Old ~**, earliest written Slavonic language, a Bulgarian dialect fixed in writing toward end of 9th c., extinct as a vernacular but remaining the liturgical language of the Orthodox Church in Slav countries.

slaw (slaw) *n.* Coleslaw.

slay (slā) *v.t.* (**slew** pr. sloo͞, **slain** pr. slān, **slay·ing**). (chiefly poet. and rhet.) Kill.

slea·zy (slē′zē) *adj.* (**-zi·er, -zi·est**). 1. Flimsy, loosely woven. 2. Shoddy, shabby. 3. Squalid. **slea'zi·ly** *adv.* **slea'zi·ness** *n.*

sled (slĕd) *n.* Any of several types of vehicles with attached runners for travel on ice or snow. ~ *v.* (**sled·ded, sled·ding**). Travel, ride, carry, etc. on sled.

sledge[1] (slĕj) *n.* Sled. ~ *v.* (**sledged, sledg·ing**). Travel, go, convey, on sled.

sledge[2] (slĕj) *n.* (also **sledge'-hammer**) Large heavy hammer usu. wielded with both hands, esp. that used by blacksmith.

sleek (slēk) *adj.* (of hair, fur, surface, etc.) Soft, smooth and glossy; sleek-haired or -skinned; of well-fed comfortable appearance. **sleek'ly** *adv.* **sleek'ness** *n.* **sleek** *v.t.* Make sleek.

sleep (slēp) *n.* Bodily condition regularly and naturally assumed by man and other animals, in which the postural and other muscles are relaxed and consciousness is largely suppressed, though it may be re-established by a sensory disturbance; period or occasion of this; inert condition of some animals in hibernation; (fig.) death; rest, quiet, peace; **sleep'walking**, somnambulism. **sleep** *v.* (**slept** pr. slĕpt, **sleep·ing**). Be in state of sleep; fall, be asleep; rest in death; spend in, affect by, sleeping; stay for the night *at, in*, etc.; **sleep'away** (*adj.*), (slang) (of summer camp) with sleeping accommodations; **sleep-in** (*adj.*), (of domestic servant) living with employer's family; **sleep'ing** *n.* (esp.) ~ **bag**, bag, usu. lined or padded, for sleeping in, esp. out of doors; ~

car, railroad car with berths or beds; ~ **pill**, pill containing drug inducing sleep; ~ **sickness**, (1) freq. fatal disease characterized by extreme lethargy, prevalent in parts of W. and S. Africa and caused by a trypanosome (*Trypanosoma gambiense*) transmitted by the bite of the tsetse fly; (2) ENCEPHALITIS lethargica. **sleep'less** *adj.* **sleep'less·ness** *n.*

sleep·er (slē'p*er*) *n.* (esp.) Horizontal wooden member resting on ground, concrete floor, etc., to support flooring; (colloq.) sleeping car; (colloq.) someone or something suddenly and unexpectedly successful; (football) player stationed at distance from teammates in hope he will be unnoticed, play involving this.

sleep·y (slē'pē) *adj.* (**sleep·i·er, sleep·i·est**). Drowsy, ready for sleep; inactive, indolent, without stir or bustle. **sleep'yhead**, sleepy or inattentive person. **sleep'i·ly** *adv.* **sleep'i·ness** *n.*

sleet (slēt) *n.* Hail or snow falling in a half melted state; thin coating of ice formed on road, trees, etc., when rain freezes. **sleet'y** *adj.* (**sleet·i·er, sleet·i·est**).

sleeve (slēv) *n.* Part of garment covering arm; tube or hollow shaft fitting over rod, spindle, etc.; wind sock, drogue; envelope for phonograph record; ~ **valve**, internal combustion engine's valve with sleeve(s) fitting interior of cylinder, sliding with piston, and so designed and controlled that inlet and exhaust ports are uncovered at proper stages in cycle. **sleeved, sleeve'less** *adjs.*

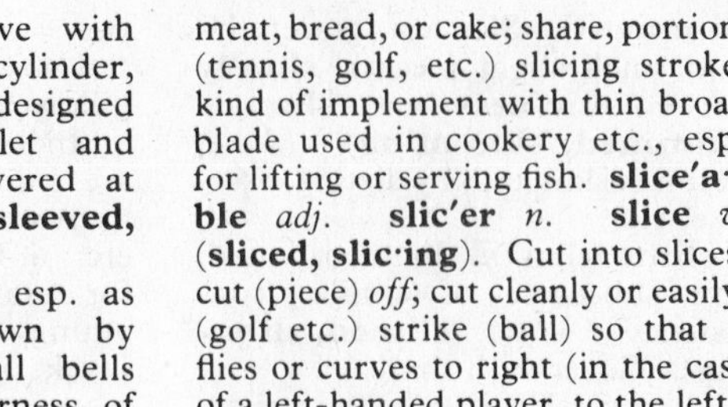

sleigh (slā) *n.* Sled, esp. as passenger vehicle drawn by horse(s); ~ **bells**, small bells attached to sleigh or harness of sleigh horse.

sleight (slīt) *n.* Dexterity, cunning, artifice (archaic exc. in) ~ **of hand**, conjuring, trick(s) displaying great dexterity, esp. performed so quickly as to deceive the eye.

slen·der (slĕn'd*er*) *adj.* Of small girth or breadth; scanty, slight, meager. **slen'der·ly** *adv.* **slen'der·ness** *n.*

sleuth (sloōth) *n.* (colloq.) Detective. **sleuth** *v.* Track, trail; play the detective.

slew[1]: see SLAY.

slew[2], **slue** (sloō) *ns.* (colloq.) Great number; lot.

slew[3]: SLOUGH[1].

slew[4]: SLUE[2].

slice (slīs) *n.* Relatively thin flat broad piece or wedge cut from esp. meat, bread, or cake; share, portion; (tennis, golf, etc.) slicing stroke; kind of implement with thin broad blade used in cookery etc., esp. for lifting or serving fish. **slice'a·ble** *adj.* **slic'er** *n.* **slice** *v.* (**sliced, slic·ing**). Cut into slices, cut (piece) *off*; cut cleanly or easily; (golf etc.) strike (ball) so that it flies or curves to right (in the case of a left-handed player, to the left).

***Sleeping sickness,** transmitted by the tsetse fly, is still prevalent in many parts of Africa, despite W.H.O. and other campaigns to eliminate the disease. In its advanced form, it is fatal.*

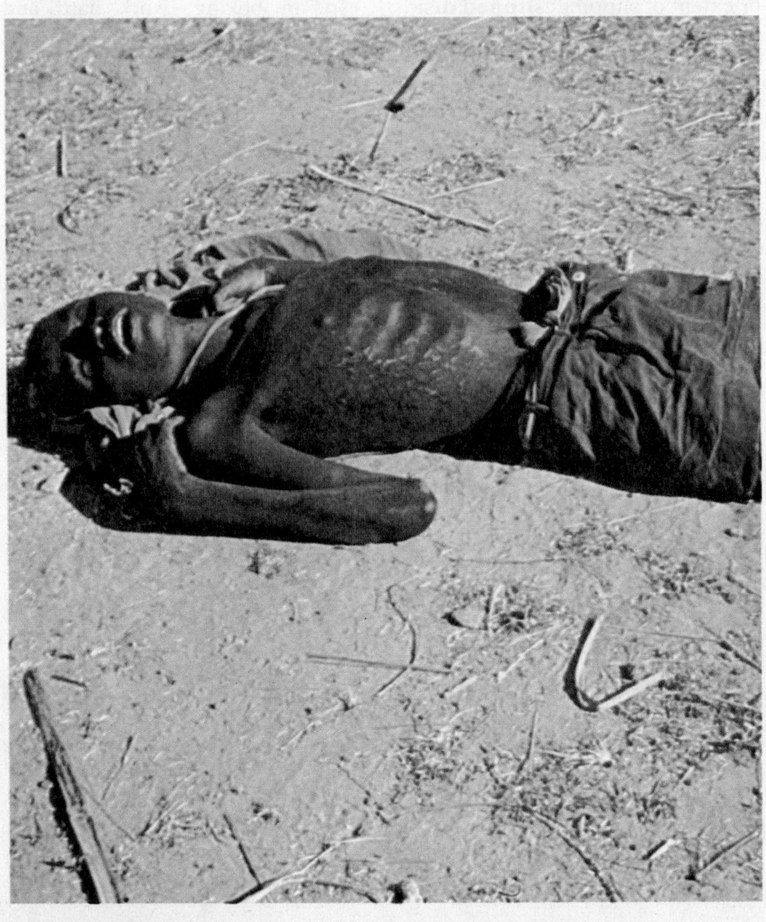

slick (slĭk) *adj.* Sleek; smooth, plausible; adroit, deft, quick, cunning. **slick'ly** *adv.* **slick'ness** *n.* **slick** *n.* (also **oil** ~) Patch or film of oil on water. **slick** *v.t.* Smooth, sleek.

slick·er (slĭk'*er*) *n.* Long loose raincoat, usu. oilskin; (colloq.) smooth, tricky person.

slide (slīd) *v.* (**slid** pr. slĭd, **slid·ing**). (Make) progress along smooth surface in continuous contact with that surface; glide over ice without skates in more or less erect posture; glide, go smoothly along, pass easily or gradually; (baseball) throw oneself down and forward, usu. feet first, toward base to avoid being tagged out; **let** ~, let (something) take its own course; ~ **rule**, rule graduated along one edge according to the logarithms of the numbers from 1 to 100 and along the other according to the logarithms of the numbers from 1 to 10 (enabling squares and square roots to be read off directly), and having a similarly graduated sliding piece along its center (enabling numbers to be multiplied or divided by adding or subtracting their logarithms); ~ **valve**, valve with sliding plate for opening and closing orifice, esp. in steam engine. **slide** *n.* Act of sliding; track on ice made by sliding; slope prepared with snow or ice for tobogganing; avalanche; inclined plane down which goods etc. slide to lower level; part(s) of machine on or between which sliding part works; part of machine or instrument that slides. **slid'a·ble** *adj.* **slid'er** *n.* (esp. baseball) Fast pitched ball with slight curve.

slid·ing (slī'dĭng) *adj.* That slides; ~ **door, lid, panel**, etc., door, lid, etc., drawn across aperture by sliding sideways instead of turning on hinges; ~ **scale**, scale (of payments, wages, etc.) rising or falling in established relation to rise or fall of some other standard.

slight (slīt) *adj.* Slender, slim, thin; not good or substantial, rather flimsy or weak; small in amount, degree, etc., unimportant, trifling. **slight'ly** *adv.* **slight'ness** *n.* **slight** *n.* Instance of slighting or being slighted; contemptuous indifference or disregard. ~ *v.t.* Treat with indifference or disrespect, disregard, disdain, ignore.

slim (slĭm) *adj.* (**slim·mer,**

slim·mest). Slender, (gracefully) thin; small, slight, meager. **slim'ly** *adv.* **slim'ness** *n.* **slim** *v.* (**slimmed, slim·ming**). Make, become, slim, esp. by dieting, exercise, etc.

slime (slīm) *n.* Fine oozy mud; any substance of similar consistency. ~ *v.t.* (**slimed, slim·ing**). Cover with slime.

slim·y (slī'mē) *adj.* (**slim·i·er, slim·i·est**). Of the consistency of slime; covered or smeared with slime; vile, disgusting; repulsively meek or flattering. **slim'i·ly** *adv.* **slim'i·ness** *n.*

sling[1] (slĭng) *n.* 1. (also **sling'shot**) Weapon, consisting of strap attached to 2 cords or to staff, for hurling stones etc. 2. Belt, rope, etc., formed into loop, with hooks and tackle, for securing bulky or heavy articles while being hoisted or lowered; strap, band, etc., supporting something suspended; bandage etc. formed into loop around neck to support injured arm. ~ *v.* (**slung** pr. slŭng, **sling·ing**). 1. Throw, cast, hurl; hurl (stone etc.) from sling, use sling. 2. Suspend with sling; hoist or transfer with sling; hang up, suspend, esp. between two points. **sling'er** *n.*

sling[2] (slĭng) *n.* Drink of gin and whiskey, sweetened and flavored with lemon.

slink (slĭngk) *v.i.* (**slunk** pr. slŭngk or archaic **slank** pr. slăngk, **slink·ing**). Move, go, in quiet, stealthy, or sneaking manner. **slink'y** *adj.* (**slink·i·er, slink·i·est**). (of woman's garment) Close-fitting and smooth, sinuous.

slip[1] (slĭp) *n.* Finely ground clay, flint, etc., mixed with water to consistency of cream and used for making, cementing, decorating, etc., pottery, tiles, etc.; **slip'ware**, pottery coated with slip.

slip[2] (slĭp) *n.* 1. Act of slipping; blunder, accidental piece of misconduct; slipstream; **give person the** ~, evade or escape from him. 2. Loose covering or garment, e.g. pillowcase, petticoat. 3. Dog leash. 4. Inclined plane on which ships are built or repaired. 5. Long narrow strip of thin wood, paper, etc. 6. Cutting taken from a plant for grafting or planting; scion, young, esp. slender, person. 7. Dock, pier; space between two piers. **slip** *v.* (**slipped, slip·ping**). 1. Slide unintentionally for short distance; lose footing, balance, etc., by unintended sliding; go with sliding motion, move easily or unperceived, glide, steal; escape restraint or capture esp. by being slippery or hard to hold; make careless mistake (also, colloq., ~ **up**). 2. Let go (hounds etc.) from restraint of some kind; pull (garment etc.) hastily *on, off*; make pass or move stealthily, casually, or with gliding motion; escape from, (naut.) allow (anchor cable) to run out when leaving anchorage hastily, drop (anchor) thus; (of animals) miscarry with, drop (young) prematurely; **slip'cover**, removable, fitted fabric covering for piece of furniture; **slip'knot**, knot that can be undone by a pull; knot that slips up and down rope etc. and tightens or loosens loop; **slip-on, slip'over**, (shoe, garment, etc.) that can be easily slipped on and off; **slip'page**, act or instance of slipping; amount or extent of slipping; **slipped disk**, rupture of an intervertebral disk of spinal column, causing lumbar pain; **slip'stick**, (slang) slide rule; **slip'stream**, current of air driven astern by propulsion unit of an aircraft producing the thrust that moves the aircraft forward.

Although some goods which need to be lifted are now built with eyes to which hooks may be attached, the use of a **sling** for material-handling is still widespread.

slip·per (slĭp'*er*) *n.* Light loose comfortable indoor shoe; light slip-on shoe for dancing etc.; **slip'per·wort**, any of numerous plants (genus *Calceolaria*) of tropical Amer., having bright slippershaped flowers.

slip·per·y (slĭp'*er*ē) *adj.* (**-per·i·er, -per·i·est**). With smooth, polished, oily, slimy, or greasy surface making foothold insecure, or making object etc. difficult to grasp or hold; (fig.) elusive, unreliable, shifty, unscrupulous; ~ **elm**, tree (*Ulmus rubra*) of eastern N. Amer., having aromatic, mucilaginous juice once used in medications. **slip'per·i·ness** *n.*

slip·shod (slĭp'shŏd) *adj.* With shoes down at heel; slovenly, careless, unsystematic.

slit (slĭt) *n.* Long incision; long narrow opening comparable to cut. ~ *v.* (**slit, slit·ting**). Cut or tear lengthwise, make slit in, cut into strips; ~ **trench**, narrow trench made to accommodate a soldier.

slith·er (slĭdh'*er*) *v.i.* Slide unsteadily, go with irregular slipping motion. **slith'er·y** *adj.*

sliv·er (slĭv'*er*) *n.* Small, thin strip cut or split off; thin strip of wood torn from tree or timber, splinter. ~ *v.* Break off as sliver, break up into slivers.

sliv·o·vitz (slĭv'*o*vĭts, -wĭts, shlĭv'*o*-) *n.* Alcoholic spirit distilled from plums esp. in Yugoslavia, plum brandy.

slob (slŏb) *n.* Stupid or careless person.

slob·ber (slŏb'*er*) *v.* & *n.* SLAVER[2], drivel. **slob'ber·y** *adj.*

sloe (slō) *n.* (Small bluish-black wild plum, fruit of) blackthorn; ~**-eyed**, having large eyes of this color; slant-eyed; **sloe gin**, gin flavored with sloes and sweetened.

slog (slŏg) *v.* (**slogged, slog·ging**). Hit hard and freq. wildly, esp. in boxing; work hard and doggedly, plod. **slog'ger** *n.*

slo·gan (slō'g*a*n) *n.* Party cry, watchword, motto; advertiser's phrase calculated to catch the eye. [Gael. *sluagh* host, *gairm* outcry]

sloop (slo͞op) *n.* Small one-masted fore-and-aft-rigged vessel having mainsail and jib.

slop (slŏp) *n.* 1. Soft mud or partly melted snow; slush. 2. Liquid carelessly splashed or

The **sloe** or blackthorn is a wild plum native to western Europe. The fruit was used to make sloe gin and the timber, which is dark brown, was often made into walking sticks.

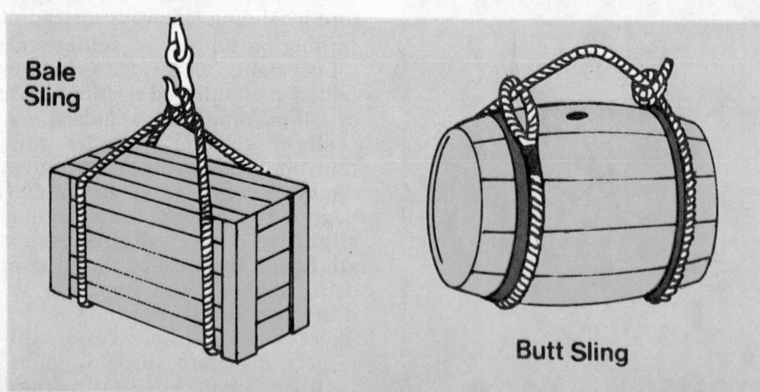

Wholly adapted to an arboreal life, although able to swim, the ***sloth*** *spends its life in the trees which provide the leaves that are its food. It is found only in Central and South America.*

spilled. 3. Unappetizing food, esp. when liquid or semiliquid. 4. (usu. pl.) Kitchen waste used for feeding pigs and other animals; swill. ~ *v.* (**slopped, slop·ping**). Spill, (allow to) flow over edge of vessel; spill or splash liquid upon.

slope (slōp) *n.* Stretch of rising or falling ground; inclined surface or way; upward or downward inclination, deviation from horizontal or perpendicular. ~ *v.* (**sloped, slop·ing**). Take, form, move in, be in, place or arrange in, a slope or inclined direction or position.

slop·py (slŏp'ē) *adj.* (**-pi·er, -pi·est**). Wet, splashed, full of puddles; messy with liquid; watery and disagreeable; weak, slovenly, maudlin. **slop'pi·ly** *adv.* **slop'pi·ness** *n.*

slosh (slŏsh) *v.* Splash about, move with splashing sound; (colloq.) pour (liquid) clumsily, pour liquid on. **sloshed** *adj.*

slot (slŏt) *n.* 1. Groove, channel, slit, long aperture, made in machine, fabric, etc., to admit some other part, esp. slit for coin; ~ **car**, miniature racing car electrically operated by remote control in competition with similar cars on slotted track; ~ **machine**, vending or gambling machine operated by putting coin in slot. 2. (fig.) Place in series etc.; position. **slot** *v.t.* (**slot·ted, slot·ting**). Provide with slot(s).

sloth (slawth, slōth) *n.* 1. Laziness, indolence. 2. Long-haired slow-moving arboreal mammal of tropical Central and S. Amer., with two toes with hooklike claws on each forefoot (genus *Choloepus*) or three toes (*Bradypus tridactylus*); ~ **bear**, common shaggy black-haired bear (*Melursus ursinus*) of India and Sri Lanka, feeding on fruit, insects, and honey. **sloth'ful** *adj.* **sloth'ful·ly** *adv.* **sloth'ful·ness** *n.*

slouch (slowch) *v.* Droop, hang down negligently; go, stand, etc., with loose ungainly stoop of head and shoulders; pull or bend down brim of hat, esp. over face. ~ *n.* Slouching gait or posture, stoop; downward bend of hat brim; ~ **hat**, soft hat with wide flexible brim. **slouch'y** *adj.* (**slouch·i·er, slouch·i·est**). **slouch'ing·ly** *adv.*

slough[1] (slow, slo͞o), **slew** (slo͞o) *ns.* Quagmire, swamp, miry place; **S~ of Despond** in Bunyan's *Pilgrim's Progress*, deep miry place between City of Destruction and wicket gate at beginning of Christian's journey; state of hopeless depression. **slough'y** *adj.*

slough[2] (slŭf) *n.* Outer skin periodically cast by snake etc.; any part cast or molted by an animal; dead tissue from surface of wound, ulcer, etc. ~ *v.* Drop off as slough; cast slough.

Slo·vak (slō'vahk, -văk) *adj.* & *n.* (Member) of a Slavic people inhabiting chiefly Slovakia and S. Moravia; (of) their language. **Slo·va·ki·a** (slōvah'kēa, -văk'ēa). Territory forming the E. part of Czechoslovakia, formerly a part of

Sailing for pleasure is a relatively recent pastime, beginning in the U.S.A. in the late 18th, early 19th centuries. The ***sloop*** *style of yacht was one of the earliest types built to race.*

*Very similar to a snail but lacking an external shell, a **slug** is usually nocturnal. Its sensitivity to light and heat prevent movement beyond a certain distance from its underground shelter.*

Hungary.

slov·en (slŭv′*e*n) *n.* Person who is careless, untidy, or dirty in personal appearance or slipshod and negligent in work etc. **slov′en·ly** *adj.* (**-li·er, -li·est**). **slov′en·li·ness** *n.*

Slo·vene (slōvēn′, slō′vēn) *adj.* & *n.* (Member, language) of the Slavonic people inhabiting chiefly Slovenia and neighboring parts of Yugoslavia. **Slo·ve·ni·a** (slōvē′nēa, -vēn′y*a*). Constituent republic of Yugoslavia, bordering on Austria and Italy; capital, Ljubljana. **Slo·ve′ni·an** *adj.* & *n.* Slovene.

slow (slō) *adj.* 1. Not quick, taking a long time to do a thing or traverse a distance; gradual; tardy, lingering; not hasty; (of clock etc.) behind true time; (of surfaces) tending to cause slowness (*a slow track*, etc.). 2. Dull-witted, stupid; deficient in liveliness or interest, dull, tedious. 3. **~-motion,** action or speed of a film in which movements appear much slower than in nature, achieved either by exposing the film at high speed or by projecting it at reduced speed; **~ neutron,** one with low kinetic energy, esp. after moderation; **~ poison,** poison of which repeated doses are injurious; **slow′poke,** person slow in action, dull of wit, or behind the times in opinions etc.; **slow-witted,** slow to understand; stupid; dull. **slow′ly** *adv.* **slow′ness** *n.* **slow** *adv.* **~** *v.* Reduce one's speed, reduce speed of; **slow′down** (*n.*), action of slowing down.

SLR *abbrev.* Single-lens reflex (camera).

sludge (slŭj) *n.* Thick greasy mud; sewage; muddy or slushy sediment or deposit; accumulation of dirty oil, esp. in sump of internal combustion engine; sea ice newly formed in small pieces. **sludg′y** *adj.* (**sludg·i·er, sludg·i·est**).

slue[1] (sloo͞): see SLEW[2].

slue[2] (sloo͞) *v.* (**slued, slu·ing**), also **slew** (sloo͞). Turn or swing around on axis; twist sideways. **~** *n.* Act of sluing.

slug[1] (slŭg) *n.* 1. Gastropod mollusk with rudimentary or no shell, many kinds of which are destructive to small plants. 2. Roughly or irregularly shaped bullet or other piece of metal; (round) bullet; disk of metal used (usu. illegally) instead of coin in slot; (colloq.) drink of straight whiskey; (printing) thick piece of metal used in spacing; line of type in linotype printing. 3. (eng., as measure in calculating acceleration) That mass to which a force of 1 lb. will impart an acceleration of 1 ft. per second per second.

Sluice gates in the power station dam on the Niagara River in Canada. They are needed to reduce water level (and pressure) behind the dam wall in times of heavy rains and floods.

slug[2] (slŭg) *n.* & *v.* (**slugged, slug·ging**). (colloq.) (Strike with) hard heavy blow, esp. with fist or baseball bat; **slug′fest,** boxing match marked by slugging and little attention to defense; baseball game marked by many extra-base hits and runs; **slug′ger** (*n.*), (esp. baseball) strong hitter; player who hits many doubles, triples, and home runs.

slug·a·bed (slŭg′*a*bĕd) *n.* (archaic) One who lies late in bed.

slug·gard (slŭg′*e*rd) *n.* Lazy sluggish person.

slug·gish (slŭg′ĭsh) *adj.* Inert, inactive, slow moving, torpid. **slug′gish·ly** *adv.* **slug′gish·ness** *n.*

sluice (sloo͞s) *n.* (Gate in) dam or embankment with sliding gate or other contrivance for controlling volume or flow of water; any device for regulating flow of water; artificial water channel, esp. in gold-washing. **~** *v.* (**sluiced, sluic·ing**). Provide with sluice(s); flood with water from sluice; rinse, pour or throw water freely upon; (of water etc.) rush (as) from sluice.

slum (slŭm) *n.* Dirty squalid overcrowded street, district, etc. inhabited esp. by the very poor; **slum′lord,** landlord of slum housing, esp. one who charges excessive rent and fails to maintain property. **slum′my** *adj.* (**-mi·er, -mi·est**). **slum** *v.i.* (**slummed, slum·ming**). Visit slums.

slum·ber (slŭm′b*e*r) *n.* & *v.i.* Sleep (chiefly poet. and rhet.). **slum′ber·ous, slum′brous** *adjs.* **slum′ber·ous·ly** *adv.* **slum′ber·er** *n.*

slump (slŭmp) *n.* Sudden decrease (esp. of commercial ventures, prices, etc.; opp. BOOM[3]); sudden or heavy fall in demand. **~** *v.i.* Undergo slump, fall in price; sit or slop down heavily and slackly.

slung: see SLING[1].

slunk: see SLINK.

slur (slėr) *v.* (**slurred, slur·ring**). 1. Smudge, blur; pro-

In overcrowded countries where there is widespread poverty, it is surprising how some people survive. This Indian child looks down on the ***slum*** *shanties which include his home.*

nounce indistinctly, with sounds running into one another; (mus.) sing, play, two or more notes smoothly and connectedly; mark with slur. 2. Pass lightly *over*, conceal, minimize. ~ *n.* 1. Slight, discredit, blame. 2. Slurred sound or utterance; (mus.) curved line (⌒, ‿) over or under two or more notes to be sung or played without a break or as smoothly as possible.

slurp (slẽrp) *n.* & *v.t.* Eat(ing) or drink(ing) noisily.

slur·ry (slẽr'ē) *n.* (pl. **-ries**). Thin sloppy cement, mud, etc; suspension of fine material in liquid, esp. water.

slush (slŭsh) *n.* Watery mud or water-saturated snow; soft greasy mixture of oil etc. or other materials, used to lubricate or protect machinery etc.; (fig.) silly sentiment; ~ **fund**, money used for corrupt purposes, esp. bribery of public officials. **slush'y** *adj.* (**slush·i·er, slush·i·est**). **slush'i·ness** *n.*

slut (slŭt) *n.* Slovenly woman; immoral woman. **slut'tish** *adj.* **slut'tish·ly** *adv.* **slut'tish·ness** *n.*

sly (slī) *adj.* (**sli·er, sli·est** or **sly·er, sly·est**). 1. Cunning, wily, deceitful; practicing concealment, working, moving, etc., in stealthy or underhand manner. 2. Knowing, arch, bantering, insinuating. **sly'ly** *adv.* **sly'ness** *n.*

Sm *symbol.* Samarium.

S.M. *abbrev.* Master of Science [L. *Scientiae Magister*]; sergeant major.

smack[1] (smăk) *n.* Flavor, taste; trace, tinge, suggestion, *of* something. ~ *v.i.* Have taste or savor *of*, suggest the presence *of*.

smack[2] (smăk) *n.* Sharp slight sound as of surface struck with palm of hand, lips parted suddenly, etc.; slap, sounding blow; loud kiss. ~ *v.* Strike with palm of hand or with something flat; part (lips) noisily, (of lips) be parted, in eager anticipation or enjoyment of food etc. ~ *adv.* (colloq.) (As) with a smack, slap; outright, exactly.

smack[3] (smăk) *n.* Single-masted sailing vessel, rigged like sloop or cutter, for coasting or fishing; fishing vessel with well for keeping fish alive.

smack[4] (smăk) *n.* (slang) Heroin.

smack·er (smăk*er*) *n.* (slang) Dollar.

At Looe in Cornwall, U.K. (left), the fishermen moor their boats in the local river. The single-masted ***smack*** *is considered highly suitable for working the inshore waters.*

small (smawl) *adj.* Not large, of comparatively little size, strength, power, or number; consisting of minute units; (of agent) not acting on large scale; poor, mean, humble; ungenerous, not much of; unimportant, trifling; petty, paltry; ~ **arms**, portable firearms, esp. rifle, pistol, light machine gun; ~ **change**, coins as opposed to bills, (fig.) trivial remarks; ~ **fry**, little children; insignificant or unimportant things or persons; **small-scale**, made or occurring on a small scale or in small amounts; **small talk**, ordinary social conversation, chat; **small-time**, (colloq.) of little matter or importance; minor; insignificant; **small-town**, (typical) of small town or village; unsophisticated; countrified. **small** *n.* Small, slender, or narrow part of anything, esp. the back. ~ *adv.* Into small pieces, on small scale, etc. **small'ish** *adj.* **small'ness** *n.*

small·pox (smawl'pŏks) *n.* (hist.) Acute contagious febrile disease (*variola*), often endemic in occurrence, characterized by pustular eruption, usu. leaving scars or pits on skin; worldwide campaign of vaccination apparently resulted by 1978 in total eradication of the disease.

smart[1] (smart̄) *n.* Sharp pain, stinging sensation. ~ *v.i.* Feel, cause, smart. **smart'ing·ly** *adv.*

smart[2] (smart̄) *adj.* 1. Severe, sharp; lively, vigorous, brisk. 2. Clever, quick, ingenious; quick at looking after one's own interests; ~ **al·eck** (ăl'ĭk), would-be clever person (~ **al·eck·y** (ăl'ĭkē) *adj.*); ~ **bomb**, (slang) air-to-surface bomb that reaches target by television or laser beam guidance. 3. Alert, brisk; neat, trim; stylish, fashionable, elegant. **smart'en** *v.* **smart'ly** *adv.* **smart'ness** *n.*

smash (smăsh) *n.* Breaking to pieces; violent fall, collision, or disaster; commercial failure, bankruptcy; violent and heavy blow; very successful thing; (tennis) hard overhand stroke; **smash'up**, complete smash; violent collision of motor vehicles; total ruin or failure. **smash** *v.* Break utterly to pieces, shatter, bash *in*; utterly rout and disorganize; break, come to grief, go bankrupt; (of vehicle etc.) crash; (tennis) hit (ball) in smash. **smash** *adv.* With a smash. **smash'er** *n.*

smat·ter·ing (smăt'erĭng) *n.* Slight superficial knowledge (*of*); small amount.

smaze (smāz) *n.* Mixture of smoke and haze.

smear (smēr) *v.* Daub with greasy or sticky substances or with something that stains, make greasy or sticky marks on; blot, obscure outlines of; blacken character of, discredit publicly; (slang) overpower or defeat. **smear'y** *adj.* (**smear·i·er, smear·i·est**). **smear** *n.* Mark, blotch, made by smearing; vilification. **smear'er** *n.*

smell (smĕl) *n.* 1. Faculty of smelling, by which odors are perceived by means of the nose; act of smelling, sniff. 2. Property of things affecting sense of smell, odor; bad odor, stench. **smell'y** *adj.* (**smell·i·er, smell·i·est**). (colloq.) Smelling strongly, evil smelling. **smell** *v.* (**smelled** or **smelt** pr. smĕlt, **smell·ing**). 1. Perceive smell of, detect presence of by smell; use sense of smell, sniff *at*; hunt *out* by smell; (fig.) discover, find *out*, as if by smell; perceive smells, have sense of smell. 2. Emit smell; suggest or recall the smell *of*; stink, be rank. 3. **smelling salts**, preparation of ammonium carbonate and scent, to be sniffed as cure for faintness etc. **smell'i·ness** *n.*

A section of the olfactory region of the nasal passage. The nerves are responsible for the sense of ***smell*** *although the exact mechanism is not fully known.*

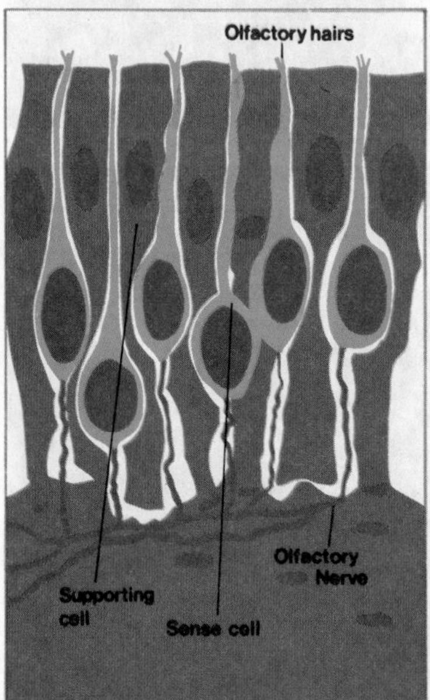

smelt[1] (smĕlt) *n.* (pl. **smelts**, collect. **smelt**). Small edible fish esp. of genus *Osmerus*, allied to salmon, with greenish back, silvery sides and belly, and delicate tender rather oily flesh.

smelt[2] (smĕlt) *v.t.* Fuse or melt (ore) to extract metal; obtain (metal) thus. **smelt'er** *n.*

smile (smīl) *v.* (**smiled, smil·ing**). Express pleasure, amusement, affection, indulgent scorn, incredulity, etc., with slight more or less involuntary movement of features, upward curving of corners of mouth, parting of lips, etc; look *at* with such expression; express by smiling; drive *away*, bring *into* or *out of* (mood), by smiling; be, appear, propitious; look pleasant, have bright aspect; **come up smiling**, (colloq.) recover from adversity and cheerfully face what is to come; **smile on**, show favor to, approve of. **smile** *n.* Act of smiling; smiling expression or aspect. **smil'er** *n.* **smi'ling** *adj.* **smil'ing·ly** *adv.*

smirch (smērch) *v.t.* & *n.* Stain, soil, smear, spot (also fig.).

smirk (smērk) *v.i.* & *n.* (Put on) affected or silly smile; simper.

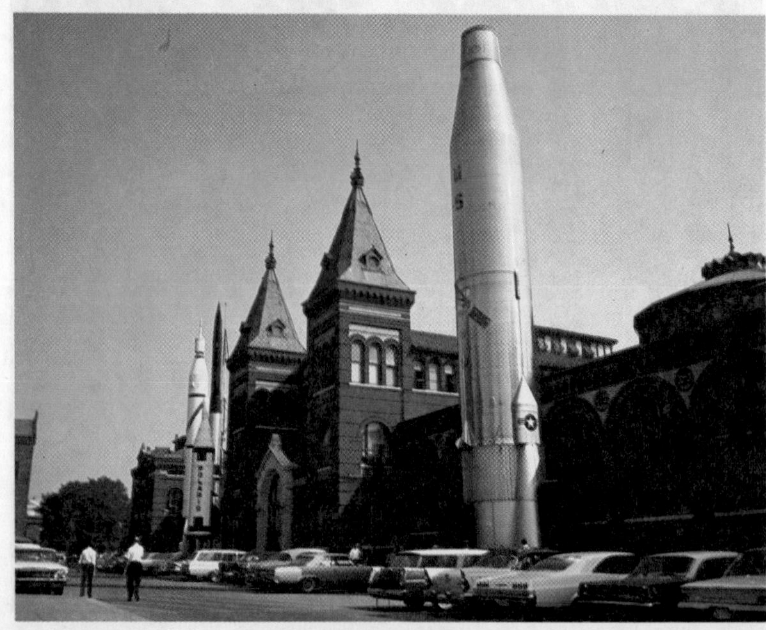

The outdoor display of missiles and rockets contrasts with the mid-Victorian architecture of the ***Smithsonian Institution*** *in Washington, D.C., the world's largest museum-gallery.*

smirk'er *n.* **smirk'ing·ly** *adv.*

smite (smīt) *v.* (**smote** pr. smōt, **smit·ten** pr. smĭt'*e*n, **smit·ing**). Strike (*upon*), hit, chastise, defeat (chiefly poet, and rhet.); (chiefly in past part. **smitten**) strike, seize, infect, possess, *with* disease, love, etc. **smit'er** *n.*

smith (smĭth) *n.* Worker in metal, esp. iron; blacksmith.

-smith (smĭth) *comb. form.* Worker in (gold, silver, etc.), *goldsmith, silversmith,* etc.

Smith[1] (smĭth), **Adam** (1723–1790). Scottish political economist, author of *The Wealth of Nations* (1776).

Smith[2] (smĭth), **John** (1580–1631). English explorer and colonist; president of Jamestown, Virginia, colony, 1608–09; captured by Indians and saved by Pocahontas, daughter of Chief Powhatan.

Smith[3] (smĭth), **Joseph** (1805–1844). Founder of the MORMON sect.

smith·er·eens (smĭdh*e*rēnz') *n.pl.* (colloq.) Small fragments.

Smith·so·ni·an (smĭthsō'nē*a*n) **Institution.** Establishment for increase and diffusion of knowledge, founded 1846 in Washington under will of an English mineralogist and chemist, James Smithson (1765–1829, earlier known as James Lewis Macie); it comprises national museums of natural history, zoology and ethnology, history and technology, air and space, fine arts, and also includes an astrophysical observatory, the John F. Kennedy Center for the Performing Arts, the Radiation Biology Laboratory, the Woodrow Wilson International Center for Scholars, and the Tropical Research Institute.

smith·y (smĭth'ē, smĭdh'ē) *n.* (pl. **smith·ies**). 1. Blacksmith's workshop, forge. 2. Blacksmith.

smock (smŏk) *n.* 1. Chemise (archaic). 2. Loose-fitting outer garment of shirtlike shape, freq. with gathered or smocked yoke. ~ *v.t.* Adorn with smocking. **smock'ing** *n.* Form of needlework with honeycomb ornamentation on basis of very close thick gathers.

smog (smŏg) *n.* Smoky fog. **smog'gy** *adv.* (**-gi·er, -gi·est**).

smoke (smōk) *n.* 1. Visible volatile product given off by burning or smoldering substances; cloud or column of this, esp. used as signal etc.; **go up in** ~, come to nothing. 2. Cigar or cigarette; act of smoking tobacco etc. 3. ~ **bomb**, bomb emitting dense clouds of smoke on bursting, for forming smoke screen; **smoke'house**, building where meat and fish are cured and flavored by smoking; **smoke screen**, dense volume of smoke diffused by funnel of vessel, smoke bomb, etc., to conceal naval or military operations etc.; also fig.; **smoke'stack**, chimney, chimney pipe. **smoke'less** *adj.* Producing little or no smoke; free from smoke. **smoke** *v.* (**smoked, smok·ing**). 1. Emit smoke or visible vapor, reek, steam; (of chimney, lamp, etc.) emit smoke, be smoky, as result of imperfect draft etc. 2. Color, darken, obscure, with smoke; preserve or cure by exposure to smoke; fumigate, suffocate, stupefy, drive *out*, insects, etc., with smoke; ~ **out,** (fig.) reveal, expose. 3. Inhale and exhale smoke of (tobacco, opium, etc.); **smoking car, compartment**, car etc. for smokers on railroad train; **smoking room,** room set apart for smoking in.

*This **smog** in Montreal, Canada is one example of the pollution we are exposed to in the modern world. A large proportion of city pollution is caused by exhaust and gasoline fumes.*

smok·er (smō'k*e*r) *n.* (esp.) Person who habitually smokes tobacco; smoking car on train; men's informal gathering.

smok·y (smō'kē) *adj.* (**smok·i·er, smok·i·est**). Emitting, veiled or filled with, obscure (as) with, smoke; stained with, colored like, smoke; ~ (**bear**), (slang, citizens' band radios) officer of the law. **smok'i·ly** *adv.* **smok'i·ness** *n.*

smol·der, Brit. **smoul·der** (smōl'd*e*r) *vbs.i.* Burn and smoke without flame (freq. fig.).

smolt (smōlt) *n.* Young salmon at stage when it migrates to sea for first time.

smooch (smo͞och) *v.* (slang) Engage in kissing and caressing.

smooth (smo͞odh) *adj.* With surface free from projections, wrinkles, lumps, or undulations; not rough, uneven, or bristly; (of ground etc.) not broken or obstructed, easily traversed; not harsh in sound, taste, etc.; pleasant, polite, unruffled; bland, insinuating, flattering; **smooth'bore,** gun with unrifled barrel; **smooth-spoken, -tongued**, smooth, plausible, flattering, in speech; soft-spoken. **smooth'ly** *adv.* **smooth'ness** *n.* **smooth** *v.* Make or become smooth; free from impediments etc.; ~ **over, away,** reduce or get rid of (differences, perplexities, difficulties, faults, etc.) in fact or appearance. **smooth** *n.* Smoothing touch or stroke. **smooth'er** *n.*

smor·gas·bord, smör·gas·bord (shmōr'g*a*sbōrd, -bōrd; *Swed.* smör'gawsboord) *ns.* Buffet meal with a variety of hors d'oeuvres and other dishes. [Swed. *smörgåsbord*]

smote: see SMITE.

smoth·er (smŭdh'*e*r) *v.* Suffocate, stifle, be suffocated or stifled, esp. with smoke; deaden or extinguish (fire) by excluding air with ashes etc.; suppress, conceal, cover (*up*); cover closely or thickly (*in*). ~ *n.* Dense or suffocating smoke, dust, fog, etc. **smoth'er·y** *adj.*

smoul·der (smōl'd*e*r): SMOLDER.

smudge[1] (smŭj) *n.* Dirty mark, smear, blur, blot. ~ *v.* (**smudged, smudg·ing**). Soil, stain, smirch, smear. **smudg'y** *adj.*

smudge[2] (smŭj) *n.* Outdoor fire with dense smoke to drive away insects, protect plants etc. against frost.

smug (smŭg) *adj.* (**smug·ger, smug·gest**). Self-satisfied, consciously virtuous. **smug'ly** *adv.* **smug'ness** *n.*

smug·gle (smŭg'*e*l) *v.* (**-gled, -gling**). Convey (goods), convey goods, clandestinely into or out of country to avoid payment of customs duties etc.; convey stealthily or secretly *in, out,* put *away* into concealment. **smug'gler** *n.*

smut (smŭt) *n.* 1. Fungous disease of cereals and other plants, with (parts of) grain covered with blackish powdery spores; any fungus causing this. 2. (Black mark, smudge, made by) flake of soot. 3. Indecent or obscene talk or publication. **smut'ty** *adj.* (**-ti·er, -ti·est**). **smut'ti·ly** *adv.* **smut'ti·ness** *n.* **smut** *v.t.* (**smut·ted, smut·ting**).

Smuts (smŭts; *Du.* smöts), **Jan Christiaan** (1870–1950). South African general and statesman; founder (1910) and prime minister (1918–24, 1939–48) of the Union of South Africa.

Smyr·na (smĕr'na). Former name of Izmir.

Sn *symbol.* Tin.

snack (snăk) *n.* Slight, casual, or hurried meal; ~ **bar**, counter where sandwiches and other snacks may be obtained.

sna·fu (snăfōō', snăf'ōō) *adj.* & *n.* (slang) (In state of) utter confusion. ~ *v.* (**-fued, -fu·ing**). (slang) Throw into confusion; jumble. [*S*(ituation) *n*(ormal), *a*(ll) *f*(ouled) *u*(p)]

snag (snăg) *n.* Jagged projecting point, as stump or branch left on tree after pruning or cutting, trunk or large branch of tree embedded in bottom of river etc., with end pointed upward; (fig.) impediment, obstacle, unexpected drawback. **snag** *v.t.* (**snagged, snag·ging**). Run upon or damage by a snag. **snag'gy** *adj.* (**-gi·er, -gi·est**).

snail (snāl) *n.* Any aquatic or terrestrial gastropod mollusk with well-developed spiral or whorled shell capable of covering whole body; slow-moving or indolent person.

snake (snāk) *n.* 1. Limbless reptile of suborder Ophidia, serpent; (also, pop.) snakelike limbless lizard or amphibian; treacherous or ungrateful person; long flexible metal band for opening blocked drains; ~ **in the grass**, lurking danger, secret enemy. 2. **S**~, Amer. Ind. of various Shoshone groups of western U.S. 3. **snake'bird**: see ANHINGA; **snake charmer**, person giving exhibition of control of venomous snake with music etc.; **snake dance**, religious ceremony and dance of Hopi Indians, in which rattlesnakes are imitated and handled; informal procession in which participants join hands as they zigzag back and forth in long line; **snake eyes**, (slang) dice throw of 2 ones; **snake fence**, zigzag fence of split rails or poles; **snake'head** = TURTLEHEAD; **snake-hipped** (*adj.*), having slim, supple hips; **snake'mouth**, orchid (*Pogonia ophioglossoides*) of eastern N. Amer., having single rose-lavender flower with tufted lip; **snake oil**, any liquid misrepresented as curative agent; **snake pit**, overcrowded mental hospital where patients are neglected; **snake plant**, any of various easily cultivated tropical plants (genus *Sansevieria*), having long, stiff, pointed leaves and popular as house plants; **snake'root**, (root of) any of various Amer. plants, esp. *Aristolochia serpentaria* and *Polygala senega*, reputed to be antidotes to snake poison, and used in medicine. **snak'y** *adj.* (**snak·i·er, snak·i·est**). Infested with snakes; snakelike; (chiefly of hair of Gorgons, Furies) composed of snakes. **snake** *v.i.* (**snaked, snak·ing**). Make twisting course.

Present on land and in water, ***snails,*** *seem omnipresent and are disliked by gardeners. However, larger varieties in France and Africa have been farmed for food since the Roman era or earlier.*

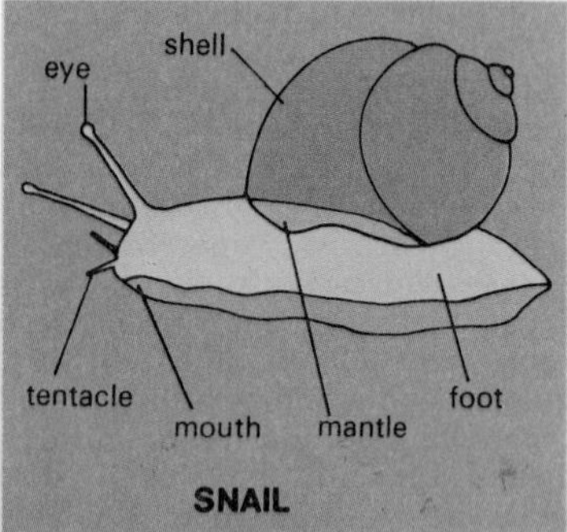

snap (snăp) *n.* 1. (Bite, cut, with) sudden quick closing of jaws or scissors; sudden break or fracture; sound of snapping, quick sharp sound. 2. Small crisp ginger cookie. 3. Spring catch or one closing with snapping sound. 4. (colloq.) Something easy. 5. Sudden, usu. brief, spell of frost or cold. 6. Alertness, vigor, energy; dash. 7. Snapshot. 8. ~ **bean** = STRING bean; **snap'-dragon**, any of various perennial plants (genus *Antirrhinum*), esp. a popular horticultural species (*A. majus*) having clusters of white, yellow, pink, crimson, etc., double-lipped closed flowers; **snap fastener**, device for fastening pieces of fabric or clothing by pressing two parts together; **snap lock**, lock shutting automatically with spring when door etc. is closed; **snap'shot** (*n.*), taken photograph, esp. with hand camera; **snap'shot** (*v.*) (**-shot·ted, -shot·ting**), take such photograph (of). **snap** *v.* (**snapped, snap·ping**). 1. Make quick or sudden bite; speak irritably; say ill-tempered or spiteful things. 2. Pick *up* (esp. bargain) hastily. 3. Break sharply; produce sudden sharp sound from, emit sharp report or crack; close with snapping sound; ~ **fingers**, make audible fillip (*at*), esp. in contempt. 4. Take snapshot of. 5. **snapping turtle**, any of various large ferocious Amer. freshwater tortoises seizing prey with snap of jaws. **snap** *adj.* (colloq.) Easy (~ *course*); made on spur of moment (*snap judgment*). **snap'per** *n.* (pl. **-pers**, collect. for *food fish* **-per**). (esp.) Snapping turtle; any of various carnivorous food fishes (family Lutianidae) of warm seas.

snap·pish (snăp'ĭsh) *adj.* Peevish, testy, malicious, ill-natured. **snap'pish·ly** *adv.* **snap'pish·ness** *n.*

snap·py (snăp'ē) *adj.* (**-pi·er, -pi·est**). 1. Snappish. 2. Quick, vigorous, lively, full of life or spring; **make it** ~, (colloq.) be quick about it.

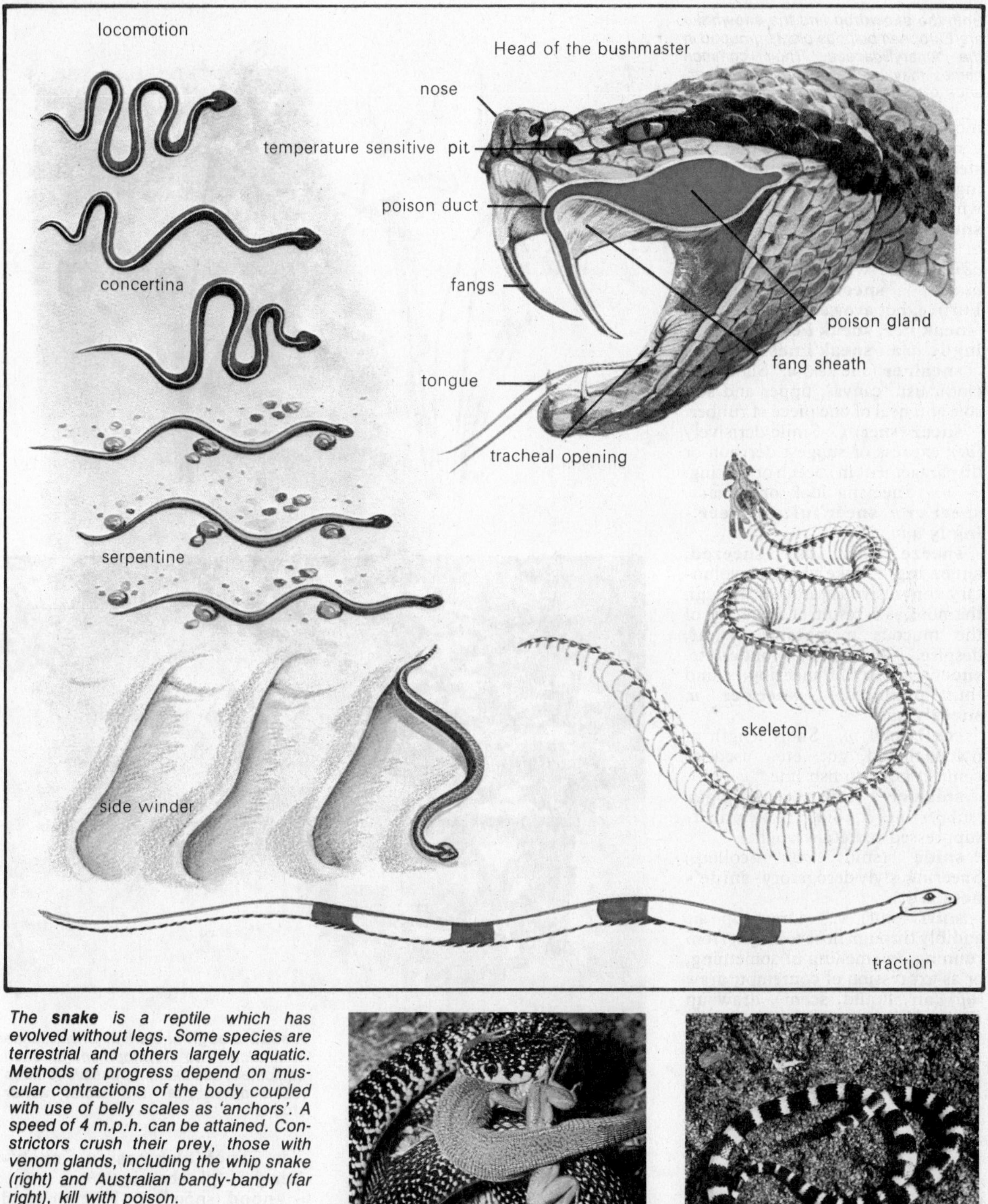

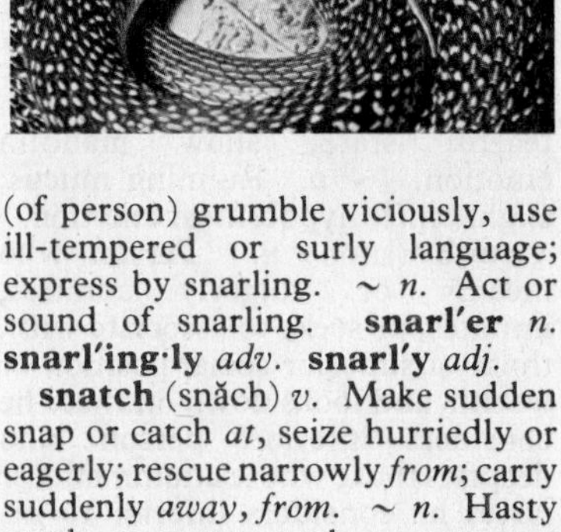

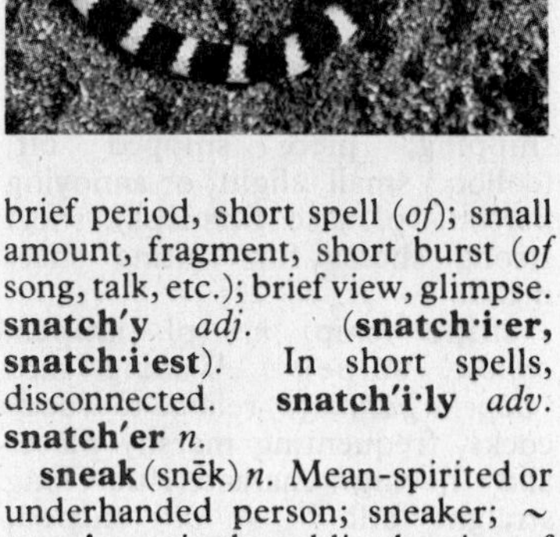

locomotion

concertina

serpentine

side winder

traction

Head of the bushmaster

nose

temperature sensitive pit

poison duct

fangs

poison gland

fang sheath

tongue

tracheal opening

skeleton

*The **snake** is a reptile which has evolved without legs. Some species are terrestrial and others largely aquatic. Methods of progress depend on muscular contractions of the body coupled with use of belly scales as 'anchors'. A speed of 4 m.p.h. can be attained. Constrictors crush their prey, those with venom glands, including the whip snake (right) and Australian bandy-bandy (far right), kill with poison.*

snare (snār) *n.* Device for catching birds or animals, esp. with running noose of cord, wire, etc. (freq. fig. of temptation etc.); gut or rawhide string stretched across lower head of drum; ~ **drum**, drum so fitted. **snare** *v.t.* (**snared, snar·ing**). Catch with snare.

snarl[1] (snārl) *n.* Tangle, esp. of wool, hair, or the like; tangled condition. ~ *v.* Tangle (*up*), mix together confusedly. **snarl'y** *adj.*

snarl[2] (snārl) *v.* (of dog etc.) Make angry sound with bared teeth; (of person) grumble viciously, use ill-tempered or surly language; express by snarling. ~ *n.* Act or sound of snarling. **snarl'er** *n.* **snarl'ing·ly** *adv.* **snarl'y** *adj.*

snatch (snăch) *v.* Make sudden snap or catch *at*, seize hurriedly or eagerly; rescue narrowly *from*; carry suddenly *away*, *from*. ~ *n.* Hasty catch or grasp, grab or snap *at*; brief period, short spell (*of*); small amount, fragment, short burst (*of* song, talk, etc.); brief view, glimpse. **snatch'y** *adj.* (**snatch·i·er, snatch·i·est**). In short spells, disconnected. **snatch'i·ly** *adv.* **snatch'er** *n.*

sneak (snēk) *n.* Mean-spirited or underhanded person; sneaker; ~ **preview**, single public showing of

*Both the **snowdrop** and the **snowflake** are European bulbous plants grouped in the Amaryllidaceae. Their common names may be based on the appearance of clumps seen at a distance.*

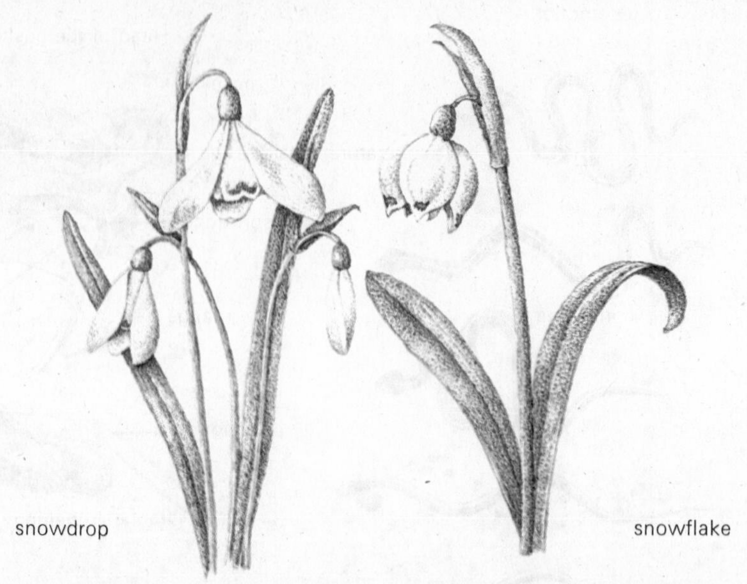

motion picture in advance of general release; ~ **thief**, one who steals without breaking into buildings, by entering open door or window. **sneak** *v.* (**sneaked, sneak·ing**). 1. Slink, go furtively. 2. (colloq.) Make off with, steal. ~ *adj.* Done without warning (~ *attack*). **sneak'ing** *adj.* (esp.) Furtive, not avowed. **sneak'y** *adj.* (**sneak·i·er, sneak·i·est**). **sneak'ing·ly** *adv.* **sneak'i·ness** *n.*

sneak·er (snē'k*er*) *n.* Shoe with cloth, usu. canvas, upper and soft sole and heel of one piece of rubber.

sneer (snēr) *v.* Smile derisively (*at*); express or suggest derision or disparagement in speech or writing. ~ *n.* Sneering look or remark. **sneer'er** *n.* **sneer'ful** *adj.* **sneer'ing·ly** *adv.*

sneeze (snēz) *v.i.* (**sneezed, sneez·ing**). Make sudden involuntary convulsive expiration through the nose as a result of irritation of the mucous membrane; ~ **at**, despise, disregard, underrate. **sneeze** *n.* Act of sneezing; sound thus produced. **sneez'er** *n.* **sneez'y** *adj.*

snell (snĕl) *n.* Short length of nylon thread, gut, etc., used to connect hook to fish line.

snick·er (snĭk'*er*), **snig·ger** (snĭg'*er*) *ns.* & *vbs.i.* (Utter) half-suppressed secretive laugh.

snide (snīd) *adj.* (colloq.) Sneering, slyly derogatory. **snide'ness** *n.*

sniff (snĭf) *v.* Draw up air audibly through nose to stop it from running, in smelling *at* something, or as expression of contempt; draw (*up*) (air, liquid, scent), draw up scent of, into nose. ~ *n.* Act or sound of sniffing; amount sniffed up. **sniff'er** *n.* **sniff'ing·ly** *adv.* [imit.]

snif·fle (snĭf'el) *v.* (**-fled, -fling**). Sniff slightly or repeatedly. ~ *n.* Act of sniffling; (pl., usu. **the ~s**) cold in the head.

snif·ter (snĭf'*ter*) *n.* 1. Brandy glass. 2. (colloq.) Shot of liquor.

snig·ger: SNICKER.

snip (snĭp) *v.* (**snipped, snip·ping**). Cut with scissors etc., esp. in small quick strokes. ~ *n.* Act of snipping; piece snipped off; (colloq.) small, slight, or annoying person; (pl. also **tinsnips**), short strong shears for cutting sheet metal.

snipe (snīp) *n.* (pl. **snipes**, collect. **snipe**). Wading bird (*Capella gallinago*) related to woodcocks, frequenting marshy places and having characteristic long straight bill. ~ *v.* (**sniped, snip·ing**). Shoot snipe; (mil.) shoot at (men) one at a time, usu. from cover and at long range; shoot, shoot *at*, thus; (colloq.) criticize. **snip'er** *n.*

*A **snow-plough** at work in Chamrousse in France. The development of such equipment has made it possible to keep roads open after the worst winter storms.*

snip·pet (snĭp'ĭt) *n.* Small piece cut off, snipping; (fig.) scrap, fragment, (pl.) odds and ends. **snip'pet·y** *adj.*

snitch (snĭch) *v.* (slang) 1. Act as informer. 2. Steal, purloin.

sniv·el (snĭv'el) *v.i.* (**-eled, -el·ing**). Run at the nose; make sniffling or snuffling sound; be in tearful state, show maudlin emotion. ~ *n.* Running mucus; slight sniff; hypocritical emotion.

snob (snŏb) *n.* Person who meanly or vulgarly admires, imitates, or seeks to associate with, those of superior social position or wealth, and looks down on those he considers inferior; person who despises those whose attainments or tastes he considers inferior to his own. **snob'bish** *adj.* **snob'bish·ly** *adv.* **snob'bish·ness** *n.* **snob'ber·y** *n.* (pl. **-ber·ies**).

snood (snōōd) *n.* Fillet or band for woman's hair; net etc. loosely confining hair at back.

snook·er (snŏŏk'*er*) *n.* (also ~ **pool**) Variety of pool played with 15 red balls and six balls of other colors.

snoop (snōōp) *v.i.* (slang) Pry inquisitively. **snoop'er** *n.* **snoop'y** *adj.* (**snoop·i·er, snoop·i·est**).

snoot·y (snōō'tē) *adj.* (**snoot·i·er, snoot·i·est**). (slang) Contemptuous, supercilious. **snoot'i·ly** *adv.* **snoot'i·ness** *n.*

snooze (snōōz) *v.i.* (**snoozed, snooz·ing**) & *n.* (Take) short sleep, esp. in daytime.

snore (snōr, snōr) *n.* & *v.* (**snored, snor·ing**). (Make) harsh or noisy respiration through mouth, or mouth and nose, during sleep.

snor·kel (snōr′kel), **schnor·kel** (shnōr′kel) *ns.* Device for supplying air to submerged submarine; breathing tube for underwater swimmer.

snort (snōrt) *n.* 1. Loud or harsh sound made by driving breath violently through nose, or noise resembling this. 2. Expression of contempt, defiance, etc., made by snorting. 3. (slang) Small drink of liquor. **snort** *v.* Make sound of snort; express by snorting, utter with snorts; (colloq.) sniff (cocaine). **snort′er** *n.*

snot (snŏt) *n.* (vulg.) Mucus of the nose; contemptible person. **snot′ty** *adj.* (**-ti·er, -ti·est**). (vulg.) Running or foul with snot; (colloq.) impudent.

snout (snowt) *n.* Projecting part of head of animal, including nose and mouth, (contempt.) person's nose; projecting part, structure, nozzle, etc., resembling snout.

snow (snō) *n.* 1. Atmospheric vapor condensed and frozen into small, usu. hexagonal, crystals, and falling in soft white clusters of these known as flakes; fall of these, layer of them on ground; (usu. pl.) fall or accumulation of snow. 2. Something resembling snow, esp. in whiteness; white hair. 3. (slang) Cocaine. 4. **snow′ball**, snow pressed into ball, esp. as missile; anything growing or increasing rapidly, like snowball rolled along ground; **snow′ball** (*v.*), pelt with, throw, snowballs; increase rapidly; **snow′berry** (pl. **-ries**) (fruit of) any of various plants or shrubs with white berries, esp. *Symphoricarpos albus*; **snow′bird**, any of various small white or partly white birds, esp. junco or snow bunting; **snow-blind**, with vision affected by glare of sun on snow; **snow blower, thrower**, motor-driven, hand-operated machine on wheels, used to remove snow from sidewalks and driveways; **snow′bound**, cut off, isolated, by snow; **snow bunting**, small finch (*Plectrophenax nivalis*) breeding in Arctic regions, migrating to Europe and N. Amer. in winter, with brown and white or black and white plumage; **snow′drift**, snow piled up in heap by action of wind; **snow′drop**, (flower of) small early-flowering bulbous plant (*Galanthus nivalis*) with white pendent flower; **snow′fall**, (esp.) amount of snow that falls on one occasion or on given area within given time; **snow fence**, temporary fencing of upright laths wired together, used to minimize drifting of snow onto sidewalks, highways, etc.; **snow′flake**, one of flakes or small crystalline masses in which

The ***snorkel,*** *a simple breathing apparatus, was first used by German submarines in the 1939–45 war so that air could be taken in and exhaust fumes emitted without surfacing. Today it is used widely, particularly by sportsmen.*

snow falls; any (white flower of) plant of bulbous genus *Leucojum*, esp. spring-flowering *L. vernum*, resembling snow drop; **snow goose**, white goose (*Chen hyperborea*) of N. Amer., breeding in Arctic regions; **snow job**, (slang) attempt to deceive by overwhelming with many details; **snow leopard**: see OUNCE²; **snow line**, boundary of a region above which snow never completely disappears; **snow′man** (pl. **-men**), mass of snow formed into figure of man; **snow′mobile**, motor vehicle used to travel over snow, esp. one with skis and caterpillar track; **snow′plow**, truck, locomotive, or device equipped with plow for clearing snow from road, railroad track, sidewalk, etc; **snow′shoe**, one of pair of racket-shaped frames of light wood strung with rawhide, enabling wearer to walk on surface of snow; **snowshoe rabbit**, hare (*Lepus americanus*) having large heavily furred feet and coat white in winter and brown in summer (hence called *varying hare*); **snow′storm**, storm with heavy fall of snow; **snow′suit**, heavy clothing for children, in cold-weather, consisting of separate jacket and pants or zippered coverall, usu. with hood, and tightly fitted at ankles, wrists, and neck; **snow tire**, tire having deep tread, and sometimes metal studs, to provide extra for wheel on snow or ice; **snow-white**, white as snow, pure white. **snow′y** *adj.* (**snow·i·er, snow·i·est**). **snow** *v.* 1. **it snows, it is snowing**, snow falls. 2. Let fall as or like snow; strew, cover, (as) with snow; bewilder, overwhelm, with impressive talk, flattery, etc.; **snow in**, block, enclose, with fallen snow; **snow under**, bury in snow, (fig.) submerge, overwhelm.

snub¹ (snŭb) *v.t.* (**snubbed, snub·bing**). 1. Rebuff, reprove, humiliate, in sharp or cutting manner. 2. Check (rope running out) suddenly (by winding it around post). ~ *n.* Snubbing, rebuff. **snub′ber** *n.*

snub² (snŭb) *adj.* (of nose) Short and turned up, hence **snub-nosed.**

snuff¹ (snŭf) *n.* Charred part of candle wick, esp. as black excrescence obscuring light. ~ *v.* Trim snuff from (candle, wick) with fingers, scissors, etc.; ~ **out**, extinguish thus; crush, suppress; destroy. **snuf′fers** *n.pl.* Scissors for snuffing candle, with box to catch snuff.

snuff² (snŭf) *n.* Powdered tobacco for sniffing up into nostrils; **snuff′box**, small box for holding this; **up to snuff**, (colloq.) reaching acceptable standard. **snuff′y** *adj.* (**snuff·i·er, snuff·i·est**). **snuff** *v.* Sniff (*up, in, at*).

snuf·fle (snŭf′el) *v.* (**-fled, -fling**). Sniff, esp. audibly or noisily; speak or say nasally, whiningly, or like one with a cold. ~ *n.* Sniff; snuffling sound or speech; **the ~s** (colloq.), = the SNIFFLES.

snug (snŭg) *adj.* (**snug·ger, snug·gest**). Sheltered, comfortable, cozy; (of ship etc.) trim, neat, well protected from bad weather. **snug′ly** *adv.* **snug′ness** *n.*

snug·gle (snŭg′el) *v.* (**-gled, -gling**). Move, lie, close *up to* for warmth; hug, cuddle.

so (sō) *adv.* To extent, in manner, with result, described or indicated; of the kind, in the condition, etc., already indicated, by that name or designation; on condition set forth or implied; indeed, as well; **just** ~, (pred.) in precise style etc.; **or** ~, or thereabouts; **so′-and-so** (*n., adj.,* & *adv.*) (pl. **so-and-sos**), used as substitute for name or expression not exactly remembered or not needing to be specified, or (colloq., euphem.) for term of abuse etc.; **so-called** (*adj.*) (epithet calling attention to, or questioning accuracy of description); indifferently, only passably. **so** *conj.* (colloq.) In order that; with the result that; therefore.

So. *abbrev.* South(ern).

s.o. *abbrev.* Strikeout.

soak (sōk) *n.* Soaking; hard drinker. ~ *v.* Place, lie, for some time in liquid, steep; make, be, saturated or wet through; (colloq.) overcharge; take *up*, suck *in*, liquid; (of liquid) make way *in(to), through*, by saturation; drink heavily; ~ **up**, absorb mentally, assimilate readily. **soak′er** *n.*

soap (sōp) *n.* Cleansing agent, essentially sodium salts of fatty acids usu. forming lather when rubbed in water; **soft ~**, kind remaining semifluid, potassium salts of fatty acids; (fig.) flattery; **soap′box**, box or rough platform for open-air orators; (attrib.) of or like open-air oratory; **soap opera**, (colloq.) sentimental radio or television serial; **soap′stone**, steatite; **soap′suds**, water impregnated with dissolved soap; **soap′wort**, herbaceous plant of genus *Saponaria*, yielding detergent substances, esp. *S. officinalis*, or bouncing Bet, with clusters of pink or white flowers. **soap** *v.t.* Rub, smear, lather, treat, with soap; (slang) flatter.

soap·y (sō′pē) *adj.* (**soap·i·er, soap·i·est**). Like, smeared or impregnated with, suggestive of, soap; ingratiating, unctuous, flattering. **soap′i·ly** *adv.* **soap′i·ness** *n.*

soar (sōr, sŏr) *v.i.* Fly at, mount to, great height; hover or sail in air without flapping of wings or use of motor power. **soar′er** *n.*

sob (sŏb) *v.* (**sobbed, sob·bing**). Draw breath in convulsive gasps, usu. with weeping; utter with sobs; bring *oneself into* state, *to sleep*, with sobbing. **~** *n.* Convulsive catching of breath, esp. in weeping; **~ sister**, writer of sentimental stories; **~ story**, narrative designed mainly to evoke sympathy. **sob′ber** *n.* **sob′bing·ly** *adv.*

so·ber (sō′ber) *adj.* Not drunk; temperate in regard to drink; moderate, well-balanced, sedate, temperate; (of color) quiet, inconspicuous. **so′ber·ly** *adv.* **sober** *v.* Make, become, sober. **so′ber·ness** *n.*

so·bri·e·ty (sobrī′etē, sō-) *n.* Being sober.

so·bri·quet (sō′brikā, -kĕt, sōbrikā′, -kĕt′) *n.* Nickname.

Soc., soc. *abbrevs.* Socialist; society.

soc·cer (sŏk′er) *n.* Type of football in which two teams of 11 players kick round ball up and down rectangular field with goal at either end [abbrev. of Association football].

so·cia·ble (sō′shabel) *adj.* Fitted or inclined for company of others, not averse to society, ready to converse; of, characterized by, friendly or pleasant companionship. **so′cia·bly** *adv.* **so·cia·bil·i·ty** (sōshabĭl′ĭtē) *n.* (pl. **-ties**). **sociable** *n.* Informal social gathering, esp. of church members.

so·cial (sō′shal) *adj.* 1. Of, marked by, friendly intercourse; enjoyed, taken, in company with others; inclined to friendly intercourse, sociable. 2. Living in companies or more or less organized communities, gregarious. 3.

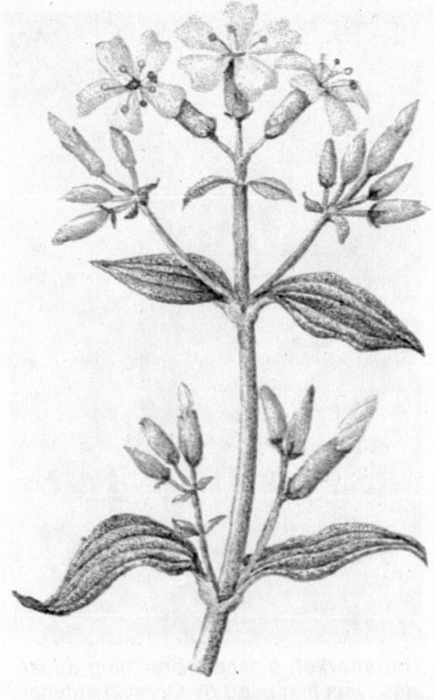

*A perennial herb, **soapwort** received its name because its leaves, when rubbed in water, produce a lather. Saponin is also obtained from the roots and has been used as a soap substitute.*

Of, concerned with, interested in, society and its constitution, or the mutual relations of men or classes of men; **~ contract**, contract assumed by Rousseau (*Contrat Social*, 1762) and other writers by which true freedom was obtained by mutual agreement to substitute a state of law for a state of individualism; **S~ Democrat**, member of socialistic political party esp. (i) that founded in Germany, 1863, by Ferdinand Lassalle, and united with Marxists 1875; (ii) Russian Marxist socialist party; (iii) moderate state socialist party in Germany after 1919; **~ disease**, venereal disease; **~ science**, study of human society regarded as a science (freq. taken to include not only sociology but economics, political science, social anthropology, and social psychology); **~ security**, (governmental provision of) financial and welfare benefits; **~ services**, welfare services provided by government; **~ work**, welfare work, work aimed at relieving poverty, improving social conditions, etc.; so **~ worker**. **so′cial·ly** *adv.* **social** *n.* Social gathering, esp. one organized by club, association, etc.

so·cial·ism (sō′shalĭzem) *n.* Political and economic principle that community as a whole should have ownership and control of all means of production and distribution (opp. CAPITALISM and INDIVIDUALISM); policy aiming at this; state of society in which this principle is accepted. **so′cial·ist** *n.* **so·cial·is·tic** (sōshalĭs′tĭk) *adj.* **so·cial·is′ti·cal·ly** *adv.*

so·cial·ite (sō′shalīt) *n.* Person prominent in fashionable society.

so·cial·ize (sō′shalīz) *v.t.* (**-ized, -iz·ing**). Make social or socialistic; **socialized medicine**, provision of medical services for all from public funds. **so·cial·i·za·tion** (sōshalīzā′shon), **so·cial·iz′er** *ns.*

so·ci·e·ty (sosī′etē) *n.* (pl. **-ties**). 1. State of living in association with other individuals; customs and organization of ordered community; any social community. 2. Leisured, well-to-do, or fashionable persons regarded as distinct part of community. 3. Association with others, companionship, company. 4. Association of persons with common interest, aim, principle, etc.; **S~ of Friends**: see QUAKER; **S~ of Jesus**: see JESUIT; **so·ci′e·tal** *adj.*

So·ci·e·ty (sosī′etē) **Islands.** Group of islands in French Polynesia, including Tahiti.

socio- *comb. form.* Of society or sociology (and), as: **sociocultural**, combining social and cultural factors.

so·ci·ol·o·gy (sōsēŏl′ojē, sōshē-) *n.* Study of human, esp. civilized, society; study of social problems, esp. with a view to solving them. **so·ci·o·log·i·cal** (sōsēolŏj′ĭkal, sōshē-), **so·ci·o·log′ic** *adjs.* **so·ci·o·log′i·cal·ly** *adv.* **so·ci·ol′o·gist** *n.*

sock[1] (sŏk) *n.* (pl. **socks**, also for sense 1 **sox**). 1. Short stocking not reaching knee. 2. Light shoe worn by comic actors on ancient Greek and Roman stage; comedy.

sock[2] (sŏk) *n.* (slang) Hard or violent blow. **~** *v.t.* Hit, strike hard; **~** (person) **one**, give him hard blow.

sock·et (sŏk′ĭt) *n.* Hollow, usu. cylindrical, part or piece for thing to fit into, revolve in, etc.; hollow or cavity in which eye, tooth, bone, etc., is contained; (elect.) device into which electric light bulb or plug fits to make an electrical connection.

sock·eye (sŏk′ī) *n.* Amer. fish, the blueback salmon (*Oncorhynchus nerka*). [Amer. Ind. *sukai*]

Soc·ra·tes (sŏk′ratēz) (469–399 B.C.). Greek philosopher, who was tried at Athens on a charge of corrupting the young by his teaching, and sentenced to death (by drinking hemlock); he left no writings, but his method and doctrines are preserved in the Dialogues of PLATO. **So·crat·ic** (sokrăt′ĭk) *adj.* & *n.* Of, like, Socrates; **~ irony**: see IRONY[1]; **~ method**, method of inquiry and instruction by series of questions. **So·crat′i·cal·ly** *adv.*

sod (sŏd) *n.* Turf, (piece of) upper layer of grassland, with grass growing on it. **~** *v.t.* (**sod·ded,**

sod·ding). Cover (ground) with sods.

so·da (sō′d*a*) *n.* 1. (also **washing ~**) Sodium carbonate (Na_2CO_3) an alkaline substance occurring naturally in mineral state or in solution, used in manufacture of glass, soap, etc., and obtained orig. from ashes of marine plants; **baking ~**, sodium bicarbonate. 2. Soda water (see below). 3. **~ biscuit, cracker**, biscuit, cracker, leavened with sodium bicarbonate; **~ fountain**, apparatus for drawing soda water kept under pressure; counter, shop, apparatus, for making and serving iced drinks, ice cream, sundaes, etc.; **~ jerk**(**er**), (slang) attendant at soda fountain; **~ pop**, (colloq.) carbonated, flavored soft drink; **~ water**, effervescent water charged under pressure with carbon dioxide and used alone or mixed with spirits, syrups, etc., as beverage; club soda.

so·dal·i·ty (sōdăl′ĭtē) *n.* (pl. **-ties**). Confraternity, association, esp. R.C. religious guild or brotherhood.

sod·den (sŏd′*e*n) *adj.* Saturated with liquid, soaked; heavy, doughy; stupid or dull with habitual drunkenness. **sod′den·ly** *adv.* **sod′den·ness** *n.* [orig. past part. of SEETHE]

so·di·um (sō′dē*u*m) *n.* (chem.) Soft silver-white lustrous metallic element, oxidizing rapidly in air and reacting violently with water, closely resembling potassium in appearance and properties; symbol Na, at. no. 11, at. wt. 22.9898; **~ bicarbonate**, substance ($NaHCO_3$), used in baking (baking soda) and medicinally as an antacid; **~ carbonate**, common washing soda (Na_2CO_3); **~ chloride**, common salt (NaCl); **~ hydroxide**, caustic soda; **~ nitrate**, odorless, crystalline salt ($NaNO_3$), used in explosives and fertilizers; **~ thiosulfate**, white, crystalline salt ($Na_2S_2O_3$), used as bleach and fixative in photography. [named by Sir H. Davy, 1807, f. *soda*]

*The **sociable** design of an open carriage was very popular for family outings in fine weather. However, an enclosed phaeton or cabriolet was also needed for protection from rain or cold.*

*Left: A Tahitian carries pandanus leaves for use in thatching and mat-weaving. The **Society Islands** are mountainous and volcanic, and export coffee, copra and vanilla.*

Sod·om (sŏd′*o*m). Ancient city near the Dead Sea, destroyed, along with Gomorrah, because of its wickedness, by fire from heaven (Gen. 18–19).

sod·om·y (sŏd′*o*mē) *n.* Unnatural sexual intercourse by a man, esp. with another male or with an animal. **sod·om·ite** (sŏd′*o*mīt) *n.* Person practicing sodomy. [f. SODOM]

so·ev·er (sōĕv′*er*) *adv.* At all, of any kind, in any way (used with generalizing or emphatic force after words or phrases preceded by *how, what, who,* etc.).

-soever *suffix.* Soever.

so·fa (sō′f*a*) *n.* Long seat with raised back and end(s). [Arab. *suffa*]

sof·fit (sŏf′ĭt) *n.* (archit.) Undersurface of architrave, lintel, arch, etc.

So·fi·a (sō′fē*a*, sōfē′*a*). Capital city of Bulgaria.

soft (sawft, sŏft) *adj.* 1. Not hard; yielding to pressure, malleable, plastic, easily cut. 2. Of smooth surface or fine texture, not rough or coarse. 3. (of water) Not containing calcium or other mineral salts that prevent formation of lather with soap. 4. Not astringent, sour, or bitter; not crude or brilliant; not sharply defined; not strident or loud; (phonet.) voiced; (of the letters *c, g*) pronounced as spirants, not stops. 5. Gentle, quiet, conciliatory; sympathetic, compassionate; maudlin, feeble, flabby, weak; silly; (of drink) nonalcoholic. 6. **soft′ball**, game similar to baseball but played on smaller diamond with larger and softer ball, which is pitched underhand; **soft-boiled**, (of egg) boiled so that yolk remains runny; **soft coal**, bituminous coal; **soft**(**-core**), (of pornography) subtle rather than overt; **soft currency**, currency not

*This experimental house in Arizona has **solar** energy panels installed which enables energy for heating to be generated by the sun. As the world's resources are dwindling, scientists have had to search for alternative methods of producing power. Harnessing the energy of the sun is one of the most feasible possibilities. A solar power station has been built in the Soviet Union.*

*Deadly nightshade (above) is one of 1,700 plants in the genus **Solanum.** Others include the potato (originally from the Andes) and the eggplant of tropical Asia.*

convertible to gold or supported by gold reserves, or not easily exchangeable for other currencies, and therefore likely to depreciate; **soft focus**, (photog.) slight, deliberate blurring of image; **soft goods**, textiles; **soft landing**, landing in which spacecraft etc. reaches ground without being destroyed or damaged; **soft line**, policy of reconciliation and co-operation, esp. in politics, international affairs, etc.; **soft on**, (colloq.) in love with; **soft palate**, rear part of palate; **soft pedal**, (in mus. instr.) foot pedal for making tone softer; **soft-pedal** (*v.*), play with soft pedal down; (fig.) tone down, refrain from emphasizing; **soft sell**, quietly persuasive salesmanship; **soft-shell**(**ed**), having a soft or flexible shell; having shell not yet hardened owing to recency of molt; **soft-shoe** (*adj.*), of or pertaining to style of tap dancing with no metal taps on shoes; **soft shoulder**, gravel, sand, dirt, etc., strip off paved surface of highway; **soft soap**: see SOAP; **soft spot**, sentimental affection for; **soft'ware**, (in computer) programs, program material, i.e., tapes, punched cards, etc.; (audio-visual aids) recorded material, such as films, film strips, records, tapes, etc., as opp. to *hardware*, the permanent equipment, such as projectors, record players, etc., in which it is used; **soft'wood**, (wood of) coniferous tree(s). **soft'ly** *adv.* **soft'ness** *n.* **soft** *adv.*

sof·ten (saw'fen, sŏf'*e*n) *v.* Become, make soft or softer; reduce strength of a defended position by bombing or bombardment (often with *up*); **softening of the brain**, morbid, esp. senile, degeneration of brain. **sof'ten·er** *n.* Person or thing that softens, esp. (i) chemical compound used in water treatment of fabrics to make them soft and light; (ii) WATER softener.

soft·y, soft·ie (sawf'tē, sŏf'-) *n.* (pl. **-ties**). (colloq.) Person who is very sentimental.

sog·gy (sŏg'ē) *adj.* (**-gi·er, -gi·est**). Sodden, saturated, heavy with moisture.

Sog·ne (sawng'n*e*) **Fjord.** Longest and deepest inlet of Norway, in the Norwegian Sea, on the W. coast; extends 127 mi. (204 km), and reaches depths of 4,081 ft. (1,244 m).

soi·gné, soi·gnée (swahnyā') *adjs.* Carefully or elegantly arranged; well-groomed.

soil[1] (soil) *n.* The ground, upper layer of earth in which plants grow, consisting of disintegrated rock usu. with admixture of organic remains. **soil'less** *adj.*

soil[2] (soil) *v.* Make dirty, smear or stain with dirt; tarnish, defile; admit of being soiled. ~ *n.* Dirty mark, smear, defilement.

soi·ree, soi·rée (swahrā', swār'ā) *ns.* Evening party, social evening.

so·journ (*n.* sō'jērn; for *v.* also sōjērn') *n.* & *v.i.* (Make) temporary stay in place. **so'journ·er** *n.* & *v.i.*

sol (sŏl, sōl) *n.* (phys. chem.) Liquid solution or suspension of colloid. [for *solution*]

sol·ace (sŏl'ĭs) *n.* Comfort, consolation. **sol'ac·er** *n.* **solace** *v.t.* (**-aced, -ac·ing**). Comfort, cheer, console.

sol·a·na·ceous (sŏlanā'sh*u*s) *adj.* Belonging to the nightshade family of plants (Solanaceae).

so·lar (sō'l*e*r) *adj.* Of, concerned with, determined by, emanating from, the sun; ~ **battery, cell**, device for converting solar radiation into electrical energy; ~ **day** = DAY sense 2; ~ **month**, exact 12th of the year; ~ **plexus**, (anat.) complex of nerves situated in abdomen behind stomach; ~ **system**, sun with the nine major planets and many minor planets, asteroids, comets, etc., held by its attraction and revolving around it; ~ **wind**, streams of ionized hydrogen and helium particles constantly radiating outward from sun at rate of about a million tons per second.

so·lar·i·um (sol*ā*r'ē*u*m) *n.* (pl. **-lar·i·a** pr. -lār'ē*a*). Room, balcony, etc., enclosed in glass or open to air, for sunbathing etc.

sold: see SELL.

sol·der (sŏd'*e*r) *n.* Fusible metal or metallic alloy used for joining metal surfaces or parts. ~ *v.t.* Join with solder. **sol'der·er** *n.*

*Practical use of **solar** energy (facing) includes a French radial house which uses the sun for heating and plant growing; use of solar radiation for air heating; and (top) solar water-heaters devised for roof-installation and now fitted in sunny States such as California and Texas.*

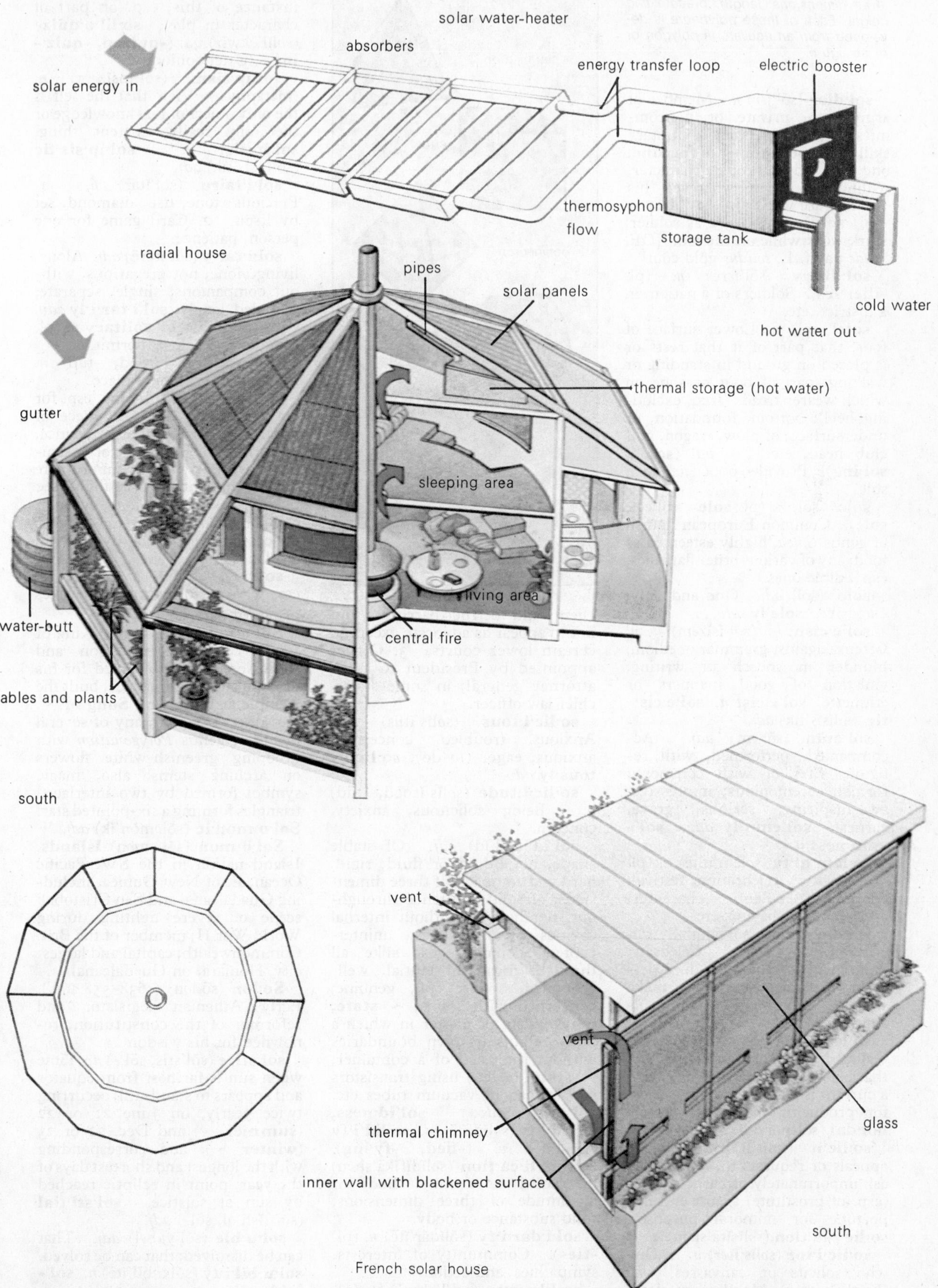
solar water-heater
absorbers
solar energy in
energy transfer loop
electric booster
thermosyphon flow
storage tank
cold water in
hot water out
radial house
pipes
solar panels
thermal storage (hot water)
gutter
sleeping area
living area
water-butt
central fire
etables and plants
south
vent
vent
thermal chimney
inner wall with blackened surface
glass
south
French solar house

*In geometry, a **solid** is an object of three dimensions: length, breadth and height. Each of these polyhedra is developed from an equilateral polygon or plane figure.*

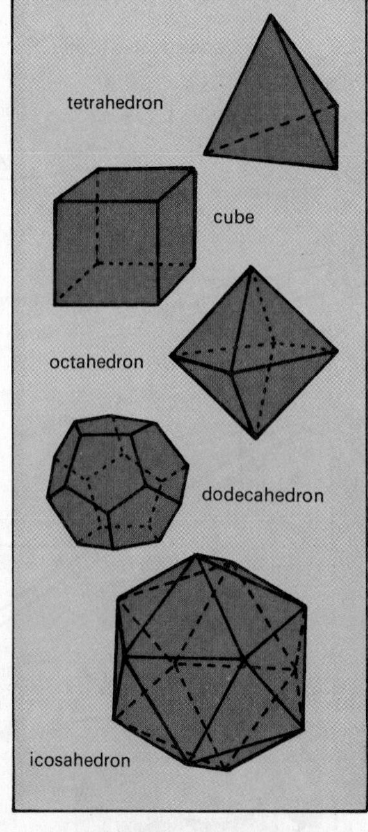

sol·dier (sōl'*jer*) *n.* Member of army, esp. private or noncommissioned officer; man of military skill and experience; ~ **of fortune,** one of adventurous character, willing to serve wherever his services are well paid. **sol'dier·ly** *adj.* **soldier** *v.* Serve as soldier; shirk work while on the job. [OF. *soude* pay f. L. *solidus* gold coin]

sol·dier·y (sōl'*jer*ē) *n.* (pl. **-dier·ies**). Soldiers of a nation, in a district, etc.

sole[1] (sōl) *n.* Lower surface of foot, that part of it that rests or is placed on ground in standing or walking; part of boot or shoe on which wearer treads (freq. excluding heel); bottom, foundation, or undersurface, of plow, wagon, golf club head, etc. ~ *v.t.* (**soled, sol·ing**). Provide (boot etc.) with sole.

sole[2] (sōl) *n.* (pl. **soles,** collect. **sole**). Common European flatfish of genus *Solea,* highly esteemed as food; any of various other flatfishes, esp. edible ones.

sole[3] (sōl) *adj.* One and only; exclusive. **sole'ly** *adv.*

sol·e·cism (sŏl'ĭsĭz*e*m) *n.* Offense against grammar or idiom, blunder in speech or writing; violation of good manners or etiquette. **sol'e·cist** *n.* **sol·e·cis·tic** (sŏlĭsĭs'tĭk) *adj.*

sol·emn (sŏl'*e*m) *adj.* Accompanied, performed, with religious rites or with ceremony; formal; ceremonious; impressive, awe-inspiring; serious, grave, earnest. **sol'emn·ly** *adv.* **sol'emn·ness** *n.*

so·lem·ni·ty (s*o*lĕm'nĭtē) *n.* (pl. **-ties**). Rite, celebration, festival, ceremony; solemn character, appearance, behavior, etc.

sol·em·nize (sŏl'*e*mnīz) *v.t.* (**-nized, -niz·ing**). Celebrate, honor with ceremonies; duly perform (marriage ceremony); make solemn. **sol·em·ni·za·tion** (sŏl*e*mnĭzā'sh*o*n) *n.*

so·le·noid (sō'l*e*noid) *n.* (elect.) Cylindrical coil of conducting wire that behaves as a bar magnet when a current is passed through it, used for producing magnets. **so·le·noi·dal** (sōl*e*noi'd*a*l) *adj.*

so·lic·it (s*o*lĭs'ĭt) *v.* Make appeals or requests to, importune; ask importunately or earnestly for; (esp. of prostitute) accost and importune for immoral purposes. **so·lic·i·ta·tion** (s*o*lĭsĭtā'sh*o*n) *n.*

so·lic·i·tor (s*o*lĭs'ĭt*e*r) *n.* 1. One who solicits or canvasses. 2. (English law) Member of legal profession qualified to advise clients and instruct barristers, but not to appear as advocate except in certain lower courts. 3. Officer appointed by President to assist attorney general; in some states, chief law officer.

so·lic·i·tous (s*o*lĭs'ĭt*u*s) *adj.* Anxious, troubled, concerned; anxious, eager (*to* do); **so·lic'i·tous·ly** *adv.*

so·lic·i·tude (s*o*lĭs'ĭto͞od, -tūd) *n.* Being solicitous, anxiety, concern.

sol·id (sŏl'ĭd) *adj.* Of stable shape, not liquid or fluid, rigid, hard and compact; of three dimensions; of solid substance throughout, not hollow, without internal cavities or interstices, uninterrupted; homogeneous, alike all through; firm, substantial, well-grounded, sober, real, genuine; concerned with solids; ~ **state,** (phys.) state of matter in which a body retains its own boundaries without the need of a container; **~-state,** (elect.) using transistors etc. instead of vacuum tubes etc. **sol'id·ly** *adv.* **sol'id·ness, so·lid·i·ty** (s*o*lĭd'ĭtē) *ns.* **so·lid·i·fy** (s*o*lĭd'ĭfī) *v.* (**-fied, -fy·ing**). **so·lid·i·fi·ca·tion** (s*o*lĭdĭfĭkā'sh*o*n) *n.* **solid** *n.* (geom.) Body or magnitude of three dimensions; solid substance or body.

sol·i·dar·i·ty (sŏlĭdăr'ĭtē) *n.* (pl. **-ties**). Community of interests, sympathies, and action.

so·lil·o·quy (s*o*lĭl'*o*kwē) *n.* (pl. **-quies**). Talking to oneself or without addressing any person; instance of this, esp. on part of character in play. **so·lil·o·quize** (s*o*lĭl'*o*kwīz) *v.i.* (**-quized, -quiz·ing**). Utter soliloquy.

sol·ip·sism (sŏl'ĭpsĭz*e*m) *n.* (metaphys.) View that the self is the only object of real knowledge or the only really existent thing. **sol'ip·sist** *n.* **sol·ip·sis·tic** (sŏlĭpsĭs'tĭk) *adj.*

sol·i·taire (sŏl'ĭtār) *n.* 1. Precious stone, usu. diamond, set by itself. 2. Card game for one person, patience.

sol·i·tar·y (sŏl'ĭtĕrē) *adj.* Alone, living alone, not gregarious, without companions; single, separate; secluded, lonely. **sol'i·tar·i·ly** *adv.* **sol'i·tar·i·ness** *n.* **solitary** *n.* (pl. **-tar·ies**). Recluse, hermit.

sol·i·tude (sŏl'ĭto͞od, -tūd) *n.* Being solitary; lonely place.

so·lo (sō'lō) *n.* (pl. **-los,** esp. for def. 1 **-li** pr. -lē). 1. Piece of vocal or instrumental music, dance, performed by 1 person or instrument, with or without subordinate accompaniment. 2. Solo flight (see below). ~ *adj.* Alone, without companion or partners; ~ **flight,** unaccompanied flight by pilot in airplane.

so·lo·ist (sō'lōĭst) *n.* Musician etc. who performs alone or takes principal part.

Sol·o·mon (sŏl'*o*m*o*n). King of Israel *c*970–933 B.C., son and successor of David; famed for his wisdom and magnificence; built the Temple at Jerusalem; **Song of** ~: see SONG; **~'s seal,** any of several plants of genus *Polygonatum* with drooping greenish-white flowers on arching stems; also, magic symbol formed by two interlaced triangles forming a six-pointed star. **Sol·o·mon·ic** (sŏl*o*mŏn'ĭk) *adj.*

Sol·o·mon (sŏl'*o*m*o*n) **Islands.** Island nation in the SW. Pacific Ocean, E. of New Guinea, including Guadalcanal and San Cristobal; scene of severe fighting during World War II; member of the Brit. Commonwealth; capital and largest city, Honiara, on Guadalcanal.

So·lon (sō'l*o*n) (*c*638–558 B.C.). Early Athenian legislator and reformer of the constitution, renowned for his wisdom.

sol·stice (sŏl'stĭs, sōl'-) *n.* Time when sun is farthest from equator and appears to stand still, occurring twice yearly, on June 21 or 22 (**summer** ~) and Dec. 22 or 23 (**winter** ~), and corresponding with the longest and shortest days of the year; point in ecliptic reached by sun at solstice. **sol·sti·tial** (sŏlstĭsh'*a*l, sōl-) *adj.*

sol·u·ble (sŏl'y*u*b*e*l) *adj.* That can be dissolved; that can be solved. **sol·u·bil·i·ty** (sŏly*u*bĭl'ĭtē) *n.* **sol'u·bly** *adv.*

sol·ute (sŏl'ūt, sōl'-) *n.* & *adj.*

*The **Solomon Islands** in the south-west Pacific are partly a British protectorate while Bougainville is included in Papua New Guinea. Above: An islander tribesman in his finery.*

*As part of his scheme to develop some form of public pride in the country, General Siad Barre, head of **Somalia,** rallied the people of Mogadishu in a mass street-cleaning campaign.*

(Of, pertaining to, designating) dissolved substance.

so·lu·tion (solo͞o′shon) *n.* 1. Solving, being solved; instance or method of solving, explanation, answer. 2. Dissolving, being dissolved, conversion of solid or gas into liquid form by mixture with solvent; dissolved state; fluid substance produced by process of solution. 3. Breaking, breach (chiefly in ~ *of continuity*).

So·lu·tre·an, So·lu·tri·an (solo͞o′trēan) *adjs.* Of the later paleolithic culture (immediately following the Aurignacian); named from remains found in a rock shelter at La Solutré, central France, with characteristic flint implements; worked by pressure flaking.

solve (sŏlv, sawlv) *v.t.* (**solved, solv·ing**). Explain, resolve, answer; (math.) find answer to (problem etc.). **solv′a·ble** *adj.* **solv·a·bil·i·ty** (sŏlvabĭl′ĭtē, sawl-), **solv′er** *ns.*

sol·ven·cy (sŏl′vensē, sawl′-) *n.* Being financially solvent.

sol·vent (sŏl′vent, sawl′-) *adj.* 1. Able to pay all one's debts or liabilities. 2. That dissolves or can dissolve. ~ *n.* Substance (usu. liquid) capable of dissolving something; dissolving or disintegrating agent.

so·ma (sō′ma) *n.* (biol.) Body of organism in contrast to germ cells.

So·ma·li (somah′lē) *adj.* & *n.* (pl. **-lis**, collect. **-li**). (Member) of a dark-skinned Muslim Hamitic people inhabiting Somalia; (of) their language, belonging to the Ethiopian group of Hamitic languages.

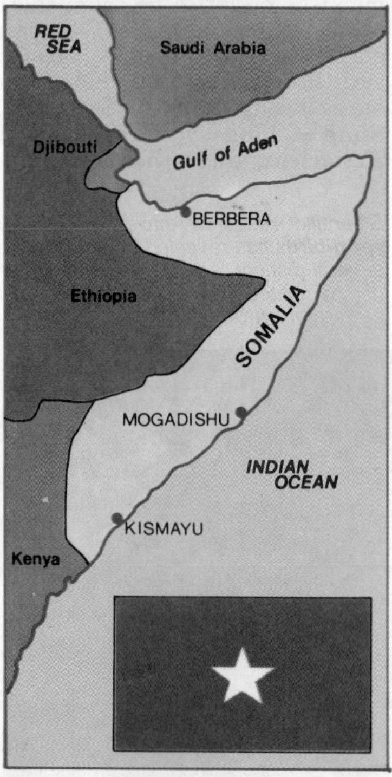

So·ma·li·a (somah′lēa, -mahl′-ya). Republic on E. coast of Africa, formed (1960) from the former protectorate British Somaliland and the former Italian colony of Somalia; capital, Mogadishu.

So·ma·li·land (somah′lēlănd). Coastal region of E. Africa on the Gulf of Aden and the Indian Ocean, covering 300,000 sq. mi. (777,000 sq. km), and including Djibouti, Somalia, and SE. Ethiopia.

so·mat·ic (sōmăt′ĭk) *adj.* Of the body, corporeal, physical; of the framework of the body as dist. from the internal organs; ~ **cell,** one of the cells forming tissues, organs, etc., of the body (dist. from GERM cell). **so·mat′i·cal·ly** *adv.*

som·ber (sŏm′ber) *adj.* Dark, gloomy, dismal. **som′ber·ly** *adv.* **som′ber·ness** *n.*

som·bre·ro (sŏmbrār′ō) *n.* (pl. **-ros**). Broad-brimmed, usu. felt, hat, of kind common in Spain and Latin Amer.

some (sŭm) *adj.* Particular but unknown or unspecified; certain quantity or number of; appreciable or considerable quantity of; (colloq., emphat.) in the fullest sense, worthy of the name. ~ *pron.* Certain persons or things; certain quantity or number. ~ *adv.* (slang) In some degree; to a great extent.

-some[1] *suffix.* Formerly used to form adjectives with sense "characterized by being" or "apt to" (*bothersome, tiresome*).

-some[2] *suffix.* Forming nouns from numerals to indicate group (*twosome*).

-some[3] *comb. form.* (biol.) Denoting portion of a body, esp. of a cell (*chromosome, ribosome*).

some·bod·y (sŭm′bŏdē, -bodē) *n.* (pl. **-bod·ies**) & *pron.* Person of some note or consequence; some person.

some·how (sŭm′how) *adv.* In some indefinite or unspecified manner, by some means or other.

some·one (sŭm′wŭn) *n.* & *pron.* Somebody.

some·place (sŭm′plās) *adv.* (colloq.) Somewhere.

som·er·sault (sŭm′*er*sawlt), **som·er·set** (sŭm′*er*sĕt) *ns.* & *vbs.i.* (Make) acrobatic movement of the body turning head over heels or the reverse, either on the ground or in the air.

some·thing (sŭm′thĭng) *n.* & *pron.* Some thing; some undetermined, unspecified, or unknown thing; important thing or person. ~ *adv.* (archaic, exc. in ~ **like**) In some degree.

some·time (sŭm′tīm) *adv.* At some time; (archaic) formerly. ~ *adj.* Former. **some′times** *adv.* At some times.

some·what (sŭm′hwŭt, -hwŏt, -wŭt, -wŏt) *adv.* In some degree.

some·where (sŭm′hwār, -wār) *adv.* In, at, to, some place.

som·nam·bu·lism (sŏmnăm′-by*u*lĭzem, s*o*m-) *n.* Walking or performing other action during sleep; state characterized by this. **som·nam′bu·list** *n.* **som·nam·bu·lis·tic** (sŏmnămbyŭlĭs′tĭk, s*o*m-) *adj.*

som·no·lent (sŏm′n*o*lent) *adj.* Sleepy, drowsy; inducing drowsiness. **som′no·lent·ly** *adv.* **som′no·lence, som′no·len·cy** *ns.*

son (sŭn) *n.* I. Male child in relation to parent; male descendant; offspring, product, native, follower; **~-in-law** (pl. **~s-in law**), daughter's husband. 2. **the S~,** second person of the Trinity; **S~ of God, S~ of Man,** Jesus Christ.

so·nant (sō′n*a*nt) *adj.* & *n.* Voiced (sound, letter).

so·nar (sō′nar̄) *n.* Device for detecting and locating submerged objects by reflection of sonic and ultrasonic waves.

so·na·ta (s*o*nah′t*a*) *n.* (orig.) Musical composition for one or two instruments, in several movements contrasted in rhythm and tempo but related in key; ~ **form,** musical composition in which two subjects are successively set forth, developed, and restated.

son·a·ti·na (sŏn*a*tē′n*a*) *n.* Shorter or simpler form of sonata.

sonde (sŏnd) = RADIOSONDE.

son et lu·mière (sawn̄′ā lümyĕr′). Entertainment recounting history connected with a building etc. and using recorded sound together with lighting effects. [Fr., = "sound and light"]

song (sawng, sŏng) *n.* Singing, vocal music; musical utterance of certain birds; short poem set to music or meant to be sung; short poem, esp. in rhymed stanzas; poetry, verse; **buy for a ~,** buy for very little; **song′bird,** bird with musical song; **Song of Solomon, Song of Songs,** poetic book of Old Testament, traditionally ascribed to Solomon; **song sparrow,** common sparrow (*Melospiza melodia*) of N. Amer. with streaked brown plumage and sweet song. **song′ful, song′less** *adjs.* **song′ful·ly** *adv.*

*Scientific research into the calls of **song-birds** has revealed that most have several distinct 'songs', and that these can be related to specific activities such as territory protection.*

*A well coordinated child learns to do a **somersault** at an early age. Gymnasts however, can turn a simple somersault into a movement of grace and fluidity. Travelling troupes of tumblers were popular entertainers for many centuries.*

song·ster (sawng′st*e*r, sŏng′-), fem. **song·stress** (sawng′strĭs, sŏng′-) *ns.* (poet.) I. Singer. 2. Songbird.

son·ic (sŏn′ĭk) *adj.* Of, using, sound waves, esp. (of apparatus) determining depth of water by reflection of sound waves; (of a mine) set off by sound vibrations; ~ **barrier,** sound barrier; ~ **boom,** explosive noise produced by aircraft flying faster than the speed of sound.

son·net (sŏn′ĭt) *n.* Poem of 14 lines arranged according to any of various definite schemes, each line having normally ten syllables in English verse (but in Italian verse 11, in French 12), of which the commonest forms in English are the **Petrarchan** or **Italian ~,** divided into an octave of eight lines rhyming *a b b a a b b a* and a sestet of six lines with three rhymes more freely arranged, and the **Shakespearian** or **English ~,** which consists of three quatrains and a final couplet.

son·ny (sŭn′ē) *n.* (pl. **-nies**). Familiar form of address to boy.

so·no·rous (s*o*nōr′*u*s, -nōr′-, sŏn′*e*r*u*s) *adj.* Resonant, (capable of) giving out esp. loud or rich sound; high-sounding. **so·no′rous·ly** *adv.* **so·no′rous·ness, so·nor·i·ty** (s*o*nōr′ĭtē, -nar̄′-) *ns.* (pl. **-ties**).

soon (so͞on) *adv.* Not long after present time or time in question, in a short time; early; willingly; **as ~**

as, the moment that, not later than, as early as; **sooner or later**, at some time or other. **soon'er** *n.* 1. Person who settled in western U.S. before land was officially open to settlement, thus winning unfair advantage in choosing location. 2. (**S~**), nickname for Oklahoman.

soot (sŏŏt) *n.* Black carbonaceous substance or deposit in fine particles formed by combustion of coal, wood, oil, etc. ~ *v.t.* Smear, smudge, cover, choke (*up*). **soot'y** *adj.* (**soot·i·er, soot·i·est**). **soot'i·ly** *adv.* **soot'i·ness** *n.*

soothe (sōōdh) *v.t.* (**soothed, sooth·ing**). Calm, tranquilize; reduce force or intensity of (passion, pain, etc.). **sooth'er** *n.* **sooth'ing** *adj.* **sooth'ing·ly** *adv.*

sooth·say·er (sōōth'sāer) *n.* One who foretells future events, diviner.

SOP, S.O.P. *abbrevs.* (mil.) Standard operating procedure.

sop (sŏp) *n.* Piece of bread etc. dipped or steeped in liquid before eating or cooking. **sop** *v.* (**sopped, sop·ping**). Soak, steep (*in* liquid), take *up* (liquid) by absorption; **sopping** (**wet**), very wet, drenched. **sop'py** *adj.* (**-pi·er, -pi·est**). Soaked, wet; (colloq.) mawkish, foolishly sentimental.

soph·ism (sŏf'ĭzem) *n.* Argument correct in form but fallacious, esp. one intended to deceive or mislead.

soph·ist (sŏf'ĭst) *n.* 1. Paid teacher of rhetoric and philosophy in ancient Greece. 2. Captious or fallacious reasoner, quibbler. **so·phis·tic** (sofĭs'tĭk), **so·phis'ti·cal** *adjs.* **so·phis'ti·cal·ly** *adv.* **soph·is·try** (sŏf'ĭstrē) *n.* (pl. **-tries**).

so·phis·ti·cate (sofĭs'tĭkāt) *v.t.* (**-cat·ed, -cat·ing**). 1. Render somewhat artificial by depriving of natural simplicity, as by education, worldly experience, etc. 2. Falsify by misstatement or alteration. **so·phis'ti·cat·ed** *adj.* (esp.) 1. (of person) Having fashionable tastes or style; (of things) satisfying such persons; (of peoples) of a fully developed culture or stage of civilization. 2. (of machinery etc.) Complex, intricate, and versatile. **so·phis'ti·cat·ed·ly** *adv.* **so·phis·ti·ca·tion** (sofĭstĭkā'shon) *n.* **sophisticate** (sofĭs'tĭkĭt, -kāt) *n.* Sophisticated person.

Soph·o·cles (sŏf'oklēz) (495–406 B.C.). Athenian tragedian; author of *Oedipus Rex, Antigone, Electra,* etc.

soph·o·more (sŏf'omōr, -mōr, sŏf'mōr, -mōr) *n.* Second-year student in high school or college. **soph·o·mor·ic** (sŏfomōr'ĭk, -măr'-) *adj.* Conceited and overly confident of one's knowledge but immature and poorly informed.

sop·o·rif·ic (sŏporĭf'ĭk, sōpo-) *adj.* & *n.* (Drug) tending to produce sleep.

Grain ***sorghum*** *N.S.W. Australia. One of the earliest grains to be cultivated, it has been used as stock feed, as a source of sugar, to ferment into alcohol and for making into a porridge.*

so·pra·no (soprah'nō) *n.* (pl. **-nos, -ni** pr. -nē). Highest singing voice in women and boys; singer with such voice; musical part for this.

Sor·bonne (sōrbŭn', -bŏn'). Orig. a theological college founded in Paris by Robert de Sorbon, chaplain and confessor to Louis IX, *c*1257; later, faculty of theology in University of Paris, suppressed 1792; now, seat of faculties of science and letters of University of Paris.

sor·cer·er (sōr'serer), fem. **sor·cer·ess** (sōr'serĭs) *ns.* User of magic arts, wizard, magician. **sor·cer·y** (sōr'serē) *n.* (pl. **-cer·ies**).

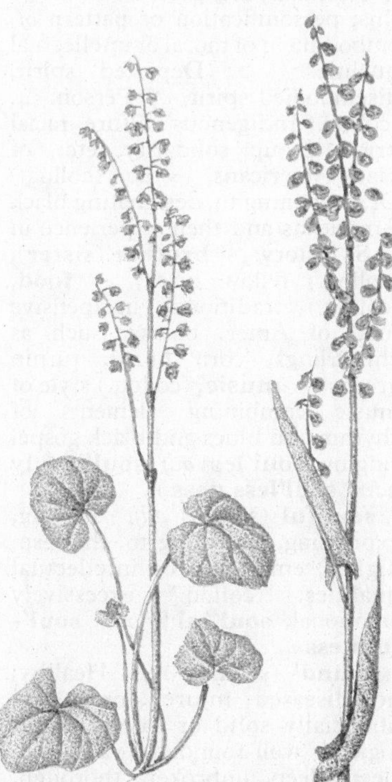

sor·did (sōr'dĭd) *adj.* Dirty, foul, squalid; ignoble, base; avaricious, mercenary. **sor'did·ly** *adv.* **sor'did·ness** *n.*

sore (sōr, sōr) *n.* Place where skin or flesh of animal body is diseased or injured so as to be painfully tender or raw. ~ *adj.* (**sor·er, sor·est**). Painful, causing pain, distressing, irritating, grievous; suffering pain; irritable, sensitive; (colloq.) irritated, annoyed; **sore'head**, (colloq.) grumpy person. **sore'ly** *adv.* **sore'ness** *n.*

sor·ghum (sōr'gum) *n.* Tropical, old-world grass (*Sorghum vulgare*) grown for grain, fodder, and as source of syrup; syrup made from juices of this plant.

so·ror·i·ty (sorōr'ĭtē, -răr'-) *n.* (pl. **-ties**). Society for women in college or university.

sorp·tion (sōrp'shon) *n.* (phys. chem.) Absorption and adsorption considered jointly.

sor·rel[1] (sōr'el, săr'-) *n.* Any of various small sour-tasting perennial plants of genera *Rumex* and *Oxalis*, freq. used in salads etc.

sor·rel[2] (sōr'el, săr'-) *adj.* & *n.* (Horse) of bright chestnut or reddish-brown color; (having) this color.

Common ***sorrel*** *is a herb, endemic to temperate parts of Europe, which has long been used as a vegetable. Mountain sorrel is an American variety and was used mainly by the Indians.*

Obviously in the best condition, this ***sorrel*** *hunter grazes in a Kentish meadow during summer while waiting for the fox-hunting season to begin at the onset of winter in the U.K.*

Each ***sorus*** *on the underneath of a fern frond contains large numbers of spores. These eventually fall to earth but only a small number germinate and grow to maturity.*

sor·row (sa͡r′ō, so͡r′-) *n.* Distress of mind caused by loss, suffering, disappointment, etc.; occasion or cause of this, misfortune, trouble. ~ *v.i.* Grieve, feel sorrow, mourn. **sor′row·ful** *adj.* **sor′row·ful·ly** *adv.* **sor′row·ful·ness** *n.*

sor·ry (sa͡r′ē, so͡r′ē) *adj.* (**-ri·er, -ri·est**). 1. Feeling regret, regretful (freq. in expressions of sympathy or apology). 2. Wretched, paltry, shabby, mean. **sor′ri·ly** *adv.* **sor′ri·ness** *n.*

sort (so͡rt) *n.* Kind, species, variety (*of*); (print., usu. pl.) any particular letter or character in font of type; **of ~s**, (colloq.) of a not very satisfactory kind; **out of ~s**, out of health, spirits, or temper; slightly unwell; ~ **of**, (slang) in a way. **sort** *v.* Separate into sorts; take *out* (certain sorts from others). **sort′er** *n.* (esp). Letter sorter at a post office.

sor·tie (so͡r′tē) *n.* Sally, esp. of beleaguered garrison; operational flight by an aircraft.

so·rus (sōr′*us*, so͡r′-) *n.* (pl. **so·ri** pr. so͡r′ī, so͡r′ī). Cluster of spore cases or spores on undersurface of fern leaves, in fungi, lichens, etc.

SOS (ĕs′ō ĕs′) *n.* International code signal (three dots, three dashes, three dots) of extreme distress, used esp. by ships at sea; (colloq.) urgent appeal for help.

sot (sŏt) *n.* Person stupefied by habitual drunkenness. **sot′tish** *adj.* **sot′tish·ly** *adv.* **sot′tish·ness** *n.*

sot·to vo·ce (sŏt′ō vō′chē; *It.* saw′taw vaw′chĕ). In an undertone, aside. [It.]

Sou·bi·rous (so͞obĕro͞o′), **Marie Bernarde**: see BERNADETTE.

sou·brette (so͞obrĕt′) *n.* Maidservant or similar character (esp. with implication of pertness, coquetry, intrigue, etc.) in comedy, opera, etc.; actress playing such parts.

souf·flé (so͞oflā′, so͞o′flā) *n.* Light spongy dish made by mixing a thick sauce or purée with the yolks and stiffly beaten whites of eggs, and baking it.

sough (sow) *n.* & *v.i.* (Make) rushing, sighing, or rustling sound, as of wind in trees.

sought (sawt) *adj.*: see SEEK; (esp.) **~-after**, much in demand.

soul (sōl) *n.* 1. Spiritual or immaterial part of man; moral and emotional part of man; vital principle and mental powers of animals, including man; animating or essential part, person viewed as this; personification or pattern *of*, embodiment of moral or intellectual qualities. 2. Departed spirit; disembodied spirit. 3. Person. 4. (colloq.) Indigenous culture, racial pride, group solidarity, etc., of black Americans. ~ *adj.* (colloq.) Of, pertaining to, designating black Americans and their experience in U.S. history: ~ **brother** (**sister**), (colloq.) fellow black; ~ **food**, (colloq.) traditional inexpensive food of Amer. blacks, such as chitterlings, corn bread, turnip greens; ~ **music**, (colloq.) style of music combining elements of rhythm and blues and black gospel singing. **soul′less** *adj.* **soul′less·ly** *adv.* **soul′less·ness** *n.*

soul·ful (sōl′*ful*) *adj.* Having, expressing, appealing to, the (esp. higher) emotional or intellectual qualities; (colloq.) excessively emotional. **soul′ful·ly** *adv.* **soul′ful·ness** *n.*

sound[1] (sownd) *adj.* Healthy; not diseased, injured, or rotten; financially solid or safe; correct, logical, well-founded, valid; (of sleep) deep, unbroken; thorough, unqualified. **sound′ly** *adv.* **sound′ness** *n.* **sound** *adv.* Deeply, profoundly (*asleep*).

sound[2] (sownd) *n.* Sensation produced in organs of hearing when surrounding air etc. vibrates so as to affect these; what is or can be heard; vibrations causing this sensation; utterance, speech, or one of the separate articulations composing this; impression produced by sound, statement, etc.; ~ **barrier**, extremely great resistance of air to object moving at speed near that of sound; **sound(ing) board**, thin resonant board in musical instrument so placed as to reinforce tones; audience whose responses serve as an indication of the effectiveness of the ideas etc. presented; **sound′box**, hollow chamber in musical instrument reinforcing resonance; **sound camera**, motion-picture camera that records sound while taking pictures; **sound effects**, sounds, other than speech or music, broadcast as part of program; **sound engineer**, one who deals with acoustics etc.; **sound film**, film for recording sound; cinema film with soundtrack; **sound′proof**, preventing passage of sound; (*v.t.*) make soundproof; **sound ranging**, determination of position by measuring time of arrival of sounds from known points; **sound′track**, (area of film carrying) sound record on cinema film; **sound truck**, truck equipped with loudspeakers that broadcast political messages, advertising slogans, etc.; **sound wave**, one of a series of progressive longitudinal vibratory disturbances in air or other medium by which the auditory nerves are stimulated. **sound′less** *adj.* **sound**

v. Give forth sound (freq. fig., with reference to impression created); cause to sound; utter, pronounce; give notice of by sound, cause to resound, declare, make known; **sound off,** (colloq.) talk loudly, express one's opinions forcefully.

sound[3] (sownd) *v.* Investigate, test depth or quality of bottom of (water), with line and lead or other apparatus; measure (depth) thus; measure temperature etc. of upper atmosphere with **sound'ing balloon** or sonde; (of whale) dive deeply; (usu. **sound out**) inquire, esp. in cautious or indirect manner, into sentiments or inclination of (person); **sounding lead,** lead attached to line (**sounding line**) used in sounding depth of water.

sound[4] (sownd) *n.* Narrow channel, esp. between island and mainland, or connecting two large bodies of water; arm of sea.

sound·ing (sown'ding) *n.* (esp. pl.) Measurement of depth of water at specific places; places where such measurements can be or have been taken.

soup (sōōp) *n.* 1. Liquid food made by stewing vegetables, meat, etc.; **in the ~,** (slang) in difficulties; **~ kitchen,** public institution where soup etc. is supplied free to the poor or in times of distress. 2. (slang) Nitroglycerine, esp. when used to open safe; **~ up** (*v.t.*), increase power of (engine), supercharge. **soup'y** *adj.* (**soup·i·er, soup·i·est**).

soup·çon (sōōpsawn', sōōp'-sawn) *n.* Trace of flavor (*of*); very small amount.

sour (sowr) *adj.* With tart or acid taste, esp. as result of unripeness or of fermentation; rendered acid esp. by fermentation; affected or spoiled thus; (of smell) suggesting fermentation; (of soil) acid; (of person etc.) harsh, peevish, morose; **sour'dough,** prospector, one who lives in the open, esp. in Alaska or Canada (from keeping piece of sour dough for making bread); fermented bread dough; **sour grapes,** scorn or affectation of distaste for something one cannot or does not have; **sour gum,** ornamental tree (*Nyssa sylvatica*) of moist areas in eastern N. Amer., having shiny, tough leaves that turn brilliant scarlet in fall; also called black gum; pepperidge, tupelo; **sour'puss,** (slang) ill-tempered or gloomy person; **sour'sop,** (large succulent, slightly acid fruit of) tropical Amer. tree (*Anona muricata*). **sour** *n.* Acid solution used in bleaching, tanning, etc.; acid drink, usu. of whiskey or other liquor with lemon or lime juice. **sour'ish** *adj.* **sour'ly** *adv.* **sour'ness** *n.* **sour** *v.* Make, become, sour.

*The **sound engineer** in a recording studio is responsible for mixing the various instrument and voice tracks together to produce a final mix for recording purposes. The work requires considerable skill.*

*Johannesburg, capital of **South Africa.** South Africa has come under intense pressure in recent years because of its policy of apartheid.*

source (sōrs, sōrs) *n.* Spring, fountainhead, of stream or river; origin, chief or prime cause, *of*; document, work, etc., giving evidence, esp. original or primary, as to fact, event, etc.; literary work(s) from which later writers have derived inspiration, plots, etc.

souse (sows) *n.* 1. Pickle made with salt; food in pickle, esp. head, feet, and ears of swine. 2. Sousing. 3. Drunkard. **~** *v.* (**soused, sous·ing**). Put in pickle; plunge (*into* water etc.), soak (*in* liquid), drench. **soused** *adj.* (slang) Drunk.

sou·tane (sōōtahn') *n.* Cassock of R.C. priest.

south (sowth) *adv.* Toward, in, the south. **~** *n.* 1. Point of horizon directly opposite north; this direction. 2. Cardinal point of the compass opposite north. 3. (usu. **the S~**) That part of a country, district, etc., that lies to the south; (esp.) Southern states of U.S. **south** *adj.* Lying, toward, in, the south; (of wind) blowing from the south; **south'paw,** (colloq.) left-handed (person), esp. in sports;

*Typical landscape in the Natal National Park, **South Africa,** with the Drakensberg Mountains in the background. Elsewhere, much of the country is devoted to agriculture and there are many mines.*

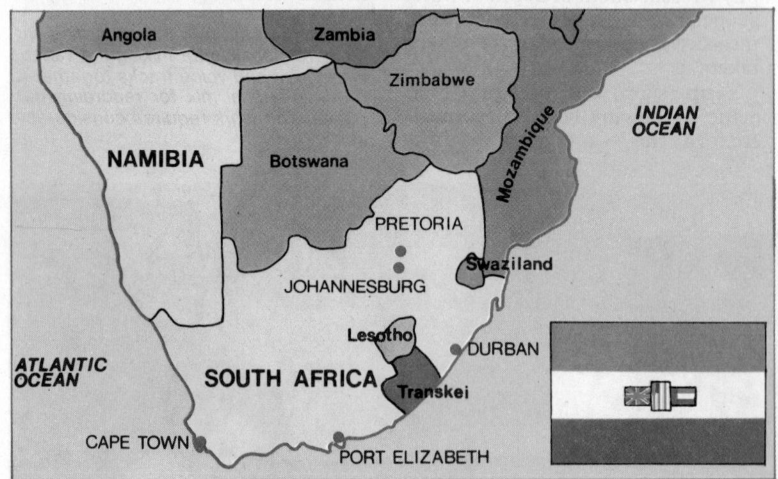

South Pole, point on Earth that is farthest south; **South Seas**, South Pacific. **south′ward** *adv., adj.,* & *n.* **south′wards** *adv.*

South (sowth) **Africa.** Republic in southern Africa; constituted in 1910 (as **Union of ~**) from the self-governing Brit. colonies Cape of Good Hope, Transvaal, Natal, and Orange Free State; member of the Brit. Commonwealth until 1961; administrative capital, Pretoria; seat of legislature, Cape Town. **South African** *adj.* & *n.*

South (sowth) **America.** Southern part of the continent of Amer., joined to Central Amer. by the isthmus of Panama. **South American** *adj.* & *n.*

South (sowth) **Carolina.** Southern state of U.S.; one of the original states of the Union (1788); capital, Columbia.

South (sowth) **Dakota.** State in N. central U.S.; admitted to the Union in 1889; capital, Pierre.

south·east (sowthēst′) *adv.* & *n.* (Direction or compass point) between south and east. ~ *adj.* Of, in, to, from, the southeast. **south·east·er** (sowthēs′*ter*; *naut.* sowē′s*ter*) *n.* Southeast wind. **south′east′er·ly** *adv., adj.,* & *n.* **south′east′ern** *adj.* **south′east′ward** *adv., adj.,* & *n.* **south′east′ward·ly** *adv.* & *adj.* **south′east′wards** *adv.*

South·east (sowthēst′) **Asia.** Region consisting of Cambodia, Indonesia, Laos, Malaysia, Singapore, Thailand, and Vietnam. **South East Asia Treaty Organization**, alliance (1954) of Australia, France, Great Britain, New Zealand, Pakistan, the Philippines, Thailand, and the United States to prevent spread of Communism in the area.

south·er·ly (sŭdh′*er*lē) *adj.* In the south; (of wind) blowing from the south. ~ *adv.* Toward the south. ~ *n.* South wind.

south·ern (sŭdh′*ern*) *adj.* Of the south; lying or directed toward the south; (poet.) coming from the south; **S~**, pertaining to the Southern states of the U.S. **S~ Cross:** see CROSS; **S~ hemisphere**: see HEMISPHERE; **~ lights**: see AURORA australis; **S~ states**, esp. those states S. of Mason-Dixon line and E. of New Mexico. **south′ern·er** *n.* (also **S~**) Native, inhabitant, of the south. **south′ern·most** *adj.*

South (sowth) **Korea.** Unofficial name for the Republic of Korea.

south·west (sowthwĕst′; *naut.* sowwĕst′) *adv.* & *n.* (Direction or compass point) between south and west. ~ *adj.* Of, in, to, from, the southwest. **south′west′er** *n.* 1. Southwest wind. 2. (usu. **sou′wester**) Waterproof hat with broad flap behind to protect the neck. **south′west′er·ly** *adv., adj.,* & *n.* **south′west′ern** *adj.* **south′west′ward** *adv., adj.,* & *n.* **south′west′ward·ly** *adv.* & *adj.* **south′west′wards** *adv.*

South-West (sowth′ wĕst) **Africa**: see NAMIBIA.

sou·ve·nir (sōōv*e*nēr′, sōō′v*e*nēr) *n.* Thing given, brought, kept, etc., for memento (*of* occasion, place, etc.). [Fr., = remember, f. L. *subvenire* occur to the mind]

sou′west·er (sowwĕs′*ter*) = SOUTHWESTER.

sov·er·eign (sŏv′rĭn, -*er*ĭn, sŭv′-) *n.* 1. Supreme ruler, esp. monarch. 2. (hist.) English gold coin worth £1. ~ *adj.* Supreme; possessing sovereign power; (of remedies etc.) very good or efficacious. **sov·er·eign·ty** *n.* (pl. **-ties**).

so·vi·et (sō′vēĕt, -ĭt, sōvēĕt′) *n.* Council, esp. elected organ of government of district, republic, etc., or (**Supreme S~**) whole, of U.S.S.R.; **the Soviet**, the U.S.S.R. **so·vi·et·ize** (sō′vēĭtīz) *v.t.* (**-ized, -iz·ing**). Change or convert to a form of government by soviets. **so′vi·et·ism** *n.* [Russ. *sovet* council]

Soviet (sō′vēĕt, -ĭt, sōvēĕt′) **Union.** Union of Soviet Socialist Republics (see entry).

sow[1] (sow) *n.* 1. Female of swine, adult female pig, esp. domestic one used for breeding. 2. Trough through which molten iron runs into side channels to form pigs; large block of iron solidified in this. 3. ~ **thistle**, plant of genus *Sonchus*, common weed with sharply toothed thistlelike leaves and milky juice.

sow[2] (sō) *v.t.* (**sowed, sown, sow·ing**). Scatter (seed) on or in the earth; plant (ground *with* seed) by sowing; (fig.) cover thickly *with*. **sow'er** *n.*

sox (sŏks): see SOCK[1].

soy (soi) *n.* (also ~ **sauce, soybean sauce**) Sauce for fish etc. made, chiefly in Japan, China, and India, from soybeans pickled in brine; soybean. [Jap. colloq. f. *sho-yu* f. Chin. *shi-yu* (*shi* salted beans, *yu* oil)]

soy·bean (soi'bēn), **soy·a** (soi'*a*) *ns.* (Seed of) a widely cultivated Asiatic bushy leguminous plant (*Soja hispida*), yielding valuable meal (**soy bean flour**), oil, fertilizer, forage, etc. [f. SOY]

Sp. *abbrev.* Spanish.

sp. *abbrev.* Spelling.

S.P. *abbrev.* Shore patrol; shore police.

spa (spah) *n.* Watering place, (place with) mineral spring. [f. *Spa*, watering place in Belgium, fashionable in 18th c.]

space (spās) *n.* 1. Continuous expanse viewed with or without reference to the existence of objects within it; (also **outer** ~) the universe beyond Earth's atmosphere, the immeasurable expanse in which the solar and stellar systems, nebulae, etc., are situated; **space'craft** (pl. **-craft**), **space'ship**, vehicle designed to travel outside Earth's atmosphere; **space'man**, astronaut or member of spaceship's crew; **space medicine**, medicine dealing with effects of space travel on human body; **space probe**, investigation of conditions in outer space; **space shuttle**, spacecraft for travel be-

__South Dakota__ is one of the midwestern states of the U.S.A. The badlands are a major tourist attraction famous for their hostile and arid landscapes, and the strange rock formations found there.

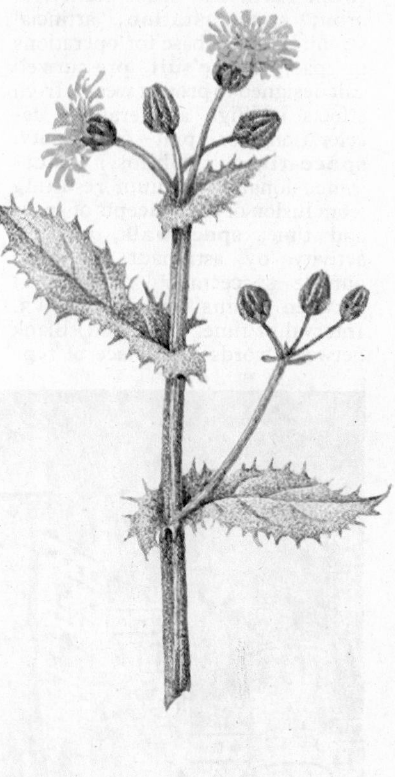

The yellow flowers of the __sow-thistle__ may be seen in Europe from June onwards each summer. In some places its leaves were used as a vegetable and they were also fed to domestic animals.

Orbiter I was the first NASA __space shuttle__ to be launched, and was thus an uncrewed space flight designed to test the shuttle method, which proved successful.

tween Earth and space station in orbit; **space station**, artificial satellite used as base for operations in space; **space'suit**, pressurized suit designed to protect wearer from effects of high acceleration, deceleration, or pull of gravity; **space-time**, (philos.) four-dimensional continuum resulting from fusion of the concepts of space and time; **space'walk**, physical activity by astronaut in space outside spacecraft. 2. Interval between points or objects. 3. Interval of time. 4. (print.) Blank between words etc., piece of type metal used to separate words etc. 5. **space bar** or **spac'er**, bar on typewriter for making space(s) between words etc.; **space heater**, self-contained unit for heating room etc. **space** *v*. (**spaced, spac·ing**). Set at intervals, put spaces between; make space between words on typewriter etc.; **spaced-out** (*adj*.), (slang) under influence of alcohol, marijuana, etc.

spa·cious (spā'shus) *adj*. Enclosing a large space, having ample space, roomy. **spa'cious·ly** *adv*. **spa'cious·ness** *n*.

spade[1] (spād) *n*. Tool for digging or cutting ground, turf, etc., usu. with flattish rectangular blade socketed on wooden handle, with grip or crosspiece at upper end, grasped with both hands while blade is pressed into ground with foot; anything resembling this in form or use; **call a ~ a ~**, call things by their names, speak plainly or bluntly; **spade'work**, (fig.) hard, preliminary work. **spade** *v.t.* (**spad·ed, spad·ing**). Dig up with spade.

spade[2] (spād) *n*. (Playing card with) black figure(s) resembling pointed spade; (pl.) suit of these cards. [Span. *espada* sword]

spa·dix (spā'dĭks) *n*. (pl. **spa·dix·es, spa·di·ces** pr. spādī'sēz, spā'dĭsēz). Inflorescence consisting of thick fleshy spike, usu. enclosed in spathe.

spa·ghet·ti (spagĕt'ē) *n*. Pasta formed into long rods, thinner than macaroni but thicker than vermicelli.

Spain (spān). Country in SW. Europe on the Iberian Peninsula, covering 194,881 sq mi. (504,742 sq. km), and including the Balearic and Canary Islands; capital, Madrid.

spake: see SPEAK.

spall (spawl) *n*. Splinter, chip. ~ *v*. Splinter; (mining) prepare (ore) for sorting by breaking it up.

span[1] (spăn) *n*. Distance from tip of thumb to tip of little finger of fully extended hand; this as measure (9 in.); short distance or time; whole extent of a period of time; full extent or stretch between abutments of arch, piers of bridge, wingtips of aircraft, etc.; arch of bridge. ~ *v.t.* (**spanned, span·ning**). Stretch from side to side of, extend across; bridge (river etc.), form arch across; measure, cover, extent of (thing) with one's grasp etc.

span[2] (spăn) *n*. (naut.) Rope with both ends made fast to afford purchase in loop, rope connecting stays or other uprights; pair of horses, mules, etc. ~ *v.t.* (**spanned, span·ning**). (naut.) Fasten, attach, draw tight. [Du. *spannen* fasten]

span·drel (spăn'drel) *n*. Space between either shoulder of arch and surrounding rectangular molding or framework, or between shoulders of adjoining arches and molding above.

span·gle (spăng'gel) *n*. Small round thin piece of glittering metal etc., esp. one of many sewn to dress etc. as ornament; any small sparkling object. **span'gly** *adj*. (**-gli·er, -gli·est**). **span'gled** *adj*. Covered

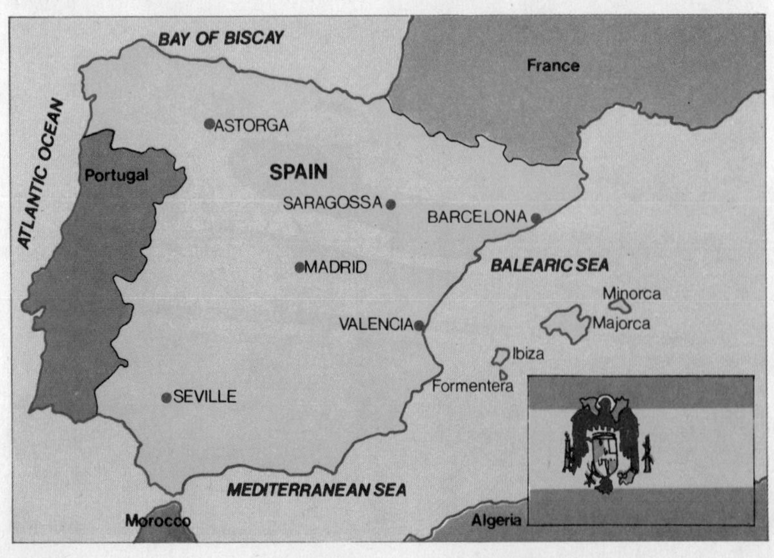

*Above left: The Episcopal Palace at Astorga in the north west of **Spain** was built in the twentieth century. However, the city is much older and the cathedral was built in the 15th century.*

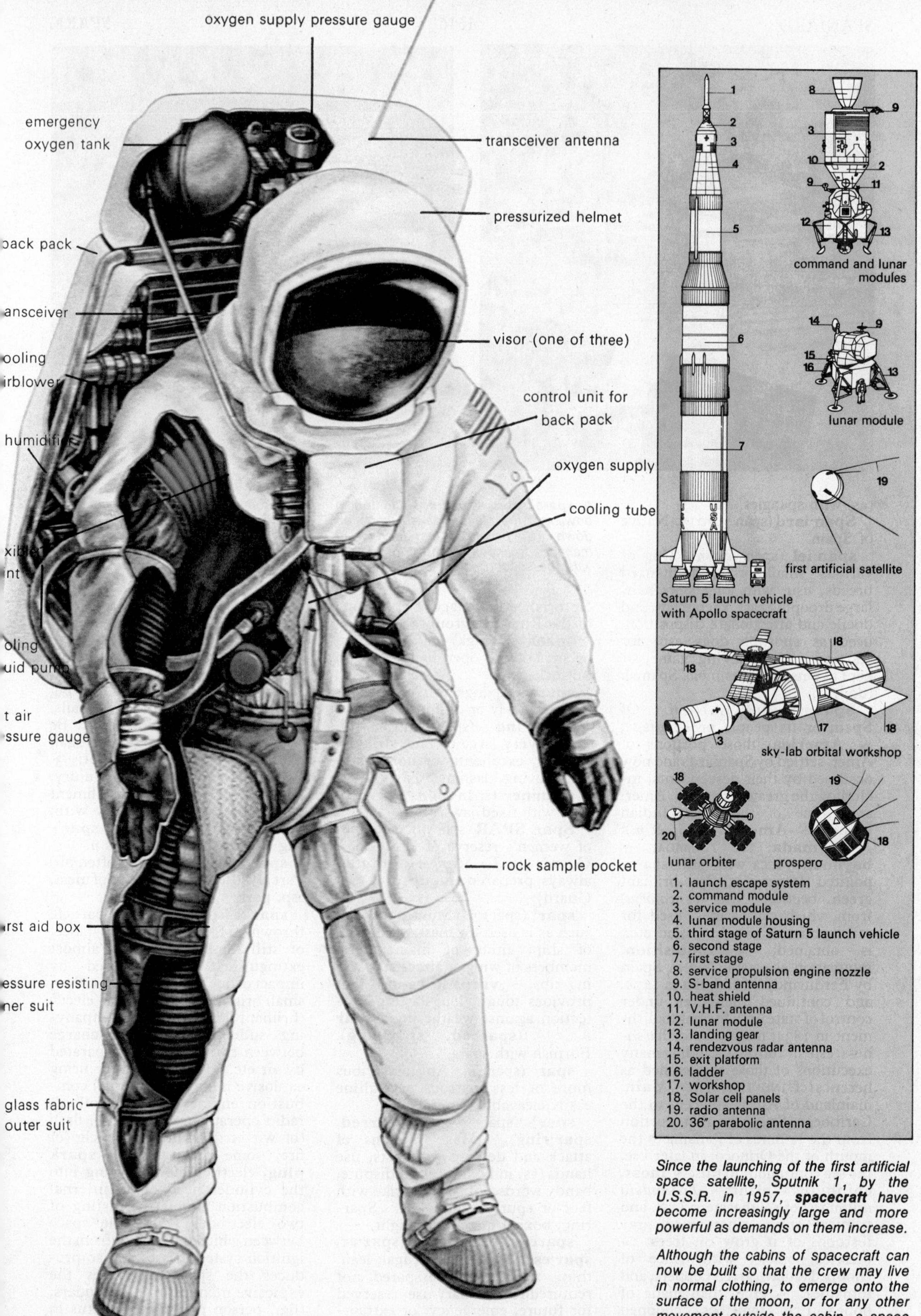

Since the launching of the first artificial space satellite, Sputnik 1, by the U.S.S.R. in 1957, ***spacecraft*** *have become increasingly large and more powerful as demands on them increase.*

Although the cabins of spacecraft can now be built so that the crew may live in normal clothing, to emerge onto the surface of the moon, or for any other movement outside the cabin, a space suit must be worn.

A **spare** score is recorded in tenpin bowling if the player has not knocked down all the pins in the first delivery but manages to knock down the remainder with the second.

The common **sparrow** has not only adapted itself to life near human habitation, but in some places, has become exceptionally tame. Elsewhere, it has reached plague proportions.

(as) with spangles.

Span·iard (spăn′*ya*rd) *n.* Native of Spain.

span·iel (spăn′y*e*l) *n.* Dog of various small or medium-sized breeds, usu. with long silky hair, large drooping ears, keen scent, and docile and affectionate disposition, used as sporting dogs esp. for starting and retrieving game, or kept as pets. [OF. *espaignol* Spanish (dog)]

Span·ish (spăn′ĭsh) *adj.* Of Spain or its people or language; ~ **America**, those portions of Amer. settled by Spaniards and now occupied by their descendants, including the greater part of S. Amer. and some of the West Indian islands; ~**-American** (*adj.* & *n.*); ~ **Armada**: see ARMADA; ~ **bayonet**, yucca with stiff sharp-pointed leaves; ~ **fly**, brilliant green beetle (*Lytta vesicatoria*) from which cantharides, used for raising blisters, as aphrodisiac, etc., is obtained; ~ **Inquisition**, inquisition as established in Spain by Ferdinand and Isabella in 1478, and continued thereafter under control of state until formal abolishment in 1834; notorious for harshness, esp. in 16th c., including many executions of those condemned as heretics (cf. INQUISITION); ~ **Main**, mainland of Amer. adjacent to the Caribbean Sea, esp. that portion from the Isthmus of Panama to the mouth of the Orinoco; in later use, the sea contiguous to this; ~ **moss**, epiphytic plant (*Tillandsia usneoides*) of southeastern U.S. and tropical Amer., where long, gray festoons of it grow on trees; ~ **omelet**, omelet with sauce of chopped onions, green peppers, and tomatoes; ~ **rice**, dish made of boiled rice, tomatoes, chopped onions and peppers, and spices.

Spanish *n.* Language of Spain, one of the Romance group.

spank[1] (spăngk) *v.t.* & *n.* Slap or smack with open hand, esp. on buttocks.

spank[2] (spăngk) *v.t.* Move or travel quickly or dashingly.

spank·ing (spăng′kĭng) *adj.* (esp.) Very large or fine, striking, notable, excellent; (of horse etc.) fast-moving, dashing, showy.

span·ner (spăn′*er*) *n.* Wrench, usu. with fixed jaws.

Spar, SPAR (spa͡r) *ns.* Member of women's reserve of U.S. Coast Guard. [f. L. *S*(*emper*) *Par*(*atus*) always prepared, motto of Coast Guard]

spar[1] (spa͡r) *n.* Stout pole, esp. such as is used for mast, yard, etc., of ship; either of main lateral members of wing of aircraft, carrying ribs; ~ **varnish**, varnish that provides tough, long-lasting protection against weathering. **spar** *v.t.* (**sparred, spar·ring**). Furnish with spars.

spar[2] (spa͡r) *n.* Any of various more or less lustrous crystalline easily cleavable minerals.

spar[3] (spa͡r) *v.i.* (**sparred, spar·ring**). Make motions of attack and defense with fists, use hands (as) in boxing; (fig.) dispute, bandy words; (of cocks) strike with feet or spurs, fight. ~ *n.* Sparring; boxing match; cockfight.

spare (spa͡r) *adj.* (**spar·er, spar·est**). 1. Scanty, frugal; lean, thin. 2. That can be spared, not required for ordinary use; reserved for future, emergency, or extraordinary use; ~ **part**, duplicate of part of machine, kept in readiness to replace one lost, broken, etc.; ~ **room**, room not ordinarily used, guest room. **spare′ly** *adv.* **spare′ness** *n.* **spare** *n.* 1. Spare part, tire, etc. 2. (bowling) Knocking down all pins with first two balls. ~ *v.* (**spared, spar·ing**). 1. Be frugal or grudging of; be frugal. 2. Dispense with, do without. 3. Refrain from inflicting injury, affliction, or damage or punishment on, deal leniently or gently with; refrain from taking (life). **spar′ing·ly** *adv.* **spar′ing·ness** *n.*

spare·rib (spa͡r′rĭb) *n.* (often pl.) Part of closely trimmed ribs of meat, esp. pork.

spark[1] (spa͡rk) *n.* Fiery particle thrown off from burning substance, or still remaining in one almost extinguished, or produced by impact of one hard body on another; small bright object or point; (elect.) (brilliant flash of light accompanying) sudden disruptive discharge between two conductors separated by air etc.; electric spark for firing explosive mixture in internal combustion engine; **sparks** (colloq.) radio operator on ship; (fig.) flash (of wit etc.); scintilla, particle (of fire, some quality, etc.); **spark plug**, electrical device fitting into the cylinder head of an internal combustion engine, consisting of two electrodes across the space between which the current from the ignition system passes and so produces the spark that fires the explosive mixture in the cylinders; (fig.) person providing impetus in an undertaking. **spark** *v.* Emit

*Left: 'Young **Spartans**' by Degas is a romantic impression of the young people of the Greek civilization which thrived from about 700–370 B.C. Their warrior class believed in austerity.*

*The collared **sparrow-hawk** is found only in Australia and New Guinea where it preys on smaller birds and mammals. Related birds are found on most continents and have similar behavior.*

spark(s) of fire or electricity; produce sparks at point where electric circuit is broken; (colloq.) begin, animate, set in motion.

spark[2] (spa͞rk) *n.* Outgoing, lively, elegant fellow; gallant. **spark'ish** *adj.* **spark** *v.i.* Play the gallant, woo.

spar·kle (spa͞r'k*e*l) *n.* Sparkling; gleam, spark. ~ *v.i.* (**-kled, -kling**). Emit sparks; glitter, glisten, scintillate. **spar'kler** *n.* (esp., colloq.) Diamond or other sparkling gem. **spar'kling** *adj.* (of wines etc.) Effervescing with small glittering bubbles of carbon dioxide.

spar·row (spăr'ō) *n.* Any of numerous species of small brownish-gray birds of genus *Passer*, commonest being the *house or English* ~ (*P. domesticus*), a native of Europe introduced into N. Amer., abundant in towns and cities; **spar'rowgrass**, (colloq. corrupt. of) asparagus; **sparrow hawk**: see FALCON, KESTREL.

sparse (spa͞rs) *adj.* (**spars·er, spars·est**). Thinly dispersed or scattered, not crowded or dense, with wide distribution or intervals. **sparse'ly** *adv.* **sparse'ness, spar·si·ty** (spa͞r'sĭtē) *ns.*

Spar·ta (spa͞r't*a*). Ancient city of Greece, capital of Laconia, a Dorian city-state of ancient Greece in SE. Peloponnesus, the inhabitants of which were noted for the military organization of their state and for their rigorous discipline, simplicity, and courage.

Spar·ta·cus (spa͞r't*a*k*u*s). Thracian leader of an army of slaves who rebelled against Rome in 73–71 B.C.

Spar·tan (spa͞r't*a*n) *adj.* Of Sparta (esp. with allusion to the characteristics of the Spartans); hence, austere, hardy. ~ *n.* Native, inhabitant, of Sparta; hardy austere person.

spasm (spăz'*em*) *n.* Involuntary sudden and violent muscular contraction; sudden convulsive movement, convulsion.

spas·mod·ic (spăzmŏd'ĭk), **spas·mod·i·cal** (spăzmŏd'ĭk*a*l) *adjs.* Of, caused by, subject to, spasm(s); occurring, done, jerkily or by fits and starts. **spas·mod'i·cal·ly** *adv.*

spas·tic (spăs'tĭk) *adj.* Of, characterized by, (esp. tonic) spasm(s). ~ *n.* Person with cerebral PALSY.

spat[1] (spăt) *n.* Spawn of shellfish, esp. oyster. ~ *v.* (**spat·ted, spat·ting**). (of oyster) Spawn.

spat[2] (spăt) *n.* (usu. pl.) Short gaiter covering instep and reaching little above ankle.

spat[3] (spăt) *n.* Tiff, quarrel.

spat[4]: see SPIT[2].

spate (spāt) *n.* River flood, esp. sudden; rush, outburst.

spathe (spādh) *n.* (bot.) Large bract, freq. bright colored, enveloping inflorescence on same axis (spadix), as in arum etc.

spa·tial (spā'sh*a*l) *adj.* Of, relating to, occupying, occurring in, space. **spa'tial·ly** *adv.*

spat·ter (spăt'*er*) *v.* Scatter (liquid, mud, etc.) here and there in small drops, splash (*with* mud, slander, etc.) thus, (of liquid) fall thus or with sound suggesting heavy drops. ~ *n.* Spattering, splash; pattering. **spat'ter·ing·ly** *adv.*

spat·u·la (spăch'*u*l*a*) *n.* Flat broad-bladed knife-shaped implement used for spreading foods, paints, etc. and for medical examination of certain organs etc. **spat'u·lar, spat·u·late** (spăch'-

ulĭt, -lāt) *adjs*.

spav·in (spăv′ĭn) *n*. Disease of hock in horses, marked by hard bony tumor or excrescence and caused by strain etc. **spav′ined** *adj*.

spawn (spawn) *n*. Minute eggs of frogs, fishes, etc., usu. extruded in large numbers and often forming coherent or gelatinous mass, fertilized by the MILT; (contempt.) brood, (numerous) offspring; mycelium of fungi. ~ *v*. Cast spawn; produce or generate as spawn or in large numbers.

spay (spā) *v.t*. Remove ovaries of (animal).

S.P.C.A. *abbrev*. Society for the Prevention of Cruelty to Animals.

S.P.C.C. *abbrev*. Society for the Prevention of Cruelty to Children.

speak (spēk) *v*. (**spoke** pr. spōk or archaic **spake** pr. spāk, **spo·ken** pr. spō′*ke*n or archaic **spoke, speak·ing**). Utter words or articulate sound in ordinary (not singing) voice; hold conversation; make oral address, deliver speech; utter (words); make known (opinion, *the truth*, etc.) thus; use (specified language) in speaking; state in words; be evidence of, indicate; ~ **for**, act as spokesman of or for; ~ **of**, mention; **speak out, up**, speak freely; speak loud(er) or so as to be distinctly heard; **speak′-easy** (pl. **-easies**), (slang) place illegally selling liquor, esp. during Prohibition in U.S. **speak′a·ble** *adj*.

speak·er (spē′*ker*) *n*. 1. One who speaks, esp. one who makes a speech. 2. **S**~, officer of U.S. House of Representatives chosen to preside over debates, preserve order, etc.; similar officer in other legislative bodies. 3. Loudspeaker (see LOUD).

speak·ing (spē′kĭng) *n*. (esp.) Speechmaking; ~ part, part in play etc. containing words to be spoken; ~ **terms**, degree of acquaintanceship allowing exchange of conversation (**not on** ~ **terms**, (usu.) estranged).

spear (spēr) *n*. Thrusting or hurling weapon with long shaft and sharp-pointed head, usu. of iron or steel; sharp-pointed and barbed instrument for catching fish etc.; ~ **grass**, grass with stiff pointed leaves; **spear′head**, (fig.) person(s) leading, anything in forefront of, attack; (*v.t.*) act as spearhead for; **spear′mint**, aromatic herb (*Mentha spicata*) used for flavoring. **spear** *v.t*. Pierce, strike, (as) with spear. **spear′er** *n*.

spec (spĕk) *n*. (colloq.) Speculation; **on** ~, experimentally, as a gamble; specification(s) (usu. pl.).

spe·cial (spĕsh′*al*) *adj*. Of a particular kind, peculiar, not general; for a particular purpose; exceptional in amount, degree, kind, etc.; ~ **delivery**, delivery of mail in advance of regular delivery; ~ **handling**, processing as expeditiously as possible of fourth-class or parcel post mail. **spe′cial·ly** *adv*. In special manner, to special degree or extent; of special purpose, expressly. **special** *n*. Special radio or television program, train, edition of magazine, etc.

spe·cial·ist (spĕsh′*al*ĭst) *n*. One who devotes himself to particular branch of profession, science, etc., esp. medicine.

spe·cial·ize (spĕsh′*al*īz) *v*. (**-ized, -iz·ing**). 1. Make specific or individual; modify, limit (idea, statement). 2. (biol.) Adapt (organ etc.) for particular purpose, differentiate; be differentiated, become individual in character. 3. Be, become, a specialist. **spe·cial·i·za·tion** (spĕsh*al*īzā′sh*o*n) *n*.

spe·cial·ty (spĕsh′*al*tē) *n*. (pl. **-ties**). Special feature or characteristic; special pursuit, product, operation, etc., thing to which person gives special attention.

spe·cie (spē′shē) *n*. Coin, coined money. [L. *in specie* in kind]

spe·cies (spē′shēz) *n*. (pl. **-cies**). 1. (logic) Group subordinate to genus, containing individuals that have common attribute(s) and are called by a common name. 2. (biol.) Group of organisms that have certain characteristics not shared by other groups, usu. a group that is believed to be reproductively isolated, i.e. whose members will breed among themselves but not normally with members of other groups; subdivision of genus. 3. (loosely) Kind, sort.

spe·cif·ic (spĭsĭf′ĭk) *adj*. 1. Definite; distinctly formulated; precise, particular. 2. Of a species; possessing, concerned with, the properties characterizing a species. 3. (med., of remedies) Specially efficacious for a particular ailment etc.; (path.) characteristic. 4. ~ **gravity**: see GRAVITY; **specific heat**: see HEAT. **spe·cif′i·cal·ly** *adv*. **specific** *n*. Specific remedy. **spec·i·fic·i·ty** (spĕsĭfĭs′ĭtē) *n*.

spec·i·fi·ca·tion (spĕsĭfĭkā′sh*o*n) *n*. Specifying; specified detail, esp. detailed description of construction, workmanship, materials, etc., of work undertaken by engineer, architect, etc.; description by applicant for patent of nature, details, and use of invention.

spec·i·fy (spĕs′ĭfī) *v.t*. (**-fied, -fy·ing**). Name expressly, mention definitely; include in specification.

spec·i·men (spĕs′*i*m*e*n) *n*. Indi-

*The **Speaker** presides over debates in the United States House of Representatives. His responsibility is to ensure that rules are obeyed. Here Speaker, Tip O'Neil, sits beside Vice-President Walter Mondale as President Carter addresses Congress.*

*The **spear** is a standard weapon carried by natives in Uganda and many other places. Broad-bladed spears are used to kill larger animals while the finer tips may be used for birds.*

vidual or part taken as example of class or whole, esp. serving as example of class or thing in question for purposes of investigation or scientific study; (med.) sample; (colloq.) person of a specified sort.

spe·cious (spē´shus) *adj.* Good in appearance but not in reality; plausible; fair or right only on the surface. **spe´cious·ly** *adv.* **spe´-cious·ness** *n.* **spe·ci·os·i·ty** (spē-shēŏs´ĭtē) *n.* (pl. **-ties**).

speck (spĕk) *n.* Small spot, dot, stain; particle (*of* dirt etc.); spot of rottenness in fruit. **speck´-less** *adj.* **speck** *v.t.* Mark with specks.

speck·le (spĕk´el) *n.* Small speck, mark, or stain. ~ *v.t.* (**-led, -ling**). Mark with speckles.

spec·ta·cle (spĕk´takel) *n.* 1. Public show, specially prepared or arranged display; object of public attention, curiosity, admiration, etc. 2. (**pair of**) ~**s**, eyeglasses. **spec´ta·cled** *adj.* Wearing spectacles; (of animals etc.) marked in way that suggests spectacles.

spec·tac·u·lar (spĕktăk´yuler) *adj.* Of, of the nature of, a spectacle or show; striking; imposing. **spec·-tac´u·lar·ly** *adv.*

spec·ta·tor (spĕk´tāter, spĕktā´-) *n.* One who looks on, esp. at show, game, etc. **spec·ta·to·ri·al** (spĕk-tatōr´ēal, -tōr´-) *adj.*

spec·ter, Brit. **spec·tre** (spĕk´-ter) *ns.* Ghost, apparition.

spec·tral (spĕk´tral) *adj.* 1. Ghostly, of ghosts. 2. Of spectra or the spectrum.

spec·tre: SPECTER.

spec·tro·gram (spĕk´trogrăm) *n.* Record obtained with spectrograph.

spec·tro·graph (spĕk´trográf, -grahf) *n.* Instrument producing representation of a spectrum usu. on a screen or photographic plate. **spec·tro·graph·ic** (spĕktrográf´ĭk) *adj.* **spec·tro·graph´i·cal·ly** *adv.*

spec·trom·e·ter (spĕktrŏm´eter) *n.* Spectroscope that can be used for measurement of observed spectra. **spec·tro·met·ric** (spĕtro-mĕt´rĭk) *adj.*

spec·tro·scope (spĕk´troskōp) *n.* Optical instrument for producing and examining spectra. **spec·-tro·scop·ic** (spĕktroskŏp´ĭk), **spec·tro·scop´i·cal** *adjs.* **spec·-tro·scop´i·cal·ly** *adv.* **spec·-tros·co·pist** (spĕktrŏs´kopĭst), **spec·tros´co·py** *ns.*

spec·trum (spĕk´trum) *n.* (pl. **-tra** pr. -tra, **-trums**). 1. Series of images formed when a beam of radiant energy is dispersed and then brought to focus, so that its component waves are arranged in order of wavelength; (esp.) colored band into which beam of light is decomposed by prism etc.; afterimage seen when eyes are turned away from bright-colored object etc.; ~ **analysis**, analysis, esp. chemical analysis, by means of spectra. 2. Range, series, of interrelated ideas or objects.

spec·u·lar: see SPECULUM.

spec·u·late (spĕk´yulāt) *v.i.* (**-lat·ed, -lat·ing**). 1. Engage in thought or reflection, esp. of confectural or theoretical kind (*on*). 2. Buy or sell commodities etc. in expectation of rise or fall in their market value; engage in commercial operation, make investment, involving risk of loss. **spec·u·la·tive** (spĕk´yulātĭv, -latĭv) *adj.* **spec´u·la·tive·ly** *adv.* **spec´u·la·tive·-ness, spec´u·la·tor** *ns.*

spec·u·la·tion (spĕkyulā´shon) *n.* 1. Meditation on, inquiry into, theory about, a subject. 2. Speculative investment or enterprise, practice of speculating, in business.

spec·u·lum (spĕk´yulum) *n.* (pl. **-la** pr. -la, **-lums**). 1. (surg.) Instrument for dilating cavities of human body for inspection. 2. Mirror, usu. of polished metal, esp. in optical instruments; ~ **metal**, alloy of copper and tin taking high polish used as a reflector in telescopes. 3. Lustrous colored patch on wing of some birds. **spec·u·lar** (spĕk´yuler) *adj.*

sped (spĕd): see SPEED.

speech (spēch) *n.* Act, faculty, or manner of speaking; thing said, remark; public address; language, dialect; ~ **therapy**, remedial treatment of defective speech.

speech·i·fy (spē´chĭfī) *v.i.* (**-fied, -fy·ing**). (mildly contempt.) Make speeches, hold forth.

speech·less (spēch´lĭs) *adj.* Dumb; temporarily deprived of speech by emotion etc. **speech´-less·ly** *adv.* **speech´less·ness** *n.*

speed (spēd) *n.* 1. Rate at which something moves, travels, proceeds, or operates; rapidity; transmission gear of motor vehicle; (photog.) sensitivity of film etc. to light; length of exposure; (slang) stimulant drug, as amphetamine. 2. (archaic) Success, prosperity. 3. **speed´ball**, (slang) mixture of cocaine and heroin; **speed´boat**, motorboat etc. capable of very high speed; **speed limit**, maximum speed permitted on road, to vehicle etc.; **speed trap**, stretch of high-

People who feel strongly about a topic often give a ***speech.*** *Some do so in formal surroundings; others, like this 'soap-box orator' in Sydney, Australia, attract an audience with their rhetoric.*

*A **speed-boat** designed for competition racing must have special lines and a very powerful motor. Other power boats, for big game fishing, are slower.*

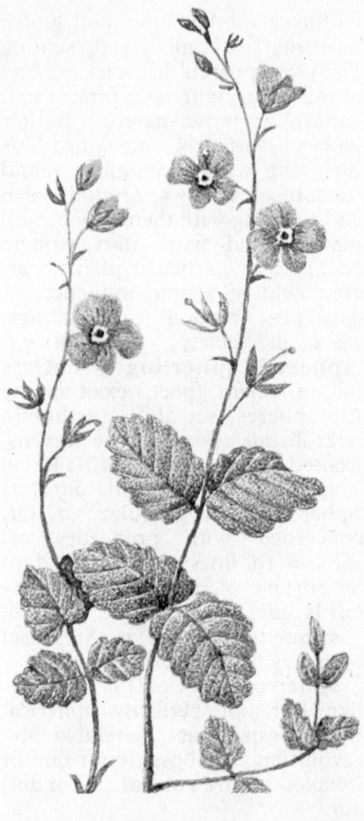

***Speedwell** or veronica is a herb found in northern Europe, Asia and North America whose leaves were used to make a decoction (or tea) said to provide relief from many ailments.*

way where police monitor traffic speed to catch drivers who exceed the speed limit; **speed'way**, track for motor racing, road intended only for fast motor vehicles. **speed** *v.* (**sped** pr. spĕd or **speed·ed, speed·ing**). I. Go fast; travel at excessive or illegal speed; (archaic) send fast, send on the way. 2. (archaic) Be, make, prosperous; succeed, give success to. 3. Regulate speed of (engine etc.), cause to go at fixed speed; ~ **up**, increase speed of, increase rate of work, production; ~**-up** (*n.*). **speed'er** *n.* **speed'ing** *adj.* & *n.*

speed·om·e·ter (spēdŏm'ĭter, spĭ-) *n.* Instrument for registering speed at which vehicle, esp. car, is moving.

speed·well (spēd'wĕl) *n.* Plant, flower, of genus *Veronica*, of small herbaceous plants with leafy stems and small usu. blue flowers.

speed·y (spē'dē) *adj.* (**speed·i·er, speed·i·est**). Rapid, swift; prompt. **speed'i·ly** *adv.* **speed'i·ness** *n.*

spe·le·ol·o·gy (spēlēŏl'ojē) *n.* Scientific study of caves. **spe·le·ol'o·gist** *n.*

spell[1] (spĕl) *n.* Words, formula, used as charm; incantation; attraction, fascination; **spell'binder**, (colloq.) political speaker who can hold audiences spellbound; **spell'bound**, bound (as) by spell, fascinated, entranced.

spell[2] (spĕl) *v.* (**spelled** or **spelt** pr. spĕlt, **spell·ing**). Name or write in order letters of (word etc.); form words etc. thus; (of letters) make up, form (word); (fig.) signify, imply, involve; ~ **out**, make out (words etc.) laboriously letter by letter; state explicitly, explain in detail. **spell'ing** *n.* (esp.) ~ **bee**, competition in spelling.

spell[3] (spĕl) *n.* Period of work, or *of* or *at* some occupation; short period. ~ *v.* (**spelled, spell·ing**). (Allow to) rest for short period.

spe·lun·ker (spĭlŭng'ker, spē'lŭng-) *n.* One who explores caves for sport. **spe·lunk'ing** *n.*

spend (spĕnd) *v.t.* (**spent, spend·ing**). Pay out (money) for a purchase etc., pay out money; use, use up, consume, exhaust, wear out; be consumed; live or stay through (period of time); **spend'thrift**, extravagant person, prodigal (freq. attrib. or as adjective). **spend'er** *n.*

Spen·ser (spĕn'ser), **Edmund** (*c*1552–99). English poet, author of *The Faerie Queene* etc. **Spen·se·ri·an** (spĕnsēr'ēan) *adj.* & *n.* Of Spenser; **S**~ **stanza**, stanza invented by Spenser, in which he wrote *The Faerie Queene*, consisting of eight 5-foot iambic lines, followed by an iambic line of 6 feet, rhyming *a b a b b c b c c*.

spent (spĕnt) *adj.*: see SPEND; (esp.) used up; exhausted.

sperm (spērm) *n.* I. Male generative fluid, semen; (biol.) spermatozoon. 2. ~ **oil**, spermaceti; ~ **whale**, large whale (*Physeter catodon*) found in warm oceans, with large head cavity containing spermaceti.

sper·ma·ce·ti (spērmasĕt'ē, -sē'tē) *n.* White soft scaly solid, a mixture of fatty esters, separating from oil found in head of sperm whale and other cetaceans, and used for ointments, candles, etc. [med. L. f. *sperma* seed, *cetus* whale (because it was thought to be whale spawn)]

sper·mat·ic (spērmăt'ĭk) *adj.* Of sperm or the organ that produces sperm, seminal; ~ **cord**, structure connecting testicles with seminal vesicles.

sper·mat·o·gen·e·sis (spērmătojĕn'esĭs, -mato-) *n.* Development of spermatozoa. **sper·mat·o·ge·net·ic** (spērmatōjenĕt'ĭk, spermătō-) *adj.*

sper·mat·o·phore (spērmăt'ofōr, -fōr, spēr'mato-) *n.* (zool.) Capsule formed by some animals containing compact mass of spermatozoa.

sper·mat·o·zo·on (spērmatozō'on, -măto-) *n.* (pl. **-zo·a**). Minute active fertilizing cell of male organism.

spew, spue (spū) *vbs.* Vomit, eject.

sphag·num (sfăg'num) *n.* Moss of genus *S*~ growing in boggy and swampy places, used as packing for plants, surgical dressings, etc.

sphe·noid (sfē'noid) *adj.* Wedge-shaped; ~ **bone**, compound bone at base of skull. **sphenoid** *n.* (anat.) Sphenoid bone. **sphe·noi·dal** (sfĭnoi'dal) *adj.*

sphere (sfēr) *n.* I. Body or space bounded by surface, every point of which is equidistant from a point within called the center; ball, globe; heavenly body; globe representing Earth or apparent heavens. 2. Any of the (orig. eight, later nine or ten) concentric transparent hollow globes formerly imagined as revolving with harmonious sound (**music of the ~s**) around Earth and carrying with them moon, sun, planets, and fixed stars; sphere occupied by particular planet, star, etc.; field of action, influence, or existence, natural surroundings, place in society. **sphere** *v.t.* (**sphered, spher·ing**). Enclose (as) in sphere; (poet.) exalt among the spheres, set aloft. **spher·ic** (sfĕr´ĭk) *adj.* (poet.) Of the heavens, exalted. **sphe·ric·i·ty** (sfĭrĭs´ĭtē) *n.*

spher·i·cal (sfĕr´ĭk*a*l) *adj.* 1. Sphere-shaped, globular. 2. Of, concerned with properties of, spheres; (of lines etc.) described in, on surface of, sphere. **spher'i·cal·ly** *adv.*

spher·ics (sfĕr´ĭks) *n.* Spherical geometry and trigonometry.

sphe·roid (sfēr´oid) *n.* Sphere-like but not perfectly spherical body, esp. one generated by revolution of ellipse about one of its axes. **sphe·roi·dal** (sfĭroi´d*a*l) *adj.*

sphinc·ter (sfĭngk´t*e*r) *n.* Ring of muscle guarding or closing an orifice in the animal body, e.g. **anal, oral, pupillary, ~; cardiac ~**, sphincter guarding upper orifice of stomach.

sphinx (sfĭngks) *n.* (pl. **sphinx·es, sphin·ges** pr. sfĭn´jēz). 1. (Gk. myth.) Winged monster with woman's head and lion's body, which infested Thebes, killing all who could not answer the riddle it propounded, until the riddle was solved by OEDIPUS; (loosely) enigmatic or mysterious person. 2. Ancient Egyptian figure of a recumbent lion with the head of a man, ram, or hawk, esp. (**the S~**) the colossal fourth-Dynasty stone, one near the Pyramids at Giza; any similar figure. 3. (also **sphinx moth**) = HAWK[1] moth.

sphyg·mo·ma·nom·e·ter (sfĭg-mōm*a*nŏm´ĭt*e*r), **sphyg·mom·e·ter** (sfĭgmŏm´ĭt*e*r) *ns.* Instrument recording graphically variations in arterial pressure.

Spi·ca (spī´k*a*) (pl. **-cas**). (astron.) Star of 1st magnitude in constellation Virgo.

spi·ca (spī´k*a*) *n.* (pl. **-cae** pr. -sē, **-cas**). (surg.) Form of spiral bandage with reversed turns, suggesting ear of wheat.

spi·cate (spī´kāt) *adj.* (bot., zool.) Pointed, spiked, spike-shaped.

spice (spīs) *n.* Any of various strong-flavored or aromatic vegetable substances obtained from tropical plants, as ginger, cinnamon, nutmeg, allspice, used to season or preserve food etc.; spices collectively; slight touch, trace, dash, *of* some quality etc.; **spice'-bush**, aromatic shrub (*Lindera benzoin*) of eastern N. Amer. with small yellow flowers and scarlet berries; aromatic shrub (*Calycanthus occidentalis*) of California, with fragrant light-brown flowers. ~ *v.t.* (**spiced, spic·ing**). Flavor or season with spice(s).

spick-and-span (spĭk´*a*nspăn´) *adj.* Smart and new; neat, trim. [extended f. ME. *span-new* (ON. *spánn* chip)]

spic·u·la (spĭk´yul*a*) *n.* (pl. **-lae** pr. -lē). Spicule; prickle.

spic·ule (spĭk´ūl) *n.* Small, slender, pointed or needlelike process or formation; esp. (zool.) small hard calcareous or siliceous body stiffening tissues of various invertebrates, as sponges etc. **spic·u·lar** (spĭk´yul*e*r), **spic·u·late** (spĭk´yulāt, -lĭt) *adjs.*

spic·y (spī´sē) *adj.* (**spic·i·er, spic·i·est**). Of, flavored or fragrant with, spice; (fig.) pungent, sensational, scandalous, somewhat improper. **spic'i·ly** *adv.* **spic'i·ness** *n.*

spi·der (spī´d*e*r) *n.* 1. Eight-legged animal of order Araneida of arachnids, many species of which spin webs esp. for capture of insects as food; (loosely) spiderlike arachnid. 2. Frying pan, orig. one with legs or feet. 3. Part of machinery with radiating arms. 4. **~ crab**, crab of group Oxyrhyncha with long slender legs; **spider monkey**, tropical Amer. monkey of genus *Ateles* with long slender limbs and prehensile tail; **spi'der-wort**, plant of Amer. genus *Tradescantia*, with ephemeral white, pink, or violet flowers and slender hairy stamens. **spi'der·y** *adj.* Spider-like, esp. long and slender like spider's legs; like cobweb.

spiel (spēl, shpēl) *n.* (slang) Talk, sales talk, speech, story (esp. glib or persuasive one). ~ *v.i.* Talk volubly. [Ger., = "game"]

spif·fy (spĭf´ē) *adj.* (**-fi·er, -fi·est**). (slang) Smart in dress; stylish; dapper. **spif'fi·ness** *n.*

spig·ot (spĭg´*o*t) *n.* Small peg or plug esp. for insertion into vent hole of cask; plain end of section of pipe fitting into socket of another; faucet.

spike (spīk) *n.* 1. Sharp point; pointed piece of metal, e.g. forming part of barrier, fixed in shoe sole to prevent slipping, etc.; (pl.) shoes

*The great **Sphinx** at Giza, Egypt, was built to represent a guardian of the tombs of the ancient pharaohs. It is 239 ft. long and was probably built about 2,550 B.C.*

***Spiderwort** is one of 60 species of a herb native to the Americas. The genus, Tradescantia, was named after a gardener of Charles I who helped to finance the colony of Virginia.*

The pink crab ***spider*** *(above) is usually colored so that it remains inconspicuous among the flowers used by it as a place for an ambush.*

Large, hairy theraphosid spiders are able to attack and kill small vertebrates. However, although their bite may hurt a human, it will not kill.

Originally from south-west Asia, **spinach** has been cultivated in most places where there is a temperate climate. It is sold fresh, canned, or deep-frozen.

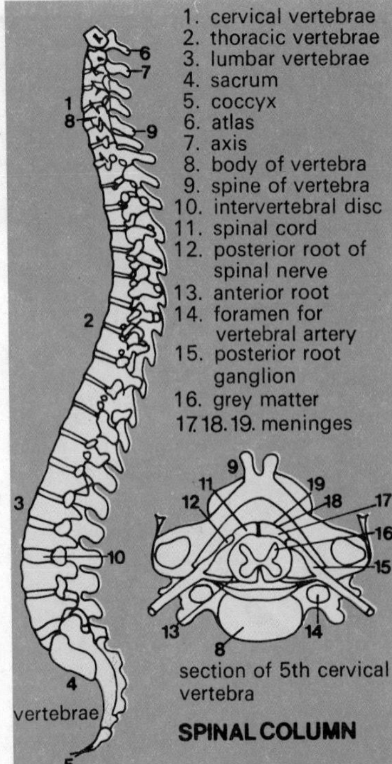

The **spine** or vertebral column consists of 26 small bones (vertebrae) in the human adult. This supports the body and also houses the spinal cord which is part of the central nervous system.

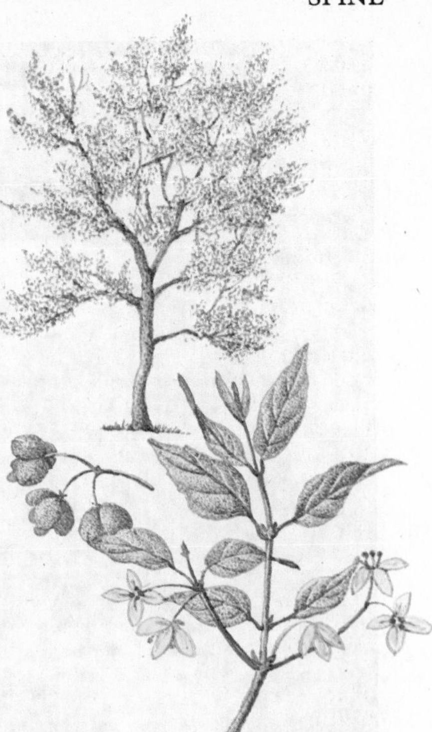

The **spindle-tree,** a member of the genus Euonymus, is native to Europe and northern Asia. Its berries were once used to produce a dye and oil from its seeds was used in soap-making.

fitted with spikes; high, tapering heel on woman's shoe; large stout nail. 2. (bot.) Inflorescence of sessile flowers on elongated simple axis. 3. Young mackerel under 6 in. long. **spik'y** *adj.* (**spik·i·er, spik·i·est**). **spike** *v.t.* (**spiked, spik·ing**). Furnish with spike(s); fix on, pierce, with spike(s); plug up vent of (gun) with spike; (fig.) make useless, put an end to (idea etc.); (colloq.) add alcohol to (drink).

spike·let (spīk'lĭt) *n.* (bot.) Small or secondary spike esp. as part of inflorescence of grasses etc.

spile (spīl) *n.* Wooden peg or plug, spigot; small spout for conducting sap from sugar maple etc. ~ *v.t.* (**spiled, spil·ing**). Provide (cask, tree, etc.) with spile.

spill[1] (spĭl) *n.* Thin strip of wood, folded or twisted piece of paper etc., for lighting candle, pipe, etc.

spill[2] (spĭl) *v.* (**spilled** or **spilt, spill·ing**). Allowing (liquid etc.) to fall or run out from vessel, esp. accidentally or wastefully, run out thus; shed (blood); empty (sail) of wind (naut.); cause to fall from horse or vehicle; **spill'way,** passageway for overflow of surplus water from reservoir etc. **spill** *n.* Throw or fall, esp. from horse or vehicle; tumble. **spill'a·ble** *adj.* **spill'age** *n.*

spin (spĭn) *v.* (**spun** pr. spŭn or archaic **span** pr. spăn, **spin·ning**). 1. Draw out and twist (wool, cotton, etc.) into threads, make (yarn) thus; be engaged in, follow, this occupation; (of insects) make (web, cocoon, etc.) by extrusion of fine viscous thread; (fig.) produce, compose (story etc.); ~ **out,** spend, consume (time etc.); prolong, extend. 2. Revolve; (of top etc.) whirl around; (of person or thing) turn *around* quickly, e.g. as result of being struck; (of person's head etc.) be in whirl through dizziness or astonishment; (aviation) make diving descent with continued rotation of aircraft; cause (minnow etc.) to revolve in water as bait for trout etc., fish thus. 3. ~ **off,** produce incidentally, esp. as benefit from industrial or technological development (**spin'off** *n.*). **spin** *n.* Spinning motion, esp. in rifle bullet, in tennis ball, etc., struck aslant, or in airplane in diving descent; brisk or short run, short excursion by automobile etc.; (phys.) intrinsic angular momentum of elementary particle. **spin'ner** *n.* **spin'ning** *n.* & *adj.*

spin·ach (spĭn'ĭch) *n.* Plant (*Spinacia oleracea*) with succulent leaves used as vegetable.

spi·nal (spī'nal) *adj.* Of the spine; ~ **anesthetic,** anesthetic that anesthetizes lower part of body when injected into spinal cord; ~ **canal,** channel formed by arches of vertebrae, containing spinal cord; ~ **column,** spine; ~ **cord,** rope-like mass of nerve cells and nerve fibers enclosed within and protected by spinal column, co-ordinating activities of limbs and trunk and transmitting impulses between the brain and the tissues of the body. **spi'nal·ly** *adv.*

spin·dle (spĭn'del) *n.* 1. Slender rounded rod tapering at both ends, used to twist fibers of wool, flax, etc., into thread in spinning frame; steel rod by which thread is twisted and wound on bobbin; varying measure of length for yarn. 2. Pin, axis, that revolves or on which something revolves. 3. Anything spindle-shaped, esp. (biol.) spindle-shaped system of fibers formed during cell division, to which the chromosomes become attached. 4. **spin'dleshanks** (pl. **-shanks**), (person with) long thin legs; **spindle tree,** ornamental European shrub of genus *Euonymus*, esp. *E. europaeus*, with hard fine-grained yellowish wood formerly much used for spindles. **spin'dling** *adj.* **spin'dly** *adj.* (**-dli·er, -dli·est**). Very thin. **spindle** *v.i.* (**-dled, -dling**). Have, grow into, long slender form.

spine (spīn) *n.* 1. Invertebrates, articulated series of vertebrae extending from skull to the hips (and in some animals continued to form the tail) and forming the supporting axis of the body, backbone. 2. (bot.) Stiff sharp-pointed woody or hardened process, usu. a shoot; (anat.) sharp-pointed slender process of various bones; (zool.) thorn-like process or appendage in certain fishes, insects, etc., prickle of hedgehog, quill of porcupine, etc. 3. Ridge, sharp projection, of rock, ground, etc., resembling backbone. 4. Part of outer cover of book that protects and encloses the back.

spine·less (spīn'lĭs) *adj.* Invertebrate; having no spines; (fig.) limp, weak. **spine'less·ness** *n.*

spin·et (spĭn'ĭt, spĭnĕt') *n.* 1. (hist.) Small keyboard instrument (17th–18th c.) of harpsichord type but smaller, and with only one string to a note. 2. (also ~ **piano**): see PIANO. [prob. f. name of Giovanni *Spinetti* of Venice (*c*1550)]

spin·na·ker (spĭn'*a*k*er*) *n.* Large three-cornered sail carried on mainmast opposite mainsail of racing yacht running before wind. [fanciful formation f. *Sphinx*, name of yacht first using it]

spin·ner (spĭn'*er*) *n.* (esp.) Spinning machine; manufacturer engaged in (esp. cotton) spinning; kind of (artificial) trout fly, spinning bait.

spin·ner·et (spĭn'*e*rĕt) *n.* 1. (zool.) Organ or process, esp. nipple-like process on spider's abdomen, tubule on lower lip of silkworm, for producing silk, gossamer, etc. 2. Contrivance of glass or metal with fine holes through which viscous solution is forced, to form filaments or threads of synthetic fiber.

spin·ning (spĭn'ĭng) *n.* (esp.) ~ **jenny**, early spinning machine with several spindles; ~ **wheel**, simple spinning apparatus in which spindle is driven by wheel worked by hand or foot.

spi·nose (spī'nōs, spīnōs'), **spi·nous** (spī'n*u*s) *adjs.* Armed or furnished with spines; slender and sharp-pointed like a spine.

Spi·no·za (spĭnō'z*a*), **Baruch** (1632–77). (also known as Benedict de Spinoza) Dutch philosopher; exponent of pantheism; rejected Cartesian dualism and held God to be the immanent cause of the universe with an infinite number of attributes, of which only two, thought and extension, are known to man, all individual things being modes of these. **Spi·no'zism, Spi·no'zist** *ns.*

spin·ster (spĭn'st*er*) *n.* Unmarried woman, usu. elderly. **spin'ster·hood** *n.*

spi·nule (spī'nūl, spĭn'ūl) *n.* (bot., zool.) Small spine. **spin·u·lose** (spĭn'y*u*lōs, spī'ny*u*-) *adj.*

spin·y (spī'nē) *adj.* (**spin·i·er, spin·i·est**). Full of spines, prickly; (fig.) perplexing, troublesome, thorny; ~ **lobster**, any of several edible marine crustaceans (family Palinuridae), similar to true lobster but having spiny shell and lacking large pincers.

spi·ra·cle (spīr'*a*k*e*l, spĭr'*a*-) *n.* (zool.) Orifice or pore that can be opened or closed for respiration in insects etc.; reduced first gill slit in fishes, blowhole of cetacean.

spi·rae·a: SPIREA.

spi·ral (spīr'*a*l) *adj.* Coiled in cylindrical or conical manner; curving continuously around fixed point in same plane at a steadily increasing (or diminishing) distance from it. **spi'ral·ly** *adv.* **spiral** *n.* Anything of spiral form; (geom. etc.) continuous curve traced by point moving around fixed point

In a sailing race, nothing is more impressive than when a yacht turns down-wind and a huge and often vivid ***spinnaker*** *is raised to catch every breath of wind.*

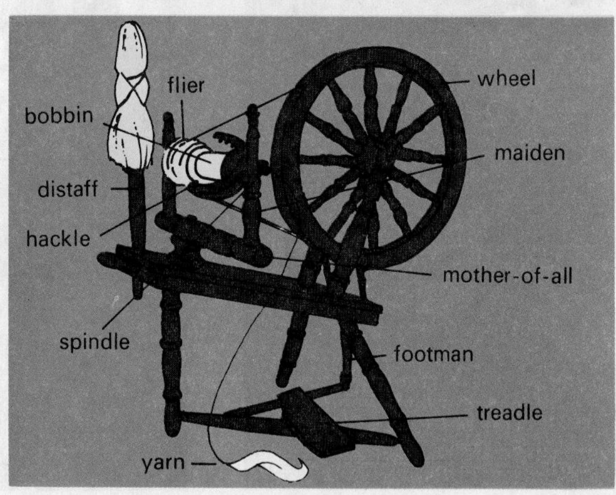

Devices for ***spinning*** *fibers into threads have been discovered in sites dated as early as 6500 B.C. The distaff and spindle were replaced by a hand-turned spinning-wheel in A.D. 1300.*

in same plane at steadily increasing or diminishing distance; curve traced by point simultaneously moving around and advancing along cylinder or cone; spiral nebula; flight in spiral path; progressive but gradual rise or fall of two or more interdependent quantities alternately, as of wages or prices. ~ *v.i.* (**-raled, -ral·ing**; Brit. **-ralled, -ral·ling**). Wind or move in spiral path, (of aircraft, pilot) descend (or ascend) in spiral path.

spi·rant (spīr′ant) *adj.* & *n.* (phonet.) Fricative.

spire[1] (spīr) *n.* Tapering structure in form of tall cone or pyramid rising above tower, esp. of church; tapering or pointed top of anything. **spir′y** *adj.*

spire[2] (spīr) *n.* Spiral, coil; single fold or convolution of this.

spi·re·a, spi·rae·a (spīrē′a) *ns.* Rosaceous plant or shrub of genus *S*~, with simple leaves and small pink or white flowers in panicles, racemes, or corymbs.

spir·it (spĭr′ĭt) *n.* 1. Animating or vital principle, intelligent or immaterial part of man, soul; person viewed as possessing this, esp. with ref. to particular mental or moral qualities; **the S~, the Holy ~** = HOLY GHOST. 2. Rational or intelligent being not connected with material body; disembodied soul; incorporeal being, ghost, elf, fairy. 3. Person's mental or moral nature or qualities; essential character or qualities, prevailing tone, general meaning, *of* something; mental or moral condition or attribute, mood; mettle, vigor, courage, energy, dash. 4. (chiefly Brit.) Strong alcoholic liquor got by distillation (usu. pl.); distilled extract, alcoholic solution *of* some substance; ~ **gum**, quick-drying gum used in fastening false hair, beard, etc., to actor's skin; ~ **level**, instrument for determining a true horizontal or vertical line or surface, usu. by centering an air bubble in a hermetically sealed glass tube filled with spirit. **spirit** *v.t.* Convey (*away, off*, etc.) rapidly and secretly (as) by agency of spirits.

spir·it·ed (spĭr′ĭtĭd) *adj.* 1. Full of spirit; animated, lively, brisk; courageous. 2. Having specified spirit(s). **spir′it·ed·ly** *adv.* **spir′it·ed·ness** *n.*

spir·it·ism (spĭr′ĭtĭzem) = SPIRITUALISM.

spir·it·less (spĭr′ĭtlĭs) *adj.* Wanting in ardor, animation, or courage. **spir′it·less·ly** *adv.* **spir′it·less·ness** *n.*

spir·it·u·al (spĭr′ĭchōōal) *adj.* Of spirit as opp. to matter; of the soul esp. as acted upon by God; of, proceeding from, God, holy, divine, inspired; concerned with sacred or religious things; ecclesiastical. **spir′it·u·al·ly** *adv.* **spir′it·u·al·ness** *n.* **spiritual** *n.* Religious song originating among or characteristic of blacks in southern U.S.

spir·it·u·al·ism (spĭr′ĭchōōalĭzem) *n.* Belief that spirits of dead can communicate with the living, esp. through a medium; system of doctrines or practices founded on this. **spir′it·u·al·ist** *n.* **spir·it·u·al·is·tic** (spĭrĭchōōalĭs′tĭk) *adj.* **spir·it·u·al·is′ti·cal·ly** *adv.*

spir·it·u·al·i·ty (spĭrĭchōōăl′ĭtē) *n.* (pl. **-ties**). 1. Spiritual quality. 2. (usu. pl.) What belongs or is due to church or to an ecclesiastic as such.

spir·it·u·al·ize (spĭr′ĭchōōalīz) *v.t.* (**-ized, -iz·ing**). Make spiritual.

spir·it·u·ous (spĭr′ĭchōōus) *adj.* Containing much alcohol; ~ **liquor**, one produced by distilla-

*A stem of **spiraea** in full blossom. The profuse blossoms, which range from white to deep red, are a desired feature of plants in this genus. Some may attain a height of ten feet.*

*Below: The **spire** of Chichester Cathedral and (top right) one at Stockbury in Kent, U.K. Below right: Several variations which show how this architectural device has been applied at different times.*

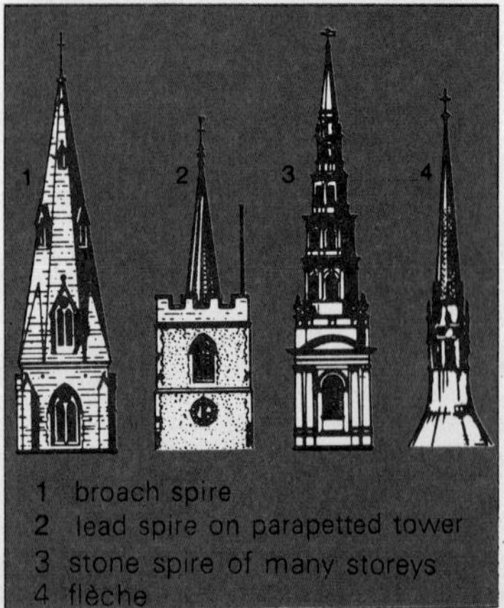

tion, not by fermentation alone.

spi·ro·chete, spi·ro·chaete (spīr′okēt) *ns.* Any of various slender flexible microorganisms with spiral bodies, many of which cause diseases (esp. syphilis and yaws) in man.

spit[1] (spĭt) *n.* 1. Slender pointed rod thrust into meat for roasting at fire. 2. Small low point of land running into water. ~ *v.t.* (**spit·ted, spit·ting**). Pierce, transfix, (as) with spit.

spit[2] (spĭt) *v.* (**spit** or **spat** pr. spăt, **spit·ting**). Eject saliva; eject (saliva, food, etc., *out*) from mouth; (fig.) utter vehemently; (of cat etc.) make noise as of spitting as sign of anger or hostility; (of rain etc.) fall thinly; (of frying pan etc.) sputter; ~ **and image** (also **spitting image**), exact counterpart of, likeness of; **spit and polish**, neat and cleanness, as for military inspections; **spit′ball**, ball of chewed paper as missile; baseball moistened by pitcher to impart spin; **spit′fire**, fiery-tempered person, esp. woman. **spit** *n.* Spittle; act, instance, of spitting.

spite (spīt) *n.* Ill will, malice; **in ~ of**, notwithstanding. **spite′ful** *adj.* **spite′ful·ly** *adv.* **spite′ful·ness** *n.* **spite** *v.t.* (**spit·ed, spit·ing**). Thwart, mortify, annoy.

Spits·ber·gen (spĭts′bĕrgen). Archipelago in the Arctic Ocean, N. of Norway, under Norwegian sovereignty.

spit·tle (spĭt′el) *n.* Saliva, spit.

spit·toon (spĭtōōn′) *n.* Receptacle for spittle.

splash (splăsh) *v.* Bespatter (*with* water etc.); dash, spatter (liquid); (of liquid) fly about in drops or scattered portions; cause liquid to do this; step, fall, etc., *into* (water etc.) so as to cause it to splash; mark, mottle, with irregular patches of color etc. **splash′down**, landing of spacecraft in sea. **splash′y** *adj.* (**splash·i·er, splash·i·est**). **splash** *n.* Act, result, or sound of splashing; quantity of fluid splashed; large irregular patch of color etc.; (colloq.) striking or ostentatious display or effect. **splash′er** *n.* **splash′i·ly** *adv.* **splash′i·ness** *n.*

splat·ter (splăt′er) *v.* & *n.* Splash, esp. with continuous and noisy action.

splay (splā) *n.* (archit.) Slope or bevel; embrasure. ~ *adj.* Wide and flat, spread or turned out; **splay′foot** (pl. **-feet**), (having) broad, flat clumsy foot turned outward. **splay** *v.* Bevel; construct (aperture) with divergent sides, be so constructed; spread out (limbs etc.) awkwardly.

spleen (splēn) *n.* Dark red abdominal organ (in mammals situated beneath diaphragm on left side) that is concerned in the formation of antibodies and the destruction of red blood cells; this as the supposed seat of the passions; moroseness, irritability, spite; **spleen′wort**, fern of genus *Asplenium*. **spleen′ful, splen·ic** (splē′nĭk) *adjs.* **spleen′ful·ly** *adv.*

*Those ferns given the common name **spleenwort** are found in many parts of the world, but those in Europe were said to possess medicinal properties, beneficial to the spleen; hence the name.*

splen·dent (splĕn′dent) *adj.* Shining, bright, brilliant.

splen·did (splĕn′dĭd) *adj.* Magnificent, grand, sumptuous, brilliant, gorgeous; excellent, very good or fine. **splen′did·ly** *adv.*

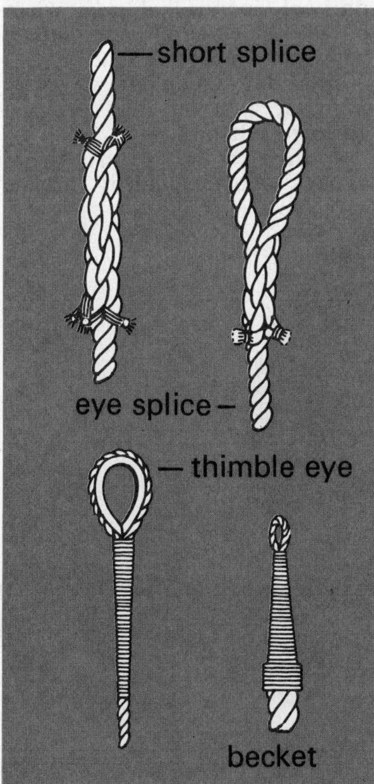

*The use of a **splice** is to join two rope ends so that there is no great increase in size, or reduction in strength. It is particularly necessary where a rope has to pass over a pulley.*

splen·dif·er·ous (splĕndĭf′erus) *adj.* (colloq.) Magnificent, splendid.

splen·dor (splĕn′der) *n.* Great brightness; magnificence; parade, pomp, brilliance. **splen′dor·ous** *adj.*

sple·net·ic (splĭnĕt′ĭk), **sple·net·i·cal** (splĭnĕt′ĭkal) *adjs.* Ill-tempered, peevish; of the spleen. **sple·net′i·cal·ly** *adv.* **splenetic** *n.* Splenetic person.

splice (splīs) *n.* Joining of two ends of rope etc. by untwisting and interweaving strands at point of junction; overlapping join of two pieces of wood etc. ~ *v.t.* (**spliced, splic·ing**). Join by splice; (colloq.) join in marriage. **splic′er** *n.*

spline (splīn) *n.* Thin strip of material inserted in grooves to join two boards etc.; one of a series of ridges on a shaft fitting into grooves of a hub to transmit torque. ~ *v.* Join by spline.

splint (splĭnt) *n.* Appliance to keep in position or protect injured part, esp. strip of more or less rigid material for holding fractured bone in position. ~ *v.t.* Put into splints, secure with splint(s).

splin·ter (splĭn′ter) *n.* Rough, sharp-edged, or thin piece of wood, bone, stone, etc., broken or split off; ~ **group, party**, (pol.) party (esp. one that is very small in numbers) that has broken away from a larger one. **splin′ter·y** *adj.* Like splinter(s); apt to splinter. **splinter** *v.* Split into splinters.

split (splĭt) *v.* (**split, split·ting**). Break forcibly, be broken, into parts, esp. with the grain or plane of cleavage; divide into parts, thicknesses, shares, etc.; divide into factions, groups, etc; ~ **hairs**, draw very subtle distinctions; ~ **the difference**, take average of two proposed amounts. **split** *adj.* (esp.) ~ **infinitive**, infinitive with adverb etc. inserted between *to* and verb, e.g. *seems to partly correspond*; **~-level**, (of building) having some room(s) part of a story higher than the adjacent part; ~ **personality**, alteration or dissociation of personality such as may occur in certain mental illnesses, esp. schizophrenia and hysteria; ~ **second**, very brief moment of time. **split** *n.* Act, result, of splitting; cleft; rupture; anything formed by splitting, as single thickness of split hide; half-bottle of mineral water; (pl.) in acrobatic dancing etc., movement in which body is lowered to floor between legs widely separated at right angles to trunk.

splotch (splŏch) *n.* Large irregular spot or patch; blot, smear. **splotch'y** *adj.* (**splotch·i·er, splotch·i·est**). **splotch** *v.t.* Cover or splash with splotches.

splurge (splẽrj) *n.* & *v.i.* (**splurged, splurg·ing**). (Make) lavish or showy expenditure. ~ *v.t.* Spend (money) lavishly.

splut·ter (splŭt'*er*) *v.* Utter, talk, hastily and indistinctly or confusedly; scatter or fly in small splashes or pieces; make sputtering sound. ~ *n.* Spluttering (noise); fuss.

Spode (spōd), **Josiah** (1754–1827). English china manufacturer; hence, china made by him.

spoil (spoil) *v.* (**spoiled** or **spoilt, spoil·ing**). 1. (archaic) Plunder, deprive (*of* thing) by force or stealth. 2. Destroy or impair good, valuable, or effective qualities of; prevent full exercise or enjoyment of; **spoil'sport**, one who spoils sport or enjoyment of others. 3. Injure character of (person) by overindulgence. 4. Deteriorate, decay, go bad. **spoil** *n.* (usu. pl. or collect. sing.) Plunder, booty, taken from enemy in war or acquired by violence; (pl.) public offices etc. distributed among supporters of successful political party; **~s system**, practice of such distribution. **spoil'age, spoil'er** *ns.*

spoke[1] (spōk) *n.* Each of set of bars or rods radiating from hub to rim of wheel; each radial handle of steering wheel; rung of ladder; **spoke'shave**, tool with blade or plane bit between two handles used for planing curved surface, shaping spokes, etc. **spoke** *v.t.* (**spoked, spok·ing**). Furnish with spokes.

spoke[2] (spōk), **spo·ken**

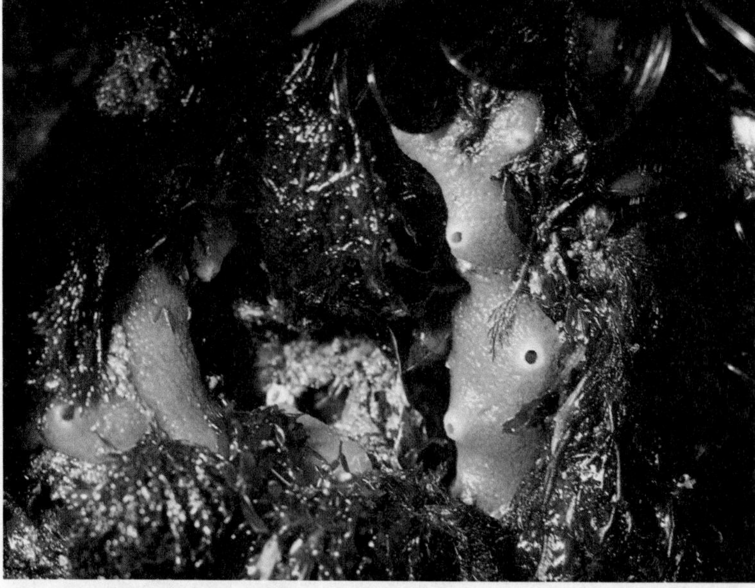

The 'crumb of bread' ***sponge,*** *commonly found as an encrustation on rocks between high and low tide levels, is small compared with others of the 2500 species.*

(spō'ken): see SPEAK.

spokes·man (spōks'm*a*n), fem. **spokes·wom·an** (spōks'wŏŏm*a*n) *ns.* (pl. **-men** pr. -m*e*n; fem. **-wom·en** pr. -wĭmĭn). One who speaks for others, representative.

spo·li·a·tion (spōlēā'sh*o*n) *n.* 1. Despoiling, plundering, pillaging. 2. (law) Destruction of, tampering with, document to destroy its value as evidence.

spon·da·ic (spŏndā'ĭk), **spon·da·i·cal** (spŏndā'ĭk*a*l) *adjs.* Composed of spondees; (of hexameter) with spondee as fifth foot.

spon·dee (spŏn'dē) *n.* (pros.) Metrical foot of two long or accented syllables, — —.

sponge (spŭnj) *n.* 1. Any of various aquatic (chiefly marine) animals of the group Porifera, with tough elastic skeleton of interlacing fibers. 2. Soft, light, porous, easily compressible, highly absorbent framework remaining after living matter has been removed from various members of this group, used in bathing, cleansing surfaces, etc.; porous rubber etc. used similarly. 3. Thing of spongelike absorbency or consistence; gauze pad to absorb fluid in surgery; soft porous leavened dough in baking. 4. Immoderate drinker, soaker; person who contrives to live at others' expense. 5. Sponging; bath, swill, with sponge. 6. ~ **cake**, very light sweet cake of flour, beaten eggs, and sugar; ~ **cloth**, loose-textured cotton fabric with wrinkled surface; ~ **rubber**, rubber made porous like a sponge. **sponge** *v.* (**sponged, spong·ing**). 1. Wipe, cleanse, with sponge, wet *with* liquid applied with sponge; wipe out, efface, (as) with sponge; absorb, take *up* (liquid) with sponge. 2. Live on others as parasite, be meanly dependent *on* (esp. ~ **on** person *for* money etc.).

spong·er (spŭn'j*er*) *n.* (esp.) One who sponges for money etc.

spon·gy (spŭn'jē) *adj.* (**-gi·er, -gi·est**). Spongelike; esp. porous, compressible, absorbent, or soft, as sponge.

spon·son (spŏn's*o*n) *n.* Projection from ship's side, as gun platform; buoyant projection from side of canoe, seaplane, etc.

spon·sor (spŏn's*er*) *n.* Person making himself responsible for another; person who presents

Josiah Spode *introduced bone into the manufacture of porcelain and this gave it added transparency and beauty. The cup and saucer (left) were made by his firm about 1815.*

candidate for baptism and makes promises on behalf of infant being baptized, godparent; supporter; advertiser paying cost of broadcast program into which advertisements of his wares are introduced; person subscribing to charity. **spon·so·ri·al** (spŏnsōr′ēal, -sōr′-) *adj.* **spon′sor·ship** *n.* **sponsor** *v.t.* Act as sponsor for; support, advocate.

spon·ta·ne·ous (spŏntā′nēus) *adj.* Acting, done, occurring, without external cause; voluntary; (of movements etc.) involuntary, not due to conscious volition; ~ **combustion**, ignition of mass of material (e.g. straw) from heat generated within itself; ~ **generation**, abiogenesis, development of living organisms from nonliving matter. **spon·ta′ne·ous·ly** *adv.* **spon·ta′ne·ous·ness** *n.* **spon·ta·ne·i·ty** (spŏntanē′ĭtē, -nā′-) *n.* (pl. **-ties**).

spoof (spōōf) *n.* & *v.t.* Swindle, hoax, parody.

spook (spōōk) *n.* (colloq.) Ghost. **spook′y** *adj.* (**spook·i·er, spook·i·est**).

spool (spōōl) *n.* Reel for winding thread, wire, photographic film, fishing line, etc., on. ~ *v.t.* Wind on spool.

spoon (spōōn) *n.* Utensil consisting of round or usu. oval bowl and a handle, used for conveying soft or liquid food to mouth, in cooking, etc.; spoon-shaped thing, esp. wooden golf club with slightly concave face; kind of artificial bait used in spinning for fish; **spoon′bill**, any of various wading birds, esp. roseate spoonbill (*Ajaja ajaja*), related to ibises, with long bill expanded and flattened at tip; **spoon′bread**, kind of bread, usu. of corn meal, so soft that it must be served with spoon; **spoon′fed**, fed with spoon like child; (fig.) pampered, coddled. **spoon** *v.* 1. Take, lift, etc., with spoon. 2. Behave amorously, make love, esp. in sentimental fashion. **spoon′ful** *n.* (pl. **-fuls**).

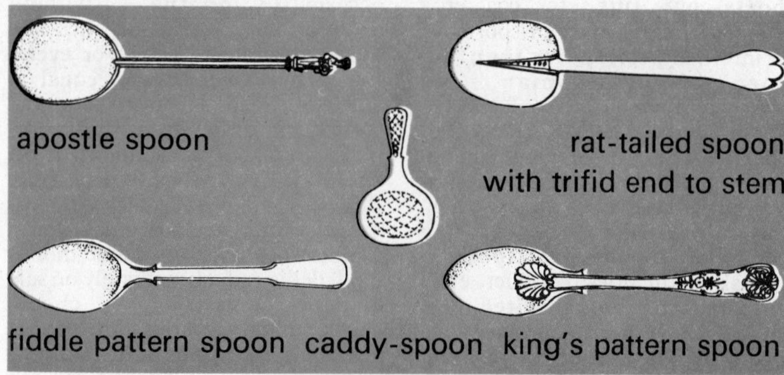

*The use of a **spoon** for eating and other purposes can be traced to the ancient world. However, silver spoons in England became a social symbol and were made for special presents.*

spoon·er·ism (spōō′nerĭzem) *n.* Accidental transposition of initial or other sounds of two or more words (e.g. *kingquering congs*, for *conquering kings*). [Rev. W. A. *Spooner* (1844–1930), Warden of New College, Oxford]

spoor (spoor, spōr, spōr) *n.* Track, trail, of animal or person. ~ *v.t.* Trace by spoor.

spo·rad·ic (sporăd′ĭk) *adj.* Occurring in isolated instances or very small numbers; scattered, dispersed; occasional. **spo·rad′i·cal·ly** *adv.* **spo·rad′i·cal·ness** *n.*

spo·ran·gi·um (sporăn′jēum) *n.* (pl. **-gi·a** pr. -jēa). (bot.) Receptacle containing spores.

spore (spōr, spōr) *n.* Minute reproductive body produced by plants and some protozoa and capable of development into new individuals independently; ~ **case**, sporangium.

sport (spōrt, spōrt) *n.* 1. Amusement, diversion, fun; jest, mockery (as in *make* ~ *of*); plaything, toy; pastime(s), game(s), esp. of athletic or open-air character; pastime afforded by taking or killing wild animals, game, or fish; (pl.) (meeting for competition in) athletic pastimes. 2. Animal, plant, etc., exhibiting abnormal variation from parent stock or type. 3. (slang) Good fellow; playboy; sportsman. 4. ~**s car, model**, etc., car of open low-built fast type; **sports′cast**, radio or television broadcast of sports news. **sports′caster** *n.*;

*Related to the ibis, the **spoonbill** inhabits marshes and estuaries where it feeds on small aquatic fauna. The roseate variety is from America while others are found in the tropics.*

sports-coat, suit, etc., coat etc. suitable for some outdoor sports or for informal wear; **sports'man** (pl. **-men**), **sports'woman** (pl. **-women**), person fond of sports, esp. hunting, shooting, etc.; good fellow; one displaying good qualities of sportsman, esp. desire for fair play, in ordinary life; **sports'manlike**, benefitting, worthy of, a sportsman: **sports'-manship**, qualities, conduct, etc., of sportsman; **sports'writer**, one who writes (esp. as journalist) on sports. **sport** *v.* 1. Divert oneself; take part in pastime. 2. (bot. etc.) Become, produce, a sport. 3. Wear, exhibit, produce, esp. ostentatiously.

sport·ing (spōr'tĭng, spŏr'-) *adj.* Interested in sport; sportsmanlike; ~ **chance**, one involving risk but offering possibility of success. **sport'ing·ly** *adv.*

spor·tive (spōr'tĭv, spŏr'-) *adj.* Playful. **spor'tive·ly** *adv.* **spor'tive·ness** *n.*

sport·y (spōr'tē, spŏr'-) *adj.* (**sport·i·er, sport·i·est**). (slang) Sporting; characteristic of a sport, showy.

spor·ule (spŏr'ūl, spăr'-) *n.* (Small) spore. **spor·u·lar** (spŏr'-yul*er*, spăr'-) *adj.*

spot (spŏt) *n.* 1. Speck, stain, small discoloring or disfiguring mark; eruptive mark on skin, pimple; dark mark on sun etc.; small, usu. roundish mark on surface; moral blemish, stain; (billiards) marked place on table, esp. that on which red ball is placed; **hit the** ~, (colloq.) satisfy a desire or need; **in a** ~ (slang) in difficulties, in an awkward situation; **in** ~**s**, now and then, off and on, occasionally; **on the** ~, without delay or change of place, then and there, at scene of action or event; (of person) wide awake, equal to situation, in good form at game etc.; (colloq.) in difficult position, compelled to take some action; **put on the** ~, place in position of great difficulty, danger; mark for assassination. 2. Particular place, definite locality. 3. ~ **cash**, money paid, delivered, immediately on sale or other transaction; ~ **check**, check made at random; **spot-check**, (*v.t.*); **spot'light**, (lamp or projector throwing) concentrated beam of light on one spot, esp. of stage (freq. fig.); (*v.t.*) illuminate (as) with spotlight, throw into relief, concentrate attention etc. on. **spot'ty** (**-ti·er, -ti·est**), **spot'less** *adjs.* **spot'less·ly** *adv.* **spot'ti·ness, spot'less·ness** *ns.* **spot** *v.* (**spot·ted, spot·ting**). 1. Mark, stain, soil, with spots; (of textile etc.) be (liable to be) marked with spots. 2. (colloq.) Single out, detect, mark out, note; esp. single out (winner in race etc.) beforehand. 3. Act as spotter.

spot·ted (spŏt'ĭd) *adj.* (esp.) Marked with spots (freq. in names of animals etc.); **Rocky Mountain** ~ **fever**: see RICKETTSIA.

spot·ter (spŏt'*er*) *n.* (esp.) Watcher on roof, observer in aircraft, etc., noting approach or position of enemy forces, effect of gunfire or bombing, etc.

spous·al (spow'z*a*l) *n.* (usu. pl.) Nuptials, wedding.

spouse (spows, spowz) *n.* Husband or wife.

spout (spowt) *n.* Projecting tube, pipe, or lip, through which rain water is carried off from roof, liquid is poured from teapot, kettle, etc., or issues from fountain, pump, etc.; jet, column, of liquid, etc.; whale's spiracle; sloping trough down which thing may be shot into receptacle. ~ *v.* Discharge, issue, forcibly in a jet; utter in declamatory manner, speechify.

S.P.Q.R., SPQR *abbrevs.* *Senatus Populusque Romanus* (L., = the senate and people of Rome).

sprain (sprān) *v.t.* Wrench (joint of body, esp. ankle or wrist) violently so as to cause pain and swelling. ~ *n.* Act, result, of spraining.

sprang: see SPRING.

sprat (sprăt) *n.* Small European herring (*clupea sprattus*), common on Atlantic coasts; any similar fish.

sprawl (sprawl) *v.* Spread oneself, spread (limbs), out in careless or ungainly way; straggle. ~ *n.* Sprawling movement or attitude; straggling group or mass. **sprawl'er** *n.*

spray[1] (sprā) *n.* Slender shoot or twig, graceful branch with flowers etc., esp. used for decoration or ornament.

spray[2] (sprā) *n.* Water or other liquid dispersed in small mistlike drops by wind, waves, atomizer, etc.; preparation intended for spraying; instrument or apparatus for applying spray. ~ *v.* Scatter, diffuse, as spray; sprinkle (as) with spray.

spread (sprĕd) *v.* (**spread, spread·ing**). Extend surface of, stretch out, cause to cover larger surface, by unrolling, unfolding, smearing, flattening out, etc.; cover surface of; show extended or extensive surface; diffuse, be diffused; prepare (table) for eating. ~ *adj.* (esp.) ~ **eagle**, representation of eagle with legs and wings extended; something resembling this; ~**-eagle** (*v.t.*) (**-gled, -gling**), extend, fix, in form of spread eagle; (attrib., in allusion to figure of spread eagle on U.S. emblems etc.) bombastic, noisily patriotic, jingoistic. **spread** *n.* Spreading; being spread; extent or expanse, breadth, compass, span; cloth cover for bed or table; (colloq.) feast, meal; food to be spread on bread or crackers; printed matter spread across two facing pages or across more than one column. **spread'a·ble** *adj.* **spread'er** *n.*

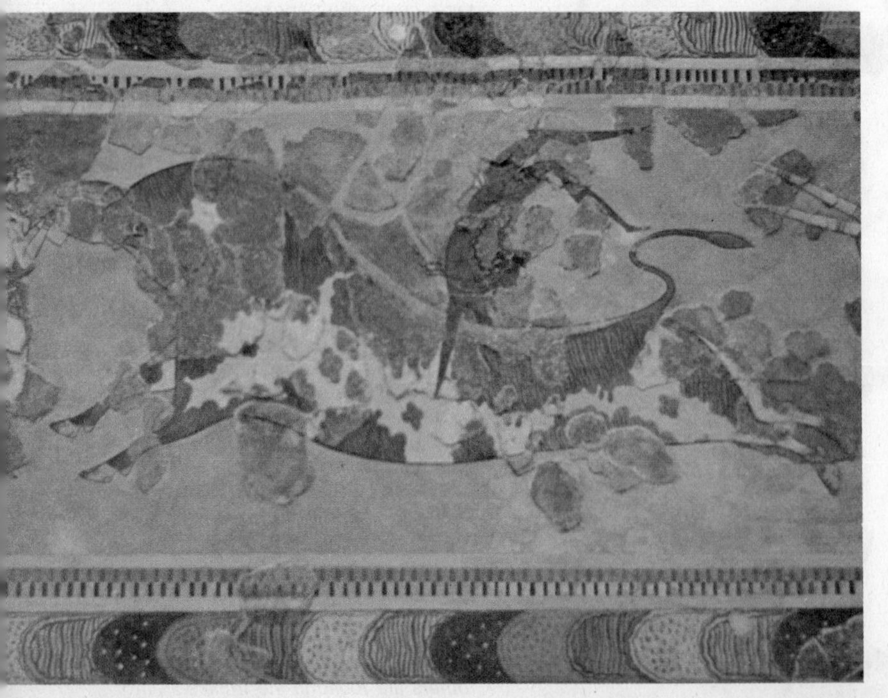

*Facing: Children specially garbed for the **Spring** Festival in Japan. Throughout the world, spring has epitomized the reawakening of life and has been a time for celebration in many ways.*

*During the bull games in Minoan Crete, as shown in this fresco from the Palace at Knossos, both boys and girls would grasp the bull's horns as it charged and **spring** into the air to complete a somersault before landing.*

spree (sprē) *n.* Lively frolic, bout of drinking, etc.

sprig (sprĭg) *n.* 1. Small branch, spray; ornament in form of sprig or spray. 2. (usu. contempt.) Youth, young man. ~ *v.t.* (**sprigged, sprig·ging**). Ornament with sprigs.

spright·ly (sprīt′lē) *adj.* Vivacious, lively, gay. **spright′li·ness** *n.*

spring (sprĭng) *v.* (**sprang** pr. sprăng or **sprung** pr. sprŭng, **sprung, spring·ing**). 1. Leap, jump, move rapidly or suddenly, esp. from constrained position or by action of a spring; arise, take rise; originate; (of wood) warp, split, crack. 2. Rouse (game) from earth or cover; cause to spring, move suddenly, etc.; cause to work by a spring; produce, develop, suddenly or unexpectedly; explode (mine etc.); develop (leak); (slang) contrive the escape of (person from confinement etc.). ~ *n.* 1. Leap; power of springing, elasticity, springiness; place from which vault or arch springs or rises. 2. Elastic contrivance possessing property of returning to normal shape after being compressed, bent, coiled, etc., used for lessening or preventing concussion, as motivating power in clockwork etc.; moving or actuating agency, motive; source, origin. 3. Place where water wells up from underground rocks; flow of water etc. rising from earth. 4. Season between winter and summer, season in which vegetation begins, popularly reckoned in N. hemisphere as comprising March, April, and May, but astronomically as lasting from vernal equinox (March 20 or 21) to summer solstice (June 21 or 22). 5. ~ **balance**, balance measuring weight by elasticity of steel spring; ~ **beauty**, any of a genus (*Claytonia*) of small plants, esp. *C. virginica* of eastern N. Amer. having white or pink flowers; **spring′board**, flexible board, esp. stout projecting board from end of which person jumps or dives; **spring fever**, feeling of laziness affecting many people during first warm days of spring; **spring lock**, lock with bolt closing by means of spring; **spring peeper**: see PEEPER[1]; **spring′tail**, wingless insect of the order Collembola, leaping by means of long elastic caudal appendages; **spring tide**, highest tide, occurring on days shortly after new and full moon; **spring′tide, spring′time**, season of spring; **spring water**, water from spring. **spring′less, spring′like** *adjs.* **spring′y** *adj.* (**spring·i·er, spring·i·est**). **spring′i·ness** *n.*

spring·bok (sprĭng′bŏk) *n.* (pl. **-boks**, collect. **-bok**). S. African species of gazelle (*Antidorcas marsupialis*), springing lightly and suddenly in air when disturbed. [S. Afr. Du., f. *springen* spring, *bok* antelope]

spring·er (sprĭng′*er*) *n.* (esp.) 1. (archit.) Support from which arch springs. 2. ~ (**spaniel**), medium-sized hunting dog with black and white or brown and white silky coat.

Spring·field (sprĭng′fēld). Capital of Illinois, in the central part; home and burial place of Abraham Lincoln.

sprin·kle (sprĭng′k*e*l) *v.* (**-kled, -kling**). Scatter in small drops or particles; subject to sprinkling (*with* liquid etc.); (of liquid etc.) fall thus on. **sprin′kler** *n.* Contrivance for sprinkling (water on soil etc.); ~ **system** (system of sprinkling devices for fire protection, actuated by heat on the sprinkler head). **sprinkle** *n.* Slight shower (*of* rain etc.). **sprin′kling** *n.*

sprint (sprĭnt) *v.i.* Run etc. at top speed, esp. for short distance. ~ *n.* Short spell of sprinting; short race run at full speed over whole distance. **sprint′er** *n.*

sprit (sprĭt) *n.* 1. Small spar reaching diagonally from mast to upper outer corner of sail; **sprit·sail** (sprĭt′sāl; *naut.* sprĭt′s*a*l). 1. Sail extended by sprit. 2. = BOWSPRIT.

sprite (sprīt) *n.* Elf, fairy, goblin.

sprock·et (sprŏk′ĭt) *n.* Projection or tooth on rim of wheel engaging with links of chain; ~ **wheel**, wheel with sprockets.

The ***springbok,*** *a white-faced gazelle, was once abundant in South Africa; but excessive hunting and use of land for agriculture has driven the remaining flocks into the Kalahari Desert.*

sprout (sprowt) *v.* Begin to grow, shoot forth, put forth shoots; spring up, grow to a height; produce by sprouting. ~ *n.* Shoot, new growth, from plant; (pl.) young and tender side shoots of plants like cabbage, Brussels sprouts.

spruce[1] (sprōōs) *n.* Any of several coniferous evergreen trees (genus *Picea*), having short needle-like leaves and soft wood; any of various similar evergreen trees, or Douglas fir and wood of these; ~ **beer**, fermented drink made from leaves and small branches of spruce.

spruce[2] (sprōōs) *adj.* (**spruc·er, spruc·est**). Trim, neat, smart in appearance. **spruce′ly** *adv.* **spruce′ness** *n.* **spruce** *v.t.* (**spruced, spruc·ing**). Smarten (*up*), make spruce.

sprue (sprōō) *n.* Tropical disease with chronic diarrhea and ulceration of mouth. [Du. *spr(o)uw* THRUSH[2]]

sprung (sprŭng) *adj.*: see SPRING; (esp.) 1. Furnished with springs. 2. ~ **rhythm**, verse rhythm invented by G. M. HOPKINS[2] in which each foot consists of a stressed first syllable followed by a varying number of unstressed syllables.

spry (sprī) *adj.* (**spri·er, spri·est** or **spry·er, spry·est**). Active, nimble, lively. **spry′ly** *adv.* **spry′ness** *n.*

spud (spŭd) *n.* 1. Small sharp narrow spade, occas. with prongs instead of blade, for digging up big-rooted weeds etc. 2. (colloq.) Potato. ~ *v.t.* (**spud·ded, spud·ding**). Dig (*up, out*) with spud.

spue: SPEW.

spume (spūm) *n.* & *v.i.* (**spumed, spum·ing**). Froth, foam. **spu′mous** *adj.* **spum′y** *adj.* (**spum·i·er, spum·i·est**).

spu·mes·cence (spūmĕs′*e*ns) *n.* Foaminess.

spu·mo·ne (sp*u*mō′nē, -nā), **spu·mo·ni** (sp*u*mō′nē) *ns.* Italian frozen dessert of different kinds of ice cream with bits of candied fruit, nuts, etc.

spun (spŭn) *adj.*: see SPIN; (esp.) that has undergone spinning; (of butter, sugar, etc.) drawn out into threads for ornamenting cakes etc.; ~ **glass**, glass drawn into thread while liquid; ~ **silk**, thread or fabric made from floss or waste silk, freq. mixed with cotton; ~ **sugar**, confection of sugar in a fluffy mass, also called cotton candy.

spunk (spŭngk) *n.* Spirit, mettle, pluck. **spunk′y** *adj.* (**spunk·i·er, spunk·i·est**). **spunk′i·ness** *n.* [orig., "spark"]

spur (spẽr) *n.* 1. Small spike or spiked wheel attached to rider's heel

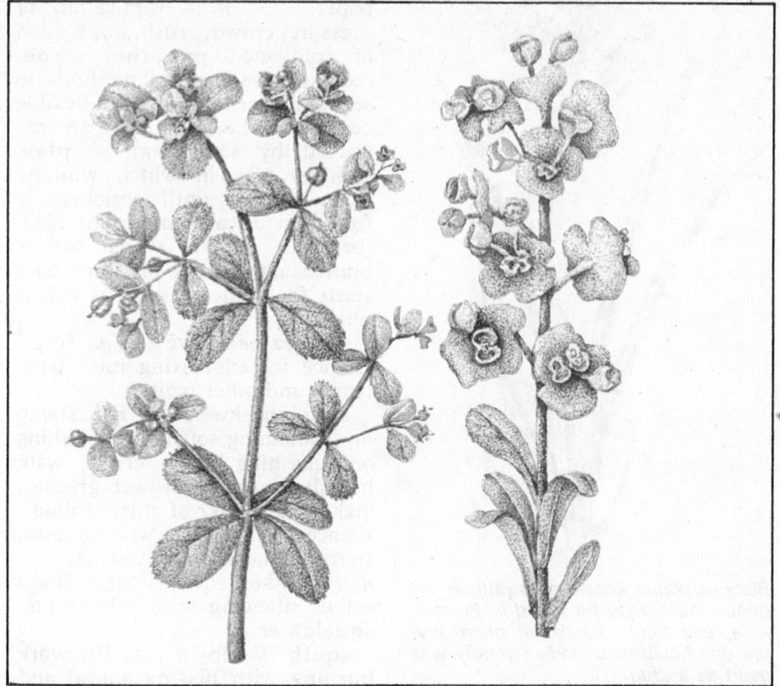

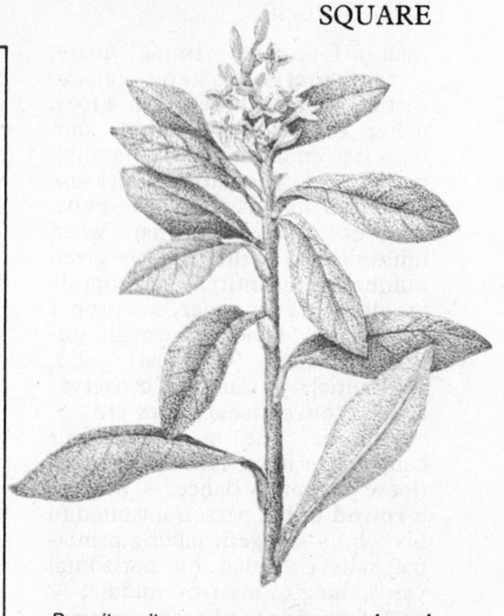

*Despite its name, **spurge laurel** (above) is not a herb but is a variety of Daphne. This plant is native to Britain and Europe but others are found in China.*

*Sun **spurge** (far left) and wood spurge (left) are two English varieties of a widespread group of herbs. Their milky sap has been used for such diverse products as rat poison, and a cosmetic.*

for urging horse etc. forward; (fig.) incentive, stimulus; **on the ~ of the moment**, without premeditation; **win one's ~s**, gain knighthood (hist.); gain distinction, make a name. 2. Spur-shaped thing; hard process or projection on cock's leg, steel point fastened to this in cock-fight; range, ridge, mountain, etc., projecting from main system or mass; short branch or shoot, esp. one bearing fruit; (bot.) tubular projecting part, usu. nectary, of corolla or calyx; short track connecting with main railroad (**spur track**). **spur** *v.* (**spurred, spurring**). Prick (horse) with spurs; incite, urge, prompt; provide with spur(s); ride hard, hasten.

spurge (spẽrj) *n.* Plant of genus *Euphorbia*, with acrid milky juice with medicinal properties; **~ laurel**, shrub of European and Asiatic genus *Daphne*.

spu·ri·ous (spūr′ēus) *adj.* Not genuine or authentic; not what it appears, claims, or pretends to be. **spu′ri·ous·ly** *adv.* **spu′ri·ous·ness** *n.*

spurn (spẽrn) *v.* Repel, thrust back, with foot; reject with disdain, treat with contempt.

spurt[1] (spẽrt) *v.i.* & *n.* (Make) short sudden violent effort, esp. in racing.

spurt[2] (spẽrt) *v.* (Cause to) gush out in a jet or stream. **~** *n.* Sudden gushing out, jet.

sput·nik (spo͝ot′nĭk, spŭt′-) *n.* Russian earth SATELLITE. [Russ., = "traveling companion"]

sput·ter (spŭt′*er*) *v.* Emit with spitting sound; spit, splutter; speak, utter, rapidly or incoherently; speak in rapid or vehement fashion. **~** *n.* Sputtering; sputtering speech. **sput′ter·er** *n.*

spu·tum (spū′*t*um) *n.* (pl. **-ta** pr. -*ta*). Expectorated saliva, spittle; thick expectorated matter, mucus, etc.

spy (spī) *n.* (pl. **spies**). Secret agent, one keeping secret watch on person, place, etc.; person employed by a government, esp. in time of war, to obtain information relating to defenses, military and naval affairs, etc., of other countries. **~** *v.* (**spied, spy·ing**). 1. Act as spy (*on, upon*). 2. Discern, make out, esp. by careful observation; **~ out**, explore secretly, discover thus; **spyglass**, small hand telescope.

sq. *abbrev.* Square; squadron.

squab (skwŏb) *n.* Young, esp. unfledged, pigeon; short fat person; thickly stuffed cushion. **~** *adj.* Short and fat, squat. **squab′by** *adj.* (**-bi·er, -bi·est**).

squab·ble (skwŏb′*el*) *v.i.* (**-bled, -bling**) & *n.* (Engage in) petty or noisy quarrel.

squad (skwŏd) *n.* (mil.) Small number of men grouped or assembled for drill etc.; small party of persons; **~ car**, police car having radio link with headquarters; **flying ~**, detachment of police or other service organized for rapid movement in emergency.

squad·ron (skwŏd′*ron*) *n.* 1. Group of naval vessels usu. of same type, esp. naval unit of two or more divisions. 2. Cavalry unit of two to four troops and certain auxiliary units. 3. (Air Force) Unit of two or more flights, usu. part of an air group; at least six aircraft in formation. 4. Any large organized group.

squal·id (skwŏl′ĭd, skwaw′lĭd) *adj.* Dirty, foul, wretched, mean in appearance. **squal′id·ly** *adv.* **squal′id·ness** *n.*

squall (skwawl) *n.* 1. Sudden violent gust (*of* wind, rain, etc.). 2. Discordant cry, scream. **squall′y** *adj.* (**-li·er, -li·est**). **squall** *v.* Scream loudly or discordantly; utter in harsh or screaming voice.

squal·or (skwŏl′*er*, skwaw′l*er*) *n.* Squalid condition.

squa·ma (skwā′m*a*) *n.* (pl. **-mae** pr. -mē). (zool., anat., bot., etc.) Scale; scalelike portion of bone etc. **squa·mose** (skwā′mōs, skwamōs′), **squa′mous** *adjs.*

squan·der (skwŏn′d*er*) *v.t.* Spend wastefully, dissipate.

square (skwār) *n.* 1. Plane rectilinear rectangular figure with four equal sides; object (approximately) of this shape; quadrilateral area, open space, esp. enclosed by buildings or houses, buildings surrounding this; block (of buildings), area, surrounded by streets; **on the ~**, at right angles; honest, genuine. 2. Instrument for determining, measuring, or setting out angles. 3. Product of number or quantity multiplied by itself. 4. (slang) Person of conservative or conventional tastes etc., one ignorant of or disliking current trends. **square** *adj.* (**squar·er, squar·est**). 1. Of the (approximate) shape of a square; rectangular; angular, not round; approximating to square section or outline, solid, sturdy; of stated length on each of four sides forming square; ~ **foot, meter**, etc. (area equal to that of) square whose side is a foot, meter, etc.; ~ **knot**, double knot with free ends paralleling standing parts; ~ **measure**, measure expressed in such units; ~ **root**, number or quantity that, when multiplied by itself, produces given number or quantity. 2. Properly arranged, in good order, on a proper footing; fair, honest; thorough, uncompromising; (of meal) solid, substantial. 3. (slang) Of conservative or conventional tastes etc. 4. ~ **dance**, one in which four couples face inward from four sides; (loosely) country dance; ~ **peg** (**in a round hole**), person unsuited to his job; ~**-rigged**, having principal sails extended by horizontal yards slung to mast by middle; ~ **sail**, four-sided sail set from yards and slung at right angles to the mast. **square'ly** *adv.* **square'ness** *n.* **squar'ish** *adj.* **square** *adv.* Squarely. ~ *v.* (**squared, squar·ing**). 1. Make square or rectangular; mark (*out*) in squares; multiply (number, quantity) by itself; ~ **the circle**, construct square equal in area to given circle (problem incapable of purely geometrical solution); freq. fig., attempt an impossibility. 2. Adjust, make or be consistent (*with*), reconcile; settle (accounts etc.), also (abs.) ~ **up**; conciliate or satisfy (person) esp. with bribe or compensation. 3. ~ **off**, assume boxing attitude.

squar·rose (skwăr'ōs, skwŏrōs') *adj.* (biol.) Rough with scalelike processes.

squash[1] (skwŏsh) *v.* Crush, squeeze flat or into pulp; be so crushed or squeezed; pack tight, crowd; (fig.) silence (person) with crushing retort. **squash'y** *adj.* (**squash·i·er, squash·i·est**). **squash'i·ness** *n.* **squash** *n.* 1. Squashing; something squashed or crushed; crush, crowd; drink made of juice of crushed fruit, freq. in compounds as **lemon** ~. 2. (also **squash rackets, racquets**): see RACQUET.

squash[2] (skwŏsh) *n.* (Gourd, used as vegetable etc., of) species of *Cucurbita*, genus of trailing herbaceous annual plants. [Amer. Ind. *askútasquash*]

squat (skwŏt) *v.* (**squat·ted, squat·ting**). 1. Sit with knees drawn up and heels close to or touching hams; crouch; put into this position; (colloq.) sit. 2. Settle on or in uncultivated or unoccupied land, building, etc., without legal title or payment of rent. ~ *adj.* In squatting posture; short and thick, dumpy. ~ *n.* Squatting posture. **squat'ness** *n.*

squat·ter (skwŏt'*er*) *n.* Person who settles on land or occupies a building, without right or per-

*Bulbous plants known as **squill,** in the genus Scilla, may be found in Europe, Asia, and South Africa. In pharmacy, the dried bulb of an Indian variety was used as a drug.*

mission.

squaw (skwaw) *n.* (usu. considered offensive) N. Amer. Ind. woman or wife. [Amer. Ind.]

squawk (skwawk) *v.i.* & *n.* (Utter) harsh cry of pain or fear; (make) complaint.

squeak (skwēk) *v.* 1. Emit short, shrill, thin sound; utter in squeaking voice. 2. ~ **by, through,** (colloq.) succeed, win, survive, etc. by slim margin. **squeak** *n.* Short, thin high-pitched sound; **narrow** ~, narrow escape. **squeak'er** *n.* 1. Person, animal, or thing that squeaks. 2. (colloq.) Game won by narrow margin. **squeak'i·ly** *adv.* **squeak'y** *adj.* (**squeak·i·er, squeak·i·est**).

squeal (skwēl) *v.* 1. Utter, emit, more or less prolonged loud shrill noise, esp. of pain or fright; utter with this sound. 2. (slang) Turn informer. ~ *n.* Sharp shrill sound. **squeal'er** *n.*

squeam·ish (skwē'mĭsh) *adj.* Fastidious; easily shocked; of delicate stomach or conscience. **squeam'ish·ly** *adv.* **squeam'ish·ness** *n.*

squee·gee (skwē'jē) *n.* Implement with rubber blade or roller for scraping, cleaning, squeezing away moisture, etc. ~ *v.t.* (**-geed, -gee·ing**). Treat with squeegee.

squeeze (skwēz) *v.* (**squeezed, squeez·ing**). Press, compress hard, esp. so as to crush, drain liquid from, etc.; force by pressure, press out; force one's way; extort money etc. from, bring pressure to bear on, constrain; obtain (money etc.) *from, out of*, by extortion or pressure; take impression of (coin etc.), esp. with sheets of damp paper. ~ *n.* Application of pressure; crowd, crush; impression of coin etc.; **put the ~ on**, (colloq.) use forceful methods to secure payment; ~ **bottle**, flexible container whose contents are extracted by squeezing; ~ **play**, (bridge) play in which winning cards are led until opponent is forced to discard important card; (baseball) play in which ball is bunted and runner on third base starts for home as soon as ball is pitched.

squeez·er (skwē'z*er*) *n.* (esp.) Device for expressing juice from lemon and other fruits.

squelch (skwĕlch) *v.* Fall, stamp on (something soft), with crushing or squashing force; crush; walk heavily in water or wet ground, make sound (as) of this; (colloq.) silence, disconcert, as with sarcasm, stern rebuke, harsh retort, etc. ~ *n.* (Sound of) squelching; (colloq.) act of silencing with rebuke etc. **squelch'er** *n.*

squib (skwĭb) *n.* 1. Firework burning with hissing sound and usu. with small explosion at end. 2. Short satirical composition, lampoon.

squid (skwĭd) *n.* (pl. **squids**, collect. **squid**). Any of various 10-armed cephalopod mollusks, esp. of genus *Loligo* or *Ommastrephes*, some of which are used for food and as fish bait.

squig·gle (skwĭg'*e*l) *n.* Curly mark. ~ *v.* (**-gled, -gling**). **squig'gly** *adj.*

squill (skwĭl) *n.* Any of several bulbous perennial plants (genus *Scilla*), having stiff, narrow leaves and blue, white, or pink bell-shaped drooping flowers.

squint (skwĭnt) *n.* Strabismus, abnormality of the eyes in which the visual axes do not coincide at the objective; stealthy or sidelong glance; (colloq.) glance, look. ~ *adj.* Squinting, looking different ways. ~ *v.* Have the eyes turned in different directions, have strabismus; look obliquely at; give cast to (eye), cause to look as though squinting. **squint'er** *n.* **squint'y** *adj.*

squire (skwīr) *n.* 1. Attendant on knight (hist.); follower; man escorting or attending on lady. 2. Country gentleman, esp. chief landed proprietor in district. ~ *v.t.* Attend upon, escort (woman).

squirm (skwẽrm) *v.i.* Wriggle, writhe (freq. fig.). ~ *n.* Squirming movement. **squirm'er** *n.*

*Species of **squirrel** are found in forests of most parts of the world excepting Australia, New Zealand and New Guinea. They range from the pigmy African variety, less than 3 inches long, to the giants of South-East Asia. Most, are diurnal although the 'flying' varieties are active at night.*

giant squirrel
grey squirrel
fox squirrel
flying squirrel
Arctic ground squirrel
red squirrel
th African
nd squirrel
Prevost's squirrel
chipmunk
thirteen-lined ground squirrel
Asiatic striped squirrel

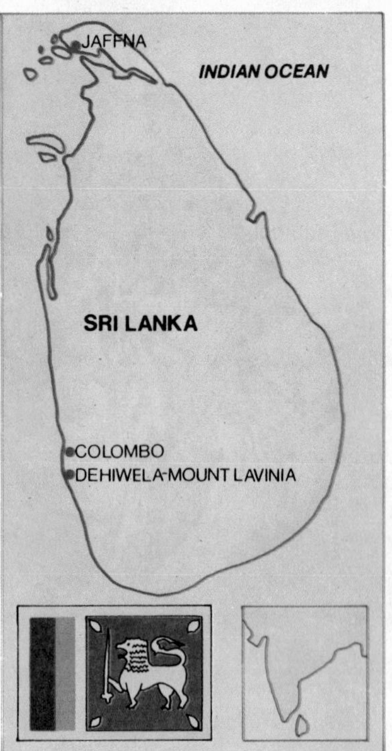

squirm'y *adj.* (**squirm·i·er, squirm·i·est**).

squir·rel (skwẽr'*e*l, skwŭr'-) *n.* (pl. **-rels**, collect. **-rel**). Any of various rodents of the family Sciuridae, small and slender with long bushy tail, many being arboreal (**red, gray, flying, ground ~**); **~ cage**, cage for squirrel etc. with revolving cylinder resembling treadmill; (fig.) repetitiveness, monotony, etc., in job or life; **squir'relfish**, any of several nocturnal fishes (genus *Holocentrus*) of shallow tropical waters; **squirrel monkey**, small soft-haired long-tailed S. Amer. monkey of genus *Saimiri*.

squirt (skwẽrt) *v.* Eject (liquid etc.) in jet as from syringe; be so ejected, spurt. **~** *n.* 1. Syringe; small jet or spray. 2. (colloq.) Insignificant person, whippersnapper.

Sr *symbol.* Strontium.

sr *abbrev.* Steradian.

Sr. *abbrev.* Senior; señor.

Sra. *abbrev.* Señora.

Sri Lan·ka (srē lăng'k*a*, shrē lahng'k*a*). Large island in Indian Ocean near S. point of India, until 1972 called Ceylon; formerly a Brit. colony; independent republic, member of the Brit. Commonwealth, since 1948; capital, Colombo. **Sri Lan'kan** *adj.* [Sanskrit name of the island]

S.R.O. *abbrev.* Standing room only.

SS. *abbrev.* Saints.

ss. *abbrev.* (baseball) Shortstop.

S.S. *abbrev.* (hist.) *Schutz Staffel* (Ger., = protection patrol; Nazi police force); steamship.

SSA *abbrev.* Social Security Act;

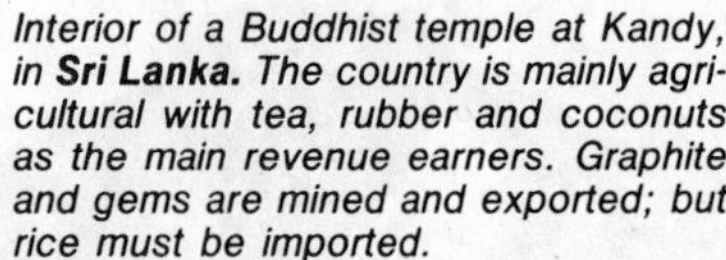
Interior of a Buddhist temple at Kandy, in ***Sri Lanka.*** *The country is mainly agricultural with tea, rubber and coconuts as the main revenue earners. Graphite and gems are mined and exported; but rice must be imported.*

Social Security Administration.

SSE, S.S.E., s.s.e. *abbrevs.* South-southeast.

SSR, S.S.R. *abbrevs.* Soviet Socialist Republic.

SSS *abbrev.* Selective Service System.

SST *abbrev.* Supersonic transport.

SSW, S.S.W., s.s.w. *abbrevs.* South-southwest.

St. *abbrev.* Saint; strait; street.

s.t. *abbrev.* Short ton.

sta. *abbrev.* Station; stationary.

stab (stăb) *v.* (**stabbed, stab·bing**). Pierce, wound, with (usu. short) pointed weapon, needle, etc.; aim blow (*at*) with such weapon etc. **~** *n.* Act of stabbing, wound made thus; short stiff stroke with billiard cue, bat, etc.; **have a ~ at,** (colloq.) make shot at, try.

sta·bile (st*a*bēl', stā'bēl; *Brit.* stā'bīl, -bĭl) *n.* Abstract sculpture or structure of wire, wood, metal, etc.

sta·bi·lize (stā'b*i*līz) *v.t.* (**-lized, -liz·ing**). Make stable, bring into a state of stability. **sta·bi·li·za·tion** (stāb*i*līzā'sh*o*n) *n.* (esp.) Maintenance of exchange rate of a country's currency.

sta·bi·liz·er (stā'b*i*līz*e*r) *n.* (esp.) 1. One of a pair of retractable fins inserted into sides of ship's hull below waterline to prevent rolling. 2. Horizontal tail surface of aircraft.

sta·ble[1] (stā'b*e*l) *n.* Building with stalls, loose boxes, mangers, etc., for keeping horses; establishment for training racehorses, horses belonging to this (also transf.); **sta'bleboy, sta'bleman** (pl. **-men**), one who works in a stable. **stable** *v.* (**-bled, -bling**). Put, keep, (horse) in stable; be stabled. **sta'bling** *n.* (esp.) Accommodation for horses etc.

sta·ble[2] (stā'b*e*l) *adj.* (**-bler, -blest**). Firmly fixed or established, not easily shaken, dislodged, decomposed, changed, destroyed, etc.; firm, resolute, steadfast. **sta·bil·i·ty** (st*a*bĭl'ĭtē) *n.* (pl. **-ties**). **sta'bly** *adv.*

stac·ca·to (st*a*kah'tō) *adv., n.* (pl. **-tos, -ti** pr. -tē) & *adj.* (mus.) (Note etc. played) in detached disconnected manner, with breaks between successive notes.

stack (stăk) *n.* 1. Circular or rectangular pile of hay, straw, sheaves of grain, etc., usu. with sloping thatched top; pile, esp. one arranged in orderly way; (colloq., pl.) large quantity. 2. Group of chimneys etc. standing together; chimney of house, factory, ship, locomotive, etc.; (pl.) area within library where books are stored; aircraft circling airfield at various altitudes while waiting their turn to land. **~** *v.t.* Pile, arrange, in stack(s); **~ up**, measure up; keep aircraft circling in air at specified altitudes until landing space is ready, weather conditions change, etc.

sta·di·um (stā'dē*u*m) *n.* (pl. **-di·ums, -di·a** pr. -dē*a*). 1. Ancient Greek and Roman measure (about 600 ft.). 2. Enclosed athletics ground with tiers of seats for spectators.

staff (stăf, stahf) *n.* (pl. **staffs, staves** pr. stāvz). 1. Stick used as aid in walking or climbing (now usu. literary); stick, rod, as sign of office or authority, as **pastoral** ~; shaft, pole, as support or handle, as **flagstaff**; rod used for measuring distances, heights, etc., in surveying etc. 2. (mus., pl. **staves**) Set of (now five) parallel horizontal lines on and between which notes are placed so as to indicate pitch. 3. (pl. **staffs**) Body of officers, not themselves in command, assisting a general or other commanding officer; body of people working under central direction, esp. in factory, educational institution, etc.; **general** ~, body of officers controlling an army from headquarters under the commander in chief; ~ **college**, (mil.) establishment for instruction and training of officers for staff appointments; **staff sergeant**, (U.S. Army and Marine Corps) noncommissioned officer ranking above sergeant and below (Army) sergeant first class and (USMC) gunnery sergeant; (U.S. Air Force) noncommissioned officer ranking above airman 1st class and below technical sergeant. **staff** *v.t.* Provide with staff of officers, teachers, servants, etc.

stag (stăg) *n.* Male of deer; (attrib., colloq.) for, of, men only, as ~ *party*; ~ *beetle*, large beetle of family Lucanidae of which males have long denticulated mandibles resembling stag's horns. **stag** *adv.* (of a man) Alone, without female companion (*go* ~).

stage (stāj) *n.* 1. Raised floor or platform, e.g. scaffold for workmen and their tools, platform used as gangway, landing place, etc., surface on which object is placed for inspection through microscope.

To counter the effect of rough seas, modern ships are fitted with some form of ***stabilizer.*** *This may be the use of fixed bilge keels; retractable fins; or by lining the hull with tanks which are filled with water and compensate for the motion of the waves.*

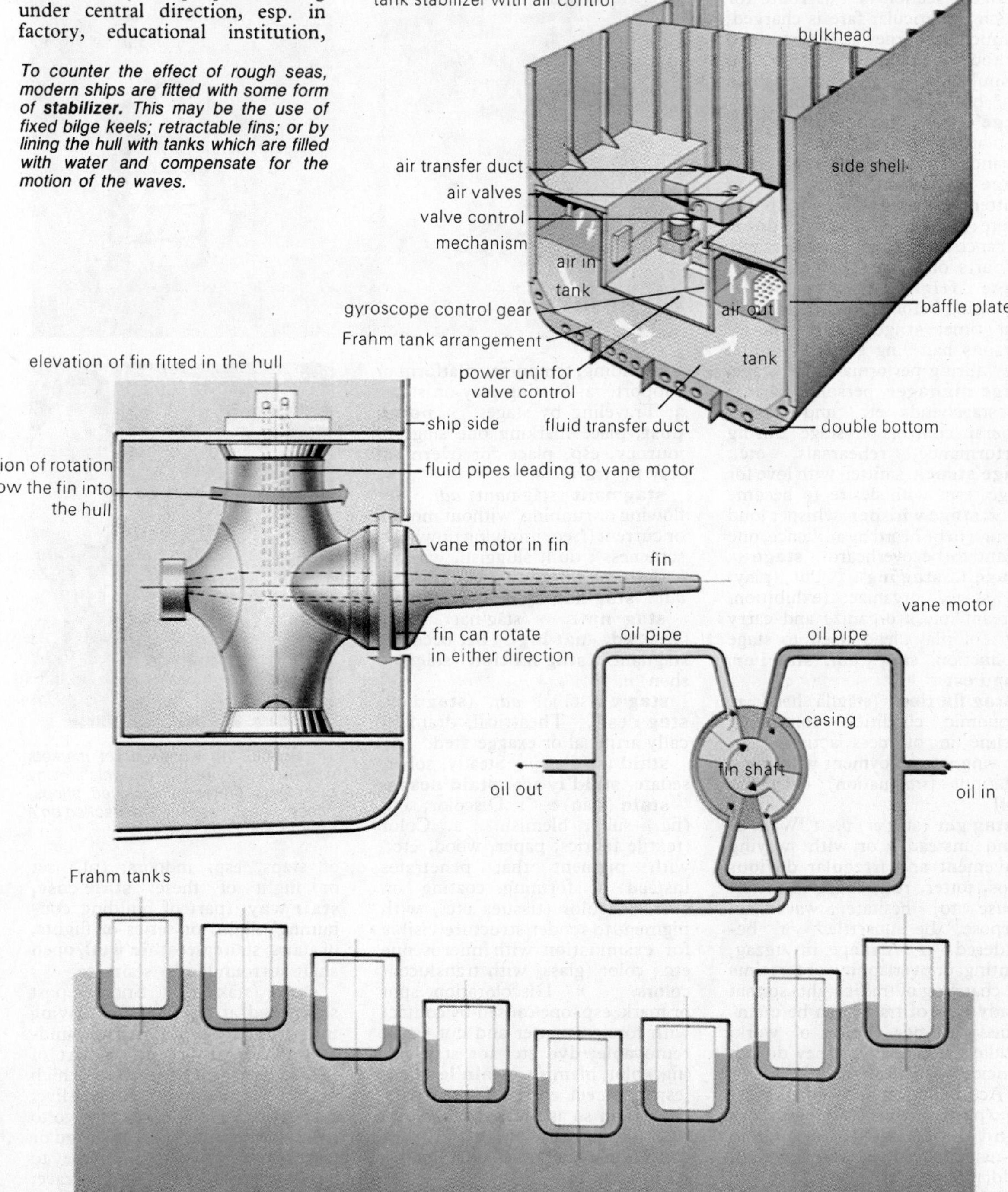

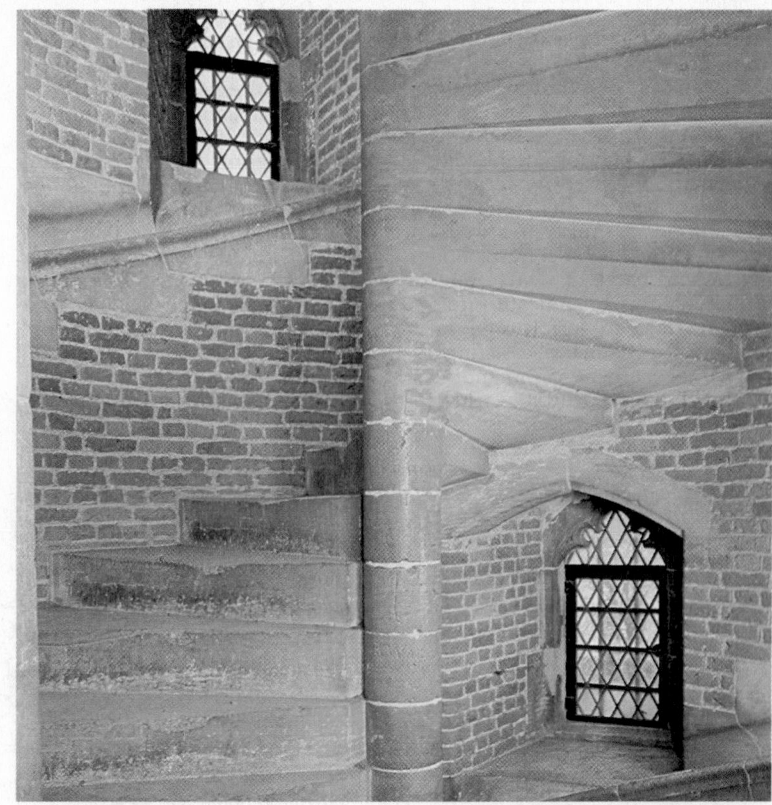

*Spiral **staircase** at Tattershall Castle, in Lincolnshire, England. Built in 1440, the building is said to represent some of the finest examples of the work of East Anglian stonemasons.*

2. Platform on which spectacles, plays, etc., are exhibited, esp. that in theater, with scenery, etc., theater, drama; actor's profession; (fig.) scene of action; **hold the ~**, dominate conversation etc. 3. Division of journey, process, development, etc.; point reached; regular stopping place on stagecoach route where horses were changed; section of bus route for which a particular fare is charged; as much of journey as is performed without stopping for rest etc. 4. Propulsion section of rocket, which can be shed after firing. 5. **stage'coach**, (hist.) coach running regularly between 2 places for conveyance of passengers, parcels, etc.; **stage direction**, instruction in written or printed play for appropriate action etc.; **stage door**, entrance from street for actors etc. to parts of theater behind stage; **stage fright**, nervousness at appearing before audience, esp. for first time; **stage hand**, one of persons handling scenery, lights, etc., during performance on stage; **stage manager**, person in charge of stagehands etc. and having general control of stage during performance, rehearsals, etc.; **stage'struck**, smitten with love for stage, esp. with desire to become actor; **stage whisper**, whisper loud enough to be heard by audience, one meant to be overheard. **stage** *v.* (**staged, stag·ing**). Put (play) on stage, organize (exhibition, pageant, etc.); organize and carry out; (of play) lend itself to stage production. **stag'y** *adj.* (**stag·i·er, stag·i·est**).

stag·fla·tion (stăgflā'sh*o*n) *n.* Economic condition combining decline in business activity and growing unemployment with rapid inflation. [*stag*(nation) + (in)*flation*]

stag·ger (stăg'*er*) *v.* 1. Walk or stand unsteadily or with swaying movement and irregular devious steps, totter, reel; cause to totter; (cause to) hesitate, waver in purpose, be unsettled or bewildered. 2. Arrange in zigzag, slanting, or overlapping order; time the changing of traffic lights so that steady flow of traffic can be maintained; arrange (hours of work, holidays, etc.) so that they do not coincide with those of others. ~ *n.* Act, effect, amount, of staggering; (pl. usu. with sing. verb, also **blind ~s**) diseased condition in animals resulting in unsteady gait, sudden falling, etc.

stag·ing (stā'jĭng) *n.* (esp.) 1. Scaffolding, temporary platform or support. 2. Putting play on stage. 3. Traveling by stages; ~ **point, post**, place marking one stage of journey, esp. place for overnight stay for travelers.

stag·nant (stăg'n*a*nt) *adj.* Not flowing or running, without motion or current (freq. implying unwholesomeness); dull, sluggish, without activity or interest. **stag'nant·ly** *adv.* **stag'nan·cy** *n.*

stag·nate (stăg'nāt) *v.i.* (**-nat·ed, -nat·ing**). Be, become, stagnant. **stag·na·tion** (stăgnā'sh*o*n) *n.*

stag·y (stā'jē) *adj.* (**stag·i·er, stag·i·est**). Theatrical, dramatically artificial or exaggerated.

staid (stād) *adj.* Steady, sober, sedate. **staid'ly** *adv.* **staid'ness** *n.*

stain (stān) *v.* 1. Discolor, soil; (fig.) sully, blemish. 2. Color (textile fabrics, paper, wood, etc.) with pigment that penetrates instead of forming coating on surface; color (tissues etc.) with pigment to render structure visible for examination with microscope etc.; color (glass) with translucent colors. ~ *n.* Discoloration, spot or mark, esp. one caused by contact with foreign matter and not easily removable; dye etc. for staining; (fig.) blot, blemish. **stain'less** *adj.* (esp. of steel etc.) Alloyed with chromium so as not to be liable to rust or tarnish under ordinary conditions; made of such metal. **stain'er** *n.*

stair (stār) *n.* Each of succession of steps, esp. indoors; (pl.) set or flight of these; **stair'case, stair'way**, (part of building containing) flight, or series of flights, of stairs; staircase; **stair'well**, open shaft surrounded by staircase.

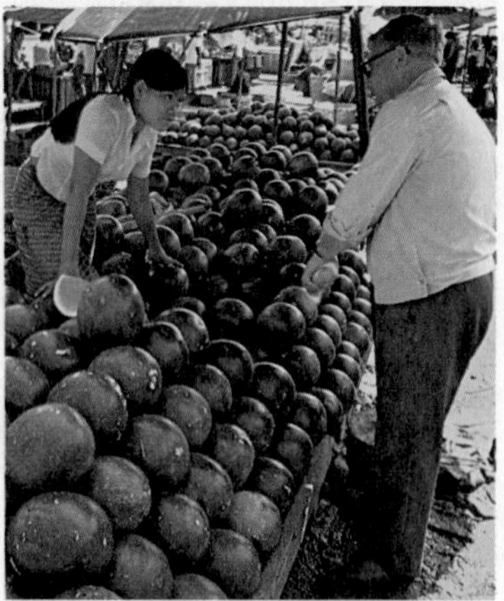

*Throughout the world, street markets provide a shopping area which many customers prefer to enclosed shops. These globular melons are stacked on a **stall** in Vientiane, Laos.*

stake (stāk) *n.* 1. Stick or post sharpened at one end for driving into ground, used to mark boundary, to support plant, as part of fence, etc.; (hist.) post to which person was tied to be burned alive; **pull up ~s**, (colloq.) depart, go to live elsewhere. 2. What is staked or wagered on an event; (pl.) money to be contended for, esp. in horse race; (pl.) such race; (fig.) interest

Colored floodlights are used to emphasize the natural beauty of a **stalagmite** and adjoining stalactites at Lake Caves in the Margaret River area of Western Australia.

involved, something to be gained or lost; **at** ~, at issue, in question, risked. 3. (Mormon Ch.) Number of wards administered by a president. **stake** *v.t.* (**staked, stak·ing**). 1. Fasten, secure, support, with stake(s); mark *off, out*, with stakes; ~ **out**, (colloq.) place under surveillance. 2. Wager, risk (*on* event etc.); (fig.) hazard, risk loss of; furnish with money, supplies, etc., esp. in order to share gains.

Sta·kha·nov·ite (st*a*kah'n*o*vīt, -χah'-) *adj.* & *n.* (Member) of Soviet Russian movement aiming at greater output in industry, initiated by Alexei Stakhanov, a Donetz miner, who in 1935 produced a phenomenal quantity of coal by a combination of new method and great energy.

sta·lac·tite (st*a*lăk'tīt, stăl'*a*k-) *n.* Icicle-like formation of crystalline calcium carbonate formed by dripping of water through overlying limestone and hanging from roof or wall of cavern etc. **stal·ac·tit·ic** (stăl*a*ktĭt'ĭk) *adj.*

sta·lag (stăl'*a*g, stah'l*a*g; *Ger.* shtah'lahk) *n.* German prison camp. [abbrev. of Ger. *Stammlager* (*Stamm* main body, *Lager* camp)]

sta·lag·mite (st*a*lăg'mīt, stăl'-*a*g-) *n.* Deposit of calcium carbonate or other material on floor of cavern etc. resembling inverted stalactite and similarly formed. **stal·ag·mit·ic** (stăl*a*gmĭt'ĭk) *adj.*

stale (stāl) *adj.* (**stal·er, stal·est**). Not fresh; insipid, musty, or otherwise the worse for age; lacking novelty, trite; (of athlete) overtrained (similarly of other persons whose vigor is impaired by overwork); **stale'mate**, (chess) position in which player can make no move without bringing his king into check, (fig.) deadlock, drawn contest; (*v.t.*) place (player, his king) in position of stalemate. **stale'ly** *adv.* **stale'ness** *n.* **stale** *n.* Urine of horses and cattle. ~ *v.* (**staled, stal·ing**). 1. Make, become, stale or common. 2. (of horse etc.) Urinate.

Sta·lin (stah'lĭn, -lēn). Name adopted by Joseph Vissarionovich Dzhugashvili (1879–1953), Soviet dictator, by birth a Georgian; worked as an underground revolutionary from 1904 until the Bolshevik revolution of 1917; by *c*1927 he was established as undisputed successor to Lenin and leader of the Communist Party and administration, retaining that position until his death; premier of U.S.S.R. 1941–53. **Sta'lin·ism** *n.* **Sta'lin·ist** *adj.* & *n.* [Russ., = "man of steel"]

Sta·lin·grad (stah'lĭngrăd). See VOLGOGRAD.

stalk[1] (stawk) *n.* Main stem of herbaceous plant, bearing flowers and leaves; attachment or support

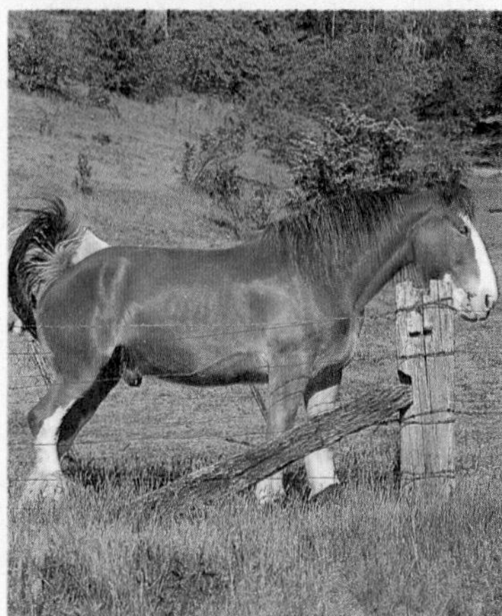

*This old **stallion** has probably been put out to pasture after a long working life. The draft horse is descended from the warhorses of the Middle Ages which had to carry the huge weight of their armored riders.*

of leaf, flower, fruit, animal organ, etc.; stem, shaft, of object. **stalked** *adj.*

stalk[2] (stawk) *v.* 1. Pursue (game) stealthily; steal up to game under cover; **stalking-horse**, horse, screen, behind which hunter approaches game; (fig.) something used to conceal intentions or efforts; (pol.) candidate put forward to conceal another's candidacy or to draw votes from a rival. 2. Walk with stiff measured steps; stride in stately or imposing manner. ~ *n.* Act of stalking game; stealthy pursuit.

stall[1] (stawl) *n.* 1. (Division for 1 animal in) stable, cattle shed, cow house. 2. Fixed seat enclosed wholly or partly at back and sides, and freq. canopied, in choir or chancel of church or in chapter-house, for clergyman, dignitary of church, knight, etc.; (fig.) office or dignity of canon etc.; (Brit.) each of set of seats in part of theater nearest stage, usu. between pit and orchestra. 3. Booth, table, stand, in market etc., compartment in building, for exposure and sale of goods. 4. Compartment for occupation by one person in shower baths etc. 5. (Condition or delay resulting from) stalling of engine or aircraft. ~ *v.* 1. Place, keep, (cattle etc.) in stall, esp. for fattening; furnish with stalls. 2. (Cause to) stick fast in mud, snow, etc.; stop (internal combustion engine) accidentally, (of engine) be accidentally stopped; (cause to) lose flying speed to point at which aircraft ceases to respond normally to controls; ~ **speed**, critical speed below which aircraft stalls.

stall[2] (stawl) *v.* (colloq.) 1. Play for time when being questioned etc. 2. Block, delay, obstruct. ~ *n.* (colloq.) Device, trick, evasion, etc. used in stalling.

stal·lion (stăl'y*o*n) *n.* Uncastrated male horse, esp. one kept for breeding.

stal·wart (stawl′wert) *adj.* (chiefly literary) Stout, strong, sturdy; valiant, courageous, resolute. ~ *n.* Resolute uncompromising partisan, esp. of political party. **stal′wart·ly** *adv.* **stal′wart·ness** *n.*

sta·men (stā′men) *n.* (pl. **sta·mens, stam·i·na** pr. stăm′ina). (bot.) Male fertilizing organ of flowering plants, with anther containing pollen supported on slender filament.

stam·i·na (stăm′ina) *n.* Staying power, power of endurance.

stam·i·nate (stăm′inĭt, -nāt) *adj.* Having stamens, esp. without pistils.

stam·mer (stăm′er) *v.* Falter or stumble in speech, esp. repeat involuntarily certain sounds in a word etc. several times in rapid succession through inability to complete the articulation; utter with stammer. ~ *n.* Stammering speech, tendency to stammer. **stam′mer·er** *n.* **stam′mer·ing·ly** *adv.*

stamp (stămp) *v.* 1. Bring down one's foot, bring down (foot), heavily on ground; ~ **out**, put an end to, crush, destroy; **stamp′ing ground**, (colloq.) animal's (or colloq., person's) habitual place of resort. 2. Impress pattern, name, mark, upon with die or similar instrument; affix postage or other stamp to (document, envelope, etc.); assign a character to, characterize; impress *on* the memory. 3. Crush, pulverize (ore etc.). **stamp** *n.* 1. Act, sound, of stamping, esp. with foot. 2. Instrument for stamping pattern or mark, mark made by this; government's embossed or impressed mark, adhesive label with distinctive device, on deed or other document etc., to certify that duty, tax, etc., has been paid; postage stamp; mark impressed on, label etc. affixed to, commodity as evidence of quality etc.; (fig.) characteristic mark, impress (*of* some quality etc.); character, kind. 3. Heavy pestle operated by machinery for crushing ores, stamp mill. 4. **S~ Act**, act of British Parliament for regulating stamp duties, esp. that of 1765 (repealed 1766) levying such duties on Amer. colonies; ~ **mill**, apparatus for crushing ore, usu. with series of stamps.

*The **stall** in the private chapel of Petworth House, near Arundel in Sussex, U.K., may have been carved by Grinling Gibbons. The chapel and house were acquired for the nation in 1947.*

stam·pede (stămpēd′) *n.* Sudden rush and flight of number of frightened horses, cattle, etc.; sudden unreasoning rush or action of persons in a body or mass. ~ *v.* (**-ped·ed, -ped·ing**). (Cause to) take part in stampede.

stance (stăns) *n.* (golf etc.) Player's position for making stroke; pose, attitude.

stanch, staunch (stawnch, stahnch, stănch) *vbs.t.* Check flow of (esp. blood); check flow from (esp. wound).

stan·chion (stăn′shon) *n.* Upright bar, stay, or support, esp. for confining cattle in stall. ~ *v.t.* Provide, strengthen, support, with stanchion(s).

stand (stănd) *v.* (**stood** pr. stŏŏd, **stand·ing**). 1. Have, take, assume, erect attitude on one's feet; be set, remain, upright; be of specified height when standing; remain stationary, stop walking or moving on; be set, placed, or situated; remain firm, secure, valid, etc., or in specified condition; present a firm front; (naut.) sail, steer, in specified direction, to sea, etc. 2. Place, set, in upright or specified position. 3. Bear the brunt of, resist; endure, undergo (trial etc.); endure without succumbing or complaining. 4. Provide at one's expense. 5. ~ **by**, uphold, support, side with; adhere to, abide by; stand near, be a bystander, stand and look on; stand ready, be on the alert; **stand′by** (pl. **bys**), thing, person, that can be depended on; **stand a chance**, have a chance or prospect (of success); **stand down**, step down from witness stand; retire, withdraw; go off duty; **stand for**, represent, signify, imply; (colloq.) tolerate, acquiesce in; **stand in**, act as deputy (*for*); be in favor (*with*); **stand-in**, person employed to take place of actor until lights, cameras, etc., are ready; deputy, substitute; **stand off**, move away, keep one's distance; **stand′off**, indecisive contest, tie; **standoff′ish**, distant, reserved, not affable; **standoff′ishly** (*adv.*), **standoff′ishness** (*n.*); **stand on**, insist on, observe scrupulously; **stand out**, hold out, persist in opposition or endurance; be prominent or conspicuous; **stand pat**, (in poker) play hand as dealt; oppose change, maintain one's position; **stand′patter**, (esp. pol.) rigid conservative, opponent of progress; **stand′pipe**, vertical pipe for conveying water, gas, etc., or with spout or nozzle for hose, for attachment to water main; **stand′point**, point of view; **stand′still**, halt, pause, cessation of movement

Claimed to be the most valuable **stamp** in the world, the 1 cent British Guiana of 1856 and the only one of its kind surviving, was insured for £200,000 when exhibited in 1965.

Possibly one of the most unusual **stamps** ever issued, a humorous cartoon figure was used in a series to introduce and demonstrate the advantages of metric conversion in Australia.

or activity; **stand to**, abide by, stick to, not desert; **stand to win, lose**, etc., be reasonably certain to win, lose, etc.; **stand up**, rise to one's feet from sitting position etc.; maintain erect position; (colloq.) fail to keep appointment with; remain durable, convincing; **stand-up**, (of theater, nightclub, etc. entertainer) delivering comic monologue without prop or costume; (of fight) fair and square, in which opponents stand up to one another without flinching or evasion; (of meal etc.) taken standing; **stand up for**, side with, maintain, support. **stand** *n.* 1. Cessation from motion or progress, stoppage; stationary condition, esp. for resistance (*against*); position taken up. 2. Table, set of shelves, rack, etc., on or in which things may be placed; stall in market etc.; standing place for vehicles etc. (as **taxi** ~); raised structure at sports events etc. for persons to sit or stand on (often pl.); (also **witness** ~) place in courtroom for giving testimony. 3. Standing growth or crop. 4. (of theatrical company, sports team, etc.) Appearance made during tour.

stand·ard (stăn′derd) *n.* 1. Distinctive flag, as (*English*) *royal* ~; banner of chief of state; flag of cavalry or armored regiment (opp. to *colors* of infantry); (fig.) rallying principle; (bot.) vexillum, uppermost petal of sweet pea or similar flower. 2. Weight or measure to which others conform or by which the accuracy of others is judged (often attrib. as in *standard pound, yard,* etc.); legal proportion of weight of fine metal and alloy in gold and silver coin (**monetary** ~) or in articles made of these metals; thing serving as basis of comparison. 3. Degree of excellence etc. required for a particular purpose; thing recognized as model for imitation etc.; (attrib. of book) recognized as possessing merit or authority; (in schools) each of several degrees of proficiency; ~ **of living**, degree of material comfort enjoyed by community, class, or person. 4. Average quality. 5. Upright support; upright water or gas pipe; upright holder for lamp in street or room; tree, shrub, trained on erect stem (not as espalier or dwarfed). 6. ~**-bearer**, soldier etc. who carries flag; (fig.) prominent leader in cause; ~ **English**, form of English used, with local variations, by the majority of cultured English-speaking people; ~ **time**, time established legally or by custom in country or region, usu. that of a specific time zone.

stand·ard·ize (stăn′derdīz) *v.t.* (**-ized, -iz·ing**). Make to conform to standard; make uniform. **stand·ard·i·za·tion** (stănderdīzā′shon) *n.*

stand·ee (stăndē′) *n.* (colloq.) Person who stands, as at theatrical performance.

stand·ing (stan′ding) *n.* (esp.) Estimation in which person is held, repute; duration. ~ *adj.* (esp.)

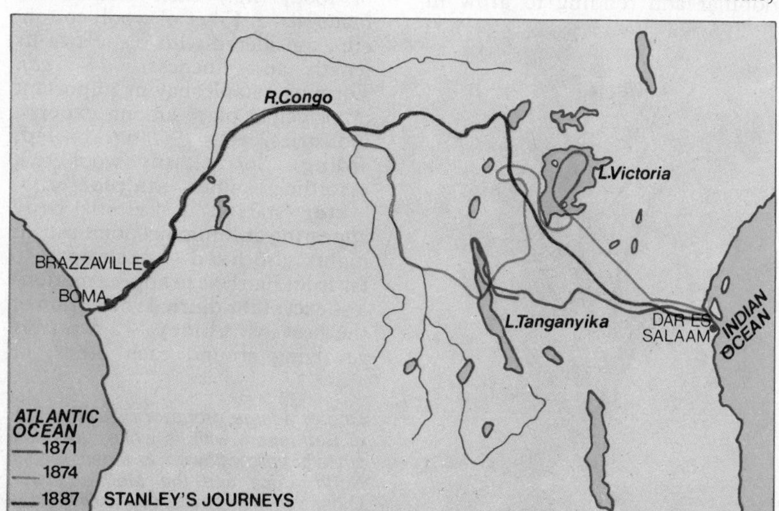

Sir Henry Stanley, the British explorer and journalist, is best known for locating David Livingstone in 1871. However, he also traced the route of the Congo on other expeditions (shown left).

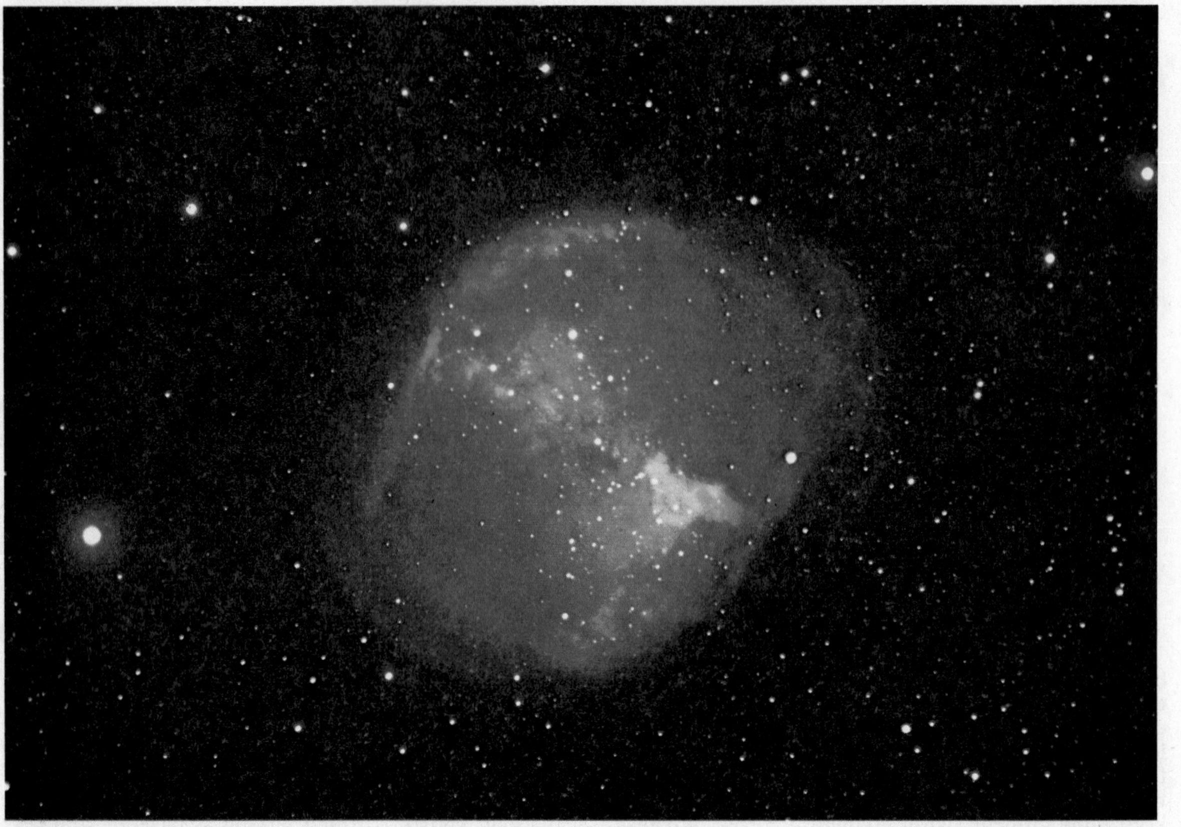

Established; permanent, not made, formed, etc., for the occasion; stagnant (of water); performed upright (of jump); ~ **orders**, series of instructions remaining in force until countermanded or repealed by a proper authority, esp. (mil.) orders not subject to change by an officer temporarily in command; ~ **room**, area in which to stand, esp. when no seats are available, as at theater.

stank: see STINK.

Stan·ley (stăn′lē), **Sir Henry Morton** (1841–1904). (orig. name John Rowlands) Welsh explorer and journalist; commissioned by the New York *Herald* to search central Africa for David Livingstone; his famous remark on finding him in 1871 was, "Dr. Livingstone, I presume?"; his explorations for Belgium in the Congo region, 1879–1884, helped in establishing the Congo Free State (Belgian Congo); **Stanley Falls**, seven cataracts of the upper Congo River, on the equator in Zaire.

stan·nate (stăn′āt) *n.* (chem.) Salt of stannic acid.

stan·nic (stăn′ĭk) *adj.* Of tin; (chem.) containing tin as quadrivalent element.

stan·nous (stăn′*u*s) *adj.* Containing tin as bivalent element.

Stan·ton (stăn′t*o*n), **Elizabeth Cady** (1815–1902). Amer. feminist leader; organized first women's rights convention, 1848; first president of National Woman Suffrage Association, 1869–90.

*When seen through a 200-inch telescope, the vast number of **stars** shows how little can be seen with the eye. Above: A small section of the Vulpecula constellation.*

stan·za (stăn′z*a*) *n.* Group of (usu. rhymed) lines forming division of song or poem.

sta·pes (stā′pēz) (pl. **sta·pes, sta·pe·des** pr. st*a*pē′dēz) = STIRRUP bone.

staph (stăf) *n.* (colloq.) Staphylococcus.

staph·y·lo·coc·cus (stăf*i*l*o*kŏk′-*u*s) *n.* (pl. **-coc·ci** pr. -kŏk′sī). Any of numerous microorganisms, globular and tending to grow in clusters, causing various conditions such as boils, carbuncles, and abscesses. **staph·y·lo·coc′cal** *adj.* [Gk. *staphulē* bunch of grapes, *kokkos* grain]

sta·ple[1] (stā′p*e*l) *n.* U-shaped bar or loop of metal with pointed ends to be driven into post, wall, etc., as hold for hook, bolt, etc.; contrivance of similar shape or function, esp. bent wire used in bookbinding for wire stitching. ~ *v.t.* (**-pled, -pling**). Furnish, fasten, with staple. **sta′pler**[1] *n.* (esp.) Device for stapling.

sta·ple[2] (stā′p*e*l) *n.* 1. Important or principal product or article of commerce; raw material; basic item of food; (fig.) chief element or material. 2. Fiber of wool, cotton, etc., considered with respect to its length and fineness. ~ *adj.* Forming a staple; having important or principal place among exports, industries, etc. ~ *v.t.* (**-pled, -pling**). Sort, classify (wool etc.), according to fiber. **sta′pler**[2] *n.*

star (stâr) *n.* 1. Celestial body appearing as luminous point esp. at night; (also **fixed** ~) such body so far from Earth as to appear motionless except for diurnal revolution of the heavens; **binary** ~, two stars revolving around each other, or

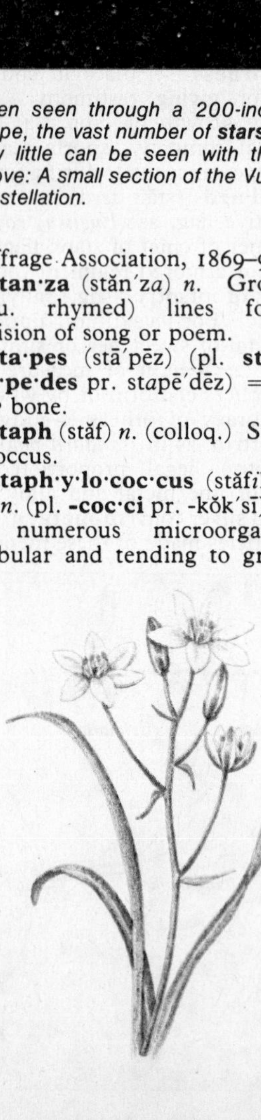

*One of a large group of lilies, the **Star of Bethlehem** with its white, greenish-white or yellow flowers is widespread in North Africa and the Mediterranean. Other varieties have been cultivated.*

around a common center; **double** ~, two fixed stars appearing to naked eye as one, esp. binary star; **multiple** ~, similar group of three to six; **falling, shooting** ~, small meteor looking like rapidly moving star. 2. (astrol.) Heavenly body, esp. planet, considered as influencing human affairs or person's fortunes. 3. Thing suggesting star by its shape, esp. figure or object with radiating points; asterisk; white spot on forehead of horse etc. 4. Actor, singer, athlete, etc., of great celebrity; brilliant or prominent person. 5. ~ **chamber**, (judgment, trial) marked by arbitrary, unjust, or clandestine procedure (from **Court of S~ Chamber**, English Privy Council court, abolished 1641); ~ **drift**, common proper motion of a number of fixed stars in same region; **star'dust**, multitude of stars looking like dust, (fig.) romantic or dreamlike mood; **star'fish**, marine echinoderm of the class Asteroidea with usu. five broad arms radiating from a central disk; **star'flower**, any of various small N. Amer. plants (genus *Trientalis*), having pink or white star-shaped flowers; **star'gazer**, esp. impractical idealist; **star'gazing** (*n.*); **star'light**, light of the stars; (*adj.*, also **star'lit**); **star-nosed mole**, mole (*Condylura cristata*) of eastern N. Amer., having ring of small fleshy tentacles encircling end of snout; **star of Bethlehem**, plant of genus *Ornithogalum*, esp. *O. umbellatum*, with white stellate flowers; any of various other plants; **Star of David**, figure of two interlaced equilateral triangles used as Jewish and Israeli symbol; **star sapphire**, cabochon sapphire giving impression of embedded star; **The Star Spangled Banner**, U.S. national anthem, with ref. to the Stars and Stripes (see below); **star stream**, either of two systematic drifts of stars (one of which comprises the nearer stars and moves toward Orion); **Stars and Stripes**, flag of the U.S. with 13 horizontal stripes, representing the 13 original states, and one star for each of the 50 states in the Union. **star'dom** *n.* Status of star performer (see *n.*, sense 4); realm, sphere, of such stars. **star'let** *n.* Young star (sense 4). **star'less** *adj.* **star'ry** *adj.* (**-ri·er, -ri·est**). **star** *adj.* Brilliant, prominent, preeminent. ~ *v.* (**starred, star·ring**). Set, adorn (as) with stars; mark with asterisk; present (actor etc.), appear, as a star (sense 4).

star·board (stär'bẽrd) *n.* Right-hand side of boat or ship or aircraft looking forward (opp. PORT[4]). ~ *v.t.* Turn, put, (helm) to starboard. [OE. *steor rudder*]

starch (stärch) *n.* White odorless tasteless carbohydrate occurring widely in plants, esp. cereals, potatoes, etc., and forming an important constituent of human food; preparation of this for stiffening linen etc.; (fig.) stiffness of manner or conduct, formality. **starch'y** *adj.* (**starch·i·er, starch·i·est**). **starch'i·ly** *adv.* **starch'i·ness** *n.* **starch** *v.t.* Stiffen with starch.

stare (stãr) *v.* (**stared, star·ing**). Gaze fixedly with eyes wide open; open eyes in astonishment, be amazed; reduce (person) to specified condition by staring; be obtrusively conspicuous; ~ (person) **in the face**, (of thing) be glaringly obvious to. **stare** *n.* Staring gaze. **star'er** *n.*

stark (stärk) *adj.* Stiff, rigid; downright, sheer. ~ *adv.* Quite, completely (now chiefly in ~ *mad, naked*). **stark'ly** *adv.* **stark'ness** *n.*

star·ling[1] (stär'lĭng) *n.* Any of various Old World birds of family Sturnidae, esp. *Sturnus vulgaris*, blackbird introduced into N. Amer. and now a gregarious, aggressive, and abundant pest.

star·ling[2] (stär'lĭng) *n.* Outwork of piles protecting pier of bridge against force of stream, damage by floating objects, etc.

*The common European **starling** is an introduced species in Australia and America where it has reached pest proportions. Other, more vividly colored varieties of this bird, are indigenous to certain tropical countries.*

start (stârt) *v.* 1. Make sudden movement from pain, surprise, etc., give start; move suddenly from one's place; rouse (game) from lair etc.; (of timbers etc.) spring from proper position, be displaced by pressure or shrinkage; cause, experience, starting of timbers etc. 2. Set out, begin journey, career, course of action, etc. (*out* or *off*); make a beginning (*on*); begin; originate, set going; cause to begin doing, cause or enable to commence course of action etc.; give signal to (persons) to start in race etc.; (also ~ **up**) cause (engine) to begin to run; (of engine) begin to operate. **start** *n.* 1. Sudden involuntary movement caused by surprise, fright, pain, etc.; (pl.) intermittent and sudden efforts or displays of energy in (esp. *by fits and starts*). 2. Beginning of journey, action, race, career, etc.; starting place of race; opportunity or assistance for starting career, course of action, etc.; advantage gained by starting first in race, journey; position in advance of competitors.

start·er (stâr′ter) *n.* (esp.) 1. Person giving signal to start in race. 2. Horse, competitor, starting in race etc. 3. Apparatus for starting engine, esp. **self-~**. 4. **for starters**, (slang) to start with, as a beginning.

start·ing (stâr′tĭng) *n.* (esp.) ~ **block**, shaped block for bracing the feet of runners at start of race; ~ **gate**, movable barrier for securing fair start in horse race.

star·tle (stâr′tel) *v.t.* (**-tled, -tling**). Cause to start with surprise or fright; alarm; take by surprise. **star′tling** *adj.*

starve (stârv) *v.* (**starved, starv·ing**). (Cause to) die of hunger; (cause to) suffer from lack of food; (colloq.) feel hungry; force *into* course of action, *out*, etc., by starvation; (fig.) (cause to) suffer mental or spiritual want. **star·va·tion** (stârvā′shon) *n.*

starve·ling (stârv′lĭng) *n.* Starving or ill-fed person or animal.

sta·sis (stā′sĭs, stăs′ĭs) *n.* (pl. **sta·ses** pr. stā′sēz, stăs′ēz). Stoppage of circulation of any body fluids, esp. blood.

state[1] (stāt) *n.* 1. Condition; manner or way of existence as determined by circumstances; (colloq.) excited or agitated condition of mind or feeling; ~ **of the art**, stage of development or knowledge of a subject. 2. Rank, dignity; pomp; **in ~**, with all due ceremony; **lie in ~**, (of dead person) be ceremoniously exhibited in public place. 3. Organized political community under one government, commonwealth, nation; such community forming part of federation with sovereign government; civil government; **the S~s**, (colloq.) the UNITED STATES OF AMERICA; **States-General**, legislative assembly of clergy, nobles, and commons of whole realm in France before the Revolution, or in Netherlands from 15th c. to 1796. 4. (attrib.) **state capitalism**, system in which capital is owned or controlled by state; **state′craft**, art of conducting affairs of state; **State Department**, department of U.S. government dealing with foreign affairs; **State′house**, building in which legislature of a state holds its sessions; **States rights, States' rights**, rights and powers not delegated to the Federal government but reserved to individual states; **state′room**, passenger's private cabin on ship, train, etc.; **state′side**, (colloq.) of or pertaining to the U.S. (as seen from overseas); **state socialism**, system of state control of industries, railroads, etc. **state′hood** *n.* **state′less** *adj.* Having no legal nationality, esp. because of change

The invention and use of a ***starting-block*** *has given runners, and especially those in short-distance sprints, the benefit of a non-slip start when the gun is fired.*

The ***starting-gate*** *was devised for horse racing so that all mounts would have an equal chance to leave the barrier at the same instant, as demonstrated at an Australian race track.*

*In Richmond, Virginia, and other States, the **Statehouse** is where the General Assembly meets. The present building replaced a more modest one which was erected in 1785.*

*'Satyr, nymph and cupid' a **statuette** molded in terracotta by the French 18th-century sculptor Clodion, and much influenced by the styles originally created in Greece and Rome.*

of government or alteration of boundaries of states. **state** *adj.* Of, for, concerned with the state (sense 3); reserved for, employed on, occasions of state or ceremony.

state[2] (stāt) *v.t.* (**stat·ed, stat·ing**). Express, esp. fully or clearly, in speech or writing; specify (number etc.).

state·ly (stāt′lē) *adj.* (**-li·er, -li·est**). Dignified, imposing, grand. **state′li·ness** *n.*

state·ment (stāt′m*e*nt) *n.* Stating, expression in words; presentation of musical theme or subject; thing stated; formal account of facts, as of liabilities and assets; account presented periodically by tradesman to customer.

states·man (stāts′m*a*n), fem. **states·wom·an** (stāts′wŏŏm*a*n) *ns.* (pl. **-men** pr. -m*e*n, **-wom·en** pr. -wĭmĭn). Person skilled or taking leading parts in management of state affairs, esp. sagacious, farsighted politician; **elder s~**: see ELDER[2].

stat·ic (stăt′ĭk) *adj.* Of forces in equilibrium or bodies at rest (contrasted with *dynamic* or *kinetic*); acting by weight without motion; passive, not active or changing; (elect.) stationary, produced by friction; (of a store of water in a tank) having no pressure of its own and requiring to be pumped. ~ *n.* Static electricity; (slang) opposition, unpleasant remarks, etc. **stat′i·cal** *adj.* Of statics. **stat′ics** *n.* Branch of physical science concerned with bodies at rest and forces in equilibrium (contrasted with *dynamics*). **stat′i·cal·ly** *adv.*

sta·tion (stā′sh*o*n) *n.* 1. Place in which person or thing stands or is placed, esp. habitually or for definite purpose or duties; building from which radio and television broadcasts are transmitted. 2. Position in life, rank, status. 3. Stopping place on railroad or long-distance bus line with buildings for passengers and freight, or freight only; these buildings. 4. One of a series of holy places, esp. Roman churches, visited in turn for devotions; **~s of the Cross**, series of 14 pictures or images of Christ's Passion (orig. crosses) in church or occas. in open air, before which devotions are performed. 5. **(station) break**, pause between or during television and radio programs for station identification, announcements, or commercials; **station house**, police station; **sta′tionmaster**, official in control of railroad station; **station wagon**, automobile with removable or folding rear seats and wide rear door with tailgate to expedite loading and unloading of luggage etc. **station** *v.* Assign station or post to; post, place, in station.

sta·tion·ar·y (stā′sh*o*nĕrē) *adj.* Remaining in one place, not moving; fixed, not movable; not changing in condition, quality, or quantity; ~ **front**, (meteorol.) motionless or nearly motionless boundary between 2 masses of air having different densities; ~ **orbit**, orbit whose period is the same as the period of Earth's rotation on its axis and oriented so that any object in it remains located over one spot on Earth; ~ **satellite**, artificial satellite in such orbit.

sta·tion·er (stā′sh*o*n*er*) *n.* Tradesman selling writing materials etc. **sta·tion·er·y** (stā′sh*o*nĕrē) *n.* Articles sold by stationer, as paper, pens, ink, etc.

sta·tis·tics (st*a*tĭs′tĭks) *n.* Branch of study concerned with collection and classification of (esp.) numerical facts; (as pl.) facts so collected and classified. **sta·tis′ti·cal** *adj.* **sta·tis′ti·cal·ly** *adv.* **stat·is·ti·cian** (stătĭstĭsh′*a*n) *n.*

sta·tor (stā′t*er*) *n.* Stationary part of machine or device.

stat·u·ar·y (stăch′ŏŏĕrē) *n.* (pl. **-ar·ies**). (Art of making) statues. ~ *adj.* Of statues; sculptured; suitable for statues.

stat·ue (stăch′ōō) *n.* Sculptural representation in the round of (esp.) deity, allegorical subject, or human being(s), usu. of life-size proportions.

stat·u·esque (stăchŏŏĕsk′) *adj.* Resembling a statue, esp. in beauty or dignity.

stat·u·ette (stăchŏŏĕt′) *n.* Small statue.

stat·ure (stăch′*er*) *n.* Height of (esp. human) body; degree of (moral, intellectual, etc.) development attained (by person).

sta·tus (stā′t*u*s, stăt′*u*s) *n.* Social or legal position or condition, rank, standing; superior social etc. position; ~ **symbol**, possession etc. thought of as indicating person's high status; ~ **quo** (**ante**), unchanged position (previous position) of affairs.

stat·ute (stăch′ōōt, -ōōt) *n.* Written law of a legislative body; ordinance of corporation etc. intended to be permanent; ~ **law**, written law as established by legislative enactment; (cf. COMMON law); ~ **mile**, unit of distance (5,280 ft.); ~ **of limitations**, statute setting time limit within which legal action may be taken; **stat′u·ta·ble** *adj.* **stat·u·to·ry** (stăch′ōōtorē, -tōrē) *adj.* Enacted, required, imposed, by statute; ~ **rape**, sexual intercourse with girl below age of consent.

staunch[1]: STANCH.

staunch[2] (stawnch, stahnch) *adj.* Trustworthy, loyal, firm; (of vessel etc.) watertight, airtight. **staunch′ly** *adv.* **staunch′ness** *n.*

stave (stāv) *n.* 1. Each of the narrow shaped pieces of wood etc. placed together vertically to form sides of cask etc. 2. Stanza, verse, of poem, song, etc. 3. (mus.) = STAFF sense 2. ~ *v.t.* (**staved** or **stove** pr. stōv, **stav·ing**). 1. Break up (cask) into staves, break into, break hole *in* (boat, cask, etc.); crush, bash (*in*). 2. Furnish, fit (cask etc.) with staves. 3. ~ **off**, ward off, defer.

stay[1] (stā) *n.* Rope supporting mast, leading down from masthead; guy or rope supporting flagstaff etc.; tie piece, crosspiece, holding parts together in aircraft etc. **stay** *v.t.* (**stayed, stay·ing**). Support, steady, with stay(s).

stay[2] (stā) *v.* (**stayed** or archaic **staid, stay·ing**). 1. Check, stop (now chiefly literary); postpone (judgment etc.); appease. 2. Support, prop (*up*), as with buttress etc. 3. Remain; dwell temporarily; pause in movement, action, speech; ~ **put**, remain in one's, or its, place. 4. Hold out, show powers of endurance; hold out for (specified distance, *the course*). 5. ~**-at-home**, (person) remaining habitually at home; **staying power**, endurance. **stay** *n.* 1. Remaining, esp. dwelling temporarily, in a place; duration of this. 2. Suspension of judicial proceedings, esp. ~ **of execution**, of judgment delivered. 3. Prop, support.

S.T.B. *abbrev.* Bachelor of Sacred Theology. [L. *Sanctae Theologiae Baccalaureus*]

St. Croix (sānt kroi′). Largest of the U.S. Virgin Islands, in the N. Lesser Antilles, in the West Indies.

S.T.D. *abbrev.* Doctor of Sacred Theology. [L. *Sanctae Theologiae Doctor*]

stead (stĕd) *n.* **stand** (person) **in good** ~, be of advantage or service to; **in person's** ~, instead of him, as his substitute.

Largely superseded by diesel-electric locomotives, the ***steamengine*** *was a direct development from the first steam locomotives designed by Richard Trevithick and George Stephenson. The fastest exceeded 125 m.p.h. in 1928.*

stead·fast (stĕd′făst, -fahst, -fast) *adj.* Constant, firm, unwavering. **stead′fast·ly** *adv.* **stead′fast·ness** *n.*

stead·y (stĕd′ē) *adj.* (**stead·i·er, stead·i·est**). Firm, not tottering, faltering, rocking, or shaking; stable; unwavering, resolute; settled, unvarying; regular, maintained at even rate of action, change, etc., not erratic. ~**-state theory**, theory that the universe is in unvarying condition and has not been created by any past event; cf. BIG bang theory. **stead′i·ly** *adv.* **stead′i·ness** *n.* **steady** *adv.* Steadily (chiefly naut.); **go** ~, (colloq.) date regularly only one girl or boy. **steady** *n.* (colloq.) Constant sweetheart. ~ *v.* (**stead·ied, stead·y·ing**). Make, become, steady.

steak (stāk) *n.* Thick slice or strip of meat (esp. beef) for grilling, frying, etc., esp. cut from hindquarters of animal; thick slice of fish cut through backbone.

steal (stēl) *v.* (**stole** pr. stōl, **stol·en** pr. stō′len, **steal·ing**). 1. Take away dishonestly, and esp. secretly, what belongs to another; obtain surreptitiously or by surprise; win, get possession of, by insidious arts, attractions, etc.; ~ **the show**, unexpectedly outshine other performers. 2. Move secretly or silently. **steal** *n.* (colloq.) Stealing, theft; thing stolen; bargain.

stealth (stĕlth) *n.* Secret, secret procedure; **by** ~, surreptitiously, clandestinely. **stealth·y** *adj.* (**stealth·i·er, stealth·i·est**).

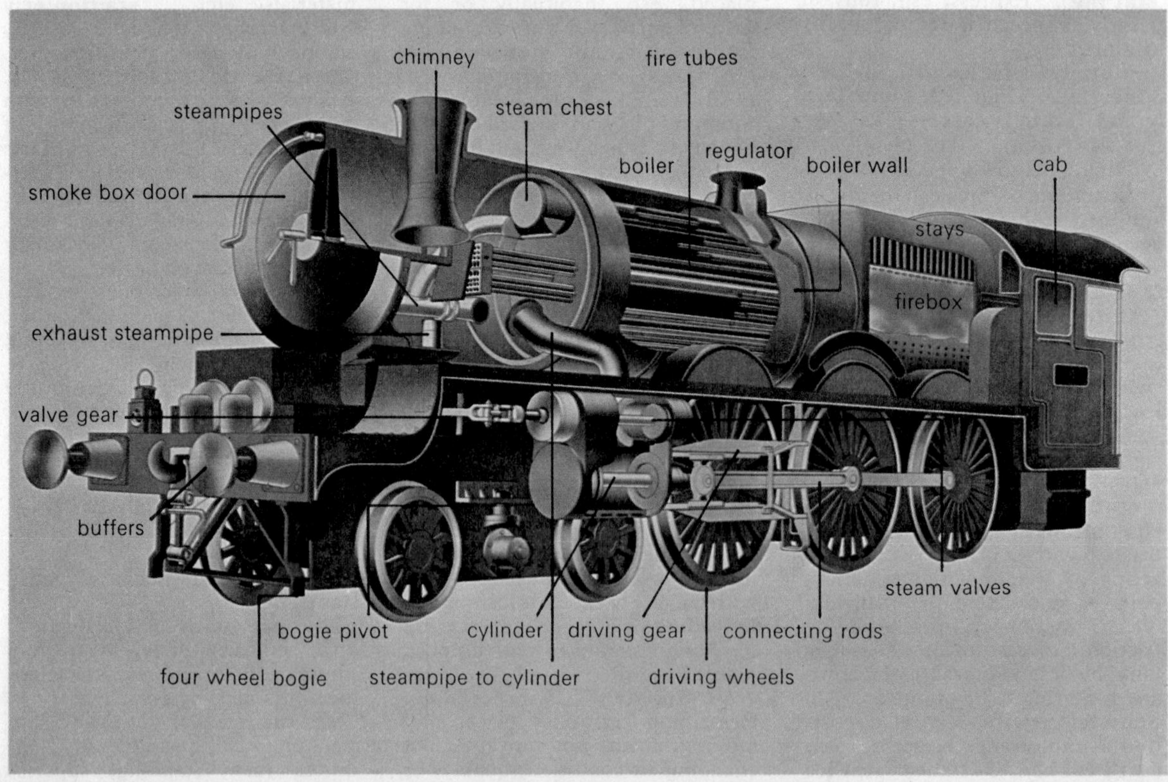

__Steam__ passes through three different cylinders in a triple-expansion steam engine (bottom). These are connected by side valves (top) which in turn are operated by eccentrics mounted on the crankshaft. Each piston is linked by a piston rod which transmits the drive to the crankshaft, which, in marine engines, provided the driving power to the propeller. The advantage of these engines, used until the late 1940s, was their high torque at low rotation.

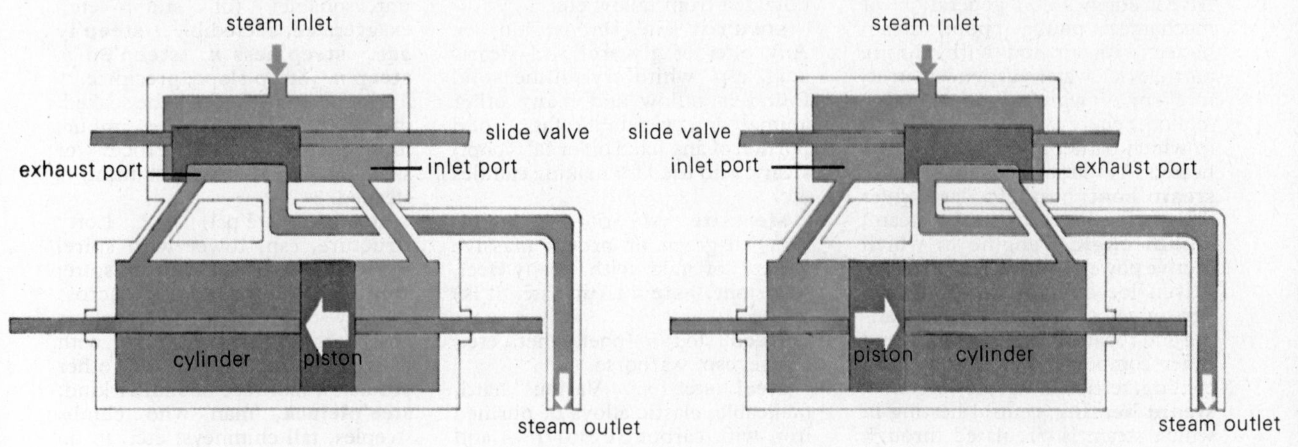

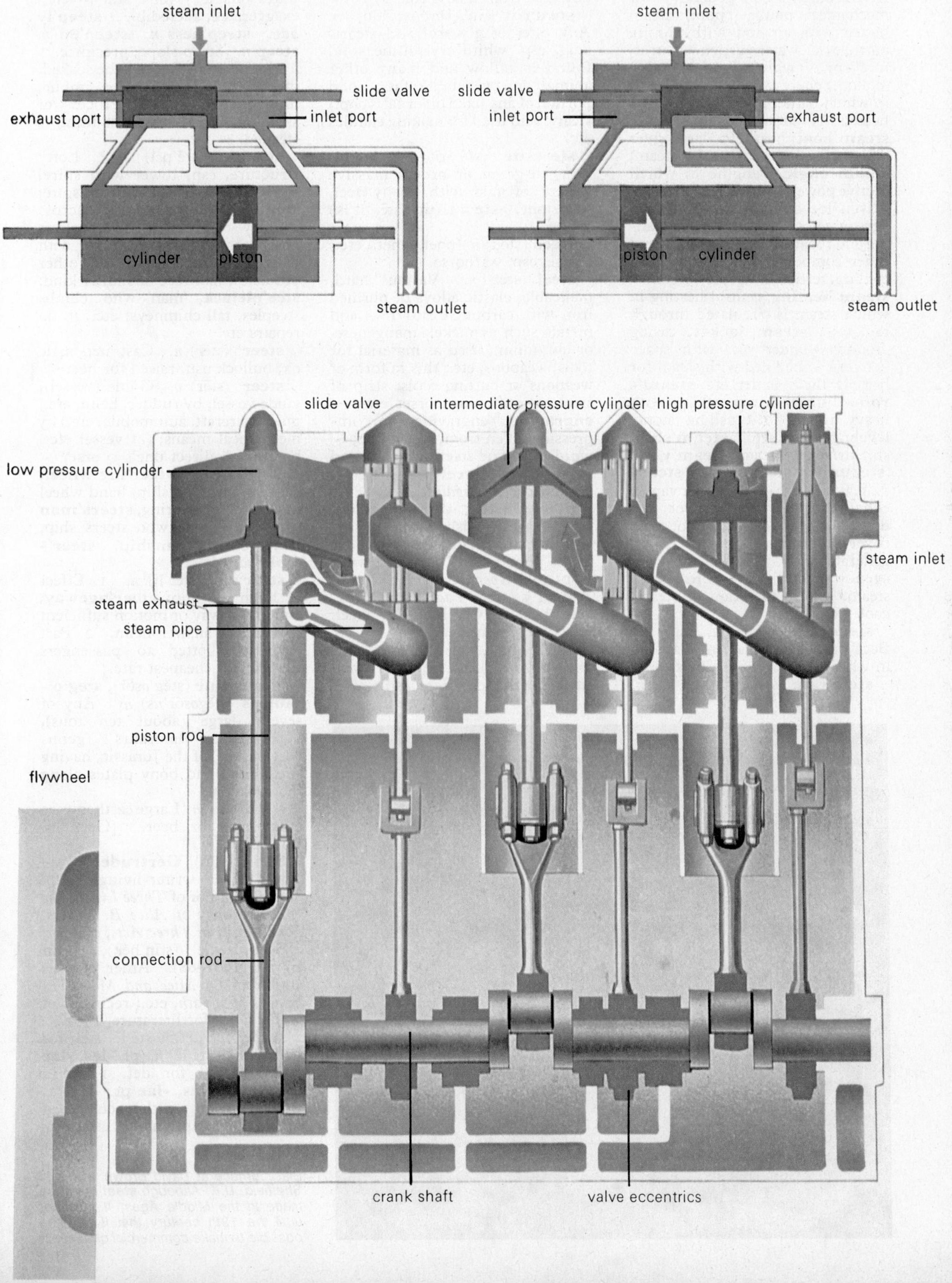

stealth'i·ly *adv.* **stealth'i·ness** *n.*

steam (stēm) *n.* Invisible vapor into which water is converted by heat; this used in specially contrived engines for generation of mechanical power; (pop.) steam mixed with air and with minute particles of water suspended in it, in form of white cloud or mist; (colloq.) energy, go; ~ **bath**, bath in which bather or substance to be heated is immersed in steam; **steam'boat**, boat, esp. large river or coasting boat, driven by steam; **steam engine**, engine in which motive power is steam; freq., steam-driven locomotive; **steam fitter**, person whose occupation is installing and repairing boilers, pipes, and other components of heating, air-cooling, refrigerating, etc., systems; **steam heating**, central heating in which steam is circulated through radiators; **steam jacket**, casing around cylinder etc. with space between to be filled with steam for heating the cylinder etc. **steam'-roller**, steam-driven vehicle with heavy roller for crushing stone, leveling roads, etc.; **steam'ship**, ship driven by steam. **steam'y** *adj.* (**steam·i·er, steam·i·est**). **steam** *v.* 1. Emit, give off, steam or vapor, exhale (steam, vapor), cover, bedew, (surface), (of surface) become covered, with condensed vapor; generate steam. 2. Travel, move, by agency of steam. 3. Treat with steam, expose to action of steam; cook by steam.

steam·er (stē'm*er*) *n.* (esp.) 1. Boat propelled by steam. 2. Pan in which food is cooked by steam.

ste·a·rate (stē'*e*rāt, stēr'āt) *n.* Salt of stearic acid.

ste·ar·ic (stēăr'ĭk, stēr'ĭk) *adj.* Derived from, containing, stearin; ~ **acid**, white crystalline fatty acid obtained from tallow etc.

ste·a·rin (stē'*e*rĭn, stēr'ĭn) *n.* Any ester of glycerol and stearic acid, esp. white crystalline solid found in tallow and many other animal and vegetable fats; solid portion of any fixed oil or fat; (pop.) stearic acid used for making candles etc.

ste·a·tite (stē'*a*tīt) *n.* (min.) Grayish-green or brown massive variety of talc with soapy feel, soapstone. **ste·a·tit·ic** (stē*a*tĭt'ĭk) *adj.*

steed (stēd) *n.* (poet., rhet., etc.) Horse, esp. warhorse.

steel (stēl) *n.* Various hard, malleable, elastic alloys of purified iron with carbon (up to 1%) and metals such as nickel, manganese, or chromium, used as material for tools, weapons, etc.; this in form of weapons or cutting tools; strip of steel for stiffening corset etc.; ~ **engraving**, engraving on, impression taken from, steel plate; ~ **wool**, very fine steel shavings used as abrasive. **steel** *v.t.* Nerve, harden, fortify (*against*).

Steele (stēl), **Sir Richard** (1672–1729). Irish essayist, playwright, and man of letters; founder of the periodicals *Tatler* and (with ADDISON[1]) *Spectator*.

steel·y (stē'lē) *adj.* (**steel·i·er, steel·i·est**). Of, hard as, steel; inflexible, obdurate.

steen·bok (stēn'bŏk, stān'-) *n.* (pl. **-boks**, collect. **-bok**). Small African antelope (*Raphicerus campestris*).

steep[1] (stēp) *adj.* With precipitous face or slope, sloping sharply; (colloq., of price etc.) exorbitant, unreasonable; (of story etc.) exaggerated, incredible. **steep'ly** *adv.* **steep'ness** *n.* **steep'en** *v.* **steep** *n.* Steep slope, precipice.

steep[2] (stēp) *v.* Soak, be soaked, in liquid; (fig.) permeate, imbue, impregnate. ~ *n.* Process of steeping; liquid in which thing is steeped.

stee·ple (stē'p*e*l) *n.* Lofty structure, esp. tower with spire, rising above roof of church; spire; **stee'plechase**, horse race across country (orig. perh. with steeple as goal) or on made course with hedges, water jumps, and other obstacles; foot race of similar kind; **stee'plejack**, man who climbs steeples, tall chimneys, etc., to do repairs etc.

steer[1] (stēr) *n.* Castrated male ox, bullock usu. raised for beef.

steer[2] (stēr) *v.* Guide (vessel), guide vessel, by rudder, helm, etc.; guide (aircraft, automobile, etc.) by mechanical means; (of vessel etc.) be guided; direct one's course; ~ **clear of**, avoid; **steer'ing wheel**, vertical wheel on ship, hand wheel in car etc. for steering; **steers'man** (pl. **-men**), one who steers ship, hence **steers'manship**. **steer'a·ble** *adj.*

steer·age (stēr'ĭj) *n.* 1. Effect of helm on ship; **steer'ageway**, amount of way or motion sufficient for ship to answer helm. 2. Part of ship allotted to passengers traveling at cheapest rate.

steg·o·saur (stĕg'*o*sôr), **steg·o·sau·rus** (stĕg*o*sôr'*u*s) *ns.* Any of several large (about ten tons), herbivorous dinosaurs (genus *Stegosaurus*) of the Jurassic, having small head and bony plates along the backbone.

stein (stīn) *n.* Large earthenware mug, esp. for beer. [Ger., = "stone"]

Stein (stīn), **Gertrude** (1874–1946). Amer. writer living chiefly in Paris; author of *Three Lives, The Autobiography of Alice B. Toklas, Four Saints in Three Acts,* etc.

Stein·beck (stīn'bĕk), **John Ernst** (1902–68). Amer. writer; author of *Of Mice and Men, The Grapes of Wrath,* etc.; recipient of Nobel Prize for literature, 1962.

ste·le (for def. 1 stē'lē, stēl; for sense 2 stēl, stē'lē) *n.* (pl. **-les, -lae** pr. -lē); also for def. 1 **ste·la** (stē'l*a*) (pl. **-las, -lae** pr. -lē). 1. Upright slab with sculptured design or inscription, esp. as grave-

*Blast furnace at David Brown works in Sheffield, U.K. Although **steel** could be made in the Middle Ages, it was not until the 19th century that it became possible to make commercial quantities.*

Unlike most antelopes, the ***steenbock*** *of east Africa tries to avoid danger by lying in the grass with the neck outstretched, rather than rely on its speed to outpace its enemies.*

stone. 2. (bot.) Axial cylinder in stems and roots of vascular plants.

stel·lar (stĕl′*er*) *adj.* Of stars; star-shaped.

stel·late (stĕl′ĭt, -āt), **stel·lat·ed** (stĕl′ātĭd) *adjs.* Star-shaped, radiating from center like rays of star.

stem[1] (stĕm) *n.* 1. Main body above ground, ascending axis, of tree, shrub, or other plant; stalk supporting leaf, flower, or fruit. 2. Stem-shaped part or object, as slender upright support of cup, wineglass, etc., long slender part or tube of key, thermometer, tobacco pipe, etc.; **stem′ware**, glasses with stems; **stem-winder**, watch wound by turning head on end of stem, not by key. 3. Part of word remaining essentially unchanged in inflection, part to which inflectional suffixes are added. 4. Line of ancestry; branch of family; stock, race. 5. (naut.) Curved upright timber or metal piece at fore end of vessel, to which ship's sides are joined; bows or forepart of vessel. **stem** *v.* (**stemmed, stem·ming**). 1. Remove stem of. 2. Make headway against (tide, current, etc.). 3. ~ **from**, originate in.

stem[2] (stĕm) *v.t.* (**stemmed, stem·ming**). Check, stop, dam up (stream etc.); (skiing) check (oneself), check progress, by forcing heel of ski(s) outward from line of run; ~ **turn**, turn made by stemming one ski.

stench (stĕnch) *n.* Foul or offensive smell.

sten·cil (stĕn′sĭl) *n.* Thin sheet of metal, cardboard, etc. with holes cut in such a way that when paintbrush etc. is passed over it, desired design is produced on surface beneath; decoration, lettering, so produced. ~ *v.t.* (**-ciled, -cil·ing**, Brit. **-cilled, -cil·ling**). Produce (pattern) on surface, ornament (surface) with pattern, by means of stencil(s).

Sten·dhal (stĕndahl′). Pen name of Henri Beyle (1783–1842),

The ***stem*** *of a plant can be distinguished from the root by the bud which is always at its tip. Its function is to provide support for the leaves and to convey food. Young stems are soft but as they age, they become hard and woody. Bulbs and rhizomes are underground stems which store food; runners, on a strawberry, are horizontal stems that produce new plants.*

transverse and longitudinal sections of stems

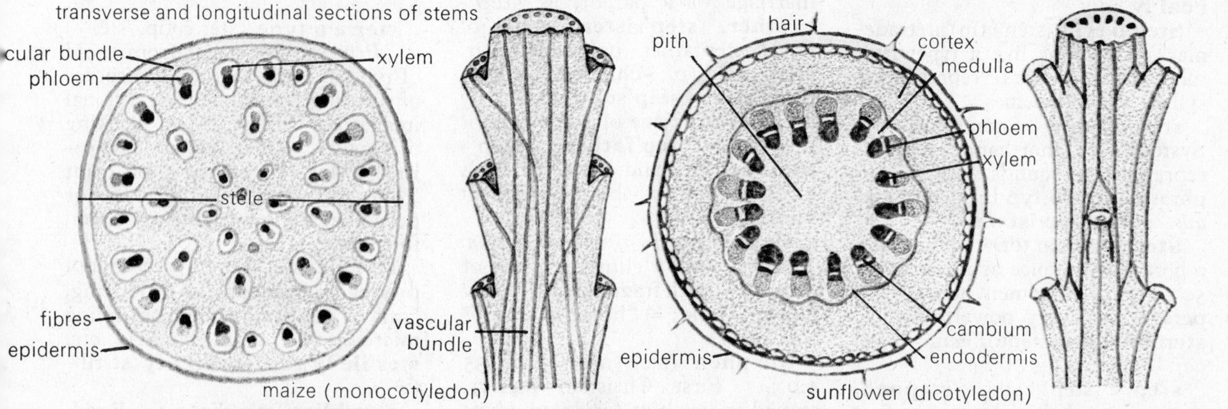

cular bundle
phloem
xylem
stele
fibres
epidermis
vascular bundle
maize (monocotyledon)
pith
hair
cortex
medulla
phloem
xylem
cambium
endodermis
epidermis
sunflower (dicotyledon)

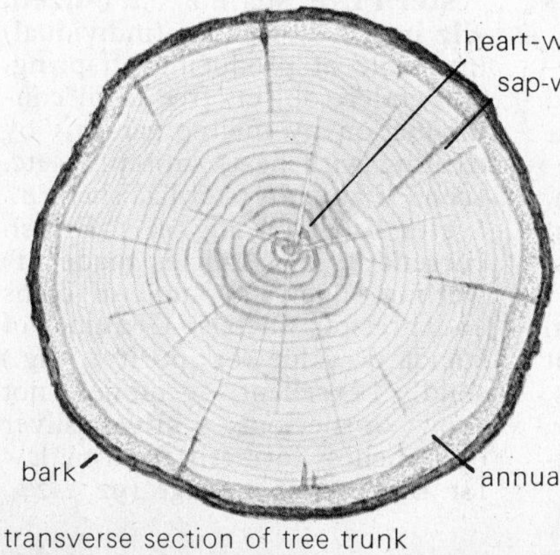

heart-wood
sap-wood
bark
annual ring
transverse section of tree trunk 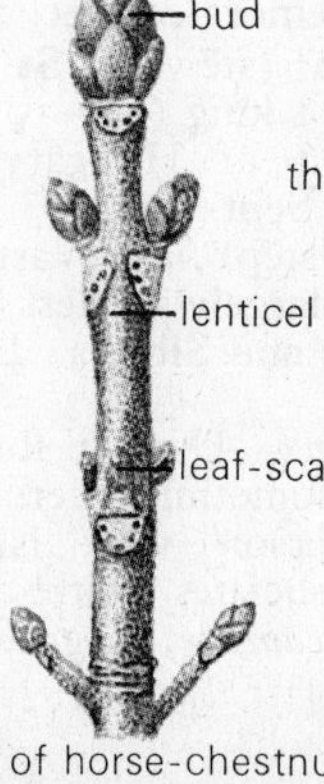
bud
lenticel
leaf-scar
twigs of horse-chestnut 
thorn
hawthorn 
true leaf
cladode
butcher's broom

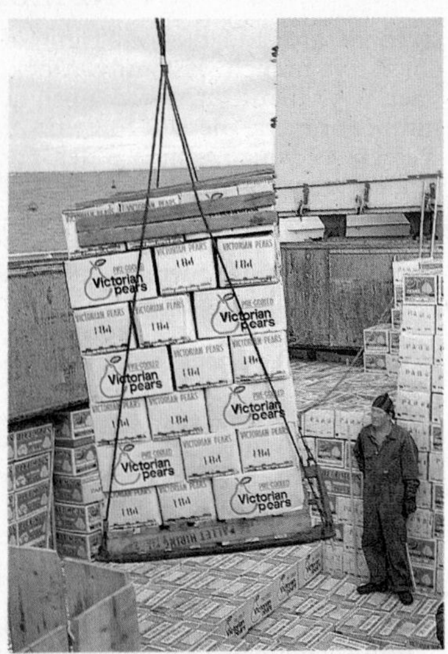

Modern lifting equipment has made the working life of a ***stevedore*** *far less taxing than in the past, when most freight had to be loaded and unloaded by hand.*

French novelist, author of *The Red and the Black* and *The Charterhouse of Parma*.

sten·o (stĕn′ō) *n.* (colloq.) Stenography; stenographer.

ste·nog·ra·phy (st*e*nŏg′r*a*fē) *n.* Art of writing in shorthand. **sten·o·graph** (stĕn′*o*grăf, -grahf) *n.* Writing, machine for writing, in shorthand. ~ *v.* Write in shorthand, act as stenographer. **ste·nog′ra·pher** *n.* **sten·o·graph·ic** (stĕn*o*grăf′ĭk), **sten·o·graph′i·cal** *adjs.* **sten·o·graph′i·cal·ly** *adv.*

Sten·o·type (stĕn′*o*tīp) *n.* (trademark) Machine like a typewriter that prints letters representing syllables or phonemes.

sten·o·typ·y (stĕn′*o*tīpē) *n.* System of shorthand symbols representing sounds, words, or phrases. **sten·o·typ·ic** (stĕn*o*tĭp′ĭk) *adj.* **sten′o·typ·ist** *n.*

Sten·tor (stĕn′tōr). In the *Iliad*, a herald with voice as powerful as 50 voices of other men; hence (**s**~), person with very powerful voice. **sten·to·ri·an** (stĕntōr′ē*a*n, -tōr′-) *adj.*

step (stĕp) *v.* (**stepped, step·ping**). Lift and set down foot or alternate feet in walking etc.; go short distance, progress in some direction, by stepping; measure (distance) by stepping; (naut.) set up (mast) in step; ~ **down**, retire, resign, take lower position; (elect.) lower voltage of (current) by means of a transformer; ~ **in**, (fig.) intervene to help or hinder; ~**-in** (*n.* & *adj.*), (garment, esp. formerly of woman's underwear) put on by being stepped into without unfastening; ~ **on the gas**: see GAS²; ~ **on it**, (slang) hurry; ~ **out**, walk vigorously, stride; behave, live, in lively, extravagant, or dissipated manner; ~ **up**, (elect.) increase voltage of (current) by means of a transformer; increase (efficiency, production) in rate, volume, etc., speed up; **stepping stone**, stone set in or projecting above water or muddy place as a help in crossing; (fig.) means of advancement or progress. **step** *n.* 1. Movement of stepping, distance gained by this; progress by stepping, course followed; manner of stepping; sound made by setting foot down; (fig.) action toward result, one of series of measures taken; **in** ~, stepping in time with other person(s) or music, stepping simultaneously and with corresponding legs with other person(s) or animal(s); **out of** ~, not in step. 2. Flat-topped structure, used singly or as one of series, to facilitate person's movement from one level to another; rung of ladder; foot piece for entering, mounting, or alighting from vehicle; notch cut for foot in climbing; (pl.) stepladder; (fig.) degree in an ascending scale, advance from one of these to another. 3. (naut.) Block or socket supporting mast etc.; (mech.) lower bearing on which vertical shaft revolves; steplike part or offset. 4. **step cut**, (of gem) cut in straight facets arranged around center of stone; **step′ladder**, kind of portable short ladder with flat steps and prop hinged to back for steadying.

step- *prefix.* Having a specified relationship resulting from remarriage of a parent, as **step′brother, step′sister**, child of one's stepfather or stepmother; **step′child** (pl. **-children**), **step′daughter, step′son**, child by previous marriage of one's wife or husband; **step′father, step′mother**, husband, wife, of one's mother, father, by subsequent marriage.

steph·a·no·tis (stĕf*a*nō′tĭs) *n.* Tropical woody climbing plant of genus *S*~ with fragrant white waxy flowers. [Gk., = "fit for a wreath" (*stephanos*)]

Ste·phen¹ (stē′v*e*n), **St.** (d. *c*35 A.D.). First Christian martyr, stoned to death at Jerusalem (Acts 6, 7; commemorated Dec. 26).

Ste·phen² (stē′v*e*n), **St.** (*c*977–1038). First king (997–1038) and patron saint of Hungary; commemorated Sept. 2.

steppe (stĕp) *n.* Vast plain, grassy and largely treeless, esp. in SE. Europe and Siberia. [f. Russ. *step′*]

-ster *suffix.* Used in formation of nouns, sometimes derog., that indicate person who is, does, creates, associates with: *oldster, prankster, teamster, songster, gangster.*

ste·ra·di·an (st*e*rā′dē*a*n) *n.* (abbrev. sr) Solid angle at center of sphere subtending a section on the surface whose area is equal to the square of the radius.

ster·co·ra·ceous (stērk*e*rā′sh*u*s), **ster·co·rous** (stēr′k*e*r*u*s) *adjs.* Of, produced by, dung or feces.

stere (stēr) *n.* One cubic meter.

ster·e·o (stēr′ēō, stēr′-) *n.* (pl. **-os**). Stereotype; stereoscopic photograph or photography; stereophonic reproduction or equipment. ~ *adj.* Stereotyped; stereoscopic; stereophonic.

stereo- *prefix.* Solid; three dimensional; stereoscopic.

ster·e·o·chem·is·try (stĕrēō-kĕm′ĭstrē, stēr-) *n.* (Branch of chemistry dealing with) spatial arrangement of atoms etc. in molecule. **ster·e·o·chem′i·cal** *adj.*

ster·e·oph·o·ny (stĕrēŏf′*o*nē, stēr-) *n.* System of separate microphones or loudspeakers designed to enhance the realism of broadcast or recorded sounds. **ster·e·o·phon·ic** (stĕrē*o*fŏn′ĭk, stēr-) *adj.* **ster·e·o·phon′i·cal·ly** *adv.*

ster·e·o·scope (stĕr′ē*o*skōp, stēr-) *n.* Instrument for obtaining single image giving impression of solidity or relief from two pictures (usu. photographs) of object from slightly different points of view. **ster·e·o·scop·ic** (stĕrē*o*skŏp′ĭk, stēr-) *adj.* Of the stereoscope or stereoscopy. **ster·e·os·co·py** (stĕrēŏs′k*o*pē, stēr-) *n.* Vision of objects as solid or in three dimensions. **ster·e·o·scop′i·cal·ly** *adv.*

ster·e·o·type (stĕr′ē*o*tīp, stēr′-) *n.* Printing plate cast from mold of type in form; method or process of printing from this; conventional image or idea; idea lacking originality. ~ *v.t.* (**-typed, -typ·ing**). Make stereotype(s) of, print from stereotype(s); (fig.) fix or perpetuate in unchanging form, formalize.

ster·ile (stĕr′*i*l) *adj.* Barren; not producing, incapable of producing, fruit or offspring; free from living microorganisms, as bacteria etc. **ster′ile·ly** *adv.* **ste·ril·i·ty** (st*e*rĭl′ĭtē) *n.*

ster·i·lize (stĕr′*i*līz) *v.t.* (**-lized, -liz·ing**). 1. Render (individual) incapable of producing offspring. 2. Render (object) free from contamination by microorganisms by treating with heat, antiseptic, etc. **ster·i·li·za·tion** (stĕr*i*līzā′sh*o*n) *n.*

ster·ling (stēr′lĭng) *n.* 1. British currency. 2. (Articles made of) sterling silver. ~ *adj.* (of coins and precious metals) Genuine, of standard value or purity; (fig.) solidly excellent, genuine, not showy or specious; ~ **silver**, silver of a fineness formerly fixed by law for Brit. silver coinage (92 1/2%

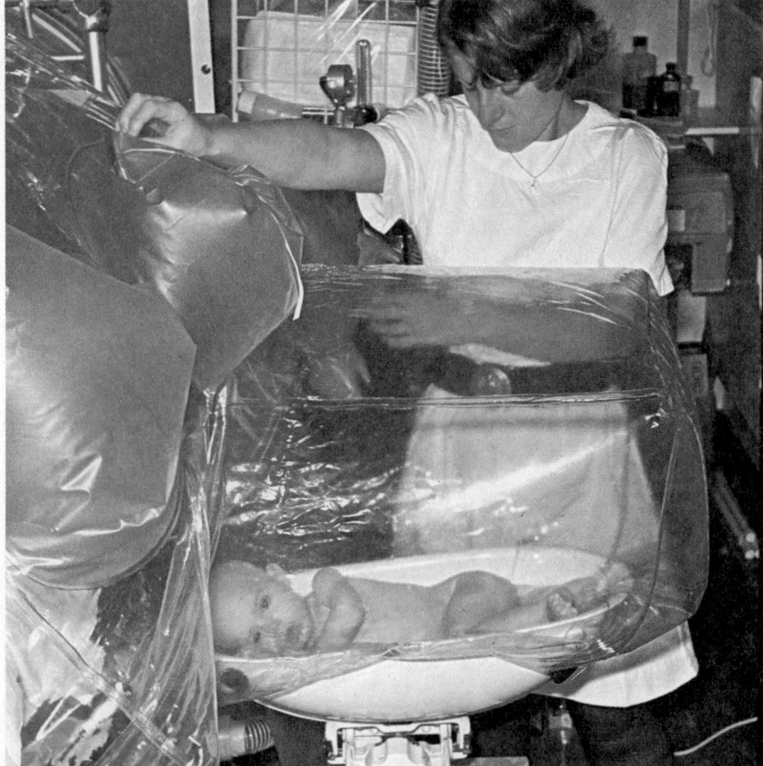

To prevent premature babies risking infection, they are kept in a **sterile** unit which is sufficiently flexible to allow them to be moved about without exposure to the atmosphere.

Of little practical use, although popular during the 19th century to give a three dimensional effect, the **stereoscope** was conceived by Wheatstone but improved by Sir David Brewster.

silver and 7 1/2% copper). [orig. as noun, = the English silver penny]

stern[1] (stẽrn) *n.* After or rear part of aircraft, ship, or boat, specif. that part of the hull abaft the sternpost; buttocks, rump; tail, esp. of foxhound; ~ **chase**, pursuit of ship by another directly in its wake; **stern'post**, central upright timber or iron of stern, attached to keel and usu. bearing rudder; **stern'-wheeler**, (hist.) steamer with 1 large paddle wheel at stern.

stern[2] (stẽrn) *adj.* Severe, strict, not lenient, rigorous in principle, punishment, or condemnation; hard, grim, harsh, gloomy. **stern'ly** *adv.* **stern'ness** *n.*

ster·nal (stẽr'nal) *adj.* Of the sternum.

Sterne (stẽrn), **Laurence** (1713–68). English novelist, author of *Tristram Shandy* and *A Sentimental Journey*.

ster·num (stẽr'num) *n.* (pl. **-nums, -na** pr. -na). Bone or series of bones running along middle line of front of trunk, usu. articulated with some of ribs; breastbone of bird; ventral plate of body segment of arthropod.

ster·nu·ta·tion (stẽrnyutā'shon) *n.* Sneezing, sneeze. **ster·nu·ta·to·ry** (sternōō'tatōrē, -tōrē, -nū'-) *adj.* & *n.* (pl. **-ries**). (Substance, e.g. snuff) causing sneezing.

ster·nu·ta·tor (stẽrn'yutāter) *n.* Chemical agent, esp. poison gas, that acts as a nose irritant.

ster·oid (stĕr'oid, stẽr'-) *adj.* & *n.* (biochem.) (One) of a class of compounds with complex 4-ring molecular structure, found in animal and plant cells or prepared synthetically and including the sterols, bile acids, and certain hormones.

ster·ol (stĕr'awl, -ŏl, -ōl, stẽr'-) *n.* (biochem.) One of a class of complex solid alcohols, as cholesterol, ergosterol, widely distributed in animals and plants.

ster·to·rous (stẽr'terus) *adj.* (of breathing etc.) Producing snoring or rasping sound. **ster'to·rous·ly** *adv.* **ster'to·rous·ness** *n.*

stet (stĕt) *n.* Direction to printer, written in margin of manuscript or proof, to cancel a correction made in the text, the letters thus restored being indicated by dots beneath them. ~ *v.t.* (**stet·ted, stet·ting**). [L., = "let it stand"]

steth·o·scope (stĕth'oskōp) *n.* Instrument, consisting of ear tubes and a main tube to be applied to chest etc. for auscultation, esp. of heart or lungs. **steth·o·scop·ic** (stĕthoskŏp'ĭk) *adj.* **steth·o·scop'i·cal·ly** *adv.* **ste·thos·co·py** (stĕthŏs'kopē) *n.*

Stet·son (stĕt'son) *n.* (trademark, colloq.) Man's felt hat with broad brim.

ste·ve·dore (stē'vedōr, -dōr) *n.* Man employed in loading and unloading ship's cargoes.

Ste·ven·son[1] (stē'venson), **Adlai Ewing** (1835–1914). Amer. statesman; member from Illinois of U.S. House of Representatives, 1875–7, 1879–81; vice president under Grover Cleveland, 1893–7; also his grandson (1900–65) of the same name, U.S. Ambassador to the United Nations from 1961.

Ste·ven·son[2] (stē'venson), **Robert Louis** (1850–94). Scottish essayist, novelist, and poet; author of *Treasure Island*, *Dr. Jekyll and Mr. Hyde*, *Kidnapped*, etc.

stew (stōō, stū) *v.* Cook by long simmering in closed vessel with liquid; (fig.) be oppressed by close or moist warm atmosphere; ~ **in one's own juice**, be left to suffer the consequences of one's own actions. **stew** *n.* Dish of stewed meat, usu. with vegetables; (fig.) state of great alarm or excitement; **stew'pan, stew'pot**, pan, covered pot, for stewing.

stew·ard (stōō'erd, stū'-), fem. **stew·ard·ess** (stōō'erdĭs, stū'-) *ns.* 1. Person entrusted with management of another's property, esp. paid manager of great house or estate. 2. Purveyor of provisions etc. for college, club, ship, etc. 3. Attendant waiting on passengers in ship or aircraft. 4. Official managing meeting, ball, show, etc.

stick (stĭk) *v.* (**stuck** pr. stŭk, **stick·ing**). 1. Thrust point of (pin, weapon, etc.) *in*(*to*), *through*; insert pointed thing(s) into, stab; fix *on* pointed thing, be fixed (as) by point *in*(*to*) or *on*; (colloq.) put in specified position. 2. ~ **out, up**, etc., protrude, (cause to) project; be, make, erect; ~ **up for**, maintain cause or character of, champion; ~ **up**, (slang) rob with violence, hold up; ~**-up** (*n.*). 3. Fix, become

or remain fixed (as) by adhesion of surfaces; (cause to) adhere or cleave; baffle, confuse; (colloq.) endure, bear; ~ **at** or **to it**, persist, not cease trying; ~ **by** or **to**, remain faithful to; ~**-to-it-ive-ness**, (colloq.) perseverance; ~**-to-it-ive** (*adj*.). 4. Lose or deprive of power of motion through friction, jamming, suction, difficulty, etc.; ~**-in-the-mud**, slow, unprogressive (person); **sticking plaster**, adhesive plaster for wounds etc.; **stick'pin**, (ornamental) pin, esp. tie pin, that is merely stuck in, as dist. from safety pin; **stick-up**, (*adj*.) that sticks up or projects.
stick *n*. 1. Short and relatively slender piece of wood; shoot or branch of tree cut to convenient length for use as walking cane, bludgeon, staff, wand, support for climbing plant, etc.; fiddlestick, drumstick, composing stick, etc.; implement used in hockey or lacrosse; twigs or small pieces of wood as fuel; (fig.) person of no liveliness or intelligence, poor actor; ~ **ball**, baseball played with broom handle and rubber ball; ~ **of furniture**, (esp. in neg. or pl.) piece of furniture; ~ **shift**, manually operated gearshift set in the floor of a car. 2. Slender more or less cylindrical piece *of* any material. 3. Number of aerial bombs released in close succession, or of parachute troops from an

*A **still life** of apples as painted by Gustave Courbet shows the painter's determination to pursue the modes of Velazquez, whom he admired, rather than follow classical trends.*

aircraft. 4. ~ **insect**, insect of family Phasmidae, usu. wingless, with long slender sticklike body resembling twigs of trees in which it lives.

stick·er (stĭk'*er*) *n*. (esp.) 1. Adhesive label or other paper gummed on back; ~ **price**, retail price for product suggested by manufacturer, esp. as pasted on window of new automobile. 2. Dogged or persistent person.

stick·le·back (stĭk'*el*băk) *n*. Any of small spiny-finned fishes (family Gasterosteidae) of N. hemisphere.

stick·ler (stĭk'l*er*) *n*. 1. (followed by *for*) One who insists on or pertinaciously supports or advocates. 2. Difficult problem.

stick·y (stĭk'ē) *adj*. (**stick·i·er, stick·i·est**). Tending to stick or adhere, glutinous, viscous; (of weather) muggy; covered with wet paint, adhesive, etc.; (slang) highly unpleasant and painful. **stick'i·ly** *adv*. **stick'i·ness** *n*.

stiff (stĭf) *adj*. 1. Rigid, not flexible; unbending, unyielding, uncompromising, obstinate; lacking ease, grace, or freedom; formal, labored, constrained, haughty; ~**-arm** (*v*. & *n*.) (make) motion with extended arm of pushing away or shoving someone; ~**-necked**, stubborn. 2. Not working freely, sticking, offering resistance; (of joints, limbs, etc.) not supple, unable to move without pain; ~ **neck**, condition in which head cannot be moved without pain. 3. Hard to cope with, trying, difficult. 4. (of moist or semiliquid substance) Thick and viscous, not fluid. **stiff'ly** *adv*. **stiff'ness** *n*. **stiff'en** *v*. **stiff'en·er** *n*. **stiff** *n*. (slang) Corpse.

sti·fle[1] (stī'f*e*l) *v*. (**-fled, -fling**). Smother; (cause to) feel oppressed or unable to breathe. **sti'fling** *adj*. **sti'fling·ly** *adv*.

sti·fle[2] (stī'f*e*l) *n*. (also ~ **joint**) Joint between femur and tibia in horse and some other quadrupeds, corresponding to knee in man.

stig·ma (stĭg'm*a*) *n*. (pl. **stig·mas, stig·ma·ta** pr. stĭg'm*ata*, stĭgmah'*ta*, -măt'*a*). Mark branded on slave, criminal, etc. (archaic); (fig.) mark of disgrace or infamy, stain on one's good name; (path.) definite characteristic of some disease, morbid red spot on skin, esp. one bleeding spontaneously; (anat., zool.) spot, pore, natural mark, esp. spot on surface of ovary where rupture of Graafian follicle will occur; insect's spiracle; (bot.) receptive surface of the floral pistil to which pollen grains adhere; (pl. **stigmata**) marks resembling wounds on crucified body of Christ, said to have developed on bodies of some saints. **stig·mat·ic** (stĭgmăt´ĭk), **stig·mat´i·cal** *adjs.*

stig·ma·tize (stĭg´matīz) *v.t.* (**-tized, -tiz·ing**). Mark with stigmata, produce stigmata upon; (fig.) use opprobrious terms of, describe by disgraceful or reproachful name. **stig·ma·ti·za·tion** (stĭgmatīzā´shon) *n.*

stil·bes·trol (stĭlbĕs´trawl, -trŏl, -trōl) *n.* Synthetic estrogen, diethylstilbestrol.

stile[1] (stīl) *n.* Arrangement of steps, rungs, etc., allowing passage to persons over or through fence or wall but excluding cattle etc.

stile[2] (stīl) *n.* Vertical bar of wainscot, sash, or other wooden framing.

sti·let·to (stĭlĕt´ō) *n.* (pl. **-tos, -toes**). Short dagger; small pointed implement for making eyelet holes etc.

still[1] (stĭl) *adj.* Without or almost without motion or sound, silent, quiet, calm; (of wine etc.) not sparkling or effervescing; **still´-birth**, delivery of dead child, so **still´born; still life**, (pl. **still lifes**) representation in painting etc. of inanimate things, as fruit, flowers, etc. **still´ness** *n.* **still** *n.* 1. Deep silence. 2. Photograph (other than motion picture), esp. single frame from motion picture film. ~ *v.* Quiet, calm, appease, make still; (rare) grow still or calm. ~ *adv.* 1. Without motion or change. 2. Now as formerly; then as before; now, in contrast with future; even then, even now; nevertheless; even, yet; always, even.

still[2] (stĭl) *n.* Distilling apparatus, consisting essentially of a closed vessel for heating substance to be distilled, and spiral tube or worm for condensing the vapor so produced.

Still·son (stĭl´son) **wrench.** (trademark) Monkey wrench having pivoted, adjustable jaw that tightens its grip on pipes etc. as pressure is applied on handle.

stilt (stĭlt) *n.* 1. Each of pair of poles, usu. held by hands or under arms, with footrest some way from lower end, for enabling person to walk over marshy ground, stream, etc., with feet raised above ground; one of set of piles or posts supporting building, etc. 2. Marsh bird of the widely distributed genus *Himantopus*, with very long slender legs and sharp slender bill.

stilt·ed (stĭl´tĭd) *adj.* (As) on stilts; (of style, language, etc.) artificially lofty, formally pompous. **stilt´ed·ly** *adv.* **stilt´ed·ness** *n.*

Stil·ton (stĭl´ton) *n.* (also ~ **cheese**) Rich blue-veined cheese, made principally in England.

stim·u·lant (stĭm´yulant) *n.* Agent producing temporary increase of activity in part of organism; such a food, beverage, as tea, coffee, etc.; (pop.) alcoholic drink.

stim·u·late (stĭm´yulāt) *v.t.* (**-lat·ed, -lat·ing**). Apply stimulus to, act as stimulus on; animate, spur on, make more vigorous or active. **stim·u·la·tion** (stĭmyulā´shon) *n.* **stim´u·la·tive** *adj.* **stim´u·lat·ing·ly** *adv.*

stim·u·lus (stĭm´yulus) *n.* (pl. **-li** pr. -lī). Something that rouses to activity or energy; rousing effect; thing that rouses organ or tissue to specific activity or function, effect of this. [L., = "goad"]

sting (stĭng) *n.* 1. Sharp-pointed organ in some insects and other animals, freq. connected with poison gland, and capable of giving painful or dangerous wound; poison fang of snake; (bot.) stiff sharp-pointed hair emitting irritating fluid when touched. 2. Stinging, being stung; wound made, pain or irritation produced, by sting; rankling or acute pain of body or mind; keenness, vigor; stimulus. 3. **sting´ray, stingaree** (stĭng´erē, stĭngerē´), ray esp. of family Dasyatidae, with long tapering tail armed with flattened sharp-pointed serrated spine(s) capable of inflicting severe wounds. **sting** *v.* (**stung** pr. stŭng, **sting·ing**). 1. Wound with sting; (of some plants) produce kind of burning or itching rash or inflammation by contact with (skin); feel acute pain; be able to sting, have a sting; **stinging hair**, sting of plant; **stinging nettle**, common NETTLE. 2. (slang, chiefly *pass.*) Charge heavily, involve in expense, swindle.

stin·gy (stĭn´jē) *adj.* (**-gi·er, -gi·est**). Meanly parsimonious. **stin´gi·ly** *adv.* **stin´gi·ness** *n.*

stink (stĭngk) *v.* (**stank** pr. stăngk or **stunk** pr. stŭngk, **stunk, stink·ing**). Have, emit, strong offensive smell; drive *out* with stench or suffocating fumes; cause to stink; (slang) be of offensively poor quality. ~ *n.* Strong offensive smell; **raise a** ~, (colloq.) cause trouble by criticizing or complaining; ~ **bomb**, small bomb giving off offensive smell on bursting; **stink´horn**, any of various ill-smelling fungi, esp. *Phallus impudicus*; **stink´wood**, any of various trees with unpleasant smelling wood.

stink·er (stĭng´ker) *n.* (colloq.) Person or thing particularly offensive or irritating.

stink·ing (stĭng´kĭng) *adj.* That stinks (freq. in names of plants etc., e.g. ~ **gum**, eucalyptus with leaves having strong, buglike smell; ~ **Roger**, wild marigold); (slang) objectionable, obnoxious; very drunk.

stint (stĭnt) *n.* Limitation of supply or effort; fixed or allotted amount (of work etc.). ~ *v.* Keep on short allowance, supply or give in niggardly amount or grudgingly. **stint´er** *n.* **stint´ing** *adj.* **stint´ing·ly** *adv.*

stipe (stīp) *n.* (bot.) Footstalk, esp. stem supporting pileus of fungus, leafstalk of fern etc.; (zool.) stipes.

*With legs longer in proportion to its body than any other wading bird, the **stilt** will feed on shrimps either in salt water estuaries or in grassy areas flooded by freshwater.*

*The greater **stitchwort** is one of a group of some 80 plants with a wide distribution. Others include common chickweed and the bog variety with large white flowers on foot-high stems.*

*Reconstructed in the 1950s, the **Stoa of Attalus** still flanks the Agora or ancient civic centre of Athens. A stoa could be a detached portico, or a frontage to a hall as in the example illustrated.*

sti·pend (stī'pĕnd) *n.* Salary or pension, esp. of clergyman.

sti·pen·di·ar·y (stīpĕn'dēĕrē) *adj.* & *n.* (Person) receiving stipend.

sti·pes (stī'pēz) *n.* (pl. **stip·i·tes** pr. stĭp'ĭtēz). (zool.) Stalklike part or organ, esp. 2nd segment of maxilla of insect, eyestalk, etc.; (bot.) stipe.

stip·ple (stĭp'*e*l) *n.* Method of painting, engraving, etc., by use of dots or small spots to produce gradations of shade or color; layer of paint applied roughly over layer of another color that shows through in places; effect, work, so produced. ~ *v.* Engrave, paint, in stipple.

stip·u·late (stĭp'yulāt) *v.* Require or insist upon as essential condition; make express demand *for* as condition of agreement. **stip·u·la·tion** (stĭpyulā'sh*o*n) *n.*

stip·ule (stĭp'ūl) *n.* One of pair of lateral appendages, freq. resembling small leaf or scale, at base of leaf in certain plants.

stir[1] (stẽr) *n.* Commotion, bustle, disturbance, excitement; slight movement; act of stirring. ~ *v.* (**stirred, stir·ring**). Set, keep, (begin to) be, in (esp. slight) motion; agitate (soft or liquid or semiliquid mass) with more or less circular motion, as with spoon, so as to mix ingredients, prevent burning in cooking, etc.; rouse (*up*), excite, animate, inspirit. **stir'ring** *adj.* Exciting, stimulating. **stir'ring·ly** *adv.*

stir[2] (stẽr) *n.* (slang) Prison.

stir·rup (stẽr'*u*p, stĭr'-, stŭr'-) *n.* Support suspended by strap from side of saddle for rider's foot, now usu. iron loop with flattened base; something resembling this, esp. U-shaped clamp or support; (naut.) rope with eye at end supporting footrope; (also ~ **bone**) stirrup-shaped bone of middle ear, stapes; ~ **cup**, (Brit.) parting cup of wine etc. handed to rider on horseback; ~ **jar, vase,** (Gk. antiq.) jar with solid neck joined to body by handle on each side; ~ **leather,** strap suspending stirrup from saddle.

stitch (stĭch) *n.* 1. Sudden sharp pain, esp. in side of the body. 2. Each movement of threaded needle in and out of fabric in sewing, or of awl in shoemaking; loop of thread etc. left in fabric by this movement; single complete movement of needle, hook, etc., in knitting, crochet, embroidery, etc.; part of work produced by this; (surg.) movement of needle in sewing up wound, loop of catgut etc. left in skin or flesh by this; method of making stitch, kind of work produced. 3. **stitch'wort,** chickweed, esp. kind with erect stem and white starry flowers. **stitch** *v.* Sew, make stitches (in); fasten, make, ornament, with stitches.

stitch·er·y (stĭch'*e*rē) *n.* Needlework.

sto·a (stō'*a*) *n.* (pl. **sto·as, sto·ai** pr. stō'ī, **sto·ae** pr. stō'ē). Portico in ancient Greek architecture.

stoat (stōt) *n.* (pl. **stoats,** collect. **stoat**). ERMINE, esp. in its brown summer coat.

stock (stŏk) *n.* 1. Trunk or stem of tree; stump, butt; plant into which graft is inserted; (bot.) rhizome; (geol.) cylindrical intrusive body of igneous rock (freq. granite) of moderate size. 2. Body piece serving as the base or holder or handle for the working parts of an implement or machine, as whip, lathe, plow, rifle, anchor, etc. 3. (Source of) family or breed; line of descent, ancestry; race, racial strain, or other related group of plants or animals; ethnic group or other major subdivision of human race; group of related (families of) languages. 4. (hist., pl.) Instrument of punishment, wooden framework set up in public place with holes for offender's feet or feet and hands. 5. (pl.) Timbers on which ship rests while building. 6. Cruciferous plant of genus *Mathiola*, with fragrant flowers. 7. Livestock. 8. Liquor or broth made by stewing meat, bones, vegetables, etc., and used as foundation for soup etc. 9. Raw material of manufacture; fund, store ready for drawing on, equipment for trade or pursuit. 10. Specified type or grade of paper; paper for specific job of printing. 11. Outstanding capital of corporation, regarded as transferable property held by subscribers or creditors and subject to fluctuations in market value; see COMMON ~, PREFERRED ~. 12. **take ~,** make inventory of merchandise etc. in hand; (fig.) make careful estimate of one's position, prospects, resources, etc.; **take ~ of,** reckon up, evaluate, scrutinize. 13. (attrib. or as *adj.*) Kept regularly in stock for sale or use; commonly used, constantly recurring in discussion etc.; ~ **company,**

Left: Present in the north-temperate forests and tundra of Europe, Asia and North America, the ***stoat*** *lives on small animals and is a swift hunter. However it in its turn is prey to hawks.*

Stocks *in Williamsburg, Virginia are a reminder of the times when vagabonds and other petty criminals were sentenced to be locked in the wooden bars and exposed to public ridicule.*

company of actors regularly performing together at particular theater; **stock'broker**, broker who buys and sells stocks for clients on commission; **stock'car**, railroad boxcar for carrying livestock; **stock car**, standard passenger automobile modified for use in racing; **stock certificate**, paper given by corporation to stockholder as proof of ownership of specified number of shares of stock; **stock dove**, Old World pigeon (*Columba oenas*) nesting in hollow trees; **stock exchange**, market, building, for buying and selling of stocks esp. *New York Stock Exchange*; association of brokers and jobbers doing business in particular place or market; **stock'fish** (pl. **-fishes**, collect. **-fish**), cod, hake, etc., split open and dried in the air without salt; **stock'holder**, holder or owner of stock etc.; shareholder; **stock in trade**, goods kept in stock, all requisites for a particular trade; **stock'man** (pl. **-men**), man employed to look after livestock; man owning and raising livestock; **stock market**, traffic in stocks and shares; **stock'pile**, raw materials purchased and accumulated; **stock'piling**, this practice; **stock-still**, quite motionless; **stock'yard**, enclosure with pens etc. for sorting or temporary keeping of cattle.

stock *v.* 1. Fit (gun etc.) with stock. 2. Provide (shop, farm, etc.) with goods, livestock, or requisites. 3. Keep (goods) in stock.

stock·ade (stŏkād′) *n.* & *v.t.* (**-ad·ed, -ad·ing**). (Fortify with) enclosure of upright stakes, posts, etc.

Stock·holm (stŏk′hōm, -hōlm; *Swed.* stawk′hawm). Capital city and port of Sweden, on the Baltic Sea.

stock·ing (stŏk′ĭng) *n.* Close-fitting, usu. knitted, covering for foot and leg up to or above knee; ~ **cap**, knitted usu. tapered cap, often having tassel at end.

stock·y (stŏk′ē) *adj.* (**stock·i·er, stock·i·est**). Thickset, short, and strongly built. **stock'i·ly** *adv.* **stock'i·ness** *n.*

stodg·y (stŏj′ē) *adj.* (**stodg·i·er, stodg·i·est**). (of food) Heavy, filling, thick or semisolid; (of person, book, etc.) dull, heavy, solid, uninspired. **stodg'i·ly** *adv.* **stodg'i·ness** *n.*

sto·gie, sto·gy (stō′gē) *ns.* (pl. **-gies**). Kind of long slender cigar or cheroot.

Sto·ic (stō′ĭk) *n.* 1. Philosopher of school founded *c*315 B.C. by ZENO[1], who taught that virtue was the highest good, and inculcated repression of emotion, indifference to pleasure or pain, and patient endurance; later Stoic writers were Seneca, Epictetus, and Marcus Aurelius. 2. (**s**~) Person of great self-control, fortitude, or austerity. **sto'i·cal** *adj.* **sto'i·cal·ly** *adv.* **sto·i·cism** (stō′ĭsĭzem) *n.* [Gk. *stoa* porch, hall in Athens where Zeno taught]

stoke (stōk) *v.* (**stoked, stok·ing**). Feed and tend (furnace), feed furnace of (engine etc.); act as stoker; **stoke'hold**, containing ship's boilers, where furnaces are tended; **stoke'hole**, space in front of furnace where stokers stand, opening through which furnace is tended, stokehold.

stok·er (stō′ker) *n.* One who feeds and tends furnace esp. of ship or steam engine.

STOL *abbrev.* Short takeoff and landing (aircraft).

stole[1] (stōl) *n.* 1. Long loose garment reaching to feet, esp. as outer dress of ancient Roman matron. 2. Ecclesiastical vestment, narrow strip of silk or linen worn over shoulders and reaching to or below knees; woman's fur etc. wrap of similar shape.

stole[2], **stol·en**: see STEAL.

stol·id (stŏl′ĭd) *adj.* Not easily excited or moved, phlegmatic, dull and impassive. **stol'id·ly** *adv.*

sto·lid·i·ty (stolĭd′ĭtē) *n.*

sto·lon (stō′lon) *n.* 1. (bot.) Reclined or prostrate branch that strikes root and develops new plant. 2. (zool.) In hydrozoa etc., extension of body wall that develops buds, giving rise to new zooids.

sto·ma (stō′ma) *n.* (pl. **sto·ma·ta** pr. stō′mata, stŏm′a-, **sto·mas**). (anat., zool.) Small mouthlike opening, esp. in lower animals; (bot.) minute orifice in epidermis of plants, esp. of leaves, affording communication between outer air and intercellular spaces in interior tissue.

stom·ach (stŭm′ak) *n.* Internal pouch or cavity in human or other animal body in which food is digested; in man, a dilatation of alimentary canal at upper left of abdomen; in some animals, esp. ruminants, one of several digestive cavities; (loosely) abdomen; (archaic) appetite *for* food; (fig.) relish, inclination, desire (*for*) danger, conflict, an undertaking, etc.; **stom′achache**, pain in belly, esp. bowels; **stomach pump**, small pump or syringe for emptying stomach or introducing liquids into it. **stomach** *v.t.* Bear without resistance, endure (insult etc.).

stom·ach·er (stŭm′aker) *n.* (hist.) In women's dress of 15th–17th centuries, ornamental piece, freq. embroidered or set with gems, covering breast and pit of stomach.

stomp (stŏmp) *n.* Lively jazz dance with heavy stamping. ~ *v.* Dance stomp; tread heavily.

stone (stōn) *n.* (pl. **stones, stone** for sense 3). 1. Piece of rock, esp. of small or moderate size; hard compact material of which stones and rocks consist, particular kind of this; gem; piece of stone of definite form and size, for special purpose, as for building, paving, grinding, as a monument, etc. 2. Hard morbid concretion in body, esp. in kidney, urinary bladder, or gall bladder, calculus; hard woodlike case of kernel in drupe; seed of grape etc. 3. (Brit.) Unit of weight, 14 lbs. 4. **S~ Age**, stage of culture marked by use of implements and weapons of stone, not metal; **stone′crop**, species of sedum, esp *Sedum acre*, with bright yellow flowers and small cylindrical fleshy leaves, growing on rocks, old walls, etc.; **stone′fish** (pl. **-fishes**, collect. **-fish**), (Austral.) tropical fish, (*Synanceja verrucosa*), with erectile dorsal spines containing deadly poison; **stone′fly** (pl. **-flies**), insect of order Plecoptera with larvae often found under stones in streams, used by anglers

*In the Black Hills of South Dakota is Mt. Rushmore, where the **stone** has been carved with the faces of 4 U.S. Presidents, Washington, Jefferson, Lincoln and Theodore Roosevelt.*

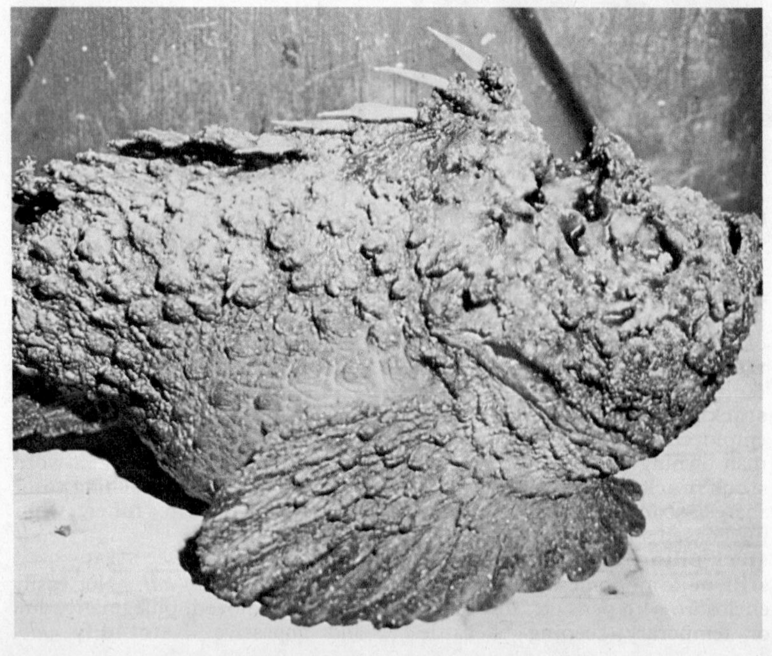

*Probably the most poisonous of all stinging fish, the **stonefish** is present in Indo-Pacific waters and off the coasts of northern Australia and South Africa. An antivenin is available.*

***Stoneware** is a particular type of pottery fired at very high temperatures, which makes it vitrified (nonporous and glossy). Because of its nonporous quality it does not require glazing.*

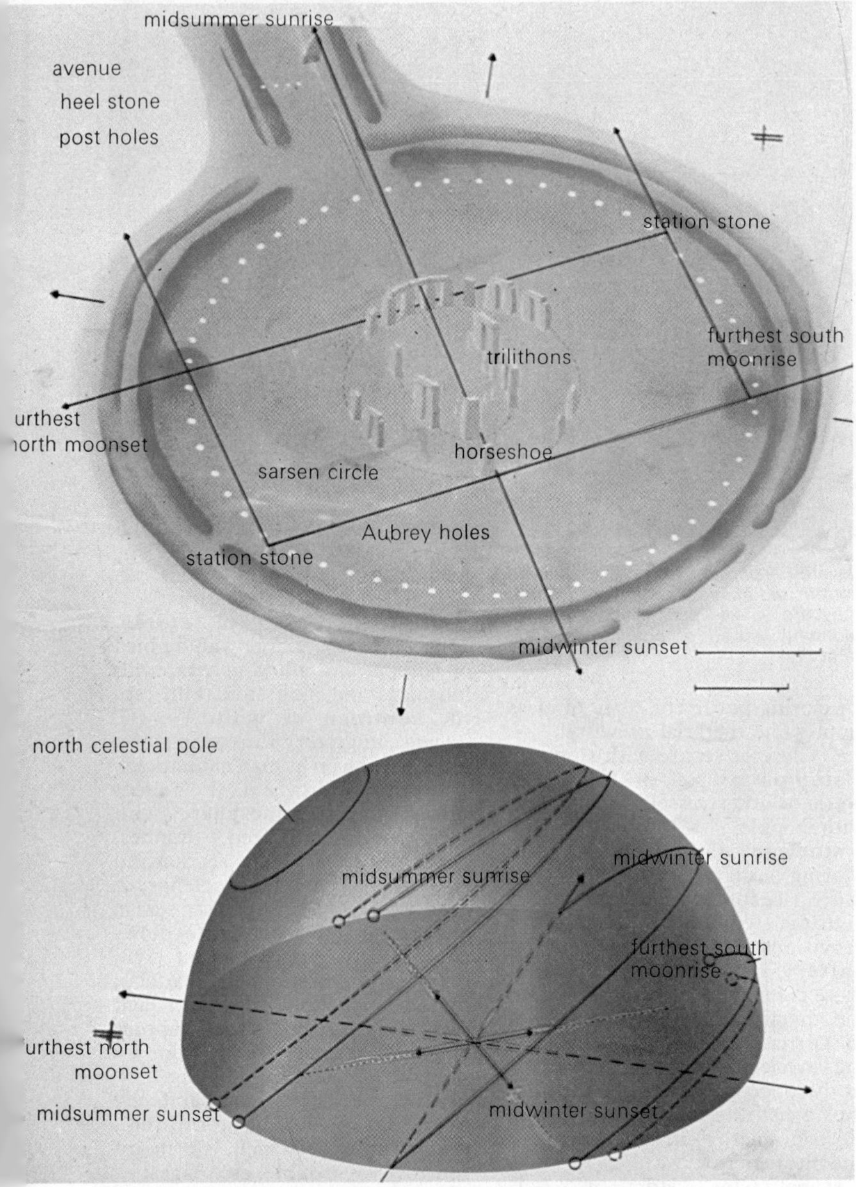

Left: Original arrangement and suggested calendar and astronomical functions of ***Stonehenge.*** *Above: The mammoth uprights and lintels. The outer bank and ditch have been carbon-dated at about 3700 years old and carvings of axheads are between 1600 and 1400 B.C. Beyond its description as 'a prehistoric ritual monument' and its construction and modification in five stages, its true function has not been determined, although it seems likely that it served a religious function.*

as bait; **stone fruit**, drupe; **stone lily**, fossil crinoid; **stone'mason**, mason; **Stone of Scone**: see SCONE; **stone's throw**, short or moderate distance; **stone'wall**, obstruct by stonewalling; **stone'walling**, (pol. slang) parliamentary obstruction; refusal to cooperate; deliberate delay; **stone'ware**, hard dense kind of pottery made from very siliceous clay or mixture of clay with much flint or sand; **stone'work**, masonry. **stone** *v.t.* (**stoned, ston·ing**). Pelt with stones, esp. put to death thus; take stones out of (fruit); face, pave, etc., with stone. ~- *adv.*. (in comb.) Completely, altogether (as *~-blind, ~-broke, ~-dead*).

Stone·henge (stōn'hĕnj). Prehistoric stone monument on Salisbury Plain, Wiltshire, England, consisting of concentric circles of huge dressed stones erected mainly in the Bronze Age; some of the larger stones carry lintels and among the smaller are blue stones that apparently come from SW. Wales.

ston·y (stō'nē) *adj.* (**ston·i·er, ston·i·est**). Full of, covered with, having many, stones; hard, rigid, fixed, as stone, obdurate, unfeeling. **ston'i·ly** *adv.* **ston'i·ness** *n.*

stood: see STAND.

stooge (stōōj) *n.* (slang) Butt, foil, esp. for comedian; person deputed to do routine or undesirable work for another. ~ *v.i.* (**stooged, stoog·ing**). (slang) Act as stooge (*for*); move, travel *about*, *around*, in vehicle or aircraft.

stool (stōōl) *n.* 1. Seat for one person, without arms or back, esp. wooden one on three or four legs; footstool. 2. Feces evacuated. 3. Stump of felled tree etc., esp. with new shoots. 4. ~ **pigeon**, decoy (freq. fig., esp. police spy, informer). **stool** *v.* Throw up young shoots or stems; act as stool pigeon.

stoop[1] (stōōp) *v.* 1. Bring one's head nearer ground by bending shoulders, trunk, etc., forward; carry head and shoulders bowed forward; incline (head, shoulders, back, etc.) forward and down; (fig.) descend from dignity, rank, etc., *to* action, *to* do. 2. (of falcon or other bird of prey) Swoop, descend steeply and swiftly, on quarry. ~ *n.* 1. Stooping carriage of back or shoulders; act of stooping. 2. Swoop of bird of prey on its quarry. **stoop'ing·ly** *adv.*

stoop[2] (stōōp) *n.* Porch, platform, small verandah, before door of house.

stop (stŏp) *v.* (**stopped, stop·ping**). 1. Close or almost close aperture or cavity by plugging, obstructing, etc.; close (organ pipe) at upper end with plug or cap; prevent or forbid passage through; make impervious or impassable. 2. Put an end to, arrest (motion etc.); check progress, motion or operation of; effectively hinder or prevent; suspend (payment etc.), give instructions to banker not to cash (check etc.). 3. (mus.) Press down (string of violin etc.) with finger to raise pitch of note, produce

The development of effective refrigeration was probably the most important development in food preservation. Today, pallets of frozen food can be stacked in cold ***storage*** *until needed.*

Elevated grain bunkers in Kansas are a modern and efficient means of ***storage.*** *They are usually built of concrete for economy, speed of construction and durability.*

(note, sound) thus. 4. Cease, come to an end, cease from, discontinue; cease from motion, speaking, or action; make halt or pause; (colloq.) remain, stay, sojourn. 5. ~ **by, in**, make short visit; ~ **off, over**, interrupt journey. 6. ~ **the clock**, continue discussions past time limit during efforts to negotiate strike settlement, conduct legislative business, etc. 7. ~ **down**, reduce aperture of (lens). **stop′page** *n.*

stop *n.* 1. Stopping, being stopped; pause, check. 2. Punctuation mark, esp. comma, semicolon, colon, or period; **full** ~, period. 3. Batten, peg, block, etc., meant to stop motion of something at fixed point; something stopping aperture, plug. 4. (optics, photog.) Aperture. 5. (mus.) ORGAN stop; closing of hole in tube of wind instrument to alter pitch of note, hole so closed, metal key closing it; pressing with finger on string of violin etc. to raise pitch of note, part of string where this pressure is applied. 6. (phonet.) Consonant in formation of which passage of breath is completely obstructed, mute. 7. **stop-**, in comb.: **stop′cock**, tap or short pipe with externally operated valve to stop or regulate passage of liquid, gas, etc.; key or handle for turning this; **stop′gap**, makeshift, temporary substitute; **stop′light**, red traffic light; light, on rear of motor vehicle, that illuminates when brakes are applied; **stop′-over**, act of stopping over; permission to passenger to break journey; **stop′watch**, watch indicating fractions of a second by a hand that can be instantly stopped at will, used in timing races etc.

stop·per (stŏp′*er*) *n.* (esp.) Plug for closing bottle etc., usu. of glass or of same material as vessel. ~ *v.t.* Close or secure with stopper.

stop·ple (stŏp′*el*) *n.* Stopper of bottle or other vessel. ~ *v.* Close with stopple.

stor·age (stōr′ĭj, stōr′-) *n.* Storing of goods, method of doing this; space for storing; cost of warehousing; **cold** ~, storing of provisions under refrigeration; ~ **battery**, electric cell (or group of these connected in series) in which the chemical action that produces the current can be reversed by passing an electric current through it in the opposite direction, and that thus constitutes a means of storing electric energy in the form of chemical energy.

store (stōr, stōr) *n.* 1. Abundance, provision, stock of something ready to be drawn upon; **in** ~ **for**, awaiting (person). 2. Building, room, for retail sale of some commodity. 3. (pl.) Articles of particular kind or for special purpose accumulated for use; supply of things needed, stocks, reserves. 4. (attrib.) **store′front**, (rooms etc. at) street front of a store; **store′house**, place where things are stored; store, treasury; **store′keeper**, person in charge of store(s); **store′room**, room for storing goods or supplies, esp. of ship or household. **store** *v.t.* (**stored, stor·ing**). Furnish, stock (*with* something); lay *up* for future use, form stock of; deposit (goods, furniture, etc.) in warehouse for temporary keeping; have storage accommodation for.

sto·rey: see STORY[2].

sto·ried (stōr′ēd, stōr′ēd) *adj.* 1. Adorned with representations of historical or legendary scenes. 2. Celebrated in history or story.

stork (stōrk) *n.* (pl. **storks**, collect. **stork**). Large wading bird of *Ciconia* and allied genera, with long legs and long stout bill, esp. the **common** or **white** ~ (*C. ciconia*), migratory European stork, often nesting on human habitations.

storm (stōrm) *n.* Violent disturbance of atmosphere, with high winds and freq. thunder, heavy rain, hail, snow, etc.; wind of particular degree of violence, of force 10 or 11 on BEAUFORT SCALE; heavy discharge or shower (*of* blows etc.); violent disturbance of civil, political, domestic, etc., affairs; tumult, agitation, dispute, etc.; assault on fortified place, capture *of* place by such assault; **take by** ~, take by assault (freq. fig.); ~ **center**, central, comparatively calm, area of cyclonic storm; (fig.) center around which storm of controversy, trouble, etc., rages; ~ **signal**, any device for signaling approach of a storm; ~ **troops**, shock troops, esp. a Nazi semi-military organization; ~ **trooper**, member of this. **storm** *v.* 1. Take by storm, rush violently, esp. to attack. 2. (of wind etc.) Rage, be violent; bluster, fume; scold.

storm·y (stōr′mē) *adj.* (**storm·i·er, storm·i·est**). Characterized, marked, by storm(s); associated or connected with storms; ~ **petrel**: see PETREL. **storm′i·ly** *adv.* **storm′i·ness** *n.*

Among the largest wading birds and found in many parts of the world, probably the best-known ***stork*** *is the white species. It winters in Africa but makes its nests on buildings in Europe during the summer. Other species nest in trees or cliffs. Their food consists of freshwater fauna and insects. In flight, they extend the neck and allow the legs to trail behind the body. They have no call but rattle their beaks.*

painted stork
pen-billed stork
saddle-billed stork
mycteria stork
od stork
black stork
white stork
yellow-billed stork

*Although this **Stradivarius** violin is among a collection of old instruments in a museum, others made by this master are still used regularly in concert performances by leading violinists.*

Stor·thing, Stor·ting (stōr′-tĭng) *ns.* Norwegian parliament. [Norw. *stor* great, *ting* assembly]

sto·ry[1] (stōr′ē, stōr′ē) *n.* (pl. **-ries**). Past course of life of person, institution, etc.; account given of incident or series of events; narrative meant to entertain hearer or reader, tale in prose or verse of actual or fictitious events; legend, myth, anecdote, novel, romance; (amusing) anecdote; plot (of novel, play, etc.); account in newspaper, material for this; (colloq.) lie.

sto·ry[2], Brit. **sto·rey** (stōr′ē, stōr′ē) *ns.* (pl. **-ries, -reys**). Each stage or portion into which house or building is divided horizontally, thing forming horizontal division.

stoup (stoop) *n.* Vessel for holy water, usu. stone basin in wall of church or near church porch; (archaic) flagon, tankard, beaker.

stout (stowt) *adj.* 1. Valiant, undaunted, resolute. 2. Of considerable thickness or strength. 3. Corpulent. **stout′ish** *adj.* **stout′ly** *adv.* **stout′ness** *n.* **stout** *n.* Heavy dark type of beer prepared with well-roasted barley or malt and sometimes caramelized sugar.

stove[1] (stōv) *n.* Portable or fixed closed apparatus to contain burning fuel or consume gas, electricity, etc., for use in warming rooms, cooking, etc.; **stove′pipe**, pipe to carry off smoke and gases from stove; (colloq.) top hat, tall silk hat. **stove** *v.t.* (**stoved, stov·ing**). Dry, heat, in stove.

stove[2]: see STAVE *v.*

stow (stō) *v.* Pack (*away*) in receptacles or convenient places, esp. (naut.) place (cargo) in proper order in hold etc.; fill (receptacle) with articles compactly arranged; (slang) desist, refrain from; ~ **away**, conceal oneself on board ship; **stow′away**, person hiding in ship, aircraft, etc. to avoid paying passage money, to escape by stealth etc. **stow′age** *n.* (Cost of) stowing.

Stowe (stō), **Mrs. Harriet Elizabeth Beecher** (1811–96). Amer. author and abolitionist; famous for novel *Uncle Tom's Cabin.*

S.T.P. *abbrev.* Standard temperature and pressure.

stra·bis·mus (strabĭz′mus) *n.* Disorder of eye muscles in which one eye fails to focus with the other on a given point at the same time. **stra·bis′mal, stra·bis′mic** *adjs.*

strad·dle (străd′el) *v.* (**-dled, -dling**). Spread legs wide apart in walking, standing, or sitting; (of legs) be wide apart; stand or sit across (thing) thus; part (legs) widely; drop shells beyond and short of a target in order to establish its range; drop bombs across (a target) beginning on one side and finishing on the opposite side; (colloq.) be noncommittal, seem to favor both sides of a controversy, vacillate. ~ *n.* 1. Action, position, of straddling. 2. (stock exch.) Contract giving holder right of either calling for or delivering stock at fixed price. **strad′dler** *n.*

Strad·i·var·i·us (strădivār′ēus). Latinized name of Antonio Stradivari (*c*1644–1737), most famous of a family of Italian makers of stringed instruments; hence, violin or other stringed instrument made by member of this family.

strafe (strāf, strahf) *v.t.* (**strafed, straf·ing**). Bombard, worry with shells, bombs, sniping, etc.; reprimand sharply, abuse, thrash. ~ *n.* Strafing attack. **straf′er** *n.* [Ger. *strafer* punish]

strag·gle (străg′el) *v.i.* (**-gled, -gling**). Stray from the main body, be dispersed or scattered, grow irregularly or loosely. **strag′gler** *n.* **strag′gling·ly** *adv.* **strag′gly** *adj.* (**-gli·er, -gli·est**). **straggle** *n.*

straight (strāt) *adj.* 1. Not crooked, not curved, bent, or angular; (geom., of line) lying evenly between any two of its points; (of hair) not curly or waving. 2. Direct, undeviating, going direct to the mark. 3. Upright, honest, candid; in proper order or place; (slang) conventional; heterosexual. 4. (of liquor) Unmixed, undiluted; (of playing cards) in sequences, without gap; (of drama) without music. 5. ~**-arm** (*v.t.*), push away (someone, as tackler in football) by stretching arm out straight; **straight′edge**, strip of wood, steel, etc., with a perfectly straight edge, for testing accuracy of plane surface, drawing straight lines, etc.; **straight face**, intentionally expressionless face, esp. avoiding smile though amused (**straight-faced** *adj.*); ~ **flush**, in poker, a hand with all five cards of the same suit and in sequence; **straight man**, entertainer who acts as foil for a comedian; **straight time**, number of working hours set as standard for specified work period; pay rate for work during such hours. **straight'ness** *n.* **straight** *n.* Straight condition; straight part of something, esp. concluding stretch of racetrack; consecutive sequence of cards in poker. **straight** *adv.* In a straight line, direct, without deviation or circumlocution; in right direction, with good aim; **straight away, straight'away**, immediately, at once; **straight off**, without hesitation, deliberation, etc.; **straight out**, frankly, outspokenly.

straight·en (strā'ten) *v.* Make straight.

straight·forward (strātfōr'-werd) *adj.* Honest, open, frank; (of task etc.) presenting no complications. **straight·for'ward·ly** *adv.*

strain[1] (strān) *n.* Breed, stock; inherited tendency or quality, moral tendency forming part of a character.

strain[2] (strān) *n.* 1. Straining, being strained, pull, tension, exertion; injury or damage due to excessive exertion, tension, or force; deformation or distortion in any body due to stress, molecular displacement. 2. Melody, tune; passage, snatch, of music, poetry, etc.; tone, mode, etc., adopted in talking or writing; tenor, drift, general tendency or character. ~ *v.* 1. Stretch tightly, make taut; stretch beyond normal degree, force to extreme effort, exert to utmost; wrest, distort, from true intention or meaning. 2. Overtask; injure, try, imperil, by overuse, by making excessive demands on, etc. 3. Make intense effort; strive intensely *after*, try *at*. 4. Clear (liquid) of solid matter by passing through sieve etc.; filter (solids) *out* from liquid; (of liquid) percolate. **strained** *adj.* (esp.) Artificial, forced, constrained.

strain·er (strā'ner) *n.* (esp.) Utensil for straining or filtering.

strait (strāt) *adj.* Narrow, limited; confined, confining; (archaic exc. in) **strait'jacket**, strong garment for upper part of body, designed to confine the arms, used to restrain violent persons in mental hospital; **strait-jacket** (*v.t.*) (fig.) restrict severely; **strait-laced**, (now only fig.) severely virtuous, puritanical. **strait** *n.* 1. Narrow passage of water connecting two seas or large bodies of water. 2. (usu. pl.) Difficult position; need, distress.

strait·en (strā'ten) *v.t.* (chiefly in past part.) Restrict in amount, scope, or range; reduce to straits; **straitened circumstances**, inadequate means of living, poverty.

strake (strāk) *n.* Section of iron rim of cartwheel; continuous line of planking or plates, of uniform breadth, from stem to stern of ship.

stra·mo·ni·um (stramō'nēum) *n.* Jimson weed; dried poisonous leaves of this, used in treatment of asthma etc.

strand[1] (strănd) *n.* Margin of sea, lake, or river, esp. part of shore between tidemarks. ~ *v.* Run aground. **strand'ed** *adj.* (esp.) Left in a helpless position or without adequate resources.

strand[2] (strănd) *n.* Each of strings or wires twisted together to form rope, cord, cable, etc.; thread of woven material, string of beads, pearls, etc.; single hair; group of hairs.

strange (strānj) *adj.* (**strang·er, strang·est**). Foreign, alien, not one's own, not familiar or well known (*to*); novel, queer, peculiar, surprising, unexpected; fresh or unaccustomed *to*, unacquainted, bewildered. **strange'ly** *adv.* **strange'ness** *n.*

stran·ger (strān'jer) *n.* Foreigner; person in place, company, etc., to which he does not belong; person unknown to or *to* one.

stran·gle (străng'gel) *v.t.* (**-gled, -gling**). Throttle, kill by external compression of throat; hinder growth of (plant) by overcrowding; (fig.) suppress; **stran'glehold**, deadly grip (usu. fig.). **stran'gler** *n.*

Chatham Strait *is a fault-formed passage of the eastern North Pacific in southeast Alaska. It is 150 miles long and was named in 1794 after the 2nd Earl of Chatham.*

stran·gles (străng'gelz) *n.* (usu. considered sing.) Infectious febrile disease, caused by a streptococcus, in equine animals.

stran·gu·late (străng'gyulāt) *v.t.* (**-lat·ed, -lat·ing**). Strangle (rare); (med.) constrict (organ, duct, etc.) so as to prevent circulation or passage of fluid; **strangulated hernia**, hernia so constricted as to arrest circulation in protuding part. **stran·gu·la·tion** (străng-gyulā'shon) *n.* Strangling, being strangled; strangulating.

strap (străp) *n.* Leather band; flat strip of leather etc. of uniform breadth with buckle or other fastening for holding things together etc.; strip of metal used to secure or connect leaf of hinge etc.; **strap'hanger**, passenger in bus, subway, etc., who must stand and hold on by strap for lack of seat. **strap'less** *adj.* Without strap(s); (esp. of dress) without shoulder straps. **strap** *v.t.* (**strapped, strap·ping**). Furnish, fasten, with strap; beat, flog, with strap; (surg.) close (wound), bind (part) up with adhesive plaster. **strapped** *adj.* (slang) Lacking money.

strap·ping (străp'ĭng) *adj.* (of persons) Strongly and stoutly built.

stra·ta: see STRATUM.

strat·a·gem (străt'ajem) *n.* Artifice, trick, trickery; device(s)

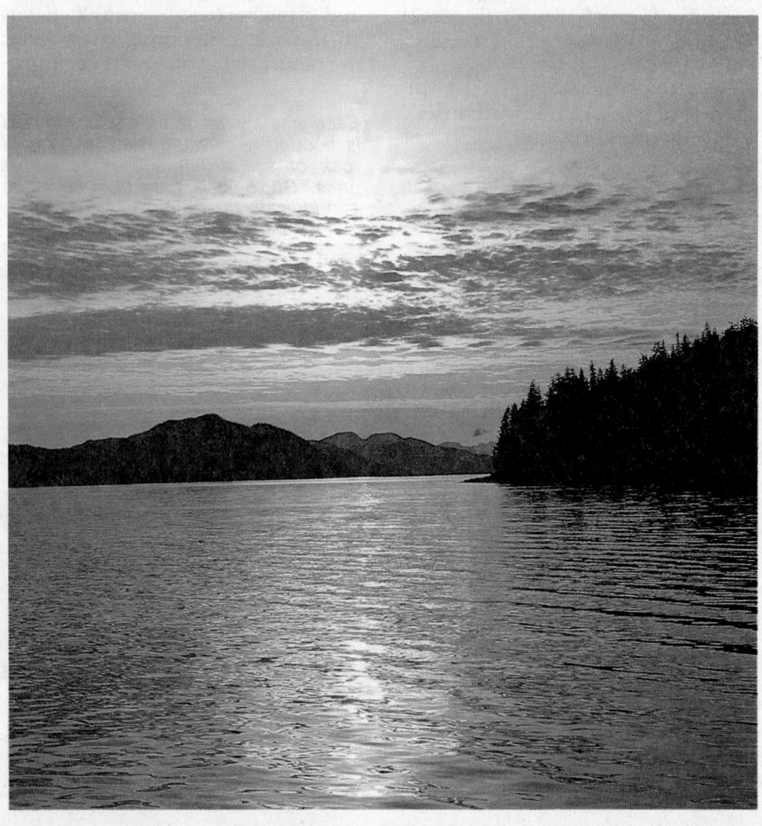

for deceiving enemy.

stra·te·gic (stratē'jĭk) *adj.* Of, dictated by, serving the ends of, strategy; ~ **bombing**, bombing designed to disrupt the enemy's internal economy, destroy morale, etc. (opp. TACTICAL bombing). **stra·te'gi·cal** *adj.* **stra·te'gi·cal·ly** *adv.*

strat·e·gy (străt'*e*jē) *n.* (pl. **-gies**). Generalship, art of war; art of planning and directing larger military movements and operations of campaign or war (opp. TACTICS); also fig. **strat'e·gist** *n.*

Strat·ford-up·on-A·von (străt'f*e*rd *u*pŏn ā'vŏn, -v*o*n). Town in Warwickshire, England, birthplace and burial place of Shakespeare.

strat·i·fy (străt'*i*fī) *v.t.* (**-fied, -fy·ing**). Arrange in strata. **strat·i·fi·ca·tion** (străt*i*fĭkā'sh*o*n) *n.*

stra·to·cu·mu·lus (strātōkū'my*ulu*s, strătō-) *n.* (meteor.) Type of low cloud, a layer of globular masses.

strat·o·sphere (străt'*o*sfēr) *n.* Region of the atmosphere lying above the troposphere, in which the temperature does not decrease with increasing height.

stra·tum (strā't*u*m, străt'*u*m, strah't*u*m) *n.* (pl. **stra·ta** pr. strā't*a*, străt'*a*, strah't*a*, rarely **stra·tums**). Layer of material, esp. one of several one on top of another; (geol.) layer or bed of sedimentary rock; (biol.) layer of tissue; (archaeol.) layer of deposits in excavation etc. indicating distinct period or form of culture; (fig.) level or grade in social position, culture, etc.

stra·tus (strā't*u*s, străt'*u*s) *n.* (pl. **stra·ti** pr. strā'tī, străt'ī, **stra·tus**). Continuous horizontal sheet of cloud.

Strauss[1] (strows). Name of a Viennese family of composers, famous esp. for dance music; **Johann** ~ (1825–99), composer of the "Blue Danube" waltz and the opera *Die Fledermaus.*

Strauss[2] (strows), **Richard Georg** (1864–1949). German composer of *Der Rosenkavalier* and other operas, and of orchestral music.

straw (straw) *n.* Dry cut stalks of various cereals used for bedding, thatching, litter for animals, plaited or woven as material for hats, beehives, etc.; stem of any cereal plant; single stalk or piece of straw; tube orig. of straw for sucking drink through; insignificant trifle; straw hat; **catch** or **grasp at ~s**, resort to utterly inadequate expedient, like drowning man; **last straw**: see LAST[2]; **straw'board**, coarse yellow cardboard made of straw pulp; **straw boss**, workman who also acts as foreman; assistant foreman; **straw color, straw-colored**, (of) the pale light yellow color of straw; **straw in the wind**, slight hint that suggests much; **straw man**, stuffed effigy; imaginary person, idea, put forward as adversary to divert attention from real issue; **straw vote**, unofficial vote, esp. as sample or indication of public opinion. **straw'y** *adj.* (**straw·i·er, straw·i·est**).

straw·ber·ry (straw'bĕrē, -b*e*rē) *n.* (pl. **-ries**). (Juicy edible pulpy, usu. red, fruit, not properly a berry, of) plant of any species of genus *Fragaria*, stemless herbs with trifoliate leaves, white flowers, and slender trailing runners; color of red strawberries; ~ **mark**, nevus birthmark, resembling strawberry; ~ **roan**, red roan; ~ **tree**, European evergreen tree (*Arbutus unedo*) with white flowers and strawberry-like fruit; spindle tree.

*Each time a volcano erupts, or the land is flooded, a new **stratum** or layer of rock or soil is left above the earlier ones. Geological study of such strata can indicate their ages.*

stray (strā) *v.i.* Wander, go aimlessly; deviate from right way or (fig.) from virtue; lose one's way; get separated from flock, companions, home, or proper place. ~ *n.* Lost or strayed domestic animal; homeless, friendless person, esp. child. ~ *adj.* Strayed; scattered, sporadic, occasional, casually met with. **stray'er** *n.*

streak (strēk) *n.* Thin irregular line of different color or substance from material or surface in which it occurs; flash (*of* lightning); vein of mineral; trait, strain, element, of character, etc. **streak'y** *adj.* (**streak·i·er, streak·i·est**). **streak'i·ly** *adv.* **streak'i·ness** *n.* **streak** *v.* Mark with streak(s); move very rapidly (like streak of lightning); (slang) run nude through public place. **streak'er, streak'ing** *ns.*

stream (strēm) *n.* Body of water flowing in bed, esp. rivulet or brook as dist. from river; current or flow of river, in sea, etc.; flow of any liquid, current of air, gas, etc.; continuous flow of persons, traffic, etc. moving in one direction, or of words, events, influences, etc.; **stream'line**, path of particle of fluid in motion, current of air, etc.; form of body (esp. car or aircraft) calculated to offer minimum of resistance to air, water, etc.; **stream'line** (*v.t.*), give this shape to (also fig.); **stream of consciousness**, (psychol.) thoughts and feelings considered as series of states constantly moving forward in time; (attrib.) applied to style of writing presenting individual's thoughts and feelings as continuous monologue. **stream'y** *adj.* (**stream·i·er, stream·i·est**). **stream** *v.* Flow or move as a stream; run with liquid; emit stream

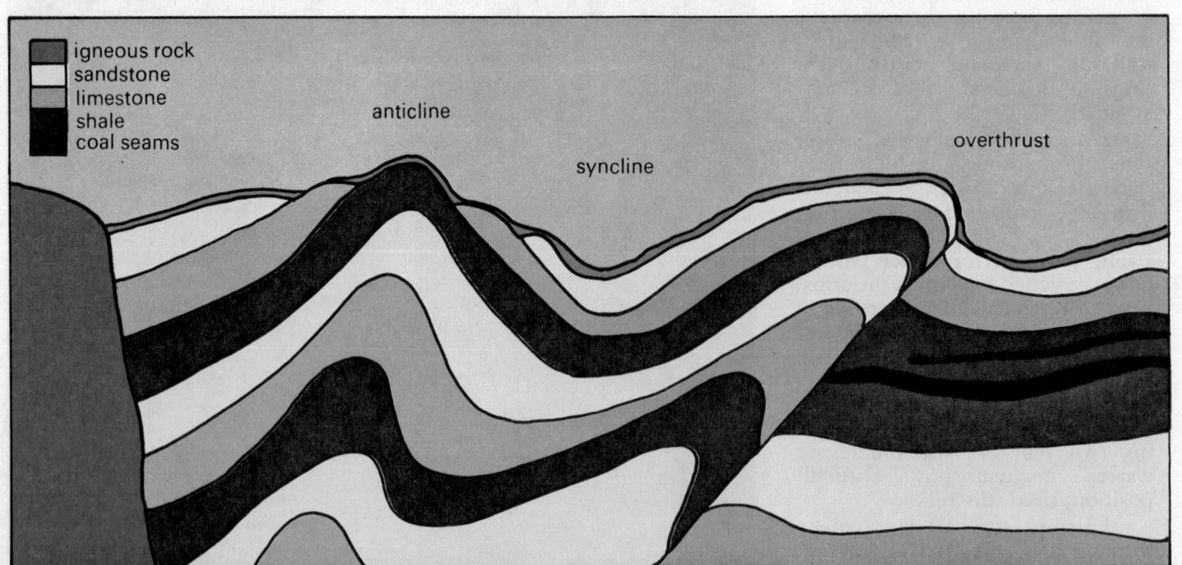

The ***streetcar*** *is a familiar sight in San Francisco, although it is largely retained as a tourist attraction. During the 1920s and 1930s the use of streetcars in the U.S.A. all but died out.*

of; float or wave in wind, current of water, etc.

stream·er (strē′m*er*) *n.* Pennon; ribbon etc. attached at one end and floating or waving at the other; (pl.) Aurora Borealis.

stream·let (strēm′lĭt) *n.* Small stream.

street (strēt) *n.* Road in town or village with houses on one side or both; this with its houses; **the S~**, (esp.) Wall Street; **on the ~**, living by prostitution; **street′car**, public electric passenger car, trolley car; **street theater**, theatrical presentation in street, park, etc., usu. with no admission charge; **street′walker**, prostitute who solicits in street.

strength (strĕngkth, strĕngth) *n.* 1. Being strong; degree in which person or thing is strong; that which makes strong; number of men in army, regiment, etc., of ships in fleet etc., men enrolled; **on the ~ of**, encouraged by, relying on, arguing from. 2. Significance; effectiveness (of argument).

strength·en (strĕngk′th*e*n, strĕng′-) *v.* Make, become, stronger. **strength′en·er** *n.*

stren·u·ous (strĕn′ūus) *adj.* Vigorous, energetic, persistently and ardently laborious (esp. of action or effort). **stren′u·ous·ly** *adv.* **stren′u·ous·ness** *n.*

strep (strĕp) *n.* (colloq.) Streptococcus; ~ **throat**, septic sore throat.

strep·to·coc·cus (strĕpt*o*kŏk′*u*s) *n.* (pl. **-coc·ci** pr. -kŏk′sī). Microorganism of genus *S~*, of bacteria that form chains, certain species of which produce infections in man, as scarlet fever, endocarditis, strep throat, etc. **strep·to·coc′cal, strep·to·coc·cic** (strĕpt*o*kŏk′sĭk) *adjs.*

strep·to·my·cin (strĕpt*o*mī′sĭn) *n.* Antibiotic drug, produced from *Actinomyces griseus*, a moldlike microorganism found in garden soil.

stress (strĕs) *n.* 1. Pressure *of* load, weight, some adverse force or influence etc.; condition of things demanding or marked by strained effort; (mech.) force exerted between contiguous bodies

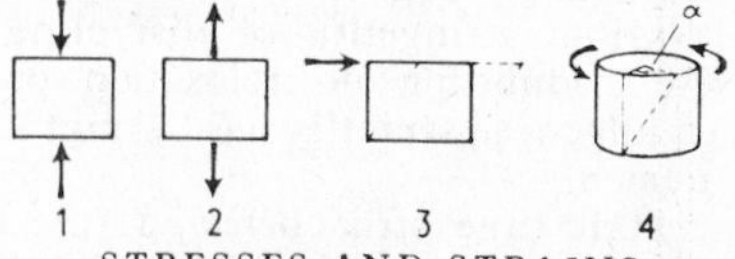

STRESSES AND STRAINS

1: Compressive stress. 2. Tensile stress. 3. Shear stress and strain. 4. Torsional stress and strain. α = angle of twist

or parts of a body. 2. Emphasis; greater relative force of utterance given to one syllable of word, one part of a syllable, word in sentence, etc. ~ *v.t.* Lay the stress on, accent, emphasize; subject to mechanical stress. **stress·or** (strĕs′*er*, -ōr) *n.*

stretch (strĕch) *v.* 1. Make taut; tighten, straighten; place in tightly drawn or outspread state; lay (person) flat; (also ~ **oneself**) extend limbs to tighten muscles after sleeping etc.; ~ **one's legs**, take walking exercise; ~ **out**, extend (hand, foot, etc.) by straightening arm or leg; reach out hand. 2. Strain; exert to utmost or beyond legitimate extent; do violence to; exaggerate. 3. Have specified length or extension; be continuous between points, to or from a point. 4. Draw, be drawn, admit of being drawn, out into greater length, extension, or size. **stretch** *n.* Stretching, being stretched; continuous expanse, tract, or spell; (slang) term of imprisonment; **stretch′out** (*n.*), practice in factory operation of having workers do extra work without adequate increase in wages. **stretch′a·ble** *adj.* **stretch′y** *adj.* (**stretch·i·er, stretch·i·est**).

stretch·er (strĕch′*er*) *n.* (esp.) 1. Brick or stone laid with length in direction of wall, bar or rod used as tie or brace, e.g. between legs of chair; board in boat against which rower presses feet. 2. Frame on which artist's canvas is spread and drawn tight by wedges etc. 3. Oblong frame, with handles at each end, for carrying sick or wounded persons on; **~-bearer**, one who helps to carry this.

strew (strōō) *v.t.* (**strewed, strewn, strew·ing**). Scatter (flowers, small objects) over a surface; cover (surface, object) *with* small objects scattered.

stri·a (strī′*a*) *n.* (pl. **stri·ae** pr. strī′ē). (anat., zool., geol., etc.) Linear mark on surface; slight ridge, furrow, or score. **stri·ate** (strī′ĭt, -āt), **stri·at·ed** (strī′ātĭd) *adjs.* **striate** (strī′āt) *v.t.* (**-at·ed, -at·ing**). **stri·a·tion** (strīā′shon) *n.*

strick·en (strĭk′en) *adj.*: see STRIKE; (esp., of deer etc.) wounded; (of person, mind, etc.) afflicted with disease, trouble, grief, etc.

strict (strĭkt) *adj.* 1. Exact, precise, accurately determined or defined. 2. Rigorous, allowing no evasion, stringent; (of discipline etc.) admitting no relaxation or indulgence. **strict′ly** *adv.* **strict′ness** *n.*

stric·ture (strĭk′cher) *n.* 1. (usu. pl.) Adverse criticism, critical remark. 2. (path.) Morbid contraction of passage of the body, esp. urethra; contracted part.

stride (strīd) *v.* (**strode** pr. strōd, **strid·den** pr. strĭd′en, **strid·ing**). Walk with long steps; pass over or *over* (obstacle etc.) with one step; bestride. ~ *n.* Striding; long step; distance covered by this; striding gait; **take in one's** ~, (of horse or rider) clear (obstacle) without changing gait; (fig.) deal with incidentally without interrupting course of action etc. **strid′er** *n.*

stri·dent (strī′dent) *adj.* Loud and harsh, grating. **stri′dent·ly** *adv.* **stri′dence, stri′den·cy** *ns.*

strid·u·late (strĭj′ulāt) *v.i.* (**-lat·ed, -lat·ing**). Make harsh grating shrill noise (esp., of grasshoppers etc.) by rubbing together hard parts of body. **strid·u·la·tion** (strĭjulā′shon) *n.*

strife (strīf) *n.* Condition of antagonism or discord; contention, struggle, dispute.

strike (strīk) *v.* (**struck** pr. strŭk, **strick·en** pr. strĭk′en, **strik·ing**). 1. Hit, hit upon or *on*, deliver blow(s) or stroke(s); afflict (with infirmity or death); (of disease etc.) attack suddenly; (of lightning) descend upon and blast. 2. Produce or record or bring into specified state by strokes or striking; impress, stamp, print (*with* device etc.); coin (money); touch (string or key of instrument), produce (note) thus; (of clock) sound (hour etc.) with stroke(s) on bell etc.; (of hour) be sounded thus; produce (fire, spark) by percussion of flint and steel, friction of match, etc. 3. Arrest attention of; occur to mind of; produce mental impression on, impress *as*. 4. Lower or take down (sail, flag, tent); signify surrender by striking flag, remove tents of (camp etc.); (theatr.) remove (scene etc.). 5. (of body of employees) Cease work by agreement among themselves or by order of labor union etc. in order to obtain remedy for grievance, better working conditions, etc. 6. (Cause to) penetrate; pierce, stab (as) with sharp weapon. 7. Turn in new direction, go *across, down, over*, etc.; take specified direction. 8. Assume (attitude) suddenly and dramatically. 9. ~ **from the record** (pp. **stricken**), (law) erase, expunge; **strike home**, (fig.) hit the mark; get blow well in; **strike off**, cancel, erase, (as) by stroke of pen; print; **strike off the register, rolls**, remove (doctor, lawyer) from official list, for misconduct; **strike out**, erase; open up (path, course) *for* oneself; lay about one with fists etc.; begin to swim or skate; (baseball) (be) put out by strikeout (see sense 4 of *n.*); **strike up**, begin to play or sing; start (acquaintance, conversation) esp. rapidly or casually; **strike zone**, (baseball) space over plate between batter's knees and armpits. **strike** *n.* 1. Concerted refusal to work by employees till some grievance is remedied; **on** ~, taking part in this; **strike′bound**, immobilized by a strike; **strike′breaker**, one who works for employer whose employees are on strike; **strike pay**, labor union's allowance to workers on strike. 2. Sudden discovery of rich ore, oil, etc.; (fig.) sudden success or piece of good fortune; (bowling) knocking down all the pins on first bowl; score thus made. 3. (geol.) Horizontal course of stratum. 4. (baseball) Pitched ball swung at and missed, or in strike zone and not swung at. **strike′out** (*n.*) (baseball), out made when batter is charged with three strikes.

strik·er (strī′ker) *n.* (esp.) Employee taking part in industrial strike.

strik·ing (strī′kĭng) *adj.* (esp.) Noticeable, arresting, impressive. **strik′ing·ly** *adv.* **strik′ing·ness** *n.*

string (strĭng) *n.* 1. Thin length of twisted fiber; piece of this or of leather, ribbon, or other material, used for tying up, lacing, drawing together, activating puppet, etc.; bowstring; (fig.) condition or limitation imposed; **first, second,**

String beans *are grown as a commercial crop throughout the U.S.A. and southern Canada. They are also popular with home gardeners, having a high yield and a relatively simple growth cycle.*

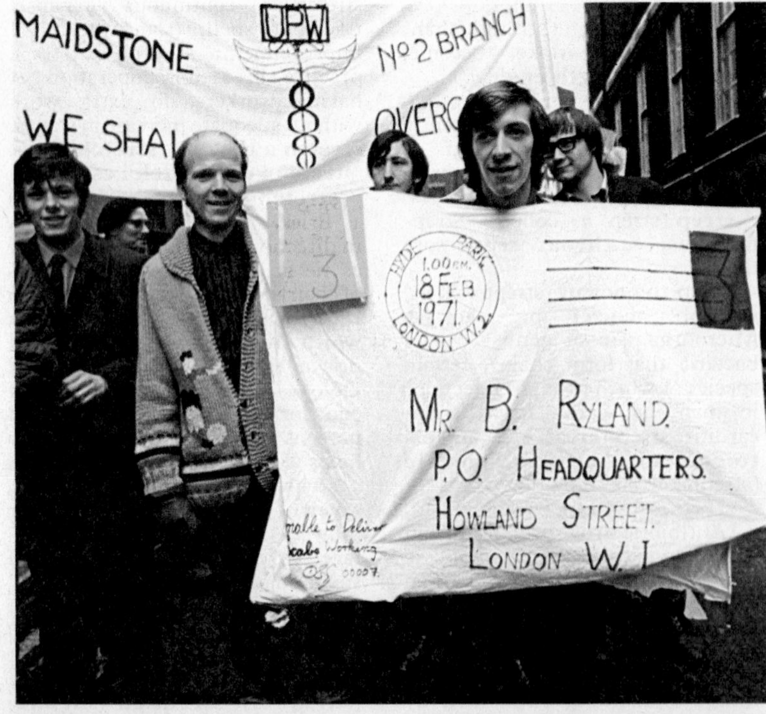

A ***striker*** *from the British Post Office during industrial unrest in 1971. Such industrial action only became effective after the formation of trade unions during the 19th century.*

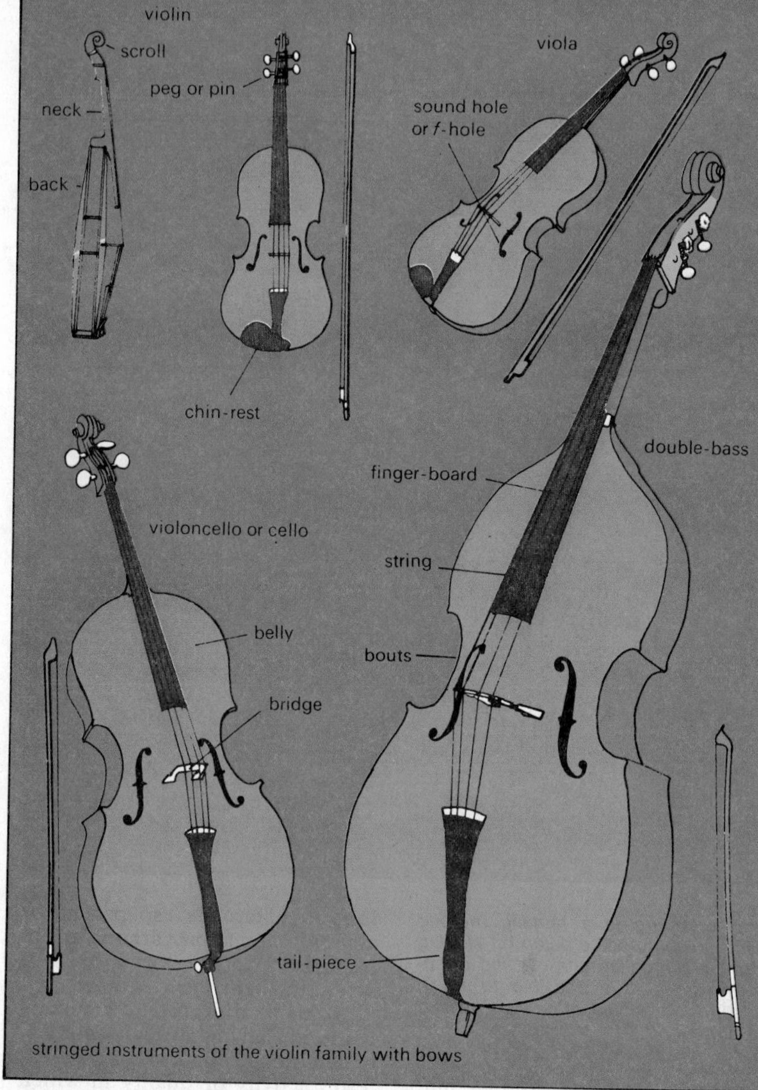

stringed instruments of the violin family with bows

*The first **stringed** instrument was a type of harp, played at Ur about 4500 years ago. The violin family, like the guitar, probably evolved from the lute, which originated in Persia.*

etc., ~, person or thing that chief, alternative, etc., reliance is placed on; **have two ~s to one's bow**, have two alternative resources; **pull strings**, control course of affairs; exert (esp. hidden) influence; **without strings**, unconditionally. 2. Tendon, nerve, elongated muscle, etc., in animal body; tough piece connecting two halves of pod in beans etc.; thread of viscid substance. 3. Catgut, wire, etc., yielding musical tone(s) when stretched, in piano, harp, violin, and other instruments; (pl.) stringed instruments played with bow, players of these in orchestra etc. 4. Set of or *of* objects strung together; number of animals etc. in single file; set or stud of horses; number of things in row or line; continuous series or succession. 5. **string bass**, double bass; **string bean**, bush or vine (*Phaseolus vulgaris*) widely grown for its slim, green edible pods; (colloq.) tall, thin person; **string quartet**, quartet of stringed instruments, esp. two violins, viola, and violoncello; music for this; **string tie**, very narrow necktie. **string** *v.* (**strung** pr. strŭng, **string·ing**). Supply, fit, tie, with string(s); thread (beads etc.) on string; make (bow) ready for use by slipping loop of bowstring into its notch; remove strings of bean pod; brace *up*, bring to specified condition of sensitiveness or tension; connect, put together in continuous series; arrange in row(s) or series; move in string or disconnected line (esp. ~ **out**); ~ **along**, (colloq.) deceive (person); ~ **up**, (colloq.) hang (person).

stringed (strĭngd) *adj.* (esp., of musical instruments) Having strings.

strin·gent (strĭn′jent) *adj.* (of regulations, obligations, etc.) Rigorous, strict, binding, requiring exact performance. **strin′gent·ly** *adv.* **strin′gen·cy** *n.* (pl. **-cies**).

string·er (strĭng′er) *n.* Longitudinal stiffening member used in construction of ships (e.g. *deck, side* ~) and aircraft; long horizontal timber.

string·y (strĭng′ē) *adj.* (**string·i·er, string·i·est**). Fibrous, like string; (of liquid) ropy. **string′i·ness** *n.*

strip[1] (strĭp) *n.* Long narrow piece or tract (of textile material, land, paper, etc.); narrow flat bar of iron or steel; iron or steel in this form; airstrip; CARTOON, COMIC, strip; ~ **cropping**, practice of planting different crops in alternating strips usu. following contours of terrain, in order to reduce erosion; ~ **lighting**, lighting with usu. tubular lamps arranged in line.

strip[2] (strĭp) *v.* (**stripped, strip·ping**). Denude, lay bare; deprive *of* covering, appurtenance, or property; undress; pull or tear off, *off* or *from* something; tear off (thread from screw, teeth from wheel); extract last milk from udder of (cow); ~ **mine**, mine in open pit formed by removal of earth and rock overlying ore etc.; **strip′tease**, entertainment in which a woman undresses in time to music before an audience. **strip′per** *n.* (esp.) 1. Performer of striptease. 2. Device or solvent for removing paint, varnish, etc.

stripe[1] (strĭp) *n.* (archaic; chiefly pl.) Stroke or lash with whip etc.

stripe[2] (strīp) *n.* Long narrow portion, usu. of uniform width, on surface, differing in color or texture from adjacent parts; narrow strip of cloth, braid, etc., sewn on garment, esp. chevron indicating rank of noncommissioned officer. **strip′y** *adj.* **stripe** *v.t.* (**striped, strip·ing**). Mark, ornament, with stripe(s). **striped** *adj.* ~ **bass**: see BASS[1]. **strip′er** *n.*

strip·ling (strĭp′lĭng) *n.* Youth approaching manhood.

strive (strīv) *v.i.* (**strove** pr. strōv, **strived, striv·en** pr. strĭv′en, **striv·ing**). Endeavor, try hard, struggle; contend, vie.

strobe (strōb) *n.* 1. Device that emits extremely short, fast flashes of high-intensity light for high-speed photography. 2. (colloq.) Stroboscope.

stro·bile (strō′bĭl, -bīl) *n.* (bot.) Cone of pine etc., inflorescence made up of imbricated scales.

stro·bo·scope (strō′boskōp, strŏb′o-) *n.* Optical instrument employing pulsed illumination to make rapidly moving, rotating, or vibrating objects appear stationary. **stro·bo·scop·ic** (strōboskŏp′ĭk, strŏbo-) *adj.*

strode: see STRIDE.

stroke[1] (strōk) *n.* 1. Blow, shock

given by blow; apoplectic or paralytic seizure; damaging or destructive discharge (of lightning). 2. Single effort put forth, one complete performance of recurrent action or movement; time or way in which such movements are performed; act or method of striking ball etc. in games; (golf) action of hitting (at) ball with club, as unit of scoring; specially successful or skillful effort; ~ **of genius**, original or strikingly successful idea; ~ **of luck**, unforeseen opportune occurrence. 3. Mark made by movement in one direction of pen, pencil, paintbrush, etc.; detail in description etc. 4. Sound made by striking clock; **on the ~ of**, exactly at specified hour. 5. Oarsman rowing nearest stern and setting time of stroke. **stroke** *v.t.* (**stroked, strok·ing**). Act as stroke to (boat, crew).

stroke[2] (strōk) *v.t.* (**stroked, strok·ing**). Pass hand etc. softly and usu. repeatedly in one direction over (hair, skin, etc.), as caress etc. ~ *n.* Act, spell, of stroking.

stroll (strōl) *n.* Leisurely walk or ramble, saunter. ~ *v.i.* Walk in leisurely fashion; **stroll'ing company, players**, etc., actors traveling about and giving performances.

strol·ler (strō'ler) *n.* 1. Person who strolls. 2. Child's light folding

***Strip cropping** is a farming method which prevents soil erosion on sloping land. By alternating shallow and deep-rooted crops it is possible to retain moisture that would otherwise be lost through runoff.*

chair on wheels.

strong (strawng, strŏng) *adj.* (**strong·er** pr. strawng'ger, strŏng'-, **strong·est** pr. strawng'gĭst, strŏng'-). 1. Physically powerful, vigorous, or robust; performed with muscular strength; having great muscular, moral, or mental power or strength; powerful in arms, numbers, equipment, authority, etc. 2. Difficult to capture, break into, invade, or escape from, capable of resisting force or strain, resistant, tough. 3. Energetic, effective, vigorous, decided. 4. Convincing, striking; powerfully affecting the senses, passions, mind, etc. 5. (of drink) Having large proportion of flavoring element, solid ingredient, alcohol, etc. 6. (gram., of verbs) Forming inflections by vowel change in root syllable, rather than by addition of suffixes. 7. **~-arm**, (colloq.) using force; **strong'box**, strongly made chest or safe for money, documents, etc.; **strong drink**, alcoholic liquors; **strong'-hold**, fortified place; secure place of refuge or retreat; center of support for cause etc.; **strong language**, forcible (esp. profane or abusive) expressions; **strong'man**, (esp.) one who performs feats of strength for entertainment; (colloq.) dictator; **strong-minded**, having strong, vigorous, or determined mind; **strong point**, (esp.) activity or quality in which person or thing excels; **strong'-point**, (mil.) specially fortified position in a defense system. **strong'ly** *adv.* **strong** *adv.* **come on ~**, act aggressively; **be going ~**, be vigorous, thriving, or prosperous.

stron·ti·um (strŏn'shēum, -shum, -tēum) *n.* Soft easily fusible metallic element (silver white when pure); symbol Sr, at. no. 38, at. wt. 87.62; ~ **90**, hazardous radioactive isotope of strontium present in fallout of nuclear fission.

strop (strŏp) *n.* Strip of leather for sharpening razor, implement or machine serving same purpose. ~ *v.t.* (**stropped, strop·ping**). Sharpen on or with strop.

stro·phe (strō'fē) *n.* (Lines recited during) movement made from right to left by chorus in ancient Greek choral dance; series of lines forming division of lyric poem. **stroph·ic** (strō'fĭk, strŏf'ĭk) *adj.*

struc·tur·al (strŭk'cheral) *adj.* Of structure; ~ **linguistics**, study of language as system of interrelated thought and sound elements, the sounds being purely arbitrary; ~ **steel**, strong steel in shapes specially suitable for structural purposes. **struc'tur·al·ly** *adv.*

struc·ture (strŭk'cher) *n.* 1. Manner in which building or other complete whole is constructed; supporting framework or whole of essential parts of something; make, construction. 2. Thing constructed; complex whole; building. ~ *v.t.* (**-tured, -tur·ing**). Arrange, organize, give a structure to.

stru·del (strōō'del, shtrōō'-) *n.* Paper-thin pastry rolled up around a filling and baked.

strug·gle (strŭg'el) *v.i.* (**-gled, -gling**). Throw one's limbs about in violent effort to escape grasp etc.; make violent or determined efforts under difficulties, strive hard; contend *with, against*, make one's way with difficulty *through, along*, etc. ~ *n.* Struggling; resolute contest, continued effort to resist force, free oneself from constraint etc.; determined effort or resistance; ~ **for existence, life**, competition between organic species, esp. as element in natural selection; continued effort to maintain life or obtain means of livelihood. **strug'gler** *n.* **strug'gling** *adj.* (esp.) Experiencing difficulty in making a living, getting recognition, etc. **strug'gling·ly** *adv.*

strum (strŭm) *v.* (**strummed, strum·ming**). Twang strings of stringed instrument; play, esp. unskillfully, *on* (guitar, etc.). ~ *n.* Sound made by strumming.

strum·pet (strŭm'pĭt) *n.* (archaic) Female prostitute.

strung: see STRING *v.*

strut[1] (strŭt) *n.* & *v.i.* (**strut·ted, strut·ting**). (Walk with) pompous or affected stiff gait.

strut[2] (strŭt) *n.* Bar, rod, etc., of wood, iron, etc., inserted in framework to resist pressure or thrust in direction of its length; brace. ~ *v.t.* (**strut·ted, strut·ting**).

strych·nine (strĭk'nĭn, -nēn, -nīn) *n.* Highly poisonous vegetable alkaloid obtained from plants of genus *Strychnos*, esp. the nux vomica, used in medicine as stimulant and tonic.

Stu·art[1] (stōō'ert, stū'-). Name of royal house of Scotland from the accession (1371) of Robert II, one of the hereditary stewards of Scotland, and of England from the accession of James VI of Scotland to the English throne as James I (1603) to the death of Queen Anne (1714). (cf. PRETENDER).

Stu·art[2] (stōō'ert, stū'-), **Gilbert Charles** (1755–1828). Amer. portrait painter; famous for portrait of George Washington.

Stu·art[3] (stōō'ert, stū'-), **James Ewell Brown** ("Jeb") (1833–64). Amer. Confederate general and cavalry leader in Civil War.

stub (stŭb) *n.* Stump of tree, tooth, etc., left projecting; short remnant *of* pencil, cigar, etc.; counterfoil of check, ticket, receipt, etc. **stub** *v.t.* (**stubbed, stub·bing**). Grub up (stubs, roots), clear (land) of stubs; hurt (toe) by striking it against something; extinguish (cigarette) by crushing lighted end against something hard. **stub'by** *adj.* (**-bi·er, -bi·est**). **stub'bi·ness** *n.*

stub·ble (stŭb'el) *n.* Lower ends of grain stalks left in ground after harvest; short stubble-like growth of hair esp. on unshaven face. **stub'bly** *adj.* (**-bli·er, -bli·est**).

stub·born (stŭb'ern) *adj.* Unreasonably obstinate, obdurate, refractory, intractable. **stub'born·ly** *adv.* **stub'born·ness** *n.*

stuc·co (stŭk'ō) *n.* (pl. **-coes, -cos**). Fine plaster used to cover walls, ceilings, etc., and for making cornices, moldings, etc.; coarse plaster or cement for covering exterior surfaces of walls in imitation of stone. ~ *v.t.* (**-coed, -co·ing**). Coat or ornament with stucco.

stuck (stŭk) *adj.*: see STICK; (esp. of animal) that has been stabbed or had throat cut; ~**-up**, (colloq.) conceited, insolently exclusive.

stud[1] (stŭd) *n.* 1. Large-headed nail, boss, or knot, projecting from surface, esp. for ornament; rivet, crosspiece in each link of chain cable; kind of two-headed button passed through one or more eyelets or buttonholes, esp. in shirt front, or to fasten collar to shirt. 2. Upright post in framing for walls, usu. two inches by four inches. ~ *v.t.* (**stud·ded, stud·ding**). Set with studs; be scattered over or about (surface). **stud'ding** *n.* (esp.) Framing woodwork of wall.

stud[2] (stŭd) *n.* Number of

*James I founded the **Stuart** dynasty in England because his mother, Mary Queen of Scots (left) and father, Lord Darnley, shared a Tudor grandmother. Below: The children of Charles I (James' grandchildren).*

horses kept for breeding, hunting, racing, etc.; place where stud, esp. for breeding, is kept; **stud'book, stud book**, book giving pedigree of thoroughbred horses; **stud farm**, place where horses are bred; **stud'horse**, stallion; **stud poker**, kind of poker in which all but first round(s) of cards are dealt with faces up.

stu·dent (stōō'dent, stū'-) *n.* Person engaged in or inclined toward study; person undergoing instruction at university or other place of education or technical training; ~ **teacher**, college student who teaches under supervision as part of requirement for degree in education.

stu·di·o (stōō'dēō, stū'-) *n.* (pl. **-di·os**). Workroom of sculptor, painter, photographer, etc.; room in which movie action is staged; room or premises used for transmission of broadcasts, or for making films or recordings; ~ **apartment**, one-room apartment with kitchenette and bath; ~ **couch**, couch that opens out to form a bed.

stu·di·ous (stōō'dēus, stū'-) *adj.* Given to study, devoted to learning; careful *to* do, anxiously desirous *of*; studied, deliberate, zealous, anxious, painstaking. **stu'di·ous·ly** *adv.* **stu'di·ous·ness** *n.*

stud·y (stŭd'ē) *n.* (pl. **stud·ies**). 1. Devotion of time and thought to acquisition of information esp. from books; (freq. pl.) pursuit of some branch of knowledge; careful examination or observation *of* (subject, question, object, etc.); reverie, deep thought, abstraction. 2. Thing to be secured by pains or attention; thing to be investigated. 3. Literary composition devoted to detailed consideration of a subject or problem or executed as exercise or experiment in style etc. 4. (painting etc.) Careful sketch made for practice in technique or as preliminary experiment for picture etc. or part of it; (mus.) composition designed to develop player's skill. 5. (theatr.) Learning of parts in play; **quick, slow,** ~, person who learns part quickly, slowly. 6. Room used for literary occupation. **study** *v.* (**stud·ied, stud·y·ing**). Make a study of, take pains to investigate or acquire knowledge of (subject) or to ensure (desired result); examine carefully, read attentively, investigate (object); apply oneself to study; take pains *to* do. **stud'ied** *adj.* (esp.) Deliberate, intentional, affected. **stud'i·er** *n.*

stuff (stŭf) *n.* 1. Material of which thing is made or that is or can be used for some purpose; available supply of something; belongings. 2. Textile material, esp. woolen fabric. 3. Valueless matter; trash, nonsense; **do one's** ~, (colloq.) do what one is expected to do; show one's skill. **stuff** *v.* Pack, cram; stop *up*, fill; distend; fill out (skin of bird, beast, etc.) with material to restore original shape; fill (inside of bird, piece of meat, etc.) with seasoned bread crumbs, herbs, etc., before cooking; cram food into, gorge (food); gorge oneself, eat greedily; ram or press into receptacle; place fraudulent votes in (ballot box); ~**ed shirt**, (colloq.) pompous, incompetent person. **stuff'ing** *n.* (esp.) Ingredients for stuffing fowl etc. in cookery; **knock the** ~ **out of** (person), reduce to state of flabbiness or weakness.

stuff·y (stŭf'ē) *adj.* (**stuff·i·er, stuff·i·est**). Lacking fresh air or ventilation, close; stopped up; without freshness, interest, etc.; easily offended or shocked, strait-laced. **stuff'i·ly** *adv.* **stuff'i·ness** *n.*

stul·ti·fy (stŭl'tifī) *v.t.* (**-fied, -fy·ing**). Reduce to foolishness or

*The term **'studfarm'** now applies to a place where different types of animals are bred. It includes the Santa Gertrudis cattle stud at Bowral, Australia, where beasts are hand fed.*

*The **studio** used by Winston Churchill at Chartwell, England. Like many other men who achieved eminence in other spheres, as a hobby, he became skilled as a naturalistic painter.*

The Royal Air Force "Red Arrows" perform highly-skilled aerobatic ***stunts*** *which involve intricate synchronized displays, requiring split-second timing and coordination.*

absurdity; render worthless or useless; exhibit in ridiculous light. **stul·ti·fi·ca·tion** (stŭlt*i*fĭkā'sh*o*n) *n.*

stum·ble (stŭm'b*e*l) *v.* (**-bled, -bling**). Lurch forward, have partial fall, from catching or striking foot or making false step; make blunder(s) in doing something; come accidentally *on* or *across*; **stumbling block**, obstacle; circumstance that causes difficulty, hesitation, or scruples; **stum'ble-bum,** (slang) inept, clumsy person, esp. third-rate boxer. **stumble, stum'bler** *ns.* **stum'bling·ly** *adv.*

stump (stŭmp) *n.* Projecting remnant of cut or fallen tree; part remaining of broken branch or tooth, broken-off mast, amputated limb, etc.; stub of cigar, pencil, etc.; stalk of plant (esp. cabbage) with leaves removed; (pl., joc.) legs; stump of tree used by orator to address meeting from; ~ **speech,** open-air speech. **stump** *v.* 1. Walk stiffly, clumsily, and noisily. 2. Nonplus, pose, cause to be at a loss. 3. Make stump speeches; traverse (district) doing this.

stump·y (stŭm'pē) *adj.* (**stump·i·er, stump·i·est**). Thickset, stocky; of small height or length in proportion to girth. **stump'i·ly** *adv.* **stump'i·ness** *n.*

stun (stŭn) *v.t.* (**stunned, stun·ning**). (of blow etc.) Knock senseless, reduce to insensibility or stupor; daze, bewilder, with strong emotion, din, etc. **stun'ner** *n.* (esp., slang) Stunning person or thing. **stunning** *adj.* (esp., slang) Splendid, delightful.

stung: see STING *v.*

stunk (stŭngk): see STINK.

stunt[1] (stŭnt) *n.* (colloq.) Special effort, feat; showy performance, skillful trick or maneuver, esp. with aircraft. ~ *v.i.* Perform stunt.

stunt[2] (stŭnt) *v.t.* Retard growth or development of, dwarf, cramp. **stunt'ed·ness** *n.*

stu·pe·fy (stōō'p*e*fī, stū'-) *v.t.* (**-fied, -fy·ing**). Make stupid or torpid, deprive of sensibility; stun with amazement, fear, etc. **stu·pe·fa·cient** (stōōp*e*fā'sh*e*nt, stū-) *adj.* **stu·pe·fac·tion** (stōōp*e*făk'sh*o*n, stū-) *n.*

stu·pen·dous (stōōpĕn'd*u*s, stū-) *adj.* Prodigious, astounding, esp. by size or degree. **stu·pen'dous·ly** *adv.* **stu·pen'dous·ness** *n.*

stu·pid (stōō'pĭd, stū'-) *adj.* In a state of stupor or lethargy; dull by nature, slow-witted, obtuse, crass, characteristic of persons of this nature; uninteresting, dull. **stu'pid·ly** *adv.* **stu·pid·i·ty** (stōōpĭd'ĭtē, stū-) *n.* (pl. **-ties**). **stupid** *n.* Stupid person.

stu·por (stōō'p*er*, stū'p*er*) *n.* Dazed state, torpidity; helpless amazement. **stu'por·ous** *adj.*

stur·dy (stẽr'dē) *adj.* (**-di·er, -di·est**). Robust, hardy, vigorous, strongly built. **stur'di·ly** *adv.* **stur'di·ness** *n.*

stur·geon (stẽr'j*o*n) *n.* (pl. **-geons,** collect. **-geon**). Any of various large fishes of rivers, lakes, and coastal waters of north temperate zone, with long almost cylindrical body and long tapering snout, esteemed as food and the source of caviar, esp. *Acipenser oxyrhynchus*, of Atlantic coastal regions of Europe and N. Amer.

stut·ter (stŭt'*er*) *v.* Stammer; speak or say with continued involuntary repetition of parts of words, esp. initial consonants. ~ *n.* Act or habit of stuttering. **stut'ter·er** *n.* **stut'ter·ing·ly** *adv.*

sty[1] (stī) *n.* (pl. **sties**). (also **pigsty**) 1. Pen or enclosure for pigs. 2. Filthy room or dwelling. **sty** *v.* (**stied, sty·ing**). Lodge in sty.

sty[2] (stī) *n.* (pl. **sties, styes**). Inflamed swelling on edge of eyelid.

Styg·i·an (stĭj'ē*a*n) *adj.* (As) of the Styx or of Hades; murky, gloomy, black as the Styx.

style (stīl) *n.* 1. Ancient writing implement, small rod with pointed end for scratching letters on wax-covered tablets, and flat broad end for erasing and smoothing tablet; (poet.) pen, pencil; stylelike thing, as engraver, blunt-pointed probe; (bot.) narrowed prolongation of ovary supporting stigma; (zool.) small slender pointed process or part; pointed sponge spicule. 2. Manner of writing, speaking, or doing, esp. as opp. to the matter expressed or thing done; manner of execution of work of art etc.; manner characteristic of person, school, period, etc.; (esp. correct or pleasing) way of doing something; kind, sort, pattern, type; mode of behavior, manner of life; fashion, mode, esp. in dress etc.; distinction, noticeably superior quality or manner, esp. with regard to appearance. 3. Descriptive formula, designation of person or thing; full title. 4. Mode of expressing dates; **New S~,** (abbrev. N.S.) according to the reformed or GREGORIAN calendar; **Old Style,** (abbrev. O.S.) according to the JULIAN[2] calendar, used by all Christian nations until 1582. **styl'ing** *n.* **style** *v.t.* (**styled, styl·ing**). Call by specified name

*Estes Park in northern Colorado is at the eastern entrance of Rocky Mountain National Park and is an example of the **sub-alpine** terrain typified by coniferous vegetation.*

or style; design, arrange, make, etc. in (esp. fashionable) style. **styl'er** *n.*

sty·let (stī'lĭt) *n.* Stiletto; engraving tool, pointed marking instrument; (surg.) slender probe, wire run through catheter for stiffening or cleaning; (zool.) piercing mouthpart of insects etc.

styl·ish (stī'lĭsh) *adj.* Noticeably conforming to fashionable standard of elegance; having good style. **styl'ish·ly** *adv.* **styl'ish·ness** *n.*

styl·ist (stī'lĭst) *n.* Person having or aiming at good style in writing or doing something. **sty·lis·tic** (stīlĭs'tĭk) *adj.* Of literary or artistic style. **sty·lis'ti·cal·ly** *adv.*

sty·lite (stī'līt) *n.* Medieval ascetic living on top of a pillar: see SIMEON STYLITES.

styl·ize (stī'līz) *v.t.* (**-ized, -iz·ing**). Conform (work of art etc., or part of it) to the rules of a conventional style. **styl·i·za·tion** (stīlīzā'sh*o*n) *n.*

sty·lo·bate (stī'l*o*bāt) *n.* Continuous base supporting row(s) of columns.

sty·loid (stī'loid) *adj.* Slender, pointed; ~ **process**, process projecting from base of temporal bone in man. **styloid** *n.* Styloid process.

sty·lus (stī'l*u*s) *n.* (pl. **-lus·es, -li** pr. -lī). Style, ancient writing implement; tracing point producing indented groove in phonograph record, or following such groove in reproducing sound.

sty·mie, sty·my (stī'mē) *ns.* (pl. **-mies**). (golf) Position on the putting green in which the opponent's ball lies in a direct line between the player's ball and the hole. ~ *v.t.* (**-mied, mie·ing, -mied, -my·ing**). Put into position of having to negotiate stymie (freq. fig.).

styp·tic (stĭp'tĭk) *adj.* & *n.* (Substance) that contracts organic tissue and checks bleeding. **styp'sis** *n.*

sty·rene (stīr'ēn) *n.* Liquid hydrocarbon ($C_6H_5CH{:}CH_2$), used as basis for many plastics.

Sty·ro·foam (stīr'*o*fōm) *n.* (trademark) Lightweight polystyrene, used in insulation, as packing, in boatbuilding, etc.

Styx (stĭks). (Gk. myth.) River of Hades over which Charon ferried the souls of the dead. **Styg·i·an** (stĭj'ēan) *adj.*

sua·sion (swā'zh*o*n) *n.* Persuasion, esp. in **moral** ~.

suave (swahv) *adj.* Bland, soothing, polite. **suave'ly** *adv.* **suav·i·ty** (swah'vĭtē, swăv'ĭ-), **suave'ness** *ns.*

sub (sŭb) *n.* (colloq.) Submarine, substitute. ~ *v.* (**subbed, sub·bing**). (colloq.) Act as substitute (*for*).

sub- *prefix.* (freq. with letter *b* changed by assimilation) 1. Under, below. 2. More or less, roughly; not quite; on the borders of. 3. Subordinate(ly); secondary; further.

sub·ac·id (sŭbăs'ĭd) *adj.* Moderately acid or tart; somewhat biting.

sub·a·cute (sŭb*a*kūt') *adj.* (med.) Between acute and chronic.

sub·al·pine (sŭbăl'pīn, -pĭn) *adj.* Of higher slopes of mountains (about 4,000–5,000 ft.), just below the timber line.

sub·al·tern (sŭbawl't*e*rn) *n.* (Brit. mil.) Junior officer below rank of captain.

sub·a·que·ous (sŭbā'kwē*u*s, -ăk'wē-) *adj.* Existing, formed, performed or taking place, underwater; adapted for use underwater.

sub·arc·tic (sŭbark'tĭk) *adj.* Of regions somewhat south of Arctic Circle or resembling these in climate etc.

sub·a·tom·ic (sŭb*a*tŏm'ĭk) *adj.* Occurring in, smaller than, an atom.

sub·cla·vi·an (sŭbklā'vēan) *adj.* Lying or extending under clavicle; ~ **artery**, main trunk of arterial system of upper extremity. **subclavian** *n.* Subclavian artery, vein, or muscle.

sub·clin·i·cal (sŭbklĭn'ĭk*a*l) *adj.* (med.) Not yet presenting definite symptoms.

sub·com·mit·tee (sŭb'k*o*mĭtē) *n.* Committee formed from main committee for special purpose.

sub·con·scious (sŭbkŏn′shus) *adj.* Of part of mind or mental field outside range of attention or imperfectly or partially conscious. ~ *n.* Subconscious part of mind. **sub·con′scious·ly** *adv.* **sub·con′scious·ness** *n.*

sub·con·ti·nent (sŭbkŏn′tinent, sŭb′kŏn-) *n.* Land mass of great extent but smaller than those generally called continents. **sub·con·ti·nen·tal** (sŭbkŏntinĕn′tal) *adj.*

sub·con·tract (sŭbkŏn′trăkt, sŭb′kŏn-) *n.* Contract for carrying out (part of) previous contract. ~ (sŭbkontrăkt′) *v.* Make subcontract (for). **sub·con·trac·tor** (sŭbkŏn′trăkter, sŭb′kŏn-, sŭbkontrăk′-) *n.*

sub·cor·ti·cal (sŭbkôr′tikal) *adj.* Situated, formed, etc., below a cortex, esp. the cortex of the brain.

sub·cu·ta·ne·ous (sŭbkūtā′nēus) *adj.* Lying, living, performed, etc., under the skin; hypodermic. **sub·cu·ta′ne·ous·ly** *adv.*

sub·dea·con (sŭbdē′kon, sŭb′dē-) *n.* Minister of order next below deacon; (R.C. Ch.) cleric or lay clerk assisting next below deacon at solemn celebration of Eucharist.

sub·deb (sŭb′dĕb) *n.* (colloq.) Girl who is about to become a debutante.

sub·di·vide (sŭbdĭvīd′, sŭb′dĭvīd) *v.* 1. Divide again after first division. 2. Divide (land) into lots for sale. **sub·di·vi·sion** (sŭb′dĭvĭzhon) *n.* Subdividing; subordinate division; tract of land subdivided into lots.

sub·due (subdōō′, -dū′) *v.t.* (**-dued, -du·ing**). Conquer, subjugate, overcome, prevail over; reduce intensity, force, or vividness of (sound, color, light).

su·ber·ic (sōōbĕr′ĭk) *adj.* Of cork; (chem.) ~ **acid**, white crystalline dibasic acid obtained by action of nitric acid on cork etc.

su·ber·ose (sōō′berōs), **su·ber·ous** (sōō′berus) *adjs.* (bot.) Of, like, cork, corky.

sub·fam·i·ly (sŭbfăm′ilē, -făm′lē) *n.* (pl. **-lies**). (zool.) Taxonomic category below family and above tribe or genus.

sub·head (sŭb′hĕd), **sub·head·ing** (sŭb′hĕdĭng) *ns.* Subordinate division of subject etc.; subordinate heading or title in chapter, article, etc.

sub·hu·man (sŭbhū′man) *adj.* Less than human; not quite human.

sub·ject (sŭb′jĭkt) *n.* 1. Person owing allegiance to government or ruling power esp. sovereign; any member of a state except the sovereign, any member of a subject state. 2. (logic, gram.) That member of a proposition or sentence about which something is predicated; substantive word, phrase, or clause governing a verb. 3. (philos.) Thinking or feeling entity, the mind, the ego, the conscious self, as opp. to all that is external to the mind; the substance of anything as opp. to its attributes. 4. Theme of or *of* discussion or description or representation; matter (to be) treated of or dealt with; department of study. 5. (chiefly med.) Person to be treated or operated on; person of specified usu. undesirable bodily or mental characteristics, as *hysterical, sensitive*, ~. 6. ~ **catalog, index**, etc., catalog, index, listing books, etc., according to subject; ~ **matter**, matter treated of in book etc. **subject** *adj.* Under government, not independent, owing obedience *to*; liable, exposed, or prone *to*; ~ *to*, conditional(ly) upon, on the assumption of. **subject** (subjĕkt′) *v.t.* Subdue, make subject, (*to* one's sway etc.); expose, make liable, treat, *to*. **sub·jec·tion** (subjĕk′shon) *n.*

sub·jec·tive (subjĕk′tĭv) *adj.* 1. Of, proceeding from, taking place within, the thinking subject, having its source in the mind; personal, individual; introspective; imaginary, illusory. 2. (gram.) Of the subject; ~ **case**, nominative. **sub·jec′tive·ly** *adv.* **sub·jec′tive·ness, sub·jec·tiv·i·ty** (sŭbjĕktĭv′ĭtē) *ns.*

sub·jec·tiv·ism (subjĕk′tĭvĭzem) *n.* Philosophical theory that all knowledge is merely subjective. **sub·jec′tiv·ist** *n.*

sub·join (subjoin′) *v.t.* Add at the end, append.

In this photograph of urban development taking over agricultural land the process of ***subdivision,*** *dividing an area of land into plots for sale, is clearly illustrated.*

sub ju·di·ce (sŭb jōō′dĭsē). (law, of case) Under judicial consideration, not yet decided. [L.]

sub·ju·gate (sŭb′jugāt) *v.t.* (**-gat·ed, -gat·ing**). Bring under the yoke or into subjection, subdue, vanquish. **sub′ju·ga·tor, sub·ju·ga·tion** (sŭbjugā′shon) *ns.*

sub·junc·tive (subjŭngk′tĭv) *adj.* (gram.) Of a verbal mood used in classical language chiefly in subordinate or subjoined clauses; obsolescent in English exc. in certain uses, e.g. to express wish (*I wish it* were *over*), imprecation (*manners* be hanged!), and contingent or hypothetical events (*if he* were *here now*). **sub·junc′tive·ly** *adv.* **subjunctive** *n.* Subjunctive mood.

sub·lease (sŭb′lēs) *n.* Lease granted to subtenant. ~ (sŭblēs′) *v.t.* (**-leased, -leas·ing**). Let to subtenant.

sub·let (sŭblĕt′) *v.t.* (**-let, -let·ting**). Sublease.

sub·li·mate (sŭb′limĭt, -māt) *n.* (chem.) Solid produced when a substance is sublimed. ~ (sŭb′limāt) *v.t.* (**-mat·ed, -mat·ing**). 1. (chem., obs.) = SUBLIME[2]. 2. Transmute into something nobler, more sublime or refined; (psychol.) divert energy of (primitive impulse) into activity more socially useful or regarded as higher in cultural or moral scale. **sub·li·ma·tion** (sŭblĭmā′shon) *n.* Action, process, of subliming or sublimating.

sub·lime[1] (sublīm′) *adj.* Of the most exalted kind, aloof from and raised far above the ordinary; inspiring awe, deep reverence, or lofty emotion by beauty, vastness, grandeur, etc. **sub·lime′ly** *adv.* **sub·lim·i·ty** (sublĭm′ĭtē), **sub·lime′ness** *ns.* **sublime** *n.* (usu. **the** ~) What is sublime, sublimity.

sub·lime[2] (sublīm′) *v.* (**-limed, -lim·ing**). 1. (chem.) Subject (substance) to action of heat so as to convert it to vapor that, on cooling, is deposited in solid form; purify (substance) by this means; (of substance) undergo this process; pass from solid to gaseous state without liquefaction. 2. (fig.) Purify or elevate, become pure, as by sublimation; make sublime.

sub·lim·i·nal (sublĭm′inal) *adj.* (psychol.) Below threshold of consciousness, too faint or rapid to be recognized; ~ **advertising**, advertising done, e.g. by rapid flashes on motion picture or television screen, which, though not consciously seen by observers, is thought to affect their subsequent behavior. **sub·lim′i·nal·ly** *adv.*

sub·lu·nar·y (sŭblōō′nerē, sŭb′lōōnĕre), **sub·lu·nar** (sŭblōō′ner) *adjs.* Beneath the moon; between orbits of moon and Earth; subject

*The conventional **submarine** such as the 'Narwhal' (right) is being replaced by nuclear-powered vessels. They have a much longer range and can fire I.C.B.Ms while submerged.*

to moon's influence; of this world, earthly, terrestrial.

sub·ma·chine (sŭbm*a*shēn') **gun.** Lightweight machine gun fired from waist or shoulder.

sub·mar·gin·al (sŭbmar̄'j*i*n*a*l) *adj.* 1. Falling below minimum standards or requirements. 2. Not producing sufficient amount; infertile.

sub·ma·rine (sŭbm*a*rēn', sŭb'-m*a*rēn) *adj.* Existing or lying under surface of sea; operating, operated, constructed, laid, intended for use, under surface of sea. ~ *n.* Vessel, esp. warship, that can be submerged and navigated underwater, used esp. for carrying and launching torpedoes and other missiles; ~ **chaser**, small highly maneuverable naval patrol boat equipped for operations against submarines. **sub·ma·rin·er** (sŭbm*a*rē'n*e*r, sŭb-măr'*i*-) *n.* Member of crew of submarine.

sub·max·il·lar·y (sŭbmăk'-s*i*lĕrē) *adj.* Beneath lower jaw.

sub·merge (s*u*bmẽrj') *v.* (**-merged, -merg·ing**). (Cause to) sink or plunge under water. **sub·mer'gence, sub·mer·sion** (s*u*bmẽr'zh*o*n, -sh*o*n) *ns.* **sub·mer·si·ble** (s*u*bmẽrs*i*b*i*l) *adj.* & *n.* **sub·mer·si·bil·i·ty** (s*u*bmẽrs*i*bĭl'-ĭtē) *n.*

sub·mi·cro·scop·ic (sŭbmīkr*o*-skŏp'ĭk) *adj.* Too small to be seen by an ordinary microscope.

sub·min·i·a·ture (sŭbmĭn'-ēach*e*r) *adj.* Of greatly reduced size; (of camera) miniature and using 16-mm film. **sub·min'i·a·tur·ize** *v.* (**-ized, -iz·ing**).

sub·mis·sion (s*u*bmĭsh'*o*n) *n.* Submissive, yielding, or deferential attitude, condition, conduct, etc.; submitting, being submitted.

sub·mis·sive (s*u*bmĭs'ĭv) *adj.* Inclined to submit, yielding to power or authority, humble, obedient. **sub·mis'sive·ly** *adv.* **sub·mis'sive·ness** *n.*

sub·mit (s*u*bmĭt') *v.* (**-mit·ted, -mit·ting**). 1. Surrender oneself, become subject, yield (*to* person, his authority, etc., or *to* judgment, criticism, correction, or condition, etc.). 2. Bring under notice or consideration of person, refer *to* his decision or judgment; urge or represent deferentially (*that*).

sub·nor·mal (sŭbnōr'm*a*l) *adj.* Less than normal, below normal. **sub·nor·mal·i·ty** (sŭbnōrmăl'ĭtē) *n.* (pl. **-ties**).

sub·or·bi·tal (sŭbōr'b*i*t*a*l) *adj.* Of less duration or distance than 1 orbit.

sub·or·der (sŭb'ōrd*e*r) *n.* (zool., bot.) Subdivision of order next below order in classification.

*A bank in Crete showing red earth above limestone **subsoil.** If it is 'double-dug,' or plowed to the surface, and then mixed with topsoil and humus, a greater depth for cultivation can be obtained.*

sub·or·di·nate (s*u*bōr'd*i*nĭt) *adj.* Of inferior importance of rank, secondary, subservient; (gram., of clause) dependent, being syntactically equivalent to noun, adjective, or adverb. ~ *n.* Person under control or orders of superior. **sub·or'di·nate·ly** *adv.* **subordinate** (s*u*bōr'd*i*nāt) *v.t.* (**-nat·ed, -nat·ing**). Make subordinate, treat or regard as of minor importance, bring or put into subservient relation (*to*). **sub·or·di·na·tion** (s*u*bōrd*i*nā'sh*o*n) *n.* **sub·or'di·na·tive** *adj.*

sub·orn (s*u*bōrn') *v.t.* Bribe, induce, or procure (person) by underhand or unlawful means to commit perjury or other unlawful act. **sub·or·na·tion** (sŭbōrnā'sh*o*n) *n.*

sub·plot (sŭb'plŏt) *n.* Secondary plot in play etc.

sub·poe·na (s*u*pē'n*a*) *n.* Writ commanding person's attendance in court of justice. ~ *v.t.* (**-naed, -na·ing**). Serve subpoena on. [L. *sub poena* = "under penalty," first words of writ]

sub·ro·ga·tion (sŭbr*o*gā'sh*o*n) *n.* (law) Substitution of one party for another as creditor so that the same rights and duties apply.

sub ro·sa (sŭb rō'z*a*). In confidence, in secret. [L., = "under the rose"]

sub·scribe (s*u*bskrīb') *v.* (**-scribed, -scrib·ing**). 1. Write (one's name) at foot of document, sign one's name to (document etc.), signify assent to by signing one's name; put one's signature *to* in token of assent, approval, etc.;

express one's agreement, acquiescence, etc. 2. Enter one's name in list of contributors; make or promise a contribution, contribute (specified sum) to or *to* common fund, society, party, etc., or *for* common object, raise or guarantee raising of by subscribing thus; ~ **to**, undertake to buy (periodical) regularly. **sub·scrib'er** *n.* **sub·scrip·tion** (s*u*bskrĭp'sh*o*n) *n.*

sub·script (sŭb'skrĭpt) *adj.* Written below or underneath (math. etc., of index written below and to right of symbol).

sub·sec·tion (sŭb'sĕksh*o*n) *n.* Subordinate division of section.

sub·se·quent (sŭb'sekw*e*nt) *adj.* Following in order, time, or succession, esp. coming immediately after. **sub'se·quent·ly** *adv.* **sub'-se·quence** *n.*

sub·ser·vi·ent (s*u*bsẽr'vē*e*nt) *adj.* 1. Serving as means to further an end or purpose. 2. Subordinate, subject (*to*); cringing, truckling, obsequious. **sub·ser'vi·ent·ly** *adv.* **sub·ser'vi·ence, sub·ser'-vi·en·cy** *ns.*

sub·side (s*u*bsīd') *v.i.* (**-sid·ed, -sid·ing**). Sink down, sink to low(er) level (esp. of liquids or soil sinking to normal level); (of swelling etc.) go down; (of person, usu. joc.) sink *into*, *onto*, chair etc.; (of storm, strong feeling, clamor, etc.) abate, become less agitated, violent, or active; cease from activity or agitation. **sub·sid·ence** (s*u*bsī'd*e*ns, sŭb'sĭ-) *n.*

sub·sid·i·ar·y (s*u*bsĭd'ēērē) *adj.* Serving to assist or supplement, auxiliary, supplementary; subordinate, secondary. ~ *n.* (pl. **-ar·ies**). Subsidiary person or thing.

sub·si·dize (sŭb'sĭdīz) *v.t.* (**-dized, -diz·ing**). Pay subsidy to. **sub·si·di·za·tion** (sŭbsĭdĭzā'-sh*o*n) *n.*

sub·si·dy (sŭb'sĭdē) *n.* (pl. **-dies**). 1. Money grant from one country to another in return for military or naval aid etc. 2. Financial aid given by government or private organization toward expenses of an undertaking or institution held to be of public utility, or (by government) to producers of commodity etc. to enable goods or services to be provided at low(er) cost to consumer.

sub·sist (s*u*bsĭst') *v.* 1. Exist as a reality; continue to exist, remain in being. 2. Maintain, support, keep, provide food or funds for, provision; maintain or support oneself.

sub·sist·ence (s*u*bsĭs'tens) *n.* Subsisting; means of supporting life, livelihood; ~ **allowance**, allowance granted to employee for living expenses while traveling on employer's business; ~ **farming**, farming in which produce is consumed by farm household, with little or no surplus for selling.

sub·soil (sŭb'soil) *n.* Soil lying immediately under surface soil.

sub·son·ic (sŭbsŏn'ĭk) *adj.* (of aircraft etc.) Having speed less than that of sound (opp. SUPERSONIC).

sub·spe·cies (sŭb'spēshēz) *n.* Subdivision of species. **sub·spe·cif·ic** (sŭbspesĭf'ĭk) *adj.* **sub·spe·cif'i·cal·ly** *adv.*

sub·stance (sŭb'st*a*ns) *n.* 1. (philos.) What underlies phenomena, permanent substratum of things, that in which accidents or attributes inhere; essential nature; essence or most important part of anything, purport, real meaning. 2. Theme, subject matter, material, esp. as opp. to form; reality, solidity, solid or real thing. 3. (archaic) Possessions, wealth. 4. Particular kind or species of matter.

sub·stand·ard (sŭbstăn'd*e*rd) *adj.* Of less than required or normal quality, size, etc.

sub·stan·tial (s*u*bstăn'sh*a*l) *adj.* 1. Having substance, actually existing, not illusory; of real importance or value, of considerable amount. 2. Of solid material or structure, not flimsy, stout; possessed of property, well-to-do, commercially sound. 3. That is such essentially, virtual, practical. **sub·stan'tial·ly** *adv.* **sub·stan·ti·al·i·ty** (s*u*bstăn-shēăl'ĭtē), **sub·stan'tial·ness** *ns.*

sub·stan·tial·ism (s*u*bstăn'-sh*a*lĭz*e*m) *n.* (philos.) Doctrine that there are substantial realities underlying phenomena.

sub·stan·ti·ate (s*u*bstăn'shēāt) *v.t.* (**-at·ed, -at·ing**). Give substantial form to; demonstrate or verify by proof or evidence. **sub·stan·ti·a·tion** (s*u*bstănshēā'sh*o*n) *n.*

sub·stan·ti·val (sŭbst*a*ntī'v*a*l) *adj.* Of, consisting of, substantive(s). **sub·stan·ti'val·ly** *adv.*

sub·stan·tive (sŭb'st*a*ntĭv) *adj.* 1. Having a separate and independent existence, not merely inferential or implicit or subservient. 2. (gram.) Expressing existence; denoting a noun or its equivalent; ~ **verb**, the verb *be*. 3. (law) Of, consisting of, rules of right administered by court as opp. to forms of procedure. **sub'stan·tive·ly** *adv.* **substantive** *n.* (gram.) Noun.

sub·sti·tute (sŭb'stĭtōōt, -tūt) *n.* Person or thing acting or serving in place of another. ~ *v.* (**-tut·ed, -tut·ing**). Put in place of another; (cause to) act as substitute *for*. **sub·sti·tu·tion** (sŭbstĭtōō'sh*o*n, -tū'-) *n.* (esp., chem.) Replacement of one atom or radical in molecule by another. **sub·sti·tut·a·bil·i·ty** (sŭbstĭ-tōōt*a*bĭl'ĭtē, -tū-) *n.* **sub·sti·tu'-tion·al, sub'sti·tu·tive** *adjs.*

sub·strat·o·sphere (sŭbstrăt'-*o*sfẽr) *n.* Layer of atmosphere immediately below stratosphere.

sub·stra·tum (sŭbstrā't*u*m, -străt'*u*m, sŭb'strāt*u*m, -străt*u*m) *n.* (pl. **-ta** pr. -t*a*, **-tums**). What underlies or forms basis of anything.

sub·struc·ture (sŭb'strŭkch*e*r) *n.* Underlying or supporting structure.

sub·sume (s*u*bsōōm') *v.t.* (**-sumed, -sum·ing**). Bring (one idea, principle, etc.) under another, a rule, or a class. **sub·sump·tion** (s*u*bsŭmp'sh*o*n) *n.* **sub·sum'a·ble** *adj.*

sub·ten·ant (sŭbtĕn'*a*nt, sŭb'-tĕn-) *n.* One who holds or leases from a tenant. **sub·ten'an·cy** *n.*

sub·tend (sŭbtĕnd') *v.t.* (geom.) (of chord, side of figure, angle) Be opposite to (angle, arc).

This road in Holtville, California has been subjected to an earthquake of 6.7 on the Richter scale, and the ensuing ***subsidence*** *is a common result of a tremor of that size.*

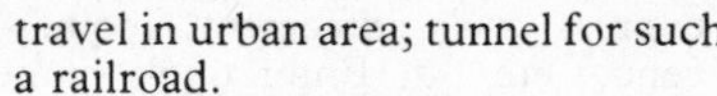

sub·ter·fuge (sŭb′terfūj) *n.* Evasion, shift; artifice or device adopted to escape or avoid force of argument, condemnation, or censure, or to justify conduct.

sub·ter·ra·ne·an (sŭbterā′nēan) *adj.* Existing, lying, situated, formed, operating, taking place, performed, under surface of the earth; underground. **sub·ter·ra′ne·ous** *adj.* Subterranean. **sub·ter·ra′ne·ous·ly** *adv.*

sub·ti·tle (sŭb′tītel) *n.* Subordinate or additional title of literary work etc.; caption for silent film; television caption; translation printed on screen for foreign-language film. ~ *v.t.* (**-ti·tled, -ti·tling**). Add subtitle(s) to.

sub·tle (sŭt′el) *adj.* (**sub·tler, sub·tlest**). Tenuous, rarefied (archaic); pervasive or elusive by reason of tenuity; fine or delicate, esp. to such an extent as to elude observation or analysis; making fine distinctions, having delicate perceptions, acute; ingenious, elaborate, clever; crafty, cunning. **sub′tly** *adv.* **sub′tle·ty** (pl. **-ties**), **sub′tle·ness** *ns.*

sub·ton·ic (sŭbtŏn′ĭk) *n.* (mus.) Note next below tonic, seventh note of ascending scale.

sub·tract (subtrăkt′) *v.t.* Deduct (part, quantity, number) from or *from* whole or from quantity or number, esp. in arithmetic and algebra. **sub·trac·tion** (subtrăk′shon) *n.* **sub·trac′tive** *adj.*

sub·tra·hend (sŭb′trahĕnd) *n.* (math.) Quantity or number to be subtracted.

sub·trop·i·cal (sŭbtrŏp′ĭkal) *adj.* (Characteristic of regions) bordering on the tropics.

sub·urb (sŭb′ẽrb) *n.* Residential area lying on or near outskirts of city. **sub·ur·ban** (subẽr′ban) *adj.* **sub·ur·ban·ite** (subẽr′banīt) *n.* Person living in a suburb.

sub·ur·bi·a (subẽr′bēa) *n.* Suburbs and their inhabitants.

sub·ven·tion (subvĕn′shon) *n.* Grant from government etc., in support of enterprise of public importance, subsidy.

sub·ver·sion (subvẽr′zhon, -shon) *n.* Overturning, ruin, overthrow from foundation, esp. overthrowing or undermining of government.

sub·ver·sive (subvẽr′sĭv) *adj.* Tending to subvert or overthrow. **sub·ver′sive·ly** *adv.*

sub·vert (subvẽrt′) *v.t.* Overthrow, overturn, upset, effect destruction or ruin of (religion, government). **sub·vert′er** *n.*

sub·way (sŭb′wā) *n.* Underground electric railroad for rapid travel in urban area; tunnel for such a railroad.

Dormouse ***suckling*** *her young. Like all mammals the young after birth rely on the mother's milk to provide their total food intake until they are old enough to digest other substances.*

suc·ceed (suksēd′) *v.* 1. Come next after and take the place of, follow in order, come next (to); be subsequent (to); come by inheritance or in due course to or *to* office, title, or property. 2. Have success, be successful; prosper; accomplish one's purpose; (of plan etc.) be brought to a successful completion or fulfillment. **suc·ceed′er** *n.*

suc·cès d'es·time (süksĕ dĕstēm′). Cordial reception by critics but not by general public. [Fr.]

suc·cess (suksĕs′) *n.* Favorable issue; attainment of object, or of wealth, fame, or position; thing or person that succeeds or is successful. **suc·cess′ful** *adj.* **suc·cess′ful·ly** *adv.*

suc·ces·sion (suksĕsh′on) *n.* 1. Following in order, succeeding; series of things in succession; **in** ~, one after another in regular sequence. 2. (Right of) succeeding to the throne or any office or inheritance; set or order of persons having such right; **apostolic** ~, uninterrupted transmission of spiritual authority through bishops from the apostles downward. **suc·ces′sion·al** *adj.*

suc·ces·sive (suksĕs′ĭv) *adj.* Coming one after another in uninterrupted sequence. **suc·ces′sive·ly** *adv.*

suc·ces·sor (suksĕs′er) *n.* Person or thing succeeding another.

suc·cinct (suksĭngkt′) *adj.* Terse, brief, concise. **suc·cinct′ly** *adv.* **suc·cinct′ness** *n.*

suc·cor (sŭk′er) *v.t.* Come to assistance of, give aid to in need or difficulty. ~ *n.* Aid given in time of need.

suc·co·tash (sŭk′otăsh) *n.* Dish of lima beans and corn kernels cooked together. [Amer. Ind. *msiquatash*]

Suc·coth: SUKKOTH.

suc·cu·ba (sŭk′yuba) (pl. **-bae** pr. -bē), **suc·cu·bus** (sŭk′yubus) (pl. **-bi** pr. -bī, **-bus·es**) *ns.* Female demon supposed to have sexual intercourse with men in their sleep.

suc·cu·lent (sŭk′yulent) *adj.* Juicy; (bot.) having juicy or fleshy tissues, as the cactus. **suc′cu·lent·ly** *adv.* **suc′cu·lence, suc′cu·len·cy** *ns.* **succulent** *n.* Plant with fleshy foliage or stems or both.

suc·cumb (sukŭm′) *v.i.* Sink under pressure, give way to superior force, authority, etc.; (esp.) yield to effects of disease, wounds, etc., die.

such (sŭch) *adj.* 1. Of the character, degree, or extent described, referred to, or implied; previously described or specified; ~ **as**, of the kind or degree that,

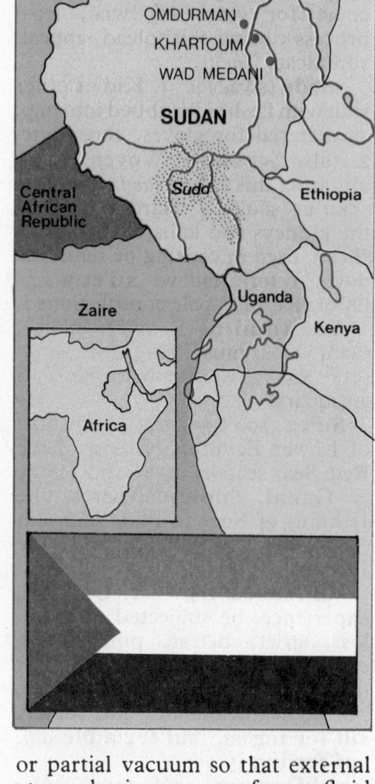

Until the 19th century, the Sudd of ***Sudan*** *remained isolated from invasion by vast papyrus swamps (above). Today the country is unified and supplies 80 percent of the world's gum arabic.*

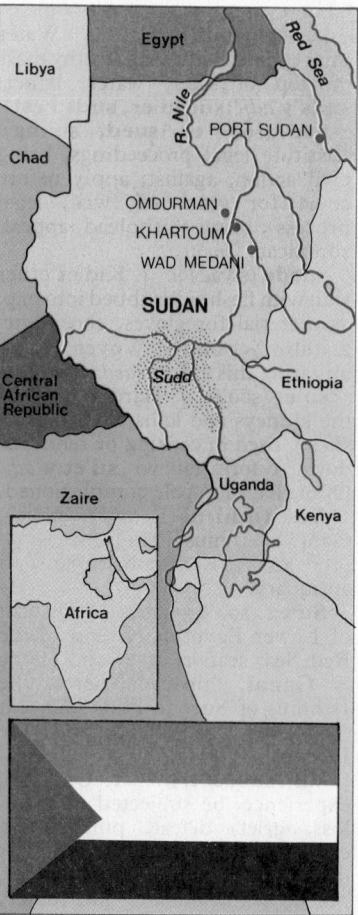

the kind of (person or thing) that; for example, e.g. 2. So great, so eminent, etc. (freq. emphatic and exclamatory); (preceding attrib. adjective, with adverbial force) so. 3. particular, but not specified; ~ **and** ~, a particular but unspecified; **such'like,** (of) such a kind. **such** *pron.* That, the action, etc., referred to; such people *as*, those *who* (chiefly archaic or rhet.); (vulg. or commerc.) the aforesaid thing(s); **as** ~, as what has been specified.

suck (sŭk) *v.* 1. Draw (liquid, esp. milk from breast) into mouth by contracting muscles of lips, tongue, and cheeks so as to produce partial vacuum; (fig.) imbibe, absorb (knowledge etc.). 2. Apply lips, lips and tongue or analogous organs, to breast, food substance, etc., to absorb nourishment. 3. Perform action of sucking, use sucking action; (of pump etc.) make sucking or gurgling sound, draw in air instead of water. 4. ~ **at,** take pull at (pipe etc.); ~ **down, in,** (of whirlpool, quicksand, etc.) engulf; ~ **dry,** exhaust of contents by sucking; ~ **in,** (slang) cheat, deceive, swindle; ~ **in, up,** (of absorbent substance) absorb; ~ **up to,** (slang) toady to, curry favor with. **suck** *n.* Action, act, spell, of sucking (**give** ~, suckle); drawing action of whirlpool etc.

suck·er (sŭk′*er*) *n.* 1. Person or thing that sucks, esp. sucking pig or young whale calf; organ adapted for sucking; any of several esp. N. Amer. fish of family Catostomidae with mouths of form that suggests feeding by suction; piston of pump, syringe, etc. 2. Part, organ, or device adapted for adhering to object by suction; fish with suctorial disk by which it adheres to foreign objects. 3. Shoot thrown out by plant, esp. root under ground; axillary shoot to tobacco plant. 4. Lollipop. 5. (slang) Person easily victimized or gulled.

suck·ing (sŭk′ĭng) *adj.* Not yet weaned; (fig.) budding, unpracticed, immature.

suck·le (sŭk′*e*l) *v.t.* (**-led, -ling**). Give suck to, feed at the breast. **suck'ling** *n.* Unweaned child or animal, as ~ *pig*.

su·crose (so͞o′krōs) *n.* Sugar ($C_{12}H_{22}O_{11}$) from cane and beet and found widely in many plants.

suc·tion (sŭk′sh*o*n) *n.* Action of sucking; production of complete or partial vacuum so that external atmospheric pressure forces fluid into vacant space or causes adhesion of surfaces; ~ **pump,** pump drawing liquid through pipe into chamber exhausted by piston. **suc'tion·al** *adj.*

suc·to·ri·al (sŭktōr′ēal, -tōr′-) *adj.* (of organ) Adapted for sucking; (of animal) having suctorial organs; of the group Suctoria of protozoa, with tubular suctorial tentacles.

Su·dan (so͞odăn′). 1. Region of Africa, S. of Sahara and Libyan deserts. 2. Republic in NE. Africa, south of Egypt; capital, Khartoum. **Su·da·nese** (so͞od*a*nēs′, -nēz′) *adj.* & *n.* (pl. **-nese**).

sud·den (sŭd′*e*n) *adj.* Happening, coming, performed, taking place, etc., without warning or unexpectedly, abrupt; ~ **death,** (sports) overtime play to settle tied game, play ending as soon as one side scores the required number of points, goals, etc. **sud'den·ly** *adv.* **sud'den·ness** *n.* **sudden** *n.* (**all**) **of a** ~, suddenly.

su·dor·if·er·ous (so͞od*e*rĭf′*e*rus) *adj.* Producing or secreting sweat. **su·dor·if·ic** (so͞od*e*rĭf′ĭk) *adj.* & *n.* (Drug) promoting or causing sweating.

Su·dra (so͞o′dr*a*) *n.* (Member of) the lowest of the four great Hindu castes, the artisans and laborers.

suds (sŭdz) *n.pl.* Water impregnated with soap; frothy mass on top of soapy water, lather. **suds'y** *adj.* (**suds·i·er, suds·i·est**).

sue (so͞o) *v.* (**sued, su·ing**). Institute legal proceedings, bring civil action, against; apply before court for grant of (writ, legal process); bring suit; plead, appeal, supplicate (*for*).

suede (swād) *n.* 1. Kid or other skin with flesh side rubbed into nap, as material for gloves, shoes, etc. 2. (also ~ **cloth**) Woven fabric imitating this. [Fr. *Suède* Sweden]

su·et (so͞o'ĭt) *n.* Hard fat around the kidneys and loins of cattle and sheep, used in cooking or rendered down to form tallow. **su'et·y** *adj.* Of or like suet; pale complexioned.

Sue·to·ni·us (swētō'nēus). Gaius Suetonius Tranquillus (*c*70–*c*100 A.D.). Roman historian and antiquary.

Su·ez (so͞o'ĕz, so͞oĕz'). District of Lower Egypt at N. end of the Red Sea; seaport at S. end of the ~ **Canal**, ship canal across the Isthmus of Suez to Port Said, cut (1859–69) by Ferdinand de Lesseps.

suf·fer (sŭf'er) *v.* 1. Undergo, experience, be subjected to (pain, loss, grief, defeat, punishment, etc.); undergo pain, grief, or damage. 2. Permit *to* do; allow, put up with, tolerate. **suf'fer·er, suf'fer·ing** *ns.* **suf'fer·a·ble** *adj.* **suf'fer·ing·ly** *adv.*

suf·fer·ance (sŭf'erans, sŭf'rans) *n.* 1. (archaic) Long-suffering, forbearance. 2. Sanction, or acquiescence, implied by absence of objection; tacit permission or toleration, esp. in **on** ~, under conditions of bare tolerance or tacit acquiescence.

suf·fice (sufīs') *v.* (**-ficed, -fic·ing**). Be enough, be adequate; satisfy, meet the needs of.

suf·fi·cien·cy (sufĭsh'ensē) *n.* (pl. **-cies**). (esp.) Sufficient supply, adequate provision.

suf·fi·cient (sufĭsh'ent) *adj.* Sufficing; adequate, esp. in amount or number; enough; (archaic) competent, adequate in ability or resources. **suf·fi'cient·ly** *adv.*

suf·fix (sŭf'ĭks) *n.* (gram.) Verbal element attached to end of word as inflectional formative or to form new word. ~ (sŭf'ĭks, sufĭks') *v.t.* Add as suffix. **suf·fix·ion** (sufĭk'shon) *n.*

suf·fo·cate (sŭk'okāt) *v.* (**-cat·ed, -cat·ing**). Kill, stifle, choke, by stopping respiration; produce choking sensation in, smother, overwhelm; feel suffocated. **suf·fo·ca·tion** (sŭfokā'shon) *n.* **suf'fo·cat·ing·ly** *adv.*

suf·fra·gan (sŭf'ragan) *adj.* ~ **bishop**, bishop appointed to assist diocesan bishop in particular part of his diocese; bishop in relation to his archbishop. **suffragan** *n.* Suffragan bishop.

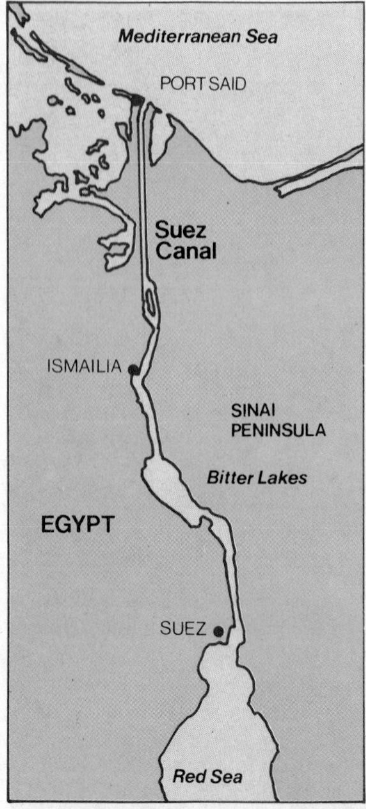

It is believed that the first ***Suez Canal,*** *while much smaller than the present one, was dug by Seti I of Egypt about 1380 B.C. Another was planned by Napoleon.*

suf·frage (sŭf'rĭj) *n.* Vote; approval or consent expressed by voting; right of voting as member of political or other body, franchise; (archaic and eccles.) intercession, prayer. **suf'frag·ism** *n.*

suf·fra·gette (sŭfrajĕt') *n.* (hist.) Woman advocating political enfranchisement of women, esp. militantly or violently.

suf·fra·gist (sŭf'rajĭst) *n.* Advocate of extension of political franchise, esp. to women.

suf·fuse (sufūz') *v.t.* (**-fused, -fus·ing**). Overspread as with a fluid, a color, a gleam of light. **suf·fu·sion** (sufū'zhon) *n.*

sug·ar (sho͝og'er) *n.* 1. Sweet crystalline substance (C_{12} H_{22} O_{11}), white when pure, obtained by evaporation from plant juices, esp. that of sugar cane and sugar beet, and forming important article of human food, saccharose; (pl.) kinds of sugar. 2. (colloq.) Sweet words, flattery, anything serving purpose of sugar put around pill in reconciling person to what is unpalatable. 3. (chem.) Any of a group of carbohydrates, soluble in water and having a sweet taste, found esp. in plants and including glucose, lactose, saccharose, etc. 4. ~ **beet**, kind of white beet from which sugar is extracted; **sug'arbush**, grove of sugar maples; **sugar cane**, perennial tropical and subtropical grass (*Saccharum officinarum*), with tall stout jointed stems, cultivated as a source of sugar; **sugar daddy**, (colloq.) elderly man who lavishes gifts on a young woman; **sug'arhouse**, place for refining or processing sugar, esp. shed or other building where maple sugar or syrup is made; **sugar loaf**, conical molded mass of hard refined sugar; anything, esp. hill, in shape of a sugar loaf; **sugar maple**, N. Amer. tree (*Acer saccharum*) yielding fine hardwood for furniture, and sweet sap which is boiled down for maple syrup and sugar; **sug'arplum**, small round or oval candy of boiled sugar; **sugar tongs**, small tongs for picking up lump sugar at table. **sug'ar·less** *adj.* **sugar** *v.t.* Sweeten, coat with sugar; make sweet or agreeable; form sugar, become crystalline or granulated like sugar; spread sugar mixed with gum etc. on (tree) to catch moths; **sug'arcoat**, coat or cover with sugar; make seem more pleasing, less disagreeable; **sugar off**, complete boiling down of maple syrup for sugar.

sug·ar·y (sho͝og'erē) *adj.* Like sugar; containing (much) sugar; (fig.) cloying, sentimental.

sug·gest (sugjĕst', sujĕst') *v.t.* Cause (idea) to be present to mind, call up idea of; prompt execution of; put forward opinion or proposition (*that*), utter as a suggestion; give hint or inkling of, give impression of existence or presence of.

sug·gest·i·ble (sugjĕs'tĭbel, sujĕs'-) *adj.* (esp.) Capable of being influenced by suggestion. **sug·gest·i·bil·i·ty** (sugjĕstĭbĭl'ĭtē, sujĕs-) *n.*

sug·ges·tion (sugjĕs'chon, sujĕs'-) *n.* Suggesting; idea, plan, or thought suggested, proposal; suggesting of prurient ideas; insinuation of belief or impulse into mind of subject by hypnosis or other means, such belief or impulse.

sug·ges·tive (sugjĕs'tĭv, sujĕs'-) *adj.* (esp.) Suggesting something indecent. **sug·ges'tive·ly** *adv.* **sug·ges'tive·ness** *n.*

su·i·cide (so͞o'ĭsīd) *n.* 1. Intentional self-slaughter; **commit** ~, kill oneself. 2. (fig.) Action destructive to one's own interests etc. 3. Person who has committed suicide. **suicide** *v.i.* (**-cid·ed, -cid·ing**). (colloq.) Commit suicide. **su·i·ci·dal** (so͞oĭsī'dal) *adj.* **su·i·ci'dal·ly** *adv.*

su·i ge·ne·ris (so͞o'ī jĕn'erĭs; *Lat.* so͞o'ē gĕ'nĕrĭs). Of its own

Sugarcane is grown on the eastern coastal plain of Australia from northern N.S.W. to north Queensland. Miniature locomotives tow canetrolleys from the fields to the crushers.

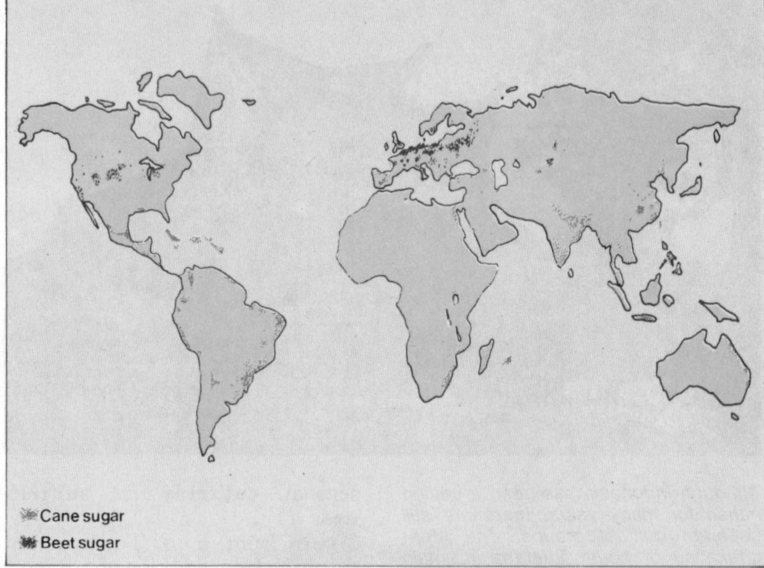

*Map showing the **sugar** production areas of the world and indicating areas where sugarcane can be grown, and cooler locations where sugarbeet is the alternative.*

kind, peculiar, unique. [L.]

suit (so͞ot) *n.* 1. Suing in court of law, legal prosecution; process instituted in court of justice, lawsuit. 2. Suing, supplication, petition; courting of a woman, courtship. 3. Set of outer garments, usu. coat (and sometimes vest), and trousers or skirt; set of sails, armor, etc.; **suit′case,** case for carrying clothes, usu. box-shaped with flat hinged lid and one handle. 4. Any of the four sets (spades, clubs, hearts, diamonds) of playing cards in pack, consisting of 13 cards (ten numbered consecutively and three face cards); **follow suit,** play card of suit led; (fig.) follow another's example. **suit** *v.* 1. Accommodate, adapt, make fitting or appropriate, *to.* 2. Be agreeable or convenient to; be fitted or adapted to; be good for, favorable to health of; go well with appearance or character of, be becoming to; be fitting or convenient; ~ **up,** put on athletic uniform or special clothing, as for underwater exploration, space travel, etc.; ~ **yourself,** do as you choose; find something that satisfies you. **suit′ing** *n.* (esp.) Material for suits of clothing.

suit·a·ble (so͞o′t*a*b*e*l) *adj.* Suited *to* or *for*; well fitted for the purpose; appropriate to the occasion. **suit′a·bly** *adv.* **suit·a·bil·i·ty** (so͞ot*a*bĭl′ĭtē), **suit′a·ble·ness** *ns.*

suite (swēt) *n.* 1. Retinue, set of persons in attendance. 2. Set, series; number of rooms forming unit used by particular person(s) or for particular purpose; set of furniture of same pattern. 3. (mus.) Old form of instrumental composition (*c*1500–*c*1750), later partly superseded by SONATA, and consisting of several (usu. four) movements based on dance tunes, in same or related keys; set of instrumental compositions related in theme etc. and freq. constituting music for ballet, incidental music for play, etc.

suit·or (so͞o′t*e*r) *n.* 1. Party to lawsuit; petitioner. 2. Wooer, one who seeks woman in marriage.

su·ki·ya·ki (so͞okēyah′kē, so͞okē-, skēyah′-) *n.* Japanese dish of sliced meat cooked with vegetables and soy sauce.

Suk·koth, Suc·coth (so͝ok′*o*s; *Heb.* so͞okawt′) *ns.* Feast of Tabernacles or Booths, Jews' autumn festival of thanksgiving for harvest, and commemoration of their wandering in the wilderness when they dwelt in tents. [Heb. *sukkôt* booths]

sul·cus (sŭl′k*u*s) *n.* (pl. **-ci** pr. -sī). Groove, furrow; esp. (anat.) fissure between two convolutions of brain.

sul·fa (sŭl′f*a*) *adjs.* ~ **drug,** sulfonamide.

sul·fa·nil·a·mide (sŭlf*a*nĭl′-*a*mīd) *n.* Synthetic organic chemical compound ($H_2NC_6H_4SO_2NH_2$), from which most of the sulfa drugs are derived.

sul·fate (sŭl′fāt) *n.* Salt of sulfuric acid. ~ *v.* (**-fat·ed, -fat·ing**). Treat, impregnate, with sulfuric acid or a sulfate; (elect.) form whitish scales of lead sulfate on plates of (storage battery), become sulfated. **sul·fa·tion** (sŭlfā′sh*o*n) *n.*

sul·fide (sŭl′fīd) *n.* Compound of sulfur with another element or a radical.

sul·fite (sŭl′fīt) *n.* Salt of sulfurous acid.

sul·fon·a·mide (sŭlfŏn′*a*mīd) *n.* Any of a group of drugs derived from amides of sulfonic acids, capable of killing or preventing the multiplication of bacteria, e.g. streptococci, used in the treatment of many different infections.

sul·fone (sŭl′fōn) *n.* Any of a group of organic compounds containing the radical SO_2 united directly to two carbon atoms. **sul·fon·ic, sul·phon·ic** (sŭlfŏn′ĭk) *adjs.*

sul·fur, sul·phur (sŭl′f*e*r) *ns.* 1. (chem.) Greenish-yellow non-metallic inflammable element,

*The fruit of the stag-horn **sumac**, known as the lemonade tree, is used to make lemonade in eastern North America. Other varieties in Europe and Asia provide tannin, resin and wax.*

burning with blue flame, widely distributed free and in combination, and used in manufacture of matches, gunpowder, and sulfuric acid, for vulcanizing rubber, as a disinfectant (as sulfur dioxide), and in medicine as a laxative, a sudorific, and an ingredient of ointments; symbol S, at. no. 16, at. wt. 32.06; **flowers of** ~, pure sulfur in form of yellow powder; ~ **dioxide**, poisonous gas formed in burning of sulfur, used in many manufacturing processes and as refrigerant, disinfectant, etc. 2. In popular belief, material of which hellfire and lightning were held to consist; (alchemy) one of the supposed ultimate elements, the principle of combustion. 3. ~ (or ~ **butterfly**), any of various yellow (or orange) butterflies of family Pieridae. 4. ~ **yellow**, (of) the bright pale-yellow color of sulfur.

sul·fu·ric (sŭlfūr′ĭk) *adj.* Of, containing, sulfur; ~ **acid**, dense highly corrosive oily fluid, oil of vitriol (H_2SO_4); ~ **ether**, ether.

sul·fur·ous (sŭl′fer*us*, sŭlfūr′-) *adj.* 1. Of, like, suggesting, sulfur; with qualities associated with (burning) sulfur; full of sulfur of hell; sulfur yellow. 2. (chem. of compounds) Containing sulfur of lower valence than sulfuric compounds; ~ **acid**, acid (H_2SO_3) present in solutions of sulfur dioxide in water.

sulk (sŭlk) *v.i.* Be sulky. ~ *n.* (usu. pl.) Sulky fit.

sulk·y[1] (sŭl′kē) *adj.* (**sulk·i·er, sulk·i·est**). Sullen, morose; silent, inactive, or unsociable from resentment or ill temper. **sulk′i·ly** *adv.* **sulk′i·ness** *n.*

sulk·y[2] (sŭl′kē) *n.* (pl. **sulk·ies**). Light two-wheeled carriage for one person, esp. one used in trotting races.

Sul·la (sŭl′*a*), **Lucius Cornelius** (138–78 B.C.). Roman dictator and general; instituted reforms of the constitution designed to increase the power of the senate and reduce that of the people and their tribunes.

sul·len (sŭl′*e*n) *adj.* Gloomy, ill-humored. **sul′len·ly** *adv.* **sul′len·ness** *n.*

Sul·li·van (sŭl′ĭv*a*n), **Sir Arthur Seymour** (1842–1900). English musical composer, in collaboration with W. S. GILBERT[3], of light satiric operas.

sul·ly (sŭl′ē) *v.t.* (**-lied, -ly·ing**). (chiefly poet.) Soil, tarnish; be stain on, discredit.

sul·tan (sŭl′t*a*n) *n.* 1. Sovereign of Muslim country, esp. (hist.) of Turkey. 2. Small white domestic fowl with heavily feathered legs and feet, orig. from Turkey. 3. (also **sweet** ~) Either of two sweet-scented annuals, *Centaurea moschata* (purple or white sweet ~) and *C. suaveolens* (yellow ~).

*Although Indonesia has been a unified nation for many years, there are still separate cultural groups. The Menangkabau of south **Sumatra** maintain huge communal houses (above).*

sul·tan·ate (sŭl′t*a*nāt) *n.* Rank, authority, of a sultan; jurisdiction, dominion, of a sultan. [Arab. *sulṭān* ruler, emperor]

sul·tan·a (sŭltăn′*a*, -tah′n*a*) *n.* 1. Wife or concubine of sultan. 2. Small light-colored seedless raisin grown esp. near Izmir; pale yellow grape from which sultanas are produced.

sul·try (sŭl′trē) *adj.* (**-tri·er, -tri·est**). Oppressively hot, sweltering; (fig.) having strong sexual attraction, passionate, sensual. **sul′tri·ly** *adv.* **sul′tri·ness** *n.*

sum (sŭm) *n.* 1. Total amount resulting from addition of 2 or more numbers, quantities, magnitudes, etc.; total number or amount *of*; **in** ~, briefly but comprehensively put; ~ **total**, total amount, aggregate (of). 2. Quantity or amount of or *of* money. 3. (Working out of) arithmetical problem. **sum** *v.* (**summed, sum·ming**). 1. Find sum of; reckon, count, or total *up*; collect (*up*) into small compass. 2. ~ **up**, summarize, epitomize; form estimate or judgment of; (of judge in trial, or counsel concluding client's case) recapitulate (evidence or arguments), with any necessary exposition of points of law, before jury considers its verdict; so **summing-up** (*n.*) (pl. **summings-up**).

su·mac, su·mach (sōō′măk, shōō′-) *ns.* Shrub or small tree of genus *Rhus*, with feathery leaves and clusters of (usu. red) berries;

one species (*R. vernix*), poison sumac, with white berries, causes acute skin rash like that from poison ivy. [Arab. *summāk*]

Su·ma·tra (sōōmah′tr*a*). Large island of Indonesia, separated from the Malay Peninsula by the Strait of Malacca.

Su·mer (sōō′m*er*). Region in ancient Mesopotamia, now part of S. Iraq. **Su·mer·i·an** (sōōmēr′ē*a*n, -mĕr′-) *adj.* & *n.* (Native, inhabitant) of Sumer; (of) the agglutinative language of the Sumerian inscriptions written in a cuneiform script.

sum·ma cum lau·de (sōōm′*a* kōōm low′dē, -d*e*, sŭm′*a* kŭm law′dē). With the greatest praise; used of diplomas awarded with highest honors for academic excellence (cf. CUM laude, MAGNA CUM LAUDE). [L.]

sum·ma·rize (sŭm′erīz) *v.t.* (**-rized, -riz·ing**). Make or constitute a summary of, sum up. **sum·ma·ri·za·tion** (sŭm*e*rīzā′-sh*o*n) *n.*

sum·ma·ry (sŭm′*e*rē) *adj.* Compendious and (usu.) brief; dispensing with needless detail, performed with dispatch; (law, of proceedings) carried out rapidly by omission of certain formalities required by common law; ~

In areas where there is geothermal activity, such as the Yellowstone National Park, strong-smelling **sulfurous** *vapors are emitted with steam from hot springs and geysers in the area.*

court-martial, court-martial comprising one commissioned officer for judging relatively minor offenses. **sum·mar·i·ly** (s*u*mĕr′*i*lē, sŭm′er-) *adv.* **summary** *n.* (pl. **-ries**). Summary account or statement, abridgment, epitome.

sum·ma·tion (sŭmā′sh*o*n) *n.* Addition, summing (up); finding of total or sum. **sum·ma′tion·al** *adj.*

sum·mer (sŭm′*er*) *n.* 1. Warmest season of year, popularly reckoned in N. hemisphere as lasting from mid-May to middle or end of August, but astronomically as lasting from summer solstice (June 21 or 22) to autumnal equinox (Sept. 22 or 23); summer weather; (pl.) years of life or age (chiefly poet.); **Indian** ~: see INDIAN. 2. (*attrib.* or as *adj.*) **sum′merhouse**, (usu. simple and light) building in park or garden providing cool shady place in summer; **summer school**, a program of courses given during summer vacation, esp. at university; **summer solstice**: see SOLSTICE; **sum′mertime**, season of summer. **summer** *v.* Pass summer (*at* or *in* place); pasture (cattle) *at*, *in*. **sum′mer·y** *adj.*

sum·mit (sŭm′ĭt) *n.* Highest point, top, apex; highest degree; ~ **conference**, meeting of heads of nations.

sum·mon (sŭm′*o*n) *v.t.* Call together by authority for action or deliberation, require presence or attendance of, bid approach; call upon *to* do; call *up* (courage, resolution, etc.) to one's aid; cite by authority to appear before court or judge to answer charge or give evidence. **sum′mon·er** *n.*

sum·mons (sŭm′*o*nz) *n.* (pl. **-mons·es**). Authoritative call or urgent invitation to attend on some occasion or to do something; citation to appear before judge or magistrate. ~ *v.t.* Take out summons against.

su·mo (sōō′mō) *n.* (Participant in) Japanese wrestling, in which defeat follows touching of ground except with feet, or failure to keep within marked area.

sump (sŭmp) *n.* Pit or well for collecting water or other fluid, esp. in mine or basement; oil reservoir at bottom of crankcase of internal combustion engine.

sump·tu·ous (sŭmp′chōō*o*s) *adj.* Costly, splendid, magnificent

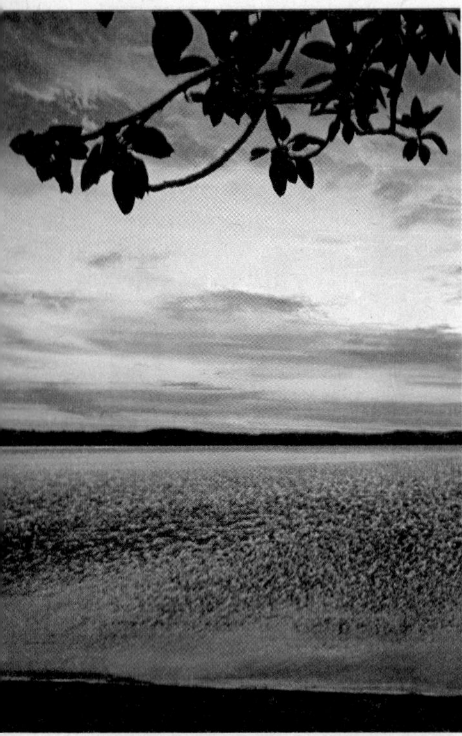

The indescribable beauty of a **sunset** is due to the refraction, reflection and scattering of light. The colors are also affected and intensified by dust particles or smoke.

Close-up of the disk florets which occupy the centre of a **sunflower.** These eventually form into large dark seeds which are a rich source of oil, used for culinary and industrial purposes.

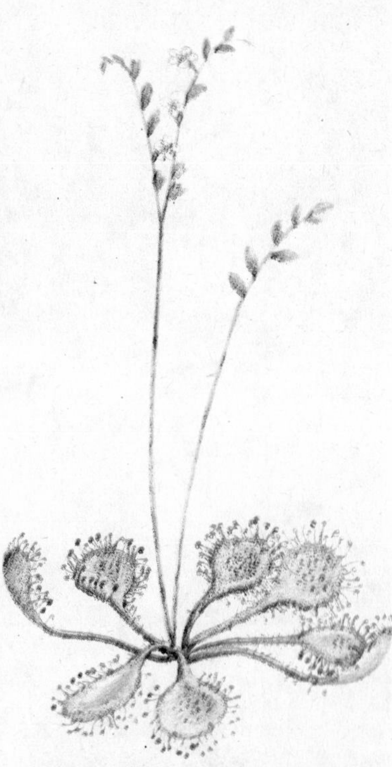

Sundew is the common name for a group of about 100 species of insectivorous plants. Prey is trapped in a sticky secretion which forms at the tips of the leaves.

in workmanship, decoration, appearance, etc. **sump'tu·ous·ly** *adv.* **sump'tu·ous·ness** *n.*

sun (sŭn) *n.* Star forming center of system of worlds or planets, esp. the central body of the solar system, around which Earth and other planets revolve, and which supplies them with light and warmth by its radiation; such light or warmth; (poet.) climate, clime; **a place in the ~**, position giving scope for development of individual or national life; **take the ~**, (naut.) make observation of meridian altitude of sun to determine latitude; **~ bath**, exposure of skin to sun's rays; **sun'bathe** (**-bathed, -bath·ing**), take sunbath; **sun'beam**, beam of sunlight; **Sun'belt**, southern and southwestern area of U.S., having more warm, sunny weather than other regions of nation and, for the past decade, rapid population and economic expansion; **sun'bonnet**, bonnet of cotton etc. shaped so as to shade eyes and neck from sun; **sun'burn**, superficial inflammation of skin caused by exposure to sun; brown color produced thus; **sun'burned, sun'burnt** (*adj.*); **sun'burst**, burst of sunlight; piece of jewelry representing sun surrounded by rays; **sun deck**, flat roof or raised open platform of house etc. for sunbathing etc.; **sun'dew**, plant of genus *Drosera* of small herbs growing in bogs, with leaves covered with glandular hairs secreting viscid drops; **sun'dial**, contrivance for showing time by shadow cast by sun on surface marked with hours; **sun disk**, (archaeol.) winged disk, symbol of sun god; **sun'dog**, parhelion, mock sun; **sun'down**, sunset; **sun'fish** (pl. **-fishes**, collect. **-fish**), large fish of family Molidae of warm seas, with round ungainly body and short fringelike caudal fin; any of various small usu. brilliantly colored Amer. freshwater fishes of family Centrarchidae; **sun'flower**, composite plant of genus *Helianthus*, chiefly native of N. Amer., with conspicuous yellow flower heads whose disk and rays suggest figure of sun; **sun'glasses**, tinted spectacles for protecting eyes from sunlight or glare; **sun'lamp**, large lamp with parabolic mirror reflector used in motion-picture photography; lamp emitting ultraviolet rays; **sun'light, sun'lit**, (illuminated by) light from sun; **sun'lit**, (illuminated by) light from sun; **sun'ray**, sunbeam; (attrib.) emitting, using, ultraviolet rays, esp. therapeutically; **sun'rise**, (time of) sun's apparent ascent above eastern horizon; **sun'roof**, sliding section of automobile roof; **sun'room**, room with walls largely of glass, designed to admit maximum amount of sunshine; **sun'set**, (time of) sun's apparent descent below western horizon at end of day; glow of light or display of color in sky at this time; (fig.) decline, close (esp. of life); **sun'set law**, law requiring periodic evaluation of need for government agencies and programs; **sun'shade**, device providing protection from sun's rays, esp. parasol or awning over window; **sun'shine**, unimpeded sunlight, fair weather; (fig.) cheerfulness, bright influence; **sun'shine law**, law making official meetings and records of most government agencies accessible to public; **sun'spot**, one of the cavities in photosphere appearing as dark spots or patches on sun's surface, lasting from a few hours to several months, recurring in greatest numbers at intervals of a little over 11 years, and freq. accompanied by magnetic disturbances etc. on Earth; **sun'stroke**, prostration or collapse caused by exposure to excessive heat of sun; **sun'tan** (*n.* & *v.*), tan(ning of) skin by exposure to sun; **sun'up**, sunrise; **sun'wise**, in direction of sun's apparent motion, clockwise. **sun'less** *adj.* **sun'less·ness** *n.* **sun** *v.* (**sunned, sun·ning**). Expose to the sun; **~ oneself**, bask in sun.

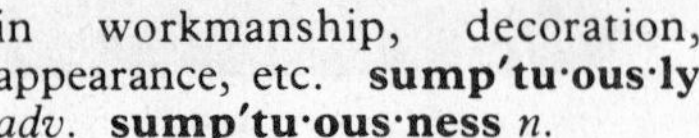

Sun. *abbrev.* Sunday.

sun·dae (sŭn'dā) *n.* Confection of ice cream with fruit, nuts, syrup, cream, etc.

Sun·day (sŭn'dā, -dē) *n.* First day of the week, observed by Christians as day of rest and worship; **a month of ~s**, a very long time; **~ best**, best clothes as worn on Sunday; **~ punch**, (slang) boxer's most powerful punch; (fig.) anything capable of maximum effectiveness against an opponent; **~ school**, school held on Sunday, now only for religious instruction, and usu. attached to parish or church congregation.

sun·der (sŭn'der) *v.* (now poet. or rhet.) Separate, sever, keep apart.

sun·dry (sŭn'drē) *adj.* Diverse, several; **all and ~**, one and all. **sundry** *n.* (pl. **-dries**). (pl.) Oddments, small items classed together without individual mention.

Sung (sōōng). Name of dynasty that ruled China 960–1279.

sung: see SING.

sunk (sŭngk), **sunk·en** (sŭng'ken) *adjs.*: see SINK[2]; (esp., of eyes, cheeks, etc.) hollow, fallen in.

Sun·na, Sun·nah (sōōn'*a*) *ns.* Traditional portion of Muslim law based on Muhammad's words or acts but not written by him, accepted as authoritative by the orthodox but rejected by the Shiites. **Sun·ni** (sōōn'ē, sŭn'ē), **Sun·nite** (sōōn'īt, sŭn'-) *adjs.* & *ns.* (Muslim) accepting the Sunna as well as Koran.

sun·ny (sŭn'ē) *adj.* (**-ni·er, -ni·est**). Bright with or as sunlight; exposed to, warm with, the sun; cheery, bright in disposition. **sun'ni·ly** *adv.* **sun'ni·ness** *n.*

Sun Yat-sen (sŭn'yăt'sĕn', sōōn'yaht'sĕn') (1866–1925). Leader of Chinese revolutionary movement, 1911–12; first president of the Chinese Republic, 1921–2.

sup (sŭp) *v.* (**supped, sup·ping**). Take supper.

su·per (sōō'per) *n.* (colloq.) Supernumerary actor; building superintendent. **~** *adj.* (colloq.) Excellent, unusually good.

super- *prefix.* On the top (of); over; beyond, besides, in addition; exceeding, going beyond, more than, transcending; of higher kind; to a degree beyond the usual.

su·per·a·bun·dant (sōōper-*a*bŭn'dant) *adj.* Very or too abundant. **su·per·a·bun'dance** *n.* **su·per·a·bun'dant·ly** *adv.*

su·per·an·nu·ate (sōōperăn'ūāt) *v.t.* (**-at·ed, -at·ing**). Dismiss or discharge as too old; discharge with pension. **su·per·an·nu·a·tion** (sōōperănūā'shon) *n.* **su·per·an'nu·at·ed** *adj.*

su·perb (sōōpĕrb') *adj.* Grand, majestic, splendid, magnificent. **su·perb'ly** *adv.*

su·per·car·go (sōōperkăr'gō, sōō'perkăr-) *n.* (pl. **-goes, -gos**). Merchant ship's officer superintending cargo and commercial transactions of voyage.

su·per·charge (sōō'perchărj) *v.t.* Charge to excess (*with* energy, emotion, etc.); use supercharger on. **su'per·charged** *adj.*

su·per·charg·er (sōō'perchărjer) *n.* Device supplying internal combustion engine with air or explosive mixture at higher pressure than normal in order to increase its efficiency.

su·per·cil·i·ar·y (sōōpersĭl'ēĕrē) *adj.* Of the eyebrow, over the eye.

su·per·cil·i·ous (sōōpersĭl'ēus) *adj.* Haughtily contemptuous, disdainful, or superior. **su·per·cil'i·ous·ly** *adv.* **su·per·cil'i·ous·ness** *n.*

su·per·con·duc·tiv·i·ty (sōōperkŏndŭktĭv'ĭtē) *n.* Extremely high conductivity shown by certain substances at very low temperatures. **su·per·con·duc·tive** (sōōperkondŭk'tĭv) *adj.* **su·per·con·duc'tor** *n.*

su·per·cool (sōōperkōōl') *v.t.* Cool below freezing point without solidification or crystallization.

su·per·e·go (sōōperē'gō, sōō'perē-) *n.* (psych.) Part of mind that exerts conscience and responds to social rules.

The ***sundial*** *was one of the earliest devices used to tell the time but, since they depend on bright sunlight to operate, sundials were replaced by clocks when these became available. Sundials are now purely decorative.*

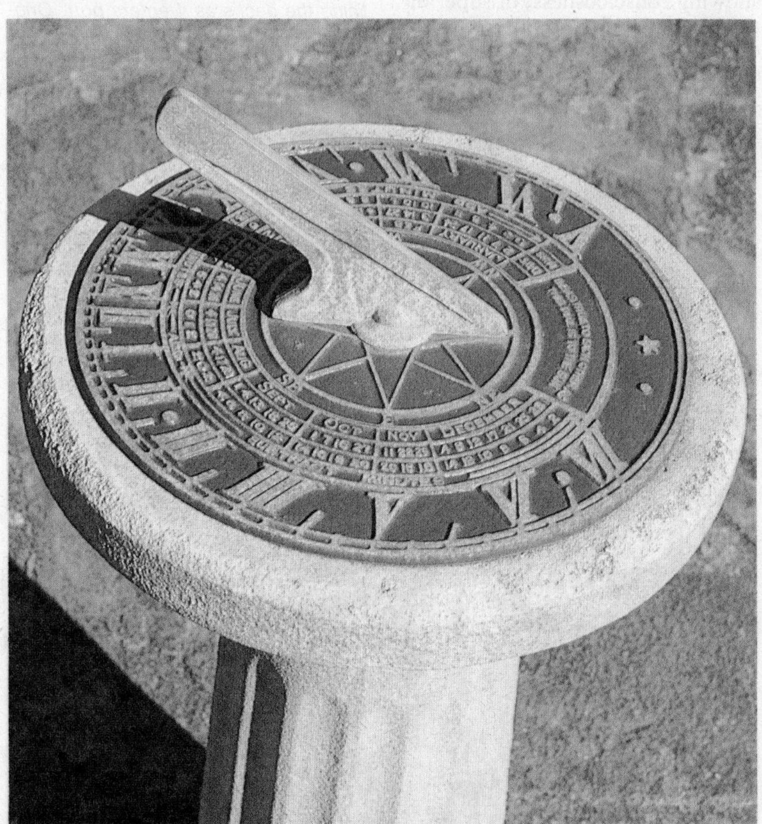

su·per·er·o·ga·tion (sōōperĕrogā'shon) *n.* Performance of more than duty or circumstances require; esp. (R.C. theol.) performance of good works beyond what God requires, which constitute a store of merit that the church may dispense to make up others' deficiencies. **su·per·e·rog·a·to·ry** (sōōpererŏg'atōrē, -tōrē) *adj.*

su·per·fam·i·ly (sōō'perfămĭlē, -fămlē) *n.* (pl. **-lies**). (biol.) Set of related families within an order.

su·per·fi·cial (sōōperfĭsh'al) *adj.* Of, on, the surface; not going deep, without depth; (of measures) involving two dimensions, of extent of surface, square. **su·per·fi'cial·ly** *adv.* **su·per·fi·ci·al·i·ty** (sōōperfĭsheăl'ĭtē), **su·per·fi'cial·ness** *n.*

su·per·flu·id (sōōperflōō'ĭd) *n.* (phys.) Fluid, as liquid helium, having frictionless flow at temperatures below 2.18° K and high heat conductivity. **su·per·flu·id·i·ty** (sōōperflōōĭd'ĭte) *n.*

su·per·flu·i·ty (sōōperflōō'ĭtē) *n.* (pl. **-ties**). Superfluous amount.

su·per·flu·ous (sōōpĕr'flōōus) *adj.* More than enough, excessive, redundant; needless, uncalled-for. **su·per'flu·ous·ly** *adv.* **su·per'flu·ous·ness** *n.*

su·per·heat (sōōperhēt') *v.t.* Heat to very high temperature; esp. raise temperature of (steam) to increase its pressure. **su·per·heat'er** *n.*

su·per·het·er·o·dyne (sōōperhĕt′erodīn) *adj.* & *n.* (Of) radio reception or receiver in which, by means of a local oscillator, a beat note is set up with the incoming signal and amplified at the resulting intermediate frequency.

su·per·high·way (sōōperhī′wā) *n.* Broad main highway for fast traffic.

su·per·hu·man (sōōperhū′man, -ū′man) *adj.* Beyond (normal) human capacity, strength, etc.; higher than (that of) man.

su·per·im·pose (sōōperĭmpōz′) *v.t.* (**-posed, -pos·ing**). Impose or place *on* or on something else. **su·per·im·po·si·tion** (sōōper-ĭmpozĭsh′on) *n.*

su·per·in·tend (sōōperĭntĕnd′) *v.* Have or exercise charge or direction (of), oversee, supervise. **su·per·in·tend′ence, su·per·in·tend′en·cy** *ns.* **su·per·in·tend′ent** *n.* Officer or official having control, oversight, or direction of business, institution, etc.; caretaker of building.

su·pe·ri·or (sōōpēr′ēer, su-) *adj.* 1. Upper, higher, situated above or farther up than something else; growing above another part or organ, that is higher than other(s) of the same kind; (printing) above the line or near the top of other figures etc. 2. Higher in rank, dignity, degree, amount, quality, status, etc.; ~ **to**, above the influence or reach of, not affected or mastered by, higher in status or quality than. 3. Conscious, showing consciousness, of superior qualities; lofty, supercilious, dictatorial, etc. **su·pe′ri·or·ly** *adv.* **su·pe·ri·or·i·ty** (sōōpērēŏr′ĭtē, -ār′-, su-) *n.* **superior** *n.* 1. Person of higher rank, dignity, or authority, superior officer or official; person or thing of higher quality or value than another. 2. Head of religious community (freq. **Father, Mother**, etc., **S**~).

Su·pe·ri·or (sōōpēr′ēer, su-), **Lake.** World's largest freshwater lake, covering 31,800 sq. mi. (82,362 sq. km) in N. central U.S. and S. Canada, northernmost and westernmost of the Great Lakes.

su·per·la·tive (sōōpēr′latĭv, su-) *adj.* 1. Raised above or surpassing all others; of the highest degree. 2. (gram., of an inflectional form of an adjective or adverb, as *highest, fastest*) Expressing the highest or very high degree of the quality etc. denoted by the simple word (e.g. *high, fast*). **su·per′la·tive·ly** *adv.* **superlative** *n.* (Word in) the superlative degree. **su·per′la·tive·ness** *n.*

su·per·man (sōō′permăn) *n.* (pl. **-men** pr. -mĕn). Ideal superior man of the future, conceived by NIETZSCHE as evolved from normal human type; man of superhuman powers or achievement. [transl. Ger. *übermensch*]

su·per·mar·ket (sōō′permārkĭt) *n.* Large self-service store selling food and household goods.

su·per·nal (sōōpēr′nal) *adj.* (poet., rhet.) Heavenly, divine; of the sky; lofty.

Crew of the German warship 'Hamburg' lining the decks as it enters port. Originally designed to provide visibility for the helmsman, the ***superstructure*** *now houses complex equipment.*

su·per·nat·u·ral (sōōpernăch′-eral) *adj.* Due to, manifesting, some agency above the forces of nature; outside the ordinary operation of cause and effect. **su·per·nat′u·ral·ly** *adv.* **su·per·nat′u·ral·ness** *n.*

su·per·nat·u·ral·ism (sōōper-năch′eralĭzem) *n.* Belief in supernatural beings, powers, events, etc. **su·per·nat′u·ral·ist** *n.* & *adj.* **su·per·nat·u·ral·is·tic** (sōōper-năcheralĭs′tĭk) *adj.*

su·per·no·va (sōōpernō′va) *n.* (pl. **-vae** pr. -vē, **-vas**). Nova of immense brightness or intensity.

su·per·nu·mer·ar·y (sōōper-nōō′merĕrē, -nū′-) *adj.* & *n.* (pl. **-ar·ies**). (Person or thing) in excess of the normal number, esp. (extra person) not belonging to the regular body or staff but associated with it in some need or emergency; (actor) employed in addition to regular company, appearing on stage or in scene but not speaking.

su·per·phos·phate (sōōperfŏs′-fāt) *n.* Fertilizer made by treating phosphate containing rock with sulfuric acid.

su·per·pose (sōōperpōz′) *v.t.* (**-posed, -pos·ing**). Place above or on something else; bring into same position so as to coincide. **su·per·pos′a·ble** *adj.* **su·per·po·si·tion** (sōōperpozĭsh′on) *n.*

su·per·pow·er (sōō′perpower) *n.* Extremely powerful nation, esp. one of only a few such.

su·per·sat·u·rate (sōōpersăch′-erāt) *v.t.* (**-rat·ed, -rat·ing**). Add to (esp. solution) beyond saturation point. **su·per·sat·u·ra·tion** (sōōpersăcherā′shŏn) *n.*

su·per·scribe (sōō′perskrīb) *v.t.* (**-scribed, -scrib·ing**). Write upon, put inscription on or over; write (inscription) at top of or outside something. **su·per·scrip·tion** (sōōperskrĭp′shon) *n.* **su·per·script** (sōō′perskrĭpt) *adj.* & *n.*

su·per·sede (sōōpersēd′) *v.* (**-sed·ed, -sed·ing**). Set aside, cease to employ; adopt or appoint another person or thing in place of; take the place of, oust, supplant. **su·per·ses·sion** (sōōper-sĕsh′on) *n.*

su·per·son·ic (sōōpersŏn′ĭk) *adj.* With a velocity greater than that of sound. **su·per·son′ics** (*n.pl.* constr. with sing. verb) (Science and application of) supersonic phenomena.

su·per·sti·tion (sōōperstĭsh′on) *n.* Irrational fear of unknown or mysterious, credulity regarding the supernatural; habit or belief based on such tendencies; religious system deemed false or irrational. **su·per·sti′tious** *adj.* **su·per·sti′tious·ly** *adv.* **su·per·sti′tious·ness** *n.*

su·per·struc·ture (sōō′per-strŭkcher) *n.* Building, upper part of building, any material or immaterial structure, resting upon something else or with some other part as a foundation; parts of warship or other vessel above main deck.

su·per·vene (sōōpervēn′) *v.i.* (**-vened, -ven·ing**). Occur as something additional or extraneous, follow closely upon some other occurrence or condition. **su·per·ven·tion** (sōōpervĕn′shon) *n.*

su·per·vise (sōō′pervīz) *v.t.* (**-vised, -vis·ing**). Oversee, superintend execution or performance of (thing), movements or work of (person). **su·per·vi·sion** (sōōpervĭzh′on), **su′per·vi·sor** *ns.* **su·per·vi·so·ry** (sōōpervī′zerē) *adj.*

su·pi·nate (sōō′pināt) *v.t.* (**-nat·ed, -nat·ing**). (physiol.) Turn (hand or forelimb) so that back of it is downward or backward (opp. PRONATE). **su·pi·na·tion** (sōōpinā′shon) *n.*

su·pine (sōōpīn′) *adj.* 1. Lying face upward; supinated. 2. Disinclined to exertion, indolent, lethargic, inert. **su·pine′ly** *adv.* **su·pine′ness** *n.*

sup·per (sŭp′er) *n.* Meal taken at end of day, esp. evening meal less formal and substantial than dinner; evening meal when dinner is taken at midday; ~ **club**, small and expensive nightclub having fine food and drink. **sup′per·less** *adj.*

suppl., supp. *abbrevs.* Supplement.

sup·plant (suplănt′, -plahnt′) *v.t.* Dispossess and take the place of, oust, esp. by dishonorable or treacherous means. **sup·plant′er** *n.*

sup·ple (sŭp′el) *adj.* Easily bent, pliant, flexible; (fig.) compliant, accommodating, artfully or servilely obliging or submissive. **sup·ply**[2], **sup·ple·ly** (sŭp′lē) *advs.* **sup′ple·ness** *n.*

sup·ple·ment (sŭp′lement) *n.* 1. Something added to supply a deficiency; part added to complete literary work etc., esp. special number or part of periodical dealing with particular item(s). 2. (math.) Amount by which arc is less than semicircle, or angle is less than 180°. ~ (sŭp′lemĕnt) *v.t.* Furnish supplement to. **sup·ple·men·tal** (sŭplemĕn′tal), **sup·ple·men·ta·ry** (sŭplemĕn′terē) *adjs.* (esp.) ~ **angle**, either of 2 angles that together make 180°. **sup·ple·men′tal·ly** *adv.*

sup·pli·ant (sŭp′lēant) *n.* Humble petitioner. ~ *adj.* Supplicating; expressing supplication. **sup′pli·ant·ly** *adv.*

sup·pli·cate (sŭp′likāt) *v.* (**-cat·ed, -cat·ing**). Make humble petition to or *to* person, for or *for* thing. **sup′pli·cant, sup·pli·ca·tion** (sŭplĭkā′shon) *ns.* **sup·pli·ca·to·ry** (sŭp′likatōrē, -tōrē) *adj.*

*'Grace Before Meat' by the 17th-century Dutch painter, Jan Steen, is typical of genre painting. He possessed a rare insight which revealed the feelings of this family as they prepared for **supper.***

sup·pli·er (suplī′er) *n.* Person, firm, etc., that supplies.

sup·ply[1] (suplī′) *v.t.* (**-plied, -ply·ing**). Furnish, provide (thing needed, or person, receptacle, etc. with or *with* thing needed); make up for (deficiency etc.). ~ *n.* (pl. **-plies**). 1. Provision of what is needed. 2. Stock, store, quantity, of or *of* something provided or available, esp. (econ.) on the market for purchase; (pl.) food and other stores necessary for armed force, expedition, etc.; ~ **and demand**, (econ.) factors regarded as regulating price of commodities.

sup·ply[2]: see SUPPLE.

sup·port (supōrt′, -pōrt′) *n.* Supporting, being supported; person or thing that supports. ~ *v.t.* 1. Carry (part of) weight of; hold up, keep from falling or sinking; keep from failing or giving way, give courage, confidence, or power of endurance to. 2. Endure, tolerate. 3. Supply with necessaries, provide for. 4. Lend assistance or countenance to; back up, second, further; bear out, substantiate; speak in favor of (resolution etc.). **sup·port′a·ble** *adj.* **sup·port′a·bly** *adv.* **sup·port′ive** *adj.* **sup·port′er** *n.*

sup·pose (supōz′) *v.t.* (**-posed, -pos·ing**). 1. Assume as a hypothesis, as ~ *it were true*; in part. or imper. = if, as *supposing white were black you would be right*; also in imper. as formula of proposal, as ~ *we try again.* 2. (of theory, result, etc.) Involve or require as condition, as *design in creation supposes a creator.* 3. Assume in default of knowledge, be inclined to think, accept as probably. 4. **be supposed**, have as a duty, as *he is supposed to clean the boots*; colloq., with neg., freq. = not be allowed, as *children are not supposed to go in.* **sup·posed′** *adj.* Believed to exist or have specified character. **sup·pos′ed·ly** *adv.* **sup·pos′a·ble** *adj.*

sup·po·si·tion (sŭpozĭsh′on),

sup·po·sal (s*u*pō′z*a*l) *ns.* What is supposed or assumed. **sup·po·si′tion·al** *adj.*

sup·po·si·tious (sŭp*o*zĭsh′*u*s) *adj.* Hypothetical, assumed.

sup·pos·i·ti·tious (s*u*pŏzĭtĭsh′*u*s) *adj.* Substituted for the real; spurious, false. **sup·pos·i·ti′tious·ly** *adv.* **sup·pos·i·ti′tious·ness** *n.*

sup·pos·i·to·ry (s*u*pŏz′ĭtōrē, -tōrē) *n.* (pl. **-ries**). (med.) Cone or cylinder of medicated easily melted substance introduced into rectum, urethra, etc.

sup·press (s*u*prĕs′) *v.t.* Put down, quell, put a stop to activity or existence of; withhold or withdraw from publication; keep secret or unexpressed, refrain from mentioning or showing; (psych.) keep out of one's consciousness; (elect.) partly or wholly eliminate (unwanted frequencies, interference), equip (device) so as to reduce interference due to it. **sup·press′i·ble** *adj.* **sup·pres·sion** (s*u*prĕsh′*o*n) *n.* **sup·pres′sive** *adj.*

sup·pres·sant (s*u*prĕs′*a*nt) *n.* Chemical or drug used for suppressing undesirable behavior or physical condition.

sup·pu·rate (sŭp′y*e*rāt) *v.t.* (**-rat·ed, -rat·ing**). Form or secrete pus, fester. **sup·pu·ra·tion** (sŭpy*e*rā′sh*o*n) *n.* **sup′pu·ra·tive** *adj.*

su·pra (sōō′pr*a*) *adv.* Above; previously, before (in a book or writing).

supra- *prefix* = SUPER-, esp. in scientific (esp. anat. and zool.) terms with senses above, higher than; on.

su·pra·or·bi·tal (sōōpr*a*ōr′bĭt*a*l) *adj.* & *n.* (Artery, vein, bone, nerve) above the orbit of the eye.

su·pra·re·nal (sōōpr*a*rē′n*a*l) *adj.* & *n.* (Gland) situated above the kidney, adrenal.

su·prem·a·cy (sōōprĕm′*a*sē) *n.* Being supreme, position of supreme authority or power. **su·prem·a·cist** (sōōprĕ′m*a*sĭst) *n.* Advocate of supremacy of a group, as *white, black, male* ~.

su·preme (sōōprēm′, s*u*-) *adj.* Highest in authority or rank; greatest, of the highest quality, degree, or amount; **the S~ (Being)**, God; **S~ Court**, (esp.) highest judicial body in U.S. Government, consisting of nine members appointed for life by President with Senate's approval; **S~ Soviet**, governing council of U.S.S.R. or one of its constituent republics. **su·preme′ly** *adv.* **su·preme′ness** *n.*

Supt., supt. *abbrevs.* Superintendent.

sur·cease (sĕrsēs′) *n.* (archaic) Cessation, esp. temporary.

sur·charge (sĕr′chārj) *n.* Additional or excessive pecuniary charge, or load or burden; additional mark printed on face of stamp, esp. to change its value. ~ (sĕrchārj′) *v.t.* (**-charged, -charg·ing**). Charge (person) additional or excessive price or payment; exact (sum) as surcharge; overload, fill or saturate to excess; print surcharge on (stamp). **sur·charg′er** *n.*

surd (sĕrd) *adj.* & *n.* 1. (math.) Irrational (quantity, esp. root of integer). 2. Voiceless (speech sound).

sure (shoor) *adj.* (**sur·er, sur·est**). 1. Certain, assured, confident, persuaded (*of*); having no doubt. 2. That may be relied on, trustworthy, unfailing, infallible; certainly true or truthful; safe; **sure′fire**, (colloq.) certain (to succeed); **sure′footed**, treading securely or firmly. 3. Certain *to* do or be; **sure of**, certain to get, keep, have, etc.; **make sure**, act so as to be certain *of*. **sure′ness** *n.* **sure** *adv.* Assuredly, undoubtedly, certainly; *as* certainly *as*.

sure·ly (shoor′lē) *adv.* 1. With certainty or safety (chiefly in **slowly but** ~). 2. Certainly, assuredly; (freq., expressing belief without absolute proof, or readiness to maintain a statement against possible denial) as may be confidently supposed, as must be the case.

sur·e·ty (shoor′ĭtē, shoor′tē) *n.* (pl. **-ties**). 1. Certainty (archaic; chiefly in **of a** ~, certainly). 2. Formal engagement,

*To ride a **surfboard** along a breaking wave and be carried inshore until all power is spent requires considerable balance, technique and practice as shown by this surfer.*

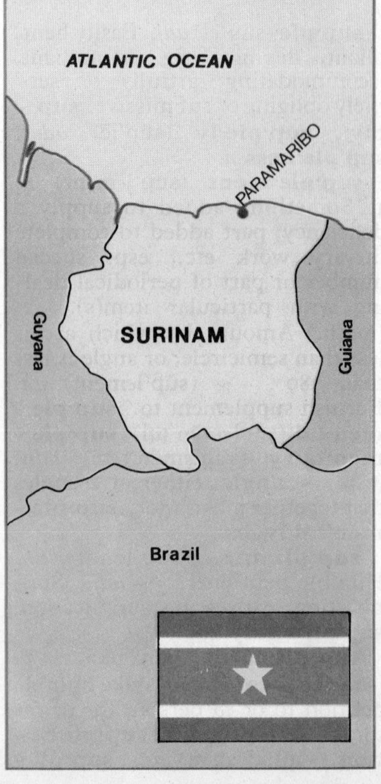

*Independent since November 1975, the former Dutch colony of **Surinam** has a population of about 410,000 people. Its main revenue comes from bauxite mining and timber felling.*

pledge, guarantee, bond, security, for fulfillment of undertaking; person undertaking to be liable for default of another, or for his appearance in court, payment of debt, etc.

surf (sẽrf) *n.* Swell and white foamy water of sea breaking on rock or (esp. shallow) shore; **surf'bird**, Pacific coast shorebird (*Aphriza virgata*) with gray plumage spotted with black and yellow legs; **surf'-board**, long narrow board for riding over heavy surf to shore; (*v.i.*) ride on surfboard; **surf casting**, fishing by casting from water's edge on beach into sea; **surf scoter**, N. Amer. sea duck (*Melanitta perspicillata*) with black plumage and with head and neck marked with white; **surf'riding**, sport of riding on surfboard. **surf'ing** *n.* Surfriding. **surf'er** *n.*

sur·face (sẽr'fĭs) *n.* 1. Outermost boundary of any material body, upper boundary on top of soil, water, etc.; superficial area; (fig.) outward aspect or appearance of anything immaterial, what is presented to casual view or consideration. 2. (geom.) Continuous extent with 2 dimensions only

Possibly the most famous work by the Belgian ***surrealist*** *painter, Paul Delvaux, 'The Call of the Night' uses psychoanalytical symbols in a dreamlike setting and reflects Chirico.*

(length and breadth, without thickness). 3. ~**-active**, (of substance) able to affect wetting properties of a liquid; ~ **craft**, ship navigable on the surface of the sea (opp. SUBMARINE); ~ **mail**, mail carried by land or sea; (opp. AIR mail); ~ **noise**, noise in playing phonograph record, due to roughness of groove; ~ **tension**, (phys.) tension of surface film of liquid, due to attraction between its particles, which tends to bring it into form with smallest superficial area. **surface** *v.* (**-faced, -fac·ing**). Put special surface on (paper etc.); raise (submarine etc.), (of submarine etc.) rise, to surface.

sur·feit (sẽr'fĭt) *n.* Excess, esp. in eating or drinking; oppression or satiety arising from excessive eating or drinking. ~ *v.* Overfeed; (cause to) take too much of something; cloy, satiate *with.*

surge (sẽrj) *v.i.* (**surged, surg·ing**). Rise and fall, toss, move to and fro (as) in waves or billows; move suddenly and powerfully (*forward, upward*); increase suddenly; (naut., of rope etc.) slip back or around with jerk. ~ *n.* Waves, a wave; surging motion; (elect.) sudden increase in current; ~ **tank**, standpipe or storage reservoir to neutralize sudden changes of water pressure.

sur·geon (sẽr'jon) *n.* Person skilled in surgery; medical officer in army, navy, or military hospital; **sur'geonfish**, fish of genus *Acanthurus* with sharp movable spine (like lancet) on each side of tail.

sur·ger·y (sẽr'jerē) *n.* (pl. for sense 2 **-ger·ies**). 1. Manual or instrumental treatment of injuries or disorders of the body, esp. (also **operative** ~) involving incision of the skin. 2. Room or department in which surgeon operates.

sur·gi·cal (sẽr'jĭkal) *adj.* Of surgeons or surgery. **sur'gi·cal·ly** *adv.*

Su·ri·name (soor*i*nahm'). Republic on the NE. coast of S. Amer., N. of Brazil and E. of Guyana; formerly Dutch Guiana until Nov., 1975; capital, Paramaribo. **Su·ri·nam'er** *n.*

sur·ly (sẽr'lē) *adj.* (**-li·er, -li·est**). Uncivil, churlishly ill-humored, rude and cross. **sur'li·ly** *adv.* **sur'li·ness** *n.*

sur·mise (s*e*rmīz', sẽr'mīz) *n.* Conjecture, idea formed without certainty and on slight evidence. ~ (s*e*rmīz') *v.* (**-mised, -mis·ing**). Infer doubtfully or conjecturally; conjecture, guess.

sur·mount (s*e*rmownt') *v.t.* 1. Prevail over, overcome, get over (obstacle etc.). 2. Cap, be on the top of. **sur·mount'a·ble** *adj.*

sur·name (sẽr'nām) *n.* Family name, name common to all members of family; (archaic) name or epithet added to person's name(s), esp. one derived from his birthplace or some quality or achievement.

sur·pass (s*e*rpăs', -pahs') *v.t.* Outdo, excel. **sur·pass'ing** *adj.* That greatly exceeds or excels others, of very high degree. **sur·pass'ing·ly** *adv.*

sur·plice (sẽr'plĭs) *n.* Loose full-sleeved white vestment worn, usu. over cassock, by some clergy.

sur·plus (sẽr'plŭs, -pl*u*s) *n.* What remains over, excess; (attrib.) that is in excess of what is taken, used, or needed; ~ **value,** (econ.) difference between value of work done and wages paid. **sur'plus·age** *n.*

sur·prise (s*e*rprīz') *n.* 1. Catching or taking of person(s) unprepared. 2. Emotion excited by the unexpected, astonishment. 3. Thing, event, that excites surprise. ~ *v.t.* (**-prised, -pris·ing**). 1. Assail, capture, by surprise; come upon unexpectedly, take unawares. 2. Affect with surprise; be a surprise to; lead unawares, betray, *into* doing something not intended. **sur·pris'er** *n.* **sur·pris'ing** *adj.* **sur·pris'ing·ly** *adv.*

Opened in 1964, the ***suspension bridge*** *over the Forth in Scotland is 1 ½ miles long and when built, had the greatest single span in Europe and the fourth-longest in the world.*

sur·re·al·ism (s*u*rē'alĭz*e*m) *n.* Movement in art and literature, which originated in France (1924), purporting to express the subconscious activities of the mind by representing the phenomena of dreams and similar experiences; art, literature, produced in accordance with this theory. **sur·re'al** *adj.* **sur·re'al·ist** *n.* & *adj.* **sur·re·al·is·tic** (s*u*rēalĭs'tĭk) *adj.* **sur·re·al·is'ti·cal·ly** *adv.*

sur·ren·der (s*u*rĕn'd*e*r) *v.* Yield up, give into another's power or control, relinquish possession of, esp. upon compulsion or demand; abandon claim under (insurance policy) in return for payment of consideration; abandon *oneself*, give *oneself* up *to* some influence, habit, emotion, etc.; (of army, fortress, etc.) yield to enemy or assailant; give oneself up, submit, cease from resistance. ~ *n.* Surrendering, being surrendered; ~ **value,** amount to which insured is entitled if he surrenders insurance policy.

sur·rep·ti·tious (sẽrĕptĭsh'*u*s, sŭrĕp-) *adj.* Underhand, secret, clandestine, done by stealth. **sur·rep·ti'tious·ly** *adv.* **sur·rep·ti'tious·ness** *n.*

sur·rey (sẽr'ē, sŭr'ē) *n.* (pl. **-reys**). (hist.) Light four-wheeled carriage with two seats facing forward.

sur·ro·gate (sẽr'*o*gāt, -gĭt, sŭr'-) *n.* Deputy, judge with jurisdiction over probate of wills and settlement of estates.

sur·round (s*u*rownd') *v.t.* Come, lie, be, all around or on all sides; invest, enclose, encompass, environ, ençircle. **sur·round'ings** *n.pl.* Things (collectively) surrounding person or thing, environs, environment.

sur·tax (sẽr'tăks) *n.* Additional tax; graduated tax on incomes exceeding the amount to which the standard rate applies. ~ (sẽr'tăks, sẽrtăks') *v.t.* Impose surtax on.

sur·veil·lance (s*e*rvā'l*e*ns) *n.* Supervision; close guard or watch, esp. over person under suspicion of wrongdoing.

sur·vey (s*e*rvā') *v.t.* 1. Take general view of, scan. 2. Consider (situation, subject, etc.) as a whole, make or present survey of. 3. Examine condition of (building etc.). 4. Determine form, extent,

The information gathered by this surveyor will be incorporated into a ***survey*** *which will establish the boundaries and contours of the area to be developed.*

etc., of (tract of ground etc.) by linear and angular measurements so as to settle boundaries or construct map, plan, or detailed description. ~ (sẽr'vā) *n.* (pl. **-veys**). General or comprehensive view of something; inspection, examination in detail, esp. for specific purpose; account given of result of this; department or persons engaged in, operations constituting, act of, surveying of land etc., map or plan setting forth results of such survey. **sur·vey'ing** *n.* (esp.) Science, method of surveying land. **sur·vey'or** *n.*

sur·viv·al (s*e*rvī'v*a*l) *n.* Surviving; person or thing remaining as relic of earlier time.

sur·vive (s*e*rvīv') *v.* (**-vived, -viv·ing**). Outlive, continue to live or exist after death or cessation of, or after the occurrence of (disaster, hardship, etc.); continue to live or exist, be still alive or existent. **sur·vi'vor** *n.* **sur·vi'vor·ship** *n.* (esp.) Right of person having some joint interest to take whole estate on death of other(s).

sus·cep·ti·ble (s*u*sĕp'tĭb*e*l) *adj.* 1. (pred.) Admitting *of*; open, liable, accessible, sensitive, *to.* 2. Impressionable; sensitive; readily touched with emotion; touchy. **sus·cep·ti·bil·i·ty** (s*u*sĕptĭbĭl'ĭte) *n.* **sus·cep'ti·bly** *adv.*

sus·pect (s*u*spĕkt') *v.t.* 1. Imagine something evil, wrong, or undesirable in, have suspicions or doubts about; imagine something, esp. something wrong, about. 2. Imagine to be possible or likely, have faint notion or inkling of; surmise. ~ (sŭs'pĕkt, s*u*spĕkt') *adj.* Regarded with suspicion or dis-

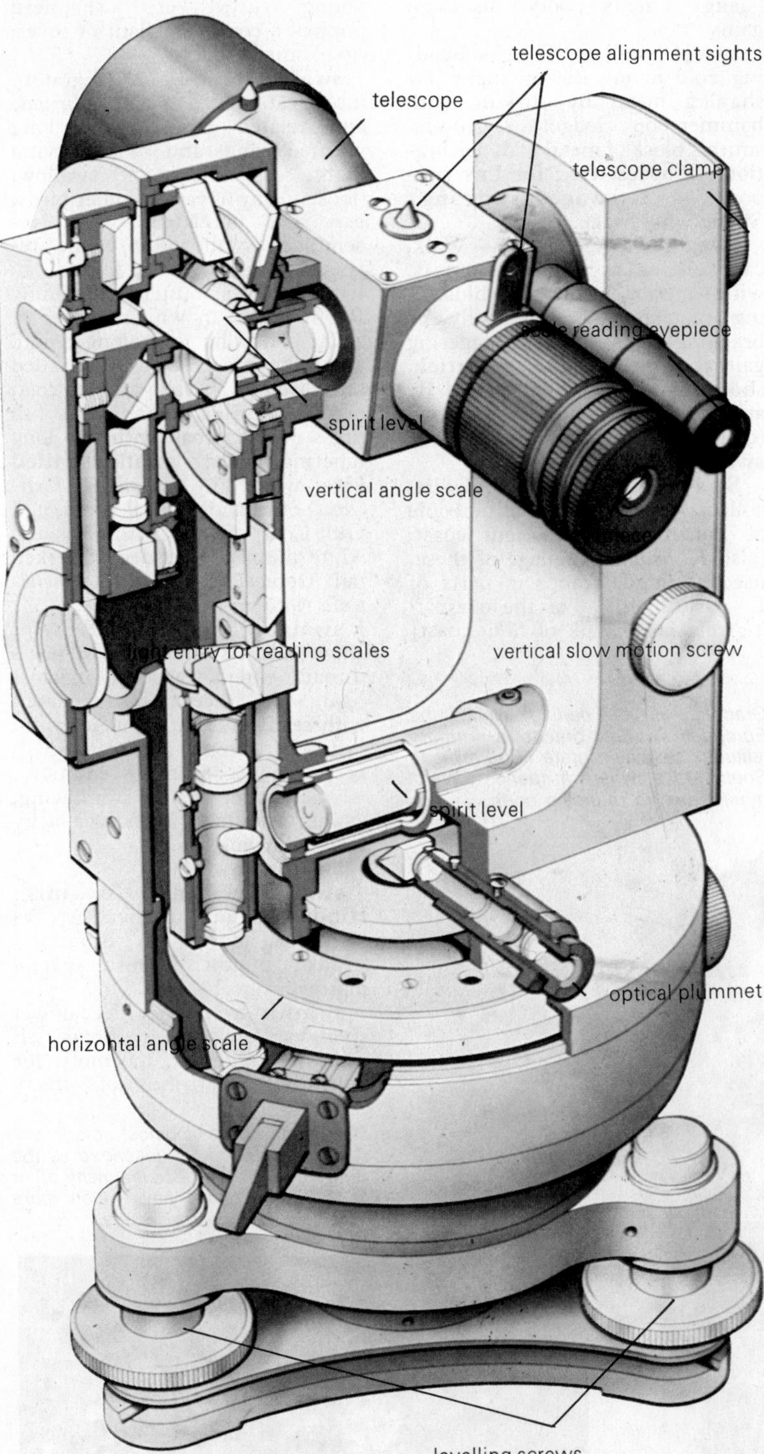

The theodolite is a major tool for a ***surveyor.*** *It enables a boundary to be located in relation to other landmarks. By measuring the angle to the top of a building and knowing its distance from himself, the surveyor can calculate its height by trigonometry.*

trust; of suspected character. ~ (sŭs′pĕkt) *n.* Suspected person.

sus·pend (s*u*spĕnd′) *v.t.* 1. Debar from exercise of function or enjoyment of privilege; deprive (temporarily) of office; put a (temporary) stop to, put in abeyance, annul for a time; defer; refrain from forming (judgment, opinion); ~ **payment,** fail to meet financial engagements; become insolvent. 2. (mus.) Prolong (1 note of chord) to following chord. 3. Hang up; hold, cause to be held, in suspension. **sus·pend′ed** *adj.* (esp.) ~ **animation**, temporary cessation of vital physical functions.

sus·pend·er (s*u*spĕn′d*er*) *n.* (esp., pl.) Straps worn over shoulders to support trousers.

sus·pense (s*u*spĕns′) *n.* State of usu. anxious uncertainty, expectation, or waiting for information; doubtfulness, uncertainty; ~ **account**, (bookkeeping) account in which items are temporarily entered until proper place is determined. **sus·pense′ful** *adj.*

sus·pen·sion (s*u*spĕn′sh*o*n) *n.* Suspending, being suspended; condition of being diffused in form of particles through fluid medium; (mus.) prolonging note of chord into following chord, dissonance so produced; ~ **bridge**, bridge in which roadway is suspended from ropes, chains, or wire cables extending between steel or masonry towers or other supports.

sus·pen·so·ry (s*u*spĕn′s*e*rē) *adj.* That suspends or holds suspended or supported (esp. some part or organ).

sus·pi·cion (s*u*spĭsh′*o*n) *n.* Suspecting; feeling or state of mind of one who suspects; being suspected; slight belief or idea, faint notion, inkling; slight trace, very small amount *of.*

sus·pi·cious (s*u*spĭsh′*u*s) *adj.* Prone to, feeling, indicating, open to, deserving of, exciting, suspicion. **sus·pi′cious·ly** *adv.* **sus·pi′cious·ness** *n.*

sus·tain (s*u*stān′) *v.t.* 1. Uphold or allow validity, rightfulness, truth, correctness, or justice of; be adequate as ground or basis for. 2. Keep from failing or giving way; keep in being, in a certain state or at the proper level or standard; keep up, keep going (sound, effort, etc.); keep up, represent (part, character) adequately. 3. Endure without failing or giving way; withstand; undergo, experience, suffer. 4. Hold up, bear weight of; be support of; bear, support (weight, pressure); **sustain′ing program**, broadcast program without commercial sponsor. **sus·tain′a·ble** *adj.*

sus·te·nance (sŭs′t*e*n*a*ns) *n.* Livelihood; means of sustaining life, food.

su·sur·ra·tion (sōōs*u*rā′sh*o*n) *n.* Whispering, rustling.

su·tra (sōō′tr*a*) *n.* 1. In Sanskrit literature, any of several collections of aphorisms dating from *c*500–200 B.C. and summarizing ritual and law of the Vedic period (*c*1500–200 B.C.). 2. (Buddhism) Any discourse of Buddha. [Sansk. *sūtra* manual of aphoristic rules]

sut·tee (sŭtē′) *n.* (hist.) Hindu widow who immolated herself on husband's funeral pyre; such immolation. **sut·tee′ism** *n.* [Sansk. *satī* virtuous wife]

su·ture (sōō′cher) *n.* 1. (surg.) Joining of edges of wound etc. by stitch(es), stitch used for this. 2. (anat.) Seamlike line of junction of two bones, esp. of skull; (zool., bot.) line of junction of contiguous parts, as of valves in shell, plant's ovary, etc. **su′tur·al** *adj.* **suture** *v.t.* (**-tured, -tur·ing**). Stitch (wound).

svelte (svĕlt, sfĕlt) *adj.* (**svelt·er, svelt·est**). Slim, willowy.

SW, S.W., s.w. *abbrevs.* Southwest(ern).

Sw. *abbrev.* Sweden, Swedish.

swab (swŏb) *n.* Mop or other absorbent mass used for cleansing or mopping up; pad of cotton wool or other absorbent material for applying medication, cleaning wound, etc.; specimen of morbid secretion etc. taken with swab. ~ *v.t.* (**swabbed, swab·bing**). Clean or wipe (as) with swab, mop *up* (as) with swab.

swad·dle (swŏd′el) *v.t.* (**-dled, -dling**). Swathe in bandages, wrappings, etc.; **swaddling clothes**, narrow bandages wrapped around newborn infant to prevent free movement (now chiefly fig.).

swag (swăg) *n.* 1. Ornamental festoon of flowers, fruit, etc., fastened up at both ends and hanging down in middle; carved or molded representation of this. 2. (slang) Thief's booty; dishonest gains.

swage (swāj) *n.* Tool for bending cold metal, die or stamp for shaping metal by striking with hammer or sledge; ~ **block**, smith's block of metal with perforations, grooves, etc., for this purpose. ~ *v.t.* (**swaged, swag·ing**). Shape with swage.

swag·ger (swăg′er) *v.i.* Walk, carry oneself, as if among inferiors, with superior, insolent, or blustering manner; talk boastfully or braggingly. ~ *n.* 1. Swaggering gait, talk, or manner. 2. ~ **stick**, short light cane often carried by army officers. **swagger** *adj.* (colloq.) Smart, fashionable. **swag′ger·er** *n.*

Swa·hi·li (swahhē′lē) *n.* (pl. **-lis**, collect. **-li**). (One of) Bantu people of Zanzibar and adjacent coast; (also *Kiswahili*) language of these, used as lingua franca in parts of E. Africa. [lit., "of the coasts," f. Arab. *sawāḥil* pl. of *sāḥil* coast]

*Graceful in its darting flight, the European **swallow** breeds in northern latitudes but may migrate 7000 miles to South Africa, where it spends several months before returning north.*

swain (swān) *n.* Countryman, young rustic, esp. shepherd (archaic); country gallant or lover; (joc.) suitor, lover.

swal·low[1] (swŏl′ō) *n.* Migratory insect-eating bird of genus *Hirundo* and related genera, with long pointed wings and swift curving flight, esp. the BARN swallow; (loosely) any of various other birds, esp. the unrelated swifts, resembling swallows in some respects; **swal′lowtail**, forked tail like swallow's; butterfly of family Papilionidae, in which border of each hind wing is prolonged into a taillike process; swallow-tailed kite; (freq. pl.) swallow-tailed coat; **swallow-tailed coat**, man's full dress evening coat, with two long tapering tails; **swallow-tailed kite**, white kite (*Elanoides forficatus*) of S. and Central Amer. and Gulf Coast of U.S., with black and white plumage and deeply forked tail; tropical African kite (*Chelictinia riocourii*).

swal·low[2] (swŏl′ō) *v.* Cause or allow (food etc.) to pass down one's throat; engulf, absorb, exhaust (usu. ~ **up**); accept (statement etc.) with ready credulity; put up with, stomach (affront); recant (words); keep down, repress (emotion). ~ *n.* Gullet; act of swallowing; amount swallowed at once; capacity for swallowing.

swam: see SWIM.

swa·mi (swah′mē) *n.* (pl. **-mis**). Hindu religious teacher (esp. as form of address to Brahmin); (transf.) pundit. [Sansk. *svāmin* master, prince]

swamp (swŏmp) *n.* Piece of wet spongy ground, marsh; tract of rich soil with trees etc., too moist for cultivation; (attrib., of many

*Despite its bright hindmost colors, this Australian butterfly is described as the **dingy swallowtail** because many other in the same genus have much more vivid and iridescent markings.*

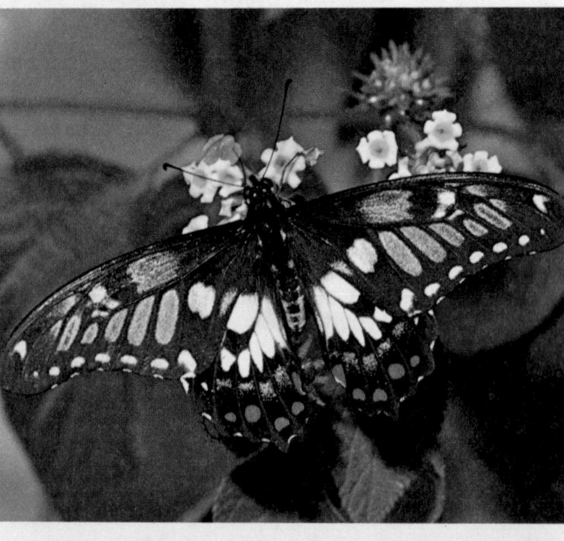

animals, birds, plants, etc.) growing, living, in swamps; ~ **boat** (or **buggy**), automotive vehicle for travel through swamps or muddy areas, usu. amphibious and having extra large tires; flat-bottomed boat driven by propeller rising over stern. **swamp′y** *adj.* (**swamp·i·er, swamp·i·est**). **swamp′i·ness** *n.* **swamp** *v.* Submerge, inundate, soak, with water; (of boat) (cause to) fill with water and sink; overwhelm with numbers or quantity of anything.

swan (swŏn) *n.* (pl. **swans**, collect. **swan**). Large web footed swimming bird usu. of genera *Cygnus* and *Olor*, with long gracefully curved neck, esp. the domestic, mute, or tame swan, *C. olor*, with pure white plumage in adult, black legs and feet and red bill with black knob, occurring wild in NE. Europe and W. Central Asia, and semidomesticated all over Amer. and Europe, formerly supposed to sing melodiously just before its death; (**S** ~, astron.) northern constellation Cygnus; ~ **dive**, forward dive in which spine is curved and arms are outspread, being moved forward and together just before hitting water; **swan's-down, swans′down**, down or fine soft feathers of swan used for powder puffs, trimmings, etc.; soft thick woolen cloth, thick cotton fabric with soft nap; **swan song**, legendary song of dying swan; last (esp. artistic) production of person etc. **swan′like** *adj.*

swank (swăngk) *n.* (colloq.) 1. Fashionable elegance in dress, appearance, etc.; smartness. 2. Ostentatious, swaggering display in speech, behavior, etc. ~ *adj.* (colloq.) Affectedly stylish.

swank·y (swăng′kē) *adj.* (**swank·i·er, swank·i·est**). (colloq.) Fashionable; ostentatious. **swank′i·ly** *adv.* **swank′i·ness** *n.* **swank** *v.i.* Show off, swagger.

swap, swop (swŏp) *ns.* & *vbs.* (**swapped, swap·ping, swopped, swop·ping**). (colloq.) Exchange by way of barter. **swap′per** *n.*

swarm[1] (swôrm, swârm) *n.* Cluster of bees leaving hive or main body with queen bee to establish new hive; large or dense body, throng, multitude of persons, insects, etc., esp. moving about. ~ *v.i.* Move in a swarm; (of bees) gather in compact cluster around queen and leave hive in a body; congregate in number, be very numerous; (of places) be overrun or crowded.

swarm[2] (swôrm, swârm) *v.* Climb *up* (rope, pole, tree) by clasping it with arms and legs alternately; climb up or *up* (any steep ascent) by clinging with hands and knees.

swarth·y (swôr′dhē, swâr′-) *adj.*

*Louisiana's **swamp** land lies along the coast area of the state on the Gulf of Mexico. Rich in oil and natural gas deposits, this lush subtropical area was not exploited until the 1890s when its economic potential was realized.*

***Swahili** is the lingua franca of East Africa, and is spoken by 11 million people in Tanzania, Kenya, Zaire, and Uganda. In market places such as this one it is a valuable adjunct to trade.*

(**swarth·i·er, swarth·i·est**). Dark complexioned, dark in color. **swarth′i·ly** *adv.* **swarth′i·ness** *n.*

swash[1] (swŏsh) *v.* (of water etc.) Wash about, make sound of washing or rising and falling; **swash′-buckler**, swaggering bravo or ruffian, bully. **swash′buckling** *adj.* & *n.* **swash** *n.* (Sound of) swashing.

swash[2] (swŏsh) *adj.* (turning etc.) Inclined obliquely to axis of work; (print., of italic capitals) having flourished strokes at top and bottom, as $\mathcal{T}$, $\mathcal{N}$; ~ **plate**, rotating circular plate set at an oblique angle to its shaft, giving reciprocating motion to rod resting on it and parallel to its shaft.

swas·ti·ka (swŏs′tĭk*a*) *n.* Primitive and ancient symbol or talisman in form of cross with equal arms, each arm having a limb of same length projecting from its end at right angles, all in same direction

*Representatives of three continents: the black-necked **swan,** a native of South America; the black variety of Australia; and the mute swan found in Europe. There are four other species.*

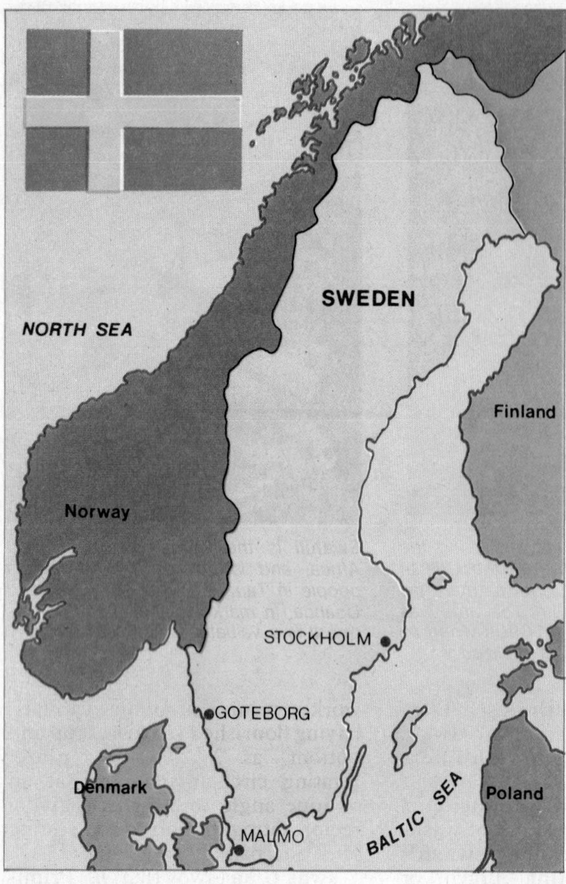

(usu. direction of sun's course, i.e. clockwise), found in various parts of the world, esp. Mexico, Peru, and Tibet, used in Germany and Austria from 1918 onward as symbol of anti-Semitism or as emblem of Nazi party. [Sansk. f. *svastika*, f. *svasti* well-being, good fortune, luck]

swat (swŏt) *v.t.* (**swat·ted, swat·ting**). Hit hard, crush (fly etc.) with blow. **swat′ter** *n.*

swatch (swŏch) *n.* Sample of cloth or fabric.

swath (swŏth, swawth), **swathe**[1] (swŏdh, swādh) *ns.* (pl. **swaths** pr. swŏdhz, swawdhz, **swathes**). Row or line of grass, corn, etc., as it falls when mown or reaped; space covered by mower's scythe, width of grass or corn so cut.

swathe[2] (swŏdh, swādh) *v.t.* (**swathed, swath·ing**). Wrap up or around, envelop, like bandage or (as) with wrapping.

sway (swā) *v.* 1. Lean unsteadily to one side or in different directions by turns; have unsteady swinging motion; oscillate irregularly; waver, vacillate; give swaying motion to. 2. Govern the motion of; wield, control direction of; have influence over; govern, rule over. 3. **swayed, sway′back, sway′-backed**, with back abnormally hollowed (esp. of horse). **sway** *n.* 1. Swaying motion or position. 2. Rule, government.

The spires of the old city of Stockholm seen beyond a foreground network of modern freeways and fly-overs. As capital of **Sweden** *it reflects both past history and present development.*

Swa·zi·land (swah′zēlănd). Kingdom in SE. Africa between Mozambique, Transvaal, and Natal; member of the Brit. Commonwealth, formerly a Brit. protectorate; independent 1968; capital, Mbabane.

swear (swār) *v.* (**swore** pr. swōr, **sworn** pr. swōrn, **swear·ing**). 1. State something, state (thing) on oath, take oath; promise or undertake something by oath; promise to observe or perform (something); confirm by oath; affirm emphatically or confidently; ~ **by**, (colloq.) profess or have great belief in; ~ **off**, forswear. 2. Utter profane oath, use profane language, to express anger or as expletive(s); (of colors) clash unpleasantly (with); **swear′word**, (colloq.) profane oath or word. 3. Cause to take oath, administer oath to; (also **swear in**), admit to office or function by administering oath; **swear out**, obtain (warrant etc.) by making charge on oath. **swear′er** *n.*

sweat (swĕt) *n.* 1. Salty fluid secreted by glands beneath the skin and exuded through the pores, perspiration; something resembling sweat, drops of moisture on a surface; condition or period of sweating; (colloq.) state of impatience or anxiety; **sweat′band**, band of leather etc. as lining of hat or cap; **sweat gland**, minute coiled tubular gland beneath skin secreting sweat; **sweat shirt**, shirt worn esp. by athletes before or after exercise. 2. (chiefly colloq.) Drudgery, toil, laborious task; **sweat′shop**, factory in which workers are made to work hard for very poor wages. **sweat′y** *adj.* (**sweat·i·er, sweat·i·est**). **sweat′i·ly** *adv.* **sweat′i·ness** *n.* **sweat** *v.* (**sweat** or **sweat·ed, sweat·ing**). 1. Exude sweat, perspire; emit or exude, ooze *out*, as or like sweat; cause (horse, athlete, etc.) to sweat by exercise etc.; exude or gather moisture in drops on surface; cause to exude moisture, force moisture out of. 2. Work hard, toil, drudge; employ (workers) at very poor wages for long hours, exploit to the utmost; (of workers) work on such terms.

sweat·er (swĕt′*er*) *n.* (esp.) Knitted, crocheted, etc., jacket, jersey, usu. of wool, for informal wear; pullover.

Swed. *abbrev.* Sweden, Swedish.

Swede (swēd) *n.* Native of Sweden.

Swe·den (swē′d*e*n). Kingdom of E. Scandinavia; capital, Stockholm.

Swe·den·borg (swē′d*e*nbôrg), **Emanuel** (1688–1772). Swedish religious mystic and philosopher; held that God, as divine man, is infinite love and infinite wisdom, and the end of creation is the approximation of man to God; he taught that there is a symbolic sense to the Scriptures, of which he was the appointed interpreter. **Swe·den·bor·gi·an** (swēd*e*nbôr′-gē*a*n) *adj.* & *n.* (Follower) of Swedenborg, (member) of the New Jerusalem Church. **Swe·den·-bor′gi·an·ism, Swe′den·borg·-ism** *ns.*

Swed·ish (swē′dĭsh) *adj.* Of Sweden or its people or language. **Swedish** *n.* Indo-European language of Sweden, one of the Norse group.

sweep (swēp) *v.* (**swept** pr. swĕpt, **sweep·ing**). 1. Glide swiftly, speed along with impetuous unchecked motion, go majestically; extend in continuous curve, line, or slope. 2. Impart sweeping motion to; carry *along, down, away, off,* in impetuous course; clear *off, away, from,* etc. 3. Traverse or range swiftly, pass lightly across or along; pass eyes or hand quickly along or over; scan, scour, graze; (of artillery etc.) include in line of fire, cover, enfilade, rake. 4. Clear everything from; clear of dust, soot, litter, with broom; win all points, games, etc.; gather *up*, collect, (as) with broom. 5. **sweep′back**, angle at which airplane's wing is set back from position at right angles to body; **sweep (second) hand**, hand on clock or watch moving on same dial as other hands; **sweep′stake(s)**, (prize won in) race or contest in which all competitors' stakes are taken by winner(s); form of gambling on horse races etc. in which sum of participators' stakes goes to holder(s) of tickets on winning or placed horse(s); **swept′back** (*adj.*), (of aircraft wing) slanted to the rear from points of connection; **swept′-wing** (*n.* & *adj.*), (aircraft) having sweptback wings. **sweep′er** *n.* **sweep′ing** *adj.* (esp., of statement etc.) General, unqualified, regardless of limitations or exceptions. **sweep′ing** *n.* (esp. pl.) Matter swept up; litter; trash. **sweep** *n.* 1. Sweeping, clearing up or away (now usu. **a clean** ~); moving in continuous curve (of an army, fleet, river, etc.); hostile reconnaissance by group of aircraft; sweeping motion or extension, curve in road, etc.; curved driveway leading to house. 2. Range or compass of something that has curving motion; extent, stretch, expanse, esp. such as can be taken in at one look. 3. Long oar worked by rower(s) standing on barge etc.; long pole mounted as lever for raising bucket from well; gear for clearing submarine mines, usu. consisting of a long wire with a cutting device attached, streamed from a vessel (**minesweeper**) at the required depth. 4. Chimney sweep. 5. Victory in all parts of a contest; winning all games in a series or match. **sweep′ing·ly** *adv.*

sweet (swēt) *adj.* 1. Tasting like sugar, honey, etc., corresponding to one of the primary sensations of taste; (of wine) tasting thus, containing unfermented natural sugar (opp. DRY). 2. Pleasing to the sense of smell, fragrant, perfumed. 3. Fresh and sound, not salt(ed) or sour or bitter or putrid. 4. Agreeable, attractive, gratifying; inspiring affection, dear, amiable, gentle, easy; (colloq.) pretty, charming, delightful; **at one's own ~ will**, as one pleases, arbitrarily; **~ on**, (colloq.) very fond of, (inclined to be) in love with. 5. **~-and-sour**, cooked or prepared with seasoning of both sugar and vinegar or lemon; **~ bay** = BAY[1], 1; (also) N. Amer. magnolia (*Magnolia virginiana*); **sweet′-bread**, pancreas or thymus gland of animal, esp. calf, used for food; **sweet′brier, sweet′briar**, eglantine (*Rosa eglanteria*, and other species), with small hooked prickles, pink flowers, and small aromatic leaves; **sweet corn**, any of several varieties of corn with sweet kernels, eaten when young; also called green corn; **sweet gum**, large tree of N. Amer. (*Liquidambar styraciflua*) having prickly fruit balls and aromatic resin; **sweet′heart**, darling; either of pair of lovers; **sweetheart contract,** (slang) contract with unfavorable terms for union members arranged by secret understanding between officials of union and management; **sweet marjoram,** aromatic cultivated herb (*Marjorana hortensis*); **sweet′meat**, = SWEET *n.* sense 2; **sweet pea**, climbing leguminous annual (*Lathyrus odoratus*) cultivated for its many-colored, sweet-scented flowers; **sweet pepper**: see PEPPER sense 2; **sweet potato**, (large sweet farinaceous tuberous root, eaten as vegetable, of) tropical climbing plant (*Ipomoea batatas*) widely cultivated in warm regions; **sweet-**

Sweet William, *a variety of plants in the genus Dianthus, is a popular garden biennial, especially in borders where the colorful array of blooms provides a vivid foreground to larger plants.*

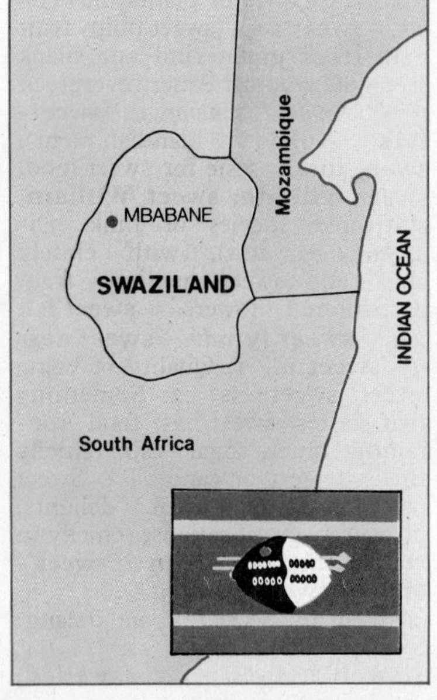

Small and land-locked, the independent Kingdom of ***Swaziland*** *benefited by being a British protectorate. This forestalled invasion by both the Boers and Zulus.*

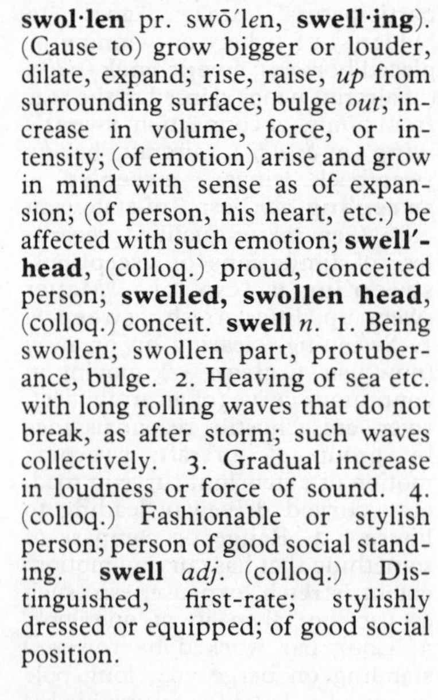

Despite its apparent similarity to the swallow, the **swift** is considered by ornithologists, to be more closely related to the hummingbird. Nests of an Asian variety are used to make soup.

scented, having a sweet scent (freq. in names of plants, flowers, etc.); **sweet′sop**, (sweet pulpy fruit with thick green rind and black seeds of) tropical Amer. evergreen tree (*Annona squamosa*); **sweet-talk**, (colloq.) blandish(ment); **sweet tooth**, taste for sweet food; **sweet william, sweet William**, cultivated species of pink (*Dianthus barbatus*), with closely clustered sweet-smelling freq. particolored flowers. **sweet′ish** *adj.* **sweet′ly** *adv.* **sweet′ness** *n.* **sweet** *n.* 1. Quality of being sweet; sweetness. 2. Something that tastes sweet, as food containing much sugar, esp. (chiefly Brit.) dessert or candy. 3. Sweet part (chiefly fig.); (pl.) delights, pleasures, gratifications; (chiefly in voc.) darling. **sweet′en** *v.* **sweet′en·ing, sweet′en·er** *ns.*

sweet·ie (swē′tē) *n.* (slang) Sweetheart.

swell (swĕl) *v.* (**swelled, swol·len** pr. swō′len, **swell·ing**). (Cause to) grow bigger or louder, dilate, expand; rise, raise, *up* from surrounding surface; bulge *out*; increase in volume, force, or intensity; (of emotion) arise and grow in mind with sense as of expansion; (of person, his heart, etc.) be affected with such emotion; **swell′-head**, (colloq.) proud, conceited person; **swelled, swollen head**, (colloq.) conceit. **swell** *n.* 1. Being swollen; swollen part, protuberance, bulge. 2. Heaving of sea etc. with long rolling waves that do not break, as after storm; such waves collectively. 3. Gradual increase in loudness or force of sound. 4. (colloq.) Fashionable or stylish person; person of good social standing. **swell** *adj.* (colloq.) Distinguished, first-rate; stylishly dressed or equipped; of good social position.

swell·ing (swĕl′ĭng) *n.* (esp.) Distention of injured or diseased part of body.

swel·ter (swĕl′ter) *v.i.* Be oppressed or oppressive with heat; sweat profusely, languish, be faint, with excessive heat.

swept: see SWEEP.

swerve (swẽrv) *v.* (**swerved, swerv·ing**). Turn aside, (cause to) deviate from straight or direct course. ~ *n.* Swerving motion; divergence from course.

swift (swĭft) *adj.* Fleet, rapid, quick; soon coming or passing, not long delayed; prompt, quick *to* do. ~ *adv.* Swiftly (chiefly in comb. as ~*-footed*). **swift′ly** *adv.* **swift′ness, swift** *ns.* Any of various swift-flying insectivorous birds of the family Apodidae, superficially resembling swallows, esp. *Chaetura pelagica*, the chimney swift.

Swift (swĭft), **Jonathan** (1667–1745). Irish satirist and clergyman, dean of St. Patrick's Cathedral, Dublin; author of *A Tale of a Tub*, *Gulliver's Travels*, etc.

swig (swĭg) *v.* (**swigged, swig·ging**). (colloq.) Take drafts (of). ~ *n.* (Act of taking) a draft of liquor.

swill (swĭl) *v.* Wash or rinse (*out*), pour water over or through, flush; drink greedily; feed (usu. pigs) with swill. ~ *n.* 1. Liquid or partly liquid food, chiefly kitchen refuse, given to swine; hogwash; inferior liquor. 2. Rinsing, swilling.

swim (swĭm) *v.* (**swam** pr. swăm, **swum** pr. swŭm, **swim·-ming**). 1. Float on or at surface of liquid. 2. Progress at or below surface of water by working legs, arms, tail, webbed feet, fins, etc.; traverse (distance etc.) thus; compete in (race) thus; cause (horse, dog, etc.) to progress thus; (fig.) go with gliding motion. 3. Appear to undulate, reel, or whirl, have dizzy effect or sensation; be flooded or overflow with or *with* or *in* moisture. 4. ~ **bladder**, air bladder of many fish. **swim** *n.* Period of swimming; (fig.) main current of affairs (**in, out of, the** ~); **swim′suit**, bathing suit. **swim′mer** *n.*

swim·mer·et (swĭmerĕt′, swĭm′erĕt) *n.* Abdominal appendage in some crustaceans.

swim·ming (swĭm′ĭng) *n.* Act, practice, or sport of one who or that which swims. ~ *adj.* 1. Being able to swim; concerning or used in swimming. 2. Flooded or brimming over with water or other liquid. 3. Affected with dizziness or faintness.

swim·ming·ly (swĭm′ĭnglē) *adv.* (esp.) With easy and unobstructed progress.

swin·dle (swĭn′del) *v.* (**-dled, -dling**). Cheat (person, *money out of* person, person *out of* money); practice fraud. **swin′dler** *n.* **swindle** *n.* Piece of swindling; fraudulent scheme, imposition; something represented as what it is not, fraud.

Best remembered for 'Gulliver's Travels', **Jonathan Swift** was a bitter man whose books all contained trenchant satire. His career as a clergyman was matched by his interest in politics.

swine (swīn) *n.* (pl. **swine**). Animal of family Tayassuidae of nonruminant hoofed mammals, with stout body, thick skin, longish snout with terminal nostrils, and small tail; hog, pig, domesticated for its flesh and regarded as type of greediness and uncleanness; person of greedy or bestial habits (used esp. as strong term of abuse); ~ **fever**, hog cholera; **swine'herd**, one who tends swine; **swine plague**, infectious bacterial disease of swine resembling swine fever but chiefly affecting lungs. **swin'ish** *adj.* **swin'ish·ly** *adv.* **swin'ish·ness** *n.*

swing (swĭng) *v.* (**swung** pr. swŭng, **swing·ing**). 1. Move with the to-and-fro or curving motion of object having fixed point(s) or side, but otherwise free; sway or so hang as to be free to sway like pendulum, door, etc.; oscillate, revolve, rock, wheel; move back and forth in swing. 2. Go with swinging gait; (slang) be sophisticated, lively, up-to-the-minute, etc., in seeking pleasurable experience; (slang) engage promiscuously in sexual intercourse (colloq.) have decisive influence on (voting, jury, etc.); (colloq.) be executed by hanging. 3. Give (music) the character of swing music. **swing** *n.* 1. Act or process of swinging; swinging gait or rhythm; movement describing curve; quick trip around country, region, etc.; **in full** ~, at height of activity. 2. Seat slung by ropes or chains for swinging in; period of swinging in either of these. 3. (also **swing music**) Kind of jazz in which the time of the melody (usu. played by single instrument) is freely varied over simple harmonic accompaniment in strict time with strongly marked rhythm. **swing shift**, (colloq.) work shift running from about midafternoon to about midnight. **swing'er** *n.* 1. Person who or thing that swings. 2. (slang) Stylish, up-to-the-minute person who seeks pleasurable experience, esp. sexual freedom.

swing·ing (swĭng'ĭng) *adj.* (superl. **-ing·est**). 1. That swings; **swinging door, gate**, door (esp. in two leaves hung separately and sprung), gate that swings in either direction and closes of itself when released. 2. (of gait, melody, etc.) Vigorously rhythmical. 3. Gay, lively. **swing'ing·ly** *adv.*

swin·gle (swĭng'gel) *n.* Wooden swordlike instrument for beating flax and removing woody parts from it; striking or swinging part of flail; **swin'gletree**, crossbar pivoted in middle, to ends of which traces are fastened in cart, plough, etc. **swingle** *v.t.* (**-gled, -gling**). Clean (flax) with swingle.

swipe (swīp) *v.* (**swiped, swip·ing**). 1. (colloq.) Strike with a hard sweeping blow. 2. (slang) Snatch, steal. ~ *n.* Hard sweeping blow.

swirl (swẽrl) *n.* Eddy, whirlpool; eddying or whirling motion; twist, convolution, curl. ~ *v.* Eddy, carry (object), be carried, with eddying or whirling motion.

swish (swĭsh) *n.* Sound of switch or similar object moved rapidly through air, of scythe cutting grass, or object moving rapidly through water. ~ *v.* Make, move with, swish; flog with birch or cane.

Swiss (swĭs) *adj.* Of Switzerland or its people; ~ **Guards**, Swiss mercenary troops employed as bodyguards formerly by sovereigns of France etc. and still at Vatican. **Swiss** *n.* Native (collect., people) of Switzerland.

swiss (swĭs) *n.* Fine cotton fabric of plain weave freq. with dots or flecks formed by extra yarns (**dotted** ~).

switch (swĭch) *n.* 1. Slender tapering whip; thin flexible shoot cut from tree, something resembling this. 2. Device for making and breaking contact or altering connections in electric circuit; (on railroad etc.) movable rail or pair of rails pivoted at one end at junction of tracks, used to deflect train etc. from one line to another. 3. Tress of real or false hair, tied at one end, used in hairdressing. 4. **switch'back**, zigzag road, railroad, climbing steep grade; **switch'blade**, pocket knife with blade released by spring; **switch'board**, board or frame with set of switches for varying connection among a number of electric circuits, as of telephone, telegraph, etc.; **switch hitter**, (baseball) player who can bat with either hand; **switch'man** (pl. **-men**), man who works switch(es), esp. on railroad. **switch** *v.* 1. Strike, whip, (as) with switch; flourish like a switch, whisk, lash, move with sudden jerk. 2.

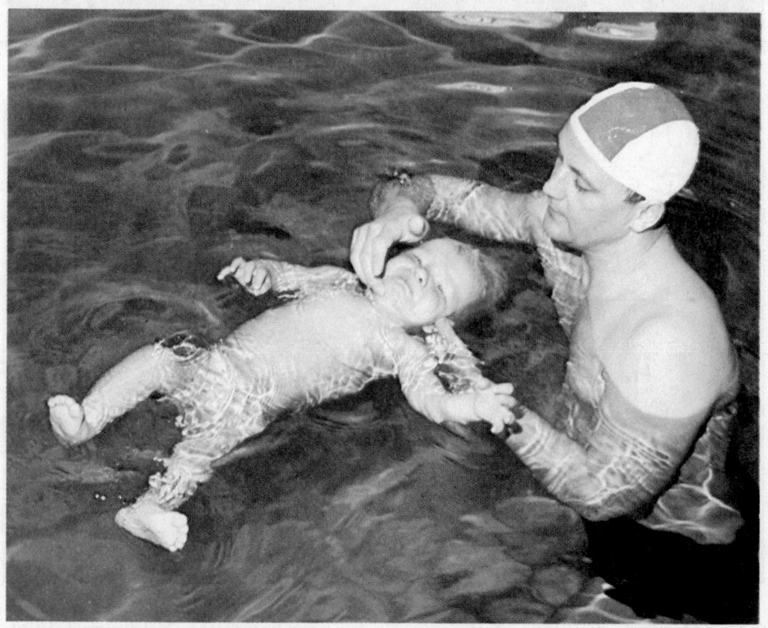

*It is believed by some that a child can easily learn to **swim** at a very early age, if an adult is nearby to assure safety (left). Swimmers must be a little more advanced to learn the breast stroke and butterfly stroke (below).*

Highland meadows backed by the snow-covered Alps near Murren in the higher part of ***Switzerland.*** *This small country has diverse and highly productive agricultural regions and its industries are specialized.*

Turn (train etc.) onto another line by means of switch; turn (electric current, light, etc.) *on, off*, by means of switch, change (connection) *over* with switch; (fig.) turn off, divert; **switch'over**, diversion of effort, activity, or production.

Switz·er·land (swĭt'serland). Republic in central Europe, S. of West Germany and N. of Italy, consisting of federation of 22 cantons; capital, Berne.

swiv·el (swĭv'el) *n.* Simple joining or coupling device made so that object fastened can turn freely upon it, or so that each half of the swivel itself can turn independently; ring or staple turning on pin, or the like; ~ **bearing, chain, coupling, gun**, etc., one provided with or mounted on swivel; **swivel chair**, chair with seat turning horizontally on pivot. **swivel** *v.* (**-eled, -el·ing,** *Brit.* **-elled, -el·ling**). Turn (as) on swivel.

swiz·zle (swĭz'el) *n.* Tall mixed drink usu. made with rum, lime, etc.; ~ **stick**, rod for stirring drinks.

swol·len: see SWELL.

swoon (swo͞on) *n.* & *v.i.* (archaic) Faint.

swoop (swo͞op) *v.* Come down or *down* with the rush of a bird of prey (often upon prey etc.); attack from a distance; (*up* or *away*) snatch, seize, the whole of. ~ *n.* Act of swooping, esp. sudden pounce of bird of prey; **at one (fell)** ~, at a single blow or stroke.

swop: SWAP.

sword (sōrd, sōrd) *n.* Offensive weapon for cutting or thrusting, consisting of long straight or curved blade with handle or hilt and cross guard, sharp point, and usu. one or two sharp edges; **at ~s' points**, ready to fight or argue; **cross swords**, fight; dispute violently; **draw, sheathe, the sword**, begin, cease from, war; **sword dance**, dance, esp. folk dance, in which performers go through evolutions with swords, or one which is danced over naked swords laid on ground; **sword'fish** (pl. **-fishes,** collect **-fish**), large sea fish used for food (*Xiphias gladius*), with upper jaw prolonged into swordlike point; **sword grass**, grass with sharp-edged leaves; plant with swordshaped leaves, as the gladiolus; **sword lily**, gladiolus; **sword'play**, fencing; **swords'man** (pl. **-men**), one skilled in use of sword; **swords'manship. sword'like** *adj.*

sworn (swōrn) *adj.*: see SWEAR; (esp.) bound by an oath; ~ **brother**, close friend; ~ **enemy, foe**, determined or irreconcilable enemy.

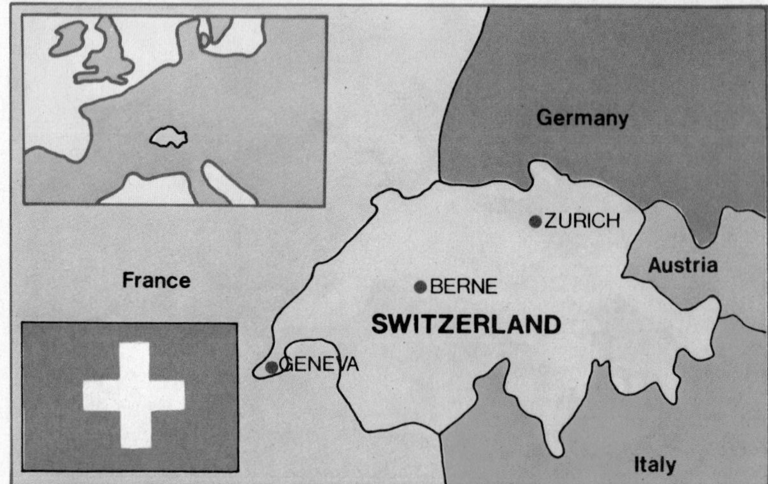

swum: see SWIM.

swung (swŭng) *adj.*: see SWING; (esp.) ~ **dash**, mark (~) used in place of (part of) word previously spelled out.

Syb·a·rite (sĭb'arīt) *n.* Inhabitant of ancient Greek colony of Sybaris in S. Italy noted for luxury; hence (**s**~), luxury-loving person. **syb·a·rit·ic** (sĭbarĭt'ĭk) *adj.*

syc·a·more (sĭk'amōr, -mōr) *n.* 1. Buttonwood or plane tree (*Platanus occidentalis*) of eastern N. Amer., with buttonlike seeds and whitish bark that flakes off in patches. 2. Large Eurasian species of maple (*Acer pseudoplatanus*) grown as shady ornamental tree and for its wood.

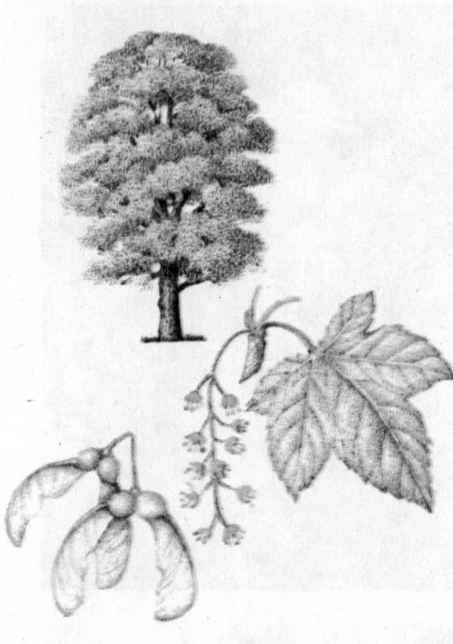

The familiar ***sycamore*** *tree that is grown in streets in England is a hybrid obtained from cross-breeding trees which were originally native to the Near East and North America.*

syc·o·phant (sĭk′*o*fant) *n.* Flatterer, parasitic person. **syc′o·phan·cy** *n.* (pl. **-cies**). **syc·o·phan·tic** (sĭk*o*făn′tĭk) *adj.* [Gk. *sukophantes* informer, f. *sukon* fig., *phainō* show (reason for name unknown)]

syl·la·bar·y (sĭl′*a*bĕrē) *n.* (pl. **-bar·ies**). Collection, system, or table of syllables, esp. of written characters each representing a syllable, such as Japanese katakana.

syl·la·bic (sĭlăb′ĭk) *adj.* Of, forming, syllable(s); (of written symbols) denoting a syllable; consisting of such symbols; (pros.) based on number of syllables. **syl·lab′i·cal·ly** *adv.*

syl·lab·i·cate (sĭlăb′*i*kāt) (**-cat·ed, -cat·ing**), **syl·lab·i·fy** (sĭlăb′*i*fī) (**-fied, -fy·ing**) *vbs.t.* Divide into syllables. **syl·lab·i·ca·tion** (sĭlăb*i*kā′sh*o*n), **syl·lab·i·fi·ca·tion** (sĭlăb*i*fĭkā′sh*o*n) *ns.*

syl·la·ble (sĭl′*a*bel) *n.* Vocal sound(s) forming a whole word or part of a word and uttered as an uninterrupted unit; character(s) representing this; least mention, hint, or trace (*of*). ~ *v.t.* (**-bled, -bling**). Pronounce by syllables; articulate distinctly; (poet.) utter, speak. **syl·lab·ic** (sĭlăb′ĭk) *adj.*

syl·la·bus (sĭl′*a*b*u*s) *n.* (pl. **-bus·es, -bi** pr. -bī). 1. Concise statement of subjects of lectures, course of study, etc. 2. (R.C. Ch.) (also called ~ **of errors**) Catalog of 80 heretical doctrines, practices, or institutions condemned by Pope Pius IX (1864).

syl·lo·gism (sĭl′*o*jĭzem) *n.* Form of reasoning in which conclusion is deduced from two premises (major and minor) containing a common or middle term that is absent from the conclusion, e.g. (major premise) *All men are mortal*; (minor premise) *Socrates is a man: therefore* (conclusion) *Socrates is mortal*; deductive as opp. to inductive reasoning. **syl·lo·gis·tic** (sĭl*o*jĭs′tĭk) *adj.* **syl·lo·gis′ti·cal·ly** *adv.*

syl·lo·gize (sĭl′*o*jīz) *v.* (**-gized, -giz·ing**). Use syllogisms; throw (facts, arguments) into syllogistic form.

sylph (sĭlf) *n.* Imaginary, delicate being supposed to inhabit the air; slender graceful woman. **sylph′like** *adj.* Slender and graceful.

syl·van, sil·van (sĭl′v*a*n) *adjs.* Of wood(s); consisting of, abounding in, furnished with, woods or trees.

sym- *prefix.* Assim. form of SYN- before *b, m, p.*

sym·bi·o·sis (sĭmbīō′sĭs, -bē-) *n.* (pl. **-ses** pr. -sēz). (biol.) Association of two different organisms living attached to one another or one as tenant of the other (used esp. of associations advantageous to both organisms, as dist. from *parasitism*). **sym·bi·ot·ic** (sĭmbīŏt′ĭk, -bē-) *adj.* **sym·bi·ot′i·cal·ly** *adv.*

sym·bol (sĭm′b*o*l) *n.* Thing standing for or representing something else, esp. material thing taken to represent immaterial or abstract thing, as an idea or quality; written

First developed in the Bronze Age, and improved and refined as metallurgy developed, the ***sword*** *remained a vital weapon for armed forces, and for dueling, until the development of rifles and revolvers.*

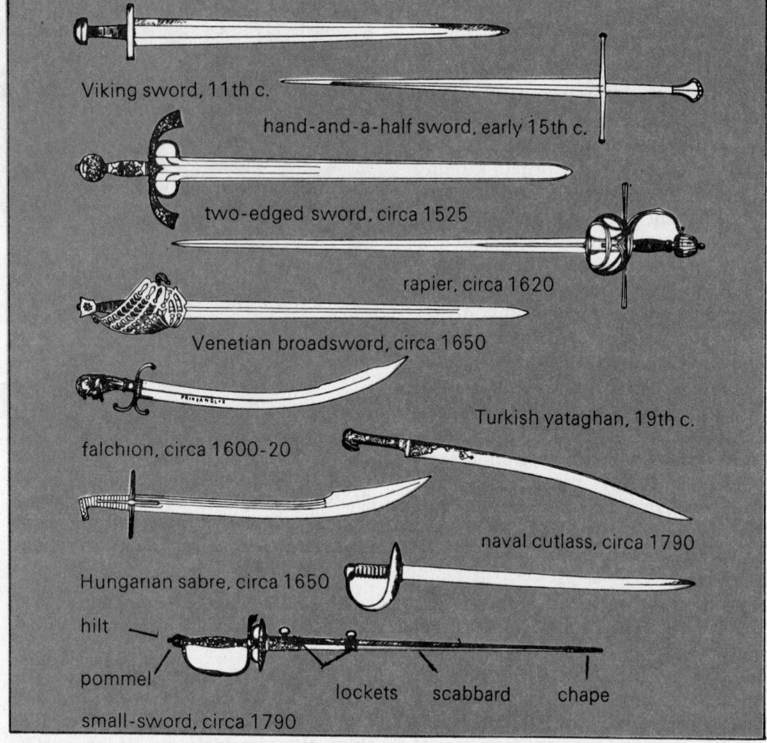

The true function of the beak of a ***swordfish*** *has yet to be determined. However, one piece of ship's timber now in the British Museum, was penetrated 22 inches by a 'sword'.*

*The **symbiosis** that exists between the sea anemone and the clown fish is illustrated by the ability of the fish to swim and feed among the anemone tentacles which prove fatal to other small fish.*

character conventionally standing for some object, process, etc. **sym·bol·ic** (sĭmbŏl′ĭk), **sym·bol′i·cal** *adjs.* **sym·bol′i·cal·ly** *adv.*

sym·bol·ism (sĭm′bolĭzem) *n.* System, use, meaning, of symbols; doctrine of the Symbolists. **sym′bol·ist** *n.* 1. One who uses symbols. 2. **S~**, member of a school of French poets (*c*1880–*c*1900) whose artistic purpose was arousal of emotions by indirect suggestion rather than by direct expression, with particular objects, words, etc. carrying symbolic meaning.

sym·bol·ize (sĭm′bolīz) *v.t.* (**-ized, -iz·ing**). Be symbol of; represent by symbol; treat as symbolic or emblematic. **sym·bol·i·za·tion** (sĭmbolīzā′shon) *n.*

sym·me·try (sĭm′etrē) *n.* (pl. **-tries**). 1. (Beauty resulting from) right proportion between the parts of the body or any whole, balance, congruity, harmony. 2. Such structure as allows of an object's being divided by a point or line or plane or radiating lines or planes into two or more parts exactly similar in size and shape and in position relatively to the dividing point etc.; repetition of exactly similar parts in contrary or equally divergent directions; **axial ~**, symmetry about an axis; **bilateral ~**, about a plane; **radial ~**, about a point. 3. Approximation to such structure; possession by a whole of corresponding parts correspondingly placed. **sym·met·ric** (sĭmĕt′rĭk), **sym·met′ri·cal** *adjs.* **sym·met′ri·cal·ly** *adv.* **sym′me·trize** *v.t.* (**-trized, -triz·ing**).

sym·pa·thet·ic (sĭmpathĕt′ĭk) *adj.* 1. Of sympathy; full of, expressing, due to, effecting sympathy; in agreement; favorably inclined (*to* or *with*); (in literary criticism) capable of evoking sympathy, appealing *to* reader. 2. (of disorder, pain, etc.) Induced in organ or part of body by a similar or corresponding one in another; **~ string**, (mus.) string that vibrates with sympathetic resonance, enriching the tone. 3. (physiol.) Of that part of the nervous system consisting principally of a pair of ganglionated nerve trunks placed alongside the vertebral column and connected with nerve fibers that extend to the blood vessels, viscera, sweat and salivary glands, and pupils. **sym·pa·thet′i·cal·ly** *adv.*

sym·pa·thize (sĭm′pathīz) *v.i.* (**-thized, -thiz·ing**). Feel or express sympathy (*with*); suffer with or like another. **sym′pa·thiz·er** *n.*

*The art of calligraphy, particularly in China and Japan, requires an understanding of the **symbolism** of each character, which can have an abundance of meanings.*

sym·pa·thy (sĭm′pathē) *n.* (pl. **-thies**). Affinity or relation between things by virtue of which they are similarly or correspondingly affected by the same influence, or affect or influence each other; tendency to share, state of sharing, emotion, sensation, or condition of another person or thing; mental participation in another's trouble, compassion, commiseration; disposition to agree (*with*) or approve, favorable attitude of mind toward person, cause etc.; **~ strike**, strike of workers not to remedy their own grievances but to support other strikers.

sym·pho·ny (sĭm′fonē) *n.* (pl. **-nies**). Musical composition written in form of SONATA but for full orchestra and usu. comprising four movements; (colloq.) concert by a symphony orchestra; **~ orchestra**, large orchestra including strings, woodwind, brass, and percussion instruments, playing chiefly symphonies or other works of serious artistic quality. **sym·phon·ic** (sĭmfŏn′ĭk) *adj.* **~ poem**, orchestral work, usu. of descriptive or rhapsodic character, freq. resembling first movement of symphony or sonata. **sym·phon′i·cal·ly** *adv.* **sym′pho·nist** *n.*

sym·po·si·um (sĭmpō′zēum) *n.* (pl. **-si·ums, -si·a** pr. -zēa). 1. Ancient Greek drinking party, convivial meeting for drinking, conversation, and intellectual entertainment; **the S~**, title of one of Plato's dialogues recording such conversation. 2. Meeting or conference for discussion of some subject; collection of opinions delivered or articles contributed by number of persons on special topic. **sym·po′si·al** *adj.*

symp·tom (sĭmp′tom) *n.* 1. Perceptible change in the body or its functions indicating presence of disease or injury, esp. (also **subjective ~**) one directly

Touro ***Synagogue*** *in Newport, Rhode Island is the oldest in the U.S.A., built in 1763 and named a national historic site in 1946.*

perceptible to the patient only; **objective ~**, one accompanied by signs (see SIGN *n.* sense 1). 2. Evidence or token of the existence of something. **symp·to·mat·ic** (sĭmptŏmăt´ĭk) *adj.* **symp·to·mat´i·cal·ly** *adv.*

symp·to·ma·tize (sĭmp´tomatīz) *v.t.* (**-tized, -tiz·ing**). Be a symptom of.

syn- *prefix.* With, together, alike.

syn·a·gogue, syn·a·gog (sĭn´agŏg, -gawg) *ns.* Regular assembly of Jews for religious instruction or worship; building where this is held. **syn·a·gog·al** (sĭnagŏg´al, -gaw´gel), **syn·a·gog·i·cal** (sĭnagŏj´ĭkal) *adjs.*

syn·apse (sĭn´ăps, sĭnăps´) *n.* (anat.). Locus where a nervous impulse passes from the axon of one neuron to the dendrites of another.

syn·ap·sis (sĭnăp´sĭs) *n.* (pl. **-ses** pr. -sēz). 1. (biol.) Fusion of pairs of chromosomes, the first process in meiotic division of germ cells. 2. (anat.) = SYNAPSE. **syn·ap·tic** (sĭnăp´tĭk) *adj.*

sync, synch (sĭngk) *ns.* (colloq.) Synchronization. ~ *v.* (colloq.) Synchronize.

syn·carp (sĭn´kārp) *n.* (bot.) Compound fruit, one arising from number of carpels in one flower. **syn·car·pous** (sĭnkār´pus) *adj.*

syn·chro·mesh (sĭng´kromĕsh) *n.* System of gearing, esp. in motor vehicles, in which the sliding gear-wheels are provided with small friction clutches that make contact with the nonsliding wheels before engagement, thus facilitating gear changing by making both wheels revolve at the same speed. [abbrev. f. *synchronized mesh*]

syn·chro·nize (sĭng´kronīz) *v.* (**-nized, -niz·ing**). Occur at the same time, be contemporary or simultaneous (*with*); keep time (*with*); cause to go at same rate or function simultaneously; cause (clocks etc.) to indicate same time; add dialogue or other sound as synchronous accompaniment to (motion picture). **syn·chro·ni·za·tion** (sĭngkronīzā´shon), **syn´chro·niz·er** *ns.*

syn·chro·nous (sĭng´kronus), **syn·chro·nal** (sĭng´kronal) *adjs.* Existing or happening at same time, contemporary, simultaneous, (*with*); keeping time, proceeding at same pace (*with*), having coincident periods; **~ orbit**, orbit whose period coincides with period of Earth's rotation on its axis and is so oriented that any body in it holds a position above one point on the surface of Earth. **syn´chro·nous·ly** *adv.*

syn·chro·tron (sĭng´krotrŏn) *n.* An adaptation of the cyclotron designed for high acceleration of particles combined with a low-frequency magnetic field.

syn·cline (sĭng´klīn, sĭn´-) *n.* (geol.) Rock bed that forms a trough (opp. ANTICLINE). **syn·cli·nal** (sĭngklī´nal, sĭng´klī-) *adj.*

syn·co·pate (sĭng´kopāt) *v.t.* (**-pat·ed, -pat·ing**). 1. (gram.) Shorten (word) by omitting syllable(s) or letter(s) in the middle. 2. (mus.) Affect, modify, by syncopation. **syn·co·pa·tion** (sĭngkopā´shon) *n.* (esp., mus.) Displacement of accent, or beat, by beginning note on normally unaccented part of bar (and freq. prolonging it into normally accented part), putting strong accent on normally weakly accented part of bar etc.

syn·co·pe (sĭng´kopē, sĭn´-) *n.* 1. (path.) Fainting, sudden temporary loss of consciousness

Beehive type huts in a village near Aleppo, ***Syria.*** *Increasing in political power in the Middle East, Syria took a major part in achieving a cease-fire in Lebanon in 1976.*

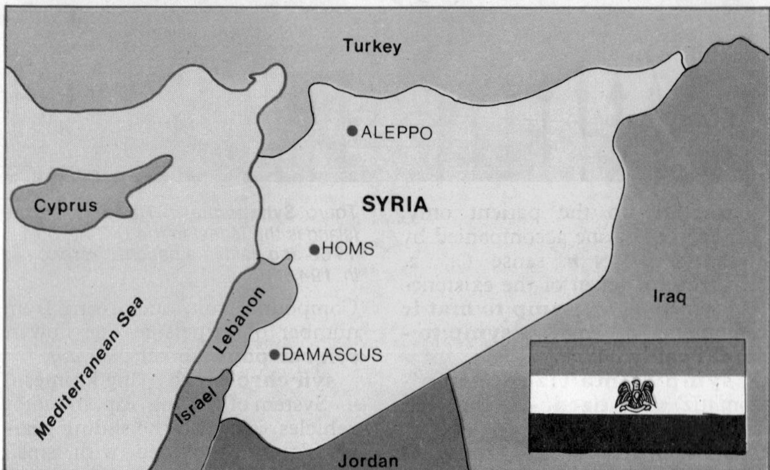

due to cerebral anemia associated with a severe disturbance of the circulation. 2. (gram.) Shortening of word by dropping of syllable(s) or letters in the middle. **syn′co·pal, syn·cop·ic** (sĭnkŏp′ĭk) *adjs.*

syn·cre·tism (sĭng′kretĭzem, sĭn′-) *n.* (Attempted) reconciliation of diverse or opposite tenets or practices, esp. in philosophy or religion. **syn·cret·ic** (sĭnkrĕt′ĭk), **syn·cre·tis·tic** (sĭngkretĭs′tĭk, sĭnkre-) *adjs.*

syn·di·cal·ism (sĭn′dĭkalĭzem) *n.* Movement, orig. and esp. in France, for transfer of control and ownership of means of production and distribution to workers' unions. **syn′di·cal·ist** *adj.* & *n.* [Fr. *syndicalisme*, f. *syndicat* trade union]

syn·di·cate (sĭn′dikĭt) *n.* Combination of financiers etc. for promotion of financial or commercial undertaking; (journalism) agency for syndicating articles etc. in newspapers; (colloq.) organization of gangsters. ~ (sĭn′dikāt) *v.* (**-cat·ed, -cat·ing**). Form into syndicate; publish simultaneously in a number of periodicals. **syn·di·ca·tion** (sĭndikā′shon), **syn′di·ca·tor** *ns.*

syn·drome (sĭn′drōm) *n.* Concurrence of several symptoms in a disease, set of concurrent symptoms characterizing it.

syn·ec·do·che (sĭnĕk′dokē) *n.* (gram., rhet.). Figure of speech in which the specific is used for the general or vice versa; or the part for the whole or vice versa, e.g. *50 sail* for *50 ships* or *the law* for *a policeman.*

syn·er·gism (sĭn′erjĭzem), **syn·er·gy** (sĭn′erjē) *ns.* (pl. **-gies**). Combined effect of drugs, organs, etc. that exceeds the sum of their individual effects. **syn·er·get·ic** (sĭnerjĕt′ĭk), **syn·er·gic** (sĭnēr′jĭk), **syn·er·gis·tic** (sĭnerjĭs′tĭk) *adjs.* **syn′er·gist** *n.* **syn·er·gis′ti·cal·ly** *adv.*

syn·od (sĭn′od) *n.* 1. Assembly of clergy of church, diocese, nation, etc., for discussing and deciding ecclesiastical affairs; in Presbyterian churches, assembly of ministers and other elders constituting ecclesiastical court next above presbytery. 2. Any convention or council. **syn′od·al, syn·od·i·cal** (sĭnŏd′ĭkal), **syn·od′ic** *adjs.* **syn·od′i·cal·ly** *adv.*

syn·o·nym (sĭn′onĭm) *n.* Word having same meaning as another in same language; another name (*for*). **syn·on·y·mous** (sĭnŏn′ĭmus) *adj.* **syn·on′y·mous·ly** *adv.*

syn·on·y·my (sĭnŏn′ĭmē) *n.* (pl. **-mies**). Being synonymous; use of synonyms, esp. for amplification or emphasis; subject or study of, a collection of, synonyms.

syn·op·sis (sĭnŏp′sĭs) *n.* (pl. **-ses** pr. -sēz). Brief general survey; summary.

syn·op·tic (sĭnŏp′tĭk) *adj.* Of, forming, furnishing, a synopsis; taking, affording, comprehensive mental view; (meteor.) of, affording, a comprehensive description of atmospheric conditions; **S~**, of the **~ Gospels**, those of Matthew, Mark, and Luke, as giving an account of events under same general aspect or from same point of view. **syn·op′ti·cal** *adj.* **syn·op′ti·cal·ly** *adv.* **Syn·op′tist** *n.* Writer of a Synoptic Gospel.

syn·tax (sĭn′tăks) *n.* (gram.) Arrangement of words in sentence showing their connection and relation; rules of grammar dealing with usages of grammatical construction. **syn·tac·tic** (sĭntăk′tĭk), **syn·tac′ti·cal** *adjs.*

syn·the·sis (sĭn′thesĭs) *n.* (pl. **-ses** pr. -sēz). Putting together of parts or elements to make up a complex whole (cf. ANALYSIS); (chem.) formation of a compound by combination of its elements or simpler compounds, esp. artificial production of organic compounds. **syn·the·size** (sĭn′thesīz) *v.t.* (**-sized, -siz·ing**).

syn·thet·ic (sĭnthĕt′ĭk), **syn·thet·i·cal** (sĭnthĕt′ĭkal) *adjs.* Produced by synthesis, artificial. **syn·thet′i·cal·ly** *adv.* Artificially produced fiber etc.

syph·i·lis (sĭf′ilĭs) *n.* Venereal disease due to the microorganism

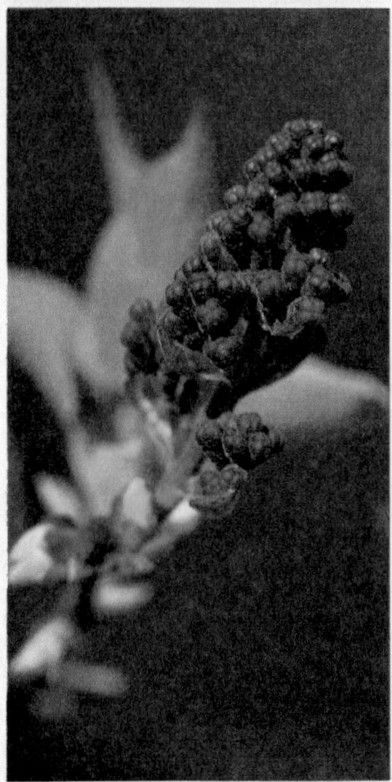

Better known as lilac, plants in the genus ***Syringa*** *also include others which have flowers with a strong perfume. The plants are believed to have originated in western Asia and southern Europe.*

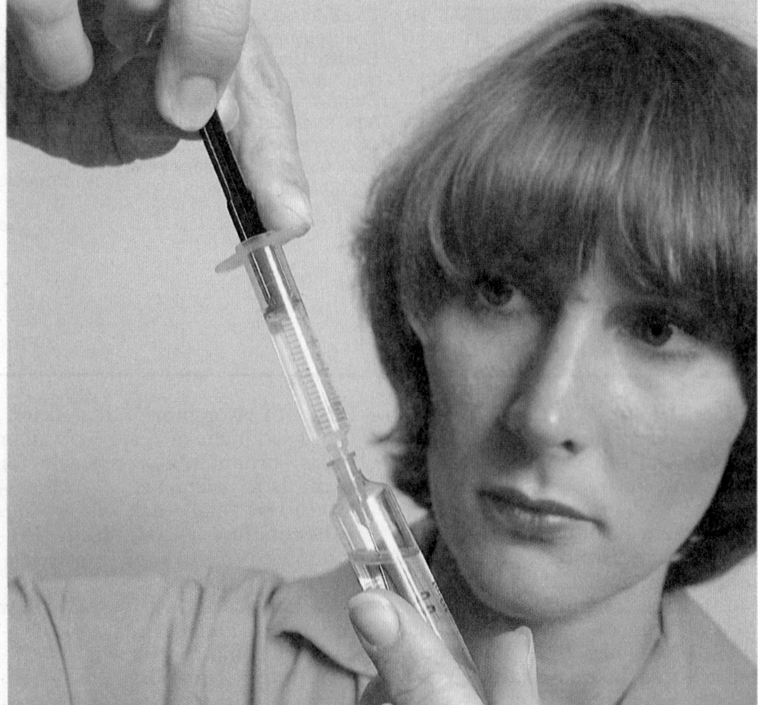

Blaise Pascal, French philosopher, physicist and mathematician, was the inventor of the ***syringe*** *in the 17th century. Injection by syringe has become the standard method of introducing fluid drugs into the body.*

Treponema pallidum, communicated by direct contact, usu. sexual intercourse, with an infected person, affecting first some local part (**primary** ~), secondly skin and mucous membrane (**secondary** ~), and thirdly bones, muscles, and brain (**tertiary** ~); **congenital** ~, condition in which an unborn child is infected through the maternal blood stream. **syph·i·lit·ic** (sĭf*i*lĭt´ĭk) *adj.* & *n.* Of (person) affected with, syphilis. [f. *Syphilus*, character in Latin poem on the subject (1530) by Girolano Fracastoro, Veronese physician]

Syr·i·a (sĭr´ēa, sēr´-). Republic in SW. Asia at E. end of Mediterranean; formed, with nearby regions, part of the Roman Empire from 64 B.C. to 36 A.D.; chiefly under Arab domination until the Ottoman conquest in 1517; French mandated territory 1918–41; capital, Damascus. **Syr´i·an** *adj.* & *n.* **Syr´i·ac** *adj.* (Of, in) the language of ancient Syria, a branch of Aramaic.

sy·rin·ga (s*i*rĭng´g*a*) *n.* 1. MOCK orange. 2. Shrub of genus *S*~, esp. *S. vulgaris*, the common lilac. [Gk. *surigx* pipe, with ref. to use of stems cleared of pith as pipestems]

sy·ringe (s*i*rĭnj´) *n.* Tube with nozzle and piston or bulb for drawing in quantity of liquid and ejecting it in stream or jet, for making injections, cleansing wounds, spraying plants, etc. ~ *v.t.* (**-ringed, -ring·ing**). Sluice, spray, with syringe.

syr·up, sir·up (sĭr´*u*p, sēr´-) *ns.* Water (nearly) saturated with sugar, this combined with flavoring as beverage or with drug(s) as medicine; condensed sugar cane juice, part of this remaining uncrystallized at various stages of refining, molasses; **maple** ~, syrup obtained by boiling down maple sap. **syr´up·y** *adj.* (esp. fig.) Sentimental, excessively sweet in style etc.

sys·tal·tic (sĭstawl´tĭk, -tăl´-) *adj.* Contracting, esp. (physiol.) with alternate contraction (*systole*) and dilatation (*diastole*).

sys·tem (sĭs´t*e*m) *n.* 1. Complex whole, set of connected things or parts, organized body of material or immaterial things; (phys.) group of bodies moving about one another in space under some dynamic law, as that of gravitation, esp. (astron.) group of heavenly bodies moving in orbits about central body; (biol.) set of organs or parts in animal body of same or similar structure or subserving same function, animal body as an organized whole; ~**s analysis**, technique of analyzing an operation in order to improve efficiency etc.; ~**s design**, organization of data for electronic processing, or of data processing equipment. 2. Body of knowledge or belief considered as organized whole; comprehensive body of doctrines, beliefs, theories, practices, etc., forming particular philosophy, religion, form of government, etc.; scheme or method of classification, notation, etc.; (cryst.) any of six general methods or types in which substances crystallize. 3. Orderly arrangement or method.

sys·tem·at·ic (sĭst*e*măt´ĭk), **sys·tem·at·i·cal** (sĭst*e*măt´ĭk*a*l) *adjs.* Methodical; arranged, conducted, according to system or organized plan; of system(s). **sys·tem·at´i·cal·ly** *adv.* **sys·tem·at´ics** *n.* (with sing. verb) Scientific study of classification of the plant and animal kingdoms, taxonomy. **sys·tem·a·tize** (sĭs´t*e*m*a*tīz) *v.t.* (**-tized, -tiz·ing**).

sys·tem·ic (sĭstĕm´ĭk) *adj.* 1. Of, affecting, a system; (esp., physiol.) of the system or body as a whole, or a particular system of bodily organs. 2. Absorbed by a plant so as to be poisonous to insects that feed on it. **sys·tem´i·cal·ly** *adv.*

sys·to·le (sĭs´t*o*lē) *n.* Contraction of heart, alternating with DIASTOLE. **sys·tol·ic** (sĭstŏl´ĭk) *adj.*

syz·y·gy (sĭz´ĭjē) *n.* (pl. **-gies**). (astron.) Point at which the heavenly bodies are in conjunction or opposition, esp. the moon with the sun.

Sze·chwan, Si·chuan (sĕ´chwahn´). Province of China on the Yangtze Kiang.

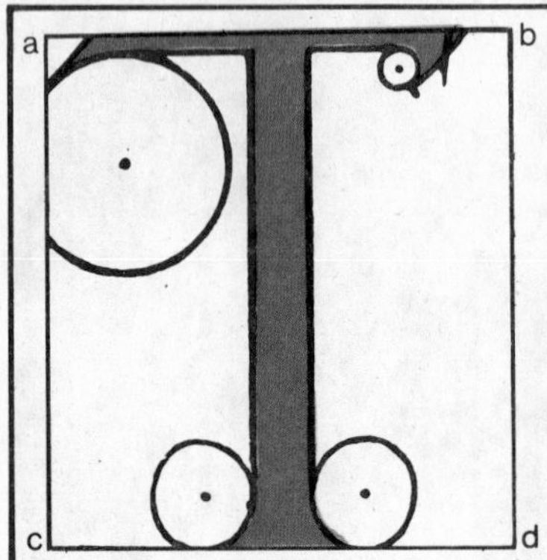

The earliest forms of the letter ***'T, t'*** *were simple crosses which, in Semitic languages, were called 'taw'. It meant a mark or sign. Somewhat surprisingly, its shape has remained relatively constant compared with the changes that have occurred to other letters during their history.*

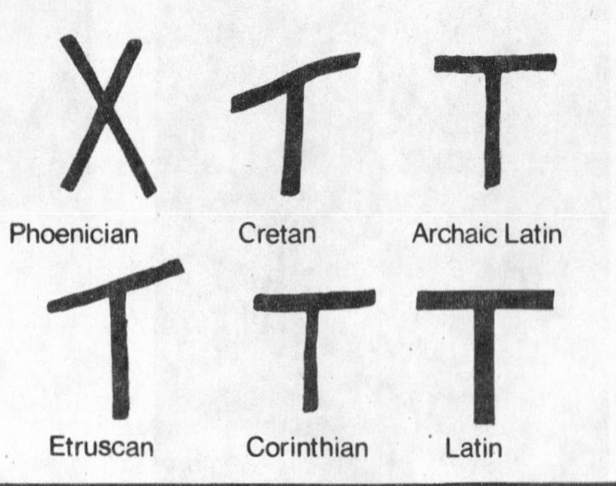

T, t (tē) (pl. **T's, t's** or **Ts, ts**). 1. Twentieth letter of modern English and 19th of ancient Roman alphabet, derived in form from Greek *T* (*tau*), from the Phoenician and ancient Semitic ✝ ✕ ✕ X, and representing a voiceless dental (or in English, rather alveolar) stop, but in some combinations, as *-tion*, *-tial*, it has the sound "sh," in *-tual*, *-tue*, *-ture* freq. the sound represented in this dictionary by "ch"; the combination -th- represents voiced and voiceless dental spirants, simple sounds for which the Roman alphabet has no single symbols; **to a T**, exactly, to a nicety. 2. Object etc. shaped like T; **T-bone steak**, beefsteak from thin end of loin, containing T-shaped bone; **T-shirt**, short-sleeved usu. collarless shirt; **T square**, T-shaped instrument for obtaining or testing right angles and parallel lines.

T *abbrev.* Tesla.

T. *abbrev.* Tablespoon, tablespoonful, tenor, tera-, territory, true, Tuesday.

t. *abbrev.* Teaspoon, teaspoonful, temperature, (grammar) tense, time, ton(s), transitive, troy.

Ta *symbol.* Tantalum.

Taal (tahl) *n.* Cape Dutch, Afrikaans. [Du., = "language"]

tab (tăb) *n.* Short broad strap, flat loop, strip, tag, attached by one end to object, or forming projecting tongue, by which thing can be taken hold of, hung up, fastened, identified, etc.; (colloq.) restaurant or bar bill, check (esp. **keep ~s on**). **tab** *v.* (**tabbed, tab·bing**).

tab·by (tăb'ē) *n.* (pl. **-bies**). Brownish, tawny, or gray cat with darker stripes (also **tabby cat**); old maid, elderly gossiping woman.

tab·er·nac·le (tăb'*er*năk*e*l) *n.* 1. Temporary or slightly built dwelling, hut, booth, tent; **Feast of Tabernacles**, Jewish festival, held in October, commemorating Israelites' sojourn in tents in the wilderness. 2. (Jewish hist.) Curtained tent containing Ark of the Covenant, which served as portable sanctuary of Jews during their wandering in the wilderness. 3. Place of worship. 4. (eccles.) Canopied niche or recess in wall or pillar; ornamental receptacle for eucharistic elements. **tab·er·nac·u·lar** (tăb*er*năk'y*u*l*er*) *adj.* **tabernacle** *v.* (**-led, -ling**). Provide with shelter or tabernacle; dwell temporarily.

ta·bes (tā'bēz) *n.* (path.) Slow progressive emaciation; ~ **dorsa'lis**, locomotor ataxia.

ta·bet·ic (t*a*bĕt'ĭk) *adj.* Of, affected with, tabes, esp. locomotor ataxia. ~ *n.* Tabetic patient.

tab·la·ture (tăb'l*a*ch*er*) *n.* Tabular space or structure.

ta·ble (tā'b*e*l) *n.* 1. Article of furniture consisting of flat top of wood or other solid material supported on legs or central pillar, esp. one on which meals are laid out, articles of use or ornament kept, work done, or games played; each half of folding backgammon board; provision or supply of food for meals, fare; company of persons at a table; **at ~**, at a meal or meals; **lay on the ~**, (in legislative debate) postpone (measure, report); **turn the ~s**, reverse relation between two persons or parties, cause a complete reversal of state of affairs. 2. Flat, usu. rectangular, horizontal or vertical surface in architecture etc.; flat part of machine tool on which work is put to be operated on; flat upper surface of faceted gem; crystal of flattened or short prismatic form; flat elevated tract of land, plateau, flat mountain top. 3. Slab of wood, stone, etc.; matter written on this; **~s of the law** (**covenant**), the Ten Commandments, the stones on which they were written; **the Twelve Tables**, laws drawn up by decemviri in Rome, 451 and 450 B.C., embodying most important rules of Roman law. 4. Tabulated statement or arrangement; arrangement of numbers, words, etc., esp. in columns and lines occupying single sheet, so as to exhibit set of facts or relations distinctly and comprehensively for study, reference, or calculation. 5. **ta'blecloth**, cloth spread on table, esp. for meals; **table cut**, (of gem) cut with flat upper surface and surrounded by small facets; **ta'ble-**

Possibly invented by British officers stationed in India during the 1890s, ***table tennis*** *was adopted in the U.S.A. about 1902. It became internationally accepted in 1926.*

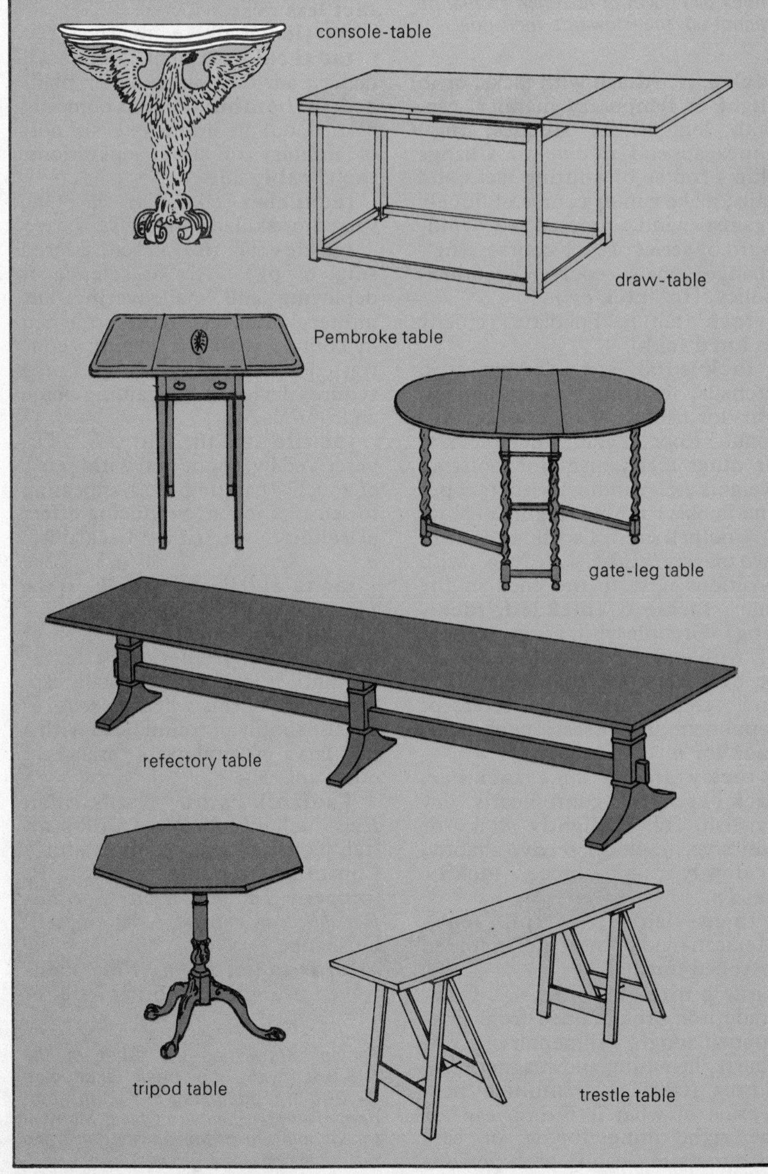

Left top: A marble-topped and gilt covered ***table*** *showing the degree of ornamentation used on furniture in the past. Below left: A range of tables showing the variations adopted for different needs.*

land, extensive elevated region with level surface, plateau; **table linen**, tablecloths, napkins, etc.; **ta′blespoon**, spoon, used at table for serving vegetables, etc.; tablespoonful; **ta′blespoonful**, amount held by tablespoon, about 4 fluid drams or 3 teaspoonfuls; **table talk**, informal conversation at table; **table tennis**, indoor game resembling lawn tennis, played with small round bats and celluloid ball on table with net stretched across it; **ta′bleware**, utensils and dishes etc. used at table; **table wine**, wine for drinking with meals, containing 8–13 percent alcohol. **table** *v.t.* (**-bled, -bling**). Lay (measure, report, etc.) on table, esp. as way of postponing indefinitely.

tab·leau (tăb′lō, tăblō′) *n.* (pl. **tab·leaux, tab·leaus** pr. tăb′lōz, tăblōz′). Presentation, esp. of group of persons etc., producing picturesque effect; striking or dramatic effect suddenly produced.

ta·bleau vi·vant (tăblō′ vēvahṅ′) (pl. **ta·bleaux vi·vants** pron. as sing.). Representation of painting, statue, scene, etc., by silent and motionless person or group.

ta·ble d'hôte (tăb′el dōt′, tah′bel; *Fr.* tăble dōt′) (pl. **ta·bles d'hôte** pr. tăb′elz dōt′, tah′belz; *Fr.* tăble dōt′). (of meal) Served at fixed price for a stated series of courses (opp. *à la carte*). [Fr., = "host's table"]

tab·let (tăb′lit) *n.* Small thin flat piece of ivory, wood, etc., for writing on, esp. each of set fastened together; pad of sheets of notepaper fastened together at top; small slab, esp. with or for inscription; small flat or compressed piece of solid confection, drug, etc., flattened lozenge.

tab·loid (tăb′loid) *n.* 1. Anything in summarized, compressed, or concentrated form. 2. Newspaper of small format, esp. one giving news in concentrated and simplified form. ~ *adj.*

ta·boo, ta·bu (tăbōō′) *adjs.* Set apart as sacred or prohibited. ~ *n.* (pl. **-boos, -bus**). Ban, prohibition. ~ *v.t.* (**-booed, -boo·ing**). Put under taboo. [Polynesian]

tab·u·lar (tăb′yuler) *adj.* 1. Of, arranged in, computed, etc., by means of, tables. 2. Broad, flat, and (usu.) comparatively thin, like a table; formed of, tending to split into, pieces of this form; (of crystal etc.) of short prismatic form with flat base and top. **tab′u·lar·ly** *adv.*

ta·bu·la ra·sa (tăb′yula rā′sa, rah′sa; *Lat.* tah′bōōlah rah′sah) (pl.

ta·bu·lae ra·sae pr. tăb'y*u*lē rā'sē, rah'sē; *Lat.* tah'bo͞olī rah'sī). Erased tablet; (fig.) human mind at birth viewed as having no innate ideas; complete obliteration, a blank. [L., = "scraped tablet," i.e. "clean slate"]

tab·u·late (tăb'y*u*lāt) *v.t.* (**-lat·ed, -lat·ing**). Arrange, summarize, exhibit, in form of a table, scheme, or synopsis. **tab·u·la·tion** (tăby*u*lā'sh*o*n) *n.* **tabulate** (tăb'y*u*lĭt, -lāt) *adj.* Having flat surface, tabular.

tab·u·la·tor (tăb'y*u*lāt*er*) *n.* (esp.) Typewriter attachment for indenting a selected number of spaces when paragraphing and tabulating.

ta·chis·to·scope (t*a*kĭs't*o*skōp) *n.* Instrument for very brief measured exposure of objects to eye. **ta·chis·to·scop·ic** (t*a*kĭst*o*skŏp'ĭk) *adj.*

tach·o·graph (tăk'*o*grăf, -grahf) *n.* Device on vehicle, measuring and recording its speed and travel time; tachometer.

ta·chom·e·ter (tăkŏm'*eter*) *n.* Instrument for measuring the velocity of machines or the rate of flow of liquids. **ta·chom'e·try** *n.*

ta·chy·car·di·a (tăk*i*kar'dē*a*) *n.* (path.) Abnormally rapid action of heart.

tac·it (tăs'ĭt) *adj.* Implied, understood, inferred, but not openly expressed or stated; saying nothing, silent. **tac'it·ly** *adv.* **tac'it·ness** *n.*

tac·i·turn (tăs'ĭtẽrn) *adj.* Reserved in speech, saying little, uncommunicative. **tac·i·tur·ni·ty** (tăsĭtẽr'nĭtē) *n.* **tac'i·turn·ly** *adv.*

Tac·i·tus (tăs'ĭt*u*s), **Publius Cornelius** (c56–117 A.D.). Roman historian, son-in-law of Agricola; author of *Agricola* (containing an account of Britain), *Germania*, *Histories*, and *Annals*.

tack[1] (tăk) *n.* 1. Small sharp nail, usu. with large flat head, for fastening thin or light object to more solid one. 2. Fastening together, esp. in slight or temporary way; long slight stitch used in fastening together seams etc. before permanent sewing. 3. Rope used for securing lower corner of some sails; lower windward corner of sail, to which tack is attached. 4. Tacking; ship's course in relation to direction of wind and position of sails; course obliquely opposed to direction of wind, one of consecutive series of such courses with wind alternately on port and starboard side; (fig.) course of action or policy; **on the wrong ~**, with mistaken idea; in error. 5. (of varnish, printing ink, etc.) Viscous condition. 6. Saddles, harness, bridles, etc. and other equipment for riding horse; **~ room**, room in or near stable where this is kept.

In football, a player receiving the ball expects to be the victim of a ***tackle.*** *Members of the opposing team either knock him down or hold him so that he cannot advance towards their goal.*

tack *v.* 1. Attach with tacks, or in slight or temporary manner, esp. with long slight stitches; (fig.) annex, append (*to, onto*). 2. Change ship's course by shifting tacks and sails; make run or course obliquely against wind, proceed to windward by series of such courses; (fig.) change one's course, conduct, policy, etc. **tack'er** *n.*

tack[2] (tăk) *n.* Foodstuff (chiefly in **hard'tack**).

tack·le (tăk'*e*l) *n.* 1. Apparatus, utensils, instruments, appliances, esp. for fishing or other sport. 2. (naut.) Rope(s) and pulley block(s) or other mechanism for hoisting weights etc.; windlass with its ropes and hooks; running rigging of ship. 3. (football etc.) Tackling; each of two players (**right ~, left ~**), with positions next to the ends in the line. **tackle** *v.* (**tack·led, tack·ling**). Grapple with, grasp, lay hold of, with endeavor to hold, manage, or overcome; (football etc.) seize and stop, obstruct, intercept (opponent in possession of ball). **tack'ler** *n.*

tack·y (tăk'ē) *adj.* (**tack·i·er, tack·i·est**). (of gum, nearly dry varnish, etc.) Slightly sticky or adhesive; (colloq.) seedy, shabby, or dowdy in appearance. **tack'i·ness** *n.*

ta·co (tah'kō) *n.* (pl. **-cos**). Mexican food of meat etc. in folded or rolled tortilla.

tac·o·nite (tăk'*o*nīt) *n.* Low-grade iron ore obtained from fine-grained, tough, sedimentary rock of quartz, hematite, and magnetite.

tact (tăkt) *n.* Intuitive perception of what is fitting, esp. of the right thing to do or say; adroitness in dealing with persons or circumstances. **tact'ful** *adj.* **tact'ful·ly** *adv.* **tact'ful·ness** *n.* **tact'less** *adj.* **tact'less·ly** *adv.* **tact'less·ness** *n.*

tac·tic (tăk'tĭk) = TACTICS.

tac·ti·cal (tăk'tĭk*a*l) *adj.* Of tactics; adroitly planning or planned; **~ bombing**, aerial bombing carried out in immediate support of military or naval operations. **tac'ti·cal·ly** *adv.*

tac·ti·cian (tăktĭsh'*a*n) *n.* One versed or skilled in tactics.

tac·tics (tăk'tĭks) *n.* (considered sing. or pl.). Art or science of deploying and maneuvering air, military, or naval forces, esp. when in contact with the enemy (contrasted with strategy); (as pl.) procedure, device(s) for gaining some end.

tac·tile (tăk'tĭl, -tīl) *adj.* Of, perceived by, connected with, sense of touch; (painting etc.) appealing to sense of touch, producing effect of solidity. **tac·til·i·ty** (tăktĭl'ĭtē) *n.*

tac·tu·al (tăk'cho͞o*a*l) *adj.* Tactile. **tac'tu·al·ly** *adv.*

tad·pole (tăd'pōl) *n.* Larva of frog or toad, from time it leaves egg until it loses gills and tail, esp. early stage of this when it seems to consist simply of round head with a tail; larva of similar appearance in other animals.

Ta·dzhik·i·stan (t*a*jĭk'ĭstăn; *Russ.* tahjĭkĭstahn'), **Ta·jik·stan** (tah'jĭkstahn; *Russ.* tahjĭkstahn'). Constituent republic of U.S.S.R. (properly *Tadzhik Soviet Socialist Republic*), in central Asia; Capital, Dushanbe.

taf·fe·ta (tăf'*e*t*a*) *n.* Fine plain-woven usu. glossy fabric of silk or

Facing: Known as the Tibet of the U.S.S.R. with one peak exceeding 24,000 ft., ***Tadzhikistan*** *is on the borders of Afghanistan and China. Many of the people are of Iranian ancestry and raise livestock and grow cotton.*

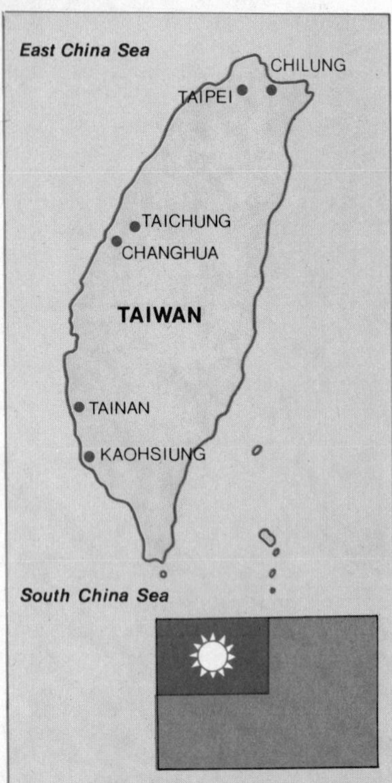

*Helped by massive aid from the U.S.A., the government of Chiang Kai-Shek was established on **Taiwan** (formerly Formosa) in 1949. Since then, it has developed a large export market.*

other material. [Pers. *tāftah* (*tāftan* twist)]

taf·fy (tăf′ē) *n.* Chewy candy of brown sugar or molasses, sometimes containing chopped nuts.

Taft (tăft), **William Howard** (1857–1930). Amer. politician; first civil governor of the Philippines, 1901–04; U.S. secretary of war, 1904–08; 27th U.S. president, 1909–13; chief justice of the U.S. Supreme Court, 1921–30.

tag[1] (tăg) *n.* Metal etc. point at end of shoelace; small hanging piece or part, as loop at back of boot for pulling it on, ragged lock of wool on sheep, address label for tying on, any loose or ragged end; brief and usu. familiar, trite or much-used quotation; refrain or catch of song etc., last words of speech in play etc.; ~ **team**, team of two wrestlers, each of whom competes against either wrestler on similar team, competitors in ring switching with those outside by tagging them. **tag** *v.* (**tagged, tag·ging**). Furnish with a tag; join (*to, onto, together*); find rhymes for (verses), string (rhymes) together; follow closely, trail or drag behind; (in baseball) to touch with the ball or with the ball held in the glove. **tag′ger** *n.*

tag[2] (tăg) *n.* Children's game in which one pursues the others until he touches one, who in turn becomes pursuer.

Ta·ga·log (tahgah′lŏg, tăg′*a*lŏg) *n.* (pl. **-logs**, collect. **-log**). (Member, language) of principal Malayan people of Philippine Islands. [native name, f. *taga* native, *ilog* river]

Ta·gore (t*a*gōr′, -gōr′, tah′gōr), **Sir Ra·bin·dra·nath** (r*a*bēn′-dr*a*naht) (1861–1941). Indian poet and writer; awarded Nobel Prize for literature 1913.

Ta·hi·ti (t*a*hē′tē, tah-). One of the Society Islands in the S. Pacific, a French protectorate since 1843. **Ta·hi·tian** (tahē′sh*a*n) *adj.* & *n.*

Tai = THAI.

tail[1] (tāl) *n.* 1. Hindmost part of animal, esp. when prolonged beyond rest of body; **turn** ~, run away. 2. Thing, part, appendage, resembling this, as luminous train of comet, twisted or braided tress of hair, stem of musical note, pendent posterior part of man's coat, esp. dress coat; appendage of string and paper at lower end of kite; rear end of column, procession, etc.; rear part of aircraft; reverse side of coin; (pl.) full-dress suit. 3. **tail′board**, usu. hinged or removable board at back of cart, truck, etc.; **tail end**, extreme end, concluding part; **tail′gate**, lower gate of canal lock; hinged or removable part of delivery truck, van, station wagon, etc.; (*v.i.*) drive too close behind another vehicle; **tail′light**, light carried at back of train, cycle, car, etc.; **tail′piece**, piece forming tail; triangular piece of wood to which lower ends of strings are fastened in violin etc.; small decoration at end of book, chapter, etc.; **tail′pipe**, exhaust pipe of motor vehicle; **tail skid**, small skid or runner supporting tail of aircraft in contact with ground; **tail′spin**, (aviation) kind of spinning dive; **tail′stock**, one of two parts (**tailstock** and **headstock**) that hold work in a lathe; **tail′wind**, wind blowing in same direction as course of aircraft etc. **tail** *v.* Furnish with tail; follow (person) inconspicuously to keep watch on him; cut or pull off what is regarded as tail, esp. of plant or fruit; ~ **away, off**, fall away in tail or straggling line; diminish and cease. **tail′less** *adj.* **tail′less·ness** *n.* **tail′like** *adj.*

tail[2] (tāl) *n.* (law) Limitation of freehold estate or fee to a person and (particular class of) the heirs of his body (freq. in phrase **in** ~). **tail** *adj.* Limited to specified heirs; being in tail.

tai·lor (tā′l*er*) *n.* Maker of men's outer garments, or of such women's garments as have similar character, e.g. coats, suits, riding clothes; **tailor-made**, made by tailor, usu. with little ornament and with special attention to exact fit. **tailor** *v.* Do tailor's work; make (garments etc.) by tailor's methods; furnish with clothes, dress. **tai′lored** *adj.* (esp., of women's clothes) Made in plain fitted style.

taint (tānt) *n.* Spot, trace, of decay, corruption, or disease; corrupt condition, infection. ~ *v.* Introduce corruption or disease into, infect, be infected. **taint′less** *adj.* **taint′less·ly** *adv.* **taint′less·ness** *n.*

*In various legal capacities, **W. H. Taft** aroused controversy due to his handling of labor–management disputes, especially secondary boycotts and the right of workers to strike.*

Memorable for the visit of the 'Bounty' and Gauguin's paintings, **Tahiti** is now the base for French nuclear tests. These provoke complaints from N.Z., Australia and other Pacific countries.

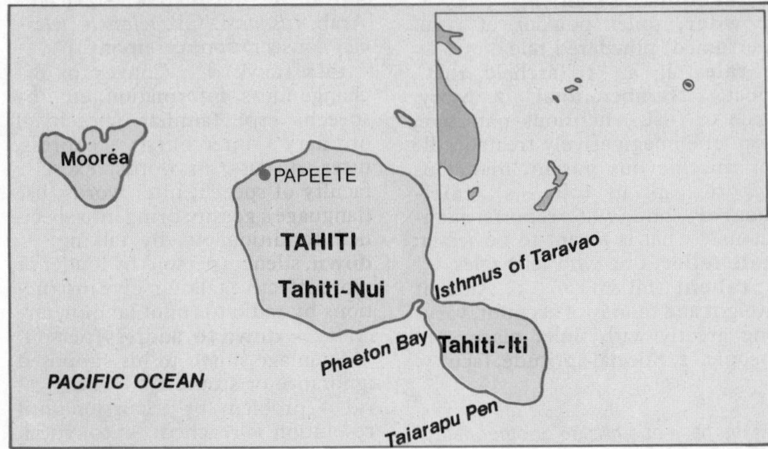

Tai·pei (tī'pā'; *Chin.* tī'bā'). Capital of Taiwan, at N. end of Taiwan Island.

Tai·wan (tī'wahn'). (formerly Formosa) Island in the Pacific Ocean, separated from the SE. coast of mainland China by ~ **Strait**; in 1949, Chiang Kai-Shek fled mainland Communists, establishing his Nationalist government there; Taiwan lost U.N. recognition as representing China, 1971, to the People's Republic of China; capital, Taipei.

Ta·jik·stan = TADZHIKISTAN.

Taj Ma·hal (tahj' mahahl', tazh'). Marble mausoleum of great splendor and beauty at Agra, India, built (1631–45) by the Mogul Emperor Shah-Jahan in memory of his favorite wife. [corrupt. of Pers. *Mumtāz-i-Mahall*, title of wife of Shah-Jahan, f. *mumtāz* distinguished, *mahall* abode]

take (tāk) *v.* (**took** pr. to͝ok, **tak·en** pr. tā'ken, **tak·ing**). 1. Seize, grasp; capture; catch; (cards) win (trick); (of plant, seed, etc.) germinate, begin to grow; catch fancy or affection of; (of inoculation etc.) be successful or effective; **be taken ill**, fall ill. 2. Receive into body, as medicine, food, drink, etc.; bring or receive (person) into some relation to oneself; appropriate, enter into possession (of); secure, get, receive, by payment, esp. regularly, as a periodical; assume, charge oneself with, undertake; perform, discharge (function, service, etc.); range oneself on, ally oneself with, (side, in contest etc.); (gram.) have as proper construction; **take it**, (colloq.) endure punishment, affliction, etc., with fortitude. 3. Choose, adopt, take into use or employment; proceed or begin to deal with in some way; proceed to occupy; use (up), consume; need (specified size) *in* shoes, gloves, etc. 4. Obtain, derive, from some source or by some process; write (*down*) (notes, spoken words, etc.); obtain likeness, esp. by photography. 5. Receive, accept, enjoy (pleasure, money, wager, hint, etc.); exact (vengeance etc.); accept as true or correct, or in some specified way; face and attempt to get over, through, etc., negotiate; admit, absorb, contract, be affected by (moisture, infection, dye, a quality, etc.). 6. Grasp with mind, apprehend, understand; suppose, assume; regard, consider (*as*); feel, experience (emotion etc.). 7. Perform, do (action, movement, etc.); raise, make (objection, exception, etc.). 8. Carry, convey, cause to go with one; **take from**, carry away, remove, deprive or rid person or thing of. 9. **take aim**, aim (*at*); **take charge**, make oneself responsible; **take care**, be careful; **take care of**, be careful of; be in charge of; deal with; **take fire**, become kindled or ignited, catch fire; **take hold** (**of**), grasp, seize,

The **tailorbird** is named after its method of stitching together leaves with fibers so that they form a pouch in which a cradle type of nest can be made.

take under one's control; **take place**, (esp. of prearranged event) occur; **take possession**, enter into possession (*of*). 10. **take after**, resemble (person, esp. parent) in character, feature, etc.; **take away**, remove, subtract, detract *from*; **take back**, retract (words); **take down**, write down; humiliate, humble; pull down (building), lower, carry or cut down; **take in**, admit, receive (lodgers etc.); undertake (work) to be done in one's own house; conduct into house, room, etc.; include, comprise; reduce (garment etc.) to smaller compass, furl (sail); understand, comprehend; deceive, cheat; believe (false statement); **take off**, remove; conduct away; deduct (part of price); mimic; jump, spring; (of aircraft or pilot) leave ground etc. at beginning of flight; **take′off** (*n.*), caricature; spot from which jump etc. is made; aircraft's leaving of ground etc.; **take on**, undertake (work, responsibility, etc.); play (person) *at* game; (colloq.) show violent emotion, be greatly agitated; **take out**, cause to come out; bring or convey out; remove; accept payment or compensation *in* specified form; procure, get issued (patent, insurance policy, etc.); buy (food etc.) at lunch counter, diner, etc. for eating elsewhere; **take it out of**, exhaust, fatigue; exact satisfaction from; **take over**, succeed to possession or control of; **take′over** (*n.*), assumption of control (esp. of business etc.); **take to**, begin, begin to occupy oneself with; conceive a liking for; **take up**, lift up; shorten (garment); absorb; occupy, engage; enter upon; pursue (occupation, subject, inquiry, etc.); secure, fasten; accept (challenge); subscribe for, subscribe amount of (shares, loan, etc.); **take up with**, begin to consort with. **take** *n.* Amount (of fish, game, etc.) taken or caught; takings; (cinemat.) scene or part of scene photographed at one time without stopping camera, photographing of this.

tak·en: see TAKE.

tak·er (tā′ker) *n.* (esp.) One who takes a bet.

tak·ing (tā′kĭng) *n.* Act of person or thing that takes; thing that is taken; (pl.) business receipts. ~ *adj.* Attractive, captivating, charming. **tak′ing·ly** *adv.*

tal·a·poin (tăl′*a*poin) *n.* 1. Buddhist priest or monk. 2. Small W. African monkey (*Cercopithecus talapoin*).

talc (tălk) *n.* Soft, translucent, white, green, or gray mineral (a hydrated magnesium silicate) with greasy feel and shining luster, freq. occurring in broad flat plates, and used in making soap, toilet powder, paper, lubricants, etc.; talcum powder.

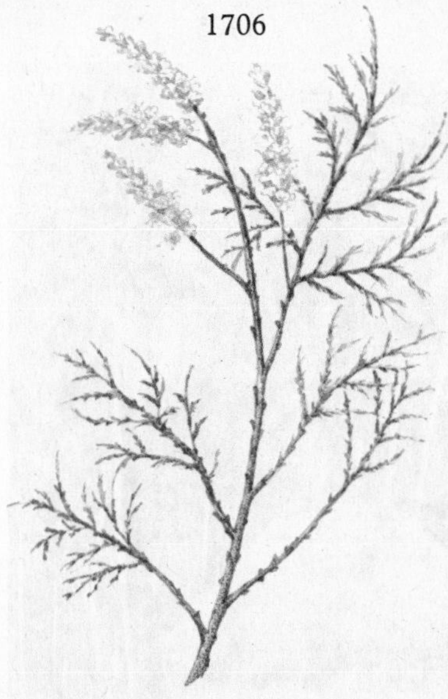

*Native to India, the **tamarisk** is now acclimatized in England where it has proved invaluable for stabilizing sand dunes. Its galls were used for tannin and a dye in Asian countries.*

tal·cum (tăl′k*u*m) *n.* Talc; ~ **powder**, toilet powder of (usu. perfumed) powdered talc.

tale (tāl) *n.* 1. (archaic, rhet., poet.) Number, total. 2. Story, true or (usu.) fictitious narrative, esp. one imaginatively treated; idle or mischievous gossip, malicious report (esp. in **tell ~s**); **tale′-bearer**, one who reports maliciously what is meant to be secret; **tale′teller**, one who tells tales.

tal·ent (tăl′*e*nt) *n.* 1. Ancient weight and money of account, varying greatly with time, place, and people. 2. Special aptitude, faculty, gift (from the parable of the talents, Matt. 25); high mental ability; ~ **scout**, person engaged in searching for talented people, esp. theatrical etc. performers; ~ **show**, theatrical show in which amateur or unknown performers display abilities as actors, singers, dancers, etc., with hope of winning recognition. **tal′-ent·ed** *adj.*

*At the base of a hillside or other natural declivity, a **talus** (or scree) will accumulate from the eroded material of the hill. The angle at which this material lies is known as the angle of repose.*

ta·les (tā′lēz) (considered sing. or pl.) *n.* (law) Writ for summoning jurors, list of persons who may be so summoned, to supply deficiency; **tales·man** (tālz′m*a*n, tā′-lēz-) (pl. **-men** pr. -m*e*n), person so summoned. [L. *tales de circumstantibus* such of the bystanders, first words of the writ]

tal·i·pes (tăl′*i*pēz) *n.* Clubfoot. **tal·i·ped** (tăl′*i*pĕd) *adj.* & *n.* Clubfooted (person).

tal·is·man (tăl′ĭsm*a*n, -ĭz-) *n.* (pl. **-mans**). Charm, amulet, esp. stone, ring, etc., inscribed with astrological figures or characters and supposed to protect its wearer or bring him good fortune. **tal·-is·man·ic** (tălĭsmăn′ĭk, -ĭz-) *adj.* [Arab. *tilsam*, f. Gk. *telesma* (*telesmos* consecration, ceremony)]

talk (tawk) *v.* Convey or exchange ideas, information, etc., by speech, esp. familiar speech of ordinary intercourse; express, utter, discuss, in words; exercise faculty of speech; utter words; use (language); gossip; bring into specified condition etc. by talking; ~ **down**, silence (person) by louder or more effective talking; give instructions by radio to (pilot landing aircraft); ~ **down to**, address (person) in language suited to his supposed ignorance or stupidity; ~ **out**, get rid of (problem) by discussion until resolution is reached; ~ **to**, speak to, (colloq.) reprove; **talk′ing-to** (*n.*, pl. **-tos**), (colloq.) scolding. **talk** *n.* Conversation; short address or lecture in conversational style, esp. one broadcast by radio; theme of gossip.

talk·a·thon (taw′k*a*thŏn) *n.* Prolonged public discussion.

talk·a·tive (taw′k*a*tĭv) *adj.* Fond of talking. **talk′a·tive·ly** *adv.* **talk′a·tive·ness** *n.*

talk·ie (taw′kē) *n.* (archaic slang) Sound motion picture. [abbrev. of talking picture]

talk·ing (taw′kĭng) *n.* & *adj.* ~ **book**, recording of reading of book, magazine, etc., for use by blind people; ~ **point**, topic for discussion or argument.

tall (tawl) *adj.* 1. (of persons) Of more than average height; (of things) high, lofty, higher than the average or than surrounding objects; of specified height; **tall′-boy**, tall chest of drawers, occas. in 2 sections, one standing above the other. 2. (of talk etc.) High-flown; exaggerated, highly colored; **tall**

drink, drink served in tall glass; **tall order**, unreasonable or excessive demand. **tall'ish** *adj.* **tall'ness** *n.*

Tal·la·has·see (tălahăs'ē). Capital of Florida, in the NW. part.

Tal·linn (tahl'lĭn). Seaport and capital of Estonian S.S.R., on the Gulf of Finland opposite Helsinki.

tal·lith (tah'lĭs; *Heb.* tahlēt') *n.* (pl. **ta·li·thim** pr. tahlē'sĭm; *Heb.* tahlētēm'). Scarf worn by Jews, esp. at prayer.

tal·low (tăl'ō) *n.* Fat of animals, esp. of sheep and cattle, separated by melting and clarifying and used for making candles, soap, etc. **tal'low·y** *adj.*

tal·ly (tăl'ē) *n.* (pl. **-lies**). 1. (obs.) Piece of wood scored across with notches representing amount of debt or payment and split lengthwise across notches, each party keeping half; account so kept. 2. Score, reckoning. 3. Distinguishing mark, ticket, label, attached to thing for identification etc. 4. Corresponding thing, counterpart, duplicate. ~ *v.* (**-lied, -ly·ing**). Record, reckon, by tally; agree, correspond (*with*).

Tal·mud (tahl'mo͝od, -m*u*d, tăl'-) *n.* Body of Jewish civil and ceremonial law, comprising the MISHNAH and the GEMARA. **Tal·mud·ic** (tahlmo͝od'ĭk, -mo͞o'dĭk, -mū'-, -mŭd'ĭk, tăl-), **Tal·mud'i·cal** *adjs.* **Tal·mud·ist** (tahl'm*u*dĭst, tăl'-) *n.*

tal·on (tăl'*o*n) *n.* Claw, esp. of bird of prey; (pinochle etc.) remainder of pack after cards have been dealt; shoulder of bolt against which key presses in turning it; handle end of sword blade.

ta·lus[1] (tā'l*u*s) *n.* (pl. **-lus·es**). Slope, esp. (fort.) sloping side of wall or earthwork; (geol.) mass of rock debris gathering at foot of a cliff.

ta·lus[2] (tā'l*u*s) *n.* (pl. **-li** pr. -lī). (anat.) Ankle bone; (path.) form of clubfoot with toes drawn up and heel resting on ground.

tam (tăm) = TAM-O'-SHANTER.

ta·ma·le (t*a*mah'lē) *n.* Mexican dish of cornmeal with pieces of meat or chicken, red pepper, etc., wrapped in corn husks and baked or steamed.

tam·a·rack (tăm'*e*răk) *n.* (Timber of) any of various Amer. larches, esp. *Larix laricina* of northern N. Amer.

tam·a·rind (tăm'*e*rĭnd) *n.* Large tropical tree (*Tamarindus indica*) with hard heavy timber, dark green pinnate leaves, and racemes of fragrant red-streaked yellow flowers; fruit of this, brown pods with seeds embedded in brown or reddish-black acid pulp, used in medicine, as relish, etc. [Arab. *tamr-hindī* date of India]

tam·a·risk (tăm'*e*rĭsk) *n.* Plant of genus *Tamarix*, esp. *T. gallica*, a graceful evergreen shrub or small tree with slender feathery branches and minute leaves, growing in sandy places.

tam·bour (tăm'boor) *n.* 1. Circular frame consisting of one hoop fitting closely within another, over which material is stretched for embroidering; embroidery worked on it; tambour lace. 2. Drum. 3. (fort.) Small defensive work of palisades, earth, etc., defending entrance or passage. ~ *v.* Decorate, embroider, on tambour.

tam·bou·rin (tam'bo͝orĭn) *n.* (pl. **-rins**). Long narrow drum used in Provence; (music for) dance accompanied by this.

tam·bou·rine (tămb*e*rēn') *n.* Musical instrument consisting of a wooden hoop with a skin stretched over one side and pairs of small cymbals in slots around the circumference, played by shaking, striking with knuckles, or drawing finger(s) across parchment.

Tam·bur·laine (tăm'b*e*rlān), **Tam·er·lane** (tăm'*e*rlān). *Timur Lenk* or *Lang* "lame Timur" (c1335–1405), Tartar conqueror of much of Asia and E. Europe; ancestor of the Mogul dynasty in India.

tame (tām) *adj.* (**tam·er, tam·est**). 1. (of animals, birds, etc.) Made tractable, domesticated, not wild; (colloq., of land or plant) cultivated. 2. Submissive, spiritless, insipid. **tame'ly** *adv.* **tame'ness** *n.* **tame** *v.t.* (**tamed, tam·ing**). Make gentle and tractable, break in, domesticate (wild beast, bird, etc.); subdue, curb, humble, reduce to submission. **tam'a·ble, tame'a·ble** *adjs.* **tam'er** *n.*

Tam·il (tăm'ĭl, tŭm'-) *n.* (pl.

Found only in the Americas and ranging in size from a tit to a finch, the 200 species of ***tanager*** *are better known for the vivid plumage of the males, especially the paradise variety.*

*Brilliantly conceived and admirably made, this ceramic lion from the **T'ang** dynasty in China demonstrates the degree of art and craftsmanship achieved in the seventh century A.D.*

*A Victor bomber, converted for use in air-to-air refuelling, acts as a **tanker** or 'mother' for the two Lightnings which carefully maneuver until the fuel supply line is attached.*

-ils, collect. **-il**). Member of people of SE. India and part of Sri Lanka; Dravidian language of this people.

Tam·ma·ny (tăm′*a*nē). Fraternal and benevolent society of New York City, founded in 1789, developed out of one of the earlier patriotic societies; political organization of the Democratic Party, identified with this society and notorious in 19th c. for corruption; ~ **Hall**, any of the successive buildings used as headquarters of Tammany; (transf.) members of Tammany. [f. name of Indian chief (late 17th c.) noted for wisdom and friendliness toward whites, and regarded (*c*1770–90) as "patron saint" of Pennsylvania and other northern colonies]

Tam·muz (tah′mo͞oz, tah-mo͞oz′). 1. (myth.) Syrian or Babylonian deity, god of agriculture and flocks, lover of Astarte, who brought him back from the lower world after his death. 2. Tenth month of Jewish calendar.

tam-o'-shan·ter (tăm *o* shăn′-*ter*) *n.* Round woolen or cloth cap of Scottish origin, with flat baggy top much wider than headband. [f. hero of Robert Burns's poem "Tam o'Shanter"]

tamp (tămp) *v.t.* Plug (blast hole etc.) with clay above firing charge; ram down with repeated light strokes.

tamp·er (tăm′p*er*) *v.i.* ~ **with**, meddle with; alter, corrupt, pervert. **tam′per·er** *n.*

tam·pi·on (tăm′pē*o*n) *n.* Plug for top of organ pipe; plug or cover for muzzle of gun.

tam·pon (tăm′pŏn) *n.* Plug inserted in wound, body cavity, or orifice, to stop hemorrhage or absorb secretions. ~ *v.t.* Plug with tampon.

tan[1] (tăn) *v.* (**tanned, tan·ning**). 1. Convert (skin or hide) into leather by soaking in a bath containing oak bark or other substance rich in tannin, or by any other process. 2. Make, become, brown by exposure to sun or weather. 3. (colloq.) Beat, thrash. ~ *n.* 1. Crushed or bruised bark of oak or other trees, used for tanning (also **tan′bark**); spent bark from tan pits used for covering riding track, circus ring, etc.; track etc. covered with this. 2. Brown color of tan; bronzed color of skin that has been exposed to sun or weather. ~ *adj.* (**tan·ner, tan·nest**). Of the color of tan or tanned leather, yellowish or reddish brown.

tan[2] *abbrev.* Tangent.

tan·a·ger (tăn′*a*j*er*) *n.* Amer. bird of family Thraupidae, with numerous species, in which males are usu. brightly colored.

Ta·nan·a·rive (tănănărēv′). Now known as Antananarivo. Capital of the Democratic Republic of Madagascar, in the E. central part.

tan·dem (tăn′d*e*m) *adv.* (of horses in harness) One behind the other; **drive** ~, drive horses so harnessed. **tandem** *n.* 1. Carriage driven tandem. 2. Bicycle

*The 'Torrey Canyon' oil **tanker** was one of the first of the larger vessels used in this service to come to grief. Its wreck provided a warning of the pollution hazards that can result.*

with 2 or more seats one behind the other, also called ~ **bicycle.** [punning use of L. *tandem* at length (of time)]

Ta·ney (taw′nē), **Roger Brooke** (1777–1864). Amer. jurist; U.S. secretary of the treasury, 1833–34, and chief justice of U.S. Supreme Court, 1836–64.

Tang, T'ang (tahng). Name of dynasty that ruled in China 618–906 A.D., a period noted for territorial conquest and great wealth, and regarded as golden age of Chinese poetry and art; hence, porcelain etc. of this period.

tang (tăng) *n.* 1. Point, projection, esp. extension of knife, chisel, or other metal tool or instrument by which it is secured to its handle. 2. Strong or penetrating taste or smell; characteristic quality; trace, touch, suggestion, *of* something. ~ *v.t.* Furnish with tang. **tang·y** (tăng′ē) *adj.* (**tang·i·er, tang·i·est**).

Tan·gan·yi·ka (tăng*a*nyē′k*a*, tăngg*a*n-). Mainland part of TANZANIA; **Lake** ~, lake in E. central Africa, 420 mi. (676 km) long and 30–45 mi. (48–72 km) wide, covering 12,700 sq. mi., (32,893 sq. km) and forming part of the border between Tanzania and Zaire; world's longest freshwater lake. **Tan·gan·yi′kan** *adj.* & *n.*

tan·ge·lo (tăn′jelō) *n.* (pl. **-los**). Hybrid between tangerine and grapefruit.

tan·gent (tăn′jent) *adj.* Of (the nature of) a tangent; (of line or surface) touching a line or surface, but not intersecting it. ~ *n.* 1. Straight line tangent to a curve; **fly, go,** etc., **off at a** ~, diverge suddenly from previous course or direction, or from matter in hand. 2. (trig., function of angle in right-angled triangle) Ratio of side opposite given acute angle to side opposite the other (abbrev. tan). 3. Upright piece that strikes string of clavichord. **tan′gen·cy** *n.* **tan·gen′tial** (tănjĕn′sh*a*l) *adj.* **tan·gen′tial·ly** *adv.* **tan·gen·ti·al·i·ty** (tănjĕnshēăl′ĭtē) *n.*

tan·ge·rine (tănj*e*rēn′) *n.* Small flattened deep-colored sweet-scented variety of orange from Tangier; deep orange-yellow color of this. ~ *adj.* Of color of tangerine.

tan·gi·ble (tăn′j*i*bel) *adj.* That can be touched, perceptible by touch; real, objective, definite. **tan′gi·ble·ness, tan·gi·bil·i·ty** (tănj*i*bĭl′ĭtē) *ns.* **tan′gi·bly** *adv.*

Tan·gier (tănjēr′). Seaport in N. Morocco, NW. Africa, at the SW. end of the Strait of Gibraltar.

tan·gle (tăng′g*e*l) *v.* (**-gled, -gling**). Intertwine, become twisted or involved, in confused mass; entangle; complicate; (colloq.) quarrel, argue, or fight. ~ *n.* Tangled condition or mass. **tan′gler** *n.*

tan·go (tăng′gō) *n.* (pl. **-gos**). Slow dance of central African origin, brought by Africans to Central Amer. and then to Argentina, where it was influenced by European rhythms, fashionable in ballrooms since *c*1910; music for this, in $\frac{2}{4}$ time. ~ *v.i.* Dance the tango.

tang·y: see TANG.

tank (tăngk) *n.* 1. Large vessel for liquid, gas, etc.; ~ **car**, railroad car with large tank for carrying liquids; ~ **truck**, truck for transporting large amounts of liquids or gases. 2. (mil.) Armored car carrying guns and mounted on

*Although first conceived in the late 19th century, the **tank** as a weapon of war was never seriously produced until Winston Churchill took the responsibility to order some during the 1914-18 war. The term 'tank' was coined as a code name, for security purposes.*

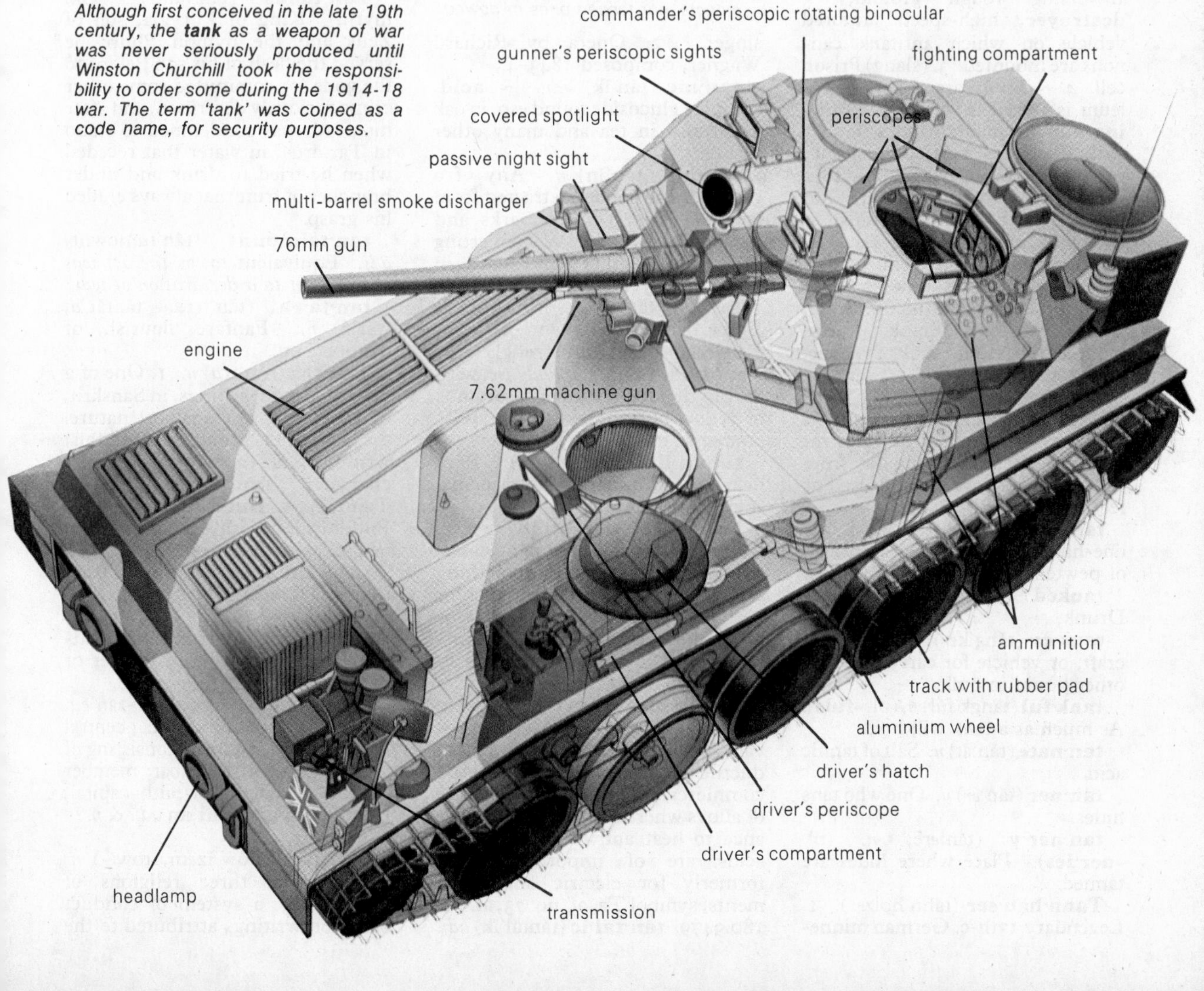

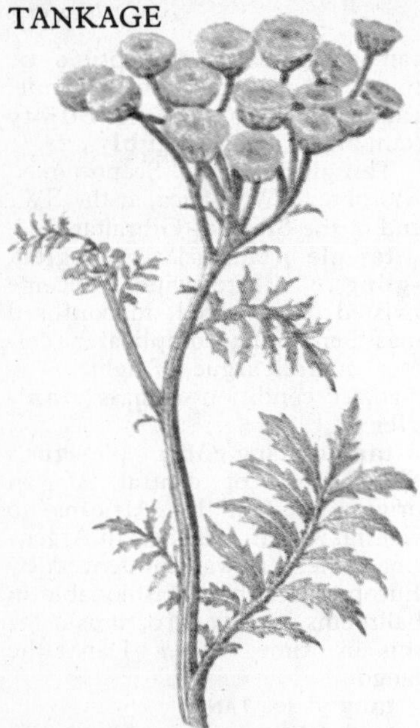

***Tansy** oil is distilled from the flowers and leaves of a plant related to the chrysanthemum. It was considered an effective remedy for intestinal worms but is toxic if over-used.*

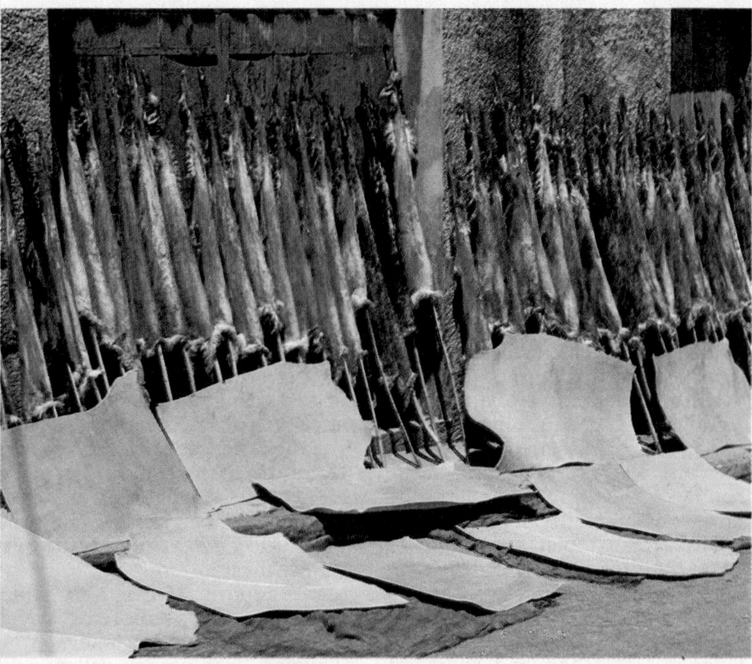

*Raw goatskins and tanned oxhides being dried in the sun outside a Cretan **tannery.** The drying process is essential if raw hides are not to be attacked by insects, nor tanned ones mildewed.*

caterpillar tracks, capable of traversing rough ground; ~ **destroyer**, high-speed armored vehicle on which antitank cannons are mounted. 3. (slang) Prison cell. 4. ~ **farm**, area where petroleum is stored in tanks; ~ **farming**, growing plants in tanks of water without soil; ~ **suit**, simple, one-piece swimsuit for women; ~ **top**, shirt similar to undershirt but having wider shoulder straps; ~ **town**, formerly stopping place on railroad where trains refilled their boilers with water; now small or unimportant town. **tank** *v.t.* Store, put, or process in tank; ~ **up**, (colloq.) fill gasoline tank of vehicle; (slang) drink heavily.

tank·age (tăng′kĭj) *n.* 1. (Charge for) storage in tanks; cubic contents of (tanks). 2. Animal residues remaining after rendering fat from slaughterhouse waste, and used as fertilizer or feed.

tank·ard (tăng′kerd) *n.* Large one-handled drinking vessel, esp. of pewter or silver, freq. with lid.

tanked (tăngkt) *adj.* (slang) Drunk.

tank·er (tăng′k*er*) *n.* Ship, aircraft, or vehicle for carrying oil or other liquid in bulk.

tank·ful (tăngk′f*u*l) *n.* (pl. **-fuls**). As much as a tank will hold.

tan·nate (tăn′āt) *n.* Salt of tannic acid.

tan·ner (tăn′*er*) *n.* One who tans hides.

tan·ner·y (tăn′*er*ē) *n.* (pl. **-ner·ies**). Place where hides are tanned.

Tann·häu·ser (tahn′hoiz*er*). 1. Legendary 13th-c. German minnesinger. 2. Opera by Richard Wagner, composed 1843–4.

tan·nic (tăn′ĭk) *adj.* ~ **acid**, complex glucoside found esp. in oak galls, also in tea and many other plants.

tan·nin (tăn′ĭn) *n.* Any of a group of substances extracted from oak galls and various barks and having the property of converting hides into leather; also used in medicine, dyeing, etc.

tan·sy (tăn′zē) *n.* (pl. **-sies**). Erect herbaceous plant of genus *Tanacetum*, esp. the strongly aromatic bitter tasting *T. vulgare*, with deeply divided leaves and corymbs of yellow buttonlike flowers. [Gk. *athanasia* immortality]

tan·ta·lite (tăn′t*a*līt) *n.* Rare heavy black mineral, the principal source of tantalum.

tan·ta·lize (tăn′t*a*līz) *v.t.* (**-lized, -liz·ing**). Torment, tease, by sight or promise of something desired that is kept out of reach or withheld. **tan·ta·li·za·tion** (tăn-t*a*līzā′sh*o*n), **tan′ta·liz·er** *ns.* **tan′-ta·liz·ing** *adj.* **tan′ta·liz·ing·ly** *adv.* [f. TANTALUS]

tan·ta·lum (tăn′t*a*l*u*m) *n.* (chem.) Rare metallic element of vanadium group, a very hard ductile grayish-white metal, used commercially in the manufacture of alloys where hardness and resistance to heat and to the action of acids are of importance, and formerly for electric lamp filaments; symbol Ta, at. no. 73, at. wt. 180.9479. **tan·tal·ic** (tăntăl′ĭk) *adj.* [f. TANTALUS, with ref. to incapacity of tantalum to absorb acids]

Tan·ta·lus (tăn′t*a*l*u*s). (Gk. myth.) King of Phrygia, son of Zeus and the nymph Pluto; he served the flesh of his son Pelops to the gods (or committed some other crime variously described) and after his death was condemned to stand in Tartarus, in water that receded when he tried to drink and under branches of fruit that always eluded his grasp.

tan·ta·mount (tăn′t*a*mownt) *adj.* Equivalent *to*, as *the act was tantamount to a declaration of war.*

tan·ta·ra (tăn′t*e*r*a*, tăntăr′*a*, -tar̄′*a*) *n.* Fanfare, flourish, of trumpets etc.

Tan·tra (tŭn′tr*a*) *n.* 1. One of a class of Hindu writings, in Sanskrit, of a mystical and magical nature. 2. One of a group of Buddhist writings of somewhat similar character. **Tan′tric** *adj.* Of the Tantras; ~ **Buddhism**, form of Buddhism, with emphasis on magic, practiced esp. in Tibet. **Tan′trism** *n.* Tantric Buddhism. [Sansk. *tantra* loom, doctrine, manual]

tan·trum (tăn′tr*u*m) *n.* Outburst or display of bad temper or petulance.

Tan·za·ni·a (tănz*a*nē′*a*, -zăn′ēa, -zā′nēa). Republic in E. central Africa, formed in 1964, consisting of Tanganyika and Zanzibar; member of the Brit. Commonwealth; capital, Dodoma. **Tan·za·ni′an** *adj.* & *n.*

Tao·ism (dow′ĭz*e*m, tow′-) *n.* One of the three religions of China, orig. a system of conduct based on writings attributed to the

Left: A young woman carries a tray of corn or maize meal from the mill at Ngala in **Tanzania.** Despite a substantial export trade, the majority of the people are subsistence gardeners.

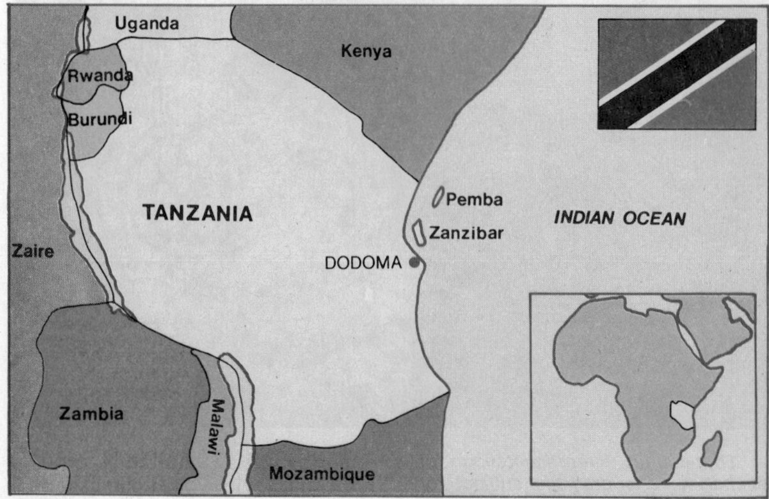

philosopher LAO-TSE and later invested with magical beliefs and a large pantheon. **Tao'ist** *n.* [f. Chin. *Tao tê king* "the way and its power"]

tap[1] (tăp) *n.* 1. Hollow or tubular plug with device for shutting off or controlling flow, through which liquid or gas can be drawn from pipe, cask, etc.; liquor from a particular tap, particular quality or kind of drink; **on ~**, on draft, ready for immediate use or consumption. 2. Tool in shape of male screw of hard steel, for cutting female screw thread. 3. **tap'room**, room in hotel etc. where liquors are kept on tap; **tap'root**, straight root growing vertically downward, thick at top and tapering to a point; **tap water**, water from a tap, esp. that supplied through system of pipes and taps to house etc. **tap** *v.t.* (**tapped, tap·ping**). 1. Furnish (cask etc.) with tap; pierce (cask, tree, etc.) so as to draw off liquid, draw liquid from (any reservoir); draw off (liquid); (surg.) release (fluid accumulated in body), operate thus on (person); (fig.) broach (subject). 2. Furnish (bolt, hole, etc.) with screw thread. 3. Connect electric circuit to (another circuit), esp. as means of intercepting telegraph or telephone message, stealing current etc. **tap'per** *n.*

tap[2] (tăp) *v.* (**tapped, tap·ping**). 1. Strike lightly; cause (thing) to strike lightly (*against* etc.); strike gentle blow, rap; do tap dancing. 2. Apply metal to (toe or heel of shoe). ~ *n.* 1. Light blow, rap; sound of this; (pl., mil.) signal sounded on drum or bugle for lights out. 2. Piece of leather or metal put on over toe or heel of shoe in shoe repairing. 3. ~ **dance**, dance in which rhythm, esp. in elaborate syncopation, is tapped out with the feet; ~ **dancer, dancing**; ~ **shoes**, shoes with metal plates attached to toes or heels for dancing.

tape (tāp) *n.* 1. Narrow woven strip of cotton etc. used as string for tying garments etc.; piece of tape stretched across race course at finish line. 2. Strip of tape, flexible metal, etc., used as measuring line etc.; paper strip on which messages are printed in tape machine (see below); strip of magnetic material on which sounds etc. are recorded. 3. ~ **deck**, tape recorder without its own amplifier or speaker; ~ **machine**, receiving instrument of recording telegraph system; ~ **measure**, strip of tape or thin flexible metal marked for use as measure; ~ **recorder**, machine for recording and reproducing sounds on magnetic tape; **tape'worm**, any of numerous cestode worms (*Taenia* and allied genera) parasitic in intestines of man and other vertebrates, and having long flat body of numerous propagative segments. **tape** *v.t.* (**taped, tap·ing**). Furnish, measure, join, with tape(s); record on tape.

ta·per (tā'pe*r*) *n.* 1. Slender wax candle; long wick coated with wax for lighting lamp etc. 2. Tapering. ~ *v.* (freq. ~ **off**) Make, become, gradually smaller toward one end; (cause to) grow gradually less. **ta'per·ing·ly** *adv.*

tap·es·try (tăp'ĭstrē) *n.* (pl. **-tries**). Thick handwoven fabric, usu. of wool, with a pictorial or ornamental design formed by the warp threads, these being carried

Though the male weighs up to 800 lb., the ***tapir*** *is defenseless and shy. There are three species present in South America and others in south-east Asian countries.*

back and forth across the parts where their respective colors are needed and not from selvage to selvage; wall-hanging of this; embroidered, painted, or machine-woven fabric imitating or resembling tapestry.

ta·pe·tum (*tapē'tum*) *n.* (pl. **-ta** pr. -*ta*). 1. (zool.) Irregular sector in eyes of certain animals (e.g. cat), which shines owing to absence of black pigment. 2. (bot.) Layer of nutritive tissue, esp. in reproductive organs.

tap·i·o·ca (tăpēō'*ka*) *n.* Starchy granular foodstuff prepared from cassava and used in puddings, as a thickener, etc. [Braz. *tipioca* juice of cassava (*tipi* dregs, *og*, *ók* squeeze out)]

ta·pir (tā'p*er*, tāpēr') *n.* (pl. **ta·pirs, ta·pir**). Hoofed piglike mammal of genus *Tapirus* of tropical Amer. and Malaya, with short flexible proboscis, related to rhinoceros.

tap·pet (tăp'ĭt) *n.* Arm, collar, cam, etc., used in machinery to impart intermittent motion.

tar[1] (tar̄) *n.* Thick viscid inflammable black or dark-colored liquid with heavy resinous or bituminous odor, obtained by distillation of wood, coal, or other organic substance, used for coating and preserving timber, cordage, etc., and as a preservative and antiseptic; source (by distillation) of a number of aromatic hydrocarbons and other substances that are starting materials for the manufacture of numerous chemicals and drugs; substances resembling this; **Tar'heel,** (colloq.) nickname for inhabitant of North Carolina; **tar'macadam** (tar̄măkăd'*a*m), **Tar'mac,** (trademark) roadmaking material of crushed stone, slag, etc., mixed or covered with tar or other bituminous binder; **tar paper,** tar-coated thick paper as building material; **tar sands,** (geol.) sandstone deposits or sands from which bituminous oil can be recovered. **tar** *v.t.* (**tarred, tar·ring**). Cover, smear, with tar; **beat (whale) the ~ out of,** (colloq.) defeat utterly, enfeeble, weaken; **~ and feather,** smear (person) with tar and cover him with feathers, as punishment or indignity.

tar[2] (tar̄) *n.* (colloq.) Sailor. [perh. f. TARPAULIN]

tar·an·tel·la (tărantĕl'*a*) *n.* Rapid whirling dance of S. Italian peasants; music for this; instrumental composition in rhythm of tarantella, now always in $\frac{6}{8}$ time, increasing in speed toward the end.

ta·ran·tu·la (t*a*răn'ch*u*l*a*) *n.* (pl.

A 16th-century representation of Jezebel made a dramatic subject for this ***tapestry.*** *Tapestries were originally woven or embroidered as wall-hangings, and their popularity has varied.*

-las, -lae pr. -lē). Large black S. European spider of genus *Lycosa*, with slight poisonous bite; any of various other large venomous spiders, esp. large hairy spiders, family Theraphosidae, of warm parts of America. [f. *Taranto* in S. Italy]

Ta·ra·wa (tahrah'wah). Capital of Kiribati. Island atoll in N. central Kiribati (previously Gilbert Islands) in the central Pacific Ocean; site of victory by U.S. Marines over Japanese during World War II, November, 1943.

ta·rax·a·cum (t*a*răk's*a*k*u*m) *n.* Plant of genus *T~* of weedy composite herbs, including dandelion, with bitter foliage and usu. yellow flowers; drug prepared from dried roots of dandelion (*T. officinale*) and used as tonic and laxative. [Pers. *talkh chakōk* bitter herb]

tar·boosh (tar̄bōōsh') *n.* Man's

brimless (usu. red) felt etc. cap resembling a fez worn alone or as part of a turban by Muslims in certain countries of E. Mediterranean.

tar·dy (tar̄′dē) *adj.* (**-di·er, -di·est**). Slow-moving, slow, sluggish; late, coming or done late. **tar′di·ly** *adv.* **tar′di·ness** *n.*

tare[1] (tar̄) *n.* Any of various vetches; vetch seed; (bibl.) a noxious weed.

tare[2] (tar̄) *n.* (Allowance made for) weight of wrapping, box, conveyance, etc., in which goods are packed; (chem.) weight of vessel in which substance is weighed. ~ *v.t.* (**tared, tar·ing**). Ascertain, allow for, tare of.

tar·get (tar̄′gĭt) *n.* Mark, esp. with concentric circles around central ring or spot, for shooting at; anything aimed at; disk-shaped railroad signal indicating position of switch.

tar·iff (tăr′ĭf) *n.* 1. List of duties or customs to be paid on imports or exports; such duties collectively; law imposing these; duty on particular class of goods. 2. List or scale of charges at hotel, on railroad, etc. [Arab. *ta'rīf* notification (*'arrafa* notify)]

Tar·mac (tar̄′măk): see TAR[1].

tarn (tar̄n) *n.* Small mountain lake.

tar·na·tion (tar̄nā′shon) *int.* & *n.* (dial. euphemism) Damnation.

tar·nish (tar̄′nĭsh) *v.* Dull or dim luster of, discolor by oxidation etc.; lose luster; (fig.) sully, taint, stain. ~ *n.* Tarnishing, being tarnished; stain, blemish, tarnished coating.

ta·ro (tăr′ō, tar̄′ō) *n.* (pl. **-ros**). Either of two plants of the arum family, *Colocasia esculenta* and *C. antiquorum*, cultivated in Pacific islands and other tropical regions for the starchy edible root; the root of these plants.

tar·ot (tăr′ō, tărō′) *n.* Any of a set of playing cards bearing allegorical representations of vices and virtues and elements of nature, used in fortunetelling.

tar·pau·lin (tar̄paw′lĭn, tar̄′pu-) *n.* Canvas made waterproof by coating or impregnating with tar and used as covering, esp. for ship's hatches, boats, etc.; other waterproof cloth used as covering; sailor's tarpaulin or oilskin hat.

tar·pon (tar̄′pon) *n.* (pl. **-pons,** collect. **-pon**). Large silvery marine game fish (*Tarpon atlanticus*) found in warmer waters of W. Atlantic.

Tar·quin (tar̄′kwĭn). Name of two semilegendary, perhaps Etruscan, kings of ancient Rome, Tarquinius Priscus and Tarquinius Superbus (~ **the Proud**); when the latter was expelled (510 B.C.), the Republic was founded.

tar·ra·gon (tăr′agŏn, -gon) *n.* Plant (*Artemisia dracunculus*) allied to wormwood, with aromatic leaves used for flavoring salads etc.; ~ **vinegar**, vinegar flavored with oil or leaves of tarragon. [Arab. *tarkhōn*, perh. f. Gk. *drakōn* dragon]

tar·ry[1] (tar̄′ē) *adj.* (**-ri·er, -ri·est**). Of, like, smeared or impregnated with, tar. **tar′ri·ness** *n.*

tar·ry[2] (tăr′ē) *v.* (**-ried, -ry·ing**). Remain, stay; wait; delay, be late. **tar′ri·er** *n.*

tar·sal (tar̄′sal) *adj.* Of the TARSUS.

tar·si·er (tar̄′sēer) *n.* Small nocturnal tree-climbing animal of E. Indies with soft fur and large prominent eyes (esp. *Tarsius spectrum*), a primate related to the lemurs. [L. *tarsus*, from formation of its foot]

Tar·sus (tar̄′sus). City in SW. corner of Turkey, home of St. Paul.

tar·sus (tar̄′sus) *n.* (pl. **-si** pr. -sī). 1. (anat.) Ankle, collection of small bones (seven in man) between metatarsus and leg; third segment of bird's leg; (entom.) terminal segment of limb. 2. Tarsal plate, plate of condensed connective tissue stiffening eyelid.

tart[1] (tar̄t) *n.* 1. Small pie containing fruit or other sweetened filling; open-faced pie of same type. 2. (chiefly Brit. slang) Girl, woman, esp. of loose morals; female prostitute.

tart[2] (tar̄t) *adj.* Sharp tasting, sour, acid; cutting, biting. **tart′ly** *adv.* **tart′ness** *n.*

tar·tan (tar̄′tan) *n.* Woolen cloth with stripes of various colors crossing at right angles, esp. in the distinctive plaid of a Highland clan; such pattern; other fabric with similar pattern. ~ *adj.* Made of, checkered like, tartan.

*Nocturnal in behavior and related to the lemurs, the **tarsier** has abnormally large eyes and a very large angle of neck rotation. It lives on insects in the forests of south-east Asian countries.*

Tar·tar (tar̄′ter) *n.* 1. (also **Tatar**) Member of any of numerous, mostly Muslim and Turkic, tribes inhabiting various parts of European and Asiatic Russian, esp. parts of Siberia, Crimea, and N. Caucasus, districts along Volga, etc.; one of the mingled horde of Mongols, Turks, Tartars, etc., who overran E. Europe under Genghis Khan. 2. (usu. **t~**) Violent tempered or intractable or savage person. [Pers. *tātār*; altered to tartar by association with TARTARUS]

tar·tar (tar̄′ter) *n.* 1. Acid potassium tartrate deposited in form of crust in wine casks etc. during fermentation of grape juice; **cream of ~**, purified tartar in form of white crystals, used in cookery; ~ **emetic**, poisonous white crystalline salt, potassium antimonyl tartrate, used in medicine, and in dyeing as mordant. 2. Hard deposit of calcium phosphate from saliva on teeth. **tar′tar·ous** *adj.*

*The genus **Taraxacum** includes the dandelion (left) whose leaves can be used in salads. Other species include one in south-eastern Europe whose latex can be used to make rubber.*

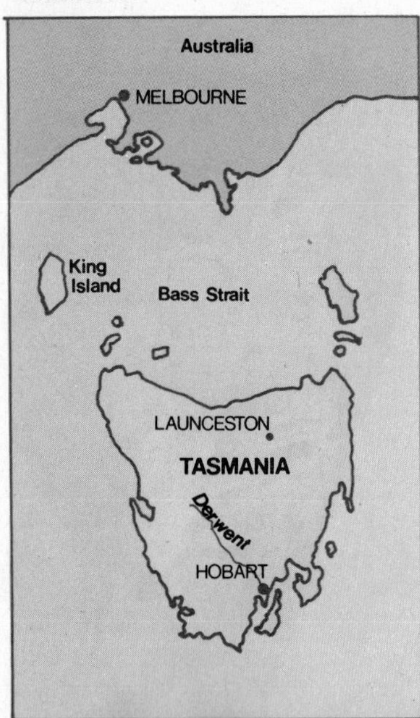

*Separated from the mainland by Bass Strait, **Tasmania** was the second place in Australia to have hydro-electricity. The first aluminum smelter was built on the island, which is also the major producer of orchard fruits.*

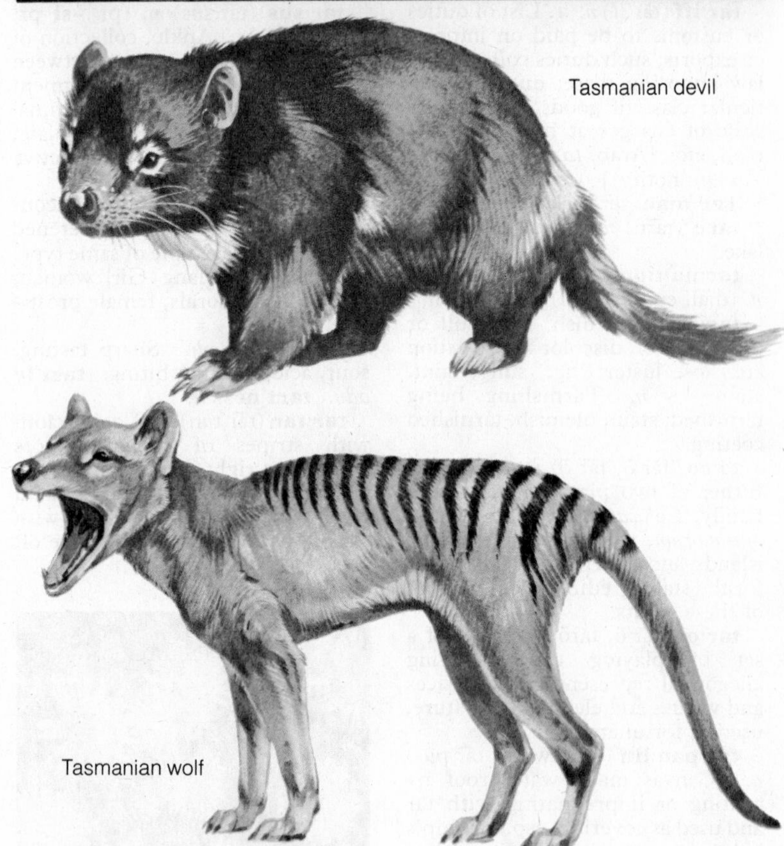

*Since Tasmania was cut off from the mainland by rising seas about 10,000 years ago, its fauna evolved in isolation. The thylacine or **Tasmanian 'wolf'** was the largest marsupial carnivore; the 'devil' is smaller but survives.*

tar·tar, tar·tare (tar̄′ter) **sauce.** Dressing consisting of mayonnaise with capers, chopped gherkins and herbs, etc., served with fish etc.

tar·tar·ic (tar̄tăr′ĭk, -tar̄′-) *adj.* Derived from tartar; ~ **acid,** organic acid present in numerous plants esp. unripe grapes, and used in photography, tanning, manufacture of baking powders and effervescent drinks, etc.

Tar·ta·rus (tar̄′terus). (Gk. myth.) Infernal regions, or lowest part of them, where the Titans were confined; place of punishment in Hades. **Tar·tar·e·an** (tar̄tār′ēan) *adj.*

tar·trate (tar̄′trāt) *n.* Salt of tartaric acid.

Ta·shi La·ma (tah′shē lah′ma). Lama second in rank to Dalai Lama; also called Panchen Lama.

task (tăsk, tahsk) *n.* Piece of work imposed or undertaken as a duty etc.; any work that has to be done; **take to** ~, find fault with, rebuke (*for*); ~ **force,** armed force organized for operations under a unified command; similar group organized by government or business to accomplish designated task; **task′master, task′mistress,** (now usu. fig.) one who sets a task, one who imposes heavy burden or labor. **task** *v.t.* Assign task to; occupy or engage fully, put strain upon.

Tas·ma·ni·a (tăzmā′nēa). State of Australia, consisting of one large and several smaller islands SE. of the continent; discovered 1642 by Abel Janszoon Tasman, Dutch navigator; formerly called Van Diemen's Land; capital, Hobart.

Tas·ma·ni·an (tăzmā′nēan) *adj.* Of Tasmania; ~ **devil,** nocturnal carnivorous marsupial (*Sarcophilus harrisii*) of savage appearance, about size of badger, with coarse black hair with white patches; ~ **wolf,** THYLACINE. **Tasmanian** *n.* Native, inhabitant, of Tasmania.

Tass (tăs, tahs). News agency of U.S.S.R. [*T*(elegrafnoye) *A*(gentsvo) *S*(ovyetskovo) *S*(oyuza)]

tas·sel (tăs′el) *n.* Tuft of loosely hanging threads or cords as ornament for cushion, cap, etc.; tassel-like head of some plants, esp. staminate inflorescence at top of stalk of corn; ribbon sewn into book to be used as bookmark. ~ *v.*

(**-seled, -sel·ing**). Furnish with tassel; remove tassels of (corn) to strengthen plant; put out tassels. [OF., perh. f. L. *taxillus* small die]

taste (tāst) *v.* (**tast·ed, tast·ing**). Learn flavor of (food etc.) by taking it into the mouth; eat small portion of; experience, have experience *of*; (of food etc.) have specified flavor, have flavor *of*. ~ *n.* 1. Sensation excited in taste buds by contact of some soluble things, flavor; ~ **bud**, one of a number of groups of narrow rod-shaped cells in epithelium of mouth, esp. of tongue. 2. Faculty of perceiving flavor of things by allowing them to touch the tongue. 3. Small portion (*of* food etc.) taken as sample. 4. Liking; predilection *for*; **to one's** ~, in the amount or proportion that gives the desired result. 5. Faculty of discerning and enjoying beauty or other excellence esp. in art and literature; sense of what is harmonious or fitting in art, language, or conduct (**in good** ~, manifesting this faculty; **in bad** ~, showing lack of it).

taste·ful (tāst'f*u*l) *adj.* Having, showing, done in, good taste (TASTE *n.* sense 5). **taste'ful·ly** *adv.* **taste'ful·ness** *n.*

taste·less (tāst'lĭs) *adj.* 1. Flavorless, insipid. 2. Lacking physical sense of taste. 3. Lacking in good taste, or critical discernment and appreciation; not in good taste. **taste'less·ly** *adv.* **taste'less·ness** *n.*

tast·er (tās'ter) *n.* (esp.) 1. Person employed to judge quality of tea, wine, etc., by taste; (hist.) person employed to taste food before it was touched by his employer, esp. to guard against poison. 2. Shallow cup for tasting wines etc.

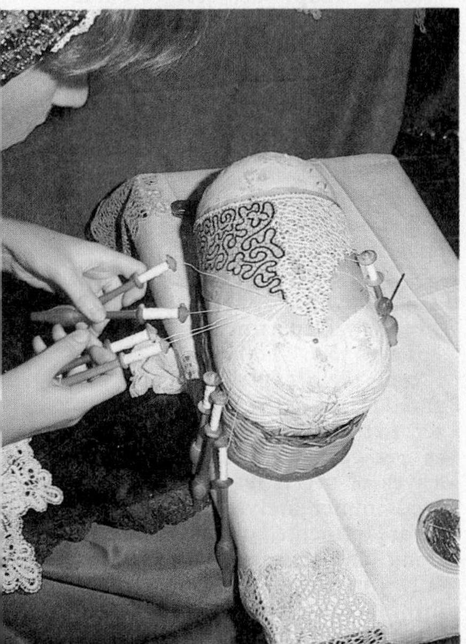

***Tatting** is not widely practiced today, but was for hundreds of years a common cottage industry. In France it is known as la frivolite, and in Italy, occhi.*

tast·y (tās'tē) *adj.* (**tast·i·er, tast·i·est**). (colloq.) Savory, appetizing. **tast'i·ly** *adv.* **tast'i·ness** *n.*

TAT *abbrev.* Thematic Apperception Test.

tat (tăt) *v.* (**tat·ted, tat·ting**). Do tatting; make by tatting.

ta·ta·mi (t*a*tah'mē) *n.* (pl. **-mi, -mis**). Japanese standard-sized straw mat, about 3 by 6 ft., used for sitting on; unit of room size in Japan.

Ta·tar (tah't*er*) = TARTAR.

tat·ter (tăt'*er*) *n.* 1. Rag, irregularly torn piece, of cloth, paper, etc. 2. (pl.) Worn, ragged clothing. **tat'tered** *adj.* Reduced to tatters.

tat·ter·de·mal·ion (tăt*er*dĭmāl'yon, -măl'-) *n.* Ragged fellow, ragamuffin.

tat·ter·sall (tăt'*er*sawl) *n.* Pattern of colored lines forming squares like tartan.

tat·ting (tăt'ĭng) *n.* Kind of notted lace made by hand from thread with small flat shuttle.

tat·tle (tăt'*e*l) *v.i.* (**-tled, -tling**). Gossip idly; inform on wrongdoer; repeat or discuss scandal. ~ *n.* Tattling; gossip. **tat'tler** *n.*

tat·too[1] (tătōō') *n.* (pl. **-toos**). 1. (mil.) Signal by drum or bugle in evening summoning soldiers to quarters; elaboration of this as military entertainment, usu. by torch or other artificial light, with music, troop exercises, etc. 2. Drumming, rapping; drumbeat. **tattoo** *v.* (**-tooed, -too·ing**). Rap quickly and repeatedly. [Du. *tap-toe*, lit. "close the tap" (of the cask)]

*To **tattoo** a man may determine his status in certain societies. This Samoan craftsman has tattooing around his lower torso and more on his legs. Elsewhere, emphasis was on the face.*

tat·too[2] (tătōō') *v.t.* (**-tooed, -too·ing**). Mark (skin) with permanent pattern or design by puncturing it and inserting pigment; make (design) thus. ~ *n.* Tattooing. **tat·too'er, tat·too'ist** *ns.* [Tahitian *tatau*]

tat·ty (tăt'ē) *adj.* (**-ti·er, -ti·est**). Tattered, shabby; vulgar.

tau (taw, tow) *n.* Letter of Greek alphabet (Τ, τ), corresponding to *t*; mark or cross (~ **cross**) in shape of this.

taught: see TEACH.

taunt (tawnt, tahnt) *v.t.* Reproach, upbraid, (*with*) insultingly or contemptuously. ~ *n.* Insulting or provoking gibe; scornful reproach. **taunt'er** *n.* **taunt'ing·ly** *adv.*

tau·rine (tōr'īn, -ĭn) *adj.* Of, like, a bull, bovine; of the zodiacal sign Taurus.

tau·rom·a·chy (tawrŏm'*a*kē) *n.* Bullfight(ing).

Tau·rus (tōr'*u*s). The Bull, a constellation; second sign (♉) of the zodiac, which the sun enters about April 21. **Tau·re·an** (tōr'ē*a*n) *adj.* & *n.*

taut (tawt) *adj.* (of rope etc.) Tightly drawn, not slack; (of ship etc.) trim, neat. **taut'ly** *adv.* **taut'ness** *n.* **taut'en** *v.*

tauto- *prefix.* Same.

tau·tol·o·gy (tawtŏl'*o*jē) *n.* (pl. **-gies**). 1. Needless repetition of same word or phrase, or of same idea etc., in different words, e.g. *arrived one after the other in succession*. 2. Instance of such repetition. **tau·tol·o·gous** (tawtŏl'*o*g*u*s), **tau·to·log·i·cal** (tawt*o*lŏj'ĭk*a*l) *adjs.* **tau·to·log'i·cal·ly** *adv.*

tau·tom·er·ism (tawtŏm'*e*rĭz*e*m) *n.* (chem.) Property possessed by some organic compounds of behaving in different reactions as if they possessed two or more different constitutions. **tau·to·mer** (taw't*o*m*er*) *n.* Compound having property of tautomerism. **tau·to·mer·ic** (tawt*o*mĕr'ĭk) *adj.*

tav·ern (tăv'*e*rn) *n.* Inn or public house; place where liquor is sold.

taw (taw) *v.t.* Make (hides or skins) into leather by steeping in solution of alum and salt.

taw·dry (taw'drē) *adj.* (**-dri·er, -dri·est**). Showy or gaudy without real value. **taw'dri·ly** *adv.* **taw'dri·ness** *n.* [f. *tawdry lace* sold at *St. Audrey's Fair*, i.e. St. Etheldreda's, in Isle of Ely]

taw·ny (taw'nē) *adj.* (**-ni·er, -ni·est**) & *n.* (Of) brown color with preponderance of yellow or orange. **taw'ni·ness** *n.*

tax (tăks) *n.* Contribution levied

on person, property, business, or articles of commerce, for the support of the government and for government services; oppressive or burdensome charge etc.; strain, heavy demand *on*; ~ **assessor**, one who assesses taxes or estimates value of property for taxation or insurance purposes; ~ **collector, tax'gatherer**, collector of taxes; **tax-deductible**, (of expenses) that may be paid out of income before deduction of income tax; **tax-exempt**, exempt from taxes, esp. from income taxes; **tax'payer**, one who pays taxes; building meant to pay expenses of a parcel of land until it can be used more profitably; **tax shelter**, any financial investment made for purpose of incurring expenses, depreciation, etc., in order to reduce one's tax obligations. **tax** *v.* 1. Impose tax on, subject to taxation; make demands on, strain, burden. 2. Accuse, charge (*with*); call to account, take to task. **tax'a·ble** *adj.* **tax·a·tion** (tăksā'sh*o*n) *n.*

tax·i (tăk'sē) *n.* (pl. **tax·is, tax·ies**). Automobile for hire, esp. one fitted with taximeter; **air** ~, aircraft plying for hire. **taxi** *v.* (**tax·ied, tax·i·ing** or **tax·y·ing**). Go, convey, in taxi; (of aircraft)

*The art of **taxidermy** is mostly restricted to preparation of fauna for museums. In the past, it was fashionable for big-game hunters to have their trophies mounted and hung at home.*

run along ground or over surface of water before taking off or after alighting.

tax·i·der·my (tăk'sĭdẽrmē) *n.* Art of preparing and mounting skins of animals with lifelike effect. **tax·i·der·mal** (tăksĭdẽr'm*a*l), **tax·i·der'mic** *adjs.* **tax'i·der·mist** *n.*

tax·i·me·ter (tăk'sēmēt*er*) *n.* Automatic device fitted to taxi indicating fare due.

tax·is (tăk'sĭs) *n.* 1. (biol.) Movement of organism in a particular direction in response to external stimulus (e.g. toward or away from light or heat). 2. (surg.) Manipulative operation to restore displaced part or reduce hernia etc.

tax·on·o·my (tăksŏn'*o*mē) *n.* (biol.) (Laws and principles of) classification. **tax·on'o·mer, tax·on'o·mist** *ns.* **tax·o·nom·ic** (tăks*o*nŏm'ĭk), **tax·o·nom'i·cal** *adjs.* **tax·o·nom'i·cal·ly** *adv.*

Tay·lor (tā'l*er*), **Zachary** (1784–1850). American soldier; 12th president of U.S., 1849–50.

TB, T.B. *abbrevs.* Tubercle bacillus, hence (colloq.) tuberculosis.

Tb *symbol.* Terbium.

T-bar (tē'bār) **lift.** Ski lift consisting of inverted T-shaped bar against which two skiers may lean as they are pulled uphill.

tbs., tbsp. *abbrevs.* Tablespoon(ful).

Tc *symbol.* Technetium.

Tchai·kov·sky (chīkawf'skē), **Peter Ilyich** (1840–93). Russian composer of ballets including *Swan Lake*, *Nutcracker*, and symphonies, esp. *Fourth Symphony in F Minor*, *Fifth Symphony in E Minor*, etc.

Tche·khov (chĕk'awf; *Russ.* chĕ*k*'awf): see CHEKHOV.

TD *abbrev.* 1. (also **td, td.**) Touchdown(s). 2. (also **T.D.**) Treasury Department.

Te *symbol.* Tellurium.

tea (tē) *n.* 1. Dried and prepared leaves of the tea plant, classed acc. to their method of manufacture as *green*, *black*, and *oolong* (the leaves of green tea are rolled and fired immediately, those of black tea are fermented or oxidized before firing, and those of oolong tea are only partially oxidized before firing); drink made by steeping tea leaves in hot water, having slightly

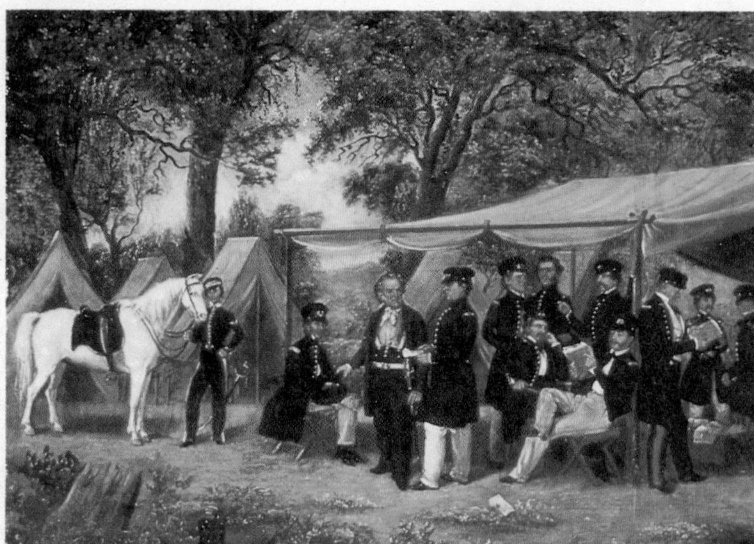

Nicknamed 'Old Rough and Ready', Zachary ***Taylor*** *(3rd from left) had a distinguished career as a soldier before becoming President, his term was marked by Whig patronage.*

bitter and aromatic flavor and moderately stimulant action, widely used as a beverage; (Brit.) meal at which this is served, esp. light meal in afternoon, or (**high** ~) early evening meal; (slang) marijuana. 2. (also ~ **plant**) Plant from which tea is obtained; shrub (*Thea*) with fragrant white flowers and evergreen lanceolate leaves, cultivated from ancient times in China and Japan and grown also in India, Sri Lanka, etc. 3. Drink made in same way as tea from leaves, blossoms, etc., of other plants, beef extract, fruit preserves, etc., and freq. used medicinally; (with defining word) plant used for tea, or the beverages prepared from this. 4. ~ **bag**, small permeable bag of tea leaves for steeping; **tea'cup**, cup from which tea is drunk; as measure, about 4 fluid ounces; ~ **dance**, afternoon tea with dancing; **tea gown**, woman's usu. flowing dress worn at tea etc.; **tea'kettle**, kettle with spout and cover for boiling water; **tea leaf** (pl. **leaves**), leaf of tea, esp. (pl. **leaves**), leaf of tea, esp. (pl.) dregs after brewing; **tea plant**: see sense 2; **tea'pot**, vessel with spout in which tea is made; **tea'room**, shop in which tea and other refreshments are served to public; **tea rose**, delicate-scented half-hardy or tender varieties of cultivated rose derived from *Rosa odorata* of China; **tea set**, set of cups and saucers, plates, etc., for tea; **tea'spoon**, small spoon used for stirring tea etc.; teaspoonful; **tea'spoonful**, amount held by teaspoon, about $1\frac{1}{3}$ fluid drams or $\frac{1}{3}$ tablespoonful; **tea'taster**, one whose business is to test quality of tea by tasting samples. [Chin. (Amoy dial.) *t'e*, Mandarin *ch'a*]

teach (tēch) *v.* (**taught** pr. tawt, **teach·ing**). Give (person) instruction or lessons in (a subject); show or make known to person (how to do something); give instruction to, educate; explain, state by way of instruction; be a teacher; ~**-in** (pl. ~**-ins**), kind of symposium on subject of topical interest.

teach·a·ble (tē'ch*a*bel) *adj.* Apt to learn, docile; (of subject etc.) that can be taught. **teach·a·bil·i·ty** (tēch*a*bĭl'ĭtē), **teach'a·ble·ness** *ns.*

teach·er (tē'ch*er*) *n.* (esp.) One who teaches in a school.

teach·ing (tē'chĭng) *n.* 1. Action or profession of one who teaches. 2. (usu. pl.) What is taught, doctrine; ~ **machine**, mechanical or electronic device that presents the user with educational material in a planned sequence of statements and questions and tells him whether his responses to questions about the material are satisfactory or not.

teak (tēk) *n.* (Yellowish-brown heavy durable oily wood of) large E. Indian tree (*Tectona grandis*) with large egg-shaped leaves and

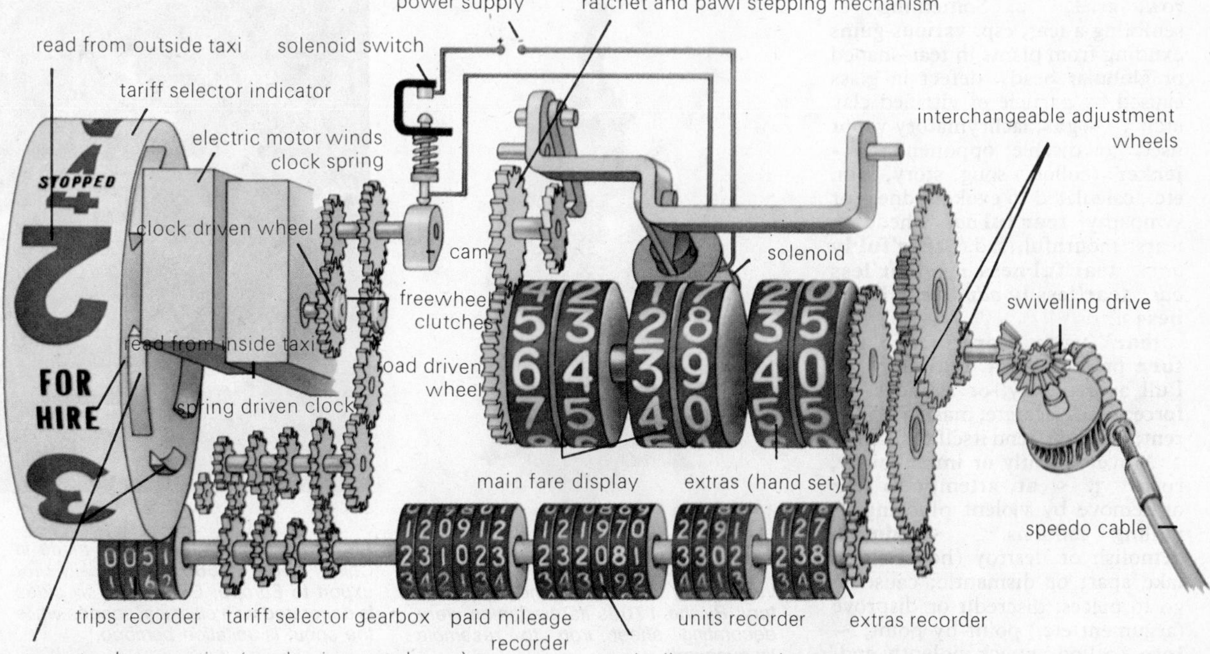

A ***taximeter*** *records the distance traveled, the periods spent waiting, and the charges for each function. It is operated by the speedometer cable and a timing device.*

Highlanders picking ***tea*** *near Mount Hagen, Papua New Guinea. Commercial tea-growing began there in the 1960s; within 15 years tea exports exceeded K2 million (about US $1.9 m).*

panicles of white flowers; (strong or durable timber of) any of various other trees; also **teak'wood**.

teal (tēl) *n.* 1. Small freshwater duck of *Anas* or other genera, widely distributed in Europe, Asia, and Amer., esp. *A. crecca*. 2. (also **teal blue**) Deep greenish blue.

team (tēm) *n.* 1. Two or more draft animals harnessed together; two or more beasts, or a single beast, with the vehicle they pull. 2. Set of players playing against opposing set in game or sport; set of persons working together; **team'mate**, fellow member of a team; **team spirit**, willingness to act for group rather than individual benefit; **team'work**, combined effort, organized cooperation. **team** *v.* Harness in team; convey, transport, with team; (also ~ **up**) join, put together in a team (*with*).

team·ster (tēm'st*er*) *n.* Driver of a team of horses or of a truck used for hauling.

Tea·pot (tē'pŏt) **Dome.** Oil producing region in Wyoming that was designated a naval oil reserve in 1915; associated with scandal, 1922, when Secretary of the Interior Albert B. Fall was found to have leased the lands to private oil concerns from whom he received bribes.

tear[1] (tēr) *n.* 1. Drop of limpid saline fluid secreted by lachrymal gland appearing in or flowing from eye, as result of emotion, esp. grief, or of physical irritation, nervous stimulus, etc.; (pl.) weeping, sorrow, grief. 2. Something resembling a tear, esp. various gums exuding from plants in tear-shaped or globular beads, defect in glass caused by particle of vitrified clay etc. 3. ~ **gas**, lachrymatory vapor used to disable opponents; ~-**jerker**, (colloq.) song, story, film, etc., calculated to evoke sadness or sympathy. **tear'ful** *adj.* Shedding tears; mournful, sad. **tear'ful·ly** *adv.* **tear'ful·ness** *n.* **tear'less** *adj.* **tear'less·ly** *adv.* **tear'less·ness** *n.*

tear[2] (tār) *v.* (**tore** pr. tōr, tōr, **torn** pr. tōrn, tōrn, **tear·ing**). 1. Pull apart, away, or asunder, by force; rend, lacerate; make a tear or rent; (of thing) lend itself to tearing. 2. Move violently or impetuously, rush. 3. ~ **at**, attempt to tear or remove by violent plucking or pulling motions. ~ **down**, demolish or destroy (house etc.); take apart or dismantle; cause to go to pieces; discredit or disprove (argument etc.) point by point; ~ **into**, (colloq.) attack violently and,

Japanned enamel metalware ***tea urn*** *made in Pontypool, Wales, U.K., an ironworking center from the 16th century. By the 1700s its craftsmen were decorating sheet iron to resemble lacquerwork.*

An ornately decorated ***teapot*** *made in China about 1680 specifically for export to Europe. Each of its six sides is decorated with classical scenes while the spout is imitation bamboo.*

often, destructively; attack with words, scold; ~ **off,** (colloq.) do or produce quickly and easily; ~ **up,** tear into small pieces, shred. **tear** *n.* Damage caused by tearing; torn part or place in cloth etc. **tear′-a·ble** *adj.* **tear′er** *n.*

tear·ing (tār′ĭng) *adj.* (esp.) Violent, overwhelming.

tear·y (tēr′ē) *adj.* (**tear·i·er, tear·i·est**). 1. Of or like tears. 2. Tearful; crying. **tear′i·ly** *adv.*

tease (tēz) *v.t.* (**teased, teas·ing**). 1. Pull asunder fibers of, comb, card (wool, flax, etc.); raise surface of (cloth etc.) into nap with teasels etc. 2. Ruffle (hair) by combing toward the scalp. 3. Assail playfully or maliciously, vex, irritate, with jests, questions, or petty annoyances. ~ *n.* Person addicted to teasing.

tea·sel, tea·zel, tea·zle (tē′zel) *ns.* Plant of genus *Dipsacus,* herbs with prickly leaves and flower heads, esp. *D. fullonum,* **fuller's ~,** heads of which have hooked prickles between flowers; dried prickly flower head of fuller's teasel used for teasing cloth etc. so as to raise nap on surface; contrivance used as substitute for this.

teas·er (tē′zer) *n.* (colloq.) Difficult question, problem, or task, thing hard to deal with; a tease.

teat (tēt, tĭt) *n.* Nipple, small protuberance at tip of breast in female mammals, upon which ducts of mammary gland open and from which milk is sucked by young; artificial structure resembling this, esp. contrivance of rubber etc. through which milk is sucked from bottle.

teaze (tēz) **tenon.** (carpentry) Steplike tenon on top of a post supporting 2 horizontal pieces of wood that meet each other at right angles.

tea·zle = TEASEL.

tech·ne·ti·um (těknē′shēum) *n.* (chem.) Radioactive metallic element not found in nature, the first otherwise unknown element to be produced artificially (1937); symbol Tc, at. no. 43, at. wt. 98.9062. [Gk. *tekhnētos* artificial]

tech·nic (těk′nĭk, sometimes těknēk′) *n.* Technical term or detail, technicality; (pl. rare) technique; (usu. pl.) technology.

tech·ni·cal (těk′nĭkal) *adj.* 1. Of or (used) in a particular art, science, profession, handicraft, etc. 2. Of, for, in, the mechanical arts and applied science generally. 3. Regarded in specified way according to a strict interpretation of law or rule(s); ~ **knockout,** referee's termination of prize fight on grounds of boxer's inability to continue, his opponent being declared winner. **tech′ni·cal·ly** *adv.* **tech′-ni·cal·ness** *n.* **tech·ni·cal·i·ty** (těknĭkăl′ĭtē) *n.* (pl. **-ties**). Technical quality or character; technical point, detail, term, etc.

tech·ni·cal (těk′nĭkal) **sergeant.** (U.S. Air Force) Enlisted man of second grade, ranking just below master sergeant and above staff sergeant.

tech·ni·cian (těknĭsh′an) *n.* Person skilled in the technique of an art or subject; person expert in the practical application of science.

Tech·ni·col·or (těk′nĭkŭler) *n.* (trademark) (cinemat.) Process of color photography in which the colors are separately but simultaneously recorded and then transferred to a single positive print.

tech·nique (těknēk′) *n.* Manner of execution or performance in painting, music, etc.; mechanical part of an art, craft, etc.; (loosely) method of achieving one's purpose.

tech·noc·ra·cy (těknŏk′rasē) *n.* (pl. **-cies**). Government or control of society by technical experts. **tech·no·crat** (těk′nokrăt) *n.* **tech·no·crat·ic** (těknokrăt′ĭk) *adj.*

tech·nol·o·gy (těknŏl′ojē) *n.* Scientific study of practical or industrial arts; practical arts collectively; terminology of particular art or subject. **tech·no·log·i·cal** (těknolŏj′ĭkal) *adj.* **tech·no·log′i·cal·ly** *adv.* **tech·nol′o·gist** *n.*

tec·ton·ic (těktŏn′ĭk) *adj.* Of building or construction; ~ **geology,** that part of geology that deals with deformation of Earth's crust or structural changes caused thereby. **tec·ton′ics** *n.pl.* (usu. considered sing.). 1. Art of producing useful and beautiful buildings, furniture, vessels, etc. 2. (geol.) Structural features as a whole.

tec·trix (těk′trĭks) *n.* (pl. **tec·tri·ces** pr. těk′trĭsēz, těktrī′-). (ornith.) = COVERT[1] sense 2.

ted (těd) *v.t.* (**ted·ded, ted·ding**). Turn over and spread out (grass, hay) to dry. **ted′der** *n.* Machine for drying hay.

ted·dy (těd′ē) **bear.** Child's toy bear. [named after *Theodore* Roosevelt]

Te De·um (tā dā′um; *Brit.* tē dē′um). Ancient Latin hymn of praise beginning *Te Deum laudamus* "We praise thee, O God," sung (usu. in English) at matins in R.C. Ch. and Church of England, and as thanksgiving on special occasions; musical setting of this.

Tectonic geology is concerned with the structure of the earth. The theory of plate tectonics, derived from that of continental drift, assumes that the plates of the crust are still moving.

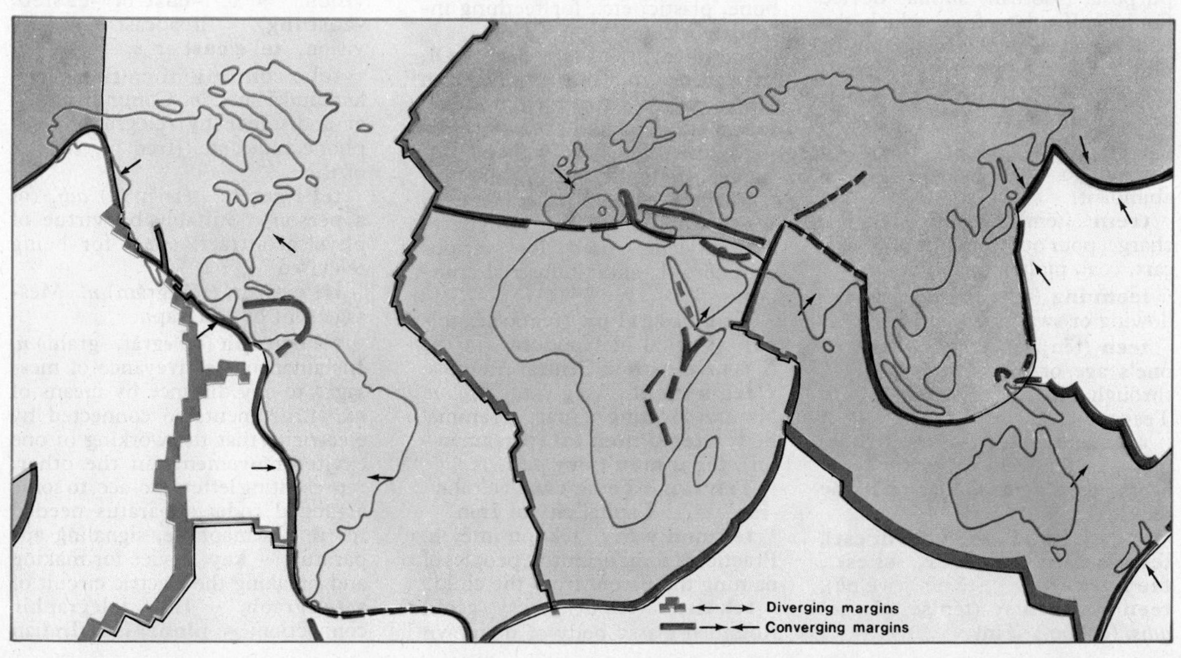

Telecommunication techniques have made possible remarkable improvements since the early 1960s. Above left, Papua New Guinea Highlanders can be connected by telephone to anywhere in the world via satellite links such as that at Ceduna, Australia (above right).

te·di·ous (tē′dē*u*s) *adj.* Tiresomely long, prolix, irksome. **te′di·ous·ly** *adv.* **te′di·ous·ness** *n.*

te·di·um (tē′dē*u*m) *n.* Weariness produced by tediousness, tedious circumstances.

tee[1] (tē) *n.* (pl. **tees**). Letter T; T-shaped thing or part; **~-shirt, ~ square** = T shirt, T square.

tee[2] (tē) *n.* (pl. **tees**). (golf) Small mound of sand on which golfer places the ball for driving off at the start and after each hole; small piece of plastic, wood, etc., for the same purpose; (football) similar device for kickoff; place from which the ball is played at the beginning of play for each hole. ~ *v.* (**teed, tee·ing**). Place (ball) on tee; ~ **off**, play ball from tee.

teem[1] (tēm) *v.i.* Be prolific, be stocked to overflowing *with*, be abundant.

teem[2] (tēm) *v.t.* Empty, discharge, pour out (contents of vessel, cart, coal, molten metal, etc.).

teem·ing (tē′mĭng) *adj.* Overflowing or swarming *with*.

teen (tēn) *n.* 1. (pl.) Years of one's age or of century from 13 through 19. 2. Teenager. ~ *adj.* Teenage.

teen·age, teen-age (tēn′āj) *adjs.* In the teens; of or for teenagers. **teen′ag·er** *n.* Person in the teens.

tee·ny (tē′nē) (**-ni·er, -ni·est**), **teen·sy** (tēn′sē) (**-si·er, -si·est**), **tee·ny-wee·ny** (tē′nē wē′nē), **teen·sy-ween·sy** (tēn′sē wēn′sē) *adjs.* (colloq.) Tiny.

tee·ter (tē′t*e*r) *v.* Move like a seesaw; move unsteadily. **tee′ter-board** *n.* Seesaw.

teeth (tēth) *n.* Pl. of TOOTH.

teethe (tēdh) *v.i.* (**teethed, teeth·ing**). Grow or cut teeth. **teeth′ing** *n.* (esp.) ~ **ring**, ring of bone, plastic, etc., for teething infant to bite on.

tee·to·tal (tētō′t*a*l) *adj.* Of, advocating, total abstinence from intoxicants. **tee·to′tal·ism** *n.* **tee·to′tal·ly** *adv.* **tee·to·tal·er** (tētō′t*a*l*e*r, tē′tō-) *n.* Total abstainer. [reduplicated form of *total*]

Tef·lon (těf′lŏn) *n.* (trademark) Waxlike, tough plastic (polytetrafluorethylene) used for various commercial and industrial purposes.

Te·gu·ci·gal·pa (tĕgōō′sēgahl-p*a*). Capital of Honduras, in the S. central part, in Central America.

teg·u·ment (tĕg′y*u*m*e*nt) *n.* Natural covering of (part of) animal body. **teg·u·men·tal** (tĕgy*u*mĕn′-t*a*l), **teg·u·men′ta·ry** *adjs.*

Teh·ran, Te·he·ran (tĕrahn′, -răn′, tā-). Capital city of Iran.

tek·non·y·my (tĕknŏn′*i*mē) *n.* Practice of some primitive peoples of naming the parent from the child.

tek·tite (tĕk′tīt) *n.* (geol.) Rounded glassy body of unknown origin, found in various parts of the world.

tel·aes·the·sia = TELESTHESIA.

tel·a·mon (tĕl′*a*mŏn) *n.* (pl. **tel·a·mo·nes** pr. tĕl*a*mō′nēz). (archit.) Male figure supporting an entablature (cf. CARYATID). [L. f. Gk. *Telamōn* myth. person]

tele- *comb. form.* Far; (esp.) in names of instruments, producing or recording results etc. at a distance; of, for, television.

tel·e·cast (tĕl′*e*kăst, -kahst) *n.* Program or item broadcast by television. ~ *v.* (**-cast** or **-casted, -cast·ing**). Broadcast by television. **tel′e·cast·er** *n.*

tel·e·com·mu·ni·ca·tion (tĕl*e*-kom*ū*n*i*kā′sh*o*n) *n.* Communication at a distance by telegraph, telephone, radio, etc.; (freq. pl.) science of this.

tel·e·gen·ic (tĕl*e*jĕn′ĭk) *adj.* (of a person) Suitable by virtue of physical attractiveness for being televised.

tel·e·gram (tĕl′*e*grăm) *n.* Message sent by telegraph.

tel·e·graph (tĕl′*e*grăf, -grahf) *n.* Instantaneous conveyance of messages to any distance by means of two instruments so connected by electricity that the working of one excites movements in the other, representing letters etc. acc. to some arranged code; apparatus needed for this; semaphore, signaling apparatus; ~ **key**, device for making and breaking the electric circuit of a telegraph; ~ **line**, telegraphic connection; ~ **plant**, East Indian plant of the bean family whose leaves have spontaneous jerking motion. **telegraph** *v.* Send (message *to* person, or abs.) by telegraph; make signals, convey by signals. **te·leg·ra·pher** (tel*ĕg'ra*-f*er*) *n.*

tel·e·graph·ese (tĕl'*e*grăfēz, -fēs, tĕl*e*grăfēz', -fēs') *n.* Elliptical style used in telegrams.

tel·e·graph·ic (tĕl*e*grăf'ĭk) *adj.* Of, by, for, the telegraph; (of style) economically worded, with unessential words omitted. **tel·e·graph'i·cal·ly** *adv.*

te·leg·ra·phy (tel*ĕg'ra*fē) *n.* Art of constructing, practice of communicating by, telegraph; **wireless** ~, transmission of signals through space by means of electromagnetic waves.

tel·e·ki·ne·sis (tĕl*e*kĭnē'sĭs) *n.* Movement at a distance from the motive cause or agent without material connection, esp. as a spiritualistic phenomenon. **tel·e·ki·net·ic** (tĕl*e*kĭnĕt'ĭk) *adj.*

Te·lem·a·chus (telĕm'*a*k*u*s). In the *Odyssey*, son of Odysseus and Penelope.

tel·e·mark (tĕl'*e*mărk) *n.* Swing turn in skiing used to change direction or to stop short. [f. *Telemark*, district in Norway]

te·lem·e·ter (telĕm'*eter*, tĕl'-*e*mē-) *v.t.* Register (temperature, pressure or other phenomena) at a distant meter, usu. by means of radio devices. ~ *n.* Instrument for this. **te·lem'e·try** *n.*

tel·e·ol·o·gy (tĕlēŏl'*o*jē, tĕlē-) *n.* Doctrine of final causes, view that developments are due to the purpose of design that is served by them. **tel·e·o·log·ic** (tĕlē*o*lŏj'ĭk, tĕlē-), **te·le·o·log'i·cal** *adjs.* **tel·e·o·log'i·cal·ly** *adv.* **tel·e·ol'o·gism, tel·e·ol'o·gist** *ns.*

te·lep·a·thy (telĕp'*a*thē) *n.* Communication of impressions from one mind to another without the aid of the known senses. **tel·e·path·ic** (tĕlepăth'ĭk) *adj.* **tel·e·path'i·cal·ly** *adv.* **te·lep'a·thist** *n.*

tel·e·phone (tĕl'*e*fōn) *n.* Instrument for converting the vibrations caused by sound, esp. those of the voice, into an electric current that passes along a wire and is reconverted into sound at the other end; system of communication by a network of telephones; ~ **exchange**: see EXCHANGE. **tel·e·phon·ic** (tĕl*e*fŏn'ĭk) *adj.* **tel·e·phon'i·cal·ly** *adv.* **telephone** *v.* (**-phoned, -phon·ing**). Send (message), speak (*to* person), by telephone.

te·leph·o·ny (telĕf'*o*nē) *n.* Art or science of constructing telephones; the working of a telephone or telephones.

tel·e·pho·to (tĕl'*e*fōtō, tĕl*e*fō'tō) *adj.* Telephotographic; ~ **lens**, lens or combination of lenses for photographing distant objects.

tel·e·pho·tog·ra·phy (tĕl*e*f*o*-tŏg'r*a*fē) *n.* Photography of objects at a distance by means of a telephoto lens. **tel·e·pho·to·graph·ic** (tĕl*e*-fōt*o*grăf'ĭk) *adj.*

tel·e·print·er (tĕl'*e*prĭnt*er*) *n.* Telegraphically operated kind of typewriter.

Tel·e·prompt·er (tĕl'*e*prŏmp-t*er*) *n.* (trademark) Electronic device for prompting television speaker by slowly unrolling his text in large letters out of sight of the audience.

tel·e·scope (tĕl'*e*skōp) *n.* 1. Optical instrument for making distant objects appear nearer and larger, consisting of one or more tubes with an arrangement of lenses, or of one or more mirrors and lenses, by which the rays of light are collected and brought to a focus and the resulting image magnified; **reflecting** ~, one in which the image is reproduced by a mirror; **refracting** ~, one in which the image is reproduced by a lens (the object glass). 2. **radio** ~, directional aerial system for collecting radio energy from different parts of the sky as an optical telescope collects light from different stars, either steerable or fixed and directed by Earth's rotation to successive points in the sky. **telescope** *v.* (**-scoped, -scop·ing**). Force or drive one into another like the sliding tubes of a hand telescope; close, slide together, in this manner; be forced one into the other (esp. of colliding railroad trains).

tel·e·scop·ic (tĕl*e*skŏp'ĭk) *adj.* Of, made with, a telescope; visible only through a telescope, as ~ **star**; consisting of sections that telescope. **tel·e·scop'i·cal·ly** *adv.*

te·les·co·pist (telĕs'k*o*pĭst) *n.* User of telescope.

te·les·co·py (telĕs'k*o*pē) *n.* Use and making of telescopes.

tel·es·the·si·a, tel·aes·the·sia (tĕlĭsthē'zh*a*, -zhē*a*, -zē*a*) *ns.*

*The design and construction of a modern **telephoto lens** is complex and calls for extreme accuracy in lens grinding and matching, and in the manufacture of the metal components, so that absolutely accurate focus can be obtained. Results revolutionized photography.*

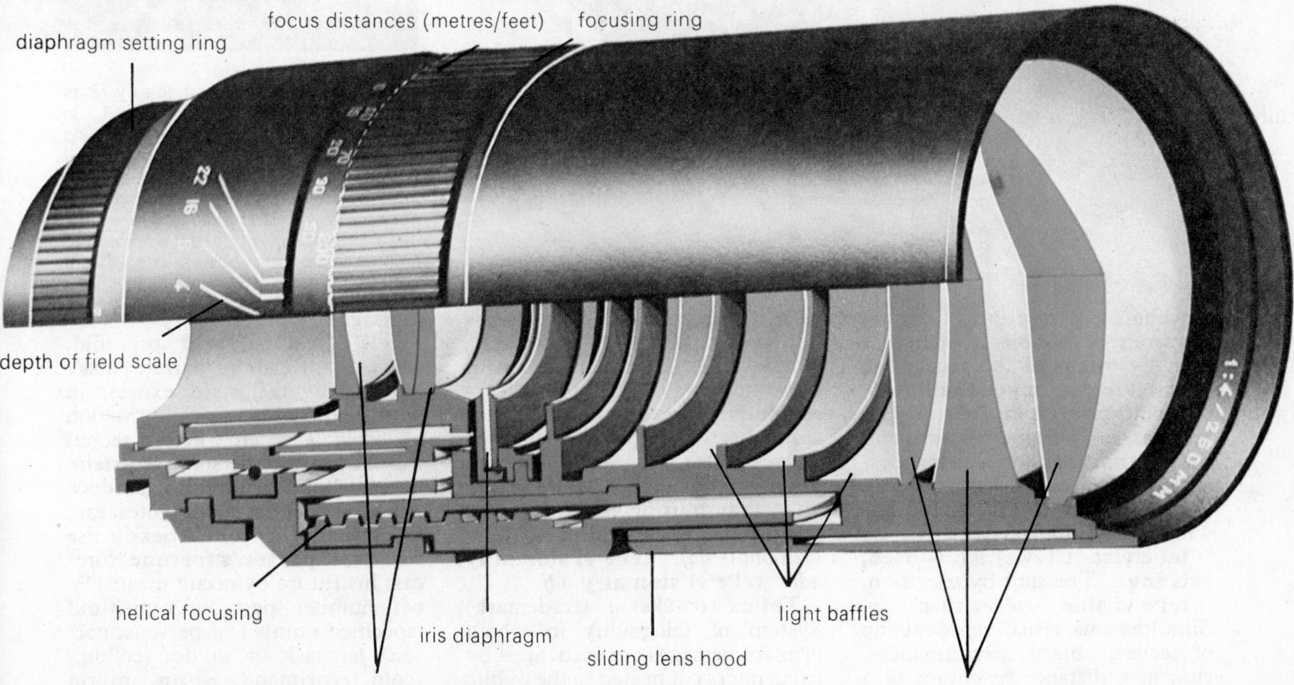

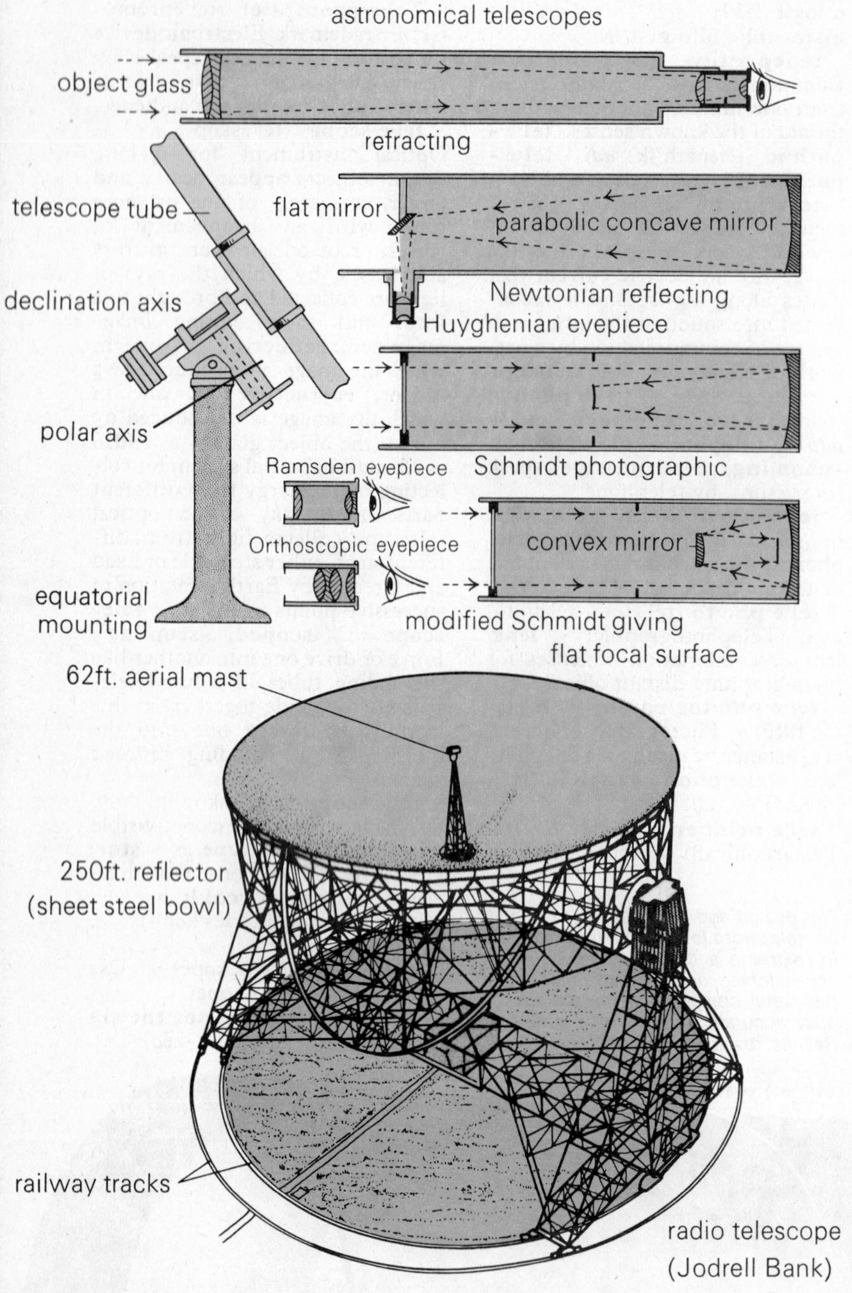

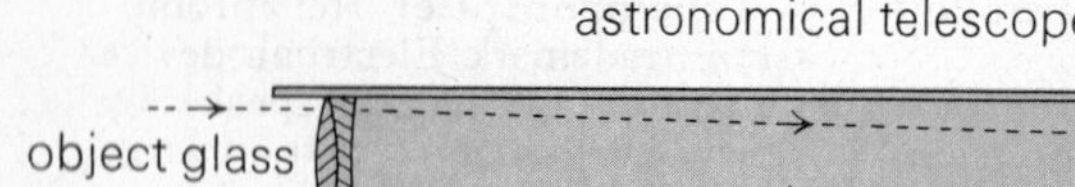

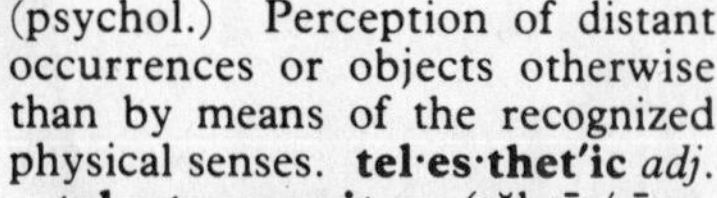

*The first **telescope** was made by Hans Lippershey in Holland in 1608. In 1668, Newton invented a reflecting telescope (top right) to overcome blurred images. Optical developments are shown (top left) while radio telescopes (lower left and right) are now used to supplement optical work and to locate signals from bodies without light sources.*

(psychol.) Perception of distant occurrences or objects otherwise than by means of the recognized physical senses. **tel·es·thet′ic** *adj.*

tel·e·type·writ·er (tĕletīp′rīter, tĕl′etīp-) *n.* Telegraph instrument for transmitting and receiving messages by typing.

tel·e·view (tĕl′evū) *v.i.* View with a television receiver.

tel·e·vise (tĕl′evīz) *v.t.* (**-vised, -vis·ing**). Transmit by television.

tel·e·vi·sion (tĕl′evĭzhon) *n.* Simultaneous visual reproduction of scenes, objects, performances, etc., at a distance by means of a camera that converts the image into electrical impulses that are transmitted by radio to a receiver, which converts them by means of a CATHODE ray tube into a corresponding image on a screen; apparatus for reception of televised images (also ~ **set**); televised program(s) or matter. **tel′e·vi·sor** *n.* Transmitting apparatus for television. **tel·e·vi·sion·al** (tĕlevĭzh′onal) *adj.* **tel·e·vi′sion·al·ly** *adv.* **tel·e·vi′sion·ar·y** *adj.*

Tel·ex (tĕl′ĕks) *n.* (trademark) System of telegraphy in which printed messages are exchanged by teleprinters connected to the public telecommunication network; **t**~, message so sent.

tell[1] (tĕl) *v.* (**told** pr. tōld, **tell·ing**). Relate or narrate; make known, divulge, state, express in words; inform or give information *of*, *about*, *how*, etc.; betray secret, inform against (person); ascertain, decide about, distinguish; produce marked effect on; count (votes, esp. in legislature); ~ **one's beads**, use rosary; ~ **person's fortune**, forecast his future by occult means; ~ **off**, number (party etc.), pick out (specified number of persons, person) *for* task or *to* do; (colloq.) scold, reprimand; ~ **on**, inform against; ~ **tales**, reveal another's

*The **telex** system evolved from an invention about 1900 and it allows typed messages to be received and recorded, from all over the world, even when the office is not staffed.*

private affairs, misconduct, etc.; tell falsehoods. **tell'a·ble** *adj.*

tell[2] (tĕl) *n.* Artificial mound found esp. in Near and Middle Eastern countries, consisting of accumulated remains of ancient settlements.

tell·er (tĕl'*er*) *n.* (esp.) Person appointed to count votes in a legislature; person appointed to receive or pay out money in bank etc.

tell·ing (tĕl'ĭng) *adj.* (esp.) Producing marked effect. **tell'ing·ly** *adv.*

tell·tale (tĕl'tāl) *n.* 1. Person who tells about another's private affairs; (fig.) thing, circumstance, that reveals person's thoughts, conduct, etc., esp. attrib., as ~ *blush, stain.* 2. Kind of automatic registering device; (naut.) index near wheel to show position of the tiller.

tel·lu·rate (tĕl'*yu*rāt) *n.* Salt of telluric acid.

tel·lu·ri·an (t*e*loor'ēan) *adj.* & *n.* (Inhabitant) of Earth.

tel·lu·ric[1] (t*e*loor'ĭk) *adj.* Of earth; obtained from earth or soil.

tel·lu·ric[2] (t*e*loor'ĭk) *adj.* Of, derived from, TELLURIUM.

tel·lu·ri·um (t*e*loor'ē*u*m) *n.* (chem.) Rare, brittle, lustrous, silver-colored element, formerly classed among the metals, but chemically belonging to the same family as sulfur and selenium; symbol Te, at. no. 52, at. wt. 127.60.

tel·lu·rous (tĕl'*yu*r*u*s, t*e*loor'-) *adj.* Of, containing, tellurium, esp. of compounds containing a greater proportion of tellurium than those called *telluric*.

Tel·lus (tĕl'*u*s). (Rom. myth.) Goddess of the Earth; Earth personified, the planet Earth.

tel·son (tĕl's*o*n) *n.* Posterior abdominal region of some crustaceans and other arthropods.

Tel·u·gu (tĕl'*u*gōō) *adj.* & *n.* (pl. **-gus**, collect. **-gu**). (Language, member) of Dravidian people in Coromandel coast region of India, N. of Madras.

tem·er·ar·i·ous (tĕm*e*rār'ē*u*s) *adj.* (literary) Rash, reckless. **tem·er·ar'i·ous·ly** *adv.*

te·mer·i·ty (t*e*mĕr'ĭtē) *n.* Rashness, audacity.

tem·per (tĕm'p*er*) *v.* Bring (clay etc.) to the desired consistency by moistening and kneading; toughen and harden (metal, esp. steel, glass) by heating, sudden cooling, and reheating; (of metal etc.) come to proper hardness and elasticity by this means; modify, mitigate (*justice* etc.) by blending *with* (*mercy* etc.). ~ *n.* 1. Consistency of clay etc. obtained by tempering; degree of hardness and elasticity in steel etc. produced by tempering. 2. Habitual or temporary disposition of mind; fit of anger; composure under provocation.

***Televisions** line the benches of this assembly plant in Singapore; most of the components are designed and built elsewhere and only come together in the final assembly.*

tem·per·a (tĕm'p*e*r*a*, -pr*a*) *n.* Painting with colors that have been mixed with a natural emulsion (e.g. egg yolk) or an artificial emulsion (e.g. oil and gum), esp. the method used for movable pictures before the development of oil painting.

tem·per·a·ment (tĕm'p*e*r*a*-m*e*nt, -pr*a*-) *n.* Characteristic combination of physical, mental, and moral qualities that together constitute the character of an individual and affect the person's manner of acting, feeling, and thinking; (also **artistic, musical** ~) emotional character of artist or musician.

tem·per·a·men·tal (tĕmp*e*r*a*-mĕn't*a*l, -pr*a*-) *adj.* Of, relating to, the temperament; liable to, marked by, variable or unaccountable moods. **tem·per·a·men'tal·ly** *adv.*

tem·per·ance (tĕm'p*e*r*a*ns, -pr*a*ns) *n.* Moderation, self-restraint, in speech, conduct, etc., esp. in eating and drinking; moderation in use of, total abstinence from, alcoholic liquors as beverages; (attrib.) nonalcoholic, aimed at the restriction or prohibition of alcoholic drinks, as in ~ **league, movement**.

tem·per·ate (tĕm'p*e*rĭt, -prĭt) *adj.* Moderate, self-restrained; abstemious; (of climate) not exhibiting extremes of heat or cold, equable; ~ **zone**, zone between either tropic and the corresponding polar circle. **tem'per·ate·ly** *adv.* **tem'per·ate·ness** *n.*

tem·per·a·ture (tĕm′pe*r*ache*r*, -pr*a*-) *n.* Degree or intensity of sensible heat of a body or of the atmosphere, esp. as shown by the thermometer; (med.) internal heat of the body in man, normally 98.6° F (37° C); (colloq.) body temperature above normal, fever; **take person's ~**, ascertain his internal heat with a clinical thermometer to detect any variation from the normal state of health; **~ chart**, one showing a temperature curve; **~ curve**, curve showing variations of temperature, esp. in clinical use.

Temperature (tĕm′pe*r*ache*r*, -pr*a*-) **-Humidity Index.** Quantity giving measure of discomfort due to combined effects of temperature and humidity of air.

tem·pest (tĕm′pĭst) *n.* Violent storm; (fig.) violent tumult or agitation; **~ in a teapot**, great excitement over trivial matter.

tem·pes·tu·ous (tĕmpĕs′-chōō*u*s) *adj.* (of weather, time, etc., and fig. of person or mood) Stormy, violent. **tem·pes′-tu·ous·ly** *adv.* **tem·pes′tu·ous·-ness** *n.*

tem·plate, tem·plet (tĕm′plĭt) *ns.* Pattern, gauge, usu. thin board or metal plate, used as a guide in cutting or drilling metal, stone, wood, etc.; timber or plate used to distribute weight in a wall or under a beam etc.; wedge for building block under ship's keel.

tem·ple[1] (tĕm′pe*l*) *n.* Edifice dedicated to service of (esp. ancient Gk., Rom., Egyptian) god; any of the three successive religious edifices of the Jews in Jerusalem; place of Christian public worship, esp. Protestant church in France; (fig.) place in which God resides.

tem·ple[2] (tĕm′pe*l*) *n.* Flat part of either side of the head between the forehead and the ear.

tem·ple[3] (tĕm′pe*l*) *n.* Device for keeping cloth taut on a loom.

tem·plet (tĕm′plĭt) = TEMPLATE.

tem·po (tĕm′pō) *n.* (pl. **-pos, -pi** pr. -pē). (mus.) Speed at which a passage is (to be) played; (transf.) rate of movement, activity, or progress.

tem·po·ral (tĕm′pe*r*a*l*, -pr*a*l) *adj.* 1. Of, in, denoting, time; (gram.) pertaining to time or tense. 2. Of this life only, secular, lay (opp. *spiritual*). 3. (anat.) Of the temples; **~ bone**, compound bone of the side of the human skull; **~ lobe**, lobe on each side of cerebral hemisphere. **tem′po·ral·ly** *adv.* **tem′-po·ral·ness** *n.* **temporal** *n.* Temporal bone.

tem·po·ral·i·ty (tĕmpe*r*ăl′ĭtē) *n.* (pl. **-ties**). Secular possessions, esp. properties and revenues of a religious body or an ecclesiastic (usu. pl.); (law) temporariness.

tem·po·rar·y (tĕm′pe*r*ĕrē) *adj.* Lasting only for a time, transient; held, occupied, during a limited time only, not permanent; **~ duty**, duty for limited period with organization to which one is not regularly assigned or attached. **tem·-po·rar·i·ly** (tĕmpe*r*âr′*i*lē, tĕm′-pe*r*ĕr-) *adv.* **tem′po·rar·i·ness** *n.* **temporary** *n.* (pl. **-rar·ies**).

tem·po·rize (tĕm′pe*r*īz) *v.i.* (**-rized, -riz·ing**). Pursue indecisive or time-serving policy; avoid committing oneself, act so as to gain time; comply temporarily with requirements of an occasion. **tem·po·ri·za·tion** (tĕmpe*r*īzā′-sho*n*), **tem′po·riz·er** *ns.*

tempt (tĕmpt) *v.t.* Entice, incite; attract; (archaic) test or try the resolution of.

temp·ta·tion (tĕmptā′sho*n*) *n.* Tempting or being tempted; thing that attracts, attractive course.

tempt·er (tĕmp′te*r*), fem. **tempt·ress** (tĕmp′trĭs) *ns.* One who tempts (chiefly in bad sense).

tempt·ing (tĕmp′tĭng) *adj.* Attractive, inviting. **tempt′ing·ly** *adv.*

ten (tĕn) *adj.* Amounting to 10; **Ten Commandments**: see COMMANDMENT; **ten-gallon hat**, cowboy's large broad-brimmed hat; **ten′penny**, designating 3-in.-long nail; **ten′pin**, pin used in **ten′pins**, game similar to ninepins, played with ten pins; **ten-spot**, (slang) playing card having ten spots; ten-dollar bill; **ten-strike**, (bowling) = STRIKE *n.* sense 2; (colloq.) wholly successful action. **ten** *n.* One more than 9; symbol for this (10, x, or X); card with ten spots; ten o'clock; size etc. indicated by 10; set of ten things or persons. **ten·fold** (tĕn′fōld) *adj.* & *adv.*

ten·a·ble (tĕn′*a*be*l*) *adj.* Capable of being maintained or defended against attack or objection; (of office etc.) that can be held *for* a specified time, *by* person, etc. **ten·a·bil·i·ty** (tĕn*a*bĭl′ĭtē), **ten′-a·ble·ness** *ns.* **ten′a·bly** *adv.*

te·na·cious (tenā′sh*u*s) *adj.* Holding fast; keeping firm hold (*of* property, rights, principles, etc.); (of memory) retentive; adhesive, sticky; strongly cohesive. **te·na′-cious·ly** *adv.* **te·na′cious·ness, te·nac·i·ty** (tenăs′ĭtē) *ns.*

te·nac·u·lum (tenăk′y*u*l*u*m) *n.* (pl. **-la** pr. -l*a*). Surgeon's sharp hook used for seizing and holding arteries etc.

ten·an·cy (tĕn′*a*nsē) *n.* (pl. **-cies**). Act of holding position or property as a tenant; period of such holding; property, land etc., held by a tenant.

ten·ant (tĕn′*a*nt) *n.* (law) Person holding real property by private ownership; person who occupies land or tenement under a landlord; inhabitant, dweller; **~ farmer**, one who cultivates farm he does not own. **tenant** *v.t.* Occupy as tenant (esp. in past part.). **ten′-**

*Before the development of oil painting, **tempera**, having egg yolk as a medium for the pigments, was used by artists such as Domenico Veneziano who painted 'A Miracle of St. Zenobus'.*

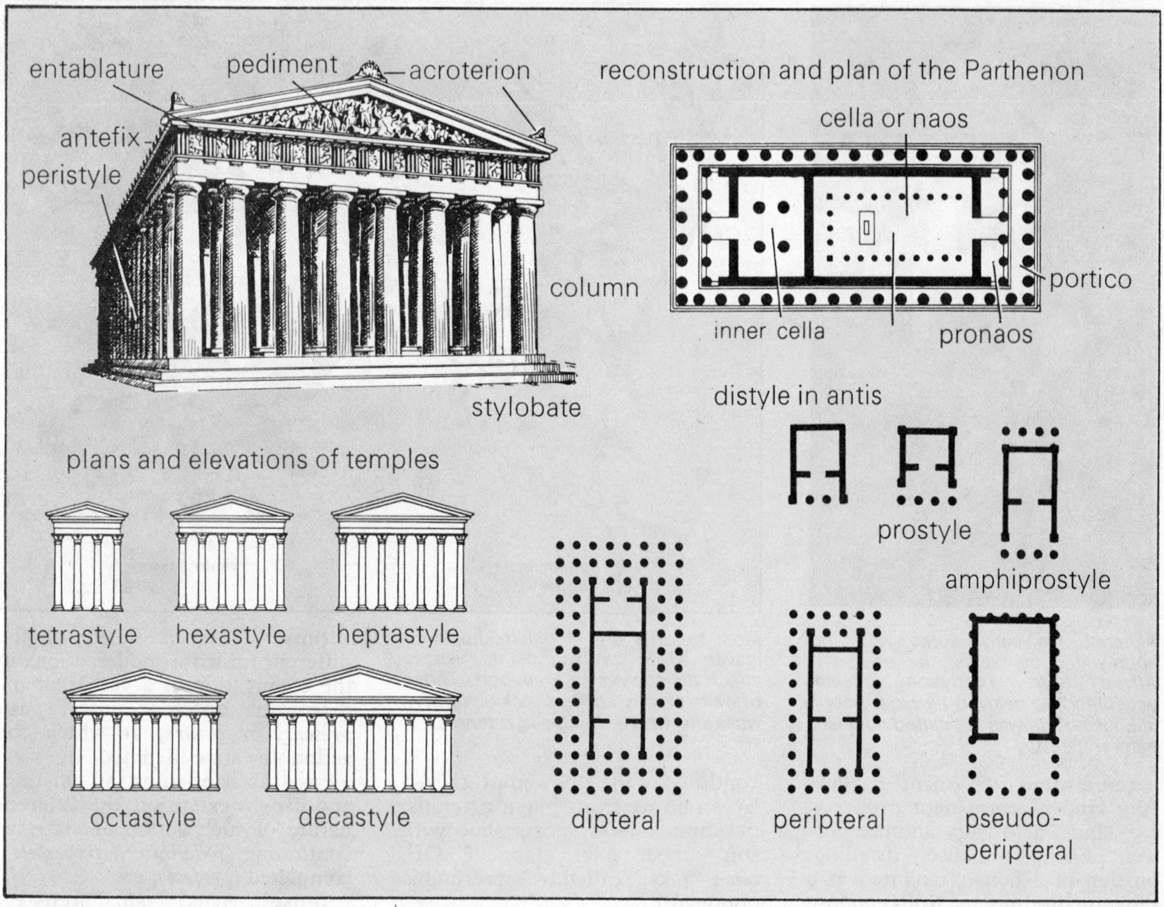

entablature
pediment
acroterion
antefix
peristyle
column
stylobate
reconstruction and plan of the Parthenon
cella or naos
portico
inner cella
pronaos
distyle in antis
prostyle
amphiprostyle
plans and elevations of temples
tetrastyle
hexastyle
heptastyle
octastyle
decastyle
dipteral
peripteral
pseudo-peripteral

ant·less, ten′ant·like *adjs.*

ten·ant·a·ble (tĕn′*ant*ab*el*) *adj.* Fit to be occupied by a tenant.

tend[1] (tĕnd) *v.i.* Move, be directed, in a certain direction; be apt or inclined, serve, conduce (*to* action, quality, etc., *to* do).

tend[2] (tĕnd) *v.* Take care of, look after (flocks, invalid, machine, etc.); wait *upon*; (naut.) watch (ship at anchor) so as to keep turns out of her cable.

tend·en·cy (tĕn′*d*ensē) *n.* (pl. **-cies**). Bent, leaning, inclination (*toward, to*, thing, *to* do).

ten·den·tious, ten·den·cious (tĕndĕn′sh*us*) *adjs.* (of writing etc.) Having an underlying purpose, calculated to advance a cause. **ten·den′tious·ly** *adv.* **ten·den′tious·ness** *n.*

ten·der[1] (tĕn′d*er*) *n.* (esp.) 1. Small ship in attendance upon a larger one to supply her with stores, convey orders, etc. 2. Car attached to a steam locomotive and carrying fuel, water, etc. [f. TEND[2]]

ten·der[2] (tĕn′d*er*) *v.* Offer, present, give in (*one's services, resignation*, etc.); offer (money etc.) as payment; make a tender (*for* supply of thing or execution of work). ~ *n.* Offer, esp. offer in writing to execute work or supply goods at a fixed price; **legal ~**, currency recognized by law as acceptable in payment of a debt.

Above: Various designs of ***temple*** *built by the Greeks. An image of the deity worshipped was housed in the cella (or naos) but the altar was often located outside. The Romans also built temples with a circular plan such as the Tempio Rotondo in Rome (right).*

ten′der·a·ble *adj.* **ten′der·er** *n.*

ten·der[3] (tĕn′d*er*) *adj.* Soft, not tough or hard; easily touched or wounded, susceptible to pain or grief; delicate, fragile, (lit. and fig., of reputation etc.); loving, affectionate, fond; solicitous, considerate; requiring careful handling, ticklish; **ten′derfoot** (pl. **-foots, -feet**), newcomer in camp, settlement, etc., novice, greenhorn; new recruit in Boy Scouts of America; **ten′derheart′ed**, susceptible to, easily moved by, pity; kindly, compassionate; **ten′derloin**, middle part of loin of pork; undercut of sirloin; **Tenderloin**, former district on W. side of Manhattan, New York City, below 42nd St., center of vice and considered a choice assignment for police accepting bribes; such a district in any U.S. city. **ten′der·ly** *adv.* **ten′der·ness** *n.* **ten·der·ize** (tĕn′d*er*īz) *v.t.* (**-ized, -iz·ing**). Make (more) tender. **ten′der·iz·er** *n.*

ten·di·nous (tĕn′d*i*n*us*) *adj.* Of, connected with, resembling, a tendon.

ten·don (tĕn′d*o*n) *n.* Tough, fibrous tissue connecting a muscle to some other part; sinew; **Achilles ~**: see ACHILLES.

ten·dril (tĕn′drĭl) *n.* Slender threadlike organ or appendage of a plant, often spiral in form, which stretches out and attaches itself to some other body so as to support the plant.

Ten·e·brae (tĕn′*e*brā) *n.pl.* or *sing.* (R.C. Ch.) Matins and lauds for the last three days of Holy Week, at which the candles are successively extinguished. [L., = "darkness"]

Although his early works were not appreciated by critics, the poems of ***Alfred Lord Tennyson*** *became accepted and beloved by most people in England. He was appointed poet laureate in 1850.*

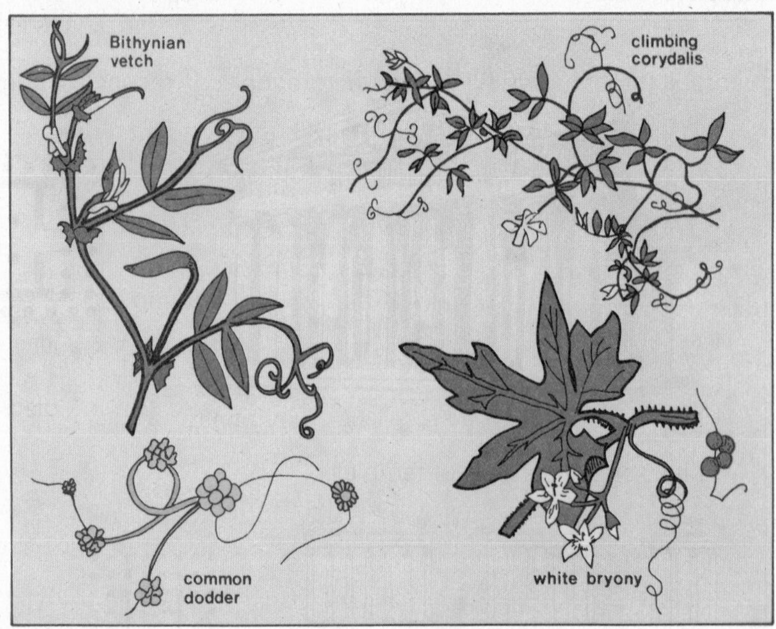

Most ***tendrils*** *are modified shoots or leaves which climbing plants use to attach themselves to a support. Those of white bryony act as shock absorbers while the whole dodder is a tendril.*

ten·e·ment (tĕn′ement) *n.* (law) Any kind of permanent property, e.g. lands, held from another person; tenement house; dwelling; portion of a house, tenanted as a separate dwelling; ~ **house**, house containing tenements, esp. in slums, that is overcrowded, dirty, badly maintained, etc. **ten·e·men·tal** (tĕnemĕn′tal) *adj.*

ten·et (tĕn′ĭt) *n.* Principle, dogma, doctrine, of a person or school. [L., = "he holds"]

Tenn., TN *abbrevs.* Tennessee.

ten·ner (tĕn′*er*) *n.* (colloq.) Ten-dollar bill; (Brit.) ten-pound note, ten pounds.

Ten·nes·see (tĕnĭsē′). State in southeastern U.S., admitted to the Union in 1796; capital, Nashville. ~ **River**, river in the SE. United States, flowing 652 mi. (1,049 km) from Knoxville, Tennessee, through Alabama, Tennessee, and Kentucky, to the Ohio. **Ten·nes·see′an** *adj.* & *n.*

Ten·nes·see (tĕnĭsē′) **Valley Authority.** U.S. Government corporation organized in 1933 to develop cheap hydroelectric power, flood control projects, and irrigation works in the entire Tennessee River basin.

ten·nis (tĕn′ĭs) *n.* Game for two or four persons played by striking ball with racket (formerly with the palm of the hand) over a net stretched across an oblong court, called **lawn tennis** when played on grass court; ~ **ball**, hollow rubber ball with fuzzy cloth covering; ~ **court**, court on which tennis is played; ~ **elbow**, inflammatory condition of the elbow joint, caused by strain as from playing tennis; ~ **shoe**, canvas sports shoe with soft rubber sole. [app. f. OF. *tenez* "take," called by server to his opponent]

Ten·ny·son (tĕn′ĭs*o*n), **Alfred, 1st Baron** (1809–92). English poet; poet laureate from 1850; author of "In Memoriam," "Maud," "Idylls of the King," etc. **Ten·ny·so·ni·an** (tĕnĭsō′nē*a*n) *adj.*

ten·on (tĕn′*o*n) *n.* Projection fashioned on the end or side of a piece of wood or other material, to fit into a corresponding cavity, or mortise, in another piece; ~ **saw**, fine saw for making tenons etc., having a thin blade, strong brass or steel back, and small teeth. **tenon** *v.t.* Cut into a tenon; join by means of a tenon.

ten·o·ni·tis (tĕnonī′tĭs) *n.* Painful inflammation of tendon.

ten·or (tĕn′*er*) *n.* 1. Settled or prevailing course or direction (esp. fig. *of one's life* etc.); general purport, drift (*of* speech, writing, etc.). 2. (mus.) (Music for, singer with) high adult male voice, usually ranging from the octave below middle C to the A above it; viola; (usu. attrib.) applied to an instrument of any kind (~ **saxophone** etc.) of which the range is approx. that of tenor voice. [L. *tenorem* holding on, (med. L.) chief melody, formerly assigned to adult male voice]

te·not·o·my (tĕnŏt′omē) *n.* (pl. **-mies**). Surgical cutting of a tendon.

tense[1] (tĕns) *n.* Any of the different forms or modifications in the conjugation of a verb that indicate the different times (*past, present,* or *future*) at which the action or state denoted by it is viewed as happening or existing, and also (by extension) the different nature of such action or state, as continuing (*indefinite*), (*imperfect*), completed (*perfect*), etc.

tense[2] (tĕns) *adj.* (**tens·er, tens·est**). (of cord, membrane, fig. of nerve, mind, emotion) Stretched tight, strained to stiffness, highly strung. **tense′ly** *adv.* **tense′ness** *n.* **tense** *v.* (**tensed, tens·ing**). Make, become, tense.

ten·si·ble (tĕn′s*i*b*e*l) *adj.* Capable of being stretched out or extended. **ten·si·bil·i·ty** (tĕnsĭbĭl′ĭtē) *n.*

ten·sile (tĕn′s*i*l; *Brit.* also tĕn′sīl) *adj.* Of tension; capable of being drawn out or stretched; ~ **strength**, maximum of lengthwise stress a material can bear without tearing apart. **ten·sil·i·ty** (tĕnsĭl′ĭtē) *n.*

ten·sion (tĕn′sh*o*n) *n.* Stretching, being stretched; tenseness; mental strain or excitement, strained (political, social, etc.) state; (phys.) effect produced by forces pulling against each other; (elect.) stress along lines of force in a dielectric, formerly used as a synonym for potential, electromotive force, and mechanical force exerted by electricity, still so applied, in industrial and commercial use, in **high** and **low** ~. **ten′sion·al** *adj.*

ten·sor (tĕn′s*er*) *n.* (anat.) Muscle that tightens or stretches a part.

tent (tĕnt) *n.* Portable shelter of canvas, cloth, etc., usu. supported by pole(s) and stretched by cords secured to pegs driven into the ground; **oxygen** ~, tentlike

French dandies in the late 18th century playing an early form of ***tennis.*** *The game had its origin in England in the 16th century but lawn tennis, as played today did not evolve until the 1870s.*

cover, enclosing head and shoulders or whole body, through which oxygen can be supplied to assist breathing; ~ **bed**, bed with a tent-like canopy; bed for use in a tent; ~ **fly**, piece of canvas pitched outside and over ridge of tent as extra protection from sun, rain, etc.; ~ **stitch**, series of parallel diagonal stitches. **tent** *v.* Cover (as) with a tent; encamp in a tent.

ten·ta·cle (tĕn′t*a*kel) *n.* Slender flexible process in animals, esp. invertebrates, serving as sensory or attachment organ, (bot.) sensitive hair or filament. **ten′ta·cled, ten·tac·u·lat·ed** (tĕntăk′y*u*lātĭd) *adjs.*

tent·age (tĕn′tĭj) *n.* Tents collectively; supply or equipment of tents.

ten·ta·tive (tĕn′t*a*tĭv) *adj.* Done by way of trial, experimental. **ten′ta·tive·ly** *adv.* **ten′ta·tive·ness** *n.*

tent (tĕnt) **caterpillar**. Any of several caterpillars (genus *Malacosoma)* that live in colonies in tent-like webs constructed among the branches of deciduous trees, which they defoliate.

ten·ter (tĕn′t*er*) *n.* Machine or frame for stretching cloth to set or dry; **ten′terhooks**, hooks to which cloth is fastened on a tenter; **on tenterhooks**, (fig.) in a state of suspense, distracted by uncertainty.

tenth (tĕnth) *adj.* Next after ninth. ~ *n.* Tenth part (see PART[1] sense 1); tenth thing etc. **tenth′ly** *adv.* In the tenth place.

ten·u·ous (tĕn′ūus) *adj.* Thin, slender; (of distinctions etc.) subtle, overrefined. **ten′u·ous·ness** *n.* **ten′u·ous·ly** *adv.*

ten·ure (tĕn′y*er*) *n.* Holding *of* a piece of property or office; conditions or period of such holding; permanent appointment after probationary period. **ten′ured** *adj.*

te·o·cal·li (tēokăl′ē) *n.* (pl. **-cal·lis**). (archaeol.) Temple of Aztec or other Mexican aborigines, usu. built on a truncated pyramidal mound. [Nahuatl, f. *teotl* god, *calli* house]

Te·o·ti·hua·cán (tāōtēwahkahn′). Town in Mexico, in the central part, 30 mi. (48 km) NE. of Mexico City; site of many ancient Indian ruins, including the Pyramid of the Sun, Pyramid of the Moon, and the Temples of Tlaloc and Quetzalcoatl.

te·pee (te′pē) *n.* Conical tent, hut, or wigwam of the Amer. Indians.

Nomadic tribes in Afghanistan follow their livestock in the search for grazing. Each family has a low black ***tent,*** *and when groups band together, they form villages of tents.*

tep·id (tĕp′ĭd) *adj.* Slightly warm, lukewarm (lit. and fig.). **te·pid·i·ty** (tĕpĭd′ĭtē), **tep′id·ness** *ns.* **tep′id·ly** *adv.*

te·qui·la (tekē′l*a*) *n.* Mescal or redistilled mescal.

ter·a·tism (tĕr′*a*tĭzem) *n.* (biol.) Monstrosity.

ter·a·tol·o·gy (tĕr*a*tŏl′*o*jē) *n.* Tale or myth concerning prodigies, marvelous tale, collection of these; (biol.) study of monstrosities or abnormal formations, esp. in man. **ter·a·to·log·i·cal** (tĕr*a*tolŏj′ĭk*a*l) *adj.*

ter·bi·um (tĕr′bē*u*m) *n.* (chem.) Metallic element of rare-earth group found in combination in gadolinite and other minerals; symbol Tb, at. no. 65, at. wt. 158.9254. [f. *Ytterby* in Sweden]

terce (tẽrs) = TIERCE sense 1.

ter·cel (tẽr′sel) *n.* Male hawk. [L. *tertius* 3rd, from belief that the 3rd egg of a hawk produced a small male bird]

ter·cen·te·nar·y (tẽrsĕn′t*e*nĕrē, tẽrsĕntĕn′*e*rē) *n.* (pl. **-nar·ies**). Three hundredth anniversary. ~ *adj.* Of 300 (esp. years). **ter·cen·ten·ni·al** (tẽrsĕntĕn′ē*a*l) *adj.* & *n.* Tercentenary.

Ter·ence (tĕr′*e*ns). Publius Terentius Afer (*c*190–*c*159 B.C.), Roman playwright, author of comedies, born at Carthage.

Te·resh·ko·va (tĕrĕshkō′v*a*), **Valentina Vladimirovna** (1937–). Soviet cosmonaut; first woman in space, 1963.

ter·gal (tẽr′g*a*l) *adj.* Of the back, dorsal.

ter·gi·ver·sate (tẽr′jĭv*e*rsāt) *v.i.* (**-sat·ed, -sat·ing**). Turn one's coat, desert one's party or principles, apostatize. **ter·gi·ver·sa·tion** (tẽrjĭv*e*rsā′sh*o*n) *n.*

ter·gum (tẽr′g*u*m) *n.* (pl. **-ga** pr. -g*a*). Dorsal surface of body segment of arthropod.

term (tẽrm) *n.* 1. Boundary, limit, esp. of time; limited period; completion of period of pregnancy, (normal) time of childbirth; (law)

Right: Soldiers of the ***termite*** *genus Psammotermes. Above: Tall* ***termitary*** *in S.W. Africa. Despite their destructive ability, termites are highly sensitive to heat and humidity and need the insulation of large nests.*

estate or interest in land, etc., for fixed period; ~ **insurance**, life insurance having specific date of expiration; ~ **paper**, research paper written by student as part of particular course requirements during school term. 2. Figure, post, stone, etc., marking boundary (= TERMINUS sense 3). 3. Each period appointed for sitting of court of law, or for instruction and study in school, university, etc. 4. (math.) Each of two quantities composing a ratio or fraction; each of the quantities forming a series of progression; each of the quantities connected by signs of addition (+) or subtraction (−) in an algebraic expression or equation. 5. (logic) Word(s), notion, that may be subject or predicate of a proposition; hence, any word or group of words expressing a definite conception, esp. in particular branch of study etc.; (pl.) language employed, mode of expression; **~s of reference**, terms defining scope of inquiry, action, etc. 6. (pl.) Conditions, esp. charge, price; **bring to ~s**, cause to accept conditions; **come to ~s**, yield, give way; in terms of, in reference to. 7. (pl.) Relation, footing. **term** *v.t.* Denominate, call.

ter·ma·gant (tẽr′m*a*g*a*nt) *n.* Brawling turbulent woman. [imaginary deity supposed in medieval times to be worshipped by Muslims]

ter·mi·na·ble (tẽr′m*i*n*a*bel) *adj.* That may be terminated (esp. after stipulated period).

ter·mi·nal (tẽr′m*i*n*a*l) *adj.* Of, forming, a limit or terminus; situated at, forming, the end or extremity of something; of, forming, a term; (med.) forming, suffering, the final stage of a fatal disease; ~ **leave**, final leave given to member of armed forces preceding discharge, equal to amount of accumulated unused leave; ~ **moraine**, (geol.) moraine formed at extreme forward edge of glacier; (med.) forming, suffering, the final stage of a fatal disease. **ter′mi·nal·ly** *adv.* **terminal** *n.* Terminating thing, extremity, esp. (structure or device forming) each of free ends of open electrical circuit, by connecting which circuit is closed; end of railroad line, terminus.

ter·mi·nate (tẽr′m*i*nāt) *v.* (**-nat·ed, -nat·ing**). Bound, limit; bring, come, to an end, end (*at, in, with*). **ter′mi·na·ble, ter′mi·na·tive** *adjs.* **ter′mi·na·tive·ly** *adv.*

ter·mi·na·tion (tẽrm*i*na′sh*o*n) *n.* 1. Act of terminating or state of being terminated. 2. End of something in space or time; boundary; conclusion. 3. Outcome or result of something. 4. Final syllable or letter(s) of word, (inflectional or derivative) ending, suffix.

ter·mi·na·tor (tẽr′m*i*nāt*e*r) *n.* 1. Person or thing that terminates. 2. Line of separation between dark and light parts of moon or planet.

ter·mi·nol·o·gy (tẽrm*i*nŏl′*o*jē) *n.* (pl. **-gies**). System of terms belonging to a science or subject; technical terms collectively. **ter·min·o·log·i·cal** (tẽrm*i*n*o*lŏj′ĭk*a*l) *adj.* **ter·min·o·log′i·cal·ly** *adv.* **ter·mi·nol′o·gist** *n.*

ter·mi·nus (tẽr′m*i*n*u*s) *n.* (pl. **-ni** pr. -nī, **-nus·es**). 1. (Brit.) Station at end of line of railroad, bus route, etc. 2. Either end of a railroad line. 3. (Rom. antiq., also **term**) Statue or bust of the god Terminus, who presided over landmarks and boundaries; figure of human bust supported on square pillar.

ter·mite (tẽr′mīt) *n.* Pale-colored soft-bodied social insect of order Isoptera, chiefly tropical, and very destructive to timber; white ant.

tern (tẽrn) *n.* Seabird esp. of genus *Sterna*, resembling gull but usu. smaller and more slender bodied, with long, pointed wing and forked tail; sea swallow.

ter·na·ry (tẽr′n*e*rē) *adj.* Of, in, set(s) of three; composed of three parts or elements.

ter·nate (tẽr′nĭt, -nāt) *adj.* Consisting of, arranged in, threes, esp. (bot.) composed of three leaflets, (of leaves) in whorls of three. **ter′nate·ly** *adv.*

Terp·sich·o·re (tẽrpsĭk′*e*rē). (Gk. and Rom. myth.) Muse of lyric poetry and dance. **Terp·si·cho·re·an** (tẽrps*i*k*o*rē′*a*n, -kōr′ē*a*n, -kōr′-) *adj.* Of Terpsichore; of

*There are more than 40 species of **tern** and the Arctic variety actually spends half the year in the northern hemisphere before flying to the Antarctic. Most of these birds live on fish that they catch by diving directly into the water after them.*

dancing.

terr. *abbrev.* Territorial; territory.

ter·ra al·ba (tĕr′*a* ăl′b*a*). Any of various white mineral substances; (esp.) pipe clay. [L.]

ter·race (tĕr′*a*s) *n.* Raised level place, natural or artificial, esp. raised walk in garden or level space in front of building on sloping ground; (geol.) horizontal shelf or beach bordering river, lake, or sea. ~ *v.t.* (**-raced, -rac·ing**). Form into, furnish with, terrace(s).

ter·ra cot·ta (tĕr′*a* kŏt′*a*). Hard unglazed pottery of fine quality used for decorative tiles, statuary, architectural decorations, etc.; statuette, figurine of this; brownish-red color of this pottery. ~ *adj.* Of, made of, of the color of, terra cotta. [It., = "baked earth"]

ter·ra fir·ma (tĕr′*a* fẽr′m*a*). Dry land, firm ground. [L.]

ter·rain[1] (t*e*rān′) *n.* Tract of country considered with regard to its natural features etc., esp. (mil.) its tactical advantages, fitness for maneuvering etc.

ter·rain[2]: see TERRANE.

ter·ra in·cog·ni·ta (tĕr′*a* ĭnkŏg′nĭt*a*, ĭnkŏgnē′-; *Lat.* tĕr′ah ĭnkŏg′nĭtah). Unknown or unexplored region. [L.]

Ter·ra·my·cin (tĕr*a*mī′sĭn) *n.* (trademark) OXYTETRACYCLINE.

tar·rane, ter·rain (t*e*rān′) *ns.* (geol.) Connected series, group, or system of rocks or formations, area over which a group of formations is prevalent.

ter·ra·pin (tĕr′*a*pĭn) *n.* Any of various N. Amer. edible tortoises of family Emydidae, found in fresh or brackish water, esp. the **diamondback ~**, (*Malaclemys*) of salt marshes of coasts of Atlantic and Gulf of Mexico, famous for its delicate flesh.

ter·raz·zo (t*e*răz′ō, -rah′zō) *n.* Flooring material of stone chips set in concrete and given a smooth surface.

ter·rene (tĕrēn′) *adj.* Of Earth, earthy; terrestrial.

ter·res·tri·al (t*e*rĕs′trē*a*l) *adj.* Of the Earth, of this world, worldly; of land as opp. to water. **ter·res′tri·al·ly** *adv.*

ter·ri·ble (tĕr′*i*bel) *adj.* Exciting, fitted to excite, terror; awful, dreadful, formidable; (colloq.) very great, excessive. **ter′ri·bly** *adv.* **ter′ri·ble·ness** *n.*

ter·ri·er (tĕr′ēer) *n.* Any of several kinds of usu. small active hardy dog orig. used to pursue quarry (fox, badger, etc.) into burrow or earth.

ter·rif·ic (t*e*rĭf′ĭk) *adj.* Causing terror; (colloq.) of great size, intensity, etc.; very good, admirable, etc. **ter·rif′i·cal·ly** *adv.*

ter·ri·fy (tĕr'ifī) *v.t.* (**-fied, -fy·ing**). Fill with terror, frighten. **ter'ri·fy·ing·ly** *adv.* **ter'ri·fi·er** *n.*

ter·rine (terēn') *n.* Earthenware vessel containing and sold with some table delicacy as pâté de foie gras.

ter·ri·to·ri·al (tĕrĭtōr'ēal, -tōr'-) *adj.* Of territory; of a particular territory or locality, local; ~ **waters**, that part of the seas adjacent to its shores over which a nation claims jurisdiction, within a minimum number of (formerly three) miles from low-water mark. **ter·ri·to'ri·al·ly** *adv.*

ter·ri·to·ri·al·ism (tĕrĭtōr'ēalĭzem, -tōr'-) *n.* System of church government under which civil rule has religious jurisdiction over the subjects of a nation; principle of predominance of land-owning classes.

ter·ri·to·ri·al·i·ty (tĕrĭtōrēăl'ĭtē, -tōr-) *n.* 1. State or quality of being territorial. 2. Behavior pattern of an animal when defending its territory.

ter·ri·to·ry (tĕr'ĭtōrē, -tōr-) *n.* (pl. **-ries**). 1. Land under jurisdiction of sovereign, nation, city, etc.; (large) tract of land, region; portion of country not yet admitted to full rights of a state or province. 2. District in which salesperson or sales supervisor operates; (zool.) area of habitat that a particular animal or group defends against others of the same species; (in games) half of field regarded as belonging to team whose goal etc. is in it. 3. (fig.) Sphere, province.

ter·ror (tĕr'er) *n.* Extreme fear; person or thing causing this; (colloq.) exasperating or tiresome person, troublesome child.

ter·ror·ist (tĕr'erĭst) *n.* Person attempting to further his views or to rule by coercive intimidation. **ter'ror·ism** *n.* **ter·ror·is·tic** (tĕrerĭs'tĭk) *adj.*

ter·ror·ize (tĕr'erīz) *v.t.* (**-ized, -iz·ing**). Fill with terror; rule or maintain power by terrorism. **ter·ror·i·za·tion** (tĕrerĭzā'shon) *n.*

ter·ry (tĕr'ē) *n.* (pl. **-ries**) & *adj.* (Pile fabric) with loops forming pile left uncut, also called ~ **cloth**.

terse (tērs) *adj.* (**ters·er, ters·est**). (of speech, style, writer) Free from cumbrousness and superfluity, smooth and concise; curt. **terse'ly** *adv.* **terse'ness** *n.*

ter·ti·ar·y (tēr'shēērē, -sherē) *adj.* 1. Of the third order, rank, class, stage, etc. 2. **T**~, (geol.) of the period subsequent to the Mesozoic, forming the earlier part of the Cenozoic, characterized by the appearance of mammals other than man. 3. (ornith., of wing feathers) Borne on humerus. 4. ~ **color**, (painting) one of the grayish hues obtained by mixing two secondary colors (e.g. purple with green). **tertiary** *n.* 1. Tertiary color; tertiary feather. 2. Member of third order of monastic body. 3. **T**~, (geol.) Tertiary period or system.

ter·va·lent (tērvā'lent) *adj.* (chem.) = TRIVALENT.

ter·za ri·ma (tērt'sa rē'ma). Form of verse in sets of three 10- or 11-syllabled lines rhyming *a b a*, *b c b*, etc., as in Dante's *Divina Commedia.* [It., = "third rhyme"]

tes·la (tĕs'la) *n.* (abbrev. T) Unit of magnetic induction in M.K.S. system. [f. N. *Tesla* (1856–1943), U.S. electrician]

tes·sel·late, tes·se·late (tĕs'elāt) *vbs.t.* (**-lat·ed, -lat·ing**). Make into mosaic, form (esp. pavement) by combining variously colored blocks into pattern. **tes'sel·lat·ed** *adj.* Composed of, ornamented with, small colored blocks arranged in pattern; (zool., bot.) marked, colored, in regularly arranged squares or patches, reticulated. **tes·sel·la·tion, tes·se·la·tion** (tĕselā'shon) *ns.*

tes·ser·a (tĕs'era) *n.* (pl. **tes·ser·ae** pr. tĕs'erē). 1. (Gk. and Rom. hist.) Small tablet of wood, bone, ivory, etc., used as token, tally, label, etc. 2. Each of small square pieces of marble, glass, tile, etc., of which mosaic pavement etc. is made up.

***Terrapin** is a name applied both to particular varieties of freshwater tortoises in eastern North America, and to freshwater tortoises in general. Tortoises in the genus Terrapene are terrestrial.*

test[1] (tĕst) *n.* 1. Critical examination or trial of qualities of person or thing; means of so examining; standard for comparison or trial, cicumstances suitable for this; (chem.) examination of substance under known conditions to determine its identity or that of one of its constituents, reagent used for this. 2. ~ **case**, (law) case in which decision is taken as settling a number of other cases involving same question of law; ~ **match**, one of series of usu. five cricket games played between sides representing England and Australia or other country, esp. of the Commonwealth, as test of superiority; ~ **meal**, meal of specified quantity and composition given to enable gastric secretions etc. to be examined; ~ **paper**, school examination paper written by student; ~ **pattern**, (television) design transmitted to receivers to test transmission quality; ~ **pilot**, one who pilots aircraft on experimental flights; ~ **stand**, device that keeps missile or rocket immobilized during test of full engine thrust; ~ **tube**, (chem.) tube of thin glass closed at one end, used to hold substance under test etc.; ~**-tube baby**, (colloq.) one conceived by artificial insemination, or developing elsewhere than in a mother's body. **test** *v.t.* Put to the test, make trial of; try severely, tax (endurance etc.); subject to chemical test.

test[2] (tĕst) *n.* External covering or shell of tunicates.

tes·ta (tĕs'ta) *n.* (pl. **-tae** pr. -tē). (bot.) Seed coat.

tes·ta·ceous (tĕstā'shus) *adj.* Having a shell, esp. a hard shell; of shells, shelly; (bot., zool.) of color of tile or red brick, brownish red.

tes·ta·cy (tĕs'tasē) *n.* Being testate.

tes·ta·ment (tĕs'tament) *n.* 1. (law) Will, esp. (formerly) disposition of personal as dist. from real property. 2. (colloq.) (Written) statement, affirmation, of (political) beliefs, principles, etc. 3. (bibl.) Covenant between God and man (archaic), hence, **Old, New, T**~, (abbrev. O.T., N.T.) main divisions of Bible consisting respectively of books of old or Mosaic, and new or Christian, dispensation; **T**~, copy of New Testament. **tes·ta·men·ta·ry** (tĕstamĕn'terē) *adj.* Of (nature of), relating to, a will.

tes·tate (tĕs'tāt) *adj.* & *n.* (Person) who has left a valid will at death.

tes·ta·tor (tĕs´tāter, tĕstā´-) *n.* Person who makes or has died leaving a will. **tes·ta·trix** (tĕstā´-trĭks) *n. fem.* (pl. **-tri·ces** pr. -trisēz).

test·er[1] (tĕs´ter) *n.* Person or thing that tests.

test·er[2] (tĕs´ter) *n.* Canopy, esp. over four-poster bed.

tes·ti·cle (tĕs´tĭkel) *n.* Testis, esp. in man and most other mammals. **tes·tic·u·lar** (tĕstĭk´yuler) *adj.*

tes·tic·u·late (tĕstĭk´yulĭt) *adj.* Having, shaped like, testicles; (bot., of some orchids) having 2 tubers of this shape.

tes·ti·fy (tĕs´tĭfī) *v.* (**-fied, -fy·ing**). Bear witness; (law) give evidence; affirm, declare, be evidence of, evince. **tes´ti·fi·er** *n.*

tes·ti·mo·ni·al (tĕstimō´nēal) *n.* Certificate of character, conduct, or qualifications; gift presented, esp. in public at ~ **dinner**, as mark of esteem, in acknowledgement of services, etc. **tes·ti·mo´ni·al·ize** *v.t.* (**-ized, -iz·ing**). Present with testimonial.

tes·ti·mo·ny (tĕs´timōnē) *n.* (pl. **-nies**). Evidence, esp. (law) statement made under oath or affirmation.

tes·tis (tĕs´tĭs) *n.* (pl. **-tes** pr. -tēz). Male organ in which sperms are produced; in man and most other mammals, each of two such organs enclosed in scrotum.

tes·tos·ter·one (tĕstŏs´terōn) *n.* Male sex hormone secreted by testes; synthetic preparation of this.

tes·tu·di·nate (tĕst o͞o´dinĭt, -nāt, -tū´-) *adj.* Arched, vaulted, like tortoise shell.

tes·ty (tĕs´tē) *adj.* (**-ti·er, -ti·est**). Irritable, touchy. **tes´ti·ly** *adv.* **tes´ti·ness** *n.*

The ***Teton Range*** *extends from the southern boundary of Yellowstone to the Teton Pass. The first European to see the mountains was John Colter in 1808 as a member of the Lewis and Clark expedition.*

Tet (tĕt) *n.* Three-day celebration of arrival of lunar new year as observed in SE. Asia.

tet·a·nus (tĕt´anus) *n.* 1. (med.) Painful and often fatal disease caused by microorganism, usu. introduced through wound, and characterized by tonic spasm and rigidity of voluntary muscles. 2. (physiol.) Prolonged contraction of muscle produced by rapidly repeated stimuli. **tet´a·noid** *adj.*

tetch·y, tech·y (tĕch´ē) *adjs.* (**tetch·i·er, tetch·i·est, tech·i·er, tech·i·est**). Peevish, irritable. **tetch´i·ly, tech´i·ly** *advs.* **tetch´i·ness, tech´i·ness** *ns.*

tête-à-tête (tā´tătāt´, tĕt´atĕt´) *n.* & *adj.* (Of) private conversation or interview between two persons. ~ *adv.* In private, without presence of third person.

The ***tetradactyl*** *structure of the potto's paws is due to the index finger being reduced to a small knob and the thumb being widely opposed to the remaining digits — an adaptation to life in trees.*

teth·er (tĕdh´er) *n.* Rope, chain, halter, by which grazing animal is confined; **end of one's ~**, extreme limit of one's resources. **tether** *v.t.* Make fast, confine, with tether (freq. fig.).

Te·thys (tē´thĭs). (Gk. myth.) Sea deity, daughter of Uranus and Ge, and wife of Oceanus.

Te·ton (tē´ton) **Range.** Range of the Rocky Mountains, in NW. Wyoming and SE. Idaho; highest peak, Grand Teton, 13,766 ft. (4,196 m) in Grand Teton National Park in Wyoming.

tet·ra (tĕt´ra) *n.* Any of various small freshwater fishes (family Characidae) of the Amer. tropics, kept in home aquariums.

tetra- *prefix.* Four.

tet·ra·cy·cline (tĕtrasī´klĭn, -klēn) *n.* Yellow crystalline compound, $C_{22}H_{24}N_2O_8$, used as a broad spectrum antibiotic.

tet·rad (tĕt´răd) *n.* The number four, set or group of four.

tet·ra·dac·tyl (tĕtradăk´til) *adj.* & *n.* (Animal) with four fingers or toes. **tet·ra·dac´ty·lous** *adj.*

tet·ra·eth·yl (tĕtraĕth´il) *adj.* (chem.) Containing four ethyl groups; ~ **lead**, heavy colorless liquid used in fuels to prevent knock in internal combustion engines.

tet·ra·flu·o·ro·eth·yl·ene (tĕt-raflo͞oerōĕth´ilēn, -floorō-, -flōrō-, -flŏrō-) *n.* (chem.) Colorless, water-insoluble inflammable gas, C_2F_4, used to synthesize various polymeric resins.

tet·ra·gram (tĕt′ragrăm) *n.* 1. Word of four letters. 2. Quadrilateral.

Tet·ra·gram·ma·ton (tĕtragrăm′atŏn) *n.* Hebrew word of four consonants (YHWH or JHVH) representing the incommunicable name of God.

tet·ra·he·dron (tĕtrahē′dron) *n.* (pl. **-drons, -dra** pr. -dra). Solid figure bounded by four plane triangles; triangular pyramid; crystal of this form. **tet·ra·he′dral** *adj.*

te·tral·o·gy (tĕtrăl′ojē) *n.* (pl. **-gies**). Series of four connected operas, plays, etc., esp. (Gk. antiq.) series of three tragedies and a satyric drama produced at Athens at festival of Dionysus.

te·tram·e·ter (tĕtrăm′ĭter) *n.* 1. (Gk. and L. pros.) Verse consisting of four measures in trochaic, iambic, or anapestic meter. 2. (Engl. pros.) Line of verse of four feet.

tet·ra·pod (tĕt′rapŏd) *adj.* & *n.* (Vertebrate) having two pairs of limbs (zool.; now more usu. than *quadruped* and not necessarily implying walking on four feet).

tet·ra·style (tĕt′rastīl) *adj.* & *n.* (Portico) of four columns.

tet·ra·syl·la·ble (tĕtrasĭl′abel) *n.* Word of four syllables. **tet·ra·syl·la·bic** (tĕtrasĭlăb′ĭk) *adj.*

tet·ra·va·lent (tĕtravā′lent) *adj.* (chem.) Having a VALENCE of four. **tet·ra·va′lence, tet·ra·va′len·cy** *ns.*

tet·rode (tĕt′rōd) *n.* Vacuum tube with four main electrodes.

Teu·ton (too͞′ton, tū′-) *n.* 1. One of the ancient **Teutones**, or **Teutoni**, a N. European people in ancient Roman times. 2. One of a N. European race of tall stature with long heads, blue eyes, and fair hair and skin, first appearing in Germany, Scandinavia, and the Netherlands. 3. German. **Teu′ton·ize** *v.* (**-ized, -iz·ing**).

Teu·ton·ic (too͞tŏn′ĭk, tū-) *adj.* Of the Teutons or their languages (see GERMANIC).

Tex. *abbrev.* Texas.

Tex·as (tĕk′sas). Second largest state in the United States, in the S. Central part, bordered on the SW. by Mexico and on the SE. by the Gulf of Mexico; discovered and explored by Spanish and by French who claimed it as part of Louisiana; acquired by U.S. with Louisiana Purchase, 1803; relinquished by treaty with Spain, 1819 and became province of Mexico; declared independence after battle of San Jacinto, 1836, and became Republic of Texas; sought annexation and became 28th state admitted to the Union, 1845; capital, Austin. **Tex′an** *adj.* & *n.*

text (tĕkst) *n.* 1. Wording of anything written or printed, esp. the very words and sentences as orig. written, as opp. to translation, commentary, notes, etc. 2. (print.) Type, as opp. to illustrations etc. 3. Passage of Scripture quoted as authority or esp. chosen as subject of sermon etc.; subject, theme. 4. **text′book**, manual of instruction in any branch of science or study, work recognized as an authority; **text hand**, fine large kind of handwriting esp. used for manuscripts.

tex·tile (tĕks′tĭl, -tīl) *adj.* Of weaving; woven, suitable for weaving. ~ *n.* Textile fabric or material.

tex·tu·al (tĕks′cho͞oal) *adj.* Of, in, the text. **tex′tu·al·ly** *adv.*

tex·tu·al·ist (teks′cho͞oalĭst) *n.* One who adheres strictly to the letter of the text; one well acquainted with text, esp. of Bible. **tex′tu·al·ism** *n.*

tex·ture (tĕks′cher) *n.* Character of textile fabric, resulting from way in which it is woven; arrangement of constituent parts, structure, constitution; representation of surface of objects in work of art, (also) character of surface of paint in picture etc. **tex′tur·al** *adj.* **tex′tur·al·ly** *adv.*

Th *symbol.* Thorium.

-th *suffix.* Forming ordinal and fractional numbers with all simple numbers from 4 on (*fourth, fifth, twentieth*).

Thack·er·ay (thăk′erē), **William Makepeace** (1811–63). English novelist, author of *Vanity Fair, Henry Esmond, The Virginians*, etc.

Thai, Tai (tī, tah′ē) *adjs.* Of Thailand or its people or languages. ~ *ns.* (pl. **Thais, Tais**, collect. **Thai, Tai**). 1. Native, inhabitant, of Thailand; (member of) a people of Mongolian stock who migrated southward from S. China (*c*10th c.) and now inhabit parts of Thailand, Burma, Vietnam, and Laos. 2. Language of Thailand. 3. Group of languages spoken over a wide area in SE. Asia. **Thai′land**. Kingdom in SE. Asia, until 1939 called Siam; capital Bangkok. **Thai′land·er** *n.* [Siamese *thai* free]

*After squandering a fortune, **Thackeray** earned his living as a journalist. He was editor of 'Punch' and founded 'Cornhill Magazine'. His novels were written as instalments for magazines.*

*The Astrodome at Houston, **Texas,** was built in 1965 and cost $US 31.6m. It was the first air-conditioned, all-purpose stadium and the roof has a diameter of 642 feet.*

*Despite the tourist image of golden temples and their dancers, **Thailand** is a major rice producer in South-East Asia. It also exports teak and rubber, and tin and gems are mined.*

Tha·ïs (tā´ĭs, tahēs´). Athenian courtesan who accompanied Alexander the Great on his Asiatic campaign and later became wife of Ptolemy Lagus, king of Egypt; hence, any cultured and intelligent courtesan.

thal·a·mus (thăl´*a*mus) *n.* (pl. **-mi** pr. -mī). 1. (anat.) Interior region of brain where certain important sensory nerves, esp. the optic nerve, originate (hence sometimes called **optic** ~). 2. (bot.) Receptacle of flower. **tha·lam·ic** (th*a*lăm´ĭk) *adj.*

tha·las·sic (th*a*lăs´ĭk) *adj.* Of sea(s), esp. of smaller or inland seas as dist. from oceans.

Tha·les (thā´lēz) (end of 7th c. B.C.). Greek philosopher of Miletus, one of the seven sages, believed to have founded the geometry of lines, discovered several theorems, and advanced the study of astronomy; he regarded water as the principle of all material things.

Tha·li·a (th*a*lī´*a*, thā´lē*a*, thāl´y*a*). (Gk. and Rom. myth.) 1. Muse of comedy. 2. One of the Graces. **Tha·li´an** *adj.*

tha·lid·o·mide (th*a*lĭd´*o*mīd) *n.* Sedative drug, the taking of which by pregnant women was followed *c*1960 by the birth of children with many defects, including malformed limbs; so ~ **child**.

thal·li·um (thăl´ēum) *n.* (chem.) Soft bluish-white leaden-lustered metallic element; symbol Tl, at. no. 81, at. wt. 204.37. **thal´lic, thal´lous** *adjs.* [Gk. *thallos* green shoot, from brilliant green line in its spectrum]

thal·lo·phyte (thăl´*o*fīt) *n.* Plant whose body is a thallus, e.g. seaweed, liverwort.

thal·lus (thăl´*u*s) *n.* (pl. **thal·li** pr. thăl´ī, **thal·lus·es**). Body of a primitive plant that is not divided into leaves, stem, and roots but consists of more or less uniform tissue. **thal´loid** *adj.*

Thames (tĕmz). Chief river of England, on which London stands, rising in Gloucestershire and flowing 210 mi. (336 km) into North Sea.

Tham·y·ris (thăm´*e*rĭs). (Gk. legend) Thracian poet and musician blinded by the muses for his arrogance.

than (dhăn, unstressed dh*a*n) *conj.* Introducing second member of comparison.

thane (thān) *n.* (Engl. hist.) One holding land of king or other superior by virtue of military service, with rank between ordinary freemen and hereditary nobles; (Sc. hist.) one, ranking with earl's son,

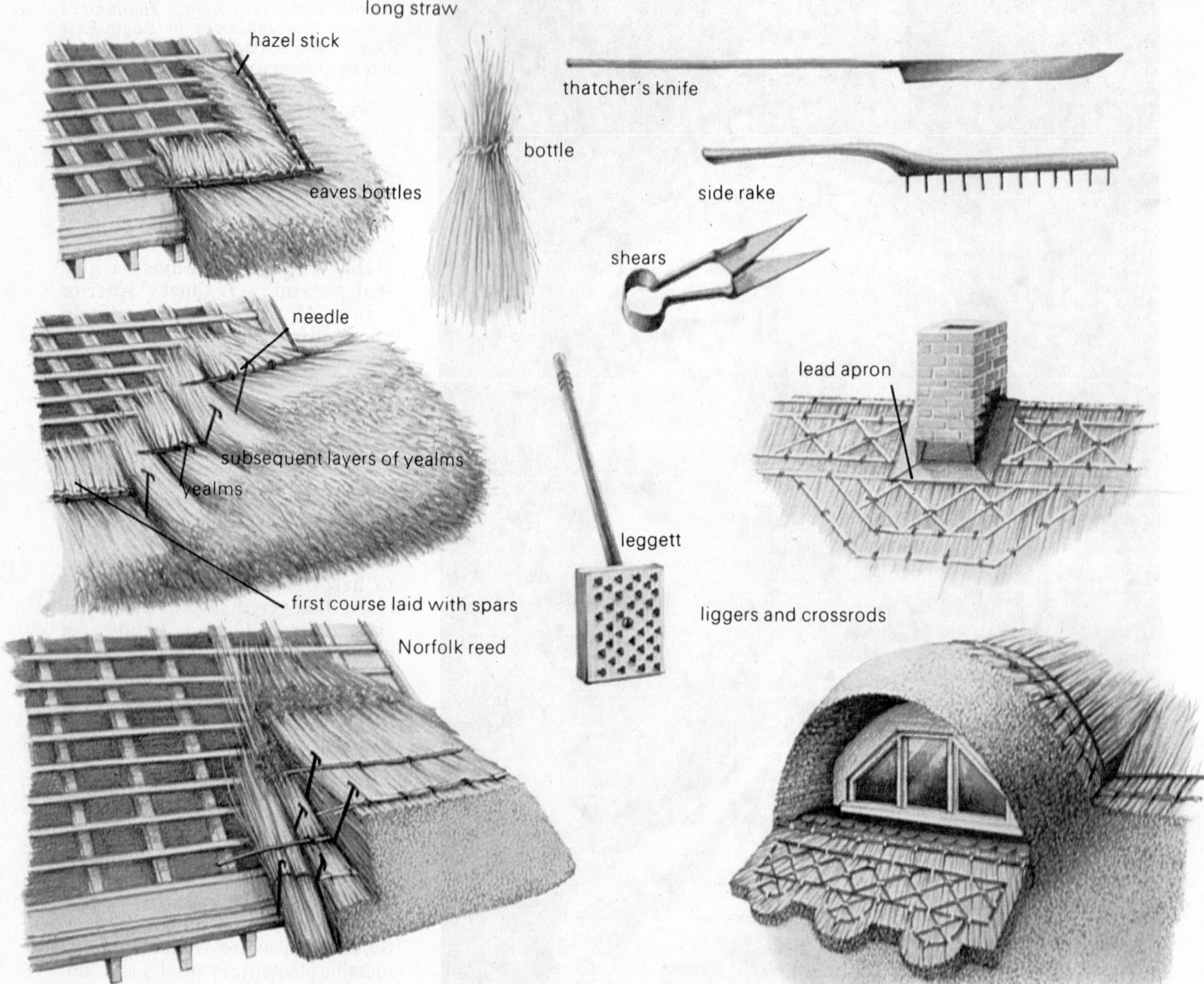

holding land of the king, chief of a clan.

thank (thăngk) *v.t.* Express gratitude to (person *for* thing); ~ **you**, I thank you (as polite formula of gratitude etc.). **thank** *n.* (now only in pl.) (Expression of) gratitude; ~**s**, thank you; ~**s to**, owing to, as the result of; **thanksgiv'ing**, expression of gratitude, esp. to God; form of words for this; **Thanksgiving** (**Day**), annual festival and legal holiday, usu. on fourth Thursday of November, first held 1621 by the Plymouth colony in thankfulness for its first harvest. **thank·ful** (thăngk'ful) *adj.* Grateful, expressive of thanks. **thank'ful·ly** *adv.* **thank'ful·ness** *n.*

thank·less (thăngk'lĭs) *adj.* Not feeling or expressing gratitude; (of task etc.) not likely to win thanks, unprofitable. **thank'less·ly** *adv.* **thank'less·ness** *n.*

that (dhăt, unstressed dh*a*t) *pron.* 1. (*demonstr.*) (pl. **those** pr. dhōz) Person or thing referred to, observed, understood, in question, etc.; (coupled or contrasted with *this*) esp., the farther, less immediate or obvious, etc., of two; **and all** ~, and so forth; **at** ~, at that standard, (even) in that capacity; too, besides; ~ **is** (**to say**), introducing explanation of preceding word, phrase, etc.; **that's that!** (colloq.) that is taken care of, completed, decided, etc.; **with that**, immediately following; at once. 2. (*rel.*) (introducing defining clause; often omitted) Who, whom, which. **that** *adj.* (pl. **those** pr. dhōz). Designating person or thing referred to etc.; the (used demonstratively not merely definitively); farther or less immediate of the two (opp. this); well known (often implying censure or dislike, but sometimes admiration). ~ *adv.* (colloq.) To the extent or degree indicated (as ~ **far, much**). **that** *conj.* Introducing dependent clause, esp. expressing result or consequence.

Cost of labor coupled with fewer men interested in learning the craft of thatching, and a shortage of reed, has resulted in a reduction in the number of buildings roofed with **thatch.** *Many that were formerly thatched have had the old straw replaced with tiles. Reeds used for this purpose had a life of 75 years but straw must be replaced in 20.*

that-a·way (dhăt'*a*wā) *adv.* (colloq.) In the direction or manner indicated.

thatch (thăch) *n.* Roof covering of straw, reeds, etc. ~ *v.t.* Roof or cover with thatch; make (roof) of thatch. **thatch'er** *n.* **thatch'ing** *n.* Thatch.

Thatch·er (thăch'*er*), **Margaret Hilda** (1925–). British Conservative stateswoman, first British woman prime minister, 1979– .

thau·ma·turge (thaw'mat*ẽ*rj) *n.* Worker of miracles, wonder-worker. **thau·ma·tur·gic** (thaw-mat*ẽ*r'jĭk), **thau·ma·tur'gi·cal** *adjs.* **thau'ma·tur·gy** *n.*

thaw (thaw) *v.* Reduce (frozen substance) to liquid state by raising its temperature above freezing point; become liquid, flexible, or limp by rise of temperature after being frozen; (fig.) free, be freed, from coldness or stiffness, (cause to) unbend or become genial. ~ *n.* Thawing, melting of ice and snow after frost; warmth of weather that thaws.

the (dh*e* preceding a consonant, dhē preceding a vowel or for emphasis) *definite article.* Denoting, defining, or singling out person(s) or thing(s) already mentioned or under discussion, actually or potentially existent, unique, familiar, or otherwise sufficiently identified; applied to singular nouns as representing species, class, etc.; used with adjectives used abs., *the just*, *the wicked*; emphatically, applied to person or thing best known or best entitled to the name. ~ *adv.* In that degree, by that amount, on that account; **the ... the**, by how much ... by so much; in what degree ... in that degree.

the·ar·chy (thē′ārkē) *n.* (pl. **-chies**). Theocracy; system or order of gods.

theat. *abbrev.* Theater.

the·a·ter, the·a·tre (thē′*a*ter) *ns.* 1. Building or outdoor area for dramatic performances etc.; (Gk. and Rom. antiq.) open-air structure in form of segment of circle rising gradually; room, hall, for lectures etc., with seats in tiers; **~-in-the-round**, dramatic performance on stage surrounded by spectators. 2. Scene, field, of action. 3. **~ of operations**, (mil.) area of military operations and their necessary support in theater of war. 4. Natural formation of land resembling ancient Greek or Roman theater. 5. Dramatic literature or art. **~ of the absurd**, avant-garde style in drama that emphasizes irrational, incongruous, and aimless elements and omits or distorts traditional ideas of character and plot development in order to raise questions about the nature of reality and to depict the alienation and anxiety of modern man.

the·at·ri·cal (thēăt′rĭk*a*l), **the·at·ric** (thēăt′rĭk) *adjs.* Of or suited to theater; of acting or actors; calculated for effect, showy, artificial. **the·at′ri·cal·ly** *adv.* **the·at′ri·cal·ism, the·at·ri·cal·i·ty** (thēătrĭkăl′ĭtē) *ns.* **the·at′ri·cals** *n.pl.* Theatrical performances, esp. by amateurs.

The·ba·id (thē′băĭd, -bē-, thēbā′-). 1. Latin epic poem (*c*92 A.D.) by Statius, concerned with legendary expedition against Thebes to recover throne for Polynices from his brother Eteocles. 2. Ancient region in Egypt surrounding Thebes.

Thebes (thēbz). 1. Ancient capital (from time of 12th dynasty) of Upper Egypt, on site of modern Luxor. 2. (Gk. *Thivai*) Ancient city of Greece, subject of many legends, including those of Cadmus, Oedipus, and Antigone; from the late 6th c. B.C., the bitter enemy of Athens, and after the Peloponnesian War the rival of Sparta for the hegemony of Greece; it was razed in 335 B.C. but rebuilt, existed throughout Roman times, and was finally destroyed in 1311. **The′ban** *adj.* & *n.*

the·ca (thē′k*a*) *n.* (pl. **-cae** pr. -sē). 1. (bot.) Part of plant serving as receptacle, as pollen sac of anther, spore case, capsule of moss, etc. 2. (zool., anat.) Case or sheath enclosing some organ or part.

thee (dhē) *pron.* Objective (accus., dat.) case of THOU; dial. and among Quakers occas. used for *thou*.

theft (thĕft) *n.* Stealing; (law) act of dishonestly appropriating another's property with intent of permanently depriving him of it.

their (dhār) *poss. pron.* Possessive case of THEY used as attrib. adj. with abs. and pred. form **theirs** (dhārz), belonging to, affecting, them.

the·ism (thē′ĭzem) *n.* Belief in gods or (esp.) a god, as opp. to ATHEISM, PANTHEISM, POLYTHEISM, esp. belief in one God as creator and supreme ruler of universe. **the′ist** *adj.* & *n.* **the·is·tic** (thēĭs′tĭk), **the·is′ti·cal** *adjs.* **the·is′ti·cal·ly** *adv.*

them (dhĕm) *pron.* Objective (accus., dat.) case of THEY.

the·mat·ic (thĭmăt′ĭk) *adj.* Of, belonging to, constituting, a theme.

The·mat·ic (thĭmăt′ĭk) **Apperception Test.** (psychol.) Projective technique using a series of standard pictures about which person being tested tells stories that presumably reveal psychological components of his or her personality.

theme (thēm) *n.* 1. Subject of discourse, conversation, composition, etc., topic; school essay. 2. (mus.) Subject, tune, or passage developed in musical composition, and recurring as a principal part of its material; tune on which variations are constructed; **~ song**, recurrent melody in a musical play, film, etc.

The·mis (thē′mĭs, thĕm′ĭs). (Gk.

John Barrymore, illustrated here by his self-portrait, was a great romantic actor of the early 1900s up until the 1940s. He had a huge following in ***theater,*** *screen and radio.*

*Excess steam being released from geothermal bores at Wairakei, New Zealand. This steam is directed to a **thermal** power station where generators can operate without furnaces.*

myth.) Goddess of law and justice.

The·mis·to·cles (th*e*mĭs′t*o*klēz) (*c*524–459 B.C.). Athenian statesman and soldier, commander of the Athenian fleet at SALAMIS.

them·selves (dhĕmsĕlvz′, dh*e*m-) *pron.* Emphatic and reflexive form corresponding to THEY, THEM.

then (dhĕn) *adv.* At that time; next, afterward, after that; **now and** ~, at one time and another, from time to time. **then** *conj.* In that case; therefore; it follows that; accordingly. ~ *adj.* Existing etc. at that time. ~ *n.* That time; **every now and** ~, from time to time.

the·nar (thē′nār) *n.* (anat.) Ball of muscle at base of thumb; palm of hand; sole of foot.

thence (dhĕns) *adv.* (archaic and literary) From that place, from there; from that source, for that reason. **thence·forth** (dhĕnsfōrth′, -fōrth′, dhĕns′fōrth, -fōrth), **thence·for·ward** (dhĕnsfōr′w*e*rd), **thence·for′wards** *advs.* & *ns.* From (*from*) that time forward.

theo- *prefix.* God.

the·o·cen·tric (thē*o*sĕn′trĭk) *adj.* Having God as its center.

the·oc·ra·cy (thēŏk′r*a*sē) *n.* (pl. **-cies**). Government by God, directly or through a priestly class etc.; state so governed; **the T**~, the Jewish commonwealth from Moses to the monarchy.

the·oc·ra·sy (thēŏk′r*a*sē) *n.* Union of the soul with God through contemplation (among Neoplatonists, Buddhists, etc.).

the·o·crat (thē′*o*krăt) *n.* Ruler in, subject under, a theocracy. **the·o·crat·ic** (thē*o*krăt′ĭk) *adj.* **the·o·crat′i·cal·ly** *adv.*

The·oc·ri·tus (thēŏk′rĭt*u*s) (3rd c. B.C.). Sicilian Greek poet; regarded as the originator of pastoral poetry.

the·od·o·lite (thēŏd′*o*līt) *n.* Surveying instrument for measuring horizontal and vertical angles; telescope rotating around a graduated circular plate and also free to swivel in vertical plane over a graduated arc. **the·od·o·lit·ic** (thēŏd*o*lĭt′ĭk) *adj.*

The·o·do·ra (thē*o*dōr′*a*, -dōr′*a*) (508?–48). Empress of the Eastern Roman Empire; married Justinian I, 523, and greatly influenced political and religious events.

The·o·dore (thē′*o*dōr, -dōr). Name of three czars of Russia: ~ **I** (1557–98), succeeded his father Ivan the Terrible 1584; ~ **II** (1589–1605), son of Boris Godunov, succeeded his father 1605 and was murdered in the same year; ~ **III** (1661–82), succeeded his father Alexey 1679.

The·od·o·ric (thēŏd′*e*rĭk) (*c*454–526). King of the Ostrogoths, invader (488–93) and conqueror of Italy, which he ruled from Ravenna; attempted to revive the Western Roman Empire.

The·o·do·si·us (thē*o*dō′shē*u*s, -sh*u*s). Name of three emperors of the Eastern Roman Empire: ~ **I** (*c*346–95), "the Great," Roman general, born in Spain, became emperor of the East 379; ~ **II** (401–50), succeeded his father Arcadius as emperor 408; ~ **III** (dates uncertain), was proclaimed emperor 715 by the rebellious Byzantine army and deposed 717 by Leo III. **The·o·do′sian** *adj.* Of Theodosius; (esp.) ~ **Code**, code of all imperial legislation since time of Constantine, promulgated in 438 by Theodosius II.

theol. *abbrev.* Theologian; theological; theology.

the·o·lo·gian (thē*o*lō′j*a*n, -jē*a*n) *n.* Person skilled in theology.

the·ol·o·gy (thēŏl′*o*jē) *n.* (pl. **-gies**). Science of religion, study of God or gods, esp. of attributes and relations with man etc.; **dogmatic** ~, that based on the authoritative teaching of the Scriptures and the church; **natural** ~, dealing with knowledge of God as gained from evidence by natural human reason without the aid of revelation; **positive, revealed** ~, based on revelation; **speculative** ~, not confined to revelation but giving scope to human speculation; systematic ~, methodical arrangement of the truths of religion in their natural connection. **the·o·log·i·cal** (thē*o*lŏj′ĭk*a*l) *adj.* **the·o·log′i·cal·ly** *adv.*

the·om·a·chy (thēŏm′*a*kē) *n.* (pl. **-chies**). Strife among the gods.

the·o·mor·phic (thē*o*mōr′fĭk) *adj.* Having the form or likeness of a god.

the·o·rem (thē′*o*r*e*m, thēr′*e*m) *n.* Universal or general proposition, not self-evident but demonstrable by chain of reasoning; algebraic or other rule, esp. expressed by symbols or formulas. **the·o·re·mat·ic** (thē*o*r*e*măt′ĭk, thēr*e*-) *adj.*

the·o·ret·i·cal (thē*o*rĕt′ĭk*a*l), **the·o·ret·ic** (thē*o*rĕt′ĭk) *adjs.* Of, consisting in, relating to, conforming to, theory; existing only in theory, hypothetical; addicted to, constructing, dealing with, theories, speculative. **the·o·ret′ics** *n.pl.* Theory, theoretical parts of science etc.

the·o·ry (thē′*o*rē, thēr′ē) *n.* (pl. **-ries**). Scheme or system of ideas or statements held to explain group of facts or phenomena, statement of general laws, principles, or causes of something known or observed; systematic conception or statement of principles of something, abstract knowledge, formulation of this; branch of art or technical subject concerned with knowledge of its principles or methods, as opp. to practice; systematic statement of general principles of some branch of mathematics; mere hypothesis, conjecture, individual view or notion. **the·o·re·ti·cian** (thēore-tĭsh′an, thēre-), **the′o·rist** *ns.* **the·o·rize** (thē′orīz) *v.* (**-rized, -riz·ing**). **the′o·riz·er** *n.*

the·os·o·phy (thēŏs′ofē) *n.* (pl. **-phies**). Philosophy professing to attain to knowledge of God by spiritual ecstasy, direct intuition, or special individual relations, now usu., doctrines of the Theosophical Society. **the·o·soph·ic** (thēosŏf′-ĭk), **the·o·soph′i·cal** *adjs.* (esp.) **T~ Society**, society founded in 1875 in New York, advocating universal brotherhood, and following esp. Brahminic and Buddhistic teachings. **the·o·soph′i·cal·ly** *adv.* **the·os′o·phist** *n.*

ther·a·peu·tic (thĕrapū′tĭk), **ther·a·peu·ti·cal** (thĕrapū′tĭkal) *adjs.* Of the healing of disease, curative; ~ **abortion**, abortion performed when health of mother is endangered by pregnancy. **ther·a·peu′tics** *n.pl.* Branch of medicine concerned with remedial treatment of disease. **ther·a·peu′-ti·cal·ly** *adv.*

ther·a·py (thĕr′apē) *n.* (pl. **-pies**). 1. Medical or physical treatment of disease or physical defects. 2. Healing quality or power. 3. Treatment of patients with psychological, social, or emotional problems, as by PSYCHOTHERAPY. **ther′a·pist** *n.*

Ther·a·va·da (thĕravah′da) *n.* One of the two great schools of Buddhism, surviving esp. in Sri Lanka, Burma, Thailand, and Kampuchea; Hinayanist name for Hinayana.

there (dhār) *adv.* In or at that place; at that point in argument, situation, progress of affairs, etc.; to that place or point; used unemphatically to introduce sentence or clause in which verb comes before its subject (also, with some form of the verb *be*, without inversion); **there′about(s)**, near that place; near that number, quantity, etc.; **thereaf′ter**, (archaic) after that; **thereat′** (archaic) there; thereupon, at that; **thereby′**, (archaic) by or through that; **thereby hangs a tale**, in that connection there is something to be told; **therefor′**, (archaic) for that, for it; for that reason, on that account; **there′fore**, in consequence of that; for that reason, accordingly, consequently; **therein′**, (archaic) in that place; in that respect; **thereinaf′ter**, (archaic) later, in same document etc.; **thereof′**, (archaic) of that, of it; **thereon′**, (archaic) to that, to it; in addition; **there′upon**, in consequence of that; soon, immediately, after that; (archaic) upon that; **therewith′**, (archaic) with that; thereupon. **there** *n.* That place or point. ~ *int.* Exclamation expressing confirmation, triumph, dismay, etc.

therm, therme (thērm) *ns.* Unit of heat, esp. 100,000 Btu as basis of charge for gas used as fuel.

therm- = THERMO-.

-therm *comb. form.* Indicating heat, as in *endotherm, megatherm.*

ther·mal (thēr′mal) *adj.* Of heat; determined, measured, operated by heat; ~ **capacity**, (of a body) number of heat units required to raise its temperature by 1 degree; ~ **spring**, hot spring; ~ **unit**, unit of heat; **British T~ Unit**, (abbrev. Btu) amount of heat required to raise the temperature of 1 pound of water at its maximum density by 1 degree Fahrenheit. **thermal** *n.* Rising current of warm air. **ther′mic** *adj.* **ther′mal·ly** *adv.*

Ther·mi·dor (thēr′mĭdōr). Eleventh month of French revolutionary calendar, covering parts of July and August. **Ther·mi·do·ri·an** (thērmĭdōr′ēan, -dōr′-) *n.* (Fr. hist.) One of those taking part in overthrow of Robespierre on 9

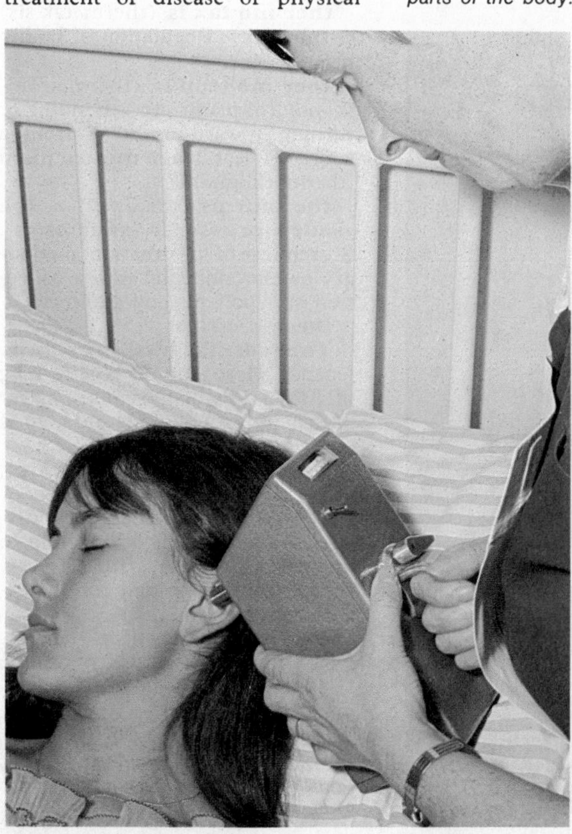

Development of new equipment has enabled much more accurate data to be obtained. An infra-red ***thermometer*** *can measure radiation from different parts of the body.*

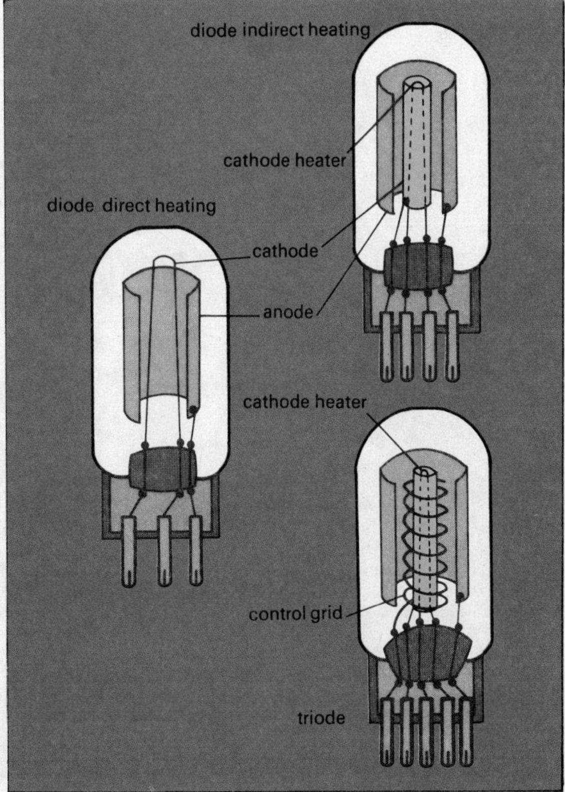

In the early days of radio, the ***thermionic valve*** *was essential. However, development of transistors and other miniature circuitry has largely eliminated valves.*

Thermidor (July 27, 1794).

therm·i·on (thẽrm´īon, thẽr´-mē-) *n.* Electrically charged particle (electron or ion) emitted from a heated body. **therm·i·on·ic** (thẽrmīŏn´ĭk, thẽrmē-) *adj.* Of, emitting, thermions; ~ **tube,** vacuum tube in which electrons emitted by a heated filament carry electric current in one direction, used as a rectifier of an alternating current and in radio receiving sets for the detection and amplification of radio waves.

therm·is·tor (th*er*mĭs´t*er*) *n.* Type of semiconductor in which the resistance decreases as the temperature rises.

ther·mite (thẽr´mīt) *n.* Mixture of finely divided aluminum and oxide of iron or oxide of other metal, producing very high temperature (*c*3,000°C) on combustion, used in smelting, welding, and for incendiary bombs.

thermo-, therm- *comb. forms.* Heat (*thermistor, thermodynamics*).

ther·mo·chem·is·try (thẽrmō-kĕm´ĭstrē) *n.* Branch of chemistry dealing with the heat changes accompanying reactions. **ther·mo·chem´i·cal** *adj.* **ther·mo·chem´ist** *n.*

ther·mo·cline (thẽr´m*o*klīn) *n.* Layer of water in ocean or certain lakes between warmer layer near surface and colder, deep-water layer below, with temperature dropping rapidly at greater depths.

ther·mo·cou·ple (thẽr´m*o*-kŭp*e*l) *n.* Device consisting of two different metals joined at two places so that when a difference of temperature exists at the junction of the metals, an electromotive force is produced that can be used to measure that difference.

ther·mo·dy·nam·ics (thẽrm*o*-dīnăm´ĭks) *n.pl.* (usu. considered sing.). Science dealing with the relationship between thermal energy (heat) and all other forms of energy (mechanical, electrical, etc.); **first law of** ~: during transformation of heat into another form of energy there is a constant relation between the amount of heat expended and energy gained; the same is true of the reverse process; **second law of** ~, heat cannot pass of its own accord from a colder to a hotter body. **ther·mo·dy·nam´ic** *adj.* **ther·mo·dy·nam´i·cal·ly** *adv.*

ther·mo·e·lec·tric·i·ty (thẽr-mōĭlĕktrĭs´ĭtē, -ēlĕk-) *n.* Electricity developed by the action of heat at the junction of two different metals. **ther·mo·e·lec·tric** (thẽrmōĭlĕk´-trĭk) *adj.*

ther·mol·y·sis (thẽrmŏl´ĭsĭs) *n.* (pl. **-ses** pr. -sēz). (chem.) Dissociation, decomposition, by action of heat.

ther·mom·e·ter (th*er*mŏm´*eter*) *n.* Instrument for measuring temperature, freq. a graduated glass tube with bulb containing a substance (as mercury, alcohol) whose expansion and contraction under the influence of temperature can be accurately measured. **ther·mo·met·ric** (thẽrm*o*mĕt´rĭk), **ther·mo·met´ri·cal** *adjs.* **ther·mo·met´ri·cal·ly** *adv.* **ther·mom´e·try** *n.* Science dealing with the measurement of temperature.

ther·mo·nu·cle·ar (thẽrmō-nōō´klēe*r*, -nū´-) *adj.* Of or concerned with reactions involving the fusion of atomic nuclei at very high temperatures, as in a hydrogen bomb.

ther·mo·pile (thẽr´m*o*pīl) *n.* Set of thermocouples arranged in series, used to detect radiant heat.

ther·mo·plas·tic (thẽrm*o*plăs´-tĭk) *adj.* & *n.* (Substance) that becomes plastic when heated, hardens when cooled, and can do this repeatedly. **ther·mo·plas·tic·i·ty** (thẽrmōplăstĭs´ĭtē) *n.*

Ther·mop·y·lae (th*er*mŏp´*i*lē). Pass in Greece from Locris into Thessaly, orig. narrow but now much widened by recession of sea; scene of the heroic defense (480 B.C.) against the Persian army of Xerxes by 6,000 Greeks, including 300 Spartans under LEONIDAS.

ther·mos (thẽr´m*o*s) *n.* (also ~ **bottle, jug**) Kind of vacuum flask. [orig. trademark]

ther·mo·set·ting (thẽr´mōsĕt-ĭng) *adj.* Becoming permanently hard and rigid when heated.

ther·mo·stat (thẽr´m*o*stăt) *n.* Device that automatically regulates temperature by cutting off and restoring the supply of heat to a piece of equipment or a room etc. **ther·mo·stat·ic** (thẽrm*o*stăt´ĭk) *adj.* **ther·mo·stat´i·cal·ly** *adv.*

ther·mo·tax·is (thẽrm*o*tăk´sĭs) *n.* (physiol.) Regulation of bodily heat.

ther·mo·trop·ic (thẽrm*o*trŏp´-ĭk) *adj.* (of plants etc.) Bending or turning toward or away from a source of heat. **ther·mot·ro·pism** (th*er*mŏt´r*o*pĭz*e*m) *n.*

the·saur·us (thĭsôr´*u*s) *n.* (pl. **-saur·i** pr. -sôr´ī, **-saur·us·es**). Storehouse of information; dictionary or encyclopedia, esp. a collection of synonyms and antonyms.

these: see THIS.

The·seus (thē´sē*u*s, -sōōs). (Gk. legend) Hero, son of Aegeus, king of Athens (or of Poseidon); slayer of the Cretan Minotaur and hero of other famous exploits.

the·sis (thē´sĭs) *n.* (pl. **-ses** pr. -sēz). Proposition laid down or stated, esp. as theme to be discussed and proved; dissertation to maintain and prove thesis, esp. submitted by candidate for university degree.

Thes·pi·an (thĕs´pē*a*n) *adj.* 1. Of Thespis; of tragedy or the

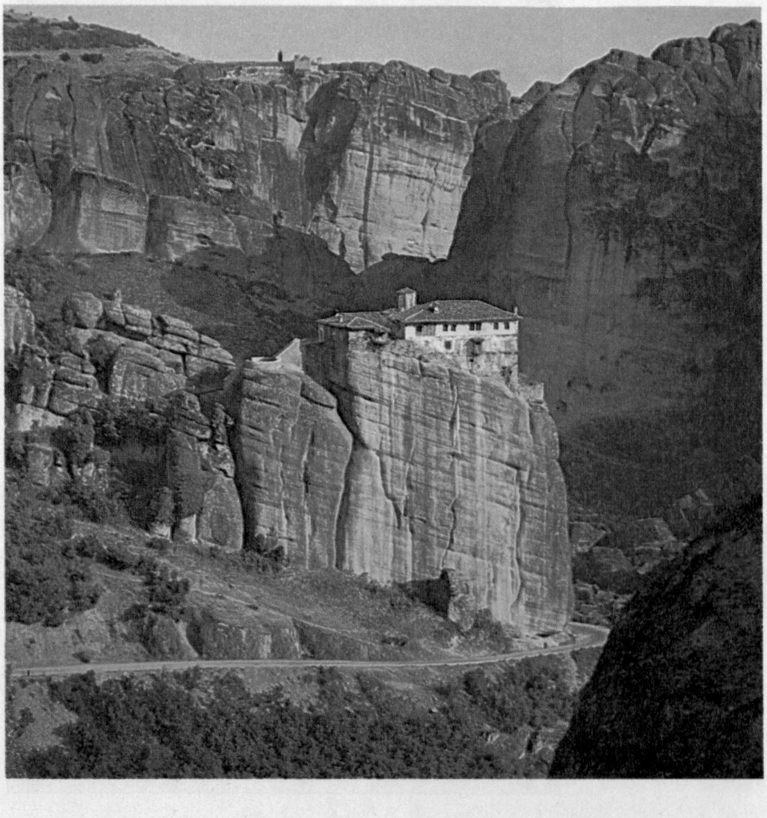

The monastery of Aghios Stephanos on a pinnacle in the modern Greek district of ***Thessaly.*** *Subject to invasion by Romans and Turks, such buildings had to be made impregnable.*

dramatic art. 2. Of Thespiae, ancient city of Greece. ~ *n.* 1. Actor or actress. 2. Native, inhabitant, of Thespiae.

Thes·pis (thĕs′pĭs) (6th c. B.C.). Greek dramatic poet, regarded as father of Greek tragedy.

Thess. *abbrev.* Thessalonians (N.T.).

Thes·sa·lo·ni·an (thĕsalō′nēan) *adj.* Of Thessalonica. ~ *n.* Native, inhabitant, of Thessalonica; (**Epistle to the**) **~s**, either of two books of the New Testament, earliest extant letters of St. Paul, written from Corinth to the new church at Thessalonica.

Thes·sa·lon·i·ca (thĕsalŏn′ĭka). Ancient city in Macedonia, founded 316 B.C. by Cassander, a general of Alexander the Great; now SALONIKA.

Thes·sa·ly (thĕs′alē). Region of Greece in the central part of the Greek peninsula bordering the Aegean.

the·ta (thā′ta, thē′-) *n.* Ninth (later 8th) letter of Greek alphabet (Θ, θ), = *th*.

The·tis (thē′tĭs). (Gk. myth.) Sea nymph, mother of ACHILLES.

they (dhā) *pron.* Third person nom. pl. pronoun, plural of HE, SHE, IT.

Thi·bet (tĭbĕt′), **Thi·bet·an** (tĭbĕt′an): see TIBET, TIBETAN.

thick (thĭk) *adj.* 1. Of great or specified depth between opposite surfaces; (of line etc.) broad, not fine. 2. Arranged closely, crowded together; numerous; abounding, packed, *with*; of great or considerable density, viscid, stiff; turbid, muddy, cloudy, not clear; (of soup) thickened. 3. Stupid, dull; (of voice) muffled, indistinct; (colloq.) intimate. 4. **thick′head**, blockhead; **thick′headed**, stupid, slow-witted; **thick′set**, set or growing close together; heavily or solidly built; **thick′skinned**, (fig.) not sensitive to criticism, reproach, insult, etc. **thick′ish** *adj.* **thick′ly** *adv.* **thick** *n.* Thick part of anything, esp. fight etc.; **through ~ and thin**, through good times and bad, under all conditions, resolutely. **thick** *adv.* Thickly.

thick·en (thĭk′en) *v.* Make or become thick; make of stiffer consistence. **thick′en·er, thick′en·ing** *ns.*

thick·et (thĭk′ĭt) *n.* Dense growth of small trees, shrubs, undergrowth, etc.

thick·ness (thĭk′nĭs) *n.* Being thick; third dimension, dist. from length and breadth; what is thick; layer.

thief (thēf) *n.* (pl. **thieves** pr. thēvz). One who steals, esp. secretly and without violence. **thieve** (thēv) *v.* (**thieved, thiev·ing**). Be a thief, practice stealing; steal (thing). **thiev·er·y** (thē′verē) *n.* (pl. **-er·ies**). **thiev′ish** *adj.* **thiev′ish·ly** *adv.* **thiev′ish·ness** *n.*

As national emblem of Scotland, the ***thistle*** *was taken by migrants to places like Australia. In the warmer climate, growth was prolific and it had to be proclaimed a noxious weed.*

thigh (thī) *n.* Upper part of human leg, from hip to knee; corresponding part (or part pop. supposed to correspond) in other animals; **thigh′bone**, bone of the thigh, femur.

thim·ble (thĭm′bel) *n.* Bell-shaped sheath of metal etc. worn on end of finger to push needle in sewing; (mech. etc.) ring, tube, sleeve, ferrule, etc.; **thim′bleful** (pl. **-fuls**), small quantity (of whiskey etc.) to drink.

Thim·phu (tĭm′po͞o). Capital of Bhutan, in the W. part.

thin (thĭn) *adj.* (**thin·ner, thin·nest**). Having opposite surfaces close together; of small diameter; slender; lean, spare, not plump; not dense; not full or closely packed; of slight density or consistency; wanting body, fullness, volume, or substance; (of lines) narrow, fine; (fig.) shallow, transparent, flimsy; **~-skinned**, (fig.) sensitive. **thin′ly** *adv.* **thin′ness** *n.* **thin′nish** *adj.* **thin** *v.* (**thinned, thin·ning**). Make or become thin; reduce in bulk or number; **~ out**, reduce number of (esp. seedlings, by pulling up the less promising). **thin** *adv.* Sparsely.

thine: see THY.

thing (thĭng) *n.* 1. What is or may be an object of perception, knowledge, or thought. 2. Entity, being, esp. inanimate object. 3. Piece of property, possession, (pl.) clothes, garments, esp. outdoor garments; (pl.) implements, utensils. 4. (pl.) Affairs, concerns, matters. 5. What is (to be) done, fact, deed, occurrence; what is said, expression, statement.

thing·um·a·jig (thĭng′umajĭg) *n.* (colloq.) Thing indicated vaguely because speaker cannot remember or does not wish to use correct word; what-d'you-call-it; also **thing·um·bob** (thĭng′umbŏb), **thing·a·ma·bob, thing·um·a·bob** (thĭng′amabŏb).

think (thĭngk) *v.* (**thought** pr. thawt, **think·ing**). Consider, be of opinion; form conception of; exercise mind in active way, form connected ideas; consider a matter, reflect; conceive notion of doing something, contemplate, intend; **~ about**, consider; **~ of**, consider; imagine; intend, contemplate; entertain idea *of*; hit upon; **~ out**, consider carefully; devise (plan etc.); **~ over**, reflect upon. **think** *n.* (colloq.) Act of thinking; **~ piece**, journalistic article dealing with general assessment and interpretation of news etc.; **~ tank**, (colloq.) organization providing advice and ideas on national, industrial, etc., problems. **think′er** *n.* (esp.) Person of skilled or powerful mind.

think·a·ble (thĭng′kabel) *adj.* Capable of being considered or thought about; conceivable; possible. **think′a·bly** *adv.*

think·ing (thĭng′kĭng) *n.* Act of one who thinks or outcome of such act; thought; opinion; judgment. ~ *adj.* Typified by thoughtfulness; rational; **put on one's ~ cap**, meditate on a problem.

thi·o (thī′ō) **acid.** Acid in which oxygen is partly or wholly replaced by sulfur.

thi·o·cy·an·ic (thīōsīăn′ĭk) *adj.* **~ acid**, colorless unstable liquid acid (HCNS) with penetrating odor. **thi·o·cy·a·nate** (thīōsī′anāt) *n.* Salt of this.

thi·o·sul·fate (thīōsŭl′fāt) *n.* Salt of thiosulfuric acid ($H_2S_2O_2$), extremely unstable acid; used in photography, formerly called *hyposulphite* (see HYPO).

third (thērd) *adj.* Next after second; (baseball) **~ base**, base between second base and home plate; (baseball) **~ baseman**, infielder near third base; **~-class**, (esp.) poor, inferior; **~ degree**, severe examination of prisoner to extort confession or information; (freemasonry) degree of master mason; **~-degree burn**, severe burn that destroys epidermis and exposes nerve endings; **~ dimension**, depth in an object as distinguished from length or width, which are the flat surface dimensions; quality of possessing or appearing to possess such depth; quality of appearing real; **~ gear**, gear next above second gear on motor vehicle or bicycle; **third′-**

Above: ***Dylan Thomas*** *as painted by Rupert Shepherd. Considered by some critics as an outstanding poet of his generation, he did not attain popular success until 'Under Milk Wood'.*

Right: The ***thorax*** *of a grasshopper is covered by the large pronotum which, on members of the Acrididae family, has conspicuous crests. Their function is not known.*

hand, (*adj.*) having had two previous owners or users; learned, acquired, etc., through two successive intermediaries; **third mate**, officer on merchant vessel next below second mate; **third party**: see PARTY; **third person**, (gram.) personal pronoun (*he, she, it, they*), verb form denoting person or thing spoken of; **third rail**, (in some electric railroads) rail through which current is conducted, lying alongside those on which train runs; **third-rate**, inferior, decidedly poor, in quality; **Third Reich**: see REICH; **Third World**, underdeveloped countries of Asia, Africa, and Latin Amer., usu. not aligned with either the communist or the Western nations. **third** *n.* Third part (see PART[1] sense 1); third thing, person, place, class, etc.; (in motor vehicle) third gear; (mus.) interval of which the span involves three alphabetical names of notes; harmonic combination of the two notes thus separated. **third'ly** *adv.* In the third place.

thirst (thẽrst) *n.* Uneasy or painful sensation caused by want of drink; desire for drink; (fig.) ardent desire, craving. **thirst'y** *adj.* (**thirst·i·er, thirst·i·est**). Feeling thirst; dry, parched, arid; (colloq.) causing thirst; (fig.) eager, greedy. **thirst'i·ly** *adv.* **thirst'i·ness** *n.* **thirst** *v.i.* Feel thirst.

thir·teen (thẽr'tēn') *adj.* & *n.* One more than 12 (13, xiii, or XIII). **thir'teenth'** *adj.* & *n.*

thir·ty (thẽr'tē) *adj.* Amounting to 30; **T~-nine Articles**, articles of religion assented to by person taking orders in Church of England; **T~ Years' War**, war (1618–48) originating between Catholics and Protestants of Germany and later involving most of Western Europe. **thirty** *n.* (pl. **-ties**). Cardinal number, 3 times 10 (30, xxx, or XXX); set of 30 things or persons; **thirties**, numbers etc. from 30 to 39; these years of century or life. **thir'ti·eth** *adj.* & *n.*

this (dhĭs) *demonstr. pron.* & *adj.* (pl. **these** pr. dhēz). The (person, thing, event, time) near, present, just mentioned (freq. opp. THAT). ~ *adv.* To the extent or degree indicated (as ~ **far, much**).

This·be (thĭz'bē). (Rom. legend) Lover of PYRAMUS.

this·tle (thĭs'el) *n.* Prickly composite herbaceous, often woody, plant of *Cirsium* and related genera, with stems, leaves, and involucres thickly armed with prickles, usu. globular flower heads and most freq. purple flowers; **this'tledown**, downy appendage of thistle (freq. as type of lightness or flimsiness). **this'tly** *adj.*

thith·er (thĭdh'*er*, dhĭdh'-) *adv.* (archaic) To that place.

tho, tho' (dhō) = THOUGH.

Thom·as[1] (tŏm'*a*s), **St.** Apostle who refused to believe that Christ had risen again unless he could see and touch his wounds (John 20); commemorated Dec. 21; **doubting** ~, skeptic.

Thom·as[2] (tŏm'*a*s), **Dylan** (1914–53). Welsh poet; author of *Under Milk Wood*, a play for voices.

Thom·as[3] (tŏm'*a*s), **Norman** (**Mattoon**) (1884–1968). Amer. socialist and politician; U.S. presidential candidate six times between 1928–48.

Thom·as[4] **à Kem·pis** (tŏm'*a*s *a* kĕm'pĭs). Thomas Hämmerken (*c*1380–1471), named for his birthplace, Kempen, near Düsseldorf; Augustinian monk, author of *De Imitatione Christi*.

Thom·as[5] **A·qui·nas** (tŏm'*a*s *a*kwī'n*a*s), **St.**: see AQUINAS.

Tho·mism (tō'mĭz*e*m, thō'-). System of theology and philosophy taught by St. Thomas AQUINAS. **Tho'mist** *n.* **Tho·mis·tic** (tōmĭs'tĭk, thō-) *adj.*

Thomp·son[1] (tŏmp's*o*n), **Francis** (1859–1907). English poet; author of "Hound of Heaven," describing the poet's flight from God, the pursuit, and the overtaking.

Thomp·son[2] (tŏmp's*o*n), **John Taliaferro** (1860–1940). U.S. general; one of the inventors of the **Thompson submachine gun**, a portable automatic weapon.

thong (thŏng) *n.* Narrow strip of hide or leather etc. used as strap etc.

Thor (thōr). (Scand. myth.) God of thunder, war, and agriculture, represented as armed with hammer.

tho·rax (thōr′ăks, thōr′-) *n.* (pl. **tho·rax·es, tho·ra·ces** pr. thōr′asēz, thōr′-). 1. (anat., zool.) Part of body of mammal between neck and abdomen that is enclosed by ribs, breastbone, and vertebrae and contains chief organs of circulation and respiration. 2. (zool.) Middle section of body of insect etc. between head and abdomen. **tho·rac·ic** (thorăs′ĭk) *adj.*

Thor·eau (thōr′ō, thōr′ō, thorō′), **Henry David** (1817–62). Amer. essayist, poet, and naturalist; author of *Walden or Life in the Woods* (1854).

tho·ri·um (thōr′ēum, thōr′-) *n.* (chem.) Radioactive metallic element that (like uranium) will undergo fission when bombarded with neutrons and is therefore a potential source of atomic energy; symbol Th, at. no. 90, at. wt. 232.0381.

thorn (thōrn) *n.* 1. Stiff sharp-pointed process on stem or other part of plant; thorn-bearing bush or tree, esp. hawthorn, whitethorn, or other species of genus *Crataegus*; ~ **in one's side** or **flesh**, constant source of annoyance (2 Cor. 12:7). 2. Name of Old English and Icelandic runic letter þ (= th). 3. ~ **apple**, poisonous plant of genus *Datura*, esp. *D. stramonium*, Jimson weed. **thorn′y** *adj.* (**thorn·i·er, thorn·i·est**). (esp., fig.) Harassing, vexatious, difficult to handle, delicate, ticklish; ~ **locust**, small tree or spiny shrub (*Robinia neomexicana*) of southwest U.S.

thor·ough (thēr′ō, thŭr′ō) *adj.* Complete, unqualified, not superficial, out-and-out; **thor′ough-bred**, (animal, esp. horse) of pure breed; (person) with attractive characteristics associated with a thoroughbred animal; **thor′ough-fare**, any public way open at both ends, esp. main road; **thor′ough-going**, extreme, thorough, out-and-out. **thor′ough·ly** *adv.* **thor′ough·ness** *n.* **thorough** *adv.* & *prep.* (archaic) Through.

those: see THAT.

Thoth (thōth, tōt). (Egyptian myth.) God of wisdom and magic, the scribe of the gods, identified with the Greek Hermes and represented in human form with head of an ibis.

thou (dhow) *pron.* Second person nom. sing. pronoun (now archaic or poet.) denoting person addressed.

though (dhō) *conj.* In spite of the fact that; even if, granting that; **as** ~, as if. **though** *adv.* (colloq.) And yet, but yet, all the same, none the less.

thought[1] (thawt) *n.* Process, power, capacity, faculty, of thinking; what one thinks, what is or has been thought; idea, notion; consideration, heed; meditation; intention, purpose, design; ~ **transference,** telepathy.

thought[2]: see THINK.

thought·ful (thawt′ful) *adj.* Engaged in, given to, meditation; showing thought or consideration; considerate (*of*), kindly. **thought′ful·ly** *adv.* **thought′ful·ness** *n.*

thought·less (thawt′lĭs) *adj.* Unthinking, heedless, imprudent; inconsiderate. **thought′less·ly** *adv.* **thought′less·ness** *n.*

thou·sand (thow′zand) *adj.* Amounting to 1,000; (loosely) very many; **T~ and One Nights**, the "ARABIAN Nights"; **T~ Island dressing**, salad dressing of mayonnaise and chili sauce with additions of chopped mixed pickles, diced hard-boiled eggs, chopped pimentos, onions, capers, etc.; **T~ Islands**, group of about 1,000 islands in St. Lawrence River at the outlet of Lake Ontario. **thousand** *n.* (pl. **-sands**, following a numeral **-sand**). Ten hundred; symbol for this (1,000, m, or M). **thou′sand·fold** *adj.* & *adv.* **thou′sandth** *adj.* & *n.*

Thrace (thrās). District of eastern Balkan peninsula, in ancient times including Bulgaria and eastern Macedonia. **Thra·cian** (thrā′shan) *adj.* & *n.* (Native, inhabitant) of Thrace; (of) its ancient Indo-European language, closely related to Illyrian, Phrygian, and Armenian.

thrall (thrawl) *n.* Slave; bondage. **thrall′dom, thral′dom** *ns.*

thrash (thrăsh) *v.t.* Beat, esp. with stick or whip; conquer, surpass; thresh; ~ **out**, (fig.) discuss exhaustively, argue thoroughly. **thrash′er**[1] *n.* One who or that which thrashes.

thrash·er[2] (thrăsh′er) *n.* 1. (esp.) Kind of shark (*Alopias vulpinus*), with very long upper division of tail, with which it lashes an enemy. 2. Any of several Amer. songbirds (genus *Toxostoma*) having a long tail and a long curving bill.

thread (thrĕd) *n.* 1. Fine cord of spun-out fibers or filaments of flax, cotton, wool, glass, etc., esp. of two or more twisted together; thread-shaped or threadlike thing, e.g. fine line or streak of color or light; spiral ridge of screw, each complete turn of this. 2. (fig.) Something represented as like thread, esp. course of human life; that which connects successive points in narrative, train of thought, etc., or on which things hang; continuous or persistent feature running through pattern of anything. 3. **thread′bare**, with nap worn off and threads of warp and woof left bare; wearing such garments, shabby, seedy; (fig.) commonplace, trite, hackneyed; **thread′fish** (pl. **-fishes**, collect. **-fish**), tropical fish of family Polycnemidae, with pectoral fin in long threads; **thread′worm**, any of various threadlike worms, any nematode, esp. the pin worm. **thread′y** *adj.* (**thread·i·er, thread·i·est**). **thread** *v.t.* Pass thread through eye of (needle); string (beads etc.) on thread, make (chain etc.) thus; pick one's way through (street, crowded place, etc.), make one's *way* thus; form screw thread on.

threat (thrĕt) *n.* Declaration of intention to punish or hurt; (law) such menace of bodily hurt or injury to reputation or property as may restrain person's freedom of action; indication of coming evil.

threat·en (thrĕt′en) *v.* Use threats (against); try to influence by threats; announce one's intention (*to* do) as punishment or in revenge etc.; be source of danger to; presage, portend. **threat′en·er** *n.* **threat′en·ing·ly** *adv.*

three (thrē) *adj.* Amounting to 3; **~-color process**, printing process in which colored picture etc. is reproduced by superposition of the three primary colors or their complementary colors; **~-cornered**, having three angles or corners; (of contest etc.) between three persons; **~-decker**, three-decked ship, esp. (hist.) line-of-battle ship with guns on three decks;

The drug daturine, which has similar properties to atropine, can be extracted from the ***thornapple*** *and other plants in the genus Datura. Other species contain anesthetic properties.*

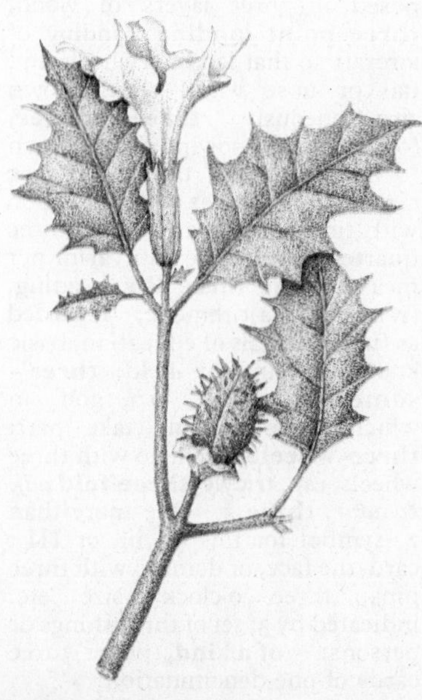

*Although powered machinery has long been used to **thresh** grain in the U.S.A. and other industrialized countries, hand-operated threshers are still used in the Spanish Pyrenees.*

***Thrift** or sea pink is found in coastal and mountainous areas in north temperate zones. Its leaves once provided a substance used for slimming.*

sandwich made with three slices of bread; anything with three layers, tiers, etc.; ~**-dimensional**, (producing effect or illusion of) having depth in space as well as height and width; realistic; ~**-legged**, (of race) run by pairs with one runner's right leg tied to the other's left leg; **T~ Mile Island**, site of nuclear power plant near Harrisburg, Pa., at which accident occurred in 1979, calling attention of the public to safety problems inherent in conventional reactor designs; ~**-master**, vessel with three masts; ~**-mile limit**, hist. the limit of zone of territorial waters, extending three miles from coast; **threepence** (thrĕp′*e*ns, thrĭp′-, thrŭp′-), (Brit.) sum of three pence; **three-ply**, having, woven with, three strands (of thread, yarn, etc.); (plywood) composed of three layers of wood; **three-point landing**, landing of aircraft so that landing wheels and tail or nose wheel touch down simultaneously; **three-quarter**, (of portraits) showing figure down to hips or knees; **three-quarter time**, (mus.) meter of composition with time signature of $\frac{3}{4}$ and three quarter notes or the equivalent per measure; **the three R's**, reading, (w)riting, (a)rithmetic, regarded as fundamentals of education; basic knowledge in any field; **three′some**, (game etc., esp. golf) in which three persons take part; **three-wheeler**, vehicle with three wheels, esp. tricyle; **three′fold** *adj.* & *adv.* **three** *n.* One more than 2; symbol for this (3, iii, or III); card, die face, or domino with three pips; three o'clock; size etc. indicated by 3; set of three things or persons; ~ **of a kind**, (poker) three cards of one denomination.

thren·o·dy (thrĕn′*o*dē) (pl. **-dies**), **thre·node** (thrē′nōd, thrĕn′ōd) *ns.* Song of lamentation, esp. for death, dirge. **thre·no·di·al** (thrĭnō′dē*a*l), **thre·nod·ic** (thrĭnŏd′ĭk) *adjs.* **thren′o·dist** *n.*

thresh (thrĕsh) *v.t.* Beat out or separate grain from (wheat etc.) on **thresh′ing floor** (prepared hard level for the purpose) or in **threshing machine**.

thresh·old (thrĕsh′ōld, -hōld) *n.* Piece of stone, timber, etc., lying below bottom of doorway; entrance; (psych.) point at which stimulus begins to produce its effect.

thrice (thrīs) *adv.* (archaic or literary) Three times.

thrift (thrĭft) *n.* 1. Frugality, economical management; ~ **shop**, store that sells discarded clothing, household wares, etc., for bargain prices to raise funds for charity. 2. Plant of genus *Armeria*, esp. *A. maritima* (sea pink), seashore and alpine plant with pink, white, or purple flowers on naked stems rising from tuft of grasslike radical leaves. **thrift′less** *adj.* **thrift′less·ly** *adv.* **thrift′less·ness** *n.* **thrift′y** *adj.* (**thrift·i·er, thrift·i·est**). **thrift′i·ly** *adv.* **thrift′i·ness** *n.*

thrill (thrĭl) *n.* Nervous tremor caused by intense emotion or sensation, wave of feeling or excitement; sensational quality (of story etc.). ~ *v.* Penetrate with wave of emotion or sensation, be thus penetrated or agitated; (of emotion etc.) pass *through*, *over*, etc.; quiver, throb, (as) with emotion. **thrill′er** *n.* (esp.) Sensational play, story, etc. **thrill′ing** *adj.* **thrill′ing·ly** *adv.*

thrips (thrĭps) *n.* (pl. **thrips**). Any minute insect, with four hair-fringed wings, of order Thysanoptera, many of which injure plants by feeding on their juices.

thrive (thrīv) *v.t.* (**thrived** or **throve** pr. thrōv, **thrived** or **thriv·en** pr. thrĭv′*e*n, **thriv·ing**). Grow or develop well and vigorously, flourish; prosper; grow rich. **thriv′er** *n.*

thro, thro′ (thrōō) = THROUGH.

throat (thrōt) *n.* 1. Front of neck between chin and collarbone, region containing pharynx and larynx; narrow passage, esp. in or near entrance of something, narrow part in a passage; **sore** ~, inflammation of lining membrane of pharynx etc. **cut one's own** ~, (fig.) bring about one's own defeat; **cut one another's** ~**s**, compete ruinously; **jump down someone's** ~, (slang) criticize or contradict someone violently and prematurely; **lump in one's** ~, tightness in the throat as emotional reaction; **ram something down someone's** ~, (colloq.) force (thing) on his attention; **stick in one's** ~, be difficult to utter; ~ **microphone**, microphone suspended at neck of speaker etc. and actuated by vibrations of larynx. 2. Forward upper corner of fore-and-aft sail. **throat** *v.t.* Groove, channel.

throat·y (thrō′tē) *adj.* (**throat·i·er, throat·i·est**). Guttural, uttered in the throat, hoarse. **throat′i·ly** *adv.* **throat′i·ness** *n.*

throb (thrŏb) *v.i.* (**throbbed, throb·bing**). (of heart etc.) Beat strongly, palpitate, pulsate, vibrate. ~ *n.* Throbbing, violent beat or pulsation.

throe (thrō) *n.* (usu. pl.) Violent pang(s); desperate or agonizing struggle, anguish.

throm·bo·sis (thrŏmbō′sĭs) *n.* (pl. **-ses** pr. -sēz). Localized clotting of blood within the heart or blood vessels. **throm·bot·ic** (thrŏmbŏt′ĭk) *adj.*

throm·bus (thrŏm′b*u*s) *n.* (pl. **-bi** pr. -bī). Blood clot formed within vascular system that may impede circulation.

throne (thrōn) *n.* Chair of state for sovereign, bishop, etc., usu. decorated and raised on dais; sovereign power; (pl.) order of angels (see ANGEL); ~ **room**, chamber or hall containing throne where monarch sits in state; (fig.) center of power in government, industrial complex, etc. **throne** *v.t.* (**throned, thron·ing**). Enthrone.

throng (thrŏng) *n.* Crowd, multitude (*of*) esp. in small space. ~ *v.* Come, go, press, in multitudes; fill with crowd or as crowd does.

throt·tle (thrŏt′*e*l) *n.* 1. Throat, gullet (of a horse etc.) 2. Valve controlling flow of steam in steam engine or of fuel in internal combustion engine. ~ *v.t.* (**-tled, -tling**). 1. Choke, strangle. 2. Control, obstruct, flow of (steam, fuel, etc.) in engine, esp. with throttle; (also ~ **down**) slow down (engine) thus.

Throt·tle-bot·tom (thrŏt′*e*l-bŏt*o*m) *n.* (sometimes **t**~) Inept, unfit public official.

through (thrōō) *prep.* From end to end or side to side of, between the sides, walls, parts, etc., of; from beginning to end of; by reason of, by agency, means, or fault of; up to and including. ~ *adv.* Through something; from end to end; to the end; ~ **and** ~, all the way through, completely, utterly; **be, get,** ~ (**with**), finish (with), come to end (of). **through** *adj.* Going, concerned with going, through; (of railroad etc.) going all the way without change of train, line, etc.; ~ **street**, street where vehicles have right of way over traffic entering from side streets or crossing at intersections; **through′put**, amount of material put through a manufacturing etc. process; work done by a computer in a period of time.

through·out (thrōōowt′) *prep.* From end to end of; in every part of. ~ *adv.* In every part or respect.

throw (thrō) *v.* (**threw** pr. thrōō, **thrown, throw·ing**). 1. Shape (pottery) on wheel; prepare and twist (silk etc.) into threads. 2. Project (thing) from hand or arm with jerking motion, esp. with sudden straightening of arm near shoulder level, so that it passes through air or free space; cast, make specified cast, (with) dice; move (esp. part of the body) quickly or suddenly. 3. (of wrestler, horse, etc.) Bring (antagonist, rider) to the ground; (of animals) bring forth (young). 4. Put carelessly or hastily *on, off*, etc. 5. (slang) Give (a party). 6. ~ **away**, (fig.) squander, waste; lose (chance etc.) by neglect; discard (card) when one cannot follow suit; **throw′away** (*n.*), printed paper, advertisement, etc., not intended to be kept; **throw back**, revert to ancestral type or character; **throw′back** (*n.*), such reversion, example of this; **throw in**, add (thing) to bargain without extra charge; interpose (word, remark) in parenthesis or casually; **throw cold water on**, discourage by raising objections, being indifferent, etc.; **throw in one's hand**, give up, withdraw from contest; **throw in one's lot with**, decide to share fortunes of; **throw-in** (*n.*), (soccer or basketball) act of throwing in ball after it has gone out of play; **throw in the sponge** or **the towel**, (slang, esp. boxing) admit defeat; give up; **throw off**, discard; get rid of; abandon (disguise); disturb, distract (person) from train of thought etc.; **throw oneself at**, try hard to gain love or favor of; **throw oneself into**, participate enthusiastically in; **throw oneself on**, place one's reliance on; **throw out**, cast out; suggest, insinuate; reject (bill in legislature); eject; (baseball) put (batter or base runners) out; **throw over**, desert, abandon; **throw the bull**, (slang) talk without point or sequence; boast; **throw up**, vomit; give up; build carelessly. **throw**

Left: The song ***thrush,*** *is originally from Europe but has been acclimatized in other parts of the world. The ground thrush, below, is an Australian bird related to others in S.E. Asia.*

n. 1. Throwing, cast; cast of dice; distance missile is or may be thrown; fall in wrestling; (geol., mining) (amount of vertical displacement caused by) fault in stratum. 2. (Extent of) action or motion of slide valve, crank, cam, etc.

throw·er (thrō′*er*) *n.* One who or that which throws.

thru (thrōō) *adv.* & *adj.* (colloq.) Through.

thrum[1] (thrŭm) *n.* Fringe of warp threads remaining on loom when web has been cut off, single thread of this; any loose thread or tuft.

thrum[2] (thrŭm) *v.* (**thrummed, thrum·ming**). Strum; sound monotonously, hum. ~ *n.* (Sound of) thrumming.

thrush[1] (thrŭsh) *n.* Small or medium-sized passerine bird of family Turdidae.

thrush[2] (thrŭsh) *n.* 1. Disease, esp. of infants, characterized by whitish vesicular specks on inside of mouth and throat etc. and caused by fungi of genus *Candida.* 2. Inflammatory pussy disease of foot in animals, esp. the frog of the foot of the horse.

thrust (thrŭst) *v.* (**thrust, thrust·ing**). Push, drive, exert force of impact on or against; pierce *through*; make sudden push *at* with pointed weapon; force oneself *through, past*, etc., make *way* thus. ~ *n.* Thrusting, lunge, stab; (mech. etc.) thrusting force of one part of structure etc. on contiguous part, esp. horizontal or diagonal pressure of part of building against abutment or support, driving force exerted by paddle, propeller shaft, or jet stream in ship or aircraft, (effect of) compressive strain in Earth's crust; ~ **augmentation**, increase in rocket or jet engine thrust, achieved by afterburning etc. ~ **bearing**, bearing in machinery that absorbs thrusts paralleling axis of revolution; ~ **stage**, (theatr.) stage extending into audience.

thrust·er, thrus·tor (thrŭs′t*er*) *ns.* (esp.) One who pushes forward in hunting field or rides too close to hounds; pusher.

thru·way (thrōō′wā) *n.* Highway for high speed traffic, with limited access to it and usu. requiring a toll.

Thu·cyd·i·des (thōōsĭd′ĭdēz) (5th c. B.C.). Athenian historian of the Peloponnesian War.

thud (thŭd) *n.* & *v.i.* (**thud·ded, thud·ding**). (Make, fall with) low dull sound as of blow on soft thing.

thug (thŭg) *n.* Vicious ruffian; **T**~, (hist.) member of an association in India (suppressed 1830–40) of professional robbers and murderers, who strangled their victims. **thug′ger·y** *n.* **Thug·gee** (thŭg′ē) *n.* (hist.) Practice of Thugs.

thu·ja (thōō′j*a*), **thu·ya** (thōō′y*a*) *ns.* Tree or shrub of coniferous genus *T*~ (the arborvitae) including the N. Amer. (*T. occidentalis*) and Chinese (*T. orientalis*) varieties.

Thu·le[1] (thōō′lē). Ancient Greek and Latin name of country six days' sail N. of Britain, supposed to be most northerly region in world; see ULTIMA THULE.

Thu·le[2] (tōō′lē) *adj.* Of or pertaining to an Eskimo culture in the Arctic from about 500 to 1400 A.D.

thu·li·um (thōō′lē*u*m) *n.* (chem.) Rare metallic element found in combination in some rare earths; symbol Tm, at. no. 69, at. wt. 168.9342. [f. THULE[1]]

thumb (thŭm) *n.* Short thick inner digit, opposable to fingers, and with only two phalanges, of human hand; any inner digit opposable to and set apart from other digits; part of glove etc. covering thumb; ~**s-down** (*n.*), act or example of disapproval, dissent; **turn** ~**s down**; ~**s up**! exhortation to cheerfulness or expression of satisfaction; **rule of** ~: see RULE; **under one's** ~, under influence or domination of; ~ **index**, reference index consisting of grooves cut in, or tabs projecting from, front edges of book, or margins so cut as to show initial letters or titles etc.; **thumb′nail**, nail of thumb; **thumbnail sketch**, small or hasty portrait, brief word picture; **thumb′screw**, screw with flattened or winged head that can be turned with thumb and fingers; instrument of torture for compressing thumb(s); **thumb-sucker**, one, esp. child, with the habit of sucking the thumb; **thumb-sucking** (*n.*); **thumb′tack**, tack with flat head that can be pushed into a soft surface. **thumb′less** *adj.* **thumb** *v.t.* Soil, wear, with thumb; handle with thumb or awkwardly or clumsily; make a request for (a ride in a vehicle) by sticking out a thumb in the direction one wishes to go; ~ **through**, turn over pages of (as if) with thumb.

thump (thŭmp) *n.* Heavy blow, bang; sound of this. ~ *v.* Beat heavily, esp. with fist; deliver heavy blows (*at, on*, etc.). **thump′ing** *adj.* (esp., colloq.) Very large, striking, impressive. **thump′er** *n.*

thun·der (thŭn′d*er*) *n.* Loud noise accompanying lightning (but appearing to follow it because of

Lemon-scented ***thyme,*** *is a cultivated variation of a herb which grows wild in the Mediterranean region. Oil extracted from thyme had culinary and therapeutic uses.*

Incorrect functioning of the ***thyroid*** *may result in an enlargement of the neck known as goiter. Sometimes, minor problems may be avoided by using foods containing iodine.*

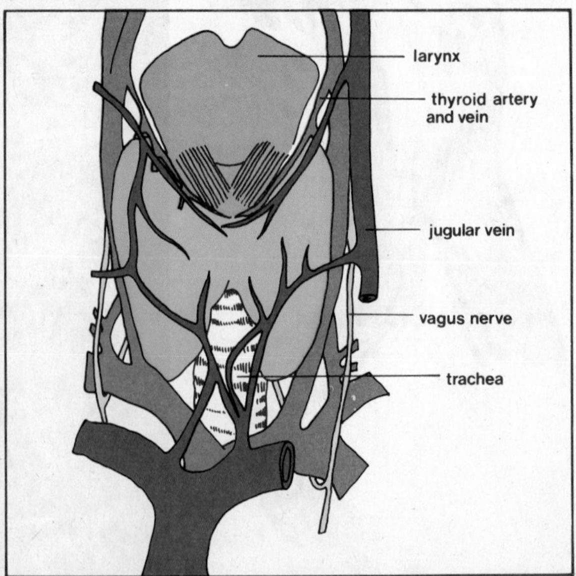

difference in speeds of light and sound) and due to sudden violent disturbance of air by the electric discharge; any loud deep rumbling or resounding noise; terrifying, threatening, or impressive utterance(s); **thun′derbird**, in the mythology of some N. Amer. Indians, a great bird that causes thunder, lightning, and rain to come from the heavens; **thun′derbolt**, imaginary bolt or dart formerly supposed to be the destructive agent when thing is struck by lightning, esp. as attribute of Thor, Jupiter, etc.; conventional representation of this; something very startling, terrible, or destructive; **thun′derclap**, loud crash of thunder; **thun′dercloud**, storm cloud charged with electricity and producing thunder and lightning; **thun′derhead**, rounded cumulus cloud near horizon projecting above general body of cloud and portending thunder; **thun′dershower, thun′dersquall**, rain accompanied by thunder and lightning; **thun′derstorm**, storm with thunder and lightning; **thun′derstruck**, (fig.) amazed, terrified, confounded. **thun′der·less, thun′der·ous, thun′der·y** *adjs*. **thunder** *v*. 1. **it ~s, it is thundering**, there is thunder. 2. Sound with or like thunder; emit (threats etc.) in loud or impressive manner; fulminate. **thun′der·er** *n*. (esp., **T~**) Jupiter. **thun′der·ing** *adj*. & *adv*. (esp., colloq.) Unusual(ly), decided(ly).

thun·der·a·tion (thŭnderā′shon) *int*. Mild oath or exclamation of surprise or irritation.

thu·ri·ble (thoor′ibel) *n*. Censer.

Thu·rin·gi·a (thurĭn′jēa). (Ger. *Thüringen*) Former state in central Germany; part of East Germany since 1945. **Thu·rin′gi·an** *adj*. & *n*. (Native, inhabitant) of Thuringia; (member) of an ancient tribe of central Germany conquered by Franks in 6th c.

Thurs., Thur. *abbrevs*. Thursday.

Thurs·day (thẽrz′dā, -dē) *n*. Fifth day of the week; **Holy ~**: see HOLY. [OE. *thur(e)sdæg* Thor's day, rendering LL. *dies Jovis* day of Jupiter]

thus (dhŭs) *adv*. In this way, like this, as follows: accordingly, consequently, and so; to this extent, number, or degree.

thwack (thwăk) = WHACK. **thwack′er** *n*.

thwart (thwôrt) *n*. Seat across boat, on which rower sits. ~ *adv*. & *adj*. (Lying) athwart. ~ *prep*. Athwart. ~ *v.t.* Frustrate, cross.

thy (dhī) *poss. pron*. Possessive case of THOU used as attrib. adjective with abs. and pred. form (also used before initial vowel and

A ***Tibetan*** *woman using a portable spinning device as she walks through the mountain meadows with her child on her back. Despite Chinese occupation, many people remain nomadic.*

silent "h") **thine** (dhīn), belonging to, affecting, thee.

Thy·es·tes (thīĕs′tēz). (Gk. legend) Brother of ATREUS. **Thy·es·te·an** (thiĕs′tēan) *adj*.

thy·la·cine (thī′lasīn, -sĭn) *n*. Tasmanian wolf (*Thylacinus cynocephalus*), a carnivorous marsupial resembling a dog in appearance, grayish brown with conspicuous black markings on the hinder half of the back.

thyme (tīm) *n*. Shrubby herb of genus *Thymus* with fragrant aromatic leaves, chiefly of Mediterranean regions, esp. **garden** ~ (*T. vulgaris*), native of Spain and Italy, cultivated as seasoning, and **wild** ~ (*T. serpyllum*), growing on dry banks etc. throughout Europe.

thym·ic (thī′mĭk) *adj*. Of the thymus.

thy·mol (thī′mōl, -mŏl) *n*. (chem.) White crystalline phenol obtained from oil of thyme, having pleasant aroma and used as antiseptic.

thy·mus (thī′mus) *n*. (pl. **-mus·es, -mi** pr. -mī). (anat.) Ductless glandular body (of uncertain function) situated near base of neck in vertebrates, in man disappearing or diminishing after childhood.

thy·roid (thī′roid) *adj*. (anat.) Of the thyroid gland; ~ **cartilage**, large cartilage of the larynx consisting of two broad plates united in front at an angle, forming the Adam's apple; ~ **gland**, large ductless gland lying near larynx and

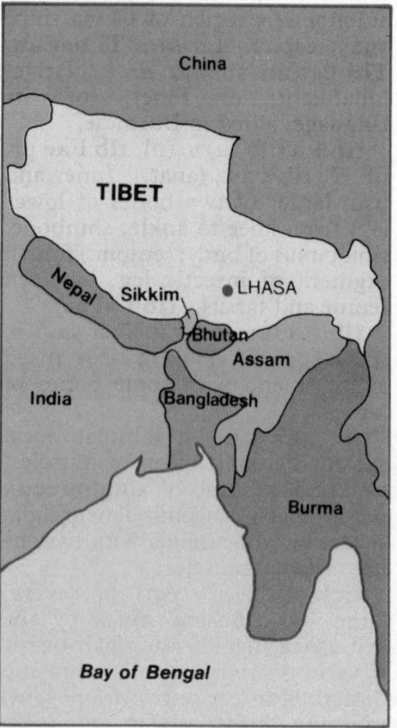

upper trachea in vertebrates and influencing growth and development, so called because of its proximity to the thyroid cartilage. **thyroid** *n*. Thyroid gland; extract prepared from thyroid gland of some animals, used in treating goiter, cretinism, etc.

thy·rox·ine (thīrŏk′sēn, -sĭn), **thy·rox·in** (thīrŏk′sĭn) *ns*. (chem.) Active hormone of thyroid gland.

thyr·sus (thẽr′sus) *n*. (pl. **-si** pr. -sī). 1. (Gk. antiq.) Staff tipped with ornament like pine cone, attribute of Dionysus. 2. (bot.) Kind of inflorescence in which primary axis is racemose and secondary etc. cymose, as in lilac and horse chestnut.

thy·self (dhīsĕlf′) *pron*. Emphatic and reflexive form corresponding to THOU, THEE.

Ti *symbol*. Titanium.

ti·ar·a (tēăr′a, -ār′a, -ar′a) *n*. Ancient Persian form of headdress; official headdress of the pope, consisting of a high pointed cap encircled by three crowns, symbolic of the temporal, spiritual, and purgatorial sovereignty claimed by the papacy; papal office; jeweled coronet worn by women.

Ti·ber (tī′ber). River of central Italy flowing from Tuscan Apennines through Rome to Mediterranean Sea at Ostia.

Ti·be·ri·as (tībēr′ēas). 1. Ancient town (built by Herod Antipas *c*21 A.D. and named after Tiberius) on W. shore of Sea of Galilee. 2. **Sea of ~**: see Sea of GALILEE.

Ti·ber·i·us (tībēr′ēus). Tiberius Claudius Nero (42 B.C.–37 A.D.), Roman emperor 14–37 A.D.

Ti·bet, Thi·bet (tĭbĕt′). Mountainous country of central Asia, an autonomous region of China since 1965; capital, Lhasa. **Ti·bet'an, Thi·bet'an** *adjs.* & *ns.* (Native, inhabitant) of Tibet; (of) its language, allied to Burmese.

tib·i·a (tĭb'ēa) *n.* (pl. **tib·i·ae** pr. tĭb'ēē, **tib·i·as**). (anat.) Inner and usu. larger of two bones of lower leg, from knee to ankle, shinbone; tibiotarsus of birds; (entom.) fourth segment of insect's leg, between femur and tarsus. **tib'i·al** *adj.*

tib·i·o·tar·sus (tĭbēōtar'*sus*) *n.* (pl. **-si** pr. -sī). Tibia of birds, fused at lower end with some bones of tarsus.

tic (tĭk) *n.* Habitual local spasmodic contraction of muscles, esp. of face; (also ~ **douloureux** pr. dōōlōōrö') trigeminal neuralgia, severe facial neuralgia with twitching of facial muscles.

tick[1] (tĭk) *n.* Any of several large bloodsucking mites of the order Acarina, infesting hair or fur of various animals; similar parasitic dipterous insect (e.g. *Melophagus*) infesting birds, sheep, etc.; ~ **fever**, fever transmitted by bite of tick.

tick[2] (tĭk) *n.* Case of mattress or pillow. **tick'ing** *n.* Strong cotton or other material for making ticks.

tick[3] (tĭk) *n.* 1. Quick light dry recurring sound, distinct but not loud, esp. of alternate check and release of movement in clock or watch. 2. Mark (dot, check, etc.) used to record review of items in a list. ~ *v.* Mark (*off* item etc.) with tick; make ticking sound; throw *off* (message or passage of time by ticking); **what makes (person)** ~, motivation; ~ **off**, (slang) annoy, exasperate.

tick[4] (tĭk) *n.* (chiefly Brit. colloq.) Credit; **on** ~, on credit. [abbrev. of TICKET]

tick·er (tĭk'*er*) *n.* (esp., colloq.) Watch; telegraphic tape machine; (joc.) heart.

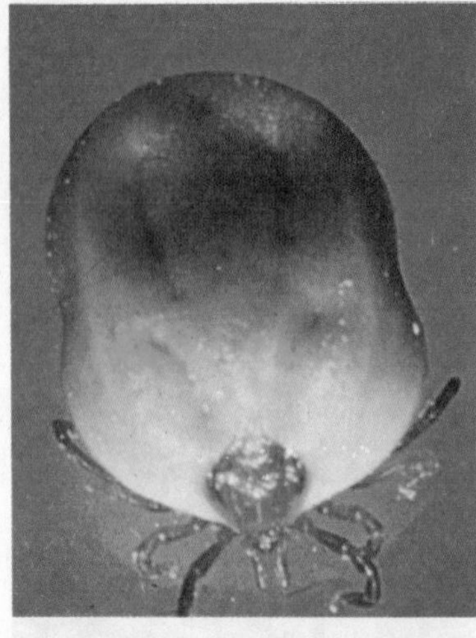

*The 700 species of **tick** can transmit more diseases to man and domestic animals than any arthropod excepting the mosquito. They are more common in tropical and subtropical regions.*

ticker (tĭk'*er*) **tape.** Paper tape from tape machine; this or similar material thrown from windows to greet a celebrity (**ticker-tape parade**).

tick·et (tĭk'ĭt) *n.* Slip, usu. of paper or cardboard, bearing evidence of holder's title to some service or privilege, as railroad journey, seat at entertainment, etc.; certificate of qualifications of pilot, ship's mate, or captain, etc.; list of candidates of one party or group put forward for election; ~ **agency**, agency in the business of selling tickets, esp. for theatrical presentations and sports events; ~ **agent**, individual selling tickets, as for theatrical and sports events, travel accommodations, etc.; ~ **office**, office where such tickets may be purchased; **parking** ~, notice from police to owner of vehicle parked in violation of regulations that fine must be paid; **the** ~, (slang) what is wanted, expected, etc. **ticket** *v.t.* Put ticket on (article for sale, illegally parked automobile, etc.).

tick·le (tĭk'*el*) *n.* Act, sensation, of tickling. ~ *v.* (**-led, -ling**). Touch or stroke (person, part of body) lightly with fingertips, feather, etc., so as to excite nerves and usu. produce laughter; cause or feel peculiar uneasy sensation as of being tickled; excite agreeably, amuse, divert; ~**d pink** or **to death**, (colloq.) highly amused or delighted.

tick·lish (tĭk'lĭsh) *adj.* Easily tickled, sensitive to tickling; (of question etc.) difficult, critical, delicate, requiring careful handling. **tick'lish·ly** *adv.* **tick'lish·ness** *n.*

tick-tack-toe, tic-tac-toe (tĭk-tăktō') *ns.* Game in which nine squares in a block are filled alternately with O's and X's by two players seeking to complete a row of three of either kind.

tick·tock (tĭk'tŏk) *n.* Repetitive sound as of a clock ticking. ~ *v.i.* Make sound of a clock ticking.

Ti·con·der·o·ga (tīkŏnderō'*ga*). Village and tourist resort in NE. New York State, on Lake Champlain; site of **Fort** ~, captured by the Americans under Ethan Allen, 1775, and then under Burgoyne, 1777, during the Revolutionary War.

tid·al (tī'd*al*) *adj.* Of tides; ~ **basin**, manmade lake or large pond

*While the gravitational forces in the sun and moon are responsible for **tides** on earth, the height and frequency may also be affected by ocean currents especially where there is a strait.*

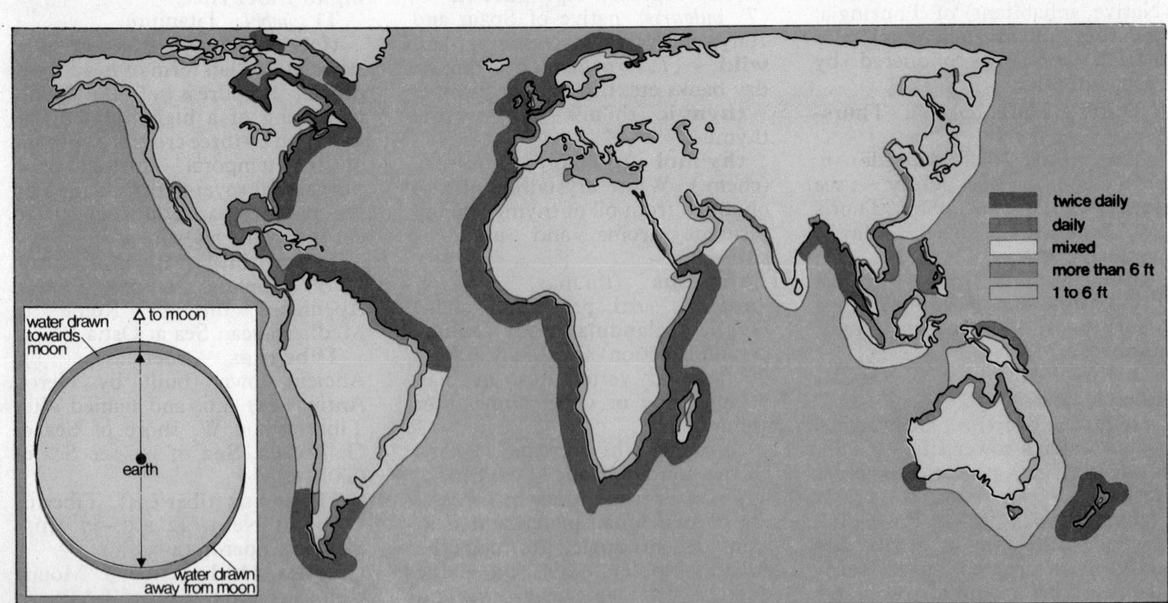

with access to a river and subject to tidal action; ~ **flat**, muddy or marshy flatland covered with water at full tide and laid bare at low tide; ~ **wave**, wave caused by movement of tide; (pop.) exceptionally large ocean wave or very high water sometimes following earthquake or other local commotion (cf. TSUNAMI); (fig.) widespread manifestation of feeling etc. **tid′al·ly** *adv.*

tid·bit (tĭd′bĭt), Brit. **tit·bit** (tĭt′bĭt) *ns.* Delicate bit, choice morsel.

tid·dly·winks (tĭd′lēwĭngks), **tid·dle·dy-winks** (tĭd′*e*ldēwĭngks) *ns.* Game in which small counters are flipped across table into receptacle.

tide (tīd) *n.* 1. Time, season (archaic exc. in **Eastertide** etc.). 2. Flowing or swelling of sea, or its alternate rising (**flood tide**) and falling (**ebb tide**), twice in each lunar day, due to the attraction of moon (and sun); (fig.) something like a tide in ebbing and flowing, turning, etc.; flood tide; **high, low tide**, completion of the flood, ebb, tide; NEAP, SPRING, **tide**: see these words; **tide gate**, gate through which water passes into dock etc. at flood, and by which it is retained during ebb; **tide lock**, double lock between tidal water and canal, basin, etc., beyond it; **tide′mark**, mark made by tide at high water; **tide′rip**, rough water caused by opposing tides; **tide table**, chart forecasting times and heights of tides for days of month at specific locations; **tide′water**, water affected by ebb and flow of tides; coastal land affected by tide; **tide′way**, channel in which tidal current runs, tidal part of river; **turn the tide**, reverse a situation. **tide′less** *adj.* **tide** *v.* (**tid·ed, tid·ing**). 1. Drift with tide. 2. ~ **over**, (enable or assist to) get through difficult time, surmount difficulty, etc.

ti·dings (tī′dĭngz) *n.pl.* (now chiefly literary) (Piece of) news.

ti·dy (tī′dē) *adj.* (**-di·er, -di·est**). Neatly arranged, neat, orderly; (colloq.) pretty large, considerable. ~ *v.t.* (**-died, -dy·ing**). Make neat, put in good order. **ti′di·ly** *adv.* **ti′di·ness** *n.*

tie (tī) *v.* (**tied, ty·ing**). 1. Attach, fasten, with cord etc.; secure (shoe etc.) by tightening and knotting lace etc.; form into knot or bow; bind (rafters etc.) by crosspiece etc.; restrict, bind (person etc.); ~ **down**, restrict one's activities, confine; restrain; ~ **in**, make or be consistent; connect; ~ **off**, tie suture around (artery etc.) so as to draw sides together and halt blood circulation within; ~ **one on**, (slang) become drunk; ~ **the knot**, (colloq.) get married; ~ **up**, restrict, esp. annex conditions to (bequest etc.) to prevent its being sold or diverted from its purpose. 2. Make same score as (competitor) in game etc.; be equal in score *with*. **tie** *n.* 1. Cord, chain, etc., used for fastening. 2. Necktie. 3. Rod, beam, etc., holding parts of structure together; transverse beam on a rail bed supporting railroad tracks. 4. (fig.) Thing that connects or unites in some way, link, bond. 5. Equality of score between competitors or sides in match or contest, drawn match; deciding match played after draw, match between victors in previous matches or heats; match between any pair of several competing players or teams. 6. ~ **beam**, horizontal beam connecting rafters; **tie′clasp, tie′pin**, ornamental pin worn on necktie; **tie-dye**, (1) Method of producing dyed patterns by tying string etc. to prevent parts of fabric from being dyed; (2) Fabric so decorated or pattern thus made; **tie-in**, of, pertaining to, or designating a sale in which purchaser must buy one or more additional and unwanted items in order to buy the item desired; **tie line**, direct connection between telephone extensions in a switchboard system; **tie-up**, link; obstructed situation, standstill, esp. obstruction of traffic on railroad etc. caused by strike, breakdown, etc.

Tie·po·lo (tēĕp′*o*lō), **Giovanni Battista** (1696–1770). Venetian painter.

Influenced by Veronese and Titian, ***Giovanni Tiepolo*** *was a master of the baroque style. His work ranged from biblical subjects (in 17th-century dress) to Tesso's epic, 'Rinaldo' (below).*

tier[1] (tēr) *n.* Row, rank, esp. one of several placed one above another as in theater. ~ *v.t.* Arrange or pile in tiers.

ti·er[2] (tī′*er*) *n.* One who ties.

tierce (tērs) *n.* 1. **T**~, (R.C. Ch.) canonical hour, (orig. said at) third hour of day (9 a.m.). 2. Position in fencing, third of eight parries or corresponding thrust. 3. (hist.) Measure of capacity, ⅓ of pipe (42 gallons); cask or vessel holding this quantity.

Tier·ra del Fue·go (tyĕr′ah dĕl fwā′gō). (Main island of) archipelago at S. tip of S. Amer., discovered 1520 by Magellan; divided between Chile and Argentina.

tiff (tĭf) *n.* Slight or petty quarrel. ~ *v.i.* Have a tiff.

Tif·fa·ny (tĭf′*a*nē), **Louis Comfort** (1848–1933). Amer. painter, stained-glass decorator, and glass manufacturer, especially of opalescent glass.

tif·fin (tĭf′ĭn) *n.* & *v.i.* (Brit.) (Take) light meal, lunch. [app. f. obs. *tiff* drink, sip]

ti·ger (tī′g*er*) *n.* (pl. **-gers**, collect. for senses 1 & 2 **-ger**). 1. Large Asiatic carnivorous feline quadruped (*Panthera tigris*), maneless, of tawny yellow color with blackish transverse stripes and white belly, proverbial for ferocity and cunning. 2. Any of various other feline animals, esp. (in Amer.) the jaguar and puma, and (in S. Africa) the leopard. 3. Fierce, cruel, or rapacious person or animal; formidable opponent in a game; paper tiger, person or thing threatening in appearance but ineffectual. 4. Loud yell at end of burst of cheering. 5. ~ **beetle**, active carnivorous voracious beetle of family Cicindelidae; ~ **cat**, any of various moderate-sized feline beasts resembling tiger in markings etc.; ~**'s eye, ti′gereye**, yellowish-brown quartz with brilliant luster, used as gem; kind of crystalline pottery glaze resembling this; **tiger lily**, tall garden lily (*Lilium tigrinum*) of Asiatic origin with orange flowers spotted with black; **tiger moth**, moth of family Arctiidae, with striped and spotted wings; **tiger shark**, any of various large voracious spotted or streaked sharks, esp. *Galeocerdo cuvier;* **tiger snake**, venomous and aggressive Australian snake, brown with dark stripes. **ti·gress** (tī′grĭs) *n.* Female tiger.

ti·ger·ish (tī′gerĭsh), **ti·grish** (tī′grĭsh) *adjs.* Like, cruel as, a tiger. **ti′ger·ish·ly** *adv.* **ti′ger·ish·ness** *n.*

tight (tīt) *adj.* 1. Close-textured,

Much of the effect of Muslim architecture was from the use of the painted ***tile.*** *Each was part of a total design. They became used increasingly in Persia from the 13th century onwards.*

firmly constructed, so as to be impervious to fluid etc. 2. Closely held, drawn, fastened, fitting, etc.; tense, taut, stretched so as to leave no slack; neat, trim, compact. 3. Produced by, requiring, great exertion or pressure; (colloq., of person) closefisted, (of money) difficult to obtain. 4. (slang) Drunk. 5. **tight′fisted**, stingy, closefisted; **tight′rope**, tightly stretched rope, wire, etc., on which acrobats perform; **tight′wad**, (colloq.) tightfisted person. **tight** *adv.* Tightly. **tight′en** *v.* **tight′en·er** *n.* **tight′ly** *adv.* **tight′ness** *n.*

The Australian ***tigermoth,*** *Rhodogastria, emits a pungent liquid from the base of its wings as a deterrent against predators.*

tights (tīts) *n.pl.* 1. (also **pair of** ~) Closely fitting garment covering legs, feet, and lower part of body. 2. Leotard with legs and feet.

Ti·gris (tī′grĭs). River of SW. Asia flowing 1,150 mi. (1,840 km) from Turkey, joining Euphrates to form Shatt al Arab, which flows into Persian Gulf.

ti·grish = TIGERISH.

Ti·jua·na (tēawah′n*a*). City and tourist center of Mexico, in the NW. part on the U.S. border.

Ti·ki (tē′kē). 1. (Polynesian myth.) First man on Earth. 2. (**t**~) (New Zealand) Maori large wooden or small ornamental greenstone image of creator of man or an ancestor.

til·de (tĭl′d*e*) *n.* Diacritical mark (˜) placed in Spanish over *n* to indicate palatalized sound (ny) and in Portuguese over *a* and *o* to indicate nasal sound; swung dash (~).

tile (tīl) *n.* 1. Thin slab of baked clay for covering roof, paving floor, lining wall, fireplace, etc.; or making drains etc.; material of this; tiles collectively. 2. Decorated piece used in mah-jongg. ~ *v.t.* Cover, line, with tiles.

tile·fish (tīl′fĭsh) *n.* (pl. **-fishes, -fish**). Large deepwater yellow-spotted food fish (*Lopholatilus chamaeleonticeps*), of Atlantic off New England etc.

till[1] (tĭl) *n.* Money drawer etc. in shop etc.

till[2] (tĭl) *n.* Boulder clay, stiff unstratified clay mixed with sand, gravel, and boulders.

till[3] (tĭl) *v.t.* Labor on (land), as by plowing etc. in order to produce crops. **till′age** *n.* 1. Cultivation of land. 2. Tilled land. **till′a·ble** *adj.* **till′er**[1] *n.* One who tills; farmer.

till[4] (tĭl) *prep.* Up to, as late as, until. ~ *conj.* To the time that; up to (the point) when.

till·er[2] (tĭl′*er*) *n.* Shoot of plant springing from bottom of original stalk; sapling; sucker.

till·er[3] (tĭl′*er*) *n.* Horizontal bar fixed to rudder head and acting as lever for steering.

till·ite (tĭl′īt) *n.* Rock composed of consolidated TILL[2].

tilt[1] (tĭlt) *n.* Covering or awning of canvas etc. esp. for cart. ~ *v.t.* Furnish with tilt.

tilt[2] (tĭlt) *v.* 1. (Cause to) incline abruptly from vertical or horizontal, (cause to) assume sloping or slanting position, heel over; (fig.) incline toward (one

Originating in prehistoric times from Siberia, the ***tiger*** *migrated southward to become the major feline in Asia. They are still present in northern regions but populations are low through hunting in India and Sumatra.*

country, person, etc. or another) in bestowing aid or encouragement; (geol., pass., of strata) be inclined. 2. Engage in tilt; strike, thrust, run, *at*, with weapon; ~ **at windmills**: see WINDMILL. 3. Forge, work, with tilt hammer. **tilt** *n.* 1. Tilting, sloping position. 2. Joust, combat between two armed men on horseback, each trying to throw opponent from saddle with lance; **full** ~, at full speed, with full force or impetus; **tilt'yard**, enclosed place for tilting, tilting ground. 3. (also **tilt hammer**) Heavy forging hammer, fixed on pivot and alternately tilted up and dropped by action of cam or eccentric gear.

tilth (tĭlth) *n.* Tillage, cultivation; depth of soil dug or cultivated.

Tim. *abbrev.* Timothy (New Testament).

tim·bal, tym·bal (tĭm'bal) *ns.* Kettledrum. [Fr. *timbale*, earlier *attabale*, f. Arab. *al tabl* the drum]

tim·bale (tĭm'bal, tĭmbahl') *n.* Dish of minced meat, fish, etc., cooked in drum-shaped mold of pastry etc. [Fr.]

tim·ber (tĭm'ber) *n.* Wood prepared for building etc.; trees suitable for this; piece of wood, beam, esp. (naut.) any curved piece forming ribs of vessel; **standing** ~, trees, woods; ~ **hitch**, knot used in attaching rope to log or spar; **tim'berland**, land covered with forest yielding timber; **tim'berline**, altitude above which no trees grow, as in mountain or polar regions; **timber wolf**, large gray wolf (*Canis lupus*) of northern N. Amer. **timber** *v.t.* Support (roof of mine or working, sides and roof of tunnel, etc.) with timber. **tim'bered** *adj.* Made of timber or wood, as a ~ **ceiling**; wooded. **tim'ber·ing** *n.*

tim·bre (tĭm'ber, tăm'bre) *n.*

*The **timber** industry is one of the main primary industries in the U.S.A. Logs removed from pine plantations, such as here in Oregon, are processed into a variety of products.*

Distinctive quality of musical or vocal sound depending on voice or instrument producing it, tone color. [Fr., = "clock bell," "drum," f. L. *tympanum*]

tim·brel (tĭm'brel) *n.* Tambourine or the like. [f. TIMBRE]

Tim·buk·tu (tĭmbŭktōō'). Town in central Mali near the Niger river; very remote place.

time (tīm) *n.* 1. Indefinite continuous duration regarded as dimension in which sequence of events takes place (freq. personified, **Father T**~, esp. as old man with scythe and hourglass); finite duration as dist. from eternity; more or less definite portion of this associated with particular events or circumstances, historical or other period; (freq. pl.) conditions of life, prevailing circumstances, of a period; allotted or available portion of time, time at one's disposal; moment or definite portion of time destined or suitable for a purpose etc., esp. period of gestation, term of imprisonment, term of apprenticeship, length of round in boxing, part of football or other game, time to begin or end this; point of time; (prison slang) period of imprisonment; season; occasion; (payment for) amount of time worked; (amount of) time as reckoned by conventional standards; STANDARD ~, DAYLIGHT saving ~: see these words; **a good** ~, period of enjoyment. 2. (mus.) Rhythm or measure of musical composition; tempo. 3. (pl.) (Preceded by numeral and followed by number or expression of quantity etc.) expressing multiplication, comparison, etc. 4. (**work**) **against** ~, with utmost speed so as to reach a goal by a specified time; **ahead of** ~, earlier than expected or promised; **all the** ~, during the whole time referred to; at all times; **at the same** ~, simultaneously; all the same; **at** ~**s**, now and then; **beat (somebody's)** ~, (slang) try to win or win favor of person, esp. woman being wooed by another; triumph over competitor; **behind the** ~**s**, out of style; old-fashioned; **for the** ~ **being**, for the moment; temporarily; **from** ~ **to** ~, occasionally; **in good** ~, at the correct time; before the correct time; **in** ~, not late; early enough; eventually, sooner or later; following the time of music etc.; **in no** ~, rapidly, in a moment; **make** ~, move rapidly, esp. to compensate for lost time; travel at specific, usu. fast, speed; (slang) date, woo, or have affair *with*; **pass the** ~, have short conversation with or greet person; ~ **of day**, hour by clock; current time; now; period of time in a day. 5. ~ **and motion study**, systematic investigation of working methods in order to increase efficiency and establish standards; ~ **bomb**, bomb with fuse or other device so adjusted that it will explode after a predetermined interval, delayed-action bomb; (fig.) precarious, threatening condition; ~ **capsule**, urn or strongbox buried in foundations of new building etc. and containing objects typical of the present time, for discovery in the future; **time'card**, card with record of time worked; **time clock**, clock with device recording times, e.g. of arrival and departure of workmen etc.; **time constant**, mathematical expression giving indication of delay involved in heating, charging, moving, etc., when the process produces an opposing effect proportional to the temperature, charge, speed, etc.; **time-consuming** (*adj.*), taking much time, wasteful of time; **time deposit**, bank deposit not repayable before set date; **time exposure**, (photog.) exposure for regulated length of time, as dist. from instantaneous exposure; **time-honored**, respected because of its antiquity; **time immemorial,** time of long ago and too early to remember; **time′keeper**, watch, clock, esp. in ref. to accuracy; one who records time, esp. of workmen; **time-lag**, interval of time between cause etc. and result or consequence; **time-lapse** (*adj.*), (of motion picture film) containing frames taken at long intervals but shown at normal pace to accelerate view of events, as growth of a plant, construction of a building, etc.; **time limit**, period within which something must be done; **timeout,** time used for rest, leisure, etc.; (football etc.) halt in play, with clock stopped, to permit substitution of players, etc.; **time′piece**, instrument for measuring time, chronometer; **time′server**, opportunist; **time′serving**, opportunism; **time sheet**, sheet of paper recording hours worked by employee(s) etc.; **time signal**, visible or audible signal, esp. radio signal, announcing the time of day; **time′table**, tabular list or schedule of times of classes in school etc., arrival and departure of trains, boats, etc.; **time zone**, one of 24 regions, each bounded by two lines of longitude 15° apart, adopting as standard the mean solar time of the meridian in it distant from Greenwich a complete number of hours. **time** *v.* (**timed, tim·ing**). Choose the time for, do at chosen time; record time of event, duration of action, etc., keep time, harmonize (*with*).

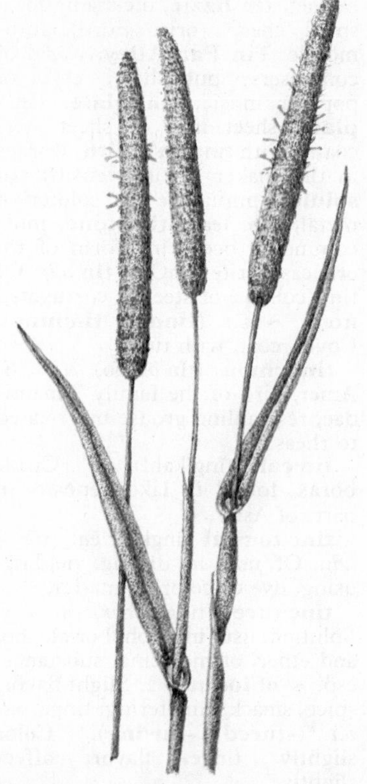
Timothy grass, with its long cylindrical spikes, is native in Britain and northern Europe. Being perennial, it has proved useful for cutting and storage as hay.

time·less (tīm′lĭs) *adj.* Unending, eternal; not subject to time. **time′less·ly** *adv.* **time′less·ness** *n.*

time·ly (tīm′lē) *adj.* (**-li·er, -li·est**). Seasonable, opportune. **time′li·ness** *n.*

Times (tīmz) **Square.** Area of Manhattan in New York City formed by Broadway crossing Seventh Avenue and extending from 42nd Street to 47th Street, center of New York theatrical district.

tim·id (tĭm′ĭd) *adj.* Easily alarmed; shy. **tim′id·ly** *adv.* **tim′id·ness, ti·mid·i·ty** (tĭmĭd′ĭtē) *ns.*

tim·ing (tī′mĭng) *n.* Regulation of speed, control, occurrence, or coordination, as in mechanics, theatrical production, sports, etc., in order to gain best results.

ti·moc·ra·cy (tīmŏk′rasē) *n.* (pl. **-cies**). 1. In the Aristotelian sense: a state with a property qualification for office. 2. In the Platonic sense: a state (like that of Sparta) in which love of honor is said to be the dominant motive among the rulers. **ti·mo·crat·ic** (tīmokrăt′ĭk), **ti·mo·crat′i·cal** *adjs.*

Ti·mon (tī′mon) (5th c. B.C.). Athenian who became a misanthrope owing to the ingratitude of his friends.

Ti·mor (tē′mōr). Island in the S. Malay Archipelago belonging to Indonesia; largest and easternmost of the Lesser Sunda Islands, covering 13,094 sq. mi. (33,913 sq. km); formerly ruled by the Netherlands in the W. part and Portugal in the E. part; ~ **Sea**, part of Indian Ocean lying between Timor and NW. Australia.

tim·or·ous (tĭm′erus) *adj.* Timid. **tim′or·ous·ly** *adv.* **tim′or·ous·ness** *n.*

Tim·o·thy (tĭm′othē). Convert and colleague of St. Paul; either of two Pauline epistles of New Testament addressed to him.

tim·o·thy (tĭm′othē) *n.* (also ~ **grass**) Meadow grass (*Phleum*

*Hauling in the fishing nets on **Timor.** Formerly divided between Portugal and Indonesia, the country has since been occupied by Indonesia which now claims control of the island.*

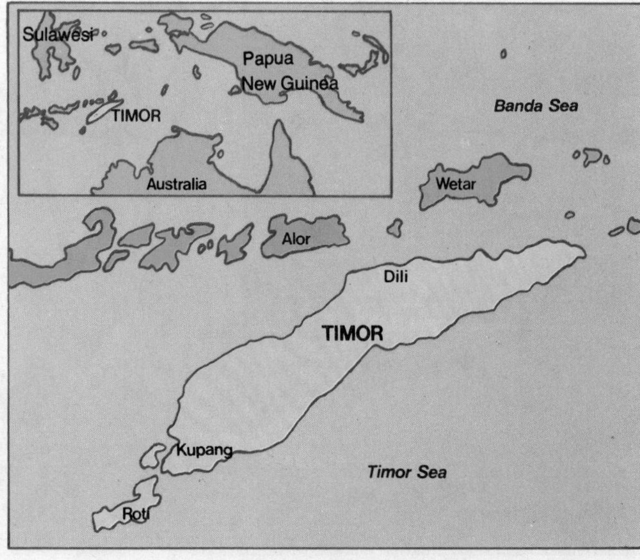

pratense), European grass with long cylindrical spikes, introduced into N. Amer. from England for cultivation for hay. [said to be f. *Timothy* Hanson, who introduced it into N. Amer. *c*1720]

tim·pa·ni, tym·pa·ni (tĭm′panē) *ns.pl.* Kettledrums. **tym′pa·nist** *n.*

tin (tĭn) *n.* 1. (chem.) Metallic element nearly approaching silver in whiteness, highly malleable, and taking a high polish, used in the manufacture of such alloys as bronze and pewter and, because of its resistance to oxidation, for making tinplate and lining culinary and other iron vessels; symbol Sn, at. no. 50, at. wt. 118.69. 2. (chiefly Brit.) Vessel made of tin, or more usu. tinned iron, esp. a vessel in which meat, fish, fruit, etc., is hermetically sealed for preservation; can tinplate, as the material for such vessels. 3. (attrib. or as adj.) **tin′foil**, tin hammered or rolled into a thin sheet; sheet of this rubbed with mercury, formerly used for backing mirrors and precious stones; similar sheet of an alloy of tin and lead used for wrapping and packing; (*v.t.*) cover, coat, with tinfoil; **tin god**, (fig.) base or unworthy object of veneration; **tin hat**, (mil. slang) steel helmet; **tin lizzie**, nickname for a small cheap (orig. Ford) automobile; **Tin Pan Alley**, world of composers, publishers, etc., of popular music; **tin plate, tin′plate**, sheet iron or sheet steel coated with tin; **tin′smith**, worker in tin, maker of tin utensils; **tin soldier**, miniature toy soldier of metal, esp. lead; **tin′stone**, most commonly occurring form of tin ore, cassiterite (SnO_2). **tin** *adj.* Of tin; (colloq.) of steel or corrugated iron. ~ *v.t.* (**tinned, tin·ning**). Cover, coat, with tin.

tin·a·mou (tĭn′amōō) *n.* S. Amer. bird of the family Tinamidae, resembling grouse but related to rheas.

tin·cal (tĭng′kahl) *n.* Crude borax, found in lake deposits in parts of Asia.

tinc·to·ri·al (tĭngktōr′ēal, -tôr′-) *adj.* Of, used in, dyeing; yielding, using, dye or coloring matter.

tinc·ture (tĭngk′cher) *n.* 1. Solution, usu. in alcohol or alcohol and ether, of medicinal substance, esp. ~ **of iodine**. 2. Slight flavor, spice, smack; smattering; tinge. ~ *v.t.* (**-tured, -tur·ing**). Color slightly; tinge, flavor; affect slightly.

tin·der (tĭn′der) *n.* Any dry inflammable substance readily taking fire from spark, esp. that formerly used in **tin′derbox** to catch spark from flint and steel for kindling fire etc. **tin′der·y** *adj.* Resembling tinder; extremely inflammable.

tine (tīn) *n.* Prong, projecting sharp point of fork etc.

tin·e·a (tĭn′ēa) *n.* (path.) Ringworm.

ting (tĭng) *n.* & *v.i.* (Make) tinkling sound.

tinge (tĭnj) *v.t.* (**tinged, tinge·ing** or **ting·ing**). Color slightly, modify tint or color of; (fig.) qualify, modify, slightly alter tone of. ~ *n.* Tint, slight coloring; flavor, touch.

tin·gle (tĭng′gel) *n.* & *v.* (**-gled, -gling**). (Feel, cause) slight pricking or stinging sensation. **tin′gler** *n.* **tin′gly** *adj.*

tin·ker (tĭng′ker) *n.* Mender (esp. itinerant) of kettles, pans, etc.; (Scotland and N. Ireland) gypsy; jack-of-all-trades; act of tinkering. ~ *v.* Repair, patch (*up*), roughly; work amateurishly or clumsily *at*, esp. in attempt to repair or improve. **tink′er·er** *n.*

tin·kle (tĭng′kel) *n.* & *v.* (**-kled, -kling**). (Make, cause to make) succession of short light sharp ringing sounds, as of small bell.

tin·ner (tĭn′er) *n.* Tinsmith.

tin·ni·tus (tĭnī′tus) *n.* (med.) Noises heard in the ear not due to external stimulation by sound waves.

tin·ny (tĭn′ē) *adj.* (**-ni·er, -ni·est**). Of or like tin; having a metallic taste; (of sound) thin and metallic.

tin·sel (tĭn′sel) *n.* Shining metallic gold- or silver-colored material used in thin sheets, strips, or threads to give sparkling effect; fabric adorned with tinsel; (fig.) anything having or giving deceptively fine or glittering appearance, gaudy or showy but worthless thing. **tin′sel·ly, tinsel** *adjs.* Showy, gaudy, cheaply splendid. ~ *v.t.* (**-seled, -sel·ing** or **-selled, -sel·ling**). Adorn with tinsel. [L. *scintilla* spark]

tint (tĭnt) *n.* Color, usu. slight or delicate, esp. one of several tones of the same color; (in painting, esp.) lighter tone of a color as dist. from shade, darker one; (engraving) effect produced by fine lines or dots set more or less closely together so as to produce an even tone. ~ *v.t.* Apply tint to, color. **tint′er** *n.*

Tin·tag·el (tĭntăj′el). Village on coast of N. Cornwall, England, with ruins of castle; traditional birthplace of King Arthur.

Tin·tern (tĭn′tern) **Abbey.**

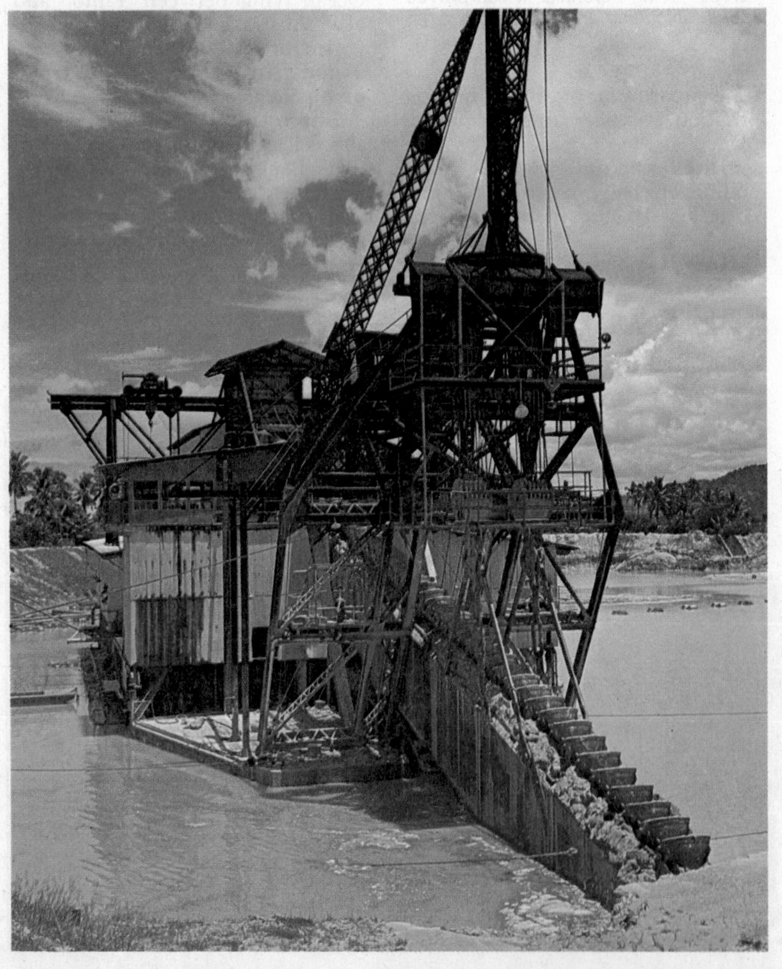

Tin *dredge working in Malaysia between Kuala Lumpur and Ipoh. Other major producers include China, Bolivia, the U.S.S.R. and Thailand. World production in 1974 was 232,400 tons.*

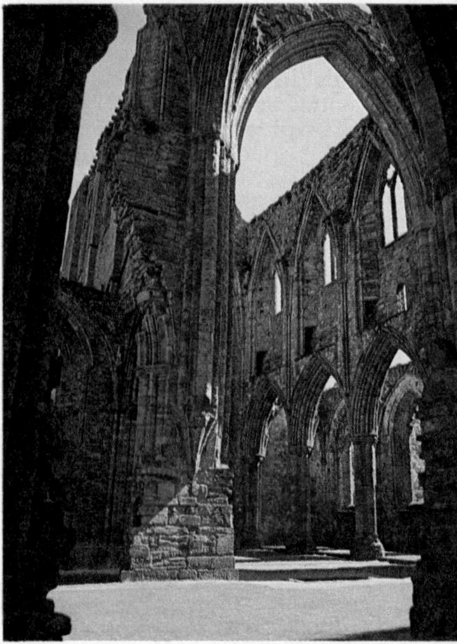

Cistercian monks built ***Tintern Abbey*** *in 1131 and the church in 1287. The establishment achieved much wealth but was abandoned during the Reformation. The Crown bought the ruins in 1901.*

Ruins, on River Wye, Wales, of a Cistercian abbey, founded 1131 and dissolved by Henry VIII.

tin·tin·nab·u·la·tion (tĭntĭnăby*u*lā'sh*o*n) *n.* Ringing or tinkling of bell(s).

Tin·to·ret·to (tĭnt*o*rĕt'ō). Jacopo Robusti (1518–94), Venetian painter.

ti·ny (tī'nē) *adj.* (**-ni·er, -ni·est**). Very small. **ti'ni·ness** *n.*

tip[1] (tĭp) *n.* Extremity, end, esp. of small or tapering thing; small piece or part attached to thing to form serviceable end; thin flat brush used for gilding; (**on**) **tip'toe** (*n.*), on the tips of the toes, standing or walking with heels raised from ground; **tip'toe** (*v.i.*) (**-toed, -toe·ing**), walk on tiptoe; **tip'top**, highest point of excellence; first-rate. **tip** *v.t.* (**tipped, tip·ping**). Furnish with tip.

tip[2] (tĭp) *v.* (**tipped, tip·ping**). 1. (Cause to) lean or slant, tilt, topple, esp. with slight effort; overturn, cause to overbalance. 2. Strike or touch lightly; (slang) forecast as winner, esp. informally; ~

Tintoretto, *a student of Titian, is said to have achieved the peak of his creativity with his paintings of Jesus Christ. Above: 'Christ Washing the Disciples' Feet' at Wilton House, England*

off, (colloq.) give private or secret information to; warn of danger etc.; **tip'off** (*n.*) (colloq.) warning, hint; **tip** (**over**), upset, overturn, topple *over*. 3. Give a tip to (see *n.*, sense 4). 4. **tip'cart**, one pivoted so that its contents can readily be tipped out; **tip sheet**, (slang) publication with up-to-the-minute facts and predictions about the stock market, various businesses, racetrack activities, etc. **tip** *n.* 1. Act of tipping or tilting. 2. Light touch or blow. 3. Piece of useful private or special information given by expert, esp. about horse racing, stock market, etc.; useful hint or idea. 4. Small present of money, esp. for service rendered or expected. **tip'per** *n.*

Tip·pe·ca·noe (tĭp*e*k*a*nōō'). River of N. Indiana, flowing SW. 166 mi. (267 km) to the Wabash River near the battlesite of ~, where Gen. William Henry Harrison defeated Indians led by Tecumseh, 1811; **"T ~ and Tyler too"** was Whig party slogan during 1840 presidential campaign, using Harrison's nickname with the last name of his vice presidential running mate.

tip·ple (tĭp'*e*l) *v.* (**-pled, -pling**). Drink intoxicating liquor habitually; take (such) continually in small quantities. **tip'pler** *n.* **tipple** *n.* Intoxicating liquor.

tip·ster (tĭp'st*e*r) *n.* (colloq.) One who gives tips about races etc.

tip·sy (tĭp'sē) *adj.* (**-si·er, -si·est**). (Partly) intoxicated; unsteady, staggering, from effects of drink. **tip'si·ly** *adv.* **tip'si·ness** *n.*

ti·rade (tī'răd, tĭrăd') *n.* Long vehement speech esp. of denunciation or abuse; long declamatory passage. [It. *tirada* volley]

Ti·ra·na (tērah'nah). Capital of Albania, in the central part.

tire[1] (tīr) *v.* (**tired, tir·ing**). Make or grow weary. **tired** *adj.* Weary (*of*); hackneyed; stale. **tired'ly** *adv.* **tired'ness** *n.* **tire'less** *adj.* **tire'less·ly** *adv.* **tire'less·ness** *n.*

tire[2] (tīr) *n.* 1. Iron or rubber rim or hoop around wheel on vehicle. 2. Air-filled or solid rubber or synthetic elastic tube on wheel of vehicle to reduce shock and supply traction.

tire[3] (tīr) *n.* (archaic) Headdress, attire. ~ *v.t.* (**tired, tir·ing**). Adorn, attire.

tire·some (tīr's*o*m) *adj.* Tending to tire, fatiguing, tedious; annoying. **tire'some·ly** *adv.*

tire′some·ness *n.*

ti·ro = TYRO.

Tir·ol = TYROL.

'tis (tĭz). (archaic, poet., or dial.) Contraction of *it is.*

Ti·siph·o·ne (tĭsĭf′onē). (Gk. myth.) One of the Furies (see FURY).

tis·sue (tĭsh′o͞o) *n.* 1. Any (esp. rich or fine) woven stuff. 2. (biol.) Substance of animal or plant body, esp. of a particular part; organized mass of cells of similar kind, as *muscle* ~ etc. 3. (fig.) Interwoven series, set, collection (*of*). 4. (also ~ **paper**) Thin soft gauzelike unsized paper for wrapping delicate articles, toilet use, etc.; piece of tissue paper.

tit[1] (tĭt): see TITMOUSE.

tit[2] (tĭt) *n.* ~ **for tat**, equivalent given in return, blow for blow, retaliation.

tit[3] (tĭt) *n.* Teat; (vulg. slang) breast.

Tit. *abbrev.* Titus (New Testament).

Ti·tan (tī′tan) *n.* (Gk. myth.) One of 12 gigantic children of Uranus and Ge (Oceanus, Coeus, Crius, Hyperion, Iapetus, Theia, Rhea, Themis, Mnemosyne, Phoebe, Tethys, Cronus), from two of whom (Cronus and Rhea) Zeus and the Olympians descended; hence, person of superhuman size, strength, etc.

Ti·ta·ni·a (tĭtā′nēa). In W. European folklore, queen of the fairies, wife of Oberon.

Ti·tan·ic (tītăn′ĭk). Brit. passenger liner that sank after collision with an iceberg on her maiden voyage, to New York in April 1912.

ti·tan·ic (tītăn′ĭk) *adj.* 1. **T**~, of the Titans. 2. Gigantic, colossal.

ti·ta·ni·um (tĭtā′nēum) *n.* (chem.) Gray metallic element widely distributed in combination in many minerals and clays, used esp. in the manufacture of alloy steels, symbol Ti, at. no. 22, at. wt. 47.90. **ti·tan′ous** *adj.*

tit·bit = TIDBIT.

ti·ter (tī′ter) *n.* (chem.) Strength of solution as determined by titration.

tithe (tīdh) *n.* 1. (hist.) Tenth of annual produce of agriculture etc. conceived as due to God and hence payable for support of priesthood, religious establishments, etc. 2. (rhet.) Tenth part. ~ *v.t.* (**tithed, tith·ing**). Subject to tithes. **tith′ing, tith′er** *ns.*

Ti·tho·nus (tĭthō′nus). (Gk. myth.) Brother of Priam, loved by the dawn goddess, Eos, who asked Zeus to make him immortal but omitted to ask for eternal youth for him.

Ti·tian (tĭsh′an, tē′shan). Tiziano Vecellio (1477–1576), Venetian painter; ~ **red**, bright golden auburn, color of the hair favored by Titian in his pictures.

tit·il·late (tĭt′ilāt) *v.t.* (**-lat·ed, -lat·ing**). Tickle, excite agreeably. **tit′il·lat·ing·ly** *adv.* **tit·il·la·tion** (tĭtilā′shon) *n.*

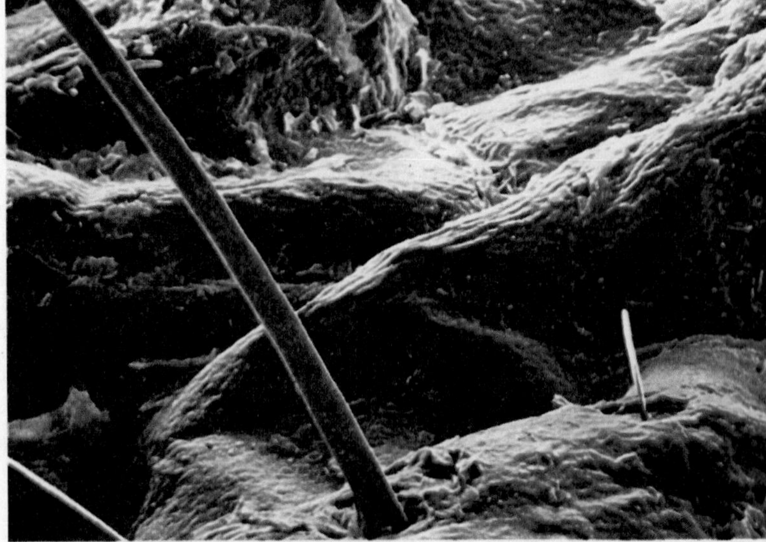

*Unrecognizable under stereoscan magnification, the **tissue** of human skin looks more like a view of a tropical swamp. The upright in the foreground is a hair.*

*Left: A blue **titmouse** collects seeds, which it may store for the winter in its nest in a hollow tree. Below: A great **titmouse** in spring looking for insects. In harsh winters these birds may migrate to milder areas.*

As an assistant to Giorgione, ***Titian*** *revealed his master's influence in such early works as 'The Three Ages of Man' (above) where the pastoral setting of this allegorical subject reflects the master's treatment.*

tit·i·vate (tĭt′*i*vāt) *v.* (**-vat·ed, -vat·ing**). (colloq.) Adorn, smarten; adorn oneself; put finishing or improving touches to appearance (of).

tit·lark (tĭt′lark) *n.* Any of several larks, esp. PIPIT.

ti·tle (tī′t*e*l) *n.* 1. Name (freq. descriptive) of book, poem, picture, piece of music, etc. 2. Distinctive name or style; personal appellation denoting or relating to rank, function, office, attainment, etc. 3. (law) Legal right to possession of (esp. real) property, title deeds as evidence of this; just or recognized right or claim (*to*). 4. (eccles.) Any of principal or parish churches in Rome, of which incumbents are cardinal priests. 5. Championship in sport. 6. ~ **deed**, document constituting evidence of ownership; **ti′tleholder**, one who holds a title, esp. as champion in some sport; **title insurance**, insurance that protects the owner of or holder of mortgage on real estate from possible legal actions because of a defective title; **title part, role**, part in play etc. from which title is taken; **title page**, page at beginning of book bearing title. **title** *v.t.* (**-tled, -tling**).

ti·tled (tī′t*e*ld) *adj.* Having a title of nobility.

tit·mouse (tĭt′mows) *n.* (pl. **-mice** pr. -mis). Any of various small birds, mostly of the common and widely distributed genus *Parus* and including chickadees, having soft, thick plumage, short, pointed bill, and, in some species, a crest on the head. [f. TUFTED TITMOUSE]

Ti·to (tē′tō), **Josip Broz, Marshal** (1892–1980). Prime minister of Yugoslavia 1945–53; president 1953–80.

ti·trate (tī′trāt, tĭt′rāt) *v.t.* (**-trat·ed, -trat·ing**). (chem.) Determine by volume quantity of constituent in (solution) by adding reagent of known strength until a point is reached at which reaction occurs or ceases. **ti·tra·tion** (tītrā′sh*o*n, tĭ-) *n.*

tit·ter (tĭt′*er*) *n.* & *v.i.* (Produce) laugh of suppressed or covert kind, giggle. **tit′ter·ing·ly** *adv.*

tit·tle-tat·tle (tĭt′*e*l tăt′*e*l) *n.* & *v.i.* (**-tled, -tling**). (Indulge in) petty gossip, chatter.

tit·u·ba·tion (tĭchoobā′sh*o*n) *n.* Staggering, reeling, unsteadiness in gait or carriage (esp. path.).

tit·u·lar (tĭch′*u*l*er*, tĭt′y*u*-) *adj.* Held by virtue of a title; such, existing, only in name; ~ **bishop**, (R.C. Ch.) bishop *in partibus* *infidelium*, one deriving his title from see lost to Roman pontificate; ~ **saint** etc., (R.C. Ch.) sacred person or thing giving name to church. **tit'u·lar·ly** *adv.* **titular** *n.* One who holds title to office, benefice, etc., esp. without performing functions thereof; (esp.) titular bishop.

Ti·tus[1] (tī'tus). Convert and helper of St. Paul; Pauline epistle of New Testament addressed to him.

Ti·tus[2] (tī'tus). Titus Flavius Sabinus Vespasianus (40–81 A.D.), Roman emperor 79–81; took Jerusalem (70 A.D.) after long siege.

tiz·zy (tĭz'ē) *n.* (pl. **-zies**). (colloq.) Dither.

TKO, T.K.O. *abbrevs.* Technical knockout.

Tl *symbol.* Thallium.

Tm *symbol.* Thulium.

tme·sis (temē'sĭs, mē'sĭs) *n.* (gram.) Separation of parts of compound word by intervening word(s), e.g. *to* us *ward*.

TN *abbrev.* Tennessee.

TNT, T.N.T. *abbrevs.* Trinitrotoluene.

to (tōō) *prep.* 1. In the direction of; as far as, not short of. 2. Used after words expressing comparison, ratio, proportion, relative position, agreement, or adaptation, correspondence, reference, etc. 3. Introducing indirect object, supplying place of dative; indicating person or thing for whose benefit, use, disposal, etc., thing is done etc. 4. Used as sign of infinitive; expressing purpose, consequence, etc. ~ *adv.* To the normal or required position or condition, esp. to a standstill; **~-and-fro**, backward and forward, up and down, from place to place.

toad (tōd) *n.* Tailless leaping amphibian (*Bufo*), resembling a frog, but terrestrial in habits except at breeding season, more squat in shape, and having a warty skin; **toad'eater**, toady; **toad'fish** (pl. **-fishes**, collect. **-fish**), any of various fishes with large heads or inflated bodies, of family Batrachoididae, of Amer. Atlantic coasts; **toad'flax**, common European and Asiatic herb (*Linaria vulgaris*) with showy spurred orange-spotted yellow flowers; various related plants; **toad'stone**, any of various small stones formerly supposed to be found in head of toad and worn as jewel or amulet; **toad'stool**, fungus with round disklike top and slender stalk, esp. of inedible or poisonous kind.

toad·y (tō'dē) *n.* (pl. **toad·ies**). Sycophant, obsequious parasite. **toad'y·ism** *n.* **toady** *v.i.* (**toad·ied, toad·y·ing**). Fawn upon, behave servilely (*to* person).

toast (tōst) *n.* 1. (Slice of) bread browned by heat. 2. Person or thing in whose honor a company is requested to drink (hist., reigning belle of season etc.); call to drink, instance of drinking, thus; **toast'master**, fem. **toast'mistress**, one who proposes or announces toasts at public dinner etc. **toast** *v.t.* 1. Brown, cook (bread, cheese, etc.) by exposure to heat of fire etc.; warm (one's feet etc.) before fire; **toasting fork**, long-handled fork for toasting bread, marshmallows, etc. 2. Drink to health or in honor of. **toast'er** *n.* Electrical etc. device for toasting bread.

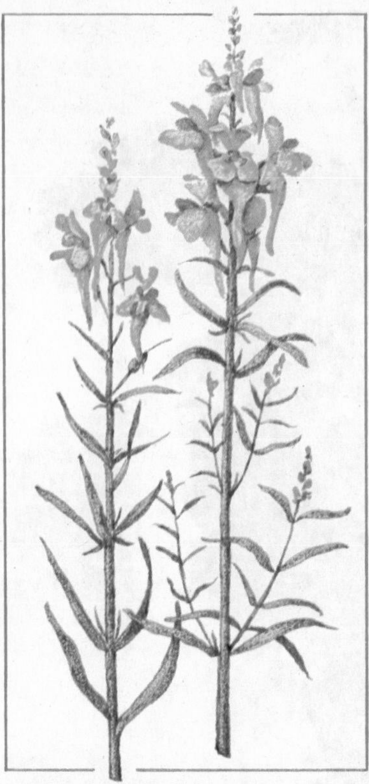

Widespread in the northern hemisphere, ***toadflax*** *(also known as 'butter and eggs' or 'flaxweed') was once made into a tisane to treat complaints of the bladder and liver.*

to·bac·co (tobăk'ō) *n.* (pl. **-cos, -coes**). Tall annual plant of genus *Nicotiana*, esp. *N. tabacum*, native of tropical Amer., with white or pink tubular flowers and large ovate leaves used for smoking or chewing or as snuff; these dried leaves, or cigars, cigarettes, etc., manufactured from them; plant resembling tobacco or used for same purposes; ~ **heart**, disease of the heart due to excessive tobacco smoking.

to·bac·co·nist (tobăk'onĭst) *n.* Dealer in tobacco.

To·ba·go: see TRINIDAD AND TOBAGO.

to-be (tobē') *adj.* Future; coming; soon to be what is named, as *bride-to-be*.

to·bog·gan (tobŏg'an) *n.* Long light narrow sled curved up at the forward end used esp. in sport of coasting down prepared slopes of snow or ice. ~ *v.t.* Ride on toboggan. **to·bog'gan·ist** *n.*

to·by (tō'bē) *n.* (pl. **-bies**). 1. (also **T~ jug**) Mug or small jug for ale etc. in form of stout old man wearing long full-skirted coat and three-cornered hat. 2. **Toby**, name of trained dog in Punch and Judy show, usu. wearing frill round neck. [dim. of name *Tobias*]

toc·ca·ta (tokah'ta) *n.* (mus.) Composition for keyboard instrument, freq. as prelude to fugue etc., designed to exhibit touch and technique of performer.

To·char·i·an, To·khar·i·an (tōkār'ēan, -kār'-) *adj.* & *n.* (Member) of fairly highly cultured people living in 1st 1,000 years of Christian era in central Asia; (of) Indo-European language of these people, recovered (1904–8) from manuscripts and inscriptions found in ruined temples of northern Chinese Turkestan.

Tocque·ville (tōk'vĭl), **Alexis Charles Henri Maurice Clérel de** (1805–59). French statesman, historian, and writer; minister of foreign affairs, 1849; author of *Democracy in America* etc.

toc·sin (tŏk'sĭn) *n.* (Bell rung as) alarm or signal. [Provençal *tocarsenh* (*tocar* touch, *senh* signal bell, f. L. *signum* sign)]

to·day, to-day (todā') *advs.* & *ns.* (On) this present day; (loosely) nowadays, (in) modern times.

The ***holy cross toad****, shown burrowing into soft mud. Although toads resemble frogs, they prefer land rather than water and have warty, rather than smooth skins.*

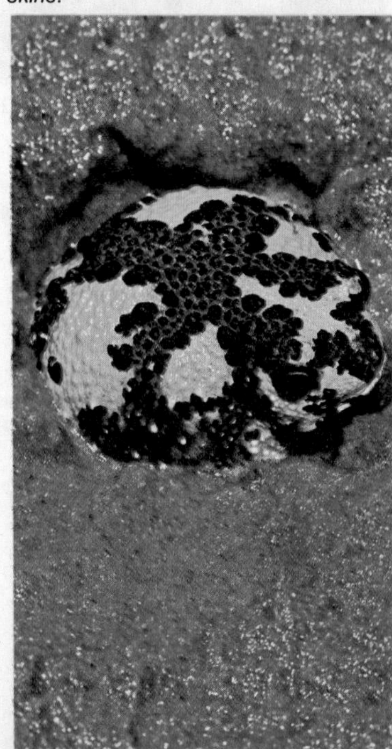

*Picking **tobacco** leaves in Kenya. They must then be cured in a drying kiln (below left) where heat and humidity are carefully controlled. After 'yellowing', the leaf is then dried and conditioned before grading for quality.*

tod·dle (tŏd′*e*l) *n.* Toddling walk. ~ *v.i.* (**-dled, -dling**). (esp. of child) Walk with short unsteady steps; take casual walk. **tod′dler** *n.* (esp.) Child just learning to walk.

tod·dy (tŏd′ē) *n.* (pl. **-dies**). 1. Fresh or fermented sap of various species of palm, used as beverage. 2. Sweetened drink of whiskey and hot water. [Hind. *tārī*, f. *tār* palm tree (Sansk. *tâla* palmyra)]

to-do (t*o*dōō′) *n.* (pl. **-dos**). Commotion.

to·dy (tō′dē) *n.* (pl. **-dies**). Small insectivorous W. Indian bird of genus *Todus*, allied to the kingfisher.

toe (tō) *n.* One of five terminal members of foot, forepart of foot; part of stocking, shoe, etc., that covers toes; forepart of hoof; something suggesting a toe by its position, shape, etc., esp. outer end of striking surface of golf club; **on one's ~s**, (fig.) alert; **toe′cap**, piece of leather covering toe of boot or shoe; **toe dance**, dance performed on extreme tips of toes; **toe dancer, dancing**; **toe′hold**, minimal foothold (also fig.); **toe-in, -out**, slight forward convergence, divergence, in setting of wheels of vehicle; **toe′nail**, nail of human toe; metal nail driven obliquely through end of board etc.; **toe′shoe**, dance slipper having wooden toe to help dancer dance on toes. **toe** *v.t.* (**toed, toe·ing**). Furnish with toe, put new toe on (stocking etc.); touch or reach with toes; ~ **the line, mark**, stand with tips of toes reaching line indicating starting point in race etc.; (fig.) conform strictly to standard or requirement, esp. under pressure.

tof·fee, tof·fy (taw′fē, tŏf′ē) *ns.* (pl. **-fees, -fies**). (chiefly Brit.) Taffy.

tog (tŏg) *v.* (**togged, tog·ging**). (colloq.) Dress (person, oneself, *out* or *up*). ~ *n.pl.* Clothes.

to·ga (tō′g*a*) *n.* (pl. **-gas, -gae** pr. -jē). Ancient Roman citizen's outer garment, flowing cloak or robe of single piece of cloth covering whole body except right arm, freq. with allusion to civil career or to its assumption at age of manhood; (transf.) gown or other garb associated with some profession. **to′gaed** *adj.*

to·geth·er (t*o*gĕdh′*e*r) *adv.* In(to) company or conjunction, so as to unite, in union; simultaneously; uninterruptedly, in unbroken succession.

to·geth·er·ness (t*o*gĕdh′*e*rnĭs) *n.* Feeling of belonging together.

tog·gle (tŏg′*e*l) *n.* Short pin put

through eye or loop of rope, link of chain etc. to keep it in place etc.; any similar crosspiece on chain etc.; rod or screw with crosspiece or device enabling it to pass through hole in one position but not in other; movable pivoted crosspiece serving as barb in harpoon; (also ~ **joint**) two plates or rods hinged together endwise, so that force applied at the elbow to straighten the joint is transmitted to the outer end of each plate or rod; ~ **bolt**, anchor bolt having folding wings that open behind wall into which it is driven when screw in center is tightened; ~ **switch**, electric switch with projecting lever to be moved usu. up and down.

To·go (tō′gō). Republic in W. Africa between Ghana and Benin; fully independent 1960; capital, Lome.

toil[1] (toil) *v.i.* Work long or laboriously; move painfully or laboriously. **toil′er** *n.* **toil** *n.* Labor, drudgery, hard and continuous work or exertion. **toil′some** *adj.* **toil′some·ness** *n.*

toil[2] (toil) *n.* (now only in pl.) Net, snare. [OF. *toile* cloth, f. L. *tela* web]

toile (twahl) *n.* Cloth esp. for garments; pattern of garment in muslin etc. for fitting or for use in making copies.

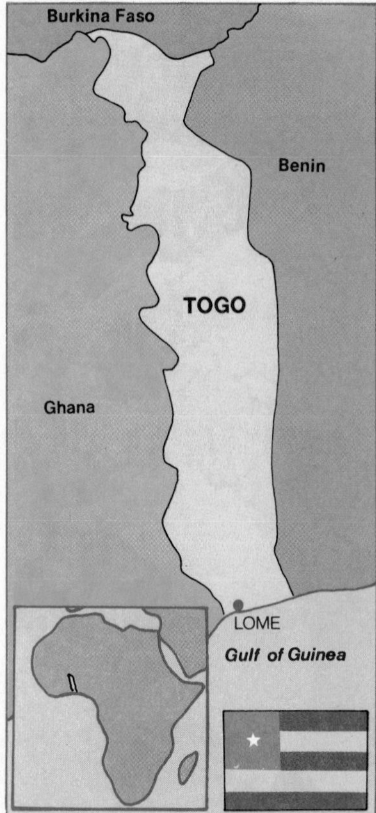

*The Republic of **Togo** in West Africa gained independence from France in 1960. The main exports are phosphate, cocoa, coffee and palm nuts but deposits of iron ore may be exploited.*

toi·let (toi′lĭt) *n.* Process of dressing, arranging hair, etc.; (style of) dress; dressing room; lavatory; toilet bowl; ~ **bowl**, ceramic bowl in toilet for urination and defecation; ~ **paper**, soft paper for use in lavatories; ~ **powder**, dusting powder used after bath, shaving, etc.; ~ **seat**, wooden or plastic seat on top of toilet bowl; ~ **set**, set of usu. matching articles used in dressing, as hand mirror, brush, comb, etc.; ~ **water**, scented liquid used after washing. [Fr. *toilette*, orig. = cloth thrown over shoulders in dressing]

toi·let·ry (toi′lĭtrē) *n.* (pl. **-ries**). (also pl.) Articles for use in making one's toilet.

To·kay (tōkā′) *n.* Rich sweet aromatic wine made near Tokay in Hungary; similar wine made elsewhere.

to·ken (tō′ken) *n.* Sign, symbol (*of*); characteristic mark; thing serving to authenticate person, message, etc.; keepsake; small flat piece of stamped metal used in vending machine, toll booth, etc. to receive goods etc.; **by the same** ~, similarly; moreover; in corroboration of what I say; **in ~ of**, in evidence of; ~ **payment**, proportionately small payment made by debtor as indication that debt or obligation is not repudiated.

to·ken·ism (tō′kenĭzem) *n.* Making outward show of meeting requirements of law, principle, etc., by small and merely symbolic gestures.

To·khar·i·an = TOCHARIAN.

To·ky·o (tō′kēō; *Jap.* taw′kyaw).

__Tokyo,__ capital of Japan, has the second-highest population in the world (8.8m) after Shanghai. At night the Ginza (below) is a blaze of lights; by day tuna is sold in the fish markets.

Capital city of Japan, at head of Tokyo Bay on SE. coast of main island; **T ~ Bay**, inlet of the W. Pacific Ocean, extending inland 30 mi. (48 km) into SE. Honshu Island, Japan.

To·le·do (tolē´dō; *Sp.* tawlĕ´-dhaw). City of Spain, Spanish capital 1087–1560 famous for manufacture of finely tempered sword blades.

tol·er·a·ble (tŏl´*e*rabel) *adj.* Endurable; fairly good, not bad. **tol′er·a·ble·ness** *n.* **tol′er·a·bly** *adv.*

tol·er·ance (tŏl´*e*rans) *n.* Willingness to tolerate, forbearance; capacity to tolerate (esp. med.); (eng.) permitted variation in dimension.

tol·er·ate (tŏl´*e*rāt) *v.t.* (**-at·ed, -at·ing**). Endure, permit; allow to exist, be practiced, etc., without interference or molestation; forbear to judge harshly; (med.) sustain use of (drug etc.) without harm. **tol′er·ant** *adj.* **tol′er·ant·ly** *adv.*

tol·er·a·tion (tŏl*e*rā´sh*o*n) *n.* Tolerating; (esp.) recognition of liberty to uphold one's religious opinions and forms of worship or to enjoy all social privileges etc. without regard to religious differences.

toll[1] (tōl) *n.* Tax, duty, charge, paid for passage along public road or over bridge or ferry, for use of telephone, for transport of goods by railroad or canal etc.; **take ~**, (fig.) abstract a portion of; **toll′gate**, bar or gate across road to prevent passage without paying toll; **toll bridge**, bridge at which toll is charged; **toll call**, telephone call for which charge is higher than for local call; **toll′house** (pl.

Above: Tula, capital of the old ***Toltec*** *people. They were noted builders and craftsmen, and gave the cults of the Feathered Serpent, the Coyote, and the Eagle to the Mayan Peoples.*

-houses pr. -howzĭz), house occupied by collector of tolls at tollgate or toll bridge; **tollhouse cookie**, cookie containing bits of chocolate and, sometimes, nuts; **toll road**, road maintained by means of tolls collected on it. **toll** *v.t.* Collect, pay, toll.

toll[2] (tōl) *v.* Cause (bell) to ring, ring bell, with slow uniform strokes, esp. for death or funeral; (of bell or clock) give out (stroke, knell, hour of day), give out measured sounds. **~** *n.* Tolling, stroke, of bell.

Tol·stoy, Tol·stoi (tŏl´stoi, tōl´-; *Russ.* tŏlstoi´), **Lev (Leo) Nikolaevich, Count** (1828–1910). Russian novelist and social reformer, author of *War and Peace*, *Anna Karenina*, etc. **Tol′stoy·an, Tol′stoi·an** *adjs.* & *ns.* (Follower) of doctrines of Tolstoy, who advocated simple living and practice of manual labor and believed that the holding of property is sinful.

Tol·tec (tŏl´tĕk) *n.* (pl. **-tecs**, collect. **-tec**). Member, language, of an Amer. Ind. people, remarkable esp. as architects, who flourished in Mexico from the 9th c. onward, having their capital at Tula, which they abandoned in 1168, when some of them moved to Yucatan and lived in association with the MAYA. **Tol′tec·an** *adj.* & *n.*

to·lu (tōlōō´) *n.* (also **balsam of ~, ~ balsam**) Fragrant brown balsam obtained by incision from tropical S. Amer. tree (*Myroxylon balsamum*) and used to flavor cough syrups and lozenges, as expectorant, and in perfumery. [f. (*Santiago de*) *Tolu* in Colombia]

tol·u·ene (tŏl´ūēn) *n.* Colorless aromatic liquid hydrocarbon (methyl benzene) with smell like benzene and burning taste, orig. obtained from tolu balsam but now esp. from coal tar, used in manufacture of explosives and other compounds. **to·lu·ic** (tolōō´ĭk, tŏl´ūĭk) *adj.* **~ acid**, any of isomeric acids derived from toluene.

tol·u·ol (tŏl´ūōl) *n.* Commercial form of toluene.

Tom (tŏm). Masculine proper name used in various collocations: **Long ~**, large gun with long range; (naut.) long gun formerly carried amidships on swivel carriage; **~ Collins**, drink of gin, sugar, lemon or lime juice, and soda water; **~, Dick, and Harry**, (usu. derog.) persons taken at random, ordinary people; **~ Thumb**, dwarf in nursery tale, no bigger than his father's thumb; any diminutive person; dwarf variety of various plants. **tom** *n.* 1. Male animal, esp. cat (**tom′cat**). 2. **tom′boy**, wild romping girl; **tom′cod** (pl. **-cods**, collect. **-cod**), any of various small Amer. fishes (*Microgradus*) resembling cod; **tom′fool′**, witless fellow; (*adj.*) stupid, senseless; (*v.i.*) play the fool; **tomfool′ery** (pl. **-er·ies**), foolish trifling, foolish knickknacks, etc.; **tom′tit**, titmouse.

tom·a·hawk (tŏm´*a*hawk) *n.* Light ax of N. Amer. Indians, used as tool and as weapon of war. **~**

A Shoshoni Indian with a modern ***tomahawk.*** *Before Europeans arrived, these plateau people used blades of stone or deer horn to butcher buffalo or gut the salmon that were their food.*

v.t. Strike, kill, with tomahawk.

tom·al·ley (tŏm′ălē) *n.* (pl. **-leys**). Fat (often called *liver*) of lobster, green when cooked.

to·ma·to (t*o*mā′tō, -mah′-) *n.* (pl. **-toes**). (Glossy red or yellow fleshy edible fruit of) S. Amer. plant (*Lycopersicon esculentum*) with weak trailing or climbing stem, irregularly pinnate leaves, and yellow flowers, widely cultivated, usu. as annual. [Mex. *tomatl*]

tomb (to͞om) *n.* Excavation, chamber, vault, in earth or rock for reception of dead body; sepulchral monument; **tomb′-stone**, memorial stone over grave.

tom·bac (tŏm′băk) *n.* Alloy of copper and zinc used as material for cheap jewelry. [Malay]

tome (tōm) *n.* Volume, book, esp. large heavy one.

to·men·tum (t*o*mĕn′t*u*m) *n.* (pl. **-ta** pr. -t*a*). (bot.) Pubescence of matted woolly hairs. **to·men′tose** *adj.*

tom·my (tŏm′ē) *n.* (pl. **-mies**). 1. **T~ (Atkins)**, private in British Army. 2. **T~ gun**, Thompson submachine gun; similar automatic weapon; **tom′myrot**, nonsense. [familiar form of *Tom*]

to·mor·row (t*o*mŏr′ō, -mar′-) *adv.* & *n.* (On) the day after today; (at) a future time.

Tomp·kins (tŏmp′kĭnz), **Daniel D.** (1774–1825). Amer. politician; governor of New York, 1807–17; U.S. vice president, 1817–25, under James Monroe.

tom-tom (tŏm′tŏm) *n.* Amer. or E. Indian drum, usu. beaten with hands; any barbaric drum; the sound of such a drum. [Hind. *tamtam*, imit.]

ton (tŭn) *n.* 1. (abbrev. t.) Measure of weight; **long ~**, 2,240 lbs. avoirdupois; **metric ~**, unit of mass equal to 1000 kilograms, 2,204.6 lbs. avoirdupois; **short ~**, 2,000 lbs. avoirdupois. 2. Measure of capacity (often varying) for timber (40 cu. ft.), stone (16 cu. ft.), salt (42 bushels), lime (40 bushels), coke (28 bushels), wheat (20 bushels), etc. 3. Unit of internal capacity of ship (for purposes of registered TONNAGE, 100 cu. ft.; for purposes of freight, usu. 40 cu. ft.). 4. (colloq., esp. pl.) Large number or amount. [var. of *tun*]

ton·al (tō′n*a*l) *adj.* Of tone or tones; (of fugue) having **tonal** (opp. real) **answer**, in which intervals are modified rather than repeated exactly.

to·nal·i·ty (tōnăl′ĭtē) *n.* (pl. **-ties**). 1. (mus.) The relation between notes in a composition that constitutes the key; strict observation of key scheme or mode of musical composition. 2. (painting) Coloring in respect of its lightness and darkness, tones of a picture in relation to one another.

On this experimental farm in California ***tomatoes*** *are tested under various conditions. The end result will, it is hoped, be bigger, tastier tomatoes.*

tone (tōn) *n.* 1. Sound, esp. with ref. to pitch, quality, and strength. 2. Particular quality, pitch, modulation, etc., of voice; intonation; pitch, inflection, of spoken sound, expressing differences of meaning, esp. (in Chinese and similar languages) any of various inflections or pitches distinguishing words that otherwise have the same sound. 3. (mus.) Sound of definite pitch and character produced by regular vibration of sounding body, musical note; each of the several tones (**fundamental ~** and **overtones**) audible in sound of bell or similar instrument; (also) musical note without overtones. 4. (mus.) Interval of major second, e.g. C-D, E-F sharp (freq. **whole tone**, as opp. to **semitone**). 5. (med.) Degree of firmness or tension proper to strong and healthy organs or tissues of body. 6. Prevailing character of morals, sentiments, etc., in society or community; state of mind, mood. 7. Degree of lightness or darkness of color(s); general effect of combination of light and shade, esp. in a picture or a scene in nature. 8. **tone arm**, phonograph pickup arm; **tone color**, (mus.) timbre; **tone deaf,**

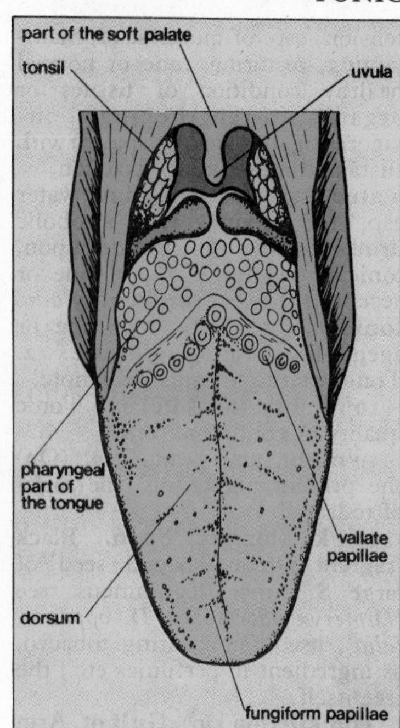

*Above: The human **tongue** is important for taste, swallowing, and pronunciation.*

*Dancers from **Tonga** in skirts made from tapa or beaten bark. Except for a small export trade of copra and bananas, the Polynesian islanders are self-supporting gardeners.*

deafness, insensitive(ness) to differences in pitch between musical tones; **tone language,** language such as Chinese or Swedish in which similar sounds are distinguished by tones (see sense 2 above); **tone poem,** orchestral composition of indeterminate form and illustrative character, based on poetic or literary rather than purely musical ideas. **tone** *v.* (**toned, ton·ing**). Give tone or quality (of sound or color) to; alter tone or color of (photographic print) in finishing it; harmonize; **tone down,** lower tone, quality, or character of; make, become, less emphatic; become lower or softer in tone or quality; **tone up,** improve tone of, give higher or stronger tone to. **ton′al·ly** *adv.*

tone·less (tōn′lĭs) *adj.* (esp.) Without distinctive quality of sound or color, dull, lifeless, unexpressive. **tone′less·ly** *adv.* **tone′less·ness** *n.*

tong (tawng, tŏng) *n.* Chinese association, esp. secret society or fraternal association of Chinese in foreign country. [Chin. *t'ang* meeting place]

Ton·ga (tŏng′g*a*). (also Tongan Islands or Friendly Islands) Group of islands in S. Pacific E. of Fiji; kingdom, member state of the Brit. Commonwealth, independent since 1970; capital, Nukualofa. **Ton′gan** *adj.* & *n.*

ton·ga (tŏng′g*a*) *n.* Light two-wheeled carriage in India.

tongs (tawngz, tŏngz) *n.pl.* (also **pair of ~**) Implement consisting of two limbs connected by hinge, pivot, or spring bringing together lower ends to grasp objects that are inconvenient to lift with hand.

tongue (tŭng) *n.* 1. Organ in floor of mouth, usu. freely movable; in man and many other vertebrates tapering, blunt tipped, muscular, soft and fleshy, used in taking in and swallowing food, as principal organ of taste, and, in people, of articulate speech; animal's tongue as article of food. 2. Action of speaking, faculty of speech, words, talk, language; speech or language of a people; **gift of ~s,** power of speaking in unknown languages, esp. as miraculously conferred on early Christians (Acts 2); **lose, find, one's tongue,** be too bashful or surprised to speak, recover power of speech after this; **hold one's tongue,** be silent; **on the tip of one's tongue,** on the point of being said; about to be said, esp. because nearly but not quite remembered; (**speak**) **with one's tongue in one's cheek,** (speak) insincerely or mockingly. 3. Thing like tongue in shape or function, as pin of buckle, narrow strip of land between two bodies of water, clapper of bell, pole of wagon or other vehicle, strip of leather or cloth closing gap in front of boot or shoe, movable tapered piece of steel in railroad switch, projecting tenon along edge of board, to be inserted into groove or mortise of another board etc. 4. **tongue and groove,** joint in which tongue on edge of one board fits into groove on another; **tongue depressor,** thin piece of wood for holding down patient's tongue during medical examination of mouth and throat; **tongue′fish,** flatfish of family Cynoglossidae; **tongue-lashing,** severe scolding or rebuke; **tongue-tie(d),** (condition of) having frenum of tongue too short, so that distinct speech is difficult or impossible; speechless, dumb, from embarrassment, shyness, etc.; **tongue twister,** sequence of words difficult to articulate quickly. **tongue** *v.* (**tongued, tongu·ing**). Utter, speak; furnish with tongue; interrupt stream of air with tongue in playing wind instrument. **tongued, tongue′less** *adjs.*

ton·ic (tŏn′ĭk) *adj.* 1. Producing

tension, esp. of muscles; of, maintaining, restoring, tone or normal healthy condition of tissues or organs; strengthening, invigorating, bracing; (of spasm) with sustained muscular contraction; ~ **water**, carbonated quinine water esp. for mixing with alcoholic drinks. 2. (mus.) Of, founded upon, tonic or keynote. 3. Of tone or accent in speech. **ton'i·cal·ly** *adv.* **tonic** *n.* 1. Tonic medicine or agent; invigorating influence. 2. Tonic water. 3. (mus.) Keynote.

to·nic·i·ty (tōnĭs'ĭtē) *n.* Tonic quality or condition, tone.

to·night (to*n*īt') *adv.* & *n.* (On) the present night, (on) the night of today.

ton·ka (tŏng'k*a*) **bean.** Black fragrant almond-shaped seed of large S. Amer. leguminous tree (*Dipteryx odorata* or *D. oppositifolia*), used for scenting tobacco, as ingredient in perfumes etc.; the tree itself.

Ton·kin (tŏn'kĭn), **Gulf of.** Arm of the China Sea, 300 mi. (483 km) long, between the E. coast of Vietnam and Hainan Island.

ton·nage (tŭn'ĭj) *n.* 1. Carrying capacity of ship expressed in tons of 100 cu. ft.; ships collectively, shipping; charge per ton on cargo or freight; **displacement** ~, weight of water displaced by a ship when loaded up to her load line, used in stating the tonnage of warships; **gross** ~, total cubic capacity of all spaces above and below the tonnage deck; **net** or **register** ~, gross tonnage less space occupied by engines, crew's quarters, etc., tonnage for which vessels are registered and on which the assessment of fees and charges on shipping are based.

to·nom·e·ter (tōnŏm'ĭt*er*) *n.* Tuning fork or other instrument for measuring the pitch of tones.

ton·sil (tŏn'sĭl) *n.* Either of a pair of small organs on either side of the root of the tongue, composed of lymphatic tissue and instrumental in protecting the throat from infection, but themselves liable to become septic. **ton'sil·lar, ton'sil·ar** *adjs.* Of, affected by, the tonsils.

ton·sil·lec·to·my (tŏnsĭlĕk'tomē) *n.* (pl. **-mies**). Surgical removal of the tonsils.

ton·sil·li·tis (tŏnsĭlī'tĭs) *n.* Inflammation of the tonsils.

ton·so·ri·al (tŏnsŏr'ēal, -sōr'-) *adj.* (usu. joc.) Of a barber or his work.

ton·sure (tŏn'sh*er*) *n.* Shaving of head (in Eastern Ch.) or part of it, esp. circular patch on crown (in R.C. Ch., until 1972), as religious practice, esp. as preparation to entering priesthood or monastic order; part of head thus shaved. ~ *v.t.* (**-sured, -sur·ing**). Shave head of, give tonsure to.

*The **tonsure** of this Benedictine monk is said to represent the 'coronal of St. Peter'. The practice was begun in monasteries in the 5th century, adopted by other clerics, but is now restricted to monks.*

ton·tine (tŏn'tēn, tŏntēn') *n.* Financial scheme by which subscribers to loan each receive an annuity for life, increasing as their number is diminished by death, until last survivor enjoys whole income; any arrangement, as form of insurance, in which benefits shared among members are increased on death or default of any of them, or in which they are distributed among all remaining members at end of fixed period. [Lorenzo *Tonti*, Neapolitan banker, who instituted scheme in France *c*1653]

To·ny (tō'nē) *n.* (pl. **-nies**). Any of several awards given each year by the American Theater Wing for outstanding work in the theater as a performer, director, writer, designer, etc.

too (tōō) *adv.* 1. In addition, moreover, besides, also. 2. In excess; more than is right or fitting, more than enough; (colloq.) extremely, very.

tool (tōōl) *n.* Implement for working on something, usu. one held in and operated by hand, but also including simple machines, as lathe; (cutting part of) machine tool; anything used in performing some operation or in any occupation or pursuit; person used as mere instrument by another; (bookbinding etc.) small stamp or roller for impressing design on leather; **tool'box**, box or chest, usu. having compartments, to hold workman's tools; **tool'house** (pl. **-houses** pr. -howzĭz), **tool'shed**, shed, as in garden, where tools are kept; **tool'maker**, machinist who makes machine tools and parts and maintains and repairs them. **tool** *v.* Work with tool; smooth surface of building stone with large chisel; ornament (leather) with tool; drive, ride, (*along*) esp. in casual or leisurely manner; ~ **up**, equip with tools.

tool·ing (tōō'lĭng) *n.* (esp.) Dressing of stone with broad chisel; impressing of ornamental design with heated tools on leather, such design(s).

toot (tōōt) *n.* Note or short blast of horn, trumpet, or other wind instrument. ~ *v.* Sound (horn or other wind instrument); give out such sound. **toot'er** *n.*

tooth (tōōth) *n.* (pl. **teeth** pr. tēth). 1. Each of the hard processes (in mammals usu. of dentine coated with cement around root and enamel in exposed part) attached, usu. in sockets, in a row to each jaw in most vertebrates except birds, with points, edges, or grinding surfaces, and used for biting, tearing, or chewing food, or as weapons of attack or defense; elephant's tusk; (fig.) sense of taste, taste, liking; **by the skin of one's teeth**, narrowly, barely; **cut one's teeth on**, do at the start of one's career, schooling, etc.; **in the teeth of**, in spite of; in opposition to; in the face of (wind etc.); **long in the tooth**, old; **put teeth in**(**to**), make (more) effective, make (law etc.) enforceable; **set one's teeth**, clench teeth firmly from indignation or fixed resolution (freq. fig.); **show one's teeth**, (usu. fig.) show hostility or malice, behave threateningly; (**armed** etc.)

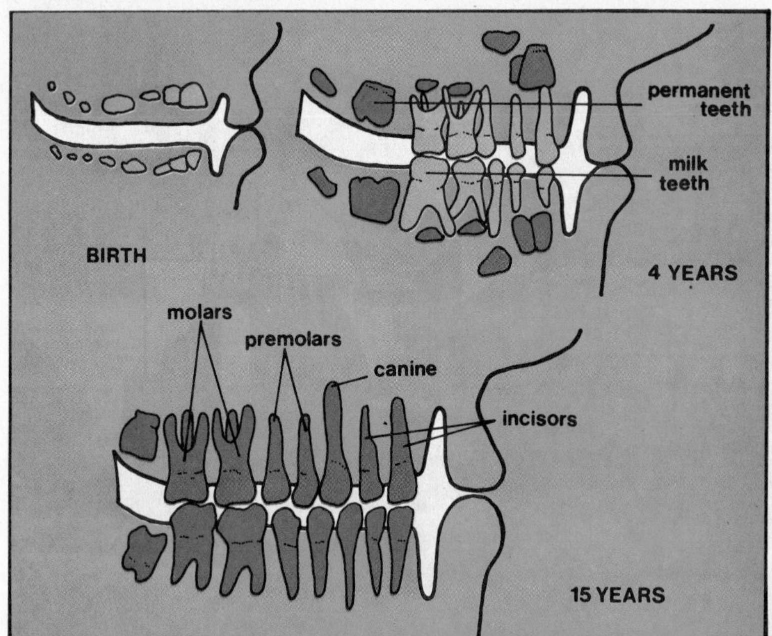

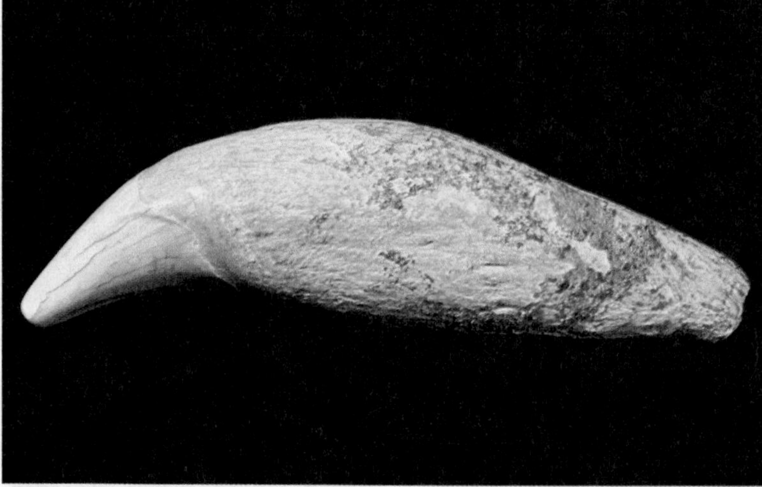

Left: Cross sections of the human mouth at various ages showing development of the teeth. Below left: The fossil canine ***tooth*** *of a bear which lived during the Pleistocene, at some time up to 3 million years ago.*

to the teeth, completely, elaborately armed, equipped, etc.; **tooth and nail**, (usu. fig.) vigorously, fiercely. 2. Projecting part or point resembling tooth, as pointed process on margin of leaf; projecting point of rock; prong or tine of comb, saw, file, rake, fork, etc.; one of series of projections on edge of wheel, pinion, etc., engaging with corresponding ones on another, cog; (sing. only) rough surface on paper, canvas, etc., to which pencil marks, colors, etc., adhere; roughness made on surfaces to be glued together. 3. **tooth'-ache**, ache in tooth or teeth; **tooth'brush**, small brush used for cleaning teeth; **fine-tooth comb**, comb with closely set teeth; **tooth'-paste, tooth powder**, paste, powder, for cleaning teeth; **tooth'-pick**, small pointed instrument of quill, wood, etc., used for removing matter lodged between teeth; **tooth shell**, (long tubular tusk-shaped shell of) mollusk of class Schaphopoda or allied genus. **toothed** (tōōdhd), **tooth'less** *adjs.* **tooth'less·ly** *adv.* **tooth'less·ness** *n.* **tooth** *v.* Furnish with tooth or teeth; give rough surface to; (of cog wheels etc.) interlock.

tooth·some (tōōth'sŏm) *adj.* Pleasant to eat. **tooth'some·ly** *adv.* **tooth'some·ness** *n.*

too·tle (tōō'tel) *v.i.* (**-tled, -tling**). Toot gently or continuously, esp. on flute.

toot·sy (tōōt'sē) *n.* (pl. **-sies**). (nursery or joc.) [also **~-wootsy** (-wōōtsē) (pl. **-woot·sies**)] Foot.

top[1] (tŏp) *n.* I. Summit, upper part, surface; highest place, rank, degree, etc.; end of anything conventionally regarded as the higher; (usu. pl.) part of plant growing above ground, esp. of vegetable grown for its root; **blow one's ~**, (slang) lose one's temper; lose one's sanity; **from ~ to toe**, from head to foot, in every part; **on ~**, (fig.) supreme, dominant; **on ~ of the world**, (colloq.) exuberant; successful; **the ~s**, (colloq.) (used predicatively) best in ability, popularity, quality, etc.; foremost; **top dog**, victor, master; **top-dog**, of the highest authority; **top'flight**, in highest rank of achievement; **top spin**, spin given to a ball, causing it to rotate forward in direction of its flight. 2. Part of piece forming upper part or covering of something, e.g. platform near head of lower mast of ship, in warship, topsail; upper part of leg of high boot, esp. broad band of material around this; gauntlet part of glove; turned-down part of leg of sock or stocking; stopper of bottle; hood of carriage, automobile, etc. **top** *adj.* Highest in position or degree, that is at or on top; **top'coat**, overcoat; **top drawer**, uppermost drawer of series; **top-drawer**, of high social position, origin, or quality; **top-dress**, apply material to surface of (land, road, etc.) without working it in; **top dressing**, material, esp. manure, so applied; **topgal'lant**, mast, sail, yard, rigging, immediately above topmast and topsail; **top hat**, tall silk hat; **top-heavy**, overweighted at top, so as to be unstable; **top'knot**, knot, bow of ribbon, tuft, crest, etc., worn or growing on top of head; **topmast** (tŏp'măst, -mahst; naut. tŏp'm*a*st), smaller mast on top of lower mast, esp. second section of mast above deck; **top'notch**, (colloq.) first-rate, excellent; **topsail** (tŏp'sāl; naut. tŏp's*a*l), in square-rigged vessel, sail next above lower sail, sometimes divided into **upper** and **lower topsails** (**double topsails**); **top-secret**, extremely secret (esp. as security classification); **top sergeant**, (colloq.) first sergeant of company or other military unit; **top'side**, upper part of ship's side, above water line or main deck. **top** *v.* (**topped, top·ping**). I. Provide with top or cap; remove top of (plant) to improve growth etc.; reach top of (hill etc.); be at top of, have highest position in; exceed in height; hit (golf ball) above center, make (stroke) thus; **~ off**, put end or finishing touch to. 2. (naut.) Tip *up*, slant, raise (yard); (of yard) rise, tip up. **top'-less** *adj.* (Seemingly) without a top; (of clothes) having no upper part, (of person) wearing such clothes, bare-breasted.

top[2] (tŏp) *n.* Toy, usu. conical, rotating on point when set in

Topiary became fashionable in the gardens of the great English homes during the reign of the Tudors. These shrubs at Leven's Hall in Cumbria are fine examples.

motion by hand, spring, or string; **sleep like a ~** sleep soundly, (with ref. to apparent stillness of top spinning on vertical axis).

to·paz (tō′păz) *n.* Silicate of aluminum usu. in yellow, white, pale blue, or pale green transparent lustrous prismatic crystals, classed as semiprecious stone; **false ~**, transparent pale yellow variety of quartz; **oriental ~**, precious stone, the yellow sapphire; **pink ~**, rose-colored kind produced by exposing yellow Brazilian topaz to great heat. **to·paz·ine** (tō′pazēn, -zīn) *adj.*

tope[1] (tōp) *n.* Small European shark, *Galeorhinus galeus*; any of various related sharks.

tope[2] (tōp) *n.* Buddhist monument, usu. a cylindrical tower surmounted by a cupola. [Sansk. *stupa* mound]

tope[3] (tōp) *v.i.* (**toped, top·ing**). (now chiefly literary) Drink to excess, esp. habitually. **top′er** *n.*

to·pee, to·pi (tōpē′, tō′pē) *ns.* Light pith hat or helmet, esp. **sola ~**. [Hind. *topī* hat]

To·pe·ka (topē′ka). Capital of Kansas, in the NE. on the Kansas River.

to·phus (tō′fus) *n.* (pl. **-phi** pr. -fī). (path.) Mineral concretion in the body, esp. on the joints or on a bone, in gout.

to·pi = TOPEE.

to·pi·ar·y (tō′pēĕrē) *adj.* & *n.* (pl. **-ar·ies**). (Of) the art of clipping and trimming shrubs etc. into ornamental or fantastic shapes. [L. *topia* landscape gardening or painting, f. Gk. *topos* place]

top·ic (tŏp′ĭk) *n.* Subject of discourse, argument, etc., theme; (rhet., logic) class of considerations from which arguments can be drawn.

top·i·cal (tŏp′ĭkal) *adj.* 1. Of topics; of topics of the day, containing local or temporary allusions. 2. (med.) Local. **top′i·cal·ly** *adv.* **top·i·cal·i·ty** (tŏpĭkăl′ĭtē) *n.*

top·most (tŏp′mōst) *adj.* Uppermost.

to·pog·ra·phy (topŏg′rafē) *n.* (pl. **-phies**). Detailed delineation or description, physical features, of place; features of locality collectively; (study of) local distribution; (anat.) regional anatomy. **to·pog′ra·pher** *n.* **top·o·graph·ic** (tŏpogrăf′ĭk), **top·o·graph′i·cal** *adjs.* **top·o·graph′i·cal·ly** *adv.*

to·pol·o·gy (topŏl′ojē) *n.* (pl. **-gies**). Branch of mathematics dealing with properties of spaces (sets of points) in respect of their being one connected piece and of forming a boundary, independently of shape and size. **top·o·log·i·cal** (tŏpolŏj′ĭkal) *adj.* **top·o·log′i·cal·ly** *adv.* **to·pol′o·gist** *n.*

top·per (tŏp′er) *n.* 1. (colloq.) Top hat. 2. One who or thing that tops. 3. (slang) Witticism, joke, etc., better than all that preceded.

top·ple (tŏp′el) *v.* (**-pled, -pling**). (Cause to) tumble or fall headlong, as if top-heavy.

top·sy-tur·vy (tŏp′sētẽr′vē) *adv.* & *adj.* With the top where the bottom should be, upside down; in(to) utter confusion or disorder.

toque (tōk) *n.* Small usu. brimless hat of folded or swathed material.

tor (tōr) *n.* Craggy or rocky hill or peak.

To·rah (tōr′a, tōr′a; *Heb.* tōrah′) *n.* Pentateuch, the Mosaic Law; scroll of this used in synagogue. [Heb. *tôrāh* instruction, direction]

torc = TORQUE.

torch (tōrch) *n.* 1. Light for carrying in hand, consisting of piece of resinous wood or length of twisted hemp or flax soaked in resin, tallow, etc.; (fig.) source of conflagration, illumination, enlightenment, etc.; **carry the ~ for**, (slang) have unrequited passion for; **pass on the ~**, pass on tradition. 2. (also **electric ~**) (Brit.) Flashlight. 3. Lamp or other portable device for producing hot flame (also **blow ~**). 4. **torch′bearer**, (esp.) one who guards or hands on light of truth, civilization, etc.; **torch singer**, singer of **torch songs**, popular, esp. jazz, songs about unrequited love.

tore[1]: see TEAR[2].

tore[2] (tōr, tōr) = TORUS, senses 1 and 3.

tor·e·a·dor (tōr′ēadōr) *n.* Bullfighter (term still current in English but not in mod. Spanish). [Sp. *toro* bull, f. L. *taurus*]

to·re·ro (torār′ō) *n.* (pl. **-ros**). Bullfighter, esp. a matador. [Sp.]

to·reu·tic (torōō′tĭk) *adj.* & *n.* (Of) the art of chasing, carving, and embossing, esp. metal. **to·reu′tics** *n.sing.*

tor·ment (tōr′mĕnt) *n.* Severe bodily or mental suffering; cause of this. ~ (tōrmĕnt′) *v.t.* Subject to torment. **tor·men′tor, tor·ment′er** *ns.* **tor·ment′ed·ly, tor·ment′ing·ly** *advs.*

tor·men·til (tōr′mĕntĭl) *n.* Low-growing yellow-flowered herb (*Potentilla tormentilla*) of Europe and Asia, common on heaths and dry pastures, with strongly astringent roots.

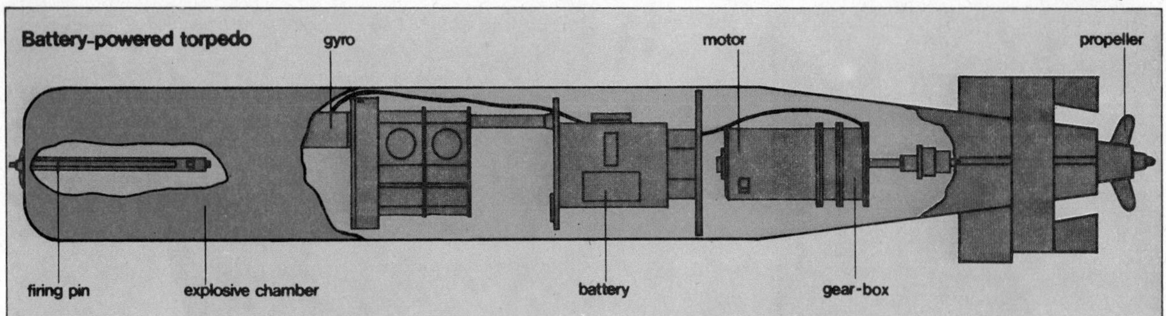

torn: see TEAR[2].

tor·na·do (tōrnā´dō) *n.* (pl. **-does, -dos**). Violent storm, usu. with heavy rain, in which wind rotates or constantly changes direction, esp., in the midwestern U.S., destructive storm with funnel-shaped (tornado) cloud like waterspout, extending toward the ground and advancing in narrow path for many miles. **tor·nad·ic** (tōrnăd´ĭk), **tor·na´do·like** *adjs.*

to·roid (tōr´oid, tōr´-) *n.* (geom.) Surface generated by the rotation of a plane closed curve about a line lying in its plane. ~ *adj.* Of, resembling, a tore or toroid. **to·roi·dal** (toroi´dal, tōr´oidal, tōr´-) *adj.*

To·ron·to (torŏn´tō). Capital city of province of Ontario, Canada.

tor·pe·do (tōrpē´dō) *n.* (pl. **-does**). 1. ELECTRIC ray, esp. *Torpedo nobiliana* found in Atlantic Ocean (also ~ **fish**). 2. Self-propelled submarine missile, usu. equipped with a homing device, cigar-shaped, carrying an explosive that is fired by impact with its objective, used for destroying or disabling ships at sea; similar missile discharged from aircraft (**aerial** ~); case containing explosive used for various military purposes, explosive cartridge for clearing obstructions etc. in oil well, detonator placed on railroad line as fog signal etc.; small firework consisting of gravel and a percussion cap wrapped in tissue paper, exploding loudly when thrown against a hard surface. 3. (slang) Gangster, thug, etc., who kills for hire; ~ **boat**, small fast lightly armored vessel carrying torpedoes; **~-boat destroyer** (now usu. *destroyer*), larger and more heavily armed torpedo boat, orig. for attacking torpedo boat (see also DESTROYER); ~ **tube**, steel tube through which torpedoes are discharged, usu. by compressed air. **torpedo** *v.t.* (**-doed, -do·ing**). Attack, damage, destroy, (as) with a torpedo. [L. name of the fish (*torpere* be numb)]

*The first guided missile was also the ancestor of the **torpedo** — a small boat filled with explosives and steered on the surface by wires. It was made by Robert Whitehead in 1866.*

tor·pid (tōr´pĭd) *adj.* Benumbed; dormant; sluggish, inactive, dull. **tor´pid·ly** *adv.* **tor·pid·i·ty** (tōrpĭd´ĭtē), **tor´pid·ness** *ns.*

tor·por (tōr´per) *n.* Torpidity. **tor·por·if·ic** (tōrporĭf´ĭk) *adj.* Causing torpor.

torque, torc (tōrk) *ns.* 1. Necklace or collar, usu. of twisted metal, worn esp. by ancient Britons and Gauls. 2. (phys. etc.) Twisting or rotary force in piece of mechanism, moment of system of forces producing rotation; ~ **converter**, device to transmit correct torque from engine to axle in motor vehicle; ~ **wrench**, wrench having dial or other indicator that shows amount of torque exerted.

*A **tor** is a term peculiar to the west of England and may refer to a small rocky hill, or to a weathered outcrop of rock such as that below, on Bodmin Moor in Cornwall.*

*The roots of **tormentil** have been found to possess useful qualities. Tannin could be obtained from them; if soaked in brandy, the infusion was used to treat stomach complaints.*

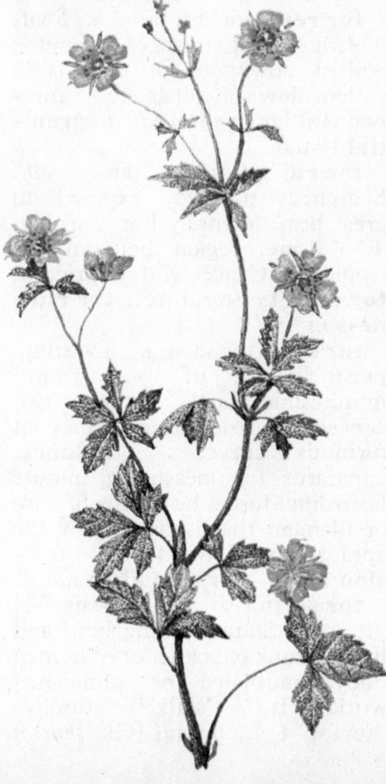

Land-dwelling ***tortoises*** *range in size from the giants of Galapagos and the Seychelles up to 4 ft. long, to the tiny spider tortoise of Madagascar which does not exceed 4 ins. Three species are native to Europe but those kept as pets in Britain are all imported from the Mediterranean countries.*

Tor·que·ma·da (tōrkĕmah′-dhah), **Tomás de** (1420–98). Spanish Dominican monk; first inquisitor general.

torr (tōr) *n.* Unit of pressure in measuring partial vacuum, equal to $\frac{1}{760}$ of standard atmosphere.

tor·rent (tōr′ent, tār′-) *n.* Swift violent rushing stream of water etc.; violent downpour of rain; (fig.) violent flow (of words etc.). **tor·ren·tial** (torĕn′sh*a*l) *adj.* **tor·ren′tial·ly** *adv.*

tor·rid (tōr′ĭd, tār′-) *adj.* Scorched, parched, exposed to great heat; intensely hot, burning; **T~ Zone**, region between the tropics of Cancer and Capricorn. **tor·rid·i·ty** (torĭd′ĭtē), **tor′rid·ness** *ns.*

tor·sion (tōr′sh*o*n) *n.* Twisting, twist; **angle of ~**, (geom.) infinitesimal angle between two consecutive osculating planes of tortuous curve; **~ balance**, apparatus for measuring minute horizontal forces by means of wire or filament that is twisted by the application of the force. **tor′sion·al** *adj.* **tor′sion·al·ly** *adv.*

tor·so (tōr′sō) *n.* (pl. **-sos, -si** pr. -sē). Statue lacking head and limbs; trunk of statue, or of human body; mutilated or unfinished work. [It., = "stalk," "stump," "torso," f. L. *thyrsus* (Gk. *thursos* shaft, wand)]

tort (tōrt) *n.* (law) Wrongful act (but not breach of contract) that results in injury to person, property, etc., making offender liable to action for damages. [med. L. *tortum* wrong f. L. *torquere* twist]

torte (tōrt) *n.* Rich cake, often layered, made with many eggs, chopped nuts, spices, and bread or cracker crumbs.

tor·ti·col·lis (tōrt*i*kŏl′ĭs) *n.* (path.) Rheumatic or other condition of muscles causing twisting and stiffness of neck.

tor·til·la (tōrtē′*a*) *n.* In Mexican cooking, thin flat cake of corn flour baked on flat plate of iron etc.

tor·tious (tōr′sh*u*s) *adj.* Of, constituting, a tort.

tor·toise (tōr′t*o*s) *n.* Slow-moving four-footed reptile of land and freshwater species of order Chelonia, with body enclosed in heavy shell, and head and legs retractile.

tortoise (tōr′t*o*s) **shell.** 1. Carapace of turtle, esp. that of the hawksbill turtle (*Chelone imbricata*), semitransparent, of rich yellowish-brown mottled color, used for ornamental articles, in inlaying, etc. 2. (also **~ butterfly**) Any of various butterflies with coloring resembling that of tortoise shell, esp. the **small tortoise shell** (*Aglais urticae*).

tor·to·ni (tōrtō′nē) *n.* Ice cream made with heavy cream, eggs, and chopped maraschino cherries and usually topped with ground almonds or macaroon crumbs.

tor·tu·ous (tōr′cho͞o*u*s) *adj.* Full of twists or turns; (geom., of curve) of which no two successive portions are in same plane; (fig.) devious, circuitous, crooked, not straightforward. **tor′tu·ous·ly** *adv.* **tor′tu·ous·ness, tor·tu·os·i·ty** (tōrcho͞oŏs′ĭtē) *ns.*

tor·ture (tōr′ch*e*r) *n.* Infliction of severe bodily pain, e.g. as punishment or to force confession or extort information; severe physical or mental pain. **~** *v.t.* (**-tured, -tur·ing**). Subject to torture; (fig.) strain, wrench, distort, pervert. **tor′tured·ly** *adv.* **tor′tur·er** *n.*

to·rus (tōr′*u*s, tōr′*u*s) *n.* (pl. **to·ri** pr. tōr′ī, tōr′ī). (also for senses 1 & 3 **tore**) 1. (archit.) Large convex molding esp. at base of column. 2. (bot.) Receptacle of flower, swollen summit of flower stalk, supporting floral organs; (also) thickening of PIT membrane. 3. (Solid enclosed by) surface described by a conic section, esp. circle, rotating about a straight line in its own plane. [L., = "protuberance," "bed"]

To·ry (tŏr′ē, tōr′ē) *adj.* & *n.* (pl. **-ries**). 1. (now chiefly in Brit. colloq. and hostile use) Conservative. 2. (hist.) (Member) of the parliamentary and political party in England that opposed the exclusion of the Duke of York (James II) from the succession, inclined to the Stuarts after 1689, accepted George III and the established order in church and state, opposed the Reform Bill of 1832, and has been known officially (since *c*1830) as "Conservative"; cf. WHIG. 3. In the Amer. Revolution, a colonist loyal to Gt. Britain. **To′ry·ism** *n.* [Ir. *tóraidhe* pursuer, applied orig. to 17th-c. Irish outlaws who robbed and killed English settlers and soldiers]

toss (taws, tŏs) *v.* Throw (*up*, *away*, *to*, etc.), esp. lightly, carelessly, or easily; (of bull etc.) throw (person etc.) up with horns; throw (coin), throw coin (*up*), into air to decide choice etc. by way it falls; settle question or dispute with (person *for* thing) thus; throw back *head*, esp. in contempt or impatience; throw about from side to side, throw oneself about thus in bed etc.; roll about restlessly; roll or swing with fitful to-and-fro motion; throw (pancake) up so that it returns to pan with other side up; ~ **off**, drink off at a draft; dispatch (work etc.) rapidly or without apparent effort; **tossed salad**, salad of mixed greens, tomatoes, sliced onions, cucumbers, etc., with dressing, mixed in large bowl. **toss** *n.* Tossing; sudden jerk, esp. of head; tossing of coin; throw from horseback etc; **toss′up**, tossing of coin; doubtful question; even chance.

tot[1] (tŏt) *n.* Tiny child; (Brit.) small quantity (*of* drink, esp. liquor), dram.

tot[2] (tŏt) *v.* (**tot·ted, tot·ting**). Add (*up*), mount *up* (*to*). [abbrev. of TOTAL or of L. *totum* whole]

to·tal (tō′tal) *adj.* Complete, comprising or involving the whole; absolute, unqualified; ~ **depravity**, Calvinistic belief that man's whole nature, including the rational aspects, has been entirely laid over with sin since the Fall, leaving man totally dependent on Christ for spiritual rebirth before he can do anything pleasing to God; ~ **eclipse**, eclipse in which whole disk of sun or moon is obscured; ~ **recall**, ability to remember every detail of one's experience clearly; ~ **war**, one in which all available resources are employed without reserve. **to′tal·ly** *adv.* **to·tal·i·ty** (tōtăl′ĭtē) *n.* (pl. **-ties**). **total** *n.* Sum of all items, total amount. **total** *v.* (**-taled, -tal·ing** or **-talled, -tal·ling**) Amount to, mount *up to*; reckon total of.

to·tal·i·tar·i·an (tōtălĭtār′ēan) *adj.* Of, pertaining to, regime that permits no rival loyalties or parties and arrogates to itself all rights, including those normally belonging to individuals. **to·tal·i·tar′i·an·ism** *n.*

*The largest of the 37 types of **toucan** has a length of 24 ins. and its beak can be a quarter of that. Despite its size, the beak is light in weight and is an adaptation which allows the bird to obtain soft fruit from stems that are too weak to carry the weight of the bird. These birds are found only in the forests of South America.*

to·tal·i·za·tor (tō′talĭzāter) *n.* Device for registering or finding total of something; esp. a parimutuel machine for registering and indicating bets on each horse, dog, etc., in a race; tote board. **to′tal·i·sa·tor, to′tal·iz·er** *ns.*

to·tal·ize (tō′talīz) *v.* (**-ized, -iz·ing**). Collect into a total, find the total of.

tote[1] (tōt) *v.t.* (**tot·ed, tot·ing**). (colloq.) 1. Carry or lug; haul, esp. in one's arms or on one's back. 2. Carry or bear on one's person. 3. Convey, transport, as on truck or boat. ~ *n.* (colloq.) 1. Act of toting. 2. Thing that is toted; burden; ~ **bag**, woman's large bag for carrying parcels etc.

tote[2] (tōt) *v.* (**tot·ed, tot·ing**). (colloq.) Total.

tote (tōt) **board.** (colloq.) Totalizator.

to·tem (tō´tem) *n.* Natural, esp. animal, object assumed as emblem of family or clan; image of this; ~ **pole**, pole or post with carved and painted representation of totem, set up in front of N. Amer. Ind. dwelling. **to'tem·ism** *n.*

toth·er, t'oth·er (tŭdh´*er*) *prons.* & *adjs.* (dial.) The other.

tot·ter (tŏt´*er*) *v.i.* Walk with unsteady steps, go shakily or feebly; rock or shake on its base, as if about to overbalance or collapse. **tot'ter·ing** *adj.* **tot'ter·ing·ly** *adv.* **totter** *n.* Tottering gait. **tot'ter·y** *adj.*

tou·can (to͞o´kăn, to͝okahn´) *n.* Tropical Amer. fruit-eating bird of *Rhamphastos* or allied genera, with huge light thin-walled beak and freq. brilliant coloring.

touch (tŭch) *v.* 1. Put hand or other part of body on or into contact with; bring (thing) into contact *with* another; be in, come into contact (with); (geom.) be tangent (to); (of king or healer) lay hand on (person) as cure for scrofula or other disease (also abs.). 2. Affect in some way by contact; strike (strings, keys) of musical instrument so as to make it sound; mark, draw (*in*), modify, alter, by touching drawing etc. with pencil or brush; add touches to; mark, modify, slightly *with* color, expression, etc.; (of ship etc.) call at (port); reach, (fig.) approach in excellence etc. 3. Affect mentally or morally; affect with tender feeling, soften; rouse painful or angry feeling in; concern. 4. Treat of (subject) lightly or in passing. 5. Affect slightly, produce slightest effect on; have to do with in the slightest degree, esp. hurt or harm in the least degree; (usu. with neg.) eat or drink the smallest quantity of. 6. ~ **at**, (of ship) call at (port); ~ **down**, land on ground from the air; ~ **(someone) for**, (slang) beg or borrow (money) from (person); ~ **off**, characterize (someone) precisely; discharge (explosive etc.); ~ **on, upon**, treat (subject) briefly; ~ **up**, give finishing, improving, or heightening touches to; jog (memory). 7. ~ **and go,** ~**-and-go**, delicate state of affairs; of uncertain result, risky; ~**-me-not**, plant of genus *Impatiens*, esp. yellow balsam (*I. noli-me-tangere*) with seed capsules that split open when touched; ~ **wood**, touch (wooden object) to avert bad luck. **touch** *n.* 1. Act or fact of touching, contact; faculty by which material things are perceived by their contact with some part of the body surface; sensation conveyed by touching, feel; light stroke with pencil, brush, etc., detail of any artistic work, slight act or effort in work of any kind; artistic skill, style of artistic work; manner of touching keys or strings of musical, esp. keyboard, instrument, manner or degree in which instrument responds to this. 2. (also ~ **mark**) Manufacturer's identifying mark on article of metal, esp. pewter. 3. Close relation of communication, agreement, sympathy, etc. (esp. **in, out of,** ~ **with; keep in, lose,** ~). 4. **touch'back**, (football) play in which player touches ball to ground behind his own goal line after opponents have caused ball to pass over the line; cf. SAFETY; **touch'down**, (football) scoring by being in possession of ball behind opponents' goal line; landing on ground by airplane; **touch football**, informal style of football played without uniforms or protective equipment and with touching, usu. with both hands, of ball carrier substituted for tackling; **touch'line**, (soccer) boundary line on each side of field of play between goal lines. 5. **touch'hole**, (hist.) small tubular hole in breech of cannon through which fire was applied to powder; **touch needle**, slender rod of gold or silver of known fineness, used with touchstone to test fineness of gold or silver; **touch paper**, paper impregnated with potassium nitrate so as to burn steadily without flame, formerly used for firing gunpowder etc.; **touch'stone**, basanite, used to test fineness of gold and silver alloys by color of streak produced by rubbing them on it; (fig.) standard, criterion; **touch system, typing**, typewriting by touch, i.e. without looking at keys; **touch'wood**, wood or woody substance in such state as to catch fire readily, used as tinder; esp. soft white long-burning substance into which wood is converted by action of some fungi, punk.

tou·ché (to͞oshā´) *int.* (fencing) Exclamation acknowledging a touch by opponent's foil; (transf.) acknowledgement of telling thrust in argument. [Fr., = "touched"]

touch·ing (tŭch´ĭng) *prep.* Concerning, about. ~ *adj.* Affecting, pathetic. **touch'ing·ly** *adv.* **touch'ing·ness** *n.*

touch·y (tŭch´ē) *adj.* (**touch·i·er, touch·i·est**). Easily taking offense, oversensitive. **touch'i·ly** *adv.* **touch'i·ness** *n.*

tough (tŭf) *adj.* Of close tenacious substance or texture; hard to break or cut, not brittle; (of food) difficult to chew; (of clay etc.) stiff, tenacious; hardy, able to endure hardship; unyielding, stubborn; difficult; (colloq., of luck etc.) hard, severe, unpleasant; (slang) vicious, rowdy. **tough'ly** *adv.* **tough'ness** *n.* **tough'en** *v.* **tough** *n.* Street ruffian, tough person.

Tou·louse-Lau·trec (to͞olo͞os´-lōtrĕk´; *Fr.* to͞olo͞oz´lōtrĕk´), **Henri de** (1864–1901). French painter and lithographer.

tou·pee (to͞opā´) *n.* 1. (hist.) Topknot of hair esp. as crowning feature of wig; wig with this. 2. Patch, front, of false hair; man's wig. [OF. *toup* tuft]

tour (toor) *n.* 1. Journey through (part of) a country from place to place; rambling excursion, short journey, walk, esp. for sake of observing what is noteworthy; **grand** ~, (hist.) journey through France, Germany, Switzerland, and Italy, fashionable esp. in 18th c. as finishing course in education of young man of rank; **on** ~, touring. 2. (esp. mil.) Period of duty in service, time to be spent at station; shift. **tour** *v.* Make tour (of); (of actor, theatrical company, etc.) travel from town to town fulfilling engagements, travel about (country) thus, take (entertainment) about thus; so **touring company**. **touring car** (*n.*), open automobile designed for touring.

tour de force (toor d*e* fōrs´, fōrs´) (pl. **tours de force** pr. toor d*e* fōrs´, fōrs´). Feat of strength or (esp.) skill or artistry. [Fr.]

tour·ism (toor´ĭzem) *n.* Organized touring; accommodation and entertainment of tourists as industry.

tour·ist (toor´ĭst) *n.* Person who makes a tour; person who travels for pleasure; ~ **class**, class of accommodation below first and second class in ships and aircraft; ~ **court**, motel; ~ **home**, private home where travelers may rent rooms; ~ **trap**, place that exploits tourists by overcharging. **tourist** *adv.* In tourist-class accommodation. **tour'ist·y** *adj.* (derog.) Suitable for or visited by tourists.

tour·ma·line (toor´malĭn, -lēn) *n.* Brittle mineral, freq. occurring as crystals, a complex silicate of boron and aluminum with vitreous luster, usu. black or blackish and opaque (*schorl*), also blue (*indicolite*), red (*rubellite*), and other colors, used in optical instruments or as gem. [Sinhalese *tòramalli* (orig. found in Sri Lanka)]

***Henri de Toulouse-Lautrec** was a caricaturist and a sensitive social commentator. This picture of a man watching a woman adjust her garter (facing) is typical of his style.*

tour·na·ment (toor′nament, tẽr′-) *n.* 1. (hist.) Medieval martial sport in which mounted combatants in armor fought with blunted weapons for prize of valor; later, meeting for knightly sports and exercises. 2. Any contest in which a number of competitors play a series of games or take part in athletic events.

tour·ne·dos (toor′nedō, toor-nedō′) *n.* (pl. **-dos**). Small slices of fillet of beef served grilled or sauteed.

tour·ney (toor′nē, tẽr′-) *n.* (pl. **-neys**) & *v.i.* (hist.) (Take part in) tournament.

tour·ni·quet (tẽr′nĭkĭt, toor′-) *n.* Bandage for arresting bleeding by compression, tightened by twisting a rigid bar put through it; surgical instrument usu. with pad and screw, for same purpose.

tou·sle (tow′zel) *v.t.* (**-sled, -sling**). Pull about, handle roughly, make (esp. hair) untidy.

Tous·saint L'Ou·ver·ture (*Fr.* tōōsăn′ lōōvĕrtür′), **François Dominique** (1743–1803). Black leader of uprising in Haiti in 1791; later became a general in French army, and governor of the island 1796–1802, but was arrested, and died a prisoner in France.

tout (towt) *v.* Solicit business, pester possible customers with calls (*for* orders); give out information on condition of racehorses in training, esp. for a fee; describe flatteringly. ~ *n.* One who touts.

to·va·rich, to·va·rish (tōvar′-ĭsh) *ns.* Comrade. [Russ. *tovarishch*]

tow[1] (tō) *n.* Coarse and broken fibers of flax or hemp, separated by hackling and ready for spinning; **tow′head(ed)**, (having) head of very light-colored straight hair. **tow′y** *adj.*

tow[2] (tō) *v.t.* Pull (boat, barge, etc.) along in water by rope or chain; pull (person, thing) along behind one; **tow′line, tow′rope**, line or rope by which something is towed; **tow′path**, path beside canal or navigable river for use in towing. **tow′age** *n.* **tow** *n.* Towing, being towed; **in ~**, being towed; **take in ~**, (fig.) take under one's guidance or patronage; **~ truck**, truck with special equipment for towing away vehicles that have broken down, are illegally parked, etc.

to·ward (tōrd, tōrd, towōrd′), **to·wards** (tōrdz, tōrdz, towōrdz′) *preps.* In the direction of; as regards, in relation to; near, approaching (in time); as contribution to.

tow·el (tow′el) *n.* Absorbent cloth, paper, etc., for drying or wiping oneself or thing after washing; **~ rack**, frame or stand on which towels are hung. **towel** *v.t.* (**-eled, -el·ing** or **-elled, -el·ling**). Wipe or dry with towel. **tow′el·ing** *n.* (esp.) Material for towels.

tow·er (tow′er) *n.* Tall, usu. square or circular structure, freq. forming part of church, castle, or other large building; such structure (or whole fortress or stronghold of which it is part) used as stronghold or prison; (fig.) place of defense, protector (**~ of strength**, (of person) champion, comforter, etc.); **the T~ (of London)**, buildings in London, orig. fortress and palace and later a prison, now used as repository of ancient armor and weapons and other objects of public

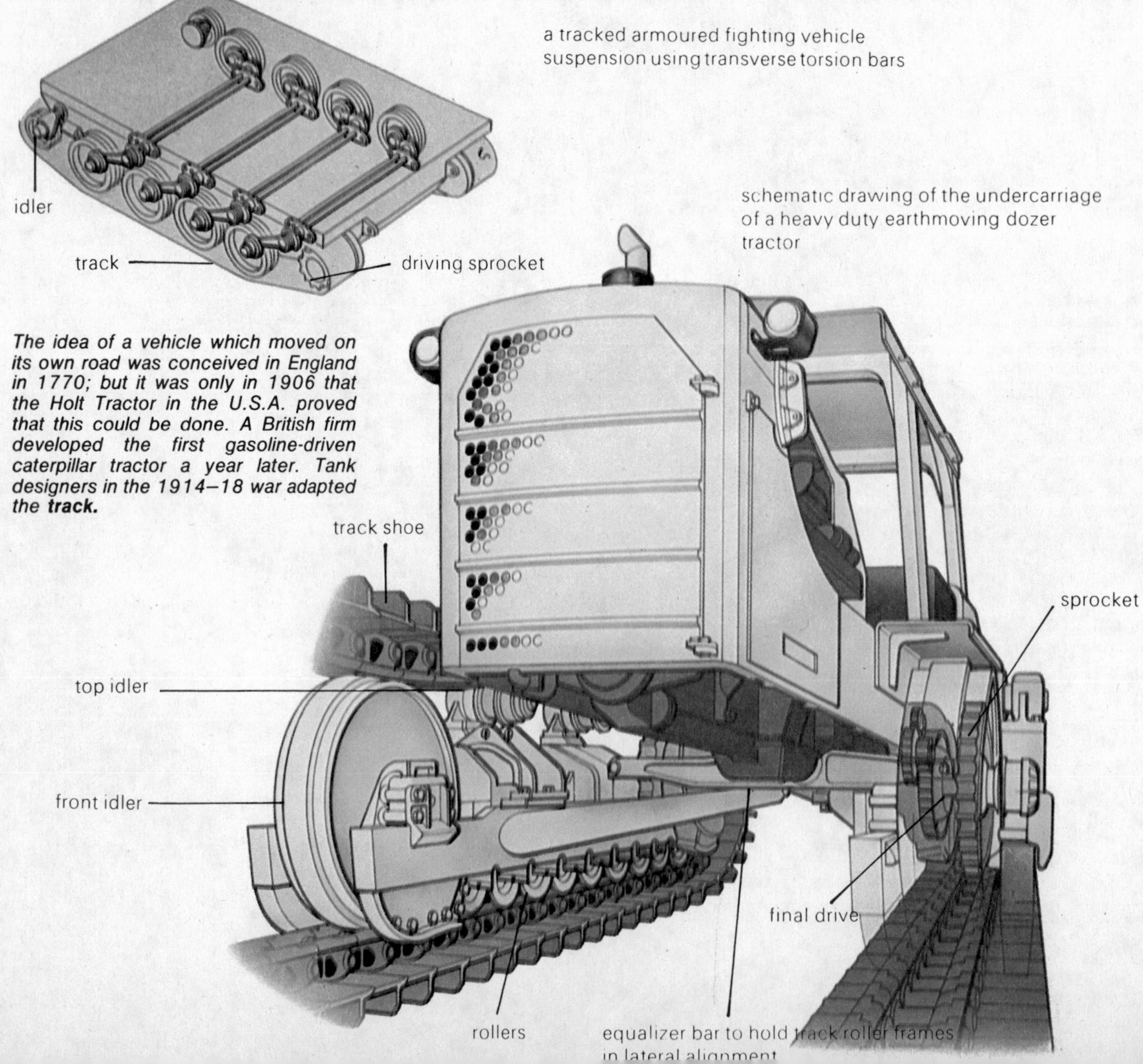

The idea of a vehicle which moved on its own road was conceived in England in 1770; but it was only in 1906 that the Holt Tractor in the U.S.A. proved that this could be done. A British firm developed the first gasoline-driven caterpillar tractor a year later. Tank designers in the 1914–18 war adapted the ***track.***

interest. **tower** *v.i.* Reach high (*above* surroundings); (of eagle etc.) soar, be poised, aloft. **tow'er·ing** *adj.* High, lofty; (fig., of rage, passion) violent. **tow'er·ing·ly** *adv.*

tow·hee (tow'hē, tō'hē) *n.* Any of various small, ground-feeding N. Amer. birds (family Fringillidae), esp. *Pipilo erythrophthalmus*, the male having black, white, and chestnut-brown plumage.

town (town) *n.* Inhabited place usu. larger than a village and smaller than a city; civic community as dist. from members of university (esp. in ~ **and gown**); **go to** ~, work enthusiastically, spend lavishly, etc. (*on*); **man about** ~, sophisticated man seen at many social functions, fashionable night spots, restaurants, theaters, etc.; playboy; **on the** ~, (slang) out for an evening of pleasure at restaurants, theaters, nightclubs, bars, etc.; **paint the** ~ **red**, (slang) celebrate boisterously, cause commotion by wild and riotous spree; ~ **clerk**, secretary to town officials, in charge of records, correspondence, etc.; ~ **hall**, building used for transaction of official business of town, often also used for public assembly; **town'-house**, town (as dist. from country) residence; (also) private house (often row house) in town; **town meeting**, meeting of voters of town for transaction of public business, with certain powers of local government; **town planning**, construction of plans for regulating the growth and extension of town(s) etc.; **towns'people, towns'folk**, people of a town; **town talk**, common talk or gossip of people of town.

town·ship (town'shĭp) *n.* Division of county with some corporate powers of local administration, district 6 miles square whether settled or not.

tox·e·mi·a, tox·ae·mi·a (tŏksē'mēa) *ns.* Diseased condition due to presence of toxic substances in blood, usu. of bacterial origin; condition of pregnancy characterized by edema and raised blood pressure. **tox·e'mic** *adj.*

tox·ic (tŏk'sĭk) *adj.* Of, affected or caused by, a poison or toxin; poisonous. **tox'i·cal·ly** *adv.* **tox·ic·i·ty** (tŏksĭs'ĭtē) *n.* [Gk. *toxikon* poison for arrows (*toxa* arrows)]

toxico-, toxic- *comb. forms.* Poison.

tox·i·col·o·gy (tŏksĭkŏl'ojē) *n.* Study of the nature and effects of poisons, their detection and treatment. **tox·i·co·log·i·cal** (tŏksĭkolŏj'ikal), **tox·i·co·log'ic** *adjs.* **tox·i·co·log'i·cal·ly** *adv.* **tox·i·col'o·gist** *n.*

tox·in (tŏk'sĭn) *n.* Poisonous substance of animal or vegetable origin; esp. (path.) one of the poisons produced in a human or animal body by microorganisms of disease, provoking the formation of antitoxins.

toy (toi) *n.* Plaything, esp. for child; knicknack, small or trifling thing, thing meant rather for amusement than for serious use; (attrib., of dogs etc.) of diminutive breed or variety. ~ *v.t.* Trifle, amuse oneself (*with*); deal *with* in trifling, fondling, or careless manner.

trace[1] (trās) *v.* (**traced, trac·ing**). 1. Delineate, mark out, sketch, write esp. laboriously. 2. Copy (drawing etc.) by following and marking its lines, using a transparent sheet placed over it or similar device. 3. Follow the track or path of (person, animal, footsteps, etc.); follow course or line of, decipher; follow course or history of; observe or find vestiges or signs of. **trace'a·ble** *adj.* **trace** *n.* 1. Track left by person or animal walking or running, footprints or other visible signs of course pursued (usu. pl.); path of indicating spot in cathode ray tube, shown as trace on a fluorescent screen. 2. Visible or other sign of what has existed or happened; minute quantity, esp. (chem.) too little to be measured; ~ **element**, substance that is essential, though only in minute amounts, to plant or animal life.

trace[2] (trās) *n.* Each of pair of ropes, chains, or straps connecting collar of draft animal with whiffletree etc. of vehicle; **kick over the** ~**s**, (fig.) become insubordinate, act recklessly.

trac·er (trā'ser) *n.* (esp.) 1. (also ~ **bullet**) Bullet etc. emitting smoke or flame which makes its course visible. 2. (also ~ **element**) Isotope that can be detected in minute quantities because of its radiations, so that the path of a molecule or radical containing it can be traced through a physical, chemical, or biological system to study the system.

trac·er·y (trā'serē) *n.* (pl. **-er·ies**). Decorative stone openwork, esp. in head of Gothic window, in which patterns are formed by placing strips of stone inside a window opening (**bar** ~) or by perforating expanses of flat stone (**plate** ~); interlaced work of vault etc.; anything resembling or suggesting this.

tra·che·a (trā'kēa) *n.* (pl. **tra·che·ae** pr. trā'kēē). 1. Musculomembranous tube from larynx to bronchial tubes, conveying air to lungs in air-breathing vertebrates. 2. Each of tubes forming respiratory organ in insects etc. 3. (bot.) Duct, vessel. **tra'che·al, tra'che·ate** *adjs.*

tra·che·id (trā'kēĭd) *n.* Water-conducting element in the wood of vascular plants.

tra·che·os·to·my (trākēŏs'tomē) *n.* (pl. **-mies**). Surgical incision to create artificial opening into trachea.

***Tracery** applied to the windows of The George and Pilgrims, an inn in Glastonbury, Somerset, U.K. This use of stonework decoration was popular in Gothic forms of architecture.*

tra·che·ot·o·my (trăkēŏt'omē) *n.* (pl. **-mies**). Incision of trachea.

tra·cho·ma (trakō'ma) *n.* Contagious form of conjunctivitis with inflammatory granulation of inner surface of eyelids, scarring of cornea, freq. causing blindness. **tra·cho·ma·tous** (trakŏm'atus, -kō'ma-) *adj.*

trac·ing (trā'sĭng) *n.* (esp.) Copy made by tracing; record of self-registering instrument; ~ **paper**, tough semitransparent paper for copying drawings etc.

track (trăk) *n.* 1. Mark, series of marks, left by passage of anything, as wheel rut, wake of ship, footprints; **in one's ~s**, on the spot, instantly; **on the ~ of**, in pursuit of, having a clue to; **cover (up) ~s**, conceal or screen actions etc. (of); **keep, lose, ~ of**, follow, fail to follow or grasp course, sequence, etc., of; **make ~s (for)**, make off, make for; **off, on, the ~**, (fig.) wandering from, sticking to, the subject; **on the wrong (right) side of the ~s**, in socially inferior (superior) part of town. 2. Path, esp. one beaten by use, rough unmade road; line of travel or motion, course; train, sequence; prepared course for racing etc.; parallel lines of rails with crossties etc.; (mech.) caterpillar track; projection on Earth's surface of route or path of airplane etc.; groove on phonograph record; strip of magnetic tape containing one sequence of signals; ~ **and field**, athletic events performed in competition on running track and adjacent field esp. running, jumping, pole vaulting, shot-putting (**~-and-field** *adj.*); ~ **man**, athlete who participates in track or field events; ~ **meet**, series of athletic contests in track-and-field events; ~ **record**, (esp. fig.) (record of) past achievements; ~ **shoe**, spiked shoe worn by runner. 3. Transverse distance between wheels of vehicle. **track'a·ble, track'less** *adjs.* **track'less·ness** *n.* **track** *v.* Follow track of (animal, person, *to* lair etc.; spacecraft etc.); pursue, follow up; (of wheels) run in same track, be in alignment; ~ **down**, find or catch by tracking; **tracking station**, station set up for the purpose of tracking path of and recording data from artificial satellite, spacecraft, etc. by means of radio or radar.

tract[1] (trăkt) *n.* Stretch, extent, region (*of*); region or area of natural structure, esp. bodily organ or system.

tract[2] (trăkt) *n.* Short treatise or discourse, esp. on religious subject.

trac·ta·ble (trăk'tabel) *adj.* (usu. of persons or animals) Easily handled, manageable, pliant, docile. **trac·ta·bil·i·ty** (trăktabĭl'-

*Many **tractors** today offer comforts that pioneer farmers could not have dreamed of — air conditioning, stereo music — and no effort required.*

ĭtē), **trac'ta·ble·ness** *ns.* **trac'ta·bly** *adv.*

Trac·tar·i·an (trăktār'ēan) *adj.* & *n.* (Adherent, promoter) of Tractarianism. **Trac·tar'i·an·ism** *n.* English high church movement of 19th c. (later called the Oxford Movement) intended to restore high church ideals of 17th c. and based on a series of *Tracts for the Times* (1833–41) by Newman and other theologians and clergy in and near Oxford.

trac·tate (trăk'tāt) *n.* Treatise.

trac·tion (trăk'shon) *n.* Drawing, pulling (esp. as dist. from pushing or pressure); drawing of vehicles or loads along road or track, esp. in ref. to form of power used for this; grip of tire on road, wheel or rail, etc.; (med.) sustained pulling on limb etc., esp. by weights and pulleys, to correct dislocation, relieve pressure, etc.; ~ **engine**, steam or diesel engine used for drawing loads on ordinary road, across fields, etc. **trac'tion·al, trac'tive** *adjs.*

trac·tor (trăk'ter) *n.* Motor vehicle for drawing heavy loads etc., esp. one for farm work; such a vehicle for drawing a trailer, **~-trailer**.

trade (trād) *n.* 1. Skilled manual or mechanical employment (opp. to PROFESSION), carried on as means of livelihood or profit; skilled handicraft. 2. Exchange of commodities for money or other commodities. 3. People engaged in a trade. 4. (usu. pl.) Trade wind(s) (see below). 5. ~ **book**, book sold in bookstores and other retail outlets patronized by general public, as dist. from textbook, limited edition, or subscription book; ~ **discount**, deduction from list price allowed by a manufacturer or wholesaler to a retailer or granted reciprocally by firms in the same business; **~-in**, used car, appliance, etc., for which credit is allowed on purchase price of new one; amount so allowed; business deal involving a trade-in; **trade'-mark**, device, word(s), etc., used by manufacturer etc. to distinguish his goods, established by use and legally registered; **trade name**, name of proprietary article; name by which a thing is called by the trade; name under which a person or firm conducts trade; **trade-off**, (also **trade'off**), exchange of one thing for another; esp. surrendering one good thing so as to get another that is thought to be even better; **trade route**, any route generally used by merchant ships, caravans, etc.; **trade secret**, formula, method, or process used by businessman and giving him an advantage over competitors who do not know or use it; **trades'man** (pl. **-men**), person engaged in trade; craftsman, man skilled in one of a number of crafts or trades; **trades'woman** (fem.) (pl. **-women**), woman engaged in trade; **trade union** = LABOR union; **trade unionism, unionist; trade wind**, one of the winds blowing constantly toward the equatorial region of calms from about the 30th parallel north and south, being deflected westward by Earth's rotation so that they blow from the northeast in the N. hemisphere and from the southeast in the S. hemisphere. **trade** *v.* (**trad·ed, trad·ing**). Buy and sell, engage in trade; have commercial transaction (*with*); carry merchandise (*to* place); exchange in commerce, barter (goods); ~ **in**, hand over (e.g. used car) in (part) payment or exchange (*for* thing); **trade on**, take (esp. unscrupulous) advantage of (person's credulity or good nature, one's knowledge of secret etc.); **trade up**, exchange object or property of less value or merit for one of greater value or merit.

trad·ing (trā'dĭng) *n.* (esp.) ~ **pòst**, station in sparsely populated area for exchanging local products for goods etc.; ~ **stamp**, stamp given by merchant to customer, exchangeable for various articles.

tra·di·tion (tradĭsh'on) *n.* Transmission of statements, beliefs, customs, etc., esp. by word of mouth or by practice without writing; what is thus handed down from generation to generation; long-established and generally accepted custom, practice, etc., an immemorial usage; (theol.) doctrine etc. held to have divine authority but not orig. committed to writing, esp., among Christians, body of teachings transmitted orally from generation to generation from earliest times and by Roman Catholics held to derive from Christ and the apostles or to have divine authority. **tra·di'tion·al** *adj.*

tra·di′tion·al·ly *adv.* **tra·di′tion·al·ism, tra·di′tion·al·ist** *ns.* **tra·di·tion·al·is′tic** *adj.*

tra·duce (trad*ōō*s′, -dūs′) *v.t.* (**-duced, -duc·ing**). Calumniate, misrepresent. **tra·duce′ment, tra·duc′er** *ns.*

traf·fic (trăf′ĭk) *n.* 1. Trade (*in* commodity); now esp. dealing or bargaining in something that should not be the subject of trade, e.g. certain drugs. 2. Transportation of goods, coming and going of persons, goods, or esp. vehicles or vessels, along road, railroad, canal, etc.; amount of this; ~ **circle**, one-way road around circular island receiving traffic from several streets, designed to expedite traffic flow; ~ **cop**, (colloq.) policeman regulating road traffic; ~ **court**, local court that deals with alleged violations of traffic laws; ~ **jam**, halt or slowdown of highway traffic as result of accident, overcrowding, detour, etc.; ~ **light, signal**, electrical or mechanical signal for controlling road traffic, esp. at junctions or crossings, by means of colored lights etc; ~ **manager**, person in charge of transportation of a firm's products; person in transportation company who establishes rates, schedules, etc., for passengers or freight; person in business office in charge of flow of routine business; ~ **pattern**: see FLIGHT. **traffic** *v.* (**-ficked, -fick·ing**). Trade (*in*), carry on commerce; barter.

trag·a·canth (trăg′*a*kănth) *n.* Gum exuded from various species of *Astragalus*, usu. obtained in dried whitish flakes, and used as vehicle for drugs, in the arts, etc. [Gk. *tragakantha* goat's thorn (*tragos* he-goat, *akantha* thorn)]

tra·ge·di·an (tr*a*jē′dē*a*n) *n.* Writer of tragedies; actor in tragedies. **tra·ge·di·enne** (tr*a*jēdēĕn′) *n.* Actress in tragedies.

trag·e·dy (trăj′*e*dē) *n.* (pl. **-dies**). Literary composition, esp. play, of serious and usu. elevated character, with fatal or disastrous conclusion; branch of dramatic art dealing with sorrowful or terrible events in serious and dignified style; sad event, calamity, disaster. [Gk. *tragōidia* app. goat song (*tragos* goat, *ōidē* song)]

trag·ic (trăj′ĭk) *adj.* 1. Of, in the style of, tragedy; ~ **irony**, used in ancient Greek tragedy of words having an inner esp. prophetic meaning for audience unsuspected by speaker. 2. Sad, calamitous, distressing. **trag′i·cal·ly** *adv.*

trag·i·com·e·dy (trăjĭkŏm′*e*dē) *n.* (pl. **-dies**). Drama of mixed tragic and comic elements. **trag·i·com′ic, trag·i·com′i·cal** *adjs.* **trag·i·com′i·cal·ly** *adv.*

trag·o·pan (trăg′*o*păn) *n.* Asiatic pheasant of genus *T*~, with erectile fleshy horns on head of male, horned pheasant. [L. f. Gk. reputed bird in Ethiopia (*tragos* goat + PAN[3])]

The ***tragopan*** *from the high mountain forests of Asia, is also known as the horned pheasant because of the two fleshy blue 'horns' on the head of the male. There are five species.*

trail (trāl) *n.* Part drawn behind or in the wake of a thing, long (real or apparent) appendage; hinder end of stock of gun carriage, resting on ground when piece is unlimbered; track left by thing that has moved or been drawn over surface; track, scent; beaten path, esp. through wild region; **at the** ~, (mil.) (of rifle etc.) being trailed. **trail** *v.* Drawn along behind one, esp. on ground, drag (one's limbs, oneself) along, walk wearily, lag, straggle; hang loosely; (of plant) grow decumbently and stragglingly to some length, esp. so as to touch or rest on the ground; (mil.) carry (rifle etc.) in horizontal or oblique position with arm extended downward; track, follow the track or wake of, shadow.

trail·er (trā′l*er*) *n.* (esp.) 1. Trailing plant. 2. Vehicle designed to be drawn along behind another, esp. **house** ~, an automobile-drawn vehicle designed to serve, when parked, as a dwelling, office, etc.; ~ **camp** (also ~ **court** or **park**), site for parking house trailers, usu. having piped water, electrical connections, etc. 3. Excerpt(s) of motion picture exhibited in advance as an advertisement.

trail·ing (trā′lĭng) *adj.* That trails; (esp.) ~ **edge**, rear edge of aircraft wing, tail, or fin.

train (trān) *v.* Bring (person, child, animal) to desired state or standard of efficiency, obedience, etc., by instruction and practice; subject, be subjected to, course of instruction and discipline (*for* profession, art, etc.); teach and accustom (*to* do, *to* action); bring, bring oneself, to physical efficiency by exercise and diet, esp. in preparation for sport or contest; cause (plant) to grow in required shape; point, aim, (firearm, camera, *on* object etc.). ~ *n.* 1. Trailing thing, esp. elongated part of skirt or robe trailing behind on ground, or sometimes carried on ceremonial occasions by page or attendant; long or conspicuous tail of bird. 2. Body of followers, retinue, suite; succession or series of persons or things; line of gunpowder or other combustible material to convey fire to explosive charge etc.; set of parts in mechanism actuating one another in series, esp. set of wheels and pinions actuating striking part or turning hands of clock or watch. 3. Number of railroad cars, coupled together (usu. including locomotive drawing them); **train′man**, member of railroad train crew or worker in railroad yard; **train sickness**, sickness or nausea caused by rail travel. **train′less** *adj.*

train·ee (trānē′) *n.* One who is being trained (for an occupation).

train·er (trā′n*er*) *n.* (esp.) One who trains persons or animals for athletic performance, as race, boxing match, etc.

train·ing (trā′nĭng) *n.* (esp.) **in** ~, undergoing physical training, physically fit as a result of this; **out of** ~, in poor condition from lack or cessation of training; ~ **pants**, extra-thick cotton shorts, often plastic-coated, for young child out of diapers but not yet ready for regular underclothing; ~ **ship**, ship on which boys are trained for naval service or merchant navy.

train (trān) **oil.** Whale blubber oil [MDu. *traen*, app. = "tear," "drop"]

traipse (trāps) *v.* (**traipsed, traips·ing**). (colloq.) Walk in trailing or untidy way, walk about aimlessly or needlessly, trudge wearily; walk over (thus). ~ *n.*

trait (trāt) *n.* Feature (of face or esp. of mind or character), distinguishing quality.

trai·tor (trā′ter), *fem.* **trai·tress** (trā′trĭs) *ns.* One who is false to his allegiance or acts disloyally (*to* his sovereign or country, his principles, religion, etc.). **trai′tor·ous** *adj.* **trai′tor·ous·ly** *adv.* **trai′tor·ous·ness** *n.*

tra·jec·to·ry (trajĕk′terē) *n.* (pl. **-ries**). Path of any body moving under action of given forces, esp. that of projectile in its flight through air; (geom.) curve or surface cutting all curves or surfaces of a given system at constant angle.

tram[1] (trăm) *n.* (also ~ **silk**) Silk thread of two or three loosely twisted strands used for woof of some velvets and silks. [L. *trama* woof]

tram[2] (trăm) *n.* 1. Small iron truck running on rails; undercarriage of this. 2. (Brit. also **tram′car**) Passenger car running on rails on public road; **tram′line**, track with rails flush with road surface on which tramcars are run. 3. **tram′way**, cable along which tram runs, esp. system (**aerial tramway**) in which cables are suspended from towers. **tram** *v.* (**trammed, tram·ming**). Convey in tram, perform (journey) in tram; travel by tram. [app. same word as LG. *traam* beam, barrow shaft]

tram·mel (trăm′el) *n.* 1. Fishing net consisting of fine net hung loosely between vertical walls of coarser net, so that fish passing through carry some of the finer net through the coarser and are caught in the pocket thus formed. 2. Shackle, esp. one used in teaching horse to amble; (fig., usu. pl.) impediment to free movement or action. 3. Instrument for drawing ellipses, esp. cross with grooves in which move pins carrying beam and pencil; kind of gauge for adjusting and aligning machine parts; kind of hook for holding kettle etc. at adjustable heights in fireplace. ~ *v.t.* (**-meled, -mel·ing** or **-melled, -mel·ling**). Confine, hamper, with trammels.

tra·mon·tane (tramŏn′tān, trăm′ontān) *adj.* (Situated, living) on other side of mountains, esp. the Alps; (fig., from Italian point of view) foreign, barbarous; (of wind) blowing from beyond mountains, esp. the Alps. ~ *n.* Tramontane person, wind.

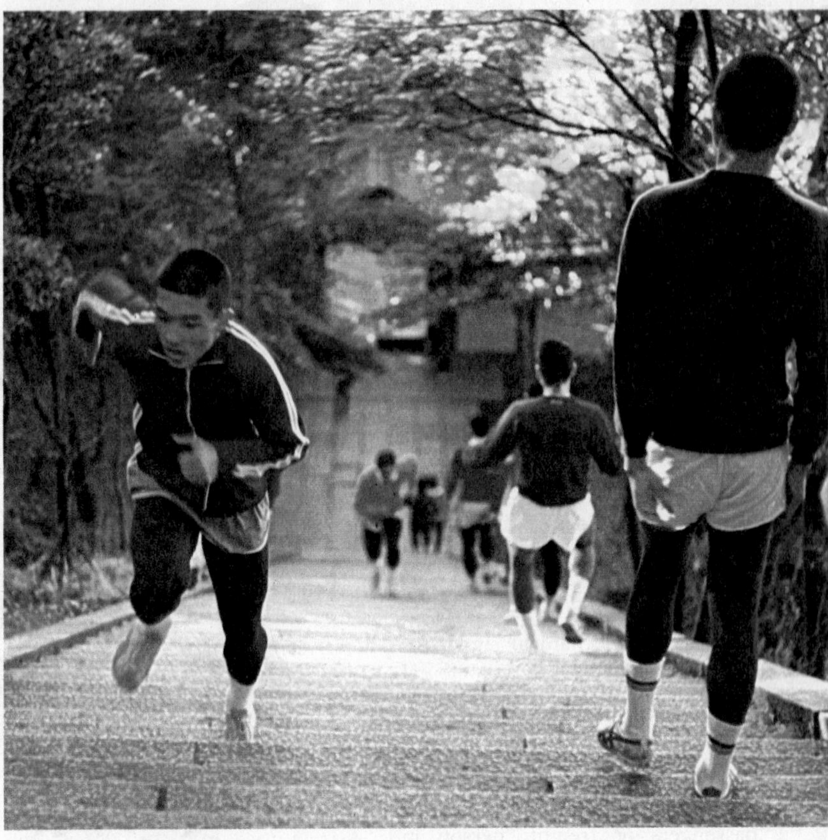

At Kyoto in Japan, athletes in ***training*** *must run up these steep steps to develop strength and stamina. Elsewhere, different techniques are used but all are designed to give the same result.*

tramp (trămp) *v.* Walk with firm heavy tread; walk, go, traverse, on foot; be a tramp. ~ *n.* 1. Measured, steady tread of body of persons or animals, sound of heavy footfalls. 2. Tramping, long or tiring walk or march; journey on foot, walking excursion. 3. Person who tramps roads in search of employment or as vagrant. 4. Immoral woman, esp. prostitute. 5. (also ~ **steamer**) Cargo vessel not trading regularly between fixed ports, but taking cargoes wherever obtainable and for any port. **tramp′er** *n.* **tramp′ish** *adj.* **tramp′ish·ly** *adv.* **tramp′ish·ness** *n.*

tram·ple (trăm′pel) *v.* (**-pled, -pling**). Tread heavily and (esp.) injuriously (upon), crush or destroy thus (freq. fig.); put (fire) *out* by trampling. ~ *n.* Trampling. **tram′pler** *n.*

tram·po·line (trămpolēn′, trăm′polēn) *n.* Canvas sheet attached to horizontal frame by springs, providing resilient platform for acrobatics etc. **tram·po·lin′er, tram·po·lin′ist** *ns.*

trance (trăns, trahns) *n.* Sleep-like state, with more or less inertness to stimulus and subsequent amnesia; hypnotic or cataleptic condition, similar state of spiritualistic medium; mental abstraction from external things, absorption, ecstasy.

tran·quil (trăng′kwĭl) *adj.* Serene, free from agitation or disturbance. **tran′quil·ly** *adv.* **tran·quil·li·ty, tran·quil·i·ty** (trăngkwĭl′ĭtē) *ns.* **tran′quil·ize, tran′quil·lize** *vbs.t.* (**-ized, -iz·ing; -lized, -liz·ing**). **tran′quil·iz·er** *n.* (esp.) Sedative drug.

trans- *prefix.* Across, beyond, over, to or on farther side of.

trans·act (trănsăkt′, -zăkt′) *v.t.* Perform, carry on, do (action, business, etc.). **trans·ac′tion** *n.* Transacting, being transacted; what is transacted, piece of business; (pl.) proceedings, dealings; (usu. pl.) learned society's, esp. published, records of its proceedings.

trans·al·pine (trănsăl′pĭn, -pīn, trănz-) *adj.* Situated, living, beyond the Alps (usu. from Italian point of view); passing across or through the Alps; **T~ Gaul**, Roman province including the present France, Switzerland, Belgium, and the Netherlands. **transalpine** *n.* Person born or living beyond the Alps.

trans·at·lan·tic (trănsatlăn′tĭk, trănz-) *adj.* Across the Atlantic; esp., from European point of view,

One **transept** and nave (the second longest in England) of St. Albans Cathedral (formerly the Abbey Church) in Hertfordshire. The original was built with Roman-made bricks and tiles.

American; (of boat, aircraft, etc.) crossing the Atlantic.

Trans·cau·ca·sia (trănzkawkā′-zha, -sha). Region of U.S.S.R. lying beyond (i.e. S. of) the Caucasus, including the republics of Armenia, Azerbaijan, and Georgia. **Trans·cau·ca′sian** *adj.* & *n.*

trans·ceiv·er (trănsē′ver) *n.* 1. Combined radio transmitter and receiver. 2. Telephonic device for transmitting and receiving facsimiles of printed material, pictures, etc.

tran·scend (trănsĕnd′) *v.t.* Go beyond, exceed, limits of; rise above, surpass, excel.

tran·scend·ent (trănsĕn′dent) *adj.* That transcends ordinary limits, preeminent, supreme, extraordinary; (Kantian philos.) transcending, altogether outside, unrealizable in, experience. **tran·scend′ent·ly** *adv.* **tran·scend′en·cy** *n.* **transcendent** *n.* Transcendent thing.

tran·scen·den·tal (trănsĕndĕn′-tal) *adj.* 1. (Kantian philos.) Not derived from experience, a priori; (of any philosophy) based on recognition of a priori element in experience; (pop., vaguely) abstract, metaphysical, obscure, visionary; ~ **meditation**, technique of meditation for purpose of inducing detachment from problems and relief from anxiety etc. 2. (math.) Not capable of being produced by a finite number of ordinary algebraical operations of multiplication, addition, subtraction, or division.

tran·scen·den·tal·ism (trănsĕndĕn′talĭzem) *n.* Transcendental philosophy, esp. idealism of Hegel and others (which does not recognize Kantian distinction between *transcendent* and *transcendental*), and religio-philosophical doctrine of Emerson and his followers, emphasizing the spiritual and intuitive rather than the empirical; extravagant, vague, or visionary quality, philosophy, language, etc. **tran·scen·den′tal·ist** *adj.* & *n.*

trans·con·ti·nen·tal (trănskŏn-tinĕn′tal) *adj.* Extending or passing across a continent.

tran·scribe (trănskrīb′) *v.t.* (**-scribed, -scrib·ing**). Copy out (esp. in writing), make copy of; write out (shorthand) in ordinary characters; (mus.) adapt (composition) for voice or instrument other than that for which it was orig. written. **tran·script** (trăn′skrĭpt) *n.* Written copy; (law) copy of legal record. **tran·scrip·tion** (trănskrĭp′shon) *n.* **tran·scrip′tive** *adj.* **tran·scrib′er** *n.*

trans·duc·er (trănsdōō′ser, -dū′-, trănz-) *n.* Device that accepts power from one part of a system and emits power in a different form to another part, as between electrical, mechanical, or acoustic parts.

tran·sept (trăn′sĕpt) *n.* (Either arm of) transverse part of cruciform church. **tran·sep·tal** (trănsĕp′tal) *adj.* **tran·sep′tal·ly** *adv.*

trans·fer (trănsfėr′, trăns′fer) *v.* (**-ferred, -fer·ring**). Convey, transmit, transport, hand over, from one person, place, etc., to another; (law) convey (title, property, etc.) by legal process; convey (design etc.) from one surface to another; change from one station, line, route, etc., to another to continue journey; transfer to another group, job, school, etc. ~ (trăns′fer) *n.* 1. Transferring, being transferred, esp. (law) conveyance of property, as shares, etc., from one person to another; means or place of transfer, esp. conveyance of passenger and luggage from one station or line to another, place where trains etc. are transferred to ferry for water transport etc.; ticket allowing journey to be continued on another line or route. 2. Transferred thing; design etc. (to be) conveyed from one surface to another, (freq. colored) design or picture on prepared paper from which it can be transferred to another surface, as with water or hot iron. 3. ~ **agent**, bank or person empowered to transfer corporation stock between legal owners; ~ **company**, company conveying passengers and luggage between stations or from station. **trans·fer·a·bil·i·ty** (trănsfėrabĭl′-ĭtē, trănsfer-), **trans·fer′al, trans·fer′ral, trans·fer′rer** *ns.* **trans·fer′a·ble** *adj.*

trans·fer·ence (trănsfėr′ens, trăns′ferens) *n.* (esp., psychol.) Transferring of emotions to new object.

trans·fig·u·ra·tion (trăns-fĭgyerā′shon) *n.* Transfiguring, being transfigured; esp. change in appearance of Jesus on the mountain (Matt. 17; Mark 9), church festival (Aug. 6) commemorating this, picture representing it.

trans·fig·ure (trănsfĭg′yer) *v.t.* (**-ured, -ur·ing**). Alter form or appearance of, transform; esp. glorify, change so as to elevate or idealize.

trans·fix (trănsfĭks′) *v.t.* (**-fixed** or **-fixt, -fix·ing**). Pierce with, impale on, sharp-pointed instrument; pierce through, render motionless (with fear, grief, horror, etc.). **trans·fix·ion** (trănsfĭk′-shon) *n.*

trans·form (trănsfôrm′) *v.t.* Change shape or form of, esp.

considerably; change in character, condition, function, nature, etc.; (phys.) change (one form of energy) into another; (elect.) change (current) in potential (as from high voltage to low) or type (as from alternating to direct).

trans·for·ma·tion (trănsfermā´shon) *n.* Transforming, being transformed; metamorphosis, as of insects; (math.) change of form without alteration of value, as substitution of one geometric figure for another of equal magnitude, or of one algebraic expression for another of same value; change of form of substance, as from solid to liquid, or of potential or type of electric current etc.; wig; (linguistics) production of an equivalent phrase or sentence from one that is grammatically different in structure.

trans·for·ma·tion·al (trănsfermā´shonal) **grammar.** Statement of linguistic transformations to account for construction of a language, as relations between sentence or phrase elements or between word forms.

trans·form·ér (trănsfōr´mer) *n.* (esp., elect.) Apparatus for changing potential or type of electric current, usu. consisting of a few turns of comparatively thick wire and a coil of fine wire wound on a laminated iron core.

trans·fuse (trănsfūz´) *v.t.* (**-fused, -fus·ing**). Cause (fluid, fig. quality etc.) to flow or pass from one vessel etc. to another; transfer (blood of one person or animal) into veins of another. **trans·fus´er** *n.* **trans·fus´i·ble** *adj.* **trans·fu·sion** (trănsfū´zhon) *n.*

trans·gress (trănsgrĕs´, trănz-) *v.t.* Violate, infringe (law, command, esp. of God). **trans·gres·sion** (trănsgrĕsh´on, trănz-), **trans·gres´sor** *ns.*

tran·ship = TRANSSHIP.

tran·sient (trăn´shent, -zhent, -zēent) *adj.* Not durable or permanent, brief, momentary, fleeting. ~ *n.* 1. Temporary visitor, worker, etc. 2. Brief oscillation of electrical current in a circuit because of voltage surge etc. **tran´sient·ly** *adv.* **tran´sience, tran´sien·cy** *ns.*

tran·sis·tor (trănzĭs´ter) *n.* Electronic device using the flow of electrons in a solid to perform most of the functions of a vacuum tube; radio set using such device; also attrib., as ~ **radio**. **tran·sis´tor·ize** *v.t.* (**-ized, -iz·ing**). Design, equip, with transistors instead of vacuum tubes.

trans·it (trăn´sĭt, -zĭt) *n.* 1. Passing, passage, journey, conveyance, from one place to another. 2. (astrol.) Passage of planet across some region or point of zodiac; (astron.) passage of inferior planet across sun's disk, or of satellite or its shadow across planet's disk; passage of celestial body across meridian. 3. Surveying instrument for measurement of horizontal and occasionally vertical angles. 4. ~ **circle**, astronomical instrument, consisting of transit instrument combined with meridian circle for determining right ascension and declination of star by observation of its transit; ~ **instrument**, astronomical telescope mounted at right angles to horizontal east-and-west axis, for determining time of transit of celestial body over meridian; also same as 3 above. **transit** *v.* 1. (of heavenly body) Make transit (across). 2. Revolve (telescope of a transit) to opposite direction.

Invented by three engineers at the Bell Telephone Laboratories and first demonstrated in 1948, the ***transistor*** *has enabled miniaturization of many electrical circuits.*

tran·si·tion (trănzĭsh´on) *n.* Passage from one condition, action, style, subject, stage of development, etc., to another; period of this; (mus.) modulation, esp. passing or brief, or into remote key. **tran·si´tion·al** *adj.* **tran·si´tion·al·ly** *adv.* **tran·si´tion·ar·y** *adj.*

tran·si·tive (trăn´sĭtĭv, -zĭ-) *adj.* & *n.* (Verb) expressing action that passes over to an object, requiring direct object to complete the sense. **tran´si·tive·ly** *adv.* **tran·si·tiv·i·ty** (trănsĭtĭv´ĭtē, -zĭ-), **tran´si·tive·ness** *ns.*

tran·si·to·ry (trăn´sĭtōrē, -tōrē, -zĭ-) *adj.* Not lasting; fleeting, momentary, brief. **tran´si·to·ri·ly** *adv.* **tran´si·to·ri·ness** *n.*

Trans-Jor·dan (trănsjōr´dan, trănz-). Major part of the Hashemite Kingdom of Jordan, E. of Jordan River.

Trans·kei (trahnz´kā), **The.** Independent enclave in SE. South Africa in E. Cape of Good Hope Province; granted independence by South Africa, 1976; capital, Umtala.

trans·late (trănslāt´, trănz-, trăns´lāt, trănz´-) *v.* (**-lat·ed, -lat·ing**). 1. Turn (word, sentence, book, etc.) from one language *into* another, express sense of it in another form of words. 2. Infer or declare the significance of, interpret (signs, movement, conduct, etc.). 3. Convey, introduce (idea, principle, design) *from* one art etc. *into* another. 4. Remove (bishop) to another see. 5. (bibl.) Convey to heaven without death. 6. (teleg.) Retransmit (message). 7. (mech.) Cause (body) to move so that all its parts follow same direction, impart motion without rotation to. **trans·lat´a·ble** *adj.* **trans·la´tor, trans·la·tion** (trănslā´shon, trănz-) *ns.* **trans·la´tion·al** *adj.*

trans·lit·er·ate (trănslĭt´erāt, trănz-) *v.t.* (**-at·ed, -at·ing**). Replace (letters of one alphabet or language) with those of another. **trans·lit·er·a·tion** (trănslĭterā´shon, trănz-) *n.*

trans·lo·ca·tion (trănslōkā´shon, trănz-) *n.* Change of location, esp. (bot.) movement of dissolved substances inside plants.

trans·lu·cent (trănslōō´sent, trănz-) *adj.* Allowing passage of light but so diffusing it as to prevent bodies lying beyond from being clearly distinguished. **trans·lu´cence, trans·lu´cen·cy** *ns.* **trans·lu´cent·ly** *adv.*

trans·lu·nar·y (trăns´lōōnĕrē, trănz´-, trănslōō´nerē, trănz-) *adj.* Lying beyond the moon; (fig.) insubstantial, visionary.

trans·ma·rine (trănsmarēn´, trănz-) *adj.* That is beyond the sea; crossing the sea.

trans·mi·grate (trănsmī´grāt, trănz-) *v.t.* (**-grat·ed, -grat·ing**). Migrate; (of soul) pass after death into another body, either human or animal. **trans·mi´grant** *n.* (esp.) Emigrant from one country passing through another in which he does not intend to settle. **trans·mi·gra·tion** (trănsmīgrā´shon, trănz-), **trans·mi´gra·tor** *ns.* **trans·mi´gra·to·ry** *adj.*

trans·mis·sion (trănsmĭsh´on, trănz-) *n.* (esp.) 1. Gears by which power is transmitted from engine to axle in automobile etc. 2. Transmitting by radio or television; program etc. so transmitted.

trans·mit (trănsmĭt´, trănz-) *v.t.* (**-mit·ted, -mit·ting**). Send, convey, cause to pass or go, to another person, place, or thing;

suffer to pass through, be medium for, serve to communicate (heat, light, sound, electricity, emotion, news). **trans·mis·si·ble** (trăns-mĭs'*i*b*e*l, trănz-), **trans·mis'sive, trans·mit'ta·ble** *adjs.* **trans·mit'tal, trans·mit'tance** *ns.*

trans·mit·ter (trănsmĭt'*e*r, trănz-) *n.* (esp.) Part of telegraphic or telephonic apparatus by means of which message etc. is transmitted; (part of) radio set or station for transmitting radio waves.

trans·mog·ri·fy (trănsmŏg'r*i*fī, trănz-) *v.t.* (**-fied, -fy·ing**). (joc.) Transform (esp. utterly, grotesquely, or strangely). **trans·mog·ri·fi·ca·tion** (trăns-mŏgr*i*fĭkā'sh*o*n, trănz-) *n.*

trans·mu·ta·tion (trănsmūtā'-sh*o*n, trănz-) *n.* Transmuting, being transmuted; (biol.) transformation of one species into another, evolution (esp. in Lamarckian theory).

trans·mute (trănsmūt', trănz-) *v.t.* (**-mut·ed, -mut·ing**). Change form, nature, or substance of; convert (one element, substance, species, etc.) into another; esp. (alchemy) change (baser metal) into gold or silver. **trans·mut'a·ble** *adj.*

trans·o·ce·an·ic (trăns-ōshēăn'ĭk, trănz-) *adj.* Situated, existing, beyond the ocean; crossing the ocean.

tran·som (trăn's*o*m) *n.* Cross-piece, esp. one spanning an opening; horizontal bar across window; crossbar separating door from fanlight above it; window above transom, esp. of door. **tran'somed** *adj.*

tran·son·ic (trănsŏn'ĭk) *adj.* Relating to speeds close to that of sound.

trans·pa·cif·ic (trănsp*a*sĭf'ĭk) *adj.* Situated, being, beyond the Pacific Ocean; crossing the Pacific.

trans·par·en·cy (trănspār'*e*nsē, -păr'-) *n.* (pl. **-cies**). Being transparent; transparent object or medium; esp. photograph or picture on transparent substance, to be viewed by transmitted light.

trans·par·ent (trănspār'*e*nt, -păr'-) *adj.* Transmitting light so that bodies lying beyond are completely visible; permeable to specified form of radiant energy, as heat rays, x-rays; easily seen through, manifest, obvious, clear; candid, frank, open. **trans·par'-ent·ly** *adv.*

tran·spire (trănspīr') *v.* (**-spired, -spir·ing**). Emit through excretory organs of skin or lungs, send off in moisture, odor; be emitted thus; (bot., of plant or leaf) exhale moisture; (of gas or liquid) move through capillary tube under pressure; (of secret etc.) come to be known; (misused for) occur, happen. **tran·spi·ra'tion** *n.*

trans·plant (trănsplănt', -plahnt') *v.* Remove (plant) from one place and plant it in another; remove and establish, esp. cause to live, in another place; (surg.) transfer (living tissue or organ) from one part of body, or one person or animal, to another; bear transplanting. ~ (trăns'plănt, -plahnt) *n.* **trans·plan·ta·tion** (trănsplăntā'sh*o*n), **trans·plant'er** *ns.* **trans·plant'a·ble** *adj.*

tran·spon·der (trănspŏn'd*e*r) *n.* Radio or radar transceiver for receiving radio signal and automatically transmitting a different signal in response.

trans·port (trănspōrt', -pōrt') *v.t.* 1. Carry, convey, from one place to another. 2. (hist.) Deport, convey (convict) to penal colony. 3. (usu. pass.) Carry away by strong emotion. ~ (trăns'pōrt, -pōrt) *n.* 1. Conveyance, carrying, of goods or passengers, from one place to another; means of conveyance, esp. vessel used in transporting troops or military stores, wagons or other vehicles carrying supplies of army etc. 2. Vehement (usu. pleasurable) emotion; (freq. pl.) fit of joy or rage. **trans·port'er** *n.* **trans·port'-a·ble** *adj.*

trans·por·ta·tion (trănsp*e*rtā'-sh*o*n) *n.* Transporting; deportation transfer to penal settlement; means of transport or conveyance.

Rice is first planted in seed beds. When the seedlings are about 8 inches tall they are ***transplanted*** *to wet paddy fields. In Kiso, Japan, (below) this arduous work is done in July.*

trans·pose (trănspōz') *v.t.* (**-posed, -pos·ing**). Alter order of (series of things) or position of (thing in series), interchange; esp. alter order of (letters) in word or (words) in sentence; (algebra) transfer (quantity) from one side of equation to the other; (mus.) put into different key, alter key of. **trans·po·si·tion** (trănsp*o*zĭsh'*o*n) *n.*

trans·ship, tran·ship (trăns-shĭp') *vbs.* (**-shipped, -ship·ping**). Transfer, change, from one ship, train, etc., to another. **trans·ship'-ment** *n.*

tran·sub·stan·ti·ate (trăn-s*u*bstăn'shēāt) *v.t.* (**-at·ed, -at·ing**). Change from one substance into another.

tran·sub·stan·ti·a·tion (trăn-s*u*bstănshēā'sh*o*n) *n.* (esp., theol.) Doctrine that in the Eucharist a change is wrought in the elements at consecration, whereby the whole substance of the bread and wine is transmuted into the body and blood of Christ, only the appearances of bread and wine remaining.

trans·u·ran·ic (trănsyoorăn'ĭk, trănz-) *adj.* (chem.) Belonging to a group of radioactive elements having atomic numbers and weights greater than those of uranium, not found in nature but produced artificially, e.g. in atomic pile.

trans·ver·sal (trănsvėr's*a*l, trănz-) *adj.* (of line) Cutting two or more lines. ~ *n.* Transversal line.

trans·verse (trănsvẽrs′, trănz-, trăns′vẽrs, trănz′-) *adj.* Situated, lying, across or athwart. **trans·verse′ly** *adv.* **transverse′** *n.* Transverse muscle, piece, etc.

trans·ves·tism (trănsvĕs′tĭzem, trănz-) *n.* Practice of dressing in clothes of opposite sex. **trans·ves·tite** (trănsvĕs′tīt, trănz-) *n.* One who practices transvestism. ~ *adj.*

trap[1] (trăp) *n.* 1. Device, as pitfall, snare, mechanical contrivance, for catching animals; (fig.) something by which one is caught, led astray, etc. 2. Trap door; movable covering of opening, falling when stepped upon; door flush with surface in floor, ceiling, etc. 3. Device for suddenly releasing bird etc. to be shot at; compartment from which greyhound is released at start of race. 4. (chiefly Brit.) Light, esp. two-wheeled horse carriage on springs. 5. Device, usu. U-shaped section of pipe with standing water, for preventing upward escape of air or noxious gases from pipe; contrivance for preventing passage of steam, water, silt, etc. 6. (slang) Mouth. 7. **speed** ~: see SPEED; **trap door,** hinged or sliding door flush with surface of floor, roof, wall, etc.; **trap-door spider,** spider living in burrow closed by one or more hinged lids; **trap′rock** = TRAP[2]; **trap′shooting,** sport of shooting clay pigeons released from spring trap. **trap** *v.* (**trapped, trap·ping**). Catch (as) in trap, snare, ensnare; set traps for game etc.; furnish with trap(s).

trap[2] (trăp) *n.* (also **traprock**) Any of various dark colored fine-grained igneous rocks, freq. columnar in structure, esp. basalt.

trap[3] (trăp) *v.t.* (**trapped, trap·ping**). (chiefly in past part.) Adorn with trappings, caparison. [OF. *drap* cloth, covering]

trap (trăp) **cut** = step cut, see STEP.

tra·peze (trăpēz′) *n.* Horizontal crossbar suspended by ropes as apparatus for acrobatics etc. **tra·pez′ist** *n.* (also **trapeze artist**) Performer on trapeze.

tra·pe·zi·um (trapē′zēum) *n.* (pl. **-zi·ums, -zi·a** pr. -zēa). 1. Quadrilateral with two sides (thought of as base and opposite side) parallel. 2. Quadrilateral with no sides parallel. 3. (anat.) Bone of carpus articulating with metacarpal bone of thumb. [Gk. *trapezion,* dim. of *trapeza* table]

tra·pe·zi·us (trapē′zēus) *n.* (pl. **-us·es**). (anat.) Each of pair of large flat triangular muscles of back, extending over back of neck etc.

trap·e·zoid (trăp′ĭzoĭd) *n.* 1. Quadrilateral with two sides parallel and two not parallel. 2. (anat.) Second bone of distal row of carpus. ~ *adj.* Of, in the form of, a trapezoid. **trap·e·zoi·dal** (trăpĭzoi′dal) *adj.*

trap·per (trăp′er) *n.* (esp.) One engaged in trapping wild animals for their furs.

trap·pings (trăp′ĭngz) *n.pl.* Ornamental housing for horse; ornaments, embellishments, ornamental accessories.

Trap·pist (trăp′ĭst) *adj.* & *n.* (Monk) of reformed Cistercian order established 1664 at monastery of La Trappe in Normandy, France, and observing extremely austere discipline and perpetual silence except with confessors and in choir.

traps (trăps) *n.pl.* (colloq.) Personal effects, portable belongings, baggage. [app. shortening of *trappings*]

trash (trăsh) *n.* Waste or worthless stuff, refuse, rubbish; stripped-off leaves and tops of sugar cane; worthless or disreputable people; ~ **can,** container for household refuse; **white** ~, (derog.) poor white population of southern U.S. **trash′y** *adj.* (**trash·i·er, trash·i·est**). **trash′i·ly** *adv.* **trash′i·ness** *n.*

trau·ma (trow′ma, traw′-) *n.* (pl. **-mas, -ma·ta** pr. -mata). Injury, wound; condition resulting from this; (psychol.) unpleasant or disturbing experience in which neurosis etc. may originate, emotional shock. **trau·mat·ic** (trowmăt′ĭk, traw-, tra-) *adj.* **trau·mat′i·cal·ly** *adv.* **trau′ma·tism** *n.* **trau′ma·tize** *v.t.* (**-tized, -tiz·ing**).

tra·vail (travāl′, trăv′āl) *n.* & *v.i.* (Suffer) pangs of childbirth; (make) painful or laborious effort. [OF. *travail,* app. f. LL. *trepalium* instrument of torture (L. *tres* three, *palus* stake)]

trav·el (trăv′el) *v.* (**-eled, -el·ing;** Brit. **-elled, -el·ling**). 1. Make journey, esp. of some length or to foreign countries; act as traveling sales representative; pass from one point or place to another, proceed; (of part of mechanism) move, be capable of moving, along fixed course; (colloq.) bear transportation, as in *this wine travels well.* 2. Journey through, pass over, traverse, cover (specified distance); cause (herds etc.) to journey. ~ *n.* 1. Traveling, esp. in foreign countries. 2. Single movement of part of mechanism; range, rate, mode of motion, of this. 3. ~ **agency, agent,** one making arrangements, supplying tickets, etc., for travelers; ~ **time,** time used to travel between home and place of employment or from one

*The true **trap-door spider** weaves a movable lid over the top of its burrow and lives in a warm climate. In the photograph, the open lid is below the hole.*

place to another as part of one's work.

trav·el·er, Brit. **trav·el·ler** (trăv'*eler*, trăv'l*er*) *ns.* One who travels; traveling sales representative; ~**'s check**, check or draft readily redeemable throughout world, sold in sets of various denominations by bank, express agency, etc., to traveler who signs it when receiving it and again when cashing it, check being valid only if signatures match; ~**'s joy**, European shrub (*Clematis alba* and other climbing species of *Clematis*) trailing over wayside hedges.

trav·el·ing, Brit. **trav·el·ling** (trăv'*el*ĭng, trăv'lĭng) *ns.* ~ **bag**, small suitcase in which traveler carries most essential items; ~ **crane**, crane that travels along esp. overhead support; ~ **salesman**, business firm's representative who visits stores and other customers to show samples and take orders.

trav·e·logue, trav·e·log (trăv'*e*lawg, -lŏg) *ns.* Illustrated narrative of travel, esp. employing motion pictures.

trav·erse (trăv'ẽrs, tr*a*vẽrs') *n.* 1. Movement or part of structure that crosses another; place at which one can cross; crossing; (mountaineering) more or less horizontal motion across face of precipice from one practicable line of ascent or descent to another, place where this is necessary; (naut.) zigzag course taken owing to contrary winds or currents, each leg of this; (surv.) single line of survey across region, tract of country so surveyed; (mil.) horizontal or lateral movement of gun; (eng.) platform for shifting engine etc. from one line of rails to another; sideways movement of part or machine; (archit.) gallery from side to side of church etc.; (hist.) curtain, partition across room etc., compartment so cut off. 2. (law) Formal denial of matter of fact alleged by other side. ~ (tr*a*vẽrs', trăv'ẽrs) *v.* (**-ersed, -ers·ing**). 1. Travel or lie across; make a traverse in climbing; determine position of points, survey (road, river, etc.) by measuring lengths and azimuths of connected series of straight lines; turn (gun); (of needle of compass etc.) turn (as on pivot); (of horse) walk crosswise; plane (wood) across grain; (of pulley) run over rope etc. that supports it. 2. (fig.) Consider, discuss, whole extent of (subject). 3. Deny, esp. (law) in pleading; thwart, frustrate (plan or opinion). **tra·vers'al** *n.*

trav·er·tine (trăv'*er*tĭn, -tēn) *n.* White or light colored crystalline concretionary limestone deposited from springs etc. and used for building. [L. *tiburtinus*, f. *Tibur*, now Tivoli, a town in central Italy]

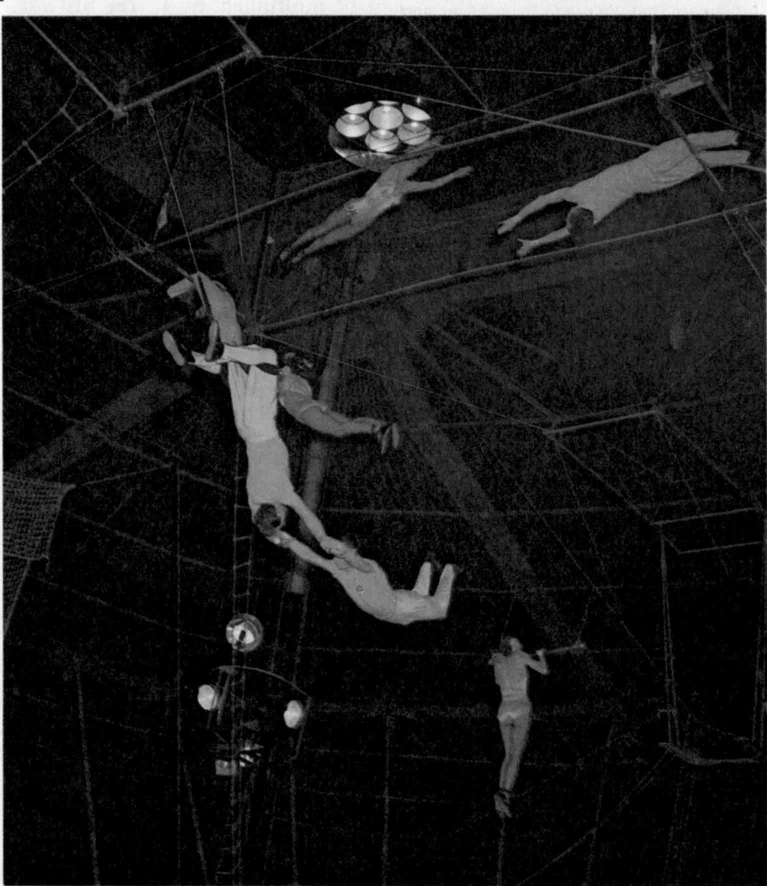

*The use of a **trapeze** as a circus act was only introduced by Leotard in 1859. Other forms of acrobatics had been performed at various locations since ancient Greece and Rome.*

trav·es·ty (trăv'ĭstē) *v.t.* (**-tied, -ty·ing**). Make ridiculous by gross parody or imitation; be ridiculous imitation of. ~ *n.* (pl. **-ties**). Ridiculing treatment; ridiculous imitation.

trawl (trawl) *n.* Large net (~ **net**) with mouth held open by beam or otherwise, dragged along bottom of sea etc. by boat; ~ **line**, long buoyed line, anchored at ends and with numerous short baited lines attached, for sea fishing. **trawl** *v.* Fish with trawl or in trawler; catch with trawl.

trawl·er (traw'l*er*) *n.* One who trawls; vessel used in fishing with trawl net.

tray (trā) *n.* Flat shallow vessel usu. with raised rim for placing or carrying small articles on, steeping specimens in laboratory, holding correspondence on desk, etc.; shallow lidless box forming compartment of trunk.

treach·er·ous (trĕch'*er*us) *adj.* Violating faith or betraying trust; perfidious; not to be relied on, deceptive. **treach'er·ous·ly** *adv.* **treach'er·ous·ness** *n.* **treach'er·y** *n.* (pl. **-er·ies**).

trea·cle (trē'k*el*) *n.* 1. (Brit.) Uncrystallized syrup produced in refining sugar; golden syrup. 2. Unrestrained or artificial sentimentality. **trea'cly** *adj.*

tread (trĕd) *v.* (**trod** pr. trŏd, **trod·den, tread·ing**). Set down one's foot, walk, (of foot) be set down; go through (dance) esp. in stately measure; press or crush with feet, trample (*on*); (of male bird) copulate with; ~ **the boards**, be an actor, appear on stage; ~ **down**, press down with feet; trample on, destroy, oppress, crush; ~ **on** someone's **toes** or **corns**, (fig.) offend against his feelings or privileges; ~ **water**, (swimming) keep body erect and head above water while moving feet as in walking upstairs; (fig.) make no progress even though working hard. **tread** *n.* 1. Manner, sound, of walking. 2. Top surface of step or stair; each step of treadmill; rung of ladder. 3. Piece of metal, rubber, or other substance placed on step to lessen wear or sound. 4. Part of wheel that touches ground or rails; part of rails that wheels touch. 5. Part of stilt on which foot rests. 6. Part of sole of shoe etc. that rests on ground. 7. Distance between pedals of bicycle. 8. (of male bird) Copulation. 9. **tread'mill**, appliance for translating motion by the stepping of man or horse etc. on steps fixed to revolving cylinder, esp. kind formerly used in prisons as punishment; (fig.) monotonous routine. **tread'er** *n.*

trea·dle (trĕd'*el*) *n.* Lever moved by foot and imparting motion to machine, e.g. lathe, sewing machine. ~ *v.* (**-dled, -dling**). Work treadle. **tread'ler** *n.*

treas., Treas. *abbrevs.* Treasurer; treasury.

trea·son (trē'*zon*) *n.* 1. (also **high** ~) Violation by subject of allegiance to sovereign or chief authority of nation (e.g. plotting or intending sovereign's death, levying war against him, or conspiring with his enemies). 2. Breach of faith, disloyalty (*to* cause, friend, etc.). **trea'son·ous** *adj.*

trea·son·a·ble (trē'*zonabel*) *adj.* Involving, guilty of, treason. **trea'son·a·ble·ness** *n.* **trea'son·a·bly** *adv.*

treas·ure (trĕzh'*er*) *n.* Wealth or riches stored, esp. in form of precious metals or gems; accumulated wealth; anything valued or preserved as precious; beloved person, esp. child; (colloq.) very efficient or satisfactory person, esp. servant; ~ **house**, place where treasure is kept, treasury; ~ **trove**, valuable discovery; gold or silver, money, etc., found hidden in ground or other place, owner of which is unknown. **treasure** *v.t.* (**-ured, -ur·ing**). Store as valuable; cherish, prize; (fig.) store (e.g. in memory).

treas·ur·er (trĕzh'*erer*) *n.* (orig.) One charged with receipt and disbursement of revenues of king, noble, nation, church, etc.; now, one responsible for funds of public body or any corporation, society, or club; officer of Treasury Department (~ **of the U.S.**) who receives and keeps the federal funds. **treas'ur·er·ship** *n.*

treas·ur·y (trĕzh'*erē*) *n.* (pl. **-ur·ies**). 1. Room, building, in which precious or valuable objects are preserved (freq. fig.); (esp. in book titles) collection of treasured writings. 2. Funds or revenue of nation, corporation, etc.; **Department of the T**~, financial agent for the U.S. government, collecting and managing public revenue and advising the president on fiscal policy; ~ **bill**, security given by U.S. government in exchange for a loan of short duration (freq. 91 days); ~ **bond**, any of various series of U.S. government bonds issued by the Treasury, usu. maturing after a long period; ~ **certificate**, bond of U.S. government, usu. maturing in one year and paying interest periodically by redemption of coupons; ~ **note**, demand note issued by the Department of the Treasury and legal tender for all debts except as otherwise provided.

Discovered in 1942-43, the Mildenhall ***treasure*** *consisted of a host of Roman tableware, mostly made from silver and dated at the 4th century A.D. The great dish (below) is heavily ornamented.*

treat (trēt) *v.* 1. Deal, negotiate (*with*), in order to settle terms. 2. Deal with (subject), deal with subject, in speech or writing; deal with in way of art, represent artistically; deal with to obtain particular result, esp. deal with disease etc. in order to relieve or cure. 3. Behave or act toward in specified way. 4. Entertain, esp. with food and drink, regale, feast. ~ *n.* Entertainment, esp. one given gratuitously, pleasure party; treating, invitation to eat or drink; a great pleasure, delight, or gratification. **treat'er** *n.*

trea·tise (trē'tĭs) *n.* Book or writing, longer than essay, treating in formal or methodical manner of particular subject.

treat·ment (trēt'*ment*) *n.* (Mode of) dealing with or behaving toward person or thing; esp. (method of) treating patient or disease; artistic or literary execution, esp. with regard to style.

trea·ty (trē'tē) *n.* (pl. **-ties**). (Document embodying) formal contract between nations relating to peace, truce, alliance, commerce, etc.

tre·ble (trĕb'*el*) *adj.* 1. Threefold, triple. 2. Soprano; high-pitched, shrill; of treble pitch; ~ **clef**: see CLEF. **treble** *n.* 1. Treble quantity, stitch, etc. 2. Treble voice, singer, string, etc. ~ *v.* (**-bled, -bling**). Multiply, be multiplied, by 3. **tre'bly** *adv.*

tre·cen·to (trāchĕn'tō) *n.* (also **T**~) Fourteenth century as period of Italian art and literature. [It., = "three hundred," short for *mil trecento* 1300]

tree (trē) *n.* Perennial plant with self-supporting woody main stem (usu. developing woody branches at some distance from ground); erect bush or shrub with single stem; piece of wood shaped for some purpose (as *shoetree*); genealogical chart like branching tree (**family** ~); **up a** ~, cornered, in difficulty; ~ **creeper**, any of various birds that creep on trunks and branches of trees, esp. *Certhia familiaris*; ~ **fern**, fern usu. of the family Cyatheaceae, with upright woody stem, growing to size of tree, found in tropics, Australia, and New Zealand; ~ **frog**, arboreal amphibian esp. of genus *Hyla*; ~ **of knowledge of good and evil**, tree in Garden of Eden bearing the forbidden fruit, which was tasted by Adam and Eve (Gen. 3); ~ **surgery**, treatment of trees having disease, damaged or decayed branches, etc., by pruning, filling cavities, spraying, feeding, bracing weak parts, etc.; ~ **toad**, tree frog. **tree** *v.t.* (**treed, tree·ing**). Cause to take refuge in tree, drive up a tree; stretch on shoetree. **tree'less** *adj.*

Cedar

Ash

Sycamore

orange
silver birch
acacia
Norway spruce
American elm
weeping willow
desert oak

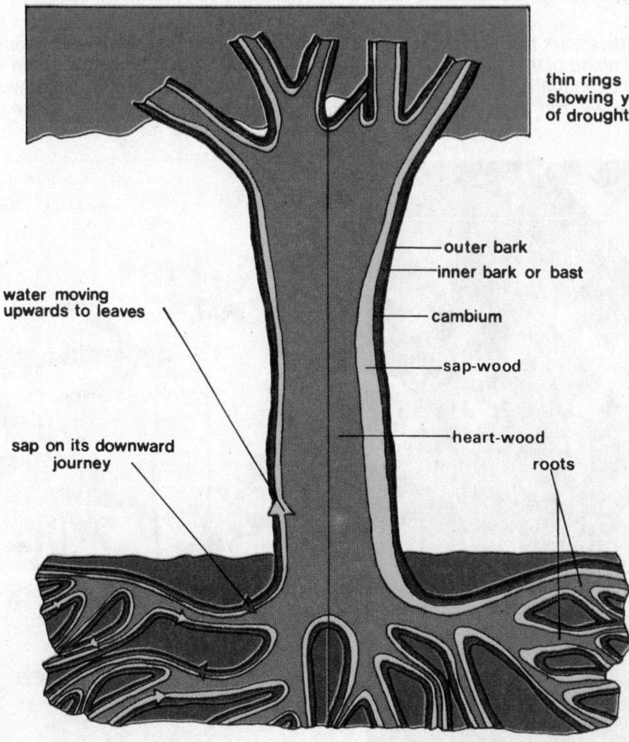

water moving upwards to leaves
sap on its downward journey
outer bark
inner bark or bast
cambium
sap-wood
heart-wood
roots

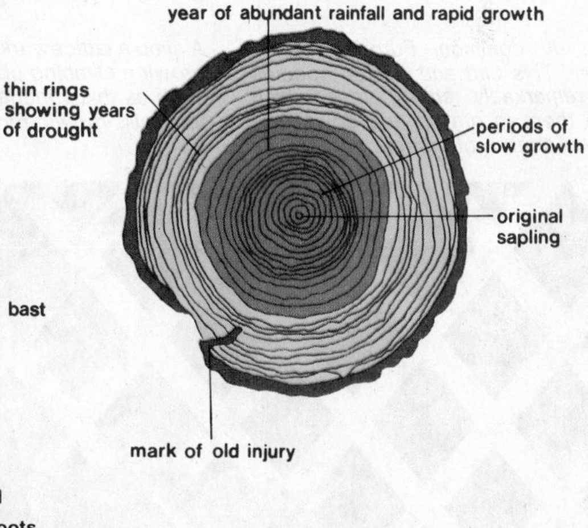

year of abundant rainfall and rapid growth
thin rings showing years of drought
periods of slow growth
original sapling
mark of old injury

Top left to right: Western red cedar, ash and sycamore are all trees now grown in northern temperate regions. Left: Every ***tree*** *has the same sort of structure but may have special provisions to guard against excessive loss of moisture in arid conditions or other special climatic conditions. By cutting through a trunk, the history of a tree can be determined with remarkable accuracy, as shown above.*

tre·foil (trē′foil, trĕf′oil) *n.* 1. Plant of genus *Trifolium* with leaves of three leaflets, clover. 2. Ornamental figure resembling cloverleaf; (archit.) opening divided by cusps suggesting three-lobed leaf.

trek (trĕk) *v.i.* (**trekked, trek·king**). (orig. S. Afr.) Travel, migrate, esp. by ox wagon; make arduous journey or expedition. ~ *n.* (Stage of) journey made by trekking. **trek′ker** *n.*

trel·lis (trĕl′ĭs) *n.* Structure of light bars crossing each other with open square or diamond-shaped spaces between, used as screen, as support for climbing plants, etc.; **trel′liswork**, trellis. **trellis** *v.t.* Furnish, support, (as) with trellis. [L. *trilix* three-ply (f. *licium* warp thread)]

trem·a·tode (trĕm′*a*tōd) *n.* Member of the Trematoda, a class of unsegmented parasitic flatworms having external suckers.

trem·ble (trĕm′b*e*l) *v.i.* (**-bled, -bling**). Shake involuntarily as with fear or other emotion, cold, or weakness; quiver; (fig.) be affected with fear, agitation, suspense, etc. ~ *n.* Trembling, quiver, tremor. **trem′bly, trem′bling** *adjs.* **trem′bling·ly** *adv.*

tre·men·dous (trĭmĕn′d*u*s) *adj.* Awe-inspiring, terrible; (colloq.) extraordinarily great, immense. **tre·men′dous·ly** *adv.* **tre·men′dous·ness** *n.*

trem·o·lo (trĕm′*o*lō) *n.* (pl. **-los**). Tremulous or vibrating effect in certain instruments or human voice; organ stop producing this effect. [It., = "trembling"]

trem·or (trĕm′*er*, trē′m*er*) *n.* Tremulous or vibratory movement or sound, vibration, shaking, quaking; (instance, fit, of) involuntary agitation of body or limbs from physical weakness, fear, etc. **trem′or·ous, trem′or·less** *adjs.*

trem·u·lous (trĕm′y*u*l*u*s) *adj.* Trembling, quivering; shaky; timid; tremblingly sensitive or responsive. **trem′u·lous·ly** *adv.* **trem′u·lous·ness** *n.*

trench (trĕnch) *n.* Long narrow usu. deep hollow cut out of ground, esp. with earth thrown up as parapet to protect soldiers under fire or from bombing; ~ **coat**, thick, usu. lined, waterproof overcoat, orig. for wearing in trenches; ~ **foot**, disease of feet resembling chilblains, sometimes with gangrene, due to exposure to extreme cold and wet and prevalent among soldiers serving in trenches; ~ **fever**, low, intermittent, infectious fever carried by lice and common among men serving in trenches; ~ **mortar**, small mortar for throwing bombs etc. into enemy trenches at short range; ~ **mouth**, disease characterized by ulceration of mucous membranes of mouth and pharynx with pain and foul smell; also called Vincent's angina (disease); ~ **warfare**, hostilities carried on from more or less permanent trenches. **trench** *v.* 1. Make trench(es) or ditch(es) in ground; make series of trenches in digging or plowing (ground) so as to bring lower soil to surface; dig

Above: A common European ***tree-creeper.*** *This bird and related species have remarkably strong feet which enable them to run up and down tree trunks in search of insects.*

A simple latticework ***trellis*** *is perfect for growing climbing plants. Many species, such as this variegated ivy, are popular for trellis-growing in the U.S.A.*

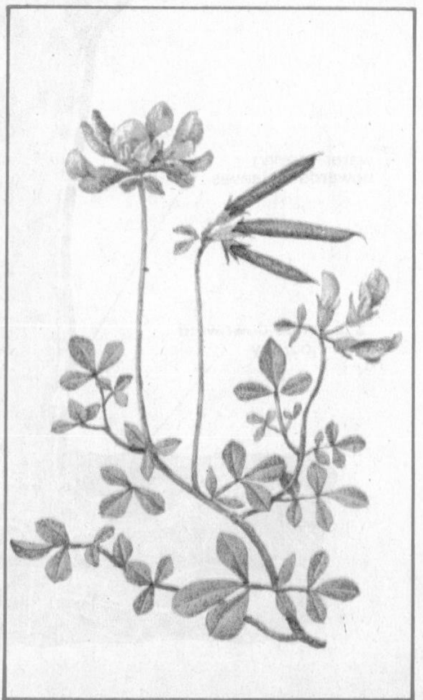

Common birdsfoot ***trefoil*** *is only one of some 300 species of plants in the genus Trifolium which is best known for a wide range of clovers. These are widely harvested for fodder.*

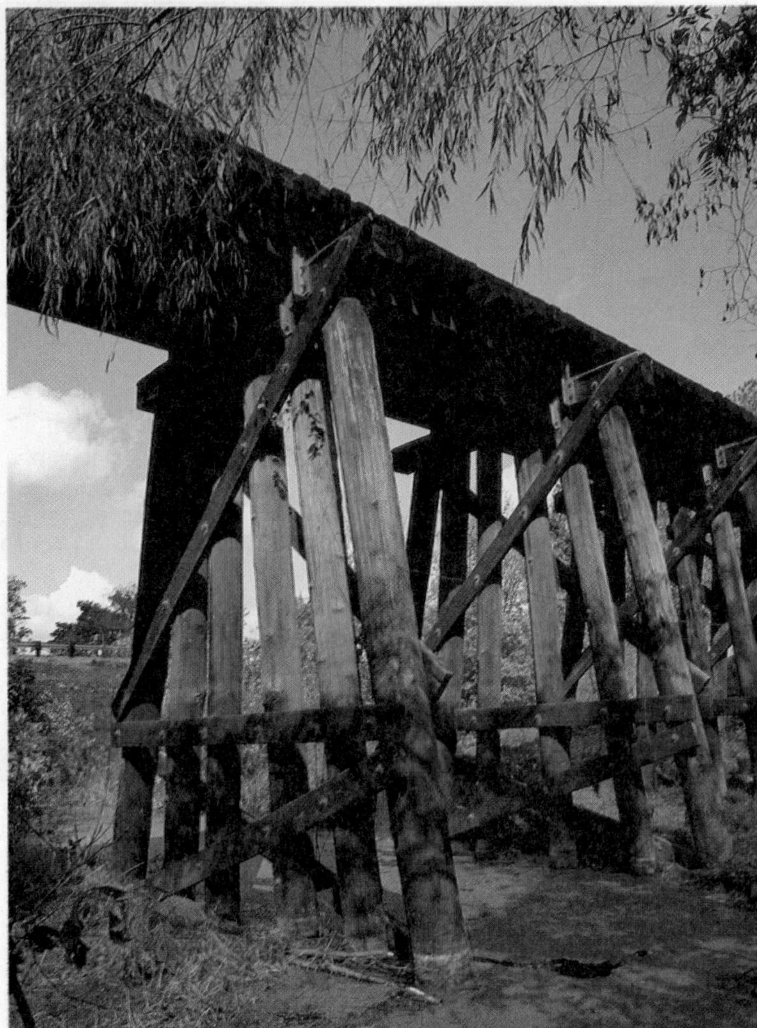

*The **trestle** bridge is a very old design, but it is still an extremely effective means of support. Dated examples add immensely to the charm of their surroundings.*

trench(es); cut (groove), cut groove in (wood etc.). 2. Encroach *on*; verge or border closely *on*.

trench·ant (trĕn′chant) *adj.* (archaic and poet.) Keen, sharp; (zool., of tooth etc.) having cutting edge; (fig.) keen, penetrating; vigorous, energetic. **trench′ant·ly** *adv.* **trench′an·cy** *n.*

trench·er (trĕn′cher) *n.* Flat square or usu. circular piece of wood on which meat etc. was formerly cut; any flat round piece of wood; **trench′erman** (pl. **-men**), heavy feeder, eater.

trend (trĕnd) *n.* General direction, course, style, tendency. **trend′y** *adj.* (**trend·i·er, trend·i·est**). (colloq.) Following latest trends of fashion etc. **trend** *v.i.* Have specified direction, course, or general tendency. **trend′i·ness** *n.*

Trent (trĕnt). (It. *Trento*) City of N. Italy; scene of Council of Trent, ecumenical council of R.C. Ch., meeting from time to time, 1545–63, which defined the doctrines of the church in opposition to those of the Reformation, reformed discipline, and strengthened the authority of the papacy.

tre·pan (trĭpăn′) *n.* 1. Surgeon's cylindrical saw (obs.; superseded by TREPHINE) for cutting holes. 2. (mining etc.) Heavy boring instrument for sinking shafts. ~ *v.t.* (**-panned, -pan·ning**). Operate on with trepan. **trep·a·na·tion** (trĕpanā′shon), **tre·pan′ner** *ns.*

tre·phine (trĭfīn′, -fēn′) *n.* Surgeon's cylindrical saw with guiding center pin, for removing part of bone of skull. ~ *v.t.* (**-phined, -phin·ing**). Operate on with trephine. **treph·i·na·tion** (trĕfĭnā′shon) *n.*

trep·i·da·tion (trĕpĭdā′shon) *n.* Agitation or alarm, flurry, perturbation.

tres·pass (trĕs′pas) *n.* Transgression, breach of law or duty; (law) actionable wrong committed against person or property of another, esp. wrongful entry upon another's lands with damage (however inconsiderable) to real property. ~ *v.i.* 1. Transgress, sin. 2. (law) Commit trespass, esp. enter unlawfully on land of another or his property or right; (fig.) make unwarrantable claim or undesired intrusion *on*, encroach *on*, infringe. **tres′pass·er** *n.*

tress (trĕs) *n.* Lock, braid of (esp. woman's long) hair; (pl.) woman's hair.

tres·tle (trĕs′el) *n.* Supporting structure for table etc. consisting of horizontal beam with diverging legs, usu. two at each end, or of two frames hinged together or fixed at an angle; open braced framework of wood or metal for supporting bridge etc.; (naut., pl.) trestletrees; ~ **bridge**, bridge supported on trestles; ~ **table**, table of board(s) laid across trestles or other supports; **tres′tletree**, either of a pair of fore-and-aft horizontal timbers on mast, supporting crosstrees, topmast, etc.

trey (trā) *n.* Three at dice or cards.

tri- *comb. form.* Three, thrice.

tri·ad (trī′ăd) *n.* Group or set of three; (mus.) chord of three notes, esp. note with its third and fifth (e.g. common chord without octave); (chem.) group of three chemical elements having similar properties, as iron, nickel, and cobalt. **tri·ad·ic** (trīăd′ĭk) *adj.* **tri′ad·ism** *n.*

tri·a·del·phous (trīadĕl′fus) *adj.* (bot.) (Having stamens) united by filaments into three bundles.

tri·age (trēahzh′, trē′ahzh) *n.* Assignment of degrees of urgency to decide priority in treatment of wounded etc.

tri·al (trī′al) *n.* 1. Examination and determination of causes at law by judicial tribunal. 2. Testing or putting to proof of qualities of thing; test, probation; experimental treatment, investigation by means of experience; examination of person, esp. for Presbyterian ministry. 3. Being tried by suffering or temptation; painful test of endurance, patience, etc.; affliction, hardship. 4. Attempt, endeavor. 5. Something serving as sample, proof, etc., piece of pottery used to test temperature or progress of firing inside kiln. 6. ~ **and error**, process of attacking a task by trying different methods and eliminating those that fail; ~ **balance**, (in double entry bookkeeping) addition of all entries on each side of ledger to establish that debits balance credits; ~ **balloon**, (fig.) experiment to see how new policy etc. will be received; ~ **marriage**, relationship of man and woman living together without legal marriage, esp. when such marriage is a possibility for the

Historic photograph of the **trial** of Nazi war criminals at Nuremberg in 1945. Methods and procedures of justice differ between countries but the principal aim remains similar.

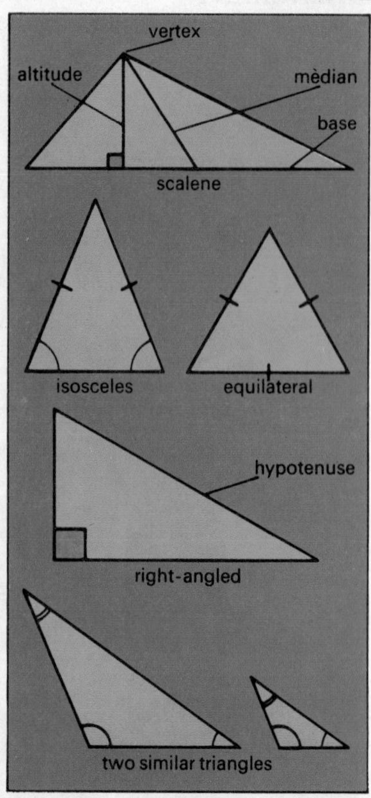

The relationship between the sides and angles of a **triangle** is the basis of trigonometry. It is invaluable in surveying and other forms of measurement where only some figures are available.

future; ~ **run**, trip to test speed and other qualities of new vessel etc.

tri·an·gle (trī′ănggel) *n.* Geometric figure, esp. plane rectilineal figure, with three angles and three sides; any system of three points not in a straight line, with the three real or imaginary lines joining them; any three-cornered body, object, or space, esp. musical percussion instrument consisting of steel rod bent into a triangle open at one corner and struck with a small steel rod; **eternal** ~: see ETERNAL.

tri·an·gu·lar (trīăng′gyuler) *adj.* Of the shape of a triangle, three-cornered; three-sided, among three persons or parties. **tri·an′gu·lar·ly** *adv.* **tri·an·gu·lar·i·ty** (trīănggyulăr′ĭtē) *n.*

tri·an·gu·late (trīăng′gyulĭt, -lāt) *adj.* Consisting of, marked with, triangles. **tri·an′gu·late·ly** *adv.* **triangulate** (trīăng′gyulāt) *v.t.* (**-lat·ed, -lat·ing**). Divide or convert into triangles; (surveying etc.) measure, map out, by measurement of sides and angles of series of triangles on determined base line(s). **tri·an·gu·la·tion** (trīănggyulā′shon) *n.*

Tri·as (trī′as) = TRIASSIC.

Tri·as·sic (trīăs′ĭk) *adj.* & *n.* (geol.) (Of) the earliest period or system (also **Trias**) of the Mesozoic. [Gk. *trias* group of three, f. threefold subdivision of Triassic strata]

tri·a·tom·ic (trīatŏm′ĭk) *adj.* Having three atoms in the molecule; having three replaceable atoms or groups.

trib·al (trī′bal) *adj.* Of tribe(s). **trib′al·ly** *adv.*

trib·al·ism (trī′balĭzem) *n.* Tribal system or organization.

tri·ba·sic (trībā′sĭk) *adj.* (chem.) Having three replaceable hydrogen atoms; containing three atoms of a univalent metal or three basic hydroxyl groups.

tribe (trīb) *n.* 1. Group of clans under recognized chiefs. 2. (Rom. hist.) Each of the political divisions of the Romans (orig. three, prob. representing clans, ultimately 35); (Gk. hist.) = PHYLE. 3. Any similar division, whether of natural or political origin; any of the 12 divisions of the people of Israel, each traditionally descended from one of the patriarchs; **Lost T~s**, the ten Israelite tribes (i.e. all but Judah and Benjamin) that revolted from the House of David and were deported by Shalmaneser, after which time their history is lost. 4. (biol.) Group ranking usu. below family and above genus (with name usu. ending in *-ini* for animals and *-eae* for plants). 5. Class, lot, set (usu. contempt.). **tribes′man** *n.* (pl. **-men**). Member of a tribe.

trib·u·la·tion (trĭbyulā′shon) *n.* Great affliction, oppression, or misery. [L. *tribulare* press, oppress, f. *tribulum* threshing sledge]

tri·bu·nal (trībū′nal, trĭbū′-) *n.* 1. Judgment seat; court of justice, judicial assembly; (fig.) place of judgment, judicial authority. 2. Board or committee appointed to adjudicate claims of a particular kind, act as arbiters, etc.

trib·une[1] (trĭb′ūn) *n.* 1. (Rom. hist.) Administrative officer, esp. one of two (later five, then ten) orig. protecting interests and rights of plebeians from patricians; one of six officers of legion, each in command for two months of year. 2. Protector of rights of people, popular leader. **trib·u·nate** (trĭb′yunĭt, -nāt), **trib′une·ship** *ns.*

trib·une[2] (trĭb′ūn) *n.* Raised floor for magistrate's chair in apse of Christian basilica; bishop's throne, apse containing this, in basilica; platform, stage, pulpit; raised and seated area or gallery.

trib·u·tar·y (trĭb′yutĕrē) *adj.* 1. Paying or subject to tribute; furnishing subsidiary supplies or aid, auxiliary, contributory; (of stream) flowing into a larger stream or a lake. ~ *n.* (pl. **-tar·ies**). Tributary person or state; tributary stream.

trib·ute (trĭb′ūt) *n.* Money or equivalent paid by one sovereign or country to another in acknowledgment of submission or for protection or peace; obligation of paying this; (fig.) contribution, offering or gift as mark of respect, affection, etc.

trice[1] (trīs) *n.* **in a** ~, in an instant.

trice[2] (trīs) *v.t.* (**triced, tric·ing**). (naut.) Hoist *up* and secure with rope or lashing, lash *up*.

tri·cen·ten·ni·al (trīsĕntĕn'ēal) *adj.* & *n.* Tercentenary.

tri·ceps (trī'sĕps) *adj.* & *n.* (pl. **-ceps·es, -ceps**). (Muscle, esp. great extensor muscle of back of upper arm) with three heads or attachments.

Tri·cer·a·tops (trīsĕr'atŏps) *n.* Gigantic dinosaur of Genus *T*~ found in parts of U.S. in the late Cretaceous era, with two large horns above eyes and one on nose.

tri·chi·na (trĭkī'na) *n.* (pl. **-nae** pr. -nē). Minute nematode worm (*Trichinella spiralis*) parasitic in muscles and intestines of man, pig, etc. **trich·i·no·sis** (trĭkinō'sĭs) *n.* Disease caused by introduction of trichinae from infected pork into alimentary canal. **trich·i·nous** (trĭk'inus) *adj.* Of trichinae or trichinosis.

tri·chot·o·my (trĭkŏt'omē) *n.* (pl. **-mies**). Division into, classification or arrangement in, three (classes etc.); division of human nature into body, soul, and spirit. **tri·chot'o·mous** *adj.*

tri·chro·ic (trīkrō'ĭk) *adj.* Having or showing three colors; esp. of crystal, presenting three different colors when viewed in three different directions. **tri·chro·ism** (trī'krōĭzem) *n.*

tri·chro·mat·ic (trīkrōmăt'ĭk) *adj.* Trichroic; esp. of or having three fundamental color sensations (red, green, violet) of normal vision; of (printing in) three colors. **tri·chro·ma·tism** (trīkrō'matĭzem) *n.*

trick (trĭk) *n.* 1. Crafty or fraudulent device or stratagem, esp. of mean or base kind; hoax, joke; capricious, foolish, or stupid act; clever device or contrivance, stratagem, feat of skill or dexterity; knack (freq. in ~(**s**) **of the trade**); **do the** ~, achieve the desired result. 2. Peculiar or characteristic practice; habit, mannerism. 3. (cards) Cards played and won in one round; such round, point(s) gained by winning it. 4. (naut.) Time, usu. two hours, of duty at helm. 5. ~ **knee**, chronic sudden weakening and collapse of knee as result of injury to tendons and ligaments; ~ **or treat**, Hallowe'en children's game of calling at houses with threat of pranks if candy or other treats are not given them. **trick** *v.* 1. Deceive by trick, cheat; cheat *out of*, beguile *into*, by trickery; practice trickery. 2. Dress, deck, decorate (usu. *out*, *up*). **trick'er·y** *n.* (pl. **-er·ies**).

trick·le (trĭk'el) *v.* (**-led, -ling**). (Cause to) flow in drops or in scanty halting stream; (of baseball) run slowly over surface of ground, cause (baseball) to do this. ~ *n.* Trickling, small fitful stream. **trick'ling·ly** *adv.*

trick·ster (trĭk'ster) *n.* One who tricks; cheat; fraud; deceiver.

trick·y (trĭk'ē) *adj.* (**trick·i·er, trick·i·est**). Crafty, given to tricks, deceitful; skilled in clever tricks or dodges, adroit, resourceful; (colloq.) requiring cautious or adroit action or handling, ticklish. **trick'i·ly** *adv.* **trick'i·ness** *n.*

tri·clin·ic (trīklĭn'ĭk) *adj.* (cryst.) Having the three axes unequal and obliquely inclined.

tri·col·or (trī'kŭler) *n.* & *adj.* (Flag, esp. that adopted as national flag of France at Revolution) having three colors.

tri·corn, tri·corne (trī'kôrn) *adjs.* & *ns.* Three-cornered (cocked hat).

tri·cos·tate (trīkŏs'tāt) *adj.* (zool.) Having three ribs, raised lines, or riblike parts.

tri·cot (trē'kō) *n.* Fabric knitted by hand or machine.

tri·cus·pid (trīkŭs'pĭd) *adj.* Having three cusps or points; ~ **valve**, (anat.) valve, consisting of three triangular segments, that guards the opening from the right atrium into the right ventricle of the heart.

tri·cy·cle (trī'sĭkel) *n.* Three-wheeled velocipede or motorcycle. ~ *v.i.* Ride tricycle.

tri·dent (trī'dent) *n.* Three-pronged instrument or weapon, esp. three-pronged fish spear or scepter as attribute of Neptune or of Britannia.

tri·en·ni·al (trīĕn'ēal) *adj.* Existing, lasting, for three years; occurring, done, every three years. **tri·en'ni·al·ly** *adv.* **tri·en'ni·al, tri·en'ni·um** *ns.* Triennial occasion, event, publication, etc.; esp. visitation of diocese by bishop every three years.

tri·fle (trī'fel) *n.* 1. Thing, fact, circumstance, of slight value or importance; small amount, esp. of

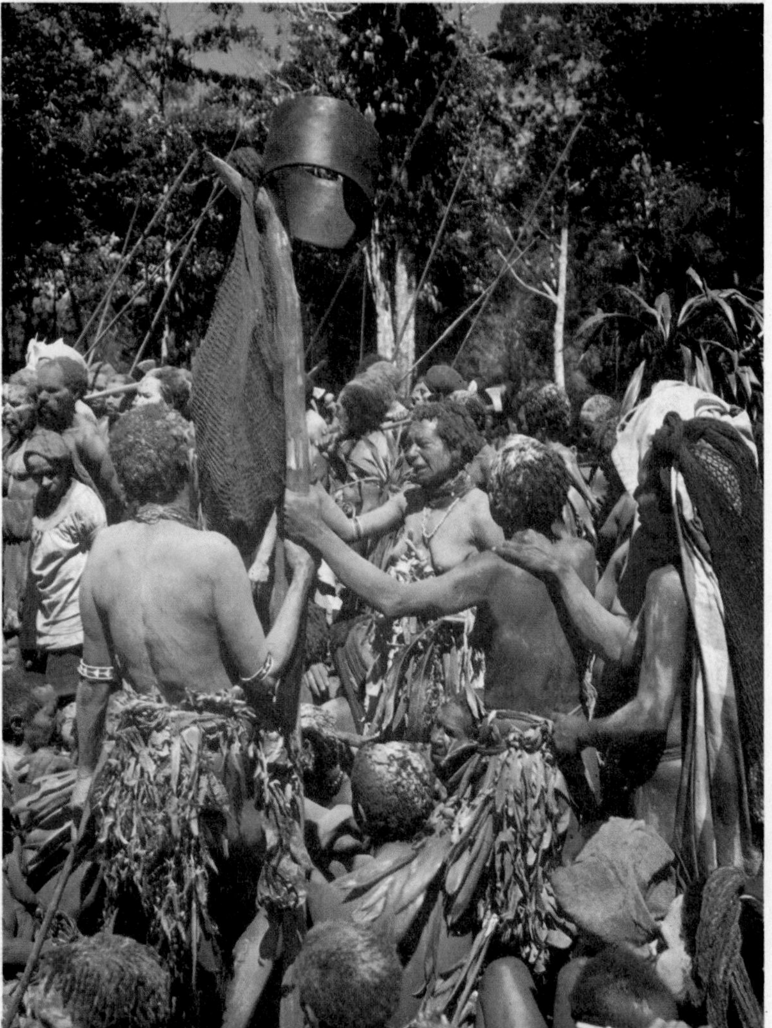

***Tribal** customs vary from one area to another. While different types of tribalism exist throughout the world it is, perhaps, more easily recognised in some developing countries. Left: a mourning ceremony in Papua New Guinea.*

The **triggerfish** of tropical seas is named because the first dorsal spine can be locked upright. This enables the fish to wedge itself in a crevice or stick in the mouth of a predator.

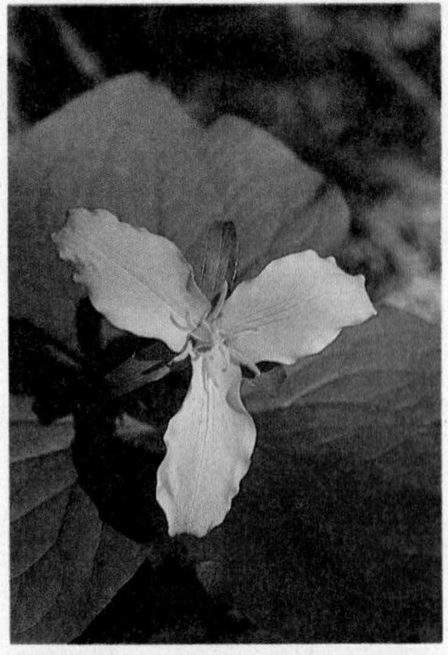

Often called wakerobin, plants of the **trillium** genus are popular in wildflower gardens in North America. Many features of these plants are similar to those of the lily.

money; small article. 2. (Brit.) Sweet dish of sponge cakes flavored with wine, jam, etc., topped with custard or whipped cream. ~ *v.i.* Toy, play, dally, fidget, *with*; act or speak idly or frivolously. **tri'fler** *n.* **tri'fling** *adj.* Unimportant, paltry, insignificant; foolish, frivolous, idle. **tri'fling·ly** *adv.*

tri·fo·li·o·late (trīfō'lēolĭt), **tri·fo·li·ate** (trīfō'lēāt) *adjs.* Three-leaved; consisting of three leaflets; having such leaves.

tri·form (trī'fōrm) *adj.* Having a triple form, existing or appearing in three forms.

trig. *abbrev.* Trigonometry.

tri·gem·i·nal (trījĕm'*i*nal) *adj.* Of the fifth and (in man) largest pair of cranial nerves, dividing into three main branches (ophthalmic, maxillary, and mandibular nerves).

trig·ger (trĭg'*er*) *n.* Movable catch or lever that is pulled or pressed to release a spring or otherwise set mechanism in motion, esp. small steel catch for releasing hammer of lock in firearm; **quick on the** ~, (fig.) quick to respond; ~ **finger**, forefinger of right hand; **trig'gerfish** (pl. **-fishes**, collect. **-fish**), fish of *Balistes* and related genera, so called because pressure on second spine of anterior dorsal fin depresses first; **trigger-happy**, apt to shoot on slight provocation; **trig'german** (*n.*), (colloq.) gangster specializing in murdering with gun. **trigger** *v.* Initiate, set *off* a reaction etc.

tri·glyc·er·ide (trīglĭs'*e*rīd, -ĭd) *n.* (chem.) Ester derived from glycerol and one to three fatty acids.

tri·glyph (trī'glĭf) *n.* (archit.) Ornament of frieze in Doric order, consisting of block or tablet with two vertical grooves and a half-groove on each side, alternating with metopes.

tri·gon (trī'gŏn) *n.* 1. (archaic) Triangle. 2. (astrol.) Set of three signs of zodiac 120° distant from each other; each of four such groups (airy, earthy, fiery, watery) into which the 12 signs are divided; triplicity, trine. 3. (zool.) Cutting region of crown of upper molar.

trig·o·nal (trĭg'*o*n*a*l) *adj.* Triangular; having triangular cross section; of a trigon; (geom., cryst., of solid) having triangular faces, having three equal and equally inclined axes. **trig'o·nal·ly** *adv.*

trig·o·nom·e·try (trĭg*o*nŏm'-*e*trē) *n.* Branch of mathematics dealing with measurement of sides and angles of triangles and with certain functions of their angles or of angles in general. **trig·o·no·met·ric** (trĭg*o*n*o*mĕt'rĭk) *adj.* ~ **function**, any of the basic functions of an angle (as sine, cosine, secant, etc.) expressed as the ratio of two of the sides of a right-angled triangle containing the angle. **trig·o·no·met'ri·cal** *adj.* **trig·o·no·met'ri·cal·ly** *adv.*

tri·graph (trī'grăf, -grahf) *n.* Combination of three letters representing one sound.

tri·he·dron (trīhē'dr*o*n, -hĕd'r*o*n) *n.* (pl. **-drons, -dra** pr. -dr*a*). Figure formed by three surfaces meeting in point. **tri·he'dral** *adj.* & *n.*

tri·ju·gate (trī'jōōgāt, trījōō'gĭt, -gāt) *adj.* (bot.) With three pairs of pinnate leaves.

tri·lat·er·al (trīlăt'*e*r*a*l) *adj.* & *n.* (Figure) having three sides; triangle, triangular.

tri·lin·e·ar (trīlĭn'ē*e*r) *adj.* (math.) Of, contained by, having some relation to, three lines.

tri·lin·gual (trīlĭng'gw*a*l) *adj.* Speaking, using, expressed in, three languages.

tri·lith (trī'lĭth), **tri·lith·on** (trīlĭth'ŏn, trī'l*i*thŏn) *ns.* Prehistoric structure of two upright stones with another resting on them as a lintel.

trill (trĭl) *n.* 1. (mus.) Rapid alternation of two notes a tone or semitone apart, shake. 2. (phon.) Pronunciation of consonant, consonant pronounced, with vibration of tongue or other part of speech organs. 3. Tremulous high-pitched sound or note(s), esp. in singing of birds. ~ *v.* Utter, sing, produce, with trill(s); make trill(s).

tril·lion (trĭl'y*o*n) *n.* Fourth power of a thousand, unit followed by 12 zeros. **tril'lionth** *adj.* & *n.*

tril·li·um (trĭl'ē*u*m) *n.* Any of several perennial plants of genus *Trillium*, having a single whorl of three leaves borne on an erect stem and one flower of three petals and various colors.

tri·lo·bate (trīlō'bāt, trī'l*o*bāt) *adj.* Having, consisting of, three lobes.

tri·lo·bite (trī'l*o*bīt) *n.* Fossil arthropod with three-lobed body found in Lower Paleozoic rocks.

tril·o·gy (trĭl'*o*jē) *n.* (pl. **-gies**). (Gk. antiq.) Series of three tragedies performed at Athens at festival of Dionysus; any series or group of three related dramatic or other literary works.

trim (trĭm) *adj.* (**trim·mer, trim·mest**). In good order; well arranged or equipped; neat, spruce. **trim'ly** *adv.* **trim'ness** *n.* **trim** *v.* (**trimmed, trim·ming**). 1. Set in good order, make neat or tidy; remove irregular, superfluous, or unsightly parts from; remove (such parts) by clipping, planing, etc. 2. Ornament (with ribbon, lace, etc.); dress (windows). 3. Adjust

Although extinct, some 10,000 species of **trilobite** existed in the seas from 450 to 200 million years ago. However, many of the known fossils consist of skins that had been molted.

balance of (vessel, aircraft) by distribution of cargo, passengers, etc.; arrange (sails etc.) to suit wind; (fig.) hold middle course in politics or opinion, adjust oneself to prevailing opinion, etc. for the sake of expediency; (colloq.) defeat, cheat. ~ *n.* 1. (naut.) State of being trimmed and rigged ready for sailing, battle (**fighting** ~), etc.; state of ship, cargo, etc., in reference to fitness for sailing, esp. proper balance in water on fore-and-aft line; difference between draft forward and draft aft; (aeron.) balance of aircraft in ref. to fore-and-aft in horizontal plane. 2. State, degree, of adjustment, readiness, or fitness; good order. 3. Trimming, being trimmed; interior furnishings of automobile; visible woodwork around openings of house etc.; window dressing. 4. Trimming or cutting off; anything cut off or out, trimmings.

tri·ma·ran (trī'mərăn) *n.* Boat resembling catamaran but with three hulls side by side.

tri·mes·ter (trīmĕs'tɘr, trī'mĕs-) *n.* Three months; division of academic year into three parts in some colleges and universities.

trim·e·ter (trĭm'ĭtɘr) *adj.* & *n.* (Verse) of three measures or feet.

trim·mer (trĭm'ɘr) *n.* 1. One who has no fixed allegiance to a political party or other institution but inclines to each of two opposite sides as interest dictates. 2. One whose business is to stow coal or cargo in loading ship. 3. Short beam framed across an opening (as a stairwell or hearth) to carry the ends of joists that cannot be extended across the opening. 4. Machine or tool for clipping shrubbery, weeds, etc.

Chelsea Pensioners U.K. wear a **tricorn** hat with their full-dress uniform. The style evolved in the 17th century from broad-brimmed hats which had their brim pinned to the crown.

trim·ming (trĭm'ĭng) *n.* (esp.) Ornamental addition to dress, hat, etc.; (pl.) accessories, usual accompaniments, esp. sauces, stuffing, condiments, etc. accompanying main course of a meal; (pl.) pieces cut off in trimming something.

tri·mor·phic (trīmŏr'fĭk), **tri·mor·phous** (trīmŏr'fus) *adjs.* (of species etc.) Having three distinct forms; (bot.) having three distinct forms of organs on individuals of same species; (cryst., of substance) crystallizing in three fundamentally distinct forms. **tri·morph** (trī'mŏrf), **tri·mor'phism** *ns.*

trine (trīn) *adj.* & *n.* Threefold, triple (group); (thing) made up of three parts; (astrol.) (aspect) of two heavenly bodies distant from each other by a third part of the zodiac (120°); ~ **immersion**, thrice sprinkling in baptism. **tri'nal, tri'na·ry** *adjs.*

Trin·i·dad (trĭn'ĭdăd) **and To·ba·go** (tōbā'gō). W. Indian islands off coast of Venezuela; member state of the Brit. Commonwealth, independent since 1962; capital, Port of Spain.

Trin·i·tar·i·an (trĭnĭtār'ēan) *adj.* & *n.* 1. (Member) of religious order of Holy Trinity, founded 1198 to redeem Christian captives from Muslims. 2. (Holder) of doctrine of Trinity. **Trin·i·tar'i·an·ism** *n.*

trin·i·tro·tol·u·ene (trīnī-trōtŏl'ūēn), **tri·ni·tro·tol·u·ol** (trīnītrōtŏl'ūōl, -awl, -ōl) *ns.* Derivative of toluene with three nitro (NO_2) groups, high explosive used as shell fillings and as ingredient of various explosives (abbrev. TNT).

*The nation of **Trinidad and Tobago** gained independence in 1962. The islands were discovered by Columbus. Trinidad is now a major producer of oil and asphalt as well as sugar.*

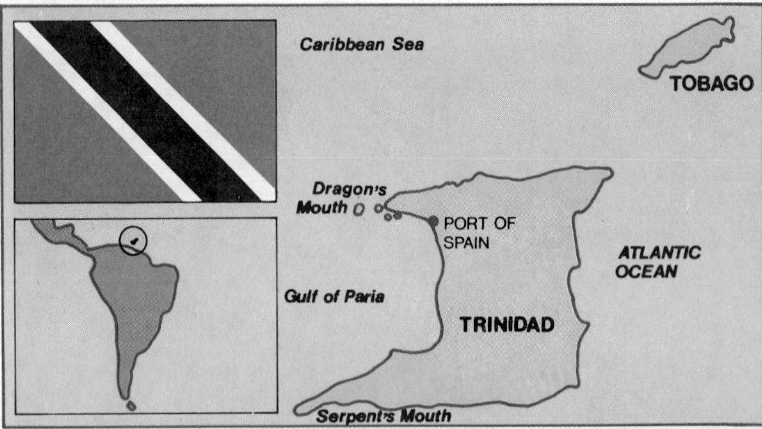

trin·i·ty (trĭn′ĭtē) *n.* (pl. **-ties**). Being three; group of three; **the T∼**, union of three persons or modes of being in the Godhead as conceived in orthodox Christian belief; Father, Son, and Holy Ghost as constituting one God; **T∼ Sunday**, Sunday after Pentecost, observed as festival in honor of the Trinity.

trin·ket (trĭng′kĭt) *n.* Small or trifling ornament or fancy article, esp. piece of jewelry.

tri·nod·al (trīnō′d*a*l) *adj.* (bot.) Having three joints or nodes.

tri·no·mi·al (trīnō′mē*a*l) *adj.* & *n.* (esp., math.) (Algebraical expression) consisting of three terms connected by plus or minus signs.

tri·o (trē′ō) *n.* (pl. **tri·os**). 1. (mus.) (Composition for) three voices or instruments in combination; composition in three parts. 2. Set of three persons or things.

tri·ode (trī′ōd) *n.* Vacuum tube with three main electrodes (anode, cathode, and grid).

tri·oe·cious (trīē′sh*u*s) *adj.* Having male, female, and bisexual flowers on different plants.

tri·ox·ide (trīŏk′sīd) *n.* (chem.) Compound of three atoms of oxygen with an element or radical.

trip (trĭp) *v.* (**tripped, trip·ping**). 1. Walk, dance, (as in ∼ **the light fantastic**), skip, etc., with quick light tread, run lightly, move freely and quickly. 2. (freq. with *up*) Make false step, stumble; cause (person) to stumble by entangling or suddenly arresting his feet; make mistake, commit fault, inconsistency, or inaccuracy; detect in stumble, inconsistency, or inaccuracy. 3. Tilt, esp. (naut.) tilt or cant (yard or mast) in lowering it; (naut.) loose (anchor) from its bed and raise it clear of bottom; (mech.) release (catch, lever, etc.) by contact with projection, operate (mechanism) thus. 4. (colloq.) Experience effects of hallucinogenic drug. **trip** *n.* 1. Short voyage or journey, esp. each of series of such journeys over particular route; excursion for pleasure, business, or health; (colloq.) experience induced by hallucinogenic or psychedelic drug. See EGO (sense 2). 2. Stumble; tripping or being tripped up. 3. Contrivance for tripping, projecting part of mechanism coming into contact with another part so as to cause or check movement; **trip′hammer, trip hammer**, massive machine

*Using the 'Adoration of the Magi' as a central theme, the Dutch painter of this **triptych** also included the man who commissioned the work, and his wife, as part of the composition.*

hammer operated by trip.

tri·par·tite (trīpar̄′tīt) *adj.* Divided into, composed of, three parts or kinds; of, involving, such division; engaged in by, concluded between, three parties.

tripe (trīp) *n.* First or second stomach of ruminant, esp. ox, prepared as food; (slang) worthless or trashy product or thing.

tri·phib·i·ous (trīfĭb′ē*u*s) *adj.* (of military operations) On land, sea, and in the air.

tri·plane (trī′plān) *n.* Aircraft with three sets of wings.

tri·ple (trĭp′*e*l) *adj.* Threefold, three times as much or as many, of three parts; **T∼ Alliance**, (1) alliance of England, Sweden, and Netherlands against France, 1668; (2) that of France, Gt. Britain, and Netherlands against Spain, 1717; (3) that of Germany, Austria, and Italy against Russia and France, 1882–3; ∼ **crown**, (horse racing) of, pertaining to, victory by same horse in Kentucky Derby, Preakness, and Belmont Stakes; **∼-decker**, sandwich having three slices of bread and two layers of filling; ∼ **play**, (baseball) putting out three runners; **T∼ Entente**: see ENTENTE; ∼ **threat**, (football) player who excels at running, passing, and kicking; any person having great ability in three fields or three skills in one field; ∼ **time**, (mus.) rhythm of three beats in the bar. **tri′ply** *adv.* **triple** *n.* Set of three; number or amount three times greater than another; (baseball) hit on which batter gets to third base without a fielding error. ∼ *v.* (**tri·pled, tri·pling**). Increase threefold; be three times as great or as many as; (baseball) make a triple.

tri·plet (trĭp′lĭt) *n.* 1. Set of three; esp. three successive lines of verse rhyming together; (mus.) group of three notes performed in the time of two of the same value. 2. Each of three children born at a birth.

tri·plex (trĭp′lĕks) *adj.* Triple, threefold; apartment occupying three floors of a building.

trip·li·cate (trĭp′l*ĭ*kĭt, -kāt) *adj.* Threefold, forming three exactly corresponding copies. ∼ *n.* Each of set of three exactly corresponding copies or parts; **in ∼**, in three exactly corresponding copies. **triplicate** (trĭp′l*ĭ*kāt) *v.t.* (**-cat·ed, -cat·ing**). Triple, multiply by three, make or provide in triplicate.

trip·li·ca·tion (trĭplĭkā'shon) *n.*

trip·loid (trĭp'loid) *adj.* & *n.* (biol.) (Organism or cell) having three times the haploid set of chromosomes.

tri·pod (trī'pŏd) *n.* Three-legged support, table, seat, etc., esp. frame or stand with three diverging legs, usu. hinged at top, for supporting camera, theodolite, etc.; (Gk. antiq.) altar at Delphi on which priestess sat to utter oracles. **tri·pod·al** (trĭp'odal) *adj.*

Trip·o·li (trĭp'olē). Seaport and capital city of Libya.

trip·per (trĭp'er) *n.* (esp.) Excursionist, one who goes on a pleasure trip.

trip·tych (trĭp'tĭk) *n.* Picture or carving, or set of three, in three compartments side by side, with lateral panels usu. hinged so as to fold over central one, used esp. as altarpiece.

tri·reme (trī'rēm) *n.* Ancient Greek or Roman warship with three banks of oars.

tri·sect (trīsĕkt', trī'sĕkt) *v.t.* Divide into three, esp. (geom.) equal parts. **tri·sec·tion** (trīsĕk'-shon) *n.*

tri·sep·al·ous (trīsĕp'alus) *adj.* (bot.) Having three sepals.

tris·mus (trĭz'mus, trĭs'-) *n.* (pl. **-mus·es**). (path.) Lockjaw.

Tris·tram (trĭs'tram). Knight, hero of a medieval legend; lover of ISEULT.

tri·syl·la·ble (trīsĭl'abel) *n.* Word of three syllables. **tri·syl·lab·ic** (trīsĭlăb'ĭk) *adj.* **tri·syl·lab'i·cal·ly** *adv.*

trite (trīt) *adj.* (**trit·er, trit·est**). Worn out by constant use or repetition, hackneyed, commonplace. **trite'ly** *adv.* **trite'ness** *n.*

trit·i·um (trĭt'ēum, trĭsh'um) *n.* (chem.) Radioactive isotope of hydrogen (at. wt. 3, half-life 12.5 years).

Tri·ton (trī'ton). (Gk. myth.) Sea god, son of Poseidon and Amphitrite, represented as a merman; one of a number of sea gods in form of mermen, freq. represented with conch shell trumpets.

tri·ton[1] (trī'ton) *n.* (zool.) Marine gastropod of family Tritonidae with large spiral shell.

tri·ton[2] (trī'tŏn) *n.* Tritium nucleus containing one proton and two neutrons.

trit·u·rate (trĭch'erāt) *v.t.* (**-rat·ed, -rat·ing**). Grind, rub, pound, etc., to powder or fine particles, pulverize. **trit·u·ra·tion** (trĭcherā'shon) *n.* **trit'u·ra·ble** *adj.* **trit'u·ra·tor** *n.*

tri·umph (trī'umf) *n.* 1. (Rom. antiq.) Entrance of commander with army and spoils in solemn procession into Rome in celebration of victory. 2. Triumphing; victory, conquest, the glory of this; rejoicing in success, elation, exultation. ~ *v.i.* Celebrate a Roman triumph; be victorious, prevail; rejoice in victory, exult (*over*); rejoice, glory.

tri·um·phal (trīŭm'fal) *adj.* Of, used in, celebrating, commemorating, a triumph or victory; ~ **arch**, arch erected, by Roman emperor or in modern times, in commemoration of victory etc.

tri·um·phant (trīŭm'fant) *adj.* Victorious, successful; triumphing, exultant. **tri·um'phant·ly** *adv.*

tri·um·vir (trīŭm'ver) *n.* (pl. **-virs, -vi·ri** pr. -verī). 1. (Rom. hist.) One of three public officers jointly charged with one department of administration; member of first or second triumvirate (see below). 2. Member of any group of three jointly exercising power.

tri·um·vi·rate (trīŭm'verĭt) *n.* Office or function of triumvir; set of triumvirs; **first** ~, coalition of Pompey, Julius Caesar, and Crassus (60 B.C.); **second** ~, administration of Mark Antony, Octavian (Augustus), and Lepidus (43 B.C.).

tri·va·lent (trīvā'lent) *adj.* (chem.) Having a valence of three. **tri·va'lence, tri·va'len·cy** *ns.*

tri·valve (trī'vălv) *adj.* & *n.* (Shell) having three valves.

triv·et (trĭv'ĭt) *n.* Stand for pot, kettle, etc., placed over fire, orig. and properly on three feet, now freq. with projection(s) by which it can be secured on top bar of grate; similar stand for hot dishes or pots at table.

triv·i·al (trĭv'ēal) *adj.* Of small value or importance, trifling, slight, inconsiderable. **triv'i·al·ly** *adv.* **triv'i·al·ness, triv'i·al·ism** *ns.* **triv·i·al·i·ty** (trĭvēăl'ĭtē) *n.* (pl. **-ties**). **triv·i·a**[1] (trĭv'ēa) *n.pl.* Matters or information of no importance or usefulness. [L. *trivialis* commonplace f. *trivium* place where three ways meet (*via* way)]

triv·i·um (trĭv'ēum) *n.* (pl.

A ***tripod*** *is essential in photography where a steady hand is required. This is especially so when the camera, such as this movie camera, is heavy.*

Backed by the ruins of the Coliseum which was completed by Titus, this ***triumphal arch*** *was erected to commemorate his capture of Jerusalem in A.D. 70. He later ruled Rome.*

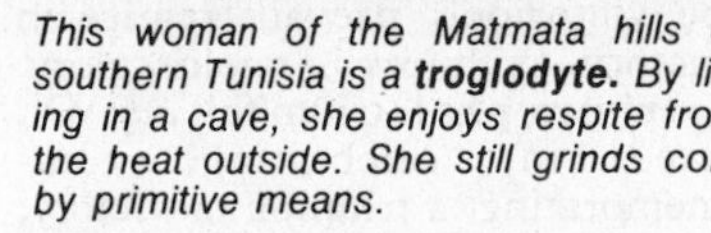

This woman of the Matmata hills of southern Tunisia is a ***troglodyte.*** *By living in a cave, she enjoys respite from the heat outside. She still grinds corn by primitive means.*

With such exact realism that artist Martin Battersby could have been playing a practical joke on his viewers, his ***trompe l'oeil*** *at Mompesson House, Salisbury U.K. is a masterpiece of its type.*

triv·i·a[2] pr. trĭv′ēa). (hist.) Grammar, rhetoric, and logic, forming the lower division (the other being the QUADRIVIUM) of the seven liberal arts in medieval schools. [see TRIVIAL]

tri·week·ly (trīwēk′lē) *adj.* & *adv.* (Occurring, appearing, etc.) every three weeks or three times a week.

-trix *suffix.* Forming fem. agent nouns corresponding to masc. nouns ending in *-tor* (*executrix, testatrix*).

tro·cha·ic (trōkā′ĭk) *adj.* Consisting of trochees, that is a trochee. ~ *n.* Trochee; (pl.) trochaic verse.

tro·chan·ter (trōkăn′ter) *n.* (anat., zool.) Prominence or protuberance (usu., as in man, two in number) in upper part of thigh bone, serving for attachment of certain muscles; (entom.) second joint of insect leg.

tro·che (trō′kē) *n.* Flat, usu. round, medicated tablet or lozenge.

tro·chee (trō′kē) *n.* (pros.) Metrical foot of two syllables, the first long or accented and the second short or unaccented (— ◡). [Gk. *trokhaios* (*pous*) running (foot) (*trekhō*, run)]

troch·i·lus (trŏk′ilus) *n.* (pl. **-li** pr. -lī). Small Egyptian bird said by ancients to pick teeth of crocodile; small bird, esp. hummingbird.

troch·le·a (trŏk′lēa) *n.* (pl. **-le·ae** pr. -lēē). (anat.) Pulley-like structure or arrangement of parts, as surface of inner condyle of humerus at elbow joint, with which ulna articulates, fibrous ring through which superior oblique muscle of eye passes etc. **troch′le·ar** *adj.* Of, connected with, a trochlea; ~ **nerve**, each of fourth pair of cranial nerves, motor nerves for trochlear muscles.

tro·choid (trō′koid) *n.* (geom.) Curve traced by a point on a circle rolling on a straight line, or by a curve rolling upon another curve; (anat.) pivot joint. ~ *adj.* (anat., of joint) In which one bone turns upon another with rotary motion. **tro·choi·dal** (trōkoi′dal) *adj.*

trod·den (trŏd′en) *adj.*: see TREAD; (esp., of path) formed by treading, beaten.

trog·lo·dyte (trŏg′lodīt) *n.* Cave dweller, cave man. **trog·lo·dyt·ic** (trŏglodĭt′ĭk) *adj.*

troi·ka (troi′ka) *n.* (Russian vehicle drawn by) three horses abreast; group of three persons, nations, etc. acting equally together to exert influence, control, etc. [Russ.]

Troi·lus (troi′lus, trō′i-). (Gk. legend) Son of Priam and Hecuba, killed by Achilles; in medieval legend, forsaken lover of CRESSIDA.

Tro·jan (trō′jan) *adj.* Of TROY or its inhabitants; ~ **horse**, see below; ~ **War**, (Gk. legend) siege of Troy by Greeks under Agamemnon, undertaken in order to recover his brother's wife, HELEN; it lasted ten years and ended in the destruction of Troy after the success of the stratagem of the ~ **horse**, a huge wooden figure of a horse concealing soldiers within it which the Greeks caused the Trojans to bring inside the city. **Trojan** *n.* 1. Native, inhabitant, of Troy. 2. Person of great energy, endurance, or bravery.

troll[1] (trōl) *v.* 1. Sing out in carefree spirit. 2. Fish for, fish in (water), fish, with rod and line and dead bait or with bait drawn along behind boat. **troll′er** *n.*

troll[2] (trōl) *n.* (Scand. myth.) One of race of supernatural beings formerly conceived as giants, later, in Denmark and Sweden, as dwarfs, inhabiting caves and subterranean dwellings.

trol·ley, trol·ly (trŏl′ē) *ns.* (pl. **-leys, -lies**). In streetcar etc., wheel running along overhead electric wire (~ **wire**), the wheel being mounted usu. on a pole (~ **pole**) down which current is conveyed to vehicle; ~ **bus**, bus with motive power derived from trolley; ~ **car**, streetcar.

trol·lop (trŏl′op) *n.* Slatternly woman, slut.

Trol·lope (trŏl′op), **Anthony** (1815–82). English novelist; author of *The Warden*, *Barchester Towers*, etc.

trom·bone (trŏmbōn′, trŏm′bōn) *n.* Large brass wind instrument, usu. of tenor or bass range, having a tube that is adjusted in

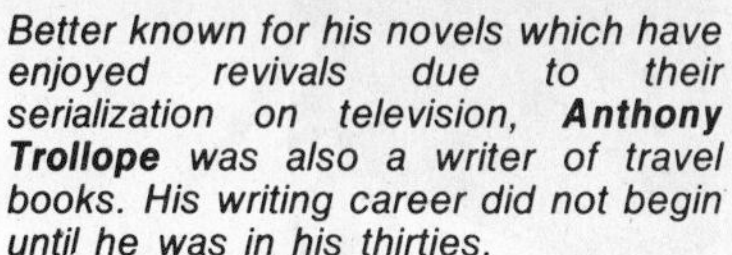

Better known for his novels which have enjoyed revivals due to their serialization on television, ***Anthony Trollope*** *was also a writer of travel books. His writing career did not begin until he was in his thirties.*

Outside the theater of war, ***troops*** *play an important part in ceremonial occasions, such as here at the opening of the new Parliament in Zimbabwe, formerly Rhodesia.*

length for different notes; organ reed stop of similar tone. **trom·-bon′ist** *n.*

trompe l'oeil (trŏmp′ lā′; *Fr.* trawn̂p löy′). Painting in which objects represented give the illusion of reality; also attrib. [Fr., = "deceives the eye"]

troop (trōōp) *n.* 1. Body of soldiers, esp. cavalry unit under a captain, artillery unit, or unit of armored vehicles; (pl.) armed forces; ~ **carrier**, aircraft or armored ground vehicle for transporting troops; **troop′ship, troop′train**, vessel, train, for conveyance of troops. 2. Number of persons or things collected together as a group. 3. Unit of Boy Scouts or Girl Scouts. **troop** *v.* Flock, assemble, move along in or as a troop; come or go in great numbers; ~ **the color**(**s**), (mil.) perform that part of ceremonial of mounting the guard in which the flag or colors are received.

troop·er (trōō′p*er*) *n.* Cavalryman, horse soldier; **state** ~, in U.S., member of police force operated by, and having authority throughout, a state; **swear like a** ~, swear vigorously and at length.

trope (trōp) *n.* Figurative (e.g. metaphorical, ironical) use of a word; (eccles.) phrase or verse introduced as embellishment into some part of the Mass.

-trope *comb. form.* Turning, changing in response to specific stimulus (*heliotrope*).

troph·ic (trŏf′ĭk) *adj.* (biol.) Of nutrition; ~ **nerves**, nerves concerned with or regulating nutrition of tissues.

troph·o·blast (trŏf′*o*blăst) *n.* Layer of cells enclosing embryo, serving to nourish it and (in mammals) to attach it to the wall of the uterus. **troph·o·blas·tic** (trŏf*o*-blăs′tĭk) *adj.*

tro·phy (trō′fē) *n.* (pl. **-phies**). (Gk. and Rom. antiq.) Arms or other spoils taken from enemy set up as memorial of victory, painted or carved figure of such memorial; (representation of) ornamental or symbolic group of objects; anything taken in war, hunting, etc., esp. if displayed as memorial token or evidence of victory, power, skill, etc.; prize, memento.

-trophy *comb. form.* Nourishment, growth (*hypertrophy, atrophy*).

trop·ic (trŏp′ĭk) *n.* Each of two circles of celestial sphere (northern ~ **of Cancer**, and southern ~ **of Capricorn**) parallel to equator and 23° 28′ north and south of it, where sun reaches its greatest declination north or south; each of two corresponding parallels of latitude on Earth's surface; (pl.) torrid zone, region lying between these parallels. **tropic** *adj.* Tropical; ~ **bird**, seabird of the chiefly tropical genus

The anemone fish is one of many bizarre ***tropical fish.*** *It is protected from predators by living amongst the poisonous anemones, to which it has developed an immunity.*

Phaethon, resembling terns, with webbed feet, rapid flight, and usu. white plumage marked with black.

trop·i·cal (trŏp′ĭk*a*l) *adj.* Of, occurring in, inhabiting, peculiar to, suggestive of, the tropics; (fig.) very hot, ardent, or luxuriant; ~ **cyclone**, cyclone that originates over tropical oceans and that can develop into severe disturbance known as hurricane, typhoon, or other names used in different regions; ~ **fish**, any of various small usually brightly colored fishes

*As its name suggests, the **tropic bird** is found mainly in the warmer parts of the world's oceans. It lives on fish and squid. The conspicuous tail streamers may be twice the body length.*

originating in tropical waters and kept in aquariums; ~ **year**: see YEAR, sense 1. **trop'i·cal·ly** *adv.*

tro·pism (trō'pĭzem) *n.* (biol.) Turning of organism or part of one in particular direction in response to external stimulus or automatically.

trop·o·pause (trŏp'*o*pawz) *n.* Boundary between the troposphere and the stratosphere.

trop·o·sphere (trŏp'*o*sfēr) *n.* Layer of atmosphere extending from surface of Earth to stratosphere, within which temperature falls with height. **trop·o·spher·ic** (trŏp*o*sfĕr'ĭk) *adj.*

trot (trŏt) *n.* Quadruped's gait between walk and gallop, in which legs move in diagonal pairs almost together; similar gait between walking and running of man etc.; (slang) = CRIB sense 7; **the ~s,** (slang) diarrhea. **trot** *v.* (**trot·ted, trot·ting**). (Make) go at a trot; cover (distance) by trotting; bring to specified condition by trotting; **~ out,** lead out and show off paces of (horse); (fig.) produce, bring forward.

troth (trawth, trōth) *n.* (archaic) Truth; faith, plighted word; **plight one's ~**: see PLIGHT[1].

Trot·sky (trŏt'skē), **Leon.** Lev Davidovich Bronstein (1877–1940), Russian revolutionary leader; advocate of world proletarian revolution; came into conflict with Stalin and was ordered to leave Russia 1929. **Trot'sky·ism, Trot'sky·ist** *ns.*

trot·ter (trŏt'*er*) *n.* (esp.) Horse specially bred and trained for trotting; animal's foot, esp. used for food.

trot·ting (trŏt'ĭng) **race.** Race at trotting pace between horses, each pulling a sulky on which the driver sits.

trou·ba·dour (trōō'b*a*dōr, -dōr, -door) *n.* One of a class of 11th–13th-c. lyric poets living in S. France, E. Spain, and N. Italy and singing in Provençal, chiefly of chivalry and gallantry. [Fr., f. Provençal *trobador*, f. *trobar* find, invent, compose in verse]

trou·ble (trŭb'*el*) *n.* Affliction, grief, vexation, bother, inconvenience; pains, exertion; thing or person that gives trouble; **get into, be in, ~,** incur censure, punishment, etc.; (euphem., of unmarried

*Fauna of the **tropical** regions are often much more vividly colored than their counterparts in cooler areas as exemplified by these sun-birds (above) from Africa.*

woman) become, be, pregnant; **troubled waters,** generally disturbed, agitated conditions; **trou'blemaker,** one who stirs up trouble, agitator; **trou'bleshooter,** person employed to trace and remove cause of defective working, discontent, etc. **trouble spot,** place where trouble frequently occurs. **trouble** *v.* (**-bled, -bling**). Disturb, agitate; distress, grieve; be disturbed or worried; subject, be subjected, to inconvenience or exertion.

trou·ble·some (trŭb'*el*s*o*m) *adj.* Causing trouble, vexatious. **trou'ble·some·ly** *adv.* **trou'ble·some·ness** *n.*

trough (trawf, trŏf) *n.* Long

*The popular concept of **tropical** areas being filled with lush vegetation applies only where there is high rainfall. The Sahara and Arabian deserts are also in the tropics; while in West Irian, there is perpetual snow on mountain peaks which are so high that the warmth of the sun has little or no effect.*

narrow open boxlike wooden or other receptacle for holding water or food for animals, kneading dough, washing ore, etc.; wooden or other channel for conveying liquid; hollow or valley resembling trough; (meteor.) elongated region of lower barometric pressure between two of higher; **feed at the public ~**, gain advantages over and above usual compensation for serving in public office.

trounce (trowns) *v.t.* (**trounced, trounc·ing**). Beat severely, castigate; defeat heavily; scold, abuse.

troupe (tro͞op) *n.* Company, troop, esp. of actors, acrobats, etc. **troup′er** *n.* 1. (esp.) Actor. 2. (colloq.) Person loyal to a task or enterprise even under adverse conditions.

trou·sers (trow′*zerz*) *n.* (usu. considered pl.) (also **pair of ~s**) Loose-fitting two-legged outer garment (sometimes sing.) extending (usu.) from waist to ankles.

trous·seau (tro͞o′sō, tro͞osō′) *n.* (pl. **-seaux, -seaus**). Bride's outfit of clothes etc.

trout (trowt) *n.* (pl. **trouts**, collect. **trout**). Any of various small usu. speckled freshwater fish of the salmon family and three genera (*Salmo, Salvelinus, Cristivomer*), inhabiting rivers and lakes of temperate or colder parts of N. hemisphere, fished for sport and esteemed as food.

trove (trōv): see TREASURE trove.

tro·ver (trōv*er*) *n.* (law) Finding and keeping of personal property; (also **action of ~**) action to recover value of personal property illegally converted by another to his own use.

ARCTIC CIRCLE
North America
Europe
Asia
TROPIC OF CANCER
India
Africa
EQUATOR
South America
TROPIC OF CAPRICORN
Australia
New Zealand
ANTARCTIC CIRCLE

*Left: Map showing the areas of the world encompassed by the **Tropics** of Capricorn and Cancer. In these regions, the sun is directly overhead on one or more days each year.*

trow (trow) *v.t.* (archaic) Think, believe.

trow·el (trow'*e*l) *n.* Flat-bladed tool with short handle used for spreading mortar etc.; gardener's short-handled tool with hollow scooplike blade. ~ *v.t.* (**-eled, -el·ing**; Brit. **-elled, -el·ling**). Spread, smooth, lay on, etc., (as) with trowel.

Troy (troi). Ancient city in NW. Asia Minor, besieged by the Greeks in the TROJAN War; believed to be a figment of Greek legend until its remains were excavated between 1870 and 1890 by Heinrich Schliemann at Hissarlik.

troy (troi) **weight.** System of weights (1 lb. = 12 ounces = 240 pennyweights = 5760 grains) used for precious metals etc. [prob. f. city of *Troyes* in France]

tru·ant (troo'*a*nt) *n.* One who absents himself from duty or business, esp. child who stays away from school without leave; **play ~**, act thus; **~ officer**, school official who deals with truants. **truant** *adj.* That plays truant or is a truant; shirking, idle, loitering, wandering. **tru'an·cy** *n.* (pl. **-cies**).

truce (troos) *n.* (Agreement for) temporary cessation of hostilities; respite or intermission from something disagreeable or painful. **truce'less** *adj.*

truck[1] (trŭk) *n.* 1. Barter; (system of) payment of wages otherwise than in money; (fig.) dealings, intercourse. 2. Small miscellaneous articles, sundries; odds and ends, trash, rubbish; vegetables raised for market, hence **~ crop(s), farming, farm**. **truck** *v.* Exchange, trade, barter; bargain, trade (*in*); pay or deal with on truck system.

truck[2] (trŭk) *n.* 1. Strong usu. four- or six-wheeled vehicle for heavy goods; **truck'driver** = TRUCKER, sense 2; barrowlike frame for moving luggage etc.; hand cart; set of wheels in framework for supporting whole or part of railroad car etc.; **truck'load**, full or nearly full load on truck; minimum weight of particular commodity legally qualified for shipment at rate below that charged for shipments weighing less than the minimum. 2. (naut.) Disk at top of mast with holes for halyards. **truck** *v.t.* Carry, convey, on truck. **truck'age** *n.* (Cost of) conveyance by truck(s).

The ***truffle*** *of Europe is esteemed by gourmets. However, as this fungus grows underground, it can only be obtained by specially trained dogs or pigs which locate it by its distinctive smell.*

truck·er (trŭk'*er*) *n.* 1. Person or company in business of trucking. 2. Person who owns and drives his own truck or serves as driver for trucking company. **truck'ing** *n.* Transportation of goods by truck.

truck·le (trŭk'*e*l) *v.i.* (**-led, -ling**). Submit obsequiously, cringe, (*to*). **truck'ler** *n.* [orig., = to sleep in truckle bed]

truck·le (trŭk'*e*l) **bed** = TRUNDLE bed.

truc·u·lent (trŭk'y*u*l*e*nt) *adj.* Showing ferocity or cruelty; aggressive, savage, harsh. **truc'u·lent·ly** *adv.* **truc'u·lence, truc'u·len·cy** *ns.*

trudge (trŭj) *v.* (**trudged, trudg·ing**). Walk laboriously, wearily, or without spirit, but steadily; perform (distance) thus. ~ *n.* Trudging; laborious or wearisome walk. **trudg'er** *n.*

trudg·en (trŭj'*e*n) *n.* (also **~ stroke**) Hand over hand or double overarm stroke in swimming with vigorous leg kicks. [f. John *Trudgen* (19th c.), English swimmer]

true (troo) *adj.* (**tru·er, tru·est**). 1. Consistent with fact or reality, not false or erroneous; **come ~**, be verified in experience, be fulfilled. 2. Agreeing with reason, correct principles, or recognized standard; real, genuine, correct, proper; not spurious, counterfeit, hybrid, or merely apparent; (of voice etc.) in good tune; conformable to the type; accurately placed, fitted, or shaped; (of ground etc.) level, smooth; **~ bill**, bill of indictment found by grand jury sufficiently well supported to justify hearing of case. 3. Steadfast in adherence (*to*), constant, loyal, faithful, sincere. 4. **~-blue**, (fig.) (person) of uncompromising loyalty or orthodoxy; **true'born'**, truly such by birth; **true'bred'**, of true or pure breed, thoroughbred; **true-life**, like what occurs in real life; corresponding to reality; **true** *adv.* Truly. *v.t.* (**trued, tru·ing** or **true·ing**) Make (piece of equipment etc.) true, adjust or shape accurately, make perfectly straight, smooth, level, etc. **true'ness** *n.*

truf·fle (trŭf'*e*l) *n.* Any of various edible fungi of genus *Tuber*, esp. the French *T. melanospora*, usu. shaped like petals, with black warty exterior and rich flavor, esteemed as delicacy. **truf'fled** *adj.*

tru·ism (troo'ĭz*e*m) *n.* Self-

Facing: To cater for anglers, especially in areas where the fish have been introduced, ***trout*** *farms have been established. This specimen leaps for its food at a New Zealand hatchery.*

Above: **Harry S. Truman** took office as President of the U.S.A. when Roosevelt died. He will always be remembered as the man who decided to drop an atom bomb on Japan.

Metal pieces forming triangular shapes, as in this **truss bridge** in New Mexico, form a highly stable structure capable of supporting heavy loads over a wide area.

evident truth, esp. of slight importance; hackneyed truth, platitude.

tru·ly (tro͞o′lē) *adv.* Sincerely, genuinely; faithfully, loyally; accurately, truthfully.

Tru·man (tro͞o′m*a*n), **Harry S.** (1884–1972). Thirty-third president of U.S., 1945–53; U.S. senator, 1933–45; U.S. vice president, 1945; formulator (1947) of the ~ **Doctrine**, providing military and economic aid to Greece and Turkey and to any nation "resisting attempted subjugation by armed minorities or outside pressures."

trump (trŭmp) *n.* (also **~s**) Playing card of suit ranking temporarily above other three; ~ **card**, card turned up to determine which suit shall be trumps; any card of this suit; (fig.) valuable resource, important means of doing something, gaining one's point, etc. **trump** *v.* Put trump on, take (trick, card) with trump; play trump, take trick with trump; excel, surpass, gain advantage; ~ **up**, fabricate, invent. **trumped-up** *adj.*

trump·er·y (trŭm′p*e*rē) *n.* (pl. **-er·ies**). Worthless stuff, trash, rubbish, nonsense. ~ *adj.* Showy but worthless, delusive, shallow. [Fr. *tromper* deceive]

trum·pet (trŭm′pĭt) *n.* Musical wind instrument of bright ringing tone, consisting of narrow cylindrical, usu. metal, straight or curved tube with bell and cup-shaped mouthpiece and now usu. with valves; organ reed stop with powerful trumpetlike tone; something shaped like trumpet, tubular corona of daffodil; sound (as) of trumpet, esp. elephant's loud cry; ~ **creeper**, creeper (*Campsis radicans*) of southern U.S., with large scarlet trumpet-shaped flowers; ~ **flower**, any of various plants with trumpet-shaped flowers; ~ **honeysuckle**, vine (*Lonicera sempervirens*) of eastern U.S. having tubular reddish blossoms; ~ **vine**, trumpet creeper; **trum′petweed**, any of several weedlike herbs, esp. of the genus *Eupatorium*. **trumpet** *v.* Proclaim (as) by sound of trumpet; celebrate, extol loudly; (of elephant) make loud sound as of trumpet.

trum·pet·er (trŭm′pĭt*e*r) *n.* 1. One who plays on or sounds trumpet, esp. cavalry soldier giving signals with trumpet. 2. Any of various large S. Amer. birds of genus *Psophia*, allied to cranes, with loud, harsh cry; ~ **swan**, large N. Amer. wild swan, *Olor buccinator*, with loud sonorous note.

trun·cate (trŭng′kāt) *adj.* Truncated. ~ *v.t.* (**-cat·ed, -cat·ing**). Cut short, cut off top or end of. **trun′cat·ed** *adj.* (esp.) (of cone or pyramid) With vertex cut off by plane section, esp. parallel to base; (of edge or solid angle) cut off by plane face, esp. one equally inclined to adjacent faces; (of crystal, solid figure, etc.) having such angles; (biol.) looking as if tip or end were cut off. **trun·ca·tion** (trŭngkā′sh*o*n) *n.*

trun·cheon (trun′ch*o*n) *n.* (chiefly Brit.) Short thick staff or club, esp. that carried by policeman. ~ *v.t.* Strike or beat with truncheon.

trun·dle (trŭn′d*e*l) *n.* 1. Small wheel; lantern wheel, device of two disks connected by cylinder of parallel staves that engage with teeth of cogwheel; roller with two arms for transmitting motion from stop knob of organ. 2. Trundling; ~ **bed**, low bed on wheels that can be pushed under another. **trundle** *v.* (**-dled, -dling**). (Cause to) roll; draw, be drawn, along on wheel(s) or in wheeled vehicle; walk with a rolling gait. **trun′dler** *n.*

trunk (trŭngk) *n.* 1. Main stem of tree as dist. from roots and branches; shaft of column; human or animal body (apart from head and limbs); main body or line of nerve, artery, etc., or of river, railroad, telegraph, telephone, road, or canal system, as dist. from branches; part of a fish between head and anus. 2. Box or chest with hinged lid for carrying clothes etc. while traveling; compartment in automobile for storing spare tire, luggage, etc. 3. Elephant's long flexible nose. 4. (pl.) Close-fitting shorts worn by swimmers, boxers, etc. 5. ~ **call**, (chiefly Brit.) long-distance telephone call involving use of trunk line; **trunk′fish** (pl. **-fishes**, collect. **-fish**), fish of *Ostracion* and related genera, with

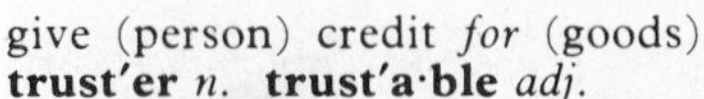

body of angular cross section and covered with bony hexagonal plates; **trunk line**, main line of railroad, telephone system, etc. **trunk'ful** *n.* (pl. **-fuls**). **trunk'less** *adj.*

trun·nion (trŭn'yon) *n.* Supporting cylindrical projection on each side of cannon; hollow structure supporting cylinder in steam engine and giving passage to steam. **trun'nioned** *adj.*

truss (trŭs) *n.* 1. Compact cluster of flowers growing on one stalk. 2. Supporting structure or framework of bridge, roof, etc.; large corbel, projecting from face of wall and freq. supporting cornice etc.; (naut.) tackle for securing yard to mast, metal ring around mast with pivoted attachment to yard at center; ~ **bridge**, bridge supported by trusses. 3. Surgical appliance, now usu. pad with belt or spring, for support in cases of hernia etc. **truss** *v.t.* 1. Tie (*up*), pack, in a bundle or parcel; tie, fasten (*up*) closely or securely; fasten limbs of (fowl etc. for cooking) to body with skewers etc.; (hist.) fasten (*up*) points or laces of (hose), tie up (points), tie up arms of (person). 2. Support or secure with truss(es). **truss'er** *n.*

trust (trŭst) *n.* 1. Confidence in, reliance on, some quality of person or thing, or truth of statement; confident expectation, hope; confidence in future payment for goods etc. supplied, credit; object of trust. 2. Condition of being trusted; obligation of one in whom confidence is placed or authority vested; (law) confidence reposed in person in whom legal ownership of property is vested to hold or use for benefit of another, property so committed, body of trustees; thing, person, duty entrusted to one or committed to one's care; **in** ~, entrusted to person or body of persons, held as trust; **investment** ~, company whose profits are drawn from investments distributed among a number of other companies and from the sale of these investments; ~ **account**, account of property opened with a trust company by depositor, to be distributed during his lifetime or after death; savings account in a bank with balance going to predesignated beneficiary upon death of depositor; ~ **company**, company formed or authorized to act as trustee or handle trusts; ~ **fund**, money, securities, etc., held in trust; ~ **territory**, one under trusteeship of (country designated by) the United Nations. 3. Illegal combination of producing or trading firms to reduce or defeat competition, control production and distribution, etc., esp. such a combination with central governing body holding majority or whole of stock of combining firms. **trust** *v.* Have faith or confidence (in); place trust in, rely or depend on; hope; believe (statement), rely on truthfulness, etc., of (person); commit care or safety of (thing) *to* or *with* person; place or allow to be *in* place or condition or *to do* something, without fear of the consequences; entrust to care, disposal, etc., of; give (person) credit *for* (goods). **trust'er** *n.* **trust'a·ble** *adj.*

trus·tee (trŭstē') *n.* Person to whom property is entrusted for benefit of another; one of number of persons appointed to manage affairs of an institution.

trus·tee·ship (trŭstē'shĭp) *n.* Position of a trustee; status of area for whose government another country is instructed by the United Nations to be responsible.

trust·ful (trŭst'*f*ul) *adj.* Full of trust, confiding. **trust'ful·ly** *adv.* **trust'ful·ness** *n.*

trust·wor·thy (trŭst'wẽrdhē) *adj.* Worthy of trust, reliable. **trust'wor·thi·ness** *n.*

trust·y (trŭs'tē) *adj.* (**trust·i·er, trust·i·est**). Trustworthy. **trust'i·ly** *adv.* **trust'i·ness** *n.* **trusty** *n.* (pl. **trust·ies**). Trustworthy convict granted special privileges.

truth (tro͞oth) *n.* (pl. **truths** pr. tro͞odhz). Quality, state, of being true; loyalty, honesty, accuracy, integrity, etc.; what is true, true statement or account, true belief or doctrine, reality, fact; ~ **or consequences**, game in which players are asked questions in turn by leader and, failing to reply or give correct answer, must pay penalty or forfeit; ~ **serum** (or **drug**), substance administered in supposition that it will make person tell the truth.

truth·ful (tro͞oth'*f*ul) *adj.* Habitually speaking truth, not deceitful; true. **truth'ful·ly** *adv.* **truth'ful·ness** *n.*

try (trī) *v.* (**tried, try·ing**). 1. Examine and determine (cause, question) judicially, determine

Found only in tropical forests in South America, the ***trumpeter*** *seldom flies although it roosts in trees. Eggs are laid in holes in a tree trunk and adults are chicken-sized.*

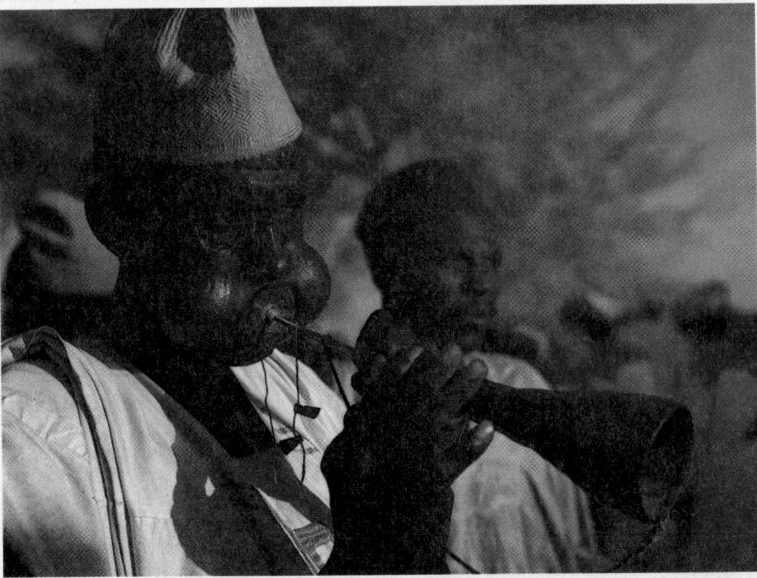

A Nigerian tribesman plays a traditional form of ***trumpet*** *at a gathering of his people. The earliest known designs of straight trumpets can be traced to the ancient Egyptians.*

*Tuba was the Roman name for a military trumpet. The modern **tuba** (above) which has the lowest notes of any brass wind instrument, only became used, in Germany, sometime after 1820.*

*Right: Actually a food storage stem, the **tuber** of many plants has been used by man for food. These include the potato, yam and Jerusalem artichoke. Inedible ones include the dahlia.*

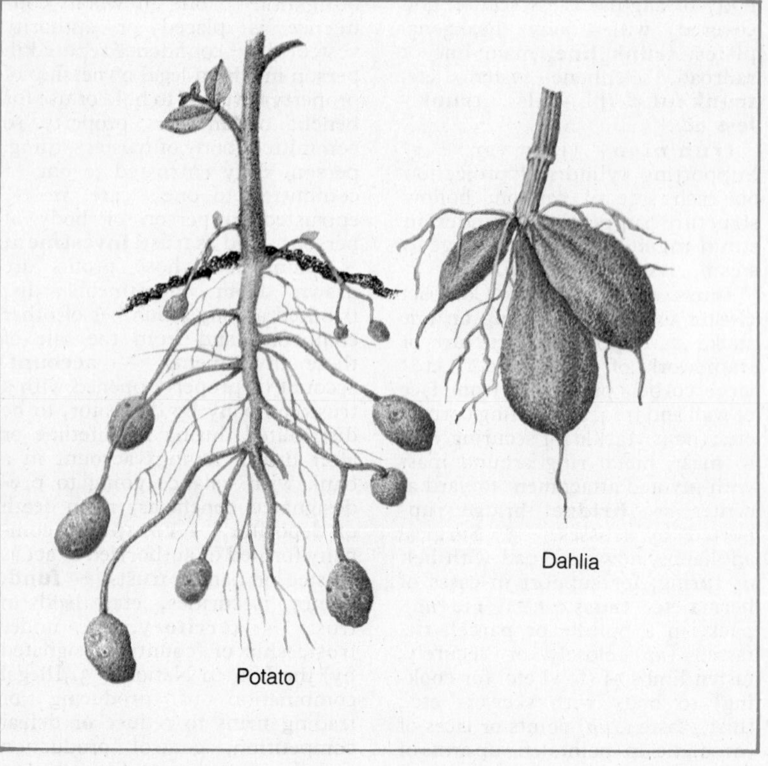

guilt or innocence of (accused person) by consideration of evidence; test (quality), test qualities of (person, thing) by experiment; test effect or operation of, experiment with; attempt to ascertain by experiment or effort; subject to severe test or strain, strain endurance or patience of; ~ **on**, test fit or style of (garment) by putting it on; ~ **out**, put to the test, test thoroughly. 2. Attempt to do, perform, or accomplish, essay; make an effort, endeavor, attempt; ~ **out for**, attempt to attain (object, position, etc.) or to reach (place); ~ **one's hand**, make attempt *at* for first time. 3. Dress (board etc.) to perfectly flat surface with plane. 4. (also ~ **out**) Extract (oil) from blubber or fat by heat, extract oil from (fat etc.) thus, render. 5. **try'out**, experimental run, esp. of a play or of an actor seeking to gain a role in a play; **try'sail**, small strongly made fore-and-aft sail used as substitute for normal sail in stormy weather; **try square**, carpenter's instrument of two straight edges fixed at right angles, for laying off short perpendiculars. **try** *n.* 1. Act of trying, attempt. 2. (football) (also ~ **for point**) attempt to score additional point(s) after touchdown by place-kicking or other means; **old college ~**, (colloq.) sincere attempt.

try·ing (trī'ĭng) *adj.* That tries; (esp.) exhausting; exasperating; difficult to bear. **try'ing·ly** *adv.*

tryp·a·no·some (trĭp'*a*nosōm, trĭpăn'*o*-) *n.* Parasite of *Trypanosoma* or allied genera of flagellate protozoa, infesting blood etc. of man and other animals and often causing disease. [Gk. *trupanon* borer, *soma* body]

tryp·sin (trĭp'sĭn) *n.* Enzyme present in pancreatic juice, converting proteins into peptones.

tryp·tic (trĭp'tĭk) *adj.* Of, produced by, trypsin.

tryst (trĭst) *n.* Appointed meeting, appointment, esp. by lovers. **tryst'ing place**, appointed place for secret meeting of lovers; rendezvous.

tsar, tzar, czar (zar̄, tsar̄) *ns.* 1. (hist.) Emperor, title assumed *c*1482 by Ivan Basilovich, Grand Duke of Muscovy, and used by emperors of Russia until 1917. 2. (usu. **czar**) Any person with great power or authority. **tsar'dom** *n.* [Russ. *tsar*, f. L. CAESAR]

tsar·e·vich, tzar·e·vitch, czar·e·vitch (zar̄'*e*vĭch, tsar̄'-) *ns.* (hist.) (Title of) son of tsar (in English usage, but erroneously, the eldest son and heir).

tsa·rev·na, tza·rev·na, cza·rev·na (zahrĕv'n*a*, tsah-) *ns.* (hist.) (Title of) daughter of tsar.

tsa·ri·na, tza·ri·na, cza·ri·na (zahrē'n*a*, tsah-) *ns.* (hist.) (Title of) empress of Russia.

tsar·ism, tzar·ism, czar·ism (zar̄'ĭzem, tsar̄'-) *ns.* (Devotion to, advocacy of) autocratic rule of tsars. **tsar'ist** *adj.* & *n.* **tsa·ris·tic** (zahrĭs'tĭk) *adj.*

tsa·rit·za, tza·rit·za, cza·rit·za (zahrĭt's*a*, tsah-) *ns.* Tsarina.

tset·se (tsĕt'sē, tsē'tsē) **fly.** Fly of genus *Glossina*, abundant in parts of central and southern Africa and carrying disease to men and animals, esp. *G. palpalis*, carrier of the trypanosome causing sleeping sickness.

tsp. *abbrev.* Teaspoon(ful).

tsu·na·mi (tso͞onah'mē) *n.* Unusually large wave produced by submarine earthquake. **tsu·na'·mic** *adj.*

Tswa·na (tswah'n*a*) *n.* (pl. **-nas**). 1. (Member of) a black people living between the Orange and Zambezi rivers in southern Africa. 2. Bantu language of this people.

Tu. *abbrev.* Tuesday.

tu·a·ta·ra (to͞oatah'r*a*) *n.* Large iguana-like reptile (*Sphaenodon punctatum*) peculiar to N.Z., having a dorsal row of yellow spines. [Maori]

tub (tŭb) *n.* Open cylindrical or slightly concave vessel, usu. of staves and hoops, with flat bottom; measure of capacity for butter or other commodities; (colloq.) bath; (joc.) slow clumsy ship; (mining) box or bucket for conveying coal etc. to surface; (derog.) short fat person. ~ *v.i.* (**tubbed, tub·bing**). (colloq.) Bathe or wash in tub.

tu·ba (to͞o'b*a*, tū'-) *n.* (pl. **-bas, -bae** pr. -bē). (mus.) Brass wind instrument, the bass of the horn family, usu. with wide conical bore and cup-shaped mouthpiece.

tub·by (tŭb'ē) *adj.* (**-bi·er, -bi·est**). Tub-shaped; short and fat, round, corpulent. **tub'bi·ness** *n.*

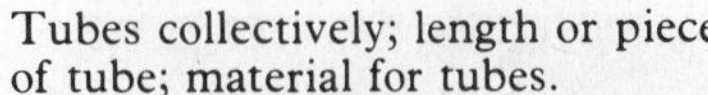

tube (to͞ob, tūb) *n.* 1. Long hollow cylinder esp. for conveying or holding liquids, pipe. 2. Main body of wind instrument. 3. Short cylinder of flexible metal with screw cap for holding semi-liquid substance, e.g. toothpaste, artists' paint. 4. Inner tube containing air in pneumatic tire. 5. Hollow cylindrical organ in animal body, as **bronchial** ~; ~ **foot**, one of the tubular projections on body of echinoderm, used for locomotion and grasping. 6. Cylindrical tunnel in which some railroads or subway trains run; such trains. 7. Vacuum tube. **tube'less** *adj.* (esp., of pneumatic tire) Having no inner tube. **tube** *v.* (**tubed, tub·ing**) Furnish with, enclose in, tube(s).

tu·ber (to͞o'b*er*, tū'b*er*) *n.* 1. Short, thick, more or less rounded, root or stem of plant, freq. bearing eyes or buds from which new plants may grow, as potato etc. 2. (anat.) Rounded swelling or protuberant part.

tu·ber·cle (to͞o'b*e*rk*e*l, tū'-) *n.* Small rounded projection or protuberance, esp. (path.) small rounded swelling on surface of body or in part or organ, esp. mass of granulation cells characteristic of tuberculosis; (bot.) small tuber, or root growth resembling this, small wartlike excrescence; ~ **bacillus**, bacillus *Myobacterium tuberculosis* causing tuberculosis. **tu·ber'cu·lar** *adj.*

tu·ber·cu·lin (to͞obẽr'ky*u*lĭn, tyo͞o-) *n.* Sterile liquid prepared from cultures of tubercle bacillus and used for diagnosis and treatment of tuberculosis, esp. in children and cattle; ~ **test**, injection of tuberculin under skin, causing inflammation in tuberculous subjects.

tu·ber·cu·lo·sis (to͞obẽrky*u*lō'-sĭs, tyo͞o-) *n.* Infectious disease in men and animals caused by tubercle bacillus and characterized by formation of tubercles in bodily tissues, esp. lungs (**pulmonary** ~). **tu·ber·cu·lous** (to͞obẽr'ky*u*-l*u*s) *adj.* (esp.) Affected with, of the nature of, tuberculosis.

tu·ber·ose (to͞o'b*e*rōs, tū'-) *adj.* Tuberous. ~ *n.* Tropical liliaceous plant (*Polianthes tuberosa*) with creamy white funnel-shaped fragrant flowers and tuberous roots. **tu·ber·os·i·ty** (to͞ob*e*rŏs'ĭtē, tū-) *n.* (pl. **-ties**). Tuberous formation or part; esp. (anat., zool.) large irregular projection of bone, usu. as attachment for muscle. [L. *tuberosus* tuberous]

tu·ber·ous (to͞o'b*e*r*u*s, tū'-) *adj.* Of the form or nature of a tuber; covered or affected with, bearing, tubers; ~ **root**, (esp.) root thickened so as to resemble tuber but bearing no buds.

tub·ing (to͞o'bĭng, tū'-) *n.* (esp.) Tubes collectively; length or piece of tube; material for tubes.

Tub·man (tŭb'm*a*n), **Harriet** (1820?–1913). Black Amer. abolitionist leader; best known for guiding many slaves to freedom via the underground railway.

tu·bu·lar (to͞o'by*u*l*er*, tū'-) *adj.* Tube-shaped; cylindrical, hollow, and open at one or both ends; constructed with, consisting of, tubes; ~ **skate**, ice skate having steel blade in aluminum tube. **tu'bu·lous** *adj.*

tu·bule (to͞o'būl, tū'-) *n.* Small tube, minute tubular structure in animal or plant.

tuck (tŭk) *n.* 1. Flattened fold in garment etc., secured by stitching, for ornament or to shorten the article. 2. (naut.) Part of vessel where ends of bottom planks meet under stern. 3. Tucking in of ends or edges, anything so tucked in; (*adj.*) (esp., of woman's blouse etc.) designed to be tucked into top of skirt etc. ~ *v.* 1. Put tuck(s) in, shorten or ornament with tuck(s); thrust or put (*away*) object into place where it is snugly held or concealed; thrust or turn (*in*) ends or edges of (anything pendent or loose, now esp. bedcovers) so as to retain or confine them; be so disposed of; draw together into small compass. 2. ~ **in, away**, (slang) eat heartily.

tuck·er[1] (tŭk'*er*) *n.* (esp.) Piece of lace, linen, etc., worn by women inside or around top of bodice in 17th–18th c. (now chiefly in **best bib and** ~, best clothing).

tuck·er[2] (tŭk'*er*) *v.t.* Tire (*out*), weary; **tuckered out**, exhausted, worn out.

Tu·dor (to͞o'd*er*, tū'-). 1. Name of English royal house from Henry VII to Elizabeth I, descended from Owen Tudor, who married Catherine, widowed queen of Henry V. 2. (attrib. or as adjective) Of the architectural style prevailing in England during the reigns of Tudors; of, resembling, imitating, the domestic architecture of this period, with much half-timbering, brickwork freq. in patterns, elaborate chimneys, many gables, rich oriel windows, much interior paneling and molded plasterwork etc.; ~ **arch**, flattened four-centered arch characteristic of the period.

Tues. *abbrev.* Tuesday.

Tues·day (to͞oz'dā, -dē, tūz'-) *n.* Third day of the week. [OE. *Tiwesdæg* (rendering L. *dies Martis*) f. *Tiw*, Germanic deity identified with MARS]

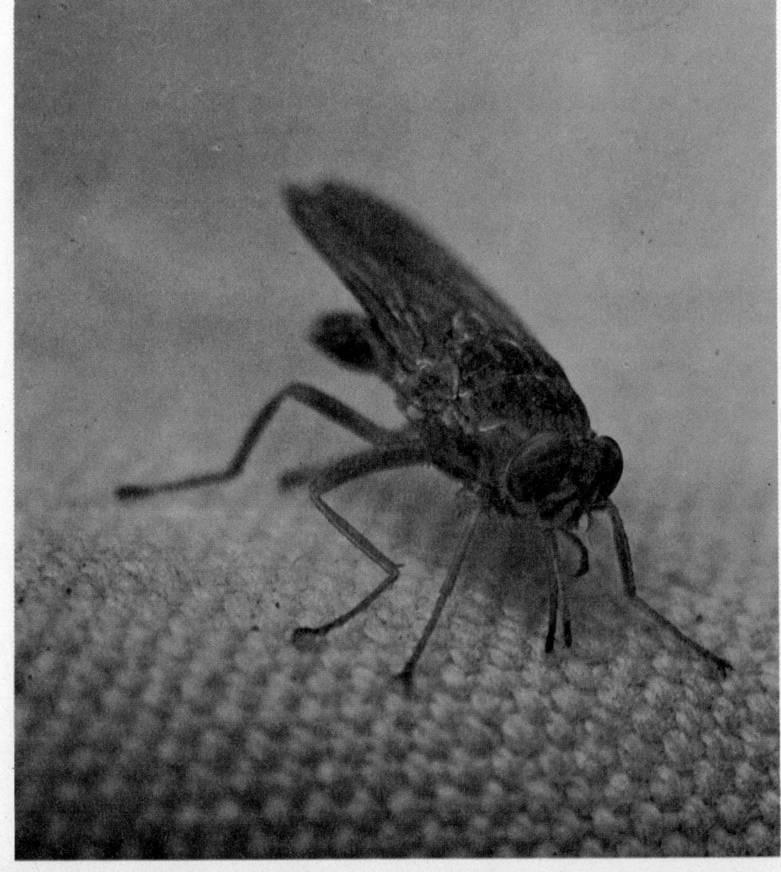

*Carrier of the deadly trypanosomes which cause sleeping sickness, the **tsetse fly** of Africa transfers these organisms to man. Its blood-sucking can also cause disease in cattle.*

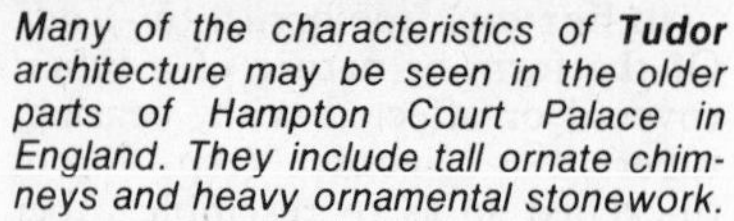

Many of the characteristics of ***Tudor*** *architecture may be seen in the older parts of Hampton Court Palace in England. They include tall ornate chimneys and heavy ornamental stonework.*

A modern high-powered ***tugboat*** *capable of maneuvering the largest ships into their berth in port. These boats may also be used to tow barges and for certain types of salvaging operations.*

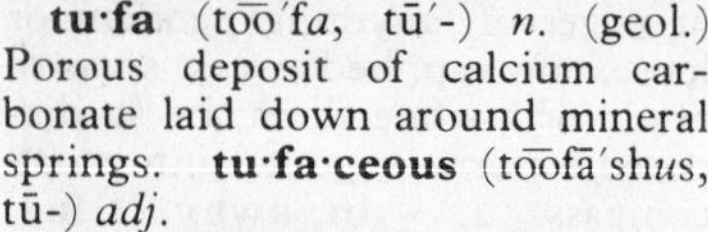

tu·fa (to͞o′fa, tū′-) *n.* (geol.) Porous deposit of calcium carbonate laid down around mineral springs. **tu·fa·ceous** (to͞ofā′sh*u*s, tū-) *adj.*

tuft (tŭft) *n.* Bunch, collection, of threads, grass, feathers, etc., held or growing together at the base. **tuft′y** *adj.* (**tuft·i·er, tuft·i·est**). **tuft** *v.t.* Furnish with tuft(s); (upholstery) secure padding of (mattress, cushion, etc.) with thread drawn through tightly at regular intervals, producing depressions in surface usu. ornamented with tuft or button. **tuft′ed** *adj.* (esp., of birds) Having tuft of feathers on head, crested; (of plants etc.) growing in tuft(s), clustered, bearing flowers in tufts; ~ **titmouse**, mouse-colored titmouse (*Parus bicolor*) ranging throughout E. and midwestern U.S. and having dull reddish-brown flanks and tufted crest on head.

tug (tŭg) *v.* (**tugged, tug·ging**). Pull with great effort or violently; make vigorous pull *at*; tow (vessel) by means of tugboat. ~ *n.* 1. Tugging, violent pull; ~ **of war**, decisive contest, struggle for supremacy; athletic contest between two teams hauling on rope, each team trying to pull other over line marked between them. 2. Trace, various other parts of harness; any chain, strap, or rope used for pulling. 3. (also **tug′boat**) Small, stoutly built, powerful vessel used to tow other vessels. **tug′ger** *n.*

Tui·ler·ies (twē′lerēz; *Fr.* twēlrē′). Royal palace on N. bank of Seine in Paris, begun 1564 by Catherine de Médicis and later joined by wings to Louvre; destroyed by fire 1871; ~ **Gardens**, grounds of the former palace, now a public park.

tu·i·tion (to͞oĭsh′*o*n, -tū-) *n.* Teaching, instruction, esp. as thing to be paid for; fee for this. **tu·i′tion·al, tu·i′tion·ar·y** *adjs.*

tu·la·re·mi·a, tu·la·rae·mi·a (to͞olerē′mē*a*) *ns.* Severe infectious bacterial disease of rodents, esp. rabbits, transmitted to man by contact with flesh of diseased animals or by insect bites and characterized by aches, irregular fever for several weeks, and inflamed lymph glands; also called rabbit fever. **tu·la·re′mic** *adj.*

tu·lip (to͞o′lĭp, tū′-) *n.* (Flower of) bulbous spring-flowering plant of genus *Tulipa*, esp. any of the numerous cultivated varieties, with showy bell-shaped or cup-shaped flowers of various colors and markings; ~ **orchid**, plant (*Cattleya citrina*) that grows in trees of tropical Amer., having single tulip-like yellow flower with white edges; ~ **tree**, large N. Amer. tree (*Liriodendron tulipifera*) with large greenish-yellow tuliplike flowers and soft white wood; any of various other trees with tuliplike flowers, as species of *Magnolia* etc.; **tu′lipwood**, light ornamental wood used for cabinetwork etc., of tulip tree; any of various colored and striped woods or trees producing these. [Turk. *tülbend-(lale)* turban (tulip)]

tulle (to͞ol) *n.* Thin soft fine silk, nylon, etc. net, used for dresses, veils, etc. [Fr., name of town]

Tul·ly (tŭl′ē). Familiar name for Marcus Tullius CICERO.

tum·ble (tŭm′b*e*l) *v.* (**-bled, -bling**). 1. (Cause to) fall, esp. helplessly or violently; roll, toss, wallow; move in headlong or blundering fashion; overthrow, demolish; be overthrown, fall into ruin; handle roughly, disorder, rumple, disarrange by tossing; (fig.) stumble, blunder (*on, into*); ~ **to**, understand, grasp (esp. something hidden or not clearly expressed). 2. Perform leaps, somersaults, and other acrobatic feats; (of spaceship etc.) turn end over end in flight. 3. **tum′blebug**, dung beetle that rolls up balls of dung in which to lay its eggs; **tum′bledown**, falling or fallen into ruin, dilapidated; **tum′bleweed**, any of various plants that in late summer are broken off and blown along by wind in light globular rolling mass. **tumble** *n.* Fall; tumbled condition, confused or tangled heap.

tum·bler (tŭm′bl*e*r) *n.* (esp.) 1. One who does somersaults, handsprings, etc., acrobat. 2. Variety of domestic pigeon turning over and over backward in flight. 3. Kind of tapering cylindrical or barrel-shaped drinking cup or (now usu.) glass without handle or foot, orig. with rounded or pointed bottom so that it would not stand upright, now with flat usu. heavy bottom. 4. Pivoted plate through which mainspring acts on hammer of gunlock; pivoted piece in lock that must be moved into proper position by key etc. before lock can be opened; any of various mechanisms or parts, as projecting piece on revolving shaft for operating another piece, movable part of tumbler gear, revolving barrel for washing hides, etc. 5. ~ **gear**, gear with one or more idle wheels on swinging frame for producing reverse motion.

tum·bling (tŭm′blĭng) **barrel.** Rotating drum in which small articles are cleaned and polished by attrition.

tum·brel, tum·bril (tŭm′brel) *ns.* 1. Dump cart, esp. for dung. 2. Cart in which condemned persons were carried to the guillotine during the French Revolution. 3. (archaic) Ammunition cart.

tu·me·fy (tōō′mefī, tū′-) *v.* (**-fied, -fy·ing**). (Cause to) swell; make, become, tumid, turgid, or bombastic. **tu·me·fac·tion** (tōōmefăk′shon, tū-) *n.*

tu·mes·cent (tōōmĕs′ent, tū-) *adj.* Swelling up, becoming tumid. **tu·mes′cence** *n.*

tu·mid (tōō′mĭd, tū′-) *adj.* Swollen, swelling, morbidly affected with swelling; inflated, turgid, bombastic. **tu′mid·ly** *adv.* **tu·mid·i·ty** (tōōmĭd′ĭtē, tū-) *n.*

tum·my (tŭm′ē) *n.* (pl. **-mies**). (esp. nursery) Stomach.

tu·mor (tōō′mer, tū′-) *n.* Abnormal or morbid swelling, overgrowth; BENIGN ~, MALIGNANT ~: see these words. **tu′mor·ous** *adj.*

tu·mult (tōō′mult, tū′-) *n.* Commotion of a multitude, esp. with confused cries and uproar, public disturbance, riot, insurrection; commotion, agitation, disorderly or noisy movement, confused and violent emotion. **tu·mul·tu·ous** (tōōmŭl′chōōus, tū-) *adj.* **tu·mul′tu·ous·ly** *adv.* **tu·mul′tu·ous·ness** *n.*

tun (tŭn) *n.* Large cask or barrel for wine, beer, etc.; measure of capacity, usu. 252 wine gallons.

tu·na (tōō′na) *n.* (pl. **-nas**, collect. **-na**). Any of various large fishes of the family *Scombridae* found in tropical and temperate seas; **yellowfin** ~, an albacore, *Thunnus albacares*.

tun·a·ble (tōō′nabel, tū′-): see TUNE.

tun·dra (tŭn′dra) *n.* Vast level treeless region of N. Europe, Asia, and N. Amer., with arctic climate and vegetation (chiefly mosses and lichens with dwarf shrubs etc.).

tune (tōōn, tūn) *n.* Rhythmical succession of musical tones, air, melody with or without harmony; being in proper pitch, correct intonation in singing or instrumental music; harmony or accordance in respect to vibrations other than those of sound; **call the** ~, have control of events; **change one's** ~, sing another tune, assume a different style of language or manner, e.g. change from insolent to respectful tone; **in, out of** ~, in or out of the proper pitch or correct intonation; in or out of order or proper condition, (not) correctly adjusted; in or out of harmony (*with*); **to the** ~ **of**, to the (considerable or exorbitant) amount or sum of; **tune′smith**, (colloq.) composer or arranger of popular music; **tune-up** (*n.*), adjusting of engine to improve operating efficiency. **tune**

Though it may appear desolate, such as here in the Rocky Mountains National Park, ***tundra*** *is home to a wide variety of plant and animal life.*

The ***tulip*** *was first brought to western Europe from Constantinople in 1556. Within 100 years tulip-breeding became an obsession and very large sums were paid for a bulb.*

Native to the eastern U.S.A. a ***tulip-tree*** *can attain a height of 200 ft. and a trunk diameter of 12 ft. The timber was used for cabinet-making and was known as whitewood or yellow poplar.*

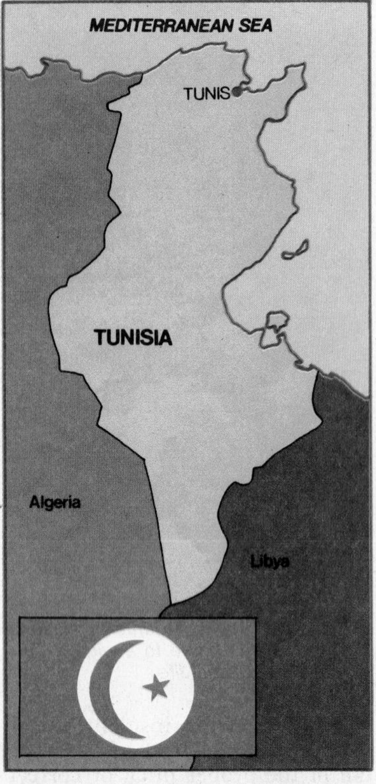

v. (**tuned, tun·ing**). Adjust tones of (musical instrument) to standard of pitch, put in tune; attune, bring into accord or harmony; bring into proper or desirable condition; adjust (engine etc.) to run smoothly and efficiently, (radio receiver) to desired wavelength etc.; ~ **in**, adjust (radio receiver) to receive transmission; ~ **out**, cut off (radio signal) by tuning receiver; ~ **up**, bring (instrument) up to proper pitch, adjust instruments for playing together; bring (engine etc.) into most efficient working order by esp. fine adjustments. **tun'a·ble, tune'a·ble** *adjs.* **tun·a·bil·i·ty** (to͞on*a*bĭl'ĭtē, tū-) *n.* **tun'a·bly** *adv.*

tune·ful (to͞on'f*u*l, tūn'-) *adj.* Melodious, musical. **tune'ful·ly** *adv.* **tune'ful·ness** *n.*

tune·less (to͞on'lĭs, tūn'-) *adj.* Untuneful, unmusical; not in tune; songless, silent. **tune'less·ly** *adv.* **tune'less·ness** *n.*

tun·er (to͞o'n*e*r, tū'-) *n.* 1. (esp.) One whose occupation is to tune pianos or organs. 2. Electronic circuit or similar device in radio receiver that selects signals of given frequency for amplifying and converting to sound.

tung·sten (tŭng'st*e*n) *n.* (chem.) Heavy steel-gray ductile metallic element, melting only at a very high temperature, occurring in combination in wolfram and other minerals, and used for electric light filaments, electric contacts, sparkplug points, hard steel alloys, etc.; symbol W (*wolfram*), at. no. 74, at. wt. 183.85. **tung·sten·ic** (tŭngstĕn'ĭk), **tung'stic** *adjs.* [Swed. *tung* heavy, *sten* stone]

Above: An oasis in the southern part of ***Tunisia*** *which borders the Sahara. The main exports are phosphates and crude oil. There is a fertile region in the north bounding the sea.*

tung (tŭng) **tree.** Subtropical Asian tree (*Aleurites fordii*) widely cultivated for its seeds, which yield tung oil, used in paints, varnishes, etc.

tu·nic (to͞o'nĭk, tū'-) *n.* 1. Ancient Greek and Roman short-sleeved body garment reaching almost to knees. 2. Close-fitting short coat of police or military uniform. 3. Woman's loose garment for upper part of body; belted frock worn by women and children at games. 4. (anat., zool.) Membranous sheath or lining of organ or part; (bot.) integument of seed etc.

tu·ni·cate (to͞o'nĭkĭt, -kāt, tū'-) *n.* Member of the subphylum Urochordata, having body enclosed in a hard test and, at least in larval stage, a notochord. ~ *adj.* 1. (zool.) Enclosed in a sheath; of the tunicates. 2. (bot.) Consisting of a series of concentric layers, as a bulb.

tun·ing (to͞o'nĭng, tū'-) **fork.** Small two-pronged steel instrument giving definite musical note of constant pitch when struck.

Tu·nis (to͞o'nĭs, tū'-). Seaport and capital of Tunisia, in the NE. part on the Mediterranean.

Tu·ni·sia (to͞onē'zh*a*, -sh*a*, -nĭzh'*a*, -nĭsh'*a*). Republic in N. Africa between Algeria and Libya; formerly a French protectorate; independent 1956; capital, Tunis. **Tu·ni'sian** *adj.* & *n.*

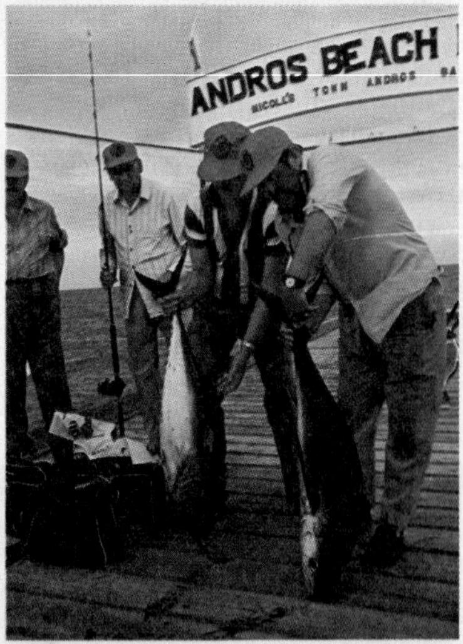

Big game fishermen with their catch of ***tunny*** *or tuna in the Bahamas. These specimens are small but the larger species may weigh up to 1800 lb. The smaller ones are canned for eating.*

tun·nel (tŭn'*e*l) *n.* Subterranean passage under hill, river, roadway, etc.; subterranean passage dug by burrowing animal; level or nearly level passage in mine etc.; ~ **of love**, amusement park ride made up of dark, narrow tube through which travel small boats or cars, usu. occupied by couples; ~ **vision**, vision defective in lateral directions. **tunnel** *v.* (**-neled, -nel·ing**). Make tunnel, make tunnel through. **tun'nel·er** *n.*

Turbans are worn today by several religious groups, including Sikhs and Muslims. In the latter group, however, this has not been an obligation since the early 19th century.

Below: Cross-section of the **Great St. Bernard Tunnel** showing how the air within this 7.25 mile road beneath Mont Blanc is kept fresh and how exhaust fumes are extracted.

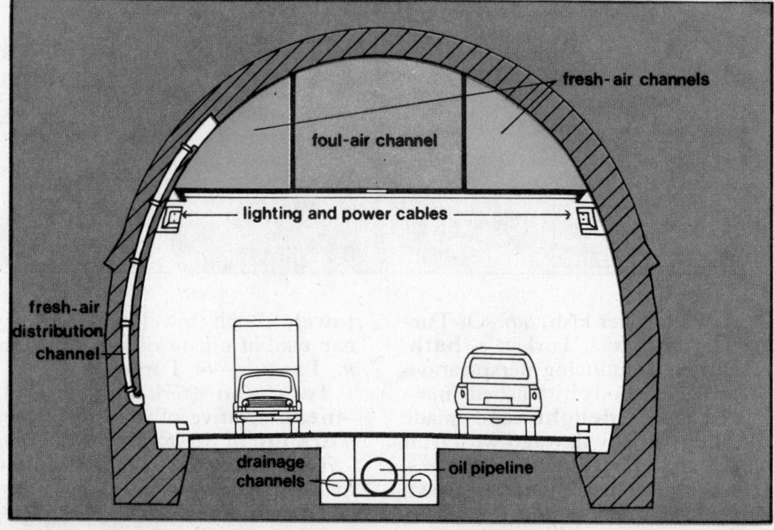

tun·ny (tŭn′ē) *n.* (pl. **-nies**, collect. **-ny**). (chiefly Brit.) Tuna.

tu·pe·lo (to͞o′pelō) *n.* (pl. **-los**). Any of various large N. Amer. trees of genus *Nyssa*, growing in swamps or on river banks in southern U.S.; wood of this.

tur·ban (tẽr′ban) *n.* Oriental men's headdress of Muslim origin consisting of cap with long band or scarf of linen, cotton, or silk wound around it; woman's hat of scarf wound or twisted around. [Turk. *tülbend*]

tur·bid (tẽr′bĭd) *adj.* Muddy, thick, not clear; (fig.) confused, disordered. **tur′bid·ly** *adv.* **tur·bid·i·ty** (tẽrbĭd′ĭtē), **tur′bid·ness** *ns.*

tur·bi·nate (tẽr′bĭnĭt, -nāt), **tur·bi·nat·ed** (tẽr′bĭnātĭd) *adjs.* (of shell) Spiral with whorls decreasing rapidly in size; (bot.) inversely conical; ~ **bone,** (anat.) one of scroll-like bones of the nose.

tur·bine (tẽr′bĭn, -bīn) *n.* Motor in which rotary motion is produced by a fluid (water, steam, gas, etc.) impinging directly upon a series of vanes on the circumference of a revolving cylinder or disk, used to drive a ship, aircraft, generators for electric power, etc.

turbo- *prefix.* Turbine, in compounds forming the name of machines driven by a turbine, or that are themselves turbines, as **tur′bofan**; **tur′bojet**, power unit of a jet-propelled aircraft; aircraft with turbojet engine; jet produced by a gas turbine.

tur·bot (tẽr′bot) *n.* (pl. **-bots**, collect. **-bot**). Large European flat fish (*Scophthalmus maximus*) much esteemed as food; (loosely) any of various similar fish.

tur·bu·lent (tẽr′byulent) *adj.* Disturbed, in commotion, disorderly, troubled, stormy; tumultuous, unruly, violent. **tur′bu·lent·ly** *adv.* **tur′bu·lence** *n.*

Tur·co·man = TURKOMAN.

turd (tẽrd) *n.* (vulg.) (Lump or piece of) excrement.

tu·reen (to͝orēn′, tyo͞o-) *n.* Deep covered dish from which soup is served.

turf (tẽrf) *n.* (pl. **turfs, turves**). Covering of grass etc. with matted roots, forming surface of grassland; sod; (slang) area defended by street gang as its own private territory; **the** ~, grassy course used for horse racing; institution, action, or practice of horse racing. **turf′y** *adj.* (**turf·i·er, turf·i·est**). **turf** *v.t.* Cover (ground) with turf.

Tur·ge·nev (to͝orgĕn′yĕf), **Ivan Sergeevich** (1818–83). Russian novelist; author of *Fathers and Sons*, *Virgin Soil*, etc.

tur·gid (tẽr′jĭd) *adj.* Swollen, distended, puffed out; (fig., of language) pompous, bombastic. **tur′gid·ly** *adv.* **tur·gid·i·ty** (tẽr-

Inhabitants of Iran and the southern U.S.S.R., ***Turkoman*** *horse dealers are renowned, as are the rugs made by their nomadic groups and then sold in the cities.*

Right: A coppersmith at Istanbul reflects the traditional crafts of ***Turkey.*** *The nation is mainly agricultural with large exports of tobacco, cotton, nuts and raisins. It is also a major source of chrome and other minerals.*

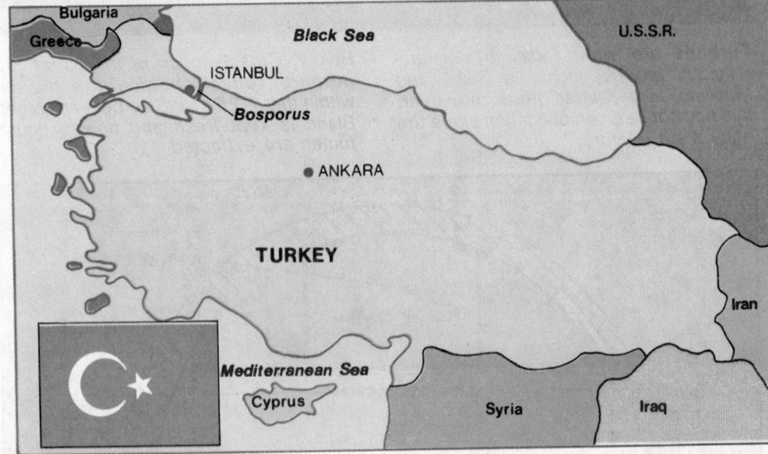

jĭd′ītē), **tur·ges·cence** (tẽrjĕs′*e*ns) *ns.* **tur·ges′cent** *adj.*

tur·gor (tẽr′g*e*r) *n.* (bot.) Rigidity due to uptake of water into living cells or tissues.

Turk (tẽrk) *n.* 1. Native of Turkey; (hist.) native or inhabitant of the Ottoman Empire. 2. Member of a people speaking a Turkic language.

Tur·key (tẽr′kē). Country of Asia Minor and Europe, formerly part of the Ottoman Empire, declared a republic in 1923; capital (since 1923), Ankara.

tur·key (tẽr′kē) *n.* (pl. **-keys,** collect. **-key**). Large gallinaceous bird of the Amer. genus *Meleagris*, with handsome plumage and naked wattled head, esp. *M. gallopavo*, found domesticated in Mexico in 16th c. and highly esteemed as table fowl, esp. for Thanksgiving feast; ~ **cock**, male of turkey; ~ **trot**, ragtime ballroom dance in vogue during World War I; ~ **vulture**, Amer. carrion vulture (*Cathartes aura*) with dark plumage and naked reddish head and neck (also ~ **buzzard**). [short for *turkey cock*, orig. guinea fowl, so-called f. being orig. imported through Turkey]

Tur·ki (tẽr′kē, toor′-) *adj.* & *n.* (Of, belonging to) a group of Ural-Altaic languages and peoples, including Turkish. **Tur′kic** *adj.*

Turk·ish (tẽr′kĭsh) *adj.* Of Turkey or the Turks; Turkic; ~ **bath**, steam bath, inducing perspiration, after which body is washed, massaged, etc.; ~ **delight**, candy made of lumps of jelly flavored with fruit juice and dusted with sugar; ~ **tobacco**, aromatic tobacco grown esp. in Turkey and Greece; ~ **towel**, rough towel with a long nap usu. of uncut loops. **Turkish** *n.* Language of Turkey.

Turk·man (tẽrk′m*a*n) *n.* (pl. **-men**). Native of Turkmenistan. **Turk·me·ni·an** (tẽrkmē′ne*a*n) *adj.*

Turk·men (tẽrk′m*e*n) *n.* Turkoman language.

Turk·me·ni·stan (tẽrkm*e*nĭstăn′, -stahn′). Constituent republic (properly *Turkmen Soviet Socialist Republic*) of U.S.S.R. lying between the Caspian Sea and Afghanistan; capital, Ashkhabad.

Tur·ko·man, Tur·co·man (tẽr′k*o*man) *ns.* (pl. **-men**). Member of a group of tribes of E. Turkic stock, living chiefly in Turkmenistan and parts of Iran and the Caucasus; Ural-Altaic language of these tribes; ~ **carpet, rug**, soft richly colored carpet made by them. [Pers. *turkumān* Turk-like person]

tur·mer·ic (tẽr′merĭk) *n.* East Indian herb (*Curcuma longa*) of ginger family; pungent aromatic rhizome of this, used as condiment, esp. as chief ingredient in curry powder and as yellow dye.

tur·moil (tẽr′moil) *n.* Agitation, commotion, trouble.

turn (tẽrn) *v.* 1. Move on or as on axis; give rotary motion to, receive such motion; shape (clay on wheel) to form pottery; execute (somersault etc.) with rotary motion; change from one side to another; invert, reverse; (fig.) revolve mentally; ~ **the tables**, (*on* person, or absolute) reverse relations (between), esp. pass from inferior to superior position; ~ **the tide**, (fig.) reverse trend of events. 2. Give new direction to, take new direction; adapt, be adapted; ~ **one's hand to**, undertake (task of new kind). 3. Move to other side of, go around, flank; pass around (*flank* etc. of army) so as to attack from flank or rear; cause to go, send, put. 4. Change in nature, form, condition, etc.; esp. change for the worse; (cause to) become; (of milk) (cause to) become sour. 5. Shape (object, material) in lathe; (of material) lend itself to treatment in lathe; give (esp. elegant) form to. 6. ~ **about**, turn so as to face in a new direction; ~ **against**, become hostile to; ~ **around**, face about; change to opposite opinion, state of mind, etc.; (of ship) discharge cargo and be ready for new voyage; ~ **down**, fold down; place upside down or face downward; reduce flame of (gas, lamp, etc.) by turning tap etc.; reject (proposal, offer, etc.); ~ **in**, fold inward; incline inward; (colloq.) go to bed; ~ **off**, check flow of (water, electricity, etc.) by turning tap, switch, etc.; (slang) cause to lose interest; ~ **on**, allow passage to (water, electricity, etc.) by turning tap etc.; depend upon; face hostilely, become hostile to; (slang) begin using illegal drugs; (slang) introduce to illegal drugs; (slang) arouse interest of; ~ **out**, expel; (cause to) point or incline outward; produce; put (contents) out of room, pocket, etc.; appear publicly; discharge from employment; extinguish (light) by turning switch etc.; (cause to) assemble for duty etc.; get out of bed; be found, prove to be so; ~ **over**, reverse, invert; (cause to) fall over, upset, hand over, make over, transfer; do business to amount of; ~ **to**, apply oneself to, set about; begin work; ~ **up**, turn (playing card) face upward; disinter; appear; happen; fold (cloth, hem, etc.); uncover, find; increase; ~ **upon**, become hostile to (someone). 7. **turn′buckle,** coupling with internal screw thread(s) for connecting metal rods, regulating their length, etc.; **turn button**, small pivoted bar engaging with catch, edge of door, etc.; **turn′coat**, one who changes his principles or party, renegade; **turn′down**, turned-down part of anything; (*adj.*) made to wear with upper part turned down; **turn′key**, (pl. **-keys**), jailer; one in charge of keys of prison; **turn′off**, small road branching off from larger one, esp. exit ramp from main highway; **turn′out**, (esp.) assemblage, muster; (style of) equipment, outfit, array; **turn′over**, kind of pie or tart in which filling is laid on half of rolled-out pastry and other half is turned over it; amount of money or merchandise turned over in business; **turn′pike**, (hist.) spiked barrier across road or passage, as defense against attack; (hist.) toll gate; (hist.) road with gates for collection of tolls; main road, highway; **turn′spit**, spit; (hist., freq. contempt.) man or boy who turned spit upon which meat was cooked; **turn′stile**, post with four radiating arms revolving horizontally as person passes through, in gateway, door, etc., similar device with mechanism for registering number passing through; **turn′table**, revolving platform, table, stand, etc., esp. one for reversing railroad cars or other wheeled vehicles; circular horizontal rotating platform that supports record or phonograph.

turn *n.* 1. Turning; rotation, esp. single revolution of wheel etc.; (single) coil or twist. 2. (mus.) Ornament consisting of note above principal note, note itself, note below and note itself, performed instead of principal note or after it. 3. Change of direction or course, change of position by rotary movement; curved or bent part of anything, bend, angle; turning back (esp. ~ **of the tide**). 4. Change, alteration; change of color, condition, etc.; (colloq.) momentary shock caused by sudden alarm etc. 5. Act of good or ill will, (**good, bad,** ~, service, disservice); attack of illness, faintness, etc. 6. Opportunity, occasion, privilege, obligation, etc., coming successively to each of several persons, etc.; public appearance on stage before or after others; **in** ~, in succession ; ~ **(and ~) about**, in turn. 7. Character, tendency, disposition, formation. 8. **at every** ~, con-

*The ocellated **turkey** is found only in Central America and has brighter plumage than the common variety of North America. This bird has minor differences in behavior from the others.*

tinually; **done to a ~**, done (esp. cooked) to just the right degree; **out of ~**, not in correct order; at an unsuitable time or in an unsuitable manner; **take ~s**, work etc. alternately.

turn·er[1] (tẽr′ner) *n.* (esp.) One who works with a lathe. **turn′er·y** *n.* (pl. **-er·ies**). Use of lathe; objects fashioned on lathe; turner's workshop.

turn·er[2] (tẽr′ner) *n.* Gymnast or tumbler, esp. one who belongs to a turnverein.

Tur·ner (tẽr′ner), **Nat** (1800–1831). Black Amer. slave leader; leader of slave uprising, Nat Turner's Rebellion, 1831.

turn·ing (tẽr′nĭng) *n.* (esp.) 1. Use of, art of using, lathe. 2. Place where road, path, etc., turns or turns off from another; such road; **~ point**, point at which decisive change takes place.

tur·nip (tẽr′nĭp) *n.* Either of two biennial cruciferous plants (*Brassica rapa* and *B. napobrassica*) with fleshy globular and spheroid root, toothed leaves, and yellow flowers; root of these, used as vegetable.

turn·ver·ein (tẽrn′verīn) *n.* Club of turners or gymnasts.

tur·pen·tine (tẽr′pentīn) *n.* Yellowish viscous liquid oleoresins, usu. solidifying on exposure (many varieties acc. to source, most having the same composition, $C_{10}H_{16}$), obtained from various coniferous trees; (also **oil of ~**) colorless or yellowish volatile inflammable oil, of pungent smell and taste, distilled from turpentines and used in mixing paints and varnishes etc.

tur·pi·tude (tẽr′pĭtōōd, -tūd) *n.* Baseness, depravity, wickedness.

turps (tẽrps) *n.* (colloq.) (Oil of) turpentine.

tur·quoise, tur·quois (tẽr′koiz, -kwoiz) *ns.* Opaque or translucent sky blue or blue-green hydrous aluminum phosphate found esp. in Persia and valued as gem; (also **~ blue**) brilliant greenish-blue color of turquoise. [OF. (*pierre*) *turquoise* Turkish (stone)]

tur·ret (tẽr′ĭt, tŭr′-) *n.* Small or subordinate tower, esp. rounded addition to angle of building, freq. commencing at some height above ground; (mil., nav.) towerlike armored usu. revolving structure in which guns are mounted in fort or tank or (usu.) warship; structure housing guns in aircraft; (mech.) rotating holder for various dies or cutting tools in lathe, drill, etc. **tur′ret·ed** *adj.*

tur·tle (tẽr′tel) *n.* (pl. **-tles**, collect. **-tle**). Reptile of any of the marine species (in U.S. also freshwater species) of the order Chelonia resembling tortoise but with limbs compressed into flippers or paddles; flesh of certain turtles as food, much used for soup; **turn ~**, turn over, capsize; **tur′tleback, tur′tledeck**, arched structure over part of deck of vessel to protect it from heavy sea; **tur′tleneck**, high close-fitting neck of knitted garment.

tur·tle·dove (tẽr′teldŭv) *n.* 1. Wild dove of genus *Streptopelia*, esp. the common European *S. turtur* with cinnamon-brown plumage and white-tipped tail feathers, noted for its soft cooing and affection for its mate. 2. = MOURNING DOVE. 3. Sweetheart.

tur·tle·head (tẽr′telhĕd) *n.* Any of several plants (genus *Chelone*), esp. *C. glabra* of eastern N. Amer., having tubular white or pink flowers; also called snakehead.

Tus·can (tŭs′kan) *adj.* Of Tuscany; (archit.) of the Tuscan order, simplest of the classical orders. **~** *n.* Native, inhabitant, language, of Tuscany.

Tus·ca·ny (tŭs′kanē). Region of W. central Italy.

Tus·ca·ro·ra (tŭskarōr′a, -rōr′a) *n.* (pl. **-ras**, collect. **-ra**). Indian of tribe orig. of North Carolina, but since admission to Iroquois confederacy living mainly in New York.

tush[1] (tŭsh) *int.*, *n.*, & *v.i.* (archaic) (Make) exclamation of impatient contempt.

tush[2] (tŭsh) *n.* Long pointed tooth, esp. horse's canine tooth; small or stunted tusk in some Indian elephants.

tusk (tŭsk) *n.* Long pointed tooth projecting beyond mouth in certain animals, as elephant, wild boar, etc.; tusklike thing, as long protruding tooth, kind of tenon, etc. **~** *v.t.* Dig (*up*), tear, wound, with tusk; furnish with tusks. **tusked** *adj.*

tus·sle (tŭs′el) *n.* & *v.i.* (**-sled, -sling**). Struggle, scuffle.

tus·sock (tŭs′ok) *n.* Tuft, clump, small hillock, of grass. **~ moth**, moth with larva covered with long tufts of hair. **tus′sock·y** *adj.*

Tut·ankh·a·men (tōōtahnkah′-men) (14th C B.C.). Egyptian king of XVIIIth dynasty who died at age of 18; successor and son-in-law of Akhnaton; his tomb at Karnak, containing remarkable treasures, was excavated in 1922.

tu·te·lage (tōō′telĭj, tū′-) *n.* Guardianship, being under this; instruction, tuition. **tu′te·lar** *adj.*

tu·te·lar·y (tōō′telĕrē, tū′-) *adj.* Serving as protector, guardian, or patron, esp. of particular person, place, etc.; of a guardian, protective.

tu·tor (tōō′ter, tū-) *n.* 1. Private teacher, esp. one having general charge of person's education; (in some Brit. universities) graduate (usu. fellow of a college) directing studies of undergraduates assigned to him; college teacher ranking below instructor. 2. (Rom. law) Guardian of a minor. **tu′tor·age, tu′tor·ship** *ns.* **tu·to·ri·al** (tōōtōr′ēal, -tōr′-, tū-) *adj.* Of a tutor. **~** *n.* Period of individual instruction given to small group or single student. **tutor** *v.* Act as tutor (to); exercise restraint over, subject to discipline.

tut·ti-frut·ti (tōō′tēfrōō′tē) *n.* & *adj.* (Preserve) made of or flavored with various fruits. [It., = "all fruits"]

tu·tu (tōō′tōō) *n.* Dancer's short skirt made of layers of stiffened frills.

Tuvalu (Tōōvah′lōō). Republic in the central Pacific Ocean, of nine islands.

tu-whit to-whoo (tōō hwĭt′ tōō hwōō′). (Make) cry of owl. [imit. of cry of owl]

tux·e·do (tŭksē′dō) *n.* Dinner jacket; man's evening dress including this. [name of fashionable country club at *Tuxedo* Park, N.Y.]

TV (tēvē′) *abbrev.* (pl. **TVs, TV's**). Television; terminal velocity.

TVA, T.V.A. *abbrevs.* Tennessee Valley Authority.

twad·dle (twŏd′el) *n.* & *v.i.* (**-dled, -dling**). (Indulge in) senseless, silly, or trifling talk or writing, (talk) nonsense. **twad′dler** *n.*

Left: The ***green turtle,*** *Chelonia mydas.*

The ***turret*** *of a warship is an armored, revolving structure, often with the purpose of protecting the breech of a large gun.*

DO NOT CLIMB
ON TURRET

twain (twān) *adj.* & *n.* (archaic) Two.

Twain (twān), **Mark.** Pseudonym of Samuel Langhorne Clemens (1835–1910), Amer. humorist, author of *Tom Sawyer* (1876), *Huckleberry Finn* (1884), etc. [call of leadsmen taking soundings on Mississippi where Clemens served as a pilot; = second mark on cable, i.e. 2 fathoms]

twang (twăng) *n.* Sharp ringing sound (as) of taut string of musical instrument or bow when plucked; nasal intonation; distinctive, esp. local, peculiarity of pronunciation. ~ *v.* (Cause to) make twanging sound; play on stringed instrument; utter, speak, with twang. **twang'y** *adj.*

tweak (twēk) *n.* Twist, sharp pull, pinch. ~ *v.t.* Seize and pull sharply with twisting movement, pull at with jerk, twitch.

tweed (twēd) *n.* Twilled woolen (or woolen mixture) cloth of usu. rough surface, dyed, freq. in several colors, before weaving. **tweed'y** *adj.* (**tweed·i·er, tweed·i·est**). [formerly a trademark originating in a misreading of *tweel*, Sc. form of TWILL, influenced by name of river Tweed, Scotland]

twee·dle·dum and twee·dle·dee (twēdeldŭm' *an* twēdeldē'). Two persons or things differing only or chiefly in name, orig. applied to the composers Handel and Bononcini in a satire by John Byrom containing the lines "Strange all this Difference should be Twixt Tweedledum and Tweedledee!"

'tween (twēn) *prep.* Between; ~ **decks**, (space) between decks.

tweet (twēt) *n.* & *v.i.* (Utter) note of small bird.

tweez·ers (twē'zerz) *n.pl.* (also **pair of** ~) Small pincerlike instrument for taking up small objects, plucking out hairs, etc. **tweeze** *v.t.* (**tweezed, tweez·ing**). Use, pull out with, tweezers.

twelfth (twĕlfth) *adj.* Next after 11th; **T~-day, -night**, 12th day after Christmas, Jan. 6, feast of Epiphany, formerly last day of Christmas festivities and observed as time of merrymaking. **twelfth** *n.* Twelfth part (see PART[1] sense 1); twelfth thing etc.

twelve (twĕlv) *adj.* Amounting to 12. ~ *n.* One more than 11 (12, xii, or XII).

twen·ty (twĕn'tē) *adj.* Amounting to 20. ~ *n.* Cardinal number, twice 10 (20, xx, or XX); set of 20 things or persons; **twenties**, numbers etc. from 20 to 29; these years of century or life. **twen'ti·eth** *adj.* & *n.* **twen'ty·fold** *adj.* & *adv.*

twice (twīs) *adv.* Two times; on two occasions; doubly, in double degree or quantity.

***Twilight** creates many dazzling effects, such as here on the St. Lawrence Seaway near Massena, New York State, where the subtly diffused light plays on the water.*

twid·dle (twĭd'el) *n.* Slight twirl, quick twist; twirled mark or sign. ~ *v.* (**-dled, -dling**). Trifle (with); twirl idly, play with idly or absently; ~ **one's fingers, thumbs**, keep turning them idly around each other (for lack of occupation); be idle. **twid'dly** *adj.* **twid'dler** *n.*

twig (twĭg) *n.* Small shoot or branch of tree or plant.

twi·light (twī'līt) *n.* Light diffused by reflection of sun's rays between daybreak and sunrise or (usu.) sunset and dark; period of this; faint light; (fig.) condition of imperfect knowledge, understanding, etc.; **T~ of the Gods**, (transl. Ger. *Götterdämmerung*; Icel. *ragna rökkr*, orig. *ragna rök* judgment of the gods) in Scand. and Ger. myth., destruction of the gods and the world in conflict with the powers of evil; hence (fig.) complete downfall of a regime etc.; ~ **sleep**, (formerly) partial narcosis for dulling pains of childbirth.

twi·lit (twī'lĭt) *adj.* Dimly illuminated (as) by twilight.

twill (twĭl) *n.* (Textile fabric with) surface of parallel diagonal ribs produced by passing filling threads over 1 and under 2 or more (not 1 as in plain weaving) warp threads. ~ *v.t.* Weave with twill (esp. in past part.). **twilled** *adj.* [Sc. and north. variant of obs. *twilly*, OE. *twili*, f. OHG. *zwilîh*, after L. *bilix* (*licium* thread)]

twin (twĭn) *adj.* Forming, being one of, a closely related pair, esp. of children born together; (bot.) growing in pairs; consisting of 2 closely connected and similar parts; **twin'flower**, species of *Linnaea* (*L. borealis* of northern Europe and Asia and *L. americana* of northern N. Amer.), prostrate plants with fragrant flowers growing in pairs; **twin-screw**, (esp., of steamer) having two screw propellers on separate shafts and revolving in opposite directions. **twin** *n.* One of two children or young carried simultaneously in uterus and born at short interval (FRATERNAL, IDENTICAL, ~**s**: see these words); each of closely related pair; exact counterpart of person or thing; **T~ Cities**, Minneapolis and St. Paul, Minnesota, in the SE. part, in the N. central U.S.; **the Twins**: see GEMINI. **twin** *v.* (**twinned, twin·ning**). Bear twins; join intimately together, couple, pair.

twine (twīn) *n.* Strong thread or string of two or more strands of hemp, cotton, etc., twisted together, used for sewing coarse materials, tying packages, making nets, etc.; twining or trailing stem, spray, etc.; coil, twist. ~ *v.* (**twined, twin·ing**). Twist (strands) together to form twine, make (thread) thus; form (garland etc.) by interlacing; wreathe, clasp, twist; coil, wind; (of plant) grow in twisting or spiral manner.

twinge (twĭnj) *n.* Sharp darting pain. ~ *v.* (**twinged, twing·ing**).

twi·night (twī′nīt) *adj.* (baseball) Of, pertaining to, designating, doubleheader that starts late in the afternoon and continues into the evening under lights. **twi′night·er** *n.* A twinight baseball game.

twin·kle (twĭng′kel) *v.* (**-kled, -kling**). Shine with rapidly intermittent light, sparkle, glitter; emit (light etc.) thus; wink, blink, quiver; move to and fro, in and out, etc., rapidly, flit, flicker; **in the twinkling of an eye, in a twinkling**, in an instant. **twinkle** *n.* Wink, blink; twitch, quiver; intermittent or transient gleam. **twin′kler** *n.*

twirl (twẽrl) *v.* Revolve rapidly, spin, whirl; turn (one's thumbs etc.) around and around idly, twiddle; twist, coil. ~ *n.* Whirling, twirling; anything that twirls, curved line, whorl of shell, etc. **twirl′er** *n.*

twist (twĭst) *v.* Wind (strands etc.) one about another; form (rope etc.) thus; interweave; give spiral form to (rod, column, etc.) as by rotating ends in opposite directions; receive, grow in, spiral form; cause (ball, esp. in baseball) to rotate while following curved path; wrench out of natural shape, distort. ~ *n.* 1. Thread, rope, etc., made by winding two or more strands etc. about one another; kinds of strong silk thread and of cotton yarn; roll of bread, tobacco, etc., in form of twist. 2. Act of twisting, condition of being twisted; manner or degree in which thing is twisted; peculiar tendency of mind, character, etc.; twisting strain, torque; angle through which thing is twisted; dance involving rhythmic gyrations. **twist′a·ble** *adj.*

twit (twĭt) *v.t.* (**twit·ted, twit·ting**). Reproach, upbraid, taunt.

twitch (twĭch) *v.* Pull with light jerk, pull at, jerk at, esp. to call attention; (of features, muscles, etc.) move or contract spasmodically. ~ *n.* Sudden sharp pull or tug, jerk; sudden involuntary, usu. slight, contraction. **twitch′er** *n.*

twitch (twĭch) **grass**: see COUCH².

twit·ter (twĭt′*er*) *v.* (of bird) Utter succession of light tremulous notes, chirp continuously (freq. fig., of person); utter, express, thus. ~ *n.* Twittering; state of tremulous excitement.

'twixt (twĭkst) *prep.* (poet.) Betwixt.

two (tōō) *adj.* Amounting to 2; ~ **or three**, a few; **two-bagger, -base hit**, (baseball) hit enabling batter to reach second base; double; **two-bit**, costing 25 cents; (fig.) petty; **two-by-four**, 2 (inches, feet) by 4, hence (colloq.) small, cramped; (*n.*) length of lumber 2 by 4 inches before trimming and, usu., approximately 1⅝ inches by 3⅝ inches trimmed; **two-dimensional,** having height and width; (of literary work) superficial, unconvincing; **two-edged**, having two cutting edges; (fig.) cutting both ways, ambiguous; **two-faced**, having two faces; deceitful, insincere; **two′fer**, (colloq.) card or coupon entitling bearer to buy theater tickets etc. at reduced price; **two-fisted**, (colloq.) vigorous; **two′fold**, double, doubly; **two-handed**, wielded with both hands; worked or wielded by hands of two persons; (of card game etc.) for two persons; **twopence** (tŭp′*e*ns), (Brit.) sum of two pence; **two′-penny**, (tŭ′p*e*nē) (Brit.) worth, costing, twopence; paltry, trifling; **two-piece**, of a suit of clothes or woman's bathingsuit comprising two separate parts; **two-ply**, of two strands, layers, or thicknesses; **two′some**, two people, couple; **two-step**, ballroom dance with sliding steps in ²⁄₄ time; **two-time** (*v.t.*) (**-timed, -tim·ing**), (slang) deceive; **two-way**, (esp.) allowing passage of fluid in either of two directions; **two-way switch**, device by which electric current can be switched on or off at either of two points. **two** *n.* One more than 1; symbol for this (2, ii, or II); card, die face, or domino with two pips; two o'clock; size etc. indicated by 2; set of two things or persons; **put ~ and ~ together**, draw inference from facts.

twp *abbrev.* Township.

TWX *abbrev.* Teletypewriter exchange.

TX *abbrev.* Texas.

-ty¹ *suffix.* Forming nouns denoting quality or condition (*cruelty, plenty, safety*).

-ty² *suffix.* Tens (*twenty, sixty, ninety*, etc.)

ty·coon (tīkōōn′) *n.* Business magnate. [Jap. *taikun* great lord, title applied by foreigners to shogun of Japan 1854–68 (Chin. *ta* great, *kuin* prince)]

ty·ing (tī′ĭng): see TIE.

tyke (tīk) *n.* Dog, cur; child, esp. young boy.

Ty·ler (tī′l*er*), **John** (1790–1862). Tenth president of U.S., 1841–5.

tym·bal = TIMBAL.

tym·pan (tĭm′p*a*n) *n.* 1. Appliance in printing press interposed between platen etc. and sheet to be printed to equalize pressure, in hand presses usu. double frame covered with sheets of parchment or strong linen, with packing of blanket, rubber, etc., between. 2. (archit.) TYMPANUM.

tym·pa·ni = TIMPANI.

A model of **twins** *in the uterus. The ones shown may be known as fraternal and result from two eggs being fertilized at the same time. Identical twins come from a single egg which divides.*

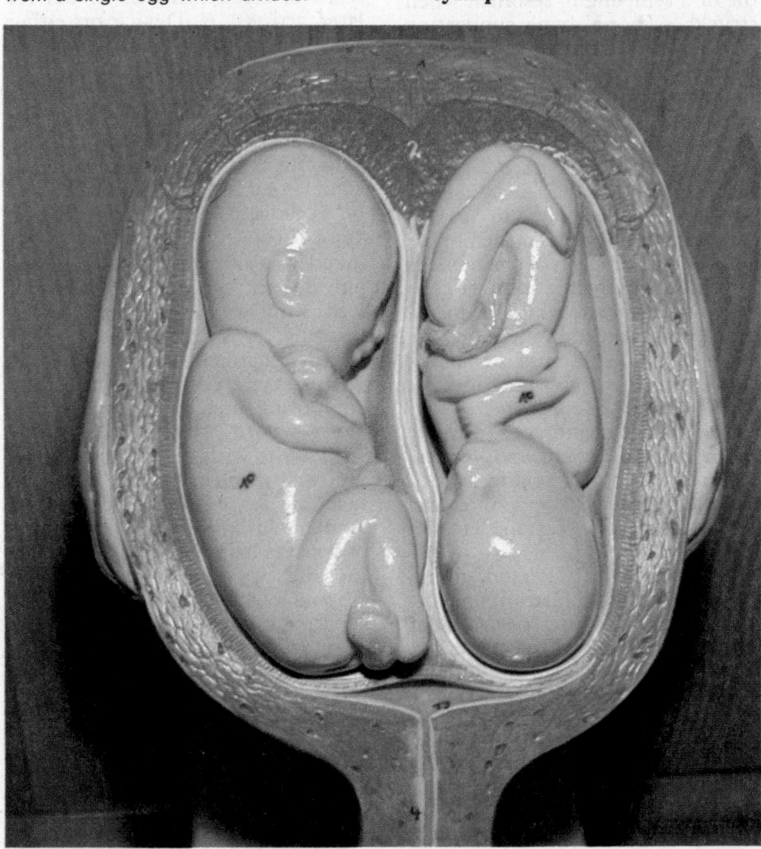

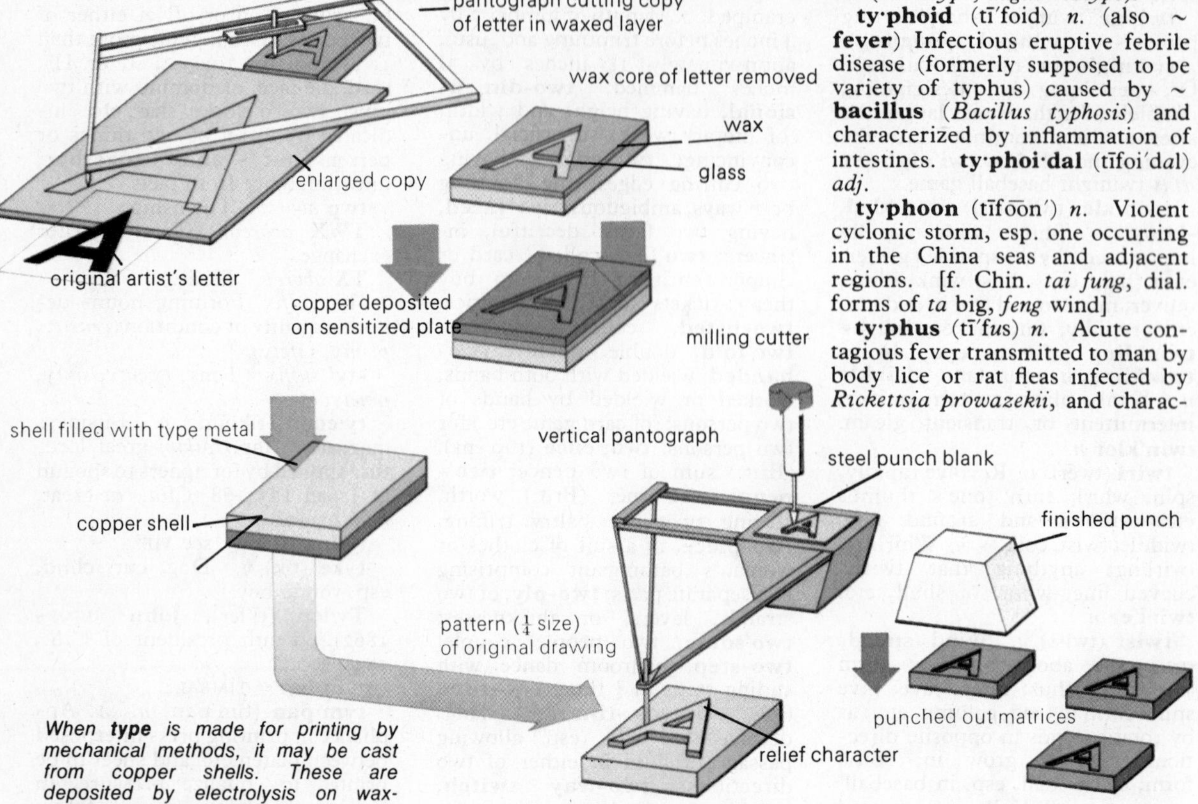

When ***type*** *is made for printing by mechanical methods, it may be cast from copper shells. These are deposited by electrolysis on wax-coated glass on which the letter was originally inscribed. Other methods are also used.*

tym·pan·ic (tĭmpăn′ĭk) *adj.* Of the or a tympanum; resonant when struck; ~ **bone**, bone supporting tympanic membrane; ~ **membrane**, thin membrane closing middle ear and serving to transmit vibrations from air to inner ear.

tym·pa·num (tĭm′p*a*n*u*m) *n.* (pl. **-nums, -na** pr. -n*a*). 1. (anat.) Eardrum, middle ear, cavity in temporal bone filled with air, closed externally by tympanic membrane and containing chain of small bones by which sound vibrations are conveyed to inner ear; tympanic membrane; similar membrane in insects covering organ of hearing in leg etc.; (ornith.) bony labyrinth at base of trachea in some ducks with resonant membranes in walls. 2. (archit.) (also **tympan**) Vertical recessed face (usu. triangular) of pediment; space between lintel and arch of door etc., carving etc. on this.

type (tīp) *n.* 1. Person, thing, event, serving as illustration, symbol, or characteristic specimen, of another thing or of a class. 2. General form, character, etc., distinguishing particular class or group; kind, class, as distinguished by particular character. 3. (biol.) Species or genus regarded as most complete example of essential characteristics of genus, family, etc., and from which family etc. is named. 4. Biblical event regarded as symbolic or as foreshadowing a later one. 5. Object, conception, work of art, serving as model for later artists. 6. Device on either side of medal or coin. 7. Small block, usu. of metal or wood, with raised letter, figure, etc., on its upper surface for use in printing; (collect.) set, supply, kind, of these. 8. **type′casting**, assignment (of actor) in certain type of role because of predisposing characteristics; **type′face**, (impression made by) inked part of type, set of types in one design; **type metal**, alloy of lead, antimony, and tin from which printing types are cast; **type′script**, (matter) written with typewriter; **type′setter**, compositor; composing machine; **type′write** (*v.*) (**-wrote, -writ·ten, -writ·ing**), write with typewriter; **type′writer**, mechanical or electrical machine for writing in characters similar to those of print, the characters being produced by striking the paper through an inked ribbon by steel types arranged on separate rods or on a wheel or ball and actuated by striking corresponding keys on a keyboard. **type** *v.* (**typed, typ·ing**). 1. Be a type of, typify. 2. Determine type or group of, classify acc. to type. 3. Write with typewriter.

-type *comb. form.* 1. Type, example, model (*prototype*). 2. Printing type, photographic process (*monotype, daguerreotype*).

ty·phoid (tī′foid) *n.* (also ~ **fever**) Infectious eruptive febrile disease (formerly supposed to be variety of typhus) caused by ~ **bacillus** (*Bacillus typhosis*) and characterized by inflammation of intestines. **ty·phoi·dal** (tīfoi′d*a*l) *adj.*

ty·phoon (tīfōōn′) *n.* Violent cyclonic storm, esp. one occurring in the China seas and adjacent regions. [f. Chin. *tai fung*, dial. forms of *ta* big, *feng* wind]

ty·phus (tī′f*u*s) *n.* Acute contagious fever transmitted to man by body lice or rat fleas infected by *Rickettsia prowazekii*, and characterized by eruption of rose-colored spots, extreme prostration, and usu. delirium. **ty′phous** *adj.*

typ·i·cal (tĭp′ĭk*a*l) *adj.* Serving as type, symbol, or representative specimen, symbolical, emblematic; distinctive, characteristic. **typ′i·cal·ly** *adv.* **typ′i·cal·ness** *n.*

typ·i·fy (tĭp′ĭfī) *v.t.* (**-fied, -fy·ing**). Represent by type or symbol, foreshadow; serve as type or example of. **typ·i·fi·ca·tion** (tĭpĭfĭkā′sh*o*n), **typ′i·fi·er** *ns.*

typ·ist (tī′pĭst) *n.* One who uses a typewriter.

ty·po (tī′pō) *n.* (pl. **-pos**). (colloq.) Mistake in printing or typewriting; typographical error.

ty·pog·ra·phy (tīpŏg′r*a*fē) *n.* Art, practice, of printing from types; style, appearance, of printed matter. **ty·pog′ra·pher** *n.* **ty·po·graph·ic** (tīp*o*grăf′ĭk), **ty·po·graph′i·cal·ly** *adv.*

ty·pol·o·gy (tīpŏl′*o*jē) *n.* 1. Classification of archaeological remains etc. according to type. 2. Doctrine, interpretation, of biblical types and antitypes, study of these. **ty·po·log·i·cal** (tīp*o*lŏj′ĭk*a*l) *adj.* **ty·po·log′i·cal·ly** *adv.*

ty·ran·ni·cal (tĭrăn′ĭk*a*l, tī-) *adj.* Acting like, characteristic of, a tyrant; despotic, arbitrary, oppressive, cruel. **ty·ran′ni·cal·ly** *adv.* **ty·ran′ni·cal·ness** *n.*

ty·ran·ni·cide (tĭrăn′ĭsīd, tī-) *n.* Killer, killing, of tyrant. **ty·ran·ni·cid·al** (tĭrănĭsī′d*a*l, tī-) *adj.*

tyr·an·nize (tĭr′anīz) *v.* (**-nized, -niz·ing**). Play the tyrant; rule despotically or cruelly (*over*).

ty·ran·no·saur (tĭrăn′osŏr, tī-) **ty·ran·no·saur·us** (tĭrănosŏr′us, tī-) *ns.* Fossil dinosaur (*Tyrannosaurus rex*), largest known carnivore, which walked erect on hind feet, of late Cretaceous period of N. Amer.

tyr·an·nous (tĭr′anus) *adj.* Ruling or acting tyrannically; oppressive, unjustly severe or cruel. **tyr′an·nous·ly** *adv.*

tyr·an·ny (tĭr′anē) *n.* (pl. **-nies**). 1. Government of, nation ruled by, tyrant or absolute ruler. 2. Oppressive or despotic government; arbitrary or oppressive exercise of power; tyrannical act or behavior.

ty·rant (tī′rant) *n.* 1. (Gk. hist.) Absolute ruler who seized sovereign power without legal right; (despotic) usurper. 2. Oppressive, unjust, or cruel ruler, despot; person exercising power or authority arbitrarily or cruelly. 3. ~ **flycatcher**, bird of Amer. passerine family Tyrannidae.

Tyre (tīr). (Arab. *Sur*) Ancient seaport of the Phoenicians on Lebanon coast.

Tyr·i·an (tĭr′ēan) *adj.* Of Tyre or its inhabitants; ~ **purple**, purple dye made from shellfish by the Tyrians and exported by them to ancient Greece and Rome. **Tyrian** *n.* Native, inhabitant, of Tyre.

ty·ro, ti·ro (tī′rō) *ns.* (pl. **-ros**). Beginner or learner in anything, novice.

Tyr·ol, Tir·ol (tĭr′ol, tĭrōl′). Alpine province of W. Austria, the S. part of which was ceded to Italy after World War I. **Tyr·o·lese, Tir·o·lese** (tĭrolēz′, -lēs′) *adjs.* & *ns.* (pl. **-lese**).

tzar = TSAR.

tzi·gane (tsĭgahn′) *adj.* Of the Hungarian gypsies or their music. ~ *n.* Hungarian gypsy.

***John Tyler** served as President from 1841-1845, gaining office after the death of W. H. Harrison. He tended to follow the philosophies of Thomas Jefferson.*

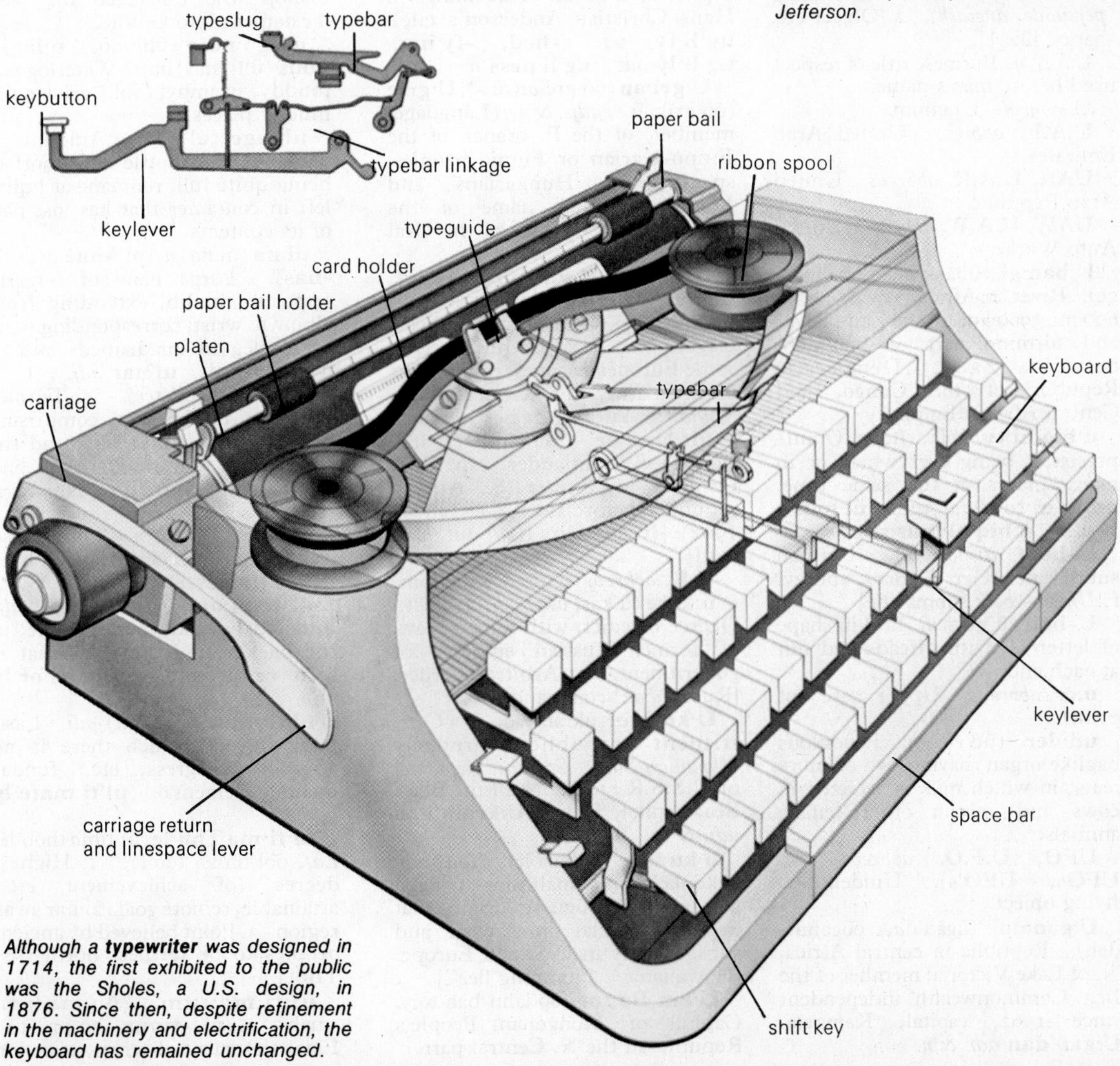

typeslug
typebar
keybutton
paper bail
typebar linkage
ribbon spool
keylever
typeguide
card holder
paper bail holder
platen
keyboard
carriage
typebar
keylever
carriage return and linespace lever
space bar
shift key

*Although a **typewriter** was designed in 1714, the first exhibited to the public was the Sholes, a U.S. design, in 1876. Since then, despite refinement in the machinery and electrification, the keyboard has remained unchanged.*

The letter U, u is derived from the Semitic 'vau' which in turn came from the hieroglyphic horned asp and a Phoenician symbol. The present sound derived from the Greeks who called it upsilon. The Romans used the shape V to signify the sounds for U and W and they were not separated until the 15th century.

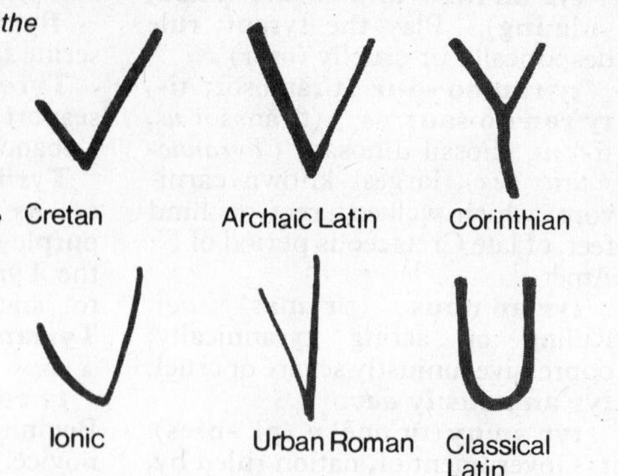

U, u (ū) (pl. **U's, u's** or **Us, us**). 1. Twenty-first letter of modern English and 20th of ancient Roman alphabet, where it was identical in form and origin with *v*; now representing a vowel sound except after *g*, where it is freq. silent (*guard*), in final *-que*, where it is always silent (*grotesque*), and after *q* in other positions, where it has the value of *w* (*quick, inquest*), as also in various words after *s* and *g* (*persuade, anguish*). 2. Object etc. shaped like U.

U (o͞o) *n.* Burmese title of respect used before man's name.

U *symbol.* Uranium.

U.A.E. *abbrev.* United Arab Emirates.

UAR, U.A.R. *abbrevs.* United Arab Republic.

UAW, U.A.W. *abbrevs.* United Auto Workers.

U·ban·gi (ūbăng′gē, o͞obahng′-gē). River in Africa flowing about 600 mi. (960 km) to the Zaire River and forming part of boundary between Zaire, Democratic Republic of the Congo, and Central African Empire.

u·biq·ui·ty (ūbĭk′wĭtē) *n.* Omnipresence; being everywhere or in many places at the same time. **u·biq′ui·tous** *adj.* **u·biq′ui·tous·ly** *adv.* **u·biq′ui·tous·ness** *n.*

U-boat (ū′bōt) *n.* German submarine. [Ger. *U-Boot*, abbrev. f. *Unterseeboot* submarine]

U-bolt (ū′bōlt) *n.* Bolt in shape of letter U, with threads and nut at each end.

u.c. *abbrev.* Upper case (of print).

ud·der (ŭd′*er*) *n.* Pendulous baglike organ, having two or more teats, in which milk is secreted in cows and certain other female animals.

UFO, U.F.O. *abbrevs.* (pl. **UFOs, UFO's**). Unidentified flying object.

U·gan·da (ūgăn′d*a*, o͞ogahn′-dah). Republic in central Africa, N. of Lake Victoria; member of the Brit. Commonwealth, independent since 1962; capital, Kampala. **U·gan′dan** *adj.* & *n.*

ugh (o͝ox, ŭx, ŭg) *int.* Exclamation expressing disgust etc.

ug·ly (ŭg′lē) *adj.* (**-li·er, -li·est**). Unpleasing or repulsive to sight or hearing; morally repulsive, vile; disquieting, threatening; extremely awkward or unpromising (task, situation); ~ **customer**, unpleasantly formidable person; ~ **duckling**, dull or plain child who becomes brilliant adult (w. ref. to cygnet in a brood of ducklings in Hans Christian Anderson's tale). **ug′li·fy** *v.t.* (**-fied, -fy·ing**). **ug′li·ly** *adv.* **ug′li·ness** *n.*

U·gri·an (o͞o′grē*an*, ū′-), **U·gric** (o͞o′grĭk, ū′-) *adjs.* & *ns.* (Language, member) of the E. branch of the Finno-Ugrian or Finnic peoples, specif. the Hungarians and Magyars. [*Ugra*, name of the country on both sides of the Ural mountains]

UHF, U.H.F., uhf, u.h.f. *abbrevs.* Ultrahigh FREQUENCY.

uh·lan (o͞o′lahn, ū′l*a*n) *n.* (hist.) Cavalryman armed with lance in some European armies, esp. former German army. [Fr., Ger., f. Polish (*h*)*ulan*, f. Turk. *oğlan* boy, servant]

uit·land·er (oit′lănd*er*, ĭt′-, -lahn-) *n.* Outlander, esp. Brit. resident in former S. African republics before Boer War (1899–1902). [(Cape) Du., f. *uit* out, *land* land]

U.K. *abbrev.* United Kingdom.

u·kase (ū′kās, ūkāz′) *n.* 1. (hist.) Decree or edict, with force of law, of former Russian emperor or government. 2. Arbitrary order. [Russ. *ukaz*′ command]

U·kraine (ūkrān′, o͞o-). Constituent republic (properly *Ukranian Soviet Socialist Republic*) of U.S.S.R., to the N. of the Black Sea; capital, Kiev. **U·krain′i·an** *adj.* & *n.*

u·ku·le·le (ūkul*ā*′lē; *Hawaiian* o͞oko͞olā′lā) *n.* Small four-stringed guitar of Portuguese origin that became popular in Hawaii and subsequently in U.S. and Europe. [Hawaiian, = "jumping flea"]

U·lan Ba·tor (o͞o′lahn bah′tōr). Capital of Mongolian People's Republic in the N. Central part.

ul·cer (ŭl′s*er*) *n.* Open sore on external or internal surface of body, secreting pus; (fig.) corroding or corrupting influence, plague spot. **ul′cer·ous** *adj.* **ul′cer·ous·ly** *adv.*

ul·cer·ate (ŭl′s*e*rāt) *v.* (**-at·ed, -at·ing**). Make, become, ulcerous. **ul·cer·a·tion** (ŭls*e*rā′sh*o*n) *n.* **ul·cer·a·tive** (ŭl′s*e*rātĭv, -*a*tĭv) *adj.*

Ul·fi·las (ŭl′fĭl*a*s), **Wul·fi·la** (wo͝ol′fĭl*a*) (*c*311–83). Gothic bishop who translated the New Testament into Gothic.

u·lig·i·nose (ūlĭj′ĭnōs), **u·lig·i·nous** (ūlĭj′ĭn*u*s) *adjs.* Waterlogged, muddy, swampy; (bot.) growing in muddy places.

ul·lage (ŭl′ĭj) *n.* Amount by which cask or bottle falls short of being quite full; remnant of liquor left in container that has lost part of its contents.

ul·na (ŭl′n*a*) *n.* (pl. **-nae** pr. -nē, **-nas**). Large bone of forearm opposite thumb, extending from elbow to wrist; corresponding bone of foreleg in quadrupeds and of wing in birds. **ul′nar** *adj.*

Ul·ster (ŭl′st*er*). Former province of Ireland, comprising present Northern Ireland and the counties of Cavan, Donegal, and Monaghan; (loosely) Northern Ireland.

ul·ster (ŭl′st*er*) *n.* Long loose freq. belted overcoat, orig. of Ulster frieze. [f. ULSTER]

ul·te·ri·or (ŭltēr′ē*er*) *adj.* Situated beyond; more remote; in the background, beyond what is seen or avowed. **ul·te′ri·or·ly** *adv.*

ul·ti·mate (ŭl′tĭmĭt) *adj.* Last, final; beyond which there is no advance, progress, etc.; fundamental, elemental. **ul′ti·mate·ly** *adv.*

ul·ti·ma Thu·le (ŭl′tĭm*a* tho͞o′lē; *Lat.* o͞ol′tĭmah to͞o′lē). 1. Highest degree (of achievement etc.) attainable; remote goal. 2. Far away region. 3. Point believed by ancient peoples to be farthest north (see THULE).

ul·ti·ma·tum (ŭltĭmā′t*u*m, -mah′-) *n.* (pl. **-tums, -ta** pr. -t*a*). Final statement of terms, rejection

Left: The Murchison Falls, ***Uganda.*** *At this point the Nile emerges from Lake Albert and drops 118 ft. through a gorge only 20 ft. wide.*

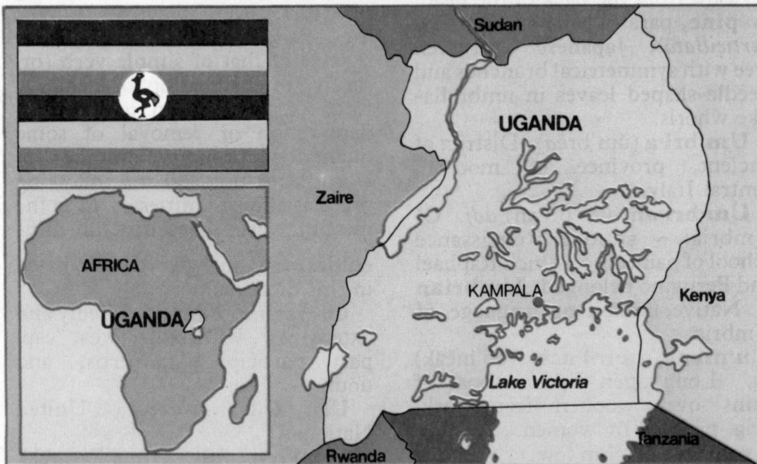

of which by opposite party may lead to rupture, declaration of war, etc.

ul·tra (ŭl′tr*a*) *adj.* & *n.* (Person) holding extreme views, esp. in religion or politics. [orig. as abbrev. of Fr. *ultra-royaliste*]

ultra- *prefix.* Lying beyond or on the other side of; (with adjectives) going beyond, surpassing; having (the quality etc. expressed by the adjective) in extreme or excessive degree.

ul·tra·con·ser·va·tive (ŭltr*a*-kons*ẽ*r′v*a*tĭv) *adj.* & *n.* (Person who is) conservative to extreme degree, esp. in political attitudes.

ul·tra·fiche (ŭl′tr*a*fēsh) *n.* Microfiche of printed material reduced in size to extreme degree.

ul·tra·high fre·quency: see FREQUENCY.

ul·tra·ma·rine (ŭltr*a*m*a*rēn′) *adj.* Situated beyond the sea; of the color of ultramarine. ~ *n.* Brilliant deep blue pigment made from lapis lazuli; imitation of this. [L. *ultra* beyond, *mare* sea (w. ref. to foreign origin of lapis lazuli)]

ul·tra·mi·cro·scope (ŭltr*a*mī′-kr*o*skōp) *n.* Microscope using beam of light at right angles to its optical axis to detect particles beyond the range of an ordinary microscope. **ul·tra·mi·cro·scop·ic** (ŭltr*a*-mīkr*o*skŏp′ĭk) *adj.*

ul·tra·mon·tane (ŭltr*a*mŏntān′) *adj.* Situated S. of the Alps; Italian; favorable to the absolute authority of the pope in matters of faith and discipline. ~ *n.* One who resides S. of the Alps; person holding ultramontane views. **ul·tra·mon·tan·ism** (ŭltr*a*mŏn′t*a*nĭz*e*m), **ul·tra·mon′tan·ist** *ns.* [L. *ultra* beyond, *mons* mountain]

ul·tra·mun·dane (ŭltr*a*mŭn′-dān, -mŭndān′) *adj.* (Of or pertaining to things) lying outside the world or beyond the limits of the solar system.

ul·tra·son·ic (ŭltr*a*sŏn′ĭk) *adj.* (of sound) So high-pitched as to be beyond the range of human hearing; (of sound frequency) above audio frequency range. **ul·tra·son′i·cal·ly** *adv.*

ul·tra·vi·o·let (ŭltr*a*vī′*o*lĭt) *adj.* (phys.) Lying immediately beyond the violet end of the visible spectrum; of, producing, electromagnetic radiation with a wavelength shorter than that of visible light rays and having powerful actinic effect.

ul·tra vi·res (ŭltr*a* vīr′ēz). Beyond one's powers; exceeding the powers granted by law. [L.]

ul·tra·vi·rus (ŭltr*a*vīr′*u*s) *n.* Ultramicroscopic virus so small that it can pass through pores of finest bacterial filter.

ul·u·late (ŭl′y*u*lāt, ŭl′-) *v.i.* (**-lat·ed, -lat·ing**). Howl, wail. **ul·u·la·tion** (ŭly*u*lā′sh*o*n, ŭl-) *n.*

Ul·ya·nov (o͞olyah′nawf), **Vladimir Ilyich**: see LENIN.

U·lys·ses (ūlĭs′ēz). Roman name for ODYSSEUS.

um·bel (ŭm′b*e*l) *n.* (bot.) Inflorescence with pedicels of nearly equal length springing from common center. **um·bel·late** (ŭm′belĭt, -lāt), **um·bel·lif·er·ous** (ŭmbelĭf′*e*r*u*s) *adjs.* [L. *umbella* sunshade, dim. of *umbra* shadow]

um·ber (ŭm′b*e*r) *n.* Brown earth (iron and manganese) used as pigment. ~ *adj.* Of the color of umber. [Fr. (*terre d'*)*ombre* or It. (*terra di*) *ombra*, either = "shadow" (L. *umbra*) f. fem. of L. *Umber* Umbrian]

um·bil·i·cal (ŭmbĭl′ĭk*a*l) *adj.* Of, affecting, situated near, forming, umbilicus; ~ **cord**, flexible tube attaching fetus to placenta, navel string (also transf.). **um·bil·i·cate** (ŭmbĭl′ĭkĭt, -kāt), **um·bil′i·cat·ed** *adjs.* Resembling a navel.

*The **umbrella bird** is found only in South America, where there are three species. It is named after its distinctive curving crest which opens to cover the head.*

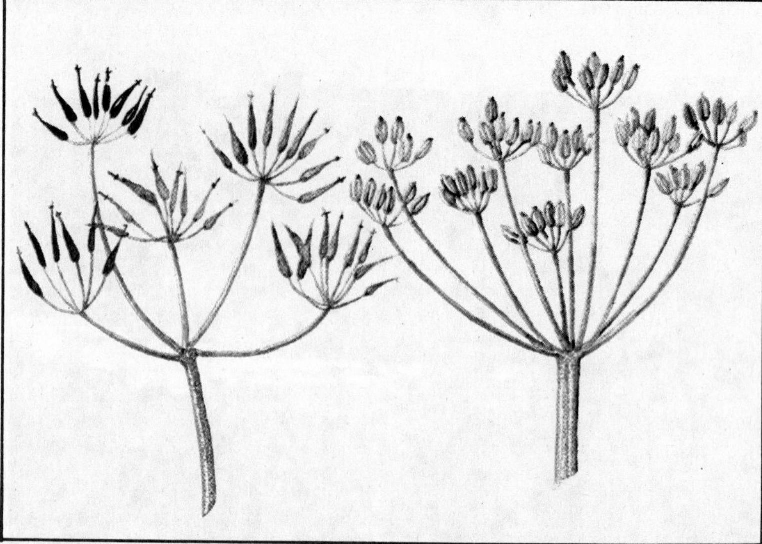

*Named after the flowers which open like sunshades, **umbelliferous** plants include many that are useful to man. They range from carrots to parsley, chervil (above) and fennel (right).*

um·bil·i·cus (ŭmbĭl′ĭkus, -bĭlī′-) *n.* (pl. **-bil·i·ci** pr. -bĭl′isī, -bĭlī′sī, **-bil·i·cus·es**). Central depression in abdomen, marking point of attachment of umbilical cord, navel; small depression or hollow suggesting this; (geom.) point in surface through which all its lines of curvature pass.

um·bra (ŭm′br*a*) *n.* (pl. **-brae** pr. -brē). Earth's or moon's shadow in an eclipse, esp. the complete shadow as dist. from the *penumbra*; dark central part of a sunspot. **um′bral** *adj.* [L., = "shade"]

um·brage (ŭm′brĭj) *n.* 1. Sense of slight or injury, offense. 2. (archaic) Shade. **um·bra·geous** (ŭmbrā′*j*us) *adj.*

um·brel·la (ŭmbrĕl′*a*) *n.* Light portable screen usu. circular and supported on central stick, used in hot countries as protection against sun, and in some Oriental and African countries as symbol of rank or state; portable protection against rain etc., made of silk or similar material fastened on slender ribs that are attached radially to stick and can be readily raised to form an arched circular canopy; structure resembling an umbrella, esp. (zool.) gelatinous disk or bellshaped structure of jellyfish; (conch.) umbrella shell, the part of its shell like an open umbrella; protective screen of fighter aircraft; (fig.) general protection, aegis; ~ **bird**, S. or Central Amer. bird of genus *Cephalopterus*, esp. Brazilian *C. ornatus*, with black plumage and large crest curving forward from the back of the head; ~ **pine**, parasol pine (*Sciadopitys verticillata*), Japanese evergreen tree with symmetrical branches and needle-shaped leaves in umbrella-like whorls.

Um·bri·a (ŭm′brē*a*). District of ancient, province of modern, central Italy.

Um·bri·an (ŭm′brē*a*n) *adj.* Of Umbria; ~ **school**, Renaissance school of painting to which Raphael and Perugino belonged. **Umbrian** *n.* Native, inhabitant, language, of Umbria.

u·mi·ak, u·mi·ack (ōō′mēăk) *ns.* Long open Eskimo boat of skins over wooden framework, orig. paddled by women.

um·laut (ŏŏm′lowt) *n.* (in Germanic languages) Vowel change due to *i*, *j*, etc. (now usu. lost or altered) in following syllable, e.g. Ger. *mann männer, fuss füsse*; diacritical sign (¨) indicating this. [Ger. *um* about, *laut* sound]

um·pire (ŭm′pīr) *n.* One who decides between disputants or contending parties and whose decision is usu. accepted as final; (law) third person called upon to settle question submitted to arbitrators who cannot agree; person chosen to enforce rules of games or contest and settle disputes or doubtful points. ~ *v.* (**-pired, -pir·ing**). Act as umpire (in). [OF. *nomper* peerless, in sense "odd man" (*non* not, *per* PEER[1])]

ump·teen (ŭmp′tēn′) *adj.* & *n.* (slang) Indeterminate but large number (of). **ump′teenth′** *adj.* [joc. formation, on analogy of *thirteen* etc.]

UMT *abbrev.* Universal Military Training.

Um·ta·ta (ōōmtah′t*a*). Capital of The Transkei.

UMW *abbrev.* United Mine Workers.

un-[1] *prefix.* Used with verbs and verbal derivatives and in forming new verbs from adjectives, nouns, etc., to signify action contrary to or reverse of that of simple verb (or, rarely, intensification of negative force of verb, as in *unloose*), or deprivation or removal of some quality or property; number of words with this and the following prefix is almost limitless, and as the meaning usu. presents no difficulties, few such words are listed in this dictionary.

un-[2] *prefix.* Not (used freely and extensively with adjectives, esp. past participles, adverbs, and nouns).

UN, U.N. *abbrevs.* United Nations.

un·al·ien·a·ble (ŭnā′lēen*a*bel, -āl′ye-) *adj.* (archaic) Inalienable.

un·al·loyed (ŭn*a*loid′) *adj.* Not mixed, pure.

un-A·mer·i·can (ŭn*a*mĕr′ĭkan) *adj.* Not American; (esp.) not of, not worthy or characteristic of, opposed to, against interests etc. of, the U.S.

u·nan·i·mous (ūnăn′ĭm*u*s) *adj.* All of one mind, agreeing in opinion; (of opinion, vote, etc.) formed, held, given, etc., with general agreement or consent. **u·nan′i·mous·ly** *adv.* **u·na·nim·i·ty** (ūn*a*nĭm′ĭtē), **u·nan′i·mous·ness** *ns.*

un·as·sum·ing (ŭnasōō´mĭng) *adj.* Modest, not pretentious. **un·as·sum′ing·ly** *adv.*

un·a·wares (ŭnawār̄z´) *adv.* Unexpectedly, unconsciously; by surprise.

un·bal·anced (ŭnbăl´anst) *adj.* (esp.) Mentally unstable or deranged.

un·be·known (ŭnbĭnōn´), **un·be·knownst** (ŭnbĭnōnst´) *adjs.* & *advs.* Unknown; ~ **to,** without the knowledge of.

un·bend (ŭnbĕnd´) *v.* (**-bent** pr. -bĕnt or **-bend·ed, -bend·ing**). Release, relax, from tension; straighten; become unconstrained or genial.

un·bend·ing (ŭnbĕn´dĭng) *adj.* Rigid, uncompromising.

un·bos·om (ŭnbŏŏz´em, -bōō´zem) *v.* Disclose, reveal; ~ **oneself,** disclose one's secrets, thoughts, etc.

un·bri·dled (ŭnbrī´deld) *adj.* Unrestrained, uncontrolled. **un·bri′dled·ly** *adv.*

un·called-for (ŭnkawld´fōr̄´) *adj.* Not required or requested; unprovoked, impertinent.

un·can·ny (ŭnkăn´ē) *adj.* Supernatural, mysterious, uncomfortably strange or unfamiliar. **un·can′ni·ly** *adv.* **un·can′ni·ness** *n.*

un·ci·al (ŭn´shēal, -shal) *adj.* Of, written in, a form of majuscule script resembling capitals but with some ascending and descending strokes, used in Greek and Latin manuscripts of the 4th–8th centuries. ~ *n.* Uncial letter; uncial manuscript. [L. *uncialis* in LL. sense "inch-high," "large," f. *uncia* 12th part of foot, inch]

un·cle (ŭng´kel) *adj.* 1. Father's or mother's brother, aunt's husband; (children's colloq.) unrelated man who is a family friend; **cry** (or **say**) ~, (slang) admit defeat, submit; **U~ Sam,** government (or people) of U.S. (perh. facetious expansion of initials *U.S.*); **U~ Tom,** (derog.) black person subservient to whites; **U~ Tomism,** kind of relationship between whites and blacks involving kindness and condescension by the former and meek submissiveness by latter. [after leading character in Harriet Beecher Stowe's novel *Uncle Tom's Cabin* (1852)]

un·com·mon (ŭnkŏm´on) *adj.* Unusual, remarkable. **un·com′mon·ly** *adv.* **un·com′mon·ness** *n.*

un·com·pro·mis·ing (ŭnkŏm´promīzĭng) *adj.* Refusing compromise; unyielding, stubborn. **un·com′pro·mis·ing·ly** *adv.*

un·con·scion·a·ble (ŭnkŏn´shonabel) *adj.* 1. Having no conscience, unscrupulous; (of actions) performed against dictates of conscience. 2. Not right or reasonable; excessive, shameless. **un·con′scion·a·bly** *adv.*

un·con·scious (ŭnkŏn´shus) *adj.* Not conscious; ~ **mind,** (psychol.) those mental processes whose existence is inferred from their effects. ~ *n.* Unconscious mind; **collective** ~, (Jungian psychol.) unconscious mental processes presumed common to all mankind.

un·con·sti·tu·tion·al (ŭnkŏnstĭtōō´shonal, -tū´-) *adj.* Not in accordance with the political constitution or with procedural rules. **un·con·sti·tu·tion·al·i·ty** (ŭnkŏnstĭtōōshonăl´ĭtē, -tū-) *n.* **un·con·sti·tu′tion·al·ly** *adv.*

un·cork (ŭnkōr̄k´) *v.* 1. Remove cork from. 2. (colloq.) Let loose; let go or propel with force.

un·couth (ŭnkōōth´) *adj.* Odd, uncomely, awkward, clumsy, in shape, sound, bearing, etc. **un·couth′ly** *adv.* **un·couth′ness** *n.* [OE. *uncuth* = "unknown," "unfamiliar"]

unc·tion (ŭngk´shon) *n.* 1. Anointing with oil etc. as religious rite or symbol (esp. of investiture with kingship or other office); unguent; **extreme** ~: see EXTREME. 2. (Manner suggesting) deep spiritual or religious feeling; simulation of this, affected enthusiasm, gush.

unc·tu·ous (ŭngk´chōōus) *adj.* 1. Of the nature or quality of an unguent, oily, greasy in feel, appearance, etc. 2. Full of (esp. simulated) unction; complacently agreeable or self-satisfied. **unc′tu·ous·ly** *adv.* **unc′tu·ous·ness, unc·tu·os·i·ty** (ŭngkchōōŏs´ĭtē) *ns.*

un·der (ŭn´der) *prep.* In or to position lower than, below, at the foot of; within, on the inside, of; inferior to, less than; supporting or sustaining; subjected to, undergoing, liable to, on condition of, subject to; governed, controlled, or bound by; in accordance with; in the form of; in the time of; (**speak** etc.) ~ **one's breath,** in a whisper; ~ **a cloud**: see CLOUD; ~ **the sun,** anywhere on Earth; ~ **way**: see

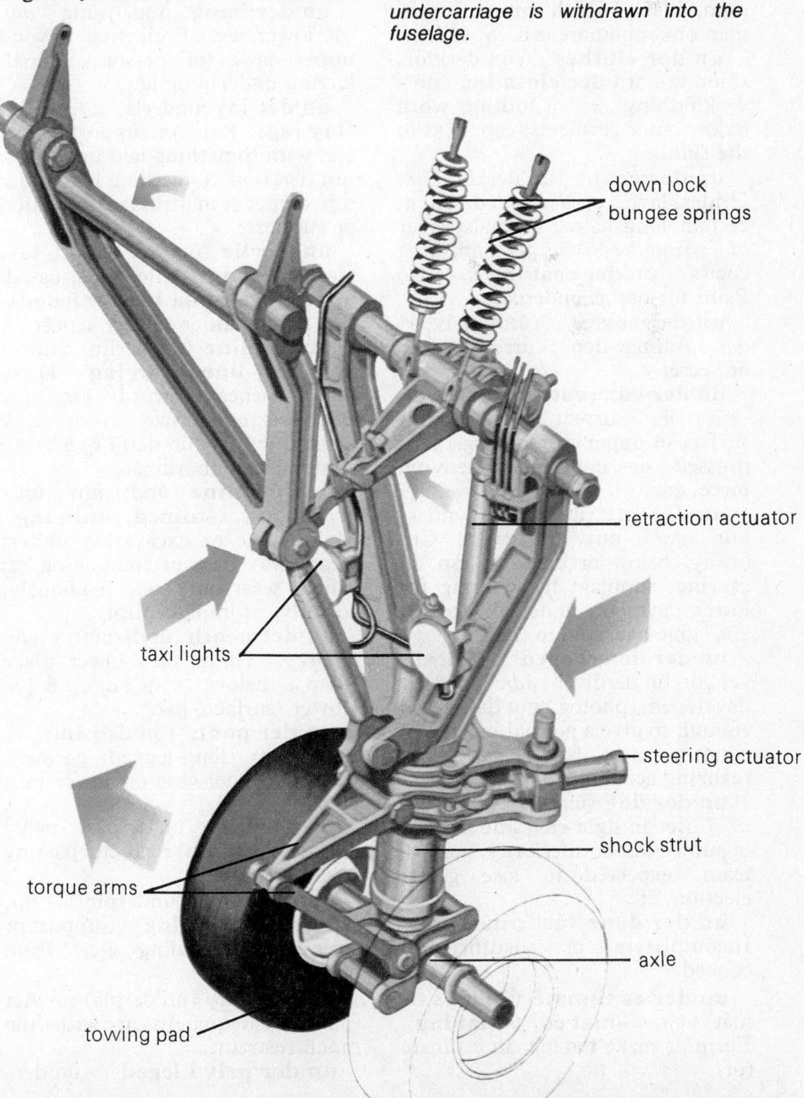

*The retractable **undercarriage** of modern aircraft takes many forms. Below: The nose wheels of a Lockheed TriStar. The arrows show the directions in which the links move when the undercarriage is withdrawn into the fuselage.*

WAY. **under** *adv.* In a lower place or subordinate condition. ~ *adj.* Lower. **un′der·most** *adj.*

under- *prefix.* Below; beneath, lower than; insufficiently, incompletely; situated beneath, subordinate.

un·der·a·chieve (ŭnd*er*achēv′) *v.* Do less or worse than was expected (esp. scholastically). **un·der·a·chiev′er** *n.*

un·der·act (ŭnd*er*akt′) *v.* Underplay.

un·der·arm (ŭn′d*er*ar̅m) *adj.* & *adv.* (Performed) with arm lower than the shoulder; of the armpit.

un·der·bid (ŭnd*er*bĭd′) *v.* (**-bid, -bid·ding**). Bid less than; bid too little (on); undercut.

un·der·brush (ŭn′d*er*brŭsh) *n.* Undergrowth in forest.

un·der·car·riage (ŭn′d*er*kărĭj) *n.* Lower framework of a vehicle that supports the superstructure.

un·der·charge (ŭn′d*er*char̅j) *v.* Charge too little for (thing) or to (person); give less than proper charge to (gun, electric battery, etc.).

un·der·class·man (ŭn′d*er*klăs-m*a*n, -klahs-) *n.* (pl. **-men**). Freshman or sophomore in U.S. college.

un·der·clothes (ŭn′d*er*klōz, -klōdhz), **un·der·cloth·ing** (ŭn′d*er*klōdhĭng) *ns.* Clothing worn below outer garments, esp. next to the skin.

un·der·coat (ŭn′d*er*kōt) *n.* Under layer of hair or down in certain long-haired animals; layer of paint used under finishing coat(s). **un′der·coat·ing** *n.* (esp.) Paint for use as undercoat.

un·der·cov·er (ŭnd*er*kŭv′*er*) *adj.* Acting, done, surreptitiously or secretly.

un·der·cur·rent (ŭn′d*er*kēr*e*nt, -kŭr-) *n.* Current flowing below surface or upper current; (fig.) suppressed or underlying activity, force, etc.

un·der·cut (ŭn′d*er*kŭt, ŭnd*er*-kŭt′) *v.t.* (**-cut, -cut·ting**). Cut (away) below or beneath, esp. in carving; supplant by working for lower payment; undersell; (tennis etc.) give backspin to (ball).

un·der·de·vel·oped (ŭnd*er*dĭ-vĕl′*o*pt, ŭn′d*er*dĭvĕl-) *adj.* Not fully developed; (photog.) not developed enough to give a normal image; (of country etc.) below not (yet) realizing economic potential.

un·der·dog (ŭn′d*er*dawg, -dŏg) *n.* Loser in fight etc.; one in state of subjection or inferiority; person, team, expected to lose game, election, etc.

un·der·done (ŭnd*er*dŭn′) *adj.* Incompletely or insufficiently cooked.

un·der·es·ti·mate (ŭnd*er*ĕs′t*i*-māt) *v.t.* (**-mat·ed, -mat·ing**). Form or make too low an estimate (of).

un·der·foot (ŭnd*er*fo͝ot′): see FOOT.

un·der·gar·ment (ŭn′d*er*gar̅-m*e*nt) *n.* Article of underwear.

un·der·go (ŭn′d*er*gō, ŭnd*er*gō′) *v.t.* (**-went, -gone, -go·ing**). Be subjected to, suffer, endure.

un·der·grad·u·ate (ŭn′d*er*grăj-o͞oĭt, ŭnd*er*grăj′-) *n.* College or university student who has not yet taken a degree.

un·der·ground (ŭn′d*er*-grownd′) *adv.* Below the surface of the ground; in(to) secrecy or concealment. ~ (ŭn′d*er*grownd) *adj.* & *n.* (group, movement, etc.) Conducted or existing in secret, esp. in resistance to established order etc.; (Brit.; usu. **the** ~) subway train or system.

un·der·growth (ŭn′d*er*grōth) *n.* Growth of plants or shrubs under trees etc.

un·der·hand (ŭn′d*er*hănd) *adj.* & *adv.* 1. Clandestine(ly), secret(ly), not aboveboard. 2. (baseball) Thrown with the arm lower than the shoulder.

un·der·hand·ed (ŭn′d*er*hăn′-dĭd) *adj.* UNDERHAND sense 1.

un·der·hung (ŭnd*er*hŭng′) *adj.* (of lower jaw) Projecting beyond upper jaw; (of person, animal) having underhung jaw.

un·der·lay (ŭnd*er*lā′) *v.t.* (**-laid, -lay·ing**). Raise or support or line etc. with something laid under. ~ (ŭn′d*er*lā) *n.* Something laid under esp. carpet or mattress as protection or support.

un·der·lie (ŭnd*er*lī′) *v.t.* (**-lay, -lain, -ly·ing**). Lie, be situated, under; (fig.) be the basis or foundation of, lie under surface aspect of.

un·der·line (ŭn′d*er*līn, ŭnd*er*-līn′) *v.t.* (**-lined, -lin·ing**). Draw line(s) beneath (words etc.) for emphasis; emphasize.

un·der·ling (ŭn′d*er*lĭng) *n.* (usu. contempt.) Subordinate.

un·der·mine (ŭnd*er*mīn′, ŭn′-d*er*mīn) *v.t.* (**-mined, -min·ing**). Make mine or excavation under; wear away base or foundation of; injure, wear out, etc., insidiously, secretly, or imperceptibly.

un·der·neath (ŭnd*er*nēth′) *adv.* & *prep.* At or to a lower place (than), below. ~ *adj.* & *n.* Lower (surface, part).

un·der·pants (ŭn′d*er*pănts) *n.* Short- or long-legged garment worn as underwear on lower part of body.

un·der·pass (ŭn′d*er*păs, -pahs) *n.* (Crossing with) road etc. passing under another.

un·der·pin (ŭnd*er*pĭn′) *v.t.* (**-pinned, -pin·ning**). Support or strengthen (building etc.) from beneath.

un·der·play (ŭn′d*er*plā) *v.* Act (part) inadequately or with too much restraint.

un·der·priv·i·leged (ŭn′d*er*-prĭv′*i*lĭjd, -prĭv′lĭjd) *adj.* Not enjoying normal living standard or rights and privileges of member of society.

un·der·rate (ŭnd*er*rāt′, ŭn′d*er*-rāt) *v.t.* (**-rat·ed, -rat·ing**). Form too low an estimate of.

un·der·score (ŭn′d*er*skōr, -skōr, ŭnd*er*skōr′, -skōr′) *v.* (**-scored, -scor·ing**). Underline.

un·der·sec·re·tar·y (ŭn′d*er*-sĕkrĭtĕrē, ŭnd*er*sĕk′-) *n.* (pl. **-tar·ies**). Official subordinate to a secretary.

un·der·sell (ŭn′d*er*sĕl, ŭnd*er*-sĕl′) *v.* (**-sold** pr. -sōld, **-sel·ling**). 1. (of person) Sell at a lower price than (another person); cut out of competition by selling at a lower rate; (of thing) be sold thus. 2. Sell (thing) at too low a price.

un·der·shoot (ŭn′d*er*sho͞ot, ŭnd*er*sho͞ot′) *v.* (**-shot** pr. -shŏt, **-shoot·ing**). (esp., of aircraft) Land short of (the runway).

un·der·shot (ŭn′d*er*shŏt) *adj.* (of wheel) Turned by water flowing under it.

un·der·signed (ŭn′d*er*sīnd) *adj.* (Whose names are) signed below; **the** ~, undersigned person(s).

un·der·sized (ŭn′d*er*sīzd) *adj.* Of less than normal size.

un·der·slung (ŭn′d*er*slŭng′) *adj.* Supported from above; (of vehicle chassis) hanging lower than axles.

un·der·stand (ŭnd*er*stănd′) *v.* (**-stood** pr. -sto͝od, **-stand·ing**). Perceive the meaning of; know how to deal with; infer, esp. from information received; take for granted. **un·der·stand′ing** *n.* (esp.) Intelligence; agreement; convention, thing agreed upon. ~ *adj.* Intelligent, having understanding. **un·der·stand′a·bly, un·der·stand′ing·ly** *advs.* **un·der·stand′a·ble** *adj.*

un·der·state·ment (ŭn′d*er*stāt-m*e*nt, ŭnd*er*stāt′-) *n.* Statement falling below or coming short of truth or fact; intentionally, ironically, restrained statement. **un·der·state** (ŭn′d*er*stāt, ŭnd*er*-stāt′) *v.t.* (**-stat·ed, -stat·ing**).

un·der·steer (ŭn′d*er*stēr, ŭnd*er*-stēr′) *v.i.* (of vehicle) Have tendency to steer toward the outer side on a curve. ~ *n.* Understeering.

un·der·stud·y (ŭn′d*er*stŭdē) *n.* (pl. **-stud·ies**). Actor who learns part in order to play it at short notice in absence of usual performer. ~ *v.t.* (**-stud·ied, -stud·y·ing**). Act as understudy to.

un·der·take (ŭn′d*er*tāk, ŭnd*er*-tāk′) *v.* (**-took** pr. -to͝ok, **-tak·en, -tak·ing**). Bind oneself to perform; engage in, enter upon (work, enterprise, etc.); promise (*to* do); guarantee; (colloq.) manage funerals. **un′der·tak·er** *n.* (esp.) One whose business is to carry out arrangements for funerals. **un·der·tak'ing** *n.* (esp.) Work etc. undertaken, enterprise; business of funeral undertaker.

un·der·tone (ŭn'dertōn) *n.* Low or subdued, underlying or subordinate, tone.

un·der·tow (ŭn'dertō) *n.* Current below sea surface moving in contrary direction to surface current.

un·der·wear (ŭn'derwār) *n.* Underclothes.

un·der·wood (ŭn'derwŏŏd) *n.* Small trees or shrubs, brushwood, growing beneath trees.

un·der·world (ŭn'derwĕrld) *n.* (esp. myth.) Abode of souls of the dead; criminal section of society.

un·der·write (ŭn'derrīt, ŭnderrīt') *v.* (**-wrote** pr. -rōt, -rōt', **-writ·ten** pr. -rĭten, -rĭt'en, **-writ·ing**). (esp.) Subscribe (insurance policy), thereby accepting risk of insurance; undertake esp. marine insurance; agree to support (venture financially); agree to buy stock not bought by public in (new company or new issue). **un'der·writ·er** *n.*

un·dies (ŭn'dēz) *n.pl.* (colloq.) Women's underclothes.

un·dis·trib·ut·ed (ŭndĭstrĭb'yutĭd) *adj.* Not distributed; ~ **middle**, (logic) fallacy resulting from failure of middle term to refer to all members of a class (e.g. *all men are mammals*; *all apes are mammals*; *therefore, all men are apes.*).

un·do (ŭndōō', ŭn'dōō) *v.t.* (**-did** pr. -dĭd, **-done** pr. -dŭn, -dŭn', **-do·ing**). Annul, cancel; open (parcel etc.); unfasten (laces, buttons, etc.); (poet.) ruin. **un·do'ing** *n.* (esp.) (Cause of) bringing to ruin. **un·done'** *adj.* (esp.) Unfastened; (poet.) ruined.

un·dress (ŭndrĕs') *v.* Take off clothes (of). ~ *n.* Ordinary dress; informal dress; negligee.

un·due (ŭndōō', -dū') *adj.* Not owed or suitable; excessive, disproportionate.

un·du·lant (ŭn'julant, -du-, -dyu-) *adj.* Undulating, rising and falling like waves; ~ **fever**, persistent remittent fever with profuse perspiration, swollen joints, and enlarged spleen, transmitted through milk esp. of diseased cows.

un·du·late (ŭn'julĭt, -lāt, -dyu-, -du-) *adj.* With wavelike markings; having waved surface or outline, arranged in wavelike curves. ~ (ŭn'julāt, -dyu-, -du-) *v.i.* (**-lat·ed, -lat·ing**). Have wavy motion or look. **un'du·lat·ing** *adj.*

un·du·la·tion (ŭnjulā'shon, -dyu-, -du-) *n.* Wavy motion or form, gentle rise and fall, each wave of this; set of wavy lines.

un·du·la·to·ry (ŭn'julatōrē, -tōrē, -dyu-, -du-) *adj.* Undulating, wavy; of, due to, undulation.

un·du·ly (ŭndōō'lē, -dū'-) *adv.* Unrightfully, improperly; excessively.

un·dy·ing (ŭndī'ĭng) *adj.* Not dying; forever or unceasing. **un·dy'ing·ly** *adv.*

un·earned (ŭnĕrnd') *adj.* (esp.) ~ **income**, revenue from interest payments etc., dist. from wages etc.

un·earth (ŭnĕrth') *v.t.* Dig up, disinter; force out of hole or burrow; (fig.) bring to light, disclose, find by searching.

un·earth·ly (ŭnĕrth'lē) *adj.* Celestial, not of Earth; supernatural, ghostly; (colloq.) not appropriate, absurdly early or inconvenient.

un·eas·y (ŭnē'zē) *adj.* (**-eas·i·er, -eas·i·est**). Restless, disturbed, uncomfortable in body or mind. **un·eas'i·ly** *adv.* **un·eas'i·ness** *n.*

un·em·ployed (ŭnĕmploid') *adj.* Not employed or occupied; not in use. **un·em·ploy'ment** *n.*

UNESCO (ūnĕs'kō) *n.* United Nations Educational, Scientific, and Cultural Organization.

un·ex·cep·tion·a·ble (ŭnĭksĕp'shonabel) *adj.* With which no fault can be found. **un·ex·cep'tion·a·bly** *adv.*

un·fair (ŭnfār') *adj.* Not equitable or honest or impartial or according to rules. **un·fair'ly** *adv.* **un·fair'ness** *n.*

un·faith·ful (ŭnfāth'ful) *adj.* Failing in loyalty; not true *to*; adulterous. **un·faith'ful·ly** *adv.*

un·fas·ten (ŭnfăs'en, -fah'sen) *v.t.* Make loose; detach; open fastening(s) of.

un·feel·ing (ŭnfē'lĭng) *adj.* Lacking sensibility, without feeling; harsh, cruel. **un·feel'ing·ly** *adv.*

un·fit (ŭnfĭt') *adj.* Not fit, unsuitable; in poor health. ~ *v.t.* (**-fit·ted, -fit·ting**). Make unsuitable (for). **un·fit'ly** *adv.* **un·fit'ness** *n.*

un·flap·pa·ble (ŭnflăp'abel) *adj.* (colloq.) Imperturbable; remaining cool in a crisis. **un·flap·pa·bil'i·ty** *n.* **un·flap'pa·bly** *adv.*

un·fold (ŭnfōld') *v.* Open out; reveal; develop.

un·for·tu·nate (ŭnfōr'chunĭt) *adj.* Unlucky; regrettable; ill-advised. **un·for'tu·nate·ly** *adv.* **un·for'tu·nate·ness** *n.*

un·frock (ŭnfrŏk') *v.t.* Deprive of priestly status.

un·gain·ly (ŭngān'lē) *adj.* Awkward, clumsy, ungraceful. **un·gain'li·ness** *n.*

un·god·ly (ŭngŏd'lē) *adj.* (**-li·er, -li·est**). Impious, wicked; (colloq.) outrageous. **un·god'li·ness** *n.*

un·gov·ern·a·ble (ŭngŭv'ernabel) *adj.* Uncontrollable.

un·gual (ŭng'gwal) *adj.* Of, like, bearing, a nail, claw, or hoof.

un·guent (ŭng'gwent) *n.* Ointment, salve. **un'guen·tar·y** *adj.*

un·gu·la (ŭng'gyula) *n.* (pl. **-lae** pr. -lē). 1. Hoof, claw, talon. 2. (math.) Cone, cylinder, with top cut off by plane oblique to base.

un·gu·late (ŭng'gyulĭt, -lāt) *adj.* Hoofshaped; (of mammals) having hoofs.

un·hal·lowed (ŭnhăl'ōd) *adj.* Not consecrated; unholy, impious, wicked.

un·hand (ŭnhănd') *v.t.* (archaic) Take one's hands off (person or thing).

un·health·y (ŭnhĕl'thē) *adj.* (**-health·i·er, -health·i·est**). Sickly; diseased; prejudicial or hurtful to health; unwholesome; (slang) dangerous. **un·health'i·ness** *n.*

un·heard (ŭnhĕrd') *adj.* Not heard; ~ **of**, unknown, unprecedented.

un·hinge (ŭnhĭnj') *v.t.* (**-hinged, -hing·ing**). (chiefly in past part.) Derange, disorder (mind).

uni- *prefix.* One; having, composed or consisting of, characterized by, etc., one (thing specified by second element).

u·ni·cam·er·al (ūnĭkăm'eral) *adj.* Having one (legislative) chamber.

UNICEF (ū'nĭsĕf) *n.* United Nations (International) Children's (Emergency) Fund.

u·ni·cel·lu·lar (ūnĭsĕl'yuler) *adj.* (esp. of organism) Having, composed of, a single cell.

u·ni·corn (ū'nĭkōrn) *n.* Fabulous animal represented as having the body of a horse with a single horn projecting from its forehead.

u·ni·cy·cle (ū'nĭsīkel) *n.* Frame mounted on one wheel with saddle for driver who propels vehicle by pushing pedals.

U·ni·fi·ca·tion (ūnĭfĭkā'shon) **Church.** Anticommunist religious (political?) group led by Rev. Sun Myung Moon (cf. MOONIE).

u·ni·form (ū'nĭfōrm) *adj.* Being or remaining the same in different places, at different times, etc., unvarying, consistent; plain, unbroken, undiversified; conforming to one standard, rule, or pattern, alike, similar. **u'ni·form·ly** *adv.* **uniform** *n.* Distinctive dress of uniform cut, material, and color worn by all members of particular military or other organization. ~ *v.* Make uniform; dress in uniform. **u'ni·form·ness** *n.*

u·ni·form·i·ty (ūnĭfōr'mĭtē) *n.* (pl. **-ties**). Being uniform, sameness, consistency, conformity.

u·ni·fy (ū'nĭfī) *v.t.* (**-fied, -fy·ing**). Reduce to unity or uniformity. **u·ni·fi·ca·tion** (ūnĭfĭkā'shon), **u'ni·fi·er** *ns.*

u·ni·lat·er·al (ūnĭlăt'eral) *adj.* One-sided; of, affecting, etc., one side (only); made by, binding on,

*The combined area of the states of the **Union of Soviet Socialist Republics** is the largest of any nation in the world. Inside its boundaries, the diversity of architecture and activity can range from traditional onion domes on village churches (top left) to huge stores in Moscow which are as large as small towns. However, small village markets still operate in some areas.*

affecting, one part only. **u·ni·lat′er·al·ly** *adv.*

un·im·peach·a·ble (ŭnĭmpē′chabel) *adj.* Giving no opportunity for censure; beyond reproach, question, or doubt. **un·im·peach′a·bly** *adv.*

un·in·hib·it·ed (ŭnĭnhĭb′ĭtĭd) *adj.* Not inhibited; free from conventional social customs or restraints. **un·in·hib′it·ed·ly** *adv.*

un·ion (ūn′yon) *n.* 1. Uniting, joining, being united, coalition, junction; marriage; concord, agreement. 2. Body formed by combination of parts or members; labor union. 3. Kind of joint or coupling for pipes etc. 4. **the Union**, the UNITED STATES OF AMERICA. 5. ~ **catalog**, library catalog combining catalogs of several libraries or several divisions; **U~ flag, Jack**, national flag of the United Kingdom; ~ **label**, identification stamped, fastened, etc., on item to show it was made by union labor; ~ **shop**, business or industry, employees of which must belong to union or agree to join within certain time after taking job.

un·ion·ist (ūn′yonĭst) *n.* 1. Member of a labor union; advocate of labor unions. 2. One who desires or advocates union, esp. particular legislative or political union, supporter of federal union of U.S., esp. (in Civil War) as opp. *secessionist.* ~ *adj.* Of, supporting, belonging to, union, unionism, or unionists. **un′ion·ism** *n.*

un·ion·ize (ūn′yonīz) *v.* (**-ized, -iz·ing**). Bring under labor union organization or rules. **un·ion·i·za·tion** (ūnyonīzā′shon) *n.*

Un·ion (ūn′yon) **of Soviet Socialist Republics.** (abbrev. U.S.S.R., USSR) Largest country in the world, stretching from E. Europe across Asia, bordered by Pacific on E., Arctic on N., Black and Caspian seas, Iran, Afghanistan, China, and Mongolia on S., and Poland and Rumania on W.; comprising 15 constituent republics (Russian Soviet Federal Socialist Republic, Ukraine, Byelorussia, Uzbekistan, Kazakhstan, Georgia, Azerbaijan, Lithuania, Moldavia, Latvia, Kirghizia, Tadzhikistan, Armenia, Turkmenistan, Estonia) and 20 autonomous republics; capital, Moscow.

u·nique (ūnēk′) *adj.* Of which there is only one; unmatched, unequaled; having no like, equal, or parallel. **u·nique′ly** *adv.* **u·nique′ness** *n.*

u·ni·sex (ū′nĭsěks) *adj.* Of fashions of dress, hairstyle, etc. designed for members of both sexes without distinction.

u·ni·son (ū′nĭson, -zon) *n.* (mus.) Coincidence in pitch; sound or note of same pitch as another; combination of voices or instruments at same pitch; **in** ~, at same pitch; in concord, agreement, or harmony. **u·nis·o·nal** (ūnĭs′onal), **u·nis′o·nant** *adjs.*

u·nit (ū′nĭt) *n.* 1. Single magnitude or number regarded as undivided whole, esp. the numeral "1"; any determinate quantity, magnitude, etc., as basis or standard of measurement for other quantities of same kind. 2. One of the individuals or groups into which a complex whole may be analyzed; that part of collective body or whole regarded as lowest or least to have separate existence; fractional interest in investment trust. 3. Device with specified function forming element in complex mechanism etc.; piece of furniture for fitting with others like it or formed of complementary elements. 4. ~ **pricing**, method of pricing items, esp. food products, that shows price for an ounce, pint, or other standard unit, thus making it easy for shoppers to compare prices of similar items; ~ **rule**, in Democratic Party national convention, rule that all the votes of a state must be given to the candidate chosen by the majority of that state's delegation. **unit** *adj.* Of, being, forming, a unit, individual.

U·ni·tar·i·an (ūnĭtār′ēan) *n.* One who maintains that the Godhead is one person, not a Trinity; member of Christian body that originated in England in 17th c. maintaining this belief; (also) one who advocates individual freedom of belief. ~ *adj.* Of Unitarians or their doctrine. **U·ni·tar′i·an·ism** *n.*

u·nite (ūnīt′) *v.* (**-nit·ed, -nit·ing**). Join together, make or become one, combine, consolidate, amalgamate; agree, combine, cooperate (*in*). **u·nit′ed** *adj.* (esp.) **U~ Brethren**, Moravians; **U~ States**, UNITED STATES OF AMERICA. **u·nit′ed·ly** *adv.*

United Arab Emirates. (abbrev. U.A.E.) Union of seven emirates in the E. part of the Arabian peninsula along Oman and Persian gulfs, comprising Abu Dhabi, Ajman, Dubai, Fujairah, Ras al Khaimah, Sharjah, and Umm al Qaiwain; capital, Abu Dhabi.

United Arab Republic. (abbrev. UAR) Former (1958–71) name of Egypt.

United Church of Christ. U.S. Protestant denomination formed by 1957 merger of Congregational Christian Church and Evangelical and Reformed Church.

United Kingdom. (abbrev. U.K.) Kingdom in W. Europe consisting of Gt. Britain (England, Scotland, and Wales) and Northern Ireland; capital, London.

United Methodist Church. Protestant church formed 1968 in U.S. by union of Methodist Church and Evangelical United Brethren.

United Nations. (orig.) Nations at war with the Axis, 1939–45; hence, international organization of these and other nations established as successor to the League of Nations by the ~ **Charter**, signed at San Francisco on June 26, 1945; its main object is the maintenance of peace and its six principal organs are the General Assembly, Security Council, Secretariat (at New York), International Court (at The Hague), Economic and Social Council, and Trusteeship Council.

United States of America. (abbrev. US, U.S., USA, U.S.A.) Republic of N. Amer. bounded on N. by Canada and on S. by Mexico; federation of 50 states and District of Columbia; capital, Washington, D.C.; colonies were established in N. Amer. beginning in 16th c. by Spanish in S. and W., followed by French in S. and N., Dutch in the E. and English along the Atlantic coast; colonies in E. were ruled by English after defeat of French during French and Indian War, 1754–63; colonies declared independence, 1776, and after defeat of English, during Revolutionary War, 1775–83, the 13 original colonies united under a constitution and chose George Washington as first president; westward expansion of this union resulted from purchase of Louisiana Territory from French, 1803; Florida purchased from Spain, 1819; Texas annexed, 1845; discovery of gold in California further extended westward expansion to Pacific coast; New Mexico and California ceded by Mexico, 1848, after Mexican War; Alaska purchased from Russia, 1867; Hawaiian Islands annexed, 1898.

u·ni·ty (ū′nĭtē) *n.* (pl. **-ties**). State of being one or single or

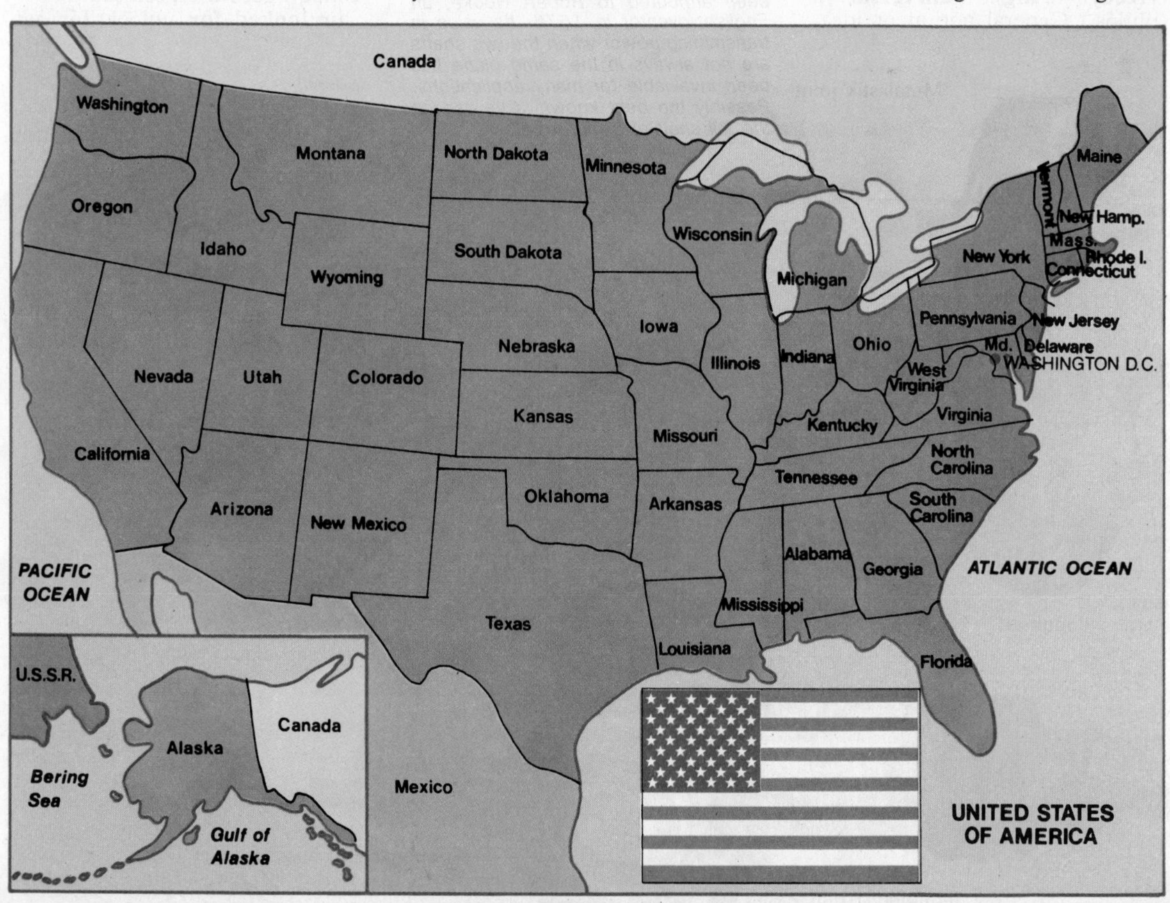

*The **United States of America** consists of the original 48 states together with Alaska (bought in 1867 but only granted statehood in 1959) and Hawaii which also joined the Union in 1959. Each state has certain policies not subject to Federal control.*

individual; being formed of parts that constitute a whole; due interconnection and coherence of parts; thing showing such unity, thing forming complex whole; (math.) the numeral 1 as basis of number; harmony, concord, between persons etc.; any of the three Aristotelian principles of dramatic composition as adapted by French classical dramatists, by which a play should consist of one main action, represented as occurring at one time and in one place.

Univ. *abbrev.* University.

u·ni·va·lent (ūnĭvā′lent) = MONOVALENT.

u·ni·valve (ū′nĭvălv) *adj.* (zool., of shell) Composed of a single valve, (of mollusk) having such shell.

u·ni·ver·sal (ūnĭvẽr′sal) *adj.* Of, belonging to, done, or used by, etc., all persons or things in the world or in the class concerned; applicable to all cases; covering many or all subjects, very broad (*universal genius*); ~ **joint**, mechanical joint or coupling permitting movement in any direction of the parts joined while transmitting rotary motion; ~ **suffrage**, suffrage extending to all persons over a specified age with the exception of certain minor categories. **u·ni·ver′sal·ly** *adv.* **u·ni·ver·sal·i·ty** (ūnĭvẽrsăl′ĭtē) *n.* (pl. **-ties**). **u·ni·ver′sal·ize** *v.t.* (**-ized, -iz·ing**). **universal** *n.* (philos.) General notion or idea, thing that by its nature may be predicated of many.

u·ni·ver·sal·ism (ūnĭvẽr′salĭzem) *n.* (theol.) Doctrine that all mankind will eventually be saved. **u·ni·ver′sal·ist** *n.* One who holds this doctrine, esp. (**U**~) member of Protestant denomination holding this doctrine, founded in U.S. in late 18th c., merged with Unitarians in 1961.

u·ni·verse (ū′nĭvẽrs) *n.* All created or existing things, all creation; = COSMOS[1]; the world or Earth; all mankind.

u·ni·ver·si·ty (ūnĭvẽr′sĭtē) *n.* (pl. **-ties**). Whole body of teachers and scholars engaged at particular place in giving and receiving instruction in higher branches of learning; such persons as corporate body with definite organization and powers (esp. of conferring degrees), forming institution for promotion of higher education; colleges, buildings, etc., of such a body.

un·kempt (ŭnkĕmpt′) *adj.* Uncombed, disheveled; untidy, looking neglected.

un·kind (ŭnkīnd′) *adj.* Lacking kindness; unpleasant, harsh. **un·kind′ness** *n.*

un·known (ŭnnōn′) *adj.* Not known; not identified; **U**~ **Soldier**, unnamed representative of a country's armed services killed in battle, buried in tomb serving as national memorial, esp. (U.S.) in Arlington National Cemetery.

un·lead·ed (ŭnlĕd′ĭd) *adj.* (of gasoline) Containing no tetraethyl lead; (printing) with no leads for spacing.

un·learn (ŭnlẽrn′) *v.* Cause to be no longer in one's knowledge, memory, or regular behavior.

un·leash (ŭnlēsh′) *v.t.* Free from leash or restraint; set free in order to pursue, attack, etc.

un·less (ŭnlĕs′) *conj.* If ... not, except when.

un·let·tered (ŭnlĕt′erd) *adj.* Not instructed in learning from books; illiterate.

un·like (ŭnlīk′, ŭn′līk) *adj.* & *prep.* Not like, different (from). **un·like′ness** *n.*

un·like·ly (ŭnlīk′lē) *adj.* Improbable; unpromising. **un·like′li·hood, un·like′li·ness** *ns.*

un·lim·it·ed (ŭnlĭm′ĭtĭd, ŭn′lĭm-) *adj.* Without limit, unrestricted, very great in number or quantity.

un·list·ed (ŭnlĭs′tĭd, ŭn′lĭs-) *adj.* Not included in list, esp. of stock exchange prices or of telephone numbers.

un·load (ŭnlōd′) *v.* Remove cargo or anything carried or conveyed (from); remove charge from (gun); relieve of burden; (colloq.) get rid of, sell (out).

un·looked-for (ŭnlo͝okt′fõr) *adj.*

Invention of the ***universal joint*** *has been attributed to Robert Hooke, an English inventor in 1676. Its value in transmitting power when the two shafts are not always in the same plane has been invaluable for many applications. Possibly the best known is its use on the tail shaft of a motor car.*

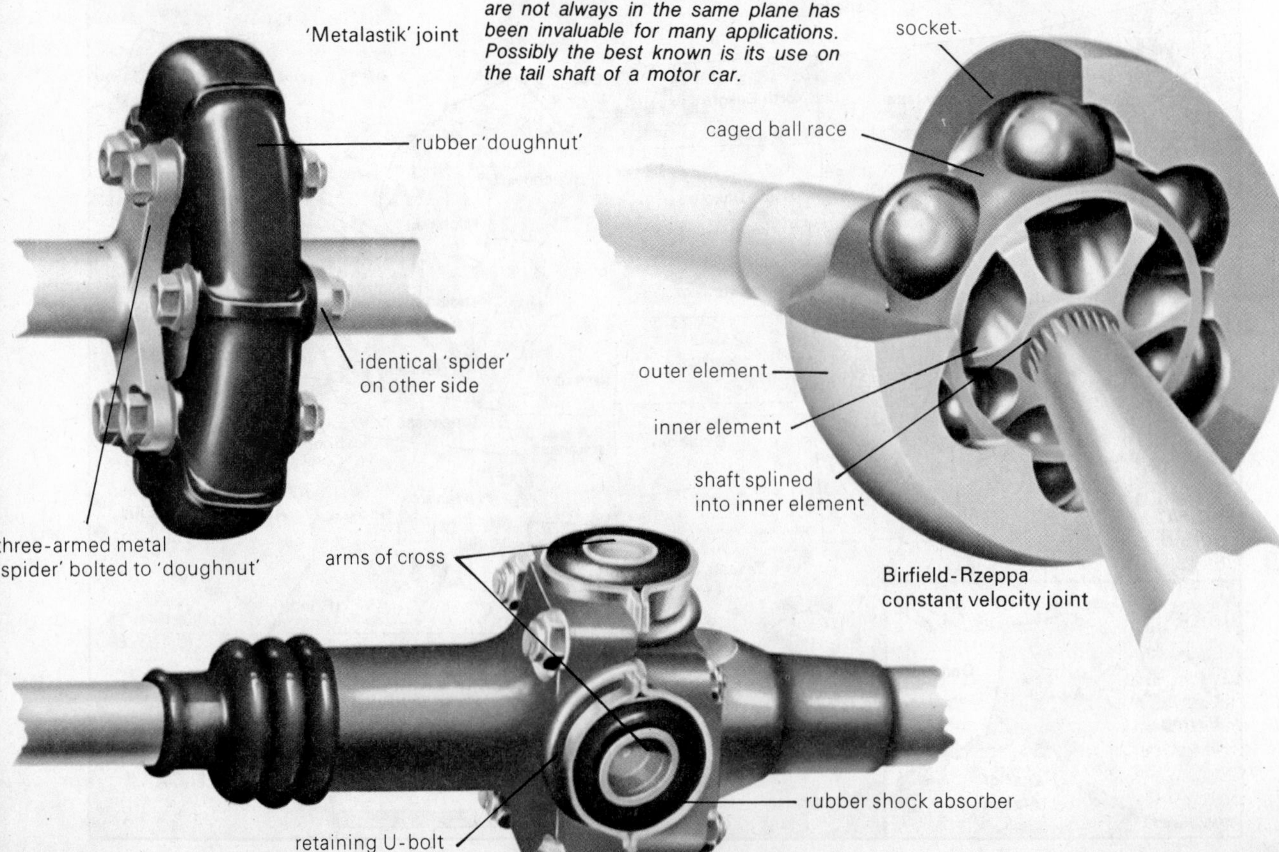

Not expected or foreseen.

un·loose (ŭnlo͞os′) *v.t.* (**-loosed, -loos·ing**). Loose, untie.

un·man (ŭnmăn′) *v.t.* (**-manned, -man·ning**). Deprive of courage, strength, firmness, etc.

un·manned (ŭnmănd′, ŭn′mănd) *adj.* (Of) pilotless spacecraft, aircraft without crew and operated by remote or automatic control.

un·mask (ŭnmăsk′, -mahsk′) *v.* Remove mask from; (fig.) expose true character of.

un·men·tion·a·ble (ŭnmĕn′sh*o*n*a*bel) *adj.* Unspeakable, that may not (properly) be mentioned.

un·mis·tak·a·ble (ŭnmĭstā′k*a*bel) *adj.* That cannot be mistaken or doubted. **un·mis·tak′a·bly** *adv.*

un·mit·i·gat·ed (ŭnmĭt′ĭgātĭd) *adj.* Unqualified, absolute. **un·mit′i·gat·ed·ly** *adv.*

un·nat·u·ral (ŭnnăch′*e*r*a*l) *adj.* Contrary or not conforming to nature; lacking natural feelings; artificial. **un·nat′u·ral·ly** *adv.* **un·nat′u·ral·ness** *n.*

un·nec·es·sar·y (ŭnnĕs′*e*sĕrē) *adj.* Not necessary; more than necessary. **un·nec·es·sar·i·ly** (ŭnnĕs*e*sār′*i*lē, -sĕr′-) *adv.* **un·nec′es·sar·i·ness** *n.*

un·nerve (ŭnnẽrv′) *v.t.* (**-nerved, -nerv·ing**). Deprive of nerve, courage, self-control, etc.

un·num·bered (ŭnnŭm′b*e*rd) *adj.* Countless; not marked etc. with a number.

un·oc·cu·pied (ŭnŏk′y*u*pīd) *adj.* 1. Having no occupant. 2. Not busy; idle.

un·or·gan·ized (ŭnōr′g*a*nīzd) *adj.* 1. Having no system or order. 2. Not acting, talking, etc. in systematic way. 3. Not part of labor union; not unionized.

un·pleas·ant (ŭnplĕz′*a*nt) *adj.* Disagreeable. **un·pleas′ant·ly** *adv.* **un·pleas′ant·ness** *n.*

un·prec·e·dent·ed (ŭnprĕs′ĭdĕntĭd) *adj.* For which there is no precedent, novel.

un·prin·ci·pled (ŭnprĭn′s*i*peld) *adj.* Not having, not based on, etc., sound or honest principles of conduct.

un·pro·fes·sion·al (ŭnpr*o*fĕsh′*o*nal) *adj.* Not professional; unworthy of a member of a profession.

un·qual·i·fied (ŭnkwŏl′*i*fīd) *adj.* Not qualified; not modified or limited. **un·qual′i·fied·ly** *adv.*

un·quote (ŭn′kwōt). Direction used in dictation to indicate the end of a quotation.

un·rav·el (ŭnrăv′*e*l) *v.* (**-eled, -el·ing**; Brit. **-elled, -el·ling**). Take out of tangled or intertwined condition (freq. fig.); undo, pull out (woven or esp. knitted fabric); come undone, become unknit or disentangled.

un·read (ŭnrĕd′) *adj.* (Of book etc.) not read; (of person) uneducated; ignorant.

un·rea·son·a·ble (ŭnrē′z*o*n*a*bel) *adj.* Not reasonable, esp. having or displaying little intelligence or judgment, irrational; immoderate, excessive. **un·rea′son·a·ble·ness** *n.* **un·rea′son·a·bly** *adv.*

un·re·con·struct·ed (ŭnrēk*o*nstrŭk′tĭd) *adj.* Holding to earlier ideas, beliefs, etc., esp. not accepting the spirit or fact of Reconstruction after the Civil War.

un·re·gen·er·ate (ŭnrĭjĕn′*e*rĭt) *adj.* Not regenerate; not reborn in spirit; unconverted to a specific belief, attitude, etc.; obstinate, stubborn. **un·re·gen′er·ate·ly** *adv.*

un·re·mit·ting (ŭnrĭmĭt′ĭng) *adj.* Incessant.

un·re·served (ŭnrĭzẽrvd′) *adj.* Not reserved; without reservations, qualifications, or exceptions; free from reserve, frank, open. **un·re·serv′ed·ly** *adv.*

un·rest (ŭnrĕst′) *n.* Disturbance, turmoil, trouble.

UNRRA, U.N.R.R.A. *abbrevs.* United Nations Relief and Rehabilitation Administration.

un·ruly (ŭnro͞o′lē) *adj.* (**-rul·i·er, -rul·i·est**). Not amenable to rule or discipline; turbulent. **un·rul′i·ness** *n.*

un·sat·u·rat·ed (ŭnsăch′*e*rātĭd) *adj.* (chem.): see SATURATE def. 2. **un·sat·u·rate** (ŭnsăch′*e*rĭt, -rāt) *n.*

un·sa·vor·y (ŭnsā′v*e*rē) *adj.* Not savory; morally offensive. **un·sa′vor·i·ness** *n.*

un·scathed (ŭnskādhd′) *adj.* Not injured or harmed.

un·scram·ble (ŭnskrăm′bel) *v.* Restore from scrambled state, esp. (electron.) restore (incoming scrambled signals) to understandable form. **un·scram′bler** *n.*

un·scru·pu·lous (ŭnskro͞o′py*u*l*u*s) *adj.* Not having scruples, shameless, unprincipled. **un·scru′pu·lous·ly** *adv.* **un·scru′pu·lous·ness** *n.*

un·sea·son·a·ble (ŭnsē′z*o*n*a*bel) *adj.* 1. Not appropriate to the season. 2. Not at the right time, inopportune. **un·sea′son·a·ble·ness** *n.* **un·sea′son·a·bly** *adv.*

un·seat (ŭnsēt′) *v.t.* 1. (of horse) Throw (rider) from saddle. 2. Dislodge, deprive of seat, esp. in legislative body etc.

un·seem·ly (ŭnsēm′lē) *adj.* Not in accordance with what is customary; improper; unbecoming. **un·seem′li·ness** *n.*

un·set·tled (ŭnsĕt′*e*ld) *adj.* Not (yet) settled; liable to or open to change or further discussion; (of bill etc.) unpaid; (of region) unpopulated. **un·set′tled·ness** *n.*

un·sight·ly (ŭnsīt′lē) *adj.* Unpleasing to the eye, ugly. **un·sight′li·ness** *n.*

un·skilled (ŭnskĭld′) *adj.* Not having or needing skill or special training.

un·so·lic·it·ed (ŭns*o*lĭs′ĭtĭd) *adj.* Not asked for; given or done voluntarily.

un·sound (ŭnsownd′) *adj.* Not sound; diseased, unhealthy, rotten, ill-founded, fallacious, unreliable. **un·sound′ly** *adv.* **un·sound′ness** *n.*

un·spar·ing (ŭnspār′ĭng) *adj.* Profuse, lavish; merciless. **un·spar′ing·ly** *adv.*

un·speak·a·ble (ŭnspē′k*a*bel) *adj.* That may not be spoken; indescribably repulsive or objectionable. **un·speak′a·bly** *adv.*

un·sta·ble (ŭnstā′bel) *adj.* Not stable; changeable; showing tendency to sudden mental or emotional changes. **un·sta′ble·ness** *n.* **un·sta′bly** *adv.*

un·stead·y (ŭnstĕd′ē) *adj.* Not steady or firm, changeable, fluctuating; not uniform or regular. **un·stead′i·ly** *adv.* **un·stead′i·ness** *n.*

un·stop (ŭnstŏp′) *v.* Remove stopper from; free from obstruction.

un·strung (ŭnstrŭng′) *adj.* 1. With strings relaxed or removed. 2. Not threaded on a string. 3. Weakened, unnerved.

un·stuck (ŭnstŭk′) *adj.* Not stuck, loosened from being stuck; **come ~**, (fig., colloq.) fail, go wrong.

un·sung (ŭnsŭng′) *adj.* Not sung; not celebrated or honored in verse or song.

un·think·a·ble (ŭnthĭng′k*a*bel) *adj.* Inconceivable.

un·ti·dy (ŭntī′dē) *adj.* (**-di·er, -di·est**). Not tidy, slovenly. **un·ti′di·ly** *adv.* **un·ti′di·ness** *n.*

un·til (ŭntĭl′) *prep* & *conj.* = TILL[4], used esp. when its clause or phrase stands first, and in formal style.

un·time·ly (ŭntīm′lē) *adj.* Occurring at time not suitable, too soon or too early. **~** *adv.* Prematurely, unseasonably, inopportunely. **un·time′li·ness** *n.*

un·to (ŭn′to͞o) *prep.* (archaic) To.

un·told (ŭntōld′) *adj.* Not told; not counted; beyond count.

un·touch·a·ble (ŭntŭch′*a*bel) *n.* Noncaste Hindu (whom a caste man may not touch).

un·to·ward (ŭntōrd′, -tōrd′, -tō′w*e*rd) *adj.* Perverse, refractory (archaic); awkward; unlucky; unseemly. **un·to′ward·ly** *adv.* **un·to′ward·ness** *n.*

un·truth (ŭntro͞oth′) *n.* Being untrue; falsehood, lie.

un·tu·tored (ŭnto͞o′t*e*rd, -tū′-) *adj.* 1. Not taught or tutored; uneducated. 2. Unsophisticated, naive.

un·used (for sense 1 ŭnūzd′; for sense 2 ŭnūst′) *adj.* 1. Not or never having been used. 2. Not

The African Republic of ***Burkina Faso*** *is 600 miles from the sea. Its people are mostly subsistence farmers though some livestock, cotton and peanuts are exported. There is also a textile plant.*

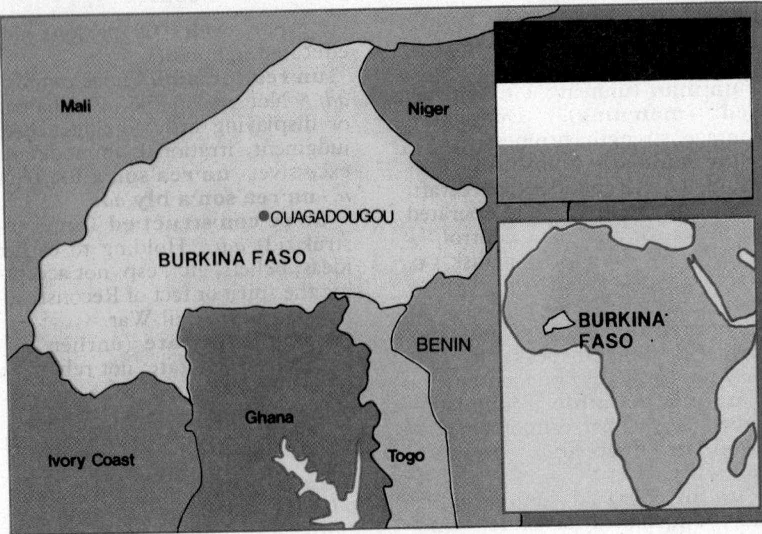

accustomed (*to*).

un·u·su·al (ŭnū′zhōōal) *adj.* Not usual; remarkable. **un·u′su·al·ly** *adv.* **un·u′su·al·ness** *n.*

un·ut·ter·a·ble (ŭnŭt′*e*rab*e*l) *adj.* That cannot be uttered; above or beyond description.

un·var·nished (ŭnvar̄′nĭsht) *adj.* Not covered (as) with varnish; not embellished, plain.

un·veil (ŭnvāl′) *v.t.* Remove veil from; remove concealing drapery from (statue etc.) as part of ceremony of first public display; (fig.) disclose, reveal, make publicly known. ~ *v.i.* Remove one's veil.

un·voiced (ŭnvoist′) *adj.* Not spoken; (phonet.) not voiced.

un·washed (ŭnwŏsht′,-wawsht′) *adj.* Not washed; not usually washed or clean; **the great** ~, the rabble.

un·well (ŭnwĕl′) *adj.* Not in good health; indisposed.

un·wept (ŭnwĕpt′) *adj.* Not wept for, not lamented.

un·whole·some (ŭnhōl′s*o*m) *adj.* Injurious to body or mind; having poor health or appearing to be in bad health; morally corrupt, loathsome. **un·whole′some·ly** *adv.* **un·whole′some·ness** *n.*

un·wield·y (ŭnwēl′dē) *adj.* Slow or clumsy of movement, awkward to handle, wield, or manage, by reason of size, shape, or weight. **un·wield′i·ness** *n.*

un·wind (ŭnwīnd′) *v.* (**-wound** pr. -wownd, **-wind·ing**). (Cause to) become drawn out at length after having been wound; (colloq.) relax.

un·wit·ting (ŭnwĭt′ĭng) *adj.* Not knowing, not aware; not intentional. **un·wit′ting·ly** *adv.*

un·wont·ed (ŭnwōn′tĭd, -wawn′-, -wŭn′-) *adv.* Not usual, customary, or habitual. **un·wont′-ed·ly** *adv.*

un·wound: see UNWIND.

un·writ·ten (ŭnrĭt′*e*n) *adj.* Not written (down); oral; traditional.

up (ŭp) *adv.* To, in, a high or higher place, position, degree, amount, value, etc.; to or in place farther north or otherwise conventionally regarded as higher; to or in the place in question or where the speaker etc. is; to or in erect or vertical position esp. as favorable to activity, out of bed, out of lying or sitting or kneeling posture, in(to) condition of efficiency or activity; (with verbs, usu.) expressing complete or effectual result etc.; **well** ~, in a high position; ~ **against**, in(to) contact or collision with; (colloq.) faced or confronted by; ~ **and down,** rising and falling; to and fro along; ~ **in,** (colloq.) expert, well-informed (in subject etc.); ~ **to,** as high or far as, up toward, so as to reach or arrive at; until; as many or much as, fit or qualified for, capable of, able to deal with, ready for; on a level with; engaged in, occupying oneself with; (colloq.) obligatory or incumbent on; **~-to-date,** extending to the present time; according to the newest ideas, styles, facts, etc.; keeping abreast of the newest styles, most recent news, etc.; **~-to-the-minute,** (colloq.) with the latest information; in the latest style etc.; ~ **with,** so as to overtake; on a level with. **up** *prep.* To a higher point of, on or along in ascending direction; at or in a higher part of; **up′stream,** against the current, farther from mouth of river. **up** *adj.* Moving, sloping, going, toward a higher point; (colloq.) optimistic, cheerful; **~-and-coming,** alert and likely to succeed; **up′beat,** (mus.) unaccented beat, esp. last beat in bar; **up′chuck,** (slang) vomit; **up′coming,** (colloq.) forthcoming, about to appear, anticipated; **up′grade,** upward slope; **on the upgrade,** (fig.) improving; **upgrade** (*v.t.*) (**-grad·ed, -grad·ing**), raise in status etc. **up** *n.* **on the** ~ **and** ~, honest(ly); **~s and downs,** rises and falls; undulating ground; alternately good and bad fortune. **up** *v.* (**upped, up·ping**). 1. Rise or raise abruptly. 2. (colloq.) Begin abruptly or boldly (to do something) (*he ~s and says ...*).

U·pan·i·shad (ōōpăn′ĭshăd, ōōpah′nĭshahd) *n.* Any of various compositions forming the final part of the Vedic literature, dealing with the nature of the soul and ultimate reality; see VEDA.

up·braid (ŭpbrād′) *v.t.* Chide, reproach.

up·bring·ing (ŭp′brĭnging) *n.* Bringing up of young persons, early rearing and training.

up·cast (ŭp′kăst, -kahst) *adj.* Turned upward. ~ *n.* (esp.) 1. (mining and geol.) (Fault caused by) upward dislocation of seam. 2. (mining) ~ **(air-)shaft,** shaft through which air passes out of mine.

up·coun·try (ŭp′kŭntrē) *n., adj.,* & *adv.* (To, in, of) inland part of country.

up·date (ŭp′dāt, ŭpdāt′) *v.t.* (**-dat·ed, -dat·ing**). Advance date of, bring up to date.

up·draft (ŭp′drăft) *n.* Upward flow of air.

up·end (ŭpĕnd′) *v.* Set, rise up, on end.

up·heave (ŭphēv′) *v.* (**-heaved, -hove** pr. -hōv, **-heav·ing**). Lift up, raise; throw up with violence, esp. by volcanic action; raise up. **up·heav′al** *n.*

up·hill (ŭp′hĭl) *adj.* Sloping upward; (fig.) arduous, difficult, laborious. **uphill** *adv.* With upward slope on hill, with slope in upward direction.

up·hold (ŭphōld′) *v.t.* (**-held** pr. -hĕld, **-hold·ing**). Hold up, keep erect, support; give support or countenance to; maintain, confirm (decision etc.). **up·hold′er** *n.*

up·hol·ster (ŭphōl′st*e*r, upōl′-) *v.t.* Furnish (room etc.) with hangings, carpets, etc.; provide (chair etc.) with textile covering, padding, etc., cover chair (*with, in*). **up·hol′ster·er** *n.* **up·hol′ster·y** *n.* (pl. **-ster·ies**). [f. obs. *upholster, upholder* one who upholds, i.e. keeps in repair; verb back formation]

UPI *abbrev.* United Press International.

up·keep (ŭp′kēp) *n.* (Cost of) maintenance in good condition or repair.

up·land (ŭp′l*a*nd, -lănd) *n.* (freq. pl.) Piece of high ground, stretch of hilly or mountainous country. ~ *adj.* Living, growing, situated, etc., on high ground; ~

plover, long-necked, long-tailed brownish bird (*Bartramia longicauda*) of Amer. prairie.

up·lift (ŭplĭft′) *v.t.* Raise up, elevate (esp. fig.). ~ (ŭp′lĭft) *n.* Raising, elevating; (colloq.) moral or intellectual edification. **up·lift′ment** *n.*

up·on (*u*pŏn′, *u*pawn′) = ON.

up·per (ŭp′*er*) *adj.* Higher in place, situated above; superior in rank, authority, dignity, etc.; ~ **case**: see CASE[2]; ~ **class**, class of people holding highest status in society, (~**-class** *adj.*); **upper-class′man**, junior or senior in college, cf. UNDERCLASSMAN; **upper crust**, (colloq.) aristocracy, highest social circles; **up′percut** (**-cut, -cut·ting**), (boxing) upward blow to the chin; **upper deck**, highest continuous deck of ship; **upper hand**, mastery, control, or advantage (*of, over*); **upper house**, higher legislative assembly, esp. U.S. Senate. **upper** *n.* Upper part of boot or shoe; (slang) any stimulant drug, esp. an amphetamine; **on one's** ~**s**, (colloq.) reduced to penury, having hard luck.

up·per·most (ŭp′*er*mōst) *adj.* Highest in place or rank. ~ *adv.* On or to the top.

Upper (ŭp′*er*) **Volta.** Now Burkina Faso. Inland republic of W. Africa, formerly part of the Ivory Coast; independent since 1960; capital, Ouagadougou.

up·pish (ŭp′ĭsh) *adj.* (colloq.) Self-assertive, pert, putting on airs. **up′pish·ly** *adv.* **up′pish·ness** *n.*

up·pi·ty (ŭp′ĭtē) *adj.* (colloq.) Arrogant, snobbish.

up·raise (ŭprāz′) *v.t.* (**-raised, -rais·ing**). Raise up, elevate, rear.

up·right (ŭp′rīt) *adj.* & *adv.* Erect, vertical; righteous, strictly honorable or honest. **up′right·ly** *adv.* **up′right·ness** *n.* **upright** *n.* Upright PIANO[2]; post or rod fixed upright esp. as support to some structure.

up·ris·ing (ŭp′rīzĭng) *n.* (esp.) Insurrection, popular rising against authority etc.

up·roar (ŭp′rōr, -rōr) *n.* Tumult, violent disturbance, clamor. **up·roar′i·ous** *adj.* **up·roar′i·ous·ly** *adv.* **up·roar′i·ous·ness** *n.*

up·root (ŭproot′, -root′) *v.t.* Tear up by the roots; eradicate, destroy.

up·set[1] (ŭpsĕt′) *v.* (**-set, -set·ting**). Overturn, be overturned; disturb the peace, composure, temper, digestion, etc., of. ~ (ŭp′sĕt, ŭpsĕt′) *n.* Upsetting, being upset.

up·set[2] (ŭp′sĕt) *adj.* ~ **price**, price fixed as lowest for which property offered at auction will be sold.

up·shot (ŭp′shŏt) *n.* Final issue, conclusion.

up·side down, up·side-down (ŭp′sīd down′) *advs.* & *adjs.* With the upper part under, inverted, in(to) total disorder. [altered from ME. *up so down* up as if down]

up·si·lon (ŭp′*s*ilŏn, ūp′-) *n.* Letter of Greek alphabet (*Y*, *υ*), corresponding to *u*.

up·stage (ŭp′stāj′) *adv.* Away from front of stage; ~ **of**, farther upstage than. **upstage** *adj.* (slang) Supercilious, haughty. ~ (ŭpstāj′) *v.t.* (**-staged, -stag·ing**). Force (another actor or actress) to face away from audience by getting or keeping upstage; (fig.) outshine; behave superciliously or haughtily toward.

up·stairs (ŭpstārz′) *adv.* Up the stairs. ~ (ŭp′stārz) *adj.* & *n.* (Of, in) upper floor of house etc.

up·stand·ing (ŭpstăn′dĭng) *adj.* Well set up, erect.

up·start (ŭp′stārt) *n.* One who has newly or suddenly risen in position or importance (freq. attrib.).

up·state (ŭp′stāt′) *adj.*, *adv.*, & *n.* (Pertaining to, in) part of state remote from large cities, esp. northern part.

up·stroke (ŭp′strōk) *n.* Upward line made in writing.

up·surge (ŭp′sĕrj) *n.* Upward surge, rise.

up·swept (ŭp′swĕpt) *adj.* 1. (of hair) Brushed upward toward top of head. 2. Curved or sloped upward.

up·take (ŭp′tāk) *n.* (colloq.) Understanding, apprehension.

up·thrust (ŭp′thrŭst) *n.* Upward thrust, esp. (geol.) one caused by volcanic or seismic action.

up-tight, up·tight (ŭptīt′) *adjs.* (slang) 1. Tense, worried; annoyed. 2. Stiffly conventional. **up·tight′ness** *n.*

up·town (ŭp′town′) *adj.* & *n.* (Pertaining to, in) higher or residential part of town or city.

up·turn (ŭp′tĕrn) *n.* Upheaval; improvement, upward trend.

up·ward (ŭp′w*er*d) *adj.* & *adv.* (Directed) toward a higher place (lit. & fig.); ~ **mobility**, capacity or tendency to move from lower to higher economic and social position. **up′wards** *adv.* (esp.) ~ **of**, more than. **up′ward·ly** *adv.* **up′ward·ness** *n.*

up·wind (ŭp′wĭnd) *adj.* & *adv.* In the direction opposite to that in which the wind is blowing.

U·ral-Al·ta·ic (ūr′*a*l ăltā′ĭk) *adj.* Of (the people of) the Urals and Altaic mountain ranges of central Asia; of a family of Finnic, Mongolian, Turkic, and other agglutinative languages of N. Europe and Asia.

Ural (ūr′*a*l) **Mountains.** (also **Urals**) Mountain range in U.S.S.R. forming a natural boundary between Europe and Asia.

U·ra·ni·a (yoorā′nē*a*). (Gk. and Rom. myth.) 1. Muse of astronomy. 2. Title of Aphrodite, in her heavenly or pure aspect.

u·ra·ni·um (yoorā′nē*u*m) *n.* (chem.) Heavy grayish metallic radioactive element, found in pitchblende and minerals, capable of nuclear fission and hence used in the production of atomic energy and atomic bombs; symbol U, at. no. 92, at. wt. 238.029. **u·ran·ic** (yoorăn′ĭk), **u·ran·ous** (ūr′*a*n*u*s, yoorăn′-) *adjs.* [f. URANUS]

U·ra·nus (ūr′*a*n*u*s, yoorā′-). 1. (Gk. myth.) Personification of the sky, the most ancient of the Greek gods and the first ruler of the universe. 2. (astron.) Seventh of the major planets, farthest from the sun except for Neptune and Pluto. **U·ra′ni·an** *adj.*

Ur·ban (ĕr′b*a*n). Name of eight popes: **Urban II**, pope 1088–99, inaugurated the first crusade; **Urban VIII**, pope 1623–44, Florentine scholar and poet.

ur·ban (ĕr′b*a*n) *adj.* Of, living or situated in, a city or town; ~ **guerrilla**, terrorist operating in cities; ~ **renewal**, slum clearance and redevelopment with new housing and facilities; ~ **sprawl**, uncontrolled expansion of town or city.

ur·bane (ĕrbān′) *adj.* Courteous, civil; bland, suave. **ur·bane′ly** *adv.* **ur·ban·i·ty** (ĕrbăn′ĭtē) *n.* (pl. **-ties**). [L. *urbanus* of the city, refined, polished (*urbs* city)]

*The smallest country in South America, **Uruguay**, once very prosperous, has suffered from political unrest and inflation. Its exports are mainly wool, meat and hides.*

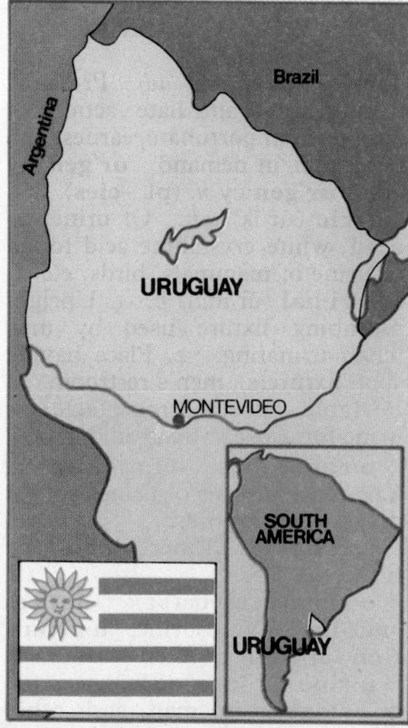

ur·ban·ize (ẽr′banīz) *v.t.* (**-ized, -iz·ing**). Render urban; remove rural character of (district or population). **ur·ban·i·za·tion** (ẽrbanīzā′shon) *n.*

ur·chin (ẽr′chĭn) *n.* 1. Hedgehog (archaic or dial.); **sea ~**: see SEA. 2. Roguish or mischievous boy; little fellow, boy. [ME. *hurcheon* hedgehog, f. L. *ericius*]

Ur·du (o͝or′do͞o, o͝ordo͞o′) *n.* Literary form of Hindustani drawing vocabulary from Persian and using Persian-Arabic script; one of the national languages of Pakistan. [Hind., lit. = "camp language"]

-ure *suffix.* Forming nouns with sense (1) (result of) action or process (*composure, enclosure, figure, seizure*); (2) function, state, rank, dignity, office (*judicature, prefecture*); (3) collective body of agents (*legislature*); (4) that by which the action is effected (*closure, ligature*).

u·re·a (yo͞orē′*a*, ūr′ē*a*) *n.* (chem.) Soluble nitrogenous crystalline compound ($CO(NH_2)_2$), present in urine of mammals, birds, and some reptiles, and also in blood, milk, etc.

u·re·mi·a (yo͞orē′mē*a*) *n.* (path.) Presence in blood of urinary matter normally excreted by kidneys; condition caused by failure of kidneys to function. **u·re′mic** *adj.*

u·re·ter (yo͞orē′t*e*r) *n.* Either of two ducts conveying urine from kidney to bladder or cloaca.

u·re·thra (yo͞orē′thr*a*) *n.* (pl. **-thrae** pr. -thrē, **-thras**). Duct through which urine is discharged from bladder. **u·re′thral** *adj.*

urge (ẽrj) *v.t.* (**urged, urg·ing**). 1. Bring forward (fact etc.) earnestly to someone's attention; state as justification etc.; advocate pressingly. 2. Entreat pertinaciously, incite. 3. Drive forcibly, impel; hasten. ~ *n.* Impelling motive, force, pressure, etc.

ur·gent (ẽr′j*e*nt) *adj.* Pressing, calling for immediate action or attention; importunate, earnest and persistent in demand. **ur′gent·ly** *adv.* **ur′gen·cy** *n.* (pl. **-cies**).

u·ric (ūr′ĭk) *adj.* Of urine; ~ **acid**, white crystalline acid found in urine of mammals, birds, etc.

u·ri·nal (ūr′*i*nal) *n.* 1. Upright plumbing fixture used by men when urinating. 2. Place having such fixture(s), men's restroom. 3. Portable vessel or receptacle for urine for use, e.g. by invalid in bed.

u·ri·nal·y·sis (ūr*i*năl′ĭsĭs) *n.* Chemical analysis of urine esp. for diagnostic purposes.

u·ri·nar·y (ūr′*i*nĕrē) *adj.* Of urine.

u·ri·nate (ūr′*i*nāt) *v.t.* (**-nat·ed, -nat·ing**). Void urine. **u·ri·na·tion** (ūr*i*nā′shon) *n.*

u·rine (ūr′ĭn) *n.* Fluid secreted by kidneys in man and other mammals, stored in bladder and voided at intervals through urethra; similar fluid in other vertebrates. **u′ri·nous** *adj.*

urn (ẽrn) *n.* 1. Vessel or vase with foot and usu. with rounded body, esp. as used for storing ashes of the dead, or as receptacle or measure. 2. Large vessel with spigot, for serving tea or coffee.

u·rol·o·gy (yo͞orŏl′*o*jē) *n.* Study of diseases of urinary system. **u·rol′o·gist** *n.*

Ur·sa (ẽr′s*a*). (astron.) ~ **Major**, the Great Bear, a northern constellation, also known as the Big Dipper; ~ **Minor**, the Little Bear or Little Dipper, northernmost constellation, containing the polestar. [L., = "she-bear"]

Ur·su·line (ẽr′s*u*lĭn, -līn, ẽrs′-y*u*-) *adj.* & *n.* (Nun) of an order founded by St. Angela Merici at Brescia in 1537 for nursing the sick and teaching girls. [named after St. Ursula, patron saint of the foundress]

ur·ti·car·i·a (ẽrtĭkār′ē*a*) *n.* (path.) Severely itching skin eruptions caused by allergic reaction to external agents (foods etc.) or emotional stimuli; also called hives and nettle rash.

U·ru·guay (oor′*u*gwā, -gwī, ūr′-). S. Amer. republic, lying to the E. of the Uruguay river, inaugurated in 1830; capital, Montevideo. **U·ru·guay·an** (oor*u*-gwā′*a*n, -gwī′-, ūr-) *adj.* & *n.*

US, U.S. *abbrevs.* United States (of America).

us (ŭs) *pron.* Objective (accus., dat.) case of WE.

USA, U.S.A. *abbrevs.* United States of America; United States Army.

USAF, U.S.A.F. *abbrevs.* United States Air Force.

us·age (ū′sĭj, ū′zĭj) *n.* Manner of using or treating, treatment; habitual or customary practice, established use (esp. of word); quantity used; (law) habitual but not necessarily immemorial practice.

USCG, U.S.C.G. *abbrevs.* United States Coast Guard.

USDA *abbrev.* United States Department of Agriculture.

use (ūz) *v.* (**used, us·ing**). 1. Employ for a purpose or as instrument or material; exercise, put into operation, avail oneself of; ~ **up**, use the whole of, find a use for what remains of; exhaust, wear out. 2. Treat in specified manner. 3. (now only in past t.) Be accustomed, have as constant or frequent practice; (past part.) accustomed; (past part.) (of clothes, vehicles, etc.) secondhand. **us·a·ble** *adj.* **use** (ūs) *n.* 1. Using, employment, application to a purpose; right or power of using; availability, utility, purpose for which thing can be used, occasion for using. 2. Ritual and liturgy of a church, diocese, etc. 3. (law) Benefit or profit of lands etc. held by another solely for the beneficiary. **us·er** (ū′z*e*r) *n.*

use·ful (ūs′f*u*l) *adj.* Of use, serviceable; suitable for use, advantageous, profitable. **use′ful·ly** *adv.* **use′ful·ness** *n.*

use·less (ūs′lĭs) *adj.* Serving no useful purpose, unavailing; of inadequate or insufficient capacity, inefficient. **use′less·ness** *n.*

USES *abbrev.* United States Employment Service.

USGS, U.S.G.S. *abbrevs.* United States Geological Survey.

ush·er (ŭsh′*e*r) *n.* Person who shows people to seats in church, theater, etc. (fem. **ush·er·ette′**); attendant of bridegroom at wedding. **usher** *v.t.* Act as usher to; precede (person) as usher, announce, show *in, out* (freq. fig.). [OF. *uissier* f. L. *ostiarius* doorkeeper (*ostium* door)]

USIA, U.S.I.A. *abbrevs.* United States Information Agency.

USMC, U.S.M.C. *abbrevs.* United States Marine Corps.

USN, U.S.N. *abbrevs.* United States Navy.

USPHS, U.S.P.H.S. *abbrevs.* United States Public Health Service.

U.S.S. *abbrev.* United States Senate; United States Ship (or Steamer, Steamship).

U.S.S.R., USSR *abbrevs.*

US Air Force Phantoms stationed at Lakenheath, England. There are many strategically positioned bases around the world used by the US Air Force.

Union of Soviet Socialist Republics.

usu. *abbrev.* Usual(ly).

u·su·al (ū'zhōōal) *adj.* Commonly or ordinarily observed, practiced, used, happening, to be found, etc.; current, ordinary, customary, wonted. **u'su·al·ly** *adv.* **u'su·al·ness** *n.*

u·su·fruct (ū'zufrŭkt, ū'su-, ūz'yu-, ūs'yu-) *n.* (law) Right of enjoying use and advantages of another's property, short of causing damage or prejudice to this; use, enjoyment (*of* something). **u·su·fruc·tu·ar·y** (ūzufrŭk'chōōĕrē, ūsu-, ūzyu-, ūsyu-) *adj.* & *n.* (pl. **-ar·ies**). Of usufruct, (person) enjoying usufruct.

u·su·rer (ū'zherer) *n.* One who lends money at exorbitant or illegal rates of interest.

u·surp (ūsẽrp', ūzẽrp') *v.* Seize, assume, (power, right, etc.) wrongfully. **u·sur·pa·tion** (ūserpā'shon, ūzer-), **u·surp'er** *ns.*

u·su·ry (ū'zherē) *n.* (pl. **-ries**). Practice of lending money at exorbitant interest, esp. at higher interest than is allowed by law; such interest. **u·su·ri·ous** (ūzhoor'ēus) *adj.* **u·su'ri·ous·ly** *adv.* **u·su'ri·ous·ness** *n.*

UT, Ut. *abbrevs.* Utah.

U·tah (ū'taw, ū'tah). Western state of U.S., admitted to the Union in 1896; capital, Salt Lake City.

u·ten·sil (ūtĕn'sĭl) *n.* Instrument, implement, vessel, esp. in domestic use.

u·ter·ine (ū'terĭn, -rīn) *adj.* 1. Having the same mother but different fathers. 2. Of, situated in, connected with, the uterus.

u·ter·us (ū'terus) *n.* (pl. **u·ter·i** pr. ū'terī). Womb, organ in which young are conceived, develop, and are protected till birth.

u·til·i·tar·i·an (ūtĭlĭtār'ēan) *adj.* Of, consisting in, based on, utility, esp., regarding the greatest good of the greatest number as the chief consideration of morality; holding utilitarian views or principles. ~ *n.* One who holds or supports utilitarian views; one devoted to mere utility or material interests.

u·til·i·tar·i·an·ism (ūtĭlĭtār'ēanĭzem) *n.* Utilitarian principles, doctrines, etc., esp. as expounded by BENTHAM and J. S. MILL.

u·til·i·ty (ūtĭl'ĭtē) *n.* (pl. **-ties**). 1. Usefulness, fitness for some desirable end or useful purpose, profitableness; power to satisfy human wants; useful thing; (**public**) **utilities**, (organizations supplying) gas, water, electricity, transport services, means of communication, etc., provided for some or all members of the community and regarded as so essential to the life of the community that they are subject to various forms of public control. 2. (attrib.) Reared, kept, made, etc., for useful ends as opp. to display or show purposes; **utility man**, (baseball) reserve player able to play several positions; **utility room**, room containing appliances (e.g. heater, washer, dryer, etc.).

u·ti·lize (ū'tilīz) *v.t.* (**-lized, -liz·ing**). Make use of, turn to account, use. **u·ti·li·za·tion** (ūtilīzā'shon) *n.*

ut·most (ŭt'mōst) *adj.* Furthest, extreme; that is such in the highest degree. ~ *n.* Utmost point, degree, limit, extent, etc.; best of one's ability, power, etc.

U·to·pi·a (ūtō'pēa). Name of the imaginary island governed under a perfect political and social system, which forms the title of a book by Sir Thomas More published in 1516; hence, any ideal or perfect social and political system. **U·to'pi·an** *adj.* & *n.* (Inhabitant) of Utopia; (usu. **u**~) (characteristic of) an ardent, but unpractical reformer. **u·to'pi·an·ism** *n.* [Gk. *ou* not + *topos* place]

U·tril·lo (ūtrĭl'ō, ōō-), **Maurice** (1883–1955). French painter known especially for scenes of villages and Paris streets.

Awesome pinnacles tower above the Rec Canyon in the Bryce Canyon Natinal Park, ***Utah****. The result of differential weathering, they will, in time, fall and add to the soil-building process below.*

ut·ter[1] (ŭt'er) *adj.* Complete, total, unqualified. **ut'ter·ly** *adv.* **ut'ter·ness** *n.* **ut'ter·most** *adj.*

ut·ter[2] (ŭt'er) *v.t.* 1. Emit audibly; express in spoken or written words. 2. Put (counterfeit money etc.) into circulation. **ut'ter·er** *n.* **ut'ter·ance** *n.* Uttering; power of speech; spoken words.

U-turn (ū'tẽrn) *n.* Turning completely around, esp. of motor vehicle on street to face in opposite direction, without reversing; complete reversal of policy etc.

u·vu·la (ūv'yula) *n.* (pl. **-las, -lae** pr. -lē). Conical fleshy prolongation hanging from middle of pendent margin of soft palate. **u'vu·lar** *adj.*

Ux·mal (ōōshmahl'). Ancient city in Yucatan, Mexico; site of Mayan ruins.

ux·o·ri·ous (ŭksōr'ēus, -sōr'-, ŭgzōr'-, -zōr'-) *adj.* Excessively, foolishly fond of one's wife; marked by such fondness. **ux·or'i·al·ly** *adv.* **ux·o'ri·ous·ness** *n.*

Uz·bek (ōōz'bĕk, ŭz'-), **Uz·beg** (ōōz'bĕg, ŭz'-) *adjs.* & *ns.* (pl. **-beks, -begs**, collect. **-bek, -beg**). (Member, language) of a Turkic people of Turkestan and Uzbekistan.

Uz·bek·i·stan (ōōzbĕk'ĭstăn, ŭz-, -stahn). Constituent republic (properly *Uzbek Soviet Socialist Republic*) of U.S.S.R., lying S. and SE. of the Aral Sea; capital, Tashkent.

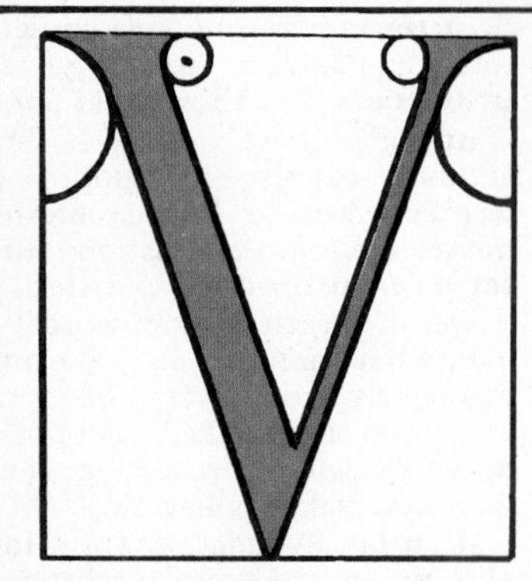

In Latin and in English, use of the letter ***V, v*** *was at first interchangeable with U. This continued in English as late as the 17th century. However, the Latin sound changed earlier (about the end of the Roman Empire) from that of W to its present usage.*

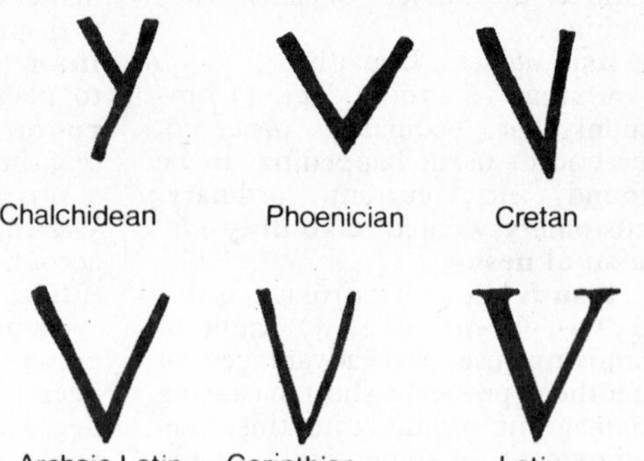

V, v (vē) (pl. **V's, v's** or **Vs, vs**). 1. Twenty-second letter of modern English and 20th of ancient Roman alphabet, adopted in form from early Greek vowel symbol **V**, in English representing a labiodental voiced spirant. 2. Roman numeral symbol for 5. 3. **V**, symbol for allied victory in World War II; **V-E Day**, May 8, 1945, day fixed for the official celebration of the end of hostilities in Europe; **V-J Day**, Aug. 15, 1945, celebrating end of hostilities in Japan. 4. Object etc. shaped like **V; V sign**, (orig. in World War II) first two fingers held up in shape of **V**, palm outward, as symbol of victory. Similar sign, palm inward, as vulgar derisory gesture.

V *symbol.* Vanadium.

V, v *abbrevs.* Volt(s).

v. *abbrev.* Verb; verse; versus; *vide.*

VA, V.A. *abbrevs.* Veterans Administration; Virginia.

Va. *abbrev.* Virginia.

V.A. *abbrev.* Vicar Apostolic; Vice Admiral.

va·can·cy (vā′kansē) *n.* (pl. **-cies**). Being vacant; vacant space, breach, gap; lack of intelligence, inanity; unoccupied office, room(s) to let, post, or dignity.

va·cant (vā′kant) *adj.* Empty, not filled or occupied; (of the mind) unoccupied with thought; without intelligence; (of person) with vacant mind. **va′cant·ly** *adv.*

va·cate (vā′kāt) *v.t.* (**-cat·ed, -cat·ing**). Leave (office, position) vacant; give up possession or occupancy of (house etc.); (law) make void, annul, cancel.

va·ca·tion (vākā′shon, va-) *n.* Vacating; part of year constituting fixed period of cessation from work (esp. while still collecting pay) or study; period of recreation, travel, etc.; time during which courts, schools, or universities are closed; cf. HOLIDAY. **va·ca′tion·er, va·ca′tion·ist** *ns.*

vac·ci·nate (văk′sināt) *v.t.* (**-nat·ed, -nat·ing**). Inoculate with a vaccine, esp. against smallpox. **vac·ci·na·tion** (văksinā′shon), **vac′ci·na·tor** *ns.*

vac·cine (văksēn′, văk′sēn) *n.* Preparation of cowpox virus used for inoculation against smallpox; any preparation of microorganisms used as an immunizing agent.

vac·il·late (văs′ilāt) *v.i.* (**-lat·ed, -lat·ing**). Swing or sway unsteadily; hover doubtfully; waver between different opinions, etc.

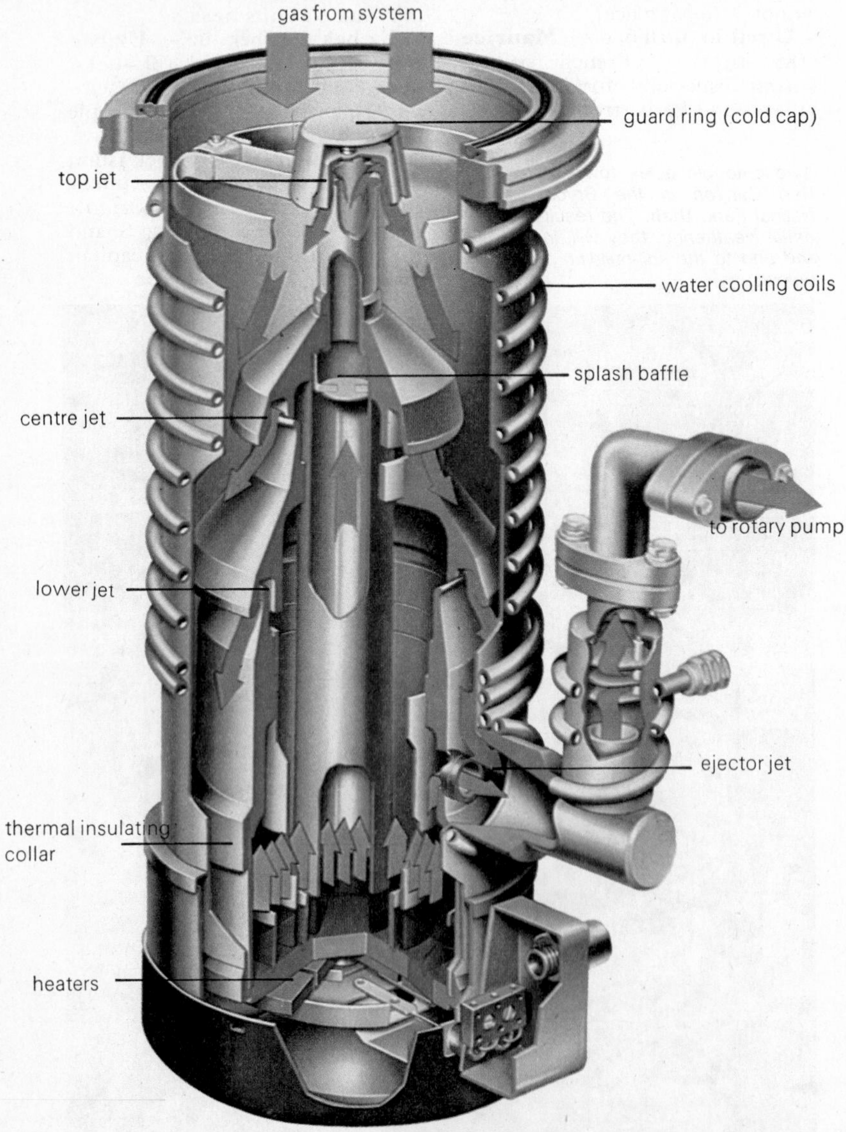

To obtain the low pressures needed to achieve a near-perfect ***vacuum,*** *a vapor-diffusion pump is often used. The rotary pump exhausts most of the air and then the heated oil gathers the remaining gas in the system.*

To prevent outbreaks of cholera and other highly-infectious diseases, mass ***vaccination*** *programs have been instituted in India and in other countries where infection is likely to occur.*

vac'il·la·tor, vac·il·la·tion (văsilā'shon) *ns.*

va·cu·i·ty (văkū'ĭtē) *n.* (pl. **-ties**). Empty space; absolute emptiness; vacuousness, vacancy.

vac·u·ole (văk'ūōl) *n.* Space within protoplasm usu. filled with liquid.

vac·u·ous (văk'ūus) *adj.* Empty; void; unintelligent, vacant. **vac'u·ous·ly** *adv.* **vac'u·ous·ness** *n.*

vac·u·um (văk'ūum, -ūm) *n.* (pl. **-u·ms, -u·a** pr. -ūa). Space entirely empty of matter; empty space; space, vessel, empty of air, esp. one from which air has been artificially withdrawn; ~ **bottle, jug**, vessel with double wall enclosing vacuum so that liquid in inner receptacle retains its heat or cold; ~ **cleaner**, apparatus for removing dust etc. from carpets, upholstery, etc., by suction; ~-**packed**, sealed after partial removal of air; ~ **pump**, pump for producing a vacuum; ~ **tube**, sealed glass or metal tube or bulb from which almost all the air has been removed, so that electrical current can flow between electrodes inside without disturbance by a gaseous atmosphere; such tube used in radio and electronics. **vacuum** *v.t.* (colloq.) Clean with vacuum cleaner.

va·de me·cum (vā'dē mē'kum, vah'-) *n.* (pl. **va·de me·cums**). Book or other thing carried constantly about the person, esp. handbook or manual. [L., = "go with me"]

Va·duz (vahdōōts', fah-). Capital of the principality of Liechtenstein.

vag·a·bond (văg'abŏnd) *adj.* Wandering, having no settled habitation or home; straying; (as) of a vagabond. ~ *n.* Vagabond person, esp. idle and worthless wanderer, vagrant; (colloq.) scamp, rascal. **vag'a·bond·age, vag'a·bond·ism** *ns.* **vag'a·bond·ish** *adj.*

va·gar·y (vagār'ē, vā'gerē) *n.* (pl. **-gar·ies**). Capricious or extravagant action, notion, etc.; freak, caprice.

va·gi·na (vajī'na) *n.* (pl. **-nas, -nae** pr. -nē). Sheathlike covering, organ, or part; membranous canal leading from vulva to uterus in female mammals; analogous structure in some other animals. **vag·i·nal** (văj'inal) *adj.*

vag·i·ni·tis (văjinī'tĭs) *n.* (pathol.) Inflammation of the vagina.

va·grant (vā'grant) *n.* One without established home or regular work, wandering from place to place, tramp, wanderer; (law) idle and disorderly person liable to arrest and imprisonment. ~ *adj.* That is a vagrant; (as) of a vagrant; roving, itinerant. **va'grant·ly** *adv.* **va·gran·cy** (vā'granse) *n.* (pl. **-cies**).

vague (vāg) *adj.* (**va·guer, va·guest**). Indistinct, not clearly expressed or perceived, of uncertain or ill-defined meaning or character or appearance; forgetful, unbusinesslike. **vague'ly** *adv.* **vague'·ness** *n.*

va·gus (vā'gus) *n.* (pl. **va·gi** pr. vā'jī). Either of tenth pair of cranial nerves, with branches to thoracic and abdominal viscera etc.

vain (vān) *adj.* Unsubstantial, empty, of no effect, unavailing; having excessively high opinion (*of* one's own appearance, qualities, possessions, etc.); **in** ~, to no effect or purpose, vainly; **take in** ~, utter, use (name, esp. of God), needlessly, casually, or idly. **vain'ly** *adv.*

vain·glo·ry (vān'glōrē, -glōrē, vānglōr'ē, -glōr'ē) *n.* Boastfulness, extreme vanity. **vain·glo'ri·ous** *adj.* **vain·glo'ri·ous·ly** *adv.* **vain·glo'ri·ous·ness** *n.*

Vais·ya (vīs'ya, vīsh'-). (Member of) the third of the four great Hindu castes, comprising merchants and agriculturalists. [Sansk. *vaiśya* peasant, laborer]

val·ance (văl'ans, vā'lans) *n.* Short curtain around frame or canopy of bedstead, above window or under shelf.

vale[1] (vāl) *n.* Valley (now chiefly poet. or in names); ~ **of tears**, the world as a scene of troubles etc.

va·le[2] (vah'lā, vā'lē; *Lat.* wah'lĕ) *int.* & *n.* Farewell. [L., = "be well!"]

val·e·dic·tion (văledĭk'shon) *n.* (Words used in) bidding farewell.

val·e·dic·to·ri·an (văledĭktōr'ean, -tōr'-) *n.* Senior student (usu. highest ranking in class) who delivers the valedictory oration on graduation etc.

val·e·dic·to·ry (văledĭk'terē) *adj.* & *n.* (pl. **-ries**). (Speech, oration) bidding farewell.

va·lence (vā'lens), **va·len·cy** (vā'lensē) (pl. **-cies**) *ns.* (chem.) 1. Power that atoms possess of combining with one another to form molecules; ~ **bond**, linkage between two atoms in a molecule, formed either by the transfer of an electron from one atom to the other (*electrovalent bond*) or by the sharing of electrons, two to each link, between the atoms (*covalent bond*). 2. Number indicating the number of atoms of hydrogen with which a single atom of a given element can combine (an element with a valence of 1 is *univalent* or *monovalent*, of 2 *bivalent* or *divalent*, of 3 *tervalent* or *trivalent*, of 4 *quadrivalent* or *tetravalent*, etc.).

Va·len·ci·a (valĕn'shēa, -sēa). Town and province of E. Spain; hence, variety of almond, raisin, orange, and other fruits, produced there.

Va·len·ci·ennes (valĕnsēĕnz'; *Fr.* vălahnsyĕn'). Town in NE. France, formerly Flemish; ~ **lace**, fine bobbin lace made at Valenciennes in 17th and 18th centuries.

va·len·cy = VALENCE.

Val·en·tine[1] (văl'entīn), **St.** Name of several saints of whom the most celebrated are two martyrs whose festivals fall on Feb. 14, both belonging to reign of the emperor

Claudius.

Val·en·tine[2] (văl′entīn) *n.* 1. St. Valentine's day, Feb. 14, on which birds were believed to mate and sweethearts were chosen. 2. Sweetheart chosen on St. Valentine's day; gift given on this occasion (archaic); (also **v~**) letter or card, of sentimental or comic nature, sent, usu. anonymously, to person of opposite sex on St. Valentine's day.

Va·le·ra (v*a*lār′*a*), **Ea·mon De** (ā′mŏn dĕ): see DE VALERA.

va·le·ri·an (v*a*lēr′ē*a*n) *n.* Any species of widely distributed herbaceous genus *Valeriana*, esp. *V. officinalis*, with small pink or white flowers and strong odor; dried roots etc. of species of valerian used as carminative etc., or in scents etc.

va·ler·ic (v*a*lĕr′ĭk, -lēr′-), **va·le·ri·an·ic** (v*a*lērēăn′ĭk) *adjs.* Derived from valerian; ~ **acid**, any of four strong-smelling isomeric fatty acids.

val·et (văl′ĭt, văl′ā, vălā′) *n.* (also ~ **de cham·bre** pr. vălā d*e* shahṅ′-br*e*) (pl. ~**s de cham·bre** pr. vălā d*e* shahṅ′br*e*). Manservant attending on man's person and having charge of clothes etc.; one who cleans, presses, and mends clothes. **val′et** *v.t.* (**-et·ed, -et·ing**). Wait on, act, as valet to.

val·e·tu·di·nar·i·an (văl*e*tōōd*i*-nār′ē*a*n, -tū-) *adj.* & *n.* (Person) of infirm health, esp. unduly solicitous or anxiously concerned about health. **val·e·tu·di·nar′i·an·ism** *n.* **val·e·tu·di·nar·y** (văl*e*tōō′d*i*-nĕrē, -tū′-) *adj.* & *n.* (pl. **-nar·ies**).

Val·hal·la (vălhăl′*a*, vahlhah′l*a*). (Scand. myth.) Hall assigned to heroes who have died in battle, in which they feast with Odin.

val·iant (văl′y*a*nt) *adj.* Brave, courageous. **val′iant·ly** *adv.* **val′-iance, val·ian·cy** (văl′y*a*nsē) *ns.*

val·id (văl′ĭd) *adj.* (of reason, argument, etc.) Sound, defensible, well-grounded; (law) sound and sufficient, executed with proper formalities. **val′id·ly** *adv.* **val′id·-ness, va·lid·i·ty** (v*a*lĭd′ĭtē) *ns.*

val·i·date (văl′ĭdāt) *v.t.* (**-dat·ed, -dat·ing**). Make valid, ratify, confirm. **val·i·da·tion** (vălĭdā′-sh*o*n) *n.*

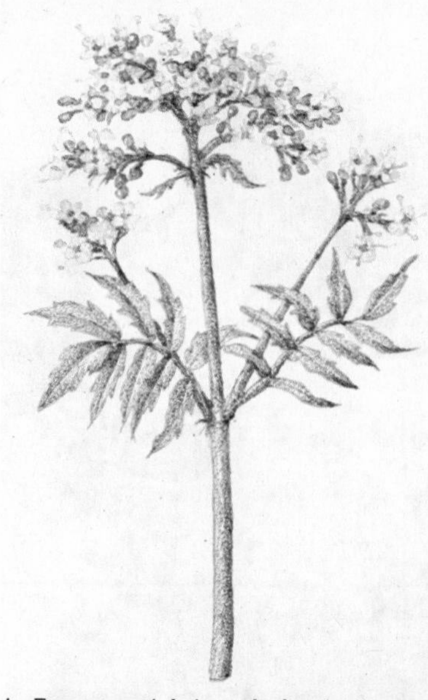

In Europe and Asia, ***valerian*** *had many uses. Its roots contained a drug used to treat nervous disorders; perfume was extracted from its leaves which were also used as a condiment.*

va·lise (v*a*lēs′; *Brit.* also v*a*lēz′) *n.* Small piece of hand luggage.

Va·li·um (văl′ē*u*m) *n.* (trademark) Drug used as tranquilizer and muscle relaxant.

Val·kyr·ie (vălkēr′ē, văl′kĭrē) *n.* (Scand. myth.) Each of 12 war maidens supposed to hover over battlefields selecting those to be slain and conducting them to Valhalla.

Val·let·ta (vahllĕt′tah). Capital city and port of Malta.

val·ley (văl′ē) *n.* (pl. **-leys**). Long depression or hollow between hills, freq. with stream or river along bottom; stretch of country drained or watered by river system; any depression or hollow resembling valley, esp. trough between waves; angle formed by intersection of two roofs or roof and wall; ~ **of the shadow of death**, experience of being near to death (Ps. 23).

The most familiar ***valve*** *used today is the domestic water faucet which is screwed down to stop the passage of water. A rotary valve is used where finer tolerances are needed, as with a gas.*

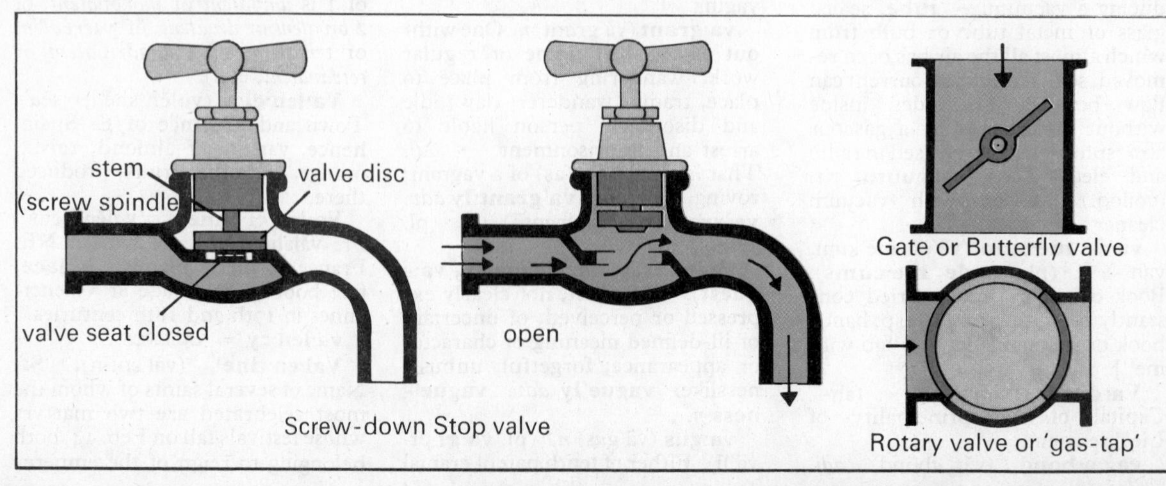

Val·ley (văl′ē) **Forge.** Village in SE. Pennsylvania where George Washington and Amer. Revolutionary army passed winter of 1777–8 in conditions of great hardship.

val·or, Brit. **val·our** (văl′*er*) *ns.* (now chiefly poet. and rhet.) Courage, esp. as shown in war or conflict. **val′or·ous** *adj.* **val′or·-ous·ly** *adv.*

Val·pa·rai·so (vălp*a*rī′sō, -zō), **Val·pa·ra·í·so** (vahlpahrahē′saw). City and major seaport of Chile on the Pacific.

valse (văls, vahls) *n.* Waltz. [Fr.]

val·u·a·ble (văl′ū*a*b*e*l, -y*a*b*e*l) *adj.* Of great value, price, or worth. ~ *n.* (usu. pl.) Valuable thing or possession esp. small article.

val·u·a·tion (vălyūā′sh*o*n) *n.* Estimation (esp. by professional valuer) of thing's worth; worth so estimated, price set on thing.

val·ue (văl′ū) *n.* 1. Amount of commodity, money, etc., considered equivalent for something else; material or monetary worth of thing; worth, desirability, utility, qualities on which these depend; (econ.) amount of commodity, money, etc., for which something else is readily available; FACE, SURPLUS, SURRENDER, ~: see these words; ~ **judgment**, (philos.) subjective estimate of quality etc.; ~ **added tax**, (abbrev. VAT, V.A.T.) tax on amount by which the value of an article is increased by each stage in its production. 2. (math. etc.) Precise number or amount represented by figure, quantity, etc. 3. (mus.) Relative duration of tone signified by note. 4. (painting) Relation of part of picture to others with respect to light and shade, part

*Second-largest city and the major port of Chile, **Valparaiso** has a population of some 300,000 people. A large percentage of the country's imports is unloaded at this deep-water port.*

*The three species of **vampire bat** live in Central and South America. They feed on the blood of birds and mammals, thus being the only parasitic mammals.*

characterized by particular tone. **value** *v.t.* (**-ued, -u·ing**). Estimate value of, appraise, esp. professionally; have high or specified opinion of, prize, esteem, appreciate.

val·ue·less (văl′ūlĭs) *adj.* Worthless. **val′ue·less·ness** *n.*

valve (vălv) *n.* 1. Device for controlling flow of any fluid, usu. acting by yielding to pressure in one direction only. 2. (anat.) Membranous fold or other device in organ or passage of body closing automatically to prevent return flow of blood or other fluid. 3. (Brit.) Vacuum tube. 4. (mus.) Device for varying length of tube in instruments of horn or trumpet kind. 5. (conch.) Each half of hinged shell, single shell of same form; (bot.) each half or section of dehiscent pod, capsule, etc. **valve′-less** *adj.*

val·vu·lar (văl′vyuler) *adj.* Of, like, acting as, furnished with, valve(s).

va·moose (vămōōs′) *v.i.* (**-moosed, -moos·ing**). (slang) Make off, decamp (from). [Span. *vamos* let us go]

vamp[1] (vamp) *n.* 1. Upper front part of boot or shoe. 2. Something vamped up or patched; (mus.) improvised accompaniment, introductory bars of song etc. ~ *v.* 1. Put new vamp to (boot, shoe); repair, patch *up*. 2. Make *up*, produce (as) by patching; compose, put together (book etc.) out of old materials; serve up (something old) as new by addition or alteration; (mus.) improvise (esp. accompaniment).

vamp[2] (vămp) *n.* (archaic slang) Adventuress, woman who exploits men. ~ *v.t.* Attract as vamp, allure. [abbrev. of *vampire*]

vam·pire (văm′pīr) *n.* 1. Reanimated corpse supposed in parts of central and E. Europe to leave grave at night and renew its life by sucking blood of sleeping persons; hence, person preying on others. 2. (also ~ **bat**) Any of various small bats of S. Amer. that make an incision with their teeth and lap blood of animals (genera *Desmodus, Diaemus,* and *Diphylla*); any of various other bats, chiefly S. American, that do not lap blood, esp. the large **false** ~ (*Vampyrus spectrum*). **vam·pir·ic** (vămpĭr′ĭk), **vam′pir·ish** *adjs.* **vam′pir·ism** *n.*

van[1] (văn) = VANGUARD.

van[2] (văn) *n.* Closed truck or wagon for carrying goods; (Brit.) baggage car, closed freight car; small closed truck with sleeping, camping facilities, usu. gaudily decorated.

va·na·di·um (vanā′dēum) *n.* (chem.) Extremely hard, steel-white metallic element found in small quantities in combination in many minerals; symbol V, at. no. 23, at. wt. 50.941; ~ **steel,** steel alloyed with vanadium (and sometimes other elements). **va·nad′ic, van′a·dous** *adjs.*

Van Al·len (văn ăl′en), **James Alfred** (1914–). U.S. physicist; ~ **(radiation) belt**, either of two zones of intense radiation surrounding Earth.

Van Bu·ren (văn būr′en), **Martin** (1782–1862). Eighth president of U.S., 1836–40.

Van·cou·ver (vănkōō′ver). City and seaport of Brit. Columbia, Canada; ~ **Island**, large island off Pacific coast, opposite Vancouver. [George *Vancouver* (1758–98), English navigator and explorer of W. coast of N. Amer.]

Van·dal (văn′dal) *n.* 1. One of an ancient Germanic people who invaded W. Europe, and settled in Gaul, Spain, etc., in 4th and 5th centuries and finally (428–9) migrated to N. Africa; in 455 they sacked Rome in a marauding expedition; their kingdom in N. Africa was overthrown by Belisarius in 533. 2. **v**~, willful or ignorant destroyer of anything beautiful, venerable, or worthy of preservation. **van′dal·ism** *n.* **van·dal·is′tic** *adj.*

Van de Graaff (văn′ de grăf) **generator.** Electrostatic generator producing potentials of over a million volts by using a fast-moving belt inside a hollow spherical conductor, often used as a particle accelerator in nuclear research. [Robert Jemison *Van de Graaf* (1901–67), U.S. physicist]

*Nicknamed the 'Little Magician' because of his astute political mind, **Martin Van Buren** was one of the founding members of the Democrat Party and later became the 8th president of the United States.*

Van Dyck, Van·dyke (văn dĭk′), **Sir Anthony** (1599–1641). Flemish portrait painter who worked for some years, and died, in England; **Vandyke beard**, neat pointed beard of kind freq. found in his paintings; **Vandyke brown**, deep brown pigment; **Vandyke collar**, broad lace or linen collar with deeply indented edge, seen in portraits by Van Dyck.

vane (vān) *n.* Thin upright plate of metal etc. often in silhouette of cock, ship, arrow, etc., pivoting freely to show direction of wind, often called *weathervane*; windmill sail; blade, wing, or other projection attached to axis etc. so as to be acted on by current of air or liquid; barbs of a feather; sight of surveying instrument.

van Gogh (văn gō′; *Du.* vahn *x*ŏ*x*′), **Vincent** (1853–90). Dutch Post-Impressionist painter, active chiefly in France.

van·guard (văn′gârd) *n.* Front part or foremost division of army, fleet, etc., moving forward or onward; (fig.) leaders of movement etc.

va·nil·la (vanĭl′*a*) *n.* (Podlike capsule of) tropical climbing orchid of genus *V*~, esp. *V. planifolia*; aromatic extract or synthetic preparation of this, used as flavoring or perfume.

va·nil·lin (văn′*i*lĭn, vanĭl′-) *n.* (chem.) Fragrant principle of vanilla (C_6H_5CHO).

van·ish (văn′ĭsh) *v.i.* Disappear from sight, esp. suddenly and mysteriously; pass, fade, away; cease to exist; (math.) become zero; **vanishing cream**, face cream that is quickly absorbed by skin; **vanishing point**, in perspective, point at which receding parallel lines appear to meet. **van′ish·er** *n.*

van·i·ty (văn′ĭtē) *n.* (pl. **-ties**). What is vain or worthless; futility, worthlessness, emptiness; empty pride, self-conceit and desire for admiration; woman's dressing table; ~ **bag, case**, woman's small handbag or case containing mirror, face powder, etc.; **V**~ **Fair**, (from Bunyan's *Pilgrim's Progress*) the world as scene of idle amusement and vain display; fashionable world of society. **van′i·tied** *adj.*

van·quish (văng′kwĭsh, văn′-) *v.t.* (now chiefly rhet.) Conquer, overcome. **van′quish·er** *n.*

van·tage (văn′tĭj, vahn′-) *n.* Advantage (esp. in lawn tennis); ~ **ground**, advantageous position for defense or attack; ~ **point**, position giving wide etc. view.

*Portrait of Henry Percy by **Sir Anthony Van Dyck.***

Vanu·atu (Vah′nōōahtōō). Independent republic; island group in W. Pacific. Capital, Vila.

vap·id (văp′ĭd) *adj.* Insipid, flat. **vap′id·ly** *adv.* **vap·id·i·ty** (văpĭd′-ĭtē) *n.* (pl. **-ties**). **vap′id·ness** *n.*

va·por, Brit. **va·pour** (vā′p*e*r) *ns.* Matter diffused or suspended in air, as mist, steam, etc., esp. form into which liquids are converted by action of heat; (phys.) gaseous form of normally liquid or solid substance; vaporized substance; ~ **lock**, blockage of fuel flow in internal combustion engine, caused by pocket of vaporized gasoline as result of excessive heat. **va·por·if·ic** (vāp*e*rĭf′ĭk), **va′por·ous, va′por·y** *adjs.* **va′por·ous·ly** *adv.* **va′por·ous·ness** *n.* **vapor** *v.i.* Emit vapor; talk fantastically or boastingly.

***Variegated** plants generally have only two colors in the leaves; this coleus has three. Variegation is rarely found in the wild, for it reduces photosynthesis.*

*'Cornfield Near Arles' is typical of the expressive brushwork of **Vincent Van Gogh** in his later years. Despite such originality, few of his paintings sold while he was alive.*

va·por·ize (vā´perīz) *v.* (**-ized, -iz·ing**). Convert, be converted, into vapor. **va´por·iz·er** *n.* (esp.) Apparatus for vaporizing liquid, fine spray. **va·por·i·za·tion** (vāperīzā´shon) *n.*

va·pour = VAPOR.

va·que·ro (vahkār´ō) *n.* (pl. **-ros**). (in Latin Amer. and Southwest U.S.) Herdsman, cowboy.

Va·ra·na·si (varah´nasē). (formerly *Benares*) City on the Ganges in India, regarded as sacred by Hindus.

var·i·a·ble (vār´ēabel) *adj.* Apt, liable, to vary or change, capable of variation; modifiable, alterable, changeable, shifting, inconstant; (of star) varying periodically in brightness or magnitude; (math. etc., of quantity etc.) that may assume a succession of values, having different values under different conditions. **var·i·a·bil·i·ty** (vārēabĭl´ĭtē), **var´i·ble·ness** *ns.* **var´i·a·bly** *adv.* **variable** *n.* Variable quantity, star, or other thing; shifting wind, (pl.) parts of sea where steady wind is not expected.

var·i·ance (vār´ēans) *n.* Disagreement, difference of opinion, lack of harmony (esp. in **at ~**); (law) discrepancy between two documents, statements, etc., that should agree; official permission to do something contrary to regulations, esp. authorization to build in contravention of real estate zoning ordinance.

var·i·ant (vār´ēant) *adj.* Differing *from* something or from standard, type, etc. ~ *n.* Variant form, spelling, reading, etc.

var·i·a·tion (vārēā´shon) *n.* 1. Varying, undergoing or making modification or alteration, esp. from normal condition, action, or amount, or from standard or type; extent of this. 2. (astron.) Deviation of heavenly body from mean orbit or motion. 3. (of magnetic needle) Declination. 4. (math.) Change in function(s) of equation due to indefinitely small change of value of constants. 5. (mus.) One of series of repetitions of theme or tune with changes that do not disguise its identity. 6. (ballet) Solo dance.

var·i·co·cele (văr´ikōsēl) *n.* Varicose swelling of spermatic veins.

var·i·col·ored (vār´ĭkŭlerd) *adj.* Of various colors, variegated in color.

var·i·cose (văr´ikōs, vār´-) *adj.* (of veins) Having permanent abnormal local dilation; affected with, resembling, of, a varix or varices. **var·i·cos·i·ty** (vărikŏs´ĭtē) *n.*

var·ied (vār´ēd) *adj.* Of differing kinds; changed; ~ **thrush**, songbird of Pacific coast (*Ixoreus naevius*), like robin but having black stripe across breast.

var·i·e·gate (vār´ēegāt, vār´e-, văr´ēe-, văr´e-,) *v.t.* (**-gat·ed, -gat·ing**). Diversify in appearance, esp. in color. **var´i·e·gat·ed** *adj.* **var·i·e·ga·tion** (vārēegā´shon, vāre-, vărēe-, văre-) *n.* Being variegated, esp. (bot.) presence of two or more colors in leaves, petals, etc.; defective or special development leading to such coloring; variegated marking.

va·ri·e·ty (varī´etē) *n.* (pl. **-ties**). 1. Being varied, diversity, absence of monotony, sameness, or uniformity; collection of different things; ~ **store**, one selling many kinds of small items. 2. Different form *of* some thing, quality, or condition; kind, sort; (biol.) (plant, animal, belonging to) group distinguished by characteristics considered too trivial to permit its classification as distinct species. 3. (also ~ **show**) Entertainment consisting of a number of different independent performances. **va·ri´e·tal·ly** *adv.*

var·i·form (vār´ifōrm) *adj.* Of various forms.

var·i·o·rum (vārēōr´um, -ōr´-) *n.* & *adj.* (Edition, esp. of classical author or text) with notes of various editors or commentators. [L. gen. pl. of *varius* various]

var·i·ous (vār´ēus) *adj.* Different, diverse; separate, several. **var´i·ous·ly** *adv.* **var´i·ous·ness** *n.*

var·ix (vār´ĭks) *n.* (pl. **var·i·ces** pr. vār´ĭsēz). 1. Permanent abnormal dilation of vein or artery, usu. with tortuous development. 2. Prominent longitudinal ridge on surface of shell.

var·let (vār´lĭt) *n.* (hist.) Knight's attendant or page; (archaic) menial, low fellow, scoundrel.

var·mint (vār´mint) *n.* (dial.) Vermin; mischievous or discreditable person or animal.

var·nish (vār´nĭsh) *n.* Resinous matter dissolved in oil or spirit, used for spreading over surface to produce a translucent and usu. glossy protective coating; preparation of certain other substances, e.g. wax, cellulose, for same purpose; surface so formed; gloss; superficial polish of manner; external appearance or display without underlying reality. ~ *v.t.* Coat with varnish; gloss (*over*), disguise.

var·si·ty (vär'sĭtē) *n.* (pl. **-ties**). Principal or first team representing college or school in any sport.

Var·u·na (vĕr'ōōna). (Hinduism) Supreme cosmic deity, creator, and ruler.

var·y (vär'ē) *v.* (**var·ied, var·y·ing**). Change, make different, modify, diversify; suffer change; be or become different in degree or quality; be of different kinds; ~ **(inversely) as**, change in quantity or value in (inverse) proportion to. **var'y·ing·ly** *adv.*

Vas·co da Ga·ma (vah'skō da gah'ma): see GAMA.

vas·cu·lar (văs'kyuler) *adj.* (biol., anat.) Of tubular vessels; containing, supplied with, these; ~ **system**, system of tubes within an organism for conveying fluid, esp. blood, sap. **vas'cu·lar·ly** *adv.*

vas de·fe·rens (văs dĕf'ĕrĕnz) (pl. **va·sa de·fe·ren·ti·a** pr. vā'sa dĕfĕrĕn'shēa). Spermatic duct. [L. *vas* vessel, *deferens* carrying down]

vase (vās, vāz, vahz) *n.* Vessel, usu. of greater height than width, used as ornament, for holding flowers, etc. or (archaeol.) as container.

vas·ec·to·my (văsĕk'tomē) *n.* (pl. **-mies**). Surgical removal of (part of) the vas deferens, for sterilization.

Vas·e·line (văs'elēn, văselēn') *n.* (trademark) Kind of petroleum jelly. [f. Ger. *Wasser* water, Gk. *elaion* oil]

vas·o·mo·tor (văsōmō'ter) *adj.* (of nerves) Acting on walls of blood vessels so as to constrict or dilate these and thus regulate flow of blood.

vas·sal (văs'al) *n.* 1. (hist., in feudal system) One holding lands on condition of homage and allegiance to superior. 2. Humble servant or subordinate, slave. **vas'sal·age** *n.* (hist.) Condition, obligations, service, of vassal; servitude, dependence; fief.

vast (văst, vahst) *adj.* Of great extent or area; of great size or amount. **vast'ly** *adv.* **vast'ness** *n.*

VAT, V.A.T. *abbrevs.* Value added tax.

vat (văt) *n.* Large tub, cask, cistern, or other vessel for holding or storing liquids. **vat** *v.* (**vat·ted, vat·ting**). Place, treat, mature, in vat.

Vat·i·can (văt'ĭkan). Pope's palace and official residence on Vatican Hill in Rome; (of or pertaining to) the papal government; ~ **City**, independent papal state in Rome, including Vatican and St. Peter's, established 1929 by Lateran Council; ~ **Council**, ecumenical council of 1869–70, that proclaimed papal infallibility; similar council held 1962–5; ~ **Hill**, hill in Rome on W. bank of Tiber, opposite ancient Rome.

vaude·ville (vawd'vĭl, vaw'de-) *n.* Variety entertainment. [Fr., prob. f. earlier (*chanson du*) *Vau de Vire* (son of) valley of the Vire, Normandy]

vault[1] (vawlt) *n.* Arched structure of masonry usu. supported by walls or pillars and serving as roof or carrying other parts of building; any arched surface resembling this, esp. apparently concave surface of sky; room or other part of building covered by vault, esp. when subterranean and used as cellar for storing food, wine, etc.; room of this kind without arched roof, underground room, strongroom; (partly) underground burial chamber in cemetery or under church. ~ *v.t.* Construct with, cover (as) with vault; form vault over; make in form of vault. **vault'ed, vault'y** *adjs.*

vault[2] (vawlt) *n.* Leap, spring, performed by vaulting. ~ *v.* Leap, spring, esp. while resting on the hand(s) or with help of pole; spring over thus.

vaunt (vawnt, vahnt) *n.* (archaic or rhet.) Boast. ~ *v.* Boast, brag, (of). **vaunt'ed** *adj.* **vaunt'ing·ly** *adv.*

V.C. *abbrev.* Vice-Chancellor; Vietcong; Victoria Cross.

VD, V.D. *abbrevs.* Venereal disease.

veal (vēl) *n.* Calf's flesh as food.

vec·tor (vĕk'ter) *n.* 1. (math.) Quantity having both magnitude and direction. 2. (path.) Carrier of disease, esp. insect that conveys pathogenic organisms from one host to another. ~ *v.t.* Direct (aircraft) on a course. **vec·to'ri·al** (vĕktōr'ēal, -tōr-) *adj.*

*Wine is kept in a **vat** for a predetermined period to mature. Once, vats were made from wood, but today stainless steel also is used, especially for white wines.*

*A **vault,** an extension of the arch, needs an elaborate structure so that it can be supported whilst being assembled. Facing, top left to right: The most complex form of ribs used at Pershore Abbey; more simplified ribs in the cloisters at Fountain Abbey; and massive supports for the groin at Norwich Cathedral, U.K.*

Ve·da (vā'da, vē-) *n.* Ancient sacred literature of the Hindus; (esp.) the four collections of hymns known as the Rig-Veda, Yarjur-Veda, Sama-Veda, and Atharva-Veda. **Ve'dic** *adj.* [Sansk. *veda* (sacred) knowledge]

Ve·dan·ta (vedahn'ta, -dăn'-) *n.* 1. Final part of the Veda, the Upanishads. 2. Later system of monistic philosophy based on the Upanishads and taught principally by Śandara Ācārya. **Ve·dan'tic** *adj.* [Sansk. VEDA, *anta* end]

vee (vē) *adj.* In the shape of the letter **V**.

veep (vēp) *n.* (colloq.) Vice president, esp. (**V**~) of the U.S.

veer (vēr) *v.* Change direction, esp. (of wind) in clockwise direction; (of ship) turn with head away from wind, cause to turn thus; (fig.) change from one state, tendency, etc., to another, be variable. **veer'ing·ly** *adv.*

veer·y (vēr'ē) *n.* (pl. **veer·ies**). Amer. thrush (*Hylocichla fuscescens*) noted for its song.

Ve·ga[1] (vē'ga). (astron.) Star in constellation Lyra, fourth brightest in the heavens. [Arab. (*al nasr*) *al wāki* "the falling (vulture)," meaning the constellation Lyra]

Ve·ga[2] (vā'ga; *Sp.* vĕ'gah), **Lo·pe de** (law'pĕ dĕ). Lope Felix de Vega Carpio (1562–1635), prolific Spanish poet and playwright, founder of Spanish drama.

veg·e·ta·ble (vĕj'tabel, vĕj'e-) *n.* Living organism belonging to plant

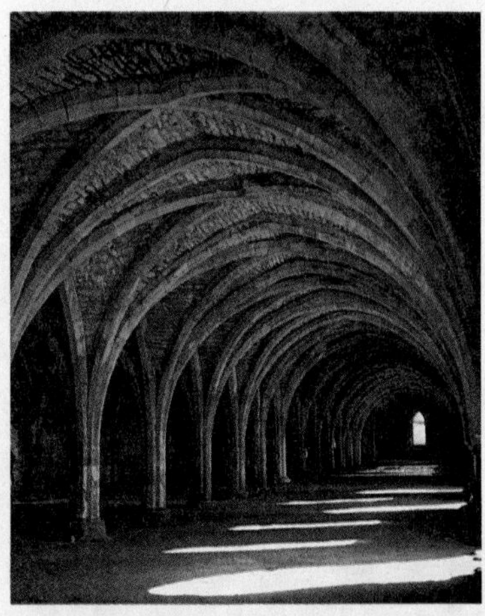

Barrel Vaults

square pins to prevent vertical slipping

boarded formwork

quadrant forms

thick continuous wall

Groin Vaulting

masonry vault

centring frame

longitudinal vault with continuous formwork

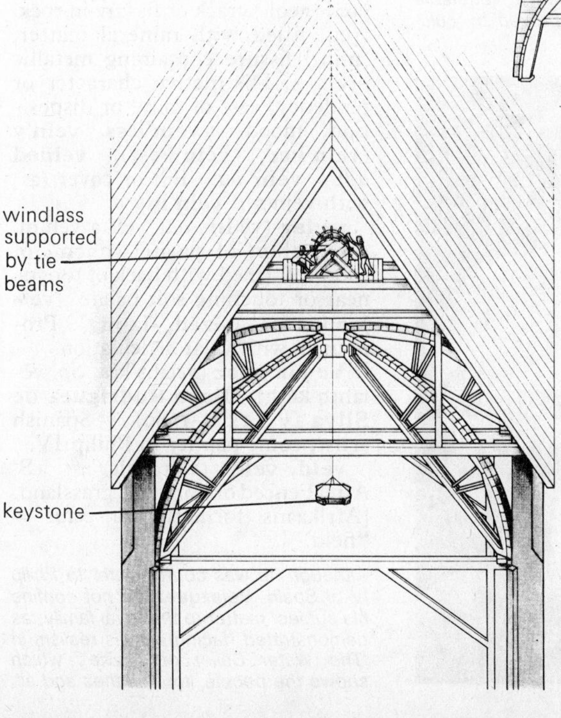

Erection of a Vault Web

windlass supported by tie beams

keystone

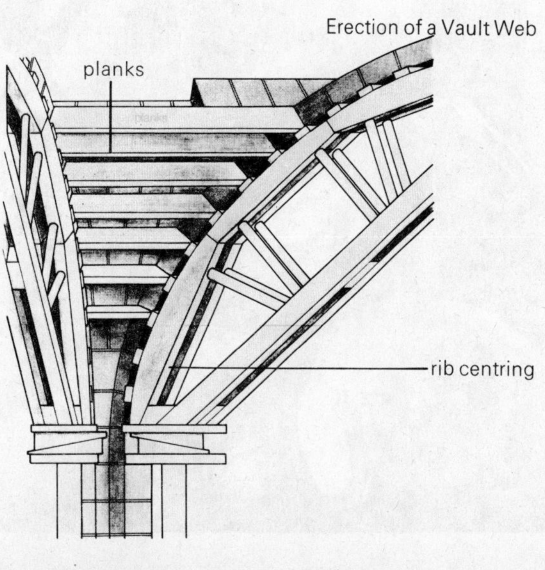

planks

rib centring

kingdom, plant; (esp.) herbaceous plant cultivated for food. ~ *adj.* Of (the nature of), derived from, concerned with, comprising, plants; ~ **kingdom**, that division of organic nature to which plants belong; ~ **marrow**: see MARROW sense 2.

veg·e·tar·i·an (vĕjetār′ean) *n.* One who eats no animal food, or none that is obtained by destruction of animal life. ~ *adj.* Of vegetarian(s); living on vegetables; consisting of vetetables. **veg·e·tar′i·an·ism** *n.*

veg·e·tate (vĕj′etāt) *v.i.* (**-tat·ed, -tat·ing**). Grow as or like plant(s); (fig.) lead dull monotonous life without intellectual activity or social intercourse. **veg′e·ta·tive** *adj.* 1. Of, concerned with, or typical of vegetation, plants, or plant growth. 2. Of or involved with growth and nutrition, rather than sexual reproduction. 3. Not consciously controlled; passive. **veg′e·ta·tive·ly** *adv.* **veg′e·ta·tive·ness** *n.*

veg·e·ta·tion (vĕjetā′shon) *n.* 1. Vegetating; plants collectively, vegetable growths. 2. (path.) Morbid growth or excrescence on part of body. **veg·e·ta′tion·al** *adj.*

ve·he·ment (vē′ement) *adj.* Intense, violent, acting with great force; exhibiting, caused by, strong feeling or excitement. **ve′he·ment·ly** *adv.* **ve′he·mence, ve′he·men·cy** *ns.*

ve·hi·cle (vē′ĭkel) *n.* 1. Carriage or conveyance for persons or goods, any means of transport, esp. by land. 2. Substance, esp. liquid, used as medium for application, administration, etc., of another substance, as drug; liquid in which pigment is suspended. 3. Thing, person, as means, channel, or instrument of expression, communication, etc. **ve·hic·u·lar** (vēhĭk′yuler) *adj.*

veil (vāl) *n.* 1. Piece of linen or other material as part of nun's headdress, falling over head and shoulders; **take the** ~, become a nun. 2. Piece of thin, usu. more or less transparent, material worn over head or face as part of headdress or to conceal the face or protect it from sun, dust, etc.; curtain; (fig.) disguise, cloak, mask, anything that conceals or covers; **draw a** ~ **over**, conceal, avoid discussing or dealing with. 3. Velum. **veil** *v.t.* Cover (as) with veil; (fig.) conceal, disguise, mask. **veil′ing** *n.* (esp.) Material for veils, net. **veiled** *adj.*

vein (vān) *n.* 1. Each of the tubular vessels in which blood is conveyed from all parts of body back to heart; (pop.) any blood vessel. 2. (bot.) One of the slender bundles of tissue forming framework of leaf. 3. (entom.) Nervure of insect's wing. 4. Anything suggesting or resembling vein, esp. streak of different color in wood, marble, etc., channel of water in ice etc.; (geol.) crack or fissure in rock, freq. filled with mineral matter; (min.) fissure containing metallic ore. 5. Distinctive character or tendency, cast of mind or disposition, mood. **vein′less, vein′y** (**vein·i·er, vein·i·est**), **veined** *adjs.* **vein** *v.t.* Fill or cover (as) with vein(s). **vein′ing** *n.*

ve·lar (vē′ler) *adj.* Of a velum, esp. velum of palate; (phon., of sound) formed with back of tongue near or touching soft palate. **ve′lar·ize** *v.t.* (**-ized, -iz·ing**). Pronounce with velar articulation.

Ve·láz·quez (velahs′kes; *Sp.* vĕlahth′kĕth), **Diego Rodriguez de Silva y** (1599–1660). Spanish artist, court painter to Philip IV.

veld, veldt (vĕlt, fĕlt) *ns.* (S. Afr.) Fenced or unfenced grassland. [Afrikaans (formerly Du. *veldt* = "field")]

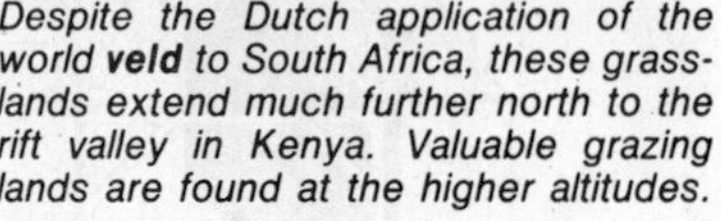

Despite the Dutch application of the world ***veld*** *to South Africa, these grasslands extend much further north to the rift valley in Kenya. Valuable grazing lands are found at the higher altitudes.*

Observations of nomadic hunter-gatherers have shown that even when man was mainly a meat-eater, he still gathered ***vegetables.*** *Most vegetable varieties have been improved by cultivation.*

Although he was court painter to Philip IV of Spain. ***Velazquez*** *did not confine his subject matter to the royal family, as demonstrated (facing) by his realism in 'The Water Seller of Seville', which shows the people, torn clothes and all.*

Street **vendors** offer a wide variety of goods. This one, in San Francisco, has a range of jewelry on sale, probably at below retail cost, but with no guarantees.

Although both skins and papyrus were used for writing in Egypt about 2000 B.C., paper was unknown in Europe before the 11th century A.D. **Vellum** was used for illuminated manuscripts.

vel·lum (vĕl′*u*m) *n.* Skin (strictly, calfskin) dressed and prepared for writing, painting, etc.; imitations of this, esp. (commerc.) smooth-surfaced writing paper.

ve·loc·i·pede (v*e*lŏs′*i*pēd) *n.* Any of various light vehicles propelled by riders, esp. early forms of bicycle and tricycle.

ve·loc·i·ty (v*e*lŏs′ĭtē) *n.* (pl. **-ties**). Rapidity of motion, operation, or action; (mech.) time rate of change of position of body in a given direction; (loosely) (esp. high) speed; **actual ~**, speed at which a body moving on a curve actually moves as distinct from its **circular ~** (speed at which it is moving around a point) and its **radial ~** (speed at which it is moving away from or toward that point); **terminal ~**, maximum speed of falling object, when resistance of air equals pull of gravity.

ve·lour, ve·lours (v*e*loor′) *ns.* (pl. **ve·lours**). Woven fabric with plushlike or velvety pile; felt with similar surface, used for hats; hat of this.

ve·lum (vē′l*u*m) *n.* (pl. **-la** pr. -l*a*). (anat., bot., zool.) Membrane or membranous partition; (esp.) soft PALATE.

vel·vet (vĕl′vĭt) *n.* Textile fabric having a dense smooth pile on one side formed by loops of additional warp threads, the loops being usu. cut through during the weaving; surface, substance, resembling this in softness or rich appearance, e.g. soft downy skin covering newly grown antlers of deer; (slang) in easy or advantageous position; (slang) gambling winnings, clear profit. **vel′vet·y** *adj.*

vel·vet·een (vĕlv*e*tēn′, vĕl′v*e*tēn) *n.* Cotton fabric resembling velvet; (pl.) velveteen trousers.

ve·na ca·va (vē′n*a* kā′v*a*) (pl. **ve·nae ca·vae** pr. vē′nē kā′vē). Each of two veins (**inferior ~** and **superior ~**) conveying blood to right atrium of heart.

ve·nal (vē′n*a*l) *adj.* (of person) That may be bribed, willing to lend support, exert influence, or sacrifice principles, from mercenary motive; (of action etc.) characteristic of venal person. **ve′nal·ly** *adv.* **ve·nal·i·ty** (vēnăl′ĭtē, v*e*-) *n.* (pl. **-ties**).

ve·na·tion (vēnā′sh*o*n, v*e*-) *n.* Arrangement of veins in a leaf or leaflike organ.

vend (vĕnd) *v.* Sell (now rare exc. law); offer (esp. small articles) for sale, hawk; **vending machine**, coin operated machine for selling small goods. **ven′dor, vend′er** *ns.* **vend′i·ble** *adj.*

ven·det·ta (vĕndĕt′*a*) *n.* Blood feud, esp. one practiced through generations, as in Corsica and parts of Italy; also fig.

ve·neer (v*e*nēr′) *v.t.* Cover, overlay, (furniture etc.) with thin sheet of finer wood or other more beautiful or valuable material; thin layer used in making plywood; (fig.) give merely specious or superficial appearance of some good quality to, gloss over. **~** *n.* Thin outer sheet used in veneering; (fig.) superficial appearance.

ven·er·a·ble (vĕn′*e*r*a*b*e*l) *adj.* Entitled to veneration because of age, character, etc.; (in Ch. of England) title of archdeacons; (in R.C. Ch.) title of one who has attained lowest of three degrees of sanctity but is not yet beatified or canonized; **V~ Bede**: see BEDE. **ven·er·a·bil·i·ty** (vĕn*e*r*a*bĭl′ĭtē), **ven′er·a·ble·ness** *ns.* **ven′er·a·bly** *adv.*

ven·er·ate (vĕn′*e*rāt) *v.t.* (**-at·ed, -at·ing**). Regard with feelings of respect and reverence; consider as exalted or sacred. **ven·er·a·tion** (vĕn*e*rā′sh*o*n) *n.*

ve·ne·re·al (v*e*nēr′ē*a*l) *adj.* Of, connected with, sexual desire or intercourse; infected with venereal disease; **~ disease**, disease, esp. gonorrhea or syphilis, contracted by sexual intercourse with person already infected. [f. VENUS]

Ve·ne·tian (v*e*nē′sh*a*n) *adj.* Of Venice; **~ blind, v~ blind**, window blind of horizontal slats that can be adjusted so as to admit or exclude light; **Venetian glass**, decorative glassware made at Murano, near Venice, since 15th c., freq. very elaborate and sometimes fusing clear glass with opaque or with glass of various colors; **Venetian lace**, one of several varieties of point lace; **Venetian red**, reddish pigment consisting of ferric oxides; **Venetian School**, school of painting centered in Venice in the 15th and 16th centuries, culminating in the work of Giorgione, Titian, Veronese, and Tintoretto; revival of this in 18th c.; **Venetian window**, PALLADIAN window. **Venetian** *n.* Native, inhabitant, of Venice.

Ven·e·zue·la (vĕn*e*zwā′l*a*, -zwē′-). S. Amer. republic on Caribbean Sea, formed 1830 after

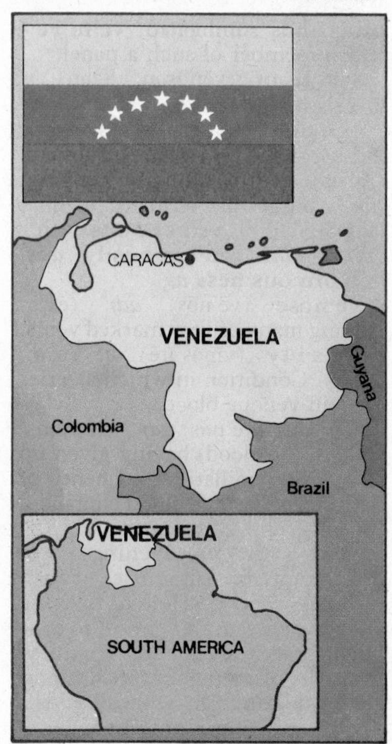

*Above left: General view of the skyscrapers and freeways of Caracas, capital of **Venezuela.** The prosperity of this country derives from huge reserves of crude oil.*

secession from the Republic of Colombia; capital, Caracas. **Ven·e·zue′lan** *adj.* & *n.* (Native, inhabitant) of Venezuela.

venge·ance (vĕn′jans) *n.* Avenging oneself on another, retributive or vindictive punishment, hurt or harm inflicted in revenge; **with a ~**, in an extreme degree, with great force or violence.

venge·ful (vĕnj′ful) *adj.* Seeking vengeance, disposed to revenge, vindictive. **venge′ful·ly** *adv.* **venge′ful·ness** *n.*

ve·ni·al (vē′nēal, vēn′yal) *adj.* (of sin or fault) Pardonable, excusable, not grave or heinous, (theol.) not MORTAL. **ve′ni·al·ly** *adv.* **ve′ni·al·ness, ve·ni·al·i·ty** (vēnēăl′ĭtē, vēnyăl′-) *ns.*

Ven·ice (vĕn′ĭs). (Ital. *Venezia*) Seaport of NE. Italy built on numerous islands in a lagoon of the Adriatic; formerly the chief European port for trade with the East, famous esp. for its beauty and (from 15th to 18th c.) as a center of art.

ven·i·punc·ture (vĕn′ipŭngkcher, vē′ni-) *n.* Puncture of vein, esp. by insertion of hollow needle for medical purposes or for extraction of blood specimen.

ve·ni·re (vĭnī′rē) *n.* (law) Writ directing sheriff to summon jury;

*Left: As an oligarchic ruler, the **Doge of Venice** built the Bridge of Sighs between his palace and the state prison. His enemies were discreetly taken across it after sentencing.*

panel thus summoned; **ve·ni're·-man**, member of such a panel.

ven·i·son (vĕn'ĭson, -zon) *n.* Deer's flesh as food.

ven·om (vĕn'om) *n.* Poisonous fluid secreted by certain snakes etc. and injected by biting or stinging; (fig.) bitter or virulent feeling, language, etc. **ven·om·ous** (vĕn'-omus) *adj.* **ven'om·ous·ly** *adv.* **ven'om·ous·ness** *n.*

ve·nose (vē'nōs) *adj.* (esp.) Having many or very marked veins. **ve·nos·i·ty** (vĭnŏs'ĭtē) *n.* (esp., med.) Condition in which arteries contain venous blood.

ve·nous (vē'nus) *adj.* Of veins; veined; (of blood) having given up oxygen in capillaries and hence of dark red color, like blood contained in veins (opp. ARTERIAL).

vent[1] (vĕnt) *n.* Opening or slit in garment, esp. slit in back of coat.

vent[2] (vĕnt) *n.* Hole or opening allowing passage out of or into confined space, as flue of chimney, fumarole of volcano, hole in top of barrel to admit air while liquid is drawn out, finger hole in musical instrument, etc.; anus, esp. of lower animals; (fig.) outlet, free passage, free play. ~ *v.t.* Make vent in; give vent or free expression to.

ven·ti·late (vĕn'tilāt) *v.t.* (**-lat·ed, -lat·ing**). Expose to fresh air, purify by air, oxygenate; provide with a vent; cause air to circulate freely in (enclosed space); make public, discuss freely. **ven·ti·la·tion** (vĕntilā'shon) *n.* **ven'ti·la·tor** *n.* (esp.) Contrivance, e.g. revolving fan, for ventilating building, ship, mine, etc.; opening in wall, freq. with grid, for same purpose. **ven·ti·la·to·ry** (vĕn'tilatōrē, -tōrē) *adj.*

ven·tral (vĕn'tral) *adj.* Of the abdomen, abdominal; of the anterior or lower surface (opp. DORSAL). **ven'tral·ly** *adv.*

ven·tri·cle (vĕn'trĭkel) *n.* (anat., zool.) Cavity of body, esp. cavity of heart from which blood is pumped into arteries (in mammals and birds) either of two such cavities; one of series of communicating cavities in brain formed by enlargements of neural canal. **ven·tric·u·lar** (vĕntrĭk'yuler) *adj.*

ven·tril·o·quism (vĕntrĭl'o-kwĭzem), **ven·tril·o·quy** (vĕntrĭl'o-kwē) *ns.* Practice of speaking etc. without visible movement of the lips and in such a manner that the voice appears to come from some other person or object. **ven·tri·lo·qui·al** (vĕntrilō'kwēal), **ven·tril·o·quis·tic** (vĕntrĭlokwĭs'tĭk) *adjs.* **ven·tril'o·quist** *n.* **ven·tril'o·quize** *v.* (**-quized, -quiz·ing**). [L. *venter* belly, *loqui speak*]

*Of all the operas composed by **Verdi,** none lends itself more to impressive production than 'Aida'. It was commissioned by an opera house in Cairo to celebrate the opening of the Suez Canal.*

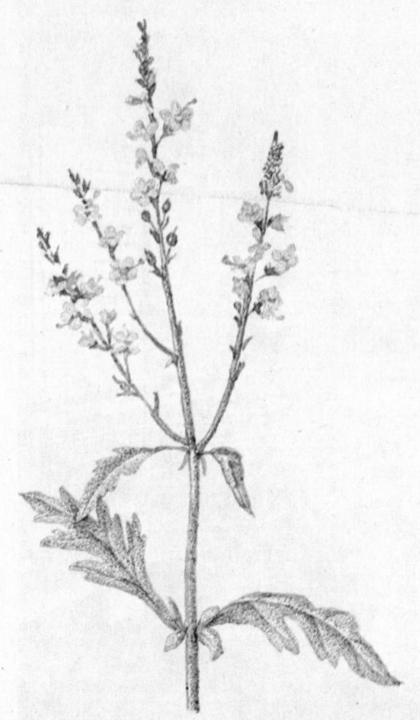

***Verbena** was used as a medicinal herb from the times of ancient Egypt. It was said to alleviate kidney complaints and induce sweating. Aromatic verbena oil is made from another plant.*

ven·ture (vĕn'cher) *n.* Undertaking of a risk, risky undertaking; (archaic) property at stake, thing risked; **at a ~**, at random. **ven'-ture·some** *adj.* **ven'ture·some·ly** *adv.* **ven'ture·some·ness** *n.* **ven-ture** *v.* (**-tured, -tur·ing**). Dare; not be afraid, make bold *to* do, hazard (opinion etc.).

ven·tu·ri (vĕntoor'ē) *n.* Short piece of tube between wider sections for measuring flow rate or exerting suction. [G.B. *Venturi* (1740–1822), It. physicist]

ven·ue (vĕn'ū) *n.* (law) County, district, where jury is summoned to come for trial of case; **change of ~**, change location of place of trial to avoid riot, prejudiced jury, etc.; (colloq.) place, rendezvous; position or ground adopted for argument.

Ve·nus (vē'nus). 1. (Rom. myth.) Ancient Italian goddess, identified by the Romans with Aphrodite; **~ de Milo**: see MELOS; **~'s flytrap**, N. Amer. insectivorous plant (*Dionaea muscipula*); **Venus's-hair**, delicate maidenhair fern. 2. (astron.) Second planet in order of distance from sun, in orbit between Mercury and Earth; the morning or evening star.

Ve·nu·si·an (venōō'sēan, -shēan, -shan) *adj.* Of, pertaining to, or characteristic of the planet Venus. ~ *n.* Imagined being living on Venus.

ve·ra·cious (verā'shus) *adj.* Speaking, disposed to speak, the truth; true, accurate. **ve·ra'-cious·ly** *adv.* **ve·rac·i·ty** (verăs'-ĭtē) *n.* (pl. **-ties**). **ve·ra'cious·ness** *n.*

ve·ran·da, ve·ran·dah (verăn'-da) *ns.* Open roofed portico or gallery along the side of house. [Hindi, f. Port. or Sp. *varanda* railing]

verb (vērb) *n.* (gram.) Part of speech that expresses action, occurrence, or being. **verb'less** *adj.*

ver·bal (vēr'bal) *adj.* 1. Of, concerned with, words; (pop.) oral, not written; verbatim. 2. Of (the nature of) a verb; **~ noun**, noun derived from verb stem and having some verbal constructions (as English

The paintings of ***Vermeer,*** *including 'A Young Woman Standing at a Virginal', are renowned for their translucent purity and richness of color. However, his work was ignored for 200 years.*

nouns ending in *-ing*). ~ *n.* Verbal noun. **ver′bal·ly** *adv.*

ver·bal·ism (vẽr′balizem) *n.* Verbal expression; predominance of merely verbal over real significance. **ver′bal·ist** *n.* One concerned with words only, apart from reality or meaning.

ver·bal·ize (vẽr′balīz) *v.t.* (**-ized, -iz·ing**). Make (noun etc.) into verb; express in words; be verbose. **ver·bal·i·za·tion** (vẽrba-līzā′shon) *n.*

ver·ba·tim (verbā′tĭm) *adv.* & *adj.* Word for word, in the exact words.

ver·be·na (verbē′na) *n.* Plant of genus *V*~, which comprises the vervains, esp. garden variety of this with blue, white, or crimson flowers.

ver·bi·age (vẽr′bēĭj) *n.* Needless abundance of words.

ver·bose (verbōs′) *adj.* Using, expressed in, too many words. **ver·bose′ly** *adv.* **ver·bose′ness, ver·bos·i·ty** (verbŏs′ĭtē) *ns.*

ver·bo·ten (verbō′ten, fer-) *adj.* Forbidden, esp. by authority. [Ger.]

Ver·cin·get·o·rix (vẽrsĭnjĕt′-erĭks, -gĕt′-). Gallic chief of the Arverni (occupants of the district now called Auvergne) in 52 B.C. in their war against Julius Caesar.

ver·dant (vẽr′dant) *adj.* Green. **ver′dant·ly** *adv.* **ver′dan·cy** *n.*

Ver·di (vār′de; *It.* vĕr′dē), **Gui·sep·pe Fortunino Francesco** (1813–1901). Italian composer of operas esp. *Aida, Falstaff, Rigoletto,* and church music, esp. *Manzoni Requiem,* etc.

ver·dict (vẽr′dĭkt) *n.* Decision of jury in civil or criminal case on issue submitted to them; decision, judgment.

ver·di·gris (vẽr′digrēs, -grĭs) *n.* Green or greenish-blue deposit forming on copper or brass as a rust; copper acetate, obtained by action of dilute acetic acid on copper and used as pigment and mordant in dyeing. [OF. *vert de Grece* green of Greece]

ver·dure (vẽr′jer) *n.* Fresh green color of flourishing vegetation; green vegetation. **ver·dur·ous** (vẽr′jerus) *adj.*

verge[1] (vẽrj) *n.* 1. Extreme edge, brink, border; grass edging of path, flower bed, etc. 2. Wand, rod, carried before bishop, dean, etc., as emblem of office.

verge[2] (vẽrj) *v.t.* (**verged, verg·ing**). Incline downward or in specified direction; border *on.*

verg·er (vẽr′jer) *n.* (chiefly Brit.) Official carrying rod or other symbol of office before dignitaries of cathedral, church, or university; one who takes care of interior of church and acts as attendant.

ver·i·fy (vĕr′ifī) *v.t.* (**-fied, -fy·ing**). Establish the truth or correctness of, examine for this purpose; (pass.) be proved true or correct by result, be borne out. **ver′i·fi·able** *adj.* **ver·i·fi·a·bil·i·ty** (vĕrifīabĭl′ĭtē), **ver·i·fi·ca·tion** (vĕrifĭkā′shon), **ver′i·fi·er** *ns.*

ver·i·ly (vĕr′ilē) *adv.* (archaic) Really, in truth.

ver·i·si·mil·i·tude (vĕrĭsĭmĭl′ĭ-tood, -tūd) *n.* Appearance of truth or reality; probability; apparent truth.

ver·i·ta·ble (vĕr′ĭtabel) *adj.* Real, properly or correctly so called. **ver′i·ta·bly** *adv.*

ver·i·ty (vĕr′ĭtē) *n.* (pl. **-ties**). Truth; true statement; reality, fact.

Ver·meer (vermēr′; *Du.* vermār′), **Jan** (1632–75). Dutch painter, of Delft.

ver·mi·cel·li (vẽrmĭsĕl′ē, -chĕl′ē) *n.* Pasta in long slender threads. [It., = "little worms" (L. *vermis* worm)]

ver·mi·cide (vẽr′mĭsīd) *n.* Substance used to kill (esp. intestinal) worms.

ver·mic·u·lar (vermĭk′yuler) *adj.* Wormlike in form or movements; of worm-eaten appearance; marked with close wavy lines; (med.) of, caused by, intestinal worms.

ver·mic·u·lat·ed (vermĭk′yu-lātĭd) *adj.* Covered or ornamented with close wavy markings like those made by gnawing of worms or their sinuous movements. **ver·mic·u·la·tion** (vermĭkyulā′shon) *n.*

ver·mic·u·lite (vermĭk′yulīt) *n.* Hydrous silicate material, usu. resulting from alteration of mica, and expandable into sponge by heating.

ver·mi·form (vẽr′mifôrm) *adj.* Worm-shaped; ~ **appendix,** small wormlike blind tube extending from cecum in man and some other

mammals.

ver·mi·fuge (vĕr′mĭfūj) *n.* Substance that expels worms from intestines.

ver·mil·ion (vermĭl′yon) *n.* Cinnabar; brilliant scarlet color of this. ~ *adj.* Of the color of vermilion. ~ *v.t.* Color (as) with vermilion.

ver·min (vĕr′mĭn) *n.* (pl. **-min**). (usu. collect.) Mammals and birds injurious to game crops, etc.; creeping or wingless insects etc. of noxious or offensive kind, esp. those infesting or parasitic on living beings or plants; noxious, vile, or offensive persons. **ver′min·ous** *adj.* (esp.) Infested with, full of, vermin; caused by vermin. **ver′min·ous·ly** *adv.* **ver′min·ous·ness** *n.*

Ver·mont (vermŏnt′). New England state; admitted to Union in 1791; capital, Montpelier. **Ver·mont′er** *n.*

ver·mouth (vermōōth′) *n.* White or red wine flavored with wormwood or other aromatic herbs, made esp. in France and Italy. [Fr., f. Ger. *Wermuth* wormwood]

ver·nac·u·lar (vernăk′yuler) *adj.* (of language, idiom, word) Of one's own native country, native, indigenous, not of foreign origin or of learned formation. **ver·nac′u·lar·ly** *adv.* **ver·nac′u·lar·ize** *v.t.* (**-ized, -iz·ing**). **vernacular** *n.* Vernacular language or dialect; homely speech.

ver·nal (vĕr′nal) *adj.* Of, appropriate to, coming or happening in, spring; ~ **equinox**: see EQUINOX. **ver′nal·ly** *adv.*

ver·ni·er (vĕr′nēer) *n.* Device consisting of graduated scale sliding along fixed scale, for measuring fractional parts of divisions of larger scale. [after Pierre *Vernier* (1580–1637), French mathematician]

Ve·ro·na (verō′na). City of N. Italy.

Trained as a sculptor and a decorative painter, and with canvases monumental in size, ***Veronese*** *preferred subjects such as 'The Family of Darius before Alexander' (above).*

Ver·o·nese[1] (vĕronēz′, -nēs′) *adj.* & *n.* (pl. **-nese**). (Native, inhabitant) of Verona.

Ve·ro·ne·se[2] (vĕrawnĕ′zē), **Paul Cagliari** (1528–88). Italian painter.

Ve·ron·i·ca (verŏn′ĭka), **St.** 1. Woman who, acc. to legend, wiped the sweat from the face of Christ on the way to Calvary. 2. (often **v**~) Representation of Christ's face in this scene; the handkerchief or veil used by Veronica to wipe Christ's face.

ve·ron·i·ca (verŏn′ĭka) *n.* 1. Speedwell. 2. Pass in bullfighting in which matador stands motionless while swinging cape away from charging bull. [f. VERONICA]

Ver·ra·za·no (vĕrazah′nō), **Giovanni da** (1485?–1528?). Florentine navigator; explored Atlantic Coast of Amer.; discovered New York Bay.

Ver·sailles (vĕrsī′, -sālz′). Town SW. of Paris that contains the royal palace built by Louis XIII and XIV; **Treaty of** ~, treaty that terminated the Amer. War of Independence in 1783; treaty signed on June 28, 1929, that terminated World War I.

ver·sa·tile (vĕr′satĭl, -tīl) *adj.* Turning easily or readily from one subject, occupation, etc., to another, showing facility in varied subjects, many-sided, **ver′sa·tile·ly** *adv.* **ver·sa·til·i·ty** (vĕrsatĭl′ĭtē) *n.*

verse (vĕrs) *n.* 1. Words arranged according to rules of prosody and forming complete metrical line (now chiefly in ref. to Gk. and Latin poetry). 2. Small number of metrical or rhythmical lines forming either a whole in themselves or a unit in a longer composition; stanza. 3. Metrical composition or structure; poetry esp. with ref. to metrical form as dist. from PROSE. 4. Each of the short sections into which the chapters of the Bible are divided. 5. Short sentence as part of liturgy.

versed[1] (vĕrst) *adj.* ~ **sine**, quantity obtained by subtracting cosine from unity.

versed[2] (vĕrst) *adj.* Experienced, practiced, skilled (*in* subject etc.).

ver·si·cle (vĕr′sĭkel) *n.* Each of a series of short sentences said or sung in liturgy, esp. sentence said by the minister or priest and followed by another (RESPONSE) from the people; (pl.) versicles and responses collectively.

ver·si·fy (vĕr′sĭfī) *v.* (**-fied, -fy·ing**). Make verses; turn into, narrate in, verse. **ver·si·fi·ca·tion** (vĕrsĭfĭkāshon), **ver′si·fi·er** *ns.*

ver·sion (vĕr′zhon, -shon) *n.* Rendering of work, passage, etc., into another language; particular form of statement, account, etc., given by one person or party.

vers li·bre (*Fr.* vĕr lē′bre) = FREE verse.

ver·so (vĕr′sō) *n.* (pl. **-sos**). Left-hand page of open book; back of leaf of book or manuscript (opp. RECTO); reverse of coin or medal.

verst (vĕrst, vĕrst) *n.* Russian measure of length, about ⅔ mi.

ver·sus (vĕr′sus) *prep.* (abbrev. v., vs.) 1. Against. 2. As compared with.

ver·te·bra (vĕr′tebra) *n.* (pl. **-brae** pr. -brā, -brē, **-bras**). Each of the bony segments composing the spinal column (pl., loosely) backbone; **cervical vertebrae**, those of neck; **thoracic**, of ribs; **lumbar**, of loins; **sacral**, of hips;

caudal, of tail. **ver′te·bral** *adj.* **ver′te·bral·ly** *adv.*

ver·te·brate (vẽr′tebrăt, -brĭt) *adj.* & *n.* (Animal) belonging to the Vertebrata, the division containing all animals having a cranium and a spinal column or a notochord and including mammals, birds, reptiles, amphibians, and fishes.

ver·te·bra·tion (vẽrtebrā′sh*o*n) *n.* Formation of, division into, vertebrae or similar segments.

ver·tex (vẽr′tĕks) *n.* (pl. **-tex·es, -ti·ces** pr. -tĭsēz). Top, highest part or point; top of the head; (math.) point opposite base of (plane or solid) figure, point where axis meets curve or surface, or where lines forming angle meet.

ver·ti·cal (vẽr′tĭk*e*l) *adj.* Of, at, passing through, vertex or zenith, having position in heavens directly above given place or point; placed, moving, perpendicularly; upright; of, at, affecting, vertex of the head; (econ.) pertaining to all successive processes of manufacture or distribution of a product, as dist. from HORIZONTAL; ~ **takeoff**, (of aircraft) takeoff directly upward (freq. attrib.); **vertical union**: see INDUSTRIAL union. **ver′ti·cal·ly** *adv.* **ver·ti·cal·i·ty** (vẽrtĭkăl′ĭtē) *n.* **vertical** *n.* Vertical line, plane, or circle. **ver′ti·cal·ness** *n.*

ver·ti·cil (vẽr′tĭsĭl) *n.* (bot.) Number of similar organs or parts arranged in circle around axis. **ver·tic·il·late** (vertĭs′*i*lĭt, -lāt, vẽrtĭsĭl′āt) *adj.*

ver·ti·go (vẽr′tigō) *n.* (pl. **ver·ti·goes**). Dizziness, condition with sensation of whirling and tendency to lose equilibrium. **ver·tig·i·nous** (vertĭj′*i*n*u*s) *adj.* Of vertigo; causing, tending to cause, giddiness. **ver·tig′i·nous·ly** *adv.* **ver·tig′i·nous·ness** *n.*

ver·vain (vẽr′vān) *n.* Common herbaceous plant of genus *Verbena*, esp. *V. hastata.*

verve (vẽrv) *n.* Vigor, enthusiasm, energy, esp. in literary work.

ver·y (vĕr′ē) *adj.* (**ver·i·er, ver·i·est**). Real, true, genuine, properly so called or designated; **the** ~, used to emphasize identity, significance, extreme degree, etc. **very** *adv.* (used with adjectives, adverbs, adjectival participles, but not other parts of verbs). In a high degree, to a great extent, extremely; ~ **high frequency**: see FREQUENCY; ~ **well**, formula of consent or approval.

Ve·sa·li·us (vĭsā′lē*u*s), **Andreas** (1514–64). Flemish anatomist and surgeon born in Brussels; considered as father of modern anatomy.

ve·si·ca (vesī′k*a*) *n.* (pl. **-cae** pr. -sē). 1. (anat.) Bladder. 2. ~ **pis·cis** (pĭs′ĭs, pī′sĭs), pointed oval (O) used as an aureole in medieval art. **ves·i·cal** (vĕs′ĭk*a*l) *adj.* [L., = "bladder of a fish"]

ves·i·cate (vĕs′ĭkāt) *v.t.* (**-cat·ed, -cat·ing**). Raise blisters on (skin etc.). **ves′i·cant, ves·i·ca·to·ry** (vĕs′ĭk*a*tōrē, -tōre) *adjs.* & *ns.* (pl. **-to·ries**). (Substance) causing formation of blisters. **ves·i·ca·tion** (vĕsĭkā′sh*o*n) *n.*

ves·i·cle (vĕs′ĭk*e*l) *n.* Small bladderlike vessel, cavity, sac; (path.) small, usu. round, elevation of cuticle containing clear watery fluid. **ve·sic·u·lar** (vesĭk′y*u*ler), **ve·sic·u·late** (vesĭk′y*u*lĭt, -lāt) *adjs.*

Ves·pa·si·an (vĕspā′zhē*a*n, -zh*a*n). Titus Flavius Vespasianus (9–79 A.D.), Roman emperor 69–79 A.D.; began building the Coliseum.

Ves·pers (vĕs′p*e*rz) *n.pl.* (R.C. Ch.) Canonical HOUR; office said or sung toward evening, evensong; **Sicilian** ~: see SICILIAN.

ves·per (vĕs′p*e*r) **sparrow.** Gray N. Amer. sparrow (*Pooecetes gramineus*), having white outer tail feathers that are conspicuous when bird is in flight, and chestnut wing patch.

Ves·puc·ci (vĕspōō′chē, -spū -), **Amerigo** (1451–1512). Florentine merchant who settled in Spain; he claimed to have made a voyage in 1497 in which he discovered the mainland of S. Amer.; this claim, in virtue of his name was given to the continent of Amer.

ves·sel (vĕs′*e*l) *n.* 1. Hollow receptacle for liquid etc., esp. domestic utensil, usu. round, used for preparing, storing, or serving food or drink; (bibl.) person regarded as containing or receiving some spiritual quality. 2. (anat., zool.) Membranous canal, duct, etc., in which body fluids are contained or circulated, esp. artery or vein (**blood** ~); (bot.) woody duct carrying or containing sap etc., (rare) seed vessel. 3. Any craft or ship, usu. one larger than rowboat.

vest[1] (vĕst) *n.* Short, sleeveless garment for men, buttoning in front and worn under jacket; similar garment worn by woman over dress or blouse; ~**-pocket**, (attrib. of

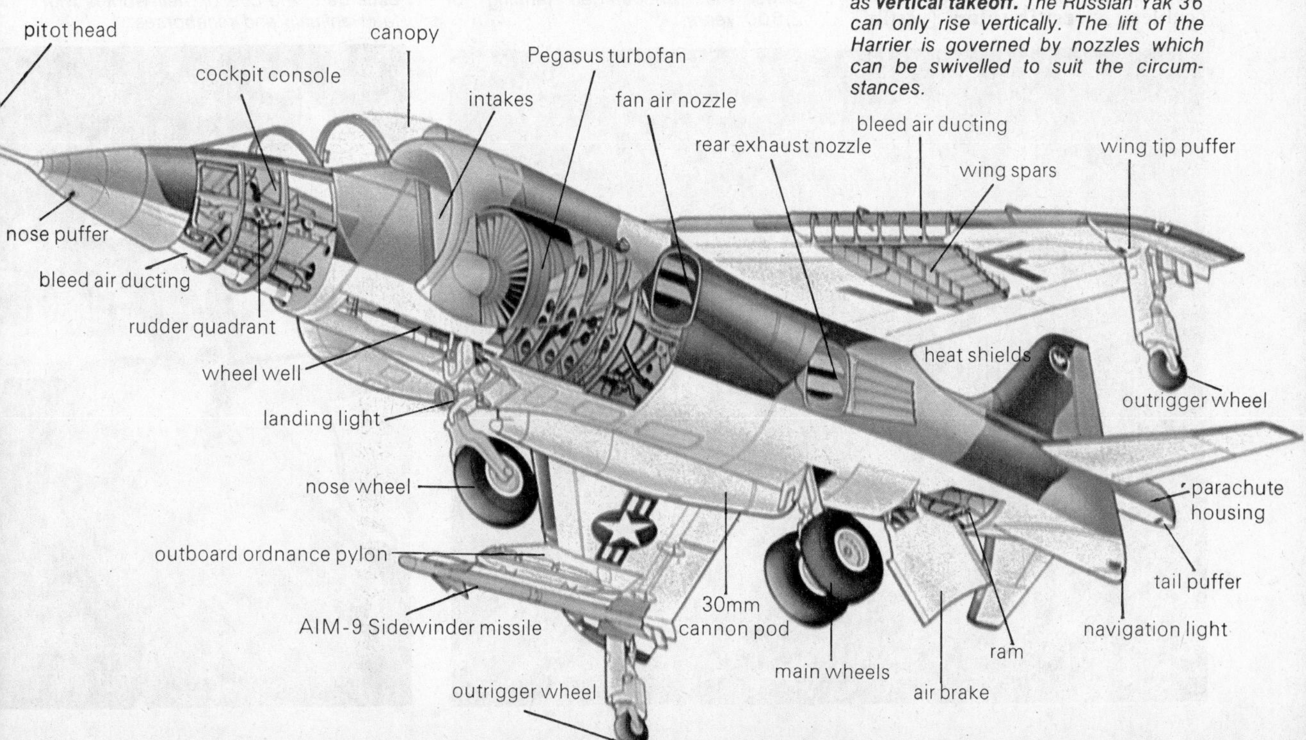

Sold to the U.S. forces, the Hawker Siddeley Harrier is the only aircraft capable of using short runways as well as ***vertical takeoff.*** *The Russian Yak 36 can only rise vertically. The lift of the Harrier is governed by nozzles which can be swivelled to suit the circumstances.*

articles etc., as cameras) of small size.

vest[2] (vĕst) *v.* 1. (chiefly pass.) Invest (person) *with* power, authority, etc.; put in full or legal possession of something, place or secure (something, freq. power or authority) in possession of person(s). 2. Become vested (*in* person), pass into possession of; **vested interests, rights**, etc., interest, rights, etc., possession of which is established in a person by right or by long association and usu. gives rise to expectation of gain; **vesting**, retention by eligible employee of all or some pension benefits, without regard to discontinuation of employment.

Ves·ta (vĕs'ta). 1. (Rom. myth.) Goddess of hearth and household, daughter of Saturn, with temple in Rome whose sacred fire was tended by vestal virgins. 2. (astron.) One of minor planets or asteroids with orbit between Mars and Jupiter.

ves·tal (vĕs'tal) *adj.* 1. Of the goodess Vesta or the vestal virgins; ~ **virgin**, (Rom. hist.) one of the (orig. two, later four, then six) virgins consecrated to the service of Vesta and vowed to chastity. 2. Chaste, virgin. **vestal** *n.* Vestal virgin; chaste unmarried woman.

ves·ti·bule (vĕs'tĭbūl) *n.* 1. Antechamber, hall, lobby, between entrance door and interior of house or other building; porch of church etc. 2. (Gk. and Rom. antiq.) Enclosed or partially enclosed space in front of main entrance of house. 3. Enclosed entrance at end of railroad car giving access to car and usu. communicating with other cars. 4. (anat.) Dilated entrance to a canal or cavity between middle ear and cochlea. **ves·tib·u·lar** (vĕstĭb'yuler) *adj.*

*Kidney **vetch** usually has yellow flowers but they may vary and become orange red in a salty atmosphere. Like other plants in the genus Vicia, it has long been used for fodder.*

ves·tige (vĕs'tĭj) *n.* Trace, track, evidence (of something no longer existing or present); (biol.) organ or part that is small or degenerate in descendants but in ancestors was fully developed. **ves·tig·i·al** (vĕstĭj'ēal) *adj.* **ves·tig'i·al·ly** *adv.*

vest·ment (vĕst'ment) *n.* Garment, esp. worn by king or official on ceremonial occasion; any of official garments of priests, assistants, etc., during church service etc., esp. chasuble.

ves·try (vĕs'trē) *n.* (pl. **-tries**). Room or part of church used for keeping vestments, vessels, records, etc., for robing of clergy and choir, for parish meeting, etc.; (Episcopal Ch.) committee of parishioners that manages business affairs of parish; **ves'tryman** (pl. **-men**), member of parochial vestry.

Ve·su·vi·us (vesōō'vēus). Active volcano in SW. Italy near Naples (3,891 ft., 1,175 m); its eruption destroyed Pompeii and Herculaneum, 79 A.D. **Ve·su'vi·an** (vesōō'vēan) *adj.*

vet[1] (vĕt) *n.* (colloq.) Veterinary surgeon. ~ *v.t.* (**vet·ted, vet·ting**). Examine, treat (animal, person) medically; work as a veterinarian; submit (scheme, book, etc.) to careful examination.

vet[2] (vĕt) *n.* (colloq.) Veteran.

vetch (vĕch) *n.* Leguminous plant of *Vicia* (esp. *V. sativa*, common tare) or related genera, many or which are valuable for fodder.

vet·er·an (vĕt'eran, vĕt'ran) *adj.* Grown old in service; experienced by long practice; (of army) composed of veteran troops; (of service) long continued. ~ *n.* Veteran person, esp. soldier; former serviceman; **Veterans Day**, national holiday honoring all veterans of armed services, orig. Armistice Day and formerly observed on Nov. 11,

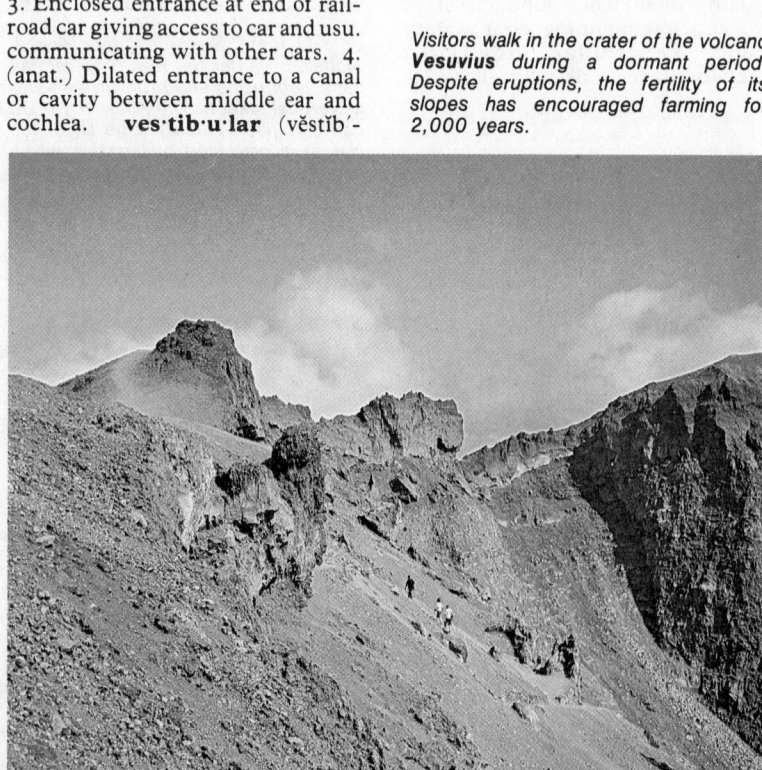

*Visitors walk in the crater of the volcano **Vesuvius** during a dormant period. Despite eruptions, the fertility of its slopes has encouraged farming for 2,000 years.*

*A **veterinarian** giving treatment to a sheep in Australia. Although most people associate these men with domestic pets, the bulk of their work is with farm animals and racehorses.*

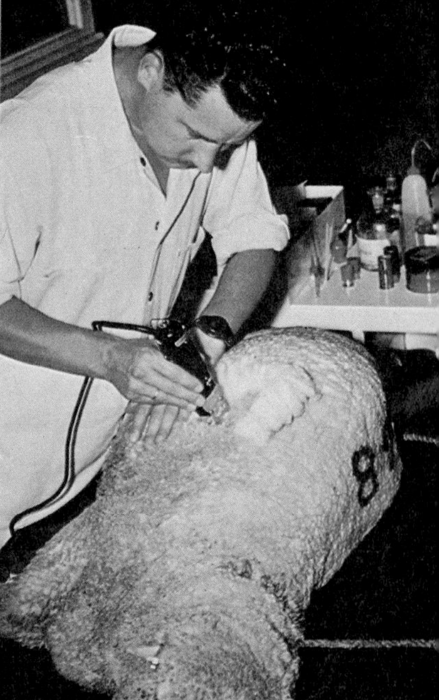

now on the fourth Monday of October.

vet·er·i·nar·y (vĕt´*er*inĕrē, vĕt´-*ri*-) *adj.* Of, for, concerned with (treatment of) diseases and injuries of cattle and other animals. ~ *n.* (pl. **-nar·ies**). **vet·er·i·nar·i·an** (vĕt*er*inār´ēan, vĕtr*i*-) *n.* Veterinary surgeon.

ve·to (vē´tō) *n.* (pl. **-toes**). Prohibition of proposed or intended act; (exercise of) constitutional right to prohibit passing or putting in force of an enactment or measure. ~ *v.t.* (**-toed, -to·ing**). Exercise veto against. **ve'to·er** *n.* [L., = "I forbid"]

vex (vĕks) *v.t.* Anger by slight or petty annoyance, irritate.

vex·a·tion (vĕksā´sh*o*n) *n.* Being vexed, irritation; vexing thing. **vex·a'tious** *adj.* **vex·a'tious·ly** *adv.* **vex·a'tious·ness** *n.*

vex·il·lum (vĕksĭl´*u*m) *n.* (pl. **vex·il·la** pr. vĕksĭl´*a*). 1. (Rom. antiq.) Banner of Roman troops; body of troops under this. 2. (eccles.) Small piece of linen or silk wound around upper part of crosier. 3. (bot.) Large upper petal of papilionaceous flower. 4. (ornith.) Vane of feather.

VFD *abbrev.* Volunteer fire department.

VFW, V.F.W. *abbrevs.* Veterans of Foreign Wars.

VHF, V.H.F., vhf, v.h.f. *abbrevs.* Very high FREQUENCY.

VI *abbrev.* Virgin Islands.

v.i. *abbrev.* Verb intransitive.

vi·a (vī´*a*, vē´*a*) *prep.* By way of, through (specified place).

vi·a·ble (vī´*a*bel) *adj.* Capable of maintaining separate existence (of child at birth etc.); able to live in particular environment; practicable; (bot., of seeds) having ability to germinate. **vi·a·bil·i·ty** (vī*a*bĭl´-ĭtē) *n.* **vi'a·bly** *adv.* [Fr., f. *vie* life]

***Viburnum** species are used mainly as decorative shrubs and include the guelder rose, the berries of which are widely used in the U.S.A. as a substitute for cranberries in jelly-making.*

vi·a·duct (vī´*a*dŭkt) *n.* Bridge-like structure carrying railroad or road over valley, river, etc.

vi·al (vī´*a*l, vīl) *n.* Small vessel for liquid medicines, now esp. small glass bottle.

vi·and (vī´*a*nd) *n.* (usu. pl.) Article(s) of food, provision(s), victual(s).

vi·at·i·cum (vīăt´*i*k*u*m) *n.* (pl. **-ca** pr. -k*a*, **-cums**). 1. Eucharist as administered to one (in danger of) dying. 2. (rare) Sum of money

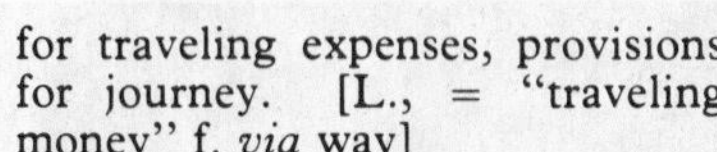

for traveling expenses, provisions for journey. [L., = "traveling money" f. *via* way]

vibes (vībz) *n.pl.* 1. (colloq.) Vibraphone. 2. (slang) (also **vibrations**) Emotional stimulus one gets from person or place.

vi·brac·u·lum (vībrăk´y*u*l*u*m) *n.* (pl. **-la** pr. -l*a*). Whiplike movable filament in some polyzoan colonies serving e.g. to prevent noxious material from settling.

vi·brant (vī´br*a*nt) *adj.* Vibrating, thrilling, resonant. **vi'brant·ly** *adv.* **vi'bran·cy** *n.*

vi·bra·phone (vī´br*a*fōn) *n.* Percussion instrument with lids of resonators kept in constant motion by electric current so as to produce a pulsating effect.

vi·brate (vī´brāt) *v.* (**-brat·ed, -brat·ing**). (Cause to) swing to and fro periodically, oscillate, quiver; set, be, in state of vibration; thrill; (of sound) strike ear with quivering or pulsating effect; (of pendulum) measure (seconds etc.) by vibration. **vi·bra·tile** (vī´br*a*tĭl, -tīl) *adj.*

vi·bra·tion (vībrā´sh*o*n) *n.* (esp., phys.) 1. Rapid reciprocating motion to and fro, up and down, etc., of particles of elastic body produced by disturbance of its equilibrium. 2. (pl.) = VIBES sense 2. **vi·bra'tion·al** *adj.*

vi·bra·to (vībrah´tō, vī-) *n.* (pl. **-tos**). (mus.) Tremulous effect in singing or of playing stringed instruments by rapid slight variation of pitch; cf. TREMOLO. [It.]

vi·bra·tor (vī´brāt*e*r) *n.* Thing, person, that vibrates. **vi·bra·to·ry** (vī´br*a*tōrē, -tōrē) *adj.* Characterized by, causing, connected with, vibration; capable of vibrating.

vi·bur·num (vībẽr´n*u*m) *n.* Shrub of widely distributed genus *V*~, which includes the cranberry bush.

Vic. *abbrev.* Victoria.

vic·ar (vĭk´*e*r) *n.* 1. Representative; substitute; assistant. 2. (Ch. of England) Parish priest formerly acting in place of rector, now in charge of parish; (Protestant Episcopal) clergyman in charge of a chapel. 3. (R.C. Ch.) Representative of pope or bishop; **V~ of Christ**, the pope as Christ's representative on Earth. **vic'ar·ship** *n.*

vic·ar·age (vĭk´*e*rĭj) *n.* Benefice, residence, of vicar.

vi·car·i·ous (vīkār´ē*u*s) *adj.* Deputed, delegated; acting, done, endured, for another. **vi·car'i·ous·ly** *adv.* **vi·car'i·ous·ness** *n.*

vice[1] (vīs) *n.* Evil, esp. grossly immoral, habit or conduct; de-

*A granite **viaduct** carrying the railway near St. Austell in Cornwall U.K. Devised by the Romans to carry their aqueducts across river valleys, this device is also used to make roads less steep.*

*Ascending the throne at the age of 18, **Queen Victoria** of England had the longest reign of any British monarch and, when she died in 1901, had been queen for 63 years.*

*Discovered by David Livingstone in 1855, the **Victoria Falls** on the Zambezi River are now used to drive a hydro-electric power station. The canyon beyond the falls is spanned by a bridge.*

pravity, serious fault; defect, blemish; fault, bad trick (of horse etc.); ~ **squad**, division of police department enforcing laws against prostitution, gambling, etc.

vice[2] (vīs) *n.* (chiefly Brit.) Vise.

vi·ce[3] (vī′sē) *prep.* In the place of, in succession to.

vice- *prefix.* Acting in place of, assistant, next in rank to.

vice ad·mi·ral (vīs′ăd′m*e*r*a*l). Naval officer ranking next below admiral.

vice·ge·rent (vīsjĕr′*e*nt) *n.* & *adj.* (Person) exercising delegated power, deputy. **vice·ge′ren·cy** *n.*

vi·cen·ni·al (vīsĕn′ēal) *adj.* Lasting, happening, every, 20 years.

vice-pres·i·dent (vīs′prĕz′ĭ-d*e*nt) *n.* 1. Officer ranking next to a president. 2. (**V ~ -P ~**) Elected officer second in rank to the President of the U.S. **vice′-pres′i·den·cy** *n.* **vice′-pres·i·den′tial** *adj.*

vice-re·gent (vīs′rē′j*e*nt) *n.* One acting in place of regent.

vice·reine (vīs′rān) *n.* Woman viceroy; wife of viceroy.

vice·roy (vīs′roi) *n.* 1. Person acting as governor of country, province, etc., in name and by authority of supreme ruler; (hist.) representative of British Crown in India. 2. Handsome red-and-black Amer. butterfly (*Limenitis archippus*); like monarch but smaller. **vice·re·gal** (vīsrē′g*a*l), **vice·roy·al** (vīsroi′*a*l) *adjs.* **vice·roy′al·ty** *n.* (pl. **-ties**).

vi·ce ver·sa (vī′s*e* vĕr′s*a*, vīs′). The other way around, conversely.

Vi·chy (vĭsh′ē; *Fr.* vēshē′). Town in central France noted for mineral waters; ~ **Government**, French government, with headquarters at Vichy, that administered S. part of France (~ **France**) and collaborated with Germans in World War II after French collapse in 1940; ~ **water**, effervescent mineral water from Vichy, freq. bottled; bottled water resembling this.

vi·chy·ssoise (vĭshēswahz′, vĭsh′ēswahz) *n.* Cream soup of potatoes and leeks, usu. served cold.

vi·cin·i·ty (vĭsĭn′ĭtē) *n.* (pl. **-ties**). Surrounding district; nearness in place; close relationship; **in the ~ (of)**, in the neighborhood (of).

vi·cious (vĭsh′*u*s) *adj.* 1. Of the nature of, addicted to, vice; evil; depraved. 2. (of language, reasoning, etc.) Incorrect, faulty, unsound, corrupt; intensifying its own causes; ~ **circle**: see CIRCLE. 3. (esp. of animals) Bad-tempered, spiteful. **vi′cious·ly** *adv.* **vi′cious·ness** *n.*

vi·cis·si·tude (vĭsĭs′ĭtōōd, -tūd) *n.* Change of circumstances, esp. of condition or fortune.

Vicks·burg (vĭks′bĕrg). Town in Mississippi, on the Mississippi River, where, in 1863, the Union forces under Grant besieged the Confederates, who surrendered on July 4; this victory and Gettysburg marked the turning point in the Civil War.

vic·tim (vĭk′tĭm) *n.* Living creature sacrificed to a deity or in performance of religious rite; person who is killed or made to suffer by cruel or oppressive treatment; (loosely) one who suffers injury, hardship, loss, etc.; **victimless crime**, legal offense, such as prostitution, considered as not having any identifiable victim.

vic·tim·ize (vĭk′t*i*mīz) *v.t.* (**-ized, -iz·ing**). Cause to suffer inconvenience, discomfort, annoyance, etc.; cheat, defraud; treat unjustly or with undue harshness, esp. dismiss (employee) for striking, etc. **vic′tim·i·zer, vic·tim·i·za·tion** (vĭkt*i*mīzā′sh*o*n) *ns.*

vic·tor (vĭk′t*e*r) *n.* Conqueror in battle or contest.

Vic·tor Em·man·u·el (vĭk′t*e*r ĭmăn′ū*e*l). Name of three kings of Sardinia, two of whom became kings of Italy: **Victor Emmanuel I** (1759–1824), king of Sardinia 1802–1821; **Victor Emmanuel II** (1820–78), first king of Italy 1861–1878; **Victor Emmanuel III** (1869–1947), king of Italy 1900–46.

Vic·to·ri·a (vĭktōr′ē*a*, -tōr-) (1819–1901). Daughter of Edward, Duke of Kent, fourth son of George III; queen of Gt. Britain and Ireland 1837–1901; empress of India 1877–1901; married Prince Albert of Saxe-Coburg-Gotha, 1840; **Lake ~**, largest lake in Africa and chief reservoir of the Nile; ~ **Cross**, (abbrev. V.C.)

Video games have gained worldwide popularity since they first appeared. Unlike many 'fads', their popularity has not waned with time.

Vienna, capital and largest city of Austria, contains many old buildings like St. Michael's Gate shown above. It is however, essentially a modern city and is an important port and major European railroad center.

decoration awarded for conspicuous bravery to members of Brit. and Commonwealth armed forces, first instituted by Queen Victoria in 1856; ~ **Falls**, African waterfall on the Zambezi, discovered by David Livingstone in 1855.

Vic·to·ri·an (vĭktōr′ēan, -tōr′-) *adj.* Of, living in, characteristic of, the reign of Queen VICTORIA. ~ *n.* Person living in the reign of Queen Victoria.

vic·to·ri·ous (vĭktōr′ēus, -tōr′-) *adj.* Triumphant, successful in contest or struggle; marked by, producing, victory. **vic·to′ri·ous·ly** *adv.* **vic·to′ri·ous·ness** *n.*

vic·to·ry (vĭk′terē) *n.* (pl. **-ries**). Supremacy achieved by battle or in war, defeat of enemy; triumph or ultimate success in any contest or enterprise.

vict·ual (vĭt′al) *n.* (usu. pl.) Food, provisions. ~ *v.* (**-ualed, -ual·ing**; *Brit.* **-ualled, -ual·ling**). Supply with victuals; lay in supply of victuals; eat.

Related to the camel and the llama, the **vicuna** of the central Andes lives at altitudes up to 16,000 ft. Its wool, the finest known to man, is rare and expensive.

vi·cu·ña (vĭkōō′na, -ku′-, vĭkōō′nya) *n.* (pl. **-ñas**, collect. **-ña**). S. Amer. mammal (*Vicugna vicugna*) of N. Andes, related to llama and alpaca, and with fine silky wool used for textiles; soft cloth made of this, imitation of it.

vi·de (vī′dē; *Lat.* wē′dĕ) *v.imp.* (as direction to reader) Refer to, consult. [L.]

vi·de·li·cet (vĭdĕl′ĭsĭt; *Lat.* wēdā′lĭkĕt) *adv.* (abbrev. viz., viz) That is to say, namely. [L.]

vid·e·o (vĭd′ēō) *n.* Television; **vid′eodisc, vid′eodisk**, disk similar to phonograph record that can record pictures and sound for reproducing on television sets; **video game**, electronic apparatus connected to television set, enabling players in game to control dots, lines, etc., on screen; **vid′eophone**, telephone transmitting picture of person speaking; **vid′eotape**, magnetic tape for recording pictures and sound for reproducing on television sets.

vie (vī) *v.i.* (**vied, vy·ing**). Contend or compete for superiority in some respect (*with*), be rivals.

Vi·en·na (vēĕn′a). (Ger. *Wien*) Capital of Austria; **Congress of** ~, conference (1814–15) of European statesmen that readjusted territories and governments throughout Europe after the Napoleonic Wars. **Vi·en·nese** (vēenēz′, -nēs′) *adj.* & *n.*

Vien·tiane (vyĕntyahn′). Capital of Laos in the NW. on the Mekong River.

Vi·et·cong, Viet Cong (vēĕtkŏng′, vyĕt-) *n.* (pl. **-cong**). Communist guerrilla (member of) force in South Vietnam who, with aid from North Vietnam, fought (1954–76) to overthrow the S. Vietnamese government.

Vi·et·nam (vēĕtnahm′, -năm, vyĕt-). Country in SE. Asia, formed 1945 from the Tongking, Annam, and Cochin-China provinces of French Indochina; divided 1954–75 into the **Democratic Republic of (North)** ~ and the **Republic of (South)** ~; since April 1975, united into the **Socialist Republic of** ~, capital

*A unified country since the civil war ended in 1975, **Vietnam** now has a 'socialist' regime with a single national assembly. Although corruption has been eliminated, work on post-war reconstruction is still behind planned targets.*

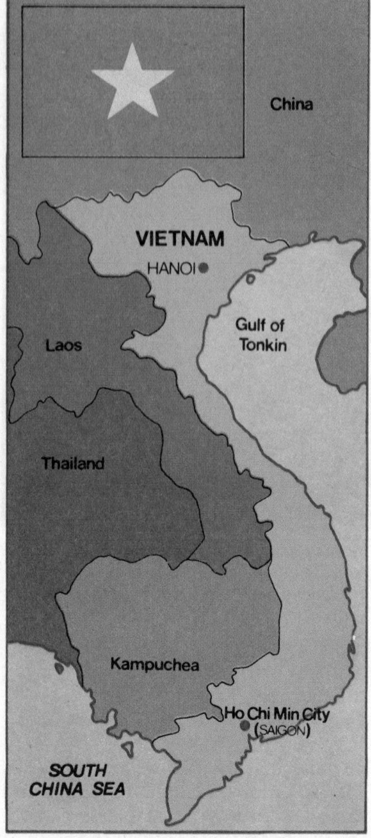

Hanoi. **Vi·et·nam·ese** (vēĕtn*a*mēz′, -mēs′, vyĕt-) *adj.* & *n.*

view (vū) *n.* Inspection by eye or mind; power of seeing, range of physical or mental vision; what is seen, scene, prospect; picture etc. representing this; mental survey, mental attitude; **in ~ of,** having regard to, considering; **on ~,** open to inspection; **point of ~,** position from which thing is viewed, way of looking at a matter; **private ~, viewing,** view of exhibition open only to invited guests, usu. on day before public opening; **with a view to,** for the purpose of, as a step toward; with an eye to, in the hope of getting; **view′finder,** attachment to camera showing view in range of camera lens; similar device used by painters; **view′point,** point of view. **view** *v.t.* Survey with eyes or mind, form impression or judgment of.

view·er (vū′*er*) *n.* (esp.) One who watches television broadcast.

vig·il (vĭj′*il*) *n.* Keeping awake during usual time for sleep; (pl.) prayers at church service, esp. for the dead; **keep ~,** keep watch.

vig·i·lance (vĭj′*i*lans) *n.* Watchfulness against danger or action of others, caution, circumspection; **~ committee,** (hist.) in 19th c. U.S. West, self-appointed committee for maintenance of justice and order, esp. for summary punishment of criminals when processes of law were considered inadequate. **vig′i·lant** *adj.* **vig′i·lant·ly** *adv.* **vig′i·lant·ness** *n.*

vig·i·lan·te (vĭj*i*lăn′tē) *n.* Member of vigilance committee.

vi·gnette (vĭnyĕt′, vē-) *n.* Decorative design, usu. small, on blank space in book, having edges shading off into surrounding paper; photograph with edges shading off into background; (fig., literary) character sketch or short description. **~** *v.t.* (**-gnet·ted, -gnet·ting**). Make vignette of esp. by shading off or softening away edges. **vig·nett′ist** *n.* [Fr., = "little vine," ornamental design at end of chapter]

vig·or, Brit. **vig·our** (vĭg′*er*) *ns.* Active physical strength or energy; flourishing physical condition, vitality; mental or moral strength, force, or energy. **vig·or·ous** (vĭg′*er*us) *adj.* **vig′or·ous·ly** *adv.* **vig′or·ous·ness** *n.*

Vik·ing (vī′kĭng) *adj.* & *n.* (One) of the Scandinavians during the period (8th–11th centuries) when they became active as traders esp. between Russia and W. Europe, and also took to piracy, plundering and temporarily occupying many of the coastal districts and river valleys of N. and W. Europe.

vile (vīl) *adj.* (**vil·er, vil·est**). Despicable on moral grounds, base, depraved; worthless, of poor or bad quality; disgusting, filthy; shameful. **vile′ly** *adv.* **vile′ness** *n.*

vil·i·fy (vĭl′*i*fī) *v.t.* (**-fied, -fy·ing**). Defame, traduce, speak evil of. **vil·i·fi·ca·tion** (vĭl*i*fĭkā′-sh*o*n) *n.*

vil·la (vĭl′*a*) *n.* 1. (hist., esp. Roman) Country estate with house(s), farm(s), etc. 2. Italian country house. 3. Large, usu. luxurious, country house or estate. [L. *villa* farmhouse]

Vil·la (vē′*a*; *Sp.* vē′yah), **Francisco ("Pancho")** (1877–1923). (orig. name Doroteo Arango) Mexican bandit and revolutionary leader; assassinated.

vil·lage (vĭl′ĭj) *n.* Assemblage of houses etc. in country district, larger than hamlet and smaller than town; small municipality with limited corporate powers. **vil′lag·er** *n.* Inhabitant of village (usu. implying rusticity).

vil·lain (vĭl′*a*n), fem. **vil·lain·ess** (vĭl′*a*nĭs, -nĕs) *ns.* Person guilty or capable of great wickedness, scoundrel; character in play, novel, etc., whose evil motives or actions are important element of plot. **vil′lain·y** *n.* (pl. **-lain·ies**).

vil·lain·ous (vĭl′*a*nus) *adj.* Worthy of a villain, wicked, vile; (colloq.) very unpleasant. **vil′lain·ous·ly** *adv.* **vil′lain·ous·ness** *n.*

vil·la·nelle (vĭl*a*nĕl′) *n.* Poem usu. of 19 lines based on two rhymes with some lines repeated.

-ville *suffix.* 1. City or town, used as part of many place names (*Pleasantville, N.Y.*). 2. (colloq.) Forming names of fictitious places with reference to particular quality etc. (*Squaresville, Endsville*).

vil·lein (vĭl′*i*n) *n.* (hist., in feudal system) Peasant cultivator entirely subject to a lord or attached to a manor. **vil′lein·age** *n.* Tenure of villein; being a villein, serfdom.

vil·lose (vĭl′ōs), **vil·lous** (vĭl′*u*s) *adjs.* Covered with (numerous close slender projections resembling) thickset hairs.

vil·lus (vĭl′*u*s) *n.* (pl. **vil·li** pr. vĭl′ī). (bot.) Long slender soft hair; (anat., zool.) slender hairlike projection, esp. of small intestine.

Vil·ni·us (vĭl′nēōōs). (also Vilna) Capital city of Lithuania.

vim (vĭm) *n.* (colloq.) Vigor, energy.

Vim·i·nal (vĭm′*i*nal). One of the Seven Hills of Rome.

vin·ai·grette (vĭn*a*grĕt′) *n.* 1. Small ornamental bottle holding aromatic salts etc., smelling bottle. 2. (also **~ sauce**) Sauce of oil,

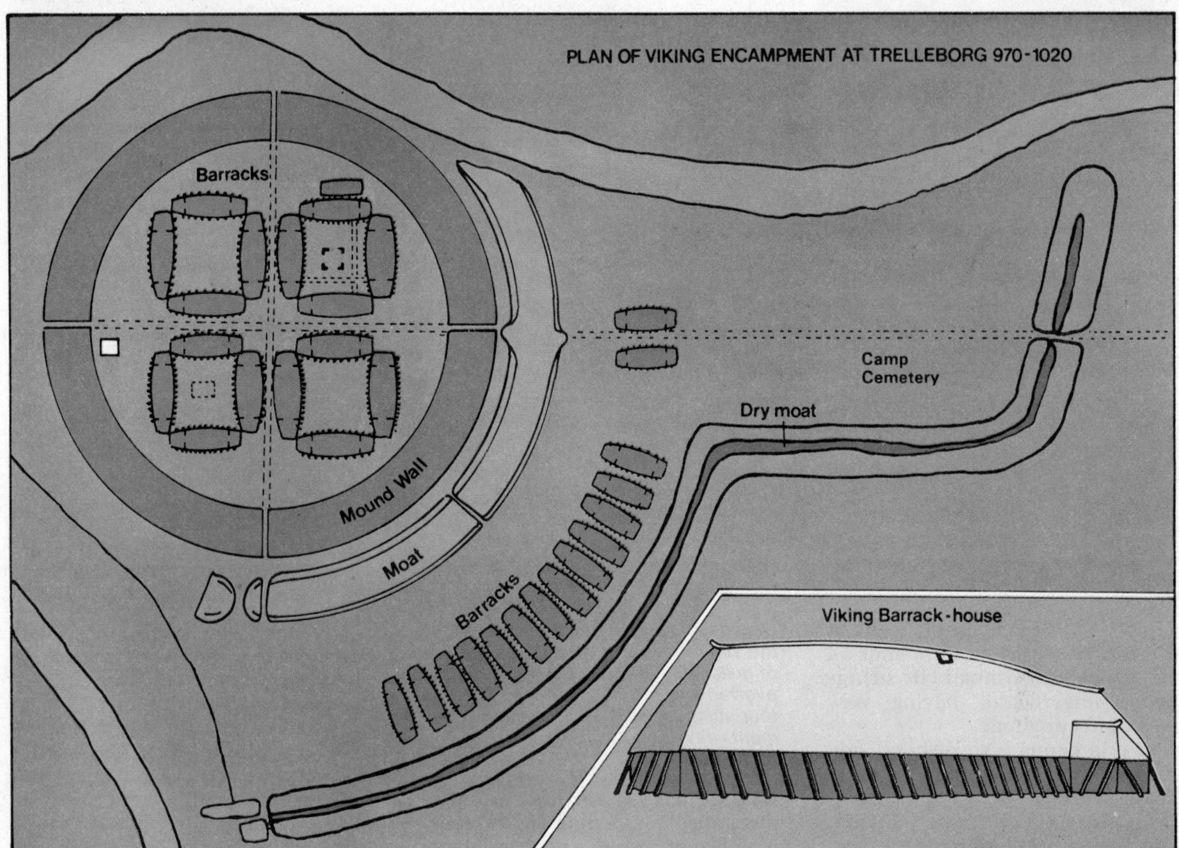

Diagram of the large ***Viking*** *stronghold at Trelleborg on the island of West Zealand in Denmark. The size of the settlement, dated between 950 and 1050 A.D. indicates that this may have been a staging post for Norse forces. Also it could have been the base for the invasion of England in A.D. 1013 by King Swein of Denmark. Earlier, the Vikings had reached the Mediterranean.*

vinegar, etc., used esp. with salads.

Vin·cent de Paul (vĭn'sent de pawl'), **St.** (1576–1660). French R.C. reformer, founder of Congregation of Priests of the Mission, now usu. known as the Lazarists, and of Sisters of Charity. **Vin·cen·tian** (vĭnsĕn'chan) *adj.* & *n.* (Member) of society founded by Vincent de Paul.

Vin·ci (vĭn'chē; *It.* vēn'chē): see LEONARDO DA VINCI.

vin·cu·lum (vĭng'kyulum) *n.* (pl. **-la** pr. -la). (math.) Straight line drawn over two or more terms denoting that these are subject to the same operations of multiplication, division, etc., by another term. [L., = "bond"]

vin·di·cate (vĭn'dikāt) *v.t.* (**-cat·ed, -cat·ing**). Maintain the cause of (person, religion, etc.) successfully; establish the existence or merits or justice of (one's veracity, courage, conduct, character, assertion). **vin·di·ca·tion** (vĭndikā'shon), **vin'di·ca·tor** *ns.*

vin·di·ca·to·ry (vĭn'dikatōrē, -tōrē) *adj.* Tending to vindicate; (of laws) punitive.

vin·dic·tive (vĭndĭk'tĭv) *adj.* Revengeful, avenging, given to revenge. **vin·dic'tive·ly** *adv.* **vin·dic'tive·ness** *n.*

vine (vīn) *n.* Trailing or climbing woody plant of genus *Vitis* (esp. *V. vinifera*, from the fruit of which wine is made) bearing grapes; grapevine; any trailing or climbing plant.

vin·e·gar (vĭn'eger) *n.* Sour liquid (dilute acetic acid) produced by acetous fermentation of wine, cider, etc., and used as condiment, preservative, etc. **vin'e·gar·y** *adj.* Sour like vinegar, acid. [OF. *vin* wine, *aigre* sour]

vin·er·y (vī'nerē) *n.* (pl. **-er·ies**). Greenhouse for growing grapes.

vine·yard (vĭn'yerd) *n.* Plantation of grapevines, esp. for wine making.

Vin·land (vĭn'land). Region of N. Amer. explored and briefly settled by Norsemen under Leif Erics(s)on in the 11th c.; remains of a settlement have been discovered at L'Anse au Meadow in Newfoundland.

vin or·di·naire (*Fr.* văn ōrdēnār') (pl. ***vins or·di·naires*** pr. vănz ōrdēnār'). Cheap usu. red wine for ordinary use.

vi·nous (vī'nus) *adj.* Of, like, due to, addicted to, wine. **vi·nos·i·ty** (vīnŏs'ĭtē) *n.*

vin·tage (vĭn'tĭj) *n.* 1. (Season of) grape harvest; wine, esp. of good quality; wine made from grapes of particular district (freq. used with ref. to the age of a wine or the year when it was made). 2. Class of antique objects, automobiles, etc. ~ *adj.* Of high quality, esp. from the past; of a past season.

vint·ner (vĭnt'ner) *n.* Wine merchant.

vi·nyl (vī'nil) *n.* 1. (chem.) Univalent radical (CH_2CH) derived from ethylene, forming the basis of many plastics. 2. Synthetic material made from a vinyl compound; ~ **chloride**, colorless, extremely toxic gas, $CH_2{:}CHCl$, used in plastics manufacture.

vi·ol (vī'ol) *n.* Late medieval stringed musical instrument (now again in use), similar in shape to violin, but usu. with six strings and held downward on or between the knees; ~ **da gamba, d'amore** = VIOLA² da gamba, d'amore.

vi·o·la¹ (vē'ola, vīō'-) *n.* Herbaceous plant of genus *V*~, which includes violets and pansies; hybrid garden plant of this genus, more uniformly and delicately colored than pansy. [L., = "violet"]

vi·o·la² (vēō'la) *n.* 1. Member of violin family of musical instruments, slightly larger than violin, of lower pitch (its lowest note being C below middle C) and with less bright, more sonorous tone. 2. ~ **da gam·ba** (da

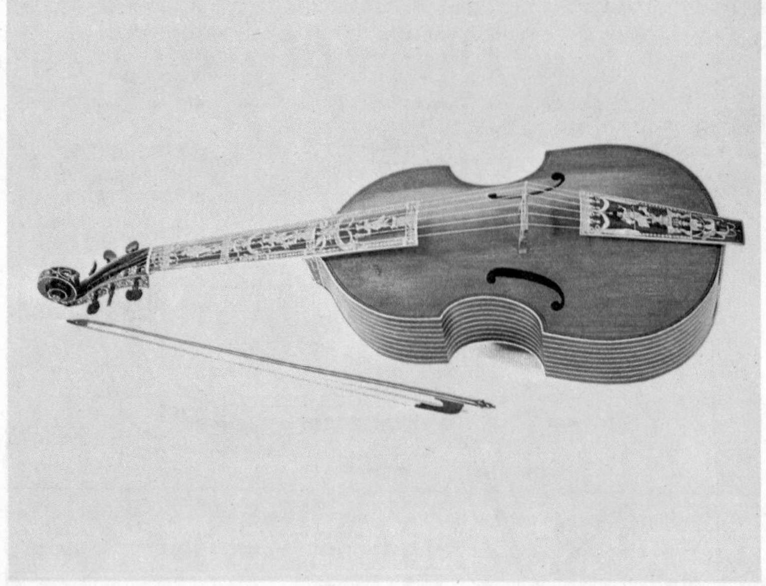

gahm′ba), bass viol; **viola d'a·mo·re** (dah mōr′ā, -mōr′ā), tenor viol with sympathetic strings under fingerboard, having very sweet affecting tone.

vi·o·la·ceous (vīolā′shus) *adj.* (bot.) Of the violet family (Violaceae).

vi·o·late (vī′olāt) *v.t.* (**-lat·ed, -lat·ing**). Break (agreement, law, oath, etc.); treat profanely, break in upon (sanctuary, privacy, etc.); rape. **vi·o·la·tion** (vīolā′shon), **vi'o·la·tor** *ns.* **vi·o·la·ble** (vī′-olabel) *adj.*

vi·o·lence (vī′olens) *n.* Violent treatment or conduct, outrage, injury; violent feeling or language, vehemence; intensity (*of*); (law) (intimidation by threat of) unlawful exercise of physical force.

vi·o·lent (vī′olent) *adj.* Involving, caused by, acting with, great physical force or unlawful exercise of force; intense in force, effect, feelings, etc. **vi'o·lent·ly** *adv.*

vi·o·let (vī′olĭt) *n.* 1. Plant of genus *Viola*, esp. (also **sweet** ~) the sweet-scented *V. odorata*, with purplish-blue, yellow, or white flowers; similar plant of various other genera. 2. Purplish-blue color of the violet, color at opposite end of spectrum to red. **violet** *adj.* Of the color violet.

vi·o·lin (vīolĭn′) *n.* Stringed musical instrument held under chin with left hand and played with bow or occas. by plucking, having a resonant curvilinear soundbox of polished wood over which are stretched four strings tuned in fifths, the lowest note being G below middle C; part for violin in instrumental composition, player of this; **first** ~, violin player performing FIRST part (see FIRST *adj.*: sense 1); leader of string quartet; **second** ~, violin player performing

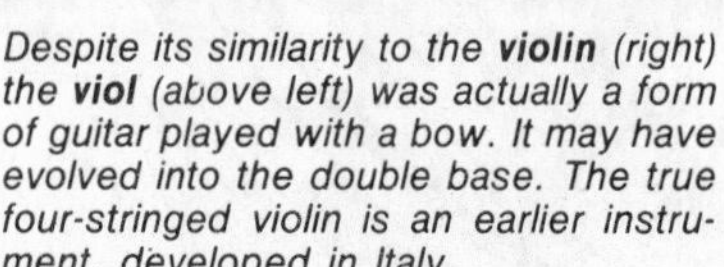

*Despite its similarity to the **violin** (right) the **viol** (above left) was actually a form of guitar played with a bow. It may have evolved into the double base. The true four-stringed violin is an earlier instrument, developed in Italy.*

SECOND part; ~ **family**, group of instruments including violin, viola, violoncello, and double bass. **vi·o·lin'ist** *n.* Player of violin. [It. *violino* little VIOLA[2]]

vi·ol·ist (vēō′lĭst) *n.* Player of viol, viola.

vi·o·lon·cel·lo (vēolonchĕl′ō) = CELLO.

VIP, V.I.P. *abbrevs.* (colloq.) Very important person.

vi·per (vī′per) *n.* Venemous snake of family Viperidae, esp. adder; (fig.) malignant or treacherous person. **vi·per·ine** (vī′perĭn, -rīn), **vi'per·ish, vi'per·ous** *adjs.*

vi·ra·go (vĭrā′gō) *n.* (pl. **-goes, -gos**). Turbulent woman, termagant. [L., = "female warrior," f. *vir* man]

vi·ral (vīr′al) *adj.* (of disease) Caused by a VIRUS.

vir·e·o (vĭr′ēō) *n.* (pl. **-os**). Any of several small N. Amer. insectivorous grayish songbirds of genus *Vireo*.

vi·res·cence (vīrĕs′ens) *n.* Greenness, esp. (bot.) in petals etc. normally of some other color. **vi·res'cent** *adj.*

Vir·gil (vēr′jil). Publius Vergilius Maro (70–19 B.C.), Roman poet whose chief works were the *Aeneid*, epic poem on the legendary ancestors of Rome, Aeneas and his Trojans; the *Georgics*, didactic poem on agriculture and rearing of cattle and bees; the *Eclogues* or *Bucolics*, pastoral poems. **Vir·gil·i·an** (verjĭl′ēan) *adj.* Of, in the style of, Virgil.

vir·gin (vēr′jĭn) *n.* 1. Person, esp. woman, who has had no sexual intercourse; (eccles.) in early Christian times, unmarried or chaste woman distinguished for piety and steadfastness in religion. 2. (**Mary**) **the V**~, the (**Blessed**) **V**~ (**Mary**): see MARY[1]; image or picture representing her. 3. **the V** ~: see VIRGO. 4. ~ **birth**, (esp.) doctrine that Jesus Christ was born to the Virgin Mary having no human father but conceived by the power of the Holy Spirit; **~'s-bower**, traveler's joy or other species of plant *Clematis*. **virgin** *adj.* That is a virgin; of, befitting, a virgin; spotless, not yet or not previously touched, handled, or employed; (of metal) made from ore by smelting; ~ **forest**, forest as yet untouched by man; **V**~ **Queen**, Elizabeth I of England; ~ **soil**, soil not yet brought into cultivation etc. **vir·gin·i·ty** (verjĭn′ĭtē) *n.* Condition or quality of a virgin.

vir·gin·al (vēr′jinal) *adj.* Being, befitting, belonging to, a virgin. **vir'gin·al·ly** *adv.* **virginal** *n.* (freq. pl.) Keyboard instrument, earliest (16th and 17th centuries) and simplest form of harpsichord, with one string to a note, in box or case, usu. without legs.

Vir·gin·ia (verjĭn′ya). South Atlantic state of U.S., one of the original 13 states of the Union (1788), and site of first English settlement (1607) in Amer.; capital, Richmond; ~ **creeper**, N. Amer. climbing plant (*Parthenocissus quinquefolia*); ~ **reel**, Amer. country dance, in which partners at the start form two lines facing one another and perform a variety of steps together. **Vir·gin'ian** *adj.* & *n.* [named in honor of Elizabeth I of England (VIRGIN Queen)]

Vir·gin (vēr′jĭn) **Islands.** Group of about 100 small islands in W. Indies, mostly uninhabited; divided between Britain (with capital Road Town) and U.S. (with capital Charlotte Amalie).

Vir·go (vẽr′gō). The Virgin, a constellation; 6th sign (♍) of the zodiac, which the sun enters about Aug. 23.

vir·gule (vẽr′gul) *n.* Slanting line (/) to mark division of words or lines; slash.

vir·i·des·cent (vĭrĭdĕs′ent) *adj.* Greenish, somewhat green. **vir·i·des′cence** *n.*

vi·rid·i·an (virĭd′ēan) *n.* 1. Yellowish-green color. 2. Chromium oxide, an emerald green pigment. ~ *adj.* Of the color viridian.

vi·rid·i·ty (virĭd′ĭtē) *n.* Greenness, esp. of foliage or grass; real or apparent youth, freshness and innocence of mind or body.

vir·ile (vĭr′il; *Brit.* vĭr′īl) *adj.* Of, characteristic of, a man; capable of procreation; having masculine vigor or strength. **vir′i·lism** *n.* (pathol.) Development of secondary male characteristics in female or precociously in male. **vi·ril·i·ty** (virĭl′ĭtē) *n.*

vi·rol·o·gy (vīrŏl′ojē, vĭ-) *n.* Study of viruses. **vi·ro·log·i·cal** (vīrolŏj′ĭkal) *adj.* **vi·rol′o·gist** *n.*

vir·tu·al (vẽr′chōōal) *adj.* That is so in essence or effect, although not formally or actually; ~ **focus** (optics) apparent focus of reflected or refracted rays of light. **vir′tu·al·ly** *adv.* **vir·tu·al·i·ty** (vẽrchōōăl′ĭtē) *n.*

vir·tue (vẽr′chōō) *n.* Moral excellence, uprightness, goodness; particular moral excellence, moral quality regarded as of special excellence or importance; chastity, esp. of women; good quality or influence, efficacy; **by, in ~ of,** on the strength or ground of; (pl.) order of angels (see ANGEL). [L. *virtus* worth, valor, f. *vir* man]

vir·tu·o·so (vẽrchōōō′sō) *n.* (pl. **-sos, -si** pr. -sē). Person with special interest in or knowledge of works of art; person skilled in technique of an art, esp. of performance on musical instrument. **vir·tu·os·i·ty** (vẽrchōōŏs′ĭtē) *n.* (pl. **-ties**). [It. *virtuoso* learned, skilled, f. L. *virtus* (see VIRTUE)]

vir·tu·ous (vẽr′chōōus) *adj.* Possessing, showing, moral rectitude; chaste. **vir′tu·ous·ly** *adv.* **vir′tu·ous·ness** *n.*

vir·u·lent (vĭr′yulent, vĭr′u-) *adj.* Poisonous; malignant, bitter; (of disease) extremely violent. **vir′u·lent·ly** *adv.* **vir′u·lence, vir′u·len·cy** *ns.*

vi·rus (vīr′us) *n.* 1. Organic particle, much smaller than bacteria or other classifiable microorganisms, existing only within cells of animal and plant bodies and capable of producing various diseases. 2. Poisonous substance, the product of disease, found in the tissues and body fluids. 3. (fig.) Moral poison, malignity. [L., = "poison"]

vi·sa (vē′za), **vi·sé** (vē′zā, vēzā′) *ns.* Endorsement on passport permitting holder to enter or cross a particular country. ~ *v.t.* (**-saed, -sa·ing; -séed, -sé·ing**). Mark with visa.

vis·age (vĭz′ĭj) *n.* (now chiefly literary) Face.

vis-à-vis (vēzavē′) *n.* Either of two persons or things facing or situated opposite each other. ~ *prep.* & *adv.* Over against, in comparison with; facing, face-to-face (with).

vis·ca·cha, viz·ca·cha (vĭskah′cha) *ns.* Large burrowing S. Amer. rodent (*Lago stomus maximus*) having long soft fur, gray on back and yellowish-white beneath.

vis·cer·a (vĭs′era) *n.pl.* (sing. **vis·cus** pr. vĭs′kus). Internal organs of principal cavities of animal body, as intestines, heart, liver, etc. **vis′cer·al** *adj.* **vis′cer·al·ly** *adv.*

vis·cid (vĭs′ĭd) *adj.* Glutinous, sticky. **vis·cid·i·ty** (vĭsĭd′ĭtē) *n.* **vis′cid·ly** *adv.*

vis·cose (vĭs′kōs) *n.* Highly viscous solution of cellulose compound obtained by treating wood pulp or cotton fiber with caustic soda and carbon disulfide, used in manufacture of rayon etc.

vis·cos·i·ty (vĭskŏs′ĭtē) *n.* (pl. **-ties**). Quality, degree, of being viscous; (phys.) body's property of resisting alteration in position of its parts relative to each other.

vis·count (vī′kownt) *n.* Member of fourth order of Brit. peerage, between earl and baron; courtesy title of earl's eldest son. **vis-**

*Growing to a length of 6 ft. the Gaboon **viper** is the largest snake in this family. All have venom which is dangerous to man and there is even a European representative, the adder.*

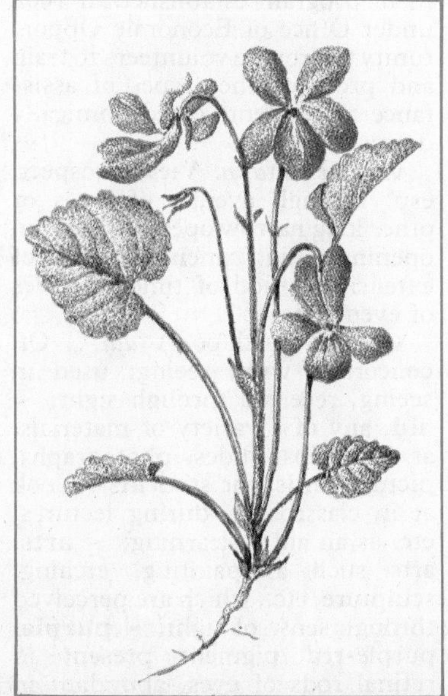

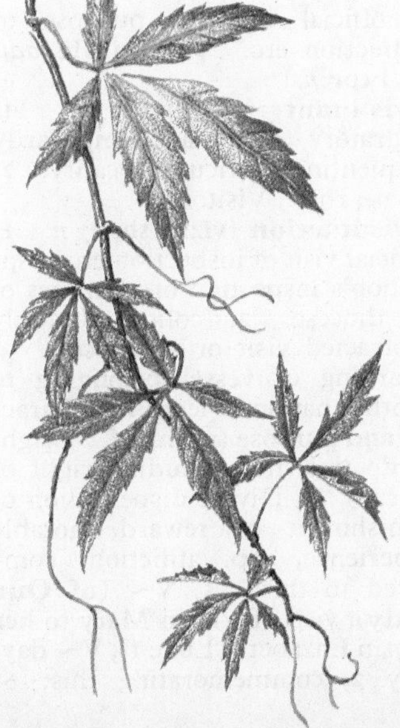

*Far left: Plants in the genus Viola include both the colorful **violet** and the pansy. The violet has long been a source of essence for the perfume industry and is also used in a liqueur.*

*Left: **Virginia creeper,** a native vine of North America, is more closely related to the grape vine than to ivy. The Indians made a dye from its berries.*

*Right: Nepalese statue of '**Vishnu** floating on the waters'. Together with Brahma and Siva, Vishnu forms part of the Hindu trinity. He is considered to act as 'preserver of the universe'.*

count·cy (vī′kowntsē), **vis·count·y** (vī′kowntē) *ns.* **vis·count·ess** (vī′kowntĭs) *n.* Wife or widow of viscount; peeress of fourth order of nobility.

vis·cous (vĭs′k*u*s) *adj.* Glutinous, gluey, sticky; having viscosity; intermediate between solid and fluid, adhesively soft. **vis′cous·ly** *adv.* **vis′cous·ness** *n.*

vis·cus (vĭs′k*u*s) *n.* (anat.) Internal organ (sing. of VISCERA).

vise, Brit. **vice** (vīs) *ns.* Tool with two jaws worked by screw for gripping firmly and holding thing being worked upon by metalworker, carpenter, etc.

vi·sé = VISA.

Vish·nu (vĭsh′nōō). (Hinduism) One of the principal deities, identified by his worshippers with the supreme deity and regarded as savior of the world. **Vish′nu·ism** *n.*

vis·i·ble (vĭz′*i*bel) *adj.* Capable of being seen; that can be seen at particular time, under certain conditions, etc.; in sight; that can be perceived or observed, apparent, open, obvious. **vis′i·bly** *adv.* **vis·i·bil·i·ty** (vĭz*i*bĭl′ĭtē) *n.* (pl. **-ties**). (esp.) Conditions of light, atmosphere, etc., with respect to distinguishing of objects by sight; possibility of seeing, range of vision, under such conditions.

Vis·i·goth (vĭz′*i*gŏth) *n.* West Goth, one of that branch of Goths that entered Roman territory toward end of 4th c. and subsequently established in Spain a kingdom overthrown by the Moors in 711–12. **Vis·i·goth·ic** (vĭzigŏth′ĭk) *adj.*

vi·sion (vĭzh′*o*n) *n.* 1. Act or faculty of seeing, sight; perception of things by means of the light coming from them, which enters the eye. 2. Power of discerning future conditions, sagacity in planning, foresight. 3. Thing, person, seen in dream or trance; supernatural apparition, phantom; thing, esp. of attractive or fantastic character, seen vividly in the imagination; person, sight, of unusual beauty.

vi·sion·ar·y (vĭzh′*o*nĕrē) *adj.* Given to seeing visions or indulging in fanciful theories; seen (only) in a vision, existing only in imagination; unreal, fantastic, unpractical. ~ *n.* (pl. **-ar·ies**). Visionary person.

vis·it (vĭz′ĭt) *v.t.* Go, come, to see (person, place, etc.) as act of friendship or social ceremony, on business, from curiosity, for official inspection, etc.; (of disease, calamity, etc.) come upon, attack; (bibl.) punish (person, sin), avenge (sins etc.) *upon* person, comfort, bless, (person *with* salvation etc.); **visiting card**, calling card; **visiting nurse**, registered or licensed practical nurse who takes care of the sick in their homes; **visiting professor**, college or university professor invited to join faculty at another institution for specified period. **visit** *n.* Call on a person or at a place; temporary residence with a person or at a place; occasion of going *to* doctor, dentist, etc., for examination or treatment, doctor's professional call on patient; formal or official call for purpose of inspection etc. **vis′it·a·ble** *adj.* **vis′i·tor** *n.*

vis·i·tant (vĭz′ĭt*a*nt) *n.* 1. Migratory bird, as temporarily frequenting particular locality. 2. (poet., rhet.) Visitor.

vis·it·a·tion (vĭzĭtā′sh*o*n) *n.* 1. Official visit of inspection etc., esp. bishop's inspection of churches of his diocese. 2. (colloq.) Unduly protracted visit or social call. 3. Boarding of vessel belonging to another nation to learn her character and purpose (**right of** ~, right to do this, not including right of search). 4. Divine dispensation of punishment or reward, notable experience, esp. affliction, compared to this. 5. **V**~ (**of Our Lady**), visit of Virgin Mary to her cousin Elizabeth (Luke I); **V**~ day, July 2, commemorating this; ~ **rights**, legally decreed right of a divorced or separated parent to visit child in custody of other parent. **vis·it·a′tion·al** *adj.*

vi·sor (vī′z*e*r) *n.* 1. (hist.) Movable front part of helmet, covering face, and with openings for seeing and breathing. 2. (hist.) Mask. 3. Projecting front part of cap. 4. Movable shield fixed inside motor vehicle above windshield to protect eyes from sunlight or glare. **vi′sor·less** *adj.*

VISTA *abbrev.* Volunteers in Service to America. (U.S. government program established in 1964 under Office of Economic Opportunity to provide volunteers to train and provide other types of assistance to residents of economically deprived areas.)

vis·ta (vĭs′t*a*) *n.* View, prospect, esp. through avenue of trees or other long narrow opening; such an opening; (fig.) mental view of extensive period of time or series of events etc.

vis·u·al (vĭzh′ōō*a*l) *adj.* Of, concerned with, seeing; used in seeing, received through sight; ~ **aid**, any of a variety of materials, as filmstrips, slides, photographs, picture cards, for students to look at in classrooms, during lectures, etc. as an aid to learning; ~ **arts**, arts such as painting, etching, sculpture, etc., which are perceived through sense of sight; ~ **purple**, purple-red pigment present in retinal rods of eyes, abundant in eyes of nocturnal animals. **vis′u·al·ly** *adv.*

vis·u·al·ize (vĭzh′ōōalīz) *v.t.* (**-ized, -iz·ing**). Make mental vision or image of (something not present or not visible), make visible to imagination. **vis·u·al·i·za·tion** (vĭzhōōalīzā′shon), **vis′u·al·iz·er** *ns.*

vi·tal (vī′tal) *adj.* Of, concerned with, essential to, organic life; essential to existence or to the matter in hand; affecting life, fatal to life or to success, etc.; ~ **parts**, parts of body essential to life, as lungs, heart, brain, etc.; ~ **signs**, bodily functions, esp. pulse, temperature, and respiration, that are measured to determine organism's efficiency; ~ **statistics**, those relating to births, deaths, health, disease, etc. **vi′tal·ly** *adv.* **vi′tals** *n.pl.* Vital parts of body.

vi·tal·ism (vī′talĭzem) *n.* (philos.) Theory that life originates in a vital principle distinct from chemical and physical forces (opp. MECHANISM). **vi′tal·ist** *n.* Adherent of vitalism. **vi·tal·is·tic** (vītalĭs′tĭk) *adj.*

vi·tal·i·ty (vītăl′ĭtē) *n.* (pl. **-ties**). Vital power, ability to sustain life; (fig.) active force or power, activity, animation, liveliness.

vi·tal·ize (vī′talīz) *v.t.* (**-ized, -iz·ing**). Put life or animation into, infuse with vitality or vigor. **vi·tal·i·za·tion** (vītalīzā′shon) *n.*

vi·ta·min (vī′tamĭn) *n.* Any of a number of substances essential for growth and nutrition, occurring in certain foodstuffs or produced synthetically; ~ **A**, present in liver oils, butterfat, green and yellow vegetables, etc.; ~ **B**, any of a group present in yeast products, whole wheat, etc., that comprises a number of separate substances concerned esp. with the formation and functioning of important enzymes in the body; ~ **C**, ASCORBIC acid; ~ **D**, present in fish liver oils and egg yolk and apparently concerned in the deposition of calcium phosphate in bones; ~ **E**, present in wheat germ oil and green leaves, its absence causing sterility; ~ **K**, present in various foodstuffs, esp. green leaves, facilitating clotting of blood. **vi·ta·min·ic** (vītamĭn′ĭk) *adj.* **vi′ta·min·ize** *v.t.* Introduce vitamin(s) into (food). [orig. named *vitamine* f. L. *vita* life and English AMINE, in the belief that an amino acid was present]

vi·tel·lin (vĭtĕl′ĭn, vī-) *n.* (biochem.) Chief protein of egg yolk.

vi·tel·lus (vĭtĕl′us, vī-) *n.* (pl. **-lus·es**). (embryol.) Yolk of an egg. **vi·tel′line** *adj.* Of the vitellus; ~ **membrane**, membrane enclosing vitellus.

vi·ti·ate (vĭsh′ēāt) *v.t.* (**-at·ed, -at·ing**). Impair the quality of, corrupt, debase; make invalid or ineffectual. **vi·ti·a·tion** (vĭshēā′shon), **vi′ti·a·tor** *ns.*

vit·i·cul·ture (vĭt′ĭkŭlcher, vī′tĭ-) *n.* Cultivation of grapes.

vit·re·ous (vĭt′rēus) *adj.* Of (the nature of) glass; resembling glass in composition, brittleness, hardness, luster, transparency, etc.; ~ **humor**: see HUMOR *n.* def 3. **vit′re·ous·ly** *adv.* **vit·re·os·i·ty** (vĭtrēŏs′ĭtē) *n.*

vit·ri·fy (vĭt′rĭfī) *v.* (**-fied, -fy·ing**). Convert, be converted, into glass or glasslike substance; render, become, vitreous. **vit·ri·fac·tion** (vĭtrĭfăk′shon), **vit·ri·fi·ca·tion** (vĭtrĭfĭkā′shon) *ns.* **vit′ri·fi·a·ble** *adj.*

vit·ri·ol (vĭt′rēol) *n.* 1. Any of various metallic sulfates used in the arts or medicinally, esp. iron sulfate; (also **oil of** ~) concentrated sulfuric acid. 2. (fig.) Causticity, acrimony, of feeling or utterance. **vit·ri·ol·ic** (vĭtrēŏl′ĭk) *adj.* (esp., fig.) Extremely caustic, scathing, bitter, or malignant.

vit·ta (vĭt′a) *n.* (pl. **vit·tae** pr. vĭt′ē). 1. (bot.) Stripe or band of color. 2. (bot.) One of a number of oil tubes in pericarp of fruit of most umbelliferous plants. **vit·tate** (vĭt′āt) *adj.*

vi·tu·per·ate (vītōō′perāt, -tū′-, vī-) *v.t.* (**-at·ed, -at·ing**). Revile. **vi·tu·per·a·tion** (vītōōperā′shon, -tū-, vī-) *n.* **vi·tu·per·a·tive** (vītōō′perātĭv, -pera-, -tū′-, vī-) *adj.* **vi·tu′per·a·tive·ly** *adv.*

Vi·tus (vī′tus), **St.** (*c*300). Child martyr of the DIOCLETIAN persecution; **St. Vitus's dance**, (pop.) = CHOREA.

vi·va (vē′va) *n.* & *int.* (Salute, greeting, cry, of) "long live ..." [It. third pers. imper. of *vivere* live]

vi·va·ce (vĭvah′chā, -chē) *adv.* & *n.* (mus.) (Passage performed) in brisk and lively manner. [It.]

vi·va·cious (vĭvā′shus, vī-) *adj.* Lively, animated. **vi·va′cious·ly** *adv.* **vi·vac·i·ty** (vĭvăs′ĭtē, vī-), **vi·va′cious·ness** *ns.*

Vi·val·di (vĭvahl′dē), **Antonio** (1680?–1743). Italian violinist and composer.

vi·var·i·um (vīvār′ēum) *n.* (pl. **-var·i·ums, -var·i·a** pr. -vār′ēa). Place or enclosure for keeping living animals etc. as far as possible under natural conditions, for interest or scientific study.

vi·va vo·ce, vi·va-vo·ce (vī′va vō′sē). Orally; by word of mouth. [L., = "with the living voice"]

vive (vēv) *int.* Cry of "long live," as in ~ **le roi** (rwah), long live the king. [Fr. third pers. sing. imperat. of *vivre* live]

vi·ver·rine (vīvĕr′ĭn, -īn, vī-) *adj.* Of the Viverridae or CIVET family.

viv·id (vĭv′ĭd) *adj.* Strong, intense, glaring (esp. of color, light, etc.); clearly or distinctly perceived or perceptible, intensely or strongly felt or expressed, (capable of) presenting subjects or ideas in clear and striking manner. **viv′id·ly** *adv.* **viv′id·ness** *n.*

viv·i·fy (vĭv′ĭfī) *v.t.* (**-fied, -fy·ing**). (chiefly fig.) Give life to, animate. **viv·i·fi·ca·tion** (vĭvĭfĭkā′shon), **viv′i·fi·er** *ns.*

vi·vip·a·rous (vīvĭp′erus) *adj.* 1. (zool.) Bringing forth young in developed state, not hatching from egg (cf. OVIPAROUS). 2. (bot.) Germinating while still attached to the parent plant; having such seeds. **vi·vip′a·rous·ly** *adv.* **vi·vip′a·rous·ness, viv·i·par·i·ty** (vĭvĭpăr′ĭtē) *ns.*

viv·i·sect (vĭv′ĭsĕkt, vĭvĭsĕkt′) *v.t.* Perform vivisection upon. **viv·i·sec·tion** (vĭvĭsĕk′shon) *n.* Performance of surgical experiments on living animals in laboratory for the advancement of (esp. medical) knowledge. **viv·i·sec′tion·ist** *n.* One who approves of or advocates this practice.

Related to the chinchilla and the guinea pig, the 2 ft. long ***vizcacha*** *has been hunted in South America for its meat and for its fur. The plains species is in Argentina.*

vix·en (vĭk′sen) *n.* 1. Female fox. 2. Ill-tempered quarrelsome woman. **vix′en·ish** *adj.* **vix′en·-ish·ly** *adv.*

viz., viz *abbrevs.* (usu. spoken as "namely") = VIDELICET.

viz·ca·cha: see VISCACHA.

vi·zier (vĭzēr′, vĭz′yer), **vi·zir** (vĭzēr′) *ns.* High administrative official in some Muslim countries, esp. (**grand ~**) chief minister of former Turkish Empire. [Arab. *wazīr* caliph's chief minister]

VL, V.L. *abbrevs.* Vulgar Latin.

VLF, V.L.F. *abbrevs.* Very low frequency.

V.M.D. *abbrev.* Doctor of Veterinary Medicine [L. *Veterinariae Medicinae Doctor*].

VOA *abbrev.* Voice of America.

voc. *abbrev.* Vocative.

vo·ca·ble (vō′kabel) *n.* Word, esp. with ref. to form rather than meaning.

vo·cab·u·lar·y (vōkăb′yulĕrē) *n.* (pl. **-lar·ies**). List of words with their meanings, glossary; sum of words used in a language, or in a particular book or branch of science etc., or by a particular person, class, profession, etc.

vo·cal (vō′kal) *adj.* Of, concerned with, uttered by, the voice; (poet.) endowed (as) with a voice; expressive, eloquent; (of music) composed for voice(s) with or without accompaniment; (phonet.) of a vowel, vocalic; ~ **cords**, voice-producing organs, two straplike membranes stretched across the larynx, each having a medial edge that is free to vibrate in the air stream, determining pitch of voice by their length and frequency of vibration, women's being shorter than men's; ~ **score**, musical score showing voice parts in full. **vo′-cal·ly** *adv.* **vocal** *n.* 1. Vocal sound. 2. Piece of music for, performance of, singing. 3. (R.C. Ch.) Person entitled to vote in certain elections.

vo·cal·ic (vōkăl′ĭk) *adj.* Of, concerning, vowel(s); of the nature of a vowel; rich in vowels.

vo·cal·ism (vō′kalĭzem) *n.* Use of voice in speech or singing; system of vowels in a language. **vo′cal·ist** *n.* Singer.

vo·cal·ize (vō′kalīz) *v.* (**-ized, -iz·ing**). Utter, make vocal; convert into, use as, vowel; furnish with vowels or vowel points; sing without words, but with vowel sound(s). **vo·cal·i·za·tion** (vōkalĭzā′shon), **vo′cal·iz·er** *ns.*

vo·ca·tion (vōkā′shon) *n.* Divine call to, sense of fitness for, a career or occupation; occupation, calling. **vo·ca′tion·al** *adj.* **vo·ca′tion·al·ly** *adv.*

voc·a·tive (vŏk′atĭv) *adj.* (gram.) Of the case used in address or invocation. ~ *n.* (Word in) vocative case. **voc′a·tive·ly** *adv.*

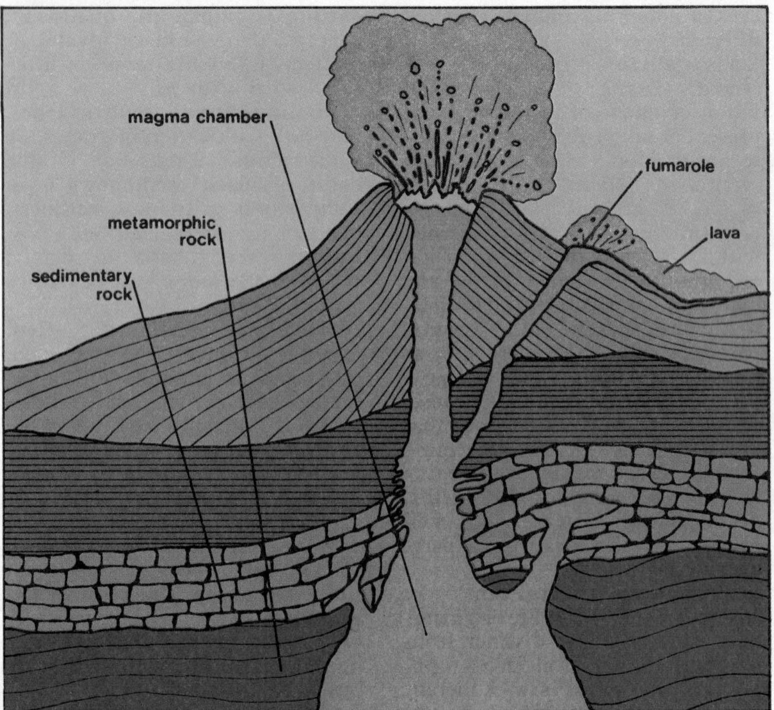

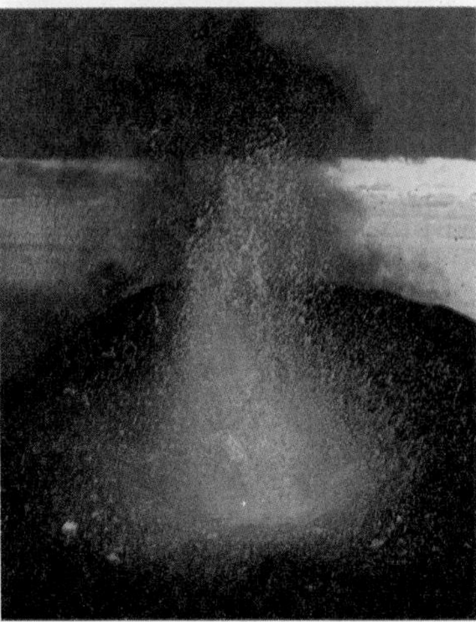

Top: Diagrammatic version of the structure of a ***volcano.*** *Above: Volcanic activity in Tenequia near the Canary Islands in the Atlantic. Above right: A form of volcanic rock sculpted in Egypt about 1800 B.C.*

vo·cif·er·ate (vōsĭf′erāt) *v.* (**-at·ed, -at·ing**). Utter, cry out, noisily; shout, bawl. **vo·cif·er·a·-tion** (vōsĭferā′shon) *n.*

vo·cif·er·ous (vōsĭf′erus) *adj.* Clamorous, noisy. **vo·cif′er·ous·ly** *adv.* **vo·cif′er·ous·ness** *n.*

vod·ka (vŏd′ka) *n.* Alcoholic spirit made esp. in Russia by distillation of rye etc. [Russ. dim. of *voda* water]

vogue (vōg) *n.* Popularity, general acceptance or currency; prevailing fashion; **in ~**, in fashion, generally current; ~ **word**, currently popular word. **vogu′ish** *adv.*

voice (vois) *n.* 1. Sound uttered by the mouth, esp. human utterance in speaking, shouting, or singing; use of the voice, esp. in spoken or (fig.) written words; opinion so expressed; right to express opinion; vote; (mus.) singing voice, quality of this; (phonet.) sound uttered with vibration or resonance of vocal cords (dist. from *breath* or *whisper*). **Voice of America**, U.S. radio network broadcasting programs to foreign countries, expressing American point-of-view; **voice-over**, voice heard without speaker in view, as in television commercials; **voice print**, graphic record of speech with respect to frequency, duration, and amplitude; **with one voice**, unanimously. 2. (gram.) Set of forms of a verb showing relation of its subject to the action (ACTIVE, PASSIVE, **voice**). **voice** *v.t.* (**voiced, voic·ing**). Give utterance to, express; (phonet.) utter with voice, change from voiceless to voiced; (mus.) regulate tone quality of organ pipes. **voiced** (voist) *adj.* (esp., phonet.) Uttered with voice, sonant. **voic·ed·ness** (voi′sĭdnĭs) *n.*

voice·less (vois′lĭs) *adj.* Speechless, dumb, mute; (phonet.) not voiced. **voice′less·ly** *adv.* **voice′less·ness** *n.*

void (void) *adj.* Empty, vacant; invalid, not binding; (poet., rhet.) ineffectual, useless; ~ **of**, lacking, free from. **void** *n.* Empty space. ~ *v.t.* Render void or invalid; emit (excrement etc.). **void′a·ble** *adj.* **void′er, void′ance** *ns.*

voi·là (*Fr.* vwălă′) *int.* There it is! There you are! [Fr.]

voile (voil) *n.* Thin semi-transparent cotton, wool, or silk dress material. [Fr., = "veil"]

vol. *abbrev.* (pl. **vols.**). Volume; volunteer.

vo·lar (vō′l*er*) *adj.* (anat.) Of palm of hand or sole of foot.

vol·a·tile (vŏl′*a*tĭl; *Brit.* vŏl′*a*tīl) *adj.* Readily evaporating at ordinary temperatures; (fig.) changeable, flighty, lively, gay; evanescent, transient; ~ **oil**, essential oil. **vol·a·til·i·ty** (vŏl*a*tĭl′ĭtē) *n.*

vol·a·til·ize (vŏl′*a*tĭlīz) *v.* (**-ized, -iz·ing**). (Cause to) evaporate; make, become, volatile. **vol·a·til·i·za·tion** (vŏl*a*tĭlĭzā′sh*o*n) *n.*

vol·can·ic (vŏlkăn′ĭk) *adj.* Of, produced by, a volcano; characterized by volcanoes; ~ **glass**, obsidian. **vol·can′i·cal·ly** *adv.*

vol·ca·no (vŏlkā′nō) *n.* (pl. **-noes, -nos**). Hill or mountain, more or less conical, composed partly or wholly of discharged matter, with crater(s) or other opening(s) in Earth's crust through which steam, gases, ashes, rocks, and freq. streams of molten material are or have been periodically ejected; (fig.) violent, esp. suppressed, feeling, passion, etc. **vol·can·ism** (vŏl′k*a*nĭzem) *n.* Volcanic activity. **vol·can·ol·o·gy** (vŏlk*a*nŏl′*o*jē) *n.* [It., f. L. *Volcanus* VULCAN]

vole (vōl) *n.* Small rodent with short ears and tail, rounded snout, and herbivorous teeth, of genus *Microtus* and related genera.

Vol·ga (vŏl′g*a*; *Russ.* vawl′gah). Longest river of Europe, 2,325 mi. (3,743 km), rising in NW. of U.S.S.R. and flowing E., then S. to the Caspian Sea.

Vol·go·grad (vŏl′g*o*grăd, *Russ.* vawl′gawgraht). City (formerly Stalingrad, 1925–61, previously Tsaritsyn) of U.S.S.R. on the Lower Volga.

vo·li·tion (v*o*lĭsh′*o*n) *n.* Act, power, of willing or resolving, exercise of the will. **vo·li′tion·al** *adj.* **vo·li′tion·al·ly** *adv.*

vol·ley (vŏl′ē) *n.* (pl. **-leys**). Salvo, shower, of missiles (or fig. of oaths etc.); (tennis etc.) return stroke at ball before it touches ground; **voll′eyball**, game in which large inflated ball is struck with hands from alternate sides of high net without touching ground. **volley** *v.* (**-leyed, -ley·ing**). Discharge (missiles etc.), return, hit, (ball), in volley; fly in volley; make sound like volleys of artillery.

volt (vōlt) *n.* Unit of electromotive force, the electrical pressure that if steadily applied to a conductor whose resistance is 1 ohm will produce a current of 1 ampere (abbrev. V, v). [f. VOLTA]

Vol·ta (vōl′t*a*; *It.* vawl′tah), **A·les·san·dro** (1745–1827). Italian physicist, a pioneer of electrical science; first devised apparatus for chemically developing electric currents.

volt·age (vōl′tĭj) *n.* Electromotive force expressed in volts.

vol·ta·ic (vŏltā′ĭk) *adj.* Producing electricity, (of electricity) generated, by chemical action, after the method discovered by VOLTA; (consisting) of, caused by, connected with, such electricity.

Vol·taire (vŏltār′, vōl-). Pen name of François Marie Arouet (1694–1778), French deist philosopher, historian, dramatist, and writer of historical and satirical poems and tales; famous for anticlericalism, witty skepticism, and influence on the leaders of the French Revolution; author of satirical novels *Candide*, and *Zadig*, and *Philosophical Letters*, etc.

volte-face (vōltfăs′, vŏlt-) *n.* (pl. **volte-face**). Complete change of front in argument, politics, etc. [Fr.]

volt·me·ter (vōlt′mēt*er*) *n.* Any instrument for measuring difference in potential in volts.

vol·u·ble (vŏl′y*u*bel) *adj.* Fluent, glib; speaking, spoken with great readiness or fluency. **vol·u·bil·i·ty** (vŏly*u*bĭl′ĭtē), **vol′u·ble·ness** *ns.* **vol′u·bly** *adv.*

vol·ume (vŏl′ūm) *n.* 1. Collection of written or esp. printed sheets bound together to form a book; division of work (intended to be) separately bound. 2. Bulk, mass, quantity, esp. large quantity; space occupied by anything, esp. as measured in cubic units; size, dimensions, amount, *of*. 3. (usu. pl.) Plume, coil, rounded mass, of smoke etc. 4. (mus. etc.) Quantity,

*Mouse-sized but with a blunter snout and shorter tail, the **vole** is present in many parts of the northern hemisphere. One species in Russia is rat-sized and has been trapped for its fur.*

*Teams from Germany and Japan play **volleyball** during the 1972 Olympic Games at Munich. This form of 'hand-tennis' was invented in the U.S.A. during the 1890s.*

power, fullness, of tone or sound.

vol·u·met·ric (vŏlyuˌmĕt′rĭk) *adj.* Of, pertaining to, measurement of volume. **vol·u·met′ri·cal·ly** *adv.*

vo·lu·mi·nous (volōō′minus) *adj.* 1. Containing, consisting of, many coils or convolutions. 2. Consisting of many volumes; (of writer) producing many books etc. 3. Of great volume, bulky, ample. **vo·lu′mi·nous·ly** *adv.* **vo·lu′mi·nous·ness, vo·lu·mi·nos·i·ty** (volōōminŏs′ĭtē) *ns.*

vol·un·tar·y (vŏl′untĕrē) *adj.* Done, acting, able to act, of one's own free will; purposed, intentional, not constrained; (of bodily action etc.) controlled by the will; brought about, produced, maintained, etc., by voluntary action; ~ **hospital**, one maintained by voluntary contributions. **vol·un·tar·i·ly** (vŏl′untĕrilē, vŏluntĕr′ilē) *adv.* **vol′un·tar·i·ness** *n.* **voluntary** *n.* (pl. **-tar·ies**). (orig.) Extempore performance, esp. as prelude to other music; (now) organ solo played before, during, or after any church service; music composed for this.

vol·un·teer (vŏlunter′) *n.* Person who voluntarily offers his services or enrolls himself for any enterprise, esp. for service in any of the armed forces. ~ *adj.* Of or pertaining to a volunteer or volunteers; made up of volunteers; serving as volunteer(s). ~ *v.* Undertake, offer, voluntarily; make voluntary offer of one's services; be a volunteer.

vo·lup·tu·ar·y (volŭp′chōōĕrē) *n.* (pl. **-ar·ies**) & *adj.* Of, concerned with, (person) given up to, indulgence in luxury and gratification of the senses.

vo·lup·tu·ous (volŭp′chōōus) *adj.* Of, derived from, marked by, addicted to, promising etc., gratification of the senses. **vo·lup′tu·ous·ly** *adv.* **vo·lup′tu·ous·ness** *n.*

vo·lute (volōōt′) *n.* 1. (archit.) Spiral scroll forming chief ornament of Ionic capital and used also in Corinthian and Composite capitals. 2. Spiral conformation; convolution, esp. of spiral shell; marine gastropod of genus *Voluta* and allied genera, chiefly tropical, and freq. with very handsome shell. ~ *adj.* Having the form of a volute, forming spiral curve(s).

vo·lu·tion (volōō′shon) *n.* Convolution, spiral turn, whorl of spiral shell; rolling or revolving movement.

vol·va (vŏl′va) *n.* (bot.) Membranous covering enclosing many fungi in early stages of growth.

vo·mer (vō′mer) *n.* (anat.) Small thin bone separating nostrils in man and most vertebrates.

vom·it (vŏm′ĭt) *v.* Eject contents of stomach through mouth; bring up, eject, (as) by vomiting, belch forth, spew out. ~ *n.* Matter ejected from stomach. **vom′it·er** *n.*

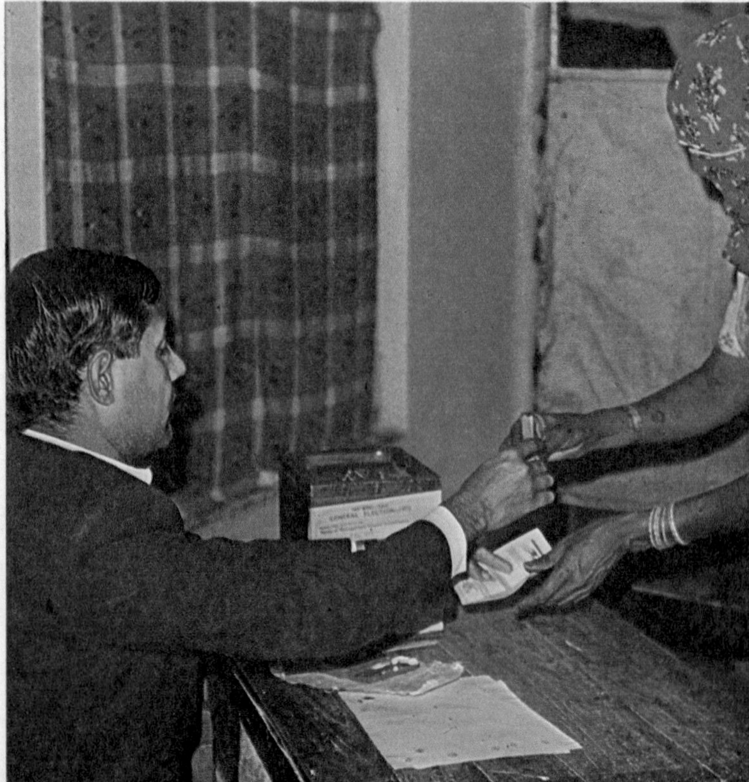

Veiled Muslim woman marks the counterfoil of her ballot paper during an election. The power to cast a ***vote*** *is the mark of equality among citizens: one vote, one person.*

voo·doo (vōō′dōō) *adj.* & *n.* (pl. **-doos**). (Of a) system of religious or magical beliefs and practices of African origin among people of West Indies and Amer.; person skilled in this; voodoo spell; fetish etc. used in voodoo. ~ *v.t.* Bewitch, put voodoo spell on. **voo′doo·ism** *n.*

vo·ra·cious (vōrā′shus, vaw-, vo-) *adj.* Greedy in eating; gluttonous. **vo·ra′cious·ly** *adv.* **vo·ra′cious·ness, vo·rac·i·ty** (vōrăs′ĭtē, vaw-, vo-) *ns.*

-vorous *suffix.* Forming adjectives (usu. with intermediate -i-) with sense "feeding on" (*carnivorous*); so **-vora**, forming names of groups of animals classified by their food (*Insectivora*); **-vore**, forming name of individual of such group (*herbivore*).

vor·tex (vōr′tĕks) *n.* (pl. **-tex·es, -ti·ces** pr. -tĭsēz). 1. Mass of fluid, esp. liquid, with rapid circular movement around axis and tendency to form vacuum or cavity in center toward which bodies are attracted, whirlpool; anything likened to this, esp. by reason of rush or excitement, rapid change, or absorbing effect. 2. Whirling mass of air or vapor; (central part of) whirlwind. **vor·ti·cal** (vōr′-tĭkal) *adj.* **vor′ti·cal·ly** *adv.*

vo·ta·ry (vō′terē), fem. **vo·ta·ress** (vō′terĭs, -rĕs) *ns.* One bound by vow(s), esp. to religious life; devotee, devoted or zealous worshipper, ardent follower (*of*).

vote (vōt) *n.* Expression of one's acceptance or rejection signified by ballot, show of hands, voice, or otherwise; right to vote; opinion expressed, resolution or decision carried, by voting; votes collectively. ~ *v.* (**vot·ed, vot·ing**). Give a vote, express choice or preference by ballot, show of hands, etc.; choose, elect, establish, ratify, grant, confer, by vote; pronounce, declare, by general consent; (colloq.) propose, suggest. **vote′-less** *adj.* **vot′er** *n.*

vo·tive (vō′tĭv) *adj.* Dedicated, offered, consecrated, etc., in fulfillment of a vow.

vouch (vowch) *v.* Confirm, uphold, (statement) by evidence or assertion; answer, be surety, *for*.

vouch·er (vow′cher) *n.* Document, receipt, etc., to attest correctness of accounts or monetary transactions, authorize or establish payment, etc.; esp. document that can be exchanged for goods or services as token of payment made or promised.

vouch·safe (vowchsāf′) *v.t.* (**-safed, -saf·ing**). Give, grant, bestow, in condescending or gracious manner; deign to give, condescend (*to* do).

vow (vow) *v.t.* Promise, or undertake solemnly, esp. by a vow; make solemn resolve to exact (vengeance), harbor (hatred), etc. ~ *n.* Solemn promise or engagement, esp. to God or to any deity or saint. **vow'er** *n.*

vow·el (vow'*e*l) *n.* Speech sound produced by vibrations of vocal cords, modified or characterized by form of vocal cavities, but without audible friction (opp. to, but not sharply divided from, CONSONANT[2]); letter or symbol representing such a sound, as a, e, i, o, u; ~ **point**, sign used to indicate vowel in certain alphabets, as Hebrew etc.

vox po·pu·li (vŏks' pŏp'y*u*lī). (abbrev. **vox pop.**) Voice of the people; public opinion, popular belief, general verdict. [L.]

voy·age (voi'ĭj) *n.* Journey, esp. to distant place or country, by sea or water. ~ *v.* (**-aged, -ag·ing**). Travel by water; traverse, travel over. **voy'ag·er** *n.*

vo·ya·geur (vwahyahzhēr', voi*a*-) *n.* (in Canada) Man employed in transportation of goods and passengers between trading posts; any guide, woodsman, or boatman of the Canadian wilderness.

vo·yeur (vwahyēr', voi-) *n.* One who derives gratification from looking at sexual organs or acts of others. **vo·yeur'ism** *n.* **voy·eur·is·tic** (vwahy*e*rĭs'tĭk, voi*e*-) *adj.*

VP, V.P. *abbrevs.* Vice president.

vs. *abbrev.* Verse; versus.

V.S. *abbrev.* Veterinary Surgeon.

V/STOL *abbrev.* Vertical/short takeoff and landing (aircraft).

VT, Vt. *abbrevs.* Vermont.

v.t. *abbrev.* Verb transitive.

VTOL *abbrev.* Vertical takeoff and landing (aircraft).

Vul·can (vŭl'k*a*n). (Rom. myth.) God of fire and patron of workers in metal, identified with Hephaestus.

vul·can·ite (vŭl'k*a*nīt) *n.* Ebonite, black variety of rubber hardened by treatment with sulfur at high temperatures.

vul·can·ize (vŭl'k*a*nīz) *v.t.* (**-ized, -iz·ing**). Harden and make (rubber etc.) more durable by chemical means, esp. by combining it with sulfur, usu. with heat and pressure. **vul·can·i·za·tion** (vŭlk*a*nīzā'sh*o*n), **vul'can·iz·er** *ns.*

Vulg. *abbrev.* Vulgate.

vul·gar (vŭl'g*e*r) *adj.* Of, characteristic of, the common people, plebeian, coarse, low; in common use, generally prevalent; ~ **tongue**, vernacular, popular or native language, esp. opp. Latin; ~ **Latin**, colloq. speech of ancient Rome, opp. of literary or classical Latin. **vul'gar·ly** *adv.* **vul'gar·ism, vul·gar·i·ty** (vŭlgăr'ĭtē) (pl. **-ties**), **vul'gar·ness** *ns.*

vul·gar·i·an (vŭlgār'ē*a*n) *n.* Vulgar (esp. rich) person.

vul·gar·ize (vŭl'g*e*rīz) *v.t.* (**-ized, -iz·ing**). Make vulgar or commonplace; reduce to level of something usual or ordinary. **vul·gar·i·za·tion** (vŭlg*e*rīzā'sh*o*n) *n.*

Vul·gate (vŭl'gāt, -gĭt). Latin version of Bible prepared (in the main) by St. Jerome, *c*382–404; recension of this published 1592 by order of Pope Clement VIII, official text of R.C. Ch. [L. *vulgare* make public]

vul·ner·a·ble (vŭl'n*e*r*a*b*e*l) *adj.* That may be wounded, open to attack, injury, or assault, not proof against weapon, criticism, etc.; (in contract bridge) that has won one game toward rubber and therefore is liable to double penalties. **vul·ner·a·bil·i·ty** (vŭln*e*r*a*bĭl'ĭtē) *n.* **vul'ner·a·bly** *adv.*

vul·pine (vŭl'pīn, -pĭn) *adj.* Of fox(es); characteristic of, like, fox; crafty, cunning.

vul·ture (vŭl'ch*e*r) *n.* Any of various large carrion-eating birds of the family Cathartidae in the New World and Accipitridae in the Old World; **turkey** ~: see TURKEY; (fig.) rapacious person. **vul·tur·ine** (vŭl'ch*e*rīn, -rĭn), **vul'tur·ous** *adjs.*

vul·va (vŭl'v*a*) *n.* (pl. **-vae** pr. -vē, **-vas**). External female genital organ, esp. external opening of vagina. **vul'val, vul'var** *adjs.*

*Below: Red-headed turkey **vulture** and king vulture of America. All have 'bald' heads and most feed on carrion, or the prey of other animals.*

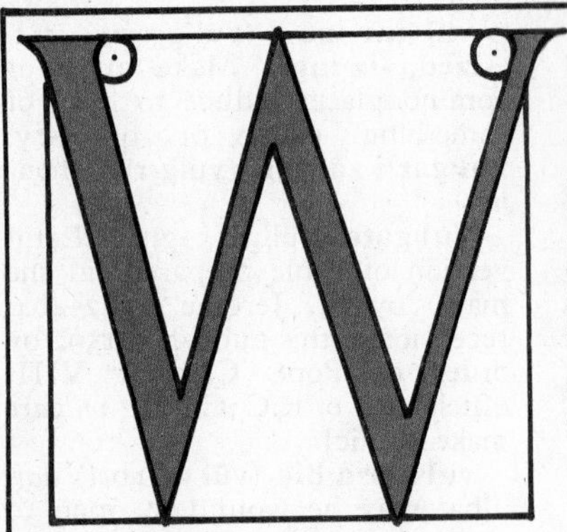

The use of a runic symbol to signify the sound of the present letter ***W, w*** *only seems to have occurred in West Saxon. The sound it represents is not known in German or Slavonic languages. Later two Us or Vs were shown together, side by side, until they were linked into a single letter.*

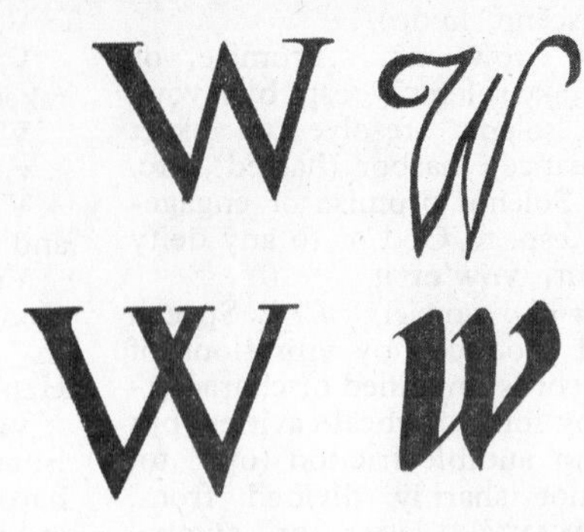

W, w (dŭb′elū) (pl. **W's, w's** or **Ws, ws**). Twenty-third letter of modern English alphabet, originally a ligatured doubling of the Roman letter represented by *u* and *v* of modern alphabets, pronounced as a voiced bilabial spirant and, after vowels, as a *u*-glide, the second element of a diphthong.

W *symbol.* Tungsten. [Ger. *wolfram*]

W. *abbrev.* Watt(s); Wednesday; west(ern).

w. *abbrev.* Watt(s); wide; wife; with.

WA. *abbrev.* Washington.

Wa·bash (waw′băsh). River in Ohio and Illinois flowing 475 mi. (760 km) to the Ohio.

WAC, W.A.C. *abbrevs.* Women's Army Corps. **Wac** (wăk) *n.* Member of WAC.

wack·y (wăk′ē) *adj.* (**wack·i·er, wack·i·est**) & *n.* (slang) Crazy (person).

wad (wŏd) *n.* Small bundle or mass of soft flexible material used as pad etc., esp. plug or disk of felt, cardboard, etc., keeping powder and shot compact in cartridge to prevent gas from passing between shot and barrel when the cartridge is fired; tight roll, esp. of bank notes, (colloq.) wealth, money. ~ *v.t.* (**wad·ded, wad·ding**). Press, compress, roll into wad; line, pad, with wadding; furnish, plug, with wad.

wad·ding (wŏd′ĭng) *n.* (Soft pliable material for making) wads; loose, soft, fibrous material for padding, stuffing, etc.

wad·dle (wŏd′*el*) *v.i.* (**-dled, -dling**). Walk with short steps and swaying motion natural to stout short-legged person or to bird with short legs set far apart. ~ *n.* Waddling gait. **wad′dler** *n.*

wade (wād) *v.* (**wad·ed, wad·ing**). Walk through water or any soft substance that impedes motion; walk through (stream etc.); ~ **into**, (colloq.) attack (person, task) vigorously; (fig.) progress slowly or with difficulty (*through* book etc.); **wading bird** = WADER sense 1. **wade** *n.* Act of wading.

wad·er (wā′d*er*) *n.* (esp.) 1. Long-legged bird, as crane, heron, sandpiper, that wades in shallow water. 2. (pl.) High waterproof boots or long waterproof garments covering feet and legs and coming up above waist, worn by fishermen etc.

wa·di, wa·dy (wah′dē) *ns.* (pl. **wa-dis, wa-dies**). In N. Africa etc., rocky ravine or watercourse, dry except in rainy season.

WAF, W.A.F. *abbrevs.* Women in the Air Force. **Waf** (wahf) *n.* Member of WAF.

wa·fer (wā′f*er*) *n.* Very thin light sweet crisp biscuit or cake; thin disk of unleavened bread used at Eucharist; small disk of gelatine, flour and gum, etc., formerly used for sealing letters; disk of red paper stuck on legal document instead of seal. **wa′fer·y** *adj.* **wafer** *v.t.* Attach or seal with wafer.

waf·fle[1] (wŏf′*el*) *n.* Small soft crisp batter cake with honeycomb surface; ~ **iron**, utensil, usu. two shallow metal pans hinged together, between which waffle is baked or fried.

waf·fle[2] (wŏf′*el*) *v.i.* (**-fled, -fling**) & *n.* (Indulge in) verbose but aimless or ignorant talk or writing.

waft (wăft, wahft) *n.* Act of waving, waving movement; whiff of odor, breath of wind; flag or some substitute, usu. knotted, hoisted as signal, etc. ~ *v.t.* Convey (as) through air or over water, sweep smoothly and lightly along.

wag[1] (wăg) *v.* (**wagged, wag·ging**). Shake or move briskly to and fro, oscillate; **wag′tail**, small Old World bird of genus *Motacilla*, with slender body and long tail that is freq. in wagging motion. **wag** *n.* Single wagging motion.

wag[2] (wăg) *n.* Facetious person, habitual joker. **wag′ger·y** *n.* (pl. **-ger·ies**). Action(s), humor, of a wag. **wag′gish** *adj.* **wag′gish·ly** *adv.* **wag′gish·ness** *n.*

wage[1] (wāj) *n.* Amount paid periodically, esp. by day or week or month, for work or service of employee (usu. pl); requital, reward (usu. pl.); (pl., econ.) that part of total production of community that is the reward of all forms of labor (as dist. from remuneration received by capital); **living** ~, pay that permits earner and family to live without fear of privation; ~ **scale**, schedule of rates of wages for related types of jobs in an industry, company, etc.; ~ **slave**, person dependent on income obtained from (esp. unpleasant) labor.

wage[2] (wāj) *v.t.* (**waged, wag·ing**). Carry on (war etc.).

wa·ger (wā′j*er*) *n.* Bet, stake; ~ **of battle**, (hist.) trial to decide guilt or innocence by personal combat. **wage** *v.t.* (**waged, wag·ing**). Bet, stake. **wa′ger·er** *n.*

wag·gle (wăg′*el*) *v.* (**-gled, -gling**). Move (something held or fixed at one end), be moved, to and fro with short quick motions. ~ *n.* Act of waggling. **wag′gly** *adj.*

wag·gon = WAGON.

Wag·ner (vahg′n*er*), **Richard** (1813–83). German composer of operas, including the Ring Cycle, *Tristan and Isolde, Parsifal*, etc. **Wag·ne·ri·an** (vahgnēr′ēan) *adj.* & *n.*

wag·on, Brit. **wag·gon** (wăg′*on*) *ns.* Four wheeled vehicle for drawing heavy loads, often with removable semi-cylindrical cover, usu. drawn by two or more horses; (Brit.) open freight car; vehicle for carrying water, hence **on the** ~, (slang) abstaining from alcohol; **tea** ~, small wheeled table for conveying tea etc.

wag·on-lit (văgawṅlē′) *n.* (pl. ***wag·ons·lits*** pr. văgawṅlē′). Sleeping car on continental railroad. [Fr. *wagon* wagon, *lit* bed]

Wah·ha·bi, Wa·ha·bi (wahhah′bē) *ns.* (pl. **-bis**). Member of Muslim sect, followers of Abd-el-Wahhab (*c*1703–91), who acquired political power in Arabia in early 20th c.

wa·hi·ne (wahhē′nā) *n.* Girl, woman. [Hawaiian and Maori]

wa·hoo (wah′hōō, wahhōō′) *n.* (pl. **-hoos**). Shrub or small tree (*Euonymus atropurpureus*) of eastern N. Amer. having brilliant red leaves in autumn.

waif (wāf) *n.* (law) Any object

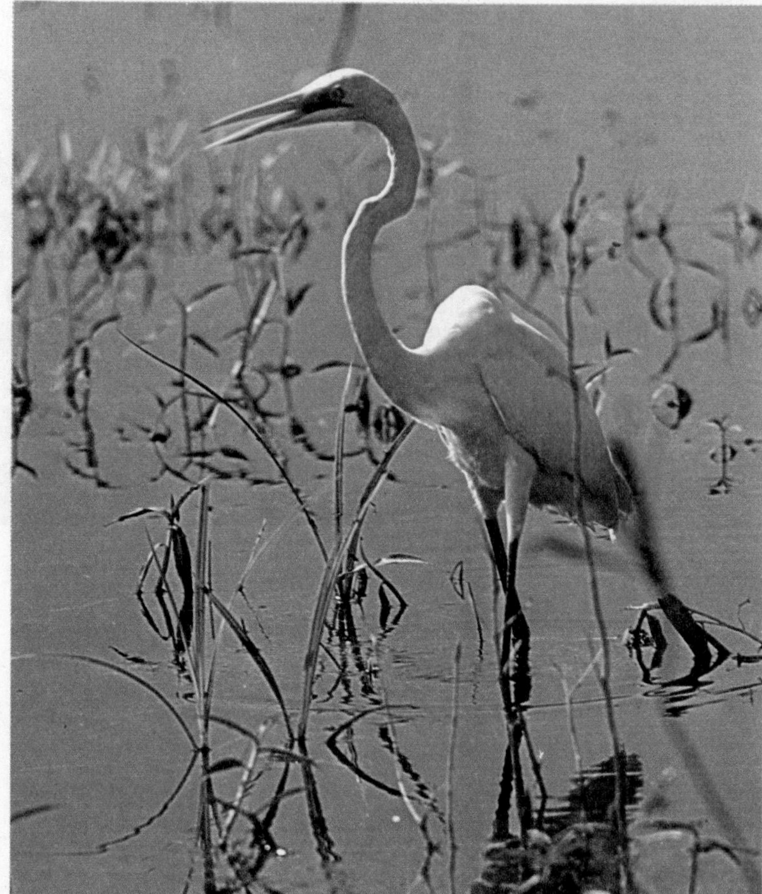

*The great white heron is a **wader** and one of a widespread group of birds mostly conspicuous for long legs and bills. These enable them to walk on mud and feed in shallow water.*

or animal found ownerless; homeless and helpless person, esp. unowned or abandoned child; **~s and strays**, odds and ends; homeless or neglected children.

Wai·ki·ki (wīkēkē′). Beach and resort area of Honolulu, on SE. Oahu, Hawaii.

wail (wāl) *n.* Prolonged plaintive inarticulate cry of pain, grief, etc.; bitter lamentation; sound resembling cry of pain. ~ *v.i.* Utter wails or persistent and bitter lamentations or complaints; bewail, lament; **Wail′ing Wall**, high wall in Jerusalem, supposed to stand on the site of Solomon's temple, to which Jews go to pray and lament. **wail′er** *n.* **wail′ful** *adj.*

wain·scot (wān′skot, -skŏt) *n.* Wooden paneling or boarding on room wall; (hist.) imported oak of fine quality. ~ *v.t.* (**-scot·ed, -scot·ing** or **-scot·ted, -scot·ting**). Line with wainscot. **wain′scot·ing, wain′scot·ting** *ns.* Wainscot or material for it.

waist (wāst) *n.* Part of human body between ribs and hip bones, normally slenderer than parts above and below it; middle narrower part of anything; part of garment covering waist, narrowed part of garment corresponding to waist (but sometimes worn higher or lower than position of this); bodice, blouse; **waist′band**, band going around waist, esp. one forming upper part of lower garment; **waist′cloth**, loincloth; **waist′coat**, (also pr. wĕs′kĭt) (Brit.) vest; **waist′line**, line of waist; measurement of this.

wait (wāt) *v.* 1. Abstain from action or departure until some expected event occurs; pause, tarry; be expectant or on the watch. 2. Await, bide. 3. Act as attendant *on* person; serve food and drink, shift plates at table; **~ on, ~ upon**, serve as attendant to; pay respectful visit to. 4. Defer (meal) till someone arrives. 5. **~-a-bit**, [f. Afrikaans *wag-'n-bietje*] any of various plants and shrubs, esp. species of *Mimosa*, with hooked and clinging thorns. **wait** *n.* Act or time of waiting; **lie in ~**, lurk in ambush.

wait·er (wā′ter), fem. **wait·ress** (wā′trĭs) *ns.* Person employed at hotel, restaurant, etc., to wait upon guests, take orders for meals, etc.

wait·ing (wā′tĭng) *n.* (esp.) (Period of) official attendance at court; **in ~**, on duty, in attendance; **~ game**, abstention from attempt to secure advantage in early part of enterprise, game, etc. in order to act more effectively at later stage; **~ list**, list of persons waiting for appointment, next chance of obtaining something etc.; **~ room**, room provided for persons to wait in, esp. at bus or railroad station or for patients waiting to consult doctor etc.

waive (wāv) *v.t.* (**waived, waiv·ing**). Relinquish, refrain from insisting on, refuse to avail oneself of (advantage, privilege, claim, opportunity, etc.). **waiv′er** *n.* (law) Waiving.

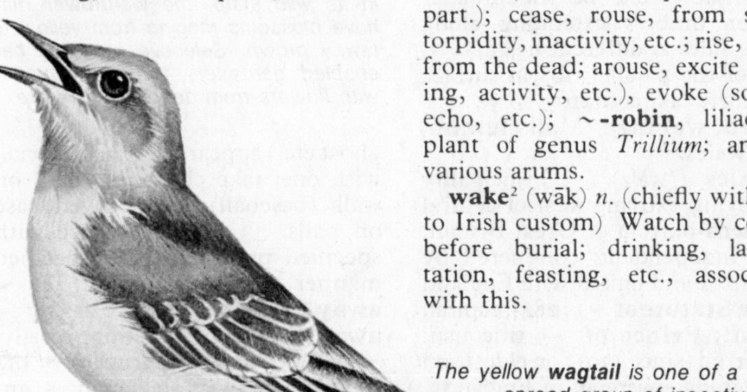

wake[1] (wāk) *v.* (**woke** pr. wōk or **waked, waked** or **wok·en** pr. wō′ken, **wak·ing**). Cease to sleep, rouse from sleep, (freq. **~ up**); be awake (archaic except in pres. part.); cease, rouse, from sloth, torpidity, inactivity, etc.; rise, raise, from the dead; arouse, excite (feeling, activity, etc.), evoke (sound, echo, etc.); **~-robin**, liliaceous plant of genus *Trillium*; any of various arums.

wake[2] (wāk) *n.* (chiefly with ref. to Irish custom) Watch by corpse before burial; drinking, lamentation, feasting, etc., associated with this.

*The yellow **wagtail** is one of a widespread group of insectivorous birds. Each has a long tail that is wagged up and down or from side to side.*

*Because of the altitude and topography, agriculture in **Wales** is confined to grazing and stock-breeding. There are also large deposits of coal.*

wake[3] (wāk) *n.* Track left on water's surface by ship or other moving object; **in the ~ of,** following close behind; in imitation of; following as a result or consequence.

wake·ful (wāk′f*u*l) *adj.* Keeping awake, esp. while others sleep; unable to sleep; marked by absence or want of sleep. **wake′ful·ly** *adv.* **wake′ful·ness** *n.*

Wake (wāk) **Island.** N. Pacific island under sovereignty of U.S.

wak·en (wā′k*e*n) *v.* Cause to be, become, awake; wake up.

Wal·bur·ga (vahlboor′gah), **St.** (*c*710–79). English missionary to Germany, abbess of Heidenheim; commemorated Feb. 25 and May 1 (see WALPURGIS).

Wal·den (wawl′d*e*n) **Pond.** Pond near Concord in NE. Massachusetts; site of Henry David Thoreau's cabin.

Wal·den·ses (wŏldĕn′sēz) *n.pl.* Puritanical religious sect that originated in S. France *c*1170 through preaching of a rich Lyons merchant, Peter Waldo; was banned in 1184 and scattered by persecution into Germany and Bohemia; became a separately organized Church that associated itself with the Protestant Reformation of the 16th c. and still exists, chiefly in N. Italy and in N. and S. Amer., though not officially tolerated until 1848. **Wal·den·si·an** (wŏldĕn′-sē*a*n) *adj.* & *n.*

wale (wāl) *n.* 1. WEAL[2]. 2. One of horizontal timbers connecting and bracing piles of trench, dam, etc.; (naut.) one of the broader thicker timbers extending along ship's sides at different heights. 3. One of the parallel ribs in surface of fabric as corduroy. ~ *v.t.* (**waled, wal·ing**). Mark, furnish, with wales.

Wales (wālz). Principality occupying extreme west of central southern portion of Great Britain; orig. independent; conquered by Edward I and united with England by the **Statute of** ~ (1284); capital, Cardiff; **Prince of** ~, title usu. conferred (since 1301) on eldest son of reigning sovereign of England.

Wal·hal·la (wahlhah′l*a*, vahl-) = VALHALLA.

walk (wawk) *v.* 1. Travel, go, on foot; perambulate, tread floor or surface of, go over or along on foot; (of bipeds) progress by alternate movements of legs so that one foot is always on the ground, (of quadrupeds) go at gait in which there are always two, and during part of step three, feet on ground (opp. to run, trot, gallop, etc.); (of ghost etc.) appear. 2. Cause to walk with one; take charge of (dog) on walk; (baseball) give, be given, base on balls. 3. (archaic) Live with specified principle or in specified manner, conduct oneself. 4. ~ **away from,** outdistance easily; ~ **away with,** win (something) easily; ~ **off,** depart, esp. abruptly; ~ **off with,** carry away, steal; win; ~ **on,** play nonspeaking (**walk-on**) part on stage; ~ **out,** (esp., colloq.) strike; hence **walk′out** (*n.*); **walk out on,** abandon, esp. without warning; **walk over,** (of horse) win race in which horse has no competitors going over (course) at walking pace; win a race or other contest with little or no effort; **walk′over** (*n.*), race in which winner walks over; **walk the plank**: see PLANK; **walk the streets,** (esp.) be a prostitute; **walk-up,** (colloq.) apartment in building without elevator. 5. **walk′ing beam,** overhead oscillating lever, pivoted in the center, for transmitting power, esp. in sidewheel steamers, pumps, etc.; **walking delegate,** (formerly) trade union official who visited sick members, interviewed employers, etc.; **walking stick,** cane; STICK insect. **walk′er** *n.* **walk** *n.* 1. Walking gait, walking pace; manner of walking, spell of walking, esp. short journey on foot for exercise or pleasure; (baseball) base on balls. 2. Place for walking, tree-bordered avenue, broad path in garden or

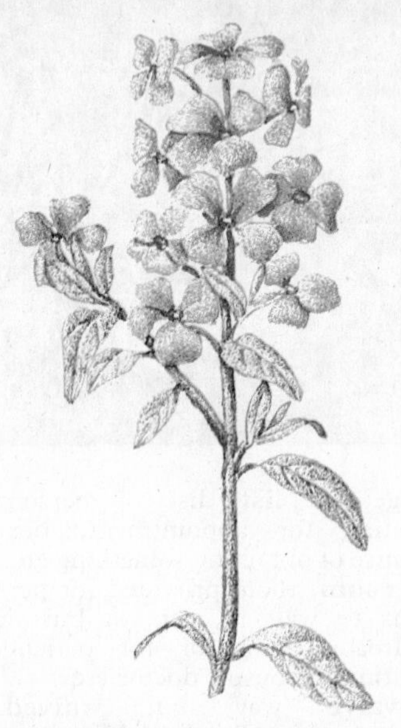

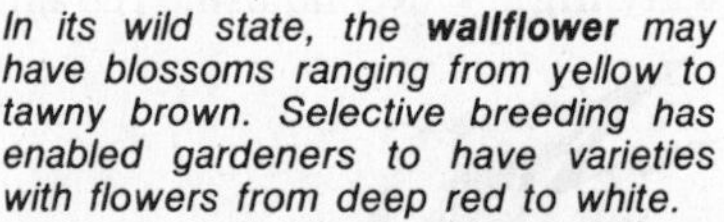

*In its wild state, the **wallflower** may have blossoms ranging from yellow to tawny brown. Selective breeding has enabled gardeners to have varieties with flowers from deep red to white.*

*There are 15 species of tree in the genus which includes the **walnut.** The most common commercial variety used in Europe was originally from Asia and Asia Minor.*

pleasure ground, sidewalk, footpath; distance to be walked; course or circuit for walking; **cock of the ~**, person whose supremacy in his own circle is undisputed. 3. Sphere of activity, calling, profession, occupation (usu. **~ of life**).

walk·ie-talk·ie (waw′kē taw′kē) *n.* (pl. **-talk·ies**). Radio transmitting and receiving set carried on the person.

Wal·kyr·ie (wălkēr′ē, wăl′kĭrē, vălkēr′ē, văl′kĭrē) = VALKYRIE.

wall (wawl) *n.* 1. Structure of stone, bricks, earth, etc., of some height, serving as rampart, embankment, defensive enclosure of city, castle, etc., or to enclose or divide off house, room, field, garden, etc.; **drive, send, up the ~**, (slang) drive to distraction. 2. Something resembling wall in appearance or function; outermost part of hollow structure, as tire etc. 3. (anat., zool., bot.) Outermost layer bounding organ, cell, etc. 4. **wall′flower**, plant of genus *Cheiranthus*, esp. *C. cheiri*, with yellow or orange-brown fragrant flowers, growing wild on old walls, rocks, etc., and cultivated in gardens; (colloq.) woman sitting out dances for lack of partners; **wall′paper**, paper for covering interior walls of rooms; **wall pennywort**: see PENNYWORT; **wall plate**, timber or other horizontal member laid on or in wall to support rafters, distribute pressure, etc. **wall** *v.t.* Provide or protect with wall; close (*up, in*), block, shut *up*, with wall(s). **walled** *adj.*

__Walruses__ live in large groups, up to 100, frequenting shallow waters in search of clams. These are shoveled out of the shells by the long tusks and whiskers.

wal·la·by (wŏl′*a*bē) *n.* (pl. **-bies,** collect. **-by**). Any of various smaller species of kangaroo.

Wal·lace[1] (wŏl′ĭs, waw′lĭs), **Henry A**(**gard**) (1888–1965). Amer. agriculturist and politician; secretary of Agriculture 1933–40; vice president of U.S. under Franklin D. Roosevelt, 1941–5; secretary of Commerce, 1945–6.

Wal·lace[2] (wŏl′ĭs, waw′lĭs), **Sir William** (1270?–1305). National hero of Scotland; resisted the English under Edward I, was captured by treachery and executed in London.

wal·let (wŏl′ĭt) *n.* 1. (archaic) Bag, esp. pilgrim's or beggar's, for holding provisions etc. on journey. 2. Flat folding case for carrying in pocket, closed by flap or opening like book, for holding money, documents, etc.

wall·eye (wawl′ī) *n.* Eye with iris whitish (or occas. streaked, particolored, or different in color from other eye) or with divergent squint. **wall′eyed** *adj.* Having walleye; (of fishes) with large prominent eyes.

The __wallaby__ differs from a kangaroo mainly in its smaller size. There are many species but all are confined to Australia and New Guinea. The pretty-faced variety (left) is found in north-eastern Australia.

Wal·loon (wŏlo͞on′) *adj.* & *n.* (Member, language) of people, of Gaulish origin and speaking a French dialect, forming chief part of population of SE. Belgium.

wal·lop (wŏl′*o*p) *n.* (colloq.) Heavy resounding blow, whack. ~ *v.t.* Thrash, beat.

wal·lop·ing (wŏl′*o*pĭng) *adj.* (esp., colloq.) Big, strapping, thumping.

wal·low (wŏl′ō) *v.i.* Roll about in mud, sand, water, etc.; (of ship) roll helplessly; (fig.) take delight in gross pleasures etc. ~ *n.* Act of wallowing; place where buffalo, elephants, etc., go to wallow; depression, mudhole, dusthole, formed by this.

Wall (wawl) **Street.** Street in New York City, on or near which are located most of the chief financial institutions of U.S.; Amer. money market.

wal·nut (wawl′nŭt, -n*u*t) *n.* Fruit, consisting of two-lobed seed enclosed in spheroidal shell covered with green fleshy husk, of various trees of genus *Juglans*, esp. *J. regia*; any tree of *Juglans* or some related genera; wood of walnut tree, used in cabinetmaking.

Wal · pur · gis (vahlpoor′gĭs) **Night.** Eve of May 1, on which, acc. to German legend, a witches' Sabbath took place on the Brocken, a peak of the Harz mountains; named after St. WALBURGA, whose feast day on May 1 coincides with an old pagan feast with rites protecting from witchcraft.

wal·rus (wawl′r*u*s, wŏl′-) *n.* (pl. **-rus·es,** collect. **-rus**). Large marine mammal (*Odobenus rosmarus*) of Arctic seas, allied to seals and sea lions, and chiefly distinguished by two long tusks; **~ mustache,** long thick mustache hanging down on both sides of mouth.

Wal·ton (wawl′t*o*n), **I·zaak** (ī′z*a*k) (1593–1683). English writer, author of *Compleat Angler* (1653) and *Lives* of several contemporary writers.

waltz (wawlts) *n.* Dance performed to music in triple time; music for this, or in its characteristic time and rhythm. ~ *v.* Dance waltz; move lightly, trippingly, etc.; move (person) as in waltz. **waltz′er** *n.*

wam·pun (wŏm′p*u*m, wawm′-) *n.* Cylindrical beads of polished ends of shells threaded to form broad belts; formerly used by N. Amer. Indians of the east coast as currency, as ornaments, or for mnemonic or symbolic purposes, recording treaties, etc.; (slang) money.

wan (wŏn) *adj.* (**wan·ner, wan·nest**). Pale, pallid, colorless, sickly. **wan′ly** *adv.* **wan′ness** *n.*

wand (wŏnd) *n.* Slender rod or staff carried as sign of office by verger, beadle, usher, etc.; staff used in enchantments by fairy or magician.

wan·der (wŏn′d*er*) *v.* Roam, ramble, move idly or restlessly or casually about, stroll, saunter; go from country to country or place to place without settled route or destination; stray, diverge from right way, get lost; wind, meander; be unsettled or incoherent in mind, purpose, talk, etc., be inattentive or delirious, rave; traverse in wandering. **wan′der·er, wan′der·ing** *ns.* **wandering** *adj.* (esp.) **W~ Jew,** (1) person who, according to medieval legend, is condemned to wander the earth without rest until Day of Judgment, as punishment for insulting Christ on way to crucifixion; (2) any of various trailing plants esp. *Tradescantia fluminensis.*

wan·der·lust (wŏn′d*er*lŭst) *n.*

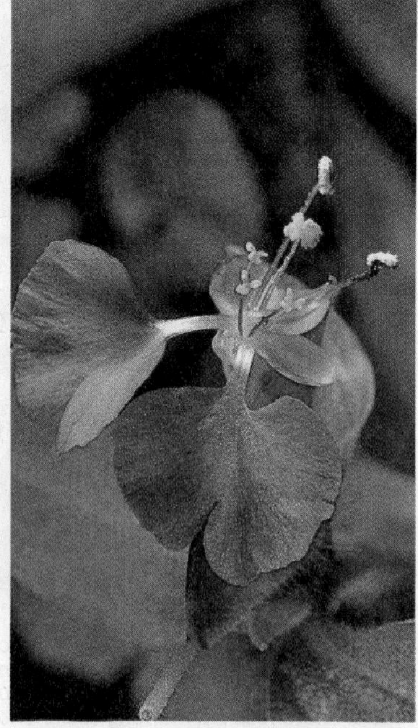

Species of ***Wandering Jew,*** *(Tradescantia) are grown all around the world. They are especially tolerant of low light levels, favoring shady positions.*

Strong desire to wander or travel. [Ger.]

wane (wān) *v.t.* (**waned, wan·ing**). Decrease in brilliance, size, or splendor, decline; lose power, vigor, importance, intensity, etc.; (of moon) undergo periodical decrease in extent of visible illuminated portion during second half of lunation. ~ *n.* (Period of) waning, decline.

wan·gle (wăng′g*e*l) *v.t.* (**-gled, -gling**). (slang) Accomplish, obtain, by scheming or contrivance; manipulate, fake, (account, report, etc.). ~ *n.* Act of wangling.

Wan·kel (vahng′k*e*l), **Felix** (1902–). German engineer, inventor of the Wankel rotary internal combustion engine.

want (wŏnt, wawnt) *n.* Lack, absence, deficiency, *of*; penury, destitution; need, condition marked by lack of necessary or desirable thing; (chiefly pl.) something needed or desired; **want ad**, newspaper advertisement by person seeking to obtain employee, buy merchandise, etc. **want** *v.* Be without or have too little of, fall short (by specified amount) *of*; be in want; require; desire, wish for possession or presence of. **want′ed** *adj.* (esp.) Sought by police as suspect. **want′ing** *adj.* (esp.) Lacking *in* quality or quantity; without; not adequate to need or expectation; (colloq.) mentally deficient.

wan·ton (wŏn′t*o*n) *adj.* Sportive, capricious; luxuriant, wild (archaic and poet.); licentious, unchaste; unprovoked, reckless, arbitrary. **wan′ton·ly** *adv.* **wan′ton·ness** *n.* **wanton** *n.* Licentious person. ~ *v.i.* (chiefly archaic and poet.) Gambol, frolic; luxuriate, revel, *in*; sport amorously or lewdly.

wap·i·ti (wŏp′ĭtē) *n.* (pl. **-tis**, collect. **-ti**). N. Amer. ELK (*Cervus canadensis*).

war (wōr) *n.* 1. Strife usu. between nations conducted by force, state of open hostility and suspension of ordinary international law prevalent during such quarrel, attack or series of attacks by armed forces; fighting as profession; (fig.) hostility between persons; **civil ~**, war between parts of one nation for supremacy; **U.S. Civil W~**: see CIVIL War; **cold ~**: see COLD; **holy ~**, war waged in support of some religious cause; **private ~**, feud between persons or families carried on in defiance of laws of murder etc.; (also) armed attack made by members of one nation upon another without government sanction; **W~ Between the States**: see CIVIL War; **W~ of (American) Independence**: see AMERICAN War of Independence; **~ of nerves**, attempt to wear down opponent by gradual destruction of morale; **W~**

REWARD!

FIFTY SOVEREIGNS, and a Conditional Pardon.

WHEREAS the three Convicts (Runaways from Port Arthur) MARTIN CASH, GEORGE JONES, and LAWRENCE KAVENAGH, whose descriptions are as under, stand charged with having committed divers Capital Felonies, and are now illegally at large: This is to give Notice, that I am authorised by His Excellency the Lieutenant-Governor to offer a Reward of Fifty Sovereigns to any person or persons who shall apprehend or cause to be apprehended and lodged in safe custody either of the said Felons; and should this service be performed by a Convict, then, in addition to such pecuniary Reward, a CONDITIONAL PARDON.

M. FORSTER,
Chief Police Magistrate.

19th January, 1843.

DESCRIPTION OF THE ABOVE-NAMED CONVICTS.

Martin Cash, per Francis Freeling, tried at Launceston Q.S. 24th March 1840, 7 years, labourer, 6 feet, age 33, native place Wexford, complexion very ruddy, head small and round, hair curly and carroty, whiskers red small, forehead low, eyebrows red, eyes blue small, nose small, mouth large, chin small. Remarks remarkably long feet, a very swift runner.

Lawrence Kavenagh, per Marian Watson, tried at Sydney, 12th April 1842, life, stonemason, 5 feet 10½, age 30, complexion pale, head long large, hair brown to grey, whiskers brown, visage long, forehead high, eyebrows brown, eyes light grey, nose long and sharp, mouth and chin medium size, native place Wicklow. Remarks A. D. above elbow joint left arm, 2 scars on palm of left hand, lost little finger on right hand.

George Jones, per Marian Watson, tried at Sydney, 14th April 1842, life, labourer, 5 feet 7, age 27, complexion ruddy fair, freckled, head long, hair brown, whiskers brown, visage long, forehead perpendicular, eyebrows brown, eyes blue, nose medium, mouth medium, chin pointed, native place Westminster. Remarks H. W. anchor on right arm, breast hairy.

JAMES BARNARD GOVERNMENT PRINTER HOBART TOWN

Less frequently used today, a ***'wanted'*** *poster may still be erected by the authorities in an attempt to obtain information on criminals.*

Facing: the most revolutionary form of internal-combustion engine to be developed since the invention of reciprocating designs, the ***Wankel*** *has a smaller number of moving parts and much smoother operation. It was first used in an NSU car in 1968 and then in the Japanese Mazdas.*

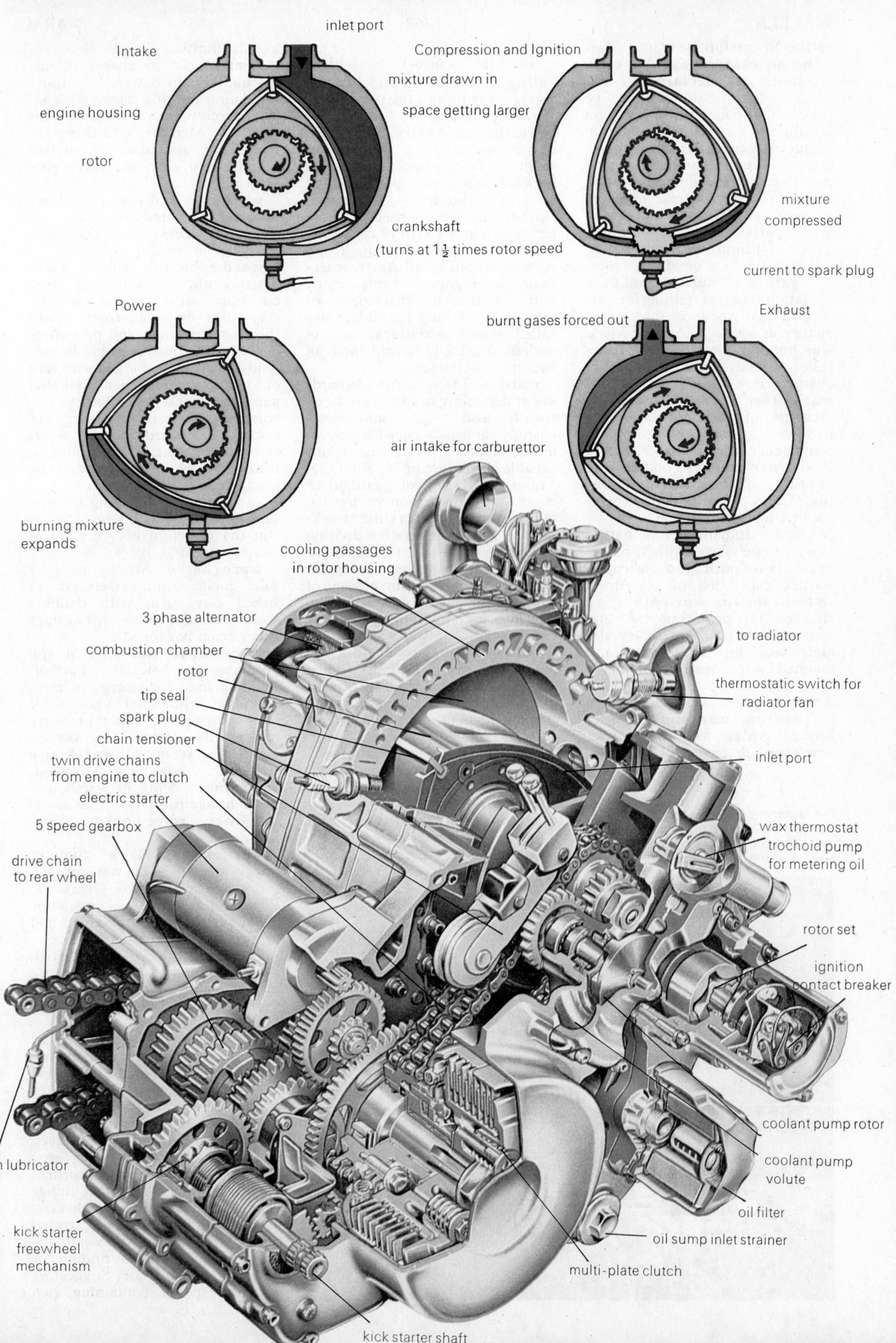

inlet port
Intake
Compression and Ignition
mixture drawn in
engine housing
space getting larger
rotor
mixture
compressed
crankshaft
(turns at 1½ times rotor speed
current to spark plug
Power
Exhaust
burnt gases forced out
air intake for carburettor
burning mixture
expands
cooling passages
in rotor housing
3 phase alternator
to radiator
combustion chamber
rotor
thermostatic switch for
radiator fan
tip seal
spark plug
chain tensioner
inlet port
twin drive chains
from engine to clutch
electric starter
5 speed gearbox
wax thermostat
trochoid pump
for metering oil
drive chain
to rear wheel
rotor set
ignition
contact breaker
coolant pump rotor
in lubricator
coolant pump
volute
oil filter
kick starter
freewheel
mechanism
oil sump inlet strainer
multi-plate clutch
kick starter shaft

of the Secession: see CIVIL War. 2. **be at, make, wage,** ~, carry on hostilities; **declare** ~, announce that hostilities may be expected (also fig.); **go to** ~, begin hostilities. 3. ~ **cloud**, condition in international affairs that threatens war; ~ **correspondent**, newspaper etc. correspondent reporting on war; ~ **cry**, phrase or name shouted in charging or rallying to attack; party catchword; ~ **dance**, dance of primitive people before warlike excursion or after victory; ~ **game**, simulated military operation as part of training for war; ~ **god**, god worshipped as giving victory in war, esp. Ares or Mars; **war'head**, explosive head of torpedo, rocket, etc.; **war'horse**, charger (now chiefly fig. in **old war'horse**, person excited by memories of past combats or controversies); **war'lord**, military commander (transl. of Ger. *Kriegsherr*); **war'monger**, one seeking to bring about war; **war'mongering** (*adj.* & *n.*); **war paint**, paint applied to face and body esp. by N. Amer. Indians before battle; (colloq.) one's best clothes, make-up, etc.; **war'path**, (route taken by) warlike expedition of N. Amer. Indians; **on the war'path**, (fig.) engaged in, preparing for, any conflict; **war'plane**, military aircraft; **war'ship**, ship armed and manned for war; **war'time**, time of war; **war whoop**, yell esp. of N. Amer. Indians in charging. **war** *v.* (**warred, war·ring**). (chiefly literary) Make war, be at war. **war'ring** *adj.* (esp.) Contending, discordant.

*The launching of a **warship.** The U.S.S. San Diego stands on the slips as guests arrive for the launching ceremony. It was designed as a combat store ship.*

war·ble[1] (wōr'bel) *v.* (**-bled, -bling**). Sing softly and sweetly, sing with trills and quavers. ~ *n.* Warbling sound.

war·ble[2] (wōr'bel) *n.* Small hard tumor produced by pressure of saddle on horse's back; swelling on back of cattle etc. produced by larva of warble fly; ~ **fly**, any of various dipterous insects whose larvae live under skin of cattle etc.

war·bler (wōr'bler) *n.* (esp.) Any of various small Amer. insectivorous, migratory birds, many with yellowish markings or plumage, of family Parulidae, also called **wood warblers**; any of various small Old World birds of subfamily Sylviinae.

ward (wōrd) *n.* 1. Act of guarding or defending (now only in **keep watch and** ~); confinement, custody (archaic); guardianship of minor or other person legally incapable of conducting his affairs. 2. Minor under care of guardian or court. 3. Separate room or division of prison or hospital or (hist.) workhouse. 4. Administrative division of city or town esp. for elections. 5. Each ridge projecting from inside plate of lock, preventing passage of any key not having corresponding incisions; each incision in bit of key corresponding to ward of lock. 6. **ward'room**, messroom or living space of naval commissioned officers below commanding officer. **ward** *v.t.* Have in keeping, protect (chiefly now of God); parry (*off* blow), keep *off* (danger etc.).

-ward *suffix*. Forming adjectives with sense "having specified direction or tendency" (e.g. *backward, downward, homeward, toward*), also used as adverbs (= -WARDS) and nouns (e.g. *to the eastward*).

war·den (wōr'den) *n.* 1. Chief administrative officer in charge of prison; official in charge of enforcing certain laws, esp. those regulating hunting (*game warden*). 2. Churchwarden. 3. (also **air-raid** ~) Member of civil organization for assistance of civilian population in air raids. **ward'en·ship** *n.*

ward·er (wōr'der) *n.* 1. (archaic) Sentinel, watchman on tower. 2. (fem. **ward'ress**) (Brit.) Official in charge of prisoners.

ward·robe (wōr'drōb) *n.* Place where clothes are kept, esp. large cupboard with hangers, movable trays, drawers, etc.; room where theatrical costumes and properties are kept; in royal or noble household, department charged with care of wearing apparel (chiefly in titles); person's stock of clothes; ~ **mistress**, woman in charge of professional wardrobe of actor, actress, or theatrical company; ~ **trunk**, upright trunk for dresses, suits, etc.

-wards *suffix*. Forming adverbs (and adjectives) with sense "to" or "in the direction of" (e.g. *backwards, towards*).

ware (wār) *n.* Articles made for sale, goods; esp., vessels etc. of baked clay (usu. with defining word, as *Wedgwood* ~); (pl.) things that person has for sale.

ware·house (wār'hows) *n.* (pl. **-hous·es** pr. -howzĭz). (Part of) building used for storage of merchandise, wholesaler's goods for sale, furniture or other property temporarily stored for owner; **bonded** ~: see BOND[1]. **warehouse** (wār'howz, -hows) *v.t.* (**-housed, -hous·ing**). Store in warehouse. **ware·house·man** (wār'howsman) (pl. **-men**), **ware·hous·er** (wār'howzer, -ser) *ns.*

war·fare (wōr'fār) *n.* State of war, being engaged in war, conflict.

war·fa·rin (wōr'ferĭn) *n.* Poisonous, colorless, crystalline powder used for killing rodents and in medicine as an anticoagulant.

war·like (wōr'līk) *adj.* Martial; skilled in, fond of, war; of, for use in, war; bellicose, threatening war.

war·lock (wōr'lŏk) *n.* (archaic) Male witch, sorcerer.

warm (wōrm) *adj.* 1. Of, at, rather high temperature, giving out considerable degree of heat (but less than that indicated by *hot*); (of persons etc.) glowing with exercise, excitement, eating and drinking, etc.; (of clothes etc.) serving to keep one warm. 2. (of feelings etc.) Sympathetic, affectionate, cordial; eager, emotionally excited, indignant; (of conflict) vigorous, harassing; (of scent or trail) fresh, strong; (in children's games) close to the object sought, or to finding or guessing. 3. (of color) Suggesting warmth; esp., of, containing, rich reds and yellows. 4. **warm´-blood´ed,** (of birds and mammals) having constant body temperature normally higher than that of surrounding medium; (fig.) amorous, emotional; **warm-hearted, warm´heart´ed,** of, showing, proceeding from, generous and affectionate disposition. **warm´ly** *adv.* **warm´ness, warmth** (wŏrmth) *ns.* **warm** *n.* Warming, being warmed; warmth of atmosphere. ~ *v.* Make warm; excite; become warm, animated, or sympathetic; ~ **up,** practice, exercise before game; make, become, warm; reheat (food etc.); (of radio, engine, etc.) come, bring, to efficient working temperature; **warmed up** or **over,** (of food, lit. or fig.) reheated, stale; **warm´up** (*n.*), action of warming up; **warm´ing pan,** long-handled covered metal (usu. brass) pan for holding live coals etc., formerly used for warming beds. **warm´er** *n.*

warn (wŏrn) *v.t.* Give timely notice to (person etc.) of impending danger or misfortune, put on guard, caution *against*; admonish; notify of something requiring attention, give previous notice to; ~ **off,** give notice to person to keep at distance, off private ground, etc.

warn·ing (wŏr´nĭng) *n.* (esp.) Thing that serves to warn; notice

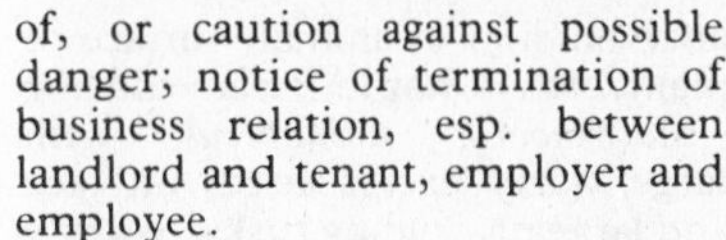

of, or caution against possible danger; notice of termination of business relation, esp. between landlord and tenant, employer and employee.

warp (wŏrp) *v.* 1. Make, become, crooked or perverted, bias, change from straight or right or natural state. 2. (naut.) Move (ship) by hauling on rope attached to fixed point; (of ship etc.) progress thus. ~ *n.* 1. Threads stretched lengthwise in loom to be crossed by woof. 2. Rope used in towing or warping. 3. Crooked state produced in lumber etc. by uneven shrinking or expansion; (fig.) perversion or perverse inclination of mind. 4. ~ **and woof,** (fig.) essential structure, base. **warp´er** *n.*

war·rant (wŏr´*a*nt, wăr´-) *n.* 1. Act, token, of authorization, sanction; justifying reason or ground for action, belief, etc.; proof, authoritative witness. 2. Document conveying authority or security; esp. written authorization to pay or receive money; executive authority's writ or order empowering officer to make arrest or search, execute judicial sentence, etc.; (mil., naval) official certificate or rank issued to ~ **officer,** officer intermediate in rank between commissioned and noncommissioned officers. **warrant** *v.t.* Serve as warrant for, justify; guarantee. **war´rant·er, war·ran·tor** (wŏr´-*a*ntŏr, wăr´-) *ns.*

war·ran·ty (wŏr´*a*ntē, wăr´-) *n.* (pl. **-ties**). Authority, justification (*for*); (esp., law) express or implied undertaking by vendor that his title is secure or that thing sold fulfills specified conditions.

war·ren (wŏr´*e*n, wăr´-) *n.* Piece of land where rabbits breed or abound; (fig.) densely populated building or district; (hist.) piece of land enclosed and preserved for breeding game.

war·ri·or (wŏr´ēer, wăr´-, -y*e*r) *n.* Fighting man, valiant or experienced soldier (now poet. or rhet.); fighting man of tribe etc.

War·saw (wŏr´saw). (Pol. *Warszawa*) Capital city of Poland; ~ **Pact,** treaty of mutual defense and military aid, signed at Warsaw May 14, 1955, by U.S.S.R., Poland, Czechoslovakia, Hungary, Rumania, Bulgaria, Albania, and East Germany.

wart (wŏrt) *n.* Small round dry tough excrescence on skin caused by abnormal growth of papillae and thickening of epidermis over them; rounded excrescence or protuber-

Top to bottom: ***Reed warbler*** *and its nest; wood warbler; Dartford warbler. Many of these birds have particularly tuneful songs. Some have a restricted range owing to individual needs but others migrate long distances.*

ance on skin of animal, surface of plant, etc.; ~ **hog**, African wild hog (*Phacochoerus aethiopicus*) with large warty excrescences on face and large protruding tusks. **wart'y** *adj.* (**wart·i·er, wart·i·est**).

war·y (wār'ē) *adj.* (**war·i·er, war·i·est**). (Habitually) on one's guard, circumspect, cautious, careful. **war·i·ly** (wār'ĭlē) *adv.* **war·i·ness** (wār'ēnĭs) *n.*

was (wŭz, wŏz): see BE.

wash (wŏsh, wawsh) *v.* 1. Cleanse with liquid; take (stain, dirt, etc.) *out, off, away*, by washing; wash oneself or esp. one's hands (and face); wash clothes; (of textile material, dye, etc.) bear washing without deterioration; (fig.) purify; ~ **down**, clean thoroughly esp. a ship; follow (food) with drink; ~ **one's hands of**, decline responsibility for; ~ **up**, wash (table utensils etc.) after use; sweep (object) on to shore etc.; clean one's face and hands. 2. Moisten; be removed by flow of water; (of sea, river, etc.) flow past, beat upon (shore, walls, etc.), sweep *over*, surge *against*; make (channel etc.) thus. 3. Sift (ore), sift ore, sand, etc. (*for* gold etc.), by action of water; brush thin coating of watery color over (wall, drawing, etc.); coat (inferior metal) thinly with gold etc. **washed** (wŏsht, wawsht) *adj.* (esp.) ~ **out**, (of fabric) faded from being washed; (fig.) enfeebled, limp, exhausted; ~ **up**, (colloq.) having failed completely, defeated. **wash'a·ble** *adj.* **wash** *n.* 1. Washing, being washed; process of being laundered (esp. **in the** ~); quantity of clothes etc. (to be) washed. 2. Lotion; liquid applied to hair esp. to cleanse it. 3. Thin even layer of transparent watercolor or diluted ink. 4. Solution applied to metal to give effect of gold or silver. 5. Visible or audible motion of agitated water, esp. waves caused by passage of vessel; disturbance in air caused by passage of aircraft. 6. Sandbank, tract of land, alternately covered and exposed by sea; low-lying often flooded ground, with shallow pools and marshes; shallow pool, backwater, etc.; dry bed of winter storm. 7. Solid particles carried away or deposited by running water; soil from which gold or diamonds may be washed out. 8. **wash-** *combining form*, **wash-and-wear** = DRIP-dry; **wash'basin**, bowl for washing hands etc.; **wash'board**, corrugated board on which clothes etc. may be scrubbed; **wash'cloth**, small cloth used to wash one's face or body; **wash'day**, day on which clothes are washed; **wash goods**, washable fabrics or clothes; **wash'-out**, (esp.) (site of) removal by flood of part of hillside, road, track, railroad, etc.; (slang) disappointing failure, fiasco; **wash'room**, room with toilet facilities, lavatory; **wash'tub**, tub for washing clothes etc.

*The **Washington Monument**, an obelisk memorial to George Washington, was built between 1848 and 1884. The design, by Robert Mills, was greatly modified. It stands 555 ft. high.*

Wash. *abbrev.* Washington.

wash·er[1] (wŏsh'*er*, waw'sh*er*) *n.* Person, thing, that washes; **wash'erman** (pl. **-men**), **wash'erwoman** (pl. **-women**), person whose occupation is washing clothes.

wash·er[2] (wŏsh'*er*, waw'sh*er*) *n.* (esp.) Disk or flattened ring of metal, leather, rubber, fiber, etc., placed between two surfaces, as under nut of bolt or tie rod etc. to relieve rotative friction or prevent lateral motion, under plunger of screw-down water tap etc. to prevent leakage, etc.

wash·ing (wŏsh'ĭng, waw'shĭng) *n.* (esp.) Clothes, linen sent to the wash; ~ **machine**, machine for washing clothes etc.; ~ **soda**, form of sodium carbonate used in washing clothes etc.

Wash·ing·ton[1] (wŏsh'ĭngt*o*n, waw'shĭng-). Most northerly of the Pacific states of U.S., admitted to the Union in 1889; capital, Olympia. **Wash·ing·to·ni·an** (wŏshĭngtō'nē*a*n, wawshĭng-) *adj.* & *n.*

Wash·ing·ton[2] (wŏsh'ĭngt*o*n, waw'shĭng-), **Booker T**(**aliaferro**) (1856–1915). Amer. black educator; established Tuskegee Institute, Alabama.

Wash·ing·ton[3] (wŏsh'ĭngt*o*n,

*Present throughout Africa, but most numerous on the open plains and their fringes, the **wart hog** is a large animal weighing up to 200 lb. It sleeps in a burrow at night, and can run at 30 m.p.h.*

waw′shĭng-), **George** (1732–99). Commander in chief of the Continental forces in the Revolutionary War and first president of U.S., 1789–97.

Wash·ing·ton[4] (wŏsh′ĭngton, waw′shĭng-) **D.C.** Administrative capital of U.S., conterminous with the District of Columbia on the NE. bank of the Potomac River; founded during presidency of George Washington and named after him.

wash·y (wŏsh′ē, waw′shē) *adj.* (**wash·i·er, wash·i·est**). (of food etc.) Diluted, weak, thin; (of color) faded looking; (of style, utterance, etc.) feeble, diffuse, lacking vigor. **wash′i·ness** *n.*

WASP, Wasp, wasp[1] (wŏsp) *ns.* & *adjs.* (usu. derog.) White Anglo-Saxon Protestant.

wasp[2] (wŏsp) *n.* Any of the superfamily Vespoidea of hymenopterous insects, often carnivorous, with slender body, abdomen attached to thorax by narrow stalk, usu. two pairs of fully developed wings, and often formidable sting; ~ **waist, -waisted,** (having) very slender waist, esp. one produced by tight lacing.

wasp·ish (wŏs′pĭsh) *adj.* Irritable, petulantly spiteful, irascible; caustic. **wasp′ish·ly** *adv.* **wasp′-ish·ness** *n.*

wasp·y (wŏs′pē) *adj.* (**wasp·i·er, wasp·i·est**). Wasplike; abounding in wasps.

was·sail (wŏs′al, wăs′-, wŏsāl′) *n.* (archaic) Salutation in presenting cup of wine to guest; festive occasion, drinking bout; liquor in which healths were drunk, esp. spiced ale drunk on Twelfth Night and Christmas Eve. ~ *v.i.* Make

Above left: ***George Washington,*** *first President of the U.S.A., was a weathy landowner whose commonsense helped to override differences between the States and unify the nation.*

merry; sit carousing and drinking healths. **was′sail·er** *n.* [ON. *ves heill* "be in good health," form of salutation]

Was·ser·man (wŏs′erman; *Ger.* vah′sermahn), **August von** (1866–1925). German pathologist; ~ **test**, blood test employed in diagnosis of syphilis.

wast·age (wās′tĭj) *n.* Loss or diminution by use, wear, decay, leakage, etc.; amount wasted.

waste[1] (wāst) *n.* 1. Desert, waste region; dreary scene or expanse. 2. Consumption, loss or diminution from use, wear and tear, etc.; wasting, useless or extravagant expenditure or consumption, squandering (*of*); **run to** ~, (of liquid) flow away so as to be wasted; (fig.) be expended uselessly. 3. Waste matter; useless remains (esp. of manufacturing process), scraps, shreds; esp. scraps, remnants, from manufacture of cotton, wool, etc., yarn or textiles, used for cleaning machinery, absorbing oil, etc.; ~ **pipe**, pipe for carrying off used or superfluous water or steam. **waste** *adj.* 1. (of land, region, etc.) Desert, uninhabited, desolate, barren; uncultivated; (fig.) monotonous, without features of interest; not built upon; **lay** ~, destroy, devastate, ruin; **waste′land**, land not utilized for cultivation or building; (fig.) time, place, society, barren of hope, culture, etc. 2. Superfluous, refuse,

Above: Nest of the ***tree wasp*** *(Vespula sylvestris). It is made of 'paper' from wood fibers and saliva, by the communal activity of workers.*

left over; no longer serving a purpose; **waste′paper, waste paper**, paper thrown away as spoiled, superfluous, useless, etc.; **wastepaper basket**, container for this; **waste product**, (usu. useless) byproduct of manufacture or physiological process.

waste[2] (wāst) *v.* (**wast·ed, wast·ing**). 1. Lay waste; (law) bring (estate) into bad condition by damage or neglect. 2. Expend to no purpose or for inadequate result, use extravagantly, squander; run to waste. 3. Wear gradually away, be used up, lose substance or volume by gradual loss, decay, etc.; wither.

waste·ful (wāst′ful) *adj.* Given to, exhibiting, waste; extravagant. **waste′ful·ly** *adv.* **waste′ful·ness** *n.*

wast·rel (wās′trel) *n.* Wasteful person, spendthrift; idler, good-for-nothing.

watch (wŏch) *v.* (archaic) Remain awake for devotion or other purpose, keep vigil; be on the alert *for*, keep watch, be vigilant; exercise protecting care *over*; keep eyes fixed on, keep under observation, follow observantly. **watch′er** *n.* **watch** *n.* 1. Watching, keeping awake and vigilant at night for guarding, attending, etc.; (hist.) each of (three, four, or five) periods into which night was anciently divided; (naut.) period of time (usu. four hours) during which each division of ship's company remains on duty, sailor's turn of duty; part, usu. half, of officers and crew who together work ship during a watch. 2. Watching, observing, with continuous attention, continued lookout, guard (**keep** ~); one who watches, lookout man; (hist.) man, body of men, charged with patrolling and guarding streets at night, proclaiming the hour, etc. 3. Small timepiece designed to be worn on wrist or carried in pocket etc. 4. **watch'band**, small band of leather, metal, cloth, etc., for securing a watch to the wrist; **watch chain**, chain attaching timepiece to one's person; **watch'dog**, dog kept to guard house, property, etc.; **watch fire**, fire burning at night as signal or for use of sentinel or other person(s) on watch; **watch'man**, (fem.) **watch'woman** (pl. **-men; -women**), formerly one who patrolled streets at night to safeguard life and property; now esp. person employed to guard building etc., esp. at night; **watch pocket**, small pocket, usu. in vest, for holding a watch; **watch'tower**, tower from which observation is kept of approach of danger; **watch'word**, (hist.) military password; (transf.) word or phrase expressing guiding principle or rule of action of party or individual.

watch·ful (wŏch'*f*ul) *adj.* Wakeful (archaic); accustomed to, engaged in, watching, vigilant; showing vigilance. **watch'ful·ly** *adv.* **watch'ful·ness** *n.*

wa·ter (waw'*t*er, wŏt'*er*) *n.* 1. Transparent, colorless, tasteless, odorless liquid (H_2O) composing seas, lakes, and rivers, falling as rain, issuing from springs, etc., and convertible into steam by heat and into ice by cold; this as supplied for domestic needs, esp. through pipes; liquid resembling (and usu. containing) water, as tears, saliva, urine, etc.; aqueous decoction, infusion, etc., used in medicine or as cosmetic or perfume; (freq. pl.) water of mineral spring(s) used medicinally for bathing or drinking; state of tide (in **high, low,** ~); **heavy** ~: see HEAVY; ~ **on the brain**, hydrocephalus; ~ **on the knee**, accumulation of inflammatory exudate in knee joint. 2. Characteristic transparency and luster of diamond or pearl; **of the first** ~, of the finest quality. 3. ~ **ballet**, synchronized movements in water by group of swimmers, usu. accompanied by music; ~ **bath**, (esp., chem.) vessel containing water in or over which vessels containing chemical preparations etc. are placed for cooling, evaporating, etc.; ~ **bed**, (bed with) rubber mattress filled with water; ~ **biscuit**, unsweetened biscuit made of flour and

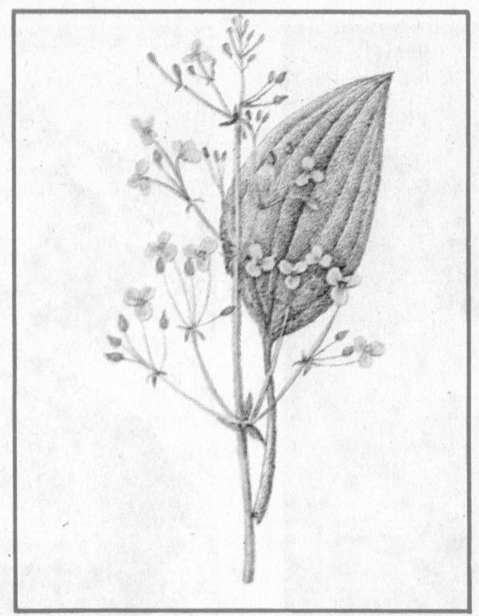

*The lower parts of the **water plantain** are poisonous. However, after boiling, the stem and root can be eaten. The leaves were once used to relieve kidney complaints.*

water; ~ **boatman**, aquatic insect (*Notonecta*) with boat-shaped body and oarlike legs, which swims upside down over surface of water; **wa'terbuck**, S. African antelope of genus *Kobus*, frequenting riverbanks; **wa'terborne**, (esp. of diseases) communicated by use of contaminated drinking water etc.; (of seaplane) having landed on water; **water buffalo**, common Asiatic buffalo (*Bubalus bubalis*), often domesticated; **Water carrier**: see AQUARIUS; **water chestnut**, Chinese sedge (*Eleocharis dulcis*) growing in thick clumps in water and having buttonlike tubers used as ingredient in Chinese dishes; flating aquatic weed (*Trapa natans*) native to Asia, bearing hard black fruit; **water clock**, water-operated machine for measuring time; **water closet**, (Brit.) (room etc. containing) flush toilet (abbrev. W.C., w.c.); **wa'tercolor**, artists' paint made of pigment mixed usu. with gum and diluted with water; esp., transparent variety of this, aquarelle; picture painted, art or method of painting, with such colors; **water-cooled**, (of internal combustion engine) cooled by means of circulating water; **water cooler**, (esp.) small tank containing cooled drinking water; **wa'tercourse**, (bed or channel of) stream of water, river, brook; **wa'tercress**, hardy perennial cress (*Nasturtium officinale*) often growing in springs and clear running streams, and with pungent leaves used as a salad; **water cure** = HYDROPATHY; **wa'terfall**, more or less perpendicular descent of water from a height, cascade; **wa'terfinder**, DOWSER; **water flag**, yellow iris; **wa'terfowl** (pl. **-fowls,** collect. **-fowl**), bird(s) frequenting water, esp. swimming game bird(s); **wa'terfront**, land or buildings abutting on river, lake, sea, etc.; **water gap**, opening in mountainous or hilly area worn down by stream flow; **water gas**, gas (mixture of hydrogen and carbon monoxide), made by forcing steam over red-hot coke and used as fuel etc.; **water glass, wa'terglass**, tube with glass bottom for observing objects under water; aqueous solution of sodium or potassium silicate, solidifying on exposure to air and used as cement, fireproof paint, for preserving eggs, etc.; **water hammer**, concussion of water made when its flow through pipe is suddenly checked; **water hen**, any of various chickenlike marsh birds, as rail and coot; **water hole**, hole or hollow containing water, esp. in desert or dry bed of stream; **water ice**, frozen dessert of flavored water and sugar; **water jacket**, casing holding water, esp. casing through which water circulates in water-cooled engines, guns, etc.; **water jump**, place where horse must jump over water in steeplechase etc.; **water level**, (height of) surface of water; upward limit of saturation by water; **wa'terlily** (pl. **-lil·ies**), aquatic plant of *Nymphaea* and related genera, and similar plants with broad floating leaves and showy fragrant flowers; **water line** (1) line on ship's side corresponding to surface of water when ship is afloat, esp. proper line of floating when ship is fully loaded; (2) line left by receding tide or flood indicating greatest height of water; **wa'terlogged**, filled or saturated with water so as to be unbuoyant, heavy and unmanageable; (of ground etc.) made useless by saturation with water; **water main**, chief pipe in system of watersupply; **wa'termark**, distinguishing mark or design in paper visible when paper is held up to light; **wa'termelon**, large fruit (*Citrullus vulgaris*) with smooth hard rind, soft pink or red pulp, and abundant sweet watery juice; plant, native of tropical Africa and widely cultivated, bearing this; **water mill**, mill driven by water; **water moccasin**: see COTTONmouth; **water nymph**, nymph inhabiting or presiding over water, naiad; **water ouzel**: see DIPPER, sense 1; **water plantain**, plant of genus *Alisma*, with plantainlike leaves, growing in ditches etc.; **water polo**, ball game played in water by teams of swimmers; **water power, wa'terpower**, mechanical force derived from weight or motion of water; **wa'terproof** (*adj.*), impervious to water; (*n.*), waterproof garment or material; (*v.t.*), make waterproof; **water rat**, (slang) waterfront vagrant or thief;

1

2

3

4

*The natural energy from a **waterfall,** such as Russell Fall in Australia (1), enabled man to drive a **water wheel** that turned a millstone, as in Lancashire U.K. (2). The **waterlily** (3) grows wild in warmer areas: and the **watermelon** (4) has been cultivated for 5,000 years.*

*The **waterbok** is a large African antelope which can weigh up to 475 lb. and have a height of nearly 5 ft. There are five species and only the males carry horns.*

water-repellent, not easily penetrated by water; **water-resistant**, resisting but not completely preventing penetration by water; **water right**, legal right, sometimes restricted, to use water of a river etc. for irrigation, navigation, etc.; **wa'tershed**, summit or boundary line separating waters flowing into different rivers or river basins; whole catchment area of river system; **water-ski** (*v.i.*) (**-skied, -ski·ing**), plane over water on water skis, towed by boat; **water ski** (*n.*), ski used on water; **water-ski·er** (*n.*); **water snake**, snake inhabiting or frequenting water, esp. nonpoisonous freshwater snake of *Natrix* and related genera; **water softener**, any of several chemical compounds used to make water soft; **water spaniel**, large spaniel of variety used for retrieving waterfowl; **wa'terspout**, (esp.) gyrating column of mist, spray, and water produced by action of whirlwind on part of sea and clouds above it; hole or spout for discharging (esp. rain) water; **water system**, river and all its tributaries; system of reservoirs, filtration plants, pipes, etc., used

for storing, treating, and supplying water to a community or region; **water table**, level at which porous rock etc. is saturated by underground water, height to which such water naturally rises in well etc.; **wa'tertight**, so closely constructed or fitted that water cannot leak through; (of argument etc.) unassailable; **watertight compartment**, each of compartments with watertight partitions into which interior of ship is divided for safety; (fig.) division of anything regarded as kept entirely separate from rest; **water tower**, structure supporting elevated tank to secure necessary pressure for water supply; fire-fighting apparatus for delivering water at considerable height; **wa'terway**, navigable channel; (naut.) channel around ship's deck to drain off water; **water wheel**, wheel rotated by action of water and driving machinery; wheel for raising water for irrigation etc. in boxes or buckets fitted on its circumference; **water wings**, inflated floats used as supports by persons learning to swim; **wa'terworks**, assemblage of machinery, buildings, engineering constructions, etc., for supplying town, ornamental fountain, etc., with water through pipes. **wa'ter·less** *adj.* **water** *v.* 1. Give (animal) water to drink, (of animals) go to pool etc. to drink; furnish (ship etc.) with, take in, supply of water; supply water to (plant, crop, etc.), esp. by pouring or sprinkling; add water to (drink etc.), dilute (freq. ~ **down**). 2. (of eyes) Fill and run with moisture; (of mouth) secrete abundant saliva in anticipation of appetizing food etc. 3. (commerc.) Increase nominal amount of (company's stock or capital) by issue of new shares without corresponding addition to assets. 4. (chiefly in past part.) Produce wavy lustrous finish on (silk or other textiles) by sprinkling with water and passing through calender. 5. **wa'tering can**, portable vessel for watering plants, with long tubular spout; **watering hole**, (slang) bar, cocktail lounge, or nightclub; **watering place**, pool, trough, etc., where animals obtain water; place where supply of water is obtained; (Brit.) spa, seaside holiday or health resort.

*At the Battle of **Waterloo,** infantry in conspicuous uniforms were cut to pieces by artillery, as they were forced to maintain rigid 'squares' conceived for fighting at close range.*

Wa·ter·gate (waw'tergāt, wŏt'-er-) *n.* Scandal involving abuse of authority and violation of public trust by elected or appointed officials who, to retain power, engage in such acts as deception, perjury, bribery, and burglary. [after *Watergate*, building complex in Washington, D.C., site of Democratic Party offices, burglarized in June 1972, at direction of government officials]

Wa·ter·loo (waw'terlōō, wŏt'er-, wawterlōō', wŏter-). Village S. of Brussels, Belgium, where on June 18, 1815, Napoleon was finally defeated by the British under the Duke of Wellington and the Prussians; hence, **meet one's** ~, suffer final defeat.

wa·ter·y (waw'terē, wŏt'erē) *adj.* Of, consisting of, water (esp. in ~ **grave**, place in which person lies drowned); full of, covered with, containing too much, water; resembling water in color, pale; washed out; (of liquids) too thin, diluted, having little or no taste; (fig.) vapid, insipid, feeble.

WATS (wŏts) *n.* Telephone service that gives customer access to long-distance lines at special monthly rate. [*w*(ide) *a*(rea) *t*(elecommunications) *s*(ervice)]

Wat·son (wŏt'son), **James Dewey** (1928–). Amer. biologist; co-discoverer of DNA molecular structure; received Nobel Prize for medicine, 1962, with CRICK and WILKINS[1].

watt (wŏt) *n.* Unit of power in M.K.S. system, equivalent to 1 joule per second (abbrev. W); **watt'meter**, instrument for measuring electric power in terms of watts. [f. WATT]

Watt (wŏt), **James** (1736–1819). Scottish inventor of the steam engine.

watt·age (wŏt'ĭj) *n.* Amount of electric power expressed in watts.

wat·tle[1] (wŏt'el) *n.* Interlaced rods and twigs or branches used for fences and walls and roofs of buildings; ~ **and daub**, this plastered with clay or mud as building material for huts etc. **wattle** *v.t.* (**-tled, -tling**). Construct of wattle; interlace (twigs etc.) to form wattle; enclose, fill up, with wattle work.

wat·tle[2] (wŏt'el) *n.* Fleshy, usu. bright colored, lobe pendent from head or neck of turkey, domestic fowl, and other birds; barb, fleshy appendage on mouth of some fishes.

Wave (wāv) *n.* Member of the WAVES.

wave (wāv) *n.* 1. Moving ridge or swell of water between two troughs; movement of sea etc. in which such waves are formed. 2. Undulating configuration or line in or on surface, as hair etc. 3. Something resembling or supposed to resemble a wave, esp. temporary heightening of emotion, influence, etc.; **heat, cold,** ~, spell of hot or cold weather. 4. (phys.) Oscillatory condition that is propagated from place to place in such manner that the same type of vibration occurs all along the path with a difference of PHASE (i.e. slightly delayed in time); **heat, light, radio, ~s**, electromagnetic waves propagated through space; ~ **band**, (radio and television) range of wavelengths between specified limits; **~-form**, shape of wave, graphical or arithmetical specification of this; ~ **front**, surface containing points affected in same way by a wave at given time; **wave'length**, distance between successive points of equal phase in the direction of propagation of a wave; specific electromagnetic wave used by radio transmitting station. 5. Act or gesture of waving. **wave** *v.* (**waved, wav·ing**). 1. Move in waves, undulate; move to and fro, shake, sway; impart waving movement to; wave hand in greeting or as signal; motion (person) *away, back, in*, etc., by movement of hand. 2. Give undulating surface, course, or appearance to, make wavy; (of hair, lines, etc.) have such appearance, be wavy. **wave'like** *adj.* **wav'er**[1] *n.*

wave·let (wāv'lĭt) *n.* Small wave, ripple.

wa·ver[2] (wā'ver) *v.i.* Change, vary, fluctuate, shake, tremble; be irresolute, show doubt or indecision; falter, show signs of giving way. **wa'ver·er** *n.* **wa'ver·ing·ly** *adv.*

WAVES (wāvz) *n. sing.* or *pl.* Women's branch of U.S. Navy. [*W*(omen) *A*(ppointed for) *V*(oluntary) *E*(mergency) *S*(ervice)]

wav·y (wā'vē) *adj.* (**wav·i·er, wav·i·est**). Undulating; forming undulating line or series of wavelike curves. **wav'i·ly** *adv.* **wav'i·ness** *n.*

wax[1] (wăks) *n.* 1. Beeswax, sticky plastic yellowish substance of low melting point secreted by bees from special abdominal glands, used as material of honeycomb; white brittle translucent odorless tasteless substance gotten from this by purifying and bleaching, and used for candles, as plastic material for modeling, as basis of polishes, as air-excluding protective coating, etc. 2. Any of class of natural substances of plant or animal origin resembling beeswax in general properties and in being composed of fatty acids and alcohols; any of various hydrocarbons resembling beeswax. 3. Compound, chiefly of lac, used to receive impression of seal, sealing wax. 4. Thick resinous composition used by shoemakers for rubbing thread, cobblers' wax. 5. Cerumen. 6. ~ **bean**, variety of string bean having long, slim yellow pods; edible seed of this plant; **wax'berry** (pl. **-ries**), (fruit of) wax myrtle; **wax candle**, candle of beeswax, paraffin wax, etc.; **wax myrtle**, shrub (*Myrica cerifera*) of southeastern U.S., with aromatic foliage and small hard berries thickly coated with a white wax; **wax, waxed, paper**, paper coated with wax used as waterproof and airtight wrapping etc.; **wax'plant**, tropical Old World vine (*Hoya carnosa*) with pink or white waxy flowers; **wax'wing**, any of various Amer. and Asiatic passerine birds of genus *Bombycilla*, esp. *B. cedrorum*, cedar waxwing, with showy crest and red waxlike tips on wing feathers; **wax'work**, modeling in wax; object modeled in wax, esp. life-size figure of person with wax head, hands, etc., colored and clothed to look lifelike; (pl.) exhibition of such figures. **wax** *v.t.* Smear, coat, polish, treat, with wax. **wax'er** *n.*

*An amazing number of uses have been found for **wax**. It is applied to surfboards to improve grip and, here, it is being used to make ornamental candles.*

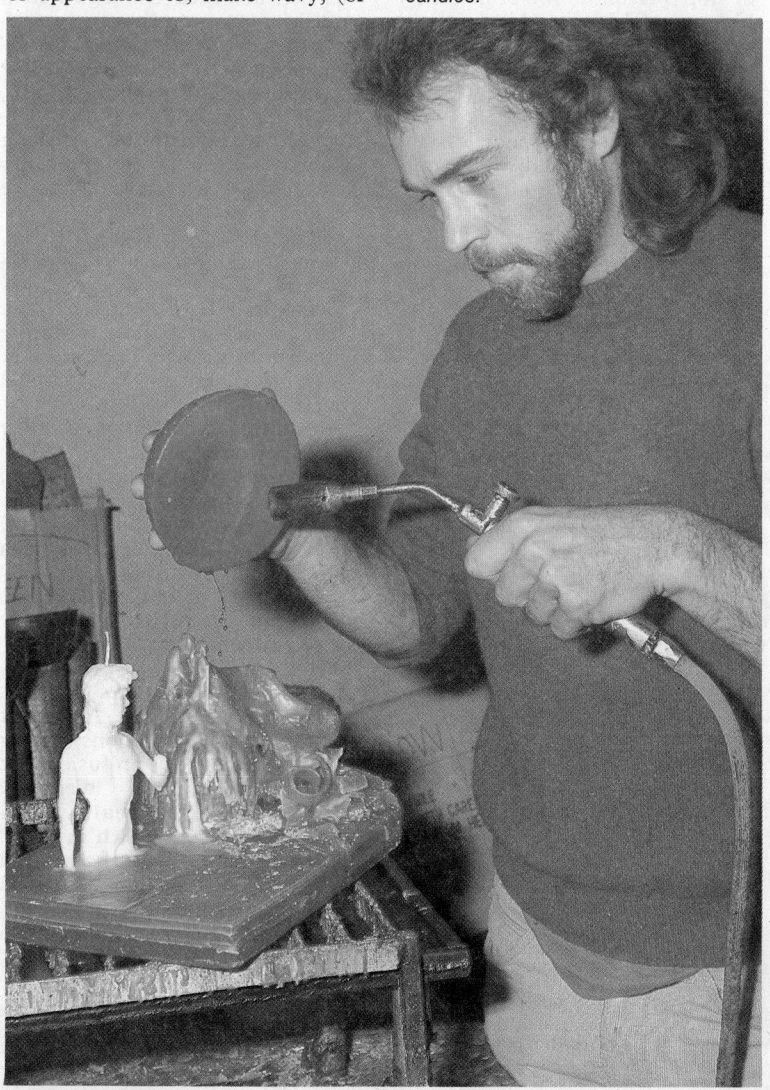

wax[2] (wăks) *v.i.* (**waxed, waxed** or **wax·en, wax·ing**). (of moon) Undergo periodical increase in extent of visible illuminated portion in first part of lunation, before full moon (opp. WANE); (archaic and poet.) grow, increase; change by growth or increase, become (*fat* etc.).

wax·en (wăk'sen) *adj.* (archaic) Made of, coated with, wax; resembling wax, esp. in smooth and lustrous surface, pallor, or softness and impressibility.

wax·y (wăk'sē) *adj.* (**wax·i·er, wax·i·est**). Resembling wax, esp. easily molded, or presenting smooth pale translucent surface; (of tissue) affected with amyloid degeneration. **wax'i·ness** *n.*

way (wā) *n.* 1. Road, track, path, street (esp. in phrases **across, over, the ~**, etc.); place of passage through door, crowd, etc.; (pl.) inclined structure, usu. of timber, on which ship is built and down which it is slid at launch; (pl.) parallel sills forming track for carriage or table of lathe or other machine; (pl.) inclined plane of parallel wooden rails or planks for sliding down heavy loads. 2. Route, line or course of travel for reaching place; opportunity for passage or advance, (fig.) freedom of action, scope, opportunity; travel or motion in particular direction, direction of motion, relative position, aspect; distance (to be) traveled, distance between places or to a place; (naut.) progress, rate of progress, through water, impetus gained by vessel in motion; **give ~**, fail to resist; be dislodged or broken under load; make concessions; allow precedence (*to*); abandon oneself (*to* grief etc.); **out of one's** or **the ~**, no longer an obstacle or impediment, disposed of, settled; (of person) imprisoned or killed; **the other ~ around**, conversely, vice versa. 3. Path or course of life or conduct, (pl.) habits of life, esp. with regard to moral conduct; course of action, device, method, means; customary or usual, habitual or characteristic, manner of acting, behaving, speaking, etc., (pl.) habits; condition regarded as hopeful or the contrary; kind, sort (now only in **in the ~ of** and similar phrases), kind *of business*; **on the ~ out**, going out of fashion or use; (slang) near death; **~s and means**, methods, esp. of providing money; **~ out**, method of solving a problem. 4. **make ~**, open a passage (*for*), move to allow person to pass; leave place vacant *for* (successor etc.); **make one's ~**, proceed in certain direction or to certain place; make progress in career, advance in wealth, reputation, etc.; **pay one's ~**, pay expenses as they arise, without incurring debts; (of business etc.) be carried on at least without loss; **see one's ~**, (esp., fig.) feel justified in deciding *to do* something. 5. **by the ~**, by the roadside; while going along; (fig.) incidentally, in passing; **by ~ of**, via; in capacity or function of, as something equivalent to; in the habit of (*doing*), making a profession of, having a reputation for (*being, doing,* something); **under ~**, (of vessel) having begun to move through water (also freq. fig.). 6. **way'bill**, list of passengers or goods on conveyance; **way'farer**, traveler, esp. on foot; **way'faring**, traveling, itinerant; **way'faring tree**, Old World shrub (*Viburnum lantana*), also grown in U.S., with dense cymes of white flowers, and green berries turning red and then black; **waylay'** (**-laid, -lay·ing**), lie in wait for; wait for and accost or stop (person) to rob or interview him; **way'side**, (land bordering) side of road or path; (*adj.*) situated on, growing at, lying near, etc., wayside. **way** *adv.* Away; (esp.) at or to a great distance, far; **way back**, (colloq.) long ago; distant past; remote or rural district; **way-out**, (slang) exotic, esoteric.

way·ward (wā'werd) *adj.* Childishly or capriciously self-willed or perverse, erratic, freakish, unaccountable. **way'ward·ly** *adv.* **way'ward·ness** *n.*

Wb *abbrev.* WEBER.

W.C., w.c. *abbrevs.* Water closet.

W.C.T.U. *abbrev.* Women's Christian Temperance Union.

we (wē) *pron.* First person nom. pl. pronoun denoting speaker and other person(s) associated with him as subject of sentence; used by sovereign or ruler, by newspaper writer or editor etc., instead of *I*.

weak (wēk) *adj.* Lacking strength, power or number; fragile, easily broken, bent, or defeated; lacking vigor, feeble, sickly; lacking resolution or power or resisting temptation, easily led; (of action etc.) not effective, showing weakness; (of argument etc.) unconvincing, logically deficient; (of liquid, esp. infusion) watery, thin; (of stress, a speech sound, etc.) having relatively little force etc., (of word or syllable, esp. final syllable or verse) unstressed; (gram., of verbs) forming past tense by addition of suffix, (of nouns or adjectives) belonging to any declension in which Old Teut. stem ended in *-n*; **~ ending**, (in verse) occurrence of unstressed monosyllable in normally stressed place at end of line; **weak-kneed**, (esp. fig.) lacking resolution or determination; **weak-minded**, lacking strength of purpose; mentally deficient; **weak sister**, ineffective person. **weak'ly**[1] *adv.*

weak·en (wē'ken) *v.* Make, become, weak or weaker. **weak'en·er** *n.*

weak·fish (wēk'fĭsh) *n.* (pl. **-fish·es,** collect. **-fish**). Marine food fish of genus *Cynoscion*, esp. *C. regalis* of eastern U.S. coastal waters.

weak·ling (wēk'lĭng) *n.* Weak or feeble person or animal.

weak·ly[2] (wēk'lē) *adj.* (**-li·er, -li·est**). Sickly, not robust, ailing.

weak·ness (wēk'nĭs) *n.* (esp.) Weak point, failing, defect, foolish or self-indulgent liking *for*.

weal[1] (wēl) *n.* (archaic) Welfare, well-being, prosperity (now chiefly in **~ and woe, common ~**).

weal[2] (wēl) *n.* = WELT sense 2. **~** *v.t.* Raise welt(s) on.

wealth (wĕlth) *n.* Abundant means, large possessions, being rich; abundance, profusion or lavish display *of*. **wealth'y** *adj.* (**wealth·i·er, wealth·i·est**). **wealth'i·ly** *adv.* **wealth'i·ness** *n.*

wean (wēn) *v.t.* Accustom (child or other young mammal) to food other than its mother's milk; (fig.) detach, alienate *from* accustomed object of pursuit or enjoyment,

*Found in the northern hemisphere, the **waxwing** is omnivorous. It eats insects in the summer and berries when available.*

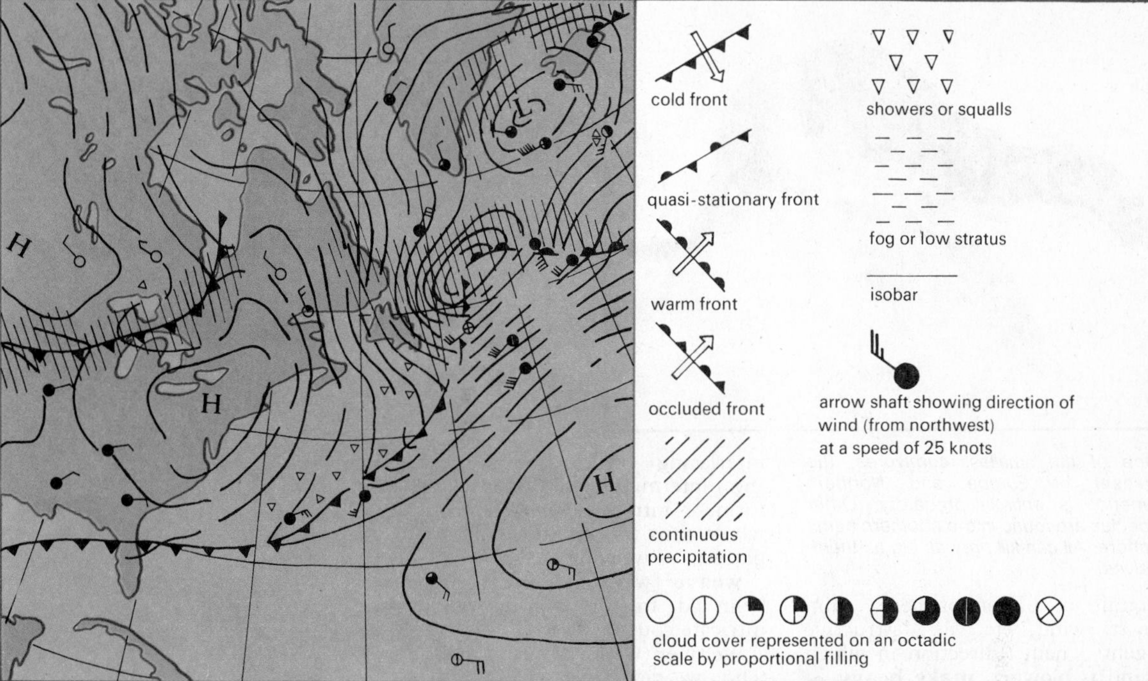

*Typical **weather map** (above left) alongside a legend of some of the more common symbols and their meaning. Coupled with satellite observation, modern weather maps must be accurate to provide data for aircraft.*

reconcile gradually to privation of something.

wean·ling (wēn′lĭng) *n.* Newly weaned child or other young mammal.

weap·on (wĕp′*o*n) *n.* Instrument used in war or combat as means of attack or defense; any part of body (esp. of bird or beast) used for similar purpose, as claw, horn, etc.; any action or means used against another in conflict.

weap·on·ry (wĕp′*o*nrē) *n.* 1. Weapons collectively. 2. Design and manufacture of weapons.

wear (wār) *v.* (**wore** pr. wōr, **worn, wear·ing**). 1. Be dressed in (habitually or on specific occasion); have on, be covered or decked with; dress (hair, beard, etc.), allow to grow, in specific fashion, or as opposed to shaving or wearing wig; (of ship etc.) fly (flag, colors); (transf. and fig.) bear, carry, exhibit, present (scar, appearance, title, etc.), carry in one's heart, mind, or memory. 2. Waste and impair, damage, deteriorate, gradually by use or attrition; suffer such waste, damage, or deterioration; come or bring into specified state by use, rub *away, down, off, out,* etc.; make (hole, groove, etc.) by attrition; exhaust, tire or be tired *out*; put *down* by persistence; endure continued use *well, badly,* etc., remain specified time in working order or presentable state, last long; ~ **out**, use, be used, until usable no longer. 3. (of time) Go slowly and tediously *on*, pass (time), be passed, gradually *away*. **wear′a·ble** *adj.* **wear′er** *n.* **wear** *n.* 1. Wearing or being worn on person, use as clothes; thing to wear, fashionable or suitable apparel. 2. Damage or deterioration due to ordinary use (freq. ~ **and tear**); capacity for resisting wear and tear.

*For all man's achievements there is still one thing he cannot control — the **weather**. The power of an electrical storm or a tornado remains unchallenged.*

wea·ri·some (wēr′ēs*o*m) *adj.* Causing weariness, monotonous, fatiguing. **wea′ri·some·ly** *adv.* **wea′ri·some·ness** *n.*

wea·ry (wēr′ē) *adj.* (**-ri·er, -ri·est**). 1. Tired, worn out with exertion, endurance, wakefulness, etc., intensely fatigued; sick or impatient *of*; dispirited, depressed. 2. Tiring, toilsome, tedious, irksome. **wea′ri·ly** *adv.* **wea′ri·ness** *n.* **weary** *v.* (**-ried, -ry·ing**). Make, grow, weary.

wea·sel (wē′zel) *n.* (pl. **-sels,** collect. **-sel**). Small slender-bodied reddish-brown carnivorous mammal (*Mustela frenata*) closely allied to stoats and polecats and remarkable for slyness, ferocity, and bloodthirstiness. **weasel** *v.i.* (colloq.) Equivocate, speak evasively; ~ **words,** (colloq.) equivocal words.

weath·er (wĕdh′*er*) *n.* Atmospheric conditions prevailing at a specified time or place with respect to heat or cold, quantity of sunshine, presence or absence of rain, snow, fog, etc., strength of wind; adverse, unpleasant, or hurtful

One of the smallest carnivores, the ***weasel*** *of Europe and Northern America is entirely predatory. Other species are found in the southern hemisphere. All can kill prey as big as themselves.*

condition of atmosphere, rain, frost, wind, etc., as destructive agents; (naut.) direction in which wind is blowing; **make heavy ~ of**, find trying or difficult; **under the ~**, (colloq.) indisposed, not very well; in adversity; **~-beaten**, worn, defaced, damaged, bronzed, hardened, etc., by exposure to weather; **weather-bound**, detained by bad weather; **weath′ercock**, (Brit.) weathervane; (fig.) changeable or inconstant person; **weather eye**, alertness to change in weather; **keep one's weather eye open**, be watchful and alert; **weath′erglass**, barometer; **weath′erman**, (1) meteorologist, esp. one who broadcasts a weather forecast; (2) (**W~**), member of violent revolutionary group in U.S. during late 1960s; **weather map**, chart or map showing state of weather over specific area at particular time; **weath′erproof**, impervious to effects of weather; **weather station**, meteorological observation post; **weath′erstrip**, **weather strip**, strip of material around window to exclude rain etc.; **weather vane**: see VANE sense 1. **weather** *adj.* (naut.) Windward. ~ *v.* 1. Expose to atmospheric changes; wear away, be worn away, disintegrate, discolor, by exposure to weather. 2. Withstand or come safely through (storm etc.); (fig.) come safely through (trouble, adversity, etc.).

weave[1] (wēv) *v.* (**wove** pr. wōv, or **weaved, wo·ven** pr. wō′vĕn, or **wove, weav·ing**). Form fabric by carrying a continuous thread or threads (the woof) back and forth across a set of lengthwise threads (the warp) so that warp and woof are interlaced; operate loom; make (thread etc.) into fabric, make (fabric) out of thread etc., thus; make (basket, wreath etc.) by interlacing reeds, flowers, etc.; (fig.) intermingle as if by weaving, form or introduce *into* connected whole thus. ~ *n.* Style, method, pattern, of weaving.

weave[2] (wēv) *v.* (Cause to) move from side to side or in devious or intricate course.

weav·er (wē′ver) *n.* (esp.) 1. One who weaves fabrics. 2. (also **weav′erbird**) Any of numerous Asiatic or African tropical birds of family Ploceidae, building elaborately interwoven nests.

web (wĕb) *n.* 1. Woven fabric, esp. whole piece in process of weaving or after coming from loom; (fig.) thing of complicated structure or workmanship, tissue. 2. Spiderweb; (freq. fig.); filmy texture spun by some caterpillars etc. 3. Tissue or membrane in animal body or plant; membrane or fold of skin connecting digits, esp. that between toes of aquatic bird or beast, forming palmate foot; vane of feather; thin flat plate or part connecting more solid parts in machinery; center part of girder between flanges; (papermaking) (large roll of paper made on) endless wire cloth on rollers carrying the pulp. 4. **web′foot** (pl. **-feet**), **web′footed**, (having) foot with webbed toes; **web′worm**, larva of various moths spinning large webs in which to feed or rest. **web** *v.t.* (**webbed, web·bing**). Cover with web or fine network; stretch threads of spider's web across (micrometer etc.); connect (fingers, toes) with web or membrane.

web·bing (wĕb′ĭng) *n.* (esp.) Stout strong closely woven material in form of narrow bands, used in upholstery etc.

Related to the sparrow, the ***weaverbird*** *is renowned for the complex nest it makes. Some gregarious species in Africa build up to 100 nests so close that they seem to be a single mass.*

we·ber (wĕb′er, vā′ber) *n.* Unit of magnetic flux in M.K.S. system, equal to 10^8 maxwells (abbrev. Wb). [f. WEBER[2]]

We·ber (wĕb′er; *Ger.* vā′ber), **Wilhelm Eduard** (1804–91). German physicist; devised the centimeter-gram-second system of measurement of electrical quantities.

Web·ster[1] (wĕb′ster), **Daniel** (1782–1852). Amer. lawyer, statesman, and orator.

Web·ster[2] (wĕb′ster), **Noah** (1758–1843). Amer. lexicographer.

wed (wĕd) *v.* (**wed·ded** or **wed, wed·ding**). Marry; unite, join, or couple intimately *with*; **be wedded to**, be obstinately attached to (pursuit etc.).

Wed. *abbrev.* Wednesday.

we'd (wēd) *contr.* We had; we should; we would.

wed·ding (wĕd′ĭng) *n.* Marriage ceremony with its attendant festivities; specified anniversary of this, as *silver* ~; ~ **cake**, highly decorated cake eaten at wedding and sent in small portions to absent friends etc.; ~ **day**, (anniversary of) day of wedding; ~ **march**, march (often Wagner's at beginning, Mendelssohn's at close) for performance at wedding; ~ **ring**, ring placed by bridegroom on bride's finger (usu. third finger of left hand) as part of wedding ceremony and usu. worn there constantly by married woman; one of pair of such rings exchanged by bride and groom at wedding.

wedge (wĕj) *n.* 1. Piece of wood, metal, etc., thick at one end and tapering to thin edge at the other, used as tool operated by percussion or pressure on thick end for splitting wood, stone, etc., forcing things apart, widening opening, rendering separate parts immovable, etc.; (fig.) something that splits or separates. 2. Anything shaped like a wedge. 3. Golf club, a heavy lofted iron used for pitching. **wedge** *v.* (**wedged, wedg·ing**). Tighten, fasten tightly, by driving in wedge(s); split *off*, force *apart*, with wedge; drive, push, squeeze (object) into position where it is held fast; pack or crowd (*together*) in close formation or limited space.

Wedg·wood (wĕj´wo͝od), **Josiah** (1730–95). Founder of pottery works near Stoke on Trent, England; hence, ware made at this factory, esp. fine porcelain with small cameo reliefs in white paste on a tinted matte ground; **Wedgwood blue**, shade of blue characteristic of Wedgwood (trademark) ware.

wed·lock (wĕd´lŏk) *n.* Married state; **born in** (or **out of**) ~, having parents married (or not).

Wednes·day (wĕnz´dā, -dē). Fourth day of the week; **Ash** ~: see ASH[2]. [OE. *wódnes daeg* day of WODEN; transl. of LL. *Mercurii dies* day of Mercury]

wee (wē) *adj.* (**we·er, we·est**). Tiny (chiefly Sc. and in nursery use).

weed (wēd) *n.* 1. Plant growing where it is not wanted. 2. (archaic) Tobacco; (colloq.) cigarette; (slang) marijuana. 3. (colloq.) Lanky and weak horse or person. 4. **weed´-killer**, substance used to destroy weeds or other plants. **weed´less** *adj.* **weed´y** *adj.* (**weed·i·er, weed·i·est**). **weed** *v.* Clear ground of weeds; free (land, a crop, etc.) from weeds, remove (weeds); eradicate, remove, clear *out* (faults, inferior or superfluous individuals, etc.). **weed´er** *n.*

weeds (wēdz) *n.pl.* Deep mourning worn by widow (usu. **widow's** ~).

week (wēk) *n.* 1. Cycle of seven days usu. understood as beginning with Sunday; period of any seven successive days; work days or hours of seven-day period, as *five-day* ~. 2. Seven days before or after a specified day. 3. **week´day**, any day other than Saturday and Sunday; **week´end**, holiday period at end of week, usu. from Friday night to Monday; (*v.i.*) make weekend visit, etc.

week·ly (wēk´lē) *adj.* Occurring, done, etc., once a week; of, for, lasting, a week. ~ *adv.* Once a week, every week. ~ *n.* (pl. **-lies**). Weekly newspaper or periodical.

ween (wēn) *v.t.* (archaic and poet.) Think, consider, deem.

wee·nie (wē´nē) *n.* (slang) Wiener, hot dog.

wee·ny (wē´nē) *adj.* (**-ni·er, -ni·est**). (colloq.) Tiny.

weep (wēp) *v.* (**wept**, pr. wĕpt, **weep·ing**). Shed tears; shed tears over, shed (tears), lament, utter, with tears; shed moisture in drops, exude drop of water, exude (water or other liquid); **weeping**, (of trees) having long, slender, drooping branches; esp. **weeping willow**, large Asiatic species of willow (*Salix babylonica*), cultivated as ornamental tree and regarded as symbolic of mourning. **weep´y** *adj.* Inclined to weep, tearful.

wee·vil (wē´vĭl) *n.* Beetle of the large family Curculionidae, usu. of small size, with head elongated into kind of snout, freq. very destructive to farm crops; any insect damaging stored grain. **wee´viled, wee´villed, wee´vil·y, wee´vil·ly** *adjs.* Infested with weevils.

weft (wĕft) *n.* Woof.

Wei (wā). Name of several dynasties that ruled in China, esp. that of 386–535.

wei·ge·la (wīgē´la, -jē´-, wī´ge-) *n.* Any of various shrubs (genus *Weigela*) of the honeysuckle family, having clusters of tubular flowers, esp. the widely grown *W. florida*, with red, pink, or white flowers.

weigh (wā) *v.* 1. Heave up (ship's anchor) before sailing; ~ **anchor**, sail; ~ **up**, raise (sunk ship etc.) from bottom of water. 2. Find weight of with scales or other machine; balance in hands (as if) to guess weight of; take definite weight of, take specified weight from larger quantity (freq. ~ **out**); be equal to or balance (specified weight) in scales; (fig.) estimate relative value or importance of (*with, against*), consider, ponder, balance in the mind; have specified importance or value, be of account, have influence (*with*); ~ **one's words**, speak deliberately and in calculated terms. 3. ~ **down**, draw, bend, force, down by pressure of weight; depress, oppress, lie heavy on; ~ **in**, (of boxer or wrestler) be weighed before contest; (of jockey) be weighed after race; have one's baggage weighed; hence ~**-in** (*n.*); ~ **in with**, (colloq.) contribute; ~ **on**, be burdensome, heavy, oppressive, on; ~ **out**, (of jockey) be weighed before race; hence ~**-out** (*n.*). 4. **weigh´bridge**, platform scale, flush with road, for weighing vehicles etc. **weigh** *n.* Process or occasion of weighing; **under** ~, corruption (from association with phrase *weigh anchor*) of *under way*

*Best known for vases that imitate those of ancient Greece with white cameos on a blue ground, **Josiah Wedgwood** originally used black as his basic color when he first made this stoneware.*

(see WAY, *n.* sense 5).

weight (wāt) *n.* 1. Force with which body is attracted to Earth; product of mass of any body and the average force of terrestrial gravitation; mass or relative heaviness as property of material substances; amount that thing etc. weighs, expressed in units of some recognized scale; portion or quantity weighing definite amount; heavy mass, burden, load; (fig.) heavy burden *of* care, responsibility, etc.; importance, influence, authority; persuasive or convincing power (of argument etc.), preponderance (*of* evidence, authority) on one side of question. 2. Any of various systems, with series of units in fixed arithmetical relations, used for stating weight of anything; piece of metal etc. of known weight, used in scales for weighing articles; heavy piece of metal etc. used to pull or press down something, give impulse to machinery (e.g. in clock), act as counterpoise, etc.; ~ **lifting**, athletic sport or exercise of lifting heavy weights; hence ~ **lifter;** ~ **watcher**, one who takes care not to become unduly fat. **weight'less** *adj.* Having little or no apparent weight as a result of gravitational pull, which has been neutralized by equal and opposing inertial force, as centrifugal force imparted initially to space capsule at launching. **weight'less·ness** *n.* **weight** *v.t.* Attach a weight to, hold down with weight(s); impede or burden with load; add weight to (textiles or other commodities) by addition of adulterant etc.; (statistics) multiply components of (average) by compensating factors.

weight·y (wā'tē) *adj.* (**weight·i·er, weight·i·est**). Heavy, weighing much; momentous, important; requiring or giving evidence of earnest thought, consideration, or application; influential, authoritative. **weight'i·ly** *adv.* **weight'i·ness** *n.*

Wei·mar (vī'mar̄). Town in Thuringia, Germany, famous as the residence of Goethe and Schiller and as the seat of the National Assembly of Germany (1919–33); ~ **Republic**, German republic (1919–33), the constitution of which was drawn up at Weimar.

weir (wēr̄) *n.* Dam or barrier across river etc. to retain water and regulate its flow; fence or enclosure of stakes etc. in river, harbor, etc., to catch or preserve fish.

weird[1] (wēr̄d) *n.* (archaic or Sc.) Fate, destiny.

weird[2] (wēr̄d) *adj.* Connected with fate; uncanny, supernatural; (colloq.) queer, fantastic. **weird'ly** *adv.* **weird'ness** *n.* [f. WEIRD[1], f. phrase ~ *sisters* the Fates, the witches, in Shakespeare's *Macbeth*]

weird·ie, weird·y (wēr̄'dē) (pl. **weird·ies**), **weird·o** (wēr̄'dō) (pl. **weird·os**) *ns.* (slang) Unusually odd, eccentric, person or thing.

wel·come (wĕl'kom) *int.* Exclamation of greeting, indicating pleasure at arrival of person(s) (often in phrases as ~ **home**, ~ **to**). **welcome** *n.* Saying "welcome" to person; kind or glad reception or entertainment of person or acceptance of offer. ~ *v.t.* (**-comed, -com·ing**). Say "welcome" to, receive gladly. ~ *adj.* Gladly received; acceptable as visitor; ungrudgingly permitted *to* do something or given right *to* thing. [OE. *wilcuma* (*wil-*) desire, pleasure, and *cuma* comer, one whose coming is pleasing, later changed to *wel-* (= WELL[2]) after OF. *bien venu*]

weld[1] (wĕld) *n.* Plant *Reseda lutea*; yellow dye yielded by this.

weld[2] (wĕld) *v.* Unite (pieces of metal) into solid mass by hammering or pressure, or by fusion using an electric arc (**arc weld'ing**), usu. when metal is soft but not melted; (of metal) admit of being welded; (fig.) unite intimately or inseparably. **weld'er** *n.* **weld** *n.* Joint made by welding.

wel·fare (wĕl'far̄) *n.* Satisfactory state, health and prosperity, well-being (usu. *of* person, society, etc.); maintenance of members of community in such condition, esp. by statutory procedure or social effort; money etc. thus received by those in need; **on** ~, receiving such aid because of poverty, loss of job, etc.; ~ **state**, country having highly

***Weir** across the Leven River at Newby Bridge, Cumbria, U.K. Adjustable openings (or sluice gates) control floods and allow a navigable depth to be maintained during droughts.*

*Rising from ensign to Field Marshal in 27 years, **Wellington** gained honors and cash rewards for his leadership in the Napoleonic campaigns. His political career was conservative.*

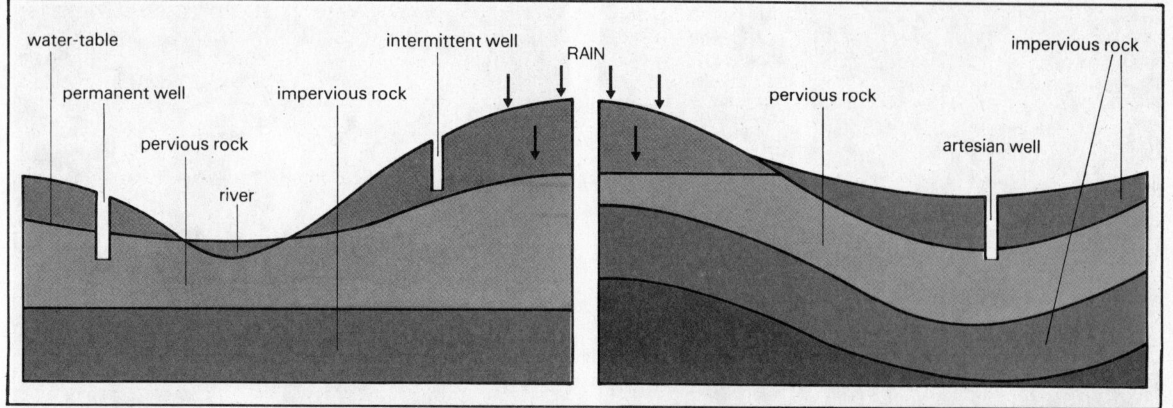

Where the watertable is close to the surface it is possible to dig a simple **well** *(left). Where it is not, artesian borings must be made, to penetrate to a pervious layer (right).*

developed social services controlled or financed by the government; ~ **work**, organized effort for welfare of class or group; hence ~ **worker**.

wel·kin (wĕl′kĭn) *n.* (archaic, poet.) Sky, firmament.

well[1] (wĕl) *n.* 1. (archaic and poet.) Spring, fountain; (fig.) source, origin. 2. Pit, esp. circular vertical excavation, usu. lined with masonry, sunk in ground to obtain supply of water; shaft sunk in ground for obtaining oil, gas, brine, etc., for storage of ice, etc. 3. Enclosed space more or less resembling well shaft, esp. central open space of winding or spiral staircase, elevator shaft, deep narrow space between surrounding walls of building(s) for light and ventilation, deep receptacle in piece of furniture, body of vehicle, etc.; receptacle for liquid, esp. for ink. 4. **well′head**, (esp. fig.) chief source, fountainhead; top of a well; **well′spring**, headspring of stream etc.; (fig.) fountainhead, source of perennial emanation or supply. **well** *v.i.* Spring (*up, out, forth*), from or as from fountain.

well[2] (wĕl) *adj.* (**bet·ter, best**). (chiefly predic.) In good health; in satisfactory state or position, satisfactory; advisable, right and proper. ~ *adv.* 1. In good manner or style, satisfactorily, rightly. 2. Thoroughly, carefully, completely, sufficiently; to a considerable degree or extent, quite. 3. Heartily, kindly, approvingly, laudatorily, on good terms. 4. Probably, easily, with reason, wisely, advisably. 5. **as** ~, with equal reason; preferably; in addition; **as** ~ **as**, (esp.) to the same extent, in the same degree, as much ... as; in addition to, both ... and, not only ... but also. 6. In comb., esp. with past and present participles of verbs, and with adjectives ending in *-ed*, as **~-advised**, (esp.) prudent, wary, wise; **~-appointed**, properly equipped or fitted out; **~-balanced**, sensible, sane; equally matched; **~-being**, happy, healthy, or prosperous condition; **well′born**, of noble or distinguished family; **well-bred**, having or displaying good manners, courteous; of good breed; **well-conditioned**, of good disposition, morals, or behavior; sound, healthy, in good physical condition; **well-defined**, clearly indicated or determined; **well-disposed**, (esp.) disposed to be friendly or favorable (*toward, to*); **well-done** (*int.*), exclamation of approval; skillfully or rightly done; (of meat etc.) cooked thoroughly; **well-favored**, good-looking; **well-fed**, appearing to be well nourished; **well-founded**, (esp.) having foundation in fact, based on reason; **well-groomed**, (esp. of persons) with hair, skin, etc., carefully tended; **well-grounded**, well-founded; well-trained in rudiments; **well-heeled**, (colloq.) rich; **well-informed**, having mind fully furnished with general or special knowledge; **well-intentioned**, having, showing, based on, good intentions; **well-knit**, (esp., of person, his frame) strongly and compactly built, not loosely made; **well-known**, widely known; fully or thoroughly known; **well-made**, (of thing) skillfully manufactured; **well-meaning**, well-intentioned (freq. with implication of inefficiency or unwisdom); **well-nigh**, very nearly, almost wholly; **well-off**, fortunately situated; sufficiently rich; **well-preserved**, kept in good condition; (of elderly person) of more youthful appearance than age merits; **well-read**, well-informed by reading, learned (*in*), versed or skilled (*in*); **well-rounded**, symmetrical, (of sentence etc.) full and well-turned; (of person) broadly educated; **well-spoken**, (esp.) having good or ready speech, refined in speech; **well-timed**, timely, opportune; **well-to-do**, prosperous, well off; **well-tried**, often tried or tested with good result; **well-turned**, (esp., of speech) neatly finished, happily expressed; **well-wisher**, one who wishes well to another, a cause, etc.; **well-worn**, (esp.) trite, hackneyed. **well** *int.* Exclamation introducing remark or statement, expressing astonishment, relief, concession, etc., or resumption of talk or subject, qualified recognition of point, expectation, resignation, etc.

we'll (wēl) *contr.* We shall; we will.

Wel·ling·ton[1] (wĕl′ĭngtən). Capital of New Zealand, in North Island.

Wel·ling·ton[2] (wĕl′ĭngtən), **Arthur Wellesley, 1st Duke of** (1769–1852). British general and statesman; led the British forces in the Peninsular War, defeated Napoleon at Waterloo (1815); prime minister 1828–30.

Welsh (wĕlsh, wĕlch) *adj.* Of Wales or its people or language; ~ **corgi**: see CORGI; **Welsh′man** (pl. **-men**), **Welsh′woman** (pl. **-women**), native of Wales; **Welsh rabbit**, dish consisting of seasoned melted or toasted cheese on buttered toast, sometimes incorrectly called **Welsh rarebit. Welsh** *n.* 1. (collect.) People of Wales. 2. Language of Wales, one of the Celtic group of languages.

welsh (wĕlsh, wĕlch) *v.* (also ~ **on**); swindle by not paying debt; fail to meet obligation; fail to pay gambling debt. **welsh′er** *n.*

welt (wĕlt) *n.* 1. Strip of leather sewn between edge of sole and turned-in edge of upper in soling boot or shoe; ribbed or reinforced border of knitted garment. 2. Ridge on flesh, esp. mark of heavy blow or healed wound, weal. ~ *v.t.* 1. Provide with welt. 2. Raise weals on, beat, flog.

wel·ter (wĕl′tər) *v.i.* Roll, wallow; be tossed or tumbled about; lie prostrate *in* (blood or gore); (fig.) be sunk or deeply involved *in*. ~ *n.* State of turmoil or upheaval; surging or confused mass.

welt·er·weight (wĕl′tərwāt) *n.* Boxer of weight between lightweight and middleweight.

The **Western Church** has developed many sects and branches, possibly more so than in any other religion. This splintering has at times, led to bloody conflict.

John Wesley founded a new movement in the church. He preached in the open and is said to have given 40,000 sermons. He founded Methodism in 1784 and had 100,000 followers.

wen (wĕn) *n.* More or less permanent benign tumor on skin, esp. of scalp.

Wen·ces·las[1], **Wen·ces·laus**[1] (wĕn′seslaws) (1361–1419). King of Bohemia (as Wenceslas IV), king of Germany and Holy Roman Emperor (1378–1419).

Wen·ces·las[2], **Wen·ces·laus**[2] (wĕn′seslaws), **St., Duke of Bohemia** (early 10th c.). National saint of Bohemia, commemorated Sept. 28.

wench (wĕnch) *n.* (now dial. or joc.) Girl or young woman. ~ *v.i.* (archaic) Associate with female prostitutes.

Wend (wĕnd) *n.* Member of a Slavonic people of eastern Germany.

wend (wĕnd) *v.* (**wend·ed** or **went, wend·ing**). Direct one's *way*; (archaic) go.

Wend·ish (wĕn′dĭsh) *adj.* Of the Wends or their language. ~ *n.* Western-Slavonic language of the Wends.

went: see GO[1].

wept: see WEEP.

were (wẽr): see BE.

we're (wẽr) *contr.* We are.

weren't (wẽr′ent) *contr.* Were not.

were·wolf, wer·wolf (wẽr′-wo͝olf, wãr′-, wẽr′-) *ns.* (pl. **-wolves** pr. -wo͝olvz). In folklore, human being who changes into a wolf.

Wes·ley (wĕs′lē, wĕz′-). **John** ~ (1703–91), Anglican clergyman, evangelist, and founder of METHODISM; **Charles** ~ (1707–88), his brother, author of many hymns.

Wes·ley·an (wĕs′lēan, wĕz′-) *adj.* & *n.* (Follower) of John Wesley or his teaching. **Wes′ley·an·ism** *n.*

Wes·sex (wĕs′ĭks). 1. Kingdom of West Saxons. 2. Those counties of SW. England, principally Dorset, that are the scene of Thomas Hardy's novels.

west (wĕst) *adv.* Toward, in, the west; **go** ~, (esp.) go to the western states; (fig.) die, perish, be destroyed. **west** *n.* 1. Point on horizon where sun sets at equinox; this direction. 2. Cardinal point of the compass lying opposite east. 3. (usu. the **W**~) That part of a country, district, etc., that lies to the west; Europe and America as dist. from Asia; (esp.) western Europe and America as dist. from communist states of Asia and eastern Europe; states of U.S. west of Mississippi River. **west** *adj.* Lying toward, in, the west; coming from the west (~ **wind**); **W**~ **Germany**: see GERMANY; **W**~ **Point**, town in SE. New York State, on west bank of Hudson River, site of the U.S. Military Academy. **west′ward** *adv.*, *adj.*, & *n.* **west′ward·ly** *adv.* & *adj.* **west′wards** *adv.*

west·er·ly (wĕs′terlē) *adj.* In the west; (of wind) blowing from the west. ~ *adv.* Toward the west. ~ *n.* (pl. **-lies**). West wind.

west·ern (wĕs′tern) *adj.* Of the west; occidental; lying or directed toward the west; (poet.) in, coming from, the west; **W**~, of the West as dist. from communist countries; **W**~ **Church**, Latin or R.C. Ch. (occas. including Anglican Church or all Churches of western Christendom) as dist. from Orthodox Church; **W**~ **Empire**: see ROMAN Empire; **W**~ **Hemisphere**, half of Earth that includes N. and S. Amer. and the surrounding islands and oceans. **western** *n.* (esp.) Film or novel about adventures of cowboys, rustlers, etc., in western parts of N. Amer. **west′ern·er** *n.* (also **W**~) Native, inhabitant, of the west, esp. of western U.S. **west′ern·most** *adj.*

West (wĕst) **Indies.** Chain of islands extending from coast of Florida to Venezuela and enclosing Caribbean Sea; **West Indies Associated States**, group of former British colonies; in 1967 became self-governing territories in association with the United Kingdom, including Antigua, Dominica, St. Lucia, St. Christopher–Nevis-Anguilla, and St. Vincent. **West Indian** *adj.* & *n.*

West (wĕst) **Malaysia.** Federation of 11 states forming part of Malaysia; formerly Malaya, in the Malay Peninsula.

Western Sahara. Arab republic bordered by Morocco and Mauritania. Capital is El-Aauin.

Western Samoa (Sah′mō*a*). Population 155 000. Capital, Apia.

West·min·ster (wĕst′mĭnst*er*). City and inner London borough containing the Houses of Parliament (**Palace of** ~) and many government offices etc.; hence, British parliamentary life or politics; ~ **Abbey**, collegiate church of St. Peter in the city of Westminster.

West Virginia became the 35th State of the U.S.A. in 1863. In the fall, deciduous trees of West Virginia turn on a magnificent display as the leaves change color.

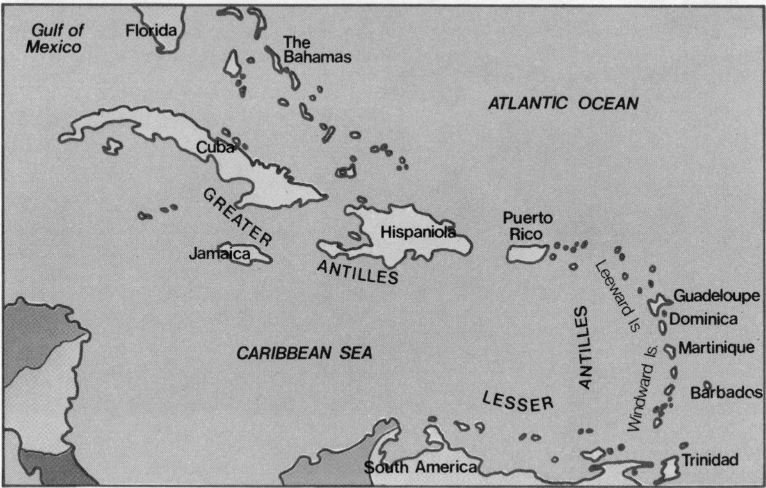

*Named because Columbus believed he had reached India, the **West Indies** is an archipelago whose islands have an area of 100,000 square miles. The Bahamas lies beyond this region.*

*Formerly controlled by the British, the **West Indies** are fast becoming a popular tourist destination. The islands have few natural resources, and arable land is minimal.*

West (wĕst) **Virginia.** South Atlantic state of U.S., admitted to the Union in 1863; capital, Charleston. **West Virginian** *adj.* & *n.*

wet (wĕt) *adj.* (**wet·ter, wet·test**). 1. Soaked, covered, supplied with, etc., water or other liquid; rainy; employing, done by means of, water or other liquid. 2. (colloq.) Permitting or favoring sale of alcoholic liquors. 3. **all ~**, (slang) completely mistaken; **wet'back**, (derog.) illegal immigrant from Mexico to U.S.; **wet blanket**: see BLANKET; **wet bulb thermometer**, one having its bulb covered with wet muslin so that the difference between its reading and that of a dry bulb thermometer indicates the amount of watei vapor in the air; **wet cell**, battery cell having electrolyte in liquid form; **wet fly**, (angling) artificial fly used under water; **wet'lands**, swamps and other damp areas of land; **wet nurse**, woman employed to suckle another's child; **wet-nurse** (*v.t.*) (**-nursed, -nurs·ing**), act as wet nurse to; foster, coddle; **wet pack**, (med.) form of bath, in which patient is wrapped in wet sheets, esp. to reduce fever. **wet'ly** *adv.* **wet'ness** *n.* **wet'tish** *adj.* **wet** *v.t.* (**wet** or **wet·ted, wet·ting**). Make wet; **wet'ting agent**, substance that helps water to spread or penetrate. **wet** *n.* Moisture, liquid that wets something, rainy weather; (colloq.) person in favor of allowing sale of alcoholic drinks. **wet'ter** *n.*

weth·er (wĕdh'*er*) *n.* Castrated male sheep.

we've (wēv) *contr.* We have.

wf., w.f. *abbrevs.* (print.) Wrong font.

WFTU, W.F.T.U. *abbrevs.* World Federation of Trade Unions.

whack (hwăk, wăk) *n.* Heavy resounding blow, esp. with stick; **have, take, a ~ at**, (colloq.) attempt; **out of ~**, (colloq.) out of order. **whack** *v.t.* Beat or strike vigorously.

whale[1] (hwāl, wāl) *n.* (pl. **whales,** collect. **whale**). Any marine mammal of order Cetacea, with short forelimbs and tail with horizontal flukes, esp. one of the larger of these, hunted for oil, whalebone, etc.; (colloq.) something impressive in size or amount, or superlative in quality (**~ of a** ...); **blue ~**, large bluish-gray whale, hunted for its oil; **Greenland ~**, whalebone whale, with very large head; **right ~**, whalebone whale, esp. of genus *Balaena*; **whale'back**, anything shaped like back of whale, esp. arched structure over deck of ship, kind of steamboat, much used on the Great Lakes in early 20th c., with spoon bow and main decks covered in and rounded over; **whale′boat**, long narrow rowboat, pointed at both ends, used in whale fishing or carried as lifeboat; **whale′bone**, elastic horny substance growing in series of thin parallel plates in upper jaw of some whales and used in feeding, baleen; strip of this, used as stiffening in clothes etc.; **whalebone whale**, whale of suborder Mysiceti having whalebone plates in upper jaw; **whale oil**, oil obtained from blubber of whales. **whale** *v.i.* (**whaled, whal·ing**). Fish for whales. **whal′er** *n.* Ship, man, engaged in whale fishing.

whale[2] (hwāl, wāl) *v.* (**whaled, whal·ing**). Beat, thrash; perform action vigorously or vehemently.

wham (hwăm, wăm) *int.* Expressing sound of forcible impact. ~ *n.* & *v.* (**whammed, wham·ming**). (Make, strike with) such sound.

wham·my (hwăm′ē, wăm′ē) *n.* (slang) (Thing with) supernatural power, esp. one bringing bad luck.

whang (hwăng, wăng) *v.* (colloq.) Strike heavily and loudly; (of drum etc.) sound (as) under heavy blow. ~ *n.* Whanging sound or blow.

wharf (hwōrf, wōrf) *n.* (pl. **wharves** pr. hwōrvz, wōrvz, **wharfs**). Substantial structure of stone, timber, etc., at water's edge for loading or unloading of ships lying alongside. ~ *v.t.* Discharge (cargo), accommodate (ships), at wharf. **wharf′age** *n.* Provision of accommodation at wharf; charge made for this; wharves collectively.

Whar·ton (hwōr′ten, wōr′-), **Edith** (1862–1937). American novelist, author of *The House of Mirth, The Age of Innocence, Ethan Frome*, etc.

what (hwŭt, hwŏt, wŭt, wŏt) *pron.* 1. (interrog.) What thing(s)?; what did you say?; ~ **about?**, what is the news concerning?; how do you dispose of the question of?; what do you think of?; ~ **for?**, for what reason or purpose?; ~ (would result) **if?**; ~ **of it?**, the fact has no immediate relevance or interest. 2. **know ~'s what**, have good judgment; know the matter in hand, know what is fitting or profitable; **what′not**, other things of the same kind, anything; some indefinite or trivial thing; (19th c.) piece of furniture with shelves for knickknacks; **what's-his** (or **-her**)-**name, what d'you-call-it**, person, thing, whose name the speaker cannot recall. 3. (exclam.) What thing(s)!; how much! 4. (rel.) That or those which; the thing(s) that; anything that; a thing that. **what** *adj.* 1. (interrog.) Asking for selection from indefinite number or for specification of amount, number, kind, etc. 2. (exclam.) How great, how strange, how remarkable in some way; (before adjectives) how. 3. The ... that, any ... that, as much or many ... as. ~ *adv.* 1. (interrog.) To what extent or degree?; how much? 2. ~ **with**, because of, considering. **what** *int.* Exclamation of surprise.

what·ev·er (hwŭtĕv′*er*, hwŏt-, wŭt-, wŏt-) *pron.* Anything that; any quantity etc. that; no matter what; something of the same kind; (colloq.) as emphatic extension of

***Whales** are renowned for their high intelligence, and are used for entertainment at places such as Sea World, San Diego, where this killer whale has been taught to perform.*

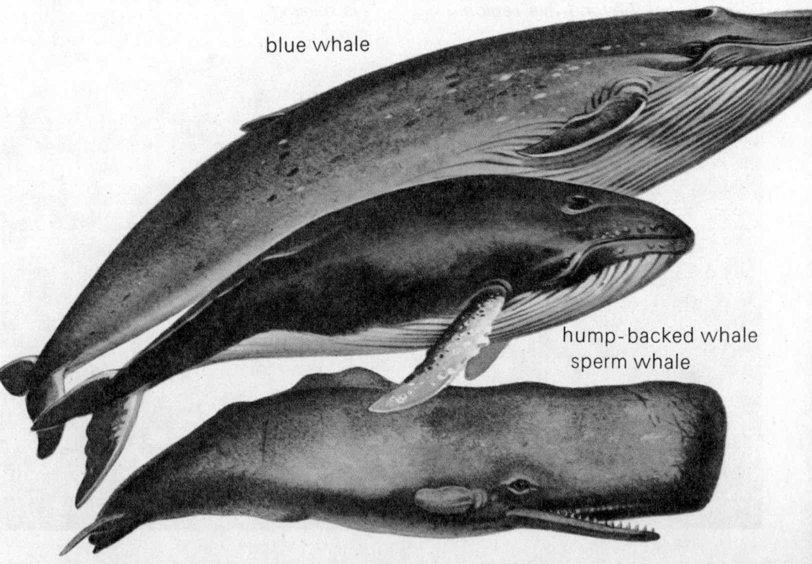

*Right from top to bottom: Blue, humpback and sperm **whales.** Populations of these huge marine mammals have been greatly reduced by modern methods of hunting. After killing, they are taken to shore bases where flensers (above) strip the blubber for making **whale oil.***

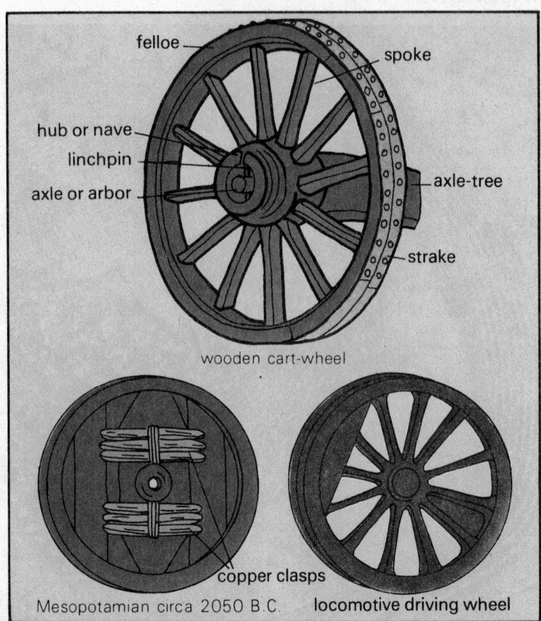

*Above left: The **wheatear** migrates to Britain each summer from tropical Africa and India. It is about 6 ins. long and is mainly insectivorous. Once they were killed for food.*

*The earliest representation of a **wheel** on a vehicle is from Uruk, Mesopotamia about 3200 B.C. It is believed that the spoked wheel may have been developed later in Syria.*

"what" implying perplexity or surprise. ~ *adj.* All; any quantity etc. of; (with negatives) at all.

what·so·ev·er (hwŭtsōĕv'*er*, hwŏt-, wŭt-, wŏt-) *pron.* & *adj.* (emphat.) Whatever.

wheat (hwēt, wēt) *n.* Cereal plant of genus *Triticum*, esp. *T. aestivum*, closely related to barley and rye; its grain, furnishing meal or flour, the chief ingredient of bread in temperate countries; ~ **germ**, embryo of wheat kernel, added to breads, cereals, etc. for additional vitamins. **wheat'en** *adj.* Of wheat, of grain or flour of wheat.

wheat·ear (hwēt'ēr, wēt'-) *n.* Small passerine bird (*Oenanthe oenanthe*) of N. parts of Europe, Asia, and Amer., with black wings and distinctive white rump and upper tail feathers. [prob. *whit eeres* white arse]

Wheat·stone (hwēt'stōn, wēt'-), **Sir Charles** (1802–75). English physicist and inventor; ~ **bridge**, device utilizing galvanometer for comparison of electrical resistances.

whee·dle (hwē'del, wē'-) *v.* (**-dled, -dling**). Entice or persuade by soft words or flattery; obtain by such action; use soft words or flattery. **whee'dler** *n.*

wheel (hwēl, wēl) *n.* 1. Circular frame or disk arranged to revolve on axis and used to facilitate motion of vehicle or for various mechanical purposes; wheellike structure or thing; instrument or appliance with wheel as essential part, e.g. bicycle; revolving firework in form of spiral; ancient instrument of torture. 2. Motion as of wheel, circular motion, motion of line as on pivoted end, esp. as military maneuver; **left, right,** ~, words of command to troops in line to swing around on left, right, flank as pivot. 3. **on ~s**, (fig.) with rapid easy motion; **~s within ~s**, intricate machinery; indirect or secret agencies. 4. **wheel'barrow**, shallow open box with shafts and one wheel for carrying small loads on; **wheel'base**, distance between points of contact with ground or rail of front and back wheels of vehicle; **wheel'chair**, invalid's chair on wheels; **wheel'horse**, horse harnessed next to wheels and behind another; (fig.) steady, reliable worker; **wheel'house**, structure enclosing large wheel, esp. (naut.) superstructure containing steering wheel; **wheel lock**, (gun with) lock in which powder was fired by friction of small wheel against flint; **wheel'wright**, one who makes or mends wooden wheels of farm vehicles. **wheel** *v.* 1. Turn on axis or pivot, (cause to) move in circle or spiral; change direction, face another way, turn *around* or *about*. 2. Push or pull (wheelchair, bicycle, etc.); ~ **and deal**, engage in political or commercial scheming. **wheeled** *adj.* (esp.) Having wheels. **wheel'less** *adj.*

wheel·er (hwē'l*er*, wē'-) *n.* (esp.) Wheel horse; (in comb.) vehicle etc. having specified no. of wheels, e.g. *three-~*; **~-dealer**, (colloq.) schemer.

Wheel·er (hwē'l*er*, wē'-), **William Almon** (1819–87). Vice president of the U.S. under Rutherford B. Hayes, 1877–81.

wheeze (hwēz, wēz) *v.* (**wheezed, wheez·ing**). Breathe hard with audible whistling or piping sound from dryness or obstruction in throat; utter with wheezing. ~ *n.* 1. Sound of wheezing. 2. (orig., theatr. slang) Joke, esp. one frequently repeated; (slang) catch phrase, trick or dodge. **wheez'y** *adj.* (**wheez·i·er, wheez·i·est**). **wheez'i·ly** *adv.* **wheez'i·ness** *n.*

whelk[1] (hwĕlk, wĕlk) *n.* Marine gastropod mollusk of *Buccinum* and allied genera, with spiral shell, esp. *B. undatum*, common in Europe and N. Amer. and much used for food.

whelk[2] (hwĕlk, wĕlk) *n.* Pimple.

whelp (hwĕlp, wĕlp) *n.* Young dog, puppy; (archaic) young of lion, tiger, bear, and wolf; (derog.) youth. ~ *v.* Bring forth (whelp(s)).

when (hwĕn, wĕn) *adv.* (interrog.) At what time, on what occasion, in what case or circumstances?; **say** ~, (in pouring drink etc.) tell me when to stop. **when** *conj.* At the time that, on the occasion etc., that; at which time etc., and (just) then; seeing that, considering that, since; whereas. ~ *pron.* What or which time.

whence (hwĕns, wĕns) *adv.* & *conj.* (literary) From where, from what or which place, source, circumstance, etc.; (with *place* etc.) from which.

when·ev·er (hwĕnĕv'*er*, wĕn-) *adv.* & *conj.* At whatever time, on whatever occasion; every time that.

when·so·ev·er (hwĕnsōĕv'*er*, wĕn-) *adv.* & *conj.* (emphat.) Whenever.

where (hwār, wār) *adv.* (interrog.) At or in what place, position,

The term **'whipsnake'** is a common name applied on the basis of appearance. Above: A southern European Coluber viridiflavus which is a constrictor. Others are venomous.

A species of curlew, the **whimbrel** is more oriented to a terrestrial existence and spends less time than the larger curlew in marshy and coastal locations.

or circumstances?; in what respect, in what, from what source, etc.?; to what place?; in comb. with prepositions, with the general meaning of the preposition followed by *what* or *which* (chiefly archaic or formal), as **whereat', whereby', where'fore, wherein', whereof', whereon', whereto', whereupon', where'-upon, wherewith'. where** *conj.* In, at, to, etc., place in or at which; and there. ~ *pron.* What place, the place in which.

where·a·bouts (hwār'*a*bowts, wār'-) *adv.* About where, in or near what place or position? ~ *n.pl.* (Approximate) position or situation (of), place in or near which person or thing is.

where·as (hwārăz', wār-) *conj.* In view or consideration of the fact that, inasmuch as (chiefly in preamble of legal or other formal document); while on the contrary, but on the other hand.

where·fore (hwār'fōr, -fōr, wār'-) *adv.* For what?; for what purpose, reason, cause, or end, why?; on which account, for which reason, and therefore; (archaic) because of which, in consequence or as a result of which.

where·so·ev·er (hwārsōĕv'*er*, wār-) *adv.* (emphat.) Wherever.

wher·ev·er (hwārĕv'*er*, wār-) *adv.* At or to whatever place etc.

where·with·al (hwār'wĭdhawl, wār'-) *adv.* (archaic) Wherewith. ~ *n.* (colloq.) Means (esp. pecuniary).

whet (hwĕt, wĕt) *n.* Sharpening; something that whets the appetite, esp. small drink of liquor as appetizer. ~ *v.t.* (**whet·ted, whet·ting**). Sharpen; make (interest, wits, appetite, etc.) (more) acute, keen, or eager; **whet'stone**, shaped stone, natural or artificial, for giving sharp edge to cutting tools; any hard fine-grained rock from which whetstones are made. **whet'ter** *n.*

wheth·er (hwĕdh'*er*, wĕdh'-) *conj.* Introducing dependent question or its equivalent expressing doubt, choice, etc., between alternations, or, freq. as ordinary sign of indirect interrogation (*if*). ~ *pron.* & *adj.* (archaic) Which of the two.

whew (hwū) *int.* Exclamation of astonishment, consternation, etc.

whey (hwā, wā) *n.* Serum or watery part remaining after separation of curd from milk, esp. in cheese-making. **whey'ey** (hwā'ē, wā-) *adj.*

which (hwĭch, wĭch) *adj.* & *pron.* 1. (interrog.) What one(s) of a stated or implied set of persons, things, or alternatives. 2. (rel.) Relative adjective and pronoun, introducing additional statement about the antecedent. = "and that (it, they, etc.)," "that."

which·ev·er (hwĭchĕv'*er*, wĭch-) *adj.* & *pron.* Any or either (of definite set of persons or things) that . . . ; no matter which.

which·so·ev·er (hwĭchsōĕv'*er*, wĭch-) *adj.* & *pron.* (emphat.) Whichever.

whiff (hwĭf, wĭf) *n.* 1. Puff, waft, of air, smoke, odor, etc. 2. Slight smell (also fig.). 3. ~ **of grapeshot**, (fig.) violent suppression of riot, protest, etc. **whiff** *v.* Blow or puff lightly; (baseball slang) strike out.

whif·fle (hwĭf'*e*l, wĭf'-) *v.* (**-fled, -fling**). 1. Puff lightly; move as if blown by puff of air. 2. Make light whistling sound. ~ *n.* Slight movement of air.

whif·fle·tree (hwĭf'*e*ltrē, wĭf'-) *n.* Crossbar pivoted in middle, to ends of which traces are fastened in cart, plow, etc.

Whig (hwĭg, wĭg) *adj.* & *n.* 1. (Member) of political party in Great Britain that, after the Revolution of 1688, aimed at subordinating the power of the Crown to that of Parliament and the upper classes, passed the 1832 Reform Bill, and in the 19th c. was succeeded by the Liberal party. 2. (Amer. hist.) Supporter of the Revolution. 3. (Member) of political party formed *c*1834 in opp. to Democratic Party and remaining one of the two chief U.S. parties until its collapse in 1852. **Whig'-ger·y, Whig'gism** *ns.* **Whig'gish** *adj.* **Whig'gish·ly** *adv.* **Whig'-gish·ness** *n.* [used earlier of Scotch Covenanters, prob. short for *whiggamer, -more*, of uncertain origin]

while (hwīl, wīl) *n.* Space of time, esp. time spent in doing something (now only in **worth (one's)** ~, worth doing, advantageous); **a** ~, (colloq.) a considerable time, some time; **all the, this,** ~, during the whole time (that). **while** *conj.* During the time that, for as long as, at the same time as; when on the contrary, whereas, although; and at the same time, besides that. ~ *v.t.* (**whiled, whil·ing**). Pass (time etc.) *away* in leisurely manner or without weariness.

whi·lom (hwī′lom, wī′-) *adv.* & *adj.* (archaic) (That existed, or was such) at some past time; former(ly).

whilst (hwīlst, wīlst) *adv.* & *conj.* (Brit.) = WHILE.

whim (hwĭm, wĭm) *n.* Sudden fancy, caprice, freakish notion.

whim·brel (hwĭm′brel, wĭm′-) *n.* Small curlew (*Numenius phaeopus*) of both Amer. and European coasts.

whim·per (hwĭm′per, wĭm′-) *v.i.* Cry querulously, whine softly. ~ *n.* Feeble whining broken cry. **whim′per·ing·ly** *adv.*

whim·si·cal (hwĭm′zĭkal, wĭm′-) *adj.* Capricious, fanciful, characterized by whims. **whim′si·cal·ly** *adv.* **whim·si·cal′i·ty** *n.* (pl. **-ties**).

whim·sy (hwĭm′zē, wĭm-) *n.* (pl. **-sies**). Crotchet, whim.

whine (hwīn, wīn) *n.* Long-drawn complaining cry (as) of dog; suppressed nasal tone; feeble, mean, or undignified complaint. ~ *v.* (**whined, whin·ing**). Utter whine(s); utter, complain, whiningly. **whin′y** *adj.* (**whin·i·er, whin·i·est**) **whin′er** *n.* **whin′ing·ly** *adv.*

whin·ny (hwĭn′ē, wĭn′-) *v.i.* (**-nied, -ny·ing**). Neigh gently or joyfully. ~ *n.* Whinnying sound.

whip (hwĭp, wĭp) *n.* 1. Instrument for flogging or beating, or for urging on horse etc., consisting usu. of lash attached to short or long stick. 2. Official, in legislative body, appointed to maintain discipline among members of his party, give them necessary information, and secure their attendance esp. when a bill is up for voting. 3. Whipping or lashing motion, esp. slight bending movement produced by sudden strain. 4. Dessert made with whipped cream or egg whites. 5. **whip′cord**, thin tough kind of hempen cord for whiplashes etc.; close-woven worsted fabric with fine close diagonal ribs, used for riding breeches etc.; **whip hand**, hand in which whip is held; (fig.) upper hand, control (*of*), advantage; **whip′lash**, lash of whip; object resembling this; **whiplash injury**, injury to neck caused by sudden jerk of head in collision of vehicle etc.; **whip′saw**, saw with very long narrow tapering blade; two-man crosscut saw; (fig.) swindle or defeat (opponent) by collusion of two poker players, political allies, etc.; **whip scorpion**, arachnid resembling scorpion but without sting and usu. with lashlike organ at end of body; **whip′snake, whip snake**, any of various slender snakes; **whip stitch**, (sew with) whipping stitch (*v.* sense 3). **whip** *v.* (**whipped, whip·ping**). 1. Move suddenly or briskly, snatch, dart; make *up* quickly or hastily. 2. Beat, drive or urge on, (as) with whip; lash, flog; beat up (eggs, cream, etc.) into froth; (angling) throw line or bait on water with movement like stroke of whip; (colloq.) overcome, defeat. 3. Bind around (rope, stick, etc.) with close covering of twine, thread, etc.; sew over and over, overcast, esp. hem, or gather (fabric) by overcasting rolled edge with fine stitches. 4. ~ **graft**, (make) graft with slit in end of both scion and stock, tongue of each being inserted in slit of the other.

whip·per·snap·per (hwĭp′er-snăper, wĭp′-) *n.* (colloq.) Small child; young and insignificant but impertinent person.

whip·pet (hwĭp′ĭt, wĭp′-) *n.* Small dog like greyhound used for racing, and orig. bred (19th c.) in N. of England from cross between greyhound and terrier or spaniel.

whip·ping (hwĭp′ĭng, wĭp′-) *n.* (esp.) Overcasting of hem; ~ **boy**, (hist.) boy educated with young prince and chastised in his stead (also fig.); ~ **post**, post to which offenders were tied to be whipped.

whip·poor·will (hwĭp′erwĭl, wĭp′-, hwĭperwĭl′, wĭp-) *n.* (pl. **-wills,** collect. **-will**). Nocturnal insectivorous bird (*Caprimulgus vociferus*) of eastern N. Amer.; an unusually skillful flier. [f. its cry]

whir (hwẽr, wẽr) *n.* & *v.i.* (**whirred, whir·ring**). (Make) continuous buzzing or vibratory sound, as of bird's rapidly fluttering wings, swiftly turning wheel, etc.

whirl (hwẽrl, wẽrl) *v.* Swing around and around, revolve rapidly; send, travel, swiftly in orbit or curve; convey, go, rapidly in wheeled conveyance; (of brain, senses, etc.) be giddy, seem to spin around; **whirl′pool**, part of river, sea, etc., where water is in constant and usu. rapid circular motion; **whirlpool bath**, therapeutic bath in which current of hot water is swirled by agitating device around immersed body or parts of body; **whirl′wind**, mass of air whirling rapidly around and around and moving progressively over surface of land or water (also fig. of violent motion); tornado; (also attrib.) hurried, intense and hasty; **whirl′ybird**, (slang) helicopter. **whirl** *n.* Whirling, swift, or violent movement; disturbance, commotion; distracted or dizzy state. **whirl′er** *n.*

whirl·i·gig (hwẽr′lĭgĭg, wẽr′-) *n.* Spinning toy like sails of windmill revolving on stick; merry-go-round; revolving motion.

whisk (hwĭsk, wĭsk) *n.* 1. Bunch of twigs, grass, hair, bristles, etc., for brushing or dusting; instrument for beating up eggs, cream, etc., into a froth; slender hairlike part or appendage, as on tails of certain insects etc.; panicle of certain plants, esp. common millet. 2. Quick sweeping movement (as) of whisk, animal's tail, etc. ~ *v.* Convey, go, move with light rapid sweeping motion; brush or sweep lightly and rapidly from surface; beat up (eggs, cream, etc.), esp. with whisk.

whisk·er (hwĭs′ker, wĭs′-) *n.* 1. (usu. pl.) Hair on cheeks or sides of face of man. 2. Each of set of projecting hairs or bristles on upper lip or about mouth of cat or other animals, birds, etc. **whisk′ered, whisk′er·y** *adjs.*

whis·key, Brit. and Canadian **whis·ky** (hwĭs′kē, wĭs′-) *ns.* (pl.

*Known by various names around the world — tornado, twister willy-willy — **whirlwinds** can be devastating in settled districts. This one in Kenya caused minimal damage.*

*Influenced by Courbet and prints of Japanese painters, **Whistler** was concerned with color as displayed in 'Stormy Sunset' (above). However, his work was noted for its individuality and was not linked to any movement.*

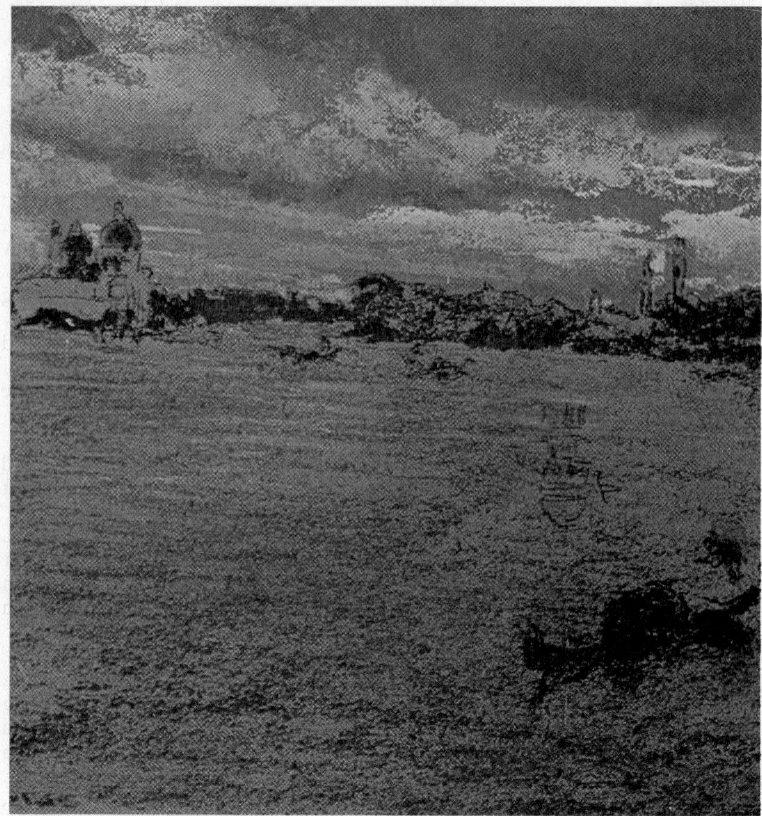

-keys, -kies). Alcoholic liquor distilled, orig. in Scotland and Ireland, from malted barley, rye, corn, or other grains; drink of whiskey; ~ **jack** = CANADA jay; ~ **sour**, cocktail of whiskey, lemon juice, and sugar.

whis·per (hwĭs′p*e*r, wĭs′-) *n.* Speech or vocal sound without vibration of vocal cords; remark uttered thus; soft rustling sound; insinuation, rumor, hint. ~ *v.* Utter in whisper, esp. for sake of secrecy; communicate etc. quietly or confidentially; (of leaves etc.) make soft rustling sound;

whist (hwĭst, wĭst) *n.* Game of cards, played (usu.) by two pairs of opponents with pack of 52 cards, in which one suit is trumps and tricks are taken by highest card of suit led or highest trump.

whis·tle (hwĭs′*e*l, wĭs′-) *n.* 1. Tubular wind instrument of wood, metal, etc., producing shrill tone by forcing air or steam against a sharp edge or into a bell and causing it to vibrate, used for giving signal or alarm; also as musical toy, usu. of tin and pierced with six holes; (joc., colloq.) mouth or throat (esp. in **wet one's** ~, take a drink); ~ **stop**, (colloq.) small unimportant town on railroad; pause of train at such a station for politician to make speech [from practice of announcing stop at country place by sounding train whistle]. 2. Whistling, clear shrill sound produced by forcing breath through lips contracted to narrow opening; similar sound made by whistle or pipe; clear shrill note of bird; any similar sound, as of wind blowing through trees or missile flying through air. **whistle** *v.* (**-tled, -tling**). Make sound of whistle with mouth, esp. as call or signal, expression of derision, contempt, astonishment, enthusiasm, etc.; utter, produce, clear shrill sound or note; blow whistle; produce, utter, by whistling; call, send, (*away, off, up*) by whistling; ~ **for**, (colloq.) seek or expect in vain, go without.

whis·tler (hwĭs′l*e*r, wĭs′-) *n.* One who whistles; (local) any of various whistling birds; (also **whistling marmot**) marmot (*Marmota caligata*) common in mountains of northwestern N. Amer.

Whis·tler (hwĭs′l*e*r, wĭs′-), **James Abbott McNeill** (1834–1903). American-born painter, etcher, and wit, active chiefly in England.

whit (hwĭt, wĭt) *n.* (chiefly with neg.) Particle, least possible amount.

white (hwīt, wīt) *adj.* (**whit·er, whit·est**). Of the color of snow or milk, of color produced by reflection or transmission of all kinds of light in proportions in which they exist in complete visible spectrum, without apparent absorption; of some color approaching this, pale, less dark than other things of the same kind; (fig.) innocent, unstained, harmless; of a light-skinned race or people; Caucasian; (pol., usu. Russian) of royalist, counterrevolutionary, or reactionary tendency (opp. RED); ~ **ant**, termite; **white′bait** (pl. **-bait**), any of various small silvery-white fish cooked and eaten whole; **white bear**, polar bear; **white′cap**, white-crested wave; **white-collar**, engaged in, being, nonmanual work; **white corpuscle**, (also **white blood cell, white blood corpuscle**) leucocyte; **white dwarf**, one of class of small stars of great density radiating white light; **white-eye** (pl. **-eyes**), Old World passerine bird (family Zosteropidae) with white ring around eye; **white elephant**, Indian elephant with pale-colored skin, venerated as rarity in Siam etc.; (fig.) burdensome or useless possession (from story that kings of Siam made presents of these animals to those whom they wished to ruin by cost of their maintenance); **white feather**, symbol or emblem of cowardice (from white feather in gamecock's tail, held to show that he is not purebred); **white′fish** (pl. **-fish, -fish·es**), any light-colored or silvery fish, as cod, haddock, whiting, etc.; lake fish of *Coregonus* and allied genera, resembling salmon and valued as food; **White Friar**, Carmelite; **white gold**, white-colored alloy of gold, esp. alloy with nickel and zinc, resembling platinum; **white-haired** (or **-headed**) **boy**, favorite; **white heat**, degree of temperature (higher than red heat) at which body radiates white light (freq. fig. of passions etc.); **white-hot**, at white heat; **White House**, official residence of U.S. president, Washington, D.C.; **white lead**, basic lead carbonate, a heavy white powder, used as white pigment; **white lie**, innocent, harmless, or trivial lie, fib; **white man's burden**, (hist.) supposed task of leading subject colonial people of dark races; **white meat**, light-colored meat of poultry; **white metal**, white or silver-colored alloy, esp. one that is easily fusible and so suitable for lining high-speed bearings; **White Nile**: see NILE; **white noise**, almost inaudible sound containing many frequencies with approximately equal energies; **white′out**, atmospheric condition, esp. in polar regions, marked by dense snow cloud and total obscuration of physical features; **white paper**,

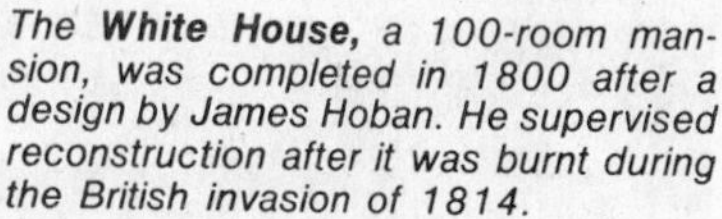

*The **White House,** a 100-room mansion, was completed in 1800 after a design by James Hoban. He supervised reconstruction after it was burnt during the British invasion of 1814.*

governmental report disclosing and explaining official position; **white race**, (loosely or pop.) Caucasian people; **White Russia**, Byelorussia; **White Russian**, (native, language) of White Russia; **white sale**: see SALE; **white sapphire**, colorless variety of sapphire; **white sauce**, sauce of flour or cornstarch, milk, and butter, variously flavored; **White Sea**, gulf of Arctic Ocean in U.S.S.R.; **white slave**, woman held unwillingly for purpose of prostitution, esp. one transported from one state or country to another; **white slaver, slavery** (*ns.*); **white-tailed deer**, N. Amer. deer (*Odocoileus virginianus*) having a tail white on the underside; **white´thorn**, hawthorn; **white´-throat, white-throated sparrow**, N. Amer. sparrow (*Zorotrichia albicollis*) with sweet plaintive song and white patch on throat; **white´wall**, rubber automobile tire with white band on outer wall; **white´wash**, liquid composition of lime and water or whiting, size, and water, for whitening walls, ceilings, etc.; (fig.) glossing over person's or institution's faults; **white´wash** (*v.*), apply whitewash to (lit. and fig.). **white´ly** *adv.* **white´ness** *n.* **whit´ish** *adj.* **white** *n.* White or light-colored part of anything; white or nearly white color; white pigment; white clothes or material; translucent viscid fluid surrounding yolk of egg, becoming white when coagulated; sclerotic coat, white part of eyeball surrounding colored iris; member of a light-skinned race or people, Caucasian; white butterfly, pigeon, pig, etc.; member of political party called "white," reactionary, legitimist, extreme conservative; player having white (or light-colored) pieces in chess etc.

White·field (hwīt´fēld, wīt´-), **George** (1714–70). English religious reformer, one of the founders of METHODISM, who engaged in evangelical preaching in N. Amer., adopted Calvinistic views, and formed a party of Calvinistic Methodists.

whit·en (hwī´ten, wī´-) *v.* Make, become, white or whiter. **whit´en·er, whit´en·ing** *ns.*

White (hwīt, wīt) **Sands National Monument.** Area 219 sq. mi. (567 sq. km) in south central New Mexico containing world's largest surface deposit of gypsum; **White Sands Proving Grounds,** area SW. of White Sands National Monument used as test range for missiles; site of explosion of first atom bomb, 1945.

whit·ey (hwī´tē, wī´-) *n.* 1. (slang) Very blond man or boy. 2. (slang, derog.) White person or white people as group.

whith·er (hwĭdh´er, wĭdh´-) *adv.* (archaic) To where.

whit·ing[1] (hwī´tĭng, wī´-) *n.* Preparation of finely powdered chalk used for paints, putty, etc.

whit·ing[2] (hwī´tĭng, wī´-) *n.* (pl. **-ings**, collect. **-ing**). Common

*The **golden whistler** (Pachycephala pectoralis) is found only in coastal regions of eastern, south-eastern and south-western Australia where it inhabits fairly dense woodland.*

*The large copper stills at Cardew Distillery in Scotland. Malted barley liquor is heated by furnaces beneath the stills and the **whiskey** produced is colorless. The color is added before bottling.*

Above left: The cricket player W. G. Grace defending his **wicket.** Dimensions of a two-stump wicket were defined in 1744 and a third was added in 1776. The size was increased later.

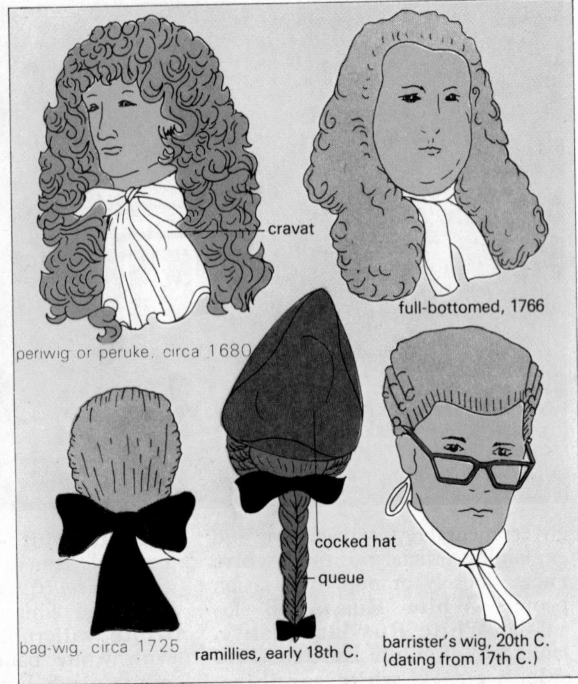

The use of a **wig** can be traced to ancient times. Probably they reached their greatest size in the late 17th and 18th centuries and then gradually became smaller and needed less attention.

small codlike fish (genus *Menticirrhus*) with pearly white flesh, used as food; fish resembling this.

Whit·man (hwĭt′m*a*n, wĭt′-), **Walt(er)** (1819–92). Amer. poet; author of *Leaves of Grass, Drum Taps*, etc.

Whit·ney[1] (hwĭt′nē, wĭt′-), **Eli** (1765–1825). Amer. inventor of cotton gin, 1793.

Whit·ney[2] (hwĭt′nē, wĭt′-), **Mount.** Highest mountain, 14,495 ft. (4,421 m), in U.S., excluding Alaska, in Sierra Nevada range in E. central California.

Whit·ti·er (hwĭt′ēer, wĭt′-), **John Greenleaf** (1807–92). Amer. poet; author of *The Barefoot Boy, Snow-Bound, Barbara Frietchie*, etc.

whit·tle (hwĭt′*e*l, wĭt′-) *v.* (**-tled, -tling**). Dress, pare, with knife; cut thin slices or shavings from surface of, make or shape thus; (fig.) reduce amount or effect of by successive abstractions, pare *down*, take *away* by degrees.

whiz, whizz (hwĭz, wĭz) *vbs.* (**whizzed, whiz·zing**). (Cause to) make sound as of body rushing through air; move swiftly (as) with such sound. **whiz** *n.* Act, sound, of whizzing; (slang) person of outstanding skill, wizard.

WHO *abbrev.* World Health Organization.

who (hōō) *pron.* (obj. **whom** pr. hōōm, poss. **whose** pr. hōōz). 1. (interrog.) What or which person(s); what sort of person(s) in regard to origin, position, authority, etc.; *Who's Who*, title of reference book of contemporary biography (first issued 1849) and of similar works. 2. (rel.) (Person or persons) that; and, but, he (she, they); (archaic) the or any person(s) that.

whoa (hwō, wō) *int.* Word of command to horse etc. to stop or stand still.

who·dun·it (hōōdŭn′ĭt) *n.* (slang) Detective or mystery story.

who·ev·er (hōōĕv′*er*) *pron.* Whatever person(s), any(one) who; no matter who.

whole (hōl) *adj.* In sound condition, uninjured, not broken or divided, intact; integral, without fractions; undiminished, without subtraction; all, all of; **with one's ~ heart**, heartily, with concentrated effort, etc., hence **whole′heart′ed, whole′heart′edly, whole′heart′edness; go the whole hog**, go to the utmost limit; act etc. without reservation; **whole milk**, milk as given by the cow, containing all its butterfat and other elements; **whole note**, note having duration of four beats; **whole number**, number that can be got from zero by adding or subtracting units; **whole-wheat**, made from the entire wheat kernel. **whole** *n.* Full, complete, or total amount (*of*); complete thing; organic unity, complex system, total made up of parts. **whole′ness** *n.*

whole·sale (hōl′sāl) *n.* Selling of articles in large quantities to be retailed by others. ~ *adj.* Selling by wholesale; pertaining to sale in bulk; unlimited, indiscriminate; doing, done, largely or profusely. ~ *adv.* In large quantities, in bulk; in abundance, extensively, indiscriminately. **whole′sal·er** *n.* One who sells wholesale. **wholesale** *v.* (**-saled, -sal·ing**).

whole·some (hōl′s*o*m) *adj.* Promoting, conducive to, health or well-being; beneficial, salutary, salubrious; not morbid, healthy. **whole′some·ly** *adv.* **whole′some·ness** *n.*

who'll (hōōl) *contr.* Who shall; who will.

whol·ly (hō′lē, hōl′lē) *adv.* Entirely, completely, to the full extent, altogether; exclusively.

whom (hōōm) *pron.* Objective (accus., dat.) case of WHO.

whom·ev·er (hōōmĕv′*er*) *pron.* Objective case of WHOEVER.

whom·so·ev·er (hōōmsōĕv′*er*) *pron.* Objective case of WHOSOEVER.

whoop (hōōp, hwōōp, wōōp) *int.* Cry expressing excitement, exultation, etc. (used esp. by N. Amer. Indians as signal or war cry). ~ *n.* Cry of "whoop"; characteristic drawing-in of breath after coughing in whooping cough. ~ *v.i.* Utter whoop; **whoop·ing** (hōō′pĭng, hōōp′ĭng) **cough**, infectious disease, esp. of children, with violent convulsive cough followed by whoop, caused by a bacillus, *Haemophilus pertussis*; **whoop'ing crane**, very large white wading bird (*Grus americana*), nearly extinct. **whoop'er** *n.*

whoop·ee (hwōōp′ē′, wōōp′ē′, hwōō′pē′, wōō′-) *int.* (slang) Exclamation of exuberant joy. ~

(hwo͝op´ē, wo͝op´ē, hwo͞o´pē, wo͞o´-) *n.* (slang) Cry of "whoopee"; **make ~**, (slang) rejoice noisily or hilariously, have a good time.

whoosh (hwo͞osh, wo͞osh, hwo͝osh, wo͝osh) *int.* Expressing sound of rushing air or water. ~ *n.* & *v.* (Make or cause) such sound.

whop (hwŏp, wŏp) *v.t.* (**whopped, whop·ping**). (slang) Thrash, defeat, overcome. **whop'ping** *adj.* Very large or great. **whop'per** *n.* Very large thing; monstrous falsehood.

whore (hōr, hōr, hoor) *n.* Female prostitute. **whore'dom** *n.* Fornication. **whore'mong·er** *n.* Fornicator; pimp. **whore** *v.i.* (**whored, whor·ing**). Have to do with whore(s), fornicate; (fig., archaic, after Deut. 31) **go a-whoring after strange gods** etc., practice idolatry or iniquity. **whor'ish** *adj.*

whorl (hwẽrl, wẽrl, hwōrl, wōrl) *n.* Small flywheel or pulley on spindle to steady its motion; convolution, coil, something suggesting whirling movement, esp. (of fingerprint) complete circle formed by central papillary ridges; each turn of spiral shell or any spiral structure; (bot.) ring of leaves, flowers, etc., springing from stem or axis at same level. **whorled** *adj.*

who's (ho͞oz) *contr.* Who has; who is.

whose (ho͞oz) *pron.* Possessive case of WHO.

who·so·ev·er (ho͞osōĕv´*er*) *pron.* (emphat.) Whoever.

why (hwī, wī) *adv.* 1. (interrog.) On what ground, for what reason, with what purpose. 2. (rel.) On account of which. ~ *n.* (pl. **whys**). Reason, cause, explanation, esp. in **~(s) and wherefore(s)**. **why** *int.* Exclamation expressing (esp. mild or slight) surprise, slight protest, etc., or emphasizing or calling attention to following statement, in opposition to possible doubt or objection.

WI *abbrev.* Wisconsin.

W.I. *abbrev.* West Indies.

wick (wĭk) *n.* Bundle of fiber, now usu. loosely twisted or woven cotton, immersed at one end in oil or grease of lamp, candle, etc., and drawing it up to maintain flame at other end.

wick·ed (wĭk´ĭd) *adj.* Sinful, iniquitous, vicious, morally depraved; (colloq., usu. joc.) very or excessively bad, malicious, mischievous, roguish; **W~ Bible**, English edition of 1632 with "not" omitted in 7th commandment. **wick'ed·ly** *adv.* **wick'ed·ness** *n.*

wick·er (wĭk´*er*) *n.* Plaited pliant twigs or reeds as material of baskets, chairs, mats, etc.; **wick'erwork**, things made of wicker; craft of making them.

***Wickerwork** abounds in Asian countries such as here in Sri Lanka. The elephants make interesting decorations while the baskets serve a practical purpose.*

wick·et (wĭk´ĭt) *n.* 1. (also **~ gate**) Small gate or door, esp. one made in or placed beside large one. 2. (cricket) Either of two sets of stumps at which bowler aims ball and which batsman defends; **wick'etkeeper**, fielder stationed behind wicket; **sticky wicket**, difficult or unpleasant situation. 3. (croquet) Small wire arch through which player tries to drive ball.

wide (wīd) *adj.* (**wid·er, wid·est**). 1. Measuring much from side to side; broad, not narrow; in width (as *20 ft.* ~). 2. Extending far, embracing much, of great extent; not tight, close, or restricted; loose, free, liberal, unprejudiced, general. 3. Open to full extent. 4. At considerable distance from point or mark, not within reasonable distance *of*. 5. **~-angle**, (of lens) having short focus and field extending through wide angle; **wide-eyed**, with eyes wide open, gazing intently; (fig.) wondering, naïve; **wide'mouthed**, with a wide mouth; with mouth opened wide in astonishment etc. **wide'ly** *adv.* **wide** *adv.* Over or through large space or region, far abroad (now only in **far and ~**); at wide interval(s), far apart; with wide opening, to full extent, at a distance to one side, so as to miss mark or way, astray; **wide-awake**, fully awake; (colloq.) on the alert, fully aware of what is going on, sharp-witted, knowing; **wide'-spread'**, widely disseminated or diffused.

wid·en (wīd*e*n) *v.* Make, become, wide or wider. **wid'en·er** *n.*

widg·eon, wi·geon (wĭj´*o*n) *ns.* (pl. **-eons,** collect. **-eon**). Either of two surface-feeding ducks, *Mareca americana* of N. Amer., having white head, or *M. penelope* of the Old World, having rusty head.

wid·ow (wĭd´ō) *n.* Woman who has lost her husband by death and has not married again; **widow's mite**: see MITE[1]; **widow's peak**, V-shaped growth of hair in center of forehead. **wid'ow·hood** *n.* **widow** *v.t.* Make widow or widower of (usu. in past part.); bereave, deprive *of*.

wid·ow·er (wĭd´ō*er*) *n.* Man who has lost his wife by death and has not married again.

width (wĭdth) *n.* Distance or measurement from side to side; large extent; piece of material of same width as when woven, esp. one of such pieces sewn together to make garment etc.

wield (wēld) *v.t.* Control, sway, hold and use, manage. **wield'er** *n.*

wie·ner (wē´n*er*) *n.* Frankfurter.

wife (wīf) *n.* (pl. **wives** pr. wīvz). 1. Married woman esp. in relation to her husband. 2. Woman, esp. one who is old and rustic or uneducated (now rare exc. in **old wives' tale**, foolish or superstitious tradition). **wife'hood** *n.* **wife'less** *adj.* **wife'ly** *adj.* (**-li·er, -li·est**).

wig (wĭg) *n.* Artificial head of hair worn esp. to conceal baldness, or as part of professional, ceremonial, or fashionable costume.

wi·geon = WIDGEON.

wig·gle (wĭg′el) *v.t.* (**-gled, -gling**). (colloq.) (Cause to) move from side to side.

wig·wag (wĭg′wăg) *v.* (**-wagged, -wag·ging**). (colloq.) Wag; esp. wave flag, light, etc., to and fro in signaling.

wig·wam (wĭg′wŏm, -wawm) *n.* Tent or cabin of N. Amer. Indian tribes of region of Great Lakes and eastward, formed of bark, matting, or hides stretched over frame of converging poles.

wild (wīld) *adj.* 1. Living or growing in state of nature, not domesticated, tame, or cultivated. 2. Uncivilized, barbarous. 3. Rebellious, lawless; not under control or restraint; tempestuous; rash, random. 4. Violently excited or agitated; passionately desirous (*to do*); elated, enthusiastic; haphazard, reckless, extravagant. 5. **wild′cat** (pl. **-cats**, collect. **-cat**), N. Amer. wild species of cat of genus *Lynx*, larger and stronger than domestic cat and similar in color and marking to tabby; any of various small undomesticated cats, as lynx, serval, ocelot, etc.; (colloq.) unsound or risky enterprise (freq. attrib.); **wildcat** (*v.t.*) (**-catted, -catting**), prospect esp. for oil in unexplored or unpromising area; **wildcat strike**, unofficial strike; **wild-eyed**, (1) having angry, distraught, or demented look in the eyes; (2) extremely foolish, irrational, or impractical; **wild′fire**, highly inflammable composition very difficult to extinguish, formerly used in warfare etc. (now chiefly in **spread like wildfire**, spread with immense rapidity); phosphorescent light; vast conflagration; **wild′fowl** (pl. **-fowls**, collect. **-fowl**), wild birds, esp. wild game; **wild goose**, any undomesticated goose, in England usu. graylag, in N. Amer. the Canada goose; **wild-goose chase**, foolish, fruitless, or hopeless quest; **wild indigo**, any of a genus (*Baptisia*) of N. Amer. leguminous plants, esp. *B. tinctoria*, having trifoliate leaves and yellow flowers; **wild man**, savage; **wild oat**, wild grass of genus *Avena*, resembling oats; **sow one's wild oats**, indulge in youthful indiscretions and escapades; **wild pitch**, (baseball) pitch that catcher cannot be expected to stop and that allows a runner to advance; **wild rice**, tall aquatic grass (*Zizania aquatica*) of eastern N. Amer. yielding edible grains; **Wild West, wild West**, western states of U.S. during period in which they were lawless frontier districts; **wild′-wood**, (chiefly poet.) uncultivated or unfrequented wood. **wild′ly** *adv.* **wild′ness** *n.* **wild** *n.* (usu. pl.) Desert, wild tract.

Wilde (wīld), **Oscar Fingal O'Flahertie Wills** (1854–1900). Irish-born author of comedies, novels, and verse; wrote *The Picture of Dorian Gray*, *The Importance of Being Ernest*, *Lady Windermere's Fan*, etc.

wil·de·beest (wĭl′debēst) *n.* (pl. **-beests**, collect. **-beest**). Gnu. [S. Afr. Du., = "wild beast"]

wil·der·ness (wĭl′dernĭs) *n.* Desert, uncultivated and uninhabited land or tract; mingled, confused, or vast assemblage *of*; **in the ~**, (of political party, with ref. to Num. 14) out of office.

wild·ing (wīl′dĭng) *n.* Wild plant, esp. wild crab apple; fruit of such plant.

wile (wīl) *n.* Trick, cunning procedure, artifice. **~** *v.t.* (**wiled, wil·ing**). Lure.

wil·ful = WILLFUL.

Wil·kins[1] (wĭl′kĭnz), **Maurice Hugh Frederick** (1916–). British physicist; co-discoverer of DNA molecular structure; received Nobel Prize for medicine, 1962, with WATSON and CRICK.

Wil·kins[2] (wĭl′kĭnz), **Roy** (1901–1981). Amer. Civil rights leader, executive secretary and director of NAACP, 1955–77.

will[1] (wĭl) *n.* 1. Faculty or function that is directed to conscious and intentional action; act, action, of willing; intention or determination that something shall be done or happen; desire, wish, inclination (*to* do); (archaic or poet.) what one desires; **against one's ~**, unwillingly; **at ~**, according to one's volition or choice, as one will; at the command or disposal (*of*); **with a ~**, resolutely, determinedly, energetically; **will′-power**, (strength of) will, esp. power to control one's own actions etc. 2. Person's formal declaration, usu. in writing, of his intention as to disposal of his property etc. after

*All species of non-domesticated ducks and geese can be termed **wildfowl.** These Canadian geese take off from a pond in North America.*

*Despite a superficial resemblance to cattle, the **wildebeest** is the largest antelope. Although fierce in the wild, youngsters raised in captivity have been domesticated.*

his death; document in which this is expressed. **will** *v.* (**willed, will·ing**). 1. Determine by the will, choose or decide to do something or that something shall be done; exercise the will; bring, get, (*into* etc.) by exercise of will; control (person), induce (another) *to do*, by exercise of one's will. 2. Direct by will or testament; dispose of by will, bequeath. **willed** *adj.*

will[2] (wĭl) *v.t.* (past **would** pr. wo͝od). Desire (thing; archaic); want, desire, choose, to; wish that; consent, be prevailed on, to; intend unconditionally; be accustomed, be observed from time to time, to; be likely to. ~ *v.aux.* Forming compound tenses or moods expressing (in second and third pers.) plain future or conditional statement or question, (in first pers.) future or conditional statement expressing speaker's will or intention.

Wil·lem·stad (wĭl′*e*mstaht). Capital of Netherlands Antilles on S. coast of Curaçao.

wil·let (wĭl′ĭt) *n.* (pl. **-lets**, collect. **-let**). Large N. Amer. shorebird of sandpiper family (*Catotrophorus semipalmatus*), with warbling call and striking wing pattern in flight.

will·ful, wil·ful (wĭl′f*u*l) *adjs.* Asserting or disposed to assert one's own will against instruction, persuasion, etc.; obstinately self-willed; deliberate, intentional, showing perversity or self-will. **will′ful·ly** *adv.* **will′ful·ness** *n.*

Wil·liam[1] (wĭl′y*a*m). Name of four kings of England: ~ **I** (*c*1027–1087), "the Conqueror," Duke of Normandy, claimed the English throne, invaded England and defeated Harold at the Battle of Hastings (1066); reigned 1066–87; ~ **II** (1056–1100), "Rufus," son of William I; reigned 1087–1100; ~ **III** (1650–1702), Prince of Orange, married Mary, daughter of James II, and reigned jointly with her 1689–94, and alone (after her death) until 1702; ~ **IV** (1765–1837), third son of George III, succeeded his brother, George IV in 1830.

Wil·liam[2] (wĭl′y*a*m). Name of three princes of Orange: ~ **I** (1533–84), "the Silent," led the insurrection of the Netherlands against Spain and became (1580) the first chief magistrate of the United Provinces of the Netherlands; ~ **II** (1626–50); ~ **III** = William III of England (see WILLIAM[1]).

Wil·liam[3] (wĭl′y*a*m). Anglicized form of name (*Wilhelm*) of two German emperors and kings of Prussia: ~ **I** (1797–1888), king of Prussia 1861–88, first German emperor 1871–88; ~ **II** (1859–1941), "the Kaiser," grandson of William I, succeeded his father, Frederick III, 1888, abdicated 1918 after the defeat of Germany, and fled to Holland.

Wil·liams[1] (wĭl′y*a*mz), **Roger** (1603?–83). English clergyman in Amer.; founded Providence, earliest settlement in Rhode Island.

Wil·liams[2] (wĭl′y*a*mz), **Tennessee** (1911–1983). (orig. name Thomas Lanier Williams) Amer. playwright; author of *A Streetcar Named Desire*, *Summer and Smoke*, etc.

wil·lies (wĭl′ēz) *n.pl.* (slang) Nervous feeling of discomfort or fear.

will·ing (wĭl′ĭng) *adj.* Consenting, disposed (*to* do); ready to be of use or service; given, rendered, performed, etc., will-

***Oscar Wilde** as portrayed by Toulouse-Lautrec in 1895, not long before he was sentenced to two years jail for homosexuality. Wilde's finest plays were written between 1891 and 1895.*

***William III** of Great Britain was born in the Netherlands. He accepted joint rule of England with Mary to obtain forces to save Holland from France.*

*Better known as the 'sailor king' of England, **William IV** reigned only for 7 years. However during the first two years of his reign, he had considerable influence on British politics.*

ingly. **will′ing·ly** *adv.* **will′ing·ness** *n.*

wil·li·waw (wĭl′*i*waw) *n.* Sudden blast of chill wind gusting down from mountains near the sea, as in Alaska and the Strait of Magellan.

will-o'-the-wisp (wĭl′*o*dh*e* wĭsp′) *n.* = IGNIS FATUUS; (fig.) person or thing that deludes or misleads by fugitive appearances. [orig. *Will with the wisp* (= handful of lighted flax etc.)]

wil·low (wĭl′ō) *n.* Tree or shrub of genus *Salix*, widely distributed in temperate and cold regions, usu. growing by water and with pliant branches and long narrow drooping leaves; ~ **herb**: see FIREWEED; **wil′lowware**, white china with blue pattern including willow tree etc., of Chinese origin, introduced into England in late 18th c. by Thomas Turner. **wil′low·y** *adj.* 1. Abounding in willows, bordered or shaded with willows. 2. Lithe and slender.

wil·ly-nil·ly (wĭl′ē nĭl′ē) *adv.* & *adj.* With or against the will of the persons concerned, whether one will or not, willing(ly) or unwilling(ly).

Wil·son[1] (wĭl′s*o*n), **Henry** (1812–75). (orig. name Jeremiah Jones Colbath) Vice president of U.S. under Ulysses S. Grant, 1873–5.

Wil·son[2] (wĭl′s*o*n), **(Thomas) Wood·row** (1856–1924). Twenty-eighth president of U.S., 1913–21; U.S. representative at the peace treaty negotiations after World War I and sponsor of the covenant of the League of Nations.

wilt[1] (wĭlt) *v.* (Cause to) fade, droop, become limp.

wilt[2] (wĭlt) *v.* (archaic) Second person sing., pres. ind. of WILL[2].

wil·y (wī′lē) *adj.* (**wil·i·er, wil·i·est**). Full of wiles, crafty, cunning. **wil′i·ly** *adv.* **wil′i·ness** *n.*

wim·ple (wĭm′pel) *n.* Cloth of linen or silk so folded as to cover head, chin, sides of face, and neck, formerly worn by women and retained in dress of nuns. ~ *v.* (**-pled, -pling**). Envelop in wimple, veil; fall in folds.

win (wĭn) *v.* (**won** pr. wŭn, **win·ning**). Be victorious in (game, battle, race, etc.); gain victory; get, gain, secure, esp. by effort or competition, as price or reward, by merit, or in gambling or betting; gain affection or allegiance of, bring *over* to one's party or cause; make one's way to, make one's way *to*, *through*, etc.; ~ **out** (colloq.), **through**, gain one's end, be successful. **win′ner** *n.* **win** *n.* (colloq.) Victory in game or contest.

wince (wĭns) *v.i.* (**winced, winc·ing**). Make involuntary shrinking movement, start, with pain, in alarm, etc., flinch. ~ *n.* Such movement. **winc′er** *n.*

winch (wĭnch) *n.* Crank of wheel or axle; hoisting or hauling apparatus consisting essentially of revolving horizontal drum worked by a crank.

wind[1] (wĭnd) *n.* 1. Air in motion, current of air of any degree of force perceptible to senses occurring naturally in atmosphere; this in reference to direction from which it blows or (naut.) its direction or position in relation to ship; air artificially put in motion by passage of missile, action of bellows, etc.; scent, esp. of person or animal in hunting etc., conveyed on wind; **get ~ of**, (fig.) begin to suspect, hear rumor of; **in the ~**, happening or ready to happen, astir, afoot; **like the ~**, swiftly; **sail** etc. **close to the ~**, (fig.) come very near indecency or dishonesty; **take ~ out of person's sails**, (fig.) put him at a disadvantage, esp. by anticipating his arguments etc. 2. Gas in stomach or intestines. 3. Breath as needed in exertion, power of drawing breath without difficulty while running etc.; **second ~**, regular breathing regained after breathlessness during continued exertion (also fig.). 4. Breath as used in speaking, esp. (fig.) empty talk. 5. Breath or air as used for sounding musical instrument, as horn, flute, organ pipe; (players of) wind instruments of orchestra collectively. 6. **wind′age**, effect of the wind in deflection of a missile; degree of such deflection; **wind′bag**, wordy talker; **wind′break**, something, esp. row of trees, used to break force of wind or as protection against it; **wind chill factor**, (meteorol) temperature of still air having same perceived effect on exposed human flesh as a specified combination of air temperature and wind velocity; **wind′fall**, something blown down by wind, esp. fruit; (fig.) piece of unexpected good fortune, esp. legacy; **wind′flower**, anemone; **wind instrument**, musical instrument in which sound is produced by current of air, esp. by breath; **wind′jammer**, (colloq.) sailing ship; **wind′pipe**, air passage between throat and bronchi or lungs, trachea; **wind′proof**, affording protection from wind; **wind′row**, row of mown grass or

Once confined to classical music, ***wind instruments*** *are finding their way into diverse forms of music including jazz, rock and even country and western.*

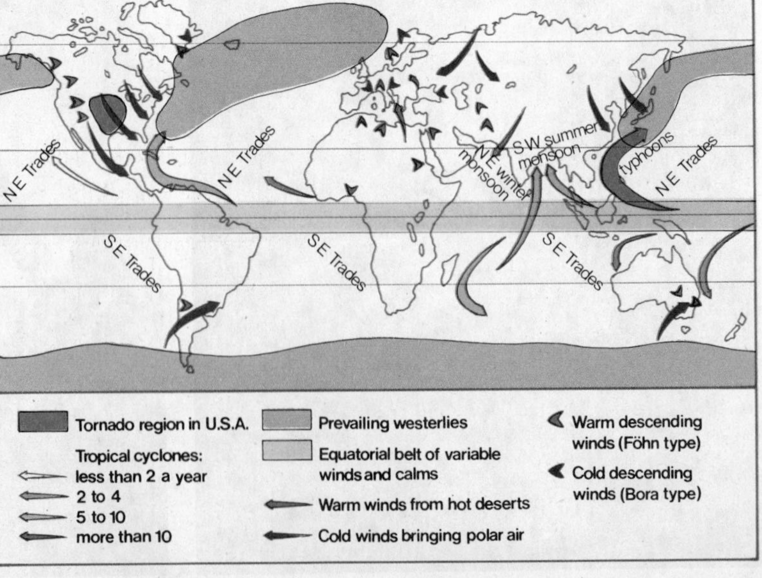

The direction and regularity of a ***wind*** *depends on topography and climatic conditions. Trade winds are due to semi-permanent anticyclones over subtropical oceans.*

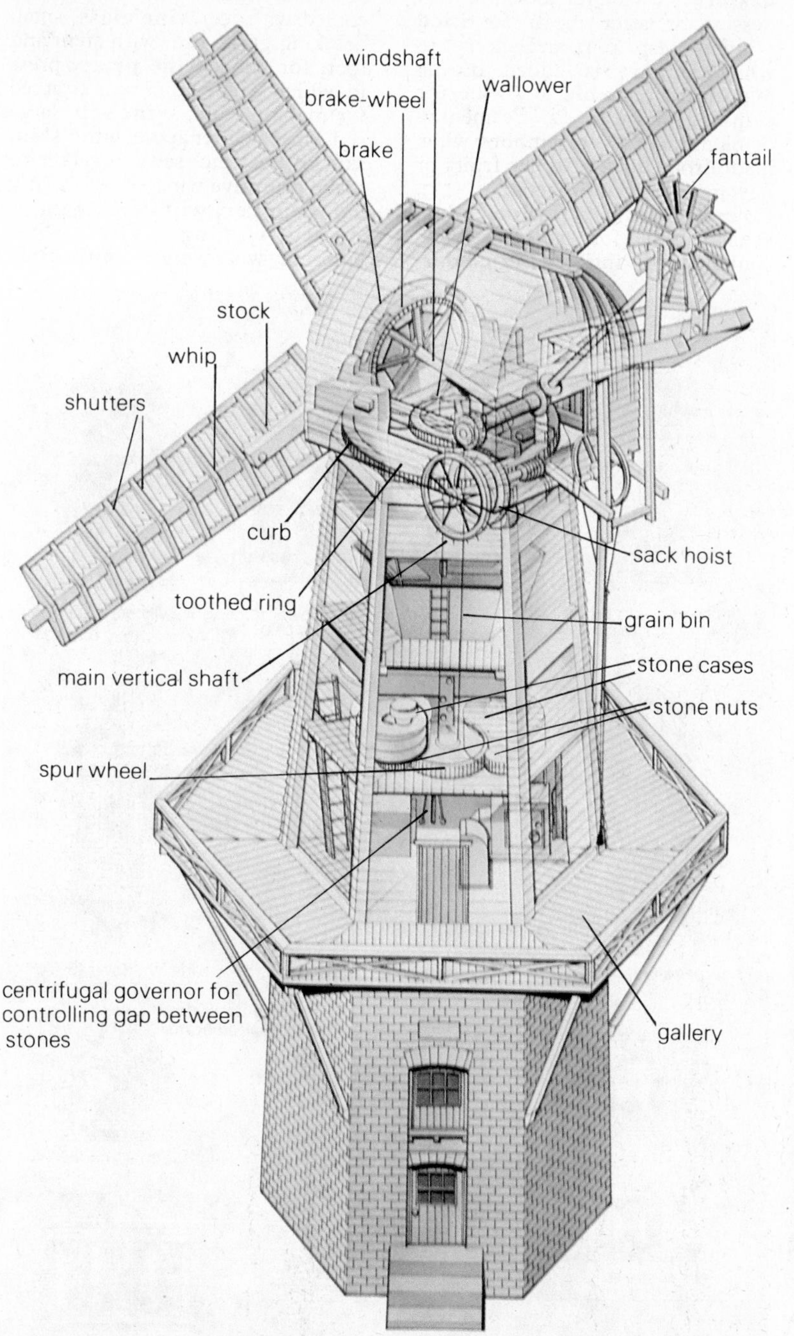

windshaft
wallower
brake-wheel
brake
fantail
stock
whip
shutters
curb
sack hoist
toothed ring
grain bin
main vertical shaft
stone cases
stone nuts
spur wheel
centrifugal governor for controlling gap between stones
gallery

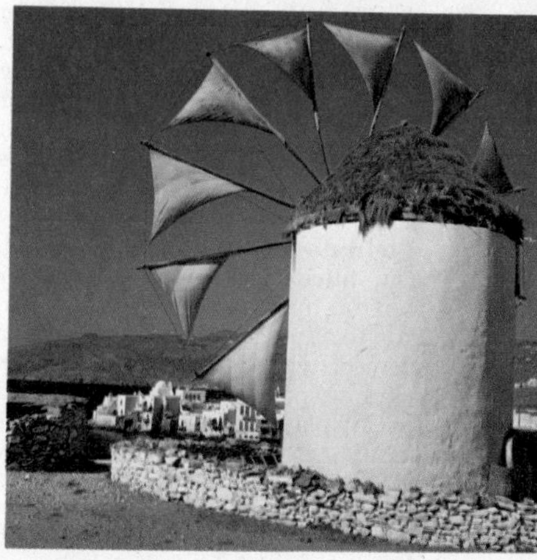

Numerous small sails are used to drive this ***windmill*** *in the Cyclades, Greece (above). Sprung shutters, similar to those on a Venetian blind, were invented by Meikle in 1772 and used in western Europe. Modern windmills (below) have much lighter machinery.*

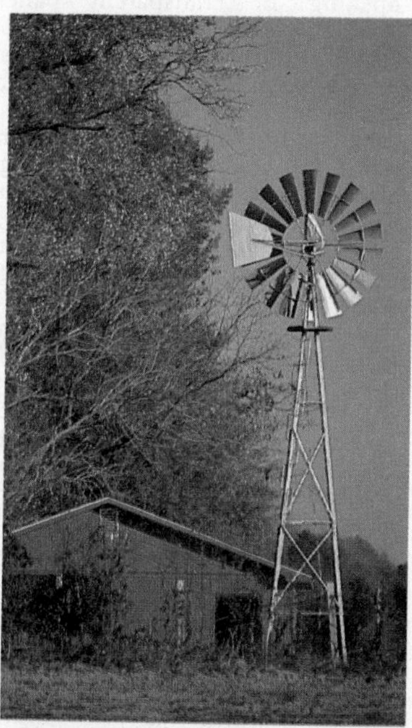

hay raked up to dry before being bundled; **wind′shield**, screen to keep off wind, esp. sheet of glass etc., in front of driver of motor vehicle etc.; **wind sleeve, wind′-sock**, piece of cloth shaped like truncated cone, held open at larger end by ring of wire and used to indicate direction of wind, drogue; **wind′swept**, swept by winds, exposed; **wind′tight**, constructed so as to keep out wind; **wind tunnel**, enclosed chamber through which wind may be blown at known velocities, for testing (models of) aircraft etc.; **wind′ward**, (region) lying in direction from which wind blows, facing the wind. **wind′less** *adj.* **wind** *v.* (**wind·ed** or for sense 1. **wound** pr. wownd, **wind·ing**). 1. Sound (horn or bugle) by blowing; blow (note, call, etc.) on horn etc. 2. Detect presence of by scent. 3. Deprive of breath, make out of breath; hence **wind′ed** (*adj.*), out of breath.

wind[2] (wīnd) *v.* (**wound** pr. wownd, **wind·ing**). Move, traverse, in curved or sinuous course; coil, wrap closely, around something or upon itself, encircle or enclose thus; haul or hoist by turning windlass etc.; tighten (*up*) coiled spring of (clock etc.), or (fig.) tension, intensity, or efficiency of; ~ **up**, bring or come to conclusion, conclude; arrange and adjust affairs of (company) on its dissolution; **wind′up**, finish, conclusion; (baseball) preparatory motions of pitcher before throwing ball to batter; **winding sheet**, shroud. **wind′er** *n.* Person, thing, that winds; winding step in staircase.

Wind·hoek (vĭnt′ho͝ok). Capital city of Namibia.

wind·lass (wĭnd′las) *n.* Mechanical contrivance for hauling or hoisting, consisting essentially of horizontal roller or beam on supports, with rope or chain wound around. ~ *v.t.* Hoist or haul with windlass.

wind·mill (wĭnd′mĭl) *n.* Mill worked by action of wind on sails; toy consisting of stick with shaped card or other light substance fixed to its end and revolving when moved through air; **fight, tilt at, ~s**, expend energy contending against imaginary opponents or difficulties (in allusion to story of Don Quixote's tilting at windmills under the delusion that they were giants).

win·dow (wĭn′dō) *n.* Opening, usu. filled with glass, in wall or roof of building, ship, car, train, etc., to admit light or air and afford view of what is outside or inside; window space or opening, esp. used for display of goods, advertisements, etc., in shop etc.; any opening resembling window in shape or function; ~ **box**, box on outside window sill in which flowers and plants are grown; ~ **dresser**, one who arranges display in store window etc.; ~ **dressing**, art of arranging such display; (fig.) adroit presentation of facts etc. to give falsely favorable impression; ~ **envelope**, envelope with opening or transparent panel through which address inside is visible; **windowpane**, pane of glass set in window frame; **window seat**, seat below window, usu. in recess or bay; **window shade**, curtain or shade for window, usu. consisting of heavy cloth, paper, or plastic on spring roller; **window-shopping**, looking at store displays without buying; **window sill**, sill of window.

Wind·sor (wĭn′*zer*). English town on bank of Thames, site of royal residence, ~ **Castle**; surname assumed by English royal house in 1917; **Duke of ~**, title conferred on Edward VIII on his abdication in 1936; ~ **chair**, kind of wooden chair with back formed of upright spokes surmounted by curved crosspiece.

Wind·ward (wĭnd′*werd*) **Islands.** 1. Group of islands in the West Indies consisting of Grenada, St. Vincent, St. Lucia, and Dominica, with their dependencies. 2. Group of islands in southern part of Lesser Antilles, including British and French territories.

wind·y (wĭn′dē) *adj.* (**wind·i·er, wind·i·est**). Windswept; exposed to, blown upon or through, by wind; in which wind is frequent or prevalent, accompanied by (much) wind; verbose, empty. **wind′i·ly** *adv.* **wind′i·ness** *n.*

wine (wīn) *n.* 1. Fermented grape juice for drinking, varying in color from *red* (usu. a purplish crimson) to *white* (pale gold); **dessert ~**, wine for drinking with dessert or after meal; **fortified ~**, wine (esp. port and sherry) to which brandy is added during manufacture; **table ~**, wine for drinking at meal. 2. Fermented drink more or less resembling wine, made from juice of other fruits or flowers or root vegetables. 3. Color of red wine. 4. **wine cellar**, cellar used for storing wine; contents of this; **wine-cooler**, vessel in which bottles of wine are cooled with ice; **wine′glass**, small drinking glass, usu. with stem and foot, for wine; **wine press**, press in which grape juice is extracted for making wine; **Wine′sap**, large red Amer. winter apple; **wine′skin**, skin of goat etc. sewn together to make primitive wine vessel. **win′y** *adj.* (**win·i·er, win·i·est**). **wine** *v.* (**wined, win·ing**). Drink wine; entertain with wine; ~ **and dine**,

*The glazed **window** was used by the Greeks and Romans but its use declined in the Middle Ages so that churches seem to have been the only buildings with glazing. Its use in private dwellings increased only with the availability of glass.*

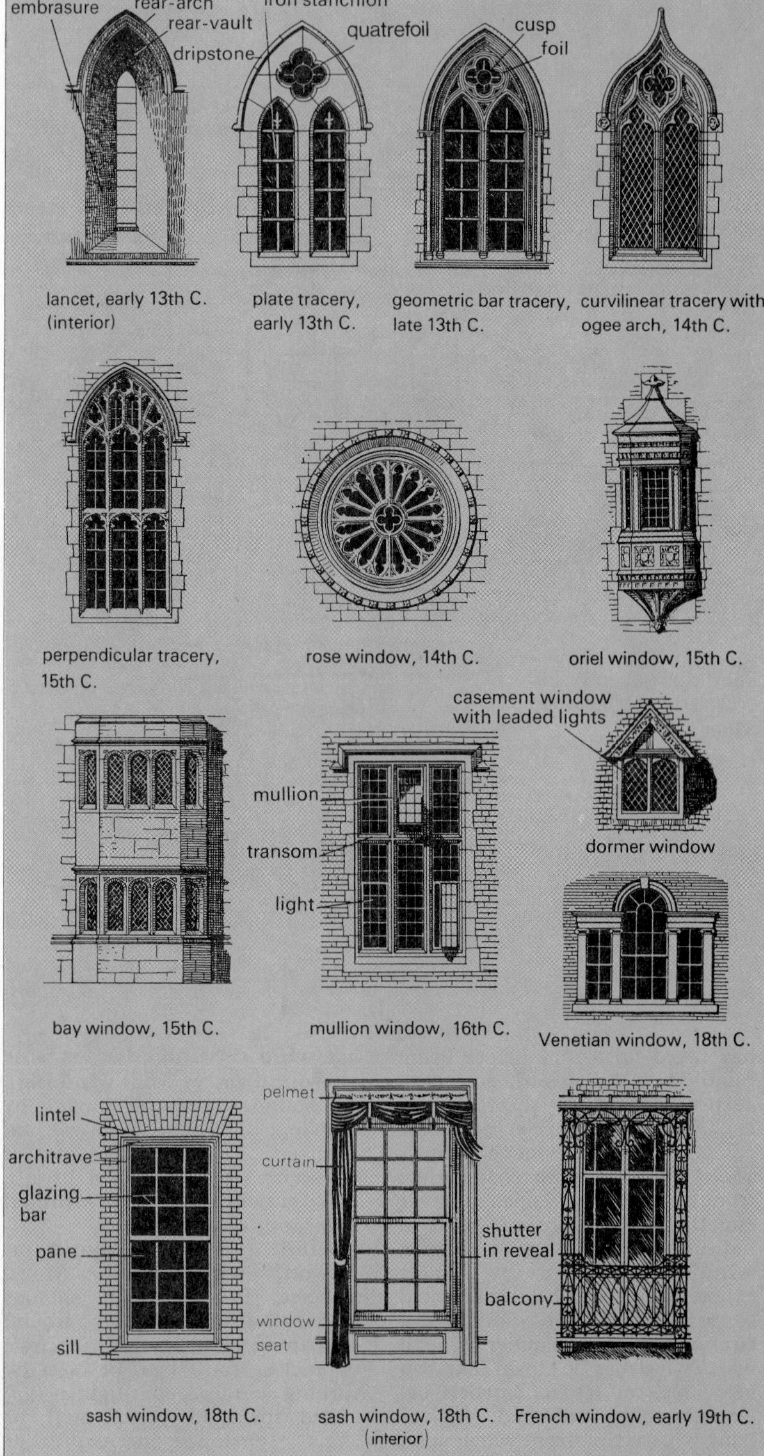

entertain generously.

wing (wĭng) *n.* 1. Organ of flight of any flying animal, in birds a specially modified forelimb; in bats, extension of skin attached to modified parts of forelimb; in insects, membranous expansions attached to thorax in addition to limbs; **on the ~**, flying; **take ~**, fly away; **take under one's ~**, treat as protégé. 2. Anything resembling wing in form or function, esp. one of the main supporting surfaces (planes) of aircraft. 3. Lateral part or appendage. 4. Either of two divisions on each side of main body of army or fleet in battle. 5. (soccer etc.) Position, player, on outside of forward line. 6. Section of political party etc. holding views deviating from center: see RIGHT wing, LEFT[1] wing. 7. Subordinate part of building on one side of main or central part. 8. (usu. pl.) Space at side of stage where actors stand before going on stage; **waiting in the ~s**, (fig.) holding oneself in readiness. 9. (anat., bot.) Lateral part or projection of some organ or structure, as lateral cartilage of nose, thin membranous appendage of seed or fruit serving for its dispersal by wind etc. 10. Division of air force, usu. comprising three groups. 11. (pl.) Representation of pair of bird's wings worn as badge by those who have passed flying tests. 12. **wing'back**, (football) back positioned on offense, flanking the end of the line; position played by this back; **wing case**, horny covering of functional wings in certain insects; **wing chair**, chair with sidepieces projecting forward at top of high back, for protection from drafts; **wing collar**, man's stiff collar with upper corners turned down; **wing covert**: see COVERT[1] sense 2; **wing load(ing)**, total weight of loaded aircraft divided by area of supporting surfaces; **wing nut**, nut with projections for thumb and fingers to turn it by; **wing'span, wing'spread**, extreme measurement between tips of wings of bird or aircraft; **wing tip**, outer end or tip of wing of bird or aircraft. **wing** *v.* Equip with wings; enable to fly or mount; send in flight, lend speed to; travel, traverse, on wings; wound (esp. game bird) in the wing.

wing·ding (wĭng'dĭng) *n.* (slang) Lively, noisy party or celebration.

winged (wĭngd; occas. wĭng'ĭd) *adj.* Having wings; swift, rapid, flying; (of speech) conveying its message swiftly and effectively; **~ god**, Mercury; **~ horse**, Pegasus; **W~ Victory**, statue of Nike, Greek goddess of victory, with wings, esp. Hellenistic statue found in Samothrace, preserved in Louvre.

wing·less (wĭng'lĭs) *adj.* Having no wings; (of birds) having rudimentary wings not used for flight.

wink (wĭngk) *v.* Blink; close one eye momentarily in flippant or frivolous manner; close (an eye, eyes) for a moment; move swiftly, (cause to) flicker like an eyelid, twinkle; give (signal, message, etc.) by flashing lights; **~ at**, shut one's eyes to, connive at. **wink** *n.* Act of winking, esp. as signal; **not a ~ (of sleep)**, no sleep at all. **wink'er** *n.*

win·ning (wĭn'ĭng) *adj.* That wins; charming, attractive. **~** *n.* 1. Act of winning. 2. (pl.) Money won by gambling or betting. **win'ning·ly** *adv.*

win·now (wĭn'ō) *v.t.* Fan (grain) free of chaff etc., fan (chaff) *away, out, from*; sift, separate, clear of worthless or inferior element, extract, select (*out*) thus.

win·o (wī'nō) *n.* (pl. **win·os**). (slang) Alcoholic.

win·some (wĭn'səm) *adj.* Attractive, charming. **win'some·ly** *adv.* **win'some·ness** *n.*

win·ter (wĭn'tər) *n.* 1. Coldest season of year, popularly reckoned in N. hemisphere as comprising December, January, and February, but astronomically as lasting from winter solstice (Dec. 21 or 22) to vernal equinox (Mar. 20 or 21); (opp. SUMMER[1]) colder half of year. 2. (*attrib.* or *adj.*) Of, characteristic of, winter; occurring, used, etc., in, lasting for, winter; (of fruit) ripening late or keeping well until or during winter; **~ aconite**, small perennial herb (*Eranthis hyemalis*) producing bright-yellow starry flowers in winter; **win'tergreen**, any of various creeping or low shrubby plants with leaves remaining green in winter, esp. N. Amer. *Gaultheria procumbens*, with drooping white flowers, edible scarlet berries, and aromatic leaves yielding oil used in medicine and for flavoring; **win'terkill**, kill or be killed by exposure to cold temperatures, ice, snow, etc.; **winter solstice**: see SOLSTICE; **win'tertide** (poet.), **win'tertime**, season of winter; **winter wheat** (**oats** etc.), wheat (oats etc.) sown in autumn and remaining in ground all winter. **winter** *v.* Spend winter (*at, in*); keep, feed, during winter.

win·ter·ize (wĭn'tərīz) *v.t.* (**-ized, -iz·ing**). Adapt for operation or for use in cold weather.

win·try (wĭn'trē) (**-tri·er, -tri·est**), **win·ter·y** (wĭn'tərē) (**-ter·i·er, -ter·i·est**) *adj.* Characteristic of winter, having the temperature, storminess, etc., appropriate to winter, cold, windy, cheerless; (of smile, greeting, etc.) devoid of warmth. **win'tri·ness** *n.*

wipe (wīp) *v.* (**wiped, wip·ing**). Clean or dry surface of by rubbing with cloth etc.; clear away (moisture, dust, etc.) thus; apply soft or liquid substance over surface by rubbing it on, esp., (plumbing) apply solder to (joint) thus; **~ out**, (colloq.) destroy, annihilate, exterminate; **~ the floor with**, (slang) humiliate (person) by defeat

*During the middle of **winter** in the high altitudes of the Canadian Rocky Mountains, nearly everything is covered with snow. Nevertheless, some animals are able to survive in such conditions without hibernating.*

*Just as a Christian may utter a prayer, followers of Shinto in Japan may express a **wish** by writing it on paper or cloth and attaching it to the fence in front of a shrine.*

or correction. **wipe** *n.* Act of wiping.

wip·er (wī′p*er*) *n.* (esp., also **windshield ~**) Mechanical device that wipes windshield of motor vehicle.

wire (wīr) *n.* (Piece of) metal drawn into slender flexible rod or thread; length or line of this used for various purposes, esp. for fencing, as conductor of electric current, etc.; wire netting, framework of wire; snare of wire etc.; (colloq.) telegram; (horse racing) the finish line; (pl.) lines by which puppets are worked (chiefly fig., in **pull (the) ~s**); **under the wire**, barely meeting the deadline; **wire cloth**, fabric (for strainers etc.) woven from wire; **wire cutter**, tool for cutting wire; **wire entanglement**, entanglement of barbed wire stretched over ground to impede enemy's advance; **wire gauge**, gauge for measuring diameter of wire etc.; standard series of sizes to which wire etc. is made; **wire-haired**, (of dogs, esp. terriers) having rough hard wiry coat; **wire′-puller**, (colloq.) politician etc. who privately influences others; **wire′-pulling** (*adj.* & *n.*); **wire service**, business organization that collects news and photographs for distribution to subscribing newspapers and broadcasting stations; **wire′tap** (*v.*) (**-tapped, -tap·ping**), make secret connection with (telephone or telegraph wire) in order to eavesdrop on telephone conversations; **wire′worm**, slender yellow larva of any click beetle destructive to plants; (also) millipede that destroys plant roots. **wire** *v.* (**wired, wir·ing**). Furnish, support, stiffen, secure, with wires; snare with wire; (colloq.) telegraph. **wir′ing** *n.* (esp.) Electrical system of building.

wire·less (wīr′lĭs) *adj.* Without wire(s), esp. (of telegraphy, telephony) with no connecting wire between transmitting and receiving stations; (archaic) radio. ~ *n.* (archaic) Radio receiver or transmitter; telegraphy or telephony. ~ *v.* Send (message etc.), inform, by wireless.

wir·y (wīr′ē) *adj.* (**wir·i·er, wir·i·est**). Made of wire; tough and flexible like wire; (of persons) tough, sinewy, untiring. **wir′i·ly** *adv.* **wir′i·ness** *n.*

Wis., Wisc. *abbrevs.* Wisconsin.

Wis·con·sin (wĭskŏn′s*i*n). State in N. central U.S., admitted to Union in 1848; capital, Madison.

wis·dom (wĭz′dom) *n.* Being wise; soundness of judgment in matters relating to life and conduct; knowledge, enlightenment, learning; **W~ of Solomon**, book of the Apocrypha; **~ of Jesus the son of Sirach**, Ecclesiasticus; **W~ literature**, biblical books of Job, Proverbs, Ecclesiastes, Wisdom of Solomon, Ecclesiasticus, and Epistle of James; **~ tooth**, hindmost molar tooth on each side of upper and lower jaws in humans, usu. appearing about age of 20.

*Although the status of a **witch doctor** (above) has declined in Africa, in some places, including Zambia, they retain an important role in tribal life and wield considerable influence.*

wise[1] (wīz) *n.* (archaic) Way, manner, guise.

wise[2] (wīz) *adj.* (**wis·er, wis·est**). Having, exercising, proceeding from, indicating, sound judgment resulting from experience and knowledge; sagacious, prudent, sensible; having knowledge (*of*); (archaic) skilled in magic or occult arts; (slang) offensively knowledgeable; insolent; **be, get, ~ to**, (colloq.) be, become, aware of; **put ~ (to)**, inform (of); **wise′crack**, smart remark, witticism; (*v.i.*) make wisecracks; **wise guy**, (slang) cocksure person; **wise man**, man of good judgment or discernment; (archaic) one skilled in magic, wizard, esp. one of the Magi; **wise woman**, witch, female soothsayer, esp. harmless or beneficent one. **wise′ly** *adv.*

-wise *suffix.* In (specified) manner, way, or respect. [f. WISE[1]]

wise·a·cre (wīz′ā′k*er*) *n.* One who pretends to, or affects an air of, wisdom. [MDu. *wijsseggher* soothsayer]

wish (wĭsh) *n.* (Expression of)

desire or aspiration; request; (pl.) expression of desire for another's welfare, success, etc.; **wish'bone**, forked bone between neck and breast of cooked bird (because when two persons have pulled it apart the holder of the larger piece is entitled to the magical fulfillment of a wish); **wish fulfillment**, (psychoanal.) gratification of unconscious wishes, esp. symbolically in dreams, fantasy, etc. **wish** *v.* Have, feel, express, a wish for; express desire or aspiration *for*; want (*to* do, person *to* do); request; (esp. in expressions of goodwill, greeting, etc.) desire (something, esp. something good) for a person etc. **wish'er** *n.*

wish·ful (wĭsh'*f*ul) *adj.* Wishing, desirous; ~ **thinking**, believing a thing to be so because it is desired or desirable. **wish'ful·ly** *adv.* **wish'ful·ness** *n.*

wish·y-wash·y (wĭsh'ē wŏshē, -wawshē) *adj.* Thin, sloppy; feeble or poor in quality or character. **wish'y-wash·i·ness** *n.*

wisp (wĭsp) *n.* Small bundle or twist of straw, hay, etc.; thin, narrow, filmy, or slight piece or scrap (*of*). **wisp'y** *adj.* (**wisp·i·er, wisp·i·est**).

wis·ter·i·a (wĭstēr'ē*a*), **wis·tar·i·a** (wĭstār'ē*a*) *ns.* Leguminous plant of genus *Wisteria* of N. Amer., Japan, and China, forming hardy climbing deciduous shrubs with pendulous racemes of blue, purple, or white papilionaceous flowers. [Caspar *Wistar* or *Wister*, Amer. anatomist (1761–1818)]

wist·ful (wĭst'*f*ul) *adj.* Yearningly or mournfully expectant or eager. **wist'ful·ly** *adv.* **wist'ful·ness** *n.*

wit[1] (wĭt) *n.* 1. (sing. or pl.) Intelligence, understanding; **at one's ~'s end**, utterly perplexed; **have one's wits about one**, be mentally alert; **live by one's wits**, get one's living by clever or crafty devices, without any settled occupation; **out of one's wits**, mad, distracted. 2. Unexpected combining or contrasting of previously unconnected ideas or expressions; power of causing surprise and delight by this; capacity for making brilliant observations in an amusing way. 3. Person with this capacity; (archaic) person of great mental ability, man of talent.

wit[2] (wĭt) *v.* (**wist, wit·ting**). (archaic) Know; **to ~**, this is to say, namely.

witch[1] (wĭch) *n.* Sorceress, woman supposed to have dealings with devil or evil spirits; (fig.) fascinating or bewitching woman; **old ~**, (colloq.) malevolent or ugly old woman; **witch'craft**, sorcery; **witch doctor**, tribal magician of primitive people; **witches' Sabbath**, midnight meeting of demons, sorcerers, and witches, presided over by the Devil, supposed in medieval times to have been held annually as orgy or festival; **witch hunt, hunting**, searching out and persecution of (formerly) supposed witches, or (now) persons suspected of unpopular or unorthodox political views, etc. **witch** *v.t.* Bewitch; (fig.) fascinate, charm; **witch'ing time (of night)**, (*Hamlet*, III. ii) time when witches are active, midnight. **witch'er·y** *n.* (pl. **-er·ies**).

witch[2]: see WYCH.

with (wĭdh, wĭth) *prep.* 1. (of conflict, rivalry, etc.) Against, in opposition to. 2. In or into company of or relation to, among, beside. 3. Agreeably or in harmonious relation to. 4. Having, carrying, possessed of, characterized by; ~ **child, young**, pregnant. 5. In the care, charge, or possession of. 6. By use of as instrument or means, by addition or supply of, by operation of, owing to. 7. In same way, direction, degree, at same time, as. 8. In regard to, concerning, in the mind or view of. 9. Despite, notwithstanding, the presence of. 10. **with it**, (colloq.) up-to-the-minute, (capable of) understanding new ideas etc.

with·al (wĭdhawl', wĭth-) *adv.* & *prep.* (archaic) With (it); in addition, moreover, as well, at the same time.

with·draw (wĭdhdraw', wĭth-) *v.* (**-drew** pr. -drōō', **-drawn, -draw·ing**). 1. Pull aside or back; take away, remove; retract. 2. Retire from presence or place, go aside or apart. **with·draw'al** *n.* **with·drawn'** *past part.* as *adj.* Shy, unresponsive.

Winter in ***Wisconsin.*** *The 35th State of the U.S.A., Wisconsin occupies 56,154 sq. miles and is bordered on the north by Lake Superior.*

Despite the short flowering season, the ***wisteria*** *is popular with gardeners for training over a pergola or along a wall, or as a standard. However, its seeds and pods are poisonous.*

*A possible ancestor of the dog, the **wolf** lives as one of a pack within which there is a complex social structure. It inhabits the cooler isolated regions of the northern hemisphere.*

*Posthumously awarded the status of hero, and romanticized in paintings (above) **James Wolfe** led his men to capture Quebec. It has been suggested that the plan came from his brigadiers.*

with·er (wĭdh′*er*) *v.* Make, become, dry or shriveled (*up*); deprive of or lose vigor, vitality, freshness, importance; decline, languish, decay; blight, paralyze (*with* look of scorn etc.). **with′er·ing** *adj.* **with′er·ing·ly** *adv.*

with·ers (wĭdh′*erz*) *n.pl.* Ridge between shoulder blades of horse and some other animals. [part that takes strain of collar, f. OE. *wither* against]

with·hold (wĭthhōld′, wĭdh-) *v.t.* (**-held, -hold·ing**). Hold back, restrain; refuse to give, grant, or allow; **withholding tax**, tax deducted from wages or salary.

with·in (wĭdhĭn′, wĭth-) *adv.* Inside, internally, inwardly; indoors. ~ *prep.* To, on, in, the inside of; enclosed by; in the limits of; not beyond, above, outside, or farther than the extent of; in the scope or sphere of action of.

with·out (wĭdhowt′, wĭth-) *adv.* (literary or archaic) Outside, externally. ~ *prep.* 1. (archaic) Outside of. 2. Not having, not with; devoid of; lacking; free from.

with·stand (wĭthstănd′, wĭdh-) *v.t.* (**-stood** pr. -stŏŏd′, **-stand·ing**). Resist, oppose.

wit·less (wĭt′lĭs) *adj.* (archaic and literary) Lacking in wits, senseless; lacking wit. **wit′less·ly** *adv.* **wit′less·ness** *n.*

wit·ness (wĭt′nĭs) *n.* 1. Testimony, evidence; confirmation. 2. Person giving sworn testimony in court or for legal purpose; person attesting execution of document by adding his signature; thing or person whose existence, position, etc., is testimony *to* or proof *of*; person present as spectator or auditor; ~ **stand**, stand from which witness gives evidence. **witness** *v.* State in evidence (archaic); give evidence, serve as evidence; indicate, serve as evidence of; see, be spectator of; sign (document) as witness.

wit·ted (wĭt′ĭd) *adj.* Having wit; usu. in comb., as *quick-*~, *slow-*~, etc.

wit·ti·cism (wĭt′ĭsĭzem) *n.* Witty saying, piece of wit; esp. jeer, witty sarcasm. [coined by Dryden from WITTY, after *criticism*]

wit·ting (wĭt′ĭng) *adj.* Knowing or intending, conscious. **wit′ting·ly** *adv.* [f. WIT[2]]

wit·ty (wĭt′ē) *adj.* (**-ti·er, -ti·est**). Capable of, given to, saying or writing brilliantly or sparklingly amusing things; full of wit. **wit′ti·ly** *adv.* **wit′ti·ness** *n.*

wive (wīv) *v.* (**wived, wiv·ing**). (archaic) Provide with, take, wife.

wives: see WIFE.

wiz·ard (wĭz′*erd*) *n.* Magician, sorcerer, male witch; extremely skillful person; person who effects seeming impossibilities. **wiz′ard·ry** *n.*

wiz·en (wĭz′*en*), **wiz·ened** (wĭz′*end*) *adjs.* Of shriveled or dried-up appearance.

wk. *abbrev.* Week.

wkly. *abbrev.* Weekly.

WL, w.l. *abbrevs.* Wavelength.

WNW, W.N.W., w.n.w. *abbrevs.* West-northwest.

WO, W.O. *abbrevs.* Warrant Officer.

w/o *abbrev.* Without.

woad (wōd) *n.* European biennial plant (*Isatis tinctoria*); blue dye formerly obtained from this.

wob·ble (wŏb′el) *v.i.* (**-bled, -bling**). Move unsteadily or with uncertain direction from side to side or backward and forward; shake, rock, quiver; (fig.) vacillate, hesitate, waver. ~ *n.* Wobbling motion. **wob′bly** *adj.* (**-bli·er, -bli·est**). **wob′bli·ness** *n.*

Wob·bly (wŏb′lē) *n.* (pl. **-blies**). (slang) Member of the Industrial Workers of the World (I.W.W.). [prob. f. mispronunciation of letter *W*]

Wo·den (wō′*den*) = ODIN.

woe (wō) *n.* (chiefly poet. or joc.) Affliction, bitter grief, distress; (pl.) calamities, troubles; ~ **is me!**, alas!; **woe′begone**, dismal looking. **woe′ful** *adj.* **woe′ful·ly** *adv.* **woe′ful·ness** *n.*

wok (wŏk) *n.* Large bowllike metal pan used in Chinese cooking.

woke: see WAKE[1].

wolf (wŏŏlf) *n.* (pl. **wolves** pr. wŏŏlvz). 1. Any of various large mammals of dog tribe (*Canis*, esp. *C. lupus*) of Europe, Asia, and N. Amer., with gray or brownish-gray fur, erect pointed ears, and bushy tail, noted for fierceness and rapacity; rapacious or greedy person; (slang) man who pursues women; **cry** ~, raise false alarm; **keep** ~ **from the door**, ward off hunger or starvation; ~ **in sheep's clothing**, person concealing malicious intentions under guise of friendliness etc. 2. ~ **dog, wolf′hound**, any of various large varieties of dog kept for hunting wolves; **wolfs′bane**, *Aconitum lycoctonum*, with yellow flowers; dried root of this, used as poison; **wolf whistle**, expressive whistle uttered by man as indication of sexual attraction to woman. **wolf′ish** *adj.* **wolf′ish·ly** *adv.* **wolf′ish·ness** *n.* **wolf** *v.t.* Devour ravenously.

Wolfe (wŏŏlf), **James** (1727–1759). English general; commanded the British forces at the siege of Quebec, in which he was killed.

wolf·ram (wŏŏlf′*ram*) *n.* Ore

($FeWO_4$) yielding tungsten.

wol·ver·ine (wo͝olverēn′) *n.* Very large voracious weasel (*Gulo gulo*) of N. Amer. and N. Europe, with shaggy black fur, white markings, and bushy tail; also called "glutton."

wom·an (wo͝om′*a*n) *n.* (pl. **wom·en** pr. wĭm′ĭn). Adult human female; female servant or attendant; (without article) the average or typical woman, the female sex; (attrib.) female, as ~ **doctor,** ~ **friend; wom′ankind**, women in general; **women's lib** (sometimes derog.), movement urging liberation of women from domestic duties and subservient status; **women's rights**, rights claimed for women of privileges and opportunities equal with those of men; **woman suffrage**, right of women to vote. **wom′an·hood** *n.* State of being a woman; womanliness; womankind.

wom·an·ish (wo͝om′*a*nĭsh) *adj.* Characteristic of woman as opp. to man; (of man) effeminate. **wom′-an·ish·ly** *adv.* **wom′an·ish·ness** *n.*

wom·an·ize (wo͝om′*a*nīz) *v.* (**-ized, -iz·ing**). Make womanish; (of men) philander. **wom′an·iz·er** *n.*

wom·an·like (wo͝om′*a*nlīk) *adj.* Like a woman.

wom·an·ly (wo͝om′*a*nlē) *adj.* Having the qualities or bearing of a woman; befitting a woman. **wom′an·li·ness** *n.*

womb (wo͞om) *n.* Uterus, (fig.) place where anything is generated or produced.

wom·bat (wŏm′băt) *n.* Burrowing herbivorous marsupial, esp. of genus *Phascolomis*, native to S. Australia and Tasmania, with thick heavy body, short legs, rudimentary tail, and general resemblance to small bear.

*A **witness** is required for almost all legal proceedings, including this naturalization ceremony.*

*The **withers** of a horse form a prominent ridge between the shoulder blades; they are quite sensitive to pressure.*

*The common **wombat** is found in eastern and south-eastern Australia from southern Queensland to the islands of Bass Strait and Tasmania. The three other species have limited distribution.*

wom·en·folk (wĭm′ĭnfōk), **wom·en·folks** (wĭm′ĭnfōks) *n.pl.* Women collectively, esp. of family or community.

won: see WIN.

won·der (wŭn′d*er*) *n.* 1 Marvel, miracle, prodigy; astonishing thing, deed, event, occurrence, etc.; **no ~**, (it is) not surprising; **Seven W~s of the World**: see SEVEN. 2. Emotion excited by something novel and unexpected, or inexplicable; astonishment mixed with perplexity, bewildered curiosity, or admiration. 3. **wonder drug**, any drug supposed to have remarkable power to relieve symptoms of or cure illness; **won′derland**, imaginary realm of wonders, fairyland; **won′derworker**, one who performs wonders or miracles. **wonder** *v.* 1. Be affected with wonder, marvel; **I shouldn't ~**, (colloq.) I should not be surprised. 2. Feel some doubt or curiosity, be desirous to know or learn. **won′der·er, won·der·ment** (wŭn′d*er*m*e*nt) *ns.*

won·der·ful (wŭn′d*er*f*u*l) *adj.* Marvelous, surprising; surprisingly large, fine, excellent, etc. **won′der·ful·ly** *adv.* **won′der·ful·ness** *n.*

won·drous (wŭn′dr*u*s) *adj.* & *adv.* (poet., rhet.) Wonderful(ly). **won′drous·ly** *adv.* **won′drous·ness** *n.*

wont (wōnt, wawnt, wŭnt) *adj.* (archaic) Accustomed, used (*to* do). ~ *n.* Custom; habit. **wont′ed** *adj.* Habitual.

won't (wōnt, wŭnt) *contr.* Will not.

woo (wōō) *v.* COURT[2]. **woo′er** *n.*

wood (wŏŏd) *n.* 1. Collection of trees growing more or less thickly together, of considerable extent; piece of ground covered with trees; (now rare) wooded country, woodland; **out of the ~s**, clear of a difficulty, danger, etc. 2. Hard compact fibrous substance making up trunks and branches of trees and shrubs between bark and pith, whether growing or cut down for use in construction or cabinetwork, for fuel, etc.; particular kind of wood. 3. Something made of wood, esp. cask in which wine etc. is stored; (mus.) wooden wind instrument, woodwind; golf club used for driving. 4. **wood alcohol**, methyl alcohol; **wood anemone**, any of various common wild anemones, abundant in woods and flowering in early spring; **wood′bine**, VIRGINIA creeper; any of various climbing plants, esp. honeysuckle of genus *Lonicera*; **wood′block**, block of wood, e.g. for paving or esp. with design for printing from; **wood′cock** (pl. **-cocks**, collect **-cock**), common European migratory bird (*Scolopax rusticola*), allied to snipe,

*Above: A common British species, the spotted **woodpecker.** Left: The Arizona woodpecker. Both may eat seeds as well as insects. Below: Autumnal leaves cast a golden glow over an English **wood.** Because land was needed for farming and houses, wooded areas in that country have been reduced.*

The ***woodcock*** *is unusual because the female carries the young in flight. The usual position is between the feet and body, but occasionally, they have also been seen on her back.*

with long bill, large eyes, and mottled plumage, esteemed as food; similar but smaller N. Amer. *Philohela minor*; **wood'craft**, knowledge of and skill in forest conditions applied to hunting, maintaining oneself, making one's way, etc.; **wood'cut**, print obtained from design cut in relief on block of wood (usu. sawn along the grain); this art; **wood'cutter**, one who fells or lops trees for timber or fuel; **wood engraving**, print obtained from design engraved on block of wood (usu. sawn across grain); this art; **wood ibis**, large wading bird of southern swampland (*Mycteria americana*), the only Amer. stork; **wood'land**, wooded country, woods; (attrib.) of, in, growing or dwelling in, consisting of, etc., woodland; **wood louse**, small terrestrial isopod crustacean of *Oniscus* or related genera, found in old wood, under stones, etc.; **wood'man** (pl. **-men**), forester, woodcutter; **wood nymph**, nymph of the woods, dryad; **wood'pecker**, any bird of numerous genera and species of family Picidae, found in most parts of world, with plumage usu. bright colored and variegated, characterized by habit of pecking holes in trunks and branches of trees to find insects for food or make cavities for laying eggs; **wood pigeon**: see PIGEON; **wood pulp**, pulp made by mechanical or chemical disintegration of wood fiber, used for making paper etc.; **wood'ruff**, low-growing European woodland herb (*Asperula odorata*) with clusters of small white flowers and whorls of strongly sweet-scented leaves; **woods'man** (pl. **-men**), man living in or frequenting woods, one skilled in woodcraft; **wood sorrel**, low-growing spring-flowering woodland plant (*Oxalis acetosella*) with delicate trifoliate leaves and small white flowers streaked with purple; other species of *Oxalis*; **wood tar**, tar obtained in dry distillation of wood; **wood warbler**: see WARBLER; **wood'wind**, wooden wind instruments of orchestra; **wood'work**, work done in wood, wooden part *of* anything, esp. wooden interior parts of building; **wood'worm**, wood-boring larva of a furniture beetle *Anobium punctatum*. **wood'ed** *adj.* Covered with growing trees; abounding in woods.

wood·chuck (wŏŏd'chŭk) *n.* Thick-bodied reddish-brown marmot (*Marmota monax*) of northeastern U.S. and Canada. [f. Amer. Ind. name, cf. Cree *wuchak, otchock*]

Modern automatic machinery at a mill in Galashiels, Scotland. Current demand for ***wool*** *has resulted in most early methods of spinning and weaving being superseded.*

wood·en (wŏŏd'*e*n) *adj.* Made, consisting, of wood; resembling wood; dull and inert, stiff and lifeless, inexpressive; **wood'en-head**, blockhead; **wooden-headed** (*adj.*); **wooden horse**, wooden figure of a horse made by Greeks in TROJAN War; **wood'enware**, kitchen utensils made of wood. **wood'en·ly** *adv.* **wood'en·ness** *n.*

wood·y (wŏŏd'ē) *adj.* (**wood·i·er, wood·i·est**). Covered with trees, abounding in woods, well wooded; of the nature of, consisting of, wood; resembling (that of) wood; (of plant) forming wood, having woody stems and branches; ~ **nightshade**: see NIGHTSHADE. **wood'i·ness** *n.*

woof (wōōf, wŏŏf) *n.* Threads crossing from side to side of web and interwoven with warp; yarn for woof threads.

wool (wŏŏl) *n.* Fine soft curly hair forming fleecy coat of domesticated sheep and similar animals, characterized by overlapping of the filaments, to which is due its property of felting, and used chiefly in prepared state for making cloth; twisted woolen yarn used for knitting etc.; woolen garment or cloth; short soft underhair or down of some animals; something resembling wool, esp. downy substance found on some plants: any fine fibrous substance naturally or artificially produced; **dyed in the** ~, dyed before spinning; (fig.) thoroughgoing, out-and-out; **pull the** ~ **over person's eyes**, hoodwink; **wool'gathering**, gathering fragments of wool torn from sheep by bushes etc.; absent-minded(ness), indulging or indulgence in idle imagining. **wool** *adj.* (commerc.) Made of wool throughout. (cf. WOOLEN).

wool·en, Brit. **wool·len** (wŏŏl'*e*n) *adjs.* Made, consisting, of wool or of yarns containing wool fibers, esp. when coarse or loosely woven. ~ *n.* (usu. pl.) Woolen clothing or fabric.

Woolf (wŏŏlf), **Virginia** (1882–1941). English novelist and critic.

wool·len = WOOLEN.

wool·ly (**-li·er, -li·est**), **wool·y** (**wool·i·er, wool·i·est**) (wŏŏl'ē) *adjs.* Bearing, naturally covered with, wool or woollike hair; resembling or suggesting wool in softness, texture, etc.; confused, blurred, hazy; (of thought) lacking clarity; (of plants) pubescent, downy; **wild and** ~, vigorous, rough, lawless (orig. applied to West of U.S. in frontier days);

woolly bear, (colloq.) large hairy caterpillar, esp. larva of tigermoth. **wool·ly** (pl. **-lies**), **wool·y** (pl. **wool·ies**) *ns.* Woolen, esp. knitted, garment. **wool'li·ness, wool'i·ness** *ns.*

word (wẽrd) *n.* 1. Vocal sound or combination of sounds, or written or printed symbols of these, constituting minimal element of speech having a meaning as such and capable of independent grammatical use; ~ **for** ~, verbatim, exact(ly); **last** ~, final utterance in conversation or esp. dispute; (pl.) last utterance before death; final or conclusive statement, latest thing. 2. Thing(s) said, speech, utterance (usu. pl.); (pl.) text of song, actor's part, etc.; verbal expression contrasted with action or thought; (pl.) contentious or violent talk, altercation; (with negative etc.) anything at all (said or written); watchword, password; report, tidings, information; command, order; promise, undertaking; declaration, assurance; **the W~ (of God)**, the Bible or some part of it; second person of Trinity; **man of his** ~, one who keeps his promises. 3. ~**-blind**, (path.) unable as result of brain injury or disease to understand written or printed words; **word'book**, book with list(s) of words, vocabulary; **word-deaf**, (path.) unable to understand speech though capable of hearing the sounds; **word painting**, vivid descriptive writing; **word'play**, joke using features of words, pun, etc.; **word square**, series of words so arranged as to read the same vertically and horizontally, puzzle of which solution is such a series. **word'less** *adj.* **word'less·ly** *adv.* **word** *v.t.* Put into words, phrase, select words to express. **word'ing** *n.* (esp.) Form of words used, phrasing.

word·age (wẽr'dĭj) *n.* 1. Words collectively, esp. number of words in story, book, etc. 2. Use of too many words; verbiage. 3. Wording.

Words·worth (wẽrdz'wẽrth), **William** (1770–1850). English Romantic lyric poet, one of the Lake poets (see LAKE[1]); poet laureate from 1843.

word·y (wẽr'dē) *adj.* (**word·i·er, word·i·est**). Verbose; in, consisting of, words. **word'i·ly** *adv.* **word'i·ness** *n.*

wore: see WEAR[2].

work (wẽrk) *n.* 1. Action involving effort or exertion, esp. as means of gaining livelihood; labor done in making something, as dist. from materials used; (phys. etc.) operation of a force in producing movement or other physical change, esp. as measurable quantity; something to do or to be done, employment, business, function; act, deed, proceeding, (pl.) doings; (theol., pl.) moral action considered in relation to justification; **at** ~, engaged in work, working, operating; **out of** ~, without work to do, unemployed; **set to** ~, set (person), apply oneself, to a task, or to do something; **the** ~ **of** ..., a proceeding occupying (a stated time).

Some modern critics tend to dismiss the poetry of ***William Wordsworth*** *yet his recommendation that the language of ordinary speech be used was a strong influence on his contemporaries.*

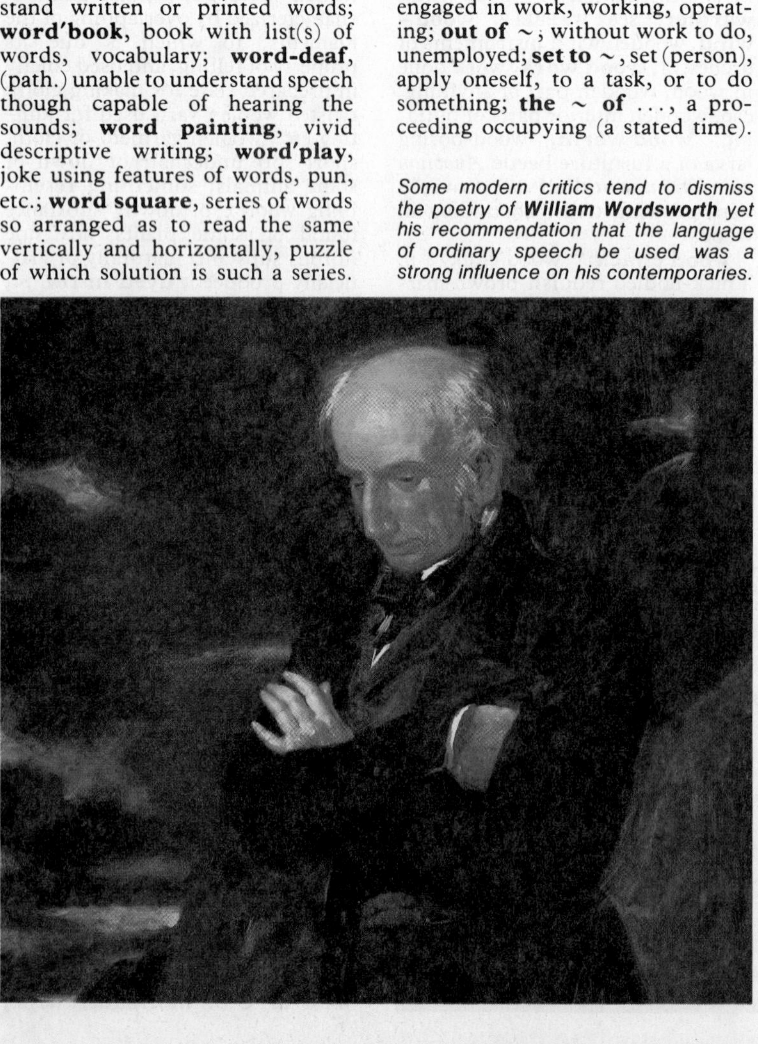

2. Product of labor, thing(s) made; result of action; (pl.) architectural or engineering operations; (mil.) fortified building, defensive structure, fortification; literary or musical composition, product of any fine art, as statue, picture, etc., (pl. or collect. sing.) person's writings, compositions, paintings, etc., as a whole; sewing, embroidery, knitting, etc. 3. (pl.) Establishment, building with machinery, etc., where industrial process, esp. manufacture, is carried on; (pl.) internal mechanism, moving parts of piece of machinery, etc., esp. clock or watch. 4. **workahol'ic**, (colloq.) person having obsessive need to work; **work'bag, work'basket, work'box**, bag etc. holding materials and implements for needlework; **work'bench**, bench for mechanical work, esp. carpentry; **work'book**, book containing instructions and suggestions for study work in the form of questions, exercises, etc.; book for recording work done or planned; handbook containing directions for workman; **work'day**, day on which work is ordinarily performed, weekday; **work'horse**, horse (or fig. person or machine etc.) that performs arduous labor; **work'house**, (hist.) public institution for maintenance of paupers, in which able-bodied were set to work; **work'load**, amount of work that can be performed by a person, machine, etc. in a specified time; **work'man** (pl. **-men**), man hired to do work or (usu.) manual labor, esp. skilled labor; craftsman; one who works in specified manner; **work'manlike, work'manly**, characteristic of a good workman, efficient; **work'manship**, skill as a workman, craftsmanship exhibited in piece of work; **work'room**, room in which work is done; **work sheet**, sheet of paper for recording work schedules, working time, instructions, etc.; sheet of paper having questions, problems, etc., to be solved by pupils; sheet of paper setting forth in preliminary form ideas, plans for action; **work'shop**, room or building in which manual work is carried on; seminar or group of meetings for sharing ideas, group study, demonstrating methods, etc.; **work'table**, table for holding working implements; **work'week**, total number of days or hours worked in a week for base pay. **work'less** *adj.* & *n.* **work** *v.* (**worked** or **wrought** pr. rawt,

Cigar packing in a Belgian factory (1) may be monotonous ***work,*** *but despite such developments as automation at the Volkswagen works in Germany (2), the need to provide work for more people is sometimes paramount. Termite* ***workers,*** *of course, act from instinct and not need.*

1

2

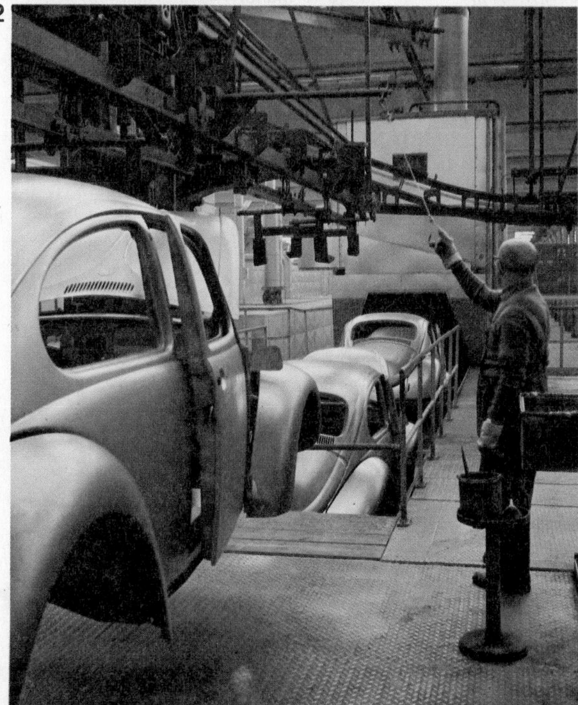

3

work·ing). 1. Engage, be engaged, in work; carry on operations; make efforts; be craftsman (*in* some material); (of machine, plan, etc.) operate, act, (of person) put or keep (machine etc.) in operation; keep (person, machine, etc.) at work or going, exact toil from; purchase (*passage* etc.) with labor instead of money. 2. Carry on, manage, control; have influence or effect, exercise influence on; bring about, effect, accomplish, produce as result. 3. Be in motion, be agitated; cause agitation; ferment. 4. (Cause to) make way, make (way etc.), slowly or with difficulty or by shifting motions; gradually become (tight, free, etc.) by motion. 5. Knead, hammer, fashion, into shape or desired consistency; artificially and gradually excite (person) *into* (a rage etc.). 6. Do, make by, needlework or the like. 7. Solve (sum) by mathematical processes. 8. ~ **off**, get rid of, free oneself from; finish working at; pass off, palm off; ~ **out**, find (amount etc.), solve (sum) by calculation, (of amount etc.) be calculated (*at*); exhaust (mine etc.) by working; accomplish, attain, with difficulty; develop, elaborate, plan or provide for details of; discharge (debt, obligation), pay for, by labor instead of money; (of athlete, team, etc.) box, play, etc., for practice and exercise not in contest; **work'-out**, exercise; practice game, bout, run, etc.; **work up**, bring gradually to efficient state; elaborate in description; advance gradually *to* (climax); excite, incite, stir up, arouse (*to*); stir up, make up (materials), compose, produce, construct; study (subject) carefully and in detail.

work·a·ble (wẽr'kabel) *adj.* That can be worked, fashioned, manipulated, managed, conducted, etc. **work·a·bil·i·ty** (wẽrkabĭl'ĭtē), **work'a·ble·ness** *ns.*

work·a·day (wẽr'kadā) *adj.* Of, characteristic of, workday or its occupations; of ordinary humdrum everyday life.

work·er (wẽr'ker) *n.* (esp.) 1. One employed for a wage, esp. in manual or industrial work; one who works either with hand or brain (opp. capitalist; see CAPITAL[2]). 2. Neuter or undeveloped female of certain social hymenopterous and other insects, as ants and bees, which supplies food and performs other services for community.

work·ing (wẽr'kĭng) *n.* (esp.) Way thing works, result of its working; action, operation; ~ **capital**, capital used in actual conduct of business, not invested in buildings, machinery, etc.; ~ **day**, workday, number of hours of work entitling workman to day's pay, portion of day devoted to work; ~ **drawing(s)**, scale drawing(s) from which workmen carry out construction; ~ **order**, (of a machine, system, etc.) working efficiently. **working** *adj.* (esp.) Engaged in manual or industrial work; ~ **class(es)**, grade(s) of society comprising those employed for wages, esp. in manual or industrial occupations; ~**-class**, of, for, the working class; **work'ingman, work'ingwoman**, (pl. **-men; -women**), person of working class; **working model**, model of machine etc. capable of doing work on small scale, or of being operated.

world (wẽrld) *n.* 1. Human existence, (also **this** ~) present life; pursuits and interests, affairs and conditions of life; secular or lay life and interests; **next, other,** ~, life after death; ~ **without end**, endlessly, eternally. 2. Earth considered as a planet; Earth and all created things upon it; planet or other heavenly body, esp. one viewed as inhabited; material universe as ordered system, system of created things; everything, all phenomena; countries of Earth and their inhabitants, all people; human society; particular section of this, esp. high or fashionable society; sphere of interest, action, or thought; (freq. pl.) great quantity, vast or infinite amount or extent; **for all the** ~, in every respect (like); **man, woman, of the** ~, one knowing the ways of society; **not for (all) the** ~, not on any account. 3. **New World**, Western Hemisphere, containing the nations of the Americas; **Old World**, Eastern Hemisphere, comprising the continents of Europe, Asia, Africa, and Australia; **World Bank**, (colloq.) International Bank for Reconstruction and Development, established in 1945 as an agency of the United Nations; **world history**, history embracing

When scientists first began to classify animals, the term ***worm*** *was even used to describe snakes. However, today, marine bristle worms (below) are in the same phylum as the earthworm.*

Plants named ***woundwort*** *include Stachys palustris whose leaves were used as a poultice; and resin from the root of Laserpitium prutenicum was used to make 'Thaspia plasters'.*

events of whole world; **world language**, artificial language intended for universal use; **world politics**, international politics, politics based upon considerations affecting whole world; **world power**, state or nation dominating world politics; **world series** (often **W ~ S ~**), annual series of baseball games between the two U.S. major league pennant winners to decide championship; **world war**, war affecting (most of) the world; **World War I, First World War**, that of 1914–18, fought mainly in Europe and the Middle East between the Allied Powers (Great Britain, U.S., France, etc.) and the Central Powers (Germany, Austria-Hungary, etc.); **World War II, Second World War**, that of 1939–45, fought between the Allies (Great Britain, U.S., France, Soviet Union) and the Axis (Germany, Italy and Japan); **world-weary**, weary of (the life of) the world; **world'wide**, spread over the world, known or found everywhere, universal.

world·ling (wẽrld'lĭng) *n.* Worldly person.

world·ly (wẽrld'lē) *adj.* (**-li·er, -li·est**). Temporal, earthly; exclusively or predominantly concerned with or devoted to affairs of this life, esp. to pursuit of wealth or pleasure; **~ goods**, property; **~-minded**, intent on worldly things; **~ wisdom**, esp. prudence in advancing one's own interests; **~ -wise**, having worldly wisdom, sophisticated. **world'li·ness** *n.*

worm (wẽrm) *n.* Slender burrowing invertebrate animal esp. of genus *Lumbricus*, usu. brown or reddish with soft body divided into segments, earthworm; any annelid (**ringed** or **segmented ~**), nematode (**round'worm**), or platyhelminth (**flat'worm**); platyhelminth or nematode living as parasite in intestine of man or other animal; (pl.) disorder characterized by presence of these; larva of insect, maggot, grub, esp. one feeding on or destructive to fruit, leaves, timber, paper, flesh, etc.; maggot supposed to eat dead bodies in the grave; SHIPworm. 2. Abject, miserable, or contemptible person. 3. (fig.) Grief or passion that preys stealthily on the heart or torments the conscience. 4. Natural or artificial object resembling earthworm; small worm-shaped ligament in dog's tongue; any of various spiral implements, esp. spiral of screw (also **worm gear**) endless or tangent screw whose thread gears with teeth of toothed wheel etc.; long spiral or coiled tube connected to head of still, in which vapor is condensed. 5. **worm-eaten**, eaten into by worm(s), full of wormholes; decayed, decrepit, antiquated; **worm gear**, see sense 4; worm wheel; **worm'hole**, hole in wood, fruit, book, etc., made by burrowing insect larva; **worm wheel**, toothed wheel gearing with worm. **worm'y** *adj.* (**worm·i·er, worm·i·est**). **worm** *v.* 1. Hunt for worms; rid (plants etc.) of worms or grubs; cure (puppies etc.) of worms; extract worm from tongue of (dog) as supposed safeguard against madness. 2. Progress or move sinuously; make one's way insidiously, insinuate *oneself*, *into* (person's confidence, secrets, etc.); **~ out**, extract (secret etc.) by insidious questioning.

*In Scotland, some types of seaweed have long been used as a vegetable. **Bladder-wrack** (above) is used as mulch and as winter feed for livestock. It was also used to combat scurvy and goiter.*

worm·wood (wẽrm'wo͝od) *n.* European woody herb (*Artemisia absinthium*) with bitter aromatic taste, yielding dark green oil, and formerly used as tonic and vermifuge and now for making vermouth and absinthe; (fig.) bitter humiliation or its cause.

Worms (wẽrmz; *Ger.* vōrmz), **Diet of**: see DIET[1].

worn (wōrn, wōrn) *adj.*: see WEAR; (esp.) impaired by use, exposure, or wear; enfeebled, exhausted, by toil, age, anxiety, etc.; **~-out**, no longer of use or service; utterly wasted in strength or vitality; stale, trite.

wor·ry (wẽr'ē, wŭr'ē) *n.* (pl. **-ries**). Harassing anxiety or solicitude; cause of this, matter for anxiety, (pl.) cares, troubles; **wor'rywart**, (colloq.) person who habitually worries unduly. **worry** *v.* (**-ried, -ry·ing**). 1. (of dog etc.) Seize by throat with teeth and tear or lacerate, kill or injure by biting and shaking; (fig.) harass, work at, get *along* or *through* with persistent aggression or dogged effort or struggle; vex or distress by inconsiderate or importunate behavior, pester with repeated demands, requests, etc. 2. Make anxious and ill at ease; give way to anxiety or mental disquietude. **wor'ri·er** *n.*

worse (wẽrs) *adj.* & *adv.* Used as comparative of *bad*, *evil*, *badly*, *ill*, or as opposite of *better*. **~** *n.* Worse thing(s); worse condition. **wors'en** *v.* Make or become worse, deteriorate.

wor·ship (wẽr'shĭp) *n.* 1. Reverence paid to being or power regarded as divine; acts, rites, or ceremonies displaying this; adoration or devotion comparable to this felt or shown to person or principle; **public ~**, church service. 2. (Brit.) Respectful form of address to or mention of certain magistrates in court, also (formerly) persons of high rank etc. **worship** *v.* (**-shiped, -ship·ing**, Brit. **-shipped, -ship·ping**). Adore as divine, pay religious homage to; idolize, regard with adoration; attend public worship; be full of adoration. **wor'ship·er**, Brit. **wor'ship·per** *ns.*

wor·ship·ful (wẽr'shĭpful) *adj.* 1. Reverent, filled with spirit of veneration. 2. (archaic) Entitled to honor and respect. **wor'ship·ful·ly** *adv.* **wor'ship·ful·ness** *n.*

worst (wẽrst) *adj.* & *adv.* Used as superlative of *bad*, *evil*, *badly*, *ill*; least good or well. **~** *n.* Worst part, feature, state, event, possible issue, action, etc.; **at (the) ~**, in the most evil or undesirable possible state; even on the most unfavorable view or surmise; **do one's ~**, do the utmost evil or harm possible; **get** (etc.) **the ~ of**, be

Sir Christopher Wren attained eminence as an astronomer before he became an architect at the age of 30. His plan for the redesign of London was never completed, but his churches still stand.

worsted in; **if (the) ~ come(s) to (the) ~**, if things turn out as badly as possible or conceivable. **worst** *v.t.* Get the better of, defeat, outdo.

wor·sted (wŏŏs′tĭd, wẽr′stĭd) *n.* Fine smooth-surfaced yarn spun from long staple wool that has been combed so that fibers lie parallel; fabric woven from this. ~ *adj.* Made of worsted. [f. *Worste(a)d* in Norfolk, England]

wort (wẽrt) *n.* Plant or herb used for food or medicine (archaic exc. as second element of plant names).

worth (wẽrth) *predic. adj.* Of the value of (a specified amount or sum); of specified or certain value in other than material respects; sufficiently valuable or important to be equivalent or good return for (something); possessed of, owning; deserving or worthy of (something); **worth′while′**, that is worth time or effort expended. **worth′less** *adj.* **worth′less·ly** *adv.* **worth′less·ness** *n.* **worth** *n.* What a thing is worth, value; equivalent *of* specified sum or amount.

wor·thy (wẽr′dhē) *adj.* (**-thi·er, -thi·est**). Estimable; having high moral standard; of sufficient worth, value, desert, or merit (*to*), deserving (*of*). ~ *n.* (pl. **-thies**). Distinguished, eminent, or famous person, esp. hero of antiquity.

would (wŏŏd): see WILL[2]; **~-be** (*adj.*) desiring or professing to be, posing as.

wound[1] (wōōnd) *n.* Injury done by cutting, stabbing, lacerating, etc., animal or vegetable tissues with hard or sharp instrument, bullet, etc. (freq. fig.); **wound′-wort**, plant used for healing or dressing wounds, esp. species of kidney vetch, goldenrod, etc. **wound** *v.* Inflict wound (on); inflict pain or hurt on, pain, grieve deeply.

wound[2]: see WIND[2].

wove (wōv) *adj.*: see WEAVE; (esp. of paper) made on mold of closely woven wire.

wo·ven: see WEAVE.

wow[1] (wow) *n.* (slang) Striking success.

wow[2] (wow) *n.* Waver, tremolo, in reproduced sound, due to fluctuations in record speed.

w.p. *abbrev.* (baseball) Wild pitch(es).

WPA *abbrev.* Works Progress Administration.

wpm, w.p.m. *abbrevs.* Words per minute.

wrack (răk) *n.* Seaweed or other marine vegetation cast up or growing on tidal seashore; (archaic) wreck; destruction (= RACK[1]); vestige.

wraith (rāth) *n.* Apparition, ghost, of dead person; spectral appearance of living person supposed to portend his death.

wran·gle (răng′gel) *v.* (**-gled, -gling**). 1. Brawl; engage in noisy, vehement, or contentious argument or quarrel; gain or bring about by wrangling. 2. Herd, round up, horses etc. ~ *n.* Noisy, vehement dispute. **wran′gler** *n.*

wrap (răp) *v.* (**wrapped** or **wrapt, wrap·ping**). Enfold, enclose, pack, swathe, (freq. *up*) in garment or folded or soft encircling material; form wrap or covering for; involve, enfold, *in* something obscuring or disguising; fold, wind, draw (covering, garment, etc.) *about, around,* etc.; **~ up**, put on wraps; (colloq.) finish, settle, summarize; **wrapped up**, (esp.) engrossed, centered, absorbed, *in*; bound up with, involved *in*. **wrap** *n.* Wrapper, covering; blanket, rug, etc., (usu. pl.) additional outer garment worn as defense against wind and weather; woman's shawl, scarf, or the like; **wrap′around**, (designating) garment, skirt, robe, etc., that wraps around body and overlaps its full length; **wrap′up**, (colloq.) brief summary.

wrap·per (răp′*er*) *n.* (esp.) Protective covering for parcel etc.; paper enclosing newspaper etc. for posting; paper cover of pamphlet or periodical; book jacket; loose enveloping robe or gown; tobacco leaf of superior grade used for outer cover of cigar.

wrap·ping (răp′ĭng) *n.* (esp. pl.) Wraps, enveloping garments; **~ paper**, paper for packing or wrapping parcels, packages, etc.

wrath (răth) *n.* (chiefly poet. or rhet.) Anger, indignation. **wrath′ful** *adj.* **wrath′ful·ly** *adv.* **wrath′ful·ness** *n.*

wreak (rēk) *v.t.* Gratify (anger etc.), inflict (vengeance etc.), *on*.

wreath (rēth) *n.* (pl. **wreaths** pr. rēdhz). Flowers or leaves strung or woven or wound together into ring for wearing on head, for Christmas ornament, or for decorating statue, building, coffin, etc.; carved imitation of this; similar ring of soft twisted material, as silk; curl *of* smoke, circular or curved band of cloud, light driftin mass of sand, snow, etc.

wreathe (rēdh) *v.* (**wreathed, wreath·ing**). Encircle as (or with, or as with) a wreath; form into wreath; entwine; wind, turn (flexible object) around or over something; (of smoke etc.) move in wreathlike shape.

wreck (rĕk) *n.* Disabling, destruction, ruin, overthrow, esp. of ship; ship that has suffered wreck; what remains *of* thing or person that has suffered ruin, waste, disablement, dilapidation, etc., anything broken down or ruined, person of undermined or shattered constitution; (law) goods etc. cast up by sea, piece of wreckage. ~ *v.* Cause wreck of (ship, train, person's constitution, undertaking, etc.); suffer wreck.

wreck·age (rĕk′ĭj) *n.* Fragments or remains of wrecked or shattered vessel, structure, etc.; (fig.) act or process of wrecking.

wreck·er (rĕk′*er*) *n.* (esp.) One who tries from shore to bring about shipwreck in order to plunder or profit by wreckage; one who steals wreckage; person employed in recovering wrecked ship or its contents; vehicle to tow wrecked car; one who obstructs undertaking etc.

wren (rĕn) *n.* Any of numerous species of genus *Troglodytes* and related genera of small songbirds, esp. the *T. aedon*, the house wren, a very small dark brown mottled bird with short erect tail.

Wren (rĕn), **Sir Christopher** (1632–1723). English architect; designer of St. Paul's Cathedral and many other London churches and buildings after the fire of 1666.

wrench (rĕnch) *n.* 1. Violent twist, turn, or pull; (fig.) pain or anguish caused by parting. 2. Instrument or tool of various forms for gripping or turning bolthead, nut, etc., consisting essentially of metal bars with (freq. adjustable) jaws. ~ *v.* Twist, turn; pull around or sideways, violently or with effort; pull *away*, *off*, *out*, thus; injure, pain, by straining or stretching.

wrest (rĕst) *v.* Twist, deflect, distort, pervert; force or wrench away from person's grasp. ~ *n.* Tuning key of wire-stringed instrument, as harp, piano; ~ **pins**, pegs to which piano strings are attached.

wres·tle (rĕs′*el*) *n.* (**-tled, -tling**). Wrestling match; hard struggle. ~ *v.* Strive to overpower and throw another to the ground, esp. in contest governed by fixed rules, by grappling with him and tripping or overbalancing him; have wrestling match with; contend, grapple, struggle, *with* thing, difficulties, feelings, forces, etc.; throw (cattle) for branding. **wres′tler, wres′tling** *ns.*

wretch (rĕch) *n.* Miserable, unhappy, or unfortunate person; contemptible or vile person, one without conscience or shame (freq. as term of playful abuse).

wretch·ed (rĕch′ĭd) *adj.* Miserable, unhappy, afflicted; inferior, of poor quality, of no merit; contemptible; unsatisfactory; causing discontent, discomfort, or nuisance. **wretch′ed·ly** *adv.* **wretch′ed·ness** *n.*

wrig·gle (rĭg′*el*) *n.* (**-gled, -gling**). Wriggling movement. ~ *v.* Twist or turn body about with short writhing movements; (fig.) be slippery, practice evasion; move (oneself, part of body, etc.) with wriggling motion, make (*way*) by wriggling. **wrig′gly** *adj.* (**-gli·er, -gli·est**). **wrig′gler** *n.* (esp.) Larva of a mosquito.

Wright[1] (rīt), **Frank Lloyd** (1869–1959). Amer. architect known for his exceptionally original and innovative designs.

Wright[2] (rīt), **Orville** (1871–1948) and **Wilbur** (1867–1912). Two brothers, Amer. technicians, who built and flew (1903) the first heavier-than-air motor-driven flying machine.

wring (rĭng) *v.t.* (**wrung** pr. rŭng, **wring·ing**). Press, squeeze, or twist, with hands or machine, esp. so as to drain or make dry, strain (moisture etc.) by squeezing or torsion from moist or wet thing; twist forcibly, break by twisting, torture, distress, rack; extort, get (money, concession, etc.) *out of* or *from* by exaction or importunity; press or clasp (person's *hand*) forcibly or with emotion; ~ **one's hands**, clasp and twist them together in distress or pain. **wring** *n.* Squeeze, act of wringing.

wring·er (rĭng′*er*) *n.* (esp.) Device for wringing water from laundered clothes etc., usu. consisting essentially of two rollers between which article is squeezed.

wrin·kle (rĭng′*kel*) *n.* 1. Furrowlike crease, depression, or ridge in skin (esp. of kind produced by age, care, etc.) or in other flexible surface. 2. (colloq.) Useful hint; clever expedient. **wrin′kly** *adj.* (**-kli·er, -kli·est**). **wrinkle** *v.* (**-kled, -kling**). Acquire or assume wrinkles; produce wrinkles in.

wrist (rĭst) *n.* Joint in man connecting hand with forearm, carpus; analogous joint in other animals; part of garment covering wrist; **wrist′band**, band of sleeve covering or fastening about wrist; wristlet; **wrist pin**, (mech.) pin, stud, joining connecting rod to piston; **wrist′watch**, small watch worn on strap or bracelet around wrist.

wrist·let (rĭst′lĭt) *n.* Band, bracelet, strap, worn on wrist to strengthen or guard it, as ornament, to hold watch, etc.

writ[1] (rĭt) *n.* 1. **Holy, Sacred, W**~, sacred writings collectively, esp. the Bible. 2. Formal written order issued by court in name of government, state, etc., directing person(s) to whom it is addressed to do or refrain from doing specified act.

writ[2] (rĭt) *v.* (archaic and poet.) Wrote, written.

write (rīt) *v.* (**wrote** pr. rōt, **writ·ten** pr. rĭt′*en*, **writ·ing**). Form symbols representing letter(s) or word(s) esp. on paper, parchment, etc., with pen, pencil, brush, etc., form (such symbols), set (words etc.) down in writing, express in writing; chronicle, make record or account of; convey (message, information, etc.) by letter; engage in writing or authorship; produce writing; ~ **down**, set down in writing; write in disparagement or depreciation of; reduce (total, assets, etc.) to lower amount; ~ **in**, add (extra name) on list of candidates when voting (so **write-in** *n.*); **write off**, record canceling of (bad debt, depreciated stock, etc.); reckon as lost or worthless; **write-off** (*n.*), something that must be regarded as total loss or wreck, failure; **write out**, make written copy of; transcribe in full or detail; **write up**, write full account

*As with many animals in the colonies the name **wren** was given to small birds which are unrelated to the true varieties. Most of these birds are insectivorous and the common wren of Europe is only 4 ins. long. In contrast, the cactus wren in the south-west U.S.A. grows to 8½ inches long.*

or record of; give full or elaborate description of; commend by appreciative writing, praise in writing; **write-up** (*n.*), review or report.

writ·er (rī′ter) *n.* One who writes; person writing books, articles, etc., esp. as profession; **~'s cramp**, painful spasmodic cramp affecting muscles of hand and fingers used in writing, and resulting from excessive writing.

writhe (rīdh) *v.* (**writhed, writh·ing**). Twist or roll oneself about (as) in acute pain, squirm; twist (*body* etc.) about, contort. ~ *n.* Act of writhing. **writh′ing·ly** *adv.*

writ·ing (rī′tĭng) *n.* (esp.) Written document; (piece of) literary work; personal script, handwriting; **put in ~**, write down; **the W~s** = HAGIOGRAPHA; **writing desk**, desk; **writing paper**, paper for writing on with ink, esp. notepaper; **writing table**, desk.

writ·ten (rĭt′en) *adj.*: see WRITE; (esp.) that is in writing, esp. opp. *oral* or *printed*.

wrong (rawng, rŏng) *adj.* 1. Not morally right or equitable, unjust; doing or prone to do evil; not correct or proper; not true, mistaken; judging, acting, etc., contrary to facts, in error; **~-headed, wrong′head′ed**, perversely or obstinately wrong, characterized by perversity of judgment; **wrong-headedness, wrong′headed′ness** (*ns.*). 2. Not in good order or condition, amiss; not what is required or intended, unsuitable, inappropriate; (of way etc.) leading in, tending to, direction other than what is intended, desired, or expected; **wrong end**, end or limit less adapted or suitable for particular purpose; **get hold of the wrong end of the stick**, (fig.) be mistaken in judgment etc.; **wrong side**, side (of fabric etc.) not meant for use or show; **on the wrong side of**, older than (specified age); under a person's disapproval or disfavor; **get up, get out of bed, on the wrong side**, be in irritable mood; (**the**) **wrong way**, in contrary or opposite way to proper or usual one. **wrong′ly** *adv.* **wrong′ness, wrong′er** *ns.* **wrong** *adv.* Amiss, in wrong course or direction; mistakenly, erroneously; in improper or unfitting manner; **get person ~**, misunderstand him; **get in ~ with person**, (colloq.) incur his dislike; **get person in ~**, bring him into disfavor; **go ~**, go astray; happen amiss or unfortunately; get out of gear or working order; take to bad ways. **wrong** *n.* What is morally wrong; wrong action; unjust action or treatment; being wrong in attitude, procedure, or belief (freq. **in the ~**); **wrong′doing**, transgression against moral or established law. **wrong** *v.t.* Treat unjustly, do wrong to; do injustice to by statement, opinion, etc.; dishonor by word or thought.

wrong·ful (rawng′ful, rŏng′-) *adj.* Marked by wrong, unfairness, injustice, etc.; contrary to law, etc., unlawful, illegal; (of persons) holding office, possession, etc., unlawfully or without legitimacy or right. **wrong′ful·ly** *adv.* **wrong′ful·ness** *n.*

*Empty hay cart in the rodeo parade at Cheyenne, **Wyoming.** This mountain State is a major center of cattle breeding although the greatest income is derived from mining, and oil and gas.*

wrote: see WRITE.

wroth (rawth, rōth; *Brit.* also rōth) *pred. adj.* (poet. and rhet.) Angry, stirred to wrath.

wrought (rawt) *adj.* Worked, processed, manufactured, worked into shape; (literary) put together, worked, made; (of metals) beaten out or shaped with hammer etc.; **~ iron**: see IRON; **wrought-up**, stirred up, excited or agitated.

wrung: see WRING.

wry (rī) *adj.* (**wri·er, wri·est**). Distorted, turned to one side; temporarily twisted or contorted in disgust, disrelish, etc.; **wry·mouth** (pr. rī′mowth) (pl. **-mouth**, collect. **-mouths** pr. -mowdhz), any of numerous large fish of family Stichaeidae, of blenny kind, the ghostfish of northern Atlantic coasts of N. Amer.; **wry′neck**, deformity with contortion of neck and face and lateral inclination of head, torticollis; species of genus *Jynx* of small migratory birds allied to woodpeckers, esp. *J. torquilla* of Europe and Asia, with peculiar manner of writhing neck and head. **wry′ly** *adv.* **wry′ness** *n.*

WSW, W.S.W., w.s.w. *abbrevs.* West-southwest.

wt. *abbrev.* Weight.

Wul·fi·la (wo͝ol′fĭla): see ULFILAS.

WV, W.Va. *abbrevs.* West Virginia.

WY *abbrev.* Wyoming.

Wy·an·dotte (wī′andŏt) *n.* (pl. **-dottes**, collect. for def. 1 **-dotte**). 1. Member of tribe of N. Amer. Indians. 2. Domestic fowl of medium-sized breed, orig. white laced with black but now bred in various colors.

wych, witch[2] (wĭch) *ns.* In names of various trees with pliant branches: **~-elm**, species of elm (*Ulmus glabra*) with broader leaves and more spreading branches than common elm; **~ hazel**, N. Amer. shrub (*Hamamelis virginiana*) with yellow flowers blooming in late autumn or winter.

Wyc·liffe, Wyc·lif (wĭk′lĭf), **John** (*c*1320–84). English religious reformer; attacked the papacy and asserted the right of every man to examine the Bible for himself; instituted the first translation into English of the whole Bible, himself translating the Gospels and probably other parts; his doctrines were taken up by the Lollards.

Wyo. *abbrev.* Wyoming.

Wy·o·ming (wīō′mĭng). State of northwestern U.S., admitted to the Union in 1890; capital, Cheyenne.

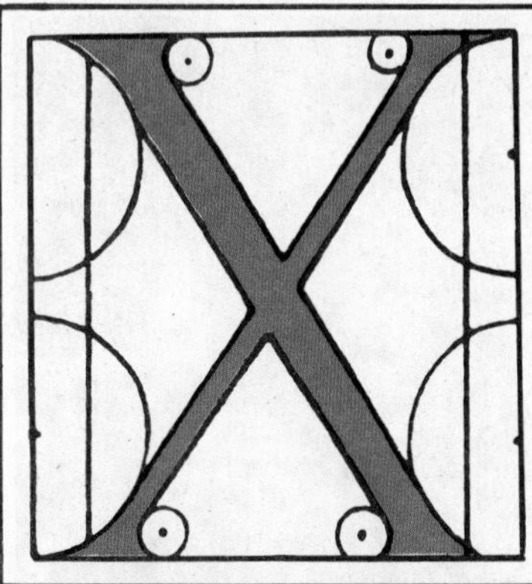

Although the letter **X, x** appeared in the Greek alphabet, about 600 B.C., it was derived from a symbol used in Egyptian hieroglyphics and a later Phoenician character. The sound attributed to it in Greek was as in 'fix' but if used at the beginning of a word, then sounded as in 'xylophone'.

X, x (ĕks) (pl. **X's, x's** or **Xs, xs**). 1. Twenty-fourth letter of modern English and 21st of ancient Roman alphabet, adopted from the Greek alphabet introduced into Italy, with the value (ks, as in lyn*x*) that it usually has in modern English except when occurring initially in words chiefly of Greek origin, when it is pronounced z. 2. Roman numeral symbol for ten; **X,** (slang) ten-dollar bill. 3. (alg. etc.) Symbol for (esp. first) unknown or variable quantity; hence, incalculable or unknown factor or influence. 4. **X,** symbol for Christ, representing the chi in Greek *ΧΡΙΣΤΟΣ*, used in abbreviations, e.g. *Xmas* (= Christmas). 5. Symbol to mark position (*X marks the spot*) or incorrectness or to symbolize a kiss or vote or as signature by illiterate person. 6. **X,** designation of motion picture for showing only to persons over 18 years. 7. **x-height,** height of an x, height of body of letter. 8. Object etc. shaped like X.

x (ĕks) *v.t.* (**x-ed** or **x'd, x-ing**). Mark with *x*; (also **x out**) delete, cross out.

xan·thate (zăn'thāt) *n.* (chem.) Salt of xanthic acid.

xan·the·in (zăn'thēĭn) *n.* (chem.) Yellow coloring matter found in plants.

xan·thic (zăn'thĭk) *adj.* (chem. etc.) Yellow; of xanthin; ~ **acid,** complex acid ($C_3H_6OS_2$), many of whose salts are yellow.

xan·thine (zăn'thēn, -thĭn) *n.* (chem.) Substance ($C_5H_4N_4O_2$) related to uric acid and found in animal secretions.

Xan·thip·pe, Xan·tip·pe (zăntĭp'ē). Wife of Socrates, reputed to be a shrew; hence, shrewish woman or wife.

xan·tho·phyll (zăn'th*o*fĭl) *n.* Dark brown crystalline compound found in plants, usu. associated with chlorophyll, and forming yellow coloring matter of autumn leaves.

xan·thous (zăn'th*u*s) *adj.* (of a people) Having yellow(ish) or red(dish) hair; having yellow skin.

Xa·vi·er (zā'vēer, zăv'ē-, zāv'y*er*), **St. Francis** (1506–52). Spanish Jesuit, one of the founders of the Society of Jesus, and a missionary in the Far East, commemorated Dec. 3.

x-ax·is (ĕks'ăksĭs) *n.* (pl. **x-ax·es** pr. ĕks'ăksēz). (math.) Horizontal axis in two-dimensional coordinate system.

X chromosome: see CHROMOSOME.

Xe *symbol.* Xenon.

xeno- *comb. form.* Foreign(er), other, as *xenolith, xenophobe.*

xen·o·lith (zĕn'*o*lĭth) *n.* (geol.) Stone or rock occurring in a system to which it does not belong. **xen·o·lith·ic** (zĕn*o*lĭth'ĭk) *adj.*

xe·non (zē'nŏn, zĕn'ŏn) *n.* (chem.) Heavy inert gaseous element present in minute quantity in the atmosphere; symbol Xe, at. no. 54, at. wt. 131.30. [Gk. *xenos* strange]

xen·o·pho·bi·a (zĕn*o*fō'bē*a*) *n.* Morbid dislike or fear of foreigners, foreign customs, etc. **xen·o·phobe** (zĕn'*o*fōb) *n.* Person showing xenophobia. **xen·o·pho'bic** *adj.*

Xen·o·phon (zĕn'*o*fon, -fŏn) (*c*428–354 B.C.). Athenian historian and philosopher; pupil of Socrates, about whom he wrote in the *Memorabilia* and the *Symposium*; he described in the *Anabasis* the expedition of Cyrus against Artaxerxes (401–399 B.C.) in which he led Greek mercenaries in their retreat to the Black Sea after they had been left in a dangerous situation between the Tigris and Euphrates.

Xe·res (*Sp.* hĕ'rĕs). Old spelling of JEREZ.

xe·rog·ra·phy (zĭrŏg'r*a*fē) *n.* Dry printing process in which colored resin adheres to those areas of the surface of paper that have been sensitized with a charge of static electricity. **xe·ro·graph·ic** (zēr*o*grăf'ĭk) *adj.*

xe·roph·a·gy (zĭrŏf'*a*jē) *n.* (pl. **-gies**). Strictest form of fast, practiced in Eastern Church esp. during Lent or Holy Week, and forbidding meat, fish, cheese, milk, butter, oil, wine, and all seasonings except salt.

xe·roph·i·lous (zĭrŏf'*i*l*u*s) *adj.* (bot.) Adapted to extremely dry conditions.

xe·roph·thal·mi·a (zērŏfthăl'mē*a*) *n.* (path.) Inflammation of the conjunctiva with abnormal dryness and corrugation.

xe·ro·phyte (zēr'*o*fīt) *n.* Plant adapted to very dry conditions, desert plant.

Xer·ox (zēr'ŏks) *n.* (trademark) Process of reproduction by xerography. **x**~ *v.t.* Reproduce by Xerox.

Xerx·es (zērk'sēz). King of Persia 486–465 B.C., son of Darius; invaded Greece and overcame the resistance of Leonidas and the Spartans at Thermopylae, but was defeated at Salamis 480 B.C.

xi (zī, sī; *Gk.* ksē) *n.* (pl. **xis**). Fifteenth (later 14th) letter of Greek alphabet (*Ξ, ξ*), corresponding to *x.*

xiph·i·ster·num (zĭfĭstēr'n*u*m) *n.* (pl. **-na** pr. -n*a*). Xiphoid process.

xiph·oid (zĭf'oid) *adj.* Sword-shaped; ~ **process,** cartilaginous or bony process at lower or posterior end of sternum in man and other animals.

Xi·zang (shē'zahng') = TIBET.

Xmas *abbrev.* Christmas (see X, x sense 4).

xo·a·non (zō'*a*nŏn) *n.* (pl. **-na** pr. -n*a*). (Gk. antiq.) Primitive usu. wooden image of deity, supposed to have fallen from heaven.

X-ra·di·a·tion (ĕks'rādēā'sh*o*n) *n.* Radiation composed of x-rays; treatment with or exposure to this.

x-ray, x ray (ĕks'rā) *ns.* Electromagnetic radiation of very short wavelength emitted by electrons whose velocity is suddenly reduced, capable of passing through opaque bodies, of acting on photographic plates, and of ionizing gases; (also ~ **photograph**) photograph, esp. showing position of bones etc., made with x-rays. **x-ray** *v.t.* Photograph, examine, with x-rays; treat (disease, patient) with x-rays. [Ger. *X-strahlen*, name given by their discoverer, ROENTGEN, to indicate that their essential nature was unknown]

xy·lem (zī'lem, -lĕm) *n.* (bot.) Woody tissue including vessels and fibers forming harder part of fibrovascular tissues of plant (opp. PHLOEM).

xy·lene (zī'lēn) *n.* (chem.) One of three colorless, oily, isomeric hydrocarbons, derivatives of benzene, obtained from wood, tar, etc.

xy·li·tol (zī'litōl, -tawl, -tŏl) *n.* Sugar substitute derived from wood.

xy·lo·graph (zī'logrăf, -grahf) *n.* Woodcut, esp. of early period.

xy·loph·a·gous (zīlŏf'agus) *adj.* (of insects) Feeding on, boring into, wood.

xy·lo·phone (zī'lofōn) *n.* Musical instrument consisting of a series of flat wooden bars, graduated in length to sound the musical scale, resting on strips of straw or felt, and played by striking with small wooden hammer(s).

Right: Rock tombs at Persepolis in southern Iran which were excavated for such kings as Darius and ***Xerxes*** *between 550 and 331 B.C. The bas relief between is Roman.*

A modern ***X-ray*** *generator used for medical work. A beam of electrons from the cathode is directed at an anode which rotates at speeds up to 10,000 r.p.m. This prevents over-heating and extends the working life of the equipment.*

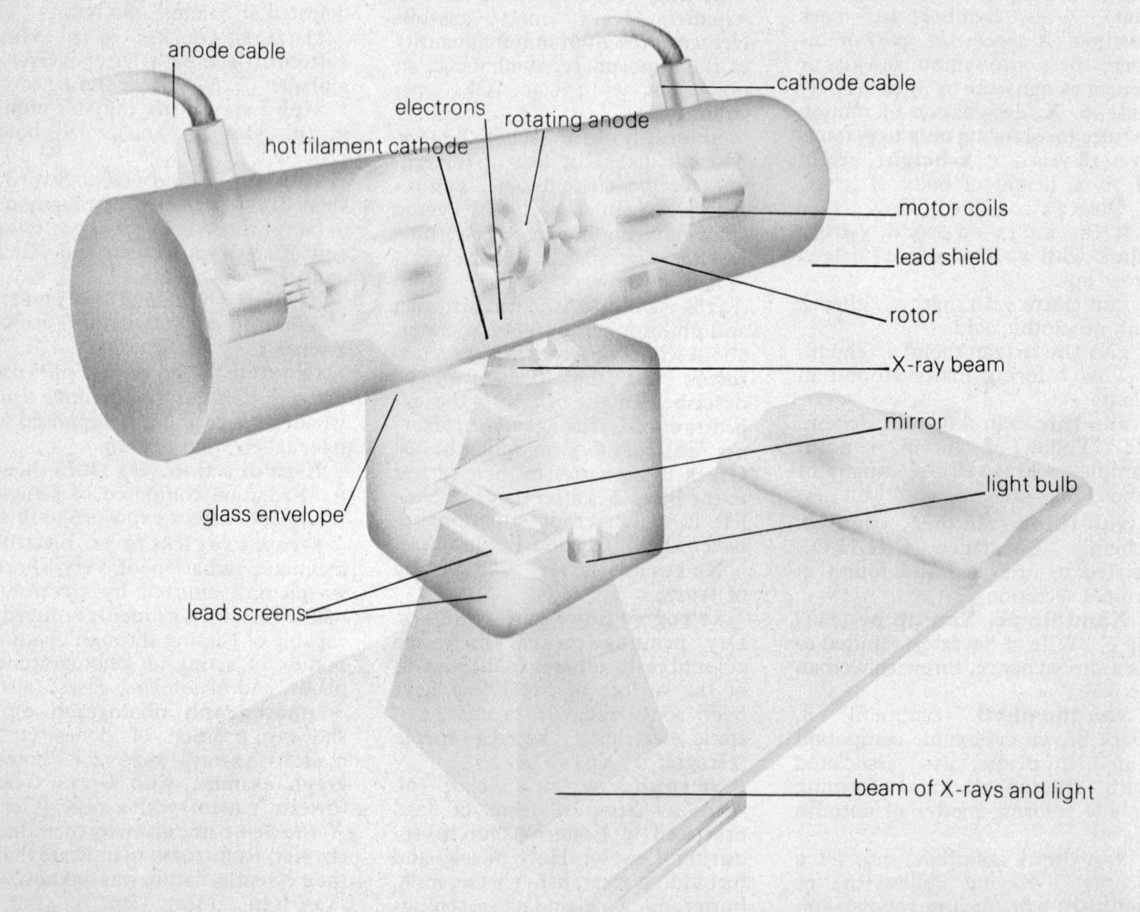

anode cable
cathode cable
electrons
rotating anode
hot filament cathode
motor coils
lead shield
rotor
X-ray beam
mirror
light bulb
glass envelope
lead screens
beam of X-rays and light
photographic film holder

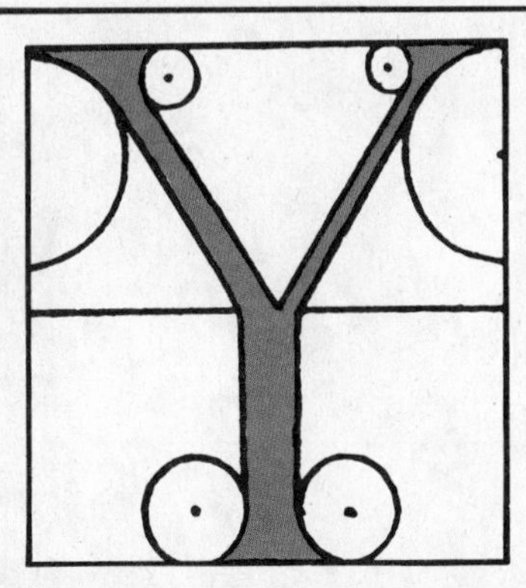

The original Roman alphabet ended with X but when the Romans conquered the Greeks, they needed **Y, y** as a letter to be equivalent of upsilon for those words that they had adopted from the Greek. This, in turn, had been adopted from a Phoenician symbol and sounded like a U.

Phoenician Early Etruscan Classical Latin

Cursive Majuscule Cursive Miniscule Italian (italic)

Y, y (wī) *n.* (pl. **Y's, y's** or **Ys, ys**). 1. Twenty-fifth letter of modern English and 23rd of ancient Roman alphabet, representing ultimately Y, *Y*, of Greek alphabet, a differentiated form of primitive V (see U, V), first adopted in Latin alphabet as V, and later readopted in form Y to represent Y of borrowed Greek works; as a vowel, representing in English all the sounds (except ē) commonly spelled with *i*, and used as the normal spelling (*a*) for final *i*-sounds, (*b*) in words of Greek origin, representing upsilon, (*c*) before *i* in inflectional forms of verbs ending in *-y* or *-ie*, (*d*) in plural of nouns ending in *-y* preceded by another vowel; as a consonant, representing a voiced palatal spirant. 2. (alg. etc.) Symbol of second of series of unknown or variable quantities (cf. x). 3. Object etc. shaped like Y; **Y-branch**, piece of piping with branch at acute angle to main.

Y *symbol.* Yttrium.

Y, Y. *abbrevs.* YMCA, YMHA, YWCA, YWHA.

y. *abbrev.* Year(s).

y- *prefix.* Used esp. with past participles, still found in a few archaic forms, as *yclad* clad, *yclept* called, *ywis* surely.

-y[1] *suffix.* Forming nouns denoting (1) state, condition, or quality (*courtesy, fury, glory*); (2) action or its result (*remedy, subsidy*); (3) activity, shop or goods specified, place of business (*bakery, company, library*).

-y[2] *suffix.* Forming adjectives with sense full of or containing, having the quality of, addicted to (*gluey, horsy, messy, slangy, thorny*).

-y[3] *suffix.* Forming diminutive nouns, pet names, etc. (*granny, Sally*).

yacht (yŏt) *n.* Light sailing vessel kept, and usu. specially built, for racing; vessel propelled by sails, steam, or any motive power other than oars, and used for private pleasure excursions, cruising, travel, etc.; ~ **club**, club esp. for yacht racing; **yachts'man**, person who yachts. **yacht** *v.i.* Race or cruise in yacht. [early mod. Du. *jaght(e)*, = *jaghtschip* (*jagen* to hunt); named f. its speed]

yah (yah) *int.* Exclamation of disgust, defiance, or derision.

ya·hoo (yah'hōō, yā'-, yahhōō') *n.* In Swift's *Gulliver's Travels*, race of brutes in human shape; hence, degraded or bestial human being.

Yah·weh, Yah·we (yah'wĕ), **Yah·veh** (yah'vĕ). Name of God in Old Testament, transliteration of the Tetragrammaton that is rendered JEHOVAH in the Authorized Version etc.

Yah·wist (yah'wĭst) *n.* Author(s) of those parts of the Hexateuch where God is referred to as *Yahweh* rather than *Elohim*. **Yah'wism** *n.* **Yah·wis·tic** (yahwĭs'tĭk) *adj.*

yak[1] (yăk) *n.* Large humped bovine mammal (*Bos grunniens*) with long silky hair on sides, tail, etc., found wild and domesticated in Tibet and other high regions of central Asia; used as a beast of burden. [Tibetan *gyag*]

yak[2] (yăk) *n.* & *v.* (**yakked, yak·king**). (Utter) steady senseless chatter.

Yale[1] (yāl) *n.* **Yale'lock**, (trademark) type of cylinder lock for doors etc. [f. Linus *Yale* (1821–68), Amer. locksmith]

Yale[2] (yāl). University at New Haven, Conn., originally called Yale College in consequence of benefactions received from Elihu Yale (1648–1721).

Yal·ta (yawl'ta). Seaport in S. Ukraine on the Black Sea, scene of wartime conference (Feb. 1945) of Churchill, Roosevelt, and Stalin, at which they made final plans to defeat Germany, and also decided to set up the United Nations Organization.

Ya·lu (yah'lōō). River in North Korea flowing 300 mi. (480 km), along Manchurian border to Yellow Sea.

yam (yăm) *n.* Starchy tuberous root, serving as a staple food in many tropical and subtropical countries; of various species of *Dioscorea*, twining herbs or shrubs with spikes of small inconspicuous flowers; any of these plants; sweet potato.

Ya·ma (yŭm'a). (Hinduism) Ruler of the world of the dead.

Yang (yăng) *n.* (Chin. philos.) Active male principle of universe (opp. YIN).

Yang·tze (yăng'sē; *Chin.* yahng'-tsĕ'). (also ~ **Kiang**) Principal river of China; rises in Tibet and flows through central China 3,602 mi. (5,797 km) to E. China Sea.

*A wild bull **yak** may have a shoulder height of 6 ft. 8 ins. and may weigh more than 1100 lb. Domesticated yaks are smaller but are useful providers of milk, meat, and even dung for fuel.*

The veiling of a woman with a **yashmak** was not introduced by Muhammad but was a continuation of an existing custom among the Arabs. Today, it has been dropped in some places.

The Yellowstone River drops more than 300 ft. over the Lower Falls—one of the most impressive sights in the **Yellowstone National Park**—to enter the Grand Canyon.

Yank (yăngk) *n.* & *adj.* (colloq.) Yankee.

yank (yăngk) *n.* & *v.* (slang) (Pull with) sudden sharp tug or jerk.

Yan·kee (yăng′kē) *n.* Native or inhabitant of New England or of northern states of U.S. generally; (applied by other peoples to) any inhabitant of U.S.; (attrib.) of Yankees, that is a Yankee. [perh. f. Du. *Janke* dim. of *Jan* John used derisively; or f. *Jengees* Indian pronunciation of *English*]

Ya·oun·dé (yahōōndā′). Capital of Cameroon in W. central Africa.

yap (yăp) *n.* & *v.i.* (**yapped, yap·ping**). (Utter) shrill or fussy bark, yelp. **yap′per** *n.* **yap′ping·ly** *adv.* [imit.]

yard[1] (yard) *n.* Piece of enclosed ground, esp. one surrounded by or attached to building(s) or used for manufacturing or other purpose; prison yard, shipyard, dockyard, stockyard, etc.; garden; ground near railroad station where rolling stock is kept, trains are made up, etc.; **the Y** ~, SCOTLAND YARD; **yard′man**, man who works in railroad or lumber yard; gardener or man doing various outdoor jobs; **yard′master**, manager of railroad yard. **yard** *v.t.* Enclose (cattle etc.) in yard.

yard[2] (yard) *n.* 1. Unit of long measure, equal to 3 feet or 36 inches (0.9144 m); measure of area (**square** ~); measure of solidity (**cubic** ~), as in *yard of gravel, lime*, etc.; yard length of material; ~ **measure**, rod, tape, etc., one yard long, usu. marked in feet and inches; **yard′stick**, stick as yard measure; (fig.) standard, criterion. 2. (naut.) Long usu. cylindrical spar, tapering to each end, slung (usu. at its center for square sail) from mast, to support and extend sail; **yard′arm**, either end of yard of square-rigged vessel. **yard′age** *n.* Number of yards of material etc.; (football) yards gained in offensive play.

yar·mul·ke (yar′mulkė) *n.* Skullcap worn by Jewish men.

yarn (yarn) *n.* 1. Fiber, as of cotton, wool, silk, flax, spun and prepared for use in weaving, knitting, etc. 2. (colloq., orig. naut.) Story, tale; **spin a** ~, tell (usu. long) tale. **yarn** *v.i.* (colloq.) Tell yarn(s).

yar·row (yăr′ō) *n.* Plant of genus *Achillea*, esp. *A. millefolium*, common on roadsides, dry meadows, and waste ground, with tough grayish stem, finely divided bipinnate leaves, and dull white or pinkish flower heads in close flat clusters.

yash·mak (yahsh′mahk, yăsh′-măk) *n.* Double veil concealing face below eyes, worn in public by Muslim women of some countries.

yat·a·ghan (yăt′agăn, -gan; *Turk.* yahtahgahn′) *n.* Short sword of Muslim countries with slight reverse curve.

yaw (yaw) *v.i.* & *n.* (naut., aeron.) (Make) deviation from straight course owing to action of heavy sea or strong winds.

yawl (yawl) *n.* Ship's boat with four or six oars; two-masted fore-and-aft sailboat with after mast much smaller than mainmast and placed abaft the rudder.

yawn (yawn) *v.* Breathe in involuntarily with mouth wide open, as from drowsiness, fatigue, boredom, etc.; utter or say with yawn; (of chasm etc.) gape, have wide opening. ~ *n.* Act of Yawning.

yaws (yawz) *n.pl.* (usu. considered sing.) Skin disease of tropical countries with raspberry-like tubercles or excrescences on skin, having many analogies with syphilis.

y-ax·is (wī′ăksĭs) *n.* (pl. **y-ax·es** pr. wī′ăksēz). (math.) Vertical axis in two-dimensional coordinate system.

Yaz·oo (yăz′ōō). River in Mississippi flowing 190 mi. (305 km), to Mississippi near Vicksburg.

Yb *symbol*. Ytterbium.

Y chromosome: see CHROMOSOME.

y·clept, y·cleped (ēklĕpt′) *adjs.* (archaic or joc.) Called (so-and-so).

yd. *abbrev.* Yard.

ye (yē) *pron.* Second person pl. (archaic, dial. or poet.) = YOU.

yea (yā) *adv.* & *n.* (archaic) Yes.

year (yēr) *n.* 1. Time occupied by Earth in one revolution around the sun (also **astronomical, equinoctial, natural, solar, tropical,** ~ = 365 days, 5 hours, 48 minutes, 46 seconds) or by the sun in recovering its previous apparent relation to the fixed stars (**astral** or **sidereal** ~, longer by 20 minutes, 23 seconds). 2. Period of days (esp. **common** ~ of 365 days reckoned from Jan. 1 or **leap** or **bissextile** ~ of 366) used by community for dating or other purposes commencing on a certain day, usu. divided into 12 months, and corresponding more or less exactly in length to the astronomical year (also called **calendar, civil,** or **legal** ~). 3. Such space of time with limits not necessarily coinciding with those of civil year, used in reckoning age, period of office, occupation, etc., or for special purpose, as taxation, payment of dividends, etc. 4. (pl.) Age (of person); (pl.) period, times, a very long time. 5. **~ in, ~ out,** successive through the years, continuously; **year'book,** annual publication containing information for the year. **year'long'** *adj.* Lasting a year. **year-round** *adj.* Existing throughout the year, through all seasons.

year·ling (yēr'lĭng) *n.* & *adj.* (Animal, esp. lamb, calf, or foal) a year old; (racing) colt one year old from Jan. 1 of year of foaling.

year·ly (yēr'lē) *adj.* & *adv.* (Occurring, observed, done, etc.) once a year or every year; annual(ly).

yearn (yērn) *v.i.* Long; be moved with compassion or tender feelings. **yearn'ing** *n.*

yeast (yēst) *n.* Minute unicellular fungus esp. of family Saccharomycetaceae; grayish-yellow substance produced as froth or sediment during alcoholic fermentation of malt brews and other saccharine fluids, consisting of aggregations of minute fungi and used in manufacture of beer, to leaven bread, etc.; dried form of this substance prepared in cakes or granules. **yeast'y** *adj.* (**yeast·i·er, yeast·i·est**). Frothy like yeast; in a ferment, working like yeast; made with yeast. **yeast'i·ness** *n.*

Yeats (yāts), **William Butler** (1865–1939). Irish lyric poet and dramatist; assisted in the creation of an Irish national theater; received Nobel Prize for literature, 1923.

yegg (yĕg) *n.* (slang) (also **yegg'-man,** pl. **-men**). Burglar, esp. one who breaks open safes. [said to be name of Amer. safe-cracker]

yell (yĕl) *n.* Sharp loud outcry of strong and sudden emotion, as rage, horror, agony; set of words or syllables shouted as an organized cheer, as by college students. ~ *v.* Make, utter with, yell.

yel·low (yĕl'ō) *adj.* Of the color of buttercup or lemon or sulfur or gold, most luminous of the primary colors, occurring in spectrum between green and orange; having a yellow skin or complexion, as the Mongolian peoples; (of newspaper etc.) recklessly or unscrupulously sensational; (slang) cowardly, craven; **yel'lowbelly,** (slang) coward; **yellow fever,** acute, often fatal febrile disease of hot climates, characterized by jaundice, vomiting, hemorrhages, etc., and transmitted by a mosquito; **yellow jack,** yellow fever; quarantine flag; **yellow jacket,** any of several small wasps (family Vespidae) having black and yellow markings; **yel'lowlegs,** either of two N. Amer. wading birds (*Totanus melanoleucus* and *T. flavipes*) with long bill and bright yellow legs; **yellow ocher**: see OCHER; **yellow pages,** section of telephone directory on yellow paper listing business subscribers according to goods or services they offer; **Yellow River,** most northerly of China's great rivers, 2,900 mi. (4,640 km) long, known as "China's Sorrow" because of its uncontrollable floods; **Yellow Sea,** arm of Pacific between China and Korea, into which the Yellow River formerly flowed; **Yel'lowstone National Park,** area of about 3,458 sq. miles (8,956 sq. km), chiefly in Wyoming, reserved since 1872 for public uses, named after the **Yellowstone River,** a tributary of the Missouri, which rises there; **yel'lowthroat,** any of several small Amer. birds of the genus *Geothlypis,* esp. *G. trichas,* having yellow breast and throat, and, in the male, a distinctive black mask on the face; **yellow-throated warbler,** wood warbler (*Dendroica dominica*) of southeastern U.S., having gray back, yellow breast, and black, gray, and white striped sides. **yellow** *n.* Yellow color, pigment, fabric, etc.; yellow species or variety of bird, butterfly, moth, flower, etc. **yellow** *v.* Turn yellow. **yel'low·ish** *adj.*

Found primarily through the northern temperate zone, the ***yarrow*** *comprises about 80 species; some are used to induce sneezing.*

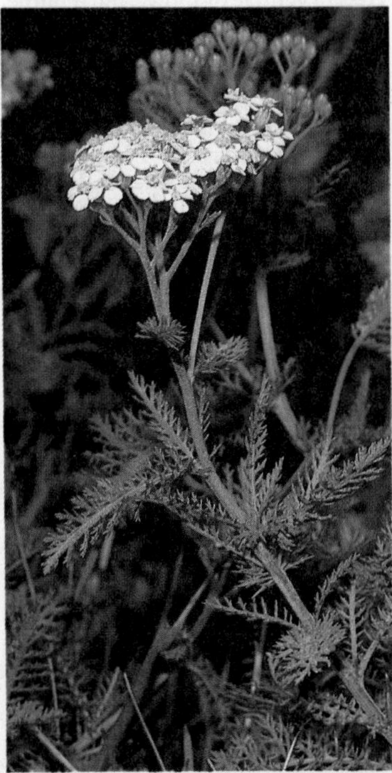

yelp (yĕlp) *n.* & *v.i.* (Utter) sharp shrill bark or cry (as) of dog in pain, excitement, etc. **yelp'er** *n.*

Yem·en (yĕm'en). Name of two republics in the Arabian peninsula: **~ Arab Republic,** a republic since 1962 (kingdom 1934–62) of SW. Arabia, the *Arabia Felix* of the ancients, freed from Turkish rule in 1918; capital, Sana'a; **People's Democratic Republic of ~,** a republic since 1967 in S. Arabia bordering on the Yemen Arab Republic; capital, Aden; administrative capital, Madinat al Shaab; **Yem·en·ite** (yĕm'enīt), **Yem·e·ni** (yĕm'enē) *adjs.* & *ns.*

yen[1] (yĕn) *n.* (pl. **yen**). Monetary unit of Japan. [Jap., f. Chin. *yüan* round, dollar]

yen[2] (yĕn) *n.* (colloq.) Passionate or impelling desire or longing. [Chin. *yen* smoke, opium]

yeo·man (yō'man) *n.* (pl. **-men**). 1. (hist.) British small landowner, person of middle class engaged in agriculture (esp. attrib., as **~ farmer**). 2. (hist.) Servant and attendant in British royal or noble household of rank between sergeant and groom or squire and page. 3. (U.S. Navy) Petty officer performing clerical duties on board ship. 4. Member of yeomanry force; **~('s) service,** help in need; efficient service. **yeo'man·ly** *adj.* Of, befitting, a yeoman or yeomen.

yeo·man·ry (yō'manrē) *n.* 1. Yeomen collectively. 2. (hist.) Volunteer cavalry force in British Army, orig. formed in 18th c. for home defense, merged in the Territorial Force in 1907.

yep (yĕp) *adv.* (dial.) = YES.

yer·ba ma·té (yēr'ba mahtā', mătā'): see MATÉ.

yes (yĕs) *adv.* Particle expressing affirmative reply to request, question, etc. ~ *n.* (pl. **yes·es**). Word, answer, "yes"; **~ man,** (colloq.) person who agrees uncritically with everything that is said to him by a superior.

ye·shi·va (yeshē'va) *n.* (pl. **-vahs** pr. -vaz, **-voth** pr. -vawt). 1. School or college for Talmudic study, esp. seminary for training orthodox rabbis. 2. Jewish day school providing religious and secular education.

yes·ter·day (yĕs'terdā, -dē) *n.* & *adv.* (On) the day immediately preceding today; (in) time not long past.

yes·ter·year (yĕs'teryēr) *n.* Last year, the past (poet.). [coined by D. G. Rossetti to translate Fr. *antan,* f. L. *ante annum*]

yet (yĕt) *adv.* 1. In addition or continuation, besides, also (archaic); (with comparative) even, still; **nor ~,** and also not. 2. Up to this or that time, till now, till then; at some time in the future, hereafter (though not hitherto), henceforth, even now (though not till now); **not** ~, still not, not by this (or that) time; **as** ~, hitherto. **yet** *adj.* That is still such, still continuing. **yet** *conj.* In spite of that, nevertheless, notwithstanding.

yet·i, Yet·i (yĕt′ē) *ns.* (pl. **yet·i, Yet·i**). (pop. the "Abominable Snowman") Either of two unidentified animals occas. seen on high slopes of Himalayas, the one being prob. the red bear (*Ursus arctos isabellinus*) and the other possibly the langur monkey (*Presbytis entellus achilles*). [Tibetan *yeh* rocky area, *teh* animal]

yew (ū) *n.* Tree of coniferous genus *Taxus*, widely distributed in north temperate zone, esp. common European *T. baccata*, with heavy elastic wood and dense dark green foliage, freq. planted in cemeteries and regarded as symbol of sadness; wood of this, formerly used for making bows.

Y·gerne (ēgĕrn′) = IGRAINE.

Yid·dish (yĭd′ĭsh) *adj.* & *n.* (Of) the language used by Jews in Europe and America, a German dialect (orig. from Middle Rhine area) written in Hebrew letters, with an admixture of Hebrew elements and of words borrowed from several modern languages. [Ger. *jüdisch* Jewish]

yield (yēld) *v.* 1. Produce or return as fruit, profit, or result. 2. Surrender or make submission (*to*); concede; give way *to* persuasion, entreaty, etc., give consent; be inferior *to*; (of vehicle or traffic) give right of way (*to*); ~ **to**, give way under, be affected by, physical action or agent, as pressure, heat, etc. **yield** *n.* Amount yielded or produced, output, return.

Yin (yĭn) *n.* (Chin. philos.) Passive female principle of universe (opp. YANG).

yip (yĭp) *v.* (**yipped, yip·ping**) & *n.* = YELP.

yip·pee (yĭp′ē) *int.* Expression of delight or excitement.

yip·pie (yĭp′ē) *n.* Politically active student in late 1960s. [Y(outh) I(nternational) P(arty), after HIPPIE]

y·lang-y·lang (ē′lahng ē′lahng) *n.* Tree (*Cananga odorata*) of Malaya, Philippines, etc., with fragrant greenish-yellow flowers; perfume distilled from these.

YMCA, Y.M.C.A. *abbrevs.* YOUNG Men's Christian Association.

YMHA, Y.M.H.A. *abbrevs.* YOUNG Men's Hebrew Association.

yo·del (yō′del) *v.* (**-deled, -del·ing,** Brit. **-delled, -del·ling**). Sing or warble with interchange of ordinary and falsetto voice in manner of Swiss and Tyrolese mountaineers. ~ *n.* Yodeling cry; yodeling match. **yo′del·er** *n.*

yo·ga (yō′ga) *n.* Hindu system of ascetic practice, abstract meditation, and mental concentration as means of attaining union with Supreme Spirit. [Sansk. *yoga* union]

yo·gi (yō′gē) *n.* (pl. **-gis** pr. -gēz). (also **yo·gin** pr. yō′gĭn). Devotee of YOGA.

yo·gurt, yo·ghurt (yō′gert) *ns.* Semisolid junketlike or curdlike food prepared from milk fermented by addition of *Lactobacillus bulgaricus*. [Turk. *yoğurt*]

yoiks (yoiks), **hoiks** (hoiks) *ints.* Exclamation used in fox hunting to urge on hounds.

yoke (yōk) *n.* (pl. **yokes** for senses 1, 3–6; **yoke** for sense 2). 1. Contrivance, usu. curved or hollowed piece of wood over animals' necks, fastened at center to chain or trace by which plow or vehicle is drawn, used from ancient times for coupling two animals, esp. oxen, for drawing vehicle etc. 2. Pair *of* oxen etc. 3. Piece of wood shaped to fit person's shoulders and support pail etc. at each end. 4. (Rom. hist.) Uplifted yoke, or arch of three spears symbolizing it, under which defeated enemy was made to march; (fig.) sway, dominion, servitude; (fig.) bond of union, esp. marriage tie. 5. Upper part of bodice; upper part of garment, from which the rest hangs. 6. Object resembling a yoke in shape, esp. crossbar on which bell swings; crossbar of rudder to whose ends steering lines are fastened; coupling piece of two pipes discharging into one; kinds of coupling or controlling piece in machinery. ~ *v.t.* (**yoked, yok·ing**). Put yoke upon; harness (ox etc.) *to* vehicle or plow; (fig.) couple, unite, join, link (*together*). **yoke′less** *adj.*

yo·kel (yō′kel) *n.* (contempt.) Country bumpkin.

Yo·ko·ha·ma (yōkohah′ma). City and seaport on Tokyo Bay in E. central Honshu Island, Japan.

yolk (yōk) *n.* Yellow(ish) internal part of egg, containing vitellin and other proteins, surrounded by white and serving as nourishment for young before hatching; (biol.) corresponding part in any animal ovum; substance from which embryo is developed.

Yom Kip·pur (yŏm kĭp′er; *Heb.* yawm′ kēpoor′). (Jewish religion) The Day of Atonement, falling on the 10th day of the month Tishri (approx. October) and observed as a solemn fast day acc. to the rites described in Lev. 16.

yon (yŏn) *adj.* & *adv.* (also **yon·der** pr. yŏn′der). (archaic or dial.) (Situated) over there, at some distance (but within sight).

yore (yōr, yo͡r) *n.* **of** ~, in or of time long past, former(ly).

York[1] (yo͡rk). Name of English royal dynasty, descending from Edmund of Langley (1341–1402), fifth son of Edward III and (from 1385) first Duke of York; included Edward IV, Edward V, and Richard III; party of the white rose in the Wars of the Roses (see ROSE sense 2); united with the House of Lancaster when Henry VII married the eldest daughter of Edward IV (1486).

York[2] (yo͡rk), **Alvin Collum** (1887–1964). Known as Sgt. York, U.S. soldier and celebrated hero of World War I, who single-handedly captured 132 German soldiers and two machine gun nests.

Yorkshire (yo͡rk′shēr, -sher). Former county of northeast England; ~ **pudding**, baked batter, usu. eaten with meat, esp. roast beef; ~ **terrier**, small, long-haired terrier.

York·town (yo͡rk′town). Town on the shore of Chesapeake Bay, where, in 1781, the British army under Lord Cornwallis was blockaded by the American army and the French fleet.

Yo·ru·ba (yar′o͞oba, -bah, yo͡r′) *n.* (pl. **-bas,** collect. **-ba**). Member, language, of a black people of the West African coast.

Yo·sem·i·te (yōsĕm′ĭtē). U.S.

Facing: Elaborate decoration on houses in Sana'a, capital of the ***Yemen Arab Republic.*** *Together with the adjoining State (which was formerly the British colony of Aden), this is a barren region with few natural resources.*

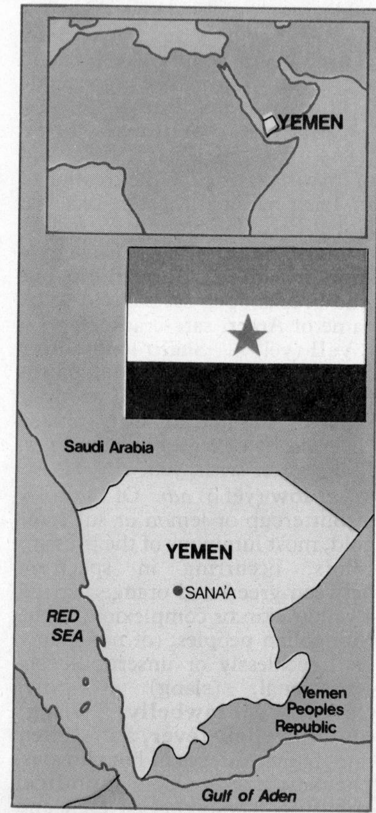

national park in E. California, named after the Yosemite River, which traverses it.

you (ū) *pron.* Second person sing. and pl. pronoun denoting person(s) or thing(s) addressed; (in general statements freq. =) one, anyone, everyone, a person.

you'd (ūd) *contr.* You had; you would.

you'll (ūl) *contr.* You will; you shall.

young (yŭng) *adj.* That has lived, existed, etc., a relatively short time; lately begun, formed, introduced, etc., recent, new; of young person(s) or youth; youthful, esp. having freshness or vigor of youth; ~ **blood**, young people; new vigorous ideas and action; **Y~ Chevalier, Y~ Pretender**: see PRETENDER; **Y~ Men's Christian Association** (YMCA), **Y~ Men's Hebrew Association** (YMHA), **Y~ Women's Christian Association** (YWCA), **Y~ Women's Hebrew Association** (YWHA), organizations for promoting spiritual, intellectual, and physical welfare of young people; **young turk**, member of any established political party or group who aggressively advocates reform: **Young Turks**, Turkish party that, in 1908, forced Sultan Abdul Hamid II to proclaim liberal constitution, and in 1909 deposed him in favor of his brother, Muhammad V. **young** *n.* Young people; young ones, offspring, of animals; **with** ~, pregnant. **young'ish** *adj.*

Young (yŭng), **Brigham** (1801–1877). MORMON leader; headed the Mormon migration to Utah (1847), founded Salt Lake City, and was appointed governor of Utah (1851).

young·ling (yŭng'lĭng) *n.* Young person, animal, or plant.

young·ster (yŭng'ster) *n.* Young person, esp. young man; child, esp. boy.

youn·ker (yŭng'ker) *n.* (archaic) Young gentleman or nobleman; youngster.

your (ūr, yōr, yo͝or) *poss. pron.* Possessive case of YOU used as attributive adjective, belonging to, affecting, you; (archaic, now usu. derog.) that you know of, familiar.

you're (ūr) *contr.* You are.

yours (ūrz, yōrz, yo͝orz) *poss. pron.* Abs. and pred. form of YOUR; used in conventional ending to letter (~ **sincerely, truly**, etc.); ~ **truly**, (also, joc.) I; **what's ~?**, what will you drink?

your·self (ūrsĕlf', yōr-, yo͝or-) *pron.* (pl. **-selves** pr. -sĕlvz'). Emphatic and reflexive form corresponding to YOU.

youth (ūth) *n.* (pl. **youths** pr. ūths, ūdhz). 1. Being young; early part of life, esp. adolescence; quality or condition characteristic of the young. 2. Young people collectively; ~ **hostel**, cheap lodging, usu. provided by an association, where young travelers put up for the night. 3. Young person, esp. young man between boyhood and maturity. **youth'ful** *adj.* **youth'ful·ly** *adv.* **youth'ful·ness** *n.*

yowl (yowl) *n.* & *v.* (Utter) loud wailing cry (as) of dog in distress, pain, etc., howl.

Below: Cattle market at Jajce, in the Bosnian region of ***Yugoslavia.*** *Despite considerable diversity among its peoples, the country has remained united and independent.*

yo-yo (yō'yō) *n.* (pl. **yo-yos**). Kind of toy, small roughly spherical object with string attached to and wound around a deep central groove, made to fall and rise as its weight causes the string to unroll rapidly and roll up again. [orig. a trademark]

yr., yrs. *abbrevs.* Year(s); your(s).

Y·seult (ĭso͞olt') = ISEULT.

yt·ter·bi·um (ĭtĕr'bēum) *n.* (chem.) Metallic element of rare-earth group; symbol Yb, at. no. 70, at. wt. 173.04. [f. *Ytterby* in Sweden]

yt·tri·um (ĭ'trēum) *n.* (chem.) Metallic element closely resembling ytterbium and found with it in gadolinite and other minerals; symbol Y, at. no. 39, at. wt. 88.9059.

Yü·an (ū'ahn'). Name of dynasty that ruled in China 1260–1368.

yu·an (ūahn') *n.* (pl. **yu·an**). Principal monetary unit of China.

Yu·ca·tan (ūkatăn'). Peninsula in SE. Mexico between the Gulf of Mexico and the Gulf of Honduras.

yuc·ca (yŭk'a) *n.* Liliaceous plant of genus *Y~*, native to Central America, Mexico, etc., with woody stem, a crown of usu. rigid narrow pointed leaves, and upright cluster of white bell-shaped flowers.

Yu·go·slav (ū'gōslahv) *n.* & *adj.* 1. (Native, inhabitant) of Yugoslavia. 2. (Member) of the southern group of Slavic peoples, comprising Serbs, Croats, and Slovenes. 3. (Branch) of the Slavonic languages spoken in Yugoslavia, Serbo-Croatian. **Yu·go·sla·vi·an** (ūgōslah'vēan) *adj.*

Yu·go·sla·vi·a (ūgōslah'vēa). State in the Balkans; formed under a monarchy in Dec., 1918, by the union of Bosnia, Croatia, Dalmatia, Montenegro, Serbia, and Slovenia, proclaimed a republic in Nov., 1945; capital, Belgrade. [f. Serbian = "South Slav"]

Yu·kon (ū'kŏn). 1. Territory of NW. Canada, constituted a separate political unit in 1898 with its capital at Dawson. 2. River of Canada flowing 1,770 mi. (2,848 km) through Alaska to the Bering Sea.

yule (ūl) *n.* (also **yule'tide**) Christmas season or festival; ~ **log**, large log burned on hearth at Christmas.

yum·my (yŭm'ē) *adj.* (**-mi·er, -mi·est**). (colloq.) Tasty, delicious.

yurt (ūrt) *n.* Mongolian nomads' circular skin- or felt-covered tent with collapsible frame.

YWCA, Y.W.C.A. *abbrevs.* Young Women's Christian Association.

YWHA, Y.W.H.A. *abbrevs.* Young Women's Hebrew Association.

In Semitic and Greek, Z, z was represented in the alphabet but fell to the sixth or seventh position. Although at first incorporated into Latin, it was dropped for several centuries there was no use for this letter until the Romans needed to transcribe Greek words. Nevertheless, it was introduced to western European languages by the Romans.

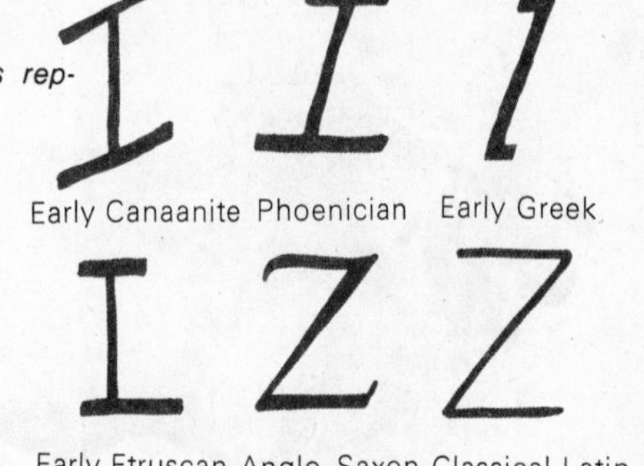

Z, z (zē; *Brit.* zĕd) (pl. **Z's, z's** or **Zs, zs**). 1. Twenty-sixth and last letter of modern English and 23rd of later Roman alphabet, derived through Latin and Greek from Phoenician and ancient Hebrew, I, Z, Z, and representing the voiced form of *s*, especially in loan words; referred to by Shakespeare in *King Lear* as "Thou whoreson zed; thou unnecessary letter"; **from A to Z**, from beginning to end, all through. 2. (alg. etc.) Symbol of third of series of unknown or variable quantities (cf. *x*, *y*). 3. Object etc. shaped like Z.

za·ba·glio·ne (zahbalyō'nē) *n.* Dessert consisting of a mixture of egg yolks, sugar, and Marsala. [It.]

Za·ire, Za·ïre (zahēr'). Republic of W. central Africa; formerly Belgian Congo; independent since 1960; capital, Kinshasa; river in central Africa flowing 2,716 mi. (4,371 km), through Zaire to Atlantic Ocean. **Za·ir'e·an** *adj.* & *n.*

Zam·bi·a (zăm'bēa, zahm'-). Republic of central Africa; formerly Northern Rhodesia; member of the British Commonwealth, independent since 1964; capital, Lusaka.

za·ny (zā'nē) *n.* (pl. **-nies**). Buffoon, simpleton; comically crazy or bizarre person; (hist.) attendant on clown or acrobat awkwardly imitating his master's acts. ~ *adj.* (**-ni·er, -ni·est**). **za'ni·ly** *adv.* **za'ni·ness** *n.* [Fr. or It. *zani* servants acting as clowns in Commedia dell' Arte (Venetian form of *Gianni* = *Giovanni* John)]

Zan·zi·bar (zăn'zibār). Island off east coast of Africa, formerly (with Pemba and some adjacent islets) a sultanate and British protectorate; since 1963 forming, with Tanganyika, the republic of TANZANIA. **Zan·zi·ba·ri** (zănzibār'ē) *n.* Native, inhabitant, of Zanzibar.

zap (zăp) *v.t.* (**zapped, zap·ping**). (slang) Kill, destroy, with gun, electric shock, etc.

Za·pa·ta (zahpah'tah), **Emiliano** (1877–1919). Mexican revolutionist; advocate of agrarian reforms.

Zar·a·thus·tra (zărathoo'stra). Old Iranian form of ZOROASTER.

zeal (zēl) *n.* Ardor, eagerness, enthusiasm, in pursuit of some end or in favor of person or cause. **zeal·ous** (zĕl'us) *adj.* **zeal'ous·ly** *adv.* **zeal'ous·ness** *n.*

Zea·land (zē'land). (Dan. *Sjoelland*) Group of islands in E. Denmark; largest island of this group, on which Copenhagen is situated.

zeal·ot (zĕl'ot) *n.* 1. Zealous person, fanatical enthusiast. 2. **Z~**, (hist.) member of Jewish sect that aimed at Jewish theocracy over the world and fiercely resisted Romans until fall of Jerusalem in 70 A.D. **zeal'ot·ry** *n.*

ze·bra (zē'bra) *n.* (pl. **-bras**, collect. **-bra**). African equine mammal of genus *Equus*, related to horse and ass, covered with black or brownish stripes on whitish or buff ground; **ze'brawood**, (ornamentally striped wood of) any of various trees and shrubs, esp. *Connarus guianensis* of tropical Amer., used in cabinetmaking.

ze·bu (zē'bū) *n.* (pl. **-bus**, collect. **-bu**). Humped species of ox (*Bos indicus*), domesticated in India, China, Japan, and parts of Africa.

Zech. *abbrev.* Zechariah (Old Testament).

Zech·a·ri·ah (zĕkerī'a). Hebrew minor prophet; book of Old Testament containing his prophecies.

zed (zĕd) *n.* (Brit.) Letter Z, z.

Zed·e·ki·ah (zĕdekī'a). Son of Josiah, and the last king of Judah; he rebelled against Nebuchadnezzar and was carried off to Babylon into captivity (2 Kings 24–25, 2 Chron. 26).

zee (zē) *n.* (pl. **zees**). Letter Z, z.

Zeit·geist (tsīt'gīst) *n.* Spirit of the times; characteristic trend of thought, culture, etc., of period. [Ger. *Zeit* time, *Geist* spirit]

Zen (zĕn) *n.* Form of Buddhism emphasizing value of meditation and intuition.

Zend (zĕnd) *n.* 1. Pahlavi translation and exposition of the Avesta. 2. (archaic, erron.) Avestan. [f. ZEND-AVESTA, because Zend was erron. thought to denote the language of the books]

Zend-A·ves·ta (zĕndavĕs'ta) *n.* Avesta together with the Zend. [properly *Avestava-Zend*, text with interpretation]

Zen·ger (zĕng'ger), **John Peter** (1697–1746). German-born printer and publisher in Amer.; central

*A major world copper producer, and with reserves of other minerals, **Zambia** also exports tobacco grown on the high plateau. Zambia has one of the highest per capita incomes in Africa.*

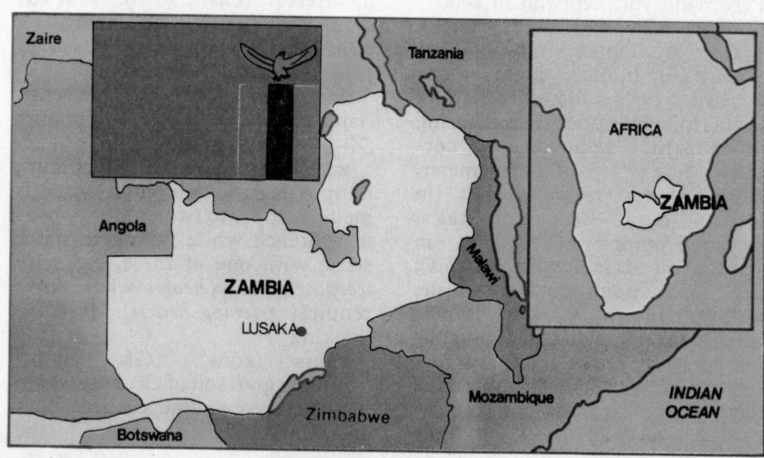

Believed to have originated in India, but to have dispersed through China and Africa, the ***zebu*** *has recently proved ideal for crossing with European cattle breeds for tropical conditions.*

Although a true member of the horse family, the ***zebra*** *has never proved suitable for domestication. It is found throughout Africa south of the Sahara and there are three species.*

figure in trial for seditious libel resulting from his attacks on British colonial administration; his acquittal established precedent for freedom of the press in America.

ze·nith (zē′nĭth; *Brit.* also zĕn′ĭth) *n.* Point of sky directly overhead (fig.) highest point or state, culmination, acme. **ze′nith·al** *adj.* **~ projection,** projection of a portion of the globe upon a plane tangent to it at its center, ensuring that all points have their true compass directions from the center of the map. [Arab. *samt (ar-rās)* way (over the head)]

Ze·no (zē′nō) (335–263 B.C.). Greek philosopher born at Citium, Cyprus, founder of STOIC School.

Zeph. *abbrev.* Zephaniah (Old Testament).

Zeph·a·ni·ah (zĕfanī′*a*) (7th c. B.C.). Hebrew minor prophet; book of Old Testament containing his prophecies.

zeph·yr (zĕf′*er*) *n.* 1. West wind, esp. personified; soft mild gentle wind or breeze. 2. Fine very thin woolen material; garment made from this.

zep·pe·lin (zĕp′*e*lĭn) *n.* Cigar-shaped rigid dirigible airship of the type constructed by Count Ferdinand von Zeppelin in 1900.

ze·ro (zēr′ō) *n.* (pl. **-ros, -roes**). Figure 0, cipher; nothing, no quantity or number; point or line marked 0 on graduated scale, esp. in thermometer or other measuring instrument; temperature corresponding to zero of thermometer, degree of heat reckoned as 0° (in Celsius and Réaumur scales, freezing point of water; in Fahrenheit scale, 32° below this); (fig.) lowest point, bottom of scale, nullity, nonentity; zero hour; **absolute ~,** lowest possible temperature; temperature (approx. −273.1 °C) at which all substances have lost their heat and can be cooled no further; **~-base budgeting,** evaluation of all items in proposed budget each fiscal year to determine their usefulness without consideration of any prior budget; **~ gravity,** (phys.) state in which gravitational attraction equals zero; weightlessness; **~ hour,** hour at which any planned military operation is timed to begin; any crucial time; **~ population growth,** condition in which a nation's population remains constant because birth and death rates are equal. **zero** *adj.* 1. Of, concerning, or being zero. 2. Lacking measurable value. 3. (aeron.) Of or pertaining to a cloud ceiling at or close to the ground and restricting vertical visibility; of or pertaining to visibility along the ground of less than a few feet. **~** *v.t.* (**-roed, -ro·ing**). Adjust (instrument etc.) to a zero point; **~ in on,** take aim at (target etc.), focus attention on. [Arab. *çifr* cipher]

zest (zĕst) *n.* Piquancy, stimulating flavor; keen enjoyment or interest, relish, gusto. **zest′ful** *adj.* **zest′ful·ly** *adv.* **zest′ful·ness** *n.* [Fr. *zeste* orange or lemon peel]

ze·ta (zā′t*a*, zē′-) *n.* Seventh (later sixth) letter of Greek alphabet (*Z*, *ζ*), corresponding to *z*.

zeug·ma (zo͞og′m*a*) *n.* Figure of speech in which single word is made to apply to two or more words in sentence while failing to make sense with one of these, e.g. *with weeping eyes and hearts* (where sense requires *grieving hearts*). [Gk., = "yoking"]

Zeus (zo͞os). (Gk. myth.) Supreme god, son of Cronus, whom he overthrew and succeeded; Zeus and his brothers divided the universe by casting lots, Zeus obtaining heaven, Poseidon the sea, and Pluto the underworld; Zeus was regarded as the king and father of gods and men, with powers over all other deities save the Fates, as the dispenser of good and evil, giver of laws and defender of house and hearth; identified by the Romans with Jupiter.

zig·gu·rat (zĭg′o͞orăt) *n.* Pyramidal tower in Ancient Mesopotamia, surmounted by a temple and with stages or a continuous ramp to the summit.

zig·zag (zĭg′zăg) *n.* Series of short lines inclined at angles in alternate directions; something having such lines or sharp turns. **~** *adj.* Having form of zigzag; with abrupt alternate left and right turns. **~** *adv.* In zigzag manner or course. **~** *v.i.* (**-zagged, -zag·ging**). Move in zigzag course.

zilch (zĭlch) *n.* (slang) Nothing or zero.

zil·lion (zĭl′yon) *n.* (colloq.) Indefinite large number.

Zim·ba·bwe (zĭmbah′bwā). Formerly Rhodesia; country in central Africa bordered by Zambia, Botswana, the Transvaal, and Mozambique; territory colonized chiefly by British settlers; declared independence from Great Britain in 1965; republic established, 1970; name changed from Rhodesia in 1980; capital, Harare.

zinc (zĭngk) *n.* (chem.) Hard bluish-white metallic element, brittle at subnormal temperatures and above 200°C. but malleable between 100° and 150°C., used for roofing, galvanizing sheet iron, to make alloys, esp. brass, and in voltaic cells etc.; symbol Zn, at. no. 30, at. wt. 65.37; **~ ointment,**

white salve made from zinc oxide; ~ **oxide**, antiseptic astringent powder used for skin irritations. **zinc** *v.t.* (**zincked, zinck·ing** or **zinced, zinc·ing**). Treat, coat, with zinc.

zing (zĭng) *n.* (colloq.) Vigor, energy. ~ *v.i.* (colloq.) Move swiftly and energetically.

zin·ni·a (zĭn'ēa) *n.* Tropical American composite plant with showy flowers, esp. *Z~ elegans*, the common garden species. [J. G. *Zinn* (1727–59), German professor of medicine]

Zin·zen·dorf (tsĭn'tsendōrf), **Count Nicholas Ludwig von** (1700–60). German religious leader; founder of Moravian Church.

Zi·on (zī'on). Hill in Jerusalem, on which the city of David was built, and which became the center of Jewish life and worship; hence, the house of God, the Jewish religion, the Christian Church, the Heavenly Jerusalem or kingdom of God, a Christian (esp. Protestant) place of worship. **Zi·on·ism** (zī'onĭzem) *n.* Movement among modern Jews, founded 1897 by Theodor HERZL, that resulted in the reestablishment of Israel. **Zi'on·ist** *adj.* & *n.* (Adherent) of Zionism. [Heb. *Tsīyón* hill]

zip[1] (zĭp) *n.* (Movement accompanied by) light sharp sound as of tearing canvas, flying bullet, etc.; (fig.) energy, force, impetus; ~ (also **Z~**) **code**, system of five-figure numbers used to identify postal delivery areas [*z*one *i*mprovement *p*lan]; ~ **gun**, crude improvised pistol, usu. made from toy pistol or piece of pipe and having a firing pin activated by an elastic band. **zip** *v.* (**zipped, zip·ping**). 1. Move or go with sound of zip or with great force or rapidity. 2. Close or fasten (up) with zipper. **zip'py** *adj.* (**-pi·er, -pi·est**). (colloq.) Full of energy and vigor.

zip[2] (zĭp) *n.* (sports slang) Zero. ~ *v.t.* (**zipped, zip·ping**). (sports slang) Shut out, defeat, (opponent) by keeping him from scoring.

zip fastener *n.* Fastening device consisting of two flexible strips with interlocking metal or plastic projections that can be closed or opened by a sliding clip pulled along them, also called slide fastener.

zir·ca·loy (zēr'kaloi) *n.* Zirconium alloy used in water-cooled nuclear reactors as cladding for fuel rods.

zir·con (zēr'kŏn) *n.* (min.) Zirconium silicate, occurring usu. in variously colored tetragonal crystals, of which translucent varieties are used as gems, esp. red or brownish kinds called HYACINTH. [Arab. *zarqūn*]

*Introduced to Europe from Mexico in 1796, the **zinnia** was rapidly adopted by gardeners because of its easy cultivation. There are now dwarf and tall varieties.*

zir·co·ni·um (zerkō'nēum) *n.* (chem.) Metallic element obtained from zircon etc. as black powder or grayish crystalline substance; symbol Zr, at. no. 40, at. wt. 91.22.

zith·er (zĭth'er) *n.* Musical instrument somewhat like dulcimer with flat soundbox and numerous strings (up to 40), held horizontally and played with fingers and plectrum. **zith'er·ist** *n.*

zlo·ty (zlaw'tē) *n.* (pl. **-tys**). Principal monetary unit of Poland. [Pol., = "golden"]

Zn *symbol.* Zinc.

zo·di·ac (zō'dēăk) *n.* Belt of the heavens limited by lines about 8° from the ecliptic on each side, including all apparent positions of the sun and planets as known to the ancient astronomers, and divided into 12 equal parts (**signs of the** ~: ARIES, TAURUS, GEMINI, CANCER, LEO[1], VIRGO, LIBRA, SCORPIO, SAGITTARIUS, CAPRICORN, AQUARIUS, PISCES) each formerly containing the similarly named constellation but now by precession of equinoxes coinciding with the constellation that bears the name of the preceding sign (e.g. the constellation Aries is now in Taurus). [Gk. *zodiakos* (*kuklos*) (circle) of figures, f. *zōdion* dim. of *zōon* animal]

zo·di·a·cal (zōdī'akal) *adj.* Of, in, the zodiac; ~ **light**, luminous tract of sky shaped like tall triangle occas. seen in east before sunrise or in west after sunset, esp. in tropics.

Zo·la (zō'la; *Fr.* zawlă'), **Émile** (1840–1902). French naturalistic novelist, author of *Germinal*, *The Earth*, *Nana*, etc.

Zöll·ner (tsawl'ner), **Johann Karl Friedrich** (1834–82). German physicist; **~'s lines**, parallel lines made to appear to converge or diverge by series of short lines parallel to each other and intersecting each of them obliquely.

Zoll·ver·ein (tsawl'fĕrīn) *n.* Union of nations having common customs tariff against outsiders and usu. free trade with one another, specif., customs union formed (1834) among the German States under the leadership of Prussia. [Ger.]

zom·bie (pl. **-bies**), **zom·bi** (pl. **-bis**) (zŏm'bē) *ns.* 1. (in voodoo) Supernatural force or spirit reanimating and controlling corpse; corpse so reanimated. 2. Person thought to resemble zombie; mindless or will-less automaton.

zone (zōn) *n.* 1. (archaic) Girdle or belt; band or ring, esp. one of series of concentric or alternate stripes of color, light or shade, etc. 2. Each of five encircling regions, distinguished by differences of climate, into which surface of Earth is divided by tropics of Cancer and Capricorn and arctic circles. 3. Area enclosed between two concentric circles; any well-defined tract or region of more

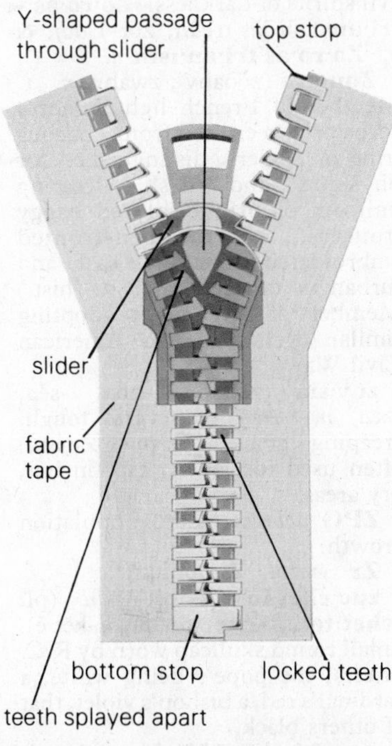

*Although the **zip fastener** was conceived by a Chicago engineer in 1893, it took Dr Gideon Sundback, a Swede, to make it reliable. It was first used on U.S. army uniforms, but Schiaparelli convinced the public of its value in 1930.*

or less beltlike form; ~ **time**, standard time in a TIME zone. 4. (geol.) = HORIZON sense 2. 5. Any part of a town or region thought of as divided off from other parts for a particular purpose (esp. in town and country planning). 6. (math.) Part of surface of sphere enclosed between two parallel planes, or of surface of any solid of revolution contained between two planes perpendicular to the axis. 7. (cryst.) Series of faces in crystal having their lines of intersection parallel. **zoned, zon'al, zon·a·ry** (zō'nerē) *adjs.* **zon'al·ly** *adv.* **zone** *v.t.* (**zoned, zon·ing**). Mark, encircle, with a zone, divide into, assign to, zones (esp. in town and country planning). **zo·na·tion** (zōnā'shon) *n.* [f. L. *zona*, f. Gr. *zōnē* girdle]

zoo (zōō) *n.* (pl. **zoos**). Zoological gardens; see ZOOLOGY.

zoo- *comb. form.* Pertaining to animals.

zo·o·ge·og·ra·phy (zōojēŏg'rafē) *n.* (Study of) the geographical distribution of animals. **zo·o·ge·og'ra·pher** *n.* **zo·o·ge·o·graph·i·cal** (zōojēogrăf'ĭkal) *adj.*

zo·og·ra·phy (zōŏg'rafē) *n.* Descriptive zoology. **zo·og'ra·pher** *n.* **zo·o·graph·i·cal** (zōogrăf'ĭkal) *adj.*

zo·oid (zō'oid) *n.* Individual member of a colony of animals joined together.

zo·ol·o·gy (zōŏl'ojē) *n.* (pl. **-gies**). Branch of biology dealing with the animal kingdom and the physiology, classification, habits, etc., of its members. **zo·ol'o·gist** *n.* **zo·o·log·i·cal** (zōolŏj'ĭkal) *adj.* **Z~ Gardens**, orig. gardens of London Zoological Society, housing the society's collection of wild animals; any garden or park in which wild animals are kept for public exhibition. **zo·o·log'ic** *adj.* **zo·o·log'i·cal·ly** *adv.*

zoom (zōōm) *v.* 1. Make loud low-pitched buzzing sound. 2. (of aircraft) Climb for short time at high speed and very steep angle; make (aircraft) climb thus. 3. (cinemat.) Cause (image) to seem to approach or recede from viewer. ~ *n.* Act of zooming; ~ **lens**, (photog.) lens that, by variation of focal length, enables continuous alteration from long shot to close-up. [imit.]

zo·o·mor·phic (zōomŏr'fĭk) *adj.* Representing or imitating animal forms; having form of an animal; attributing form or nature of animal to something, esp. deity.

zo·o·phyte (zō'ofīt) *n.* Any of various animals of low organization, usu. fixed, and freq. resembling plants or flowers in having branched or radiating structure, as crinoids, sea anemones, corals, sponges, etc. **zo·o·phyt·ic**

*Originally designed more for public entertainment than for an animal's comfort, **zoos** today are trying to strike a balance between the two.*

(zōofĭt'ĭk) *adj.*

zo·o·spore (zō'ospōr, -spŏr) *n.* Spore occurring in certain algae, fungi, etc., having power of locomotion.

Zo·ro·as·ter (zōrōăs'ter, zŏr-). (also **Zarathustra**) Persian believed to have lived in the 6th c. B.C., founder of the dualistic religious system of the Magi and ancient Persia, which survives among the Parsees; its scriptures, the ZEND-AVESTA, teach that Ormazd, lord of goodness and light and creator of mankind, is ceaselessly at war with Ahriman and the evil spirits of darkness. **Zo·ro·as·tri·an** (zōrōăs'trēan, zŏr-) *adj.* & *n.* **Zo·ro·as'tri·an·ism** *n.*

Zou·ave (zōōahv', zwahv) *n.* 1. Member of French light infantry corps orig. recruited from Zouaoua tribe of Algiers, distinguished for physique and dash, wearing uniform of bright-colored baggy trousers, short open-fronted embroidered jacket, wide sash, and turban or tasseled cap. 2. (hist.) Member of any corps adopting similar dress, esp. in American Civil War.

zoy·sia (zoi'sha, -zha, -sēa, -zēa) *n.* Any of several tough, creeping grasses (genus *Zoysia*) often used for lawns, esp. in hot, dry areas.

ZPG *abbrev.* Zero population growth.

Zr *symbol.* Zirconium.

zuc·chet·to (zōōkĕt'ō) *n.* (pl. **-chet·tos, -chet·ti** pr. -kĕt'ē). Small round skullcap worn by R.C. priests, the pope's being white, a cardinal's red, a bishop's violet, that of others black.

zuc·chi·ni (zōōkē'nē) *n.* (pl. **-ni, -nis**). Summer squash that resembles a cucumber.

Zui·der Zee, Zuy·der Zee (zī'der zē'; *Du.* zöĭ'der zā'). Large shallow inlet of the North Sea in the Netherlands, the reclamation of which was begun in 1924 for the purpose of forming a new province. [Du., = "southern sea"]

Zu·lu (zōō'lōō) *n.* (pl. **-lus**, collect. **-lu**) & *adj.* (Member, language) of a South African Bantu people inhabiting NE. part of Natal; **Zu·lu·land** (zōō'lōōlănd), region inhabited by Zulus, annexed to Natal in 1897.

Zu·ñi (zōō'nyē, -nē, sōō'-) *n.* (pl. **-ñis**, collect. **-ñi**). (Member, language) of a New Mexico tribe of Pueblo Indians. **Zu'ñi·an** *adj.*

zwie·back (zwī'băk, -bahk, zwē'-, swī'-) *n.* Kind of biscuit or sweet cake toasted in slices.

Zwing·li (zwĭng'lē), **Ulrich** or **Huldreich** (1484–1531). Swiss religious reformer; his doctrines contain elements of Reformed as distinguished from Lutheran doctrine. **Zwing'li·an** *adj.* & *n.* (Follower) of Zwingli. **Zwing'li·an·ism** *n.*

zwit·ter·i·on (tsvĭt'erīon) *n.* Molecule or ion having separate positively and negatively charged groups.

zy·go·dac·tyl (zīgodăk'tĭl, zĭgo-) *adj.* & *n.* (Bird) with toes arranged in pairs, two before and two behind, e.g. parrot.

zy·go·ma (zīgō'ma, zĭ-) *n.* (pl. **-ma·ta** pr. -mata). Bony arch on each side of skull of vertebrates, joining cranial and facial bones, and consisting of cheekbone and its connections. **zy·go·mat·ic** (zīgomăt'ĭk, zĭgo-) *adj.*

zy·go·spore (zī'gospōr, -spŏr, zĭg'o-) *n.* (in some algae and fungi) Spore or germ cell arising from fusion of two similar cells.

zy·gote (zī'gōt, zĭg'ot) *n.* (biol.) Cell arising from union of two reproductive cells or gametes, fertilized ovum. **zy·got·ic** (zīgŏt'ĭk, zĭ-) *adj.*

zy·mase (zī'mās) *n.* (biochem.) Any of a group of enzymes converting glucose and a few other carbohydrates, in the presence of oxygen, into carbon dioxide and water, or, in the absence of oxygen, into alcohol and carbon dioxide, or into lactic acid.

zy·mol·y·sis (zīmŏl'ĭsĭs) *n.* Action of enzymes, changes produced by this. **zy·mo·lyt·ic** (zīmolĭt'ĭk) *adj.*

zy·mo·sis (zīmō'sĭs) *n.* (pl. **-ses**). Fermentation; zymotic disease. **zy·mot·ic** (zīmŏt'ĭk) *adj.* Of fermentation.

zy·mur·gy (zī'merjē) *n.* Branch of applied chemistry dealing with science of wine making, brewing, and distilling.

APPENDIX I

Presidents of the United States of America

1.	George Washington	1789
2.	John Adams	1797
3.	Thomas Jefferson	1801
4.	James Madison	1809
5.	James Monroe	1817
6.	John Quincy Adams	1825
7.	Andrew Jackson	1829
8.	Martin Van Buren	1837
9.	William H. Harrison	1841
10.	John Tyler	1841
11.	James K. Polk	1845
12.	Zachary Taylor	1849
13.	Millard Fillmore	1850
14.	Franklin Pierce	1853
15.	James Buchanan	1857
16.	Abraham Lincoln	1861
17.	Andrew Johnson	1865
18.	Ulysses S. Grant	1869
19.	Rutherford B. Hayes	1877
20.	James A. Garfield	1881
21.	Chester A. Arthur	1881
22.	Grover Cleveland	1885
23.	Benjamin Harrison	1889
24.	Grover Cleveland	1893
25.	William McKinley	1897
26.	Theodore Roosevelt	1901
27.	William H. Taft	1909
28.	T. Woodrow Wilson	1913
29.	Warren G. Harding	1921
30.	Calvin Coolidge	1923
31.	Herbert C. Hoover	1929
32.	Franklin D. Roosevelt	1933
33.	Harry S. Truman	1945
34.	Dwight D. Eisenhower	1953
35.	John F. Kennedy	1961
36.	Lyndon B. Johnson	1963
37.	Richard M. Nixon	1969
38.	Gerald Ford	1974
39.	James Carter	1977
40.	Ronald Reagan	1980–

APPENDIX II

Prime Ministers of Canada since 1867

1.	Sir John A. Macdonald	1867–1873
2.	Alexander Mackenzie	1873–1878
3.	Sir John A. Macdonald	1878–1891
4.	Sir John J. Abbott	1891–1892
5.	Sir John S. D. Thompson	1892–1894
6.	Sir Mackenzie Bowell	1894–1896
7.	Sir Charles Tupper	1896
8.	Sir Wilfrid Laurier	1896–1911
9.	Sir Robert L. Borden	1911–1917
10.	Sir Robert L. Borden	1917–1920
11.	Arthur Meighen	1920–1921
12.	William Lyon Mackenzie King	1921–1926
13.	Arthur Meighen	1926
14.	William Lyon Mackenzie King	1926–1930
15.	Richard Bedford Bennett	1930–1935
16.	William Lyon Mackenzie King	1935–1948
17.	Louis Stephen St. Laurent	1948–1957
18.	John G. Diefenbaker	1957–1963
19.	Lester Bowles Pearson	1963–1968
20.	Pierre Elliott Trudeau	1968–1979
21.	Charles Joseph Clark	1979–1980
22.	Pierre Elliott Trudeau	1980–1984
23.	John Napier Turner	1984
24.	Martin Brian Mulroney	1984–

APPENDIX III

Rulers of England and the United Kingdom

House of Normandy

William I (the Conqueror)	1066–1087
William II	1087–1100
Henry I	1100–1135
Stephen	1135–1154

House of Plantagenet

Henry II	1154–1189
Richard I	1189–1199
John	1199–1216
Henry III	1216–1272
Edward I	1272–1307
Edward II	1307–1327
Edward III	1327–1377
Richard II	1377–1399

House of Lancaster

Henry IV	1399–1413
Henry V	1413–1422
Henry VI	1422–1461

House of York

Edward IV	1461–1483
Edward V	1483
Richard III	1483–1485

House of Tudor

Henry VII	1485–1509
Henry VIII	1509–1547
Edward VI	1547–1553
Mary I	1553–1558
Elizabeth I	1558–1603

House of Stuart

James I of England and VI of Scotland	1603–1625
Charles I	1625–1649

Commonwealth (*declared* 1649)

Oliver Cromwell, Lord Protector	1653–1658
Richard Cromwell	1658–1659

House of Stuart

Charles II	1660–1685
James II	1685–1688
William III and Mary II (Mary d. 1694)	1689–1702
Anne	1702–1714

House of Hanover

George I	1714–1727
George II	1727–1760
George III	1760–1820
George IV	1820–1830
William IV	1830–1837
Victoria	1837–1901

House of Saxe-Coburg-Gotha

Edward VII	1901–1910

House of Windsor

George V	1910–1936
Edward VIII	1936
George VI	1936–1952
Elizabeth II	1952–

APPENDIX IV

Prime Ministers of Great Britain

Sir Robert Walpole	1730–1741
Earl of Wilmington	1741–1743
Henry Pelham	1743–1754
Duke of Newcastle	1754–1756
Duke of Devonshire	1756–1757
Duke of Newcastle	1757–1762
Earl of Bute	1762–1763
George Grenville	1763–1765
Marquis of Rockingham	1765–1766
Earl of Chatham	1766–1768
Duke of Grafton	1768–1770
Lord North	1770–1782
Marquis of Rockingham	1782
Earl of Shelburne	1782–1783
Duke of Portland	1783
William Pitt	1783–1801
Henry Addington	1801–1804
William Pitt	1804–1806
Lord William Grenville	1806–1807
Duke of Portland	1807–1809
Spencer Perceval	1809–1812
Earl of Liverpool	1812–1827
George Canning	1827
Viscount Goderich	1827–1828
Duke of Wellington	1828–1830
Earl Grey	1830–1834
Viscount Melbourne	1834
Duke of Wellington	1834
Sir Robert Peel	1834–1835
Viscount Melbourne	1835–1841
Sir Robert Peel	1841–1846
Lord John Russell	1846–1852
Earl of Derby	1852
Earl of Aberdeen	1852–1855
Viscount Palmerston	1855–1858
Earl of Derby	1858–1859
Viscount Palmerston	1859–1865
Earl Russell	1865–1866
Earl of Derby	1866–1868
Benjamin Disraeli	1868
William Ewart Gladstone	1868–1874
Benjamin Disraeli Earl of Beaconsfield	1874–1880
William Ewart Gladstone	1880–1885
Marquis of Salisbury	1885–1886
William Ewart Gladstone	1886
Marquis of Salisbury	1886–1892
William Ewart Gladstone	1892–1894
Earl of Rosebery	1894–1895
Marquis of Salisbury	1895–1902
Arthur James Balfour	1902–1905
Sir Henry Campbell-Bannerman	1905–1908
Herbert Henry Asquith	1908–1916
David Lloyd George	1916–1922
Andrew Bonar Law	1922–1923
Stanley Baldwin	1923–1924
James Ramsay MacDonald	1924
Stanley Baldwin	1924–1929
James Ramsay MacDonald	1929–1935
Stanley Baldwin	1935–1937
Neville Chamberlain	1937–1940
Winston Spencer Churchill	1940–1945
Clement Richard Attlee	1945–1951
Sir Winston Spencer Churchill	1951–1955
Sir Anthony Eden	1955–1957
Harold Macmillan	1957–1963
Sir Alexander Douglas-Home	1963–1964
Harold Wilson	1964–1970
Edward Heath	1970–1974
Harold Wilson	1974–1976
James Callaghan	1976–1979
Margaret Thatcher	1979–

APPENDIX V

WEIGHTS AND MEASURES

MEASURES OF WEIGHT

In scientific usage the units of weight are units of mass

Avoirdupois weight

	grain	0·0648 gramme
	dram	1·772 grammes
16 drams	ounce (oz)	28·35 grammes
16 ounces or 7000 grains	pound (lb)	0·454 kilogramme
14 pounds	stone	6·35 kilogrammes
28 pounds	quarter	12·7 kilogrammes
25 pounds	U.S. quarter	11·34 kilogrammes
4 quarters or 112 pounds	hundredweight (cwt)	50·80 kilogrammes
4 quarters or 100 pounds	U.S. hundredweight (cwt)	45·36 kilogrammes
20 hundredweight or 2240 pounds	long ton	1016·05 kilogrammes
20 hundredweight or 2000 pounds	U.S. short ton	907·19 kilogrammes

Troy weight

	grain	0·0648 gramme
24 grains	pennyweight (dwt)	1·555 grammes
20 pennyweights or 480 grains	ounce	31·1035 grammes
12 ounces or 5760 grains	pound (not a legal measure but used for convenience)	373·27 grammes

Apothecaries' weight

	grain	0·0648 gramme
20 grains	scruple	1·296 grammes
3 scruples or 60 grains	drachm or (U.S.) dram	3·888 grammes
8 drachms or 480 grains	ounce (= troy ounce)	31·1035 grammes

Apothecaries' fluid measure

	minim	0·0059 centilitre
60 minims	fluid drachm	0·355 centilitre
8 fluid drachms	fluid ounce	0·284 decilitre
20 fluid ounces	pint	0·568 litre
8 pints	gallon	4·546 litres

BRITISH MEASURES OF CAPACITY

	fluid ounce	0·284 decilitre
	gill	1·42 decilitres
4 gills or 20 fluid ounces	pint	0·568 litre
2 pints	quart	1·136 litres
4 quarts	gallon (imperial gallon, 277·274 cubic inches)	4·546 litres
2 gallons	peck	9·092 litres
4 pecks or 8 gallons	bushel	0·364 hectolitre
8 bushels	quarter	2·909 hectolitres

AMERICAN MEASURES OF CAPACITY

Liquid measure

	minim	0·059 millilitre
60 minims	fluid dram	3·6966 millilitres
8 fluid drams	fluid ounce	0·296 decilitre
16 fluid ounces	pint	0·473 litre
2 pints	quart	0·946 litre
4 quarts	gallon (Winchester or wine gallon, 231 cubic inches)	3·785 litres

Dry measure

	pint	0·551 litre
2 pints	quart	1·101 litres
8 quarts	peck	8·809 litres
4 pecks	bushel	35·328 litres

LINEAR MEASURES

	inch	2·54 centimetres (4 in = approx. 10 cm)
7·92 inches	link	0·201 metre
12 inches	foot	0·3048 metre
3 feet	yard	0·9144 metre
6 feet	fathom	1·8288 metres
5½ yards	rod, pole, or perch	5·0292 metres
22 yards or 4 rods or 100 links	chain	20·11678 metres
10 chains or 220 yards	furlong	201·1678 metres
8 furlongs or 1760 yards or 5280 feet	statute mile	1·60934 kilometres (5 miles = approx. 8 km.)
6080 feet	nautical mile	1·8533 kilometres

SQUARE MEASURES

	square inch	6·452 square centimetres
144 square inches	square foot	0·0929 square metre
9 square feet	square yard	0·8361 square metre
30¼ square yards	square rod, pole, or perch	25·29 square metres
40 square rods	rood	0·101 hectare
4 roods or 10 square chains or 4 840 square yards	acre	0·405 hectare
640 acres or 3 097 600 square yards	square mile	2·59 square kilometres

CUBIC MEASURES

	cubic inch	16·387 cubic centimetres
1728 cubic inches	cubic foot	0·0283 cubic metre
27 cubic feet	cubic yard	0·765 cubic metre
100 cubic feet	register ton	2·832 cubic metres

METRIC SYSTEM

Measures of length

1000 microns	millimetre	0·039 inch
10 millimetres	centimetre	0·3937 inch
10 centimetres	decimetre	3·397 inches
10 decimetres	metre	39·37 inches
10 metres	decametre	32 feet 10 inches (nearly 11 yards)
10 decametres	hectometre	328 feet 1 inch (about $\frac{1}{16}$ mile)
10 hectometres or 1000 metres	kilometre	0·621 mile (roughly $\frac{5}{8}$), or 3280 feet 10 inches

Square measures

100 square millimetres	square centimetre	0·155 square inch
100 square centimetres	square decimetre	15·50 square inches
100 square decimetres	square metre or centiare	1·196 square yards or 1550 square inches
100 square metres	are	119·6 square yards
100 acres	hectare	2·4711 acres

Cubic measures

1000 cubic millimetres	cubic centimetre	0·061 cubic inch
1000 cubic centimetres	cubic decimetre	61·024 cubic inches
1000 cubic decimetres	cubic metre or stere	35·31 cubic feet or 1·308 cubic yards
100 cubic metres	hectostere	130·8 cubic yards

Measures of capacity

	millilitre	16·894 minims
10 millilitres	centilitre	2 fluid drachms 49 minims
10 centilitres	decilitre	3 fluid ounces, 4 drachms, 10·4 minims (about 3½ fluid ounces)
10 decilitres	litre	1·7598 pints or about 35 fluid ounces
10 litres	decalitre	2·2 imperial gallons
10 decalitres	hectolitre	22 imperial gallons

Measures of weight

	milligramme	0·015 grain
10 milligrammes	centigramme	0·154 grain (about $\frac{1}{7}$)
10 centigrammes	decigramme	1·543 grains
10 decigrammes	gramme	15·432 grains or 0·035 ounce
10 grammes	decagramme	0·353 ounce (about $\frac{1}{3}$)
10 decagrammes	hectogramme	3·527 ounces
10 hectogrammes or 1000 grammes	kilogramme	2·205 pounds (5 kilogrammes = approx. 11 pounds)
100 kilogrammes	quintal	220·46 pounds or 1·968 hundredweights
1000 kilogrammes	tonne	2204·6 pounds

ANGULAR MEASURES

	second (″)
60 seconds	minute (′)
60 minutes	degree (°)
90 degrees	right angle or quadrant
4 quadrants or 360 degrees	circle

TEMPERATURES

CENTIGRADE FAHRENHEIT

Centigrade	*Fahrenheit*
—17·8°	0°
—10°	14°
0°	32°
10°	50°
20°	68°
30°	86°
40°	104°
50°	122°
60°	140°
70°	158°
80°	176°
90°	194°
100°	212°

To convert Centigrade into Fahrenheit: multiply by 9, divide by 5, and add 32.

To convert Fahrenheit into Centigrade: subtract 32, multiply by 5, and divide by 9.

APPENDIX VI

THE CHEMICAL ELEMENTS

Atomic number		*Atomic weight*	*Symbol*
1	Hydrogen	1·0080	H
2	Helium	4·00260	He
3	Lithium	6·941	Li
4	Beryllium	9·01218	Be
5	Boron	10·811	B
6	Carbon	12·011	C
7	Nitrogen	14·0067	N
8	Oxygen	15·9994	O
9	Fluorine	18·9984	F
10	Neon	20·179	Ne
11	Sodium	22·9898	Na
12	Magnesium	24·305	Mg
13	Aluminium	26·9815	Al
14	Silicon	28·086	Si
15	Phosphorus	30·9738	P
16	Sulphur	32·06	S
17	Chlorine	35·453	Cl
18	Argon	39·948	Ar
19	Potassium	39·102	K
20	Calcium	40·98	Ca
21	Scandium	44·9559	Sc
22	Titanium	47·90	Ti
23	Vanadium	50·941	V
24	Chromium	51·996	Cr
25	Manganese	54·9380	Mn
26	Iron	55·847	Fe
27	Cobalt	58·9332	Co
28	Nickel	58·71	Ni
29	Copper	63·546	Cu
30	Zinc	65·37	Zn
31	Gallium	69·72	Ga
32	Germanium	72·59	Ge
33	Arsenic	74·9216	As
34	Selenium	78·96	Se
35	Bromine	79·904	Br
36	Krypton	83·80	Kr
37	Rubidium	85·678	Rb
38	Strontium	87·62	Sr
39	Yttrium	88·9059	Y
40	Zirconium	91·22	Zr
41	Niobium	92·9064	Nb
42	Molybdenum	95·94	Mo
43	Technetium	98·9062	Tc
44	Ruthenium	101·07	Ru
45	Rhodium	102·9055	Rh
46	Palladium	106·4	Pd
47	Silver	107·868	Ag
48	Cadmium	112·40	Cd
49	Indium	114·82	In
50	Tin	118·69	Sn
51	Antimony	121·75	Sb
52	Tellurium	127·60	Te
53	Iodine	126·9045	I
54	Xenon	131·30	Xe
55	Caesium	132·9054	Cs
56	Barium	137·34	Ba
57	Lanthanum	138·9055	La
58	Cerium	140·12	Ce
59	Praesodymium	140·9077	Pr
60	Neodymium	144·24	Nd
61	Promethium	147*	Pm
62	Samarium	150·4	Sm
63	Europium	151·96	Eu
64	Gadolinium	157·25	Gd
65	Terbium	158·9254	Tb
66	Dysprosium	162·50	Dy
67	Holmium	164·9340	Ho
68	Erbium	167·26	Er
69	Thulium	168·9342	Tm
70	Ytterbium	173·04	Yb
71	Lutetium	174·97	Lu
72	Hafnium	178·49	Hf
73	Tantalum	180·9479	Ta
74	Tungsten	183·85	W
75	Rhenium	186·2	Re
76	Osmium	190·2	Os
77	Iridium	192·2	Ir
78	Platinum	195·09	Pt
79	Gold	196·9665	Au
80	Mercury	200·59	Hg
81	Thallium	204·371	Tl
82	Lead	207·12	Pb
83	Bismuth	208·9806	Bi
84	Polonium	210*	Po
85	Astatine	211*	At
86	Radon	222*	Rn
87	Francium	223*	Fr
88	Radium	226·0254	Ra
89	Actinium	227*	Ac
90	Thorium	232·0381	Th
91	Protactinium	231·0359	Pa
92	Uranium	238·029	U
93	Neptunium	237·0482	Np
94	Plutonium	239*	Pu
95	Americium	241*	Am
96	Curium	242*	Cm
97	Berkelium	243*	Bk
98	Californium	244*	Cf
99	Einsteinium	253*	E
100	Fermium	256*	Fm
101	Mendeleviumt†		Md
102	Nobelium†		No
103	Lawrencium†		Lw

† Isotopic weight not yet known.

* Principal isotope.